Wörterbuch
Deutsch ▸ Englisch
Englisch ▸ Deutsch

German ▸ English
English ▸ German
Dictionary

German–English
English–German
Dictionary

HarperResource

An Imprint of Harper**Collins***Publishers*

fourth edition 2003

© William Collins Sons & Co. Ltd. 1987
© HarperCollins Publishers 1994, 1998, 2003

HarperCollins Publishers
Westerhill Road, Bishopbriggs, Glasgow G64 2QT
Great Britain

www.collinsdictionaries.com

Collins® and Bank of English® are registered trademarks of
HarperCollins Publishers Limited

ISBN 0-00-470710-9

HarperCollins Publishers, Inc.
10 East 53rd Street, New York, NY 10022

ISBN 0-06-051532-5

Library of Congress Cataloging-in-Publication Data has been applied for

www.harpercollins.com

First HarperCollins edition published 1995

HarperCollins books may be purchased for educational, business, or sales
promotional use. For information, please write to: Special Markets Department,
HarperCollins Publishers Inc., 10 East 53rd Street, New York, NY 10022

Acknowledgements

We would like to thank those authors and publishers who
kindly gave permission for copyright material to be used
in the Bank of English. We would also like to thank
Times Newspapers Ltd for providing valuable data.

Note

Entered words that we have reason to believe constitute
trademarks have been designated as such. However, neither
the presence nor absence of such designation should be
regarded as affecting the legal status of any trademark.

A catalogue record for this book is available from the British Library

Typeset by Thomas Callan, HarperCollins Publishers, Glasgow, Great Britain

Printed and bound in Great Britain by The Bath Press, Bath

FOURTH EDITION   VIERTE AUFLAGE

Editors / Redakteure
Stuart Fortey Horst Kopleck
Helen Galloway Veronika Schnorr

Editorial Coordination / Koordination
Susie Beattie
Joyce Littlejohn

Computing and Typesetting / Datenverarbeitung und Schriftsatz
Thomas Callan

SECOND AND THIRD EDITIONS   ZWEITE UND DRITTE AUFLAGE

Prepared by / Bearbeitet von
Eva Vennebusch
Robin Sawers

with / mit
Horst Kopleck

Editorial Staff/Verlagsangestellte
Joyce Littlejohn
Christine Bahr
Nicola Cooke

FIRST EDITION   ERSTE AUSGABE
Peter Terrell Horst Kopleck

Assistant Editors / Bearbeitung
Jimmy Burnett   Philip Ladd
Andrea Ender   Reinhold Trott

Copy Editor / Redaktionsassistentin
Daphne Trotter

based on / auf der Basis von
Collins German Dictionary

by / von
Peter Terrell Veronika Calderwood-Schnorr
Wendy V.A. Morris Roland Breitsprecher

INHALT

CONTENTS

Einleitung

Dieses Wörterbuch ist insbesondere für Benutzer geeignet, die bereits Grundkenntnisse in der Fremdsprache besitzen und ein handliches Wörterbuch mittlerer Größe benötigen, welches ihnen jedoch eine umfassende Darstellung der modernen englischen und deutschen Alltagssprache bieten soll. Dieses Ziel wird erreicht, indem der Schwerpunkt auf den heutigen Sprachgebrauch — ob Umgangssprache oder förmlichere Ausdrucksweise — gelegt wird und alle Sachbereiche, die in der Welt von heute wichtig sind, wie z.B. Handel, Computertechnik und Sport, ausführlich abgedeckt werden. Aus diesem Grund ist dieses Wörterbuch gleichermaßen für Büro und Geschäftswelt, für die Schule, die Universität, sowie zum allgemeinen Gebrauch zu Hause geeignet.

Dieses Wörterbuch soll jedoch nicht nur ein Verständnis der Fremdsprache vermitteln, sondern dem Benutzer darüber hinaus ihren sicheren Gebrauch in Wort und Schrift ermöglichen. Zu diesem Zweck wird die Verwendungsweise der angegebenen Übersetzungen auf vielfache Art aufgezeigt, z.B. durch Indikatoren zur Unterscheidung verschiedener Bedeutungen, durch Angabe typischer Subjekte und Objekte bei Verben sowie typischer Substantive, die gemeinsam mit Adjektiven verwendet werden; daneben wird eine Fülle von Beispielen gegeben, die Verwendungs- und Übersetzungsvarianten je nach Kontext aufzeigen. Überdies werden elementare, am häufigsten verwendete Wörter besonders ausführlich behandelt, da gerade sie häufig Schwierigkeiten bei der Kommunikation und Ausdrucksweise in der Fremdsprache bereiten. Dieses Wörterbuch folgt durchweg der reformierten deutschen Rechtschreibung.

Introduction

This dictionary is intended especially for users who already have a grasp of the basics of the language and who require a handy dictionary of medium size, which will nonetheless provide them with a comprehensive survey of modern everyday German and English. It achieves this by placing the emphasis on current usage — from the colloquial to the more formal — and by giving extensive treatment of subjects such as commerce, computer technology and sport which are relevant to the modern world. Hence the dictionary is equally suitable for the business person at the office, the student both at school and at college, and the interested general reader at home.

However, the dictionary is designed to enable the user not only to understand the foreign language, but also to write and speak it with confidence. To this end there are numerous features which show how the translations given are used, such as the guiding system of indicating words to distinguish between alternatives, the typical subjects and objects for verbs and nouns that go with adjectives, and the rich store of examples, all of which show how usage and hence translation vary according to context. Also the basic, most frequently used words are treated in depth, as these so often cause problems when trying to communicate or express oneself in the foreign language. In addition, the German Spelling Reform has been fully implemented.

The new-look fourth edition of the Collins Concise German Dictionary helps you make even more effective use of the text. The innovative "German in Action" supplement in the middle of the book draws on the wealth of lexicographic information to

Die vierte Auflage des Collins Handwörterbuchs Englisch präsentiert sich in neuer Aufmachung und ermöglicht Ihnen eine noch effektvollere Handhabung Ihrer Texte. Der Zusatzteil „Englisch aktiv" in der Mitte des Buches ist eine innovative Zusammenstellung von authentischen Beispielsätzen aus unseren gegenwärtig mehr als 650 Millionen Wörter umfassenden Textdatenbanken des heutigen Englisch und Deutsch. Die „Bank of English" sowie die „Deutsche Textbörse" enthalten Artikel aus Zeitungen und Zeitschriften, literarische Texte, Gesprächsmitschnitte und vieles mehr. In „Englisch aktiv" finden Sie weiterhin nützliche Tips zum Telefonieren in der Fremdsprache, und Geschäfts- und Privatbriefe helfen Ihnen in vielen Situationen, von der Bewerbung bis zur Hochzeitseinladung. „Englisch aktiv" mit Hunderten von thematisch geordneten Mustersätzen ist damit ein umfassender und kompakter Ratgeber für alle wichtigen Sprechhandlungen.

Unsere erklärenden Einträge zu wichtigen kulturellen Aspekten des Alltags, der Literatur, in Politik, Geschichte, Bildungswesen sowie verschiedenen Organisationen in Deutschland, Großbritannien und den USA sollen zum besseren Verständnis kultureller Unterschiede zwischen diesen Nationen beitragen. Die Einträge erscheinen jeweils in der Muttersprache desjenigen Wörterbuchbenutzers, für den diese Hinweise gedacht sind. Daher werden deutsche Besonderheiten auf Englisch, britische und amerikanische jedoch auf Deutsch beschrieben. Der Inhalt dieses Wörterbuchs basiert auf der vierten Auflage unseres berühmten Großwörterbuchs, dem Maßstab, an dem andere gemessen werden. Diese Ausgabe besitzt dieselben Vorzüge wie das Großwörterbuch, darunter eine außergewöhnlich klare Anordnung der Einträge und eine moderne Sprachauffassung.

be found in our databases of authentic German and English, both written and spoken, from such diverse sources as contemporary literature, press articles and recordings of real-life conversations currently totalling over 650 million words. In "German in Action" we have also included sections on the telephone, business and personal correspondence with authentic sample letters which cover every situation from applying for a job to accepting a wedding invitation. Together they provide a comprehensive guide to self-expression in German, with hundreds of example phrases grouped thematically to help you communicate in fluent, natural German.

Our encyclopaedic entries on key aspects of German, British and American culture such as everyday life, literature, politics, history, education and organization attempt to bridge the gap between the differing cultures. These entries are written in the native language of the user they are designed to benefit; this means that entries on German items are in English and entries on British and American items are in German. The content of the dictionary is based on the fourth edition of our famous large dictionary which has become the market leader and the standard by which others are judged. This dictionary shares the outstanding features of the larger edition, including exceptional clarity of layout and modernity of approach.

Using the Dictionary

Hinweise zur Benutzung des Wörterbuchs

1. Layout and order

1. Aufbau und Anordnung der Einträge

Alphabetical order is followed throughout. Where a letter occurs in brackets in a headword, this letter is counted for the alphabetical order, eg **enc(l)** will be found in the place of **encl**.

Die alphabetische Anordnung der Einträge ist durchweg gewahrt. In Klammern stehende Buchstaben in einem Stichwort unterliegen ebenfalls der Alphabetisierung, so findet man z.B. **enc(l)** an der Stelle von **encl**.

Abbreviations, acronyms and **proper nouns** will be found in their alphabetical place in the word list.

Abkürzungen, Akronyme und **Eigennamen** sind in alphabetischer Ordnung im Wörterverzeichnis zu finden.

Superior numbers are used to differentiate between words spelt the same way.

Hochgestellte Ziffern werden verwendet, um zwischen Wörtern gleicher Schreibung zu unterscheiden.

> **rowing¹** [ˈrəʊɪŋ] N Rudern *nt*
> **rowing²** [ˈraʊɪŋ] N (*esp Brit*: *= quarrelling*) Streiterei *f*

Roman numerals are used to distinguish between the different parts of speech of the headword and to subdivide verbs (*vt, vi, vr, vi impers, vt impers, vi + prep obj* etc.)

Die römischen Ziffern dienen zur Unterscheidung der verschiedenen Wortarten, denen ein Stichwort angehört, und zur Gliederung der Verben (*vt, vi, vr, vi impers, vt impers, vi + prep obj* etc.)

> **südwestlich** **1** ADJ *Gegend* southwestern; *Wind* southwest(erly) **2** ADV (to the) southwest (*von* of) **3** PREP +GEN (to the) southwest of

Arabic numerals are used to distinguish meanings which are fundamentally different.

Grundlegend verschiedene Bedeutungen eines Stichworts sind durch arabische Ziffern differenziert.

> **moonshine** N **(a)** (*= moonlight*) Mondschein *m* **(b)** (*inf*: *= nonsense*) Unsinn *m* **(c)** (*inf*: *= illegal whisky*) illegal gebrannter Whisky

Nouns which are always used in the plural are entered in the plural form.

Substantive, die stets im Plural verwendet werden, sind in der Pluralform angegeben.

> **Ferien** [ˈfeːriən] PL holidays *pl* (*Brit*), vacation *sing* (*US, Univ*); (*= ~reise*) holiday *sing* (*esp Brit*), vacation *sing* (*US*); (*= Parlamentsferien, Jur*) recess *sing*

Compounds will be found in their alphabetical place in the word list. The term "compound" is taken to cover not only those written in one word or hyphenated (eg **tablecloth, LCD-Anzeige**) but also attributive uses of English nouns (eg **defence mechanism**) and other set word combinations (eg **ad absurdum**) which function in a similar way. Where possible a general translation has been given for the first element.

Zusammengesetzte Wörter stehen an ihrer Stelle im Alphabet. Der Begriff „zusammengesetzte Wörter" bezeichnet nicht nur zusammengeschriebene oder durch Bindestrich verbundene Komposita (z. B. **tablecloth, LCD-Anzeige**) sondern auch die attributive Verwendung englischer Substantive (z. B. **defence mechanism**) und andere feste Verbindungen (z. B. **ad absurdum**), die eine ähnliche Funktion haben. Wo immer möglich, ist für das erste Element eine allgemeine Übersetzung angegeben.

coral IN CPDS Korallen-

From this the user can derive the translation for compounds not given in the word list.

Daraus kann der Benutzer die Übersetzung hier nicht angegebener Zusammensetzungen erschließen.

Where alphabetical order permits, compounds are run on in blocks. Illustrative phrases appear in a semibold typeface so that they can easily be distinguished from compounds.

Wo die alphabetische Ordnung es gestattet, werden die Zusammensetzungen in Blöcken angeordnet. Für Wendungen wird eine halbfette Schrift verwendet, um dem Benutzer die schnelle Identifizierung von Wendungen und zusammengesetzten Wörtern zu erleichtern.

Kurs-: Kursrisiko NT market risk; **Kursrückgang** M fall in prices; **Kursschwankung** F fluctuation in exchange rates; (*St Ex*) fluctuation in market rates; **Kurssystem** NT (*Sch, Univ*) course system; **Kursverlust** M (*Fin*) loss (on the stock exchange *or* foreign exchange market); **das Pfund musste ~e hinnehmen** the pound suffered losses on the foreign exchange market; **Kurswagen** M (*Rail*) through coach

Phrasal verbs (marked ◆) will be found immediately after the main headword entry.

Phrasal verbs (feste Verb-Partikel-Verbindungen im Englischen, durch ◆ bezeichnet) folgen unmittelbar auf das Hauptstichwort.

Idioms and set phrases will normally be found under the first meaningful element or the first word in the phrase which remains constant despite minor variations in the phrase itself. Thus, 'jdm einen Denkzettel verpassen' is included under **'Denkzettel'** whereas 'to lend sb a hand' is treated under **'hand'** because it is equally possible to say 'to give sb a hand'.

Redensarten und feste Wendungen sind im Allgemeinen unter dem ersten bedeutungstragenden Element oder dem ersten Wort der Wendung, das trotz leichter Abwandlungen in der Wendung selbst unverändert bleibt, zu finden. So ist ‚jdm einen Denkzettel verpassen' unter ‚**Denkzettel**' aufgenommen, ‚to lend sb a hand' dagegen wird unter ‚**hand**' abgehandelt, weil es ebenfalls möglich ist, ‚to give sb a hand' zu sagen.

Certain very common verbs such as 'be, have, make, bringen, haben, machen', which form the basis of a great many phrases e.g. 'to make sense', 'etw in Ordnung bringen' have been considered as having a diminished meaning and in such cases the set phrase will be found under the most significant element in the phrase.

Bei als Funktionsverben gebrauchten Verben wie ‚be, have, make, bringen, haben, machen' werden die meisten festen Wendungen, wie z. B. ‚to make sense', ‚etw in Ordnung bringen', unter dem bedeutungstragenden Bestandteil der Wendung behandelt.

2. Explanatory material

2. Erklärende Zusätze

General explanatory notes or 'signposts' in the dictionary are printed in italics and take the following forms:

Allgemeine erklärende Zusätze im Wörterbuch sind kursiv gedruckt und erscheinen in folgender Form:

Indicators in brackets ( ):
explanations and clarification

Indikatoren, in Klammern stehend ( ):
Erklärungen und Erläuterungen

> **pad** N (*for comfort etc*) Polster *nt*; (*for protection*) Schützer *m*; (*in bra*) Einlage *f*

synonyms and partial definitions

Synonyme und Teildefinitionen

> **Kanal** [ka'naːl] M **-s, Kanäle** [ka'nɛːlə] (= *Schifffahrtsweg*) canal; (= *Wasserlauf*) channel

within verb entries, typical subjects of the headword

in Verb-Einträgen typische Substantiv-Ergänzungen

> ➤ **ice up** VI (*aircraft wings, windscreen etc*) vereisen; (*pipes etc*) einfrieren

within noun entries, typical noun complements of the headword

typische Substantiv-Ergänzungen des Stichworts in Substantiv-Einträgen

> **Herbheit** F **-**, NO PL (*von Geruch*) sharpness; (*von Parfüm*) tanginess; (*von Geschmack*) sharpness, tanginess; (*von Wein*) dryness

Collocators or typical complements, not in brackets:

Kollokatoren oder typische Ergänzungen, ohne Klammern stehend:

in transitive verb entries, typical objects of the headword

typische Objekte des Stichworts bei transitiven Verb-Einträgen

> **conquer** ['kɒŋkə'] VT **(a)** (*lit*) *country* erobern; *enemy, nation* besiegen **(b)** (*fig*) *difficulties, feelings, disease, mountain* bezwingen

in adjective entries, typical nouns modified by the headword

typische, durch das Stichwort näher bestimmte Substantive in Adjektiv-Einträgen

> **blühend** ADJ *Baum* blossoming; *Blume, Pflanze auch* blooming; *Garten, Wiese, Feld* full of flowers; (*fig*) *Aussehen* radiant; *Geschäft, Handel, Industrie, Kultur, Stadt* flourishing, thriving; *Fantasie* vivid; *Unsinn* absolute

in adverb entries, typical verbs or adjectives modified by the headword

typische, durch das Stichwort näher bestimmte Verben oder Adjektive bei Adverb-Einträgen

absolutely [ˌæbsəˈluːtlɪ] ADV absolut; *true* völlig; *amazing, fantastic* wirklich; *deny, refuse* strikt; *forbidden* streng; *necessary* unbedingt; *prove* eindeutig

Field labels are used:

Sachbereichsangaben werden verwendet:

to differentiate various meanings of the headword

um die verschiedenen Bedeutungen des Stichworts zu unterscheiden

Membran [mɛmˈbraːn] F -, -en, **Membrane** [mɛmˈbraːnə] F -, -n
(a) (*Anat*) membrane **(b)** (*Phys, Tech*) diaphragm

when the meaning may be ambiguous in the source language or in the target language

wenn die Bedeutung in der Ausgangssprache oder in der Zielsprache mehrdeutig sein könnte

bishop [ˈbɪʃəp] N **(a)** (*Eccl*) Bischof *m* **(b)** (*Chess*) Läufer *m*

Style labels are used to mark all words and phrases which are not neutral in style level or which are no longer current in the language. This labelling is given for both source and target languages and serves primarily as an aid to the non-native speaker.

Stilangaben werden verwendet zur Kennzeichnung aller Wörter und Wendungen, die keiner neutralen Stilebene oder nicht mehr dem modernen Sprachgebrauch angehören. Die Angaben erfolgen sowohl in der Ausgangs- als auch in der Zielsprache und sollen in erster Linie dem Nichtmuttersprachler helfen.

When a style label is given at the beginning of an entry or category it covers all meanings and phrases in that entry or category.

Stilangaben zu Beginn eines Eintrages oder einer Kategorie beziehen sich auf alle Bedeutungen und Wendungen innerhalb dieses Eintrages oder dieser Kategorie.

(*inf*) denotes colloquial language typically used in an informal conversational context or a chatty letter, but which would be inappropriate or could even cause offence in more formal speech or writing.

(*inf*) bezeichnet umgangssprachlichen Gebrauch, wie z. B. in einer Unterhaltung unter Freunden oder einem zwanglosen Brief, der in förmlicherer Rede oder förmlicherem Schriftverkehr jedoch unangebracht wäre oder sogar Anstoß erregen könnte.

(*sl*) indicates that the word or phrase is highly informal and usually restricted in its use to members of a particular social or age group. It may also be misunderstood or seen as offensive by members of other social or age groups. When combined with a field label eg (*Mil sl*), (*Sch sl*) it denotes that the expression belongs to the jargon of that group.

(*sl*) soll anzeigen, dass das Wort oder die Wendung äußerst salopp ist und häufig nur von Mitgliedern einer bestimmten sozialen oder Altersgruppe verwendet wird und von anderen sozialen oder Altersgruppen möglicherweise entweder nicht verstanden oder als anstößig empfunden wird. In Verbindung mit einer Sachgebietsangabe, z. B. (*Mil sl*), (*Sch sl*), wird auf die Zugehörigkeit des Ausdrucks zum Jargon dieser Gruppe hingewiesen.

(*vulg*) denotes words regarded as taboo which generally cause offence.

(*geh*) denotes an elevated style of spoken or written German such as might be used by an educated speaker choosing his words with care.

(*form*) denotes formal language such as that used on official forms, for official communications and in formal speeches.

(*spec*) indicates that the expression is a technical term restricted to the vocabulary of specialists.

(*dated*) indicates that the word or phrase, while still occasionally being used especially by older speakers, now sounds somewhat old-fashioned.

(*old*) denotes language no longer in current use but which the user will find in reading.

(*obs*) denotes obsolete words which the user will normally only find in classical literature.

(*liter*) denotes language of a literary style level. It should not be confused with the field label (*Liter*) which indicates that the expression belongs to the field of literary studies, or with the abbreviation (*lit*) which indicates the literal as opposed to the figurative meaning of a word.

Style labels used in this dictionary are given inside the front and back covers.

also used after explanatory material denotes that the translation(s) following it can be used in addition to the first translation given in the respective entry, category or phrase.

(*vulg*) bezeichnet Wörter, die als tabu gelten und an denen allgemein Anstoß genommen wird.

(*geh*) bezeichnet einen gehobenen Stil sowohl im gesprochenen wie geschriebenen Deutsch, wie er von gebildeten, sich gewählt ausdrückenden Sprechern verwendet werden kann.

(*form*) bezeichnet förmlichen Sprachgebrauch, wie er uns auf Formularen, im amtlichen Schriftverkehr oder in förmlichen Ansprachen begegnet.

(*spec*) gibt an, dass es sich um einen Fachausdruck handelt, der ausschließlich dem Wortschatz von Fachleuten angehört.

(*dated*) weist darauf hin, dass das Wort bzw. die Wendung heute recht altmodisch klingen, obwohl sie besonders von älteren Sprechern noch gelegentlich benutzt werden.

(*old*) bezeichnet nicht mehr geläufiges Wortgut, das dem Benutzer jedoch noch beim Lesen begegnet.

(*obs*) bezeichnet veraltete Wörter, die der Benutzer im Allgemeinen nur in der klassischen Literatur antreffen wird.

(*liter*) bezeichnet literarischen Sprachgebrauch. Es sollte nicht mit der Sachbereichsangabe (*Liter*) verwechselt werden, die angibt, dass der betreffende Ausdruck dem Gebiet der Literaturwissenschaft angehört, und ebenso wenig mit der Abkürzung (*lit*), die die wörtliche im Gegensatz zur übertragenen Bedeutung eines Wortes bezeichnet.

In diesem Wörterbuch verwendete Stilangaben und ihre Bedeutungen befinden sich auf den Umschlag-Innenseiten.

also nach erklärenden Zusätzen gibt an, dass die folgende(n) Übersetzung(en) zusätzlich zu der ersten Übersetzung, die in dem Eintrag oder der Kategorie angegeben ist, benutzt werden kann/können.

3. Grammatical Information

Gender

All German **nouns** are marked for gender.

Where a German translation consists of an adjective plus a noun, the adjective is given in the indefinite form which shows gender and therefore no gender is given for the noun.

3. Grammatische Angaben

Geschlecht

Alle deutschen **Substantive** sind mit der Geschlechtsangabe versehen.

Wenn eine deutsche Übersetzung aus einem Adjektiv und einem Substantiv besteht, wird das Adjektiv in der unbestimmten Form angegeben, die das Geschlecht erkennen lässt. Für das Substantiv erfolgt daher keine Geschlechtsangabe.

high court N oberstes *or* höchstes Gericht

Nouns listed in the form **Angestellte(r)** *mf* can be either masculine or feminine and take the same endings as adjectives.

Substantive nach dem Muster **Angestellte(r)** *mf* können sowohl männlich wie weiblich sein und haben die gleichen Deklinationsendungen wie Adjektive.

Angestellte(r) *mf* = der Angestellte
ein Angestellter
die Angestellte
eine Angestellte

Nouns listed in the form **Beamte(r)** *m* take the same endings as adjectives.

Substantive nach dem Muster **Beamte(r)** *m* haben die gleichen Deklinationsendungen wie Adjektive.

Beamte(r) *m* = der Beamte, ein Beamter
Gute(s) *nt* = das Gute, ein Gutes

Adjectives listed in the form **letzte(r, s)** do not exist in an undeclined form and are only used attributively.

Adjektive nach dem Muster **letzte(r, s)** haben keine unflektierte Form und werden nur attributiv verwendet.

**der letzte Mann, ein letzter Mann
die letzte Frau, eine letzte Frau
das letzte Kind, ein letztes Kind**

The **feminine forms** are shown, where relevant, for all German nouns

Where the feminine noun is formed by adding '-in' to the masculine, '-in' is given in brackets and the gender is marked *m(f)*.

Für alle deutschen Substantive, die ein natürliches Geschlecht haben, wird die **weibliche** neben der **männlichen Form** angegeben.

Wird bei einer weiblichen Form ein ‚-in' an die männliche angehängt, steht ‚-in' in Klammern und das Geschlecht wird mit *m(f)* gekennzeichnet.

murderer ['mɜːdərə'] N Mörder(in) *m(f)*

4. Nouns

Nouns marked *no pl* are not normally used in the plural or with an indefinite article or with numerals.

4. Substantive

Substantive mit der Angabe *no pl* werden im Allgemeinen nicht im Plural, mit dem unbestimmten Artikel oder mit Zahlwörtern verwendet.

no pl is used:

(a) to give warning to the non-native speaker who might otherwise use the word wrongly;

(b) as an indicator to distinguish the uncountable meanings of a headword in the source language.

Nouns marked *no art* are not normally used with either a definite or an indefinite article except when followed by a relative clause.

Irregular plural forms of English nouns are given.

Most English nouns take *-s* in the plural.

bed -s, site -s, key -s, roof -s

Nouns ending in *-s, -z, -x, -sh, -ch* take *-es*.

gas -es, box -es, patch -es

Nouns ending in *-y* preceded by a consonant change the *-y* to *-ie* and add *-s* in the plural, except in the case of proper nouns.

lady — ladies, berry — berries
Henry — two Henrys

The **genitive and plural endings** are given for all German noun headwords. The genitive and plural endings of German compound nouns are only given where the final element does not exist as a headword in its own right.

5. Prepositions

Prepositions used in combination with verbs, nouns and adjectives and their translation are given in brackets.

no pl dient:

(a) als Warnung an den Nicht-Muttersprachler, der das Wort sonst falsch benutzen könnte;

(b) zur Unterscheidung der unzählbaren und zählbaren Bedeutungen in der Ausgangssprache.

Mit *no art* bezeichnete Substantive stehen im Allgemeinen weder mit dem unbestimmten noch mit dem bestimmten Artikel, außer wenn ein Relativsatz von ihnen abhängig ist.

Unregelmäßige Pluralformen englischer Substantive sind angegeben.

Die meisten englischen Substantive bilden den Plural durch Anhängen von *-s*.

Substantive, die auf *-s, -z, -x, -sh, -ch* enden, erhalten die Endung *-es*.

Substantive, die auf Konsonant + *-y* enden, verwandeln im Plural das auslautende *-y* in *-ie*, auf das die Pluralendung *-s* folgt. Ausnahmen bilden Eigennamen.

Bei allen deutschen Substantiv-Stichwörtern sind **Genitivendung und Plural** angegeben, bei zusammengesetzen Substantiven jedoch nur dann, wenn das letzte Element der Zusammensetzung nicht als eigenes Stichwort vorkommt.

5. Präpositionen

Bei Verben, Substantiven und Adjektiven, die mit bestimmten Präpositionen verbunden werden, ist die zugehörige Präposition und ihre Übersetzung in Klammern angegeben.

research [rɪˈsɜːtʃ] N Forschung *f* (*into, on* über *+acc*)

6. Adjectives and adverbs

English adverbs have been accorded the status of headwords in their own right.

German adverbs have been treated as separate grammatical entries distinct from adjective entries whenever their use is purely adverbial (e.g. **höchst, wohl, sehr**) or when the adverbial use is also common.

7. Phrasal verbs

Phrasal verbs are covered in separate entries marked ◆ following the main headword.

Verb + adverb and verb + preposition combinations have been treated as phrasal verbs:
- (a) where either the meaning or the translation is not simply derivable from the individual constituents;
- (b) for clarity in the case of the longer verb entries.

Where a combination consists simply of a verb plus an adverb or preposition of direction it will frequently be covered under the main headword.

6. Adjektive und Adverbien

Englische Adverbien sind als selbstständige Stichwörter aufgeführt.

Deutsche Adverbien sind immer dann als selbstständige grammatische Einträge von Adjektiven unterschieden worden, wenn es sich um echte Adverbien handelt (z. B. **höchst, wohl, sehr**) oder wenn ein adverbialer Gebrauch wahrscheinlich ist.

7. Phrasal verbs

Phrasal verbs (feste Verb-Partikel-Verbindungen) sind in eigenen Einträgen abgehandelt. Sie sind durch ◆ gekennzeichnet und folgen dem Stichworteintrag für das Verb.

Die Zusammensetzungen Verb + Adverb und Verb + Präposition werden als *phrasal verbs* abgehandelt:
- (a) wo entweder die Bedeutung oder die Übersetzung sich nicht aus den Einzelbestandteilen ergibt;
- (b) aus Gründen der Übersichtlichkeit bei längeren Verbeinträgen.

Bei einfachen Kombinationen von Verb + Adverb oder Präposition der Richtung ist unter dem Haupteintrag zu suchen.

> **dash** [dæʃ] VI sausen (*inf*); **to ~ into/across a room** in ein Zimmer/quer durch ein Zimmer stürzen *or* stürmen; **to ~ away/back/up** fort-/zurück-/hinaufstürzen

Irregular preterites and past participles are only given in phrasal verb entries in the rare cases where they differ from those given in the main entry.

Phrasal verbs are treated in four grammatical categories:

Unregelmäßige Formen des Präteritums und des 2. Partizips werden in Einträgen, die *phrasal verbs* behandeln, nur in den seltenen Fällen angegeben, wo sie von den im Haupteintrag angegebenen abweichen.

Phrasal verbs werden unter vier grammatischen Kategorien abgehandelt:

i *vi (intransitive verb)*

i *vi (intransitives Verb)*

> ➤ **grow apart** VI (*fig*) sich auseinander entwickeln

ii *vi +prep obj*
This indicates that the verbal element is intransitive but that the particle requires an object.

ii *vi +prep obj*
Hiermit soll gezeigt werden, dass das Verbelement intransitiv ist, dass aber die Partikel ein Objekt erfordert.

> **deal in** VI +PREP OBJ (*Comm*) *goods* handeln mit

iii *vt (transitive verb)*
This indicates that the verbal element is transitive. In most cases the object can be placed either before or after the particle; these cases are marked *sep*.

iii *vt (transitives Verb)*
Dies gibt an, dass das Verbelement transitiv ist. In den meisten Fällen kann das Objekt vor oder hinter der Partikel stehen; diese Fälle sind mit *sep* bezeichnet.

> **kill off** VT SEP **(a)** vernichten, töten; *whole race* ausrotten; *cows, pigs, elephants* abschlachten; *weeds* vertilgen; *character in TV series* sterben lassen **(b)** (*fig*) *hopes* zerstören; *speculation* ein Ende machen (+*dat*)

In some cases the object must precede the particle; these cases are marked *always separate*.

In einigen Fällen muss das Objekt der Partikel vorangehen; solche Fälle sind durch *always separate* bezeichnet.

> **get over with** VT ALWAYS SEPARATE hinter sich (*acc*) bringen; **let's get it over with** bringen wirs hinter uns

Occasionally the object must come after the particle, these cases are marked *insep*.

Gelegentlich muss das Objekt der Partikel nachgestellt werden; solche Fälle sind durch *insep* bezeichnet.

> **give off** VT INSEP *heat, gas* abgeben; *smell* verbreiten

iv *vt +prep obj*
This indicates that both the verbal element and the particle require an object.

iv *vt +prep obj*
Hiermit wird gezeigt, dass sowohl das Verbelement als auch die Partikel ein Objekt verlangen.

> **take upon** VT +PREP OBJ **he took that job upon himself** er hat das völlig ungebeten getan; **he took it upon himself to answer for me** er meinte, er müsse für mich antworten

In cases where a prepositional object is optional its translation is covered under *vi* or *vt*.

In Fällen, wo ein Präpositionalobjekt möglich, aber nicht nötig ist, findet man die entsprechende Übersetzung unter *vi* oder *vt*.

> **go by** VI (*person, opportunity*) vorbeigehen (*prep obj* an +*dat*); (*procession*) vorbeiziehen (*prep obj* an +*dat*); (*vehicle*) vorbeifahren (*prep obj* an +*dat*); (*time*) vergehen; **as time went by** mit der Zeit; **in days gone by** in längst vergangenen Tagen

8. Cross-references

8. Querverweise

Cross-references are used in the following instances:

Querverweise sind gelegentlich verwendet worden:

to refer the user to the spelling variant treated in depth;

um den Benutzer auf diejenige Schreibweise zu verweisen, wo die ausführliche Darstellung des Stichworts zu finden ist;

to refer the user to the headword where a particular construction or idiom has been treated;

to draw the user's attention to the full treatment of such words as numerals, languages, days of the week and months of the year under certain key words.

9. Punctuation and Symbols

, between translations indicates that the translations are interchangeable; between alternative phrases to be translated indicates that the phrases have the same meaning.

; between translations indicates a difference in meaning which is clarified by explanatory material unless:

(a) the distinction has already been made within the same entry;

(b) in the case of some compounds the distinction is made under the simple form;

(c) the distinction is self-evident.

/ between translations indicates parallel structure but different meanings, e.g. **to feel good/bad**.

(a) in a source language phrase it will normally be paralleled in the translation; where this is not the case, the translation covers both meanings

(b) in a target language phrase where it is not paralleled by an oblique in the source language the distinction will either be made clear earlier in the entry or will be self-evident

(c) in compounds it may be used to reflect a distinction made under the simple form.

um den Benutzer auf das Stichwort zu verweisen, wo eine bestimmte Konstruktion oder Wendung abgehandelt wird;

um die Aufmerksamkeit des Benutzers auf die ausführliche Behandlung solcher Wortklassen wie Zahlwörter, Sprachbezeichnungen, Wochentage und Monate unter bestimmten Schlüsselwörtern zu lenken.

9. Satzzeichen und Symbole

, zwischen Übersetzungen zeigt an, dass die Übersetzungen gleichwertig sind; zwischen Wendungen in der Ausgangssprache zeigt an, dass die Wendungen die gleiche Bedeutung haben.

; zwischen Übersetzungen zeigt einen Bedeutungsunterschied an, der durch erklärende Zusätze erläutert ist, außer:

(a) wenn die Unterscheidung innerhalb desselben Eintrags schon gemacht worden ist;

(b) bei Komposita, wo die Unterscheidung schon unter dem Simplex getroffen wurde

(c) wenn die Unterscheidung offensichtlich ist.

/ zwischen Übersetzungen zeigt an, dass es sich um analoge Strukturen aber verschiedene Übersetzungen handelt, z. B. **to feel good/bad.**

(a) der Schrägstrich in einer ausgangssprachlichen Wendung wird im Allgemeinen seine Entsprechung in der Übersetzung finden; wo das nicht der Fall ist, gilt die Übersetzung für beide Bedeutungen;

(b) hat ein Schrägstrich in der Zielsprache kein Äquivalent in der Ausgangssprache, geht die getroffene Unterscheidung entweder aus in dem Eintrag bereits Gesagtem hervor oder sie ist offensichtlich;

(c) bei Zusammensetzungen kann der Schrägstrich verwendet werden, um an eine für das Simplex getroffene Unterscheidung anzuknüpfen.

is used within an entry to represent the headword whenever it occurs in an unchanged form even if it consists of two or more words.	~	wird innerhalb von Einträgen verwendet, um das unveränderte Stichwort zu ersetzen, auch wenn dieses aus zwei oder mehr Wörtern besteht.
Phrasal verbs are not replaced with a swung dash (~).		*Phrasal verbs* werden nicht mit einer Tilde ersetzt.
separates two speakers.	—	unterscheidet zwischen zwei Sprechern.
indicates that the translation is approximate or the cultural equivalent of the term and may not have exactly the same sense; in the case of institutions, they are those of the country indicated and obviously not the same.	≈	weist darauf hin, dass die Übersetzung eine Entsprechung ist oder aufgrund kultureller Unterschiede nicht genau die gleiche Bedeutung hat. Bei Institutionen werden die des jeweiligen Landes angegeben, die natürlich nicht identisch sind.
is used to separate parts of a word or phrase which are semantically interchangeable.	*or*	wird verwendet, um Bestandteile einer Wendung zu unterscheiden, die semantisch austauschbar sind.
used after indicating material denotes that the translation(s) following it can be used in addition to the first translation(s) given in the respective entry, category or phrase.	*also*	nach erklärenden Zusätzen gibt an, dass die folgende(n) Übersetzung(en) zusätzlich zu der ersten Übersetzung oder Folge von austauschbaren Übersetzungen, die in dem Eintrag oder der Kategorie angegeben sind, benutzt werden kann/können.
in a phrase or translation indicate that the word is stressed.	CAPITALS GROSS-BUCHSTABEN	in Wendungen und Übersetzungen geben an, dass das Wort betont ist.

Zeichen der Lautschrift

Phonetic Symbols

Die Lautschrift wird für alle Hauptstichwörter im englisch-deutschen Teil angegeben, außer dann, wenn Wörter in Schreibweise und Aussprache genau übereinstimmen.

Phonetic transcriptions in square brackets are given for all headwords in the English-German section, apart from compounds and from words spelt the same way and with the same pronunciation.

Vokale/Vowels

matt	[a]	
Fahne	[aː]	
Vater	[ɐ]	
	[ɑː]	calm, part
	[æ]	sat
Chanson	[ã]	
Chance	[ɑ̃]	
	[ɑ̃ː]	double entendre
Etage	[e]	egg
Seele, Mehl	[eː]	
Wäsche, Bett	[ɛ]	
zählen	[ɛː]	
Teint	[ɛ̃ː]	
mache	[ə]	above
	[ɜː]	burn, earn
Kiste	[ɪ]	pit, awfully
Vitamin	[i]	
Ziel	[iː]	peat
Oase	[o]	
oben	[oː]	
Fondue	[õ]	
Chanson	[õː]	
Most	[ɔ]	
	[ɒ]	cot
	[ɔː]	born, jaw
ökonomisch	[ø]	
blöd	[øː]	
Götter	[œ]	
Parfum	[œ̃ː]	
	[ʌ]	hut
zuletzt	[u]	
Mut	[uː]	pool
Mutter	[ʊ]	put
Typ	[y]	
Kübel	[yː]	
Sünde	[ʏ]	

Konsonanten/Consonants

Ball	[b]	ball
mich	[ç]	
	[tʃ]	child
fern	[f]	field
gern	[g]	good
Hand	[h]	hand
ja, Million	[j]	yet, million
	[dʒ]	just
Kind	[k]	kind, catch
links, Pult	[l]	left, little
matt	[m]	mat
Nest	[n]	nest
lang	[ŋ]	long
Paar	[p]	put
rennen	[r]	run
fast, fassen	[s]	sit
Chef, Stein, Schlag	[ʃ]	shall
Tafel	[t]	tab
	[θ]	thing
	[ð]	this
wer	[v]	very
	[w]	wet
Loch	[x]	loch
fix	[ks]	box
singen	[z]	pods, zip
Zahn	[ts]	
genieren	[ʒ]	measure

Andere Zeichen/Other signs

|	glottal stop/Knacklaut
[r]	[r] pronounced before a vowel/vor Vokal ausgesprochenes [r]
[']	main stress/Hauptton
[ˌ]	secondary stress/Nebenton

Diphthonge/Diphthongs

weit	[ai]	
	[aɪ]	buy, die, my
Haus	[au]	
	[aʊ]	house, now
	[eɪ]	pay, mate
	[ɛə]	pair, mare
	[əʊ]	no, boat
	[ɪə]	mere, shear
Heu, Häuser	[ɔy]	
	[ɔɪ]	boy, coin
	[ʊə]	tour, poor

NB: Vokale und Konsonanten, die häufig elidiert (nicht ausgesprochen) werden, sind *kursiv* dargestellt:

Vowels and consonants which are frequently elided (not spoken) are given in *italics:*

convention [kən'venʃən]
attempt [ə'tempt]

Abkürzungen   Abbreviations

Abkürzung	*abbr*	abbreviation
Akkusativ	*acc*	accusative
Adjektiv	*adj*	adjective
Verwaltung	*Admin*	administration
Adverb	*adv*	adverb
Landwirtschaft	*Agr*	agriculture
Anatomie	*Anat*	anatomy
Archäologie	*Archeol*	arch(a)eology
Architektur	*Archit*	architecture
Artikel	*art*	article
Kunst	*Art*	art
Astrologie	*Astrol*	astrology
Astronomie	*Astron*	astronomy
attributiv	*attr*	attributive
österreichisch	*Aus*	Austrian
australisch	*Austral*	Australian
Kraftfahrzeugwesen	*Aut*	automobiles
Hilfsverb	*aux*	auxiliary
Luftfahrt	*Aviat*	aviation
Kindersprache	*baby-talk*	
biblisch	*Bibl*	biblical
Biologie	*Biol*	biology
Botanik	*Bot*	botany
britisch	*Brit*	British
Hoch- und Tiefbau	*Build*	building
Kartenspiel	*Cards*	
Chemie	*Chem*	chemistry
Schach	*Chess*	
Handel	*Comm*	commerce
Komparativ	*comp*	comparative
Computer	*Comput*	computers
Konjunktion	*conj*	conjunction
Zusammenziehung	*contr*	contraction
Kochen	*Cook*	cooking
Kompositum	*cpd*	compound
Dativ	*dat*	dative
altmodisch	*dated*	
Deutsche Demokratische Republik (1949–90)	*DDR*	German Democratic Republic (1949–90)
dekliniert	*decl*	declined
bestimmt	*def*	definite
demonstrativ	*dem*	demonstrative
Dialekt	*dial*	dialect
Verkleinerung	*dim*	diminutive
Akkusativobjekt	*dir obj*	direct object
kirchlich	*Eccl*	ecclesiastical
Volkswirtschaft	*Econ*	economics
ostdeutsch	*E Ger*	East German
Elektrizität	*Elec*	electricity
betont	*emph*	emphatic
besonders	*esp*	especially
etwas	*etw*	something
Euphemismus	*euph*	euphemism
Femininum	*f*	feminine
Mode	*Fashion*	
übertragen	*fig*	figurative
Finanzen	*Fin*	finance
Fischerei	*Fishing*	
Forstwesen	*Forest*	forestry
förmlich	*form*	formal
Fußball	*Ftbl*	football
gehoben	*geh*	elevated
Genitiv	*gen*	genitive
Geographie	*Geog*	geography
Geologie	*Geol*	geology
Deutschland	*Ger*	Germany
Grammatik	*Gram*	grammar

Abkürzungen

Abbreviations

Heraldik	*Her*	heraldry
Geschichte	*Hist*	history
Gartenbau	*Hort*	horticulture
scherzhaft	*hum*	humorous
Jagd	*Hunt*	hunting
Imperativ	*imper*	imperative
unpersönlich	*impers*	impersonal
Industrie	*Ind*	industry
unbestimmt	*indef*	indefinite
Dativobjekt	*indir obj*	indirect object
umgangssprachlich	*inf*	informal
Infinitiv	*infin*	infinitive
untrennbar	*insep*	inseparable
Versicherungswesen	*Insur*	insurance
Interjektion	*interj*	interjection
interrogativ	*interrog*	interrogative
unveränderlich	*inv*	invariable
irisch	*Ir*	Irish
ironisch	*iro*	ironical
unregelmäßig	*irreg*	irregular
jemand, jemandes,	*jd, jds*	somebody,
jemandem, jemanden	*jdm, jdn*	somebody's
Rechtswesen	*Jur*	law
Sprachwissenschaft	*Ling*	linguistics
wörtlich	*lit*	literal
literarisch	*liter*	literary
Literatur	*Liter*	literature
Maskulinum	*m*	masculine
Mathematik	*Math*	mathematics
Maß	*Measure*	
Mechanik	*Mech*	mechanics
Medizin	*Med*	medicine
Meteorologie	*Met*	meteorology
Metallurgie	*Metal*	metallurgy
militärisch	*Mil*	military
Bergbau	*Min*	mining
Mineralogie	*Miner*	mineralogy
Straßenverkehr	*Mot*	motoring and transport
Musik	*Mus*	music
Mythologie	*Myth*	mythology
Substantiv	*n*	noun
nautisch	*Naut*	nautical
verneint	*neg*	negative
nordenglisch	*N Engl*	Northern English
norddeutsch	*N Ger*	North German
Nationalsozialismus	*NS*	Nazism
Neutrum	*nt*	neuter
Zahlwort	*num*	numeral
Objekt	*obj*	object
obsolet	*obs*	obsolete
veraltet	*old*	
Optik	*Opt*	optics
Vogelkunde	*Orn*	ornithology
Parlament	*Parl*	parliament
Passiv	*pass*	passive
pejorativ	*pej*	pejorative
persönlich/Person	*pers*	personal/person
Pharmazie	*Pharm*	pharmacy
Philosophie	*Philos*	philosophy
Phonetik	*Phon*	phonetics
Fotografie	*Phot*	photography
Physik	*Phys*	physics
Physiologie	*Physiol*	physiology
Plural	*pl*	plural
poetisch	*poet*	poetic
Dichtung	*Poet*	poetry
Politik	*Pol*	politics

Abkürzungen   Abbreviations

Possessiv-	*poss*	possessive
prädikativ	*pred*	predicative
Vorsilbe	*pref*	prefix
Präposition	*prep*	preposition
Präsens	*pres*	present
Presse	*Press*	
Präteritum, Imperfekt	*pret*	preterite, imperfect
Pronomen	*pron*	pronoun
sprichwörtlich	*prov*	proverbial
Sprichwort	*Prov*	proverb
Partizip Präsens	*prp*	present participle
Psychologie	*Psych*	psychology
Partizip Perfekt	*ptp*	past participle
Warenzeichen	®	trademark
Rundfunk	*Rad*	radio
Eisenbahn	*Rail*	railways
selten	*rare*	
regelmäßig	*reg*	regular
Relativ-	*rel*	relative
Religion	*Rel*	religion
jemand(em, -en)	*sb*	somebody
Schulwesen	*Sch*	school
Naturwissenschaften	*Sci*	science
schottisch	*Scot*	Scottish
Bildhauerei	*Sculpt*	sculpture
trennbar, veränderbare Folge	*sep*	separable
Handarbeiten	*Sew*	sewing
süddeutsch	*S Ger*	South German
Singular	*sing*	singular
Skisport	*Ski*	skiing
Slang, Jargon	*sl*	slang
Sozialwissenschaften	*Sociol*	social sciences
Raumfahrt	*Space*	space flight
Fachausdruck	*spec*	specialist term
Börse	*St Ex*	Stock Exchange
etwas	*sth*	something
Konjunktiv	*subjunc*	subjunctive
Nachsilbe	*suf*	suffix
Superlativ	*superl*	superlative
Landvermessung	*Surv*	surveying
schweizerisch	*Sw*	Swiss
Technik	*Tech*	technology
Nachrichtentechnik	*Telec*	telecommunications
Textilien	*Tex*	textiles
Theater	*Theat*	theatre
Fernsehen	*TV*	television
Typographie, Buchdruck	*Typ*	typography and printing
Hochschule	*Univ*	university
(nord)amerikanisch	*US*	(North) American
gewöhnlich	*usu*	usually
Verb	*vb*	verb
Tiermedizin	*Vet*	veterinary medicine
intransitives Verb	*vi*	intransitive verb
reflexives Verb	*vr*	reflexive verb
transitives Verb	*vt*	transitive verb
vulgär	*vulg*	vulgar
westdeutsch	*W Ger*	West German
Zoologie	*Zool*	zoology

A, a [aː] NT **-, -** or (inf) **-s, -s** A, a; **das A und (das) O** (fig) the be-all and end-all; (eines Wissensgebietes) the basics pl; **von A bis Z** (fig inf) from A to Z; **wer A sagt, muss auch B sagen** (prov) in for a penny, in for a pound (esp Brit prov); (moralisch) if you start something, you should see it through

à [a] PREP (esp Comm) at

Aa [ˈaːla] NT **-**, NO PL (baby-talk) **Aa machen** to do a number two (baby-talk)

AA [aːˈlaː] M **-s, -s** ABBR von **Anonyme Alkoholiker** AA

Aal [aːl] M **-(e)s, -e** eel

aalglatt (pej) **1** ADJ slippery (as an eel), slick **2** ADV slickly; **sich ~ herauswinden** to worm one's way out of it

a. a. O. ABBR von **am angegebenen** or **angeführten Ort** loc. cit.

Aargau [ˈaːrgau] M **-s der ~** Aargau

Aas [aːs] NT **-es, -e** [-zə] **(a)** (= Tierleiche) carrion, rotting carcass **(b)** pl **Äser** [ˈɛːzə] (inf: = Luder) bugger (Brit inf), jerk (sl); **kein ~** not a single soul

aasen [ˈaːzn] VI (inf) to be wasteful; **mit etw ~** to waste sth

Aas-: Aasfresser M scavenger, carrion eater; **Aasgeier** M (lit, fig) vulture

ab [ap] **1** ADV off, away; (Theat) exit sing, exeunt pl; **die nächste Straße rechts ab** the next street on the right; **ab Zoologischer Garten** from Zoological Gardens; **ab Hamburg** after Hamburg; **München ab 12.20 Uhr** (Rail) leaving Munich 12.20; **ab wann?** from when?; **as of when?**; **ab nach Hause** go home; **Mütze/Helm ab!** caps/hats off; **ab durch die Mitte** (inf) beat it! (inf); **ab und zu** or (N Ger) **an** now and again, now and then

2 PREP +DAT **(a)** (räumlich) from; (zeitlich) from, as of, as from; **Kinder ab 14 Jahren** children from (the age of) 14 up; **ab Werk** (Comm) ex works; **ab sofort** as of now **(b)** (Sw: in Zeitangaben) past; **Viertel ab 7** a quarter past or after (US) 7

abändern VT SEP to alter (in +acc to); Gesetzentwurf to amend (in +acc to); Strafe, Urteil to revise (in +acc to)

abarbeiten SEP **1** VT **(a)** Schuld to work off; Vertragszeit to work **(b)** (Comput) Programm to run; Befehl to execute **2** VR to slave (away); siehe auch **abgearbeitet**

Abart F variety (auch Biol)

abartig **1** ADJ abnormal, unnatural; (= widersinnig) perverse **2** ADV (inf: = widerlich) abnormally; **das tut ~ weh** that hurts like hell (inf); **mir ist ~ schlecht** I feel terribly sick

Abbau M, NO PL **(a)** (= Förderung) (über Tage) quarrying; (unter Tage) mining **(b)** (lit, fig: = Demontage) dismantling **(c)** (Chem) decomposition; (im Körper) breakdown **(d)** (= Verringerung) (von Personal, Produktion, Privilegien) reduction (+gen of), cutback (+gen in); (von Vorurteilen) breaking down (+gen of)

abbaubar ADJ (Chem) degradable; **schwer ~e Chemikalien** chemicals that are difficult to break down; **biologisch ~** biodegradable

abbauen SEP **1** VT **(a)** (= fördern) (über Tage) to quarry; (unter Tage) to mine **(b)** (= demontieren) to dismantle; Kulissen, Zelt to take down; Lager to strike **(c)** (Chem) to break down **(d)** (= verringern) Produktion, Personal, Bürokratie, Privilegien to cut back; Arbeitsplätze, Arbeitskräfte to reduce the number of **2** VI (Sportler etc) to go downhill; (Patient) to deteriorate

abbeißen VT SEP IRREG to bite off; **sich (dat) die Zunge ~** to bite one's tongue off

abbekommen ptp **abbekommen** VT SEP IRREG (= erhalten) to get; **etwas ~** to get some (of it); (= beschädigt werden) to get damaged; (= verletzt werden) to get hurt; (= Prügel ~) to catch or cop it (Brit inf); **to get yours** (US inf); **das Auto/er hat dabei ganz schön was ~** (inf) the car/he really copped it (Brit inf) or got it (inf); **nichts ~** not to get any (of it); (= nicht beschädigt werden) not to get damaged; (= nicht verletzt werden) to come off unscathed; **sein(en) Teil ~** (lit, fig) to get one's fair share

abberufen ptp **abberufen** VT SEP IRREG to recall

abbestellen ptp **abbestellt** VT SEP to cancel; Telefon to have disconnected

abbezahlen ptp **abbezahlt** VT SEP to pay off

abbiegen SEP IRREG **1** VT **(a)** Ellbogen, Knie to bend; (= abbrechen) to bend off **(b)** (inf: = verhindern) Thema, Verfahren to head off; Frage to deflect; **das Gespräch ~** to change the subject; **zum Glück konnte ich das ~** luckily I managed to stop that **2** VI AUX SEIN to turn off (in +acc into); (Straße) to veer

Abbiegespur F (Mot) filter (Brit) or turning (US) lane

Abbild NT (= Nachahmung, Kopie) copy; (= Spiegelbild) reflection; (= Wiedergabe) picture

abbilden VT SEP (lit, fig) to depict, to portray; (= wiedergeben) to reproduce; **auf der Titelseite ist ein Teddybär abgebildet** there's a picture of a teddy bear on the front page

Abbildung F (= das Abbilden) depiction, portrayal; (= Wiedergabe) reproduction; (= Illustration) illustration; (= Schaubild) diagram

abbinden SEP IRREG **1** VT **(a)** (= abmachen) to undo, to untie; **sich (dat) die Schürze ~** to take off one's apron **(b)** (Med) Arm, Bein etc to ligature **2** VI (Beton, Mörtel) to set

Abbitte F apology; **(bei jdm wegen etw) ~ tun** or **leisten** to make or offer one's apologies (to sb for sth)

abblasen VT SEP IRREG (inf: = absagen) to call off

abblättern VI SEP AUX SEIN to flake (off)

abblenden SEP **1** VT (Aut) to dip (Brit), to dim (esp US) **2** VI (Aut) to dip (Brit) or dim (esp US) one's headlights; **es wurde abgeblendet** (Film) the scene (was) faded out

Abblendlicht NT (Aut) dipped (Brit) or dimmed (esp US) headlights pl; **mit ~ fahren** to drive on dipped (Brit) or dimmed (esp US) headlights

abblitzen VI SEP AUX SEIN (inf) to be sent packing (bei by) (inf); **jdn ~ lassen** to send sb packing (inf)

abbrausen SEP **1** VT to give a shower; Körperteil to wash under the shower; **sich ~** to have or take a shower **2** VI AUX SEIN (inf) to roar off or away

abbrechen SEP IRREG **1** VT to break off; Bleistift to break, to snap; Zelt to take down; Lager to strike; (= niederreißen) to demolish; Raumflug, Rennstart, Experiment to abort; (Comput) Operation to abort; Veranstaltung, Verfahren, Verhandlung, Therapie to stop; Streik, Suche, Mission to call off; **Schwangerschaft** to terminate; **die diplomatischen Beziehungen ~** to break off diplomatic relations; **die Schule ~** to stop going to school; **etw von etw ~** to break sth off sth; **(nun) brich dir (mal) keinen ab!** (inf) don't make such a palaver (inf); **sich (dat) einen ~** (inf) (= Umstände machen) to make a fuss about it; (= sich sehr anstrengen) to go to a lot of bother; siehe auch **abgebrochen** **2** VI **(a)** AUX SEIN to break; (Eisscholle) to break off **(b)** (Kontakt) to break off; (Student) to break off one's studies; (Comput) to abort; **mitten im Satz ~** to break off in the middle of a sentence; **wir müssen jetzt leider ~** we have to stop now **(c)** (= abtreiben) to abort

Abbrecher(in) M(F) (= Student) dropout

abbrennen VTI SEP IRREG (VI: AUX SEIN) to burn down; Feuerwerk, Rakete to let off; Kerze etc to burn; **ein Feuerwerk ~** to have a firework display; **unser Gehöft ist abgebrannt** our farm was burned down; **wir sind abgebrannt** our house/farm etc was burned down; siehe auch **abgebrannt**

abbringen VT SEP IRREG **jdn davon ~, etw zu tun** to stop sb (from) doing sth; **jdn von etw ~** to make sb change his/her mind about sth; **sich von etw ~ lassen** to be dissuaded from sth; **ich lasse mich von meiner Meinung nicht ~** nothing will make me change my mind; **jdn vom Thema ~** to get sb off the subject; **vom Kurs ~** to throw or put off course

abbröckeln VI SEP AUX SEIN to crumble away; (fig) to fall off (auch St Ex)

Abbruch M **(a)** NO PL (= das Niederreißen) demolition; (von Schwangerschaft) termination; (von Beziehungen, Verhandlungen, Reise) breaking off; (von Raumflug etc) abortion, aborting; (von Veranstaltung) stopping; **warmer ~** (inf: = Brandstiftung) torch job (inf); **einem Land mit ~ der diplomatischen Beziehungen drohen** to threaten to break off diplomatic relations with a country; **einer Sache (dat) ~ tun** (= schaden) to do (some) harm or damage to sth; **das tut der**

Liebe keinen ~ it doesn't harm or hurt their/our relationship **(b)** (= *Schwangerschaftsabbruch*) termination

Abbruch-: Abbrucharbeiten PL demolition work; **Abbruchbirne** F wrecking ball; **Abbruchfirma** F demolition firm; **abbruchreif** ADJ only fit for demolition; (= *zum Abbruch freigegeben*) condemned

abbrühen VT SEP to scald; *Mandeln* to blanch; *siehe auch* **abgebrüht**

abbuchen VT SEP to debit (*von* to, against); (*durch Dauerauftrag*) to pay by standing order (*von* from); (*fig*: = *abschreiben*) to write off

Abbuchung F debit; (*durch Dauerauftrag*) (payment by) standing order; (*durch Einzugsermächtigung*) (payment by) direct debit

Abbuchungsauftrag M direct debit; **jdm einen ~ erteilen** to instruct sb to pay by direct debit

abbügeln VT SEP (*inf*: = *heruntermachen*) to pooh-pooh (*inf*)

abbummeln VT SEP (*inf*) *Stunden* to take off; **Überstunden ~** to take time off for overtime worked

abbürsten VT SEP to brush; *Staub* to brush off (*von etw* sth)

abbüßen VT SEP *Strafe* to serve

Abc [abeːtseː, aːbeːˈtseː] NT **-, -** (*lit, fig*) ABC; **Wörter/Namen nach dem ~ ordnen** to arrange words/names in alphabetical order

ABC- IN CPDS (*Mil*) atomic, biological and chemical, Abc

abdanken VI SEP to resign; (*König etc*) to abdicate

Abdankung F **-, -en (a)** (= *Thronverzicht*) abdication; (= *Rücktritt*) resignation **(b)** (*Sw.* = *Trauerfeier*) funeral service

abdecken VT SEP to cover; *Dach* to take off; *Haus* to take the roof off; *Tisch* to clear

abdichten VT SEP (= *isolieren*) to insulate; *Loch, Leck, Rohr* to seal (up); *Ritzen* to fill; **gegen Luft/Wasser ~** to make airtight/watertight; **gegen Feuchtigkeit ~** to damp-proof

Abdichtung F (= *Isolierung*) insulation; (= *Verschluss, Dichtung*) seal; (= *das Verschließen*) sealing; (*von Ritzen*) filling; **~ gegen Feuchtigkeit** damp-proofing; **~ gegen Wasser** waterproofing

abdrängen VT SEP to push away (*von* from); *Menschenmenge* to force back; (*fig*) *Verfolger etc* to shake off; **ein Auto von der Straße ~** to force a car off the road; **jdn in eine bestimmte Richtung ~** to push sb in a certain direction; **einen Spieler vom Ball ~** to push or barge a player off the ball; **vom Wind abgedrängt werden** to be blown off course (by the wind); **jdn an den Rand der Gesellschaft ~** to marginalize sb to the fringes of society

abdrehen SEP **1** VT **(a)** *Gas, Wasser, Hahn* to turn off **(b)** *Film* to shoot, to film **2** VI AUX SEIN or HABEN (= *Richtung ändern*) to change course; **nach Osten ~** to turn east

abdriften VI SEP AUX SEIN (*Naut, Aviat, fig*) to drift off

Abdruck[1] M, *pl* **-drücke** imprint, impression; (= *Stempelabdruck*) stamp; (= *Fingerabdruck, Fußabdruck*) print; (= *Gebissabdruck*) mould (*Brit*), mold (*US*), impression; **einen ~ abnehmen** or **machen** (*inf*) to take or make an impression

Abdruck[2] M, *pl* **-drucke** (= *das Nachdrucken*) reprinting; (= *Nachdruck*) reprint

abdrucken VT SEP to print; **wieder ~** to reprint

abdrücken SEP **1** VT **(a)** *Gewehr* to fire **(b)** (*inf*) *jdn* to squeeze, to hug **(c)** *Vene* to constrict; **jdm die Luft ~** (*lit, inf*) to squeeze all the breath out of sb **2** VI to pull or squeeze the trigger **3** VR to leave an imprint or impression; **sich (durch etw) ~** to show through (sth)

abdunkeln VT SEP *Lampe* to dim; *Zimmer, Farbe* to darken

abduschen VT SEP to give a shower; *Körperteil* to wash under the shower; **sich ~** to have or take a shower

abebben ['aplɛbn] VI SEP AUX SEIN to die or fade away

abend ['aːbnt] ADV *siehe* **Abend**

Abend ['aːbnt] M **-s, -e** [-də] evening; **am ~** in the evening; (= *jeden*) in the evening(s); **am ~ des 4. April** on the evening or night of April 4th; **heute/gestern/morgen/Mittwoch ~** this/yesterday/tomorrow/Wednesday evening, tonight/last night/tomorrow night/Wednesday night; **jeden ~** every evening or night; **gegen ~** toward(s) (the) evening; **am nächsten ~, den nächsten ~** the next evening; **am ~ vor der Schlacht** on the eve of the battle; **eines ~s** one evening; **es wird ~** evening is approaching; **es wurde ~**

evening came; **guten ~** good evening; **zu ~ essen** to have supper or dinner; **je später der ~, desto schöner** or **netter die Gäste** (*prov*) the best guests always come late; **es ist noch nicht aller Tage ~** it's early days still or yet; **man soll den Tag nicht vor dem ~ loben** (*Prov*) don't count your chickens before they're hatched (*Prov*)

Abend- IN CPDS evening; **Abendanzug** M dinner jacket or suit, tuxedo (*US*); **Abendblatt** NT evening (news)paper; **Abendbrot** NT supper, tea (*Scot, N Engl*); **~ essen** to have supper or tea; **Abenddämmerung** F dusk, twilight

abendelang ADJ ATTR, ADV night after night

Abend-: Abendessen NT supper, evening meal; **abendfüllend** ADJ taking up the whole evening; *Film, Stück* full-length; **~ sein** to take up the whole evening; **Abendgesellschaft** F soirée; **Abendkasse** F (*Theat*) box office; **Abendkleid** NT evening dress or gown; **Abendland** NT, NO PL (*geh*) West; **das christliche ~** the Christian West; **abendländisch** ['aːbntlɛndɪʃ] (*geh*) **1** ADJ western, occidental (*liter*) **2** ADV in a western way or fashion

abendlich ['aːbntlɪç] **1** ADJ NO PRED evening *attr*; **die ~e Stille** the quiet or still of the evening; **die ~e Kühle** the cool of the evening **2** ADV **es war schon um drei Uhr ~ kühl** at three it was already as cool as (in the) evening

Abendmahl NT (*Eccl*) Communion, Lord's Supper; **das ~ nehmen** or **empfangen** to take or receive Communion; **zum ~ gehen** to go to (Holy) Communion; **das (Letzte) ~** the Last Supper

Abendmahlsgottesdienst M (Holy) Communion, Communion service

Abend-: Abendmahlzeit F evening meal; **Abendprogramm** NT (*Rad, TV*) evening('s) programmes *pl* (*Brit*) or programs *pl* (*US*); **Abendrot** NT, **Abendröte** F (*liter*) sunset

abends ['aːbnts] ADV in the evening; (= *jeden Abend*) in the evening(s); **spät ~** late in the evening

Abend-: Abendstille F still or quiet of the evening; **Abendstunde** F evening (hour); **zu dieser späten ~** at this late hour of the evening; **die frühen ~n** the early hours of the evening; **sich bis in die ~n hinziehen** to go on (late) into the evening; **Abendvorstellung** F evening performance; (*Film auch*) evening showing; **Abendzeitung** F evening paper

Abenteuer ['aːbntɔye] NT **-s, -** adventure; **ein militärisches/politisches/verbrecherisches ~** a military/political/criminal venture; **auf ~ aus sein** to be looking for adventure

Abenteuer- IN CPDS adventure; **Abenteuerferien** PL adventure holiday (*esp Brit*) or vacation (*US*)

Abenteurerin ['aːbntɔyerɪn] F **-, -nen** adventuress

abenteuerlich ['aːbntɔyelɪç] **1** ADJ adventurous; (= *erlebnishungrig*) adventuresome; (= *fantastisch*) bizarre; *Erzählung* fantastic; (*inf*) *Preis* outrageous; *Argument* ludicrous **2** ADV *klingen, sich anhören* bizarre; *gekleidet* bizarrely

Abenteuer-: Abenteuerlust F thirst for adventure; **Abenteuerspielplatz** M adventure playground; **Abenteuerurlaub** M adventure holiday (*esp Brit*) or vacation (*US*)

Abenteurer ['aːbntɔyre] M **-s, -** adventurer

aber ['aːbe] **1** CONJ but; **~ dennoch** or **trotzdem** but still; **schönes Wetter heute, was? – ja, ~ etwas kalt** nice weather, eh? – yes but it's a bit cold; **oder ~** or else; **~ ja!** oh, yes!; (= *sicher*) but of course; **~ selbstverständlich** or **gewiss (doch)!** but of course; **~ nein!** oh, no!; (= *selbstverständlich nicht*) of course not!; **~ Renate!** but Renate!; **~, ~!** now, now!; **das ist ~ schrecklich!** but that's awful!; **das mach ich ~ nicht!** I will NOT do that!; **dann ist er ~ wütend geworden** then he really got mad; **das ist ~ heiß/schön!** that's really hot/nice; **bist du ~ braun!** aren't you brown!; **das geht ~ zu weit!** that's just or really going too far!; **schreib das noch mal ab, ~ sauber!** write it out again, and do it neatly! **2** ADV **~ und ~mals** again and again, time and again; *siehe auch* **abertausend**

Aber ['aːbe] NT **-s, -** or (*inf*) **-s** but; **kein ~!** no buts (about it); **die Sache hat ein ~** there's just one problem or snag

Aberglaube(n) M superstition; (*fig auch*) myth

abergläubisch ['aːbeɡlɔybɪʃ] **1** ADJ superstitious **2** ADV **er fürchtet sich ~ vor ...** he has a superstitious fear of ...

aberkennen *ptp* **aberkannt** VT SEP or *(rare)* INSEP IRREG **jdm etw ~** to deprive or strip sb of sth; **jdm den Sieg ~** (*Sport*) to disallow sb's victory

abermals ['aːbɐmaːls] ADJ (*geh*) once again or more

abernten VTI SEP to harvest

abertausend ADJ thousands upon thousands of; **tausend und ~, Tausend und Abertausend** thousands and or upon thousands

Abessinien [abɛˈsiːniən] NT **-s** Abyssinia

Abessinier [abɛˈsiːniɐ] M **-s, -**, **Abessinierin** [-iərɪn] F **-, -nen** Abyssinian

abessinisch [abɛˈsiːnɪʃ] ADJ Abyssinian

Abf. ABBR *von* **Abfahrt** departure, dep.

abfackeln VT (= *verbrennen*) to burn off; *Dschungel, Wald* to burn; (= *in Brand stecken*) to torch

abfahren SEP IRREG AUX SEIN **1** VI **(a)** (*Bus, Zug, Auto, Reisende*) to leave; (*Ski:* = *zu Tal fahren*) to ski down; **der Zug fährt um 8 Uhr in** *or* **von Bremen ab** the train leaves Bremen at 8 o'clock; **der Zug ist abgefahren** (*lit*) the train has left or gone; (*fig*) we've/you've *etc* missed the boat; **wir müssen schon um 7 Uhr ~** we must set off or leave at 7 o'clock
(b) (*inf*) **auf jdn/etw ~** to be into sb/sth (*inf*); **sie fährt voll auf ihn ab** she's into him (*Brit*) or she's fallen for him in a big way (*inf*)
2 VT **(a)** AUX SEIN or HABEN *Strecke* (= *bereisen*) to cover, to do (*inf*); (= *überprüfen, ausprobieren*) to go over
(b) (= *abtrennen*) *Körperteil* to cut off, to sever
(c) (= *abnutzen*) *Schienen, Reifen* to wear out; (= *benutzen*) *Fahrkarte* to use; **abgefahrene Reifen/Schienen** worn tyres (*Brit*) or tires (*US*)/rails

Abfahrt F **(a)** (*von Zug, Bus etc*) departure; **bis zur ~ sind es noch fünf Minuten** there's still five minutes before the train/bus *etc* leaves or goes; **Vorsicht bei der ~ des Zuges!** stand clear, the train is about to leave! **(b)** (*Ski*) (= *Talfahrt*) descent; (= *Abfahrtsstrecke*) (ski) run **(c)** (*inf:* = *Autobahnabfahrt*) exit; **die ~ Gießen** the Gießen exit, the exit for Gießen

abfahrtbereit ADJ ready to leave

Abfahrtszeit F departure time

Abfall M **(a)** (= *Müll*) refuse; (= *Hausabfall*) rubbish (*Brit*), garbage (*US*), trash (*US*); (= *Straßenabfall*) litter; (= *Rückstand*) waste *no pl*; **in den ~ kommen** to be thrown away or out; **Fleisch-/Stoffabfälle** scraps of meat/material **(b)** NO PL (= *Rückgang*) drop (+*gen* in), falling off; (= *Verschlechterung*) deterioration

Abfall-: Abfallbeseitigung F refuse or garbage (*US*) or trash (*US*) disposal; **Abfalleimer** M rubbish bin (*Brit*), waste bin, garbage can (*US*), trash can (*US*)

abfallen VI SEP IRREG AUX SEIN **(a)** (= *herunterfallen*) to fall or drop off; (*Blätter, Blüten etc*) to fall; **von etw ~** to fall or drop off (from) sth
(b) (*Gelände*) to fall or drop away; (*Druck, Temperatur*) to fall, to drop; **der Weg talwärts verläuft sacht ~d** the path down to the valley slopes gently
(c) (*fig:* = *übrig bleiben*) to be left (over); **das, was in der Küche abfällt** the kitchen leftovers; **der Stoff, der beim Schneidern abfällt** the leftover scraps of material
(d) (= *schlechter werden*) to fall or drop off, to go downhill; (*Sport:* = *zurückbleiben*) to drop back; **gegen etw ~** to compare badly with sth
(e) (*fig:* = *sich lösen*) to melt away; **alle Unsicherheit/Furcht fiel von ihm ab** all his uncertainty/fear left him
(f) (*von einer Partei*) to break (*von* with); (*Fraktion*) to break away (*von* from); **vom Glauben ~** to break with the faith
(g) (*inf:* = *herausspringen*) **wie viel fällt bei dem Geschäft für mich ab?** how much do I get out of the deal?; **es fällt immer ziemlich viel Trinkgeld ab** you/they *etc* always get quite a lot of tips (out of it)

Abfall-: Abfallerzeugnis NT waste product; **Abfallhaufen** M rubbish or refuse dump, garbage dump (*US*)

abfällig **1** ADJ *Bemerkung, Kritik* disparaging, derisive; *Lächeln* derisive; *Urteil* adverse **2** ADV **über jdn ~ reden** or **sprechen** to be disparaging of or about sb; **über jdn/etw ~ urteilen** to be disparaging about sb/sth

Abfall-: Abfallprodukt NT waste product; (*von Forschung*) by-product, spin-off; **Abfallverwertung** F waste utilization

abfangen VT SEP IRREG *Flugzeug, Funkspruch, Brief, Ball* to intercept; *Menschen* to catch (*inf*); *Schlag* to block

Abfangjäger M (*Mil*) interceptor

abfärben VI SEP **(a)** (*Wäsche*) to run; **pass auf, die Wand färbt ab!** be careful, the paint rubs off the wall **(b)** (*fig*) **auf jdn ~** to rub off on sb

abfassen VT SEP (= *verfassen*) to write; *Erstentwurf* to draft

abfaulen VI SEP AUX SEIN to rot away or off

abfeiern VT SEP (*inf*) **Überstunden ~** to take time off in lieu (of overtime) (*Brit*), to use up overtime without pay(ment) (*US*)

abfertigen SEP VT **(a)** *Pakete, Waren* to prepare for dispatch; *Gepäck* to check (in); (= *be- und entladen*) *Flugzeug* to make ready for takeoff; *Schiff* to make ready to sail; **die Schauerleute fertigen keine Schiffe aus Chile mehr ab** the dockers won't handle any more ships from Chile
(b) (= *bedienen*) *Kunden, Antragsteller, Patienten* to attend to, to deal with; (*inf: Sport*) *Gegner* to deal with; **jdn kurz** or **schroff ~** (*inf*) to snub sb; **ich lasse mich doch nicht mit 10 Euro ~** I'm not going to be fobbed off (*esp Brit*) with 10 euros
(c) (= *kontrollieren*) *Waren, Reisende* to clear; **beim Zoll/an der Grenze abgefertigt werden** to be cleared by customs/at the border; **die Zöllner fertigten (die Reisenden) sehr zügig ab** the customs officers dealt with the travellers (*Brit*) or travelers (*US*) very quickly; **die Zollbeamten hatten den Zug fast abgefertigt, als …** the customs officials had almost finished checking the train when …

Abfertigung F **(a)** (*von Paketen, Waren*) getting ready for dispatch; (*von Gepäck*) checking; (*von Flugzeug*) getting ready for takeoff; (*von Schiff*) making ready to sail **(b)** (= *Bedienung*) (*von Kunden*) service; (*von Antragstellern*) dealing with **(c)** (*von Waren, Reisenden*) clearance; **die ~ an der Grenze** customs clearance

Abfertigungshalle F (*Aviat*) terminal building

Abfertigungsschalter M dispatch counter; (*von Zollamt*) customs clearance; (*im Flughafen*) check-in desk

abfeuern VT SEP to fire; (*Ftbl inf*) to let fire with

abfinden SEP IRREG **1** VT to pay off; (= *entschädigen*) to compensate; **er wurde von der Versicherung mit 20.000 Euro abgefunden** he was paid 20,000 euros (in) compensation by the insurance company **2** VR **sich mit jdm/etw ~** to come to terms with sb/sth; **er konnte sich nie damit ~, dass …** he could never accept the fact that …; **sich mit jdm/etw schwer ~** to find it hard to accept sb/sth

Abfindung ['apfɪndʊŋ] F **-, -en (a)** (*von Gläubigern*) paying off; (= *Entschädigung*) compensation **(b)** (= *Summe*) payment, (sum in) settlement; (= *Entschädigung*) compensation *no pl*, indemnity; (*bei Entlassung*) severance pay; (*wegen Rationalisierung*) redundancy payment (*Brit*), buyout (*US*)

abflauen ['apflauən] VI SEP AUX SEIN (*Wind*) to drop, to die down; (*fig*) (*Empörung, Erregung, Interesse*) to fade; (*Börsenkurse*) to fall, to drop; (*Geschäfte*) to fall or drop off

abfliegen SEP IRREG **1** VI AUX SEIN (*Aviat*) to take off (*nach* for); (*Zugvögel*) to migrate; **sie sind gestern nach München/von Hamburg abgeflogen** they flew to Munich/from Hamburg yesterday **2** VT *Gelände* to fly over; *Verwundete* to fly out (*aus* of)

abfließen VI SEP IRREG AUX SEIN (= *wegfließen*) to drain or run away; (*Verkehr*) to flow away; (*fig:* = *Geld*) to flow out of the country; **der Ausguss fließt nicht ab** the water isn't running or draining out of the sink (at all)

Abflug M takeoff; (*von Zugvögeln*) migration; (*inf:* = *~stelle*) departure point; **~ Glasgow 8.00 Uhr** departure Glasgow 8.00 a.m.

Abflug-: abflugbereit ADJ ready for takeoff; **Abflughalle** F departure lounge; **Abflugschalter** M check-in desk

Abfluss M **(a)** (= *Abfließen*) draining away; **dem ~ von Kapital ins Ausland Schranken setzen** to impose limits on the (out)flow of capital out of the country **(b)** (= *~stelle*) drain; (*von Teich etc*) outlet **(c)** (= *~rohr*) drainpipe; (*von sanitären Anlagen*) waste pipe

Abfluss-: Abflussreiniger M drain cleaner; **Abflussrinne** F gutter; **Abflussrohr** NT outlet; (*im Gebäude*) waste pipe; (*außen am Gebäude*) drainpipe

Abfolge F (*geh*) sequence, succession

abfordern VT SEP **jdm etw ~** to demand sth from sb

Abfrage F (*Comput*) query

abfragen VT SEP **(a)** (*Comput*) *Information* to call up; *Datenbank* to query, to interrogate **(b)** (*esp Sch*) **jdn** *or* **jdm etw** ~ to question sb on sth; (*Lehrer*) to test sb orally on sth; **eine Lektion** ~ to give an oral test on a lesson

abfressen VT SEP IRREG *Blätter, Gras* to eat

abfretten ['apfrɛtn] VR SEP (*Aus inf*) to struggle along

abfrieren SEP IRREG **1** VI AUX SEIN to get frostbitten; **ihm sind die Zehen abgefroren** he got frostbite in his toes; **abgefroren sein** (*Körperteil*) to be frostbitten **2** VT **sich** (*dat*) **etw** ~ to get frostbite in sth; **sich** (*dat*) **einen** ~ (*sl*) to freeze to death (*inf*)

Abfuhr ['apfuːɐ] F **-, -en (a)** NO PL (= *Abtransport*) removal **(b)** (*inf*: = *Zurückweisung*) snub, rebuff; **jdm eine ~ erteilen** to snub *or* rebuff sb; **sich** (*dat*) **eine ~ holen** to be snubbed; **sich** (*dat*) **(gegen jdn) eine ~ holen** (*Sport*) to be given a thrashing (by sb) (*inf*)

abführen SEP **1** VT **(a)** (= *wegführen*) to take away **(b)** *Betrag* to pay (*an +acc* to) **2** VI **(a)** (= *wegführen*) **der Weg führt hier (von der Straße) ab** the path leaves the road here; **das würde vom Thema ~** that would take us off the subject **(b)** (= *den Darm anregen*) to have a laxative effect

abführend **1** ADJ *Mittel* laxative *no adv* **2** ADV ~ **wirken** to have a laxative effect

Abführmittel NT laxative

abfüllen VT SEP **(a)** (= *abziehen*) *Wein etc* to draw off (*in +acc* into); (*in Flaschen*) to bottle; *Flasche* to fill; **Wein in Flaschen** ~ to bottle wine **(b)** **jdn** ~ (*inf*) to get sb sloshed (*inf*)

abfüttern VT SEP *Vieh* to feed; (*hum*) *jdn* to feed

Abgabe F **(a)** NO PL (= *Abliefern*) handing *or* giving in; (*von Gepäck*) depositing; (= *Übergabe: von Brief etc*) delivery, handing over; **zur ~ von etw aufgefordert werden** to be told to hand sth in **(b)** NO PL (= *Verkauf*) sale; **~ von Prospekten kostenlos** leaflets given away free **(c)** NO PL (*von Wärme etc*) giving off, emission **(d)** NO PL (*von Schuss, Salve*) firing; **nach ~ von vier Schüssen** after firing four shots **(e)** (= *Steuer*) tax; (= *soziale ~*) contribution **(f)** NO PL (*von Erklärung, Urteil, Meinungsäußerung etc*) giving; (*von Gutachten*) submission; (*von Stimme*) casting **(g)** (*Sport*) (= *Abspiel*) pass; **nach ~ von zwei Punkten ...** after conceding two points ...

Abgabe(n)-: **abgabe(n)frei** ADJ (= *steuerfrei, beitragsfrei*) not liable for tax/for social security contributions (*Brit*), exempt from tax/welfare contributions (*US*); **abgabe(n)pflichtig** [-pflɪçtɪç] ADJ liable for tax/for social security contributions (*Brit*) *or* welfare contributions (*US*)

Abgabetermin M closing date; (*für Dissertation etc*) submission date

Abgang M, *pl* **-gänge (a)** NO PL (= *Absendung*) dispatch; **vor ~ der Post** before the post (*Brit*) *or* mail goes **(b)** NO PL (*aus einem Amt, von Schule*) leaving; **seit seinem ~ von der Schule** since he left school; **einen ~ machen** (*sl*: = *verschwinden*) to split (*sl*) **(c)** NO PL (*Theat, fig*) exit; **sich** (*dat*) **einen guten/glänzenden ~ verschaffen** to make a grand exit **(d)** (*Sport*) dismount **(e)** (*Med*: = *Ausscheidung*) passing; (= *Fehlgeburt*) miscarriage, abortion (*form*) **(f)** (= *Person*) (*Sch*) leaver (*Brit*), high school graduate (*US*); (*Med, Mil*) death

Abgänger ['apgɛŋɐ] M **-s, -, Abgängerin** [-ərɪn] F **-, -nen** (*Sch*) (school) leaver (*Brit*), graduate (*US*)

Abgangszeugnis NT leaving certificate (*Brit*), high school diploma (*US*)

Abgas NT exhaust *no pl*, exhaust fumes *pl*; **Luftverschmutzung durch ~e** exhaust gas pollution

Abgas-: **abgasarm** ADJ *Fahrzeug* low-pollution; **das Auto ist ~** the car has a low level of exhaust emissions; **abgasfrei** **1** ADJ exhaust-free; **~es Fahrzeug** zero-emission vehicle, ZEV; **~e Produktionsverfahren** production methods which produce no waste gases **2** ADV ~ **verbrennen** to burn without producing exhaust fumes; **Abgasnorm** F exhaust emission standard; **Abgas(sonder)untersuchung** F (*Aut*) emissions test

abgaunern VT SEP (*inf*) **jdm etw** ~ to con *or* trick sb out of sth (*inf*)

ABGB [aːbeːgeːˈbeː] NT **-** (*Aus*) ABBR *von* **Allgemeines Bürgerliches Gesetzbuch**

abgearbeitet ADJ (= *verbraucht*) work-worn; (= *erschöpft*) worn out, exhausted; *siehe auch* **abarbeiten**

abgeben SEP IRREG **1** VT **(a)** (= *abliefern*) to hand *or* give in; (= *hinterlassen*) to leave; *Gepäck, Koffer* to leave, to deposit; (= *übergeben*) to hand over, to deliver **(b)** (= *weggeben*) to give away; (= *verkaufen*) to sell; (*an einen anderen Inhaber*) to hand over; **Matratze preisgünstig abzugeben** mattress for sale at (a) bargain price **(c)** (= *verschenken*) to give away; **jdm etw** ~ to give sth to sb; **jdm etwas von seinem Kuchen** ~ to give sb some of one's cake **(d)** (= *überlassen*) *Auftrag* to hand *or* pass on (*an +acc* to); (= *abtreten*) *Posten* to relinquish (*an +acc* to) **(e)** (*Sport*) *Punkte, Rang* to concede; (= *abspielen*) to pass **(f)** (= *ausströmen*) *Wärme, Sauerstoff* to give off, to emit **(g)** (= *abfeuern*) *Schuss, Salve* to fire **(h)** (= *äußern*) *Erklärung* to give; *Gutachten* to submit; *Meinung* to express; *Stimme* to cast **(i)** *Rahmen, Hintergrund, Stoff, Material* to give, to provide **(j)** (= *verkörpern*) to make; **er würde einen guten Schauspieler** ~ he would make a good actor **2** VR **sich mit jdm/etw** ~ (= *sich beschäftigen*) to concern oneself with sb/sth; (= *sich einlassen*) to associate with sb/sth

abgebrannt ADJ PRED (*inf*: = *pleite*) broke (*inf*); *siehe auch* **abbrennen**

abgebrochen ADJ (= *nicht beendet*) *Studium* uncompleted; **er ist ~er Mediziner** (*inf*) he broke off his medical studies; *siehe auch* **abbrechen**

abgebrüht ['apgəbryːt] ADJ (*inf*) callous; *siehe auch* **abbrühen**

abgedroschen ['apgədrɔʃn] ADJ (*inf*) hackneyed (*Brit*), well-worn; *Witz auch* corny (*inf*); **eine ~e Phrase** a cliché; **eine ~e Redensart** a hackneyed (*Brit*) *or* trite saying

abgefeimt ['apgəfaimt] ADJ cunning, wily

abgegriffen ['apgəgrɪfn] ADJ *Buch* (well-)worn; *Leder* worn; (*fig*) *Klischees, Phrasen etc* well-worn

abgehackt ['apgəhakt] **1** ADJ *Sprechweise* clipped **2** ADV ~ **sprechen** to speak in a clipped manner; *siehe auch* **abhacken**

abgehalftert ['apgəhalftɐt] ADJ haggard; **ein ~er Politiker** a political has-been

abgehärmt ['apgəhɛrmt] ADJ careworn

abgehärtet ['apgəhɛrtət] ADJ tough, hardy; (*fig*) hardened; **gegen Erkältungen ~ sein** to be immune to colds; *siehe auch* **abhärten**

abgehen SEP IRREG AUX SEIN **1** VI **(a)** (= *abfahren*) to leave, to depart (*nach* for); **der Zug ging in** *or* **von Frankfurt ab** the train left from Frankfurt **(b)** (*Sport*: = *abspringen*) to jump down **(c)** (*Theat*: = *abtreten*) to exit **(d)** (*von Schule*) to leave; **von der Schule** ~ to leave school **(e)** (= *sich lösen*) to come off; **an meiner Jacke ist ein Knopf abgegangen** a button has come off my jacket **(f)** (= *abgesondert werden*) to pass out; (*Fötus*) to be aborted **(g)** (= *abgesandt werden*) to be sent *or* dispatched **(h)** (*inf*: = *fehlen*) **jdm geht Verständnis/Taktgefühl ab** sb lacks understanding/tact **(i)** (= *abgezogen werden*) (*vom Preis*) to be taken off; (*von Verdienst*) to be deducted; (**von etw**) ~ (*von Preis*) to be taken off (sth); **davon gehen 5% ab** 5% is taken off that **(j)** (= *abzweigen*) to branch off **(k)** (= *abweichen*) **von einem Plan/einer Forderung** ~ to give up *or* drop a plan/demand; **von seiner Meinung** ~ to change one's opinion **(l)** (= *verlaufen*) to go; **gut/glatt/friedlich** ~ to go well/smoothly/peacefully; **es ging nicht ohne Streit ab** there was an argument **(m)** (*sl*) **das geht gut ab** it's really great; **da geht aber was ab** it's a really happening place (*inf*); **was geht ab?** what's doing? (*inf*) **2** VT (= *entlanggehen*) to go *or* walk along; (*hin und zurück*) to walk *or* go up and down; (*Mil*) to patrol; (= *inspizieren*) to inspect

abgehend ADJ *Post, Anruf, Daten* outgoing; *Zug, Schiff* departing; **die morgen ~e Post** the mail which will go out tomorrow

abgehoben ADJ (*inf*) *Mensch, Politik* out of touch with the real world; *siehe auch* **abheben**

abgekämpft [ˈapgəkɛmpft] ADJ exhausted, worn-out

abgekartet [ˈapgəkartət] ADJ fixed (inf), rigged (inf); **eine ~e Sache, ein ~es Spiel** a fix (inf)

abgeklärt [ˈapgəklɛːɐt] ADJ Mensch worldly-wise; Urteil well-considered; Sicht detached; **~ sein** to stand above things; siehe auch **abklären**

Abgeklärtheit F -, NO PL detachment

abgelegen ADJ (= entfernt) Dorf, Land remote; (= einsam) isolated; siehe auch **abliegen**

Abgelegenheit F remoteness; (= Einsamkeit) isolation

abgelten VT SEP IRREG Ansprüche to satisfy; Gefallen to return; **Umweltschäden mit Geldzahlungen ~** to provide financial compensation for environmental damage; **sein Urlaub wurde durch Bezahlung abgegolten** he was given payment in lieu of holiday (Brit) or instead of vacation (US)

abgemacht [ˈapgəmaxt] **1** INTERJ OK, that's settled; (bei Kauf) it's a deal, done **2** ADJ **eine ~e Sache** a fix (inf); **das war doch schon vorher eine ~e Sache** it was all arranged beforehand; siehe auch **abmachen**

abgemagert [ˈapgəmaːgɐt] ADJ (= sehr dünn) thin; (= ausgemergelt) emaciated; (fig: = reduziert) scaled down; siehe auch **abmagern**

abgeneigt ADJ averse pred (+dat to); **ich wäre gar nicht ~** (inf) actually I wouldn't mind; **einer Sache nicht ~ sein** not to be averse to sth; **jdm ~ sein** to dislike sb

abgenutzt [ˈapgənʊtst] ADJ Möbel, Teppich worn; Bürste, Besen worn-out; Reifen worn-down; (fig) hackneyed (Brit), well-worn; siehe auch **abnutzen**

Abgeordnete(r) [ˈapgəɔrdnətə] MF DECL AS ADJ (elected) representative; (von Nationalversammlung) member of parliament; **Herr ~r!** sir; **Frau ~!** madam

Abgesandte(r) [ˈapgəzantə] MF DECL AS ADJ envoy

abgeschieden [ˈapgəʃiːdn] **1** ADJ (geh: = einsam) secluded **2** ADV **~ leben** to live a secluded life; **~ wohnen** to live in seclusion

Abgeschiedenheit F -, NO PL seclusion

abgeschlafft [ˈapgəʃlaft] ADJ (inf: = erschöpft) exhausted; siehe auch **abschlaffen**

abgeschlagen [ˈapgəʃlaːgn] **1** ADJ (= zurück) behind; (= besiegt) well beaten; **auf einem ~en 8. Platz** in a poor 8th place **2** ADV **weit ~ liegen** to be way behind; **er landete ~ auf dem 8. Platz** he finished up way down in 8th place; siehe auch **abschlagen**

abgeschlossen ADJ (= einsam) isolated; (attr: = geschlossen) Wohnung self-contained; Grundstück, Hof enclosed; siehe auch **abschließen**

abgeschmackt [ˈapgəʃmakt] ADJ outrageous; Witz corny

Abgeschmacktheit F -, -en (a) NO PL tastelessness (b) (= Bemerkung) platitude; **alberne Witze und ähnliche ~en** stupid jokes and similar corny things

abgesehen [ˈapgəzeːən] **1** PTP **es auf jdn ~ haben** to have it in for sb (inf); **es auf jdn/etw ~ haben** (= interessiert sein) to have one's eye on sb/sth; **du hast es nur darauf ~, mich zu ärgern** you're only trying to annoy me **2** ADV **~ von jdm/etw** apart from sb/sth; **~ davon, dass ...** apart from the fact that ...; siehe auch **absehen**

abgespannt ADJ weary, tired; siehe auch **abspannen**

abgestanden [ˈapgəʃtandn] **1** ADJ Luft, Wasser stale; Bier, Limonade etc flat **2** ADV **~ schmecken** to taste flat; (Wasser) to taste stale; siehe auch **abstehen**

abgestorben [ˈapgəʃtɔrbn] ADJ Glieder numb; Pflanze, Ast, Gewebe dead; (fig) defunct; Gefühle that have/had died; siehe auch **absterben**

abgestraft [ˈapgəʃtraːft] ADJ (Aus) = **vorbestraft**

abgestumpft [ˈapgəʃtʊmpft] ADJ Mensch insensitive; Gefühle, Gewissen dulled; siehe auch **abstumpfen**

abgetan ADJ PRED (= erledigt) finished or done with; **damit ist die Sache ~** that settles the matter; **damit ist es (noch) nicht ~** that's not the end of the matter; siehe auch **abtun**

abgetragen ADJ worn; **~e Kleider** old clothes; siehe auch **abtragen**

abgewinnen VT SEP IRREG **jdm etw ~** (lit) to win sth from sb; **einer Sache etwas/nichts ~ können** (fig) to be able to see some/no attraction in sth; **jdm/einer Sache keinen Reiz ~ können** to be unable to see anything attractive in sb/sth;

einer Sache (dat) **Geschmack ~** to acquire a taste for sth; **jdm Achtung ~** to win sb's respect; **dem Meer Land ~** to reclaim land from the sea

abgewirtschaftet [ˈapgəvɪrtʃaftət] ADJ (pej) rotten; Firma run-down; **einen total ~en Eindruck machen** to be on its last legs; siehe auch **abwirtschaften**

abgewogen ADJ Urteil, Worte balanced; siehe auch **abwägen**

abgewöhnen VT SEP **jdm etw ~** to cure sb of sth; das Rauchen, Trinken to get sb to give up sth; **sich** (dat) **etw ~** to give up sth; **das/die ist ja zum Abgewöhnen** (inf) that/she is enough to put anyone off

abgewrackt [ˈapgəvrakt] ADJ Mensch washed-up

abgießen VT SEP IRREG Flüssigkeit to pour off or away; Kartoffeln, Gemüse to strain

Abglanz M reflection (auch fig); **nur ein schwacher** or **matter ~** (fig) a pale reflection

Abgleich [ˈapglaiç] M -s, NO PL comparison

abgleichen VT SEP IRREG (fig) Termine, Vorgehensweise to coordinate; Dateien, Einträge to compare

abgleiten VI SEP IRREG AUX SEIN (geh) (= abrutschen) to slip; (Gedanke) to wander; (Fin: Kurs) to drop, to fall; **von etw ~** to slip off sth; **in Nebensächlichkeiten ~** to wander off into side issues; **in Anarchie ~** to descend into anarchy; **an** or **von jdm ~** (fig: = abprallen) to bounce off sb

abgöttisch [ˈapgœtiʃ] **1** ADJ idolatrous; **~e Liebe** blind adoration **2** ADV **jdn ~ lieben/verehren** to idolize sb

abgrenzen SEP **1** VT Grundstück, Gelände to fence off; (fig) to delimit (gegen, von from); **etw durch einen Zaun/ein Seil/eine Mauer/eine Hecke ~** to fence/rope/wall/hedge sth off; **diese Begriffe lassen sich nur schwer (gegeneinander) ~** it is hard to distinguish (between) these two concepts **2** VR to dis(as)sociate oneself (gegen from)

Abgrenzung F -, -en (a) NO PL (von Gelände) fencing off; (fig) delimitation (b) (= Distanzierung) dis(as)sociation (gegen from); **Politik der ~** politics of separation (c) (= Umzäunung, Zaun) fencing no pl

Abgrund M precipice; (= Schlucht, fig) abyss; **sich am Rande eines ~es befinden** (fig) to be on the brink (of disaster); **diese Politik bedeutet ein Wandeln am Rande des ~es** this policy is an exercise in brinkmanship; **in einen ~ von Verrat/Gemeinheit blicken** (fig) to stare into a bottomless pit of treason/baseness; **die menschlichen Abgründe** the darkest depths of the human soul

abgrundhässlich ADJ loathsome

abgründig [ˈapgrʏndiç] **1** ADJ Humor, Ironie cryptic **2** ADV lächeln cryptically

abgrundtief **1** ADJ Hass, Verachtung profound **2** ADV hassen, verachten profoundly

abgucken VTI SEP to copy; **jdm etw ~** to copy sth from sb; **bei jdm (etw) ~** (Sch) to copy (sth) from or off (inf) sb; **ich guck dir nichts ab!** (inf) don't worry, I've seen it all before

abhaben VT SEP IRREG (inf) (a) (= abgenommen haben) Brille, Hut to have off; (= abgemacht haben) to have got off; (= abgerissen haben) to have off (b) (= abbekommen) to have; **willst du ein Stück/etwas (davon) ~?** do you want a bit/some (of it)?

abhacken VT SEP to hack off; siehe auch **abgehackt**

abhaken VT SEP (= markieren) to tick (Brit) or check (esp US) off; (fig) to cross off

abhalten VT SEP IRREG (a) (= hindern) to stop, to prevent; (= fern halten) to keep off; **jdn von etw/vom Trinken/von der Arbeit ~** to keep sb from sth/drinking/working; **jdn davon ~, etw zu tun** to stop sb (from) doing sth, to prevent sb (from) doing sth; **lass dich nicht ~!** don't let me/us etc stop you (b) (= veranstalten) to hold

Abhaltung F, NO PL (= Durchführung) holding; **nach ~ der Wahlen** after the elections (were held)

abhandeln VT SEP (a) Thema to treat, to deal with (b) (= abkaufen) **jdm etw ~** to do or strike a deal with sb for sth; **sie wollte sich** (dat) **das Armband nicht ~ lassen** she didn't want to let her bracelet go

abhanden [apˈhandn] ADV **~ kommen** to get lost; **jdm ist etw ~ gekommen** sb has lost sth

Abhandlung F treatise, discourse (über +acc (up)on); (= das Abhandeln) treatment

Abhang M slope, incline

abhängen SEP ◆ VT (a) *Bild* to take down; *Schlafwagen, Kurswagen* to uncouple; *Wohnwagen, Anhänger* to unhitch; **(gut) abgehangen** *Fleisch* well-hung **(b)** (*inf*: = *hinter sich lassen*) *jdn* to shake off (*inf*) ◆ VI (a) IRREG (*Fleisch etc*) to hang **(b)** IRREG AUX HABEN or (*S Ger, Aus*) SEIN **von etw ~** to depend (up)on sth; **das hängt ganz davon ab** it all depends; **davon hängt viel/zu viel ab** a lot/too much depends on it; **von jdm (finanziell) ~** to be (financially) dependent on sb

abhängig ['aphɛŋɪç] ADJ **(a)** (= *bedingt durch*) dependent (*auch Math*); **etw von etw ~ machen** to make sth conditional (up)on sth **(b)** (= *angewiesen auf*, euph: = *süchtig*) dependent (*von* on); **~ Beschäftigte(r)** employee **(c)** (*Gram*) *Satz* subordinate; *Rede* indirect; *Kasus* oblique; **von etw ~ sein** to be governed by sth

-abhängige(r) MF DECL AS ADJ SUF (= *-süchtiger*) addict; **ein Heroinabhängiger** a heroin addict

Abhängigkeit F **-, -en (a)** NO PL (= *Bedingtheit*) dependency *no pl* (*von* on); (*Gram*: *von Sätzen*) subordination (*von* to) **(b)** (= *Angewiesensein*, euph: = *Sucht*) dependence (*von* on)

abhärten SEP ◆ VT to toughen up ◆ VI **das härtet (gegen Erkältung) ab** that toughens you up (and stops you catching cold) ◆ VR to toughen oneself up; **sich gegen etw ~** to toughen oneself against sth; (*fig*) to harden oneself to sth; *siehe auch* **abgehärtet**

Abhärtung F toughening up; (*fig*) hardening

abhauen SEP ◆ *ptp* **abgehauen** VI AUX SEIN (*inf*) to clear out; **hau ab!** get lost! (*inf*) ◆ VT (a) *pret* **hieb** or (*inf*) **haute ab**, *ptp* **abgehauen** *Kopf* to chop or cut off; *Baum* to chop or cut down **(b)** *pret* **haute ab**, *ptp* **abgehauen** (= *wegschlagen*) *Verputz, Schicht* to knock off

abhäuten VT SEP to skin

abheben SEP IRREG ◆ VT (a) (= *anheben*) to lift (up), to raise; (= *abnehmen*) to take off; *Telefonhörer* to pick up; *Telefon* to answer; (*beim Stricken*) *Masche* to slip; (*Cards*) to take, to pick up; *Geld* to withdraw ◆ VI (a) (*Flugzeug*) to take off; (*Rakete*) to lift off **(b)** (= *ans Telefon gehen*) to answer; (*beim Stricken*) to slip; **lass es doch klingeln, du brauchst nicht abzuheben** let it ring, you don't have to answer (it) **(c)** (= *Geld ~*) to withdraw money; **wenn Sie ~ wollen** if you wish to make a withdrawal **(d)** (*Cards*) (= *schneiden*) to cut; (= *Karte nehmen*) to take a card; *siehe auch* **abgehoben** ◆ VR **sich von jdm/etw ~** to stand out from sb/sth; **sich gegen jdn/etw ~** to stand out against sb/sth; **sich wohltuend gegen etw ~** to contrast pleasantly with sth

Abhebung F **-, -en** (*von Geld*) withdrawal

abheften VT SEP **(a)** *Rechnungen, Schriftverkehr* to file away **(b)** (*Sew*) to tack, to baste

abhelfen VI SEP IRREG +DAT to remedy; **dem ist leicht abzuhelfen** that can be or is easily remedied

Abhilfe F, NO PL remedy, cure; **~ schaffen** to take remedial action; **in einer Angelegenheit ~ schaffen** to remedy a matter

abhin [ap'hɪn] ADV (*Sw*) **vom 18.9.2002 ~** from 18.9.2002 onwards

abholen VT SEP to collect (*bei* from); *Fundsache* to claim (*bei* from); *jdn* to call for; (euph: = *verhaften*) to take away; **jdn am Bahnhof/Flughafen ~** to collect sb from or to meet sb at the station/airport; **etw ~ lassen** to have sth collected; **„Geldbörse gefunden, abzuholen bei ...“** "purse found, claim from ..."

Abholmarkt M warehouse (*selling furniture/drinks etc*)

Abholung F **-, -en** collection

abholzen VT SEP *Wald* to clear; *Baumreihe* to fell

abhorchen VT SEP to sound, to listen to; *Brust auch, Patienten* to auscultate (*form*)

Abhöreinrichtung F bugging device; (= *System*) bugging system

abhören VT SEP **(a)** AUCH VI (= *überwachen*) *Raum, Gespräch* to bug; (= *mithören*) to listen in on; *Telefon* to tap; **abgehört werden** (*inf*) to be bugged **(b)** (*Med*) to sound, to listen to; **jdm das Herz ~** to listen to or sound sb's heart **(c)** (*Sch*: = *abfragen*) **einen** or **einem Schüler etw ~** to test a pupil orally

on sth; **kannst du mir mal Vokabeln ~?** can you test my vocabulary?

Abhörgerät NT bugging device

abhörsicher ADJ *Raum* bug-proof; *Telefon* tap-proof

abhungern VT SEP **er musste sich** (*dat*) **sein Studium ~** he had to starve himself to pay for his studies; **sich** (*dat*) **Gewicht/10 Kilo ~** to lose weight/10 kilos by going on a starvation diet

abi ['abi] (*Aus inf*) = **hinunter**

Abi ['abi] NT **-s, -s** (*Sch inf*) ABBR *von* **Abitur**

Abitur [abi'tuːɐ] NT **-s,** (*rare*) **-e** *school-leaving exam and university entrance qualification*, ≈ A levels *pl* (*Brit*), ≈ Highers *pl* (*Scot*), ≈ high-school diploma (*US*); **(sein** or **das) ~ machen** to do (one's) school-leaving exam (*Brit*), ≈ to do one's A levels (*Brit*) or Highers (*Scot*), ≈ to take one's high-school diploma (*US*)

ABITUR

In Germany the **Abitur** examination is taken by pupils at a **Gymnasium** after thirteen years at school. The **Abitur** consists of written and oral tests in four core subjects, although the overall mark takes account of a student's performance in various courses throughout their **Kollegstufe**. The **Abitur** is also known as the *allgemeine Hochschulreife*, since it is a prerequisite for acceptance on a university course.

The Austrian equivalent is the **Matura**, taken after twelve years at school.

In Switzerland the **Maturität** is taken after twelve or thirteen years at school. Success in the examination entitles the student to be admitted to university. ▶ GYMNASIUM, KOLLEGSTUFE

Abiturient [abitu'rient] M **-en, -en, Abiturientin** [-'rientɪn] F **-, -nen** *person who is doing/has done the Abitur*

Abitur-: Abiturklasse F *final-year class at school which will take the Abitur*, ≈ sixth form (*Brit*), ≈ twelfth grade (*US*); **Abiturzeugnis** NT certificate of having passed the Abitur, ≈ A level (*Brit*) or Highers (*Scot*) certificate, ≈ high-school diploma (*US*)

Abk. ABBR *von* **Abkürzung** abbreviation, abbr

abkämmen VT SEP (*fig*) to comb, to scour

abkanzeln ['apkantsln] VT SEP (*inf*) **jdn ~** to give sb a dressing-down

abkapseln ['apkapsln] VR SEP (*lit*) to become encapsulated; (*fig*) to shut or cut oneself off

abkassieren *ptp* **abkassiert** SEP ◆ VT *Fahrgäste* to collect money from; *Geldsumme, Schutzgelder, Maut* to collect; (= *ausnehmen*) to clean out (*inf*) ◆ VI (= *großes Geld machen*) to make a killing (*inf*); **darf ich mal (bei Ihnen) ~?** could I ask you to pay now?

abkaufen VT SEP **jdm etw ~** to buy sth from or off (*inf*) sb; (*inf*: = *glauben*) to buy sth off

Abkehr ['apkeːɐ] F **-,** NO PL turning away (*von* from); (*von Glauben, von der Welt etc*) renunciation (*von* of); (*von der Familie*) estrangement (*von* from)

abkehren SEP ◆ VT (*geh*: = *abwenden*) *Blick, Gesicht* to turn away; **sie musste den Blick (davon) ~** she had to look away (from it) ◆ VR (*fig*) to turn away (*von* from); (*von einer Politik*) to give up; **sich von Gott ~** to renounce God; **die von uns abgekehrte Seite des Mondes** the far side of the moon

abklappern VT SEP (*inf*) *Läden, Gegend, Straße* to scour, to comb (*nach* for); *Kunden, Museen* to do (*inf*)

abklären SEP ◆ VT *Angelegenheit* to clear up, to clarify ◆ VR (= *sich setzen*) to clarify; (= *sich beruhigen*) to calm down; *siehe auch* **abgeklärt**

Abklatsch M (*fig pej*) poor imitation or copy

abklatschen VT SEP **er klatschte sie ab** he cut in on her partner; **es wird abgeklatscht** it's an excuse-me (*Brit*), you can cut in

abklemmen VT SEP to clamp

Abklingbecken NT spent fuel storage bay

abklingen VI SEP IRREG AUX SEIN **(a)** (= *leiser werden*) to die or fade away **(b)** (= *nachlassen*) to abate; (*radioaktives Material*) to decay

abklopfen VT SEP **(a)** (= *herunterklopfen*) to knock off; (= *klopfend säubern*) to brush down; *Staub etc* to brush off; *Teppich, Polstermöbel* to beat; **er klopfte die Asche von der**

Zigarre ab he tapped the ash off his cigar **(b)** (= *beklopfen*) to tap; (*Med*) to sound

abknabbern VT SEP (*inf*) to nibble off; *Knochen* to gnaw at

abknacken VI SEP (*sl*: = *schlafen*) to crash (out) (*inf*)

abknallen VT SEP (*inf*) to shoot down (*inf*)

abknappen ['apknapn], **abknapsen** VT SEP (*inf*) **sich** (*dat*) **etw ~** to scrape together sth; **sich** (*dat*) **jeden Pfennig ~ müssen** to have to scrimp and save; **er hat mir 20 Euro abgeknapst** he got 20 euros off me

abkneifen VT SEP IRREG to nip off

abknicken SEP 1 VT (= *abbrechen*) to break *or* snap off; (= *einknicken*) to break 2 VI AUX SEIN (= *abzweigen*) to fork *or* branch off; **~de Vorfahrt** traffic turning left/right has priority

abknöpfen VT SEP **(a)** (= *abnehmen*) to unbutton **(b)** (*inf*: = *ablisten*) **jdm etw ~** to get sth off sb; **jdm Geld ~** to get money out of sb

abknutschen VT SEP (*inf*) to canoodle (*Brit inf*) *or* cuddle with; **sich ~** to canoodle (*Brit inf*), to cuddle

abkochen VT SEP to boil; (= *keimfrei machen*) to sterilize (by boiling)

abkommandieren *ptp* **abkommandiert** VT SEP (*Mil*) (*zu anderer Einheit*) to post; (*zu bestimmtem Dienst*) to detail (*zu* for); **jdn ins Ausland ~** to post sb abroad

abkommen VI SEP IRREG AUX SEIN **(a) von etw ~** (= *abweichen*) to leave sth; (= *abirren*) to wander off sth; **vom Kurs ~** to deviate from one's course; **(vom Thema) ~** to digress; **vom rechten Weg ~** (*fig*) to stray *or* wander from the straight and narrow **(b)** (= *aufgeben*) **von etw ~** to give sth up; *von Idee, Plan* to abandon sth; **von einer Meinung ~** to revise one's opinion; **von diesem alten Brauch kommt man immer mehr ab** this old custom is dying out more and more

Abkommen ['apkɔmən] NT **-s, -** agreement (*auch Pol*)

abkömmlich ['apkœmlıç] ADJ available; **nicht ~ sein** to be unavailable

abkönnen VT SEP IRREG (*inf*) **(a)** (= *trinken*) **der kann ganz schön was ab** he can put it away (*inf*); **er kann nicht viel ab** he can't take much (alcohol) **(b)** (= *vertragen*) to bear, to stand; **er kann nichts ab** he can't take it **(c)** (= *mögen*) **das kann ich überhaupt nicht ab** I can't stand *or* abide it; **ich kann ihn einfach nicht ab** I just can't stand *or* abide him

abkoppeln VT SEP (*Rail*) to uncouple; *Pferd* to untie; *Raumfähre* to undock; *Anhänger* to unhitch

abkratzen SEP 1 VT *Schmutz etc* to scratch off; (*mit einem Werkzeug*) to scrape off; *Wand, Gegenstand* to scratch, to scrape; **die Schuhe ~** to scrape the mud/snow *etc* off one's shoes 2 VI AUX SEIN (*inf*: = *sterben*) to kick the bucket (*inf*)

abkriegen VT SEP (*inf*) = **abbekommen**

abkühlen SEP 1 VT (*lit, fig*) to cool 2 VI AUX SEIN to cool down; (*fig*) *Freundschaft etc* to cool off; (*Begeisterung*) to cool 3 VR to cool down *or* off; (*Wetter*) to become cool(er); (*fig*) to cool

Abkühlung F cooling

abkupfern ['apkʊpfɐn] VT SEP (*inf*) to crib (*inf*)

abkuppeln VT SEP = **abkoppeln**

abkürzen VT SEP **(a)** (= *verkürzen*) to cut short; *Verfahren* to shorten; (= *verkürzt schreiben*) *Namen* to abbreviate; **Kilohertz wird kHz abgekürzt** kilohertz is abbreviated to kHz; **den Weg ~** to take a short cut

Abkürzung F **(a)** (*Weg*) short cut; **durch die ~ haben wir eine Stunde gespart** we've saved an hour by taking the short cut **(b)** (*von Aufenthalt, Vortrag*) cutting short; (*von Verfahren*) shortening; **gibt es keine ~ dieses Verfahrens?** isn't there any way of shortening this process? **(c)** (*von Wort*) abbreviation

Abkürzungsverzeichnis NT list of abbreviations

abladen SEP IRREG 1 VT *Last, Wagen* to unload; *Schutt* to dump; (*esp Comm*) *Passagiere, Ware* to off-load; (*fig inf*) *Kummer, Ärger* to vent (*bei jdm* on sb); *Verantwortung* to off-load (*auf +acc* onto); **seine Kinder/Arbeit auf jdn ~** (*fig inf*) to dump one's children/work on sb (*inf*); **sie lud ihren ganzen Kummer bei ihrem Mann ab** (*inf*) she unburdened herself *or* all her worries on her husband

2 VI (= *entladen*) to unload; **bei jdm ~** (*fig inf*: = *Sorgen loswerden*) to offload on sb

Abladeplatz M unloading area; (*für Schrott, Müll etc*) dump, dumping ground

Ablage F **(a)** (= *Gestell*) place to put sth; (*zur Aufbewahrung*) place to keep sth; (= *~korb*) filing tray; (= *Gepäckablage*) luggage (*Brit*) *or* baggage (*US*) rack; **der Tisch dient als ~ für ihre Bücher** her books are kept on the table; **etw als ~ benutzen** (*für Akten, Bücher etc*) to use sth for storage **(b)** (= *Aktenordnung*) filing **(c)** (*Sw*) = **Annahmestelle, Zweigstelle**

Ablagekorb M filing tray

ablagern SEP 1 VT **(a)** (= *anhäufen*) to deposit **(b)** (= *deponieren*) to leave, to store 2 VI AUX SEIN *or* HABEN (= *ausreifen*) to mature; **~ lassen** to allow to mature; **abgelagert** *Wein* mature; *Holz, Tabak* seasoned 3 VR to be deposited; **in einem Wasserkessel lagert sich Kalk ab** a chalk deposit builds up *or* forms in a kettle

Ablagerung F (= *Vorgang*) depositing; (*von Wein*) maturation; (*von Holz*) seasoning; (= *abgelagerter Stoff*) deposit

ablassen VT SEP IRREG **(a)** *Wasser, Luft* to let out; *Motoröl* to drain off; *Dampf* to let off **(b)** *Teich, Schwimmbecken* to drain, to empty **(c)** (= *ermäßigen*) to knock off (*inf*)

Ablassventil NT outlet valve

Ablauf M **(a)** (= *Abfluss*) drain; (= *~stelle*) outlet; (= *~rohr*) drain(pipe); (*im Haus*) waste pipe; (= *Rinne*) drainage channel **(b)** (= *Ablaufen*) draining *or* running away **(c)** (= *Verlauf*) course; (*von Empfang, Staatsbesuch*) order of events (*+gen* in); (*von Verbrechen*) sequence of events (*+gen* in); (*von Handlung im Buch etc*) development; **er sprach mit uns den ~ der Prüfung durch** he took us through the exam; **er hat den ~ des Unglücks geschildert** he described the way the accident happened; **es gab keinerlei Störungen im ~ des Programms** the programme (*Brit*) *or* program (*US*) went off without any disturbances **(d)** (*von Frist etc*) expiry; **nach ~ der Frist** after the deadline had passed *or* expired **(e)** (*von Zeitraum*) passing; **nach ~ von 4 Stunden** after 4 hours (have/had gone by *or* passed); **nach ~ des Jahres/dieser Zeit** at the end of the year/this time

ablaufen SEP IRREG 1 VT **(a)** (= *abnützen*) *Schuhsohlen, Schuhe* to wear out; *Absätze* to wear down; **sich** (*dat*) **die Beine** *or* **Hacken** *or* **Absätze** *or* **Schuhsohlen nach etw ~** (*inf*) to walk one's legs off looking for sth **(b)** AUX SEIN *or* HABEN (= *entlanglaufen*) *Strecke* to go *or* walk over; (*hin und zurück*) to go *or* walk up and down; *Stadt, Straßen, Geschäfte* to comb, to scour 2 VI AUX SEIN **(a)** (= *abfließen: Flüssigkeit*) to drain *or* run away *or* off; **aus der Badewanne ~** to run out of the bath; **an ihm läuft alles ab** (*fig*) he just shrugs everything off **(b)** (= *vonstatten gehen*) to go off; **wie ist das bei der Prüfung abgelaufen?** how did the exam go (off)?; **zuerst sah es sehr gefährlich aus, aber dann ist die Sache doch glimpflich abgelaufen** at first things looked pretty dangerous but it was all right in the end **(c)** (*Pass, Visum, Frist etc*) to expire; **die Frist ist abgelaufen** the period is up

Ableben NT, NO PL (*form*) demise (*form*)

ablecken VT SEP to lick; *Blut, Marmelade* to lick off; **sich** (*dat*) **etw von der Hand ~** to lick sth off one's hand

ablegen SEP 1 VT **(a)** (= *niederlegen*) to put down; (*Zool*) *Eier* to lay **(b)** (= *abheften*) *Schriftwechsel, Dokumente* to file (away); (*Comput*) *Daten* to store **(c)** (= *ausziehen*) to take off **(d)** (= *nicht mehr tragen*) *Anzug, Kleid* to cast off; *Trauerkleidung, Ehering* to take off **(e)** (= *aufgeben*) *Misstrauen, Scheu, Stolz* to lose; *schlechte Gewohnheit* to give up; *kindische Angewohnheit* to put aside; *Namen* to give up **(f)** (= *ableisten, machen*) *Schwur, Eid* to swear; *Gelübde* to make; *Zeugnis* to give; *Bekenntnis, Beichte, Geständnis* to make; *Prüfung* to take, to sit; (*erfolgreich*) to pass **(g)** (*Cards*) to discard 2 VI **(a)** (= *abfahren: Schiff*) to cast off **(b)** (*Garderobe ~*) to take one's things off **(c)** (*Cards*) to discard

Ableger ['aple:gɐ] M **-s, -** (*Bot*) layer; (*fig*: = *Zweigunternehmen*) branch, subsidiary; (*iro*: = *Sohn*) son; **durch ~** by layering

ablehnen SEP 1 VT **(a)** (= *zurückweisen, nein sagen*) to decline, to refuse; *Antrag, Angebot, Vorschlag, Bewerber, Stelle* to turn

down, to reject; (Parl) Gesetzentwurf to throw out; **es ~, etw zu tun** to decline or refuse to do sth
(b) (= missbilligen) to disapprove of; **jede Form von Gewalt ~** to be against any form of violence
2 VI to decline, to refuse; **drei der erfolgreichen Bewerber haben abgelehnt** three of the successful applicants have declined the job offer; **eine ~de Antwort** a negative answer; **ein ~der Bescheid** a rejection; **dankend ~** to decline with thanks

Ablehnung F -, -en **(a)** (= Zurückweisung) refusal; (von Antrag, Bewerber etc) rejection; **auf ~ stoßen** to meet with a refusal/a rejection **(b)** (= Missbilligung) disapproval; **auf ~ stoßen** to meet with disapproval

ableitbar ADJ (= herleitbar) derivable, deducible; Wort derivable (aus from)

ableiten SEP **1** VT **(a)** (= herleiten) to derive; (= logisch folgern) to deduce (aus from); (Math) Gleichung to differentiate
(b) Bach, Fluss to divert; Rauch, Dampf, Flüssigkeit to draw off or out; Blitz to conduct **2** VR (= sich herleiten) to be derived (aus from); (= logisch folgen) to be deduced (aus from)

Ableitung F **(a)** NO PL (= das Herleiten) derivation; (= Folgerung) deduction; (Math: von Gleichung) differentiation **(b)** (= Wort, Math) derivative

ablenken SEP **1** VT **(a)** (= ab-, wegleiten) to deflect (auch Phys), to turn aside or away; Wellen, Licht to refract; Schlag to parry; Katastrophe to avert
(b) (= zerstreuen) to distract; **er ließ sich durch nichts ~** he wouldn't let anything distract him; **wir mussten die Kinder ~** we had to find something to take the children's minds off things; **jdn von seinem Schmerz/seinen Sorgen ~** to take sb's mind off his/her pain/worries
(c) (= abbringen) to divert; Verdacht to avert; **jdn von der Arbeit ~** to distract sb from his/her work
2 VI **(a)** (= ausweichen) (vom Thema) **~** to change the subject
(b) (= zerstreuen) to create a distraction; **sie geht jede Woche Schwimmen, das lenkt ab** she goes swimming every week, which takes her mind off things
3 VR to take one's mind off things

Ablenkung F **(a)** (= Zerstreuung) diversion, distraction; **~ brauchen** to need something to take one's mind off things; **sich** (dat) **~ verschaffen** to provide oneself with a distraction; **zur ~ einen Spaziergang machen** to take one's mind off things by going for a walk **(b)** (= Störung) distraction

Ablenkungsmanöver NT diversionary tactic

ablesen VT SEP IRREG **(a)** AUCH VI (vom Blatt) to read; **(jdm) etw von den Lippen ~** to lip-read sth (that sb says)
(b) AUCH VI (= registrieren) Messgeräte, Barometer, Strom to read; Barometerstand to take; **nächste Woche wird abgelesen** the meter(s) will be read next week
(c) (= herausfinden, erkennen, folgern) to see; **jdm etw vom Gesicht** or **von der Stirn ~** to see or tell sth from sb's face; **das konnte man ihr vom Gesicht ~** it was written all over her face; **aus der Reaktion der Presse war die Stimmung im Volke deutlich abzulesen** the mood of the people could be clearly gauged from the press reaction; **jdm jeden Wunsch an** or **von den Augen ~** to anticipate sb's every wish

Ableser(in) M(F) meter-reader

ableugnen SEP **1** VT to deny; Glauben to renounce **2** VI **er hat weiter abgeleugnet** he continued to deny it

abliefern VT SEP (bei einer Person) to hand over (bei to); Examensarbeit auch to hand in; (bei einer Dienststelle) to hand in (bei to); (= liefern) to deliver (bei to); (inf) Kinder, Freundin to deposit (inf); (= nach Hause bringen) to take home

Ablieferung F (bei einer Person) handing-over no pl; (bei einer Dienststelle) handing-in no pl; (= Lieferung) delivery

abliegen VI SEP IRREG (= entfernt sein) to be at a distance; (fig) to be removed; **das Haus liegt weit ab** the house is a long way off or away; **das liegt sehr weit ab von unserem Thema** that is very far removed from the topic we are dealing with; siehe auch **abgelegen**

ablocken VT SEP **jdm etw ~** to get sth out of sb; **diese Äußerung lockte ihm nur ein müdes Lächeln ab** this statement only got a tired smile out of him; **er lockte seiner Geige süße Töne ab** he coaxed sweet sounds from his violin

ablöschen VT SEP (Cook) to add water to

Ablöse ['aplø:zə] F -, -n **(a)** (= Abstand) key money
(b) (= Ablösungssumme) transfer fee

ablösen SEP **1** VT **(a)** (= abmachen) to take off
(b) (Fin) (= kapitalisieren) Rente to get paid in a lump sum; (= auszahlen) to pay (off) in a lump sum; (= tilgen) Schuld, Hypothek to pay off, to redeem
(c) (= ersetzen) Wache to relieve; Kollegen to take over from; **drei Minister wurden abgelöst** (euph) three ministers were relieved of their duties
(d) (fig: = an Stelle treten von) to take the place of; Methode, System to supersede
2 VR **(a)** (= abgehen) to come off; (Lack etc auch) to peel off; (Netzhaut) to become detached
(b) (auch **einander ablösen**) to take turns; (Wachen) to relieve each other; **wir lösen uns alle drei Stunden beim Babysitten ab** we each do three-hour shifts of babysitting
(c) (auch **einander ablösen**: = alternieren) to alternate; **bei ihr lösen sich Fröhlichkeit und Trauer ständig ab** she constantly alternates between being happy and being miserable

Ablösesumme F (Sport) transfer fee

Ablösung F **(a)** (Fin) (von Rente) lump payment; (von Hypothek, Schuld) paying off, redemption
(b) (= Wachwechsel) relieving; (= Wache) relief; (= Entlassung) replacement; **wann findet die ~ der Wache statt?** when will the guard be relieved?; **er kam als ~** he came as a replacement; **bei dieser Arbeit braucht man alle zwei Stunden eine ~** you need relieving every two hours in this work

ablotsen, abluchsen VT SEP (inf) **jdm etw ~** to get or wangle (inf) sth out of sb

ABM [a:be:'lɛm] ABBR von **Arbeitsbeschaffungsmaßnahme**

ABM

ABM is an abbreviation of Arbeitsbeschaffungsmaßnahme. So-called ABM-Stellen are jobs sponsored by the employment office, which are designed to give certain groups of people the chance to work - groups such as the over-55s, the severely disabled and the long-term unemployed in areas of high unemployment. An **ABM** is normally restricted to one year and must involve work that benefits the community. It must be a genuinely new job, so that no existing posts are filled.

---

abmachen VT SEP **(a)** (inf: = entfernen) to take off; (= herunternehmen) to take down; **er machte dem Hund die Leine ab** he took the dog's lead (Brit) or leash off
(b) (= vereinbaren) to agree (on); **wir haben abgemacht, dass wir das tun werden** we've agreed to do it, we've agreed on doing it; **es ist noch nichts abgemacht worden** nothing's been agreed (on) yet; siehe auch **abgemacht**
(c) (= besprechen) to sort out, to settle; **etw mit sich allein ~** to sort sth out for oneself; **etw mit seinem Gewissen ~** to square sth with one's conscience

Abmachung ['apmaxʊŋ] F -, -en agreement

abmagern ['apma:gɐn] VI SEP AUX SEIN to get thinner, to lose weight; **sehr ~** to lose a lot of weight; **er war bis zum Skelett abgemagert** he was nothing but skin and bone(s); siehe auch **abgemagert**

Abmagerungskur F diet; **eine ~ machen** to be on a diet, to be dieting; (anfangen) to go on a diet, to diet

abmahnen VT SEP (form) to caution

Abmahnung F (form) caution

Abmahnungsschreiben NT (form) formal letter of caution

Abmarsch M departure

abmarschbereit ADJ ready to set or move off; (Mil) ready to move off or march

abmarschieren ptp **abmarschiert** VI SEP AUX SEIN to set or move off; (Mil) to march or move off

Abmelde-: Abmeldebestätigung F document confirming that one has cancelled one's registration with the local authorities; **Abmeldeformular** NT form to be filled in when one cancels one's registration with the local authorities

abmelden SEP **1** VT **(a)** Zeitungen etc to cancel; Telefon to have disconnected; (bei Verein) jdn to cancel the membership of; **sein Auto ~** to take one's car off the road; **seinen Fernsehapparat ~** to cancel one's television licence (Brit); **ein Kind von einer Schule ~** to remove a child from a school
(b) (inf) abgemeldet sein (Sport) to be outclassed; **jd/etw ist bei jdm abgemeldet** sb has lost interest in sb/sth; **er/sie ist bei mir abgemeldet** I don't want anything to do with him/her

2 VR to ask for permission to be absent; (*vor Abreise*) to announce one's departure; (*im Hotel*) to check out; **sich bei jdm ~** to tell sb that one is leaving; **sich bei einem Verein ~** to cancel one's membership of a club

Abmeldung F (*von Zeitungen etc*) cancellation; (*von Telefon*) disconnection; (*beim Einwohnermeldeamt*) cancellation of one's registration; (*inf.* = *Formular*) form to be filled in so that one's registration with the local authorities is cancelled; **seit der ~ meines Autos** since I took my car off the road; **die ~ eines Kindes von einer Schule** the removal of a child from a school

abmessen VT SEP IRREG (= *ausmessen*) to measure; (= *genaue Maße feststellen von*) to measure up; (= *abschätzen*) *Verlust, Schaden* to measure

Abmessung F USU PL measurement; (= *Ausmaß*) dimension

abmildern VT SEP *Geschmack* to tone down; *Aufprall* to cushion; *Schock* to lessen

abmontieren *ptp* **abmontiert** VT SEP *Räder, Teile* to take off (*von etw* sth); *Maschine* to dismantle

ABM-Stelle [aːbeːˈlɛm-] F temporary position (through job creation scheme)

abmühen VR SEP to struggle (away)

abnabeln [ˈapnaːbln] SEP **1** VT **ein Kind ~** to cut a baby's umbilical cord **2** VR to cut oneself loose; **sich vom Elternhaus ~** to leave the nest (*inf*)

abnagen VT SEP to gnaw off; *Knochen* to gnaw

Abnäher [ˈapnɛːɐ] M **-s, -** dart

Abnahme [ˈapnaːmə] F **-, -n** (a) (= *Wegnahme*) removal; (= *Herunternehmen*) taking down; (= *Amputation*) amputation (b) (= *Verringerung*) decrease (+*gen* in); (*von Niveau, Kräfte, Energie, Interesse*) decline (+*gen* in); (*von Aufmerksamkeit*) flagging (c) (*von Prüfung*) holding; (*von Neubau, Fahrzeug etc*) inspection; (*von TÜV*) carrying out; (*von Eid*) administering; **die ~ der Prüfung kann erst erfolgen, wenn ...** the exam can only be held if ... (d) (*Comm*) purchase; **bei ~ von 50 Kisten** if you/we *etc* purchase *or* take 50 crates; **keine ~ finden** to find no market; **gute ~ finden** to sell well

abnehmbar ADJ removable, detachable

abnehmen SEP IRREG **1** VT (a) (= *herunternehmen*) to take off, to remove; *Hörer* to pick up; (= *lüften*) *Hut* to raise; *Vorhang, Bild, Wäsche* to take down; *Maschen* to decrease; (= *abrasieren*) *Bart* to take *or* shave off; (= *amputieren*) to amputate; (*Cards*) *Karte* to take from the pile; **das Telefon ~** to answer the telephone

(b) (= *an sich nehmen*) **jdm etw ~** to take sth from sb; (*fig*) *Arbeit, Sorgen* to relieve sb of sth; **darf ich Ihnen den Mantel/die Tasche ~?** can I take your coat/bag?; **kann ich dir etwas ~?** (= *tragen*) can I take something for you?; (= *helfen*) can I do anything for you?; **jdm die Beichte ~** to hear confession from sb; **jdm einen Eid ~** to administer an oath to sb; **jdm eine Besorgung ~** to do some shopping for sb

(c) (= *wegnehmen*) to take away (*jdm* from sb); (= *rauben, abgewinnen*) to take (*jdm* off sb)

(d) (= *begutachten*) *Gebäude, Wohnung, Auto* to inspect; (= *abhalten*) *Prüfung* to hold; *TÜV* to carry out

(e) (= *abkaufen*) to take (+*dat* off), to buy (+*dat* from, off)

(f) *Fingerabdrücke* to take; *Totenmaske* to make (+*dat* of)

(g) (*fig inf:* = *glauben*) to buy (*inf*); **dieses Märchen nimmt dir keiner ab!** (*inf*) nobody will buy that tale! (*inf*)

2 VI (a) (= *sich verringern*) to decrease; (*Niveau, Kräfte, Energie, Interesse, Nachfrage*) to decline; (*Fieber*) to go down; (*Aufmerksamkeit*) to flag; (*Mond*) to wane; (*Tage*) to grow *or* get shorter; (*beim Stricken*) to decrease; **(an Gewicht) ~** to lose weight; **in letzter Zeit hast du im Gesicht abgenommen** your face has got thinner recently

(b) (*Telec*) to answer; **es hat keiner abgenommen** no-one answered

Abnehmer(in) M(F) (*Comm*) buyer, customer; **keine ~ finden** not to sell; **viele/wenige ~ finden** to sell well/badly

Abneigung F dislike (*gegen* of); (= *Widerstreben*) aversion (*gegen* to)

abnorm [apˈnɔrm], **abnormal** [ˈapnɔrmaːl, apnɔrˈmaːl] **1** ADJ abnormal **2** ADV abnormally

abnutzen, (*esp S Ger, Aus, Sw*) **abnützen** VTR SEP to wear out; *siehe auch* **abgenutzt**

Abnutzung F, (*esp S Ger, Aus, Sw*) **Abnützung** F **-, -en** wear (and tear); **die normale ~ ist im Mietpreis berücksichtigt** general wear and tear is included in the rent

Abnutzungserscheinung F sign of wear (and tear)

Abo [ˈabo] NT **-s, -s** (*inf*) ABBR *von* **Abonnement**

Abonnement [abɔnəˈmãː, (*Sw*) abɔnɔˈment, abɔnˈmãː] NT **-s, -s** *or* (*Sw*) **-e** (a) (*von Zeitung, Fernsehsender*) subscription; **eine Zeitung im ~ beziehen** to subscribe to a newspaper (b) (= *Theaterabonnement*) season ticket

Abonnent [abɔˈnent] M **-en, -en**, **Abonnentin** [-ˈnentɪn] F **-, -nen** (*von Zeitung, Fernsehsender*) subscriber; (= *Theaterabonnent*) season-ticket holder

abonnieren [abɔˈniːrən], *ptp* **abonniert** VT SEP *Zeitung, Fernsehsender* to subscribe to; *Konzertreihe, Theater* to have a season ticket for

abordnen VT SEP to delegate

Abordnung F delegation

abpacken VT SEP to pack; **ein abgepacktes Brot** a wrapped loaf

abpassen VT SEP (a) (= *abwarten*) *Gelegenheit, Zeitpunkt* to wait for; (= *ergreifen*) to seize; **den richtigen Augenblick or Zeitpunkt ~** (= *abwarten*) to wait for the right time; (= *ergreifen*) to move at the right time; **ich habe den Zeitpunkt nicht richtig abgepasst** I mistimed it; **etw gut ~** to manage *or* arrange sth well; (*zeitlich auch*) to time sth well (b) (= *auf jdn warten*) to catch; (= *jdm auflauern*) to waylay

abpfeifen SEP IRREG (*Sport*) **1** VI (*Schiedsrichter*) to blow one's whistle **2** VT **das Spiel/die erste Halbzeit ~** to blow the whistle for the end of the game/for half-time

Abpfiff M (*Sport*) final whistle; **~ zur Halbzeit** half-time whistle

Abprall M (*von Ball*) rebound; (*von Geschoss, Kugel*) ricochet (*von* off)

abprallen VI SEP AUX SEIN (*Ball*) to bounce off; (*Kugel*) to ricochet (off); **von or an etw** (*dat*) **~** to bounce/ricochet off sth; **an jdm ~** (*fig*) to make no impression on sb; (*Beleidigungen*) to bounce off sb

abpumpen VT SEP *Teich, Schwimmbecken* to pump dry; *Wasser, Öl* to pump off; *Muttermilch* to express

abputzen VT SEP to clean; *Schmutz* to clean off *or* up; **sich** (*dat*) **die Nase/den Mund/die Hände ~** to wipe one's nose/mouth/hands; **sich** (*dat*) **den Hintern ~** to wipe *or* clean one's bottom; **putz dir die Schuhe ab** wipe your feet

abqualifizieren *ptp* **abqualifiziert** VT SEP to dismiss, to write off

abrackern VR SEP (*inf*) to struggle; **sich für jdn ~** to slave away for sb

Abraham [ˈaːbraham] M **-s** Abraham; **sicher wie in ~s Schoß** safe and secure

Abrakadabra [aːbrakaˈdaːbra, ˌabrakaˈdaːbra] NT **-s**, NO PL (= *Zauberwort*) abracadabra

abrasieren *ptp* **abrasiert** VT SEP to shave off

abraten VTI SEP IRREG **jdm (von) etw ~** to advise sb against sth; **jdm davon ~, etw zu tun** to warn *or* advise sb against doing sth

abräumen SEP **1** VT (a) *Geschirr, Frühstück* to clear up *or* away; **den Tisch ~** to clear the table (b) (= *entfernen*) *Sitzblockierer* to remove (c) *Konten* to clean out; *Preise, Medaillen* to walk off with (d) (*inf:* = *stehlen*) to pinch (*inf*) **2** VI (a) (= *den Tisch ~*) to clear up (b) (= *sich bereichern*) to clean up

abreagieren *ptp* **abreagiert** SEP **1** VT *Spannung, Wut* to work off; **seinen Ärger an anderen ~** to take it out on others **2** VR to work it off; **er war ganz wütend, aber jetzt hat er sich abreagiert** he was furious, but he's simmered down now; **sich an der Katze ~** to take it out on the cat

abrechnen SEP **1** VI (a) (= *Kasse machen*) to cash up; **der Kellner wollte ~** the waiter was wanting us/them to pay our/their bill; **darf ich ~?** would you like to settle your bill now? (b) **mit jdm ~** to settle up with sb; (*fig*) to settle the score with sb **2** VT (= *abziehen*) to deduct, to take off

Abrechnung F (a) (= *Aufstellung*) statement (*über* +*acc* for); (= *Rechnung*) bill, invoice; (= *das Kassemachen*) cashing up; (*fig:* = *Rache*) revenge; **ich bin gerade bei der ~** I'm just working it out now; **bei der ~ der Konten** when the accounts are/were being balanced; **er muss noch die ganzen ~en machen** he still has to do all the accounts *or* the bookwork;

der Tag der ~ (*fig*) the day of reckoning **(b)** (= *Abzug*) deduction; **nach ~ von** after the deduction of; **in ~ bringen** *or* **stellen** (*form*) to deduct

Abrechnungsstelle F (*Fin*) clearing house

abreichern ['aprαiçɐn] VT SEP to deplete

Abreise F departure (*nach* for); **bei der** *or* **meiner ~** on my departure

abreisen VI SEP AUX SEIN to leave (*nach* for); **wann reisen Sie ab?** when will you be leaving?

abreißen SEP IRREG **1** VT **(a)** (= *abtrennen*) to tear *or* rip off; *Tapete* to strip off; *Plakat* to tear *or* rip down; **den Kontakt nicht ~ lassen** to stay in touch **(b)** (= *niederreißen*) *Gebäude* to pull down **2** VI AUX SEIN (= *sich lösen*) to tear *or* come off; (*Schnürsenkel*) to break (off); (*fig:* = *unterbrochen werden*) to break off; **das reißt nicht ab** (*fig*) there is no end to it

abrichten VT SEP (= *dressieren*) to train; **der Hund ist nur auf Einbrecher abgerichtet** the dog is trained to go only for burglars; **darauf abgerichtet sein, etw zu tun** to be trained to do sth

abriegeln ['apriːgln] VT SEP *Tür* to bolt; *Straße, Gebiet* to seal *or* cordon off

abringen VT SEP IRREG **jdm etw ~** to wring sth out of sb; **sich** (*dat*) **ein Lächeln ~** to force a smile; **sich** (*dat*) **eine Entscheidung ~** to force oneself into (making) a decision; **sich** (*dat*) **ein paar Worte ~** to manage to produce a few words

Abriss M **(a)** (= *Abbruch*) demolition **(b)** (= *Übersicht*) outline, summary

Abriss-: Abrissarbeiten PL demolition work; **Abrissbirne** F wrecking ball; **Abrissliste** F (*inf*) demolition list; **auf der ~ stehen** to be condemned; **abrissreif** ADJ only fit for demolition; (= *zum Abriss freigegeben*) condemned

abrollen SEP **1** VT *Papier, Stoff* to unroll; *Film, Bindfaden, Kabel, Tau* to unwind **2** VI AUX SEIN **(a)** (*Papier, Stoff*) to unroll, to come unrolled; (*Film, Bindfaden*) to unwind, to come unwound; (*Kabel, Tau*) to uncoil, to come uncoiled **(b)** (*inf*) (= *vonstatten gehen*) (*Programm*) to run; (*Veranstaltung*) to go off; (*Ereignisse*) to unfold; **etw rollt vor jds Augen ab** sth unfolds *or* unwinds before sb's (very) eyes; **mein ganzes Leben rollte noch einmal vor meinen Augen ab** my whole life passed before me again

Abruf M **sich auf ~ bereithalten** to be ready to be called (for); **Ihr Wagen steht jederzeit auf ~ bereit** your car will be ready at any time; **auf ~ zur Verfügung stehen** to be available on call; **etw auf ~ bestellen/kaufen** (*Comm*) to order/buy sth (to be delivered) on call

Abruf-: abrufbar ADJ **(a)** (*Comput*) *Daten* retrievable **(b)** (*Fin*) ready on call **(c)** (*fig*) accessible; **abrufbereit** ADJ **(a)** *Mensch* ready to be called (for); (= *einsatzbereit*) ready (and waiting); (= *abholbereit*) ready to be called for **(b)** (*Comm, Fin*) ready on call

abrufen VT SEP IRREG **(a)** (= *wegrufen*) to call away; **jdn aus dem Leben ~** (*euph*) to gather sb to his fathers (*euph*) **(b)** (*Comm*) to request delivery of; (*Fin:* = *abheben*) to withdraw; *staatliche Zuschüsse* to call **(c)** *Daten, Informationen* to call up, to retrieve

abrunden VT SEP (*lit, fig*) to round off; **eine Zahl nach oben/ unten ~** to round a number up/down; **wir haben die Summe abgerundet** we made it a round sum; **EUR 13,12, also abgerundet EUR 13,10** EUR 13.12, so call it EUR 13.10

abrupt [ap'rʊpt, a'brʊpt] **1** ADJ abrupt **2** ADV abruptly

abrüsten SEP **1** VI **(a)** (*Mil, Pol*) to disarm **(b)** (*Build*) to take down the scaffolding **2** VT **(a)** (*Mil, Pol*) to disarm **(b)** *Gebäude* to take down the scaffolding from *or* on

Abrüstung F, NO PL **(a)** (*Mil, Pol*) disarmament **(b)** (*Build*) removal of the scaffolding

Abrüstungs-: Abrüstungsabkommen NT disarmament treaty; **Abrüstungskonferenz** F disarmament conference

abrutschen VI SEP AUX SEIN (= *abgleiten*) to slip; (*nach unten*) to slip down; (*Wagen*) to skid; (*Aviat*) to sideslip; (*fig*) (*Mannschaft, Schüler*) to drop (down) (*auf +acc* to); (*Leistungen*) to go downhill

ABS [aːbeːˈʔɛs] NT -, NO PL (*Aut*) ABBR *von* **Antiblockiersystem** ABS

Abs. ABBR *von* **Absatz, Absender**

absacken VI SEP AUX SEIN (= *sinken*) to sink; (*Flugzeug, Blutdruck*) to drop, to fall; (*inf:* = *verkommen*) to go to pot (*inf*);

sie ist in ihren Leistungen sehr abgesackt her performance has dropped off a lot

Absage F refusal; **das ist eine ~ an die Demokratie** that's a denial of democracy; **jdm/einer Sache eine ~ erteilen** to reject sb/sth

absagen SEP **1** VT (= *rückgängig machen*) *Veranstaltung, Besuch* to cancel, to call off; (= *ablehnen*) *Einladung* to turn down; **er hat seine Teilnahme abgesagt** he decided to withdraw his participation **2** VI to cry off (*Brit*), to cancel; **jdm ~** to tell sb that one can't come; **wenn ich ihn einlade, sagt er jedes Mal ab** whenever I invite him he says no

absägen VT SEP **(a)** (= *abtrennen*) to saw off **(b)** (*fig inf*) to chuck *or* sling out (*inf*); *Minister, Beamten* to oust; *Schüler* to make fail

absahnen ['apzaːnən] SEP **1** VT *Milch* to skim; (*fig inf*) *Geld* to rake in; (= *sich verschaffen*) to cream off; *das Beste* to take **2** VI (*fig inf*) to take the best; (*in Bezug auf Geld*) to clean up (*inf*)

Absatz M **(a)** (= *Abschnitt*) paragraph; (*Typ*) indention; (*Jur*) section; **einen ~ machen** to start a new paragraph/to indent **(b)** (= *Treppenabsatz*) half landing **(c)** (= *Schuhabsatz*) heel; **spitze Absätze** stilettos **(d)** (= *Verkauf*) sales *pl*; **um den/ unseren ~ zu steigern** to increase sales/our sales; **~ finden** *or* **haben** to sell; **guten/begeisterten** *or* **starken** *or* **reißenden ~ finden** to sell well/like hot cakes

Absatz-: Absatzchance F sales potential *no pl*; **Absatzflaute** F slump in sales; **Absatzgebiet** NT sales area; **Absatzlage** F sales situation; **Absatzmarkt** M market; **Absatzrückgang** M decline *or* decrease in sales; **Absatzschwierigkeiten** PL sales problems *pl*; **auf ~ stoßen** to meet with sales resistance; **Absatzsteigerung** F increase in sales

absatzweise **1** ADJ in paragraphs **2** ADV paragraph by paragraph

absaugen VT SEP *Flüssigkeit, Gas, Staub* to suck out *or* off; *Teppich, Sofa* to hoover® (*Brit*), to vacuum

ABS- [aːbeːˈʔɛs-]: **ABS-Bremse** F ABS brakes *pl*; **ABS-Bremssystem** NT ABS braking system

abschaben VT SEP to scrape off; (= *säubern*) to scrape (clean); *Stoff* to wear thin

abschaffen SEP **1** VT **(a)** *Gesetz, Regelung* to abolish **(b)** (= *nicht länger halten*) to get rid of; *Auto etc* to give up **2** VR (*S Ger inf*) to slave away (*inf*)

Abschaffung F **(a)** (*von Gesetz, Regelung*) abolition **(b)** (= *Loswerden*) getting rid of; (*von Auto etc*) giving up

abschalten SEP **1** VT to switch off; *Kontakt* to break **2** VI (*fig*) to unwind **3** VR to switch itself off

abschätzen VT SEP to assess; **ein ~der Blick** an appraising look

abschätzig ['apʃɛtsɪç] **1** ADJ disparaging **2** ADV disparagingly; **sich ~ über jdn äußern** to make disparaging remarks about sb

Abschaum M, NO PL scum; **der ~ der Menschheit, der ~ der menschlichen Gesellschaft** the scum of the earth

Abscheu M -(e)s *or* f -, NO PL repulsion (*vor +dat* at); **vor jdm/ etw ~ haben** *or* **empfinden** to loathe *or* detest sb/sth; **~ erregend** *siehe* **abscheuerregend**

abscheuerregend ADJ repulsive, loathsome

abscheulich [ap'ʃɔylɪç] **1** ADJ atrocious, loathsome; (*inf*) awful, terrible **2** ADV *behandeln, zurichten* atrociously, abominably; *sich anziehen* terribly, awfully; **es ist ~ kalt** it's hideously cold; **~ riechen/schmecken** to smell/taste horrible; **das tut ~ weh** it hurts terribly

abschicken VT SEP to send; *Paket, Brief* to send off, to dispatch

Abschiebehaft F (*Jur*) remand pending deportation; **jdn in ~ nehmen** to put sb on remand pending deportation

abschieben VT SEP IRREG **(a)** (= *ausweisen*) *Ausländer, Häftling* to deport **(b)** (*inf:* = *loswerden*) to get rid of; **jdn in eine andere Abteilung ~** to shunt sb off to another department **(c)** (*fig*) *Verantwortung, Schuld* to push *or* shift (*auf +acc* onto)

Abschiebung F (= *Ausweisung*) deportation

Abschied ['apʃiːt] M -(e)s, -e [-də] farewell, parting; **von jdm/ etw ~ nehmen** to say goodbye to sb/sth; **ein Kuss zum ~** a farewell *or* goodbye kiss; **zum ~ überreichte er ihr einen Blumenstrauß** on parting, he presented her with a bunch of flowers; **ein trauriger ~** a sad farewell; **es war für beide schwerer ~** parting was hard for both of them; **ich hasse ~e** I hate farewells *or* goodbyes; **es war ein ~ für immer** *or* **fürs Leben** it was goodbye for ever; **beim ~ meinte er, ...** as he was leaving he said ...; **beim ~ auf Bahnhöfen ...** saying goodbye at stations ...; **der ~ von der Heimat fiel ihm schwer** it was hard for him to say goodbye to the land of his birth; **ihr ~ von der Bühne/vom Film** her farewell to the stage/to films; (= *letzte Vorstellung*) her farewell performance; **der ~ von der Vergangenheit** breaking *or* the break with the past

Abschieds- IN CPDS farewell; **Abschiedsbrief** M farewell letter; **Abschiedsfeier** F farewell *or* leaving party; **Abschiedsgeschenk** NT (*für Kollegen etc*) leaving present; (*für Freund*) going-away present; **Abschiedsgesuch** NT (*Pol*) letter of resignation; **sein ~ einreichen** to tender one's resignation; **Abschiedskuss** M farewell *or* goodbye kiss; **Abschiedsstimmung** F mood of parting *or* farewell

abschießen VT SEP IRREG **(a)** (= *losschießen*) Geschoss, Gewehr, Kanone to fire; Pfeil to shoot (off); Rakete to launch; (*auf ein Ziel*) to fire; (*fig*) Fragen, Befehle, Bemerkung to fire (*auf +acc* at) **(b)** Flugzeug, Pilot to shoot down; Bein etc to shoot off **(c)** (= *totschießen*) Wild to shoot; (*inf*) Menschen to shoot down

abschinden VR SEP IRREG (*inf*) to tire oneself out; (= *schwer arbeiten*) to work one's fingers to the bone

Abschirmdienst M (*Mil*) counterespionage service

abschirmen [ˈapʃɪrmən] SEP **1** VT to shield; Lampe to cover; **jdn vor etw** (*dat*) ~ to shield *or* protect sb from sth; **etw gegen die Sonne ~** to screen *or* shield sth from the sun **2** VR to shield oneself (*gegen* from); (= *sich schützen*) to protect oneself (*gegen* from *or* against); (= *sich isolieren*) to cut oneself off (*gegen* from)

abschlachten VT SEP to slaughter

abschlaffen [ˈapʃlafn] VI SEP AUX SEIN (*inf*) to flag; *siehe auch* **abgeschlafft**

Abschlag M **(a)** (= *Preisnachlass*) reduction; (= *Abzug*) deduction **(b)** (= *Zahlung*) part payment (*auf +acc* of) **(c)** (*Ftbl*) kickout, punt; (*Hockey*) bully(-off); (*Golf*) tee-off; (= *~fläche*) tee

abschlagen VT SEP IRREG **(a)** (*mit Hammer etc*) to knock off; (*mit Schwert etc*) Fuß, Kopf, Hand to cut off; (*mit Beil*) to cut *or* chop off; (= *herunterschlagen*) to knock down **(b)** (= *ablehnen*) to refuse; **jdm etw ~** to refuse sb sth (*Ftbl*) to punt; (*Hockey*) to bully off; (*Golf*) to tee off; *siehe* **abgeschlagen**

abschlägig [ˈapʃlɛːgɪç] **1** ADJ negative; **~er Bescheid** rejection; (*bei Sozialamt, Kredit etc*) refusal **2** ADV **jdn/etw ~ bescheiden** (*form*) to turn sb/sth down

Abschlag(s)zahlung F part payment

abschleifen SEP IRREG **1** VT Kanten, Ecken, Unebenheiten to grind down; Rost to polish off; Messer to grind; Holz, Holzboden to sand (down) **2** VR to get worn off, to wear down; (*fig*) (Angewohnheit etc) to wear off

Abschleppdienst M breakdown *or* recovery service

abschleppen SEP **1** VT **(a)** (= *wegziehen*) to drag off *or* away; Fahrzeug, Schiff to tow; (*Behörde*) to tow away sb (*inf*) Menschen to drag along; (= *aufgabeln*) to pick up (*inf*) **2** VR **sich mit etw ~** (*inf*) to struggle with sth

Abschlepp-: **Abschleppfahrzeug** NT breakdown *or* recovery vehicle; **Abschleppkosten** PL recovery costs *pl*; **Abschleppöse** F tow loop; **Abschleppseil** NT towrope; **Abschleppstange** F towbar

abschließbar ADJ (= *verschließbar*) lockable

abschließen SEP IRREG **1** VT **(a)** (= *zuschließen*) to lock; Auto, Raum, Schrank to lock (up) **(b)** (= *beenden*) Sitzung, Vortrag etc to conclude, to bring to a close; (*mit Verzierung*) to finish off; Kursus to complete; **sein Studium ~** to take one's degree, to graduate; **mit abgeschlossenem Studium** with a degree **(c)** (= *vereinbaren*) Geschäft to conclude, to transact; Versicherung to take out; Vertrag to conclude; Wette to place **(d)** (*Comm*: = *abrechnen*) Bücher to balance; Konto to settle; Geschäftsjahr to close; Inventur to complete; Rechnung to make up **2** VR (= *sich isolieren*) to shut oneself away; **sich von der Außenwelt ~** to cut *or* shut oneself off from the outside world; *siehe auch* **abgeschlossen** **3** VI **(a)** (= *zuschließen*) to lock up; **sieh mal nach, ob auch abgeschlossen ist** will you see if everything's locked? **(b)** (= *enden*) to come to a close, to conclude **(c)** (= *Schluss machen*) to finish, to end; **mit allem/dem Leben ~** to finish with everything/life; **mit der Vergangenheit ~** to break with the past

abschließend 1 ADJ concluding **2** ADV in conclusion

Abschluss M **(a)** (= *Beendigung*) end; (*von Untersuchung*) conclusion; (*inf*: = *~prüfung*) final examination; (*Univ*) degree; **zum ~ von etw** at the close *or* end of sth; **zum ~ möchte ich ...** finally *or* to conclude I would like ...; **seinen ~ finden** (*geh*), **zum ~ kommen** to come to an end; **etw zum ~ bringen** to finish sth; **ein Wort zum ~** a final word; **kurz vor dem ~ stehen** to be in the final stages; **seinen ~ machen** (*Univ*) to do one's final exams; **nach ~ des Studiums/der Lehre** after finishing university/one's apprenticeship; **sie hat die Universität ohne ~ verlassen** she left the university without taking her degree **(b)** NO PL (= *Vereinbarung*) conclusion; (*von Wette*) placing; (*von Versicherung*) taking out; **bei ~ des Vertrages** on conclusion of the contract **(c)** (*Comm*: = *Geschäft*) business deal; **zum ~ kommen** to make a deal **(d)** NO PL (*Comm*) (*der Bücher*) balancing; (*von Konto*) settlement; (*von Geschäftsjahr*) close; (*von Inventur*) completion

Abschluss-: **Abschlussball** M (*von Tanzkurs*) final ball; **Abschlussfeier** F (*Sch*) speech *or* prize-giving day; **Abschlussklasse** F (*Sch*) final class *or* year; **Abschlussprüfung** F **(a)** (*Sch*) final examination; (*Univ*) finals *pl* (*Brit*), final exam **(b)** (*Comm*) audit; **Abschlussrechnung** F final account; **Abschlusszahlung** F final payment; (*Schlussrate*) final instalment (*Brit*) *or* installment (*US*); **Abschlusszeugnis** NT (*Sch*) leaving certificate (*Brit*), diploma (*US*)

abschmettern VT SEP (*inf*) (*Sport*) to smash; (*fig*: = *zurückweisen*) to throw out

abschmieren SEP **1** VT (*Tech*) Auto to grease, to lubricate **2** VI AUX SEIN (*Aviat*) to go down

Abschmierpresse F grease gun

abschminken SEP **1** VT **(a)** Gesicht, Haut to remove the make-up from **(b)** (*inf*: = *aufgeben*) sich (*dat*) **etw ~** to get sth out of one's head **2** VR to take off *or* remove one's make-up

abschmirgeln VT SEP to sand down

abschnallen SEP **1** VT to unfasten, to undo **2** VR to unfasten one's seat belt **3** VI (*sl*: = *nicht mehr folgen können*) to give up

abschneiden SEP IRREG **1** VT (*lit, fig*) to cut off; Blumen, Scheibe to cut (off); Zigarre to cut the end off; Haar to cut; **jdm die Rede** *or* **das Wort ~** to cut sb short **2** VI **bei etw gut/schlecht ~** (*inf*) to come off well/badly in sth

Abschnitt M section; (*Math*) segment; (*Mil*) sector, zone; (= *Geschichtsabschnitt, Zeitabschnitt*) period; (= *Kontrollabschnitt*) (*von Scheck etc*) counterfoil

abschöpfen VT SEP to skim off; (*fig*) Kaufkraft to absorb; (= *für sich gewinnen*) to cream off; **den Gewinn ~** to siphon off the profits

Abschöpfung F (*Fin: von Kaufkraft*) absorption

abschotten [ˈapʃɔtn] VT SEP (*Naut*) to separate with a bulkhead, to bulkhead off; **sich gegen etw ~** (*fig*) to cut oneself off from sth; **etw ~** to shield *or* screen sth

abschrägen VT SEP to slope; Holz, Brett to bevel; **ein abgeschrägtes Dach** a sloping roof

Abschrägung F **-, -en** slope; (*von Brett*) bevel

abschrauben VT SEP to unscrew

abschrecken SEP **1** VT **(a)** (= *fern halten*) to deter, to put off; (= *verjagen: Hund, Vogelscheuche*) to scare off; **jdn von etw ~** to put sb off sth; **ich lasse mich dadurch nicht ~** that won't deter me **(b)** (= *abkühlen*) Stahl to quench; (*Cook*) to rinse with cold water **2** VI (*Strafe*) to act as a deterrent

abschreckend ADJ (= *warnend*) deterrent; **ein ~es Beispiel** a warning; **eine ~e Wirkung haben**, **~ wirken** to act as a deterrent

Abschreckung [ˈapʃrɛkʊŋ] F **-, -en** (= *das Fernhalten*) (*Mil*) deterrence; (= *das Verjagen*) scaring off; (= *Abschreckungsmittel*) deterrent

Abschreckungs-: **Abschreckungsmittel** NT deterrent; **Abschreckungstheorie** F (*Jur*) theory of deterrence; **Abschreckungswaffe** F deterrent weapon

abschreiben SEP IRREG **1** VT **(a)** (= *kopieren*) to copy out; (= *plagiieren, Sch*) to copy (*bei, von* from) **(b)** (*Comm*) (= *absetzen, abziehen*) to deduct; (= *im Wert mindern*) to depreciate **(c)** (= *verloren geben*) to write off; **er ist bei mir**

abgeschrieben I'm through or finished with him **2** VI (Sch) to copy, to crib (Brit inf)

Abschreibung F (= Steuerabschreibung) tax write-off; (Comm) deduction; (= Wertverminderung) depreciation

Abschrift F copy

abschrubben VT SEP (inf) Schmutz to scrub off or away; Rücken, Kleid, Fußboden to scrub (down)

abschuften VR SEP (inf) to slog one's guts out (inf)

abschuppen SEP **1** VT Fisch to scale **2** VR to flake off

abschürfen VT SEP to graze

Abschürfung F -, -en (= Wunde) graze

Abschuss M (a) (= das Abfeuern) firing, shooting; (von Pfeil) shooting; (von Rakete) launch(ing); (auf ein Ziel) firing (b) (= das Außer-Gefecht-Setzen) shooting down; (von Panzer) knocking out; **die Luftwaffe erzielte zwölf Abschüsse** the air force shot or brought down twelve planes (c) (von Wild) shooting; **die Zahl der Abschüsse** the number of kills; **Fasanen sind jetzt zum ~ freigegeben** pheasant-shooting is now permitted; **jdn zum ~ freigeben** (fig) to throw sb to the wolves; **durch ~ des Ministers** (fig inf) by getting rid of the minister (d) (Sport) (goal) kick

Abschussbasis F launching base

abschüssig ['apʃʏsɪç] ADJ sloping

Abschuss-: Abschussliste F (inf) **er steht auf der ~** his days are numbered; **jdn auf die ~ setzen** to put sb on the hit list (inf); **auf jds ~ stehen** to be on sb's hit list (inf); **Abschussrampe** F launching pad

abschwächen SEP **1** VT to weaken; Behauptung, Formulierung, Kontrast to tone down; Schock, Aufprall to lessen; Stoß, Eindruck to soften **2** VR to drop or fall off, to diminish; (Lärm) to decrease; (Met: Hoch, Tief) to disperse; (Preisauftrieb, Andrang) to ease off; (St Ex: Kurse) to weaken

Abschwächung F weakening; (von Behauptung, Formulierung) toning down; (von Schock, Aufprall) lessening; (von Eindruck) softening; (= Rückgang: von Lärm) decrease; (Met: von Hoch, Tief) dispersal; (von Andrang, Preisauftrieb) easing off

abschwatzen, (S Ger) abschwätzen VT SEP (inf) **jdm etw ~** to talk sb into giving one sth

abschweifen VI SEP AUX SEIN (lit, fig) to stray, to wander (off); (Redner auch) to digress; **er schweifte vom Thema ab** he wandered off the subject

abschwellen VI SEP IRREG AUX SEIN (Entzündung, Fluss) to go down; (Lärm) to die away

abschwören VI SEP IRREG to renounce (+dat sth); **einer Sache** (dat) ~, **dem Alkohol ~** (inf) to give up drinking

Abschwung M (Comm) downward trend

absegeln VI SEP AUX SEIN (= lossegeln) to sail off, to set sail; (inf: = weggehen) to sail off

absegnen VT SEP (inf) Vorschlag, Plan to give one's blessing to; **von jdm abgesegnet sein** to have sb's blessing

absehbar ADJ foreseeable; **in ~er/auf ~e Zeit** in/for the foreseeable future; **das Ende seines Studiums ist noch nicht ~** the end of his studies is not yet in sight; **die Folgen sind noch gar nicht ~** there's no telling what the consequences will be

absehen SEP IRREG **1** VT (a) (= abgucken) **(bei) jdm etw ~** to pick sth up from sb; (= abschreiben) to copy sth from sb (b) (= voraussehen) to foresee; **es ist noch gar nicht abzusehen, wie lange die Arbeit dauern wird** there's no telling yet how long the work will take; **es ist ganz klar abzusehen, dass ...** it's easy to see that ...; **das Ende lässt sich noch nicht ~** the end is not yet in sight **2** VI **von etw ~** (= verzichten) to refrain from sth; (= nicht berücksichtigen) to disregard sth; **davon ~, etw zu tun** to refrain from doing sth; siehe auch **abgesehen**

abseilen ['apzailən] SEP **1** VT to let or lower down on a rope **2** VR to let or lower oneself down on a rope; (Bergsteiger) to abseil (down) (Brit), to rappel (US); (fig inf) to skedaddle (inf)

ab sein VI IRREG AUX SEIN (inf) (a) (= weg sein) to be off; **die Farbe/der Knopf ist ab** the paint/button has come off (b) (= abgelegen sein) to be far away

abseits ['apzaits] **1** ADV to one side; (= abgelegen) out of the way; (Sport) offside; **~ liegen** to be out of the way; **~ vom Wege** off the beaten track; **~ von der Straße** away from the road; **~ stehen** (fig) to be on the outside; (Sport) to be offside;

~ bleiben (fig), **sich ~ halten** (fig) to keep to oneself **2** PREP +GEN away from; **~ des Weges** off the beaten track

Abseits ['apzaits] NT -, - (Sport) offside; **im ~ stehen** to be offside; **ein Leben im ~ führen** (fig), **im ~ leben** (fig) to live in the shadows; **ins politische ~ geraten** to end up on the political scrapheap

absenden VT SEP to send; Brief, Paket to send off, to dispatch; (mit der Post) to send, to post (Brit), to mail (esp US)

Absender M (= Adresse) (sender's) address

Absender(in) M(F) sender

Absentismus [apzɛn'tɪsmʊs] M -, NO PL (Ind, Sociol) absenteeism

Absenz [ap'zɛnts] F -, -en (Sch: Aus, Sw) absence

abservieren ptp **abserviert** SEP **1** VI to clear the table **2** VT (a) Geschirr, Tisch to clear (b) (inf: = entlassen, kaltstellen) **jdn ~** to get rid of sb (c) (Sport sl: = besiegen) to thrash (inf)

absetzbar ADJ Ware saleable; Betrag deductible; **steuerlich ~** tax-deductible

absetzen SEP **1** VT (a) (= abnehmen) Hut, Brille to take off, to remove; (= hinstellen) Gepäck, Glas to set or put down; Geigenbogen, Feder to lift; Gewehr to unshoulder (b) (= aussteigen lassen) to drop (c) Theaterstück, Oper to take off; Fußballspiel, Turnier, Versammlung, Termin to cancel; **etw vom Spielplan ~** to take sth off the programme (Brit) or program (US) (d) (= entlassen) to dismiss; König, Kaiser to depose (e) (= entwöhnen) Jungtier to wean; (Med) Medikament, Tabletten to come off; Behandlung to discontinue; (Mil) Ration etc to stop; **die Tabletten mussten abgesetzt werden** I/she etc had to come off the tablets (f) (Comm) Waren to sell; **sich gut ~ lassen** to sell well (g) (= abziehen) Betrag, Summe to deduct; **das kann man (von der Steuer) ~** that is tax-deductible (h) (= kontrastieren) to contrast; **etw gegen etw ~** to set sth off against sth **2** VR (a) (Chem, Geol) to be deposited; (Feuchtigkeit, Staub etc) to collect (b) (inf: = weggehen) to get or clear out (aus of) (inf); **sich nach Brasilien ~** to clear off to Brazil (inf) **3** VI to put one's glass down; **er trank das Glas aus ohne abzusetzen** he emptied his glass in one

Absetzung F -, -en (a) (= Entlassung) dismissal; (von König) deposition (b) (Fin: = Abschreibung) deduction (c) (von Theaterstück etc) withdrawal; (von Fußballspiel, Termin etc) cancellation (d) (Med) discontinuation

absichern SEP **1** VT to safeguard; (= garantieren) to cover; Bauplatz, Gefahrenstelle to make safe; Dach to support; (= schützen) to protect; **jdn über die Landesliste ~** (Pol) to give sb a safe seat **2** VR (= sich schützen) to protect oneself; (= sich versichern) to cover oneself

Absicht F -, -en (= Vorsatz) intention; (= Zweck) purpose; (Jur) intent; **in der besten ~, in bester ~** with the best of intentions; **die ~ haben, etw zu tun** to intend to do sth; **eine ~ mit etw verfolgen** to have something in mind with sth; **etw mit/ohne ~ tun** to do/not to do sth on purpose or deliberately; **ernste ~en haben** (inf) to have serious intentions; **das war nicht meine ~!** I didn't intend that; **das war doch keine ~!** (inf) it wasn't deliberate or intentional

absichtlich **1** ADJ deliberate, intentional **2** ADV deliberately, intentionally

Absichtserklärung F declaration of intent

absinken VI SEP IRREG AUX SEIN to fall, to drop; (Boden) to subside, to sink; (Temperatur, Wasserspiegel, Kurs) to fall, to go down; (Interesse, Leistungen) to fall or drop off

absitzen SEP IRREG **1** VT (= verbringen) Zeit to sit out; (= verbüßen) Strafe to serve **2** VI AUX SEIN (vom Pferd) ~ to dismount (from a horse); **abgesessen!** dismount!

absolut [apzo'luːt] **1** ADJ (alle Bedeutungen) absolute **2** ADV absolutely; **~ genommen** or **betrachtet** considered in the absolute; **ich sehe ~ nicht ein, warum ...** I just don't understand why ...

Absolution [apzolu'tsioːn] F -, -en (Eccl) absolution; **jdm die ~ erteilen** to grant or give sb absolution

Absolutismus [apzolu'tɪsmʊs] M -, NO PL absolutism

absolutistisch [apzolu'tɪstɪʃ] **1** ADJ absolutist **2** ADV **~ herrschen** or **regieren** to be an absolute monarch

Absolvent [apzɔl'vɛnt] M **-en, -en, Absolventin** [-'vɛntɪn] F **-, -nen** (*Univ*) graduate; **die ~en eines Lehrgangs** the students who have completed a course

absolvieren [apzɔl'viːrən], *ptp* **absolviert** VT INSEP (= *durchlaufen*) *Studium, Probezeit* to complete; *Schule* to finish, to graduate from (*US*); *Prüfung* to pass; **er hat die technische Fachschule absolviert** he completed a course at technical college

absonderlich ☐ ADJ peculiar, strange ☐ ADV peculiarly, strangely

absondern SEP ☐ VT (a) (= *trennen*) to separate; (= *isolieren*) to isolate (b) (= *ausscheiden*) to secrete (c) (*inf*: = *von sich geben*) to come out with (*inf*) ☐ VR (a) (*Mensch*) to cut oneself off; **sie sondert sich immer sehr ab** she always keeps herself very much to herself (b) (= *ausgeschieden werden*) to be secreted

Absonderung F **-, -en** (a) (= *das Trennen*) separation; (= *Isolierung*) isolation; (= *Ausscheidung*) secretion (b) (*von Menschen*) segregation (c) (= *abgeschiedener Stoff*) secretion

absorbieren [apzɔr'biːrən], *ptp* **absorbiert** VT INSEP (*lit*, *fig*) to absorb

abspalten VTR SEP to split off; (*Chem*) to separate (off)

Abspann ['apʃpan] M **-s, -e** (*TV, Film*) final credits *pl*

abspannen SEP ☐ VT *Pferd, Wagen* to unhitch; *Ochsen* to unyoke ☐ VI (*fig*: = *entspannen*) to relax; *siehe auch* **abgespannt**

Abspannung F (= *Erschöpfung*) weariness

absparen VT SEP **sich** (*dat*) **Geld von etw ~** to save money from sth; **sich** (*dat*) **ein Auto vom Lohn ~** to save up for a car from one's wages; **sich** (*dat*) **etw vom** *or* **am Munde** *or* **am eigenen Leib ~** to scrimp and save for sth

abspecken ['apʃpɛkn] SEP (*inf*) ☐ VT to shed; (*fig*: = *verkleinern*) to trim ☐ VI to lose weight

abspeichern VT SEP *Daten* to store (away)

abspeisen VT SEP **jdn mit etw ~** to fob sb off with sth (*esp Brit*)

abspenstig ['apʃpɛnstɪç] ADJ **jdm jdn/etw ~ machen** to lure sb/sth away from sb; **jdm die Freundin ~ machen** to steal sb's girlfriend (*inf*)

absperren SEP ☐ VT (a) (= *abriegeln*) to block *or* close off (b) (= *abdrehen*) *Wasser, Strom, Gas etc* to turn *or* shut off (c) (= *verschließen*) to lock ☐ VI to lock up

Absperr-: Absperrgitter NT barrier; **Absperrkette** F chain

Absperrung F (a) (= *Abriegelung*) blocking *or* closing off (b) (= *Sperre*) barrier; (= *Kordon*) cordon

abspielen SEP ☐ VT (a) *Schallplatte, Tonband* to play (through); *Nationalhymne* to play; (*vom Blatt*) *Musik* to sight-read (b) (*Sport*) *Ball* to pass; (*beim Billard*) to play ☐ VR (= *sich ereignen*) to happen; (= *stattfinden*) to take place; **wie mein Leben sich abspielt** what my life is like; **da spielt sich (bei mir) nichts ab!** (*inf*) nothing doing! (*inf*)

absplittern VI SEP AUX SEIN (*Farbe*) to drip off; (*fig*: *Gruppe*) to break away

Absprache F arrangement; **eine ~ treffen** to make *or* come to an arrangement; **ohne vorherige ~** without prior consultation

absprechen SEP IRREG ☐ VT (a) **jdm etw ~** *Recht* to deny *or* refuse sb sth; *Begabung* to deny *or* dispute sb's sth (b) (= *verabreden*) *Termin* to arrange; **die Zeugen hatten ihre Aussagen vorher abgesprochen** the witnesses had agreed on what to say in advance ☐ VR **sich mit jdm ~** to make an arrangement with sb; **die beiden hatten sich vorher abgesprochen** they had agreed on what to do/say *etc* in advance; **ich werde mich mit ihr ~** I'll arrange *or* fix things with her

abspringen VI SEP IRREG AUX SEIN (a) (= *herunterspringen*) to jump down (*von* from); (*Aviat*) to jump (*von* from); (*bei Gefahr*) to bale out; **mit dem rechten Bein ~** to take off on the right leg (b) (= *sich lösen*) to come off; (*esp Farbe, Lack*) to flake *or* peel off; (= *abprallen*) to bounce off (*von etw* sth) (c) (*fig* *inf*: = *sich zurückziehen*) to opt out; (*von Partei, Kurs etc*) to back out; **von etw ~** to get *or* back out of sth

Absprung M jump (*auch Aviat*), leap; (*Sport*) takeoff; (= *Abgang*) dismount; **den ~ schaffen** (*fig*) to make it (*inf*); **er hat den ~ gewagt** (*fig*) he took the jump

abspülen SEP ☐ VT *Hände, Geschirr* to rinse; *Fett etc* to rinse off ☐ VI to wash up (*Brit*), to wash the dishes

abstammen VI SEP NO PTP to be descended (*von* from); (*Ling*) to be derived (*von* from)

Abstammung F **-, -en** descent; (*Ling*) origin, derivation; **ehelicher/unehelicher ~** (*Jur*) of legitimate/illegitimate descent

Abstand M (a) (= *Zwischenraum*) distance; (= *kürzerer ~*) gap, space; (= *Zeitabstand*) interval; (= *Punkteabstand*) gap; **mit ~** by far; **~ von etw gewinnen** (*fig*) to distance oneself from sth; **in regelmäßigen Abständen/Abständen von 10 Minuten** at regular/10 minute intervals; **~ halten** to keep one's distance; **mit großem ~ führen/gewinnen** to lead/win by a wide margin (b) (*form*: = *Verzicht*) **von etw ~ nehmen** to dispense with sth; **von Meinung, Absicht, Forderung** to abandon sth; **davon ~ nehmen, etw zu tun** to refrain from doing sth

Abstandssumme F (*form*) indemnity

abstatten ['apʃtatn] VT SEP (*form*) **jdm einen Besuch ~** to pay sb a visit; **jdm seinen Dank ~** to give thanks to sb

abstauben VTI SEP (a) *Möbel etc* to dust (b) (*inf*) (= *wegnehmen*) to pick up; (= *schnorren*) to cadge (*von, bei, +dat* off, from); **er will immer nur ~** he's always on the scrounge (c) (*Ftbl inf*) (**ein Tor** *or* **den Ball**) **~** to put the ball into (the back of) the net

abstechen SEP IRREG ☐ VT (a) **ein Tier ~** to cut an animal's throat; **jdn ~** (*inf*) to knife sb (*inf*) (b) (= *abtrennen*) *Torf* to cut; *Rasen* to trim (the edges of) ☐ VI **gegen jdn/etw ~, von jdm/etw ~** to stand out against sb/sth

Abstecher ['apʃtɛçɐ] M **-s, -** (= *Ausflug*) excursion, trip; (= *Umweg*) detour; (*fig*) sortie

abstecken VT SEP (a) *Gelände, Grenze, Trasse* to mark out; (*mit Pflöcken*) to peg *or* stake out; (*fig*) to work out (b) *Kleid, Naht* to pin

abstehen VI SEP IRREG (= *entfernt stehen*) to stand away; (= *nicht anliegen*) to stick out; **~de Ohren** ears that stick out; *siehe auch* **abgestanden**

Absteige F (*inf*) cheap hotel

absteigen VI SEP IRREG AUX SEIN (a) (= *heruntersteigen*) to get off (*von etw* sth); **„Radfahrer ~!"** "cyclists dismount" (b) (= *abwärts gehen*) to make one's way down; (*esp Bergsteiger*) to climb down; **auf dem ~den Ast sein** (*inf*) to be going downhill (c) (*Sport*: *Mannschaft*) to be relegated

Absteiger(in) M(F) (*Sport*) relegated team; (*vom Abstieg bedroht*) team facing relegation

abstellen SEP ☐ VT (a) (= *hinstellen*) to put down (b) (= *unterbringen*) to put; (*Aut*: = *parken*) to park (c) (= *abkommandieren*) to detail; (*fig*: = *abordnen*) to assign (d) (= *ausrichten auf*) **etw auf jdn/etw ~** to gear sth to sb/sth (e) (= *abdrehen*) *Gas, Geräte, Licht* to switch *or* turn off; *Gas, Strom* to cut off; *Telefon* to disconnect (f) (= *sich abgewöhnen*) to give up, to stop (g) (= *unterbinden*) *Mangel, Unsitte etc* to bring to an end; **das lässt sich nicht/lässt sich ~** nothing/something can be done about that; **lässt sich das nicht ~?** couldn't that be changed? ☐ VI **auf etw** (*acc*) **~** to be geared to sth; (= *etw berücksichtigen*) to take sth into account

Abstell-: Abstellgleis NT siding; **jdn aufs ~ schieben** (*fig*) to push *or* cast sb aside; **Abstellkammer** F boxroom; **Abstellplatz** M (*für Auto*) parking space; **ein ~ für Fahrräder** a place for leaving bicycles

abstempeln VT SEP to stamp; *Post* to postmark; (*fig*) to stamp (*zu, als* as)

absterben VI SEP IRREG AUX SEIN to die; (= *gefühllos werden*: *Glieder*) to go numb; (*fig*) (*Gefühle*) to die; (= *untergehen*: *Industriezweig, Sprachgruppe*) to die out; **mir sind die Zehen abgestorben** my toes have gone numb; *siehe auch* **abgestorben**

Abstieg ['apʃtiːk] M **-(e)s, -e** [-ɡə] (= *das Absteigen*) way down, descent; (= *Weg*) descent; (= *Niedergang*) decline; (*Sport*) relegation; **vom ~ bedroht** (*Sport*) threatened by relegation

abstimmen SEP ☐ VI to take a vote; **über etw** (*acc*) **~** to vote *or* take a vote on sth; **über etw** (*acc*) **~ lassen** to put sth to the vote; **geheim ~** to have a secret ballot ☐ VT *Instrumente* to tune (*auf +acc* to); *Radio* to tune (in) (*auf +acc* to); *Farben, Kleidung* to match (*auf +acc* with); *Termine* to coordinate (*auf +acc* with); (= *anpassen*) to suit (*auf +acc* to); **gut auf etw** (*acc*)**/aufeinander abgestimmt sein** (*Instrumente*) to be in tune with sth/with each other; (*Farben, Speisen etc*) to go well with sth/with each other *or* together; (*Termine*) to fit in well with sth/with each other; (= *einander angepasst* *sein*) to be well-suited to sth/(to each other); **etw miteinander ~** (= *vereinbaren*) to settle sth amongst ourselves/themselves *etc*; **abgestimmt** (= *vereinbart*) *Politik, Aktionen etc* agreed; **(aufeinander) abgestimmt** *Pläne, Strategien* mutually agreed **3** VR **sich (mit jdm/miteinander) ~** to come to an agreement (with sb/amongst ourselves/themselves *etc*)

Abstimmung F **(a)** (= *Stimmabgabe*) vote; (= *geheime* ~) ballot; (= *das Abstimmen*) voting; **eine ~ durchführen** *or* **vornehmen** to take a vote; to hold a ballot; **zur ~ bringen** (*form*) to put to the vote **(b)** (*von Instrumenten*) tuning; (*von Farben, Kleidung*) matching; (*von Terminen*) coordination; (= *das Anpassen*) suiting

Abstimmungs-: Abstimmungsergebnis NT result of the vote; **Abstimmungsniederlage** F **eine ~ erleiden** to be defeated in a/the vote; **Abstimmungssieg** M **einen ~ erringen** to win a/the vote

abstinent [apsti'nɛnt] **1** ADJ teetotal; (*geschlechtlich*) abstinent; **sie sind politisch ~** they don't engage in politics **2** ADV **~ leben** to live a life of abstinence

Abstinenz [apsti'nɛnts] F **-**, NO PL abstinence

abstinken VI SEP IRREG (*sl: = einpacken*) **damit kannst du ~** you can forget it (*inf*)

abstoßen SEP IRREG **1** VT **(a)** (= *wegstoßen*) *Boot* to push off *or* out; (= *abschlagen*) *Ecken* to knock off; *Möbel* to batter; **sich** (*dat*) **die Ecken und Kanten ~** (*fig*) to have the rough edges knocked off one **(b)** (= *zurückstoßen*) to repel; (*Comm*) *Ware, Aktien* to sell off; (*Med*) *Organ* to reject; (*fig: = anwidern*) to repulse, to repel; **dieser Stoff stößt Wasser ab** this material is water-repellent **2** VR **(a)** (= *abgeschlagen werden*) to get broken; (*Möbel*) to get battered **(b)** (*esp Sport: Mensch*) to push oneself off; **sich mit den Füßen vom Boden ~** to push oneself off **(c)** (*Phys*) to repel; **die beiden Pole stoßen sich ab** the two poles repel each other **3** VI (= *anwidern*) to be repulsive; **sich von etw abgestoßen fühlen** to find sth repulsive

abstoßend 1 ADJ *Aussehen, Äußeres* repulsive; **sein Wesen hat etwas Abstoßendes** there's something repulsive about him **2** ADV repulsively; **~ aussehen/riechen** to look/smell repulsive

Abstoßung F **-**, **-en** (*Phys*) repulsion; (*Med: von Organ*) rejection

Abstoßungsreaktion F (*Med*) rejection

abstottern VT SEP (*inf*) to pay off

abstrahieren [apstra'hiːrən], *ptp* **abstrahiert** VTI INSEP to abstract (*aus* from)

abstrahlen VT SEP *Wärme, Energie, Programm etc* to emit

abstrakt [ap'strakt] **1** ADJ abstract; **~e Kunst** abstract art **2** ADV abstractly

Abstraktum [ap'straktʊm] NT **-s**, **Abstrakta** [-ta] (*Ling*) abstract noun

abstrampeln VR SEP (*fig inf*) to sweat (away) (*inf*)

abstreifen VT SEP **(a)** (= *abtreten*) *Schuhe, Füße* to wipe; *Schmutz* to wipe off **(b)** (= *abziehen*) *Kleidung, Schmuck* to take off; (= *entfernen*) *Haut* to cast, to shed; (*fig*) *Gewohnheit, Fehler* to get rid of

abstreiten VT SEP IRREG (= *streitig machen*) to dispute; (= *leugnen*) to deny; **das kann man ihm nicht ~** you can't deny it

Abstrich M **(a)** (= *Kürzung*) cutback; **~e machen** to cut back (*an +dat* on); (= *weniger erwarten etc*) to lower one's sights **(b)** (*Med*) swab; (= *Gebärmutterabstrich*) smear; **einen ~ machen** to take a swab/smear

abstrus [ap'struːs] (*geh*) **1** ADJ abstruse **2** ADV abstrusely; **das ~ anmutende Drehbuch** the abstruse (film) script

abstufen VT SEP *Gelände* to terrace; *Haare* to layer; *Farben* to shade; *Gehälter, Steuern, Preise* to grade

Abstufung F **-**, **-en** (*von Gelände*) terracing; (= *Nuancierung*) shading; (= *Nuance*) shade; (= *Staffelung*) grading; (= *Stufe*) grade

abstumpfen ['apʃtʊmpfn] SEP **1** VI AUX SEIN (*fig: Geschmack etc*) to become dulled; **wenn man ewig dasselbe machen muss, stumpft man nach und nach ab** always having to do the same thing dulls the mind; **gegen etw ~** to become inured to sth **2** VT **(a)** *Menschen, Sinne* to deaden; *Gerechtigkeitssinn,*

Gewissen, Urteilsvermögen to dull; *siehe auch* **abgestumpft (b)** (*lit*) to blunt

Abstumpfung F **-**, NO PL (*von Menschen, Sinnen*) deadening; (*von Gewissen, Gerechtigkeitssinn*) dulling

Absturz M crash; (*sozial*) ruin; (*von Politiker etc*) downfall; (*Comput*) crash; **ein Flugzeug zum ~ bringen** to bring a plane down

abstürzen VI SEP AUX SEIN **(a)** (*Flugzeug*) to crash; (*Bergsteiger*) to fall **(b)** (*inf: sozial*) to go to ruin **(c)** (*inf: psychisch*) to come a cropper (*Brit inf*), to fall flat on one's face **(d)** (*sl: = betrunken werden*) to go on a bender (*Brit inf*), to go on a binge (*inf*) **(e)** (*Comput*) to crash **(f)** (*sl*) **mit jdm ~** (*sich sexuell betätigen*) to have a fumble with sb (*inf*)

abstützen SEP **1** VT to support (*auch fig*) **2** VR to support oneself

absuchen VT SEP to search; (*Med, Sci*) *Körper, Flüssigkeit* to scan; **jdn/etw nach etw ~** to search sb/sth for sth; **wir haben den ganzen Garten abgesucht** we searched all over the garden

absurd [ap'zʊrt] ADJ absurd; **das Absurde** the absurd

Absurdität [apzʊrdi'tɛːt] F **-**, **-en** absurdity

Abszess [aps'tsɛs] M **-es**, **-e** abscess

Abszisse [aps'tsɪsə] F **-**, **-n** abscissa

Abt [apt] M **-(e)s**, **ˆe** ['ɛptə] abbot

Abt. ABBR *von* Abteilung dept

abtasten VT SEP to feel; (*Med auch*) to palpate; (*Elec*) to scan; (*bei Durchsuchung*) to frisk (*auf +acc* for); (*fig: = erproben*) *jdn* to sound out

abtauchen VI SEP AUX SEIN **(a)** (*U-Boot*) to dive **(b)** (*inf*) to go underground

abtauen SEP **1** VT to thaw out; *Kühlschrank* to defrost **2** VI AUX SEIN to thaw

Abtei [ap'tai] F **-**, **-en** abbey

Abteil [ap'tail, 'ap-] NT compartment; **~ für Mutter und Kind, Mutter-(und-)Kind-~** *compartment reserved for mothers with young children*; **~ für Raucher** smoking compartment; **~ für Nichtraucher** no-smoking compartment

abteilen VT SEP **(a)** (= *einteilen*) to divide up; **fünf Stücke ~** to cut off five pieces **(b)** (= *abtrennen*) to divide off

Abteilung [ap'tailʊŋ] F (*in Firma, Kaufhaus, Hochschule*) department; (*in Krankenhaus*) (*Jur*) section; (*Mil*) unit, section

Abteilungsleiter(in) M(F) head of department; (*in Kaufhaus*) department manager/manageress

abtippen VT SEP (*inf*) to type out

Äbtissin [ɛp'tɪsɪn] F **-**, **-nen** abbess

abtönen VT SEP *Farbe* to tone down

abtöten VT SEP (*lit, fig*) to destroy, to kill (off); *Nerv* to deaden; *sinnliche Begierde* to mortify

abtragen VT SEP IRREG **(a)** AUCH VI *Geschirr, Speisen* to clear away **(b)** *Boden, Gelände* to level **(c)** *Kleider, Schuhe* to wear out; *siehe auch* **abgetragen**

abträglich ['aptrɛːklɪç], (*Sw*) **abträgig** ['aptrɛːgɪç] ADJ detrimental, harmful; *Bemerkung, Kritik etc* unfavourable (*Brit*), unfavorable (*US*); **einer Sache** (*dat*) **~ sein** to be detrimental *or* harmful to sth

Abtransport M transportation; (*aus Katastrophengebiet*) evacuation; **beim ~ der Gefangenen** when the prisoners were being taken away

abtransportieren *ptp* **abtransportiert** VT SEP *Waren* to transport; *Personen* to take away; (*aus Katastrophengebiet*) to evacuate

abtreiben SEP IRREG **1** VT *Kind* to abort; **sie hat das Kind abgetrieben** *or* **~ lassen** she had an abortion **2** VI **(a)** AUX SEIN (**vom Kurs**) (*Flugzeug*) to be sent off course; (*Boot auch, Schwimmer*) to be carried off course **(b)** (= *Abort vornehmen*) to carry out an abortion; (*generell*) to do abortions; (= *Abort vornehmen lassen*) to have an abortion

Abtreibung ['aptraibʊŋ] F **-**, **-en** abortion; **eine ~ vornehmen lassen** to have an abortion

Abtreibungs-: Abtreibungsbefürworter(in) M(F) pro-abortionist; **Abtreibungsgegner(in)** M(F) anti-abortionist, pro-lifer (*inf*); **Abtreibungsklinik** F abortion clinic;

Abtreibungspille F abortion pill; **Abtreibungspraxis** F (= *Klinik*) abortion clinic; **Abtreibungstourismus** M (*inf*) *going to another country/state to have an abortion*; **Abtreibungsversuch** M attempt at an abortion

abtrennbar ADJ (= *lostrennbar*) detachable; (= *abteilbar*) separable; *Verfahren* severable (*form*)

abtrennen VT SEP **(a)** (= *lostrennen*) to detach; *Knöpfe, Besatz etc* to remove, to take off; (= *abschneiden*) to cut off; *Bein, Finger etc* (*durch Unfall*) to sever; **„hier ~"** "detach here" **(b)** (= *abteilen*) to separate off; (*mit Trennwand etc*) to divide or partition off

abtreten SEP IRREG **1** VT **(a)** (= *überlassen*) (*jdm or an jdn to sb*) to hand over; *Rechte, Ansprüche, Haus, Geldsumme* to transfer **(b)** *Teppich* to wear; (*völlig*) to wear out; *Schnee, Schmutz* to stamp off; **sich** (*dat*) **die Füße** *or* **Schuhe ~** to wipe one's feet **2** VI AUX SEIN (*Theat*) to go off (stage); (*Mil*) to dismiss; (*inf*: = *zurücktreten*) (*Politiker*) to step down (*inf*), to resign; (*Monarch*) to abdicate

Abtretung F **-, -en** (*an +acc to*) transfer; (*von Rechten, Ansprüchen auch, von Gebiet*) ceding (*form*); **durch ~ aller Ansprüche an seinen Teilhaber** by transferring all rights to his partner

Abtrieb M **(a)** (= *Viehabtrieb*) **im Herbst beginnt der ~ des Viehs von den Bergweiden** in autumn (*esp Brit*) *or* fall (*US*) they start to bring the cattle down from the mountain pastures **(b)** (*Tech*) output **(c)** (*Aus*) mixture

abtrocknen SEP **1** VT to dry (off); *Geschirr* to dry **2** VI to dry (up)

abtropfen VI SEP AUX SEIN to drip; (*Geschirr*) to drain; **etw ~ lassen** *Wäsche etc* to let sth drip; *Salat* to drain sth; *Geschirr* to let sth drain

abtrünnig ['aptrʏnɪç] ADJ renegade, apostate (*form, esp Eccl*); (= *rebellisch*) rebel; **jdm/einer Gruppe** *etc* **~ werden** to desert sb/a group *etc*; (= *sich erheben gegen*) to rebel against sb/a group *etc*

abtun VT SEP IRREG **(a)** (*fig*: = *beiseite schieben*) to dismiss; **etw mit einem Achselzucken/einem Lachen ~** to shrug/laugh sth off; **etw kurz ~** to brush sth aside; *siehe auch* **abgetan (b)** (*dial*: = *ablegen*) to take off

abtupfen VT SEP *Tränen, Blut* to dab away; *Gesicht, Mundwinkel* to dab; *Wunde* to swab

abverlangen *ptp* **abverlangt** VT SEP = **abfordern**

abwägen ['apvɛːgn], *pret* **wog ab** [voːk ap], *ptp* **abgewogen** ['apgəvoːgn] VT SEP IRREG to weigh up; *Worte* to weigh; *siehe auch* **abgewogen**

abwählen VT SEP to vote out (of office); (*Sch*) *Fach* to give up

abwälzen VT SEP *Schuld, Verantwortung* to shift (*auf +acc* onto); *Arbeit* to unload (*aus* out of); *Kosten* to pass on (*auf +acc* to)

abwandern VI SEP AUX SEIN to move (away) (*aus* from); (*Kapital*) to be transferred (*aus* out of); **viele Spieler/Abonnenten** *etc* **wandern ab** a lot of players/subscribers *etc* are transferring

Abwärme F waste heat

Abwart ['apvart] M **-(e)s, -e**, **Abwartin** [-tɪn] F **-, -nen** (*Sw*) concierge, caretaker

abwarten SEP **1** VT to wait for; **das Gewitter ~** to wait till the storm is over; **er kann es nicht mehr ~** he can't wait any longer; **das bleibt abzuwarten** that remains to be seen **2** VI to wait; **warten Sie ab!** just wait a bit!; **~ und Tee trinken** (*inf*) to wait and see; **eine ~de Haltung einnehmen** to adopt a policy of wait-and-see

abwärts ['apvɛrts] ADV down; (= *nach unten auch*) downwards; **den Fluss/Berg ~** down the river/mountain; **„~!"** (*im Fahrstuhl*) "going down!"

Abwärts-: Abwärtsfahrt F journey down; **abwärts gehen** VI IMPERS IRREG AUX SEIN (*fig*) **mit ihm/dem Land geht es abwärts** he/the country is going downhill; **abwärtskompatibel** ADJ (*Comput*) downward compatible; **Abwärtstrend** M downwards trend

Abwasch¹ ['apvaʃ] M **-s**, NO PL washing-up (*Brit*), dirty dishes *pl*; **den ~ machen** to wash the dishes; **... dann kannst du das auch machen, das ist (dann) ein ~** (*inf*) ... then you could do that as well and kill two birds with one stone

Abwasch² F **-, -en** (*Aus*: = *Spülbecken*) sink

abwaschbar ADJ *Tapete* washable; *Kleidung* wipeable; *Tinte* non-permanent

abwaschen SEP IRREG **1** VT *Gesicht, Geschirr* to wash; *Farbe, Schmutz* to wash off; *Pferd, Auto* to wash down; **den Schmutz (vom Gesicht) ~** to wash the dirt off (one's face) **2** VI to wash the dishes

Abwaschwasser NT, *pl* **-wässer** dishwater

Abwasser NT, *pl* **-wässer** sewage *no pl*; **industrielle Abwässer** industrial effluents *pl or* waste *sing*

Abwasser-: Abwasseraufbereitung F reprocessing of sewage; (*von Industrieabwässern*) reprocessing of effluents; **Abwasserkanal** M sewer

abwechseln VIR SEP to alternate; **sich** *or* **einander ~** to alternate; (*Menschen auch*) to take turns; **sich mit jdm ~** to take turns with sb; **Regen und Schnee wechselten (sich) miteinander ab** it rained and snowed alternately

abwechselnd **1** ADV alternately; **wir haben ~ Klavier gespielt** we took turns playing the piano; **er war ~ fröhlich und traurig** he alternated between being happy and sad **2** ADJ alternate

Abwechslung ['apvɛkslʊŋ] F **-, -en** change; (= *Zerstreuung*) diversion; **eine angenehme/schöne ~** a pleasant/nice change; **zur ~** for a change; **hier haben wir wenig ~** there's not much variety in life here; **da gibt es mehr ~** there's more going on there

abwechslungsreich **1** ADJ varied **2** ADV **den Unterricht ~ gestalten** to give interesting and varied lessons

Abweg ['apveːk] M (*fig*) mistake, error; **jdn auf ~e führen** to mislead sb; (*moralisch*) to lead sb astray; **auf ~e geraten** *or* **kommen** to go astray

abwegig ['apveːgɪç] ADJ absurd; *Verdacht* unfounded

Abwehr F, NO PL **(a)** (*Biol, Psych, Med*) defence (*Brit*), defense (*US*) (+*gen* against); (= *Schutz*) protection (+*gen* against); **der ~ von etw dienen** to give protection against sth **(b)** (= *Spionageabwehr*) counterintelligence (service); **die ~ des Feindes** the repulsing of the enemy; **auf ~ stoßen** to be repulsed **(c)** (*Sport*) defence (*Brit*), defense (*US*); (= *~aktion*) piece of defence (*Brit*) or defense (*US*) (work)

Abwehrdienst M counterintelligence service

abwehren SEP **1** VT **(a)** *Gegner* to fend off; *Angriff, Feind* to repulse; *Flugzeug, Rakete* to repel; *Ball* to clear; *Schlag* to parry; **hervorragend, wie der Torwart den Ball abwehrte** that was a really good save the goalkeeper made (there) **(b)** (= *fern halten*) to keep away; *Krankheitserreger* to protect against; *Gefahr, üble Folgen, Krise* to avert; *Inflation* to fight against **2** VI **(a)** (*Sport*) to clear; (*Torwart*) to save; **mit dem Kopf ~** to head clear; **zur Ecke ~** to clear the ball (*so that a corner is given away*) **(b)** (= *ablehnen*) to refuse; **nein, wehrte sie ab** no, she said in refusal

Abwehr-: Abwehrkräfte PL (*Physiol*) (the body's) defences *pl* (*Brit*) or defenses *pl* (*US*); **Abwehrmechanismus** M (*Psych*) defence (*Brit*) or defense (*US*) mechanism; **Abwehrrakete** F anti-aircraft missile

abweichen VI SEP IRREG AUX SEIN (= *sich entfernen*) to deviate; (= *sich unterscheiden*) to differ; **vom Kurs ~** to deviate or depart from one's course; **vom Thema ~** to digress; **vom rechten Weg ~** (*fig*) to wander from the straight and narrow

Abweichung ['apvaiçʊŋ] F **-, -en** (*von Kurs etc*) deviation; (= *Unterschied*) difference; (*von zwei Theorien, Auffassungen etc*) divergence; (*von Magnetnadel*) declination; **~ von der Norm/Wahrheit** departure from the norm/truth; **~ von der Parteilinie** failure to toe the party line, deviation from the party line; **zulässige ~** (*Tech*) tolerance; (*zeitlich, zahlenmäßig*) allowance

abweisen VT SEP IRREG to turn down; (= *wegschicken*) to turn away; (*Jur*) *Klage* to dismiss; **er lässt sich nicht ~** he won't take no for an answer

abweisend **1** ADJ *Ton, Blick, Mensch* cold **2** ADV negatively

abwendbar ADJ avoidable

abwenden SEP REG *or* IRREG **1** VT **(a)** (= *verhindern*) *Unheil, Folgen* to avert **(b)** (= *zur Seite wenden*) to turn away; *Blick* to avert; *Kopf* to turn **2** VR to turn away

abwerben VT SEP IRREG to woo away (+*dat* from)

abwerfen SEP IRREG **1** VT to throw off; *Reiter* to throw; *Bomben, Flugblätter etc* to drop; *Ballast* to jettison; *Geweih* to shed, to cast; *Blätter, Nadeln* to shed; (*Cards*) to throw away; (*Sport*) *Ball, Speer* to throw; *Latte* to knock off *or* down; (*Comm*)

Gewinn to yield, to return; *Zinsen* to bear, to yield **2** VI (*Ftbl*) to throw

abwerten SEP **1** VT (a) *Währung* to devalue (b) (*fig*) *Ideale, Sprache, Kultur* to debase; *jds Leistung* to devalue **2** VI (*Fin*) to devalue

abwertend 1 ADJ derogatory, pejorative; *Blick* dismissive **2** ADV derogatorily, pejoratively

Abwertung F (a) (*von Währung*) devaluation; **eine ~ vornehmen** to devalue (the currency) (b) (*fig*) debasement; **solche Ideale erfahren eine immer stärkere ~** such ideals are valued less and less

abwesend ['apveːznt] ADJ absent; (*von zu Hause auch*) away *pred*; (*iro: = zerstreut auch*) far away; *Blick* absent-minded; **die Abwesenden** the absentees

Abwesenheit ['apveːznhait] F **-, -en** absence; (*fig: = Geistesabwesenheit*) abstraction; **in ~** (*Jur*) in absentia; **durch ~ glänzen** (*iro*) to be conspicuous by one's absence

abwickeln VT SEP (a) (*= abspulen*) to unwind; *Verband* to take off, to remove (b) (*fig: = erledigen*) to deal with; *Geschäft* to complete, to conclude; *Kontrolle* to carry out; (*Comm: = liquidieren*) to wind up

Abwicklung ['apvɪkluŋ] F **-, -en** (*= Erledigung*) completion, conclusion; (*Comm: = Liquidation*) winding up; **die Polizei sorgte für eine reibungslose ~ der Veranstaltung** the police made sure that the event passed off smoothly

abwiegeln ['apviːgln] SEP **1** VT to appease **2** VI to calm things down; **das Abwiegeln** appeasement

abwiegen VT SEP IRREG to weigh out

abwimmeln VT SEP (*inf*) *jdn* to get rid of (*inf*); *Auftrag* to get out of (*inf*); **die Sekretärin hat mich abgewimmelt** his secretary turned me away; **lass dich nicht ~** don't let them get rid of you (*inf*)

abwinken VI SEP (*inf*) (*abwehrend*) to wave it/him *etc* aside; (*resignierend*) to groan; (*fig: = ablehnen*) to say no; **der Chef winkt bei so einem Vorschlag bestimmt gleich ab** the boss is bound to say no to a suggestion like that; **bis zum Abwinken** (*= massenhaft*) galore

abwirtschaften VI SEP (*inf*) to go downhill; **abgewirtschaftet haben** to have reached rock bottom; *siehe auch* **abgewirtschaftet**

abwischen VT SEP *Staub, Schmutz etc* to wipe off *or* away; *Hände, Nase etc* to wipe; *Augen, Tränen* to dry; **er wischte sich** (*dat*) **den Schweiß von der Stirn ab** he mopped (the sweat from) his brow

Abwurf M throwing off; (*von Reiter*) throw; (*von Bomben etc*) dropping; (*von Ballast*) jettisoning; (*Sport: des Speers etc*) throwing; **ein ~ vom Tor** a goal throw

abwürgen VT SEP (*inf*) *Motor* to stall; **etw von vornherein ~** to nip sth in the bud

abzahlen VT SEP to pay off

abzählen SEP **1** VT to count; **bitte das Fahrgeld abgezählt bereithalten** please tender exact *or* correct fare (*form*) **2** VI to number off

Abzählreim M counting-out rhyme (*such as "eeny meeny miney mo", for choosing a person*)

Abzahlung F (a) (*= Rückzahlung*) repayment, paying off (b) (*= Ratenzahlung*) hire purchase (*Brit*), HP (*Brit*), installment plan (*US*); (*= Rate*) (re)payment

Abzahlungsgeschäft NT hire purchase (*Brit*), HP (*Brit*), installment plan (*US*)

Abzählvers M = **Abzählreim**

Abzeichen NT badge; (*Mil*) insignia *pl*; (*= Orden, Auszeichnung*) decoration

abzeichnen SEP **1** VT (a) (*= abmalen*) to draw (b) (*= signieren*) to initial **2** VR (*= sichtbar sein*) to stand out; (*fig*) (*= deutlich werden*) to emerge; (*= drohend bevorstehen*) to loom; **sich gegen etw ~** (*= kontrastieren*) to stand out against sth

abzgl. ABBR *von* **abzüglich**

Abziehbild NT transfer

abziehen SEP IRREG **1** VT (a) *Tier* to skin; *Fell, Haut* to remove; *grüne Bohnen* to string
(b) *Bett* to strip; *Bettzeug* to strip off
(c) (*Sw: = ausziehen*) to take off; *Hut* to raise
(d) *Schlüssel* to take out
(e) (*= zurückziehen*) *Truppen, Kapital* to withdraw
(f) (*= subtrahieren*) *Zahlen* to take away; *Steuern* to deduct;

2 Euro vom Preis ~ to take 2 euros off the price; **man hatte mir zu viel abgezogen** they'd deducted too much
(g) (*Typ: = vervielfältigen*) to run off; (*Phot*) *Bilder* to make prints of; **etw zwanzigmal ~** to run off twenty copies of sth **2** VI (a) AUX SEIN (*Rauch, Dampf*) to escape; (*Sturmtief etc*) to move away
(b) AUX SEIN (*Soldaten*) to pull out (*aus* of); (*inf: = weggehen*) to go off *or* away; **zieh ab!** (*inf*) beat it! (*inf*)
(c) (*sl: = schnell fahren*) **das Auto zieht ganz schön ab** that car can really move (*inf*) **3** VR (*Sw: = sich ausziehen*) to undress

abzielen VI SEP **auf etw** (*acc*) **~** (*Mensch*) to aim at sth; (*in Rede*) to get at sth; (*Bemerkung, Maßnahme etc*) to be aimed at sth

abzinsen VT SEP (*Fin*) to discount; **abgezinste Sparbriefe** savings certificates sold at discounted interest

Abzinsung F **-, -en** (*Fin*) discounting

abzischen VI SEP AUX SEIN (*inf: = abhauen*) to beat it (*inf*)

abzocken VT SEP (*inf*) *jdn* **~** to rip sb off (*inf*); **hier wird man nur abgezockt** they just rip you off here (*inf*)

Abzug ['aptsuːk] M (a) NO PL (*= Weggang*) departure; (*= Weggang von Truppen, Kapital etc*) withdrawal; **jdm freien ~ gewähren** to give sb (a) safe-conduct
(b) (*usu pl: vom Lohn etc*) deduction; (*= Rabatt*) discount; **ohne ~** (*Comm*) net terms only; **er verdient ohne Abzüge ...** before deductions *or* stoppages he earns ...; **etw in ~ bringen** (*form*) to deduct sth
(c) (*Typ*) copy; (*= Korrekturfahne*) proof; (*Phot*) print
(d) (*am Gewehr*) trigger

abzüglich ['aptsyːklɪç] PREP +GEN (*Comm*) minus, less

Abzugs-: **abzugsfähig** ADJ (*Fin*) (tax-)deductible; **abzugsfrei** ADJ (*Fin*) tax-free; **Abzugshaube** F extractor hood; **Abzugsrohr** NT flue (pipe)

abzweigen ['aptsvaign] SEP **1** VI AUX SEIN to branch off **2** VT (*inf*) to put on one side

Abzweigung F **-, -en** turn-off; (*= Gabelung*) fork

abzwicken VT SEP to pinch *or* nip off

abzwitschern VI SEP AUX SEIN (*inf*) to go off

a cappella [a kaˈpela] ADV (*Mus*) a cappella

Accessoires [aksɛˈsoaːɐ(s)] PL accessories *pl*

Acetat [atseˈtaːt] NT **-s, -e** acetate

Aceton [atseˈtoːn] NT **-s, -e** acetone

Acetylen [atsetyˈleːn] NT **-s,** NO PL acetylene

Acetylen(sauerstoff)brenner M oxyacetylene burner

ach [ax] INTERJ oh; **~ nein!** oh no!; (*überrascht*) no!, really!; (*ablehnend*) no, no!; **~ nein, ausgerechnet der!** well, well, him of all people; **~ so!** I see!, aha!; (*= ja richtig*) of course!; **~ was** *or* **wo!** of course not; **~ was** *or* **wo, das ist doch nicht so schlimm!** come on now, it's not that bad; **~ was** *or* **wo, das ist nicht nötig!** no, no that's not necessary

Ach [ax] NT **mit ~ und Krach** (*inf*) by the skin of one's teeth (*inf*); **eine Prüfung mit ~ und Krach bestehen** to scrape through an exam (by the skin of one's teeth)

Achillesferse [aˈxɪlɛsˌfɛrzə] F Achilles heel

Achse ['aksə] F **-, -n** (a) axis; **die ~** (*Rom-Berlin*) (*Hist*) the (Rome-Berlin) Axis (b) (*Tech*) axle; (*= Propellerachse*) shaft; **auf (der) ~ sein** (*inf*) to be out (and about); (*Kraftfahrer, Vertreter etc*) to be on the road

Achsel ['aksl] F **-, -n** (a) shoulder; **die ~n** *or* **mit den ~n zucken** to shrug (one's shoulders) (b) (*= -höhle*) armpit

Achsel-: **Achselhöhle** F armpit; **Achselzucken** NT **-s,** NO PL shrug; **mit einem ~** with a shrug (of one's shoulders); **achselzuckend 1** ADJ shrugging **2** ADV with a shrug of one's shoulders; **er stand ~ da** he stood there shrugging his shoulders

Achsenkreuz NT (*Math*) coordinate system

acht [axt] NUM eight; **für** *or* **auf ~ Tage** for a week; **in ~ Tagen** in a week('s time); **heute/morgen in ~ Tagen** a week today/tomorrow; **heute vor ~ Tagen war ich ...** a week ago today I was ...; **vor ~ Tagen werden sie wohl nicht fertig sein** they won't be ready for a week at least; *siehe auch* **vier**

Acht¹ [axt] F **-, -en** eight; (*bei Fahrrad*) buckled wheel; (*beim Eislaufen etc*) figure (of) eight; *siehe auch* **Vier**

Acht² F **sich in ~ nehmen** to be careful, to take care; **etw außer ~ lassen** to leave sth out of consideration; **~ geben, ~ haben**

(geh) to take care (auf +acc of); (= aufmerksam sein) to pay attention (auf +acc to); **auf jdn/etw ~ geben** (= beaufsichtigen) to look after sb/sth; **wenn man im Straßenverkehr nur einen Augenblick nicht ~ gibt, ...** if your attention wanders for just a second in traffic ...

Acht³ F -, NO PL (Hist) outlawry; **jdn in ~ und Bann tun** to outlaw sb; (fig) to ostracize sb

Achteck NT octagon

achteckig ADJ octagonal, eight-sided

achtel ['axtl] ADJ eighth; siehe auch **viertel**

Achtel ['axtl] NT -s, - eighth; siehe auch **Viertel¹**

Achtel-: Achtelfinale NT round before the quarterfinal, 2nd/3rd etc round; **ein Platz im ~** a place in the last sixteen; **Achtelnote** F quaver, eighth note (US); **Achtelpause** F quaver rest (Brit), eighth note rest (US)

achten ['axtn] **1** VT **(a)** (= schätzen) to respect, to think highly of; **geachtete Leute** respected people **(b)** (= respektieren) to respect **2** VI **auf etw** (acc) **~** to pay attention to sth; **auf die Kinder ~** to keep an eye on the children; **darauf ~, dass ...** to be careful or to take care that ...

ächten ['ɛçtn] VT (Hist) to outlaw; (fig) to ostracize

achtens ['axtns] ADV in the eighth place

achtenswert ['axtnsveːrt] ADJ worthy

Achte(r) ['axtə] MF DECL AS ADJ eighth; siehe auch **Vierte(r)**

Achter ['axtɐ] M -s, - (Rudern) eight; (Eislauf etc) figure (of) eight; siehe auch **Vierer**

achte(r, s) ['axtə] ADJ eighth; siehe auch **vierte(r, s)**

Achterbahn F roller coaster

achtern ['axtɐn] ADV (Naut) aft, astern

achtfach [-fax] **1** ADJ eightfold; **in ~er Ausfertigung** with seven copies; siehe auch **vierfach 2** ADV eightfold, eight times

achtgeben VI siehe **Acht²**

achthundert ['axt'hʊndɐt] NUM eight hundred

achtlos 1 ADJ careless, thoughtless **2** ADV durchblättern casually; wegwerfen thoughtlessly; sich verhalten carelessly; **viele gehen ~ daran vorbei** many people just pass by without noticing it

achtmal ['axtmaːl] ADV eight times

Acht-: Achtstundentag M eight-hour day; **achttägig** ADJ week-long; **mit ~er Verspätung** a week late; **der ~e Streik ist ...** the week-long strike is ...; **achttausend** ['axt'tauznt] NUM eight thousand; **ein Achttausender** a mountain eight thousand metres in height; **Achtundsechziger** [axtlʊnt'zɛçtsɪgɐ] M -s, -, **Achtundsechzigerin** [-ərɪn] F -, -nen, **68er(in)** M(F) member of the '68 generation; **die ~** the '68 generation

Achtung ['axtʊŋ] F -, NO PL **(a)** (= Vorsicht) **~!** watch or look out!; (Mil: Befehl) attention!; **~, ~!** (your) attention please!; **"~ Hochspannung!"** "danger, high voltage"; **"~ Lebensgefahr!"** "danger"; **"~ Stufe!"** "mind the step"; **~, fertig, los!** ready, steady or get set, go!
(b) (= Wertschätzung) respect (vor +dat for); **die ~ vor sich selbst** one's self-respect; **bei aller ~ vor jdm/etw** with all due respect to sb/sth; **sich** (dat) **~ verschaffen** to make oneself respected; **alle ~!** good for you/him etc!

Achtungsapplaus M polite applause

Achtungserfolg M succès d'estime

achtzehn ['axtseːn] NUM eighteen

achtzig ['axtsɪç] NUM eighty; **auf ~ sein** (inf) to be livid; **da war er gleich auf ~** (inf) then he got livid; siehe auch **vierzig**

ächzen ['ɛçtsn] VI to groan (vor +dat with); **~ und stöhnen** to moan and groan

Acker ['akɐ] M -s, ⁼ ['ɛkɐ] (= Feld) field; **einen ~ bebauen** or **bewirtschaften** to work the land; **sich vom ~ machen** (sl: = verschwinden) to split (sl)

Acker-: Ackerbau M, NO PL agriculture, arable farming; **~ betreiben** to farm the land; **~ treibend** farming; **~ und Viehzucht** farming; **Ackergaul** M (pej) farm horse, old nag (pej); **Ackerland** NT arable land

ackern ['akɐn] VI (inf) to slog away (inf)

Ackersalat M (S Ger) lamb's lettuce (Brit), corn salad

a conto [a 'kɔnto] ADV (Comm) on account

Acryl [a'kryːl] NT -s, NO PL acrylic

Acryl- IN CPDS acrylic; **Acrylfarbe** F acrylic paint; **Acrylglas** NT acrylic glass

Action ['ɛkʃn] F -, NO PL (sl) action

Actionfilm ['ɛkʃən-] M action film

a. D. [aːˈdeː] ABBR von außer Dienst ret(d)

Adabei ['aːdabai] M -s, -s (Aus inf) limelighter (inf)

ad absurdum [at ap'zʊrdʊm] ADV **~ führen** to make a nonsense of; Argument etc to reduce to absurdity

ADAC [aːdeːlaː'tseː] -, NO PL ABBR von Allgemeiner Deutscher Automobil-Club ≈ AA (Brit), ≈ RAC (Brit), ≈ AAA (US)

ad acta [at 'akta] ADV **etw ~ legen** (fig) to consider sth finished; Frage, Problem to consider sth closed

Adam ['aːdam] M -s Adam; **bei ~ und Eva anfangen** (inf) to start right from square one (inf)

Adamsapfel M (inf) Adam's apple

Adapter [a'daptɐ] M -s, - adapter, adaptor

adaptieren [adap'tiːrən], ptp **adaptiert** VT **(a)** (= anpassen) to adapt **(b)** (Aus: = herrichten) to fix up

adäquat [adɛ'kvaːt, atlɛ'kvaːt] **1** ADJ adequate; Stellung, Verhalten suitable; Kritik valid; **einer Sache** (dat) **~ sein** to be adequate to sth **2** ADV adequately

addieren [a'diːrən], ptp **addiert 1** VT to add (up) **2** VI to add

Addition [adi'tsioːn] F -, -en addition

Additiv [adi'tiːf] NT -s, -e [-və] additive

ade [a'deː] INTERJ (old, S Ger) farewell (old, liter); **jdm ~ sagen** to bid sb farewell

Adel ['aːdl] M -s, NO PL nobility; (esp Brit) peerage; (esp hoher ~) aristocracy; **eine Familie von ~** an aristocratic family; **er stammt aus altem ~** he comes from an old aristocratic family; **der niedere ~** the lesser nobility, the gentry; **der hohe ~** the higher nobility, the aristocracy; **~ verpflichtet** noblesse oblige

adelig ['aːdəlɪç] ADJ = **adlig**

adeln ['aːdln] VT to make a (life) peer (Brit), to ennoble; (= den Titel „Sir" verleihen) to knight; (= niedrigen Adel verleihen) to bestow a title on; (fig geh: = auszeichnen) to ennoble

Adelstitel M title

Ader ['aːdɐ] F -, -n (Bot, Geol) vein; (Physiol) blood vessel; (Elec: = Leitungsdraht) core; (fig: = Veranlagung) bent; **das spricht seine künstlerische/musikalische ~ an** that appeals to the artist/musician in him; **eine/keine ~ für etw haben** to have feeling/no feeling for sth; **eine poetische/musikalische ~ haben** to have a poetic/musical streak

Äderchen ['ɛːdɐçən] NT -s, - DIM von Ader

Aderlass [-las] M -es, **Aderlässe** [-lɛsə] (old Med) blood-letting (auch fig); **die Abwanderung der Akademiker ist ein ~, den sich das Land nicht länger leisten kann** the country can no longer afford the bleeding of its resources through the exodus of its academics

Adhäsion [athɛ'zioːn] F -, -en (Phys) adhesion

Adhäsionsverschluss M adhesive seal

ad hoc [at 'hɔk, at 'hoːk] ADV (geh) ad hoc; **~ wurde ein Komitee gebildet** an ad hoc committee was set up

Ad-hoc- [at'hɔk-, at'hoːk-] IN CPDS ad hoc;

Adjektiv ['atjɛktiːf] NT -s, -e [-və] adjective

adjektivisch ['atjɛktiːvɪʃ, atjɛk'tiːvɪʃ] **1** ADJ adjectival **2** ADV adjectivally

Adjutant [atju'tant] M -en, -en, **Adjutantin** [-'tantɪn] F -, -nen adjutant; (von General) aide(-de-camp)

Adler ['aːdlɐ] M -s, - eagle

Adler-: Adlerauge NT (fig) eagle eye; **~n haben** to have eyes like a hawk; **Adlerblick** M (fig) eagle eye; **Adlerfarn** M bracken; **Adlerhorst** M (eagle's) eyrie; **Adlernase** F aquiline nose

adlig ['aːdlɪç] ADJ (lit, fig) noble; **~ sein** to be of noble birth

Adlige ['aːdlɪgə] F DECL AS ADJ member of the nobility, noblewoman

Adlige(r) ['aːdlɪgə] M DECL AS ADJ member of the nobility, nobleman

Administration [atminɪstra'tsioːn] F -, -en administration

administrativ [atminɪstra'tiːf] **1** ADJ administrative **2** ADV administratively

Admiral [atmi'raːl] M -s, -e or **Admiräle** [-'rɛːlə], **Admiralin** [-'raːlɪn] F -, -nen admiral

Adonis [a'do:nɪs] M -, -se (geh) Adonis
adoptieren [adɔp'tiːrən], ptp **adoptiert** VT to adopt
Adoption [adɔp'tsioːn] F -, -en adoption
Adoptiv- [adɔp'tiːf-]: **Adoptiveltern** PL adoptive parents pl; **Adoptivkind** NT adopted child
Adrenalin [adrena'liːn] NT -s, NO PL adrenalin
Adrenalin-: **Adrenalinschub** M surge of adrenalin; **Adrenalinspiegel** M, NO PL adrenalin level; **Adrenalinstoß** M surge of adrenalin
Adressat [adrɛ'saːt] M -en, -en, **Adressatin** [-'saːtɪn] F -, -nen (geh) addressee; (Comm auch) consignee (form); **~en** (fig) target group
Adressbuch NT directory; (privat) address book
Adresse [a'drɛsə] F -, -n (a) (= Anschrift, Comput) address; **eine Warnung an jds ~** (acc) **richten** (fig) to address a warning to sb; **da sind Sie bei mir an der richtigen/falschen** or **verkehrten ~** (inf) you've come to the right/wrong person; **eine erste/ feine ~** (inf) a top-class/prominent establishment **(b)** (form: = Botschaft) address
Adressen-: **Adressenaufkleber** M address label; **Adressenverwaltung** F (Comput) address filing system
adressieren [adrɛ'siːrən], ptp **adressiert** VT to address (an +acc to)
adrett [a'drɛt] (dated) **1** ADJ smart **2** ADV smartly
Adria ['aːdria] F - Adriatic (Sea)
Adstringens [at'strɪŋgɛns] NT -, **Adstringenzien** [-tsiən] astringent
Advent [at'vɛnt] M -s, -e Advent; **im ~** in Advent; **erster/vierter ~** first/fourth Sunday in Advent
Adventist [atvɛn'tɪst] M -en, -en, **Adventistin** [-'tɪstɪn] F -, -nen (Rel) (Second) Adventist
Advents-: **Adventskalender** M Advent calendar; **Adventskranz** M Advent wreath; **Adventssonntag** M Sunday in Advent; **Adventszeit** F (season of) Advent
Adverb [at'vɛrp] NT -s, **Adverbien** [-biən] adverb
adverbial [atvɛr'biaːl] **1** ADJ adverbial **2** ADV adverbially
Adverbialbestimmung F adverbial qualification; **mit ~** qualified adverbially
Advocatus Diaboli [atvo'kaːtʊs di'aːboli] M - -, **Advocati -** [-ti] (geh) devil's advocate
Advokat [atvo'kaːt] M -en, -en, **Advokatin** [-'kaːtɪn] F -, -nen (Aus, Sw, auch pej) lawyer
Advokaturbüro NT (Sw), **Advokaturskanzlei** F (Aus) lawyer's office
Aero- [a'eːro, 'ɛːro] IN CPDS aero
Aerobic [ɛ'roːbɪk] NT -(s), NO PL aerobics sing
Aero-: **Aerodynamik** [aerody'naːmɪk] F aerodynamics sing or (bei Flugzeug etc) pl; **aerodynamisch** [aerody'naːmɪʃ] **1** ADJ aerodynamic **2** ADV aerodynamically; **aeronautisch** [aero'nautɪʃ] ADJ aeronautic(al)
Afa ['aːfa] F -, NO PL (Fin, Comm) ABBR von **Absetzung für Abnutzung**
Affäre [a'fɛːrə] F -, -n (a) (= Angelegenheit) affair, business no pl; (= Liebesabenteuer) affair; **sich aus der ~ ziehen** (inf) to get (oneself) out of it (inf) **(b)** (= Zwischenfall) incident, episode
Affe ['afə] M -n, -n (a) monkey; (= Menschenaffe) ape; **der Mensch stammt vom ~n ab** man is descended from the apes; **an jdm einen ~n gefressen haben** (inf) to have been really taken by sb **(b)** (sl: = Kerl) clown (inf); **ein eingebildeter ~** a conceited ass (inf)
Affekt [a'fɛkt] M -(e)s, -e emotion, affect (form); **ein im ~ begangenes Verbrechen** a crime committed under the influence of emotion; **im ~ handeln** to act in the heat of the moment
Affekthandlung F act committed under the influence of emotion
affektiert [afɛk'tiːrt] (pej) **1** ADJ affected **2** ADV affectedly
Affektiertheit F -, -en affectation
Affen-: **affenartig** ADJ like a monkey; (= menschenaffenartig) apelike; **mit ~er Geschwindigkeit** (inf) like greased lightning (inf); **Affenbrotbaum** M monkey bread (tree), baobab; **Affenhaus** NT ape house; **Affenhitze** F (inf) sweltering heat (inf); **gestern war eine ~** yesterday was a scorcher (inf); **Affenkäfig** M siehe **Affe** monkey's/ape's cage; **Affenliebe** F blind adoration (zu of); **Affenschande** F (inf) crying shame

(inf); **Affentempo** NT (inf) breakneck (Brit) or neck-breaking (US) speed (inf); **in** or **mit einem ~** at breakneck (Brit) or neck-breaking (US) speed (inf); **Affentheater** NT (inf) carry-on (inf), fuss; **ein ~ aufführen** to make a fuss; **Affenweibchen** NT siehe **Affe** female monkey/ape
affig ['afɪç] (inf) **1** ADJ (= eitel) stuck-up (inf); (= geziert) affected; (= lächerlich) ridiculous **2** ADV **sich ~ anstellen** or **haben** to be stuck-up (inf)/affected/ridiculous; **~ wirken** to seem ridiculous
Äffin ['ɛfɪn] F -, -nen female monkey; (= Menschenäffin) female ape
Affinität [afini'tɛːt] F -, -en affinity
Affront [a'frõː] M -s, -s (geh) affront (gegen to)
Afghane [af'gaːnə] M -n, -n, **Afghanin** [-'gaːnɪn] F -, -nen Afghan
afghanisch [af'gaːnɪʃ] ADJ Afghan; **Afghanischer Windhund** Afghan (hound)
Afghanistan [af'gaːnɪstaːn, -tan] NT -s Afghanistan
Afrika ['aːfrika, 'afrika] NT -s Africa
Afrikaans [afri'kaːns] NT - Afrikaans
Afrikaner [afri'kaːnɐ] M -s, -, **Afrikanerin** [-ərɪn] F -, -nen African
afrikanisch [afri'kaːnɪʃ] ADJ African
Afro- ['aːfro-]: **Afroamerikaner(in)** M(F) Afro-American; **Afrolook** M Afro-look
After ['aftɐ] M -s, - (form) anus
Aftershave ['aːftɐʃeːv] NT -(s), -s aftershave
AG [aː'geː] F -, -s ABBR von **Aktiengesellschaft** ≈ plc (Brit), ≈ corp. (US), ≈ inc. (US)
Ägäis [ɛ'gɛːɪs] F - Aegean (Sea)
ägäisch [ɛ'gɛːɪʃ] ADJ Aegean
AGB ABBR von **Allgemeine Geschäftsbedingungen**
Agenda [a'gɛnda] F -, **Agenden** [-dn] (= Tagesordnung) agenda; (= Aktionsplan) plan of action
Agent [a'gɛnt] M -en, -en, **Agentin** [a'gɛntɪn] F -, -nen agent; (= Spion) secret agent
Agententätigkeit F espionage; **ihre ~** her activity as a secret agent
Agentin F -, -nen siehe **Agent**
Agentur [agɛn'tuːɐ] F -, -en agency
Agenturbericht M (news) agency report
Aggregat [agre'gaːt] NT -(e)s, -e (Geol) aggregate; (Tech) unit, set of machines; (Aut: = Motor) engine
Aggregatzustand M state; **die drei Aggregatzustände** the three states of matter
Aggression [agrɛ'sioːn] F -, -en aggression (gegen towards); **~en gegen jdn empfinden** to feel aggression toward(s) sb
aggressiv [agrɛ'siːf] **1** ADJ aggressive **2** ADV aggressively
Aggressivität [agrɛsivi'tɛːt] F -, -en aggressivity
agieren [a'giːrən], ptp **agiert** VI to act
agil [a'giːl] ADJ (körperlich) agile; (geistig) **~** mentally agile
Agio ['aːdʒo, 'aːʒio] NT -s, **Agien** ['aːdʒən, 'aːʒiən] (Fin) (von Wertpapier) premium; (von Geldsorte) agio
Agitation [agita'tsioːn] F -, -en (Pol) agitation
agitatorisch [agita'toːrɪʃ] (Pol) **1** ADJ agitational; Rede, Inhalt inflammatory **2** ADV **~ argumentieren** to have an inflammatory style of arguing; **sich ~ betätigen** to be an agitator
agitieren [agi'tiːrən], ptp **agitiert** VI to agitate
Agrar- [a'graːe] IN CPDS agrarian; **Agrarfabrik** F factory farm; **Agrargesellschaft** F agrarian society; **Agrarland** NT agrarian country; **Agrarmarkt** M agricultural commodities market; **Agrarpolitik** F agricultural policy
Ägypten [ɛ'gʏptn] NT -s Egypt
Ägypter [ɛ'gʏptɐ] M -s, -, **Ägypterin** [-ərɪn] F -, -nen Egyptian
ägyptisch [ɛ'gʏptɪʃ] ADJ Egyptian
Ägyptologie [ɛgʏptolo'giː] F -, NO PL Egyptology
äh [ɛ] INTERJ (beim Sprechen) er, um; (Ausdruck des Ekels) ugh
aha [a'haː, a'ha] INTERJ aha; (verstehend auch) I see
Aha-Erlebnis [a'haː-, a'ha-] NT sudden insight
ähneln ['ɛːnln] VI +DAT to be like, to be similar to, to resemble; **sich** or **einander** (geh) **~** to be alike or similar; **die beiden Systeme ~ einander nicht sehr/~ sich wenig** the two systems are not very similar or alike/have little in common

ahnen ['aːnən] **1** VT (= *voraussehen*) to foresee, to know; *Gefahr, Tod etc* to have a presentiment *or* premonition of; (= *vermuten*) to suspect; (= *erraten*) to guess; **das kann ich doch nicht ~!** I couldn't be expected to know that!; **nichts Böses ~** to be unsuspecting; **nichts Böses ~d** unsuspectingly; **da sitzt man friedlich an seinem Schreibtisch, nichts Böses ~d ...** (*hum*) there I was sitting peacefully at my desk minding my own business ... (*hum*); **ohne zu ~, dass ...** without suspecting (for one minute) that ...; **ohne es zu ~** without suspecting; **davon habe ich nichts geahnt** I didn't suspect it for one moment; **so etwas habe ich doch geahnt** I did suspect something like that; **(ach), du ahnst es nicht!** (*inf*) would you believe it! (*inf*); **du ahnst es nicht, wen ich gestern getroffen habe!** you'll never guess *or* believe who I met yesterday!

2 VI (*geh*) **mir ahnt etwas Schreckliches** I have a dreadful foreboding; **mir ahnt nichts Gutes** I have a premonition that all is not well

Ahnen-: Ahnenforschung F genealogy; **Ahnengalerie** F ancestral portrait gallery; **Ahnentafel** F genealogy

ähnlich ['ɛːnlɪç] **1** ADJ similar (+*dat* to); **ein dem Rokoko ~er Stil** a style similar to rococo; **das dem Vater ~e Kind** the child that resembles his father; **~ wie er/sie** like him/her; **~ wie damals** as then; **~ wie vor 10 Jahren** as 10 years ago; **sie sind sich ~** they are similar *or* alike; **(etwas) Ähnliches** something similar, something like it/that

2 ADV **ein ~ aussehender Gegenstand** a similar-looking object; **~ kompliziert/intelligent** just as complicated/intelligent; **eine ~ komplizierte Sachlage** a similarly complicated state of affairs; **ich denke ~** I feel the same way (about it); **er hat sie ~ hintergegangen wie seine frühere Freundin** he cheated on her just as he did with his former girlfriend; **jdm ~ sehen** to be like sb, to resemble sb; **das sieht ihm (ganz) ~!** (*inf*) that's just like him!

3 PREP +DAT similar to, like

Ähnlichkeit F -, -en (*mit* to) (= *Vergleichbarkeit*) similarity; (= *ähnliches Aussehen*) similarity, resemblance; **mit jdm/etw ~ haben** to resemble sb/sth

Ahnung ['aːnʊŋ] F -, -en **(a)** (= *Vorgefühl*) hunch, presentiment; (*düster*) premonition

(b) (= *Vorstellung, Wissen*) idea; (= *Vermutung*) suspicion, hunch; **eine ~ von etw vermitteln** to give an idea of sth; **keine ~ (davon) haben, dass/wie/was** *etc* to have no idea that/how/what *etc*; **keine ~!** (*inf*) no idea! (*inf*); **er hat keine blasse** *or* **nicht die geringste ~** he hasn't a clue *or* the faintest idea (*inf*); **hast du eine ~, wo er sein könnte?** have you any idea where he could be?; **hast du eine ~!** (*iro inf*) a (fat) lot you know (about it)! (*inf*)

ahnungslos **1** ADJ (= *nichts ahnend*) unsuspecting; (= *unwissend*) clueless (*inf*) **2** ADV unsuspectingly

Ahnungslosigkeit F -, NO PL (= *Unwissenheit*) cluelessness (*inf*); **er bewies seine völlige ~ darüber, dass ...** he showed how totally unsuspecting he was of the fact that ...

ahoi [aˈhɔy] INTERJ **Schiff ~!** ship ahoy!

Ahorn ['aːhɔrn] M -s, -e maple

Ähre ['ɛːrə] F -, -n (= *Getreideähre*) ear; (*allgemeiner, = Grasähre*) head; **~n lesen** to glean (corn)

AHV [aːhaːˈfau] F -, NO PL (*Sw*) ABBR *von* **Alters- und Hinderungsversicherung** age and disability insurance

Aids [eːds] NT -, NO PL Aids

Aids- ['eːds] IN CPDS Aids; **Aids-Erreger** M Aids virus; **Aidshilfe** F Aids support; **die Münchener ~** the Munich Aids support group; **aidsinfiziert** [-ɪmfitsiːɐt] ADJ infected with Aids; **Aidsinfizierte(r)** [-ɪmfitsiːɐtə] MF DECL AS ADJ person infected with Aids; **aidskrank** ADJ suffering from Aids; **Aidskranke(r)** MF DECL AS ADJ Aids sufferer; **Aidstest** M Aids test; **Aidstote(r)** MF DECL AS ADJ person/man/woman who died of Aids; **2000 ~ pro Jahr** 2000 Aids deaths *or* deaths from Aids per year

Air- ['ɛːɐ-]: **Airbag** ['ɛːɐbɛg] M -s, -s (*Aut*) airbag; **Airbus** ['ɛːɐbʊs] M (*Aviat*) airbus

ais, Ais ['aːɪs] NT -, - A sharp

Ajatollah [aja'tɔla] M -(s), -s ayatollah

Akademie [akade'miː] F -, -n [-'miːən] academy; (= *Fachschule*) college, school

Akademiker [aka'deːmikɐ] M -s, -, **Akademikerin** [-ərɪn] F -, -nen person with a university education; (= *Student*) (university) student; (= *Hochschulabsolvent*) (university) graduate; (= *Universitätslehrkraft*) academic

akademisch [aka'deːmɪʃ] **1** ADJ (*lit, fig*) academic; **die ~e Jugend** (the) students *pl*; **das ~e Proletariat** (the) jobless graduates *pl*; **das ~e Viertel** (*Univ*) the quarter of an hour allowed between the announced start of a lecture etc and the actual start **2** ADV **~ gebildet sein** to have (had) a university education

Akazie [aˈkaːtsiə] F -, -n acacia

Akelei [akəˈlai, ˈaːkəlai] F -, -en aquilegia, columbine

akklimatisieren [aklimatiˈziːrən], *ptp* **akklimatisiert** **1** VR (*lit, fig*) (*in* +*dat* to) to become acclimatized, to acclimatize oneself **2** VT to acclimatize

Akklimatisierung F -, -en acclimatization

Akkord [aˈkɔrt] M -(e)s, -e [-də] **(a)** (*Mus*) chord **(b)** (= *Stücklohn*) piece rate; **im** *or* **in** *or* **auf ~ arbeiten** to do piecework

Akkord-: Akkordarbeit F piecework; **Akkordarbeiter(in)** M(F) pieceworker

Akkordeon [aˈkɔrdeɔn] NT -s, -s accordion

Akkordeonspieler(in) M(F) accordionist

Akkord-: Akkordlohn M piece wages *pl*, piece rate; **Akkordsatz** M piece rate; **Akkordzuschlag** M piece rate bonus

akkreditieren [akrediˈtiːrən], *ptp* **akkreditiert** VT *Botschafter, Journalisten* to accredit (*bei* to, at)

Akkreditiv [akrediˈtiːf] NT -s, -e [-və] **(a)** (*Pol*) credentials *pl* **(b)** (*Fin*) letter of credit; **jdm ein ~ eröffnen** to open a credit in favour (*Brit*) *or* favor (*US*) of sb

Akkreditiv-: Akkreditivbedingungen PL (*Fin*) conditions *pl* of the documentary credit; **Akkreditivbetrag** M (*Fin*) amount of the documentary credit

Akku ['aku] M -s, -s (*inf*) ABBR *von* **Akkumulator** accumulator

Akkumulation [akumulaˈtsioːn] F -, -en accumulation

Akkumulator [akumuˈlaːtoːɐ] M -s, **Akkumulatoren** [-'toːrən] accumulator

akkumulieren [akumuˈliːrən], *ptp* **akkumuliert** VTIR to accumulate

akkurat [akuˈraːt] **1** ADJ precise; (= *sorgfältig auch*) meticulous **2** ADV precisely, exactly; (= *tatsächlich*) naturally, of course

Akkusativ ['akuzatiːf] M -s, -e [-və] accusative; **im ~ stehen** to be in the accusative

Akkusativobjekt NT accusative object

Akne ['aknə] F -, -n acne

Akontozahlung [a'kɔnto-] F payment on account

AKP [a:ka'pe:] F ABBR *von* **Afrika, Karibik und pazifischer Raum** ACP; **die ~-Staaten** the ACP countries

akquirieren [akviˈriːrən], *ptp* **akquiriert** **1** VT *Spenden* to collect; **Inserate ~** to sell advertising space; **Kunden ~** to canvass for customers **2** VI (*Comm*) to canvass for custom

Akquisiteur [akvizi'tøːɐ] M -s, -e, **Akquisiteurin** [-'tøːrɪn] F -, -nen agent, canvasser

Akquisition [akviziˈtsioːn] F -, -en (*Comm*) (customer) canvassing

akribisch [a'kriːbɪʃ] (*geh*) **1** ADJ meticulous, precise **2** ADV meticulously

Akrobat [akroˈbaːt] M -en, -en, **Akrobatin** [-'baːtɪn] F -, -nen acrobat

Akrobatik [akroˈbaːtɪk] F -, NO PL acrobatics *pl*; (= *Geschicklichkeit*) acrobatic skill

akrobatisch [akroˈbaːtɪʃ] ADJ acrobatic

Akronym [akro'nyːm] NT -s, -e acronym

Akt¹ [akt] M -(e)s, -e **(a)** act; (= *Zeremonie*) ceremony, ceremonial act **(b)** (*Art*: = *~bild*) nude **(c)** (= *Geschlechtsakt*) sexual act

Akt² M -(e)s, -en (*Aus*) = **Akte**

Akt-: Aktaufnahme F nude (photograph); **Aktbild** NT nude (picture *or* portrait)

Akte ['aktə] F -, -n file, record; **die ~ Schmidt** the Schmidt file; **etw zu den ~n legen** to file sth away, to put sth on file; (*fig*) *Fall etc* to drop sth

Akten-: Aktendeckel M folder; **Akteneinsicht** F (*form*) inspection of records *or* files; **Aktenkoffer** M attaché case; **aktenkundig** ADJ on record; **~ werden** to be put on record;

Aktenlage F **nach** or **laut ~** according to the files; **die ~ prüfen** to examine the files; **Aktenmappe** F **(a)** (= *Tasche*) briefcase **(b)** (= *Umschlag*) folder, file; **Aktennotiz** F memo(randum); **Aktenordner** M file; **Aktenschrank** M filing cabinet; **Aktentasche** F briefcase; **Aktenvermerk** M memo(randum); **Aktenzeichen** NT reference

Aktfoto NT nude (photograph)

AktG ABBR von **Aktiengesetz**

Aktie ['aktsiə] F **-, -n** share; (= *Aktienschein*) share certificate; **in ~n anlegen** to invest in (stocks and) shares; **die ~n fallen/ steigen** share prices are falling/rising; **die ~n stehen gut/ schlecht** (*lit*) share prices are looking good/bad; (*fig*) things are looking good/bad; **wie stehen die ~n?** (*hum inf*) how are things?; (= *wie sind die Aussichten*) what are the prospects?

Aktien-: Aktienaufteilung F split; **Aktienbesitz** M shareholdings *pl*, shares *pl* held; **Aktienbesitzer(in)** M(F) shareholder, stockholder (*esp US*); **Aktienbörse** F stock exchange; **Aktienemission** F share issue; **Aktiengesellschaft** F ≈ public limited company (*Brit*), ≈ corporation (*US*); **Aktiengesetz** NT ≈ Stock Corporation Act; **Aktienindex** M (*Fin*) share index; **Aktienkapital** NT share capital; (*von Gesellschaft auch*) (capital) stock; **Aktienkurs** M share price; **Aktienmantel** M share certificate; **Aktienmarkt** M stock market; **Aktienoption** F share or stock option; **Aktienpaket** NT block of shares; **ein ~ von 20 Prozent** a shareholding of 20 per cent (*Brit*) or percent (*US*); **Aktientausch** M share exchange; **Aktienurkunde** F share or stock certificate

Aktion [ak'tsio:n] F **-, -en** action; (= *Kampagne*) campaign; (= *Werbeaktion*) promotion; (= *geplantes Unternehmen, Einsatz*) operation; **in ~** in action; **sie muss ständig in ~ sein** she always has to be active; **in ~ treten** to go into action

Aktionär [aktsio'nɛ:ɐ] M **-s, -e**, **Aktionärin** [-'nɛ:rɪn] F **-, -nen** shareholder, stockholder (*esp US*)

Aktionärsversammlung F shareholders' or stockholders' (*esp US*) meeting

Aktionismus [aktsio'nɪsmʊs] M **-**, NO PL (*Pol*) actionism

Aktions-: Aktionsart F (*Gram*) aspect; **aktionsfähig** ADJ capable of action; **Aktionsradius** M (*Aviat, Naut*) range, radius; (*fig*: = *Wirkungsbereich*) scope (for action); **aktionsunfähig** ADJ incapable of action

aktiv [ak'ti:f, 'akti:f] **1** ADJ active; (*Econ*) *Bilanz* positive, favourable (*Brit*), favorable (*US*) **2** ADV actively; **sich ~ an etw** (*dat*) **beteiligen** to take an active part in sth

Aktiv ['akti:f] NT **-s,** (*rare*) **-e** [-və] (*Gram*) active

Aktiva [ak'ti:va] PL assets *pl*; **~ und Passiva** assets and liabilities

Aktivgeschäft NT (*Fin*) lending business

aktivieren [akti'vi:rən], *ptp* **aktiviert** VT (*Sci*) to activate; (*fig*) *Arbeit, Kampagne* to step up; *Mitarbeiter* to get moving; (*Comm*) to enter on the assets side

Aktivismus [akti'vɪsmʊs] M **-**, NO PL activism

Aktivist [akti'vɪst] M **-en, -en**, **Aktivistin** [-'vɪstɪn] F **-, -nen** activist

Aktivität [aktivi'tɛ:t] F **-, -en** activity

Aktiv-: Aktivkohlefilter F activated carbon filter; **Aktivposten** M (*lit, fig*) asset; **Aktivsaldo** M credit balance; **Aktivseite** F assets side; **Aktivurlaub** M activity holiday (*esp Brit*) or vacation (*US*); **Aktivvermögen** NT realizable assets *pl*; **Aktivzinsen** PL interest receivable *sing*

Akt-: Aktmalerei F nude painting; **Aktmodell** NT nude model; **Aktstudie** F nude study

aktualisieren [aktuali'zi:rən], *ptp* **aktualisiert** VT to make topical; *Datei, Nachschlagewerk* to update

Aktualisierung F **-,** updating

Aktualität [aktuali'tɛ:t] F **-, -en** topicality

aktuell [ak'tuɛl] ADJ relevant (to the current situation); *Thema* topical; *Buch, Film auch* of topical interest; (= *gegenwärtig*) *Problem, Theorie* current; (= *modern*) *Mode, Stil* latest *attr*; (*Econ*) *Bedarf, Kaufkraft* actual; **von ~em Interesse** of topical interest; **von ~er Bedeutung** of relevance to the present situation; **dieses Problem ist nicht mehr ~** this is no longer a (current) problem; **das Buch ist wieder ~ geworden** the book is topical again; **eine ~e Sendung** (*Rad, TV*) a current affairs

programme (*Brit*) or program (*US*); **~e Stunde** (*Parl*) ≈ question time *no art* (*Brit*)

> *Vorsicht!* **aktuell** *wird nicht mit dem englischen Wort* **actual** *übersetzt.*

Akupressur [akuprɛ'su:ɐ] F **-, -en** acupressure

Akupunkteur [akupʊŋk'tø:ɐ] M **-s, -e**, **Akupunkteurin** [-'tø:rɪn] F **-, -nen** acupuncturist

akupunktieren [akupʊŋk'ti:rən], *ptp* **akupunktiert** **1** VT to acupuncture **2** VI to perform acupuncture

Akupunktur [akupʊŋk'tu:ɐ] F **-, -en** acupuncture

Akustik [a'kʊstɪk] F **-**, NO PL (*von Gebäude etc*) acoustics *pl*; (*Phys*: = *Lehre*) acoustics *sing*

akustisch [a'kʊstɪʃ] **1** ADJ acoustic **2** ADV acoustically; **rein ~ ist die Stereoanlage prima** the acoustics of that stereo are fantastic; **etw ~ verbessern** to improve the acoustics of sth; **ich habe dich rein ~ nicht verstanden** I simply didn't catch what you said (properly)

akut [a'ku:t] **1** ADJ (*Med, fig*) acute **2** ADV acutely; **ihr Zustand ist ~ lebensgefährlich** her condition is listed as critical

Akut [a'ku:t] M **-(e)s, -e** acute (accent)

AKV (a) ABBR von **Allgemeine Kreditvereinbarungen (b)** ABBR von **Auslandskassenverein**

AKW [a:ka've:] NT **-s, -s** ABBR von **Atomkraftwerk**

Akzent [ak'tsɛnt] M **-(e)s, -e** (= *Zeichen, Aussprache*) accent; (= *Betonung, fig auch*) stress; **den ~ auf etw** (*acc*) **legen** (*lit*) to stress sth; **dieses Jahr liegen die (modischen) ~e bei ...** this year the emphasis is on ...

Akzent-: Akzentbuchstabe M accented letter; **akzentfrei** ADJ, ADV without any or an accent

Akzept [ak'tsɛpt] NT **-(e)s, -e** (*Comm*) acceptance

akzeptabel [aktsɛp'ta:bl] ADJ acceptable

Akzeptanz [aktsɛp'tants] F **-**, NO PL acceptance; **unsere Produkte haben keine ~ auf dem deutschen Markt** our products have not been accepted by the German market; **um die ~ unserer Produkte zu erhöhen** to make our products more acceptable

akzeptieren [aktsɛp'ti:rən], *ptp* **akzeptiert** VT to accept

AL [a:'lɛl] F **-, -s** ABBR von **Alternative Liste**

à la [a la] ADV à la

Alabaster [ala'bastɐ] M **-s, -** alabaster

Alarm [a'larm] M **-(e)s, -e** (= *Warnung*) alarm; (= *Fliegeralarm*) air-raid warning; (= *Zustand*) alert; **bei ~** following an alarm/ air-raid warning; (*während ~*) during an alert; **~!** fire!/air raid! *etc*; **~ schlagen** to give or raise or sound the alarm

Alarm-: Alarmanlage F alarm system; **alarmbereit** ADJ on the alert; *Feuerwehr, Polizei auch* standing by; **sich ~ halten** to be on the alert/standing by; **Alarmbereitschaft** F alert; **erhöhte ~** high alert; **in ~ sein** or **stehen** to be on the alert; (*Feuerwehr, Polizei auch*) to be standing by; **in ~ versetzen** to put on the alert

alarmieren [alar'mi:rən], *ptp* **alarmiert** VT *Polizei etc* to alert; (*fig*: = *beunruhigen*) to alarm; **~d** (*fig*) alarming; **aufs höchste** or **Höchste alarmiert** (*fig*) highly alarmed

Alarm-: Alarmstufe F alert stage; **Alarmzustand** M alert; **im ~ sein** to be on the alert

Alaska [a'laska] NT **-s** Alaska

Alb [alp] M **-(e)s, -e** [-bə] **wie ein ~ auf jdm lasten** (*fig geh*) to lie or weigh heavily (up)on sb

Albaner [al'ba:nɐ] M **-s, -**, **Albanerin** [-ərɪn] F **-, -nen** Albanian

Albanien [al'ba:niən] NT **-s** Albania

albanisch [al'ba:nɪʃ] ADJ Albanian

Albatros ['albatrɔs] M **-, -se** albatross

Albdruck M, *pl* **-drücke** (*lit, fig*) nightmare; **wie ein ~ auf jdm lasten** to weigh sb down

Alben PL von **Album**

Alberei [albə'rai] F **-, -en** silliness; (= *das Spaßmachen*) fooling about (*Brit*) or around (*US*); (= *Tat*) silly prank; (= *Bemerkung*) inanity

albern ['albɐn] **1** ADJ silly, stupid; **~es Zeug** (silly) nonsense **2** ADV *klingen* silly; **sich ~ benehmen** to act silly; (= *Quatsch machen*) to fool around; **~ fragen** to ask a silly question **3** VI to fool around

Albernheit F -, -en (a) NO PL (= *albernes Wesen*) silliness; (= *Lächerlichkeit*) ridiculousness (b) (= *Tat*) silly prank; (= *Bemerkung*) inanity

Albino [al'bi:no] M **-s, -s** albino

Albtraum M (*lit, fig*) nightmare

Album ['album] NT **-s, Alben** ['albn] album

al dente [al 'dɛntə] ADJ al dente

Alemanne [alə'manə] M **-n, -n, Alemannin** [-'manɪn] F -, **-nen** Alemannic

alemannisch [alə'manɪʃ] ADJ Alemannic

Aleuten [ale'u:tn] PL **die ~** the Aleutians

Alexandriner [aleksan'dri:nɐ] M **-s, -** (*Poet*) alexandrine

Alge ['algə] F -, **-n** alga

Algebra ['algebra] F -, NO PL algebra

algebraisch [alge'bra:ɪʃ] ADJ algebraic(al)

Algen-: Algenblüte F algae *or* algal bloom; **Algenpest** F algae plague; **Algenteppich** M algae slick

Algerien [al'ge:riən] NT **-s** Algeria

Algerier [al'ge:riɐ] M **-s, -, Algerierin** [-iərɪn] F -, **-nen** Algerian

algerisch [al'ge:rɪʃ] ADJ Algerian

Algier ['alʒi:ɐ] NT **-s** Algiers

algorithmisch [algo'rɪtmɪʃ] ADJ algorithmic

Algorithmus [algo'rɪtmʊs] M **-, Algorithmen** [-mən] algorithm

Ali ['a:li] M **-s, -s** (*pej sl:* = *Araber*) wog (*Brit pej sl*), Arab

alias ['a:lias] ADV alias, also *or* otherwise known as

Alibi ['a:libi] NT **-s, -s** (*Jur, fig*) alibi

Alibi-: Alibifrau F token woman; **Alibifunktion** F **~ haben** (*fig*) to be used as an alibi

Alimente [ali'mɛntə] PL maintenance *sing*

Alkali [al'ka:li, 'alkali] NT **-s, Alkalien** [-'ka:liən] alkali

alkalisch [al'ka:lɪʃ] ADJ alkaline

Alki ['alki] M **-s, -s, Alkie** M **-s, -s** (*sl*) alkie (*inf*)

Alkohol ['alkoho:l, alko'ho:l] M **-s, -e** alcohol; (= *alkoholische Getränke auch*) drink; **seinen Kummer im ~ ertränken** to drown one's sorrows; **unter ~ stehen** to be under the influence (of alcohol *or* drink)

Alkohol-: alkoholarm ADJ low in alcohol (content); **~es Bier** low-alcohol beer; **Alkoholausschank** M sale of alcohol(ic drinks); **Alkoholeinfluss** M, **Alkoholeinwirkung** F influence of alcohol *or* drink; **Alkoholfahne** F (*inf*) smell of alcohol; **eine ~ haben** to smell of alcohol *or* drink; **alkoholfrei** ADJ *Bier* alcohol-free, nonalcoholic; *Getränk auch* soft; *Gegend, Stadt* dry; **ein ~er Tag** a day without drink *or* alcohol; **Alkoholgehalt** M alcohol(ic) content; **Alkoholgenuss** M consumption of alcohol; **alkoholhaltig** ADJ alcoholic

Alkoholika [alko'ho:lika] PL alcoholic drinks *pl*

Alkoholiker [alko'ho:likɐ] M **-s, -, Alkoholikerin** [-ərɪn] F -, **-nen** alcoholic

alkoholisch [alko'ho:lɪʃ] ADJ alcoholic

alkoholisiert [alkoholi'zi:ɐt] ADJ (= *betrunken*) inebriated; **in ~em Zustand** in a state of inebriation

Alkoholismus [alkoho'lɪsmʊs] M -, NO PL alcoholism

Alkohol-: Alkoholkonsum [-kɔnzu:m] M consumption of alcohol; **Alkoholkontrolle** F roadside breath test; **Alkoholmissbrauch** M alcohol abuse; **Alkoholpegel** M (*hum*), **Alkoholspiegel** M **jds ~** the level of alcohol in sb's blood; **alkoholsüchtig** ADJ addicted to alcohol; **Alkoholsünder(in)** M(F) (*inf*) drunk(en) driver; **Alkoholtest** M breath test; **Alkoholtestgerät** NT Breathalyzer®, drunkometer (*US hum*); **Alkoholverbot** NT ban on alcohol; **Alkoholvergiftung** F alcohol(ic) poisoning

all [al] INDEF PRON **~ das/mein ...** *etc* all the/my *etc*; *siehe auch* **alle(r, s)**

All NT **-s**, NO PL (*Sci, Space*) space *no art*; (*außerhalb unseres Sternsystems*) outer space; (*litergeh*) universe; **Spaziergang im ~** space walk

all-: allabendlich ❶ ADJ (which takes place) every evening; **der ~e Spaziergang** the regular evening walk ❷ ADV every evening; **alldem** [al'de:m] PRON = **alledem**; **alldieweil** [aldi:'vail] CONJ (*old, hum:* = *weil*) because

alle ['alə] ❶ PRON *siehe* **alle(r, s)** ❷ ADV (*inf*) all gone; **die Milch ist ~** the milk's all gone, there's no milk left; **etw/jdn ~ machen** (*inf*) to finish sth/sb off; **~ werden** to be finished

alledem [alə'de:m] PRON **bei/trotz** *etc* **~** with/in spite of *etc* all that; **von ~ stimmt kein Wort** there's no truth in any of that *or* it; **zu ~** moreover

Allee [a'le:] F -, **-n** [-'le:ən] avenue

> *Vorsicht!* **Allee** *wird nicht mit dem englischen Wort* **alley** *übersetzt.*

Allegorie [alego'ri:] F -, **-n** [-'ri:ən] allegory

allegorisch [ale'go:rɪʃ] ❶ ADJ allegorical ❷ ADV allegorically

Allegro [a'le:gro] NT **-s, -s** *or* **Allegri** [-gri] allegro

allein [a'lain] ❶ ADJ PRED (*esp inf: auch* **alleine**) alone; *Gegenstand, Wort auch* by itself, on its own; (= *ohne Gesellschaft, Begleitung, Hilfe auch*) by oneself, on one's own; (= *einsam*) lonely; **für sich ~** by oneself, on one's own, alone; **von ~** by oneself/itself; **ich tue es schon von ~e** I'll do that in any case; **das weiß ich von ~(e)** you don't have to tell me (that); **ganz ~** (= *einsam*) quite *or* all alone; (= *ohne Begleitung, Hilfe*) all by oneself, all on one's own; **auf sich** (*acc*) **~ angewiesen sein** to be left to cope on one's own ❷ ADV (= *nur*) alone; **nicht ~, ... sondern auch** not only ... but also; **~ schon der Gedanke, (schon) der Gedanke ...** the very *or* mere thought ...; **~ erziehend** *Mutter, Vater* single; **~ Erziehende(r)** single parent; **~ stehend** living alone *or* on one's own; **~ Stehende(r)** single person

Allein-: Alleinerbe M, **Alleinerbin** F sole heir; **alleinerziehend** ADJ *siehe* **allein**; **Alleinerziehende(r)** [-ɛɐtsi:əndə] MF DECL AS ADJ single parent; **Alleingang** M, *pl* **-gänge** (*inf*) (*Sport*) solo run; (*von Bergsteiger*) solo climb; (*fig:* = *Tat*) solo effort; **etw im ~ machen** (*fig*) to do sth on one's own; **die Möglichkeit eines ~s** the possibility of going it alone

alleinig [a'lainɪç] ADJ ATTR sole, only; (*Aus, S Ger*) (= *allein stehend*) single; (= *ohne Begleitung*) unaccompanied; **die ~e Führung übernehmen** to go alone into the lead

Allein-: Alleinsein NT being on one's own *no def art*, solitude; (= *Einsamkeit*) loneliness; **alleinstehend** ADJ *siehe* **allein**; **Alleinstehende(r)** [-ʃte:əndə] MF DECL AS ADJ single person; **Alleinunterhalter(in)** M(F) solo entertainer; **Alleinverkaufsrecht** NT exclusive right of sale; **das ~ für etw haben** to have the exclusive right to sell sth; **Alleinvertretung** F (*Comm*) sole agency; (*Pol*) sole representation; **Alleinvertretungsanspruch** M (*Pol*) claim to sole representation

alleluja [ale'lu:ja] INTERJ halleluja(h)

allemal ['alə'ma:l] ADV every *or* each time; (= *ohne Schwierigkeit*) without any problem; **was er kann, kann ich noch ~** anything he can do I can do too; **~!** no problem! (*inf*); *siehe* **Mal²**

allenfalls ['alən'fals, 'alənfals] ADV (= *nötigenfalls*) if need be; (= *höchstens*) at most; (= *bestenfalls*) at best

aller- ['alɐ] IN CPDS WITH SUPERL (*zur Verstärkung*) by far; **das Allergrößte** by far the biggest, the biggest by far

alle(r, s) ['alə] ❶ INDEF PRON (a) ATTR all; (*bestimmte Menge, Anzahl*) all the; (= *all sein*) *Geld, Liebe, Freunde, Erfahrungen* all one's; **~ Kinder unter 10 Jahren** all children under 10; **~ Kinder dieser Stadt** all the children in this town; **die Eltern fuhren mit ~n Kindern weg** the parents went off with all their children; **~ meine Kinder** all (of) my children; **wir haben ~n Hass vergessen** we have forgotten all (our *or* the) hatred; **~ Anwesenden/Beteiligten/Betroffenen** all those present/taking part/affected; **mit ~m Nachdruck** with every emphasis; **trotz ~r Mühe** in spite of every effort; **ohne ~n Grund** for no reason at all; **mit ~r Deutlichkeit** quite distinctly; **ohne ~n Zweifel** without any doubt; *siehe auch* **all** (b) **alles** SING (*substantivisch*) everything; (*inf:* = *~ Menschen*) everybody, everyone; **~s, was ...** all *or* everything that ...; everybody *or* everyone who ...; **das ~s** all that; **~s Schöne** everything beautiful; **„~s für das Baby/den Heimwerker"** "everything for (the) baby/the handyman"; **(ich wünsche dir) ~s Gute** (I wish you) all the best; **~s und jedes** anything and everything; **in ~m** (= *in jeder Beziehung*) in everything; **~s in ~m** all in all; **trotz ~m** in spite of everything; **über ~s** above all else; (= *mehr als alles andere*) more than anything else; **vor ~m** above all; **das ist ~s, das wäre ~s** that's all, that's it (*inf*); **das ist ~s andere als ...** that's anything but ...; **er ist ~s, nur kein Vertreter** he's anything but a salesman; **das ist mir ~s gleich** it's all the same to me; **was soll das ~s?** what's all this supposed to mean?; **~s schon mal da gewesen!** (*inf*) it's all been done before!; **was habt ihr ~s gemacht?** what did you

get up to?; **wer war ~s da?** who was there?; **was er (nicht) ~s weiß/kann!** the things he knows/can do!; **was es nicht ~s gibt!** well I never (*inf*)
(c) alle PL (*substantivisch*) all; (= *alle Menschen auch*) everybody, everyone; **sie sind ~ alt** they're all old; **die haben mir ~ nicht gefallen** I didn't like any of them; **~ beide** both of them; **~ drei** all three of them; **diese ~** all (of) these; **der Kampf ~r gegen ~** the free-for-all; **~ für einen und einer für ~!** all for one and one for all; **sie kamen ~** they all came, all of them came; **sie haben ~ kein Geld mehr** none of them has any money left; **redet nicht ~ auf einmal!** don't all talk at once!
(d) (*mit Zeit-, Maßangaben*) USU PL every; **~ fünf Minuten/halbe Stunde/fünf Meilen** every five minutes/half-hour/five miles; **~ Jahre wieder** year after year
2 ADV *siehe* **alle**

alleraller- [ˈaleˈale] IN CPDS WITH SUPERL (*inf: zur Verstärkung*) far and away; **das Allerallergrößte** far and away the biggest

aller-: allerbeste(r, s) [ˈaleˈbestə] ADJ very best, best of all, best ... of all; (= *exquisit*) *Waren, Qualität* very best; **ich wünsche dir das Allerbeste** (I wish you) all the best; **der/die/das Allerbeste** the very best, the best of all; **es ist das Allerbeste** *or* **am ~, zu .../wenn ...** the best thing would be to .../if ...; **allerdings** [ˈaleˈdɪŋs] ADV **(a)** (*einschränkend*) though; **das ist ~ wahr, aber ...** that may (well) be true, but ... **(b)** (*bekräftigend*) certainly; **~!** (*most*) certainly!; **allererste(r, s)** [ˈaleˈleːestə] ADJ very first; **allerfrühestens** [ˈaleˈfryːastns] ADV at the very earliest

Allergen [aleɐˈgeːn] NT -s, -e (*Med*) allergen

Allergie [aleɐˈgiː] F -, -n [-ˈgiːən] (*Med*) allergy; (*fig*) aversion (*gegen* to); **eine ~ gegen etw haben** to be allergic to sth (*auch fig hum*)

Allergieschock M (*Med*) anaphylactic shock

Allergiker [aˈlergikɐ] M -s, -, **Allergikerin** [-ərɪn] F -, -nen person suffering from an allergy

allergisch [aˈlergɪʃ] **1** ADJ (*Med, fig*) allergic (*gegen* to) **2** ADV **auf etw** (*acc*) **~ reagieren** to have an allergic reaction to sth; (*fig*) to react oversensitively to sth; **~ bedingt sein** to be caused by an allergy

Allergologe [alergoˈloːgə] M -n, -n, **Allergologin** [-ˈloːgɪn] F -, -nen allergist

Allergologie [alergoloˈgiː] F -, NO PL (*Med*) allergology

Aller-: allerhand [ˈaleˈhant] ADJ INV (*substantivisch*) (= *allerlei*) all kinds of things; (= *ziemlich viel, attributiv*) all kinds *or* sorts of; **das ist ~!** (*zustimmend*) that's quite something!; **das ist ja** *or* **doch ~!** (*empört*) that's too much!; **Allerheiligen** [ˈaleˈhailɪgn] NT -s All Saints' Day, All Hallows (Day) (*Brit*);

ALLERHEILIGEN

Allerheiligen (All Saints' Day, celebrated on November 1st) is a holiday in Catholic areas of Germany and in Austria. The following day, November 2nd, is Allerseelen (All Souls' Day) when the dead are commemorated. It is traditional on these days to visit cemeteries and place flowers, wreaths and lighted candles on the graves of loved ones. In Alpine regions children traditionally go from house to house asking for Seelenwecken (bread rolls).

In the Protestant Church Totensonntag falls on the last Sunday before Advent and is devoted to the remembrance of the dead.

Aller-: allerhöchstens [ˈaleˈhøːçstns] ADV at the very most; **allerhöchste(r, s)** [ˈaleˈhøːçstə] ADJ *Berg etc* highest of all, highest ... of all; *Betrag, Belastung, Geschwindigkeit* maximum; *Funktionäre* highest, top *attr*; *Instanz, Kreise* very highest; **es wird ~ Zeit, dass ...** it's really high time that ...; **allerlei** [ˈaleˈlai] ADJ INV (*substantivisch*) all sorts *or* kinds of things; (*attributiv*) all sorts *or* kinds of; **allerletzte(r, s)** [ˈaleˈletstə] ADJ very last; (= *allerneueste*) very latest; (*inf: = unmöglich*) most awful *attr* (*inf*); **in ~r Zeit** very recently; **der/die/das Allerletzte** the very last (person)/thing; **der/das ist (ja) das Allerletzte** (*inf*) he's/it's the absolute end! (*inf*); **allerliebste(r, s)** [ˈaleˈliːpstə] ADJ (= *Lieblings-*) most favourite *attr* (*Brit*) *or* favorite *attr* (*US*); **sie ist mir die Allerliebste** she's my absolute favourite (*Brit*) *or* favorite (*US*); **es wäre mir das Allerliebste** *or* **am ~n, wenn ...** I would much prefer it if ...; **am ~n geh ich ins Kino** I like going to the cinema most *or* best of all; **allermeiste(r, s)** [ˈaleˈmaistə] ADJ most of all, most ... of all; (= *weitaus beste*) by far the most; **am ~n** most of all; **die**

Allermeisten the vast majority; **allerneueste(r, s)** [ˈaleˈnɔyastə], **allerneuste(r, s)** [ˈaleˈnɔystə] ADJ very latest; **Allerseelen** [ˈaleˈzeːlən] NT -s All Souls' Day; **allerseits** [ˈaleˈzaits] ADV on all sides; **guten Abend ~!** good evening everybody; **allerspätestens** [ˈaleˈʃpeːtəstns] ADV at the very latest

Allerwelts- [ˈaleˈvelts] IN CPDS (= *Durchschnitts-*) ordinary; (= *nichts sagend*) general; **Allerweltsthema** NT general subject

Aller-: allerwenigstens [ˈaleˈveːnɪçstns] ADV at the very least; **allerwenigste(r, s)** [ˈaleˈveːnɪçstə] ADJ least of all, least ... of all; (*pl*) fewest of all, fewest ... of all; (= *äußerst wenig*) very little; (*pl*) very few; (= *geringste*) *Mühe* least possible; **die ~n Menschen wissen das** very (very) few people know that; **das ist doch das Allerwenigste, was man erwarten könnte** but that's the very least one could expect; **er hat von uns allen das ~** *or* **am ~n Geld** he has the least money of any of us; **sie hat von uns allen die ~n** *or* **am ~n Sorgen** she has the fewest worries of any of us; **das am ~n!** least of all that!; **Allerwerteste(r)** [ˈaleˈveːɐtəstə] M DECL AS ADJ (*hum*) posterior (*hum*)

alles [ˈaləs] INDEF PRON *siehe* **alle(r, s)**

allesamt [aləˈzamt] ADV all (of them/us *etc*), to a man; **ihr seid ~ Betrüger!** you're all cheats!

Alles-: Allesfresser M omnivore; **Alleskleber** [-kleːbɐ] M -s, - all-purpose adhesive *or* glue

allfällig [ˈalfelɪç, aˈfelɪç] (*Aus, Sw*) **1** ADJ possible **2** ADV (= *eventuell*) possibly

allgegenwärtig [alˈgeːgnvertɪç] ADJ omnipresent

allgemein [ˈalgəˈmain] **1** ADJ general; *Feiertag* public; *Regelungen, Wahlrecht* universal; *Wehrpflicht* compulsory; **im Allgemeinen** in general, generally; **im ~en Interesse** in the common interest; **von ~em Interesse** of general interest; **~e Redensarten** (= *idiomatische Ausdrücke*) set expressions; (= *Phrasen*) commonplaces; **das ~e Wohl** the common good; **~es Aufsehen erregen** to cause a sensation; **wir sind ganz ~ geblieben** (*inf*) we stayed on a general level; **das Allgemeine und das Besondere** the general and the particular **2** ADV generally; (= *ausnahmslos von allen*) universally; (= *nicht spezifisch*) in general terms; **seine Thesen sind so ~ abgefasst, dass ...** his theses are worded in such general terms that ...; **du kannst doch nicht so ~ behaupten, dass ...** you can't generalize like that and say that ...; **es ist ~ bekannt** it's common knowledge; **~ bildend** providing (a) general education; **~ verständlich** (*adjektivisch*) generally intelligible; (*adverbial*) in a way intelligible to all; **etw ~ verständlich ausdrücken** to express sth in a way which everyone can understand; **~ verbreitet** widespread; **~ zugänglich** open to all

Allgemein-: Allgemeinbefinden NT general condition; **Allgemeinbildung** F general education; **Allgemeingut** NT, NO PL (*fig*) common property; **Allgemeinheit** F -, -en **(a)** NO PL (= *Öffentlichkeit*) general public; (= *alle*) everyone, everybody **(b)** (= *Unbestimmtheit*) generality; **~en** generalities; **Allgemeinmedizin** F general medicine; **Arzt für ~** general practitioner, GP; **Allgemeinplatz** M (*pej*) commonplace, platitude; **allgemeinverständlich** ADJ *siehe* **allgemein**; **Allgemeinwissen** NT general knowledge; **Allgemeinwohl** NT public welfare

Allheilmittel [alˈhailmɪtl] NT cure-all

Allianz [aˈliants] F -, -en **(a)** alliance **(b)** (= *NATO*) Alliance

Alligator [aliˈgaːtoːɐ] M -s, **Alligatoren** [-ˈtoːrən] alligator

alliiert [aliˈiːɐt] ADJ ATTR allied; (*im 2. Weltkrieg*) Allied

Alliierte(r) [aliˈiːɐtə] MF DECL AS ADJ ally; **die ~n** (*im 2. Weltkrieg*) the Allies

Alliteration [alɪteraˈtsioːn] F -, -en (*Poet*) alliteration

All-: alljährlich [ˈalˈjeːɐlɪç] **1** ADJ annual, yearly **2** ADV annually, yearly; **allmächtig** [alˈmeçtɪç] ADJ all-powerful; *Gott* almighty

allmählich [alˈmeːlɪç] **1** ADJ ATTR gradual **2** ADV gradually; (*inf: = endlich*) at last; **es wird ~ Zeit** (*inf*) it's about time; **ich werde (ganz) ~ müde** (*inf*) I'm beginning to get tired; **wir sollten ~ gehen** (*inf*) shall we think about going?

All-: allmonatlich [ˈalˈmoːnatlɪç] ADJ, ADV monthly; **allmorgendlich** [ˈalˈmɔrgntlɪç] **1** ADJ which takes place every morning; **die ~e Eile** the regular morning rush **2** ADV every morning

Allparteienregierung F (*Pol*) all-party government

Allradantrieb [ˈalraːt-] M (*Aut*) four-wheel drive
Allround- [ˈɔːlraʊnd] IN CPDS all-round (*Brit*), all-around (*US*)
Allrounder [ˈɔːlraʊndɐ] M **-s, -**, **Allrounderin** [-ərɪn] F **-, -nen** all-rounder (*Brit*), multi-talent (*US*)
allseitig [ˈalzaɪtɪç] **1** ADJ (= *allgemein*) general; (= *ausnahmslos*) universal; (= *vielseitig*) all-round *attr* (*Brit*), all-around *attr* (*US*); **zur ~en Zufriedenheit** to the satisfaction of everyone **2** ADV ~ **begabt sein** to be an all-rounder (*Brit*) or a multi-talent (*US*); **jdn ~ ausbilden** to provide sb with a general education; **er wurde ~ informiert** he was informed about every (possible) area; **~ interessiert sein** to be interested in everything
allseits [ˈalzaɪts] ADV (= *überall*) everywhere, on all sides; (= *in jeder Beziehung*) in every respect; **~ beliebt/unbeliebt** universally popular/unpopular
Alltag [ˈaltaːk] M (a) (= *Werktag*) weekday; **mitten im ~** in the middle of the week (b) (*fig*) everyday life; **im ~** in everyday life; **der ~ der Ehe** the mundane side of married life
alltäglich [ˈalˈtɛːklɪç, ˈalteːklɪç, alˈtɛːklɪç] ADJ (= *tagtäglich*) daily; (= *üblich*) everyday *attr*, ordinary; *Gesicht, Mensch* ordinary; *Bemerkung* commonplace; **es ist ganz ~** it's nothing unusual; **das ist nichts Alltägliches, dass/wenn ...** it doesn't happen every day that ...; **was ich suche, ist nicht das Alltägliche** I'm looking for something a bit out of the ordinary
Alltags- [ˈaltaːks-] IN CPDS everyday; **Alltagsleben** NT everyday life; **danach begann wieder das ~** after that life got back to normal again; **Alltagsrhythmus** M daily rhythm; **Alltagstrott** M (*inf*) treadmill of everyday life
Allüren [aˈlyːrən] PL behaviour (*Brit*), behavior (*US*); (= *geziertes Verhalten*) affectations *pl*; (*eines Stars etc*) airs and graces *pl*
All-: **allwissend** [ˈalvɪsnt] ADJ omniscient; **allwöchentlich** [ˈalvœçntlɪç] **1** ADJ weekly **2** ADV every week; **allzeit** [ˈalˈtsaɪt] ADV (*geh*) always; **~ bereit!** be prepared!
allzu [ˈaltsuː] ADV all too; (+*neg*) too; **~ viele Fehler** far too many mistakes; **nur ~** only or all too; **~ früh** far too early; (+*neg*) too early; **~ gern** mögen only too much; (= *bereitwillig*) only too willingly; (+*neg*) all that much, too much; all that willingly, too willingly; **~ sehr** too much; *mögen* all too much; (+*neg*) too much, all that much; *sich freuen, erfreut sein* only too; (+*neg*) too; *versuchen* too hard; *sich ärgern, enttäuscht sein* too; **~ viel** too much; **~ viel ist ungesund** (*Prov*) you can have too much of a good thing (*prov*)
Allzweck- [ˈaltsvɛk] IN CPDS general purpose; **Allzweckhalle** F multipurpose hall; **Allzweckreiniger** M multipurpose cleaner
Alm [alm] F **-, -en** alpine pasture
Almosen [ˈalmoːzn] NT **-s, -** (a) (*geh*: = *Spende*) alms *pl* (*old*) (b) (= *geringer Lohn*) pittance
Aloe [ˈaːloe] F **-, -n** [ˈaːloən] aloe
Alp¹ [alp] F **-, -en** (= *Alm*) alpine pasture
Alp² M **-(e)s, -e** (*old*: = *Nachtmahr*) *siehe* **Alb**
Alpdruck M, *pl* **-drücke** *siehe* **Albdruck**
Alpen [ˈalpn] PL Alps *pl*
Alpen- IN CPDS alpine; **Alpenland** NT alpine country; **alpenländisch** [-lɛndɪʃ] ADJ *Literatur, Kulturgut etc* of the alpine region; *Mensch* from the alpine region; **Alpenpass** M alpine pass; **Alpenrepublik** F **die ~** (*hum*) Austria; **Alpenrose** F Alpine rose *or* rhododendron; **Alpenveilchen** NT cyclamen; **Alpenvorland** NT foothills *pl* of the Alps
alph. ABBR *von* **alphabetisch**
Alpha [ˈalfa] NT **-(s), -s** alpha
Alphabet [alfaˈbeːt] NT **-(e)s, -e** alphabet; **nach dem ~** alphabetically, in alphabetical order
alphabetisch [alfaˈbeːtɪʃ] **1** ADJ alphabetical **2** ADV alphabetically
alphabetisieren [alfabetiˈziːrən], *ptp* **alphabetisiert** VT to make literate
Alphabetisierung F **-, -en ein Programm zur ~ Indiens** a programme (*Brit*) *or* program (*US*) against illiteracy in India; **die ~ Kubas ist abgeschlossen** the population of Cuba is now largely literate
Alpha-: **alphanumerisch** [alfanuˈmeːrɪʃ] **1** ADJ alphanumeric **2** ADV alphanumerically; **Alphastrahlen** PL alpha rays *pl*
alpin [alˈpiːn] ADJ alpine (*auch Ski*)

Alpinist [alpiˈnɪst] M **-en, -en**, **Alpinistin** [-ˈnɪstɪn] F **-, -nen** alpinist
Alptraum M *siehe* **Albtraum**
als [als] CONJ (a) (*nach comp*) than; **ich kam später ~ er** I came later than he (did) *or* him; **mehr ~ arbeiten kann ich nicht** I can't do more than work
(b) (*bei Vergleichen*) **so ... ~ ...** as ... as ...; **so viel/so weit ~ möglich** as much/far as possible; **~ wie** as; **nichts/niemand/nirgend anders** nothing/nobody/nowhere but; **eher** *or* **lieber ... ~** rather ... than; **anders sein ~** to be different from; **das machen wir anders ~ ihr** we do it differently to you; **alles andere ~** anything but
(c) **es sieht aus, ~ würde es bald schneien** it looks as if *or* though it will snow soon; **~ ob ich das nicht wüsste!** as if I didn't know!; **~ (da sind) ...** (*in Aufzählung*) that is to say ...; **sie ist zu alt, ~ dass sie das noch verstehen könnte** she is too old to understand that; **das ist umso trauriger, ~ es nicht das erste Mal war** that's all the sadder in that it wasn't the first time
(d) (*in Temporalsätzen*) when; (= *gleichzeitig*) as; **gleich, ~ as** soon as; **damals, ~** (in the days) when; **gerade, ~** just as
(e) (= *in der Eigenschaft*) as; **~ Beweis** as proof; **~ Antwort/Warnung** as an answer/a warning; **sich ~ wahr/falsch erweisen** to prove to be true/false; **~ Kind/Mädchen** *etc* as a child/girl *etc*; **~ Rentner will er ein Buch schreiben** when he retires he is going to write a book
also [ˈalzo] **1** CONJ (= *folglich*) so, therefore; **er war Künstler, ein hochsensibler Mensch ~** he was an artist, (and) therefore a highly sensitive person
2 ADV so; (*nach Unterbrechung anknüpfend*) well; (*zusammenfassend, erklärend*) that is; **~ doch** so ... after all; **du machst es ~?** so you'll do it then?; **~ wie ich schon sagte** well (then), as I said before
3 INTERJ (*verwundert, entrüstet, auffordernd*) well; (*drohend*) just; **~, dass du dich ordentlich benimmst!** (you) just see that you behave yourself!; **~ doch!** so he/they *etc* did!; **na ~!** there you are!, you see?; **~, ich habs doch gewusst!** I knew it!; **~ gut** *or* **schön** well all right then; **~ dann!** right then!; **~ so was!** well (I never)!; **~ so eine Frechheit!** what impudence!

> *Vorsicht!* **also** *wird nicht mit dem englischen Wort* **also** *übersetzt.*

Alsterwasser [ˈalstɐ-] NT, *pl* **-wässer** (*N Ger*) shandy (*Brit*), radler (*US*), beer and lemonade
alt [alt] ADJ, *comp* **äer** [ˈɛltə], *superl* **äeste(r, s)** [ˈɛltəstə] (a) old; (= *sehr ~*) *Mythos, Sage, Aberglaube, Griechen, Geschichte* ancient; *Sprachen* classical; **das ~e Rom** ancient Rome; **Alt und Jung** (everybody) old and young; **ein drei Jahre ~es Kind** a three-year-old child; **wie ~ bist du?** how old are you?; **etw ~ kaufen** to buy sth second-hand; **man ist so ~, wie man sich fühlt** you're only as old as you feel; **~ und grau werden** to grow old and grey (*Brit*) *or* gray (*US*); **ich werde heute nicht ~ (werden)** (*inf*) I won't last long tonight (*inf*); **hier werde ich nicht ~** (*inf*) this isn't my scene (*inf*); **in ~er Freundschaft, dein ...** yours as ever ...; **~ aussehen** (*inf*: = *dumm dastehen*) to look stupid
(b) (= *dieselbe, gewohnt*) same old; **sie ist ganz die ~e Ingrid** *or* **die Alte** she's the same old Ingrid, she hasn't changed a bit; **er ist nicht mehr der Alte** he's not the man he was; **es ist nicht mehr das ~e Glasgow** it's not the (same old) Glasgow I/we *etc* knew; **alles bleibt beim Alten** everything stays as it was; **alles beim Alten lassen** to leave everything as it was
Alt¹ [alt] M **-s, -e** (*Mus*) alto; (*von Frau auch*) contralto; (*Gesamtheit der Stimmen*) altos *pl*, contraltos *pl*
Alt² NT **-s, -** (= *Bier*) top-fermented German dark beer
Altar [alˈtaːɐ] M **-s, Altäre** [-ˈtɛːrə] altar; **eine Frau zum ~ führen** to lead a woman to the altar
Alt-: **Altauto** NT old car (*ready to be scrapped or recycled*); **altbacken** [-bakn] ADJ (a) stale (b) (*fig*) old-fashioned; **Altbatterie** F used battery; **Altbau** M, *pl* **-bauten** old building; **Altbauwohnung** F flat (*Brit*) *or* apartment in an old building; **Altbier** NT top-fermented German dark beer; **Altbundeskanzler(in)** M(F) former German/Austrian Chancellor; **Altbundesland** NT **die Altbundesländer** the former West German states; **altdeutsch** ADJ old German; *Möbel, Stil* German Renaissance

Alte ['altə] F DECL AS ADJ (= *alte Frau*) (*inf*: = *Ehefrau, Mutter*) old woman; (*inf*: = *Vorgesetzte*) boss; *siehe auch* **Alte(r)**

Alt-: **Alteigentümer(in)** M(F) (*von Land, Gebäude*) original owner; **Alteisen** NT scrap metal; **altenglisch** ADJ old English; **Altenglisch(e)** NT Old English, Anglo-Saxon

Alten-: **Altenheim** NT old people's home; **Altenhilfe** F old people's welfare; **Altenpflege** F care (*for the elderly*); **Altenpflegeheim** NT nursing home for the elderly; **Altenpfleger(in)** M(F) old people's nurse; **Altenwohnheim** NT sheltered housing complex (for the elderly); **sie lebt in einem ~** she lives in sheltered housing

Alte(r) ['altə] M DECL AS ADJ (= *alter Mann*) (*inf*: = *Ehemann, Vater*) old man; (*inf*: = *Vorgesetzter*) boss; **die ~n** (= *Eltern*) the folk(s) *pl* (*inf*); (= *Tiereltern*) the parents *pl*; (= *ältere Generation*) the old people *pl* or folk *pl*; (*aus klassischer Zeit*) the ancients *pl*; *siehe auch* **Alte**

älter ['ɛltɐ] ADJ **(a)** COMP *von* **alt** older; *Bruder, Tochter etc auch* elder; **werden Frauen ~ als Männer?** do women live longer than men? **(b)** ATTR (= *nicht ganz jung*) elderly; **die ~en Herrschaften** the older members of the party

Alter ['altɐ] NT **-s, -** age; (= *letzter Lebensabschnitt, hohes*) ~) old age; **im ~** in one's old age; **in deinem ~** at your age; **er ist in deinem ~** he's your age; **im ~ von 18 Jahren** at the age of 18; **von mittlerem ~, mittleren ~s** middle-aged; **57 ist doch kein ~, um in Rente zu gehen** 57 is no age to retire; **er hat keinen Respekt vor dem ~** he has no respect for his elders; **~ schützt vor Torheit nicht** (*Prov*) there's no fool like an old fool (*Prov*)

Ältere(r) ['ɛltərə] MF DECL AS ADJ **(a)** (= *älterer Mensch*) older man/woman *etc*; **die ~n** the older ones **(b)** (*bei Namen*) Elder; **Holbein der ~** Holbein the Elder

altern ['altɐn] VI AUX SEIN or (*rare*) HABEN to age; (*Mensch auch*) to get older; (*Wein*) to mature; **vorzeitig ~** to grow old before one's time; **~d** ageing

alternativ [alterna'ti:f] **1** ADJ alternative; **Alternative Liste** (*Pol*) electoral pact of alternative political groupings **2** ADV **~ leben** to live an alternative lifestyle; **~ eingestellt sein** to have alternative political views

Alternativ- IN CPDS alternative

Alternative [alterna'ti:və] F **-n, -n** alternative (*etw zu tun* of doing sth)

Alternative(r) [alterna'ti:və] MF DECL AS ADJ (*Pol*) person with alternative views; (= *alternativ lebender Mensch*) proponent of the alternative society; **die ~n** those who favour (*Brit*) or favor (*US*) the alternative society

Alternativmedizin F alternative medicine

Alternsforschung F gerontology

Alters-: **Altersabstand** M age difference; **Altersasyl** NT (*Sw*) old people's home; **altersbedingt** ADJ age-related; **Altersbeschwerden** PL complaints *pl* of old age; **Alterserscheinung** F sign of old age; **Altersfleck** M blotch; **Altersforschung** F gerontology; **Altersfreibetrag** M age-related allowance; **Altersgenosse** M, **Altersgenossin** F contemporary; (*Kind*) child of the same age; (*Psych, Sociol*) peer; **wir sind ja ~n** we are the same age; **Altersgrenze** F age limit; (= *Rentenalter*) retirement age; **Altersgründe** PL **aus ~n** for reasons of age; **Altersgruppe** F age group; **Altersheim** NT old people's home; **Alterspyramide** F age pyramid *or* diagram; **Altersrente** F old age pension; **altersschwach** ADJ *Mensch* old and infirm; *Tier* old and weak; *Auto, Möbel etc* decrepit; **Altersschwäche** F (*von Mensch*) infirmity (*due to advancing years*); (*von Tier*) weakness (*due to old age*); (*hum*: *von Auto, Möbel etc*) decrepitude; **Altersschwachsinn** M senility; **Alterssitz** M **sein ~ war München** he spent his retirement in Munich; **Altersstufe** F age group; (= *Lebensabschnitt*) age, stage in life; **Altersteilzeit** F *part-time working for people approaching retirement*; **in (die) ~ gehen** to switch to part-time working (*when approaching retirement*); **Altersversorgung** F provision for (one's) old age; **betriebliche ~** ≈ company pension scheme

Altertum ['altətu:m] NT **-s,** NO PL antiquity *no art*

Altertümer ['altəty:mɐ] PL antiquities *pl*

altertümlich ['altəty:mlɪç] ADJ (= *aus dem Altertum*) ancient; (= *veraltet*) antiquated

Alterung ['altərʊŋ] F **-,** NO PL (= *das Altern*) ageing; (*von Wein*) maturation

Alte(s) ['altə] NT DECL AS ADJ **das ~** (= *das Gewohnte, Traditionelle*) the old; (= *alte Dinge*) old things *pl*; **er hängt sehr am ~n** he clings to the past; **sie hat Freude an allem ~n** she gets a lot of pleasure from anything old

Ältestenrat M council of elders; (*Ger Pol*) parliamentary advisory committee, ≈ think-tank (*Brit*)

älteste(r, s) ['ɛltəstə] ADJ SUPERL *von* **alt** oldest; *Sohn, Bruder etc auch* eldest

Alt-: **Altflöte** F treble recorder; (= *Querflöte*) bass *or* alto flute; **Altgerät** NT old appliance; **Altglas** NT, NO PL waste glass; **Altglasbehälter** M, **Altglascontainer** M bottle bank; **altgriechisch** ADJ ancient Greek; (*Ling auch*) classical Greek; **althergebracht, altherkömmlich** ADJ traditional; *Tradition* long-established; **althochdeutsch** ADJ Old High German

Altist [al'tɪst] M **-en, -en, Altistin** [-tɪstɪn] F **-, -nen** (*Mus*) alto

Alt-: **altjüngferlich** [alt'jʏŋfɛlɪç] ADJ old-maidish, spinsterish; **Altkanzler(in)** M(F) former chancellor; **altkatholisch** ADJ Old Catholic; **Altkleidersammlung** F collection of old clothes; **altklug** **1** ADJ precocious **2** ADV precociously; **Altlast** F USU PL (*Ökologie*) dangerous waste (*accumulated over the years*)

ältlich ['ɛltlɪç] ADJ oldish

Alt-: **Altmaterial** NT scrap; **Altmetall** NT scrap metal; **altmodisch** **1** ADJ old-fashioned; (= *rückständig*) outmoded **2** ADV **sie kleidet sich sehr ~** the way she dresses is very old-fashioned; **~ klingen** to sound old-fashioned; **sie denken ~** their ideas are old-fashioned; **Altöl** NT used oil; **Altpapier** NT wastepaper; **Altpapiercontainer** M (waste)paper bank; **Altpapiersammlung** F wastepaper collection; **Altphilologe** M, **Altphilologin** F classical philologist; **Altphilologie** F classical philology; **altphilologisch** ADJ *Abteilung* of classical philology; *Bücher, Artikel* on classical philology; **altrosa** ADJ INV old rose; **Altsängerin** F contralto (singer); **Altschlüssel** M (*Mus*) alto clef; **Altschnee** M old snow; **Altsein** NT being old *no art*; **Altsprachler** [-ʃpra:xlɐ] M **-s, -, Altsprachlerin** [-ərɪn] F **-, -nen** classicist; (= *Sprachwissenschaftler*) classical philologist; **altsprachlich** ADJ *Zweig, Abteilung* classics *attr*; **~es Gymnasium** ≈ grammar school (*Brit*) *or* high school (*US*) teaching classical languages; **Altstadt** F old (part of a/the) town; **die Ulmer ~** the old part of Ulm; **Altstimme** F (*Mus*) alto; (*von Frau auch*) contralto, contralto voice; (*Partie*) alto/contralto part; **Altstoff** M USU PL waste material; **~e sammeln** to collect (recyclable) waste; **gefährliche ~e** dangerous waste

Alt-Taste F (*Comput*) Alt key

Altweibersommer M **(a)** (= *Nachsommer*) Indian summer **(b)** (= *Spinnfäden*) gossamer

Alu ['a:lu] NT **-s,** NO PL (*inf*: = *Aluminium*) aluminium (*Brit*), aluminum (*US*)

Alufolie F tin *or* kitchen foil

Aluminium [alu'mi:niʊm] NT **-s,** NO PL (*abbr* **Al**) aluminium (*Brit*), aluminum (*US*)

Alzheimerkranke(r) ['altshaimɐ-] MF DECL AS ADJ person/man/woman suffering from Alzheimer's (disease); (= *Patient*) Alzheimer's patient

Alzheimerkrankheit F Alzheimer's (disease)

am [am] PREP **(a)** CONTR *von* **an dem** **(b)** (*zur Bildung des Superlativs*) **er war am tapfersten** he was (the) bravest; **sie hat es am besten/schönsten gemalt** she painted it best/(the) most beautifully; **am seltsamsten war ...** the strangest thing was ... **(c)** (*als Zeitangabe*) on; **am letzten Sonntag** last Sunday; **am 8. Mai** on the eighth of May, on May (the (*Brit*)) eighth; (*geschrieben*) on May 8th; **am Morgen/Abend** in the morning/evening; **am Tag darauf/zuvor** (on) the following/previous day **(d)** (*als Ortsangabe*) on the; (*bei Gebirgen*) at the foot of the **(e)** (*inf*: *als Verlaufsform*) **ich war gerade am Weggehen** I was just leaving **(f)** (*Aus*: = *auf dem*) on the

Amalgam [amal'ga:m] NT **-s, -e** amalgam

Amaryllis [ama'rʏlɪs] F **-, Amaryllen** [-lən] amaryllis

Amateur [ama'tø:ɐ] M **-s, -e, Amateurin** [-'tø:rɪn] F **-, -nen** amateur

Amateur- [ama'tø:ɐ] IN CPDS amateur; **Amateurfunker(in)** M(F) radio amateur *or* ham (*inf*)

amateurhaft [ama'tø:ɐ-] **1** ADJ amateurish **2** ADV amateurishly

Amateurin [amaˈtøːrɪn] F -, **-nen** amateur

Amazonas [amaˈtsoːnas] M - Amazon

Ambiente [amˈbiɛntə] NT -, NO PL (geh) ambience

Ambition [ambiˈtsioːn] F -, **-en** ambition; **~en auf etw** (acc) **haben** to have ambitions of getting sth

Amboss [ˈambɔs] M **-es, -e** anvil

ambulant [ambuˈlant] **◼** ADJ (a) (Med: in Arztpraxis, Krankenhaus) outpatient attr; **~e Patienten** outpatients (b) (= wandernd) itinerant **◼** ADV **~ behandelt werden** (Patient) to be treated as an outpatient; (Fall) to be treated in the outpatient department; **~ operieren/arbeiten** or **tätig sein** to operate on/treat outpatients

Ambulanz [ambuˈlants] F -, **-en** (a) (= Klinikstation) outpatient department, outpatients sing (inf) (b) (= ~wagen) ambulance

Ameise [ˈaːmaizə] F -, **-n** ant

Ameisen-: Ameisenbär M anteater; (größer) giant anteater; **Ameisenhaufen** M anthill; **Ameisensäure** F formic acid; **Ameisenstaat** M ant colony

amen [ˈaːmən] INTERJ amen

Amen [ˈaːmən] NT **-s, -** amen; **sein ~ zu etw geben** to give one's blessing to sth; **das ist so sicher wie das ~ in der Kirche** (prov) you can bet your bottom dollar on that (inf)

Amerikaner [ameriˈkaːnɐ] M **-s, -, Amerikanerin** [-ərɪn] F -, **-nen** American

amerikanisch [ameriˈkaːnɪʃ] ADJ American

amerikanisieren [amerikaniˈziːrən], ptp **amerikanisiert** VT to Americanize

Amerikanismus [amerikaˈnɪsmʊs] M -, **Amerikanismen** [-mən] Americanism

Amerikanist [amerikaˈnɪst] M **-en, -en, Amerikanistin** [-ˈnɪstɪn] F -, **-nen** specialist in American studies

Amerikanistik [amerikaˈnɪstɪk] F -, NO PL American studies pl

Amethyst [ameˈtʏst] M **-s, -e** amethyst

Ami [ˈami] M **-s, -s** (inf) Yank (inf)

Aminosäure [aˈmiːno-] F amino acid

Ammann [ˈaman] M, pl **-männer** (Sw) (a) mayor (b) (Jur) local magistrate

Ammenmärchen NT fairy tale or story

Ammoniak [amoˈniak, ˈamoniak] NT **-s**, NO PL ammonia

Amnestie [amnɛsˈtiː] F -, **-n** [-ˈtiːən] amnesty

amnestieren [amnɛsˈtiːrən], ptp **amnestiert** VT to grant an amnesty to

Amöbe [aˈmøːbə] F -, **-n** (Biol) amoeba

Amöbenruhr F (Med) amoebic dysentery

Amok [ˈaːmɔk, aˈmɔk] M **~ laufen** to run amok (esp Brit) or amuck; **~ fahren** to drive like a madman or lunatic

Amok-: Amokfahrer(in) M(F) mad or lunatic driver; **Amokfahrt** F mad or crazy ride; **Amoklauf** M **einen ~ aufführen** to run amok (esp Brit) or amuck; **Amokläufer** M madman; **Amokläuferin** F madwoman; **Amokschütze** M crazed gunman; **Amokschützin** F crazed gunwoman

Amortisation [amɔrtizaˈtsioːn] F -, **-en** amortization

amortisieren [amɔrtiˈziːrən], ptp **amortisiert ◼** VT **eine Investition ~** to ensure that an investment pays for itself **◼** VR to pay for itself

Ampel [ˈampl] F -, **-n** (= Verkehrsampel) (traffic) lights pl; **halte an der nächsten ~** stop at the next (set of) (traffic) lights

Ampel-: Ampelanlage F (set of) traffic lights pl; **Ampelkoalition** F (Pol inf) coalition formed by SPD, FDP and Green Party; **Ampelphase** F traffic light sequence; **die langen ~n an dieser Kreuzung** the length of time the lights take to change at this junction

Amphetamin [amfetaˈmiːn] NT **-s, -e** amphetamine

Amphibie [amˈfiːbiə] F -, **-n** (Zool) amphibian

Amphibienfahrzeug NT amphibious vehicle

Amputation [amputaˈtsioːn] F -, **-en** amputation

amputieren [ampuˈtiːrən], ptp **amputiert** VT to amputate; **jdm den Arm ~** to amputate sb's arm; **amputiert werden** (Mensch) to have an amputation

amputiert ADJ Körperteil amputated; (fig) truncated

Amputierte(r) [ampuˈtiːɐtə] MF DECL AS ADJ amputee

Amsel [ˈamzl] F -, **-n** blackbird

Amsterdam [amstɐˈdam, ˈamstɐdam] NT **-s** Amsterdam

Amt [amt] NT **-(e)s, ⸚er** [ˈɛmtɐ] (a) (= Stelle) post (Brit), position; (öffentlich) office; **im ~ sein** to be in or hold office; **in ~ und Würden** in an exalted position; **von ~s wegen** (= aufgrund von jds Beruf) because of one's job; **kraft seines ~es** (geh) by virtue of one's office

(b) (= Aufgabe) duty, task

(c) (= Behörde) (= Fürsorgeamt) welfare department; (= Sozialamt) department of social security; (= Einwohnermeldeamt) registration office; (= Passamt) passport office; (= Finanzamt) tax office; (= Stadtverwaltung) council offices pl; **zum zuständigen ~ gehen** to go to the relevant authority; **die Ämter der Stadt** the town authorities; **von ~s wegen** (= auf behördliche Anordnung hin) officially

amtieren [amˈtiːrən], ptp **amtiert** VI (a) (= Amt innehaben) to be in office; **~d** incumbent; **der ~de Bürgermeister** the (present) mayor; **der ~de Weltmeister** the reigning world champion (b) (= Amt vorübergehend wahrnehmen) to act; **er amtiert als Bürgermeister** he is acting mayor

amtl. ABBR von amtlich

amtlich [ˈamtlɪç] **◼** ADJ official; (= wichtig) Miene, Gebaren officious; (inf: = sicher) certain; **~es Kennzeichen** registration (number), license number (US) **◼** ADV officially; **etw ~ haben** to have official confirmation of sth

Amts-: Amtsanmaßung F unauthorized assumption of authority; (= Ausübung eines Amtes) fraudulent exercise of a public office; **Amtsantritt** M siehe **Amt** assumption of office/one's post (Brit) or position; **Amtsblatt** NT gazette; **Amtsdauer** F term of office; **Amtsdiener(in)** M(F) clerk; (= Bote) messenger; **Amtseinführung** F, **Amtseinsetzung** F installation, inauguration; **Amtsenthebung** [-lɛntheːbʊŋ] F -, **-en** (Sw, Aus) **Amtsentsetzung** [-lɛntzɛtsʊŋ] F -, **-en** dismissal or removal from office; **Amtsgeheimnis** NT (= geheime Sache) official secret; (= Schweigepflicht) official secrecy; **Amtsgericht** NT ≈ county (Brit) or district (US) court; **Amtshandlung** F official duty; **seine erste ~ bestand darin, ...** the first thing he did in office was ...; **Amtshilfe** F cooperation between authorities; **Amtskanzlei** F (Aus) office; **Amtsleitung** F (Telec) exchange line; **Amtsniederlegung** F resignation; **Amtsperiode** F term of office; **Amtsperson** F official; **Amtsrichter(in)** M(F) ≈ county (Brit) or district (US) court judge; **Amtsschimmel** M (hum) officialdom; **den ~ reiten** to do everything by the book; **der ~ wiehert** officialdom rears its ugly head; **Amtssprache** F official language; **Amtsübergabe** F handing-over of office; **bei der ~ an seinen Nachfolger** when handing over his office to his successor; **Amtsübernahme** F siehe **Amt** assumption of office/a post (Brit) or position; **Amtsvergehen** NT malfeasance (form); **Amtsweg** M official channels pl; **den ~ beschreiten** to go through the official channels; **Amtszeichen** NT (Telec) dialling tone (Brit), dial tone (US); **Amtszeit** F period of office

Amulett [amuˈlɛt] NT **-(e)s, -e** amulet, charm

amüsant [amyˈzant] **◼** ADJ amusing **◼** ADV amusingly; **er hat ~ geplaudert** he talked in an amusing way; **wir haben ~ geplaudert** we had an amusing conversation

amüsieren [amyˈziːrən], ptp **amüsiert ◼** VT to amuse; **was amüsiert dich denn so?** what do you find so amusing or funny?; **lassen Sie sich ein bisschen ~** have some fun; **amüsiert zuschauen** to look on amused **◼** VR (= sich vergnügen) to enjoy oneself, to have fun; **sich mit etw ~** to amuse oneself with sth; (iro) to keep oneself amused with sth; **sich über etw** (acc) **~** to find sth funny; (= über etw lachen) to laugh at sth; (unfreundlich) to make fun of sth; **sich darüber ~, dass ...** to find it funny that ...; **sich mit jdm ~** to have fun or a good time with sb; **amüsiert euch gut** have fun, enjoy yourselves

Amüsier- [amyˈziːr-]: **Amüsierlokal** NT nightclub; **Amüsierviertel** NT nightclub district

an [an] **◼** PREP +DAT (a) (räumlich: wo?) at; (= an etw dran) on; **am Haus/Bahnhof** at the house/station; **an dieser Schule** at this school; **an der Wand stehen** to stand by the wall; **an der Tür/Wand** on the door/wall; **an der Donau/Autobahn/am Ufer/am Rhein** by or (direkt an gelegen) on the Danube/motorway/bank/Rhine; **Frankfurt an der Oder** Frankfurt on (the) Oder; **zu nahe an etw stehen** to be too near to sth; **etw an etw festmachen** to fasten sth to sth; **oben am Berg** up the mountain; **unten am Fluss** down by the river; **Haus an Haus** one house after the other; **an etw vorbeigehen** to go past sth,

to pass sth
(b) (*zeitlich*) on; **an diesem Abend** (on) that evening; **am Tag zuvor** the day before, the previous day; **an dem Abend, als ich ...** the evening I ...; **an Ostern/Weihnachten** (*dial*) at Easter/Christmas; *siehe* **am**
(c) (*fig*) **jung an Jahren sein** to be young in years; **fünf an der Zahl** five in number; **an etw arbeiten/schreiben/kauen** to be working on/writing/chewing sth; **an etw sterben/leiden** to die of/suffer from sth; **was haben Sie an Weinen da?** what wines do you have?; **unübertroffen an Qualität** unsurpassed in quality; **es an der Leber** *etc* **haben** (*inf*) to have liver *etc* trouble; **was findet sie an dem Mann?** what does she see in that man?; **sie hat etwas an sich, das ...** there is something about her that ...; **es ist an ihm, etwas zu tun** (*geh*) it's up to him to do something
2 PREP +ACC **(a)** (*räumlich: wohin?*) to; (= *gegen*) on, against; **etw an die Wand/Tafel schreiben** to write sth on the wall/blackboard; **die Zweige reichten (bis) an den Boden/mein Fenster** the branches reached down to the ground/up to my window; **er ging ans Fenster** he went (over) to the window; **An den Vorsitzenden ...** (*bei Anschrift*) The Chairman ...
(b) (*zeitlich: woran?*) **an die Zukunft/Vergangenheit denken** to think of the future/past; **bis an mein Lebensende** to the end of my days
(c) (*fig*) **ich habe eine Bitte/Frage an Sie** I have a request to make of you/a question to ask you; **an (und für) sich** actually; **wie war es? – an (und für) sich ganz schön** how was it? – on the whole it was quite nice
3 ADV **(a)** (= *ungefähr*) about; **an (die) hundert** about a hundred
(b) (*Ankunftszeit*) **Frankfurt an: 18.30 Uhr** arriving Frankfurt 18.30
(c) **von diesem Ort an** from here onwards; **von diesem Tag an** from this day on(wards); **von heute an** from today onwards
(d) (*inf: = angeschaltet, angezogen*) on; **Licht an!** lights on!; **ohne etwas an** with nothing on; *siehe auch* **an sein**
anabol [ana'boːl] ADJ anabolic
Anabolikum [ana'boːlikʊm] NT **-s, Anabolika** [-ka] anabolic steroid
anal [a'naːl] **1** ADJ (*Psych, Anat*) anal **2** ADV **Fieber messen** anally; **einführen into the anus;** ~ **untersucht werden** to undergo an anal examination; ~ **fixiert sein** to have an anal fixation
analog [ana'loːk] **1** ADJ **(a)** analogous (+*dat, zu* to) **(b)** (*Telec*) analogue (*Brit*), analog (*US*) **(c)** (*Comput*) analog **2** ADV **(a)** analogously **(b)** (*Telec, Comput*) in analogue (*Brit*) *or* analog format
Analog-: Analogrechner M analog computer; **Analoguhr** F analogue (*Brit*) *or* analog (*US*) clock
Analphabet [anlalfa'beːt, 'an-] M **-en, -en, Analphabetin** [-'beːtɪn] F **-, -nen** illiterate (person)
Analphabetentum [anlalfa'beːntuːm] NT **-s,** NO PL, **Analphabetismus** [anlalfabe'tɪsmʊs] M **-,** NO PL illiteracy
Analverkehr M anal intercourse
Analyse [ana'lyːzə] F **-, -n** analysis (*auch Psych*)
analysieren [analy'ziːrən], *ptp* **analysiert** VT to analyze
Analyst [ana'lʏst] M **-en, -en, Analystin** [-'lʏstɪn] F **-, -nen** (*St Ex*) investment analyst
Analytiker [ana'lyːtike] M **-s, -, Analytikerin** [-ərɪn] F **-, -nen** analyst; (= *analytischer Denkender*) analytical thinker
analytisch [ana'lyːtɪʃ] **1** ADJ analytical **2** ADV analytically; ~ **begabt sein** to have a talent for analytical thinking
Anamnese [anam'neːzə] F **-, -n** case history
Ananas ['ananas] F **-, -** *or* **-se** pineapple
Anarchie [anar'çiː] F **-, -n** [-'çiːən] anarchy
anarchisch [a'narçɪʃ] ADJ anarchic
Anarchismus [anar'çɪsmʊs] M **-,** NO PL anarchism
Anarchist [anar'çɪst] M **-en, -en, Anarchistin** [-'çɪstɪn] F **-, -nen** anarchist
anarchistisch [anar'çɪstɪʃ] ADJ anarchistic; (= *den Anarchismus vertretend auch*) anarchist *attr*
Anästhesie [anlɛste'ziː] F **-, -n** [-'ziːən] anaesthesia (*Brit*), anesthesia (*US*)
anästhesieren [anlɛste'ziːrən], *ptp* **anästhesiert** VT to anaesthetize (*Brit*), to anesthetize (*US*)

Anästhesist [anlɛste'zɪst] M **-en, -en, Anästhesistin** [-'zɪstɪn] F **-, -nen** anaesthetist (*Brit*), anesthesiologist (*US*)
Anatolien [ana'toːliən] NT **-s** Anatolia
Anatomie [anato'miː] F **-, -n** [-'miːən] anatomy; (= *Institut*) anatomical institute
anatomisch [ana'toːmɪʃ] ADJ anatomical
anbaggern VT SEP (*inf*) to chat up (*esp Brit inf*), to flirt with
anbahnen SEP **1** VT to initiate **2** VR (= *sich andeuten*) to be in the offing; (*Unangenehmes*) to be looming; (*Möglichkeiten, Zukunft etc*) to be opening up; **zwischen den beiden bahnt sich etwas an** (*Liebesverhältnis*) there is something going on between those two
Anbau¹ M, NO PL **(a)** (= *Anpflanzung*) cultivation, growing **(b)** (*von Gebäuden*) building
Anbau² M, *pl* **-bauten** (= *Nebengebäude*) extension
anbauen SEP **1** VT **(a)** Kartoffeln, Weizen, Hanf etc to cultivate, to grow; (= *anpflanzen*) to plant; (= *säen*) to sow **(b)** (*Build*) to add, to build on; **etw ans Haus** ~ to build sth onto the house **2** VI to build an extension; **Möbel zum Anbauen** unit furniture
Anbau-: Anbaugebiet NT cultivable area; **ein gutes** ~ **für etw** a good area for cultivating sth; **Anbaumöbel** PL unit furniture; **Anbauschrank** M cupboard unit
anbehalten *ptp* **anbehalten** VT SEP IRREG to keep on
anbei [an'bai, 'anbai] ADV (*form*) enclosed; ~ **schicken wir Ihnen ...** please find enclosed ...
anbeißen SEP IRREG **1** VI (*Fisch*) to bite; (*fig*) to take the bait **2** VT Apfel etc to bite into; **ein angebissener Apfel** a half-eaten apple; **sie sieht zum Anbeißen aus** (*inf*) she looks good enough to eat
anbekommen *ptp* **anbekommen** VT SEP IRREG (*inf*) to (manage to) get on; Feuer to (manage to) get going
anbelangen *ptp* **anbelangt** VT SEP to concern; **was das/mich anbelangt ...** as far as that is/I am concerned ...
anberaumen ['anbərauman], *ptp* **anberaumt** VT SEP *or* (*rare*) INSEP (*form*) to arrange, to fix
anbeten VT SEP to worship
Anbetracht M in ~ (+*gen*) in consideration *or* view of; **in ~ dessen, dass ...** in consideration *or* view of the fact that ...
anbiedern ['anbiːden] VR SEP (*pej*) **sich (bei jdm)** ~ to try to get pally (with sb) (*inf*)
Anbiederung F **-, -en** currying favour (*Brit*) *or* favor (*US*) (+*gen* with)
Anbiederungsversuch M **einen** ~ **bei jdm unternehmen** to attempt to curry favour (*Brit*) *or* favor (*US*) with sb
anbieten SEP IRREG **1** VT to offer (*jdm etw* sb sth); (*Comm*) Waren to offer for sale; **jdm das Du** ~ *to suggest sb uses the familiar form of address*
2 VR (*Mensch*) to offer one's services; (*Ftbl*) to be in position; (= *in Betracht kommen: Gelegenheit*) to present itself; **sich für die Arbeit** ~, **sich** ~, **die Arbeit zu tun** to offer to do the work; **der Ort bietet sich für die Konferenz an** that is the obvious place for the conference; **das Fahrrad bietet sich geradezu zum Mitnehmen an** that bicycle is just asking to be taken; **das bietet sich als Lösung an** that would provide a solution; **es bieten sich mehrere Lösungsmöglichkeiten an** there are several possible solutions; **es bietet sich an, das Museum zu besuchen** the thing to do would be to visit the museum
Anbieter(in) M(F) supplier
anbinden VT SEP IRREG (*an* +*acc* or *dat* to) (= *festbinden*) to tie (up); **jdn** ~ (*fig*) to tie sb down; *siehe auch* **angebunden**
Anblick M sight; **beim ersten** ~ at first sight; **beim** ~ **des Hundes** when he *etc* saw the dog
anblicken VT SEP to look at
anblinzeln VT SEP **(a)** (= *blinzelnd ansehen*) to squint at **(b)** (= *zublinzeln*) to wink at
Anbot ['anboːt] NT **-(e)s, -e** (*Aus*) = **Angebot**
anbraten VT SEP IRREG to brown; Steak etc to sear; **etw zu scharf** ~ to brown sth too much
anbräunen VT SEP (*Cook*) to brown (lightly)
anbrechen SEP IRREG **1** VT **(a)** Packung, Flasche etc to open; Vorrat to broach; Ersparnisse, Geldsumme, Geldschein to break into **(b)** (= *teilweise brechen*) Brett, Gefäß, Knochen etc to crack; **angebrochen sein** to be cracked; *siehe auch* **angebrochen 2** VI

AUX SEIN (*Epoche etc*) to dawn; (*Tag auch*) to break; (*Nacht*) to fall; (*Jahreszeit*) to begin; (*Winter*) to close in

anbrennen VI SEP IRREG AUX SEIN to start burning, to catch fire; (*Holz, Kohle etc*) to catch light; (*Essen*) to burn, to get burned; (*Stoff*) to scorch, to get scorched; **mir ist das Essen angebrannt** I burned the food; **nichts ~ lassen** (*inf*: = *keine Zeit verschwenden*) to be quick; (= *sich nichts entgehen lassen*) not to miss out on anything; *siehe auch* **angebrannt**

anbringen VT SEP IRREG **(a)** (= *befestigen*) to fix, to fasten (*an +dat* (on)to); (= *aufstellen, aufhängen*) to put up; *Telefon, Feuermelder etc* to install; *Stiel an Besen* to put on **(b)** (= *äußern*) to make (*bei* to); *Kenntnisse, Wissen* to display; *Argument* to use; **er konnte seine Kritik nicht mehr ~** he wasn't able to get his criticism in; *siehe auch* **angebracht** **(c)** (= *hierher bringen*) to bring (with one); (*nach Hause*) to bring home (with one)

Anbringung F -, NO PL (= *das Befestigen*) fixing, fastening; (= *das Aufstellen, Aufhängen*) putting up; (*von Telefon, Feuermelder etc*) installing

Anbruch M, NO PL (*geh*: = *Anfang*) beginning; (*von Zeitalter, Epoche*) dawn(ing); **bei ~ des Tages** *or* **Morgens** at daybreak; **bei ~ der Nacht** *or* **Dunkelheit** at nightfall

anbrüllen SEP **1** VT (*inf*: *Mensch*) to shout *or* bellow at **2** VI **gegen etw ~** to shout above (the noise of)

Andacht ['andaxt] F -, **-en** (= *Gottesdienst*) prayers *pl*

andächtig ['andɛçtɪç] **1** ADJ **(a)** (*im Gebet*) in prayer; **die ~en Gläubigen** the worshippers at their devotions *or* prayers **(b)** (= *versunken*) rapt; (= *ehrfürchtig*) reverent **2** ADV (= *inbrünstig*) raptly; (*hum*: = *ehrfürchtig*) reverently

Andalusien [anda'luːziən] NT **-s** Andalusia

andauern VI SEP to continue; (= *anhalten*) to last; **der Regen dauert noch an** the rain hasn't stopped; **das schöne Wetter wird nicht ~** the fine weather won't last

andauernd **1** ADJ (= *ständig*) continuous; (= *anhaltend*) continual **2** ADV constantly, continuously, continually; **wenn du mich ~ unterbrichst ...** if you keep on interrupting me ...

Anden ['andn] PL Andes *pl*

Andenken ['andɛŋkn] NT **-s, -** **(a)** NO PL memory; **das ~ von etw feiern** to commemorate sth; **zum ~ an jdn** *an Verstorbenen etc* in memory of sb; **zum ~ an etw** *an Urlaub etc* to remind you/us *etc* of sth **(b)** (= *Reiseandenken*) souvenir (*an +acc* of); (= *Erinnerungsstück*) memento (*an +acc* from)

anderenfalls ADV otherwise

andere(r, s) ['andərə] **1** INDEF PRON (*adjektivisch*) **(a)** different; (= *weiterer*) other; **jede ~ Frau hätte ...** any other woman would have ...; **das machen wir ein ~s Mal** we'll do that another time; **das ~ Geschlecht** the other sex; **er ist ein ~r Mensch geworden** he is a changed *or* different man; **~ Länder, ~ Sitten** (*prov*) different countries have different customs **(b)** (= *folgend*) next, following **2** INDEF PRON (*substantivisch*) **(a)** (= *Ding*) **ein ~r** a different one; (= *noch einer*) another one; **etwas ~s** something *or* (*jedes, in Fragen*) anything else; **alle ~n** all the others; **er hat noch drei ~** he has three others *or* (*von demselben*) more; **ja, das ist etwas ~s** yes, that's a different matter; **das ist etwas ganz ~s** that's something quite different; **hast du etwas ~s gedacht?** did you think otherwise?; **ein Mal ums ~** every single time; **ich habe ~s gehört** I heard differently; **nichts ~s** nothing else; **nichts ~s als ...** nothing but ...; **es blieb mir nichts ~s übrig, als selbst hinzugehen** I had no alternative but to go myself; **und ~s mehr** and more besides; **und vieles ~ mehr** and much more besides; **alles ~** (= *alle ~n Dinge*) everything else; **alles ~ als zufrieden** anything but pleased; **bist du müde? – nein, alles ~ als das** are you tired? – no, far from it *or* anything but; **unter ~m** among other things; **es kam eins zum ~n** one thing led to another; **... man kann doch eines tun, ohne das ~ zu lassen** ... but you can have the best of both worlds; **sie hat sich eines ~n besonnen** she changed her mind; **von einem Tag zum ~n** overnight; **von etwas ~m sprechen** to change the subject; **eines besser als das ~** each one better than the next **(b)** (= *Person*) **ein ~r/eine ~** a different person; (= *noch einer*) another person; **er/sie und ~** he/she and others; **jeder ~/kein ~** anyone/no-one else; **es war kein ~r als ...** it was none other than ...; **niemand ~s** no-one else; **jemand ~s** somebody else; **das haben mir ~ auch schon gesagt** other people *or* others have told me that too; **die ~n** the others; **alle ~n** all the

others, everyone else; **jemand ~s** *or* (*S Ger*) **~r** somebody *or* (*jeder, in Fragen*) anybody else; **wer ~s?** who else?; **wir/ihr ~n** the rest of us/you; **sie hat einen ~n** she has someone else; **der eine oder der ~ von unseren Kollegen** one or other of our colleagues; **es gibt immer den einen oder den ~n, der faulenzt** there is always someone who is lazy; **der eine ..., der ~ ...** this person ..., that person...; **einer nach dem ~n** one after the other; **eine schöner als die ~** each one more beautiful than the next

andererseits ADV on the other hand

Anderkonto NT fiduciary account, trust account (*Brit*)

andermal ['andɐmaːl] ADV **ein ~** some other time

andern- IN CPDS = **anderen-**

ändern ['ɛndɐn] **1** VT to change, to alter; *Meinung, Richtung* to change; *Kleidungsstück* to alter; **ich kann es nicht ~** I can't do anything about it; **das ist nicht zu ~, das lässt sich nicht (mehr) ~** nothing can be done about it; **das ändert nichts an der Tatsache, dass ...** that doesn't alter the fact that ... **2** VR to change; **wenn sich das nicht ändert ...** if things don't improve ...

anders ['andɐs] ADV **(a)** (= *sonst*) else; **jemand/niemand ~** somebody *or* anybody/nobody else; **wer/wo ~?** who/where else?

(b) (= *verschieden, besser, schöner*) differently; (= *~artig*) sein, aussehen, klingen, schmecken different (*als* to); **~ denkend** of a different opinion; **~ Denkende(r)** = **Andersdenkende(r)**; **~ als jd aussehen** to look different from sb; **~ geartet sein als jd** to be different from *or* to sb; **~ gesinnt** of a different opinion; **~ ausgedrückt** in other words; **sie ist ~ geworden** she has changed; **wie könnte es ~ sein?** how could it be otherwise?; **es geht nicht ~** there's no other way; **ich kann nicht ~** (= *kann es nicht lassen*) I can't help it; (= *muss leider*) I have no choice; **~ lautend** (*form*) contrary; **es sich** (*dat*) **~ überlegen** to change one's mind; **da wird mir ganz ~** I start to feel funny; **ich kann auch ~** (*inf*) you'd/he'd *etc* better watch it (*inf*); **das klingt schon ~** (*inf*) now that's more like it

Anders-: **andersartig** ADJ NO COMP different; **andersdenkend** ADJ ATTR *siehe* **anders**; **Andersdenkende(r)** [-dɛŋkndə] MF DECL AS ADJ person of a different opinion; (= *Dissident*) dissident, dissenter; **andersfarbig** ADJ of a different colour (*Brit*) *or* color (*US*); **Andersgesinnte(r)** [-gəzɪntə] MF DECL AS ADJ person of a different opinion; **andersgläubig** ADJ of a different faith *or* religion *or* creed; **~ sein** to be of *or* have a different faith *etc*; **andersherum** ADV the other way (a)round; **~ gehen** to go the other way (a)round; **dreh die Schraube mal ~** turn the screw the other way; **anderslautend** ADJ ATTR *siehe* **anders**; **andersrum** (*inf*) ADV, ADJ = **andersherum**; **anderswie** ADV (*inf*) (= *auf andere Weise*) some other way; (= *unterschiedlich*) differently; **anderswo** ADV elsewhere; **das gibt es nicht ~** you don't get that anywhere else; **anderswoher** ADV from elsewhere; **anderswohin** ADV elsewhere; **ich gehe nicht gerne ~** I don't like going anywhere else

anderthalb ['andɐt'halp] NUM one and a half; **~ Pfund Kaffee** a pound and a half of coffee; **~ Stunden** an hour and a half

Änderung ['ɛndərʊŋ] F -, **-en** change, alteration (*an +dat, +gen* in, to); (*in jdm*) change (*in +dat* in); (*an Kleidungsstück, Gebäude*) alteration (*an +dat* to); (*der Gesellschaft, der Politik etc*) change (*+gen* in)

Änderungs-: **Änderungskündigung** F *dismissal with the option of altered conditions of employment*; **Änderungsschneider(in)** M(F) tailor/dressmaker (who does alterations); **Änderungsvorschlag** M suggested change *or* alteration; **einen ~ machen** to suggest a change *or* alteration

anderweitig ['andɐ'vaɪtɪç] **1** ADJ ATTR other **2** ADV (= *anders*) otherwise; (= *an anderer Stelle*) elsewhere; **~ vergeben/besetzt werden** to be given to/filled by someone else; **etw ~ verwenden** to use sth for a different purpose

andeuten SEP **1** VT (= *zu verstehen geben*) to hint, to intimate (*jdm etw* sth to sb); (= *kurz erwähnen*) *Problem* to mention briefly; (*Art, Mus*) to suggest; (= *erkennen lassen*) to indicate **2** VR to be indicated; (*Melodie etc*) to be suggested; (*Gewitter*) to be looming

Andeutung F (= *Anspielung, Anzeichen*) hint; (= *flüchtiger Hinweis*) brief mention; (*Art, Mus*) suggestion *no pl*; (= *Spur*) sign, trace; **eine ~ machen** to hint (*über +acc* at), to drop a hint (*über +acc* about)

andeutungsweise ADV (= *als Anspielung, Anzeichen*) by way of a hint; (= *als flüchtiger Hinweis*) in passing; **jdm ~ zu verstehen geben, dass ...** to hint to sb that ...; **man kann die Mauern noch ~ erkennen** you can still see traces of the walls

andienen SEP (*pej*) **1** VT **jdm etw ~** to press sth on sb; **man diente ihm einen hohen Posten im Ausland an, um ihn loszuwerden** they tried to get rid of him by palming him off with a high position abroad **2** VR **sich jdm ~** to offer sb one's services (*als* as)

andocken SEP **1** VI (*Schiff*) to dock (*an* +dat at); (*Raumfähre*) to dock (*an* +dat with) **2** VT (a) *Raumfähre* to dock (*an* +dat or acc at) (b) (*Comput*) to connect up (*an* +dat or acc to)

Andorra [an'dɔra] NT **-s** Andorra

Andrang M, NO PL (a) (= *Zustrom, Gedränge*) crowd, crush; **es herrschte großer ~** there was a great crowd or crush (b) (*von Blut*) rush; (*von Wassermassen*) onrush

andrehen VT SEP (a) (= *anstellen*) to turn on (b) (*inf*) **jdm etw ~** to palm sth off on sb

andre(r, s) ['andrə] ADJ = **andere(r, s)**

androgyn [andro'gyːn] ADJ androgynous

androhen VT SEP to threaten (*jdm etw* sb with sth)

Androhung F threat; **unter der ~, etw zu tun** with the threat of doing sth; **unter ~** (*Jur*) under penalty (*von*, +gen of)

Android [andro'iːt] M **-en, -en** [-dn], **Androide** [andro'iːdə] M **-n, -n** android

anecken ['anɛkn] VI SEP AUX SEIN (*inf*) (**bei jdm/allen**) **~** to rub sb/everyone up the wrong way

aneignen VT SEP **sich** (*dat*) **etw ~** (= *etw erwerben*) to acquire sth; (= *etw wegnehmen*) to appropriate sth; (= *sich mit etw vertraut machen*) to learn sth

Aneignung F (= *Erwerb*) acquisition; (= *Wegnahme*) appropriation; (= *Lernen*) learning; **widerrechtliche ~** (*Jur*) misappropriation

aneinander [anlai'nandə] ADV (a) (= *gegenseitig, an sich*) **~ denken** to think of each other; **sich ~ gewöhnen** to get used to each other; **sich ~ stoßen** (*lit*) to knock into each other; **Freude ~ haben** to enjoy each other's company (b) (*mit Richtungsangabe*) **~ vorübergehen** or **vorbeigehen** to go past each other; **~ vorbeireden** to talk at cross-purposes (c) (= *einer am anderen, zusammen*) **befestigen** together; **die Häuser stehen zu dicht ~** the houses are built too close together

aneinander: aneinander fügen 1 VT to put together **2** VR to join together; **aneinander geraten** VI IRREG AUX SEIN to come to blows (*mit* with); (= *streiten*) to have words (*mit* with); **aneinander grenzen** VI to border on each other; **in Istanbul grenzen Orient und Okzident aneinander** in Istanbul East and West meet; **aneinander hängen** IRREG **1** VI (a) (= *zusammenhängen*) to be linked (together) (b) (*fig: Menschen*) to be attached to each other **2** VT to link together; **aneinander koppeln** VT to couple; *Raumschiffe* to link up; **aneinander reihen 1** VT to string together **2** VR to be strung together; (*zeitlich: Tage etc*) to run together; **aneinander stoßen** IRREG **1** VT to bang together **2** VI AUX SEIN to collide; (*Fahrzeuge, Köpfe auch, Menschen*) to bump into each other; (= *aneinander grenzen*) to meet

Anekdote [anɛk'doːtə] F **-, -n** anecdote

anekeln VT SEP (= *anwidern*) to disgust; **die beiden ekeln sich nur noch an** they just make each other sick; *siehe auch* **angeekelt**

Anemone [ane'moːnə] F **-, -n** anemone

anerkannt ['anlɛrkant] ADJ recognized; *Tatsache auch* established; *Werk* standard; *Bedeutung* accepted; *Experte* acknowledged; *siehe auch* **anerkennen**

anerkennen *ptp* **anerkannt** VT SEP or INSEP IRREG *Staat, König, Rekord* to recognize; *Forderung auch, Rechnung* to accept; *Vaterschaft* to acknowledge; (= *würdigen*) *Leistung, Bemühung* to appreciate; *Meinung* to respect; (= *loben*) to praise; **..., das muss man ~** (= *zugeben*) admittedly, ...; (= *würdigen*) ..., one has to appreciate that; **als gleichwertiger Partner anerkannt sein** to be accepted as an equal partner; **ihr ~der Blick** her appreciative look; *siehe auch* **anerkannt**

anerkennenswert ADJ commendable

Anerkennung F recognition; (*von Forderung auch, von Rechnung*) acceptance; (*von Vaterschaft*) acknowledgement;

(= *Würdigung*) appreciation; (*von Meinung*) respect; (= *Lob*) praise

anfahren SEP IRREG **1** VI AUX SEIN (= *losfahren*) to start (up); **angefahren kommen** (*Wagen, Fahrer*) to drive up; (*Fahrrad*) to ride up; (*Zug*) to pull up; (= *ankommen*) to arrive; **beim Anfahren** when starting (up); **das Anfahren am Berg üben** to practise (*Brit*) or practice (*US*) a hill start **2** VT (a) (= *ansteuern*) *Ort, Hafen* to stop or call at; (*Aut*) *Kurve* to approach (b) *Passanten, Baum etc* to hit; (*fig: ausschelten*) to shout at

Anfahrt F (= *Anfahrtsweg, Anfahrtszeit*) journey; (= *Zufahrt*) approach; (= *Einfahrt*) drive; **„nur ~ zum Krankenhaus"** "access to hospital only"

Anfall M (a) attack; (= *Wutanfall, epileptischer ~*) fit; **einen ~ haben/bekommen** (*lit*) to have a fit; (*fig inf*) to have or throw a fit (*inf*); **in einem ~ von** (*fig*) in a fit of (b) (= *Ertrag, Nebenprodukte*) yield (*an* +dat of) (c) (*von Reparaturen, Kosten*) amount (*an* +dat of); **bei ~ von Reparaturen** if repairs are necessary

anfallen SEP IRREG **1** VT (= *überfallen*) to attack; (*Sittenstrolch etc*) to assault **2** VI AUX SEIN (= *sich ergeben*) to arise; (*Zinsen*) to accrue; (*Nebenprodukte*) to be obtained; (= *sich anhäufen*) to accumulate; **die ~den Kosten/Reparaturen/Probleme** the costs/repairs/problems incurred; **die ~de Arbeit** the work which comes up

anfällig ADJ delicate; *Motor, Maschine* temperamental; **für etw ~ sein** to be susceptible to sth; **für eine Krankheit ~ sein** to be prone to an illness

Anfälligkeit F delicate health; (*von Motor, Maschine etc*) temperamental nature

Anfang ['anfaŋ] M **-(e)s, Anfänge** [-fɛŋə] (= *Beginn*) beginning, start; (= *erster Teil*) beginning; (= *Ursprung*) beginnings *pl*, origin; **zu or am ~** to start with; (= *anfänglich*) at first; **gleich zu ~ darauf hinweisen, dass ...** to mention right at the beginning or outset that ...; **am ~ schuf Gott Himmel und Erde** (*Bibl*) in the beginning God created the heaven(s) and the earth; **~ fünfzig** in one's early fifties; **~ Juni/1998** *etc* at the beginning of June/1998 *etc*; **von ~ an** (right) from the beginning or start; **von ~ bis Ende** from start to finish; **den ~ machen** to start or begin; (= *den ersten Schritt tun*) to make the first move; **einen neuen ~ machen** to make a new start; (*im Leben*) to turn over a new leaf; **aller ~ ist schwer** (*Prov*) the first step is always the most difficult; **der ~ vom Ende** the beginning of the end

anfangen SEP IRREG **1** VT (a) (= *beginnen*) to start, to begin; *Streit, Verhältnis, Fabrik* to start (b) (= *anstellen, machen*) to do; **das musst du anders ~** you'll have to go about it differently; **was soll ich damit ~?** what am I supposed to do with that?; (= *was nützt mir das?*) what's the use of that?; **damit kann ich nichts ~** (= *nützt mir nichts*) that's no good to me; (= *verstehe ich nicht*) it doesn't mean a thing to me; **nichts mit sich/jdm anzufangen wissen** not to know what to do with oneself/sb; **mit dir ist heute (aber) gar nichts anzufangen!** you're no fun at all today! **2** VI to begin, to start; **wer fängt an?** who's going to start or begin?; **du hast angefangen!** you started!; (*bei Streit*) you started it!; **es fing zu regnen an** or **an zu regnen** it started raining or to rain; **das fängt ja schön** or **heiter an!** (*iro*) that's a good start!; **fang nicht wieder davon** or **damit an!** don't start all that again!; **mit etw ~** to start sth

Anfänger(in) M(F) beginner; (= *Neuling*) novice; (*Aut*) learner; (*inf: = Nichtskönner*) amateur (*pej*)

Anfängerkurs M beginners' course

anfänglich ['anfɛŋlɪç] **1** ADJ ATTR initial **2** ADV at first, initially

anfangs ['anfaŋs] **1** ADV at first, initially; **wie ich schon ~ erwähnte** as I mentioned at the beginning; **gleich ~ auf etw** (*acc*) **hinweisen** to mention sth right at the beginning or outset **2** PREP +GEN **~ der zwanziger Jahre** or **Zwanzigerjahre** in the early twenties; **~ des Monats** at the beginning of the month

Anfangs- IN CPDS initial; **Anfangsbuchstabe** M first letter; **kleine/große ~n** small/large or capital initials; **Anfangsgehalt** NT initial or starting salary; **Anfangskapital** NT starting capital; **Anfangskurs** M (*Fin*) opening price; **Anfangsstadium** NT initial stage; **im ~ dieser Krankheit/dieses Projekts** in the initial stages of this illness/project; **meine Versuche sind**

schon im ~ stecken geblieben my attempts never really got off the ground; **Anfangszeit** F starting time

anfassen SEP **1** VT **(a)** (= *berühren*) to touch; **fass mal meinen Kopf an** just feel my head **(b)** (= *bei der Hand nehmen*) **jdn ~** to take sb's hand; **fasst euch an!** hold hands!; **angefasst gehen** to walk holding hands **(c)** (*fig*) (= *anpacken*) *Problem* to tackle; (= *behandeln*) *Menschen* to treat **2** VI **(a)** (= *berühren*) to feel; **nicht ~!** don't touch! **(b)** (= *mithelfen*) **mit ~** to lend a hand **(c)** (*fig*) **zum Anfassen** *Sache* accessible; *Mensch auch* approachable; **Politik zum Anfassen** grassroots politics **3** VR (= *sich anfühlen*) to feel; **es fasst sich weich an** it feels *or* is soft (to the touch)

anfauchen VT SEP (*Katze*) to spit at; (*fig inf*) to snap at

anfechtbar ADJ contestable; (*moralisch*) questionable (*form*)

anfechten VT SEP IRREG **(a)** (= *nicht anerkennen*) to contest; *Urteil, Entscheidung* to appeal against **(b)** (= *beunruhigen*) to trouble; **das ficht mich gar nicht an** that doesn't concern me in the slightest

Anfechtung ['anfɛçtʊŋ] F **-, -en (a)** (= *das Nichtanerkennen*) contesting; (*von Meinung, Aussage*) challenging; (*von Urteil, Entscheidung*) appeal (+*gen* against) **(b)** (= *Versuchung*) temptation; (= *Selbstzweifel*) doubt

anfeinden ['anfaindn] VT SEP to treat with hostility

Anfeindung F **-, -en** hostility; **trotz aller ~en** although he/she *etc* had aroused so much animosity

anfertigen VT SEP to make; *Arznei* to make up; *Schriftstück* to draw up; *Hausaufgaben, Protokoll* to do; **jdm etw ~** to make sth for sb; **sich** (*dat*) **einen Anzug** *etc* **~ lassen** to have a suit *etc* made

Anfertigung F making; (*von Arznei*) making up; (*von Schriftstück*) drawing up; (*von Protokoll, Hausaufgaben*) doing; **die ~ dieser Übersetzung/der Arznei hat eine halbe Stunde gedauert** it took half an hour to do the translation/to make up the prescription

anfeuchten ['anfɔyçtn] VT SEP to moisten

anfeuern VT SEP *Ofen* to light; (*Ind*) to fire; (*fig:* = *ermutigen*) to spur on

anfixen VT SEP (*sl*) **jdn ~** to give sb his/her first fix (*inf*); (= *abhängig machen*) to get sb hooked (on drugs) (*inf*)

anflehen VT SEP to implore (*um* for); **ich flehe dich an, tu das nicht!** I beg you, don't do it!

anfliegen SEP IRREG **1** VI AUX SEIN (*auch* **angeflogen kommen**) (*Flugzeug*) to come in to land; (*Vogel, Geschoss*) to come flying up **2** VT (*Flugzeug*) to approach; (= *landen*) to land (*in* +*dat* in, *auf* +*dat* on); **diese Fluggesellschaft fliegt Bali an** this airline flies to Bali

Anflug M **(a)** (= *Flugweg*) flight; (= *das Heranfliegen*) approach; **wir befinden uns im ~ auf Paris** we are now approaching Paris **(b)** (= *Spur*) trace

anfordern VT SEP to request, to ask for

Anforderung F **(a)** (= *Anspruch*) requirement; (= *Belastung*) demand; **große ~en an jdn/etw stellen** to make great demands on sb/sth; **hohe/zu hohe ~en stellen** to demand a lot/too much (*an* +*acc* of) **(b)** **Anforderungen** PL (= *Niveau*) standards *pl* **(c)** NO PL (= *das Anfordern*) request (+*gen, von* for)

Anforderungsprofil NT (*für Personen*) job description; (*für Software etc*) product profile; **dem ~ entsprechen** to fit the job description/product profile

Anfrage F (*auch Comput*) inquiry; (*Parl*) question; **kleine ~** *Parliamentary question dealt with in writing*; **große ~** *Parliamentary question dealt with at a meeting of the Lower House*

anfragen VI SEP to ask (*bei jdm* sb)

anfreunden ['anfrɔyndn] VR SEP to become friends; **sich mit etw ~** (*fig*) to get to like sth

anfügen VT SEP to add

anfühlen VTR SEP to feel

anführen VT SEP **(a)** (= *vorangehen, befehligen*) to lead **(b)** (= *zitieren*) to quote; *Einzelheiten, Grund, Beweis* to give; *Umstand* to cite **(c)** (*Typ*) to mark with quotation marks **(d) jdn ~** (*inf*) to have sb on (*inf*)

Anführer(in) M(F) (= *Führer*) leader; (*pej:* = *Anstifter*) ringleader

Anführung F **(a)** (= *das Vorangehen*) leadership; (= *Befehligung*) command; **unter ~ von ...** under the leadership of ... **(b)** (= *das Zitieren*) quotation; (*von Tatsachen, Beispiel*) citation; (*von Umstand*) citing; (*von Grund, Beweis*) giving; (= *Zitat*) quotation; **die ~ von Zitaten/Einzelheiten** giving quotations/details

Anführungszeichen NT quotation mark, inverted comma; **das habe ich in ~ gesagt** I was saying that in inverted commas

Angabe ['anga:-] F **(a)** USU PL (= *Aussage*) statement; (= *Anweisung*) instruction; (= *Zahl, Detail*) detail; **~n über etw** (*acc*) **machen** to give details about sth; **laut ~n** (+*gen*) according to; **nach Ihren eigenen ~n** by your own account; **nach ~n des Zeugen** according to (the testimony of) the witness; **~n zur Person** (*form*) personal details *or* particulars; **~n zur Sache machen** (*Jur*) to give details of the case **(b)** (= *Nennung*) giving; **wir bitten um ~ der Einzelheiten/Preise** please give details/prices; **vergessen Sie nicht die ~ des Datums auf dem Brief** don't forget to put the date on the letter **(c)** NO PL (*inf:* = *Prahlerei*) showing off; (*esp durch Reden*) bragging **(d)** (*Sport:* = *Aufschlag*) service, serve; **wer hat ~?** whose service *or* serve is it?

angaffen ['anga-] VT SEP (*pej*) to gape at

angeben ['ange:-] SEP IRREG **1** VT **(a)** (= *nennen*) to give; (*als Zeugen*) to cite; (*schriftlich*) to indicate; (= *erklären*) to explain; (*beim Zoll*) to declare; (= *anzeigen*) *Preis, Temperatur etc* to indicate; (= *aussagen*) to state; (= *behaupten*) to maintain; *siehe auch* **angegeben** **(b)** (= *bestimmen*) *Tempo, Kurs* to set; (*Mus*) *Tempo, Note* to give; **den Takt ~** (= *klopfen*) to beat time **2** VI **(a)** (= *prahlen*) to show off; (*esp durch Reden*) to brag (*mit* about) **(b)** (*Tennis etc*) to serve

Angeber(in) ['ange:-] M(F) (= *Prahler*) show-off; (*esp durch Reden*) bragger

Angeberei [ange:bə'rai] F **-, -en** (*inf*) **(a)** NO PL (= *Prahlerei*) showing off (*mit* about); (*esp verbal*) bragging (*mit* about) **(b)** USU PL (= *Äußerung*) boast

angeberisch ['ange:bərıʃ] **1** ADJ *Reden* boastful; *Aussehen, Benehmen, Tonfall* pretentious **2** ADV pretentiously; **sich ~ benehmen** to be pretentious

angeblich ['ange:plıç] **1** ADJ ATTR alleged **2** ADV supposedly, allegedly; **er ist ~ Musiker** he says he's a musician

angeboren ['angə-] ADJ innate; (*Med, fig inf*) congenital (*bei* to)

Angebot ['angə-] NT offer; (*bei Auktion*) bid; (*Comm* = *Sonderangebot*) special offer; (*Comm, Fin*) supply (*an* +*dat, von* of); **im ~** (*preisgünstig*) on special offer; **~ und Nachfrage** supply and demand

angebracht ['angəbraxt] ADJ appropriate; (= *sinnvoll*) reasonable; *siehe auch* **anbringen**

angebrannt ['angə-] **1** ADJ burned **2** ADV **~ riechen/ schmecken** to smell/taste burned; *siehe auch* **anbrennen**

angebrochen ['angə-] ADJ *Packung, Flasche* open(ed); **wie viel ist von den ~en hundert Euro übrig?** how much is left from the 100 euros we'd started using?; **ein ~er Abend/Nachmittag** (*hum*) the rest of an evening/afternoon; **das Parken kostet für jede ~e Stunde einen Euro** parking costs one euro for every hour or part of an hour; *siehe auch* **anbrechen**

angebunden ['angə-] ADJ (= *beschäftigt*) tied (down); **kurz ~ sein** (*inf*) to be abrupt *or* curt; *siehe auch* **anbinden**

angeekelt ['angəle:klt] **1** ADV in disgust **2** ADJ disgusted; *siehe auch* **anekeln**

angegammelt ['angəgamlt] ADJ (*inf*) **~e Lebensmittel** food that is going bad

angegeben ['angəge:bn] ADJ stated; **die ~e Telefonnummer** the phone number given; **am ~en Ort** loco citato; *siehe auch* **angeben**

angegossen ['angəgɔsn] ADV **wie ~ sitzen** *or* **passen** to fit like a glove

angegraut ['angəgraut] ADJ grey (*Brit*), gray (*US*)

angegriffen ['angəgrıfn] ADJ *Gesundheit* weakened; *Mensch, Aussehen* frail; (= *erschöpft*) exhausted; (*nervlich*) strained; **sie ist nervlich immer noch ~** her nerves are still strained; **sie ist gesundheitlich immer noch ~** she is still weak *or* frail; *siehe auch* **angreifen**

angehalten ['angəhaltn] ADJ ~ **sein, etw zu tun** to be required to do sth; **zu Pünktlichkeit ~ sein** to be required to be punctual; *siehe auch* **anhalten**

angehaucht ['angəhauxt] ADJ **links/rechts ~ sein** to have or show left-wing/right-wing tendencies

angeheitert ['angəhaitɐt] ADJ tipsy

angehen ['ange-] SEP IRREG **1** VI AUX SEIN **(a)** (*inf*: = *beginnen*) to start; (*Feuer*) to start burning; (*Radio, Licht*) to come on **(b)** (= *entgegentreten*) **gegen jdn ~** to fight sb; **gegen etw ~** to fight sth; *gegen Flammen, Hochwasser* to fight sth back; *gegen Missstände, Zustände* to take measures against sth; **dagegen muss man ~** something must be done about it **2** VT **(a)** AUX HABEN or (*S Ger*) SEIN (= *anpacken*) to tackle; *Gegner* to attack; *Kurve* to take **(b)** AUX HABEN or (*S Ger*) SEIN (= *bitten*) to ask (**jdn um etw** sb for sth) **(c)** AUX SEIN (= *betreffen*) to concern; **was mich angeht** for my part; **was geht das ihn an?** (*inf*) what's that got to do with him?; **das geht ihn gar nichts** or **einen Dreck an** (*inf*) that's none of his business **3** VI IMPERS AUX SEIN **das geht nicht/keinesfalls an** that's not on/quite out of the question

angehend ADJ *Musiker, Künstler, Manager etc* budding; *Lehrer, Ehemann, Vater* prospective

angehören ['angə-], *ptp* **angehört** VI SEP +DAT to belong to

Angehörige(r) ['angəhø:rɪgə] MF DECL AS ADJ **(a)** (= *Mitglied*) member **(b)** (= *Familienangehörige*) relative, relation; **der nächste ~** the next of kin

Angeklagte(r) ['angəkla:ktə] MF DECL AS ADJ accused, defendant

angeknackst ['angəknakst] ADJ *Wirbel, Bandscheibe* damaged; (*inf*) *Mensch* (*seelisch*) uptight (*inf*); *Selbstvertrauen, Selbstbewusstsein* weakened; **er/seine Gesundheit ist ~** he is in a bad way; **sie ist noch immer etwas ~** she still hasn't got over it yet; *siehe auch* **anknacksen**

Angel ['aŋl] F **-, -n (a)** = *Türangel, Fensterangel*) hinge; **die Welt aus den ~n heben** (*fig*) to turn the world upside down **(b)** (= *Fischfanggerät*) (fishing) rod and line (*Brit*), fishing pole (*US*); **jdm an die ~ gehen** (*fig*) to fall for sb's line

Vorsicht! **Angel** *wird nicht mit dem englischen Wort* **angel** *übersetzt.*

Angelegenheit ['angə-] F matter; (*politisch, persönlich*) affair; (= *Aufgabe*) concern; **das ist meine/nicht meine ~** that's my/not my concern or business; **sich um seine eigenen ~en kümmern** to mind one's own business; **in einer dienstlichen ~** on official business; **in eigener ~** on a private or personal matter

angelegt ['angəle:kt] ADJ (= *ausgerichtet*) calculated (*auf* +*acc* for); **künstlich ~** *Hügel, Landschaft* man-made; **breit ~** *Wissenschaft, Strategie* wide-ranging; *siehe auch* **anlegen**

angelernt ['angə-] ADJ **(a)** *Arbeiter* semiskilled; **der Lohn für Angelernte** the wage for semiskilled workers **(b)** *Verhalten* acquired; *Wissen* superficially acquired; *siehe auch* **anlernen**

Angel- ['aŋl-]: **Angelhaken** M fish-hook; **Angelleine** F fishing line

angeln ['aŋln] **1** VI to fish; **nach etw ~** to fish for sth **2** VT *Fisch* to fish for; (= *fangen*) to catch; **sich** (*dat*) **einen Mann ~** (*inf*) to catch (oneself) a man (*inf*)

Angeln ['aŋln] PL (*Hist*) Angles pl

Angel-: Angelpunkt M crucial or central point; (= *Frage*) key or central issue; **Angelrute** F fishing rod

Angelsachse ['aŋl-] M, **Angelsächsin** F Anglo-Saxon

angelsächsisch ADJ Anglo-Saxon

angemessen ['angə-] **1** ADJ (= *passend, entsprechend*) appropriate (*dat* to, for); (= *adäquat*) adequate (+*dat* for); *Preis* reasonable; **eine der Leistung ~e Bezahlung** payment commensurate with performance **2** ADV appropriately; **jds Einsatz ~ würdigen** to give sb enough credit for his/her efforts

angenehm ['angə-] **1** ADJ pleasant, agreeable; **das wäre mir sehr ~** I should be very or most grateful; **es ist mir gar nicht ~, wenn ich früh aufstehen muss** I don't like getting up early; **es ist mir gar nicht ~, dass er mich besuchen will** I don't like the idea of him wanting to visit me; **ist es Ihnen so ~?** is that all right for you?; **wenn Ihnen das ~ ist** if you prefer; **~e Ruhe/Reise!** *etc* have a pleasant rest/journey *etc*; **(sehr) ~!**

(*form*) delighted (to meet you); **das Angenehme mit dem Nützlichen verbinden** to combine business with pleasure **2** ADV pleasantly, agreeably

angenommen ['angənɔmən] **1** ADJ assumed; *Name auch, Kind* adopted **2** CONJ assuming; *siehe auch* **annehmen**

angepasst ['angəpast] **1** ADJ *Mensch* conformist; **gesellschaftlich ~** conformist **2** ADV **sich ~ verhalten** to conform; *siehe auch* **anpassen**

angeregt ['angəre:kt] **1** ADJ animated **2** ADV **sie diskutierten ~** their discussion was animated; **sie unterhielten sich ~** they had an animated conversation; *siehe auch* **anregen**

angesäuselt ['angəzɔyzlt] ADJ (*inf*) tipsy

angeschlagen ['angəʃla:gn] ADJ (*inf*) *Mensch, Aussehen, Nerven* shattered (*inf*); *Gesundheit* poor (*inf*); *Ruf* tarnished; *Ehe, Unternehmen, Volkswirtschaft* failing; *siehe auch* **anschlagen**

angeschmiert ['angəʃmi:ɐt] ADJ PRED (*inf*) in trouble; **mit dem/ der Waschmaschine bist du ganz schön ~** he/the washing machine is not all he/it is cracked up to be (*inf*); **der/die Angeschmierte sein** to have been had (*inf*)

angeschmutzt ['angəʃmʊtst] ADJ soiled; (*Comm*) shopsoiled (*Brit*), damaged

angeschrieben ['angəʃri:bn] ADJ (*inf*) **bei jdm gut/schlecht ~ sein** to be in sb's good/bad books; *siehe auch* **anschreiben**

Angeschuldigte(r) ['angəʃʊldɪçtə] MF DECL AS ADJ suspect

angesehen ['angəze:ən] ADJ respected; *siehe auch* **ansehen**

angesichts ['angəzɪçts] PREP +GEN in the face of; (= *im Hinblick auf*) in view of

angespannt ['angəʃpant] **1** ADJ **(a)** (= *angestrengt*) *Nerven* strained; *Aufmerksamkeit* close; **aufs höchste** or **Höchste ~ sein** to be very tense **(b)** (= *bedrohlich*) *politische Lage* tense; (*Comm*) *Markt, Lage* overstretched **2** ADV **dasitzen, verfolgen** tensely; *zuhören* attentively; **~ wirken** to seem tense; *siehe auch* **anspannen**

angestellt ['angəʃtɛlt] ADJ PRED **~ sein** to be an employee (*bei* of); **er ist bei Collins ~** he works for Collins; **fest ~ sein** to be on the permanent staff; *siehe auch* **anstellen**

Angestellten-: Angestelltengewerkschaft F white-collar union; **Angestelltenverhältnis** NT employment (without permanent tenure); **im ~** in non-tenured employment

Angestellte(r) ['angəʃtɛltə] MF DECL AS ADJ (salaried) employee; (= *Büroangestellte*) office worker, white-collar worker; (= *Behördenangestellte*) public employee (without tenure)

angestrengt ['angəʃtrɛŋt] **1** ADJ *Gesicht* strained; *Arbeiten, Denken* hard **2** ADV *diskutieren, nachdenken* carefully; *siehe auch* **anstrengen**

angetan ['angəta:n] ADJ PRED **von jdm/etw ~ sein** to be taken with sb/sth; **es jdm ~ haben** to have made quite an impression on sb; **das Mädchen hat es ihm ~** he has fallen for that girl; *siehe auch* **antun**

angetrunken ['angətrʊŋkn] ADJ inebriated; **in ~em Zustand Auto fahren** to drive under the influence (of alcohol); *siehe auch* **antrinken**

angewiesen ['angəvi:zn] ADJ **auf jdn/etw ~ sein** to be dependent on sb/sth; **auf sich selbst ~ sein** to have to fend for oneself; (*Kind*) to be left to one's own devices; **er war auf sich selbst und sein eigenes Wissen ~** he had to rely on himself and his own knowledge; **darauf bin ich nicht ~** I don't need it; *siehe auch* **anweisen**

angewöhnen ['angə-], *ptp* **angewöhnt** VT SEP **jdm etw ~** to get sb used to sth; **sich** (*dat*) **etw ~** to get into the habit of sth; **es sich** (*dat*) **~, etw zu tun** to get into the habit of doing sth

Angewohnheit ['angə-] F habit

angiften ['angı-] VT SEP (*pej inf*) to snap at

Angina [an'gi:na] F **-, Anginen** [-nən] (*Med*) angina; **~ pectoris** angina (pectoris)

angleichen ['angl-] SEP IRREG **1** VT to bring into line (+*dat, an* +*acc* with) **2** VR (*Kulturen, Geschlechter, Methoden*) to grow closer together; **sich jdm/einer Sache ~** (*einseitig*) to become like sb/sth; **die beiden haben sich (aneinander) angeglichen** the two of them have become more alike

Angler ['aŋlɐ] M **-s, -, Anglerin** [-ərɪn] F **-, -nen** angler (*esp Brit*), fisherman

anglikanisch [aŋli'ka:nɪʃ] ADJ Anglican; **die ~e Kirche** the Anglican Church, the Church of England

anglisieren [aŋgli'zi:rən], *ptp* **anglisiert** VT to anglicize

Anglist [aŋ'glɪst] M **-en, -en, Anglistin** [-'glɪstɪn] F **-, -nen** Anglicist; (= *Student*) student of English

Anglistik [aŋ'glɪstɪk] F **-, NO PL** English (language and literature)

Anglizismus [aŋgli'tsɪsmʊs] M **-, Anglizismen** [-mən] anglicism

Anglo- ['aŋglo] IN CPDS Anglo; **Angloamerikaner(in)** M(F) Anglo-American; **anglophil** [aŋglo'fiːl] ADJ Anglophile; **anglophob** [aŋglo'foːp] ADJ Anglophobic

anglotzen ['aŋgl-] VT SEP (*inf*) to gawk at (*inf*)

Angola [aŋ'goːla] NT **-s** Angola

Angora- [aŋ'goːra] IN CPDS Angora; **Angorakatze** F Angora cat; **Angorawolle** F Angora (wool)

angreifbar ADJ open to attack

angreifen ['aŋgr-] SEP IRREG **1** VT (a) (= *überfallen, kritisieren, Sport*) to attack (b) (= *schwächen*) *Organismus, Organ, Nerven* to weaken; *Gesundheit, Pflanzen* to affect; (= *ermüden, anstrengen*) to strain; *Lack, Farbe* to attack; **das hat ihn sehr angegriffen** that affected him greatly; *siehe auch* **angegriffen** (c) (= *anbrechen*) *Vorräte, Geld* to break into **2** VI (*Mil, Sport, fig*) to attack

Angreifer ['aŋgraifɐ] M **-s, -, Angreiferin** [-ərɪn] F **-, -nen** attacker (*auch Sport, fig*)

angrenzen ['aŋgr-] VI SEP **an etw** (*acc*) **~** to border on sth

angrenzend ADJ ATTR adjacent (*an +acc* to)

Angriff ['aŋgr-] M (*Mil, Sport, fig*) attack (*gegen, auf +acc* on); (= *Luftangriff*) (air) raid; **~ ist die beste Verteidigung** (*prov*) attack is the best means of defence (*Brit*) *or* defense (*US*); **etw in ~ nehmen** to tackle sth

angriffig ['aŋgr-] ADJ (*Sw*) aggressive

Angriffs-: Angriffsfläche F target; **jdm/einer Sache eine ~ bieten** (*lit, fig*) to provide sb/sth with a target; **eine ~ bieten** to present a target; **Angriffskrieg** M war of aggression; **Angriffswaffe** F offensive weapon

angrinsen ['aŋgr-] VT SEP to grin at

angst [aŋst] ADJ PRED afraid; **ihr wurde ~ (und bange)** she became worried *or* anxious; *siehe auch* **Angst**

Angst [aŋst] F **-, ̈e** ['ɛŋstə] (= *innere Unruhe*) (*Psych*) anxiety (*um* about); (= *Sorge*) worry (*um* about); (= *Befürchtung, Furcht*) fear (*um* for, *vor +dat* of); (= *Existenzangst*) angst; **(vor jdm/etw) ~ haben** to be afraid *or* scared (of sb/sth); **~ um jdn/etw haben** to be worried *or* anxious about sb/sth; **~ bekommen** *or* **kriegen** to become afraid, to get scared; (= *erschrecken*) to take fright; **das machte ihm ~ (und Bange)** that worried him; **aus ~, etw zu tun** for fear of doing sth; **keine ~!** don't be afraid; **keine ~, ich sage es ihm schon** don't you worry, I'll tell him; **jdm ~ machen** to scare sb; **jdm ~ einflößen** *or* **einjagen** to frighten sb; **jdn in ~ und Schrecken versetzen** to terrify sb; **in tausend Ängsten schweben** to be terribly worried *or* anxious

Angsthase M (*inf*) scaredy-cat (*inf*)

ängstigen ['ɛŋstɪgn] **1** VT to frighten; (= *unruhig machen*) to worry **2** VR to be afraid; (= *sich sorgen*) to worry; **sich wegen etw ~** to worry about sth

ängstlich ['ɛŋstlɪç] **1** ADJ (= *verängstigt*) anxious, apprehensive; (= *schüchtern*) timid **2** ADV **~ darauf bedacht sein, etw zu tun** to be at pains to do sth

Ängstlichkeit F **-, NO PL** (= *das Verängstigtsein*) anxiety, apprehension; (= *Schüchternheit*) timidity

Angst-: Angstschrei M cry of fear; **Angstschweiß** M cold sweat; **mir brach der ~ aus** I broke out in a cold sweat; **angstverzerrt** [-fɛɐtsɛrt] ADJ *Gesicht* petrified; **Angstzustand** M state of panic; **Angstzustände bekommen** to get into a state of panic

angucken ['aŋgʊ-] VT SEP (*inf*) to look at

angurten ['aŋgʊrtn] VT SEP = **anschnallen**

anhaben VT SEP IRREG (a) (= *angezogen haben*) to have on, to wear (b) (= *zuleide tun*) to do harm; **jdm etwas ~ wollen** to want to harm sb; **die Kälte kann mir nichts ~** the cold doesn't bother me (c) (= *am Zeuge flicken*) **Sie können/die Polizei kann mir nichts ~!** (*inf*) you/the police can't touch me

Anhalt M (= *Hinweis*) clue (*für* about); (*für Verdacht*) grounds *pl* (*für* for)

anhalten SEP IRREG **1** VI (a) (= *stehen bleiben*) to stop; **mit dem Sprechen ~** to stop talking (b) (= *fortdauern*) to last (c) (= *werben*) **(bei jdm) um ein Mädchen** *or* **um die Hand eines Mädchens ~** to ask (sb) for a girl's hand in marriage **2** VT (a) (= *stoppen*) to stop (b) (= *anlegen*) *Lineal* to use; **sie hielt mir/sich das Kleid an** she held the dress up against me/herself (c) (= *anleiten*) to urge, to encourage; *siehe auch* **angehalten**

anhaltend 1 ADJ continuous **2** ADV continuously

Anhalter(in) M(F) hitchhiker; **per ~ fahren** to hitchhike

Anhaltspunkt M (= *Vermutung*) clue (*für* about); (*für Verdacht*) grounds *pl*; **ich habe keinerlei ~e** I haven't a clue (*inf*)

anhand [an'hant], **an Hand** PREP +GEN with an example; **~ dieses Berichts/dieser Unterlagen** from this report/these documents

Anhang M (a) (= *Nachtrag*) appendix (b) NO PL (= *Gefolgschaft*) following; (= *Angehörige*) family; **Witwe, 62, ohne ~** widow, 62, no family

anhängen SEP **1** VT (a) (= *ankuppeln*) to attach (*an +acc* to); (*Rail*) to couple on (*an +acc* -to); *Anhänger* to hitch up (*an +acc* to); (*fig*: = *anfügen*) to add (*+dat, an +acc* to) (b) (*inf*) **jdm etw ~** (= *verkaufen*) to palm sth off on sb; (= *andrehen*) to foist sth on sb; *Krankheit* to pass sth on to sb; (= *nachsagen, anlasten*) to blame sth on sb; *schlechten Ruf, Spitznamen* to give sb sth; *Verdacht, Schuld* to pin sth on sb **2** VR (*lit*) to hang on (*+dat, an +acc* to); (*fig*) to tag along (*+dat, an +acc* with); (= *jdm hinterherfahren*) to follow (*+dat, an +acc* sth)

Anhänger M (a) (= *Wagen*) trailer; (= *Straßenbahnanhänger*) second car; **die Straßenbahn hatte zwei ~** the tram (*esp Brit*) *or* streetcar (*US*) had two extra cars (b) (= *Schmuckstück*) pendant (c) (= *Kofferanhänger etc*) label

Anhänger(in) M(F) supporter

anhänglich ['anhɛŋlɪç] ADJ **mein Sohn/Hund ist sehr ~** my son/dog is very attached to me

Anhänglichkeit F **-, NO PL die ~ an etw** (*acc*) one's attachment to sth

Anhängsel ['anhɛŋzl] NT **-s, -** (a) (= *Überflüssiges, Mensch*) appendage (*an +dat* to); **das ist ein ~ am Wort** that is added onto the word (b) (= *Schildchen*) tag (c) (= *Zusatz*) addition; (= *Nachtrag*) appendix

anhauen VT SEP (a) (*inf*: = *ansprechen*) to accost (*um* for); **jdn um etw ~** to be on the scrounge for sth from sb (*inf*) (b) (*auch irreg*) *Baum* to cut a notch in

anhäufen SEP **1** VT to accumulate, to amass; *Vorräte, Geld* to hoard **2** VR to accumulate

Anhäufung F accumulation, amassing; (*von Geld*) hoarding

anheben VT SEP IRREG (= *erhöhen*) to raise

Anhebung F increase (*+gen, von* in); **eine ~ der Gehälter um 5%** an increase of 5% in salaries

anheimelnd ['anhaimlnt] ADJ (*geh*) homely; *Klänge* familiar

anheizen VT SEP (a) *Ofen* to light (b) (*fig inf*: = *ankurbeln*) *Wirtschaft, Wachstum* to stimulate; (= *verschlimmern*) *Krise* to aggravate; *Inflation* to fuel

anheuern VTI SEP (*Naut, fig*) to sign on *or* up

Anhieb M **auf (den ersten) ~** (*inf*) straight *or* right away; **das kann ich nicht auf ~ sagen** I can't say offhand

anhimmeln ['anhɪmln] VT SEP (*inf*) to worship; (= *schwärmerisch ansehen*) to gaze adoringly at

anhin ['anhɪn] ADV **bis ~** (*Sw*: = *bisher*) until now

Anhöhe F hill

anhören SEP **1** VT (a) (= *Gehör schenken*) to hear; *Schallplatten, Konzert* to listen to; **jdn ganz ~** to hear sb out; **sich** (*dat*) **etw ~** to listen to sth (b) (= *zufällig mithören*) to overhear; **ich kann das nicht mehr mit ~** I can't listen to that any longer (c) (= *anmerken*) **man konnte ihr** *or* **ihrer Stimme die Verzweiflung ~** one could hear the despair in her voice; **das hört man ihm aber nicht an!** you can't tell that from hearing him speak; **man hört ihm sofort den Ausländer an** you can hear at once that he's a foreigner **2** VR (= *klingen*) to sound; **das hört sich ja gut an** (*inf*) that sounds good

Anhörung ['anhøːrʊŋ] F **-, -en** hearing

animalisch [ani'maːlɪʃ] ADJ animal; (*pej auch*) bestial

Animateur [anima'tøːɐ] M **-s, -e** host

Animateurin [anima'tøːrɪn] F **-, -nen** hostess

Animation [anima'tsioːn] F **-, -en** (*Film*) animation

Animierdame F nightclub hostess

animieren [aniˈmiːrən], *ptp* **animiert** VT **(a)** (= *anregen*) to encourage; **jdn zu einem Streich ~** to put sb up to a trick; **sich animiert fühlen, etw zu tun** to feel prompted to do sth **(b)** (*Film*) to animate

animierend (*geh*) **1** ADJ stimulating **2** ADV **~ wirken** to have a stimulating effect

Animo [ˈaːnimo] NT **-s**, NO PL (*Aus*) **(a)** (= *Vorliebe*) liking **(b)** (= *Schwung*) **mit ~ mitmachen** to join in with gusto

Animosität [animoziˈtɛːt] F **-, -en** (*geh*) (*gegen* towards) (= *Feindseligkeit, Abneigung*) hostility; (= *Äußerung*) hostile remark

Anion [ˈanioːn] NT (*Chem*) anion

Anis [aˈniːs, (*S Ger, Aus*) ˈaːnis] M **-(es), -e** (= *Gewürz*) aniseed; (= *Schnaps*) aniseed brandy; (= *Pflanze*) anise

Ank. ABBR *von* **Ankunft** arr.

ankämpfen [ˈankɛ-] VI SEP **gegen etw ~** to fight sth; **gegen die Elemente, Strömung** to battle with sth; **gegen jdn ~** to fight (against) sb; **gegen die Tränen ~** to fight back one's tears

Ankauf [ˈankauf] M purchase; **An- und Verkauf von ...** we buy and sell ...; **An- und Verkauf(s-Geschäft)** ≈ second-hand shop

Anker [ˈaŋkɐ] M **-s, -** anchor; (*Elec*) armature; **~ werfen, vor ~ gehen** to drop anchor; **vor ~ liegen** *or* **treiben** to lie at anchor

ankern [ˈaŋkɐn] VI (= *Anker werfen*) to anchor; (= *vor Anker liegen*) to be anchored

anketten [ˈankɛ-] VT SEP to chain up (*an +acc or dat* to); **angekettet sein** (*fig*) to be tied up

Anklage [ˈankl-] F **(a)** (*Jur*) charge; (= *~vertretung*) prosecution; **gegen jdn ~ erheben** to bring *or* prefer charges against sb; **jdn unter ~ stellen** to charge sb (*wegen* with); **(wegen etw) unter ~ stehen** to have been charged (with sth); **als Vertreter der ~ fragte Herr Stein ...** acting for the prosecution Mr Stein asked ... **(b)** (*fig*) (= *Verurteilung*) condemnation (*gegen +gen* of); (= *Beschuldigung*) accusation; (= *Anprangerung*) indictment (*an +acc* of)

Anklagebank F, *pl* **-bänke** dock; **auf der ~ (sitzen)** (*lit, fig*) (to be) in the dock

anklagen [ˈankl-] VT SEP **(a)** (*Jur*) to charge; **jdn einer Sache** (*gen*) *or* **wegen etw ~** to charge sb with sth, to accuse sb of sth **(b)** (*fig*) (= *verurteilen*) to condemn; (*Buch, Rede*) to be a condemnation of; (= *anprangern*) to be an indictment of; **jdn einer Sache** (*gen*) **~** (= *beschuldigen*) to accuse sb of sth; **jdn ~, etw getan zu haben** to accuse sb of having done sth

anklagend **1** ADJ *Ton* accusing, accusatory; *Blick* reproachful; *Buch, Bild etc* that cries out in condemnation **2** ADV reproachfully

Anklagepunkt M charge

Ankläger(in) [ˈankl-] M(F) (*Jur*) prosecutor

Anklage-: **Anklageschrift** F indictment; **Anklagevertreter(in)** M(F) counsel for the prosecution

Anklang [ˈankl-] M **(a)** NO PL (= *Beifall*) approval; **~ (bei jdm) finden** to meet with (sb's) approval; **großen/wenig/keinen ~ finden** to be very well/poorly/badly received **(b)** (= *Reminiszenz*) **Anklänge an etw** (*acc*) **enthalten** to be reminiscent of sth; **die Anklänge an Mozart sind unverkennbar** the echoes of Mozart are unmistakable

ankleben [ˈankl-] SEP **1** VT to stick up (*an +acc or dat* on) **2** VI AUX SEIN to stick

Ankleide- [ˈankl-]: **Ankleidekabine** F changing cubicle; **Ankleideraum** M, **Ankleidezimmer** NT dressing room; (*im Schwimmbad, Geschäft*) changing room

anklicken [ˈankl-] VT (*Comput*) to click on

anklingen [ˈankl-] VI SEP IRREG AUX SEIN (= *erinnern*) to be reminiscent (*an +acc* of); (= *angeschnitten werden*) to be touched (up)on; (= *spürbar werden*) to be discernible

anklopfen [ˈankl-] VI SEP to knock (*an +acc or dat* at on); **bei jdm wegen etw ~** (*fig inf*) to go knocking on sb's door for sth; **Anklopfen** (*Telec*) call waiting (service)

anknabbern [ˈankn-] VT SEP (*inf*) (= *annagen*) to nibble (at); (*fig*) *Ersparnisse etc* to gnaw away at

anknacksen [ˈanknaksn] VT SEP (*inf*) **(a)** *Knochen* to crack; *Fuß, Gelenk etc* to crack a bone in **(b)** (*fig*) *Gesundheit* to affect; *Stolz* to deal a blow to; **sein Selbstvertrauen/Stolz wurde dadurch angeknackst** that was a blow to his self-confidence/pride; *siehe auch* **angeknackst**

anknüpfen [ˈankn-] SEP **1** VT to tie on (*an +acc or dat* -to); *Beziehungen* to establish; *Verhältnis* to form; *Gespräch* to start up **2** VI **an etw** (*acc*) **~** to take sth up

anknurren [ˈankn-] VT SEP (*lit, fig*) to growl at

ankommen [ˈankɔ-] SEP IRREG AUX SEIN **1** VI **(a)** (= *eintreffen*) to arrive; **bei etw angekommen sein** to have reached sth **(b)** (= *Anklang, Resonanz finden*) (*bei* with) to go down well; (*Mode, Neuerungen*) to catch on; **mit deinem dummen Gerede kommst du bei ihm nicht an!** you won't get anywhere with him with your stupid talk!; **ein Lehrer, der bei seinen Schülern ausgezeichnet ankommt** a teacher who is a great success with his pupils **(c)** (*inf*) (= *auftreten, erscheinen*) to come along; (= *wiederholt erwähnen*) to come up (*mit* with); **jdm mit etw ~** to come to sb with sth; **komm mir nachher nicht an und verlange, dass ich ...** don't come running to me afterwards wanting me to ...; **komm mir nur nicht wieder damit an, dass du Astronaut werden willst** don't start up again with this business about (your) wanting to be an astronaut **(d)** (= *sich durchsetzen*) **gegen etw ~** *gegen Gewohnheit, Sucht etc* to be able to fight sth; **gegen jdn ~** to be able to cope with sb; **gegen diese Konkurrenz kommen wir nicht an** we can't fight this competition; **er ist zu stark, ich komme gegen ihn nicht an** he's too strong, I'm no match for him **2** VI IMPERS **(a)** (= *wichtig sein*) **es kommt auf etw** (*acc*) **an** sth matters; **darauf kommt es (uns) an** that is what matters (to us); **es kommt darauf an, dass wir ...** what matters is that we ...; **auf eine halbe Stunde kommt es jetzt nicht mehr an** it doesn't matter about the odd half-hour; **darauf soll es mir nicht ~** that's not the problem **(b)** (= *abhängig sein*) to depend (*auf +acc* on); **es kommt darauf an** it (all) depends; **es käme auf einen Versuch an** we'd have to give it a try **(c)** (*inf*) **es darauf ~ lassen** to take a chance; **lass es nicht drauf ~!** don't push your luck! (*inf*); **lassen wirs darauf ~** let's chance it; **er ließ es auf einen Streit/einen Versuch ~** he was prepared to argue about it/to give it a try; **lass es doch nicht deswegen auf einen Prozess ~** for goodness' sake don't let it get as far as the courts

ankoppeln [ˈankɔ-] VT SEP to hitch up (*an +acc* to) *or* on (*an +acc* -to); (*Rail*) to couple up (*an +acc* to) *or* on (*an +acc* -to); (*Space*) to link up (*an +acc* with, to)

ankotzen [ˈankɔ-] VT SEP (*sl*: = *anwidern*) to make sick (*inf*)

ankratzen [ˈankr-] VT SEP to scratch; (*fig*) *jds Ruf etc* to damage

ankreiden [ˈankraidn] VT SEP (*fig*) **jdm etw (dick** *or* **übel) ~** to hold sth against sb; **jdm sein Benehmen als Frechheit/Schwäche ~** to regard sb's behaviour (*Brit*) *or* behavior (*US*) as impertinence/weakness

ankreuzen [ˈankr-] SEP **1** VT *Stelle, Fehler, Antwort* to put a cross beside **2** VI AUX SEIN *or* HABEN (*Naut*) **gegen den Wind ~** to sail into the wind

ankündigen [ˈanky-] VT SEP **(a)** (= *ansagen, anmelden*) to announce; (*auf Plakat, in Zeitung etc*) to advertise; **heute kam endlich der angekündigte Brief** today the letter I/we had been expecting finally arrived; **er besucht uns nie, ohne sich (nicht) vorher anzukündigen** he never visits us without letting us know in advance **(b)** (= *auf etw hindeuten*) to be a sign of

Ankunft [ˈankʊnft] F **-, Ankünfte** [-kʏnftə] arrival; **bei** *or* **nach ~** on arrival

Ankunfts-: **Ankunftshalle** F arrivals lounge; **Ankunftstafel** F arrivals (indicator) board; **Ankunftszeit** F time of arrival

ankuppeln [ˈankʊ-] VT SEP = **ankoppeln**

ankurbeln [ˈankʊ-] VT SEP *Maschine* to wind up; (*Aut*) to crank; (*fig*) *Wirtschaft, Konjunktur* to reflate

Anl. ABBR *von* **Anlage** encl.

anlächeln VT SEP to smile at; **der Kuchen lächelte mich förmlich an** (*hum*) the cake sat there just asking to be eaten

anlachen VT SEP to smile at; **sich** (*dat*) **jdn ~** (*inf*) to pick sb up (*inf*)

Anlage F **(a)** (= *Fabrikanlage*) plant **(b)** (= *Grünanlage, Parkanlage*) (public) park; (*um ein Gebäude herum*) grounds *pl* **(c)** (= *Einrichtung*) (*Mil, Elec*) installation(s *pl*); (= *sanitäre Anlagen*) sanitary installations *pl* (*form*); (= *Sportanlage etc*) facilities *pl* **(d)** (*inf*: = *Stereoanlage*) (stereo) system *or* equipment; (= *EDV-*

Anlage) system
(e) USU PL (= *Veranlagung*) aptitude, talent (*zu* for);
(= *Neigung*) tendency (*zu* to)
(f) (= *das Anlegen*) (*von Park*) laying out; (*von Stausee etc*)
construction; **die ~ einer Kartei veranlassen** to start a file
(g) (= *Kapitalanlage*) investment
(h) (= *Beilage zu einem Schreiben*) enclosure; **als ~ or in der ~**
erhalten Sie ... please find enclosed ...

anlagebedingt ADJ inherent; **Krampfadern sind ~** some
people have a predisposition to varicose veins

Anlage-: Anlageberater(in) M(F) investment advisor;
Anlageberatung F investment advice; **Anlagefonds** M
investment fund; **Anlagekapital** NT investment capital;
Anlagepolitik F investment policy; **Anlagevermögen** NT
fixed assets *pl*

Anlass ['anlas] M **-es, Anlässe** [-lɛsə] **(a)** (= *Veranlassung*)
(immediate) cause (*zu* for); **zum ~ von etw werden** to bring
sth about; **welchen ~ hatte er, das zu tun?** what prompted
him to do that?; **er hat keinen ~ zur Freude** he has no cause
or reason for rejoicing; **es besteht kein ~ ...** there is no
reason ...; **es besteht ~ zur Hoffnung** there is reason for hope;
das ist kein ~ zu feiern that's no reason to celebrate; **etw zum**
~ nehmen, zu ... to use sth as an opportunity to ...; **beim**
geringsten ~ for the slightest reason; **bei jedem ~** at every
opportunity
(b) (= *Gelegenheit*) occasion; **aus ~** (+*gen*) on the occasion of;
aus gegebenem ~ in view of the occasion; **aus diesem ~** on
this occasion
(c) (*Sw: = Lustbarkeit*) social

anlassen SEP IRREG **1** VT **(a)** *Motor, Wagen* to start (up) **(b)** (*inf*)
Schuhe, Mantel to keep on; *Licht, Radio, Motor* to leave on;
Kerze, Feuer to leave burning **2** VR **sich gut/schlecht ~** to get
off to a good/bad start; **das Wetter lässt sich gut an** the
weather looks promising; **wie lässt er sich in der Sache denn**
an? what sort of start has he made on it?

Anlasser ['anlasɐ] M **-s, -** (*Aut*) starter

anlässlich ['anleslɪç] PREP +GEN on the occasion of

anlasten VT SEP **jdm etw ~** to blame sb for sth; **jdm die Schuld**
für etw ~ to lay the blame for sth on sb; **jdm etw als Schwäche**
~ to regard sth as a weakness on sb's part

Anlauf M **(a)** (*Sport*) run-up; **mit ~** with a run-up; **ohne ~** from
standing; **Sprung mit/ohne ~** running/standing jump; **~**
nehmen to take a run-up; **~ zu etw nehmen** (*fig*) to pluck up
courage to do sth **(b)** (*fig: = Versuch*) attempt, try; **beim**
ersten/zweiten ~ at the first/second attempt

anlaufen SEP IRREG **1** VI AUX SEIN **(a)** (= *beginnen*) to begin, to
start; (*Film*) to open; (*Motor*) to start **(b) angelaufen kommen**
to come running along *or* (*auf einen zu*) up **(c)** (= *beschlagen*)
(*Brille, Spiegel etc*) to mist up; (*Metall*) to tarnish; **rot/blau ~** to
turn *or* go red/blue **(d) gegen etw ~** (*fig*) to stand up to sth
2 VT (*Naut*) *Hafen etc* to put into

Anlauf-: Anlaufhafen M port of call; **Anlaufphase** F initial
stage; **in der ~** in the initial stages; **Anlaufstelle** F shelter,
refuge

Anlaut M (*Phon*) initial sound; **im ~ stehen** to be in initial
position

anläuten VTI SEP (*dial: = anrufen*) **jdn** *or* **bei jdm ~** to call *or*
phone sb

anlegen SEP **1** VT **(a)** *Leiter* to put up (*an* +*acc* against); *Brett,*
Karte, Dominostein to lay (down) (*an* +*acc* next to, beside);
Lineal to position; **das Gewehr ~** to raise the gun to one's
shoulder; **das Gewehr auf jdn/etw ~** to aim the gun at sb/sth;
den Säugling ~ to put the baby to one's breast; **strengere**
Maßstäbe ~ to lay down stricter standards (*bei* in)
(b) *Kartei, Akte* to start; *Vorräte* to lay in; *Garten, Gelände,*
Aufsatz, Bericht, Schaubild to lay out; *Liste, Plan, Statistiken* to
draw up; *Roman, Drama* to structure
(c) (= *investieren*) *Geld, Kapital* to invest; (= *ausgeben*) to
spend (*für* on)
(d) es darauf ~, dass ... to be determined that ...; **du legst es**
wohl auf einen Streit mit mir an you're determined to have a
fight with me, aren't you?; *siehe auch* **angelegt**
2 VI **(a)** (*Naut*) to berth, to dock
(b) (*Cards*) to lay down cards/a card (*bei jdm* on sb's hand)
3 VR **sich mit jdm ~** to pick a fight with sb

Anlegeplatz M berth

Anleger ['anle:gɐ] M **-s, -, Anlegerin** [-ərɪn] F **-, -nen** (*Fin*)
investor

Anlege-: Anlegesteg M jetty; **Anlegestelle** F mooring

anlehnen SEP **1** VT to lean *or* rest (*an* +*acc* against); *Tür, Fenster*
to leave ajar; **angelehnt sein** (*Tür, Fenster*) to be ajar **2** VR
to lean (*an* +*acc* against); **sich an etw** (*acc*) **~** (*fig*) to follow sth

Anlehnung F **-, -en** (= *Imitation*) following (*an jdn/etw* sb/sth);
in ~ an jdn/etw following sb/sth

Anlehnungs-: Anlehnungsbedürfnis NT need of loving care;
anlehnungsbedürftig ADJ in need of loving care

anleiern VT SEP (*inf*) to get going

Anleihe F, (*Sw*) **Anleihen** ['anlaiən] NT **-s, -** **(a)** (*Fin*)
(= *Geldaufnahme*) loan; (= *Wertpapier*) bond **(b)** (*von*
geistigem Eigentum) borrowing; **bei jdm eine ~ machen** (*hum*
inf) to borrow from sb

anleinen ['anlainən] VT SEP (= *festmachen*) to tie up; **den Hund ~**
to put the dog on the lead (*esp Brit*) *or* leash; **den Hund an etw**
(*acc or dat*) **~** to tie the dog to sth

anleiten VT SEP to teach; **jdn zu etw ~** to teach sb sth

Anleitung F (= *Erklärung, Hilfe*) instructions *pl*; **unter der ~**
seines Vaters under his father's guidance

anlernen VT SEP (= *ausbilden*) to train; *siehe auch* **angelernt**

anlesen VT SEP IRREG **(a)** *Buch, Aufsatz* to begin *or* start reading;
das angelesene Buch the book I have/he has *etc* started
reading **(b)** (= *aneignen*) **sich** (*dat*) **etw ~** to learn sth by
reading; **angelesenes Wissen** knowledge which comes
straight out of books

anliefern VT SEP to deliver

Anlieferung F delivery

anliegen VI SEP IRREG **(a)** (= *anstehen, vorliegen*) to be on
(b) (*Kleidung*) to fit tightly (*an etw* (*dat*) sth); (*Haar*) to lie flat
(*an* +*dat* against, on)

Anliegen ['anli:gn] NT **-s, -** **(a)** (= *Bitte*) request **(b)** (= *wichtige*
Angelegenheit) matter of concern

Anlieger ['anli:gɐ] M **-s, -, Anliegerin** [-ərɪn] F **-, -nen** neighbour
(*Brit*), neighbor (*US*); (= *Anwohner*) (local) resident; **die ~ der**
Nordsee the countries bordering (on) the North Sea; **~ frei,**
frei für ~ residents only

Anlieger-: Anliegerstaat M **die ~en des Schwarzen Meers** the
countries bordering (on) the Black Sea; **Anliegerverkehr** M
(local) residents' vehicles *pl*; **„~ frei"** "residents only"

anlocken VT SEP to attract

anlöten VT SEP to solder on (*an* +*acc or dat* -to)

anlügen VT SEP IRREG to lie to

Anm. ABBR *von* **Anmerkung**

Anmache F (*sl*) chatting-up (*Brit inf*), flirting; (= *Spruch*) chat-
up line (*inf*); **sexuelle ~** advances *pl*

anmachen VT SEP **(a)** (*inf: = befestigen*) to put up (*an* +*acc or dat*
on)
(b) (= *zubereiten*) to mix; *Salat* to dress
(c) (= *anstellen*) *Radio, Licht, Heizung etc* to put *or* turn on;
Feuer to light
(d) (*inf*) (= *ansprechen*) to chat up (*Brit inf*), to put the moves
on (*US inf*); (= *scharf machen*) to turn on (*inf*); (*sl: = belästigen*)
to harass; **mach mich nicht an** leave me alone

anmailen ['anme:ln] VT SEP to e-mail

anmalen SEP **1** VT (= *bemalen, anzeichnen*) to paint (*an* +*acc*
on); (= *ausmalen*) to colour (*Brit*) *or* color (*US*) in; **sich** (*dat*) **die**
Lippen *etc* **~** to paint one's lips *etc* **2** VR (*pej: = schminken*) to
paint one's face

anmaßen ['anma:sn] VT SEP **sich** (*dat*) **etw ~** *Befugnis, Recht* to
claim sth (for oneself); *Kritik* to take sth upon oneself; *Titel,*
Macht, Autorität to assume sth; **sich** (*dat*) **ein Urteil/eine**
Meinung über etw (*acc*) **~** to presume to pass judgement on/
have an opinion about sth; **sich** (*dat*) **~, etw zu tun** to
presume to do sth

anmaßend ADJ presumptuous

Anmaßung F **-, -en** presumptuousness; **es ist eine ~ zu**
meinen, ... it is presumptuous to maintain that ...

Anmelde-: Anmeldeformular NT application form;
Anmeldefrist F registration period; **Anmeldegebühr** F
registration fee

anmelden SEP **1** VT **(a)** (= *ankündigen*) *Besuch* to announce;
einen Freund bei jdm ~ to let sb know that a friend is coming
to visit

(b) (*bei Schule, Kurs etc*) to enrol (*Brit*), to enroll (*US*) (*bei* at, *zu* for)
(c) *Patent* to apply for; *neuen Wohnsitz, Auto, Untermieter* to register (*bei* at); *Fernseher* to get a licence (*Brit*) *or* license (*US*) for; *Waffe* to register; **Konkurs ~** to declare oneself bankrupt
(d) (= *vormerken lassen*) to make an appointment for
(e) *Recht, Ansprüche* (*zu Steuerzwecken, bei Zoll*) to declare; *Bedenken, Zweifel, Protest* to register; *Wünsche, Bedürfnisse* to make known; **ich melde starke Bedenken an** I have serious doubts about that
2 VR **(a)** (*Besucher*) to announce one's arrival; (*im Hotel*) to book (in); (*fig: Probleme, Zweifel etc*) to appear on the horizon; **sich bei jdm ~** to tell sb one is coming
(b) (*an Schule, zu Kurs etc*) to enrol (*Brit*) *or* enroll (*US*) (oneself) (*an +dat* at, *zu* for); **sich polizeilich ~** to register with the police
(c) (= *sich einen Termin geben lassen*) to make an appointment; **sich beim Arzt** *etc* **~** to make an appointment at the doctor's *etc*

Anmeldung F **(a)** (*von Besuch*) announcement; (*im Hotel*) booking; (*an Schule, zu Kurs etc*) enrolment (*Brit*), enrollment (*US*) (*an +dat* at, *zu* for); (*bei Einwohnermeldeamt*) registration; (*beim Arzt etc*) making an appointment; **nur nach vorheriger ~** by appointment only **(b)** (*von Patent*) application (*von, +gen* for); (*von Auto*) registration; (*von Fernseher*) licensing **(c)** (= *Anmelderaum*) reception

anmerken VT SEP (= *sagen*) to say; (= *anstreichen*) to mark; (*als Fußnote*) to note; **sich** (*dat*) **etw ~** to make a note of sth; **jdm seine Verlegenheit** *etc* **~** to notice sb's embarrassment *etc*; **sich** (*dat*) **etw ~ lassen** to let sth show; **man merkt ihm nicht an, dass ...** you can't tell that he ...

Anmerkung ['anmɛrkʊŋ] F -, -en (= *Erläuterung*) note; (= *Fußnote*) (foot)note; (*iro: = Kommentar*) remark

anmieten VT SEP to rent

anmit ['anmɪt] ADV (*Sw*) herewith

Anmut ['anmuːt] F -, NO PL grace; (= *Schönheit*) beauty

anmuten SEP **1** VT (*geh*) to appear, to seem (*jdn* to sb) **2** VI **es mutet sonderbar an** it seems curious; **eine eigenartig ~de Geschichte** a story that strikes one as odd

anmutig ADJ (*geh*) graceful; (= *hübsch anzusehen*) lovely

annageln VT SEP to nail on (*an +acc or dat* -to)

annagen VT SEP to gnaw (at)

annähen VT SEP to sew on (*an +acc or dat* -to)

annähern SEP **1** VT to bring closer (*+dat, an +acc* to); **zwei Standpunkte so weit als möglich ~** to bring two points of view as much into line (with each other) as possible **2** VR **(a)** (*lit, fig: = sich nähern*) to approach (*einer Sache* (*dat*) sth) **(b)** (= *sich angleichen, näher kommen*) to come closer (*+dat, an +acc* to)

annähernd **1** ADJ (= *ungefähr*) approximate, rough **2** ADV (= *etwa*) roughly; (= *fast*) almost; **können Sie mir den Betrag ~ nennen?** can you give me a rough idea of the amount?; **nicht ~** not nearly, nothing like; **nicht ~ so viel** not nearly *or* nothing like as much

Annäherung F (*lit: = das Näherkommen*) (*fig: = Angleichung*) approach (*an +acc* towards); (*von Standpunkten*) convergence (*+dat, an +acc* with); **die ~ zwischen Ost und West** the rapprochement of East and West; **die ~ von zwei Menschen** two people coming closer together; **die ~ an den Partner** coming closer to one's partner

Annäherungs-: **Annäherungsversuch** M overtures *pl*; **annäherungsweise** ADV approximately

Annahme ['anaːmə] F -, -n **(a)** (= *Vermutung, Voraussetzung*) assumption; **in der ~, dass ...** on the assumption that ...; **gehe ich recht in der ~, dass ...?** am I right in assuming that ...?; **der ~ sein, dass ...** to assume that ...
(b) (= *das Annehmen*) acceptance; (*von Rat, Telegramm, Gespräch, Reparaturen*) taking; (*von Arbeit, Auftrag, Bewerber*) acceptance, taking on; (*von Herausforderung, Angebot*) taking up; (= *Billigung*) approval; (*von Gesetz*) passing; (*von Resolution, Staatsangehörigkeit*) adoption; (*von Gestalt, Name*) assuming; **~ an Kindes statt** (child) adoption
(c) = **Annahmestelle**

Annahme-: **Annahmeschluss** M closing date; **Annahmestelle** F (*für Pakete, Telegramme*) counter; (*für Wetten, Lotto, Toto etc*) place where bets *etc* are accepted; (*für Reparaturen*) reception; (*für Material*) delivery point; **die ~ für Autobatterien ist ...**

please bring your old car batteries to ...;
Annahmeverweigerung F refusal; **bei ~** when delivery is refused

annehmbar **1** ADJ acceptable; (= *nicht schlecht*) reasonable **2** ADV reasonably well

annehmen SEP IRREG **1** VT **(a)** (= *entgegennehmen, akzeptieren*) to accept; *Nahrung, einen Rat, Telegramm, Gespräch, Telefonat, Lottoschein, Reparaturen* to take; *Arbeit, Auftrag* to take on
(b) (= *billigen*) to approve; *Gesetz* to pass; *Resolution* to adopt; *Antrag* to accept
(c) (= *sich aneignen*) to adopt; *Akzent, Tonfall, Gestalt, Namen* to take on; **ein angenommener Name** an assumed name
(d) *Patienten, Bewerber* to take on
(e) (= *adoptieren*) to adopt; **jdn an Kindes statt ~** to adopt sb
(f) (= *vermuten*) to presume; **von jdm etw ~** (= *erwarten*) to expect sth of sb; (= *glauben*) to believe sth of sb; **er ist nicht so dumm, wie man es von ihm ~ könnte** he's not as stupid as you might think
(g) (= *voraussetzen*) to assume; **wir wollen ~, dass ...** let us assume that ...; **etw als gegeben** *or* **Tatsache ~** to take sth as read; **das kann man wohl ~** you can take that as read; *siehe auch* **angenommen**
(h) (*Sport*) to take
2 VR **sich jds ~** to look after sb; **sich einer Sache** (*gen*) **~** to see to a matter

Annehmlichkeit F -, -en (= *Bequemlichkeit*) convenience; (= *Vorteil*) advantage **Annehmlichkeiten** PL comforts *pl*

annektieren [anɛk'tiːrən], *ptp* **annektiert** VT to annex

anno ['ano] ADV in (the year); **der härteste Winter seit ~ zwölf** the coldest winter since 1912; **ein harter Winter, wie ~ 81** a cold winter, like the winter of '81; **von ~ dazumal** *or* **dunnemals** *or* **Tobak** (*all inf*) from the year dot (*Brit inf*), forever; **das war im Deutschland von ~ dazumal so üblich** that was the custom in Germany in olden days; **~ dazumal** *or* **dunnemals war alles viel billiger** (*inf*) in those days everything was much cheaper

Anno Domini ['ano 'doːmini] ADV in the year of Our Lord

Annonce [a'nɔ̃sə] F -, -n advertisement

Annonceteil [a'nɔ̃sn-] M classified (advertisement) section

annoncieren [anɔ̃'siːrən, anɔŋ'siːrən], *ptp* **annonciert** VTI to advertise

annullieren [anʊ'liːrən], *ptp* **annulliert** VT (*Jur*) to annul

Anode [a'noːdə] F -, -n anode

anöden ['anøːdn] VT SEP (*inf*) to bore stiff (*inf*)

Anomalie [anoma'liː] F -, -n [-'liːən] anomaly; (*Med:* = *Missbildung*) abnormality

anonym [ano'nyːm] **1** ADJ anonymous; **Anonyme Alkoholiker** Alcoholics Anonymous **2** ADV anonymously; **~ angerufen werden** to get anonymous phone calls

Anonymität [anonymi'tɛːt] F -, NO PL anonymity

Anorak ['anorak] M -s, -s anorak

anordnen VT SEP **(a)** (= *befehlen, festsetzen*) to order
(b) (= *aufstellen*) to arrange; (*systematisch*) to order

Anordnung F **(a)** (= *Befehl*) order; **laut (polizeilicher) ~ by** order (of the police); **auf ~ des Arztes** on doctor's orders
(b) (= *Aufstellung*) arrangement; (= *systematische ~*) order; (= *Formation*) formation; **in welcher ~ wollen Sie die Tische für die Konferenz?** how do you want the tables arranged for the conference?

Anorexie [anɔre'ksiː] F -, -n [-'ksiːən] anorexia (nervosa)

anorganisch ['anlɔrganɪʃ, anlɔr'ganɪʃ] ADJ (*Chem*) inorganic

anpacken SEP (*inf*) **1** VT **(a)** (= *anfassen*) to grab (hold of)
(b) *Problem, Thema* to tackle **(c)** (= *umgehen mit*) to treat **2** VI (= *helfen*) *auch* **mit anpacken** to lend a hand

anpassen SEP **1** VT **(a)** *Kleidung* to fit (*+dat* on); *Bauelemente* to fit (*+dat* to) **(b)** (= *abstimmen*) **etw einer Sache** (*dat*) **~** to suit sth to sth (*+dat*); (= *angleichen*) **etw einer Sache** (*dat*) **~** to bring sth into line with sth **2** VR to adapt (oneself) (*+dat* to); (*gesellschaftlich*) to conform; **wir mussten uns ihren Wünschen ~** we had to fit in with their wishes; *siehe auch* **angepasst**

Anpassung F -, -en (*an +acc* to) adaptation; (*von Gehalt etc*) adjustment; (*an Gesellschaft, Normen etc*) conformity

Anpassungs-: **anpassungsfähig** ADJ adaptable; **Anpassungsschwierigkeiten** PL difficulties *pl* in adapting; **Anpassungsvermögen** NT (*Sociol*) adaptability

anpfeifen SEP IRREG **1** VI (*Sport*) to blow the whistle **2** VT **(a)** (*Sport*) **das Spiel ~** to start the game (by blowing one's whistle) **(b)** (*inf*) to bawl out (*inf*)

Anpfiff M **(a)** (*Sport*) (starting) whistle; (= *Spielbeginn*) (*Ftbl*) kickoff; (*Eishockey*) face-off **(b)** (*inf*) bawling out (*inf*)

anpflanzen VT SEP (= *bepflanzen*) to plant; (= *anbauen*) to grow

anpiepsen VT SEP (*Telec inf*) to bleep (*Brit*), to beep (*US*)

anpinseln VT SEP to paint

anpirschen VR SEP to creep up (*an +acc* on)

anpöbeln VT SEP (*inf*) to be rude to

Anprall M impact; **beim ~ gegen** on impact with

anprangern ['anpraŋɐn] VT SEP to denounce

anpreisen VT SEP IRREG to extol (*jdm etw* sth to sb); **sich (als etw) ~** to sell oneself (as sth)

anpressen VT SEP to press on (*an +acc* -to)

Anprobe F **(a)** fitting **(b)** (= *Raum*) (*im Kaufhaus*) changing room; (*beim Schneider*) fitting room

anprobieren *ptp* **anprobiert** SEP **1** VT to try on; *jdm etw* **~** (*inf*) to try sth on sb **2** VI (*beim Schneider*) to have a fitting; **kann ich mal ~?** can I try this/it *etc* on?

anpumpen VT SEP (*inf*) to borrow from; **jdn um 50 Euro ~** to borrow 50 euros from sb

anpusten VT SEP (*inf*) to blow at; *Feuer* to blow on

anquatschen ['ankvatʃn] VT SEP (*inf*) to speak to; *Mädchen* to chat up (*Brit inf*), to put the moves on (*US inf*)

Anrainer ['anrainɐ] M **-s, -**, **Anrainerin** [-ərɪn] F **-, -nen** **(a)** neighbour (*Brit*), neighbor (*US*); **die ~ der Nordsee** the countries bordering (on) the North Sea **(b)** (*esp Aus*: = *Anwohner*) (local) resident

Anrainerstaat M **die ~en des Mittelmeers/der Donau** the countries bordering (on) the Mediterranean/the Danube

anrechenbar ADJ countable; **auf etw** (*acc*) **~ sein** to count toward(s) sth

anrechnen VT SEP **(a)** (= *in Rechnung stellen*) to charge for (*jdm* sb)
(b) (= *gutschreiben*) to count, to take into account (*jdm* for sb); **das alte Auto rechnen wir (Ihnen) mit 500 Euro an** we'll allow (you) 500 euros for the old car; **den alten Fernseher ~** to allow something on the old television
(c) (= *bewerten*) **dem Schüler wird die schlechte Arbeit nicht angerechnet** the pupil's bad piece of work is not being taken into account; **jdm etw hoch ~** to think highly of sb for sth; **jdm etw als Fehler ~** (*Lehrer*) to count sth as a mistake for sb; (*fig*) to consider sth as a fault on sb's part; **ich rechne es ihr als Verdienst an, dass ...** I think it is greatly to her credit that ...; **ich rechne es mir zur Ehre an** (*form*) I consider it an honour (*Brit*) *or* honor (*US*)

Anrechnung F allowance; (*fig*: = *Berücksichtigung*) counting (*auf +acc* towards); **jdm etw in ~ bringen** *or* **stellen** (*form*) to charge sb for sth

Anrecht NT (= *Anspruch*) right, entitlement (*auf +acc* to); **ein ~ auf etw** (*acc*) **haben** *or* **besitzen** to be entitled to sth

Anrede F form of address

anreden SEP **1** VT to address; **jdn mit seinem Titel ~** to address sb by his title **2** VI **gegen jdn ~** to argue against sb; **gegen etw ~** to make oneself heard against sth

anregen VT SEP **(a)** (= *ermuntern*) to prompt (*zu* to); **jdn zum Denken ~** to make sb think **(b)** (*geh*: = *vorschlagen*) *Verbesserung* to propose **(c)** (= *beleben*) to stimulate; *Appetit* to sharpen; **Kaffee etc regt an** coffee *etc* has a stimulating effect; *siehe auch* **angeregt**

anregend 1 ADJ stimulating; **ein ~es Mittel** a stimulant; **die Verdauung/den Kreislauf ~e Mittel** stimulants to the digestion/circulation **2** ADV **~ wirken** to have a stimulating effect

Anregung F **(a)** (= *Antrieb, Impuls*) stimulus; **jdm eine ~ zum Denken geben** to make sb think **(b)** (= *Vorschlag*) idea; **auf ~ von** *or* +*gen* at *or* on the suggestion of **(c)** (= *Belebung*) stimulation

anreichern ['anraiçɐn] SEP **1** VT (= *gehaltvoller machen*) to enrich; (= *vergrößern*) *Sammlung* to increase; **hoch/niedrig** *or* **schwach angereichertes Uran** high/low enriched uranium; **das Gemisch mit Sauerstoff ~** (= *zufügen*) to add oxygen to

the mixture; **angereichert werden** (*Chem*: = *gespeichert werden*) to be accumulated **2** VR (*Chem*) to accumulate

Anreise F **(a)** (= *Anfahrt*) journey there/here; **die ~ zu diesem abgelegenen Ort ist sehr mühsam** it is very difficult to get to this remote place **(b)** (= *Ankunft*) arrival

anreisen VI SEP AUX SEIN **(a)** (= *ein Ziel anfahren*) to make a/the journey *or* trip (there/here); **über welche Strecke wollen Sie ~?** which route do you want to take (there/here)? **(b)** (= *eintreffen*: *auch* **angereist kommen**) to come

anreißen VT SEP IRREG **(a)** (= *einreißen*) to tear, to rip **(b)** (*inf*: = *anbrechen*) to start, to open **(c)** (*Tech*) to mark (out) **(d)** (= *kurz zur Sprache bringen*) to touch on **(e)** *Streichholz* to strike

anreiten SEP IRREG **1** VI AUX SEIN **angeritten kommen** to come riding along *or* (*auf einen zu*) up **2** VT *Ziel etc* to ride toward(s)

Anreiz M incentive; **ein ~ zum Lernen** *etc* an incentive to learn *etc*; **jdm den ~ nehmen, etw zu tun** to take away sb's incentive for doing sth

anreizen SEP **1** VT (= *anspornen*) to encourage; **jdn zum Kauf ~** to encourage sb to buy **2** VI to act as an incentive (*zu* to); **dazu ~, dass jd etw tut** to act as an incentive for sb to do sth

anrempeln VT SEP (= *anstoßen*) to bump into; (*absichtlich*) *Menschen* to jostle

anrennen VI SEP IRREG AUX SEIN **gegen etw ~** *gegen Wind etc* to run against sth; (*Mil*) to storm sth; (*Sport*) to attack sth; (= *sich stoßen*) to run into sth; (*fig*: = *bekämpfen*) to fight against sth; **angerannt kommen** (*inf*) to come running

Anrichte ['anrɪçtə] F **-, -n (a)** (= *Schrank*) dresser; (= *Büfett*) sideboard **(b)** (= *Raum*) pantry

anrichten VT SEP **(a)** (= *zubereiten*) *Speisen* to prepare; (= *servieren*) to serve; *Salat* to dress; **es ist angerichtet** (*form*) dinner *etc* is served (*form*)
(b) (*fig*: = *verursachen*) *Schaden, Unheil* to bring about; **etwas ~** (*inf*: = *anstellen*) to get up to something (*inf*); **da hast du aber etwas angerichtet!** (*inf*: = *verursachen*) you've started something there all right; (= *anstellen*) you've really made a mess there

anrosten VI SEP AUX SEIN to get (a bit) rusty

anrüchig ['anryçɪç] ADJ **(a)** (= *von üblem Ruf*) *Geschäfte, Lokal* disreputable **(b)** (= *anstößig*) offensive; (= *unanständig*) indecent

anrücken VI SEP AUX SEIN (*Truppen*) to advance; (*Polizei etc*) to move in; (*hum*: *Essen, Besuch*) to turn up

Anruf M (*Telec*) (phone) call

Anrufbeantworter [-bəlantvɔrtɐ] M **-s, -** answering machine

anrufen SEP IRREG **1** VT **(a)** (= *zurufen*) to shout to; (*Telec*) to ring (*esp Brit*), to phone, to call; **darf ich dich ~?** can I give you a ring? (*esp Brit*), can I call you?; **kann man Sie ~?** (= *haben Sie Telefon?*) are you on the phone? **(b)** (*fig*: = *appellieren an*) (*um* for) to appeal to; *Gott* to call on **2** VI (= *telefonieren*) to phone; **bei jdm ~** to phone sb; **ins Ausland/nach Amerika ~** to phone abroad/America

Anrufer ['anru:fɐ] M **-s, -**, **Anruferin** [-ərɪn] F **-, -nen** caller

Anrufumleitung F (*Telec*) call diversion

anrühren VT SEP **(a)** (= *berühren, sich befassen mit*) to touch; (*fig*) *Thema* to touch upon **(b)** (= *mischen*) *Farben* to mix; *Sauce* to blend; (= *verrühren*) to stir

ans [ans] CONTR *von* **an das**; **sich ~ Arbeiten machen** *or* (*geh*) **begeben** to set to work; **wenn es ~ Sterben geht** when it comes to dying

Ansage F announcement; (*Cards*) bid; **er übernimmt bei diesem Programm die ~** he is doing the announcements for this programme (*Brit*) *or* program (*US*)

ansagen SEP **1** VT **(a)** (= *ankündigen*) to announce; **jdm den Kampf ~** to declare war on sb
(b) (*Cards*) (*Bridge*) to bid; (*Skat*) to declare
(c) (*inf*) **angesagt sein** (= *modisch sein*) to be in; (= *erforderlich sein*) to be called for; (= *auf dem Programm stehen*) to be the order of the day; **Spannung ist angesagt** we are in for a bit of excitement
2 VR (= *Besuch ankündigen*) to say that one is coming; (*Zeit, Frühling*) to announce itself (*liter*)

ansägen VT SEP to saw into

Ansager ['anza:gɐ] M **-s, -**, **Ansagerin** [-ərɪn] F **-, -nen** (*Rad etc*) announcer; (*im Kabarett*) compère (*Brit*), emcee (*US*)

ansammeln SEP **1** VT (a) (= *anhäufen*) to accumulate; *Reichtümer, Erfahrung* to amass; *Vorräte* to build up (b) (= *zusammenkommen lassen*) to gather together **2** VR (a) (= *sich versammeln*) to gather, to collect (b) (= *sich aufhäufen*) to accumulate; (*Staub, Flüssigkeit, Schadstoffe, Fragen*) to collect; (*Zinsen*) to build up; (*fig: Wut, Frust, Misstrauen*) to build up

Ansammlung F (= *Auflauf*) gathering; (*von Truppen*) concentration

ansässig ['anzɛsɪç] ADJ (*form*) resident; **eine in München ~e Firma** a firm based in Munich; **sich in London ~ machen** to settle in London

Ansatz M (a) (*von Hals, Arm, Henkel etc*) base; (*an Stirn*) hairline; (= *Haarwurzeln*) roots *pl* (b) (*Tech*) (= *Zusatzstück*) attachment; (*zur Verlängerung*) extension; (= *Naht*) join (c) (= *erstes Anzeichen, Beginn*) first sign(s *pl*); (= *Versuch*) attempt (*zu etw* at sth); (= *Ausgangspunkt*) starting point; **einen neuen ~ zu etw machen** to make a fresh attempt at sth; **Ansätze zeigen, etw zu tun** to show signs of doing sth; **die ersten Ansätze** the initial stages; **im ~** basically (d) (*Math*) formulation (e) (*Mus*) intonation; (= *Lippenstellung*) embouchure (f) (*Econ form*) estimate; (= *Fonds für Sonderzwecke*) appropriation; **außer ~ bleiben** to be left out of account; **etw für etw in ~ bringen** to appropriate sth for sth

ansaufen VT SEP IRREG (*inf*) **sich** (*dat*) **einen (Rausch) ~** to get smashed (*inf*)

anschaffen SEP **1** VT (**sich** *dat*) **etw ~** to get oneself sth; (= *kaufen*) to buy sth; **sich** (*dat*) **Kinder ~** (*inf*) to have children **2** VI (a) (*Aus, S Ger*) to give orders; **jdm ~** to order sb about (b) (*sl: durch Prostitution*) **~ gehen** to be on the game (*inf*); **für jdn ~ gehen** to go on the game for sb (*inf*); **jdn ~ or zum Anschaffen schicken** to send sb out on the game (*inf*)

Anschaffung F acquisition; (*gekaufter Gegenstand*) purchase, buy; **ich habe mich zur ~ eines Autos entschlossen** I have decided to get a new car; **~en machen** to acquire things; (= *kaufen*) to make purchases

Anschaffungs-: Anschaffungskosten PL cost *sing* of purchase; **Anschaffungspreis** M purchase price

anschalten VT SEP to switch on

anschauen VT SEP (*esp dial*) to look at; (*prüfend*) to examine; **sich** (*dat*) **etw ~** to have a look at sth; (da) **schau einer an!** (*inf*) well I never! (*inf*)

anschaulich ['anʃaulɪç] **1** ADJ clear; (= *lebendig, bildhaft*) vivid; *Beschreibung* graphic; *Beispiel* concrete; **etw ~ machen** to illustrate sth; **den Unterricht sehr ~ machen** to make teaching come alive **2** ADV clearly; (= *lebendig*) vividly

Anschauung ['anʃauʊŋ] F **~, -en** (= *Ansicht, Auffassung*) view; (= *Meinung*) opinion; **nach neuerer ~** according to the current way of thinking; **aus eigener ~** from one's own experience

Anschauungsmaterial NT illustrative material

Anschein M appearance; (= *Eindruck*) impression; **dem ~ nach** apparently; **allem ~ nach** to all appearances; **den ~ erwecken, als ...** to give the impression that ...; **sich** (*dat*) **den ~ geben, als ob man informiert sei** to pretend to be informed; **es hat den ~, als ob ...** it appears that ...

anscheinend **1** ADV apparently **2** ADJ apparent

anschieben VT SEP IRREG (a) *Fahrzeug* to push; **können Sie mich mal ~?** can you give me a push? (b) (*fig*) *Wirtschaft, Konjunktur* to kick-start

anschießen SEP IRREG **1** VT (a) (= *verletzen*) to shoot (and wound) (b) (*Sport*) *Rennen* to start (c) *Tor* to shoot at; *Spieler* to hit; (= *treffen*) *Schiff, Billardkugel* to hit **2** VI AUX SEIN (= *heranrasen*) to shoot up; **angeschossen kommen** to come shooting along *or* (*auf einen zu*) up

Anschiss M **-es, -e** (*inf*) bollocking (*Brit sl*), ass-kicking (*US sl*)

Anschlag M (a) (*Plakat*) poster; (= *Bekanntmachung*) notice; **einen ~ machen** to put up a poster/notice (b) (= *Überfall*) attack (*auf +acc* on); (= *Attentat*) attempt on sb's life; **einen ~ auf jdn verüben** to make an attempt on sb's life; **einem ~ zum Opfer fallen** to be assassinated; **einen ~ auf jdn vorhaben** (*hum: = etwas von jdm wollen*) to have a favour (*Brit*) *or* favor (*US*) to ask of sb (c) (= *Kostenanschlag*) estimate; **etw in ~ bringen** (*form*) to take sth into account; **eine Summe in ~ bringen** (*form*) to

calculate an amount (d) (*Sport*) (*beim Schwimmen*) touch; (*beim Versteckspiel*) home (e) (*von Klavier(spieler), Schreibmaschine*) touch; **200 Anschläge in der Minute** ≈ 40 words per minute (f) (*bei Hebel, Knopf etc*) stop; **etw bis zum ~ durchdrücken** to push sth right down; **etw bis zum ~ drehen** to turn sth as far as it will go

anschlagen SEP IRREG **1** VT (a) (= *befestigen*) to fix on (*an +acc* to); (*mit Nägeln*) to nail on (*an +acc* to); (= *aushängen*) *Plakat* to put up (*an +acc* on) (b) *Stunde, Taste, Akkord* to strike; (*Mus*) to play; **eine schnellere Gangart ~** (*fig*) to speed up (c) (= *beschädigen, verletzen*) *Geschirr* to chip; **sich** (*dat*) **den Kopf** *etc* **~** to knock one's head *etc*; *siehe auch* **angeschlagen** (d) (*Aus*: = *anzapfen*) *Fass* to tap (e) (= *aufnehmen*) *Maschen* to cast on **2** VI (a) (*Welle*) to beat (*an +acc* against); **mit etw gegen/an etw** (*acc*) **~** to strike *or* knock sth against/on sth (b) (*Sport, Tennis etc*) to serve; (*beim Schwimmen*) to touch (c) (*Hund*) to give a bark; (*Vogel*) to give a screech (d) (= *wirken: Arznei etc*) to take effect (e) (*inf: = dick machen*) **bei jdm ~** to make sb put on weight

anschleichen SEP IRREG **1** VI AUX SEIN to creep along *or* (*auf einen zu*) up; **angeschlichen kommen** (*inf*) to come creeping along/up **2** VR **sich an jdn/etw ~** to creep up on sb/sth; (= *sich anpirschen*) to stalk sb/sth

anschleifen VT SEP (*inf*: = *herbeischleppen*) to drag along; **was schleifst du denn da für einen Plunder an?** what's that junk you're carting up? (*inf*)

anschleppen VT SEP (a) *Auto* to tow-start (b) (*inf*) (= *unerwünscht mitbringen*) to bring along; (*nach Hause*) to bring home; (= *mühsam herbeibringen*) to drag along (*inf*); (*hum*: = *hervorholen, anbieten*) to bring out

anschließen SEP IRREG **1** VT (a) (*an +acc* to) (*Tech, Elec, Telec etc*: = *verbinden*) to connect; (*in Steckdose*) to plug in; **angeschlossen** connected(-up) (b) (*fig*: = *hinzufügen*) to add; **angeschlossen** *Organisation etc* affiliated (*dat* to *or* (*US*) with), associated (*dat* with) **2** VR **sich jdm** *or* **an jdn ~** (= *folgen*) to follow sb; (= *zugesellen*) to join sb; (= *beipflichten*) to side with sb; **sich einer Sache** (*dat*) *or* **an etw** (*acc*) **~** (= *folgen*) to follow sth; (= *beitreten, sich beteiligen*) to join sth; (= *beipflichten*) to endorse sth; (= *angrenzen*) to adjoin sth; **dem Vortrag** *or* **an den Vortrag schloss sich ein Film an** the lecture was followed by a film **3** VI **an etw** (*acc*) **~** to follow sth

anschließend **1** ADV afterwards **2** ADJ following; **Essen mit ~em Tanz** dinner dance

Anschluss M (a) (= *Verbindung*) connection; (= *Beitritt*) entry (*an +acc* into); (*Hist euph*) Anschluss; **~ haben nach** (*Rail*) to have a connection to; **den ~ verpassen** (*Rail etc*) to miss one's connection; (*fig*) to miss the boat *or* bus; **ihm gelang der ~ an die Spitze** (*Sport*) he managed to catch up with the leaders (b) (*Telec, Comput*) connection; (= *Anlage*) telephone (connection); (= *weiterer Apparat*) extension; (= *Wasseranschluss*) supply point; (*für Waschmaschine*) point; **elektrischer ~** power point; **einen ~ beantragen** (*Telec*) to apply for a telephone to be connected; **~ bekommen** (*Telec*) to get through; **der ~ ist besetzt** (*Telec*) the line is engaged (*Brit*) *or* busy (*esp US*); **kein ~ unter dieser Nummer** (*Telec*) number unobtainable (*Brit*), this number is not in service (*US*) (c) **im ~** (*an +acc* = *nach*) subsequent to, following (d) (*fig*) (= *Kontakt*) contact (*an +acc* with); (= *Bekanntschaft*) friendship; (= *Aufnahme*) integration; **~ finden** to make friends (*an +acc* with); **er sucht ~** he wants to make friends

Anschluss-: Anschlussflug M connecting flight; **Anschlusskonkurs** M bancruptcy (*after failure to agree on composition*); **Anschlusszug** M (*Rail*) connection

anschmiegen VR SEP **sich an jdn/etw ~** (*Kind, Hund*) to snuggle up to sb/sth; (*Kleidung*) to cling to sb/sth; (*geh: Dorf an Berg etc*) to nestle against sth

anschmiegsam ['anʃmiːkzaːm] ADJ *Wesen* affectionate; *Material* smooth

anschnallen SEP **1** VR (*Aut, Aviat*) to fasten one's seat belt; **bitte ~!** fasten your seat belts, please! **2** VT (a) *Skier* to clip on (b) *Person, Kind* to strap up; (*in etw*) to strap in; **jdn ~** (*Aviat, Aut*) to fasten sb's seat belt

Anschnallpflicht F, NO PL mandatory wearing of seat belts; **für Kinder besteht ~** children must wear seat belts

anschnauzen VT SEP (inf) to yell at

anschneiden VT SEP IRREG (a) Brot etc to (start to) cut (b) (fig) Frage, Thema to touch on (c) (Aut) Kurve to cut; (Sport) Ball to cut

Anschnitt M (= Schnittfläche) cut part; (= erstes Stück) first slice; (= Ende) cut end

anschnorren VT SEP (pej inf) to (try to) cadge (Brit inf) or bum (US inf); **jdn um etw ~** to cadge (Brit inf) or bum (US inf) sth from sb

anschrauben VT SEP to screw on (an +acc -to); (= festschrauben) to screw tight or up

anschreiben SEP IRREG **1** VT (a) Behörde, Versandhaus etc to write to; **es antworteten nur 20% der Angeschriebenen** only 20% of the people written to replied (b) (= aufschreiben) to write up (an +acc on); **angeschrieben stehen** to be written up; siehe auch **angeschrieben** (c) (inf: = in Rechnung stellen) to chalk up (inf) **2** VI (inf) **unser Kaufmann schreibt an** our grocer doesn't give anything on tick (Brit inf) or on credit; **sie lässt immer ~** she always buys on tick (Brit inf) or on credit

anschreien VT SEP IRREG to shout or yell at

Anschrift F address

Anschubfinanzierung [ˈanʃuːp-] F (Econ) start-up funds pl

anschwärzen VT SEP (fig inf) **jdn ~** to blacken sb's name (bei with); (= denunzieren) to run sb down (bei to)

anschweigen VT SEP IRREG to say nothing to; (demonstrativ) to refuse to speak to; **sich gegenseitig ~** to say nothing to each other

anschweißen VT SEP (Tech) to weld on (an +acc -to)

anschwellen VI SEP IRREG AUX SEIN to swell (up); (Wasser auch, Lärm) to rise; **dick angeschwollen** very swollen

anschwemmen SEP **1** VT to wash up **2** VI AUX SEIN to be washed up

anschwindeln VT SEP (inf) **jdn ~** to tell sb fibs (inf)

ansegeln SEP **1** VT (= zusegeln auf) to sail for; (= anlegen in) Hafen to put into **2** VI AUX SEIN **angesegelt kommen** (inf: lit, fig) to come sailing along or (auf einen zu) up

ansehen VT SEP IRREG (a) (= betrachten) to look at; **er sah mich ganz groß an** he stared at me; **er sah mich ganz böse an** he gave me an angry look; **jdn nicht mehr ~** (fig inf) not to want to know sb any more; **sieh mal einer an!** (inf) well, I never! (inf) (b) (fig) to regard, to look upon (als, für as); **ich sehe es als meine Pflicht an** I consider it to be my duty; **sie sieht ihn nicht für voll an** she doesn't take him seriously; siehe auch **angesehen** (c) (sich dat) **etw ~** (= besichtigen) to (have a) look at sth; Fernsehsendung to watch sth; Film, Stück, Sportveranstaltung to see sth; **sich** (dat) **jdn/etw gründlich ~** (lit, fig) to take a close look at sb/sth (d) **das sieht man ihm an** he looks it; **das sieht man ihm nicht an** he doesn't look it; **das sieht man ihm an der Gesichtsfarbe an** you can tell (that) by the colour (Brit) or color (US) of his face; **man kann ihm die Strapazen der letzten Woche ~** he's showing the strain of the last week; **man sieht ihm sein Alter nicht an** he doesn't look his age; **jdm etw (an den Augen or an der Nasenspitze** (hum)**) ~** to tell sth by looking at sb; **jeder konnte ihm sein Glück ~** everyone could see that he was happy (e) **etw (mit) ~** to watch sth; **das kann man doch nicht mit ~** you can't stand by and watch that; **ich kann das nicht länger mit ~** I can't stand it any more; **das habe ich (mir) lange genug (mit) angesehen!** I've had enough of that!

Ansehen NT -s, NO PL (= guter Ruf) (good) reputation; (= Prestige) prestige; **großes ~ genießen** to enjoy a good reputation; **zu ~ kommen** to acquire a good reputation; **(bei jdm) in hohem ~ stehen** to be held in high regard (by sb); **an ~ verlieren** to lose credit or standing

ansehnlich [ˈanzeːnlɪç] ADJ (= beträchtlich) considerable; Leistung impressive; **ein ~es Sümmchen** (hum) a tidy little sum

anseilen [ˈanzailən] VT SEP **jdn/sich ~** to rope sb/oneself up; **etw ~ und herunterlassen** to fasten sth with a rope and let it down

an sein VI IRREG AUX SEIN (inf) to be on

ansetzen SEP **1** VT (a) (= anfügen) to attach (an +acc to); (= annähen) to sew on (b) (= in Ausgangsstellung bringen) to place in position; **eine Leiter an etw** (acc) **~** to put a ladder up against sth; **den Bleistift/die Feder ~** to put pencil/pen to paper; **die Flöte/ Trompete** etc **~** to raise the flute/trumpet to one's mouth; **das Glas ~** to raise the glass to one's lips; **an welcher Stelle muss man den Wagenheber ~?** where should the jack be put? (c) (mit, auf +acc at) (= festlegen) Kosten, Termin to fix; (= veranschlagen) Kosten, Zeitspanne to estimate (d) (= einsetzen) **jdn auf jdn/etw ~** to put sb on(to) sb/sth; **Hunde (auf jdn/jds Spur) ~** to put dogs on sb/sb's trail (e) (= entstehen lassen) Blätter etc to put out; Frucht to produce; **Fett ~** (Mensch) to put on weight; (Tier) to get fatter; **Rost ~** to get rusty (f) (Cook: = vorbereiten) to prepare; Bowle to start **2** VI (= beginnen) to start, to begin; **zur Landung ~** (Aviat) to come in to land; **zum Sprung/Start ~** to get ready to jump/ start; **er setzte immer wieder an, aber ...** (zum Sprechen) he kept opening his mouth to say something but ...

Ansicht F -, -en (a) view; **von hinten/vorn** rear/front view; **~ von oben/unten** view from above/below (b) (= das Betrachten, Prüfen) inspection; **bei ~ (von unten** etc) on inspection (from below etc); **zur ~** (Comm) for (your/our etc) inspection; **jdm Waren zur ~ schicken** (Comm) to send sb goods on approval (c) (= Meinung) opinion, view; **nach ~** +gen in the opinion of; **meiner ~ nach** in my opinion or view; **ich bin der ~, dass ... ** I am of the opinion that ...; **anderer/der gleichen ~ sein** to be of a different/the same opinion; **über etw** (acc) **anderer ~ sein** to have a different opinion about sth; **ich bin ganz Ihrer ~** I entirely agree with you

Ansichts(post)karte F picture postcard

Ansichtssache F **das ist ~** that is a matter of opinion

ansonsten [anˈzɔnstn] ADV otherwise; **~ gibts nichts Neues** (inf) there's nothing new apart from that; **~ hast du nichts auszusetzen?** (iro) have you any more complaints?

anspannen VT SEP (a) (= straffer spannen) to tauten, to tighten; Muskeln to tense (b) (= anstrengen) to strain, to tax; **jdn zu sehr ~** to overtax sb; **alle seine Kräfte ~** to exert all one's energy; siehe auch **angespannt** (c) Wagen to hitch up; Pferd to harness; Ochsen to yoke up (zu for); **es ist angespannt!** the carriage is ready

Anspannung F (fig) strain

anspeien VT SEP IRREG to spit at

Anspiel NT (Sport) start of play; (Cards) lead; (Chess) first move

anspielen SEP **1** VT (Sport) to play the ball etc to; Spieler to pass to **2** VI (a) (= Spiel beginnen) to start; (Ftbl) to kick off; (Cards) to lead; (Chess) to open (b) **auf jdn/etw ~** to allude to sb/sth; **worauf wollen Sie ~?** what are you getting at?; **spielst du damit auf mich an?** are you trying to insinuate something?

Anspielung [ˈanʃpiːluŋ] F -, -en allusion (auf +acc to); (böse) insinuation, innuendo (auf +acc regarding)

anspitzen VT SEP Bleistift etc to sharpen

Ansporn M, NO PL incentive; **ihm fehlt der innere ~** he has no motivation

anspornen VT SEP Pferd to spur (on); (fig auch) to encourage (zu to); Mannschaft to cheer on; **Kinder zum Lernen ~** to encourage children to learn

Ansprache F (= Rede) address; **eine ~ halten** to give an address, to make a speech

ansprechbar ADJ (= bereit, jdn anzuhören) approachable; (= gut gelaunt) amenable; Patient responsive; **er ist beschäftigt/wütend und zurzeit nicht ~** he's so busy/angry that no-one can talk to him just now; **auf etw** (acc) **~ sein** to respond to sth

ansprechen SEP IRREG **1** VT (a) (= anreden) to speak to; (= das Wort an jdn richten, mit Titel, Vornamen etc) to address; (belästigend) to accost; **jdn auf etw** (acc)**/um etw ~** to approach sb about/for sth; **damit sind Sie alle angesprochen** this is directed at all of you (b) (= gefallen) to appeal to (c) (= erwähnen) to mention **2** VI (a) (auf +acc to) (= reagieren) (Patient, Gaspedal etc) to respond; **diese Tabletten sprechen bei ihr nicht an** these tablets don't have any effect on her; **leicht ~de Bremsen** very responsive brakes

(b) (= *Anklang finden*) to go down well

ansprechend ■ ADJ (= *reizvoll*) *Äußeres, Verpackung etc* attractive, appealing; (= *angenehm*) *Umgebung etc* pleasant ② ADV attractively; **~ wirken** to be attractive

Ansprechpartner(in) M(F) (*form*) contact

anspringen SEP IRREG ■ VT (= *anfallen*) to jump; (*Raubtier*) to pounce (up)on; (*Hund:* = *hochspringen*) to jump up at ② VI AUX SEIN **(a)** (*Motor*) to start **(b) angesprungen kommen** to come bounding along *or* (*auf einen zu*) up; **auf etw** (*acc*) **~** (*fig inf*) to jump at sth (*inf*); **gegen etw ~** to jump against sth **(c)** (*Sport*) to jump

anspritzen VT SEP (= *bespritzen*) to splash; (*mit Spritzpistole, -düse etc*) to spray

Anspruch M **(a)** (*esp Jur*) claim; (= *Recht*) right (*auf +acc* to); **~ auf etw** (*acc*) **haben** to be entitled to sth; **~ auf Schadenersatz erheben** to make a claim for damages

(b) (= *Anforderung*) demand; (= *Standard*) standard, requirement; **an jdn dauernd Ansprüche stellen** to make constant demands on sb; **große** *or* **hohe Ansprüche stellen** to be very demanding; (= *hohes Niveau verlangen*) to demand high standards; **den erforderlichen Ansprüchen gerecht werden** to meet the necessary requirements

(c) (= *Behauptung*) claim, pretension; **diese Theorie erhebt keinen ~ auf Unwiderlegbarkeit** this theory does not claim to be irrefutable

(d) etw in ~ nehmen *Recht* to claim sth; *jds Hilfe, Dienste* to enlist sb; *Möglichkeiten, Kantine etc* to take advantage of sth; *Zeit, Aufmerksamkeit, Kräfte* to take up sth; **jdn völlig in ~ nehmen** to take up all of sb's time; (*jds Aufmerksamkeit, Gedanken*) to engross *or* preoccupy sb completely; **sehr in ~ genommen** very busy/preoccupied

Anspruchs-: Anspruchsdenken NT high expectations *pl* (of one's entitlements); **anspruchslos** ■ ADJ undemanding; (= *geistig nicht hoch stehend*) lowbrow; (= *minderwertig*) *Produkte* down-market ② ADV simply; **~ leben** to lead a modest life; **anspruchsvoll** ■ ADJ (= *viel verlangend*) demanding; (= *übertrieben ~*) hard to please; (= *wählerisch*) discriminating; (= *kritisch*) critical; *Stil, Buch* ambitious; *Geschmack, Musik* highbrow; (= *kultiviert*) sophisticated; (= *hochwertig*) high-quality; **eine Zeitung für Anspruchsvolle** a newspaper for the discriminating reader ② ADV (= *kultiviert*) in a sophisticated manner

anspucken VT SEP to spit at *or* on

anstacheln VT SEP to spur (on); (= *antreiben*) to drive *or* goad on

Anstalt ['anʃtalt] F **-, -en (a)** institution (*auch euph*); (= *Institut*) institute; **eine ~ öffentlichen Rechts** a public institution **(b) Anstalten** PL (= *Maßnahmen*) measures *pl*; (= *Vorbereitungen*) preparations *pl*; **für** *or* **zu etw ~en treffen** to take measures/make preparations for sth; **~en/keine ~en machen, etw zu tun** to make a/no move to do sth

Anstand[1] M **(a)** NO PL (= *Schicklichkeit*) decency, propriety; (= *Manieren*) (good) manners *pl* **(b)** (*geh:* = *Einwand*) **ohne ~** without hesitation; **~/keinen ~ an etw** (*dat*) **nehmen** to object/not to object to sth

Anstand[2] M (*Hunt*) raised hide

anständig ■ ADJ decent; *Witz auch* clean; (= *ehrbar*) respectable; (*inf:* = *beträchtlich*) sizeable; **das war nicht ~ von ihm** that was pretty bad of him; **bleib ~!** behave yourself!; **eine ~e Tracht Prügel** (*inf*) a good hiding ② ADV decently; **sich ~ benehmen** to behave oneself; **sich ~ hinsetzen** to sit properly; **jdn ~ bezahlen** (*inf*) to pay sb well; **~ essen/ausschlafen** (*inf*) to have a decent meal/sleep; **sie hat sich ~ gestoßen** (*inf*) she really took a knock (*inf*)

anständigerweise ADV out of decency; **du könntest ihm die zerbrochene Vase ~ bezahlen** you could in all decency pay him for the broken vase

Anstands-: Anstandsbesuch M formal call; (*aus Pflichtgefühl*) duty visit; **Anstandsdame** F chaperon(e); **anstandshalber** ADV out of politeness; **anstandslos** ADV without difficulty

anstarren VT SEP to stare at

anstatt [an'ʃtat] ■ PREP +GEN instead of ② CONJ **~ zu arbeiten** instead of working; **~, dass er das tut, ...** instead of doing that, he ...

anstechen VT SEP IRREG to make a hole in; *Kartoffeln, Fleisch* to prick; *Reifen* to puncture; *Blase* to pierce; *Fass* to tap

anstecken SEP ■ VT **(a)** (= *befestigen*) to pin on; *Ring* to put on **(b)** (= *anzünden*) to light; (= *in Brand stecken*) to set fire to **(c)** (*Med, fig*) to infect; **ich will dich nicht ~** I don't want to give it to you ② VR **sich (mit etw) ~** to catch sth (*bei* from) ③ VI (*Med*) (*fig*) to be infectious; (*durch Berührung, fig*) to be contagious

ansteckend ADJ (*Med*) (*fig*) infectious; (*durch Berührung, fig*) contagious

Anstecker M (*inf*) (= *Button*) badge (*Brit*), button (*US*); (= *Schmuck*) small brooch

Ansteckung ['anʃtekʊŋ] F **-, -en** (*Med*) infection; (*durch Berührung*) contagion

Ansteckungsgefahr F risk of infection

anstehen VI SEP IRREG AUX HABEN *or* (*S Ger, Aus, Sw*) SEIN **(a)** (*in Schlange*) to queue (up) (*Brit*), to stand in line (*nach* for) **(b)** (= *auf Erledigung warten*) to be due to be dealt with; (*Verhandlungspunkt*) to be on the agenda; **~de Probleme** problems facing us/them *etc*

ansteigen VI SEP IRREG AUX SEIN to rise

anstelle [an'ʃtɛlə] PREP +GEN instead of, in place of

anstellen SEP ■ VT **(a)** (= *daneben stellen*) to place; (= *anlehnen*) to lean (*an +acc* against) **(b)** (= *dazustellen*) to add (*an +acc* to) **(c)** (= *beschäftigen*) to employ, to take on; **jdn zu etw ~** (*inf*) to get sb to do sth; *siehe auch* **angestellt** **(d)** (= *anmachen, andrehen*) to turn on; (= *in Gang setzen*) to start **(e)** *Betrachtung, Vermutung, Vergleich* to make; **(neue) Überlegungen ~(, wie ...)** to (re)consider (how ...) **(f)** (= *machen, unternehmen*) to do; (= *fertig bringen*) to manage; **ich weiß nicht, wie ich es ~ soll** *or* **kann** I don't know how to do/manage it **(g)** (*inf:* = *Unfug treiben*) to get up to; **etwas ~** to get up to mischief; **was hast du da wieder angestellt?** what have you been up to now? ② VR **(a)** (= *Schlange stehen*) to queue (up) (*Brit*), to stand in line **(b)** (*inf:* = *sich verhalten*) to act; **sich dumm/ungeschickt ~** to be stupid/clumsy; **sich geschickt ~** to go about sth well **(c)** (*inf:* = *sich zieren*) to make a fuss; **stell dich nicht so an!** don't make such a fuss!; (= *sich dumm ~*) don't act so stupid!

Anstellung F employment

Anstellungsverhältnis NT contractual relationship between employer and employee; **im** *or* **mit ~** under contract; **im ~ sein** to be under contract

ansteuern VT SEP to make *or* head (*auch hum*) for; (*lit, fig*) *Kurs* to follow

Anstich M (*von Fass*) tapping; (= *erstes Glas*) first draught (*Brit*) *or* draft (*US*); (= *erster Spatenstich*) digging the first sod

Anstieg ['anʃti:k] M **-(e)s, -e** [-gə] **(a)** (= *Aufstieg*) ascent **(b)** (*von Straße*) incline; (*von Temperatur, Kosten, Preisen etc*) rise, increase (*+gen* in)

anstiften VT SEP (= *anzetteln*) to instigate; (= *verursachen*) to cause; **jdn zu etw ~** to incite sb to (do) sth

anstimmen SEP ■ VT **(a)** (*singen*) to begin singing; (*Chorleiter*) *Grundton* to give; (*spielen*) to start playing; (*Kapelle*) to strike up **(b)** (*fig*) **ein Geheul/Geschrei/Proteste** *etc* **~** to start whining/crying/protesting *etc* ② VI to give the keynote

Anstoß M **(a) den (ersten) ~ zu etw geben** to initiate sth; **den ~ zu weiteren Forschungen geben** to give the impetus to further research; **jdm den ~ geben, etw zu tun** to induce sb to do sth; **den ~ zu etw bekommen, den ~ bekommen, etw zu tun** to be encouraged to do sth; **es bedurfte eines neuen ~es** new impetus was needed **(b)** (*Sport*) kickoff; (*Hockey*) bully-off **(c)** (= *Ärgernis*) annoyance (*für* to); **~ erregen** to cause offence (*Brit*) *or* offense (*US*) (*bei* to); **ein Stein des ~es** (= *umstrittene Sache*) a bone of contention; **die ungenaue Formulierung des Vertrags war ein ständiger Stein des ~es** the inexact formulation of the contract was a constant obstacle

anstoßen SEP IRREG ■ VI **(a)** AUX SEIN **an etw** (*acc*) **~** to bump into sth; **mit dem Kopf an etw** (*acc*) **~** to bump one's head on sth; **mit der Zunge ~** to lisp **(b) (mit den Gläsern) ~** to clink glasses; **auf jdn/etw ~** to drink to sb/sth

(c) (*Sport*) to kick off; (*Hockey*) to bully off
(d) (= *angrenzen*) **an etw** (*acc*) ~ to adjoin sth
2 VT *jdn* to knock (into); (*mit dem Fuß*) to kick; (= *in Bewegung setzen*) to give a push; *Kugel, Ball* to hit; **sich** (*dat*) **den Kopf/ Fuß** *etc* ~ to bang one's head/foot *etc*

Anstößer [ˈanʃtøːsɐ] M **-s, -**, **Anstößerin** [-ərɪn] F **-, -nen** (*Sw:* = *Anwohner*) (local) resident

anstößig [ˈanʃtøːsɪç] **1** ADJ offensive; *Kleidung* indecent **2** ADV offensively; *gekleidet, aufgemacht* shockingly

anstrahlen VT SEP to floodlight; (*im Theater*) to spotlight; (= *strahlend ansehen*) to beam at; **das Gebäude wird rot/von Scheinwerfern angestrahlt** the building is lit with a red light/ is floodlit

anstreben VT SEP to strive for

anstreichen VT SEP IRREG **(a)** (*mit Farbe etc*) to paint
(b) (= *markieren*) to mark; **(jdm) etw als Fehler** ~ to mark sth wrong (for sb); **er hat das angestrichen** (*als Fehler*) he marked it wrong; **er hat nichts angestrichen** he didn't mark anything wrong

Anstreicher [ˈanʃtraiçɐ] M **-s, -**, **Anstreicherin** [-ərɪn] F **-, -nen** (house) painter

anstrengen [ˈanʃtrɛŋən] SEP **1** VT **(a)** *Augen* to strain; *Muskel, Gehirn, Geist* to exert; *jdn* to tire out; *esp Patienten* to fatigue; **das viele Lesen strengt meine Augen/mich an** all this reading puts a strain on my eyes/is a strain (for me); **alle Kräfte** ~ to use all one's strength *or* (*geistig*) faculties; **sein Gedächtnis** ~ to rack one's brains; **streng doch mal deinen Verstand ein bisschen an** think hard; *siehe auch* **angestrengt**
(b) (*Jur*) **eine Klage/einen Prozess** ~ to institute proceedings (*gegen* against)
2 VR to make an effort; **sich mehr/sehr** ~ to make more of an effort/a big effort; **unsere Gastgeberin hatte sich sehr angestrengt** our hostess had gone to a lot of trouble

anstrengend ADJ (*körperlich*) strenuous; (*geistig*) demanding; (= *erschöpfend*) exhausting; **das ist ~ für die Augen** it's a strain on the eyes

Anstrengung F **-, -en** effort; (= *Strapaze*) strain; **große ~en machen** to make every effort; **~en machen, etw zu tun** to make an effort to do sth; **mit äußerster/letzter** ~ with very great/one last effort

Anstrich M (= *das Anmalen, Tünchen*) painting; (= *Farbüberzug*) paint; **ein zweiter** ~ a second coat of paint

anstückeln VT SEP *Stück* to attach (*an* +*acc* to); **etw (an etw** *acc*) ~ to add sth (onto sth)

Ansturm M onslaught; (= *Andrang: auf Kaufhaus etc*) rush; (= *Menschenmenge*) crowd

ansuchen VI SEP (*dated, Aus*) **bei jdm um etw** ~ (= *bitten um*) to ask sb for sth; (= *beantragen*) to apply to sb for sth

Ansuchen [ˈanzuːxn] NT **-s, -** (*dated, Aus*) request; (= *Gesuch*) application; **auf jds** (*acc*) at sb's request

Antagonismus [antagoˈnɪsmʊs] M **-**, **Antagonismen** [-mən] antagonism

antagonistisch [antagoˈnɪstɪʃ] ADJ antagonistic

antanzen VI SEP AUX SEIN (*fig inf*) to turn up (*inf*)

Antarktika [antˈlarktika] F **-**, NO PL Antarctica

Antarktis [antˈlarktɪs] F **-**, NO PL Antarctic

antarktisch [antˈlarktɪʃ] ADJ antarctic

antasten VT SEP **(a)** (= *verletzen*) *Ehre, Würde* to offend; *Rechte* to infringe; (= *anbrechen*) *Vorräte, Ersparnisse etc* to break into
(b) (= *berühren*) to touch; (*fig*) *Thema, Frage* to touch on

Anteil M **(a)** (*auch Fin*) share; **er hat bei dem Unternehmen ~e von 30%** he has a 30% share in the company
(b) (= *Beteiligung*) ~ **an etw** (*dat*) **haben** (= *beitragen*) to make a contribution to sth; (= *teilnehmen*) to take part in sth
(c) (= *Teilnahme: an Leid etc*) sympathy (*an* +*dat* with); **an etw** (*dat*) ~ **nehmen** *an Leid etc* to be deeply sympathetic over sth; *an Freude etc* to share in sth; **sie nahmen alle an dem Tod seiner Frau** ~ they all felt deeply for him when his wife died; **sie nahmen alle an seinem Leid** ~ they all felt for him in his sorrow
(d) (= *Interesse*) interest (*an* +*dat* in); **regen ~ an etw** (*dat*) **nehmen/zeigen** *or* **bekunden** (*geh*) to take/show a lively interest in sth

anteilig, anteilmäßig **1** ADJ proportionate **2** ADV proportionately

Anteilnahme [-naːmə] F **-**, NO PL (= *Beileid*) sympathy (*an* +*dat* with)

Anteilschein M (*Fin:* = *Aktie*) share certificate

Anteilseigner [-aignɐ] M **-s, -**, **Anteilseignerin** [-ərɪn] F **-, -nen** (*Fin:* = *Aktionär*) shareholder, stockholder (*esp US*)

anteilsmäßig ADJ, ADV = **anteilig**

Antenne [anˈtɛnə] F **-, -n** (*Rad*) aerial; (*Zool*) feeler, antenna; **eine/keine** ~ **für etw haben** (*fig inf*) to have a/no feeling for sth

Anthropologe [antropoˈloːgə] M **-n, -n**, **Anthropologin** [-ˈloːgɪn] F **-, -nen** anthropologist

Anthropologie [antropoloˈgiː] F **-**, NO PL anthropology

anthropologisch [antropoˈloːgɪʃ] **1** ADJ anthropological **2** ADV anthropologically

Anthroposoph [antropoˈzoːf] M **-en, -en**, **Anthroposophin** [-ˈzoːfɪn] F **-, -nen** anthroposophist

Anthroposophie [antropozoˈfiː] F **-**, NO PL anthroposophy

anthroposophisch [antropoˈzoːfɪʃ] **1** ADJ anthroposophic **2** ADV **jdn** ~ **erziehen** to raise sb according to anthroposophic ideals; ~ **angehaucht** influenced by anthroposophy

Anti- [anti] PREF anti; **Antialkoholiker(in)** M(F) teetota(l)ler; **Antiamerikanismus** M, NO PL anti-Americanism; **antiautoritär** **1** ADJ anti-authoritarian **2** ADV ~ **eingestellt sein** to be anti-authoritarian; **jdn** ~ **erziehen** to raise sb using anti-authoritarian methods; **Antibabypille** F (*inf*) contraceptive pill; **Antibiotikum** [antiˈbioːtikʊm] NT **-s, Antibiotika** [-ka] antibiotic; **Antiblockier(brems)system** [antiblɔˈkiːɐ-] NT (*Aut*) antilock braking system; **antidemokratisch** ADJ antidemocratic; **Antidepressivum** [antidepreˈsiːvʊm] NT **-s, Antidepressiva** [-va] antidepressant

Antifa [ˈantifa] ABBR *von* **Antifaschismus** antifascism

Anti-: Antifaschismus M antifascism; **antifaschistisch** **1** ADJ antifascist **2** ADV ~ **erzogen werden** to be raised to be antifascist; ~ **orientiert sein** to be antifascist; **sich** ~ **geben** to pose as an antifascist; **Antihistamin** NT antihistamine

antik [anˈtiːk] ADJ **(a)** (*Hist*) ancient; **der ~e Mensch** man in the ancient world **(b)** (*Comm inf*) antique

Antike [anˈtiːkə] F **-**, NO PL antiquity; **die Kunst der** ~ the art of the ancient world

Anti-: Antiklopfmittel [antiˈklɔpf-] NT (*Tech*) antiknock (mixture); **antikommunistisch** **1** ADJ anti-Communist **2** ADV ~ **eingestellt** *or* **gesinnt sein** to be anti-Communist; **Antikörper** M (*Med*) antibody

Antilope [antiˈloːpə] F **-, -n** antelope

Antipathie [antipaˈtiː] F **-, -n** [-ˈtiːən] antipathy (*gegen* to)

Antipode [antiˈpoːdə] M **-n, -n** (*lit*) antipodean; (*fig*) adversary; **die Engländer sind die ~n Australiens** the English live on the opposite side of the world from Australia

antippen VT SEP to tap; *Pedal, Bremse* to touch; (*fig*) *Thema* to touch on; **jdn** ~ to tab sb on the shoulder/arm *etc*; **bei jdm** ~**(, ob ...)** (*inf*) to sound sb out (as to whether ...)

Antiquariat [antikvaˈriaːt] NT **-(e)s, -e** (= *Laden*) antiquarian *or* (*modernerer Bücher*) second-hand bookshop; (= *Abteilung*) antiquarian/second-hand department; **modernes** ~ remainder bookshop/department

antiquarisch [antiˈkvaːrɪʃ] **1** ADJ antiquarian; (*von moderneren Büchern*) second-hand **2** ADV second-hand

antiquiert [antiˈkviːɐt] ADJ (*pej*) antiquated

Antiquität [antikviˈtɛːt] F **-, -en** USU PL antique

Antiquitäten-: Antiquitätengeschäft NT antique shop; **Antiquitätenhandel** M antique trade; **Antiquitätenhändler(in)** M(F) antique dealer

Anti-: Antirakete F, **Antiraketenrakete** F anti(missile) missile; **Antisatellitenwaffe** F antisatellite weapon; **Antisemit(in)** M(F) anti-Semite; **antisemitisch** **1** ADJ anti-Semitic **2** ADV anti-Semitically; ~ **eingestellt sein** to be anti-Semitic; **sich** ~ **äußern** to make anti-Semitic remarks; **Antisemitismus** [antizemiˈtɪsmʊs] M **-**, NO PL antisemitism; **antiseptisch** **1** ADJ antiseptic **2** ADV antiseptically; **antistatisch** **1** ADJ antistatic **2** ADV **etw** ~ **behandeln** to treat sth with an antistatic agent; **Antiteilchen** NT (*Phys*) antiparticle

Antiterror- IN CPDS antiterrorist; **Antiterroreinheit** F antiterrorist unit

Anti-: Antithese F antithesis; **Anti-Viren-Software** [antiˈviːrən-] F (*Comput*) anti-virus software; **antizyklisch 1** ADJ anticyclical **2** ADV ~ **verlaufen** to be anticyclical

Antonym [antoˈnyːm] NT **-s, -e** antonym

antörnen [ˈantœrnən] SEP (*sl*) **1** VT (*Drogen, Musik*) to turn on (*inf*) **2** VI **das törnt an** it turns you on (*inf*)

Antrag [ˈantraːk] M **-(e)s, Anträge** [-trɛːɡə] **(a)** (*auf +acc* for) application; (= *Gesuch*) request; (= *Formular*) application form; **einen ~ auf etw** (*acc*) **stellen** to make an application for sth; **auf ~ +gen** at the request of **(b)** (*Jur*) petition; (= *Forderung bei Gericht*) claim; **einen ~ auf etw** (*acc*) **stellen** to file a petition/claim for sth **(c)** (*Parl*) motion; **einen ~ auf etw** (*acc*) **stellen** to propose a motion for sth **(d)** (= *Heiratsantrag*) proposal; **jdm einen ~ machen** to propose (marriage) to sb

Antragsformular NT application form

Antragsteller [-ʃtɛle] M **-s, -, Antragstellerin** [-ərɪn] F **-, -nen** claimant; (*für Kredit etc*) applicant

antreffen VT SEP IRREG to find; **er ist schwer anzutreffen** it's difficult to catch him in

antreiben SEP IRREG **1** VT **(a)** (= *vorwärts treiben, bewegen*) to drive; (*fig*) to urge; **jdn zur Eile/Arbeit ~** to urge sb to hurry up/to work; **ich lasse mich nicht ~** I won't be pushed **(b)** (= *anschwemmen*) to wash up; **etw ans Ufer ~** to wash up (up) on to the bank **2** VI AUX SEIN to wash up

antreten SEP IRREG **1** VT *Reise, Strafe* to begin; *Stellung* to take up; *Lehrzeit* to start; *Erbe, Erbschaft* to come into; **den Beweis ~** to offer proof; **den Beweis ~, dass ...** to prove that ...; **seine Amtszeit ~** to take office; **die Regierung ~** to come to power **2** VI AUX SEIN **(a)** (= *sich aufstellen*) to line up **(b)** (= *erscheinen*) to assemble; (*bei einer Stellung*) to start; (*zum Dienst*) to report **(c)** (*zum Wettkampf*) to compete

Antrieb M **(a)** impetus *no pl*; (*innerer*) drive; **jdm ~/neuen ~ geben, etw zu tun** to give sb the impetus/a new impetus to do sth; **aus eigenem ~** on one's own initiative **(b)** (= *Triebkraft*) drive; **Auto mit elektrischem ~** electrically powered car; **welchen ~ hat das Auto?** how is the car powered?

Antriebs-: Antriebsaggregat NT (*Tech*) drive unit; **antriebslos** ADJ (= *träge*) lacking in drive; **Antriebsrad** NT drive wheel; **antriebsschwach** ADJ (*Psych*) lacking in drive; **Antriebsschwäche** F (*Med*) lack of drive *or* motivation; **antriebsstark** ADJ (*Psych*) full of drive; **Antriebswelle** F drive shaft

antrinken VT SEP IRREG (*inf*) to start drinking; **sich** (*dat*) **einen** *or* **einen Rausch/Schwips ~** to get (oneself) drunk/tipsy; **sich** (*dat*) **Mut ~** to give oneself Dutch courage; **eine angetrunkene Flasche** an opened bottle; *siehe auch* **angetrunken**

Antritt M, NO PL (= *Beginn*) beginning; **bei ~ der Reise** when beginning one's journey; **nach ~ der Stellung/des Amtes/der Erbschaft/der Regierung** after taking up the position/ assuming office/coming into the inheritance/coming into power

antun VT SEP IRREG **(a)** (= *erweisen*) **jdm etw ~** to do sth for sb; **jdm etwas Gutes ~** to do sb a good turn **(b)** (= *zufügen*) **jdm etw ~** to do sth to sb; **das könnte ich ihr nicht ~** I couldn't do that to her; **sich** (*dat*) **etwas ~** (*euph*) to do away with oneself; **tu mir das nicht an!** don't do this to me! **(c)** (*Aus*) **sich** (*dat*) **etwas ~** (= *sich aufregen*) to get excited; (= *sich Mühe geben*) to take a lot of trouble; *siehe auch* **angetan**

Antwort [ˈantvɔrt] F **-, -en (a)** answer; **sie gab mir keine ~** she didn't reply (to me) *or* answer (me); **sie gab mir keine ~ auf die Frage** she didn't reply to *or* answer my question; **in ~ auf etw** (*acc*) (*form*) in reply to sth; **etw zur ~ bekommen** to receive sth as a response; **etw zur ~ geben** to give sb sth as a response; **um umgehende ~ wird gebeten** please reply by return; **um ~ wird gebeten** (*auf Einladungen*) RSVP; **keine ~ ist auch eine ~** (*Prov*) your silence is answer enough **(b)** (= *Reaktion*) response; **als ~ auf etw** (*acc*) in response to sth; **die deutsche ~ auf Hollywood** (= *Entsprechung*) Germany's answer to Hollywood

Antwortbrief M reply, answer

antworten [ˈantvɔrtn] VI **(a)** (= *Antwort geben*) to answer, to reply; **jdm ~** to answer sb, to reply to sb; **auf etw** (*acc*) **~** to

answer sth, to reply to sth; **was soll ich ihm ~?** what should I tell him?; **jdm auf eine Frage ~** to reply to *or* answer sb's question; **mit Ja/Nein ~** to answer yes/no **(b)** (= *reagieren*) to respond (*auf +acc* to, *mit* with)

Antwort-: Antwortschein M (international) reply coupon; **Antwortschreiben** NT reply, answer

anvertrauen *ptp* **anvertraut** SEP **1** VT **(a)** (= *übergeben, anheim stellen*) **jdm etw ~** to entrust sth to sb **(b)** (= *vertraulich erzählen*) **jdm etw ~** to confide sth to sb; **etw seinem Tagebuch ~** to confide sth to one's diary **2** VR **sich jdm ~** (= *sich mitteilen*) to confide in sb; (= *sich in jds Schutz begeben*) to entrust oneself to sb

anwachsen VI SEP IRREG AUX SEIN **(a)** (= *festwachsen*) to grow on; (*Haut*) to take; (*Pflanze etc*) to take root **(b)** (= *zunehmen*) to increase (*auf +acc* to)

Anwalt [ˈanvalt] M **-(e)s, Anwälte** [-vɛltə], **Anwältin** [-vɛltɪn] F **-, -nen (a)** *siehe* **Rechtsanwalt (b)** (*fig*: = *Fürsprecher*) advocate

Anwaltsbüro NT **(a)** lawyer's office **(b)** (= *Firma*) firm of solicitors (*Brit*) *or* lawyers

Anwalts-: Anwaltsgebühr F lawyer's fees *pl*; **Anwaltskammer** F professional association of lawyers, ≈ Law Society (*Brit*); **Anwaltskosten** PL legal expenses *pl*; **Anwaltspraxis** F legal practice; (= *Räume*) lawyer's office

Anwandlung F (*von Furcht etc*) feeling; (= *Laune*) mood; (= *Drang*) impulse; **aus einer ~ heraus** on (an) impulse; **in einer ~ von Freigebigkeit** *etc* in a fit of generosity *etc*; **dann bekam er wieder seine ~en** (*inf*) then he had one of his fits again

anwärmen VT SEP to warm up

Anwärter(in) M(F) (= *Kandidat*) candidate (*auf +acc* for); (*Sport*) contender (*auf +acc* for); (= *Thronanwärter*) heir (*auf +acc* to)

Anwartschaft [ˈanvartʃaft] F **-, NO PL** candidature; (*Sport*) contention; **seine ~ auf den Titel anmelden** to say one is in contention for the title; **~ auf den Thron** claim to the throne

anweisen VT SEP IRREG **(a)** (= *anleiten, beauftragen, befehlen*) to instruct **(b)** (= *zuweisen*) (*jdm etw* sb sth) to allocate; *Zimmer* to give; **jdm einen Platz ~** to show sb to a seat **(c)** *Geld* to transfer; *siehe auch* **angewiesen**

Anweisung F **(a)** (*Fin*) payment; (*auf Konto etc*) transfer; (= *Formular*) payment slip; (= *Postanweisung*) postal order **(b)** (= *Anordnung*) instruction; **eine ~ befolgen** to follow an instruction; **~ haben, etw zu tun** to have instructions to do sth **(c)** (= *Zuweisung*) allocation **(d)** (= *Anleitung*) instructions *pl*

anwendbar ADJ *Produkt* usable; *Theorie, Regel* applicable (*auf +acc* to); **die Methode ist auch hier ~** the method can also be applied here; **das ist in der Praxis nicht ~** that is not practicable

anwenden VT SEP AUCH IRREG **(a)** (= *gebrauchen*) *Methode, Mittel, Technik, Gewalt* to use (*auf +acc* on); *Sorgfalt, Mühe* to take (*auf +acc* over) **(b)** *Theorie, Prinzipien, Regel* to apply (*auf +acc* to); *Erfahrung, Einfluss* to use (*auf +acc* on); **sich auf etw** (*acc*) **~ lassen** to be applicable to sth

Anwender [ˈanvɛndɐ] M **-s, -, Anwenderin** [-ərɪn] F **-, -nen** (*Comput*) user

Anwender-: Anwenderprogramm NT user *or* application program; **Anwendersoftware** F user *or* applications software

Anwendung F **(a)** (= *Gebrauch*) use (*auf +acc* on); (*von Sorgfalt, Mühe*) taking; **zur ~ gelangen** *or* **kommen** (*form*), **~ finden** (*form*) to be applied **(b)** (*von Theorie, Prinzipien, Regel*) application (*auf +acc* to); (*von Erfahrung, Einfluss*) bringing to bear (*auf +acc* on) **(c)** (*Comput*) application

anwerben VT SEP IRREG to recruit (*für* to); **sich ~ lassen** to enlist

anwerfen VT SEP IRREG (*Tech*) to start up; *Propeller* to swing; (*inf*) *Gerät* to switch on

Anwesen NT (*geh*) estate

anwesend [ˈanveːznt] ADJ present; **die nicht ~en Mitglieder** the members who are not present; **~ sein** to be present (*bei, auf +dat* at); **ich war nicht ganz ~** (*hum inf*) my thoughts were elsewhere

Anwesende(r) [ˈanveːzndə] MF DECL AS ADJ person present; **die ~n** those present; **jeder ~** everyone present; **alle ~n** all those present; **~ ausgenommen** present company excepted

Anwesenheit [ˈanveːznhaɪt] F **-, NO PL** presence; **in ~ +gen** *or* **von** in the presence of

Anwesenheits-: Anwesenheitsliste F attendance list; **Anwesenheitspflicht** F obligation to attend

anwidern ['anviːdɐn] VT SEP **jdn ~** (*Essen, Anblick*) to make sb feel sick; **es/er widert mich an** I can't stand it/him; **er wandte sich angewidert ab** he turned away in disgust

Anwohner ['anvoːnɐ] M **-s, -**, **Anwohnerin** [-ərɪn] F **-, -nen** resident; **die ~ des Rheins** the people who live on the Rhine

anwurzeln VI SEP AUX SEIN to take root; **wie angewurzelt dastehen/stehen bleiben** to stand rooted to the spot

Anzahl F, NO PL number; **eine ganze ~** quite a number

anzahlen VT SEP *Ware* to pay a deposit on; **einen Betrag/100 Euro ~** to pay an amount/100 euros as a deposit

Anzahlung F deposit (*für, auf +acc* on); (= *erste Rate*) first instalment (*Brit*) *or* installment (*US*); **eine ~ machen** *or* **leisten** (*form*) to pay a deposit

anzapfen VT SEP *Fass* to broach; *Fluss* to breach; *Baum, Telefon, elektrische Leitung* to tap; **jdn ~** (*Telec inf*) to tap sb's phone

Anzeichen NT sign; (*Med auch*) symptom; **alle ~ deuten darauf hin, dass ...** all the signs are that ...

Anzeige ['antsaigə] F **-, -n** (a) (*bei Behörde*) report (*wegen* of); (*bei Gericht*) legal proceedings *pl*; **gegen jdn ~ erstatten** to report sb to the authorities; **wegen etw (eine) ~ bei der Polizei erstatten** *or* **machen** to report sth to the police **(b)** (= *Bekanntgabe*) (*auf Karte, Brief*) announcement; (*in Zeitung*) notice; (= *Inserat, Reklame*) advertisement **(c)** (= *das Anzeigen: von Temperatur, Geschwindigkeit etc*) indication; (= *Messwerte*) reading; (*auf Informationstafel*) information **(d)** (= *~tafel, Comput*) display

anzeigen VT SEP **(a)** (= *angeben*) to show **(b)** (= *bekannt geben*) to announce; *Richtung* to indicate **(c)** (*Comput*) to display **(d) jdn ~** (*bei der Polizei*) to report sb (to the police); (*bei Gericht*) to institute legal proceedings against sb; **sich selbst ~** to give oneself up

Anzeigen-: Anzeigenbeilage F advertising supplement; **Anzeigenblatt** NT advertiser, freesheet; **Anzeigenkampagne** F advertising campaign; **Anzeigenteil** M advertisement section

Anzeiger M **(a)** (*Tech*) indicator **(b)** (= *Zeitung*) advertiser

Anzeigetafel F indicator board; (*Sport*) scoreboard

anzetteln ['antsetln] VT SEP to instigate; *Unsinn* to cause

anziehen SEP IRREG ![1] VT **(a)** *Kleidung* to put on; **sich** (*dat*) **etw ~** to put sth on; **angezogen** dressed **(b)** (= *straffen*) to pull (tight); *Bremse* (= *betätigen*) to put on; (= *härter einstellen*) to adjust; *Zügel* to pull; *Saite, Schraube* to tighten **(c)** (*lit*) *Geruch, Feuchtigkeit* to absorb; (*Magnet, fig*) to attract; **sich von etw angezogen fühlen** to feel drawn by sth ![2] VI **(a)** (= *sich in Bewegung setzen*) to start moving; (= *beschleunigen*) to accelerate **(b)** (*Fin: Preise, Aktien*) to rise **(c)** AUX SEIN (= *heranziehen*) to approach; **aus vielen Ländern angezogen kommen** to come from far and near ![3] VR **(a)** (= *sich kleiden*) to get dressed **(b)** (*fig*) (*Menschen*) to be attracted to each other; (*Gegensätze*) to attract

anziehend ADJ (= *ansprechend*) attractive; (= *sympathisch*) pleasant

Anziehung F, NO PL attraction; **die Stadt hat eine große ~ für sie** she is very attracted to the town

Anziehungskraft F (*Phys*) force of attraction; (*fig*) attraction; **eine große ~ auf jdn ausüben** to attract sb strongly

Anzug M **(a)** (= *Herrenanzug*) suit **(b)** (*Sw: = Bezug*) cover **(c)** (= *das Heranrücken*) approach; **im ~ sein** to be coming; (*Mil*) to be advancing; (*fig*) (*Gewitter, Gefahr*) to be imminent; (*Krankheit*) to be coming on **(d)** (*von Auto etc*) acceleration

anzüglich ['antsyːklɪç] ![1] ADJ suggestive; **~ werden** to start making suggestive remarks; **er ist mir gegenüber immer so ~** he always makes suggestive remarks to me ![2] ADV suggestively

anzünden VT SEP *Feuer* to light; **das Haus** *etc* **~** to set fire to the house *etc*

Anzünder M lighter

anzweifeln VT SEP to question

anzwinkern VT SEP to wink at

AOK [aːloːˈkaː] F **-, -s** ABBR *von* **Allgemeine Ortskrankenkasse**

AOK

The **AOK** - short for *Allgemeine Ortskrankenkasse* - is the largest state health insurance scheme in Germany. Almost half of all employees are insured by it. In every large town there is an independently run **AOK** office. Foreign nationals may also receive help from these offices if they fall ill while in Germany.

Aorta [aˈɔrta] F **-, Aorten** [-tn] aorta

apart [aˈpart] ![1] ADJ distinctive ![2] ADV (= *schick*) stylishly

Apartheid [aˈpaːethait] F **-, NO PL** apartheid

Apartment [aˈpartmənt] NT **-s, -s** flat (*Brit*), apartment

Apartment-: Apartmenthaus NT block of flats (*Brit*), apartment house (*esp US*); **Apartmentwohnung** F flat (*Brit*), apartment

Apathie [apaˈtiː] F **-, -n** [-ˈtiːən] apathy; (*von Patienten*) listlessness

apathisch [aˈpaːtɪʃ] ![1] ADJ apathetic; *Patient* listless ![2] ADV apathetically; (= *matt*) listlessly

aper ['aːpɐ] ADJ (*Sw, Aus, S Ger*) snowless

Aperitif [aperiˈtiːf] M **-s, -s** *or* **-e** aperitif

Apfel ['apfl] M **-s, -̈** ['ɛpfl] apple; **in den sauren ~ beißen** (*fig inf*) to bite the bullet; **etw für einen ~ und ein Ei kaufen** (*inf*) to buy sth dirt cheap (*inf*); **der ~ fällt nicht weit vom Stamm** (*Prov*) it's in the blood

Apfel- IN CPDS apple; **Apfelbaum** M apple tree; **Apfelblüte** F **(a)** apple blossom **(b)** (= *das Blühen*) blossoming of the apple trees; **zur Zeit der ~ geboren** born when the apple trees were in blossom; **Apfelkompott** NT stewed apple, apple compote; **Apfelkuchen** M apple cake; **Apfelmost** M apple juice; **Apfelmus** NT apple purée *or* (*als Beilage*) sauce; **Apfelsaft** M apple juice; **Apfelsaftschorle** F *apple juice and sparkling mineral water*

Apfelsine [apflˈziːnə] F **-, -n** orange; (= *Baum*) orange tree

Apfel-: Apfelstrudel M apple strudel; **Apfeltasche** F apple turnover; **Apfelwein** M cider

Aphorismus [afoˈrɪsmʊs] M **-, Aphorismen** [-mən] aphorism

aphoristisch [afoˈrɪstɪʃ] ADJ aphoristic

Aphrodisiakum [afrodiˈziːakʊm] NT **-s, Aphrodisiaka** [-ka] aphrodisiac

Apokalypse [apokaˈlʏpsə] F **-, -n** apocalypse

apokalyptisch [apokaˈlʏptɪʃ] ADJ apocalyptic

Apostel [aˈpɔstl] M **-s, -** apostle

Apostel-: Apostelbrief M epistle; **Apostelgeschichte** F Acts of the Apostles *pl*

Apostroph [apoˈstroːf] M **-s, -e** apostrophe

apostrophieren [apostroˈfiːrən], *ptp* **apostrophiert** VT (*Gram*) to apostrophize

Apotheke [apoˈteːkə] F **-, -n** **(a)** (dispensing) chemist's (*Brit*), pharmacy **(b)** (= *Hausapotheke*) medicine cupboard; (= *Reiseapotheke, Autoapotheke*) first-aid box

apothekenpflichtig [-pflɪçtɪç] ADJ available only at a chemist's shop (*Brit*) *or* pharmacy

Apotheker [apoˈteːkɐ] M **-s, -**, **Apothekerin** [-ərɪn] F **-, -nen** pharmacist, (dispensing) chemist (*Brit*)

Apparat [apaˈraːt] M **-(e)s, -e** **(a)** apparatus *no pl*, appliance; (= *esp kleineres, technisches, mechanisches Gerät*) gadget; (= *Röntgenapparat etc*) machine **(b)** (= *Radio*) radio; (= *Fernseher*) set; (= *Rasierapparat*) razor; (= *Fotoapparat*) camera **(c)** (= *Telefon*) (tele)phone; (= *Anschluss*) extension; **am ~** on the phone; (*als Antwort*) speaking; **wer war am ~?** who did you speak to?; **jdn am ~ verlangen** to ask to speak to sb; **bleiben Sie am ~!** hold the line **(d)** (*inf: = unbestimmter Gegenstand*) thing **(e)** (*sl: = Penis*) tool (*sl*); **einen geilen ~ haben** to be well-hung (*inf*) **(f)** (= *Personen und Hilfsmittel*) setup; (= *Verwaltungsapparat, Parteiapparat, technischer etc*) apparatus

Apparatemedizin F (*pej*) hi-tech medicine

Apparatur [apaˈratuːɐ] F **-, -en** **(a)** equipment *no pl*, apparatus *no pl*; **~en** pieces of equipment; **eine ~** a piece of equipment **(b)** (*fig Pol*) apparatus

Appartement [apartə'mãː] NT **-s, -s (a)** (= *Wohnung*) flat (*Brit*), apartment **(b)** (= *Zimmerflucht*) suite

Appel ['apl] M **-s,** ⁼ ['epl] (*N Ger*: = *Apfel*) apple; **für 'n ~ und 'n Ei** (*inf*) for peanuts (*inf*)

Appell [a'pɛl] M **-s, -e (a)** (= *Aufruf*) appeal (*an* +*acc* to, *zu* for); **einen ~ an jdn richten** to (make an) appeal to sb **(b)** (*Mil*) roll call; **zum ~ antreten** to line up for roll call

Appellation [apela'tsioːn] F **-, -en** (*Sw Jur*) appeal

appellieren [apɛ'liːrən], *ptp* **appelliert** VI to appeal (*an* +*acc* to)

Appenzell [apn'tsɛl, 'apntsɛl] NT **-s** Appenzell

Appetit [ape'tiːt] M **-(e)s,** NO PL (*lit, fig*) appetite; **~ auf etw** (*acc*) **haben** (*lit, fig*) to feel like sth; **jdm ~ auf etw** (*acc*) **machen** to whet sb's appetite for sth; **guten ~!** enjoy your meal; **jdm den ~ verderben** to spoil sb's appetite; (*inf: Witz etc*) to make sb feel sick; **jdm den ~ an etw** (*dat*) **verderben** (*fig*) to put sb off sth; **der ~ kommt beim** *or* **mit dem Essen** (*prov*) appetite grows with the eating (*prov*)

Appetit-: appetitanregend ⚊ ADJ *Speise etc* appetizing; **~es Mittel** appetite stimulant ⚋ ADV **~ wirken** to stimulate the appetite; **Appetithappen** M canapé; **appetithemmend** ⚊ ADJ appetite-suppressing; **~es Mittel** appetite suppressant ⚋ ADV **~ wirken** to curb the appetite; **appetitlich** [ape'tiːtlɪç] ⚊ ADJ (= *lecker*) appetizing; (= *verlockend aussehend, riechend*) tempting; (= *hygienisch*) hygienic, savoury (*Brit*), savory (*US*); (*fig*) *Mädchen, Anblick* attractive ⚋ ADV appetizingly; **Appetitlosigkeit** F **-,** NO PL lack of appetite; **Appetitzügler** [-tsyːgle] M **-s, -** appetite suppressant

applaudieren [aplau'diːrən], *ptp* **applaudiert** VI to applaud; **jdm/einer Sache ~** to applaud sb/sth

Applaus [a'plaus] M **-es** [-zəs], NO PL applause

Applikation [aplika'tsioːn] F **-, -en (a)** (*Comput*) application **(b)** (*Sew*) appliqué

Applikator [apli'kaːtoːɐ] M **-s, Applikatoren** [-'toːrən] (*für Salbe, Make-up*) applicator

apportieren [apɔr'tiːrən], *ptp* **apportiert** VTI to retrieve

appretieren [apre'tiːrən], *ptp* **appretiert** VT (*Tex*) to starch; (= *imprägnieren*) to waterproof; *Holz* to dress; *Papier* to glaze

Appretur [apre'tuːɐ] F **-, -en** (= *Mittel*) finish; (*Tex*) starch; (= *Imprägnierung*) waterproofing; (*für Papier*) glaze

Approbation [aproba'tsioːn] F **-, -en** (*von Arzt, Apotheker*) certificate (*enabling a doctor etc to practise*); **einem Arzt die ~ entziehen** to take away a doctor's licence to practise (*Brit*) *or* license to practice (*US*)

approbiert [apro'biːɐt] ADJ *Arzt, Apotheker* registered

Après-Ski [apre'ʃiː] NT **-, -s** après-ski; (= *Kleidung*) après-ski clothes *pl*

Aprikose [apri'koːzə] F **-, -n** apricot

April [a'prɪl] M **-(s), -e** April; **~, ~!** April fool!; **jdn in den ~ schicken** to make an April fool of sb; *siehe auch* **März**

April-: Aprilscherz M April fool's trick; **das ist doch wohl ein ~** (*fig*) you/they *etc* must be joking; **Aprilwetter** NT April weather

apropos [apro'poː] ADV by the way; **~ Afrika** talking about Africa

Apsis ['apsɪs] F **-, Apsiden** [a'psiːdn] (*Archit*) apse

Aquadrom [akva'droːm] NT **-s, -e** aquadrome

Aquädukt [akvɛ'dʊkt] NT **-(e)s, -e** aqueduct

Aqua-: Aquamarin [akvama'riːn] NT **-s, -e** aquamarine; **aquamarinblau** ADJ aquamarine; **Aquaplaning** [akva'plaːnɪŋ] NT **-s,** NO PL (*Aut*) aquaplaning

Aquarell [akva'rɛl] NT **-s, -e** watercolour (*Brit*) *or* watercolor (*US*) (painting); **~ malen** to paint in watercolours (*Brit*) *or* watercolors (*US*)

Aquarell-: Aquarellfarbe F watercolour (*Brit*), watercolor (*US*); **Aquarellmaler(in)** M(F) watercolourist (*Brit*), watercolorist (*US*); **Aquarellmalerei** F watercolour (*Brit*) *or* watercolor (*US*) (painting)

Aquarien- [a'kvaːriən] IN CPDS aquarium; **Aquarienfisch** M aquarium fish

Aquarium [a'kvaːriʊm] NT **-s, Aquarien** [-riən] aquarium

Äquator [ɛ'kvaːtoːɐ] M **-s,** NO PL equator

äquatorial [ɛkvato'riaːl] ADJ equatorial

Äquatortaufe F (*Naut*) crossing-the-line ceremony

äquivalent [ɛkviva'lɛnt] ADJ equivalent

Äquivalent [ɛkviva'lɛnt] NT **-s, -e** equivalent; (= *Ausgleich*) compensation

Äquivalenz [ɛkviva'lɛnts] F equivalence

Ar [aːɐ] NT *or* M **-s, -e** (*Measure*) are (*100 m²*)

Ära ['ɛːra] F **-, Ären** ['ɛːrən] era; **die ~ Adenauer** the Adenauer era

Araber¹ ['arabɐ, 'aːrabɐ, a'raːbɐ] M **-s, -** (= *Pferd*) Arab

Araber² ['arabɐ, 'aːrabɐ, a'raːbɐ] M **-s, -, Araberin** [-ərɪn] F **-, -nen** Arab

Arabien [a'raːbiən] NT **-s** Arabia

arabisch [a'raːbɪʃ] ADJ Arab; *Ziffer, Sprache, Schrift etc* Arabic; **die Arabische Halbinsel** (*Geog*) the Arabian Peninsula, Arabia

Arabisch(e) [a'raːbɪʃ] NT Arabic; *siehe auch* **Deutsch(e)**

Arabist [ara'bɪst] M **-en, -en, Arabistin** [-'bɪstɪn] F **-, -nen** specialist in Arabic studies; (= *Student*) student of Arabic

Aralsee ['aːra(ː)l-] M Aral Sea

aramäisch [ara'mɛːɪʃ] ADJ Aramaic

Arbeit ['arbait] F **-, -en (a)** (= *Tätigkeit*) (*Phys, Sport*) work; (*Pol, Econ*) labour (*Brit*), labor (*US*); **~ und Kapital** capital and labo(u)r; **Tag der ~** Labo(u)r Day; **die ~en am Stadium** the work on the stadium; **es kann mit den ~en begonnen werden** work can begin; **bei der ~ mit Kindern** when working with children; **~ sparend** labour-saving (*Brit*), labor-saving (*US*); **viel ~ machen** to be a lot of work (*jdm* for sb); **an** *or* **bei der ~ sein** to be working; **sich an die ~ machen, an die ~ gehen** to get down to work; **an die ~!** to work!; **jdm bei der ~ zusehen** to watch sb working; **etw ist in ~** work on sth is in progress; **Ihr Bier ist in ~** (*inf*) your beer is on its way; **etw in ~ haben** to be working on sth; **die ~ läuft dir nicht davon** (*hum*) the work will still be there when you get back; **erst die ~, dann das Vergnügen** (*prov*) business before pleasure (*prov*); **~ schändet nicht** (*Prov*) work is no disgrace **(b)** NO PL (= *Ausführung*) work; **gute** *or* **ganze** *or* **gründliche ~ leisten** (*lit, fig iro*) to do a good job **(c)** NO PL (= *Mühe*) trouble; **jdm ~ machen** to put sb to trouble; **machen Sie sich keine ~!** don't go to any trouble; **das war vielleicht eine ~!** what hard work that was! **(d)** (= *Berufstätigkeit*) (*inf*: = *Arbeitsplatz, Arbeitsstelle, Arbeitszeit*) work *no indef art*; (= *Arbeitsverhältnis*) employment; (= *Position*) job; **eine ~ als etw** work *or* a job as sth; **~ suchend** looking for work *or* a job; **~ Suchende(r)** person/man/woman looking for work *or* a job; **einer (geregelten) ~ nachgehen** to have a (steady) job; **ohne ~ sein** to be out of work; **zur** *or* **auf** (*inf*) **~ gehen** to go to work; **von der ~ kommen** to come back from work **(e)** (= *Aufgabe*) job; **seine ~ besteht darin, zu …** his job is to … **(f)** (= *Produkt*) work; (*handwerkliche*) piece of work; (= *Prüfungsarbeit*) (examination) paper; (*wissenschaftliche*) paper **(g)** (*Sch*) test; **~en korrigieren** to mark test papers; **eine ~ schreiben/schreiben lassen** to do/set a test

arbeiten ['arbaitn] ⚊ VI **(a)** (= *sich betätigen*) to work (*an* +*dat* on); **der Sänger hat viel an sich** (*dat*) **gearbeitet** the singer has worked hard; **~ wie ein Pferd/Wilder** (*inf*) to work like a Trojan/like mad (*inf*); **die Zeit arbeitet für uns** time is on our side; **die Zeit arbeitet gegen uns** time is against us; **er arbeitet für zwei** (*inf*) he does the work of two **(b)** (= *funktionieren: Organ, Maschine*) to work; **die Anlage arbeitet automatisch** the plant is automatic; **die Anlage arbeitet elektrisch/mit Kohle** the plant runs *or* operates on electricity/coal **(c)** (= *berufstätig sein*) to work; **~ gehen** (= *zur Arbeit gehen*) to go to work; (= *einen Arbeitsplatz haben*) to have a job; **für eine** *or* **bei einer Firma/Zeitung ~** to work for a firm/newspaper ⚋ VR **(a) sich krank/müde ~** to make oneself ill/tire oneself out with work; **sich zu Tode ~** to work oneself to death **(b)** (= *sich fortbewegen*) to work oneself (*in +acc* into, *durch* through, *zu* to); **sich in die Höhe** *or* **nach oben/an die Spitze ~** (*fig*) to work one's way up/(up) to the top **(c)** IMPERS **es arbeitet sich gut/schlecht** you can/can't work well; **es arbeitet sich hier auch nicht besser** it's no better working here either; **mit ihr arbeitet es sich angenehm** it's nice working with her ⚌ VT **(a)** (= *herstellen*) to make **(b)** (= *tun*) to do; **was arbeitest du dort?** what are you doing there?; (*beruflich*) what do you do there?; **ich habe heute noch nichts gearbeitet** I haven't done any work today; **du**

kannst auch ruhig mal was ~! (*inf*) it wouldn't hurt you to do some work either!

Arbeiter ['arbaitɐ] M **-s, -**, **Arbeiterin** [-ǝrın] F **-, -nen** worker; (*im Gegensatz zum Angestellten*) blue-collar worker; (*auf Bau, Bauernhof*) labourer (*Brit*), laborer (*US*); (*bei Straßenbau, im Haus*) workman; **~ und ~innen** male and female workers

Arbeiter-: Arbeiterbewegung F labour (*Brit*) or labor (*US*) movement; **arbeiterfeindlich** ADJ anti-working-class; **arbeiterfreundlich** ADJ pro-working-class; **Arbeitergewerkschaft** F blue-collar (trade) union, labor union (*US*)

Arbeiterin F **-, -nen** (a) *siehe* **Arbeiter** (b) (*Zool*) worker

Arbeiter-: Arbeiterklasse F working class(es *pl*); **Arbeiterorganisation** F labour (*Brit*) or labor (*US*) organization; **Arbeiterschaft** ['arbaitɐʃaft] F **-, -en** workforce; **Arbeiterselbstverwaltung** F workers' control; **Arbeiter-und-Bauern-Staat** M (*DDR Hist*) workers' and peasants' state; **Arbeiterviertel** NT working-class area; **Arbeiterwohlfahrt** F workers' welfare association

Arbeitgeber(in) M(F) employer

Arbeitgeber-: Arbeitgeberanteil M employer's contribution; **Arbeitgeberseite** F employers' side; **Arbeitgeberverband** M employers' federation

Arbeitnehmer(in) M(F) employee

Arbeitnehmer-: Arbeitnehmeranteil M employee's contribution; **Arbeitnehmerfreibetrag** M, **Arbeitnehmerpauschale** F (*Fin*) personal or income tax allowance; **Arbeitnehmerschaft** ['arbaitne:mɐʃaft] F **-, -en** employees *pl*; **Arbeitnehmerseite** F employees' side; **Arbeitnehmer(spar)zulage** F bonus on employee saving scheme; **Arbeitnehmervertreter(in)** M(F) employees' representative

Arbeitsablauf M work routine; (*von Fabrik*) production *no art*

arbeitsam ['arbaitzam] ADJ industrious

Arbeits-: Arbeitsamt NT job centre (*Brit*), unemployment office (*US*); **Arbeitsanleitung** F instructions *pl*; **Arbeitsantritt** M commencement of work (*form*); **beim ~** when starting work; **Arbeitsauffassung** F attitude to work; **Arbeitsaufwand** M labour (*Brit*), labor (*US*); **mit geringem/großem ~** with little/a lot of work; **Arbeitsausfall** M loss of working hours; **Arbeitsbedingungen** PL working conditions *pl*; **Arbeitsbeginn** M start of work; **bei ~** when one starts work; **Arbeitsbereich** M (= *Arbeitsgebiet*) field of work; (= *Aufgabenbereich*) area of work; **das gehört nicht in meinen ~** that's not my job; **Arbeitsbeschaffung** F (a) (= *Arbeitsplatzbeschaffung*) job creation (b) (= *Auftragsbeschaffung*) bringing work in *no art*; **Arbeitsbeschaffungsmaßnahme** F (*Admin*) job creation scheme; **Arbeitsbescheinigung** F certificate of employment; **Arbeitseifer** M enthusiasm for one's work; **Arbeitseinheit** F (a) (*Ind*) work group (b) (*Phys*) unit of work (c) (*Comput*) work unit; **Arbeitserlaubnis** F (= *Recht*) permission to work; (= *Bescheinigung*) work permit; **Arbeitserleichterung** F **das bedeutet eine große ~** that makes the work much easier; **Arbeitsersparnis** F labour-saving *no pl* (*Brit*), labor-saving *no pl* (*US*); **die neuen Maschinen bedeuten eine große ~** the new machines are very labour-saving (*Brit*) or labor-saving (*US*); **Arbeitsessen** NT (*mittags*) working lunch; (*abends*) working dinner; **arbeitsfähig** ADJ *Person* able to work; (= *gesund*) fit for work; *Regierung* etc viable; **im ~en Alter sein** to be of working age; **Arbeitsfläche** F work surface; **Arbeitsfriede(n)** M peaceful labour (*Brit*) or labor (*US*) relations *pl*, *no art*; **Arbeitsgang** M, *pl* **-gänge** (a) = *Abschnitt*) operation (b) (= *Arbeitsablauf*) work routine; (*von Fabrik*) production *no art*; **Arbeitsgemeinschaft** F team; (*Sch, Univ*) study group; (*in Namen*) association; **Arbeitsgenehmigung** F (= *Recht*) permission to work; (= *Bescheinigung*) work permit; **Arbeitsgerät** NT (a) (*einzeln*) tool (b) NO PL (*Gesamtheit*) tools *pl*, equipment *no pl*; **Arbeitsgericht** NT industrial tribunal (*Brit*), labor court (*US*); **Arbeitsgruppe** F team; **Arbeitshypothese** F working hypothesis; **Arbeitsinspektion** F (*Aus, Sw*) factory supervision; **arbeitsintensiv** ADJ labour-intensive (*Brit*), labor-intensive (*US*); **Arbeitskampf** M industrial action; **Arbeitskampfmaßnahmen** PL industrial action *sing*; **Arbeitskleidung** F working clothes *pl*; **Arbeitsklima** NT work(ing) atmosphere; **Arbeitskollege** M, **Arbeitskollegin** F (*bei Angestellten etc*) colleague; (*bei Arbeitern auch*) workmate; **Arbeitskosten** PL labour (*Brit*) or labor (*US*)

costs *pl*; **Arbeitskraft** F (a) NO PL capacity for work; **die menschliche ~ ersetzen** to replace human labour (*Brit*) or labor (*US*); **seine ~ verkaufen** to sell one's labour (*Brit*) or labor (*US*) (b) (= *Arbeiter*) worker; **Arbeitskräfte** PL workforce; **Arbeitskreis** M team; (*Sch, Univ*) study group; (*in Namen*) association; **Arbeitslager** NT labour (*Brit*) or labor (*US*) camp; **Arbeitslohn** M wages *pl*, earnings *pl*

arbeitslos ADJ *Mensch* unemployed

Arbeitslosen-: Arbeitslosengeld NT earnings-related unemployment benefit; **Arbeitslosenhilfe** F unemployment benefit; **Arbeitslosenquote** F rate of unemployment; **Arbeitslosenunterstützung** F (*dated*) unemployment benefit, dole (money) (*Brit inf*); **Arbeitslosenversicherung** F ≈ National Insurance (*Brit*), ≈ social insurance (*US*); **Arbeitslosenzahlen** PL, **Arbeitslosenziffer** F unemployment figures *pl*

Arbeitslose(r) ['arbaitslo:zǝ] MF DECL AS ADJ unemployed person/man/woman etc; **die ~n** the unemployed

Arbeitslosigkeit F **-**, NO PL unemployment

Arbeits-: Arbeitsmangel M lack of work; **Arbeitsmarkt** M labour (*Brit*) or labor (*US*) market; **arbeitsmäßig** ① ADJ with respect to work ② ADV professionally; **er ist ~ stark engagiert** he's very involved in his work; **~ ist der Job okay** the work I do is okay; **Arbeitsmaterial** NT material for one's work; (*Sch*) teaching aids *pl*; **Arbeitsmoral** F work ethic; **Arbeitsniederlegung** F walkout; **Arbeitsort** M, *pl* **-orte** place of work; **Arbeitspapier** NT (a) (*esp Pol*) working paper (b) (*von Arbeitnehmer*) **Arbeitspapiere** PL cards *pl*

arbeitsparend ADJ *siehe* **Arbeit**

Arbeits-: Arbeitspensum NT quota of work; **Arbeitsplatte** F worktop

Arbeitsplatz M (a) (= *Arbeitsstätte*) workplace; **am ~** at work; **Demokratie am ~** industrial democracy (b) (*in Fabrik*) work station; (*in Büro*) workspace; **die Bibliothek hat 75 Arbeitsplätze** the library has room for 75 people to work (c) (= *Stelle*) job; **freie Arbeitsplätze** vacancies

Arbeitsplatz-: Arbeitsplatzabbau M job cuts *pl*; **Arbeitsplatzbeschreibung** F job description; **Arbeitsplatzsicherung** F safeguarding of jobs; **Arbeitsplatzteilung** F job sharing

Arbeits-: Arbeitsprobe F sample of one's work; **Arbeitsprozess** M work process; **Arbeitsraum** M workroom; (*für geistige Arbeit*) study; **Arbeitsrecht** NT industrial law; **arbeitsrechtlich** ADJ *Streitfall, Angelegenheit* concerning industrial law; *Verbot* in accordance with industrial law; **~e Konsequenzen/Literatur** consequences in terms of/literature in industrial law; **arbeitsreich** ADJ *Leben, Wochen etc* busy; **Arbeitsrichter(in)** M(F) judge in an industrial tribunal (*Brit*) or labor court (*US*); **arbeitsscheu** ADJ workshy; **Arbeitsscheu** F workshyness; **Arbeitsschluss** M end of work; **~ ist um 17.00 Uhr** work finishes at 5 pm; **nach ~** after work

Arbeitsschutz M maintenance of industrial health and safety standards

Arbeitsschutz-: Arbeitsschutzbestimmung F health and safety regulation; **Arbeitsschutzvorschriften** PL health and safety regulations *pl*

Arbeits-: Arbeitssitzung F working session; **Arbeitsspeicher** M (*Comput*) main memory; **Arbeitssprache** F (*bei Konferenz etc*) working language; **Arbeitsstelle** F (a) place of work (b) (= *Stellung*) job; **Arbeitsstunde** F man-hour; **~n werden extra berechnet** labour (*Brit*) or labor (*US*) will be charged separately; **Arbeitssuche** F search for work *or* a job; **auf ~ sein**

to be looking for work *or* a job; **Arbeitstag** M working day; **ein harter ~** a hard day; **Arbeitstätigkeit** F work; **Arbeitsteam** NT team; **arbeitsteilig** 🚹 ADJ based on the division of labour (*Brit*) *or* labor (*US*) 🚺 ADV on the principle of the division of labour (*Brit*) *or* labor (*US*); **Arbeitsteilung** F division of labour (*Brit*) *or* labor (*US*); **Arbeitstempo** NT rate of work; **Arbeitstier** NT **(a)** (*lit*) working animal **(b)** (*fig inf*) workaholic (*inf*); **Arbeitstisch** M worktable; (*für geistige Arbeit*) desk; (*für handwerkliche Arbeit*) workbench; **Arbeitstitel** M provisional *or* draft title

Arbeit-: Arbeitsuche F = **Arbeitssuche; arbeitsuchend** ADJ ATTR *siehe* **Arbeit; Arbeitsuchende(r)** [-zuːxndə] MF DECL AS ADJ person/man/woman *etc* looking for work *or* a job

Arbeits-: arbeitsunfähig ADJ unable to work; (= *krank*) unfit for work; *Regierung etc* non-viable; **Arbeitsunfähigkeitsbescheinigung** F certificate of unfitness for work; **Arbeitsunfall** M industrial accident; **Arbeitsunterlage** F work paper; (*Buch etc*) source for one's work; **Arbeitsverdienst** M earned income; **Arbeitsverfahren** NT process; **Arbeitsverhältnis** NT **(a)** employee-employer relationship; **ein ~ eingehen** to enter employment **(b) Arbeitsverhältnisse** PL working conditions *pl*; **Arbeitsvermittlung** F **(a)** (= *Vorgang*) arranging employment **(b)** (= *Amt*) employment exchange; (*privat*) employment agency; **Arbeitsvertrag** M contract of employment; **Arbeitsvorbereitung** F preparation for the/one's work; (*Ind*) production planning; **Arbeitsweise** F (= *Praxis*) working method; (*von Maschine*) mode of operation; **die ~ dieser Maschine** the way this machine works; **Arbeitswelt** F working world; **die industrielle ~** the world of industry; **arbeitswillig** ADJ willing to work; **Arbeitswillige(r)** [-vɪlɪgə] MF DECL AS ADJ person/man/woman *etc* willing to work; **Arbeitswoche** F working week; **Arbeitswut** F work mania; **ihn hat die ~ gepackt** he's turned into a workaholic (*inf*)

Arbeitszeit F **(a)** working hours *pl*; **während der ~** during working hours; **eine wöchentliche ~ von 35 Stunden** a working week of 35 hours **(b)** (= *benötigte Zeit*) **die ~ für etw** the time spent on sth; (*in Fabrik*) the production time for sth; **er ließ sich die ~ bezahlen** he wanted to be paid for his time

Arbeitszeit-: Arbeitszeitkonto NT record of hours worked; **Überstunden auf dem ~ gutschreiben** to record hours worked as overtime; **Arbeitszeitordnung** F working-time regulations *pl*; **Arbeitszeitverkürzung** F reduction in working hours

Arbeits-: Arbeitszeug NT, *pl* -zeuge (*inf*) **(a)** (= *Arbeitskleidung*) working clothes *pl* **(b)** (= *Werkzeug*) tools *pl*; **Arbeitszeugnis** NT reference from one's employer; **Arbeitszimmer** NT study

archaisch [ar'çaːɪʃ] ADJ archaic

Archäologe [arçeoˈloːgə] M -n, -n, **Archäologin** [-ˈloːgɪn] F -, -nen archaeologist (*Brit*), archeologist (*US*)

Archäologie [arçeoloˈgiː] F -, NO PL archaeology (*Brit*), archeology (*US*)

archäologisch [arçeoˈloːgɪʃ] 🚹 ADJ archaeological (*Brit*), archeological (*US*) 🚺 ADV archaeologically (*Brit*), archeologically (*US*); **~ interessiert** interested in arch(a)eology

Arche [ˈarçə] F -, -n **die ~ Noah** Noah's Ark

Archipel [arçiˈpeːl] M -s, -e archipelago

Architekt [arçiˈtɛkt] M -en, -en, **Architektin** [-ˈtɛktɪn] F -, -nen (*lit, fig*) architect

architektonisch [arçitɛkˈtoːnɪʃ] 🚹 ADJ architectural; (*geh*) *Aufbau* (*von Kunstwerk*) architectonic (*form*) 🚺 ADV architecturally

Architektur [arçitɛkˈtuːɐ] F -, -en architecture (*auch Comput*); (= *Bau*) piece of architecture

Archiv [arˈçiːf] NT -s, -e [-və] archives *pl*

Archiv-: Archivbild NT photo from the archives; **Archivexemplar** NT file copy

archivieren [arçiˈviːrən], *ptp* **archiviert** VT to archive (*auch Comput*)

Archivmaterial NT records *pl*

ARD [aːlɐˈdeː] F -, NO PL ABBR *von* **Arbeitsgemeinschaft der öffentlich-rechtlichen Rundfunkanstalten der Bundesrepublik Deutschland**

ARD

ARD is an amalgamation of the broadcasting stations of the Länder. Since 1954 it has run the Erstes Deutsches Fernsehen, the first German national TV channel. The individual stations produce programmes for the network and for the regional channels, which concentrate on local interest and educational programming. They also control up to five regional radio stations each. ARD is financed through licence fees and strictly controlled advertising. It concentrates on information, news and educational programmes.

Are [ˈaːrə] F -, -n (*Sw:* = Ar) are (*100 m²*)

Areal [areˈaːl] NT -s, -e area

Ären PL *von* **Ära**

Arena [aˈreːna] F -, **Arenen** [-nən] (*lit, fig*) arena; (= *Zirkusarena, Stierkampfarena*) ring

arg [ark] 🚹 ADJ, *comp* **=er** [ˈɛrgə], *superl* **=ste(r, s)** [ˈɛrkstə] (*esp S Ger*) **(a)** (= *schlimm*) bad; *Gestank, Katastrophe, Verlust, Blamage, Verlegenheit, Schicksal* terrible; *Enttäuschung, Feind* bitter; *Säufer, Raucher* inveterate; **sein ärgster Feind** his worst enemy; **das Ärgste befürchten** to fear the worst; **etw liegt im Argen** sth is at sixes and sevens; **das ist mir ~** (*dial*) I'm very sorry about that
(b) ATTR (= *stark, groß*) terrible; (*dial*) *Freude, Liebenswürdigkeit etc* tremendous
🚺 ADV, *comp* **=er**, *superl* **am =sten** (= *schlimm*) badly; (*dial inf*: = *sehr*) terribly (*inf*); **es geht ihr ~ schlecht** (*inf*) she's in a really bad way; **er hat sich ~ vertan** (*inf*) he's made a bad mistake; **es zu ~ treiben** to go too far

Argentinien [argɛnˈtiːniən] NT -s Argentina, the Argentine

Argentinier [argɛnˈtiːniɐ] M -s, -, **Argentinierin** [-iərɪn] F -, -nen Argentine, Argentinian

argentinisch [argɛnˈtiːnɪʃ] ADJ Argentine, Argentinian

ärger COMP *von* **arg**

Ärger [ˈɛrgə] M -s, NO PL **(a)** annoyance; (*stärker*) anger; **~ über etw** (*acc*) **empfinden** to feel annoyed about sth; **zu jds ~, jdm zum ~** to sb's annoyance
(b) (= *Unannehmlichkeiten, Streitigkeiten, ärgerliche Erlebnisse*) trouble; (= *Sorgen*) worry; **jdm ~ machen** *or* **bereiten** to cause sb a lot of trouble; **der tägliche ~ im Büro** the hassle in the office every day (*inf*); **~ bekommen** *or* **kriegen** (*inf*) to get into trouble; **~ mit jdm haben** to be having trouble with sb; **mach keinen ~!** (*inf*) don't make trouble!; **mach mir keinen ~** (*inf*) don't make (any) trouble for me; **so ein ~!** (*inf*) what a pain! (*inf*); **es gibt ~** (*inf*) there'll be trouble

ärgerlich [ˈɛrgəlɪç] 🚹 ADJ **(a)** (= *verärgert*) annoyed; *Tonfall, Handbewegung* angry; **~ über** *or* **auf jdn/über etw sein** to be annoyed with sb/about sth **(b)** (= *unangenehm*) annoying; (*stärker*) infuriating; **eine ~e Tatsache** an unpleasant fact 🚺 ADV crossly; (= *böse*) angrily; **~ klingen** to sound cross/angry; **jdn ~ ansehen** to give sb an angry look

ärgern [ˈɛrgɐn] 🚹 VT **(a)** (= *ärgerlich machen*) to annoy; (*stärker*) to make angry; **jdn krank** *or* **zu Tode ~** to drive sb mad; **das ärgert einen doch!** but it's so annoying! **(b)** (= *necken*) to torment 🚺 VR (= *ärgerlich sein/werden*) to be/get annoyed; (*stärker*) to be/get angry (*über jdn/etw* with sb/about sth); **du darfst dich darüber nicht so ~** you shouldn't let it annoy you so much; **nicht ~, nur wundern!** (*inf*) that's life

Ärgernis [ˈɛrgənɪs] NT -ses, -se **(a)** NO PL (= *Anstoß*) offence (*Brit*), offense (*US*); **~ erregen** to cause offence (*Brit*) *or* offense (*US*); **bei jdm ~ erregen** to offend sb; **wegen Erregung öffentlichen ~ses angeklagt werden** to be charged with offending public decency
(b) (= *etwas Anstößiges*) outrage; (= *etwas Ärgerliches*) terrible nuisance; **es ist ein ~ für sie, wenn ...** it annoys her (terribly) when ...; **um ~se zu vermeiden** to avoid upsetting anybody

ärgste(r, s) SUPERL *von* **arg**

Argument [arguˈmɛnt] NT -(e)s, -e argument; **das ist kein ~** that's no argument; (= *keine Entschuldigung*) that's no excuse

Argumentation [argumɛntaˈtsioːn] F -, -en **(a)** argument; (= *Darlegung*) argumentation *no pl* **(b)** (*Sch:* = *Aufsatz*) critical analysis

argumentieren [argumɛnˈtiːrən], *ptp* **argumentiert** VI to argue; **mit etw ~** to use sth as an argument

Argwohn ['arkvoːn] M **-s**, NO PL suspicion; **mit** or **voller ~** suspiciously

argwöhnen ['arkvøːnən] VT INSEP (geh) to suspect

argwöhnisch ['arkvøːnɪʃ] **1** ADJ suspicious **2** ADV suspiciously

Arie ['aːriə] F **-, -n** (Mus) aria

Arier ['aːriɐ] M **-s, -**, **Arierin** [-iərɪn] F **-, -nen** Aryan

arisch ['aːrɪʃ] ADJ **(a)** (Ling) Indo-European **(b)** (NS) Aryan

Aristokrat [arɪstoˈkraːt] M **-en, -en**, **Aristokratin** [-ˈkratɪn] F **-, -nen** aristocrat

Aristokratie [arɪstokraˈtiː] F **-, -n** [-ˈtiːən] aristocracy

aristokratisch [arɪstoˈkratɪʃ] ADJ aristocratic

Arithmetik [arɪtˈmeːtɪk] F **-**, NO PL arithmetic

arithmetisch [arɪtˈmeːtɪʃ] ADJ arithmetic(al); (Comput) arithmetic

Arktis ['arktɪs] F **-**, NO PL Arctic

arktisch ['arktɪʃ] **1** ADJ arctic **2** ADV **~ kalt** cold as the arctic

arm [arm] **1** ADJ, comp **-er** ['ɛrmɐ], superl **-ste(r, s)** ['ɛrmstə] (lit, fig) poor; **Arm und Reich** rich and poor; **die Armen** the poor pl; **du machst mich noch mal ~** (inf) you'll ruin me yet; **~ an etw** (dat) **sein** to be somewhat lacking in sth; **der Boden ist ~ an Nährstoffen** the soil is poor in nutrients; **~ an Vitaminen** low in vitamins; **um jdn/etw ärmer werden** to lose sb/sth; **um jdn/ etw ärmer sein** to have lost sb/sth; **um 10 Euro ärmer sein** to be 10 euros poorer; **ach, du/Sie Armer!** (auch iro) you poor thing!; **~es Schwein** (inf) poor so-and-so (inf); **~er Irrer** (inf) mad fool (inf); (= bedauernswert) poor fool **2** ADV, comp **-er**, superl am **-sten du isst mich noch mal ~!** (inf) you'll eat me out of house and home!; **~ dran sein** (inf) to have a hard time of it

Arm [arm] M **-(e)s, -e** (Anat, Tech, fig) arm; (von Fluss, Baum) branch; (von Waage) beam; (= Ärmel) sleeve; **~ in ~** arm in arm; **~ voll** armful; **zwei ~ voll Holz** two armfuls of wood; **die ~e voll haben** to have one's arms full; **jdn im ~** or **in den ~ halten** to hold sb in one's arms; **jdn am ~ führen** to lead sb by the arm; **jdn in die ~e nehmen** to take sb in one's arms; **jdn in die ~e schließen** to clasp sb in an embrace; **sich in den ~en liegen** to lie in each other's arms; **jdn auf den ~ nehmen** to take sb onto one's arm; (fig inf) to pull sb's leg (inf); **jdm unter die ~e greifen** (fig) to help sb out; **jdm in die ~e laufen** (fig inf) to run into sb; **jdn mit offenen ~en empfangen** (fig) to welcome sb with open arms; **jdm in den ~ fallen** (fig) to spike sb's guns (Brit), to throw sb a curve ball (US); **jdn jdm/einer Sache in die ~e treiben** (fig) to drive sb into sb's arms/to sth; **der ~ des Gesetzes** the long arm of the law; **jds verlängerter ~** an extension of sb

-arm ADJ SUF **(a)** (= wenig enthaltend) low in; **vitaminarm** low in vitamins; **salzarm** low in salt **(b)** (= gering an) lacking in; **emotionsarm** lacking in emotion **(c)** (Elec, Phys etc) low-; **rauscharm** low-noise; **strahlungsarm** low-radiation

Armatur [armaˈtuːɐ] F **-, -en** USU PL (Tech) (= Hahn, Leitung etc) fitting; (= Instrument) instrument

Armaturen-: Armaturenbeleuchtung F (Aut) dash light; **Armaturenbrett** NT instrument panel; (Aut) dashboard

Arm-: Armband [-bant] NT, pl **-bänder** bracelet; (von Uhr) (watch)strap; **Armbanduhr** F wristwatch; **Armbinde** F armband; (Med) sling; **Armbruch** M (Med) broken or fractured arm; **Armbrust** F crossbow

Armee [arˈmeː] F **-, -n** [-ˈmeːən] (Mil) (fig) army; (= Gesamtheit der Streitkräfte) (armed) forces pl; **bei der ~** in the army/forces

Ärmel ['ɛrml] M **-s, -** sleeve; **sich** (dat) **die ~ hochkrempeln** or **aufkrempeln** (lit, fig) to roll up one's sleeves; **etw aus dem ~ schütteln** to produce sth just like that

Ärmelaufschlag M cuff

-ärmelig [ɛrməlɪç] ADJ SUF -sleeved; **kurzärmelig** short-sleeved

Ärmelkanal M (English) Channel

ärmellos ADJ sleeveless

Ärmelschoner [-ʃoːnɐ] M **-s, -** oversleeve

Armenhaus NT (oldfig) poorhouse

Armenien [arˈmeːniən] NT **-s** Armenia

Armenier [arˈmeːniɐ] M **-s, -**, **Armenierin** [-iərɪn] F **-, -nen** Armenian

armenisch [arˈmeːnɪʃ] ADJ Armenian

Armensünder- [armən'zyndɐ] IN CPDS (Aus) = **Armsünder-**

Armenviertel NT poor district

ärmer COMP von arm

Armesünder- IN CPDS = **Armsünder-**

Armgelenk NT elbow joint

armieren [arˈmiːrən] ptp **armiert** VT (Tech) Kabel to sheathe; Beton to reinforce

-armig [armɪç] ADJ SUF -armed; **einarmig** one-armed; **ein siebenarmiger Leuchter** a seven-branched candelabra

Arm-: Armlehne F armrest; **Armleuchter** M **(a)** chandelier **(b)** (pej inf: = Mensch) twerp (inf)

ärmlich ['ɛrmlɪç] **1** ADJ (lit, fig) poor; Kleidung, Wohnung shabby; Essen meagre (Brit), meager (US); Verhältnisse humble; **einen ~en Eindruck machen** to look poor/shabby; **aus ~en Verhältnissen** from a poor family **2** ADV poorly, shabbily; **~ leben** to live in poor conditions

-ärmlig [ɛrmlɪç] ADJ SUF = **-ärmelig**

Arm-: Armmuskel M biceps; **Armreif** M, **Armreifen** M bangle

armselig ADJ miserable; (= jämmerlich) pathetic; Summe, Ausrede paltry; **für ~e zwei Euro** for two paltry euros; **das ist wirklich ~!** it's really pathetic!

Armsessel M armchair

ärmste(r, s) SUPERL von arm

Armsünder- [arm'zyndɐ]: **Armsünderbank** F, pl **-bänke**, **Armsünderbänkchen** NT (hum) (beim Essen) small table at which children sit; (bei Prüfung, Quiz etc) hot seat; **dasitzen wie auf dem Armsünderbänkchen** to be sitting there looking as though the world were about to end; **Armsündermiene** F (hum) hangdog expression

Armut ['armuːt] F **-**, NO PL (lit, fig) poverty; **geistige ~** intellectual poverty; (von Mensch) lack of intellect; **neue ~** new poverty

-armut F SUF IN CPDS lack of

Armutszeugnis NT (fig) **jdm/sich (selbst) ein ~ ausstellen** to show sb's/one's (own) shortcomings; **das ist ein ~ für ihn** that shows him up

Armvoll M **-, -** siehe **Arm**

Arnika ['arnika] F **-, -s** arnica

Aroma [aˈroːma] NT **-s, Aromen** or **-s (a)** (= Geruch) aroma **(b)** (= Geschmack) flavour (Brit), flavor (US)

Aromatherapie F (Med) aromatherapy

aromatisch [aroˈmatɪʃ] **1** ADJ **(a)** (= wohlriechend) aromatic **(b)** (= wohlschmeckend) savoury (Brit), savory (US) **2** ADV **~ schmecken** to taste savoury (Brit) or savory (US)

aromatisieren [aromatiˈziːrən] ptp **aromatisiert** VT to give aroma to; **aromatisiert** aromatic; **zu stark aromatisiert sein** to have too strong an aroma

Arrangement [arãʒəˈmãː] NT **-s, -s** (alle Bedeutungen) arrangement

arrangieren [arãˈʒiːrən] ptp **arrangiert** **1** VTI (alle Bedeutungen) to arrange (jdm for sb) **2** VR **sich mit jdm ~** to come to an arrangement with sb; **sich mit etw ~** to come to terms with sth

Arrest [aˈrɛst] M **-(e)s, -s** (Sch, Mil, Jur: = Jugendarrest) detention; **seine Eltern bestraften ihn mit ~** his parents punished him by grounding him

arretieren [areˈtiːrən] ptp **arretiert** VT (Tech) to lock (in place)

arrogant [aroˈgant] **1** ADJ arrogant **2** ADV arrogantly

Arroganz [aroˈgants] F **-**, NO PL arrogance

Arsch [arʃ, aːʃ] M **-(e)s, -e** ['ɛrʃə, 'ɛːrʃə] **(a)** (vulg) arse (Brit sl), ass (US sl); **jdm** or **jdn in den ~ treten** to give sb a kick up the arse (Brit sl) or ass (US sl); **den ~ voll kriegen** to get a bloody good hiding (Brit inf), to get an ass-kicking (US sl); **leck mich am ~!** (= lass mich in Ruhe) fuck off! (vulg); (= verdammt noch mal) bugger! (Brit sl), fuck it! (vulg); (sl: überrascht) fuck me! (vulg); **jdm in den ~ kriechen** (inf) to lick sb's arse (Brit sl) or ass (US sl); **du hast wohl den ~ offen!** (sl) you're out of your tiny mind (inf); **am ~ der Welt** (inf) in the back of beyond; **im** or **am ~ sein** (sl) to be screwed up (sl); **fürn ~ sein** (sl) to be crap (inf); **sich** (dat) **den ~ aufreißen** (sl) to bust a gut (inf); **das geht mir am ~ vorbei** (sl: = ist mir egal) I don't give a shit (about it) (sl); **sich** (dat) **den ~ abfrieren** (sl) to freeze one's arse (Brit sl) or ass (US sl) off

(b) (sl: = Mensch) bastard (sl); (= Dummkopf) stupid bastard (sl); **kein ~ war da** nobody fucking turned up (vulg)

Arsch-: Arschbacke F (sl) buttock, cheek; **Arschficker** [-fɪkɐ] M **-s, -** (vulg) **(a)** (lit) bum-fucker (Brit vulg), butt-fucker (US vulg) **(b)** (fig) slimy bastard (sl); **arschkalt** ADJ (inf) bloody (Brit inf) or damn (inf) cold; **Arschkriecher** [-kriːçɐ] M **-s, -**,

Arschkriecherin [-ərɪn] F **-, -nen** (sl) ass-kisser (sl);
Arschkriecherei F (sl) ass-kissing (sl); **Arschloch** NT (vulg)
(a) (lit) arsehole (Brit sl), asshole (US sl) (b) = **Arsch** (b);
Arschtritt M (sl) kick up the arse (Brit sl) or ass (US sl)

Arsen [arˈzeːn] NT **-s**, NO PL (abbr **As**) arsenic

Arsenal [arzeˈnaːl] NT **-s, -e** (lit, fig) arsenal

Art [aːɐt] F **-, -en** (a) kind, sort; **diese ~ Leute/Buch** that kind or
sort of person/book; **jede ~ (von) Buch/Terror** any kind or sort
of book/terrorism; **einzig in seiner ~ sein** to be unique; **aus
der ~ schlagen** not to take after anyone in the family
(b) (Biol) species
(c) (= Methode) way; **auf die ~** in that way; **auf die ~ geht es
am schnellsten** that is the quickest way; **auf diese ~ und
Weise** in this way
(d) (= Wesen) nature; (= übliche Verhaltensweise) way; **es
entspricht nicht meiner ~** it's not my nature; **das ist
eigentlich nicht seine ~** it's not like him
(e) (= Stil) style; **nach bayrischer ~** Bavarian style; **Schnitzel
nach ~ des Hauses** schnitzel à la maison
(f) (= Benehmen) behaviour (Brit), behavior (US); **das ist doch
keine ~!** that's no way to behave!; **was ist das (denn) für eine
~?** what sort of a way to behave is that?

Art. ABBR von **Artikel**

Artangabe F (Gram) adverb of manner;
(= Adverbialbestimmung) adverbial phrase of manner

Arten-: artenreich ADJ Lebensraum, Wald etc species-rich; **diese
Tierklasse ist sehr ~** this class of animal contains a large
number of species; **Artenreichtum** M (Biol) diversity of
species; **Artenschutz** M protection of species; **Artenschwund**
M extinction of species; **Artensterben** NT extinction of
species; **Artenvielfalt** F species diversity; **pflanzliche ~**
diversity of plant species

Arterie [arˈteːriə] F **-, -n** artery

arteriell [arteˈriɛl] ADJ arterial

Arterienverkalkung F (inf) hardening of the arteries; **~ haben**
(fig) to be senile

Arteriosklerose [arterioskleˈroːzə] F arteriosclerosis

Art-: artfremd ADJ (Biol) foreign (to the species); **Artgenosse** M,
Artgenossin F (= Tier/Pflanze) animal/plant of the same
species; (= Mensch) person of the same type; **artgerecht** ADJ
appropriate to the species; **eine ~e Tierhaltung** livestock
farming methods which are appropriate for each species

Arthritis [arˈtriːtɪs] F **-, Arthritiden** [artriˈtiːdn] arthritis

arthritisch [arˈtriːtɪʃ] ADJ arthritic

Arthrose [arˈtroːzə] F **-, -n** arthrosis

artig [ˈaːɐtɪç] ADJ Kind, Hund etc good; **sei schön ~** be good!

-artig ADJ SUF -like; **gummiartig** rubbery

Artikel [arˈtiːkl, -ˈtɪkl] M **-s, -** (alle Bedeutungen) article

Artikulation [artikulaˈtsioːn] F **-, -en** articulation; (Mus)
phrasing

artikulationsfähig ADJ articulate; (Phon) able to articulate

artikulieren [artikuˈliːrən], ptp **artikuliert** ■ VTI to articulate;
(Mus) to phrase; **sich artikuliert ausdrücken** to be articulate
■ VR (fig geh) to express oneself

Artillerie [ˈartɪləriː, artɪləˈriː] F **-, -n** [-ˈriːən] artillery

Artischocke [artiˈʃɔkə] F **-, -n** (globe) artichoke

Artischockenboden M USU PL artichoke bottom

Artischockenherz NT artichoke heart

Artist [arˈtɪst] M **-en, -en**, **Artistin** [-ˈtɪstɪn] F **-, -nen** (circus or (im
Varietee) variety) performer

*Vorsicht! **Artist** wird nicht mit dem englischen Wort **artist**
übersetzt.*

artistisch [arˈtɪstɪʃ] ADJ (a) sein **~es Können** his ability as a
performer; **eine ~e Glanzleistung/~ einmalige Leistung** (in
Zirkus/Varietee) a miraculous/unique feat of circus/variety
artistry; **eine ~e Sensation** a sensational performance
(b) (= geschickt) masterly no adv (c) (= formalkünstlerisch)
artistic

Art-: artverschieden ADJ of different species; **artverwandt** ADJ
of the same type; (Biol) species-related; **Artwort** NT, pl **-wörter**
(Gram) adjective

Arznei [aːɐtsˈnai, artsˈnai] F **-, -en** (lit, fig) medicine; **das war für
ihn eine bittere/heilsame ~** (fig) that was a painful/useful
lesson for him

Arzneimittel NT drug

Arzneimittelmissbrauch M drug abuse

Arzneischränkchen NT medicine cupboard

Arzt [aːɐtst, artst] M **-es, ~e** [ˈɛːɐtstə, ˈɛrtstə], **Ärztin** [ˈɛːɐtstɪn, ˈɛrtstɪn]
F **-, -nen** doctor; (= Facharzt) specialist; (= Chirurg) surgeon;
praktische ~, praktische Ärztin general practitioner, GP;
eine Ärztin a (woman or female) doctor

Arztberuf M medical profession

Ärzteschaft [ˈɛːɐtstəʃaft, ˈɛrtstə-] F **-, -en** medical profession

Arzt-: Arztfrau F doctor's wife; **Arzthelfer(in)** M(F), **Arzthilfe** F
(doctor's) receptionist

Ärztin F siehe **Arzt**

ärztlich [ˈɛːɐtstlɪç, ˈɛrtst-] ■ ADJ medical ■ ADV beraten,
untersuchen medically; **er ließ sich ~ behandeln** he went to a
doctor for treatment; **~ empfohlen** recommended by doctors

Arzt-: Arztpraxis F doctor's practice; **Arztrechnung** F doctor's
bill; **Arztwahl** F choice of doctor

As¹ [as] NT **-es, -e** siehe **Ass**

As² NT **-, -** (Mus) A flat

Asbest [asˈbɛst] NT **-(e)s**, NO PL asbestos

Asbestose [asbɛsˈtoːzə] F **-, -n** asbestosis

Aschantinuss [aˈʃanti-] F (Aus) peanut, groundnut

aschblond ADJ ash blond

Asche [ˈaʃə] F **-, -n** ash(es pl); (von Zigarette, Vulkan) ash; (nach
Feuer, = sterbliche Überreste) ashes pl

Äsche [ˈɛʃə] F **-, -n** grayling

Aschen-: Aschenbahn F cinder track; **Aschenbecher** M
ashtray; **Ascheneimer** M ash can (esp US), ash bin;
Aschenkasten M ash pan; **Aschenplatz** M (Ftbl) cinder pitch;
(Tennis) clay court; **Aschenputtel** [-pʊtl] NT **-s, -** (Liter, fig)
Cinderella; **Aschenregen** M shower of ash

Aschermittwoch [aʃɐˈmɪtvɔx] M Ash Wednesday

Asch-: aschfahl ADJ ashen; **aschgrau** ADJ ash-grey (Brit), ash-
gray (US)

ASCII- [ˈaski-]: **ASCII-Datei** F ASCII file; **ASCII-Kode** M ASCII
code

Ascorbinsäure [askɔrˈbiːn-] F ascorbic acid

ASEAN [ˈɛsien] F or M - ABBR von **Association of South East Asian
Nations** ASEAN; **~-Staat** ASEAN country or state

A-Seite [ˈaː-] F (von Schallplatte) A-side

aseptisch [aˈzɛptɪʃ] ■ ADJ aseptic ■ ADV aseptically

Äser PL von **Aas**

Aserbaidschan [azɛrbaiˈdʒaːn] NT **-s** Azerbaijan

aserbaidschanisch [azɛrbaiˈdʒaːnɪʃ] ADJ Azerbaijani

Asiat [aˈziaːt] M **-en, -en**, **Asiatin** [aˈziaːtɪn] F **-, -nen** Asian

asiatisch [aˈziaːtɪʃ] ADJ Asian, Asiatic; **der ~-pazifische Raum** the
Pacific Rim

Asien [ˈaːzien] NT **-s** Asia

asketisch [asˈkeːtɪʃ] ■ ADJ ascetic ■ ADV ascetically

Askorbinsäure [askɔrˈbiːn-] F ascorbic acid

Äskulap- [ɛskuˈlaːp-]: **Äskulapschlange** F snake of Aesculapius;
Äskulapstab M staff of Aesculapius

asozial [ˈaːzotsiaːl, azoˈtsiaːl] ■ ADJ asocial ■ ADV asocially

Asoziale(r) [ˈaːzotsiaːlə] MF DECL AS ADJ (pej) antisocial person/
man/woman etc; **Asoziale** pl antisocial elements

Aspekt [asˈpɛkt] M **-(e)s, -e** aspect; **unter diesem ~ betrachtet**
looking at it from this aspect

Asphalt [asˈfalt, ˈasfalt] M **-(e)s, -e** asphalt

asphaltieren [asfalˈtiːrən], ptp **asphaltiert** VT to asphalt

asphaltiert [asfalˈtiːɐt] ADJ asphalt

Asphaltstraße F asphalt road

Aspik [as'piːk, as'pɪk] M or (AUS) NT **-s, -e** aspic

aspirieren [aspi'riːrən], *ptp* **aspiriert** VT (*Phon*) to aspirate

aß PRET *von* **essen**

Ass [as] NT **-es, -e** (*lit, fig*) ace

Assel ['asl] F **-, -n** isopod (*spec*); (= *Rollassel, Kellerassel, Landassel auch*) woodlouse

Assessor [a'sɛsɔːɐ] M **-s, Assessoren** [-'soːrən], **Assessorin** [-'soːrɪn] F **-, -nen** *graduate civil servant who has completed his/her traineeship*

assimilieren [asimi'liːrən], *ptp* **assimiliert** **1** VTI to assimilate **2** VR to become assimilated; **sich an etw** (*acc*) **~** (*Mensch*) to adjust to sth

Assistent [asɪs'tɛnt] M **-en, -en**, **Assistentin** [-'tɛntɪn] F **-, -nen** assistant

Assistenz [asɪs'tɛnts] F **-,** (*rare*) **-en** assistance; **unter ~ von ...** with the assistance of ...

Assistenzarzt M, **Assistenzärztin** F junior doctor (*Brit*), intern (*US*)

assistieren [asɪs'tiːrən], *ptp* **assistiert** VI to assist (*jdm* sb)

Assoziation [asotsia'tsioːn] F **-, -en** association

assoziativ [asotsia'tiːf] (*Psych, geh*) **1** ADJ associative **2** ADV **verbunden** through association; **Erinnerungen ~ hervorrufen** to evoke memories through association; **etw ~ mit etw verbinden** to associate sth with sth

assoziieren [asotsi'iːrən], *ptp* **assoziiert** (*geh*) **1** VT to associate; **mit Grün assoziiere ich Ruhe** I associate green with peace **2** VI to make associations; **frei ~** to make free associations

assoziiert [asotsi'iːrt] ADJ associated; *Mitgliedschaft* associate; **mit der EU ~ sein** to be an associate member of the EU

Assyrien [a'syːriən] NT **-s** Assyria

assyrisch [a'syːrɪʃ] ADJ Assyrian

Ast [ast] M **-(e)s, ¨e** ['ɛstə] (**a**) branch, bough; (*fig: von Nerv*) branch; **sich in Äste teilen** to branch; **den ~ absägen, auf dem man sitzt** (*fig*) to dig one's own grave (**b**) (*im Holz*) knot

AStA ['asta] M **-s, Asten** ['astn] (*Univ*) ABBR *von* **Allgemeiner Studentenausschuss**

Aster ['aste] F **-, -n** aster

Asteroid [astero'iːt] M **-en, -en** [-dn] (*Astron*) asteroid

Astgabel F fork (of a branch)

Ästhet [ɛs'teːt] M **-en, -en**, **Ästhetin** [-'teːtɪn] F **-, -nen** aesthete

Ästhetik [ɛs'teːtɪk] F **-, NO PL** (**a**) (= *Wissenschaft*) aesthetics *sing* (**b**) (= *Schönheit*) aesthetics *pl* (**c**) (= *Schönheitssinn*) aesthetic sense

ästhetisch [ɛs'teːtɪʃ] ADJ aesthetic

Asthma ['astma] NT **-s, NO PL** asthma

Asthmatiker [ast'maːtike] M **-s, -**, **Asthmatikerin** [-ərɪn] F **-, -nen** asthmatic

asthmatisch [ast'maːtɪʃ] ADJ asthmatic

astig ['astɪç] ADJ *Holz* gnarled

Astigmatismus [astɪgma'tɪsmʊs] M **-, NO PL** (*Med*) astigmatism, astigmia

Astralkörper M, **Astralleib** M (*Philos*) astral body; (*iro inf*) heavenly body

astrein **1** ADJ (**a**) *Holz, Brett* free of knots (**b**) (*fig inf*: = *moralisch einwandfrei*) above board (**c**) (*fig inf*: = *echt*) genuine (**d**) (*dated sl*: = *prima*) fantastic (*inf*) **2** ADV (*dated sl*: = *prima*) fantastically (*inf*)

Astro-: **Astrologe** [astro'loːgə] M **-n, -n**, **Astrologin** [-'loːgɪn] F **-, -nen** astrologer; **Astrologie** [astrolo'giː] F **-, NO PL** astrology; **astrologisch** [astro'loːgɪʃ] **1** ADJ astrological **2** ADV **~ interessiert sein** to be interested in astrology; **Astronaut** [astro'naut] M **-en, -en**, **Astronautin** [-'nautɪn] F **-, -nen** astronaut; **Astronautik** [astro'nautɪk] F **-, NO PL** astronautics *sing*; **astronautisch** [astro'nautɪʃ] ADJ astronautic(al); **Astronom** [astro'noːm] M **-en, -en**, **Astronomin** [-'noːmɪn] F **-, -nen** astronomer; **Astronomie** [astrono'miː] F **-, NO PL** astronomy; **astronomisch** [astro'noːmɪʃ] ADJ (*lit*) astronomical; (*fig auch*) astronomic; **~e Navigation** astronavigation; **Astrophysik** F astrophysics *sing*

ASU ['aːzu] F **-, NO PL** ABBR *von* **Abgassonderuntersuchung**

ASW [aːɛs'veː] NO ART **-, NO PL** ABBR *von* **außersinnliche Wahrnehmung** ESP

Asyl [a'zyːl] NT **-s, -e** (= *Schutz*) sanctuary *no art* (*liter*); (= *politisches ~*) (political) asylum *no art* (*liter*); um ~ bitten *or* nachsuchen (*form*) to ask *or* apply (*form*) for (political) asylum

Asylant [azy'lant] M **-en, -en**, **Asylantin** [-'lantɪn] F **-, -nen** asylum seeker

Asylantenwohnheim NT hostel for asylum seekers

Asyl-: **Asylantrag** M application for (political) asylum; **asylberechtigt** ADJ entitled to (political) asylum; **Asylbewerber(in)** M(F) asylum seeker; **Asylrecht** NT (*Pol*) right of (political) asylum; **Asylsuchende(r)** [-zuːxndə] MF DECL AS ADJ asylum seeker; **Asylverfahren** NT *court hearing to determine a person's right to political asylum*; **Asylwerber(in)** M(F) (*Aus*) asylum seeker

Asymmetrie [azyme'triː] F asymmetry

asymmetrisch ['azymetrɪʃ, azy'meːtrɪʃ] **1** ADJ asymmetric(al); (*Comput*) asymmetric; (*fig*) *Gespräch* one-sided **2** ADV asymmetrically

Asymptote [azym'ptoːtə] F **-, -n** asymptote

asynchron ['azynkroːn, azyn'kroːn] ADJ, ADV (*Comput*) out of synchronism

Aszendent [astsɛn'dɛnt] M **-en, -en** (*Astrol*) ascendant

at [a:'teː] ABBR *von* **Atmosphäre**

A. T. ABBR *von* **Altes Testament** OT

ata ['ata] ADV (*baby-talk*) **~ (~) gehen** to go walkies (*baby-talk*)

Atelier [ate'lieː, atə'lieː] NT **-s, -s** studio

Atem ['aːtəm] M **-s, NO PL** (**a**) (= *das Atmen*) breathing; **den ~ anhalten** (*lit, fig*) to hold one's breath; **außer ~ sein** to be out of breath; **wieder zu ~ kommen** to get one's breath back; **einen langen/den längeren ~ haben** (*fig*) to have a lot of/more staying power; **jdn in ~ halten** to keep sb in suspense; **das verschlug mir den ~** that took my breath away (**b**) (*lit, fig*: = *~luft*) breath; **~ holen** *or* **schöpfen** (*lit*) to take a breath; (*fig*) to get one's breath back

Atem-: **atemberaubend** **1** ADJ breathtaking **2** ADV breathtakingly; **Atembeschwerden** PL trouble *sing* in breathing; **Atemgerät** NT breathing apparatus; (*Med*) respirator; **Atemgeräusch** NT respiratory sounds *pl*; **Atemlähmung** F respiratory paralysis; **atemlos** **1** ADJ (*lit, fig*) breathless **2** ADV breathlessly; **Atemmaske** F breathing mask; **Atemnot** F difficulty in breathing; **Atempause** F (*fig*) breathing space; **eine ~ einlegen/brauchen** to take/need a breather; **Atemschutzgerät** NT breathing apparatus; **Atemschutzmaske** F breathing mask; **Atemwege** PL (*Anat*) respiratory tracts *pl*; **Atemwegserkrankung** F respiratory disease; **Atemzug** M breath; **in einem/im selben ~** (*fig*) in one/the same breath

Atheismus [ate'ɪsmʊs] M **-, NO PL** atheism

Atheist [ate'ɪst] M **-en, -en**, **Atheistin** [-'ɪstɪn] F **-, -nen** atheist

atheistisch [ate'ɪstɪʃ] ADJ atheist(ic)

Athen [a'teːn] NT **-s** Athens

Äther ['ɛːtə] M **-s, NO PL** ether; (*Rad*) air; **über den ~** over the air

ätherisch [ɛ'teːrɪʃ] ADJ (*Liter*) ethereal; (*Chem*) essential

Äthiopien [ɛ'tioːpiən] NT **-s** Ethiopia

äthiopisch [ɛ'tioːpɪʃ] ADJ Ethiopian

Athlet [at'leːt] M **-en, -en**, **Athletin** [-'leːtɪn] F **-, -nen** athlete

Athletik [at'leːtɪk] F **-, NO PL** athletics *sing*

athletisch [at'leːtɪʃ] **1** ADJ athletic **2** ADV athletically; **~ aussehen** to look athletic

Äthylalkohol [ɛ'tyːl-] M ethyl alcohol

Atlanten PL *von* **Atlas**

Atlantik [at'lantɪk] M **-s** Atlantic

atlantisch [at'lantɪʃ] ADJ Atlantic; **ein ~es Hoch** a high-pressure area over the Atlantic; (*vom Atlantik kommend*) a high-pressure area from the Atlantic; **der Atlantische Ozean** the Atlantic Ocean

Atlas ['atlas] M **- or -ses, -se** *or* **Atlanten** [at'lantn] atlas

atmen ['aːtmən] VTI to breathe

Atmosphäre [atmo'sfɛːrə] F (*Phys, fig*) atmosphere

Atmosphären-: **Atmosphärendruck** M, *pl* **-drücke** atmospheric pressure; (= *Maßeinheit*) atmosphere; **Atmosphärenüberdruck** M (**a**) (= *Maßeinheit*) atmospheric excess pressure (**b**) (= *Maßeinheit*) atmosphere (of pressure) above atmospheric pressure

atmosphärisch [atmo'sfɛːrɪʃ] **1** ADJ atmospheric; **~e Störungen** atmospherics *pl* **2** ADV **die Beziehungen zwischen den beiden Ländern haben sich ~ verbessert** the atmosphere between the two countries has improved

Atmung ['aːtmʊŋ] F -, NO PL breathing; (*Med*) respiration

Atmungs-: atmungsaktiv ADJ *Material, Stoff* breathable; **Atmungsorgane** PL respiratory organs *pl*

Atoll [a'tɔl] NT -s, -e atoll

Atom [a'toːm] NT -s, -e atom

Atom- IN CPDS atomic; *siehe auch* **Kern-**; **Atomabfall** M nuclear waste; **Atomanlage** F atomic plant; **Atomantrieb** M nuclear propulsion; **ein U-Boot mit ~** a nuclear-powered submarine

atomar [ato'maːɐ] **1** ADJ atomic, nuclear; *Struktur* atomic; *Drohung* nuclear **2** ADV *bedrohen, vernichten* with a nuclear attack; **~ bestückt** armed with nuclear warheads; **~ angetrieben** nuclear-powered

Atom-: Atombehörde F Atomic Energy Authority (*Brit*) *or* Commission (*US*); **Atombombe** F atomic *or* atom (*esp Brit*) bomb; **Atombombenexplosion** F nuclear explosion; **atombombensicher** **1** ADJ nuclear blast-proof **2** ADV **~ gebaut** capable of withstanding a nuclear attack; **~ untergebracht** protected against nuclear attack; **Atombombenversuch** M nuclear test; **Atombunker** M nuclear blast-proof bunker; **Atomenergie** F nuclear energy; **Atomenergiebehörde** F **die (Internationale) ~** the (International) Atomic Energy Agency; **Atomforscher(in)** M(F) nuclear scientist; **Atomforschung** F nuclear research; **Atomforschungszentrum** NT nuclear research centre (*Brit*) *or* center (*US*); **Atomgegner(in)** M(F) **~ sein** to be antinuclear; **aktiver ~** antinuclear activist; **atomgetrieben** [-gətriːbn] ADJ nuclear-powered; **Atomgewicht** NT atomic weight

atomisch [a'toːmɪʃ] ADJ (*Sw*) = **atomar**

atomisieren [atomi'ziːrən], *ptp* **atomisiert** VT to atomize; (*fig*) to smash to smithereens

Atom-: Atomkern M atomic nucleus; **Atomkraft** F nuclear power *or* energy; **Atomkraftwerk** NT nuclear power station; **Atomkrieg** M nuclear war; **Atommacht** F nuclear power; **Atommeiler** M nuclear reactor; **Atommüll** M nuclear waste; **Atomphysik** F nuclear physics *sing*; **Atomphysiker(in)** M(F) nuclear physicist; **Atompilz** M mushroom cloud; **Atomrakete** F (= *Waffe*) nuclear missile; **Atomrüstung** F nuclear armament; **Atomspaltung** F nuclear fission; **die erste ~** the first splitting of the atom; **Atomsperrvertrag** M nuclear weapons nonproliferation treaty; **Atomsprengkopf** M nuclear warhead; **Atomstopp** M nuclear ban; **Atomstreitmacht** F nuclear capability; **Atomstrom** M (*inf*) electricity generated by nuclear power

Atomtest M nuclear test

Atomtest-: Atomteststopp M nuclear test ban; **Atomteststoppabkommen** NT nuclear test ban treaty

Atom-: Atom-U-Boot NT nuclear submarine; **Atomversuch** M nuclear test

Atomwaffe F nuclear weapon

Atomwaffen-: atomwaffenfrei ADJ nuclear-free; **Atomwaffensperrvertrag** M nuclear weapons nonproliferation treaty; **Atomwaffentest** M, **Atomwaffenversuch** M nuclear test

Atrium ['aːtriʊm] NT -s, **Atrien** [-riən] (*Archit, Anat*) atrium

ätsch [ɛːtʃ] INTERJ (*inf*) ha-ha

Attacke [a'takə] F -, -n (= *Angriff*) attack; (*Mil Hist*) (cavalry) charge; **eine ~ gegen jdn/etw reiten** (*lit*) to charge sb/sth; (*fig*) to attack sb/sth

attackieren [ata'kiːrən], *ptp* **attackiert** VT (= *angreifen*) to attack; (*Mil Hist*) to charge

Attentat ['atntaːt, atɛn'taːt] NT -(e)s, -e assassination; (= *Attentatsversuch*) assassination attempt; **ein ~ auf jdn verüben** to assassinate sb; (*bei gescheitertem Versuch*) to make an attempt on sb's life; **ich habe ein ~ auf dich vor** (*hum*) listen, I've got a great idea

Attentäter(in) M(F) assassin; (*bei gescheitertem Versuch*) would-be assassin

Attest [a'tɛst] NT -(e)s, -e certificate

attestieren [atɛs'tiːrən], *ptp* **attestiert** VT (*form*) to certify; **jdm seine Dienstuntauglichkeit** *etc* **~** to certify sb as unfit for duty *etc*

Attraktion [atrak'tsioːn] F -, -en attraction

attraktiv [atrak'tiːf] ADJ attractive

Attraktivität [atraktivi'tɛːt] F -, NO PL attractiveness

Attrappe [a'trapə] F -, -n dummy; **bei ihr ist alles ~** everything about her is false

Attribut [atri'buːt] NT -(e)s, -e (*also Gram*) attribute

atü [a'tyː] ABBR *von* **Atmosphärenüberdruck**

atypisch ['aːtypɪʃ, a'tyːpɪʃ] ADJ (*geh*) atypical

At-Zeichen ['ɛt-] NT At sign

ätzen ['ɛtsn] VTI (*Säure*) to corrode

ätzend ADJ (a) (*lit*) *Säure* corrosive; (*Med*) caustic (b) *Geruch* pungent; *Rauch* choking; *Spott, Kritik* caustic (c) (*inf:* = *furchtbar*) lousy (*inf*); **der Typ ist echt ~** that guy really grates on you (*inf*)

au [au] INTERJ (a) ow, ouch; **au, das war knapp!** oh, that was close! (b) (*Ausdruck der Begeisterung*) oh

AU [aː'luː] F -, NO PL ABBR *von* **Abgasuntersuchung**

aubergine [ober'ʒiːnə] ADJ PRED, **auberginefarben** [-farbn] ADJ aubergine

Aubergine [ober'ʒiːnə] F -, -n aubergine, eggplant (*esp US*)

auch [aux] ADV (a) (= *zusätzlich, gleichfalls*) also, too, as well; **~ die Engländer müssen ...** the English too must ...; **das ist ~ möglich** that's also possible; **ja, das ~** yes, that too; **~ gut** that's OK too; **du ~?** you too?; **~ nicht** not ... either; **das ist ~ nicht richtig** that's not right either; **er kommt – ich – ich** I want one – so am I *or* me too; **ich will eins – ich –** I want one – so do I *or* me too; **er kommt nicht – ich – nicht** he's not coming – nor *or* neither am I; **~ das noch!** that's all I needed! (b) (= *tatsächlich*) too, as well; **wenn sie sagt, sie geht, dann geht sie** if she says she's going then she'll go; **Frechheit! – ja, das ist es ~** what impudence! – you can say that again; **du siehst müde aus – das bin ich ~** you look tired – (so) I am; **das ist er ja ~** (and so) he is; **so ist es ~** (so) it is (c) (= *sogar*) even; **ohne ~ nur zu fragen** without even asking (d) (*emph*) **so was Ärgerliches aber ~!** it's really too annoying!; **wozu ~?** whatever for? (e) (= *immer*) **wie dem ~ sei** be that as it may; **was er ~ sagen mag** whatever he might say; **und mag er ~ noch so klug sein, wenn er ~ noch so klug ist** however clever he may be

Audienz [au'diɛnts] F -, -en audience

Audimax [audi'maks, 'audimaks] NT -, NO PL (*Univ sl*) main lecture hall

audiovisuell [audiovi'zuɛl] **1** ADJ audiovisual **2** ADV audiovisually; *gestalten* using audiovisual aids; *werben* using audiovisual media

Audit ['auːdit] M *or* NT -s, -s (*esp Sw*) audit

Auditorium [audi'toːriʊm] NT -s, **Auditorien** [-riən] (a) (= *Hörsaal*) lecture hall; **~ maximum** (*Univ*) main lecture hall (b) (*geh:* = *Zuhörerschaft*) audience

Auerhahn ['auɐ-] M, *pl* **Auerhähne** *or* (*Hunt*) **-en** capercaillie

Auerhenne F, **Auerhuhn** NT capercaillie (hen)

Auerochse M aurochs

---

auf [auf]

| **1** PRÄPOSITION (+DAT) | **3** ADVERB |
| **2** PRÄPOSITION (+ACC) | **4** BINDEWORT |

In Verbindung mit Substantiven, Verben etc siehe auch dort.

---

1 PRÄPOSITION (+DAT)
(a) (*Ort*) on; **auf einem Stuhl sitzen** to sit on a chair; **auf den Orkneyinseln** in the Orkney Islands; **auf See** at sea; **auf der Bank/Post/dem Rathaus** at the bank/post office/town hall; **mein Geld ist auf der Bank** my money is in the bank; **auf meinem Zimmer** in my room; **auf der Straße** on *or* in the street; **Greenwich liegt auf 0 Grad** Greenwich lies at 0 degrees (b) (*andere Wendungen*) **auf der Geige spielen** to play the violin; **etw auf dem Klavier spielen** to play sth on the piano;

auf einem Ohr taub sein to be deaf in one ear; **das hat nichts auf sich, damit hat es nichts auf sich** it doesn't mean anything; **was hat es damit auf sich?** what does it mean?

2 PRÄPOSITION (+ACC)

(a) (*Ort*) on; **etw auf etw stellen** to put sth on(to) sth; **etw auf etw heben** to lift sth onto sth; **sich auf die Straße setzen** to sit down in the road; **das Wrack ist auf den Meeresgrund gesunken** the wreck sank to the bottom of the sea; **er ist auf die Orkneyinseln gefahren** he has gone to the Orkney Islands; **man konnte nicht weiter als auf zehn Fuß herankommen** you couldn't get any nearer than ten feet; **geh mal auf die Seite** move aside; **Geld auf die Bank bringen** to take money to the bank; (= *einzahlen*) to put money in the bank; **auf sein Zimmer/die Post/die Polizei gehen** to go to one's room/the post office/the police; **aufs Gymnasium gehen** ≈ to go to grammar school (*Brit*), ≈ to go to high school (*US*); **auf eine Party/eine Hochzeit gehen** to go to a party/wedding

(b) (*Zeit*) **Heiligabend fällt auf einen Dienstag** Christmas Eve falls on a Tuesday; **die Sitzung auf morgen verschieben** to postpone the meeting until tomorrow; **auf drei Tage** for three days; **die Nacht (von Montag) auf Dienstag** Monday night; **auf morgen/bald!** see you tomorrow/soon!

(c) (*Häufung*) **Niederlage auf Niederlage** defeat after defeat; **einer auf den anderen** one after another

(d) (= *für*) **auf 10 km** for 10 km; **auf eine Tasse Kaffee** for a cup of coffee; **ein Manuskript auf Fehler prüfen** to check a manuscript for errors

(e) (= *pro*) **auf einen Polizisten kommen 1.000 Bürger** there is one policeman for every 1,000 citizens; **auf jeden kamen zwei Flaschen Bier** there were two bottles of beer (for) each

(f) (*andere Wendungen*) **auf ihn!** get him!; **auf unseren lieben Onkel Egon/ein glückliches Gelingen!** here's to dear Uncle Egon/a great success!; **auf deine Gesundheit!** (your very) good health!; **auf das** *or* **aufs schändlichste/liebenswürdigste** *or* **Schändlichste/Liebenswürdigste** (*geh*) most shamefully/kindly; **auf die elegante/ehrliche Art** elegantly/honestly

◆**auf etw** (*acc*) **hin** (*als Reaktion*) at; **auf seinen Vorschlag/seine Bitte (hin)** at his suggestion/request; **auf meinen Brief hin** on receiving my letter

◆**auf jdn/etw zu** er kam auf mich zu und sagte ... he came up to me and said ...; **während er auf mich zukam** as he was coming toward(s) me; **es geht auf Weihnachten zu** Christmas is approaching

3 ADVERB

(a) (= *offen*) open; **ist das Fenster auf oder zu?** is the window open or shut?; **Mund/Fenster auf!** open your mouth/the window!; *siehe auch* **auf sein**

(b) (*andere Wendungen*) **Helm auf!** helmets on!; **nachmittags Unterricht, und dann noch so viel auf!** (*inf*) school in the afternoon, and all that homework too!; **auf, an die Arbeit!** right, let's get down to work!; **auf nach Chicago!** let's go to Chicago!; **auf gehts!** let's go!; **auf und ab** up and down; **sie ist auf und davon** she has disappeared

4 BINDEWORT

◆**auf dass** (*liter*) that (*old, liter*); **auf dass wir niemals vergessen mögen** lest we forget

Auf [auf] NT INV **das ~ und Ab** *or* **Nieder** the up and down; (*fig*) the ups and downs; **das ~ und Ab des Kolbens** the up(ward) and down(ward) movement of the piston

aufarbeiten VT SEP **(a)** (= *erneuern*) to do up; *Möbel etc* to recondition **(b)** *Vergangenheit* to reappraise **(c)** (= *erledigen*) *Korrespondenz, Liegengebliebenes* to catch up with **(d)** (*Phys*) *Brennelemente* to reprocess

aufatmen VI SEP (*lit, fig*) to breathe a sigh of relief; **ein Aufatmen** a sigh of relief

aufbacken VT SEP to crisp up

Aufbau M, *pl* **-bauten (a)** NO PL (= *das Aufbauen*) construction; (*von neuem Staat*) building; (*von Netzwerk, System*) setting up; (= *das Wiederaufbauen*) reconstruction; **der ~ Ost** the rebuilding of East Germany **(b)** (= *Aufgebautes, Aufgesetztes*) top; (*von Auto, LKW*) body; *siehe auch* **Aufbauten (c)** NO PL (= *Struktur*) structure

aufbauen SEP **1** VT **(a)** (= *errichten*) to put up; *Verbindung, Netzwerk, System* to set up; (= *hinstellen*) *Ausstellungsstücke, kaltes Büfett, Brettspiel etc* to set out

(b) (= *darauf bauen*) *Stockwerk* to add (on); *Karosserie* to mount

(c) (*fig:* = *gestalten*) *Organisation, Geschäft, Druck, Verbindung* to build up; *Zerstörtes* to rebuild; *Theorie, Plan, System* to construct; **sich** (*dat*) **eine (neue) Existenz** *or* **ein Leben ~** to build (up) a new life for oneself

(d) (*fig:* = *fördern, weiterentwickeln*) *Gesundheit, Kraft* to build up; *Star, Politiker* to promote; *Beziehung* to build; **jdn/etw zu etw ~** to build sb/sth up into sth

(e) (*fig:* = *gründen*) **etw auf etw** (*dat or acc*) **~** to base *or* found sth on sth

(f) (= *strukturieren, konstruieren*) to construct; *Aufsatz, Rede, Organisation* to structure

2 VI (= *sich gründen*) to be based *or* founded (*auf +dat or acc* on)

3 VR **(a)** (*inf:* = *sich postieren*) to take up position; **er baute sich vor dem Lehrer auf und ...** he stood up in front of the teacher and ...; **sich vor jdm drohend ~** to plant oneself in front of sb (*inf*)

(b) (= *bestehen aus*) **sich aus etw ~** to be composed of sth

Aufbaukurs M continuation course

Aufbauprinzip NT structural principle; **die Motoren sind alle nach demselben ~ konstruiert** the engines are all constructed on the same principle

aufbauschen VTR SEP to blow out; (*fig*) to blow up

Aufbau-: Aufbaustudium NT (*Univ*) course of further study; **Aufbaustufe** F (*Sch*) school class leading to university entrance

Aufbauten PL (*Naut*) superstructure

aufbehalten *ptp* **aufbehalten** VT SEP IRREG *Hut, Brille etc* to keep on

aufbekommen *ptp* **aufbekommen** VT SEP IRREG (*inf*)
(a) (= *öffnen*) to get open **(b)** *Aufgabe* to get as homework; **habt ihr keine Hausarbeiten ~?** didn't you get any homework? **(c)** *Essen* to (manage to) eat up

aufbereiten *ptp* **aufbereitet** VT SEP to process; *Erze* to prepare; *Daten* to edit; *Text etc* to work up; **etw dramaturgisch ~** to adapt sth for the theatre (*Brit*) *or* theater (*US*)

Aufbereitung F -, -en processing; (*von Erz, Kohle*) preparation; (*von Daten*) editing; (*von Texten*) working up; (*fürs Theater*) adaptation

Aufbereitungsanlage F processing plant

aufbessern VT SEP to improve

aufbewahren *ptp* **aufbewahrt** VT SEP to keep; **ein Dokument gut ~** to keep a document in a safe place; **kann ich hier meinen Koffer ~ lassen?** can I leave my suitcase here?

Aufbewahrung F **(a)** (= *das Aufbewahren*) keeping; (*von Lebensmitteln*) storage; **jdm etw zur ~ übergeben** to give sth to sb for safekeeping; **einen Koffer in ~ geben** to deposit a suitcase (at the left-luggage (*Brit*) *or* checkroom (*US*)) **(b)** (= *Stelle*) left-luggage (office) (*Brit*), checkroom (*US*)

Aufbewahrungs-: Aufbewahrungsfrist F (*für Geschäftsunterlagen*) retention period; **Aufbewahrungsort** M, *pl* **-orte** place where something is to be kept; **etw an einen sicheren ~ bringen** to put sth in a safe place; **einen ~ für etw finden** to find a place to keep sth; **Aufbewahrungspflicht** F (*für Geschäftsunterlagen*) obligation to retain business records

aufbieten VT SEP IRREG **(a)** *Menschen, Mittel* to muster; *Kräfte, Fähigkeiten* to summon (up); *Militär, Polizei* to call in **(b)** *Brautpaar* to call the banns of

Aufbietung F -, NO PL (*von Menschen, Mitteln*) mustering; (*von Kräften, Fähigkeiten*) summoning (up); (*von Polizei, Militär*) calling in; **unter** *or* **bei ~ aller Kräfte ...** summoning (up) all his/her *etc* strength ...

aufbinden VT SEP IRREG (a) (= öffnen) Schuh etc to undo (b) (= hochbinden) Haare to put up; Pflanzen, Zweige etc to tie (up) straight (c) (= befestigen) to tie on; **etw auf etw** (acc) ~ to tie sth on(to) sth (d) **lass dir doch so etwas nicht** ~ (fig) don't fall for that; **jdm eine Lüge** ~ to tell sb a lie

aufblasbar ADJ inflatable

aufblasen SEP IRREG ◼ VT Ballon to blow up ◼ VR (fig pej) to puff oneself up; siehe auch **aufgeblasen**

aufbleiben VI SEP IRREG AUX SEIN (a) (= nicht schlafen gehen) to stay up; **wegen jdm** ~ to wait up for sb (b) (= geöffnet bleiben) to stay open

aufblenden SEP ◼ VI (Phot) to open up the lens; (Film) to fade in; (Aut) to turn the headlights on full (beam); **er fährt aufgeblendet** he drives on full beam ◼ VT (Aut) Scheinwerfer to turn on full (beam); (Film) Einstellung to fade in

aufblicken VI SEP to look up; **zu jdm/etw** ~ (lit, fig) to look up to sb/sth

aufblitzen VI SEP (a) (Licht, Strahl, Blitz, Augen) to flash (b) AUX SEIN (fig) (Emotion, Hass etc) to flare up; (Gedanke, Erinnerung) to flash through one's mind

aufblühen VI SEP AUX SEIN (a) (Knospe) to blossom (out); (Blume) to bloom (b) (fig) (Mensch) to blossom out; (Wissenschaft, Kultur) to (begin to) flourish; **das ließ sie/die Stadt** ~ it allowed her/the town to flourish

aufbocken VT SEP Auto to jack up; Motorrad to put on its stand

aufbohren VT SEP to drill a hole in

aufbrauchen VT SEP to use up

aufbrausen VI SEP AUX SEIN (a) (Brandung etc) to surge; (Brausetablette, Brause etc) to fizz up; (fig: Beifall, Jubel) to break out (b) (fig: Mensch) to flare up

aufbrausend ADJ irascible

aufbrechen SEP IRREG ◼ VT to break open; Tresor auch, Auto to break into; Deckel to prise off; Boden, Asphalt, Oberfläche to break up; (fig) System, soziale Struktur etc to break down ◼ VI AUX SEIN (a) (= sich öffnen) (Straßenbelag etc) to break up; (Knospen, Wunde) to open (b) (= sich auf den Weg machen) to set off

aufbringen VT SEP IRREG (a) (= beschaffen) to find (b) (= erzürnen) to make angry; **jdn gegen jdn/etw** ~ to set sb against sb/sth; siehe auch **aufgebracht**

Aufbruch M, NO PL departure; **das Zeichen zum** ~ **geben** to give the signal to set off; **der** ~ **ins 21. Jahrhundert** the emergence into the 21st century; **eine Zeit des** ~**s** a time of new departures

Aufbruchs-: aufbruchsbereit ADJ ready to set off; **Aufbruch(s)stimmung** F (a) **hier herrscht schon** ~ (bei Party etc) it's (all) breaking up; (in Gastwirtschaft) they're packing up; **es herrschte allgemeine** ~ (unter den Gästen) the party was breaking up; **bist du schon in** ~? are you ready to go already? (b) (= Euphorie) euphoric mood; **es herrscht** ~ there is a spirit of optimism

aufbrühen VT SEP to brew up

aufbürden VT SEP (geh) **jdm etw** ~ (lit) to load sth onto sb; (fig) to encumber sb with sth

auf dass CONJ siehe **auf 4**

aufdecken SEP VT (a) jdn to uncover; Bett(decke) to turn down; Gefäß to open; Spielkarten to show (b) (fig) Wahrheit, Verschwörung, Zusammenhänge to uncover; Verbrechen to expose; Schwäche to lay bare; Geheimnis, Rätsel to solve

Aufdeckung F (fig) (von Wahrheit, Verschwörung, Zusammenhängen) uncovering; (von Verbrechen) exposure; (von Schwäche) laying bare; (von Geheimnis, Rätsel) solving

aufdonnern VR SEP (pej inf) to get tarted up (Brit pej inf), to deck oneself out (US inf); siehe auch **aufgedonnert**

aufdrängen SEP ◼ VT **jdm etw** ~ to impose or force sth on sb ◼ VR to impose; **sich jdm** ~ (Mensch) to force one's company on sb; (fig: Erinnerung) to come involuntarily to sb's mind; **dieser Gedanke/Verdacht drängte sich mir auf** I couldn't help thinking/suspecting that

aufdrehen SEP ◼ VT Wasserhahn, Wasser etc to turn on; Ventil to open; Schraubverschluss, Schraube to unscrew; Lautstärke to turn up; (Aus: = einschalten) Licht, Radio etc to turn on ◼ VI (inf: = beschleunigen) to put one's foot down hard; (fig: = loslegen) to get going; (fig: = ausgelassen werden) to let it all hang out (inf); siehe auch **aufgedreht**

aufdringlich ADJ Mensch, Benehmen pushy (inf); Farbe loud; Geruch, Parfüm overpowering; **die** ~**e Art meines Mitreisenden** the way my fellow passenger forced his company upon me; **dieser** ~**e Kerl kam einfach auf mich zu** this guy just forced his company on me (inf); **beim Tanzen wurde er** ~ when we/they were dancing he kept trying to get frisky (inf)

Aufdringlichkeit F (von Mensch) pushiness (inf); **die** ~ **meiner Nachbarin** the way my neighbour (US) neighbor forces her company on you; **die** ~ **ihres Parfüms** her overpowering perfume

aufdröseln ['aufdrø:zln] VT SEP (lit, fig) to unravel; Strickarbeit to undo

aufdrücken VT SEP (a) **etw (auf etw** acc) ~ to press sth on (sth); **den Bleistift nicht so fest** ~! don't press (on) your pencil so hard (b) (= aufdrucken) **etw auf etw** (acc) ~ to stamp sth on sth; **ein Siegel auf einen Brief** ~ to impress a seal on a letter (c) (= öffnen) Tür etc to push open; **er drückte die Tür auf** (inf: durch Knopfdruck) he pressed the button and the door opened

aufeinander [auflai'nandə] ADV (a) on (top of) each other (b) ~ **folgend** (zeitlich) successive; **drei schnell** ~ **folgende Tore** three goals in quick succession; **sich** ~ **verlassen können** to be able to rely on each other; ~ **zufahren** to drive toward(s) each other

aufeinander-: aufeinander beißen VT IRREG Zähne to clench; **aufeinander drücken** VT to press together; **aufeinander fahren** VI IRREG AUX SEIN to drive into each other; **Aufeinanderfolge** F, NO PL sequence; (zeitlich auch) succession; **in schneller** ~ in quick succession; **aufeinander folgen** VI SEP AUX SEIN to follow each other; **aufeinander knallen** (inf) ◼ VI AUX SEIN (lit, fig) to collide ◼ VT to bang together; **aufeinander legen** ◼ VT to lay on top of each other ◼ VR to lie on top of each other; **aufeinander liegen** VI IRREG AUX SEIN or HABEN to lie on top of each other; **aufeinander prallen** VI AUX SEIN (Autos etc) to collide; (Truppen etc, Meinungen) to clash; **aufeinander pressen** VT to press together; **aufeinander schichten** VT to put in layers one on top of the other; **aufeinander sitzen** VI IRREG AUX SEIN or HABEN (a) (Gegenstände) to lie on top of each other (b) (inf: Menschen) to sit on top of each other (inf); (= eng wohnen) to live on top of each other (inf); **aufeinander stellen** VT to put on top of each other ◼ VR to get on top of each other; **aufeinander treffen** VI IRREG AUX SEIN (Mannschaften, Gruppen etc) to meet; (Meinungen) to clash; (Kugeln, Gegenstände etc) to hit each other; **aufeinander türmen** VT to pile on top of each other

Aufenthalt ['auflenthalt] M stay; (esp Rail) stop; (bei Anschluss) wait; **der** ~ **im Aktionsbereich des Krans ist verboten** do not stand within the radius of the crane; **der Zug hat 20 Minuten** ~ the train stops for 20 minutes; **wie lange haben wir** ~? how long do we stop for?; (bei Anschluss) how long do we have to wait?

Aufenthalter(in) M(F) (Sw) foreign resident, resident alien (form)

Aufenthalts-: Aufenthaltsberechtigung F right of residence; **Aufenthaltsdauer** F length of stay; **Aufenthaltserlaubnis** F, **Aufenthaltsgenehmigung** F residence permit; **Aufenthaltsraum** M day room; (in Betrieb) recreation room; (auf Flughafen) lounge

auferlegen ptp **auferlegt** VT SEP or INSEP (geh) to impose (jdm on sb)

Auferstandene(r) ['auflɛɐʃtandnə] M DECL AS ADJ (Rel) **der** ~ the risen Christ

auferstehen ptp **auferstanden** VI SEP or INSEP IRREG AUX SEIN to rise from the dead; **Christus ist auferstanden** Christ is (a)risen

Auferstehung ['auflɛɐʃte:ʊŋ] F -, -en resurrection

aufessen SEP IRREG ◼ VT to eat up ◼ VI to eat (everything) up

auffächern SEP ◼ VT to fan out; (fig) to arrange neatly ◼ VR to fan out

auffädeln VT SEP to thread or string (together)

auffahren SEP IRREG ◼ VI AUX SEIN (a) (= aufprallen) **auf jdn/etw** ~ to run into sb/sth; **auf eine Sandbank** ~ to run onto a sandbank (b) (= näher heranfahren) to drive up; **zu dicht** ~ to drive too close behind (the car in front); **mein Hintermann fährt dauernd so dicht auf** the car behind me is right on my tail

all the time
(c) (= *aufschrecken*) to start; **aus dem Schlaf ~** to awake with a start
2 VT (*inf*) *Getränke etc* to serve up; *Speisen, Argumente* to dish up (*inf*); **lass mal eine Runde ~** (*inf*) how about buying us a round? (*inf*)

auffahrend ADJ irascible

Auffahrt F **(a)** (= *das Hinauffahren*) ascent **(b)** (= *Zufahrt*) approach (road); (*bei Haus etc*) drive; (= *Rampe*) ramp **(c)** (*Sw*) = **Himmelfahrt**

Auffahrunfall M (*von zwei Autos*) collision; (*von mehreren Autos*) pile-up

auffallen SEP IRREG VI AUX SEIN **(a)** (= *sich abheben*) to stand out; (= *unangenehm ~*) to attract attention; (= *sich hervortun*) to be remarkable (*durch* for); **er fällt durch seine roten Haare auf** his red hair makes him stand out; **er ist schon früher als unzuverlässig/Extremist aufgefallen** it has been noticed before that he is unreliable/an extremist; **angenehm/ unangenehm ~** to make a good/bad impression; **nur nicht ~!** just don't be conspicuous
(b) (= *bemerkt werden*) **jdm fällt etw auf** sb notices sth; **so etwas fällt doch nicht auf** that will never be noticed; **der Fehler fällt nicht besonders auf** the mistake is not all that noticeable; **das muss dir doch aufgefallen sein!** surely you must have noticed (it)!

auffallend 1 ADJ noticeable; *Schönheit, Ähnlichkeit, Farbe, Kleider* striking **2** ADV noticeably; (= *besonders*) *schön, nett* strikingly; **stimmt ~!** (*hum*) too true!

auffällig 1 ADJ conspicuous; *Farbe, Kleidung* striking; **~ werden** (*Mensch*) to get oneself noticed; **~ ist, dass/wie ...** it's striking that/how ...
2 ADV conspicuously; (= *besonders*) *lang, kurz* amazingly; **sich ~ verhalten** to get oneself noticed; **er hat sich ~ genau erkundigt** he made a point of inquiring precisely; **er hat ~ wenig mit ihr geredet** it was conspicuous how little he talked with her; **~er gehts nicht mehr** they/he *etc* couldn't make it more obvious if they/he *etc* tried

auffangen VT SEP IRREG **(a)** *Ball, Gesprächsfetzen* to catch; *Wagen, Flugzeug* to get under control; **jds Blick** ~ to catch sb's eye **(b)** (= *abfangen*) *Aufprall etc* to cushion; *Faustschlag* to block; (*fig*) *Preissteigerung, Verluste* to offset

Auffanglager NT reception camp

auffassen SEP **1** VT **(a)** (= *interpretieren*) to interpret, to understand; **etw als etw** (*acc*) ~ to take sth as sth; **die Planeten als Götter ~** to conceive of the planets as gods; **etw falsch/richtig ~** to take sth the wrong way/in the right way **(b)** (= *geistig aufnehmen*) to grasp **2** VI to understand

Auffassung F **(a)** (= *Meinung, Verständnis*) opinion; (= *Begriff*) conception; **nach meiner ~** in my opinion; **nach christlicher ~** according to Christian belief **(b)** (= *Auffassungsgabe*) perception

Auffassungs-: **Auffassungsgabe** F **er hat eine große ~** he has a tremendous grasp of things; **Auffassungssache** F (*inf*) question of interpretation; (= *Ansichtssache*) matter of opinion

auffegen SEP **1** VT to sweep up **2** VI to sweep (up)

auffi [ˈaufi] ADV (*Aus*) = **herauf, hinauf**

auffindbar ADJ **es ist nicht/ist ~** it can't/can be found; **es ist schwer ~** it's hard to find

auffinden VT SEP IRREG to find

auffischen VT SEP (*a*) *Gegenstand* to fish up; (*inf*) *Schiffbrüchige* to fish out **(b)** (*fig inf*) to find

aufflackern VI SEP AUX SEIN (*lit, fig*) to flare up

auffliegen VI SEP IRREG AUX SEIN **(a)** (= *hochfliegen*) to fly up **(b)** (= *sich öffnen*) to fly open **(c)** (*fig inf*: = *jäh enden*) (*Konferenz etc*) to break up; (*Rauschgiftring, Verbrecher etc*) to be busted (*inf*); **einen Schmugglerring ~ lassen** to bust a ring of smugglers (*inf*); **eine Konferenz ~ lassen** to break up a meeting

auffordern VT SEP **(a)** (= *ersuchen*) to ask; **wir fordern Sie auf, ...** you are required to ... **(b)** (= *bitten*) to ask; (*zum Wettkampf etc*) to challenge **(c)** (= *zum Tanz bitten*) to ask to dance

Aufforderung F request; (*nachdrücklicher*) demand; (= *Einladung*) invitation; (*Jur*) incitement

aufforsten VT SEP *Gebiet* to reafforest; *Wald* to retimber

auffressen SEP IRREG **1** VT (*lit, fig*) to eat up; **ich könnte dich ~** (*inf*) I could eat you (*inf*); **er wird dich deswegen nicht gleich ~** (*inf*) he's not going to eat you (*inf*) **2** VI (*Tier*) to eat all its food up

auffrischen SEP **1** VT to freshen (up); *Möbel etc* to renovate; (= *ergänzen*) *Vorräte* to replenish; (*fig*) *Erinnerungen* to refresh; *Kenntnisse* to polish up; *Sprachkenntnisse* to brush up; *persönliche Beziehungen* to renew; *Impfung* to boost **2** VI AUX SEIN or HABEN (*Wind*) to freshen **3** VI IMPERS AUX SEIN to get fresher

Auffrischungsimpfung F booster

aufführen SEP **1** VT **(a)** *Theaterstück, Ballett* to put on; *Drama, Oper* to stage; *Musikwerk, Komponist* to perform; **ein Theater ~** (*fig*) to make a scene **(b)** (= *auflisten*) to list; (= *nennen*) *Beispiel* to quote; **einzeln ~** to itemize **2** VR to behave; **sich wie ein Betrunkener ~** to act like a drunkard; **wie er sich wieder aufgeführt hat!** what a performance!

Aufführung F **(a)** (*Theat*) putting on; (*von Drama, Oper*) staging; (= *Vorstellung*) performance; **etw zur ~ bringen** (*form*) to perform sth; **zur ~ kommen** or **gelangen** (*form*) to be performed **(b)** (= *Auflistung*) listing; (= *Liste*) list; **einzelne ~** itemization

auffüllen VT SEP **(a)** (= *vollständig füllen*) to fill up; (= *nachfüllen*) to top up; **darf ich Ihr Glas ~?** can I top you up? **(b)** (= *ergänzen*) *Vorräte* to replenish; *Öl* to top up (*Brit*) or off (*US*); **Benzin ~** to fill up

Aufgabe F **(a)** (= *Arbeit, Pflicht*) job, task; **es ist nicht ~ der Regierung, ...** it is not the job of the government to ...; **sich** (*dat*) **etw zur ~ machen** to make sth one's business **(b)** (= *Zweck, Funktion*) purpose, job **(c)** (*esp Sch*) (= *Problem*) question; (*zur Übung*) exercise; (*usu pl:* = *Hausaufgabe*) homework *no pl* **(d)** (*von Koffer, Gepäck*) registering; (*Aviat*) checking (in); (*von Brief, Postsendung*) handing in; (*von Anzeige*) placing *no pl* **(e)** (*Sport*) retirement; (*Mil*) surrender; **die Polizei forderte die Geiselnehmer zur ~ auf** the police appealed to the kidnappers to surrender **(f)** (*von Gewohnheit, Geschäft*) giving up; (*von Plänen, Forderungen*) dropping; (*von Hoffnung, Studium*) abandonment

aufgabeln VT SEP (*fig inf*) *jdn* to pick up (*inf*); **wo hat er denn die aufgegabelt?** where did he dig her up? (*inf*)

Aufgaben-: **Aufgabenbereich** M, **Aufgabengebiet** NT area of responsibility; **Aufgabenheft** NT (*Sch*) homework book; **Aufgabenstellung** F **(a)** (= *Formulierung*) formulation **(b)** (= *Aufgabe*) type of problem; **Aufgabenverteilung** F allocation of responsibilities

Aufgang M, *pl* **-gänge (a)** (*von Sonne, Mond, Stern*) rising; (*fig: von Stern*) emergence **(b)** (= *Treppenaufgang*) stairs *pl*, staircase; **im ~** on the stairs *or* staircase

aufgeben SEP IRREG **1** VT **(a)** *Hausaufgaben* to give; *schwierige Frage, Problem* to pose (*jdm* for sb); **jdm viel/nichts ~** (*Sch*) to give sb a lot of/no homework
(b) *Koffer, Gepäck* to register; *Fluggepäck* to check in; *Brief, Paket* to post (*Brit*), to mail (*esp US*); *Anzeige, Bestellung* to place **(c)** *Kampf, Hoffnung, Arbeitsstelle, Freund etc* to give up; **gibs auf!** why don't you give up?
(d) (= *verloren geben*) *Patienten, Schüler* to give up **2** VI **(a)** (= *sich geschlagen geben*) to give up or in; (*Mil*) to surrender
(b) (*inf: bei Tisch*) to serve (*jdm* sb); **kann ich dir noch mal ~?** can I give you some more?

aufgeblasen [ˈaufɡəblaːzn] ADJ (*fig*) self-important; *siehe auch* **aufblasen**

Aufgebot NT **(a)** (*zur Eheschließung*) notice of intended marriage; (*Eccl*) banns *pl*; **das ~ bestellen** to give notice of one's intended marriage; (*Eccl*) to post the banns **(b)** (= *Ansammlung*) (*von Menschen*) contingent; (*von Material etc*) array

Aufgebotsverfahren NT (*Jur, Fin*) judicial call procedure; (*bei Wertpapieren*) public notification procedure

aufgebracht [ˈaufɡəbraxt] ADJ outraged; *siehe auch* **aufbringen**

aufgedonnert [ˈaufɡədɔnɐt] ADJ (*pej inf*) tarted-up (*Brit pej inf*), decked-out (*US inf*); *siehe auch* **aufdonnern**

aufgedreht [ˈaufɡədreːt] ADJ (*inf*) in high spirits; *siehe auch* **aufdrehen**

aufgedunsen ADJ bloated

aufgehen VI SEP IRREG AUX SEIN **(a)** (*Sonne, Mond, Sterne*) to come up **(b)** (= *sich öffnen*) to open; (*Theat: Vorhang*) to go up; (*Knopf, Knoten, Reißverschluss, Jacke etc*) to come undone **(c)** (*Cook*) to rise **(d)** (= *klar werden*) **jdm geht etw auf** sth dawns on sb **(e)** (*Math: Rechnung etc*) to work out; (*fig*) to work (out); **wenn man 20 durch 6 teilt, geht das nicht auf** 20 divided by 6 doesn't go **(f)** (= *seine Erfüllung finden*) **in etw** (*dat*) **~** to be taken up with sth; **er geht ganz in der Familie auf** his whole life revolves around his family

aufgehoben ['aufgəhoːbn] ADJ **(bei jdm) gut/schlecht ~ sein** to `be/not to be in good hands (with sb); *siehe auch* **aufheben**

aufgeilen ['aufgailən] VR SEP (*sl*) **er geilt sich an diesen Fotos auf** he gets off on these photos (*inf*)

aufgeklärt ['aufgəkleːɐt] ADJ **(a)** enlightened (*auch Philos*) **(b)** (*sexualkundlich*) **~ sein** to know the facts of life; *siehe auch* **aufklären**

aufgekratzt ['aufgəkratst] ADJ (*inf*) in high spirits; *siehe auch* **aufkratzen**

aufgelegt ['aufgəleːkt] ADJ **gut/schlecht** *etc* **~** in a good/bad *etc* mood; **(dazu) ~ sein, etw zu tun** to feel like doing sth; *siehe auch* **auflegen**

aufgelöst ['aufgəløːst] ADJ (= *außer sich*) beside oneself (*vor +dat* with), distraught; (= *bestürzt*) upset; **in Tränen ~** in tears; *siehe auch* **auflösen**

aufgeregt ['aufgəreːkt] **1** ADJ (= *erregt*) excited; (= *nervös*) nervous; (= *durcheinander*) flustered **2** ADV excitedly; *siehe auch* **aufregen**

aufgeschlossen ['aufgəʃlɔsn] ADJ (= *nicht engstirnig*) open-minded (*für, gegenüber* as regards, about); (= *empfänglich*) open (*für, gegenüber* to); **ich bin Vorschlägen gegenüber** *or* **für Vorschläge jederzeit ~** I'm always open to suggestion(s); **einer Sache** (*dat*) **~ gegenüberstehen** to be open-minded about sth; *siehe auch* **aufschließen**

Aufgeschlossenheit F -, NO PL open-mindedness (*für, gegenüber* as regards, about); (= *Empfänglichkeit*) openness (*für, gegenüber* to)

aufgeschmissen ['aufgəʃmɪsn] ADJ PRED (*inf*) in a fix (*inf*), stuck (*inf*)

aufgeschossen ['aufgəʃɔsn] ADJ **(hoch** *or* **lang) ~ Mensch** who has shot up; **ein lang ~er Junge** a tall lanky boy; *siehe auch* **aufschießen**

aufgesetzt ADJ (= *geheuchelt*) *Sprüche* hypocritical; *Laune, Mimik* put on; **~ wirken** (= *unecht*) to seem false; *siehe auch* **aufsetzen**

aufgestellt ADJ (*Sw*) convivial; *siehe auch* **aufstellen**

aufgeweckt ['aufgəvɛkt] ADJ bright; *siehe auch* **aufwecken**

aufgewühlt ['aufgəvyːlt] ADJ (*geh*) agitated; *Wasser, Meer* turbulent; **völlig ~** (*fig*) in a complete turmoil; *siehe auch* **aufwühlen**

aufgießen VT SEP IRREG *Kaffee, Tee* to make

aufgliedern ['aufgliːdɐn] **1** VT (*in +acc* into) to split up; (= *analysieren, in Kategorien auch*) to break down **2** VR (*in +acc* into) to break down

aufgraben VT SEP IRREG to dig up

aufgreifen VT SEP IRREG **(a)** (= *festnehmen*) to pick up **(b)** (= *weiterverfolgen*) *Thema, Gedanken* to take up; (= *fortsetzen*) *Gespräch* to continue

aufgrund [auf'grʊnt], **auf Grund** PREP +GEN on the basis of; **~ einer Verwechslung/seiner Eifersucht** because of a mistake/his jealousy

aufgucken VI SEP (*inf*) to look up (*von* from)

Aufguss M brew, infusion (*auch Sci*); (*in Sauna*) pouring of water onto hot coals; (*fig pej*) rehash

Aufgussbeutel M sachet (containing coffee/herbs *etc*) for brewing; (= *Teebeutel*) tea bag

aufhaben SEP IRREG **1** VT **(a)** *Hut, Brille* to have on **(b)** *Tür, Augen, Laden, Jacke* to have open **(c)** (*Sch: als Hausaufgabe*) **etw ~** to have sth (to do); **ich habe heute viel auf** I've got a lot of homework today **(d)** (*inf: = aufgegessen haben*) to have eaten up **2** VI (*Laden etc*) to be open

aufhalsen ['aufhalzn] VT SEP (*inf*) **jdm/sich etw ~** to land sb/oneself with sth (*inf*); **sich** (*dat*) **etw ~ lassen** to get oneself landed with sth (*inf*)

aufhalten SEP IRREG **1** VT **(a)** *Fahrzeug, Entwicklung* to stop; *Inflation etc* to check; (= *verlangsamen*) to hold up; (= *abhalten, stören*) to hold back (*bei* from); **ich will dich nicht länger ~** I don't want to hold you back any longer **(b)** (*inf:* = *offen halten*) to keep open; **die Hand ~** to hold one's hand out **2** VR **(a)** (= *an einem Ort bleiben*) to stay **(b)** (= *sich verzögern*) to stay on; (*bei der Arbeit etc*) to take a long time (*bei* over) **(c)** (= *sich befassen*) **sich bei etw ~** to dwell on sth; **sich mit jdm/etw ~** to spend time dealing with sb/sth **(d)** (= *sich entrüsten*) **sich über etw** (*acc*) **~** to rail against sth

aufhängen SEP IRREG **1** VT **(a)** *Kleidung, Bild* to hang up; (*Aut*) *Rad* to suspend; **etw an einer Frage/einem Thema ~** to use a question/subject as a peg to hang sth on **(b)** (= *töten*) to hang (*an +dat* from); **(c)** (*inf*) **jdm etw ~** (= *aufschwatzen*) to palm sth off on sb; (= *aufbürden*) to land sb with sth (*inf*) **2** VR (= *sich töten*) to hang oneself (*an +dat* from); (*hum:* = *seine Kleider ~*) to hang one's things up

Aufhänger M tag, loop; **ein ~ für etw** (*fig inf*) a peg to hang sth on (*fig*)

Aufhängung ['aufhɛŋʊŋ] F -, -en (*Tech*) suspension

aufhäufen VTR SEP to accumulate

aufheben SEP IRREG **1** VT **(a)** (*vom Boden*) to pick up; *größeren Gegenstand* (= *in die Höhe heben*) to lift up; *Deckel* to lift off **(b)** (= *nicht wegwerfen*) to keep; **jdm etw ~** to put sth aside for sb; *siehe auch* **aufgehoben** **(c)** (= *ungültig machen*) to abolish; *Vertrag* to cancel; *Urteil* to quash; *Verlobung* to break off; **dieses Gesetz hebt das andere auf** this law supersedes the other **(d)** (= *beenden*) *Blockade, Belagerun, Beschränkung* to lift; *Sitzung* to close **(e)** (= *ausgleichen*) to offset; *Widerspruch* to resolve; *Schwerkraft* to cancel out **2** VR (= *sich ausgleichen*) to offset each other; (*Math*) to cancel (each other) out

Aufheben NT -s, NO PL fuss; **viel ~(s) machen** to make a lot of fuss (*von, um* about); **ohne (jedes) ~** without any fuss; **ohne viel** *or* **großes ~** without much *or* a big fuss

Aufhebung F **(a)** (= *Abschaffung*) abolition; (*von Vertrag*) cancellation; (*von Urteil*) quashing; (*von Verlobung*) breaking off **(b)** (= *Beendigung*) (*von Blockade, Beschränkung etc*) lifting; (*von Sitzung*) closing **(c)** (*von Widerspruch*) resolving; (*von Schwerkraft*) cancelling out

aufheitern ['aufhaitɐn] SEP **1** VT *jdn* to cheer up; *Rede, Leben* to brighten up (*jdm* for sb) **2** VR (*Himmel*) to clear; (*Wetter*) to clear up

Aufheiterung F -, -en (= *Erheiterung*) cheering up; (*von Rede, Leben*) brightening up; (*Met*) brighter period; **zunehmende ~** gradually brightening up

aufhellen ['aufhɛlən] SEP **1** VT to brighten (up); *Haare* to lighten; (*fig:* = *klären*) to shed light upon **2** VR (*Himmel, Wetter, fig: Miene*) to brighten (up)

aufhetzen VT SEP to stir up; **jdn gegen jdn/etw ~** to stir up sb's animosity against sb/sth; **jdn zu etw ~** to incite sb to (do) sth

aufheulen VI SEP to howl (*vor* with); (*Sirene*) to (start to) wail; (*Motor, Menge*) to (give a) roar; (= *weinen*) to start to howl

aufholen SEP **1** VT to make up; *Lernstoff* to catch up on; **Versäumtes ~** to make up for lost time **2** VI to catch up; (*Zug etc*) to make up time; (= *Versäumnisse ~*) to make up for lost time

aufhorchen VI SEP to sit up (and take notice); **das ließ ~** that made people sit up (and take notice)

aufhören VI SEP to stop; (*Musik, Lärm, Straße auch, Freundschaft, Korrespondenz*) to (come to an) end; (*bei Arbeitsstelle*) to finish; **nicht ~/~, etw zu tun** to keep on/stop doing sth; **hör doch endlich auf!** (will you) stop it!; **mit etw ~** to stop sth; **da hört sich doch alles auf!** that's the (absolute) limit!; **da hört bei ihm der Spaß auf** (*inf*) he's not amused by that

Aufkauf M buying up

aufkaufen VT SEP to buy up

Aufkäufer(in) M(F) buyer

aufkeimen VI SEP AUX SEIN to sprout; (*fig*) (*Hoffnung, Liebe, Sympathie*) to bud; (*Zweifel*) to (begin to) take root

aufklappbar ADJ *Fenster, Tafel* hinged; *Truhe, Schreibpult* with a hinged lid; *Klappe* which lets down; *Verdeck* which folds back

aufklappen SEP **1** VT to open up; *Klappe* to lift up; *Verdeck* to fold back; *Messer* to unclasp; *Fensterläden, Buch, Landkarte* to open **2** VI AUX SEIN to open

aufklaren ['aufklaːrən] SEP (*Met*) **1** VI IMPERS to clear (up) **2** VI (*Wetter*) to brighten (up); (*Himmel*) to clear

aufklären SEP **1** VT **(a)** *Missverständnis, Irrtum* to clear up; *Verbrechen, Rätsel* to solve; *Ereignis, Vorgang* to shed light upon
(b) *jdn* to enlighten; **Kinder ~** (*sexualkundlich*) to tell children the facts of life; (*in der Schule*) to give children sex education; **jdn über etw** (*acc*) **~** to inform sb about sth; **klär mich mal auf, wie ...** (*inf*) (can you) enlighten me as to how ...; *siehe auch* **aufgeklärt**
2 VR (*Irrtum, Geheimnis etc*) to resolve itself; (*Himmel*) to clear; (*fig: Miene, Gesicht*) to brighten (up)

Aufklärung F **(a)** (*Philos*) **die ~** the Enlightenment **(b)** (*von Missverständnis*) clearing up; (*von Verbrechen, Rätsel*) solution; (*von Ereignis, Vorgang*) elucidation **(c)** (= *Information*) enlightenment; (*von offizieller Stelle*) informing (*über +acc* about); (*Pol*) instruction **(d)** (**sexuelle**) **~** (*in Schulen*) sex education; **die ~ von Kindern** explaining the facts of life to children **(e)** (*Mil*) reconnaissance

Aufklärungs-: **Aufklärungsbuch** NT sex education book; **Aufklärungsfilm** M sex education film; **Aufklärungsflugzeug** NT reconnaissance plane; (*klein*) scout (plane); **Aufklärungsquote** F (*in Kriminalstatistik*) percentage of cases solved; **Aufklärungssatellit** M spy satellite; **Aufklärungsschiff** NT (*Mil*) reconnaissance ship

aufkleben VT SEP (*auf +acc* to) to stick on; (*mit Kleister*) to paste on

Aufkleber [-kleːbɐ] M **-s, -** sticker

aufknacken VT SEP *Nüsse etc* to crack (open); (*inf*) *Tresor, Auto* to break into

aufknoten VT SEP to untie

aufknüpfen SEP **1** VT **(a)** (= *aufhängen*) to hang (*an +dat* from) **(b)** (= *aufknoten*) to untie **2** VR to hang oneself (*an +dat* from)

aufkochen SEP **1** VT **(a)** (= *zum Kochen bringen*) to bring to the (*Brit*) *or* a (*US*) boil **(b)** (= *erneut kochen lassen*) to boil up again **2** VI **(a)** AUX SEIN to come to the (*Brit*) *or* a (*US*) boil; (*fig*) to begin to boil; **etw ~ lassen** to bring sth to the (*Brit*) *or* a (*US*) boil **(b)** (*Aus*) to prepare a fine spread

aufkommen VI SEP IRREG AUX SEIN **(a)** (*lit, fig*: = *entstehen*) to arise; (*Nebel*) to come down; (*Wind*) to get up; (= *auftreten*: *Mode etc*) to appear (on the scene); **etw ~ lassen** (*fig*) *Zweifel, Kritik* to give rise to sth; *üble Stimmung* to allow sth to develop **(b)** **~ für** (= *Kosten tragen*) to bear the costs of; (= *Verantwortung tragen*) to be responsible for; (= *Haftung tragen*) to be liable for; **für die Kinder ~** (*finanziell*) to pay for the children's upkeep; **für die Kosten ~** to bear the costs; **für den Schaden ~** to pay for the damage **(c)** (= *aufsetzen, auftreffen*) to land (*auf +dat* on) **(d)** (*dial: Schwindel, Diebstahl etc*) to come out

Aufkommen NT **-s, -** **(a)** NO PL (= *das Auftreten*) appearance; (*von Methode, Mode etc*) advent; **~ frischer Winde gegen Abend** fresh winds will get up toward(s) evening **(b)** (*Fin*) (= *Summe, Menge*) amount; (*von Steuern*) revenue (*aus, +gen* from) **(c)** NO PL (*von Flugzeug*) landing; **beim ~** on touchdown

aufkratzen SEP **1** VT (= *zerkratzen*) to scratch; *Wunde* to scratch open; *siehe auch* **aufgekratzt** **2** VR to scratch oneself sore

aufkreuzen VI SEP **(a)** AUX SEIN (*inf*: = *erscheinen*) to show up (*inf*) **(b)** AUX SEIN *or* HABEN **gegen den Wind ~** (*Naut*) to tack

aufkriegen VT SEP (*inf*) = **aufbekommen**

Aufl. ABBR *von* **Auflage**

auflachen VI SEP to (give a) laugh; (*schallend*) to burst out laughing

aufladbar ADJ chargeable; (= *neu ~*) rechargeable; **~e Geldkarte** electronic cash card

aufladen SEP IRREG **1** VT **(a)** **etw (auf etw** *acc*) **~** to load sth on(to) sth; **jdm/sich etw ~** to load sb/oneself down with sth; (*fig*) to saddle sb/oneself with sth **(b)** (*elektrisch*) to charge;

(= *neu ~*) to recharge; *Geldkarte* to reload; **emotional aufgeladen** (*fig*) emotionally charged **2** VR (*Batterie etc*) to be charged; (*neu*) to be recharged; (= *elektrisch/elektrostatisch geladen werden*) to become charged

Auflage F **(a)** (= *Ausgabe*) edition; (= *Druck*) impression; (= *Auflagenhöhe*) number of copies; (*von Zeitung*) circulation; **das Buch hat hohe ~n erreicht** a large number of copies of this book have been published; **die Zeitung hat hohe ~n erreicht** this paper has attained a large circulation **(b)** (*Ind*: = *Fertigungsmenge*) production; **limitierte ~** limited edition **(c)** (= *Bedingung*) condition; **jdm etw zur ~ machen** to impose sth on sb as a condition; **jdm zur ~ machen, etw zu tun** to make it a condition for sb to do sth; **die ~ haben, etw zu tun** to be obliged to do sth

Auflage(n)höhe F (*von Buch*) number of copies published; (*von Zeitung*) circulation; **das Buch hatte eine Auflagehöhe von 12.000** 12,000 copies of the book were published; **die Zeitung hatte eine Auflagehöhe von ...** the paper had a circulation of ...

Auflage-: **Auflagepunkt** M point of support; **auflageschwach** ADJ low-circulation *attr*; **auflagestark** ADJ high-circulation *attr*

auflassen VT SEP IRREG **(a)** (*inf*: = *offen lassen*) to leave open; (= *aufbehalten*) *Hut* to keep on; **das Kind länger ~** to let the child stay up (longer) **(b)** (= *schließen*) to close down; **eine aufgelassene Grube** an abandoned mine

auflauern VI SEP +DAT to lie in wait for; (*und angreifen, ansprechen*) to waylay

Auflauf M **(a)** (= *Menschenauflauf*) crowd **(b)** (*Cook*) (baked) pudding (*sweet or savoury*)

auflaufen VI SEP IRREG AUX SEIN **(a)** (*Schiff*) to run aground (*auf +acc or dat* on); **jdn ~ lassen** to drop sb in it (*inf*) **(b)** (= *aufprallen*) **auf jdn/etw ~** to run into sb/sth; **jdn ~ lassen** (*Ftbl*) to bodycheck sb

Auflaufform F (*Cook*) ovenproof dish

aufleben VI SEP AUX SEIN to revive; (= *munter, lebendig werden*) to liven up; (= *neuen Lebensmut bekommen*) to find a new lease of life; **Erinnerungen wieder ~ lassen** to revive memories

auflecken VT SEP to lick up

auflegen SEP **1** VT **(a)** *Tischdecke, Schallplatte etc* to put on; *Gedeck* to set; *Kompresse* to apply; *Hörer* to replace; **jdm die Hand ~** (*Rel*) to lay hands on sb
(b) (= *herausgeben*) *Buch* to bring out; **ein Buch neu ~** to reprint a book; (*neu bearbeitet*) to bring out a new edition of a book
(c) (*zur Einsichtnahme*) to display
(d) (*Econ*) *Serie* to launch
(e) (*Fin*) *Aktien* to issue; *Fonds* to set up
(f) *siehe* **aufgelegt**
2 VI (= *Telefonhörer ~*) to hang up

auflehnen VR SEP **sich gegen jdn/etw ~** to rebel against sb/sth

auflesen VT SEP IRREG (*lit, fig inf*) to pick up

aufliegen SEP IRREG **1** VI **(a)** (= *auf etw sein*) to lie on top; (*Schallplatte*) to be on the turntable; (*Hörer*) to be on; **auf etw** (*dat*) **~** to lie *or* be on sth **(b)** (= *ausliegen*) (*zur Ansicht*) to be displayed; (*zur Benutzung*) to be available **2** VR (*inf: Patient*) to get bedsores **3** VT (*inf*) **sich** (*dat*) **den Rücken** *etc* **~** to get bedsores on one's back *etc*

Auflieger ['aufliːgɐ] M **-s, -** (*von Lkw*) trailer

auflisten ['auflɪstn] VT SEP to list

auflockern SEP **1** VT **(a)** *Boden* to loosen (up); **die Muskeln ~** to loosen up (one's muscles) **(b)** (= *abwechslungsreicher machen*) to make less monotonous; (= *weniger streng machen*) to make less severe **(c)** (= *entspannen, zwangloser machen*) to make more relaxed; *Verhältnis, Atmosphäre* to ease; **in aufgelockerter Stimmung** in a relaxed mood **2** VR **(a)** (*Sport*) to limber up **(b)** (*Bewölkung*) to disperse

Auflockerung F **(a)** (*von Boden*) loosening (up); (*von Muskeln*) loosening up; **... trägt zur ~ des Stoffes/des strengen Musters bei** ... helps to make the material less monotonous/the pattern less severe **(b)** (*Sport*) limbering up **(c)** (*von Bewölkung*) dispersal, dispersing

auflösen SEP **1** VT **(a)** (*in Flüssigkeit*) to dissolve; (= *in Bestandteile zerlegen*) (*Phot*) to resolve (*in +acc* into); (*Math*) *Klammern* to eliminate; *Gleichung* to (re)solve; *siehe auch*

aufgelöst
(b) (Widerspruch, Missverständnis) to clear up; Rätsel to solve
(c) (= zerstreuen) Wolken, Versammlung to disperse
(d) (= aufheben) to dissolve (auch Parl); Einheit, Gruppe to disband; Firma to wind up; Verlobung to break off; Vertrag to cancel; Konto to close; Haushalt to break up
2 VR **(a)** (in Flüssigkeit) to dissolve; (= sich zersetzen: Zellen, Reich, Ordnung) to disintegrate; (Zweifel, Probleme) to disappear; **all ihre Probleme haben sich in nichts aufgelöst** all her problems have disappeared
(b) (= sich zerstreuen) to disperse
(c) (= auseinander gehen) (Verband) to disband; (Firma) to cease trading; (= sich formell ~: esp Parl) to dissolve
(d) (= sich aufklären) to be resolved
(e) sich in etw (acc) ~ (= verwandeln) to turn into sth; (= undeutlich werden) to dissolve into sth

Auflösung F **(a)** (= das Auflösen) (in Bestandteile) resolution; (von Widerspruch, Missverständnis) clearing up; (von Rätsel) solving; (von Wolken, Versammlung) dispersal; (von Einheit, Gruppe) disbanding; (von Firma) winding up; (von Verlobung) breaking off; (von Vertrag) cancellation; (von Konto) closing; (von Haushalt) breaking up; (von Reich, Ordnung, Zellen) disintegration; (von Parlament) dissolution
(b) (= Lösung) (von Problem etc) resolution; (von Rätsel) solution (+gen, von to)
(c) (Phot, Comput, von Bildschirm) resolution

Auflösungszeichen NT (Mus) natural

aufmachen SEP **1** VT **(a)** (= öffnen) to open; (= lösen, aufknöpfen, aufschnallen) to undo; Haar to loosen
(b) (= eröffnen, gründen) to open (up)
(c) (= gestalten) Buch, Zeitung to make up; (= zurechtmachen) jdn to dress; (in Presse) Ereignis, Prozess etc to feature; **der Prozess wurde groß aufgemacht** the trial was given a big spread
2 VI (= Tür öffnen) to open up; (= Geschäft (er)öffnen) to open (up)
3 VR **(a)** (= sich zurechtmachen) to get oneself up (inf)
(b) (= sich anschicken) to get ready; (= aufbrechen) to set out; **sich zu einem Spaziergang ~** to set out on a walk

Aufmacher M (Press) lead

Aufmachung ['aufmaxʊŋ] F -, -en **(a)** (= Kleidung) turnout; **in großer ~ erscheinen** to turn up in full dress **(b)** (= Gestaltung) presentation; (von Seite, Zeitschrift) layout; **der Artikel erschien in großer ~** the article was given a big spread

Aufmaß NT (Build) dimension

aufmerksam ['aufmɛrkzaːm] **1** ADJ **(a)** Zuhörer, Beobachter, Schüler attentive; Augen keen; (= scharf beobachtend) observant; **jdn auf etw** (acc) **~ machen** to draw sb's attention to sth; **jdn darauf ~ machen, dass ...** to draw sb's attention to the fact that ...; **auf jdn/etw ~ werden** to become aware of sb/sth; **~ werden** to sit up and take notice
(b) (= zuvorkommend) attentive; **(das ist) sehr ~ von Ihnen** (that's) most kind of you
2 ADV zusehen carefully; zuhören attentively; **Felix beteiligt sich ~ am Unterrichtsgeschehen** Felix pays attention in class

Aufmerksamkeit F -, -en **(a)** NO PL attention, attentiveness; **das ist meiner ~ entgangen** that escaped my notice **(b)** NO PL (= Zuvorkommenheit) attentiveness **(c)** (= Geschenk) token (gift); **(nur) eine kleine ~** (just) a little something or gift; **kleine ~en** little gifts

aufmöbeln ['aufmøːbln] VT SEP (inf) Gegenstand to do up (inf); jdn to buck up (inf)

aufmotzen VT SEP (inf) to zap up (inf)

aufmucken, aufmucksen VI SEP (inf) to protest (gegen at, against)

aufmuntern ['aufmʊntɐn] VT SEP (= aufheitern) to cheer up; (= beleben) to liven up; (= ermutigen) to encourage; **jdn zu etw ~** to encourage sb to do sth; **ein ~des Lächeln** an encouraging smile

Aufmunterung F -, -en **(a)** NO PL cheering up; (= Belebung) livening up **(b)** (= Ermutigung) encouragement

aufmüpfig ['aufmʏpfɪç] ADJ (inf) rebellious

Aufnahme ['aufnaːma] F -, -n **(a)** (= Empfang, fig: = Reaktion) reception; **bei jdm freundliche ~ finden** (lit, fig) to meet with a warm reception from sb; **die ~ in ein Krankenhaus** admission (in)to hospital; **wie war die ~ beim Publikum?** how did the audience receive it?

(b) (in Verein, Orden etc) admission (in +acc to)
(c) NO PL (lit) (fig: = Absorption) absorption; (= Nahrungsaufnahme) taking
(d) NO PL (= Einbeziehung) inclusion
(e) NO PL (von Geldern, Kapital, Hypothek) raising
(f) NO PL (von Protokoll, Diktat, Personalien) taking down; **die ~ eines Unfalls** taking down details of an accident
(g) NO PL (= Beginn) (von Gespräch etc) start; (von Tätigkeit) taking up; (von Beziehung, Verbindung) establishment
(h) NO PL (= das Fotografieren) photographing; (= das Filmen) filming, shooting (inf); **Achtung, ~!** action!
(i) (= Fotografie) photo(graph); (= Schnappschuss, Amateuraufnahme) snap (inf); **eine ~ machen** to take a photo(graph)
(j) (auf Tonband) recording

Aufnahme-: aufnahmefähig ADJ **(a)** für etw ~ sein to be able to take sth in; **ich bin nicht mehr ~** I can't take anything else in **(b)** Markt receptive; **Aufnahmegebühr** F enrolment (Brit) or enrollment (US) fee; (in Verein) admission fee; **Aufnahmeland** NT host country (für to); **Aufnahmeleiter(in)** M(F) (Film) production manager; (Rad, TV) producer; **Aufnahmeprüfung** F entrance examination; **Aufnahmestopp** M (für Flüchtlinge etc) ban on immigration; **Aufnahmevermögen** NT
(a) (= Aufnahmefähigkeit) receptiveness (für to)
(b) (= Fassungsvermögen) capacity; **Aufnahmewagen** M (Rad) recording van

Aufnahmsprüfung F (Aus) entrance examination

aufnehmen VT SEP IRREG **(a)** (vom Boden) to pick up; (= heben) to lift up
(b) (lit: = empfangen, fig: = reagieren auf) to receive
(c) (= unterbringen) to take (in); (= fassen) to take; Arbeitskräfte, Einwanderer to absorb
(d) (in Verein, Orden, Schule etc) to admit (in +acc to); (Aus: = anstellen) to take on
(e) (= absorbieren) to absorb; (= im Körper ~) to take; (fig) Eindrücke to take in; **etw in sich** (dat) **~** to take sth in
(f) (= mit einbeziehen) to include; (fig: = aufgreifen) to take up
(g) (= beginnen) to begin; Tätigkeit, Studium to take up; Verbindung, Beziehung to establish; **Kontakt or Fühlung mit jdm ~** to contact sb
(h) Kapital to borrow; Kredit, Hypothek to take out
(i) Protokoll, Diktat, Personalien to take down; Telegramm to take
(j) (= fotografieren) to take (a photo(graph) of); (= filmen) to film, to shoot (inf)
(k) (auf Tonband) to record
(l) **es mit jdm/etw ~/nicht ~ können** to be a/no match for sb/sth

äufnen ['ɔyfnən] VT (Sw) Geld etc to accumulate

aufnötigen VT SEP **jdm etw ~** to force sth on sb

aufopfern VR SEP to sacrifice oneself

aufopfernd **1** ADJ Mensch self-sacrificing; Liebe, Tätigkeit, Arbeit devoted; **ein ~es Leben** a life of self-sacrifice **2** ADV self-sacrificingly

aufopferungsvoll **1** ADJ self-sacrificing **2** ADV self-sacrificing

aufpäppeln VT SEP (inf) (mit Nahrung) to feed up; (durch Pflege) to nurse back to health

aufpassen VI SEP **(a)** (= beaufsichtigen) **auf jdn/etw ~** to keep an eye on sb/sth; (= hüten) to look after sb/sth; (= Aufsicht führen) to supervise sb/sth; (bei Examen) to invigilate sb
(b) (= aufmerksam sein, Acht geben) to pay attention; **pass auf!, aufgepasst!** look, watch; (= sei aufmerksam) pay attention; (= Vorsicht) watch out

Aufpasser ['aufpasɐ] M -s, -, **Aufpasserin** [-ərɪn] F -, -nen (pej: = Aufseher, Spitzel) spy (pej); (für VIP etc) minder; (= Beobachter) supervisor; (bei Examen) invigilator; (= Wächter) guard

aufpeitschen VT SEP Meer, Wellen to whip up; (fig) Sinne to inflame; Menschen to work up; (stärker) to whip up into a frenzy; **eine ~de Rede** an inflammatory speech

aufpeppen ['aufpɛpn] VT SEP (inf) to jazz up (inf)

aufpfropfen VT SEP (lit) to graft on (+dat -to); (fig) to superimpose (+dat on)

aufplatzen VI SEP AUX SEIN to burst open; (Lack) to crack; (Wunde) to open up

aufplustern SEP **1** VT *Federn* to ruffle up; (*fig*) *Vorfall, Ereignis* to blow up **2** VR (*Vogel*) to puff itself up; (*Mensch*) to puff oneself up

aufpolieren ptp **aufpoliert** VT SEP (*lit, fig*) to polish up

Aufprall M impact

aufprallen VI SEP AUX SEIN **auf etw** (*acc*) ~ to strike sth; (*Fahrzeug*) to collide with sth

Aufpreis M extra charge; **gegen** ~ for an extra charge

aufprobieren ptp **aufprobiert** VT SEP to try (on)

aufpumpen VT SEP *Reifen, Ballon* to inflate; *Fahrrad* to pump up the tyres (*Brit*) *or* tires (*US*) of

aufputschen SEP **1** VT **(a)** (= *aufwiegeln*) to rouse; *Gefühle, öffentliche Meinung* to stir up (*gegen* against); **jdn zu etw** ~ to incite sb to (do) sth **(b)** (*durch Reizmittel*) to stimulate; **~de Mittel** stimulants **2** VR to pep oneself up (*inf*), to dope oneself (*Sport inf*)

Aufputschmittel NT stimulant

aufquellen VI SEP IRREG AUX SEIN to swell (up); **aufgequollen** swollen; *Gesicht auch* puffy; *Mensch* bloated(-looking); **etw ~ lassen** to soak sth (to allow it to swell up)

aufraffen VR SEP **sich ~, etw zu tun** (*inf*), **sich zu etw ~** (*inf*) to rouse oneself to do sth

aufragen VI SEP AUX SEIN *or* HABEN to rise; **die hoch ~den Türme** the soaring towers; **die hoch ~den Fabrikkamine/Tannen** the towering factory chimneys/fir trees

aufrappeln VR SEP (*inf*) **(a)** = *aufraffen* **(b)** (= *wieder zu Kräften kommen*) to get over it; **er hat sich nach seiner Krankheit endlich wieder aufgerappelt** he at last recovered from *or* got over his illness

aufrauen VT SEP to roughen (up); (*Tex*) *Stoff* to nap

aufräumen SEP **1** VT to tidy up; **aufgeräumt** *Zimmer* tidy **2** VI **(a) mit etw** ~ to do away with sth **(b)** (*pej*: = *dezimieren*) **unter der Bevölkerung (gründlich)** ~ (*Seuche etc*) to decimate the population; (*Tyrann etc*) to slaughter the population wholesale

Aufräumungsarbeiten PL clear(ing)-up operations *pl*

Aufrechnung F (*Fin*) set-off (*Brit*), setoff (*US*); **~ mit einem Anspruch** setting off of a claim; **gegenseitige ~** (*Insur*) knock for knock (arrangement)

aufrecht [ˈaufrɛçt] **1** ADJ (*lit, fig*) upright; **in** *or* **mit ~em Gang** (*fig*) with one's head held high **2** ADV upright; **~ sitzen** to sit up(right); **halte dich ~!** stand up straight!

aufrechterhalten ptp **aufrechterhalten** VT SEP IRREG to maintain; *Verein* (= *moralisch stützen*) *jdn* to keep going

aufregen SEP **1** VT (= *ärgerlich machen*) to annoy; (= *nervös machen*) to make nervous; (= *beunruhigen*) to agitate; (= *bestürzen*) to upset; (= *erregen*) to excite; **du regst mich auf!** you're getting on my nerves; **er regt mich auf** he drives me mad (*inf*) **2** VR to get worked up (*inf*) (*über +acc* about); *siehe auch* **aufgeregt**

aufregend ADJ exciting

Aufregung F excitement *no pl*; (= *Beunruhigung*) agitation *no pl*; **nur keine ~!** don't get excited; **die Nachricht hat das ganze Land in ~ versetzt** the news caused a great stir throughout the country; **jdn in ~ versetzen** to get sb in a state (*inf*); **alles war in heller ~** everything was in utter confusion

aufreiben SEP IRREG **1** VT **(a)** (= *wund reiben*) *Haut etc* to chafe **(b)** (*fig*: = *zermürben*) to wear down **2** VR to wear oneself out

aufreibend ADJ (*fig*) wearing; (*stärker*) stressful; **nervlich ~** stressful

aufreihen SEP **1** VT (*in Linie*) to line up; *Perlen* to string; (*fig*: = *aufzählen*) to list **2** VR to line up

aufreißen SEP IRREG **1** VT **(a)** (= *durch Reißen öffnen, aufbrechen*) to tear open; *Straße* to tear up **(b)** *Tür, Fenster* to fling open; *Augen, Mund* to open wide **(c)** (*inf*) *Mädchen* to pick up (*inf*) **2** VI AUX SEIN (*Naht*) to split; (*Hose*) to tear; (*Wunde*) to tear open; (*Wolkendecke*) to break up

aufreizen VT SEP **(a)** (= *herausfordern*) to provoke; (= *aufwiegeln*) to incite **(b)** (= *erregen*) to excite; (*stärker*) to inflame

aufreizend **1** ADJ provocative **2** ADV provocatively

aufribbeln [ˈaufrɪbln] VT SEP (*inf*) to unpick

aufrichten SEP **1** VT **(a)** (= *in aufrechte Lage bringen*) *Gegenstand* to set upright; *jdn* to help up; *Oberkörper* to raise (up) **(b)** (= *aufstellen*) to erect; (*fig*) to set up **(c)** (*fig*:

moralisch) to lift **2** VR (= *gerade stehen*) to stand up (straight); (= *gerade sitzen*) to sit up (straight); (*aus gebückter Haltung*) to straighten up; (*fig: moralisch*) to pick oneself up; **sich im Bett ~** to sit up in bed

aufrichtig **1** ADJ sincere (*zu, gegen* towards) **2** ADV sincerely; *hassen, verabscheuen* truly

Aufrichtigkeit F sincerity (*zu, gegen* towards)

Aufrisszeichnung F (*Tech, Archit*) elevation

aufrollen VT SEP **(a)** (= *zusammenrollen*) *Teppich, Ärmel* to roll up; *Kabel* to wind up **(b)** (= *entrollen*) to unroll; *Fahne* to unfurl; *Kabel* to unwind **(c)** (*fig*) to go into; **einen Fall/Prozess wieder ~** to reopen a case/trial

aufrücken VI SEP AUX SEIN **(a)** (= *weiterrücken, aufschließen*) to move up **(b)** (= *befördert werden*) to be promoted; (*Schüler*) to move up; **zum Geschäftsleiter ~** to be promoted to manager

Aufruf M **(a)** appeal (*an +acc* to); **einen ~ an jdn richten** to appeal to sb; **~ zum Streik/Handeln** call for a strike/for negotiations **(b)** (*von Namen*) **seinen ~ abwarten** to wait to be called; **nach ~** on being called; **letzter ~ für Flug LH 1615** last call for flight LH 1615 **(c)** (*Comput*) call

aufrufen SEP IRREG **1** VT **(a)** *Namen* to call; *Wartenden* to call (the name of); **Sie werden aufgerufen** your name will be called; **einen Schüler ~** to ask a pupil (to answer) a question **(b)** (= *auffordern*) **jdn zu etw** ~ *zu Mithilfe, Unterstützung etc* to appeal to sb for sth; **jdn ~, etw zu tun** to appeal to sb to do sth; **Arbeiter zum Streik/zu einer Demonstration ~** to call upon workers to strike/to attend a demonstration **(c)** (*Jur*) *Zeugen* to summon **(d)** (*Comput*) to call up **2** VI **zum Widerstand/Streik** *etc* ~ to call for resistance/a strike *etc*

Aufruhr [ˈaufruːɐ] M -(e)s, -e **(a)** (= *Auflehnung*) rebellion **(b)** (= *Bewegtheit, fig*: = *Erregung*) turmoil; **in ~ sein** to be in turmoil; **in ~ geraten** to get into a state of turmoil; **jdn in ~ versetzen** to throw sb into turmoil

Aufrührer [ˈaufryːrɐ] M -s, -, **Aufrührerin** [-ərɪn] F -, -nen rabble-rouser

aufrührerisch [ˈaufryːrərɪʃ] **1** ADJ **(a)** (= *aufwiegelnd*) *Rede, Pamphlet* rabble-rousing **(b)** ATTR (= *in Aufruhr*) rebellious; (= *meuternd*) mutinous **2** ADV *fragen, sagen* provocatively

aufrunden VT SEP to round up (*auf +acc* to)

aufrüsten VT SEP **(a)** AUCH VI (*Mil*) to arm; **ein Land atomar ~** to give a country nuclear arms; **wieder ~** to rearm **(b)** (*Tech*) *Gerät, Computer* to upgrade **(c)** (*fig*) **jdn moralisch ~** to boost sb's morale

Aufrüstung F **(a)** (*Mil*) arming; **atomare ~** acquiring nuclear armaments **(b)** (*Tech: von Gerät, Computer*) upgrading

aufrütteln VT SEP to rouse (*aus* from); **jdn/jds Gewissen ~** to stir sb/sb's conscience

aufs [aufs] CONTR *von* **auf das**

aufsagen VT SEP **(a)** *Gedicht etc* to recite **(b)** (*geh*: = *für beendet erklären*) **jdm die Freundschaft ~** to break off one's friendship with sb; **jdm den Dienst/Gehorsam ~** to refuse to serve/obey sb

aufsammeln VT SEP (*lit, fig*) to pick up

aufsässig [ˈaufzɛsɪç] ADJ rebellious

Aufsässigkeit F -, NO PL rebelliousness

Aufsatz M **(a)** (= *Abhandlung*) essay; (*Sch*) essay **(b)** (= *oberer Teil*) top part; (*zur Verzierung*) bit on top; (*von Kamera etc*) attachment

Aufsatzthema NT essay subject

aufsaugen VT SEP IRREG *or* REG *Flüssigkeit* to soak up; (*fig*) to absorb; **etw mit dem Staubsauger ~** to vacuum sth up; **etw in sich** (*dat*) **~** (*Mensch*) to absorb sth

aufschauen VI SEP (*dial*) = **aufblicken**

aufscheuchen VT SEP to startle; **jdn aus etw ~** to jolt sb out of sth; **jdn von seiner Arbeit/Lektüre ~** to disturb sb when he is working/reading

aufscheuern SEP **1** VT *Fuß etc* to rub sore; *Haut* to chafe; **sich** (*dat*) **die Hände/Füße ~** to take the skin off one's hands/feet **2** VR to rub oneself sore

aufschichten VT SEP to stack; *Stapel* to build up

aufschieben VT SEP IRREG *Fenster, Tür* to slide open; *Riegel* to push back; (*fig*: = *verschieben*) to put off; **aufgeschoben ist**

nicht aufgehoben (*prov*) putting something off doesn't mean it won't happen

Aufschlag M **(a)** (= *das Aufschlagen*) impact; (= *Geräusch*) crash **(b)** (*Tennis etc*) serve; **wer hat ~?** whose serve is it? **(c)** (= *Preisaufschlag*) surcharge **(d)** (= *Ärmelaufschlag*) cuff; (= *Hosenaufschlag*) turn-up (*Brit*), cuff (*US*); (= *Mantelaufschlag etc*) lapel

aufschlagen SEP IRREG ◼ VI **(a)** AUX SEIN (= *auftreffen*) **auf etw** (*dat*) ~ to hit sth; **das Flugzeug schlug in einem Waldstück auf** the plane crashed into a wood; **mit dem Kopf** *etc* **auf etw** (*acc or dat*) ~ to hit one's head *etc* on sth; **dumpf ~** to thud (*auf +acc* onto)
(b) AUX HABEN or (*rare*) SEIN (*Waren, Preise*) to go up (*um* by)
(c) (*Tennis etc*) to serve; **du musst ~** it's your service or serve
◼ VT **(a)** (= *durch Schlagen öffnen*) to crack; *Eis* to crack a hole in; **jdm/sich den Kopf ~** to crack open sb's/one's head; **jdm/sich die Augenbraue ~** to cut open sb's/one's eyebrow
(b) (= *aufklappen*) to open; *Bett, Bettdecke* to turn back; *Kragen etc* to turn up; *Schleier* to lift up; **schlagt Seite 111 auf** open your books at page 111
(c) *Augen* to open
(d) (= *aufbauen*) *Bett, Liegestuhl* to put up; *Zelt* to pitch, to put up; (*Nacht*)*lager* to set up; **er hat seinen Wohnsitz in Wien aufgeschlagen** he has taken up residence in Vienna
(e) (*Comm*) *Preise* to put up; **10% auf etw** (*acc*) ~ to put 10% on sth

Aufschläger(in) M(F) (*Tennis etc*) server

aufschließen SEP IRREG ◼ VT (= *öffnen*) to unlock; **jdm die Tür** *etc* ~ to unlock the door *etc* for sb ◼ VR (*geh*) **sich jdm ~** to be open with sb ◼ VI **(a)** (= *öffnen*) (**jdm**) ~ to unlock the door (for sb) **(b)** (= *heranrücken*) to close up; (*Sport*) to catch up (*zu* with); *siehe auch* **aufgeschlossen**

aufschlitzen VT SEP (= *lösen*) to rip (open); (*mit Messer auch*) to slit (open); *Gesicht* to slash; *Bauch* to slash open

Aufschluss M (= *Aufklärung*) information *no pl*; (**jdm**) ~ **über etw** (*acc*) **geben** to give (sb) information about sth; ~ **über etw** (*acc*) **verlangen** to demand an explanation of sth

aufschlussreich ADJ informative

aufschnappen SEP ◼ VT to catch; (*inf*) *Wort etc* to pick up ◼ VI AUX SEIN to snap open

aufschneiden SEP IRREG ◼ VT **(a)** (= *öffnen*) to cut open; (= *tranchieren*) *Braten* to carve; *Buch* to cut; (*Med*) *Geschwür* to lance **(b)** (= *in Scheiben schneiden*) to slice ◼ VI (*inf* = *prahlen*) to boast

Aufschneider(in) M(F) (*inf*) boaster

Aufschnitt M, NO PL (assorted) sliced cold meat; (= *Käse*) (assorted) sliced cheeses *pl*; **kalter ~** (assorted) sliced cold meat

aufschnüren VT SEP (= *lösen*) to untie

aufschrauben VT SEP **(a)** *Schraube etc* to unscrew; *Flasche etc* to take the top off **(b)** (= *festschrauben*) to screw on (*auf +acc -to*)

aufschrecken SEP pret **schreckte auf**, ptp **aufgeschreckt** ◼ VT to startle; (*aus Gleichgültigkeit*) to jolt (*aus* out of); **jdn aus dem Schlaf ~** to rouse sb from sleep ◼ VI, pret auch **schrak auf** AUX SEIN to be startled; **aus dem Schlaf ~** to wake up with a start; **aus seinen Gedanken ~** to start

Aufschrei M yell; (*schriller ~*) scream; **ein ~ der Empörung/ Entrüstung** (*fig*) an outcry

aufschreiben VT SEP IRREG **(a)** (= *niederschreiben*) **etw ~** to write sth down **(b)** (= *notieren*) **sich** (*dat*) **etw ~** to make a note of sth **(c)** (*inf* = *polizeilich ~*) **jdn ~** to take sb's particulars; **das Auto ~** to take the car's number

aufschreien VI SEP IRREG to yell out; (*schrill*) to scream out

Aufschrift F (= *Beschriftung*) inscription; (= *Etikett*) label; **eine Flasche mit der ~ "Vorsicht Gift" versehen** to label a bottle "Danger - Poison"

Aufschub M (= *Verzögerung*) delay; (= *Vertagung*) postponement; **jdm ~ gewähren** (= *Zahlungsaufschub*) to allow sb grace

aufschürfen VT SEP **sich** (*dat*) **die Haut/das Knie ~** to graze oneself/one's knee

aufschütten VT SEP **(a)** *Flüssigkeit* to pour on; **Wasser auf etw** (*acc*) ~ to pour water on sth; *Kaffee* ~ to make coffee
(b) (= *nachfüllen*) *Kohle* to put on (the fire) **(c)** *Stroh, Steine* to spread; *Damm, Deich* to throw up

aufschwatzen, (*dial*) **aufschwätzen** VT SEP (*inf*) **jdm etw ~** to talk sb into taking sth

aufschweißen VT SEP to cut open (with an oxyacetylene torch)

aufschwemmen VT SEP **jdn ~** to make sb bloated; **jds Gesicht ~** to make sb's face bloated; **aufgeschwemmt** bloated

Aufschwung M **(a)** (= *Antrieb*) lift; (*der Fantasie*) upswing; (*der Seele*) uplift; (*der Wirtschaft etc*) upturn (*+gen* in); **das gab ihr (einen) neuen ~** that gave her a lift; **der ~ Ost** the economic upturn in Eastern Germany **(b)** (*Turnen*) swing-up

aufsehen VI SEP IRREG to look up; **zu jdm/etw ~** (*lit*) to look up at sb/sth; (*fig*) to look up to sb/sth

Aufsehen NT **-s**, NO PL sensation; **~ erregend** sensational; **großes ~ erregen** to cause a sensation; **ohne großes ~** without any fuss; **ich möchte jedes ~ vermeiden** I want to avoid any fuss

aufsehenerregend ADJ *siehe* **Aufsehen**

Aufseher [-zeːɐ] M **-s**, **-**, **Aufseherin** [-ərɪn] F **-**, **-nen** (*allgemein*) supervisor; (*bei Prüfung*) invigilator; (= *Sklavenaufseher*) overseer; (= *Gefängnisaufseher*) warder (*Brit*), guard (*US*); (= *Parkaufseher, Museumsaufseher etc*) attendant

auf sein VI IRREG AUX SEIN **(a)** (= *aufgestanden sein*) to be up **(b)** (= *geöffnet sein*) to be open

aufseiten [aufzaitn], **auf Seiten** PREP +GEN on the part of

aufsetzen SEP ◼ VT **(a)** (= *auf etw setzen*) to put on; *Tonarm* to lower; *Fuß* to put down; (*fig*) *Lächeln, Miene etc* to put on; **ich kann den Fuß nicht richtig ~** I can't put any weight on my foot; **sich** (*dat*) **den Hut ~** to put on one's hat; *siehe auch* **aufgesetzt**
(b) *Flugzeug* to land; *Boot* to pull up; (*unabsichtlich*) to run aground
(c) (= *aufrichten*) *Kranken etc* to sit up
(d) (= *verfassen*) to draft
◼ VR to sit up
◼ VI (*Flugzeug*) to touch down

aufseufzen VI SEP (**tief/laut**) **~** to heave a (deep/loud) sigh

Aufsicht [ˈaufzɪçt] F **-**, **-en (a)** NO PL (= *Überwachung*) supervision (*über +acc* of); (= *Obhut*) charge; **unter polizeilicher/ärztlicher ~** under police/medical supervision; **~ über jdn/etw führen** to be in charge of sb/sth; **bei einer Prüfung ~ führen** to invigilate an exam; **im Pausenhof ~ führen** to be on duty during break; **der Kranke darf niemals ohne ~ sein** the patient must be kept under constant supervision
(b) (= ~ *Führender*) person in charge; (= *Aufseher*) supervisor; **~ führend** *Behörde* supervisory; *Beamter* supervising; *Lehrer* on duty *pred*; (*bei Prüfung*) invigilating; **~ Führende(r)** person in charge; (= *Aufseher*) supervisor; (= *Lehrer*) teacher on duty; (*in Examen*) invigilator

aufsichtführend ADJ ATTR *siehe* **Aufsicht**

Aufsichts-: Aufsichtsbehörde F supervisory authority; **Aufsichtspersonal** NT supervisory staff; **Aufsichtspflicht** F (*Jur*) legal responsibility to care for sb *esp* a child; **die elterliche ~, die ~ der Eltern** (legal) parental responsibility; **Aufsichtsrat**[1] M (supervisory) board; **im ~ einer Firma sitzen** to be on the board of a firm; **Aufsichtsrat**[2] M, **Aufsichtsrätin** F member of the board; **Aufsichtsratsvorsitzende(r)** MF DECL AS ADJ chairman/chairwoman of the board

aufsitzen VI SEP IRREG **(a)** (= *aufgerichtet sitzen, aufbleiben*) to sit up **(b)** AUX SEIN (*auf Reittier*) to mount; (*auf Fahrzeug*) to get on; **aufs Pferd ~** to mount the horse **(c)** (= *ruhen auf*) to sit on (*auf etw* (*dat*) sth) **(d)** AUX SEIN (*inf*: = *hereinfallen*) **jdm/einer Sache ~** to be taken in by sb/sth

aufspalten VTR SEP to split; (*fig auch*) to split up

aufsparen VT SEP to save (up); **sich** (*dat*) **eine Bemerkung bis zum Ende ~** to save a remark until the end

aufspielen VR SEP (*inf*) **(a)** (= *sich wichtig tun*) to give oneself airs **(b)** (= *sich ausgeben als*) **sich als etw ~** to set oneself up as sth; **sich als Boss ~** to play the boss

aufspießen VT SEP to spear; (= *durchbohren*) to run through; (*mit Hörnern*) to gore; *Schmetterlinge* to pin; *Fleisch* (*mit Spieß*) to skewer; (*mit Gabel*) to prong

aufsplitten [ˈaufʃplɪtn, ˈaufsp-] VT SEP (*inf*) *Unternehmen, Einnahmen* to divide up

aufspringen VI SEP IRREG AUX SEIN **(a)** (= *hochspringen*) to jump up; **auf etw** (*acc*) **~** to jump onto sth **(b)** (= *sich öffnen*: *Tür*) to burst open; (= *platzen*) to burst; (*Rinde, Lack, Haut, Lippen etc*) to crack

aufsprühen VT SEP **etw (auf etw** *acc*) ~ to spray sth on (sth)

aufspulen VT SEP to wind on a spool

aufspüren VT SEP (*lit, fig*) to track down

aufstacheln VT SEP to spur (on); (= *antreiben*) to goad on; **jdn ~, etw zu tun** (= *aufwiegeln*) to goad sb into doing sth

aufstampfen VI SEP to stamp; **mit dem Fuß ~** to stamp one's foot

Aufstand M rebellion; **im ~** in rebellion; **den ~ proben** (*fig*) to flex one's muscles

aufständisch ADJ rebellious

Aufständische(r) [ˈaʊfʃtɛndɪʃə] MF DECL AS ADJ rebel

aufstapeln VT SEP to stack up

aufstauen SEP **1** VT *Wasser* to dam; **etw in sich** (*dat*) ~ (*fig*) to bottle sth up inside (oneself) **2** VR to accumulate; (*fig: Ärger*) to become bottled up

aufstechen VT SEP IRREG to puncture; (*Med*) to lance

aufstehen VI SEP IRREG AUX SEIN (a) (= *sich erheben, aus dem Bett*) to get up; **aus dem Bett ~** to get out of bed; **vor jdm/für jdn ~** to stand up for sb; **~ dürfen** (*Kranker*) to be allowed (to get) up; **da musst du früher** *or* **eher ~!** (*fig inf*) you'll have to do better than that! (b) (*inf*: = *offen sein*) to be open

aufsteigen VI SEP IRREG AUX SEIN (a) (*auf Berg, Leiter*) to climb (up); (*Vogel, Drachen*) to soar (up); (*Flugzeug*) to climb; (*Stern, Sonne, Nebel, Gefühl*) to rise; **einen Ballon ~ lassen** to release a balloon; **in einem Ballon ~** to go up in a balloon; **auf ein Fahrrad/Motorrad ~** to get on(to) a bicycle/motorbike; **auf ein Pferd ~** to mount a horse; **in jdm ~** (*Hass, Verdacht, Erinnerung etc*) to well up in sb (b) (*fig: im Rang etc*) to rise (*zu* to); (*esp beruflich, Sport*) to be promoted (*in +acc* to); **zum Abteilungsleiter ~** to rise to be head of department

Aufsteiger [ˈaʊfʃtaɪɡə] M **-s, -**, **Aufsteigerin** [-ərɪn] F **-, -nen** (*Sport*) league climber; (*in höhere Liga*) promoted team; **(sozialer) ~** social climber

aufstellen SEP **1** VT (a) (= *aufrichten, aufbauen*) to put up (*auf +dat* on); *etw Liegendes* to stand up; *Zelt* to pitch; *Kegel* to set up; *Maschine* to install; *Falle* to set; *Wachposten* to post; *Wagen* to line up; *Kragen* to turn up; *Ohren, Stacheln* to prick up
(b) *Essen etc* (*auf Herd*) to put on
(c) (*fig*: = *zusammenstellen*) *Truppe* to raise; (*Sport*) *Spieler* to select; *Mannschaft* to draw up
(d) (= *benennen*) *Kandidaten* to nominate
(e) (= *erzielen*) *Rekord* to set (up)
(f) *Forderung, Behauptung, Vermutung* to put forward; *System* to establish; *Programm, Satzungen, Rechnung* to draw up; *Liste* to make
(g) (*Sw*) *siehe* **aufgestellt**
2 VR (a) (= *sich postieren*) to stand; (*hintereinander*) to line up; **sich im Karree/Kreis** *etc* ~ to form a square/circle *etc*
(b) (*Ohren etc*) to prick up

Aufstellung F (a) NO PL (= *das Aufstellen*) putting up; (*von Zelt*) pitching; (*von Verkehrsampel, Maschine*) installation; (*von Wachposten*) posting; (*von Wagen*) lining up
(b) NO PL (= *das Zusammenstellen*) (*von Truppen*) raising; (*von Spielern*) selecting; (*von Mannschaft*) drawing up
(c) NO PL (*von Kandidaten*) nominating; (*von Rekord*) setting
(d) NO PL (*von Forderung, Behauptung, Vermutung*) putting forward; (*von System*) establishing; (*von Programm, Satzung, Rechnung, Liste*) drawing up
(e) (= *Liste*) list; (= *Tabelle*) table; (= *Inventar*) inventory
(f) (= *Mannschaft*) line-up (*inf*), team

Aufstieg [ˈaʊfʃtiːk] M **-(e)s, -e** [-ɡə] (a) NO PL (*auf Berg, von Ballon, Flugzeug, Rakete*) climb (b) (*fig*: = *Aufschwung*) rise; (*beruflich, politisch, sozial*) advancement; (*Sport: von Mannschaft*) rise; (*in höhere Liga*) promotion (*in +acc* to); **den ~ ins Management schaffen** to work one's way up into the management
(c) (= *Weg*) way up (*auf etw* (*acc*) sth)

Aufstiegschance F, **Aufstiegsmöglichkeit** F prospect of promotion

aufstocken SEP **1** VT (a) *Haus* to build another storey (*Brit*) *or* story (*US*) onto (b) *Kapital, Kredit, Armee* to increase (*um* by); *Vorräte* to stock up **2** VI to build another storey (*Brit*) *or* story (*US*)

aufstören VT SEP to disturb; *Wild* to start; **jdn aus dem** *or* **im Schlaf ~** to disturb sb while he/she is sleeping

aufstoßen SEP IRREG **1** VT (a) (= *öffnen*) to push open; (*mit dem Fuß*) to kick open
(b) (= *verletzen*) **sich** (*dat*) **das Knie ~** to graze one's knee
2 VI (a) AUX SEIN **auf etw** (*acc*) ~ to hit (on *or* against) sth
(b) AUX HABEN (= *rülpsen*) to burp
(c) AUX SEIN *or* HABEN (*Speisen*) to repeat; **Radieschen stoßen mir auf** radishes repeat on me; **das könnte dir noch sauer** *or* **übel ~** (*fig inf*) you might have to pay for that; **das ist mir sauer aufgestoßen** (*fig inf*) it left a nasty taste in my mouth
3 VR to graze oneself

aufstrebend ADJ *Land, Volk* striving for progress, aspiring; *Stadt* up-and-coming; *Persönlichkeit* ambitious; *Bürgertum, Volkswirtschaft* rising

Aufstrich M (*auf Brot*) spread; **was möchten Sie als ~?** what would you like on your bread/toast *etc*?

aufstülpen VT SEP (= *draufstülpen*) to put on; (*fig*: = *aufzwingen*) to force on; **etw auf etw** (*acc*) ~ to put sth on sth; **sich** (*dat*) **den Hut/eine Perücke ~** to put on one's hat/a wig

aufstützen SEP **1** VT *Kranken etc* to prop up; *Ellbogen, Arme* to rest (*auf +acc or dat* on); **den Kopf ~** to rest one's head on one's hand **2** VR to support oneself; (*im Bett, beim Essen*) to prop oneself up

aufsuchen VT SEP *Bekannten* to call on; *Arzt, Ort, Toilette* to go to

auftakeln VT SEP (*Naut*) to rig up; **sich ~** (*pej inf*) to tart oneself up (*Brit pej inf*), to do oneself up (*esp US inf*)

Auftakt M (= *Beginn*) start; (= *Vorbereitung*) prelude; **den ~ von** *or* **zu etw bilden** to mark the beginning of sth/to form a prelude to sth

auftanken VTI SEP to fill up; (*Aviat*) to refuel; *500 Liter* to take on; *10 Liter* to put in; *Benzin* ~ to fill up with petrol (*Brit*) *or* gas (*US*)

auftauchen VI SEP AUX SEIN (a) (*aus dem Wasser*) to surface
(b) (*fig*) (= *sichtbar werden*) to appear; (*Zweifel, Problem*) to arise (c) (= *gefunden werden, sich zeigen, kommen*) to turn up

auftauen VTI SEP (VI: AUX SEIN) to thaw

Auftaustufe F (*von Mikrowellengerät*) defrost setting

aufteilen VT SEP (a) (= *aufgliedern*) to divide up (*in +acc* into)
(b) (= *verteilen*) to share out (*an +acc* between)

Aufteilung F (= *Aufgliederung*) division (*in +acc* into); (= *Verteilung*) sharing out (*an +acc* between)

auftischen [ˈaʊftɪʃn] VT SEP to serve up; (*fig inf*) to come up with; **jdm etw ~** (*lit*) to serve sb (with) sth; **jdm Lügen** *etc* ~ (*inf*) to tell sb a lot of lies *etc*

Auftrag [ˈaʊftraːk] M **-(e)s, Aufträge** [-trɛːɡə] (a) NO PL (= *Anweisung*) orders *pl*, instructions *pl*; (= *zugeteilte Arbeit*) job; (*Jur*) brief; **jdm den ~ geben, etw zu tun** to instruct sb to do sth; **einen ~ ausführen** to carry out an order; **ich habe den ~, Ihnen mitzuteilen ...** I have been instructed to tell you ...; **in jds ~** (*dat*) (= *für jdn*) on sb's behalf; (= *auf jds Anweisung*) on sb's instructions; **i. A.** *or* **im ~ - G. W. Kurz** pp G. W. Kurz
(b) (*Comm*) order (*über +acc* for); (*bei Künstlern, Freischaffenden etc*) commission (*über +acc* for); **etw in ~ geben** to order/commission sth (*bei* from); **im ~ und auf Rechnung von** by order and for account of

auftragen SEP IRREG **1** VT (a) (= *servieren*) to serve; **es ist aufgetragen!** (*geh*) lunch/dinner *etc* is served!
(b) *Farbe, Salbe, Schminke* to apply (*auf +acc* to)
(c) **jdm etw ~** (*form*) to instruct sb to do sth; **er hat mir Grüße an Sie aufgetragen** he has asked me to give you his regards
2 VI (a) (*Kleider*) to make sb look fat; **die Jacke trägt auf** the jacket is not very flattering to your/her/his figure
(b) (= *übertreiben*) **dick** *or* **stark ~** (*inf*) to lay it on thick (*inf*)

Auftrag-: **Auftraggeber(in)** M(F) client; (*von Firma, Freischaffenden etc*) customer; **Auftragnehmer(in)** M(F) (*Comm*) firm accepting the order; (*Build*) contractor

Auftrags-: **Auftragsbestätigung** F confirmation of order; **Auftragsbuch** NT USU PL order book; **Auftragseingang** M **bei ~** on receipt of order; **hohe Auftragseingänge** a high number of orders; **auftragsgemäß** ADJ, ADV as instructed; (*Comm*) as per order; **Auftragslage** F order situation

auftreffen VI SEP IRREG AUX SEIN **auf etw** (*dat or acc*) ~ to hit sth; (*Rakete*) to land on sth; **er traf mit dem Kopf auf die Kante auf** he hit his head on the edge

auftreiben VT SEP IRREG (*inf*) (= *beschaffen*) *Geld, Heroin, Geräte* to get hold of; (= *ausfindig machen*) *Wohnung, Geschenk, Sponsor, Mieter, Täter* to find

auftrennen VT SEP to undo

auftreten SEP IRREG **1** VI AUX SEIN **(a)** (*lit*) to tread; **der Fuß tut so weh, dass ich (mit ihm) nicht mehr ~ kann** my foot hurts so much that I can't walk on it
(b) (= *erscheinen*) to appear; **als Zeuge/Kläger ~** to appear as a witness/as plaintiff; **zum ersten Mal (im Theater) ~** to make one's first (stage) appearance; **er tritt zum ersten Mal in Köln auf** he is appearing in Cologne for the first time; **gegen jdn/ etw ~** to stand up against sb/sth; **geschlossen ~** to put up a united front
(c) (*fig*: = *eintreten*) to occur; (*Schwierigkeiten etc*) to arise
(d) (= *sich benehmen*) to behave; **bescheiden/arrogant ~** to have a modest/arrogant manner; **vorsichtig ~** to tread warily
(e) (= *handeln*) to act; **als Vermittler/Friedensstifter** *etc* ~ to act as (an) intermediary/(a) peacemaker *etc*
2 VT *Tür etc* to kick open

Auftreten NT -s, NO PL **(a)** (= *Erscheinen*) appearance
(b) (= *Benehmen*) manner **(c)** (= *Vorkommen*) occurrence; **bei ~ von Schwellungen ...** in case swelling occurs ...

Auftrieb M **(a)** NO PL (*Phys*) buoyancy (force); (*Aviat*) lift
(b) NO PL (*fig*) (= *Aufschwung*) impetus; (= *Preisauftrieb*) upward trend (+*gen* in); (= *Ermunterung*) lift; **das wird ihm ~ geben** that will give him a lift

Auftritt M **(a)** (= *Erscheinen*) entrance; **ich habe meinen ~ erst im zweiten Akt** I don't go on until the second act **(b)** (*Theat*: = *Szene*) scene **(c)** (= *Streit*) row

auftürmen SEP **1** VT to pile up; (*Geol*) to build up (in layers)
2 VR (*Gebirge etc*) to tower up; (*Schwierigkeiten*) to mount up

aufwachen VI SEP AUX SEIN (*lit, fig*) to wake up; **aus seiner Lethargie ~** to snap out of one's lethargy; **aus einer Narkose ~** to come out of an anaesthetic (*Brit*) or anesthetic (*US*)

aufwachsen VI SEP IRREG AUX SEIN to grow up

Aufwand ['aufvant] M -(e)s [-dəs], NO PL **(a)** (*von Geld*) expenditure (*an* +*dat* of); **das erfordert einen ~ von 10 Millionen Euro** that will cost 10 million euros; **das erfordert einen großen ~ (an Zeit/Energie/Geld)** that requires a lot of time/energy/money **(b)** (= *Luxus, Prunk*) extravagance; **(großen) ~ treiben** to be (very) extravagant; **was da für ~ getrieben wurde!** the extravagance!

aufwändig ['aufvɛndɪç] **1** ADJ (= *teuer*) costly; (= *üppig*) lavish
2 ADV extravagantly

Aufwandsentschädigung F expense allowance

aufwärmen SEP **1** VT to heat up; (*inf*: = *wieder erwähnen*) to drag up (*inf*) **2** VR to warm oneself up; (*Sport*) to warm up

aufwärts ['aufvɛrts] ADV up, upward(s); (= *bergauf*) uphill; **den Fluss ~** upstream; **von einer Million ~** from a million up(wards); *siehe auch* **aufwärtsgehen**

Aufwärts-: **Aufwärtsbewegung** F upward movement; (*Tech*) upstroke; **aufwärts gehen** VI IMPERS IRREG AUX SEIN **mit jdm geht es aufwärts** (*finanziell, beruflich*) things are looking up for sb; (*in der Schule, gesundheitlich*) sb is doing better; **mit seinen Leistungen geht es aufwärts** he's doing better; **aufwärtskompatibel** ADJ (*Comput*) upward compatible; **Aufwärtstrend** M upward trend

Aufwasch ['aufvaʃ] M -(e)s, NO PL (*dial*) = **Abwasch**[1]

aufwecken VT SEP to wake (up); (*fig*) to rouse; *siehe auch* **aufgeweckt**

aufweichen SEP **1** VT to make soft; *Weg, Boden* to make sodden; *Brot* to soak; (*durch Wärme*) to soften; (*fig*: = *lockern*) to weaken; *Doktrin, Gesetz* to water down **2** VI AUX SEIN to get soft; (*Weg, Boden*) to get sodden; (*fig*) (= *sich lockern*) to be weakened; (*Doktrin, Gesetz*) to get watered down

aufweisen VT SEP IRREG to show; **die Leiche wies keinerlei Verletzungen auf** the body showed no signs of injury; **das Buch weist einige Fehler auf** the book contains some mistakes; **etw aufzuweisen haben** to have sth to show for oneself

aufwenden VT SEP IRREG or REG to use; *Zeit, Energie* to expend; *Mühe* to take; *Geld* to spend

aufwendig ADJ, ADV = **aufwändig**

Aufwendung F **(a)** NO PL using; (*von Zeit, Energie*) expenditure; (*von Mühe*) taking; (*von Geld*) spending; **unter ~ von ...** by using/expending/taking/spending ...
(b) (= *Ausgaben*) **Aufwendungen** PL expenditure

aufwerfen SEP IRREG **1** VT *Frage, Probleme, Thema, Verdacht* to raise **2** VR **sich zu etw ~** to set oneself up as sth

aufwerten VT SEP **(a)** AUCH VI *Währung* to revalue **(b)** (*fig*) to increase the value of; *Menschen, Ideal* to enhance the status of

Aufwertung F (*von Währung*) revaluation; (*fig*) increase in value

auf Wiedersehen [auf 'viːdezeːən], (*geh, S Ger, Aus, Sw*) **auf Wiederschauen** [auf 'viːdeʃauan] INTERJ goodbye

aufwiegeln ['aufviːgln] VT SEP to stir up; **jdn zum Streik/ Widerstand ~** to incite sb to strike/resist

aufwiegen VT SEP IRREG (*fig*) to offset; **das ist nicht mit Geld aufzuwiegen** that can't be measured in terms of money

Aufwind M (*Aviat*) upcurrent; (*Met*) upwind; **(durch etw) neuen ~ bekommen** (*fig*) to get new impetus (from sth); **einer Sache** (*dat*) **~ geben** (*fig*) to give sth impetus

aufwirbeln SEP **1** VI AUX SEIN *Staub, Schnee* to swirl up **2** VT to swirl up; *Staub auch* to raise; **(viel) Staub ~** (*fig*) to cause a (big) stir

aufwischen VT SEP *Wasser etc* to wipe up; *Fußboden* to wipe; **die Küche (feucht) ~** to wash the kitchen floor

aufwühlen VT SEP **(a)** (*lit*) *Erde, Meer* to churn (up) **(b)** (*geh*) to stir; (*schmerzhaft*) to churn up; *Leidenschaften* to rouse; **das hat seine Seele zutiefst aufgewühlt** that stirred him to the depths of his soul; **~d** stirring; *siehe auch* **aufgewühlt**

aufzahlen VT SEP (*S Ger Aus*) **10 Euro/einen Zuschlag ~** to pay an additional 10 euros/a surcharge (on top)

aufzählen VT SEP to list; *Beispiele, Details, Namen auch, Liste* to give; **er hat mir alle meine Fehler aufgezählt** he listed all my faults for me; **man kann die Fälle an den Fingern einer Hand ~** the instances can be counted on the fingers of one hand

aufzäumen VT SEP to bridle; **etw verkehrt ~** to go about sth the wrong way

aufzehren VT SEP to exhaust; (*fig*) to sap

aufzeichnen VT SEP **(a)** *Plan etc* to draw **(b)** (= *notieren, Rad, TV*) to record

Aufzeichnung F **(a)** (= *Zeichnung*) sketch **(b)** USU PL (= *Notiz*) note; (= *Niederschrift*) record **(c)** (= *Tonaufzeichnung, Filmaufzeichnung*) recording

aufzeigen VT SEP to show

aufziehen SEP IRREG **1** VT **(a)** (= *hochziehen*) to pull up; *Flagge, Segel* to hoist; *Jalousien* to let up; (*Med*) *Spritze* to fill; *Flüssigkeit* to draw up
(b) (= *öffnen*) *Reißverschluss* to undo; *Schublade* to (pull) open; *Gardinen* to draw (back)
(c) (= *aufspannen*) *Foto etc* to mount; *Leinwand, Stickerei* to stretch; *Saite, Reifen* to fit; **Saiten/neue Saiten auf ein Instrument ~** to string/restring an instrument
(d) (= *spannen*) *Feder, Uhr etc* to wind up
(e) *Kind* to bring up; *Tier* to rear
(f) (*inf*: = *veranstalten*) to set up; *Fest* to arrange; (= *gründen*) *Unternehmen* to start up
(g) (= *verspotten*) **jdn ~** (*inf*) to tease sb (*mit* about)
2 VI AUX SEIN (*dunkle Wolke*) to come up; (*Gewitter, Wolken auch*) to gather; (= *aufmarschieren*) to march up; **die Wache zog vor der Kaserne auf** the soldiers mounted guard in front of the barracks
3 VR to wind; **sich von selbst ~** to be self-winding

Aufzinsung ['auftsɪnzʊŋ] F -, -en (*Fin*) accumulation

Aufzucht F, NO PL rearing

Aufzug M **(a)** (= *Fahrstuhl*) lift (*Brit*), elevator (*US*) **(b)** (*Theat*) act **(c)** NO PL (*pej inf*: = *Kleidung*) get-up (*inf*)

aufzwingen SEP IRREG **1** VT **jdm etw ~** to force sth on sb; **jdm seinen Willen ~** to impose one's will on sb **2** VR to force itself on one; **sich jdm ~** to force itself on sb; (*Gedanke*) to strike sb forcibly; **das zwingt sich einem doch förmlich auf** the conclusion is unavoidable

Augapfel M eyeball; **jdn/etw wie seinen ~ hüten** to cherish sb/ sth like life itself

Auge ['aʊgə]

gen **Auges**, *pl* **Augen**

SUBSTANTIV (NT)
(a) (= *Sehorgan*) eye; **ganz Auge und Ohr sein** to be all ears; **Augen zu und durch!** (*inf*) grit your teeth and get on with it!

✦**Auge(n) + haben gute/schlechte Augen haben** to have good/bad eyesight; **da muss man seine Augen überall** *or* **hinten und vorn** (*inf*) **haben** you need eyes in the back of your head; **haben Sie keine Augen im Kopf?** (*inf*) haven't you got eyes in your head?; **er hatte nur Augen für sie** he only had eyes for her; **ein Auge auf jdn/etw haben** (= *aufpassen*) to keep an eye on sb/sth; **ein Auge auf jdn/etw (geworfen) haben** to have one's eye on sb/sth

✦**Auge(n) + andere Verben die Augen aufmachen** *or* **aufsperren** (*inf*) *or* **auftun** (*inf*) to open one's eyes; **sich** (*dat*) **die Augen ausweinen** to cry one's eyes out; **da blieb kein Auge trocken** (*hum*) there wasn't a dry eye in the house; (*vor Lachen*) everyone laughed till they cried; **die Augen offen halten** to keep one's eyes open; **große Augen machen** to be wide-eyed; **jdm schöne** *or* **verliebte Augen machen** to make eyes at sb; **jdm die Augen öffnen** (*fig*) to open sb's eyes; **so weit das Auge reicht** as far as the eye can see; **ein Auge riskieren** (*hum*) to have a peep (*inf*); **die Augen vor etw** (*dat*) **verschließen** to close one's eyes to sth; **ein Auge** *or* **beide Augen zudrücken** (*inf*) to turn a blind eye; **ich habe kein Auge zugetan** I didn't sleep a wink

(b) (*mit Präposition*)

✦**aufs Auge jdm etw aufs Auge drücken** (*inf*) to force sth on sb

✦**aus + Augen aus den Augen, aus dem Sinn** (*Prov*) out of sight, out of mind (*Prov*); **ich konnte kaum aus den Augen sehen** *or* **gucken** I could hardly see straight; **geh mir aus den Augen!** get out of my sight!; **sie ließen ihn nicht aus den Augen** they didn't let him out of their sight; **jdn/etw aus den Augen verlieren** to lose sight of sb/sth; (*fig*) to lose touch with sb/sth

✦**im Auge etw im Auge haben** (*lit*) to have sth in one's eye; (*fig*) to have one's eye on sth; **jdn im Auge behalten** (= *beobachten*) to keep an eye on sb; (= *vormerken*) to keep sb in mind; **etw im Auge behalten** to keep sth in mind

✦**ins Auge dem Tod ins Auge sehen** to look death in the eye; **etw ins Auge fassen** to contemplate sth; **das springt** *or* **fällt einem gleich ins Auge** it strikes one immediately; **ins Auge stechen** (*fig*) to catch the eye; **das kann leicht ins Auge gehen** (*fig inf*) it might easily go wrong

✦**in + Auge(n) in den Augen der Leute/Öffentlichkeit** in the eyes of most people/the public; **in meinen Augen** in my opinion; **jdm in die Augen sehen** to look sb in the eye(s); **Auge in Auge** face to face

✦**mit + Auge(n) mit den Augen zwinkern** to wink; **mit den Augen blinzeln** to blink; **jdn/etw mit den Augen verschlingen** to devour sb/sth with one's eyes; **jdn/etw mit anderen Augen (an)sehen** to see sb/sth with different eyes; **etw mit eigenen Augen gesehen haben** to have seen sth with one's own eyes; **mit bloßem** *or* **nacktem Auge** with the naked eye; **mit offenen Augen schlafen** to daydream; **mit verbundenen Augen** (*lit, fig*) blindfold; **mit einem lachenden und einem weinenden Auge** with mixed feelings

✦**vor + Auge(n) jdm etw vor Augen führen** (*fig*) to make sb aware of sth; **das muss man sich** (*dat*) **mal vor Augen führen!** just imagine it!; **etw noch genau** *or* **lebhaft vor Augen haben** to remember sth clearly *or* vividly; **vor aller Augen** in front of everybody; **vor meinem geistigen** *or* **inneren Auge** in my mind's eye

(c) (= *Knospenansatz*) (*bei Kartoffel*) eye
(d) (= *Fettauge*) little globule of fat

Augen-: **Augenarzt** M, **Augenärztin** F ophthalmologist; **Augenaufschlag** M look; **Augenbank** F, *pl* **-banken** eyebank; **Augenbinde** F eye bandage; (= *Augenklappe*) eye patch

Augenblick M moment; **alle -e** constantly; **jeden ~** any minute; **einen ~, bitte** one moment please!; **~ mal!** (*inf*) just a minute!, just a sec! (*inf*); **im ~** at the moment; **in diesem** *or* **im selben ~...** at that moment ...; **im letzten/richtigen** *etc* **~** at

the last/right *etc* moment; **im ersten ~** for a moment; **im nächsten ~** the (very) next moment

augenblicklich ['aʊgnblɪklɪç, aʊgn'blɪklɪç] **1** ADJ **(a)** (= *sofortig*) immediate **(b)** (= *gegenwärtig*) present **(c)** (= *vorübergehend*) temporary; (= *einen Augenblick dauernd*) momentary **2** ADV **(a)** (= *sofort*) immediately **(b)** (= *zurzeit*) at the moment

Augen-: **Augenblinzeln** NT **-s**, NO PL wink; **Augenbraue** F eyebrow; **Augenentzündung** F inflammation of the eyes; **Augenfarbe** F colour (*Brit*) *or* color (*US*) of the eyes; **Menschen mit einer dunklen ~** people with dark eyes; **Augenfehler** M eye defect; **Augenflimmern** NT **-s**, NO PL flickering before the eyes; **augenfreundlich** ADJ *Bildschirm, Größe der Buchstaben etc* easy on the eyes; **Augengläser** PL (*esp Aus*) glasses *pl*; **Augenheilkunde** F ophthalmology; **Augenhöhe** F **in ~** at eye level; **Augenklappe** F **(a)** eye patch **(b)** (*für Pferde*) blinker, blinder (*US*); **Augenkrankheit** F eye disease; **Augenleiden** NT eye complaint; **Augenlicht** NT, NO PL (eye)sight; **Augenlid** NT eyelid; **Augenmaß** NT, NO PL (*für Entfernungen*) eye for distance(s); (*fig*) perceptiveness; **nach ~** by eye; **~ haben** (*lit*) to have a good eye (for distance(s)); (*fig*) to be able to assess things; **ein ~ für etw haben** (*fig*) to have an eye for sth; **Augennerv** M optic nerve; **Augenpartie** F eye area; **Augenränder** PL rims *pl* of the/one's eyes; **er hatte rote ~, seine ~ waren gerötet** the rims of his eyes were red; **Augenringe** PL rings *pl* under the/one's eyes; **Augenschein** M, NO PL **(a)** (= *Anschein*) appearance; **dem ~ nach** by all appearances; **der ~ trügt** appearances are deceptive **(b)** **jdn/etw in ~ nehmen** to look closely at sb/sth; **augenscheinlich** ['aʊgnʃaɪnlɪç, aʊgn'ʃaɪnlɪç] **1** ADJ obvious **2** ADV obviously; **Augenschmaus** M **-es**, NO PL (*hum*) feast for the eyes; **Augenweide** F, NO PL feast for the eyes; **nicht gerade eine ~** (*iro*) a bit of an eyesore; **Augenwimper** F eyelash; **Augenwischerei** [-vɪʃə'raɪ] F **-, -en** (*fig*) eyewash; **Augenzeuge** M, **Augenzeugin** F eyewitness (*bei* to); **augenzwinkernd** **1** ADJ winking *attr*; (*fig*) sly **2** ADV with a wink; **sie sahen sich ~ an** they winked at each other; **jdm etw ~ zu verstehen geben** to let sb know sth with a wink

-äugig [ɔygɪç] ADJ SUF -eyed; **braunäugig** brown-eyed

August¹ [au'gʊst] M **-(e)s** *or* **-, -e** August; *siehe auch* **März**

August² ['aʊgʊst] M **-s** Augustus; **der dumme ~** (*inf*) the clown

Augustfeier F (*Sw*) August public holiday

Auktion [aʊk'tsioːn] F **-, -en** auction

Auktionator [aʊktsio'naːtoːɐ] M **-s, Auktionatoren**, **Auktionatorin** [-'toːrɪn] F **-, -nen** auctioneer

Auktionshaus NT auction house

Aula ['aʊla] F **-, Aulen** [-lən] (*Sch, Univ etc*) (assembly) hall; (= *Atrium*) atrium

Au-pair- [o'pɛːɐ-]: **Au-pair-Junge** M, **Aupairjunge** M (male) au pair; **Au-pair-Mädchen** NT, **Aupairmädchen** NT au pair (girl); **als ~ arbeiten** to work (as an) au pair; **Au-pair-Stelle** F, **Aupairstelle** F au pair job

Aura ['aʊra] F **-, NO PL** (*Med, geh*) aura

aus [aʊs] **1** PREP +DAT **(a)** (*räumlich*) from; (= *~ dem Inneren von*) out of; **~ dem Fenster/der Tür** out of the window/door; **~ unserer Mitte** from our midst; **~ der Flasche trinken** to drink out of the bottle; **jdm ~ einer Verlegenheit helfen** to help sb out of a difficulty
(b) (*Herkunft, Quelle bezeichnend*) from; **~ guter Familie** from a good family
(c) (*auf Ursache deutend*) out of; **~ Hass/Gehorsam/Mitleid** out of hatred/obedience/sympathy; **~ Erfahrung** from experience; **~ Furcht vor/Liebe zu** for fear/love of; **~ einer Laune heraus** on (an) impulse; **~ Spaß** for a laugh (*inf*); **~ Unachtsamkeit** due to carelessness; **~ Versehen** by mistake; **ein Mord ~ Berechnung** a calculated murder; **ein Mord** *or* **ein Verbrechen ~ Leidenschaft** a crime of passion
(d) (*zeitlich*) from; **~ dem Barock** from the Baroque period
(e) (= *beschaffen ~*) (made out) of
(f) (*Herstellungsart*) out of, from; (*fig: Ausgangspunkt*) out of; **einen Soldaten/Pfarrer ~ jdm machen** to make a soldier/minister (out) of sb; **einen anständigen Menschen ~ jdm machen** to make sb into a decent person; **was ist ~ ihm/dieser Sache geworden?** what has become of him/this?; **~ der Sache ist nichts geworden** nothing came of it
(g) **~ dem Gleichgewicht** out of balance; *Mensch, Gegenstand* off balance; **~ der Mode** out of fashion
(h) (*Aus*: = *in*) in; **eine Prüfung ~ Geschichte** an examination

in history
2 ADV *siehe auch* **aus sein (a)** (*Sport*) out; (*Ftbl, Rugby*) out (of play)
(b) (*inf:* = *vorbei, zu Ende*) over; **~ jetzt!** that's enough!
(c) (= *gelöscht*) out; (*an Geräten*) off; **Licht ~!** lights out!
(d) (*in Verbindung mit von*) **vom Fenster ~** from the window; **von München ~** from Munich; **von sich ~** of one's own accord; **von ihm ~** as far as he's concerned; **ok, von mir ~** OK, if you like

Aus [aus] NT **-,** **- (a)** NO PL (*Ftbl, Rugby*) touch *no art;* **ins ~ gehen** to go out of play; (*seitlich*) to go into touch; **ins politische ~ geraten** to end up in the political wilderness **(b)** (= *Ende*) end; **das ~ für die Firma ist unabwendbar** the company is doomed to close down

ausarbeiten SEP **1** VT to work out; (= *vorbereiten*) to prepare; (= *formulieren*) to formulate **2** VR (*Sport*) to have a work-out

Ausarbeitung F **-, -en** working out; (= *Vorbereitung*) preparation; (= *Formulierung*) formulation

ausarten VI SEP AUX SEIN **(a)** (*Party etc*) to get out of control; **~ in** (+*acc*) *or* **zu** to degenerate into **(b)** (= *ungezogen etc werden*) to get out of hand; (= *pöbelhaft, ordinär etc werden*) to misbehave

ausatmen VTI SEP to breathe out, to exhale

ausbaden VT SEP (*fig inf*) to take the rap for (*inf*); **ich muss jetzt alles ~** I have to take the rap (*inf*)

ausbalancieren *ptp* **ausbalanciert** SEP (*lit, fig*) **1** VT to balance (out) **2** VR to balance (each other out)

Ausbau M, NO PL (= *das Ausbauen*) removal; (*lit, fig:* = *Erweiterung*) extension (*zu* into); (= *Umbau*) conversion (*zu* (in)to); (= *Festigung: von Position, Vorsprung*) consolidation

ausbauen VT SEP **(a)** (= *herausmontieren*) to remove (*aus* from) **(b)** (*lit, fig:* = *erweitern, vergrößern*) to extend (*zu* into); (= *umbauen*) to convert (*zu* (in)to); (= *innen ~*) to fit out; *Beziehungen, Freundschaft* to build up; *Plan* to elaborate; (= *festigen*) *Position, Vorsprung* to consolidate; **ausgebaut** (= *umgebaut*) converted; (= *erweitert*) *Schul-, Verkehrssystem etc* fully developed; **ein ausgebautes Dachgeschoss** a loft conversion

ausbaufähig ADJ *Position* with good prospects; *Geschäft, Produktion, Markt, Computer* expandable; *Beziehungen* that can be built up; *Machtstellung* that can be consolidated; (*inf*) *Schüler, Mitarbeiter* promising

ausbedingen *ptp* **ausbedungen** VT SEP IRREG **sich** (*dat*) **etw ~** to make sth a condition; **ich bin dazu bereit, aber ich bedinge mir aus, ...** I'm prepared to do it but (only) on condition that ...; **sich** (*dat*) **das Recht ~, etw zu tun** to reserve the right to do sth

ausbessern VT SEP to repair; *Roststelle etc* to remove; *Gemälde etc* to restore; *Fehler* to correct

ausbeulen VT SEP **(a)** *Kleidung* to make baggy; *Hut* to make floppy; **ausgebeult** *Kleidung* baggy; *Hut* battered **(b)** (= *Beule entfernen*) to remove a dent/dents in; (*Tech: durch Hämmern*) to beat out

Ausbeute F (= *Gewinn*) profit; (= *Ertrag einer Grube etc*) yield (*an +dat* in); (*fig*) result(s *pl*); (= *Einnahmen*) proceeds *pl*

ausbeuten ['ausbɔytn] VT SEP (*lit, fig*) to exploit

Ausbeuter ['ausbɔytɐ] M **-s, -,** **Ausbeuterin** [-ərɪn] F **-, -nen** exploiter; **~ und Ausgebeutete** the exploiters and the exploited

ausbeuterisch ['ausbɔytərɪʃ] **1** ADJ exploitative **2** ADV **die Arbeiter ~ zu Überstunden antreiben** to exploit the workers by forcing them to work overtime

Ausbeutung F **-, -en** (*lit, fig*) exploitation

ausbezahlen *ptp* **ausbezahlt** VT SEP *Geld* to pay out; *Arbeitnehmer* to pay off; (= *abfinden*) *Erben etc* to buy out; **in bar ausbezahlt** paid in cash; **wie viel kriegst du pro Woche ausbezahlt?** what is your weekly take-home pay?

ausbilden SEP **1** VT **(a)** (*beruflich, Sport, Mil*) to train; (*akademisch*) to educate; **sich in etw** (*dat*)/**als** *or* **zu etw ~ lassen** (*esp Arbeiter, Lehrling*) to train in sth/as sth; (= *Qualifikation erwerben*) to qualify in sth/as sth **(b)** *Fähigkeiten* to develop; (*Mus*) *Stimme* to train **2** VR **sich in etw** (*dat*) **~** (*esp Arbeiter, Lehrling*) to train in sth; (= *studieren*) to study sth; (= *Qualifikation erwerben*) to qualify in sth

Ausbilder ['ausbɪldɐ] M **-s, -,** **Ausbilderin** [-ərɪn] F **-, -nen** instructor; (*Frau auch*) instructress

Ausbildung F (*beruflich*) (*Sport, Mil*) training; (*akademisch*) education; **er ist noch in der ~** he hasn't finished his education

Ausbildungs-: **Ausbildungsbeihilfe** F (*für Schüler*) (education) grant; (*für Lehrling*) training allowance; **Ausbildungsberuf** M occupation that requires training; **Ausbildungsbetrieb** M company that takes on trainees; **Ausbildungsgang** M, *pl* **-gänge** training; **Ausbildungsjahr** NT year of training; **Ausbildungsplatz** M place to train; (= *Stelle*) training vacancy; **Ausbildungsstätte** F place of training; **Ausbildungsvergütung** F payment made during training; **Ausbildungsvertrag** M articles *pl* of apprenticeship; **Ausbildungszeit** F period of training; **nach zweijähriger ~** after a two-year training period

ausbitten VT SEP IRREG **sich** (*dat*) **(von jdm) etw ~** (*geh*) to ask (sb) for sth; **das möchte ich mir (auch) ausgebeten haben!** I should think so too!; **ich bitte mir Ruhe aus!** I must have silence!

ausblasen VT SEP IRREG to blow out; *Ei* to blow

ausbleiben VI SEP IRREG AUX SEIN (= *fortbleiben*) to stay out; (*Gäste, Schüler, Schneefall*) to fail to appear; (*Erwartung, Befürchtung*) to fail to materialize; (*Puls, Atmung etc*) to stop; **die Strafe/ein Krieg wird nicht ~** punishment/a war is inevitable; **es kannte nicht ~, dass ...** it was inevitable that ...

Ausbleiben NT **-s,** NO PL (= *Fehlen*) absence; (= *das Nichterscheinen*) nonappearance; **bei ~ der Periode** if your period doesn't come

ausbleichen *pret* **bleichte aus,** *ptp* **ausgebleicht** *or* **ausgeblichen** VTI SEP IRREG (VI: AUX SEIN) to fade, to bleach

Ausblick M **(a)** view (*auf +acc* of), outlook (*auf +acc* over, onto); **ein Zimmer mit ~ auf die Straße/aufs Meer** a room overlooking the street/with a view of the sea **(b)** (*fig*) prospect, outlook (*auf +acc, in +acc* for); **einen ~ auf etw** (*acc*) **geben** to give the prospects for sth

ausbomben VT SEP to bomb out; **die Ausgebombten** people who have been bombed out (of their homes)

ausborgen VT SEP (*inf*) **sich** (*dat*) **etw (von jdm) ~** to borrow sth (from sb); **jdm etw ~** to lend sb sth

ausbrechen SEP IRREG **1** VI AUX SEIN **(a)** (= *beginnen*) (*Krieg, Seuche, Feuer*) to break out; (*Konflikt, Gewalt, Hysterie, Unruhen, Jubel, Zorn, Frust*) to erupt; (*Zeitalter*) to arrive; **in Gelächter/Tränen** *or* **Weinen ~** to burst out laughing/into tears; **in Jubel ~** to erupt with jubilation; **in Beifall ~** to break into applause; **in Schweiß ~** to break out in a sweat; **bei dir ist wohl der Wohlstand ausgebrochen** (*fig inf*) have you struck it rich? (*inf*) **(b)** (*aus Gefangenschaft*) to break out (*aus* of); (*Tier*) to escape (*aus* from); (*fig:* = *sich befreien*) to get out (*aus* of), to escape (*aus* from); **aus dem Gefängnis ~** to escape from prison **(c)** (*Vulkan*) to erupt **2** VT *Zahn* to break; *Steine* to break off; **sich** (*dat*) **einen Zahn ~** to break a tooth

ausbreiten SEP **1** VT to spread; *Arme* to stretch out; (= *ausstellen, fig:* = *zeigen*) to display; **einen Plan vor jdm ~** to unfold a plan to sb; **sein Leben vor jdm ~** to lay one's whole life before sb **2** VR **(a)** (= *sich verbreiten*) to spread **(b)** (= *sich erstrecken*) to extend **(c)** (*inf:* = *sich breit machen*) to spread oneself out **(d)** **sich über etw** (*acc*) **~** (*fig*) to dwell on sth; **darüber will ich mich jetzt nicht ~** I'd rather not go into that now

ausbrennen VI SEP IRREG AUX SEIN **(a)** (= *zu Ende brennen*) to burn out **(b)** (= *völlig verbrennen*) to be burned out; **ausgebrannt** burned-out; *Brennstab* spent; *siehe auch* **ausgebrannt**

Ausbruch M **(a)** (*aus* from) (*aus Gefängnis*) break-out (*auch Mil*), escape (*auch fig*) **(b)** (= *Beginn*) outbreak; (*von Vulkan*) eruption; **zum ~ kommen** to break out **(c)** (*fig*) outburst; (*stärker*) explosion; **zum ~ kommen** to erupt

ausbrüten VT SEP to hatch; (*esp in Brutkasten*) to incubate; (*fig inf*) *Plan etc* to cook up (*inf*); **eine Erkältung ~** to be coming down with a cold

Ausbuchtung ['ausbʊxtʊŋ] F **-, -en** bulge; (*von Strand*) (small) cove

ausbuddeln VT SEP (*inf*) to dig up (*auch fig inf*)

ausbuhen VT SEP (*inf*) to boo

ausbürgern [ˈausbʏrgɐn] VT SEP to expatriate
Ausbürgerung [ˈausbʏrgərʊŋ] F **-, -en** expatriation
ausbürsten VT SEP to brush out (*aus* of); *Anzug* to brush
ausbüxen [ˈausbʏksn] VI SEP AUX SEIN (*hum inf*) to run off; **jdm ~** to run away from sb
Ausdauer F, NO PL stamina; (*im Ertragen*) endurance; (= *Beharrlichkeit, Hartnäckigkeit*) persistence; **beim Lernen/Lesen keine ~ haben** to have no staying power when it comes to learning/reading
ausdauernd ■ ADJ *Mensch* with stamina; (*im Ertragen*) with endurance; (= *beharrlich*) tenacious; (= *hartnäckig*) persistent; *Bemühungen* untiring ■ ADV diligently
ausdehnen SEP ■ VT (a) (= *vergrößern*) to expand; (= *dehnen*) to stretch
(b) (*fig*) to extend
■ VR (a) (= *größer werden*) to expand; (*durch Dehnen*) to stretch; (= *sich erstrecken*) to extend (*bis* as far as); **die Seuche dehnte sich über das ganze Land aus** the epidemic spread over the whole country
(b) (*über +acc* over, *bis* as far as, to); (*zeitlich*) to go on (*bis* until); *siehe auch* **ausgedehnt**
ausdenken VT SEP IRREG **sich** (*dat*) **etw ~** (= *erfinden*) to think sth up; (*in Einzelheiten*) to think sth out; *Wunsch* to think of sth; *Überraschung* to plan sth; (= *sich vorstellen*) to imagine sth; (= *durchdenken*) to think sth through; **das ist nicht auszudenken** (= *unvorstellbar*) it's inconceivable; (= *zu schrecklich etc*) it doesn't bear thinking about; **da musst du dir schon etwas anderes ~!** (*inf*) you'll have to think of something better than that!
ausdeutschen [ˈausdɔytʃn] VT SEP (*Aus inf*) **jdm etw ~** to explain sth to sb in words of one syllable
ausdienen VI SEP **ausgedient haben** (*fig inf*) to have had its day; (*Kugelschreiber etc*) to be used up
ausdiskutieren *ptp* **ausdiskutiert** VT SEP *Thema* to discuss fully
ausdörren SEP ■ VT to dry up; *Kehle* to parch; *Pflanzen* to shrivel ■ VI AUX SEIN to dry up; *siehe auch* **ausgedörrt**
Ausdruck[1] M, *pl* **-drücke** (a) NO PL (= *Gesichtsausdruck*) expression
(b) NO PL **als ~ meiner Dankbarkeit** as an expression of my gratitude; **ohne jeden ~ singen/spielen** to sing/play without any expression; **etw zum ~ bringen, einer Sache** (*dat*) **~ geben** *or* **verleihen** (*form*) to express sth
(c) (= *Wort*) expression; (= *Fachausdruck, Math*) term; **das ist gar kein ~!** that's not the word for it; **sich im ~ vergreifen** to use the wrong word
Ausdruck[2] M, *pl* **-drücke** (*von Computer etc*) print-out
ausdrucken VT SEP (*Comput*) to print out
ausdrücken SEP ■ VT (a) (= *zum Ausdruck bringen*) to express (*jdm* to sb); (*Verhalten, Gesicht*) *Trauer etc* to reveal; **um es anders/gelinde auszudrücken** to put it another way/mildly; **anders ausgedrückt** in other words; **einfach ausgedrückt** put simply
(b) *Frucht, Schwamm, Lappen* to squeeze out; *Tube, Pickel* to squeeze; (= *ausmachen*) to put out; *Zigarette* to stub out; **den Saft einer Zitrone ~** to squeeze a lemon
■ VR (*Mensch*) to express oneself; (*Emotion*) to be expressed; **in ihrem Gesicht/Verhalten drückte sich Verzweiflung aus** her face/behaviour (*Brit*) *or* behavior (*US*) showed her despair; **er kann sich gewandt ~** he is very articulate
ausdrücklich [ˈausdrʏklɪç, ausˈdrʏklɪç] ■ ADJ ATTR *Wunsch, Genehmigung* express ■ ADV expressly; (= *besonders*) particularly
Ausdrucks-: Ausdrucksfähigkeit F expressiveness; (= *Gewandtheit*) articulateness; **Ausdruckskraft** F, NO PL expressiveness; (*von Schriftsteller*) articulateness; **ausdruckslos** ADJ inexpressive; *Gesicht, Blick auch* expressionless; **Ausdrucksmöglichkeit** F mode of expression; **ausdrucksvoll** ADJ expressive; **Ausdrucksweise** F way of expressing oneself; **was ist denn das für eine ~!** what sort of language is that to use!
ausdünnen VT SEP (a) *Pflanzen, Haare* to thin out (b) *Verkehr, Kapital* to reduce
Ausdünstung [ˈausdʏnstʊŋ] F **-, -en** (a) (= *das Ausdünsten*) evaporation; (*von Körper, Pflanze*) transpiration (b) (= *Geruch*) fume; (*von Tier*) scent; (*von Mensch*) smell; (*fig*) emanation

auseinander [ausˈlaɪˈnandɐ] ADV (= *voneinander entfernt, getrennt*) apart; **weit ~** far apart; **Augen, Beine etc** wide apart; **Zähne** widely spaced; **Meinungen** very different; **etw ~ schreiben** to write sth as two words; **zwei Kinder ~ setzen** to separate two children; **sich ~ setzen** to sit apart; **die beiden sind (im Alter) ein Jahr ~** there is a year between the two of them; *siehe auch* **auseinander setzen**
auseinander: auseinander bekommen VT IRREG to be able to get apart; **auseinander biegen** VT IRREG to bend apart; **auseinander brechen** VI IRREG AUX SEIN (*lit, fig*) to break up; **auseinander bringen** VT IRREG (*inf*) to manage to get apart (*auch fig*); **auseinander driften** VI AUX SEIN to drift apart; **auseinander entwickeln** VR to grow apart (from each other); (*Partner*) to drift apart; **auseinander falten** VT to unfold; **auseinander gehen** VI IRREG AUX SEIN (a) (*lit, fig*) to part; (*Menge*) to disperse; (*Versammlung, Ehe etc*) to break up; (= *auseinander fallen: Schrank etc*) to fall apart (b) (*fig: Ansichten etc*) to differ (c) (*inf: = dick werden*) to get fat; **auseinander halten** VT IRREG to keep apart; (= *unterscheiden*) *Begriffe* to distinguish between; *esp Zwillinge etc* to tell apart; **auseinander klamüsern** *ptp* **auseinander klamüsert** VT (*dialhum*) to sort out; **jdm etw ~** to spell sth out for sb; **auseinander kriegen** VT (*inf*) to be able to get apart; **auseinander laufen** VI IRREG AUX SEIN (a) (= *zerlaufen*) to melt; (*Farbe*) to run; (= *sich ausbreiten*) to spread (b) (*inf: = sich trennen*) to break up; (*Menge*) so disperse; **auseinander leben** VR to drift apart (*mit* from); **auseinander machen** VT (*inf*) (a) (= *auseinander nehmen*) to take apart (b) (= *auseinander falten*) to unfold (c) (= *spreizen*) *Arme, Beine* to spread (apart); **auseinander nehmen** VT IRREG to take apart; (*kritisch*) to tear to pieces; **auseinander setzen** ■ VT (*fig*) to explain (*jdm* so sb) ■ VR **sich mit etw ~** (= *sich befassen*) to have a good look at sth; **sich kritisch mit etw ~** to have a critical look at sth; **sich damit ~, was/weshalb ...** to tackle the problem of what/why ...; **sich mit jdm ~** to talk *or* (*sich streiten*) to argue with sb; **sich mit jdm gerichtlich ~** to take sb to court
Auseinandersetzung [ausˈlaɪˈnandɐzetsʊŋ] F **-, -en** (a) (= *Diskussion*) discussion (*über +acc* about, on); (= *Streit*) argument (b) (= *das Befassen*) examination (*mit* of); (*kritisch*) analysis (*mit* of)
auseinander: auseinander springen VI IRREG AUX SEIN to shatter; **auseinander stieben** *pret* **stob auseinander**, *ptp* **auseinander gestoben** VI IRREG AUX SEIN to scatter; **auseinander treiben** VT IRREG (= *trennen*) to drive apart; (= *auseinander jagen*) to scatter; *Demonstranten* to disperse
auserlesen ■ ADJ select ■ PTP **zu etw ~ (worden) sein** to be chosen for sth
auserwählen *ptp* **auserwählt** VT SEP (*geh*) to choose
auserwählt ADJ (*geh*) chosen; (= *ausgesucht*) select
ausessen SEP IRREG ■ VT *Speise* to eat up; *Schüssel* to empty; *Pampelmuse* to eat ■ VI to finish eating
ausfahrbar ADJ extendable; *Antenne, Fahrgestell, Klinge* retractable
ausfahren SEP IRREG ■ VT (a) *jdn* (*im Kinderwagen, Rollstuhl*) to take for a walk; (*im Auto*) to take for a drive (b) (= *ausliefern*) *Waren* to deliver (c) (= *abnutzen*) *Weg* to wear out; **sich in ausgefahrenen Bahnen bewegen** (*fig*) to keep to well-trodden paths (d) (*Aut*) *Kurve* to (drive) round (e) **ein Auto etc** (*voll*) **~** to drive a car *etc* at full speed (f) (*Tech*) to extend; *Fahrgestell etc* to lower ■ VI AUX SEIN (a) (= *spazieren fahren*) to go for a ride *or* (*im Auto auch*) drive; **mit dem Baby ~** to take the baby out in the pushchair (*Brit*) *or* stroller (*US*) (b) (= *abfahren*) (*Zug*) to pull out (*aus* of); (*Schiff*) to sail; **aus dem Hafen ~** to leave harbour (*Brit*) *or* harbor (*US*)
Ausfahrt F (a) NO PL (= *Abfahrt*) departure (b) (= *Spazierfahrt*) drive, ride; **eine ~ machen** to go for a drive *or* ride (*im Auto auch*) drive (c) (= *Ausgang, Autobahnausfahrt*) exit; **~ Gütersloh** Gütersloh exit; **„~ freihalten"** "keep clear"
Ausfall M (a) (= *Verlust, Fehlbetrag*) (*Mil*) loss; (= *das Versagen*) (*Tech, Med*) failure; (*von Motor*) breakdown; (= *Produktionsstörung*) stoppage; **bei ~ des Stroms ...** in case of a power failure ... (b) NO PL (*von Sitzung, Unterricht etc*) cancellation (c) (*Sport*) (*Fechten*) thrust; (*Gewichtheben*) jerk (d) (*fig: = Angriff*) attack

ausfallen VI SEP IRREG AUX SEIN **(a)** (= *herausfallen*) to fall out; (*Chem*) to be precipitated; (*Ling*) to be dropped; **mir fallen die Haare aus** my hair is falling out
(b) (= *nicht stattfinden*) to be cancelled (*Brit*) *or* canceled (*US*); **etw ~ lassen** to cancel sth; **die Schule/die erste Stunde fällt morgen aus** there's no school/first lesson tomorrow
(c) (= *nicht funktionieren*) to fail; (*Motor*) to break down
(d) (= *wegfallen: Verdienst*) to be lost
(e) gut/schlecht *etc* **~** to turn out well/badly *etc*; **die Rede ist zu lang ausgefallen** the speech turned out to be too long; **die Bluse fällt zu eng aus** the blouse is too tight
(f) *siehe* **ausgefallen**

ausfallend, ausfällig ◼ ADJ abusive; **~ werden** to become abusive ◼ ADV abusively

Ausfallstraße F arterial road

Ausfallzeit F (*Insur*) time which counts toward(s) pension although no payments were made

ausfeilen VT SEP to file; (*fig*) to polish

ausfertigen VT SEP (*form*) *Dokument* to draw up; *Rechnung, Lieferschein* to make out; *Pass* to issue

Ausfertigung F (*form*) **(a)** NO PL (*von Dokument*) drawing up; (*von Rechnung, Lieferschein*) making out; (*von Pass*) issuing
(b) (= *Abschrift*) copy; **ein Dokument in einfacher ~** a single copy of a document; **in doppelter/dreifacher ~** in duplicate/triplicate; **Zeugnisse in vierfacher** *etc* **~** four *etc* copies of references

ausfindig ADJ **~ machen** to find; (= *Aufenthaltsort feststellen*) to locate

ausfliegen SEP IRREG ◼ VI AUX SEIN (= *wegfliegen*) to fly away; (*aus Gebiet etc*) to fly out (*aus* of); (= *flügge werden*) to leave the nest; (*fig inf*: = *weggehen*) to go out; **ausgeflogen sein** (*fig inf*) to be out; **der Vogel ist ausgeflogen** (*fig inf*) the bird has flown ◼ VT (*Aviat*) *Verwundete etc* to evacuate (by air) (*aus* from)

ausfließen VI SEP IRREG AUX SEIN (= *herausfließen*) to flow out (*aus* of); (*Eiter etc*) to be discharged; (= *auslaufen: Öl etc, Fass*) to leak (*aus* out of)

ausflippen ['ausflɪpn] VI SEP AUX SEIN (*inf*) to freak out (*inf*); *siehe auch* **ausgeflippt**

Ausflucht ['ausflʊxt] F **-,** **Ausflüchte** [-flʏçtə] excuse; **keine Ausflüchte!** (I want) no excuses!

Ausflug M trip; (*esp mit Reisebüro*) excursion; (= *Betriebsausflug, Schulausflug*) outing; (= *Wanderung*) walk, hike; (*fig*) excursion; **einen ~ machen** to go on a trip *etc*

Ausflugs-: Ausflugsdampfer M pleasure steamer; **Ausflugslokal** NT tourist café; (*am Meer*) seaside café; **Ausflugsziel** NT destination (*of one's outing*)

Ausfluss M **(a)** (= *das Herausfließen*) outflow; (= *das Auslaufen*) leaking **(b)** (= *~stelle*) outlet **(c)** (*Med*) discharge

ausfolgen VT SEP (*Aus form*) to hand over (*jdm* to sb)

ausformulieren *ptp* **ausformuliert** VT SEP to formulate; *Rede* to tidy up

ausforschen VT SEP **(a)** *Sache* to find out; (= *erforschen*) to investigate **(b)** (*Aus*) *Täter* to apprehend

ausfragen VT SEP to question (*nach* about); (*strenger*) to interrogate; **so fragt man die Leute aus** (*inf*) that would be telling (*inf*)

ausfransen VTI SEP (VI: AUX SEIN) to fray

ausfressen VT SEP IRREG **(a)** (= *auffressen*) to eat up **(b)** (*inf*: = *anstellen*) **etwas ~** to do something wrong; **was hat er denn wieder ausgefressen?** what's he (gone and) done now? (*inf*)

Ausfuhr ['ausfuːɐ] F **-, -en (a)** NO PL (= *das Ausführen*) export; (= *~handel*) exports *pl* **(b)** **Ausfuhren** PL (= *~güter*) exports *pl*

Ausfuhr- IN CPDS *siehe auch* **Export-** export; **Ausfuhranmeldung** F (*Comm*) export notification *or* declaration; **Ausfuhrartikel** M export

ausführbar ADJ **(a)** *Plan* feasible; (*Comput*) *Programm* executable; **schwer ~** difficult to carry out **(b)** (*Comm*) exportable

Ausfuhrbestimmungen PL export regulations *pl*

ausführen VT SEP **(a)** (*zu Spaziergang, ins Theater etc*) to take out; *Hund* to take for a walk **(b)** (= *durchführen*) to carry out; *Gesetz* to implement; *Bauarbeiten* to undertake; (*Sport*) *Freistoß etc* to take; (*Comput*) *Programm* to execute
(c) (= *erklären*) to explain; (= *darlegen*) to set out;

(*argumentierend*) to argue; (= *sagen*) to say **(d)** (*Comm*) *Waren* to export

Ausfuhr-: Ausfuhrerklärung F (*Comm*) export declaration; **Ausfuhrfinanzierung** F (*Comm*) export financing; **Ausfuhrförderung** F (*Comm*) measures *pl* to encourage exports; **Ausfuhrgenehmigung** F (*Comm*) export licence (*Brit*) *or* license (*US*); **Ausfuhrgüter** PL export goods *pl*; **Ausfuhrhafen** M port of exportation; **Ausfuhrhandel** M export trade; **Ausfuhrland** NT **(a)** (= *Land, das ausführt*) exporting country; **ein ~ für Jute** a jute-exporting country **(b)** (= *Land, in das ausgeführt wird*) export market

ausführlich ['ausfyːɐlɪç, (*Aus*) aus'fyːɐlɪç] ◼ ADJ detailed ◼ ADV in detail; **sehr ~** in great detail

Ausfuhr-: Ausfuhrschein M (*Comm*) export permit; **Ausfuhrsperre** F export ban; **Ausfuhrüberschuss** M export surplus

Ausführung F **(a)** NO PL (= *Durchführung*) carrying out; (*von Gesetz*) implementation; (*von Freistoß*) taking; **zur ~ gelangen** *or* **kommen** to be carried out **(b)** (= *Erklärung*) explanation; (*von Thema etc*) exposition; (= *Bemerkung*) remark; (*usu pl*: = *Bericht*) report **(c)** (*von Waren*) design; (*Tech*: = *äußere ~*) finish; (= *Qualität*) quality; (= *Modell*) model

ausfüllen VT SEP to fill; *Ritze* to fill in; *Platz* to take up; *Formular* to fill in (*Brit*) *or* out; **jdn** (*voll or ganz*) **~** (= *befriedigen*) to satisfy sb (completely); (= *Zeit in Anspruch nehmen*) to take (all) sb's time; **er füllt den Posten nicht/gut aus** he is not fitted/well-fitted for the position; **seine Zeit mit etw ~** to pass one's time doing sth; **ein ausgefülltes Leben** a full life

Ausgabe F **(a)** NO PL (= *Austeilung*) (*von Proviant, Decken etc*) distribution; (*von Befehl, Fahrkarten, Dokumenten etc*) issuing; (*von Essen*) serving
(b) (= *Schalter*) issuing counter; (*in Bibliothek*) issue desk; (*in Kantine*) serving counter; (= *Stelle, Büro*) issuing office
(c) (*von Buch, Zeitung, Zeitschrift, Sendung*) edition; (*von Aktien*) issue
(d) (= *Ausführung*) version
(e) Ausgaben PL (= *Geldverbrauch*) expenditure *sing* (*für* on); (= *Kosten*) expenses *pl*
(f) (*Comput*) (= *Ausdruck*) print-out; (*am Bildschirm*) output

Ausgabe-: Ausgabepreis M (*Fin*) issue price; (*von Investmentanteilen*) offering price; **Ausgabeschalter** M issuing counter; (*in Bibliothek etc*) issue desk; **Ausgabetermin** M date of issue

Ausgang M, *pl* **-gänge (a)** (= *Weg nach draußen*) exit (+*gen, von* from); (= *Dorfausgang*) end; (*von Wald*) edge; (*Med*) (*von Organ*) opening (+*gen* out of); (*Aviat*) gate
(b) (= *Erlaubnis zum Ausgehen*) permission to go out; (*Mil*) pass; **~ haben** to have the day off *or* (*am Abend*) the evening off; (*Mil*) to have a pass; **bis 10 Uhr ~ haben** to be allowed out/to have a pass till 10 o'clock
(c) (= *Spaziergang*) walk (*under supervision*)
(d) NO PL (= *Ende*) end; (*esp von Epoche*) close; (*von Roman, Film*) ending; (= *Ergebnis*) outcome; **ein Unfall mit tödlichem ~** a fatal accident; **ein Ausflug mit tragischem ~** an excursion with a tragic outcome
(e) NO PL (= *Abschicken von Post*) mailing
(f) Ausgänge PL (*Post*) outgoing mail *sing*; (*Waren*) outgoing goods *pl*

Ausgangs-: Ausgangsbasis F starting point; **Ausgangsposition** F initial position; **Ausgangspunkt** M starting point; **Ausgangssperre** F ban on going out; (*esp bei Belagerungszustand*) curfew; (*für Soldaten*) confinement to barracks; **~ haben** (*Soldat*) to be confined to barracks; (*Schüler*) to be banned from going out; **Ausgangssprache** F source language; **Ausgangsverbot** NT = **Ausgangssperre**; **Ausgangszustand** M initial condition; (= *Lage*) initial position; (*esp Pol*) status quo

ausgeben SEP IRREG ◼ VT **(a)** (= *austeilen*) *Proviant, Decken etc* to distribute; (= *aushändigen*) *Dokumente, Fahrkarten, Aktien etc* to issue; *Befehl* to issue, to give; *Essen* to serve; (= *ausdrucken*) *Text* to print out
(b) *Geld* to spend (*für* on); **eine Runde ~** to stand a round (*inf*); **ich gebe heute Abend einen aus** (*inf*) it's my treat this evening; **unser Chef hat einen ausgegeben** our boss treated us; **darf ich dir einen/einen Whisky ~?** may I buy you a drink/a whisky?; **er gibt nicht gern einen aus** he doesn't like buying people drinks
(c) jdn/etw als *or* **für jdn/etw ~** to pass sb/sth off as sb/sth; **sich**

als jd/etw ~ to pass oneself off as sb/sth ◪ *VR* to exhaust oneself

ausgebrannt ADJ (*fig*) burned-out (*inf*); **geistig ~** mentally exhausted; **er ist ~** he's burned out (*inf*); *siehe auch* **ausbrennen**

ausgebucht ['ausgəbu:xt] ADJ booked up

Ausgeburt F (*pej*) (*der Fantasie etc*) monstrous product; (= *Geschöpf, Kreatur, Institution*) monster; **eine ~ der Hölle** a fiendish monster; **sie ist eine ~ von Eitelkeit und Dummheit** she is a monstrous combination of vanity and stupidity

ausgedehnt ['ausgəde:nt] ADJ *Gummiband* (over)stretched; (= *breit, groß*) (*fig*: = *weit reichend*) extensive; (*zeitlich*) lengthy; *Spaziergang* long; *siehe auch* **ausdehnen**

ausgedörrt ['ausgədœrt] ADJ dried up; *Boden, Kehle* parched; *Pflanzen* shrivelled (*Brit*), shriveled (*US*); *Land, Gebiet* arid; (*fig*) *Hirn* ossified; **mein Hirn ist völlig ~** (*fig*) I can't think straight any more; *siehe auch* **ausdörren**

ausgefallen ['ausgəfalən] ADJ **(a)** *Unterrichtsstunde etc* cancelled (*Brit*), canceled (*US*) **(b)** (= *ungewöhnlich*) unusual; (= *übertrieben*) extravagant; *Mensch* eccentric; *siehe auch* **ausfallen**

Ausgefallenheit F -, -en **(a)** (= *Ungewöhnlichkeit*) unusualness **(b)** (= *Übertriebenheit*) extravagance; (*von Mensch*) eccentricity

ausgeflippt ['ausgəflɪpt] ADJ (*inf*) freaky (*inf*); **er ist ein richtig ~er Typ** he's really freaky (*inf*); *siehe auch* **ausflippen**

ausgefuchst ['ausgəfukst] ADJ (*inf*) clever; (= *listig*) crafty (*inf*); *Kartenspieler* cunning

ausgeglichen ['ausgəglıçn] ADJ balanced; *Spiel, Klima* even; *Torverhältnis* equal; (= *gleich bleibend*) consistent; *siehe auch* **ausgleichen**

Ausgeglichenheit F -, NO PL balance; (*von Spiel, Klima*) evenness; **ihre ~** her even nature

ausgehen SEP IRREG AUX SEIN ◪ VI **(a)** (= *weggehen, zum Vergnügen*) to go out; **er geht selten aus** he doesn't go out much
(b) (= *ausfallen: Haare, Federn, Zähne*) to fall out; **ihm gehen die Haare aus** his hair is falling out; **ihm gehen die Zähne aus** he is losing his teeth
(c) (= *seinen Ausgang nehmen*) to start (*von* at); (= *herrühren*: *Idee, Anregung etc*) to come (*von* from); **von dem Platz gehen vier Straßen aus** four streets lead off (from) the square; **etw geht von jdm/etw aus** (= *wird ausgestrahlt*) sb/sth radiates sth
(d) (= *zugrunde legen*) to start out (*von* from); **gehen wir einmal davon aus, dass ...** let us assume that ...; **davon kann man nicht ~** you can't go by that
(e) (*esp Sport*) to end; (= *ausfallen*) to turn out; **gut/schlecht ~** to turn out well/badly; (*Film etc*) to end happily/unhappily; (*Abend, Spiel*) to end well/badly
(f) **straffrei** *or* **straflos ~** to receive no punishment; **leer ~** (*inf*) to come away empty-handed
(g) (= *zu Ende sein: Vorräte etc*) to run out; **mir ging die Geduld aus** I lost (my) patience; **mir ging das Geld aus** I ran out of money; **ihm ist die Luft** *or* **die Puste** *or* **der Atem ausgegangen** (*inf*) (*lit*) he ran out of breath; (*fig*) he ran out of steam (*inf*); (*finanziell*) he ran out of funds
(h) (= *aufhören zu brennen*) to go out
◪ VR **es geht sich aus** (*Aus*) it works out all right; (*Vorräte, Geld etc*) there is enough

ausgehend ADJ ATTR **(a)** **im ~en Mittelalter** toward(s) the end of the Middle Ages; **das ~e 20. Jahrhundert** the end of the 20th century **(b)** **die ~e Post** the outgoing mail

ausgehungert ['ausgəhoŋət] ADJ starved; (= *abgezehrt*) *Mensch etc* emaciated

ausgeklügelt ['ausgəkly:glt] ADJ (*inf*) *System* cleverly thought-out; (= *genial*) ingenious; *siehe auch* **ausklügeln**

ausgekocht ['ausgəkɔxt] ADJ (*pej inf*) (= *durchtrieben*) cunning; **er ist ein ~er Bursche** he's a thoroughly bad character

ausgelassen ['ausgəlasn] ◪ ADJ (= *heiter*) lively; *Stimmung* happy; (= *wild*) *Kinder* boisterous; *Stimmung, Party* mad ◪ ADV wildly; **dort geht es ~ zu** things are wild there; *siehe auch* **auslassen**

Ausgelassenheit F (= *Heiterkeit*) liveliness; (= *Wildheit: von Kindern*) boisterousness

ausgelastet ['ausgəlastət] ADJ *Mensch* fully occupied; *Maschine, Anlage* working to capacity; **mit dem Job ist er nicht (voll) ~**

he is not working at his full capacity in that job; **mit den vier Kindern ist sie voll ~** her four children keep her fully occupied; **unsere Kapazitäten sind voll ~** we're working at full capacity; *siehe auch* **auslasten**

ausgelatscht ['ausgəla:tʃt] ADJ (*inf*) *Schuhe* worn; **meine Schuhe sind völlig ~** my shoes have gone completely out of shape

ausgemacht ADJ **(a)** (= *abgemacht*) agreed; **es ist eine ~e Sache, dass ...** it is agreed that ... **(b)** ATTR (*inf*: = *vollkommen*) complete; *siehe auch* **ausmachen**

ausgenommen ['ausgənɔmən] CONJ except; **niemand/alle, ~ du** *or* **dich** no-one/everyone except (for) you; **täglich ~ sonntags** daily except for Sundays; **~ wenn/dass ...** except when/that ...; *siehe auch* **ausnehmen**

ausgepowert ['ausgəpauet] ADJ (*inf*) *Mensch* done in (*inf*)

ausgeprägt ['ausgəprɛːkt] ADJ distinctive; *Interesse* marked; **ein (stark) ~er Sinn für alles Schöne** a well-developed sense for everything beautiful

ausgerechnet ['ausgərɛçnət] ADV **~ du/er** *etc* you/he *etc* of all people; **~ mir muss das passieren** why does it have to happen to me (of all people)?; **~ heute/gestern** today/yesterday of all days; **~ jetzt kommt er** he would have to come just now; **~ dann kam er** he would have to come just at that moment; **~, als wir spazieren gehen wollten, ...** just when we wanted to go for a walk ...; *siehe auch* **ausrechnen**

ausgeschlossen ADJ PRED (= *unmöglich*) impossible; (= *nicht infrage kommend*) out of the question; **es ist nicht ~, dass ...** it's just possible that ...; **diese Möglichkeit ist nicht ~** it's not impossible; **jeder Irrtum ist ~** there is no possibility of a mistake; *siehe auch* **ausschließen**

ausgeschnitten ['ausgəʃnɪtn] ADJ *Bluse, Kleid* low-cut; **ein weit** *or* **tief ~es Kleid** a dress with a plunging neckline; *siehe auch* **ausschneiden**

ausgespielt ['ausgəʃpiːlt] ADJ **~ haben** to be finished; **er hat bei mir ~** (*inf*) I'm finished with him; *siehe auch* **ausspielen**

ausgesprochen ['ausgəʃprɔxn] ◪ ADJ *Schönheit, Qualität, Vorliebe* definite; *Begabung* particular; *Ähnlichkeit* marked; *Geiz, Großzügigkeit* extreme; *Pech, Freundlichkeit, Hilfsbereitschaft etc* real; **eine ~e Frohnatur** a very sunny person; **ein ~er Chauvi** (*inf*) an out-and-out male chauvinist; **~es Pech haben** to be really unlucky ◪ ADV really; *siehe auch* **aussprechen**

ausgestellt ADJ *Rock etc* flared; *siehe auch* **ausstellen**

ausgestorben ['ausgəʃtɔrbn] ADJ *Tierart* extinct; (*fig*) deserted; **der Park war wie ~** the park was deserted; *siehe auch* **aussterben**

ausgesucht ◪ ADJ **(a)** (= *besonders groß*) extreme **(b)** (= *erlesen*) select ◪ ADV (= *überaus, sehr*) extremely; *siehe auch* **aussuchen**

ausgetreten ['ausgətreːtn] ADJ *Schuhe* well-worn; *Pfad* well-trodden; *Stufe* worn down; *siehe auch* **austreten**

ausgewachsen ADJ fully grown; (*inf*) *Blödsinn* utter; *Skandal* huge

ausgewählt ADJ select; *Satz etc* well-chosen; *Werke* selected; *siehe auch* **auswählen**

ausgewogen ADJ balanced; *Maß* equal; **ein ~es Kräfteverhältnis** a balance of powers

Ausgewogenheit F balance

ausgezeichnet ◪ ADJ excellent ◪ ADV excellently; **sie kann ~ schwimmen/tanzen** she is an excellent swimmer/dancer; **es geht mir ~** I'm feeling marvellous (*Brit*) *or* marvelous (*US*); *siehe auch* **auszeichnen**

ausgiebig ['ausgi:bɪç] ◪ ADJ *Mahlzeit etc* substantial; *Mittagsschlaf, Gespräch* (good) long; *Gebrauch* extensive ◪ ADV **~ frühstücken** to have a substantial breakfast; **~ schlafen/schwimmen** to have a (good) long sleep/swim; **etw ~ gebrauchen** to use sth extensively

ausgießen VT SEP IRREG **(a)** (*aus einem Behälter*) to pour out; (= *weggießen*) to pour away; *Behälter* to empty; (= *verschütten*) to spill **(b)** (= *füllen*) *Gussform* to fill; *Ritzen, Fugen* to fill in

Ausgleich ['ausglaiç] M -(e)s, (*rare*) -e (= *Gleichgewicht*) balance; (*von Konto*) balancing; (*von Schulden*) settling; (*von Verlust, Fehler, Mangel*) compensation; (*von Abweichung, Unterschieden*) balancing out; (*von Meinungsverschiedenheiten, Konflikten*) evening out; **zum** *or* **als ~ für etw** in order to compensate for sth; **er treibt zum ~ Sport** he does sport for exercise; **zum ~ Ihres Kontos** to balance your account

ausgleichen SEP IRREG **1** VT *Ungleichheit, Unterschiede* to even out; *Konto* to balance; *Schulden* to settle; *Verlust, Fehler* to make good; *Mangel* to compensate for; *Meinungsverschiedenheiten, Konflikte* to reconcile; **etw durch etw ~** to compensate for sth with sth/by doing sth; **~de Gerechtigkeit** poetic justice; *siehe auch* **ausgeglichen**
2 VI **(a)** (*Sport*) to equalize; **zum 1:1 ~** to equalize the score at 1 all (*Brit*), to even up the score to 1 all (*US*)
(b) (= *vermitteln*) to act as a mediator; **~des Wesen** conciliatory manner
3 VR to balance out; (*Einnahmen und Ausgaben*) to balance; **das gleicht sich dadurch aus, dass ...** it's balanced out by the fact that ...

Ausgleichs-: Ausgleichsanspruch M (*von Handelsvertreter*) compensation claim; (*im Länderfinanzausgleich*) equalization claim; **Ausgleichsposten** M (*Comm, Fin*) adjustment item; **~ aus der Konsolidierung** adjustment from consolidation; **Ausgleichssport** M keep-fit activity; **als ~** to keep fit; **Ausgleichstor** NT, **Ausgleichstreffer** M equalizer (*Brit*), tying goal (*US*)

ausgraben VT SEP IRREG to dig up; *Grube, Loch* to dig out; *Altertümer* to excavate; (*fig*) to dig up; (= *hervorholen*) to dig out; *alte Geschichten* to bring up

Ausgrabung F (= *das Ausgraben*) excavation; (*Ort*) excavation site; (= *Fund*) (archaeological (*Brit*) or archeological (*US*)) find

ausgrenzen VT SEP to exclude

Ausgrenzung F **-, -en** exclusion

Ausguck ['ausgʊk] M **-(e)s, -e** lookout; **~ halten** to keep a lookout

ausgucken VT SEP (*inf*) **(a)** (*suchend*) **sich** (*dat*) **die Augen nach jdm ~** to look everywhere for sb **(b)** (= *aussuchen, entdecken*) **sich** (*dat*) **jdn ~** to set one's sights on sb

Ausguss M **(a)** (= *Becken*) sink; (= *Abfluss*) drain; (= *Tülle*) spout **(b)** (*Tech*) tap hole

aushaben SEP IRREG (*inf*) **1** VT (= *fertig sein mit*) *Buch, Essen etc* to have finished; (= *ausgezogen haben*) to have taken off **2** VI (*Arbeit, Schule etc*) to finish

aushaken SEP **1** VT *Fensterladen, Kette* to unhook; *Reißverschluss* to undo **2** VI (*inf*) **es hat bei ihm ausgehakt** (= *nicht begreifen*) he gave up (*inf*); (= *wild werden*) something in him snapped (*inf*)

aushalten SEP IRREG **1** VT **(a)** (= *ertragen können, standhalten*) to bear; *Druck* to stand; *jds Blick* to return; **es lässt sich ~** it's bearable; **hier lässt es sich ~** this is not a bad place; **das ist nicht auszuhalten** or **zum Aushalten** it's unbearable; **ich halte es vor Hitze/zu Hause nicht mehr aus** I can't stand the heat/being at home any longer; **er hält es in keiner Stellung lange aus** he never stays in one job for long; **hältst dus noch bis zur nächsten Tankstelle aus?** (*inf*) can you hold out till the next garage?; **er hält viel aus** he can take a lot; **er hält nicht viel aus** he can't take much
(b) (*inf:* = *unterhalten*) to keep; **sich von jdm ~ lassen** to be kept by sb
2 VI (= *durchhalten*) to hold out; **hältst du noch aus?** can you hold out (any longer)?

aushandeln VT SEP to negotiate

aushändigen ['aushɛndɪɡn] VT SEP **jdm etw ~** to hand sth over to sb; **jdm einen Preis ~** to give sb a prize

Aushang M (= *Bekanntmachung*) notice; (= *das Aushängen*) posting; **etw durch ~ bekannt geben** to put up a notice about sth

aushängen SEP **1** VT **(a)** (= *bekannt machen*) to put up **(b)** *Tür* to unhinge; *Haken* to unhook **2** VI IRREG (*Anzeige, Aufgebot*) to have been put up; (*inf:* *Brautleute*) to have the banns up (*Brit*), to have the official wedding notice up (*US*); **am schwarzen Brett ~** to be on the notice (*Brit*) or bulletin (*US*) board

Aushängeschild NT, pl **-schilder** (*lit:* = *Reklametafel*) sign; (*fig:* = *Reklame*) advertisement

aushäusig ['aushɔyzɪç] ADJ (= *außer Haus*) outside the home; (= *unterwegs*) away from home

ausheben VT SEP IRREG **(a)** *Tür etc* to take off its hinges **(b)** *Erde* to dig out; *Graben, Grab* to dig **(c)** *Vogelnest* to rob; *Vogeleier, Vogeljunge* to steal; (*fig*) *Diebesnest* to raid; *Bande* to make a raid on; (*Aus:* = *leeren*) to empty

aushecken ['aushɛkn] VT SEP (*inf*) *Plan* to cook up (*inf*); **neue Streiche ~** to think up new tricks

ausheilen SEP **1** VT *Krankheit* to cure; *Organ, Wunde* to heal **2** VI AUX SEIN (*Krankheit*) to be cured; (*Organ, Wunde*) to heal

aushelfen VI SEP IRREG to help out (*jdm* sb)

Aushilfe F **(a)** help; **jdn zur ~ haben** to have sb to help out; **Stenotypistin zur ~ gesucht** shorthand typist wanted for temporary work **(b)** (*Mensch*) temporary worker; (*esp im Büro*) temp (*inf*)

Aushilfs-: Aushilfskraft F temporary worker; (*esp im Büro*) temp (*inf*); **Aushilfslehrer(in)** M(F) supply (*Brit*) or substitute (*US*) teacher; **aushilfsweise** ADV on a temporary basis; (= *vorübergehend*) temporarily

aushöhlen ['aushøːlən] VT SEP to hollow out; *Ufer, Steilküste* to erode

ausholen VI SEP **(a)** (*zum Schlag*) to raise one's hand/arm *etc*; (*zum Wurf*) to reach back; (*mit Schläger, Boxer*) to take a swing; **weit ~** (*zum Schlag, beim Tennis*) to take a big swing; (*zum Wurf*) to reach back a long way; (*fig: Redner*) to go far afield; **bei einer Erzählung weit ~** to go a long way back in a story; **zum Gegenschlag ~** (*lit, fig*) to prepare for a counterattack
(b) (= *ausgreifen*) to stride out; **er ging mit weit ~den Schritten** he walked with long strides

aushorchen VT SEP (*inf*) *jdn* to sound out

auskehren SEP **1** VT *Schmutz* to sweep away; *Zimmer* to sweep out **2** VI to do the sweeping

auskeimen VI SEP AUX SEIN (*Getreide*) to germinate; (*Kartoffeln*) to sprout

auskennen VR SEP IRREG (*an einem Ort*) to know one's way around; (*auf einem Gebiet*) to know a lot (*auf* or *in* +*dat* about); **sich bei Männern/Frauen (gut) ~** to know (a lot) about men/women; **man kennt sich bei ihm nie aus** you never know where you are with him

auskippen VT SEP (*inf*) to empty (out); *Flüssigkeit* to pour out

ausklammern VT SEP *Problem* to leave aside; (*Math*) *Zahl* to put outside the brackets

ausklamüsern ptp **ausklamüsert** VT SEP (*inf*) to work out

Ausklang M (*geh*) conclusion; (*esp Mus*) finale; **zum ~ des Abends ...** to conclude the evening ...

ausklappbar ADJ folding; *Blatt* fold-out; **dieser Tisch ist ~** this table can be opened out

ausklappen VT SEP to open out; *Fußstütze etc* to pull out

ausklingen VI SEP IRREG **(a)** (*Glocken*) to finish ringing **(b)** AUX SEIN (*Lied*) to finish; (*Abend, Feier etc*) to end (*in* +*dat* with); **das ~de Jahrhundert** (*geh*) the close of the century

ausklinken ['ausklɪŋkn] SEP **1** VT *Bombe, Seil* to release **2** VR (*Mensch*) to withdraw; **sich aus etw ~** to withdraw from sth; *aus dem Alltag, dem Beruf* to get away from sth; *aus dem Solidaritätsprinzip* to reject sth; **sich aus seiner Zeit ~** to reject modern technology

ausklopfen VT SEP *Teppich* to beat; *Pfeife* to knock out; *Kleider* to beat the dust out of

ausknipsen VT SEP (*inf*) to switch off

ausknöpfbar ADJ *Futter* detachable

auskochen VT SEP **(a)** (*Cook*) *Knochen* to boil **(b)** (*Med*) *Instrumente* to sterilize (*in boiling water*); *siehe auch* **ausgekocht**

auskommen VI SEP IRREG AUX SEIN **(a)** (= *genügend haben, zurechtkommen*) to get by (*mit* on), to manage (*mit* on, with); **das Auto kommt mit sieben Litern auf 100 km aus** the car only uses seven litres (*Brit*) or liters (*US*) every 100 kilometres (*Brit*) or kilometers (*US*); **ohne jdn/etw ~** to manage without sb/sth **(b)** **mit jdm (gut) ~** to get on (well) with sb; **mit ihm ist nicht auszukommen** he's impossible to get on with

Auskommen NT **-s**, NO PL (= *Einkommen*) livelihood; **sein ~ haben/finden** to get by; **mit ihr ist kein ~** she's impossible to get on with

auskramen VT SEP (*inf*) *Gegenstand* to dig out; (*fig*) *alte Geschichten etc* to bring up; *Schulkenntnisse* to dig up

auskratzen VT SEP to scrape out

auskristallisieren ptp **auskristallisiert** VTIR SEP (*vi:* aux sein) to crystallize

auskugeln VT SEP **sich** (*dat*) **den Arm/die Schulter** ~ to dislocate one's arm/shoulder

auskühlen VI SEP AUX SEIN (= *abkühlen*) to cool down; (*Körper, Menschen*) to chill through; **etw** ~ **lassen** to leave sth to cool

Auskühlung F cooling; (*von Mensch*) loss of body heat

auskundschaften VT SEP *Weg, Lage* to find out; *Versteck* to spy out; *Geheimnis* to ferret out; (*esp Mil*) to reconnoitre (*Brit*), to reconnoiter (*US*)

Auskunft ['auskʊnft] F -, **Auskünfte** [-kʏnftə] **(a)** (= *Mitteilung*) information *no pl* (*über* +*acc* about); **nähere** ~ more information; **jdm eine** ~ **erteilen** *or* **geben** to give sb some information; **eine** ~ *or* **Auskünfte einholen** *or* **einziehen** to make (some) inquiries (*über* +*acc* about) **(b)** (= *Informationsstelle*) information office; (= *Schalter*) information desk; (*am Bahnhof*) inquiry office/desk; (*Telec*) directory inquiries *no art*

Auskunftei [auskʊnf'tai] F -, **-en** credit inquiry agency

Auskunfts-: Auskunftsperson F informer; (= *Beamter*) information clerk; **Auskunftspflicht** F (*Jur*) obligation to give information; **die Bank hat gegenüber der Polizei** ~ the bank is obliged to inform the police authorities; **auskunftspflichtig** [-pfliçtiç] ADJ (*Jur*) required to give information; **Auskunftsschalter** M information desk; (*am Bahnhof*) inquiry desk

auskurieren *ptp* **auskuriert** SEP (*inf*) 🖪 VT to cure 🖪 VR to get better

auslachen VT SEP *jdn* to laugh at

ausladen SEP IRREG 🖪 VT **(a)** *Ware, Ladung* to unload **(b)** (*inf*) **jdn** ~ to tell sb not to come 🖪 VI (*Äste*) to spread; (*Dach, Balkon*) to protrude

ausladend ADJ *Kinn etc* protruding; *Dach* projecting; *Gebärden, Bewegung* sweeping

Auslage F **(a)** (*von Waren*) display; (= *Schaufenster*) (shop) window; (= *Schaukasten*) showcase **(b)** USU PL expense; **seine ~n für Verpflegung** his outlay for food

auslagern VT SEP to evacuate

Ausland NT, NO PL foreign countries *pl*; (*fig*: = *die Ausländer*) foreigners *pl*; **ins/im** ~ abroad; **aus dem** *or* **vom** ~ from abroad; **wie hat das** ~ **darauf reagiert?** what was the reaction abroad?; **Handel mit dem** ~ foreign trade; **das feindliche** ~ enemy countries; **im benachbarten/europäischen** ~ in neighbouring (*Brit*) *or* neighboring (*US*)/other European countries

Ausländer ['aʊslɛndɐ] M -**s**, -, **Ausländerin** [-ərɪn] F -, **-nen** foreigner; (*Admin, Jur*) alien

Ausländerbeauftragte(r) MF DECL AS ADJ official looking after foreign immigrants

ausländerfeindlich 🖪 ADJ xenophobic; *Anschlag* on foreigners 🖪 ADV ~ **motivierte Straftaten** crimes with a racist motive

Ausländerfeindlichkeit F xenophobia

ausländerfreundlich ADJ friendly to foreigners

Ausländerhass M xenophobia

Ausländerin F *siehe* **Ausländer**

Ausländerwahlrecht NT **allgemeines/kommunales** ~ foreigners' right to vote in general/local elections

ausländisch ['aʊslɛndɪʃ] ADJ **(a)** ATTR foreign; (*Bot*) exotic **(b)** (*fig*: = *fremdländisch*) exotic

Auslands- IN CPDS foreign; **Auslandsanleihe** F foreign loan; **Auslandsaufenthalt** M stay abroad; **Auslandsbeziehungen** PL foreign relations *pl*; **Auslandsbrief** M overseas (*Brit*) *or* foreign letter; **Auslandsdeutsche(r)** MF DECL AS ADJ expatriate German; **Auslandsgeschäft** NT foreign business; **Auslandsgespräch** NT international call; **Auslandskassenverein** M (*Fin*) foreign security clearing association; **Auslandskonto** NT foreign account; **Auslandskorrespondent(in)** M(F) foreign correspondent; **Auslandskrankenschein** M (*Med*) certificate of entitlement to benefits in kind (*during a stay abroad*); **Auslandsschulden** PL foreign exchange debts *pl*; **Auslandsschule** F British/ German *etc* school (abroad); **die ~n in Brüssel** the foreign schools in Brussels; **Auslandsschutzbrief** M international travel cover; (= *Dokument*) certificate of entitlement for international travel cover; **Auslandsvertretung** F agency abroad; (*von Firma*) foreign branch; **Auslandswechsel** M foreign bill (of exchange)

auslassen SEP IRREG 🖪 VT **(a)** (= *weglassen, aussparen, übergehen*) to leave out; (= *versäumen*) *Chance, Gelegenheit* to miss **(b)** (= *abreagieren*) to vent (*an* +*dat* on) **(c)** *Butter, Fett* to melt; *Speck* to render (down) **(d)** (*inf*) *Radio, Motor, Ofen, Licht, Kleidung* to leave off **(e)** (*Aus*) (= *los-, freilassen*) to let go; (= *in Ruhe lassen*) to leave alone **(f)** *siehe* **ausgelassen** 🖪 VR to talk (*über* +*acc* about); **sich über jdn/etw** ~ (*pej*) to go on about sb/sth (*pej*); **er hat sich nicht näher darüber ausgelassen** he didn't say any more about it

Auslassung F -, **-en** (= *Weglassen*) omission

Auslassungspunkte PL suspension points *pl*

auslasten VT SEP **(a)** *Fahrzeug, Maschine* to make full use of **(b)** *jdn* to occupy fully; *siehe auch* **ausgelastet**

Auslauf M **(a)** NO PL (= *Bewegungsfreiheit*) exercise; (*für Kinder*) room to run about **(b)** (*Gelände*) run **(c)** (*Stelle*) outlet

auslaufen SEP IRREG 🖪 VI AUX SEIN **(a)** (*Flüssigkeit*) to run out (*aus* of); (*Behälter*) to empty; (= *undicht sein*) to leak; (*Wasserbett, Blase, Auge*) to drain **(b)** (*Naut*: *Schiff, Besatzung*) to sail **(c)** (= *nicht fortgeführt werden*: *Modell, Serie*) to be discontinued; (= *ausgehen*: *Vorräte, Lager*) to run out; **etw** ~ **lassen** *Produkt etc* to phase sth out **(d)** (*Farbe, Stoff*) to run 🖪 VR to have some exercise; **sich** ~ **können** (*Kinder*) to have room to run about

auslaufend ADJ *Vertrag, Frist* expiring; **~es Modell** = **Auslaufmodell**

Ausläufer M **(a)** (*Bot*) runner **(b)** (*Met*) (*von Hoch*) ridge; (*von Tief*) trough **(c)** (= *Vorberge*) foothill *usu pl* **(d)** (*Sw*: = *Bote*) delivery boy/man

Ausläuferin F (*Sw*: = *Botin*) delivery girl/woman

Auslaufmodell NT **(a)** (*lit*) discontinued model **(b)** (*fig inf*: *Person*) old model (*hum inf*); **ein** ~ **sein** (*fig inf*: *Konzept, Idee*) to be old hat (*inf*)

auslaugen ['aʊslaʊgn] VT SEP (*lit*) *Boden* to exhaust; *Haut* to dry out; (*fig*) to exhaust

Auslaut M (*Ling*) final position

auslauten VI SEP to end (*auf* +*dat* in); **~der Konsonant** final consonant

ausleben SEP 🖪 VR (*Mensch*) to live it up; (*Fantasie etc*) to run free 🖪 VT (*geh*) to realize

auslecken VT SEP to lick out

ausleeren VT SEP to empty

auslegen VT SEP **(a)** (= *ausbreiten*) to lay out; *Waren etc* to display; *Köder* to put down; *Kabel, Minen* to lay **(b)** (= *bedecken*) to cover; (= *auskleiden*) to line; **den Boden (mit Teppichen)** ~ to carpet the floor **(c)** (= *erklären*) to explain; (= *deuten*) to interpret **(d)** *Geld* to lend (*jdm etw* sb sth); **sie hat die 5 Euro für mich ausgelegt** she paid the 5 euros for me **(e)** (*Tech*) to design (*auf* +*acc*, *für* for); **straff ausgelegt sein** (*Federung*) to be tightly set

Ausleger ['aʊsle:gɐ] M -**s**, - **(a)** (*von Kran etc*) jib, boom **(b)** (*an Ruderboot*) rowlock; (= *Kufe gegen Kentern*) outrigger

Auslegung ['aʊsle:gʊŋ] F -, **-en** (= *Deutung*) interpretation; (= *Erklärung*) explanation (*zu* of); **falsche** ~ misinterpretation

ausleiden VI SEP IRREG **sie hat ausgelitten** her suffering is at an end

ausleiern SEP 🖪 VT (*inf*) **etw** ~ *Gummiband, Gewinde, Feder* to wear sth out; *Hosen, Pullover* to make sth go baggy 🖪 VI AUX SEIN to wear out; (*Pullover*) to go baggy

Ausleihbibliothek F, **Ausleihbücherei** F lending library

Ausleihe F (= *das Ausleihen*) lending; (= *Schalter*) issue desk; **eine** ~ **ist nicht möglich** it is not possible to lend out anything

ausleihen VT SEP IRREG (= *verleihen*) to lend (*jdm, an jdn* to sb); (= *von jdm leihen*) to borrow; **sich** (*dat*) **etw** ~ to borrow sth (*bei, von* from)

auslernen VI SEP (*Lehrling*) to finish one's apprenticeship; (*inf*: *Schüler, Student etc*) to finish school/college *etc*; **ausgelernt** qualified; **man lernt nie aus** (*prov*) you live and learn (*prov*)

Auslese F **(a)** NO PL (= *Auswahl*) selection; (*Liter*: *verschiedener Autoren*) anthology; **natürliche** ~ natural selection

(b) (= *Elite*) **die** ~ the élite **(c)** (= *Wein*) *high-quality wine made from selected grapes*

auslesen SEP IRREG ▌ VT **(a)** (= *auswählen*) to select; (= *aussondern*) *Schlechtes* to pick out; *Erbsen, Linsen etc* to pick over **(b)** *Buch etc* to finish reading; **er legte das ausgelesene Buch beiseite** he put away the book he had finished reading ▐ VI (= *zu Ende lesen*) to finish reading; **hast du bald ausgelesen?** will you finish (reading) it soon?

Ausleseverfahren NT selection procedure

ausliefern VT SEP **(a)** *Waren* to deliver **(b)** *jdn* to hand over (*an* +*acc* to); (*an anderen Staat*) to extradite (*an* +*acc* to); (*fig:* = *preisgeben*) to leave (*jdm* in the hands of sb); **sich der Polizei/Justiz** ~ to give oneself up to the police/to justice; **jdm/einer Sache ausgeliefert sein** to be at sb's mercy/the mercy of sth

Auslieferung F **(a)** (*von Ware*) delivery **(b)** (*von Menschen*) handing over; (*von Gefangenen*) extradition

Auslieferungs-: **Auslieferungsantrag** M (*Jur*) application for extradition; **Auslieferungslager** NT (*Comm*) distribution centre (*Brit*) *or* center (*US*)

ausliegen VI SEP IRREG (*Waren*) to be displayed; (*Zeitschriften, Liste etc*) to be available (to the public)

Auslinie F (*Sport*) (*Ftbl*) touchline; (*bei Tennis, Hockey etc*) sideline; **die ~n** (*Tennis*) the tramlines *pl*

auslöffeln VT SEP *Suppe etc* to eat up completely; *Teller* to empty; **etw** ~ **müssen** (*inf*) to have to take the consequences of sth; ~ **müssen, was man sich eingebrockt hat** (*inf*) to have to take the consequences

ausloggen [ˈauslɔgn] VR (*Comput*) to log out; **sich aus dem System** ~ to log out of the system

auslöschen VT SEP **(a)** *Feuer, Licht* to extinguish **(b)** *Spuren* to obliterate; (*mit Schwamm etc*) to wipe out; *Schrift* to erase (*an* +*dat* from); *Erinnerung, Schmach* to blot out; **ein Menschenleben** ~ (*geh*) to destroy a human life

auslosen VT SEP to draw lots for; *Preis, Gewinner* to draw

auslösen VT SEP *Mechanismus, Alarm, Reaktion* to trigger; *Kameraverschluss, Bombe* to release; (*fig*) *Wirkung* to produce; *Begeisterung, Mitgefühl, Überraschung* to arouse; *Aufstand, Beifall* to trigger off

Auslöser [ˈausløːzɐ] M **-s, -** **(a)** trigger; (*für Bombe*) release button; (*Phot*) shutter release **(b)** (= *Anlass*) cause; **der ~ für etw sein** to trigger sth off

Auslosung [ˈausloːzʊŋ] F **-, -en** draw

auslüften VTI SEP to air

auslutschen VT SEP (*inf*) *Orange, Zitrone etc* to suck; *Saft* to suck out; (*fig*) to suck dry

ausmachen VT SEP **(a)** *Feuer, Kerze, Zigarette* to put out; *elektrisches Licht, Radio, Gas* to turn off
(b) (= *ermitteln, sichten*) to make out; (= *ausfindig machen*) to locate; (= *feststellen*) to determine
(c) (= *vereinbaren*) to agree; *Streitigkeiten* to settle; **einen Termin** ~ to agree (on) a time; **wir müssen nur noch ~, wann wir uns treffen** we only have to arrange when we should meet; **etw mit sich selbst** ~ (**müssen**) to (have to) sort sth out for oneself; *siehe auch* **ausgemacht**
(d) (= *bewirken, darstellen*) (to go) to make up; **alles, was das Leben ausmacht** all that is a part of life; **der Hintergrund macht den Reiz an diesem Bild aus** the background makes this picture attractive
(e) (= *betragen*) to come to
(f) (= *bedeuten*) **viel** ~ to make a big difference; **wenig** *or* **nicht viel** ~ not to make much difference; **das macht nichts aus** that doesn't matter
(g) (= *stören*) to matter (*jdm* to); **macht es Ihnen etwas aus, wenn ...?** would you mind if ...?; **es macht mir nichts aus, den Platz zu wechseln** I don't mind changing places

ausmalen VT SEP **sich** (*dat*) **etw** ~ to imagine sth; **sich** (*dat*) **sein Leben** ~ to picture one's life

Ausmaß NT **(a)** (*von Gegenstand, Fläche*) size; (*von Katastrophe, Liebe*) extent; (= *Grad*) degree; (= *Größenordnung: von Änderungen, Verlust etc*) scale; **ein Verlust in diesem** ~ a loss on this scale **(b)** **Ausmaße** PL proportions *pl*; **erschreckende ~e annehmen** to assume alarming proportions

ausmergeln [ˈausmɛrɡl̩n] VT SEP *Gesicht, Körper etc* to emaciate; *Boden* to exhaust

ausmerzen [ˈausmɛrtsn̩] VT SEP (*lit, fig*) to eradicate; (= *aussondern*) *schwache Tiere* to cull

ausmessen VT SEP IRREG to measure (out)

Ausmessung F **(a)** (= *das Messen*) measuring (out)
(b) (= *Maße*) dimensions *pl*

ausmisten SEP ▌ VT *Stall* to muck out (*Brit*), to clear (*US*); (*fig inf*) *Schrank, Zimmer etc* to clean out ▐ VI (*lit*) to muck out (*Brit*), to clear of dung (*US*); (*fig*) to have a clean-out

ausmustern VT SEP *Maschine, Fahrzeug etc* to take out of service; (*Mil*: = *entlassen*) to discharge

Ausnahme [ˈausnaːmə] F **-, -n** exception; **mit ~ von** *or* +*gen* with the exception of; **ohne** ~ without exception; **~n bestätigen die Regel** (*prov*), **keine Regel ohne** ~ (*prov*) the exception proves the rule (*prov*)

Ausnahme-: **Ausnahmebestimmung** F special regulation; **Ausnahmeerscheinung** F exception; **Ausnahmefall** M exceptional case; **Ausnahmesituation** F special situation; **Ausnahmezustand** M (*Pol*) state of emergency; **den** ~ **verhängen** to declare a state of emergency

ausnahmslos ADV without exception

ausnahmsweise ADV **darf ich das machen? – ~** may I do that? – just this once; **wenn er – auch mal einen Fehler macht** when he makes a mistake too just for once; **sie hat es mir** ~ **einmal erlaubt** she let me do it once as a special exception; **er darf heute** ~ **früher von der Arbeit weggehen** as an exception he may leave work earlier today

ausnehmen VT SEP IRREG **(a)** (*fig*) *Verbrecherbande, Diebesnest etc* to raid; (*Mil*) *Stellung* to take out; **das Nest** ~ to remove the eggs from the nest
(b) *Fisch, Kaninchen etc* to gut; *Geflügel* to draw; *Hammel, Rind etc* to dress
(c) (= *ausschließen*) *jdn* to make an exception of; (= *befreien*) to exempt; **ich nehme keinen aus** I'll make no exceptions; *siehe auch* **ausgenommen**
(d) (*inf: finanziell*) *jdn* to fleece (*inf*); (*beim Kartenspiel*) to clean out (*inf*)
(e) (*Aus:* = *erkennen*) to make out

ausnehmend ADV exceptionally; **das gefällt mir** ~ **gut** I like that very much indeed

ausnüchtern [ˈausnʏçtɐn] VTIR SEP to sober up

Ausnüchterungszelle F drying-out cell

ausnutzen, (*esp S Ger, Aus, Sw*) **ausnützen** VT SEP to use; *jdn* to use; (= *ausbeuten*) to exploit; *Gelegenheit* to make the most of; *jds Gutmütigkeit, Leichtgläubigkeit etc* to take advantage of

auspacken SEP ▌ VTI *Koffer* to unpack; *Geschenk* to unwrap ▐ VI (*inf*) (= *alles sagen*) to talk (*inf*)

auspfeifen VT SEP IRREG to boo at; *Stück, Schauspieler* to boo off the stage

ausplaudern VT SEP to let out

ausplündern VT SEP *Dorf etc* to pillage; *Kasse, Laden* (*hum*) *Speisekammer etc* to raid; *jdn* to clean out (*inf*)

ausposaunen ptp **ausposaunt** VT SEP (*inf*) to broadcast (*inf*)

auspressen VT SEP *Saft, Schwamm etc* to squeeze out; *Zitrone etc* to squeeze

ausprobieren ptp **ausprobiert** VT SEP to try out

Auspuff M, *pl* **-puffe** exhaust

Auspuff-: **Auspuffgase** PL exhaust fumes *pl*; **Auspuffkrümmer** [-krʏmɐ] M **-s, -** (*Aut*) exhaust manifold; **Auspuffrohr** NT exhaust pipe; **Auspufftopf** M silencer (*Brit*), muffler (*US*)

auspumpen VT SEP (= *leeren*) to pump out

auspusten VT SEP (*inf*) to blow out

Ausputzer [ˈausputsɐ] M **-s, -**, **Ausputzerin** [-ərɪn] F **-, -nen** (*Ftbl*) sweeper; (*fig inf*) troubleshooter

ausquartieren [ˈauskvartiːrən], ptp **ausquartiert** VT SEP to move out; (*Mil*) to billet out

ausquatschen [ˈauskvatʃn̩] VR SEP (*inf*) to have a heart-to-heart (*bei jdm* with sb)

ausquetschen VT SEP *Saft etc* to squeeze out; *Zitrone etc* to squeeze; (*inf:* = *ausfragen*) (*Polizei etc*) to grill (*inf*); (*aus Neugier*) to pump (*inf*)

ausradieren ptp **ausradiert** VT SEP to rub out; (*fig:* = *vernichten*) to wipe out

ausrangieren ptp **ausrangiert** VT SEP (*inf*) *Kleider* to throw out; *Maschine, Auto* to scrap; **ein altes ausrangiertes Auto** an old disused car

ausrasten SEP ■ VI AUX SEIN **(a)** (*Tech*) to come out **(b)** (*hum inf*: = *zornig werden*) to do one's nut (*Brit inf*) ■ VI IMPERS (*inf*) **es rastet bei jdm aus** something snaps in sb (*inf*)

ausrauben VT SEP to rob

ausräuchern VT SEP *Zimmer* to fumigate; *Tiere, Schlupfwinkel, Bande* to smoke out

ausraufen VT SEP to tear out; **ich könnte mir die Haare ~** I could kick myself

ausräumen VT SEP to clear out; *Möbel* to move out; (*fig*) *Missverständnisse, Konflikt* to clear up; *Vorurteile, Bedenken* to dispel

ausrechnen VT SEP to work out; (= *ermitteln*) *Gewicht, Länge etc* to calculate; **sich** (*dat*) **etw ~ können** (*fig*) to be able to work sth out (for oneself); **sich** (*dat*) **große Chancen/einen Vorteil ~** to reckon that one has a good chance/an advantage; *siehe auch* **ausgerechnet**

Ausrede F excuse

ausreden SEP ■ VI to finish speaking ■ VT **jdm etw ~** to talk sb out of sth ■ VR (*esp Aus*) (= *sich aussprechen*) to have a heart-to-heart (talk); (= *Ausflüchte machen*) to make excuses

ausreichen VI SEP to be sufficient; **die Zeit reicht nicht aus** there is not sufficient time

ausreichend ■ ADJ sufficient; (*Sch*) satisfactory ■ ADV sufficiently

Ausreise F **bei der ~** on leaving the country; (= *Grenzübertritt*) on crossing the border; **jdm die ~ verweigern** to prohibit sb from leaving the country

ausreisen VI SEP AUX SEIN to leave (the country); **ins Ausland/ nach Frankreich ~** to go abroad/to France

ausreißen SEP IRREG ■ VT *Haare, Blatt* to tear out; *Unkraut, Blumen, Zahn* to pull out; **einem Käfer die Flügel/Beine ~** to pull a beetle's wings/legs off; **er hat sich** (*dat*) **kein Bein ausgerissen** (*inf*) he didn't exactly overstrain himself ■ VI AUX SEIN (+*dat* from) (*inf*: = *davonlaufen*) to run away; (*Sport*) to break away

Ausreißer ['ausraɪsɐ] M **-s, -**, **Ausreißerin** [-ərɪn] F **-, -nen** (*inf*) runaway

ausreiten VI SEP IRREG AUX SEIN to go for a ride

ausrenken ['ausrɛŋkn] VT SEP to dislocate; **sich/jdm den Arm ~** to dislocate one's/sb's arm

ausrichten SEP ■ VT **(a)** (= *aufstellen*) to line up; **jdn/etw auf etw** (*acc*) **~** (= *einstellen*) to align sb/sth with sth; (= *abstellen*) to gear sb/sth to sth
(b) (= *veranstalten*) to organize
(c) (= *erreichen*) to achieve; **ich konnte bei ihr nichts ~** I couldn't get anywhere with her
(d) (= *übermitteln*) to tell; *Nachricht* to pass on; **jdm ~, dass ...** to tell sb (that) ...; **jdm etwas ~** to give sb a message; **kann ich etwas ~?** can I give him/her *etc* a message?; **bitte richten Sie ihm einen Gruß aus** please give him my regards
(e) (*Aus*: = *schlecht machen*) to run down
■ VR to line up in a straight row; (*Mil*) to dress ranks; **sich nach dem Nebenmann/Vordermann/Hintermann ~** to line up (exactly) with the person next to/in front of/behind one; **sich an etw** (*dat*) **~** (*fig*) to orientate oneself to sth

Ausrichtung F **(a)** (*fig*) (*auf an Ideologie etc*) orientation (*auf* +*acc* towards, *an* +*dat* to); (*auf Bedürfnisse etc*) gearing (*auf* +*acc* to) **(b)** (*von Veranstaltung*) organization
(c) (= *Aufstellung*) lining up; (= *Einstellung*) alignment (*auf* +*acc* with)

Ausritt M ride (out); (= *das Ausreiten*) riding out

ausrollen VT SEP *Teig, Teppich* to roll out; *Kabel* to run out

ausrotten ['ausrɔtn] VT SEP to wipe out; *Wanzen etc* to destroy; *Religion, Ideen* to stamp out

ausrücken SEP ■ VI SEP AUX SEIN **(a)** (*Mil*) to move out; (*Polizei, Feuerwehr*) to turn out **(b)** (*inf*: = *ausreißen*) to make off; (*von zu Hause*) to run away ■ VT **(a)** (*Tech*) to disengage **(b)** (*Typ*) *Zeilen etc* to move out

Ausruf M **(a)** (= *Ruf*) cry **(b)** (= *Bekanntmachung*) proclamation

ausrufen VT SEP IRREG to exclaim; *Schlagzeilen* to cry out; *Waren* to cry; (*auf Auktion*) to start; (= *verkünden*) to call out; *Haltestellen, Streik* to call; **jdn zum** *or* **als König ~** to proclaim sb king; **jdn** *or* **jds Namen ~ (lassen)** (*über Lautsprecher etc*) to put out a call for sb; (*im Hotel*) to page sb

Ausrufezeichen NT, **Ausrufungszeichen** NT exclamation mark (*Brit*), exclamation point (*US*)

ausruhen VTIR SEP to rest; (*Mensch*) to have a rest; **ausgeruht** (well) rested; **meine Augen müssen (sich) ein wenig ~** I shall have to rest my eyes a little

ausrüsten VT SEP (*lit, fig*) to equip; *Fahrzeug, Schiff* to fit out; **ein Fahrzeug mit etw ~** to fit a car with sth

Ausrüstung F **(a)** NO PL (= *das Ausrüsten*) equipping; (*von Fahrzeug, Schiff*) fitting out **(b)** (= *Ausrüstungsgegenstände*) equipment; (= *esp Kleidung*) outfit

ausrutschen VI SEP AUX SEIN to slip; **das Messer/die Hand ist mir ausgerutscht** my knife/my hand slipped

Ausrutscher ['ausrotʃɐ] M **-s, -** (*inf: lit, fig*) slip; (= *schlechte Leistung*) slip-up

Aussaat F **(a)** NO PL (= *das Säen*) sowing **(b)** (= *Saat*) seed

aussäen VT SEP (*lit, fig*) to sow

Aussage F statement; (= *Behauptung*) opinion; (= *Bericht*) report; (*Jur*) (*eines Beschuldigten, Angeklagten*) statement; (= *Zeugenaussage*) evidence *no pl*, testimony; (*fig: von Roman etc*) message; **eine eidliche/schriftliche ~** a sworn/written statement; **hier steht ~ gegen ~** it's one person's word against another's; **nach ~ seines Chefs** according to his boss

Aussage-: Aussagekraft F, NO PL meaningfulness; **aussagekräftig** ADJ meaningful

aussagen SEP ■ VT to say (*über* +*acc* about); (= *behaupten*) to state; (*unter Eid*) to testify; **was will der Roman ~?** what message does this novel try to convey? ■ VI (*Jur*) (*Zeuge*) to give evidence; (*Angeklagter*) (*schriftlich*) to make a statement; (*unter Eid*) to testify; **eidlich** *or* **unter Eid ~** to give evidence under oath; **für/gegen jdn ~** to give evidence for/against sb

Aussage-: Aussagesatz M statement; **aussagestark** ADJ powerful; *Bewerbung* strong

Aussätzige(r) ['ausɛtsɪgə] MF DECL AS ADJ (*lit, fig*) leper

aussaugen VT SEP *Saft etc* to suck out; *Frucht* to suck (dry); *Wunde* to suck the poison out of

ausschaben VT SEP to scrape out; (*Med*) to curette

Ausschabung F **-, -en** (*Med*) curettage

ausschachten ['ausʃaxtn] VT SEP to excavate; *Brunnen* to sink

ausschaffen VT SEP (*Sw form*) to deport

Ausschaffung F (*Sw form*) deportation

ausschalten VT SEP **(a)** (= *abstellen*) to switch off; **sich (automatisch) ~** to switch (itself) off (automatically) **(b)** (*fig*) to eliminate

Ausschank[1] M **-(e)s, Ausschänke** [-ʃɛŋkə] **(a)** (= *Schankraum*) bar, pub (*Brit*); (= *Schanktisch*) bar **(b)** (*no pl*: = *Getränkeausgabe*) serving of drinks; **„~ von 9.00 Uhr bis 14.00 Uhr"** "open from 9.00 to 14.00"; **„kein ~ an Jugendliche unter 16 Jahren"** "drinks not sold to persons under the age of 16"

Ausschank[2] F **-, Ausschänke** (*Aus*) = **Ausschank**[1] **(a)**

Ausschau F, NO PL **~ halten** to look out

ausschaufeln VT SEP *Grube, Grab* to dig; *Erde* to dig out; *Leiche* to dig up

ausschäumen VT SEP (*Tech*) to foam

ausscheiden SEP IRREG ■ VT (= *aussondern*) to take out; *esp Menschen* to remove; (*Physiol*) to excrete ■ VI AUX SEIN **(a)** (*aus einem Amt*) to retire (*aus* from); (*aus Klub, Firma*) to leave (*aus etw* sth); (*Sport*) to be eliminated; (*in Wettkampf*) to drop out **(b)** (= *nicht in Betracht kommen*) to be ruled out; **das/ er scheidet aus** that/he has to be ruled out

Ausscheidung F **(a)** NO PL (= *das Aussondern*) removal; (*Physiol*) excretion **(b) Ausscheidungen** PL (*Med*) excretions *pl* **(c)** (*Sport*) elimination; (= *Vorkampf*) preliminary (round)

Ausscheidungs- IN CPDS (*Physiol*) excretory; (*Sport*) qualifying (*Brit*), preliminary; **Ausscheidungskampf** M (*Sport*) preliminary (round); (*Leichtathletik, Schwimmen*) heat

ausschenken VTI SEP to pour (out); (*am Ausschank*) to serve

ausscheren VI SEP AUX SEIN (*aus Kolonne*) (*Soldat*) to break rank; (*Fahrzeug, Schiff*) to leave the line; (*Flugzeug*) to break formation; (*zum Überholen*) to pull out; (= *ausschwenken, von gerader Linie abweichen*) to swing out; (*fig*) to step out of line

ausschiffen SEP ■ VT to disembark; *Ladung, Waren* to unload ■ VR to disembark

ausschildern VT SEP to signpost

ausschl. ABBR *von* **ausschließlich** excl.

ausschlachten VT SEP **(a)** *Tier, Beute* to dress **(b)** *(fig) Fahrzeuge, Maschinen etc* to cannibalize **(c)** *(fig inf: = ausnutzen) Skandal, Ereignis* to exploit; *Buch, Werk etc* to get everything out of

ausschlafen SEP IRREG **1** VT *Rausch etc* to sleep off **2** VIR to have a good sleep

Ausschlag M **(a)** *(Med)* rash; **(einen) ~ bekommen** to come out in *or* get a rash **(b)** *(von Zeiger etc)* swing; *(von Kompassnadel)* deflection **(c)** *(fig)* decisive factor; **den ~ geben** *(fig)* to be the decisive factor

ausschlagen SEP IRREG **1** VT **(a)** *(= herausschlagen)* to knock out; **jdm die Zähne ~** to knock sb's teeth out
(b) *Feuer* to beat out
(c) *(= verkleiden)* to line
(d) *(= ablehnen)* to turn down; *Erbschaft* to waive; **jdm etw ~** to refuse sb sth
2 VI **(a)** AUX SEIN or HABEN *(Baum, Strauch)* to start to bud
(b) *(Pferd)* to kick
(c) AUX SEIN or HABEN *(Zeiger, Nadel, Pendel)* to swing; *(Kompassnadel)* to be deflected; *(Wünschelrute etc)* to dip; **nach oben/unten ~** *(Börsenkurse etc)* to go up/down

ausschlaggebend ADJ decisive; *Stimme auch* deciding; **~ sein** to be the decisive factor; **das ist von ~er Bedeutung** that is of prime importance

ausschließen VT SEP IRREG **(a)** *(= aussperren)* to lock out **(b)** *(= entfernen)* to exclude; *(aus Gemeinschaft)* to expel; *(vorübergehend)* to suspend; *(Sport)* to disqualify; *Panne, Fehler, Möglichkeit etc* to rule out; **ich will nicht ~, dass er ein Dieb ist, aber ...** I don't want to rule out the possibility that he's a thief but ...; **die Öffentlichkeit ~** *(Jur)* to exclude the public; *siehe auch* **ausgeschlossen**

ausschließlich ['aʊsʃliːslɪç, 'aʊsʃl-, aʊsˈʃl-] **1** ADJ ATTR exclusive; *Rechte auch* sole **2** ADV exclusively **3** PREP +GEN excluding

Ausschließlichkeit F -, NO PL exclusiveness

Ausschluss M *(= Entfernung)* exclusion; *(aus Gemeinschaft)* expulsion; *(vorübergehend)* suspension; *(Sport)* disqualification; **unter ~ der Öffentlichkeit stattfinden** to be closed to the public

ausschmücken VT SEP to decorate; *(fig) Erzählung* to embellish; **~de Details** embellishments

ausschneiden VT SEP IRREG **(a)** *(= herausschneiden)* to cut out; *Zweige etc* to cut away **(b)** *(Comput)* to cut; **~ und einfügen** to cut and paste; *siehe auch* **ausgeschnitten**

Ausschnitt M **(a)** *(= Zeitungsausschnitt)* cutting **(b)** *(Math)* sector **(c)** *(= Kleidausschnitt)* neck; **ein tiefer ~** a low neckline **(d)** *(fig: = Teil)* part; *(aus einem Bild)* detail; *(aus einem Roman)* excerpt; *(aus einem Film)* clip; **ich kenne das Buch nur in ~en** I only know parts of the book

ausschnittweise **1** ADJ partial; *Veröffentlichung* in extracts **2** ADV *wahrnehmen, vermitteln, erfassen* partially; **etw ~ sehen/hören/zitieren** to see/hear/quote parts of sth

ausschöpfen VT SEP **(a)** *(= herausschöpfen) Wasser etc* to ladle out *(aus of)*; *(aus Boot)* to bale out *(aus of)* **(b)** *(= leeren)* to empty; *Fass etc* to drain; *Boot* to bale out; *(fig)* to exhaust; **die Kompetenzen voll ~** to do everything within one's power

ausschreiben VT SEP IRREG **(a)** *(in Buchstaben) Zahlen* to write out; *(= ungekürzt schreiben) Namen, Abkürzung* to write (out) in full
(b) *(= ausstellen) Rechnung etc* to make out; *Rezept, Überweisung* to write out
(c) *(= bekannt machen)* to announce; *Versammlung, Wahlen* to call; *Stellen, Grundstück (zum Verkauf)* to advertise; *Projekt, Auftrag* to invite tenders for; **etw öffentlich/europaweit ~** to advertise sth to the general public/throughout Europe; **jdn zur Fahndung/Festnahme ~** to put sb on the wanted list

Ausschreibung F *(= Bekanntmachung)* announcement; *(von Versammlung, Wahlen)* calling; *(von Projekt)* invitation of tenders *(+gen* for); *(von Stellen)* advertising

Ausschreitung F -, -en USU PL riot, rioting *no pl*

Ausschuss M **(a)** NO PL *(Comm)* rejects *pl*; *(fig inf)* trash **(b)** *(= Komitee)* committee

Ausschuss-: Ausschussmitglied NT committee member; **Ausschusssitzung** F committee meeting; **Ausschussware** F *(Comm)* rejects *pl*

ausschütteln VT SEP to shake out

ausschütten SEP **1** VT **(a)** *(= auskippen)* to tip out; *Eimer, Glas, Füllhorn* to empty; **jdm sein Herz ~** *(fig)* to pour out one's heart to sb **(b)** *(= verschütten)* to spill **(c)** *(Fin) Dividende etc* to distribute **2** VR **sich (vor Lachen) ~** *(inf)* to split one's sides laughing

ausschweifend ADJ *Leben* dissipated; *Fantasie* wild

ausschweigen VR SEP IRREG to remain silent *(über +acc, zu* about); **sich eisern ~** to maintain a stony silence

aussehen VI SEP IRREG to look; **gut ~** to look good; *(hübsch)* to be good looking; *(gesund)* to look well; **es sieht nach Regen aus** it looks like rain; **wie jd/etw ~** to look like sb/sth; **wie siehts aus?** *(inf: = wie stehts)* how's things? *(esp Brit inf)*, how are things going?; **wie siehst du denn (bloß) aus?** just look at you!; **ich habe (vielleicht) ausgesehen!** you should have seen me!; **er sieht nach nichts aus** he doesn't look (like) anything special; **es sieht nach etwas ~** it's got to look good; **es sieht danach or so aus, als ob ...** it looks as if ...; **seh ich so or danach aus?** *(inf)* what do you take me for?; **so siehst du (gerade) aus!** *(inf)* that's what you think!; **er sieht ganz so or danach aus** he looks it; **es sieht nicht gut mit ihm aus** things don't look good for him; **bei mir sieht es gut aus** I'm doing fine

Aussehen NT -s, NO PL appearance; **dem ~ nach urteilen** to go by appearances

aus sein IRREG AUX SEIN **1** VI *(inf)* **(a)** *(Schule)* to have finished; *(Krieg, Stück)* to have ended; *(Feuer, Ofen)* to be out; *(Radio, Fernseher etc)* to be off; *(Sport)* to be out
(b) **auf etw** *(acc)* **~** to be (only) after sth; **auf jdn ~** to be after sb *(inf)*; **nur auf eins ~** to be interested only in one thing
(c) *(= ausgehen)* **ich war gestern Abend (mit ihr) aus** I went out (with her) last night
2 VI IMPERS **es ist aus (und vorbei) zwischen uns** it's (all) over between us; **es ist aus mit ihm** he is finished; **es ist aus (und vorbei) mit dem bequemen Leben** the life of leisure is (all) over

außen ['aʊsn] ADV **(a)** **die Tasse ist ~ bemalt** the cup is painted on the outside; **~ an der Windschutzscheibe** on the outside of the windscreen *(Brit)* or windshield *(US)*; **von ~ sieht es gut aus** on the outside it looks good; **er läuft ~** he's running on the outside; **das Fenster geht nach ~ auf** the window opens outwards; **nach ~ hin** *(fig)* outwardly; **~ stehend** *Beobachter etc* outside *attr*
(b) **~ vor sein** to be left out; **etw ~ vor lassen** *(= etw ausschließen)* to leave sth out
(c) *(Aus)* = **draußen**

Außen-: Außenabmessung F external dimensions *pl*; **Außenantenne** F outdoor aerial *(Brit)* or antenna *(esp US)*; **Außenaufnahme** F outdoor shot; **Außenbahn** F outside lane; **Außenbeitrag** M *(Fin)* net visble and invisible exports *pl*; **Außenbezirk** M outlying district; **Außenbordmotor** M outboard motor; **Außendienst** M external duty; **im ~ sein** to work outside the office; **~ machen** *or* **haben** to work outside the office; **Außendienstmitarbeiter(in)** M(F) sales representative; **Außenfinanzierung** F external financing; **Außenhandel** M foreign trade; **Außenhandelsbeziehungen** PL foreign trade relations *pl*; **Außenhandelsbilanz** F balance of trade; **Außenhandelsdefizit** NT trade deficit; **Außenminister(in)** M(F) foreign secretary *(Brit)*, secretary of state *(US)*; **Außenministerium** NT Foreign Office *(Brit)*, State Department *(US)*; **Außenpolitik** F *(Gebiet)* foreign politics *sing*; *(bestimmte)* foreign policy; **Außenpolitiker(in)** M(F) foreign affairs politician; **außenpolitisch** **1** ADJ *Debatte, Einfluss, Sprecher* on foreign affairs; *Schaden* to foreign affairs; *Fehler* as regards foreign affairs; *Berichterstattung* of foreign affairs; *Schulung, Erfahrung* in foreign affairs; **~e Angelegenheiten** foreign affairs; **aus ~er Sicht** from the point of view of foreign affairs **2** ADV in terms of foreign policy; **~ sinnvoll sein** to be sensible foreign policy; **~ gesehen** from the point of view of foreign affairs; **Außenprüfung** F *(= Betriebsprüfung)* tax field audit; **Außenseite** F outside; **Außenseiter** ['aʊsnzaɪtɐ] M -s, -, **Außenseiterin** [-ərɪn] F -, -nen *(Sport, fig)* outsider; **Außenspiegel** M *(Aut)* outside mirror; **Außenstände** PL *(esp Comm)* outstanding debts *pl*; **wir haben noch 2.000 Euro ~** we still have 2,000 euros outstanding; **außenstehend** ADJ *siehe* **außen**; **Außenstehende(r)** ['aʊsnʃteːəndə] MF DECL AS ADJ outsider; **Außenstelle** F branch; **Außentemperatur** F outside temperature; *(außerhalb Gebäude)* outdoor temperature; **wir haben 20° ~ the**

temperature outdoors is 20°; **Außenwand** F outer wall; **Außenwert** M (Fin) exchange value; **außenwirtschaftlich** ADJ external, relating to foreign trade and payments; **~e Beziehungen** external trade relations pl; **~es Gleichgewicht** external balance; **~ bedingt** due to foreign trade and payments; **Außenwirtschaftsgesetz** NT Foreign Trade and Payments Act

außer ['ausɐ] 𝟙 PREP +DAT or (rare) +GEN **(a)** (räumlich) out of; **~ sich** (acc) **geraten** to go wild; **~ sich** (dat) **sein** to be beside oneself; **~ Haus** or **Hauses sein/essen** to be/eat out; **~ Atem** out of breath
(b) (= ausgenommen) except (for); (= abgesehen von) apart from; **~ ihm habe ich keine Verwandten mehr** I have no relatives left apart from him
(c) (= zusätzlich zu) in addition to
𝟚 CONJ except; **~ dass ...** except that ...; **~ wenn ...** except when ...; **~ sonntags** except Sundays

außerbetrieblich 𝟙 ADJ (= nicht dienstlich) private; Tätigkeiten, Arbeitsplätze outside; Berufsbildungsstätte external 𝟚 ADV veranstalten, regeln privately; ausbilden externally; **sie treffen sich auch ~** they also meet outside work

außerbörslich ADJ, ADV over the counter

außerdem ['ausədeːm, ausɐ'deːm] ADV besides; (= dazu) in addition; (= überdies) anyway; **er ist Professor und ~ noch Gutachter** he's a professor and a consultant as well

außerdienstlich 𝟙 ADJ (= nicht dienstlich) private; (= außerhalb der Arbeitszeit) social 𝟚 ADV **ich bin heute ~ unterwegs** I'm not on business today; **dürfte ich Sie mal ~ sprechen?** could I speak to you privately?

äußere(r, s) ['ɔysərə] 𝟙 ADJ outer; Durchmesser, Verletzung external; (= außenpolitisch) external; Schein, Eindruck outward **Äußere(s)** ['ɔysərə] NT DECL AS ADJ exterior, outward appearance; **das ~ täuscht oft** appearances are often deceptive; **Minister des ~n** (form) foreign secretary (Brit), secretary of state (US)

Außer-: außereuropäisch ADJ ATTR non-European; Raum outside Europe; **außerfahrplanmäßig** 𝟙 ADJ nonscheduled 𝟚 ADV **dieser Zug verkehrt ~** this train is running outside of the normal timetable; **außergerichtlich** ADJ, ADV out of court; **außergewöhnlich** 𝟙 ADJ unusual; (= sehr groß) remarkable; **Außergewöhnliches leisten** to do some remarkable things 𝟚 ADV (= sehr) extremely

außerhalb ['ausɐhalp] 𝟙 PREP +GEN outside; **~ der Stadt** outside the town 𝟚 ADV (= außen) outside; (= ~ der Stadt) out of town; **nach ~** outside; (der Stadt) out of town; **von ~** from outside/out of town

Außer-: Außerirdische(r) ['ausɐʔɪrdɪʃə] MF DECL AS ADJ extraterrestrial; **Außerkraftsetzung** [ausɐ'kraftzetsʊŋ] F -, -en repeal

äußerlich ['ɔyslɪç] 𝟙 ADJ **(a)** external; „nur ~!", „nur zur ~en Anwendung!" for external use only **(b)** (fig: = oberflächlich) superficial; (= scheinbar) outward 𝟚 ADV **(a)** externally; **~ schien er unverletzt** he seemed to have no external injuries **(b)** (fig: = oberflächlich) outwardly; **rein ~ betrachtet** on the face of it

äußern ['ɔysn] 𝟙 VT (= sagen) to say; Wunsch etc to express; Worte to voice; Kritik to voice; **seine Meinung ~** to give one's opinion 𝟚 VR (Mensch) to speak; (Krankheit, Symptom) to show itself; **sich dahin gehend ~, dass ...** to make a comment to the effect that ...; **ich will mich dazu nicht ~** I don't want to say anything about that

Außer-: außerordentlich ['ausɐʔɔrdntlɪç] 𝟙 ADJ extraordinary; (= ungewöhnlich, bemerkenswert) remarkable; Professor associate; **Außerordentliches leisten** to achieve some remarkable things 𝟚 ADV (= sehr) exceptionally; **außerorts** ['ausɐʔɔrts] ADV (Sw, Aus) out of town; **außerparlamentarisch** ADJ extraparliamentary; **außerplanmäßig** ADJ Besuch, Treffen, Sitzung unscheduled; Mahlzeit additional; Ausgabe unbudgeted; Defizit unplanned; **außerschulisch** ADJ Aktivitäten, Interessen extracurricular; **außersinnlich** ADJ extrasensory; **~e Wahrnehmung** extrasensory perception

äußerst ['ɔysɛst] ADV extremely

außerstande [ausɐ'ʃtandə, 'ausɐʃtandə], **außer Stande** ADV (= unfähig) incapable; (= nicht in der Lage) unable; **~ sein, etw zu tun** to be incapable of doing sth/unable to do sth

äußerste(r, s) ['ɔysɛstə] ADJ SUPERL von **äußere(r, s)** (räumlich) furthest; Planet, Schicht outermost; Norden etc extreme;

(zeitlich) latest possible; (fig) utmost; **der ~ Preis** the last price; **mein ~s Angebot** my final offer; **im ~n Falle** if the worst comes to the worst; **mit ~r Kraft** with all one's strength; **von ~r Dringlichkeit/Wichtigkeit** of (the) utmost urgency/importance

Äußerste(s) ['ɔysəstə] NT DECL AS ADJ **bis zum ~n gehen** to go to extremes; **er hat sein ~s gegeben** he gave his all; **ich bin auf das ~ gefasst** I'm prepared for the worst

außertariflich 𝟙 ADJ Regelung nonunion; Zuschlag supplementary to agreed union rates 𝟚 ADV **~ bezahlt werden** to be paid nonunion rates

Äußerung ['ɔysərʊŋ] F -, -en (= Bemerkung) remark; (Ling) (= Behauptung) statement; (= Zeichen) expression

aussetzen SEP 𝟙 VT **(a)** Kind, Haustier to abandon; Wild, Fische to release; Pflanzen to plant out; (Naut) Passagiere to maroon; Boot to lower
(b) (= preisgeben) jdn/etw einer Sache (dat) **~** to expose sb/sth to sth; **jdm/einer Sache ausgesetzt sein** (= ausgeliefert) to be at the mercy of sb/sth
(c) (= festsetzen) Belohnung, Preis to offer; **auf jds Kopf** (acc) **1000 Dollar ~** to put 1,000 dollars on sb's head
(d) (= unterbrechen) to interrupt; Debatte, Prozess to adjourn; Zahlung to break off
(e) an jdm/etw etwas auszusetzen haben to find fault with sb/sth; **daran ist nichts auszusetzen** there is nothing wrong with it; **daran habe ich nur eines auszusetzen** I've only one objection to make to that; **was haben Sie daran auszusetzen?** what don't you like about it?
𝟚 VI (= aufhören) to stop; (bei Spiel) to sit out; (= versagen) to give out; **mit etw ~** to stop sth; **mit der Pille ~** to stop taking the pill; **mit der Behandlung ~** to interrupt the treatment; **ich setze besser mal aus** I'd better have a break; (bei Spiel) I'd better sit this one out

Aussetzung F -, -en **(a)** (von Kind, Tier) abandonment; (von Fischen, Wild) release; (von Pflanzen) planting out; (Naut) (von Passagieren) marooning; (von Boot) lowering **(b)** (von Belohnung) offer; **durch ~ einer Belohnung** by offering a reward **(c)** (= Unterbrechung) interruption; (von Debatte, Prozess) adjournment; (von Zahlung) breaking off

Aussicht F -, -en **(a)** (= Blick) view (auf +acc of); **ein Zimmer mit ~ auf den Park** a room overlooking the park
(b) (fig) prospect (auf +acc of); **die ~, dass etw geschieht** the chances of sth happening; **gute ~en haben** to have good prospects; **keine ~** no prospect; **nicht die geringste ~** not the slightest prospect; **etw in ~ haben** to have good prospects of sth; **jdm etw in ~ stellen** to promise sb sth; **in ~ stehen** to be in prospect; **das sind ja schöne ~en!** (iro inf) what a prospect!

Aussichts-: aussichtslos ADJ hopeless; (= zwecklos) pointless; **eine ~e Sache** a lost cause; **aussichtsreich** ADJ promising; Stellung with good prospects

Aussiedler(in) M(F) (= Auswanderer) emigrant

aussitzen VT SEP IRREG Problem to sit out

aussöhnen ['auszøːnen] SEP 𝟙 VT **jdn mit jdm/etw ~** to reconcile sb with sb/to sth; **jdn ~** to appease sb 𝟚 VR **sich mit jdm/etw ~** to become reconciled with sb/to sth; **wir haben uns wieder ausgesöhnt** we have made it up again 𝟛 VI **mit etw ~** to compensate for sth

Aussöhnung F -, -en reconciliation

aussondern VT SEP (= auslesen) to select; Schlechtes to pick out; (euph) Menschen to single out

aussorgen VI SEP **ausgesorgt haben** to have no more money worries

aussortieren ptp **aussortiert** VT SEP to sort out

ausspannen SEP 𝟙 VT **(a)** Tuch, Netz to spread out **(b)** (= ausschirren) to unharness; Ochsen to unyoke; (aus Schreibmaschine) Bogen to take out **(c)** (fig inf) **jdm etw ~** to do sb out of sth (inf); **jdm die Freundin** etc ~ to steal sb's girlfriend etc **2** VI (= sich erholen) to have a break

aussparen VT SEP Fläche to leave blank; (fig) to omit

aussperren VT SEP to lock out

Aussperrung F (Ind) lockout

ausspielen SEP **1** VT (a) Karte to play; (am Spielanfang) to lead with; **seinen letzten Trumpf ~** (fig) to play one's last card (b) (fig: = einsetzen) Überlegenheit etc to display (c) (fig) **jdn/etw gegen jdn/etw ~** to play sb/sth off against sb/sth **2** VI (a) (Cards) to play a card; (als erster) to lead (b) (= zu Ende spielen) to finish playing; siehe auch **ausgespielt**

Aussprache F (a) pronunciation; (= Art des Artikulierens) articulation; (= Akzent) accent (b) (= Meinungsaustausch) discussion; (= Gespräch) talk; **es kam zu einer offenen ~ zwischen den beiden** they talked things out; **eine ~ herbeiführen** to bring things out into the open

Ausspracheangabe F (Ling) phonetic transcription

aussprechbar ADJ pronounceable; **leicht/schwer ~** easy/difficult to pronounce; **nicht ~** unpronounceable

aussprechen SEP IRREG **1** VT Wort, Urteil etc to pronounce; Scheidung to grant; (= zu Ende sprechen) Satz to finish; (= äußern) to express (jdm to sb); Verdächtigung to voice; Warnung to give

2 VR (a) (Partner) to talk things out; (= sein Herz ausschütten, seine Meinung sagen) to say what's on one's mind; **sich mit jdm (über etw** acc**) ~** to have a talk with sb (about sth); **sich für/gegen etw ~** to declare oneself in favour (Brit) or favor (US) of/against sth

(b) (Wort) to be pronounced **3** VI (= zu Ende sprechen) to finish (speaking); siehe auch **ausgesprochen**

Ausspruch M remark; (= geflügeltes Wort) saying

ausspucken SEP **1** VT to spit out; (fig) Produkte to spew out; (hum inf) Geld to cough up (inf); Gelerntes to regurgitate; **sie hat das ganze Essen wieder ausgespuckt** (inf: = erbrochen) she vomited the whole meal back up again **2** VI to spit

ausspülen VT SEP to rinse (out); (kräftiger) to flush (out); (Med, Geol) to wash out; **sich** (dat) **den Mund ~** to rinse one's mouth (out)

ausstaffieren ['ausʃtafiːrən], ptp **ausstaffiert** VT SEP (inf) to equip; jdn to rig out; (= herausputzen) to dress up

Ausstand M (a) (= Streik) strike, industrial action (Brit); **im ~ sein** to be on strike; **in den ~ treten** to (go on) strike (b) USU PL (Comm) outstanding debt (c) **seinen ~ geben** to throw a leaving party

ausständig ADJ (esp Aus) outstanding

ausstatten ['ausʃtatn] VT SEP to equip; (= versorgen) to provide; (= möblieren) to furnish; Buch to produce; **mit Intelligenz** etc **ausgestattet sein** to be endowed with intelligence etc

Ausstattung F -, -en (a) (= Ausrüstung) equipment; (= Kapital) provisions pl; (von Zimmer etc) furnishings pl; (Theat) décor and costumes pl; (von Buch) presentation (b) (= das Ausstatten) equipping; (= Versorgung) provision; (= das Möblieren) furnishing; (von Buch) production

ausstechen VT SEP IRREG (a) Pflanzen, Unkraut to dig up; Torf, Plätzchen to cut out; Apfel to core (b) Augen (esp als Strafe) to gouge out (c) (fig) jdn (= verdrängen) to push out; (= übertreffen) to outdo

ausstehen SEP IRREG **1** VT (= ertragen) to endure; Sorge, Angst to go through; **ich kann ihn/so etwas nicht ~** I can't bear him/anything like that; **jetzt ist es ausgestanden** now it's all over **2** VI (= fällig sein) to be due; (Antwort) to be still to come; (Entscheidung) to be still to be taken; (Lösung) to be still to be found; (= noch zu erwarten sein) to be still expected

aussteigen VI SEP IRREG AUX SEIN (a) (aus Fahrzeug) to get out (aus of); (aus Bus, Zug etc auch) to get off (aus etw sth); (fig: aus Gesellschaft) to opt out; **alles ~!** everybody out!; (von Schaffner) all change! (b) (inf: aus Geschäft etc) to get out (aus of)

Aussteiger ['ausʃtaigɐ] M -s, -, **Aussteigerin** [-ərɪn] F -, -nen (aus Gesellschaft) person who opts out; (aus Terroristenszene, Sekte) dropout

ausstellen SEP **1** VT (a) (= zur Schau stellen) to display; (auf Messe, in Museum etc) to exhibit

(b) (= ausschreiben) to make out (jdm to sb); (= behördlich ausgeben) to issue (jdm etw sb with sth, sth to sb); **einen Scheck auf jdn ~** to make out a cheque (Brit) or check (US) to sb; **eine Rechnung über 500 Euro ~** to make out a bill for 500 euros

(c) (= ausschalten) Gerät to turn off

(d) siehe **ausgestellt**

2 VI to exhibit

Aussteller ['ausʃtelɐ] M -s, -, **Ausstellerin** [-ərɪn] F -, -nen (a) (auf Messe) exhibitor (b) (von Dokument) issuer; (von Scheck) drawer

Ausstellung F (a) (= Kunstausstellung, Messe) exhibition; (= Blumenausstellung, Hundeausstellung etc) show (b) NO PL (von Scheck, Rezept, Rechnung etc) making out; (behördlich) issuing

Ausstellungs-: **Ausstellungsdatum** NT date of issue; **Ausstellungsgelände** NT exhibition site; **Ausstellungshalle** F exhibition hall; **Ausstellungsstück** NT (in Ausstellung) exhibit; (in Schaufenster etc) display item

aussterben VI SEP IRREG AUX SEIN to die out; siehe auch **ausgestorben**

Aussterben NT extinction; **im ~ begriffen** dying out; **vom ~ bedroht sein** to be threatened by extinction

Aussteuer F dowry

Ausstieg ['ausʃtiːk] M -(e)s, -e [-gə] (a) NO PL (= das Aussteigen) climbing out (aus of); (aus Bus, Zug etc) getting off; (fig: aus Gesellschaft) opting out (aus of); **der ~ aus der Kernenergie** abandoning nuclear energy (b) (auch **Ausstiegluke**) escape hatch

ausstopfen VT SEP Kissen etc, Tiere to stuff

Ausstoß M (= Produktion) output, production

ausstoßen VT SEP IRREG (a) (= äußern) to utter; Schrei to give; Seufzer to heave (b) (= ausschließen: aus Verein, Armee etc) to expel (aus from); (= verbannen) to banish (aus from); **jdn aus der Gesellschaft ~** to banish sb from society; siehe **Ausgestoßene(r)** (c) (= herausstoßen) to eject; Gas etc to give off; (= herstellen) Teile, Stückzahl to turn out

ausstrahlen VT SEP to radiate; (Rad, TV) to broadcast

Ausstrahlung F radiation; (Rad, TV) broadcast(ing); (fig: von Ort) aura; (von Mensch) charisma

ausstrecken SEP **1** VT to extend (nach towards); Fühler auch to put out; Hand auch, Beine etc to stretch out **2** VR to stretch (oneself) out

ausstreichen VT SEP IRREG (a) Geschriebenes to cross out; **jds Namen auf einer Liste ~** to cross sb's name off a list (b) (= glätten) Falten to smooth out

ausströmen VI SEP AUX SEIN (= herausfließen) to stream out (aus of); (= entweichen) to escape (aus from)

aussuchen VT SEP (= auswählen) to choose; (esp iro) to pick; **such dir was aus!** choose what you want; siehe auch **ausgesucht**

Austausch M exchange; (= Ersatz) replacement; (Sport) substitution; **im ~ für** or **gegen** in exchange for

austauschbar ADJ exchangeable; (= untereinander ~) interchangeable; (= ersetzbar) replaceable

austauschen VT SEP (lit, fig) to exchange (gegen for); (= untereinander ~) to interchange; (= ersetzen) to replace (gegen with); **er ist wie ausgetauscht** (fig) he's (become) a different person

Austausch-: **Austauschlehrer(in)** M(F) exchange teacher; **Austauschmotor** M replacement engine; **Austauschschüler(in)** M(F) exchange student or pupil; **Austauschstudent(in)** M(F) exchange student

austeilen VT SEP to distribute (unter +dat, an +acc among); Spielkarten to deal (out); Essen to serve; Prügel to administer

Auster ['austɐ] F -, -n oyster

Austern-: **Austernbank** F, pl -bänke oyster bed; **Austernfischer** M (Orn) oystercatcher; **Austernpark** M oyster farm; **Austernpilz** M oyster mushroom; **Austernzucht** F oyster farm; (= Austernzüchtung) oyster farming

austoben SEP **1** VT to work off (an +dat on) **2** VR (Mensch) to let off steam; (= sich müde machen) to tire oneself out; (= ein wildes Leben führen) to have one's fling; **ein Garten, wo sich die Kinder ~ können** a garden where the children can romp about

austragen SEP IRREG **1** VT (a) Problem, Frage to deal with; Duell, Wettkampf etc to hold; **einen Streit mit jdm ~** to have it out with sb (b) Waren, Post etc to deliver (c) **ein Kind ~** to carry a child (through) to full term; (= *nicht abtreiben*) to have a child **2** VR to sign out

Austräger M delivery man/boy; (*von Zeitungen*) newspaper man/boy; **wir suchen Studenten als** ~ we are looking for students to deliver newspapers

Austrägerin F delivery woman/girl; (*von Zeitungen*) newspaper woman/girl

Austragung ['austra:gʊŋ] F **-, -en** (*Sport*) holding

Austragungsort M, *pl* **-orte** (*Sport*) venue

Australien [aus'tra:liən] NT **-s** Australia; ~ **und Ozeanien** Australasia

Australier [aus'tra:liɐ] M **-s, -**, **Australierin** [-iərɪn] F **-, -nen** Australian

australisch [aus'tra:lɪʃ] ADJ Australian; **Australischer Bund** the Commonwealth of Australia

austreiben SEP IRREG **1** VT (= *vertreiben*) to drive out; *Teufel etc* to exorcise; **jdm etw** ~ to cure sb of sth; (*esp durch Schläge*) to knock sth out of sb **2** VI (= *sprießen*) to sprout

austreten SEP IRREG **1** VI AUX SEIN (a) (= *herauskommen*) to come out (*aus* of); (*esp Blut*) to issue (*aus* from); (= *entweichen: Gas etc*) to escape (*aus*, through) (b) (= *ausscheiden*) to leave (*aus etw* sth); (*formell*) to resign (*aus* from); (*aus politischer Gemeinschaft*) to withdraw (*aus* from) (c) (= *zur Toilette gehen*) to go to the toilet (*esp Brit*); (*Sch*) to be excused (*euph*) **2** VT *Spur, Feuer etc* to tread out; *Schuhe* to wear out of shape; *siehe auch* **ausgetreten**

austricksen VT SEP (*inf: Sport, fig*) to trick

austrinken VTI SEP IRREG to finish; **trink (deine Milch) aus!** drink (your milk) up

Austritt M (a) NO PL (= *das Heraustreten*) (*von Flüssigkeit*) outflow; (= *das Entweichen*) escape; (*von Kugel*) exit (b) (= *das Ausscheiden*) leaving *no art* (*aus etc* sth); (*formell*) resignation (*aus* from); (*aus politischer Gemeinschaft*) withdrawal (*aus* from); **die ~e aus der Kirche häufen sich** there are more and more people leaving the church

austrocknen SEP **1** VI AUX SEIN to dry out; (*Fluss etc*) to dry up; (*Kehle*) to become parched **2** VT to dry out; *Fluss etc* to dry up; *Kehle* to make parched; (= *trockenlegen*) *Sumpf* to drain

austüfteln VT SEP (*inf*) to work out; (= *ersinnen*) to think up

ausüben VT SEP (a) *Beruf, Kunst* to practise (*Brit*), to practice (*US*); *Aufgabe, Funktion, Amt* to perform; (= *innehaben*) *Amt* to hold (b) *Druck, Einfluss* to exert (*auf +acc* on); *Macht, Recht* to exercise; *Wirkung* to have (*auf +acc* on); **einen Reiz auf jdn** ~ to have an attraction for sb

Ausübung F (a) (*von Beruf, Kunst*) practice; (*von Aufgabe, Funktion, Amt*) performance; (= *das Innehaben: von Amt*) holding; **in** ~ **seines Dienstes/seiner Pflicht** (*form*) in the execution of his duty; **in** ~ **seines Berufs** (*form*) in pursuance of one's profession (*form*) (b) (*von Druck*) exertion; (*von Macht*) exercising

ausufern ['auslu:fɐn] VI SEP AUX SEIN (*fig*) to get out of hand; (*Konflikt etc*) to escalate (*zu* into)

Ausverkauf M (clearance) sale; (*wegen Geschäftsaufgabe*) closing-down sale; (*fig: = Verrat*) sellout; **etw im** ~ **kaufen** to buy sth at the sale(s)

ausverkauft ['ausfɛɐkauft] ADJ sold out; **vor ~em Haus spielen** to play to a full house

Auswahl F selection (*an +dat* of); (= *Angebot auch*) range; (= *Wahl*) choice; (= *die Besten*) pick; (= *Vielfalt*) variety; (*Sport*) representative team; **viel/eine reiche** ~ a large/wide selection; **hier gibt es keine** ~ there is no choice; **drei Bewerber stehen zur** ~ there are three applicants to choose from; **jdm drei Sachen zur ~ vorlegen** to offer sb a choice of three things; **eine ~ treffen** (= *eines auswählen*) to make a choice; (= *einige auswählen*) to make a selection

auswählen VT SEP to select (*unter +dat* from among); **sich** (*dat*) **etw** ~ to select sth (for oneself); *siehe auch* **ausgewählt**

Auswanderer M, **Auswanderin** F emigrant

auswandern VI SEP AUX SEIN to emigrate (*nach, in +acc* to); (*Volk*) to migrate

Auswanderung F emigration; (= *Massenauswanderung*) migration

auswärtig ['ausvɛrtɪç] ADJ ATTR (a) (= *nicht ansässig*) nonlocal; *Schüler, Mitglied* from out of town (b) (*Pol*) foreign; **der ~e**

Dienst the foreign service; **das Auswärtige Amt** the Foreign Office (*Brit*), the State Department (*US*); **der Minister des Auswärtigen** (*form*) the foreign secretary (*Brit*), the secretary of state (*US*)

auswärts ['ausverts] ADV (a) (= *nach außen*) outwards (b) (= *außerhalb des Hauses*) away from home; (= *außerhalb der Stadt*) out of town; (*Sport*) away; **von** ~ **anrufen** to call long distance; ~ **essen** to eat out

Auswärtsspiel NT (*Sport*) away (game)

auswechseln VT SEP to change; (*esp gegenseitig*) to exchange; (= *ersetzen*) to replace; (*Sport*) to substitute (*gegen* for); **sie ist wie ausgewechselt** (*fig*) she's a different person

Ausweg M way out; **der letzte** ~ a last resort; **er sieht** *or* **weiß keinen anderen ~ als ...** he can see no other way out but ...; **sich** (*dat*) **einen ~ offen lassen** *or* **offen halten** to leave oneself a way out

Ausweg-: ausweglos ADJ (*fig*) hopeless; **Ausweglosigkeit** F **-**, NO PL (*fig*) hopelessness

ausweichen VI SEP IRREG AUX SEIN to get out of the way (*+dat* of); (= *Platz machen*) to make way (*+dat* for); (*fig: = nicht Stellung nehmen*) to evade the issue; **nach rechts** ~ to get out of the way/to make way by going to the right; **einer Sache** (*dat*) ~ (*lit*) to avoid sth; (*fig*) to evade sth; **jdm/einer Begegnung** ~ to avoid sb/a meeting; **eine ~de Antwort** an evasive answer; **auf etw** (*acc*) ~ (*fig*) to switch to sth

Ausweis ['ausvais] M **-es, -e** [-zə] (= *Mitglieds-/Leser-/Studentenausweis etc*) (membership/library/student *etc*) card; (= *Personalausweis*) identity card; (= *Berechtigungsnachweis*) pass; ~, **bitte** your papers please

ausweisen SEP IRREG **1** VT (a) (*aus dem Lande*) to expel (b) (= *für bestimmten Zweck vorsehen*) *Gebiet, Fläche* to designate **2** VR (*mit Ausweis, Pass*) to identify oneself; **können Sie sich ~?** do you have any means of identification?; *siehe auch* **ausgewiesen**

Ausweisung F expulsion

ausweiten SEP **1** VT to widen; *esp Dehnbares* to stretch; (*fig*) to expand (*zu* into) **2** VR to widen; (*esp Dehnbares*) to stretch; (*fig*) (*Thema, Bewegung*) to expand (*zu* into); (= *sich verbreiten*) to spread

auswendig ADV by heart; **etw ~ können/lernen** to know/learn sth (off) by heart; **das kann ich schon** ~ (*fig inf*) I know it backwards (*inf*); **ein Musikstück ~ spielen** to play a piece (of music) from memory

Auswendiglernen NT **-s**, NO PL (*von Geschichtszahlen, Fakten*) learning by heart; **ein Gedicht zum** ~ a poem to learn by heart

auswerfen VT SEP IRREG (a) *Anker, Netz, Leine* to cast (b) (= *hinausschleudern*) *Lava, Asche* to throw out; *Geschosshülsen* to eject (c) *Dividende* to pay out (d) (= *produzieren*) to produce

auswerten VT SEP (= *bewerten*) to evaluate; (= *analysieren*) to analyse

Auswertung F (= *Bewertung*) evaluation; (= *Analyse*) analysis

auswickeln VT SEP *Paket, Bonbon etc* to unwrap

auswildern VT SEP *Tiere* to release into the wild

auswirken VR SEP to have an effect (*auf +acc* on); **sich günstig/negativ** ~ to have a favourable (*Brit*) *or* favorable (*US*)/negative effect; **sich in etw** (*dat*) ~ to result in sth; **sich zu jds Vorteil** ~ to work out to sb's advantage

Auswirkung F (= *Folge*) consequence; (= *Wirkung*) effect; (= *Rückwirkung*) repercussion

auswischen VT SEP to wipe out; *Glas etc, Wunde* to wipe clean; *Schrift etc* to rub out; **jdm eins** ~ (*inf*) to get (*Brit*) *or* pull (*esp US*) one over on sb (*inf*); (*aus Rache*) to get back at sb

auswringen VT SEP IRREG to wring out

Auswuchs ['ausvu:ks] M **-es, Auswüchse** [-vy:ksə] (a) (out)growth; (*Med, Bot auch*) excrescence (*form*); (= *Missbildung*) deformity (b) (= *Erzeugnis*) product; (= *Missstand, Übersteigerung*) excess

auswuchten VT SEP *Räder* to balance

auszahlen SEP **1** VT *Geld etc* to pay out; *Arbeiter, Gläubiger* to pay off; *Kompagnon, Miterben* to buy out; **er bekommt 500 Euro die Woche ausgezahlt** his net pay is 500 euros a week **2** VR (= *sich lohnen*) to pay (off)

auszählen SEP **1** VT *Stimmen* to count (up); (*Boxen*) to count out **2** VI (*bei Kinderspielen*) to count out

Auszahlung F (*von Geld*) paying out; (*von Arbeiter, Gläubiger*) paying off; (*von Kompagnon*) buying out; **zur ~ kommen** (*form*) *or* **gelangen** (*form*) to be paid out

Auszählung F (*von Stimmen etc*) counting (up)

auszeichnen SEP ❚ VT (a) (= *mit Zeichen versehen*) to mark; *Waren* to label; (*Typ*) *Manuskript* to mark up
(b) (= *ehren*) to honour (*Brit*), to honor (*US*); **jdn mit einem Orden ~** to decorate sb (with a medal)
(c) (= *hervorheben*) to distinguish (from all others); (= *kennzeichnen*) to be a feature of
❷ VR to stand out (*durch* due to), to distinguish oneself (*durch* by) (*auch iro*); **dieser Wagen zeichnet sich durch gute Straßenlage aus** one of the remarkable features of this car is its good roadholding; *siehe auch* **ausgezeichnet**

Auszeichnung F (a) (*no pl*: = *das Auszeichnen*) (*von Waren*) labelling (*Brit*), labeling (*US*); (*mit Preisschild*) pricing
(b) (*no pl*: = *das Ehren*) honouring (*Brit*), honoring (*US*); (*mit Orden*) decoration
(c) (= *Markierung*) marking (+*gen*, *an* +*dat* on); (*an Ware*) ticket
(d) (= *Ehrung*) honour (*Brit*), honor (*US*); (= *Orden*) decoration; (= *Preis*) award; **mit ~ bestehen** to pass with distinction

ausziehen SEP IRREG ❚ VT (a) *Kleider, Schuhe, Handschuhe* to take off; *jdn* to undress; **jdm die Jacke ~** to take off sb's jacket *etc*; **sich** (*dat*) **etw ~** to take off sth
(b) (= *herausziehen*) to pull out; (= *verlängern auch*) to extend
(c) (= *nachzeichnen*) *Linie* to trace (*mit Tusche* in ink)
❷ VR (= *sich entkleiden*) to undress; **sich nackt ~** to take off one's clothes; (*bei Leibesvisitation*) to strip naked
❸ VI AUX SEIN (= *aufbrechen, abreisen*) to set out; (*demonstrativ*) to walk out; (*aus einer Wohnung*) to move (*aus* out of); **auf Abenteuer ~** to set off in search of adventure

Auszubildende(r) [ˈaʊstsubɪldndə] MF DECL AS ADJ trainee

Auszug M (a) (= *das Weggehen*) departure; (*demonstrativ*) walkout; (*zeremoniell*) procession; (*aus der Wohnung*) move
(b) (= *Ausschnitt, Exzerpt*) excerpt; (*aus Buch*) extract; (= *Zusammenfassung*) abstract; (= *Kontoauszug*) statement; **etw in Auszügen drucken** to print extracts of sth

auszugsweise ADV in extracts; (= *gekürzt*) in an/the abridged version; **~ aus etw lesen** to read extracts from sth

autark [aʊˈtark] ADJ self-sufficient (*auch fig*), autarkic (*Econ*)

Autarkie [aʊtarˈkiː] F -, -n [-ˈkiːən] self-sufficiency (*auch fig*), autarky (*Econ*)

authentisch [aʊˈtɛntɪʃ] ADJ authentic

Autismus [aʊˈtɪsmʊs] M -, NO PL autism

autistisch [aʊˈtɪstɪʃ] ❚ ADJ autistic ❷ ADV autistically

Auto [ˈaʊto] NT -s, -s car; **~ fahren** (*selbst*) to drive (a car); (*als Mitfahrer*) to go by car; **mit dem ~ fahren** to go by car

Autobahn F motorway (*Brit*), interstate (highway *or* freeway) (*US*); (*esp in Deutschland*) autobahn; (*gebührenpflichtig*) turnpike (*US*)

AUTOBAHN

*There is no general speed limit on German **Autobahnen** (motorways), although there is a recommended limit of 130kph (80mph). In actual fact there are very few sections of road that are not subject to speed restrictions, introduced for reasons of safety and reduced exhaust emissions. No special charge is made for using the **Autobahnen** in Germany. However, in Austria and Switzerland one must purchase a **Vignette**. An additional toll, a **Maut**, is payable on some sections.*
▶ VIGNETTE

Autobahn- IN CPDS motorway (*Brit*), interstate (highway *or* freeway) (*US*); **Autobahnausfahrt** F motorway *etc* exit; **Autobahndreieck** NT motorway *etc* merging point; **Autobahngebühr** F toll; **Autobahnkreuz** NT motorway *etc* intersection; **Autobahnrasthof** M, **Autobahnraststätte** F motorway service area (*Brit*), rest area (*US*); **Autobahnzubringer** M motorway approach road (*Brit*), highway *or* freeway approach (*US*)

Auto-: Autobatterie F car battery; **Autobiografie** F autobiography; **autobiografisch** ❚ ADJ autobiographical ❷ ADV autobiographically; **Autobombe** F car bomb; **Autobus** M bus; (= *Reiseomnibus*) coach (*Brit*), bus; **einstöckiger/zweistöckiger ~** single-decker/double-decker (bus); **Autocar** M (*Sw*) coach (*Brit*), bus; **Autodidakt** [aʊtodiˈdakt] M -en, -en, **Autodidaktin** [-ˈdaktɪn] F -, -nen self-

educated person; **autodidaktisch** [aʊtodiˈdaktɪʃ] ADJ autodidactic (*form*), self-taught *no adv*; **Autodieb(in)** M(F) car thief; **Autodiebstahl** M car theft; **Autofähre** F car ferry; **Autofahren** NT -s, NO PL driving (a car); (*als Mitfahrer*) driving in a car; **Autofahrer(in)** M(F) (car) driver; **Autofahrt** F drive;; **autofrei** ADJ car-free; **Autofriedhof** M (*inf*) car dump

autogen [aʊtoˈgeːn] ADJ autogenous; **~es Training** (*Psych*) relaxation through self-hypnosis

Autogramm [aʊtoˈgram] NT, *pl* -gramme autograph

Auto-: Autokarte F road map; **autokratisch** [aʊtoˈkraːtɪʃ] ❚ ADJ autocratic ❷ ADV autocratically

Automat [aʊtoˈmaːt] M -en, -en (*auch fig*: = *Mensch*) machine; (= *Verkaufsautomat*) vending machine; (= *Roboter*) robot; (= *Musikautomat*) jukebox; (= *Spielautomat*) slot machine

Automatik¹ [aʊtoˈmaːtɪk] M -s, -s (*Aut*) automatic

Automatik² F -, -en (a) automatic mechanism (*auch fig*)
(b) (= *Gesamtanlage*) automatic system; (*Rad*) automatic frequency control; (*Aut*) automatic transmission

Automatik-: Automatikschaltung F automatic transmission; **Automatikwagen** M automatic

automatisch [aʊtoˈmaːtɪʃ] ❚ ADJ automatic ❷ ADV automatically

Automechaniker(in) M(F) car mechanic

Automobil-: Automobilausstellung F motor show; (= *ständige ~*) car exhibition; **Automobilindustrie** F automotive industry

Auto-: autonom [aʊtoˈnoːm] ADJ autonomous (*auch fig*); *Nervensystem* autonomic; **Autonome(r)** [aʊtoˈnoːmə] MF DECL AS ADJ (*Pol*) independent; **Autonomie** [aʊtonoˈmiː] F -, -n [-ˈmiːən] autonomy (*auch fig*); **Autonummer** F (car) number; **Autopilot** M (*Aviat*) autopilot; **vom ~en gesteuert werden** to be on autopilot

Autopsie [aʊtoˈpsiː] F -, -n [-ˈpsiːən] (*Med*) autopsy

Autor [ˈaʊtoːɐ] M -s, Autoren [aʊˈtoːrən] author

Auto-: Autoradio NT car radio; **Autoreifen** M car tyre (*Brit*) *or* tire (*US*); **Autoreisezug** M *train carrying holidaymakers' cars*; **mit dem ~ fahren** to go by motorail (*Brit*); **Autorennen** NT (motor) race; (*Rennsport*) motor racing; **Autorennsport** M motor racing

Autorin [aʊˈtoːrɪn] F -, -nen author, authoress

autoritär [aʊtoriˈtɛːɐ] ❚ ADJ authoritarian ❷ ADV in an authoritarian manner; **ein ~ geführtes Land** a country ruled by an authoritarian government

Autorität [aʊtoriˈtɛːt] F -, -en (*alle Bedeutungen*) authority

Auto-: Autoschalter M drive-in counter; **Autoschlange** F queue (*Brit*) *or* line of cars; **Autoschlosser(in)** M(F) panel beater; **Autoschlosserei** F body shop; **Autoskooter** [ˈaʊtoskuːtɐ] M -s, - bumper car; **Autosport** M motor sport; **Autostopp** M hitchhiking; **~ machen, per ~ fahren** to hitchhike; **Autostrich** M (*inf*) prostitution to car drivers; (= *Gegend*) kerb-crawling (*Brit*) *or* curb-crawling (*US*) area (*inf*); **Autostunde** F hour's drive; **Autotelefon** NT car phone; **Autounfall** M car accident; **Autoverleih** M, **Autovermietung** F car hire (*esp Brit*) *or* rental (*esp US*); (= *Firma*) car hire (*esp Brit*) *or* rental (*esp US*) firm; **Autoversicherung** F car insurance; **Autowerkstatt** F garage, car repair shop (*US*)

Aval [aˈval] M -s, -e (*Comm*) guarantee of a bill (of exchange); **per ~** as guarantor of payment

Avant-: Avantgarde [aˈvãːɡardə, avãˈɡardə] F (*geh*) (*Art*) avant-garde; (*Pol*) vanguard; **Avantgardist** [avãɡarˈdɪst, avant-] M -en, -en, **Avantgardistin** [-ˈdɪstɪn] F -, -nen member of the avant-garde; **avantgardistisch** [avãɡarˈdɪstɪʃ, avant-] ADJ avant-garde

Aversion [avɛrˈzioːn] F -, -en aversion (*gegen* to)

Avocado [avoˈkaːdo] F -, -s avocado

AWG [aːveːˈɡeː] NT ABBR *von* **Außenwirtschaftsgesetz**

Axt [akst] F -, ⸚e [ˈɛkstə] axe (*Brit*), ax (*US*); **sich wie eine** *or* **die ~ im Wald benehmen** (*fig inf*) to behave like a peasant; **die ~ im Haus erspart den Zimmermann** (*Prov*) self-help is the best help

Ayatollah [ajaˈtɔla] M -s, -s ayatollah

Azalee [atsaˈleːə] F -, -n azalea

Azoren [aˈtsoːrən] PL (*Geog*) Azores *pl*

aztekisch [atsˈteːkɪʃ] ADJ Aztec

Azubi [aˈtsuːbiː, ˈa(ː)tsubi] M -s, -s *or* f -, -s ABBR *von* **Auszubildende(r)**

azyklisch [ˈaʦyːklɪʃ, aˈʦyːklɪʃ] ADJ acyclic

Bb

B, b [beː] NT **-, -** B, b; (*Mus*) (= *Ton*) B flat; (= *Versetzungszeichen*) flat; **B-Dur** (the key of) B flat major; **b-Moll** (the key of) B flat minor

babbeln ['babln] VI (*inf*) to babble

Baby ['beːbi] NT **-s, -s** baby

Baby- ['beːbi-] IN CPDS baby; **Babyausstattung** F layette; **Babyboom** M baby boom; **Babyjahr** NT (*für Mutter nach Geburt*) maternity leave (*for one year*); (*Insur*) *year of pension contributions credited to women for each child*; **Babyklappe** ['beːbi-] F *anonymous drop-off point for unwanted babies*

babylonisch [baby'loːnɪʃ] ADJ Babylonian; **eine ~e Sprachverwirrung** a Babel of languages

Baby- ['beːbi-]: **Babynahrung** F baby food; **babysitten** ['beːbizɪtn] VI INSEP to babysit; **Babysitter** ['beːbizɪtɐ] M **-s, -**, **Babysitterin** [-ərɪn] F **-, -nen** babysitter; **Babytragetasche** F carrycot (*Brit*), traveling baby bed (*US*)

Bach [bax] M **-(e)s, ¨e** ['beçə] stream (*auch fig*), brook; **den ~ heruntergehen** (*inf*: *Firma etc*) to go down the tubes (*inf*)

bachab [bax'lap] ADV (*Sw*) downstream; **etw ~ schicken** (*fig inf*) to throw sth away; **~ gehen** (*fig inf*) to go up the spout (*inf*)

Bachblütentherapie F (*Med*) Bach flower remedies *pl*

Bächlein ['beçlaɪn] NT **-s, -** DIM *von* Bach (small) stream

Backblech NT baking tray (*Brit*), baking pan (*US*)

Backbord NT, NO PL (*Naut*) port (side)

backbord(s) ['bakbɔrt(s)] ADV (*Naut*) on the port side; **(nach) ~** to port

Backe ['bakə] F **-, -n** (a) (= *Wange*) cheek (b) (*inf*: = *Hinterbacke*) buttock (c) (*von Schraubstock*) jaw; (= *Bremsbacke*) (*bei Auto*) shoe; (*bei Fahrrad*) block

backen ['bakn], *pret* **backte** *or* (*old*) **buk** ['baktə, buːk], *ptp* **gebacken** [gə'bakn] **1** VT to bake, to make; *Brot, Kuchen* to bake; **frisch/knusprig gebackenes Brot** fresh/crusty bread; **wir ~ alles selbst** we do all our own baking; **gebackener Fisch** fried fish; (*im Ofen*) baked fish **2** VI (*Brot, Kuchen*) to bake; **sie bäckt gern** she enjoys baking

Backenzahn M molar

Bäcker ['beke] M **-s, -**, **Bäckerin** [-ərɪn] F **-, -nen** baker; **~ lernen** to learn the baker's trade; **beim ~** at the baker's; **zum ~ gehen** to go to the baker's

Bäckerei [bekə'raɪ] F **-, -en** (a) (= *Bäckerladen*) baker's (shop); (= *Backstube*) bakery (b) (= *Gewerbe*) baking trade (c) (*Aus*) (= *Gebäck*) pastries *pl*; (= *Kekse*) biscuits *pl* (*Brit*), cookies *pl* (*US*)

Bäckerin F *siehe* Bäcker

Back-: **backfertig** ADJ oven-ready; **Backfett** NT cooking fat; **Backform** F baking tin (*Brit*) *or* pan (*US*); (*für Kuchen*) cake tin (*Brit*) *or* pan (*US*)

Background ['bekgraunt] M **-s, -s** background

Back-: **Backhähnchen** NT, **Backhendl** NT (*S Ger, Aus*) roast chicken; **Backmischung** F cake mix; **Backobst** NT dried fruit; **Backofen** M oven; **backofenfest** ADJ ovenproof; **Backpflaume** F prune; **Backpulver** NT baking powder

Backslash ['bekslɛʃ] M **-s, -s** (*Comput*) backslash

Backspacetaste ['bekspeːs-] F, **Backspace-Taste** F (*Comput*) backspace key

Backstein M brick

bäckt [bekt] 3. PERS SING PRES *von* backen

Back-up ['bekap] NT **-s, -s** (*Comput*) backup

Backwaren PL bread, cakes and pastries *pl*

Bad [baːt] NT **-(e)s, ¨er** ['beːdə] (a) (= *Wannenbad, Badewanne*) (*Phot*) bath; (= *das Baden*) bathing; **ein ~ nehmen** to have a bath; **(sich** *dat*) **ein ~ einlaufen lassen** to run (oneself) a bath; **ein ~ in der Menge nehmen** to go (on a) walkabout (b) (*im Meer etc*) swim; (= *das Baden*) bathing, swimming (c) (= *Badezimmer*) bathroom; **Zimmer mit ~** room with (private) bath (d) (= *Schwimmbad*) (swimming) pool; **die städtischen Bäder** the public baths (*Brit*) *or* pools (*US*); **türkisches ~** Turkish bath (e) (= *Heilbad*) spa; (= *Seebad*) (seaside) resort; **~ Doberan** Bad Doberan

Bade-: **Badeanzug** M swimsuit, bathing suit (*esp US*); **Badegelegenheit** F gibt es dort eine ~? can you swim there?;

Badehose F (swimming *or* bathing) trunks *pl*; **eine ~** a pair of (swimming *or* bathing) trunks; **Badekappe** F swimming cap; **Bademantel** M beach robe; (= *Morgenmantel*) bathrobe, dressing gown (*Brit*); **Bademeister(in)** M(F) (*im Schwimmbad*) (pool) attendant; **Bademütze** F swimming cap

baden ['baːdn] **1** VI (a) (*in der Badewanne*) to have a bath; **hast du schon gebadet?** have you had your bath already?; **warm/ kalt ~** to have a hot/cold bath (b) (*im Meer, Schwimmbad etc*) to swim; **die Badenden** the bathers; **~ gehen** to go swimming; (*einmal*) to go for a swim (c) (*inf*) **~ gehen** to come a cropper (*inf*) **2** VT (a) *Kind etc* to bath (*Brit*), to bathe (*US*); **er ist als Kind zu heiß gebadet worden** (*hum*) he was dropped on the head as a child (*hum*); **in Schweiß gebadet** bathed in sweat (b) *Augen, Wunde etc* to bathe

Baden-Württemberg ['baːdn'vʏrtəmberk] NT **-s** Baden-Württemberg

Bade-: **Badeofen** M boiler; **Badeort** M, *pl* **-orte** (= *Kurort*) spa; (= *Seebad*) (seaside) resort; **Badesachen** PL swimming gear; **Badesalz** NT bath salts *pl*; **Badeschaum** M bubble bath; **Badewanne** F bath(tub); **Badewetter** NT weather warm enough for swimming; **Badezeug** NT, NO PL swimming gear; **Badezimmer** NT bathroom; **Badezusatz** M *bath salts, bubble bath etc*

badisch ['baːdɪʃ] ADJ Baden *attr*; *Wein etc auch* from Baden; **das Dorf ist ~** *or* **im Badischen** the village is in Baden

Badminton ['betmɪntən] NT **-**, NO PL badminton

baff [baf] ADJ PRED (*inf*) **~ sein** to be flabbergasted

BAföG ['baːføk] NT **-**, NO PL, **Bafög** NT **-**, NO PL ABBR *von* **Bundesausbildungsförderungsgesetz; er kriegt ~** he gets a grant

Bagatelldelikt NT petty offence (*Brit*) *or* offense (*US*)

Bagatelle [baga'tɛlə] F **-, -n** trifle

Bagatell-: **Bagatellsache** F (*Jur*) petty case; **Bagatellschaden** M minor damage

Bagger ['bage] M **-, -** excavator; (*für Schlamm*) dredger

baggern ['bagen] **1** VTI *Graben* to excavate; *Fahrrinne* to dredge **2** VI (*sl*: = *Mädchen/Jungen anmachen*) to pick up (*inf*)

Baggersee M *artificial lake in quarry etc*

Baguette [ba'gɛt] NT **-s, -s** *or* f **-, -n** baguette

Bahamainseln [ba'haːma-] PL, **Bahamas** [ba'haːmas] PL Bahamas *pl*

Bahn [baːn] F **-, -en** (a) (= *Weg*) (*fig*) path; (*von Fluss*) course; (= *Fahrbahn*) carriageway; **~ frei!** make way!; **jdm/einer Sache die ~ ebnen/frei machen** (*fig*) to pave/clear the way for sb/ sth; **die ~ ist frei** (*fig*) the way is clear; **in gewohnten ~en verlaufen** (*fig*) to go on in the same old way; **von der rechten ~ abkommen** (*fig*) to stray from the straight and narrow; **jdn auf die rechte ~ bringen** (*fig*) to put sb on the straight and narrow; **etw in die richtige ~** *or* **die richtigen ~en lenken** (*fig*) to channel sth properly; **jdn aus der ~ werfen** *or* **schleudern** (*fig*) to shatter sb (b) (= *Eisenbahn*) railway (*Brit*), railroad (*US*); (= *Zug*) (*der Eisenbahn, U-Bahn*) train; (= *Straßenbahn, Zug*) tram (*esp Brit*), streetcar (US); (= *Bahnhof*) station; **mit der** *or* **per** ~ by train *or* rail/tram (*esp Brit*) *or* streetcar (US); **frei** ~ (*Comm*) free on rail **(c)** (*Sport*) track; (*in Schwimmbecken*) pool; (= *Kegelbahn*) (bowling) alley; (*für einzelne Teilnehmer*) lane; (= *Schlittenbahn, Bobbahn*) run **(d)** (*Phys, Astron*) orbit; (= *Raketenbahn, Geschossbahn*) trajectory **(e)** (= *Stoffbahn, Tapetenbahn*) length

Bahn-: **Bahnanschluss** M railway (*Brit*) *or* railroad (US) connection; ~ **haben** to be connected to the railway (*Brit*) *or* railroad (US) (system); **Bahnarbeiter(in)** M(F) rail worker, railroader (US); **bahnbrechend** 🚂 ADJ pioneering; **Bahnbrechendes leisten** to pioneer new developments; ~ **sein** to be pioneering; (*Erfinder etc*) to be a pioneer 🚂 ADV ~ **wirken** to be pioneering; (*Erfinder etc*) to be a pioneer; **Bahnbus** M *bus run by railway company*; **BahnCard**® [-ka:ɐd] F **-, -s** ≈ railcard

bahnen [ˈbaːnən] VT *Pfad* to clear; *Flussbett* to carve out; **jdm/einer Sache den/einen Weg** ~ to clear the/a way for sb/sth; (*fig*) to pave the way for sb/sth; **sich** (*dat*) **einen Weg** ~ to fight one's way

Bahn-: **Bahnfahrt** F rail journey; **Bahnfracht** F rail freight; **Bahnfrachtbrief** M railway (*Brit*) *or* railroad (US) bill (of lading), railway consignment note; **Bahngleis** NT railway (*Brit*) *or* railroad (US) line; (*von Straßenbahn*) tram (*esp Brit*) *or* streetcar (US) line

Bahnhof M (railway (*Brit*) *or* railroad (US)) station; (= *Busbahnhof*) bus station; **am** *or* **auf dem** ~ at the station; ~ **Schöneberg** Schöneberg station; **ich verstehe nur** ~ (*hum inf*) it's as clear as mud (to me) (*Brit inf*)

Bahnhof- IN CPDS (*esp Sw*) = Bahnhofs-

Bahnhofs- IN CPDS station; **Bahnhofsgaststätte** F station restaurant; **Bahnhofshalle** F (station) concourse; **in der** ~ in the station; **Bahnhofsmission** F *charitable organization for helping needy passengers*

Bahn-: **bahnlagernd** ADJ, ADV (*Comm*) to be picked up at the station (*esp Brit*); **etw** ~ **schicken** to send sth to be picked up at the station (*esp Brit*); **Bahnpolizei** F railway (*Brit*) *or* railroad (US) police; **Bahnschranke** F, (*Aus*) **Bahnschranken** M level (*Brit*) *or* grade (US) crossing barrier; **Bahnsteig** [-ʃtaik] M **-(e)s, -e** [-gə] platform; **Bahntransport** M rail transport; (= *Güter*) consignment sent by rail; **Bahnübergang** M level (*Brit*) *or* grade (US) crossing; **beschrankter** ~ level (*Brit*) *or* grade (US) crossing with gates; **unbeschrankter** ~ unguarded level (*Brit*) *or* grade (US) crossing; **Bahnverbindung** F train service; **nach einer** ~ **fragen** to inquire about a train connection

Bahre [ˈbaːrə] F **-, -n** (= *Krankenbahre*) stretcher; (= *Totenbahre*) bier

Bahrein [baˈrain, baxˈrain] NT **-s** Bahrain

Baiser [bɛˈze:] NT **-s, -s** meringue

Baisse [ˈbɛːs(ə)] F **-, -n** (*St Ex*) fall; (*plötzliche*) slump; **auf (die)** ~ **spekulieren** to bear

Baissespekulant(in) [ˈbɛːs(ə)-] M(F), **Baissier** [bɛˈsie:] M **-s, -s** (*St Ex*) bear

Bakterie [bakˈteːriə] F **-, -n** USU PL germ; ~**n** *pl* germs *pl*, bacteria *pl*

bakteriell [bakteˈriɛl] 🚂 ADJ bacterial 🚂 ADV bacterially; ~ **verursacht** caused by germs *or* bacteria

bakteriologisch [bakterioˈloːgɪʃ] ADJ *Forschung, Test* bacteriological; *Krieg* biological

Balance [baˈlãːsə] F **-, -n** balance; **die** ~ **halten/verlieren** to keep/lose one's balance

Balanceakt [baˈlãːs(ə)-] M (*lit, fig*) balancing act

balancieren [balãˈsiːrən], *ptp* **balanciert** 🚂 VI AUX SEIN to balance; (*fig*) to achieve a balance (**zwischen** +*dat* between); **über etw** (*acc*) ~ to balance one's way across sth 🚂 VT to balance

bald [balt] 🚂 ADV, *comp* **eher** *or* ⁼**er** [ˈbɛldə] (*olddial*), *superl* **am ehesten** **(a)** (= *schnell, in Kürze*) soon; **er kommt** ~ he'll be coming soon; ~ **darauf** soon afterwards; **so** ~ **wie** *or* **als möglich, möglichst** ~ as soon as possible; **wirds** ~**?** get a move on; **bis** ~**!** see you soon **(b)** (= *fast*) almost; **das ist** ~ **nicht mehr schön** that's going too far 🚂 CONJ (*geh*) ~ **...,** ~ **...** one moment ..., the next ...; ~ **hier,** ~ **da** now here, now there

Baldachin [ˈbaldaxiːn, baldaˈxiːn] M **-s, -e** canopy; (*Archit*) baldachin

Bälde [ˈbɛldə] F **in** ~ in the near future.

baldig [ˈbaldɪç] ADJ ATTR NO COMP quick; *Antwort, Wiedersehen* early; **wir hoffen auf Ihr** ~**es Kommen** we hope you will come soon; **auf** ~**es Wiedersehen!** (hope to) see you soon!

baldmöglichst ADV as soon as possible

Baldrian [ˈbaldriaːn] M **-s, -e** valerian

Baldriantropfen PL valerian (drops *pl*)

Balearen [baleˈaːrən] PL **die** ~ the Balearic Islands *pl*

Balg¹ [balk] M **-(e)s,** ⁼**e** [ˈbɛlgə] **(a)** (= *Tierhaut*) pelt; (*von Vogel*) skin **(b)** (= *Blasebalg, Phot, Rail*) bellows *pl*

Balg² M *or* NT **-(e)s,** ⁼**er** [ˈbɛlgə] (*pej inf*: = *Kind*) brat (*pej inf*)

balgen [ˈbalgn] VR to scrap (**um** over)

Balgerei [balgəˈrai] F **-, -en** scrap; **hört jetzt auf mit der** ~**!** stop scrapping!

Balkan [ˈbalkaːn] M **-s (a)** (= ~*halbinsel, ~länder*) **der** ~ the Balkans *pl*; **auf dem** ~ in the Balkans; **vom** ~ from the Balkans; **dort herrschen Zustände wie auf dem** ~ (*fig inf*) things are in a terrible state there **(b)** (= ~*gebirge*) Balkan Mountains *pl*

Balkanhalbinsel F Balkan Peninsula

Balkanländer PL Balkan States

Balken [ˈbalkn] M **-s, -** **(a)** (= *Holzbalken, Schwebebalken*) beam; (= *Stützbalken*) prop; (= *Querbalken*) joist **(b)** (= *Strich*) bar **(c)** (*an Waage*) beam

Balken-: **Balkendiagramm** NT bar chart; **Balkenkode** M bar code (*Brit*), universal product code (US); **Balkenüberschrift** F (*Press*) banner headline

Balkon [balˈkɔŋ, balˈkoːn] M **-s, -s** *or* (*bei dt. Aussprache*) **-e** (*auch Theat*) balcony

Balkon- [balˈkɔŋ-, balˈkoːn-]: **Balkonmöbel** PL garden furniture *sing*; **Balkonpflanze** F balcony plant; **Balkontür** F French window(s *pl*)

Ball¹ [bal] M **-(e)s,** ⁼**e** [ˈbɛlə] ball; ~ **spielen** to play (with a) ball; **am** ~ **sein** (*lit*) to have the ball; **immer am** ~ **sein** (*fig*) to be on the ball; **am** ~ **bleiben** (*lit*) to keep (possession of) the ball; (*fig*: = *auf dem neuesten Stand bleiben*) to stay on the ball

Ball² M **-(e)s,** ⁼**e** [ˈbɛlə] (= *Tanzfest*) ball; **auf dem** ~ at the ball

Ballade [baˈlaːdə] F **-, -n** ballad

Ballast [ˈbalast, baˈlast] M **-(e)s,** (*rare*) **-e** (*Naut, Aviat*) ballast; (*fig*) burden; (*in Büchern*) padding; ~ **abwerfen,** ~ **über Bord werfen** (*lit*) to discharge ballast; (*fig*) to get rid of a burden; **mit** ~ **beladen** *or* **beschweren** to ballast; **jdn/etw als** ~ **empfinden** to find sb/sth (to be) a burden

Ballaststoffe PL (*Med*) roughage *sing*

ballen [ˈbalən] 🚂 VT *Faust* to clench; *Papier* to crumple (into a ball); *Lehm etc* to press (into a ball); *siehe auch* **geballt** 🚂 VR (*Menschenmenge*) to crowd; (*Wolken*) to gather; (*Verkehr*) to build up; (*Faust*) to clench

Ballen [ˈbalən] M **-s, -** **(a)** bale; (= *Kaffeeballen*) sack; **in** ~ **verpacken** to bale **(b)** (*Anat*: *an Daumen, Zehen*) ball; (*an Pfote*) pad

ballenweise ADV in bales

Ballerei [baləˈrai] F **-, -en** (*inf*) shoot-out (*inf*)

Ballerina [baləˈriːna] F **-, Ballerinen** [-ˈriːnən] ballerina

ballern [ˈbalɐn] **1** VI (*inf*) to shoot; (*Schuss*) to ring out; **gegen die Tür ~** to hammer on the door **2** VT *Stein etc* to hurl; *Tür etc* to slam

Ballett [baˈlɛt] NT **-(e)s, -e** ballet; **beim ~ sein** (*inf*) to be a ballet dancer; **zum ~ gehen** to become a ballet dancer

Ballett- IN CPDS ballet; **Balletttröckchen** NT tutu; **Balletttänzer(in)** M(F) ballet dancer; **Balletttruppe** F ballet (company)

Ballistik [baˈlɪstɪk] F **-**, NO PL ballistics *sing*

ballistisch [baˈlɪstɪʃ] ADJ ballistic

Ball-: Balljunge M (*Tennis*) ball boy; **Ballkleid** NT ball dress; **Ballmädchen** NT (*Tennis*) ball girl

Ballon [baˈlɔŋ, baˈlɔːn, baˈlɔː] M **-s, -s** *or* (*bei dt. Aussprache*) **-e** (**a**) balloon (**b**) (*Chem*) carboy

Ball-: Ballsaal M ballroom; **Ballschani** [ˈbalʃaːni] M **-s, -** (*Aus inf*) ball boy; **Ballspiel** NT ball game; **Ballspielen** NT **-s**, NO PL playing ball; **„~ verboten"** "no ball games"

Ballung [ˈbalʊŋ] F **-, -en** concentration

Ballungs-: Ballungsgebiet NT, **Ballungsraum** M conurbation; **Ballungszentrum** NT centre (*Brit*) *or* center (*US*) (*of population, industry etc*)

Ballwechsel M (*Sport*) rally

Balsaholz [ˈbalza-] NT balsa wood

Balsam [ˈbalzaːm] M **-s, -e** balsam; (*fig*) balm

Balsamessig M balsamic vinegar

Balte [ˈbaltə] M **-n, -n**, **Baltin** [-tɪn] F **-, -nen** person from the Baltic; **er ist ~** he comes from the Baltic

Baltenstaat M Baltic state

Baltikum [ˈbaltikʊm] NT **-s das ~** the Baltic States *pl*

Baltin F *siehe* **Balte**

baltisch [ˈbaltɪʃ] ADJ Baltic *attr*

Balz [balts] F **-, -en** (**a**) (= *Paarungsspiel*) courtship display (**b**) (= *Paarungszeit*) mating season

balzen [ˈbaltsn] VI to perform the courtship display

Bambi[1] [ˈbambi] NT **-s, -s** (*inf*: = *Rehkitz*) young deer

Bambi[2] M **-s, -s** Bambi (*German film award*)

Bambus [ˈbambʊs] M **-ses** *or* **-, -se** bamboo

Bambus- IN CPDS bamboo; **Bambusrohr** NT bamboo cane; **Bambussprossen** PL bamboo shoots *pl*

Bammel [ˈbaml] M **-s**, NO PL (*inf*) (**einen**) **~ vor jdm/etw haben** to be nervous *or* (*stärker*) scared of sb/sth

banal [baˈnaːl] **1** ADJ banal **2** ADV banally; **~ klingen, sich ~ anhören** to sound banal

banalisieren [banaliˈziːrən], *ptp* **banalisiert** VT to trivialize

Banalität [banaliˈtɛːt] F **-, -en** (**a**) NO PL banality (**b**) USU PL (*Äußerung*) platitude

Banane [baˈnaːnə] F **-, -n** banana

Bananen-: Bananenrepublik F (*Pol pej*) banana republic; **Bananenschale** F banana skin; **Bananenstecker** M jack plug

Banause [baˈnauzə] M **-n, -n**, **Banausin** [-ˈnauzɪn] F **-, -nen** (*pej*) peasant (*inf*); (= *Kulturbanause auch*) Philistine

band PRET *von* **binden**

Band[1] [bant] NT **-(e)s, ¨er** [ˈbɛndə] (**a**) (= *Seidenband etc*) ribbon; (= *Isolierband, Maßband, Zielband*) tape; (= *Haarband, Hutband*) band; (= *Schürzenband*) string; (*Tech: zur Verpackung*) (metal) band; (= *Fassband*) hoop (**b**) (= *Tonband*) (recording) tape; **etw auf ~ aufnehmen** to tape sth; **etw auf ~ sprechen** to record sth on tape; **etw auf ~ diktieren** to dictate sth onto tape (**c**) (= *Fließband*) conveyor belt; (*als Einrichtung*) production line; (= *Montageband*) assembly line; (*in Autowerk*) track (*inf*); **am ~ arbeiten** *or* **stehen** to work on the production line *etc*; **durchs ~ (weg)** (*Sw*) every single one (without exception); **am laufenden ~** (*fig*) nonstop; **etw am laufenden ~ tun** to keep on doing sth (**d**) (*Rad*) wavelength, frequency band; **auf dem 44m-~ senden** to broadcast on the 44m band (**e**) (*Anat*) USU PL ligament

Band[2] NT **-(e)s, -e** [-də] (*liter*) **das ~ der Freundschaft/Liebe** *etc* the ties of friendship/love *etc*; **familiäre -e** family ties; **mit jdm freundschaftliche -e anknüpfen** to become friends with sb

Band[3] M **-(e)s, ¨e** [ˈbɛndə] (= *Buchband*) volume; **darüber könnte man Bände schreiben** *or* **erzählen** you could write a book about that; **das spricht Bände** that speaks volumes

Band[4] [bɛnt] F **-, -s** (*Mus*) band; (= *Beatband auch*) group

Bandage [banˈdaːʒə] F **-, -n** bandage; **mit harten ~n kämpfen** (*fig inf*) to fight with no holds barred

bandagieren [bandaˈʒiːrən], *ptp* **bandagiert** VT to bandage (up)

Bandbreite F (**a**) (*Rad*) waveband (**b**) (*fig*) range (**c**) (*Fin*) (range of) fluctuation

Bande[1] [ˈbandə] F **-, -n** gang; (= *Schmugglerbande*) band; (*inf*: = *Gruppe*) bunch (*inf*)

Bande[2] F **-, -n** (*Sport*) (*von Eisbahn, Reitbahn*) barrier; (*Billard*) cushion; (*von Kegelbahn*) edge; **die Kugel an die ~ spielen** to play the ball off the cushion/edge

Banderole [bandəˈroːlə] F **-, -n** revenue seal

Bänder- (*Med*): **Bänderriss** M torn ligament; **Bänderzerrung** F pulled ligament

-bändig [bɛndɪç] ADJ SUF **-volume**; **eine dreibändige Ausgabe** a three-volume edition

bändigen [ˈbɛndɪɡn] VT (= *zähmen*) to tame; (= *niederhalten*) *Menschen, Tobenden etc* to subdue; (= *zügeln*) *Leidenschaften etc, Kinder* to (bring under) control; *Wut* to control; *Naturgewalten* to harness

Bandit [banˈdiːt] M **-en, -en**, **Banditin** [-ˈdiːtɪn] F **-, -nen** bandit; **einarmiger ~** one-armed bandit

Bandlaufwerk NT (*Comput*) tape streamer

Band-: Bandmaß NT tape measure; **Bandnudeln** PL ribbon noodles *pl*; **Bandscheibe** F (*Anat*) (intervertebral) disc; **er hat sich an** *or* **mit der ~** (*inf*) he has a slipped disc; **Bandscheibenschaden** M, **Bandscheibenvorfall** M slipped disc; **Bandwurm** M tapeworm; **ein ~ von einem Satz** (*hum*) an endless sentence

bang [baŋ] ADJ, *comp* **-er** *or* **¨er** [ˈbɛŋɐ], *superl* **-ste(r, s)** *or* **¨ste(r, s)** [ˈbɛŋstə] (**a**) PRED (= *ängstlich*) scared; **mir ist ~ vor ihm** I'm scared of him (**b**) (*geh*: = *beklommen*) uneasy; *Augenblicke, Stunden auch* anxious (*um* about); **es wurde ihr ~ ums Herz** her heart sank; **ihr wurde ~ und bänger** she became more and more afraid

bange [ˈbaŋə] ADJ = **bang**

Bange [ˈbaŋə] F **-**, NO PL (*esp N Ger*) **~ haben** to be scared (*vor* +*dat* of); **jdm ~ machen** to scare sb; **~ machen gilt nicht** (*inf*) you can't scare me; **nur keine ~!** (*inf*) don't worry

bangen [ˈbaŋən] VI (*geh*: = *sich sorgen*) to worry (*um* about); **um jds Leben ~** to fear for sb's life

bänger COMP *von* **bang**

Bangladesch [baŋglaˈdɛʃ] NT **-s** Bangladesh

Bangladescher [baŋglaˈdɛʃɐ] M **-s, -**, **Bangladescherin** [-ərɪn] F **-, -nen** Bangladeshi

bängste (r, s) SUPERL *von* **bang**

Banjo [ˈbanjo, ˈbɛndʒo, ˈbandʒo] NT **-s, -s** banjo

Bank[1] [baŋk] F **-, ¨e** [ˈbɛŋkə] (**a**) (= *Sitzbank*) bench; (*mit Lehne*) seat; (= *Kirchenbank*) pew; (= *Parlamentsbank*) bench; (= *Anklagebank*) dock; **auf** *or* **in der ersten/letzten ~** on the front/back bench *etc*; (**alle**) **durch die ~ (weg)** (*inf*) the whole lot of them (*inf*); **etw auf die lange ~ schieben** (*inf*) to put sth off (**b**) (= *Arbeitstisch*) (work)bench; (= *Drehbank*) lathe (**c**) (= *Sandbank*) sandbank; (= *Nebelbank, Wolkenbank*) bank; (= *Austernbank*) bed; (= *Korallenbank*) reef; (*Geol*) layer

Bank[2] F **-, -en** (*Fin, Comm, bei Glücksspielen*) bank; **Geld auf der ~ (liegen) haben** to have money in the bank; **bei der ~** at the bank; **ein Konto bei einer ~ eröffnen** to open an account with a bank; **bei der ~ arbeiten** *or* **sein** (*inf*) to work for the bank; **(die) ~ halten** (*inf*) to be banker; **die ~ sprengen** to break the bank

Bank-: Bankangestellte(r) MF DECL AS ADJ bank employee; **Bankanweisung** F banker's order; **Bankautomat** M cash dispenser (*Brit*), ATM; **Bankbilanz** F (*Bilanz einer Bank*) bank accounts *pl*; **Bankbürgschaft** F (*Fin*) bank guarantee

Bänkel- [ˈbɛŋkl-]: **Bänkellied** NT street ballad; **Bänkelsang** M **-(e)s**, NO PL ballad; **Bänkelsänger** M ballad singer

Banken-: Bankenaufsicht F (*Fin*) (**a**) (*Behörde*) banking regulatory authority (**b**) (*Kontrolle*) banking regulation; **Bankenaufsichtsbehörde** F banking regulatory authority;

Bankenclearing NT bank clearing; **Bankenkonsortium** NT banking syndicate, consortium of banks

Banker ['bɛŋkɐ] M **-s, -**, **Bankerin** [-ərɪn] F **-, -nen** (*inf*) banker

Bankett[1] [baŋ'kɛt] NT **-(e)s, -e** (= *Festessen*) banquet

Bankett[2] NT **-(e)s, -e**, **Bankette** [baŋ'kɛtə] F **-, -n** (a) (*an Straßen*) verge (*Brit*), shoulder (*US*); (*an Autobahnen*) (hard) shoulder; „**~e nicht befahrbar**", „**weiche ~e**" "soft verges (*Brit*) or shoulder (*US*)" (b) (*Build*) footing

Bank-: **Bankfach** NT (a) (= *Beruf*) banking; **im ~** in banking (b) (= *Schließfach*) safety-deposit box; **Bankgarantie** F bank or banker's guarantee; **Bankgebühr** F bank charge; **Bankgeheimnis** NT confidentiality in banking; **Bankgeschäft** NT (a) banking transaction (b) NO PL (= *Bankwesen*) banking world; **Bankgiro** NT bank giro; **Bankhalter(in)** M(F) (*bei Glücksspielen*) banker

Bankier [baŋ'kie:] M **-s, -s** banker

Bank-: **Bankkarte** F bank card; **Bankkauffrau** F, **Bankkaufmann** M (qualified) bank clerk; **Bankkonto** NT bank account; **Banklehre** F training as a bank clerk; **eine ~ machen** to train as a bank clerk; **Bankleitzahl** F (bank) sort code (*Brit*); **Banknachbar(in)** M(F) (*Sch*) **sie ist meine ~in** I sit next to her (at school); **Banknote** F banknote, bill (*US*); **Bankrate** F **=Diskontsatz**; **Bankraub** M bank robbery; **Bankräuber(in)** M(F) bank robber

bankrott [baŋ'krɔt] ADJ bankrupt; *Mensch, Politik* discredited; *Kultur* debased; (*moralisch*) bankrupt; **jdn ~ machen** to bankrupt sb

Bankrott [baŋ'krɔt] M **-(e)s, -e** bankruptcy; (*fig*) breakdown; (*moralisch*) bankruptcy; **~ gehen** or **machen** to go bankrupt; **den ~ anmelden** or **ansagen** or **erklären** to declare oneself bankrupt

Bankrotterklärung F declaration of bankruptcy; (*fig*) sellout (*inf*)

Bank-: **Bankschuldverschreibung** F (*Fin*) (bank) bond; **Bankspesen** PL bank charges *pl* or expenses *pl*; **Banküberfall** M bank raid; **banküblich** ADJ **es ist ~** it is normal banking practice; **Bankverbindung** F banking arrangements *pl*; **geben Sie bitte Ihre ~ an** please give your account details; **Bankverkehr** M bank transactions *pl*; **Bankwesen** NT **das ~** banking

Bann [ban] M **-(e)s, -e** (a) NO PL (*geh*: = *magische Gewalt*) spell; **im ~ eines Menschen/einer Sache stehen** or **sein** to be under sb's spell/the spell of sth (b) (*Hist*: = *Kirchenbann*) excommunication; **jdn mit dem ~ belegen** to excommunicate sb

bannen ['banən] VT (a) (*geh*: = *bezaubern*) to bewitch; **jdn/etw auf die Platte** (*inf*)/**die Leinwand ~** (*geh*) to capture sb/sth on film/canvas; *siehe auch* **gebannt** (b) (= *vertreiben*) böse *Geister, Teufel* to exorcize; (= *abwenden*) *Gefahr* to avert

Bann-: **Bannkreis** M (*fig*) **in jds ~** (*dat*) **stehen** to be under sb's influence; **Bannmeile** F inviolable precincts *pl* (*of city, Parliament etc*)

Bantamgewicht NT bantamweight

Baptist [bap'tɪst] M **-en, -en**, **Baptistin** [-'tɪstɪn] F **-, -nen** Baptist

bar [ba:ɐ] ADJ NO COMP (a) cash; **~es Geld** cash; **(in) ~ bezahlen** to pay (in) cash; **~ auf die Hand** cash on the nail; (*Verkauf*) **nur gegen ~** cash (sales) only; **etw für ~e Münze nehmen** (*fig*) to take sth at face value (b) ATTR (= *rein*) *Zufall* pure; *Unsinn auch* utter

Bar [ba:ɐ] F **-, -s** (a) (= *Nachtlokal*) nightclub (b) (= *Theke*) bar

Bär [bɛ:ɐ] M **-en, -en** bear; **stark wie ein ~** (*inf*) (as) strong as an ox; **der Große/Kleine ~** (*Astron*) Ursa Major/Minor, the Big/Little Dipper; **jdm einen ~en aufbinden** (*inf*) to have (*Brit*) or put (*US*) sb on (*inf*)

Baracke [ba'rakə] F **-, -n** shack

Barausschüttung ['ba:ʔ-] F (*Fin*) cash distribution

Barbar [bar'ba:ɐ] M **-en, -en**, **Barbarin** [-'ba:rɪn] F **-, -nen** (*pej*) barbarian

barbarisch [bar'ba:rɪʃ] ◼ ADJ (a) (*pej*) (= *unmenschlich*) *Grausamkeit, Folter, Sitten* barbarous; (= *ungebildet*) *Benehmen, Mensch* barbaric (b) (*Hist*) *Volk, Stamm* barbarian ◼ ADV (a) *misshandeln, quälen* brutally (b) (= *entsetzlich*) *heiß, kalt* terribly

Barbestand M (*Comm*) cash; (*Buchführung*) cash in hand

Barbiturat [barbitu'ra:t] NT **-s, -e** barbiturate

Bar-: **Bardame** F barmaid; (*euph*: = *Prostituierte*) hostess (*euph*); **Bardepot** NT (*der Bundesbank*) cash deposit; **Bareinzahlung** F cash deposit

Bären-: **Bärendienst** M **jdm/einer Sache einen ~ erweisen** to do sb/sth a disservice; **Bärenhunger** M (*inf*) **einen ~ haben** to be famished (*inf*); **Bärenjagd** F bear hunt; **Bärenklau** F **-, -** or M **-s, -** (*Bot*) (= *Heracleum*) hogweed; (= *Akanthus*) bear's-breech; **Bärenkräfte** PL the strength *sing* of an ox; **bärenstark** ADJ (a) *strapping* (b) (*inf*) terrific; **ein ~es Buch** an amazing book

Barentssee ['ba:rənts-] F (*Geog*) Barents Sea

Barfrau F barmaid

barfuß ['ba:ʔfu:s] ADJ PRED barefoot(ed); **~ gehen** to go/walk barefoot(ed)

barfüßig ADJ barefooted

barg PRET *von* **bergen**

Bar-: **Bargeld** NT cash; **bargeldlos** ◼ ADJ cashless; **~er Zahlungsverkehr** payment by money transfer ◼ ADV without using cash; **Bargeschäft** NT cash transaction; **Barhocker** M (bar) stool

bärig ['bɛ:rɪç] (*Aus inf*) ◼ ADJ tremendous ◼ ADV tremendously

Bärin ['bɛ:rɪn] F **-, -nen** (she-)bear

Bariton ['ba:rɪtɔn] M **-s, -e** [-to:nə] baritone

Barium ['ba:rɪʊm] NT **-s**, NO PL (*abbr* **Ba**) barium

Barkeeper ['ba:ɐki:pɐ] M **-s, -** barman, bartender

Barmann M, *pl* **-männer** barman

barmherzig [barm'hɛrtsɪç] ADJ (*liter, Rel*) merciful; (= *mitfühlend*) compassionate; **der ~e Samariter** (*lit, fig*) the good Samaritan

Barmittel PL cash (reserves *pl*)

Barmixer M barman

Barmixerin F barmaid

barock [ba'rɔk] ADJ baroque; (*fig*) (= *überladen auch, verschnörkelt*) ornate; *Sprache* florid; (= *seltsam*) *Einfälle* bizarre; **sie hat eine sehr ~e Figur** (*hum*) she has a very ample figure (*esp Brit*)

Barock [ba'rɔk] NT or M **-(s)**, NO PL baroque; **das Zeitalter des ~** the baroque age

Barock- IN CPDS baroque; **Barockzeit** F baroque period

Barometer [baro'me:tɐ] NT **-s, -** (*lit, fig*) barometer; **das ~ steht auf Sturm** the barometer is on stormy; (*fig*) things look stormy

Barometerstand M barometer reading

Baron [ba'ro:n] M **-s, -e** (a) baron; **Herr ~** my lord (b) (*fig*: = *Industriebaron etc*) baron

Baronesse [baro'nɛsə] F **-, -n** daughter of a baron; **Fräulein Baroness** my lady

Baronin [ba'ro:nɪn] F **-, -nen** baroness; **Frau ~** my lady

Barrel ['bɛrəl] NT **-s, -s** or **-** barrel

Barren ['barən] M **-s, -** (a) (= *Metallbarren*) bar; (= *esp Goldbarren*) ingot (b) (*Sport*) parallel bars *pl*

Barreserve F (*Fin*) cash reserve; **~ der Banken** till money

Barriere [ba'rie:rə] F **-, -n** (*lit, fig*) barrier

Barrikade [bari'ka:də] F **-, -n** barricade; **auf die ~n gehen** (*lit, fig*) to go to the barricades

barsch [barʃ] ◼ ADJ brusque ◼ ADV brusquely; **jdn ~ anfahren** to snap at sb

Barsch [barʃ] M **-(e)s, -e** bass; (= *Flussbarsch*) perch

Barscheck M uncrossed cheque (*Brit*), open check (*US*)

Barschheit F **-, -en** brusqueness

Barsortiment NT book wholesaler's

barst PRET *von* **bersten**

Bart [ba:ɐt] M **-(e)s, ⸚e** ['bɛ:ɐtə] (a) (*von Mensch, Ziege, Vogel, Getreide*) beard; (*von Katze, Maus, Robbe etc*) whiskers *pl*; **sich** (*dat*) **einen ~ wachsen** or **stehen lassen** to grow a beard; **ein drei Tage alter ~** three days' growth (on one's chin) (b) (*fig inf*) (**sich** *dat*) **etw in den ~ murmeln** or **brumme(l)n** to mutter sth in one's boots or beard (*inf*); **jdm um den ~ gehen**, **jdm Honig um den ~ streichen** or **schmieren** to butter sb up (*inf*); **der Witz hat einen ~** that's an old chestnut (c) (= *Schlüsselbart*) bit

Bärtchen ['bɛ:ɐtçən] NT **-s, -** (= *Kinnbärtchen*) (small) beard; (= *Oberlippenbärtchen*) toothbrush moustache (*Brit*) or mustache (*US*); (= *Menjoubärtchen*) pencil moustache (*Brit*) or mustache (*US*)

Bart-: Bartfäden PL (*Zool*) barbels *pl*; **Bartflechte** F (a) (*Med*) sycosis (b) (*Bot*) beard lichen

bärtig ['bɛːɛtɪç] ADJ bearded

Bart-: bartlos ADJ beardless; (= *glatt rasiert*) clean-shaven; **Bartnelke** F sweet william; **Bartstoppel** F piece of stubble; **Bartstoppeln** PL stubble *sing*; **Bartwuchs** M beard; (*esp weiblicher*) facial hair *no indef art*; **er hat starken ~** he has a heavy growth of beard

Bar-: Barverkauf M cash sales *pl*; **ein ~** a cash sale; **Barvermögen** NT liquid assets *pl*; **Barwert** M (*Fin*) (net) present value; **~ der Rückflüsse** present value of net cash inflows; **Barzahlung** F payment in cash; (**Verkauf**) **nur gegen ~** cash (sales) only; **bei ~ 3% Skonto** 3% discount for cash

Basalt [ba'zalt] M **-(e)s, -e** basalt

Basar [ba'zaːɐ] M **-s, -e** bazaar; **auf dem ~** in the bazaar

Base F **-, -n** (*Chem*) base

Baseball ['beːsboːl] M **-s**, NO PL baseball

Baseballschläger ['beːsboːl-] M baseball bat

Basedow ['baːzədo] M **-s**, NO PL (*inf*), **Basedowkrankheit** F, **basedowsche Krankheit** ['baːzədoʃə] F (exophthalmic) goitre (*Brit*) *or* goiter (*US*)

Basel ['baːzl] NT **-s** Basle, Basel

Basen PL *von* **Basis, Base**

basieren [ba'ziːrən], *ptp* **basiert** [1] VI to be based (*auf +dat* on) [2] VT to base (*auf +acc or (rare) +dat* on)

Basilika [ba'ziːlika] F **-, Basiliken** [-kn] basilica

Basilikum [ba'ziːlikum] NT **-s**, NO PL basil

Basis ['baːzɪs] F **-, Basen** ['baːzn] basis; (*Archit, Mil, Math*) base; **auf breiter ~** on a broad basis; **~ und Überbau** (*Pol, Sociol*) foundation and superstructure; **die ~** (*inf*) the grass roots (level); (= *die Leute*) (those at) the grass roots

Basiscamp NT base camp

basisch ['baːzɪʃ] (*Chem*) [1] ADJ basic [2] ADV **~ reagieren** to show a basic reaction

Basis-: Basisdemokratie F grass-roots democracy; **Basisgruppe** F action group; **Basislager** NT base camp; **Basiswissen** NT basic knowledge

Baskenland NT Basque region

Baskenmütze F beret

Basketball ['baːskət-, 'baskət-] M **-s**, NO PL basketball

baskisch ['baskɪʃ] ADJ Basque

Basrelief ['barelief, bare'lief] NT (*Archit, Art*) bas-relief

Bass [bas] M **-es, ⸚e** ['bɛsə] (a) (= *Stimme, Sänger*) bass; **hoher/tiefer or schwarzer ~** basso cantante/profundo; **einen hohen/tiefen ~ haben** to be a basso cantante/profundo (b) (= *Instrument*) double bass; (*im Jazz auch*) bass (c) (= *~partie*) bass (part)

Bassin [ba'sɛː] NT **-s, -s** (= *Schwimmbassin*) pool; (= *Gartenbassin*) pond

Bassist¹ [ba'sɪst] M **-en, -en** (= *Sänger*) bass (singer)

Bassist² [ba'sɪst] M **-en, -en, Bassistin** [-'sɪstɪn] F **-, -nen** (*im Orchester etc*) (double) bass player; **~ sein** to be a (double) bass player

Bass-: Bassklarinette F bass clarinet; **Basspartie** F bass part; **Bassschlüssel** M bass clef; **Bassstimme** F bass (voice); (= *Partie*) bass part

Bast [bast] M **-(e)s**, (*rare*) **-e** (a) (*zum Binden, Flechten*) raffia; (*Bot*) bast (b) (*an Geweih*) velvet

basta ['basta] INTERJ (**und damit**) **~!** (and) that's that

Bastelei [bastə'lai] F **-, -en** (*inf*) handicraft

basteln ['bastln] [1] VI (a) (*als Hobby*) to make things with one's hands; (= *Handwerksarbeiten herstellen*) to do handicrafts; **sie kann gut ~** she is good with her hands (b) **an etw** (*dat*) **~** to make sth; *an Modellflugzeug etc* to build sth; (= *an etw herumbasteln*) to mess around with sth [2] VT to make; *Geräte etc auch* to build

Basteln NT **-s**, NO PL handicraft, handicrafts *pl*

Bastion [bas'tioːn] F **-, -en** bastion

Bastler ['bastlɐ] M **-s, -, Bastlerin** [-ərɪn] F **-, -nen** (*von Modellen etc*) modeller (*Brit*), modeler (*US*); (*von Möbeln etc*) do-it-yourselfer; **ein guter ~ sein** to be good with one's hands

bat PRET *von* **bitten**

BAT [beːlaːˈteː] ABBR *von* **Bundesangestelltentarif**

Bataillon [batal'joːn] NT **-s, -e** (*Mil, fig*) battalion

Batchbetrieb ['bɛtʃ-] M (*Comput*) batch processing

batiken ['baːtɪkn] [1] VI to do batik [2] VT to decorate with batik; **eine gebatikte Bluse** a batik blouse

Batist [ba'tɪst] M **-(e)s, -e** batiste

Batterie [batə'riː] F **-, -n** [-'riːən] (*Elec, Mil*) (= *Legebatterie*) battery; (= *Mischbatterie etc*) regulator; (= *Reihe: von Flaschen etc*) row

batteriebetrieben [-bətriːbn] ADJ battery-powered

Bau [bau] M (a) **-(e)s**, NO PL (= *das Bauen*) building; **im** *or* **in ~** under construction; **sich im ~ befinden** to be under construction; **der ~ des Hauses dauerte ein Jahr** it took a year to build the house; **mit dem ~ beginnen, an den ~ gehen** to begin building
(b) **-(e)s**, NO PL (= *Aufbau*) structure; **von kräftigem/schwächlichem ~ sein** to be powerfully/slenderly built
(c) **-s**, NO PL (= *~stelle*) building site; **auf dem ~ arbeiten, beim ~ sein** to work on a building site
(d) **-(e)s, -ten** [-tn] (= *Gebäude*) building; (= *~werk*) construction; **~ten** (*Film*) sets
(e) **-(e)s, -e** (= *Erdhöhle*) burrow; (= *Biberbau*) lodge; (= *Fuchsbau*) den; (= *Dachsbau*) set(t)

Bau-: Bauarbeiten PL building work *sing*; (= *Straßenbau*) roadworks *pl* (*Brit*), road construction (*US*); **Bauarbeiter(in)** M(F) building worker

Bauch [baux] M **-(e)s, Bäuche** ['bɔyçə] (a) (*von Mensch*) stomach; (*Anat*) abdomen; (*von Tier*) belly; (= *Fettbauch*) paunch; **ihm tat der ~ weh** he had stomach ache; **sich** (*dat*) **den ~ voll schlagen** (*inf*) to stuff oneself (*inf*); **ein voller ~ studiert nicht gern** (*Prov*) you can't study on a full stomach; **einen dicken ~ haben** (*sl:* = *schwanger sein*) to have a bun in the oven (*inf*); **etw aus dem ~ heraus entscheiden** to decide sth according to (a gut) instinct; **mit etw auf den ~ fallen** (*inf*) to fall flat on one's face with sth (*inf*)
(b) (= *Wölbung, Hohlraum*) belly

Bauch-: Bauchansatz M beginning(s) of a paunch; **Bauchbinde** F (a) (*für Frack*) cummerbund; (*Med*) abdominal bandage (b) (*um Zigarre, Buch*) band; **Bauchfell** NT (*Anat*) peritoneum; **Bauchfellentzündung** F peritonitis; **Bauchfleck** M (*Aus inf*) belly flop (*inf*); **Bauchflosse** F ventral fin; **Bauchgegend** F abdominal region; **Bauchgrimmen** [-grɪmən] NT **-s**, NO PL (*inf*) tummy ache (*inf*); **Bauchhöhle** F abdominal cavity; **Bauchhöhlenschwangerschaft** F ectopic pregnancy

bauchig ['bauxɪç] ADJ *Gefäß* bulbous

Bauchklatscher [-klatʃɐ] M **-s, -** (*inf*) belly flop (*inf*)

Bauchlandung F (*inf*) (*Aviat*) belly landing; (*bei Sprung ins Wasser*) belly flop (*inf*)

Bäuchlein ['bɔyçlain] NT **-s, -** tummy (*inf*); (*hum*: = *Fettbäuchlein*) bit of a tummy (*inf*)

Bauch-: Bauchmuskel M stomach muscle; **Bauchnabel** M navel, bellybutton (*inf*); **Bauchredner(in)** M(F) ventriloquist; **Bauchschmerzen** PL stomach ache; (*fig*) anguish; **jdm ~ bereiten** (*fig*) to cause sb major problems; **wegen etw ~ haben** (*fig*) to feel uncomfortable because of sth; **Bauchspeicheldrüse** F pancreas; **Bauchtanz** M belly dancing; (*einzelner Tanz*) belly dance; **bauchtanzen** VI SEP USU INFIN *to* belly-dance; **Bauchtänzerin** F belly dancer; **Bauchweh** [-veː] NT **-s**, NO PL stomach ache

Baucontainer M Portakabin®, prefabricated hut

Baud [baut, boːt] NT **-(s), -** (*Comput*) baud

Baudenkmal NT historical monument

Baud-Rate ['baut-, 'boːt-] F (*Comput*) baud rate

Bauelement NT component part

bauen ['bauən] [1] VT (a) (= *erbauen*) to build; (= *anfertigen auch*) to make; *Höhle* to dig; **sich** (*dat*) **ein Haus ~** to build oneself a house; **sich** (*dat*) **ein Nest ~** to make oneself a nest (*auch fig*); **seine Hoffnung auf jdn/etw ~** to build one's hopes on sb/sth; *siehe auch* **gebaut**

(b) (inf: = verursachen) Unfall to cause; **da hast du Scheiße gebaut** (inf) you really messed that up (inf)

2 VI **(a)** (= Gebäude errichten) to build; **wir haben neu/auf Sylt gebaut** we built a new house/a house on Sylt; **an etw** (dat) ~ to be working on sth, to be building sth (auch fig); **hier wird viel gebaut** there is a lot of building going on around here **(b)** (= vertrauen) **auf jdn/etw** ~ to rely on sb/sth

Bauer[1] ['bauɐ] M **-n** or (rare) **-s, -n (a)** (= Landwirt) farmer; (als Vertreter einer Klasse) peasant; (pej: = ungehobelter Mensch) (country) bumpkin; **die dümmsten ~n haben die größten** or **dicksten Kartoffeln** (prov inf) fortune favours (Brit) or favors (US) fools (prov); **was der ~ nicht kennt, das frisst er nicht** (prov inf) some people won't try anything new **(b)** (Chess) pawn; (Cards) jack, knave

Bauer[2] ['bauɐ] M **-s, -,** **Bäuerin** [-ərɪn] F **-, -nen** (= Erbauer) builder; (fig auch) architect

Bauer[3] NT or M **-s, -** (= Käfig) (bird)cage

Bäuerchen ['bɔyɐçən] NT **-s, -** **(a)** DIM von **Bauer**[1] **(b)** (baby-talk) burp; **(ein)** ~ **machen** to (do a) burp

Bäuerin ['bɔyərɪn] F **-, -nen (a)** (= Frau des Bauern) farmer's wife **(b)** (= Landwirtin) farmer; (als Vertreterin einer Klasse) peasant (woman)

bäuerlich ['bɔyɐlɪç] ADJ rural; (= ländlich) Fest, Bräuche, Sitten country attr; **~e Klein- und Großbetriebe** small and large farms

Bauern-: Bauernbrot NT coarse rye bread; **Bauernfänger** M (inf) con man (inf); **Bauernfängerei** [-fɛŋəˈraɪ] F **-, -en** (inf) con (inf); **Bauernfängerin** F (inf) con woman (inf); **Bauernfrühstück** NT bacon and potato omelette; **Bauernhaus** NT farmhouse; **Bauernhof** M farm; **Bauernopfer** NT (fig) (= Mensch) fall guy; (= Sache) necessary sacrifice; **Bauernregel** F country saying; **Bauernschaft** ['bauɐnʃaft] F **-, NO PL** farming community; (ärmlich) peasantry; **Bauernverband** M farmers' organization

Bauersfrau F farmer's wife

Bauersleute PL farmers pl

Bau-: Bauerwartungsland NT (Admin) development area; **Baufach** NT construction industry; **baufällig** ADJ dilapidated; Decke, Gewölbe unsound; **Baufälligkeit** F dilapidation; **wegen** ~ **gesperrt** closed because building unsafe; **Baufirma** F building contractor; **Baugelände** NT land for building; (= Baustelle) building site; **Baugenehmigung** F planning and building permission; **Baugerüst** NT scaffolding; **Baugeschäft** NT building firm; **Baugewerbe** NT building and construction trade; **baugleich** ADJ Modell, Ausführung structurally identical; **Bauhaus** NT (Archit, Art) Bauhaus; **Bauherr(in)** M(F) client (for whom sth is being built); **seitdem er ~ ist ...** since he has been having a house built ...; ~ **Ministerium des Innern** under construction for the Ministry (Brit) or Department (US) of the Interior; **Bauholz** NT building timber; **Bauindustrie** F building and construction industry; **Bauingenieur(in)** M(F) civil engineer

Bauj. ABBR von **Baujahr**

Bau-: Baujahr NT year of construction; (von Auto) year of manufacture; **VW ~ 98** 1998 VW; **welches ~?** what year?; **Baukasten** M building kit; (mit Holzklötzen) box of bricks; (= Chemiebaukasten) set; **Baukastensystem** NT (Tech) modular construction system; **Bauklotz** M (building) brick; **Bauklötze(r) staunen** (inf) to gape (in astonishment); **Bauklötzchen** NT (building) block; **Baukredit** M construction loan; **Bauland** NT building land; (für Stadtplanung) development area; **baulich** ['baulıç] **1** ADJ structural; **in gutem/schlechtem ~em Zustand** structurally sound/unsound **2** ADV structurally; **Baulücke** F empty site

Baum [baum] M **-(e)s, Bäume** ['bɔymə] tree; **auf dem** ~ in the tree

Bau-: Baumangel M USU PL construction defect; (strukturell) structural defect; **Baumarkt** M property market; (= Geschäft für Heimwerker) DIY superstore; **Baumaschine** F piece of building machinery; **Baumaschinen** PL building machinery; **Baumaterial** NT building material

Bäumchen ['bɔymçən] NT **-s, -** small tree; ~**, wechsle dich spielen** to play tag; (hum: = Partnertausch) to swap partners

baumeln ['baumln] VI to dangle (an +dat from); **jdn** ~ **lassen** (sl) to let sb swing (inf)

Baum-: Baumfarn M tree fern; **Baumgrenze** F tree line; **Baumgruppe** F coppice; **baumhoch** ADJ tree-high; **Baumkrone** F treetop; **baumlos** ADJ treeless; **baumreich** ADJ wooded; **Baumschere** F (tree) pruning shears pl; **Baumschule** F tree nursery; **Baumstamm** M tree trunk; **Baumstruktur** F (Comput) tree structure

Baumwoll- IN CPDS cotton

Baumwolle F cotton; **ein Hemd aus** ~ a cotton shirt

baumwollen ADJ ATTR cotton

Baumwollspinnerei F cotton mill

Bau-: Bauplan M building plan; (Biol: genetischer, biologischer etc) blueprint; **Bauplatz** M site (for building); **Baupolizei** F building control department (Brit), Board of Works (US); **Baupreis** M building price; **Baureihe** F (von Auto) model range; (von Flugzeug, Computer) series

bäurisch ['bɔyrɪʃ] ADJ (pej) boorish

Bausatz M kit

Bausch [bauʃ] M **-es, Bäusche** or **-e** ['bɔyʃə] (= Wattebausch) ball; (Med auch) swab; **in** ~ **und Bogen** lock, stock and barrel

bauschen ['bauʃn] **1** VR **(a)** (= sich aufblähen) to billow (out) **(b)** (Kleidungsstück) to puff out; (ungewollt) to bunch (up) **2** VT **(a)** Segel, Vorhänge to fill, to swell **(b)** (= raffen) to gather; **gebauschte Ärmel** puffed sleeves

bauschig ['bauʃıç] ADJ Wolken billowing; Rock, Vorhänge full; Watte fluffy

Bauschutt M building rubble

Bauschuttmulde F skip

bausparen VI SEP USU INFIN to save with a building society (Brit) or building and loan association (US)

Bausparer(in) M(F) saver with a building society (Brit) or building and loan association (US)

Bauspar-: Bausparkasse F building society (Brit), building and loan association (US); **Bausparvertrag** M savings contract with a building society (Brit) or building and loan association (US)

Bau-: Baustein M stone (for building); (Spielzeug) brick; (= elektronischer ~) chip; (fig: = Bestandteil) building block; (Tech) module; **Baustelle** F building site; (bei Straßenbau) roadworks pl (Brit), road construction (US); (bei Gleisbau) railway (Brit) or railroad (US) construction site; **„Achtung, ~!"** "danger, roadworks (Brit) or road construction (US)"; **„Betreten der ~ verboten"** "unauthorized entry prohibited"; **Baustellenverkehr** M heavy traffic (from a building site); **„Achtung, ~!"** "construction traffic"; **Baustil** M architectural style; **Baustopp** M **einen ~ verordnen** to impose a halt on building (projects); **Bausubstanz** F fabric; **die ~ ist gut** the house is structurally sound; **bautechnisch** ADJ structural; **eine ~e Glanzleistung** a superb feat of structural engineering; **Bauteil** NT (= Bauelement) component

Bauten PL von **Bau**

Bau-: Bauträger(in) M(F) builder; **Bauunternehmen** NT (= Firma) building contractor; **Bauunternehmer(in)** M(F) building contractor; **Bauvorhaben** NT building project; **Bauweise** F type of construction; (= Stil) style; **in konventioneller ~** built in the conventional way/style; **offene ~** detached houses; **geschlossene ~** terraced (Brit) or row (US) houses; **Bauwerk** NT construction; (= Gebäude auch) edifice

Bauxit [bau'ksi:t] M **-s, -e** bauxite

Bau-: Bauzaun M hoarding, fence; **Bauzeit** F time taken for building; **die ~ betrug drei Jahre** it took three years to build

Bayer ['baiɐ] M **-n, -n, Bayerin** ['baiərın] F **-, -nen** Bavarian

bayerisch ['baiərıʃ] ADJ Bavarian; **der Bayerische Wald** the Bavarian Forest

Bayern ['baien] NT **-s** Bavaria

bayrisch ['bairıʃ] ADJ = **bayerisch**

Bazi ['ba:tsi] M **-, -** (Aus inf) blighter (Brit inf)

Bazille [ba'tsılə] F **-, -n (a)** (inf: = Bazillus) bacillus; (= Krankheitserreger) germ **(b) linke ~** (sl: = übler Typ) sly git (Brit sl)

Bazillenträger(in) M(F) carrier

Bd. ABBR von **Band**

BDI [be:de:'li:] M **-, NO PL** ABBR von **Bundesverband der Deutschen Industrie** manufacturing industries' association, ≈ CBI (Brit)

BDM [be:de:'lɛm] M **-, NO PL** (NS) ABBR von **Bund Deutscher Mädel**

BE ABBR von **Broteinheit**

beabsichtigen [bə'lapzıçtıgn] ptp **beabsichtigt** VT to intend; **eine Reise/Steuererhöhung ~** (form) to intend to go on a journey/to increase taxes; **das hatte ich nicht beabsichtigt** I didn't mean it to happen; **das war beabsichtigt** that was deliberate; **die beabsichtigte Wirkung** the desired effect

beachten ptp **beachtet** VT **(a)** (= *befolgen*) to heed; *Vorschrift, Verbot, Verkehrszeichen* to comply with; *Regel, Gebrauchsanweisung* to follow; **etw besser ~** to pay more attention to sth **(b)** (= *berücksichtigen*) to take into consideration; **es ist zu ~, dass ...** it should be taken into consideration that ... **(c)** (= *Aufmerksamkeit schenken*) jdn to notice; (*bei Bilderklärungen, Reiseführung etc*) to observe; **jdn nicht ~** to ignore sb; **von der Öffentlichkeit kaum beachtet** scarcely noticed by the public; **das Ereignis wurde in der Öffentlichkeit kaum/stark beachtet** the incident aroused little/considerable public attention

beachtenswert [bəˈaxtnsveːɐt] ADJ remarkable

beachtlich [bəˈaxtlɪç] **1** ADJ **(a)** (= *beträchtlich*) considerable; *Verbesserung, Zu- or Abnahme* marked; *Erfolg* notable; *Talent* remarkable **(b)** (= *bedeutend*) *Ereignis* significant; (= *lobenswert*) *Leistung* considerable; **er hat im Leben/Beruf Beachtliches geleistet** he has achieved a considerable amount in life/his job **2** ADV (= *sehr*) significantly

Beachtung F **(a)** (= *das Befolgen*) heeding; (*von Ratschlag, Gebrauchsanweisung*) following; (*von Vorschrift, Regel, Verbot, Verkehrszeichen*) observance, compliance (+gen with); **unter ~ der Vorschriften** in accordance with the regulations **(b)** (= *Berücksichtigung*) consideration; **unter ~ aller Umstände** taking into consideration all the circumstances **(c)** (= *das Beachten*) attention (+gen to); „**zur ~**" please note; **~ finden/verdienen** to receive/deserve attention; **jdm/einer Sache ~ schenken** to pay attention to sb/sth; **jdm keine ~ schenken** to ignore sb

Beachvolleyball [ˈbiːtʃvɔli-] M beach volleyball

beamen [ˈbiːmən] **1** VT to beam **2** VR to beam oneself

Beamte M = **Beamte(r)**

Beamten-: **Beamtenanwärter(in)** M(F) civil service trainee; **Beamtenapparat** M bureaucracy; **Beamtenbeleidigung** F insulting an official; **Beamtenbestechung** F bribing an official; **Beamtenmentalität** F bureaucratic mentality; **Beamtenschaft** [bəˈamtnʃaft] F -, NO PL civil servants pl; **Beamtenstatus** M civil servant status; **Beamtentum** [bəˈamtntuːm] NT **-s**, NO PL civil service; **Beamtenverhältnis** NT **im ~ stehen** to be a civil servant; **ins ~ übernommen werden** to become a civil servant

Beamte(r) [bəˈamtə] M DECL AS ADJ, **Beamtin** F -, **-nen** official; (= *Staatsbeamte*) civil servant; (= *Zollbeamte*) official; (= *Polizeibeamte*) officer; **er ist ein typischer ~r** (pej) he is a typical bureaucrat

beängstigend **1** ADJ alarming; **sein Zustand ist ~** his condition is giving cause for concern **2** ADV alarmingly

beanspruchen [bəˈanʃpruxn], ptp **beansprucht** VT **(a)** (= *fordern*) to claim; *Gebiet auch* to lay claim to; **etw ~ können** to be entitled to sth **(b)** (= *erfordern*) to take; *Kräfte auch, Aufmerksamkeit* to demand; (= *benötigen*) to need **(c)** (= *ausnützen*) to use; *jds Gastfreundschaft* to take advantage of; *jds Geduld* to demand; *jds Hilfe* to ask for; **ich möchte Ihre Geduld nicht zu sehr ~** I don't want to try your patience **(d)** (= *strapazieren*) *Maschine etc* to use; jdn to occupy; **jdn stark** or **sehr ~** to keep sb very busy; **ihr Beruf beansprucht sie ganz** her job is extremely demanding

beanstanden [bəˈanʃtandn], ptp **beanstandet** VT to query; **das ist beanstandet worden** there has been a query about that; **er hat an allem etwas zu ~** he has complaints about everything; **die beanstandete Ware** the goods complained about

beantragen [bəˈantraːgn], ptp **beantragt** VT to apply for (*bei* to); (*Jur*) *Strafe* to demand; (= *vorschlagen: in Debatte etc*) to move; **er beantragte, versetzt zu werden** he applied for a transfer

beantworten ptp **beantwortet** VT to answer; *Anfrage, Brief auch* to reply to; **jdm eine Frage ~** to answer sb's question; **eine Frage mit Nein ~** to answer a question in the negative; **leicht zu ~** easily answered

bearbeiten ptp **bearbeitet** VT **(a)** (= *behandeln*) to work on; *Stein, Holz* to work; (inf: *mit Chemikalien*) to treat; **etw mit dem Hammer/Meißel ~** to hammer/chisel sth

(b) (= *sich befassen mit*) to deal with; *Fall* to handle; *Bestellungen etc* to process **(c)** (= *redigieren*) to edit; (= *neu ~*) to revise; (= *umändern*) *Roman etc* to adapt; *Musikstück* to arrange **(d)** (inf: = *einschlagen auf*) *Klavier, Trommel etc* to hammer away at; *Geige* to saw away at; **jdn mit Fußtritten ~** to kick sb about (inf); **jdn mit Fäusten ~** to thump sb **(e)** (inf: = *einreden auf*) jdn to work on

Bearbeiter(in) M(F) **(a)** (*von Angelegenheit*) person dealing with sth; (*von Bestellung*) person processing sth **(b)** (= *Redakteur*) editor; (*von Neubearbeitung*) reviser; (*von Umänderung*) adapter; (*von Musik*) arranger

Bearbeitung [bəˈarbaɪtʊŋ] F -, **-en (a)** (= *Behandlung*) working (on); (*von Stein, Holz*) dressing; (inf: *mit Chemikalien*) treating; **die ~ von Granit ist schwierig** it is difficult to dress granite **(b)** (*von Angelegenheit, Antrag etc*) dealing with; (*von Fall*) handling; (*von Bestellung*) processing; **die ~ meines Antrags hat lange gedauert** it took a long time to deal with my claim **(c)** (= *Redigieren*) editing; (= *Neubearbeitung*) revising; (= *Umänderung*) adapting; (*von Musik*) arrangement; (= *bearbeitete Ausgabe etc*) edition; revision; adaptation; arrangement; **neue ~** (*von Film etc*) new version; **die deutsche ~** the German version

Bearbeitungsgebühr F handling charge

Beat [biːt] M **-(s)**, NO PL (= *Musik*) beat music

Beatband [ˈbiːtbɛnt] F, pl **-bands** beat group

beatmen ptp **beatmet** VT *Ertrunkenen* to give artificial respiration to; *Gewässer* to oxygenate; **jdn künstlich ~** to keep sb breathing artificially

Beatmung F -, **-en** artificial respiration; (*von Gewässer*) oxygenation

Beatmusik [ˈbiːt-] F beat music

beaufsichtigen [bəˈaʊfzɪçtɪgn], ptp **beaufsichtigt** VT to supervise; *Kind* to look after; *Prüfung* to invigilate at; **staatlich beaufsichtigt** state-controlled

beauftragen [bəˈaʊftraːgn], ptp **beauftragt** VT **(a)** (= *heranziehen*) to engage; *Firma auch* to hire; *Architekten, Künstler etc, Forschungsinstitut* to commission; *Ausschuss etc* to appoint; **jdn mit etw ~** to engage etc sb to do sth **(b)** (= *anweisen*) *Untergebenen etc* to instruct; **wir sind beauftragt, das zu tun** we have been instructed to do that

Beauftragte(r) [bəˈaʊftraːktə] MF DECL AS ADJ representative

bebaubar ADJ **(a)** *Boden* cultiv(at)able **(b)** *Grundstück* suitable for building; (= *zum Bau freigegeben*) available for building

bebauen ptp **bebaut** VT **(a)** *Grundstück* to develop; **das Viertel war dicht bebaut** the area was heavily built-up; **ein Gelände mit etw ~** to build sth on a piece of land **(b)** (*Agr*) to cultivate; *Land* to farm

Bebauungsplan M development plan

Bébé [beˈbeː] NT **-s**, **-s** (*Sw*) baby

beben [ˈbeːbn] VI to shake; (*Stimme auch*) to quiver (*vor* +dat with)

Beben [ˈbeːbn] NT **-s**, **-** (= *Zittern*) shaking; (*von Stimme auch*) quivering; (= *Erdbeben*) earthquake

bebildern [bəˈbɪldɐn], ptp **bebildert** VT to illustrate

Becher [ˈbɛçɐ] M **-s**, **-** cup; (= *Glasbecher*) glass; (= *esp aus Porzellan, Ton, mit Henkel*) mug; (= *Joghurtbecher etc*) carton; (= *Eisbecher*) (*aus Pappe*) tub; (*aus Metall*) sundae dish

bechern [ˈbɛçɐn] VI (hum inf) to have a few (inf)

Becken [ˈbɛkn] NT **-s**, **- (a)** (= *Brunnenbecken, Hafenbecken, Waschbecken*) (*Geol*) basin; (= *Abwaschbecken*) sink; (= *Toilettenbecken*) bowl; (= *Schwimmbecken*) pool; (= *Staubecken*) reservoir; (= *Fischbecken*) pool; (= *Taufbecken*) font **(b)** (*Anat*) pelvis; **ein breites ~** broad hips **(c)** (*Mus*) cymbal

bedacht [bəˈdaxt] ADJ **(a)** (= *überlegt*) prudent, cautious **(b) auf etw** (acc) **~ sein** to be concerned about sth; **darauf ~ sein, etw zu tun** to be concerned about doing sth; *siehe auch* **bedenken**

Bedacht [bəˈdaxt] M **-s**, NO PL (geh) **mit ~** (= *vorsichtig*) prudently; (= *absichtlich*) deliberately

Bedachte(r) [bəˈdaxtə] MF DECL AS ADJ (*Jur*) beneficiary

bedächtig [bəˈdɛçtɪç] **1** ADJ deliberate; (= *besonnen*) thoughtful **2** ADV **langsam und ~ sprechen** to speak in slow, measured tones

Bedachung F -, **-en** roofing

bedanken ptp **bedankt** VR (a) to say thank you; **sich bei jdm (für etw) ~** to thank sb (for sth); **ich bedanke mich herzlich** thank you very much; **dafür können Sie sich bei Herrn Weitz ~** (iro inf) you've got Mr Weitz to thank for that (iro) (b) (iro inf) **ich bedanke mich, dafür bedanke ich mich (bestens)** no thank you (very much); **dafür** or **für dergleichen wird er sich ~** he'll just love that (iro)

Bedarf [bəˈdarf] M **-(e)s, -e,** NO PL (a) (= Bedürfnis) need (an +dat for); (= Bedarfsmenge) requirements pl; **bei ~** as required; **der Bus hält hier nur bei ~** the bus stops here only on request; **Dinge des täglichen ~s** basic necessities; **alles für den häuslichen ~** all household requirements; **seinen ~ an Wein/ Lebensmitteln** etc **einkaufen** to buy one's supply of wine/ food etc; **an etw** (dat) **~ haben** to need sth; **danke, kein ~** (iro inf) no thank you
(b) (Comm: = Nachfrage) demand (an +dat for); (je) **nach ~** according to demand; **den ~ übersteigen** to exceed demand; **über ~** in excess of demand

Bedarfs-: Bedarfsartikel M requisite; **bedarfsgerecht** ① ADJ Politik designed to meet people's needs; **ein ~es Warenangebot** a range of goods which meets consumer demands ② ADV as needed; **~ produzieren** to match production to demand; **Bedarfsgüter** PL consumer goods pl; **Bedarfshaltestelle** F request (bus) stop

bedauerlich [bəˈdauəlɪç] ADJ regrettable, unfortunate; **~!** how unfortunate

bedauerlicherweise ADV regrettably

bedauern [bəˈdauən], ptp **bedauert** VT (a) etw to regret; **wir ~, Ihnen mitteilen zu müssen, ...** we regret to have to inform you ...; **er hat sehr bedauert, dass ...** he was very sorry that ...; **(ich) bedau(e)re!** I am sorry (b) (= bemitleiden) jdn to feel sorry for; **sich selbst ~** to feel sorry for oneself; **sie ist zu ~** one or you should feel sorry for her

Bedauern [bəˈdauən] NT **-s,** NO PL regret; **(sehr) zu meinem ~** (much) to my regret; **zu meinem ~ kann ich nicht kommen** I regret that I will not be able to come; **zu meinem größten ~ muss ich Ihnen mitteilen ...** it is with the deepest regret that I must inform you ...; **mit ~ habe ich ...** it is with regret that I ...

bedauernswert, bedauernswürdig (geh) ADJ Mensch pitiful; Zustand deplorable

bedecken ptp **bedeckt** ① VT (= zudecken) to cover; **von etw bedeckt sein** to be covered in sth ② VR (a) (= sich zudecken) to cover oneself (b) (Himmel) to become overcast; **der Himmel bedeckte sich mit Wolken** it or the sky became overcast; siehe auch **bedeckt**

bedeckt [bəˈdɛkt] ADJ (a) (= zugedeckt) covered (b) (= bewölkt) overcast (c) **sich ~ halten** (fig) to keep a low profile; siehe auch **bedecken**

bedenken ptp **bedacht** [bəˈdaxt] IRREG ① VT (a) (= überlegen) Sache, Lage, Maßnahme etc to consider; **das will wohl bedacht sein** (geh) that calls for careful consideration; **wenn man es recht bedenkt, ...** if you think about it properly ...
(b) (= in Betracht ziehen) Umstand, Folgen etc to take into consideration; **man muss ~, dass ...** one must take into consideration the fact that ...; **das hättest du früher** or **vorher ~ sollen** you should have thought about that sooner or before; **ich gebe zu ~, dass ...** I would ask you to consider that ...
(c) (in Testament) to remember; **jdn mit einem Geschenk ~** (geh) to give sb a present; **jdn reich ~** (geh) to be generous to sb; **ich wurde auch diesmal reich bedacht** (geh) I did very well this time; **mit etw bedacht werden** to receive sth ② VR (geh) to think (about it); **ohne sich lange zu ~** without stopping to think; siehe auch **bedacht**

Bedenken [bəˈdɛŋkn] NT **-s, -** USU PL (= Zweifel, Einwand) doubt; **moralische ~** moral scruples; **~ haben** to have one's doubts (bei about); **ihm kommen ~** he is having second thoughts

bedenkenlos ① ADJ (a) (= ohne Zögern) Zustimmung unhesitating (b) (= skrupellos) heedless of others; (= unüberlegt) thoughtless ② ADV (a) (= ohne Zögern) unhesitatingly; **ich würde ~ hingehen** I would not hesitate to go (b) (= skrupellos) unscrupulously; **etw ~ tun** (= unüberlegt) to do sth without thinking

bedenkenswert ADJ worth thinking about

bedenklich [bəˈdɛŋklɪç] ① ADJ (a) (= zweifelhaft) Geschäfte, Mittel etc dubious

(b) (= Besorgnis erregend) Lage, Verschlimmerung etc alarming; Gesundheitszustand serious; **der Zustand des Kranken ist ~** the patient's condition is giving cause for concern
(c) (= besorgt) apprehensive; **ein ~es Gesicht machen** to look apprehensive ② ADV (a) (= Besorgnis erregend) alarmingly; **~ zunehmen** to rise alarmingly
(b) (= besorgt) apprehensively; **~ mit dem Kopf schütteln** to shake one's head apprehensively; **jdn ~ stimmen** to make sb (feel) apprehensive

Bedenkzeit F jdm zwei Tage/bis Freitag **~ geben** or **einräumen** to give sb two days/until Friday to think about it; **sich** (dat) **(eine) ~ ausbitten** or **erbitten, um ~ bitten** to ask for time to think about it

bedeuten ptp **bedeutet** VT to mean; (Math, Ling) to stand for; (= versinnbildlichen) to symbolize; **was bedeutet dieses Wort?** what does this word mean?; **was soll das ~?** what does that mean?; **was soll denn das ~?** what's the meaning of that?; **das hat nichts zu ~** it doesn't mean anything; (= macht nichts aus) it doesn't matter; **das bedeutet nichts Gutes** that spells trouble; **Geld bedeutet mir nichts** money means nothing to me; **sein Name bedeutet etwas in der Medizin** he is a name in the field of medicine

bedeutend ① ADJ (a) (= wichtig, bemerkenswert) important; **etwas Bedeutendes leisten** to achieve something important (b) (= groß) Summe, Erfolg considerable ② ADV (= beträchtlich) considerably

bedeutsam [bəˈdɔytzaːm] ① ADJ (a) (= wichtig) Gespräch, Fortschritt etc important; (= folgenschwer) significant (für for) (b) (= viel sagend) Rede eloquent ② ADV meaningfully; **jdm ~ zulächeln** to smile meaningfully at sb

Bedeutung F (a) (= Sinn, Wortsinn) meaning; **in wörtlicher/ übertragener ~** in the literal/figurative sense (b) (= Wichtigkeit) importance; (= Tragweite) significance; **von ~ sein** to be important; **von (großer** or **tiefer/geringer) ~ sein** to be of (great/little) importance; **ein Mann von ~** an important figure; **nichts von ~** nothing of any importance; **ohne ~** of no importance; **an ~ gewinnen/verlieren** to gain/ lose in importance

Bedeutungs-: bedeutungslos ADJ (a) (= unwichtig) insignificant (b) (= nichts besagend) meaningless; **Bedeutungslosigkeit** F -, NO PL insignificance; **zur ~ verurteilt sein** to be condemned to insignificance; **Bedeutungswandel** M (Ling) change in meaning

bedienbar ADJ leicht/schwer **~** easy/hard to use; **elektrisch ~** electrically operated

bedienen ptp **bedient** ① VT (a) (Verkäufer) to serve; (Kellner, Diener etc) to wait on; **werden Sie schon bedient?** are you being served?; **hier wird man gut bedient** the service is good here; **er lässt sich gern ~** he likes to be waited on; **mit diesem Ratschlag war ich schlecht bedient** I was ill-served by that advice; **mit dieser Ware/damit sind Sie sehr gut bedient** these goods/that should serve you very well; **ich bin bedient!** (inf) I've had enough; (Aus sl) I'm smashed (inf)
(b) (Verkehrsmittel) to serve; **diese Flugroute wird von X bedient** X operate (on) this route
(c) (= handhaben) to operate; Telefon to answer
(d) (Fin) Schulden to service
(e) (Cards) **(eine) Farbe ~** to follow suit; **Karo ~** to follow suit in diamonds ② VI (a) (in Geschäft, bei Tisch) to serve; (Kellner auch) to wait (at table (Brit) or a table (US)) (b) (Cards) **du musst ~** you must follow suit ③ VR (a) (bei Tisch) to help oneself (mit to); **bitte ~ Sie sich** please help yourself
(b) (geh: = gebrauchen) **sich jds/einer Sache ~** to use sb/sth

Bedienung [bəˈdiːnʊŋ] F -, **-en** NO PL (in Restaurant etc) service; (von Maschinen) operation; **die ~ der Kunden** serving the customers; **ein Restaurant mit ~** a restaurant with waiter service; **die ~ des Geräts erlernen** to learn how to operate the machine
(b) (Fin: von Schulden) servicing
(c) (= Bedienungsgeld) service (charge)
(d) (= Bedienungspersonal) staff; (= Kellner etc) waiter; (weiblich) waitress; **kommt denn hier keine ~?** isn't anyone serving here?; **hallo, ~!, ~ bitte!** waiter/waitress!

Bedienungs-: Bedienungsanleitung F, **Bedienungsanweisung** F operating instructions pl; **Bedienungsfehler** M mistake in operating a/the machine; **Bedienungskomfort** M (*Comput, Tech*) ease of operation

bedingen *ptp* **bedingt** VT (a) (= *bewirken*) to cause; (= *notwendig machen*) to necessitate; (*Psych, Physiol*) to condition; (= *logisch voraussetzen*) to presuppose; **sich gegenseitig ~** to be mutually dependent; *siehe auch* **bedingt** (b) (= *voraussetzen, verlangen*) to call for

bedingt [bəˈdɪŋt] **1** ADJ (a) (= *eingeschränkt*) limited; *Lob auch* qualified (b) (= *an Bedingung geknüpft*) *Annahme, Straferlass, Strafaussetzung* conditional (c) (*Physiol*) *Reflex* conditioned **2** ADV (a) (= *eingeschränkt*) partly; **~ tauglich** (*Mil*) fit for limited duties; **gefällt es Ihnen hier? – ~!** do you like it here? – with some reservations; **(nur) ~ richtig** (only) partly valid; **(nur) ~ gelten** to be (only) partly valid; *siehe auch* **bedingen** (b) (*Sw, Aus*) conditionally

Bedingung [bəˈdɪŋʊŋ] F **-, -en** (a) (= *Voraussetzung*) condition; (= *Erfordernis*) requirement; **die erste ~ für etw** the basic requirement for sth; **mit** *or* **unter der ~, dass ...** on condition that ...; **unter keiner ~** under no circumstances; **(nur) unter einer ~** (only) on one condition; **unter jeder anderen ~** in any other circumstances; **von einer ~ abhängen** *or* **abhängig sein** to be conditional on one thing; **etw zur ~ machen** to make sth a condition; **es zur ~ machen, dass ...** to stipulate that ...; **~en (für etw)** stellen to place conditions (on sth) (b) (= *Forderung*) term, condition; **zu günstigen ~en** (*Comm*) on favourable (*Brit*) *or* favorable (*US*) terms (c) **Bedingungen** PL (= *Umstände*) conditions *pl*; **unter guten/ harten ~en arbeiten** to work in good/under *or* in difficult conditions

Bedingungs-: **bedingungslos** **1** ADJ *Kapitulation* unconditional; *Hingabe, Gehorsam, Gefolgschaft* unquestioning **2** ADV unconditionally; **~ für etw eintreten** to support sth without reservation; **Bedingungssatz** M conditional clause

bedrohen *ptp* **bedroht** VT to threaten; (= *gefährden*) to endanger; **den Frieden ~** to be a threat to peace; **von Überschwemmung bedroht** in danger of being flooded; **vom Aussterben bedroht** in danger of becoming extinct

bedrohlich [bəˈdroːlɪç] **1** ADJ (= *gefährlich*) alarming; (= *Unheil verkündend*) menacing; **in ~e Nähe rücken** *or* **kommen** to get dangerously close **2** ADV dangerously; **sich ~ verschlechtern** to deteriorate alarmingly; **der Himmel war ~ schwarz** the sky was an ominous black

Bedrohung F threat (+*gen* to); **in ständiger ~ leben** to live under a constant threat

bedrucken *ptp* **bedruckt** VT to print on; **ein bedrucktes Kleid** a print dress; **bedruckter Stoff** printed fabric; **etw mit einem Muster ~** to print a pattern on sth

bedrücken *ptp* **bedrückt** VT to depress; **was bedrückt dich?** what is (weighing) on your mind?; **Sorgen bedrückten ihn** cares were weighing upon him; *siehe auch* **bedrückt**

bedrückend ADJ *Anblick, Nachrichten, Vorstellung* depressing; (= *lastend*) oppressive; *Sorge, Not* pressing

bedrückt [bəˈdrʏkt] ADJ depressed; *Schweigen* oppressive; *siehe auch* **bedrücken**

Beduine [beduˈiːnə] M **-n, -n**, **Beduinin** [-ˈiːnɪn] F **-, -nen** Bedouin

bedürfen *ptp* **bedurft** VI IRREG +GEN (*geh*) to need; **das bedarf keiner weiteren Erklärung** there's no need for any further explanation; **es hätte nur eines Wortes bedurft, um ...** it would only have taken a word to ...; **es bedarf nur eines Wortes von Ihnen** you only have to say the word; **ohne dass es eines Hinweises bedurft hätte, ...** without having to be asked ...

Bedürfnis [bəˈdʏrfnɪs] NT **-ses, -se** (a) (= *Notwendigkeit*) need; (*no pl*: = *Bedarf auch*) necessity; **die ~se des täglichen Lebens** everyday needs (b) NO PL (= *Verlangen*) need; (*form*: = *Anliegen*) wish; **es war ihm ein ~, ...** it was his wish to ...; **es ist mir ein wirkliches ~** it is my sincere wish; **ich hatte das ~/das dringende ~, das zu tun** I felt the need/an urgent need to do that; **das ~ nach Schlaf haben** *or* **fühlen** to be *or* feel in need of sleep

bedürftig [bəˈdʏrftɪç] ADJ (a) (= *hilfsbedürftig*) needy; **die Bedürftigen** the needy *pl* (b) **einer Sache** (*gen*) **~ sein** (*geh*) to be in need of sth

Bedürftigkeit F **-**, NO PL need; **jds ~ (amtlich) feststellen** to give sb a means test

Beefsteak [ˈbiːfsteːk] NT steak; **deutsches ~** hamburger

beeiden [bəˈlaɪdn], *ptp* **beeidet** VT *Sache, Aussage* to swear to; *Dolmetscher, Experten* to swear in

beeidigen [bəˈlaɪdɪgn], *ptp* **beeidigt** VT (a) (= *beeiden*) to swear to (b) (*Jur*: = *vereidigen*) to swear in; **jdn auf etw** (*acc*) **~** to have sb swear on sth; **beeidigte Dolmetscherin** sworn interpreter

beeilen *ptp* **beeilt** VR to hurry (up); **sich sehr** *or* **mächtig** (*inf*) **~** to get a real move on (*inf*); **er beeilte sich hinzuzufügen ...** (*form*) he hastened to add ...

Beeilung [bəˈlaɪlʊŋ] INTERJ **~!** get a move on! (*inf*)

beeindrucken [bəˈlaɪndrʊkn], *ptp* **beeindruckt** VT to impress; **davon lasse ich mich nicht ~** I won't be impressed by that

beeindruckend **1** ADJ impressive **2** ADV impressively

beeinflussbar ADJ *Mensch* impressionable; **diese Vorgänge sind nicht ~** these events cannot be influenced

beeinflussen [bəˈlaɪnflʊsn], *ptp* **beeinflusst** VT to influence; **jdn günstig/nachhaltig ~** to have a favourable (*Brit*) *or* favorable (*US*)/lasting influence on sb; **er ist leicht/schwer zu ~** he is easily influenced/hard to influence; **kannst du deinen Freund nicht ~?** can't you persuade your friend?; **durch etw beeinflusst sein** to be *or* to have been influenced *or* affected by sth

beeinträchtigen [bəˈlaɪntrɛçtɪgn], *ptp* **beeinträchtigt** VT (a) (= *stören*) to spoil; *Rundfunkempfang* to interfere with; **sich gegenseitig ~** (*Empfangsgeräte*) to interfere with one another (b) (= *schädigen*) *jds Ruf* to damage; (= *vermindern*) *Gesundheit, Sehvermögen etc* to impair; *Appetit, Energie, Qualität, Absatz, Wert* to reduce; **den Wettbewerb ~** to restrict competition; **sich gegenseitig ~** (*Entwicklungen, Interessen*) to have an adverse effect on one another; **das beeinträchtigt die Interessen unserer Firma** this is detrimental to our firm's interests (c) (= *hemmen*) *Entscheidung* to interfere with; (= *einschränken*) *Freiheit, Entschlusskraft* to restrict

Beeinträchtigung F **-, -en** (a) (= *Stören*) spoiling; (*von Konzentration*) disturbance; (*von Rundfunkempfang*) interference (+*gen* with) (b) (= *Schädigen: von Ruf*) damage (+*gen* to); (= *Verminderung: von Appetit, Energie, Qualität*) reduction (+*gen* of, in); (*von Gesundheit, Sehvermögen, Leistung, Reaktion*) impairment

beelenden [bəˈleːlɛndn], *ptp* **beelendet** VT (*Sw, S Ger*) to upset

beenden *ptp* **beendet** VT to end; *Arbeit, Aufgabe etc* to finish; *Studium* to complete; **der Abend wurde mit einer Diskussion beendet** the evening ended with a discussion; **etw vorzeitig ~** to cut sth short; **sein Leben ~** (*geh*) to end one's days; (*durch Selbstmord*) to take one's life; **damit ist unser Konzert/ unser heutiges Programm beendet** that concludes our concert/our programmes (*Brit*) *or* programs (*US*) for today

Beendigung [bəˈlɛndɪgʊŋ] F **-**, NO PL, **Beendung** F, NO PL ending; (= *Ende*) end; (= *Fertigstellung*) completion; (= *Schluss*) conclusion; **zur ~ des heutigen Abends ...** to round off this evening ...; **nach ~ des Unterrichts** after school (ends)

beengen [bəˈlɛŋən], *ptp* **beengt** VT (*lit*) *Bewegung* to restrict; (*fig*) to stifle, to inhibit; **das Zimmer beengt mich** the room is too cramped for me; **~de Kleidung** restricting clothing

beengt [bəˈlɛŋt] **1** ADJ cramped, confined; **sich ~ fühlen** to feel confined *etc*; **~e Verhältnisse** (*fig*) restricted circumstances **2** ADV **~ wohnen** to live in cramped conditions

Beengtheit F **-**, NO PL confinement; (*von Räumen*) cramped conditions *pl*

beerben *ptp* **beerbt** VT **jdn ~** to inherit sb's estate; (*inf*: *bezüglich Stelle, Posten*) to succeed sb

beerdigen [bəˈleːrdɪgn], *ptp* **beerdigt** VT to bury; **jdn kirchlich ~** to give sb a Christian burial

Beerdigung F **-, -en** burial; (= *Beerdigungsfeier*) funeral

Beere [ˈbeːrə] F **-, -n** berry; (= *Weinbeere*) grape; **~n tragen** to bear fruit

Beeren-: **Beerenauslese** F (= *Wein*) wine made from specially selected grapes; **Beerenlese** F fruit picking

Beet [beːt] NT **-(e)s, -e** (= *Blumenbeet, Spargelbeet*) bed; (= *Gemüsebeet*) patch; (= *Rabatte*) border (*mit* of)

befähigen [bə'fɛːɪgn], *ptp* **befähigt** VT to enable; (*Ausbildung*) to qualify; **jdn zu etw ~** to enable sb to do sth; to qualify sb to do sth

Befähigung F -, NO PL **(a)** (*durch Ausbildung, Voraussetzung*) qualifications *pl*; **die ~ zum Richteramt** the qualifications to be a judge **(b)** (= *Können, Eignung*) capability; **~ zu etw zeigen** to show talent for sth

befahl PRET *von* **befehlen**

befahrbar ADJ *Straße, Weg* passable; *Seeweg, Fluss* navigable; **~ sein** (*Straße*) to be open to traffic; **nicht ~ sein** (*Straße, Weg*) to be closed (to traffic); (*wegen Schnee etc auch*) to be impassable; (*Seeweg, Fluss*) to be unnavigable

befahren¹ [bə'faːrən], *ptp* **befahren** VT IRREG **(a)** *Straße, Weg* to use; *Passstraße* to drive over; *Gegend, Land* to travel through; *Kreuzung, Seitenstreifen* to drive onto; *Eisenbahnstrecke* to travel on; **der Pass kann nur im Sommer ~ werden** the pass is only open to traffic in summer; **die Staße darf nur in einer Richtung ~ werden** this road is only open in one direction; **die Straße darf nicht ~ werden** the road is closed; **diese Straße wird stark/wenig ~** this road is used a lot/isn't used much **(b)** (*Schiff, Seemann*) to sail; *Fluss* to sail up/down; *Seeweg* to navigate; *Küste* to sail along; **diese Route wird nicht mehr von Schiffen ~** ships no longer sail this route

befahren² ADJ *Straße, Seeweg, Kanal* used; **eine viel** *or* **stark/ wenig ~e Straße** *etc* a much/little used road *etc*

Befall M, NO PL attack; (*mit Schädlingen*) infestation; **es kam zum ~ aller Organe** all organs were affected; **der ~ (des Kohls) mit Raupen** the blight of caterpillars (on the cabbage)

befallen¹ [bə'falən], *ptp* **befallen** VT IRREG **(a)** (= *angreifen, infizieren*) to affect; (*Schädlinge, Ungeziefer*) to infest **(b)** (*geh*: = *überkommen*) to overcome; (*Angst*) to grip; (*Durst, Hunger*) to grip; (*Fieber, Krankheit, Seuche*) to strike; **eine Schwäche befiel sie** she felt faint

befallen² ADJ affected (*von* by); (*von Schädlingen*) infested (*von* with)

befangen [bə'faŋən] ADJ **(a)** *Mensch, Lächeln* diffident; *Schweigen, Stille* awkward **(b)** (*esp Jur*: = *voreingenommen*) prejudiced; **als ~ gelten** to be considered (to be) prejudiced; (*Jur*) to be considered (to be) an interested party; **sich für ~ erklären** (*Jur*) to declare oneself disqualified due to a conflict of interests; **jdn als ~ erklären** to claim that sb is not qualified due to a conflict of interests; **jdn als ~ ablehnen** (*Jur*) to object to sb on grounds of suspected bias

Befangenheit F -, NO PL **(a)** (= *Verlegenheit*) diffidence **(b)** (= *Voreingenommenheit*) bias, prejudice; (*Jur*) interest; **jdn wegen (Besorgnis der) ~ ablehnen** (*Jur*) to object to sb on grounds of suspected bias

befassen *ptp* **befasst** VR **(a)** (= *sich beschäftigen*) **sich mit etw ~** to deal with sth; *mit Arbeit auch, mit Forschungsbereich etc* to work on sth; **sich mit jds Vorleben ~** to look into sb's past; **damit haben wir uns jetzt lange genug befasst** we have spent long enough on that; **mit solchen Kleinigkeiten hat sie sich nie befasst** she has never bothered with such trivialities **(b)** (= *sich annehmen*) **sich mit jdm ~** to deal with sb; **sich mit jdm sehr ~** to give sb a lot of attention

Befehl [bə'feːl] M -(e)s, -e **(a)** (= *Anordnung*) order (*an +acc* to, *von* from); (*Comput, Physiol*) command; **einen ~ verweigern** to refuse to obey an order *etc*; **er gab (uns) den ~, ...** he ordered us to ...; **auf seinen ~ (hin)** on his orders; **auf ~** to order; (= *sofort*) at the drop of a hat (*inf*); **auf ~ handeln** to act under orders; **auf höheren ~** on orders from above (*inf*); **~, Herr Hauptmann** (*Mil*) yes, sir; (*nach erhaltenem ~ auch*) very good, sir; **zu ~, Herr Kapitän** aye aye, sir; **~ ausgeführt!** mission accomplished; **~ ist ~** orders are orders; **~ von oben** orders from above; **vom Chef!** boss's orders; **dein Wunsch ist mir ~** (*hum*) your wish is my command **(b)** (= *Befehlsgewalt*) command; **den ~ haben** *or* **führen** to be in command (*über +acc* of)

befehlen [bə'feːlən], *pret* **befahl** [bə'faːl], *ptp* **befohlen** [bə'foːlən] **1** VT **(a)** (= *anordnen*) to order; **er befahl, den Mann zu erschießen, er befahl die Erschießung des Mannes** he ordered the man to be shot; **du hast mir gar nichts zu ~, von dir lasse ich mir nichts ~** I won't take orders from you **(b)** (= *beordern*) (*an die Front etc*) to order, to send; (*zu sich auch*) to summon

2 VI **(a)** (= *Befehle erteilen*) to give orders; **schweigen Sie, befahl er** be quiet, he ordered; **er befiehlt gern** he likes giving orders; **hier habe nur ich zu ~** I give the orders around here; **wie Sie ~** as you wish **(b)** (*Mil*: = *den Befehl haben*) to be in command (*über +acc* of); **über Leben und Tod ~** to be in absolute command

befehligen [bə'feːlɪgn], *ptp* **befehligt** VT (*Mil*) to command, to be in command of

Befehls-: **Befehlsempfänger(in)** M(F) recipient of an order; **~ sein** to follow orders (*+gen* from); **jdn zum ~ degradieren** (*fig*) to lower sb to the level of just following orders; **Befehlsform** F (*Gram*) imperative; **befehlsgemäß** ADJ, ADV as ordered; **er muss sich ~ um 9 Uhr dort einfinden** his orders are to report there at 9 o'clock; **Befehlshaber** [-haːbɐ] M -s, -, **Befehlshaberin** [-ərɪn] F -, -nen commander; **Befehlsschaltfläche** F (*Comput*) command button; **Befehlssprache** F (*Comput*) command language; **Befehlston** M, NO PL peremptory tone; **Befehlsverweigerung** F (*Mil*) refusal to obey orders; **Befehlszeile** F (*Comput*) command line

befeinden [bə'faɪndn], *ptp* **befeindet** VR to be hostile (towards each other)

befestigen *ptp* **befestigt** VT **(a)** (*an +dat* to) (= *anbringen*) to fasten; *Boot* to tie up; **etw durch Nähen/Kleben** *etc* **~** to sew/ glue *etc* sth; **etw an der Wand/Tür ~** to attach sth to the wall/ door; **ein loses Brett ~** to secure a loose board **(b)** *Böschung, Deich* to reinforce; *Fahrbahn, Straße* to make up

Befestigung F **(a)** (= *das Befestigen*) fastening; (*von Boot*) tying up; **zur ~ des Plakats ...** in order to attach the poster ... **(b)** (= *Vorrichtung zum Befestigen*) fastening **(c)** (= *das Haltbarmachen*) reinforcement; (*fig*: = *Stärkung*) consolidation; **zur ~ der Macht des ...** in order to consolidate the power of ... **(d)** (*Mil*) fortification

Befestigungsanlage F, **Befestigungsbau** M, *pl* **-bauten**, **Befestigungswerk** NT fortification

befeuchten [bə'fɔʏçtn], *ptp* **befeuchtet** VT to moisten; *Finger auch* to wet; *Wäsche* to damp(en)

befeuern *ptp* **befeuert** VT **(a)** (= *beheizen*) to fuel **(b)** (*Naut, Aviat*) *Wasserstraße, Untiefen* to light with beacons; *Start- und Landebahn* to light **(c)** (*lit, fig*: *mit Geschossen*) to bombard

Befeuerung F (*Aviat, Naut*) beacons *pl*

befiehlt [bə'fiːlt] 3. PERS SING PRES *von* **befehlen**

befinden *ptp* **befunden** [bə'fʊndn] IRREG **1** VR **(a)** (= *sein*) to be; (= *liegen auch*) to be situated; (*in Maschine, Körper etc*) to be (situated *or* located); **sich auf Reisen ~** to be away; **unter ihnen befanden sich einige, die ...** there were some amongst them who ...; **die Abbildung befindet sich in diesem Buch** the illustration can be found in this book; **sich in Verwirrung/ guter Laune/im Irrtum ~** to be confused/in a good mood/ mistaken; **sich auf dem Weg der Besserung ~** to be on the road to recovery; **wenn man sich in schlechter Gesellschaft befindet ...** if you find yourself in bad company ... **(b)** (*form*: = *sich fühlen*) to feel; **wie ~ Sie sich heute?** how are you (feeling) today?

2 VT (*form*: = *erachten*) to deem (*form*); **etw für nötig/ angemessen/für als gut ~** to deem sth (to be) necessary/ appropriate/good; **jdn für schuldig ~** to find sb guilty

3 VI (*geh*: = *entscheiden*) to decide (*über +acc* about, *in +dat* on); **darüber habe ich nicht zu ~** that is not for me to decide; **über jdn/etw ~** to pass judgement on sb/sth

Befinden [bə'fɪndn] NT -s, NO PL (*form*: = *Gesundheitszustand*) (state of) health; (*eines Kranken*) condition; **seelisches ~** mental state; **wie ist das (werte)** *or* **Ihr (wertes) ~?** (*form*) how are you (feeling)?

befindlich [bə'fɪntlɪç] ADJ USU ATTR (*form*) **(a)** (*an einem Ort*) *Gebäude, Park* situated; (*in Behälter*) contained; **alle in der Bibliothek ~en Bücher** all the books in the library **(b)** (*in einem Zustand*) **das im Umbau ~e Hotel** the hotel which is being renovated; **das im Umlauf ~e Geld** the money in circulation

Befindlichkeit F -, -en sensitivities *pl*; **nationale ~en** national sensitivities

beflecken [bə'flɛkn], *ptp* **befleckt** VT **(a)** (*lit*) to stain; **er hat sich** *or* **seine Hände mit Blut befleckt** (*fig*) he has blood on his hands **(b)** (*fig geh*) *Ruf, Ehre* to cast a slur on

befleißigen [bə'flaɪsɪgn], *ptp* **befleißigt** VR (*geh*) **sich einer Sache** (*gen*) **~** to cultivate sth; **sich ~, etw zu tun** to make a great effort to do sth; **sich größter** or **der größten Höflichkeit ~** to go out of one's way to be polite

Beflissenheit F -, NO PL (= *Bemühtheit*) zeal; (= *Unterwürfigkeit*) obsequiousness

beflügeln [bəˈflyːgln], *ptp* **beflügelt** VT (*geh*) to inspire; **der Gedanke an Erfolg beflügelte ihn** the thought of success spurred him on

befohlen PTP *von* **befehlen**

befolgen *ptp* **befolgt** VT *Vorschrift, Befehl etc* to obey; *grammatische Regel* to follow; *Ratschlag* to take

Befolgung [bəˈfɔlgʊŋ] F -, NO PL obeying, compliance (*+gen* with); (*von grammatischer Regel*) following; (*von Ratschlag*) taking; **~ der Vorschriften** obeying the rules

befördern *ptp* **befördert** VT **(a)** *Waren, Gepäck* to transport; *Personen* to carry; *Post* to handle; **etw mit der Post/per Luftpost/Bahn/Schiff ~** to send sth by mail/airmail/rail/ship; **jdn/etw von A nach B ~** to transport sb/sth from A to B; **jdn an die (frische) Luft** or **zur Tür hinaus** or **ins Freie ~** (*fig*) to chuck sb out (*inf*); **jdn ins Jenseits ~** (*inf*) to bump sb off (*inf*) **(b)** (= *dienstlich aufrücken lassen*) to promote; **er wurde zum Major befördert** he was promoted to (the rank of) major

Beförderung F **(a)** (= *Transport*) transportation; (*von Personen*) carriage; (*von Post*) handling; **für die ~ von 35 Personen zugelassen** permitted to carry 35 persons; **für die ~ der Kursteilnehmer wird gesorgt** transport will be arranged for course participants; **~ zu Lande/zur Luft/per Bahn** land/ air/rail transportation **(b)** (*beruflich*) promotion

befrachten [bəˈfraxtn], *ptp* **befrachtet** VT *Fahrzeug, Schiff* to load; (*fig geh auch*) to burden; **seine übermäßig mit Emotionen befrachtete Rede** his speech, overladen with emotion

befragen *ptp* **befragt** VT **(a)** (*über +acc, zu, nach* about) to question; *Zeugen auch* to examine; **jdn im Kreuzverhör ~** (*esp Jur*) to cross-examine sb; **auf Befragen** when questioned **(b)** (= *um Stellungnahme bitten*) to consult (*über +acc, nach* about); **jdn um Rat/nach seiner Meinung ~** to ask sb's advice/ opinion; **jdn in einer Angelegenheit ~** to consult sb about a matter

Befragte(r) [bəˈfraːktə] MF DECL AS ADJ person asked; (*in Umfrage auch*) interviewee; **alle ~n** all those asked

Befragung [bəˈfraːgʊŋ] F -, **-en (a)** (= *das Befragen*) questioning; (*von Zeugen auch*) examining **(b)** (*von Fachmann*) consultation (*+gen* with or of) **(c)** (= *Umfrage*) survey

befreien *ptp* **befreit** **1** VT **(a)** (= *frei machen*) to free; *Volk, Land* to liberate; (= *freilassen*) *Gefangenen, Tier, Vogel* to set free; **jdn aus einer schwierigen Lage ~** to rescue sb from a tricky situation
(b) (= *freistellen*) (*von* from) to excuse; (*von Militärdienst, Steuern*) to exempt; (*von Pflicht*) to release; **sich vom Religionsunterricht ~ lassen** to be excused religious instruction
(c) (= *erlösen: von Schmerz etc*) to release, to free; **jdn von einer Last ~** to take a weight off sb's mind; **ein ~des Lachen** a healthy laugh; *siehe auch* **befreit**
(d) (*von* of) (*von Ungeziefer etc*) to rid; (*von Schnee, Eis*) to free; **seine Schuhe von Schmutz ~** to remove the dirt from one's shoes
2 VR to free oneself; (= *entkommen*) to escape (*von, aus* from); **sich aus einer schwierigen Lage ~** to get oneself out of a difficult situation

befreit [bəˈfrait] **1** ADJ (= *erleichtert*) relieved **2** ADV *lächeln* with relief; **~ aufatmen/aufseufzen** to breathe a sigh of relief; **die Bevölkerung kann endlich ~ aufatmen** the people can finally breathe easy again; *siehe auch* **befreien**

Befreiung [bəˈfraiʊŋ] F -, **-en (a)** (= *das Befreien*) freeing; (*von Volk, Land*) liberation; (*von Gefangenen, Tieren*) setting free **(b)** (= *Freistellung*) excusing; (*von Militärdienst, Steuern*) exemption; (*von Pflichten*) releasing; **um ~ von etw bitten** to ask to be excused/exempted from sth **(c)** (*von Schmerz*) releasing **(d)** (*von Ungeziefer*) ridding; (*von Schnee, Eis*) freeing

Befreiungs-: Befreiungsbewegung F liberation movement; **Befreiungsfront** F liberation front; **Befreiungskrieg** M war of liberation; **Befreiungsorganisation** F liberation organization; **Befreiungsschlag** M (*Eishockey*) (*Ftbl*) clearance; (*fig*) coup

befremden [bəˈfrɛmdn], *ptp* **befremdet** **1** VT to disconcert; **es befremdet mich, dass ...** I'm rather taken aback that ...; **das befremdet mich an ihr** that (side of her) disconcerts me **2** VI to cause disconcertment

Befremden [bəˈfrɛmdn] NT **-s**, NO PL disconcertment; **nicht ohne ~ ...** it is with some disconcertment that ...

befreunden [bəˈfrɔyndn], *ptp* **befreundet** VR **(a)** (= *sich anfreunden*) to make or become friends **(b)** (*fig*) **sich mit etw ~** (*mit Gedanken etc*) to get used to sth

befreundet [bəˈfrɔyndət] ADJ **wir/sie sind schon lange (miteinander) ~** we/they have been friends for a long time; **gut** or **eng ~ sein** to be good or close friends; **alle ~en Familien** all the families we *etc* are friendly with; **ein uns ~er Staat** a friendly nation; **das ~e Ausland** friendly (foreign) countries; **ein uns ~er Arzt** a doctor (who is a) friend of ours

befriedigen [bəˈfriːdɪɡn], *ptp* **befriedigt** **1** VT to satisfy; *Ansprüche, Forderungen, Verlangen auch* to meet; **jdn (sexuell) ~** to satisfy sb (sexually); **er ist leicht/schwer zu ~** he's easily/ not easily satisfied; *siehe auch* **befriedigt** **2** VI to be satisfactory; **Ihre Leistung hat nicht befriedigt** your performance was unsatisfactory **3** VR **sich (selbst) ~** to masturbate

befriedigend **1** ADJ satisfactory; *Gefühl* satisfying; (*als Schulnote*) fair **2** ADV satisfactorily

befriedigt [bəˈfriːdɪçt] **1** ADJ satisfied; **bist du nun endlich ~?** are you satisfied at last? **2** ADV with satisfaction; *siehe auch* **befriedigen**

Befriedigung F -, **-en (a)** (= *das Befriedigen*) satisfaction, satisfying; **sexuelle ~** sexual satisfaction; **zur ~ deiner Neugier ...** to satisfy your curiosity ... **(b)** (= *Genugtuung*) satisfaction

befristen [bəˈfrɪstn], *ptp* **befristet** VT to limit, to restrict (*auf +acc* to); *Aufgabe, Projekt* to put a time limit on

befristet [bəˈfrɪstət] ADJ *Genehmigung, Visum* restricted (*auf +acc* to); *Arbeitsverhältnis, Anstellung* temporary; **~ sein** (*Pass etc*) to be valid for a limited time; **auf zwei Jahre ~ sein** (*Visum etc*) to be valid for two years; **mein Arbeitsverhältnis ist auf zwei Jahre ~** my appointment is restricted to two years

Befristung F -, **-en** limitation, restriction (*auf +acc* to)

befruchten *ptp* **befruchtet** VT **(a)** (*lit*) *Eizelle* to fertilize; *Blüte* to pollinate; **künstlich ~** to inseminate artificially **(b)** (*fig: = geistig anregen*) to stimulate

Befruchtung [bəˈfrʊxtʊŋ] F -, **-en** fertilization; (*von Blüte*) pollination; **künstliche ~** artificial insemination

Befugnis [bəˈfuːknɪs] F -, **-se** (*form*) authority *no pl*; (= *Erlaubnis*) authorization *no pl*; **besondere ~se erhalten** to be given special authority

befugt [bəˈfuːkt] ADJ (*form*) **~ sein(, etw zu tun)** to have the authority or (= *ermächtigt worden sein*) be authorized (to do sth)

befühlen *ptp* **befühlt** VT to feel

Befund M results *pl*; **der ~ war positiv/negativ** (*Med*) the results were positive/negative; **ohne ~** (*Med*) (results) negative

befürchten *ptp* **befürchtet** VT to fear; **ich befürchte das Schlimmste** I fear the worst; **es ist** or **steht zu ~, dass ...** it is (to be) feared that ...; **dabei sind Komplikationen zu ~** it is feared there may be complications

Befürchtung [bəˈfʏrçtʊŋ] F -, **-en** fear *usu pl*; **~en** or **die ~ haben, dass ...** to fear that ...; **die schlimmsten ~en haben** or **hegen** (*geh*) to fear the worst

befürworten [bəˈfyːɛvɔrtn], *ptp* **befürwortet** VT to approve

Befürworter [bəˈfyːɛvɔrtɐ] M **-s**, -, **Befürworterin** [-ərɪn] F -, **-nen** supporter

begabt [bəˈgaːpt] ADJ talented; (*esp geistig, musisch auch*) gifted; **für etw ~ sein** to be talented at sth; **für Musik, Kunst etc auch** to have a gift for sth

Begabte(r) [bəˈgaːptə] MF DECL AS ADJ talented person/man/ woman *etc*

Begabung F -, **-en (a)** (= *Anlage*) talent; (*geistig, musisch*) gift; **er hat eine ~ dafür, immer das Falsche zu sagen** he has a knack of always saying the wrong thing; **er hat ~ zum Lehrer** he has a gift for teaching; **mangelnde ~** a lack of talent **(b)** (= *begabter Mensch*) talented person; **sie ist eine musikalische ~** she has a talent for music

begaffen *ptp* **begafft** VT (*pej inf*) to gape at (*inf*)

begann PRET *von* **beginnen**

begeben ptp **begeben** IRREG **1** VR **(a)** (geh: = gehen) to go; **sich nach Hause ~, sich auf den Heimweg ~** to make one's way home; **sich auf eine Reise ~** to undertake a journey; **sich zur Ruhe ~** to retire; **sich an seinen Platz ~** to take one's place; **sich in ärztliche Behandlung ~** to undergo medical treatment; **sich an die Arbeit ~** to commence work **(b)** (= sich einer Sache aussetzen) **sich in Gefahr ~** to expose oneself to danger; **sich in jds Schutz** (acc) **~** to place oneself under sb's protection **2** VT (Fin) to issue

Begebenheit [bəˈgeːbnhait] F -, -en (geh) occurrence, event

begegnen [bəˈgeːgnən], ptp **begegnet** VI AUX SEIN +DAT **(a)** (= treffen) to meet; **sich or einander** (gen) **~** to meet; **ihre Augen or Blicke begegneten sich** their eyes met **(b)** (= stoßen auf) **einer Sache** (dat) **~** to encounter sth; **dieses Wort wird uns später noch einmal ~** we will encounter this word again later **(c)** (= widerfahren) **jdm ist etw begegnet** sth has happened to sb

Begegnung F -, -en **(a)** (= Treffen) meeting; (fig: mit Idee etc) encounter; **bei der ersten/letzten ~ der beiden** at the first/last meeting between the two; **ein Ort internationaler ~** an international meeting place **(b)** (Sport) encounter, match; **die ~ Spanien-Italien findet nächsten Monat statt** Spain and Italy meet next month

Begegnungsstätte F meeting place

begehen ptp **begangen** VT IRREG **(a)** (= verüben) to commit; Fehler to make; **eine Indiskretion (gegenüber jdm) ~** to be indiscreet (about sb); **einen Mord an jdm ~** to murder sb; **eine Dummheit/Taktlosigkeit/Unvorsichtigkeit ~** to do something stupid/tactless/careless; **die Dummheit/Taktlosigkeit/ Unvorsichtigkeit ~, ...** to be so stupid/tactless/careless as to ...; **ein oft begangener Fehler** a frequent mistake **(b)** (= entlanggehen) Weg to use; **der Weg wird viel begangen** the path is used a lot; „**Begehen der Brücke auf eigene Gefahr**" "persons using this bridge do so at their own risk" **(c)** (geh: = feiern) to celebrate

begehren [bəˈgeːrən], ptp **begehrt** VT (geh) to desire; Gegenstände, Besitz eines andern to covet; **du sollst nicht ~ ...** (Bibl) thou shalt not covet ... (Bibl); siehe auch **begehrt**

begehrenswert ADJ desirable

begehrt [bəˈgeːrt] ADJ much sought-after; Partner etc auch, Ferienziel popular; Junggeselle eligible; siehe auch **begehren**

begeistern ptp **begeistert** **1** VT jdn to fill with enthusiasm; (= inspirieren) to inspire; **er begeistert alle durch sein or mit seinem Talent** everybody is enthusiastic about his talent; **sie ist für nichts zu ~** she's never enthusiastic about anything **2** VR to be enthusiastic (an +dat, für about); siehe auch **begeistert**

begeistert [bəˈgaistɐt] **1** ADJ enthusiastic (von about) **2** ADV enthusiastically; siehe auch **begeistern**

Begeisterung F -, NO PL enthusiasm (über +acc about, für for); **etw mit ~ tun** to do sth enthusiastically; **in ~ geraten** to become enthusiastic

Begeisterungs-: begeisterungsfähig ADJ able to get enthusiastic; Publikum etc quick to show one's enthusiasm; **sie ist zwar ~, aber ...** her enthusiasm is easily aroused but ...; **Begeisterungsfähigkeit** F capacity for enthusiasm; **ein Pessimist, dem jegliche ~ abgeht** a pessimist who never shows enthusiasm for anything

begierig [bəˈgiːrɪç] **1** ADJ (= voll Verlangen) greedy; (= gespannt) eager; Leser avid; **auf etw** (acc) **~ sein** to be eager for sth; **~ (darauf) sein, etw zu tun** to be eager to do sth **2** ADV (= verlangend) greedily; (= gespannt) eagerly

begießen ptp **begossen** [bəˈgɔsn] VT IRREG **(a)** (mit Wasser) to pour water on; Blumen, Beet to water; (mit Fett) Braten etc to baste; siehe auch **begossen (b)** (fig inf) freudiges Ereignis, Vereinbarung to celebrate; **das muss begossen werden!** that calls for a drink!

Beginn [bəˈgɪn] M -(e)s, NO PL beginning; **am or bei or zu ~** at the beginning; **mit ~ der Verhandlungen** at the beginning of the negotiations; **gleich zu ~** right at the beginning

beginnen [bəˈgɪnən], pret **begann** [bəˈgan], ptp **begonnen** [bəˈgɔnən] **1** VI to start; **mit einer Arbeit ~** to start (to do) a job; **mit der Arbeit ~** to start work; **es beginnt zu regnen** it's starting to rain **2** VT to start, to begin

beginnend ADJ ATTR incipient (form); **eine ~e Erkältung** the beginnings of a cold; **im ~en 19. Jahrhundert** in the early 19th century

beglaubigen [bəˈglaubɪgn], ptp **beglaubigt** VT Testament, Unterschrift to witness; Zeugnisabschrift to authenticate; Echtheit to attest (to); **etw behördlich/notariell ~ lassen** to have sth witnessed etc officially/by a notary

Beglaubigung F -, -en (von Testament, Unterschrift) witnessing; (von Zeugnisabschrift) authentication; (von Echtheit) attestation

Beglaubigungsschreiben NT credentials pl

begleichen ptp **beglichen** [bəˈglɪçn] VT IRREG (lit: = bezahlen) to settle; (fig) Schuld to pay (off); **mit Ihnen habe ich noch eine Rechnung zu ~** (fig) I've a score to settle with you

Begleitbrief M covering letter (Brit), cover letter (US)

begleiten ptp **begleitet** VT (auch Mus) to accompany; **ein paar ~de Worte** a few accompanying words

Begleiter [bəˈglaitɐ] M -s, -, **Begleiterin** [-ərɪn] F -, -nen companion; (zum Schutz) escort; (von Reisenden) courier; (Mus) accompanist; **ständiger ~** constant companion

Begleit-: Begleiterscheinung F concomitant (form); (Med) side effect; **ist Jugendkriminalität eine ~ der Wohlstandsgesellschaft?** does juvenile delinquency go hand in hand with an affluent society?; **Begleitpapiere** PL (Comm) accompanying documents pl; **Begleitschreiben** NT covering letter (Brit), cover letter (US); **Begleitumstände** PL attendant circumstances pl

Begleitung [bəˈglaitʊŋ] F -, -en **(a)** NO PL company; **er bot ihr seine ~ an** he offered to accompany her; **in ~ seines Vaters** accompanied by his father; **in Peters ~** accompanied by Peter; **ich bin in ~** hier I'm with someone **(b)** (= Begleiter) companion; (zum Schutz) escort; (= Gefolge) entourage; **ohne ~** unaccompanied **(c)** (Mus) accompaniment; (= Begleitstimme) harmony; **ohne ~ spielen** to play unaccompanied

beglücken ptp **beglückt** VT jdn ~ to make sb happy; **er hat uns gestern mit seinem Besuch beglückt** (iro) he honoured (Brit) or honored (US) us with a visit yesterday; **Casanova hat tausende or Tausende von Frauen beglückt** (hum) Casanova bestowed his favours (Brit) or favors (US) upon thousands of women; **ein ~des Gefühl/Erlebnis** a cheering feeling/ experience; **beglückt lächeln** to smile happily

beglückwünschen [bəˈglʏkvʏnʃn], ptp **beglückwünscht** VT to congratulate (zu on); **lass dich ~!** congratulations!

begnadigen [bəˈgnaːdɪgn], ptp **begnadigt** VT to reprieve; (= Strafe erlassen) to pardon

Begnadigung F -, -en reprieve; (= Straferlass) pardon; **um (jds) ~ ersuchen** to seek a reprieve (for sb)

begnügen [bəˈgnyːgn], ptp **begnügt** VR **sich mit etw ~** to be content with sth; **damit begnüge ich mich nicht** I'm not satisfied with that

Begonie [beˈgoːniə] F -, -n begonia

begonnen PTP von **beginnen**

begossen ADJ **er stand da wie ein ~er Pudel** (inf) he looked so sheepish; siehe auch **begießen**

begraben ptp **begraben** VT IRREG **(a)** (= beerdigen) to bury; **dort möchte ich nicht ~ sein** (inf) I wouldn't like to be stuck in that hole (inf); **der kann sich ~ lassen** (inf) he is worse than useless **(b)** (= verschütten) to bury; **beim Einsturz begrub das Gebäude alle Bewohner unter sich** when the building collapsed all the residents were buried **(c)** Hoffnung, Wunsch to abandon; Streit, Angelegenheit, Feindschaft to end; **diese Angelegenheit ist längst ~** this matter was over (and done with) long ago

Begräbnis [bəˈgrɛːpnɪs] NT -ses, -se burial; (= ~feier) funeral

begrabschen VT (inf) to grope (inf)

begradigen [bəˈgraːdɪgn], ptp **begradigt** VT to straighten

Begradigung F -, -en straightening

begrapschen VT (inf) to grope (inf)

begreifen ptp **begriffen** [bəˈgrɪfn] IRREG **1** VT **(a)** (= verstehen) to understand; (= einsehen) to realize that ...; **er begriff nicht, worum es ging** he didn't understand what it was about; **hast du mich begriffen?** did you understand what I said?; **es ist kaum zu ~** it's almost incomprehensible; **ich begreife mich selbst nicht** I don't understand myself

(b) (= *auffassen, interpretieren*) to view, to see
2 VI to understand; **leicht** *or* **schnell/schwer** *or* **langsam** ~ to be quick/slow on the uptake
3 VR to be understandable; **eine solche Tat lässt sich nicht leicht** ~ such an action cannot be easily understood; *siehe auch* **begriffen**

begreiflich [bə'graiflıç] ADJ understandable; **es wird mir allmählich** ~, **warum** ... I'm beginning to understand why ...; **ich kann mich ihm nicht** ~ **machen** I can't make myself clear to him; **ich habe ihm das** ~ **gemacht** I've made it clear to him

begreiflicherweise ADV understandably

begrenzen *ptp* **begrenzt** VT to restrict (*auf +acc* to)

begrenzt [bə'grɛntst] **1** ADJ (= *beschränkt*) restricted; (= *geistig beschränkt*) limited; **meine Aufenthaltsdauer ist nicht zeitlich** ~ there's no time limit on (the length of) my stay; **eine genau** ~**e Aufgabe** a clearly defined task **2** ADV (*zeitlich*) for a limited time; **sich nur** ~ **bewegen können** to be restricted in one's movements; ~ **Einfluss nehmen** to exert limited influence

Begriff M **(a)** (*objektiv*) (= *Bedeutungsgehalt*) concept; (= *Terminus*) term; **in neuen** ~**en denken** to think in new terms; **sein Name ist mir ein/kein** ~ his name means something/doesn't mean anything to me; **sein Name ist in aller Welt ein** ~ his name is known all over the world **(b)** (*subjektiv*: = *Vorstellung, Eindruck*) idea; **sein** ~ **von** *or* **der Freiheit** his idea of freedom; **sich** (*dat*) **einen** ~ **von etw machen** to imagine sth; **du machst dir keinen** ~ **(davon)** (*inf*) you've no idea (about it) (*inf*); **das geht über meine** ~**e** that's beyond me; **nach unseren heutigen** ~**en** by today's standards; **für meine** ~**e** in my opinion **(c)** **im** ~ **sein** *or* **stehen** (*form*), **etw zu tun** to be on the point of doing sth **(d)** **schwer** *or* **langsam/schnell von** ~ **sein** (*inf*) to be slow/quick on the uptake; **sei doch nicht so schwer von** ~! (*inf*) don't be so dense (*inf*)

begriffen ADJ **in etw** (*dat*) ~ **sein** (*form*) to be in the process of doing sth; **ein noch in der Entwicklung** ~**er Plan** a plan still in the process of being developed; *siehe auch* **begreifen**

begrifflich [bə'grıflıç] **1** ADJ ATTR (= *bedeutungsmäßig*) conceptual; ~**e Klärung** clarification of one's terms **2** ADV (= *bedeutungsmäßig*) conceptually; ~ **bestimmen** to define (in clear terms); ~ **ordnen** to arrange according to conceptual groups

Begriffs-: **Begriffsbestimmung** F definition; **begriffsstutzig**, (*Aus*) **begriffsstützig** [-ʃtʏtsıç] ADJ (*inf*) thick (*inf*); **Begriffsstutzigkeit** F -, NO PL (*inf*) **von einer unglaublichen** ~ unbelievably thick (*inf*); ~ **mimen** to act dumb (*inf*); **ich kann mich nur über deine** ~ **wundern** I can't believe how thick you are! (*inf*)

begründen *ptp* **begründet** VT **(a)** (= *Gründe anführen für*) to give reasons for; (*rechtfertigend*) *Forderung, Meinung, Ansicht* to justify; *Verhalten* to account for; *Verdacht, Behauptung* to substantiate; **etw eingehend/näher** ~ to give detailed/specific reasons for sth; **ein** ~**der Satz** (*Gram*) a causal clause; *siehe* **begründet (b)** (= *beginnen, gründen*) to establish

begründet [bə'grʏndət] ADJ well-founded; (= *berechtigt*) justified; **es besteht** ~**e/keine** ~**e Hoffnung, dass** ... there is reason/no reason to hope that ...; **das halte ich für nicht** ~ I think that's unfounded/unjustified; **sachlich** ~ founded on fact; **etw liegt** *or* **ist in etw** (*dat*) ~ sth has its roots in sth

Begründung F **(a)** grounds *pl* (*für*, +*gen* for); **etwas zur** *or* **als** ~ **sagen** to say something in explanation **(b)** (= *Gründung*) establishment; (*von Hausstand*) setting up

begrüßen *ptp* **begrüßt** VT **(a)** *jdn* to greet; **jdn herzlich** ~ to give sb a hearty welcome; **es ist mir eine große Ehre, Sie bei mir** ~ **zu dürfen** (*form*) it's a great honour (*Brit*) *or* honor (*US*) to (be able to) welcome you here; **wir würden uns freuen, Sie bei uns** ~ **zu dürfen** (*form*) we would be delighted to have the pleasure of your company (*form*) **(b)** (= *gut heißen*) to welcome; (*esp iroform*) to appreciate; **es ist zu** ~, **dass** ... it's a good thing that ... **(c)** (*Sw:* = *um Erlaubnis fragen*) to ask (*um* for, *wegen* about)

begrüßenswert ADJ welcome; **es wäre** ~, **wenn** ... it would be desirable if ...

Begrüßung [bə'gryːsʊŋ] F -, -en greeting; (*der Gäste*) (= *das Begrüßen*) welcoming; (= *Zeremonie*) welcome; **jdm einen**

Blumenstrauß zur ~ **überreichen** to welcome sb with a bouquet of flowers

begucken *ptp* **beguckt** VT (*inf*) to look at; **lass dich mal** ~ let's (have a) look at you!

begünstigen [bə'gʏnstɪgn], *ptp* **begünstigt** VT to favour (*Brit*), to favor (*US*); *Wachstum, Handel* to encourage; *Pläne, Beziehungen* to further; (*Jur*) to aid and abet

Begünstigte(r) [bə'gʏnstɪçtə] MF DECL AS ADJ beneficiary; (*von Akkreditiv*) payee; (*von Altersversorgungsplan*) participant; (*Jur*) accessory after the fact

Begünstigung F -, -en **(a)** (*Jur*) aiding and abetting; **persönliche** ~ aiding and abetting; **sachliche** ~ (acting as an) accessory; ~ **im Amt** connivance **(b)** (= *Bevorzugung*) preferential treatment; (= *Vorteil*) advantage **(c)** (= *Förderung*) favouring (*Brit*), favoring (*US*); (*von Wachstum, Handel*) encouragement; (*von Plänen, Beziehungen*) furthering

begutachten *ptp* **begutachtet** VT to give expert advice about; *Kunstwerk, Stipendiaten* to examine; *Projekte, Leistung* to judge; *Gelände, Haus* to survey; (*inf:* = *ansehen*) to have a look at; **etw** ~ **lassen** to get expert advice about sth

begütigend **1** ADJ *Worte etc* soothing **2** ADV soothingly; **auf jdn** ~ **einreden** to calm sb down

behaart [bə'haːɐt] ADJ hairy; **stark** ~ very hairy; **dicht** ~ (thickly) covered with hair

Behaarung [bə'haːrʊŋ] F -, -en hairs *pl* (+*gen, an* +*dat* on)

behäbig [bə'hɛːbɪç] **1** ADJ *Mensch* portly; (= *phlegmatisch, geruhsam*) stolid; (*fig*) *Leben, Möbel, Auto* comfortable; *Architektur* solid; *Sprache, Ton* complacent **2** ADV **(breit und)** ~ **herumsitzen** to sit on one's fat backside (*inf*)

Behäbigkeit F -, NO PL (*von Mensch*) portliness; (= *Geruhsamkeit*) stolidity; (*von Architektur*) solidness; (*von Sprache, Ton*) complacency

behagen [bə'haːgn], *ptp* **behagt** VI **etw behagt jdm** sb likes sth; **etw behagt jdm nicht** (= *nicht gefallen*) sb doesn't like sth; (= *beunruhigen*) sb feels uneasy about sth; **er behagt ihr nicht** she doesn't like him

Behagen [bə'haːgn] NT -s, NO PL contentment; **mit sichtlichem** ~ with obvious pleasure; **mit** ~ **essen** to eat with relish

behaglich [bə'haːklıç] **1** ADJ cosy; (= *bequem*) comfortable; (= *zufrieden*) contented **2** ADV (= *gemütlich*) comfortably; (= *genussvoll*) contentedly; **es sich** (*dat*) ~ **machen** to make oneself comfortable

Behaglichkeit F -, NO PL cosiness; (= *Bequemlichkeit*) comfort; (= *Zufriedenheit*) contentment

behalten *ptp* **behalten** VT IRREG **(a)** to keep; *Mitarbeiter* to keep on; ~ **Sie (doch) Platz!** please don't get up!; **der Kranke kann nichts bei sich** ~ the patient can't keep anything down; **jdn bei sich** ~ to keep sb with one; **einen Gast zum Abendbrot bei sich** ~ to invite a guest to stay for supper; **die Ruhe** ~ to keep one's cool (*inf*); **die Nerven** ~ to keep one's nerve (*Brit*), to keep one's nerves under control (*US*); **wenn wir solches Wetter** ~ if this weather lasts; **sie muss immer ihren Willen** ~ she always has to have her own way; **etw für sich** ~ to keep sth to oneself; **jdn/etw in guter/schlechter Erinnerung** ~ to have happy/unhappy memories of sb/sth **(b)** (= *nicht vergessen*) to remember; **im Gedächtnis/im Kopf** ~ to remember, to keep in one's head; **ich habe die Zahl/seine Adresse nicht** ~ I've forgotten the number/his address **(c)** (= *zurückbehalten, nicht loswerden*) to be left with; *Schock, Schaden* to suffer; **vom Unfall hat er ein steifes Knie** ~ after the accident he was left with a stiff knee

Behälter [bə'hɛltɐ] M -s, - container

behandeln *ptp* **behandelt** VT *Material, Stoff, Materie, Menschen* to treat; (= *verfahren mit*) to handle; *Zähne* to attend to; *Thema, Frage, Problem, Antrag* to deal with; **jdn/etw gut/ schlecht** ~ to treat sb/sth well/badly; **er weiß, wie man Kinder/ die Maschine** ~ **muss** he knows how to handle children/the machine; **eine Angelegenheit diskret** ~ to handle a matter with discretion; **jdn/etw operativ** ~ to operate on sb/sth; **der** ~**de Arzt** the doctor in attendance

behändigen [bə'hɛndɪgn], *ptp* **behändigt** VT (*Sw*) to take

Behandlung F treatment; (*von Angelegenheit*) handling; (*von Zähnen*) attention (+*gen* to); **um schnelle** ~ **des Antrags wird gebeten** please deal with the application as quickly as possible; **die schlechte** ~ **seiner Frau** the ill-treatment of his wife; **waren Sie deswegen schon früher in ~?** have you had treatment for this before?; **bei wem sind Sie in ~?** who's treating you?

behängen *ptp* **behängt** *or* **behangen** ◧ VT to decorate ◨ VR (*pej*) to deck oneself out (*mit in or* with)

beharren [bəˈharən], *ptp* **beharrt** VI **(a)** (= *hartnäckig sein*) to insist (*auf +dat* on); (= *nicht aufgeben*) to persist (*bei* in) **(b)** (= *bleiben*) **in etw** (*dat*) **~** (*in Zustand*) to persist in sth; (*an Ort*) to remain in sth

beharrlich [bəˈharlıç] ◧ ADJ (= *hartnäckig*) insistent; (= *ausdauernd*) persistent; *Glaube, Liebe* steadfast; **~er Fleiß** perseverance ◨ ADV (= *hartnäckig*) insistently; (= *ausdauernd*) persistently; *glauben* steadfastly; **~ fortfahren, etw zu tun** to persist in doing sth

Beharrlichkeit F -, NO PL (= *Hartnäckigkeit*) insistence; (= *Ausdauer*) persistence; (*von Glaube, Liebe*) steadfastness

Beharrung F -, NO PL (*Phys*) inertia

behaupten [bəˈhauptn], *ptp* **behauptet** ◧ VT **(a)** (= *sagen*) to claim; (= *bestimmte Aussage aufstellen*) to maintain; **steif und fest ~** to insist; **von jdm ~, dass ...** to say of sb that ...; **es wird behauptet, dass ...** it is said that ... **(b)** (= *erfolgreich verteidigen*) *Stellung, Recht* to maintain; *Meinung* to assert; *Markt* to keep one's share of ◨ VR to assert oneself; (*bei Diskussion*) to hold one's own (*gegenüber, gegen* against); **sich auf dem Markt ~** to maintain one's hold on the market

Behauptung F -, -en **(a)** claim; (= *esp unerwiesene ~*) assertion **(b)** (= *Aufrechterhaltung*) assertion; (*von Stellung*) successful defence (*Brit*) *or* defense (*US*) **(c)** (= *das Sichbehaupten*) assertion

Behausung [bəˈhauzʊŋ] F -, -en (*gehhum*) dwelling

beheben *ptp* **behoben** [bəˈhoːbn] VT IRREG **(a)** (= *beseitigen*) to remove; *Mängel, Missstände* to rectify, to remedy; *Schaden* to repair; *Störung* to clear **(b)** (*Aus*) *Geld* to withdraw

beheizbar ADJ heatable; *Heckscheibe, Außenspiegel* heated

beheizen *ptp* **beheizt** VT to heat

behelfen *ptp* **beholfen** [bəˈhɔlfn] VR IRREG to manage; **sich mit Ausreden ~** to resort to excuses; **sich mit Ausflüchten ~** to be evasive; **er weiß sich allein nicht zu ~** he can't manage alone

Behelfs- IN CPDS temporary; **Behelfsausfahrt** F (*auf Autobahn*) temporary exit; **behelfsmäßig** ◧ ADJ makeshift; (*zeitlich begrenzt*) *Straßenbelag, Ausweis* temporary ◨ ADV temporarily; **etw ~ reparieren** to make makeshift repairs to sth

behelligen [bəˈhelıgn], *ptp* **behelligt** VT to bother

beherbergen [bəˈhɛrbergn], *ptp* **beherbergt** VT (*lit, fig*) to house; *Gäste* to accommodate

beherrschen *ptp* **beherrscht** ◧ VT **(a)** (= *herrschen über*) to rule; (*fig*: *Gefühle, Vorstellungen*) to dominate **(b)** (*fig*) *Stadtbild, Landschaft, Ebene, Markt* to dominate **(c)** (= *zügeln*) *Zunge* to curb **(d)** (= *gut können*) to master **(e)** (= *bewältigen*) *Situation* to have control of ◨ VR to control oneself; **ich kann mich ~!** (*iro inf*) not likely! (*inf*); *siehe auch* **beherrscht**

beherrscht [bəˈhɛrʃt] ◧ ADJ (*fig*) self-controlled ◨ ADV with self-control; *siehe auch* **beherrschen**

Beherrschung [bəˈhɛrʃʊŋ] F -, NO PL control; (= *Selbstbeherrschung*) self-control; (*des Markts*) domination; (*eines Fachs*) mastery; **die ~ verlieren** to lose one's temper

beherzigen [bəˈhɛrtsıgn], *ptp* **beherzigt** VT to heed

behilflich [bəˈhılflıç] ADJ helpful; **jdm (bei etw) ~ sein** to help sb (with sth)

behindern *ptp* **behindert** VT to hinder; *Sicht* to impede; (*bei Sport, im Verkehr*) to obstruct; **jdn bei etw ~** to hinder sb in sth

behindert ADJ **(a)** (*mit einer Behinderung*) disabled; (*geistig/körperlich* = mentally/physically handicapped **(b)** (*sl*: = *blöd*) stupid; **~es Auto** shitheap (*sl*); **ein ~er Typ** a tosser (*sl*)

Behinderten-: **Behindertenausweis** M *disabled person card or* ID; **behindertengerecht** ADJ adapted to the needs of the disabled; **etw ~ umbauen/gestalten** to alter/design sth to fit the needs of the disabled; **Behindertenolympiade** F Paralympics *pl*; **Behindertensport** M disabled sport; **Behindertenwerkstatt** F sheltered workshop

Behinderte(r) [bəˈhındetə] MF DECL AS ADJ disabled *or* handicapped person/man/woman *etc*; **die ~n** handicapped *or* disabled people

Behinderung F hindrance; (*im Sport, Verkehr*) obstruction; (*körperlich, = Nachteil*) handicap; **mit ~en muss gerechnet werden** delays are likely to occur

Behörde [bəˈhøːɐdə] F -, -n authority *usu pl*; (= *Amtsgebäude*) office *usu pl*; **die ~n** the authorities; **die zuständige ~** the proper authorities

behüten *ptp* **behütet** VT to look after; (*esp Engel etc*) to watch over; **jdn vor etw** (*dat*) **~** to protect sb from sth; *siehe auch* **behütet**

behütet [bəˈhyːtət] ◧ ADJ *Mädchen* carefully brought up; *Jugend, Alltag* sheltered ◨ ADV **~ aufwachsen** to have a sheltered upbringing; *siehe auch* **behüten**

behutsam [bəˈhuːtzaːm] ◧ ADJ cautious; (= *zart*) gentle ◨ ADV carefully; *streichen* gently; **man muss es ihr ~ beibringen** it will have to be broken to her gently

bei [bai] PREP +DAT **(a)** (*Nähe*) near; **sie wohnt ~m Rathaus** she lives near the town hall; **wir treffen uns ~m Leuchtturm/~ der Kirche** we'll meet by the lighthouse/the church; **ich stand/saß ~ ihm** I stood/sat beside him; **er bot sich an, ~m Gepäck zu bleiben** he offered to stay by the luggage; **ich bleibe ~ den Kindern** I'll stay with the children; **~ X schneiden sich die ~den Geraden** the two lines bisect at X; **der Wert liegt ~ tausend Euro** the value is around a thousand euros; **nicht ~ sich sein** (*inf*) to be out of one's mind (*inf*) **(b)** (*Aufenthalt*) at; **ich war ~ meiner Tante** I was at my aunt's; **ich bin ~ Gabriele zum Kaffee eingeladen** I'm invited to Gabriele's for coffee; **er wohnt ~ seinen Eltern** he lives with his parents; **~ jdm übernachten** to spend the night at sb's; **~ Müller** (*auf Briefen*) care of *or* c/o Müller; **~ uns zu Hause** (*im Haus*) at our house; (*im Land, in Familie*) at home, back home (*US*); **~ uns in Deutschland** in Germany; **~ uns fängt man um 8 Uhr zu arbeiten an** (here) we start work at 8 o'clock; **~ uns ist um 12.30 Uhr Mittagspause** we have our lunch break at 12.30; **~ jdm arbeiten** to work for sb; **~ Siemens angestellt sein** to work at Siemens; **er ist** *or* **arbeitet ~ der Post** he works for the post office; **~m Film/Fernsehen sein** to be in films/TV; **~m Fleischer/Friseur** at the butcher's/hairdresser's; **~m Militär** in the army; **~ Collins erschienen** published by Collins; **~ jdm Unterricht haben** to have lessons with sb; **~ Shakespeare liest man ...** Shakespeare says ...; **ich habe keine Taschentücher ~ mir** I haven't got a hanky; **hast du Geld ~ dir?** have you any money with you?; **~ Tisch** at table **(c)** (*Berührung*) by; **er nahm mich ~ der Hand** he took me by the hand; **jdn ~m Arm/~ den Schultern packen** to grab sb by the arm/shoulder **(d)** (= *zusammen mit*) among; **~ meiner Post sind immer mehr Rechnungen als Privatbriefe** there are always more bills than letters in my mail **(e)** (*Teilnahme*) at; **~ einer Hochzeit sein** to be at a wedding; **~ der Ausstellungseröffnung eine Rede halten** to give a speech at the opening of an exhibition; **machst du ~ der Demonstration mit?** are you taking part in the demonstration?; **ich habe ~ der Party mitgeholfen** I helped with the party **(f)** (= *betreffend*) **~ ihm ist es 8 Uhr** he makes it *or* he has (*US*) 8 o'clock; **das war ~ ihm der Fall** that was the case with him; **man weiß nicht, woran man ~ ihm ist** (*inf*) you never know where you are with him; **~ mir hast du damit kein Glück** you won't get anywhere with me; **~ Kühen findet man Maul- und Klauenseuche** you get foot-and-mouth in cows **(g)** (*Zeit*) **~m letzten Ton des Zeitzeichens ...** at the last pip ...; **~m letzten Gewitter** during the last storm; **~ meiner Ankunft** on my arrival; **Vorsicht ~ der Abfahrt (des Zuges)!** stand clear, the train is about to leave!; **~m Erwachen** on waking; **~m Erscheinen der Königin** when the queen appeared; **~ Beginn und Ende der Vorstellung** at the beginning and end of the performance; **~ Nacht** by night; **~ Tag** by day; **~ Tag und Nacht** day and night **(h)** (*Umstand*) **~ dieser Schlacht** during this battle; **~ dem Zugunglück starben viele Menschen** a lot of people died in the train crash; **ich habe ihm ~m Arbeiten** *or* **~ der Arbeit geholfen** I helped him with the work; **~ der Arbeit solltest du keine Musik hören** you shouldn't listen to music while you're working; **er verliert ~m Kartenspiel immer** he always loses at cards; **ich gehe gerne ~ Regen spazieren** I love walking in the rain; **~ Kerzenlicht essen** to eat by candlelight; **~ offenem Fenster schlafen** to sleep with the window open; **etw ~ einer Flasche Wein bereden** to discuss sth over a bottle of wine; **~ zehn Grad unter null** when it's ten degrees below zero; **~ guter Gesundheit sein** to be in good health

(l) (*Bedingung*) in case of; **~ Feuer Scheibe einschlagen** in case of fire break glass; **~ Nebel und Glatteis muss man vorsichtig fahren** when there is fog and ice you have to drive carefully; **~ Regen findet die Veranstaltung im Saale statt** if it rains the event will take place in the hall

(j) (*Grund*) with; **~ seinem Talent** with his talent; **~ reiflicher Überlegung** upon mature reflection; **~ solcher Hitze** when it's as hot as this

(k) (*Einschränkung*) in spite of, despite; **~ aller Vorsicht** in spite of all one's caution; **es geht ~m besten Willen nicht** with the best will in the world, it's not possible

(l) (*in Schwurformeln*) by; **~ Gott** by God; **~ meiner Ehre** (up)on my honour (*Brit*) *or* honor (*US*); **~m Zeus!** by Jove!

beibehalten *ptp* **beibehalten** VT SEP IRREG to keep; *Leitsatz, Richtung* to keep to; *Gewohnheit* to keep up

Beibehaltung F, NO PL keeping; (*von Leitsatz, Richtung*) keeping to; (*von Gewohnheit*) keeping up

beibringen VT SEP IRREG **(a)** *jdm etw ~* (= *mitteilen*) to break sth to sb; (= *zu verstehen geben*) to get sth across to sb **(b)** (= *unterweisen in*) to teach (*jdm etw* sb sth) **(c)** (= *zufügen*) to inflict (*jdm etw* sth on sb) **(d)** (= *herbeischaffen*) to produce; *Dokumente, Beweis, Geld etc* to supply

Beichte ['baɪçtə] F **-, -n** confession; **zur ~ gehen** to go to confession; **(bei jdm) die ~ ablegen** to make one's confession (to sb); **jdm die ~ abnehmen** to hear sb's confession

beichten ['baɪçtn] VTI (*lit, fig*) to confess (*jdm etw* sth to sb); **~ gehen** to go to confession

Beicht-: Beichtgeheimnis NT seal of confession *or* of the confessional; **Beichtstuhl** M confessional

beidbeinig ◼1 ADJ with both legs; *Lähmung of or* in both legs; *Absprung* double-footed ◼2 ADV **~ abspringen** to take off with both feet; **ein ~ gelähmter Mann** a man paralyzed in both legs

beide ['baɪdə] PRON **(a)** (*adjektivisch*) (*ohne Artikel*) both; (*mit Artikel*) two; **alle ~n Teller** both plates; **seine ~n Brüder** both his brothers; **~ Mal** both times

(b) (*als Apposition*) both; **ihr ~(n)** the two of you; **euch ~** the two of you; **euch ~n herzlichen Dank** many thanks to both of you; **wer von uns ~n** which of us (two); **wie wärs denn mit uns ~n?** (*inf*) how about it? (*inf*)

(c) (*substantivisch*) (*ohne Artikel*) both (of them); (*mit Artikel*) two (of them); **alle ~** both (of them); **alle ~ wollten gleichzeitig Geld haben** both of them wanted money at the same time; **keiner/keines etc von ~n** neither of them; **ich habe ~ nicht gesehen** I haven't seen either of them

(d) **~s** (*substantivisch: zwei verschiedene Dinge*) both; **(alles) ~s ist erlaubt** both are permitted

beider-: beiderlei ['baɪdəlaɪ] ADJ ATTR INV both; **beiderseitig** ['baɪdəzaɪtɪç] ADJ (= *auf beiden Seiten*) on both sides; (= *gegenseitig*) *Abkommen, Vertrag etc* bilateral; *Versicherungen, Einverständnis etc* mutual; **beiderseits** ['baɪdəzaɪts] ◼1 ADV on both sides ◼2 PREP +GEN on both sides of

beidhändig ◼1 ADJ (= *mit beiden Händen gleich geschickt*) ambidextrous; (= *mit beiden Händen zugleich*) two-handed ◼2 ADV **~ schießen/schreiben können** to be able to shoot/write with either hand *or* both hands

beidrehen VI SEP (*Naut*) to heave to

beidseitig ['baɪtzaɪtɪç] ◼1 ADJ (= *auf beiden Seiten*) on both sides; (= *gegenseitig*) mutual ◼2 ADV on both sides

beieinander [baɪaɪˈnandə] ADV together

beieinander-: beieinander haben VT IRREG (*inf*) to have together; **du hast sie nicht richtig** *or* **alle beieinander** you can't be all there (*inf*); **beieinander sein** VI IRREG AUX SEIN (*inf*) (*gesundheitlich*) to be in good shape (*inf*); (*geistig*) to be all there (*inf*); **gut ~** to be in good shape; to be all there (*inf*); (*S Ger. = dick sein*) to be a bit chubby (*inf*)

Beifahrer(in) M(F) (*Aut*) (front-seat) passenger; (*bei einem Motorrad, im Beiwagen*) sidecar passenger; (*auf dem Soziussitz*) pillion passenger; (= *berufsmäßiger Mitfahrer, Sport*) co-driver

Beifahrerairbag M (*Aut*) passenger airbag

Beifahrersitz M passenger seat; (*auf Motorrad*) pillion

Beifall M, NO PL (= *Zustimmung*) approval; (= *das Händeklatschen*) applause; (= *Zuruf*) cheering, cheers *pl*; **~**

finden to meet with approval; **~ spenden/klatschen/klopfen** *etc* to applaud

Beifalls-: Beifallsäußerung F expression of (one's) approval; **Beifallsbekundung** F show of (one's) approval; **Beifallsruf** M cheer; **Beifallssturm** M storm of applause

Beifangquote F (*Fischerei*) quota of unwanted catch

beifügen VT SEP (= *mitschicken*) to enclose (+*dat* with); (= *beiläufig sagen*) to add

Beifügung F **(a)** NO PL (*form*) enclosure; **unter ~ eines Fotos** enclosing a photo **(b)** (*Gram*) attribute

Beifuß M, NO PL (*Bot*) mugwort

Beigabe F addition; (= *Beilage: Gemüse, Salat etc*) side dish; (*Comm*: = *Zugabe*) free gift; (= *Grabbeigabe*) burial gift; **unter ~ eines Löffels Senf** adding a spoonful of mustard

beige [beːʃ, 'beːʒə, 'beːʒə] ADJ (*geh: inv*) beige

Beige[1] [beːʃ, 'beːʒə, 'beːʒə] NT **-,** - *or* (*inf*) **-s** beige

Beige[2] ['baɪɡə] F **-, -n** (*S Ger, Aus, Sw*) pile

beigeben SEP IRREG ◼1 VT to add (+*dat* to); (= *mitgeben*) *jdn* to assign (*jdm* to sb) ◼2 VI **klein ~** (*inf*) to give in

Beigeschmack M aftertaste; (*fig: von Worten*) flavour (*Brit*), flavor (*US*); **es hat einen unangenehmen ~** (*lit, fig*) it has an unpleasant taste (to it)

Beihilfe F **(a)** (= *finanzielle Unterstützung*) financial assistance no *indef art*; (= *Zuschuss, Kleidungsbeihilfe*) allowance; (*für Arztkosten*) contribution; (= *Studienbeihilfe*) grant; (= *Subvention*) subsidy **(b)** (*Jur*) abetment; **wegen ~ zum Mord** because of acting as an accessory to the murder

beikommen VI SEP IRREG AUX SEIN *jdm* (= *zu fassen bekommen*) to get hold of sb; (= *fertig werden mit*) to get the better of sb; *einer Sache* (*dat*) **~** (= *bewältigen*) to deal with sth

Beil [baɪl] NT **-(e)s, -e** axe (*Brit*), ax (*US*); (*kleiner*) hatchet; (= *Fleischerbeil*) cleaver

beil. ABBR *von* **beiliegend**

Beilage F **(a)** (= *Gedrucktes*) insert; (= *Beiheft*) supplement **(b)** (= *das Beilegen*) enclosure; (*in Buch*) insertion; (*Aus*: = *Anlage zu Brief*) enclosure **(c)** (*Cook*) side dish; (= *Gemüsebeilage*) vegetables *pl*; (= *Salatbeilage*) side salad; **Erbsen und Kartoffeln als ~ zum Hähnchen** chicken with peas and potatoes

beiläufig ◼1 ADJ **(a)** casual **(b)** (*Aus*: = *ungefähr*) approximate ◼2 ADV **(a)** *erwähnen, bemerken* in passing **(b)** (*Aus*) approximately

beilegen VT SEP **(a)** (= *hinzulegen*) to insert (+*dat* in); (*einem Brief, Paket*) to enclose (+*dat* with, in) **(b)** (= *beimessen*) to attribute (+*dat* to); **einer Sache** (*dat*) **Bedeutung** *or* **Gewicht/Wert ~** to attach importance/value to sth **(c)** (= *schlichten*) to settle

Beilegung ['baɪleːɡʊŋ] F **-, -en** settlement

beileibe [baɪˈlaɪbə] ADV **~ nicht!** certainly not; **das darf ~ nicht passieren** that mustn't happen under any circumstances; **~ kein ...** by no means a ...

Beileid NT condolence(s), sympathy; **jdm sein ~ aussprechen** *or* **ausdrücken** *or* **bezeigen** to offer sb one's condolences; **mein ~!** (*iro*) you have my sympathy!

Beileids-: IN CPDS of condolence *or* sympathy; **Beileidsbekundung** F expression of sympathy; **Beileidskarte** F condolence card

beiliegen VI SEP IRREG (= *beigefügt sein*) to be enclosed (+*dat* with, in); (*einer Zeitschrift etc*) to be inserted (+*dat* in)

beiliegend ADJ, ADV enclosed; **~ senden wir Ihnen ...** please find enclosed ...

beim [baɪm] CONTR *von* **bei dem**

beimengen VT SEP to add (+*dat* to)

beimessen VT SEP IRREG *jdm/einer Sache* **Bedeutung** *or* **Gewicht/Wert ~** to attach importance/value to sb/sth

Bein [baɪn] NT **-(e)s, -e** (*a*) leg; **mit übereinander geschlagenen ~en** cross-legged; **von einem ~ aufs andere treten** to shift from one leg *or* foot to the other; **sich kaum auf den ~en halten können** to be hardly able to stay on one's feet; **er ist noch gut auf den ~en** he's still sprightly; **schwach auf den ~en sein** to be a bit shaky; **jdm ein ~ stellen** (*lit, fig*) to trip sb up; **jdm wieder auf die ~e helfen** (*lit, fig*) to help sb back on his feet; **auf den ~en sein** (= *nicht krank, in Bewegung*) to be on one's feet; (= *unterwegs sein*) to be out and about; **jdm ~e machen** (*inf*) (= *antreiben*) to make sb get a move on (*inf*);

(= *wegjagen*) to make sb clear off (*inf*); **sich** (*dat*) **die ~e in den Bauch** *or* **Leib stehen** (*inf*) to stand around until one is fit to drop (*inf*); **mit beiden ~en im Leben** *or* **auf der Erde stehen** (*fig*) to have both feet (firmly) on the ground; **mit einem ~ im Grab stehen** (*fig*) to have one foot in the grave; **mit einem ~ im Gefängnis stehen** to be likely to end up in jail; **das steht auf schwachen ~en** (*fig*) that isn't very sound; **auf eigenen ~en stehen** (*fig*) to be able to stand on one's own two feet; **auf einem ~ kann man nicht stehen!** (*fig inf*) you can't stop at one!; **wieder auf die ~e kommen** (*fig*) to get back on one's feet again; **etw auf die ~e stellen** (*fig*) to get sth off the ground; *Geld etc* to raise sth; **die ~e breit machen** (*sl: zum Geschlechtsverkehr*) to spread one's legs (*sl*); **sich** (*dat*) **etw ans ~ binden** (*fig*) to saddle oneself with sth; **jdn/etw am ~ haben** (*fig inf*) to have sb/sth (a)round one's neck (*inf*)

(b) (= *Knochen*) bone; **der Schreck ist ihm in die ~e gefahren** the shock went right through him

beinah ['baina:, bai'na:], **beinahe** ['baina:ə, bai'na:ə, bai'na:ə] ADV almost; **~(e) in allen Fällen**, **in ~(e) allen Fällen** in almost every case; **das kommt ~(e) auf dasselbe heraus** that comes to almost the same thing

Bein-: Beinamputation F leg amputation; **Beinarbeit** F (*Sport*) footwork; (*beim Schwimmen*) legwork; **Beinbruch** M fracture of the leg; **das ist kein ~** (*fig inf*) it could be worse (*inf*); **Beinfreiheit** F, NO PL legroom

beinhalten [bə'ɪnhaltn], *ptp* **beinhaltet** VT INSEP (*form*) to comprise

-beinig [bainɪç] ADJ SUF -legged; **zweibeinig** two-legged

beiordnen VT SEP **(a)** (*Gram*) to coordinate **(b)** (= *beigeben*) **jdm/einer Sache beigeordnet sein** to be assigned to sb/appointed to sth; **bei einer Prüfung beigeordnet sein** to sit in on an examination

Beipack M additional consignment; (= *Frachtgut*) part load (*zu* with)

beipacken VT SEP to enclose; *Frachtgut* to add (+*dat* to)

Beipackzettel M instruction leaflet; (= *Inhaltsverzeichnis*) table of contents

beipflichten VI SEP **jdm/einer Sache (in etw** (*dat*)) **~** to agree with sb/sth (on sth)

beirren [bə'ɪrən], *ptp* **beirrt** VT to disconcert; **sich nicht in etw** (*dat*) **~ lassen** not to let oneself be swayed in sth; **sich (durch etw) ~/nicht ~ lassen** to let/not to let oneself be put off (by sth); **er lässt sich nicht ~** he won't be put off; **nichts konnte ihn (in seinem Vorhaben) ~** nothing could shake him (in his intentions)

beisammen [bai'zamən] ADV together

beisammen- PREF together; **beisammenhaben** VT SEP IRREG (*inf*) *Geld, Leute* to have got together; **seine Gedanken ~** to have one's wits about one; **seinen Verstand** *or* **seine fünf Sinne ~** to have all one's wits about one; **(sie) nicht alle ~** not to be all there; **beisammen sein** VI IRREG AUX SEIN (*fig*) (*körperlich*) to be in good shape; (*geistig*) to be all there; **gut ~** to be in good shape; (= *kräftig gebaut sein*) to be well built; **Beisammensein** NT get-together

Beisatz M (*Gram*) appositive

Beischlaf M (*Jur*) sexual intercourse

Beisein NT presence; **in jds ~** in sb's presence; **ohne jds ~** without sb being present

beiseite [bai'zaitə] ADV aside (*auch Theat*); **Spaß** *or* **Scherz ~!** joking aside!; **jdn/etw ~ schaffen** *or* **bringen** to get rid of sb/hide sth away

Beisel ['baizl] NT -s, -n (*Aus inf*) bar

beisetzen VT SEP to bury; *Urne* to install (in its resting place)

Beisetzung ['baizɛtsʊŋ] F -, -en funeral; (*von Urne*) installing in its resting place

Beisl ['baizl] NT -s, -n (*Aus inf*) bar

Beispiel NT example; **zum ~** for example; **wie zum ~** such as; **jdm ein ~ geben** to set sb an example; **sich** (*dat*) **ein ~ an jdm nehmen** to take a leaf out of sb's book; **sich** (*dat*) **ein ~ an etw** (*dat*) **nehmen** to take sth as an example; **mit gutem ~ vorangehen** to set a good example

Beispiel-: beispielhaft 🅱 ADJ exemplary 🅱 ADV exemplarily; **beispiellos** ADJ unprecedented; (= *unerhört*) outrageous; **Beispielsatz** M example

beispielsweise ADV for example

beißen ['baisn], *pret* **biss** [bɪs], *ptp* **gebissen** [gə'bɪsn] 🅱 VTI to bite; (= *brennen*) to sting; (= *kauen*) to chew; **ich kann dieses Brot nicht ~** this bread is too hard for me; **der Hund hat mich** *or* **mir ins Bein gebissen** the dog has bitten my leg *or* me in the leg; **der Rauch/Wind beißt in den Augen/mich in die Augen** (*inf*) the smoke/wind makes one's/my eyes sting; **er wird dich schon nicht ~** (*fig*) he won't bite you; **etwas/nichts zu ~** (= *inf: essen*) something/nothing to eat; **an etw** (*dat*) **zu ~ haben** to have sth to chew over on

🅱 VR (*Farben*) to clash; **sich** (*acc or dat*) **auf die Zunge/Lippen ~** to bite one's tongue/lips; **sich in den Arsch** (*vulg*) *or* **Hintern** (*sl*) **~** to kick oneself (*inf*)

beißend ADJ (*lit, fig*) biting; *Wind auch, Bemerkung* cutting; *Geschmack, Geruch* pungent; *Schmerz* gnawing; *Ironie, Hohn, Spott* bitter

Beißzange ['bais-] F (pair of) pincers *pl*; (*pej inf*) shrew

Beistand M **(a)** NO PL (= *Hilfe*) help; (= *Unterstützung*) support; (*von Priester*) attendance; **jdm ~ leisten** to give sb help; to lend sb one's support **(b)** (*Jur*) legal adviser

Beistandskredit M (*des IWF*) stand-by credit

beistehen VI SEP IRREG **jdm ~** to stand by sb

Beistell-: Beistellherd M auxiliary cooker (*Brit*) *or* kitchen range (*US*); **Beistellmöbel** PL occasional (*Brit*) *or* extra (*US*) furniture *sing*; **Beistelltisch** M occasional table

beisteuern VT SEP to contribute

Beistrich M (*esp Aus*) comma

Beitel ['baitl] M -s, - chisel

Beitrag ['baitra:k] M -(e)s, -¨e [-trɛːgə] **(a)** (= *Anteil*) contribution; **einen ~ zu etw leisten** to make a contribution to sth **(b)** (= *Betrag*) contribution; (= *Versicherungsbeitrag*) premium; (= *Mitgliedsbeitrag*) fee (*Brit*), dues *pl*

beitragen VTI SEP IRREG to contribute (*zu* to); **das trägt nur dazu bei, die Lage zu verschlimmern** that only helps to make the position worse

Beitrags-: beitragspflichtig [-pflɪçtɪç] ADJ *Arbeitsentgelt* contributory; **~ sein** (*Mensch*) to have to pay contributions; **Beitragssatz** M membership rate

beitreten VI SEP IRREG AUX SEIN +DAT to join; *einem Pakt, Abkommen* to enter into; *einem Vertrag* to accede to

Beitritt M joining (*zu etw* sth); (*zu einem Pakt, Abkommen*) agreement (*zu* to); (*zu einem Vertrag*) accession (*zu* to); **seinen ~ erklären** to become a member

Beitritts-: Beitrittserklärung F confirmation of membership; **Beitrittsgesuch** NT application for membership

beiwilligen ['baivɪlɪɡn] VI SEP (*Sw*) = **zustimmen**

Beiwort NT, *pl* -wörter **(a)** (= *Adjektiv*) adjective **(b)** (= *beschreibendes Wort*) epithet

Beiz [baits] F -, -en (*Sw, S Ger. inf*) bar

Beize ['baitsə] F -, -n **(a)** (= *Beizmittel*) corrosive fluid; (= *Metallbeize*) pickling solution; (= *Holzbeize*) stain; (*zum Gerben*) lye; (*Cook*) marinade **(b)** (= *das Beizen*) steeping in a/the corrosive fluid *etc*

beizeiten [bai'tsaitn] ADV in good time

beizen ['baitsn] VT *Holz* to stain; *Häute* to bate; (*Cook*) to marinate

bejahen [bə'jaːən], *ptp* **bejaht** VTI to answer in the affirmative; (= *gutheißen*) to approve of; **das Leben ~** to have a positive attitude toward(s) life

bejahend 🅱 ADJ positive, affirmative; *Einstellung* positive 🅱 ADV affirmatively; **etw ~ beantworten** (*form*) to answer sth in the affirmative

bejubeln *ptp* **bejubelt** VT to cheer; *Ereignis* to rejoice at; **sie wurden als Befreier bejubelt** they were acclaimed as liberators

bekämpfen *ptp* **bekämpft** VT to fight; *Ungeziefer* to control; **sich gegenseitig ~** to fight one another

Bekämpfung [bə'kɛmpfʊŋ] F -, (*rare*) -en fight (*von*, +*gen* against); (*von Ungeziefer*) controlling; **zur ~ der Terroristen** to fight the terrorists

bekannt [bə'kant] ADJ **(a)** (= *allgemein gekannt, gewusst*) well-known (*wegen* for); **die ~eren Spieler** the better-known players; **wie ist er ~ geworden?** how did he become famous?; **sie ist in Wien ~** she is (well-)known in Vienna; **er ist ~ dafür, dass er seine Schulden nicht bezahlt** he is well-known for not paying his debts; **das ist mir ~** I know about that; **sie ist**

mir ~ I know her; **es ist allgemein/durchaus ~, dass ...** it is common knowledge/a known fact that ...; **ich darf diese Tatsachen als ~ voraussetzen** I assume that these facts are known

(b) (= *nicht fremd*) familiar; **jdn mit etw ~ machen** *mit Aufgabe etc* to show sb how to do sth; *mit Gebiet, Fach etc* to introduce sb to sth; *mit Problem* to familiarize sb with sth; **sich mit etw ~ machen** to familiarize oneself with sth; **jdn/sich (mit jdm) ~ machen** to introduce sb/oneself (to sb); *siehe auch* **bekennen**

Bekanntenkreis M circle of acquaintances

Bekannte(r) [bəˈkantə] MF DECL AS ADJ friend; (= *entfernter Bekannter*) acquaintance

Bekanntgabe F announcement; (*in Zeitung etc*) publication

bekannt geben VT IRREG to announce; (*in Zeitung etc*) to publish; **ihre Verlobung geben bekannt ...** the engagement is announced between ...

Bekanntheit F -, NO PL fame; (*von Fakten*) knowledge; **aufgrund der ~ dieser Tatsachen** because these facts are known

bekanntlich [bəˈkantlɪç] ADV **~ gibt es ...** it is known that there are ...; **er hat ~ eine Schwäche für Frauen** he is known to have a weakness for women; **London ist ~ die Hauptstadt Englands** London is known to be the capital of England

bekannt machen VT to announce; (= *der Allgemeinheit mitteilen*) to publicize; *siehe auch* **bekannt**

Bekanntmachung [bəˈkantmaxʊŋ] F -, -en announcement; (= *Veröffentlichung*) publicizing

Bekanntschaft [bəˈkantʃaft] F -, -en **(a)** (= *das Bekanntwerden*) acquaintance; (*mit Materie, Gebiet*) knowledge (*mit* of); **jds ~ machen** to make sb's acquaintance; **mit etw ~ machen** to come into contact with sth; **bei näherer ~** on closer acquaintance **(b)** (*inf.* = *Bekannte*) acquaintance; **meine ganze ~** all my acquaintances; **ich habe gestern eine nette ~ gemacht** I met a nice person yesterday

bekannt werden VI IRREG AUX SEIN to become known; (*Geheimnis*) to leak out

bekehren *ptp* **bekehrt** ◆ VT to convert (*zu* to) ◆ VR to be(come) converted (*zu* to)

Bekehrung [bəˈkeːrʊŋ] F -, -en conversion

bekennen *ptp* **bekannt** [bəˈkant] IRREG ◆ VT to confess; *Wahrheit* to admit ◆ VR **sich (als** *or* **für) schuldig ~** to admit *or* confess one's guilt; **sich zum Christentum /zu einem Glauben/ zu Jesus ~** to profess Christianity/a faith/one's faith in Jesus; **sich zu jdm/etw ~** to declare one's support for sb/sth; **sich nicht zu jdm ~** to deny sb

bekennend ADJ *Katholik, Homosexueller* professed

Bekennerbrief M letter claiming responsibility

Bekenntnis [bəˈkɛntnɪs] NT -ses, -se **(a)** (= *Geständnis*) confession (*zu* of); **sein ~ zum Sozialismus** his declared belief in socialism; **ein ~ zur Demokratie ablegen** to declare one's belief in democracy **(b)** (*Rel.* = *Konfession*) denomination

bekenntnislos ADJ uncommitted to any religious denomination

beklagen *ptp* **beklagt** ◆ VT to lament; *Los* to bewail; *Tod, Verlust* to mourn; **Menschenleben sind nicht zu ~** there are no casualties; *siehe auch* **beklagt** ◆ VR to complain (*über +acc, wegen* about)

beklagenswert ADJ *Mensch* pitiful; *Zustand* lamentable; *Misserfolg, Vorfall, Scheitern* regrettable; *Unfall* terrible

beklagt [bəˈklaːkt] ADJ (*Jur*) **die ~e Partei** the defendant; (*bei Scheidung*) the respondent; **der ~e Ehegatte** the respondent; *siehe auch* **beklagen**

Beklagte(r) [bəˈklaːktə] MF DECL AS ADJ (*Jur*) defendant; (*bei Scheidung*) respondent

beklauen *ptp* **beklaut** VT (*inf*) **jdn** to rob

bekleben *ptp* **beklebt** VT **etw (mit Papier/Plakaten** *etc*) **~** to stick paper/posters *etc* on(to) sth

bekleckern *ptp* **bekleckert** (*inf*) ◆ VT to stain; **ich habe mir das Kleid bekleckert** I've made a mess on my dress ◆ VR **sich (mit Saft** *etc*) **~** to spill juice *etc* all down *or* over oneself; **er hat sich nicht gerade mit Ruhm bekleckert** (*inf*) he didn't exactly cover himself with glory

bekleidet [bəˈklaɪdət] ADJ dressed (*mit* in); **sie war nur leicht ~** she was only lightly *or* (*spärlich*) scantily dressed; **nur mit einer Hose ~ sein** to be wearing only a pair of trousers

Bekleidung F **(a)** (= *Kleider*) clothes *pl*; (= *Aufmachung*) dress; **ohne ~** without any clothes on **(b)** (*form: eines Amtes*) tenure

beklemmen *ptp* **beklemmt** VT (*fig*) to oppress

beklemmend ◆ ADJ (= *beengend*) constricting; (= *beängstigend*) oppressive ◆ ADV oppressively; **der Raum war ~ eng** the room was so small it was oppressive; **~ wirken** to be oppressive

Beklemmung [bəˈklɛmʊŋ] F -, -en USU PL feeling of oppressiveness; (= *Gefühl der Angst*) feeling of apprehension; **~en haben** to be full of apprehension; (*bei enger Kleidung*) to feel restricted

beklommen [bəˈklɔmən] ◆ ADJ apprehensive; *Schweigen* uneasy ◆ ADV apprehensively; **sie saß da und schwieg ~** she sat there in uneasy silence; **~ klingen** to sound troubled

bekloppt [bəˈklɔpt] ADJ (*inf*) *Mensch* mad (*inf*); *Sache* lousy (*inf*)

beknackt [bəˈknakt] (*sl*) ◆ ADJ *Mensch, Frage, Idee* stupid; *Spruch, Frage* idiotic ◆ ADV like a total idiot (*inf*); **~ fragen** to ask stupid questions

beknien *ptp* **bekniet** VT (*inf*) **jdn** to beg

bekommen *ptp* **bekommen** IRREG ◆ VT **(a)** (= *erhalten*) to get; *Schlaganfall, Junges, ein Kind, Besuch* to have; *Spritze, Tadel* to be given; **ein Jahr Gefängnis ~** to be given one year in prison; **wir ~ Kälte/anderes Wetter** the weather is turning cold/is changing; **wir ~ Regen/Schnee** we're going to have rain/ snow; **einen Stein/Ball** *etc* **an den Kopf ~** to be hit on the head by a stone/ball *etc*; **kann ich das schriftlich ~?** can I have that in writing?; **wir haben das große Bett nicht nach oben ~** we couldn't get the big bed upstairs; **was ~ Sie(, bitte)?** what will you have, sir/madam?; **ich bekomme bitte ein Glas Wein** I'll have a glass of wine, please; **was ~ Sie dafür?** how much is that?; **was ~ Sie von mir?** how much do I owe you?; **jdn dazu ~, etw zu tun** to get sb to do sth; **ich bekomme den Deckel nicht abgeschraubt** (*inf*) I can't unscrew the lid

(b) (= *entwickeln*) *Fieber, Schmerzen, Vorliebe, Komplexe* to develop; *Zähne* to get; *Übung, neue Hoffnung* to gain; **Rost/ Risse ~** to get rusty/cracked; **Heimweh ~** to get homesick; **Sehnsucht ~** to develop a longing (*nach* for); **graue Haare/ eine Glatze ~** to go grey (*Brit*) *or* gray (*US*)/bald; **Hunger/Durst ~** to get hungry/thirsty; **Angst ~** to get afraid; **einen roten Kopf ~** to go red

(c) (*mit Infinitivkonstruktion*) to get; **etw zu essen ~** to get sth to eat; **was muss ich denn da zu hören ~?** what's all this I've been hearing?; **es mit jdm zu tun ~** to get into trouble with sb; **etw zu fassen ~** to catch hold of sth; **wenn ich ihn zu fassen bekomme ...** if I get my hands on him ...

(d) (*mit ptp oder adj*) **etw gemacht ~** to get sth done; **etw geschenkt ~** to be given sth (as a present); **etw bezahlt ~** to get paid for sth; **einen Wunsch erfüllt ~** to have a wish fulfilled; **etw satt ~** to have enough of sth

(e) (*in Verbindung mit n*) **Lust ~, etw zu tun** to feel like doing sth; **es mit der Angst/Wut ~** to become afraid/angry; **Ärger ~** to get into trouble; **eine Ohrfeige** *or* **eine** (*inf*) **~** to get it (*inf*); **Prügel** *or* **sie** (*inf*) *or* **es** (*inf*) **~** to get a hiding ◆ VI **(a)** AUX SEIN +DAT (= *zuträglich sein*) **jdm (gut) ~** to do sb good; (*Essen*) to agree with sb; **jdm nicht** *or* **schlecht ~** not to do sb any good; (*Essen*) not to agree with sb; **wie bekommt ihm die Ehe?** how is he enjoying married life?; **es ist ihm schlecht ~, dass er nicht gearbeitet hat** not working did him no good; **wohl bekomms!** your health!

(b) (= *bedient werden*) **~ Sie schon?** are you being attended to *or* served?

> *Vorsicht!* **bekommen** *wird nicht mit dem englischen Wort* **to become** *übersetzt.*

bekömmlich [bəˈkœmlɪç] ADJ *Speisen* (easily) digestible; *Luft, Klima* beneficial; **leicht ~ sein** to be easily digestible; **schwer/ besser ~ sein** to be difficult/easier to digest

Bekömmlichkeit F -, NO PL (*von Speisen*) digestibility; (*von Luft, Klima*) beneficial qualities *pl*

bekräftigen *ptp* **bekräftigt** VT to confirm; *Vorschlag* to back up; **etw nochmals ~** to reaffirm sth; **eine Vereinbarung mit einem Handschlag ~** to seal an agreement by shaking hands

bekriegen *ptp* **bekriegt** VT to wage war on; (*fig*) to fight; **sie ~ sich (gegenseitig) schon seit Jahren** they have been at war with one another for years; **bekriegt werden** to be attacked

bekümmern *ptp* **bekümmert** VT to worry

bekümmert [bə'kʏmɛt] ADJ worried (*über +acc* about)

bekunden [bə'kʊndn], *ptp* **bekundet** VT to show; (*Jur:* = *bezeugen*) to testify to

belabern *ptp* **belabert** VT (*inf*) **jdn ~** to keep on at sb; **er hat mich belabert** (= *überreden*) he talked me into it

belächeln *ptp* **belächelt** VT to smile at

beladen[1] [bə'la:dn], *ptp* **beladen** IRREG **1** VT *Schiff, Zug* to load (up); (*fig: mit Sorgen etc*) **jdn** to burden; **ein Tier mit einer schweren Last ~** to put a heavy load on an animal **2** VR (*mit Gepäck etc*) to load oneself up; **sich mit Verantwortung/Sorgen ~** to take on responsibilities/worries; **sich mit Schuld ~** to incur guilt

beladen[2] [bə'la:dn] ADJ loaded; *Mensch* laden; (*mit Schuld*) burdened; **mit etw ~ sein** to be loaded with sth; (*Mensch*) to be loaded down with sth

Beladung F -, -en loading, lading; (= *Fracht*) load; **höchste zulässige ~** maximum permitted load

Belag [bə'la:k] M -(e)s, -̈e [-'lɛ:gə] coating; (= *Schicht*) layer; (= *Ölfilm etc, auf Zahn*) film; (*auf Pizza, Brot*) topping; (*auf Tortenboden, zwischen zwei Brotscheiben*) filling; (= *Zungenbelag*) fur; (= *Bremsbelag*) lining; (= *Fußbodenbelag*) covering; (= *Straßenbelag*) surface

belagern *ptp* **belagert** VT to besiege

Belagerung F siege

Belagerungszustand M state of siege

belämmert [bə'lɛmɐt] **1** ADJ (= *betreten*) sheepish; (= *niedergeschlagen*) miserable; (*= scheußlich*) *Wetter, Angelegenheit* lousy (*inf*) **2** ADV (= *dumm*) like an idiot

Belang [bə'laŋ] M -(e)s, -e (a) (*no pl:* = *Wichtigkeit*) importance; **von/ohne ~ (für jdn/etw) sein** to be of importance/of no importance (to sb/for *or* to sth) (b) **Belange** PL interests

belangen *ptp* **belangt** VT (*Jur*) to prosecute (*wegen* for); (*wegen Beleidigung, Verleumdung*) to sue

belanglos ADJ inconsequential; **das ist für das Ergebnis ~** that is irrelevant to the result

Belanglosigkeit F -, -en triviality

belassen *ptp* **belassen** VT IRREG to leave; **wir wollen es dabei ~** let's leave it at that; **jdn in dem Glauben ~, dass ...** to allow sb to go on believing that ...; **etw an seinem Ort ~** to leave sth in its place

belastbar ADJ (a) (*mit Last, Gewicht*) **bis zu 50 Tonnen ~ sein** to have a load-bearing capacity of 50 tons; **wie hoch ist diese Brücke ~?** what is the maximum load of this bridge? (b) (*fig*) **daran habe ich bemerkt, wie ~ ein Mensch ist** that made me see how much a person can take; **weiter waren seine Nerven nicht ~** his nerves could take no more (c) (= *beanspruchbar*) (*Med*) resilient; **der Steuerzahler ist nicht weiter ~** the tax payer cannot be burdened any more; **da wird sich zeigen, wie ~ das Stromnetz/unser Wasserhaushalt ist** that will show how much pressure our electricity/water supply will take (d) **wie hoch ist mein Konto ~?** what is the limit on my account?; **der Etat ist nicht unbegrenzt ~** the budget is not unlimited

Belastbarkeit [bə'lastba:ɐkait] F -, -en (a) (*von Brücke, Aufzug*) load-bearing capacity (b) (*von Menschen, Nerven*) ability to cope with stress; (*von Gedächtnis*) capacity (c) (*von Stromnetz etc*) maximum capacity; (*von Mensch, Organ*) maximum resilience; **die höhere physische ~ eines Sportlers** an athlete's higher degree of physical resilience (d) (*von Haushalt*) (maximum) limit (+*gen* of, on)

belasten *ptp* **belastet** **1** VT (a) (*lit*) (*mit Gewicht*) to put weight on; (*mit Last*) to load; **etw mit 50 Tonnen ~** to put a 50 ton load on sth; **den Träger gleichmäßig ~** to distribute weight evenly over the girder; **das darf nur mit maximal 5 Personen/ Tonnen belastet werden** its maximum load is 5 people/tons (b) (*fig*) **jdn mit etw ~** *mit Arbeit* to load sb with sth; *mit Verantwortung, Sorgen, Wissen* to burden sb with sth; **das Gedächtnis mit unnützem Wissen ~** to burden one's memory with useless knowledge; **jdn ~** (= *nervlich, körperlich anstrengen*) to put a strain on sb; **jdn mit zu viel Arbeit ~** to overload sb with work; **jdn mit zu viel Verantwortung** *etc* **~** to overburden sb with responsibility *etc*; **jdn/jds Gewissen/ Seele mit etw ~** (*Mensch*) to burden sb/sb's conscience/soul with sth; **jdn ~** (*Schuld etc*) to weigh upon sb's mind; **jds Gewissen ~** to weigh upon sb's conscience; **das belastet ihn**

sehr that is weighing heavily on his mind (c) (= *beanspruchen*) *Wasserhaushalt, Stromnetz, Leitung* to put pressure on; *Atmosphäre* to pollute; (*Med*) to put a strain on; *Nerven* to strain; *Steuerzahler* to burden; **jdn/etw zu sehr** *or* **stark ~** to overstrain sb/sth; *Wasserhaushalt etc* to put too much pressure on sth (d) (*Jur*) *Angeklagten* to incriminate; **~des Material** incriminating evidence (e) (*Fin*) *Konto* to charge; *Etat* to be a burden on; (*steuerlich*) *jdn* to burden; **etw (mit einer Hypothek) ~** to mortgage sth; **das Konto mit einem Betrag ~** to debit a sum from the account; **jdn mit den Kosten ~** to charge the costs to sb; **dafür werden wir Sie mit 50 Euro ~** we will charge you 50 euros for that **2** VR (a) **sich mit etw ~** *mit Arbeit* to take sth on; *mit Verantwortung* to take sth upon oneself; *mit Sorgen* to burden oneself with sth; **sich mit Schuld ~** to incur guilt; **damit belaste ich mich nicht** (*mit Arbeit, Verantwortung*) I don't want to take that on; **ich will mich nicht ~** (*mit Wissen*) I don't want to know (about it) (b) (*Jur*) to incriminate oneself

belästigen [bə'lɛstɪɡn], *ptp* **belästigt** VT to bother; (= *zudringlich werden*) to pester; (*körperlich*) to molest; (*Licht, Geräusch, Geruch*) to irritate

Belästigung F -, -en annoyance; (*durch Lärm etc*) irritation; (= *Zudringlichkeit*) pestering; **etw als eine ~ empfinden** to find sth a nuisance; **sie beklagte sich über die ~en durch ihren Chef** she complained about being harassed by her boss; **sexuelle ~** sexual harassment

Belastung [bə'lastʊŋ] F -, -en (a) (= *das Belasten*) putting weight on; (*von Fahrzeug, Fahrstuhl*) loading; (= *Last, Gewicht*) weight; (*in Fahrzeug, Fahrstuhl etc*) load; **die erhöhte ~ der Brücke** the increased weight put on the bridge; **maximale ~ der Brücke** weight limit of the bridge; **maximale ~ des Fahrstuhls** maximum load of the lift (b) (*fig*) (= *das Belasten*) (*mit Arbeit*) loading; (*mit Verantwortung etc*) burdening; (= *Anstrengung*) strain; (= *Last, Bürde*) burden (c) (= *Bedrückung*) burden (+*gen* on) (d) (= *Beeinträchtigung*) pressure (+*gen* on); (*von Atmosphäre*) pollution (+*gen* of); (*von Kreislauf, Magen*) strain (+*gen* on) (e) (*Jur*) incrimination (f) (*Fin*) (*von Konto*) charge (+*gen* on); (*von Etat, steuerlich*) burden (+*gen* on); (*mit Hypothek*) mortgage (+*gen* on)

Belastungs-: Belastungsgrenze F (*von Brücke, Balken etc*) weight limit; (*von Fahrzeug*) maximum load; (*von Atmosphäre, Wasserhaushalt*) maximum capacity; (*seelisch, physisch*) limit; (*Elec*) level of peak load; **ich habe meine ~ erreicht** I've reached my limit; **ich habe meine ~ überschritten** I've overdone it; **Belastungsmaterial** NT (*Jur*) incriminating evidence; **Belastungsprobe** F endurance test; **Belastungszeuge** M, **Belastungszeugin** F (*Jur*) witness for the prosecution

belauern *ptp* **belauert** **1** VT to watch (secretly); **jdn misstrauisch ~** to eye sb suspiciously **2** VR to eye each other

belaufen *ptp* **belaufen** VR IRREG **sich auf etw** (*acc*) **~** to come to sth

belauschen *ptp* **belauscht** VT to eavesdrop on

beleben *ptp* **belebt** **1** VT (a) (= *anregen*) to liven up; *Absatz, Konjunktur, jds Hoffnungen* to stimulate (b) (= *lebendiger gestalten*) to brighten up; *siehe auch* **belebt 2** VI **das belebt** that livens you up

belebend **1** ADJ invigorating; **ein ~es Element in etw** (*acc*) **einbringen** to liven sth up **2** ADV **~ wirken** to have a stimulating effect

belebt [bə'le:pt] ADJ *Straße, Stadt etc* busy; *siehe auch* **beleben**

Belebung [bə'le:bʊŋ] F -, -en revival; (*der Wirtschaft, Konjunktur*) stimulation

Beleg [bə'le:k] M -(e)s, -e [-gə] (a) (= *Beweis*) instance, piece of evidence; (= *Quellennachweis*) reference; **~e für den Gebrauch eines Wortes** instances of the use of a word (b) (= *Quittung*) receipt

belegen *ptp* **belegt** VT (a) (= *bedecken*) to cover; *Brote, Tortenboden* to fill; **etw mit Fliesen/Teppich ~** to tile/carpet sth; *siehe auch* **belegt** (b) (= *besetzen*) *Wohnung, Hotelbett, Sitzplatz* to occupy; (*Univ*) *Fach* to take; *Seminar, Vorlesung* to enrol (*Brit*) *or* enroll (*US*) for; **den fünften Platz ~** to take fifth place **(c)** (= *beweisen*) to verify

Belegschaft [bə'le:kʃaft] F **-, -en** (= *Beschäftigte*) staff; (*esp in Fabriken etc*) workforce

Belegschafts-: Belegschaftsaktien PL employees' shares; **Belegschaftsmitglied** NT employee; **Belegschaftsrabatt** M staff discount

belegt [bə'le:kt] ADJ *Zunge* furred; *Stimme* hoarse; *Zimmer, Bett, Wohnung* occupied; **~e Brote** open (*Brit*) *or* open-faced (*US*) sandwiches; *siehe auch* **belegen**

belehren *ptp* **belehrt** VT (= *unterweisen*) to teach; (= *aufklären*) to inform (*über +acc* of); **jdn eines anderen ~** to teach sb otherwise; **sich eines anderen ~ lassen** to learn otherwise

Belehrung [bə'le:rʊŋ] F **-, -en** explanation, lecture (*inf*); (*von Zeugen, Angeklagten*) caution; **deine ~en kannst du dir sparen** there's no need to lecture me

beleidigen [bə'laidɪgn], *ptp* **beleidigt** VT *jdn* to insult; (*Verhalten, Anblick, Geruch etc*) to offend; (*Jur*) (*mündlich*) to slander; (*schriftlich*) to libel

beleidigt [bə'laidɪçt] **1** ADJ insulted; (= *gekränkt*) offended; *Gesicht, Miene* hurt; **die ~e Leberwurst spielen** (*inf*) to be in a huff (*inf*); **bist du jetzt ~?** have I offended you?; **jetzt ist er ~** now he's in a huff (*inf*) **2** ADV in a huff (*inf*), offended

Beleidigung F **-, -en** insult; (*Jur*) (*mündliche*) slander; (*schriftliche*) libel; **eine ~ für den Geschmack** an insult to one's taste; **eine ~ für das Auge** an eyesore; **etw als ~ auffassen** to take sth as an insult

beleihen *ptp* **beliehen** [bə'li:ən] VT IRREG (*Comm*) to lend money on; *Haus, Grundstück* to give a mortgage on

Beleihung F **-, -en** (*Fin*) lending money (*gen* on); (*von Grundstück*) mortgage (*gen* on); **~ einer Versicherung** policy loan; **~ des Vermögens** lending on the property; **~ von Wertpapieren** pledging of securities; **~ von festverzinslichen Wertpapieren** loan on bonds

Beleihungssatz M (*Fin*) lending rate

belemmert [bə'lemɐt] ADJ, ADV *siehe* **belämmert**

belesen [bə'le:zn] ADJ well-read

Belesenheit F **-**, NO PL **eine gewisse ~** wide reading

beleuchten *ptp* **beleuchtet** VT to light up; *Straße, Bühne etc* to light; (*fig* = *betrachten*) to examine

Beleuchtung [bə'bɔyçtʊŋ] F **-, -en (a)** (= *das Beleuchten*) lighting; (= *das Bestrahlen*) illumination; (*fig*) examination **(b)** (= *Licht*) light; (= *das Beleuchtetsein*) lighting; (= *Lichter*) lights *pl*; **die ~ der Straßen** street lighting; **die ~ der Fahrzeuge** lights *pl* on vehicles

beleumdet [bə'lɔymdət], **beleumundet** [bə'lɔymʊndət] ADJ **gut/schlecht ~ sein** to have a good/bad reputation

Belgien ['bɛlgiən] NT **-s** Belgium

Belgier ['bɛlgiɐ] M **-s, -, Belgierin** [-iərɪn] F **-, -nen** Belgian

belgisch ['bɛlgɪʃ] ADJ Belgian

Belgrad ['bɛlgra:t] NT **-s** Belgrade

belichten *ptp* **belichtet** VT (*Phot*) to expose

Belichtung F (*Phot*) exposure

Belichtungs-: Belichtungsdauer F exposure (time); **Belichtungsmesser** M **-s, -** light meter; **Belichtungstabelle** F exposure chart; **Belichtungszeit** F exposure (time)

Belieben [bə'li:bn] NT **-s**, NO PL **nach ~** any way you *etc* want (to); **das steht *or* liegt in Ihrem ~** that is up to you

beliebig [bə'li:bɪç] **1** ADJ any; **(irgend)eine/jede ~e Zahl** any number at all *or* you like; **nicht jede ~e Zahl** not every number; **jeder Beliebige** anyone at all; **eine ganz ~e Reihe von Beispielen** a quite arbitrary series of examples; **in ~er Reihenfolge** in any order whatever; **alles Beliebige** anything whatever; **die Auswahl ist ~** the choice is free **2** ADV as you *etc* like; **Sie können ~ lange bleiben** you can stay as long as you like; **die Zahlen können ~ ausgewählt werden** you can choose any number you like

beliebt [bə'li:pt] ADJ popular (*bei* with); **sich bei jdm ~ machen** to make oneself popular with sb

Beliebtheit F **-**, NO PL popularity

beliefern *ptp* **beliefert** VT to supply

Belladonna [bɛla'dɔna] F **-, Belladonnen** [-'dɔnən] belladonna

bellen ['bɛlən] VI to bark; **etw ins Telefon/Mikrofon ~** to yell sth into the telephone/microphone

bellend ADJ *Husten* hacking; *Stimme* gruff

Belletristik [bɛle'trɪstɪk] F **-**, NO PL fiction and poetry

belletristisch [bɛle'trɪstɪʃ] ADJ *Zeitschrift, Neigung* literary; **~e Literatur** fiction and poetry

belobigen [bə'lo:bɪgn], *ptp* **belobigt** VT to commend

Belobigung F **-, -en** (*form*) commendation

belohnen *ptp* **belohnt**, (*Sw*) **belöhnen** *ptp* **belöhnt** VT to reward; **starker Beifall belohnte den Schauspieler** the actor received hearty applause

Belohnung [bə'lo:nʊŋ] F **-, -en** (*Sw*) **Belöhnung** [bə'lø:nʊŋ] F **-, -en** reward; (= *das Belohnen*) rewarding; **zur *or* als ~ (für)** as a reward (for); **zur ~ der Kinder für ihr gutes Benehmen** in order to reward the children for their good behaviour (*Brit*) *or* behavior (*US*)

belügen *ptp* **belogen** [bə'lo:gn] VT IRREG to lie to; **sich selbst ~** to deceive oneself

belustigen [bə'lʊstɪgn], *ptp* **belustigt** **1** VT to amuse **2** VR (*geh*) **sich über jdn/etw ~** to make fun of sb/sth; **sich an etw** (*dat*) **~** to laugh at sth; **sich mit etw ~** to amuse oneself by (doing) sth

belustigt [bə'lʊstɪçt] **1** ADJ amused **2** ADV in amusement

bemächtigen [bə'mɛçtɪgn], *ptp* **bemächtigt** VR (*geh*) **sich eines Menschen/einer Sache ~** to seize hold of sb/sth; **sich jds ~** (*Gefühl, Gedanke*) to come over sb

bemäkeln *ptp* **bemäkelt** VT to find fault with

bemalen *ptp* **bemalt** VT to paint; **etw mit Blumen ~** to paint flowers on sth; **bemalt sein** (*pej*) to be heavily made up

Bemalung [bə'ma:lʊŋ] F **-, -en** painting

bemängeln [bə'mɛŋln], *ptp* **bemängelt** VT to find fault with; **was die Kritiker an dem Buch ~, ist ...** the fault the critics find with the book is ...

bemannen [bə'manən], *ptp* **bemannt** VT *U-Boot, Raumschiff* to man

Bemannung F **-, -en** manning

Bembel ['bɛmbl] M **-s, -** (*dial*) pitcher

bemerkbar ADJ noticeable; **sich ~ machen** (= *sich zeigen*) to become noticeable; (= *auf sich aufmerksam machen*) to draw attention to oneself

bemerken *ptp* **bemerkt** VT **(a)** (= *wahrnehmen*) to notice; **er bemerkte rechtzeitig/zu spät, dass ...** he realized in time/too late that ... **(b)** (= *äußern*) to remark (*zu* on); **ganz richtig, bemerkte sie** quite right, she said; **nebenbei bemerkt** by the way; **ich möchte dazu ~, dass ...** I would like to say *or* add, that ...; **er hatte einiges zu ~** he had quite a few comments to make

bemerkenswert **1** ADJ remarkable **2** ADV remarkably

Bemerkung [bə'mɛrkʊŋ] F **-, -en** remark (*zu* on)

bemessen *ptp* **bemessen** IRREG **1** VT (= *zuteilen*) to allocate; (= *einteilen*) to calculate; **der Raum ist für eine kleine Gruppe ~** the room is designed for a small group of people; **reichlich ~ generous; knapp ~** not very generous; **meine Zeit ist kurz** *or* **knapp ~** my time is limited **2** VR (*form*) to be proportionate (*nach* to)

Bemessung F (= *Zuteilung*) allocation; (= *Einteilung*) calculation

Bemessungsgrundlage F (*Fin*) basis of assessment

bemitleiden [bə'mɪtlaidn], *ptp* **bemitleidet** VT to pity, to feel sorry for; **er ist zu ~** he is to be pitied; **sich selbst ~** to feel sorry for oneself

bemühen [bə'my:ən], *ptp* **bemüht** **1** VT to bother; *Rechtsanwalt etc* to engage; **jdn zu sich ~** to call in sb **2** VR **(a)** (= *sich Mühe geben*) to try hard; **sich um gute Beziehungen/eine Stelle ~** to try to establish good relations/get a job; **sich um eine Verbesserung der Lage ~** to try to improve the situation; **sich um jdn ~** (*für eine Stelle*) to try to get sb; (*um Kranken etc*) to look after sb; (*um jds Gunst*) to court sb; **bitte ~ Sie sich nicht** please don't trouble yourself; **sich redlich ~** to make a genuine effort; *siehe auch* **bemüht** **(b)** (*geh*: = *gehen*) to proceed (*form*); **sich zu jdm ~** to go to sb

bemüht [bə'my:t] ADJ **~ sein**, *etw zu tun* to try hard to do sth; **um etw ~ sein, darum ~ sein,** *etw zu tun* to be at pains to do sth; *siehe auch* **bemühen**

Bemühung F **-, -en** effort; **vielen Dank für Ihre (freundlichen) ~en** (*form*) thank you for your efforts

bemüßigen [bə'my:sɪgn], *ptp* **bemüßigt** VR (*geh*) **sich einer Sache** (*gen*) ~ to avail oneself of sth; **sich bemüßigt fühlen/ sehen/finden** (*usu iro*) to feel called upon

bemuttern [bə'mʊtɐn], *ptp* **bemuttert** VT to mother

benachbart [bə'naxba:ɐt] ADJ neighbouring *attr* (*Brit*), neighboring *attr* (*US*); **die Häuser sind** ~ the houses are next (door) to one another

benachrichtigen [bə'na:xrɪçtɪgn], *ptp* **benachrichtigt** VT to inform (*von* of)

Benachrichtigung F -, -en (= *Nachricht*) notification; (*Comm*) advice note; **die ~ der Eltern ist in solchen Fällen vorgeschrieben** the parents must be notified in such cases

benachteiligen [bə'na:xtaɪlɪgn], *ptp* **benachteiligt** VT to put at a disadvantage; (*wegen Geschlecht, Klasse, Rasse, Glauben etc*) to discriminate against; **benachteiligt sein** to be at a disadvantage

Benachteiligung F -, -en (= *das Benachteiligen*) disadvantaging; (*wegen Geschlecht, Rasse, Glauben*) discrimination (+*gen* against); (*Zustand*) disadvantage; discrimination *no pl*

benannt ADJ specified

benebeln [bə'ne:bln], *ptp* **benebelt** VT (*inf*) **jdn** *or* **jds Sinne** *or* **jds Kopf** ~ to make sb's head swim; (*Narkose, Sturz*) to make sb feel dazed; **benebelt sein** to be feeling dazed *or* (*von Alkohol*) woozy (*inf*)

Benefiz-: **Benefizspiel** NT benefit match; **Benefizvorstellung** F charity performance

benehmen *ptp* **benommen** [bə'nɔmən] VR IRREG to behave; **benimm dich!** behave yourself!; **sich schlecht** ~ to misbehave

Benehmen [bə'ne:mən] NT -s, NO PL (a) behaviour (*Brit*), behavior (*US*); **kein** ~ **haben** to have no manners (b) (*form*: = *Einvernehmen*) **sich mit jdm ins** ~ **setzen** to get in touch with sb

beneiden *ptp* **beneidet** VT to envy; **jdn um etw** ~ to envy sb sth; **er ist nicht zu** ~ I don't envy him

beneidenswert [bə'naidnsve:ɐt] ❶ ADJ enviable ❷ ADV wonderfully; **reich** enviably; ~ **naiv** (*iro*) amazingly naïve

Benelux ['be:nɛlʊks, bene'lʊks] ABBR *von* **Belgien, Niederlande, Luxemburg**

Beneluxländer ['be:nɛlʊks-, bene'lʊks-] PL, **Beneluxstaaten** PL Benelux countries *pl*

benennen *ptp* **benannt** [bə'nant] VT IRREG to name; **jdn/etw nach jdm** ~ to call sb/sth after *or* for (*US*) sb

bengalisch [bɛŋ'ga:lɪʃ] ADJ Bengalese; *Mensch, Sprache auch* Bengali; **~es Feuer** Bengal light; **~es Hölzchen** Bengal match

Bengel ['bɛŋl] M -s, -(s) boy; (= *frecher Junge*) rascal; **ein süßer** ~ (*inf*) a dear little boy

Benimm [bə'nɪm] M -s, NO PL (*inf*) manners *pl*

Benin [be'ni:n] M -s Benin

Benjamin ['bɛnjami:n] M -s, -e Benjamin; **er ist der** ~ he is the baby of the family

benommen [bə'nɔmən] ADJ dazed; *siehe auch* **benehmen**

Benommenheit F -, NO PL daze

benoten [bə'no:tn], *ptp* **benotet** VT to mark (*Brit*), to grade (*esp US*); **etw mit „gut"** ~ to mark (*Brit*) *or* grade (*esp US*) sth "good"

benötigen *ptp* **benötigt** VT to need; **das benötigte Geld** *etc* the necessary money *etc*

Benotung F -, -en mark (*Brit*), grade (*esp US*); (= *das Benoten*) marking (*Brit*), grading (*esp US*)

benutzbar ADJ usable; *Weg* passable

benutzen *ptp* **benutzt**, (*esp S Ger, Aus, Sw*) **benützen**, *ptp* **benützt** VT to use; *Literatur* to consult; **das benutzte Geschirr** the dirty dishes

Benutzer M -s, -, **Benutzerin** F -, -nen user; (*von Leihbücherei*) borrower

Benutzer-: **benutzerdefiniert** ADJ (*Comput*) user-defined; **benutzerfreundlich** ❶ ADJ user-friendly ❷ ADV **etw** ~ **gestalten** to make sth user-friendly; ~ **konzipiert/designt sein** to be conceived/designed to be user-friendly; **Benutzerfreundlichkeit** F user-friendliness; **Benutzerhandbuch** NT user's guide; **Benutzerkennung** F user ID; **Benutzeroberfläche** F, **Benutzerschnittstelle** F (*Comput*) user interface; **Benutzerpasswort** NT user password

Benutzung F, (*esp S Ger, Aus, Sw*) **Benützung** [bə'nytsʊŋ] F -, -en use; **etw in ~ haben/nehmen** to be/start using sth; **jdm etw zur ~ überlassen** to put sth at sb's disposal

Benutzungsgebühr F charge

Benzin [bɛn'tsi:n] NT -s, -e (*für Auto*) petrol (*Brit*), gas (*US*); (= *Reinigungsbenzin*) benzine; (= *Feuerzeugbenzin*) lighter fuel

Benzin-: **Benzinfeuerzeug** NT petrol lighter (*Brit*), gasoline lighter (*US*); **Benzinkanister** M petrol can (*Brit*), gasoline can (*US*); **Benzinleitung** F fuel pipe, gasoline pipe (*US*); **Benzinpumpe** F (*Aut*) fuel pump; (*an Tankstellen*) petrol pump (*Brit*), gasoline pump (*US*); **Benzinuhr** F fuel gauge; **Benzinverbrauch** M fuel consumption

beobachten [bə'lo:baxtn], *ptp* **beobachtet** VT to observe; **etw an jdm** ~ to notice sth in sb; **jdn** ~ **lassen** (*Polizei etc*) to put sb under surveillance; **er wird von der Polizei beobachtet** he's under police surveillance; **sich beobachtet fühlen** to feel (as if) one is being watched

Beobachter [bə'lo:baxtɐ] M -s, -, **Beobachterin** [-ərɪn] F -, -nen observer

Beobachtertruppen PL (*Mil*) observer force *sing*

Beobachtung F -, -en observation; (*polizeilich*) surveillance; **die ~ habe ich oft gemacht** I've often noticed that

Beobachtungsgabe F talent for observation; **er hat eine gute** ~ he has a very observant eye

beordern *ptp* **beordert** VT to order; (= *kommen lassen*) to summon; (*an andern Ort*) to instruct (to go); **jdn zu sich** ~ to send for sb

bepflanzen *ptp* **bepflanzt** VT to plant

Bepflanzung F (= *das Bepflanzen*) planting; (= *Gesamtheit der Pflanzen*) plants *pl* (+*gen* in)

bepinkeln *ptp* **bepinkelt** (*inf*) ❶ VT to pee on (*inf*) ❷ VR to wet oneself (*inf*)

bepinseln *ptp* **bepinselt** VT to paint (*auch fig*); (*Cook, Med*) to brush; *Zahnfleisch* to paint; (= *voll schreiben*) to scribble on

bepissen *ptp* **bepisst** ❶ VT (*vulg*) to piss on (*sl*) ❷ VR (a) (*vulg*: = *urinieren*) to wet oneself (b) (*sl*: = *sich amüsieren*) to piss oneself (laughing) (*sl*)

bequatschen *ptp* **bequatscht** VT (*inf*) (a) *etw* to talk over (b) (= *überreden*) *jdn* to persuade; **wir haben sie bequatscht, dass sie kommt** we talked her into coming

bequem [bə'kve:m] ❶ ADJ (= *angenehm*) comfortable; *Gast, Schüler* easy; (= *leicht, mühelos*) *Weg, Methode* easy; *Ausrede* convenient; (= *träge*) *Mensch* idle; **es** ~ **haben** to have an easy time of it; **es sich** (*dat*) ~ **machen** to make oneself comfortable; **machen Sie es sich** ~ make yourself at home ❷ ADV (= *leicht*) easily; (= *angenehm*) comfortably; **auf dem Stuhl sitzt es sich** ~ this chair is comfortable to sit in

Bequemlichkeit F -, -en, NO PL (= *Behaglichkeit*) comfort; (= *Trägheit*) laziness

berappen [bə'rapn], *ptp* **berappt** VTI (*inf*) to fork out (*inf*)

beraten *ptp* **beraten** IRREG ❶ VT (a) **jdn** ~ to advise sb; **gut/ schlecht** ~ **sein** to be well-advised/ill-advised; **jdn gut/ schlecht** ~ to give sb good/bad advice; **sich von jdm** ~ **lassen(, wie ...)** to ask sb's advice (on how ...)
(b) (= *besprechen*) to discuss ❷ VI to discuss; **mit jdm über etw** (*acc*) ~ to discuss sth with sb; **sie** ~ **noch** they are still in discussion ❸ VR (= *gegenseitig Rat spenden*) to give each other advice; (= *sich besprechen*) to discuss; **sich mit jdm** ~ to consult (with) sb (*über* +*acc* about); **das Kabinett tritt heute zusammen, um sich zu** ~ the cabinet meets today for talks

beratend ❶ ADJ advisory; *Ingenieur* consultant; **~es Gespräch** consultation ❷ ADV in an advisory capacity; **jdm** ~ **zur Seite stehen** to act in an advisory capacity to sb

Berater [bə'ra:tɐ] M -s, -, **Beraterin** [-ərɪn] F -, -nen adviser

Berater-: **Beratertätigkeit** F consultancy work; **Beratervertrag** M consultancy contract

Beratung [bə'ra:tʊŋ] F -, -en (a) (= *das Beraten*) advice; (*bei Rechtsanwalt, Arzt etc*) consultation (b) (= *Besprechung*) discussion

Beratungs-: **Beratungsgebühr** F consultancy fee; **Beratungsstelle** F advice centre (*Brit*) *or* center (*US*)

berauben *ptp* **beraubt** VT to rob; **jdn einer Sache** (*gen*) ~ to rob sb of sth; *seiner Freiheit, seines Rechtes* to deprive sb of sth; **aller Hoffnung beraubt** having lost all hope

berauschen *ptp* **berauscht** █ VT to intoxicate; (*Geschwindigkeit*) to exhilarate; (*Blut, Gräueltat etc*) to put in a frenzy; **von Glück/Leidenschaft berauscht ...** in transports of happiness/passion ... █ VR **sich an etw** (*dat*) ~ an Wein, *Drogen* to become intoxicated with sth; *an Geschwindigkeit* to be exhilarated by sth; *an Blut, Gräueltat etc* to be in a frenzy over sth

berauschend ADJ *Getränke, Drogen* intoxicating; **das war nicht sehr ~** (*iro*) that wasn't very enthralling

Berber[1] ['bɛrbɐ] M **-s, -** (*auch* **Berberteppich**) Berber carpet

Berber[2] ['bɛrbɐ] M **-s, -, Berberin** [-ərɪn] F **-, -nen** (a) (*in Nordafrika*) Berber (b) (*sl:* = *Penner*) tramp

berechenbar ADJ *Kosten* calculable; *Verhalten etc* predictable

Berechenbarkeit [bə'rɛçnbaːɐkait] F **-**, NO PL (*von Kosten*) calculability; (*von Verhalten etc*) predictability

berechnen *ptp* **berechnet** VT (a) (= *ausrechnen*) to calculate; (= *schätzen*) to estimate; *Worte, Gesten* to calculate the effect of (b) (= *in Rechnung stellen*) to charge; **das ~ wir Ihnen nicht** we will not charge you for it (c) (= *vorsehen*) to intend; **alle Rezepte sind für 4 Personen berechnet** all the recipes are (calculated) for 4 persons

berechnend ADJ (*pej*) calculating

Berechnung F (a) (= *das Berechnen*) calculation; (= *Schätzung*) estimation; **meiner ~ nach, nach meiner ~** according to my calculations (b) (*Comm*) charge; **ohne ~** without any charge (c) (*pej*: = *Eigennutz*) **aus ~ handeln** to act in a calculating manner; **mit kühler ~ vorgehen** to act in a cool and calculating manner; **er ist nur aus ~ so freundlich** (= *weil er etwas will*) he's only being so friendly because he wants something

berechtigen [bə'rɛçtɪɡn], *ptp* **berechtigt** VTI to entitle; (**jdn**) **zu etw ~** to entitle sb to sth; **diese Karte berechtigt nicht zum Eintritt** this ticket does not entitle the bearer to admittance; **er/seine Begabung berechtigt zu den größten Hoffnungen** he/his talent gives grounds for the greatest hopes; **das berechtigt zu der Annahme, dass ...** this justifies the assumption that ...

berechtigt [bə'rɛçtɪçt] ADJ justifiable; *Frage, Hoffnung, Anspruch* legitimate; ~ **sein, etw zu tun** to be entitled to do sth

berechtigterweise [bə'rɛçtɪçtɐ'vaizə] ADV legitimately; (= *verständlicherweise*) justifiably

Berechtigung F **-, -en** (a) (= *Befugnis*) entitlement; (= *Recht*) right; **die ~/keine ~ haben, etw zu tun** to be entitled/not to be entitled to do sth (b) (= *Rechtmäßigkeit*) legitimacy; (= *Verständlichkeit*) justifiability

bereden *ptp* **beredet** █ VT (a) (= *besprechen*) to discuss (b) (= *überreden*) **jdn zu etw ~** to talk sb into sth; **jdn dazu ~, etw zu tun** to talk sb into doing sth (c) (*inf:* = *beklatschen*) to gossip about █ VR **sich mit jdm über etw** (*acc*) ~ to talk sth over with sb

Bereich [bə'raiç] M **-(e)s, -e** (a) area; **in nördlicheren ~en** in more northern regions; **im ~ der Kaserne** inside the barracks; **im ~ des Domes** in the precincts of the cathedral; **im ~ der Innenstadt** in the city centre (*Brit*) *or* center (*US*) (area) (b) (= *Einflussbereich, Aufgabenbereich*) sphere; (= *Sachbereich*) area; (= *Sektor*) sector; **im ~ des Möglichen liegen** to be within the realms of possibility; **in jds ~** (*acc*) **fallen** to be within sb's province

bereichern [bə'raiçɐn], *ptp* **bereichert** █ VT (*lit, fig*) to enrich; (= *vergrößern*) to enlarge; **das Gespräch hat mich sehr bereichert** I gained a great deal from the conversation █ VR **sich auf Kosten anderer ~** to feather one's nest at the expense of other people

Bereicherung F **-, -en** (a) (= *das Bereichern*) enrichment; (= *Vergrößerung*) enlargement; **persönliche ~** (*Jur*) personal gain (b) (= *das Reichwerden*) moneymaking; **seine eigene ~** making money for oneself (c) (= *Gewinn*) boon; **das Gespräch mit Ihnen war mir eine ~** I gained a lot from my conversation with you; **das ist eine wertvolle ~** that is a valuable addition

Bereifung [bə'raifʊŋ] F **-, -en** (*Aut*) set of tyres (*Brit*) *or* tires (*US*); **eine neue ~** a new set of tyres (*Brit*) *or* tires (*US*); **die ~ bei diesem Auto** the tyres (*Brit*) *or* tires (*US*) on this car

bereinigen *ptp* **bereinigt** VT to clear up; **ich habe mit ihr noch etwas zu ~** I have something to clear up with her; **den Markt ~** (*Comm euph*) to remove the competition from the market

bereinigt [bə'rainɪçt] ADJ *Statistik, Quote* adjusted

bereisen *ptp* **bereist** VT *ein Land* to travel around; (*Comm*) *Gebiet* to travel; **die Welt/fremde Länder ~** to travel the world/in foreign countries

bereit [bə'rait] ADJ USU PRED (a) (= *fertig*) ready; **es ist alles zum Aufbruch ~** we're all ready to go; **zum Einsatz ~e Truppen** troops ready to go into action; *siehe* **bereithaben**, **bereithalten** (b) (= *willens*) willing; **zu Zugeständnissen/Verhandlungen ~ sein** to be prepared to make concessions/to negotiate; ~ **sein, etw zu tun** to be willing to do sth; **sich ~ erklären, etw zu tun** to agree to do sth

bereiten [bə'raitn], *ptp* **bereitet** VT (a) (= *zubereiten*) (+*dat* for) to prepare; *Arznei* to make up (b) (= *verursachen*) to cause; *Überraschung, Empfang, Freude, Kopfschmerzen* to give; **er hat mir Schwierigkeiten bereitet** he made difficulties for me; **das bereitet mir Schwierigkeiten** it causes me difficulties; **einer Sache** (*dat*) **ein Ende ~** to put an end to sth

bereit-: **bereithaben** VT SEP IRREG *eine Antwort/Ausrede* ~ to have an answer/excuse ready; **bereithalten** SEP IRREG █ VT *Fahrkarten etc* to have ready; (*für den Notfall*) to keep ready; *Überraschung* to have in store █ VR **sich ~** to be ready; **bereitlegen** VT SEP to lay out ready; **bereitliegen** VI SEP IRREG to be ready; **bereitmachen** VT SEP to get ready

bereits [bə'raits] ADV already; ~ **vor drei Wochen/vor 100 Jahren** even three weeks/100 years ago; ~ **damals/damals, als ...** even then/when ...; **das haben wir ~ gestern** *or* **gestern ~ gemacht** we did that yesterday; **ich warte ~ seit einer Stunde** I've (already) been waiting for an hour; **das hat man mir ~ gesagt** I've been told that already; ~ **am nächsten Tage** on the very next day

Bereitschaft [bə'raitʃaft] F **-, -en** (a) NO PL readiness; **in ~ sein** to be ready; (*Polizei, Feuerwehr, Soldaten etc*) to be on stand-by; (*Arzt*) to be on call *or* (*im Krankenhaus*) on duty; **etw in ~ haben** to have sth ready (b) NO PL (= *Bereitschaftsdienst*) ~ **haben** (*Arzt etc*) to be on call *or* (*im Krankenhaus*) on duty; (*Apotheke*) to be open 24 hours; (*Polizei etc*) to be on stand-by

Bereitschafts-: **Bereitschaftsdienst** M emergency service; ~ **haben** *siehe* Bereitschaft (b); **Bereitschaftspolizei** F riot police

Bereit-: **bereitstehen** VI SEP IRREG to be ready; (*Flugzeug auch, Truppen*) to stand by; **etw ~ haben** to have sth ready; **Ihr Wagen steht bereit** your car is waiting; **zur Abfahrt ~** to be ready to depart; **bereitstellen** VT SEP to get ready; *Material, Fahrzeug, Mittel* to supply; **Bereitstellung** F preparation; (*von Auto, Material, Mitteln*) supply; **Bereitstellungsprovision** F (*Fin*) commitment fee; **bereitwillig** █ ADJ willing; (= *eifrig*) eager █ ADV willingly; *annehmen, Auskunft erteilen* gladly; **Bereitwilligkeit** F willingness; (= *Eifer*) eagerness

bereuen *ptp* **bereut** █ VT to regret; *Schuld, Sünden* to repent of; **das wirst du noch ~!** you will be sorry (for that)! █ VI to repent

Berg [bɛrk] M **-(e)s, -e** [-gə] (a) hill; (*größer*) mountain; **wenn der ~ nicht zum Propheten kommt, muss der Prophet zum ~ kommen** (*Prov*) if the mountain won't come to Mahomet, then Mahomet must go to the mountain (*Prov*); **mit etw hinterm ~ halten** (*fig*) to keep sth to oneself; **mit seinem Alter hinterm ~ halten** (*fig*) to be cagey about sth; **in die ~e fahren** to go to the hills *etc*; **über ~ und Tal** up hill and down dale; **über den ~ sein** (*inf*) to be out of the woods; **über alle ~e sein** (*inf*) to be long gone; **da stehen einem ja die Haare zu ~e** it's enough to make your hair stand on end; **am ~ sein** (*Sw fig:* = *ratlos*) to be in the dark (b) (= *große Menge*) heap; (*von Sorgen*) mass; (*von Papieren*) mountain

Berg- IN CPDS mountain; (= ~*bau-*) mining; **bergab** [bɛrk'|ap] ADV downhill; **es geht mit ihm ~** (*fig*) he is going downhill; **Berghorn** M sycamore (tree); **Bergarbeiter(in)** M(F) miner; **bergauf(wärts)** [bɛrk'|auf(vɛrts)] ADV uphill; **es geht wieder bergauf** (*fig*) things are looking up; **es geht mit seinem Geschäft/seiner Gesundheit wieder bergauf** his business/health is looking up; **Bergbahn** F mountain railway; (= *Seilbahn*) funicular *or* cable railway; **Bergbau** M, NO PL mining

bergen ['bɛrgn], *pret* **barg** [bark], *ptp* **geborgen** [gə'bɔrgn] VT (a) (= *retten*) *Menschen* to save; *Leichen* to recover; *Ladung, Schiff, Fahrzeug* to salvage; **aus dem Wasser tot/lebend geborgen werden** to be brought out of the water dead/alive (b) (*geh:* = *enthalten*) to hold; **diese Möglichkeit birgt die**

Gefahr/das Risiko in sich, dass ... this possibility involves the danger/risk that ...; *siehe auch* **geborgen**

Berg-: **Bergführer(in)** M(F) mountain guide; **Berggipfel** M mountain top; **Berghang** M mountain slope; **Berghütte** F mountain hut

bergig ['bɛrgɪç] ADJ hilly; (= *mit hohen Bergen*) mountainous

Berg-: **Bergkamm** M mountain crest; **Bergkette** F mountain range; **Bergkristall** M rock crystal; **Bergkuppe** F (round) mountain top; **Bergmann** M, *pl* **-leute** miner; **Bergnot** F **in ~ sein/geraten** to be in/get into difficulties while climbing; **jdn aus ~ retten** to rescue sb who was in difficulties while climbing; **Bergrettungsdienst** M mountain rescue service; **Bergrücken** M mountain ridge; **Bergschuh** M climbing boot; **Bergstation** F top station; **bergsteigen** VI SEP IRREG AUX SEIN or HABEN, INFIN AND PTP ONLY to go mountaineering; **(das) Bergsteigen** mountaineering; **Bergsteiger** [-ʃtaɪɡɐ] M **-s, -**, **Bergsteigerin** [-ərɪn] F **-, -nen** mountaineer; **Bergsteigerei** [bɛrkʃtaɪɡə'raɪ] F **-, -en** (*inf*) mountaineering; **bergsteigerisch** ['bɛrkʃtaɪɡərɪʃ] **1** ADJ mountaineering **2** ADV from a mountaineering point of view; **Bergtour** F trip round the mountains; (= *Bergbesteigung*) (mountain) climb; **Berg-und-Tal-Bahn** F roller coaster

Bergung F **-, -en** (*von Menschen*) rescue; (*von Leiche*) recovery; (*von Ladung, Schiff, Fahrzeug*) salvage, salvaging

Bergungs-: **Bergungsarbeit** F rescue work; (*bei Schiffen etc*) salvage work; **Bergungsmannschaft** F, **Bergungstrupp** M rescue team

Berg-: **Bergvolk** NT mountain race; **Bergwacht** F mountain rescue service; **Bergwand** F mountain face; **Bergwanderung** F walk in the mountains; **Bergwelt** F mountains *pl*; **Bergwerk** NT mine; **im ~ arbeiten** to work down the mine

Beriberi [beri'beːri] F **-, NO PL** (*Med*) beriberi

Bericht [bə'rɪçt] M **-(e)s, -e** report (*von* on, *über* +*acc* about, on); (*Sch* = *Aufsatzform*) commentary; **der ~ eines Augenzeugen** an eyewitness account; **~e zum Tagesgeschehen** news reports; **eigener ~** from our correspondent; (*über etw acc*) **~ erstatten** to report (on sth); **jdm über etw** (*acc*) **~ erstatten** to give sb a report on sth

berichten *ptp* **berichtet** VTI to report; (= *erzählen*) to tell; **jdm über etw** (*acc*) **~** to report to sb about sth; (= *erzählen*) to tell sb about sth; **mir ist (darüber) berichtet worden, dass ...** I have been told that ...; **uns wird soeben berichtet, dass ...** (*Rad, TV*) news is just coming in that ...; **wie unser Korrespondent berichtet** according to our correspondent; **gibt es Neues zu ~?** has anything new happened?; **sie hat bestimmt viel(es) zu ~** she is sure to have a lot to tell us

Bericht-: **Berichterstatter** [bə'rɪçtʔɛɐ̯ʃtatɐ] M **-s, -**, **Berichterstatterin** [-ərɪn] F **-, -nen** reporter; (= *Korrespondent*) correspondent; **Berichterstattung** F reporting; **eine objektive ~ objective** reporting; **~ durch Presse/Rundfunk** press/radio reporting; **die ~ über diese Vorgänge in der Presse** press coverage of these events

berichtigen [bə'rɪçtɪɡn], *ptp* **berichtigt** VT to correct; (*Jur*) to rectify

Berichtigung F **-, -en** correction; (*von Fehler auch, Jur*) rectification

Berichtsjahr NT (*Comm*) year under review

beriechen *ptp* **berochen** [bə'rɔxn] VT IRREG to sniff at, to smell; **sich (gegenseitig) ~** (*fig inf*) to size each other up

berieseln *ptp* **berieselt** VT **(a)** (*mit Flüssigkeit*) to spray with water *etc*; (*durch Sprinkleranlage*) to sprinkle **(b)** (*fig inf*) **von etw berieselt werden** (*fig*) to be exposed to a constant stream of sth; **sich von Musik ~ lassen** to have a (constant stream of) music going on in the background

Berieselung [bə'riːzəlʊŋ] F **-, -en** watering; **die ständige ~ der Kunden mit Musik/Werbung** exposing the customers to a constant stream of music/advertisements

Berieselungsanlage F sprinkler (system)

Berlin [bɛr'liːn] NT **-s** Berlin

Berliner[1] [bɛr'liːnɐ] ADJ ATTR Berlin; **~ Weiße (mit Schuss)** light, fizzy beer (with fruit juice added)

Berliner[2] [bɛr'liːnɐ] M **-s, -** (*auch* **Berliner Pfannkuchen**) doughnut (*Brit*), donut (*US*)

berlinerisch [bɛr'liːnərɪʃ] ADJ (*inf*) *Dialekt* Berlin *attr*

berlinern [bɛr'liːnɐn], *ptp* **berlinert** VI (*inf*) to speak in the Berlin dialect

Bermudadreieck [bɛr'muːda-] NT Bermuda triangle

Bermudainseln [bɛr'muːda-] PL, **Bermudas** [bɛr'muːdas] PL Bermuda *sing, no def art*; **auf den ~** in Bermuda

Bermudas [bɛr'muːdas] PL, **Bermudashorts** [bɛr'muːda-] PL Bermuda shorts *pl*

Bern [bɛrn] NT **-s** Bern(e)

Berner ['bɛrnɐ] ADJ ATTR Berne(se)

Bernhardiner [bɛrnhar'diːnɐ] M **-s, -** Saint Bernard (dog)

Bernstein ['bɛrnʃtaɪn] M, NO PL amber

bernsteinfarben [-farbn], **bernsteingelb** ADJ amber

Berserker [bɛr'zɛrkɐ, 'bɛrzɛrkɐ] M **-s, -** (*Hist*) berserker; **wie ein ~ arbeiten/kämpfen** to work/fight like mad (*inf*); **wie ein ~ toben** to go berserk

bersten ['bɛrstn], *pret* **barst** [barst], *ptp* **geborsten** [ɡə'bɔrstn] VI AUX SEIN (*geh*) to crack; (= *aufbersten, zerbrechen*) to break; (= *zerplatzen*) to burst; (*fig: vor Wut etc*) to burst (*vor* with); **zum Bersten voll** (*auch inf*) full to bursting

berüchtigt [bə'rʏçtɪçt] ADJ notorious

berückend [bə'rʏkənt] ADJ charming; **das ist nicht gerade ~** (*iro inf*) it's not exactly stunning

berücksichtigen [bə'rʏkzɪçtɪɡn], *ptp* **berücksichtigt** VT (= *beachten, bedenken*) to take into account; *Mangel, Alter, geringe Erfahrung, körperliches Leiden* to make allowances for; (= *in Betracht ziehen*) *Antrag, Bewerbung, Bewerber* to consider; **meine Vorschläge wurden nicht berücksichtigt** my suggestions were disregarded

Berücksichtigung F **-, -en** consideration; **in** *or* **unter ~ der Umstände/der Tatsache, dass ...** in view of the circumstances/the fact that ...

Beruf [bə'ruːf] M (= *Tätigkeit*) occupation; (*akademischer auch*) profession; (*handwerklicher*) trade; (= *Stellung*) job; **was sind Sie von ~?** what do you do for a living?; **von ~ Arzt/Bäcker/Hausfrau sein** to be a doctor by profession/a baker by trade/ a housewife by occupation; **ihr stehen viele ~e offen** many careers are open to her; **seinen ~ verfehlt haben** to have missed one's vocation; **von ~s wegen** on account of one's job

berufen[1] [bə'ruːfn], *ptp* **berufen** IRREG **1** VT **(a)** (= *ernennen, einsetzen*) to appoint **(b)** (*inf: = beschwören*) **ich will/wir wollen** *etc* **es nicht ~** touch wood (*Brit inf*), knock on wood (*US inf*); **ich will es nicht ~, aber ...** I don't want to tempt fate, but ... **2** VR **sich auf jdn/etw ~** to refer to sb/sth **3** VI (*Aus Jur:* = *Berufung einlegen*) to appeal

berufen[2] ADJ **(a)** (= *befähigt*) *Kritiker* competent; **von ~er Seite, aus ~em Mund** from an authoritative source; **zu etw ~ sein, etw zu tun** to be competent to do sth **(b)** (= *ausersehen*) **zu etw ~ sein** to have a vocation for sth; (*esp Rel*) to be called to sth; **sich zu etw ~ fühlen** to feel one has a mission to be/ do sth

beruflich [bə'ruːflɪç] **1** ADJ professional; **sein ~er Werdegang** his career; **meine ~en Probleme** my problems at work **2** ADV professionally, jobwise; **~ ist sie sehr erfolgreich** she is very successful in her career; **sich ~ weiterbilden** to undertake further job *or* professional training; **er ist ~ viel unterwegs** he is away a lot on business; **sich ~ verbessern** to get a better job; **was machen Sie ~?** what do you do for a living?

Berufs- IN CPDS professional; **Berufsanfänger(in)** M(F) **sie ist ~in** she has just entered the job market; **wir suchen Lexikografen, keine ~** vacancies for lexicographers, experience necessary; **Berufsausbildung** F training (*for an occupation*); (*für Handwerk*) vocational training; **Berufsaussichten** PL job prospects *pl*; **berufsbedingt** ADJ occupational; **Berufsberater(in)** M(F) careers adviser; **Berufsberatung** F careers guidance; **Berufsbezeichnung** F job title; **berufsbezogen** [-batso:gn] **1** ADJ relevant to one's job; *Unterricht* vocationally orientated **2** ADV practically orientated; **Berufserfahrung** F (professional) experience; **Berufsfachschule** F training college (*attended full-time*); **Berufsfeuerwehr** F fire service; **berufsfremd** ADJ *Tätigkeit* unconnected with one's occupation; *Mensch* from outside the/a profession/trade; **Berufsfußball** M professional football (*Brit*) *or* soccer (*US*); **Berufsgeheimnis** NT professional secret; **Berufsgenossenschaft** F *siehe* **Beruf** professional/trade association; **Berufsgruppe** F occupational group; **Berufsheer** NT professional army; **Berufskleidung** F working clothes *pl*; **Berufskrankheit** F occupational disease; **Berufsleben** NT working life; **im ~ stehen** to be working; **berufsmäßig** **1** ADJ professional **2** ADV professionally; **etw ~ betreiben** to do sth

professionally; **Berufsrisiko** NT occupational hazard;
Berufsschule F vocational school, ≈ technical college (Brit);
Berufsschüler(in) M(F) student at a vocational school, ≈
student at a technical college (Brit); **Berufssoldat(in)** M(F)
professional soldier; **Berufsspieler(in)** M(F) professional
player; **berufstätig** ADJ working; **~ sein** to be working, to
work; **halbtags ~ sein** to work part-time; **ich bin auch ~** I go
out to work too; **nicht mehr ~ sein** to have left work;
Berufstätige(r) [-tɛːtɪɡə] MF DECL AS ADJ working person;
Berufstätigkeit F occupation; **während meiner ~** during my
working life; **Frauen** (dat) **die ~ ermöglichen** to enable
women to go out to work; **Bewerber sollten eine dreijährige
~ nachweisen können** applicants should be able to provide
proof of three years' work experience; **berufsunfähig** ADJ
occupationally disabled; **Berufsunfähigkeit** F inability to
practise one's profession; **Berufsunfähigkeitsrente** F
disability pension (Brit), disability (US); **Berufsverband** M siehe
Beruf professional/trade organization or association;
Berufsverbot NT exclusion from a civil service profession by
government ruling; **jdm ~ erteilen** to ban sb from a profession;
Berufsverkehr M commuter traffic; **Berufswahl** F siehe **Beruf**
choice of occupation/profession/trade

Berufung [bəˈruːfʊŋ] F -, **-en (a)** (Jur) appeal; **in die ~ gehen**, **~
einlegen** to appeal (bei to) **(b)** (in ein Amt etc) appointment
(auf or an +acc to) **(c)** (= innerer Auftrag) vocation **(d)** (form)
die ~ auf jdn/etw reference to sb/sth; **unter ~ auf etw** (acc)
with reference to sth

beruhen ptp **beruht** VI to be based (auf +dat on); **das beruht
auf Gegenseitigkeit** (inf) the feeling is mutual; **etw auf sich ~
lassen** to let sth rest

beruhigen [bəˈruːɪɡn], ptp **beruhigt** ◼ VT to calm (down); Baby
to quieten (Brit), to quiet (US); (= trösten) to comfort;
(= versichern) to reassure; Magen to settle; Nerven, Verkehr to
calm; Gewissen, Schmerzen to ease; **na, dann bin ich ja
beruhigt** well I must say I'm quite relieved; **dann kann ich ja
beruhigt schlafen/nach Hause gehen** then I can go to sleep/
go home with my mind at rest; **~d** (körperlich)
(= beschwichtigend) soothing; (= tröstlich) reassuring
◼ VR to calm down; (Gewissen) to be eased; (Andrang, Verkehr,
Kämpfe) to subside; (Börse, Preise, Magen) to settle down;
(Krämpfe, Schmerzen) to ease; (Meer) to become calm; (Sturm)
to die down; **beruhige dich doch!** calm down!

Beruhigung F -, NO PL **(a)** (= das Beruhigen) calming (down);
(von Baby) quietening (Brit), quieting (US); (= das Trösten)
comforting; (von Magen) settling; (von Nerven) soothing;
(von Verkehr) calming; (von Gewissen, Schmerzen) easing; **zu
Ihrer ~ kann ich sagen ...** you'll be reassured to know that ...
(b) (= das Sichberuhigen) calming down; (von Gewissen)
easing; (von Andrang, Verkehr, Kämpfen) subsiding; (von Börse,
Preisen, Magen) settling down; (von Meer) calming; (von
Sturm) abatement; **ein Gefühl der ~** a reassuring feeling

Beruhigungs-: **Beruhigungsmittel** NT sedative;
Beruhigungsspritze F sedative (injection);
Beruhigungstablette F tranquillizer (Brit), tranquilizer (US),
downer (inf)

berühmt [bəˈryːmt] ADJ famous; **wegen** or **für etw ~ sein** to be
famous for sth; **das war nicht ~** (inf) it was nothing to write
home about (inf)

berühmt-berüchtigt ADJ notorious

Berühmtheit F -, **-en (a)** fame; **~ erlangen** to become famous;
zu trauriger ~ gelangen to become notorious **(b)** (= Mensch)
celebrity

berühren ptp **berührt** ◼ VT **(a)** (= anfassen, streifen) (Math) to
touch; (= grenzen an) to border on; (= erwähnen) Thema,
Punkt to touch on; **Berühren verboten** do not touch
(b) (= seelisch bewegen) to move; (= auf jdn wirken) to affect;
(= betreffen) to concern; **das berührt mich gar nicht!** that's
nothing to do with me; **von etw peinlich/schmerzlich berührt
sein** to be embarrassed/pained by sth; **es berührt mich
angenehm/seltsam, dass ...** I am pleased/surprised that ...
◼ VR to touch; (Ideen, Vorstellungen, Interessen) to coincide

Berührung F -, **-en** touch; (zwischen Drähten etc)
(= menschlicher Kontakt) contact; (= Erwähnung) mention; **mit
jdm/etw in ~ kommen** to come into contact with sb/sth;
körperliche ~ physical contact

Berührungs-: **Berührungsangst** F USU PL reservation (mit
about); **die Berührungsängste vor diesem Thema sind noch
groß** there is still great reluctance to deal with this subject;

Berührungsbildschirm M touch screen; **berührungssensitiv**
ADJ (Comput) touch-sensitive; **~er Bildschirm** touch screen
bes. ABBR von besonders

besagen ptp **besagt** VT to say; (= bedeuten) to mean; **das
besagt nichts** that does not mean anything; **das besagt viel**
that means a lot; **das besagt nicht, dass ...** that does not
mean (to say) that ...

besagt [bəˈzaːkt] ADJ ATTR (form) said (form)

Besan [beˈzaːn, ˈbeːzaːn] M **-s, -e** (Naut) mizzen

besänftigen [bəˈzɛnftɪɡn], ptp **besänftigt** VT to calm down; jds
Zorn, Erregung, Gemüt to soothe; **er war nicht zu ~** it was
impossible to calm him down

Besatzung F **(a)** (= Mannschaft) crew; (= Verteidigungstruppe)
garrison (by (= Besatzungsarmee) occupying army

besaufen ptp **besoffen** [bəˈzɔfn] VR IRREG (inf) to get plastered
(inf); siehe auch **besoffen**

Besäufnis [bəˈzɔyfnɪs] NT **-ses, -se** (inf) booze-up (inf), chug-a-
lug (US inf)

beschädigen ptp **beschädigt** VT to damage

Beschädigung [bəˈʃɛːdɪɡʊŋ] F -, **-en** damage (von to)

beschaffen[1] [bəˈʃafn], ptp **beschafft** VT to get (hold of); **jdm
etw ~** to get (hold of) sth for sb; **jdm/sich eine Stelle ~** to get
sb/oneself a job

beschaffen[2] ADJ (form) **wie ist es mit seiner Gesundheit ~?**
what about his health?; **mit jdm/damit ist es gut/schlecht ~**
sb/it is in a good/bad way; **so ~ sein wie ...** to be the same
as ...; **das ist so ~, dass ...** that is such that ...

Beschaffenheit F -, NO PL composition; (körperlich)
constitution; (seelisch) nature

Beschaffung F -, NO PL obtaining

Beschaffungskriminalität F drug-related crime

beschäftigen [bəˈʃɛftɪɡn], ptp **beschäftigt** ◼ VR **sich mit etw ~**
to occupy oneself with sth; (= sich befassen, abhandeln) to
deal with sth; **sich mit dem Tod ~** to think about death; **sich
mit Literatur ~** to study literature; **sich mit der Frage ~, ob ...**
to consider the question of whether ...; **sich mit jdm ~** to
devote one's attention to sb; **sie beschäftigt sich viel mit den
Kindern** she devotes a lot of her time to the children; **sie
beschäftigt sich gerade mit den Kindern** she is busy with the
children just now
◼ VT **(a)** (= innerlich ~) **jdn ~** to be on sb's mind
(b) (= anstellen) to employ
(c) (= eine Tätigkeit geben) to occupy; **jdn mit etw ~** to give sb
sth to do

beschäftigt [bəˈʃɛftɪçt] ADJ busy; **mit dem Nähen/jdm ~ sein**
to be busy sewing/with sb; **mit sich selbst/seinen Problemen
~ sein** to be preoccupied with oneself/one's problems
(b) (= angestellt) employed (bei by, at)

Beschäftigte(r) [bəˈʃɛftɪçtə] MF DECL AS ADJ employee

Beschäftigung F -, **-en (a)** (= berufliche Arbeit) work no indef
art, job; (= Anstellung, Angestelltsein) employment; **eine ~
suchen** to be looking for work; **einer ~ nachgehen** (form) to
be employed; **ohne ~ sein** to be unemployed
(b) (= Tätigkeit) activity, occupation; **jdm eine ~ geben** to
give sb something to do
(c) (= geistige ~) preoccupation; (mit Frage) consideration;
(mit Thema) treatment (mit of); (mit Literatur) study (mit of)
(d) (von Kindern, Patienten etc) occupying

Beschäftigungs-: **Beschäftigungsgrad** M level of
employment; **beschäftigungslos** ADJ unoccupied;
(= arbeitslos) unemployed; **Beschäftigungsprogramm** NT job
creation scheme; **Beschäftigungstherapeut(in)** M(F)
occupational therapist; **Beschäftigungstherapie** F
occupational therapy

beschämen ptp **beschämt** VT to shame; (jds Großzügigkeit) to
embarrass; **es beschämt mich, zu sagen ...** I feel ashamed to
have to say ...; **beschämt** ashamed

beschämend ADJ **(a)** (= schändlich) shameful; **es war ~ für
seine ganze Familie** it brought shame on his whole family
(b) (= vorbildlich) shaming; Großzügigkeit embarrassing
(c) (= demütigend) humiliating

Beschämung [bəˈʃɛːmʊŋ] F -, (rare) **-en** shame; (= Verlegenheit)
embarrassment; **zu meiner ~** to my shame

beschatten [bəˈʃatn], ptp **beschattet** VT to (= überwachen) to tail;
jdn ~ lassen to have sb tailed

Beschattung F -, **-en** tailing

beschaulich [bəˈʃaulɪç] **1** ADJ (= geruhsam) *Leben, Abend* quiet; *Charakter, Mensch* pensive **2** ADV (= geruhsam) quietly; ~ **dasitzen** to sit contemplating; ~ **leben** to lead a simple life

Bescheid [bəˈʃait] M -(e)s, -e [-də] (a) (= *Auskunft*) information; (= *Nachricht*) notification; (= *Entscheidung auf Antrag etc*) decision; **wir erwarten Ihren** ~ we look forward to hearing from you; **ich warte noch auf** ~ I am still waiting to hear; **jdm (über etw** (*acc*) *or* **von etw)** ~ **sagen** *or* **geben** to let sb know (about sth); **jdm ordentlich** ~ **sagen, jdm gründlich** ~ **stoßen** (*inf*) to tell sb where to get off (*inf*); ~ **hinterlassen** to leave word
(b) (**über etw** *acc or* **in etw** *dat*) ~ **wissen** to know (about sth); **weißt du** ~ **wegen Samstagabend?** do you know about Saturday evening?; **ich weiß hier nicht** ~ I don't know about things around here; **er weiß gut** ~ he is well informed; **auf dem Gebiet weiß ich nicht** ~ I don't know much about that sort of thing; **weißt du schon** ~? do you know?, have you heard?; **sag ihr, Egon habe angerufen, dann weiß sie schon** ~ if you tell her Egon phoned she'll understand

bescheiden [bəˈʃaidn] **1** ADJ (a) modest; **in** ~**en Verhältnissen leben** to live modestly; **eine** ~**e Frage** one small question; **aus** ~**en Anfängen** from humble beginnings (b) (*euph*: = *beschissen*) awful; (*inf*: = *mäßig*) mediocre **2** ADV (a) *leben* modestly; **darf ich mal** ~ **fragen, ob** ... may I venture to ask whether ... (b) (*euph*) *sich fühlen* terrible; *spielen* terribly

Bescheidenheit F -, NO PL modesty; **nur keine falsche** ~ no false modesty now

bescheinigen [bəˈʃainɪgn], *ptp* **bescheinigt** VT to certify; *Gesundheit, Tauglichkeit* to confirm in writing; *Empfang* to confirm; (*durch Quittung*) to give a receipt for; (*inf*: = *mündlich bestätigen*) to confirm; **sich** (*dat*) **die Arbeit/Überstunden** ~ **lassen** to get written confirmation of having done the work/overtime; **können Sie mir** ~, **dass** ... can you give me written confirmation that ...; **hiermit wird bescheinigt, dass** ... this is to certify that ...; **jdm äußerste Kompetenz** ~ to confirm sb's extreme competence

Bescheinigung F -, -en (= *das Bescheinigen*) certification; (*der Gesundheit, Tauglichkeit*) confirmation; (= *Schriftstück*) certificate; written confirmation; (= *Quittung*) receipt

bescheißen *ptp* **beschissen** [bəˈʃisn] VTI IRREG (*inf*) to cheat (*um* out of); *siehe auch* **beschissen**

beschenken *ptp* **beschenkt** VT *jdn* to give presents/a present to; **jdn mit etw** ~ to give sb sth (as a present); (**gegenseitig**) ~ to give each other presents; **jdn reich** ~ to shower sb with presents; **damit bin ich reich beschenkt** that's very generous

Bescherung [bəˈʃeːrʊŋ] F -, -en (a) (= *Feier*) giving out of Christmas presents (b) (*iro inf*) **das ist ja eine schöne** ~! this is a nice mess; **die (ganze)** ~ the (whole) mess; **da haben wir die** ~! what did I tell you!

bescheuert [bəˈʃɔyɐt] (*inf*) **1** ADJ stupid **2** ADV **sich** ~ **anstellen** to act stupidly; **wie** ~ **putzen** to clean like crazy (*inf*); ~ **aussehen** to look ridiculous; ~ **fragen** to ask idiotic questions

beschichten *ptp* **beschichtet** VT (*Tech*) to coat; **mit Kunststoff beschichtet** laminated; **PVC-beschichtet** PVC-coated

beschießen *ptp* **beschossen** [bəˈʃɔsn] VT IRREG to shoot at; (*mit Geschützen, Phys*) to bombard

beschildern *ptp* **beschildert** VT to put a sign *or* notice/signs *or* notices on; (*mit Schildchen*) to label; (*mit Verkehrsschildern*) to signpost

Beschilderung F -, -en (*mit Schildchen*) labelling (*Brit*), labeling (*US*); (*mit Verkehrsschildern*) signposting; (= *Schilder*) signs *pl*; (= *Schildchen*) labels *pl*; (= *Verkehrsschilder*) signposts *pl*

beschimpfen *ptp* **beschimpft** VT *jdn* to swear at, to abuse; **jdn als Nazi** ~ to accuse sb of being a Nazi

Beschimpfung [bəˈʃɪmpfʊŋ] F -, -en (a) (= *das Beschimpfen*) abusing, swearing (+*gen* at); (*Jur*) slander (+*gen* on) (b) (= *Schimpfwort*) insult

Beschiss [bəˈʃɪs] M -es, -e (*inf*) rip off (*inf*); **das ist** ~ it's a swindle

beschissen [bəˈʃisn] (*inf*) **1** ADJ lousy (*inf*), shitty (*inf*) **2** ADV **das schmeckt** ~ that tastes lousy (*inf*); **mir gehts** ~ I feel shitty (*sl*); **jdn** ~ **verhalten** to behave like a louse (*inf*); **jdn** ~ **behandeln** to treat sb like a (piece of) shit (*sl*); **wir werden** ~ **bezahlt** our pay is lousy (*inf*); **ich komme mir echt** ~ **vor** I feel really shitty (*inf*); *siehe auch* **bescheißen**

Beschlag M (a) (*an Koffer, Truhe, Buch*) (ornamental) fitting; (*an Tür, Fenster, Möbelstück, Sattel*) (ornamental) mounting; (*von Pferd*) shoes *pl* (b) (*auf Metall*) tarnish; (*auf Glas, Spiegel etc*) condensation (c) (*das* ~) **belegen, jdn/etw in** ~ **nehmen** to monopolize sb/sth; **mit** ~ **belegt sein** to be being used; (*Mensch*) to be occupied

beschlagen¹ *ptp* **beschlagen** IRREG **1** VT *Truhe, Möbel, Tür* to put (metal) fittings on; *Huftier* to shoe **2** VIR (*vi: aux sein*) (*Brille, Glas, Wand*) to get steamed up; (*Silber etc*) to tarnish

beschlagen² ADJ (= *erfahren*) well-versed; **in etw** (*dat*) (**gut**) ~ **sein** to be well-versed in sth; **auf einem Gebiet** ~ **sein** to be well-versed in a subject

Beschlagenheit F -, NO PL sound knowledge (*in* +*dat* of)

beschlagnahmen [bəˈʃlaːknaːmən], *ptp* **beschlagnahmt** VT (a) (= *konfiszieren*) to confiscate; *Vermögen, Grundbesitz, Drogen* to seize; *Kraftfahrzeug, Boot* to impound (b) (*inf*: = *in Anspruch nehmen*) (*Mensch*) to monopolize; (*Arbeit*) *Zeit* to take up

beschleunigen [bəˈʃlɔynɪgn], *ptp* **beschleunigt** **1** VT to accelerate; *Verfall, wirtschaftlichen Zusammenbruch etc* to hasten; **die Angst beschleunigte ihre Schritte** fear quickened her steps; *siehe auch* **beschleunigt** **2** VR to accelerate; (*Verfall, Zusammenbruch*) to be hastened **3** VI (*Fahrzeug, Fahrer*) to accelerate

beschleunigt [bəˈʃlɔynɪçt] ADJ faster; ~**es Verfahren** (*Jur*) summary proceedings *pl*; *siehe auch* **beschleunigen**

Beschleunigung F -, -en acceleration (*auch Aut, Phys*); (*von Verfall etc*) hastening

beschließen *ptp* **beschlossen** [bəˈʃlɔsn] IRREG **1** VT (a) (= *Entschluss fassen*) to decide on; *Gesetz* to pass; *Statuten* to establish; ~, **etw zu tun** to decide to do sth (b) (= *beenden*) to end **2** VI **über etw** (*acc*) ~ to decide on sth; *siehe auch* **beschlossen**

beschlossen [bəˈʃlɔsn] ADJ decided; **das ist** ~**e Sache** that's settled; *siehe auch* **beschließen**

Beschluss M (= *Entschluss*) decision; **einen** ~ **fassen** to pass a resolution; **auf** ~ **des Gerichts** by order of the court; **wie lautete der** ~ **des Gerichts?** what was the court's decision?

Beschluss-: **beschlussfähig** ADJ ~ **sein** to have a quorum; ~**e Anzahl** quorum; **Beschlussfähigkeit** F, NO PL quorum; **beschlussunfähig** ADJ ~ **sein** not to have a quorum; **Beschlussunfähigkeit** F lack of a quorum

beschmeißen *ptp* **beschmissen** [bəˈʃmɪsn] VT IRREG (*inf*) to bombard

beschmunzeln *ptp* **beschmunzelt** VT to smile (quietly) at

beschmutzen *ptp* **beschmutzt** **1** VT to (make *or* get) dirty; (*fig*) *Ruf, Namen* to sully; *Ehre* to stain **2** VR to get oneself dirty

beschneiden *ptp* **beschnitten** [bəˈʃnɪtn] VT IRREG (a) (= *stutzen*) to trim; *Sträucher, Reben, Bäume* to prune; *Flügel* to clip (b) (*Med, Rel*) to circumcise (c) (*fig*: = *beschränken*) to curtail

Beschneidung [bəˈʃnaidʊŋ] F -, -en (*Med, Rel*) circumcision

beschneien *ptp* **beschneit** VT to cover with artificial snow

beschneit [bəˈʃnait] ADJ snow-covered

beschnüffeln *ptp* **beschnüffelt** **1** VT to sniff at; (*fig*) *jdn* to size up; (= *bespitzeln*) to spy out **2** VR (*Hunde*) to have a sniff at each other; (*fig*) to size each other up

beschnuppern *ptp* **beschnuppert** VTR = **beschnüffeln**

beschönigen [bəˈʃøːnɪgn], *ptp* **beschönigt** VT to gloss over; ~**der Ausdruck** euphemism; ... **sagte er** ~**d** ... he said, trying to make things seem better

beschränken [bəˈʃrɛŋkn], *ptp* **beschränkt** **1** VT (*auf* +*acc* to) to limit, to restrict **2** VR (*auf* +*acc* to) to limit, to restrict; (= *sich einschränken*) to restrict oneself

beschrankt [bəˈʃraŋkt] ADJ *Bahnübergang* with gates

beschränkt [bəˈʃrɛŋkt] **1** ADJ limited; **wir sind räumlich/zeitlich/finanziell** ~ we have only a limited amount of space/time/money; ~**e Haftung** limited liability; **wie kann man nur so** ~ **sein?** how can anyone be so stupid? **2** ADV (a) (= *knapp*) ~ **leben** to live on a limited income; ~ **wohnen** to live in cramped conditions (b) (*pej*) like an idiot

Beschränktheit F -, NO PL (a) (*Knappheit*) **die** ~ **der Plätze/unserer Mittel** the limited (number of) places/our limited means (b) (*geistig*) limited intelligence; (= *Engstirnigkeit*) narrowness; **er konnte in seiner** ~ **nicht begreifen, dass** ... his simple mind could not grasp that ...

Beschränkung F -, -en restriction (*auf +acc* to); **jdm ~en auferlegen** to impose restrictions on sb

beschreiben *ptp* **beschrieben** [bəˈʃriːbn] VT IRREG (a) (= *darstellen*) to describe; **sein Glück/Schmerz war nicht zu ~** his happiness/pain was indescribable; **ich kann dir nicht ~, wie erleichtert ich war** I can't tell you how relieved I was; **~de Psychologie/Grammatik** descriptive psychology/grammar (b) (= *voll schreiben*) to write on (c) *Kreis, Bahn* to describe

Beschreibung F description

beschreiten *ptp* **beschritten** [bəˈʃrɪtn] VT IRREG (*fig*) to follow

beschriften [bəˈʃrɪftn], *ptp* **beschriftet** VT to write on; *Grabstein, Sockel etc* to inscribe; (*mit Aufschrift*) to label; *Umschlag* to address; **die Funde waren mit Tusche beschriftet** the finds were marked with ink

Beschriftung F -, -en (a) (= *das Beschriften*) inscribing; (*mit Etikett*) labelling (*Brit*), labeling (*US*); (*von Umschlag*) addressing; (*von Funden*) marking (b) (= *Aufschrift*) writing; (*auf Grabstein, Sockel*) inscription; (= *Etikett*) label

beschuldigen [bəˈʃʊldɪgn], *ptp* **beschuldigt** VT to accuse

Beschuldigung F -, -en accusation; (*esp Jur auch, liter*) charge

beschummeln *ptp* **beschummelt** VTI (*inf*) to cheat

Beschuss M -es, NO PL (*Mil*) fire; (*Phys*) bombardment; **jdn/etw unter ~ nehmen** (*Mil*) to (start to) bombard *or* shell sb/sth; (*fig*) to attack sb/sth; **unter ~ geraten** (*Mil, fig*) to come under fire

beschützen *ptp* **beschützt** VT to protect (*vor +dat* from); **~d** protective

Beschützer [bəˈʃʏtsɐ] M -s, -, **Beschützerin** [-ərɪn] F -, -nen protector; (*Frau auch*) protectress

beschwatzen *ptp* **beschwatzt**, (*esp S Ger*) **beschwätzen**, *ptp* **beschwätzt** VT (*inf*) (a) (= *überreden*) to talk over; **jdn zu etw ~** to talk sb into sth; **sich zu etw ~ lassen** to get talked into sth (b) (= *bereden*) to chat about

Beschwerde [bəˈʃveːɐdə] F -, -n (a) (= *Klage*) complaint; (*Jur*) appeal; **eine ~ gegen jdn** a complaint about sb; **~ führen** *or* **einlegen** *or* **erheben** (*form*) to lodge a complaint (b) (= *Leiden*) **Beschwerden** PL trouble; **das macht mir immer noch ~n** it's still giving me trouble; **mit etw ~n haben** to have trouble with sth; **wenn Sie wieder ganz ohne ~n sind** when the trouble's cleared up completely

beschwerdefrei ADJ (*Med*) fit and healthy; **er war nie wieder ganz ~** the symptoms never completely disappeared

beschweren [bəˈʃveːrən], *ptp* **beschwert** ■ VT (*mit Gewicht*) to weigh(t) down; (*fig: = belasten*) to weigh on; **von Kummer beschwert** weighed down with sorrow ■ VR (= *sich beklagen*) to complain

beschwerlich [bəˈʃveːɐlɪç] ADJ arduous; **das Gehen/Atmen ist für ihn ~** he finds walking/breathing hard work

beschwichtigen [bəˈʃvɪçtɪgn], *ptp* **beschwichtigt** VT to appease; *Kinder* to calm down

beschwindeln *ptp* **beschwindelt** VT (*inf*: = *belügen*) **jdn ~** to tell sb a lie *or* a fib (*inf*)

beschwingt [bəˈʃvɪŋt] ADJ elated; *Musik, Mensch* vibrant; **sich ~ fühlen** to walk on air; **ein ~es Gefühl** a feeling of elation

beschwipst [bəˈʃvɪpst] ADJ (*inf*) tipsy

beschwören *ptp* **beschworen** [bəˈʃvoːrən] VT IRREG (a) (= *beeiden*) to swear to (b) (= *anflehen*) to implore, to beseech; **sie hob ~d die Hände** she raised her hands imploringly *or* beseechingly (c) (= *erscheinen lassen*) to conjure up; *Verstorbene* to raise; *Schlangen* to charm

Beschwörung [bəˈʃvøːrʊŋ] F -, -en (a) (= *das Flehen*) entreaty (b) (= *das Heraufbeschwören*) conjuring up; (*von Verstorbenen*) raising; (*von Schlangen*) charming (c) (*auch* **Beschwörungsformel**) incantation

besehen *ptp* **besehen** IRREG VT (*auch* **sich** *dat* **besehen**) to take a look at

beseitigen [bəˈzaɪtɪgn], *ptp* **beseitigt** VT (a) (= *entfernen*) to remove; *Abfall, Schnee* to clear (away); *Atommüll* to dispose of; *Schwierigkeiten* to sort out; *Fehler* to eliminate; *Missstände* to do away with (b) (*euph*: = *umbringen*) to get rid of

Beseitigung F -, NO PL (a) (= *das Entfernen*) removal; (*von Abfall, Schnee*) clearing (away); (*von Atommüll*) disposal; (*von Schwierigkeiten*) sorting out; (*von Fehlern*) elimination; (*von Missständen*) doing away with (b) (*euph*: *von Menschen*) getting rid of

Besen [ˈbeːzn] M -s, - broom; (*von Hexe*) broomstick; **ich fresse einen ~, wenn das stimmt** (*inf*) if that's right, I'll eat my hat (*inf*); **neue ~ kehren gut** (*Prov*) a new broom sweeps clean (*Prov*)

Besen-: **besenrein** ■ ADJ well-swept ■ ADV **eine Wohnung ~ verlassen** to leave an apartment in a clean and tidy condition (for the next tenant); **Besenschrank** M broom cupboard

besessen [bəˈzɛsn] ADJ (*von bösen Geistern*) possessed (*von* by); (*von einer Idee, Leidenschaft etc*) obsessed (*von* with); **wie ~** like a thing possessed; *siehe auch* **besitzen**

Besessenheit F -, NO PL (*mit bösen Geistern*) possession; (*mit Idee, Leidenschaft etc*) obsession

besetzen *ptp* **besetzt** VT (a) (= *belegen*) to occupy; (= *reservieren*) to reserve; (= *füllen*) *Plätze, Stühle* to fill; **ist hier** *or* **dieser Platz besetzt?** is this place taken?; *siehe auch* **besetzt** (b) (*mit Person*) to fill; (*Theat*) *Rolle* to cast; (*mit Tieren*) to stock; **eine Stelle** *etc* **neu ~** to find a new person to fill a job (c) (*esp Mil*: = *eingenommen haben*) to occupy; (*Hausbesetzer*) to squat in

besetzt [bəˈzɛtst] ADJ *Telefon, Nummer, Leitung* engaged (*Brit*), busy (*esp US*); *WC* occupied, engaged; *Abteil, Tisch* taken; *Gebiet* occupied; (*voll*) *Bus, Wagen, Abteil etc* full (up); **eine international ~e Jury** an international jury; **ein negativ ~es Thema** a very negative subject; *siehe auch* **besetzen**

Besetztton M, *pl* **-töne**, **Besetztzeichen** NT (*Telec*) engaged (*Brit*) *or* busy (*esp US*) tone

Besetzung [bəˈzɛtsʊŋ] F -, -en (a) (= *das Besetzen*) (*von Stelle*) filling; (*von Rolle*) casting; (*mit Tieren*) stocking; (*Theat*: = *Schauspieler*) cast; (*Sport*: = *Mannschaft*) team, side; **die Nationalelf in der neuen ~** the new line-up for the international team; **das Stück in der neuen ~** the play with the new cast; **zweite ~** (*Theat*) understudy (b) (*Mil*: *von Gebäude, durch Hausbesetzer*) occupation

besichtigen [bəˈzɪçtɪgn], *ptp* **besichtigt** VT *Kirche, Sehenswürdigkeit, Stadt* to visit; *Betrieb* to have a look (a)round; (*zur Prüfung*) *Haus* to view; *Ware* to have a look at; (*hum*) *Baby, zukünftigen Schwiegersohn etc* to inspect

Besichtigung F -, -en (*von Sehenswürdigkeiten*) sightseeing tour; (*von Museum, Kirche, Betrieb*) tour; (*zur Prüfung*) (*von Haus*) viewing; (*von Waren, Schule, Baby*) inspection; **nach einer kurzen ~ der Kirche/des Museums/Betriebs** *etc* after a short look (a)round the church/museum/factory *etc*

besiedeln *ptp* **besiedelt** VT (= *ansiedeln*) to populate, to settle (*mit* with); (= *sich niederlassen in*) to settle; (= *kolonisieren*) to colonize; **dicht/dünn/schwach besiedelt** densely/thinly/sparsely populated

Besiedelung [bəˈziːdəlʊŋ] F -, -en, **Besiedlung** F -, -en settlement; (= *Kolonisierung*) colonization; **dichte/dünne/schwache ~** dense/thin/sparse population

besiegen *ptp* **besiegt** VT (= *schlagen*) to defeat; (= *überwinden*) to overcome

Besiegte(r) [bəˈziːktə] MF DECL AS ADJ **die ~n** the conquered

besinnen *ptp* **besonnen** [bəˈzɔnən] VR IRREG (= *überlegen*) to reflect; (= *erinnern*) to remember (*auf jdn/etw* sb/sth); (= *es sich anders überlegen*) to have second thoughts; **sich anders** *or* **eines anderen ~** to change one's mind; **sich eines Besseren ~** to think better of it; **er hat sich besonnen** he has seen the light; **ohne sich (viel) zu ~, ohne langes Besinnen** without a moment's thought; *siehe auch* **besonnen**

besinnlich ADJ contemplative; *Texte, Worte* reflective; **eine ~e Zeit** a time of contemplation; **~ werden** to become thoughtful

Besinnlichkeit F -, reflection

Besinnung [bəˈzɪnʊŋ] F -, NO PL (a) (= *Bewusstsein*) consciousness; **bei/ohne ~ sein** to be conscious/ unconscious; **die ~ verlieren** to lose consciousness; **wieder zur ~ kommen** to regain consciousness; (*fig*) to come to one's senses; **jdn zur ~ bringen** to bring sb to his senses (b) (= *das Nachdenken*) reflection

Besinnungsaufsatz M discursive essay

Besitz [bəˈzɪts] M, NO PL (a) (= *das Besitzen*) possession; **im** *or* **von etw sein** to be in possession of sth; **ich bin im ~ Ihres Schreibens** I am in receipt of your letter; **etw in ~ nehmen** to take possession of sth; **von etw ~ ergreifen** to seize possession of sth; **von jdm ~ ergreifen** to take hold of sb;

(*Zweifel, Wahnsinn etc*) to take possession of sb's mind; **in privatem ~** in private ownership

(b) (= *Eigentum*) property; (= *Landgut*) estate; **in jds ~** (*acc*) **übergehen** to become sb's property

besitzanzeigend ADJ (*Gram*) possessive

besitzen *ptp* **besessen** [bə'zesn] VT IRREG to have, to possess; *käufliche Güter* to own; *Vermögen* to possess; *Wertpapiere, Narbe, grüne Augen* to have; *Rechte, jds Zuneigung etc* to enjoy; *siehe auch* **besessen**

Besitzer [bə'zɪtsɐ] M **-s, -**, **Besitzerin** [-ərɪn] F **-, -nen** owner; (*von Wertpapieren auch, von Führerschein etc*) holder; **den ~ wechseln** to change hands

Besitzwechsel M change of owner(ship)

besoffen [bə'zɔfn] ADJ (*inf*) smashed (*inf*); *siehe auch* **besaufen**

Besoffene(r) [bə'zɔfnə] MF DECL AS ADJ (*inf*) drunk

besohlen *ptp* **besohlt** VT to sole; (= *neu ~*) to resole

Besoldung [bə'zɔldʊŋ] F **-, -en** pay

besondere(r, s) [bə'zɔndərə] ADJ special; (= *bestimmt*) particular; (= *hervorragend*) *Qualität, Schönheit etc* exceptional; **er ist ein ganz ~r Freund** he is a very special friend; **das sind ~ Umstände** those are special circumstances; **das ist ein ganz ~s Gemälde** that is a very unusual painting; **unser ~s Interesse gilt ...** we are particularly interested in ...; **ohne ~ Begeisterung** without any particular enthusiasm; **es ist mein ganz ~r Wunsch, dass ...** it is my very special wish that ...; **in diesem ~n Fall** in this particular case

Besondere(s) [bə'zɔndərə] NT DECL AS ADJ **etwas/nichts ~s** something/nothing special; **er möchte etwas ~s sein** he thinks he's something special; **das ~ daran** the special thing about it; **das ~ und das Allgemeine** the particular and the general; **im ~n** (= *im Einzelnen*) in particular cases; (= *vor allem*) in particular

Besonderheit [bə'zɔndɐhait] F **-, -en** unusual quality; (= *besondere Eigenschaft*) peculiarity

besonders [bə'zɔndɐs] ADV *gut, hübsch, teuer etc* particularly, (e)specially; (= *gesondert*) separately; (= *speziell*) *anfertigen etc* specially; **nicht ~ viel Geld** not a particularly large amount of money; **das Essen/der Film war nicht ~** (*inf*) the food/film was nothing special; **wie gehts dir? – nicht ~** (*inf*) how are you? – not too hot (*inf*); **~ wenig Fehler** an exceptionally low number of mistakes; **er hat ~ viel/wenig gearbeitet** he did a particularly large/small amount of work; **er hat ~ wenig gegessen** he ate particularly little

besonnen [bə'zɔnən] ADJ level-headed; **ihre ruhige, ~e Art** her calm and collected way ADV in a careful and thoughtful manner; *siehe auch* **besinnen**

Besonnenheit F **-, NO PL** level-headedness; **durch seine ~ hat er eine Katastrophe verhindert** by staying calm and collected he avoided a disaster; **zur ~ aufrufen/mahnen** to call for/urge calm

besorgen *ptp* **besorgt** VT **(a)** (= *kaufen, beschaffen etc*) to get; (*euph inf*: = *stehlen*) to acquire (*euph inf*); **jdm/sich etw ~** to get sth for sb/oneself **(b)** (= *erledigen*) to see to; **was du heute kannst, das verschiebe nicht auf morgen** (*Prov*) never put off until tomorrow what you can do today **(c)** (= *sich kümmern um*) to take care of **(d)** (*inf*) **es jdm ~** to sort sb out (*inf*)

Besorgnis [bə'zɔrknɪs] F **-, -se** anxiety, worry; **~ erregend** (*adjektivisch*) alarming; (*adverbial*) alarmingly

besorgt [bə'zɔrkt] ADJ anxious (*wegen* about); **um jdn/etw ~ sein** to be concerned about sb/sth ADV anxiously

Besorgung [bə'zɔrgʊŋ] F **-, -en (a)** (= *das Kaufen*) purchase **(b)** (= *Erledigung*) **jdn mit der ~ seiner Geschäfte betrauen** to entrust sb with looking after one's affairs **(c)** (= *Einkauf*) errand; **~en machen** to do some shopping

bespielbar ADJ *Rasen etc* playable; *Kassette* capable of being recorded on

bespielen *ptp* **bespielt** VT **(a)** *Schallplatte, Tonband* to record on; **das Band ist mit klassischer Musik bespielt** the tape has a recording of classical music on it **(b)** (*Sport*) to play on

bespitzeln *ptp* **bespitzelt** VT to spy on

besprechen *ptp* **besprochen** [bə'ʃprɔxn] IRREG VT (= *über etw sprechen*) to discuss; (= *rezensieren*) to review; **wie besprochen** as arranged VR **sich mit jdm ~** to consult (with) sb (*über +acc* about); **sich über etw** (*acc*) **~** to discuss sth

Besprechung [bə'ʃprɛçʊŋ] F **-, -en (a)** (= *Unterredung*) discussion; (= *Konferenz*) meeting; **nach ~ mit ...** after

---

discussion with ...; **er ist bei einer ~, er hat eine ~** he's in a meeting **(b)** (= *Rezension*) review

bespritzen *ptp* **bespritzt** VT to spray; (= *beschmutzen*) to splash

besprühen *ptp* **besprüht** VT to spray

bespucken *ptp* **bespuckt** VT to spit at *or* (up)on

besser ['bɛsɐ] **🔳** ADJ COMP *von* gut better; **~e Leute** better class of people; **er hat ~e Tage** *or* **Zeiten gesehen** (*iro*) he has seen better days; **das Essen war nur ein ~er Imbiss** the meal was just a glorified snack; **du willst wohl etwas Besseres sein!** (*inf*) I suppose you think you're better than other people; **soll es etwas Besseres sein?** did you want something of rather better quality in mind?; **~ werden** to improve; **das ist auch ~ so** it's better that way; **das wäre noch ~** (*iro*) no way; **Besseres zu tun haben** (*inf*) to have better things to do; **eine Wendung zum Besseren nehmen** to take a turn for the better; **jdn eines Besseren belehren** to teach sb otherwise

🔳 ADV COMP *von* gut, **wohl (a)** better; **~ ist ~** (it is) better to be on the safe side; **umso ~!** (*inf*) so much the better!; **~ (gesagt)** *or* rather; **~ gestellt** better-off; **sie will immer alles ~ wissen** she always thinks she knows better; **es kommt noch ~** (*iro*) there's worse *or* more to come; **es ~ haben** to have a better life

(b) (= *lieber*) **lass das ~ bleiben** you had better leave well alone; **das solltest du ~ nicht tun** you had better not do that; **du tätest ~ daran ...** you would do better to ...; **dann geh ich ~ then I'd better go

besser gehen VI IMPERS IRREG AUX SEIN **es geht jdm besser** sb is feeling better; **jetzt gehts der Firma wieder besser** the firm is doing better again now

bessern ['bɛsɐn] **🔳** VT (= *besser machen*) to improve; *Verbrecher etc* to reform **🔳** VR to mend one's ways; **bessere dich** (*hum inf*) mend your ways!

besser: **besser stehen** VR IRREG (*inf*) to be better off; **besser stellen 🔳** VT **jdn ~** to improve sb's financial position **🔳** VR to be better off

Besserung ['bɛsərʊŋ] F **-, NO PL** improvement; (*von Verbrecher etc*) reformation; (= *Genesung*) recovery; **(ich wünsche dir) gute ~!** I hope you get better soon; **auf dem Wege der ~ sein** to be getting better

Besser-: **Besserwisser** ['bɛsɐvɪsɐ] M **-s, -**, **Besserwisserin** [-ərɪn] F **-, -nen** (*inf*) know-all (*Brit inf*), know-it-all (*US inf*); **Besserwisserei** [bɛsɐvɪsə'rai] F **-, NO PL** (*inf*) know(it)-all manner; **besserwisserisch** ['bɛsɐvɪsərɪʃ] (*inf*) **🔳** ADJ know(-it)-all *attr* **🔳** ADV in a superior *or* know(-it)-all manner

best- [bɛst] IN CPDS MIT ADJ best

Bestand M **(a)** (= *Fortdauer*) continued existence; **von ~ sein, ~ haben** to be permanent; **das Gesetz hat noch immer ~** the law still continues to exist; **zum 100-jährigen ~ des Vereins** (*Aus*) on the (occasion of the) 100th anniversary of the society

(b) (= *vorhandene Menge, Tiere*) stock (*an +dat* of); (= *Forstbestand*) forest *or* timber (*US*) stand; **~ aufnehmen** to take stock

(c) (*Aus*: = *Pacht*) lease, tenure; **in ~ geben** to let (out)

bestanden [bə'ʃtandn] ADJ **(a)** (= *bewachsen*) covered with trees; *Allee* lined with trees; **mit Bäumen ~** *Allee* tree-lined; *Abhang* tree-covered **(b)** **nach ~er Prüfung** after passing the/ an exam; **bei nicht ~er Prüfung** if you *etc* don't pass the exam; **sie feiert die ~e Prüfung** she's celebrating passing her exam; *siehe auch* **bestehen**

beständig [bə'ʃtɛndɪç] **🔳** ADJ **(a)** ATTR (= *dauernd*) constant **(b)** (= *gleich bleibend*) constant; *Mitarbeiter* steady; *Wetter* settled **(c)** (= *widerstandsfähig*) resistant (*gegen* to); (= *dauerhaft*) *Freundschaft, Beziehung* lasting **🔳** ADV **(a)** (= *dauernd*) constantly **(b)** (= *gleich bleibend*) consistently

-beständig ADJ SUF -resistant; **hitzebeständig** heat-resistant

Beständigkeit F **-, NO PL (a)** (= *gleich bleibende Qualität*) constant standard; (*von Mitarbeiter*) steadiness; (*von Liebhaber*) constancy; (*von Wetter*) settledness

(b) (= *Widerstandsfähigkeit*) resistance; (= *Dauerhaftigkeit*: *von Freundschaft*) durability

Bestands-: **Bestandsaufnahme** F stocktaking; **Bestandskonto** NT real account

Bestandteil M component; (*fig*) integral part; **sich in seine ~e auflösen** to fall to pieces; **etw in seine ~e zerlegen** to take sth to pieces

bestärken *ptp* **bestärkt** VT to confirm; **jdn in seinem Vorsatz/ Wunsch ~** to make sb's intention/desire stronger; **das hat mich nur darin bestärkt, es zu tun** that merely made me all the more determined to do it

bestätigen [bə'ʃtɛːtɪgn], *ptp* **bestätigt** 🔳 VT **(a)** *Aussage, Verdacht, jdn* to confirm; *Theorie, Alibi etc* to corroborate; *(Jur) Urteil* to uphold; **sich in etw** *(dat)* **bestätigt finden** to be confirmed in sth; **~d** *des Kopfnicken* a nod of confirmation; **... sagte er ~d** ... he said in confirmation
(b) *(Comm) Empfang, Brief* to acknowledge (receipt of)
(c) *(= beurkunden)* to confirm; **hiermit wird bestätigt, dass ...** this is to certify that ...; **jdn (im Amt) ~** to confirm sb's appointment
🔳 VR to be confirmed, to be proved true; **das tut er nur, um sich selbst zu ~** he only does it to boost his ego

Bestätigung F -, -en **(a)** confirmation *(auch Dokument)*; *(von Theorie, Alibi)* corroboration; *(Jur. von Urteil)* upholding
(b) *Empfangsbestätigung)* acknowledgement (of receipt)
(c) *(= Beurkundung)* certification; *(im Amt)* confirmation of appointment

bestatten [bə'ʃtatn], *ptp* **bestattet** VT to bury

Bestattung F -, -en burial; *(= Feuerbestattung)* cremation; *(= Feier)* funeral

Bestattungsunternehmen NT undertaker's, mortician's *(US)*

bestäuben *ptp* **bestäubt** VT to dust *(auch Cook)*; *(Bot)* to pollinate

Bestäubung [bə'ʃtɔybʊn] F -, -en dusting; *(Bot)* pollination

bestaunen *ptp* **bestaunt** VT to gaze at in admiration; *(verblüfft)* to gape at; **lass dich ~** let's have a good look at you

beste *siehe* **beste(r, s)**

bestechen *ptp* **bestochen** [bə'ʃtɔxn] IRREG 🔳 VT **(a)** *(mit Geld, Geschenken etc)* to bribe; **ich lasse mich nicht ~** I'm not open to bribery **(b)** *(= beeindrucken)* to captivate 🔳 VI *(= Eindruck machen)* to be impressive *(durch because of)*; **ein Mädchen, das durch Schönheit besticht** a girl of captivating beauty

bestechend 🔳 ADJ *Schönheit, Eindruck* captivating; *Angebot* tempting; *Klarheit* irresistible; *Geist, Kondition* winning 🔳 ADV *(= beeindruckend)* impressively; **schön, logisch** incredibly

bestechlich [bə'ʃtɛçlɪç] ADJ bribable, corruptible

Bestechlichkeit F -, NO PL corruptibility

Bestechung [bə'ʃtɛçʊn] F -, -en bribery

Besteck [bə'ʃtɛk] NT -(e)s, -e **(a)** *(= Essbesteck)* knives and forks *pl*; *(= Set, für ein Gedeck)* set of cutlery *(Brit)* or flatware *(US)*; **ein silbernes ~** a set of silver cutlery *(Brit)* or flatware *(US)*
(b) *(= Instrumentensatz)* set of instruments; *(= Drogenbesteck)* needles *pl*; **chirurgisches ~** (set of) surgical instruments

bestehen *ptp* **bestanden** [bə'ʃtandn] IRREG 🔳 VT **(a)** *Examen, Probe* to pass; **eine Prüfung mit Auszeichnung/„sehr gut"~** to get a distinction/"very good" (in an exam); *siehe auch* **bestanden**
(b) *(= durchstehen) Schicksalsschläge* to withstand; *schwere Zeit* to come through; *Gefahr* to overcome; *Kampf* to win 🔳 VI **(a)** *(= existieren)* to exist; **~ bleiben** *(Frage, Hoffnung etc)* to remain; **es besteht die Aussicht/der Verdacht/die Hoffnung, dass ...** there is a prospect/a suspicion/(a) hope that ...
(b) *(= Bestand haben)* to continue to exist
(c) *(= sich zusammensetzen)* to consist *(aus of)*; **in etw** *(dat)* **~** to consist in sth; *(Aufgabe)* to involve sth; **seine einzige Chance besteht darin, ...** his only chance is to ...; **das Problem besteht darin, zu zeigen ...** the problem consists in showing ...
(d) *(= standhalten, sich bewähren)* to hold one's own *(in +dat* in)*; **vor etw** *(dat)* **~** to stand up to sth
(e) *(= durchkommen)* to pass; **(in einer Prüfung) mit „sehr gut" ~** to get a "very good" (in an exam)
(f) **auf etw** *(dat)* **~** to insist on sth; **ich bestehe darauf** I insist

Bestehen NT -s, NO PL **(a)** *(= Vorhandensein, Dauer)* existence; **seit ~ der Firma/des Staates** ever since the firm/state came into existence; **das 100-jährige ~ von etw feiern** to celebrate the hundredth anniversary of (the existence of) sth
(b) *(= Beharren)* insistence *(auf +dat* on)*
(c) *(von Prüfung)* passing; *(von Schicksalsschlägen)* withstanding; *(von schwerer Zeit)* coming through; *(von Gefahr)* overcoming; **bei ~ der Prüfung** on passing the exam

bestehen bleiben VI IRREG AUX SEIN to last; *(Hoffnung)* to remain; *(Versprechen, Vereinbarungen)* to hold good

bestehend ADJ existing; *Preise* current; **die seit 1887 ~en Gesetze** the laws which have existed since 1887

bestehen lassen VT IRREG to keep

bestehlen *ptp* **bestohlen** [bə'ʃtoːlən] VT IRREG to rob; **jdn (um etw) ~** *(lit, fig)* to rob sb of sth

besteigen *ptp* **bestiegen** [bə'ʃtiːgn] VT IRREG *Berg, Turm, Leiter* to climb (up); *Fahrrad, Pferd* to get on(to); *Bus, Flugzeug* to get on; *Auto, Segelflugzeug, Hubschrauber* to get into; *Schiff* to go aboard; *Thron* to ascend

bestellen *ptp* **bestellt** 🔳 VT **(a)** *(= anfordern, in Restaurant)* to order; **sich** *(dat)* **etw ~** to order sth; **wie bestellt und nicht abgeholt** *(hum inf)* like orphan Annie *(inf)*
(b) *(= reservieren)* to book
(c) *(= ausrichten)* **bestell ihm (von mir), dass ...** tell him (from me) that ...; **soll ich irgendetwas ~?** can I take a message? **~ Sie ihm schöne Grüße von mir** give him my regards; **er hat nicht viel/nichts zu ~** he doesn't have much/any say here
(d) *(= kommen lassen)* **jdn** to send for, to summon; **jdn zu jdm/ an einen Ort ~** to summon sb to sb/a place; **ich bin um** *or* **für 10 Uhr bestellt** I have an appointment for *or* at 10 o'clock
(e) *(= bearbeiten) Land* to till
(f) *(fig)* **es ist schlecht um ihn/mit seinen Finanzen bestellt** is/his finances are in a bad way; **damit ist es schlecht bestellt** that's rather difficult
🔳 VI to order

Besteller [bə'ʃtɛlɐ] M -s, -, **Bestellerin** [-ərɪn] F -, -nen customer

Bestell-: **Bestellkarte** F order form; **Bestellmenge** F order quantity; **Bestellnummer** F order number; **Bestellschein** M order form

Bestellung F **(a)** *(= Anforderung, das Angeforderte)* order; *(= das Bestellen)* ordering **(b)** *(= das Reservieren)* booking
(c) *(= Nachricht)* message

Bestellzettel M order form

besten ADV **am ~** *siehe* **beste(r, s) 2**

bestenfalls ['bɛstnfals] ADV at best

bestens ['bɛstns] ADV *(= sehr gut)* very well; **danken** very warmly; **sie lässt ~ grüßen** she sends her best regards

beste(r, s) ['bɛstə] 🔳 ADJ SUPERL *von* **gut (a)** ATTR best; **im ~n Fall** at (the) best; **im ~n Alter, in den ~n Jahren** in the prime of (one's) life; **mit (den) ~n Grüßen/Wünschen** with best wishes; **in ~n Händen** in the best of hands; **das kommt in den ~n Familien vor** *(hum)* that can happen in the best of families; **jds ~s Stück, jds ~r Freund** *(hum sl: = Penis)* sb's John Thomas *(Brit hum inf)*, sb's Johnnie *(US hum sl)*
(b) **der/die/das Beste** the best; **der/die Beste sein** to be the best; **zu deinem Besten** for your good; **ich will nur dein Bestes** I've your best interests at heart; **sein Bestes tun** to do one's best; **wir wollen das Beste hoffen** let's hope for the best; **der/ die/das erste** *or* **nächste Beste** the first (person/job *etc*) that comes along; **the first (hotel/cinema *etc*) one comes to; **ich hielte es für das Beste, wenn ...** I thought it (would be) best if ...; **das Beste wäre, wir ...** the best thing would be for us to ...; **aufs** *or* **auf das Beste** very well; **zum Besten** for the best; **es steht nicht zum Besten** it does not look too promising; **etw zum Besten geben** *(= erzählen)* to tell sth
🔳 ADV **am ~n best; ich hielt es für am ~n, wenn ...** I thought it (would be) best if ...; **am ~n würden wir gleich gehen** we'd be best to go immediately; **am ~n gehe ich jetzt** I'd best be going now

besteuern *ptp* **besteuert** VT to tax; **Luxusartikel sind sehr hoch besteuert** luxury goods are heavily taxed

Besteuerung F taxation; *(= Steuersatz)* tax

Besteuerungsgrundlage F *(für Firmen)* tax base

Bestform F *(esp Sport)* top form

bestialisch [bɛs'tiaːlɪʃ] 🔳 ADJ bestial; *(inf)* awful 🔳 ADV *(inf)* terribly; *stinken, zurichten* dreadfully; **wehtun** like hell *(inf)*; **~ stinken** to stink to high heaven *(inf)*

Bestie ['bɛstiə] F -, -n beast; *(fig)* animal

bestimmen *ptp* **bestimmt** 🔳 VT **(a)** *(= festsetzen)* to determine; *Pflanze, Tier, Funde* to classify; **sie will immer alles ~** she always wants to decide the way things are to be done; *siehe auch* **bestimmt**
(b) *(= prägen) Stadtbild, Landschaft* to characterize; *(= beeinflussen) Preis, Anzahl* to determine; *Entwicklung, Werk,*

Stil etc to have a determining influence on; (*Gram*) *Kasus, Tempus* to determine; **näher ~** (*Gram*) to qualify
(c) (= *vorsehen*) to intend, to mean (*für* for); **jdn zu etw ~** to choose sb as sth; **er ist zu Höherem bestimmt** he is destined for higher things; **wir waren füreinander bestimmt** we were meant for each other
2 VI **(a)** (= *entscheiden*) to decide (*über* +*acc* on); **du hast hier nicht zu ~** you don't make the decisions here
(b) (= *verfügen*) **er kann über sein Geld allein ~** it is up to him what he does with his money; **du kannst nicht über ihn/seine Zeit ~** it's not up to you to decide what he's going to do/ how his time is to be spent

bestimmt [bə'ʃtɪmt] **1** ADJ **(a)** (= *gewiss, nicht genau genannt*) certain; (= *speziell, genau genannt*) particular, definite; (= *festgesetzt*) *Preis, Tag* fixed; (= *klar, deutlich*) *Angaben, Ausdruck* precise; (*Gram*) *Artikel, Zahlwort* definite; **suchen Sie etwas Bestimmtes?** are you looking for anything in particular?; **den ganz ~en Eindruck gewinnen, dass ...** to get *or* have the distinct impression that ...; *siehe auch* **bestimmen**
(b) (= *entschieden*) *Auftreten, Ton, Mensch* firm, decisive; **höflich, aber ~** polite but firm
2 ADV **(a)** (= *sicher*) definitely; **ich weiß ganz ~, dass ...** I know for sure that ...; **kommst du? – ja – ~?** are you coming? – yes – definitely?; **ich schaffe es ~** I'll manage it all right; **er schafft es ~ nicht** he definitely won't manage it
(b) (= *wahrscheinlich*) no doubt; **das hat er ~ verloren** he's bound to have lost it; **er kommt ~ wieder zu spät** he's bound to be late again

Bestimmtheit F -, NO PL **(a)** (= *Sicherheit*) certainty; **ich kann mit ~ sagen, dass ...** I can say definitely that ...; **ich weiß aber mit ~, dass ...** but I know for sure that ...
(b) (= *Entschiedenheit*) firmness; **in** *or* **mit aller ~** quite categorically

Bestimmung F **(a)** (= *Vorschrift*) regulation; **gesetzliche ~en** legal requirements **(b)** NO PL (= *Zweck*) purpose; **eine Brücke/ Straße ihrer ~ übergeben** to open a new bridge/road officially **(c)** (= *Schicksal*) destiny **(d)** (*Gram*) modifier; **adverbiale ~** = adverbial modifier **(e)** (= *das Bestimmen*) determining; (*von Grenze, Zeit etc*) fixing; (*von Pflanze, Tier, Funden*) classification; **nähere ~** (*durch Adverb*) qualifying

Bestimmungs-: Bestimmungshafen M (port of) destination; **Bestimmungsland** NT (country of) destination; **Bestimmungsort** M, *pl* **-orte** (place of) destination

Best-: Bestleistung F (*esp Sport*) best performance; **seine persönliche ~** his personal best; **Bestmarke** F best possible; **bestmöglich 1** ADJ NO PRED best possible; **wir haben unser Bestmögliches getan** we did our (level (*Brit*)) best **2** ADV in the best way possible

Best. Nr. ABBR *von* **Bestellnummer**

bestrafen *ptp* **bestraft** VT to punish; (*Jur*) *jdn* to sentence (*mit* to); (*Sport*) *Spieler, Foul* to penalize; **der Schiedsrichter bestrafte das Foul mit einem Elfmeter** the referee awarded a penalty for the foul

Bestrafung F -, **-en** punishment; (*Jur*) sentencing; (*Sport*) penalization; **wir fordern eine strengere ~ von ...** we demand more severe punishments *or* (*Jur auch*) sentences for ...

bestrahlen *ptp* **bestrahlt** VT to shine on; (*Med*) to give radiotherapy to; *Lebensmittel* to irradiate; **er ließ sich von der Sonne ~** he was soaking up the sun

Bestrahlung F illumination; (*Med*) radiotherapy; (= *von Lebensmitteln*) irradiation

Bestreben NT endeavour (*Brit*), endeavor (*US*); **im** *or* **in seinem ~, dem Fußgänger auszuweichen** in his efforts to avoid the pedestrian

bestrebt [bə'ʃtreːpt] ADJ **~ sein, etw zu tun** to endeavour (*Brit*) *or* endeavor (*US*) to do sth

bestreichen *ptp* **bestrichen** [bə'ʃtrɪçn] VT IRREG (*mit Salbe, Flüssigkeit*) to spread; (*mit Butter*) to butter; (*Cook*) (*mit Milch etc*) to coat; (*mit Farbe*) to paint; **etw mit Butter/Fett/Öl ~** to butter/grease/oil sth; **etw mit Butter/Salbe/Klebstoff ~** to spread butter/ointment/glue on sth; **etw mit Farbe ~** to put a coat of paint on sth

bestreiken *ptp* **bestreikt** VT to boycott; **bestreikt** strikebound; **die Fabrik wird zurzeit bestreikt** there's a strike on in the factory at the moment

bestreitbar ADJ disputable, contestable

bestreiten *ptp* **bestritten** [bə'ʃtrɪtn] VT IRREG **(a)** (= *abstreiten*) to dispute; (= *leugnen*) to deny; **das möchte ich nicht ~** I'm not disputing it **(b)** (= *finanzieren*) to pay for; *Kosten* to carry **(c)** (= *tragen, gestalten*) to carry; **er hat das ganze Gespräch allein bestritten** he did all the talking

bestreuen *ptp* **bestreut** VT to cover (*mit* with); (*Cook*) to sprinkle

Bestseller ['bɛstzɛlɐ] M -s, - bestseller

Bestseller-: Bestsellerautor(in) M(F) bestselling author; **Bestsellerliste** F bestseller list

bestücken [bə'ʃtʏkn], *ptp* **bestückt** VT to fit, to equip; (*Mil*) to arm; *Lager* to stock

Bestuhlung [bə'ʃtuːlʊŋ] F -, **-en** seating *no indef art*

bestürmen *ptp* **bestürmt** VT to storm; (*mit Fragen, Bitten*) to bombard; (*mit Anfragen, Briefen, Anrufen*) to inundate

bestürzen *ptp* **bestürzt** VT to shake; *siehe auch* **bestürzt**

bestürzend 1 ADJ alarming; **ich finde es ~, wie wenig die Schüler wissen** it dismays me to see how little the children know **2** ADV *hoch, niedrig* alarmingly

bestürzt [bə'ʃtʏrtst] **1** ADJ filled with consternation; **sie machte ein ~es Gesicht** a look of consternation came over her face **2** ADV in consternation; *siehe auch* **bestürzen**

Best-: Bestwert M (*Fin*) top value; (*Tech, Sport*) best performance; **Bestzeit** F (*esp Sport*) best time

Besuch [bə'zuːx] M -(e)s, -e **(a)** (= *das Besuchen*) visit (*des Museums etc* to the museum *etc*); (*von Schule, Veranstaltung*) attendance (+*gen* at); **zu seinen Aufgaben gehört auch der ~ der Klienten** his jobs include visiting clients; **bei jdm auf** *or* **zu ~ sein** to be visiting sb; **(von jdm) ~ erhalten** *or* **bekommen** to have *or* get a visit (from sb); **jdm einen ~ abstatten, einen ~ bei jdm machen** to pay sb a visit **(b)** (= *Besucher*) visitor; visitors *pl*; **er hat ~** he has company; **er bekommt viel ~** he has a lot of visitors

besuchen *ptp* **besucht** VT *jdn* to visit; *Vortrag, Schule, Seminar, Gottesdienst* to attend; *Kino, Theater, Lokal, Bordell, Museum* to go to; *siehe auch* **besucht**

Besucher(in) M(F) visitor; (*von Kino, Theater*) patron (*form*); **etwa 1.000 ~ waren zu der Veranstaltung/dem Vortrag gekommen** about 1, 000 people attended the function/ lecture

Besuchs-: Besuchsrecht NT (*Jur: nach Scheidung*) (right of) access; **das ~ bei ihrem Sohn** the right to visit her son; **Besuchszeit** F visiting time; **jetzt ist keine ~** it's not visiting time

besucht [bə'zuːxt] ADJ **gut/schlecht/schwach ~ sein** to be well/ badly/poorly attended; (*Schloss etc*) to get a lot of/not many/ only a handful of visitors; *siehe auch* **besuchen**

Betablocker ['beːtablɔkɐ] M -s, - (*Med*) beta-blocker

betagt [bə'taːkt] ADJ (*geh*) aged, well advanced in years

betanken *ptp* **betankt** VT *Fahrzeug* to fill up; *Flugzeug* to refuel

betasten *ptp* **betastet** VT to feel

Beta- ['beːta]: **Betastrahlen** PL beta rays *pl*; **Betastrahlung** F beta radiation; **Betateilchen** NT beta particle

betätigen *ptp* **betätigt 1** VT *Muskeln, Gehirn, Auslöser* to activate; *Bremse* to apply; *Mechanismus, Hebel* to operate; *Taste, Knopf* to press; (= *drehen*) to turn; *Schalter, Blinker* to turn on; *Sirene* to sound
2 VR to busy oneself; (*körperlich*) to get some exercise; **sich politisch ~** to be active in politics; **sich wissenschaftlich/ literarisch ~** to do (some) scientific work/some writing; **sich künstlerisch ~** to do (some) painting/sculpture *etc*; **sich sportlich ~** to do sport; **sich geistig und körperlich ~** to stay active in body and mind; **wenn man sich längere Zeit nicht geistig betätigt hat** if you haven't used your mind for months

Betätigung F -, **-en (a)** (= *Tätigkeit*) activity; **an ~ fehlt es mir nicht** I've no lack of things to do **(b)** (= *Aktivierung*) operation; (*von Muskel, Gehirn, Darm*) activation; (*von Bremsen*) applying; (*von Mechanismus*) operation; (*von Knopf*) pressing; (*durch Drehen*) turning; (*von Schalter*) turning on; (*von Hebel*) moving; (*von Sirene*) sounding

betatschen *ptp* **betatscht** VT (*inf*) to paw (*inf*)

betäuben [bə'tɔybn], *ptp* **betäubt** VT *Körperteil* to (be)numb; *Nerv* to deaden; *Schmerzen* to kill; (*durch Narkose*) to anaesthetize; (*mit einem Schlag*) (*fig* = *benommen machen*) to stun; (fig) Kummer, Gewissen to ease; **er versuchte, seinen Kummer mit Alkohol zu ~** he tried to drown his sorrows with alcohol; **ein ~der Duft** an overpowering smell

Betäubung F -, -en **(a)** (= das Betäuben) (be)numbing; (von Nerv, Schmerz) deadening; (von Schmerzen) killing; (durch Narkose) anaesthetization; (durch Schlag) stunning; (von Gewissen, Kummer) easing **(b)** (= Narkose) anaesthetic; **örtliche** or **lokale ~** local anaesthetic

Betäubungsmittel NT anaesthetic; (= Droge) narcotic

Betäubungsmittelgesetz NT law concerning drug abuse, narcotics law (US)

Bete ['be:tə] F -, (rare) -n beet; **Rote ~** beetroot

beteiligen [bə'tailɪgn], ptp **beteiligt** ■ VT jdn an etw (dat) to involve sb in sth; (finanziell) to give sb a share in sth ■ VR to participate (an +dat in); (finanziell) to have a share (an +dat in); **sich an den Unkosten ~** to contribute to the expenses; **ich möchte mich bei** or **an dem Geschenk ~** I would like to put something toward(s) the present

beteiligt [bə'tailɪçt] ADJ an etw (dat) **~ sein/werden** to be involved in sth; (finanziell) to have a share in sth; **am Gewinn** to have a slice of sth; **an einem Unfall/einer Schlägerei ~ sein** to be involved in an accident/a fight; **er war an dem Gelingen der Aktion maßgeblich ~** he made a major contribution to the success of the campaign; **er ist an dem Geschäft (mit 500.000 Euro) ~** he has a (500,000-euro) share in the business

Beteiligte(r) [bə'tailɪçtə] MF DECL AS ADJ person involved; (= Teilhaber) partner; (Jur) party; **die am Unfall ~n** those involved in the accident; **an alle ~n** to all concerned

Beteiligung F -, -en **(a)** (= Teilnahme) (an +dat in) participation; (finanziell) share; (an Unfall) involvement **(b)** (= das Beteiligen) involvement (an +dat in); **die ~ der Arbeiter am Gewinn** giving the workers a share in the profits

Beteiligungsfinanzierung F equity financing

beten ['be:tn] ■ VI to pray (um, für, zu to); (bei Tisch) to say grace ■ VT to say

beteuern [bə'tɔyɐn], ptp **beteuert** VT to declare; Unschuld auch to protest

Beteuerung F declaration; (von Unschuld auch) protestation

betiteln [bə'ti:tln] ptp **betitelt** VT to entitle; (= anreden) jdn to address as; (= beschimpfen) to call

Beton [be'tɔ̃, be'tɔ̃ŋ, (esp Aus) be'to:n] M -s, (rare) -s concrete

Beton- [be'tɔ̃ŋ-, be'tõ:-, (esp Aus) be'to:n-] IN CPDS concrete; **Betonbau** M, pl -bauten concrete building; **Betonburg** F (pej) pile of concrete

betonen ptp **betont** VT **(a)** (= hervorheben) to emphasize; siehe auch **betont (b)** (Ling, Mus: = einen Akzent legen auf) to stress; (= Tonfall gebrauchen) to intonate (form)

betonieren [beto'ni:rən], ptp **betoniert** VT (lit) to concrete; **betoniert** concrete

Beton- [be'tɔ̃ŋ-, be'tõ:-, (esp Aus) be'to:n-]: **Betonklotz** M (pej) concrete block; **Betonkopf** M (pej inf) reactionary die-hard; **Betonmischmaschine** F concrete mixer

betont [bə'to:nt] ■ ADJ Höflichkeit emphatic; Kühle, Sachlichkeit pointed; Eleganz pronounced ■ ADV knapp, kühl pointedly; **~ sparsam leben** to live a markedly modest life; **sich ~ einfach kleiden** to dress with marked simplicity; siehe auch **betonen**

Betonung F -, -en **(a)** NO PL (= das Betonen) emphasis; (von Hüften, Augen) accentuation **(b)** (= Akzent) stress; (fig: = Gewicht) emphasis; **die ~ liegt auf der ersten Silbe** the stress is on the first syllable

Betonungszeichen NT stress mark

betr. ABBR von **betreffend, betrifft, betreffs**

Betr. ABBR von **Betreff**

Betracht [bə'traxt] M -(e)s, NO PL **außer ~ bleiben** to be left out of consideration; **etw außer ~ lassen** to leave sth out of consideration; **in ~ kommen** to be considered; **nicht in ~ kommen** to be out of the question; **jdn/etw in ~ ziehen** to take sb/sth into consideration

betrachten ptp **betrachtet** VT to look at; **sich** (dat) **etw ~** to have a look at sth; **bei näherem Betrachten** on closer examination; **als jd** or **jdn/etw ~** (= halten für) to regard as sb/sth

Betrachter [bə'traxtɐ] M -s, -, **Betrachterin** [-ərɪn] F -, -nen observer; **der aufmerksame ~ wird bei diesem Bild festgestellt**

haben ... to the alert eye it will have become apparent that in this picture ...

beträchtlich [bə'trɛçtlɪç] ■ ADJ considerable; **um ein Beträchtliches** considerably ■ ADV considerably

Betrachtung [bə'traxtʊŋ] F -, -en **(a)** (= das Betrachten) contemplation; **bei näherer ~** on closer examination; **eine neuartige ~ des Problems** a new way of looking at the problem **(b)** (= Überlegung, Untersuchung) reflection; **über etw** (acc) **~en anstellen** to reflect on sth

Betrachtungsweise F verschiedene ~n der Lage different ways of looking at the situation; **er hat eine völlig andere ~** he has a completely different way of looking at things

Betrag [bə'tra:k] M -(e)s, ~e [-'trɛ:gə] amount; **der gesamte ~** the total (amount); **~ dankend erhalten** (payment) received with thanks

betragen ptp **betragen** IRREG ■ VT to be; (Kosten, Rechnung auch) to come to ■ VR to behave; **sich gut/schlecht ~** to behave (oneself) well/badly

Betragen NT -s, NO PL behaviour (Brit), behavior (US); (esp im Zeugnis) conduct

betrauen ptp **betraut** VT jdn mit etw ~ to entrust sb with sth; **jdn damit ~, etw zu tun** to give sb the task of doing sth; **jdn mit einem öffentlichen Amt ~** to appoint sb to public office

betrauern ptp **betrauert** VT to mourn

beträufeln ptp **beträufelt** VT **den Fisch mit Zitrone ~** to sprinkle lemon juice over the fish; **die Wunde mit der Lösung ~** to put drops of the solution on the wound

Betreff [bə'trɛf] M -(e)s, -e (form) ~: **Ihr Schreiben vom ...** re your letter of ...; **den ~ angeben** to state the reference

betreffen ptp **betroffen** [bə'trɔfn] VT IRREG (= angehen) to concern; **von dieser Regelung werde ich nicht betroffen** this rule does not concern or affect me; **was mich betrifft ...** as far as I'm concerned ...; **was das betrifft ...** as far as that is concerned ...; **betrifft** re; siehe auch **betreffend, betroffen**

betreffend ADJ ATTR (= erwähnt) in question; (= zuständig, für etw relevant) relevant; **das ~e Wort richtig einsetzen** to insert the appropriate word in the right place

betreffs [bə'trɛfs] PREP +GEN (form) concerning, re (esp Comm)

betreiben ptp **betrieben** [bə'tri:bn] VT IRREG Gewerbe, Handwerk to carry on; Geschäft to conduct; Handel auch, Sport to do; Studium, Politik to pursue; **auf jds Betreiben** (acc) **hin** at sb's instigation

Betreiber(in) M(F) operating authority

betreten¹ [bə'tre:tn], ptp **betreten** VT IRREG (= hineingehen in) to enter; Rasen, Spielfeld etc to walk on; Brücke, Bühne to walk onto; Podium to step (up) onto; **wir ~ damit ein noch unerforschtes Gebiet** we are here entering unknown territory; **„Betreten (des Rasens) verboten!"** "keep off the grass"; **„Betreten für Unbefugte verboten"** "no entry to unauthorized persons"

betreten² ■ ADJ embarrassed ■ ADV with embarrassment; **er sah ~ zu Boden** he looked at the floor, embarrassed

betreuen [bə'trɔyən], ptp **betreut** VT to look after; **betreutes Wohnen** assisted living

Betreuung F -, -en looking after; (von Patienten, Tieren etc) care; **er wurde mit der ~ der Gruppe beauftragt** he was put in charge of the group

Betrieb M **(a)** (= Firma) business, company; (= Fabrik) factory, works sing or pl; (= Arbeitsstelle) place of work; **wir kommen um 5 Uhr aus dem ~** we leave work at 5 o'clock **(b)** (= Tätigkeit) work; (von Maschine, Fabrik) working, operation; **den ~ stören** to be disruptive; **er hält den ganzen ~ auf** he's holding everything up; **der ganze ~ stand still** everything stopped; **außer ~** out of order; **die Maschinen sind in ~** the machines are running; **eine Maschine in ~ setzen** to start a machine up; **eine Maschine außer ~ setzen** to stop a machine; **eine Maschine/Fabrik in ~ nehmen** to put a machine/factory into operation **(c)** (= Betriebsamkeit) bustle; **in den Geschäften herrscht großer ~** the shops are very busy; **auf den Straßen ist noch kein ~** there is nobody about in the streets yet; **bei dem ~ soll sich ein Mensch konzentrieren können!** how can anybody concentrate with all that (bustle) going on?

betrieblich [bə'tri:plɪç] ■ ADJ ATTR company attr; Nutzungsdauer etc operational ■ ADV **eine Sache ~ regeln** to settle a matter within the company; **~ bedingte**

Entlassungen/Rationalisierungen redundancies/ rationalization measures caused by company restructuring

Betriebs- IN CPDS (= *Fabrik-*) factory, works; (= *Firmen-*) company; **Betriebsabrechnung** F operational accounting

betriebsam [bəˈtriːpzaːm] ADJ busy, bustling *no adv*

Betriebsamkeit F -, NO PL bustle; (*von Mensch*) active nature

Betriebs-: Betriebsanalyse F operational analysis; **Betriebsangehörige(r)** MF DECL AS ADJ employee; **Betriebsanleitung** F operating instructions *pl*; **Betriebsausgaben** PL operating expenses *pl*; **betriebsbedingt** ADJ **es gab 50 ~e Kündigungen** 50 people were made redundant because of restructuring; **betriebsbereit** ADJ operational; **betriebsblind** ADJ blind to the shortcomings of one's (own) company; **Betriebsbuchhaltung** F internal cost accounting; **betriebseigen** ADJ company *attr*; **Betriebseinnahmen** PL operating income; **Betriebsergebnis** NT (*Fin*) trading result; **Betriebsferien** PL (annual) holiday (*esp Brit*), vacation close-down (*US*); **wegen ~** closed for holidays (*esp Brit*) *or* vacation (*US*); **betriebsfremd** ADJ outside; **~e Personen** people visiting a/the company; **Betriebsgeheimnis** NT trade secret; **betriebsintern** ▮ ADJ internal company *attr*; *Ausbildung, Kenntnisse* in-house *attr* ▮ ADV **etw ~ regeln** to settle sth within the company; **Betriebsklima** NT atmosphere at work; **Betriebskosten** PL (*von Firma etc*) overheads *pl*; (*von Maschine*) running costs *pl*; **Betriebskrankenkasse** F company health insurance scheme; **Betriebsleiter(in)** M(F) (works *or* factory) manager; **Betriebsleitung** F management; **Betriebsnudel** F (*inf*) live wire (*inf*); (= *Witzbold*) office/club *etc* clown; **Betriebsoptimum** M optimum scale of operations; **Betriebsprüfung** F (government) audit; **Betriebsrat**[1] M (= *Gremium*) works *or* factory committee; **Betriebsrat**[2] M, **Betriebsrätin** F works *or* factory committee member; **Betriebsratsvorsitzende(r)** MF DECL AS ADJ chair of works *or* factory committee; **Betriebsstörung** F breakdown; **Betriebssystem** NT (*Comput*) operating system; **Betriebsunfall** M industrial accident; (*hum inf*) accident; **Betriebsvereinbarung** F internal agreement; **Betriebsvergleich** M inter-firm comparison; **Betriebsvermögen** NT operating assets *pl*, business capital; **gesamtes ~** aggregate assets *pl*; **landwirtschaftliches ~** farming stock; **Betriebsversammlung** F company meeting; **Betriebswirt(in)** M(F) management expert; **Betriebswirtschaft** F, NO PL business management; **betriebswirtschaftlich** ▮ ADJ business management *attr* ▮ ADV in terms of business management; **Betriebszugehörigkeit** F **nach zehnjähriger ~** after ten years of employment with the company

betrinken *ptp* **betrunken** [bəˈtrʊŋkn] VR IRREG to get drunk; *siehe auch* **betrunken**

betroffen [bəˈtrɔfn] ▮ ADJ (a) affected (*von* by) (b) (= *bestürzt*) sad; *Schweigen* awkward ▮ ADV (= *bestürzt*) in consternation; (= *betrübt*) in dismay; **jdn ~ ansehen** to look at sb in consternation; *siehe auch* **betreffen**

Betroffene(r) [bəˈtrɔfnə] MF DECL AS ADJ person affected; **schließlich sind wir die ~n** after all we are the ones who are affected

Betroffenheit F -, NO PL sadness; **stumme ~** awkward silence

betrog PRET *von* **betrügen**

betrogen PTP *von* **betrügen**

betrüben *ptp* **betrübt** VT to sadden, to distress; *siehe* **betrübt**

betrüblich [bəˈtryːplɪç] ▮ ADJ sad, distressing; *Zustände, Unwissenheit, Unfähigkeit* deplorable ▮ ADV **die Lage sieht ~ aus** things look bad

betrüblicherweise [bəˈtryːplɪçɐˈvaɪzə] ADV lamentably

betrübt [bəˈtryːpt] ADJ saddened

Betrug [bəˈtruːk] M -(e)s, NO PL deceit, deception; (*Jur*) fraud; **das ist ja (alles) ~** it's (all) a fraud; **das ist ja ~, du hast geguckt!** that's cheating, you looked!

betrügen [bəˈtryːgn], *pret* **betrog** [bəˈtroːk], *ptp* **betrogen** [bəˈtroːgn] ▮ VT to deceive; *Freund, Ehepartner* to be unfaithful to; (*Jur*) to defraud; **jdn um etw ~** to cheat sb out of sth; (*Jur*) to defraud sb of sth; **sie betrügt mich mit meinem besten Freund** she is having an affair with my best friend; **ich fühle mich betrogen** I feel betrayed; **sich um etw betrogen sehen** to feel deprived of sth; **sich in seinen Hoffnungen betrogen**

sehen to be disappointed in one's hopes ▮ VR to deceive oneself

Betrüger [bəˈtryːgɐ] M -s, -, **Betrügerin** [-ərɪn] F -, -nen (*beim Spiel*) cheat; (*geschäftlich*) swindler; (*Jur*) defrauder; (= *Hochstapler*) confidence trickster (*esp Brit*)

Betrügerei [bəˈtryːgəˈraɪ] F -, -en deceit; (*geschäftlich*) swindling *no pl*; (*von Ehepartner*) deceiving *no pl*; (*Jur*) fraud

betrügerisch [bəˈtryːgərɪʃ] ADJ deceitful; (*Jur*) fraudulent; **in ~er Absicht** with intent to defraud

betrunken [bəˈtrʊŋkn] ADJ drunk *no adv*, drunken *attr*; **Fahren in ~em Zustand** driving while under the influence alcohol (form); *siehe auch* **betrinken**

Betrunkene(r) [bəˈtrʊŋknə] MF DECL AS ADJ drunk

Betrunkenheit F -, NO PL drunkenness

Bett [bɛt] NT -(e)s, -en (*alle Bedeutungen*) bed; **das ~ machen** to make the bed; *Frühstück ans ~* breakfast in bed; **im ~** in bed; **ins** *or* **zu ~ gehen** to go to bed; **jdn ins** *or* **zu ~ bringen** to put sb to bed; **mit jdm ins ~ gehen/steigen** (*euph*) to go to/jump into bed with sb; **er hat sich ins gemachte ~ gelegt** (*fig*) he had everything handed to him on a plate

Bett-: Bettbezug M duvet cover; **Bettcouch** F bed settee (*Brit*), pullout couch (*US*); **Bettdecke** F blanket; (*gesteppt*) quilt

Bettel [ˈbɛtl] M -s, NO PL **den (ganzen) ~ hinschmeißen** (*inf*) to chuck the whole thing (*inf*)

Bettelei [bɛtəˈlaɪ] F -, -en begging

betteln [ˈbɛtln] VI to beg; **„Betteln verboten"** "no begging"; **(bei jdm) um etw ~** to beg (sb) for sth

betten [ˈbɛtn] ▮ VT (= *legen*) to make a bed for; *Kopf* to lay; **jdn weich ~** to put sb on a soft bed; **jdn flach ~** to lay sb down flat ▮ VR to make a bed for oneself; **wie man sich bettet, so liegt man** (*Prov*) as you make your bed so you must lie on it (*Brit Prov*), you make the bed you lie in (*US Prov*)

Bett-: Bettgeschichte F (love) affair; **~n** bedroom antics; **Bettgestell** NT bedstead; **bettlägerig** [-lɛːgərɪç] ADJ bedridden; **Bettlaken** NT sheet

Bettler [ˈbɛtlɐ] M -s, -, **Bettlerin** [-ərɪn] F -, -nen beggar

Bett-: Bettnässen NT -s, NO PL bed-wetting; **Bettnässer** [ˈbɛtnɛsɐ] M -s, -, **Bettnässerin** [-ərɪn] F -, -nen bed-wetter; **bettreif** ADJ ready for bed; **Bettrost** M (bed) base; **Bettschwere** F (*inf*) **die nötige ~ haben/bekommen** to be/get tired enough to sleep; **Betttuch** NT, *pl* **-tücher** sheet; **Bettüberwurf** M bedspread; **Bettvorleger** M bedside rug; **Bettwäsche** F bed linen; **Bettzeug** NT, NO PL bedding

betucht [bəˈtuːxt] ADJ (*inf*) well-to-do

betulich [bəˈtuːlɪç] ▮ ADJ (a) (= *übertrieben besorgt*) fussing *attr*; *Redeweise* old-womanish; **sei doch nicht so ~** don't be such an old mother hen (*inf*) (b) (= *beschaulich*) leisurely *no adv* ▮ ADV (a) (= *überbesorgt*) fussily; *reden* like an old woman (b) (= *gemächlich*) in a calm, unhurried fashion

Betulichkeit F -, NO PL (a) (= *übertriebene Besorgtheit*) fussing; **er redet mit einer schrecklichen ~** he talks in such a dreadfully old-womanish way (b) (= *Gemächlichkeit*) leisureliness; (= *Biederkeit*) staidness

betupfen *ptp* **betupft** VT to dab; (*Med*) to swab

Beuge [ˈbɔʏgə] F -, -n bend; (*von Arm auch*) crook; (= *Rumpfbeuge*) forward bend; (*seitlich*) sideways bend; (= *Kniebeuge*) knee bend; **in die ~ gehen** to bend

beugen [ˈbɔʏgn] ▮ VT (a) (= *krümmen*) to bend; **das Recht ~** to pervert the course of justice; **vom Alter gebeugt** bent by age; **von Kummer/Gram gebeugt** bowed down with grief/sorrow; *siehe auch* **gebeugt** (b) (*Gram*) to decline; *Verb* to conjugate ▮ VR to bend; (*fig*) to submit (*+dat* to); **sich nach vorn ~** to bend forward; **sich aus dem Fenster ~** to lean out of the window; **er beugte sich zu mir herüber** he leaned across to me; **über seine Bücher/seinen Teller gebeugt** hunched over his books/his plate; **sich der Mehrheit ~** to bow to the will of the majority

Beugung F -, -en (a) (= *Krümmung*) bending; **eine ~ des Rechts** a perversion of (the course of) justice (b) (*Gram*) declension; (*von Verb*) conjugation

Beule [ˈbɔʏlə] F -, -n (*von Stoß etc*) bump; (*eiternd*) boil; (= *Delle*) dent

beunruhigen [bəˈʊnruːɪgn], *ptp* **beunruhigt** ▮ VT to worry; **es ist ~d** it's worrying ▮ VR to worry (oneself) (*über +acc, um, wegen* about)

beurkunden [bəˈʔuːɛkʊndn], *ptp* **beurkundet** VT to certify; *Vertrag* to record; *Geschäft* to document

Beurkundung F (= *Dokument*) documentary evidence *no indef art, no pl*

beurlauben *ptp* **beurlaubt** VT to give leave (of absence); (*Univ*) *Studenten* to give time off; *Lehrpersonal* to give *or* grant sabbatical leave; (= *von Pflichten befreien*) to excuse (*von* from); **beurlaubt sein** to be on leave, to have leave of absence; to have time off; to be on sabbatical leave; (= *suspendiert sein*) to have been relieved of one's duties; **sich ~ lassen** to take leave (of absence)/time off/sabbatical leave

Beurlaubung [bəˈʔuːɛlaʊbʊŋ] F -, -en (= *das Beurlaubtsein*) leave (of absence); (*von Studenten*) time off; (*von Lehrpersonal*) sabbatical leave; **seine ~ vom Dienst** (= *Befreiung*) his being excused (from) his duties; (= *Suspendierung*) his being relieved of his duties

beurteilen *ptp* **beurteilt** VT to judge (*nach* by, from); *Buch, Bild etc* to give an opinion of; *Leistung, Wert* to assess; **etw falsch ~** to misjudge sth; **du kannst das doch gar nicht ~** you are not in a position to judge

Beurteilung F (= *das Beurteilen*) judging; (*von Leistung, Wert*) assessing; (= *Urteil*) assessment; (= *Kritik: von Stück etc*) review

Beute [ˈbɔʏtə] F -, NO PL (= *Kriegsbeute*) (*auch fig hum*) spoils *pl*, loot *no indef art*; (= *Diebesbeute*) haul; (*von Raubtieren etc*) prey; (*getötete*) kill; (= *Jagdbeute*) bag; (*beim Fischen*) catch

Beutekunst F, NO PL *works of art taken by the occupying forces during a war*

Beutel [ˈbɔʏtl] M -s, - (a) (= *Behälter*) bag; (= *Tasche*) (drawstring) bag *or* purse; (= *Tragetasche*) carrier bag; (= *Tabaksbeutel*) (*Zool*) pouch; (= *Päckchen*) packet (b) (*inf*: = *Geldbeutel*) (*von Frau*) purse; (*von Mann*) wallet; **jds ~ ist leer** sb is broke (*inf*); (*von Staat etc*) sb's coffers are empty

Beutel-: **Beutelratte** F opossum; **Beuteltier** NT marsupial

bevölkern [bəˈfœlkɐn], *ptp* **bevölkert** 1 VT (= *bewohnen*) to inhabit; (= *beleben*) to fill; (= *besiedeln*) to populate; **schwach/ stark** *or* **dicht bevölkert** sparsely/densely populated; **tausende** *or* **Tausende bevölkerten den Marktplatz** the marketplace was crowded with thousands of people 2 VR to become inhabited; (*fig*) to fill up

Bevölkerung F -, -en (= *die Bewohner*) population

Bevölkerungs-: **Bevölkerungsdichte** F population density; **Bevölkerungsexplosion** F population explosion; **Bevölkerungsschicht** F social class; **Bevölkerungszahl** F (total) population

bevollmächtigen [bəˈfɔlmɛçtɪɡn], *ptp* **bevollmächtigt** VT to authorize (*zu etw* to do sth)

Bevollmächtigte(r) [bəˈfɔlmɛçtɪçtə] MF DECL AS ADJ authorized representative; (*Pol*) plenipotentiary

bevor [bəˈfoːɛ] CONJ before; **~ Sie (nicht) die Rechnung bezahlt haben** until you pay *or* you have paid the bill

bevormunden [bəˈfoːɛmʊndn], *ptp* **bevormundet** VT to treat like a child; **jdn ~** to make sb's decisions (for him/her)

Bevormundung [bəˈfoːɛmʊndʊŋ] F -, -en **seine Schüler/ Untergebenen** *etc* **wehren sich gegen die ständige ~** his pupils/subordinates *etc* object to his constantly making up their minds for them

bevorstehen VI SEP IRREG to be imminent; (*Winter etc*) to approach; **jdm ~** to be in store for sb; **das Schlimmste steht uns noch bevor** the worst is yet to come

bevorstehend ADJ forthcoming; *Gefahr, Krise* imminent; *Winter* approaching

bevorzugen [bəˈfoːɛtsuːɡn], *ptp* **bevorzugt** VT to prefer; (= *begünstigen*) to favour (*Brit*), to favor (*US*); **hier wird niemand bevorzugt** there's no favouritism (*Brit*) *or* favoritism (*US*) here

bevorzugt [bəˈfoːɛtsuːkt] 1 ADJ preferred; *Behandlung* preferential; (= *privilegiert*) privileged 2 ADV **jdn ~ abfertigen/ bedienen** *etc* to give sb preferential treatment; **etw ~ abfertigen/bedienen** *etc* to give sth priority

Bevorzugung F -, -en preference (+*gen* for); (= *vorrangige Behandlung*) preferential treatment (*bei* in)

bewachen *ptp* **bewacht** VT to guard

Bewachung F -, -en guarding; (= *Wachmannschaft*) guard; **jdn unter ~ halten/stellen** to keep/put sb under guard

bewaffnen *ptp* **bewaffnet** 1 VT to arm 2 VR (*lit, fig*) to arm oneself

Bewaffnung [bəˈvafnʊŋ] F -, -en (a) NO PL (= *das Bewaffnen*) arming; **man hat die ~ der Polizei beschlossen** it was decided to arm the police (b) (= *Waffen*) weapons *pl*

bewahren *ptp* **bewahrt** VT (a) (= *beschützen*) to protect (*vor* +*dat* from); (**i** *or* **Gott**) **bewahre!** (*inf*) heaven forbid! (b) (*geh*: = *aufbewahren*) to keep; **jdn/etw in guter Erinnerung ~** to have happy memories of sb/sth (c) (= *beibehalten*) to keep; **sich** (*dat*) **etw ~** to keep sth

bewähren *ptp* **bewährt** VR (*Mensch*) to prove oneself; (*Gerät etc*) to prove its worth; (*Methode, Plan, Investition, Sparsamkeit, Fleiß*) to pay off; (*Auto*) to prove (to be) a good investment; **sich im Leben ~** to make something of one's life; **wenn sich der Straftäter bewährt** if the offender proves he has reformed; **es bewährt sich immer, das zu tun** it's always worthwhile doing that; **ihre Freundschaft hat sich bewährt** their friendship stood the test of time; *siehe auch* **bewährt**

bewahrheiten [bəˈvaːɛhaɪtn], *ptp* **bewahrheitet** VR (*Befürchtung, Hoffnung, Gerücht*) to prove (to be) well-founded; (*Prophezeiung*) to come true

bewährt [bəˈvɛːɛt] ADJ proven, tried and tested; *Geldanlage* worthwhile; *Rezept* tried and tested; **vielfach ~** tried and tested; **seit langem ~** well-established; *siehe auch* **bewähren**

Bewährung F (a) (*von Menschen*) proving oneself; (*von Gerät*) proving its worth; (*von Methode, Plan, Investition*) proving itself worthwhile (b) (*Jur*) probation; **eine Strafe zur ~ aussetzen** to impose a suspended sentence; **ein Jahr Gefängnis mit ~** a suspended sentence of one year; **ohne ~** without probation; **er hat noch ~** he is still on probation

Bewährungs-: **Bewährungsfrist** F (*Jur*) probation(ary) period; **Bewährungshelfer(in)** M(F) probation officer; **Bewährungsprobe** F test; **etw einer ~** (*dat*) **unterziehen** to put sth to the test

bewältigen [bəˈvɛltɪɡn], *ptp* **bewältigt** VT *Schwierigkeiten, Problem* to cope with; *Arbeit, Aufgabe auch, Strecke* to manage; *Vergangenheit, Erlebnis etc* to get over; (= *erledigen, beenden*) to deal with; (= *aufessen*) to manage

bewandert [bəˈvandɐt] ADJ experienced; **in etw** (*dat*) **~ sein** to be familiar with *or* well-versed in sth; **auf einem Gebiet ~ sein** to be experienced in a field

Bewandtnis [bəˈvantnɪs] F -, -se reason; **damit hat es** *or* **das hat eine andere ~** there's another reason for that; **damit hat es** *or* **das hat seine eigene ~** that's a long story; **damit hat es** *or* **das hat folgende ~** the fact of the matter is this/the facts of the matter are these

bewässern *ptp* **bewässert** VT to irrigate; (*mit Sprühanlage*) to water

Bewässerungssystem NT irrigation system

bewegen¹ [bəˈveːɡn], *ptp* **bewegt** 1 VT (a) (= *Lage verändern, regen*) to move; *Hund, Pferd* to exercise (b) (= *innerlich ~*) to move; (= *beschäftigen, angehen*) to concern; **dieser Gedanke bewegt mich seit langem** this has been on my mind a long time; **~d** moving; *siehe auch* **bewegt** (c) (= *bewirken, ändern*) to change 2 VR (a) (= *in Bewegung sein*) to move; **beide Reden bewegten sich in der gleichen Richtung** both speeches were along the same lines (b) (= *Bewegung haben: Mensch*) to get some exercise (c) (*fig*: = *variieren, schwanken*) to vary (*zwischen* between); **der Preis bewegt sich um die 50 Euro** the price is about 50 euros; **die Verluste ~ sich in den tausenden** *or* **Tausenden** losses are in the thousands (d) (= *sich ändern, Fortschritte machen*) to change; **es bewegt sich etwas** things are beginning to happen

bewegen² *pret* **bewog** [bəˈvoːk], *ptp* **bewogen** [bəˈvoːɡn] VT **jdn zu etw ~** to persuade sb to do sth; **was hat dich dazu bewogen?** what persuaded you to do that?

Beweggrund M motive

beweglich [bəˈveːklɪç] ADJ (a) (= *bewegbar*) movable (b) (= *wendig*) agile; *Fahrzeug* manoeuvrable (*Brit*), maneuverable (*US*); (= *geistig ~*) nimble-minded; *Geist* nimble; **mit einem Kleinwagen ist man in der Stadt ~er** you're more mobile in town with a small car

bewegt [bəˈveːkt] ADJ (a) (= *unruhig*) *Wasser, See* choppy; *Zeiten, Vergangenheit, Leben* eventful; **die See war stark ~/ kaum ~** the sea was rough/fairly calm (b) (= *gerührt*) *Stimme*,

Worte, Stille emotional; ~ **sein** to be moved; *siehe auch* **bewegen**

Bewegung [bə'veːɡʊŋ] F -, -en (a) movement; (*Sci, Tech*) movement, motion; **eine falsche ~!** one false move!; **keine ~!** freeze! (*inf*); **in ~ sein** (*Fahrzeug*) to be moving; (*Menge*) to mill around; **sich in ~ setzen** to start moving; **etw in ~ setzen** *or* **bringen** to set sth in motion; **Himmel und Hölle** *or* **alle Hebel in ~ setzen** to move heaven and earth (b) (= *körperliche ~*) exercise; **sich** (*dat*) **~ verschaffen** *or* **machen** to get (some) exercise (c) (= *Unruhe*) agitation; **diese Nachricht ließ die ganze Stadt in ~ geraten** this news threw the whole town into a state of agitation; **plötzlich kam ~ in die Menschenmenge** the crowd suddenly became agitated (d) (= *Entwicklung*) progress; **etw kommt in ~** sth gets moving; **endlich kam ~ in die Verhandlungen** at last there was some progress in the negotiations (e) (= *Ergriffenheit*) emotion (f) (*Pol, Art etc*) movement

Bewegungs-: **Bewegungsdrang** M urge to be active; **Bewegungsfreiheit** F freedom of movement; (*fig*) freedom of action; **bewegungslos** **1** ADJ motionless **2** ADV without moving; *liegen, sitzen, stehen* motionless; **Bewegungsmelder** [-mɛldɐ] M -s, - sensor (*which registers movement*); **bewegungsunfähig** ADJ unable to move; (= *gehunfähig*) unable to move about

beweinen *ptp* **beweint** VT to mourn (for)

Beweis [bə'vais] M -es, -e [-zə] proof (*für* of); (= *Zeugnis*) evidence *no pl*; **als** *or* **zum ~** as proof *or* evidence; **ein eindeutiger ~** clear evidence; **etw unter ~ stellen** to prove sth; **den ~ antreten, einen/den ~ führen** to offer evidence *or* proof; **~ erheben** (*Jur*) to hear evidence; **jdm einen ~ seiner Hochachtung geben** to give sb a token of one's respect

Beweis-: **Beweisaufnahme** F (*Jur*) hearing of evidence; **beweisbar** ADJ provable

beweisen *ptp* **bewiesen** [bə'viːzn] IRREG VT (a) (= *nachweisen*) to prove; **was zu ~ war** QED; **was noch zu ~ wäre** that remains to be seen (b) (= *erkennen lassen*) to show

Beweis-: **Beweisführung** F (*Jur*) presentation of one's case; (*Math*) proof; (= *Argumentation*) line of argument; **Beweiskraft** F value as evidence; **beweiskräftig** ADJ evidential (*Brit*), evidentiary (*US*); **Beweislage** F (*Jur*) body of evidence; **Beweismaterial** NT (body of) evidence; **Beweisstück** NT exhibit

bewenden VT IMPERS **es bei** *or* **mit etw ~ lassen** to be content with sth; **wir wollen es dabei ~ lassen** let's leave it at that

bewerben *ptp* **beworben** [bə'vɔrbn] IRREG **1** VR to apply (*um* for, *als* for the position *or* job of); **sich bei einer Firma ~** to apply to a firm (for a job) **2** VT *Produkte, Firmen* to promote

Bewerber(in) M(F) applicant

Bewerbung F application

Bewerbungs-: **Bewerbungsgespräch** NT (job) interview; **Bewerbungsschreiben** NT (letter of) application; **Bewerbungsunterlagen** PL application documents *pl*

bewerfen *ptp* **beworfen** [bə'vɔrfn] VT IRREG (a) **jdn/etw mit etw ~** to throw sth at sb/sth (b) (*Build*) to face; (*mit Rauputz*) to roughcast; **mit Kies beworfen** pebble-dashed

bewerkstelligen [bə'vɛrkʃtelɪɡn], *ptp* **bewerkstelligt** VT to manage; *Geschäft* to bring off; **es ~, dass jd etw tut** to manage to get sb to do sth

bewerten *ptp* **bewertet** VT *jdn* to judge; *Leistung auch, Schularbeit* to assess; *Gegenstand* to value; **etw zu hoch/niedrig ~** to overvalue/undervalue sth; **etw nach einem Maßstab ~** to judge sb/measure sth against a yardstick; **etw mit der Note 5 ~** to give sth a mark (*Brit*) or grade (*US*) of 5

Bewertung F judgement; (*von Leistung auch, von Schularbeit*) assessment; (*von Gegenstand*) valuation

Bewertungsmaßstab M set of criteria

bewiesenermaßen [bə'viːznɐ'maːsn] ADV **was er sagt, ist ~ unwahr** there is evidence to show that what he is saying is untrue; **er ist ~ ein Betrüger** he has been proved to be a fraud

bewilligen [bə'vɪlɪɡn], *ptp* **bewilligt** VT to allow; *Planstelle auch, Etat, Steuererhöhung etc* to approve; *Stipendium* to award

Bewilligung F -, -en allowing; (*von Etat, Steuererhöhung*) approving, approval; (*von Stipendium*) awarding; (= *Genehmigung*) approval; **dafür brauchen Sie eine ~** you

need approval for that; **die ~ für einen Kredit bekommen** to be granted credit

bewirken *ptp* **bewirkt** VT (a) (= *verursachen*) to cause; **~, dass etw passiert** to cause sth to happen (b) (= *erreichen*) to achieve

bewirten [bə'vɪrtn], *ptp* **bewirtet** VT **jdn ~** to feed sb; (*bei offiziellem Besuch etc*) to entertain sb (*by giving them a meal*); **jdn mit Kaffee und Kuchen ~** to entertain sb to coffee and cakes

bewirtschaften *ptp* **bewirtschaftet** VT (a) *Betrieb etc* to manage; **die Berghütte wird im Winter nicht bewirtschaftet** the mountain hut is not serviced in the winter (b) *Land* to farm (c) (= *staatlich kontrollieren*) *Waren* to ration; *Devisen, Wohnraum* to control

Bewirtschaftung [bə'vɪrtʃaftʊŋ] F -, -en (a) (*von Betrieb*) management (b) (*von Land*) farming (c) (= *staatliche Kontrolle*) rationing; (*von Devisen, Wohnraum*) control

Bewirtung F -, -en (= *das Bewirten*) hospitality; (*im Hotel*) (food and) service; **die ~ so vieler Gäste** catering for so many guests

Bewirtungskosten PL entertainment expenses *pl*

bewog PRET *von* **bewegen²**

bewogen PTP *von* **bewegen²**

bewohnbar ADJ habitable

bewohnen *ptp* **bewohnt** VT to live in; (*Volk*) to inhabit; **das Haus war jahrelang nicht bewohnt** the house was unoccupied for years; *siehe auch* **bewohnt**

Bewohner [bə'voːnɐ] M -s, -, **Bewohnerin** [-ərɪn] F -, -nen (*von Land, Gebiet*) inhabitant; (*von Haus etc*) occupier; **dieser Vogel ist ein ~ der Wälder** this bird is a forest dweller

Bewohnerschaft [bə'voːnɐʃaft] F -, -en occupants *pl*

bewohnt [bə'voːnt] ADJ inhabited; *siehe auch* **bewohnen**

bewölken [bə'vœlkn], *ptp* **bewölkt** VR (*lit, fig*) to cloud over; **bewölkt** cloudy; **bewölkt bis bedeckt** (*Met*) cloudy, perhaps overcast

Bewölkung F -, -en (= *das Bewölken*) clouding over; **wechselnde bis zunehmende ~** (*Met*) variable amounts of cloud

Bewunderer [bə'vʊndərɐ] M -s, -, **Bewunderin** [bə'vʊndərɪn] F -, -nen admirer

bewundern *ptp* **bewundert** VT to admire (*wegen* for); **~d** admiring

bewundernswert, bewundernswürdig **1** ADJ admirable **2** ADV admirably

Bewunderung [bə'vʊndərʊŋ] F -, (*rare*) -en admiration

Bewurf M (*Build*) facing; (= *Rauputz*) roughcast; (= *Kiesbewurf*) pebble dash

bewusst [bə'vʊst] **1** ADJ (a) (*auch Philos, Psych*) conscious; *Mensch* self-aware; **sie führte ein sehr ~es Leben** she lived a life of total awareness; **sich** (*dat*) **einer Sache** (*gen*) **~ sein/werden** to be/become aware of sth, to realize sth; **etw ist jdm ~** sb is aware of sth; **es wurde ihm allmählich ~, dass ...** he gradually realized (that) ... (b) ATTR (= *willentlich*) deliberate (c) ATTR (= *bekannt, besagt*) in question; *Zeit* agreed **2** ADV consciously; *leben* in total awareness; (= *willentlich*) deliberately

Bewusst-: **bewusstlos** **1** ADJ unconscious; **~ werden** to lose consciousness **2** ADV **jdn ~ prügeln/schlagen** to beat sb unconscious *or* senseless; **~ zusammenbrechen** to collapse unconscious; **Bewusstlose(r)** [bə'vʊstloːzə] MF DECL AS ADJ unconscious man/woman/person *etc*; **die ~n** the unconscious; **Bewusstlosigkeit** F -, NO PL unconsciousness; **bis zur ~** (*inf*) ad nauseam

Bewusstsein NT consciousness; **etw kommt jdm zu(m) ~** sb becomes aware of sth; **das allgemeine ~** general awareness; **im ~** (+*gen*)**/, dass ...** in the knowledge of that ...; **das ~ verlieren/wiedererlangen** to lose/regain consciousness; **bei ~ sein** to be conscious; **zu(m) ~ kommen** to regain consciousness; **bei vollem ~** fully conscious; **er tat es mit (vollem)/ohne ~** he was (fully) aware/he was not aware of what he was doing

Bewusstseins-: **bewusstseinserweiternd** ADJ **~e Drogen** mind-expanding drugs; **Bewusstseinsspaltung** F (*Med, Psych*) splitting of the consciousness

bez. ABBR (a) *von* **bez**a**hlt** paid (b) *von* **bezüglich** with reference to, re

beza**hlbar** ADJ payable; **das ist für die meisten durchaus ~** most people can certainly afford it

beza**hlen** ptp **bez**a**hlt** ☷ VT to pay; *Sache, Leistung, Schaden* to pay for; **etw an jdn ~** to pay sb sth; **etw bezahlt bekommen** or **kriegen** (*inf*) to get paid for sth; **jdm etw ~** (= *für jdn kaufen*) to pay for sth for sb; (= *Geld geben für*) to pay sb for sth; **er hat seinen Fehler mit dem Leben bezahlt** he paid for his mistake with his life; **Liebe ist nicht mit Geld zu ~** money can't buy love

☶ VI to pay; **Herr Ober, ~ bitte!** waiter, the bill (*Brit*) or check (*US*) please!

Beza**hlfernsehen** NT pay TV

beza**hlt** [bə'tsaːlt] ADJ paid; **sich ~ machen** to be worth it

Beza**hlung** F (a) (= *das Bezahlen*) payment; (*von Rechnung, Schulden*) paying off; (*von Leistung, Schaden*) paying for (*einer Sache* gen) sth (b) (= *Lohn, Gehalt*) pay; (*für Dienste*) payment; **ohne/gegen** or **für ~** without/for payment

beza**ubern** ptp **bez**a**ubert** ☷ VT (*fig*) to charm ☶ VI to be captivating

beza**ubernd** ADJ enchanting

beze**ichnen** ptp **bez**e**ichnet** VT (a) (= *kennzeichnen*) (*durch, mit* by) to mark; *Takt, Tonart* to indicate (b) (= *genau beschreiben*) to describe (c) (= *benennen*) to call, to describe; **ich weiß nicht, wie man das bezeichnet** I don't know what that's called; **jd/etw wird mit dem Wort ... bezeichnet** the word ... describes sb/sth; **er bezeichnet sich gern als Künstler** he likes to call himself an artist

beze**ichnend** ADJ (*für* of) characteristic; **es ist ~ für ihre Unfähigkeit, dass ...** it's indicative of her incompetence that ...

beze**ichnenderweise** [bə'tsaiçnəndɐ'vaizə] ADV **die Regierung hat ~ die Wahlversprechen wieder nicht eingehalten** typically (enough), the government hasn't kept its election promises again

Beze**ichnung** F (a) (= *Kennzeichnung*) marking; (*von Tonart, Takt*) indication; (= *Beschreibung, Benennung*) description (b) (= *Ausdruck*) expression

beze**ugen** ptp **bez**e**ugt** VT (*Sache*) to attest; (*Person auch*) to testify to; **~, dass ...** to attest the fact that...; to testify that ...

bezi**chtigen** [bə'tsɪçtɪɡn̩] ptp **bez**i**chtigt** VT to accuse; **jdn einer Sache** (gen) **~** to accuse sb of sth

bezi**ehbar** ADJ (a) *Wohnung etc* ready to move into (b) *Waren etc* obtainable

bezi**ehen** ptp **bezogen** [bə'tsoːɡn̩] IRREG ☷ VT (a) *Polster, Regenschirm* to (re)cover; *Bettdecke, Kissen* to put a cover on; *Geige etc* to string; **die Betten frisch ~** to change the beds (b) (= *einziehen in*) *Wohnung* to move into (c) *Posten, Position, Stellung* to take up (d) (= *sich beschaffen, erhalten*) to get (e) (= *in Beziehung setzen*) **etw auf jdn/etw ~** to apply sth to sb/sth; **warum bezieht er (bloß) immer alles auf sich?** why does he always take everything personally?; **auf jdn/etw bezogen** referring to sb/sth (f) (*Sw: = einfordern*) *Steuern* to collect

☶ VR (a) (*Himmel*) to cloud over (b) (= *betreffen, sich berufen*) **sich auf jdn/etw ~** to refer to sb/sth

Bezi**ehung** F (a) (= *Verhältnis*) relationship; (*Philos, Math*) relation (b) USU PL (= *Kontakt*) relations pl; **diplomatische ~en** diplomatic relations; **intime ~en zu jdm haben** to have intimate relations with sb; **menschliche ~en** human relations (c) (= *Zusammenhang*) connection (*zu* with), relation; **etw zu etw in ~ setzen** to relate sth to sth; **in keiner ~ zueinander stehen** to have no connection (with each other); **etw hat keine ~ zu etw** sth has no bearing on sth (d) USU PL (= *Verbindung*) connections pl (*zu* with); **seine ~en spielen lassen** to pull strings; **~en haben** to have connections; **~en muss/müsste man haben** you need to know the right people (e) (= *Sympathie*) (*zu etw*) feeling (*zu* for); (*zu jdm*) affinity (*zu* for), rapport (*zu* with); **er hat überhaupt keine ~ zu seinen Kindern** he just doesn't relate to his children

(f) (= *Hinsicht*) **in einer/keiner ~** in one/no respect; **in jeder ~** in every respect; **in mancher ~** in some respects

Bezi**ehungs-**: **Bez**i**ehungskiste** F (*inf*) relationship; **bez**i**ehungsreich** ADJ rich in associations

bezi**ehungsweise** CONJ (a) (= *oder aber*) or (b) (= *im anderen Fall*) and ... respectively; **zwei Briefmarken, die 50 ~ 70 Cent kosten** two stamps costing 50 and 70 cents respectively; **geben Sie in Ihrer Bestellung rot ~ blau als gewünschte Farbe an** state your choice of colour (*Brit*) or color (*US*) in your order: red or blue (c) (= *genauer gesagt*) or rather

Bezi**ehungswort** NT, pl **-wörter** (*Gram*) antecedent

bezi**ffern** [bə'tsɪfɐn] ptp **bez**i**ffert** ☷ VT (= *mit Ziffern versehen*) to number; *Bass* to figure; (= *angeben*) to estimate (*auf +acc, mit* at) ☶ VR **sich ~ auf** (+*acc*) (*Verluste, Schaden, Gewinn*) to amount to; (*Teilnehmer, Besucher*) to number

Bezi**rk** [bə'tsɪrk] M **-(e)s, -e** (a) (= *Gebiet*) district; (*fig: = Bereich*) sphere (b) (= *Verwaltungseinheit*) (*von Stadt*) ≈ district; (*von Land*) ≈ region

Bezi**rks-**: **Bez**i**rksgericht** NT (*Aus, Sw*) district court; **Bez**i**rkshauptmann** M (*Aus*) head official of local government; **Bez**i**rksrichter(in)** M(F) (*Aus, Sw*) district court judge; **Bez**i**rksspital** NT (*esp Sw*) district hospital

bezi**rzen** [bə'tsɪrtsn̩] ptp **bez**i**rzt** VT (*inf*) to bewitch

Bezogene(r) [bə'tsoːɡnə] MF DECL AS ADJ (*Fin*) (*von Scheck*) drawee; (*von Wechsel*) acceptor

Bezug M (a) (*für Kissen, Polster etc*) cover; (*für Kopfkissen*) pillowcase (b) (= *Erwerb*) (*von Waren etc*) buying; (*von Zeitung*) taking; **der ~ der diversen Magazine kostet uns ...** the various magazines we subscribe to cost (us) ... (c) (*Erhalt: von Einkommen, Rente etc*) drawing **Bezüge** PL (= *Einkünfte*) income (d) (= *Zusammenhang*) = **Beziehung (c)** (e) (*form: = Berufung*) reference; **~ nehmen auf** (+*acc*) to make reference to; **~ nehmend auf** (+*acc*) referring to; **mit** or **unter ~ auf** (+*acc*) with reference to (f) (= *Hinsicht*) **in ~ auf** (+*acc*) regarding; **in ~ darauf** regarding that

bezü**glich** [bə'tsyːklɪç] ☷ PREP +GEN (*form*) regarding, re (*Comm*) ☶ ADJ (= *sich beziehend*) **das ~e Fürwort** (*Gram*) the relative pronoun; **auf etw** (*acc*) **~** relating to sth

Bezugnahme [-naːmə] F **-, -n** (*form*) reference; **unter ~ auf** (+*acc*) with reference to

Bezugs-: **bezugsberechtigt** ADJ entitled to draw; **Bezugsberechtigte(r)** [-bərɛçtɪçtə] MF DECL AS ADJ (*von Rente etc*) authorized drawer; (*von Versicherung*) beneficiary; **bezugsfertig** ADJ *Haus etc* ready to move into; **Bezugsperson** F **die wichtigste ~ des Kleinkindes** the person to whom the small child relates most closely

bezuschussen [bə'tsuːʃʊsn̩] ptp **bezuschusst** VT to subsidize

bezwecken [bə'tsvɛkn̩] ptp **bezweckt** VT to aim at; **etw mit etw ~** (*Mensch*) to intend sth by sth; **das bezweckt doch gar nichts** that doesn't get you anywhere (at all); **was soll das ~?** what's the point of that?

bezweifeln ptp **bezweifelt** VT to doubt, to question; **das ist nicht zu ~** that's beyond question

bezwingen ptp **bezwungen** [bə'tsvʊŋən] VT IRREG to conquer; (*Sport*) to beat; *Festung* to capture; *Zorn, Gefühle* to overcome; *Strecke* to do

Bf. ABBR *von* **Bahnhof, Brief**

BfA [beːʔɛfʔaː] F **-** ABBR *von* **Bundesversicherungsanstalt für Angestellte** *federal pensions office for salaried employees*

BGH [beːɡeːʔhaː] M **-s** ABBR *von* **Bundesgerichtshof**

BH [beːˈhaː] M **-(s), -(s)** ABBR *von* **Büstenhalter** bra

Bhf. ABBR *von* **Bahnhof**

bi [biː] ADJ PRED (*inf*) bi (*inf*)

bi- [biː], **Bi-** PREF bi-; **bidirektional** (*Comput*) bidirectional

Bia**thlet(in)** M(F) biathlete

Bia**thlon** [ˈbiːatlɔn] NT **-s, -s** (*Sport*) biathlon

bibbern [ˈbɪbɐn] VI (*inf*) (*vor Angst*) to tremble; (*vor Kälte*) to shiver; **um jdn/etw ~** to fear for sb/sth

Bibel [ˈbiːbl̩] F **-, -n** (*lit*) Bible; (*fig*) bible

Bibel-: **bibelfest** ADJ well versed in the Bible; **Bibelspruch** M biblical saying; **Bibelwort** NT, pl **-worte** biblical saying

Biber ['bi:bɐ] M **-s, -** (a) (= Tier, Pelz, Tuch) beaver (b) AUCH NT (= Tuch) flannelette sheet (esp Brit)

Biber-: Biberbau M, pl **-baue** beaver's lodge; **Biberbetttuch** NT flannelette sheet (esp Brit); **Biberburg** F beaver's lodge; **Biberpelz** M beaver (fur); **Bibertuch** NT, NO PL flannelette sheet (esp Brit)

Bibliograf [biblio'gra:f] M **-en, -en, Bibliografin** [-'gra:fɪn] F **-, -nen** bibliographer

Bibliografie [bibliogra'fi:] F **-, -n** [-'fi:ən] bibliography

bibliografisch [biblio'gra:fɪʃ] **1** ADJ bibliographic(al) **2** ADV bibliographically

bibliophil [biblio'fi:l] **1** ADJ Mensch bibliophil(e) (form), book-loving attr; Ausgabe for book-lovers **2** ADV ausgestattet for collectors of books

Bibliothek [biblio'te:k] F **-, -en** library

Bibliothekar [bibliote'ka:ɐ] M **-s, -e, Bibliothekarin** [-'ka:rɪn] F **-, -nen** librarian

bibliothekarisch [bibliote'ka:rɪʃ] **1** ADJ library attr; **~e Ausbildung** training as a librarian **2** ADV **~ ausgebildet sein** to be a trained/qualified librarian

biblisch ['bi:blɪʃ] ADJ biblical; **ein ~es Alter** a great age

Bidet [bi'de:] NT **-s, -s** bidet

bieder ['bi:dɐ] **1** ADJ (a) (= rechtschaffen) honest (b) (pej) conventional **2** ADV (pej) conventionally

Biederkeit F **-,** NO PL (a) (= Rechtschaffenheit) honesty (b) (pej) conventionality

Biedermeier ['bi:dɐmaiɐ] NT **-s,** NO PL Biedermeier period

Biedermeier- IN CPDS Biedermeier; **Biedermeiersträußchen** NT posy (with paper frill)

biegbar ADJ flexible

Biegefestigkeit F (Tech) bending strength

biegen ['bi:gn], pret **bog** [bo:k], ptp **gebogen** [gə'bo:gn] **1** VT (a) Draht, Rohr etc to bend; Glieder to flex; **auf Biegen und oder Brechen** (inf) by hook or by crook (inf); siehe auch **gebogen** (b) (Aus Gram: = flektieren) to inflect **2** VI AUX SEIN (Mensch, Wagen) to turn **3** VR to bend; **sich vor Lachen ~** (fig) to double up with laughter

biegsam ['bi:kza:m] ADJ flexible; Material auch pliable; Glieder, Körper supple; (fig) pliable

Biegung F **-, -en** (a) bend; (von Weg, Fluss) bend (+gen in); **der Fluss/die Straße macht eine ~** the river/road bends (b) (Aus Gram) inflection

Biene ['bi:nə] F **-, -n** bee

Bienen-: Bienengift NT bee poison; **Bienenhaltung** F beekeeping; **Bienenhaus** NT apiary; **Bienenhonig** M real honey; **Bienenkönigin** F queen bee; **Bienenschwarm** M swarm (of bees); **Bienensprache** F language of bees; **Bienenstich** M (a) bee sting (b) (Cook) cake coated with sugar and almonds and filled with custard or cream; **Bienenstock** M (bee)hive; **Bienenvolk** NT bee colony; **Bienenwachs** NT beeswax

Biennale [biɛ'na:lə] F **-, -n** biennial film/art festival

Bier [bi:ɐ] NT **-(e)s, -e** beer; **zwei ~, bitte!** two beers, please; **dunkles/helles ~** dark/light beer; **~ vom Fass** draught (Brit) or draft (US) beer; **das ist mein** etc **~** (fig inf) that's my etc business

Beer has a particularly long tradition in Germany and is of two main types: top-fermented beers (**Weizenbier**, made from wheat and barley) and bottom-fermented beers (lager beers that are stored in the barrel for four to six weeks). These are further divided into light, medium and dark. Some beers, such as **Kölsch** or **Berliner Weiße**, are drunk mainly in the region in which they are produced, but **Pilsener** or **Pils** - a light beer with a strong bitter taste, served in traditional tulip glasses - is found everywhere. Light beers such as **Dortmunder**, which is also called **Helles** or **Export** depending on the region and the brewing method, have a slightly bitter taste. Medium beers include **Märzen** and **Wiener Bier**. Dark beers taste more strongly of malt and are therefore somewhat sweet.

Bier- IN CPDS beer; **Bierbauch** M (inf) beer belly (inf); **Bierbrauerei** F (= das Brauen) (beer-)brewing; (= Betrieb) brewery

Bierchen ['bi:ɐçən] NT **-s, -** (glass of) beer

Bier-: Bierdeckel M beer mat (Brit) or coaster (US); **Bierdose** F beer can; **Bierfass** NT keg; **Bierfilz** M beer mat; **Bierflasche** F beer bottle; **Biergarten** M beer garden

Biergärten are unpretentious open-air bars that serve mainly beer and simple food. Most of them are located in the gardens and backyards of pubs. However, some bars operate exclusively as **Biergärten** and these are closed in the winter. **Biergärten** are originally a Bavarian institution but can now be found all over Germany.

Bier-: Bierkeller M (= Lager) beer cellar; (= Gaststätte auch) bierkeller; **Bierkrug** M tankard (esp Brit); (aus Steingut) (beer) stein; **Bierwurst** F ham sausage; **Bierzelt** NT beer tent

Biest [bi:st] NT **-(e)s, -er** (pej inf) (a) (= Tier) creature; (= Insekt) bug (b) (= Mensch) (little) wretch; (= Frau) bitch (sl)

Biet [bi:t] NT **-(e)s, -e** (Sw) area

bieten ['bi:tn], pret **bot** [bo:t], ptp **geboten** [gə'bo:tn] **1** VT (a) (= anbieten) to offer (jdm etw sb sth, sth to sb); (bei Auktion) to bid (auf +acc for); **wer bietet mehr?** will anyone offer me etc more?; (bei Auktion) any more bids?; **mehr bietet dir niemand** no-one will offer you more; **diese Stadt/dieser Mann hat nichts zu ~** this town/man has nothing to offer (b) (= geben) to give (jdm etw sb sth); Asyl to grant (jdm etw sb sth) (c) (= haben, aufweisen) to have; Problem, Schwierigkeit to present; **das Hochhaus bietet Wohnungen für fünfzig Familien** the tower block (Brit) or apartment building (US) provides accommodation for fifty families (d) (= zeigen, darbieten) Anblick, Bild to present; Film to show; Leistung to give; **die Mannschaft bot den Zuschauern ein hervorragendes Spiel** the team put on an excellent game for the spectators (e) (= zumuten) **sich** (dat) **etw ~ lassen** to stand for sth; **so etwas könnte man mir nicht ~** I wouldn't stand for that sort of thing; siehe **geboten 2** VI (Cards) to bid; (bei Auktion auch) to make a bid (auf +acc for) **3** VR (Gelegenheit, Lösung, Anblick etc) to present itself (jdm to sb); **ein grauenhaftes Schauspiel bot sich unseren Augen** a terrible scene met our eyes

Bieter ['bi:tɐ] M **-s, -, Bieterin** [-ərɪn] F **-, -nen** bidder

Bifokalbrille [bifo'ka:l-] F bifocals pl

Bigamie [biga'mi:] F **-, -n** [-'mi:ən] bigamy

Biker ['baikɐ] M **-s, -, Bikerin** ['baikərɪn] F **-, -nen** (inf: = Motorradfahrer) biker

Bikini [bi'ki:ni] M **-s, -s** bikini

bikonkav [bikɔn'ka:f, bikɔŋ'ka:f] ADJ biconcave

bikonvex [bikɔn'vɛks] ADJ biconvex

Bilanz [bi'lants] F **-, -en** (a) (Econ, Comm) balance; (= Abrechnung) balance sheet; **eine ~ aufstellen** to draw up a balance sheet; **~ machen** (fig inf) to check one's finances (b) (fig: = Ergebnis) end result; (die) **~ ziehen** to take stock (aus of)

Bilanz-: Bilanzanalyse F (Comm, Fin) balance sheet analysis; **Bilanzbuchhalter(in)** M(F) company accountant (who balances end-of-year accounts); **Bilanzgewinn** M (Comm, Fin) declared profit, balance sheet profit; **Bilanzklarheit** F (Comm, Fin) balance sheet clarity; **Bilanzkontinuität** F (Comm, Fin) principle of balance sheet consistency; **Bilanzstichtag** M (Comm, Fin) balance sheet date; **Bilanzverlust** M (Comm, Fin) accumulated loss; (= Verlustvortrag) loss carried forward; **Bilanzwert** M (Comm, Fin) book value

bilateral ['bi:latera:l, bilate'ra:l] ADJ bilateral

Bild [bɪlt] NT **-(e)s, -er** ['bɪldɐ] (a) (lit, fig) picture; (= Fotografie) photo; (Film) frame; (Art) (= Zeichnung) drawing; (= Gemälde) painting; **ein ~ machen** to take a photo; **etw im ~ festhalten** to photograph/paint/draw sth as a permanent record; **sie ist ein ~ von einer Frau** she's a fine specimen of a woman; **ein ~ des Elends** a picture of misery; **~: Hans Schwarz** (TV, Film) camera: Hans Schwarz (b) (= Abbild) image; (= Spiegelbild auch) reflection (c) (= Metapher) metaphor; **um mit einem or im ~ zu sprechen ...** to use a metaphor ...; **im ~ bleiben** to use the same metaphor (d) (= Erscheinungsbild) character; **das äußere ~ der Stadt** the appearance of the town; **sie gehören zum ~ dieser Stadt** they are part of the scene in this town

(e) (*fig*: = *Vorstellung*) image, picture; **im ~e sein** to be in the picture (*über +acc* about); **jdn ins ~ setzen** to put sb in the picture (*über +acc* about); **sich** (*dat*) **von jdm/etw ein ~ machen** to get an idea of sb/sth; **du machst dir kein ~ davon, wie schwer das war** you've no idea how hard it was; **das ~ des Deutschen/Amerikaners** the image of the German/American

Bild-: Bildatlas M pictorial atlas; **Bildauflösung** F (*TV, Comput*) resolution; **Bildausfall** M (*TV*) loss of vision; **Bildband** M, *pl* **-bände** illustrated book, coffee-table book; **Bildbeschreibung** F (*Sch*) description of a picture

bilden ['bɪldn] **1** VT **(a)** (= *formen, hervorbringen, Gram, Geometrie*) to form; *Körper, Figur* to shape; **sich** (*dat*) **ein Urteil/ eine Meinung ~** to form a judgement/an opinion
(b) *Kabinett, Regierung* to form; *Ausschuss, Gruppe auch, Fonds, Institution etc* to set up; *Vermögen* to acquire
(c) (= *ausmachen*) *Höhepunkt, Regel, Ausnahme, Problem, Gefahr etc* to constitute; **die Teile ~ ein Ganzes** the parts make up a whole; **die drei ~ ein hervorragendes Team** the three of them make (up) an excellent team
(d) (= *erziehen*) to educate
2 VR **(a)** (= *entstehen*) to form
(b) (= *lernen*) to educate oneself; (*durch Lesen etc*) to improve one's mind; (*durch Reisen etc*) to broaden one's mind; *siehe auch* **gebildet**
3 VI (= *der Bildung dienen*) to be educational; (*Lesen*) to improve the mind; (*Reisen*) to broaden the mind

bildend ADJ **die ~e Kunst** art; **die ~en Künste** the fine arts; **~er Künstler** artist

Bilderbuch NT picture book; **eine Landschaft wie im ~** a picturesque landscape

Bilderbuch- IN CPDS (*lit*) picture-book; (*fig*) perfect; **Bilderbuchlandung** F **eine ~** a perfect *or* textbook landing

Bilder-: Bilderrahmen M picture frame; **Bilderrätsel** NT picture puzzle; **bilderreich 1** ADJ *Buch etc* full of pictures; (*fig*) *Sprache* rich in imagery **2** ADV **~ sprechen** to use a lot of images

Bild-: Bildfernsprecher M videophone; **Bildfläche** F (*fig inf*) **auf der ~ erscheinen** to appear on the scene; **von der ~ verschwinden** to disappear (from the scene); **Bildfolge** F sequence of pictures; (*Film*) sequence of shots; **Bildfrequenz** F filming speed; **Bildgeschichte** F strip cartoon; **bildhaft 1** ADJ pictorial; *Beschreibung, Vorstellung, Sprache* vivid **2** ADV vividly; **Bildhauer(in)** M(F) sculptor; (*Frau auch*) sculptress; **Bildhauerei** [bɪlthaʊəˈraɪ] F -, NO PL sculpture; **bildhauerisch** ['bɪlthaʊərɪʃ] ADJ sculptural; **bildhübsch** ADJ *Mädchen* (as) pretty as a picture; *Kleid, Garten etc* really lovely; **Bildjournalist(in)** M(F) photojournalist; **Bildkonserve** F film recording; **Bildlaufleiste** F (*Comput*) scroll bar

bildlich ['bɪltlɪç] **1** ADJ pictorial; *Ausdruck etc* metaphorical **2** ADV pictorially; *meinen, gebrauchen, verwenden* metaphorically; **sich** (*dat*) **etw ~ vorstellen** to picture sth in one's mind's eye; **stell dir das mal ~ vor!** just picture it

Bild-: Bildmaterial NT pictures *pl*; (*für Vortrag*) visual material; (*für Buch*) pictorial material; (*Sch*) visual aids *pl*; **Bildplattenspieler** M video disc player; **Bildpunkt** M pixel; **Bildqualität** F (*TV, Film*) picture quality; (*Phot*) print quality; **Bildredakteur(in)** M(F) picture editor

Bildschirm M (*TV, Comput*) screen

Bildschirm-: Bildschirmabstrahlung F, NO PL screen radiation; **Bildschirmfilter** M (*Comput*) screen filter; **Bildschirmschoner** [-ʃoːnɐ] M -s, - (*Comput*) screen saver; **Bildschirmtext** M Viewdata® *sing*, Prestel®

Bild-: bildschön ADJ beautiful; **Bildstelle** F educational film hire service; **Bildstörung** F (*TV*) interference (on the picture); **Bildsuchlauf** M picture search; **Bildtafel** F plate

Bildung ['bɪldʊŋ] F -, **-en (a)** (= *Erziehung*) education; (= *Kultur*) culture; **zu seiner ~ macht er Abendkurse** he does evening classes to try and educate himself; **zu seiner ~ liest er viel** he reads to improve his mind; **die allgemeine ~** general education; (*eines Menschen*) one's general education; **höhere ~** higher education; (= *Kultur*) culture; **zu seiner ~ macht er Abendkurse** he does evening classes to try and educate himself; **zu seiner ~ liest er viel** he reads to improve his mind; **die allgemeine ~** general education; (*eines Menschen*) one's general education; **höhere ~** higher education; **~ haben** to be educated
(b) NO PL (= *das Formen*) formation; (*von Figuren etc*) fashioning; (*fig: von Charakter etc*) shaping; **zur ~ des Passivs** to form the passive
(c) NO PL (= *Entstehung: von Rost etc*) formation
(d) NO PL (*von Kabinett, Regierung*) formation; (*von Ausschuss,*

Gruppe, Fonds, Institution) setting up; (*von Vermögen*) acquisition

Bildungs-: bildungsbeflissen ADJ eager to improve one's mind; **Bildungsbürger(in)** M(F) member of the educated classes; **Bildungsbürgertum** NT educated classes *pl*; **Bildungschancen** PL educational opportunities *pl*; **Bildungseinrichtung** F educational institution; **bildungsfähig** ADJ educable; **bildungsfeindlich** ADJ anti-education; **Bildungsgang** M, *pl* **-gänge** school (and university) career; **Bildungsgrad** M level of education; **Bildungslücke** F gap in one's education; **Bildungsnotstand** M chronic shortage of educational facilities; **Bildungspolitik** F education policy; **bildungspolitisch 1** ADJ *Maßnahmen, Fehlentscheidung* with regard to educational policy; *Sprecher* on educational policy **2** ADV in terms of educational policy; **Bildungsreform** F educational reform; **Bildungsreise** F educational trip; **Bildungsstand** M level of education; **Bildungsstufe** F level of education; **eine hohe/niedrige ~ haben** to be highly/not very educated; **Bildungsurlaub** M educational holiday (*esp Brit*) *or* vacation (*US*); (*in Firma*) study leave; **Bildungsweg** M **jds ~** the course of sb's education; **auf dem zweiten ~** through night school; **einen anderen ~ einschlagen** to opt for a different type of education

> **ZWEITER BILDUNGSWEG**
>
> The school system in Germany is strictly regulated and relatively inflexible. Pupils who decide after leaving school that the certificate they gained does not reflect their true abilities or allow them to pursue their desired career in the way they would wish can correct this by following the **zweiter Bildungsweg**. The courses on offer range from the **mittlere Reife** and **Abitur** - in evening and half-day classes held by means of distance teaching - to short courses and courses for gaining extra qualifications. ▶ MITTLERE REIFE, ABITUR

Bildungswesen NT education system

Bild-: Bildunterschrift F caption; **Bildwiederholfrequenz** F, **Bildwiederholrate** F (*TV, Comput*) refresh rate; **Bildwörterbuch** NT pictorial dictionary; **Bildzuschrift** F reply enclosing photograph

Billard ['bɪljart] NT -s, -e [-də] *or* (*Aus*) -s (= *Spiel*) billiards *sing*

Billard- IN CPDS billiard; **Billardkugel** F billiard ball; **Billardtisch** M billiard table

Billeteur [bɪljeˈtøːɐ] M -s, -e **(a)** (*Aus*) usher **(b)** (*Sw*: = *Schaffner*) conductor

Billeteurin [bɪljeˈtøːrɪn] F -, -nen (*Aus*) usherette

Billeteuse [bɪljeˈtøːzə] F -, -n (*Sw*) conductress

Billett [bɪlˈjɛt] NT -(e)s, -e *or* -s **(a)** (*Sw, dated*: = *Fahrschein, Eintrittskarte*) ticket **(b)** (*Aus, obs*: = *Schreiben*) note; (= *Briefkarte*) letter (*Brit*) *or* correspondence (*US*) card

Billiarde [bɪlˈjardə] F -, -n million billion (*Brit*), thousand trillion (*US*)

billig ['bɪlɪç] ADJ **(a)** (= *preisgünstig*) cheap; *Preis* low; (= *minderwertig*) cheap; **~ abzugeben** going cheap; (*inf*: = *leicht verdient*) easy money; **etw für ~es Geld kaufen** to buy sth cheap; **~ davonkommen** (*inf*) to get off lightly **(b)** (*pej*) cheap; *Ausrede* feeble

Billig- IN CPDS cheap; **Billiganbieter(in)** M(F) supplier of cheap goods

billigen ['bɪlɪɡn] VT to approve; **etw stillschweigend ~** to condone sth

Billig-: Billigflagge F (*Naut*) flag of convenience; **Billigland** NT country with low production costs; **Billiglohnland** NT low-wage country

Billion [bɪˈljoːn] F -, -en thousand billion (*Brit*), trillion (*US*)

Bimbo ['bɪmbo] M -s, -s (*pej sl*: = *Schwarzer*) wog (*Brit pej sl*), nigger (*pej sl*)

Bimetall ['bɪ-] NT (= *Material*) bimetal; (= *~streifen*) bimetal strip

Bimmel ['bɪml] F -, -n (*inf*) bell

bimmeln ['bɪmln] VI (*inf*) to ring

Bimsstein M **(a)** pumice stone **(b)** (*Build*) breeze block

bin [bɪn] 1. PERS SING PRES *von* **sein**

binär [biˈnɛːɐ] ADJ binary

Binärkode M binary code

Binde ['bɪndə] F -, -n **(a)** (*Med*) bandage; (= *Schlinge*) sling **(b)** (= *Armbinde*) armband; (= *Augenbinde*) blindfold

(c) (= *Monatsbinde*) (sanitary) towel *or* (*esp US*) napkin
(d) sich (*dat*) **einen hinter die ~ gießen** *or* **kippen** (*inf*) to put a few drinks away

Binde-: Bindegewebe NT (*Anat*) connective tissue; **Bindeglied** NT connecting link; **Bindehaut** F (*Anat*) conjunctiva; **Bindehautentzündung** F conjunctivitis

binden ['bɪndn], *pret* **band** [bant], *ptp* **gebunden** [gə'bʊndn] **1** VT
(a) (= *zusammenbinden*) to tie; (= *festbinden*) to bind; (*fig geh*) to bind; **etw zu etw** *or* **in etw** (*acc*) **~** to tie sth into sth
(b) (= *durch Binden herstellen*) to bind; *Strauß, Kranz* to make up; *Knoten etc* to tie
(c) (= *zubinden*) *Schal* to tie; *Krawatte* to knot; **sich** (*dat*) **die Schuhe ~** to tie (up) one's shoelaces
(d) (= *fesseln, befestigen*) (*an* +acc to) to tie (up); *Boot* to moor; (*fig*) *Menschen* to tie; *Geldmittel* to tie up; (*Versprechen, Vertrag, Eid etc*) to bind; **jdn an Händen und Füßen ~** to bind sb hand and foot; **mir sind die Hände gebunden** (*fig*) my hands are tied; **nichts bindet mich an Glasgow** I have no special ties to keep me in Glasgow; **sie versuchte, ihn an sich zu ~** she tried to tie him to her; *siehe auch* **gebunden**
(e) *Staub, Erdreich, Farbe, Soße* to bind; (*Chem*) (= *aufnehmen*) to absorb; (= *sich verbinden mit*) to combine with
2 VI (*Mehl, Zement, Soße etc*) to bind; (*Klebstoff*) to bond; (*fig*) to tie one down; (*Erlebnisse*) to create a bond
3 VR (= *sich verpflichten*) to commit oneself (*an* +acc to); **ich will mich nicht ~** I don't want to get involved

bindend ADJ binding (*für* on); *Zusage* definite
Bindestrich M hyphen
Bindfaden M string; **ein (Stück) ~** a piece of string; **es regnet Bindfäden** (*inf*) it's sheeting down (*Brit inf*), it's coming down in buckets (*US inf*)
Bindung ['bɪndʊŋ] F -, -en **(a)** (= *Beziehung zu einem Partner*) relationship (*an* +acc with); (= *Verbundenheit mit einem Menschen, Ort*) tie, bond (*an* +acc with); (= *Verpflichtung*) commitment (*an* +acc to) **(b)** (= *Skibindung*) binding **(c)** (*Chem*) bond **(d)** (*Tex*) weave
Bindungsangst F USU PL fear of commitment *no pl*

binnen ['bɪnən] PREP +DAT or (*GEH*) +GEN (*form*) within; **~ kurzem** shortly
Binnen-: Binnendeich M inner dyke (*Brit*) *or* dike (*esp US*); **binnendeutsch** ADJ *Ausdruck, Wort* used in Germany; *Sprache, Dialekt* spoken in Germany; **Binnenfischerei** F freshwater fishing; **Binnengewässer** NT inland waters; **Binnengrenze** F internal border; **Binnenhafen** M river port; **Binnenhandel** M domestic trade; **Binnenland** NT **(a)** (= *Landesinneres*) interior **(b)** (*N Ger*: = *eingedeichtes Gebiet*) dyked (*Brit*) *or* diked (*esp US*) land; **Binnenmarkt** M home market; **der europäische ~** the European Single Market; **Binnenschiffer** [-ʃɪfɐ] M -s, -, **Binnenschifferin** [-ərɪn] F -, -nen sailor on inland waterways; (*auf Schleppkahn*) bargeman/-woman; **Binnenschifffahrt** F inland navigation; **Binnenwährung** F internal currency; **Binnenwirtschaft** F domestic economy
Binse ['bɪnzə] F -, -n USU PL rush; **in die ~n gehen** (*fig inf*: = *misslingen*) to be a washout (*inf*)
Binsenwahrheit F, **Binsenweisheit** F truism
Bio ['bi:o] F -, NO PL (*Sch inf*) biol (*inf*), bio (*esp US inf*)
bio- [bio, 'bi:o], **Bio-** IN CPDS bio-; **bioaktiv** [biolak'ti:f, 'bi:o-] ADJ *Waschmittel* biological; **Biochemie** [bioçe'mi:] F biochemistry; **biochemisch** [-'çe:mɪʃ] **1** ADJ biochemical **2** ADV biochemically; **Biodiesel** ['bi:o-] M biodiesel; **biodynamisch** [biody'na:mɪʃ] **1** ADJ biodynamic **2** ADV biodynamically; **Bioethik** ['bi:ole:tɪk] F, NO PL bioethics *sing or pl*; **Bioethiker** ['bi:ole:tikɐ] M -s, -, **Bioethikerin** [-ərɪn] F -, -nen bioethicist; **Biogas** ['bi:o-] NT methane gas
Biograf [bio'gra:f] M -en, -en, **Biografin** [-'gra:fɪn] F -, -nen biographer
Biografie [biogra'fi:] F -, -n [-'fi:ən] biography
biografisch [bio'gra:fɪʃ] **1** ADJ biographical **2** ADV biographically
Bioladen ['bi:o-] M wholefood shop

Biologe [bio'lo:gə] M -n, -n, **Biologin** [-'lo:gɪn] F -, -nen biologist
Biologie [biolo'gi:] F -, NO PL biology
biologisch [bio'lo:gɪʃ] **1** ADJ biological; *Anbau* organic; **~-technische Assistentin, ~-technischer Assistent** laboratory technician **2** ADV biologically; *anbauen* organically
Bio-: Biomasse ['bi:o-] F, NO PL (*Chem*) organic substances *pl*; **Biomüll** ['bi:o-] M organic waste; **Biophysik** [biofy'zi:k, 'bi:o-] F biophysics *sing*
Biopsie [bio'psi:] F -, -n [-'psi:ən] (*Med*) biopsy
Bio-: Bioreaktor ['bi:o-] M bioreactor; **Biorhythmus** ['bi:o-] M biorhythm; **das verlangt mein ~** my internal clock tells me it's necessary
BIOS ['bi:ɔs] NT - (*Comput*) ABBR *von* **Basic Input/Output System** BIOS
Bio-: Biosphäre [bio'sfe:rə, 'bi:o-] F, NO PL biosphere; **Biotechnik** [bio'tɛçnɪk, 'bi:o-] F biotechnology; **Biotechniker(in)** [bio'tɛçnikɐ, 'bi:o-, -ərɪn] M(F) bioengineer; **biotechnisch** [bio'tɛçnɪʃ, 'bi:o-] ADJ biotechnological; **Biotechnologie** [biotɛçnolo'gi:, 'bi:o-] F **(a)** NO PL (*Wissenschaft*) biotechnology **(b)** (*Verfahren*) biotechnological method; **Bioterrorismus** M bioterrorism; **Biotonne** ['bi:o-] F organic waste bin; **Biotop** [bio'to:p] NT -s, -e biotope
BIP [be:li:'pe:] NT - ABBR *von* **Bruttoinlandsprodukt** GDP
birgt [bɪrkt] 3. PERS SING PRES *von* **bergen**
Birke ['bɪrkə] F -, -n birch; (= *Baum auch*) birch tree
Birk- ['bɪrk-]: **Birkhahn** M black cock; **Birkhuhn** NT black grouse
Birma ['bɪrma] NT -s Burma
birmanisch [bɪr'ma:nɪʃ] ADJ Burmese
Birnbaum M (*Baum*) pear tree; (*Holz*) pear wood
Birne ['bɪrnə] F -, -n **(a)** pear **(b)** (= *Glühlampe*) (light) bulb
birst 3. PERS SING PRES *von* **bersten**

bis [bɪs]	
1 PRÄPOSITION	**2** BINDEWORT

1 PRÄPOSITION (+ACC)
(a) (*zeitlich*) until

Im Sinne von **bis spätestens** *wird* **bis** *meist mit* **by** *übersetzt.*

das muss bis Ende Mai warten that will have to wait until *or* till the end of May; **bis zum Schluss war unklar, wie der Prozess ausgehen würde** the outcome of the trial was in doubt right up to the end; **bis jetzt hat er nichts gesagt** up to now he has said nothing; **bis spätestens Montag darfst du es behalten** you can keep it until Monday, no longer; **bis zu diesem Zeitpunkt** up to this time; **dieser Brauch hat sich bis ins 19. Jahrhundert gehalten** this custom continued into the 19th century; **bis in den Sommer/die Nacht hinein** into the summer/night; **bis 5 Uhr kann ich das unmöglich machen/ gemacht haben** I can't possibly do it/get it done by 5 o'clock; **bis Ende Mai bin ich wieder in Berlin** I'll be in Berlin again by the end of May; **das sollte bis zum nächsten Sommer fertig sein** it should be finished by next summer; **bis gegen 5 Uhr ist das fertig** it'll be ready by about 5 o'clock; **Montag bis Freitag** Monday to *or* through (*US*) Friday; **bis einschließlich 5. Mai** up to and including 5th May; **bis ausschließlich 5. Mai** up to but not including 5th May; **bis bald/später/morgen!** see you soon/later/tomorrow!; **bis wann gilt der Fahrplan?** when is the timetable valid till?; **bis wann bleibt ihr hier?** how long are you staying here?; **bis wann ist das fertig?** when will that be finished?; **bis wann können Sie das machen?** when can you do it by?; **bis auf weiteres** until further notice; **sie geht bis auf weiteres auf die Schule in der Kantstraße** for the time being, she'll continue going to the school on Kantstraße
✦bis dahin *or* **dann** bis dahin *or* dann **muss die Arbeit fertig sein** the work must be finished by then; **bis dahin hatte sie noch nie etwas von Schröder gehört** up to then she hadn't heard anything about Schröder; **bis dahin ist noch viel Zeit** that's still a long time off; **bis dahin bin ich alt und grau** I'll be old and grey (*Brit*) *or* gray (*US*) by then; **bis dahin ist er**

längst **weg** he will have gone long before then; **bis dann!** see you then!

✦**von ... bis ...** from ... to *or* through (*US*) ...; (*mit Uhrzeiten*) from ... till ...; **von 10 Uhr bis 17 Uhr** from 10am till 5pm **(b)** (*räumlich*) to; (*in Buch, Film, Erzählung*) up to; **bis durch/über/unter** right through/over/under; **bis an unsere Mauer** up to our wall; **es sind noch 10 km bis nach Schlüchtern** it's another 10 km to Schlüchtern; **bis ins Letzte** *or* **Kleinste** down to the smallest detail; **bis wo/wohin?** how far?; **bis dort** *or* **dahin** (to) there; **wie weit ist es zum nächsten Supermarkt? – bis dorthin sind es nur 5 km** how far is the nearest supermarket? – it's only 5km (away); **bis hierher** this far; **bis hierher und nicht weiter** (*lit, fig*) this far and no further; **höchstens bis Carlisle** to Carlisle at the furthest; **bis mindestens Carlisle** at least as far as Carlisle; **bis einschließlich** up to and including; **bis einschließlich Kapitel 3** up to the end of chapter 3; **bis ausschließlich** up to but not including
(c) (*mit Maßangaben*) up to; **Kinder bis sechs Jahre** children up to the age of six
(d) (*andere Wendungen*)

✦**bis zu** (= *bis zu einer oberen Grenze von*) up to; (= *bis zu einer unteren Grenze von*) (down) to

✦**bis auf** (+*acc*) (= *außer*) except (for); (= *einschließlich*) (right) down to; **bis auf Sandra** they all came, except Sandra; **alle ertranken, bis auf den letzten Mann** every single one of them drowned

Ⅱ BINDEWORT
(a) (*beiordnend*) to; **zehn bis zwanzig Stück** ten to twenty; **bewölkt bis bedeckt** cloudy or overcast
(b) (*unterordnend*) (*zeitlich*) until, till; (= *nicht später als*) by the time; **ich warte noch, bis es dunkel wird** I'll wait until it gets dark; **bis es dunkel wird, möchte ich zu Hause sein** I want to get home before it gets dark; **das muss gemacht sein, bis ich nach Hause komme** it must be done by the time I come home; **bis das einer merkt!** it'll be ages before anyone realizes (*inf*)
(c) (= *sobald*) (*Aus inf*) when; **gleich bis er kommt** the moment he comes (*inf*)

Bischof [ˈbɪʃɔf, ˈbɪʃoːf] M **-s, ̈-e** [ˈbɪʃøfə, ˈbɪʃøːfə], **Bischöfin** [ˈbɪʃœfɪn, ˈbɪʃøːfɪn] F **-, -nen** bishop
bischöflich [ˈbɪʃøːflɪç, ˈbɪʃøːflɪç] ADJ episcopal
Bischofs-: Bischofssitz M diocesan town; **Bischofsstab** M crosier
Bisexualität [bizɛksualiˈtɛːt, ˈbiː-] F bisexuality
bisexuell [bizɛˈksuɛl, ˈbiː-] ADJ bisexual

bisher [bɪsˈheːɐ] ADV until now; (= *und immer noch*) up to now; **~ nicht** not until now, not before; (= *und immer noch nicht*) not as yet; **das wusste ich ~ nicht** I didn't know that before; **~ habe ich es ihm nicht gesagt** I haven't told him as yet; **ein ~ unbekannter Stern** a previously unknown star; **alle ~ bekannten Sterne** all the known stars
bisherig [bɪsˈheːrɪç] ADJ ATTR (= *vorherig*) previous; (= *momentan*) present; **wir müssen unsere ~en Anschauungen revidieren** we will have to revise our present views; **das ist mir in meiner ~en Karriere noch nicht vorgekommen** I've never known that in my career up to now

Biskaya [bɪsˈkaːja] F **- die** = (the) Biscay; **Golf von** = Bay of Biscay
Biskuit [bɪsˈkviːt, bɪsˈkuiːt] NT *or* M **-(e)s, -s** *or* **-e** (fatless) sponge
Biskuit-: Biskuitgebäck NT sponge cake/cakes; **Biskuitteig** M sponge mixture
bislang [bɪsˈlan] ADV = **bisher**
Bismarckhering [ˈbɪsmark-] M Bismarck herring
Bison [ˈbiːzɔn] M **-s, -s** bison
biss PRET *von* **beißen**
Biss [bɪs] M **-es, -e** bite; (*fig*) vigour (*Brit*), vigor (*US*); **mit einem ~ war das Törtchen verschwunden** the tart disappeared in one mouthful; **Spag(h)etti/Bohnen mit ~** spaghetti/beans al dente; **~ haben** (*inf*) to have punch
bisschen [ˈbɪsçən] **Ⅰ** ADJ INV **ein ~ Geld/Liebe/Wärme** a bit of money/love/warmth; **ein ~ Milch/Wasser** a drop of milk/water; **ein klein ~ ...** a little bit/drop of ...; **kein ~ ...** not one (little) bit/not a drop of ...; **das ~ Geld/Whisky** that little bit

of money/drop of whisky; **ich habe kein ~ Hunger** I'm not a bit hungry
Ⅱ ADV **ein ~ a** bit, a little; **ein klein ~ a** little bit; **ein ~ wenig** not very much; **ein ~ mehr/viel/teuer** *etc* a bit more/much/expensive *etc*; **ein ~ zu wenig** not quite enough
Ⅲ NT INV **ein ~ a** bit, a little; (*von Flüssigkeit*) a drop; **ein ganz ~** (*inf*) just a tiny bit/drop
Bissen [ˈbɪsn] M **-s, -** mouthful; (= *Imbiss*) bite (to eat); **er will keinen ~ anrühren** he won't eat a thing; **sich** (*dat*) **jeden ~ vom** *or* **am Munde absparen** to watch every penny one spends
bissig [ˈbɪsɪç] ADJ **(a)** (*lit, fig*) vicious; **~ sein** to bite; „**Vorsicht, ~er Hund**" "beware of the dog" **(b)** (= *übellaunig*) waspish; **du brauchst nicht gleich ~ zu werden** there's no need to bite my *etc* head off
Bisswunde F bite
bist [bɪst] 2. PERS SING PRES *von* **sein**
biste [ˈbɪsta] (*dial inf*) CONTR *von* **bist du**
Bistum [ˈbɪstuːm] NT **-s, ̈-er** [-tyːmɐ] diocese
Bit [bɪt] NT **-(s), -(s)** (*Comput*) bit
Bittbrief M petition
bitte [ˈbɪtə] INTERJ **(a)** (*bittend, auffordernd*) please; **~ schön** please; **wo ist ~ das nächste Telefon?** could you please tell me where the nearest telephone is?; **~ nicht!** no, please!, please don't!; **ja ~!, ~ ja!** yes please; **~ ~ machen** (*inf*) (*Kind*) ≈ to say pretty please; **~ zahlen, zahlen ~!** (could I/we have) the bill (*Brit*) *or* check (*US*), please; **~ nach Ihnen!** after you; **~ schön?, ~(, was darf es sein)?** (*in Geschäft*) can I help you?; (*in Gaststätte*) what would you like?; **~(, Sie wünschen)?** what can I do for you?; **~(schön** *or* **sehr), Ihr Bier/Kaffee!** here's your beer/coffee; **ja ~?** yes?; **~(, treten Sie ein)!** come in!; **~(, nehmen Sie doch Platz)!** (*form*) please sit down; **Entschuldigung! – ~!** I'm sorry! – that's all right; **~, mit (dem größten) Vergnügen!** (*form*) with pleasure; **aber ~!** please do; **~, nur zu!** help yourself; **na ~!** there you are!
(b) (*sarkastisch:* = *nun gut*) all right; **~, wie du willst** (all right,) just as you like
(c) (*Dank erwidernd*) you're welcome; **~ sehr** *or* **schön** you're welcome, not at all (*Brit*); **~(, gern geschehen)** (not at all,) my pleasure; **~, keine Ursache** it was nothing; **~, nichts zu danken** don't mention it; **aber ~!** there's no need to thank me
(d) (*nachfragend*) **(wie) ~?** (I beg your) pardon? (*auch iro*), sorry(, what did you say?)
Bitte [ˈbɪtə] F **-, -n** request; (*inständig*) plea; **auf seine ~** his request; **ich habe eine große ~ an dich** I have a (great) favour (*Brit*) *or* favor (*US*) to ask you; **sich mit einer ~ an jdn wenden** to make a request to sb; **er kann ihr keine ~ ausschlagen** *or* **abschlagen** he can't refuse her anything
bitten [ˈbɪtn] *pret* **bat** [baːt], *ptp* **gebeten** [ɡəˈbeːtn] **Ⅰ** VT **(a)** jdn to ask; (*inständig*) to beg; (*Eccl*) to beseech; **jdn um etw ~** to ask/beg/beseech sb for sth; **darf ich Sie um Ihren Namen ~?** might I ask your name?; **um Ruhe wird gebeten** silence is requested; (*auf Schild*) silence please; **darf ich Sie um den nächsten Tanz ~?** may I have the pleasure of the next dance?; **wir ~ dich, erhöre uns!** (*Eccl*) we beseech Thee to hear us; (*katholisch, anglikanisch*) Lord hear us; **ich bitte dich um alles in der Welt** I beg you; **er lässt sich gerne ~** he likes people to keep asking him; **er lässt sich nicht (lange) ~** you don't have to ask him twice; **aber ich bitte dich!** not at all; **wenn ich ~ darf** (*form*) if you please, if you wouldn't mind; **darum möchte ich doch sehr gebeten haben!** (*form*) I should hope so indeed; **ich muss doch (sehr) ~!** well I must say!
(b) (= *einladen*) to ask, to invite; **jdn auf ein Glas Wein ~** to invite sb to have a glass of wine; **jdn zu Tisch ~** to ask sb to come to table
(c) (= *bestellen*) **jdn an einen Ort ~** to ask sb (to come) somewhere; **jdn zu sich ~** to ask sb to come and see one **Ⅱ** VI **(a)** (= *eine Bitte äußern*) to ask; (*inständig*) to plead, to beg; **um etw ~** to ask (for) *or* request sth; (*inständig*) to plead for sth; **bei jdm um etw ~** to beg sb for sth; **~ und betteln** to beg and plead
(b) (= *einladen*) **der Herr Professor lässt ~** the Professor will see you now; **ich lasse ~** he/she can come in now; **darf ich zu Tisch ~?** lunch/dinner is served; **darf ich (um den nächsten Tanz) ~?** may I have the pleasure (of the next dance)?
bitter [ˈbɪtɐ] **Ⅰ** ADJ (*lit, fig*) bitter; **Schokolade** plain; (*fig*) **Geschmack** nasty; **Wahrheit, Lehre, Verlust** painful; **Zeit,**

Schicksal hard; *Not, Notwendigkeit* dire; *Leid, Unrecht* grievous; *Ernst, Feind* deadly; *Hohn, Spott* cruel; **bis zum ~en Ende** to the bitter end; **jdn ~ machen** to embitter sb, to make sb bitter; **~e Klagen führen** to complain bitterly **2** ADV (= *sehr*) bereuen bitterly; *bezahlen, büßen* dearly; **~ schmecken** to taste bitter; **etw ~ nötig haben** to be in dire need of sth

Bitter-: bitterböse 1 ADJ furious **2** ADV furiously; **bitterernst** ADJ *Situation etc* extremely serious; *Mensch* very serious; **damit ist es mir ~** I am very serious; **bitterkalt** ADJ bitterly cold; **Bitterkeit** F -, NO PL (*lit, fig*) bitterness; **bitterlich** ['bɪtəlɪç] **1** ADJ bitter **2** ADV bitterly

Bitumen [bi'tu:mən] NT **-s, -** *or* **Bitumina** [-'tu:mina] bitumen

bivalent [biva'lɛnt] ADJ bivalent

Biwak ['bi:vak] NT **-s, -s** *or* **-e** bivouac

biwakieren [biva'ki:rən], *ptp* **biwakiert** VI to bivouac

BIZ F (a) ABBR *von* **Bank für internationalen Zahlungsausgleich** (b) ABBR *von* **Berufsinformationszentrum**

bizarr [bi'tsar] **1** ADJ bizarre **2** ADV bizarrely

Bizeps ['bi:tseps] M **-(es), -e** biceps

Bj. ABBR *von* **Baujahr**

BK [be:'ka:] F -, NO PL ABBR *von* **bildende Kunst** (*Sch inf*) art

BKA [be:ka:'la:] NT -, ABBR *von* **Bundeskriminalamt**

blabla [bla'bla:] INTERJ (*inf*) blah blah blah (*inf*)

Blabla [bla'bla:] NT **-s**, NO PL (*inf*) waffle (*inf*)

Blackbox ['blɛkbɔks] F -, **-es, Black Box** F -, **-es** (*Aviat, Telec, Comput*) black box

Black-out [blɛk'aut] NT or M **-(s), -s, Blackout** NT or M **-(s), -s** blackout

blähen ['blɛːən] **1** VTR to swell; *Nasenflügel, Nüstern* to flare **2** VI to cause flatulence *or* wind

blähend ADJ (*Med*) flatulent (*form*)

Blähung F -, **-en** USU PL (*Med*) wind *no pl*

blamabel [bla'ma:bl] ADJ shameful

Blamage [bla'ma:ʒə] F -, **-n** disgrace

blamieren [bla'mi:rən], *ptp* **blamiert** **1** VT to disgrace **2** VR to make a fool of oneself; (*durch Benehmen*) to disgrace oneself

---

Vorsicht! **blamieren** *wird nicht mit dem englischen Wort* **to blame** *übersetzt.*

---

blanchieren [blã'ʃiːrən], *ptp* **blanchiert** VT (*Cook*) to blanch

blank [blaŋk] **1** ADJ (a) (= *glänzend, sauber*) shiny, shining; (= *abgescheuert*) *Hosenboden etc* shiny (b) (= *nackt*) bare; (*Aus:* = *ohne Mantel*) coatless; (*inf:* = *ohne Geld*) broke (c) (= *rein*) pure; *Hohn* utter **2** ADV *scheuern, polieren* till it shines; **~ gewetzt** (worn) shiny; **~ poliert** brightly polished

Blanko- IN CPDS (*Fin*) blank; **Blankoakzept** NT blank acceptance; **Blankoindossament** NT blank indorsement; **Blankokredit** [-kredi:t] M open credit; **Blankoscheck** M blank cheque (*Brit*) *or* check (*US*); **Blankoverkauf** M (*St Ex*) short sale; **Blankovollmacht** F carte blanche; **Blankowechsel** M blank bill *or* draft

Blankvers M blank verse

Bläschen ['blɛːsçən] NT **-s, -** (a) DIM *von* **Blase** (b) small blister

Blase ['bla:zə] F -, **-n** (a) (= *Seifenblase, Luftblase*) bubble; (= *Sprechblase*) balloon; **~n werfen** *or* **ziehen** (*Farbe*) to blister; (*Teig*) to become light and frothy (b) (*Med*) blister; **sich** (*dat*) **~n laufen** to get blisters from walking *etc* (c) (*Anat*) bladder; **sich** (*dat*) **die ~ erkälten** to get a chill on the bladder

Blasebalg M (pair of) bellows

blasen ['bla:zn], *pret* **blies** [bliːs], *ptp* **geblasen** [gə'bla:zn] **1** VI to blow; (*Posaunenbläser etc*) to play; (*auf Essen*) to blow on it; (*auf Wunde etc*) ≈ to kiss it better; **zum Rückzug ~** (*lit, fig*) to sound the retreat **2** VT (a) *Melodie, Posaune etc* to play; **dir/ ihm werd ich was ~!** (*inf*) I'll give you/him a piece of my mind (b) (*sl:* = *fellieren*) **jdm einen ~** to give sb a blow job (*sl*)

Blasen-: Blasenbildung F formation of bubbles; (*bei Anstrich, an Fuß etc*) blistering; **Blasenentzündung** F, **Blasenkatarr(h)** M cystitis; **Blasenleiden** NT bladder trouble *no art*; **Blasenstein** M bladder stone; **Blasentee** M herb tea beneficial in cases of bladder trouble

Bläser ['blɛːzɐ] M **-s, -, Bläserin** [-ərɪn] F -, **-nen** (*Mus*) wind player; **die ~** the wind (section)

Bläserquartett NT wind quartet

---

blasiert [bla'ziːɐt] ADJ (*pej geh*) blasé

Blasiertheit F -, **-en** (*pej geh*) blasé attitude

Blas-: Blasinstrument NT wind instrument; **Blaskapelle** F brass band; **Blasmusik** F brass band music; **Blasrohr** NT (a) (= *Waffe*) blowpipe (b) (*Tech*) blast pipe

blass [blas] ADJ (a) *Gesicht, Haut, Schrift, Licht* pale; **~ werden** to grow pale; **~ wie Kreide** white as a sheet; **~ vor Neid werden** to go green with envy (b) (*fig*) faint; *Ausdruck, Sprache, Schilderung* colourless (*Brit*), colorless (*US*); **ich habe keinen ~en Schimmer** *or* **Dunst (davon)** (*inf*) I haven't a clue (about it) (*inf*)

blass- IN CPDS pale; **blassblau** ADJ pale blue

Blässe ['blɛsə] F -, **-n** paleness; (*von Haut, Gesicht etc*) pallor

Blässhuhn ['blɛs-] NT coot

blässlich ['blɛslɪç] ADJ rather pale

bläst [blɛːst] 3. PERS SING PRES *von* **blasen**

Blatt [blat] NT **-(e)s, ̈er** ['blɛtə] (a) (*Bot*) leaf; **kein ~ vor den Mund nehmen** not to mince one's words (b) (*Papier etc*) sheet; **ein ~ Papier** a sheet of paper; **(noch) ein unbeschriebenes ~ sein** (= *unerfahren*) to be inexperienced; (= *ohne Image*) to be an unknown quantity; **er ist kein unbeschriebenes ~** he's been around (*inf*); (*Krimineller*) he's got a record (c) (= *Seite*) page; **das steht auf einem anderen ~** (*fig*) that's another story; **ein neues ~ in der Geschichte** *or* **im Buch der Geschichte** a new chapter of history (d) (= *Notenblatt*) sheet; **vom ~ singen/spielen** to sight-read (e) (= *Zeitung*) paper (f) (*von Messer, Ruder, Propeller*) blade (g) (*Cards*) hand; (= *Einzelkarte*) card; **das ~ hat sich gewendet** (*fig*) the tables have been turned

blätterig ['blɛtərɪç] ADJ *Teig* flaky; *Farbe etc* flaking

-blätterig ADJ SUF -leaved; **ein vierblätteriges Kleeblatt** a four-leaved clover

Blättermagen M (*Zool*) omasum (*spec*)

blättern ['blɛtɐn] **1** VI (*in Buch*) to leaf *or* (*schnell*) flick through it/them; (*Comput*) to scroll; **in etw** (*dat*) **~** to leaf *or* (*schnell*) flick through sth **2** VT *Geldscheine, Spielkarten* to put down one by one

Blätter-: Blätterpilz M agaric; **Blätterteig** M puff pastry; **Blätterteiggebäck** NT puff pastry; (= *Backwaren*) puff pastries *pl*

Blatt-: Blattfeder F (*Tech*) leaf spring; **Blattform** F (*Bot*) leaf shape; **Blattgemüse** NT greens *pl*, leaf vegetables *pl* (*form*); **ein ~ a leaf vegetable; **Blattgold** NT gold leaf; **Blattgrün** NT chlorophyll; **Blattlaus** F greenfly; **Blattsalat** M green salad; **Blattschuss** M (*Hunt*) shot through the shoulder to the heart; **Blattspinat** M leaf spinach; **blattweise** ADV leaf by leaf; (*bei Papier*) sheet by sheet; **Blattwerk** NT, NO PL foliage

blau [blau] ADJ (a) blue; **Forelle** *etc* **~** (*Cook*) trout *etc* au bleu; **~er Anton** (*inf*) workman's overalls *pl*; **ein ~es Auge** (*inf*) a black eye; **ich tu das nicht wegen deiner schönen ~en Augen** (*fig*) I'm not doing it for the sake of your bonny blue eyes; **mit einem ~en Auge davonkommen** (*fig*) to get off lightly; **ein ~er Brief** (*Sch*) letter informing parents that their child must repeat a year; (*von Hauswirt*) notice to quit; (*von der Firma*) one's cards; **ein ~er Fleck** a bruise; **~e Flecken haben** to be bruised; **er wird sein ~es Wunder erleben** (*inf*) he won't know what's hit him (*inf*) (b) USU PRED (*inf:* = *betrunken*) drunk (c) (*inf:* = *geschwänzt*) **einen ~en Montag machen** to skip work on Monday (*inf*)

Blau [blau] NT **-s, -** *or* (*inf*) **-s** blue

Blau-: blauäugig [-ɔygɪç] ADJ blue-eyed; (*fig*) naïve; **Blaubeere** F bilberry, blueberry (*esp US*); **blaublütig** ADJ blue-blooded

Blaue ['blauə] M = **Blaue(s)**

Bläue ['blɔyə] F -, NO PL blueness

Blaue(s) ['blauə] NT DECL AS ADJ **(a)** (= *Farbe*) **das ~** the blue; **es spielt ins ~** it has a touch of blue in it; **das ~ vom Himmel (herunter) lügen** (*inf*) to tell a pack of lies; **jdm das ~ vom Himmel (herunter) versprechen** (*inf*) to promise sb the moon **(b)** (*ohne Ziel*) **ins ~ hinein** (*inf*) at random; **wir wollen ins ~ fahren** we'll just set off and see where we end up; **eine Fahrt ins ~** a trip to nowhere in particular; (= *Veranstaltung*) a mystery tour

Blau-: Blaufelchen M whitefish; **blaugrau** ADJ blue-grey (*Brit*), blue-gray (*US*), bluey grey (*Brit*) *or* gray (*US*); **blaugrün** ADJ blue-green; **Blauhelm** M UN soldier, blue helmet

bläulich ['blɔylɪç] ADJ bluish

Blau-: Blaulicht NT (*von Polizei etc*) flashing blue light; **mit ~** with its blue light flashing; **blaumachen** SEP (*inf*) **1** VI to skip work **2** VT **das Freitag/zwei Tage ~** to skip work on Friday/for two days; **Blaumann** M, *pl* **-männer** (*inf*) workman's overalls *pl*; **Blaumeise** F bluetit; **Blaupause** F blueprint; **Blausäure** F prussic acid; **Blauschimmelkäse** M blue cheese; **Blaustich** M (*Phot*) blue cast; **blaustichig** [-ʃtɪçɪç] ADJ (*Phot*) with a blue cast; **Blaustrumpf** M bluestocking; **Blauwal** M blue whale

Blazer ['bleːzɐ] M **-s, -**, **Blazerjacke** F blazer

Blech [blɛç] NT **-(e)s, -e (a)** NO PL (sheet) metal; (*von Auto*) body; **eine Dose aus ~** a tin (*Brit*), a metal container; **das ist doch nur ~** it's just ordinary metal **(b)** (= *~stück*) metal plate **(c)** (= *Backblech*) baking sheet **(d)** NO PL (*inf*: = *~instrumente*) brass **(e)** NO PL (*inf*: = *Unsinn*) rubbish *no art* (*inf*); **red kein ~** don't talk crap (*inf*)

Blech-: Blechbläser(in) M(F) brass player; **die ~** the brass (section); **Blechblasinstrument** NT brass instrument; **Blechdose** F tin container; (*esp für Konserven*) tin (*Brit*), can

blechen ['blɛçn̩] VTI (*inf*) to cough up (*inf*)

blechern ['blɛçɐn] **1** ADJ **(a)** ATTR metal **(b)** *Geräusch, Stimme etc* tinny **2** ADV tinnily; *klingen, tönen, scheppern* tinny

Blech-: Blechgeschirr NT metal pots and pans *pl*; **Blechinstrument** NT brass instrument; **Blechkanister** M metal can; **Blechlawine** F (*pej inf*) vast column of cars; **Blechlehre** F metal gauge; **Blechmusik** F (*usu pej*) brass (band) music; **Blechnapf** M metal bowl; **Blechschaden** M damage to the bodywork; **Blechtrommel** F tin drum

blecken ['blɛkn̩] VT **die Zähne ~** to bare one's teeth

Blei [blaɪ] NT **-(e)s, -e (a)** NO PL (*abbr* Pb) lead; **die Müdigkeit/Anstrengung lag ihm wie ~ in den Gliedern** *or* **Knochen** his whole body ached with tiredness/the exertion **(b)** (= *Lot*) plumb

Blei- IN CPDS lead; **Bleiader** F lead vein

Bleibe ['blaɪbə] F **-, -n** (= *Unterkunft*) place to stay; **eine/keine ~ haben** to have somewhere/nowhere to stay

bleiben ['blaɪbn̩] *pret* **blieb** [bliːp], *ptp* **geblieben** [gə'bliːbn̩] VI AUX SEIN **(a)** (= *sich nicht verändern, zu Besuch ~*) to stay; **unbeachtet/unbestraft ~** to go unnoticed/unpunished; **unbeantwortet ~** to be left unanswered; **unvergessen ~** to continue to be remembered; **an Samstagen bleibt unser Geschäft geschlossen** this shop is closed on Saturdays; **in Übung/Form ~** to keep in practice/form; **ruhig/still ~** to keep calm/quiet; **wach ~** to stay awake; **sitzen/stehen ~** to remain seated/standing; **bitte, ~ Sie doch sitzen** please don't get up; **wo bleibst du so lange?** (*inf*) what's keeping you (all this time)?; **wo bleibt er so lange?** (*inf*) where has he got to?; **wo sind denn all die alten Häuser geblieben?** what (has) happened to all the old houses?; **bei etw ~** (*fig*) to keep *or* stick (*inf*) to sth; **das bleibt unter uns** that's (just) between ourselves; **wir möchten für** *or* **unter uns ~** we want to keep ourselves to ourselves **(b)** (= *übrig*) to be left; **es blieb mir keine andere Wahl/Möglichkeit** I had no other choice/possibility; **es blieb keine andere Wahl/Möglichkeit** there was no other choice/possibility **(c)** (= *sein*) **es bleibt abzuwarten** it remains to be seen; **es bleibt zu hoffen** *or* **wünschen, dass ...** I/we can only hope that ... **(d)** (*inf*: = *versorgt werden*) **sie können (selber) sehen, wo sie ~** they'll just have to look out for themselves (*inf*); **und wo bleibe ich?** and what about me?; **sieh zu, wo du bleibst!** you're on your own! (*inf*)

bleibend ADJ *Wert, Erinnerung etc* lasting; *Schaden, Zähne* permanent

bleiben lassen *ptp* **bleiben lassen** VT IRREG (*inf*) **(a)** (= *unterlassen*) **etw ~** to give sth a miss (*inf*); **das werde ich/wirst du ganz schön ~** I'll/you'll do nothing of the sort! **(b)** (= *aufgeben*) to give up; **das Rauchen ~** to give up smoking

Bleiberecht NT, NO PL right of residence

bleich [blaɪç] ADJ pale

bleichen ['blaɪçn̩] VT to bleach

Bleich-: Bleichgesicht NT **(a)** (*inf*: = *blasser Mensch*) pasty-face (*inf*) **(b)** (= *Weißer*) paleface; **bleichgesichtig** [-gəzɪçtɪç] ADJ (*inf*) pasty-faced (*inf*); **Bleichmittel** NT bleach, bleaching agent

bleiern ['blaɪɐn] **1** ADJ (= *aus Blei*) lead; (*fig*) leaden; *Beine* like lead; *Müdigkeit* heavy **2** ADV (*fig*) heavily

Blei-: Bleierz NT lead ore; **bleifrei** **1** ADJ *Benzin etc* unleaded **2** ADV **~ fahren** to use unleaded petrol (*Brit*) *or* gas (*US*); **mein Auto fährt ~** my car runs on unleaded petrol (*Brit*) *or* gas (*US*); **Bleigewicht** NT lead weight; (*Angeln*) sinker; **Bleigießen** NT **-s**, NO PL New Year's Eve custom of telling fortunes by the shapes made by molten lead dropped into cold water; **bleihaltig** ADJ containing lead; *Erz, Gestein* plumbiferous (*spec*); *Benzin etc* leaded; **~/zu ~ sein** to contain lead/too much lead; **Bleikristall** NT lead crystal; **Bleisatz** M (*Typ*) hot-metal setting; **Bleischürze** F lead apron; **Bleisoldat** M ≈ tin soldier

Bleistift M pencil; (*zum Malen*) crayon; **mit/in ~** with a/in pencil

Bleistift- IN CPDS pencil; **Bleistiftabsatz** M stiletto heel; **Bleistiftspitzer** M pencil sharpener

Blei-: Bleivergiftung F lead poisoning; **bleiverglast** ADJ leaded; **Bleiweiß** NT white lead

Blende ['blɛndə] F **-, -n (a)** (= *Lichtschutz*) shade, screen; (*Aut*) (sun) visor; (*an Fenster*) blind **(b)** (*Opt*) filter **(c)** (*Phot*) (= *Öffnung*) aperture; (= *Einstellungsposition*) f-stop; (= *Vorrichtung*) diaphragm; **die ~ schließen** to stop down; **bei** *or* **mit ~ 2.8** at (an aperture setting of) f/2.8

blenden ['blɛndn̩] **1** VT (*lit, fig*) to dazzle; (= *blind machen, täuschen*) to blind **2** VI (*Licht, Scheinwerfer*) to be dazzling; (*fig*: = *täuschen*) to dazzle; **~d weiß (sein)** (to be) dazzling white

blendend **1** ADJ splendid; *Pianist, Schüler etc* brilliant; *Laune, Stimmung* sparkling **2** ADV splendidly; **es geht mir ~** I feel wonderful; **sich ~ amüsieren** to have a wonderful time

Blend-: blendfrei ADJ dazzle-free (*esp Brit*); *Glas, Fernsehschirm* nonreflective; **Blendschutz** M **(a)** protection against dazzle (*Brit*) *or* glare **(b)** (= *Vorrichtung*) antidazzle (*Brit*) *or* antiglare (*US*) device

Blick [blɪk] M **-(e)s, -e (a)** (= *das Blicken*) look; (= *flüchtiger ~*) glance; **auf den ersten ~** at first glance; **Liebe auf den ersten ~** love at first sight; **mit einem ~, auf einen ~** at a glance; **jds ~ (dat) ausweichen** to avoid sb's eye; **jds ~ erwidern** to return sb's gaze; **~e miteinander wechseln** to exchange glances; **jdn mit (seinen) ~en verschlingen** to devour sb with one's eyes; **sie zog alle ~e auf sich** everybody's eyes were drawn to her; **einen ~ auf etw** (*acc*) **tun** *or* **werfen** to throw a glance at sth; **einen ~ hinter die Kulissen tun** *or* **werfen** (*fig*) to take a look behind the scenes; **sie würdigte ihn keines ~es** she did not deign to look at him; **wenn ~e töten könnten!** if looks could kill! **(b)** (= *~richtung*) eyes *pl*; **mein ~ fiel auf sein leeres Glas** my eye fell on his empty glass; **den ~ heben** to look up; **den ~ senken** to look down **(c)** (= *Augenausdruck*) look in one's eyes; **den bösen ~ haben** to have the evil eye; **in ihrem ~ lag Verzweiflung** there was a look of despair in her eyes **(d)** (= *Ausblick*) view; **ein Zimmer mit ~ auf den Park** a room overlooking the park; **etw aus dem ~ verlieren** to lose sight of sth; **mit ~ auf, im ~ auf** (= *hinsichtlich*) in view of **(e)** (= *Verständnis*) **seinen ~ für etw schärfen** to increase one's awareness of sth; **einen klaren ~ haben** to see things clearly; **einen (guten) ~ für etw haben** to have an eye *or* a good eye for sth; **er hat keinen ~ dafür** he doesn't notice that sort of thing

blickdicht ADJ *Strümpfe* opaque

blicken ['blɪkn̩] **1** VI (*auf +acc* at) to look; (= *flüchtig*) to glance; (*fig*: = *hervorsehen*) to peep; **sich ~ lassen** to put in an appearance; **lass dich hier ja nicht mehr ~!** don't show your face here again!; **lass dich doch mal wieder ~!** why don't you drop in some time?; **danach hat er sich nie wieder ~ lassen**

after that he was never seen again; **das lässt tief ~** that's very revealing **2** VT (*inf:* = *verstehen*) to get

Blick-: Blickkontakt M eye contact; **Blickpunkt** M **im ~ der Öffentlichkeit stehen** to be in the public eye; **Blickwinkel** M angle of vision; (*fig*) viewpoint

blind [blɪnt] **1** ADJ **(a)** (*li, fig*) blind (*für* to); *Zufall* sheer; *Alarm* false; **~ für etw sein, ~ in Bezug auf etw** (*acc*) **sein** (*fig*) to be blind to sth; **ich bin doch nicht ~!** (*fig*) I'm not blind; **~ geboren** blind from birth; **ein ~es Huhn findet auch mal ein Korn** (*Prov*) anyone can be lucky now and again; **~e Gewalt** brute force; **~er Eifer** blind enthusiasm; **ein ~er Passagier** a stowaway
(b) (= *getrübt*) dull; *Spiegel, Glasscheibe* clouded; *Fleck* blind
(c) (*sl:* = *betrunken*) plastered (*inf*)
2 ADV **(a)** (= *wahllos*) at random
(b) (= *ohne zu überlegen*) blindly
(c) (= *ohne zu sehen*) without being able to see; **~ landen** (*Aviat*) to make a blind landing

Blind-: Blindband M, *pl* **-bände** (*Typ*) dummy; **Blindbewerbung** F unsolicited application

Blinddarm M (*Anat*) caecum (*Brit*), cecum (*US*); (*inf:* = *Wurmfortsatz*) appendix

Blinddarm-: Blinddarmentzündung F appendicitis; **Blinddarmreizung** F grumbling appendix

Blindekuh NO ART (= *Spiel*) blind man's buff

Blinden-: Blindenhund M guide dog; **Blindenschrift** F braille

Blinde(r) ['blɪndə] MF DECL AS ADJ blind person/man/woman *etc*; **die ~n** the blind; **das sieht doch ein ~r** (*mit dem Krückstock*) (*hum inf*) any fool can see that; **unter den ~n ist der Einäugige König** (*Prov*) in the country of the blind the one-eyed man is king (*prov*)

Blind-: Blindflug M blind flight; (= *das Blindfliegen*) blind flying; **Blindgänger** [-ɡɛŋɐ] M **-s, -** (*Mil*) dud (shot); **Blindgeborene(r)** [-ɡəboːrənə] MF DECL AS ADJ person blind from birth; **blindgläubig** **1** ADJ credulous **2** ADV *folgen, vertrauen* blindly; **Blindheit** F **-,** NO PL (*lit, fig*) blindness; **wie mit ~ geschlagen** (*fig*) as though blind; **mit ~ geschlagen sein** (*fig*) to be blind; **Blindlandung** F blind landing; **blindlings** ['blɪntlɪŋs] ADV blindly; **Blindschleiche** [-ʃlaɪçə] F **-, -n** slowworm; **blindwütig** **1** ADJ *Mensch* in a blind rage; *Angriff* furious **2** ADV in a blind rage

blinken ['blɪŋkn̩] **1** VI (= *funkeln*) to gleam; (*Boje, Leuchtturm*) to flash; (*Aut*) to indicate **2** VT *Signal* to flash; **SOS ~** to flash an SOS (signal)

Blinker ['blɪŋkɐ] M **-s, -** **(a)** (*Aut*) indicator (*esp Brit*), turn signal (*US*) **(b)** (*Angeln*) spinner

Blink-: Blinklicht NT flashing light; (*inf:* = *Blinkleuchte*) indicator (*esp Brit*), turn signal (*US*); **Blinklichtanlage** F warning light system; **Blinkzeichen** NT signal

blinzeln ['blɪntsl̩n] VI to blink; (= *zwinkern*) to wink; (*geblendet*) to squint

Blitz [blɪts] M **-es, -e** **(a)** (= *das Blitzen*) lightning *no pl, no indef art*; (= *~strahl*) flash of lightning; (= *Lichtstrahl*) flash (of light); **vom ~ getroffen/erschlagen werden** to be struck by lightning; **wie vom ~ getroffen** (*fig*) thunderstruck; **einschlagen wie ein ~** (*fig*) to be a bombshell; **wie ein ~ aus heiterem Himmel** (*fig*) like a bolt from the blue; **wie der ~** (*inf*) like lightning; **laufen wie ein geölter ~** (*inf*) to run like greased lightning
(b) (*Phot inf*) flash; (= *~lichtgerät*) flash(gun)

Blitz-: IN CPDS (*esp Mil:* = *schnell*) lightning; **Blitzableiter** M lightning conductor; **blitzartig** **1** ADJ lightning *attr* **2** ADV *reagieren* like lightning; *verschwinden* in a flash

blitzen ['blɪtsn̩] **1** VI IMPERS **es blitzt** there is lightning; **es blitzt und donnert** there is thunder and lightning; **hat es eben geblitzt?** was that (a flash of) lightning? **2** VI **(a)** (= *strahlen*) to flash; (*Gold, Zähne*) to sparkle; **vor Sauberkeit ~** to be sparkling clean **(b)** (*Phot inf*) to use (a) flash **3** VT (*inf:* in *Radarfalle*) to flash

Blitz-: Blitzgerät NT (*Phot*) flash(gun); **Blitzkarriere** F rapid rise; **eine ~ machen** to rise rapidly; **Blitzkrieg** M blitzkrieg

Blitzlicht NT (*Phot*) flash(light)

Blitzlicht-: Blitzlichtbirne F flashbulb; **Blitzlichtgewitter** NT popping of flashbulbs; **Blitzlichtwürfel** M flashcube

Blitz-: Blitzmerker [-mɛrkɐ] M **-s, -, Blitzmerkerin** [-ərɪn] F **-, -nen** (*inf: usu iro*) bright spark (*inf*); **blitzsauber** **1** ADJ spick and

span **2** ADV *putzen, polieren* until it shines; **Blitzschlag** M flash of lightning; **vom ~ getroffen** struck by lightning; **blitzschnell** **1** ADJ lightning *attr* **2** ADV like lightning; *verschwinden* in a flash; **Blitzstrahl** M flash of lightning; **Blitzumfrage** F quick poll

Block [blɔk] M **-(e)s, -s** or **¨e** ['blœkə] **(a)** block (*von, aus* of); (*von Seife, Schokolade*) bar **(b)** (= *Papierblock*) pad; (= *Briefmarkenblock*) block; (*von Fahrkarten*) book **(c)** (*Pol:* = *Staatenblock*) bloc **(d)** (*NS*) *smallest organizational unit of Nazi party based on a block of houses*

Blockade [blɔˈkaːdə] F **-, -n** (= *Absperrung*) blockade

Block-: Blockbildung F (*Pol*) formation of blocs; (= *Fraktionsbildung*) formation of factions; **Blockbuchstabe** M block capital; **Blockfloating** NT (*Fin*) common float; **Blockflöte** F recorder; (*Pol sl:* = *Person*) fellow traveller (*Brit*) or traveler (*US*); **blockfrei** ADJ nonaligned; **Blockhaus** NT log cabin; **Blockheizkraftwerk** NT block heating and generating plant; **Blockhütte** F log cabin

blockieren [blɔˈkiːrən], *ptp* **blockiert** **1** VT **(a)** (= *sperren, hemmen*) to block; *Verkehr, Verhandlung* to obstruct; *Flugverkehr* to halt; *Gesetz* to block the passage of; *Rad, Lenkung* to lock **(b)** (= *mit Blockade belegen*) to blockade **2** VI *(Bremsen, Rad etc*) to lock

Block-: Blocksatz M (*Typ*) justification; **Blockschrift** F block capitals *pl*; **Blockstunde** F (*Sch*) double period; **Blockunterricht** M (*Sch*) teaching by topics; **Blockwart** [-vart] M **-(e)s, -e, Blockwartin** [-vartɪn] F **-, -nen** (*NS*) block leader

blöd [bløːt], **blöde** ['bløːdə] (*inf*) **1** ADJ **(a)** (= *dumm*) stupid, idiotic; *Wetter* terrible; *Gefühl* funny; **das Blöde daran ist, dass ...** the stupid thing about it is that ... **(b)** (*Sw:* = *schüchtern*) shy **(c)** (*S Ger:* = *abgescheuert*) worn **2** ADV (= *dumm*) stupidly, idiotically; **~ fragen** to ask stupid questions

Blödelei [bløːdəˈlai] F **-, -en** (*inf*) (= *Albernheit*) messing around (*inf*); (= *Witz*) joke; (= *dumme Streiche*) pranks *pl*; **lass die ~** stop messing around (*inf*)

blödeln ['bløːdl̩n] VI (*inf*) to mess around (*inf*); (= *Witze machen*) to make jokes; **mit jdm ~** to have fun with sb

blöderweise ['bløːdɐˈvaizə] ADV (*inf*) stupidly

Blödheit F **-, -en** **(a)** (= *Dummheit*) stupidity **(b)** (= *blödes Verhalten*) stupid thing; (= *alberne Bemerkung*) stupid remark; **es ist eine ~, das zu machen** it's stupid to do that **(c)** (*Sw:* = *Schüchternheit*) shyness

Blödmann M, *pl* **-männer** (*inf*) stupid fool (*inf*)

Blödsinn M, NO PL (= *Unsinn*) nonsense; (= *Unfug*) stupid tricks *pl*; **so ein ~** what nonsense/how stupid; **~ machen** to mess around; **wer hat diesen ~ hier gemacht?** what fool did this?; **mach keinen ~** don't mess around

blödsinnig ADJ (= *dumm*) stupid, idiotic

blöken ['bløːkn̩] VI (*Schaf*) to bleat; (*geh: Rinder*) to low

blond [blɔnt] **1** ADJ **(a)** *Frau* blonde, fair(-haired); *Mann, Menschenrasse* blond, fair(-haired) **(b)** (*hum inf:* = *hellfarbig*) light-coloured (*Brit*), light-colored (*US*); *Bier* light, pale **2** ADV **~ gefärbt** dyed blond; (*bei Frauen*) dyed blonde; **~ gelockt sein** to have fair curly hair

Blonde(s) ['blɔndə] NT DECL AS ADJ (*inf:* = *Bier*) ≈ lager (*Brit*)

blondieren [blɔnˈdiːrən], *ptp* **blondiert** VT to bleach

Blondine [blɔnˈdiːnə] F **-, -n** blonde

bloß [bloːs] **1** ADJ **(a)** (= *unbedeckt*) bare; **etw auf der ~en Haut tragen** to wear sth without anything on underneath; **mit ~en Füßen** barefoot; **siehe Oberkörper**
(b) ATTR (= *alleinig*) mere; *Neid, Dummheit* sheer; (= *allein schon*) *Gedanke, Anblick* very; **er kam mit dem ~en Schrecken davon** he got off with no more than a fright
2 ADV only; **ich möchte es schon machen, ~ weiß ich nicht wie** I'd like to but I don't know how; **wie kann so etwas ~ geschehen?** how on earth can something like that happen?; **was er ~ hat?** what on earth is wrong with him?; **tu das ~ nicht wieder!** don't you dare do that again; **geh mir ~ aus dem Weg** just get out of my way; **nicht ~ ..., sondern auch ...** not only ... but also ...

Blöße ['bløːsə] F **-, -n** (*geh*) (= *Unbedecktheit*) bareness; (= *Nacktheit*) nakedness; **jdm eine ~ bieten** (*lit*) to drop one's guard with sb; (*fig*) to show sb one's ignorance; **sich** (*dat*) **eine ~ geben** (*fig*) to show one's ignorance

bloßstellen SEP **1** VT *jdn* to show up; *Lügner, Betrüger* to expose **2** VR to show oneself up

Blouson [blu'zõː] M or NT **-(s), -s** bomber jacket

blubbern ['blʊbɐn] VI (*inf*) to bubble

Bluejeans ['bluː dʒiːns] PL, **Blue Jeans** PL (pair of) (blue) jeans *pl*

Blues [bluːs] M **-, -** blues *sing or pl*; **(einen) ~ tanzen** to smooch (*inf*)

blühen ['blyːən] VI **(a)** (*Blume*) to (be in) bloom; (*Bäume*) to (be in) blossom; (*Garten, Wiese*) to be full of flowers; (*fig*: = *gedeihen*) to flourish, to thrive; **weiß ~** to have white flowers **(b)** (*inf*: = *bevorstehen*) to be in store (*jdm for sb*); **... dann blüht dir aber was ...** then you'll be (in) for it (*inf*); **das kann mir auch noch ~** that may happen to me too

blühend ADJ *Baum* blossoming; *Blume, Pflanze auch* blooming; *Garten, Wiese, Feld* full of flowers; (*fig*) *Aussehen* radiant; *Geschäft, Handel, Industrie, Kultur, Stadt* flourishing, thriving; *Fantasie* vivid; *Unsinn* absolute; **~e Landschaften** green pastures; **wie das ~e Leben aussehen, ~ aussehen** to look the very picture of health

Blume ['bluːmə] F **-, -n (a)** (= *Blüte, Pflanze*) flower; **vielen Dank für die ~n** (*iro*) thanks for nothing; **jdm etw durch die ~ sagen/ zu verstehen geben** to say/put sth in a roundabout way to sb **(b)** (*von Wein, Weinbrand*) bouquet; (*von Bier*) head

Blumen- IN CPDS flower; **Blumenerde** F potting compost; **Blumengeschäft** NT florist's; **Blumenhändler(in)** M(F) florist; **Blumenkohl** M, NO PL cauliflower; **Blumenkübel** M flower tub; **Blumenmuster** NT floral pattern; **blumenreich 1** ADJ *Stil, Sprache etc* flowery **2** ADV (*fig*) *sprechen* in a flowery way; *schreiben* in a flowery style; **Blumenständer** M flower stand; **Blumenstrauß** M, *pl* **-sträuße** bouquet *or* bunch of flowers; **Blumentopf** M flowerpot; (= *Pflanze*) flowering plant; **damit ist kein ~ zu gewinnen** (*inf*) that's nothing to write home about (*inf*); **Blumenvase** F (flower) vase; **Blumenzwiebel** F bulb

blumig ['bluːmɪç] ADJ (*lit, fig*) flowery

Bluse ['bluːzə] F **-, -n** blouse

Blut [bluːt] NT **-(e)s**, NO PL (*lit, fig*) blood; **jdm ~ abnehmen** to take blood from sb; **es ist viel ~ vergossen worden** *or* **geflossen** there was a lot of bloodshed; **er kann kein ~ sehen** he can't stand the sight of blood; **~ lecken** (*fig*) to develop a taste for it; **böses ~ machen** *or* **schaffen** *or* **geben** to cause bad blood; **blaues ~ haben** (= *adelig sein*) to have blue blood; **heißes** *or* **feuriges ~ haben** to be hot-blooded; **etw im ~ haben** to have sth in one's blood; **das liegt mir im ~** it's in my blood; **(nur) ruhig ~** keep your shirt on (*inf*); **jdn/sich bis aufs ~ bekämpfen** to fight sb/fight bitterly; **jdn bis aufs ~ reizen** (*inf*) to make sb's blood boil; **frisches ~** (*fig*) new blood; **~ und Wasser schwitzen** (*inf*) to sweat blood; **~ stillend =** **blutstillend**

Blut-: Blutalkohol(gehalt) M blood alcohol level; **Blutapfelsine** F blood orange; **blutarm** ADJ anaemic (*Brit*), anemic (*US*); **Blutarmut** F anaemia (*Brit*), anemia (*US*); **Blutbad** NT bloodbath; **Blutbahn** F bloodstream; **Blutbank** F, *pl* **-banken** blood bank; **Blutbeutel** M (*Med*) blood bag; **Blutbild** NT blood count; **Blutblase** F blood blister; **Blutbuche** F copper beech; **Blutdruck** M, NO PL blood pressure; **Blutdruckmesser** M **-s, -**, **Blutdruckmessgerät** NT blood pressure gauge; **blutdrucksenkend** ADJ hypotensive; *Mittel* antihypertensive; **~ sein** *or* **wirken** to reduce high blood pressure

Blüte ['blyːtə] F **-, -n (a)** (*von Blume*) flower, bloom; (*von Baum*) blossom; **seltsame ~n treiben** to produce strange effects; (*Fantasie, Angst*) to produce strange ideas **(b)** (= *das Blühen, ~zeit*) **zur ~ des Klees** when the clover is in flower; **zur ~ der Kirschbäume** when the cherry trees are in blossom; **in (voller) ~ stehen** to be in (full) bloom; (*Bäume*) to be in (full) blossom; (*Kultur, Geschäft*) to be flourishing; **sich zur vollen ~ entfalten** to come into full flower; (*Mädchen, Kultur*) to blossom; **seine ~ erreichen** *or* **erleben** (*Kultur etc*) to reach its peak; **ein Zeitalter kultureller ~** an age of cultural ascendency; **in der ~ seiner Jahre** in his prime **(c)** (*inf*: = *gefälschte Note*) dud (*inf*)

Blutegel M leech

bluten ['bluːtn] VI to bleed (*an +dat, aus* from); **mir blutet das Herz** my heart bleeds; **für etw (schwer) ~** (*inf*) to cough up a lot of money for sth (*inf*)

Blüten-: Blütenblatt NT petal; **Blütenstand** M inflorescence; **Blütenstaub** M pollen

Blutentnahme F taking of a blood sample

Bluter ['bluːtɐ] M **-s, -** (*Med*) haemophiliac (*Brit*), hemophiliac (*US*)

Bluterguss ['bluːtleɐɡʊs] M haematoma (*Brit spec*), hematoma (*US spec*); (= *blauer Fleck*) bruise

Bluterkrankheit ['bluːtɐ-] F haemophilia (*Brit*), hemophilia (*US*)

Blütezeit F **(a) die ~ der Obstbäume ist vorbei** the fruit trees are no longer in blossom **(b)** (*fig*) heyday; (*von Mensch*) prime

Blut-: Blutfleck M bloodstain; **Blutgefäß** NT blood vessel; **Blutgerinnsel** NT blood clot; **Blutgerinnung** F clotting of the blood; **Blutgerinnungsfaktor** M (*Med*) blood clotting factor; **Blutgruppe** F blood group; **die ~ 0 haben** to be blood group 0; **jds ~ bestimmen** to type sb's blood

blutig ['bluːtɪç] **1** ADJ **(a)** (*lit, fig*) bloody **(b)** (*inf*) *Anfänger* absolute; *Ernst* unrelenting **2** ADV bloodily; **er wurde ~ geschlagen** he was beaten until he bled

-blütig [blyːtɪç] ADJ SUF *Tier, Mensch* -blooded; **kaltblütig** cold-blooded

Blut-: blutjung ADJ very young; **Blutkonserve** F unit of stored blood; **Blutkörperchen** [-kœrpəçən] NT **-s, -** blood corpuscle; **Blutkreislauf** M blood circulation; **Blutorange** F blood orange; **Blutpass** M *card giving blood group etc*; **Blutpfropf** M clot of blood; **Blutplasma** NT blood plasma; **Blutplättchen** NT platelet; **Blutprobe** F blood test; **blutrünstig** [-rʏnstɪç] ADJ bloodthirsty; **Blutsauger(in)** M(F) (*lit, fig*) bloodsucker; (= *Vampir*) vampire

Blutsbruder M blood brother

Blut-: Blutsenkung F (*Med*) sedimentation of the blood; **eine ~ machen** to test the sedimentation rate of the blood; **Blutserum** NT, NO PL blood serum; **Blutspenden** NT **-s**, NO PL giving blood *no art*; **zum ~ aufrufen** to appeal for blood donors; **Blutspendepass** M blood donor card; **Blutspender(in)** M(F) blood donor; **Blutspur** F trail of blood; **~en** traces of blood; **blutstillend 1** ADJ styptic **2** ADV **~ wirken** to have a styptic effect

Bluts-: Blutstropfen M drop of blood; **blutsverwandt** ADJ related by blood; **Blutsverwandte(r)** MF DECL AS ADJ blood relation

Blut-: Bluttat F bloody deed; **Bluttransfusion** F blood transfusion; **bluttriefend** ADJ bloody, dripping with blood; **Blutübertragung** F blood transfusion

Blutung ['bluːtʊŋ] F **-, -en** bleeding *no pl*; (*starke*) haemorrhage (*Brit*), hemorrhage (*US*); (*monatliche*) period

Blut-: blutunterlaufen ADJ suffused with blood; *Augen* bloodshot; **Blutvergießen** NT **-s**, NO PL blood *no indef art*; **Blutvergiftung** F blood poisoning *no indef art*; **Blutverlust** M loss of blood; **Blutwurst** F blood sausage; **Blutzucker** M blood sugar; **Blutzuckerspiegel** M blood sugar level

BLZ [beːlɛlˈtset] F **-, -s** ABBR *von* Bankleitzahl

BMX-Rad [beːˈlɛmˈliːks-] NT BMX bike

BND [beːlɛnˈdeː] M **-(s)** ABBR *von* Bundesnachrichtendienst

Bö [bøː] F **-, -en** (*bøːən*) gust (of wind); (*stärker, mit Regen*) squall

Boa [ˈboːa] F **-, -s** (= *Schlange, Schal*) boa

Bob [bɔp] M **-s, -s** bob(sleigh) (*Brit*), bobsled

Bob-: Bobbahn F bob(sleigh) (*Brit*) *or* bobsled run; **Bobfahrer(in)** M(F) bobber (*inf*)

Boccia [ˈbɔtʃa] NT **-(s)** *or* f **-**, NO PL bowls *sing*

Bock¹ [bɔk] M **-(e)s, ²e** [ˈbœka] **(a)** (= *Rehbock, Kaninchenbock*) buck; (= *Schafsbock*) ram; (= *Ziegenbock*) billy goat; **alter ~** (*inf*) old goat (*inf*); **sturer ~** (*inf*) stubborn old devil (*inf*); **geiler ~** (*inf*) horny old goat (*inf*); **den ~ zum Gärtner machen** (*fig*) to be asking for trouble **(b)** (= *Gestell*) stand; (= *Stützgerät*) support; (*aus Holzbalken, mit Beinen*) trestle; (= *Sägebock*) sawhorse **(c)** (*sl*: = *Lust, Spaß*) **null ~!** I don't feel like it; **~ auf etw** (*acc*) **haben** to fancy sth (*esp Brit inf*); **~ haben, etw zu tun** to fancy doing sth (*esp Brit inf*); **null ~ auf nichts** pissed off with everything (*inf*)

Bock² NT or M **-s, -** bock (beer) (*type of strong beer*)

bocken [ˈbɔkn] VI **(a)** (*Zugtier etc*) to refuse to move; (*Pferd*) to refuse; **vor einer Hürde ~** to refuse a jump **(b)** (*inf*: = *trotzen*) to act up (*inf*) **(c)** (*sl*: = *Spaß machen*) **das bockt** that's the business (*sl*)

bockig ['bɔkɪç] ADJ (inf) awkward

Bockigkeit F -, -en awkwardness

Bock-: Bockleiter F stepladder; **Bockmist** M (inf) (= dummes Gerede) bullshit (sl); ~ **machen** to make a big blunder (inf)

Bocks- ['bɔks-]: **Bocksbeutel** M wide, rounded bottle containing Franconian wine; **Bockshorn** NT sich von jdm ins ~ **jagen lassen** to let sb upset one; **sie ließ sich nicht ins ~ jagen** she didn't let herself get into a state

Bock-: Bockspringen NT -s, NO PL leapfrog; (Sport) vaulting; ~ **machen** to play leapfrog; **Bocksprung** M (= Sprung über Menschen) leapfrog; (Sport) vault; **Bockwurst** F bockwurst (type of sausage)

Boden ['boːdn] M -s, ˷ ['bøːdn] (a) (= Erde, Grundfläche) ground; (= Erdreich auch) soil; (= Fußboden) floor; (= Grundbesitz) land; (no pl: = Terrain) soil; **auf spanischem** ~ on Spanish soil; **festen** ~ **unter den Füßen haben** to be on firm ground; **den** ~ **unter den Füßen verlieren** (lit) to lose one's footing; **keinen Fuß auf den** ~ **bekommen** (fig) to be unable to find one's feet; (in Diskussion) to get out of one's depth; **ihm wurde der** ~ **(unter den Füßen) zu heiß** (fig) things were getting too hot for him; **ich hätte (vor Scham) im** ~ **versinken können** (fig) I was so ashamed that I wished the ground would (open and) swallow me up; **am** ~ **zerstört sein** (inf) to be devastated; **(an)** ~ **gewinnen/verlieren** (fig) to gain/lose ground; **etw aus dem** ~ **stampfen** (fig) to conjure sth out of nothing; **Häuser** aus dem ~ **stampfen** to build sth overnight; **auf fruchtbaren** ~ **fallen** (fig) to fall on fertile ground

(b) (von Behälter) bottom; (von Hose) seat; (= Tortenboden) base

(c) (= Dachboden, Heuboden) loft; (für Getreide) drying floor; (für Wäsche) drying room

(d) (fig: = Grundlage) **auf dem** ~ **der Wissenschaft/Tatsachen/ Wirklichkeit stehen** to base oneself on scientific fact/on fact/ on reality; (Behauptung) to be based on scientific fact/on fact/on reality; **sie wurde hart auf den** ~ **der Wirklichkeit zurückgeholt** she was brought down to earth with a bump; **auf dem** ~ **der Tatsachen bleiben** to stick to the facts; **sich auf unsicherem** ~ **bewegen** to be on shaky ground

Boden-: Bodenbelag M floor covering; **Bodenfrost** M ground frost; **bodengestützt** [-gəʃtʏtst] ADJ Flugkörper ground-launched; **Bodengruppe** F (Aut) floorpan; **Bodenhaftung** F (Aut) road holding no indef art; **Bodenhaltung** F (Agr: von Hühnern etc) keeping (of hens etc) in free-range conditions; **„aus** ~**"** "free-range"; **Bodenkontrolle** F (Space) ground control; **bodenlos** ❶ ADJ bottomless; (inf: = unerhört) incredible ❷ ADV (inf) incredibly; **Bodennebel** M ground mist; **Bodenpersonal** NT (Aviat) ground personnel pl; **Bodenschätze** PL mineral resources pl; **Bodensee** M der ~ Lake Constance; **bodenständig** ADJ (= lang ansässig) long-established; (fig: = unkompliziert) down-to-earth; **Bodenstation** F (Space) ground station; **Bodenstreitkräfte** PL ground forces pl; **Bodenturnen** NT floor exercises pl

Body ['bɔdi] M -s, -s body

Body-: Bodybuilder ['bɔdibɪldɐ] M -s, -, **Bodybuilderin** [-ərɪn] F -, -nen bodybuilder; **Bodybuilding** ['bɔdibɪldɪŋ] NT -s, NO PL bodybuilding; ~ **machen** to do bodybuilding exercises

Böe ['bøːə] F -, -n gust (of wind); (stärker, mit Regen) squall

bog PRET von biegen

Bogen ['boːgn] M -s, - or ˷ ['bøːgn] (a) (= gekrümmte Linie) curve; (= Kurve) bend; (Math) arc; (Mus, Ski) turn; **den** ~ **heraushaben** (inf) to have got the hang of it (inf); **einen** ~ **machen** (Fluss etc) to curve; (= einen Umweg machen) to make a detour; **einen großen** ~ **um jdn/etw machen** (= meiden) to keep well clear of sb/sth; **jdn in hohem** ~ **hinauswerfen** (inf) to send sb flying out

(b) (Archit) arch

(c) (= Waffe, Mus: = Geigenbogen etc) bow; **den** ~ **überspannen** (fig) to go too far

(d) (= Papierbogen) sheet (of paper)

Bogen-: Bogengang M, pl -gänge (Archit) arcade; **Bogenlampe** F arc lamp; **Bogenschießen** NT -s, NO PL archery; **Bogenschütze** M, **Bogenschützin** F archer

Bohle ['boːlə] F -, -n (thick) board; (Rail) sleeper

Böhme ['bøːmə] M -n, -n, **Böhmin** ['bøːmɪn] F -, -nen Bohemian (inhabitant of Bohemia)

Böhmen ['bøːmən] NT -s Bohemia

Böhmerwald ['bøːmɐ-] M Bohemian Forest

böhmisch ['bøːmɪʃ] ❶ ADJ Bohemian; **das sind für mich ~e Dörfer** (inf) that's all Greek to me (inf) ❷ ADV ~ **einkaufen** (Aus inf) to shoplift

Bohne ['boːnə] F -, -n bean; **dicke/grüne/weiße** ~ broad/green or French or runner/haricot (Brit) or string or navy (US) beans; **rote** ~**n** kidney beans; **nicht die** ~ (inf) not one little bit; **du hast wohl** ~**n in den Ohren** (inf) are you deaf?

Bohnen-: Bohneneintopf M bean stew; **Bohnenkaffee** M real coffee; **gemahlener** ~ ground coffee; **Bohnenkraut** NT savoury (Brit), savory (US); **Bohnenstange** F bean support; (fig inf) beanpole (inf)

Bohrarbeiten PL drillings pl

bohren ['boːrən] ❶ VT to bore; (mit Bohrer, Bohrmaschine auch) to drill; Brunnen to sink; Stange, Pfahl, Schwert etc to sink (in +acc into)

❷ VI (a) (mit Bohrer) to bore (in +dat into), to drill (nach for); **in einem Zahn** ~ to drill a tooth; **in der Nase** ~ to pick one's nose

(b) (fig) (= drängen) to keep on; (Schmerz, Zweifel etc) to gnaw

❸ VR **sich in/durch etw** (acc) ~ to bore its way into/through sth

bohrend ADJ (fig) Blick piercing; Schmerz, Zweifel, Hunger, Reue gnawing; Frage probing

Bohrer ['boːrɐ] M -s, - (elektrisch, = Drillbohrer) drill; (= Handbohrer) gimlet

Bohr-: Bohrfeld NT oil/gas field; **Bohrinsel** F drilling rig; (für Öl auch) oil rig; **Bohrloch** NT borehole; (in Holz, Metall etc) drill hole; **Bohrmaschine** F drill; **Bohrturm** M derrick

Bohrung F -, -en (a) (= das Bohren) boring; (mit Bohrer, Bohrmaschine auch) drilling; (von Brunnen) sinking

(b) (= Loch) bore(hole); (in Holz, Metall etc) drill hole

böig ['bøːɪç] ADJ gusty; (stärker, mit Regen) squally

Boiler ['bɔylɐ] M -s, - (hot-water) tank

Boje ['boːjə] F -, -n buoy

bolivianisch [boliviˈaːnɪʃ] ADJ Bolivian

Bolivien [boˈliːviən] NT -s Bolivia

Bolzen ['bɔltsn] M -s, - (Tech) pin; (esp mit Gewinde, = Geschoss) bolt

Bolzenschneider M bolt cutters pl

Bombardement [bɔmbardəˈmãː, (Aus) bɔmbardˈmãː] NT -s, -s bombardment; **ein** ~ **von** (fig) a deluge of

bombardieren [bɔmbarˈdiːrən] ptp **bombardiert** VT to bomb; (= mit Granaten beschießen, fig) to bombard

Bombast [bɔmˈbast] M -(e)s, NO PL bombast

bombastisch [bɔmˈbastɪʃ] ❶ ADJ Sprache bombastic; Architektur, Hauseinrichtung overdone pred; Aufwand ostentatious ❷ ADV (= schwülstig) bombastically; (= pompös) ostentatiously

Bombe ['bɔmbə] F -, -n bomb; **wie eine** ~ **einschlagen** to come as a (real) bombshell; **eine/die** ~ **platzen lassen** (fig) to drop a/the bombshell

Bomben- IN CPDS (Mil) bomb; (inf: = hervorragend) fantastic (inf); **Bombenalarm** M bomb scare; **Bombenangriff** M, **Bombenanschlag** M bomb attack; **Bombenerfolg** M (inf) smash hit (inf); **Bombengeschäft** NT (inf) **ein** ~ **sein** to be a gold mine (fig inf); **ein** ~ **machen** to do a roaring trade (inf) (mit in); **Bombenleger** [-leːgɐ] M -s, -, **Bombenlegerin** [-ərɪn] F -, -nen bomber; **bombensicher** ❶ ADJ (a) (Mil) bombproof (b) (inf) dead certain (inf); Landung absolutely safe ❷ ADV (a) (Mil) lagern, unterbringen in a bombproof place (b) (inf) **das steht** ~ **fest** that's absolutely certain; **Bombensplitter** M bomb fragment; **Bombenteppich** M **einen** ~ **legen** to blanket-bomb an/the area; **Bombentrichter** M bomb crater

Bomberjacke F bomber jacket

Bon [bɔŋ, bõː] M -s, -s voucher, coupon; (= Kassenzettel) receipt

Bonbon [bɔŋˈbɔŋ, bõˈbõː] NT or M -s, -s sweet (Brit), candy (US); (fig) treat

bonbonfarben [bɔŋˈbɔŋfarbn, bõˈbõː-], **bonbonfarbig** ADJ candy-coloured (Brit), candy-colored (US)

Bonbonniere [bɔŋbɔˈniːərə, bõ-] F -, -n box of chocolates

bongen ['bɔŋən] VT (inf) Betrag etc to ring up; **das ist gebongt** (inf) okey-doke (inf)

Bonität [boniˈtɛːt] F -, -en (Fin) financial standing

Bonitätsprüfung F (Fin) credit investigation

Bonsai ['bɔnzai] NT -s, -s bonsai

Bonus ['boːnʊs] M - *or* -ses, - *or* -se (Comm, fig) bonus; (Univ, Sport: = Punktvorteil) bonus points pl

Bonusmeile F air mile (Brit), bonus mile (US)

Bonze ['bɔntsə] M -n, -n (a) (Rel) bonze (b) (pej) bigwig (inf)

Boom [buːm] M -s, -s boom

boomen ['buːmən] VI to boom

Boot [boːt] NT -(e)s, -e boat; ~ **fahren** to go out in a boat; (zum Vergnügen) to go boating; **wir sitzen alle in einem** *or* **im gleichen** ~ (fig) we're all in the same boat

booten ['buːtn] VTI (Comput) to boot (up)

Bootsektor ['buːt-] M (Comput) boot sector

Boots-: Bootsfahrt F boat trip; **Bootsflüchtlinge** PL boat people; **Bootsverleih** M boat hire business

Bor [boːɐ] NT -s, NO PL (abbr B) boron

Bord[1] [bɔrt] M -(e)s [-dəs], NO PL an ~ (eines Schiffes/der „Bremen") on board (a ship/the "Bremen"); **alle Mann an** ~! all aboard!; **an** ~ **gehen** to board (the ship/plane), to go on board; **Mann über** ~! man overboard!; **über** ~ **werfen** (lit, fig) to throw overboard!; **die Vorsicht über** ~ **werfen** to throw caution to the winds; **von** ~ **gehen** to leave (the) ship/the plane; (esp Passagiere am Ziel) to disembark

Bord[2] NT -(e)s, -e (= Wandbrett) shelf

Bord-: Bordbuch NT log(book); **Bordcomputer** M on-board computer; **bordeigen** ADJ ship's/plane's etc

Bordell [bɔr'dɛl] NT -s, -e brothel

Bord-: Bordfunk M (Naut) (ship's) radio; (Aviat) (aircraft) radio equipment; **Bordfunker(in)** M(F) (Naut, Aviat) radio operator; **Bordkante** F kerb (Brit), curb (US); **Bordkarte** F boarding pass; **Bordkonnossement** NT on-board *or* shipped bill of lading; **Bordstein** M kerb (Brit), curb (US); **den** ~ **mitnehmen** (inf) to hit the kerb (Brit) *or* curb (US); **Bordsteinkante** F kerb (Brit), curb (US)

borgen ['bɔrgn] VTI (a) (= erhalten) to borrow (von from) (b) (= geben) to lend (jdm etw sb sth, sth to sb)

Borke ['bɔrkə] F -, -n bark

Borkenkäfer M bark beetle

borniert [bɔr'niːɐt] ADJ bigoted

Borretsch ['bɔrɛtʃ] M -(e)s, NO PL borage

Borsalbe F boric acid ointment

Börse ['bœrzə, 'bøːrzə] F -, -n (a) (= Geldbörse) (für Frauen) purse; (für Männer) wallet (Brit), billfold (US) (b) (= Wertpapierhandel) stock market; (Ort) stock exchange; **an die** ~ **gehen** to be floated on the stock exchange

Börsen- (St Ex): **Börsenagent(in)** M(F) broker; **Börsenaufsicht** F (a) (Behörde) stock market regulator (b) NO PL (Kontrolle) regulation of the stock market; **Börsenauftrag** M stock exchange order; **limitierter** ~ limited order; **unlimitierter** ~ unlimited order, market order (US); **Börsenbeginn** M opening of the stock market; **bei** ~ when the stock market opens; **Börsenbericht** M stock market report; **Börseneinführung** F flotation on the stock exchange; **börsenfähig** ADJ negotiable on the stock exchange; **Börsengang** M, pl -gänge stock market flotation; **Börsengeschäft** NT (= Wertpapierhandel) stockbroking; (= Transaktion) stock market transaction; **Börsenindex** M stock exchange index; **Börsenkrach** M stock market crash; **Börsenkurs** M stock market price; **Börsenmakler(in)** M(F) stockbroker; **börsennotiert** [-notiːɐt] ADJ Firma listed; **Börsennotierung** F quotation (on the stock exchange); **Börsenplatz** M stock exchange; **Börsenschluss** M, NO PL close of the stock market; **Börsenspekulation** F speculation on the stock market; **Börsentendenz** F stock market trend; **Börsentipp** M market tip; **Börsenumsatzsteuer** F stock exchange tax; **Börsenverkehr** M stock market dealings pl; **Börsenzulassung** F admission to the stock exchange, listing (esp US); ~ **beantragen** to apply for listing

Börsianer [bœr'ziaːnɐ] M -s, -, **Börsianerin** [-ərɪn] F -, -nen (inf) (= Makler) broker; (= Spekulant) speculator

Borste ['bɔrstə] F -, -n bristle

borstig ['bɔrstɪç] ADJ bristly; (fig) snappish

Borte ['bɔrtə] F -, -n braid trimming

Borwasser NT, NO PL boric acid lotion

bös [bøːs] ADJ, ADV = **böse**

bösartig ADJ Mensch, Wesen malicious; Tier vicious; (Med) Geschwür malignant

Böschung ['bœʃʊŋ] F -, -en (von Straße, Bahndamm) embankment; (von Fluss) bank

böse ['bøːzə] ADJ ADJ (a) (= sittlich schlecht, unangenehm) bad; (inf: = unartig) naughty; Überraschung, Streich, Geschichte nasty; **die** ~ **Fee/Stiefmutter** the Wicked Fairy/Stepmother; **ein** ~**r Geist** an evil spirit; **das war keine** ~ **Absicht** there was no harm intended; **eine** ~ **Zunge haben** to have a wicked tongue; **ein** ~**s Erwachen** a rude awakening; ~ **Folgen** dire consequences

(b) (= verärgert) angry (+dat, auf +acc, mit with); **ein** ~**s Gesicht machen** to scowl

(c) (inf: = schmerzend, entzündet) bad

(d) (inf: verstärkend) real (inf); Enttäuschung, Gewitter, Sturz terrible

ADV (a) (= übel gesinnt) nastily; (stärker) evilly

(b) (= schlimm) nastily; verprügeln badly; **das/es sieht** ~ **aus** things look/it looks bad

Böse(r) ['bøːzə] MF DECL AS ADJ wicked *or* evil person; (Film, Theat) villain, baddy (inf); **die** ~**n** the wicked

Böse(s) ['bøːzə] NT DECL AS ADJ evil; (= Schaden, Leid) harm; **im** ~**n auseinander gehen** to part on bad terms; **mir schwant** ~**s** it sounds/looks ominous (to me); **ich dachte an gar nichts** ~**s, als …** I was quite unsuspecting when …; **ich habe mir gar nichts** ~**s dabei gedacht, als ich das sagte** I didn't mean any harm when I said that

boshaft ['boːshaft] ADJ malicious, nasty ADV grinsen, lächeln maliciously, nastily

Boshaftigkeit ['boːshaftɪçkait] F -, -en (a) NO PL maliciousness, nastiness (b) (Bemerkung) malicious *or* nasty remark

Bosheit ['boːshait] F -, -en malice; (Bemerkung) malicious remark; (Handlung) malicious thing to do

Boskop ['bɔskɔp] M -s, - ≈ russet

Bosnien ['bɔsniən] NT -s Bosnia

Bosnien-Herzegowina ['bɔsniənhɛrtse'goːvina, -hɛrtsego'viːna] NT -s Bosnia-Herzegovina

bosnisch ['bɔsnɪʃ] ADJ Bosnian

Bosporus ['bɔspoʊrʊs] M - der ~ the Bosporus

bot PRET *von* **bieten**

Botanik [bo'taːnɪk] F -, NO PL botany

Botaniker [bo'taːnikɐ] M -s, -, **Botanikerin** [-ərɪn] F -, -nen botanist

botanisch [bo'taːnɪʃ] ADJ botanic

Bote ['boːtə] M -n, -n, **Botin** ['boːtɪn] F -, -nen (usu mit Nachricht) messenger; (= Kurier) courier; (= Gerichtsbote) messenger-at-arms

Botschaft ['boːtʃaft] F -, -en (a) (= Mitteilung) message; (esp amtlich) communication; (= Neuigkeit) (piece of) news; (= Aussage) message (b) (Pol: = Vertretung) embassy

Botschafter ['boːtʃaftɐ] M -s, -, **Botschafterin** [-ərɪn] F -, -nen ambassador

Bottich ['bɔtɪç] M -(e)s, -e tub

Bouclé [bu'kleː] NT -s, -s bouclé (yarn)

Bouillon [bʊl'jɔn, bʊl'jõː, (Aus) bu'jõː] F -, -s bouillon

Bouillonwürfel M bouillon cube

Boulevard- [bulə'vaːɐ, bul'vaːɐ]: **Boulevardblatt** NT (inf) tabloid (auch pej); **Boulevardpresse** F (inf) popular press; **Boulevardstück** NT (Theat) light comedy; **Boulevardtheater** NT light theatre (Brit) *or* theater (US)

Boutique [bu'tiːk] F -, -n boutique

Bovist ['boːvɪst, bo'vɪst] M -s, -e (Bot) puffball

Bowle ['boːlə] F -, -n (= Getränk) punch

Bowlenservice [-zɛrviːs] NT punch set (punchbowl and cups)

Bowling ['boːlɪŋ] NT -s, -s (= Spiel) (tenpin) bowling; (= Ort) bowling alley; ~ **spielen gehen** to go bowling

Bowlingkugel F bowl

Box [bɔks] F -, -en (a) (= abgeteilter Raum) compartment; (für Pferde) box; (in Großgarage) (partitioned-off) parking place; (für Rennwagen) pit; (bei Ausstellungen) stand (b) (= Behälter) box (c) (= Lautsprecherbox) speaker (unit)

boxen ['bɔksn] VI (Sport) to box; (zur Übung) to spar; (= zuschlagen) to punch; **gegen jdn** ~ to fight sb VT (= schlagen) to punch VR (a) (inf: = sich schlagen) to have a fight (b) (= sich einen Weg bahnen) to fight one's way; **sich durchs Leben/nach oben** ~ (fig inf) to fight one's way through life/up

Boxen NT -s, NO PL (*Sport*) boxing
Boxenstopp M pit stop
Boxer[1] ['bɔksɐ] M -s, - (= *Hund*) boxer
Boxer[2] ['bɔksɐ] M -s, -, **Boxerin** [-ərɪn] F -, -nen (= *Sportler*) boxer
Boxer-: Boxermotor M (*Tech*) opposed cylinder engine (*Brit*), boxer engine (*US*); **Boxershorts** PL boxer shorts *pl*
Box-: Boxhandschuh M boxing glove; **Boxkampf** M (= *Disziplin*) boxing *no art*; (= *Einzelkampf*) fight, bout; **Boxring** M boxing ring
Boy [bɔy] M -s, -s pageboy (*Brit*), bellhop (*esp US*)
Boykott [bɔy'kɔt] M -(e)s, -e *or* -s boycott
boykottieren [bɔykɔ'tiːrən], *ptp* **boykottiert** VT to boycott
brach PRET *von* brechen
Brach-: Brachland NT fallow (land); **brachliegen** VI SEP IRREG to lie fallow; (*fig*) to be left unexploited; **~de Kenntnisse/Kräfte** unexploited knowledge/powers
brachte PRET *von* bringen
brackig ['brakɪç] ADJ brackish
Brahmane [bra'maːnə] M -n, -n, **Brahmanin** [-'maːnɪn] F -, -nen Brahman, Brahmin
brahmanisch [bra'maːnɪʃ] ADJ Brahman *attr*
Brainstorming ['breːnstɔːmɪŋ] NT -s, -s brainstorming session
Branche ['brãːʃə] F -, -n (= *Fach*) field; (= *Gewerbe*) trade; (= *Geschäftszweig*) area of business; (= *Wirtschaftszweig*) (branch of) industry
Branchen- ['brãːʃn-]: **Branchenadressbuch** NT classified directory, Yellow Pages® *sing*; **branchenfremd** ADJ *siehe* **Branche** Waren foreign to the trade/industry; *Kollege* not familiar with the trade; **Branchenführer(in)** M(F) market leader; **Branchenkenner(in)** M(F) *siehe* **Branche**; **er ist ~ he** knows the trade/industry; **Branchenrisiko** NT (*Comm*) systematic risk; **branchenüblich** ADJ *siehe* **Branche** usual in the trade/industry; **Branchenverzeichnis** NT classified directory, Yellow Pages® *sing*
Brand [brant] M -(e)s, ⸚e ['brɛndə] (a) (= *Feuer*) fire; **in ~ geraten** to catch fire; **etw in ~ setzen** *or* **stecken** to set fire to sth; **einen ~ legen** to set a fire (b) (*fig inf*: = *großer Durst*) raging thirst
Brand-: Brandblase F (burn) blister; **Brandbombe** F firebomb, incendiary device
branden ['brandn] VI to surge (*auch fig*); **an** *or* **gegen etw** (*acc*) **~ to** break against sth
Brandenburg ['brandnbʊrk] NT -s Brandenburg
Brand-: Brandfleck M burn; **Brandgefahr** F danger of fire; **bei ~ when** there is danger of fire; **Brandherd** M source of the fire; (*fig*) source; **Brandloch** NT burn hole; **brandmarken** ['brantmarkn] VT INSEP to brand; (*fig*) to denounce; **jdn als etw ~** (*fig*) to brand sb (as) sth; **brandneu** ADJ (*inf*) brand-new; **Brandrodung** F slash-and-burn; **Brandschutz** M protection against fire; **Brandstifter(in)** M(F) fire raiser (*esp Brit*), arsonist (*esp Jur*); **Brandstiftung** F arson (*auch Jur*)
Brandung ['brandʊŋ] F -, -en surf
Brand-: Brandwache F (a) (= *Überwachung der Brandstelle*) firewatch (b) (= *Personen*) firewatch team; **Brandwunde** F burn; (*durch Flüssigkeit*) scald; **Brandzeichen** NT brand
brannte PRET *von* brennen
Branntwein M spirits *pl*
Branntwein-: Branntweinbrennerei F distillery; (= *Branntweinbrennen*) distillation of spirits; **Branntweinschank** [-ʃaŋk] F -, -en (*Aus*) ≈ public house (*Brit*), ≈ bar; **Branntweinsteuer** F tax on spirits
brasilianisch [brazi'liaːnɪʃ] ADJ Brazilian
Brasilien [bra'ziːliən] NT -s Brazil
brät [brɛːt] 3. PERS SING PRES *von* braten
Brät [brɛːt] NT -s, NO PL sausage meat
Bratapfel M baked apple
braten ['braːtn], *pret* **briet** [briːt], *ptp* **gebraten** [gə'braːtn] ❶ VT I to roast; (*im Ofen: ohne Fett*) to bake; (*in der Pfanne*) to fry; **etw braun ~** to roast/fry sth until it is brown ❷ VI (*inf: in der Sonne*) to roast oneself (*inf*); **sich ~ lassen** to roast oneself (*inf*)
Braten ['braːtn] M -s, - ≈ pot roast meat *no indef art, no pl*; (*im Ofen gebraten*) joint (*Brit*), roast; **kalter ~** cold meat; **den ~ riechen** (*inf*) to smell a rat (*inf*); **einen ~ in der Röhre haben** (*inf*) to have a bun in the oven (*inf*)

Braten-: Bratensoße F gravy; **Bratenwender** [-vɛndɐ] M -s, - fish slice
Brat-: bratfertig ADJ oven-ready; **Bratfett** NT fat for roasting; (*für die Pfanne*) fat for frying; **Bratfisch** M fried fish; **Brathähnchen** NT, (*Aus, S Ger*) **Brathendl** NT roast chicken; **Brathering** M fried herring (*sold cold*); **Brathuhn** NT, **Brathühnchen** NT roast chicken; (= *Huhn zum Braten*) roasting chicken; **Bratkartoffeln** PL sauté potatoes *pl*; **Bratkartoffelverhältnis** NT (*hum*) **er hat ein ~ mit ihr** he only sees her because she feeds and waters him (*hum*); **er sucht ein ~** he's looking for a meal ticket; **Bratofen** M oven; **Bratpfanne** F frying pan; **Bratröhre** F oven; **Bratrost** M grill
Bratsche ['braːtʃə] F -, -n viola
Bratschist [bra'tʃɪst] M -en, -en, **Bratschistin** [-'tʃɪstɪn] F -, -nen violist
Brat-: Bratspieß M skewer; (= *Teil des Grills*) spit; (= *Gericht*) kebab; **Bratwurst** F (*zum Braten*) (frying) sausage; (*gebraten*) (fried) sausage
Brauch [braux] M -(e)s, **Bräuche** ['brɔyçə] custom, tradition; **nach altem ~** according to (established) custom *or* tradition; **etw ist ~** sth is traditional; **das ist bei uns so ~** (*inf*) that's traditional with us
brauchbar ADJ (a) (= *benutzbar*) useable; *Plan* workable; (= *nützlich*) useful (b) (= *ordentlich*) decent
brauchen ['brauxn] ❶ VT (a) (= *nötig haben*) to need (*für, zu* for); **Zeit/zwei Minuten** *etc* **~** to need time/two minutes *etc*; **normalerweise brauche ich zwei Stunden dafür** I normally take two hours to do it; **wenn 5 Männer 3 Stunden ~, ...** if 5 men take 3 hours ...; **da braucht seine Zeit** that takes time; **wie lange braucht man, um ...?** how long does it take to ...? (b) (*inf.* = *nützlich finden*) **das könnte ich ~** I could do with that; **das kann ich gerade ~!** (*iro*) that's all I need!; **kannst du die Sachen ~?** have you any use for the things?; **er ist zu allem zu ~** (*inf*) he's a really useful type (to have around) (*inf*); **heute bin ich zu nichts zu ~** (*inf*) I'm useless today (*inf*) (c) (= *benutzen*) to use; *siehe auch* **gebraucht** (d) (*inf.* = *verbrauchen*) to use ❷ V AUX to need; **du brauchst das nicht tun** you don't have *or* need to do that; **du hättest das nicht (zu) tun ~** you didn't have *or* need to do that; **es braucht nicht besonders betont zu werden, dass ...** there's no need to stress the fact that ...
Brauchtum ['brauxtuːm] NT -s, (*rare*) **-tümer** [-tyːmɐ] customs *pl*, traditions *pl*
Brauchwasser NT process water
Braue ['brauə] F -, -n (eye)brow
brauen ['brauən] VT *Bier* to brew; *Zaubertrank, Punsch etc* to concoct
Brauer ['brauɐ] M -s, -, **Brauerin** [-ərɪn] F -, -nen brewer
Brauerei [brauə'rai] F -, -en (a) brewery (b) NO PL (= *das Brauen*) brewing
braun [braun] ADJ brown; (*von Sonne auch*) (sun)tanned; (*inf.* = *~haarig*) brown-haired; (*pej:* = *Nazibraun*) Nazi; **~ gebrannt** (sun)tanned, brown; **von der Sonne ~ gebrannt sein** to be tanned (by the sun)
Braun [braun] NT -s, - brown
Braun-: braunäugig [-ɔygɪç] ADJ brown-eyed; **Braunbär** M brown bear
Bräune ['brɔynə] F -, NO PL (= *braune Färbung*) brown(ness); (*von Sonne*) (sun)tan
bräunen ['brɔynən] ❶ VT (*Cook*) to brown; (*Sonne etc*) to tan; *siehe auch* **gebräunt** ❷ VI (*Cook*) to go brown; (*Sonne*) to tan; **sich in der Sonne ~ lassen** to get a (sun)tan
Braun-: braungebrannt ADJ ATTR *siehe* **braun**; **braunhaarig** ADJ brown-haired; *Frau auch* brunette; **Braunkohle** F brown coal
bräunlich ['brɔynlɪç] ADJ brownish
Braunschweig ['braunʃvaik] NT -s Brunswick
Brause ['brauzə] F -, -n (a) (= *Dusche, Duschvorrichtung*) shower (b) (= *~aufsatz*) shower attachment; (*an Schlauch, Gießkanne*) rose (c) (= *Getränk*) pop; (= *Limonade*) (fizzy) lemonade; (= *~pulver*) sherbet
brausen ['brauzn] VI (a) (= *tosen*) to roar; (*Orgel, Beifall*) to thunder; **es brauste mir in den Ohren** my ears were ringing (b) AUX SEIN (= *rasen, rennen, schnell fahren*) to race (c) AUCH VR (= *duschen*) to (have a) shower

Brause-: Brausepulver NT sherbet; **Brausetablette** F effervescent tablet; **Brausewürfel** M tablet of lemonade powder

Braut [braut] F **-, Bräute** ['brɔʏtə] **(a)** (*bei Hochzeit*) bride **(b)** (*sl: = Frau, Mädchen*) bird (*esp Brit inf*), chick (*esp US inf*)

Bräutigam ['brɔʏtigam, 'brɔʏtigam] M **-s, -e** (bride)groom

Braut-: Brautjungfer F bridesmaid; **Brautkleid** NT wedding dress; **Brautpaar** NT bride and (bride)groom

brav [braːf] **1** ADJ **(a)** (= *gehorsam*) *Kind* good; **sei schön ~!** be a good boy/girl
(b) (= *bieder*) *Frisur, Kleid* plain
2 ADV **(a)** (= *artig*) **~ (gemacht)!** (*zu Tier*) good boy!; **iss das ~ leer** be a good boy/girl and eat it up
(b) (= *ganz ordentlich*) **~ seine Pflicht tun** to do one's duty without complaining; **etw zu ~ spielen** (*pej*) to give an uninspired rendition of sth

> *Vorsicht!* **brav** *wird nicht mit dem englischen Wort* **brave** *übersetzt.*

bravo ['braːvo] INTERJ well done; (*für Künstler*) bravo
Bravoruf M cheer
BRD [beːʔɛrˈdeː] F **-** ABBR *von* **Bundesrepublik Deutschland** FRG

Break [breːk] NT *or* M **-s, -s** (*Tennis*) break
Break-even-Point [breːkˈliːvnpɔint] M **-s, -s** (*Econ*) breakeven point

Brech-: Brechbohnen PL French beans *pl*; **Brechdurchfall** M diarrhoea (*Brit*) *or* diarrhea (*US*) and sickness; **Brecheisen** NT crowbar; (*von Dieb*) jemmy (*Brit*), jimmy (*US*)

brechen ['brɛçn], *pret* **brach** [braːx], *ptp* **gebrochen** [gəˈbrɔxn]
1 VT **(a)** (= *zerbrechen, herausbrechen*) to break; *Schiefer, Stein, Marmor* to cut; *Widerstand* to overcome; *Licht* to refract; **sich/jdm den Arm ~** to break one's/sb's arm; **das wird ihm das Genick** *or* **den Hals ~** (*fig*) that will bring about his downfall
(b) (= *erbrechen*) to bring up
2 VI **(a)** AUX SEIN to break; **mir bricht das Herz** it breaks my heart; **~d voll sein** to be full to bursting
(b) **mit jdm/etw ~** to break with sb/sth
(c) (= *sich erbrechen*) to be sick
3 VR (*Wellen*) to break; (*Lichtstrahl*) to be refracted; (*Schall*) to rebound (*an +dat* off)

Brecher ['brɛçɐ] M **-s, -** (= *Welle*) breaker
Brech-: Brechmittel NT emetic; **er/das ist das reinste ~ (für mich)** he/it makes me feel sick; **Brechreiz** M nausea; **ein leichter ~** a slight touch of nausea; **Brechstange** F crowbar; **mit der ~** (*fig*) using the sledgehammer approach
Brechung ['brɛçʊŋ] F **-, -en** (*der Wellen*) breaking; (*des Lichts*) refraction; (*des Schalls*) rebounding
Bredouille [breˈdʊljə] F **-**, NO PL **in der ~ sein** *or* **sitzen** to be in a scrape (*inf*); **in die ~ geraten** *or* **kommen** to get into a scrape (*inf*)

Brei [brai] M **-(e)s, -e** mush, paste; (*für Kinder, Kranke*) semi-solid food; (= *Haferbrei*) porridge; (= *Grießbrei*) semolina; (= *Reisbrei*) rice pudding; (= *Papierbrei*) pulp; **verrühren Sie die Zutaten zu einem dünnen ~** mix the ingredients to a thin paste; **jdn zu ~ schlagen** (*inf*) to beat sb to a pulp (*inf*); **um den heißen ~ herumreden** (*inf*) to beat about (*Brit*) *or* around the bush (*inf*); **jdm ~ um den Mund** *or* **ums Maul schmieren** (*inf*) to soft-soap sb (*inf*)

breit [brait] **1** ADJ **(a)** broad; (*esp bei Maßangabe*) wide; *Bekanntenkreis, Publikum, Interessen, Angebot* wide; **etw ~er machen** to broaden *or* widen sth; **er hat ein ~es Lachen** he guffaws; **die ~e Masse** the masses *pl*; **die ~e Öffentlichkeit** the public at large; **er hat einen ~en Rücken** *or* **Buckel** (*fig inf*) his shoulders are broad
(b) (*sl: = betrunken, unter Drogen*) high (*inf*)
2 ADV **den Stoff ~ nehmen** to take the material widthways; **~ lachen** to guffaw; **~ sprechen** to speak with a broad accent;

~ gebaut sturdily built; **~ gefächert** *Firmengruppe, Messe, Kritik* wide-ranging; **ein ~ gefächertes Angebot** a wide range

Breitband-: Breitbandkabel NT broadband cable; **Breitband(kommunikations)netz** NT (*Telec*) broadband (communications) network

breitbeinig **1** ADJ **in ~er Stellung** with one's legs apart; **~er Gang** rolling gait **2** ADV with one's legs apart

Breite ['braitə] F **-, -n (a)** breadth; (*von Dialekt, Aussprache*) broadness; (*esp bei Maßangaben*) width; (*von Angebot*) breadth; (*von Interessen*) wide range; **der ~ nach** widthways; **etw in aller ~ erklären** to explain sth in great detail; **in die ~ gehen** to go into detail; (*inf: = dick werden*) to put on weight **(b)** (*Geog*) latitude; (= *Gebiet*) part of the world; **in südlichere ~n fahren** (*inf*) to travel to more southerly climes; **es liegt (auf) 20° nördlicher/südlicher ~** it lies 20° north/south; **in unseren ~n** in our area

breiten ['braitn] VTR to spread

Breiten-: Breitengrad M (degree of) latitude; **Breitenkreis** M parallel; **Breitensport** M popular sport

Breit-: breitgefächert [-gəfɛçɐt] ADJ *siehe* **breit**; **breit machen** VR (*inf*) (*Mensch*) to make oneself at home; (*Gefühl, Angst, Skepsis, Befürchtung*) to spread; **wenn er sich auf dem Sofa breit macht …** when he plants himself on the sofa …; **mach dich doch nicht so breit!** don't take up so much room; **die Touristen haben sich im Hotel breit gemacht** the tourists in the hotel were behaving as if they owned the place; **breitschlagen** VT SEP IRREG (*inf*) **jdn (zu etw) ~** to talk sb round (*Brit*) *or* around (*US*) (to sth); **sich ~ lassen** to let oneself be talked round (*Brit*) *or* around (*US*); **breitschultrig, breitschulterig** ADJ broad-shouldered; **Breitseite** F (*Naut, fig*) broadside; (*von Tisch*) short end; **eine ~ abgeben** to fire a broadside (*auch fig*); **breitspurig** [-ʃpuːrɪç] **1** ADJ *Bahn* broad-gauge *attr*; *Straße* wide-laned **2** ADV (*fig*) showily; **~ reden/auftreten** to speak/behave in a showy manner; **breittreten** VT SEP IRREG (*inf*) to go on about (*inf*); *Thema, Witz* to flog to death (*inf*)

Brems-: Bremsanlage F braking system; **Bremsbacke** F brake block; **Bremsbelag** M brake lining

Bremse¹ ['brɛmzə] F **-, -n** (*bei Fahrzeugen*) brake
Bremse² F **-, -n** (= *Insekt*) horsefly

bremsen ['brɛmzn] **1** VI **(a)** (*Fahrer, Auto*) to brake; (*Vorrichtung*) to function as a brake; **der Dynamo bremst** the dynamo acts as a brake; **der Wind bremst** the wind slows you *etc* down
(b) (*inf: = zurückstecken*) to ease off; **mit etw ~** to cut down (on) sth
2 VT **(a)** *Fahrzeug* to brake
(b) (*fig*) to restrict; *Entwicklung* to slow down; *Begeisterung* to dampen; (*inf*) *jdn* to check; **er ist nicht zu ~** (*inf*) there's no stopping him
3 VR (*inf*) **ich kann** *or* **werd mich ~!** not likely! (*inf*)

Brems-: Bremsfallschirm M brake parachute; **Bremsflüssigkeit** F brake fluid; **Bremskraft** F braking power; **Bremskraftverstärker** M servo brake; **Bremslicht** NT brake light; **Bremspedal** NT brake pedal; **Bremsspur** F skid mark *usu pl*

Bremsung F **-, -en** braking

Bremsweg M braking distance

Brenn-: brennbar ADJ inflammable, flammable; **leicht ~** highly inflammable; **Brennelement** NT fuel element

brennen ['brɛnən], *pret* **brannte** ['brantə], *ptp* **gebrannt** [gəˈbrant]
1 VI to burn; (*elektrisches Gerät, Glühbirne etc*) to be on; (*Zigarette, Sparflamme*) to be alight; (*Stich*) to sting; **das Streichholz/Feuerzeug brennt nicht** the match/lighter won't light; **auf der Haut ~** to burn the skin; **in den Augen ~** to sting the eyes; **das Licht ~ lassen** to leave the light on; **es brennt!** fire, fire!; (*fig*) it's urgent; **wo brennts denn?** (*inf*) what's the panic?; **darauf ~, etw zu tun** to be dying to do sth; **es brennt mir unter den Nägeln, zu erfahren, ob …** I am dying to know if …
2 VT to burn; *Branntwein* to distil (*Brit*), to distill (*US*); *Mandeln, Kaffee* to roast; *Porzellan, Ton, Ziegel* to fire; **eine CD ~** to burn a CD
3 VR (*lit*) to burn oneself (*an +dat* on); (*inf: = sich täuschen*) to be very much mistaken

brennend 🔢 ADJ (*lit, fig*) burning; *Zigarette* lighted 🔢 ADV (*inf*: = *sehr*) terribly; *interessieren* really; **ich wüsste ja ~ gern ...** I'm dying to know ...

Brenner [ˈbrenɐ] M **-s, -** (*Tech*) burner; (*für CDs*) CD burner

Brennerei [brenəˈrai] F **-, -en** distillery; (= *Kaffeebrennerei*) coffee-roasting plant

Brennessel F = **Brennnessel**

Brenn-: Brennglas NT burning glass; **Brennholz** NT firewood; **Brennmaterial** NT fuel (for heating); **Brennnessel** F stinging nettle; **Brennofen** M kiln; **Brennpunkt** M (*Math, Opt*) focus; **im ~ des Interesses stehen** to be the focal point; **Brennspiritus** [-ˈʃpiːritʊs] M methylated spirits *sing or pl*; **Brennstab** M fuel rod; **Brennstoff** M fuel; **Brennstoffzelle** F fuel cell

brenzlig [ˈbrɛntslɪç] ADJ (a) **ein ~er Geruch** a smell of burning (b) (*inf*) *Situation, Angelegenheit* precarious; **die Sache/die Lage wurde ihm zu ~** things got too hot for him (*inf*)

Bretagne [breˈtanjə] F **- die ~** Brittany

bretonisch [breˈtoːnɪʃ] ADJ Breton

Brett [bret] NT **-(e)s, -er** [ˈbretɐ] (a) (= *Holzplatte, Spielbrett*) board; (*länger und dicker*) plank; (= *Regalbrett*) shelf; **schwarzes ~** notice board (*Brit*), bulletin board (*US*); **ich habe heute ein ~ vor dem Kopf** (*inf*) I can't think straight today (b) (*fig*) **Bretter** PL (= *Bühne*) stage, boards *pl*; (= *Boden des Boxrings*) canvas; (= *Skier*) planks *pl* (*inf*); **die ~er, die die Welt bedeuten** the stage

Brettchen [ˈbretçən] NT **-s, -** (*inf*) platter; (*zum Schneiden*) board

brettern [ˈbretɐn] VI AUX SEIN (*inf*) to race (along)

Bretter-: Bretterwand F wooden wall; (= *Trennwand*) wooden partition; (= *Zaun, für Reklame*) hoarding; **Bretterzaun** M wooden fence

Brettspiel NT board game

Brezel [ˈbreːtsl] F **-, -n** pretzel

brich [brɪç] IMPER SING *von* **brechen**

Brief [briːf] M **-(e)s, -e** letter; (*Bibl*) epistle

Brief- IN CPDS letter; **Briefbombe** F letter bomb; **Brieffreund(in)** M(F) pen friend; **Brieffreundschaft** F correspondence with a pen friend; **eine ~ mit jdm haben** to be pen friends with sb; **Briefgrundschuld** F (*Fin*) certified land charge; **Briefhypothek** F (*Fin*) certified mortgage; **Briefkasten** M (*am Haus*) letter box (*Brit*), mailbox (*US*); (*der Post*) postbox (*Brit*), mailbox (*US*); **elektronischer ~** (*Comput*) electronic mailbox; **Briefkopf** M letterhead; (*handgeschrieben*) heading; **Briefkurs** M (*St Ex*) offer price

brieflich [ˈbriːflɪç] 🔢 ADJ by letter; **wir bitten um ~e Mitteilung** please inform us by letter; **~er Verkehr** correspondence 🔢 ADV by letter

Briefmarke F stamp

Briefmarken- IN CPDS stamp; **Briefmarkenautomat** M stamp machine; **Briefmarkensammler(in)** M(F) stamp collector; **Briefmarkensammlung** F stamp collection

Brief-: Brieföffner M letter opener; **Briefpapier** NT writing paper; **Brieftasche** F wallet, billfold (*US*); **Brieftaube** F carrier pigeon; **Briefträger** M postman (*Brit*), mailman (*US*); **Briefträgerin** F postwoman (*Brit*), mailwoman (*US*); **Briefumschlag** M envelope; **Briefverkehr** M correspondence; **Briefwaage** F letter scales *pl*; **Briefwahl** F postal vote; **seine Stimme durch ~ abgeben** to use the postal vote; **Briefwechsel** M correspondence; **im ~ mit jdm stehen, einen ~ mit jdm führen** to be in correspondence with sb

Bries [briːs] NT **-es, -e** [-zə] (*Cook*) sweetbread

briet PRET *von* **braten**

Brigade [briˈgaːdə] F **-, -n** (*Mil*) brigade

Brikett [briˈket] NT **-s, -s** *or* (*rare*) **-e** briquette

brillant [brɪlˈjant] 🔢 ADJ brilliant 🔢 ADV brilliantly

Brillant [brɪlˈjant] M **-en, -en** diamond

Brille [ˈbrɪlə] F **-, -n** (a) (*Opt*) glasses *pl*, spectacles *pl*, specs *pl* (*inf*); (= *Schutzbrille*) goggles *pl*; (= *Sonnenbrille*) glasses *pl*; **eine ~** a pair of glasses *etc*; **eine ~ tragen** to wear glasses *etc* (b) (= *Klosettbrille*) (toilet) seat

Brillen-: Brillenetui NT glasses case; **Brillenglas** NT lens

---

bringen [ˈbrɪŋən]

pret **brachte** [ˈbraxtə], *ptp* **gebracht** [gəˈbraxt]

TRANSITIVES VERB

> *Im Sinne von* **herbringen** *wird* **bringen** *im Englischen mit* **to bring** *übersetzt, im Sinne von* **woanders hinbringen** *mit* **to take**.

(a) (= *herbringen*) to bring; **sich** (*dat*) **etw bringen lassen** to have sth brought to one; **der letzte Sommer brachte uns viel Regen** last summer brought us a lot of rain; **jdn/etw unter** *or* **in seine Gewalt bringen** to gain control over *or* of sb/sth; **er bringt es nicht übers Herz** *or* **über sich** he can't bring himself to do it; **etw an sich** (*acc*) **bringen** to acquire sth

✦**etw mit sich bringen** **der Frühling bringt viele prächtige Blüten mit sich** spring brings lots of wonderful flowers; **seine Vergesslichkeit bringt viele Probleme mit sich** his forgetfulness causes a lot of problems; **die Liebe bringt es mit sich, dass man alles durch eine rosarote Brille sieht** love means you see everything through rose-coloured spectacles (*Brit*) *or* rose-colored glasses (*US*)

(b) (= *woanders hinbringen*) to take; **jdn ins Krankenhaus/zum Bahnhof/nach Hause bringen** to take sb to hospital/to the station/home; **bring das Auto in die Garage** put the car in the garage; **jdm eine Nachricht bringen** to give sb some news; **etw hinter sich** (*acc*) **bringen** to get sth over and done with

(c) (= *einbringen*) *Geld, Gewinn* to bring in, to make; (*Boden, Mine etc*) to produce; *Ärger* to cause; *Vorteile* to bring; **das Bild brachte 500 Euro** the picture went for 500 euros; **Freude bringen** to bring joy; **(jdm) Glück/Unglück bringen** to bring (sb) luck/bad luck; **Unglück über jdn bringen** to bring sb unhappiness; **das bringt nichts** (*inf*) it's pointless

(d) (= *lenken, versetzen*) **in die richtige Form bringen** to get in the right form; **jdn/sich in Gefahr bringen** to put sb/oneself in danger; **das bringt dich vors Gericht/ins Gefängnis** you'll end up in court/prison if you do that; **das Gespräch/die Rede auf etw** (*acc*) **bringen** to bring the conversation/talk (a)round to sth; **jdn wieder auf den rechten Weg bringen** (*fig*) to get sb back on the straight and narrow; **jdn zum Lachen/Weinen bringen** to make sb laugh/cry; **jdn zur Verzweiflung bringen** to drive sb to despair; **jdn dazu bringen, etw zu tun** to get sb to do sth

✦**so weit bringen, dass** **sie bringt ihn mit ihrer Nörgelei noch so weit, dass er kündigt** her nagging will make him hand in his notice; **du wirst es noch so weit bringen, dass man dich hinauswirft** you will make them throw you out

(e) (= *veröffentlichen*) (*Verlag*) to publish; (*Zeitung*) to print; (= *senden*) *Bericht etc* to broadcast; **die Zeitung/das Fernsehen brachte nichts darüber** there was nothing in the paper/on television about it; **die Zeitung brachte einen Artikel darüber** there was an article in the paper about it; **alle Zeitungen brachten es auf der ersten Seite** all the papers had it on the front page; **wir bringen einen Sonderbericht aus Kuba** we now have a special report from Cuba; **wir bringen Nachrichten** here is the news

(f) (= *aufführen*) *Stück* to do; **welche Lieder bringt sie auf ihrer Tournee?** what songs is she doing on her tour?

(g) (= *schaffen, leisten*) (*sl*) **ich bringe diese Übung nicht** I can't do this exercise; **das bringt er nicht** he's not up to it; **hat er das tatsächlich gebracht?** did he really do it?; **er bringt's** he's got what it takes; **das Auto bringt 180 km/h** (*inf*) the car can do 180 km/h; **der Motor bringts nicht mehr** the engine has had it (*inf*); **das kannst du doch nicht bringen** that's not on (*inf*)

(h) (*andere Wendungen*)

✦**es bringen** (= *erreichen*) **es auf 80 Jahre bringen** to reach the age of 80; **der Motor hat es auf 180.000 km gebracht** the engine has done 180,000 km; **er hat auf 25 Punkte gebracht** he got 25 points; **es zu etwas/nichts bringen** to get somewhere/nowhere; **es (im Leben) weit bringen** to do very well; **es zu Ehren bringen** to win honours (*Brit*) *or* honors (*US*); **er hat es bis zum Hauptmann/Direktor gebracht** he made it to captain/director

✦**jdn um etw bringen** to do sb out of sth; **das bringt mich noch um den Verstand** it's driving me crazy; **der Lärm hat mich um den Schlaf gebracht** the noise stopped me getting any sleep; **jdn/sich ums Leben bringen** to kill sb/oneself

brisant [bri'zant] ADJ (*lit, fig*) explosive

Brisanz [bri'zants] F **-, -en** explosive force; (*fig*) explosive nature; **ein Thema von äußerster ~** an extremely explosive subject

Brise ['bri:zə] F **-, -n** breeze

Britannien [bri'taniən] NT **-s** (*Hist*) Britain, Britannia (*Hist*); (*Press: = Großbritannien*) Britain

britannisch [bri'taniʃ] ADJ (*Hist*) Britannic

Brite ['brɪtə, 'brɪːtə] M **-n, -n, Britin** ['brɪtɪn, 'briːtɪn] F **-, -nen** Briton, Brit (*inf*); **er ist ~** he is British; **die ~n** the British

britisch ['brɪtɪʃ, 'briːtɪʃ] ADJ British; **die Britischen Inseln** the British Isles

bröckelig ['brœkəlɪç] ADJ crumbly; *Mauer, Putz* crumbling; **~ werden** to (start to) crumble

bröckeln ['brœkln] VI AUX SEIN (*Haus, Fassade*) to crumble; (*Preise, Kurse*) to tumble; (*Argwohn, Vertrauen etc*) to disintegrate

Brocken ['brɔkn] M **-s, -** lump, chunk; (*fig: = Bruchstück*) scrap; (*inf: Person*) lump (*inf*); **das Baby ist ein richtiger ~** the baby's a right little dumpling (*Brit inf*) *or* as plump as a dumpling (*US inf*); **ein paar ~ Spanisch** a smattering of Spanish; **ein harter ~** (*= Person*) a tough cookie (*inf*); **das ist ein harter** *or* **dicker ~** that's a tough nut to crack

brodeln ['bro:dln] VI to bubble; (*Dämpfe*) to swirl; **es brodelt** (*fig*) there is seething unrest

Brokat [bro'ka:t] M **-(e)s, -e** brocade

Broker ['bro:kɐ] M **-s, -, Brokerin** [-ərɪn] F **-, -nen** (*St Ex*) (stock)broker; (*Comm*) broker

Brokerfirma F (*St Ex*) brokerage firm

Brokkoli ['brɔkoli] PL broccoli *sing*

Brom [bro:m] NT **-s**, NO PL (*abbr* **Br**) bromine

Brombeere ['brɔm-] F blackberry, bramble

Brombeerstrauch M blackberry *or* bramble bush

Bronchial-: Bronchialasthma NT bronchial asthma; **Bronchialkatarr(h)** M bronchial catarrh

Bronchie ['brɔnçiə] F **-, -n** USU PL bronchial tube

Bronchitis [brɔn'çi:tis] F **-, Bronchitiden** [-çi'ti:dn] bronchitis

Brontosaurus [brɔnto'zaurus] M **-, -se, Brontosaurier** M brontosaurus

Bronze ['brõ:sə] F **-, -n** bronze

Bronzemedaille ['brõ:sə-] F bronze medal

bronzen ['brõ:sn] ADJ bronze

Bronzezeit ['brõ:sə-] F, NO PL Bronze Age

Brosche ['brɔʃə] F **-, -n** brooch

Broschüre [brɔ'ʃy:rə] F **-, -n** brochure

Brösel ['brø:zl] M **-s, -** crumb

bröselig ['brø:zəlɪç] ADJ crumbly

bröseln ['brø:zln] VI (*Kuchen, Stein*) to crumble; (*Mensch*) to make crumbs

Brot [bro:t] NT **-(e)s, -e** bread; (*= Laib*) loaf (of bread); (*= Scheibe*) slice (of bread); (*= Butterbrot*) (slice of) bread and butter *no art, no pl*; (*= Stulle*) sandwich; (*fig: = Unterhalt*) living; **belegte ~** open (*Brit*) *or* open-face (*US*) sandwiches; **das ist ein hartes** *or* **schweres ~** (*fig*) that's a hard way to earn one's living

---

BROT

Bread plays an important nutritional role in German-speaking countries - at least one meal a day is based around bread or rolls - and consequently there are many different varieties of bread. There are two basic sorts: pale bread made exclusively or mainly from wheat flour, and darker bread made principally from rye flour. Vollkornbrot is produced using wholemeal flour and is coarse-textured. A particular speciality is Laugengebäck: pretzels, rolls and crescent shapes that are made from a special wheat dough and dipped in caustic soda before baking, thus acquiring their typical brown crust and distinctive taste.

Brot-: Brotaufstrich M spread (*for bread*); **Brotbelag** M topping (*for bread*)

Brötchen ['brø:tçən] NT **-s, -** roll; (**sich** *dat*) **seine ~ verdienen** (*inf*) to earn one's living; **kleine ~ backen** (*inf*) to set one's sights lower

Brot-: Broteinheit F carbohydrate exchange (*Brit*), bread unit (*US*); **Brotkasten** M breadbin (*Brit*), breadbox (*US*); **Brotkorb** M bread basket; **jdm den ~ höher hängen** (*fig*) to keep sb short; **brotlos** ADJ out of work; **jdn ~ machen** to put sb out of work; **Brotmesser** NT bread knife; **Brotrinde** F crust; **Brotschneidemaschine** F bread slicer; **Brotzeit** F (**a**) (*S Ger: = Pause*) tea break (*Brit*), snack break (*US*) (**b**) (*= Essen*) sandwiches *pl*

browsen ['brauzn] VI (*Comput*) to browse

Browser ['brauzɐ] M **-s, -** (*Comput*) browser

Bruch [brux] M **-(e)s, ̈e** ['bryçə] (**a**) (*= -stelle*) break; (*in Porzellan etc*) crack; (*in Damm*) breach; **zu ~ gehen** to get broken; **zu ~ fahren** to smash (**b**) (*fig*) (*von Vertrag, Eid etc*) breaking; (*mit Vergangenheit, Partei, in einer Entwicklung, im Stil*) break; (*des Vertrauens*) breach; (*von Freundschaft*) break-up; (*von Verlöbnis*) breaking off; **in die Brüche gehen** (*Ehe, Freundschaft*) to break up (**c**) (*Med*) (*= Knochenbruch*) fracture, break; (*= Eingeweidebruch*) hernia; **sich** (*dat*) **einen ~ heben** to give oneself a hernia (**d**) (*Math*) fraction (**e**) (*sl: = Einbruch*) break-in; **einen ~ machen** to do a break-in

Bruch-: Bruchbude F (*pej*) hovel; **bruchfest** ADJ unbreakable

brüchig ['bryçıç] ADJ *Material, Knochen, Fingernägel* brittle; *Gestein, Mauerwerk* crumbling; *Leder* cracked; (*fig*) *Stimme* cracked

Brüchigkeit F **-**, NO PL (*von Material, Knochen*) brittleness; (*von Gestein etc*) crumbliness

Bruch-: Bruchlandung F crash-landing; **eine ~ machen** to crash-land; **bruchrechnen** VI INFIN ONLY to do fractions; **Bruchrechnen** NT fractions *sing or pl*; **Bruchrechnung** F fractions *sing or pl*; (*= Aufgabe*) sum with fractions; **Bruchschaden** M (*Comm*) breakage; **Bruchstelle** F break; (*von Knochen auch*) fracture; **Bruchstrich** M (*Math*) line (of a fraction); **Bruchstück** NT fragment; **bruchstückhaft** ❶ ADJ fragmentary ❷ ADV in a fragmentary way; **ich kenne die Geschichte nur ~** I only know parts of the story; **Bruchteil** M fraction; **im ~ einer Sekunde** in a split second; **Bruchteilgemeinschaft** F (*Comm, Fin*) common ownership; **Bruchzahl** F (*Math*) fraction; **Bruchzins** M accrued interest

Brücke ['brykə] F **-, -n** (**a**) (*lit, fig*) bridge; **alle ~n hinter sich** (*dat*) **abbrechen** (*fig*) to burn one's bridges; **jdm goldene ~n bauen** to make things easy for sb (**b**) (*Naut*) bridge; (*= Landungsbrücke*) gangway (**c**) (*= Zahnbrücke*) bridge (**d**) (*= Teppich*) rug

Brücken-: Brückengebühr F toll; **Brückengeländer** NT parapet; **Brückenkopf** M (*Mil, fig*) bridgehead; **Brückentag** M extra day off (*taken between two public holidays or a public holiday and a weekend*)

Bruder ['bru:dɐ] M **-s, ̈** ['bry:dɐ] (**a**) brother; **unter Brüdern** (*inf*) between friends (**b**) (*= Mönch*) friar, brother; **~ Franziskus** (*als Anrede*) Brother Francis (**c**) (*inf: = Mann*) guy (*inf*); **ein zwielichtiger ~** a shady character

Brüderchen ['bry:dɐçən] NT **-s, -** little brother

Bruder-: Bruderherz NT (*hum*) dear brother; **Bruderkuss** M (*fig*) brotherly kiss; **Bruderland** NT (*sozialistisch*) brother nation

Brüderlein ['bry:dɐlain] NT **-s, -** little brother

brüderlich ['bry:dɐlıç] ❶ ADJ fraternal ❷ ADV like brothers; **~ teilen** to share and share alike; **mit jdm ~ teilen** to share generously with sb

Brüderschaft ['bry:dɐʃaft] F **-, -en** (*= Freundschaft*) close friendship (*in which the familiar "du" is used*); **mit jdm ~ trinken** to agree over a drink to use the familiar "du"

Brügge ['brʏɡə] NT **-s** Bruges

Brühe ['bry:ə] F **-, -n** (*= Suppe*) (clear) soup; (*als Suppengrundlage*) stock; (*pej*) (*= schmutzige Flüssigkeit*) sludge; (*= Getränk*) muck (*inf*)

Brüh-: brühwarm ADV (*inf*) **er hat das sofort ~ weitererzählt** he promptly went away and spread it around; **Brühwürfel** M stock cube; **Brühwurst** F sausage (*to be heated in water*)

brüllen ['brʏlən] **1** VI to shout, to roar; (*pej:* = *laut weinen*) to bawl; (*Stier*) to bellow; (*Elefant*) to trumpet; **brüll doch nicht so!** don't shout!; **er brüllte vor Schmerzen** he screamed with pain; **vor Lachen ~** to roar with laughter; **wie am Spieß** to scream blue (*Brit*) *or* bloody murder (*inf*); **das ist zum Brüllen** (*inf*) it's a scream (*inf*)
2 VT to shout, to roar; **jdm seine Wut ins Gesicht ~** to shout furiously at sb

brummeln ['brɔmln] VTI (*inf*) to mumble, to mutter

brummen ['brɔmən] **1** VI (a) (*Insekt*) to buzz; (*Bär*) to growl; (*Motor, Bass*) to drone; **mir brummt der Kopf** *or* **Schädel** my head is throbbing (b) (*Wirtschaft, Geschäft*) to boom **2** VT (= *brummeln*) to mumble, to mutter

Brummer ['brɔmɐ] M **-s, -** (= *Schmeißfliege*) bluebottle

Brummi ['brɔmi] M **-s, -s** (*inf:* = *Lastwagen*) lorry (*Brit*), truck

brummig ['brɔmɪç] ADJ grumpy

Brummschädel M (*inf*) thick head (*inf*)

Brunch [brantʃ, branʃ] M **-(e)s, -(e)s** *or* **-e** brunch

brünett [brʏ'nɛt] ADJ dark(-haired); **sie ist ~** she is (a) brunette

Brunft [brɔnft] F **-, ̈e** ['brʏnftə] (*Hunt*) rut; **in der ~ sein** to be rutting

brunftig ['brɔnftɪç] ADJ (*Hunt*) rutting

Brunft-: Brunftschrei M mating call (*auch fig*); **Brunftzeit** F rutting season

Brunnen ['brɔnən] M **-s, -** well; (= *Springbrunnen*) fountain; **den ~ erst zudecken, wenn das Kind hineingefallen ist** (*fig*) to lock the stable door after the horse has bolted (*prov*); **erst, wenn das Kind in den ~ gefallen ist** (*fig*) but not until things had gone wrong

Brunnen-: Brunnenbecken NT basin (of a well); (*von Springbrunnen*) basin (of a fountain); **Brunnenfigur** F (decorative) sculpture on a fountain; **Brunnenkresse** F watercress; **Brunnenschacht** M well shaft; **Brunnenvergiftung** F well poisoning; **politische ~** political calumny

Brunst [brɔnst] F **-, ̈e** ['brʏnstə] (*von männlichen Tieren*) rut; (*von weiblichen Tieren*) heat; (= *~zeit*) rutting season; heat; **in der ~** rutting; *on* (*Brit*) *or* in (*esp US*) heat

brünstig ['brʏnstɪç] ADJ *männliches Tier* rutting; *weibliches Tier* on (*Brit*) *or* in (*esp US*) heat

Brunst-: Brunstschrei M mating call; **Brunstzeit** F rutting season

brüsk [brʏsk] **1** ADJ brusque, abrupt **2** ADV brusquely, abruptly; **sich ~ abwenden** to turn away abruptly

brüskieren [brʏs'kiːrən], *ptp* **brüskiert** VT to snub

Brüssel ['brʏsl] NT **-s** Brussels

Brust [brɔst] F **-, ̈e** ['brʏstə] (a) (= *Körperteil*) chest; **einen zur ~ nehmen** (*inf*) to have a quick one (*inf*); **~ (he)raus!** chest out!; **sich** (*dat*) **jdn zur ~ nehmen** to have a word with sb; **schwach auf der ~ sein** (*inf*) to have a weak chest (b) (= *weibliche ~*) breast; **einem Kind die ~ geben, ein Kind an die ~ legen** to breast-feed a baby (c) (*Cook*) breast

Brust-: Brustbein NT (*Anat*) breastbone; **Brustbeutel** M money bag (*worn around the neck*); **Brustdrüse** F mammary gland

brüsten ['brʏstn] VR to boast (*mit* about)

Brust-: Brustfell NT (*Anat*) pleura; **Brustfellentzündung** F pleurisy; **Brustflosse** F pectoral fin; **Brustgegend** F thoracic region; **Brustkasten** M (*inf*), **Brustkorb** M (*Anat*) thorax; **Brustkrebs** M breast cancer; **Brustlage** F prone position; **in ~ schwimmen** to swim in the prone position; **Brustmuskel** M pectoral muscle; **Brustpanzer** M breastplate; **brustschwimmen** VI INFIN ONLY to do the breaststroke; **Brustschwimmen** NT breaststroke; **Bruststück** NT (*Cook*) breast; **Brusttee** M herbal tea (*for infections of the respiratory tract*); **Brustton** M, *pl* **-töne** (*Mus*) chest note; **im ~ der Überzeugung(, dass ...)** in a tone of utter conviction (that ...); **Brustumfang** M chest measurement; (*von Frau*) bust measurement

Brüstung ['brʏstʊŋ] F **-, -en** parapet; (= *Fensterbrüstung*) breast

Brust-: Brustwarze F nipple; **Brustweite** F chest measurement; (*von Frau*) bust measurement; **Brustwirbel** M thoracic vertebra

Brut [bruːt] F **-, -en (a)** NO PL (= *das Brüten*) incubating (b) (= *die Jungen*) brood; (*pej*) mob (*inf*)

brutal [bru'taːl] **1** ADJ brutal **2** ADV (a) *zuschlagen* brutally; *behandeln* cruelly (b) (*inf:* = *sehr*) incredibly; **das tut ~ weh** (*inf*) that hurts like hell (*inf*)

brutalisieren [brutali'ziːrən], *ptp* **brutalisiert** VT to brutalize

Brutalität [brutali'tɛːt] F **-, -en** brutality; (= *Gewalttat*) act of brutality

Brutalo [bru'taːlo] M **-s, -s** (*inf*) bruiser (*inf*)

Brutapparat M incubator

brüten ['bryːtn] VI to incubate; (*fig*) to ponder (*über* +*dat* over); **~de Hitze** stifling heat; **~d heiß** sweltering

Brüter ['bryːtɐ] M **-s, -** (*Tech*) breeder (reactor); **schneller ~** fast-breeder (reactor)

Brut-: Brutkasten M (*Med*) incubator; **hier ist eine Hitze wie in einem ~** (*inf*) it's like an oven in here (*inf*); **Brutstätte** F breeding ground (+*gen* for)

brutto ['bruto] ADV gross

Brutto-: Bruttoeinkommen NT gross income; **Bruttoertrag** M gross profit; **Bruttogehalt** NT gross salary; **Bruttogewicht** NT gross weight; **Bruttoinlandsprodukt** NT gross domestic product, GDP; **Bruttoinvestition** F gross investment; **Bruttolohn** M gross wage(s pl); **Bruttonationalprodukt** NT (*Aus Econ*) gross national product, GNP; **Bruttoregistertonne** F register ton; **Bruttorendite** F gross yield; **Bruttosozialprodukt** NT gross national product, GNP

Brutzeit F incubation (period)

brutzeln ['brʊtsln] (*inf*) **1** VI to sizzle (away) **2** VT to fry (up)

BSE [beːʔɛsˈʔeː] ABBR *von* Bovine Spongiforme Enzephalopathie BSE

BSE- [beːʔɛsˈʔeː-] IN CPDS BSE; **BSE-Erreger** M BSE virus; **BSE-frei** ADJ free from BSE

B-Seite ['beː-] F (*von Schallplatte*) B-side

BSP [beːʔɛsˈpeː] NT - ABBR *von* Bruttosozialprodukt GNP

BTA [beːteˈʔaː] M **-s, -s** *or* F **-, -s** ABBR *von* biologisch-technischer Assistent, biologisch-technische Assistentin

Btx [beːteˈʔiːks] M **-, NO PL** ABBR *von* Bildschirmtext

Bub [buːp] M **-en, -en** [-bn] (*S Ger, Aus, Sw*) boy

Bube ['buːbə] M **-n, -n** (*Cards*) jack

Bubi ['buːbi] M **-s, -s** (*inf*) little boy *or* lad (*Brit*); (*pej inf*) (school)boy; (*als Anrede*) (little) boy

Bubikopf M bob

Buch [buːx] NT **-(e)s, ̈er** ['byːçɐ] (a) book (*auch Bibl*); **über den Büchern sitzen** to pore over one's books; **er redet wie ein ~** (*inf*) he never stops talking; **ein Gentleman, wie er im ~e steht** a perfect example of a gentleman; **ein Tor, wie es im ~e steht** a textbook goal; **ein ~ mit sieben Siegeln** (*fig*) a closed book (b) USU PL (*Comm:* = *Geschäftsbuch*) books *pl*; **über etw** (*acc*) **~ führen** to keep a record of sth; **jdm die Bücher führen** to keep sb's books; **zu ~ (e) schlagen** to make a (significant) difference; **das schlägt mit 1000 Euro zu ~(e)** that gives you 1000 euros; **zu ~ stehen mit** to be valued at

Buch-: Buchbesprechung F book review; **Buchbinderei** F (= *Betrieb*) bookbindery; (= *Handwerk*) bookbinding; **Buchdeckel** M book cover; **Buchdruck** M, NO PL letterpress (printing); **Buchdrucker(in)** M(F) printer; **Buchdruckerei** F (= *Betrieb*) printing works *sing or pl*; (= *Handwerk*) printing

Buche ['buːxə] F **-, -n** (= *Baum*) beech (tree); (= *Holz*) beech(wood)

Buchecker ['buːxʔɛkɐ] F **-, -n** beechnut

Bucheinband M binding, (book) cover

buchen ['buːxn] VT (a) (*Comm*) to enter; (*Kasse*) to register; **einen Erfolg für sich ~** to chalk up a success (for oneself) (*inf*); **etw als Erfolg ~** to put sth down as a success (b) (= *vorbestellen*) to book

Bücher-: Bücherbord NT, **Bücherbrett** NT bookshelf; **Bücherbus** M mobile library

Bücherei [byːçəˈrai] F **-, -en** (lending) library

Bücher-: Bücherfreund(in) M(F) book-lover; **Bücherregal** NT bookshelf; **Bücherschrank** M bookcase; **Büchersendung** F consignment of books; (*im Postwesen*) books *pl* (sent) at printed paper rate; **Bücherverzeichnis** NT bibliography; **Bücherwand** F wall of book shelves; (*als Möbelstück*) (large) set of book shelves; **Bücherweisheit** F book learning; **Bücherwurm** M (*lit, fig hum*) bookworm

Buchfink M chaffinch

Buchführung F book-keeping, accounting; **einfache/ doppelte ~** single/double entry book-keeping

Buchführungs-: Buchführungspflicht F duty to keep books; **Buchführungssystem** NT accounting system

Buch-: Buchgeld NT (*Fin*) bank deposit money; **Buchgewinn** M (*Comm, Fin*) accounting gain; **Buchgrundschuld** F (*Fin*) uncertificated land charge; **Buchhalter(in)** M(F) book-keeper; **buchhalterisch** [-haltərɪʃ] **1** ADJ book-keeping **2** ADV **sich ~ ausbilden lassen** to be trained to be a book-keeper; **Ihre Abrechnung ist ~ korrekt** your book-keeping is correct; **sie ist ~ versiert** she is good at book-keeping; **~ kompliziert** complicated in terms of book-keeping; **Buchhaltung** F (a) book-keeping, accounting (b) (*Abteilung einer Firma*) accounts department; **Buchhandel** M book trade; **im ~ erhältlich** available in bookshops; **Buchhändler(in)** M(F) bookseller; **buchhändlerisch** [-hɛndlərɪʃ] **1** ADJ connected with the book trade; **eine ~e Ausbildung haben** to be a trained bookseller **2** ADV **~ tätig sein** to be a bookseller; **Buchhandlung** F bookshop, bookstore (*US*); **Buchhülle** F dust jacket; **Buchladen** M bookshop, bookstore (*US*); **Buchmacher(in)** M(F) bookmaker, bookie (*inf*); **Buchmesse** F book fair; **Buchprüfer(in)** M(F) auditor; **Buchprüfung** F audit; **Buchrücken** M spine

Buchs [bʊks] M **-es, -e**, **Buchsbaum** M box (tree)

Buchse [ˈbʊksə] F **-, -n** (*Elec*) socket; (*Tech*) (*von Zylinder*) liner; (*von Lager*) bush

Büchse [ˈbʏksə] F **-, -n (a)** tin; (= *Konservenbüchse*) can, tin (*Brit*); (= *Sammelbüchse*) collecting box **(b)** (= *Gewehr*) rifle, (shot)gun

Buchstabe [ˈbuːxʃtaːbə] M **-n(s), -n** letter; (= *esp Druckbuchstabe*) character; **kleiner ~** small letter; **großer ~** capital (letter); **ein fetter ~** a character in bold (face); **in fetten ~n** in bold (face); **Betrag in ~n** amount in words; **dem ~n nach** (*fig*) literally

buchstabieren [buːxʃtaˈbiːrən], *ptp* **buchstabiert** VT to spell

buchstäblich [ˈbuːxʃtɛːplɪç] **1** ADJ literal **2** ADV literally

Buchstütze F book end

Bucht [bʊxt] F **-, -en** (*im Meer*) bay; (*kleiner*) cove

Buchteln [ˈbʊxtln] PL (*Aus Cook*) sweet bread roll with jam filling

buchtenreich, buchtig [ˈbʊxtɪç] ADJ *Küste* indented

Buch-: Buchtitel M (book) title; **Buchumschlag** M dust jacket

Buchung [ˈbuːxʊŋ] F **-, -en** (*Comm*) entry; (= *Reservierung*) booking

Buchungscomputer M computerized booking system; **ich kann Sie im ~ nicht finden** I can't find your booking on the computer

Buch-: Buchverlust M (*Comm, Fin*) accounting loss; **Buchweizen** M buckwheat; **Buchwert** M (*Comm*) book value; **Buchwissen** NT (*pej*) book learning

Buckel [ˈbʊkl] M **-s, -** hump(back), hunchback; (*inf*: = *Rücken*) back; **einen ~ machen** (*Katze*) to arch its back; (*Mensch*) to hunch one's shoulders; **er kann mir den ~ (he)runterrutschen** (*inf*) he can (go and) take a running jump (*inf*); **seine 80 Jahre auf dem ~ haben** (*inf*) to be 80 (years old)

buckelig [ˈbʊkəlɪç] ADJ hunchbacked, humpbacked

Buckelige(r) [ˈbʊkəlɪgə] MF DECL AS ADJ hunchback

buckeln [ˈbʊkln] VI (*pej*) to bow and scrape; **nach oben ~ und nach unten treten** to bow to superiors and tread inferiors underfoot

Buckel-: Buckelpiste F (*Ski*) mogul piste; **Buckelrind** NT zebu; **Buckelwal** M humpback whale

bücken [ˈbʏkn] VR to bend (down); **sich nach etw ~** to bend down to pick sth up; *siehe auch* **gebückt**

bucklig [ˈbʊklɪç] ADJ ETC = **buckelig**

Bückling [ˈbʏklɪŋ] M **-s, -e** (*Cook*) smoked herring

Budapest [ˈbuːdapɛst] NT **-s** Budapest

Buddel [ˈbʊdl] F **-, -n** (*N Ger inf*) bottle

Buddelei [bʊdəˈlai] F **-, -en** (*im Sand*) digging; (*inf*: = *Tiefbauarbeiten*) constant digging (up) (*of road etc*)

buddeln [ˈbʊdln] VI (*inf*) to dig; **in der Straße wird dauernd gebuddelt** they're always digging up the road

Buddha [ˈbʊda] M **-s, -s** Buddha

Buddhismus [bʊˈdɪsmʊs] M **-, NO PL** Buddhism

Buddhist [bʊˈdɪst] M **-en, -en**, **Buddhistin** [-ˈdɪstɪn] F **-, -nen** Buddhist

buddhistisch [bʊˈdɪstɪʃ] **1** ADJ Buddhist(ic) **2** ADV **jdn ~ erziehen** to bring sb up (as) a Buddhist; **~ beeinflusst** influenced by Buddhism

Bude [ˈbuːdə] F **-, -n (a)** (= *Bretterbau*) hut; (= *Baubude*) (workmen's) hut; (= *Marktbude, Verkaufsbude*) stall; (= *Zeitungsbude*) kiosk **(b)** (*pej inf*: = *Laden, Lokal etc*) dump (*inf*) **(c)** (*inf*: = *Zimmer*) room; (= *Wohnung*) pad (*inf*); **Leben in die ~ bringen** to liven up the place; **jdm die ~ einrennen** or **einlaufen** to pester sb

Budget [byˈdʒeː] NT **-s, -s** budget

budgetär [bydʒeˈtɛːr] ADJ budgetary

Budget-: [byˈdʒeː-] (*Pol*): **Budgetberatung** F budget debate; **Budgetentwurf** M draft budget

Büfett [byˈfɛt] NT **-(e)s, -e** or **-s (a)** (= *Geschirrschrank*) sideboard **(b) kaltes ~** cold buffet **(c)** (*Sw: = Bahnhofsgaststätte*) (station) buffet

Büffel [ˈbʏfl] M **-s, -** buffalo

Büffelei [bʏfəˈlai] F **-, -en** (*inf*) cramming (*inf*)

büffeln [ˈbʏfln] (*inf*) **1** VI to cram (*inf*) **2** VT *Lernstoff* to swot up (*Brit inf*), to bone up on (*US inf*)

Büffet [bʏˈfeː] NT **-s, -s**, **Büffett** [bʏˈfeː] NT **-s, -s** (*esp Aus*) = **Büfett**

Bug [buːk] M **-(e)s, ⸗e** or **-e** [ˈbyːgə, ˈbuːgə] (= *Schiffsbug*) bow *usu pl*; (= *Flugzeugbug*) nose; **jdm eins vor den ~ knallen** (*inf*) to sock sb one (*inf*)

Bügel [ˈbyːgl] M **-s, - (a)** (= *Kleiderbügel*) (coat) hanger **(b)** (= *Steigbügel*) stirrup **(c)** (= *Brillenbügel*) side piece; (*am Lift*) T-bar

Bügel-: Bügel-BH M underwired bra; **Bügelbrett** NT ironing board; **Bügeleisen** NT iron; **Bügelfalte** F crease in one's trousers (*esp Brit*) or pants (*esp US*); **Bügelflasche** F flip-top bottle; **bügelfrei** ADJ noniron

bügeln [ˈbyːgln] VTI *Wäsche* to iron; *Hose* to press

Buggy [ˈbagi] M **-s, -s** buggy

Bugrad NT (*Aviat*) nose wheel

bugsieren [bʊˈksiːrən], *ptp* **bugsiert** VT **(a)** (*Naut*) to tow **(b)** (*inf*) *Möbelstück etc* to manoeuvre (*Brit*), to maneuver (*US*); **jdn aus dem Zimmer ~** to steer sb out of the room

buh [buː] INTERJ boo

buhen [ˈbuːən] VI (*inf*) to boo

Buhfrau F bogeywoman (*inf*)

buhlen [ˈbuːlən] VI (*pej*) **um jdn/jds Gunst ~** to woo sb/sb's favour (*Brit*) or favor (*US*)

Buhmann [ˈbuːman] M, *pl* **-männer** (*inf*) bogeyman (*inf*)

Bühne [ˈbyːnə] F **-, -n (a)** (*lit, fig*) stage; **über die ~ gehen** to go off; **wie haben Sie Ihren ersten Elternabend über die ~ gebracht?** how did you manage your first parents' evening?; **hinter der ~** (*lit, fig*) behind the scenes **(b)** (= *Theater*) theatre (*Brit*), theater (*US*); **an** or **bei der ~ sein** to be on the stage

Bühnen-: Bühnenanweisung F stage direction; **Bühnenausbildung** F dramatic training; **Bühnenaussprache** F standard pronunciation; **Bühnenausstattung** F stage props *pl*; **Bühnenautor(in)** M(F) playwright; **Bühnenbearbeitung** F stage adaptation; **Bühnenbeleuchtung** F stage lighting; **Bühnenbild** NT (stage) set; **Bühnenbildner** [-bɪltnɐ] M **-s, -**, **Bühnenbildnerin** [-ərɪn] F **-, -nen** set designer; **bühnengerecht** **1** ADJ suitable for the stage **2** ADV **etw ~ bearbeiten** to adapt sth for the stage; **Bühnenmaler(in)** M(F) scene painter; **Bühnenmalerei** F scene painting; **Bühnenpräsenz** F stage presence; **Bühnenraum** M stage and backstage area; **bühnenreif** ADJ ready for the stage; **Bühnensprache** F standard pronunciation; **bühnenwirksam** **1** ADJ effective on the stage **2** ADV effectively for the stage; **lässt sich dieser Stoff ~ gestalten?** would this material be effective on the stage?; **Bühnenwirkung** F dramatic effect

Buhruf M boo

buk (*old*) PRET *von* **backen**

Bukarest [ˈbuːkarɛst] NT **-s** Bucharest

Buklee [buˈkleː] NT **-s, -s** bouclé (yarn)

Bulette [buˈlɛtə] F **-, -n** (*dial*) meat ball; **ran an die ~n** (*inf*) go right ahead!

Bulgarien [bʊlˈgaːriən] NT **-s** Bulgaria

bulgarisch [bʊlˈgaːrɪʃ] ADJ Bulgarian

Bulimie [buliˈmiː] F **-, NO PL** (*Med*) bulimia

Bullauge [ˈbʊl-] NT (*Naut*) porthol

Bulldogge ['bʊl-] F bulldog

Bulldozer ['bʊldoːzɐ] M **-s, -** bulldozer

Bulle ['bʊlə] M **-n, -n** (a) bull (b) (inf: = starker Mann) great ox of a man (c) (pej sl: = Polizist) cop (inf)

Bulletin [bʏl'tɛ̃ː] NT **-s, -s** bulletin

Bulletinboard ['bʊlətɪn'bɔːɐd] NT **-s, -s** (Comput) bulletin board

bullig ['bʊlɪç] ADJ (inf) (a) beefy (inf) (b) Hitze boiling (inf)

Bullterrier ['bʊl-] M bull terrier

bum [bʊm] INTERJ bang; (tiefer) boom

Bumerang ['buːməraŋ, 'bʊməraŋ] M **-s, -s** or **-e** (lit, fig) boomerang

Bumerangeffekt M boomerang effect

Bummel ['bʊml] M **-s, -** stroll; (durch Lokale) tour (durch of); **einen ~ machen, auf einen ~ gehen** to go for a stroll; **einen ~ durch die Nachtlokale machen** to take in a few nightclubs

Bummelant [bʊmə'lant] M **-en, -en**, **Bummelantin** [-'lantɪn] F **-, -nen** (inf) (a) (= Trödler) dawdler (b) (= Faulenzer) loafer (inf)

Bummelei [bʊmə'laɪ] F **-, -en** (inf) (= Trödelei) dawdling; (= Faulenzerei) loafing around (inf)

bummeln ['bʊmln] VI (a) AUX SEIN (= spazieren gehen) to stroll; (= ausgehen) to go out on the town; **im Park ~ gehen** to go for a stroll in the park (b) (= trödeln) to dawdle (c) (= faulenzen) to fritter one's time away

Bummel-: Bummelstreik M go-slow; **Bummelzug** M (inf) slow train

Bummerl ['bʊmɐl] NT **-s, -(n)** (Aus inf) point against

Bummler ['bʊmlɐ] M **-s, -**, **Bummlerin** [-ərɪn] F **-, -nen** (a) (= Spaziergänger) stroller (b) (= Trödler) dawdler

bums [bʊms] INTERJ thump, thud; **~, da fiel der Kleine hin** bang! down went the little one

Bums [bʊms] M **-es, -e** (inf: = Schlag) bang, thump

bumsen ['bʊmzn] **1** VI IMPERS (inf: = dröhnen) **...**, **dass es bumste** ... with a bang; **er schlug gegen die Tür, dass es bumste** he thumped on the door; **es bumste, als ...** there was a thump when ...; **es hat gebumst** (von Fahrzeugen) there's been a crash

2 VI (a) (= schlagen) to thump (b) AUX SEIN (= prallen, stoßen) to bump, to bang; (= fallen) to fall with a bang or bump (c) (inf: = koitieren) to do it (inf)

3 VT (inf) **jdn ~** to do it with sb (inf); **gebumst werden** to get laid (sl)

Bumserei [bʊmzə'raɪ] F **-, -en** (inf) screwing (sl)

Bund¹ [bʊnt] M **-(e)s, ⁻e** ['bʏndə] (a) (= Vereinigung, Gemeinschaft) bond; (= Bündnis) alliance; **mit jdm im ~e stehen** or **sein** to be in league with sb; **den ~ der Ehe eingehen** to enter (into) the bond of marriage; **den ~ fürs Leben schließen** to take the marriage vows (b) (= Organisation) association, (con)federation; (= Staatenbund) league, alliance (c) (Pol: = Bundesstaat) Federal Government; **~ und Länder** the Federal Government and the/its Länder (d) (inf: = Bundeswehr) **der ~** the army (e) (an Kleidern) waistband

Bund² NT **-(e)s, -e** ['bʊndə] (von Stroh, Flachs, Reisig etc) bundle; (von Radieschen, Spargel etc) bunch

Bündchen ['bʏntçən] NT **-s, -** (am Hals) neckband; (am Ärmel) sleeve band

Bündel ['bʏndl] NT **-s, -** bundle, sheaf; (= Strohbündel) sheaf; (von Banknoten) wad; (von Karotten, Radieschen etc) bunch; (Opt: = Strahlenbündel) pencil; (fig) (von Fragen, Problemen etc) cluster; (von Vorschlägen etc) set; **ein schreiendes ~** a howling (little) bundle; **jeder hat sein ~ zu tragen** everybody has his/her cross to bear

bündeln ['bʏndln] VT Zeitungen etc to bundle up; Garben, Stroh to sheave; Karotten etc to tie into bunches/a bunch; (Opt) Strahlen to focus; (fig) to consolidate; siehe auch **gebündelt**

bündelweise ADV in bundles; **er holte ~ Banknoten aus der Tasche** he pulled wads of banknotes out of his pocket

Bünden ['bʏndn] NT **-s** (= Graubünden) the Grisons

Bundes- IN CPDS federal; **Bundesamt** NT Federal Office; **Bundesangestelltentarif** M (Ger) statutory salary scale;

Bundesanleihe F (Ger) government bond; **Bundesanstalt** F (Ger) Federal Institute; **~ für Arbeit** Federal Institute of Labour (Brit) or Labor (US); **Bundesanwalt** M, **Bundesanwältin** F (a) (Ger) attorney of the Federal Supreme Court (b) (Sw) ≈ Public Prosecutor; **Bundesanwaltschaft** F (Ger) Federal Prosecutor's Office; (= Gesamtheit der Anwälte) Federal bar; **Bundesanzeiger** M (Ger) Federal legal gazette; **Bundesaufsicht** F (Ger) Government supervision; **Bundesaufsichtsamt** NT Federal Regulator; **Bundesausbildungsförderungsgesetz** NT law regarding grants for higher education; **Bundesbahn** F (Ger, Aus, Sw) Federal Railway(s pl); **Bundesbank** F, NO PL (Ger) Federal bank; **Deutsche ~** Federal Bank of Germany; **Bundesbehörde** F Federal authority; **Bundesblatt** NT (Sw) Federal Law Gazette; **Bundesbürger(in)** M(F) (Ger) German, citizen of Germany; **bundesdeutsch** ADJ German; **Bundesdeutsche(r)** MF DECL AS ADJ German; **Bundesebene** F **auf ~** at a national level; **bundeseigen** ADJ Federal(-owned), national; **bundeseinheitlich 1** ADJ Federal, national **2** ADV nationally; **etw ~ regeln** to regulate sth at national level

The **Bundesfeier** is celebrated in Switzerland on the evening of August 1st, the national holiday. It commemorates the so-called **Rütlischwur**, a pledge under which the very first cantons - Uri, Schwyz and Unterwalden - formed an alliance. This is regarded as the official founding of modern Switzerland.

Bundes-: Bundesgebiet NT (Ger) Federal territory; **Bundesgenosse** M, **Bundesgenossin** F ally; **Bundesgericht** NT (a) (Ger, Aus) Federal Court (b) (Sw) Federal Appeal Court; **Bundesgerichtshof** M, NO PL (Ger) Federal Supreme Court; **Bundesgeschäftsführer(in)** M(F) (von Partei, Verein) general secretary; **Bundesgesetzblatt** NT (Ger, Aus) Federal Law Gazette; **Bundesgrenzschutz** M (Ger) Federal Border Guard; **Bundeshauptstadt** F Federal capital; **Bundeshaus** NT (Ger, Sw) Federal Houses of Parliament pl; **Bundesheer** NT (Aus) services pl, army; **Bundeskanzlei** F (Sw) Federal Chancellery; **Bundeskanzler(in)** M(F) (a) (Ger, Aus) Chancellor (b) (Sw) Head of the Federal Chancellery; **Bundeskanzleramt** NT (Ger, Aus) Federal Chancellery

The **Bundeskanzler** of the Federal Republic of Germany is the head of government. He is responsible for the government's general policy and it is on his recommendation that the **Bundespräsident** appoints and dismisses ministers. The **Bundeskanzler** is generally elected for a period of four years (corresponding to the four-year **Bundestag** mandate) by a majority of members of parliament and on the recommendation of the **Bundespräsident**.

In Austria, too, the **Bundeskanzler** is the head of government, appointed by the **Bundespräsident**. He has no legal responsibility for general policy, but he nominates ministers and thereby determines the composition of the government.

In Switzerland, on the other hand, the **Bundeskanzler** is the head of the Federal Chancellery, a department of the **Bundesversammlung** and the **Bundesrat**. His responsibilities include the organization of Federal elections and ballots and the publication of Federal laws.
▶ BUNDESPRÄSIDENT, BUNDESRAT, BUNDESTAG, BUNDESVERSAMMLUNG

Bundes-: Bundeskartellamt NT ≈ Monopolies and Mergers Commission (Brit), ≈ Federal Trade Commission (US); **Bundeskriminalamt** NT (Ger) Federal Criminal Police Office; **Bundesland** NT state; (Ger auch) Land of the Federal Republic of Germany; **die neuen Bundesländer** the former East German states; **die alten Bundesländer** the former West German states; **Bundesliga** F (Ger Sport) national league; **Bundesminister(in)** M(F) (Ger, Aus) Federal Minister; **Bundesministerium** NT (Ger, Aus) Federal Ministry; **Bundesmittel** PL Federal funds pl; **Bundesnachrichtendienst** M (Ger) Federal Intelligence Service; **Bundesobligation** F (Fin) federal bond (with a five-year term); **Bundespost** F (Ger Hist) **die (Deutsche) ~** the (German) Federal Post (Office);

Bundespräsident(in) M(F) (*Ger, Aus*) (Federal) President; (*Sw*) President of the Federal Council

*The **Bundespräsident** is the head of state of the Federal Republic of Germany. He is elected by the **Bundesversammlung**, his term of office is five years and he can be re-elected only once. The **Bundespräsident**'s main task is to represent Germany at home and abroad. Since his office requires him to be above party politics, he can make use of his status to draw attention to social problems and abuses of power.*

*The Austrian **Bundespräsident** is also the head of state, but he is elected by the people. His term of office is six years and he too can be re-elected only once. He can dissolve the **Nationalrat** and appoints and dismisses the **Bundeskanzler**.*

*In Switzerland the **Bundespräsident** is the chairman of the **Bundesrat** and is in office for a period of one year only. He is not actually head of state, but he represents the country abroad.* ▶ BUNDESKANZLER, BUNDESRAT, BUNDESVERSAMMLUNG, NATIONALRAT

Bundesrat[1] M (*Ger*) Bundesrat, *upper house of the German Parliament*; (*Sw*) Council of Ministers

Bundesrat[2] M, **Bundesrätin** F (*Sw*) Minister of State

*The **Bundesrat** is the second chamber of the Federal Republic of German, representing the **Länder**. It has 69 members, who are not elected but delegated by the 16 **Land** governments. The most important of the **Bundesrat**'s duties concerns legislation: Federal laws that impinge upon the responsibilities of the **Länder** require its approval. The **Bundesrat** may also object to other laws, although the **Bundestag** can overrule the objection. As a result, Federal policy can be influenced by parties who are in opposition in the **Bundestag** if these parties hold a majority in most of the **Land** parliaments.*

*In Austria the **Bundesrat** has 63 members. Apart from being able to introduce its own proposals for legislation, the **Bundesrat** has certain rights of veto and approval with regard to laws passed by the **Nationalrat**.*

*In Switzerland, however, the **Bundesrat** is the executive body, i.e. the government. The Bundesversammlung appoints seven **Bundesräte** (ministers), who must come from different cantons, for a period of four years. Each of these ministers is then placed in charge of a **Departement**.* ▶ BUNDESTAG, BUNDESVERSAMMLUNG, NATIONALRAT

Bundes-: **Bundesregierung** F (*Ger, Aus*) Federal Government; **Bundesrepublik** F Federal Republic; ~ **Deutschland** Federal Republic of Germany; **Bundesschatzbrief** M (*Ger Fin*) Federal treasury bill; **Bundesstaat** M federal state; **Bundesstraße** F (*Ger*) Federal road (*maintained by the Federal Government*)

Bundestag M, NO PL (*Ger*) Bundestag, *lower house of the German Parliament*

*The German **Bundestag** is the representative body of the Federal Republic of Germany and is elected by the people every four years. There are at least 656 elected representatives, of whom half are directly elected (**Erststimme**) and half taken from the parties' **Landeslisten** (**Zweitstimme**). The **Bundestag** passes Federal laws, elects the **Bundeskanzler**, exercises parliamentary control over the Federal government and sets the Federal budget. Although the General Assembly is its public face, the **Bundestag** carries out most of its work in committees, composition of which reflects that of the **Bundestag**.*

*At the **Land** level there is usually a similar body, the **Landtag**.* ▶ BUNDESKANZLER, ERSTSTIMME/ZWEITSTIMME

Bundestags- (*Ger*): **Bundestagsabgeordnete(r)** MF DECL AS ADJ member of the Bundestag; **Bundestagsfraktion** F group *or* faction in the Bundestag; **Bundestagspräsident(in)** M(F) President of the Bundestag

Bundes-: **Bundestrainer(in)** M(F) (*Ger Sport*) national coach; **Bundesverband** M federal association; **Bundesverdienstkreuz** NT (*Ger*) order of the Federal Republic of Germany, ≈ OBE (*Brit*); **Bundesverfassung** F Federal constitution; **Bundesverfassungsgericht** NT (*Ger*) Federal

Constitutional Court; **Bundesversammlung** F (**a**) (*Ger, Aus*) Federal Convention (**b**) (*Sw*) Federal Assembly

*In Germany the **Bundesversammlung** is the body that elects the **Bundespräsident**. Half of the **Bundesversammlung** is made up of members of the **Bundestag** and half of delegates from the **Landtage**.*

*In Austria the **Bundesversammlung** is the joint body of the **Nationalrat** and **Bundesrat**. Its most important function is the swearing-in of the **Bundespräsident**.*

*The Swiss **Bundesversammlung** is a two-chamber parliament (**Nationalrat** and **Ständerat**) responsible for legislation. It also elects the **Bundesrat**, the **Bundeskanzler** and, every year, the **Bundespräsident**. The two chambers discuss the various bills independently of one another.* ▶ BUNDESKANZLER, BUNDESPRÄSIDENT, BUNDESRAT, BUNDESTAG, NATIONALRAT, STÄNDERAT

Bundes-: **Bundesversicherungsanstalt** F ~ **für Angestellte** federal pensions office for salaried employees; **Bundesverwaltungsgericht** NT (*Ger*) Supreme Administrative Court; **Bundeswehr** F, NO PL (*Ger*) services *pl*, army

*The **Bundeswehr** is the name for the German armed forces. It came into being in 1955, originally as a volunteer army. However, since 1956 every male between the ages of 18 and 30 has been liable for **Wehrdienst** (military service). The Defence Minister has control over the **Bundeswehr**, although in time of war this would pass to the **Bundeskanzler**. Currently the **Bundeswehr** is composed of men performing their military service, soldiers serving voluntarily for a set period of between 2 and 15 years, and professional soldiers.* ▶ BUNDESKANZLER, WEHRDIENST

bundesweit ADJ, ADV nationwide; **sie bewarb sich** ~ **bei verschiedenen Firmen** she applied to different companies all over the country

Bund-: **Bundfaltenhose** F pleated trousers *pl* (*esp Brit*) *or* pants *pl* (*esp US*); **Bund-Futures** PL (*Fin*) Federal Government Futures *pl*, Bunds *pl*; **Bundhose** F knee breeches *pl*

bündig ['bʏndɪç] **1** ADJ (**a**) (= *kurz, bestimmt*) succinct (**b**) (= *in gleicher Ebene*) flush *pred*, level **2** ADV succinctly

Bündnis ['bʏntnɪs] NT **-ses, -se** alliance; (= *Nato*) (NATO) Alliance; ~ **90** *political alliance of civil rights campaigners from the former GDR*; ~ **für Arbeit** *informal alliance between employers and unions to help create jobs*

*In 1993 the West German party **Die Grünen** joined forces with the East German grouping **Bündnis 90**, which had emerged from civil rights groups of the former DDR. The present party **Bündnis 90/Die Grünen** sees itself as a party of ecological reform. In addition to its environmental concerns, the party aims to increase social justice through a restructuring of the tax, social security and pension systems. It also demands an equitable sharing of burdens and interests between West and East Germany.*

Bundweite F waist measurement

Bungalow ['bʊŋgalo] M **-s, -s** bungalow

Bungee-Springen ['bandʒi-] NT, **Bungeespringen** NT bungee jumping

Bunker ['bʊŋkɐ] M **-s, -** (*Mil, Golf*) bunker; (= *Luftschutzbunker*) air-raid shelter

bunkern ['bʊŋkɐn] VTI (**a**) *Kohle* to bunker; *Öl* to refuel (**b**) (*sl*: = *anhäufen, verwahren*) to stash (away) (*inf*)

Bunsenbrenner ['bʊnzn-] M Bunsen burner

bunt [bʊnt] **1** ADJ (**a**) (= *farbig*) coloured (*Brit*), colored (*US*); (= *mehrfarbig*) colo(u)rful; (= *vielfarbig*) multicolo(u)red; **zu** ~**e Kleidung** loud clothing; ~**e Farben** bright colo(u)rs; ~**es Glas** stained glass

(**b**) (*fig*: = *abwechslungsreich*) varied; **eine** ~**e Menge** a motley crowd; **ein** ~**er Abend** a social; (*Rad, TV*) a variety programme (*Brit*) *or* program (*US*)

2 ADV (**a**) (= *farbig*) *anmalen, gekleidet* colourfully (*Brit*), colorfully (*US*); *bemalt, bemalen* in bright colo(u)rs; **etw** ~ **bekleben** to stick colo(u)red paper on sth; ~ **geblümt** *Stoff,*

Kleid with a colo(u)rful flower design; **~ gefärbt** multicolo(u)red; **~ gemischt** *Programm* varied; *Truppe, Team* diverse; **~ gestreift** with colo(u)red stripes; **~ schillernd** iridescent; (= *farbig, fig*) colo(u)rful **(b)** (= *ungeordnet*) **~ durcheinander** (= *unordentlich*) higgledy-piggledy (*inf*); **es geht ~ durcheinander** it's all a complete mess **(c)** (*inf*: = *wild*) **jetzt wird es mir zu ~** I've had enough of this; **es geht hier ~ zu** it's lively here; **es zu ~ treiben** to overstep the mark

Bunt-: Buntheit F -, NO PL colourfulness (*Brit*), colorfulness (*US*); **Buntmetall** NT nonferrous metal; **Buntpapier** NT coloured (*Brit*) *or* colored (*US*) paper; **Buntsandstein** M new red sandstone; **buntscheckig** ADJ spotted; *Pferd* dappled; (*fig*) motley; **Buntspecht** M spotted woodpecker; **Buntstift** M coloured (*Brit*) *or* colored (*US*) pencil; **Buntwäsche** F coloureds *pl* (*Brit*), coloreds *pl* (*US*)

Bürde ['bʏrdə] F -, -n (*geh*) load, weight; (*fig*) burden

Bure ['buːrə] M -n, -n, **Burin** ['buːrɪn] F -, -nen Boer

Burg [bʊrk] F -, -en [-gn] castle; (= *Strandburg*) wall of sand (*built by holiday-maker to mark his spot*)

Bürge ['bʏrgə] M -n, -n, **Bürgin** ['bʏrgɪn] F -, -nen guarantor; **für jdn ~ sein** to be sb's guarantor; **einen ~n stellen** (*Fin*) to offer surety

bürgen ['bʏrgn] VI **für etw ~** to guarantee sth; **für jdn ~** (*Fin*) to stand surety for sb; (*fig*) to vouch for sb; **Sie ~ mir persönlich dafür, dass ...** you are personally responsible to me that ...

Bürger ['bʏrgɐ] M -s, -, **Bürgerin** [-ərɪn] F -, -nen (*von Staat, Gemeinde*) citizen; (*Sociol, pej*) bourgeois; **die ~ von Ulm** the townsfolk of Ulm

Bürger-: Bürgerbeauftragte(r) MF DECL AS ADJ ombudsman/-woman; **Bürgerbegehren** NT -s, - (*Ger*) public petition; **Bürgerentscheid** M (*Ger*) public decision

Bürgerin F *siehe* **Bürger**

Bürger-: Bürgerinitiative F citizens' action group; **Bürgerkrieg** M civil war; **bürgerkriegsähnlich** ADJ civil war-like *attr*; **~e Zustände** civil war conditions

bürgerlich ['bʏrgɐlɪç] **I** ADJ **(a)** ATTR *Ehe, Recht etc* civil; *Pflicht* civic; **Bürgerliches Gesetzbuch** Civil Code **(b)** (= *dem Bürgerstand angehörend*) middle-class (*auch pej*); (*Hist*) bourgeois **II** ADV **diese Stadt ist ~ geprägt** this town is very middle-class; **ein ~ orientierter Politiker** a politician who aims for the middle-class vote

Bürgerliche(r) ['bʏrgɐlɪçə] MF DECL AS ADJ commoner

Bürger-: Bürgermeister M mayor; **Bürgermeisteramt** NT **(a)** (= *Aufgabe*) office of mayor **(b)** (= *Behörde, Gebäude*) town hall; **Bürgermeisterin** F mayor(ess); **bürgernah** ADJ populist; **Bürgernähe** F populism; **Bürgerpflicht** F civic duty; **Ruhe ist die erste ~** the first duty of the citizen is law and order; **Bürgerrecht** NT USU PL civil rights *pl*; **jdm die ~e aberkennen** *or* **entziehen** to strip sb of his/her civil rights; **Bürgerrechtler** [-rɛçtlɐ] M -s, -, **Bürgerrechtlerin** [-ərɪn] F -, -nen civil rights campaigner; **Bürgerrechtsbewegung** F civil rights movement; **Bürgerschaft** ['bʏrgɐʃaft] F -, -en citizens *pl*; **Bürgerschreck** M bog(e)y of the middle classes; **Bürgersteig** [-ʃtaɪk] M -(e)s, -e [-gə] pavement (*Brit*), sidewalk (*US*); **die ~e hochklappen** (*inf*) to shut down (for the night); **Bürgertum** ['bʏrgɐtuːm] NT -s, NO PL (*Hist*) bourgeoisie (*Hist*)

Bürgin F *siehe* **Bürge**

Bürgschaft ['bʏrkʃaft] F -, -en (*Jur*) (*gegenüber Gläubigern*) surety; (= *Haftungssumme*) penalty; **~ für jdn leisten** to act as guarantor for sb; (*fig*) to vouch for sb

Bürgschafts-: Bürgschaftserklärung F declaration of suretyship; **Bürgschaftskredit** M guaranteed credit; **Bürgschaftsnehmer(in)** M(F) creditor

Burgund [bʊr'gʊnt] NT -s Burgundy

burgunderfarben [-farbn], **burgunderrot** ADJ burgundy (red)

burgundisch [bʊr'gʊndɪʃ] ADJ Burgundian; **die Burgundische Pforte** the Belfort Gap

Burin F *siehe* **Bure**

Burkina Faso [bʊr'kiːna 'faːzo] NT -s Burkina-Faso

Burma ['bʊrma] NT -s Burma

burmesisch [bʊr'meːzɪʃ] ADJ Burmese

Burnout ['bœrnaʊt, ˌbøː'ɛnaʊt] M -s, NO PL, **Burn-out** M -s, NO PL (*Med*) burnout

Burnout-Syndrom ['bœrnaʊt-, ˌbøː'ɛnaʊt-] NT (*Med*) burnout

Büro [by'roː] NT -s, -s office

Büro- IN CPDS office; **Büroangestellte(r)** MF DECL AS ADJ office worker; **Büroarbeit** F office work; **Büroartikel** M item of office equipment; (*pl*) office supplies *pl*; **Bürobedarf** M office supplies *pl*; **Bürogebäude** NT office building; **Bürohochhaus** NT high-rise office block; **Bürokauffrau** F, **Bürokaufmann** M office administrator; **Büroklammer** F paper clip; **Bürokraft** F (office) clerk

Bürokrat [byro'kraːt] M -en, -en, **Bürokratin** [-'kraːtɪn] F -, -nen bureaucrat

Bürokratie [byrokra'tiː] F -, NO PL bureaucracy

bürokratisieren [byrokrati'ziːrən] *ptp* **bürokratisiert** VT to bureaucratize

Büro-: Büroleiter(in) M(F) office manager; **Büromaschine** F office machine; **Büromaterial** NT office supplies *pl*; (= *Schreibwaren*) stationery *no pl*; **Büromensch** M (*inf*) office worker; **Büromöbel** PL office furniture; **Büropersonal** NT office personnel *or* staff; **Büroschluss** M office closing time; **nach ~** after office hours; **Bürostunden** PL office hours *pl*; **Bürozeit** F office hours *pl*

Bürschchen ['bʏrʃçən] NT -s, - DIM *von* **Bursche** little boy; **freches ~** cheeky (*Brit*) *or* fresh (*US*) little devil (*inf*); **mein ~!** young man!

Bursche ['bʊrʃə] M -n, -n **(a)** (*olddial*) boy, lad (*Brit*); **ein toller ~** quite a young man **(b)** (*inf*: = *Kerl*) fellow; **ein übler ~** a shady character

Burschenschaft ['bʊrʃnʃaft] F -, -en student fraternity

BURSCHENSCHAFT

Burschenschaften are student organizations similar to the American fraternities. They continue a tradition going back to the early 19th century, when they were politically very active and influential. Prior to the 1980s they were either banned or - during times of student unrest - marginalized, being regarded as deeply conservative and nationalistic. Typical *Burschenschaftler* are recognizable by their bright sashes and peaked caps and are most often seen in university cities such as Heidelberg or Tübingen. Even when they have completed their studies, former students tend to remain loyal to their *Burschenschaft* and to offer it their support. In so-called *schlagende Verbindungen*, the *Mensur*, a fencing bout, is compulsory.

---

burschikos [bʊrʃi'koːs] **I** ADJ **(a)** (= *jungenhaft*) (tom)boyish **(b)** (= *unbekümmert*) casual **II** ADV (tom)boyishly; **benimm dich doch nicht so ~** stop behaving like a tomboy

Bürste ['bʏrstə] F -, -n brush

bürsten ['bʏrstn] VT to brush

Bürsten-: Bürstenhaarschnitt M crew cut; **Bürstenmassage** F brush massage

Burundi [bu'rʊndi] NT -s Burundi

burundisch [bu'rʊndɪʃ] ADJ Burundian

Bus[1] [bʊs] M -ses, -se bus

Bus[2] M -, -se (*Comput*) bus

Busbahnhof M bus station

Busch [bʊʃ] M -(e)s, *·*e ['bʏʃə] **(a)** (= *Strauch*) bush; **etwas ist im ~** (*inf*) there's something up; **mit etw hinter dem ~ halten** (*inf*) to keep sth quiet **(b)** (*Geog*: *in den Tropen*) bush

Buschbohne F dwarf bean

Büschel ['bʏʃl] NT -s, - (*von Gras, Haaren*) tuft; (*von Heu, Stroh*) bundle; (*von Blumen, Rettichen*) bunch

büschelweise ADV (*von Gras, Haaren*) in tufts; (*von Heu, Stroh*) in bundles; (*von Blumen, Rettichen*) in bunches; (*von Blumenpflanzen*) in clumps

Buschfeuer NT (*lit*) bush fire; **sich wie ein ~ ausbreiten** to spread like wildfire

Buschi ['bʊʃi] NT -s, -s (*Sw*) baby

buschig ['bʊʃɪç] ADJ bushy

Busch-: Buschmann M, *pl* -männer *or* -leute bushman; **Buschmannfrau** F bushwoman; **Buschmesser** NT machete; **Buschwerk** NT bushes *pl*

Busen ['buːzn] M -s, - (*von Frau*) bust

Busen-: busenfrei **I** ADJ topless **II** ADV **sich ~ sonnen** to sunbathe topless; **Busenfreund(in)** M(F) (*iro*) bosom friend; **Busengrapscher** M (*inf*) groper (*inf*)

Bus-: **Busfahrer(in)** M(F) bus driver; **Busfahrt** F bus ride; **Bushaltestelle** F bus stop

Businessclass ['bɪznɪskla:s] F -, NO PL, **Businessklasse** ['bɪznɪs-] F -, NO PL business class

Buslinie F bus route; **welche ~ fährt zum Bahnhof?** which bus goes to the station?

Bussard ['busart] M -s, -e [-də] buzzard

Buße ['bu:sə] F -, -n (a) (Rel) (= Reue) repentance; (= Bußauflage) penance; **~ tun** to do penance; **zur ~** as a penance **(b)** (Jur) (= Schadenersatz) damages pl; (= Geldstrafe) fine; **eine ~ von 100 Euro** a 100-euro fine; **jdn zu einer ~ verurteilen** to fine sb

busseln ['busln], **bussen** ['busn] VTI (S Ger, Aus) to kiss

büßen ['by:sn] **1** VT to pay for; Sünden to atone for; **das wirst or sollst du mir ~** I'll make you pay for that **2** VI **für etw ~** (auch Rel) to atone for sth; (= wieder gutmachen) to make amends for sth; für Leichtsinn etc to pay for sth; **schwer (für etw) ~ müssen** to have to pay dearly (for sth)

Busserl ['busel] NT -s, -(n) (Aus) kiss

busserln ['buseln] VTI (Aus) to kiss

Bußgeld NT fine

Bußgeld-: **Bußgeldbescheid** M notice of payment due (for traffic violation etc); **Bußgeldkatalog** M list of offences (Brit) or offenses (US) punishable by fines; **Bußgeldverfahren** NT fining process

Bußspur F bus lane

Buß- und Bettag M day of prayer and repentance

Büste ['bystə] F -, -n bust; (= Schneiderbüste) tailor's dummy; (weibliche) dressmaker's dummy

Büstenhalter M bra

Bustier [bys'tie:] NT -s, -s (ohne Träger) bustier, boob tube (Brit inf); (mit Trägern) bra top

Busverbindung F bus connection

Butan [bu'ta:n] NT -s, -e, **Butangas** NT butane (gas)

Butt [but] M -(e)s, -e flounder, butt

Bütt [byt] F -, -en (dial) speaker's platform; **in die ~ steigen** to mount the platform

Bütten(papier) ['bytn-] NT -s, NO PL handmade paper (with deckle edge)

Butter ['bute] F -, NO PL butter; **braune ~** browned (melted) butter; **gute ~** real butter; **es schmolz wie ~ in der Sonne** (fig) it vanished into thin air; **alles (ist) in ~** (inf) everything is hunky-dory (inf); **jdm die ~ auf dem Brot nicht gönnen** (fig inf)

to begrudge sb the very air he/she breathes; **wir lassen uns** (dat) **nicht die ~ vom Brot nehmen** (inf) we're not going to let somebody put one over on us (inf)

Butter- IN CPDS butter; **Butterberg** M (inf) butter mountain; **Butterblume** F buttercup; **Butterbrot** NT (slice of) bread and butter no art, no pl; (inf: = Sandwich) sandwich; **für ein ~** (inf) for next to nothing; **das musst du mir nicht ständig aufs ~ streichen** or **schmieren** there's no need to keep rubbing it in; **Butterbrotpapier** NT greaseproof paper; **Butterdose** F butter dish; **Butterfett** NT butterfat

Butterfly(stil) ['batɛflai-] M -s, NO PL butterfly (stroke)

Butterflymesser ['batɛflai-] NT butterfly knife

Butter-: **Butterkäse** M (full fat) hard cheese; **Butterkeks** M ≈ rich tea biscuit (Brit), ≈ butter cookie (US); **Buttermilch** F buttermilk

buttern ['buten] **1** VT **(a)** Brot to butter **(b)** Milch to make into butter **(c)** (inf: = investieren) to put (in +acc into) **2** VI to make butter

Butter-: **Butterpilz** M boletus luteus (form); **Butterschmalz** NT clarified butter; **butterweich 1** ADJ Frucht, Landung beautifully soft; (Sport inf) gentle **2** ADV landen softly; formuliert vaguely

Button ['batn] M -s, -s badge (Brit), button (US)

Butzemann ['butsa-] M, pl **-männer** (= Zwerg) hobgoblin; (= Schreckgestalt) bog(e)yman

Butzenscheibe ['butsn-] F bulls'-eye (window) pane

Büx [byks] F -, -en, **Buxe** ['buksa] F -, -n (N Ger) trousers pl (esp Brit), pants pl (esp US)

Buxtehude [buksta'hu:də] NT -s **(a)** Buxtehude (town near Hamburg) **(b)** (inf) **aus/nach/in ~** from/to/in the back of beyond (inf)

Buy-out ['baiaut] M -s, -s, **Buyout** M -s, -s buyout

BVG [be:fau'ge:] NT - ABBR von Bundesverfassungsgericht

b. w. ABBR von bitte wenden pto

BWL [be:ve:'lɛl] F - ABBR von Betriebswirtschaftslehre

Bypass ['baipas] M -(es), -es or Bypässe [-pɛsə] (Med) bypass

Bypass-Operation ['baipas-] F bypass operation

Byte ['bait] NT -s, -s byte

Byzanz [by'tsants] NT -' Byzantium

B-Zelle ['be:-] F (Med) B-cell

bzgl. ABBR von bezüglich

bzw. ABBR von beziehungsweise

Cc

C, c [tse:] NT **-,** - C, c
C ABBR *von* **Celsius**
ca. ABBR *von* **circa** approx
Cabrio ['ka:brio] NT **-s, -s** (*Aut inf*) convertible
CAD [tse:la:'de:] NT **-s,** NO PL ABBR *von* **computer aided design** CAD
Cadmium ['katmiʊm] NT **-s,** NO PL (*abbr* Cd) cadmium
Café [ka'fe:] NT **-s, -s** café
Cafeteria [kafetə'ri:a] F **-, -s** cafeteria
cal ABBR *von* (**Gramm**)**kalorie** (gram) calorie
Calcium ['kaltsiʊm] NT **-s,** NO PL calcium
Call- ['kɔ:l-]: **Callboy** M male prostitute; **Callcenter** NT call centre (*Brit*) *or* center (*US*); **Callgirl** NT **-s, -s** call girl; **Call-Option** F (*St Ex*) call option
CAM [tse:la:'lem] NT **-s,** NO PL ABBR *von* **computer-aided manufacture** CAM
Camcorder ['kamkɔrdɐ] M **-s, -** camcorder
Camembert ['kaməmbɐ, kama'bɐ] M **-s, -s** Camembert
Camion ['kamiɔ:] M **-s, -s** (*Sw*) lorry (*Brit*), truck
Camp [kɛmp] NT **-s, -s** camp
campen ['kɛmpn] VI to camp
Camper ['kɛmpɐ] M **-s, -, Camperin** ['kɛmpərɪn] F **-, -nen** camper
Camping ['kɛmpɪŋ] NT **-s,** NO PL camping *no art*; **zum ~ fahren** to go camping
Camping- ['kɛmpɪŋ] IN CPDS camping; **Campingartikel** M piece of camping equipment; (*pl*) camping equipment *sing*; **Campingbus** M camper; **Campinggas** NT camping gas; **Campingkocher** M camping stove; **Campingplatz** M camp site; **Campingzubehör** NT camping equipment
Campus ['kampʊs] M **-,** NO PL (*Univ*) campus
Cannabis ['kanabɪs] M **-,** NO PL cannabis
Cannelloni [kane'lo:ni] PL cannelloni *sing or pl*
Canyoning ['kɛnjanɪŋ] NT **-s** canyoning
Cape [ke:p] NT **-s, -s** cape
Capuccino [kapu'tʃi:no] M **-s, -s** cappuccino
Car [ka:ɐ] M **-s, -s** (*Sw*) ABBR *von* **Autocar**
Caravan ['ka(:)ravan, kara'va:n] M **-s, -s** caravan (*Brit*), trailer (*US*)
Carnet [kar'ne:] NT **-s, -s** carnet; **~ TIR** TIR carnet
Carpool ['ka:rpu:l] M car pool
Carport ['ka:ɐpɔrt] M **-s, -s** carport
Carrier [ˈkɛriɐ] M **-s, -s** (*Aviat, Comm, Telec*) carrier
Car-Sharing ['ka:ɐʃɛːrɪŋ] NT **-s,** NO PL, **Carsharing** NT **-s,** NO PL car sharing
Cartoon [kar'tu:n] M or NT **-(s), -s** cartoon
Cartoonist [kartu'nɪst] M **-en, -en, Cartoonistin** [-'nɪstɪn] F **-, -nen** cartoonist
Carving ['ka:ɐvɪŋ] NT **-s,** NO PL (*Ski*) carving
Carvingski ['ka:ɐvɪŋʃi:] M (*Ski*) carver (ski)
Cäsar ['tse:zar] M **-en, -en** [tse'za:rən] Caesar
cash [kɛʃ] ADV (*inf*) cash; **~ zahlen** to pay in cash
Cashewnuss ['kɛʃu-] F cashew (nut)
Cash-Flow ['kɛʃflo:] M **-s,** NO PL, **Cashflow** M **-s,** NO PL cash flow
Cäsium ['tse:ziʊm] NT **-s,** NO PL (*abbr* Cs) caesium (*Brit*), cesium (*US*)
Casting ['ka:stɪŋ] NT **-s, -s** (*für Filmrolle etc*) casting session
Castor® ['kasto:ɐ] M **-s, -, Castor-Behälter** M spent fuel rod container

Catch-as-catch-can ['kɛtʃəz'kɛtʃˌkɛn] NT **-,** NO PL (*lit*) catch-as-catch-can, all-in wrestling (*esp Brit*); (*fig*) free-for-all

catchen ['kɛtʃn] VI to do catch *or* all-in (*esp Brit*) wrestling; **er catcht gegen X** he has an all-in (*esp Brit*) *or* catch bout against X
Catcher ['kɛtʃɐ] M **-s, -, Catcherin** ['kɛtʃərɪn] F **-, -nen** catch(-as-catch-can) wrestler, all-in wrestler (*esp Brit*)
Catering ['ke:tərɪŋ] NT **-(s),** NO PL catering
Catering-Service ['ke:tərɪŋzø:ɐvɪs, -zœrvɪs] M, **Cateringservice** M catering service
Cayennepfeffer [ka'jɛn-] M cayenne (pepper)
CB-Funk [tse:'be:-] M, NO PL Citizens' Band, CB (radio)
CB-Funker(in) [tse:'be:-] M(F) CB (radio) user
ccm ABBR *von* **Kubikzentimeter** cc, cubic centimetre (*Brit*) *or* centimeter (*US*)
CD [tse:'de:] F **-, -s** ABBR *von* **Compact Disc** CD
CD- [tse:'de:] IN CPDS CD; **CD-Brenner** M CD burner; **CD-Gerät** NT CD player; **CD-I** [tse:de:'li:] F **-, -s,** ABBR *von* **Compact Disc - Interactive** (*Comput*) CD-I; **CD-ROM** [tse:de:'rɔm] F **-, -s** CD-ROM; **CD-ROM-Laufwerk** [tse:de:'rɔm-] NT CD-ROM drive; **CD-Spieler** M CD player
CDU [tse:de:'lu:] F - ABBR *von* **Christlich-Demokratische Union** Christian Democratic Union

CD- [tse:'de:-]: **CD-Video** F video disc; **CD-Videogerät** NT video disc player, CD video; **CD-Wechsler** [-vɛkslɐ] M **-s, -** CD changer
Cellist [tʃɛ'lɪst] M **-en, -en, Cellistin** [-'lɪstɪn] F **-, -nen** cellist
Cello ['tʃɛlo] NT **-s, -s** *or* **Celli** ['tʃɛli] cello
Cellophan® [tsɛlo'fa:n] NT **-s,** NO PL, **Cellophanpapier** NT (*inf*) cellophane (paper)
Cellulite [tsɛlu'li:tə] F **-,** NO PL (*Med*) cellulite
Celsius ['tsɛlziʊs] NO ART INV Celsius, centigrade
Cembalo ['tʃɛmbalo] NT **-s, -s** cembalo
Cent [(t)sɛnt] M **-(s), -(s)** cent
Center[1] ['sɛntɐ] NT **-s, -** (= *Einkaufscenter*) shopping centre (*Brit*) *or* center (*US*)
Center[2] ['sɛntɐ] M **-s, -(s), Centerin** [-ərɪn] F **-, -nen** (*Sw Sport:* = *Mittelstürmer*) centre (*Brit*) *or* center (*US*) forward
ces [tsɛs] NT **-, -, Ces** NT **-, -** (*Mus*) C flat
Ceylon ['tsailɔn] NT **-s** (*Hist*) Ceylon
Cha-Cha-Cha ['tʃa'tʃa'tʃa] M **-(s), -s** cha-cha(-cha)
Chalet ['ʃale] NT **-s, -s** chalet
Chamäleon [ka'mɛ:leɔn] NT **-s, -s** (*lit, fig*) chameleon
chamäleonartig ADJ (*lit, fig*) chameleon-like
Champ [tʃɛmp] M **-s, -s** (*inf: Sport, fig*) champ
Champagner [ʃam'panjɐ] M **-s, -** champagne
Champignon ['ʃampɪnjɔn, 'ʃaːpɪnjɔ] M **-s, -s** mushroom
Champion ['tʃɛmpiən] M **-s, -s** champion; (= *Mannschaft*) champions *pl*
Champions League ['tʃɛmpiənsli:k] F **-, -s** (*Sport*) Champions' League
Chance ['ʃã:sə, (*Aus*) ʃã:s] F **-, -n** (**a**) chance; (*bei Wetten*) odds *pl*; **keine ~ haben** not to stand a chance; **ich sehe keine ~, das noch rechtzeitig zu schaffen** I don't see any chance of being able to do it in time; **die ~, von einem Auto überfahren zu werden** the chances of being run over by a car; **die ~n stehen nicht schlecht, dass...** there's a good chance that...; **die ~n stehen 100:1** the odds are a hundred to one
(**b**) (= *Aussichten*) **Chancen** PL prospects *pl*; **im Beruf ~n haben** to have good career prospects; (**bei jdm**) **~n haben** (*inf*) to stand a chance (with sb)
Chancen- ['ʃã:sn-]: **chancengleich** ADJ *Aufstiegsmöglichkeiten* equal; **sie waren ~** they had equal opportunities;

Chancengleichheit F equal opportunities *pl*; **chancenlos** ADJ *Spieler, Partei* bound to lose; *Plan, Produkt* bound to fail

Chanson [ʃãˈsõ] NT **-s, -s** (political/satirical) song

Chansonette [ʃãsoˈnɛtə] F **-, -n, Chansonnette** [ʃãsˈnɛtə] F **-, -n** singer of political/satirical songs

Chansonnier [ʃãsoˈnie:] M **-s, -s** singer of political/satirical songs; (= *Dichter*) political/satirical songwriter

Chaos [ˈkaːɔs] NT **-, NO PL** chaos; **einem ~ gleichen, ein einziges ~ sein** to be in utter chaos

Chaosforschung [ˈkaːɔs-] F research into the chaos theory

Chaot [kaˈoːt] M **-en, -en, Chaotin** [kaˈoːtɪn] F **-, -nen** (*Pol pej*) anarchist (*pej*); (= *unordentlicher Mensch*) scatterbrain; **er ist ein richtiger ~** he's completely chaotic

chaotisch [kaˈoːtɪʃ] **1** ADJ chaotic; **~e Zustände** a state of (utter) chaos **2** ADV chaotically; **es geht ~ zu** there is utter chaos; **in deinem Zimmer sieht es ~ aus** your room looks chaotic

Charakter [kaˈraktɐ] M **-s, -e** [-ˈteːrə] character; **er ist ein Mann von ~** he is a man of character; **die Party bekam immer mehr den ~ einer Orgie** the party became more and more like an orgy; **der vertrauliche ~ dieses Gespräches** the confidential nature of this conversation; **sie sind ganz gegensätzliche ~e** their characters are entirely different

Charakter-: **Charakteranlage** F characteristic; **angeborene ~n** innate characteristics; **charakterbildend** ADJ character-forming; **Charakterbildung** F character formation; **Charakterdarsteller(in)** M(F) character actor/actress; **Charaktereigenschaft** F character trait; **Charakterfehler** M character defect; **charakterfest** ADJ of strong character

charakterisieren [karakteriˈziːrən], *ptp* **charakterisiert** VT to characterize

Charakterisierung F **-, -en** characterization

Charakteristik [karakteˈrɪstɪk] F **-, -en** description; (= *typische Eigenschaften*) characteristics *pl*

charakteristisch [karakteˈrɪstɪʃ] ADJ characteristic (*für* of)

charakteristischerweise ADV characteristically

Charakter-: **charakterlich** [kaˈraktɐlɪç] **1** ADJ (of) character; **~e Stärke** strength of character; **~e Mängel** character defects; **~e Qualitäten** personal qualities **2** ADV in character; **sie hat sich ~ sehr verändert** her character has changed a lot; **jdn ~ stark prägen** to have a strong influence on sb's character; **charakterlos** ADJ (a) (= *niederträchtig*) unprincipled (b) (= *ohne Prägung*) characterless; **Charakterlosigkeit** F **-, -en** (a) (= *Niederträchtigkeit*) lack of principles; (*Handlung*) unprincipled behaviour (*Brit*) or behavior (*US*) *no pl* (b) NO PL (= *Prägungslosigkeit*) characterlessness; **Charaktersache** F (*inf*) **das ist ~** it's a matter of character; **Charakterschauspieler(in)** M(F) character actor/actress; **charakterschwach** ADJ weak; **Charakterschwäche** F weakness of character; **Charakterschwein** NT (*inf*) unprincipled character; **charakterstark** ADJ strong; **Charakterstärke** F strength of character; **Charakterzug** M characteristic; **es ist kein sehr schöner ~ von ihm, ...** it is not very nice of him ...

Charge [ˈʃarʒə] F **-, -n** (a) (*Mil, fig*: = *Dienstgrad, Person*) rank; **die unteren ~n** the lower ranks (b) (*Theat*) minor character part

Charisma [ˈçaːrɪsma, ˈçarɪsma, çaˈrɪsma] NT **-s, Charismen** or **Charismata** [-mən, -mata] (*Rel, fig*) charisma

Charismatiker [çarɪsˈmaːtikɐ] M **-s, -, Charismatikerin** [-ərɪn] F **-, -nen** (*fig*) charismatic person

charismatisch [çarɪsˈmaːtɪʃ] **1** ADJ charismatic **2** ADV charismatically

charmant [ʃarˈmant] **1** ADJ charming **2** ADV charmingly

Charme [ʃarm] M **-s, NO PL** charm

Charmeur [ʃarˈmøːɐ] M **-s, -e** charmer; (= *Schmeichler*) flatterer; **du alter ~!** you old smoothy! (*inf*)

Chart [tʃart] M or NT **-, -s** (*Comput*) chart; **die ~s** (= *Hitparade*) the charts

Charta [ˈkarta] F **-, -s** charter; **Magna ~** Magna Carta

Charterer [ˈtʃartərə] M **-s, -** charterer

Charter- [ˈtʃartɐ]: **Charterflug** M charter flight; **Charter(flug)gesellschaft** F charter (flight) company; **Chartermaschine** F charter plane

chartern [ˈtʃartɐn] VT to charter

Chassis [ʃaˈsiː] NT **-, -** [-iː(s), -iːs] chassis

Chat [tʃɛt] M **-s, -s** (*Comput inf*) chat

Chatikette, Chatiquette [tʃɛtiˈkɛtə] F **-** (*Comput*) chatiquette

Chat- [ˈtʃɛt-]: **Chatprogramm** NT chat program; **Chatroom** [-ruːm] M **-s, -s** chatroom

chatten [ˈtʃɛtn] VI (*Comput inf*) to chat

Chauffeur [ʃɔˈføːɐ] M **-s, -e, Chauffeurin** [-ˈføːrɪn] F **-, -nen** chauffeur

Chauvi [ˈʃoːvi] M **-s, -s** (*inf*) male chauvinist pig (*pej inf*)

Chauvinismus [ʃoviˈnɪsmʊs] M **-, Chauvinismen** [-mən] chauvinism; (= *männlicher ~*) male chauvinism

Chauvinist [ʃoviˈnɪst] M **-en, -en, Chauvinistin** [-ˈnɪstɪn] F **-, -nen** (*Pol*) chauvinist; (= *männlicher ~*) male chauvinist (pig)

chauvinistisch [ʃoviˈnɪstɪʃ] **1** ADJ (a) (*Pol*) chauvinist(ic); **er ist sehr ~** he is a real chauvinist (b) (= *männlich-~*) male chauvinist(ic) **2** ADV (a) (*Pol*) chauvinistically (b) (= *männlich-~*) in a male chauvinist way; **sich ~ verhalten** to behave like a male chauvinist

checken [ˈtʃɛkn] **1** VT (a) (= *überprüfen*) to check (b) (*inf*: = *verstehen*) to get (*inf*) (c) (*inf*: = *merken*) to catch on to (*inf*) **2** VTI (*Eishockey*) to block; (= *anrempeln*) to barge

Check- [ˈtʃɛk-]: **Check-in** [ˈtʃɛkɪn] NT **-s, -s** check-in; **Check-in-Schalter** M check-in desk; **Checkliste** F check list; **Check-up** [ˈtʃɛkap] M or NT **-(s), -s** (*Med*) checkup

Chef [ʃɛf, (*Aus*) ʃeːf] M **-s, -s** boss; (*von Bande, Delegation etc*) leader; (*von Organisation*) head; (*der Polizei*) chief; (*Mil: von Kompanie*) commander; **er ist der ~ vom Ganzen** he's in charge here

> *Vorsicht!* **Chef** *wird nicht mit dem englischen Wort* **chef** *übersetzt.*

Chefarzt M, **Chefärztin** F senior consultant

Chefin [ˈʃɛfɪn, (*Aus*) ˈʃeːfɪn] F **-, -nen** (a) boss; (*von Delegation etc*) head (b) (*inf*: = *Frau des Chefs*) boss's wife

Chef-: **Chefkoch** M, **Chefköchin** F chef; **Chefredakteur(in)** M(F) editor in chief; (*einer Zeitung*) editor; **Chefsache** F **etw zur ~ erklären** to make sth a matter for decision at the top level; **das ist ~** it's a matter for the boss; **Chefsekretär(in)** M(F) personal assistant

chem. ABBR *von* **chemisch**

Chemie [çeˈmiː, (*esp S Ger*) keˈmiː] F **-, NO PL** (*lit, fig*) chemistry; (*inf*: = *Chemikalien*) chemicals *pl*; **was die so essen, ist alles ~** they just eat synthetic food

Chemie-: **Chemiefaser** F synthetic fibre (*Brit*) or fiber (*US*); **Chemieunterricht** M chemistry

Chemikalie [çemiˈkaːliə, (*esp S Ger*) ke-] F **-, -n** USU PL chemical

Chemiker [ˈçeːmike, (*esp S Ger*) ˈkeː-] M **-s, -, Chemikerin** [-ərɪn] F **-, -nen** chemist

Cheminée [ˈʃmmne] NT **-s, -s** (*Sw*) fireplace

chemisch [ˈçeːmɪʃ, (*esp S Ger*) ˈkeː-] **1** ADJ chemical **2** ADV chemically; **etw ~ reinigen** to dry-clean sth

Chemo- [ˈçemo-, (*esp S Ger*) ke-]: **Chemotherapeutikum** [-teraˈpɔytikʊm] NT **-s, -therapeutika** [-ka] (*Pharm*) chemotherapeutic drug; **chemotherapeutisch** **1** ADJ chemotherapeutic **2** ADV **jdn ~ behandeln** to give sb chemotherapy; **Chemotherapie** F chemotherapy

-chen [çən] NT SUF DIM little; **Hündchen** little dog; **ein Löffelchen** a small spoon

chic [ʃɪk] ADJ, ADV = **schick**

Chicorée [ˈʃikore, ʃikoˈreː] F **-** or **m -s, NO PL** chicory

Chiffre [ˈʃɪfə, ˈʃɪfrə] F **-, -n** (*in Zeitung*) box number

Chiffreanzeige F advertisement with a box number

chiffrieren [ʃɪˈfriːrən], *ptp* **chiffriert** VTI to encipher; **chiffriert** coded

Chiffrierschlüssel M code key

Chiffrierung F **-, -en** coding, cyphering

Chile [ˈtʃiːle, ˈçiːlə] NT **-s** Chile

Chilene [tʃiˈleːnə, çiˈleːnə] M **-n, -n, Chilenin** [-ˈleːnɪn] F **-, -nen** Chilean

chilenisch [tʃiˈleːnɪʃ, çiˈleːnɪʃ] ADJ Chilean

Chili [ˈtʃiːli] M **-s, NO PL** chil(l)i (pepper)

chillen [ˈtʃɪlən] VI (*sl*) to chill (out) (*inf*)

China [ˈçiːna, (*esp S Ger*) ˈkiːna] NT **-s** China

China-: **Chinakohl** M Chinese cabbage; **Chinarestaurant** NT Chinese restaurant

Chinese [çi'ne:zə, (esp S Ger) ki-] M **-n, -n** Chinese (man)

Chinesin [çi'ne:zɪn, (esp S Ger) ki-] F **-, -nen** Chinese (woman)

chinesisch [çi'ne:zɪʃ, (esp S Ger) ki-] ADJ Chinese; **die Chinesische Mauer** the Great Wall of China

Chinin [çi'ni:n] NT **-s,** NO PL quinine

Chip [tʃɪp] M **-s, -s (a)** (= Spielchip) chip **(b)** (usu pl: = Kartoffelchip) (potato) crisp (Brit), potato chip (US) **(c)** (Comput) chip

Chipkarte F smart card

Chirurg [çi'rʊrk] M **-en, -en** [-gn], **Chirurgin** [çi'rʊrgɪn] F **-, -nen** surgeon

Chirurgie [çirʊr'gi:] F **-, -n** [-'gi:ən] surgery; **er liegt in der ~** he's in surgery

chirurgisch [çi'rʊrgɪʃ] **1** ADJ surgical; **ein ~er Eingriff** surgery **2** ADV surgically; **~ tätig sein** to be a surgeon

Chitin [çi'ti:n] NT **-s,** NO PL chitin

Chlor [klo:ɐ] NT **-s,** NO PL (abbr **Cl**) chlorine

Chlorakne F chloracne

chloren [ˈkloːrən], **chlorieren** [kloˈriːrən], ptp **chloriert** VT to chlorinate

chlorfrei ADJ chlorine-free

Chlorid [kloˈriːt] NT **-s, -e** [-də] chloride

Chlorkohlenwasserstoff M (Chem) chlorinated hydrocarbon

Chloro- [kloro-]: **Chloroform** [-ˈfɔrm] NT **-s,** NO PL chloroform; **Chlorophyll** [-ˈfyl] NT **-s,** NO PL chlorophyll

Chlorwasser NT, NO PL (Chem) chlorine water; (im Hallenbad) chlorinated water

Cholera [ˈkoːlera] F **-,** NO PL cholera

Choleriker [koˈleːrikɐ] M **-s, -, Cholerikerin** [-ərɪn] F **-, -nen** choleric person; (fig) irascible person

cholerisch [koˈleːrɪʃ] ADJ choleric

Cholesterin [çolɛstəˈriːn, ko-] NT **-s,** NO PL cholesterol

Cholesterinspiegel M cholesterol level

Chor [koːɐ] M **-(e)s, ≈e** [ˈkøːrə] **(a)** (= Sängerchor) choir; **im ~ sprechen/rufen** to speak/shout in chorus **(b)** (Theat) chorus **(c)** (Archit: = Altarraum) chancel

Choreo- [koreo-]: **Choreograf** [-ˈgraːf] M **-en, -en, Choreografin** [-ˈgraːfɪn] F **-, -nen** choreographer; **Choreografie** [-graˈfiː] F **-, -n** [-ˈfiːən] choreography; **choreografieren** [-graˈfiːrən], ptp **choreografiert 1** VT to choreograph **2** VI to do the (the) choreography; **choreografisch** [-ˈgraːfɪʃ] ADJ choreographic(al)

Chor-: Chorgestühl NT choir stalls pl; **Chorknabe** M choirboy; **Chorstuhl** M choir stall

Chose [ˈʃoːzə] F **-, -n** (inf: = Angelegenheit) business

Chow-Chow [tʃaʊˈtʃaʊ] M **-s, -s** chow

Chr. ABBR von **Christus**

Christ [krɪst] M **-en, -en, Christin** [ˈkrɪstɪn] F **-, -nen** Christian

Christbaum [ˈkrɪst-] M Christmas tree

Christbaumschmuck M Christmas tree decorations pl

Christ-: Christdemokrat(in) M(F) Christian Democrat; **christdemokratisch 1** ADJ Christian Democratic **2** ADV **eine ~ geführte Regierung** a Christian Democrat-led government; **~ wählen** to vote Christian Democrat

Christen- [ˈkrɪstn-]: **Christenheit** F **-,** NO PL Christendom; **Christentum** [ˈkrɪstntuːm] NT **-s,** NO PL Christianity; **Christenverfolgung** F persecution of the Christians

Christi GEN von **Christus**

Christin F siehe **Christ**

Christ-: Christkind(chen) NT, NO PL baby Jesus; (= Sinnbild für Weihnachten) Christmas; (das Geschenk bringt) ≈ Father Christmas; (fig inf: = Dummerchen) little innocent; **Christkindl** [-kɪndl] NT **-s, -(n)**, **Christkindle** [-kɪndlə] NT **-s, -** (dial) **(a)** = Christkind(chen) **(b)** (dial: = Geschenk) Christmas present; **zum ~** for Christmas

christlich [ˈkrɪstlɪç] **1** ADJ Christian; **Christlicher Verein Junger Männer** Young Men's Christian Association **2** ADV like or as a Christian; **~ leben** to live a Christian life; **~ handeln** to act like a Christian; **jdn ~ erziehen** to bring sb up as a Christian; **eine ~ orientierte Moral** a Christian(-orientated) morality

Christ-: Christmette [-mɛtə] F **-, -n** (katholisch) Midnight Mass; (evangelisch) Midnight Service; **Christrose** F Christmas rose; **Christsoziale(r)** [-zotsiaːlə] MF DECL AS ADJ member of the CSU

Christus [ˈkrɪstʊs] M, gen **Christi** [ˈkrɪsti], dat **-** or (form) **Christo** [ˈkrɪsto], acc **-** or (form) **Christum** [ˈkrɪstʊm] Christ; **vor Christi Geburt, vor Christo** (form) or **~ before Christ, BC; nach Christi Geburt, nach Christo** (form) or **~ AD, Anno Domini; Christi Himmelfahrt** the Ascension of Christ; (= Himmelfahrtstag) Ascension Day

Chrom [kroːm] NT **-s,** NO PL chrome; (Chem) (abbr **Cr**) chromium

Chromosom [kromoˈzoːm] NT **-s, -en** chromosome

Chronik [ˈkroːnɪk] F **-, -en** chronicle

chronisch [ˈkroːnɪʃ] **1** ADJ (Med, fig) chronic **2** ADV chronically

Chronologie [kronoloˈgiː] F **-, -n** [-ˈgiːən] chronology

chronologisch [kronoˈloːgɪʃ] **1** ADJ chronological **2** ADV chronologically

Chrysantheme [kryzanˈteːmə] F **-, -n** chrysanthemum

circa [ˈtsɪrka] ADV = **zirka**

Circulus vitiosus [ˈtsɪrkulʊs viˈtsioːzʊs] M **-, Circuli vitiosi** [ˈtsɪrkuli viˈtsioːzi] (geh) vicious circle

cis [tsɪs] NT, **Cis** NT **-, -** (Mus) C sharp

City [ˈsɪti] F **-, -s** city centre (Brit) or center (US)

CJK [tseːjɔtˈkaː] ABBR von **Creuzfeldt-Jakob-Krankheit** CJD

Clavicembalo [klaviˈtʃɛmbalo] NT **-s, -s** or **Clavicembali** [-li] clavicembalo

clean [kliːn] ADJ PRED (inf) clean (inf); **~ werden** to get clean (inf)

Clearing [ˈkliːrɪŋ] NT **-s, -s** (Econ) clearing

Clearing- [ˈkliːrɪŋ-]: **Clearingabkommen** [ˈkliːrɪŋ-] NT clearing agreement; **Clearingstelle** [ˈkliːrɪŋ-] F (Fin) clearing house

Clematis [kleˈmaːtɪs, ˈkleːmatɪs] F **-, -** (Bot) clematis

clever [ˈklɛvɐ] **1** ADJ clever; (= raffiniert) sharp; (= gerissen) crafty **2** ADV (= raffiniert) sharply; (= gerissen) craftily; **sich ~ verhalten** to be crafty

Cleverness [ˈklɛvɐnɛs] F **-,** NO PL cleverness; (= Raffiniertheit) sharpness; (= Gerissenheit) craftiness

Clinch [klɪntʃ] M **-(e)s,** NO PL (Boxen, fig) clinch; **in den ~ gehen** (lit, fig) to go into a clinch; (fig: Verhandlungspartner) to get stuck into each other (inf); **mit jdm im ~ liegen** (fig) to be at loggerheads with sb

Clip [klɪp] M **-s, -s** (= Haarclip, am Füller etc) clip; (= Ohrclip) (clip-on) earring

Clique [ˈklɪkə] F **-, -n (a)** (= Freundeskreis) group, set; **wir fahren mit der ganzen ~ weg** the whole gang of us are going away together; **Thomas und seine ~** Thomas and his set **(b)** (pej) clique

Clochard [klɔˈʃaːr] M **-s, -s** tramp

Clou [kluː] M **-s, -s** (von Geschichte) (whole) point; (von Show) highlight; (von Begebenheit) show stopper; (= Witz) real laugh (inf); **und jetzt kommt der ~ der Geschichte** and now, wait for it, ...; **das wäre der ~** that'd be a real laugh (inf)

Clown [klaun] M **-s, -s** (lit, fig) clown; **den ~ spielen** to clown around; **sich/jdn zum ~ machen** to make a clown of oneself/sb

Clownin [ˈklaunɪn] F **-, -nen** (lit, fig) clown

Club [klʊp] M **-s, -s** siehe **Klub**

cm ABBR von **Zentimeter** cm

C-Netz [ˈtseː-] NT (Telec) cellular (analogue) network

Co-, co- [ˈkoː] IN CPDS co-

Co. ABBR von **Kompagnon, Kompanie** Co

Coautor(in) [ˈkoː-] M(F) coauthor

Cockerspaniel [ˈkɔkɐ-] M cocker spaniel

Cockpit [ˈkɔkpɪt] NT **-s, -s** cockpit

Cocktail [ˈkɔkteːl] M **-s, -s** (= Getränk) (fig) cocktail; (= Empfang) reception

Cocktail-: Cocktailkleid NT cocktail dress; **Cocktailparty** F cocktail party; **Cocktailtomate** F cherry tomato

Code [koːt] M **-s, -s** siehe **Kode**

Codein [kodeˈiːn] NT **-s,** NO PL codeine

Codierung [koˈdiːrʊŋ] F **-, -en** (en)coding

Cognac® [ˈkɔnjak] M **-s, -s** cognac

Coiffeur [koaˈføːɐ] M **-s, -e, Coiffeuse** [-ˈføːzə] F **-, -n** (Sw) hairdresser; (geh) hair stylist

Cola [ˈkoːla] F **-, -s** (inf) Coke® (inf)

Coladose F Coke® can

Colloquium [kɔ'lɔkviʊm] NT -s, **Colloquien** [-kviən] colloquium; (Aus Univ: = Prüfung) examination

Colonia- [ko'loːnia-]: **Coloniakübel** M (Aus) dustbin (Brit), trash can (US); **Coloniawagen** M (Aus) refuse truck

Come-back [kam'bɛk] NT -(s), -s, **Comeback** NT -(s), -s comeback

Comecon ['kɔmekɔn] M or NT, **COMECON** M or NT - (Hist) Comecon

Comic ['kɔmɪk] M -s, -s comic strip

Coming-out ['kamɪŋaʊt] NT -s, NO PL (inf: als Homosexueller) coming out

Compactdisc [kɔm'pakt 'dɪsk] F -, -s, **Compact Disc** F -, -s compact disc

Compiler [kɔm'paile] M -s, - (Comput) compiler

Computer [kɔm'pjuːte] M -s, - computer; **auf ~** on computer; **per ~** by computer

Computer- IN CPDS computer-; **Computerarbeitsplatz** M computer work station; **Computerausdruck** M computer printout; **Computerdiagnostik** F computer diagnosis; **computergerecht** ① ADJ computer-compatible ② ADV übertragen in computer-compatible form; **computergesteuert** [-gəʃtɔyɐt] ADJ controlled by computer; **computergestützt** [-gəʃtʏtst] ADJ computer-based; **~es Design** computer-aided design; **Computergrafik** F computer graphics pl

computerisieren [kɔmpjutəri'ziːrən], ptp **computerisiert** VT to computerize

Computer-: **Computerkasse** F computer cash register; **computerlesbar** ADJ machine-readable; **Computerlinguistik** F computational linguistics sing; **Computersatz** M computer typesetting; **Computersicherheit** F computer security; **Computerspiel** NT computer game; **Computersprache** F computer language; **Computertomograf** M computer tomograph; **Computertomografie** F computer tomography; **Computertomogramm** NT computer tomogram; **computerunterstützt** ADJ Fertigung, Kontrolle computer-aided

Conditio sine qua non [kɔn'diːtsio 'ziːnə 'kva: 'noːn] F - - - -, NO PL (geh) sine qua non

Conférencier [kõferã'sieː] M -s, -s compère

Confiserie [kõfizə'riː] F -, -n [-'riːən] (Sw) (a) (= Konfekt) confectionery (b) (= Konditorei) cake shop; (mit Café) café

Container [kɔn'teːne] M -s, - container; (= Blumentrog) plant box; (= Bauschuttcontainer) skip; (= Wohncontainer) prefabricated hut

Container- [kɔn'teːne] IN CPDS container; **Containerbahnhof** M container depot; **Containerhafen** M container port; **Containerschiff** NT container ship; **Containerterminal** M or NT container terminal; **Containerverkehr** M container traffic; **auf ~ umstellen** to containerize

Containment [kɔn'teːnmənt] NT -s, -s containment

Contergankind NT (inf) thalidomide child

Contra ['kɔntra] M -s, -s (Pol) Contra

Controller¹ [kɔn'troːle] M -s, - (Comput) controller

Controller² [kɔn'troːle] M -s, -, **Controllerin** [-ərɪn] F -, -nen (Fin) cost controller

Controlling [kɔn'troːlɪŋ] NT -s, NO PL (Fin) cost control

Cookie ['kʊki] NT -s, -s (Comput) cookie

cool ['kuːl] ADJ (a) (inf: = gefasst) cool (inf) (b) (sl: = angenehm) cool (inf); **die Party war ~** the party was (real) cool (inf)

Coolness ['kuːlnɛs] F -, NO PL (inf) coolness

Copilot(in) ['ko-] M(F) copilot

Copyright ['kɔpirait] NT -s, -s copyright

Copyshop ['kɔpiʃɔp] M -s, -s copy shop

Cord [kɔrt] M -s, -e [-də] or -s (Tex) cord

Corner ['kɔːrne] M -s, - (Aus Sport) corner

Cornflakes ['kɔːrnfleːks] PL cornflakes pl

Cornichon [kɔrni'ʃõː] NT -s, -s gherkin

Corps [koːr] M -, - (Mil) corps; (Univ) (duelling (Brit) or dueling (US)) corps

Corpus ['kɔrpʊs] NT -, **Corpora** ['kɔrpora] siehe **Korpus²**

Corpus Delicti ['kɔrpʊs de'lɪkti] NT -, **Corpora** - ['kɔrpora] corpus delicti; (hum) culprit (inf)

cos ABBR von Kosinus cos

Costa Rica ['kɔsta 'riːka] NT -s Costa Rica

costa-ricanisch [kɔstari'kaːnɪʃ] ADJ Costa Rican

Couch [kautʃ] F -, -s or -en or (Sw) m -s, -(e)s couch

Couch- [kautʃ-]: **Couchgarnitur** F three-piece suite; **Couchpotato** [-poteːto] F -, -es (inf) couch potato (inf); **Couchtisch** M coffee table

Count-down ['kaunt'daun] M or NT -s, -s, **Countdown** M or NT -s, -s (Space, fig) countdown

Coup [kuː] M -s, -s coup; **einen ~ (gegen jdn/etw) landen** to pull off a coup (against sb/sth) (inf)

Coupon [ku'põː] M -s, -s (a) (= Zettel) coupon (b) (Fin) (interest) coupon

Courtage [kʊr'taːʒə] F -, -n (Fin) commission

Cousin [ku'zɛ̃ː] M -s, -s, **Cousine** [ku'ziːnə] F -, -n cousin

Cover ['kave] NT -s, -s cover

Covergirl ['kavegœrl] NT -s, -s cover girl

Cowboy ['kaubɔy] M cowboy

Cowboystiefel ['kaubɔy-] M cowboy boot

Cox Orange ['kɔks o'rãːʒə] M or F - -, - - or - -n Cox's (Orange) Pippin

Crack¹ [krɛk] M -s, -s (= Sportler) ace

Crack² NT -, NO PL (= Droge) crack

Cracker ['krɛkɐ] M -s, -(s) (= Keks) cracker

Crash [krɛʃ] M -s, -s (inf: = Unfall, St Ex, Comput) crash

Crash- ['krɛʃ-]: **Crashkid** NT -s, -s (inf) joyrider; **Crashkurs** M crash course; **Crashtest** M (Aut) crash test

Creme [kreːm, krɛːm] F -, -s cream; **die ~ de la ~** the crème de la crème

Crème fraîche [krɛm 'frɛʃ] F -, NO PL crème fraîche

Cremetorte F cream gateau

cremig ['kreːmɪç] ① ADJ creamy ② ADV like cream; **rühren** until creamy

Creutzfeldt-Jakob-Krankheit [krɔytsfɛlt'jakɔp-] F Creutzfeldt-Jakob disease

Crew [kruː] F -, -s crew

Croissant [kroa'sãː] NT -s, -s croissant

Cromargan® [kromar'gaːn] NT -s, NO PL stainless steel

Cross [krɔs] M -s, -s, **Cross-Country** ['krɔs'kantri] NT -, NO PL (Sport) cross-country; (= Motorradrennen) motocross

Cross(ball) ['krɔs-] M -, - (Tennis) cross-court shot

Croupier [kru'pieː] M -s, -s croupier

Crux [krʊks] F -, NO PL (= Schwierigkeit) trouble, problem; **die ~ bei der Sache ist, ...** the trouble or problem (with that) is ...

C-Schlüssel ['tseː-] M alto clef

CS-Gas [tseː'lɛs-] NT CS gas

CSU [tseː'lɛs'uː] F - ABBR von Christlich-Soziale Union Christian Social Union

---

CSU

*The **CSU** (Christlich-Soziale Union) is the sister party of the **CDU** and contests elections only in Bavaria. Founded in 1945, it emphasizes Christian, conservative values and a social market economy. It also champions the sovereignty of the Länder, especially Bavaria. The **CSU** frequently receives an absolute majority in Landtag elections and so can rely on a broad basis of support.* ▶ CDU

---

c. t. [tseː'teː] ADV ABBR von cum tempore within fifteen minutes of the time stated; **18.30 ~ 6.30** for 6.45

Curry ['kari] M or NT -s, -s curry

Currywurst ['kari-] F curried sausage

Cursor ['kɔːɐse, 'kœɐse] M -s, -s (Comput) cursor

Cursortaste ['kɔːɐse-, 'kœɐse-] F cursor key

cutten ['katn] VTI to cut

Cutter ['kate] M -s, -, **Cutterin** ['katərɪn] F -, -nen editor

CVJF [tseː'faʊyt'lef] M -s ABBR von Christlicher Verein Junger Frauen YWCA

CVJM [tseː'faʊyt'lem] M -s ABBR von Christlicher Verein Junger Männer YMCA

Cyan [tsy'aːn] NT -s, NO PL cyan

Cyanid [tsya'niːt] NT -s, -e [-də] cyanide

Cyber- ['saibe] IN CPDS cyber-; **Cybergeld** NT e-cash, electronic cash; **Cybernaut** ['saibenɔːt] M -en, -en, **Cybernautin** [-nɔːtɪn] F -, -nen cybernaut; **Cyberspace** ['saibespeːs] M -, NO PL cyberspace

Dd

D, d [de:] NT **-, -** D, d

da [da:] **1** ADV **(a)** (örtlich) (= dort) there; (= hier) here; **hier und da, da und dort** here and there; **wer da?** who goes there?; **he, Sie da!** hey, you there!; **die Frau da** that woman (over) there; **da bin ich/sind wir** here I am/we are; **da bist du ja!** there you are!; **da kommt er ja** here he comes; **wir sind gleich da** we'll soon be there; **da, wo ...** where ...; **ach, da war der Brief!** so that's where the letter was; **da haben wirs** or **den Salat** (inf) that had to happen; **da hast du deinen Kram/dein Geld!** (there you are,) there's your stuff/money; **da, nimm schon!** here, take it!

(b) (zeitlich: = dann, damals) then; **ich ging gerade aus dem Haus, da schlug es zwei** I was just going out of the house when the clock struck two; **vor vielen, vielen Jahren, da lebte ein König** (liter) long, long ago there lived a king; **da kommen Sie mal gleich mit** (inf) you just come along with me; **da siehst du, was du angerichtet hast** now see what you've done

(c) (daraufhin) sagen to that; lachen at that; **sie weinte, da ließ er sich erweichen** when she started to cry he softened; **als er das Elend der Leute sah, da nahm er sich vor ...** when he saw the people's suffering he decided ...

(d) (= folglich) so; (= dann) then; **wenn ich schon gehen muss, da gehe ich lieber gleich** if I have to go, (then) I'd rather go straight away

(e) (inf: = in diesem Fall) there; **da haben wir aber Glück gehabt!** we were lucky there!; **was gibts denn da zu lachen?** what's funny about that?; **da kann man** or **da lässt sich nichts machen** nothing can be done about it; **da kann man nur lachen/sich nur fragen, warum** you can't help laughing/asking yourself why; **und da fragst du noch?** and you still have to ask?; **und da soll einer** or **ein Mensch wissen, warum!** and you're meant to know why!; **da fragt man sich (doch), ob ...** it makes you wonder if ...; **da hat doch jemand gelacht** somebody laughed

(f) (zur Hervorhebung) **wir haben da eine neue Mitschülerin** we've got this new girl in our school; **da fällt mir gerade ein ...** it's just occurred to me ...

(g) (N Ger) siehe **dabei, dafür** etc

2 CONJ (= weil) as, since

DAAD [de:laːlaː'deː] M - ABBR von **Deutscher Akademischer Austauschdienst** German Academic Exchange Service

dabehalten ptp **dabehalten** VT SEP IRREG to keep (here/there); Schüler to keep behind

dabei [da'baɪ, (emph) 'daːbaɪ] ADV **(a)** (örtlich) with it; (bei Gruppe von Menschen, Dingen) there; **ein Häuschen mit einem Garten ~** a little house with a garden (attached to it); **ist die Lösung ~?** is the solution given (there)?; **nahe ~** nearby

(b) (zeitlich) (= gleichzeitig) at the same time; (= währenddessen, wodurch) in the course of this; **er aß weiter und blätterte ~ in dem Buch** he went on eating, leafing through the book at the same time; **warum arbeiten Sie im Stehen? Sie können doch auch ~ sitzen** why are you working standing up? you can sit down while you're doing it; **nach der Explosion entstand eine Panik; ~ wurden drei Kinder verletzt** there was a general panic after the explosion, in the course of which three children were injured

(c) (= außerdem) as well; **sie ist schön und ~ auch noch klug** she's pretty, and clever as well

(d) (wenn, während man etw tut) in the process; ertappen, erwischen at it; **~ darf man nicht vergessen, dass ...** it shouldn't be forgotten that ...; (Einschränkung eines Arguments) it should not be forgotten here that ...; **die ~ entstehenden Kosten** the expenses arising from this/that; **als er das tat, hat er ~ ...** when he did that he ...; **wir haben ihn ~ ertappt, wie er über den Zaun stieg** we caught him in the act of climbing over the fence

(e) (= in dieser Angelegenheit) **das Schwierigste ~** the most difficult part of it; **wichtig ~ ist ...** the important thing here or about it is ...; **~ kann man viel Geld verdienen** there's a lot of money in that; **er hat ~ einen Fehler gemacht** he's made a mistake; **es kommt doch nichts ~ heraus** nothing will come of it

(f) (einräumend: = doch) (and) yet; **er hat mich geschlagen, ~ hatte ich gar nichts gemacht** he hit me and I hadn't even done anything

(g) (in Wendungen mit Verben) **du gehst sofort nach Hause, und ~ bleibt es!** you're going straight home and that's that!; **es bleibt ~, dass ihr morgen alle mitkommt** we'll stick to that, you're all coming tomorrow; **ich bleibe ~** I'm not changing my mind; **er bleibt ~, dass er es nicht gewesen ist** he still insists that he didn't do it; **aber ~ sollte es nicht bleiben** but it shouldn't stop there or at that; **lassen wir es ~** let's leave it at that!; **was ist schon ~?** so what? (inf), what of it? (inf); **was ist schon ~, wenn man das tut** (inf) what harm is there in doing that?; **ich finde gar nichts ~** I don't see any harm in it; **es ist nichts ~, wenn man das tut** (= schadet nichts) there's no harm in doing that; (= will nichts bedeuten) doing that doesn't mean anything; **ich habe mir nichts ~ gedacht, als ich den Mann aus der Bank kommen sah** I didn't think anything of it when I saw the man coming out of the bank; **was hast du dir denn ~ gedacht?** what were you thinking of?

dabeibleiben VI SEP IRREG AUX SEIN to stay with it; siehe auch **dabei** (g)

dabeihaben VT SEP IRREG (inf) to have with one

dabei sein VI IRREG AUX SEIN **(a)** (= anwesend sein) to be there (bei at); (= mitmachen) to be involved (bei in); **ich bin dabei!** count me in!; **er will überall ~** he wants to be in on everything; **mit 5 Euro sind Sie dabei** take part for just 5 euros **(b)** (= im Begriff sein) **~, etw zu tun** to be just doing sth; **ich bin (gerade) dabei** I'm just doing it

Dabeisein NT **~ ist alles** it's all about taking part

dableiben VI SEP IRREG AUX SEIN to stay (on); (= nachsitzen) to stay behind; **(jetzt wird) dageblieben!** (you just) stay right there!

da capo [da 'kaːpo] ADV da capo; **~ rufen** to call for an encore

Dach [dax] NT **-(e)s, ⁻er** ['dɛçə] **(a)** roof; **mit jdm unter einem ~ wohnen** to live under the same roof as sb; **unterm ~ wohnen** (inf) to live in an attic room/flat (Brit) or apartment; (im obersten Stock) to live right on the top floor; **unter ~ und Fach sein** (= abgeschlossen) to be all wrapped up; **etw unter ~ und Fach bringen** to get sth all wrapped up; **unter dem ~** +gen (fig) under the umbrella of

(b) (fig inf) **jdm eins aufs ~ geben** (= schlagen) to smash sb on the head (inf); (= ausschimpfen) to give sb a (good) talking-to; **eins aufs ~ bekommen** or **kriegen** (= geschlagen werden) to get hit on the head; (= ausgeschimpft werden) to be given a (good) talking-to; **jdm aufs ~ steigen** (inf) to get onto sb (inf)

Dach- IN CPDS roof; **Dachbalken** M roof joist; **Dachboden** M attic; (von Scheune) loft; **auf dem ~** in the attic; **Dachfenster** NT skylight; (ausgestellt) dormer window; **Dachfirst** M ridge of the roof; **Dachgarten** M roof garden; **Dachgepäckträger** M (Aut) roof rack; **Dachgeschoss** NT attic storey (Brit) or story (US); (= oberster Stock) top floor; **Dachgesellschaft** F parent company; **Dachgestühl** NT roof truss; **Dachgiebel** M gable; **Dachlatte** F tile batten; **Dachlawine** F snowfall from a/the roof; **Dachluke** F skylight; **Dachorganisation** F umbrella or (Comm) parent organization; **Dachpappe** F roofing paper; **Dachrinne** F gutter

Dachs [daks] M **-es, -e** (Zool) badger

Dachsbau M, pl **-baue** badger's sett

Dachschaden M **(a)** (lit) damage to the roof **(b)** (inf) **einen (kleinen) ~ haben** to have a slate loose (inf)

Dächsin ['dɛksɪn] F **-, -nen** female badger

dachte PRET von **denken**

Dach-: Dachterrasse F roof terrace; **Dachträger** M (Aut) roof rack; **Dachverband** M umbrella organization; **Dachwohnung** F attic apartment; **Dachziegel** M roofing tile

Dackel ['dakl] M **-s, -** dachshund; (inf: = Person) silly clot (Brit inf), ninny (US inf)

Dackelbeine PL (inf) short stumpy legs pl

Dadaismus [dada'ɪsmʊs] M **-**, NO PL Dadaism

dadaistisch [dada'ɪstɪʃ] ADJ Dadaist

dadurch [da'dʊrç, (emph) 'daːdʊrç] ADV **(a)** (örtlich) through there; (wenn Bezugsobjekt vorher erwähnt) through it **(b)** (kausal) thereby (form); (= mithilfe von, aus diesem Grund auch) because of this/that, through this/that; (= durch diesen

Umstand, diese Tat etc auch) with that; (= *auf diese Weise*) in this/that way; **meinst du, ~ wird alles wieder gut?** do you think that will make everything all right again?; **~, dass er das tat, hat er ...** (= *durch diesen Umstand, diese Tat*) by doing that he ...; (= *deswegen, weil*) because he did that he ...; **~, dass das Haus isoliert ist, ist es viel wärmer** the house is much warmer because it's insulated

dafür [da'fyːɐ, *(emph)* 'daːfyːɐ] ADV **(a)** (= *für das, diese Tat etc*) for that/it; **der Grund ~ ist, dass ...** the reason for that is (that) ...; **warum ist er so böse? er hat doch keinen Grund ~** why is he so angry? he has no reason to be; **~ war er nicht zu haben** it wasn't his scene (*inf*); (= *erlaubte es nicht*) he wouldn't have it; **~ ist er immer zu haben** he never says no to that; **ich bin nicht ~ verantwortlich** I'm not responsible for what my brother does; **~ bin ich ja hier** that's what I'm here for **(b)** (*Zustimmung*) for that/it; **ich bin (ganz) ~, dass wir/sie das machen** I'm (all) for doing that/them doing that; **~ stimmen** to vote for it **(c)** (*als Ersatz*) instead; (*als Bezahlung*) for that/it; (*bei Tausch*) in exchange; (*als Gegenleistung*) in return; **... ich mache dir ~ deine Hausaufgaben ...** and I'll do your homework in return **(d)** (*zum Ausgleich*) but ... to make up; **in Physik ist er schlecht, ~ kann er gut Golf spielen** he's very bad at physics but he makes up for it at golf **(e)** (= *im Hinblick darauf*) **der Junge ist erst drei Jahre, ~ ist er sehr klug** the boy is only three, (so) considering that he's very clever; **~, dass er erst drei Jahre ist, ist er sehr klug** considering that he's only three he's very clever **(f)** (*in Verbindung mit n, vb etc siehe auch dort*) **er interessiert sich nicht ~** he's not interested in that/it; **~ interessiert er sich nicht** he's not interested in that sort of thing; **ein Beispiel ~ wäre ...** an example of that would be ...; **sie ist dreißig – ~ hätte ich sie nicht gehalten** she's thirty – I would never have thought it

dafür können VT IRREG **er kann nichts dafür** he can't help it; **er kann nichts dafür, dass es kaputtgegangen ist** it's not his fault that it broke; **als ob ich was dafür könnte!** as if I could help it!

DAG [deːaːˈgeː] F - ABBR *von* **Deutsche Angestellten-Gewerkschaft** Trade Union of German Employees

dagegen [da'geːgn, *(emph)* 'daːgeːgn] ADV **(a)** (*örtlich*) against it; **mache das Licht an und halte das Dia ~** put the light on and hold the slide up to it **(b)** (*als Einwand, Ablehnung*) against that/it; **~ sein** to be against it; **etwas ~ haben** to object; **nichts ~ haben** not to object; **haben Sie was ~, wenn ich rauche?** do you mind if I smoke?; **sollen wir ins Kino gehen? – ich hätte nichts ~ (einzuwenden)** shall we go to the cinema? – that's okay by me (*inf*); **ich hätte nichts ~, wenn er nicht kommen würde** I wouldn't mind at all if he didn't come **(c)** (*als Gegenmaßnahme*) *tun, unternehmen* about it; *Medikamente einnehmen etc* for it; **~ lässt sich nichts machen** nothing can be done about it **(d)** (= *verglichen damit*) in comparison **(e)** (*als Ersatz, Gegenwert*) for that/it/them ◼ CONJ (= *im Gegensatz dazu*) on the other hand; **er sprach fließend Französisch, ~ konnte er kein Deutsch** he spoke French fluently, but (on the other hand) he could not speak any German

dagegen-: dagegenhalten VT SEP IRREG (= *vergleichen*) to compare it/them with; **dagegensprechen** VI SEP IRREG to be against it; **was spricht dagegen?** what is there against it?; **was spricht dagegen, dass wir es so machen?** why shouldn't we do it that way?; **es spricht nichts dagegen, es so zu machen** there's no reason not to do it that way

dahaben VT SEP IRREG **(a)** (= *vorrätig haben*) to have here/there; (*in Geschäft etc*) to have in stock **(b)** (= *zu Besuch haben*) to have here/there; (*zum Essen etc*) to have in

daheim [da'haim] ADV (*esp S Ger, Aus, Sw*) at home; (*nach prep*) home; **bei uns ~** back home (where I/we come from); **wir haben bei mir ~ or ~ bei mir gefeiert** we had a celebration at my place; **~ sein** (*lit, fig*) to be at home; (*nach Reise*) to be home; **wo bist du ~?** where's your home?; **~ ist ~** (*Prov*) there's no place like home (*prov*)

Daheim NT, NO PL (*esp S Ger, Aus, Sw*) home

daher [da'heːɐ, *(emph)* 'daːheːɐ] ◼ ADV **(a)** (= *von dort*) from there; **von ~** from there; **~ habe ich das** that's where I got it

from **(b)** (= *durch diesen Umstand*) that is why; **~ weiß ich das** that's how *or* why I know that; **der Name X** that's why it's/he's *etc* called X; **~ kommt es, dass ...** that is (the reason) why ...; **das kommt** *or* **rührt ~, dass ...** that is because ... ◼ CONJ (= *deshalb*) that is why; **~ die Verspätung** that's what is causing the delay

daher-: daherbringen VT SEP IRREG (*Aus*) to produce; **dahergelaufen** ADJ **jeder Dahergelaufene, jeder ~e Kerl** any Tom, Dick or Harry, any guy who comes/came along; **diese ~en Kerle in der Politik** these self-important nobodies in politics; **sie hat so einen ~en Kerl geheiratet** she married some fellow who just happened along (*inf*); **daherreden** SEP ◼ VI to talk away; **red doch nicht so (dumm) daher!** don't talk such nonsense! ◼ VT to say without thinking; **was er alles/für ein blödes Zeug daherredet** the things/the nonsense he comes out with! (*inf*); **das war nur so dahergeredet** I/he *etc* just said that

daherum ['daːherʊm] ADV (a)round there

dahin [da'hɪn, *(emph)* 'daːhɪn] ◼ ADV **(a)** (*räumlich*) there; (= *hierhin*) here; **kommst du auch ~?** are you coming too?; **bis ~ as far as there**, up to that point; **ist es noch weit bis ~?** is it still a long way?; **bis ~ dauert es noch zwei Stunden** it'll take us another two hours to get there; **es steht mir bis ~** I've had it up to here (*inf*) **(b)** (*fig: so weit*) **~ kommen** to come to that; **es ist ~ gekommen, dass ...** things have got to the stage where ...; **du wirst es ~ bringen, dass ...** you'll bring things to such a pass that ... **(c)** (= *in dem Sinne, in die Richtung*) **er äußerte sich ~ gehend, dass ...** he said something to the effect that ...; **eine ~ gehende Aussage/Änderung** *etc* a statement/change *etc* to that effect; **wir sind ~ gehend verblieben, dass ...** we agreed that ... **(d)** (*zeitlich*) then ◼ ADJ PRED **~ sein** to have gone; **das Auto ist ~** (*hum inf*) the car has had it (*inf*)

da-: dahinab [dahr'nap] ADV = **dorthinab; dahinauf** [dahr'nauf] ADV = **dorthinauf; dahinaus** [dahr'naus] ADV there; *transportieren, bringen* out that way

dahindämmern VI SEP AUX SEIN to lie/sit there in a stupor

dahinein [dahr'nain] ADV = **dorthinein**

dahingegen [dahɪn'geːgn] ADV on the other hand

dahin-: dahingehen VI SEP IRREG AUX SEIN (*geh*) to pass; **dahingestellt** [-gəʃtɛlt] ADJ **~ sein lassen, ob ...** to leave it open whether ...; **es bleibt** *or* **sei ~, ob ...** it is an open question whether ...; **dahinleben** VI SEP to exist, to vegetate (*pej*); **dahinsagen** VT SEP to say without (really) thinking; **das war nur so dahingesagt** I/he *etc* just said that (without thinking); **dahinschleppen** VR SEP (*fig: Verhandlungen, Zeit*) to drag on; **dahinstehen** VI SEP IRREG to be debatable

dahinten [da'hɪntn, *(emph)* 'daːhɪntn] ADV over there; (*hinter Sprecher*) back there; **ganz weit ~** way over there (*inf*)

dahinter [da'hɪntɐ, *(emph)* 'daːhɪntɐ] ADV **(a)** (*räumlich*) behind (it/that/him *etc*); **was sich wohl ~ verbirgt?** (*lit, fig*) I wonder what's behind that?; **(da ist) nichts ~** (*fig*) there's nothing behind it **(b)** (= *danach*) beyond

dahinterher [dahɪntɐˈheːɐ] ADJ **~ sein** (*inf*) to push (*dass* to see that); **die Polizei ist ~, die Jugendkriminalität einzudämmen** the police are pretty hot on keeping juvenile delinquency under control (*inf*)

dahinter: dahinter klemmen, dahinter knien VR (*inf*) to get one's finger out (*inf*); **klemm** *or* **knie dich mal ein bisschen dahinter** make a bit of an effort; **dahinter kommen** VI IRREG AUX SEIN (*inf*) to find out; (= *langsam verstehen*) to get it (*inf*); **dahinter stecken** VI (*inf*) to be behind it/that; **dahinter stehen** VI IRREG (= *unterstützen*) to back it/that, to be behind it/that

dahinunter [dahi'nʊntɐ, *(emph)* 'daːhɪnʊntɐ] ADV = **dorthinunter**

dahinvegetieren *ptp* **dahinvegetiert** VI SEP to vegetate

Dahlie ['daːliə] F -, -n dahlia

DAK [deːaːˈkaː] F - ABBR *von* **Deutsche Angestellten-Krankenkasse** Employees' Health Insurance

Dakapo [da'kaːpo] NT -s, -s encore

Dakaporuf M call for an encore

Dalai-Lama ['daːlaiˈlaːma] M -(s), -s (*Rel*) Dalai Lama

da-: dalassen VT SEP IRREG to leave (here/there); **daliegen** VI SEP IRREG to lie there; **... sonst liegst du nachher da mit einer schweren Grippe** (inf) ... otherwise you'll be in bed with a bad dose of (the) flu

dalli ['dalɪ] ADV (inf) **~, ~!** on the double! (inf); **mach ein bisschen ~!** get a move on! (inf); **verzieh dich, aber ~!** beat it, go on, quick!

Dalmatiner [dalmaˈtiːnɐ] M **-s, -** (Hund) dalmatian

damalig ['daːmaːlɪç] ADJ ATTR at that time

damals ['daːmaːls] ADV at that time; **seit ~** since then; **von ~** of that time; **~, als ...** at the time when ...

Dame ['daːmə] F **-, -n (a)** lady; **sehr verehrte** (form) or **meine ~n und Herren!** ladies and gentlemen!; **„~n"** (= Toilette) "Ladies" **(b)** (= Tanzpartnerin, Begleiterin) lady; (auf einen bestimmten Herrn bezogen) partner; (bei Cocktailparty, Theaterbesuch etc) (lady) companion; **bringen Sie ruhig Ihre ~n mit** do by all means bring your wives and girlfriends **(c)** (Sport) woman; **Hundert-Meter-Staffel der ~n** women's hundred metre (Brit) or meter (US) relay **(d)** (Spiel) draughts sing (Brit), checkers sing (US); (= Doppelstein) king

Damebrett NT draughtboard (Brit), checkerboard (US)

Damen- IN CPDS ladies'; **Damenbart** M facial hair; **Damenbegleitung** F **- erwünscht** please bring a lady or (bei Ball) partner; **in ~** in the company of a lady; **Damenbinde** F sanitary towel (Brit) or napkin (US); **Damendoppel** NT (Tennis etc) ladies' doubles sing; **Dameneinzel** NT (Tennis etc) ladies' singles sing; **damenhaft** 🄵 ADJ ladylike 🄶 ADV in a ladylike way; **Damenmangel** M shortage of ladies; **Damensattel** M side-saddle; **im ~ reiten** to ride side-saddle; **Damenschneider(in)** M(F) dressmaker; **Damenschneiderei** F dressmaking; (= Werkstatt) dressmaker's; **Damensitz** M side-saddle style of riding; **im ~** side-saddle; **Damentoilette** F (= WC) ladies' toilet or restroom (US); **Damenwahl** F ladies' choice

Dame-: Damespiel NT draughts sing (Brit), checkers sing (US); **Damestein** M draughtsman (Brit), checker (US)

damit [da'mɪt, (emph) 'daːmɪt] 🄵 ADV **(a)** (= mit diesem Gegenstand, dieser Tätigkeit, mit Hilfe davon) with it/that; **was will er ~?** what does he want with that?; **was soll ich ~?** what am I meant to do with that?; **ist Ihre Frage ~ beantwortet?** does that answer your question? **(b)** (= mit, in dieser Angelegenheit) **meint er mich ~?** does he mean me?; **weißt du, was er ~ meint?** do you know what he means by that?; **was ist ~?** what about it?; **wie wäre es ~?** how about it?; **er konnte mir nicht sagen, was es ~ auf sich hat** he couldn't tell me what it was all about; **wie sieht es ~ aus?** what's happening about it?; **das/er hat gar nichts ~ zu tun** that/he has nothing to do with it; **~ ist nichts** (inf) it's no go (inf); **hör auf ~!** (inf) lay off! (inf); **~ hat es noch Zeit** there's no hurry for that **(c)** (bei Verben) **was willst du ~ sagen?** what's that supposed to mean?; **~ will ich nicht sagen, dass ...** I don't mean to say that ...; **sind Sie ~ einverstanden?** do you agree to that? **(d)** (bei Befehlen) with it; **weg/heraus ~!** away/out with it; **her ~!** give it here! (inf); **Schluss** or **genug ~!** that's enough (of that)! **(e)** (begründend) therefore; **er verlor den zweiten Satz und ~ das Spiel** he lost the second set and therefore the match; **~ ist es klar, dass er es war** from that it's clear that it was him **(f)** (= daraufhin, dann, jetzt) with that; **~ schließe ich für heute** I'll close with that for today; **~ kommen wir zum Ende des Programms** that brings us to the end of our programmes (Brit) or programs (US) 🄶 CONJ so that; **~ er nicht fällt** so that he does not fall

dämlich ['dɛːmlɪç] (inf) 🄵 ADJ stupid 🄶 ADV stupidly; **guck nicht so ~** don't give me that dumb look (inf); **~ fragen** to ask dumb questions/a dumb question (inf)

Damm [dam] M **-(e)s, -̈e** ['dɛmə] **(a)** (= Deich) dyke (Brit), dike (esp US); (= Staudamm) dam; (= Hafendamm) wall; (= Uferdamm, Bahndamm) embankment; (fig) barrier; **wenn wir das kleinste bisschen nachgeben, werden alle Dämme brechen** if we give way at all, the floodgates will open **(b)** (Anat) perineum **(c)** (fig inf) **wieder auf dem ~ sein** to be back to normal; **geistig auf dem ~ sein** to be with it (inf); **nicht recht auf dem ~ sein** not to be up to the mark (inf)

dämmen ['dɛmən] VT **(a)** (Tech) Wärme to keep in; Schall to absorb **(b)** (fig: = eindämmen) to contain

dämmerig ['dɛmərɪç] ADJ Licht dim; Zimmer gloomy; **es wird ~** (abends) dusk is falling; (morgens) dawn is breaking

Dämmerlicht NT twilight; (= Halbdunkel) half-light

dämmern ['dɛmən] 🄵 VI **(a)** (Tag, Morgen) to dawn; (Abend) to fall **(b)** (= im Halbschlaf sein) to doze 🄶 VI IMPERS **es dämmert** (morgens) dawn is breaking; (abends) dusk is falling; **jetzt dämmerts (bei) mir!** (inf) now it's dawning (on me)!; **es dämmerte ihm, dass ...** (inf) he began to realize that ...

Dämmerung ['dɛmərʊŋ] F **-, -en** twilight; (= Abenddämmerung auch) dusk; (= Morgendämmerung auch) dawn; (= Halbdunkel) half-light; **bei** or **mit Anbruch der ~** when dusk began/begins to fall; when dawn began/begins to break; **in der ~** at dusk/dawn

Dämmerzustand M (= Halbschlaf) dozy state; (= Bewusstseinstrübung) dopey state

dämmrig ['dɛmrɪç] ADJ = **dämmerig**

Dämmstoffe PL insulating materials pl

Dämmung ['dɛmʊŋ] F **-, -en** insulation

Dammweg M causeway

Damnum ['damnʊm] NT **-s, Damna** [-na] (Fin) debt discount

Dämon ['dɛːmɔn] M **-s, Dämonen** [dɛ'moːnən] demon; **ein böser ~** an evil spirit

dämonisch [dɛ'moːnɪʃ] 🄵 ADJ demonic 🄶 ADV demonically

Dampf [dampf] M **-(e)s, -̈e** ['dɛmpfə] vapour (Brit), vapor (US); (= Wasserdampf) steam; **~ ablassen** (lit, fig) to let off steam; **unter ~ sein** or **stehen** to have (its) steam up; **jdm ~ machen** (inf) to make sb get a move on (inf)

Dampf- IN CPDS steam; **Dampfantrieb** M steam drive; **Maschine mit ~** steam-driven engine; **Dampfbad** NT steam bath; **Dampfbügeleisen** NT steam iron

dampfen ['dampfn] VI **(a)** (= Dampf abgeben) to steam; (Badezimmer etc) to be full of steam **(b)** AUX SEIN (Zug, Schiff) to steam

dämpfen ['dɛmpfn] VT **(a)** (= abschwächen) to muffle; Geige, Trompete, Farbe to mute; Licht, Stimme to lower; Freude, Begeisterung, Stimmung to dampen; Aufprall to deaden; (fig) jdn to subdue; Konjunktur to depress; siehe auch **gedämpft (b)** (Cook) to steam

Dampfer ['dampfɐ] M **-s, -** steamer; **auf dem falschen ~ sein** or **sitzen** (fig inf) to have got the wrong idea

Dämpfer ['dɛmpfɐ] M **-s, -** (Mus: bei Klavier) damper; (bei Geige, Trompete) mute; **dadurch hat er/sein Optimismus einen ~ bekommen** that dampened his spirits/optimism; **jdm einen ~ aufsetzen** to dampen sb's spirits; **einer Sache** (dat) **einen ~ aufsetzen** (inf) to put a damper on sth (inf)

dampfig ['dampfɪç] ADJ steamy

Dampf-: Dampfkochtopf M pressure cooker; **Dampfkraft** F steam power; **Dampflokomotive** F, **Dampflok** F (inf) steam engine; **Dampfmaschine** F steam(-driven) engine; **Dampfnudel** F (Cook) sweet yeast dumpling cooked in milk and sugar; **aufgehen wie eine ~** (fig inf) to blow up like a balloon (inf); **Dampfschiff** NT steamship; **Dampfschifffahrt** F steam navigation; **Dampfturbine** F steam turbine; **Dampfwalze** F steamroller

danach [da'naːx, (emph) 'daːnaːx] ADV **(a)** (zeitlich) after that/it; (= nachher auch) afterwards; **ich las das Buch zu Ende, erst ~ konnte ich einschlafen** only when I had finished reading the book could I get to sleep; **zehn Minuten ~ war sie schon wieder da** ten minutes later she was back **(b)** (in der Reihenfolge) (örtlich) behind (that/it/him/them etc; (zeitlich) after that/it/him/them etc; **als Erster ging der Engländer durchs Ziel und gleich ~ der Russe** the Englishman finished first, immediately followed by the Russian; **bei ihm kommt als Erstes die Arbeit, ~ lange nichts und dann das Privatleben** work comes first with him, and then, a long, long way behind, his private life **(c)** (= dementsprechend) accordingly; (= laut diesem) according to that; (= im Einklang damit) in accordance with that/it; **sie hat den Aufsatz in zehn Minuten geschrieben – ~ ist er auch** (inf) she wrote the essay in ten minutes – it looks like it too; **sie sieht auch/nicht ~ aus** she looks/doesn't look (like) it; (= als ob sie so was getan hätte) she looks/doesn't look the type; **~ siehst du gerade aus** (iro) I can just see that (iro); **lesen Sie Paragraph 218; ~ ist es verboten** read paragraph 218, under that it is illegal; **~ zu urteilen** judging by that; **mir war nicht ~** (inf) or **~ zumute** or **zu Mute** I didn't feel like it

(d) (in bestimmte Richtung) toward(s) it; **er griff schnell ~** he grabbed at it

(e) (in Verbindung mit n, vb etc siehe auch dort) **sie sehnte sich ~** she longed for that/it; **er hatte großes Verlangen ~, wieder einmal die Heimat zu sehen** he felt a great desire to see his home again; **~ kann man nicht gehen** you can't go by that; **wenn es ~ ginge, was ich sage/was mir Spaß macht, dann ...** if it were a matter of what I say/enjoy then ...; **sich ~ erkundigen, ob ...** to inquire whether ...

Däne ['dɛ:nə] M **-n, -n** Dane

daneben [da'ne:bn, (emph) 'da:ne:bn] ADV **(a)** (räumlich) (= in unmittelbarer Nähe von jdm/etw) next to him/her/that/it etc; (zum Vergleich) beside him/her/that/it etc; **links/rechts ~** (neben Sache) to the left/right of it; (neben Mensch) to his/her etc left/right; **wir wohnen im Haus ~** we live in the house next door **(b)** (= verglichen damit) in comparison **(c)** (= außerdem) besides that; (= gleichzeitig) at the same time

daneben-: danebenbenehmen ptp **danebenbenommen** VR SEP IRREG (inf) to make an exhibition of oneself; **danebengehen** VI SEP IRREG AUX SEIN **(a)** (Schuss etc) to miss **(b)** (inf: = scheitern) to go wrong; (Witz) to fall flat; **danebengreifen** VI SEP IRREG **(a)** (beim Fangen) to miss (the mark) **(b)** (fig inf: mit Schätzung, Prognose etc) to be wide of the mark; **im Ton ~** to strike the wrong note; **im Ausdruck ~** to put things the wrong way; **mit seiner Bemerkung hat er aber ganz schön danebengegriffen** he really put his foot in it with that remark (inf); **danebenhalten** VT SEP IRREG **jdn/etw** ~ to compare him/her/it etc with sb/sth; **danebenhauen** VI SEP IRREG **(a)** (beim Schlagen) to miss **(b)** (fig inf: = sich irren) to be wide of the mark; **danebenliegen** VI SEP IRREG (inf: = sich irren) to be quite wrong; **danebenschießen** VI SEP IRREG **(a)** (= verfehlen) to miss **(b)** (= absichtlich vorbeischießen) to shoot to miss; **danebensein** VI IRREG AUX SEIN (inf) **(a)** (= verwirrt sein) to be completely confused; (= sich nicht wohl fühlen) not to feel up to it (inf) **(b)** (= unangebracht sein) to be out of order (inf); **danebentreffen** VI SEP IRREG to miss; **danebenzielen** VI SEP to aim to miss

Dänemark ['dɛ:nəmark] NT **-s** Denmark

Dänin ['dɛ:nɪn] F **-, -nen** Dane

dänisch ['dɛ:nɪʃ] ADJ Danish

dank [daŋk] PREP +GEN or DAT thanks to

Dank [daŋk] M **-(e)s**, NO PL (ausgedrückt) thanks pl; (= Gefühl der Dankbarkeit) gratitude; **besten** or **herzlichen** or **schönen** or **vielen ~** thank you very much, thanks a lot (inf); **vielen herzlichen/tausend ~!** many/very many thanks!; **~ sagen** (Aus) to express one's thanks; (Eccl) to give thanks; **jdm ~ schulden** (form) to owe sb a debt of gratitude; **mit bestem ~ zurück!** many thanks for lending it/them to me; (iro: = Retourkutsche) thank you, the same to you!; **das ist der (ganze) ~ dafür** that's all the thanks one gets; **als ~ für seine Dienste** in grateful recognition of his service; **zum ~ (dafür)** as a way of saying thank you

dankbar [1] ADJ **(a)** (= dankerfüllt) grateful; (= erleichtert, froh) thankful; Publikum, Zuhörer appreciative; **jdm ~ sein** to be grateful to sb (für for); **sich ~ erweisen** or **zeigen** to show one's gratitude (gegenüber to); **ich wäre dir ~, wenn du ...** I would appreciate it if you ... **(b)** (= lohnend) Arbeit, Aufgabe, Rolle rewarding [2] ADV (= voller Dank) gratefully

Dankbarkeit ['daŋkba:rkait] F **-**, NO PL gratitude (gegen, gegenüber to)

Dankbrief M thank-you letter

danke ['daŋkə] INTERJ **(a)** thank you, thanks (inf); (ablehnend) no thank you; **~ ja, ja, ~** yes please, yes, thank you; **~ nein, nein, ~** no thank you; **~ schön** or **sehr** thanks very much (inf); **(zu jdm) ~ (schön) sagen** to say thank you (to sb); **~ vielmals** many thanks; (iro) thanks a million (inf); **wie gehts? – ~, ich kann nicht klagen** how's it going? – (I) can't complain **(b)** (inf) **mir gehts ~** I'm OK (inf); **sonst gehts dir (wohl) ~!** (iro) are you feeling all right?

danken ['daŋkn] [1] VI **(a)** (= Dankbarkeit zeigen) to express one's thanks; **jdm ~** to thank sb (für for); **ich danke dir für das Geschenk/die Gastfreundschaft etc** thank you for your or the present/your hospitality etc; **(ich) danke!** yes please; (ablehnend) no thanks (inf); **(ich) danke bestens** (iro) thanks

for nothing (inf); **man dankt** (inf) thanks (inf); **jdm ~ lassen** to send sb one's thanks; **bestellen Sie bitte Ihrem Vater, ich lasse herzlich ~** please give your father my thanks; **nichts zu ~** don't mention it; **na, ich danke** (iro) no thank you; **etw ~ annehmen/ablehnen** to accept/decline sth with thanks **(b)** (= ablehnen) to decline

[2] VT **(a)** (geh: = verdanken) **jdm/einer Sache etw ~** to owe sth to sb/sth; **nur dem rechtzeitigen Erscheinen der Polizei ist es zu ~, dass ...** it was only thanks to the prompt turnout of the police that ...

(b) (= dankbar sein für) **jdm etw ~** to thank sb for sth; **man wird es dir nicht ~** you won't be thanked for it; **man wird es nicht zu ~ wissen** it won't be appreciated; **man hat es mir schlecht gedankt, dass ich das getan habe** I didn't get a lot of thanks for doing it

dankenswert ADJ Bemühung, Hingabe commendable; Hilfe kind; (= lohnenswert) Aufgabe, Arbeit rewarding; **in ~er Weise** (= löblich) (most) commendably; (= freundlicherweise) very kindly

dankenswerterweise ['daŋksve:ɐtə'vaizə] ADV thankfully; **Herr Kopleck hat uns ~ informiert** Mr Kopleck was kind enough to inform us

Dankeschön NT **-s**, NO PL thank you

Dankschreiben NT letter of thanks

dann [dan] ADV **(a)** (Reihenfolge ausdrückend, = später) then; **und ~** (a)round about then; **von ~ bis** for some time (a)round then; **und wann** now and then; **gerade ~, wenn ...** just when ...; **wenn das gemacht ist, ~ kannst du gehen** when that's done you can go

(b) (= unter diesen Umständen) then; **wenn ..., ~** if ..., (then); **selbst ~/selbst ~ nicht, wenn ...** even/not even if ...; **erst ~, wenn ...** only when ...; **ja, ~!** (oh) well then!; **ich habe keine Lust mehr – ~ hör doch auf!** I'm not in the mood any more – well stop then!; **und wie es ~ so geht or ist, kommt natürlich Besuch** and you know how it is, I got visitors; **~ eben nicht** well, in that case (there's no more to be said); **~ erst recht nicht!** in that case no way (inf); **~ ist ja alles in Ordnung** (oh well,) everything's all right then; **ja ~, auf Wiedersehen** well then, goodbye; **also ~ bis morgen** see you tomorrow then **(c)** (= außerdem) **~ ... noch** on top of that; **strohdumm und ~ auch noch frech** as thick as they come and cheeky into the bargain (Brit), as dumb as they come and a smart alec too (esp US); **kommandiert mich herum und meint ~ auch noch ...** orders me around and then on top of that thinks ...

daran [da'ran, (emph) 'da:ran] ADV **(a)** (räumlich) on it/that; schieben, lehnen, stellen against it/that; legen next to it/that; kleben, befestigen, machen, gehen to it/that; **sich setzen** at it/that; **nahe** or **dicht ~** right up against it; **nahe ~ sein, etw zu tun** or to be on the point of doing sth; **zu nahe ~** too close (to it); **~ vorbei** past it; **er hat dicht ~ vorbeigeschossen** his shot just missed it; **~ kommen** or **fassen/riechen/schlagen** to touch/smell/hit it/that

(b) (zeitlich) **im Anschluss ~, ~ anschließend** following that/this; **im Anschluss ~ findet eine Diskussion statt** it/this/that will be followed by a discussion

(c) (inf) **sie ist schlecht ~** she's in a bad way (inf); **sie ist gut ~** she's OK (inf); **ich weiß nie, wie ich (bei ihm) ~ bin** I never know where I am with him; **sie sind sehr arm ~** (= haben wenig Geld) they're not at all well-off; (= sind bedauernswert) they are poor creatures

(d) (in Verbindung mit n, adj, vb siehe auch dort) arbeiten on it/that; sterben, erinnern, Bedarf, Mangel of it/that; interessieren, sich beteiligen, arm, reich in it/that; sich klammern to it/that; **sticken/bauen** to embroider/build it/that; **was macht der Aufsatz? – ich bin zur Zeit ~** how's the essay doing? – I'm (working) on it now; **ich zweifle nicht ~** I don't doubt it; **ich zweifle nicht ~, dass ...** I don't doubt that ...; **wir haben großen Anteil ~ genommen** we sympathized deeply; **wird sich etwas ~ ändern?** will that change at all?; **~ sieht man, wie ...** there you (can) see how ...; **das Beste/Schönste/Schlimmste etc ~** the best/nicest/worst etc thing about it; **es ist nichts ~** (= ist nicht fundiert) there's nothing in it; (= ist nichts Besonderes) it's nothing special; siehe auch **dran**

daran-: darangehen VI SEP IRREG AUX SEIN to set about it; **~, etw zu tun** to set about doing sth; **daranmachen** VR SEP (inf) to set about it; (= endlich in Angriff nehmen) to get down to it; **sich ~, etw zu tun** to set about doing it; **daransetzen** SEP [1] VT (= einsetzen) to exert; (= aufs Spiel setzen) to stake; **seine**

ganzen Kräfte ~, **etw zu tun** to spare no effort to do sth **2** VR to sit down to it

darauf ['daːrauf, (emph) 'daːrauf] ADV **(a)** (räumlich) on it/that/ them etc; (in Richtung) toward(s) it/that/them etc; **schießen, zielen, losfahren** at it/that/them etc; (fig) **fußen, basieren, aufbauen** on it/that; **zurückführen, beziehen** to it/that; **er schlug mit dem Hammer ~** he hit it with the hammer; **seine Behauptungen stützen sich ~, dass der Mensch von Natur aus gut ist** his claims are based on the supposition that man is naturally good
(b) (Reihenfolge: zeitlich, örtlich) after that; **die Tage, die ~ folgten** the days which followed; **~ folgte ...** that was followed by ...; **~ folgend** after him/it/that etc; Tag etc following; Wagen etc behind pred; **am Tag/Abend/Jahr ~** the next day/evening/year
(c) (= infolgedessen) because of that
(d) (als Reaktion) **sagen, reagieren** to that; **~ antworten** to answer that; **eine Antwort ~** an answer to that; **~ wurde er ganz beschämt** that made him feel quite ashamed; **~ haben sich viele Interessenten gemeldet** a lot of people have shown an interest in it/that; **~ steht die Todesstrafe** that carries the death penalty
(e) (in Verbindung mit n, adj, vb siehe auch dort) **bestehen, verlassen, wetten, Zeit/Mühe verschwenden, Einfluss** on that/it; **hoffen, warten, sich vorbereiten, gefasst sein, reinfallen** for that/ it; **trinken** to that/it; **stolz sein** of that/it; **ich bestehe ~, dass du kommst** I insist that you come; **ich möchte ~ hinweisen, dass ...** I would like to point out that ...; **~ freuen wir uns schon** we're looking forward to it already; **~ willst du hinaus!** that's what you're getting at!; **er war nur ~ aus** he was only interested in that; **er war nur ~ aus, möglichst viel Geld zu verdienen** he was only interested in earning as much money as possible

darauffolgend ADJ ATTR siehe **darauf (b)**

daraufhin ['darauf'hɪn, (emph) 'daːraufhɪn] ADV **(a)** (= aus diesem Anlass, deshalb) as a result (of that/this); (= danach) after that, thereupon; **(b)** (= im Hinblick darauf) with regard to that/this; **wir müssen es ~ prüfen, ob es für unsere Zwecke geeignet ist** we must test it with a view to whether it is suitable for our purposes

daraus [da'raus, (emph) 'daːraus] ADV **(a)** (räumlich) out of that/it/ them; ~ **kann man nicht trinken!** you can't drink out of that/ it! **(b)** (= aus diesem Material etc) from that/it/them; ~ **kann man Wein herstellen** you can make wine from that **(c)** (= aus dieser Sache, Beziehung) from that/it/them; ~ **ergibt sich/ folgt, dass ...** it follows from that that ...

darbieten ['daːr-] VT SEP IRREG (geh) **(a)** (= vorführen) Tänze, Schauspiel to perform; (= vortragen) Lehrstoff to present **(b)** (= anbieten) etwer; Speisen to serve

Darbietung ['daːr-] F -, -en (= das Darbieten) performance; (= das Dargebotene) act

darf [darf] 3. PERS SING PRES von **dürfen**

darin [da'rɪn, (emph) 'daːrɪn] ADV **(a)** (räumlich) in there; (wenn Bezugsobjekt vorher erwähnt) in it/them **(b)** (= in dieser Beziehung) in that respect; **~ ist er ganz groß** (inf) he's very good at that; **die beiden unterscheiden sich ~, dass ...** the two of them differ in that ...; **~ liegt der Unterschied** that is where the difference is; **der Unterschied liegt ~, dass ...** the difference is that ...; **wir stimmen ~ überein, dass ...** we agree that ...

darlegen ['daːr-] VT SEP to explain (jdm to sb)

Darlehen ['daːrleːən] NT -s, - loan; **als ~** as a loan

Darlehens-: Darlehensgeber(in) M(F) lender; **Darlehenskonto** NT loan account; **Darlehensnehmer(in)** M(F) borrower; **Darlehensschuld** F loan; **Darlehenssumme** F **die ~** the amount of the/a loan; **eine ~** a loan

Darm [darm] M -(e)s, ⁿe ['dɛrmə] intestine(s pl), bowel(s pl); (für Wurst) (sausage) skin; (für Saiten, Schläger etc) gut

Darm- IN CPDS intestinal; **Darmausgang** M anus; **Darmentleerung** F evacuation of the bowels; **Darmgrippe** F gastric flu; **Darmkrebs** M cancer of the intestine; **Darmleiden** NT intestinal trouble no art; **Darmsaite** F gut string; **Darmtätigkeit** F peristalsis no art; **die ~ fördern/regulieren** to stimulate/regulate the movement of the bowels

darstellbar ['daːr-] ADJ portrayable; (durch Diagramm etc) representable; **schwer/leicht ~** hard/easy to portray/show;

dieses Phänomen ist grafisch ~ this phenomenon can be shown on a graph

darstellen ['daːr-] VT SEP **(a)** (= abbilden) to show; (= ein Bild entwerfen von, Theat) to portray; (= beschreiben) to describe; **etw kurz** or **knapp ~** to give a short description of sth; **die ~den Künste** (= Theater) the dramatic arts; (= Malerei, Plastik) the visual arts; **sie stellt etwas/nichts dar** (fig) she has a certain air/doesn't have much of an air about her **(b)** (= bedeuten) to constitute

Darsteller ['daːrʃtɛlɐ] M -s, - (Theat) actor; **der ~ des Hamlet** the actor playing Hamlet

Darstellerin ['daːrʃtɛlərɪn] F -, -nen (Theat) actress

darstellerisch ['daːrʃtɛlərɪʃ] **1** ADJ dramatic; **eine ~e Höchstleistung** a magnificent piece of acting **2** ADV in terms of acting; **~ war die Weber der Klein weit überlegen** as an actress Weber was much superior to Klein

Darstellung ['daːr-] F portrayal; (durch Diagramm etc) representation; (= Beschreibung) description; (= Bericht) account; **an den Wänden fand man ~en der Heldentaten des Königs** on the walls one could see the King's heroic deeds depicted; **eine falsche ~ der Fakten** a misrepresentation of the facts

Darts [daːts] NT -, NO PL darts sing

darüber [da'ryːbɐ, (emph) 'daːryːbɐ] ADV **(a)** (räumlich) over that/ it/them; (= quer ~) across or over there; (wenn Bezugsobjekt vorher erwähnt) across or over it/them; (= höher als etw) above (there/it/them); (= direkt auf etw) on top (of it/them); ~ **hinweg sein** (fig) to have got over it; **~ hinaus** apart from this/ that; **~ hinaus kann ich nichts sagen** over and above that I can't say anything; **~ hinaus log sie mich auch noch an** on top of that she also lied to me
(b) (= deswegen, in dieser Beziehung) about that/it; **sich ~ beschweren/beklagen** etc to complain/moan etc about it; **sich ~ beschweren/beklagen** etc, **dass ...** to complain/moan etc that ...; **wir wollen nicht ~ streiten, ob ...** we don't want to argue about whether ...
(c) (= davon) about that/it; **Rechenschaft ~ ablegen** to account for it; **sie führt eine Liste ~** she keeps a list of it **(d)** (= währenddessen) in the meantime
(e) (= mehr, höher) above that; **21 Jahre/4 Euro und ~** 21 years/4 euros and above; **~ hinaus** over and above that; **es geht nichts ~** there is nothing to beat it

darüber: darüber fahren VI IRREG AUX SEIN (fig) to run over it; **wenn du mit der Hand darüber fährst, ...** if you run your hand over it ...; **darüber liegen** VI IRREG (fig) to be higher; **darüber schreiben** VT IRREG to write above it; **darüber stehen** VI IRREG (fig) to be above such things

darum [da'rʊm, (emph) 'daːrʊm] ADV **(a)** (räumlich) (a)round that/it/him/her/them; **~ herum** (a)round about (it/him/her/ them)
(b) (= um diese Angelegenheit) (in Verbindung mit n, vb siehe auch dort) **es geht ~, dass ...** the thing is that ...; **~ geht es gar nicht** that isn't the point; **~ geht es** that is what it is about; **~ geht es mir** that's my point; **~ geht es mir nicht** that's not the point for me; **es geht mir ~, Ihnen das klarzumachen** I'm trying to make it clear to you; **wir kommen leider nicht ~ herum, die Preise heraufzusetzen** unfortunately we cannot avoid raising prices; **wir wollen nicht lange ~ herumreden** we don't want to spend a long time talking around the subject; **ich habe ihn schon ein paar Mal ~ gebeten, aber ...** I've asked him a few times (for it/to do it), but ...
(c) (= deshalb) that's why, because ...; **~, dass** or **weil ...** because ...; **eben ~** that is exactly why; **ach ~!** so that's why!; **~?** because of that?; **warum willst du nicht mitkommen? – ~!** (inf) why don't you want to come? – (just) 'cos! (inf); siehe auch **drum**

darunter [da'rʊntɐ, (emph) 'daːrʊntɐ] ADV **(a)** (räumlich) under that/it/them; (= niedriger als etw) below (that/it/them); **~ hervorkommen** to appear from underneath
(b) (= weniger) under that; **Leute im Alter von 35 Jahren und ~** people aged 35 and under; **~ macht sies nicht** (inf) she won't do it for less
(c) (= dabei) among them
(d) (= unter dieser Angelegenheit) (in Verbindung mit n, vb siehe auch dort) **was verstehen Sie ~?** what do you understand by that/it?; **~ kann ich mir nichts vorstellen** that doesn't mean anything to me; siehe auch **drunter**

darunter: **darunter bleiben** VI IRREG AUX SEIN (*fig*) to be lower; **Sie kennen die Anforderungen, wenn Sie mit** *or* **in Ihrer Leistung ~, werden Sie entlassen** you are aware of the requirements, if you fail to meet them you will be dismissed; **darunter fallen** VI IRREG AUX SEIN (*fig*) (= *dazugerechnet werden*) to be included; (= *davon betroffen werden*) to come under it/them; **darunter mischen** [8] VT *Mehl etc* to mix in [2] VR (*Mensch*) to mingle with them

das [das] *siehe* **der²**

da sein VI IRREG AUX SEIN (*lit, fig inf*) to be there; **noch ~** to be still there; **wieder ~** to be back; **sind Sie schon lange da?** have you been here/there long?; **ist Post/sind Besucher für mich da?** is there any mail/are there visitors for me?; **war der Briefträger schon da?** has the postman (*Brit*) *or* mailman (*US*) been yet?; **für jdn ~** to be there for sb; **ein Arzt, der immer für seine Patienten da ist** a doctor who always has time for his patients; **voll ~** (*inf*) to be all there (*inf*); **so etwas ist noch nie da gewesen** it's quite unprecedented; **es ist alles schon mal da gewesen** it's all been done before; **das übertrifft alles bisher da Gewesene** that beats everything; **ein nie da gewesener Erfolg** an unprecedented success

Dasein NT existence; (= *das Anwesendsein*) presence

Daseinsberechtigung F right to exist; **hat die UNO noch eine ~?** can the UN still justify its existence?

dasitzen VI SEP IRREG AUX HABEN or SEIN to sit there; **ohne Hilfe/einen Pfennig ~** (*inf*) to be left without any help/without a penny (*Brit*) *or* cent (*US*)

dasjenige [dasjeːnɪgə] DEM PRON *siehe* **derjenige**

dass [das] CONJ that; **ich bin überzeugt, ~ du das Richtige getan hast** I'm sure (that) you have done the right thing; **ich sehe nicht ein, ~ wir hungern sollen** I don't see why we should starve; **angenommen/vorausgesetzt, ~ ...** given/provided that ...; **das kommt daher, ~ ...** that comes because ...; **das liegt daran, ~ ...** that is because ...; **er verbringt seine Freizeit damit, ~ er Rosen züchtet** he spends his free time breeding roses

dasselbe [dasˈzɛlbə] DEM PRON *siehe* **derselbe**

dastehen VI SEP IRREG AUX HABEN or SEIN **(a)** (= *da sein*) to stand there; **steh nicht so dumm da!** don't just stand there looking stupid **(b)** (*fig*) **anders/glänzend/gut/schlecht ~** to be in a different/splendid/good/bad position; **allein ~** to be on one's own; **jetzt stehe ich ohne Mittel/als Lügner da** now I'm left with no money/looking like a liar; **wenn die Sache schief geht, stehst du dumm da** if things go wrong you'll be left looking stupid

DAT [deːlaːˈteː, dat] NT **-, -s** DAT

Datei [daˈtai] F **-, -en** (*Comput*) file

Datei- IN CPDS file; **Dateiattribut** NT file attribute; **Dateiendung** F, **Dateierweiterung** F file extension; **Dateimanager** M file manager; **Dateiname** M file name; **Dateiverwaltung** F file management; **Dateiverwaltungsprogramm** NT file manager; **Dateiverzeichnis** NT directory

Daten [ˈdaːtn] **(a)** PL *von* **Datum (b)** PL (*Comput*) data *sing*

Daten- IN CPDS data; **Datenaufbereitung** F data preparation; **Datenaustausch** M data exchange; **Datenautobahn** F information highway; **Datenbank** F, *pl* **-banken** database; (= *Zentralstelle*) data bank; **Datenbankverwaltung** F database management; **Datenbestand** M database; **Dateneingabe** F data input; **Datenerfassung** F data capture; **Datenfernübertragung** F data transmission; **Datenfernverarbeitung** F teleprocessing; **Datenklau** [-klau] M **-s, -s** (*inf*) theft of data; **Datenkompressionsprogramm** NT data compression program; **Datenmissbrauch** M misuse of data; **Datenmüll** M (*aus dem Internet*) Internet buildup; (*auf Festplatte*) hard disk clutter; **Datensatz** M record; **Datenschrott** M (*inf*) rubbish data; **Datenschutz** M data protection; **Datenschutzbeauftragte(r)** MF DECL AS ADJ data protection official; **Datenschützer** [-ˌʃʏtsɐ] M **-s, -**, **Datenschützerin** [-ərɪn] F **-, -nen** data protectionist; **Datenschutzgesetz** NT data protection act; **Datensicherung** F data storage; **Datenträger** M data carrier; **Datenträgeraustausch** M data carrier exchange; **Datentypist** [-typɪst] M **-en, -en**, **Datentypistin** [-pɪstɪn] F **-, -nen** keyboarder; **Datenübertragung** F data transmission; **Datenverarbeitung** F data processing

datieren [daˈtiːrən], *ptp* **datiert** VTI to date (*aus* from); **dieser Brief datiert vom 1. Januar** this letter is dated January 1st

Dativ [ˈdaːtiːf] M **-s, -e** [-və] (*Gram*) dative (case)

Dativobjekt NT (*Gram*) indirect object

DAT-Kassette [ˈdat-] F DAT *or* digital audio tape cassette

dato ADV **bis ~** (*Comm inf*) to date

Datowechsel M (*Comm*) time bill

DAT-Rekorder [ˈdat-] M DAT recorder

DAT-Streamer [ˈdat-] M DAT streamer

Dattel [ˈdatl] F **-, -n** date; **Dattelpalme** F date palm

Datum [ˈdaːtʊm] NT **-s, Daten** [ˈdaːtn] **(a)** date; **was für ein ~ haben wir heute?** what is the date today?; **das heutige/gestrige/morgige ~** today's/yesterday's/tomorrow's date; **etw mit dem ~ versehen** to date sth; **der Brief trägt das ~ vom 1. April** the letter is dated 1st April; **ein Brief ohne ~** an undated letter; **~ des Poststempels** date as postmark; **ein Nachschlagewerk neueren/älteren ~s** a recent/an old reference work **(b)** USU PL (= *Faktum*) fact; (= *statistische Zahlenangabe etc*) piece of data; **technische Daten** technical data *pl*

Dauer [ˈdauɐ] F **-**, NO PL (= *das Andauern*) duration; (= *Zeitspanne*) period; (= *Länge: einer Sendung etc*) length; **während der ~ des Vertrages/Krieges** for the duration of the contract/war; **für die ~ Ihres Aufenthaltes in unserem Hause** for the duration of your stay with us (*form*); **für die ~ eines Monats** *or* **von einem Monat** for a period of one month; **ein Gefängnisaufenthalt von zehnjähriger ~** a ten-year term of imprisonment; **von ~ sein** to be long-lasting; **keine ~ haben** to be short-lived; **von langer ~ sein** to last a long time; **von kurzer ~ sein** not to last long; **auf die ~** in the long term; **auf ~** permanently

Dauer- IN CPDS permanent; **Dauerarbeitslose(r)** MF DECL AS ADJ long-term unemployed person; **die ~n** the long-term unemployed; **Dauerauftrag** M (*Fin*) standing order; **Dauerbelastung** F continual pressure *no indef art*; (*von Maschine*) constant load; **Dauerbetrieb** M continuous operation; **Dauerbrenner** M (*inf*) (= *Dauererfolg*) long runner; (= *Dauerthema*) long-running issue; (*hum* = *Kuss*) long passionate kiss; **Dauerfrost** M freeze-up; **Dauerfrostboden** M permafrost; **Dauergast** M permanent guest; (= *häufiger Gast*) regular visitor

dauerhaft [8] ADJ *Zustand, Einrichtung, Farbe* permanent; *Bündnis, Frieden, Beziehung* lasting *attr*, long-lasting [2] ADV (= *für immer*) permanently; **durch eine Impfung sind Sie ~ geschützt** one vaccination gives you lasting immunity

Dauer-: **Dauerkarte** F season ticket; **Dauerlauf** M (*Sport*) jog; (= *das Laufen*) jogging; **Dauerlutscher** M lollipop

dauern [ˈdauɐn] VI **(a)** (= *andauern*) to last; **die Verhandlungen ~ schon drei Wochen** the negotiations have already been going on for three weeks **(b)** (= *Zeit benötigen*) to take a while; (*lange*) to take a long time; **das dauert noch** (*inf*) it'll be a while yet; **warum dauert das Anziehen bei dir immer so lange?** why do you always take so long to get dressed?; **es dauerte lange, bis er sich befreit hatte** it took him a long time to get free; **das dauert mir zu lange** it takes too long for me; **das dauert und dauert** (*inf*) it takes forever (*inf*); **es dauert jetzt nicht mehr lange** it won't take much longer; **das dauert heute vielleicht wieder einmal** (*inf*) it's taking ages again today (*inf*)

dauernd [8] ADJ (= *anhaltend*) *Frieden, Regelung* lasting; (= *ständig*) *Wohnsitz, Ausstellung* permanent; (= *fortwährend*) constant [2] ADV **etw ~ tun** to keep doing sth; (*stärker*) to be always *or* forever (*inf*) doing sth; **sie musste ~ auf die Toilette** she had to keep going to the toilet (*Brit*) *or* bathroom (*esp US*)

Dauer-: **Dauerparker** [-ˌparkɐ] M **-s, -**, **Dauerparkerin** [-ərɪn] F **-nen** long-stay (*Brit*) *or* long-term (*US*) parker; **Parkplatz für ~** long-stay car park (*Brit*), long-term parking lot (*US*); **Dauerregen** M continuous rain; **Dauersitzung** F prolonged session; **Dauerstellung** F permanent position; **in ~ beschäftigt** employed on a permanent basis; **Dauerstress** M **im ~ sein** to be in a state of permanent stress; **Dauertest** M long-term test; **Dauerthema** NT long-running issue; **Dauerwelle** F perm; **Dauerwirkung** F (long-)lasting effect; **Dauerwohnrecht** NT permanent right of tenure; **Dauerwurst** F German salami; **Dauerzustand** M permanent state of affairs; **ich möchte das nicht zum ~ werden lassen** I don't want that to become permanent

Däumchen ['dɔʏmçən] NT **-s, -** (*inf*) **~ drehen** to twiddle one's thumbs; **und da mussten wir ~ drehen** and we were left twiddling our thumbs

Daumen ['daumən] M **-s, -** thumb; **am ~ lutschen** to suck one's thumb; **jdm** *or* **für jdn die ~ drücken** *or* **halten** to keep one's fingers crossed for sb

Daumen-: Daumenkino NT flicker book; **Daumenlutscher(in)** M(F) thumb-sucker; **Daumennagel** M thumbnail; **Daumenregister** NT thumb index; **Daumenschraube** F (*Hist*) thumbscrew; **jdm die ~n anlegen** (*lit, fig inf*) to put the (thumb)screws on sb

Däumling ['dɔʏmlɪŋ] M **-s, -e (a)** (*im Märchen*) **der ~** Tom Thumb **(b)** (*von Handschuh*) thumb; (*Med*) thumbstall

Daune ['daunə] F **-, -n** down feather; **~n** down *sing*

Daunen-: Daunenbett NT, **Daunendecke** F (down-filled) duvet (*Brit*) *or* quilt; **Daunenjacke** F quilted jacket

David(s)stern ['da:fɪt(s)-, 'da:vɪt(s)-] M star of David

Daviscup ['de:vɪskap] M, **Davispokal** ['de:vɪs-] M Davis cup

davon [da'fɔn, (*emph*) 'da:fɔn] ADV **(a)** (*räumlich*) from there; (*wenn Bezugsobjekt vorher erwähnt*) from it/them; (*mit Entfernungsangabe*) away (from there/it/them); **~ zweigt ein Weg ab** a path branches off it

(b) (*fig*) (*in Verbindung mit n, vb siehe auch dort*) **es unterscheidet sich ~ nur in der Länge** it only differs from it in the length; **nein, weit ~ entfernt!** no, far from it!; **ich bin weit ~ entfernt, Ihnen Vorwürfe machen zu wollen** the last thing I want to do is reproach you; **wenn wir einmal ~ absehen, dass ...** if for once we overlook the fact that ...; **in ihren Berechnungen sind sie ~ ausgegangen, dass ...** they made their calculations on the basis that ...

(c) (*fig*: = *dadurch*) *leben, abhängen* on that/it/them; *sterben* of that/it; *krank/braun werden* from that/it/them; **... und ~ kommt das hohe Fieber** ... and that's where the high temperature comes from; **das kommt ~!** that's what you get; **~ stirbst du nicht** it won't kill you; **was habe ICH denn ~?** what do I get out of it?; **was HABE ich denn ~?** why should I?; **was hast du denn ~, dass du so schuftest?** what do you get out of slaving away like that?

(d) (*mit Passiv*) by that/it/them; **~ betroffen werden** *or* **sein** to be affected by that/it/them

(e) (*Anteil, Ausgangsstoff*) of that/it/them; **~ essen/trinken/ nehmen** to eat/drink/take some of that/it/them; **nehmen Sie doch noch etwas ~!** do have some more!; **er hat drei Schwestern, ~ sind zwei älter als er** he has three sisters, two of whom are older than he is

(f) (= *darüber*) *hören, wissen, sprechen* about that/it/them; *verstehen, halten* of that/it/them; **genug ~!** enough of this!; **nichts mehr ~!** no more of that!; **nichts ~ halten** not to think much of it; **ich halte viel ~** I think it is quite good

davon-: davonfahren VI SEP IRREG AUX SEIN (*Fahrer, Fahrzeug*) to drive away; (*auf Fahrrad etc*) to ride away; (*Zug*) to pull away; **jdm ~** to pull away from sb; **davonfliegen** VI SEP IRREG AUX SEIN to fly away; **davonkommen** VI SEP IRREG AUX SEIN (= *entkommen*) to get away; (= *nicht bestraft werden*) to get away with it; (= *freigesprochen werden*) to get off; **mit dem Schrecken/dem Leben ~** to escape with no more than a shock/with one's life; **mit einer Geldstrafe ~** to get off with a fine; **davonlassen** VT SEP IRREG **die Hände** *or* **Finger ~** (*inf*) to leave it/them well alone; **du sollst die Hände** *or* **Finger ~** keep your hands *or* fingers off (it/them); **davonlaufen** VI SEP IRREG AUX SEIN **(a)** (= *weglaufen*) to run away (*jdm/vor jdm* from sb); (= *verlassen*) to walk out (*jdm* on sb); **es ist zum Davonlaufen!** (*inf*) it's all too much! **(b)** (= *außer Kontrolle geraten*) to get out of hand; **davonmachen** VR SEP to make off; **davonrennen** VI SEP IRREG AUX SEIN (*inf*) = **davonlaufen (a)**; **davonschwimmen** VI SEP IRREG AUX SEIN **jdm ~** to outswim sb; **davontragen** VT SEP IRREG (= *erringen*) *Preis* to carry off; *Sieg, Ruhm* to win; *Schaden, Verletzung* to suffer

davor [da'fo:ɐ, (*emph*) 'da:fo:ɐ] ADV **(a)** (*räumlich*) in front (of that/it/them); (*wenn Bezugsobjekt vorher erwähnt*) in front of it/them

(b) (*zeitlich*) before that; (= *bevor man etw tut*) beforehand

(c) (*in Verbindung mit n, vb siehe auch dort*) *bewahren, schützen* from that/it; *warnen* of *or* about that/it; *Angst haben* of that/ it; *sich ekeln* by that/it; **ich habe Angst ~, das zu tun** I'm afraid of doing that; **sein Ekel ~** his disgust of it; **ich warne Sie ~!** I

warn you!; **ich habe ihn ~ gewarnt, sich in Gefahr zu begeben** I warned him not to get into danger

davor: davor legen VT to put in front of it/them; **leg doch eine Kette davor** put a chain on it/them; **davor stehen** VI IRREG AUX HABEN *or* SEIN to stand in front of it/them; **davor stellen** ■ VT to put in front of it/them ② VR to stand in front of it/them

DAX® [daks] M **-, NO PL** ABBR *von* **Deutscher Aktienindex** DAX index

---

DAX

The **DAX** is the German share index, introduced in 1988 and comprising the 30 strongest German shares. Once a year the evaluation and selection of these shares is checked and, if necessary, updated.

---

dazu [da'tsu:, (*emph*) 'da:tsu:] ADV **(a)** (*räumlich*) there **(b)** (= *dabei, damit*) with it; **sie ist hübsch und ~ nicht unintelligent** she's pretty and not unintelligent either; **noch ~ as well, too; noch ~, wo ...** when ... too; **er singt und spielt Gitarre ~** he sings and accompanies himself on the guitar **(c)** (= *dahin*) to that/it; **auf dem besten Wege ~ sein, etw zu tun** to be well on the way to doing sth; **er ist auf dem besten Wege ~** he's well on the way to it; **das führt ~, dass weitere Forderungen gestellt werden** that will lead to further demands being made; **~ führt das dann** that's what it leads to; **wie konnte es nur ~ kommen?** how could that happen?; **wer weiß, wie sie ~ gekommen ist** (*zu diesem Auto etc*) who knows how she came by it; **wie komme ich ~?** (*empört*) why on earth should I?; **... aber ich bin nicht ~ gekommen ...** but I didn't get (a)round to it **(d)** (= *dafür, zu diesem Zweck*) for that/it; **ich habe ihm ~ geraten** I advised him to (do that); **~ fähig sein, etw zu tun** *or* **~ bereit sein, etw zu tun** to be capable of doing sth; **er war nicht ~ fähig/bereit** he wasn't capable of it/prepared to; **~ gehört viel Geld** that takes a lot of money; **~ ist er da** that's what he's there for; **die Erlaubnis/ die Mittel/das Recht ~** permission/the means/the right to do it **(e)** (= *darüber, zum Thema*) about that/it; **was sagst/meinst du ~?** what do you say to/think about that?; **..., ~ hören Sie jetzt einen Kommentar ...** we now bring you a commentary; **er hat sich nur kurz ~ geäußert** he only commented briefly on that/it **(f)** (*in Wendungen*) **im Gegensatz ~** in contrast to that; **im Vergleich ~** in comparison with that; **~ wird man nicht gewählt, sondern ernannt** one is appointed rather than elected to that

dazu-: dazugeben VT SEP IRREG to add; **dazugehören** ptp **dazugehört** VI SEP to belong (*to it/us etc*); (*als Ergänzung*) to go with it/them; (= *eingeschlossen sein*) to be included (in it/them); **bei einer Familienfeier gehört Onkel Otto auch dazu** Uncle Otto should be part of any family gathering too; **das gehört mit dazu** that belongs to/goes with/is included in it; (= *versteht sich von selbst*) it's all part of it; **es gehört schon einiges dazu** that takes a lot; **dazugehörig** ADJ ATTR which goes/go with it/them; *Schlüssel etc* belonging to it/them; *Werkzeuge, Material* necessary; **dazukommen** VI SEP IRREG AUX SEIN **(a)** (= *ankommen*) to arrive (on the scene); **er kam zufällig dazu** he happened to arrive on the scene **(b)** (= *hinzugefügt werden*) to be added; **es kamen noch mehrere Straftaten dazu** there were several other offences (*Brit*) *or* offenses (*US*); **kommt noch etwas dazu?** is there anything else?; **es kommt noch dazu, dass er faul ist** on top of that he's lazy **(c)** (*Aus, Sw*: = *Zeit dafür finden*) to get (a)round to it; **dazulernen** VT SEP **viel/nichts ~** to learn a lot more/nothing new; **man kann immer was ~** there's always something to learn; **schon wieder was dazugelernt!** you learn something (new) every day!; **dazurechnen** VT SEP **(a)** *Kosten, Betrag, Zahl* to add on **(b)** (= *mit berücksichtigen*) to consider also; **dazuschreiben** VT SEP IRREG to add; **dazusetzen** SEP ■ VT **(a)** **können wir den Jungen hier noch ~?** could the boy sit here too? **(b)** (= *dazuschreiben*) to add ② VR to join him/us *etc*; **komm, setz dich doch dazu** come and join us; **dazutun** VT SEP IRREG (*inf*) to add; **Dazutun** NT **er hat es ohne dein ~ geschafft** he managed it without your doing/saying anything; **ohne dein ~ hätte er es nicht geschafft** he wouldn't have managed it if you hadn't done/said something

dazwischen [daˈtsvɪʃn, (emph) ˈdaːtsvɪʃn] ADV (räumlich, zeitlich) in between; (in der betreffenden Menge, Gruppe) amongst them; **es hing nur ein Vorhang ~** there was only a curtain between them

dazwischen-: dazwischenfunken VI SEP (inf: = eingreifen) to put one's oar in (inf); (= etw vereiteln) to put a spoke in it (inf); **dazwischenkommen** VI SEP IRREG AUX SEIN **(a) mit der Hand/der Hose** etc ~ to get one's hand/trousers etc caught in it/them **(b)** (= störend erscheinen) to get in the way; **... wenn nichts dazwischenkommt!** ... if all goes well; **leider ist** or **mir ist leider etwas dazwischengekommen** something has come up; **dazwischenlegen** VT SEP to put in between; **dazwischenreden** VI SEP (= unterbrechen) to interrupt (jdm sb)

DB [deːˈbeː] F - ABBR von **Deutsche Bahn**

DCC [deːtseːˈtseː] F -, -s ABBR von **Digitale Compact Cassette** DCC®

DDR [deːdeːˈɛr] F - (Hist) ABBR von **Deutsche Demokratische Republik** GDR

DDR

DDR is the abbreviated name of the former East Germany (Deutsche Demokratische Republik). The DDR was created in 1949 out of the Soviet occupation zone in Germany and evolved into a Warsaw Pact state. Its economy, government and society were closely based on those of the Soviet Union.

In 1961 the DDR cut itself off even further from West Germany and the West in general with the construction of the Berlin Wall. By the end of the 1980s increasing numbers of civil rights groups were protesting against the harsh regime and were demanding reforms. The huge pressure exerted by this "velvet revolution" brought about the collapse of the economically weak socialist system in the autumn of 1989. On October 3rd 1990 Germany was re-unified and the DDR became part of the Bundesrepublik Deutschland. ▶ BRD

DDR-Bürger(in) [deːdeːˈɛr-] M(F) (Hist) East German

DDT® [deːdeːˈteː] NT - ABBR von **Dichlordiphenyltrichloräthan** DDT

deaktivieren ptp **deaktiviert** VT (Comput) to disable; Kontrollkästchen to uncheck

Deal [diːl] M -s, -s (inf) deal

dealen [ˈdiːlən] (inf) **1** VI **er dealt** he is a dealer; **mit etw ~** to deal in sth **2** VT to deal in; Drogen auch to push

Dealer [ˈdiːle] M -s, -, **Dealerin** [ˈdiːlərɪn] F -, -nen (inf) (drug) dealer

Debakel [deˈbaːkl] NT -s, - debacle

Debatte [deˈbatə] F -, -n debate; **etw in die ~ werfen** to throw sth into the discussion; **etw zur ~ stellen** to put sth up for discussion or (Parl) debate; **das steht hier nicht zur ~** that's not the issue; **sich in** or **auf eine ~ (über etw** acc**) einlassen** to enter into a discussion (about sth)

debattieren [debaˈtiːrən], ptp **debattiert** VTI to debate; **über etw** (acc) **(mit jdm) ~** to discuss sth (with sb); **mit ihm kann man schlecht ~** you can't have a good discussion with him

Debet [ˈdeːbet] NT -s, -s (Fin) debits pl

Debetseite F (Fin) debit side

debitieren [debiˈtiːrən], ptp **debitiert** VT (Fin) to debit

debuggen [diːˈbagn], ptp **debuggt** [diːˈbakt] VT (Comput) to debug

Debüt [deˈbyː] NT -s, -s debut; **sein ~ als etw geben** to make one's debut as sth

dechiffrieren [deʃiˈfriːrən], ptp **dechiffriert** VT to decode; Text, Geheimschrift auch to decipher

Deck [dɛk] NT -(e)s, -s deck; (in Parkhaus) level; **auf ~** on deck; **an ~ gehen** to go on deck; **alle Mann an ~!** all hands on deck!; **unter** or **von ~ gehen** to go below deck

Deckbett NT feather quilt

Deckchen [ˈdɛkçən] NT -s, - mat; (auf Tablett) tray cloth; (= Tortendeckchen) doily

Decke [ˈdɛkə] F -, -n **(a)** cloth; (= Wolldecke) blanket; (kleiner) rug; (= Steppdecke) quilt; (= Bettdecke) cover; **unter die ~ kriechen** to pull the bedcovers up over one's head; **mit jdm unter einer ~ stecken** (fig) to be in league with sb **(b)** (= Zimmerdecke) ceiling; (Min) roof; **an die ~ gehen** (inf) to hit the roof (inf); **mir fällt die ~ auf den Kopf** (fig inf) I don't like my own company **(c)** (= Schicht) layer

Deckel [ˈdɛkl] M -s, - lid; (von Schachtel, Glas auch, von Flasche) top; (= Buchdeckel, Uhrdeckel) cover; **eins auf den ~ kriegen** (inf) (= geschlagen werden) to get hit on the head; (= ausgeschimpft werden) to be given a (good) talking-to (inf); **jdm eins auf den ~ geben** (inf) (= schlagen) to hit sb on the head; (= ausschimpfen) to give sb a (good) talking-to (inf)

decken [ˈdɛkn] **1** VT **(a)** (= zudecken) to cover; **ein Dach mit Schiefer/Ziegeln ~** to roof a building with slate/tiles; **ein Dach mit Stroh/Reet ~** to thatch a roof (with straw/reeds); siehe auch **gedeckt**
(b) Tisch, Tafel to set; **sich an einen gedeckten Tisch setzen** (lit) to find one's meal ready and waiting; (fig) to be handed everything on a plate
(c) (= breiten) **die Hand/ein Tuch über etw** (acc) **~** to cover sth with one's hand/a cloth
(d) (= schützen) to cover; (Ftbl) Spieler auch to mark; Komplizen to cover up for
(e) Kosten, Schulden, Bedarf to cover, to meet; **mein Bedarf ist gedeckt** I have all I need; (fig inf) I've had enough (to last me some time); **damit ist unser Bedarf gedeckt** that will meet our needs
(f) (Comm, Fin: = absichern) Scheck, Darlehen to cover; Defizit to offset; **der Schaden wird voll durch die Versicherung gedeckt** the cost of the damage will be fully met by the insurance
2 VI to cover; (Ftbl: = Spieler ~) to mark
3 VR **(a)** (Standpunkte, Interessen, Begriffe) to coincide; (Aussagen) to correspond; (Math: Dreiecke, Figur) to be congruent; **sich ~de Begriffe/Interessen** concepts/interests which coincide
(b) (= sich schützen) to defend oneself; (mit Schild etc) to protect oneself; (Boxer etc) to cover oneself

Deck-: Deckfarbe F opaque watercolour (Brit) or watercolor (US); **Deckladung** F deck cargo; **Deckmantel** M (fig) mask; **unter dem ~ von ...** under the guise of ...; **Deckname** M assumed name; (Mil) code name; **Deckplane** F (Aut) tarpaulin

Deckung [ˈdɛkuŋ] F -, (rare) -en **(a)** (= Schutz) cover; (Ftbl, Chess) defence (Brit), defense (US); (Boxen, Fechten) guard; **in ~ gehen** to take cover; **jdm ~ geben** to cover sb
(b) (= Verheimlichung) **die ~ von etw** covering up of sth; **er kann mit ~ durch den Minister rechnen** he can count on the minister covering up for him
(c) (Comm, Fin) (von Scheck, Wechsel) cover; (von Darlehen) security; (= das Decken) covering; (= das Begleichen) meeting; **der Scheck ist ohne ~** the cheque (Brit) or check (US) is not covered; **ein Darlehen ohne ~** an unsecured loan; **zur ~ seiner Schulden** to cover his debts; **dafür ist auf meinem Konto keine ~** there are no funds to cover that in my account
(d) (= Befriedigung) meeting; **eine ~ der Nachfrage ist unmöglich** demand cannot possibly be met
(e) (= Übereinstimmung) (Math) congruence; **zur ~ bringen** (Math) to make congruent

Deckungs-: Deckungsbeitrag M contribution margin; **Deckungsbeitragsrechnung** F contribution costing; **Deckungsfehler** M (Ftbl) error by the defence (Brit) or defense (US); **Deckungsgeschäft** NT covering or hedging transaction; **ein ~ abschließen** to hedge; **deckungsgleich** ADJ (Math) congruent; **~ sein** (fig) to coincide; (Aussagen) to agree; **Deckungskapital** NT (Insur) covering funds pl; **Deckungskauf** M cover purchase; (St Ex) short covering; **Deckungslücke** F (Fin) shortfall no pl, deficit; **Deckungszusage** F (von Versicherung) cover note

Deckweiß NT opaque white

Decoder [deˈkoːde] M -s, - decoder

Deduktion [dedʊkˈtsioːn] F -, -en deduction

deduktiv [dedʊkˈtiːf] **1** ADJ deductive **2** ADV deductively

deduzieren [deduˈtsiːrən], ptp **deduziert** VT to deduce (aus from)

Deeskalation [deleskalaˈtsioːn] F (Mil) de-escalation

de facto [de ˈfakto] ADV de facto

Defätismus [defeˈtɪsmʊs] M -, NO PL defeatism

defekt [deˈfɛkt] ADJ Gerät etc faulty; Gen defective

Defekt [deˈfɛkt] M -(e)s, -e fault; (Med) deficiency; **körperlicher ~** physical defect; **geistiger ~** mental deficiency; **einen ~ haben** to be faulty; (inf: Mensch) to be a bit lacking (inf)

defensiv [defen'ziːf] **1** ADJ *Maßnahmen, Taktik* defensive; *Fahrweise* non-aggressive **2** ADV defensively; **sich ~ verhalten** to be on the defensive

Defensiv- IN CPDS defensive

Defensive [defen'ziːvə] F -, *(rare)* -n defensive; **in der ~ bleiben** to remain on the defensive; **jdn in die ~ drängen** to force sb onto the defensive

definierbar ADJ definable; **schwer/leicht ~** hard/easy to define

definieren [defi'niːrən], *ptp* **definiert** VT to define; **etw neu ~** to redefine sth

Definition [defini'tsioːn] F -, -en definition

definitiv [defini'tiːf] **1** ADJ definite **2** ADV (= *bestimmt*) definitely

Defizit ['deːfitsɪt] NT -s, -e (= *Fehlbetrag*) deficit; (= *Mangel*) deficiency (*an* +*dat* of)

defizitär [defitsi'tɛːɐ] **1** ADJ in deficit; **die ~e Entwicklung der Organisation** the trend in the organization to run to a deficit; **eine ~e Haushaltspolitik führen** to follow an economic policy which can only lead to deficit **2** ADV **das Bankwesen entwickelt sich immer ~er** the banks have a larger deficit every year

Deflation [defla'tsioːn] F -, -en (*Econ*) deflation

Deformation [deformа'tsioːn] F deformation; (= *Missbildung*) deformity

deformieren [defor'miːrən], *ptp* **deformiert** VT to deform

defragmentieren *ptp* **defragmentiert** VT (*Comput*) to defragment

Defroster [de'frɔstɐ] M -s, - (*Aut*) heated windscreen (*Brit*), defroster (*US*)

deftig ['deftɪç] **1** ADJ *Mahlzeit, Wurst etc* substantial; *Witz, Humor* ribald; *Lüge* huge; *Ohrfeige* cracking (*inf*); *Preis* extortionate; **~e Hausmannskost** good plain cooking **2** ADV (= *tüchtig*) really; **~ schmecken** to taste well-seasoned; **sich ~ ausdrücken** to speak bluntly

Degen ['deːgn] M -s, - rapier; (*Sportfechten*) épée

Degeneration [degenera'tsioːn] F degeneration

Degenerationserscheinung F sign of degeneration

degenerieren [degene'riːrən], *ptp* **degeneriert** VI AUX SEIN to degenerate (*zu* into)

degeneriert [degene'riːɐt] ADJ degenerate

degradieren [degra'diːrən], *ptp* **degradiert** VT (*Mil*) to demote (*zu* to); (*fig* = *herabwürdigen*) to degrade; **jdn/etw zu etw ~** (*fig*) to lower sb/sth to the level of sth

Degradierung F -, -en (*Mil*) demotion (*zu* to); (*fig*) degradation

degressiv [degre'siːf] ADJ (*Fin*) degressive

dehnbar ADJ (*lit*) elastic; (*fig auch*) flexible; *Metall* ductile; **ein ~er Vokal** a vowel which can be lengthened

Dehnbarkeit ['deːnbaːɐkait] F -, NO PL (*lit*) elasticity; (*fig auch*) flexibility; (*von Metall*) ductility

dehnen ['deːnən] **1** VT to stretch; *Laut, Silbe* to lengthen **2** VR to stretch; **er dehnte und streckte sich** he had a good stretch; **der Weg dehnte sich endlos** the road seemed to go on for ever

Dehnung F -, -en stretching; (*von Laut, Silbe*) lengthening

dehydrieren [dehy'driːrən], *ptp* **dehydriert** VT (*Chem*) to dehydrate

Dehydrierung F -, -en (*Chem*) dehydration

Deich [daiç] M -(e)s, -e dyke (*Brit*), dike (*esp US*)

Deich-: Deichbau M, NO PL dyke (*Brit*), dike (*esp US*); (= *das Bauen*) dyke (*Brit*) or dike (*esp US*) building; **Deichbruch** M breach in the dyke (*Brit*) or dike (*esp US*)

Deichsel ['daiksl] F -, -n shaft, whiffletree (*US*); (= *Doppeldeichsel*) shafts *pl*

deichseln ['daiksln] VT (*inf*) to wangle (*inf*)

dein [dain] POSS PRON (*adjektivisch*) your; **herzliche Grüße, ~e Elke** with best wishes, yours or (*herzlicher*) love Elke

deiner ['dainɐ] PERS PRON GEN *von* **du** (*geh*) of you; **wir werden ~ gedenken** we will remember you

deine(r, s) ['dainə] POSS PRON (*substantivisch*) yours; **der/die/das ~** or **Deine** (*geh*) yours; **tu du das ~** or **Deine** (*geh*) you do your bit or part (*esp US*); **die ~n** or **Deinen** (*geh*) your family, your people; **du und die ~n** or **Deinen** (*geh*: = *Familie*) you and yours; **das ~** or **Deine** (*geh*: = *Besitz*) what is yours

deinerseits ['dainɐ'zaits] ADV (= *auf deiner Seite*) for your part; (= *von deiner Seite*) on your part; **den Vorschlag hast du ~ gemacht** you made the suggestion yourself

deinesgleichen ['dainəs'glaiçn] PRON INV people like you; (*pej auch*) your sort or type

deinet-: deinetwegen ['dainət've:gn] ADV (= *wegen dir*) because of you; (= *dir zuliebe*) for your sake; (= *um dich*) about you; (= *für dich*) on your behalf; **deinetwillen** ['dainət'vɪlən] ADV **um ~** for your sake

deins [dains] POSS PRON yours

deinstallieren *ptp* **deinstalliert** VT *Programm* to uninstall

Deismus [de'ɪsmʊs] M -, NO PL (*Philos*) deism

deistisch [de'ɪstɪʃ] ADJ (*Philos*) deistic

Déjà-vu-Erlebnis [deʒa'vyː-] NT (*Psych*) sense of déjà vu

Deka ['deka] NT -(s), - (*Aus*) = **Dekagramm**

dekadent [deka'dɛnt] ADJ decadent

Dekadenz [deka'dɛnts] F -, NO PL decadence

dekadisch [de'kaːdɪʃ] ADJ *Zahlensystem* decimal; **~er Logarithmus** common logarithm

Deka-: Dekaeder [deka'le:dɐ] M -s, - decahedron; **Dekagramm** ['deka-, 'dɛka-] NT decagram(me); **10 ~ Schinken** (*Aus*) 100 grams of ham; **Dekaliter** ['deka-, 'dɛka-] M decalitre (*Brit*), decaliter (*US*); **Dekameter** ['deka-, 'dɛka-] M decametre (*Brit*), decameter (*US*)

Dekan [de'kaːn] M -s, -e (*Univ, Eccl*) dean

Dekanat [deka'naːt] NT -(e)s, -e (a) (*Univ, Eccl* = *Amt, Amtszeit*) deanship (b) (= *Amtssitz*) (*Univ*) office of the dean; (*Eccl*) deanery

Dekanin [de'kaːnɪn] F -, -nen (*Univ*) dean

deklamieren [dekla'miːrən], *ptp* **deklamiert** VTI to declaim

Deklaration [deklara'tsioːn] F -, -en (*alle Bedeutungen*) declaration

deklarieren [dekla'riːrən], *ptp* **deklariert** VT (*alle Bedeutungen*) to declare

Deklination [deklina'tsioːn] F -, -en (a) (*Gram*) declension (b) (*Astron, Phys*) declination

deklinierbar ADJ (*Gram*) declinable

deklinieren [dekli'niːrən], *ptp* **dekliniert** VT (*Gram*) to decline

dekodieren [deko'diːrən], *ptp* **dekodiert** VT to decode

Dekolleté [dekɔl'teː] NT -s, -s, **Dekolletee** NT -s, -s low-cut neckline; **ein Kleid mit einem tiefen/gewagten ~** a very/daringly low-cut dress; **ihr ~ war so tief, ...** she was wearing such a plunging neckline ...

dekolletiert [dekɔl'tiːɐt] ADJ *Kleid* low-cut; **eine ~e Dame** a woman in a low-cut dress

Dekompression [dekɔmpre'sioːn] F decompression

Dekompressionskammer F decompression chamber

dekomprimieren [dekɔmpri'miːrən], *ptp* **dekomprimiert** VT (*Comput*) to decompress

dekontaminieren [dekɔntami'niːrən], *ptp* **dekontaminiert** VT to decontaminate

Dekor [de'koːɐ] M or NT -s, -s or -e decoration; (= *Muster*) pattern

Dekorateur [dekora'tøːɐ] M -s, -e, **Dekorateurin** [-'tøːrɪn] F -, -nen (= *Schaufensterdekorateur*) window-dresser; (*von Innenräumen*) interior designer

Dekoration [dekora'tsioːn] F -, -en (a) NO PL (= *das Ausschmücken*) decorating (b) (= *Einrichtung*) décor *no pl*; (= *Fensterdekoration*) window-dressing; **zur ~ dienen** to be decorative; **zu Weihnachten haben viele Kaufhäuser schöne ~en** many department stores are beautifully decorated for Christmas

Dekorations-: Dekorationsarbeiten PL decorating *no pl*; **Dekorationsstoff** M (*Tex*) furnishing fabric

dekorativ [dekora'tiːf] **1** ADJ decorative **2** ADV decoratively; **~ wirken** or **aussehen** to look decorative

dekorieren [deko'riːrən], *ptp* **dekoriert** VT to decorate; *Schaufenster* to dress

Dekostoff ['deko-] M furnishing fabric

Dekret [de'kreːt] NT -(e)s, -e decree

Delegation [delega'tsioːn] F -, -en (*alle Bedeutungen*) delegation

Delegationschef(in) M(F) head of a delegation

delegieren [dele'giːrən], *ptp* **delegiert** VT (*alle Bedeutungen*) to delegate (*an* +*acc* to)

Delegierte(r) [dele'giːɐtə] MF DECL AS ADJ delegate

Delete-Taste [di'liːt-] F delete key

Delfin etc [del'fiːn] = **Delphin** etc

delikat [deli'kaːt] **1** ADJ **(a)** (= wohlschmeckend) exquisite **(b)** (= behutsam) delicate **(c)** (= heikel) delicate; (= gewagt) risqué **2** ADV zubereitet exquisitely; **~ schmecken** to taste exquisite

Delikatess- [delika'tɛs] IN CPDS (top-)quality

Delikatesse [delika'tɛsə] F **-, -n** (= Leckerbissen, fig) delicacy; **ein Geschäft für Obst und ~n** a fruit shop and delicatessen

Delikatessengeschäft NT delicatessen

Delikatess-: Delikatessgurke F gherkin; **Delikatesssenf** M (top-)quality mustard

Delikt [de'lɪkt] NT **-(e)s, -e** (Jur) offence (Brit), offense (US)

delinquent [delɪŋ'kvɛnt] ADJ delinquent

Delinquent [delɪŋ'kvɛnt] M **-en, -en, Delinquentin** [-'kvɛntɪn] F **-, -nen** (geh) offender

Delinquenz [delɪŋ'kvɛnts] F **-, NO PL** delinquency

Delirium [de'liːriʊm] NT **-s, Delirien** [-riən] delirium; **im ~ sein** to be delirious; **im ~ redete der Kranke wirr und konfus** the sick man raved deliriously; **~ tremens** the DT's

Delkredere [dɛl'kreːdərə] NT **-, -** (Econ) (= Gewährleistung) del credere; (= Wertberichtigung) provision for doubtful debts; **~ anbieten** to offer guarantee; **~ stellen** to stand surety; **~ übernehmen** to assume the credit risk; **individuelles ~** individual contingency reserve

Delkredererisiko NT del credere or collection risk

Delle ['dɛlə] F **-, -n** (inf) dent; **eine ~ bekommen** to get dented

delogieren [delo'ʒiːrən], ptp **delogiert** VT (Aus) Mieter to evict

Delphi ['dɛlfi] NT **-s** Delphi; **das Orakel von ~** the Delphic oracle

Delphin¹ [dɛl'fiːn] M **-s, -e** (Zool) dolphin

Delphin² NT **-s, NO PL** (= ~schwimmen) butterfly (stroke)

Delta ['dɛlta] NT **-s, -s** or **Delten** ['dɛltn] (Geog) delta

Delta-: deltaförmig ADJ delta-shaped; Muskel deltoid; **Deltamündung** F delta estuary

de Luxe [də 'lyks] ADJ (Comm) de luxe

dem [deːm] **1** DEF ART DAT von **der, das** to the; (mit Präposition) the; **es ist nicht an ~** that is not the case; **wenn ~ so ist** if that is the way it is; **wie ~ auch sei** be that as it may **2** DEM PRON DAT von **der, das (a)** ATTR to that; (mit Präposition) that **(b)** (substantivisch) to that one; that one; (Menschen) to him; (von mehreren) to that one; that one **3** REL PRON DAT von **der, das** to whom, that or who(m) ... to; (mit Präposition) who(m); (von Sachen) to which, which or that ... to; which; **~ der Fehler unterlaufen ist, ...** whoever made that mistake ...

Demagoge [dema'goːgə] M **-n, -n, Demagogin** [-goːgɪn] F **-, -nen** demagogue

Demagogie [demago'giː] F **-, -n** [-'giːən] demagoguery

demagogisch [dema'goːgɪʃ] **1** ADJ Rede etc demagogic **2** ADV **leider lassen sich die Wähler immer noch ~ beeinflussen** sadly voters can still be swayed by demagogues; **er hat in seiner Rede die Tatsachen ~ verzerrt** in his speech he twisted the facts to demagogic ends

demaskieren [demas'kiːrən], ptp **demaskiert 1** VT to unmask, to expose; **jdn als etw ~** to expose sb as sth **2** VR to unmask oneself; **sich als etw ~** to show oneself to be sth

Dementi [de'mɛnti] NT **-s, -s** denial

dementieren [demɛn'tiːrən], ptp **dementiert 1** VT to deny **2** VI to deny it

dementsprechend ['deːmɛnt'ʃprɛçnt] **1** ADV correspondingly; (= demnach) accordingly; bezahlt commensurately **2** ADJ appropriate; Gehalt commensurate; Vertrag on this matter

Demenz [de'mɛnts] F **-, -en** (Med) dementia

demilitarisieren [demilitari'ziːrən], ptp **demilitarisiert** VT to demilitarize

Demission [demɪ'sioːn] F (Pol) (= Rücktritt) resignation; (= Entlassung) dismissal; **um seine ~ bitten** to ask to be relieved of one's duties; **er wurde zur ~ gezwungen** he was forced to resign

demissionieren [demɪsio'niːrən], ptp **demissioniert** VI (Pol, Sw: = kündigen) to resign

dem-: demnach ['deːmnaːx] ADV therefore; (= dementsprechend) accordingly; **demnächst** ['deːmnɛːçst, deːm'nɛːçst] ADV soon; **~ (in diesem Kino)** coming soon

Demo ['deːmo] F **-, -s** (inf) demo (inf)

Demodiskette ['deːmo-] F (Comput) demo disk

Demografie [demogra'fiː] F **-, -n** [-'fiːən] demography

demografisch [demo'graːfɪʃ] ADJ demographic

Demokrat [demo'kraːt] M **-en, -en, Demokratin** [-'kraːtɪn] F **-, -nen** democrat; (US Pol) Democrat

Demokratie [demokra'tiː] F **-, -n** [-'tiːən] democracy

Demokratieverständnis NT understanding of (the meaning of) democracy

demokratisch [demo'kraːtɪʃ] **1** ADJ democratic **2** ADV democratically

demolieren [demo'liːrən], ptp **demoliert** VT to wreck; **nach dem Unfall war das Auto total demoliert** after the accident the car was a complete wreck; **er sah ganz schön demoliert aus** (inf) he was a real mess

Demonstrant [demɔn'strant] M **-en, -en, Demonstrantin** [-'strantɪn] F **-, -nen** demonstrator

Demonstration [demɔnstra'tsioːn] F **-, -en** (alle Bedeutungen) demonstration; **eine ~ für/gegen etw** a demonstration in support of/against sth

Demonstrations-: Demonstrationsmaterial NT teaching material; **Demonstrationsrecht** NT right to demonstrate

demonstrativ [demɔnstra'tiːf] **1** ADJ demonstrative (auch Gram); Beifall acclamatory; Protest, Fehlen pointed; Beispiel clear **2** ADV pointedly; **~ Beifall spenden** to make a point of applauding

Demonstrativpronomen NT demonstrative pronoun

demonstrieren [demɔn'striːrən], ptp **demonstriert** VTI (alle Bedeutungen) to demonstrate; **für/gegen etw ~** to demonstrate in support of/against sth

Demontage [demɔn'taːʒə] F (lit, fig) dismantling

demontieren [demɔn'tiːrən], ptp **demontiert** VT (lit, fig) to dismantle; Räder to take off

demoralisieren [demorali'ziːrən], ptp **demoralisiert** VT (= entmutigen) to demoralize; (= korrumpieren) to corrupt; **die römische Gesellschaft war am Ende so demoralisiert, dass ...** ultimately Roman society had suffered such a moral decline that ...

Demoskop [demo'skoːp] M **-en -en, Demoskopin** [-'skoːpɪn] F **-, -nen** (opinion) pollster

Demoskopie [demosko'piː] F **-, NO PL** (public) opinion research

demoskopisch [demo'skoːpɪʃ] ADJ Daten, Erkenntnisse opinion poll attr; **~es Institut** (public) opinion research institute; **alle ~en Voraussagen waren falsch** all the predictions in the opinion polls were wrong; **eine ~e Untersuchung** a (public) opinion poll

demselben [deːm'zɛlbn] DAT von **derselbe, dasselbe**

Demut ['deːmuːt] F **-, NO PL** humility; **in ~** with humility

demütig ['deːmyːtɪç] **1** ADJ humble **2** ADV humbly

demütigen ['deːmyːtɪgn] **1** VT to humiliate; (= eine Lektion erteilen) stolzen Menschen etc to humble **2** VR to humble oneself (vor +dat before)

Demütigung F **-, -en** humiliation; **jdm ~en/eine ~ zufügen** to humiliate sb

demzufolge ['deːmtsu'fɔlgə] ADV therefore

den [deːn] **1** DEF ART **(a)** ACC von **der** the **(b)** DAT PL von **der, die, das** the; to the **2** DEM PRON ACC von **der (a)** ATTR that **(b)** (substantivisch) that one; (Menschen) him; (von mehreren) that one **3** REL PRON ACC von **der** who(m), that; (von Sachen) which, that

denen ['deːnən] **1** DEM PRON DAT PL von **der, die, das** to them; (mit Präposition) them **2** REL PRON DAT PL von **der, die, das** to whom, that or who(m) ... to; (mit Präposition) whom; (von Sachen) to which, that or which ... to; which

Denim® ['deːnɪm, dɛ'niːm] M or NT **-(s), NO PL** (Tex) denim

Denk- [dɛŋk-]: **Denkanstoß** M something to start one thinking; **jdm Denkanstöße geben** to give sb something to think about; **Denkaufgabe** F brain-teaser; **denkbar 1** ADJ conceivable; **es ist durchaus ~, dass er kommt** it's very possible that he'll come **2** ADV extremely; (= ziemlich) rather; **den ~ schlechtesten/besten Eindruck machen** to make the worst/best possible impression

Denke ['dɛŋkə] F -, NO PL (inf) (way of) thinking

denken ['dɛŋkən]

1 INTRANSITIVES VERB	**2** TRANSITIVES VERB

pret **dachte** ['daxtə], ptp **gedacht** [gə'daxt]

1 INTRANSITIVES VERB
(a) (= überlegen) to think; **das gibt einem zu denken** it makes you think; **langsam/schnell denken** to be a slow/quick thinker; **solange ich denken kann** (for) as long as I can remember; **wo denken Sie hin!** what an idea!
(b) (= urteilen) to think (über +acc about); **wie denken Sie darüber?** what do you think about it?; **schlecht von jdm** or **über jdn denken** to think badly of sb; **ich denke genauso** I think the same (way); **wie viel soll ich spenden? – wie Sie denken** how much should I give? – it's up to you; **ich dächte, ...** I would have thought ...; **ich denke schon** I think so; **ich denke nicht** I don't think so
(c) (= gesinnt sein) to think; **edel denken** to be noble-minded; **kleinlich denken** to be petty-minded; **alle, die liberal denken** all liberally-minded people; **da muss man etwas großzügiger denken** one must be more generous-minded
♦**denken an** to think of or about; **denk mal an mich, wenn ...** think of me when ...; **an das Geld habe ich gar nicht mehr gedacht** I had forgotten about the money; **wenn ich so an früher denke** when I think back; **an die Prüfung morgen denke ich mit gemischten Gefühlen** I've got mixed feelings about the exam tomorrow; **das Erste, woran ich dachte** the first thing I thought of; **daran ist gar nicht zu denken** that's (quite) out of the question; **ich denke nicht daran!** no way! (inf); **ich denke nicht daran, das zu tun** there's no way I'm going to do that (inf); **die viele Arbeit, ich darf gar nicht daran denken** all that work, it doesn't bear thinking about; **denk daran!** don't forget!

2 TRANSITIVES VERB
(a) to think; **sagen was man denkt** to say what one thinks; **was denkst du jetzt?** what are you thinking (about)?; **wie viel Trinkgeld gibt man? – so viel, wie Sie denken** how big a tip does one give? – it's up to you
♦**für jdn/etw gedacht sein** (= vorgesehen) to be intended for sb/sth; **so war das nicht gedacht** that wasn't what I/he etc had in mind
(b) (= annehmen, glauben) to think; **was sollen bloß die Leute denken!** what will people think!; **wer hätte das (von ihr) gedacht!** who'd have thought it (of her)!; **(nur) Schlechtes/Gutes von jdm denken** to think ill/well of sb; **denkste!** (inf) that's what you think!
♦**sich** (dat) **etw denken** to imagine sth; **sich** (dat) **etw bei etw denken** to mean sth by sth; **ich habe mir nichts Böses dabei gedacht** I meant no harm (by it); **das kann ich mir denken** I can imagine; **ich könnte ihn mir gut als Direktor denken** I can just imagine him as director; **wie denkst du dir das eigentlich?** (inf) what's the big idea? (inf); **ich habe mir das so gedacht ...** this is what I'd thought ...; **das habe ich mir gleich gedacht** I thought that from the first; **das habe ich mir gedacht** I thought so; **das habe ich mir beinahe gedacht** I thought as much; **dachte ich mirs doch!** I knew it!; **ich denke mir mein Teil** I have my own thoughts on the matter; **sie denkt sich nichts dabei** (= findet es okay) she thinks nothing of it; **siehe gedacht**

Denken NT -s, NO PL (= Gedankenwelt) thought; (= Denkweise) thinking; **ich kann seinem ~ nicht folgen** I can't follow his thinking; **abstraktes ~** abstract thought or thinking; **klares ~** clear thinking; **positives ~** positive thinking

Denker ['dɛŋkɐ] M -s, -, **Denkerin** [-ərɪn] F -, -nen thinker; **das Volk der Dichter und ~** the nation of poets and philosophers

Denk-: Denkfabrik F think tank; **Denkfähigkeit** F ability to think; **denkfaul** ADJ (mentally) lazy; **sei nicht so ~!** get your brain working!; **Denkfaulheit** F mental laziness; **Denkfehler** M flaw in the/one's reasoning

Denkmal ['dɛŋkmaːl] NT -s, -e (liter) or ⁼er [-mɛːlɐ] (= Gedenkstätte) monument (für to); (= Standbild) statue; **er**

hat sich (dat) **ein ~ gesetzt** he has left a memorial (to himself)

Denkmal(s)-: Denkmal(s)pflege F preservation of historical monuments; **Denkmal(s)schutz** M protection of historical monuments; **etw unter ~ stellen** to classify sth as a historical monument; **unter ~ stehen** to be classified as a historical monument

Denk-: Denkmodell NT (= Entwurf) plan for further discussion; (wissenschaftlich) working hypothesis; **Denkmuster** NT thought pattern; **Denkprozess** M thought-process; **Denkschrift** F memo (inf)

denkste ['dɛŋkstə] INTERJ siehe **denken 2(b)**

Denk-: Denkvermögen NT capacity for thought; **denkwürdig** ADJ memorable; **Denkzettel** M (inf) warning; **jdm einen ~ verpassen** to give sb a warning

denn [dɛn] **1** CONJ **(a)** (kausal) because
(b) (geh: vergleichend) than; **schöner ~ je** more beautiful than ever
(c) (konzessiv) **es sei ~, (dass)** unless **2** ADV **(a)** (verstärkend) **wann/woran/wer/wie/wo ~?** when/why/who/how/where?; **wieso ~?** why?, how come?; **warum ~ nicht?** why not?; **wie gehts ~?** how are you then?; **wo bleibt er ~?** where has he got to?; **was soll das ~?** what's all this then?; **das ist ~ doch die Höhe!** (well,) that really is the limit!
(b) (N Ger inf: = dann) then; **na, ~ man los!** right then, let's go!; **na, ~ prost!** well, cheers (then)

dennoch ['dɛnɔx] ADV nevertheless; **~ liebte er sie** yet he still loved her; **er hat es ~ getan** (but or yet) he still did it; **und ~, ...** and yet ...; **schön und ~ hässlich** beautiful and yet ugly

denselben [de:n'zɛlbn] DEM PRON **1** ACC von **derselbe 2** DAT von **dieselben**

dental [dɛn'taːl] ADJ (Med, Ling) dental

Dental(laut) [dɛn'taː-] M -s, -e (Ling) dental

Denunziant [denʊn'tsiant] M -en, -en, **Denunziantin** [-'tsiantɪn] F -, -nen (pej) informer

Denunziantentum [denʊn'tsiantntuːm] NT -s, NO PL (pej) informing

Denunziation [denʊntsia'tsioːn] F -, -en (pej) informing no pl (von on, against); (= Anzeige) denunciation (von of)

denunzieren [denʊn'tsiːrən] ptp **denunziert** VT to denounce

Deo ['deːo] NT -(s), -s ABBR von **Deodorant**

Deodorant [delodo'rant] NT -s, -s or -e deodorant

Deo-: Deoroller M roll-on (deodorant); **Deospray** NT or M deodorant spray; **Deostift** M stick deodorant

Departement [departə'mãː] NT -s, -s (esp Sw) department

Dependance [depã'dãːs] F -, -n **(a)** (geh) branch
(b) (= Hoteldependance) annexe (Brit), annex (US)

deplaciert [depla'siːɐt], **deplatziert** [depla'tsiːɐt], **deplaziert** [depla'tsiːɐt] ADJ out of place

Deponie [depo'niː] F -, -n [-'niːən] dump

deponieren [depo'niːrən] ptp **deponiert** VT (geh) to deposit

Deportation [depɔrta'tsioːn] F -, -en deportation

deportieren [depɔr'tiːrən] ptp **deportiert** VT to deport

Deportierte(r) [depɔr'tiːɐtə] MF DECL AS ADJ deportee

Depositen [depo'ziːtn] PL (Fin) deposits pl

Depositen- (Fin): Depositenbank F, pl **-banken** deposit bank; **Depositengelder** PL deposits pl; **Depositengeschäft** NT deposit banking; **Depositenkonto** NT deposit account; **Depositenzertifikat** NT certificate of deposit

Depot [de'poː] NT -s, -s **(a)** depot; (= Aufbewahrungsort auch, Wertpapierdepot) depository; (in Bank) strongroom; (= Schließfach) safety deposit box; (Med) deposit **(b)** (Sw: = Pfand) deposit

Depot-: Depotbank F, pl **-banken** custodian bank; **Depotbewertung** F portfolio evaluation; **Depotgebühr** F (bei Bank) custodian fees pl; **Depotwechsel** M (Fin) collateral bill

Depp [dɛp] M -en or -s, -e(n) (S Ger, Aus, Sw: pej) twit (inf)

Depression [deprɛ'sioːn] F (alle Bedeutungen) depression; **~en haben** to suffer from depression

depressiv [deprɛ'siːf] ADJ depressive; (Econ) depressed

Depressivität [deprɛsivi'tɛːt] F -, NO PL depressiveness

deprimieren [depri'miːrən] ptp **deprimiert** VT to depress

deprimierend 1 ADJ depressing **2** ADV depressingly

deprimiert [depriˈmiːɐt] ADJ depressed

Deprimiertheit F -, NO PL depression

der¹ [deːɐ] **1** DEF ART **(a)** GEN SING, PL *von* **die** of the **(b)** DAT SING *von* **die** to the; (*mit Präposition*) the **2** DEM PRON DAT SING *von* **die (a)** (*adjektivisch*) to that; (*mit Präpositionen*) that **(b)** (*substantivisch*) to her; her **3** REL PRON DAT SING *von* **die** to whom, that *or* who(m) ... to; (*mit Präposition*) who(m); (*von Sachen*) to which, which ... to; which

der² [deːɐ], **die** [diː], **das** [das], *pl* **die 1** DEF ART, *gen* **des, der, des,** *pl* **der** *dat* **dem, der, dem,** *pl* **den** *acc* **den, die, das,** *pl* **die** the; **der/die Arme!** the poor man/woman *or* girl; **die Engländer** the English *pl*; **der Faust** Faust; **der Hans** (*inf*) Hans; **der kleine Hans** little Hans; **der Rhein** the Rhine; **der Michigansee** Lake Michigan; **die Domstraße** Cathedral Street; **der Lehrer/die Frau** (*im Allgemeinen*) teachers *pl*/ women *pl*; **der Tod/die Liebe/das Leben** death/love/life; **der Tod des Sokrates** the death of Socrates; **das Viktorianische England** Victorian England; **das Singen macht ihm Freude** singing gives him pleasure; **wascht euch** (*dat*) **mal das Gesicht!** wash your faces; **er nimmt den Hut ab** he takes his hat off; **ein Euro das Stück** one euro apiece; **40 Euro die Stunde** 40 euros an hour; **der und der Wissenschaftler** such and such a scientist

2 DEM PRON, *gen* **dessen** *or* (*old*) **des, deren, dessen,** *pl* **deren** *dat* **dem, der, dem,** *pl* **denen** *acc* **den, die, das,** *pl* **die (a)** (*attr*) (= *jener, dieser*) that; (*pl*) those, them (*inf*); **zu der und der Zeit** at such and such a time; **an dem und dem Ort** at such and such a place

(b) (*substantivisch*) he/she/it; (*pl*) those, them (*inf*); **der/die war es** it was him/her; **der/die mit der großen Nase** the one *or* him/her (*inf*) with the big nose; **die** *pl* **mit den roten Haaren** those with red hair; **der und schwimmen?** him, swimming?; **der/die hier** (*von Menschen*) he/she, this man/ woman *etc*; (*von Gegenständen*) this (one); (*von mehreren*) this one; **der/die da** (*von Menschen*) he/she, that man/woman *etc*; (*von Gegenständen*) that (one); (*von mehreren*) that one; **die hier/da** *pl* these/those; **der, den ich meine** the one I mean; **der und der/die und die** so-and-so; **das und das** such and such **3** REL PRON DECL AS DEM PRON (*Mensch*) who, that; (*Gegenstand, Tier*) which, that **4** REL +DEM PRON DECL AS DEM PRON **der/die dafür verantwortlich war, ...** the man/woman who was responsible for it; **die so etwas tun, ...** those who do that sort of thing ...

derart [deːɐˈlaːɐt] ADV **(a)** (*Art und Weise*) in such a way; **er hat sich ~ benommen, dass ...** he behaved so badly that ...; **sein Benehmen war ~, dass ...** his behaviour (*Brit*) *or* behavior (*US*) was so bad that ...; **~ vorbereitet, ...** thus prepared ... **(b)** (*Ausmaß*) (*vor adj*) so; (*vor vb*) so much; **ein ~ unzuverlässiger Mensch** such an unreliable person

derartig [deːɐˈlaːɐtɪç] **1** ADJ such; **(etwas) Derartiges** something like that **2** ADV = **derart**

derb [dɛrp] **1** ADJ **(a)** (= *kräftig*) strong; *Kost* coarse **(b)** (= *grob*) coarse; *Sprache, Witz, Ausdrucksweise* crude **2** ADV **(a)** (= *heftig*) roughly; **jdn ~ anfassen** to manhandle sb; (*fig*) to be rough with sb **(b)** (= *grob*) crudely

Derby [ˈdɛrbi] NT **-s, -s** horse race for three-year-olds, derby (*US*); **das (englische) ~** the Derby

deregulieren [dereguˈliːrən], *ptp* **dereguliert** VT (*Econ*) to deregulate

deren [ˈdeːrən] **1** DEM PRON GEN PL *von* **der, die, das** their **2** REL PRON **(a)** GEN SING *von* **die** whose **(b)** GEN PL *von* **der, die, das** whose, of whom; (*von Sachen*) of which

derentwegen [ˈdeːrəntveːgn] ADV because of whom; (*von Sachen*) because of which; (= *um welche*) about whom; (*von Sachen*) about which; (= *für welche*) on whose behalf

derentwillen [ˈdeːrəntvɪlən] ADV **um ~** (*rel*) for whose sake; (*von Sachen*) for the sake of which; (*dem*) (*sing*) for her/its sake; (*pl*) for their sake

derer [ˈdeːrɐ] DEM PRON GEN PL *von* **der, die, das** of those

deret- IN CPDS = **derent-**

dergleichen [deːɐˈglaɪçn] DEM PRON INV **(a)** (*adjektivisch*) of that kind; **~ Dinge** things of that kind **(b)** (*substantivisch*) that sort of thing; **nichts ~** nothing of that kind; **er tat nichts ~** he did nothing of the kind; **und ~ (mehr)** and suchlike

Derivat [deriˈvaːt] NT **-(e)s, -e** derivative

Derivativ [derivaˈtiːf] NT **-s, -e** [-və] (*Ling*) derivative

derjenige [ˈdeːɐjeːnɪgə], **diejenige, dasjenige** *pl* **diejenigen** DEM PRON **(a)** (*substantivisch*) the one; (*pl*) those; **sie ist immer diejenige, welche** (*inf*) it's always her; **du warst also ~, welcher!** (*inf*) so you're the one! **(b)** (*adjektivisch*) the; (*pl*) those

derlei [ˈdeːɐlai] DEM PRON INV **(a)** (*adjektivisch*) like that **(b)** (*substantivisch*) that sort of thing; **und ~ (mehr)** and suchlike

dermaßen [ˈdeːɐmaːsn] ADV (*mit adj*) so; (*mit vb*) so much; **ein ~ dummer Kerl** such a stupid fellow; **er hat sich geärgert und zwar ~, dass ...** he was angry, so much so that ...

Dermatologe [dɛrmatoˈloːgə] M **-en, -en, Dermatologin** [-ˈloːgɪn] F **-, -nen** dermatologist

Dermatologie [dɛrmatoloˈgiː] F **-,** NO PL dermatology

derselbe [deːɐˈzɛlbə], **dieselbe, dasselbe** *pl* **dieselben** DEM PRON **(a)** (*substantivisch*) the same; **er sagt in jeder Vorlesung dasselbe** he says the same (thing) in every lecture; **jedes Jahr kriegen dieselben mehr Geld** every year the same people get more money; **noch mal dasselbe, bitte!** (*inf*) same again, please **(b)** (*adjektivisch*) the same; **ein und ~ Mensch** one and the same person

derweil [deːɐˈvail], **derweilen** [deːɐˈvailən] ADV in the meantime

derzeit [ˈdeːɐˈtsait] ADV (= *jetzt*) at present

derzeitig [ˈdeːɐˈtsaitɪç] ADJ ATTR (= *jetzig*) present, current

des¹ [dɛs] DEF ART GEN *von* **der, das** of the; **das Bellen ~ Hundes** the dog's barking

des² [dɛs] NT **-, -, Des** NT **-, -** (*Mus*) D flat

Desaster [deˈzastɐ] NT **-s, -** disaster

desensibilisieren [dezɛnzibiliˈziːrən], *ptp* **desensibilisiert** VT (*Phot, Med*) to desensitize

Deserteur [dezɛrˈtøːɐ] M **-s, -e, Deserteurin** [-ˈtøːrɪn] F **-, -nen** (*Mil, fig*) deserter

desertieren [dezɛrˈtiːrən], *ptp* **desertiert** VI AUX SEIN *or* (*rare*) HABEN (*Mil, fig*) to desert

desgleichen [ˈdɛsˈglaiçn] ADV (= *ebenso*) likewise; **er ist Vegetarier, ~ seine Frau** he is a vegetarian, as is his wife

deshalb [ˈdɛsˈhalp] ADV, CONJ therefore; (= *aus diesem Grunde, darüber*) because of that; (= *dafür*) for that; **es ist schon spät, ~ wollen wir anfangen** it is late, so let us start; **~ bin ich hergekommen** that is what I came here for; **ich bin ~ hergekommen, weil ich dich sprechen wollte** what I came here for was to speak to you; **also!** so that's why!; **~ muss er nicht dumm sein** that does not (necessarily) mean (to say) he is stupid; **~ frage ich ja** that's exactly why I'm asking

Design [diˈzain] NT **-s, -s** design

designen [diˈzainən], *ptp* **designt** [diˈzaint] VT to design

Designer [diˈzainɐ] M **-s, -, Designerin** [diˈzainərɪn] F **-, -nen** designer

Designer- [diˈzainɐ] IN CPDS designer *attr*; **Designerdroge** F designer drug; **Designerjeans** PL designer jeans *pl*; **Designermode** F designer fashion

designieren [dezɪˈgniːrən], *ptp* **designiert** VT to designate (*jdn zu etw* sb as sth)

designiert [dezɪˈgniːɐt] ADJ ATTR **der ~e Vorsitzende** the chairman elect

desillusionieren [dɛsɪluzioˈniːrən, dezi-], *ptp* **desillusioniert** VT to disillusion

Desinfektion [dɛsɪnfɛkˈtsioːn, dezi-] F disinfection

Desinfektions-: **Desinfektionslösung** F antiseptic solution; **Desinfektionsmittel** NT disinfectant

desinfizieren [dɛsɪnfiˈtsiːrən, dezi-], *ptp* **desinfiziert** VT *Zimmer, Bett etc* to disinfect; *Spritze, Gefäß etc* to sterilize

Desinformation [dɛsɪnfɔrmaˈtsioːn, dezi-] F (*Pol*) disinformation *no pl*

Desinteresse [dɛsɪntəˈrɛsə, dezi-] NT lack of interest (*an +dat* in)

desinteressiert [dɛsɪntərɛˈsiːɐt, dezi-] ADJ uninterested; *Gesicht* bored

deskriptiv [dɛskrɪpˈtiːf] ADJ descriptive

Desktop-Publishing [ˈdɛsktɔpˈpablɪʃɪŋ] NT **-,** NO PL, **Desktoppublishing** NT **-,** NO PL desktop publishing

desolat [dezoˈlaːt] ADJ (*geh*) desolate; *Zustand, wirtschaftliche Lage* desperate; **die ~en Staatsfinanzen** the desperate state of the public finances

desorientieren [dɛsloriɛn'tiːrən, dezo-], *ptp* **desorientiert** VT to disorient(ate)

Desorientiertheit F -, NO PL, **Desorientierung** F disorientation

Desoxyribonukleinsäure [dɛslɔksyribonukle'iːnzɔyrə, dezo-] F (*abbr* **DNS**) deoxyrybonucleic acid, DNA

Despot [dɛs'poːt] M **-en, -en**, **Despotin** ['-poːtɪn] F **-, -nen** despot

despotisch [dɛs'poːtɪʃ] ADJ despotic

desselben [dɛs'zɛlbn] DEM PRON GEN *von* **derselbe, dasselbe**

dessen ['dɛsn] ◼ DEM PRON GEN *von* **der², das** his; (*von Sachen, Tieren*) its ◼ REL PRON GEN *von* **der², das** whose; (*von Sachen*) of which, which ... of; **~ ungeachtet** (*geh*) nevertheless

dessentwillen ['dɛsnt'vɪlən] ADV **um ~** (*rel*) for whose sake; (*dem*) for his/its sake

Dessert [dɛ'seːɐ] NT **-s, -s** dessert

Dessert- [dɛ'seːɐ] IN CPDS dessert; **Dessertlöffel** M dessertspoon

Dessin [dɛ'sɛ:] NT **-s, -s** (*Tex*) pattern

destabilisieren [destabili'ziːrən, -ʃt-], *ptp* **destabilisiert** VT to destabilize

Destillation [destɪla'tsioːn] F **-, -en (a)** (*Chem*) distillation **(b)** (= *Branntweinbrennerei*) distillery

destillieren [destɪ'liːrən], *ptp* **destilliert** VT to distil (*Brit*), to distill (*US*)

desto ['dɛsto] CONJ **~ mehr/besser** all the more/better; **~ grausamer** all the more cruel; **~ schneller** all the faster; **~ wahrscheinlicher ist es, dass wir ...** that makes it all the more probable that we ...; *siehe* **je**

destruktiv [destrʊk'tiːf] ADJ destructive

deswegen ['dɛs've:gn] ADV = **deshalb**

Detail [de'tai, de'ta:j] NT **-s, -s** detail; **ins ~ gehen** to go into detail(s); **im ~** in detail; **bis ins kleinste ~** (right) down to the last detail; **in allen ~s** in the greatest detail; **etw mit allen ~s berichten** to give a fully detailed account of sth; **die Schwierigkeiten liegen im ~** it is the details that are most difficult

detaillieren [deta'jiːrən], *ptp* **detailliert** VT to specify

detailliert [deta'jiːrt] ◼ ADJ detailed ◼ ADV in detail; **~er in** greater detail

Detektei [detɛk'tai] F **-, -en** (private) detective agency; „**~ R. B. von Halske**" "R.B. von Halske, private investigator"

Detektiv [detɛk'tiːf] M **-s, -e** [-və], **Detektivin** ['-tiːvɪn] F **-, -nen** private investigator

Detektivbüro NT = **Detektei**

detektivisch [detɛk'tiːvɪʃ] ◼ ADJ *Arbeit, Aufgabe* detective *attr*; **man braucht dazu ~en Scharfsinn/~e Neugierde** you need the astuteness/inquisitiveness of a detective for this; **in ~er Kleinarbeit** with detailed detective work ◼ ADV like a detective; *aufdecken* through detailed detective work

Detektivroman M detective novel

Detektor [de'tɛktoːɐ] M **-s, Detektoren** [-'toːrən] (*Tech*) detector

Detonation [detona'tsioːn] F **-, -en** explosion; **etw zur ~ bringen** to detonate sth

detonieren [deto'niːrən], *ptp* **detoniert** VI AUX SEIN to explode

Deut ['dɔyt] M **um keinen ~** not one iota; **er versteht nicht einen ~ davon** he does not know the first thing about it; **daran ist kein ~ wahr** there is not a grain of truth in it

deutbar ADJ interpretable; **nicht/schwer ~** impossible/difficult to interpret; **es ist nicht anders ~** it cannot be explained in any other way

deuteln ['dɔytln] VI (*geh*) to quibble; **daran gibt es nichts zu ~!** there are no ifs and buts about it! (*Brit*), there are no ifs, ands or buts about it! (*US*)

deuten ['dɔytn] ◼ VT (= *auslegen*) to interpret; **etw falsch ~** to misinterpret sth ◼ VI (a) (= *zeigen*) (**mit dem Finger**) **auf etw** (*acc*) **~** to point (one's finger) at sth **(b)** (*fig*: = *hinweisen*) to indicate; **alles deutet auf Regen/Schnee** everything points to rain/snow; **alles deutet darauf, dass ...** all the indications are that ...

deutlich ['dɔytlɪç] ◼ ADJ clear; **eine ~e Sprache mit jdm reden** to speak plainly with sb; **~ werden** to make oneself clear; **das war ~!** (= *taktlos*) that was clear enough; **muss ich ~er werden?** have I not made myself clear enough?
◼ ADV (a) (= *klar*) clearly; **~ zu erkennen/sehen/hören** easy to recognize/see/hear; **~ fühlen** to feel distinctly; **ich fühle ~, dass ...** I have the distinct feeling that ...

(b) (= *unmissverständlich*) explicitly; **sich ~ ausdrücken** to make oneself clear; **ich muss es einmal ~ sagen** let me make myself perfectly clear; **jdm ~ zu verstehen geben, dass ...** to make it clear to sb that ...

Deutlichkeit F -, NO PL clarity; **etw mit aller ~ sagen** to make sth perfectly clear; **seine Antwort ließ an ~ nichts zu wünschen übrig** his answer was perfectly clear and left no possible doubt

deutsch [dɔytʃ] ◼ ADJ German; **Deutscher Schäferhund** German shepherd; **~e Gründlichkeit** *etc* German efficiency *etc*; **die Deutsche Bucht** the German Bight; **mit jdm ~ reden** (*fig inf*: *deutlich*) to speak bluntly with sb ◼ ADV **etw ~ aussprechen** to pronounce sth as it is said in German; **~ denken** to think in German; **sich ~ unterhalten** to speak (in) German; **der Text ist ~ geschrieben** the text is written in German

Deutsch [dɔytʃ] NT **-(s)**, *dat* -, NO PL German; **~ sprechend** German-speaking; **sich auf ~ unterhalten** to speak (in) German; **auf** *or* **zu ~ heißt das ...** in German it means ...; **der Text ist in ~ geschrieben** the text is written in German; **der Vortrag wird auf ~ gehalten** the lecture will be given in German; **der Unterricht in ~** German lessons *pl*; **die Schulnote in ~** school mark (*Brit*) *or* grade (*US*) in German; **auf gut ~ (gesagt)** (*fig inf*) in plain English; *siehe auch* **deutsch**

Deutsch(e) NT **-n**, *dat* **-n**, NO PL **(a)** (*Ling*) German; **aus dem ~en/ins ~e übersetzt** translated from/into (the) German; **die Aussprache des ~en** German pronunciation **(b)** (= *Charakteristik*) Germanness

Deutsche Demokratische Republik F (*abbr* **DDR**) (*Hist*) German Democratic Republic

Deutschen-: Deutschenfeind(in) M(F), **Deutschenfresser(in)** M(F) (*inf*) Germanophobe; **Deutschenfreund(in)** M(F) Germanophile

deutsch-englisch ADJ (*Pol*) Anglo-German; (*Ling*) German-English

Deutschen-: Deutschenhass M Germanophobia; **Deutschenhasser** [-hasɐ] M **-s, -**, **Deutschenhasserin** [-ərɪn] F **-, -nen** Germanophobe, German-hater

Deutsche(r) [dɔytʃə] MF DECL AS ADJ **er ist ~r** he is (a) German; **die ~n** the Germans; **der hässliche ~** the obnoxious German

Deutsch-: deutschfeindlich ADJ anti-German; **Deutschfeindlichkeit** F Germanophobia; **deutsch-französisch** ADJ (*Pol*) Franco-German; (*Ling*) German-French; **der Deutsch-Französische Krieg** the Franco-Prussian war; **deutschfreundlich** ADJ pro-German; **Deutschfreundlichkeit** F Germanophilia

Deutschland ['dɔytʃlant] NT **-s** Germany

Deutsch-: Deutschlehrer(in) M(F) German teacher; **Deutschschweiz** F **die ~** German-speaking Switzerland; **Deutschschweizer(in)** M(F) German Swiss; **deutschschweizerisch** ADJ German-Swiss; **deutschsprachig** ADJ *Bevölkerung, Gebiete* German-speaking; *Zeitung, Ausgabe* German language; *Literatur* German; **deutschsprachlich** ADJ German(-language); **deutschstämmig** ADJ of German origin; **Deutschstämmige(r)** [-ʃtɛmɪgə] MF DECL AS ADJ ethnic German; **Deutschstunde** F German lesson

Deutung ['dɔytʊŋ] F **-, -en** interpretation; **eine falsche ~** a misinterpretation

Devise [de'viːzə] F **-, -n (a)** (= *Wahlspruch*) motto **(b)** (*Fin*) **Devisen** PL foreign exchange

Devisen-: Devisenausgleich M foreign exchange offset; **Devisenausländer(in)** M(F) (*bei Bank*) non-resident; **Devisenbeschränkungen** PL foreign exchange restrictions *pl*; **Devisenbestimmungen** PL foreign exchange control regulations *pl*; **Devisenhandel** M foreign exchange dealings *pl*; **Devisenknappheit** F shortage of foreign exchange; **Devisenkonto** NT foreign exchange account; **Devisenkontrolle** F foreign exchange control; **Devisenkurs** M exchange rate; **Devisenmarkt** M foreign exchange market; **Devisenoption** F currency option; **Devisenreserve** F foreign exchange reserve; **Devisenschmuggel** M currency smuggling; **devisenschwach** ADJ ~e Länder countries with limited foreign currency reserves; **Devisenvorschriften** PL foreign exchange control regulations pl

Dextrose [dɛks'troːzə] F -, NO PL dextrose

Dezember [de'tsɛmbɐ] M -(s), - December; siehe auch **März**

dezent [de'tsɛnt] **1** ADJ discreet; Kleidung subtle; Einrichtung refined **2** ADV andeuten, hinweisen discreetly; ~ **gekleidet sein** to be dressed unobtrusively; ~ **eingerichtet sein** to have refined furnishings

> Vorsicht! **dezent** wird nicht mit dem englischen Wort *decent* übersetzt.

dezentral [detsɛn'traːl] **1** ADJ decentralized **2** ADV verwalten decentrally; **Müll ~ entsorgen** to have a decentralized waste disposal system

Dezernat [detsɐ'naːt] NT -(e)s, -e (Admin) department

Dezibel [de'tsiːbɛl, -'beːl] NT -s, - decibel

Dezi- [deːtsi-] (Aus): **Dezigramm** NT decigram(me); **Deziliter** M or NT decilitre (Brit), deciliter (US)

dezimal [detsi'maːl] ADJ decimal

Dezimalbruch M decimal fraction

dezimalisieren [detsimali'ziːrən], ptp **dezimalisiert** VT to decimalize; **als in Großbritannien dezimalisiert wurde** when Great Britain went decimal

Dezimalisierung F -, -en decimalization

Dezimal-: **Dezimalstelle** F decimal place; **auf zwei ~n genau** correct to two decimal places; **Dezimalsystem** NT decimal system

Dezimeter [detsi'meːtɐ, 'deːtsimeːtɐ] M or NT decimetre (Brit), decimeter (US)

dezimieren [detsi'miːrən], ptp **dezimiert** **1** VT to decimate **2** VR to be decimated

DFB [deːʔɛf'beː] M -s ABBR von **Deutscher Fußball-Bund** German Football Association

DFÜ [deːʔɛf'y:] F - ABBR von **Datenfernübertragung**

DGB [deːgeː'beː] M -s ABBR von **Deutscher Gewerkschaftsbund** Federation of German Trade Unions

dgl. ABBR von **dergleichen, desgleichen** the like

d. Gr. ABBR von **der Große**

d. h. ABBR von **das heißt** i.e.

Dia [ˈdiːa] NT -s, -s (Phot) slide

Diabetes [dia'beːtɛs] M -, NO PL diabetes

Diabetiker [dia'beːtikɐ] M -s, -, **Diabetikerin** [-ərɪn] F -, -nen diabetic

diabetisch [dia'beːtɪʃ] ADJ diabetic

Diabetrachter M slide viewer

diabolisch [dia'boːlɪʃ] ADJ (geh) diabolical

Diagnose [dia'gnoːzə] F -, -n diagnosis; **eine ~ stellen** to make a diagnosis

Diagnosestand M diagnostic test bay

Diagnostik [dia'gnɔstɪk] F -, NO PL diagnosis

diagnostisch [dia'gnɔstɪʃ] ADJ diagnostic

diagnostizieren [diagnɔsti'tsiːrən], ptp **diagnostiziert** VTI (Med, fig) to diagnose

diagonal [diago'naːl] **1** ADJ diagonal **2** ADV diagonally; **ein Buch ~ lesen** (inf) to skim through a book

Diagonale [diago'naːlə] F -, -n diagonal

Diagramm NT, pl -gramme diagram

Diakoniestation F community care centre (Brit) or center (US)

diakritisch [dia'kriːtɪʃ] ADJ diacritic; ~**e Zeichen** diacritics

Dialekt [dia'lɛkt] M -(e)s, -e dialect

dialektal [dialɛk'taːl] ADJ dialectal

dialektfrei **1** ADJ dialect-free **2** ADV ~ **sprechen** to speak standard German/English etc

Dialog [dia'loːk] M -(e)s, -e [-gə] dialogue (Brit), dialog (US)

Dialog-: **Dialogautor(in)** M(F) (Film) scriptwriter; **Dialogbetrieb** M (Comput) conversation mode; **dialogfähig** ADJ (Comput) ~ **sein** to be capable of two-way communication; **Dialogfähigkeit** F ability to engage in meaningful conversation; (Comput) two-way communication capability

Dialyse [dia'lyːzə] F -, -n (Med) dialysis

Dialysegerät [dia'lyːzə-] NT dialysis machine

Diamant [dia'mant] M -en, -en diamond

diamanten [dia'mantn] ADJ ATTR diamond; ~**e Hochzeit** diamond wedding

diametral [diame'traːl] **1** ADJ diametral; (fig) Ansichten diametrically opposed; Gegensatz exact **2** ADV ~ **entgegengesetzt sein, sich ~ gegenüberliegen** to be diametrically opposite; ~ **entgegengesetzt** (fig) diametrically opposed

Diaphragma [dia'fragma] NT -s, **Diaphragmen** [-mən] (Tech, Med) diaphragm

Dia- (Phot): **Diapositiv** NT slide; **Diaprojektor** M slide projector; **Diarahmen** M slide frame

Diät [di'ɛːt] F -, -en (Med) diet; ~ **kochen/essen** to cook/to eat according to a diet; ~ **halten** to keep to a diet; **nach einer ~ leben** to be on a diet or (wegen Krankheit) special diet; **jdn auf ~ setzen** (inf) to put sb on a diet; **auf ~ sein** (inf) to be on a diet

Diätassistent(in) M(F) dietician

Diäten PL (Parl) parliamentary allowance

Diavortrag M slide presentation

dich [dɪç] **1** PERS PRON ACC von **du** you **2** REFL PRON yourself; **wie fühlst du ~?** how do you feel?

dicht [dɪçt] **1** ADJ **(a)** Gefieder, Haar, Hecke thick; Wald, (Menschen)menge, Gewühl dense; Verkehr heavy; Gewebe close; Stoff closely-woven; (fig = konzentriert) Stil dense; **in ~er Folge** in rapid succession

(b) (= undurchlässig) Vorhänge thick; Rollladen heavy; (= wasserdicht) watertight; (= luftdicht) airtight; ~ **machen** to seal; **er ist nicht ganz ~** (inf) he's nuts (inf)

(c) (sl: = betrunken, high) out of it (inf)

2 ADV **(a)** (= nahe) closely; (~ **an**) ~ **stehen** to stand close together

(b) (= fest) zuziehen, schließen tightly; weben densely; ~ **halten** to be watertight; ~ **verhängen** to curtain heavily

(c) (= sehr stark) bevölkert, bepflanzt densely; ~ **mit etw übersät** covered with sth; ~ **behaart** very hairy; ~ **bewölkt** heavily overcast; ~ **gedrängt** closely packed; Programm packed

(d) (mit Präpositionen) ~ **an/bei** close to; ~ **dahinter/darüber/davor** right behind/above/in front; ~ **daneben** close beside it; ~ **daran** hard by it; ~ **hintereinander** close(ly) behind one another; ~ **beieinander** or **beisammen** close together

dichtbehaart [-bəha:ɐt] ADJ ATTR siehe **dicht**

Dichte [ˈdɪçtə] F -, -n, NO PL **(a)** (von Gefieder, Haar, Hecke) thickness; (von Laub, Nebel, Wald, Menschenmenge, fig) denseness; (von Verkehr) heaviness **(b)** (Phys) density

dichten¹ [ˈdɪçtn] **1** VT to write; **sein Glückwunsch war gedichtet** his congratulations were (written) in verse **2** VI to write poems/a poem

dichten² VT (= undurchlässig machen) to seal

Dichter [ˈdɪçtɐ] M -s, -, **Dichterin** [-ərɪn] F -, -nen poet; (= Schriftsteller) writer

dichterisch [ˈdɪçtərɪʃ] ADJ poetic; (= schriftstellerisch) literary; ~**e Freiheit** poetic licence (Brit) or license (US)

Dicht-: **dichtgedrängt** ADJ ATTR siehe **dicht**; **dichthalten** VI SEP IRREG (inf) to keep one's mouth shut (inf); **Dichtheit** F -, NO PL = **Dichte** (a); **Dichtkunst** F art of poetry; (= Schriftstellerei) creative writing; **dichtmachen** VTI SEP (inf) Laden etc to shut up; Fabrik, Betrieb etc to close down; (den Laden) ~ to shut up shop (and go home) (inf)

Dichtung¹ ['dıçtʊŋ] F -, -en **(a)** NO PL (= *Dichtkunst, Gesamtwerk*) literature; (*in Versform*) poetry; **~ und Wahrheit** (*fig*) fact and fiction **(b)** (= *Dichtwerk*) poem; literary work; **dramatische ~** dramatic poem

Dichtung² F -, -en (*Tech*) seal; (*in Wasserhahn etc*) washer; (*Aut: von Zylinder, Vergaser*) gasket

Dichtungs-: Dichtungsmaterial NT, **Dichtungsmittel** NT sealing compound; **Dichtungsring** M, **Dichtungsscheibe** F seal; (*in Wasserhahn*) washer

dick [dık] 🟦 ADJ **(a)** thick; *Mensch, Körperteil, Band, Buch, Brieftasche* fat; (*inf*) *Gehalt, Belohnung, Gewinn* hefty; **~e Milch** sour milk; **3 m ~e Wände** walls 3 metres (*Brit*) *or* meters (*US*) thick; **einen ~en Mercedes fahren** (*inf*) to drive a big Mercedes; **eine ~e Zigarre** a big fat cigar; **~ machen** (*Speisen*) to be fattening; **~ werden** (*Mensch: = zunehmen*) to get fat; **durch ~ und dünn** through thick and thin **(b)** (*inf: = schwerwiegend*) *Fehler, Verweis* big; **das ist ein ~er Tadel/ein ~es Lob** that's heavy criticism/high praise; **das ist ein ~er Hund** *or* **ein ~es Ei** (*inf: = unerhört*) that's a bit much (*inf*) **(c)** (= *geschwollen*) swollen; *Beule* big **(d)** (*inf: = herzlich*) *Freundschaft, Freund* close; **mit jdm ~e sein** to be thick with sb (*inf*)

🟦 ADV **(a)** (= *warm*) warmly **(b)** *anstreichen, unterstreichen* heavily **(c)** (= *reichlich*) thickly; **etw ~ mit Butter bestreichen** to spread butter thickly on sth; **~(e)** (*inf: = ausreichend*) easily; **er hat es ~(e)** (*inf: = hat es satt*) he's had enough of it; (= *hat viel*) he's got enough and to spare; **jdn/etw ~(e) haben** (*inf: = von jdm/ etw genug haben*) to have had one's fill of sb/sth (*inf*) **(d)** (*inf: = eng*) **mit jdm ~ befreundet sein** to be thick with sb (*inf*)

Dick-: dickbäuchig [-bɔyçıç] ADJ *Mensch* potbellied; **Dickdarm** M (*Anat*) colon

Dicke ['dıkə] F -, -n **(a)** (= *Stärke, Durchmesser*) thickness **(b)** (*von Menschen, Körperteilen*) fatness

Dicke(r) ['dıkə] MF DECL AS ADJ (*inf*) fatso (*inf*)

Dickerchen ['dıkəçən] NT **-s, -** (*inf*) chubby

dicketun VR SEP IRREG (*inf*) = **dicktun**

Dick-: dickfellig [-fɛlıç] ADJ (*inf*) thick-skinned; **dickflüssig** ADJ thick, viscous (*Tech*); **Dickhäuter** [-hɔytɐ] M **-s, -** pachyderm; (*fig*) thick-skinned person

Dickicht ['dıkıçt] NT **-(e)s, -e** (= *Gebüsch*) thicket; (*fig*) jungle

Dick-: Dickkopf M **(a)** (= *Starrsinn*) obstinacy; **einen ~ haben** to be obstinate; **sie setzt ihren ~ immer durch** she always gets what she wants **(b)** (= *Mensch*) mule (*inf*); **dickköpfig** ADJ (*fig*) stubborn; **Dickköpfigkeit** F **-**, NO PL stubbornness; **dicklich** ['dıklıç] ADJ plump; **Dickmilch** F (*Cook*) sour milk; **Dickschädel** M (*inf*) = **Dickkopf**; **dicktun** VR SEP IRREG (*inf*) to swank (*inf*); **(sich) mit etw ~** to swank about sth (*inf*)

Didaktik [di'daktık] F -, -en didactics *sing* (*form*), teaching methods *pl*

didaktisch [di'daktıʃ] 🟦 ADJ didactic 🟦 ADV didactically

die [di:] *siehe* **der²**

Dieb [di:p] M **-(e)s, -e** [-bə], **Diebin** ['di:bın] F -, -nen thief; **haltet den ~!** stop thief!

Dieberei [di:bə'rai] F -, -en thievery *no pl*

Diebes-: Diebesbande F gang of thieves; **Diebesgut** NT, NO PL stolen property; **Diebespack** NT (*pej*) thieving riffraff (*pej*)

Diebin *siehe* **Dieb**

diebisch ['di:bıʃ] ADJ **(a)** *Gesindel, Elster* thieving *attr* **(b)** (*inf*) *Freude, Vergnügen* mischievous

Diebstahl ['di:pʃta:l] M **-(e)s, ⸚e** [-ʃtɛ:lə] theft; **bewaffneter ~** armed robbery; **geistiger ~** plagiarism

Diebstahl-: diebstahlsicher ADJ theft-proof; **Diebstahlsicherung** F (*Aut*) antitheft device

diejenige ['di:je:nıgə] DEM PRON *siehe* **derjenige**

Diele ['di:lə] F -, -n **(a)** (= *Fußbodenbrett*) floorboard **(b)** (= *Vorraum*) hall

dienen ['di:nən] VI to serve (*jdm/einer Sache* sb/sth); (= *Militärdienst leisten*) to do (one's) military service; *dem Fortschritt, der Erforschung* to aid; *dem Verständnis* to promote; (= *nützlich sein*) to be of use (*jdm* to sb); **als/zu etw ~** to serve as/for sth; **es dient einem guten Zweck** it serves a useful purpose; **es dient einer guten Sache** it is for a good cause; **womit kann ich Ihnen ~?** what can I do for you?; (*im Geschäft*

auch) can I help you?; **damit kann ich leider nicht ~** I'm afraid I can't help you there; **damit ist mir wenig gedient** that's no use to me

Diener ['di:nɐ] M **-s, -** **(a)** (= *Mensch: lit, fig*) servant **(b)** (*inf: = Verbeugung*) bow

Dienerin ['di:nərın] F -, -nen maid

Dienerschaft ['di:nɐʃaft] F -, -en servants *pl*

dienlich ['di:nlıç] ADJ useful; (= *ratsam*) advisable; **jdm/einer Sache ~ sein** to be of use *or* help to sb/sth

Dienst [di:nst] M **-(e)s, -e** **(a)** (= *Arbeitsverhältnis, Tätigkeitsbereich*) service; (= *Arbeitsstelle*) position; **diplomatischer/öffentlicher ~** diplomatic/civil service; **Oberst etc außer ~** (*abbr* **a. D.**) retired colonel etc; **den ~ quittieren, aus dem ~ (aus)scheiden** to resign one's post; (*Mil*) to leave the service; **~ mit der Waffe** (*Mil*) armed service; **im ~ ergraut sein** to have many years of faithful service behind one **(b)** (= *Berufsausübung, Amtspflicht*) duty; (= *Arbeit, Arbeitszeit*) work; **im ~ sein, haben** (*Arzt, Feuerwehrmann etc*) to be on duty; (*Apotheke*) to be open; **~ habend** *Arzt, Offizier etc* duty *attr*, on duty; **im ~ sein** (*Angestellter etc*) to be working; **außer ~ sein** to be off duty; **nach ~** after work; **~ tun** to serve (*bei* in, *als* as); **tuend** *Arzt* duty *attr*, on duty; **jdn vom ~ beurlauben** to grant sb leave of absence; **jdn vom ~ befreien** to exempt sb from his duties; **Tellerwäscher/Kindermädchen vom ~** (*hum*) resident dishwasher/babysitter (*hum*); **~ nach Vorschrift** work to rule; **~ ist ~ und Schnaps ist Schnaps** (*Prov inf*) you can't mix business with pleasure **(c)** (= *Tätigkeit, Leistung, Hilfe*) service; **im ~(e) einer Sache/der Menschheit** in the service of sth/humanity; **sich in den ~ der Sache stellen** to embrace the cause; **jdm einen ~/einen schlechten ~ erweisen** to do sb a good/bad turn; **jdm gute ~e leisten** *or* **tun** to serve sb well; **die Stimme etc versagte ihr den ~** her voice *etc* failed (her) *or* gave way; **~ am Vaterland** service to one's country; **~ am Kunden** customer service

-dienst M SUF IN CPDS service; (*für Hausarbeit etc*) duty; **Militärdienst** military service; **Küchendienst haben** to be on kitchen duty

Dienstag ['di:nsta:k] M Tuesday; **~ Abend/Morgen/Nachmittag** (on) Tuesday evening/morning/afternoon; **~ abends/nachts/ vormittags** on Tuesday evenings/nights/mornings; **am ~** on Tuesday; **an einem ~, eines ~s** one Tuesday; **hast du ~ Zeit?** have you time on Tuesday?; **heute ist ~, der 10. Juni** today is Tuesday the tenth of June; **jeden ~, alle ~e** every Tuesday; **ab nächsten** *or* **nächstem ~** from next Tuesday; **in acht Tagen** *or* **in einer Woche** a week on Tuesday; **~ vor einer Woche** *or* **vor acht Tagen** a week (ago) last Tuesday

Dienstag-: Dienstagabend M Tuesday evening; **Dienstagnachmittag** M Tuesday afternoon

dienstags ['di:nsta:ks] ADV on Tuesdays, on a Tuesday; **~ abends** on Tuesday evenings, on a Tuesday evening

Dienst-: Dienstalter NT length of service; **Dienstauffassung** F conception of one's duties; **haben Sie für eine ~!** have you no sense of duty?; **Dienstaufsicht** F supervision; **die ~ über etw** (*acc*) **haben** to be in charge of sth; **Dienstaufsichtsbeschwerde** F complaint about a ruling; **dienstbeflissen** ADJ zealous; **dienstbereit** ADJ *Apotheke* open *pred*; *Arzt* on call *pred*; **Dienstbote** M, **Dienstbotin** F servant; **Dienstboteneingang** M tradesmen's entrance; **Dienstgeheimnis** NT official secret; **Dienstgrad** M (*Mil*) **(a)** (= *Rangstufe*) rank **(b)** (= *Mensch*) **ein höherer ~** a person of higher rank; **diensthabend** ADJ ATTR *siehe* **Dienst**; **Dienstkleidung** F uniform; (*Mil*) service dress; **Dienstleistung** F service

Dienstleistungs-: Dienstleistungsbetrieb M service company; **Dienstleistungsgewerbe** NT services trade; **Dienstleistungsbilanz** F balance of invisible trade

dienstlich ['di:nstlıç] 🟦 ADJ *Angelegenheiten* business *attr*; *Schreiben, Befehl* official; **~ werden** (*inf*) to become businesslike 🟦 ADV on business; **wir haben hier ~ zu tun** we have business here

Dienst-: Dienstmädchen NT maid; **Dienstpistole** F service revolver; **Dienstplan** M duty roster; **Dienstrang** M grade; (*Mil*) rank; **Dienstreise** F business trip; **auf ~** on a business trip; **Dienstschluss** M end of work; **nach ~** after work; **wir haben jetzt ~** we finish work now; **Dienstsiegel** NT, **Dienststempel** M official stamp; **Dienststelle** F (*Admin*) department;

Dienststunden PL working hours *pl*; **diensttauglich** ADJ (*Mil*) fit for duty; **diensttuend** [-tuənt] ADJ *siehe* **Dienst**;
Dienstverhältnis NT im **~ stehen** to be a public employee; **in ein ~ übernommen werden** to become a public employee;
Dienstwagen M company car; (*von Beamten*) official car; (*Mil*) staff car; (*Rail*) ≈ guard's carriage, ≈ conductor's car (*US*);
Dienstweg M **den ~ einhalten** to go through the proper channels *pl*

dies [diːs] DEM PRON INV this; (*pl*) these; **~ sind** these are; **~ und das** this and that; **~ alles, alles ~** all this/that; *siehe auch* **dieser**

diesbezüglich (*form*) 🔢 ADJ regarding this 🔢 ADV **sich ~ äußern** to give one's views on this matter

diese ['diːzə] DEM PRON *siehe* **dieser**

Diesel ['diːzl̩] M **-s, -** (*inf*) diesel

dieselbe [diː'zɛlbə] DEM PRON *siehe* **derselbe**

Diesel-: Diesellok F, **Diesellokomotive** F diesel locomotive; **Dieselmotor** M diesel engine; **Dieselöl** NT diesel oil

dieser, diese, dieses *pl* **diese** DEM PRON
(a) (*substantivisch*) this; (*pl*) these; (= **~ dort, da**) that; (*pl*) those; **diese(r, s) hier** this (one); **diese hier** *pl* these (ones); **diese(r, s) da** that (one); **diese da** *pl* those (ones); **~ ...,** **jener ...** the latter ..., the former ...; **schließlich fragte ich einen Polizisten; ~ sagte mir ...** in the end I asked a policeman; he told me ...; **dieses und jenes** this and that; **~ und jener** this person and that; **~ oder jener** someone or other
(b) ATTR this; (*pl*) these; (= **~ dort, da**) that; (*pl*) those; **Anfang dieses Jahres/Monats** at the beginning of the *or* this year/month; **am 5. dieses Monats** on the 5th of this month; **~ Tage** (*vergangen*) the other day; (*zukünftig*) one of these days; **(nur) dieses eine Mal** just this/that once; **~ Maier** (*inf*) that *or* this Maier

dieses ['diːzəs] DEM PRON *siehe* **dieser**

diesig ['diːzɪç] ADJ *Wetter, Luft* hazy

dies-: diesjährig ADJ ATTR this year's; **diesmal** ADV this time; **diesseitig** [-zaitɪç] ADJ **(a)** *Ufer* near(side) *attr*, (on) this side **(b)** (= *irdisch*) of this world; *Leben* in this world; **diesseits** ['diːszaits] PREP +GEN on this side of; **Diesseits** ['diːszaits] NT **-,** NO PL **das ~** this life

Dietrich ['diːtrɪç] M **-s, -e** skeleton key

diffamieren [dɪfa'miːrən], *ptp* **diffamiert** VT to defame

Differential [dɪfəren'tsiaːl] NT **-s, -e** = **Differenzial**

Differenz [dɪfə'rɛnts] F **-, -en (a)** (= *Unterschied, fehlender Betrag*) (*Math*) difference; (= *Abweichung*) discrepancy **(b)** USU PL (= *Meinungsverschiedenheit*) difference (of opinion)

Differenzbetrag M difference

Differenzial [dɪfəren'tsiaːl] NT **-s, -e (a)** (*Math*) differential **(b)** (*Aut: auch* **Differenzialgetriebe**) differential (gear)

Differenzial- IN CPDS (*Tech, Math*) differential;

differenzieren [dɪfərɛn'tsiːrən], *ptp* **differenziert** 🔢 VT
(a) (= *unterscheiden*) to make distinctions/a distinction in; *Behauptung, Urteil* to be discriminating in
(b) (*Math*) to differentiate 🔢 VI to make distinctions/a distinction (*zwischen +dat* between, *bei* in); (= *den Unterschied verstehen*) to differentiate (*zwischen +dat* between, *bei* in); (*bei Behauptung, Urteil*) to be discriminating; **~de Methoden** discriminative methods

differenziert [dɪfərɛn'tsiːɐt] 🔢 ADJ (= *fein unterscheidend*) subtly differentiated; (= *verfeinert*) sophisticated; *Charakter, Mensch, Gefühlsleben* complex 🔢 ADV *gestalten, sich ausdrücken* in a sophisticated manner; **ein Problem ~ sehen/betrachten** to look at/examine a problem from all angles; **ich sehe das etwas ~er** I think it's a bit more complex than that

Differenzierung F **-, -en (a)** (= *Unterscheidung*) distinction; (*zwischen zwei Dingen*) differentiation **(b)** (*Math*) differentiation

diffus [dɪ'fuːs] ADJ *Licht* diffuse; *Gedanken, Ausdrucksweise* confused; *Rechtslage* unclear

digital [digi'taːl] 🔢 ADJ digital 🔢 ADV digitally

Digital- IN CPDS digital; **Digitalbaustein** M integrated circuit element; **Digitalfernsehen** NT digital television

digitalisieren [digitali'ziːrən], *ptp* **digitalisiert** VT to digitalize

Digitalisierung F **-, -en** digitalization

Digital-: Digitalkamera F digital camera; **Digitalrechner** M (*Comput*) digital calculator; **Digitaltechnik** F (*Comput*) digital

technology; **Digitaltonband** NT (*abbr* **DAT**) digital audio tape; **Digitaluhr** F digital clock; (= *Armbanduhr*) digital watch

Diktat [dɪk'taːt] NT **-(e)s, -e** dictation (*also Sch*); **ein ~ schreiben** (*Sch*) to do (a) dictation; **etw nach ~ schreiben** to write sth from dictation; **Frau Wengel, bitte zum ~!** take a letter please, Ms Wengel; **nach ~ verreist** dictated by X and signed in his/her absence

Diktator [dɪk'taːtoːɐ] M **-s, Diktatoren** [-'toːrən], **Diktatorin** [-'toːrɪn] F **-, -nen** dictator

diktatorisch [dɪkta'toːrɪʃ] ADJ dictatorial

Diktatur [dɪkta'tuːɐ] F **-, -en** dictatorship

diktieren [dɪk'tiːrən], *ptp* **diktiert** VT (*lit, fig*) to dictate

Diktiergerät NT, **Diktiermaschine** F dictating machine

Dilemma [di'lɛma] NT **-s, -s** *or* (*geh*) **-ta** [-ta] dilemma

Dilettant [dile'tant] M **-en, -en**, **Dilettantin** [-'tantɪn] F **-, -nen** amateur

dilettantisch [dile'tantɪʃ] 🔢 ADJ amateurish 🔢 ADV amateurishly; **~ vorgehen** to act like an amateur

Dill [dɪl] M **-(e)s, -e** (*Bot, Cook*) dill

Dimension [dimɛn'zioːn] F **-, -en** dimension

-dimensional [dimɛnzionaːl] ADJ SUF -dimensional; **dreidimensional** three-dimensional

Diminutiv [diminu'tiːf] NT **-s, -e** [-və] diminutive (*zu, von* of)

Dimmer ['dɪmɐ] M **-s, -** dimmer (switch)

DIN® [dɪn, diːn] F **-,** NO PL ABBR *von* **Deutsche Industrie-Norm** German Industrial Standard; **~ A4** A4; **~-Format** German standard paper size

Ding [dɪŋ] NT **-(e)s, -e** *or* (*inf*) **-er (a)** (= *Sache, Gegenstand*) thing; **das ist ein ~ der Unmöglichkeit** that is quite impossible; **das ist nicht sein ~** (*inf*) that's not really his thing (*inf*); **guter ~e sein** (*geh*) to be in good spirits; **die ~e beim (rechten) Namen nennen** to call a spade a spade (*Brit prov*), to be frank; **gut ~ will Weile haben** (*Prov*) it takes time to do a thing well
(b) (= *Gegebenheit*) thing; **in diesen ~en** about these things; **berufliche ~e** professional matters; **reden wir von andern ~en** let's talk about something else; **wir harrten der ~e, die da kommen sollten** we waited to see what would happen; **so wie die ~e liegen** as things are; **wie ich die ~e sehe** as I see things; **vor allen ~en** above all (things); **es müsste nicht mit rechten ~en zugehen, wenn ...** it would be more than a little strange if ...
(c) (*inf: auch* **Dings**) (= *unbestimmtes Etwas*) thing; **was ist das für ein ~?** what's that thing?; **das ~(s) da** (*inf*) that thing (over) there; **das ist ein ~!** now there's a thing!; **ein tolles ~!** great! (*inf*)
(d) *pl* **-er** (*inf:* = *Verbrechen*) job; **sich** (*dat*) **ein ~ leisten** to be up to something; **~er machen** to be up to all sorts of tricks (*inf*); **was macht ihr bloß für ~er?** the things you do! (*inf*); **das war vielleicht ein ~** (*inf*) that was quite something (*inf*)
(e) (= *Mädchen*) thing
(f) (*sl:* = *Busen*) **~er** boobs *pl* (*inf*)

dinglich ['dɪŋlɪç] 🔢 ADJ material 🔢 ADV (*Fin*) **~ gesicherte Forderungen** claims *pl* covered by assets

Dings [dɪŋs] NT **-,** NO PL, **Dingsbums** ['dɪŋsbʊms] NT **-,** NO PL, **Dingsda** ['dɪŋsdaː] NT **-,** NO PL (*inf*) (= *Sache*) whatsit (*inf*); **der/die ~** (= *Person*) what's-his/her-name (*inf*)

Dinkel ['dɪŋkl̩] M **-s, -** (*Bot*) spelt

Dinosaurier [dino-] M (*lit, fig*) dinosaur

Diode [di'loːdə] F **-, -n** diode

Dioptrie [dɪɔp'triː] F **-, -n** [-'triːən] (*Opt*) (*abbr* **dpt**) diopter

Dioxid [dɪb'ksiːt] NT **-s, -e** [-də] dioxide

Dioxin [dɪb'ksiːn] NT **-s, -e** dioxin

dioxinhaltig ADJ dioxinated

Diözese [diø'tseːzə] F **-, -n** diocese

Diphtherie [dɪfte'riː] F **-, -n** [-'riːən] diphtheria

Diphthong [dɪf'tɔŋ] M **-s, -e** diphthong

Dipl. ABBR *von* **Diplom**

Dipl.-Ing. ABBR *von* **Diplomingenieur**

Dipl.-Kfm. ABBR *von* **Diplomkaufmann**

Diplom [di'ploːm] NT **-s, -e** diploma

Diplom- IN CPDS (*vor Berufsbezeichnung*) qualified

Diplomarbeit F dissertation (*submitted for a diploma*)

Diplomat [diplo'maːt] M **-en, -en**, **Diplomatin** [-'maːtɪn] F **-, -nen** diplomat

Diplomatenkoffer M executive case

Diplomatie [diploma'tiː] F **-**, NO PL (*lit, fig*) diplomacy

diplomatisch [diplo'maːtɪʃ] (*Pol, fig*) **1** ADJ diplomatic **2** ADV diplomatically; **sie hat sich nicht sehr ~ verhalten** she wasn't very diplomatic

diplomiert [diplo'miːɐt] ADJ qualified

Diplom-: **Diplomingenieur(in)** M(F) qualified engineer; **Diplomkauffrau** F, **Diplomkaufmann** M business school graduate

DIP-Schalter ['dɪp-] M (*Comput*) dip switch

dir [diːɐ] PERS PRON DAT *von* **du** to you; (*nach Präpositionen*) you; *siehe auch* **ihm**

Dir. ABBR *von* **Direktion, Direktor, Dirigent**

direkt [di'rɛkt] **1** ADJ (a) (= *unmittelbar, gerade*) direct; *Erledigung* immediate; **eine ~ Verbindung** (*mit Zug*) a through train; (*mit Flugzeug*) a direct flight
(b) (= *unverblümt*) direct; (= *genau*) *Vorstellungen, Antwort, Auskunft* clear
(c) (*inf*: = *ausgesprochen*) sheer; **es war keine ~e Katastrophe** it wasn't exactly a catastrophe
2 ADV (a) (= *unmittelbar*) directly; **~ aus** *or* **von/zu** *or* **nach** straight from/to; **~ an/neben/unter/über** right by/next to/under/over; **jdm ~ ins Gesicht/in die Augen sehen** to look sb straight in the face/the eyes; **~ übertragen** *or* **senden** to transmit live
(b) (= *unverblümt*) bluntly; **jdm etw ~ ins Gesicht sagen** to tell sb sth (straight) to his face; **~ fragen** to ask outright
(c) (*inf*: = *geradezu*) really; **nicht ~** not exactly

Direkt- IN CPDS direct; (*Rad, TV*) live; **Direktbank** F, *pl* **-banken** (*Fin*) direct bank

Direktion [dirɛk'tsioːn] F **-, -en** (a) (= *Leitung*) management; (*von Schule*) headship (*Brit*), principalship (*esp US*)
(b) (= *Direktoren, Vorstand*) management

Direktmandat NT (*Pol*) direct mandate

Direktor [di'rɛktoːɐ] M **-s, Direktoren** [-'toːrən], **Direktorin** [-'toːrɪn] F **-, -nen** director; (*von Gefängnis*) governor, warden (*US*); (*von Schule*) headmaster/-mistress (*esp Brit*), principal (*esp US*)

Direktorat [dirɛkto'raːt] NT **-(e)s, -e** (a) (= *Amt*) directorship; (*von Schule*) headship (*Brit*), principalship (*esp US*)
(b) (= *Diensträume*) (*von Firma, Museum*) director's office; (*von Schule*) head(master/mistress)'s (*esp Brit*) *or* principal's (*esp US*) study

Direkt-: **Direktübertragung** F (*Rad, TV*) live transmission; **Direktverbindung** F (*Rail*) through train; (*Aviat*) direct flight; **Direktverkauf** M (*Comm*) direct selling; (= *Haustürverkauf*) door-to-door selling; **Direktversicherung** F (*Insur*) direct insurance; **Direktvertrieb** M direct marketing

Dirigent [diri'gɛnt] M **-en, -en**, **Dirigentin** [-'gɛntɪn] F **-, -nen** (*Mus*) conductor; (*fig*) leader

dirigieren [diri'giːrən], *ptp* **dirigiert** VT (a) AUCH VI (*Mus*) to conduct; (*fig*) to lead (b) (= *leiten, einweisen*) *Verkehr etc* to direct

Dirndl ['dɪrndl] NT **-s, -** (*auch* **Dirndlkleid**) dirndl

Dirne ['dɪrnə] F **-, -n** prostitute

dis NT **-, -**, **Dis** [dɪs] NT **-, -** (*Mus*) D sharp

Disagio [dɪs'laːdʒo, dɪs'laːʒio] NT **-s, -s** *or* **Disagien** [-'laːdʒən, -laːʒiən] (*Fin*) discount

Disc-Kamera ['dɪsk-] F disc camera

Discman® ['dɪskmən] M **-s, -s** Discman®

Disco ['dɪsko] F **-, -s** disco

Discount- [dɪs'kaunt] IN CPDS discount; **Discounthändler(in)** M(F) discount dealer; **Discountladen** M discount shop

Diskette [dɪs'kɛtə] F **-, -n** disk

Disketten-: **Diskettenfehler** M disk error; **Diskettenlaufwerk** NT disk drive

Diskjockey ['dɪskdʒɔke] M **-s, -s** disc jockey

Disko ['dɪsko] F **-, -s** disco

Diskont [dɪs'kɔnt] M **-s, -e** (*Fin*) discount

Diskontgeschäft NT (*von Bank*) discounting

diskontieren [dɪskɔn'tiːrən], *ptp* **diskontiert** VT (*Fin*) to discount

Diskont-: **Diskontgeschäft** NT (*von Bank*) discounting; **Diskontkredit** M discount credit; **Diskontpolitik** F discount rate policy; **Diskontsatz** M (*Fin*) discount rate (*Brit*), bank rate (*US*)

Diskothek [dɪsko'teːk] F **-, -en** (= *Tanzbar*) discotheque

Diskrepanz [dɪskre'pants] F **-, -en** discrepancy

diskret [dɪs'kreːt] **1** ADJ discreet; (= *vertraulich*) confidential **2** ADV discreetly

Diskretion [dɪskre'tsioːn] F **-**, NO PL discretion; (= *vertrauliche Behandlung*) confidentiality; **~ üben** to be discreet; **jdn um ~ in einer Angelegenheit bitten** to ask sb to treat an affair as a matter of confidence

diskriminieren [dɪskrimi'niːrən], *ptp* **diskriminiert** VT to discriminate against

diskriminierend ADJ discriminatory

Diskriminierung F **-, -en** discrimination

Diskus ['dɪskʊs] M **-, -se** *or* **Disken** ['dɪskn] discus

Diskussion [dɪsko'sioːn] F **-, -en** discussion; **zur ~ stehen** to be under discussion; **etw zur ~ stellen** to put sth up for discussion

Diskussions-: **Diskussionsbeitrag** M contribution to the discussion; **Diskussionsteilnehmer(in)** M(F) participant (in a discussion)

Diskus-: **Diskuswerfen** NT **-s**, NO PL throwing the discus; **Diskuswerfer(in)** M(F) discus thrower

diskutabel [dɪsku'taːbl], **diskutierbar** ADJ worth discussing; **das ist überhaupt nicht ~** that's not even worth talking about

diskutieren [dɪsku'tiːrən], *ptp* **diskutiert** VTI to discuss; **über etw** (*acc*) **~** to discuss sth; **darüber lässt sich ~** that's debatable; **wir haben stundenlang diskutiert** we've spent hours in discussion; **was gibts denn da zu ~?** what is there to talk about?

Dispersionsfarbe F emulsion (paint)

Display [dɪs'pleɪ] NT **-s, -s** display

Dispokredit ['dɪspokrediːt] M (*Fin inf*) overdraft

Disposition [dɪs-] F (*geh*) (a) (= *Verfügung*) **zur ~ stehen** to be up for consideration; **jdm zur** *or* **zu jds ~ stehen** to be at sb's disposal; **jdm etw zur ~ stellen** to place sth at sb's disposal; **etw zur ~ stellen** to put sth up for consideration
(b) (= *Anordnung*) arrangement

Dispositionskredit [-krediːt] M (*Fin*) overdraft

Disqualifikation [dɪs-] F disqualification

disqualifizieren [dɪs-], *ptp* **disqualifiziert** VT to disqualify

dissen ['dɪsn] (*sl*) VT to slag off (*Brit inf*), to diss (*esp US inf*)

Dissertation [dɪsɛrta'tsioːn] F **-, -en** dissertation; (= *Doktorarbeit*) (doctoral) thesis

dissertieren [dɪsɛr'tiːrən], *ptp* **dissertiert** VI *siehe* **Dissertation** to write a dissertation/(doctoral) thesis (*über +acc* on)

Dissident [dɪsi'dɛnt] M **-en, -en**, **Dissidentin** [-'dɛntɪn] F **-, -nen** dissident

Dissonanz [dɪso'nants] F **-, -en** (*Mus*) dissonance; (*fig*) (note of) discord

Distanz [dɪs'tants] F **-, -en** (*lit*) distance; (*fig*) (= *Abstand, Entfernung*) detachment; (= *Zurückhaltung*) reserve; **~ halten** *or* **wahren** (*lit, fig*) to keep one's distance; (**zu jdm/etw**) **auf ~ gehen** (*lit, fig*) to distance oneself from sb/sth; **die nötige ~ zu etw finden/haben** to become/be sufficiently detached from sth

distanzieren [dɪstan'tsiːrən], *ptp* **distanziert** **1** VR **sich von jdm/etw ~** to distance oneself from sb/sth **2** VT (*Sport*) to outdistance

distanziert [dɪstanˈtsiːɐt] **1** ADJ *Verhalten* distant **2** ADV **sich ~ verhalten** to act distant; **~ wirken** to seem distant

Distanziertheit F -, NO PL distance

Distel [ˈdɪstl] F -, -n thistle

Disziplin [dɪstsiˈpliːn] F -, -en discipline; **~ halten** (*Lehrer*) to maintain discipline; (*Klasse*) to behave in a disciplined manner

Disziplinar- [dɪstsipliˈnaːɐ] IN CPDS disciplinary

disziplinarisch [dɪstsipliˈnaːrɪʃ] **1** ADJ disciplinary **2** ADV **jdn ~ bestrafen, ~ gegen jdn vorgehen** to take disciplinary action against sb; **sein Regelverstoß wurde ~ geahndet** he was disciplined for an infringement of the rules; **jdm ~ unterstellt sein** to be answerable to sb

Disziplinar-: Disziplinarstrafe F punishment; **mit einer ~ rechnen** to expect disciplinary action; **eine ~ bekommen** to be disciplined; **Disziplinarverfahren** NT disciplinary proceedings *pl*

diszipliniert [dɪstsipliˈniːɐt] **1** ADJ disciplined **2** ADV in a disciplined manner

dito [ˈdiːto] ADV (*Comm, hum*) ditto

Diva [ˈdiːva] F -, -s *or* **Diven** [ˈdiːvn] star; (*Film*) screen goddess

Divergenz [diverˈgɛnts] F -, -en **(a)** NO PL divergence **(b)** USU PL (= *Meinungsverschiedenheit*) difference (of opinion)

divergieren [diverˈgiːrən], *ptp* **divergiert** VI to diverge

divers [diˈvɛrs] ADJ ATTR various; **die ~esten ...** the most diverse ...; **~es Angebot von ...** an assortment of ...; **~e** (= *mehrere der gleichen Art*) several; **„Diverses"** "miscellaneous"; **wir haben noch Diverses zu erledigen** we still have various things to see to

Diversifikation [diverzifikaˈtsioːn] F -, -en diversification

diversifizieren [diverzifiˈtsiːrən], *ptp* **diversifiziert** VTI to diversify

Dividende [diviˈdɛndə] F -, -n (*Fin*) dividend

Dividenden-: Dividendenausschüttung F (*Fin*) distribution of dividends; **Dividendenkupon** M, **Dividendenschein** M dividend coupon

dividieren [diviˈdiːrən], *ptp* **dividiert** VTI to divide (*durch* by)

Division [diviˈzioːn] F -, -en (*Math, Mil*) division

Divisionskalkulation F (*Fin*) process costing

DJ [ˈdiːdʒeː] M -s, -s ABBR *von* Diskjockey DJ

d. J. ABBR **(a)** *von* **dieses Jahres** of this year **(b)** *von* **der Jüngere** jun.

DJH [deːjɔtˈhaː] NT -(s) ABBR *von* **Deutsches Jugendherbergswerk** German Youth Hostel Association

DKP [deːkaːˈpeː] F - ABBR *von* **Deutsche Kommunistische Partei**

DM [deːˈʔɛm] F -, - (*Hist*) ABBR *von* **Deutsche Mark** DM

d. M. ABBR *von* **dieses Monats** inst

D-Mark [ˈdeːmark] F, *pl* -Mark (*Hist*) Deutschmark

D-Netz [ˈdeː-] NT (*Telec*) digital cellular phone network

DNS- [deːʔɛnˈʔɛs] F - ABBR *von* **Desoxyribonukleinsäure** DNA

DNS- [deːʔɛnˈʔɛs-]: **DNS-Kode** M DNA code; **DNS-Strickleiter** F DNA ladder; **DNS-Zeile** F line of DNA

doch [dɔx] **1** CONJ (= *aber, allein*) but; (= *jedoch, trotzdem*) but still; **und ~ hat er es getan** but he still did it

2 ADV **(a)** (*betont*) (= *dennoch*) after all; (= *trotzdem*) anyway; (= *sowieso*) anyway; **du weißt es ja ~ besser** you always know better than I do anyway; **das geht denn ~ zu weit!** that really is going too far; **und ~, ...** and yet ...

(b) (*betont* = *tatsächlich*) really; **ja ~!** of course!; **nein ~!** of course not!; **also ~!** so it IS/so he DID! *etc*; **er hat es gestohlen – also ~!** he stole it – so it WAS him!; **das ist ~ interessant, was er da sagt** what he's saying is really interesting; **was es ~ alles für Leute gibt!** the people you get!

(c) (*als bejahende Antwort*) yes I do/it does *etc*; **hat es dir nicht gefallen? – (~,) ~!** didn't you like it? – (oh) yes I did!; **will er nicht mitkommen? – ~!** doesn't he want to come? – (oh) yes, he does; **~, schon, aber ...** yes it does/I do *etc*, but ...

(d) (*auffordernd: nicht übersetzt, aber emphatisches „to do"* wird oft gebraucht*) **komm ~** do come; **kommen Sie ~ bitte morgen wieder** won't you come back tomorrow?; **gib ~ mal her** (come on,) give it to me; **seid ~ endlich still!** keep quiet, can't you?; **lass ihn ~!** just leave him!; **soll er ~!** well let him!; **nicht ~!** don't (do that!)

(e) (*verstärkend*) but; (*Bestätigung erwartend*) isn't it/haven't you *etc*?; **sie ist ~ noch so jung** but she's still so young; **es**

wäre ~ schön, wenn ... (but) it WOULD be nice if ...; **das ist ~ die Höhe** *or* **das Letzte!** that really is the limit!; **das ist ~ gar nicht wahr!** (but) that's just not true!; **das ist ~ wohl nicht wahr?** that's not true, is it?; **du hast ~ nicht etwa ...?** you haven't ..., have you?

(f) (= *eigentlich*) really, actually; **hier ist es ~ ganz nett** it's actually quite nice here

(g) (*als bekannt Angenommenes wiederholend: nicht übersetzt*) **Sie wissen ~, wie das so ist** (well,) you know how it is, don't you?; **du kennst dich ~ hier aus, wo ist denn ...?** you know your way around here, where is ...?; **wie war ~ Ihr Name?** (I'm sorry,) WHAT was your name?

(h) (*in Wunschsätzen*) **wenn ~** if only; **o wäre es ~ schon Frühling!** oh if only it were spring!

Docht [dɔxt] M -(e)s, -e wick

Dock [dɔk] NT -s, -s *or* -e dock

Dockgebühren PL wharfage

Dogge [ˈdɔɡə] F -, -n mastiff; **Englische ~** (English) mastiff; **Deutsche ~** great Dane

Dogma [ˈdɔɡma] NT -s, **Dogmen** [-mən] dogma

Dogmatik [dɔˈɡmaːtɪk] F -, -en dogmatics *sing*; (*fig: usu pej*) dogmatism

Dogmatiker [dɔˈɡmaːtikɐ] M -s, -, **Dogmatikerin** [-ərɪn] F -, -nen dogmatist

dogmatisch [dɔˈɡmaːtɪʃ] ADJ (*Rel, fig*) dogmatic

Doktor [ˈdɔktoːɐ] M -s, **Doktoren** [-ˈtoːrən], **Doktorin** [-ˈtoːrɪn, ˈdɔktorɪn] F -, -nen (*auch inf:* = *Arzt*) doctor; **ja, Herr/Frau ~** yes, Doctor; **sie hat den ~, sie ist ~** she has a doctorate; **den** *or* **seinen ~ machen** *or* **bauen** (*inf*) to do a doctorate; **~ spielen** (*inf*) to play doctors and nurses

Doktorand [dɔktoˈrant] M -en, -en [-dn], **Doktorandin** [-ˈrandɪn] F -, -nen graduate student studying for a doctorate

Doktorarbeit F doctoral *or* PhD thesis

Doktorin F *siehe* **Doktor**

Doktor-: Doktorprüfung F examination for a/one's doctorate; **Doktorspiele** PL doctors and nurses *sing*; **Doktortitel** M doctorate; **den ~ haben** to have the title of doctor; **Doktorvater** M (*Univ*) supervisor

Doktrin [dɔkˈtriːn] F -, -en doctrine

doktrinär [dɔktriˈnɛːɐ] ADJ doctrinal; (*pej:* = *stur*) doctrinaire

Dokument [dokuˈmɛnt] NT -(e)s, -e document; (*fig:* = *Zeugnis*) record

Dokumentar- IN CPDS documentary; **Dokumentarfilm** M documentary (film)

dokumentarisch [dokumɛnˈtaːrɪʃ] **1** ADJ documentary; **von ~em Interesse sein** to be of interest as documentation **2** ADV **etw ~ belegen/festhalten** to provide documentary evidence for *or* of sth; **etw ~ festhalten** to document sth

Dokumentation [dokumɛntaˈtsioːn] F -, -en documentation

Dokumenten-: Dokumentenakkreditiv NT documentary (letter of) credit; **Dokumenteninkasso** NT documentary collection

dokumentieren [dokumɛnˈtiːrən], *ptp* **dokumentiert** **1** VT to document; (*fig:* = *zu erkennen geben*) to reveal **2** VR (*fig*) to become evident

Dolch [dɔlç] M -(e)s, -e dagger; (*inf:* = *Messer*) knife

Dolchstich M, **Dolchstoß** (*esp fig*) M stab (*auch fig*)

Dolchstoßlegende F (*Hist*) myth of the stab in the back (*betrayal of Germany in the first World War by its own politicians*)

Dolde [ˈdɔldə] F -, -n umbel

doll [dɔl] (*dialinf*) **1** ADJ **(a)** = **toll** **(b)** (= *unerhört*) incredible **2** ADV **(a)** = **toll** **(b)** (= *sehr*) really; **das hat ~ wehgetan** that hurt like hell (*inf*)

Dollar [ˈdɔlar] M -(s), -s *or* (*nach Zahlenangaben*) - dollar; **hundert ~** a hundred dollars

Dollar-: Dollarkurs M dollar rate; **Dollarnote** F dollar bill; **Dollarzeichen** NT dollar sign

dolmetschen [ˈdɔlmɛtʃn] VTI to interpret; **jdm** *or* **für jdn ~** to interpret for sb

Dolmetscher [ˈdɔlmɛtʃɐ] M -s, -, **Dolmetscherin** [-ərɪn] F -, -nen interpreter

Dolmetscher-: Dolmetscherinstitut NT institute of interpreting; **Dolmetscherkabine** F interpreter's booth

Dolomiten [doloˈmiːtn] PL (*Geog*) **die ~** the Dolomites *pl*

Dom [doːm] M **-(e)s, -e** cathedral

Vorsicht! **Dom** *wird nicht mit dem englischen Wort* **dome** *übersetzt.*

Domäne [doˈmɛːnə] F **-, -n** domain

domestizieren [domɛstiˈtsiːrən], *ptp* **domestiziert** VT to domesticate

Domina [ˈdoːmina] F **-, -s** dominatrix

dominant [domiˈnant] ADJ dominant

Dominant- IN CPDS (*Mus*) dominant

Dominantakkord M (*Mus*) dominant chord

Dominante [domiˈnantə] F **-, -n (a)** (*Mus*) dominant **(b)** (= *wichtigster Faktor*) dominant feature

dominieren [domiˈniːrən], *ptp* **dominiert** 🔳 VI (= *vorherrschen*) to be (pre)dominant; (*Mensch*) to dominate 🔳 VT to dominate

dominierend ADJ dominating

dominikanisch [dominiˈkaːnɪʃ] ADJ (*Geog*) **die Dominikanische Republik** the Dominican Republic

Domino NT **-s, -s** (= *Spiel*) dominoes *sing*

Domino-: Dominoeffekt M domino effect; **einen ~ auslösen** to have a domino effect; **Dominospiel** NT dominoes *sing*; (= *Spielmaterial*) set of dominoes; (= *Partie*) game of dominoes; **Dominostein** M domino

Dompfaff [ˈdɔmpfaf] M **-en** *or* **-s, -en** (*Orn*) bullfinch

Dompteur [dɔmpˈtøːɐ] M **-s, -e**, **Dompteurin** [-ˈtøːrɪn] F **-, -nen**, **Dompteuse** [-ˈtøːzə] F **-, -n** trainer; (*von Raubtieren*) tamer

Donau [ˈdoːnau] F **- die ~** (the) Danube

Donauschwaben PL *Swabian settlers on the Danube in Hungary*

Döner [ˈdøːnɐ] M **-s, -**, **Dönerkebab** [dønɐkeˈbap] M **-(s), -s** doner kebab

Donner [ˈdɔnɐ] M **-s**, (*rare*) - (*lit, fig*) thunder *no indef art, no pl*; (= *~schlag*) clap of thunder; **wie vom ~ gerührt** (*fig inf*) thunderstruck

Donner-: Donnergott M god of thunder; **Donnergrollen** NT **-s**, NO PL rolling thunder; **Donnerkeil** M (*Geol*) thunderstone; (*Archeol*) flintstone

donnern [ˈdɔnɐn] 🔳 VI IMPERS to thunder; **es donnerte in der Ferne** there was (the sound of) thunder in the distance 🔳 VI AUX HABEN *or* (*bei Bewegung*) SEIN to thunder; **gegen etw ~** (= *prallen*) to crash into sth; (= *schlagen*) to hammer on sth

donnernd ADJ (*fig*) thunderous

Donnerschlag M clap of thunder; **die Nachricht traf mich wie ein ~** the news left me thunderstruck

Donnerstag [ˈdɔnɐstaːk] M Thursday; *siehe auch* **Dienstag**

donnerstags [ˈdɔnɐstaːks] ADV on Thursdays

Donnerwetter NT (*fig inf*: = *Schelte*) row; **das wird ein schönes ~ geben** *or* **setzen** (*inf*) all hell will be let loose (*inf*); **~!** (*inf*: *anerkennend*) my word!; **(zum) ~!** (*inf*: *zornig*) damn (it)! (*inf*)

doof [doːf] (*inf*) 🔳 ADJ dumb (*inf*) 🔳 ADV **aussehen** dumb; **~ fragen** to ask a dumb question

Doofheit F **-**, NO PL (*inf*) dumbness (*inf*)

Doofi [ˈdoːfi] M **-(s), -s** (*inf*) dummy (*inf*); **wie Klein ~ mit Plüschohren aussehen** to look a proper fool

Doofmann M, *pl* **-männer** (*inf*) blockhead (*inf*)

Dopamin [dopaˈmiːn] NT **-s**, NO PL (*Med*) dopamine

Dope [doːp] NT **-s, -s** (*sl*) dope (*inf*)

dopen [ˈdɔpn, ˈdoːpn] (*Sport*) 🔳 VT to dope; **er war gedopt** he had taken drugs 🔳 VIR to take drugs

Doping [ˈdɔpɪŋ, ˈdoːpɪŋ] NT **-s, -s** (*Sport*) drug-taking; (*bei Pferden*) doping

Doping- [ˈdɔpɪŋ-, ˈdoːpɪŋ-]: **Dopingkontrolle** F (*Sport*) drug(s) test; **Dopingsünder(in)** M(F) (*Sport*) drug-taker; **Dopingtest** M (*Sport*) drug(s) test; **Dopingverdacht** M (*Sport*) **bei ihm besteht ~** he is suspected of having taken drugs

Doppel [ˈdɔpl] NT **-s, - (a)** (= *Duplikat*) duplicate (copy) (+*gen*, *zu* of) **(b)** (*Tennis etc*) doubles *sing*

Doppel- IN CPDS double; **Doppelagent(in)** M(F) double agent; **Doppelbelastung** F double burden (+*gen* on); **steuerliche ~** double taxation; **Doppelbesteuerung** F double taxation; **Doppelbesteuerungsabkommen** NT double tax treaty; **Doppelbett** NT double bed; (= *zwei Betten*) twin beds *pl*; **Doppelbrief** M *letter weighing over 20 g*; **Doppelbuchstabe** M

double letter; **Doppeldecker** [-dɛkɐ] M **-s, - (a)** (*Aviat*) biplane **(b)** (*auch* **Doppeldeckerbus**) double-decker (bus); **doppeldeutig** [-dɔytɪç] ADJ ambiguous; **Doppeldeutigkeit** F **-en** ambiguity; **Doppelfehler** M (*Tennis*) double fault; **Doppelfenster** NT double window; **~ haben** to have double glazing; **Doppelfunktion** F dual function; **Doppelgänger** [-gɛŋɐ] M **-s, -**, **Doppelgängerin** [-ərɪn] F **-, -nen** double; **doppelgleisig** 🔳 ADJ (*Rail*) double-track; (*fig*) double; **~ sein** (*lit*) to have two tracks 🔳 ADV **~ fahren** (*fig*) to play a double game; **Doppelhaus** NT semi (*Brit inf*), duplex (house) (*US*); **er bewohnt eine Hälfte eines ~es** he lives in a semi(detached house *etc*); **Doppelhaushälfte** F semidetached house (*Brit*), duplex (house) (*US*); **Doppelheft** NT (*von Zeitschrift*) double edition; (*Sch*) exercise book of double thickness; **Doppelkinn** NT double chin; **Doppelklebeband** NT double-sided adhesive tape; **Doppelklick** M (*Comput*) double click (*auf +acc* on); **doppelklicken** VI SEP (*Comput*) to double-click (*auf +acc* on); **Doppelkonsonant** M double consonant; **Doppellaut** M (*Ling*) (*Konsonant*) double consonant; (*Vokal*) double vowel; (= *Diphthong*) diphthong; **Doppelleben** NT double life; **Doppelmoral** F double (moral) standard(s *pl*)

doppeln [ˈdɔpln] VT **(a)** (= *verdoppeln*) to double **(b)** (*Aus*: = *besohlen*) to resole

Doppel-: Doppelname M (= *Nachname*) double-barrelled (*Brit*) *or* double-barreled (*US*) name; (= *Vorname*) double name; **Doppelnummer** F (*von Zeitschrift*) double issue; **Doppelpartner(in)** M(F) (*Sport*) doubles partner; **Doppelpunkt** M colon; **doppelseitig** [-zaɪtɪç] ADJ two-sided; **Lungenentzündung** double; **~e Anzeige** double page spread; **~e Lähmung** diplegia; **Doppelspiel** NT **(a)** (*Tennis*) (game of) doubles *sing* **(b)** (*fig*) double game; **Doppelsteckdose** F double socket; **Doppelstecker** M two-way adaptor; **Doppelsteuerabkommen** NT reciprocal taxation agreement; **doppelstöckig** ADJ *Haus* two-storey (*Brit*), two-story (*US*); *Bus* double-decker *attr*; **ein ~es Bett** bunk beds *pl*; **Doppelstockwagen** M (*Rail*) double-deck carriage (*Brit*) *or* car (*US*); **Doppelstudium** NT joint course (of study) (*Brit*), double major (*US*); **Doppelstunde** F (*esp Sch*) double period

doppelt [ˈdɔplt] 🔳 ADJ double; (= *verstärkt*) *Enthusiasmus* redoubled; (= *mit zwei identischen Teilen*) twin *attr*; (= *zweimal so viel*) twice; (*Comm*) *Buchführung* double-entry; *Staatsbürgerschaft* dual; **die ~e Freude/Länge/Menge** double the pleasure/length/amount; **~e Negation** *or* **Verneinung** double negative; **~er Boden** (*von Koffer*) false bottom; (*von Boot*) double bottom; **~e Moral, eine Moral mit ~em Boden** double standards *pl*, a double standard; **in ~er Hinsicht** in two respects; **ein ~es Spiel spielen** *or* **treiben** to play a double game

🔳 ADV *sehen, zählen* double; (= *zweimal*) twice; (*direkt vor Adjektiv*) doubly; **~ so schön/so viel** twice as nice/much; **das/die Karte habe ich ~** I have two of them/these cards; **das freut mich ~** that gives me double the pleasure; **~ gemoppelt** (*inf*) saying the same thing twice over; **~ und dreifach bereuen, Leid tun** deeply; **sich entschuldigen** profusely; **prüfen** thoroughly; **versichern** absolutely; **seine Schuld ~ und dreifach bezahlen** to pay back one's debt with interest; **~ (genäht) hält besser** (*prov*) ≈ better safe than sorry (*prov*)

Doppelte(s) [ˈdɔpltə] NT DECL AS ADJ double; **um das ~ größer** twice as large; **auf das ~ steigen** to double; **das ~ bezahlen** to pay twice as much; **etw um das ~ erhöhen** to double sth

Doppelung [ˈdɔpləʊŋ] F **-, -en** doubling

Doppel-: Doppelverdiener(in) M(F) person with two incomes; (*pl*: = *Paar*) double-income couple; **Doppelvergaser** M twin carburettors *pl* (*Brit*) *or* carburetors *pl* (*US*); **Doppelvokal** M double vowel; **Doppelwährungsanleihe** F dual currency bond *or* loan; **Doppelwährungsphase** F dual currency phase; **Doppelzentner** M 100 kilos; **Doppelzimmer** NT double room; **doppelzüngig** [-tsʏŋɪç] 🔳 ADJ (*fig*) devious 🔳 ADV **~ reden** to say one thing and mean another

Dopplereffekt [ˈdɔplɐ-] M (*Phys*) Doppler effect

Dorado [doˈraːdo] NT **-s, -s** El Dorado

Dorf [dɔrf] NT **-(e)s, -er** [ˈdœrfɐ] village; (*fig*) backwater; **auf dem ~(e)** (= *in einem bestimmten ~*) in the village; (= *auf dem Land*) in the country; **das Leben auf dem ~e** village life; **nie aus seinem ~ herausgekommen sein** (*fig*) to be parochial; **das olympische ~** the Olympic Village

Dorf- IN CPDS village; **Dorfbewohner(in)** M(F) villager

Dörfchen [ˈdœrfçən] NT **-s, -** DIM *von* **Dorf** small village

dörflich ['dœrflɪç] ADJ village attr; (= ländlich) rural

Dorf-: Dorfplatz M village square; **Dorfschaft** ['dɔrfʃaft] F **-, -en** (Sw) hamlet; **Dorfschöne** [-ʃø:nə] F **-n, -n, Dorfschönheit** F (iro) village beauty; **Dorftrottel** M (inf) village idiot

dorisch ['do:rɪʃ] ADJ (Archit) Doric; (Hist auch, Mus) Dorian

Dorn [dɔrn] M **-(e)s, -en** or (inf) **-e** or **=er** ['dœrnə] (a) (Bot, fig) thorn; **das ist mir ein ~ im Auge** (fig) that is a thorn in my side (esp Brit); (Anblick) I find that an eyesore (b) PL **-e** (= Sporn) spike; (von Schnalle) tongue

Dornen-: Dornengestrüpp NT thorny bushes pl; **Dornenhecke** F thorn(y) hedge; **dornenreich** ADJ thorny; (fig) fraught with difficulty

Dornfortsatz M (Anat) spiny process

dornig ['dɔrnɪç] ADJ thorny

Dorn-: Dornröschen ['-rø:sçən] NT Sleeping Beauty; **Dornröschenschlaf** ['-rø:sçən-] F (fig) slumber

dörren ['dœrən] VTI (VI: AUX SEIN) to dry

Dörr- IN CPDS dried; **Dörrfisch** M dried fish; **Dörrfleisch** NT dried meat; **Dörrobst** NT dried fruit; **Dörrpflaume** F prune

Dorsch [dɔrʃ] M **-(e)s, -e** fish of the cod group; (= Kabeljau) cod(fish)

dort [dɔrt] ADV there; **~ zu Lande** in that country; **~ behalten** to keep there; **~ bleiben** to stay there

dorten ['dɔrtn] ADV (old, Aus) there

dort-: dorther ['dɔrt'he:ɐ, dɔrt'he:ɐ, (emph) 'dɔrthe:ɐ] ADV **von ~** from there; **dortherum** ['dɔrthe'rɔm, dɔrthe'rɔm, (emph) 'dɔrtherʊm] ADV (a)round (there); **dorthin** ['dɔrt'hɪn, dɔrt'hɪn, (emph) 'dɔrthɪn] ADV as far as there; **wie komme ich ~?** how do I get there?; **dorthinab** ['dɔrthɪ'nap, dɔrthɪ'nap, (emph) 'dɔrthɪnap] ADV down there; **dorthinauf** ['dɔrthɪ'nauf, dɔrthɪ'nauf, (emph) 'dɔrthɪnauf] ADV up there; **dorthinaus** ['dɔrthɪ'naus, dɔrthɪ'naus, (emph) 'dɔrthɪnaus] ADV out there; **frech bis ~** (inf) really cheeky (Brit) or fresh (US inf); **dorthinein** ['dɔrthɪ'nain, dɔrthɪ'nain, (emph) 'dɔrthɪnain] ADV in there; **dorthinunter** ['dɔrthɪ'nʊntə, dɔrthɪ'nʊntə, (emph) 'dɔrthɪnʊntə] ADV down there

dortig ['dɔrtɪç] ADJ there (nachgestellt)

dortzulande ['dɔrttsulandə] ADV in that country

DOS [dɔs] NT **-**, NO PL ABBR von **Disk Operating System** (Comput) DOS

Dose ['do:zə] F **-, -n** (a) (= Blechdose) tin; (= Konservendose, Bierdose) can; (mit Deckel) jar; (= Pillendose) (für Schmuck, aus Holz) box; (= Butterdose) dish; (= Plastikdose, Streudose) pack (inf); **in ~n** (Konserven) canned (b) (Elec) socket

> *Vorsicht!* Dose *wird nicht mit dem englischen Wort* **dose** *übersetzt.*

dösen ['dø:zn] VI (inf) to doze

Dosen- IN CPDS canned; **Dosenbier** NT canned beer; **Dosenöffner** M can-opener; **Dosenpfand** NT deposit on drink cans; (allgemein: = Einwegpfand) deposit on drink cans and disposable bottles

dosierbar ADJ **leichter ~ sein** to be more easily measured into exact doses; **etw in ~en Mengen verabreichen** to administer sth in exact doses

dosieren [do'zi:rən], ptp **dosiert** VT Arznei to measure into doses; Menge to measure out; (fig) Rat, Liebe, Geschenke, Lob, Stoff, Hinweise to dispense; **ein Medikament genau ~** to measure out an exact dose of a medicine; **etw dosiert verteilen** (fig) to dispense etc sth in small amounts

Dosierung F **-, -en** (a) (= Dosis) dose (b) (von Arznei) measuring into doses; (von Menge) measuring out

Dosis ['do:zɪs] F **-, Dosen** ['do:zn] dose; **in kleinen Dosen** (lit, fig) in small doses

Dotationskapital NT endowment capital

dotieren [do'ti:rən], ptp **dotiert** VT Posten to remunerate (mit with); Preis to endow (mit with); **eine gut dotierte Stellung** a remunerative position

Dotter ['dɔtɐ] M or NT **-s, -** yolk

Dotter-: Dotterblume F globe flower; (= Sumpfdotterblume) marsh marigold; **dottergelb** ADJ golden yellow

doubeln ['du:bln] **1** VT jdn to stand in for; Szene to shoot with a stand-in; **er lässt sich nie ~** he never has a stand-in; **ein Stuntman hat die Szene für ihn gedoubelt** a stuntman doubled for him in the scene **2** VI to stand in; (= als Double arbeiten) to work as a stand-in

Double ['du:bl] NT **-s, -s** (Film etc) stand-in

Dow-Jones-Index ['dau'dʒo:nz-] M, NO PL (Econ) Dow-Jones Index

down [daun] ADJ PRED (inf) **~ sein** to be (feeling) down

Download ['daunlo:t] M **-s, -s** (Comput) download

downloaden ['daunlo:dn] VTI (Comput) to download

Downsyndrom ['daun-] NT, NO PL (Med) Down's syndrome; **ein Kind mit ~** a Down's (syndrome) child

Dozent [do'tsɛnt] M **-en, -en, Dozentin** [-'tsɛntɪn] F **-, -nen** lecturer (für in), (assistant) professor (US) (für of)

Dozentur [dotsɛn'tu:ɐ] F **-, -en** lectureship (für in), (assistant) professorship (US) (für of)

dozieren [do'tsi:rən], ptp **doziert** **1** VI to lecture (über +acc on, an +dat at) **2** VT to lecture in

dpa [de:pe:'la:] F **-** ABBR von **Deutsche Presse-Agentur**

Dr. ABBR von **Doktor**; **~ rer. nat./rer. pol./phil.** PhD; **~ theol./jur.** DD/LLD; **~ med.** MD

Drache ['draxə] M **-n, -n** (Myth) dragon; siehe auch **Drachen**

Drachen ['draxn] M **-s, -** (a) (= Papierdrachen) kite; (Sport: = Fluggerät) hang-glider; **einen ~ steigen lassen** to fly a kite (b) (pej inf: = zänkisches Weib) dragon (inf)

Drachen-: Drachenfliegen NT **-s,** NO PL (Sport) hang-gliding; **Drachenflieger(in)** M(F) (Sport) hang-glider

Dragee [dra'ʒe:] NT **-s, -s, Dragée** [dra'ʒe:] NT **-s, -s** (= Nussdragee, Mandeldragee) (Pharm) dragee; (= Bonbon) sugar-coated chocolate sweet

Draht [dra:t] M **-(e)s, =e** ['drɛ:tə] wire; **auf ~ sein** (inf) to be on the ball (inf); **einen guten ~ zu jdm haben** to be on good terms with sb

Draht- IN CPDS wire; **Drahtbürste** F wire brush; **Drahtgitter** NT wire netting; **Drahthaardackel** M wire-haired dachshund; **Drahthaarterrier** M wire-haired terrier

drahtig ['dra:tɪç] ADJ Haar, Mensch wiry

Draht-: drahtlos ADJ Telegrafie wireless; Telefon, Nachrichtenübermittlung cordless; **Drahtsaite** F (Mus) steel string; **Drahtschere** F wire cutters pl

Drahtseil NT wire cable; **Nerven wie ~e** (inf) nerves of steel

Drahtseil-: Drahtseilakt M (lit, fig) balancing act; **Drahtseilbahn** F cable railway; **Drahtseilkünstler(in)** M(F) tightrope artist

Draht-: Drahtverhau M wire entanglement; (= Käfig) wire enclosure; **Drahtzaun** M wire fence; **Drahtzieher** [-tsi:ɐ] M **-s, -, Drahtzieherin** [-ərɪn] F **-, -nen** (fig) wirepuller (esp US)

Drainage [drɛ'naːʒə, drɛ'na:ʒ] F **-, -n** (esp Aus, Sw) drainage (auch Med etc)

drainieren [drɛ'ni:rən], ptp **drainiert** VTI (esp Aus, Sw) to drain (auch Med)

drakonisch [dra'ko:nɪʃ] ADJ Draconian

drall [dral] ADJ Mädchen, Arme strapping; Busen, Hintern ample

Drall [dral] M **-(e)s, -e** (von Kugel, Ball) spin; (= Abweichung von Bahn) swerve; **einen ~ nach links haben** (Auto) to pull to the left

Drama ['dra:ma] NT **-s, Dramen** [-mən] drama

Dramatik [dra'ma:tɪk] F **-,** NO PL (lit, fig) drama

Dramatiker [dra'ma:tikɐ] M **-s, -, Dramatikerin** [-ərɪn] F **-, -nen** dramatist

dramatisch [dra'ma:tɪʃ] (lit, fig) **1** ADJ dramatic **2** ADV dramatically; **machs nicht so ~!** don't be so dramatic!

dramatisieren [dramati'zi:rən], ptp **dramatisiert** VT (lit, fig) to dramatize

Dramatisierung F **-, -en** dramatization

Dramaturg [drama'tʊrk] M **-en, -en** [-gn], **Dramaturgin** [-'tʊrgɪn] F **-, -nen** literary manager

Dramaturgie [dramatʊr'gi:] F **-, -n** [-'gi:ən] dramaturgy; (= Abteilung) drama department

dramaturgisch [drama'tʊrgɪʃ] ADJ dramatic; Abteilung drama attr

dran [dran] ADV (inf) siehe auch **daran** (a) (= an der Reihe) **jetzt bist du ~** it's your turn now; **(wenn er erwischt wird,) dann ist er ~** or (hum) **am ~sten** (if he gets caught) he'll be for it (inf); **morgen ist Englisch ~** we've got English tomorrow (b) **schlecht ~ sein** to be in a bad way; **gut ~ sein** to be well off; (= glücklich) to be fortunate; (gesundheitlich) to be well; **früh/spät ~ sein** to be early/late

(c) an ihm ist nichts ~ (= *sehr dünn*) he's nothing but skin and bone; (= *nicht attraktiv, nicht interessant*) there is nothing to him; **an dem Hühnchen ist nichts ~** there is no meat on that chicken; **was ist an ihm ~, dass ...?** what is there about him that ...?; **da wird schon etwas (Wahres) ~ sein** there must be some truth in that; **an den Gerüchten ist nichts ~** there's nothing in those rumours; **ich weiß nicht, wie ich (bei ihm) ~ bin** I don't know where I stand (with him)

Dränage [drɛˈnaːʒə] F **-, -n** drainage

dranbleiben VI SEP IRREG AUX SEIN (*inf*) **(a)** (= *sich nicht entfernen*) to stay close; (*am Apparat*) to hang on; (*an der Arbeit*) to stick at it; **am Gegner/an der Arbeit ~** to stick to one's opponent/at one's work **(b)** (= *sterben*) to kick the bucket (*inf*); **er ist bei der Operation drangeblieben** the operation did for him (*inf*)

drang PRET *von* **dringen**

Drang [draŋ] M **-(e)s, ⸚e** [ˈdrɛŋə] (= *Antrieb*) urge (*auch Physiol*), impulse; (= *Sehnsucht*) yearning (*nach* for); (*nach Wissen*) thirst (*nach* for); **ich habe einen ~** (*inf: zur Toilette*) I'm dying to go (*inf*)

drangeben VT SEP IRREG (*inf*) **(a)** (= *zufügen*) to add (*an +acc* to); **ich geb noch 10 Minuten dran** I'll wait another ten minutes **(b)** (= *opfern*) to give up; **sein Leben für etw ~** to give one's life for sth

drangehen VI SEP IRREG AUX SEIN (*inf*) **(a)** (= *anfassen*) to touch (*an etw acc* sth); **an etw** (*acc*) **(zu nahe) ~** to go (too) close to sth; **das Telefon klingelte, er ging aber nicht dran** the phone rang but he didn't answer it **(b)** (= *in Angriff nehmen*) **~, etw zu tun** to get down to doing sth

Drängelei [drɛŋəˈlai] F **-, -en** (*inf*) pushing; (*im Verkehr*) jostling; (= *Bettelei*) pestering

drängeln [ˈdrɛŋln] (*inf*) **1** VI to push; (*im Verkehr*) to jostle **2** VTI (= *betteln*) to pester **3** VR **sich nach vorne** *etc* **~** to push one's way to the front *etc*; **sich ~, etw zu tun** (*fig*) to fall over oneself to do sth

drängen [ˈdrɛŋn] **1** VI to press; **darauf ~, eine Antwort zu erhalten, auf Antwort ~** to press for an answer; **darauf ~, dass jd etw tut/dass etw getan wird** to press for sb to do sth/for sth to be done; **zum Aufbruch/zur Eile ~** to be insistent that one should leave/hurry; **die Zeit drängt** time is pressing; **es drängt nicht** it's not pressing
2 VT **(a)** (*mit Ortsangabe*) to push
(b) (= *auffordern*) to urge; **es drängt mich, das zu tun** I feel the urge to do that
3 VR (*Menge*) to throng; (*fig: Termine etc*) to mount up; **sich nach vorn ~** to push one's way to the front; *siehe auch* **gedrängt**

Drängen NT **-s,** NO PL urging; (= *Bitten*) requests *pl*

drängend ADJ pressing

Drängler(in) M(F) **-s, -** (*Aut*) tailgater

drangsalieren [dranzaˈliːrən] *ptp* **drangsaliert** VT (= *plagen*) to pester; (= *unterdrücken*) to oppress

dranhalten SEP IRREG (*inf*) **1** VT to hold up (*+dat, an +acc* to); **etw näher an etw** (*acc*) **~** to hold sth closer to sth **2** VR (= *sich beeilen*) to get a move on (*inf*); (= *sich anstrengen*) to make an effort

dränieren [drɛˈniːrən], *ptp* **dräniert** VT to drain

drankommen VI SEP IRREG AUX SEIN (*inf*) **(a)** (= *berühren*) to touch (*an etw* sth) **(b)** (= *erreichen können*) to be able to reach (*an etw* (*acc*) sth) **(c)** (= *an die Reihe kommen*) to have one's turn; (*Sch*) (*beim Melden*) to be called; (*Frage, Aufgabe etc*) to come up; **jetzt kommst du dran** now it's your turn/go; **du kommst als Erster/Nächster dran** you're first/next

drankriegen VT SEP IRREG (*inf*) **jdn ~** to get sb (*inf*); (*zu einer Arbeit*) to get sb to do it/sth; (*mit Witz, Streich*) to catch sb out

dranlassen VT SEP IRREG (*inf*) **etw (an etw** *dat*) **~** to leave sth on (sth)

dranmachen SEP (*inf*) **1** VR = **daranmachen 2** VT **etw (an etw** *acc*) **~** to put sth on (sth)

drannehmen VT SEP IRREG (*inf*) *Schüler* to ask; *Patienten* to take

dransetzen SEP (*inf*) **1** VT **(a)** (= *anfügen*) **ein Stück/ein Teil (an etw** *acc*) **~** to add a piece/part (to sth) **(b)** (= *einsetzen*) **seine Kraft/sein Vermögen ~** to put one's effort/money into it; **alles ~** to make every effort; **jdn ~** to put sb onto the job or it **2** VR (= *Arbeit anfangen*) to get down to work or it

drapieren [draˈpiːrən], *ptp* **drapiert** VT to drape

Drapierung F **-, -en (a)** (= *das Drapieren*) draping **(b)** (= *Schmuck, Falten*) drape

Drastik [ˈdrastɪk] F **-,** NO PL (= *Derbheit*) drasticness; (= *Deutlichkeit*) graphicness; **etw mit besonderer ~ beschreiben** to describe sth particularly graphically

drastisch [ˈdrastɪʃ] **1** ADJ (= *derb*) drastic; (= *deutlich*) graphic **2** ADV (= *energisch*) **kürzen** drastically; (= *deutlich*) explicitly; **~ vorgehen** to take drastic measures; **sich ~ ausdrücken** to use strong language

drauf [drauf] ADV (*inf*) *siehe auch* **darauf**; **~ und dran sein, etw zu tun** to be on the verge of doing sth

Drauf-: Draufgänger [-gɛŋɐ] M **-s, -, Draufgängerin** [-ərɪn] F **-, -nen** daredevil; (= *Mann: bei Frauen*) predator; **draufgängerisch** [-gɛŋərɪʃ] ADJ daring; (*negativ*) reckless; (*bei Frauen, Männern*) predatory; **Draufgängertum** NT **-s,** NO PL daring; (*negativ*) recklessness; (*bei Frauen, Männern*) predatory ways *pl*; **draufgeben** VT IRREG SEP **(a)** (= *dazugeben*) **noch etwas ~** to add some extra (*inf*) **(b)** (*Aus:* = *als Zugabe anfügen*) to sing/play *etc* as an encore; **draufgehen** VI SEP IRREG AUX SEIN (*inf*) (= *sterben*) to bite the dust (*inf*); (*Geld*) to disappear; **draufhaben** VT SEP IRREG (*inf*) *Sprüche, Antwort* to come out with; **zeigen, was man draufhat** to show what one is made of; **den Chauvi ~** to be a real chauvinist; **etw ~** (*sl*) (= *können*) to be able to do sth no bother (*inf*); *Witze, Sprüche* to have sth off pat (*inf*); **es** *or* **schwer was ~** (*sl*) to know one's stuff (*inf*); **160 Sachen ~** (*inf*) to be doing 160; **draufhauen** SEP IRREG VI (*inf:* = *schlagen*) to hit hard; **draufkommen** VI SEP IRREG AUX SEIN (*inf*) (= *sich erinnern*) to remember; (= *begreifen*) to catch on; **draufkriegen** VT SEP (*inf*) **etw (auf etw** *acc*) **~** to get sth on/on(to); **eins ~** (= *getadelt werden*) to be told off; (= *geschlagen werden*) to be given a smack; (= *besiegt werden*) to be given a thrashing (*inf*); **drauflassen** VT SEP IRREG (*inf*) **etw (auf etw** *dat*) **~** to leave sth on (sth); **drauflegen** SEP (*inf*) **1** VT **(a)** *Geld, Betrag* to lay out; **20 Euro ~** to lay out an extra 20 euros **(b)** (*lit*) **etw (auf etw** *acc*) **~** to put sth on(to sth) **2** VI (= *mehr bezahlen*) to pay more

drauflos [draufˈloːs] ADV **(nur) immer feste** *or* **munter ~!** (just) keep at it!

drauflos-: drauflosarbeiten VI SEP (*inf*) to work away; (= *anfangen*) to start working; **drauflosgehen** VI SEP IRREG AUX SEIN (*inf*) (*mit Ziel*) to make straight for it; (*ohne Ziel*) to set off; **drauflosreden** VI SEP (*inf*) to talk away; (= *anfangen*) to start talking; **drauflosschlagen** VI SEP IRREG (*inf*) to hit out

drauf-: draufmachen VT SEP (*inf*) **etw (auf etw** *acc*) **~** to put sth on(to sth); **einen ~** to make a night of it (*inf*); **draufsatteln** VT SEP (*inf*) to slap on (top); **drauf sein** VI IRREG AUX SEIN (*inf*) **schlecht/gut ~** to be in a bad/good mood; **wie ist der denn drauf?** what kind of trip is he on? (*inf*); **draufsetzen** VT SEP (*fig inf*) **eins** *or* **einen ~** to go one step further; **draufstoßen** SEP IRREG (*inf*) **1** VI AUX SEIN to come upon it; (= *finden*) to come across it **2** VT **jdn ~** to point it out to sb; **draufzahlen** VTI SEP (*inf*) *siehe auch* **drauflegen**

drauskommen VI SEP IRREG AUX SEIN (*dial, Aus:* = *aus dem Konzept kommen*) to lose track **(b)** (*Sw:* = *verstehen*) to get it (*inf*)

draußen [ˈdrausn] ADV outside; (= *da ~, weit weg von hier*) out there; **~ auf dem Lande/dem Balkon/im Garten** out in the country/on the balcony/in the garden; **~ (auf dem Meer)** out at sea; **da/hier ~** out there/here; **ganz da ~** way out there; **(vor der Tür) ~** at the door; **nach ~** outside; (*ferner weg*) out there; **weit/weiter ~** far/further out; **„Hunde müssen ~ bleiben"** "no dogs (please)"

Drechselbank F, *pl* **-bänke** wood(turning) lathe

drechseln [ˈdrɛksln] **1** VT to turn (*on a wood lathe*); (*fig pej*) to overelaborate; *Vers* to turn; *siehe auch* **gedrechselt 2** VI to work the (wood) lathe

Drechslerei [drɛkslaˈrai] F **-, -en** (= *Werkstatt*) (wood)turner's workshop; (= *Handwerk*) (wood)turning

Dreck [drɛk] M **-(e)s,** NO PL **(a)** (= *Schmutz*) dirt; (*esp ekelhaft*) filth; (*fig*) (= *Schund*) rubbish; **~ machen** (*inf*) to make a mess; **in** *or* **mit ~ und Speck** (= *ungewaschen*) unwashed; **jdn wie den letzten ~ behandeln** (*inf*) to treat sb like dirt; **der letzte ~ sein** (*inf: Mensch*) to be the lowest of the low; **am Stecken haben** (*fig*) to have a skeleton in the cupboard; **etw in den ~ ziehen** (*fig*) to drag sth through the mud
(b) (*inf*) (= *Angelegenheit, Kram*) business, stuff (*inf*); (= *Kleinigkeit*) little thing; **sich einen ~ um jdn/etw kümmern** *or*

scheren not to give a damn about sb/sth (*inf*); **mach deinen ~ alleine!** do it yourself; **das geht ihn einen ~** an that's none of his business; **einen ~ ist er/hast du** like hell he is/you have (*inf*)

Dreck-: Dreckarbeit F (*inf*) dirty work; **Dreckfinger** PL (*inf*) dirty fingers *pl*

dreckig ['drekɪç] **1** ADJ (*lit, fig*) dirty; (*stärker*) filthy **2** ADV (*inf*) **~ lachen** to give a dirty laugh; **es geht mir ~** I'm in a bad way; (*finanziell*) I'm badly off; **wenn man ihn erwischt, geht es ihm ~** if they catch him, he'll be in for it (*inf*)

Dreck-: Dreckloch NT (*pej*) hole (*inf*); **Drecknest** NT (*pej*) dump (*inf*); **Drecksack** M (*pej inf*) dirty bastard (*sl*); **Drecksau** F (*vulg*) filthy swine (*inf*); **Dreckschleuder** F (*pej*) (= *Mundwerk*) foul-mouthed person; (= *Kraftwerk, Auto*) environmental hazard; **Dreckschwein** NT (*inf*) dirty pig (*inf*)

Dreckskerl M (*inf*) dirty swine (*inf*)

Dreckspatz M (*inf*) (= *Kind*) grubby kid; (*Schimpfwort*) filthy beggar (*inf*)

Dreh [dre:] M **-s, -s** *or* **-e (a)** (= *List*) dodge; (= *Kunstgriff*) trick; **den ~ heraushaben, etw zu tun** to have got the knack of doing sth; **den (richtigen) ~ heraushaben** *or* **weghaben** (*inf*) to have got the hang of it **(b)** = **Drehe**

Dreh-: Dreharbeiten PL (*Film*) shooting *sing*; **Drehbank** F, *pl* -bänke lathe; **Drehbeginn** M (*Film*) start of shooting; **Drehbleistift** M propelling (*Brit*) *or* mechanical (*US*) pencil; **Drehbuch** NT (*Film*) (film) script; **Drehbuchautor(in)** M(F) scriptwriter

Drehe ['dre:ə] F -, NO PL (*inf*) **(so) um die ~** (*zeitlich*) (a)round about then

drehen ['dre:ən] **1** VT to turn (*auch Tech: auf Drehbank*); *Zigaretten, Pillen* to roll; *Film* to shoot; (*inf*: = *schaffen*) to fix (*inf*); **Fleisch durch den Wolf ~** to put meat through the mincer (*Brit*) *or* meat grinder (*US*); **ein Ding ~** (*sl*) to play a prank; (*Verbrecher*) to pull a job (*inf*); **wie man es auch dreht und wendet** no matter how you look at it

2 VI to turn; (*Wind*) to change; (*Film*) to shoot; **an etw** (*dat*) **~** to turn sth; **am Radio ~** to turn a knob on the radio; **daran ist nichts zu ~ und deuteln** (*fig*) there are no two ways about it **3** VR **(a)** (= *sich umdrehen, kreisen*) to turn (*um* about); (*um Achse auch*) to rotate; (*sehr schnell: Kreisel*) to spin; (*Wind*) to change; **sich auf den Rücken ~** to turn on(to) one's back; **sich um etw ~** to revolve around sth; **sich um sich (selbst) ~** to rotate, to revolve on its own axis; (*Mensch*) to turn round (*Brit*), to turn around (*US*); (*Auto*) to spin; **sich im Kreise ~** to turn (a)round and (a)round; **mir drehte sich alles** everything's spinning about me; **mir dreht sich alles im Kopf** my head is spinning; **sich ~ und winden** (*fig*) to twist and turn

(b) (= *betreffen*) **sich um etw ~** to concern sth; (*um zentrale Frage*) to centre (*Brit*) *or* center (*US*) on sth; **alles dreht sich um sie** everything revolves (a)round her; (*steht im Mittelpunkt*) she's the centre (*Brit*) *or* center (*US*) of attention *or* interest; **es dreht sich darum, dass ...** the point is that ...; **in dieser Sendung drehte es sich um ...** the broadcast was about ...

Dreh-: Drehknopf M knob; **Drehkreuz** NT turnstile; **Drehleiter** F turntable ladder; **Drehmoment** NT torque; **Drehorgel** F barrel organ; **Drehorgelspieler(in)** M(F) organ-grinder; **Drehort** M, *pl* **-orte** (*Film*) location; **Drehpause** F (*Film*) break in shooting; **Drehschalter** M rotary switch; **Drehscheibe** F **(a)** (*Rail*) turntable **(b)** (= *Töpferscheibe*) potter's wheel **(c)** (*fig*) nerve centre (*Brit*) *or* center (*US*); **Drehstrom** M three-phase current; **Drehstuhl** M swivel chair; **Drehtür** F revolving door; **Dreh- und Angelpunkt** M *siehe* **Angelpunkt**

Drehung ['dre:ʊŋ] F -, **-en** turn; (= *ganze ~ um eigene Achse auch*) rotation; (*um einen Punkt auch*) revolution; **eine ~ um 180°** a 180° turn

Drehwurm M (*inf*) **einen** *or* **den ~ kriegen/haben** to get/feel giddy

Drehzahl F number of revolutions; (*pro Minute*) revs *pl* per minute

Drehzahl-: Drehzahlbereich M (*Aut*) engine speed range; **im niederen/hohen ~** at low/high revs; **Drehzahlmesser** M **-s, -** rev counter

drei [drai] NUM three; **von uns ~en** from the three of us; **die (Heiligen) Drei Könige** the Three Kings; **die ~ Weisen aus dem Morgenland** the Three Wise Men from the East; **aller guten Dinge sind ~!** (*prov*) all good things come in threes!; (*nach*

zwei missglückten Versuchen) third time lucky!; **er arbeitet/isst für ~** (*inf*) he does the work of/eats enough for three; **ehe man bis ~ zählen konnte** (*inf*) in a trice (*esp Brit*); **sie sieht aus, als ob sie nicht bis ~ zählen könnte** (*inf*) she looks pretty empty-headed; (= *unschuldig*) she looks as if butter wouldn't melt in her mouth; *siehe auch* **vier**

Drei [drai] F -, **-en** three; *siehe auch* **Vier**

drei-, Drei- IN CPDS three-, tri-; **dreiad(e)rig** ['draiad(ə)rɪç] ADJ (*Elec*) three-core; **dreibeinig** ADJ three-legged

Drei-D- [drai'de:] IN CPDS 3-D; **Drei-D-Brille** F 3-D glasses *pl*

dreidimensional ADJ three-dimensional

Dreieck ['draiɛk] NT triangle; (= *Zeichendreieck*) set square

dreieckig ADJ triangular

Dreiecksverhältnis NT (eternal) triangle; **ein ~ haben** to be involved in an eternal triangle

Dreier ['draie] M **-s, - (a)** (*Aus, S Ger.* = *Ziffer, Note*) three **(b)** (*Sport*) (*Eislauf etc*) three; (*Golf*) threesome; **ein flotter ~** (*inf: Sex*) a threesome (*inf*)

dreifach ['draifax] **1** ADJ triple; **die ~e Menge** three times the amount; **ein ~es Hoch!** three cheers! **2** ADV three times; **~ abgesichert/verstärkt** three times as *or* trebly secure/ reinforced; *siehe auch* **vierfach**

Dreifache(s) ['draifaxə] NT DECL AS ADJ **das ~** three times as much; **9 ist das ~ von 3** 9 is three times 3; **etw um das ~ vermehren** to multiply sth three times *or* (*Zahl auch*) by three; **auf das ~ steigen** to treble

Dreifachstecker M three-way adapter

Drei-: dreifarbig, dreifärbig [-ferbɪç] (*Aus*) ADJ three-coloured (*Brit*), three-colored (*US*); **Dreifelderwirtschaft** F three-field system; **Dreifuß** M tripod; (= *Gestell für Kessel*) trivet; (= *Schemel*) three-legged stool

Dreigang M, NO PL (*inf*) = **Dreigangschaltung**

Dreigang-: Dreiganggetriebe NT three-speed gear; **Dreigangrad** NT three-speed bike; **Dreigangschaltung** F three-speed gear; **ein Fahrrad mit ~** a three-speed bicycle

Drei-: dreihundert ['drai'hʊndet] NUM three hundred; **Dreikampf** M three-part competition (*100m sprint, long jump and shot put*); **Dreikäsehoch** ['drai'kɛːzahoːx] M **-s, -s** (*inf*) tiny tot (*inf*); **Dreiklang** M (*Mus*) triad; **Dreikönige** PL Epiphany *sing*; **Dreikönigsfest** NT (feast of) Epiphany; **Dreiländereck** NT place where three countries meet; **Dreiliterauto, Drei-Liter-Auto** NT three-litre (*Brit*) *or* three-liter (*US*) car

dreimal ['draimaːl] ADV three times; *siehe auch* **viermal**

Drei-: Dreimaster ['draimaste] M **-s, -** three-master; **Dreimeterbrett** NT three-metre (*Brit*) *or* three-meter (*US*) board

drein-: dreinblicken VI SEP **traurig** *etc* **~** to look sad *etc*; **dreinfügen** VR SEP to resign oneself (to it); **dreinreden** VI SEP (*inf*) (= *dazwischenreden*) to interrupt; (= *sich einmischen*) to interfere (*bei in*, with); **ich lasse mir in dieser Angelegenheit von niemandem ~** I won't have anyone interfering (with this); **er ließ sich nirgends ~** he would never be told

Drei-: Dreipunkt(sicherheits)gurt M lap and diagonal seat belt; **Dreirad** NT tricycle; (*inf:* = *Auto*) three-wheeler; **dreiräderig, dreirädrig** ADJ three-wheeled

Dreisatz M (*Math*) rule of three

Drei-: Dreisatzaufgabe F problem using the rule of three; **Dreisatzrechnung** F calculation using the rule of three; **Dreisatztisch** M nest of tables

Drei-: Dreispitz M three-cornered hat; **Dreisprung** M triple jump

dreißig ['draisɪç] NUM thirty; *siehe auch* **vierzig**

dreißigjährig ADJ (= *dreißig Jahre dauernd*) thirty years' *attr*, lasting thirty years; (= *dreißig Jahre alt*) thirty years old, thirty-year-old *attr*; **der Dreißigjährige Krieg** the Thirty Years' War

Dreißigstel ['draisɪçstl] NT **-s, -** thirtieth; *siehe auch* **Viertel¹**

dreißigste(r, s) ['draisɪçstə] ADJ thirtieth

dreist [draist] ADJ bold

Dreistigkeit ['draistɪçkait] F -, **-en (a)** NO PL boldness **(b)** (*Bemerkung*) bold remark; (*Handlung*) bold act

Drei-: dreistufig ADJ *Rakete* three-stage *attr*, with three stages; *Plan auch* three-phase *attr*; **Dreitagebart** M stubble; **dreiteilig** ADJ *Kostüm etc* three-piece *attr*; (= *in 3 Teile geteilt*) three-part *attr*; **Dreiteilung** F division into three; **die ~ der Streitkräfte** dividing the armed forces into three

drei viertel ['drai 'fɪrtl] ADJ, ADV *siehe* **viertel, Viertel[1]**

Dreiviertel ['drai'fɪrtl] NT three-quarters; **in einem ~ der Zeit** in three-quarters of the time; **der Saal war zu einem ~ leer** the room was three-quarters empty

Dreiviertel-: Dreiviertelmehrheit [-'fɪrtl-] F three-quarters majority; **Dreiviertelstunde** F three-quarters of an hour *no indef art*; **Dreivierteltakt** [-'fɪrtl-] M three-four time

Dreiweg- IN CPDS (*Elec*) three-way; **Dreiwegekatalysator** M (*Aut*) three-way catalytic converter; **geregelter ~** computer-controlled three-way catalytic converter; **ungeregelter ~** open-loop three-way catalytic converter

Drei-: dreiwertig [-veːrtɪç] ADJ (*Chem*) trivalent; (*Ling*) three-place; **dreiwöchig** [-vœçɪç] ADJ ATTR three-week; **Dreizack** [-tsak] M **-s, -e** trident; **dreizackig** ADJ three-pointed

dreizehn ['draitseːn] NUM thirteen; **jetzt schlägts aber ~** (*inf*) that's a bit much; *siehe auch* **vierzehn**

Dresche ['drɛʃə] F **-**, NO PL (*inf*) thrashing; **~ kriegen** to get a thrashing

dreschen ['drɛʃn], *pret* **drosch** [drɔʃ], *ptp* **gedroschen** [gə'drɔʃn]
◆1 VT (**a**) *Korn* to thresh; (*inf*) *Phrasen* to bandy; **leeres Stroh ~** (*fig*) to talk a lot of hot air (*inf*); **Skat ~** (*inf*) to play skat
(**b**) (*inf*: = *prügeln*) to thrash
◆2 VI (**a**) (= *Korn ~*) to thresh
(**b**) (*inf*: = *schlagen, treten*) to hit violently; **auf die Tasten ~** to thump the keys
◆3 VR (*inf*: = *sich prügeln*) to have a fight

Dress [drɛs] M **-es, -e,** *or* (*Aus*) f **-, -en** (*Sport*) (sports) kit; (*für Fußball auch*) strip

dressierbar ADJ trainable; **leicht/schwer ~** easy/difficult to train

dressieren [drɛ'siːrən], *ptp* **dressiert** VT to train; **auf jdn/etw dressiert sein** to be trained to respond to sb/sth; **auf den Mann dressiert sein** to be trained to attack people; **zu etw dressiert sein** to be trained to do sth

Dressing ['drɛsɪŋ] NT **-s, -s** (*Cook*) dressing

Dressman ['drɛsmən] M **-s, Dressmen** male model

Dressur [drɛ'suːr] F **-, -en** training; (*für ~reiten*) dressage

dribbeln ['drɪbln] VI to dribble; **mit dem Ball ~** to dribble the ball

driften ['drɪftn] VI AUX SEIN (*Naut, fig*) to drift

Drill [drɪl] M **-(e)s**, NO PL (*Mil, fig*) drill

Drillbohrer M drill

drillen ['drɪlən] VT to drill; **jdn auf etw** (*acc*) **~** to drill sb in sth; **auf etw** (*acc*) **gedrillt sein** (*fig inf*) to be practised (*Brit*) *or* practiced (*US*) at doing sth

Drilling ['drɪlɪŋ] M **-s, -e** triplet

Drillingsgeburt F triple birth

drin [drɪn] ADV (**a**) (*inf*) = **darin, drinnen** (**b**) (= *innen ~*) in it; **er/ es ist da ~** he/it is in there; **in der Flasche ist noch etwas ~** there's still something in the bottle (**c**) (*inf:* in *Redewendungen*) **das ist** *or* **liegt bei der alles ~** anything's possible with her; **bis jetzt ist** *or* **liegt noch alles ~** everything is still quite open; **~ sein** (*in der Arbeit*) to be into it; **das ist doch nicht ~** (= *geht nicht*) that's not on (*inf*)

dringen ['drɪŋən], *pret* **drang** [draŋ], *ptp* **gedrungen** [gə'drʊŋən] VI (**a**) AUX SEIN to penetrate; (*fig: Nachricht, Geheimnis*) to get through (*an* or *in* +*acc* to); (**durch etw**) **~** to come through (sth); **an** *or* **in die Öffentlichkeit ~** to leak out; **durch eine Menschenmenge ~** to push (one's way) through a crowd of people; **in jdn ~** (*geh*) to press sb
(**b**) **auf etw** (*acc*) **~** to insist on sth; **er drang darauf, einen Arzt zu holen** *or* **dass man einen Arzt holte** he insisted that a doctor should be sent for

dringend ['drɪŋənt] **◆1** ADJ (= *eilig, wichtig*) urgent; (= *nachdrücklich, zwingend*) strong; *Gründe* compelling; **etw ~ machen** (*inf*) to treat sth as urgent; **ein ~er Fall** (*Med*) an emergency **◆2** ADV (= *unbedingt*) urgently; (= *nachdrücklich*) *warnen, empfehlen, abraten* strongly; **jdn ~ bitten, etw zu unterlassen** to urge sb to stop doing sth; **~ notwendig** *or* **erforderlich** urgently needed; **~ verdächtig** strongly suspected

dringlich ['drɪŋlɪç] ADJ urgent

Dringlichkeit F **-**, NO PL urgency

Dringlichkeits-: Dringlichkeitsantrag M (*Parl*) emergency motion; **Dringlichkeitsstufe** F priority; **~ 1** top priority

Drink [drɪŋk] M **-s, -s** drink

drinnen ['drɪnən] ADV inside; (= *im Haus auch*) indoors; **hier/ dort ~** in here/there; **ich gehe nach ~** (*inf*) I'm going in(side)

drinstecken VI SEP (*inf*) (**a**) (= *verborgen sein*) to be (contained); **auch bei ihm muss ein guter Kern ~** there must be some good even in him (**b**) (= *investiert sein*) **da steckt eine Menge Geld/Arbeit** *etc* **drin** a lot of money/work *etc* has gone into it (**c**) (= *verwickelt sein*) to be involved in it; **er steckt bis über die Ohren drin** he's up to his ears in it

drischt [drɪʃt] 3. PERS SING PRES *von* **dreschen**

dritt [drɪt] ADV **wir kommen zu ~** three of us are coming together

dritt- IN CPDS third; **drittälteste(r, s)** ADJ third oldest

Drittel ['drɪtl] NT **-s, -** third; *siehe auch* **Viertel[1]**

dritteln ['drɪtln] VT to divide into three (parts); *Zahl* to divide by three

drittens ['drɪtns] ADV thirdly

Dritte(r) ['drɪtə] MF DECL AS ADJ third person/man/woman *etc*; (= *Unbeteiligter*) third party; **der lachende ~** the third party who benefits from a division between two others; **in dieser Angelegenheit ist er der lachende ~** he comes off best from this matter; **wenn zwei sich streiten, freut sich der ~** (*prov*) when two people quarrel a third one rejoices; *siehe auch* **Vierte(r)**

dritte(r, s) ['drɪtə] ADJ third; **der ~ Fall** (*Gram*) the dative case; **an einem ~n Ort** on neutral territory; **von ~r Seite** (**eine Neuigkeit erfahren**) (to learn a piece of news) from a third party; **Menschen ~r Klasse** third-class citizens; **ein Drittes** a third thing; *siehe auch* **vierte(r, s)**

Dritte-Welt- IN CPDS Third World

Dritt-: drittgrößte(r, s) ADJ third-biggest; **dritthöchste(r, s)** ADJ third-highest; **drittklassig** ADJ third-rate (*pej*), third-class; **Drittland** NT third country; **drittletzte(r, s)** ADJ third from last; **an ~r Stelle** third from last; **drittrangig** [-raŋɪç] ADJ third-rate

DRK [deːleːr'kaː] NT - ABBR *von* **Deutsches Rotes Kreuz**

Droge ['droːgə] F **-, -n** drug

dröge ['drøːgə] ADJ (*N Ger*) = **trocken**

Drögeler ['drøːgələ] M **-s, -, Drögelerin** [-ərɪn] F **-, -nen** (*Sw*) drug addict

Drogen-: drogenabhängig ADJ addicted to drugs; **er ist ~** he's a drug addict; **Drogenabhängige(r)** MF DECL AS ADJ drug addict; **Drogenabhängigkeit** F drug addiction *no art*; **Drogenfahnder** [-faːndɐ] M **-s, -, Drogenfahnderin** [-ərɪn] F **-, -nen** drugs squad officer (*Brit*), narcotics officer (*US*); **Drogenhandel** M drug trade; **Drogenkonsum** [-kɔnzuːm] M drug consumption; **Drogenkurier(in)** M(F) drug courier; **Drogenmissbrauch** M drug abuse *no art*; **Drogensucht** F drug addiction; **drogensüchtig** ADJ addicted to drugs; **er ist ~** he's a drug addict; **Drogensüchtige(r)** MF DECL AS ADJ drug addict; **Drogenszene** F drugs scene; **Drogentote(r)** MF DECL AS ADJ person who died from drug abuse; **200 ~ pro Jahr** 200 drug deaths per year

Drogerie [drogə'riː] F **-, -n** [-'riːən] chemist's (shop) (*nondispensing*), drugstore (*US*)

Drogist [dro'gɪst] M **-en, -en, Drogistin** [-'gɪstɪn] F **-, -nen** chemist, druggist (*US*)

Drögler ['drøːglɐ] M **-s, -, Dröglerin** [-ərɪn] F **-, -nen** (*Sw*) drug addict

Drohbrief M threatening letter

drohen ['droːən] **◆1** VI to threaten (*jdm* sb); (*Gewitter*) to be imminent; (*Streik, Krieg*) to be looming; **er drohte dem Kind mit erhobenem Zeigefinger** he raised a warning finger to the child; (*jdm*) **mit etw ~** to threaten (sb with) sth; (*jdm*) **~, etw zu tun** to threaten to do sth; **jdm droht etw** sb is being threatened by sth; **jdm droht Gefahr/der Tod** sb is in danger of/in danger of dying; **es droht Gefahr/ein Streik** there is the threat of danger/a strike
◆2 V AUX to threaten; **das Schiff drohte zu sinken** the ship was in danger of sinking

drohend ADJ *Handbewegung, Haltung, Blick, Wolken* threatening; (= *bevorstehend*) *Unheil, Gefahr, Krieg, Krise* imminent

dröhnen ['drøːnən] VI (**a**) (*Flugzeug, Motor, Straßenlärm*) to roar; (*Donner*) to rumble; (*Lautsprecher, Musik, Bass, Stimme, Fernseher*) to boom; **etw dröhnt jdm in den Ohren/im Kopf** sth roars *etc* in sb's ears/head **(b)** (*Raum etc*) to resound; **mir ~ die Ohren/dröhnt der Kopf** my ears are/head is ringing **(c)** AUX SEIN (= *sich ~d fortbewegen: Lkw etc*) to rumble **(d)** (*sl: = high machen*) to give a buzz (*inf*)

dröhnend ◨ ADJ *Lärm, Applaus* resounding; *Musik, Stimme* booming; *Gelächter* roaring ◩ ADV **~ lachen** to roar with laughter

Dröhnung ['drøːnʊŋ] F **-, -en** (*sl*) **(a)** (= *laute Musik*) booming music **(b)** (= *Rausch*) high (*inf*); (= *Dosis*) fix (*inf*); **sich** (*dat*) **voll die ~ or die volle ~ geben** to get stoned (*sl*)

Drohung ['droːʊŋ] F **-, -en** threat

drollig ['drɔlɪç] ADJ **(a)** funny **(b)** (= *seltsam*) odd; **werd nicht ~!** don't be funny!

Dromedar [drome'daːɐ, 'droː-] NT **-s, -e** dromedary

Drops [drɔps] M or NT **-, -** or **-e** fruit drop

drosch PRET *von* **dreschen**

Drosophila [dro'zoːfila] F **-, Drosophilae** [-lɛ] (*Biol*) drosophila

Drossel[1] ['drɔsl] F **-, -n** (*Orn*) thrush

Drossel[2] F **-, -n** (= *~spule*) choking coil; (= *~ventil*) throttle valve

drosseln ['drɔsln] VT *Motor, Dampf etc* to throttle; *Heizung, Wärme* to turn down; *Strom* to reduce; *Tempo, Produktion etc* to cut down

Drosselung F **-, -en** (*von Motor, Dampf*) throttling; (*von Heizung, Wärme*) turning down; (*von Strom*) reducing; (*von Tempo, Produktion*) cutting down

Drosselventil NT throttle valve

drüben ['dryːbn] ADV over there; (= *auf der anderen Seite*) on the other side; (*inf: auf Amerika bezogen*) over the water; **hier/dort** *or* **da ~** over here/there; **nach ~** over there; **bei der Nachbarin ~** over at my neighbour's (*Brit*) *or* neighbor's (*US*); **~ über dem Rhein** on the other side of the Rhine

drüber ['dryːbɐ] ADV (*inf*) = **darüber, hinüber**

Druck[1] [drʊk] M **-(e)s, ¨e** ['drʏkə] **(a)** (*Phys, fig*) pressure; **unter ~ stehen** (*lit, fig*) to be under pressure; **jdn unter ~ setzen** (*fig*) to put pressure on sb; **(fürchterlich) in ~ sein** (*fig*) to be under (terrible) pressure; **~ machen** (*inf*) to put the pressure on (*inf*); **~ hinter etw** (*acc*) **machen** (*inf*) to put some pressure on sth; **ein ~ im Kopf/Magen** a feeling of pressure in one's head/stomach; **einen ~ haben** (*sl: = Lust auf Sex*) to be dying for it (*sl*) **(b)** (= *das Drücken*) pressure (+*gen* from); **durch einen ~ auf den Knopf** by pressing the button

Druck[2] M **-(e)s, -e** (= *das Drucken*) printing; (*Art des Drucks*, = *Schriftart, Kunstdruck*) print; **~ und Satz** setting and printing; **das Buch ist im ~** the book is being printed; **in ~ gehen** to go into print; **etw in ~ geben** to send sth to be printed

Druck-: **Druckabfall** M drop in pressure; **Druckanstieg** M rise in pressure; **Druckanzug** M pressure suit; **Druckausgleich** M pressure balance; **Druckbehälter** M pressure vessel; **Druckbleistift** M retractable pencil; **Druckbuchstabe** M printed character; **in ~n schreiben** to print

Drückeberger ['drʏkəbɛrɡɐ] M **-s, -**, **Drückebergerin** [-ərɪn] F **-, -nen** (*pej inf*) shirker; (= *Feigling*) coward

drucken ['drʊkn] VTI (*Typ, Tex*) to print; **ein Buch ~ lassen** to have a book printed; *siehe auch* **gedruckt**

drücken ['drʏkn] ◨ VT **(a)** *Hand, Klinke, Hebel* to press; *Obst, Saft, Eiter* to squeeze; **jdn ~** to squeeze sb; (= *umarmen*) to hug sb; **jdn/etw an sich/ans Herz ~** to press sb/sth to one/one's breast; **jdn zur Seite/nach hinten ~** to push sb aside/back; **etw in or auf den Markt ~** to push sth **(b)** (*geh: = bedrücken*) to weigh heavily upon; **was drückt dich denn?** what's on your mind? **(c)** (*Schuhe, Korsett etc*) to pinch; **jdn im Magen ~** (= *Essen*) to lie heavily on sb's stomach **(d)** (= *verringern, herabsetzen*) to force down; *Leistung, Niveau* to lower **(e)** (*inf: = unterdrücken*) *jdn* to keep down; *Stimmung* to dampen

◩ VI **(a)** (*auf Gegenstand, Klinke, Knopf etc*) to press; (*Wetter, Hitze*) to be oppressive; (*Brille, Schuhe, Korsett etc*) to pinch; (*Essen*) to lie (on one's stomach); „**bitte ~**" "push"; **auf etw** (*acc*) **/an etw** (*acc*) **~** to press sth; **aufs Gemüt ~** to get one down; **auf die Stimmung ~** to dampen one's mood; *siehe auch*

gedrückt
(b) (= *drängeln, stoßen*) to push **(c)** (*bei Stuhlleerung*) to strain **(d)** (*inf: = Heroin injizieren*) to shoot up ◨ VR **(a)** (*mit Ortsangabe*) (*in +acc* into, *an +acc* against) (= *sich quetschen*) to squeeze; (*Schutz suchend*) to huddle **(b)** (*inf: = kneifen*) to shirk; (*vor Militärdienst*) to dodge; **sich vor etw** (*dat*) **~** to shirk sth; **sich (um etw) ~** to get out of sth

drückend ◨ ADJ *Last, Steuern* heavy; *Sorgen, Probleme* serious; *Wetter, Hitze, Enge, Atmosphäre* oppressive ◩ ADV **(es ist) ~ heiß** (it's) oppressively hot

Drucker ['drʊkɐ] M **-s, -** printer

Drücker[1] ['drʏkɐ] M **-s, -** (= *Knopf*) (push) button; (*inf: von Pistole etc*) trigger; (*von Klingel*) push; **die Hand am ~ haben** (*fig inf*) to be ready to act; **am ~ sein** *or* **sitzen** (*fig inf*) (*in Machtposition*) to be in a key position; (*an der Quelle*) to be ideally placed; **auf den letzten ~** (*fig inf*) at the last minute

Drücker[2] ['drʏkɐ] M **-s, -**, **Drückerin** [-ərɪn] F **-, -nen** (*inf: = Hausierer*) hawker (*inf*)

Druckerei [drʊkə'raɪ] F **-, -en** **(a)** printing works *pl*; (= *Firma*) printer's **(b)** (= *Druckwesen*) printing *no art*

Druckerkolonne F (*inf*) door-to-door sales team

Druckerlaubnis F imprimatur

Drucker-: **Druckerschwärze** F printer's ink; **Druckertreiber** M (*Comput*) printer driver

Druck-: **Druckerzeugnis** NT printed material; **Druckfehler** M misprint, typographical error; **druckfrisch** ADJ hot off the press; *Geldscheine* newly printed; **Druckkabine** F pressurized cabin; **Druckknopf** M **(a)** (*Sew*) press stud **(b)** (*Tech*) push button

Druckluft F compressed air

Druckluft-: **Druckluftbohrer** M pneumatic drill; **Druckluftbremse** F air brake

Druck-: **Druckmenü** NT (*Comput*) print menu; **Druckmesser** M **-s, -** pressure gauge; **Druckmittel** NT (*fig*) means of exerting pressure; **als politisches ~** as a means of exerting political pressure; **Druckplatte** F printing plate; **Druckpresse** F printing press; **Druckpumpe** F pressure pump; **druckreif** ◨ ADJ ready for printing, passed for press; (*fig*) polished ◩ ADV **~ sprechen** to speak in a polished style; **Drucksache** F (*Post*) business letter; (= *Werbematerial*) circular; (*als Portoklasse*) printed matter; **Druckschrift** F (= *Schriftart*) printing; **in ~ schreiben** to print

drucksen ['drʊksn] VI (*inf*) to hum and haw (*inf*)

Druck-: **Drucksorten** PL (*Aus*) printed forms *pl*; **Drucktaste** F push button; **druckunempfindlich** ADJ insensitive to pressure; **Druckunterschied** M difference in pressure; **Druckverband** M (*Med*) pressure bandage; **Druckverlust** M (*Tech*) loss of pressure; **Druckvorlage** F (*Typ*) setting copy; **Druckwasserreaktor** M pressurized water reactor; **Druckwelle** F shock wave

drum [drʊm] ADV (*inf*) (a)round; **~ (he)rum** all (a)round; **~ (he)rumreden** to beat about the bush; **da wirst du nicht ~ (he)rumkommen** there's no getting out of it; **seis ~!** (*geh*) never mind; **das (ganze) Drum und Dran** the paraphernalia; (= *Begleiterscheinungen*) the fuss and bother; **mit allem Drum und Dran** with all the bits and pieces (*inf*); *Mahlzeit* with all the trimmings *pl*; *siehe auch* **darum**

drunter ['drʊntɐ] ADV under(neath); **~ und drüber** upside down; **alles ging** *or* **es ging alles ~ und drüber** everything was upside down; **das Drunter und Drüber** the confusion; *siehe auch* **darunter**

Drüse ['dryːzə] F **-, -n** gland

Drüsen-: **Drüsenfieber** NT glandular fever; **Drüsenfunktion** F glandular function; **Drüsenkrankheit** F, **Drüsenleiden** NT glandular disorder; **Drüsenschwellung** F swollen glands *pl*

Dschungel ['dʒʊŋl] M **-s, -** (*lit, fig*) jungle; **sich im ~ der Paragrafen zurechtfinden** to wade one's way through the verbiage

Dschungelkrieg M jungle warfare

Dschunke ['dʒʊŋkə] F **-, -n** (*Naut*) junk

DTP [deːteː'peː] NT, ABBR *von* **Desktoppublishing** DTP

DTP- [deːteː'peː] IN CPDS DTP; **DTP-Anwender(in)** M(F) DTP user; **DTP-Fachfrau** F, **DTP-Fachmann** M DTP specialist; **DTP-Software** F DTP software

dt(sch). ABBR *von* **deutsch**

Dtzd. ABBR *von* **Dutzend**

du [duː] PERS PRON, *gen* **deiner**, *dat* **dir**, *acc* **dich** you (*familiar form of address*); (= *man*) you; **du (zu jdm) sagen**, **jdn mit Du anreden** to use the familiar form of address (with sb); **du, der du es erlebt hast** you who have experienced it; **mit jdm auf Du und Du stehen** to be pals with sb; **mit jdm per du sein** to be on familiar terms with sb; **du bist es** it's you; **bist du es** *or* **das?** is that you?; **Vater unser, der Du bist im Himmel** our Father, who art in heaven; **mach du das doch!** YOU do it!; **du Glücklicher!** lucky you; **du Idiot!** you idiot; **du (Mutti), kannst du mir mal helfen?** hey (mummy), can you help me?; **du, ich muss jetzt aber gehen** listen, I have to go now; **du, du!** (*hum: drohend*) naughty, naughty

Du [duː] NT **-(s), -(s)** "du", familiar form of address; **jdm das Du anbieten** to suggest that sb uses "du"

dual [duˈaːl] ADJ dual

DUALES SYSTEM

The **duales System** *is a waste disposal system which has operated in Germany since 1991. Packaging materials that can be recycled - paper, glass, metal, plastics - are marked with the* **Grüner Punkt**. *Licences for using this symbol must be obtained from* DSD (**Duales System Deutschland GmbH**), *the company responsible for operating the system. The recyclable waste thus marked is collected separately, then sorted and sent for recycling. Although there is no charge for collecting waste for recycling, the cost of obtaining the licence from DSD is often included in the retail price. Austria has a similar system, for which the company* ARA (**Altstoff Recycling Austria AG**) *is responsible.*

▶ GRÜNER PUNKT

Dualismus [duaˈlɪsmʊs] M **-**, NO PL dualism

dualistisch [duaˈlɪstɪʃ] ADJ dualistic

Dualsystem NT (*Math*) binary system

Dübel [ˈdyːbl] M **-s, -** Rawlplug®; (= *Holzdübel*) dowel

Dübelmasse F filler

dübeln [ˈdyːbln] VTI to plug

dubios [duˈbioːs], **dubiös** [duˈbiøːs] ADJ (*geh*) dubious

Dublee [duˈbleː] NT **-s, -s** rolled gold *no pl*; (= *Gegenstand*) article made of rolled gold

Dublette [duˈblɛta] F **-, -n** duplicate

ducken [ˈdʊkn] VR to duck; (*fig pej*) to cringe; *siehe auch* **geduckt** VT *Kopf, Menschen* to duck; (*fig*) to humiliate

Duckmäuser [ˈdʊkmɔyzɐ] M **-s, -**, **Duckmäuserin** [-ərɪn] F **-, -nen** (*pej*) moral coward

Duckmäusertum [ˈdʊkmɔyzɐtuːm] NT **-s**, NO PL (*pej*) moral cowardice; **jdn zum ~ erziehen** to bring sb up to be a moral coward

Dudelei [dudəˈlai] F **-, -en** (*pej*) humming; (*auf Flöte*) tooting

dudeln [ˈduːdln] VTI (*pej inf*) to hum; (*auf Flöte*) to tootle (*auf +dat* on)

Dudelsack M bagpipes *pl*

Dudelsackpfeifer(in) M(F), **Dudelsackspieler(in)** M(F) (bag)piper

Duell [duˈɛl] NT **-s, -e** (*lit, fig*) duel (*um* over); **ein ~ (mit jdm) austragen** to fight a duel (with sb); **jdn zum ~ (heraus)fordern**, **jdn ins ~ fordern** to challenge sb to a duel

Duellant [duɛˈlant] M **-en, -en**, **Duellantin** [-ˈlantɪn] F **-, -nen** dueller

duellieren [duɛˈliːrən], *ptp* **duelliert** VR to (fight a) duel

Duett [duˈɛt] NT **-(e)s, -e** (a) (*Mus, fig*) duet; **im ~ singen** to sing a duet; **etw im ~ singen** to sing sth as a duet (b) (*fig inf:* = *Paar*) duo (*inf*)

Duft [dʊft] M **-(e)s, ⁼e** [ˈdʏfta] smell; (= *Absonderung von Tieren*) scent; **den ~ der großen weiten Welt verspüren** (*usu iro*) to get a taste of the big wide world

Duftdrüse F scent gland

dufte [ˈdʊfta] ADJ, ADV (*dated inf*) great (*inf*)

duften [ˈdʊftn] VI to smell; **nach etw ~** to smell of sth VI IMPERS **hier duftet es nach Kaffee** there is a smell of coffee here

duftend ADJ ATTR nice-smelling; *Parfüm, Blumen etc* fragrant; *Kaffee, Kräuter* aromatic

duftig [ˈdʊftɪç] ADJ *Kleid, Stoff* gossamery; *Spitzen* frothy; *Wolken* fluffy

Duft-: duftlos ADJ odourless (*Brit*), odorless (*US*); **Duftmarke** F scent mark; **Duftnote** F (*von Parfüm*) scent; (*von Mensch*) smell; **Duftstoff** M scent; (*für Parfüm, Waschmittel etc*) fragrance; **Duftwasser** NT, *pl* **-wässer** toilet water; (*hum:* = *Parfüm*) perfume; **Duftwolke** F (*iro*) fragrance (*iro*); (*von Parfüm*) cloud of perfume

dulden [ˈdʊldn] VI (*geh:* = *leiden*) to suffer VT to tolerate; **ich dulde das nicht** I won't tolerate that; **die Sache duldet keinen Aufschub** the matter cannot be delayed; **etw stillschweigend ~** to connive at sth; **er ist hier nur geduldet** he's only here on sufferance

duldsam [ˈdʊltzaːm] ADJ tolerant (*gegenüber* of, *jdm gegenüber* towards sb); (= *geduldig*) forbearing ADV tolerantly; (= *geduldig*) with forbearance

Duldung F **-**, (*rare*) **-en (a)** toleration; **solche Zustände erlauben keine weitere ~** such conditions can be tolerated no longer; **unter** *or* **bei** *or* **mit stillschweigender ~ der Behörden** *etc* with the (tacit) connivance of the authorities *etc* **(b)** (= *Aufenthaltsgenehmigung*) short-term residence permit

Dulliäh [dʊliˈɛː] M **-**, NO PL (*Aus inf*) tipsiness (*inf*); **im ~** (when one is/was) tipsy

dumm [dʊm] ADJ, *comp* **⁼er** [ˈdʏmɐ], *superl* **⁼ste(r, s)** [ˈdʏmstə] **(a)** stupid; **~e Gans** silly goose; **~es Zeug (reden)** (to talk) nonsense; **jdn wie einen ~en Jungen behandeln** (*inf*) to treat sb like a child; **jdn für ~ verkaufen** (*inf*) to think sb is stupid; **du willst mich wohl für ~ verkaufen** you must think I'm stupid; **ich lasse mich nicht für ~ verkaufen** I'm not so stupid (*inf*); **das ist gar nicht (so) ~** that's not a bad idea; **er ist dümmer als die Polizei erlaubt** (*inf*) he's as stupid as they come (*inf*); **jetzt wirds mir zu ~** I've had enough **(b)** (= *ärgerlich, unangenehm*) annoying; **es ist zu ~, dass er nicht kommen kann** it's too bad that he can't come; **etwas Dummes** a silly thing; **so etwas Dummes** how silly; (= *wie ärgerlich*) what a nuisance

ADV, *comp* **⁼er**, *superl* **am ⁼sten ~ gucken** to look stupid; **dümmer hättest du dich wirklich nicht anstellen können** you couldn't have made things worse if you'd tried; **sich ~ anstellen** to behave stupidly; **sich ~ stellen** to act stupid; **~ fragen** to ask a silly question/silly questions; **~ dastehen** to look stupid; **sich ~ und dämlich reden** (*inf*) to talk till one is blue in the face (*inf*); **sich ~ und dämlich verdienen** (*inf*) to earn the earth (*inf*); **jdm ~ kommen** to get funny with sb (*inf*); **das ist ~ gelaufen** (*inf*) that hasn't gone to plan; **~ gelaufen!** (*inf*) that's life!; **~ geboren, nichts dazugelernt** (*prov*) he/she *etc* hasn't got the sense he/she *etc* was born with (*prov*)

dummdreist ADJ insolent; *Idee* impertinent ADV *grinsen, antworten* insolently

Dummejungenstreich M silly prank

Dummenfang M **das ist der reinste ~** that's just a con (*inf*); **auf ~ ausgehen** to try to catch fools

Dumme(r) [ˈdʊma] MF DECL AS ADJ (*inf*) fool; **der/die ~ sein** to be left to carry the can (*inf*)

Dummerchen [ˈdʊmeçən] NT **-s, -** (*inf*) ninny (*inf*)

dummerweise ADV unfortunately; (= *aus Dummheit*) stupidly

Dummheit F **-, -en (a)** NO PL stupidity **(b)** (= *dumme Handlung*) stupid thing; **mach bloß keine ~en!** just don't do anything stupid

Dummkopf M (*inf*) idiot

dümmlich [ˈdʏmlɪç] ADJ silly; **eine ~e Blondine** a dumb blonde

Dummschwätzer(in) M(F) (*inf*) bullshitter (*vulg*)

Dummy [ˈdami] M **-s, -s** (= *Attrappe, bei Unfalltests*) dummy

dümpeln [ˈdʏmpln] VI (a) (*Naut*) to bob up and down **(b)** (*fig*) to hover; **die Partei dümpelt bei 40%** the party is hovering around the 40% mark

dumpf [dʊmpf] ADJ (a) *Geräusch, Ton* muffled **(b)** *Luft, Geruch, Keller etc* musty **(c)** *Gefühl, Ahnung, Erinnerung* vague; *Schmerz* dull; (= *bedrückend*) gloomy **(d)** (= *stumpfsinnig*) dull ADV (a) *aufprallen* with a thud; **~ klingen** to sound dull; (*weil hohl*) to sound hollow **(b)** (= *stumpfsinnig*) **~ glotzen** to have a mindless look on one's face; **~ vor sich hin brüten** to be completely apathetic

Dumpfbacke F (*sl*) nerd (*inf*)

Dumpfheit F **-**, NO PL (a) (*von Geräusch, Ton*) muffled quality **(b)** (*von Luft, Geruch, Keller etc*) mustiness **(c)** (= *Stumpfsinnigkeit*) dullness

Dumping [ˈdampɪŋ] NT **-s**, NO PL (*Econ*) dumping

Dumpingpreis [ˈdampɪŋ-] M giveaway price

Düne [ˈdyːnə] F **-, -n** (sand) dune

Dung [dʊŋ] M **-(e)s**, NO PL dung

Düngemittel NT fertilizer

düngen [ˈdʏŋən] 🟦 VT to fertilize 🟦 VI (*Stoff*) to act as a fertilizer; (*Mensch*) to apply fertilizer; **im Garten ~** to put fertilizer on the garden

Dünger [ˈdʏŋɐ] M **-s**, **-** fertilizer

dunkel [ˈdʊŋkl] 🟦 ADJ **(a)** (= *finster, farblich*) dark; **im Zimmer ~ machen** (*inf*) to make the room dark; **im Dunkeln** in the dark; **im Dunkeln tappen** (*fig*) to grope (about) in the dark; **ein Dunkles, bitte!** ≈ a dark beer, please; **in dunkler Vergangenheit** *or* **Vorzeit** in the dim and distant past
(b) (= *tief*) *Stimme, Ton* deep
(c) (*pej*: = *zweifelhaft, zwielichtig*) shady (*inf*)
🟦 ADV (= *in dunklen Farben*) in a dark colour (*Brit*) *or* color (*US*), in dark colours (*Brit*) *or* colors (*US*); **~ gefärbt sein** to be a dark colo(u)r; **sich ~ kleiden** to dress in dark colo(u)rs; **etw ~ anmalen** to paint sth a dark colo(u)r; **sich ~ erinnern** to remember vaguely

Dunkel [ˈdʊŋkl] NT **-s**, NO PL (*lit, fig*) darkness; **das verliert sich im ~ der Geschichte** it is lost in the mists of history; **in ~ gehüllt sein** (*fig*) to be shrouded in mystery

Dünkel [ˈdʏŋkl] M **-s**, NO PL (*pej geh*) conceit

dunkel- IN CPDS dark; **dunkelblau** ADJ dark blue; **dunkelblond** ADJ light brown; **dunkelhaarig** ADJ dark-haired

dünkelhaft ADJ (*pej geh*) conceited

Dunkel-: dunkelhäutig ADJ dark-skinned; **Dunkelheit** F **-**, (*rare*) **-en** (*lit, fig*) darkness; **bei Einbruch** *or* **Eintritt der ~** at nightfall; **Dunkelkammer** F (*Phot*) darkroom; **dunkelrot** ADJ dark red; **Dunkelwerden** NT **-s**, NO PL nightfall; **Dunkelziffer** F *estimated number of unreported/undetected cases*

dünken [ˈdʏŋkn] (*geh*) 🟦 VTI IMPERS **das dünkt mich gut, mich dünkt, dass das gut ist** it seems good to me; **mich dünkt, er kommt nicht mehr** I think he will not come 🟦 VR to think (oneself); **sie dünkt sich sehr klug** she thinks herself very clever

dünn [dʏn] 🟦 ADJ thin; *Kaffee, Tee* weak; (= *fein*) *Schleier, Regen, Strümpfe* fine; **sich ~ machen** (*hum*) to breathe in; *siehe auch* **dünnmachen** 🟦 ADV besiedelt, bevölkert sparsely; **~ behaart** *Mensch* with thin hair; *Haupt* thinly covered in hair; **~ gesät** (*fig*) few and far between

Dünn-: Dünndarm M small intestine; **dünnflüssig** ADJ *Farbe, Öl* thin; *Teig, Honig* runny; **Dünnflüssigkeit** F (*von Farbe, Öl*) thinness; (*von Teig, Honig*) runniness; **dünnhäutig** ADJ thin-skinned; **dünnmachen** VR SEP (*inf*: = *weglaufen*) to make oneself scarce; **Dünnpfiff** M (*inf*) the runs (*inf*); **Dünnsäure** F dilute acid; **Dünnsäureverklappung** F dumping of dilute acids; **dünnschalig** [-ʃaˑlɪç] ADJ *Obst* thin-skinned; *Nüsse, Ei etc* thin-shelled; **Dünnschiss** M (*inf*) the runs (*inf*); **dünnwandig** ADJ thin-walled

Dunst [dʊnst] M **-(e)s**, **¨e** [ˈdʏnstə] (= *leichter Nebel*) haze; (= *Dampf*) steam; **blauer ~** (*fig inf*) sheer invention; **jdm blauen ~ vormachen** (*inf*) to throw dust in sb's eyes

Dunstabzugshaube F extractor hood (*over a cooker*)

dünsten [ˈdʏnstn] VT to steam; *Obst* to stew

Dunstglocke F, **Dunsthaube** F (= *Nebel*) haze; (= *Smog*) pall of smog

dunstig [ˈdʊnstɪç] ADJ hazy

Dunst-: Dunstkreis M atmosphere; (*von Mensch*) society; **Dunstschicht** F layer of haze; **Dunstschwaden** PL clouds *pl* of haze; (= *Nebel*) haze *sing*; (= *Dampf*) clouds *pl* of steam; (= *Rauch*) clouds *pl* of smoke; **Dunstwolke** F cloud of smog

Duo [ˈduːo] NT **-s**, **-s** duo

Duodezimalsystem [duodetsiˈmaːl-] NT duodecimal system

Duplikat [dupliˈkaːt] NT **-(e)s**, **-e** duplicate (copy)

duplizieren [dupliˈtsiːrən], *ptp* **dupliziert** VT (*geh*) to duplicate

Duplostein® [ˈduplo-] M Duplo® brick

Dur [duːɐ] NT **-**, NO PL (*Mus*) major; **ein Stück in ~/in G-~** a piece in a major key/in G major

durch [dʊrç] 🟦 PREP +ACC **(a)** (*räumlich*: = *hindurch*) through; **quer ~** right across; **~ den Fluss waten** to wade across the river; **~ die ganze Welt reisen** to travel all over the world
(b) (= *mittels, von, wegen*) through; (*in Passivkonstruktion*:

= *von*) by; **Tod ~ Ertrinken/den Strang** death by drowning/hanging; **Tod ~ Erfrieren/Herzschlag** *etc* death from exposure/a heart attack *etc*; **neun (geteilt) ~ drei** nine divided by three; **~ Zufall/das Los** by chance/lot
(c) (= *aufgrund, infolge von*) due to
🟦 ADV **(a)** (= *hindurch*) through; **es ist 4 Uhr ~** it's gone 4 o'clock; **~ und ~ kennen, ehrlich** through and through; **verlogen, überzeugt** completely; **~ und ~ nass** wet through; **das geht mir ~ und ~** that goes right through me
(b) (*Cook inf*) *Steak* well-done; *siehe auch* **durch sein**

durch- (*in Verbindung mit Verben*) through

durchackern SEP (*inf*) 🟦 VT to plough (*Brit*) *or* plow (*US*) through 🟦 VR to plough (*Brit*) *or* plow (*US*) one's way through (*durch etw sth*)

durcharbeiten SEP 🟦 VT **(a)** *Buch, Stoff etc* to work through
(b) (= *ausarbeiten*) to work out (in detail) 🟦 VI to work through 🟦 VR **sich durch etw ~** to work one's way through sth

durchatmen VI SEP to take deep breaths

durchaus [dʊrçˈlaus, ˈdʊrçˌlaus, ˈdʊrçlaus] ADV **(a)** (*in bejahten Sätzen*: = *unbedingt*) **das muss ~ sein** that definitely has to be; **sie wollte ~ mitgehen/ein neues Auto haben** she insisted on going too/having a new car; **das ist ~ nötig** that is absolutely necessary; **hat er sich anständig benommen? – ja** – did he behave himself properly? – yes, absolutely
(b) (*bekräftigend in bejahten Sätzen*) quite; *verständlich, richtig, korrekt, möglich* perfectly; *passen, annehmen* perfectly well; *sich freuen, gefallen* really; **das könnte man ~ machen, das lässt sich ~ machen** that sounds feasible; **ich hätte ~ Lust ...** I would like to ...; **ich hätte ~ Zeit** I would have time; **es ist ~ anzunehmen, dass sie kommt** it's highly likely that she'll be coming
(c) (*in bejahten Sätzen*: = *ganz und gar*) *ehrlich, zufrieden, unerfreulich* thoroughly
(d) (*in verneinten Sätzen*) **~ nicht** (*als Verstärkung*) by no means; (*als Antwort*) not at all; (*stärker*) absolutely not; **etw ~ nicht tun wollen** to refuse absolutely to do sth; **das braucht ~ nicht schlecht zu sein** that does not HAVE to be bad; **das ist ~ kein Witz** that's no joke at all

durchbeißen SEP IRREG 🟦 VT (*in zwei Teile*) to bite through 🟦 VR (*inf*) (*durch etw sth*) to struggle through; (*mit Erfolg*) to win through

durchbekommen *ptp* **durchbekommen** VT SEP IRREG (*inf*) to get through

durchbiegen SEP IRREG 🟦 VT *Knie* to bend 🟦 VR to sag

durchblasen SEP IRREG 🟦 VT (= *Luft etc hindurchblasen*) to blow through (*durch etw sth*); *Eileiter, Rohr, Ohren etc* to clear (by blowing) 🟦 VI to blow through (*durch etw sth*)

durchblättern [ˈdʊrçblɛtɐn] VT SEP *Buch etc* to leaf through

Durchblick M *vista* (*auf +acc* of); (= *Ausblick*) view (*auf +acc* of); (*fig inf*: = *Verständnis, Überblick*) knowledge; **den ~ haben** (*inf*) to know what's what (*inf*); **den ~ verlieren** to lose track (*bei* of)

durchblicken VI SEP **(a)** (*lit*) to look through (*durch etw sth*); (= *zum Vorschein kommen*) to shine through **(b)** (*fig*) **etw ~ lassen** to hint at sth **(c)** (*fig inf*: = *verstehen*) to understand; **blickst du da durch?** do you get it? (*inf*)

durchbluten *ptp* **durchblutet** VT INSEP to supply with blood

durchblutet [dʊrçˈbluːtət] ADJ supplied with blood; **gut/schlecht ~e Körperteile** parts of the body in which circulation is good/bad

Durchblutung F circulation (of the blood) (+*gen* to)

Durchblutungsstörung F circulatory disturbance

durchbohren¹ [dʊrçˈboːrən], *ptp* **durchbohrt** VT INSEP *Wand, Brett* to drill through; (*mit Schwert etc*) to run through; (*Kugel*) to go through; **jdn mit Blicken ~** (*fig*) to look piercingly at sb; (*hasserfüllt*) to look daggers at sb

durchbohren² [ˈdʊrçboːrən] SEP 🟦 VT **etw durch etw ~** *Loch, Tunnel* to drill sth through sth; *Nagel* to pierce sth through sth 🟦 VI to drill through (*durch etw sth*) 🟦 VR (*durch etw sth*) to bore one's way through; (*Speer*) to go through

durchbohrend ADJ piercing

durchboxen SEP (*fig inf*) (*durch etw sth*) 🟦 VT to push through 🟦 VR to fight one's way through

durchbraten VTI SEP IRREG to cook through; **durchgebraten** well-done

durchbrechen¹ [ˈdʊrçbrɛçn̩] SEP IRREG **1** VT (*in zwei Teile*) to break (in two) **2** VI AUX SEIN **(a)** (*in zwei Teile*) to break (in two) **(b)** (= *einbrechen: Mensch*) to fall through (*durch etw* sth) **(c)** (*Med: Blinddarm etc*) to perforate

durchbrechen² [dʊrçˈbrɛçn̩] ptp **durchbrochen** [dʊrçˈbrɔxn̩] VT INSEP IRREG *Schallmauer* (*fig*) to break; *Mauer, Blockade etc* to break through

durchbrennen VI SEP IRREG **(a)** (= *nicht ausgehen*) to stay alight **(b)** AUX SEIN (*Sicherung, Glühbirne*) to blow; (*inf:* = *davonlaufen*) to run away; **jdm ~** (*inf*) to run away from sb

durchbringen SEP IRREG **1** VT **(a)** (*durch etw* sth) (*durch Prüfung, Kontrolle*) to get through; (*durch Krankheit*) to pull through; (= *für Unterhalt sorgen*) to provide for **(b)** *Geld* to get through **2** VR to get by

Durchbruch M **(a)** (*von Blinddarm etc*) perforation; **zum ~ kommen** (*fig*) (*Gewohnheit*) to assert itself; (*Natur*) to reveal itself **(b)** (*Mil, Sport, fig*) breakthrough; **jdm/einer Sache zum ~ verhelfen** to help sb/sth on the road to success **(c)** (= *durchbrochene Stelle*) breach; (= *Öffnung*) opening

durchbürsten VT SEP to brush thoroughly

durchchecken VT SEP to check through

durchdacht [dʊrçˈdaxt] ADJ properly thought-out; **gut/schlecht ~** well/badly thought-out

durchdenken [dʊrçˈdɛŋkn̩], ptp **durchdacht** [dʊrçˈdaxt] VT INSEP, **durchdenken** [ˈdʊrçdɛŋkn̩] VT SEP IRREG to think through

durchdiskutieren ptp **durchdiskutiert** VT SEP to talk through

durchdrehen SEP **1** VT *Fleisch etc* to mince **2** VI **(a)** (*Rad*) to spin **(b)** (*inf*) to do one's nut (*Brit inf*); (*nervlich*) to crack up (*inf*); **ganz durchgedreht sein** (*inf*) to be really uptight (*inf*) or (*aus dem Gleichgewicht*) confused

durchdringen¹ [ˈdʊrçdrɪŋən] VI SEP IRREG AUX SEIN **(a)** (= *hindurchkommen*) to penetrate (*durch etw* sth); (*Flüssigkeit, Kälte, Sonne*) to come through (*durch etw* sth); (*Stimme, Geräusch*) to be heard (*durch etw* through sth); **bis zu jdm ~** (*fig*) to get as far as sb **(b)** (= *sich durchsetzen, sich verständlich machen*) to get through; **zu jdm ~** to get through to sb; **mit einem Vorschlag ~** to get a suggestion accepted (*bei, in +dat* by)

durchdringen² [dʊrçˈdrɪŋən], ptp **durchdrungen** [dʊrçˈdrʊŋən] VT INSEP IRREG *Materie, Dunkelheit etc* to penetrate; (*Gefühl, Idee, Gedanke*) to pervade; *siehe auch* **durchdrungen**

durchdringend [ˈdʊrçdrɪŋənt] ADJ piercing; *Geruch* pungent

durchdrücken VT SEP **(a)** (*durch Sieb*) to rub through; (*durch Presse*) to press through; *Creme, Teig* to pipe **(b)** (*fig*) *Gesetz, Reformen, Neuerungen etc* to push through; *seinen Willen* to get; **es ~, dass ...** to get the decision through that ... **(c)** *Knie, Ellbogen etc* to straighten

durchdrungen [dʊrçˈdrʊŋən] ADJ PRED imbued (*von* with); **ganz von einer Idee ~ sein** to be taken with an idea; *siehe auch* **durchdringen²**

durchdürfen VI SEP IRREG (*inf*) to be allowed through; **darf ich mal durch?** can I get through?; **Sie dürfen hier nicht durch** you can't come through here

durcheinander [dʊrçaɪˈnandɐ] **1** ADV mixed up; **Gemüse ~** vegetable stew; **alles ~ essen/trinken** to eat/drink indiscriminately **2** ADJ PRED **~ sein** (*inf*) (*Mensch*) to be confused; (= *aufgeregt*) to be in a state (*inf*); (*Zimmer, Papier*) to be in a mess

Durcheinander [dʊrçaɪˈnandɐ, ˈdʊrçaɪnandɐ] NT **-s**, NO PL (= *Unordnung*) mess; (= *Wirrwarr*) confusion; **in dem Zimmer herrscht ein wüstes ~** the room is in a terrible mess

durcheinander: **durcheinander bringen** VT IRREG to muddle up; (= *verwirren*) *jdn* to confuse; **durcheinander geraten** VI IRREG AUX SEIN to get mixed up; **durcheinander kommen** VI IRREG AUX SEIN to get mixed up; **durcheinander laufen** VI IRREG AUX SEIN to run about all over the place; **durcheinander reden** VI to all speak at once; **durcheinander rufen**, **durcheinander schreien** VI IRREG to all shout out at once; **durcheinander werfen** VT IRREG to muddle up; (*fig inf*: = *verwechseln*) to mix up

durchexerzieren ptp **durchexerziert** VT SEP to rehearse

durchfahren¹ [ˈdʊrçfaːrən] VI SEP IRREG AUX SEIN **(a)** (*durch einen Ort, Tunnel etc*) to go through (*durch etw* sth) **(b)** (= *nicht anhalten/umsteigen*) to go straight through (without

stopping/changing); **er ist bei Rot durchgefahren** he jumped the lights; **die Nacht ~** to travel through the night

durchfahren² [dʊrçˈfaːrən], ptp **durchfahren** VT INSEP IRREG to travel through; (*fig: Schreck, Zittern etc*) to shoot through; **ein Gedanke durchfuhr sie blitzartig** a (sudden) thought flashed through her mind

Durchfahrt F **(a)** (= *Durchreise*) way through; **auf der ~ sein** to be passing through **(b)** (= *Passage*) thoroughfare; **~ bitte freihalten!** please keep access free; **~ verboten!** no thoroughfare; **der Polizist gab endlich die ~ frei/gab das Zeichen zur ~** the policeman finally allowed/signalled the traffic through

Durchfall M (*Med*) diarrhoea no art (*Brit*), diarrhea no art (*US*)

durchfallen VI SEP IRREG AUX SEIN **(a)** (*durch Loch, Lücke etc*) to fall through (*durch etw* sth) **(b)** (*inf:* = *nicht bestehen*); (*Wahlkandidat*) to lose; **in** or **bei der Prüfung ~** to fail the exam; **jdn ~ lassen** to fail sb; **beim Publikum/bei der Kritik ~** to be a flop with the public/critics

durchfechten VT SEP IRREG **etw ~** to fight to get sth through

durchfeiern VI SEP to stay up all night celebrating

durchfinden VIR SEP IRREG (*lit, fig*) to find one's way through (*durch etw* sth); **ich finde (mich) hier nicht mehr durch** (*fig*) I am simply lost

durchfliegen¹ [ˈdʊrçfliːgn̩] VI SEP IRREG AUX SEIN **(a)** (*mit Flugzeug*) to fly through (*durch etw* sth); (*ohne Landung*) to fly nonstop **(b)** (*inf: durch Prüfung*) to fail (*durch etw, in etw dat* (in) sth)

durchfliegen² [dʊrçˈfliːgn̩], ptp **durchflogen** [dʊrçˈfloːgn̩] VT INSEP IRREG *Luft, Wolken* to fly through; *Luftkorridor* to fly along; *Strecke* to cover; (= *flüchtig lesen*) to skim through

durchfließen VI SEP IRREG AUX SEIN to flow through (*durch etw* sth)

durchforschen ptp **durchforscht** VT INSEP *Gegend* to search; *Land, Wissensgebiet* to explore; *Akten, Bücher* to search through

durchforsten [dʊrçˈfɔrstn̩], ptp **durchforstet** VT INSEP *Wald* to thin out; (*fig*) *Bücher, Akten etc* to go through

Durchfrachtkonnossement NT through bill of lading

durchfragen VR SEP to ask one's way

durchfressen VR SEP IRREG (*Säure, Rost, Tier*) to eat (its way) through (*durch etw* sth) **sich (bei jdm) ~** (*pej inf*) to live on sb's hospitality

Durchfuhr [ˈdʊrçfuːɐ] F **-, -en** transit

durchführbar ADJ feasible

Durchführbarkeit [ˈdʊrçfyːɐbaːɐkaɪt] F **-**, NO PL feasibility

Durchführbarkeitsstudie F feasibility study

durchführen SEP **1** VT **(a)** (= *durchleiten*) (*durch etw* sth) *jdn, Fluss* to lead through; *Leitung, Rohr* to run through; *Straße* to build through; *Kanal, Tunnel* to dig through; **jdn durch eine Stadt/ein Haus ~** to show sb (a)round a town/a house **(b)** (= *verwirklichen, veranstalten*) to carry out; *Gesetz* to implement; *Test, Kurs* to run; *Expedition, Reise* to undertake; *Messung* to take; *Wahl, Prüfung* to hold **(c)** (= *konsequent zu Ende bringen*) to carry through **2** VI (*durch etw* sth) to lead through; (*Straße*) to go through; **zwischen etw** (*dat*) **~** to lead between sth; **unter etw** (*dat*) **~** to go under sth

Durchführung F **(a)** (= *das Verwirklichen*) carrying out; (*von Gesetz*) implementation; (*von Experiment, Untersuchung, Reise, Expedition*) undertaking; (*von Messung*) taking; (*von Kurs, Test*) running; (*von Wahl, Prüfung*) holding **(b)** (= *konsequentes Beenden*) carrying through

durchfüttern VT SEP (*inf*) to feed; **sich von jdm ~ lassen** to live off sb

Durchgabe F announcement; (*von Hinweis, Bericht*) giving; (*telefonisch*) message (over the telephone); **bei der ~ von Zahlen übers Telefon** when numbers are given over the telephone

Durchgang M, pl **-gänge (a)** (= *Weg, Passage*) way; (*schmal*) passage(way); (= *Torweg*) gateway; **kein ~!**, **~ verboten!** no right of way; **der ~ zur Höhle ist beschwerlich** it's difficult to get through to the cave; **er hat mir den ~ versperrt** he blocked my passage **(b)** (*von Experiment, bei Arbeit, Parl*) stage **(c)** (*bei Wettbewerb, von Wahl, Sport*) round; (*beim Rennen*) heat

durchgängig **1** ADJ universal; **eine ~e Eigenschaft in ihren Romanen** a constant feature in her novels **2** ADV generally;

feststellbar universally; **die Kandidaten wurden ~ abgelehnt** every single one of the candidates was rejected

Durchgangs-: Durchgangslager NT transit camp; **Durchgangsstraße** F through road; **Durchgangsverkehr** M (*Mot*) through traffic; (= *Transitverkehr*) transit traffic

durchgeben VT SEP IRREG (**a**) (= *durchreichen*) to pass through (*durch etw sth*) (**b**) (*Rad, TV*) to give; *Nachricht, Lottozahlen* to announce; **jdm etw telefonisch ~** to let sb know sth by telephone; **ein Telegramm telefonisch ~** to telephone a telegram; **jdm ~, dass ...** to let sb know that ...; **wir geben (Ihnen) nun den Wetterbericht durch** and now we bring you the weather forecast

durchgefroren ADJ *Mensch* frozen stiff

durchgehen SEP IRREG AUX SEIN **1** VI (**a**) (*lit*) (*durch etw sth*) to go through; (*durch Kontrolle, Zoll*) to pass through; (= *weitergehen, durchpassen, inf*: = *sich hinstecken lassen*) to go through; **zwischen/unter etw** (*dat*) **~** to go (through) between/under sth; **bitte ~!** (*im Bus*) move right down (the bus) please!
(**b**) (*Fluss, Weg, Linie etc, fig: Thema*) to run through (*durch etw sth*)
(**c**) (= *durchdringen*) to come through (*durch etw sth*)
(**d**) (*Gesetz, Antrag*) to go through
(**e**) (= *toleriert werden*) to be tolerated; **jdm etw ~ lassen** to let sb get away with sth; **das lasse ich noch mal ~** I'll let it pass
(**f**) (*ohne Unterbrechung*) to go straight through; (*Flug*) to be nonstop; **die ganze Nacht ~** (*Mensch*) to walk all night (long); (*Party*) to last all night (long)
(**g**) (*Pferd etc*) to bolt; (*inf*: = *sich davonmachen*) to run off; **seine Frau ist ihm durchgegangen** his wife has run off and left him
(**h**) (= *außer Kontrolle geraten*) **mit jdm ~** (*Temperament, Nerven*) to get the better of sb; (*Gefühle auch*) to run away with sb
2 VT AUCH AUX HABEN (= *durchsehen, -sprechen etc*) to go through

durchgehend 1 ADJ *Öffnungszeiten* round-the-clock *attr* (*Brit*), around-the-clock *attr* (*US*), continuous; *Straße* straight; *Verkehrsverbindung, Zug* direct; *Fahrkarte* through *attr* **2** ADV throughout; **~ geöffnet** open 24 hours

durchgeknallt [-gəknalt] ADJ (*inf*: = *verrückt*) crazy (*inf*)

durchgeschwitzt [-gəʃvɪtst] ADJ *Mensch* bathed in sweat; *Kleidung* soaked in sweat; *siehe auch* **durchschwitzen**

durchgestalten *ptp* **durchgestaltet** VT SEP to work out (down) to the last detail

durchgießen VT SEP IRREG to pour through (*durch etw sth*)

durchglühen VI SEP AUX SEIN to glow red-hot; (*Lampe, Draht, Sicherung*) to burn out

durchgreifen VI SEP IRREG to reach through (*durch etw sth*); (*fig*) to resort to drastic measures

durchgreifend 1 ADJ *Änderung, Maßnahme* drastic; (= *weit reichend*) *Änderung* far-reaching

durchhaben VT SEP IRREG (*inf*) **etw ~** (= *durchgelesen, zerteilt etc haben*) to have got (*Brit*) or gotten (*US*) through sth

Durchhalteappell M appeal to hold out

durchhalten SEP IRREG **1** VT (= *durchstehen*) *Zeit, Ehe, Kampf etc* to survive; *Streik* to see through; *Belastung* to (with)stand; (*Sport*) *Strecke* to stay; *Tempo* (= *beibehalten*) to keep up; (= *aushalten*) to stand; **das Rennen ~** to stay the course **2** VI to stick it out (*inf*); (= *beharren*) to persevere; (*bei Rennen*) to stay the course; **eisern ~** to hold out grimly

Durchhalte-: Durchhalteparole F rallying call; **Durchhaltevermögen** NT, NO PL staying power

durchhängen VI SEP IRREG AUX HABEN or SEIN to sag; (*fig inf*) (= *deprimiert sein*) to be down (in the mouth) (*inf*); (= *schlappmachen*) to wilt; **du solltest dich nicht so ~ lassen** you shouldn't let yourself go like that

Durchhänger M (*inf*: = *schlechte Phase*) bad patch; (*an bestimmtem Tag*) off day (*inf*)

durchhauen VT SEP IRREG or (*INF*) REG (= *entzweischlagen*) to chop in two; (= *spalten*) to split

durchhecheln VT SEP (*fig inf*) to gossip about; **in allen Zeitungen durchgehechelt** dragged through all the papers

durchhören VT SEP *etw* (**durch etw**) **~** to hear sth (through sth); **ich konnte ~, dass ...** I could tell that ...

durchkämmen [ˈdʊrçkɛmən] VT SEP (**a**) *Haare* to comb out (**b**) (= *absuchen*) to comb (through)

durchkämpfen SEP **1** VT (= *durchsetzen*) to push through **2** VR (*durch etw sth*) to fight one's way through; (*fig*) to struggle through **3** VI (*Soldaten*) to battle on; **es wurde selbst über die Weihnachtszeit durchgekämpft** the fighting continued even over Christmas

durchkauen VT SEP *Essen* to chew (thoroughly); (*inf*: = *besprechen*) to go over

durchklettern VI SEP AUX SEIN to climb through (*durch etw sth*)

durchklingen VI SEP IRREG AUX HABEN or SEIN (*durch etw sth*) to sound through; (*fig*) to come through

durchkneifen VT SEP IRREG *Draht* to snip through

durchkneten VT SEP *Teig etc* to knead thoroughly; (*bei Massage*) to massage thoroughly; **sich ~ lassen** to have a thorough massage

durchkommen VI SEP IRREG AUX SEIN (**a**) (*durch etw sth*) to get through; (*Sonne, Wasser, Farbe etc*) to come through; (*Charakterzug*) to show through; (= *sichtbar werden: Sonne*) to come out; **kommst du durch?** can you get through?
(**b**) (= *durchfahren*) to come through (*durch etw sth*)
(**c**) (*lit, fig*: = *mit Erfolg ~*) to get through (*durch etw sth*); (*finanziell*) to get by; (= *Prüfung bestehen*) to pass; (= *überleben*) to come through; **mit etw ~** *Forderungen etc* to succeed with sth; *mit Betrug, Schmeichelei etc* to get away with sth; **damit kommt er bei mir nicht durch** he won't get away with that with me

durchkönnen VI SEP IRREG (*inf*) to be able to get through (*durch etw sth*)

Durchkonnossement NT through bill of lading

durchkreuzen¹ [dʊrçˈkrɔytsn], *ptp* **durchkreuzt** VT INSEP *Land, Wüste, Ozean* to cross; (*fig*) *Pläne etc* to thwart

durchkreuzen² [ˈdʊrçkrɔytsn] VT SEP (*mit Strichen*) to cross out

durchkriechen VI SEP IRREG AUX SEIN to crawl through (*durch etw sth*)

durchkriegen VT SEP (*inf*) to get through

durchladen VTI SEP IRREG *Gewehr* to reload

Durchlass [ˈdʊrçlas] M **-es, Durchlässe** [-lɛsə] (**a**) (= *Durchgang*) passage; (*für Wasser*) duct (**b**) NO PL (*geh*) permission to pass; **sich** (*dat*) **~ verschaffen** to obtain permission to pass; (*mit Gewalt*) to force one's way through

durchlassen VT SEP IRREG (*durch etw sth*) (= *passieren lassen*) to allow through; *Licht, Wasser etc* to let through; (= *eindringen lassen*) to let in; (*inf*) *Fehler etc* to overlook

durchlässig ADJ *Material* permeable; (= *porös*) porous; *Zelt, Regenmantel, Schuh* that lets water in; *Zelt, Schuh* leaky; *Grenze* open; **eine ~e Stelle** (*fig*) a leak; **die Bildungswege ~ machen** to make the elements of the education programme (*Brit*) or program (*US*) interchangeable

Durchlässigkeit F permeability; (= *Porosität*) porosity; **die ~ der Bildungswege** the interchangeability of the elements of the education programme (*Brit*) or program (*US*)

Durchlauf M (**a**) (= *das Durchlaufen*) flow (**b**) (*TV, Rad, Comput*) run (**c**) (*Sport*) heat

durchlaufen¹ [ˈdʊrçlaufn] SEP IRREG **1** VT *Schuhe, Sohlen* to wear through **2** VI AUX SEIN (**a**) (*durch etw sth*) (= *durch Straße/Öffnung etc gehen*) to go through; (*Straße, Rohr etc, Flüssigkeit*) to run through (**b**) (*ohne Unterbrechung: Mensch*) to run without stopping

durchlaufen² [dʊrçˈlaufn], *ptp* **durchlaufen** VT INSEP IRREG *Gebiet* to run through; *Strecke* to cover; (*Astron*) *Bahn* to describe; *Lehrzeit, Schule, Phase* to pass or go through; (*Gefühl*) to run through; **es durchlief mich heiß** I felt hot all over

durchlaufend [ˈdʊrçlaufnt] ADJ continuous

Durchlauferhitzer [-lɛhɪtsɐ] M **-s, -** continuous-flow water heater

durchlavieren *ptp* **durchlaviert** [dʊrçlaˈviːrən] VR SEP to steer or manoeuvre (*Brit*) or maneuver (*US*) one's way through (*durch etw sth*)

durchleben [dʊrçˈleːbn], *ptp* **durchlebt** VT INSEP to go through

durchleiten VT SEP to lead through (*durch etw sth*)

durchlesen VT SEP IRREG to read through; **etw ganz ~** to read sth all the way through; **etw flüchtig ~** to skim through sth;

etw auf Fehler (hin) ~ to read sth through (looking) for mistakes; **sich** (*dat*) **etw** ~ to read sth through

durchleuchten¹ [dʊrçˈbʏçtn̩], *ptp* **durchleuchtet** VT INSEP *Patienten* to X-ray; *Eier* to candle; (*fig*) *Angelegenheit etc* to investigate

durchleuchten² [ˈdʊrçbʏçtn̩] VI SEP to shine through (*durch etw* sth)

durchliegen SEP IRREG **1** VT *Matratze, Bett* to wear down (in the middle) **2** VR to get bedsores

durchlöchern [dʊrçˈlœçən], *ptp* **durchlöchert** VT INSEP to make holes in; (*Motten auch, Rost*) to eat holes in; *Socken etc* to wear holes in; (*fig*) to undermine completely; **(mit Schüssen)** ~ to riddle with bullets

durchlotsen VT SEP (*durch etw* sth) *Schiff* to pilot through; *Autofahrer* to guide through; (*fig*) to steer through

durchlüften VTI SEP to air thoroughly

durchmachen SEP **1** VT **(a)** (= *erdulden, durchlaufen*) to go through; *Krankheit* to have; *Operation, Entwicklung, Wandlung* to undergo; *Lehre* to serve; **sie hat viel durchgemacht** she has been through a lot **(b)** (*inf*) (= *durcharbeiten*) to work through; **eine ganze Nacht/Woche** ~ (= *durchfeiern*) to make a night/week of it (*inf*) **2** VI (*inf*) (= *durcharbeiten*) to work right through; (= *durchfeiern*) to keep going all night

Durchmarsch M **(a)** march(ing) through; (*fig*) (*Sport, von Politiker*) walkover; (*von Partei*) landslide; (*von Parteí*) landslide; (*von Partei*) landslide; when marching through **(b)** (*inf*: = *Durchfall*) the runs *pl* (*inf*)

durchmarschieren *ptp* **durchmarschiert** VI SEP AUX SEIN to march through (*durch etw* sth)

Durchmesser M **-s, -** diameter; **120 cm im** ~ 120 cm in diameter

durchmischen¹ [ˈdʊrçmɪʃn̩] VT SEP to mix thoroughly

durchmischen² [dʊrçˈmɪʃn̩], *ptp* **durchmischt** VT INSEP to (inter)mix; **etw mit etw** ~ to mix sth with sth

durchmogeln VR SEP (*inf*) to wangle one's way through (*inf*)

durchmüssen VI SEP IRREG (*inf*) (*durch schwere Zeit*) to have to go through (*durch etw* sth) (*durch Unangenehmes*) to have to go through with (*durch etw* sth) **da musst du eben durch** (*fig*) you'll just have to see it through

durchnagen SEP **1** VT to gnaw through **2** VR to gnaw one's way through (*durch etw* sth)

durchnässen¹ [dʊrçˈnɛsn̩], *ptp* **durchnässt** VT INSEP to soak; **völlig durchnässt** soaking wet

durchnässen² [ˈdʊrçnɛsn̩] VI SEP (*Flüssigkeit*) to come through (*durch etw* sth)

durchnehmen VT SEP IRREG (*Sch*) to do (*inf*)

durchnummerieren *ptp* **durchnummeriert** VT SEP to number consecutively (all the way through)

durchorganisieren *ptp* **durchorganisiert** VT SEP to organize down to the last detail

durchpauken VT SEP (*inf*) *Gesetz, Änderungen* to force through; *Schüler* to push through; **dein Anwalt wird dich schon irgendwie** ~ your lawyer will get you off somehow

durchpausen VT SEP to trace

durchpeitschen VT SEP to flog; (*fig*) to rush through

durchpressen VT SEP to press through; *Knoblauch* to crush; *Kartoffeln* to mash (*by pushing through a press*); *Teig* to pipe

durchproben VT SEP to rehearse right through

durchprobieren *ptp* **durchprobiert** VT SEP to try one after the other

durchpusten VT SEP (*inf*) to blow through

durchqueren [dʊrçˈkveːrən], *ptp* **durchquert** VT INSEP to cross

durchrasseln VI SEP AUX SEIN (*inf*) to flunk (*inf*) (*durch etw, in etw* (*dat*) sth)

durchrechnen VT SEP to calculate; **eine Rechnung noch einmal** ~ to go over a calculation (again)

durchregnen VI IMPERS SEP **(a)** (= *durchkommen*) **hier regnet es durch** the rain is coming through here; **es regnet durchs Dach durch** the rain is coming through the roof **(b)** (= *ununterbrochen regnen*) to rain continuously; **während des ganzen Festivals hat es durchgeregnet** it rained throughout the whole festival; **es hat die Nacht durchgeregnet** it rained all night long

Durchreiche [ˈdʊrçraɪçə] F **-, -n** (serving) hatch, pass-through (*US*)

Durchreise F journey through; **auf der** ~ **sein** to be passing through

durchreisen¹ [ˈdʊrçraɪzn̩] VI SEP AUX SEIN to travel through (*durch etw* sth)

durchreisen² [dʊrçˈraɪzn̩], *ptp* **durchreist** VT INSEP to travel through

Durchreisende(r) MF DECL AS ADJ traveller (*Brit*) *or* traveler (*US*) (passing through); ~ **nach München** through passengers to Munich

durchreißen SEP IRREG **1** VT to tear in two **2** VI AUX SEIN to tear in two; (*Seil*) to snap (in two)

durchreiten SEP IRREG **1** VI AUX SEIN to ride through (*durch etw* sth); **die Nacht** ~ to ride all night long **2** VT *Hose* to wear out (through riding)

durchringen VR SEP IRREG to make up one's mind finally; **er hat sich endlich durchgerungen** after much hesitation, he has finally made up his mind; **sich zu einem Entschluss** ~ to force oneself to make a decision; **sich dazu** ~, **etw zu tun** to bring oneself to do sth

Durchritt M ride through

durchrosten VI SEP AUX SEIN to rust through

durchrühren VT SEP to mix thoroughly

durchrutschen VI SEP AUX SEIN (*lit, fig*: *Fehler*) to slip through (*durch etw* sth); (*bei Prüfung*) to scrape through; **zwischen etw** (*dat*) ~ to slip between sth

durchrütteln VT SEP to shake about

durchs [dʊrçs] CONTR *von* **durch das**

durchsacken VI SEP AUX SEIN **(a)** (= *durchhängen: Bett etc*) to sag; (= *nach unten sinken*) to sink; **durch etw** ~ (*Mensch*) to fall (down) through sth **(b)** (*Aviat: Flugzeug*) to pancake

Durchsage F message; (*im Radio*) announcement; **eine** ~ **der Polizei** a police announcement

durchsagen VT SEP **(a)** = **durchgeben (b)** *Parole, Losung* to pass on

durchsägen VT SEP to saw through

Durchsatz M (*Ind, Comput*) throughput

durchsaufen SEP IRREG (*inf*) **1** VI to booze the whole night long (*inf*); **die Nacht** ~ to booze all night long (*inf*) **2** VR to booze at somebody else's expense (*inf*)

durchschaubar [dʊrçˈʃaʊbaːɐ] ADJ (*fig*) *Hintergründe, Plan, Ereignisse* clear; *Lüge* transparent; **gut** *or* **leicht** ~ (= *verständlich*) easily comprehensible; (= *erkennbar, offensichtlich*) perfectly clear; **eine leicht ~e Lüge** a lie that is easy to see through; **schwer ~er Charakter/Mensch** inscrutable character/person

durchschauen *ptp* **durchschaut** VT INSEP *Absichten, Lüge, jdn, Spiel* to see through; *Sachlage* to see clearly; (= *begreifen*) to understand; **du bist durchschaut!** I've/we've seen through you

durchscheinen VI SEP IRREG (*durch etw* sth) to shine through; (*Farbe, Muster*) to show through

durchscheinend [ˈdʊrçʃaɪnənt] ADJ transparent; *Bluse etc* see-through

durchscheuern VTR SEP to wear through

durchschieben SEP IRREG **1** VT to push through (*durch etw* sth) **2** VR to push (one's way) through (*durch etw* sth)

durchschießen¹ [ˈdʊrçʃiːsn̩] VI SEP IRREG **(a) durch etw** ~ to shoot through sth; **zwischen etw** (*dat*) ~ to shoot between sth **(b)** AUX SEIN (= *schnell fahren, rennen*) to shoot through

durchschießen² [dʊrçˈʃiːsn̩], *ptp* **durchschossen** [dʊrçˈʃɔsn̩] VT INSEP IRREG **(a)** (*mit Kugeln*) to shoot through; (*fig*) to flash through; **ein Gedanke durchschoss mich/mein Gehirn** a thought flashed through my mind **(b)** (*Typ: = Zeilenabstand vergrößern*) to set out

durchschiffen [dʊrçˈʃɪfn̩], *ptp* **durchschifft** VT INSEP to sail across

durchschimmern VI SEP (*durch etw* sth) to shimmer through; (*Farbe, fig*) to show through

durchschlafen VI SEP IRREG to sleep through

Durchschlafproblem NT USU PL sleep problem

Durchschlag M **(a)** (= *Kopie*) carbon (copy) **(b)** (= *Küchengerät*) sieve

durchschlagen SEP IRREG **1** VT **etw** ~ (= *entzweischlagen*) to chop through sth; (= *durchtreiben*) to knock sth through (*durch etw* sth); (*Cook*) to sieve sth

2 VI **(a)** AUX SEIN (= *durchkommen*) (*durch etw* sth) to come through; (*fig: Charakter, Eigenschaft, Untugend*) to show through; **bei ihm schlägt der Vater durch** you can see his father in him

(b) AUX SEIN (= *Wirkung haben*) to catch on; **auf etw** (*acc*) ~ to make one's/its mark on sth; **auf jdn** ~ to rub off on sb; **alte Werte schlagen wieder voll durch** old values are reasserting themselves in a big way; **Investitionen schlagen auf die Nachfrage durch** investments have a marked effect on demand

3 VR to fight one's way through; (*im Leben*) to struggle through

durchschlagend [ˈdʊrçʃlaːgn̩t] ADJ *Sieg, Erfolg* sweeping; *Maßnahmen* effective; *Argument, Beweis* conclusive; **eine ~e Wirkung haben** to be totally effective

Durchschlagpapier NT copy paper; (= *Kohlepapier*) carbon paper

durchschleppen VT SEP to drag through (*durch etw* sth); (*fig*) *jdn* to drag along; *Kollegen, Mitglied etc* to carry (along) (with one)

durchschleusen VT SEP (*durch etw* sth) (*durch schmale Stelle*) to guide through; (= *durchschmuggeln*) to smuggle through; **ein Schiff ~** to pass a ship through a lock

Durchschlupf [ˈdʊrçʃlʊpf] M **-(e)s, Durchschlüpfe** [-ʃlʏpfə] way through

durchschlüpfen VI SEP AUX SEIN to slip through (*durch etw* sth); **er ist der Polizei durchgeschlüpft** he slipped through the fingers of the police

durchschmuggeln VT SEP to smuggle through (*durch etw* sth)

durchschneiden VT SEP IRREG to cut through; **etw in der Mitte ~** to cut (down) through the middle; **etw mitten ~** to cut sth in two

Durchschnitt M (= *Mittelwert, Mittelmaß*) average; (*in Statistik*) mean; (*Math*) average, (arithmetic) mean; **der ~** (= *normale Menschen*) the average person; (= *die Mehrheit*) the majority; **im ~** on average; **im ~ 100 km/h fahren** to average 100 kmph; **über/unter dem ~** above/below average; **~ sein** to be average; **guter ~ sein, zum guten ~ gehören** to be a good average

durchschnittlich [ˈdʊrçʃnɪtlɪç] **1** ADJ average **2** ADV on (an) average; **~ begabt/groß** *etc* of average ability/height *etc*; **gut** good on average; **die Mannschaft hat sehr ~ gespielt** the team played a very average game

Durchschnittlichkeit F -, NO PL ordinariness

Durchschnitts- IN CPDS average; **Durchschnittsalter** NT average age; **Durchschnittsbürger(in)** M(F) average citizen; **Durchschnittsgesicht** NT ordinary face; **Durchschnittsmensch** M average person; **Durchschnittsschüler(in)** M(F) average pupil; **Durchschnittswert** M average *or* mean (*Math*) value; **Durchschnittszeit** F average time

durchschnüffeln VT SEP (*pej inf*) to nose through (*inf*); *Wohnung* to sniff around in (*inf*)

Durchschrift F (carbon) copy

Durchschuss M **(a)** (= *durchgehender Schuss*) shot passing right through; **bei einem ~ ...** when a shot passes right through ... **(b)** (= *Loch*) bullet hole; (= *Wunde*) gunshot wound (*where the bullet has passed right through*); **ein ~ durch den Darm** a gunshot wound right through the intestine **(c)** (*Typ*: = *Zwischenraum*) leading; **ohne ~** unleaded

durchschütteln VT SEP *Mischung* to shake thoroughly; *jdn* (*zur Strafe*) to give a good shaking; (*in Auto, Bus etc*) to shake about

durchschwimmen[1] [ˈdʊrçʃvɪmən] VI SEP IRREG AUX SEIN **(a)** (*durch etw* sth) to swim through; (*Dinge*) to float through; **unter/zwischen etw** (*dat*) ~ to swim/float under/between sth **(b)** (= *ohne Pause schwimmen*) to swim without stopping

durchschwimmen[2] [ˈdʊrçʃvɪmən], *ptp* **durchschwommen** [dʊrçˈʃvɔmən] VT INSEP IRREG to swim through; *Strecke* to swim

durchschwitzen VT SEP to soak with sweat; *siehe auch* **durchgeschwitzt**

durchsehen SEP IRREG **1** VI (= *hindurchschauen*) to look through (*durch etw* sth); **ein Stoff, durch den man ~ kann** material one can see through **2** VT **(a)** (= *nachsehen, überprüfen*) **etw** ~ to look sth through; **etw flüchtig ~** to glance through sth **(b)** (*durch etw hindurch*) to see through (*durch etw* sth)

durchseihen VT SEP (*Cook*) to strain

durch sein VI IRREG AUX SEIN (*inf*) **(a)** (= *hindurchgekommen sein*) to be through (*durch etw* sth); (= *vorbeigekommen sein*) to have gone

(b) (= *fertig sein*) to have finished, to be through (*esp US*); **durch etw ~** to have got (*Brit*) *or* gotten (*US*) through sth

(c) (= *durchgetrennt sein*) to be in half; (= *durchgescheuert sein*) to have worn through

(d) (*Gesetz, Antrag*) to have gone through

(e) (= *eine Krankheit überstanden haben*) to have pulled through; (= *eine Prüfung bestanden haben*) to have got (*Brit*) *or* gotten (*US*) through; **durch die Krise ~** to be over the crisis

(f) (*Cook*) to be done

durchsetzen[1] [ˈdʊrçzɛtsn̩] SEP **1** VT *Maßnahmen, Reformen, Vorschlag, Plan, Vorhaben* to carry through; *Forderung* to push through; *Ziel* to achieve; **etw bei jdm ~** to get sb to agree to sth; **etw beim Aufsichtsrat ~** to get sth through the board; **seinen Willen (bei jdm) ~** to get one's (own) way (with sb)

2 VR **(a)** (*Mensch*) to assert oneself (*bei jdm/gegen jdn* with/against sb); (*Partei etc*) to win through; **sich gegen etw ~** to win through against sth; **sich mit etw ~** to be successful with sth

(b) (*Idee, Meinung, Neuheit*) to be (generally) accepted

durchsetzen[2] [dʊrçˈzɛtsn̩], *ptp* **durchsetzt** VT INSEP **etw mit etw ~** to intersperse sth with sth; **ein Land mit Spionen ~** to infiltrate spies into a country

Durchsetzung [ˈdʊrçzɛtsʊŋ] F -, NO PL (*von Maßnahmen, Reformen, Vorschlag, Plan, Vorhaben*) carrying through; (*von Anspruch, Forderung*) pushing through; (*von Ziel*) achievement

Durchsetzungsvermögen NT, NO PL ability to assert oneself

Durchseuchung [ˈdʊrçzɔʏçʊŋ] F -, **-en** spread of infection; **die ~ der Bevölkerung** the spread of the infection throughout the population

Durchseuchungs-: **Durchseuchungsgrad** M degree of infection; **Durchseuchungsrate** F rate of infection

Durchsicht F examination; (*von Examensarbeiten*) checking through; **jdm etw zur ~ geben/vorlegen** to give sb sth to look through *or* over; **bei ~ der Bücher** on checking the books

durchsichtig [-zɪçtɪç] ADJ *Material* transparent; *Bluse etc auch* see-through; *Wasser, Luft* clear; (*fig*) transparent; *Stil* clear

Durchsichtigkeit F -, NO PL (*von Material*) transparency; (*von Wasser, Luft*) clarity; (*fig*) transparency; (*von Stil*) clarity

durchsickern VI SEP AUX SEIN (*lit, fig*) to trickle through; (*fig: trotz Geheimhaltung*) to leak out; **Informationen ~ lassen** to leak information

durchsieben VT SEP to sieve, to sift

durchsitzen VT *Sessel* SEP IRREG to wear out (the seat of); **ich habe mir die Hose durchgesessen** I've worn through the seat of my trousers

durchsoffen [ˈdʊrçzɔfn̩] ADJ ATTR (*inf*) boozy (*inf*)

durchspielen VT SEP *Szene, Spiel, Stück* to play through; *Rolle* to act through; (*fig*) to go through

durchsprechen SEP IRREG **1** VI **durch etw ~** to speak through sth **2** VT *Problem, Möglichkeiten, Taktik* to talk over; (*Theat*) *Rolle* to read through

durchspülen VT SEP to rinse (out) thoroughly

durchstarten SEP **1** VI (*Aviat*) to overshoot; (*Aut*) to accelerate off again; (*beim, vorm Anfahren*) to rev up; (*fig*) to get going again **2** VT *Flugzeug* to pull up; *Motor, Auto* to rev (up)

durchstechen VT SEP IRREG *Nadel, Spieß* to stick through (*durch etw* sth); *Ohren* to pierce; *Deich, Damm, Grassode* to cut through; *Kanal, Tunnel* to build through (*durch etw* sth)

Durchstecherei [dʊrçʃtɛçəˈraɪ] F (*inf*) sharp practice

durchstecken VT SEP (*durch etw* sth) to put through; *Nadel etc* to stick through

durchstehen [ˈdʊrçʃteːən] SEP, **durchstehen** [dʊrçˈʃteːən] *ptp* **durchstanden** [dʊrçˈʃtandn̩] INSEP VT IRREG *Zeit, Prüfung* to get through; *Krankheit* to pull through; *Tempo, Test, Qualen* to (with)stand; *Abenteuer* to have; *Schwierigkeiten, Situation* to get through

durchsteigen VI SEP IRREG AUX SEIN to climb through (*durch etw* sth); (*fig inf*) to get it (*inf*)

durchstellen VT SEP to put through; **einen Moment, ich stelle durch** one moment, I'll put you through

Durchstich M (= *Vorgang*) cut(ting); (= *Öffnung*) cut

durchstöbern [dʊrç'ʃtøːbən], *ptp* **durchstöbert** VT INSEP to rummage through (*nach* for); *Stadt, Gegend* to scour (*nach* for); (= *durchwühlen*) to ransack (*nach* looking for)

durchstoßen[1] [dʊrç'ʃtoːsn], *ptp* **durchstoßen** VT INSEP IRREG to break through

durchstoßen[2] ['dʊrçʃtoːsn] SEP IRREG **1** VI AUX SEIN (*zu einem Ziel gelangen*) to break through (*esp Mil*) **2** VT (= *durchbrechen*) to break through; **etw** (*durch etw*) ~ to push sth through (sth); *Tunnel* to drive sth through (sth)

durchstreichen VT SEP IRREG to cross out

durchstreifen [dʊrç'ʃtraifn], *ptp* **durchstreift** VT INSEP (*geh*) to roam *or* wander through

durchstrukturieren *ptp* **durchstrukturiert** VT SEP *Aufsatz* to give a good structure to; *Gesetzesvorlage* to work out in detail; **ein gut durchstrukturierter Aufsatz** a well-structured essay

durchstylen VT SEP to give style to; **durchgestylt** fully styled

durchsuchen *ptp* **durchsucht** VT INSEP (*nach* for) to search (through); *jdn* to search

Durchsuchung F -, -en search (*auf +acc* for)

Durchsuchungsbefehl M search warrant; **richterlicher ~** official search warrant

durchtanzen ['dʊrçtantsn] SEP **1** VI to dance through; **die Nacht ~** to dance all night **2** VT *Schuhe* to wear out (by *or* with) dancing

durchtesten VT SEP to test out

durchtrainieren *ptp* **durchtrainiert** SEP **1** VT to get fit; **(gut) durchtrainiert** *Sportler* completely fit; *Muskeln, Körper* in superb condition **2** VI (= *ohne Pause trainieren*) to train nonstop

durchtränken [dʊrç'trɛŋkn], *ptp* **durchtränkt** VT INSEP to soak (completely); **mit/von etw durchtränkt sein** (*fig geh*) to be imbued with sth

durchtrennen ['dʊrçtrɛnən] VT SEP *Stoff, Papier* to tear (through); (= *schneiden*) to cut (through); *Nerv, Sehne* to sever; *Nabelschnur* to cut (through)

durchtreten SEP IRREG **1** VT **(a)** *Pedal* to step on; (*am Fahrrad*) to press down; *Starter* to kick **(b)** (= *durchkicken*) to kick through (*durch etw* sth) **2** VI **(a)** (*Aut*: = *Gas geben*) to step on the accelerator; (*Radfahrer*) to pedal (hard) **(b)** AUX SEIN (= *durchsickern, durchdringen*) to come through (*durch etw* sth) **3** VR to wear through

durchtrieben [dʊrç'triːbn] ADJ cunning

Durchtriebenheit F -, NO PL cunning

durchtropfen VI SEP AUX SEIN to drip through (*durch etw* sth)

durchwachsen[1] ['dʊrçvaksn] VI SEP IRREG AUX SEIN to grow through (*durch etw* sth)

durchwachsen[2] [dʊrç'vaksn] ADJ **(a)** (*lit*) *Speck* streaky; *Fleisch, Schinken* with fat running through it **(b)** PRED (*hum inf*: = *mittelmäßig*) so-so (*inf*); **ihm geht es ~** he's having his ups and downs

durchwagen VR SEP to venture through (*durch etw* sth)

Durchwahl F (*Telec*) direct dialling

durchwählen VI SEP to dial direct; **nach London ~** to dial London direct

Durchwahlnummer F dialling code (*Brit*), dial code (*US*); (*in Firma*) extension

durchwandern *ptp* **durchwandert** VT INSEP *Gegend* to walk through; (*hum*) *Zimmer, Straßen etc* to wander through; **die halbe Welt ~** to wander halfway round the world

durchwaschen VT SEP IRREG to wash through

durchwaten VI SEP AUX SEIN to wade through (*durch etw* sth)

durchweg ['dʊrçvɛk, dʊrç'vɛk], (*esp Aus*) **durchwegs** ['dʊrçveːks, dʊrç'veːks] ADV (*bei adj*) (= *ausnahmslos*) without exception; (= *in jeder Hinsicht*) in every respect; (*bei n*) without exception; (*bei vb*) (= *völlig*) totally; (= *ausnahmslos*) without exception; **~ gut** good without exception/in every way *or* respect

durchweichen SEP **1** VI AUX SEIN (= *sehr nass werden*) to get wet through; (*Karton, Boden*) to go soggy **2** VT *Kleidung, jdn* to soak; *Boden, Karton* to make soggy

durchwetzen VTR SEP to wear through

durchwinden VR SEP IRREG (*Fluss*) to meander (*durch etw* through sth); (*Mensch*) to worm one's way through (*durch etw* sth)

durchwitschen [-vɪtʃn] VI SEP AUX SEIN (*inf*) to slip through (*durch etw* sth)

durchwollen VI SEP (*inf*) to want to go/come through (*durch etw* sth); **zwischen/unter etw** (*dat*) ~ to want to pass between/under sth; **der Bohrer/Faden will nicht** (**durch den Beton/das Öhr**) **durch** the drill/thread doesn't want to go through (the concrete/eye)

durchwühlen ['dʊrçvyːlən] SEP, **durchwühlen** [dʊrç'vyːlən], *ptp* **durchwühlt** INSEP VT to rummage through

durchwurschteln [-vʊrʃtln], **durchwursteln** VR SEP (*inf*) to muddle through

durchzählen SEP **1** VT to count through **2** VI to count off

durchzeichnen VT SEP to trace

durchziehen[1] ['dʊrçtsiːən] SEP IRREG **1** VT **(a)** (*lit, fig*) to pull through (*durch etw* sth) **(b)** (*inf*: = *erledigen, vollenden*) to get through **(c)** (= *durchbauen*) (*durch etw* sth) *Graben* to dig through; *Mauer* to build through **2** VI AUX SEIN **(a)** (= *durchkommen*) (*durch etw* sth) to pass through; (*Truppe*) to march through **(b)** (*in Flüssigkeit*) to soak; **etw in etw** (*dat*) **~ lassen** to steep sth in sth; (*in Marinade*) to marinate sth in sth **3** VR to run through (*durch etw* sth)

durchziehen[2] [dʊrç'tsiːən], *ptp* **durchzogen** [dʊrç'tsoːgn] VT INSEP IRREG (= *durchwandern*) to pass through; (*Straße, Fluss*) (*fig*: *Thema*) to run through; (*Geruch*) to fill; (*Graben*) to cut through

durchzucken [dʊrç'tsʊkn], *ptp* **durchzuckt** VT INSEP (*Blitz*) to flash across; (*fig*: *Gedanke*) to flash through

Durchzug M **(a)** NO PL (= *Luftzug*) draught (*Brit*), draft (*US*); **~ machen** to create a draught (*Brit*) or draft (*US*); (*zur Lüftung*) to get the air moving; (**die Ohren**) **auf ~ stellen** or **schalten** (*fig*) to switch off (*inf*) **(b)** (*durch ein Gebiet*) passage; (*von Truppen*) march through; **auf dem/beim ~ durch ein Land** while passing through a country

durchzwängen SEP (*durch etw* sth) **1** VT to force through **2** VR to force one's way through

dürfen ['dʏrfn], *pret* **durfte** ['dʊrftə], *ptp* **gedurft** *or* (*bei modal aux vb*) **dürfen** [gə'dʊrft, 'dʏrfn] VI, MODAL AUX VB **(a)** (= *Erlaubnis haben*) **etw tun ~** to be allowed to do sth; **darf ich/man das tun?** may I/one do it?, am I/is one allowed to do it?; **darf ich? – ja, Sie ~** may I? – yes, you may; **darf ich ins Kino?** may I go to the cinema?; **er hat nicht gedurft** he wasn't allowed to **(b)** (*verneint*) **man darf etw nicht** (**tun**) (= *sollte, muss nicht*) one must not do sth; (= *hat keine Erlaubnis*) one isn't allowed to do sth; (= *kann nicht*) one may not do sth; **hier darf man nicht rauchen** (= *ist verboten*) smoking is prohibited here; **diesen Zug darf ich nicht verpassen** I must not miss this train; **die Kinder ~ hier nicht spielen** the children aren't allowed to play here; **das darf doch nicht wahr sein!** that can't be true!; **da darf er sich nicht wundern** that shouldn't surprise him **(c)** (*in Höflichkeitsformeln*) **darf ich das tun?** may I do that?; **Ruhe, wenn ich bitten darf!** quiet, (if you) please!; **darf ich Sie bitten, das zu tun?** could I ask you to do that?; **was darf es sein?** can I help you?; (*vom Gastgeber gesagt*) what can I get you?; **dürfte ich bitte Ihren Ausweis sehen** (*als Aufforderung*) may I see your identity card, please **(d)** (= *Veranlassung haben, können*) **wir freuen uns, Ihnen mitteilen zu** ~ we are pleased to be able to tell you; **ich darf wohl sagen, dass ...** I think I can say that ...; **man darf doch wohl fragen** one can ask, surely?; **Sie ~ mir das ruhig glauben** you can take my word for it **(e)** (*im Konjunktiv*) **das dürfte ...** (*als Annahme*) that must ...; (= *sollte*) that should ...; (= *könnte*) that could ...; **das dürfte Emil sein** that must be Emil; **das dürfte wohl das Beste sein** that is probably the best thing; **das dürfte reichen** that should be enough

dürftig ['dʏrftʊç] **1** ADJ **(a)** (= *ärmlich*) wretched; *Essen* meagre (*Brit*), meager (*US*) **(b)** (*pej*: = *unzureichend*) miserable; *Kenntnisse* sketchy; *Ausrede* feeble; *Ersatz* poor *attr*; *Bekleidung* skimpy; **ein paar ~e Tannen** a few scrawny fir trees **2** ADV (= *kümmerlich*) beleuchtet poorly; gekleidet scantily; **die**

Ernte ist ~ ausgefallen the harvest turned out to be quite meagre (Brit) or meager (US)

Dürftigkeit F -, NO PL **(a)** (= Ärmlichkeit) wretchedness; (von Essen) meagreness (Brit), meagerness (US) **(b)** (von Kenntnissen) sketchiness; (von Ausrede) feebleness; (von Ersatz) poorness; (von Bekleidung) skimpiness; **die ~ seines Einkommens/seiner Leistung** (pej) his miserable salary/performance

dürr [dʏr] ADJ **(a)** (= trocken) dry; Boden arid; Ast, Strauch dried up **(b)** (pej: = mager) scrawny **(c)** (fig: = knapp, dürftig) Auskunft meagre (Brit), meager (US); Handlung einer Oper etc thin; **mit ~en Worten** in plain terms

Dürre ['dʏrə] F -, -n **(a)** (= Zeit der ~) drought **(b)** = Dürrheit

Dürre-: Dürrejahr NT year of drought; **Dürrekatastrophe** F catastrophic drought; **Dürreperiode** F (period of) drought; (fig) barren period

Dürrheit F -, NO PL **(a)** (= Trockenheit) dryness **(b)** (pej: = Magerkeit) scrawniness

Durst [dʊrst] M -(e)s, NO PL (lit, fig) thirst (nach for); **~ haben** to be thirsty; **~ bekommen** or **kriegen** (inf) to get thirsty; **den ~ löschen** or **stillen** to quench one's thirst; **das macht ~** that makes you thirsty; **ein Glas** or **einen über den ~ getrunken haben** (inf) to have had one too many (inf)

dürsten ['dʏrstn] VI, VT IMPERS (geh) **es dürstet ihn** or **er dürstet nach Rache/Wissen/Wahrheit** he thirsts for revenge/knowledge/(the) truth

durstig ['dʊrstɪç] ADJ thirsty; **diese Arbeit macht ~** this work makes you thirsty; **sie ist eine ~e Seele** (hum inf) she likes the bottle (Brit hum), she likes to tip the bottle (US hum inf)

Durst-: durstlöschend, durststillend ADJ thirst-quenching; **Durststrecke** F hard times pl; (= Mangel an Inspiration) barren period

Dur-: Durtonart ['duːetɔn-] F major key; **Durtonleiter** F major scale

Dusche ['duʃə] F -, -n shower; **unter der ~ sein** or **stehen** to be in the shower; **das war eine kalte ~** (fig) that really brought him/her etc down to earth (with a bump); **bei ihrem Enthusiasmus wirkten seine Worte wie eine kalte ~** (fig) his words poured cold water on her enthusiasm

duschen ['duʃn] **①** VIR to have a shower; **(sich) kalt ~** to have a cold shower **②** VT **jdn ~** to give sb a shower; **jdm/sich den Kopf/Rücken ~** to spray sb's/one's head/back

Dusch-: Duschgel NT shower gel; **Duschgelegenheit** F shower facilities pl; **Duschkabine** F shower (cubicle); **Duschraum** M shower room; **Duschvorhang** M shower curtain; **Duschwanne** F shower tray

Düse ['dyːzə] F -, -n nozzle; (Mech auch: von Flugzeug) jet

Dusel ['duːzl] M -s, NO PL (inf) **(a)** (= Glück) luck; **~ haben** to be lucky; **so ein ~!** that was a fluke! (inf) **(b)** (= Trancezustand) daze; (durch Alkohol) fuddle

düsen ['dyːzn] VI AUX SEIN (inf) to dash; (mit Flugzeug) to jet; **nach Hause ~** to dash off home; **durch die Welt ~** to jet (a)round the world

Düsen-: Düsenantrieb M jet propulsion; **Düsenflugzeug** NT jet; **düsengetrieben** [-gətriːbn] ADJ jet-propelled; **Düsenjäger** M (Mil) jet fighter; (inf: = Düsenflugzeug) jet; **Düsentreibstoff** M jet fuel; **Düsentriebwerk** NT jet power-unit

Dussel ['dʊsl] M -s, - (inf) dope (inf)

dusselig ['dʊsəlɪç], **dusslig** ['dʊslɪç] (inf) **①** ADJ stupid **②** ADV **(a)** (= dumm) **sich ~ anstellen** to be stupid **(b)** (= sehr viel) **sich ~ reden** to talk till one is blue in the face (inf); **sich ~ verdienen** to make a killing (inf); **sich ~ arbeiten** to work like a horse

duster ['duːstə] ADJ = dunkel

düster ['dyːstə] ADJ gloomy; Miene, Stimmung dark; (= unheimlich) Gestalten, Stadtteil sinister

Düsterkeit F -, NO PL gloominess; (= Unheimlichkeit) sinister character; (= Dunkelheit) gloom

Dutte ['dʊtə] F -, -n (Aus) teat

Duty-free-Shop ['djuːtiːfriːʃɔp] M -s, -s, **Dutyfreeshop** M -s, -s duty-free shop

Dutzend ['dʊtsnt] NT -s, -e [-də] dozen; **ein halbes ~** half-a-dozen; **zwei/drei ~** two/three dozen; **ein ~ frische** or **frischer (geh) Eier kostet** or **kosten ...** a dozen fresh eggs cost(s) ...; **~e pl** (inf) dozens pl; **sie kamen in** or **zu dutzenden** or **~en** they came in (their) dozens; **dutzend(e) Mal** dozens of times

Dutzend-: dutzendfach **①** ADJ dozens of **②** ADV in dozens of ways; **dutzendmal** ADV (inf) siehe Dutzend; **Dutzendpreis** M price per dozen; **Dutzendware** F (pej) (cheap) mass-produced item; **~n** (cheap) mass-produced goods; **dutzendweise** ADV by the dozen

Duzbruder M good friend

duzen ['duːtsn] VT to address with the familiar "du"-form; **wir ~ uns** we use "du" (to each other)

DV [deːˈfau] F - ABBR von Datenverarbeitung DP

DVD [deːfauˈdeː] F -, -s ABBR von Digital Versatile Disk DVD

d. Verf. ABBR von der Verfasser

Dynamik [dyˈnaːmɪk] F -, NO PL (Phys) dynamics sing; (fig) dynamism

Dynamiker [dyˈnaːmɪkɐ] M -s, -, **Dynamikerin** [-ərɪn] F -, -nen go-getter

dynamisch [dyˈnaːmɪʃ] **①** ADJ (lit, fig) dynamic; Renten ≈ index-linked; **~e Gesetze** laws of dynamics **②** ADV (= schwungvoll) dynamically

dynamisieren [dynamiˈziːrən], ptp **dynamisiert** VT Renten, Sozialhilfe ≈ to index-link

Dynamit [dynaˈmiːt] NT -s, NO PL (lit, fig) dynamite

Dynamo [dyˈnaːmo, ˈdyːnamo] M(F) -s, -s dynamo

D-Zug [deː-] M express train; (hält nur in großen Städten) non-stop train; **ein alter Mann/eine alte Frau ist doch kein ~** (inf) I am going as fast as I can

Ee

E, e [eː] NT **-, -** E, e

Ebbe ['ɛbə] F **-, -n** (= ablaufendes Wasser) ebb tide; (= Niedrigwasser) low tide; ~ **und Flut** the tides; **bei ~ baden** to swim when the tide is going out; (bei Niedrigwasser) to swim at low tide; **die ~ tritt um 15.30 Uhr ein** the tide starts to go out at 3.30 p.m; **es ist ~** the tide is going out; (= es ist Niedrigwasser) it's low tide; **bei mir** or **in meinem Geldbeutel ist** or **herrscht ~** my finances are at a pretty low ebb at the moment

eben ['eːbn̩] **1** ADJ (= glatt) smooth; (= gleichmäßig) even; (= gleich hoch) level; (= flach) flat; (Math) plane; **zu ~er Erde** at ground level; **auf ~er Strecke** on the flat **2** ADV (a) (= soeben) just; (= schnell, kurz) for a minute; **das wollte ich ~ sagen** I was just about to say that; **mein Bleistift war doch ~ noch da** my pencil was there (just) a minute ago; **ich gehe ~ zur Bank** I'll just pop to (Brit) or by (US) the bank (inf) (b) (= gerade or genau das) exactly; (na)**~!** exactly!; **das ist es ja ~!** that's just it!; **das ~ nicht!** no, not that!; **das ist es ~ nicht!** that's exactly what it isn't!; **nicht ~ billig/viel** etc not exactly cheap/a lot etc (c) (= gerade noch) just; **das reicht so** or **nur ~ aus** it's only just enough (d) (= nun einmal, einfach) just; **dann bleibst du ~ zu Hause** then you'll just have to stay at home

Ebenbild NT image; **dein ~** the image of you; **das genaue ~ seines Vaters** the spitting image of his father

ebenbürtig ['eːbn̩byrtɪç] ADJ (= gleichwertig) equal; Gegner evenly matched; **jdm an Kraft/Ausdauer ~ sein** to be sb's equal in strength/endurance; **sie war ihm an Kenntnissen ~** her knowledge was equal to his; **wir sind einander ~** we are equal(s)

eben-: ebenda ['eːbn̩daː, (emph) eːbn̩'daː] ADV (a) (= gerade dort) ~ **will auch ich hin** that is exactly where I am bound too (b) (bei Zitat) ibid; **ebendann** ['eːbn̩dan, (emph) eːbn̩'dan] ADV **soll ich zum Arzt** that is exactly when I have to go to the doctor; **ebendarum** ['eːbn̩darʊm, (emph) eːbn̩'darʊm] ADV that is why; **~!** (zu Kind) because I say so!; **ebendeshalb** ['eːbn̩dɛshalp, (emph) eːbn̩'dɛshalp], **ebendeswegen** ['eːbn̩dɛsveːgn̩, (emph) eːbn̩'dɛsveːgn̩] ADV that is exactly why

Ebene ['eːbənə] F **-, -n** (= Tiefebene) plain; (= Hochebene) plateau; (Math, Phys) plane; (fig) level; **auf höchster ~** (fig) at the highest level

ebenerdig ADJ at ground level

ebenfalls ADV likewise; (bei Verneinungen) either; **danke, ~!** thank you, the same to you!

Ebenholz NT ebony

ebenso ['eːbn̩zoː] ADV (= genauso) just as; (= auch, ebenfalls) as well; **das kann doch ~ eine Frau machen** a woman can do that just as well; **viele Leute haben sich ~ wie wir beschwert** a lot of people complained just like we did; **er freute sich ~ wie ich** he was just as pleased as I was; **ich mag sie ~ gern** I like her just as much; **ich komme ~ gern morgen** I'd just as soon come tomorrow; **~ gut** (just) as well; **~ lang** just as long; **~ oft** or **häufig** just as often or frequently; **~ sehr/viel** just as much

Eber ['eːbɐ] M **-s, -** boar

Eberesche F rowan

ebnen ['eːbnən] VT to level (off); **jdm/einer Sache den Weg ~** (fig) to smooth the way for sb/sth

Ebola- ['eːbola-]: **Ebola-Epidemie** F, **Ebola-Seuche** F Ebola epidemic; **Ebola-Virus** M or NT Ebola virus

EC [eː'tseː] M **-, -s** (Rail) ABBR von **Eurocityzug**

E-Cash ['iːkæʃ] M e-cash

Echo ['ɛço] NT **-s, -s** echo; (fig) response (auf +acc to); **ein starkes** or **lebhaftes ~ finden** (fig) to meet with a lively or positive response (bei from)

Echo-: Echolot ['ɛçoloːt] NT (Naut) echo sounder; (Aviat) sonic altimeter; **Echoortung** F echolocation

Echse ['ɛksə] F **-, -n** (Zool) lizard

echt [ɛçt] **1** ADJ, ADV (a) real; Unterschrift, Geldschein, Gemälde genuine; Haarfarbe natural; **das Gemälde war nicht ~** the painting was a forgery; **~er Bruch** (Math) proper fraction (b) (= typisch) typical; **ein ~er Bayer** a real Bavarian **2** ADV (a) (= typisch) typically; **~ Tiroler Trachten** original Tyrolean costumes; **~ Shakespeare** typical of Shakespeare; **~ Franz/Frau** typical of Franz/a woman (b) (= rein) **der Ring ist ~ golden/silbern** the ring is real gold/silver (c) (inf: = wirklich) really; **der spinnt doch ~** he must be out of his mind; **ich habs ~ eilig** I'm really in a hurry

Echtheit F **-, NO PL** genuineness

Echtzeit F (Comput) real time

Eck [ɛk] NT **-(e)s, -e** (a) (esp Aus, S Ger) = Ecke (b) (Sport) **das kurze/lange ~** the near/far corner of the goal (c) **über ~** diagonally across; **die Schrauben über ~ anziehen** to tighten the nuts working diagonally across; **im ~ sein** (Aus) to be out of form; **da hats ein ~** (Aus inf) you've/he's/she's etc got problems there

EC-Karte [eː'tseː-] F = Euroscheckkarte

Eck-: Eckball M (Sport) corner; **einen ~ schießen** or **treten/geben** to take/give a corner; **Eckbank** F, pl **-bänke** corner seat; **Eckdaten** PL key figures pl

Ecke ['ɛkə] F **-, -n** (a) corner; (= Kante) edge; (von Kragen) point; (Sport: = Eckball) corner; (= Käseecke, Kuchenecke) wedge; **Kantstraße ~ Goethestraße** at the corner of Kantstraße and Goethestraße; **er wohnt gleich um die ~** he lives just (a)round the corner; **ein Kind in die ~ stellen** to make a child stand in the corner; **er wurde in die reaktionäre ~ gestellt** he was pigeon-holed as a reactionary; **an allen ~n und Enden sparen** to pinch and scrape (inf); **jdm um die ~ bringen** (inf) to bump sb off (inf); **mit jdm um ein paar** or **um sieben ~n herum verwandt sein** (inf) to be distantly related to sb; **~n und Kanten** (fig) rough edges (b) (inf: = Gegend) corner; (von Stadt) area; (= Strecke) way; **eine ~** (fig: = viel) quite a bit; **eine ganze ~ entfernt** quite a (long) way away; **eine (ganze) ~ älter/billiger** (quite) a bit older/cheaper

Eck-: Eckfahne F (Sport) corner flag; **Eckhaus** NT house on the corner; (= Reiheneckhaus) end house

eckig ['ɛkɪç] ADJ angular; Tisch, Brot, Klammer, Kinn, Mund square; (= spitz) sharp; (fig) Bewegung, Gang jerky

-eckig ADJ SUF (fünf- und mehreckig) -cornered; **achteckig** eight-cornered

Eck-: Ecklohn M basic rate of pay; **Eckpfeiler** M corner pillar; (fig) cornerstone; **Eckpfosten** M corner post; **Eckstoß** M (Sport) corner; **einen ~ ausführen** to take a corner; **Eckstunde** F (Sch) first/last lesson of the day; **~n** lessons at the start and end of the day; **Eckwert** M (Econ) benchmark figure; (fig) basis; **Eckzahn** M canine tooth; **Eckzins** M (Fin) base rate

E-Commerce ['iːkɔmɐs] M e-commerce

Economyklasse [i'kɔnəmi-] F economy class

EC-Scheck [eː'tseː-] M = Euroscheck

Ecstasy ['ɛkstəzi] NT **-, NO PL** (= Droge) ecstasy

Ecuador [ekua'doːɐ] NT **-s** Ecuador

ecuadorianisch [ekuado'riaːnɪʃ] ADJ Ecuadorian

Edamer (Käse) ['eːdamɐ] M **-s, -** Edam (cheese)

edel ['eːdl̩] **1** ADJ noble; (= hochwertig) precious; Rosen, Speisen, Wein fine; Nase regal **2** ADV eingerichtet classically; dinieren exclusively; **~ gestylt** with a classic design; **~ geformte Züge** classic features; **er denkt ~** he has noble thoughts

Edel- IN CPDS (a) (= hochwertig) high-grade (b) (pej) fancy (pej inf); **Edelgas** NT rare gas; **Edelkastanie** F sweet chestnut; **Edelkitsch** M (iro) pretentious rubbish; **Edelmetall** NT precious metal; **Edelnutte** F (iro) high-class tart; **Edelstahl** M high-grade steel; **Edelstein** M precious stone; (geschliffener auch) gem; **Edelweiß** ['eːdlvaɪs] NT **-(es), -e** edelweiss

editieren [edi'tiːrən], ptp **editiert** VT to edit

Edition [edi'tsioːn] F **-, -en** (= das Herausgeben) editing; (= die Ausgabe) edition

Editor ['eːdito:ɐ] M **-s, -en** [-'toːrən] (Comput) editor

Edutainment [edu'teːnmənt] NT **-s, NO PL** edutainment

EDV [eːdeːˈfau] F - ABBR *von* **elektronische Datenverarbeitung** EDP

EDV- [eːdeːˈfau-]: **EDV-Anlage** F EDP system; **EDV-Branche** F data-processing business

EEG [eːleːˈgeː] NT **-, -s** ABBR *von* **Elektroenzephalogramm** EEG

Efeu [ˈeːfɔy] M **-s**, NO PL ivy

Effeff [ɛfˈlɛf, ˈɛfˈlɛf, ˈɛflɛf] NT **-**, NO PL (*inf*) **etw aus dem ~ können** to be able to do sth standing on one's head (*inf*); **etw aus dem ~ beherrschen/kennen** to know sth inside out

Effekt [ɛˈfɛkt] M **-(e)s, -e** effect

Effekten [ɛˈfɛktn] PL (*Fin*) stocks and bonds *pl*

Effekten-: **Effektenabrechnung** F securities trading statement; **Effektenbörse** F stock exchange; **Effektengeschäft** NT (*von Bank*) securities business; (= *einzelnes Geschäft*) securities transaction; **Effektenhandel** M stock dealing; **Effektenmakler(in)** M(F) stockbroker; **Effektenmarkt** M stock market

Effekthascherei [-haʃəˈrai] F **-, -en** (*inf*) cheap showmanship

effektiv [ɛfɛkˈtiːf] **1** ADJ **(a)** (= *wirksam, tüchtig*) effective **(b)** (= *tatsächlich*) actual; **~e Verzinsung** *or* **Rendite** net yield **2** ADV (= *bestimmt*) actually; **ich weiß ~, dass ...** I know for a fact that ...; **~ nicht/kein** absolutely not/no

Effektivgeschäft NT (*Comm*) spot transaction

Effektivität [ɛfɛktiviˈtɛːt] F **-**, NO PL effectiveness

Effektiv-: **Effektivklausel** F (actual) currency clause; (*im Tarifrecht*) actual wage clause; **Effektivlohn** M actual wage; **Effektivverzinsung** F redemption yield

effektvoll ADJ effective

effizient [ɛfiˈtsiənt] **1** ADJ efficient **2** ADV efficiently

Effizienz [ɛfiˈtsiɛnts] F **-, -en** efficiency

EFTA [ˈɛfta] F ABBR *von* **European Free Trade Association** EFTA

EG [eːˈgeː] F - ABBR *von* **Europäische Gemeinschaft** EC

egal [eˈgaːl] ADJ, ADV PRED **das ist ~** that doesn't matter; **das ist mir ganz ~** it's all the same to me; (= *beides ist mir gleich*) it doesn't make any difference to me; (= *es kümmert mich nicht*) I don't care; **~ ob/wo/wie no** matter whether/where/how; **ihm ist alles ~** he doesn't care about anything

Egel [ˈeːgl] M **-s, -** (*Zool*) leech

Egge [ˈɛgə] F **-, -n** (*Agr*) harrow

eggen [ˈɛgn] VT (*Agr*) to harrow

Ego [ˈeːgo] NT **-s, -s** (*Psych*) ego

Egoismus [egoˈɪsmʊs] M **-, Egoismen** [-mən] ego(t)ism

Egoist [egoˈɪst] M **-en, -en, Egoistin** [-ˈɪstɪn] F **-, -nen** ego(t)ist

egoistisch [egoˈɪstɪʃ] **1** ADJ ego(t)istical **2** ADV ego(t)istically

Ego-: **Egotrip** [ˈeːgo-] M (*inf*) ego trip (*inf*); **egozentrisch** [egoˈtsɛntrɪʃ] ADJ egocentric

eh [eː] **1** INTERJ hey **2** CONJ = **ehe 3** ADV **(a)** (= *früher, damals*) **seit eh und je** for ages (*inf*); **wie eh und je** just as before; **es war alles wie eh und je** everything was just as it always had been **(b)** (*esp S Ger, Aus*: = *sowieso*) anyway

ehe [ˈeːə] CONJ (= *bevor*) before; **~ (dass) ich mich auf andere verlasse** rather than rely on others

Ehe [ˈeːə] F **-, -n** marriage; **er versprach ihr die ~** he promised to marry her; **in den Stand der ~ treten** (*form*), **die ~ eingehen** (*form*) to enter into matrimony (*form*); **die ~ vollziehen** to consummate a/their/the marriage; **eine glückliche/ unglückliche ~ führen** to have a happy/an unhappy marriage; **die ~ brechen** (*form*) to commit adultery; **sie hat drei Kinder aus erster ~** she has three children from her first marriage; **ihre ~ ist 1975 geschieden worden** they were divorced in 1975; **sie leben in wilder ~** (*datedhum*) they are living in sin; **~ ohne Trauschein** common-law marriage; **sie leben in einer ~ ohne Trauschein** they live together

Ehe-: **eheähnlich** ADJ (*form*) similar to marriage; **in einer ~en Gemeinschaft leben** to cohabit (*form*); **Eheanbahnungsinstitut** NT marriage bureau; **Eheberater(in)** M(F) marriage guidance counsellor (*Brit*) *or* counselor (*US*); **Eheberatung** F (= *das Beraten*) marriage guidance (counselling (*Brit*) *or* counseling (*US*)); (= *Stelle*) marriage guidance council; **Ehebett** NT double bed; (*fig*) marital bed; **ehebrechen** VI INFIN ONLY to commit adultery; **Ehebrecher** M adulterer; **Ehebrecherin** [-brɛçərɪn] F **-, -nen** adulteress; **Ehebruch** M adultery; **Ehefrau** F wife; **~en haben es nicht leicht** married women have a hard time; **Ehekrach** M marital row; **Ehekrise** F marital crisis; **Ehekrüppel** M (*hum inf*)

casualty of married life (*hum*); **Eheleben** NT married life; **Eheleute** PL (*form*) married couple; **ich vermiete diese Wohnung an die ~ A. und P. Meier** I hereby let this apartment to Mr and Mrs Meier; **die jungen ~** the young couple

ehelich [ˈeːəlɪç] ADJ (*Kind*) legitimate; **das ~e Leben** married life; **die ~en Freuden** the joys of marriage

Ehelosigkeit F **-**, NO PL unmarried state; (*Rel*) celibacy; **~ hat auch ihre Vorteile** being unmarried also has its advantages

ehem., ehm. ABBR *von* **ehemals**

ehemalig [ˈeːəmaːlɪç] ADJ ATTR former; **die Ehemaligen einer Schulklasse** the ex-pupils pupils of a class; **die Ehemaligen seiner Klasse** his former classmates; **ein ~er Häftling** an ex-convict; **mein Ehemaliger/meine Ehemalige** (*hum inf*) my ex (*inf*)

ehemals [ˈeːəmals] ADV (*form*) formerly

Ehe-: **Ehemann** M, *pl* **-männer** husband; **seitdem er ~ ist** since he has been married; **Ehename** M married name; **Ehepaar** NT (married) couple; **Ehepartner(in)** M(F) (= *Ehemann*) husband; (= *Ehefrau*) wife; **beide ~** both partners (in the marriage)

eher [ˈeːɐ] ADV **(a)** (= *früher*) earlier; **je ~, je** *or* **desto lieber** the sooner the better; **nicht ~ als bis/als** not until/before **(b)** (= *lieber*) rather; (= *wahrscheinlicher*) more likely; (= *leichter*) more easily; **alles ~ als das!** anything but that!; **~ verzichte ich** *or* **will ich verzichten, als dass ...** I would rather do without than ...; **umso ~, als** (all) the more because; **das lässt sich schon ~ hören** that sounds more like it (*inf*); **das könnte man schon ~ sagen, das ist ~ möglich** that is more likely; **diese Prüfung kannst du ~ bestehen** this exam will be easier for you to pass **(c)** (= *vielmehr*) more; **er ist ~ faul als dumm** he's more lazy than stupid

Ehe-: **Eherecht** NT marriage law; **Ehering** M wedding ring; **Ehescheidung** F divorce; **Eheschließung** F marriage ceremony

ehest [ˈeːəst] ADV (*Aus*) as soon as possible

Ehestand M, NO PL matrimony

ehestens [ˈeːəstns] ADV **(a)** (= *frühestens*) **~ morgen** tomorrow at the earliest **(b)** (*Aus*: = *baldigst*) as soon as possible

eheste(r, s) [ˈeːəstə] ADV **am ~n** (= *am liebsten*) best of all; (= *am wahrscheinlichsten*) most likely; (= *am leichtesten*) the easiest; (= *zuerst*) first; **am ~n würde ich mir ein Auto kaufen** what I'd like best (of all) would be to buy myself a car; **keins der Kleider gefällt mir so richtig, am ~n würde ich noch das rote nehmen** I don't really like any of the dresses, but if I had to choose I'd take the red one; **das geht wohl am ~n** that's probably the best way; **er ist am ~n gekommen** he was the first (person) to come

Ehe-: **Ehestreit** M marital row; **Ehevermittlung** F marriage-broking; (= *Büro*) marriage bureau; **Ehevertrag** M prenuptial agreement

ehrbar ADJ (= *achtenswert*) respectable; (= *ehrenhaft*) honourable (*Brit*), honorable (*US*); *Beruf* reputable

Ehre [ˈeːrə] F **-, -n** honour (*Brit*), honor (*US*); (= *Ruhm*) glory; **etw in ~n halten** to treasure sth; **damit/mit ihm können Sie ~ einlegen** that/he is a credit to you; **jdm ~ machen** to do sb credit; **jdm wenig ~ machen** not to do sb any credit; **zu seiner ~ muss ich sagen, dass ...** in his favour (*Brit*) *or* favor (*US*) I must say (that) ...; **etw um der ~ willen tun** to do sth for the hono(u)r of it; **ein Mann von ~** a man of hono(u)r; **er ist in ~n ergraut** (*geh*), **er ist in ~n alt geworden** he has had a long and hono(u)rable life; **sein Wort/seine Kenntnisse in allen ~n, aber ...** I don't doubt his word/his knowledge, but ...; **sich** (*dat*) **etw zur ~ anrechnen** to count sth an hono(u)r; **mit wem habe ich die ~?** (*iroform*) with whom do I have the pleasure of speaking? (*form*); **was verschafft mir die ~?** (*iroform*) to what do I owe the hono(u)r (of your visit)?; **es ist mir eine besondere ~, ...** (*form*) it is a great hono(u)r for me ...; **um der Wahrheit die ~ zu geben ...** (*geh*) to be perfectly honest ...; **wir geben uns die ~, Sie zu ... einzuladen** (*form*) we request the hono(u)r of your company at ... (*form*); **zu ~n** (+*gen*) in hono(u)r of; **Habe die ~!** (*dated Aus*) (*als Gruß*) hello; (*beim Abschied*) goodbye; (*als Ausdruck des Erstaunens*) good heavens; **~, wem ~ gebührt** (*prov*) credit where credit is due (*prov*)

ehren [ˈeːrən] VT to honour (*Brit*), to honor (*US*); **etw ehrt jdn** sth does sb credit; **dein Besuch/Ihr Vertrauen ehrt mich** I am hono(u)red by your visit/trust; **der Präsident ehrte den**

Preisträger in einer Rede the president made a speech in hono(u)r of the prizewinner; **jdm ein ~des Andenken bewahren** to treasure sb's memory; *siehe auch* **geehrt**

Ehren-: Ehrenamt NT honorary office; **ehrenamtlich 1** ADJ honorary; *Helfer, Tätigkeit* voluntary; **~er Richter** ≈ member of the jury **2** ADV in an honorary capacity

Ehrenbürger(in) M(F) honorary citizen; **er wurde zum ~ der Stadt ernannt** he was given the freedom of the city

Ehrenbürgerrecht NT freedom

Ehren-: Ehrendoktor(in) M(F) honorary doctor; **Ehrendoktorwürde** F honorary doctorate; **Ehrengast** M guest of honour (*Brit*) *or* honor (*US*); **ehrenhaft** ADJ honourable (*Brit*), honorable (*US*); **Ehrenhaftigkeit** [ˈeːrənhaftɪçkaɪt] F **-**, NO PL sense of honour (*Brit*) *or* honor (*US*); **ehrenhalber** ADV **er wurde ~ zum Vorsitzenden auf Lebenszeit ernannt** he was made honorary president for life; **Doktor ~** (*abbr* **e. h.**) honorary doctor; **Ehrenkarte** F complimentary ticket; **Ehrenloge** F VIP box; (*für königliche Gäste*) royal box; (*in Stadion*) directors' box; **Ehrenmann** M, *pl* **-männer** man of honour (*Brit*) *or* honor (*US*); **ein sauberer ~** (*pej*) a scoundrel; **Ehrenmitglied** NT honorary member; **Ehrenmitgliedschaft** F honorary membership; **Ehrenplatz** M (*lit*) place of honour (*Brit*) *or* honor (*US*); (*fig*) special place; **Ehrenrechte** PL (*Jur*) civil rights *pl*; **Verlust/Aberkennung der bürgerlichen ~** loss/forfeiture of one's civil rights; **Ehrenrettung** F, NO PL retrieval of one's honour (*Brit*) *or* honor (*US*); **eine ~ versuchen** to attempt to retrieve one's hono(u)r; **zu seiner ~ sei gesagt, dass ...** in his favour (*Brit*) *or* favor (*US*) it must be said that ...; **ehrenrührig** ADJ defamatory; **etw als ~ empfinden** to regard sth as an insult to one's honour (*Brit*) *or* honor (*US*); **Ehrenrunde** F (*Sport*) lap of honour (*Brit*) *or* honor (*US*); (*fig inf*: = *wiederholtes Schuljahr*) repeat year; **Ehrensache** F matter of honour (*Brit*) *or* honor (*US*); **~!** (*inf*) you can count on me; **Ehrensalut** M, **Ehrensalve** F salute; **Ehrentag** M (= *Geburtstag*) birthday; (= *großer Tag*) big day; **zum heutigen ~** on this special day; **Ehrenurkunde** F certificate (*for outstanding performance in sport*); **ehrenvoll** ADJ honourable (*Brit*), honorable (*US*); **Ehrenvorsitzende(r)** MF DECL AS ADJ honorary chairman/-woman; **Ehrenwache** F guard of honour (*Brit*) *or* honor (*US*); **ehrenwert** ADJ honourable (*Brit*), honorable (*US*); **die ~e Gesellschaft** (*hum*) the Mafia; **Ehrenwort** NT, *pl* **-worte** word of honour (*Brit*) *or* honor (*US*); (*großes*) **~!** (*inf*) cross my heart (and hope to die)! (*inf*); **~?** (*inf*) cross your heart? (*inf*); **mein ~!** you have my word; **sein ~ geben/halten/brechen** to give/keep/break one's word

Ehrfurcht F great respect (*vor* +*dat* for); (= *fromme Scheu*) reverence (*vor* +*dat* for); **vor jdm/etw ~ haben** to respect/ revere sb/sth; **von ~ ergriffen** overawed; **~ gebietend** awe-inspiring; *Stimme, Geste* authoritative

ehrfürchtig [ˈfʏrçtɪç], **ehrfurchtsvoll** ADJ reverent; *Distanz* respectful

Ehrgefühl NT sense of honour (*Brit*) *or* honor (*US*); (= *Selbstachtung*) self-respect

Ehrgeiz M ambition

ehrgeizig ADJ ambitious

ehrlich [ˈeːrlɪç] **1** ADJ honest; *Name* good; *Absicht, Zuneigung* sincere; **der ~e Finder bekommt 100 Euro** a reward of 100 euros will be given to anyone finding and returning this; **eine ~e Haut** (*inf*) an honest soul; **ich hatte die ~e Absicht zu kommen** I honestly did intend to come; **er hat ~e Absichten** (*inf*) his intentions are honourable (*Brit*) *or* honorable (*US*); **~ währt am längsten** (*Prov*) honesty is the best policy (*Prov*) **2** ADV **(a)** (= *ohne Betrug*) **~ verdientes Geld** hard-earned money; **~ teilen** to share fairly; **~ gesagt ...** quite frankly ...; **er meint es ~ mit uns** he is being honest with us; **~ spielen** (*Cards*) to play straight **(b)** (= *wirklich*) honestly; **ich bin ~ begeistert** I'm really thrilled; **~! honestly!**

ehrlicherweise [ˈeːrlɪçɐˈvaɪzə] ADV honestly

Ehrlichkeit F **-**, NO PL honesty; (*von Absicht, Zuneigung*) sincerity

ehrlos ADJ dishonourable (*Brit*), dishonorable (*US*)

Ehrung [ˈeːrʊŋ] F **-, -en** honouring (*Brit*), honor (*US*)

ehrwürdig [ˈeːrvʏrdɪç] ADJ venerable; **~e Mutter** (*Eccl*) Reverend Mother; **~er Vater** (*Eccl*) Reverend Father

Ei [aɪ] NT **-(e)s, -er (a)** (*auch Physiol*) egg; **das Ei des Kolumbus finden** to come up with just the thing; **das Ei will klüger sein**

als die Henne you're trying to teach your grandmother to suck eggs (*prov*); **jdn wie ein rohes Ei behandeln** (*fig*) to handle sb with kid gloves; **wie auf Eiern gehen** (*inf*) to step gingerly; **wie aus dem Ei gepellt aussehen** (*inf*) to look spruce; **sie gleichen sich** *or* **einander wie ein Ei dem anderen** they are as alike as two peas (in a pod); **das sind ungelegte Eier!** (*inf*) we'll cross that bridge when we come to it (*prov*) **(b)** (*sl*) (= *Hoden*) **Eier** PL balls *pl* (*sl*); **ein Tritt in die Eier** a kick in the balls (*sl*); **dicke Eier haben** (*sl*: = *Lust auf Sex*) to be dying for it (*sl*)

Eibe [ˈaɪbə] F **-, -n** (*Bot*) yew

Eich-: Eichamt NT ≈ Weights and Measures Office (*Brit*), ≈ Bureau of Standards (*US*); **Eichblattsalat** M oak-leaf lettuce

Eiche [ˈaɪçə] F **-, -n** oak

Eichel [ˈaɪçl] F **-, -n (a)** (*Bot*) acorn **(b)** (*Anat*) glans

Eichelhäher M jay

eichen¹ [ˈaɪçn] ADJ oak

eichen² VT to calibrate; **darauf bin ich geeicht!** (*inf*) that's right up my street (*inf*)

Eichen-: Eichenholz NT oak; **ein Tisch aus ~** an oak table; **Eichenlaub** NT oak leaves *pl*

Eichhörnchen NT, **Eichkätzchen** [-kɛtsçən] NT **-s, -** squirrel; **mühsam nährt sich das ~** (*inf*) one struggles on and little by little

Eich-: Eichmaß NT standard measure; (= *Gewicht*) standard weight; **Eichstrich** M official calibration; (*an Gläsern*) line measure; **ein Glas mit ~** a lined glass

Eichung [ˈaɪçʊŋ] F **-, -en** calibration

Eid [aɪt] M **-(e)s, -e** [-də] oath; **einen ~ ablegen** *or* **leisten** *or* **schwören** to take *or* swear an oath; **darauf kann ich einen ~ schwören** I can swear to that; **unter ~** under oath; **eine Erklärung an ~es statt abgeben** (*Jur*) to make a declaration in lieu of oath; **ich erkläre an ~es statt, dass ...** I do solemnly declare that ...

Eidechse [ˈaɪdɛksə] F **-, -n** (*Zool*) lizard

Eider- [ˈaɪdə-]: **Eiderdaunen** PL eiderdown *no pl*; **Eiderente** F eider (duck)

eidesstattlich 1 ADJ **eine ~e Erklärung** *or* **Versicherung abgeben** to make a declaration in lieu of an oath **2** ADV **etw ~ erklären** to declare sth in lieu of an oath

Eidgenosse [ˈaɪt-] M, **Eidgenossin** F confederate; (= *Schweizer ~*) Swiss citizen

Eidgenossenschaft F confederation; **Schweizerische ~** Swiss Confederation

eidgenössisch [-gənœsɪʃ] ADJ confederate; (= *schweizerisch*) Swiss

eidlich [ˈaɪtlɪç] **1** ADJ given under oath; **er gab eine ~e Erklärung ab** he made a declaration under oath; (*schriftlich*) he swore an affidavit **2** ADV under oath; **~ gebunden** bound by (one's) oath

Eidotter M *or* NT egg yolk

Eier- [ˈaɪə-]: **Eierbecher** M eggcup; **Eierlaufen** NT **-s**, NO PL egg and spoon race; **~ machen** to have an egg and spoon race; **Eierlikör** M advocaat; **Eierlöffel** M eggspoon

eiern [ˈaɪɐn] VI (*inf*) to wobble

Eier-: Eierschale F eggshell; **eierschalenfarben** [-farbn] ADJ off-white; **Eierschaum** M, **Eierschnee** M (*Cook*) beaten egg white; **Eierschneider** M egg slicer; **Eierspeise** F **(a)** egg dish (*b*) (*Aus*: = *Rührei*) scrambled egg; **Eierstock** M (*Anat*) ovary; **Eiertanz** M tortuous manoeuvring (*Brit*) *or* maneuvering (*US*); **einen regelrechten ~ aufführen** (*fig inf*) to go through all kinds of contortions; **Eieruhr** F egg timer

Eifer [ˈaɪfɐ] M **-s**, NO PL (= *Begeisterung*) enthusiasm; (= *Eifrigkeit*) eagerness; **mit ~** enthusiastically; **mit großem ~ bei der Sache sein** to put one's heart into it; **im ~ des Gefechts** (*fig inf*) in the heat of the moment

Eifersucht F jealousy (*auf* +*acc* of); **aus/vor (lauter) ~** out of/for (pure) jealousy

Eifersüchtelei [aɪfɐzʏçtəˈlaɪ] F **-, -en** petty jealousy

eifersüchtig ADJ jealous (*auf* +*acc* of)

Eifersuchtsszene F ihr Mann hat ihr wieder eine ~ gemacht her husband's jealousy caused another scene

eiförmig ADJ egg-shaped

eifrig [ˈaɪfrɪç] **1** ADJ eager; *Leser, Sammler, Kinobesucher* keen; *Schüler* industrious; **die Eifrigen** the eager beavers (*inf*) **2** ADV *üben* religiously; *an die Arbeit gehen* enthusiastically; *teilnehmen* gladly; ~ **lernen** to apply oneself; ~ **bemüht sein** to make a sincere effort; **sie diskutierten** ~ they were involved in an animated discussion

Eigelb NT **-s, -e** or *(bei Zahlenangabe)* **-** egg yolk

eigen [ˈaign] ADJ **(a)** own; (= *selbstständig*) separate; **etw sein Eigen nennen** *(geh)* to have sth to call one's own; **~er Bericht** *(Press)* from our (own) correspondent; **Zimmer mit ~em Eingang** room with its own entrance; **San Marino ist ein ~er Staat** San Marino is an independent state; **sich** *(dat)* **etw zu Eigen machen** to adopt sth; (= *zur Gewohnheit machen*) to make a habit of sth; **übergeben Sie diesen Brief dem Anwalt zu ~en Händen** *(form)* give this letter to the lawyer in person; **ich habe das Papier auf ~e Rechnung gekauft** I paid for the paper myself; **ich möchte kurz in ~er Sache sprechen** I would like to say something on my own account **(b)** (= *typisch, kennzeichnend*) typical; **das ist ihm ~** that is typical of him; **er antwortete mit dem ihm ~en Zynismus** he answered with (his) characteristic cynicism **(c)** (= *seltsam*) strange; **es ist eine Landschaft von ganz ~em Reiz** the country is strangely attractive in its own way **(d)** (= *ordentlich*) particular; (= *übergenau*) fussy; **in Gelddingen** *or* **was Geld anbetrifft ist er sehr ~** he is very particular about money matters

Eigenantrieb M **Fahrzeuge mit** ~ self-propelled vehicles; ~ **haben** to be self-propelled

Eigenart F (= *Besonderheit*) peculiarity; (= *Eigenschaft*) characteristic; (= *Individualität*) individuality; (= *Eigentümlichkeit von Personen*) idiosyncrasy; **das gehört zur** ~ **der Bayern** that's a typically Bavarian characteristic

eigenartig **1** ADJ peculiar; (= *persönlich kennzeichnend*) idiosyncratic **2** ADV peculiarly; ~ **aussehen/klingen** to look/sound strange

Eigen-: Eigenbedarf M *(von Mensch)* personal use; *(von Staat)* domestic requirements *pl*; **zum** ~ for (one's own) personal use; **der Hausbesitzer machte** ~ **geltend** the landlord showed that he needed the house/flat *(Brit)* or apartment for himself; **Eigenbericht** M *(Press)* **diese Zeitung bringt kaum ~e** this paper rarely carries articles by its own journalists; **Eigenblut** NT *(Med)* (own) blood; **Eigenblutbehandlung** F *(Med)* autohaemotherapy *(Brit)*, autohemotherapy *(US)*; **Eigenbrötler** [ˈaignbrøːtlɐ] M **-s, -**, **Eigenbrötlerin** [-ərɪn] F **-, -nen** *(inf)* loner; (= *komischer Kauz*) queer fish *(inf)*; **eigenbrötlerisch** [ˈaignbrøːtlərɪʃ] ADJ *(inf)* solitary; (= *komisch*) eccentric; **Eigendynamik** F momentum; **eine ~ entwickeln** to gather momentum; **Eigenfinanzierung** F self-financing; **wir bauen die neue Fabrik in ~** we are financing the building of the new factory ourselves; **Eigengeschäfte** PL principal *or* proprietary trading; **Eigengewicht** NT *(von LKW etc)* unladen weight; *(Comm)* net weight; *(Sci)* dead weight; **Eigengoal** NT *(Aus Sport)* own goal; **eigenhändig** **1** ADJ **Brief, Unterschrift etc** in one's own hand; **Übergabe** personal **2** ADV oneself; **Eigenheim** NT one's own home; **sparen Sie für ein ~!** save for a home of your own!; **Eigenheit** F **-, -en** = **Eigenart**; **Eigeninitiative** F initiative of one's own; **auf ~** on one's own initiative; **Eigenkapital** NT *(von Person)* personal capital; *(von Firma)* company capital; **10.000 Euro ~** 10,000 euros of one's own capital; **Eigenkapitalbestimmungen** PL capital resources *pl*, equity *sing*; **Eigenleben** NT, NO PL one's own life; **Eigenleistung** F *(Fin: bei Hausbau)* borrower's own funding, personal contribution; **Eigenlob** NT self-importance; ~ **stinkt!** *(inf)* don't blow your own trumpet! *(prov)*; **eigenmächtig** **1** ADJ (= *selbstherrlich*) high-handed; (= *eigenverantwortlich*) taken/done *etc* on one's own authority; (= *unbefugt*) unauthorized **2** ADV high-handedly; (entirely) on one's own authority; without any authorization; **Eigenmächtigkeit** F **-, -en** (= *Selbstherrlichkeit*) high-handedness *no pl*; (= *unbefugtes Handeln*) unauthorized behaviour *(Brit)* or behavior *(US)* *no pl*; **die ~ seines Vorgehens wurde von allen kritisiert** everyone criticized him for having acted high-handedly/without authorization; **Eigenmittel** PL *(form)* one's own resources; **man braucht nur 20%** ~ you only need to find 20% yourself; **Eigenname** M proper name; **Eigennutz** [-nʊts] M **-es**, NO PL self-interest; **das habe ich ohne jeden ~ getan** I did that with no thought of myself; **eigennützig** [-nʏtsɪç] ADJ selfish; **Eigenproduktion** F **das ist eine ~** we/they *etc* made it ourselves/themselves *etc*; **etw in ~ herstellen** to make sth oneself; **aus ~** (= *hausgemacht*) home-

made; *Tabak etc* home-grown; **das war eine ~ des Irischen Fernsehens** that was one of Irish Television's own productions

eigens [ˈaigns] ADV (e)specially

Eigenschaft [ˈaignʃaft] F **-, -en** (= *Attribut*) quality; *(Chem, Phys etc)* property; (= *Merkmal*) characteristic; (= *Funktion*) capacity

Eigen-: Eigensinn M, NO PL stubbornness; **eigensinnig** ADJ stubborn; **eigenständig** ADJ original; (= *unabhängig*) independent; **Eigenständigkeit** [-ʃtɛndɪçkait] F **-**, NO PL originality; (= *Unabhängigkeit*) independence

eigentlich [ˈaigntlɪç] **1** ADJ (= *wirklich, tatsächlich*) real; *Wert* true; (= *ursprünglich*) original; **im ~en Sinne bedeutet das ...** that really means ...; **im ~en Sinne des Wortes ...** in the original meaning of the word ... **2** ADV actually; (= *tatsächlich, wirklich*) really; (= *überhaupt*) anyway; **was willst du ~ hier?** what do you want here anyway?; **wissen Sie ~, wer ich bin?** do you know who I am?; **was ist ~ mit dir los?** what's the matter with you (anyway)?; **~ müsstest du das wissen** you should really know that; **~ dürftest du das nicht tun** you shouldn't really do that

Eigentor NT *(Sport, fig)* own goal; **ein ~ schießen** to score an own goal

Eigentum NT **-s**, NO PL property; **unbewegliches ~** immovables *pl*; ~ **an etw** *(dat)* **erwerben** to acquire possession of sth

Eigentümer [ˈaigntyːmɐ] M **-s, -**, **Eigentümerin** [-ərɪn] F **-, -nen** owner

Eigentümergrundschuld F land charge for the benefit of the owner

eigentümlich [ˈaigntyːmlɪç] ADJ (= *sonderbar, seltsam*) strange

eigentümlicherweise ADV strangely enough

Eigentümlichkeit F **-, -en (a)** (= *Kennzeichen, Besonderheit*) characteristic **(b)** (= *Eigenheit*) peculiarity

Eigentums-: Eigentumsdelikt NT *(Jur)* offence against property; **Eigentumsübertragung** F transfer of ownership; *(von Grundbesitz)* transfer of title; **Eigentumsverhältnisse** PL distribution *sing* of property; **Eigentumswohnung** F owner-occupied flat *(Brit)*, ≈ condominium *(US)*; **er kaufte sich** *(dat)* **eine ~** he bought a flat *(Brit)* or an apartment (of his own); **~en bauen** to build flats *(Brit)* or apartments for owner-occupation

Eigen-: eigenverantwortlich **1** ADJ autonomous **2** ADV on one's own authority; ~ **für etw sorgen müssen** to be personally responsible for sth; **er hat ~ dafür gesorgt** he saw to it personally; **Eigenverantwortlichkeit** F autonomy; **jds ~ für etw** sb's personal responsibility for sth; **Eigenverbrauch** M personal consumption; *(von Unternehmen)* own consumption; **Eigenverlag** M private publisher; **sein im ~ erschienenes Buch** the book which he published himself; **Eigenwechsel** M promissory note; **eigenwillig** ADJ with a mind of one's own; (= *eigensinnig*) self-willed; (= *unkonventionell*) unconventional; **sie ist in allem recht ~** she has a mind of her own in everything; **Eigenwilligkeit** [-vɪlɪçkait] F **-, -en** independence of mind; (= *Eigensinnigkeit*) self-will; (= *Unkonventionalität*) unconventionality

eignen [ˈaignən] VR to be suitable *(für, zu* for, *als* as); **er würde sich nicht zum Lehrer ~** he wouldn't make a good teacher; *siehe auch* **geeignet**

Eignung [ˈaignʊŋ] F **-, -en** suitability; (= *Befähigung*) aptitude

Eignungstest M aptitude test

Eiklar [ˈaiklaːɐ] NT **-s, -** *(Aus, S Ger)* egg white

Eil-: Eilauftrag M rush order; **Eilbote** M, **Eilbotin** F messenger; **per** *or* **durch ~n** express; **Eilbrief** M express letter; **ich schicke diesen Brief als ~** I am sending this letter express

Eile [ˈailə] F **-**, NO PL hurry; **in ~ sein** to be in a hurry; **damit hat es keine ~, das hat keine ~** it's not urgent; **er trieb uns zur ~ an** he hurried us up; **in aller ~** hurriedly; **in der ~** in the hurry; **in meiner ~** in my haste; **nur keine ~!** don't rush!

Eileiter M *(Anat)* Fallopian tube

Eileiterschwangerschaft F ectopic pregnancy

eilen [ˈailən] **1** VI **(a)** AUX SEIN to hurry; **eile mit Weile** *(Prov)* more haste less speed *(Prov)* **(b)** (= *dringlich sein*) to be urgent; **eilt!** *(auf Briefen etc)* urgent **2** VI IMPERS **es eilt** it's urgent

eilends [ˈailənts] ADV hurriedly

Eilfracht F, **Eilgut** NT, NO PL express freight

eilig ['aɪlɪç] **1** ADJ **(a)** (= *schnell, rasch*) hurried; **es ~ haben** to be in a hurry; **nur nicht so ~!** don't be in such a hurry! **(b)** (= *dringend*) urgent; **er hatte nichts Eiligeres zu tun, als ...** (*iro*) he had nothing better to do than ... (*iro*) **2** ADV as quickly as possible

Eil-: Eilpaket NT express parcel; **Eilsendung** F express delivery; **~en** *pl* express mail; **Eiltempo** NT **etw im ~ machen** to do sth in a real rush; **Eilüberweisung** F rapid money transfer

Eimer ['aɪmɐ] M **-s, -** bucket; (= *Mülleimer*) (rubbish) bin (*Brit*), garbage can (*US*); **ein ~ (voll) Wasser** a bucket(ful) of water; **es gießt wie mit** *or* **aus ~n** (*inf*) it's bucketing down (*Brit inf*), it's coming down in buckets (*US inf*); **im ~ sein** (*inf*) to be up the spout (*Brit inf*), to be down the drain (*US inf*)

eimerweise ADV by the bucket(ful)

ein¹ [aɪn] ADV (*an Geräten*) **Ein/Aus** on/off; **~ und aus gehen** to come and go; **er geht bei uns ~ und aus** he is always (a)round at our place; **ich weiß (mit ihm) nicht mehr ~ noch aus** I'm at my wits' end (with him)

ein², eine, ein 1 NUM one; **~ Uhr** one (o'clock); **~ Uhr zwanzig** twenty past one; **~ für alle Mal** once and for all; **~ und derselbe/dieselbe/dasselbe** one and the same; **er ist ihr Ein und Alles** he means everything to her; *siehe auch* **eins 2** INDEF ART a; (*vor Vokalen*) an; **~ Europäer** a European; **~ Hotel** a *or* an hotel; **~e Hitze ist das hier!** the heat here!; **was für ~ Wetter/Lärm!** some weather/noise; **wir hatten ~en Durst!** (*inf*) were we thirsty!; *siehe auch* **eine(r, s)**

einander [aɪ'nandɐ] PRON one another; **zwei ~ widersprechende Zeugenberichte** two (mutually) contradictory eyewitness reports

einarbeiten SEP **1** VR to get used to the work; **sie muss sich in ihr neues Gebiet ~** she has to get used to her new area of work **2** VT **(a)** *jdn* to train **(b)** (= *einfügen*) to incorporate

Einarbeitung ['aɪnarbaɪtʊŋ] F **-, -en** (*von Menschen*) training

Einarbeitungszeit F training period

einarmig ADJ one-armed; *Turnübungen* single-arm; **~er Bandit** one-armed bandit

einatmen VTI SEP to breathe in

Einäugige(r) ['aɪnɔʏgɪgə] MF DECL AS ADJ one-eyed person/man/woman *etc*

Einbahnstraße F one-way street

einbalsamieren *ptp* **einbalsamiert** VT SEP to embalm

Einband M, *pl* **-bände** book cover

einbändig ADJ one-volume *attr*, in one volume

Einbau M, *pl* **-bauten (a)** NO PL (= *das Einbauen*) installation **(b)** (*usu pl*: = *Schrank etc*) fixture

einbauen VT SEP to install; *Motor auch* to fit; (*inf*: = *einfügen*) *Zitat etc* to work in; **eingebaut** built-in

Einbauküche F (fully-)fitted kitchen

Einbaum M dug-out (canoe)

Einbau-: Einbaumöbel PL fitted furniture; (= *Schränke*) fitted cupboards *pl*; **Einbauschrank** M fitted cupboard

einbegriffen ['aɪnbəgrɪfn] ADJ included

einbehalten *ptp* **einbehalten** VT SEP IRREG to keep back

einbeinig ADJ one-legged

einberufen *ptp* **einberufen** VT SEP IRREG *Parlament* to summon; *Versammlung* to convene; (*Mil*) to call up, to draft (*US*)

Einberufung F **(a)** (*einer Versammlung*) convention; (*des Parlaments*) summoning **(b)** (*Mil*) conscription; (= *Einberufungsbescheid*) call-up, draft call (*US*)

Einberufungsbescheid M, **Einberufungsbefehl** M (*Mil*) call-up *or* draft (*US*) papers *pl*

einbetonieren *ptp* **einbetoniert** VT SEP to cement in (*in +acc -* to)

einbetten VT SEP to embed (*in +acc* in); *Rohr, Kabel* to lay (*in +acc* in); *siehe auch* **eingebettet**

Einbettzimmer NT single room

einbeulen VT SEP to dent (in)

einbeziehen *ptp* **einbezogen** VT SEP IRREG to include (*in +acc* in)

einbiegen SEP IRREG **1** VI AUX SEIN to turn (off) (*in +acc* into); **du musst hier links ~** you have to turn (off to the) left here; **diese Straße biegt in die Hauptstraße ein** this road joins the main road **2** VT to bend in

einbilden VT SEP **(a)** (= *sich vorstellen*) **sich** (*dat*) **etw ~** to imagine sth; **er bildet sich** (*dat*) **ein, dass ...** he's got hold of the idea that ...; **sich** (*dat*) **steif und fest ~, dass ...** (*inf*) to get it fixed in one's head that ... (*inf*); **das bildest du dir nur ein** that's just your imagination; **ich bilde mir nicht ein, ich sei ...** I don't have any illusions about being ...; **er bildet sich** (*dat*) **viel ein!** he imagines a lot of things!; **bilde dir (doch) nichts ein!** don't kid yourself! (*inf*); **was bildest du dir eigentlich ein?** what's got (*Brit*) *or* gotten (*US*) into you?; **bilde dir bloß nicht ein, dass ich das glaube!** don't kid yourself that I believe that! (*inf*) **(b)** (= *stolz sein*) **sich** (*dat*) **viel auf etw** (*acc*) **~** to be conceited about sth; **darauf kann ich mir etwas ~** (*iro*) praise indeed!; **darauf können Sie sich etwas ~!** that's something to be proud of!; **darauf brauchst du dir nichts einzubilden!** that's nothing to be proud of; *siehe auch* **eingebildet**

Einbildung F **(a)** (= *Vorstellung*) imagination; (= *irrige Vorstellung*) illusion; **das ist alles nur ~** it's all in the mind; **krank ist er bloß in seiner ~** he just imagines he's ill **(b)** (= *Dünkel*) conceit; **~ ist auch eine Bildung** (*hum inf*) he's/she's too conceited for words

Einbildungskraft F, **Einbildungsvermögen** NT, NO PL (powers *pl* of) imagination

einbinden VT SEP IRREG *Buch* to bind; (*in Schutzhülle*) to cover; (*fig*: = *einbeziehen*) to integrate; **neu ~** to rebind

Einbindung F (*fig*) integration

einbläuen ['aɪnblɔʏən] VT SEP (*inf*) **jdm etw ~** (*durch Schläge*) to beat sth into sb; (= *einschärfen*) to drum sth into sb; **ich habe ihm eingebläut, das ja nicht zu vergessen** I told him time and again not to forget it

einblenden (*Film, TV, Rad*) **1** VT to insert; (*allmählich*) to fade in; (*nachträglich*) *Musik etc* to dub over **2** VR **sich in etw** (*acc*) **~** to link up with sth; **sich bei jdm/etw ~** to go over to sb/sth

einbleuen VT SEP *siehe* **einbläuen**

Einblick M (*fig*: = *Kenntnis*) insight; **~ in etw** (*acc*) **gewinnen** to gain an insight into sth; **~ in die Akten nehmen** to look at the files; **jdm ~ in etw** (*acc*) **gewähren** to allow sb to look at sth; **er hat ~ in diese Vorgänge** he has some knowledge of these events

einbrechen SEP IRREG **1** VT *Tür, Wand etc* to break down **2** VI **(a)** AUX SEIN (= *einstürzen*) to fall in; **er ist (auf dem Eis) eingebrochen** he went through the ice **(b)** AUX SEIN *or* HABEN (= *Einbruch verüben*) to break in; **in unser** *or* **unserem Haus sind Diebe eingebrochen** thieves broke into our house; **bei mir ist eingebrochen worden, man hat bei mir eingebrochen** I've had a break-in; **in neue Absatzmärkte** *etc* **~** to make inroads into new markets *etc* **(c)** AUX SEIN (*Nacht*) to fall; (*Winter*) to set in **(d)** AUX SEIN (*inf*: = *Verluste machen*) to come a cropper (*Brit inf*), to fall apart (*US*)

Einbrecher(in) M(F) burglar

einbringen VT SEP IRREG **(a)** (*Parl*) *Gesetz* to introduce **(b)** (= *Ertrag bringen*) *Geld, Nutzen* to bring in; *Ruhm* to bring; *Zinsen* to earn; **jdm etw ~** to bring/earn sb sth; **das bringt nichts ein** (*fig*) it's not worth it **(c)** (= *beteiligen*) **sich in etw** (*acc*) **~** to play a part in sth; **sie brachte ihre Kenntnisse in die Diskussion ein** she brought her knowledge to bear in the discussion

einbrocken ['aɪnbrɔkn] VT SEP to crumble (*in +acc* into); **jdm/sich etwas ~** (*inf*) to land sb/oneself in it (*inf*); **da hast du dir etwas Schönes eingebrockt!** (*inf*) you've really let yourself in for it there; **was man sich eingebrockt hat, das muss man auch auslöffeln** (*prov*) you've made your bed, now you must lie in it (*prov*)

Einbruch M **(a)** (= *~diebstahl*) burglary (*in +acc* in); **ein ~ a** break-in; **der ~ in die Bank** the bank break-in **(b)** (*von Wasser*) penetration; **~ kühler Meeresluft** (*Met*) a stream of cold air moving inland **(c)** (= *Verlust*) setback; **der Kurse/der Konjunktur** (*Fin*) stock exchange/economic crash **(d)** (*der Nacht*) fall; (*des Winters*) onset; **bei/vor ~ der Nacht/Dämmerung** at/before nightfall/dusk

einbuddeln VT SEP (*inf*) to bury (*in +acc* in)

einbürgern ['aɪnbʏrgɐn] SEP **1** VT *Person* to naturalize; *Fremdwort, Gewohnheit, Pflanze* to introduce; **er ist in die** *or* **der Türkei eingebürgert worden** he has become a naturalized Turk

2 VR (*Person*) to become naturalized; (*Brauch, Tier, Pflanze, Fremdwort*) to become established; **das hat sich so eingebürgert** (*Brauch*) it's just the way we/they *etc* have come to do things; **es hat sich bei uns so eingebürgert, dass wir uns abwechseln** we've got into the habit of taking turns

Einbürgerung F -, -en (*von Menschen*) naturalization

Einbuße F loss (*an* +*dat* to); **der Skandal hat seinem Ansehen schwere ~ getan** he lost a considerable amount of respect because of the scandal

einbüßen SEP **1** VT to lose; (*durch eigene Schuld*) to forfeit **2** VI to lose something; **an Klarheit** (*dat*) **~** to lose some of its clarity

Eincentstück NT one-cent piece

einchecken VTI SEP to check in (*an* +*dat* at)

eincremen ['aɪnkreːmən] VT SEP to put cream on

eindämmen VT SEP *Fluss* to dam; (*fig*) (= *vermindern*) to check; (= *im Zaum halten*) to contain

eindecken SEP **1** VR **sich** (**mit etw**) ~ to stock up (with sth); (*für den Haushalt*) to get in supplies (of sth); **wir haben uns ausreichend mit Geld eingedeckt** we've got enough money; **ich bin gut eingedeckt, ich habe mich eingedeckt** I am well supplied **2** VT (*inf*: = *überhäufen*) to inundate; **mit Arbeit eingedeckt sein** to be snowed under with work

Eindecker ['aɪndɛkɐ] M -s, - (*Aviat*) monoplane; (= *Autobus*) single decker

eindellen ['aɪndɛlən] VT SEP (*inf*) to dent (in)

eindeutig ['aɪndɔʏtɪç] **1** ADJ clear; (= *nicht zweideutig*) unambiguous; *Witz* explicit **2** ADV (= *klar*) clearly; (= *unmissverständlich*) unambiguously; **jdm etw ~ sagen** to tell sb sth straight (*inf*)

Eindeutigkeit F -, NO PL clearness; (= *Unzweideutigkeit*) unambiguity; (*von Witz*) explicitness

eindeutschen ['aɪndɔʏtʃn] VT SEP to Germanize

eindicken ['aɪndɪkn] VTI SEP (*vi: aux sein*) to thicken

eindimensional ADJ one-dimensional

eindosen ['aɪndoːzn] VT SEP to can

eindösen VI SEP AUX SEIN (*inf*) to doze off

eindrehen VT SEP (a) (= *einschrauben*) to screw in (*in* +*acc* -to) (b) *Haar* to put in rollers

eindreschen VI SEP IRREG (*inf*) **auf jdn ~** to lay into sb (*inf*)

eindringen VI SEP IRREG AUX SEIN (a) (= *einbrechen*) **in etw** (*acc*) **~** to force one's way into sth; **in das Land ~** (*Mil*) to penetrate into the country (b) (= *hineindringen*) **in etw** (*acc*) **~** to go into sth; (*Fremdwort, Amerikanismus*) to find its way into sth (c) (= *bestürmen*) **auf jdn ~** to go for sb (*mit* with); (*mit Fragen, Bitten etc*) to besiege sb

eindringlich **1** ADJ (= *nachdrücklich*) insistent; *Schilderung* vivid **2** ADV *warnen* urgently; **ich habe ihn ~ gebeten, zu Hause zu bleiben** I urged him to stay at home; **jdm ~ nahe legen, etw zu tun** to urge sb to do sth

Eindringling ['aɪndrɪŋlɪŋ] M -s, -e intruder; (*in Gesellschaft etc*) interloper

Eindruck M, *pl* -drücke impression; **den ~ erwecken, als ob** *or* **dass ...** to give the impression that ...; **die Eindrücke, die wir gewonnen hatten** our impressions; **ich habe den ~, dass ..., ich kann mich des ~s nicht erwehren, dass ...** (*geh*) I have the impression that ...; **großen ~ auf jdn machen** to make a great impression on sb; **sie macht einen heiteren ~/den ~ eines heiteren Menschen** she gives the impression of being cheerful/of being a cheerful person; **er will ~ (bei ihr) machen** *or* **schinden** (*inf*) he's out to impress (her); **ich stehe noch ganz unter dem ~ der Ereignisse** I'm still too close to it all

eindrücken SEP **1** VT *Fenster* to break; *Tür, Mauer* to push down; (*Sturm, Explosion*) to blow in/down; (= *einbeulen*) to dent **2** VR to make an impression

eindübeln VT SEP *Haken* to plug (*in* +*acc* into)

eine ['aɪnə] *siehe* **ein²**, **eine(r, s)**

einebnen VT SEP (*lit*) to level (off); (*fig*) to level (out)

eineiig ['aɪnlaɪɪç] ADJ *Zwillinge* identical

eineinhalb ['aɪnlaɪn'halp] NUM one and a half; **~ Mal** one and a half times; *siehe auch* **anderthalb**

Eineltern(teil)familie F single-parent family

einengen ['aɪnlɛŋən] VT SEP (*lit*) to constrict; (*fig*) *Begriff, Freiheit* to restrict; **jdn in seiner Freiheit ~** to curb sb's freedom;

eingeengt sitzen/stehen/liegen to sit/stand/lie (all) squashed up

einer ['aɪnɐ] ADV (*Aus*) = **herein**

Einer ['aɪnɐ] M -s, - (a) (*Math*) unit (b) (= *Ruderboot*) single scull

eine(r, s) ['aɪnɐ] INDEF PRON (a) one; (= *jemand*) somebody; **der/die/das Eine** the one; **das ~ Gute war ...** the one good thing was ...; **sein ~r Sohn** (*inf*) one of his sons; **weder der ~ noch der andere** neither (one) of them; **die ~n sagen so, die anderen gerade das Gegenteil** some (people) say one thing and others say just the opposite; **~r für alle, alle für ~n** (*Prov*) all for one and one for all (*Prov*); **das ist ~r!** (*inf*) he's a (right) one! (*inf*); **du bist mir vielleicht ~r!** (*inf*) you're a fine one (*inf*); **sieh mal ~r an!** (*iro*) well what do you know! (*inf*); **in ~m fort** (*inf*), **in ~r Tour** (*inf*) non-stop

(b) (= *man*) one (*form*), you; **und das soll ~r glauben!** (*inf*) and we're/you're meant to believe that!; **wie kann ~r nur so unklug sein!** how could anybody be so stupid!

(c) **~s** (*auch* **eins**) one thing; **~s gefällt mir nicht an ihm** (there's) one thing I don't like about him; **~s sag ich dir** I'll tell you one thing; **noch ~s!** another one!; (*Lied etc*) more!; **noch ~s, bevor ichs vergesse** (there's) one other thing before I forget; **es kam ~s nach dem** *or* **zum anderen** it was (just) one thing after another; **es läuft alles auf ~s hinaus** it all comes to the same (thing) in the end

(d) (*inf*) **sich** (*dat*) **~n genehmigen** to have a quick one (*inf*); **jdm ~ kleben** to punch sb

einerlei ['aɪnɐ'laɪ] ADJ INV PRED (= *gleichgültig*) all the same; **das ist mir ganz ~** it's all the same to me; **~ ob er kommt** no matter whether he comes or not; **~ was/wer ...** it doesn't matter what/who ...

Einerlei ['aɪnɐ'laɪ] NT -s, NO PL monotony

einerseits ['aɪnɐzaɪts] ADV **~ ... andererseits ...** on the one hand ... on the other hand ...

Einerstelle F (*Math*) unit (place)

einesteils ['aɪnəstaɪls] ADV **~ ... ander(e)nteils** on the one hand ... on the other hand ...

Eine-Welt-Laden M ≈ OXFAM shop (*Brit*), ≈ thrift store (*US*), ≈ charity shop for the Third World

einfach ['aɪnfax] **1** ADJ simple; *Fahrkarte, Fahrt* one-way, single (*Brit*); *Buchführung* single-entry; *Mensch* ordinary; *Essen* plain; **einmal ~!** (*in Bus etc*) single please (*Brit*), one-way ticket please (*US*); **das ist nicht so ~ zu verstehen** that is not so easy to understand

2 ADV (a) (= *schlicht*) simply

(b) (= *nicht doppelt*) once; **~ gefaltet** folded once; **die Wolle ~ nehmen** to use one strand of wool

(c) (*verstärkend*: = *geradezu*) simply; **~ gemein** downright mean

(d) (= *ohne weiteres, mit Verneinung*) just

Einfachheit F -, NO PL simplicity; (*von Mensch*) ordinariness; (*von Essen*) plainness; **der ~ halber** for the sake of simplicity

einfädeln SEP **1** VT (a) *Nadel, Faden* to thread (*in* +*acc* through); *Nähmaschine* to thread up; *Film* to thread (b) (*inf*) *Intrige, Plan etc* to set up (*inf*) **2** VR **sich in eine Verkehrskolonne ~** to filter into a stream of traffic

einfahren SEP IRREG **1** VI AUX SEIN (*Zug, Schiff*) to come in (*in* +*acc* -to)

2 VT (a) (= *kaputtfahren*) *Mauer, Zaun* to knock down

(b) *Fahrgestell, Periskop* to retract

(c) (= *ans Fahren etc gewöhnen*) to break in; *Wagen* to run in (*Brit*), to break in (*US*); **„wird eingefahren"** "running in" (*Brit*), "being broken in" (*US*)

(d) *Verluste* to make; *Gewinne auch* to bring in

3 VR to get used to driving; **das hat sich so eingefahren** (*fig*) it has just become a habit; *siehe auch* **eingefahren**

Einfahrt F (a) NO PL (= *das Einfahren*) entry (*in* +*acc* to); (*Min*) descent; **Vorsicht bei (der) ~ des Zuges!** stand well back, the train is arriving; **der Zug hat noch keine ~** the train can't enter the station (b) (= *Eingang*) entrance; (= *Toreinfahrt*) entry; **„~ freihalten"** "keep clear"

Einfall M (a) (= *plötzlicher Gedanke*) idea; (= *Grille, Laune*) notion; **jdn auf den ~ bringen, etw zu tun** to give sb the idea of doing sth; **auf den ~ kommen, etw zu tun** to get the idea of doing sth; **es war ein bloßer** *or* **nur so ein ~** it was just an idea (b) (*Mil*) invasion (*in* +*acc* of)

einfallen VI SEP IRREG AUX SEIN **(a)** (*Gedanke*) **jdm ~** to occur to sb; **mir fällt nichts ein, was ich schreiben kann** I can't think of anything to write; **jetzt fällt mir ein, wie/warum ...** I've just thought of how/why ...; **ihm fällt immer eine Ausrede ein** he can always think of an excuse; **das fällt mir nicht im Traum ein!** I wouldn't dream of it!; **sich** (*dat*) **etw ~ lassen** to think of sth; **hast du dir etwas ~ lassen?** have you had any ideas?; **da musst du dir schon etwas anderes/Besseres ~ lassen!** you'll really have to think of something else/better; **was fällt Ihnen ein!** what are you thinking of!
(b) (= *in Erinnerung kommen*) **jdm ~** to come to sb; **dabei fällt mir mein Onkel ein, der ...** that reminds me of my uncle, who ...; **es fällt mir jetzt nicht ein** I can't think of it at the moment; **es wird Ihnen schon wieder ~** it will come back to you
(c) (= *einstürzen*) to collapse; (*Gesicht, Wangen*) to become sunken; *siehe auch* **eingefallen**
(d) (= *eindringen*) **in ein Land ~** to invade a country
(e) (*Lichtstrahlen*) to fall; (*in ein Zimmer etc*) to come in (*in +acc -to*)
(f) (= *mitsingen, mitreden*) to join in; (= *einsetzen: Chor, Stimmen*) to come in

Einfalls-: **einfallslos** ADJ unimaginative; **einfallsreich** ADJ imaginative; **Einfallswinkel** M (*Phys*) angle of incidence
einfältig ['ainfɛltɪç] ADJ (= *arglos*) simple; (= *dumm*) simple(-minded)
Einfaltspinsel ['ainfalts-] M (*inf*) simpleton
Einfamilienhaus NT single-family house
einfarbig, (*Aus*) **einfärbig** ADJ all one colour (*Brit*) *or* color (*US*); (*Tex*) self-coloured (*Brit*), self-colored (*US*)
einfassen VT SEP *Beet, Grab* to border; *Kleid, Naht, Knopfloch* to trim
einfetten VT SEP to grease; *Leder, Schuhe* to dubbin; *Haut, Gesicht* to rub cream into
einfinden VR SEP IRREG to come; (= *eintreffen*) to arrive; (*zu Prüfung etc*) to present oneself; **ich bitte alle, sich pünktlich in meinem Büro einzufinden** I would ask you all to be in my office punctually
einfliegen SEP IRREG **1** VT **(a)** *Flugzeug* to test-fly **(b)** *Proviant, Truppen* to fly in (*in +acc -to*) **(c)** *Verluste* to make; *Gewinne* to bring in **2** VI AUX SEIN to fly in (*in +acc -to*)
einfließen VI SEP IRREG AUX SEIN to flow in; (*fig*) to have some influence (*in +acc* on); **er ließ nebenbei ~, dass er Professor sei** he let it drop that he was a professor
einflößen VT SEP **jdm etw ~** to pour sth down sb's throat; *Medizin* to give sb sth; *Ehrfurcht, Mut etc* to instil (*Brit*) *or* instill (*US*) sth into sb
Einflugschneise F (*Aviat*) approach path
Einfluss M **(a)** influence; **unter dem ~ von jdm/etw** under the influence of sb/sth; **~ auf jdn haben/ausüben** to have/exert an influence on sb; **~ nehmen** to bring an influence to bear; **das Wetter steht unter dem ~ eines atlantischen Tiefs** the weather is being affected by an Atlantic depression; **darauf habe ich keinen ~** I can't influence that **(b)** (*lit*: = *das Einfließen*) (*von Luft*) (*fig*) influx; (*von Gas, Abwässern*) inflow
Einfluss-: **Einflussbereich** M, **Einflussgebiet** NT sphere of influence; **England liegt im ~ eines atlantischen Tiefs** England is being affected by an Atlantic depression; **Einflussmöglichkeit** F influence; **unsere ~en sind begrenzt** we don't have much scope for influence; **einflussreich** ADJ influential
einfordern VT SEP to demand; *Schulden* to demand payment of; *Versprechen, Zusage* to demand fulfilment (*Brit*) *or* fulfillment (*US*) of
einförmig ADJ uniform; (= *eintönig*) monotonous
Einförmigkeit F -, *no* uniformity; (= *Eintönigkeit*) monotony
einfrieren SEP IRREG **1** VI AUX SEIN to freeze; (*Wasserleitung, Schiff*) to freeze up; **die Beziehungen ~ lassen** to suspend relations **2** VT (*lit, fig*) *Nahrungsmittel, Löhne etc* to freeze; (*Pol*) *Beziehungen* to suspend; **sich ~ lassen** to allow oneself to be put into deep-freeze
Einfügemodus M (*Comput*) insert mode
einfügen SEP **1** VT *Steine, Maschinenteile* to fit (*in +acc* into); (*Comput*) to insert (*in +acc* in); (= *nachtragen*) to add (*in +acc* in); **darf ich an dieser Stelle ~, dass ...** may I add at this point

that ... **2** VR to fit in (*in +acc -to*); (= *sich anpassen*) to adapt (*in +acc* to)
Einfügetaste F (*Comput*) insert key
einfühlen VR SEP **sich in jdn ~** to empathize with sb; (*Theat*) to feel oneself into (the role of) sb; **sich in etw** (*acc*) **~** to understand sth; **sich in die Atmosphäre des 17. Jahrhunderts ~** to get into the atmosphere of the 17th century
einfühlsam ['ainfy:lza:m] **1** ADJ sensitive **2** ADV sensitively
Einfühlsamkeit F -, NO PL sensitivity
Einfühlungsvermögen NT, NO PL capacity for understanding, empathy; **ein Buch mit großem ~ interpretieren** to interpret a book with a great deal of sensitivity
Einfuhr ['ainfu:ɐ] F -, **-en** import; (= *das Einführen*) importing
Einfuhr- IN CPDS import; **Einfuhrartikel** M import; **Einfuhrbeschränkung** F import restriction; **mengenmäßige ~en** import quotas *pl*
einführen SEP **1** VT **(a)** (= *hineinstecken*) to insert (*in +acc* into) **(b)** (= *bekannt machen*) to introduce (*in +acc* into); (*Comm*) *Firma, Artikel* to establish; **jdn in sein Amt ~** to install sb (in office); **~de Worte** introductory words
(c) (*als Neuerung*) to introduce; *neue Mode* to set; *Sitte* to start **(d)** (*Comm*) *Waren, Devisen* to import **(e)** (*St Ex*) to list (*an +dat* on) **2** VR to introduce oneself; **sich gut/nicht gut ~** to make a good/bad (initial) impression
Einfuhr-: **Einfuhrerklärung** F import declaration, bill of entry; **Einfuhrgenehmigung** F import permit; **Einfuhrland** NT importing country; **Einfuhrlizenz** F import licence (*Brit*) *or* license (*US*); **Einfuhrrestriktion** F import restriction; (*mengenmäßig*) import quota; **Einfuhrumsatzsteuer** F import VAT
Einführung F introduction (*in +acc* to); (= *Amtseinführung*) installation; (= *Börseneinführung*) listing
Einführungs- IN CPDS introductory; **Einführungskurs** M (*Univ etc*) introductory course; (*St Ex*) introductory rate; **Einführungspreis** M introductory price
Einfuhrverbot NT ban on imports; **ein ~ für etw** a ban on the import of sth
Einfüllstutzen M (*Aut*) filler pipe
Eingabe F **(a)** (*form*: = *Gesuch*) petition (*an +acc* to) **(b)** (*von Medizin*) administration **(c)** (*Comput*) input
Eingabe-: **Eingabedaten** PL input data *sing*; **Eingabetaste** F (*Comput*) enter key
Eingang M, *pl* **-gänge (a)** entrance (*in +acc* to); (= *Zutritt, Aufnahme*) entry; **„kein ~!"** "no entrance" **(b)** (*Comm*) (= *Wareneingang, Posteingang*) delivery; (= *Erhalt*) receipt; **wir bestätigen den ~ Ihres Schreibens vom ...** we acknowledge receipt of your communication of the ...; **die Waren werden beim ~ gezählt** the goods are counted on delivery; **den ~** *or* **die Eingänge bearbeiten** to deal with the in-coming mail
eingängig ADJ *Melodie, Spruch* catchy; *Theorie* neat
eingangs ['aingaŋs] ADV at the start
Eingangs-: **Eingangsbestätigung** F (*Comm*) acknowledgement of receipt; **Eingangsdatum** NT date of receipt; **Eingangsstempel** M (*Comm*) receipt stamp; **mit einem ~ versehen** stamped with the date of receipt; **Eingangsvermerk** M (*Comm*) notice of receipt
eingeben VT SEP IRREG **(a)** (= *verabreichen*) to give **(b)** (*Comput*) *Text, Befehl* to enter
eingebettet [-gebetət] ADJ embedded; **in** *or* **zwischen Wäldern/ Hügeln ~** nestling among the woods/hills; *siehe auch* **einbetten**
eingebildet ADJ **(a)** (= *hochmütig*) conceited **(b)** (= *imaginär*) imaginary; *Schwangerschaft* phantom; **ein ~er Kranker** a hypochondriac; *siehe auch* **einbilden**
eingeboren ADJ (= *einheimisch*) native
Eingeborenensprache F native language
Eingeborene(r) ['aingəbo:rənə] MF DECL AS ADJ native (*auch hum*)
Eingebung ['ainge:bʊŋ] F -, **-en** inspiration
eingefahren [-gefa:rən] ADJ *Verhaltensweise* well-worn; **die Diskussion bewegte sich in ~en Gleisen** the discussion covered the same old well-worn topics; *siehe auch* **einfahren**
eingefallen ADJ *Wangen* hollow; *Augen* deep-set; *siehe auch* **einfallen**

eingefleischt [-gəflaɪʃt] ADJ ATTR (= *überzeugt*) confirmed; (= *unverbesserlich*) dyed-in-the-wool; **~er Junggeselle** (*hum*) confirmed bachelor

eingehen SEP IRREG AUX SEIN **1** VI **(a)** (= *ankommen*) (*Briefe, Waren etc*) to arrive; (*Meldung, Spenden, Bewerbungen*) to come in; **~de Post/Waren** incoming mail/goods; **eingegangene Post/Spenden** mail/donations received **(b)** (= *Aufnahme finden: Wort, Sitte*) to be adopted (*in +acc* in); **in die Geschichte ~** to go down in (the annals of) history **(c) etw geht jdm ein** (= *wird verstanden*) sb grasps sth; **es will mir einfach nicht ~, wie ...** I just cannot understand how ... **(d)** (= *wirken*) **diese Musik geht einem leicht ein** this music is very catchy **(e)** (*fig*: = *einfließen*) to have some influence (*in +acc* on) **(f)** (= *einlaufen: Stoff*) to shrink **(g)** (= *sterben: Tiere, Pflanze*) to die (*an +dat* of); (*inf: Firma etc*) to fold; **bei dieser Hitze/Kälte geht man ja ein!** (*inf*) this heat/cold is just too much (*inf*) **(h)** (= *behandeln*) **auf etw** (*acc*) **~ auf Frage, Punkt etc** to go into sth; **darauf gehe ich noch näher ein** I will go into that in more detail; **niemand ging auf meine Frage/mich ein** nobody took any notice of my question/me; **auf jdn/etw ~** (= *sich widmen, einfühlen*) to give (one's) time and attention to sb/sth; **auf einen Vorschlag/Plan ~** (= *zustimmen*) to agree to a suggestion/plan **2** VT (= *abmachen, abschließen*) to enter into; *Risiko* to take; *Wette* to make

eingehend 1 ADJ (= *ausführlich*) detailed; (= *gründlich*) thorough; *Bericht, Studien, Untersuchungen* in-depth *attr* **2** ADV (= *ausführlich*) in detail; (= *gründlich*) thoroughly

eingekeilt ['aɪngəkaɪlt] ADJ hemmed in; *Auto* boxed in; *siehe auch* **einkeilen**

Eingemachte(s) ['aɪngəmaxtə] NT DECL AS ADJ bottled fruit/vegetables; (= *Marmelade*) preserves *pl*; (*inf*: = *Erspartes*) one's own resources *pl*; **ans ~ gehen** (*fig inf*) to dig deep into one's reserves

eingenommen ['aɪngənɔmən] ADJ **für jdn/etw ~ sein** to be taken with sb/sth; **gegen jdn/etw ~ sein** to be prejudiced against sb/sth; **er ist sehr von sich selbst ~** he thinks a lot of himself; *siehe auch* **einnehmen**

eingeschnappt [-gəʃnapt] ADJ (*inf*) cross; **~ sein** to be in a huff; *siehe auch* **einschnappen**

eingeschossig, (*Aus, S Ger*) **eingeschoßig** ADJ *Haus* single-storey (*Brit*), single-story (*US*)

eingeschränkt [-gəʃrɛŋkt] ADJ (= *eingeengt*) restricted; (= *sparsam*) careful; **in ~en Verhältnissen leben** to live in straitened circumstances; *siehe auch* **einschränken**

eingeschrieben [-gəʃriːbn] ADJ *Mitglied, Brief* registered; *siehe auch* **einschreiben**

eingesessen [-gəzɛsn] ADJ established

Eingesottene(s) ['aɪngəzɔtənə] NT DECL AS ADJ (*Aus*) bottled fruit

eingespannt ADJ busy; *siehe auch* **einspannen**

eingespielt [-gəʃpiːlt] ADJ *Mannschaft* used to playing together; *Arbeitsteam, Kollegen* used to working together; **aufeinander ~ sein** to be used to one another; *siehe auch* **einspielen**

Eingeständnis NT admission, confession

eingestehen *ptp* **eingestanden** VT SEP IRREG to admit; **sich** (*dat*) **~, dass ...** to admit to oneself that ...

eingestellt ['aɪngəʃtɛlt] ADJ **materialistisch/fortschrittlich ~ sein** to be materialistic/progressive; **links/rechts ~ sein** to have leanings to the left/right; **die links/rechts Eingestellten** left-/right-wingers; **wer so ~ ist wie er** anyone who thinks as he does; **ich bin im Moment nicht auf Besuch ~** I'm not prepared for visitors; **wir sind nur auf kleinere Reisegesellschaften ~** we can only cater for small parties; *siehe auch* **einstellen**

eingetragen [-gətraːgn] ADJ *Mitglied, Warenzeichen, Verein* registered; *siehe auch* **eintragen**

Eingeweide ['aɪngəvaɪdə] NT **-s, -** USU PL entrails *pl*

Eingeweidebruch M (*Med*) hernia

eingewöhnen *ptp* **eingewöhnt** VR SEP (*in +dat* in)

Eingewöhnung F settling down

eingießen VT SEP IRREG to pour in (*in +acc* -to); (= *einschenken*) to pour (out)

eingipsen VT SEP *Arm, Bein* to put in plaster; *Dübel etc* to plaster in (*in +acc* -to)

eingleisig 1 ADJ single-track **2** ADV **der Zug fährt hier nur ~** the railway (*Brit*) *or* railroad (*US*) line is only single-track here; **er denkt sehr ~** (*fig*) he's completely single-minded

eingliedern SEP **1** VT *Firma, Gebiet* to incorporate (*+dat* into, with); **jdn** to integrate (*in +acc* into) **2** VR to fit in (*+dat, in +acc* -to, in)

eingraben SEP IRREG **1** VT *Pfahl, Pflanze* to dig in (*in +acc* -to) **2** VR to dig oneself in (*auch Mil*); **der Fluss hat sich ins Gestein eingegraben** the river carved itself a channel in the rock

eingreifen VI SEP IRREG **(a)** (= *einschreiten, Mil*) to intervene; **in jds Rechte** (*acc*) **~** to intrude (up)on sb's rights; **Eingreifen** intervention **(b)** (*Tech*) to mesh (*in +acc* with)

Eingreiftruppe F strike force

eingrenzen VT SEP (*lit*) to enclose; (*fig*) *Problem, Thema* to delimit; (= *verringern*) to narrow down

Eingriff M **(a)** (*Med*) operation **(b)** (= *Übergriff*) intervention; **ein ~ in jds Rechte/Privatsphäre** (*acc*) an intrusion (up)on sb's rights/privacy

eingruppieren *ptp* **eingruppiert** VT SEP to group (*in +acc* in)

Eingruppierung F grouping

einhaken SEP **1** VT to hook in (*in +acc* -to) **2** VI (*inf*: = *Punkt aufgreifen*) to intervene; **wenn ich an diesem Punkt vielleicht ~ darf** if I might just take up that point **3** VR **sie hakte sich bei ihm ein** she put her arm through his; **eingehakt gehen** to walk arm in arm

Einhalt M, NO PL **jdm/einer Sache ~ gebieten** to stop sb/sth

einhalten SEP IRREG **1** VT (= *beachten*) to keep; *Spielregeln* to follow; *Diät, Vertrag* to keep to; *Verpflichtungen* to carry out; **die Zeit ~** to keep to time; **den Kurs ~** (*Aviat, Naut*) to stay on course; **er hält seine Zahlungsverpflichtungen immer pünktlich ein** he's always prompt about payments **2** VI (*geh*) (= *aufhören*) to stop; (= *innehalten*) to pause; **halt ein!** stop!

Einhaltung F (= *Beachtung*) keeping (*+gen* of); (*von Spielregeln*) following (*+gen* of); (*von Diät, Vertrag*) keeping (*+gen* to); (*von Verpflichtungen*) carrying out (*+gen* of); **ich werde ihn zur ~ des Vertrages zwingen** I will force him to keep (to) the contract

einhandeln VT SEP **(a)** to trade (*gegen, für* for) **(b)** (= *bekommen*) **sich** (*dat*) **etw ~** (*inf*) to get sth

einhändig ADJ one-handed

einhängen SEP **1** VT *Tür* to hang; *Fenster* to put in **2** VR **sich bei jdm ~** to slip one's arm through sb's; **sie gingen eingehängt** they walked arm in arm

einhauen SEP IRREG **1** VT **(a)** *Nagel etc* to knock in (*in +acc* -to) **(b)** (= *zertrümmern*) to smash in **2** VI **auf jdn ~** to lay into sb; **auf etw** (*acc*) **~** to go at sth

einheimisch ['aɪnhaɪmɪʃ] ADJ *Mensch, Tier, Pflanze* native; *Produkt, Industrie, Mannschaft* local

Einheimische(r) ['aɪnhaɪmɪʃə] MF DECL AS ADJ local

einheimsen ['aɪnhaɪmzn] VT SEP (*inf*) to collect; **er hat den Ruhm für sich allein eingeheimst** he took the credit himself

Einheit ['aɪnhaɪt] F **-, -en (a)** (*von Land etc, Einheitlichkeit*) unity; (= *das Ganze*) whole; **eine geschlossene ~ bilden** to form an integrated whole; **~ von Forschung und Lehre** indivisibility of teaching and research; **die (deutsche) ~** (German) unity **(b)** (*Mil, Sci, Telec*) unit

einheitlich ['aɪnhaɪtlɪç] **1** ADJ (= *gleich*) the same, uniform; (= *genormt*) standard(ized); (= *in sich geschlossen*) unified **2** ADV uniformly; **~ gekleidet** dressed alike; **wir müssen ~ vorgehen** we must act consistently with one another

Einheitlichkeit F **-**, NO PL (= *Gleichheit*) uniformity; (= *Genormtheit*) standardization; (= *innere Geschlossenheit*) unity

Einheits-: **Einheitskleidung** F uniform; **Einheitskurs** M (*St Ex*) standard price; **Einheitspreis** M standard price; **Einheitstarif** M flat rate

einheizen SEP ■ VI to put the heating on; **jdm (tüchtig)** ~ (*inf*) (= *die Meinung sagen*) to haul sb over the coals; (= *zu schaffen machen*) to make things hot for sb ■ VT *Ofen* to put on; *Zimmer* to heat (up)

einhellig ['ainhɛlɪç] ■ ADJ unanimous ■ ADV unanimously

einher [ain'heːɐ] ADV (*Aus*) = **herein**

einher- PREF (= *entlang*) along; (= *hin und her*) up and down; **~reiten** to ride along/up and down

einhergehen VI SEP IRREG AUX SEIN **mit etw ~** (*fig*) to be accompanied by sth

einhin [ain'hɪn] ADV (*Aus*) = **hinein**

einhöckerig ['ainhœkərɪç], **einhöckrig** [-hœkrɪç] ADJ *Kamel* one-humped

einholen VT SEP (a) (= *einziehen*) *Boot, Netz, Tau* to pull in; *Fahne, Segel* to lower (b) *Rat, Gutachten, Erlaubnis* to obtain; **bei jdm Rat ~** to obtain advice from sb (c) (= *erreichen, nachholen*) *Laufenden, Auto* to catch up; *Vorsprung, Versäumtes, Zeit* to make up; *Verlust* to make good; **der Alltag/ die Vergangenheit hat mich eingeholt** the daily routine/the past has caught up with me (d) AUCH VI (*dial*) = **einkaufen**

Einhorn NT (*Myth, Astron*) unicorn

einhundert ['ain'hʊndɐt] NUM (*form*) = **hundert**

eini ['aini] ADV (*Aus*) = **hinein**

einig ['ainɪç] ADJ (a) (= *geeint*) united (b) (= *einer Meinung*) agreed, in agreement (*über +acc* on, about, *in +dat* on); **sich** (*dat*) **über etw** (*acc*) ~ **werden** to agree on sth; **wir werden schon miteinander ~ werden** we will manage to come to an agreement; **ich bin mir selbst noch nicht ganz ~, was ...** I am still somewhat undecided as to what ...

einige ['ainɪɡə] INDEF PRON = **einige(r, s)**

einigeln ['ainiːɡln] VR SEP (*fig*) to hide (oneself) away

einigemal ['ainiɡəmaːl] ADV *siehe* **einige(r, s)**

einigen ['ainɪɡn] ■ VT *Volk etc* to unite; *Streitende* to reconcile ■ VR to reach (an) agreement (*über +acc* about); **sich auf einen Kompromiss/Vergleich ~** to agree to a compromise/ settlement; **sich dahin (gehend) ~, dass ...** to agree that ...

einige(r, s) ['ainɪɡə] INDEF PRON (a) SING (= *etwas*) some; (= *ziemlich viel*) (quite) some; **nach ~r Zeit** after a while; **ich könnte dir ~s über ihn erzählen, was ...** I could tell you a thing or two about him that ...; **das wird ~s kosten** that will cost something; **dazu ist noch ~s zu sagen** there are still one or two things to say about that; **dazu gehört schon ~s** that really takes something; **dazu gehört schon ~ Frechheit/~r Mut** that takes some nerve/some courage (b) PL some; (= *mehrere*) several; (= *ein paar*) a few, some; **mit ~n anderen** with several/a few others; (= *wenige*) a few; ~ **Mal(e)** a few times; ~ **hundert** or **Hundert Menschen** a few hundred people; ~ **hunderte** or **Hunderte von Flaschen** several hundred bottles; **an ~n Stellen** in some places; **in ~n Tagen** in a few days

einigermaßen ['ainiɡə'maːsn] ■ ADV (= *ziemlich*) rather; (*vor adj*) fairly; (= *ungefähr*) to some extent; ~ **Bescheid wissen** to have a fair idea; **er hat die Prüfung so ~ geschafft** he did so-so in (*Brit*) or on (*US*) the exam; **wie gehts dir?** – ~ how are you? – all right ■ ADJ PRED (*inf*: = *leidlich*) all right

einiges ['ainɪɡəs] INDEF PRON = **einige(r, s)**

Einigkeit F ~, NO PL (= *Eintracht*) unity; (= *Übereinstimmung*) agreement; **in diesem** or **über diesen Punkt herrschte** or **bestand** ~ there was agreement on this point; ~ **macht stark** (*Prov*) strength through unity (*prov*)

Einigung F ~, **-en (a)** (*Pol*) unification (b) (= *Übereinstimmung*) agreement; (*Jur*: = *Vergleich*) settlement; **über etw** (*acc*) ~ **erzielen** to come to an agreement on sth

einjagen VT SEP **jdm Furcht ~** to frighten sb; **jdm einen Schrecken ~** to give sb a fright

einjährig ADJ *Kind, Tier* one-year-old; *Pflanze* annual; *Amtszeit, Studium* one-year *attr*; **nach ~er Pause** after a break of one year

einkalkulieren *ptp* **einkalkuliert** VT SEP to reckon with; *Kosten* to include

Einkammersystem NT (*Pol*) single-chamber system

Einkauf M (a) (= *das Einkaufen*) buying (*auch Comm*), purchase; **Einkäufe machen** to go shopping; **ich muss noch ein paar Einkäufe machen** I still have a few things to buy (b) (*usu pl*: = *Gekauftes*) purchase; **ein guter** or **vorteilhafter/ schlechter** ~ a good/bad buy; **sie packte ihre Einkäufe aus** she unpacked her shopping (c) NO PL (*Comm*: = *Abteilung*) buying (department)

einkaufen SEP ■ VT to buy ■ VI to shop; (*Comm*) to buy; ~ **gehen** to go shopping ■ VR to buy one's way (*in +acc* into)

Einkäufer(in) M(F) (*Comm*) buyer

Einkaufs- IN CPDS shopping; **Einkaufsabteilung** F purchasing department; **Einkaufsbummel** M shopping spree; **einen ~ machen** to go on a shopping spree; **Einkaufsleiter(in)** M(F) (*Comm*) chief buyer; **Einkaufsnetz** NT string bag; **Einkaufspassage** F shopping arcade; **Einkaufstasche** F shopping bag; **Einkaufswagen** M shopping trolley (*Brit*) or cart (*US*); **Einkaufszentrum** NT shopping centre (*Brit*) or center (*US*)

einkehren VI SEP AUX SEIN (a) (*in Gasthof*) to stop off (*in +dat* at) (b) (*Ruhe, Friede*) to come (*bei* to); **wieder ~** to return (*bei* to)

einkeilen VT SEP to hem in; *Mensch auch, Auto* (*fig*) to box in; *siehe auch* **eingekeilt**

einkerben VT SEP to notch; (= *schnitzen*) to cut

einkesseln ['ainkɛsln] VT SEP to encircle

einklagbar ADJ *Schulden* (legally) recoverable; *Anspruch, Recht* (legally) enforceable

einklagen VT SEP *Schulden* to sue for (the recovery of); *Anspruch, Recht* to take legal action to enforce

einklammern VT SEP to put in brackets or parentheses; (*fig*) *Thema, Frage* to leave aside

Einklang M (a) (*Mus*) unison (b) (*geh*: = *Übereinstimmung*) harmony; **in ~ bringen** to bring into line; **in** or **im ~ mit etw stehen** to be in accord with sth

einkleben VT SEP to stick in (*in +acc* -to)

einkleiden VT SEP *Soldaten* to fit out (with a uniform); (*fig*) *Gedanken* to couch; **jdn/sich völlig neu ~** to buy sb/oneself a completely new wardrobe

einklemmen VT SEP (= *quetschen*) to jam; *Finger etc* to catch; **er hat sich/mir die Hand in der Tür eingeklemmt** he caught his/ my hand in the door; **der Fahrer war hinter dem Steuer eingeklemmt** the driver was pinned behind the wheel

einknicken SEP ■ VT *Papier* to crease (over); *Streichholz, Äste* to snap ■ VI AUX SEIN (*Strohhalm*) to get bent; (*Äste*) to snap; (*Knie*) to give way; (*fig*: = *umfallen*) to give way; **mein Knöchel** or **Fuß knickt dauernd ein** I'm always going over on my ankle (*Brit*), I'm always turning my ankle (*esp US*)

einknöpfbar ADJ *Futter* attachable

einknöpfen VT SEP *Futter* to button in

einknüppeln VI SEP **auf jdn ~** to beat sb (up) with cudgels; (*Polizei*) to beat sb (up) with truncheons; (*fig*) to lash sb

einkochen SEP ■ VT *Gemüse* to preserve; *Marmelade* to make ■ VI AUX SEIN (*Marmelade etc*) to boil down; (*Wasser*) to boil away; (*Soße*) to thicken

Einkommen ['ainkɔmən] NT **-s,** - income

Einkommens-: **Einkommensausfall** M loss of income *no pl*; **Einkommenseinbuße** F USU PL loss of income *no pl*; **Einkommensgefälle** NT income differential; **Einkommensklasse** F income bracket; **einkommensschwach** ADJ low-income *attr*; **einkommensstark** ADJ high-income *attr*; **die Einkommensstarken** people in a high-income bracket

Einkommen(s)steuer F income tax

Einkommen(s)steuer-: **Einkommen(s)steuererklärung** F income tax return; **einkommen(s)steuerpflichtig** [-pflɪçtɪç] ADJ liable to income tax

einkreisen VT SEP *Feind, Wild* to surround; (*fig*) *Frage, Problem* to consider from all sides; (*Pol*) to isolate

einkremen VT SEP = **eincremen**

einkriegen SEP (*inf*) ■ VT to catch up ■ VR **sie konnte sich gar nicht mehr darüber ~, wie/dass ...** she couldn't get over how/ the fact that ...

Einkünfte ['ainkynftə] PL income *sing*

einladen VT SEP IRREG (a) *Waren* to load (*in +acc* into) (b) *jdn* to invite; **jdn zu einer Party ~** to invite sb to a party; **jdn ins Kino ~** to ask sb to the cinema; **jdn auf ein Bier ~** to invite sb for a beer; **lass mal, ich lade dich ein** come on, this one's on me; **er traut sich nicht, das Mädchen einzuladen** he doesn't dare ask the girl out; **dieses hübsche Plätzchen lädt**

zum Bleiben ein it's very tempting to linger in this pretty spot; **das lädt ja geradezu zum Stehlen/Einbrechen ein** that's asking to be stolen/broken into **(c)** (Sw) = **auffordern**

einladend ADJ inviting; Speisen appetizing

Einladung F **(a)** invitation; **einer ~ Folge leisten** (form) to accept an invitation; **eine ~ aussprechen** (sl: = aufs Klo gehen) to go for a Jimmy (Brit) or Jerry (US) Riddle (sl) **(b)** (Sw) = **Aufforderung**

Einladungs-: Einladungskarte F invitation (card); **Einladungsschreiben** NT (official) invitation

Einlage F **(a)** (= Zahneinlage) temporary filling **(b)** (= Schuheinlage) insole; (zum Stützen) (arch) support **(c)** (Cook) noodles, vegetables, egg etc added to a clear soup **(d)** (= Zwischenspiel) interlude **(e)** (Fin: = Kapitaleinlage) investment

Einlagen- (Fin): **Einlagensicherung** F protection for savers; **Einlagenzertifikat** NT certificate of deposit

einlagern VT SEP to store

Einlass ['aɪnlas] M **-es,** ⸚e [-lɛsə] **(a)** NO PL (= Zutritt) admission; **jdm ~ gewähren** to admit sb; **sich** (dat) **~ in etw** (acc) **verschaffen** to gain entry to sth **(b)** (Tech: = Öffnung) inlet

einlassen SEP IRREG ■ VT **(a)** (= eintreten lassen) to let in **(b)** (= einlaufen lassen) Wasser to run (in +acc into); **er ließ sich** (dat) **ein Bad ein** he ran himself a bath **(c)** (= einpassen, einfügen) to let in (in +acc -to); **eingelassene Schraube** countersunk screw **(d)** (Aus) Boden, Möbel to varnish ■ VR **sich auf etw** (acc) **~** to get involved in sth; (= sich zu etw verpflichten) to let oneself in for sth; **sich auf einen Kompromiss ~** to agree to a compromise; **ich lasse mich auf keine Diskussion ein** I'm not having any discussion about it; **darauf lasse ich mich nicht ein!** (bei Geschäft, Angelegenheit) I don't want anything to do with it; (bei Kompromiss, Handel etc) I'm not agreeing to that; **da habe ich mich aber auf etwas eingelassen!** I've let myself in for something there!; **sich mit jdm ~** (pej) to get involved with sb; **sie lässt sich mit jedem ein!** she'll go with anyone

Einlauf M **(a)** NO PL (Sport) (am Ziel) finish; (ins Stadion etc) entry; **beim ~ in die Zielgerade ...** coming into the final straight ... **(b)** (Med) enema; **jdm einen ~ machen** to give sb an enema

einlaufen SEP IRREG ■ VI AUX SEIN **(a)** (= hineinlaufen) to come in (in +acc -to); (durchs Ziel) to finish; **das Schiff läuft (in den Hafen) ein** the ship is coming into the harbour (Brit) or harbor (US) **(b)** (= hineinlaufen: Wasser) to run in (in +acc -to) **(c)** (= eingehen: Stoff) to shrink; **garantiert kein Einlaufen** guaranteed non-shrink ■ VT Schuhe to wear in ■ VR (Sport) to warm up

einläuten VT SEP Sonntag etc to ring in; (Sport) Runde to sound the bell for; (fig) Revolution to herald the start of; Wende to usher in

einleben VR SEP to settle down (in or an +dat in)

Einlegearbeit F inlay work no pl

einlegen VT SEP **(a)** (in Holz etc) to inlay; **eingelegte Arbeit** inlay work **(b)** (= hineintun) to insert (in +acc in); Film to load (in +acc into); **einen Pfeil (in den Bogen) ~** to fit an arrow (into the bow) **(c)** Sonderschicht, Spurt, Sonderzug to put on; Lied, Kunststück, Pause to have; (Aut) Gang to engage **(d)** (fig: = geltend machen) Protest to register; **ein gutes Wort für jdn ~** to put in a good word for sb (bei with); **sein Veto ~** to exercise one's veto **(e)** (Cook) Heringe, Gurken etc to pickle

Einlegesohle F insole

einleiten SEP ■ VT **(a)** (= in Gang setzen) to initiate; Maßnahmen, Schritte to introduce; neues Zeitalter to inaugurate; (Jur) Verfahren to institute; (Med) Geburt to induce **(b)** (= beginnen) to start; (= eröffnen) to open **(c)** Buch (durch Vorwort) to write an introduction to; (Mus) to prelude **(d)** Abwässer etc to discharge (in +acc into) ■ VI to give an introduction (in +acc to)

einleitend ■ ADJ introductory ■ ADV **er sagte ~, dass ...** he said by way of introduction that ...

Einleitung F **(a)** (= Vorwort) introduction; (Mus) prelude **(b)** (= das Einleiten) initiation; (von Maßnahmen auch, von Schritten) introduction; (von neuem Zeitalter) inauguration; (von Verfahren) institution; (von Geburt) induction **(c)** (von Abwässern) discharge (in +acc into)

einlenken VI SEP (= nachgeben) to yield; **jdn zum Einlenken bewegen** to get sb to change his/her mind

einlesen SEP IRREG ■ VR **sich in ein Buch/Gebiet** etc **~** to get into a book/subject etc ■ VT Daten to read in (in +acc -to)

einleuchten VI SEP to be clear (jdm to sb); **der Grund seiner Abneigung leuchtet mir nicht ein** I don't understand why he doesn't like me; **ja, das leuchtet mir ein!** yes, I see that; **das will mir nicht ~** I just don't understand that

einleuchtend ADJ reasonable

einliefern VT SEP Waren to deliver; **jdn ins Krankenhaus ~** to admit sb to hospital

Einlieferungsschein M certificate of posting (Brit) or mailing (esp US)

einloggen ['aɪnlɔgn] VR (Comput) to log in; **sich in das System ~** to log into the system

einlösen VT SEP Pfand to redeem; Scheck, Wechsel to cash (in); (fig) Wort, Versprechen to keep

Einlösung F (von Pfand) redemption; (von Scheck, Wechsel) cashing (in); (von Wort, Versprechen) keeping

einlullen ['aɪnlʊlən] VT SEP (inf) Misstrauen, Wachsamkeit to allay; **jdn mit Versprechungen/schönen Worten ~** to lull sb with promises/soft words

einmachen VT SEP Obst, Gemüse to preserve; (in Gläser auch) to bottle; (in Dosen) to can

Einmach-: Einmachglas NT bottling jar; **Einmachtopf** M preserving pan; **Einmachzucker** M preserving sugar

einmal ['aɪnmaːl] ADV **(a)** (= ein einziges Mal) once; (= erstens) first of all, for a start; **~ eins ist eins** one times one is one; **~ sagt er dies, ~ das** sometimes he says one thing, sometimes another; **~ sagte sie, wir sollten bleiben, ~ wir sollten gehen** first of all she says that we should stay, then that we should go; **auf ~** (= plötzlich) suddenly; (= zugleich) at once; **~ mehr** once again; **~ und nicht or nie wieder** once and never again; **noch ~** again; **noch ~ so groß wie** as big again as; **wenn sie da ist, ist es noch ~ so schön** it's twice as nice when she's there; **~ ist keinmal** (Prov) (= schadet nicht) once won't hurt or do any harm; (= zählt nicht) once doesn't count **(b)** (= früher, vorher) once; (= später, in Zukunft) one day; **waren Sie schon ~ in Rom?** have you ever been to Rome?; **er hat schon ~ bessere Zeiten gesehen** he has seen better days; **es war ~ ...** once upon a time there was ...; **das war ~!** that was then; **besuchen Sie mich doch ~!** come and visit me some time! **(c)** (verstärkend, eingrenzend: meist nicht übersetzt) **nicht ~** not even; **auch ~** also, too; **wieder ~** again; **ich bin/die Frauen sind nun ~ so** that's the way I am/women are; **wenn er nun ~ hier ist ...** seeing he's here ...; **alle ~ herhören!** listen everyone!; **sag ~, ist das wahr?** tell me, is it true?

Einmaleins [aɪnmaːlˈʔaɪns] NT **-,** NO PL (multiplication) tables pl; (fig) ABC, basics pl; **das kleine/große ~** (multiplication) tables up to/over ten

Einmalhandtuch NT disposable towel

einmalig ['aɪnmaːlɪç, (emph) ˈaɪnˈmaːlɪç] ■ ADJ **(a)** Gelegenheit, Angebot, Fall, Leistung unique **(b)** (= nur einmal erforderlich) single; Anschaffung, Zahlung one-off attr; **beim ~en Durchlesen des Textes** on reading the text through once **(c)** (inf: = hervorragend) fantastic; **dieser Film ist etwas Einmaliges** this film is really something (inf) ■ ADV (inf: = besonders) absolutely; **~ gut/schlecht** incredibly good/bad

Einmalspritze F = **Einwegspritze**

Einmarsch M entry (in +acc into); (in ein Land) invasion (in +acc of)

einmarschieren ptp **einmarschiert** VI SEP AUX SEIN to march in (in +acc -to)

einmassieren ptp **einmassiert** VT SEP to massage in (in +acc -to)

einmauern VT SEP **(a)** (= ummauern) to wall in (in +acc in) **(b)** (= einfügen) to fix into the wall

einmeißeln VT SEP to chisel in (in +acc -to)

Einmeterbrett [aɪnˈmeːtə-] NT one-metre (Brit) or one-meter (US) (diving) board

einmischen VR SEP to interfere (*in +acc* in); **wenn ich mich kurz ~ darf ...** if I can butt in a moment ...

Einmischung F interference (*in +acc* in)

einmonatig ADJ ATTR one-month

einmonatlich ADJ monthly

einmontieren *ptp* **einmontiert** VT SEP (*Tech*) to fit in (*in +acc -to*)

einmotorig ADJ *Flugzeug* single-engine(d)

einmotten ['ainmɔtn] VT SEP to mothball

einmummeln ['ainmʊmln], **einmummen** ['ainmʊmən] VT SEP (*inf*) to muffle up

einmünden VI SEP AUX SEIN (*Fluss*) to flow in (*in +acc -to*); (*Straße*) to run in (*in +acc -to*); **in etw** (*acc*) ~ to join sth; (*fig*) to end up in sth; (*Elemente, Einflüsse*) to go into sth

Einmündung F (*von Fluss*) confluence; (*von Straße*) junction; **die ~ der Isar in die Donau** the confluence of the Isar and the Danube

einmütig ['ainmy:tɪç] **1** ADJ unanimous **2** ADV unanimously; **~ zusammenstehen** to stand together as one

Einmütigkeit F -, NO PL unanimity; **darüber besteht ~** there is complete agreement on that

einnachten ['ainnaxtn] VI IMPERS SEP (*Sw*) **es nachtet ein** it's getting dark

Einnahme ['ainna:mə] F -, -n (a) (*Mil*) seizure (b) (= *Ertrag*) receipt **Einnahmen** PL income *sing*; (= *Geschäftseinnahme*) takings *pl*; (*aus Einzelverkauf*) proceeds *pl*; (= *Gewinn*) earnings *pl*; (*eines Staates*) revenue *sing*; **~n und Ausgaben** income and expenditure (c) (= *das Einnehmen*) taking; **durch ~ von etw** by taking sth

Einnahmequelle F source of income; (*eines Staates*) source of revenue

einnehmen VT SEP IRREG (a) *Geld* (*Geschäft etc*) to take; (*Freiberufler*) to earn; *Steuern* to collect; **die eingenommenen Gelder** the takings (b) (*Mil*: = *erobern*) to take (c) (*lit, fig*) *Platz etc* to take (up); *Stelle* (= *innehaben*) to have; *Haltung, Standpunkt etc* to take up; **bitte, nehmen Sie Ihre Plätze ein!** (*form*) please take your seats!; **die Plätze ~** (*Sport*) to take one's marks (d) (= *zu sich nehmen*) *Mahlzeit, Arznei* to take (e) (= *beeinflussen*) **er nahm uns alle für sich ein** he won us all over; **er hat alle für seine Pläne eingenommen** he won everyone over to his plans; **jdn gegen sich/jdn/etw ~** to set sb against oneself/sb/sth; **das nimmt mich sehr für sie ein** that makes me think highly of her; *siehe auch* **eingenommen**

einnisten VR SEP (*lit*) to nest; (*Parasiten, Ei*) to lodge; (*fig*) to park oneself (*bei* on)

Einödbauer M, *pl* **-bauern**, **Einödbäuerin** F farmer of an isolated farm

Einöde ['ainø:də] F *Moore und* ~ moors and wasteland; **Wüsten und ~** deserts and barren wastes *pl*; **die weiße ~ der Antarktis** the white wastes of the Antarctic; **er lebt in der ~ des schottischen Hochlands** he lives in the wilds of the Scottish Highlands

Einödhof M ≈ croft

einölen VT SEP to oil

einordnen SEP **1** VT (a) (*der Reihe nach*) *Bücher etc* to (put in) order; *Akten, Karteikarten* to file (b) (= *klassifizieren*) to classify **2** VR (a) (*in Gemeinschaft etc*) to fit in (*in +acc -to*) (b) (*Aut*) to get in(to) lane; **sich links/rechts ~** to get into the left/right lane

einpacken SEP **1** VT (a) (= *einwickeln*) to wrap (up) (*in +acc* in); **jdn warm ~** (*fig*) to wrap sb up warmly (b) (= *hineintun*) to pack (*in +acc* in) **2** VI to pack; **dann können wir ~** (*inf*) in that case we may as well pack it all in (*inf*)

einparken VTI SEP to park; (**in eine Parklücke**) ~ to get into a parking space

Einparteien- [ainpar'taiən] IN CPDS one-party;

einpassen VT SEP to fit in (*in +acc -to*)

Einpeitscher ['ainpaitʃɐ] M -s, -, **Einpeitscherin** [-ərɪn] F -, -nen (*Pol*) whip (*Brit*), floor leader (*US*)

einpendeln VR SEP (*fig*) to settle down

einpennen VI SEP AUX SEIN (*sl*) to drop off (*inf*)

Einpersonen- [ainpɛr'zo:nən-]: **Einpersonenhaushalt** M single-person household; **Einpersonenstück** NT (*Theat*) one-man play

einpflanzen VT SEP to plant (*in +dat* in); (*Med*) to implant (*jdm* in(to) sb); **jdm eine fremde Niere ~** to give sb a kidney transplant

einphasig ADJ single-phase

einpinseln VT SEP to paint; (*Cook*) to brush

einplanen VT SEP to plan (on); *Verzögerungen, Verluste* to allow for; *Baby* to plan

einpolig ['ainpo:lɪç] ADJ single-pole

einprägen SEP **1** VT *Inschrift* to stamp; **ein Muster in Papier ~** to emboss paper with a pattern; **sich** (*dat*) **etw ~** (= *auswendig lernen*) to memorize sth **2** VR **sich jdm ins Gedächtnis ~** to make an impression on sb's mind; **sich jdm ~** to make an impression on sb; **die Worte haben sich mir unauslöschlich eingeprägt** the words made an indelible impression on me

einprägsam ['ainprɛ:kza:m] **1** ADJ catchy **2** ADV **er kann sehr ~ formulieren** he can put things in a way that is easy to remember

einprogrammieren *ptp* **einprogrammiert** VT SEP *Daten* to feed in; (*fig*) to take into account; **jdm etw ~** (*fig*) to inculcate sth in sb

einprügeln SEP (*inf*) **1** VT **jdm etw ~** to drum sth into sb **2** VI **auf jdn ~** to lay into sb

einpudern SEP **1** VR to powder oneself **2** VT to powder

einquartieren ['ainkvarti:rən], *ptp* **einquartiert** SEP **1** VT to quarter; **Gäste bei Freunden ~** to put visitors up with friends **2** VR to be quartered (*bei* with); (*Gäste*) to stop (*bei* with); (*inf*) **er hat sich bei uns anscheinend für ewig einquartiert** he seems to have dumped himself on us for good (*inf*)

einquetschen VT SEP = **einklemmen**

einrahmen VT SEP (*lit, fig*) to frame; **von zwei Schönen eingerahmt** with a beauty on either side

einrasten VTI SEP (VI: AUX SEIN) to engage

einräuchern VT SEP (a) (= *in Rauch hüllen*) to envelop in smoke; **die Polizei räucherte die Demonstranten mit Tränengas ein** the police used tear gas against the demonstrators (b) (*inf*) *Zimmer* to fill with smoke

einräumen VT SEP (a) *Wäsche, Bücher etc* to put away; *Schrank, Regal etc* to fill; *Wohnung, Zimmer* to arrange; *Möbel* to move in (*in +acc -to*); **Bücher ins Regal ~** to put books on the shelf; **er war mir beim Einräumen behilflich** he helped me sort things out; (*der Wohnung*) he helped me move in (b) (= *zugestehen*) to concede; *Freiheiten etc* to allow; *Frist, Kredit, Recht* to give

einrechnen VT SEP to include; **ihn (mit) eingerechnet** including him; **Mehrwertsteuer eingerechnet** including VAT

einreden SEP **1** VT **jdm etw ~** to talk sb into believing sth; **das lasse ich mir nicht ~** you're not going to make me believe that; **wer hat dir denn diesen Unsinn eingeredet?** who put that nonsense into your head?; **er will mir ~, dass ...** he wants me to believe that ...; **sich** (*dat*) **etw ~** to make oneself believe sth; **das redest du dir nur ein!** you're only imagining it **2** VI **auf jdn ~** to keep on and on at sb

einreiben VT SEP IRREG **er rieb sich** (*dat*) **das Gesicht mit Schnee/Creme ein** he rubbed snow over/cream into his face

einreichen VT SEP (a) *Antrag, Unterlagen* to submit (*bei* to); (*Jur*) *Klage* to file (b) (= *bitten um*) to apply for

Einreichung ['ainraiçʊŋ] F -, (*rare*) -en (*von Antrag, Unterlagen*) submission; (*Jur. von Klage*) filing

einreihen SEP **1** VT (= *einordnen, einfügen*) to put in (*in +acc -to*); (= *klassifizieren*) to class **2** VR **sich in etw** (*acc*) ~ to join sth

Einreiher ['ainraiɐ] M -s, - (= *Anzug*) single-breasted suit; (= *Jackett*) single-breasted jacket

Einreise F entry (*in +acc* into, to); **bei der ~ in die Schweiz** when entering Switzerland

Einreise-: **Einreiseformular** NT form for entry into the country; **Einreisegenehmigung** F entry permit

einreisen VI SEP AUX SEIN to enter the country; **er reiste in die Schweiz ein** he entered Switzerland; **ein- und ausreisen** to enter and leave the country

Einreise-: **Einreiseverbot** NT refusal of entry; **~ haben** to have been refused entry; **Einreisevisum** NT entry visa

einreißen SEP IRREG **1** VT **(a)** *Papier, Stoff, Nagel* to tear **(b)** *Gebäude, Zaun, Barrikaden* to tear down **2** VI AUX SEIN (*Papier*) to tear; (*fig inf: Unsitte etc*) to catch on (*inf*)

einreiten SEP IRREG **1** VT *Pferd* to break in **2** VI AUX SEIN (*in die Manege etc*) to ride in (*in +acc* -to)

einrenken ['ainrɛŋkn] SEP **1** VT *Gelenk, Knie* to put back in place; (*fig inf*) to sort out **2** VR (*fig inf*) to sort itself out

einrichten SEP **1** VT **(a)** (= *möblieren*) to furnish; (= *ausstatten*) to fit out; **ein Haus antik/modern ~** to furnish a house in an old/a modern style; **sein Haus neu ~** to refurnish one's house; **Wohnungen im Dachgeschoss ~** to convert the attic into flats (*Brit*) *or* apartments **(b)** (= *gründen, eröffnen*) to set up; *Lehrstuhl* to establish; *Konto* to open; *Buslinie etc* to start **(c)** (*fig: = arrangieren*) to arrange; **ich werde es ~, dass wir um zwei Uhr da sind** I'll see to it that we're there at two; **das lässt sich ~** that can be arranged; **auf Tourismus eingerichtet sein** to be geared to tourism; **auf warme Speisen eingerichtet sein** to be equipped for hot meals **2** VR **(a)** (= *sich möblieren*) **sich ~/neu ~** to furnish/refurnish one's house/one's flat (*Brit*) *or* apartment **(b)** (= *sich der Lage anpassen*) to get along; (= *sparsam sein*) to cut down; **er hat sich im bürgerlichen Leben eingerichtet** he has settled down into middle-class life **(c)** (= *sich einstellen*) **sich auf etw** (*acc*) **~** to prepare oneself for sth; **sich auf eine lange Wartezeit ~** to be prepared for a long wait

Einrichtung F **(a)** (= *das Einrichten*) furnishing; (*von Hobbyraum, Spielzimmer, Labor, Praxis*) equipping **(b)** (= *Wohnungseinrichtung*) furnishings *pl*; (= *Geschäftseinrichtung etc*) fittings *pl*; (= *Laboreinrichtung etc*) equipment *no pl* **(c)** (= *Gründung, Eröffnung*) setting-up; (*von Lehrstuhl*) establishment; (*von Konto*) opening; (*von Katalog, Busverkehr*) starting **(d)** (*behördlich, wohltätig*) institution; (= *Schwimmbäder, Transportmittel etc*) facility

Einrichtungsgegenstand M item of furniture; (= *Geschäftseinrichtung*) fixture

Einritt M entry (*in +acc* into)

einritzen VT SEP to carve in (*in +acc* -to)

einrollen VR SEP to roll up

einrosten VI SEP AUX SEIN to rust up; (*fig: Glieder*) to stiffen up; **mein Latein ist ziemlich eingerostet** my Latin has got pretty rusty

einrücken SEP **1** VT *Zeile* to indent; *Anzeige* (*in Zeitung*) to insert **2** VI AUX SEIN (*Mil*) **(a)** (*in ein Land*) to move in (*in +acc* -to) **(b)** (= *eingezogen werden*) to report for duty; (*nach Urlaub etc*) to report back

einrühren VT SEP to stir in (*in +acc* -to); (*Cook*) *Ei* to beat in (*in +acc* -to)

eins [ains] NUM one; **es ist/schlägt ~** it's one/just striking one (o'clock); **um ~** at one (o'clock); **gegen ~** at around one (o'clock); **~, zwei, drei** (*lit*) one, two, three; (*fig*) in an instant; **~ zu ~** (*Sport*) one all; **~ mit jdm sein** to be one with sb; (= *übereinstimmen*) to be in agreement with sb; **das ist doch alles ~** (*inf*) it's all one; **sehen und handeln waren ~** to see was to act; **~ a** (*inf*) A 1 (*inf*), first-rate (*inf*); *siehe auch* **ein²**, **eine(r, s)**, **vier**

Eins [ains] F **-, -en** one; (*Sch auch*) A; **eine ~ schreiben/ bekommen** to get an A or a one; *siehe auch* **Vier**

einsacken¹ VT SEP **(a)** (= *in Säcke füllen*) to put in sacks **(b)** (*inf*) (= *erbeuten*) to grab (*inf*); *Geld, Gewinne* to rake in (*inf*)

einsacken² VI SEP AUX SEIN (= *einsinken*) to sink

einsalben VT SEP to rub with ointment

einsalzen VT SEP IRREG *Fisch, Fleisch* to salt

einsam ['ainzaːm] **1** ADJ **(a)** (= *allein, verlassen*) lonely; (= *einzeln*) solitary; **um sie wird es ~** she is becoming a lonely figure **(b)** (= *abgelegen*) *Haus, Insel* secluded; *Dorf* isolated; (= *menschenleer*) empty; *Strände* lonely **(c)** (*inf.: = hervorragend*) **~e Klasse** *or* **Spitze** absolutely fantastic (*inf*) **2** ADV **(a)** (= *allein*) lonely; **~ leben** to live a lonely/solitary life; **~ überragt dieser Gipfel die anderen** this peak towers over the others in solitary grandeur **(b)** (= *abgelegen*) isolated; **~ liegen** to be secluded/isolated

Einsamkeit F **-**, NO PL **(a)** (= *Verlassenheit*) loneliness; (= *das Einzelnsein*) solitariness; **er liebt die ~** he likes solitude **(b)** (= *Abgelegenheit*) (*von Haus, Insel*) seclusion; (*von Dorf*) isolation; (= *Menschenleere*) emptiness; (*von Strand*) loneliness; **die ~ der Bergwelt** the solitude of the mountains

einsammeln VT SEP to collect (in); *Obst* to gather (in)

Einsatz M **(a)** (= *~teil*) inset; (= *Schubladeneinsatz, Koffereinsatz*) tray; (= *Topfeinsatz*) compartment **(b)** (= *Spieleinsatz*) stake; (= *Kapitaleinsatz*) investment; **den ~ erhöhen** to raise the stakes **(c)** (*Mus*) entry; **der Dirigent gab den ~** the conductor raised his baton and brought in the orchestra/solist *etc*; **der Dirigent gab den Geigern den ~** the conductor brought in the violins; **der ~ der Streicher war verfrüht** the strings came in too early **(d)** (= *Verwendung*) use; (*esp Mil*) deployment; (*von Arbeitskräften*) employment; **im ~** in use; **die Ersatzspieler kamen nicht zum ~** the substitutes weren't put on; **unter ~ von Schlagstöcken** using truncheons; **unter ~ aller Kräfte** by making a supreme effort **(e)** (= *Aktion*) (*Mil*) action, operation; (*von Polizei, Feuerwehr*) operation; **im ~** in action; **wo war er im ~?** where did he see action?; **bei seinem ersten ~** the first time he went into action **(f)** (= *Hingabe*) commitment; **in selbstlosem ~ ihres Lebens** with a complete disregard for her own life; **etw unter ~ seines Lebens tun** to risk one's life to do sth

Einsatz-: Einsatzbefehl M order to go into action; **einsatzbereit** ADJ ready for use; (*Mil*) ready for action; *Rakete etc* operational; **Einsatzbereitschaft** F readiness for use; (*Mil*) readiness for action; (= *Bereitschaftsdienst*) stand-by (duty); **Einsatzfahrzeug** NT = **Einsatzwagen**; **Einsatzleiter(in)** M(F) head of operations; **Einsatzwagen** M (*von Polizei*) police car; (*von Feuerwehr*) fire engine; (= *Krankenwagen*) ambulance; (= *Straßenbahn/Bus*) extra tram (*esp Brit*) *or* streetcar (*US*)/bus

einscannen VT SEP to scan in

einschalten SEP **1** VT **(a)** *Licht, Radio, Gerät* to switch on; *Sender* to tune in to **(b)** (= *einfügen*) to interpolate **(c)** *jdn ~* to call sb in; **jdn in etw** (*acc*) **~** to bring sb in on sth **2** VR to intervene; (= *teilnehmen*) to join in; **wir schalten uns jetzt in die Sendungen von Radio Bremen ein** we now go over to Radio Bremen

Einschaltquote F (*Rad, TV*) viewing figures *pl*

einschärfen VT SEP **jdm etw ~** to impress sth (up)on sb; *Höflichkeit, Rücksichtnahme etc* to inculcate sth in sb; **er hat uns Vorsicht eingeschärft** he impressed on us the need for caution; **schärf dir das ein!** get that firmly fixed in your mind

einschätzen VT SEP to assess (*auch Fin*), to evaluate; **falsch ~** to misjudge; (= *falsch schätzen*) to miscalculate; **wie ich die Lage einschätze** as I see the situation; **etw zu hoch/niedrig ~** to overestimate/underestimate sth

Einschätzung F assessment (*auch Fin*), evaluation; **falsche ~** misjudgement; (= *falsche Schätzung*) miscalculation; **nach meiner ~** in my estimation

einschenken VT SEP to pour (out); **darf ich Ihnen noch Wein ~?** can I give you some more wine?

einschicken VT SEP to send in (*an +acc* to)

einschieben VT SEP IRREG **(a)** (= *hineinschieben*) to put in (*in +acc* -to) **(b)** (= *einfügen*) to put in; *Diskussion, Schüler, Patienten* to fit in (*in +acc* -to); **eine Pause ~** to have a break

einschießen SEP IRREG **1** VT **(a)** (= *zertrümmern*) *Fenster* to shoot in; (*mit Ball etc*) to smash in; **(b)** *Gewehr* to try out and adjust **(c)** (*Fußball*) to kick in; **Müller schoss den Ball zum 2:0 ein** Müller scored to make it 2-0 **(d)** (*Comm*) *Geld* to inject (*in +acc* into) **2** VR to find one's range; **sich auf ein Ziel ~** to get the range of a target; **sich auf jdn ~** (*fig*) to line sb up for the kill **3** VI **(a)** (*Sport*) to score; **er schoss zum 1:0 ein** he scored to make it 1-0 **(b)** AUX SEIN (*Med*) **die Milch schießt in die Brust ein** the milk comes in

einschiffen SEP **1** VT to ship **2** VR to embark; **er schiffte sich in London nach Amerika ein** he boarded a ship in London for America

einschl. ABBR *von* **einschließlich** incl

einschlafen VI SEP IRREG AUX SEIN to fall asleep; (*Bein, Arm*) to go to sleep; (*euph.* = *sterben*) to pass away; (*fig: Gewohnheit, Freundschaft*) to peter out; **ich kann nicht ~** I can't get to sleep; **bei** *or* **über seiner Arbeit ~** to fall asleep over one's work; **vor dem Einschlafen zu nehmen** *Medizin* to be taken before retiring

einschläfern ['ainʃlɛːfɐn] VT SEP (a) (= *zum Schlafen bringen*) to send to sleep; (= *schläfrig machen*) to make sleepy; (*fig*) *Gewissen* to soothe (b) (= *narkotisieren*) to give a soporific (c) (= *töten*) *Tier* to put down

einschläfernd ADJ soporific; (= *langweilig*) monotonous; **ein ~es Mittel** a soporific (drug)

Einschlafstörung F problem in getting to sleep

einschlagen SEP IRREG **1** VT (a) *Nagel* to hammer in; *Pfahl* to drive in
(b) (= *zertrümmern*) to smash (in); *Tür* to smash down; *Zähne* to knock out; **mit eingeschlagenem Schädel** with one's head bashed in (*inf*)
(c) (= *einwickeln*) *Ware* to wrap up; *Buch* to cover
(d) (*Aut*) *Räder* to turn
(e) (= *wählen*) *Weg* to take; *Kurs* (*lit*) to follow; (*fig*) to pursue; *Laufbahn etc* to enter on; **das Schiff änderte den eingeschlagenen Kurs** the ship changed from its previous course; **die Regierung schlägt einen weicheren/härteren Kurs ein** the government is taking a softer/harder line
2 VI (a) (**in etw** *acc*) **~** (*Blitz*) to strike (sth); (*Geschoss etc auch*) to hit (sth); **es muss irgendwo eingeschlagen haben** something must have been struck by lightning; **auf jdn/etw ~** to hit out at sb/sth; **gut ~** (*inf*) to be a big hit (*inf*)
(b) (*zur Bekräftigung*) to shake on it

einschlägig ['ainʃlɛːgɪç] **1** ADJ appropriate; *Literatur, Paragraf auch, Erfahrung* relevant **2** ADV **er ist ~ vorbestraft** (*Jur*) he has a previous conviction for a similar offence (*Brit*) or offense (*US*); **in der Drogenszene ~ bekannt** well-known especially on the drugs scene

einschleichen VR SEP IRREG to creep in (*in* +*acc* -to); **sich in jds Vertrauen ~** (*fig*) to worm one's way into sb's confidence

einschließen VT SEP IRREG (a) (= *wegschließen*) to lock up (*in* +*acc* in) (b) (= *umgeben*) to surround (c) (*fig:* = *beinhalten*) to include

einschließlich ['ainʃliːslɪç] **1** PREP +GEN including; **~ Porto** postage included; **Preis ~ Porto** price including postage **2** ADV **er hat das Buch bis S. 205 ~ gelesen** he has read up to and including p205; **vom 1. bis ~ 31. Oktober** *or* **bis 31. Oktober ~ geschlossen** closed from 1st to 31st October inclusive

einschmeicheln VR SEP **sich bei jdm ~** to ingratiate oneself with sb; **~de Musik** enticing music; **~de Stimme** silky voice

einschmieren VT SEP (*mit Fett*) to grease; (*mit Öl*) to oil; *Gesicht* (*mit Creme*) to put cream on; **er schmierte mir den Rücken mit Heilsalbe/Sonnenöl ein** he rubbed my back with ointment/suntan lotion

einschmuggeln VT SEP to smuggle in (*in* +*acc* -to); **er hat sich in den Saal eingeschmuggelt** he sneaked into the hall

einschnappen VI SEP AUX SEIN (a) (*Schloss, Tür*) to click shut (b) (*inf.* = *beleidigt sein*) to go into a huff (*inf*); *siehe auch* **eingeschnappt**

einschneiden SEP IRREG **1** VT *Stoff, Papier* to cut **2** VI to cut in (*in* +*acc* -to)

einschneidend ADJ (*fig*) drastic; *Bedeutung, Wirkung, Folgen* far-reaching

einschneien VI SEP AUX SEIN to get snowed up; **eingeschneit sein** to be snowed up

Einschnitt M cut; (*Med*) incision; (*im Tal, Gebirge*) cleft; (= *Zäsur*) break; (*im Leben*) decisive point

einschnüren SEP **1** VT (= *einengen*) to cut into; **dieser Kragen schnürt mir den Hals ein** this collar is nearly choking me **2** VR to lace oneself up

einschränken ['ainʃrɛŋkn] SEP **1** VT to reduce; *Bewegungsfreiheit, Recht* to restrict; *Wünsche* to moderate; *Behauptung* to qualify; **jdn in seinen Rechten ~** to restrict sb's rights; **~d möchte ich sagen, dass ...** I'd like to qualify that by saying ...; **das Rauchen/Trinken/Essen ~** to cut down on smoking/on drinking/on what one eats **2** VR (= *sparen*) to economize; *siehe auch* **eingeschränkt**

Einschränkung F **-, -en** (a) (= *das Einschränken*) reduction; (*von Bewegungsfreiheit, Recht*) restriction; (*von Wünschen*) moderation; (*von Behauptung*) qualification; (= *Vorbehalt*) reservation; **ohne ~** without reservation
(b) (= *Sparmaßnahme*) economy; (= *das Einsparen*) economizing

einschrauben VT SEP to screw in (*in* +*acc* to)

Einschreibe-: **Einschreibebrief** M recorded delivery (*Brit*) *or* certified (*US*) letter; **Einschreibegebühr** F (a) (*Univ*) registration fee (b) (*für Verein*) membership fee

einschreiben VR SEP IRREG (*in Verein, für Abendkurse etc*) to enrol (*Brit*), to enroll (*US*); (*Univ*) to register; **er schrieb sich in die Liste ein** he put his name on the list; *siehe auch* **eingeschrieben**

Einschreiben NT recorded delivery (*Brit*) *or* certified (*US*) letter/parcel (*Brit*) *or* package; **~ pl** recorded delivery (*Brit*) *or* certified (*US*) mail *sing*; **einen Brief als** *or* **per ~ schicken** to send a letter recorded delivery (*Brit*) *or* certified mail (*US*)

einschreiten VI SEP IRREG AUX SEIN to take action (*gegen* against); (= *dazwischentreten*) to intervene

Einschreiten NT **-s**, NO PL intervention

einschüchtern ['ainʃʏçtɐn] VT SEP to intimidate

Einschüchterungsversuch M attempt at intimidation

einschulen VT SEP **eingeschult werden** (*Kind*) to start school; **wir müssen unseren Sohn dieses Jahr ~** our son has to start school this year; **wir schulen dieses Jahr weniger Kinder ein** we have fewer children starting school this year

Einschulung F first day at school; **die ~ findet im Alter von 6 Jahren statt** children start school at the age of 6

Einschuss M (a) (= *~stelle*) bullet hole; (*Med*) point of entry (b) (*St Ex*) margin

einschwärzen VT SEP to blacken

einschweißen VT SEP (*Tech*) to weld in (*in* +*acc* -to); *Buch, Schallplatte* to shrink-wrap

Einschweißfolie F shrink-wrapping

einschwören VT SEP IRREG **jdn auf etw** (*acc*) **~** to swear sb to sth

einsegnen VT SEP (= *konfirmieren*) to confirm

Einsegnung F (= *Konfirmation*) confirmation

einsehbar ADJ (a) (= *verständlich*) understandable (b) *Akten, Dateien etc* accessible; *Straße, Kreuzung, Eingang* visible

einsehen SEP IRREG **1** VT (a) *Gelände* to see (b) (= *prüfen*) *Akte* to see (c) (= *verstehen, begreifen*) to see; *Fehler, Schuld auch* to recognize; **das sehe ich nicht ein** I don't see why; (= *verstehe ich nicht*) I don't see that; **es ist nicht einzusehen, warum/dass ...** it is incomprehensible why/that ... **2** VI (a) **in etw** (*acc*) **~** to see sth (b) (= *prüfen*) to look (*in* +*acc* at)

Einsehen NT **ein ~ haben** to have some understanding (*mit, für* for); (= *Vernunft, Einsicht*) to see reason; **hab doch ein ~!** be reasonable!; **hast du kein ~?** can't you see sense?

einseifen ['ainzaifn] VT SEP to soap; (*inf.* = *betrügen*) to con (*inf*); (*inf: mit Schnee*) to rub with snow

einseitig ['ainzaitɪç] **1** ADJ (a) on one side; (*Jur, Pol*) unilateral; **~e Lungenentzündung** single pneumonia; **~e Lähmung** paralysis of one side of the body
(b) *Freundschaft, Zuneigung, Ausbildung* one-sided; (= *parteiisch*) *Bericht, Standpunkt, Zeitung* biased; *Ernährung* unbalanced
2 ADV (a) (= *auf einer Seite*) on one side
(b) (= *unausgewogen*) **sich ~ ernähren** to have an unbalanced diet; **jdn ~ ausbilden** to give sb a one-sided education; **etw ~ schildern** to portray sth one-sidedly
(c) (= *parteiisch*) subjectively; **jdn ~ informieren** to give sb biased information

einsenden VT SEP IRREG to send in (*an* +*acc* to)

Einsender(in) M(F) sender; (*bei Preisausschreiben*) competitor; **wir bitten die ~ von Artikeln ...** we would ask those (people) who send in *or* submit articles ...

Einsendeschluss M closing date

Einsendung F (a) NO PL (= *das Einsenden*) submission (b) (= *das Eingesandte*) letter/article/manuscript *etc*; (*bei Preisausschreiben*) entry

einsetzen SEP **1** VT (a) (= *einfügen*) to put in (*in* +*acc* -to); *Stück Stoff* to let in (*in* +*acc* -to); (= *einschreiben*) to enter (*in* +*acc* in)
(b) (= *ernennen, bestimmen*) to appoint; *Ausschuss* to set up;

Erben, Nachfolger to name; **jdn in ein Amt ~** to appoint sb to an office

(c) (= *verwenden*) to use (*auch Sport*); *Truppen, Polizei, Feuerwehr* to deploy; *Busse, Sonderzüge* to put on

(d) (*beim Glücksspiel*) to stake; **seine ganze Kraft für etw ~** to devote all one's energies to sth

2 VI (= *beginnen*) to start; (*Mus*) to come in; (*am Anfang*) to start to play/sing; **die Ebbe/Flut setzt um 3 Uhr ein** the tide turns at 3 o'clock; **gegen Abend setzte stärkeres Fieber ein** the fever increased toward(s) evening

3 VR **sich (voll) ~** to show (complete) commitment (*in +dat* to); **die Mannschaft setzte sich bis an den Rand ihrer Kraft ein** the team did their absolute utmost; **sich für jdn ~** to fight for sb; (= *sich verwenden für*) to give sb one's support; **sie hat sich so sehr für ihn eingesetzt** she did so much for him; **sich für etw ~** to support sth; **ich werde mich dafür ~, dass ...** I will do what I can to see that ...

Einsicht F **(a)** (*in Akten, Bücher*) **~ in etw** (*acc*) **haben/nehmen/verlangen** to look/take a look/ask to look at sth; **sie legte ihm die Akte zur ~ vor** she gave him the file to look at **(b)** (= *Vernunft*) sense; (= *Erkenntnis*) insight; (= *Kenntnis*) knowledge; (= *Verständnis*) understanding; (*euph*: = *Reue*) remorse; **zur ~ kommen** to come to one's senses; **ich bin zu der ~ gekommen, dass ...** I have come to the conclusion that ...; **jdn zur ~ bringen** to bring sb to his/her senses; **er hat ~ in die internen Vorgänge der Firma** he has some knowledge of the internal affairs of the firm

einsichtig [ˈaɪnzɪçtɪç] ADJ **(a)** (= *vernünftig*) reasonable; (= *verständnisvoll*) understanding **(b)** (= *verständlich, begreiflich*) understandable; **jdm etw ~ machen** to make sb understand sth

Einsichtnahme [-naːmə] F **-, -n** (*form*) inspection; **nach ~ in die Akten** after inspecting the files; **„zur ~"** "for inspection"

Einsiedler(in) M(F) hermit

einsilbig ADJ **(a)** *Wort* monosyllabic; *Reim* masculine, single **(b)** (*fig*) *Mensch* uncommunicative; *Antwort, Erklärung* monosyllabic

einsinken VI SEP IRREG AUX SEIN (*im Morast, Schnee*) to sink in (*in +acc or dat* -to); (*Boden etc*) to subside; **er sank bis zu den Knien im Schlamm ein** he sank up to his knees in the mud

einspaltig [-ʃpaltɪç] **1** ADJ (*Typ*) single-column **2** ADV **etw ~ setzen** to set sth in a single column/in single columns

einspannen VT SEP **(a)** (*in Rahmen*) *Leinwand* to fit in (*in +acc* -to); (*in Schraubstock*) to clamp in (*in +acc* -to); (*in Kamera, Schreibmaschine*) to put in (*in +acc* -to) **(b)** *Pferde* to harness **(c)** (*fig*: = *arbeiten lassen*) to rope in (*für etw* to do sth); **jdn für seine Zwecke ~** to use sb for one's own ends; *siehe auch* **eingespannt**

einsparen VT SEP to save; *Kosten, Ausgaben* to cut down on; *Posten* to dispense with

Einsparung F **-, -en** economy; (= *das Einsparen*) saving (*von* of); (*von Kosten, Ausgaben*) reduction; (*von Posten*) elimination

einspeisen VT SEP to feed in (*in +acc* -to)

einsperren VT SEP to lock in (*in +acc or dat* -to); (*inf*: *ins Gefängnis*) to lock up

einspielen SEP **1** VR (*Mus, Sport*) to warm up; (*nach Sommerpause etc*) to get into practice; (*Regelung, Arbeit*) to work out; **... aber das spielt sich alles noch ein** ... but things should sort themselves out all right; **sich aufeinander ~** to become attuned to one another; *siehe auch* **eingespielt 2** VT (*Film, Theat*) to bring in; *Kosten* to recover

Einsprache F (*Aus, Sw*) = **Einspruch**

einsprachig ADJ monolingual

einsprechen VI SEP IRREG **auf jdn ~** to harangue sb

einspringen VI SEP IRREG AUX SEIN (*inf*: = *aushelfen*) to stand in; (*mit Geld etc*) to help out

Einspritz- IN CPDS (*Aut, Med*) injection

Einspritzdüse F (*Aut*) injector

einspritzen VT SEP **(a)** (*Aut, Med*) to inject **(b)** (= *einsprengen*) *Wäsche* to dampen

Einspritzer M (*Aut*) fuel injection engine

Einspritz-: Einspritzmotor M (*Aut*) fuel injection engine; **Einspritzpumpe** F (*Aut*) fuel injection pump

Einspruch M objection (*auch Jur*); **~ einlegen** (*Admin*) to file an objection; **gegen etw ~ erheben** to object to sth; **ich erhebe**

~! (*Jur*) objection!; **~ abgelehnt!** (*Jur*) objection overruled!; **(dem) ~ (wird) stattgegeben!** (*Jur*) objection sustained!

einspurig [-ʃpuːrɪç] **1** ADJ (*Rail*) single-track; (*Aut*) single-lane **2** ADV **die Straße ist nur ~ befahrbar** only one lane of the road is open; **er denkt sehr ~** he has a one-track mind

einst [aɪnst] ADV **(a)** (= *früher, damals*) once; **Preußen ~ und heute** Prussia past and present **(b)** (*geh*: = *in ferner Zukunft*) one day

einstampfen VT SEP *Papier, Buch, Auflage* to pulp

Einstand M **(a)** **ein guter ~** a good start to a new job; **er hat gestern seinen ~ gegeben** *or* **gefeiert** yesterday he celebrated starting his new job **(b)** (*Tennis*) deuce

Einstands- (*Comm*): **Einstandspreis** M introductory price; **Einstandswert** M (= *Anschaffungskosten*) acquisition cost

einstecken VT SEP **(a)** (= *in etw stecken*) to put in (*in +acc* -to); *Stecker auch, Gerät* to plug in **(b)** (*in die Tasche etc*) (**sich** *dat*) **etw ~** to take sth; **hast du deinen Pass eingesteckt?** have you got your passport with you?; **ich habe kein Geld eingesteckt** *or* (*incorrect*) ~ I haven't any money on me; **kannst du meinen Lippenstift für mich ~?** can you take my lipstick for me?; **steck deine Pistole wieder ein** put your pistol away **(c)** (*in den Briefkasten*) to post (*Brit*), to mail (*esp US*) **(d)** (*inf*) *Kritik etc* to take; *Beleidigung* to swallow; (= *verdienen*) *Geld, Profit* to pocket (*inf*); **der Boxer musste viel ~** the boxer had to take a lot of punishment

einstehen VI SEP IRREG AUX SEIN **für jdn/etw ~** (= *sich verbürgen*) to vouch for sb/sth; **ich stehe dafür ein, dass ...** I will vouch that ...; **für etw ~** (= *Ersatz leisten*) to make good sth; (= *sich bekennen*) to answer for sth; **für jdn ~** to assume responsibility for sb; **ich habe das immer behauptet und dafür stehe ich auch ein** I've always said that, and I'll stand by it

Einsteigekarte F (*Aviat*) boarding pass

einsteigen VI SEP IRREG AUX SEIN **(a)** (*in ein Fahrzeug etc*) to get in (*in +acc* -to); (*in Bus*) to get on (*in +acc* -to); **~!** (*Rail etc*) all aboard! **(b)** (*in ein Haus etc*) to climb in (*in +acc* -to) **(c)** (*inf*) **in die Politik/ins Verlagsgeschäft ~** to go into politics/publishing; **er ist mit einer Million in diese Firma eingestiegen** he put a million into this firm; **er ist ganz groß in dieses Geschäft eingestiegen** he's (gone) into that business in a big way (*inf*); **der Verlag ist jetzt in Wörterbücher eingestiegen** the publishing company has branched out into dictionaries

Einsteiger [ˈaɪnʃtaɪɡɐ] M **-s, -**, **Einsteigerin** [-ərɪn] F **-, -nen** (*inf*) beginner; **ein Modell für PC-~** an entry-level PC

einstellbar ADJ adjustable

Einstellbereich M (*Aut*) adjustment range

einstellen SEP **1** VT **(a)** (= *hineinstellen*) to put in **(b)** (= *anstellen*) *Arbeitskräfte* to take on; **„wir stellen ein: Sekretärinnen"** "we have vacancies for secretaries" **(c)** (= *beenden*) to stop; *Expedition, Suche* to call off; (*Mil*) *Feindseligkeiten, Feuer* to cease; (*Jur*) *Prozess, Verfahren* to abandon; **die Arbeit ist eingestellt worden** work has stopped; **die Zeitung hat ihr Erscheinen eingestellt** the paper has ceased publication; **die Arbeit ~** (*Kommission etc*) to stop work; (= *in den Ausstand treten*) to withdraw one's labour (*Brit*) *or* labor (*US*) **(d)** (= *regulieren*) to adjust (*auf +acc* to); *Fernglas, Fotoapparat* (*auf Entfernung*) to focus (*auf +acc* on); *Wecker, Zünder* to set (*auf +acc* for); *Radio* to tune in (*auf +acc* to); *Sender* to tune in to **(e)** (*Sport*) *Rekord* to equal **2** VR **(a)** (*Besucher etc, Symptome, Folgen*) to appear; (*Fieber, Regen*) to set in; (*Wort, Gedanke*) to come to mind **(b)** **sich auf jdn/etw ~** (= *sich richten nach*) to adapt oneself to sb/sth; (= *sich vorbereiten auf*) to prepare oneself for sb/sth; *siehe auch* **eingestellt 3** VI to take on staff; (*Fabrik*) to take on workers

einstellig [-ʃtɛlɪç] ADJ *Zahl* single-digit

Einstellung F **(a)** (= *Anstellung*) employment **(b)** (= *Beendigung*) stopping; (*von Expedition, Suche*) calling-off; (*Mil*) cessation; (*Jur*) abandonment; **die Lackierer beschlossen die ~ der Arbeit** the paint-sprayers decided to down tools **(c)** (= *Regulierung*) adjustment; (*von Fernglas, Fotoapparat*) focusing; (*von Wecker, Zünder*) setting; (*von Radio*) tuning (in); (*Film*: = *Szene*) take

(d) (= *Gesinnung, Haltung*) attitude; (*politisch, religiös etc*) views *pl*; **er hat eine falsche ~ zum Leben** he doesn't have the right attitude to life; **das ist doch keine ~!** what kind of attitude is that!

Einstellungs-: Einstellungsgespräch NT interview; **Einstellungsstopp** M halt in recruitment; **Einstellungstermin** M starting date; **Einstellungstest** M recruitment test

Einstich M (= *~stelle*) puncture; (= *Vorgang*) insertion

Einstieg [ˈainʃtiːk] M **-(e)s, -e** [-gə] **(a)** NO PL (= *das Einsteigen*) getting in; (*in Bus*) getting on; (*von Dieb: in Haus etc*) entry; (*fig: zu einem Thema etc*) lead-in (*zu* to); **~ nur vorn!** enter only at the front **(b)** (*von Bahn, von Bus*) door

Einstiegsdroge F starter drug

einstig [ˈainstɪç] ADJ ATTR former

einstimmen VI SEP (*in ein Lied*) to join in; (*fig*) (= *beistimmen*) to agree (*in +acc* with); (= *zustimmen*) to agree (*in +acc* to); **in den Gesang/die Buhrufe (mit) ~** to join in the singing/booing

einstimmig ADJ **(a)** *Lied* for one voice **(b)** (= *einmütig*) unanimous

Einstimmigkeit F **-, -en** unanimity

einstöckig ADJ *Haus* two-storey (*Brit*), two-story (*US*); **~ (gebaut) sein** to have two storeys (*Brit*) or stories (*US*)

einstöpseln VT SEP (*Elec*) to plug in (*in +acc* -to)

einstrahlen VI SEP to shine

Einstrahlung F (= *Sonneneinstrahlung*) shining

einstreichen VT SEP IRREG **(a) eine Wunde (mit Salbe) ~** to put ointment on a wound; **eine Kuchenform (mit Fett) ~** to grease a baking tin (*Brit*) or pan (*US*) **(b)** (*inf*) *Geld, Gewinn* to pocket (*inf*)

einströmen VI SEP AUX SEIN to pour in (*in +acc* -to); **kältere Luftschichten strömen nach Bayern ein** a stream of cooler air is moving in towards (*Brit*) or toward (*US*) Bavaria; **~de Kaltluft** a stream of cold air

einstrophig [ˈainʃtroːfɪç] ADJ one-verse *attr*

einstudieren *ptp* **einstudiert** VT SEP *Lied, Theaterstück* to rehearse; **einstudierte Antworten** (*fig*) well-rehearsed answers

einstufen VT SEP to classify; **in eine Klasse/Kategorie** *etc* **~ to** put into a class/category *etc*

einstufig ADJ single-stage

Einstufung F classification; **nach seiner ~ in eine höhere Gehaltsklasse** after he was put into a higher salary bracket

einstündig [ˈainstyndɪç] ADJ ATTR one-hour; **mehr als ~e Verspätungen** delays of more than an hour

einstürmen VI SEP AUX SEIN **auf jdn ~** (*Mil*) to storm sb; (*fig*) to assail sb; **mit Fragen auf jdn ~** to bombard sb with questions

Einsturz M collapse

einstürzen VI SEP AUX SEIN to collapse; **auf jdn ~** (*fig*) to overwhelm sb

Einsturzgefahr F danger of collapse

einstweilig [ˈainstˈvailɪç] ADJ ATTR temporary; **~e Verfügung/ Anordnung** (*Jur*) temporary injunction/order

eintägig ADJ ATTR one-day

Eintagsfliege F (*Zool*) mayfly; (*fig*) nine-day wonder; (= *Mode, Idee*) passing craze

eintauchen SEP **1** VT to dip (*in +acc* in, into); (*völlig*) to immerse (*in +acc* in); *Brot* to dunk (*in +acc* in) **2** VI AUX SEIN (*Schwimmer*) to dive in; (*Springer*) to enter the water; (*U-Boot*) to dive; **das U-Boot ist jetzt ganz eingetaucht** the submarine is now completely submerged

Eintausch M exchange; **„~ von Gutscheinen"** "coupons exchanged here"

eintauschen VT SEP to exchange (*gegen, für* for); (= *umtauschen*) *Devisen* to change

eintausend [ˈainˈtauznt] NUM (*form*) = **tausend**

einteilen VT SEP **(a)** (= *aufteilen*) to divide (up) (*in +acc* into); (= *aufgliedern*) to split (up) (*in +acc* into) **(b)** (= *sinnvoll aufteilen*) *Zeit, Arbeit* to plan (out); *Geld auch* to budget **(c)** (= *dienstlich verpflichten*) to detail (*zu* for); **er ist heute als Aufseher eingeteilt** he has been allocated the job of supervisor today

Einteiler M (*Fashion*) one-piece (swimsuit)

einteilig ADJ *Badeanzug* one-piece *attr*

Einteilung F **(a)** (= *das Aufteilen*) division **(b)** (*von Zeit, Arbeit*) planning; (*von Geld*) budgeting **(c)** (= *dienstliche Verpflichtung*) assignment

Eintel [ˈaintl] NT (SW AUCH M) **-s, -** (*Math*) whole

eintönig [ˈaintøːnɪç] **1** ADJ monotonous **2** ADV monotonously; **~ reden** to talk in a monotone

Eintönigkeit F **-,** NO PL monotony; (*von Stimme*) monotonousness

Eintopf M stew

Eintracht F, NO PL harmony; **~ X** (*Sport*) ≈ X United

einträchtig **1** ADJ peaceable **2** ADV peaceably

Eintrag [ˈaintraːk] M **-(e)s, ~e** [-trɛːgə] (*schriftlich*) entry (*in +acc* in) **(b)** (= *Schadstoffeinleitung*) discharge

eintragen SEP IRREG **1** VT (*in Liste, auf Konto etc*) to enter; (= *amtlich registrieren*) to register; **jdm Hass/Undank/Gewinn ~** to bring sb hatred/ingratitude/profit; *siehe auch* **eingetragen 2** VR to sign; (= *sich vormerken lassen*) to put one's name down; **er trug sich ins Gästebuch ein** he signed the visitors' book; **er trug sich in die Warteliste ein** he put his name (down) on the waiting list

einträglich [ˈaintrɛːklɪç] ADJ profitable

Eintragung [ˈaintraːgʊŋ] F **-, -en** entry (*in +acc* in)

eintreffen VI SEP IRREG AUX SEIN **(a)** (= *ankommen*) to arrive; **„Bananen frisch eingetroffen"** "bananas - just in" **(b)** (*fig: = Wirklichkeit werden*) to come true

eintreibbar ADJ *Schulden* recoverable; *Steuern, Zinsen* exactable

eintreiben VT SEP IRREG *Geldbeträge* to collect; *Schulden* to recover

Eintreibung [ˈaintraibʊŋ] F **-, -en** (*von Geldbeträgen*) collection; (*von Schulden auch*) recovery

eintreten SEP IRREG **1** VI (*in Zimmer etc*) to go/ come in (*in +acc* -to); (*in Verein, Partei etc*) to join (*in etw* (*acc*) sth); **in eine Firma ~** to join a firm; **in den Krieg ~** to enter the war; **in Verhandlungen ~** (*form*) to enter into negotiations; **die Verhandlungen sind in eine kritische Phase eingetreten** the negotiations have entered a critical phase; **die Rakete trat in ihre Umlaufbahn ein** the rocket went into its orbit; **bitte treten Sie ein!** (*form*) (please) do come in **(b) auf jdn ~** to kick sb **(c)** AUX SEIN (= *sich ereignen*) (*Tod*) to occur; (*Zeitpunkt*) to come; (= *beginnen*) (*Dunkelheit, Nacht*) to fall; (*Besserung, Tauwetter*) to set in; **bei Eintreten der Dunkelheit** at nightfall; **gegen Abend trat starkes Fieber ein** toward(s) evening the patient started to run a high temperature; **es ist eine Besserung eingetreten** there has been an improvement; **wenn der Fall eintritt, dass ...** if it happens that ...; **es ist der Fall eingetreten, den wir befürchtet hatten** what we had feared has in fact happened **(d)** AUX SEIN **für jdn/etw ~** to stand up for sb/sth; **sein mutiges Eintreten für seine Überzeugung** his courageous defence (*Brit*) or defense (*US*) of his conviction **(e)** (*Sw*) **auf etw** (*acc*) **~** to follow sth up **2** VT (= *zertrümmern*) to kick in

eintrichtern [ˈaintrɪçtən], **eintrimmen** VT SEP (*inf*) **jdm etw ~** to drum sth into sb

Eintritt M **(a)** (= *das Eintreten*) entry (*in +acc* (in)to); (*in Verein, Partei etc*) joining (*in +acc* of); **„~ im Sekretariat"** "entrance through the office"; **der ~ in den Staatsdienst** entry (in)to the civil service; **der ~ in die EU** entry to the EU; **der ~ ins Gymnasium** starting at grammar school (*Brit*) or high school (*US*); **seit seinem ~ in die Armee** since joining the army **(b)** (= *Einlass, ~sgeld*) admission (*in +acc* to); **was kostet der ~?** how much is the admission?; **~ frei!** admission free; **„~ verboten"** "no admittance" **(c)** (*von Winter, Dunkelheit*) onset; **bei ~ eines solchen Falles** in such an event; **der ~ des Todes** the moment when death occurs; **bei ~ der Dunkelheit** at nightfall

Eintritts-: Eintrittsgeld NT entrance money; **die Zuschauer verlangten ihr ~ zurück** the audience asked for their money back; **Eintrittskarte** F ticket (of admission); **Eintrittspreis** M admission charge

eintrüben VR SEP (*Met*) to cloud over

eintrudeln VI SEP AUX SEIN (*inf*) to drift in (*inf*); **... bis alle eingetrudelt sind** ... until everyone has turned up

eintunken VT SEP *Brot* to dunk (*in +acc* in)

einüben VT SEP to practise (*Brit*), to practice (*US*); *Theaterstück, Rolle etc* to rehearse; *Rücksichtnahme, Solidarität* to learn (through practice); **sich** (*dat*) **etw ~** to practise (*Brit*) *or* practice (*US*) sth

Einübung F practice; (*Theat etc*) rehearsal

einverleiben [ˈainfɐˌlaibn], *ptp* **einverleibt** VT SEP AND INSEP *Gebiet, Land* to annex (*dat* to); *Firma, Ministerium* to incorporate (*dat* into)

einvernehmen *ptp* **einvernommen** VT INSEP IRREG (*Jur: esp Aus, Sw*) = **vernehmen**

Einvernehmen NT **-s, -** (= *Eintracht*) harmony; (= *Übereinstimmung*) agreement; **wir arbeiten in gutem ~ (miteinander)** we work in perfect harmony (together); **im ~ mit jdm** in agreement with sb; **in gegenseitigem** *or* **beiderseitigem ~** by mutual agreement

einvernehmlich (*form*) **1** ADJ *Regelung, Lösung* consensual **2** ADV consensually

Einvernehmung F (*Jur: esp Aus, Sw*) = **Vernehmung**

einverstanden [ˈainfɐˌʃtandn] ADJ **~!** agreed!; **~ sein** to agree; **ich bin ~** that's okay by me (*inf*); **mit jdm/etw ~ sein** to agree to sb/sth; (= *übereinstimmen*) to agree with sb/sth; **ich bin mit deinem Verhalten/mit dir gar nicht ~** I don't approve of your behaviour (*Brit*) *or* behavior (*US*); **sich mit etw ~ erklären** to give one's agreement to sth

einverständlich 1 ADJ mutually agreed; *Ehescheidung* by mutual consent **2** ADV **diese Frage wurde ~ geklärt** this question was settled to the satisfaction of both/all parties

Einverständnis NT agreement; (= *Zustimmung*) consent; **wir haben uns in gegenseitigem ~ scheiden lassen** we were divorced by mutual consent; **das geschieht mit meinem ~** that has my consent; **im ~ mit jdm handeln** to act with sb's consent

Einw. ABBR *von* **Einwohner**

Einwaage F, NO PL (*Comm*: = *Reingewicht*) weight of contents of can or jar excluding juice etc; **Frucht-~/Fleisch-~ 200 g** fruit/ meat content 200g

Einwahl F (*Telec: ins Internet*) dial-up; **bei der ~** when dialling (*Brit*) *or* dialing (*US*) in

Einwahlknoten M (*Telec, Comput*) point of presence, POP

Einwand [ˈainvant] M **-(e)s, ¨e** [-vɛndə] objection; **einen ~ erheben** *or* **vorbringen** *or* **geltend machen** (*form*) to raise an objection

Einwanderer M, **Einwanderin** F immigrant

einwandern VI SEP AUX SEIN (*nach, in +acc* to) to immigrate; (*Volk*) to migrate

Einwanderung F immigration (*nach, in +acc* to)

Einwanderungs- IN CPDS immigration; **Einwanderungsbehörde** F immigration authorities *pl*; **Einwanderungsland** NT immigration country

einwandfrei 1 ADJ **(a)** (= *ohne Fehler*) perfect; *Benehmen, Leumund* impeccable; *Lebensmittel* perfectly fresh; **ethisch ~** ethically acceptable
(b) (= *unzweifelhaft*) indisputable; *Beweis auch* definite **2** ADV **(a)** (= *fehlerlos*) perfectly; *sich verhalten* impeccably; **er arbeitet sehr genau und ~** his work is very precise and absolutely faultless
(b) (= *unzweifelhaft*) indisputably; **etw ~ beweisen** to prove sth beyond doubt; **es steht ~ fest, dass ...** it is quite indisputable that ...; **das ist ~ Betrug/Unterschlagung** that is a clear case of fraud/embezzlement

einwärts [ˈainvɛrts] ADV inwards

einwechseln VT SEP *Geld* to change (*in +acc, gegen* into); **jdm Geld ~** to change money for sb

einwecken VT SEP to preserve

Einweck-: **Einweckglas** NT preserving jar; **Einweckgummi** M or NT, **Einweckring** M rubber seal (*for preserving jar*)

Einweg- [ˈainveːk] IN CPDS (= *Wegwerf-*) disposable; **Einwegflasche** F non-returnable bottle; **Einwegpfand** NT deposit on drink cans and disposable bottles; **Einwegscheibe** F one-way glass; **Einwegspiegel** M one-way mirror; **Einwegspritze** F disposable syringe

einweichen VT SEP to soak

einweihen VT SEP **(a)** (= *feierlich eröffnen*) to open (officially); (*fig*) to christen **(b) jdn in etw** (*acc*) **~** to initiate sb into sth; **er ist eingeweiht** he knows all about it

Einweihung [ˈainvaiʊŋ] F **-, -en**, **Einweihungsfeier** F (official) opening

einweisen VT SEP IRREG **(a)** (*in Krankenhaus, Heilanstalt*) to admit (*in +acc* to) **(b)** (= *in Arbeit unterweisen*) **jdn ~** to introduce sb to his/her job; **er wurde von seinem Vorgänger (in die Arbeit) eingewiesen** his predecessor showed him what the job involved **(c)** (*Aut*) to guide in (*in +acc* -to)

Einweisung F **(a)** (*in Krankenhaus, Anstalt*) admission (*in +acc* in) **(b) die ~ der neuen Mitarbeiter übernehmen** to assume responsibility for introducing new employees to their jobs

einwenden VT SEP IRREG **etwas/nichts gegen etw einzuwenden haben** to have an objection/no objection to sth; **dagegen lässt sich ~, dass ...** one objection to this is that ...; **er hat immer etwas einzuwenden** he always has some objection to make

einwerfen SEP IRREG **1** VT **(a)** *Fensterscheibe etc* to break **(b)** (*Sport*) *Ball* to throw in **(c)** *Brief* to post (*Brit*), to mail (*esp US*); *Münze* to insert **(d)** (*fig*) *Bemerkung* to make; **er warf ein, dass ...** he made the point that ... **2** VI (*Sport*) to throw in

einwickeln VT SEP **(a)** (= *einpacken*) to wrap (up) **(b)** (*inf*: = *übervorteilen, überlisten*) to fool (*inf*); (*durch Schmeicheleien*) to butter up (*inf*)

Einwickelpapier NT wrapping paper

einwilligen [ˈainvɪlɪɡn] VI SEP to consent (*in +acc* to)

Einwilligung F **-, -en** consent (*in +acc* to)

einwirken VI SEP **auf jdn/etw ~** to have an effect on sb/sth; (= *beeinflussen*) to influence sb/sth; **etw ~ lassen** (*Med*) to let sth work in; **einen Anblick auf sich** (*acc*) **~ lassen** to take a sight in

Einwirkung F influence; (*eines Katalysators*) effect; **Bayern steht unter ~ eines atlantischen Hochs** Bavaria is being affected by an anticyclone over the Atlantic; **unter (der) ~ von Drogen** *etc* under the influence of drugs *etc*; **nach ~ der Salbe ...** when the ointment has worked in ...

einwöchig [-vœçɪç] ADJ one-week *attr*

Einwohner [ˈainvoːnɐ] M **-s, -**, **Einwohnerin** [-ərɪn] F **-, -nen** inhabitant

Einwohner-: **Einwohnermeldeamt** NT *residents' registration office*; **sich beim ~ (an)melden** ≈ to register with the police; **Einwohnerschaft** [ˈainvoːnɐʃaft] F **-,** (*rare*) **-en** population; **Einwohnerzahl** F population

Einwurf M **(a)** (*von Münze*) insertion; (*von Brief*) posting (*Brit*), mailing (*esp US*); **~ 2 Euro** insert 2 euros **(b)** (*Sport*) throw-in; **falscher ~** foul throw **(c)** (= *Schlitz*) slot; (*von Briefkasten*) slit **(d)** (*fig*) interjection; (= *Einwand*) objection

Einzahl F singular

einzahlen VT SEP to pay in; **Geld auf ein Konto ~** to pay money into an account

Einzahlung F payment; (*auf Bankkonto auch*) deposit (*auf +acc* into)

einzäunen [ˈaintsɔynən] VT SEP to fence in

einzeichnen VT SEP to draw in; **ist der Ort eingezeichnet?** is the place marked?

Einzeiler [ˈaintsailɐ] M **-s, -** (*Liter*) one-line poem, one-liner (*inf*)

einzeilig ADJ one-line *attr*

Einzel [ˈaintsl] NT **-s, -** (*Tennis*) singles *sing*

Einzel-: **Einzelaufhängung** F (*Aut*) independent suspension; **Einzelaufstellung** F (*Comm*) itemized list; **Einzelblatteinzug** M cut-sheet feed; **Einzelerscheinung** F isolated occurrence; **Einzelfahrschein** M one-way ticket; **Einzelfall** M individual case; (= *Sonderfall*) isolated case; **Einzelfertigung** F special order; **in ~ hergestellt** made to order; **Einzelgänger** [-ɡɛŋɐ] M **-s, -**, **Einzelgängerin** [-ərɪn] F **-, -nen** loner; (= *Elefant*) rogue; **Einzelhaft** F solitary confinement

Einzelhandel M retail trade; **im ~ erhältlich** available retail; **im ~ kostet das ...** it retails at ...

Einzelhandels-: **Einzelhandelsgeschäft** NT retail shop; **Einzelhandelskauffrau** F trained retail saleswoman; **Einzelhandelskaufmann** M trained retail salesman; **Einzelhandelspreis** M retail price

Einzel-: **Einzelhaus** NT detached house (*Brit*), self-contained house (*US*); **Einzelheit** [ˈaintslhait] F **-, -en** detail; **auf ~en eingehen** to go into detail(s); **etw in allen/bis in die kleinsten ~en schildern** to describe sth in great detail/right down to the last detail; **sich in ~en verlieren** to get bogged down in details; **Einzelkabine** F (individual) cubicle; **Einzelkind** NT

only child; **Einzelkosten** PL direct costs *pl*;
Einzelkundengeschäft NT (*von Bank*) retail banking;
Einzelplatzlizenz F single source code licence (*Brit*) *or* license (*US*)

Einzeller ['aintsɛlə] M **-s, -** (*Biol*) single-cell(ed) *or* unicellular organism

einzellig [-tselɪç] ADJ single-cell(ed) *attr*

einzeln ['aintsln] **1** ADJ (a) individual; (= *getrennt*) separate; (*von Paar*) odd; **im ~en Fall** in the particular case
(b) (= *allein stehend*) *Baum, Haus* single; **~ stehend** solitary; **ein paar ~ stehende Bäume** a few scattered trees
(c) (*mit pl n:* = *einige, vereinzelte*) some; (*Met*) *Schauer* scattered; **~e Besucher kamen schon früher** a few visitors came earlier
2 ADV (a) (= *separat*) separately
(b) (= *nicht zusammen*) individually; **wir kamen ~** we came separately; **bitte ~ eintreten** please come in one (person) at a time

Einzelne(r) ['aintslnə] MF *decl as adj* **der/die ~** the individual; **ein ~r** an individual; (= *ein einziger Mensch*) one single person; **~ some** (people); **jeder ~/jede ~** each individual; **jeder ~ muss dabei helfen** (each and) every one of you/them *etc* must help

Einzelne(s) ['aintslnə] NT *decl as adj* (a) **~s** some; **~s hat mir gefallen** I liked parts of it; **~ haben mir gefallen** I liked some of them **(b) das ~** the particular; **er kam vom ~n zum Allgemeinen** he went from the particular to the general; **jedes ~** each one; **im ~n auf etw** (*acc*) **eingehen** to go into detail(s) about sth; **etw im ~n besprechen** to discuss sth in detail; **bis ins ~** right down to the last detail

einzelnstehend ADJ ATTR *siehe* **einzeln**

Einzel-: Einzelperson F single person; **~en haben es auf Reisen meist schwer, ein Hotelzimmer zu bekommen** people travelling (*Brit*) *or* traveling (*US*) alone usually find it hard to get a hotel room; **Einzelpreis** M price, unit price (*Comm*); (*von Zeitung*) price per copy; **Einzelradaufhängung** F (*Aut*) independent suspension; **Einzelteil** NT individual part; (= *Ersatzteil*) spare part; **etw in seine ~e zerlegen** to take sth to pieces; **Einzeltherapie** F individual therapy; **Einzelunterricht** M private tuition; **Einzelverbindungsnachweis** M (*Telec*) itemized call listing; **Einzelzimmer** NT single room

einzementieren ptp **einzementiert** VT SEP *Stein* to cement; *Safe* to set into (the) concrete

einziehen SEP IRREG **1** VT (a) *Gummiband, Faden* to thread; (*in einen Bezug etc*) to put in; *Wand, Balken* to put in; (*Kopiergerät*) *Papier* to take in
(b) (= *zurückziehen*) *Fühler, Krallen, Fahrgestell, Antenne* to retract; *Bauch, Netz* to pull in; *Periskop, Flagge, Segel* to lower; *Ruder* to take in; **den Kopf ~** to duck (one's head); **zieh den Bauch ein!** tuck your tummy in (*inf*); **mit eingezogenem Schwanz** (*lit, fig*) with its/his/her tail between its/his/her legs
(c) (*Mil*) (*zu* into) *Personen* to conscript, to draft (*US*); *Fahrzeuge etc* to requisition
(d) (= *kassieren*) *Steuern, Gelder* to collect; (*fig*) *Erkundigungen* to make (*über* +acc about)
(e) (= *aus dem Verkehr ziehen*) *Banknoten, Münzen* to withdraw (from circulation); (= *beschlagnahmen*) *Führerschein* to take away
(f) (*Typ*) *Wörter, Zeilen* to indent
2 VI AUX SEIN (a) (*in Wohnung, Haus*) to move in; **ins Parlament ~** (*Partei*) to enter parliament; (*Abgeordneter*) to take one's seat (in parliament)
(b) (= *einmarschieren*) to march in (*in* +acc into)
(c) (= *einkehren*) to come in (*in* +dat to); **wenn der Friede im Lande einzieht** when peace comes to our country; **Ruhe und Ordnung zogen wieder ein** law and order returned
(d) (= *eindringen*) to soak in (*in* +acc -to)

einzig ['aintsɪç] **1** ADJ (a) ATTR only; **ich sehe nur eine ~e Möglichkeit** I can see only one (single) possibility; **ich habe nicht einen ~en Brief bekommen** I haven't had a single letter; **kein** *or* **nicht ein ~es Mal** not once; **das Einzige** the only thing
(b) (*emphatisch*) absolute; **dieses Rugbyspiel war eine ~e Schlammschlacht** this rugby match was just one big mudbath
(c) PRED (= *~artig*) unique; **es ist ~ in seiner Art** it is quite unique; **sein Können steht ~ da** his skill is unmatched
2 ADV (a) (= *allein*) only; **seine Beförderung hat er ~ dir zu**

verdanken he owes his promotion entirely to you; **die ~ mögliche Lösung** the only possible solution; **~ und allein** solely; **~ und allein deshalb hat er gewonnen** he owes his victory solely to that; **das ~ Wahre** *or* **Senkrechte** (*inf*) the only thing; (= *das Beste*) the real McCoy (*inf*); **jetzt Ferien machen/ein Bier trinken, das wäre das ~ Wahre** *etc* to take a holiday (*esp Brit*) *or* vacation (*US*)/have a beer, that would be just the job (*inf*)
(b) (*inf*: = *außerordentlich*) fantastically

einzigartig **1** ADJ unique **2** ADV *beleidigend, gerissen* incredibly; **die Landschaft war ~ schön** the scenery was astoundingly beautiful

Einzige(r) ['aintsɪgə] MF *decl as adj* **der/die ~** the only one; **ein ~r hat geantwortet** only one (person) answered; **kein ~r wusste es** not a single person knew; **die ~n, die es wussten ...** the only ones who knew ...; **Hans ist unser ~r** Hans is our only child

Einzimmer- IN CPDS one-room; **Einzimmerwohnung** F one-room flat (*Brit*) *or* apartment

Einzug M (a) (*in Haus etc*) move (*in* +acc into); **vor dem ~** before moving in; **der ~ ins Parlament** (*von Partei*) entering parliament; (*von Abgeordnetem*) taking one's seat (in parliament) **(b)** (= *Einmarsch*) entry (*in* +acc into); **der ~ kühlerer Meeresluft ...** a low trough moving in from the sea ... **(c)** (*von Steuern, Geldern*) collection; (*von Banknoten*) withdrawal **(d)** (*Typ*) indentation

Einzugs-: Einzugsauftrag M (*Fin*) direct debit; **Einzugsbereich** M catchment area (*Brit*), service area (*US*); **Einzugsermächtigung** F (*Fin*) direct debit instruction; **eine ~ erteilen** to set up a direct debit; **Einzugsgebiet** NT catchment area (*Brit*), service area (*US*); **Einzugsverfahren** NT (*Fin*) direct debit

Eis [ais] NT **-es, -** (a) NO PL (= *gefrorenes Wasser*) ice; **zu ~ gefrieren** to freeze; **vom ~ eingeschlossen sein** to be iced in; **~ laufen** to ice-skate; **das ~ brechen** (*fig*) to break the ice; **etw auf ~ legen** (*lit, fig inf*) to put sth on ice **(b)** (= *Speiseeis*) ice (cream); **er kaufte 3 ~** he bought 3 ice creams; **~ am Stiel** ice(d) lolly (*Brit*), Popsicle® (*US*)

Eis-: Eisbahn F ice rink; **Eisbär** M polar bear; **Eisbecher** M (*aus Pappe*) ice-cream tub; (*aus Metall*) sundae dish; (= *Eis*) sundae; **Eisbein** NT (*Cook*) knuckle of pork (*boiled and served with sauerkraut*); **Eisbereiter** M **-s, -** ice-maker; **Eisberg** M iceberg; **die Spitze des ~s** (*fig*) the tip of the iceberg; **Eisbergsalat** M iceberg lettuce; **Eisbeutel** M ice pack

Eisschnee ['ai-] M (*Cook*) beaten white of egg

Eis-: Eiscreme F ice (cream); **Eisdecke** F sheet of ice; **Eisdiele** F ice-cream parlour (*Brit*) *or* parlor (*US*)

Eisen ['aizn] NT **-s, -** (a) NO PL (*Chem*) (*abbr* Fe) iron; **~ verarbeitend** iron-processing; **mehrere/noch ein ~ im Feuer haben** (*fig*) to have more than one/another iron in the fire; **zum alten ~ gehören** *or* **zählen** (*fig*) to be on the scrap heap; **man muss das ~ schmieden, solange es heiß** *or* **warm ist** (*Prov*) one must strike while the iron is hot (*prov*) **(b)** (= *Bügeleisen, Golfschläger*) iron; (= *~beschlag*) iron fitting; (= *Hufeisen*) shoe

Eisenbahn F railway (*Brit*), railroad (*US*); (= *~wesen*) railways *pl* (*Brit*), railroad (*US*); (*inf*: = *Zug*) train; (= *Spielzeugeisenbahn*) toy train; (= *Spielzeugeisenbahnanlage*) train set; **ich fahre lieber (mit der) ~ als (mit dem) Bus** I prefer to travel by train than by bus; **es ist (aller)höchste ~** (*inf*) it's getting late

Eisenbahn-: Eisenbahnabteil NT (railway (*Brit*) *or* railroad (*US*)) compartment; **Eisenbahnanlagen** PL railway (*Brit*) *or* railroad (*US*) installations *pl*; **Eisenbahnbrücke** F railway (*Brit*) *or* railroad (*US*) bridge

Eisenbahner [-ba:nɐ] M **-s, -**, **Eisenbahnerin** [-ərɪn] F **-, -nen** railway employee (*Brit*), railroader (*US*)

Eisenbahn-: Eisenbahnfähre F train ferry; **Eisenbahnnetz** NT railway (*Brit*) *or* railroad (*US*) network; **Eisenbahnschiene** F railway (*Brit*) *or* railroad (*US*) track; **Eisenbahnschwelle** F railway sleeper (*Brit*), (railroad) tie (*US*); **Eisenbahnstrecke** F railway line (*Brit*), railroad (*US*); **Eisenbahnüberführung** F (railway (*Brit*) *or* railroad (*US*)) footbridge; **Eisenbahnunglück** NT train crash; **Eisenbahnunterführung** F railway (*Brit*) *or* railroad (*US*) underpass; **Eisenbahnverbindung** F rail link; (= *Anschluss*) connection; **Eisenbahnverkehr** M railway (*Brit*) *or* railroad (*US*) traffic; **Eisenbahnwagen** M (= *Personenwagen*) railway carriage (*Brit*), railroad car (*US*); (= *Güterwagen*) goods truck (*Brit*), freight car (*US*)

Eisen-: Eisenbergwerk NT iron mine; **Eisenbeschlag** M ironwork *no pl*; (*zum Verstärken*) iron band; **eisenbeschlagen** ADJ with iron fittings; *Stiefel* steel-tipped; **Eisenblech** NT sheet iron; **Eisenerz** NT iron ore; **eisenhaltig** ADJ *Gestein* iron-bearing; *Medikament* containing iron; **das Wasser ist ~** the water contains iron; **Eisenhut** M (*Bot*) monkshood; **Eisenhütte** F ironworks *pl or sing*; **Eiseninudstrie** F iron industry; **Eisen- und Stahlindustrie** iron and steel industry; **Eisenlegierung** F iron alloy; **Eisenmangel** M iron deficiency; **Eisenoxid** NT ferric oxide; **Eisenpräparat** NT (*Med*) (*flüssig*) iron tonic; (*Tabletten*) iron tablets *pl*; **Eisenspäne** PL iron filings *pl*; **Eisenstange** F iron bar; **Eisenträger** M iron girder; **eisenverarbeitend** ADJ ATTR *siehe* Eisen; **Eisenverbindung** F (*Chem*) iron compound; **Eisenwaren** PL hardware *sing*; **Eisenwarenhändler(in)** M(F) hardware dealer; **Eisenwarenhandlung** F hardware store; **Eisenwerk** NT (a) (*Art*) ironwork (b) (= *Eisenhütte*) ironworks *pl or sing*; **Eisenzeit** F, NO PL (*Hist*) Iron Age

eisern ['aizǝn] **1** ADJ (a) ATTR (= *aus Eisen*) iron; **der ~e Vorhang** (*Theat*) the safety curtain; **der Eiserne Vorhang** (*Pol*) the Iron Curtain
(b) (= *fest, unnachgiebig*) *Disziplin* iron *attr*, strict; *Wille* iron *attr*, of iron; *Energie* indefatigable; **~e Gesundheit** iron constitution; **mit ~er Faust** with an iron hand; **ein ~es Regiment führen** to rule with an iron fist; **in etw** (*dat*) **~ sein/bleiben** to be/remain resolute about sth; **da bin or bleibe ich ~!** (*inf*) that's definite; **mit ~em Besen (aus)kehren** to make a clean sweep
(c) ATTR (= *unantastbar*) *Reserve* emergency
2 ADV resolutely; *trainieren* with iron determination; **er schwieg ~** he remained resolutely silent; **er ist ~ bei seinem Entschluss geblieben** he stuck steadfastly to his decision; **(aber) ~!** (*inf*) (but) of course!

Eiseskälte F icy cold

Eis-: Eisfach NT freezer compartment; **eisfrei** ADJ ice-free *attr*, free of ice *pred*; **eisgekühlt** ADJ chilled; **Eisgetränk** NT iced drink; **Eisglätte** F black ice; **Eisheiligen** PL **die drei ~** *three Saints' Days, 12th-14th May, which are usually particularly cold and after which further frost is rare*; **Eishockey** NT ice hockey, hockey (*US*)

eisig ['aiziç] **1** ADJ (a) (= *kalt*) icy (cold); *Kälte* icy (b) (*fig*: = *abweisend*) icy, glacial; *Ablehnung* cold; *Blick* icy; *Lächeln, Empfang* frosty **2** ADV (= *abweisend*) icily; **~ lächeln** to give a frosty smile; **er wurde ~ empfangen** he was given a frosty reception

Eis-: Eiskaffee M iced coffee; **eiskalt** ADJ (a) icy-cold (b) (*fig*) (= *abweisend*) icy; (= *kalt und berechnend*) cold-blooded; (= *dreist*) cool **2** ADV (a) = eisig (b) (= *kalt und berechnend*) cold-blooded; **sie hat auf seine Drohung ~ reagiert** her reaction to his threat was ice cool; **Eiskappe** F icecap; **Eiskeller** M cold store; **unser Schlafzimmer ist ein ~** our bedroom is like an icebox; **Eiskristall** NT ice crystal; **Eiskunstlauf** M figure skating; **Eiskunstläufer(in)** M(F) figure skater; **Eislauf** M ice-skating; **eislaufen** VI SEP IRREG AUX SEIN *siehe* **Eis; Eisläufer(in)** M(F) ice-skater; **Eismeer** NT polar sea; **Nördliches/Südliches ~** Arctic/Antarctic Ocean; **Eispickel** M ice axe (*Brit*)

Eisprung ['ai-] M (*Physiol*) ovulation *no art*

Eis-: Eisregen M sleet; **Eisrevue** F ice show; **Eisriegel** M ice-cream bar; **Eisschießen** NT **-s**, NO PL curling; **Eisschnelllauf** M speed skating; **Eisscholle** F ice floe; **Eisschrank** M refrigerator; **Eissport** M ice sports *pl*; **Eis(sport)stadion** NT ice rink; **Eistanz** M ice-dancing; **Eisverkäufer(in)** M(F) ice-cream seller; (*Mann auch*) ice-cream man (*inf*); **Eisvogel** M kingfisher

Eiswein is a very sweet, alcoholic wine, made - as the name suggests - from grapes which have been exposed to frost. To make it, selected grapes are left on the vine in autumn. Then, provided there have been constant temperatures of below -5°C for at least a week, the frozen grapes are picked at night and immediately pressed. Care must be taken that they do not thaw, so that only the best part of the grape goes into the wine. Since the yield from this process is very small and there is a risk that the temperatures will not be low enough for the process to take place, *Eiswein* is very expensive.

Eis-: Eiswürfel M ice cube; **Eiszapfen** M icicle; **Eiszeit** F Ice Age; (*fig*) cold war; **eiszeitlich** ADJ ice-age

eitel ['aitl] ADJ (a) *Mensch* vain; **~ wie ein Pfau** vain as a peacock (b) INV **es herrschte ~ Freude** there was absolute joy; **er denkt, das ganze Leben sei ~ Freude und Sonnenschein** he thinks the whole of life is nothing but a bed of roses

Eitelkeit F **-, -en** (*von Mensch*) vanity

Eiter ['aite] M **-s**, NO PL pus

Eiter-: Eiterbeule F boil; (*fig*) canker; **Eiterherd** M suppurative focus (*spec*)

eiterig ['aitǝriç] ADJ *Ausfluss* purulent; *Wunde* festering; *Binde* pus-covered

eitern ['aiten] VI to fester

Eiweiß ['aivais] NT **-es, -e** or **-** (egg) white; (*Chem*) protein

Eiweiß-: eiweißarm ADJ low in protein; **~e Kost** a low-protein diet; **eiweißhaltig** ADJ protein-containing *attr*; **Fleisch ist sehr ~** meat is high in protein; **Eiweißmangel** M protein deficiency

Eizelle F (*Biol*) egg cell

Ejakulation [ejakula'tsio:n] F **-, -en** ejaculation

ejakulieren [ejaku'li:rǝn], *ptp* **ejakuliert** VI to ejaculate

EKD [e:ka:'de:] F **-** ABBR *von* **Evangelische Kirche in Deutschland**

Ekel[1] ['e:kl] M **-s**, NO PL disgust; (= *Übelkeit*) nausea; **vor jdm/etw einen ~ haben** or **empfinden** to loathe sb/sth; **~ erregend** disgusting; **diese Heuchelei ist mir ein ~** I find this hypocrisy nauseating

Ekel[2] NT **-s**, **-** (*inf*) obnoxious person

ekelhaft, ekelig ['e:kǝliç] **1** ADJ disgusting; (*inf*) *Schmerzen, Problem, Chef* nasty; **sei nicht so ~ zu ihr!** don't be so nasty to her **2** ADV (= *widerlich*) *riechen, schmecken* disgusting; (*inf*: = *unangenehm*) *sich benehmen* terribly

ekeln ['e:kln] **1** VT to disgust **2** VT IMPERS **es ekelt mich vor diesem Geruch/Anblick, mich** or **mir ekelt vor diesem Geruch/Anblick** this smell/sight is disgusting **3** VR to be or feel disgusted; **sich vor etw** (*dat*) **~** to find sth disgusting

EKG, Ekg [e:ka:'ge:] NT **-s, -s** ABBR *von* **Elektrokardiogramm** ECG; **ein ~ machen lassen** to have an ECG

eklatant [ekla'tant] ADJ *Fall* sensational; *Beispiel* striking; *Verletzung* flagrant

eklig ['e:kliç] ADJ, ADV = ekelig

Ekstase [ek'sta:zǝ, eks'ta:zǝ] F **-, -n** ecstasy; **in ~ geraten** to go into ecstasies; **jdn in ~ versetzen** to send sb into ecstasies

Ekzem [ek'tse:m] NT **-s, -e** (*Med*) eczema

Elan [e'la:n, e'lã:] M **-s**, NO PL zest

Elastikbinde [e'lastık-] F elasticated bandage

elastisch [e'lastıʃ] **1** ADJ elastic; *Gang, Metall, Holz* springy; *Binde* elasticated **2** ADV supply; **er federte ~** he bent supply at the knees; **der Bügel schnellte ~ zurück** the bow sprang back

Elastizität [elastitsi'tɛ:t] F **-, (rare) -en** elasticity; (*von Metall, Holz*) flexibility

Elbe ['ɛlbǝ] F **- die ~** the (river) Elbe

Elch [ɛlç] M **-(e)s, -e** elk, moose (*esp US*)

Elchtest M (*inf*) (*Aut*) high-speed swerve (*to test a car's roadholding*); (*fig*: = *entscheidender Test*) make-or-break test

Eldorado [ɛldo'ra:do] NT **-s, -s** (*lit, fig*) eldorado

Electronic Banking [elek'trɔnık 'bɛŋkıŋ] NT **-**, NO PL electronic banking

Electronic Cash [elek'trɔnık 'kɛʃ] NT **-**, NO PL electronic cash

Elefant [ele'fant] M **-en, -en** elephant; **wie ein ~ im Porzellanladen** (*inf*) like a bull in a china shop (*prov*)

Elefanten-: Elefantenbaby NT (*inf*) baby elephant (*auch fig hum*); **Elefantenbulle** M bull elephant; **Elefantenhochzeit** F (*Comm inf*) mega-merger (*inf*); **Elefantenkuh** F cow elephant; **Elefantenrobbe** F elephant seal

elegant [ele'gant] **1** ADJ elegant **2** ADV elegantly

Eleganz [ele'gants] F **-**, NO PL elegance

Elegie [ele'gi:] F **-, -n** [-'gi:ǝn] elegy

elektrifizieren [elektrifi'tsi:rǝn], *ptp* **elektrifiziert** VT to electrify

Elektrik [e'lektrık] F **-, -en** (a) (= *elektrische Anlagen*) electrical equipment (b) NO PL (*inf*: = *Elektrizitätslehre*) electricity

Elektriker [e'lektrıke] M **-s, -**, **Elektrikerin** [-ǝrın] F **-, -nen** electrician

elektrisch [e'lektrıʃ] **1** ADJ electric; *Entladung, Feld, Widerstand* electrical; **~e Geräte** electrical appliances; **~er Schlag/Strom** electric shock/current; **der ~e Stuhl** the electric chair; **bei**

uns ist alles ~ we're all electric 🔢 ADV electrically; *kochen, heizen* with electricity; **sich ~ rasieren** to use an electric razor

elektrisieren [elɛktri'ziːrən], *ptp* **elektrisiert** VT (*lit, fig*) to electrify; (*Med*) to treat with electricity; **die elektrisierte Atmosphäre** the electrically-charged atmosphere; **wie elektrisiert** (as if) electrified

Elektrizität [elɛktritsi'tɛːt] F -, NO PL electricity

Elektrizitäts-: Elektrizitätsversorgung F (electric) power supply; **Elektrizitätswerk** NT (electric) power station; (= *Gesellschaft*) electric power company

Elektro- [e'lɛktro] IN CPDS electro- (*auch Sci*), electric; **Elektroanalyse** [elɛktroana'lyːzə, e'lɛktro-] F electroanalysis; **Elektroantrieb** M electric drive; **Elektroartikel** M electrical appliance; **Elektroauto** NT electric car

Elektrode [elɛk'troːdə] F -, -n electrode

Elektro-: Elektrodiagnostik [elɛktrodia'gnɔstɪk, e'lɛktro-] F (*Med*) electrodiagnosis; **Elektroenzephalogramm** [elɛktroɛtsefalo'gram] NT (*Med*) electroencephalogram, EEG; **Elektrofahrzeug** NT electric vehicle; **Elektrogerät** NT electrical appliance; **Elektrogeschäft** NT electrical shop (*Brit*) or store (*US*); **Elektrogitarre** F (*Mus*) electric guitar; **Elektroherd** M electric cooker; **Elektroindustrie** F electrical industry; **Elektroingenieur(in)** M(F) electrical engineer; **Elektroinstallateur(in)** M(F) electrician; **Elektrokardiogramm** [elɛktrokardio'gram] NT (*Med*) electrocardiogram, ECG; **Elektrolok** F electric locomotive; **Elektrolyse** [elɛktro'lyːzə] F -, -n electrolysis; **Elektrolyt** [elɛktro'lyːt] M -en, -en electrolyte; **elektrolytisch** [elɛktro'lyːtɪʃ] ADJ electrolytic; **elektromagnetisch** [elɛktroma'gneːtɪʃ, e'lɛktro-] ADJ electromagnetic; **Elektromotor** M electric motor

Elektron [e'lɛktron, e'lɛktrɔn, elɛk'troːn] NT -s, -en [elɛk'troːnən] electron

Elektronen-: Elektronenblitz M, **Elektronenblitzgerät** NT (*Phot*) electronic flash; **Elektronenlaser** M electron laser; **Elektronenmikroskop** NT electron microscope; **Elektronenschleuder** F (*Phys*) electron accelerator; **Elektronenstrahlen** PL electron *or* cathode rays *pl*

Elektronik [elɛk'troːnɪk] F -, -en electronics *sing*; (= *elektronische Teile*) electronics *pl*

Elektronik- IN CPDS electronic; **Elektronikgerät** NT electronic device; **Elektronikschrott** M electronic waste

elektronisch [elɛk'troːnɪʃ] 🔢 ADJ electronic; **~er Briefkasten** electronic mailbox; **~e Geldbörse** smartcard-based electronic wallet 🔢 ADV **~ gesteuert** electronically controlled

Elektro-: Elektroofen M (*Metal*) electric furnace; (= *Heizofen*) electric heater; **Elektrorasenmäher** M electric lawn mower; **Elektrorasierer** [-razi:rɐ] M **-s**, - electric shaver; **Elektroschock** M (*Med*) electric shock; **Elektroschockbehandlung** F electric shock treatment; **Elektrosmog** M electromagnetic radiation; **elektrostatisch** [elɛktro'ʃtaːtɪʃ] 🔢 ADJ electrostatic 🔢 ADV electrostatically; **Elektrotechnik** [elɛktro'tɛçnɪk, e'lɛktro-] F electrical engineering; **Elektrotherapie** [elɛktrotera'piː, e'lɛktro-] F (*Med*) electrotherapy

Element [ele'mɛnt] NT **-(e)s**, -e element (*auch Chem*); (*Elec*) cell, battery; **kriminelle ~e** (*pej*) criminal elements; **in seinem ~ sein** to be in one's element

elementar [elemɛn'taːɐ] 🔢 ADJ (= *grundlegend, wesentlich*) elementary; (= *naturhaft, urwüchsig*) *Gewalt, Trieb* elemental; *Hass* strong 🔢 ADV **~ hervorbrechen** to erupt with elemental force

Elementar- IN CPDS (= *grundlegend*) elementary; (= *naturhaft*) elemental; **Elementarkenntnisse** PL elementary knowledge *sing*; **Elementarladung** F (*Phys*) elementary charge; **Elementarteilchen** NT (*Phys*) elementary particle

elend ['eːlɛnt] 🔢 ADJ **(a)** (= *unglücklich, jämmerlich*) (*pej*: = *gemein*) wretched; (= *krank*) awful (*inf*), ill *pred*; **mir ist ganz ~** I feel really awful (*inf*); **mir wird ganz ~, wenn ich daran denke** I feel quite ill when I think about it **(b)** (*inf*: = *sehr groß, schlecht*) dreadful 🔢 ADV **(a)** (= *schlecht*) wretchedly; **~ aussehen** to look awful (*inf*); **sich ~ fühlen** to feel awful (*inf*) **(b)** (*inf*: = *schlimm*) dreadfully; **ich habe ~ gefroren** I was terribly cold; **da bin ich ~ betrogen worden** I was cheated terribly

Elend ['eːlɛnt] NT **-(e)s** [-dəs], NO PL (= *Unglück, Not*) misery; (= *Verwahrlosung*) squalor; (= *Armut*) poverty; **ein Bild des ~s**

a picture of misery/squalor; **ins ~ geraten** to fall into poverty; **jdn/sich (selbst) ins ~ stürzen** to plunge sb/oneself into misery/poverty; **(wie) ein Häufchen ~** (*inf*) (looking) a picture of misery; **das heulende ~** (*inf*) the blues *pl* (*inf*); **da kann man das heulende ~ kriegen** (*inf*) it's enough to make you scream (*inf*); **es ist ein ~ mit ihm** (*inf*) he makes you want to weep (*inf*); **es ist ein ~, ...** (*inf*) it's heartbreaking ...

elendig(lich) [e:'lɛndɪk(lɪç), (*emph*) e:'lɛndɪk(lɪç)] ADV (*geh*) miserably; **~ zugrunde** *or* **zu Grunde gehen** *or* **verrecken** (*sl*) to come to a wretched end

Elendsviertel NT slums *pl*

elf NUM eleven; *siehe auch* **vier**

Elf[1] [ɛlf] F -, -en (*Sport*) team, eleven

Elf[2] [ɛlf] M -en, -en, **Elfe** ['ɛlfə] F -, -n elf

Elfenbein ['ɛlfnbain] NT ivory

elfenbeinern 🔢 ADJ ivory 🔢 ADV ivory-like

Elfenbein-: elfenbeinfarben [-farbn], **elfenbeinfarbig** ADJ ivory-coloured (*Brit*), ivory-colored (*US*); **Elfenbeinküste** F Ivory Coast; **Elfenbeinturm** M (*fig*) ivory tower

elf-: elffach ['ɛlffax] ADJ elevenfold; *siehe auch* **vierfach**; **elfmal** ['ɛlfmaːl] ADV eleven times; *siehe auch* **viermal**

Elfmeter ['ɛlfmeːtɐ] M (*Ftbl*) penalty (kick) (*für* to, for); **einen ~ schießen** to take a penalty

Elfmeter-: Elfmeterschießen NT **-s**, - (*Ftbl*) penalty shoot-out; **durch ~ entschieden** decided on penalties; **Elfmeterschuss** M (*Ftbl*) penalty (kick); **Elfmeterschütze** M, **Elfmeterschützin** F (*Ftbl*) penalty-taker

Elftel ['ɛlftl] NT **-s**, - eleventh; *siehe auch* **Viertel**[1]

elftens ['ɛlftns] ADV eleventh, in the eleventh place

elfte(r, s) ['ɛlftə] ADJ eleventh; *siehe auch* **vierte(r, s)**

eliminieren [elimi'niːrən], *ptp* **eliminiert** VT to eliminate (*auch Math*)

elisabethanisch [elizabe'taːnɪʃ] ADJ Elizabethan

elitär [eli'tɛːɐ] 🔢 ADJ elitist 🔢 ADV in an elitist fashion

Elite [e'liːtə] F -, -n elite

Elixier [elɪ'ksiːɐ] NT **-s**, -e tonic

Ellbogen ['ɛlboːgn] M = **Ellenbogen**

Elle ['ɛlə] F -, -n **(a)** (*Anat*) ulna (*spec*) **(b)** (*Hist*) (*Measure*) cubit; (= *Maßstock*) ≈ yardstick

Ellenbogen ['ɛlənboːgn] M elbow; (*fig*) push; **die ~ gebrauchen** (*fig*) to use one's elbows; **er hat keine ~** (*fig*) he's not ruthless enough

Ellenbogen-: Ellenbogenfreiheit F (*fig*) elbow room; **Ellenbogengesellschaft** F dog-eat-dog society

ellenlang ADJ (*fig inf*) incredibly long (*inf*); *Kerl* incredibly tall (*inf*)

Ellipse [ɛ'lɪpsə] F -, -n (*Math*) ellipse; (*Gram*) ellipsis

elliptisch [ɛ'lɪptɪʃ] ADJ (*Math, Gram*) elliptic(al)

E-Lok ['eːlɔk] F ABBR *von* **elektrische Lokomotive** electric locomotive

Elsass ['ɛlzas] NT - *or* **-es das ~** Alsace

elsässisch ['ɛlzɛsɪʃ] ADJ Alsatian

Elsass-Lothringen ['ɛlzas'loːtrɪŋən] NT Alsace-Lorraine

Elster ['ɛlstɐ] F -, -n magpie; **wie eine ~ stehlen** to be always stealing things; **eine diebische ~ sein** (*fig*) to be a thief

elterlich ['ɛltɐlɪç] ADJ parental

Eltern ['ɛltɐn] PL parents *pl*; **nicht von schlechten ~ sein** (*inf*) to be quite something (*inf*)

Eltern-: Elternabend M (*Sch*) parents' evening; **Elternbeirat** M ≈ PTA, parent-teacher association; **Elternhaus** NT (*lit, fig*) (parental) home; **aus gutem ~ stammen** to come from a good home; **Elternliebe** F parental love; **elternlos** 🔢 ADJ orphaned 🔢 ADV **~ aufwachsen** to grow up as an orphan; **Elternschaft** ['ɛltɐnʃaft] F -, -en parents *pl*; **Elternsprechstunde** F (*Sch*) consultation hour (for parents); **Elternsprechtag** M open day (for parents); **Elternteil** M parent

Email [e'mai, e'maːj] NT **-s**, -s enamel

E-Mail ['iːmeːl] F -, -s (*Comput*) E-mail, e-mail

E-Mail-Adresse ['iːmeːl-] F (*Comput*) E-mail *or* e-mail address

emaillieren [ema'jiːrən, emal'jiːrən], *ptp* **emailliert** VT to enamel

Emanze [e'mantsə] F -, -n (*usu pej*) women's libber (*inf*)

Emanzipation [emantsipa'tsioːn] F -, -en emancipation

emanzipatorisch [emantsipa'toːrɪʃ] ADJ emancipatory

emanzipieren [emantsi'piːrən], *ptp* **emanzipiert** ▮ VT to emancipate ▮ VR to emancipate oneself

Embargo [ɛm'bargo] NT **-s, -s** embargo

Embolie [ɛmbo'liː] F **-, -n** [-'liːən] (*Med*) embolism

Embryo ['ɛmbryo] M (AUS AUCH NT) **-s, -s** *or* **-nen** [-'oːnən] embryo

Embryonenforschung F embryo research

embryonal [ɛmbryo'naːl] ADJ ATTR (*Biol, fig*) embryonic

Embryonenschutzgesetz NT embryo protection law

Emigrant [emi'grant] M **-en, -en**, **Emigrantin** [-'grantɪn] F **-, -nen** emigrant; (= *politischer Flüchtling*) émigré

Emigration [emigra'tsioːn] F **-, -en** emigration; **in der ~ leben** to live in (self-imposed) exile; **in die ~ gehen** to emigrate

emigrieren [emi'griːrən], *ptp* **emigriert** VI AUX SEIN to emigrate

eminent [emi'nɛnt] (*geh*) ▮ ADJ *Person* eminent; *Kenntnis* remarkable; **von ~er Bedeutung** of the utmost significance ▮ ADV eminently; **~ wichtig** of the utmost importance

Emir ['eːmɪr, e'miːr] M **-s, -e** emir

Emirat [emi'raːt] NT **-(e)s, -e** emirate

Emission [emi'sioːn] F **(a)** (*Fin*) issue **(b)** (*Phys*) emission **(c)** (*Sw:* = *Radiosendung*) (radio) broadcast

Emissions-: Emissionsbank F, *pl* **-banken** issuing bank; **Emissionsgeschäft** NT underwriting business; **Emissionskonsortium** NT underwriting syndicate; **Emissionskurs** M rate of issue

Emittent [emi'tɛnt] M **-en, -en** issuer; (= *Finanzunternehmen*) corporate issuer, issuing house

emittieren [emi'tiːrən], *ptp* **emittiert** VT **(a)** (*Fin*) to issue **(b)** (*Phys*) to emit

Emmentaler ['ɛməntaːlɐ] M **-s, -** (= *Käse*) Emment(h)aler

Emotion [emo'tsioːn] F **-, -en** emotion

emotional [emotsio'naːl] ▮ ADJ emotional; *Ausdrucksweise* emotive ▮ ADV emotionally

emotionalisieren [emotsionali'ziːrən], *ptp* **emotionalisiert** VT to emotionalize

Emotionalität F **-, -en** emotionality

emotions-: emotionsarm ADJ lacking in emotion; **emotionsgeladen** ADJ emotionally charged; **emotionslos** ▮ ADJ unemotional ▮ ADV unemotionally

Empf. ABBR *von* **Empfänger**

empfahl PRET *von* **empfehlen**

empfand PRET *von* **empfinden**

Empfang [ɛm'pfaŋ] M **-(e)s, ⸚e** [-'pfɛŋə] reception; (*von Brief, Ware etc*) receipt; **einen ~ geben** *or* **veranstalten** to give *or* hold a reception; **jdn/etw in ~ nehmen** to receive sb/sth; (*Comm*) to take delivery of sth; (**zahlbar**) **nach/bei ~** (+*gen*) (payable) on receipt (of); **auf ~ bleiben** (*Rad*) to stand by

empfangen [ɛm'pfaŋən], *pret* **empfing** [ɛm'pfɪŋ], *ptp* **empfangen** ▮ VT to receive; (= *begrüßen*) to greet; (*herzlich*) to welcome; (= *abholen*) *Besuch* to meet; **die Polizisten wurden mit einem Steinhagel ~** the police were greeted by a shower of stones ▮ VTI (= *schwanger werden*) to conceive

Empfänger¹ [ɛm'pfɛŋɐ] M **-s, -** (*Rad*) receiver

Empfänger² [ɛm'pfɛŋɐ] M **-s, -**, **Empfängerin** [-ərɪn] F **-, -nen** recipient; (= *Adressat*) addressee; (= *Warenempfänger*) consignee; **~ unbekannt** (*auf Briefen*) not known at this address; **~ verzogen** gone away

empfänglich [ɛm'pfɛŋlɪç] ADJ (= *aufnahmebereit*) receptive (*für* to); (= *beeinflussbar, anfällig*) susceptible (*für* to)

Empfängnis [ɛm'pfɛŋnɪs] F **-, -se** conception

Empfängnis-: empfängnisverhütend ADJ contraceptive; **~e Mittel** *pl* contraceptives *pl*; **Empfängnisverhütung** F contraception

Empfangs-: Empfangsanzeige F advice *or* notice of receipt; **Empfangsbereich** M (*Rad, TV*) reception area; **Empfangsbescheinigung** F, **Empfangsbestätigung** F (acknowledgment of) receipt; **Empfangschef(in)** M(F) (*von Hotel*) head porter; **Empfangsdame** F receptionist; **Empfangsgerät** NT (*Rad, TV*) (radio/TV) set; **Empfangsschüssel** F (*TV, Rad, Telec*) receiving dish; **Empfangsspediteur** M receiving forwarder

empfehlen [ɛm'pfeːlən], *pret* **empfahl** [ɛm'pfaːl], *ptp* **empfohlen** [ɛm'pfoːlən] ▮ VT to recommend; (**jdm**) **etw/jdn ~** to recommend sth/sb (to sb); **jdm ~, etw zu tun** to recommend sb to do sth; *siehe auch* **empfohlen** ▮ VR **sich für Reparaturen/**

als Experte *etc* **~** to offer one's services for repairs/as an expert *etc*; **es empfiehlt sich, das zu tun** it is advisable to do that

empfehlenswert ADJ to be recommended

Empfehlung F **-, -en** recommendation; (= *Referenz*) reference; **auf ~ von** on the recommendation of; **mit freundlichen** *or* **den besten ~en** (*am Briefende*) with best regards

Empfehlungsschreiben NT letter of recommendation

empfiehlt [ɛm'pfiːlt] 3. PERS SING PRES *von* **empfehlen**

empfinden [ɛm'pfɪndn], *pret* **empfand** [ɛm'pfant], *ptp* **empfunden** [ɛm'pfʊndn] VT to feel; **etw als kränkend** *or* **als Beleidigung ~** to find sth insulting; **er hat noch nie Hunger empfunden** he has never experienced hunger; **er empfand einen solch starken Hunger, dass …** his hunger was so great that …; **bei Musik Freude ~** to experience pleasure from music; **ich habe dabei viel Freude empfunden** it gave me great pleasure; **viel/nichts für jdn ~** to feel a lot/nothing for sb

Empfinden [ɛm'pfɪndn] NT **-s**, NO PL feeling; **meinem ~ nach** to my mind

empfindlich [ɛm'pfɪntlɪç] ▮ ADJ **(a)** sensitive (*auch Phot, Tech*); *Gesundheit, Stoff, Glas, Keramik etc* delicate; (= *leicht reizbar*) touchy (*inf*); **~e Stelle** (*lit*) sensitive spot; (*fig auch*) sore point; **gegen etw ~ sein** to be sensitive to sth; **Kupfer ist sehr ~** copper is easily damaged **(b)** (= *spürbar, schmerzlich*) *Verlust, Kälte, Strafe, Niederlage* severe; *Mangel* appreciable ▮ ADV (= *sensibel*) sensitively; **~ reagieren** to be sensitive (*auf* +*acc* to); (= *spürbar*) severely; **deine Kritik hat ihn ~ getroffen** your criticism cut him to the quick (*esp Brit*) *or* bone (*US*); **es ist ~ kalt** it is bitterly cold

Empfindlichkeit F **-, -en** sensitivity (*auch Phot, Tech*), sensitiveness; (*von Gesundheit, Stoff, Glas, Keramik*) delicateness; (= *leichte Reizbarkeit*) touchiness (*inf*)

Empfindung [ɛm'pfɪndʊŋ] F **-, -en** feeling

empfing PRET *von* **empfangen**

empfohlen ▮ PTP *von* **empfehlen** ▮ ADJ (**sehr** *or* **gut**) **~** (highly) recommended

empfunden PTP *von* **empfinden**

Emphysem [ɛmfy'zeːm] NT **-s, -e** (*Med*) emphysema

Empire¹ [ã'piːɐ̯] NT **-(s)**, NO PL (*Hist*) Empire; (= *~stil*) Empire style

Empire² ['ɛmpaɪɐ] NT **-(s)**, NO PL (British) Empire

Empirik [ɛm'piːrɪk] F **-**, NO PL empirical experience

Empiriker [ɛm'piːrɪkɐ] M **-s, -**, **Empirikerin** [-ərɪn] F **-, -nen** empiricist

empirisch [ɛm'piːrɪʃ] ADJ empirical

Empore [ɛm'poːrə] F **-, -n** (*Archit*) gallery

empören [ɛm'pøːrən], *ptp* **empört** ▮ VT to fill with indignation; (*stärker*) to incense; *siehe auch* **empört** ▮ VR (*über* +*acc* at) to be indignant; (*stärker*) to be incensed

empörend ADJ outrageous

empor-: emporheben VT SEP IRREG (*geh*) to raise; **emporkommen** VI SEP IRREG AUX SEIN (*geh*) to rise (up); (*fig*) (= *aufkommen*) to come to the fore; (= *vorankommen*) to go up in the world; **nur an sein Emporkommen denken** (*fig*) to think only of one's advancement; **Emporkömmling** [ɛm'poːrœmlɪŋ] M **-s, -e** (*pej*) upstart; **emporragen** VI SEP AUX HABEN or SEIN (*geh: lit, fig*) to tower (*über* +*acc* above); **emporschweben** VI SEP AUX SEIN (*geh*) to float upwards; **emporschwingen** VR SEP IRREG (*geh*) to soar upwards; (*Turner*) to swing upwards; **sich zu etw ~** (*fig*) to (come to) achieve sth; *zu einer Stellung* to reach sth; **emporsteigen** VI SEP IRREG AUX SEIN (*geh*) to climb (up); (*Mond, Angst etc*) to rise (up); **emporstreben** VI SEP AUX SEIN (*geh*) to soar upwards; (*fig*) AUX HABEN to be ambitious

empört [ɛm'pøːɐ̯t] ▮ ADJ outraged (*über* +*acc* at) ▮ ADV indignantly; *siehe auch* **empören**

Empörung [ɛm'pøːrʊŋ] F **-**, NO PL (= *Entrüstung*) indignation (*über* +*acc* at)

emsig ['ɛmzɪç] ▮ ADJ busy; (= *eifrig*) eager ▮ ADV busily; (= *eifrig*) eagerly

Emu ['eːmu] M **-s, -s** emu

emulgieren [emʊl'giːrən], *ptp* **emulgiert** VTI to emulsify

Emulsion [emʊl'zioːn] F **-, -en** emulsion

E-Musik ['eː-] F serious music

End- IN CPDS final; **Endabnehmer(in)** M(F) end buyer; **Endabrechnung** F final account; **Endbahnhof** M terminus, terminal; **Endbenutzer(in)** M(F) end user; **Endbetrag** M final amount

Ende ['ɛndə] NT **-s, -n** end; (= *Ausgang, Ergebnis*) outcome; (= *Ausgang eines Films, Romans etc*) ending; (*inf*: = *Stückchen*) (small) piece; (*inf*: = *Strecke*) way, stretch; ~ **Mai/der Woche** at the end of May/the week; ~ **der zwanziger Jahre** *or* **Zwanzigerjahre** in the late twenties; **er ist** ~ **vierzig** he is in his late forties; **er wohnt am** ~ **der Welt** (*inf*) he lives at the back of beyond; **bis ans** ~ **der Welt** to the ends of the earth; **das** ~ **vom Lied** the final outcome; **das** ~ **der Fahnenstange** (*fig inf*) the end of the road; **ein** ~ **mit Schrecken** a terrible end; **lieber ein** ~ **mit Schrecken als ein Schrecken ohne** ~ (*Prov*) it's best to get unpleasant things over and done with; **Probleme/ Leiden ohne** ~ endless problems/suffering; **letzten** ~**s** when all is said and done; (= *am* ~) in the end; (**bei** *or* **mit etw**) **kein** ~ **finden** (*inf*) to be unable to stop (sth *or* telling/doing *etc* sth); **damit muss es jetzt ein** ~ **haben** this must stop now; **das nimmt** *or* **findet gar kein** ~ (*inf*) there's no end to it; **ein böses** ~ **nehmen** to come to a bad end; **da ist das** ~ **von weg!** (*N Ger inf*) it's incredible! (*inf*); **... und kein** ~ ... without end; **es ist noch ein gutes** *or* **ganzes** ~ (*inf*) there's still quite a way to go (yet); **am** ~ at the end; (= *schließlich*) in the end; (*inf*: = *möglicherweise*) perhaps; (**am**) ~ **des Monats** at the end of the month; **am** ~ **sein** (*fig*) to be at the end of one's tether (*Brit*) *or* rope (*US*); **mit etw am** ~ **sein** to have reached the end of sth; (*Vorrat*) to have run out of sth; **ich bin mit meiner Weisheit am** ~ I'm at my wits' end; **meine Geduld ist am** ~ my patience is at an end; **zu** ~ finished; **etw zu** ~ **bringen** *or* **führen** to finish (off) sth; **ein Buch/einen Brief zu** ~ **lesen/ schreiben** to finish (reading/writing) a book/letter; **zu** ~ **gehen** to come to an end; (*Vorräte*) to run out; ~ **gut, alles gut** (*Prov*) all's well that ends well (*Prov*)

Endeffekt M **im** ~ (*inf*) in the end

enden ['ɛndn] VI to end; (*Frist auch*) to run out; (*Zug*) to terminate; (= *sterben*) to meet one's end; **auf etw** (*acc*) *or* **mit etw** ~ (*Wort*) to end with sth; **mit den Worten ...** ~ (*bei Rede*) to close with the words ...; **es endete damit, dass ...** the outcome was that ...; **er endete im Gefängnis** he ended up in prison; **wie wird das noch mit ihm** ~**?** what will become of him?; **das wird böse** ~**!** no good will come of it!; **nicht** ~ **wollend** unending

End-: Endergebnis NT final result; **Endfassung** F (*von Text, Film*) final version; **Endgehalt** NT final salary; **endgeil** ADJ (*sl*) wicked (*sl*); **Endgerät** NT (*Telec etc*) terminal

endgültig 🔟 ADJ final; *Antwort* definite; **etwas Endgültiges lässt sich noch nicht sagen** I/we *etc* cannot say anything definite at this stage 🔟 ADV finally; **damit ist die Sache** ~ **entschieden** that settles the matter once and for all; **das ist** ~ **aus** *or* **vorbei** that's (all) over and done with; **sie haben sich jetzt** ~ **getrennt** they've separated for good; **jetzt ist** ~ **Schluss!** that's it!

Endgültigkeit F, NO PL finality

Endhaltestelle F terminus, final stop (*US*)

Endivie [ɛn'diːviə] F **-, -n** endive

End-: Endlager NT (*für Atommüll etc*) permanent (waste) disposal site; **Endlagerung** F (*von Atommüll etc*) permanent (waste) disposal

endlich ['ɛntlɪç] 🔟 ADV finally; **na** ~**!** at (long) last!; **hör** ~ **damit auf!** will you stop that!; **komm doch** ~**!** come on, get a move on!; ~ **kam er doch** he eventually came after all 🔟 ADJ (*Math, Philos*) finite

endlos 🔟 ADJ endless 🔟 ADV forever; **ich musste** ~ **lange warten** I had to wait for ages (*inf*)

Endlospapier NT, NO PL continuous paper

Endo- IN CPDS endo-; **endogen** [ɛndo'geːn] ADJ endogenous; **endokrin** [ɛndo'kriːn] ADJ (*Med*) endocrine

Endorphin [ɛndɔr'fiːn] NT **-s, -e** endorphin

Endo- IN CPDS endo-; **Endoskop** [ɛndo'skoːp] NT **-s, -e** (*Med*) endoscope; **Endoskopie** [ɛndosko'piː] F **-, -n** [-'piːən] (*Med*) endoscopy; **operative** ~ endosurgery; **endoskopisch** [ɛndo'skoːpɪʃ] (*Med*) 🔟 ADJ endoscopic 🔟 ADV **jdn** ~ **operieren/ untersuchen** to operate on/examine sb using endoscopy

End-: Endphase F final stage(s *pl*); **Endpreis** M final price; **Endprodukt** NT end product; **Endrunde** F (*Sport*) finals *pl*; (*Leichtathletik, Autorennen*) final lap; (*Boxen, fig*) final round;

Endsilbe F final syllable; **Endspiel** NT (*Sport*) final; (*Chess*) end game; **Endspurt** M (*Sport, fig*) final spurt; **Endstadium** NT final *or* (*Med*) terminal stage; **Endstation** F (*Rail etc*) terminus, terminal; (*fig*) end of the line

Endung ['ɛndʊŋ] F **-, -en** (*Gram*) ending

End-: Endverbraucher(in) M(F) end user; **Endzeitstimmung** F apocalyptic mood

energetisch [ɛnɛr'geːtɪʃ] ADJ (*Phys*) energetic

Energie [ɛnɛr'giː] F **-, -n** [-'giːən] (*Sci, fig*) energy; ~ **sparend** energy-saving; **seine ganze** ~ **für etw einsetzen** *or* **aufbieten** to devote all one's energies to sth; **mit aller** *or* **ganzer** ~ with all one's energy; **kriminelle** ~ criminal resolve

Energie-: Energiebedarf M energy requirement; **energiebewusst** ADJ energy-conscious; **energiegeladen** ADJ full of energy; **Energiegewinnung** F generation of energy; **Energieknappheit** F energy shortage; **Energiekrise** F energy crisis; **energielos** ADJ lacking in energy; **Energielosigkeit** F -, NO PL lack of energy; **Energiepolitik** F energy policy; **energiepolitisch** ADJ energy-policy *attr*; *Konsens, Parteilinie, Sprecher* on energy policy; **Energiequelle** F energy source; **energiesparend** ADJ *siehe* **Energie**; **Energiesparlampe** F energy-saving bulb; **Energiesparmaßnahmen** PL energy-saving measures *pl*; **Energieträger** M energy source; **Energieverbrauch** M energy consumption; **Energieversorgung** F supply of energy; **Energieversorgungsunternehmen** NT energy supply company; **Energiewirtschaft** F (= *Wirtschaftszweig*) energy industry; **energiewirtschaftlich** ADJ relating to the energy industry; **Energiezufuhr** F energy supply

energisch [ɛ'nɛrgɪʃ] 🔟 ADJ (= *voller Energie*) energetic; (= *entschlossen, streng*) forceful; *Griff, Maßnahmen* firm; *Worte* strong; ~ **werden** to assert oneself; **wenn das nicht aufhört, werde ich** ~**!** if this doesn't stop I'll have to put my foot down! 🔟 ADV *dementieren* strongly; *sagen* forcefully; *verteidigen* vigorously; ~ **durchgreifen** to take firm action

eng [ɛŋ] 🔟 ADJ (a) (*lit*: = *schmal, fig*: = *beschränkt*) *Straße etc* narrow; (= *beengt*) *Raum* cramped; (= ~ *anliegend*) *Kleidung* tight; **ein Kleid** ~**er machen** to take a dress in; **im** ~**eren Sinne** in the narrow sense; **in die** ~**ere Wahl kommen** to be shortlisted; **es wird** ~ **für ihn** (*fig inf*) he doesn't have much room for manoeuvre (*Brit*) *or* maneuver (*US*) (b) (= *nah, dicht, vertraut*) close; **eine Feier im** ~**sten Kreise** a small party for close friends; **die Hochzeit fand im** ~**sten Kreise der Familie statt** the wedding was celebrated with just the immediate family present 🔟 ADV (a) (= *mit wenig Platz*) ~ **beisammen stehen** to stand close together; (*Bäume etc*) to be close together; ~ **anliegend** tight(-fitting); ~ **anliegen** to fit tightly; ~ **sitzen** to be tight; ~ **begrenzt** restricted; ~ **gebaute Frauen** women with narrow hips; ~ **zusammengedrängt sein** to be crowded together (b) (= *dicht*) *tanzen* close together; ~ **bedruckt** densely printed; ~ **beschrieben** closely written; ~ **nebeneinander** *or* **zusammen** close together (c) (= *intim*) ~ **befreundet sein** to be close friends; **mit jdm** ~ **befreundet sein** to be a close friend of sb (d) (*inf*: = *verkniffen*) **das darfst du nicht so** ~ **sehen** (*fig inf*) don't take it so seriously; **solche Dinge sehe ich sehr** ~ I'm very particular about that type of thing

Engadin ['ɛŋgadiːn] NT **-s das** ~ the Engadine

Engagement [ãgaʒə'mãː] NT **-s, -s** (a) (*Theat*) engagement (b) (*geh*: = *Aktivität*) involvement; (= *politisches* ~) commitment (*für* to)

engagieren [ãga'ʒiːrən] *ptp* **engagiert** 🔟 VT to engage 🔟 VR to be/become committed (*für* to); (*in einer Beziehung*) to become involved

engagiert [ãga'ʒiːɐt] ADJ committed

eng-: enganliegend ADJ ATTR *siehe* **eng**; **engbrüstig** [-brʏstɪç] ADJ narrow-chested

Enge ['ɛŋə] F **-, -n** (a) NO PL (*von Straße etc*) narrowness; (*von Wohnung*) confinement; (= *Gedrängtheit*) crush; (*von Kleid etc*) tightness (b) (= *Meerenge*) strait; (= *Engpass*) pass; **jdn in die** ~ **treiben** (*fig*) to drive sb into a corner

Engel ['ɛŋl] M **-s, -** (*lit, fig*) angel; **ein rettender** ~ (*fig*) a saviour (*Brit*) *or* savior (*US*); **sie ist auch nicht gerade ein** ~ (*inf*) she's no angel (*inf*); **wir sind alle keine** ~ (*prov*) none of us is perfect

Engelmacher(in) M(F) (*euph inf*) backstreet abortionist

Engels-: Engelsgeduld F saintly patience; **sie hat eine ~** she has the patience of a saint; **Engelszungen** PL **(wie) mit ~ reden** to use all one's powers of persuasion

Engerling ['ɛŋɐlɪŋ] M **-s, -e** (Zool) grub of the cockchafer

engl. ABBR von **englisch**

England ['ɛŋlant] NT **-s** England

Engländer ['ɛŋlɛndɐ] M **-s, - (a)** Englishman; English boy; **die ~ pl** the English, the Brits (inf); **er ist ~** he's English **(b)** (Tech) monkey wrench

Engländerin ['ɛŋlɛndərɪn] F **-, -nen** Englishwoman; English girl

Englein ['ɛŋlain] NT **-s, -** little angel

englisch ['ɛŋlɪʃ] ADJ English; Steak rare; siehe auch **deutsch**

Englisch(e) ['ɛŋlɪʃ] NT English; siehe auch **Deutsch(e)**

Englisch-: Englischhorn NT (Mus) cor anglais; **englischsprachig** ADJ Gebiet, Minderheit English-speaking; Zeitung English-language attr

Eng-: engmaschig [-maʃɪç] **1** ADJ close-meshed; (fig) close; **ein ~es soziales Netz** a comprehensive social welfare network **2** ADV **~ stricken** to knit to a fine tension; **Engpass** M (narrow) pass; (= Fahrbahnverengung, fig) bottleneck

en gros [ã ˈgro] ADV wholesale; (fig) en masse

Engrossist(in) [ãgrɔˈsɪst(ɪn)] M(F) (Aus) wholesaler

engstirnig ['ɛŋʃtɪrnɪç] ADJ narrow-minded; (= mit begrenztem Horizont) insular

Engstirnigkeit F narrow-mindedness; (= begrenzter Horizont) insularity

Enkel ['ɛŋkl] M **-s, -** (= ~kind) grandchild; (= ~sohn) grandson; (fig) heir

Enkelin ['ɛŋkəlɪn] F **-, -nen** granddaughter

Enklave [ɛnˈklaːvə] F **-, -n** enclave

en masse [ã ˈmas] ADV en masse

enorm [eˈnɔrm] **1** ADJ (= riesig) enormous; (inf: = herrlich, kolossal) tremendous (inf) **2** ADV (= riesig) enormously; (inf: = herrlich, kolossal) tremendously; (= enorm viel) an enormous amount; **er verdient ~** (inf), **er verdient ~ viel (Geld)** (inf) he earns an enormous amount (of money)

en passant [ã paˈsã] ADV en passant

Enquetekommission [ãˈkeːt-, ãˈkɛːt-] F commission of inquiry

Ensemble [ãˈsãːbl] NT **-s, -s** ensemble; (= Besetzung) cast

entarten [ɛntˈaːrtn], ptp **entartet** VI AUX SEIN to degenerate (zu into)

entartet [ɛntˈaːrtət] ADJ degenerate

entbehren [ɛntˈbeːrən], ptp **entbehrt** VT **(a)** (= vermissen) to miss; (= zur Verfügung stellen) to spare **(b)** AUCH VI (= verzichten) to do without; **wir können ihn heute nicht ~** we cannot spare him/it today

entbehrlich [ɛntˈbeːrlɪç] ADJ dispensable

Entbehrung F **-, -en** privation; **~en auf sich** (acc) **nehmen** to make sacrifices

entbinden [ɛntˈbɪndn], ptp **entbunden** [ɛntˈbʊndn] IRREG **1** VT **(a)** Frau to deliver; **sie ist von einem Sohn entbunden worden** she has given birth to a son **(b)** (= befreien) to release (von from) **2** VI (Frau) to give birth

Entbindung F delivery; (von Amt etc) release

Entbindungs-: Entbindungsklinik F maternity clinic; **Entbindungspfleger(in)** M(F) obstetric nurse; **Entbindungsstation** F maternity ward

entblöden [ɛntˈbløːdn], ptp **entblödet** VR (geh) **sich nicht ~, etw zu tun** to have the effrontery to do sth

entblößen [ɛntˈbløːsn], ptp **entblößt** VT (form) Körperteil to bare; (fig) sein Innenleben to lay bare; **er hat sich entblößt** (Exhibitionist) he exposed himself; (seinen wahren Charakter) he showed his true colours (Brit) or colors (US)

Entchen ['ɛntçən] NT **-s, -** DIM von **Ente** duckling

entdecken [ɛntˈdɛkn], ptp **entdeckt** VT (= finden) to discover; (in der Ferne, in einer Menge) to spot

Entdecker [ɛntˈdɛkɐ] M **-s, -, Entdeckerin** [-ərɪn] F **-, -nen** discoverer

Entdeckung F discovery

Ente ['ɛntə] F **-, -n** duck; (Press inf) canard; (Aut inf) Citroën 2CV, deux-chevaux

entehren [ɛntˈeːrən], ptp **entehrt** VT to dishonour (Brit), to dishonor (US); (= entwürdigen) to degrade; **~d** degrading

enteignen [ɛntˈaignən], ptp **enteignet** VT to expropriate; Besitzer to dispossess

Enteignung F expropriation; (von Besitzer) dispossession

enteisen [ɛntˈaizn], ptp **enteist** VT to de-ice; Kühlschrank to defrost

entemotionalisieren [ɛnt|emotionaliˈziːrən], ptp **entemotionalisiert** VT to de-emotionalize

Enten-: Entenbraten M roast duck; **Entenei** [-lai] NT duck's egg; **Entenküken** NT duckling

Entente [ãˈtãːt(ə)] F **-, -n** (Pol) entente

enterben [ɛntˈɛrbn], ptp **enterbt** VT to disinherit

Enterich ['ɛntərɪç] M **-s, -e** drake

entern ['ɛntɐn] **1** VT (= stürmen) Schiff, Haus to storm **2** VI AUX SEIN (Naut) to board

Entertainer [ɛntɐˈteːnɐ] M **-s, -, Entertainerin** [-ərɪn] F **-, -nen** entertainer

Enter-Taste ['ɛntɐ-] F (Comput) enter key

entfahren [ɛntˈfaːrən], ptp **entfahren** VI IRREG AUX SEIN **jdm ~** to slip out; **Blödsinn! entfuhr es ihm** nonsense, he cried inadvertently; **ihr ist ein kleiner Furz ~** (inf) she accidentally let off a little fart (sl)

entfallen [ɛntˈfalən], ptp **entfallen** VI IRREG AUX SEIN **(a)** (fig: aus dem Gedächtnis) **jdm ~** to slip sb's mind **(b)** (= nicht in Betracht kommen) not to apply; (= wegfallen) to be dropped **(c)** **auf jdn/etw ~** (Geld, Kosten) to be allotted to sb/sth; **auf jeden ~ 100 Euro** (= erhalten) each person will receive 100 euros; (= bezahlen müssen) each person will pay 100 euros

entfalten [ɛntˈfaltn], ptp **entfaltet** **1** VT (= auseinander legen) to unfold; (fig) Kräfte, Begabung, Theorie to develop; Tätigkeit to launch into; Plan, Gedankengänge to set out; Pracht, Prunk to display **2** VR (Knospe, Blüte) to open; (fig) to develop; **hier kann ich mich nicht ~** I can't make full use of my abilities here

Entfaltung F **-, -en** unfolding; (= Entwicklung) development; (einer Tätigkeit) launching into; (eines Planes, Gedankens) setting out; (von Prunk, Tatkraft) display; **zur ~ kommen** to develop

entfärben [ɛntˈfɛrbn], ptp **entfärbt** VT to decolour (Brit), to decolor (US); (= bleichen) to bleach; **das Entfärben** the removal of colour (Brit) or color (US)

Entfärber M, **Entfärbungsmittel** NT colour (Brit) or color (US) remover

entfernen [ɛntˈfɛrnən], ptp **entfernt** **1** VT to remove (von, aus from); **jdn aus der Schule ~** to expel sb from school; **das entfernt uns (weit) vom Thema** that takes us a long way from our subject **2** VR **(a)** (= weggehen) **sich (von** or **aus etw) ~** to go away (from sth); (= abfahren, abziehen) to depart (from sth); **sich von seinem Posten/Arbeitsplatz ~** to leave one's post/position; **sich zu weit ~** to go too far away **(b)** (fig) (von from) (von jdm) to become estranged; (von Thema) to digress; (von Wahrheit) to depart

entfernt [ɛntˈfɛrnt] **1** ADJ Ort, Verwandter distant; (= abgelegen) remote; (= gering) Ähnlichkeit vague; **10 km ~ von** 10 km (away) from; **das Haus liegt 2 km ~** the house is 2 km away **2** ADV remotely; **nicht einmal ~ (so gut/hübsch** etc) not even remotely (as good/pretty etc); **~ verwandt** distantly related; **das hat nur ~ mit dieser Angelegenheit zu tun** that has only a distant bearing on this matter; **nicht im Entferntesten!** not in the slightest!

Entfernung F **-, -en (a)** distance; (Mil: bei Waffen) range; **aus kurzer/großer ~ (schießen)** (to fire) at or from close/long range; **aus einiger ~** from a distance; **in einiger ~** at a distance; **in acht Kilometer(n) ~** eight kilometres (Brit) or kilometers (US) away **(b)** (= das Entfernen) removal; (aus der Schule) expulsion; **unerlaubte ~ vom Posten** etc absence from one's post etc without permission

Entfernungsmesser M **-s, -** (Mil, Phot) rangefinder

Entfernungstaste F (Comput) delete key

entfesseln [ɛntˈfɛsln], ptp **entfesselt** VT (fig) to unleash

entfesselt [ɛntˈfɛslt] ADJ unleashed; Leidenschaft, Trieb unbridled; Mensch wild; Naturgewalten raging

entfetten [ɛntˈfɛtn], ptp **entfettet** VT to remove the grease from; Wolle to scour

entflammbar ADJ inflammable

entflammen [ɛntˈflamən], *ptp* **entflammt** ① VT (*fig*) to (a)rouse; *Begeisterung* to fire ② VI AUX SEIN to burst into flames; (*fig*) (*Zorn, Streit*) to flare up; (*Leidenschaft, Liebe*) to be (a)roused; **in Liebe ~/entflammt sein** to fall/be passionately in love

entflechten [ɛntˈflɛçtn], *ptp* **entflochten** [ɛntˈflɔxtn] VT IRREG *Konzern, Kartell etc* to break up

entfliehen [ɛntˈfliːən], *ptp* **entflohen** [ɛntˈfloːən] VI IRREG AUX SEIN (*geh*: = *entkommen*) to escape (+*dat or aus* from); **dem Lärm/ der Unrast** *etc ~* to escape (from) the noise/unrest *etc*

entfremden [ɛntˈfrɛmdn], *ptp* **entfremdet** ① VT to alienate (*auch Sociol, Philos*), to estrange; **etw seinem Zweck ~** not to use sth for its intended purpose ② VR to become alienated (*dat* from)

Entfremdung F -, -en estrangement; (*Sociol, Philos*) alienation

entfrosten [ɛntˈfrɔstn], *ptp* **entfrostet** VT to defrost

Entfroster [ɛntˈfrɔstɐ] M -s, - defroster

entführen [ɛntˈfyːrən], *ptp* **entführt** VT *jdn* to kidnap; *LKW, Flugzeug* to hijack; *Mädchen* (*mit Zustimmung zur Heirat*) to elope with; (*hum inf:* = *wegnehmen*) to borrow (*often hum*); **sie ließ sich von ihrem Liebhaber ~** she eloped with her lover

Entführer(in) M(F) kidnapper; (*von Fahrzeug*) hijacker; (*von Flugzeug*) hijacker, skyjacker (*inf*)

Entführung F kidnapping; (*von Flugzeug, LKW*) hijacking; „**Die ~ aus dem Serail**" "The Abduction from the Seraglio"

entgegen [ɛntˈgeːɡn] ① PREP +DAT contrary to; **~ allen Erwartungen, allen Erwartungen** ~ contrary to all expectation(s) ② ADV (*geh*) **dem Licht/der Zukunft** *etc* **~!** on toward(s) the light/future *etc*!; **neuen Ufern/Abenteuern ~!** on to new shores/adventures!

entgegenbringen VT SEP IRREG **jdm etw ~** to bring sth to sb; (*fig*) *Achtung, Freundschaft etc* to show sth for sb

entgegenfahren VI SEP IRREG AUX SEIN +DAT to travel toward(s); (*um jdn zu treffen*) to travel to meet; (*mit dem Auto*) to drive toward(s)/to meet

entgegengehen VI SEP IRREG AUX SEIN +DAT to go toward(s); (*um jdn zu treffen*) to go to meet; (*fig*) to face; **dem Ende ~** (*Leben, Krieg*) to draw to a close; **seinem Untergang/ Schwierigkeiten ~** to be heading for disaster/difficulties; **seiner Vollendung ~** to near completion

entgegengesetzt ① ADJ opposite; (*fig:* = *einander widersprechend*) opposing *attr*, conflicting *attr*; **einander ~e Interessen/Meinungen** *etc* opposing interests/views *etc* ② ADV **genau ~ denken/handeln** *etc* to think/do *etc* exactly the opposite; *siehe auch* **entgegensetzen**

entgegenhalten VT SEP IRREG +DAT **jdm etw ~** (*lit*) to hold sth out toward(s) sb; **einer Sache ~, dass ...** (*fig*) to object to sth that ...

entgegenkommen VI SEP IRREG AUX SEIN +DAT to come toward(s); (*um jdn zu treffen*) to (come to) meet; (*fig*) to accommodate; **jdm auf halbem Wege ~** (*lit, fig*) to meet sb halfway; **das kommt unseren Plänen/Vorstellungen** *etc* **sehr entgegen** that fits in very well with our plans/ideas *etc*; **Ihr Vorschlag kommt mir sehr entgegen** I find your suggestion very congenial; **können Sie uns preislich etwas ~?** can you adjust your price a little?

Entgegenkommen NT (= *Gefälligkeit*) kindness; (= *Zugeständnis*) concession

entgegenkommend ADJ (a) *Fahrzeug* oncoming (b) (*fig*) obliging

entgegenkommenderweise ADV obligingly; (*als Zugeständnis*) as a concession

entgegenlaufen VI SEP IRREG AUX SEIN +DAT to run toward(s); (*um jdn zu treffen*) to run to meet; (*fig*) to run contrary to

Entgegennahme [-naːmə] F -, NO PL (*form*) (= *Empfang*) receipt; (= *Annahme*) acceptance; **bei ~** on receipt/acceptance

entgegennehmen VT SEP IRREG (= *empfangen*) to receive; (= *annehmen*) to accept

entgegensehen VI SEP IRREG (*fig*) **einer Sache** (*dat*) **~** to await sth; (*freudig*) to look forward to sth; **einer Sache ~ müssen** to have to face sth; **Ihrer baldigen Antwort ~d** (*form*) in anticipation of your early reply

entgegensetzen VT SEP +DAT **etw einer Sache ~** to set sth against sth; **wir können diesen Forderungen nichts ~** we have nothing to counter these claims with; **dem habe ich entgegenzusetzen, dass ...** against that I'd like to say that ...; **die Gewerkschaften hatten den Regierungsvorschlägen nichts**

entgegenzusetzen the unions had nothing to offer in reply to the government's suggestions; *siehe auch* **entgegengesetzt**

entgegenstellen SEP +DAT ① VT = **entgegensetzen** ② VR **sich** *jdm/einer Sache* ~ to oppose sb/sth

entgegenstrecken VT SEP **jdm etw ~** to hold out sth to sb

entgegentreten VI SEP IRREG AUX SEIN +DAT to step up to; **dem Feind** to go into action against; **einer Politik, Forderungen** to oppose; **Behauptungen, Vorurteilen** to counter; **einer Gefahr, Unsitten** to take steps against

entgegenwirken VI SEP +DAT to counteract

entgegnen [ɛntˈgeːɡnən], *ptp* **entgegnet** VTI to reply; (*kurz, barsch*) to retort (*auf* +*acc* to); **er entgegnete nichts** he made no reply

Entgegnung F -, -en reply

entgehen [ɛntˈgeːən], *ptp* **entgangen** [ɛntˈgaŋən] VI IRREG AUX SEIN +DAT **(a)** (= *entkommen*) *Verfolgern, dem Feind* to elude; *dem Schicksal, der Gefahr, Strafe* to escape **(b)** (*fig:* = *nicht bemerkt werden*) **dieser Fehler ist mir entgangen** I failed to notice this mistake; **mir ist kein Wort entgangen** I didn't miss a word (of it); **es ist meiner Aufmerksamkeit nicht entgangen, dass ...** it has not escaped my attention that ...; **ihr entgeht nichts** she doesn't miss a thing; **sich** (*dat*) **etw ~ lassen** to miss sth

entgeistert [ɛntˈgaɪstɐt] ① ADJ thunderstruck; *Lachen* astonished ② ADV **er starrte mich ganz ~ an** he stared at me quite thunderstruck; **er reagierte ~** he reacted with complete astonishment

Entgelt [ɛntˈgɛlt] NT -(e)s, -e (*form*) **(a)** (= *Bezahlung*) remuneration (*form*); (= *Entschädigung*) recompense (*form*); (= *Anerkennung*) reward **(b)** (= *Gebühr*) fee, consideration; **jdm etw gegen ~ abgeben** to give sb sth for a consideration

entgiften [ɛntˈgɪftn], *ptp* **entgiftet** VT to decontaminate; (*Med*) to detoxicate

Entgiftung F -, -en decontamination; (*Med*) detoxication

entgleisen [ɛntˈglaɪzn], *ptp* **entgleist** VI AUX SEIN **(a)** (*Rail*) to be derailed; **einen Zug zum Entgleisen bringen** *or* **~ lassen** to derail a train **(b)** (*fig: Mensch*) to misbehave

Entgleisung F -, -en derailment; (*fig*) faux pas

entgleiten [ɛntˈglaɪtn], *ptp* **entglitten** [ɛntˈglɪtn] VI IRREG AUX SEIN +DAT to slip; **jdm** *or* **jds Hand** ~ to slip from sb's grasp; **jdm/ einer Sache** ~ (*fig*) to slip away from sb/sth

entgräten [ɛntˈgrɛːtn], *ptp* **entgrätet** VT *Fisch* to fillet

enthaaren [ɛntˈhaːrən], *ptp* **enthaart** VT to remove unwanted hair from

Enthaarungs-: Enthaarungscreme F depilatory cream; **Enthaarungsmittel** NT depilatory

enthalten [ɛntˈhaltn], *ptp* **enthalten** IRREG ① VT to contain; (**mit**) **~ sein in** (+*dat*) to be included in ② VR **sich einer Sache** (*gen*) ~ (*geh*) to abstain from sth; **sich nicht ~ können, etw zu tun** (*geh*) to be unable to refrain from doing sth; **sich (der Stimme)** ~ to abstain

enthaltsam [ɛntˈhaltzaːm] ① ADJ abstemious; (*sexuell*) chaste; (= *mäßig*) moderate ② ADV **~ leben** to be abstinent; (= *sexuell*) to be celibate

Enthaltsamkeit F -, NO PL abstinence; (*sexuell*) chastity; (= *Mäßigkeit*) moderation

Enthaltung F abstinence; (= *Stimmenthaltung*) abstention

enthärten [ɛntˈhɛrtn], *ptp* **enthärtet** VT *Wasser* to soften

enthaupten [ɛntˈhaʊptn], *ptp* **enthauptet** VT to decapitate; (*als Hinrichtung auch*) to behead

entheben [ɛntˈheːbn], *ptp* **enthoben** [ɛntˈhoːbn] VT IRREG **jdn einer Sache** (*gen*) ~ to relieve sb of sth

enthemmen [ɛntˈhɛmən], *ptp* **enthemmt** VTI **jdn ~** to make sb lose his inhibitions; **Alkohol wirkt ~** alcohol has a disinhibiting effect; **moralisch** *etc*) **völlig enthemmt sein** to have no (moral *etc*) inhibitions whatsoever

enthüllen [ɛntˈhʏlən], *ptp* **enthüllt** ① VT to uncover; *Denkmal, Gesicht* to unveil; *Geheimnis, Plan, Hintergründe* to reveal ② VR (*lithum*) to reveal oneself

Enthüllung F -, -en uncovering; (*von Denkmal, Gesicht*) unveiling; **noch eine sensationelle ~** another sensational revelation

Enthüllungs- IN CPDS investigative; **Enthüllungsbuch** NT exposé; **Enthüllungsjournalismus** M investigative journalism

enthülsen [ɛntˈhʏlzn], *ptp* **enthülst** VT to shell; *Getreide* to husk

Enthusiasmus [ɛntuˈziasmɔs] M -, NO PL enthusiasm

enthusiastisch [ɛntuˈziastɪʃ] **1** ADJ enthusiastic **2** ADV enthusiastically

entjungfern [ɛntˈjʊŋfɐn], *ptp* **entjungfert** VT to deflower

Entjungferung F -, -en defloration

entkalken [ɛntˈkalkn], *ptp* **entkalkt** VT to decalcify

entkernen [ɛntˈkɛrnən], *ptp* **entkernt** VT **(a)** *Orangen etc* to remove the pips from; *Kernobst* to core; *Steinobst* to stone; *(Biol) Zellen* to denucleate **(b)** *Gebäude* to gut; *Wohngebiet* (= *Dichte reduzieren*) to reduce the density of

entkoffeiniert [ɛntkɔfeiˈniːɐt] ADJ decaffeinated

entkommen [ɛntˈkɔmən], *ptp* **entkommen** VI IRREG AUX SEIN to escape (+*dat, aus* from)

Entkommen NT escape

entkorken [ɛntˈkɔrkn], *ptp* **entkorkt** VT *Flasche* to uncork

entkräften [ɛntˈkrɛftn], *ptp* **entkräftet** VT (= *schwächen*) to weaken; (= *erschöpfen*) to exhaust; (*fig:* = *widerlegen*) to refute

Entkräftung F -, -en weakening; (= *Erschöpfung*) exhaustion; (*fig:* = *Widerlegung*) refutation

entkrampfen [ɛntˈkrampfn], *ptp* **entkrampft** VT (*fig*) to relax; *Lage* to ease; **eine entkrampfte Atmosphäre** a relaxed atmosphere

Entkrampfung F -, -en (*fig*) relaxation

entkriminalisieren [ɛntkriminaliˈziːrən], *ptp* **entkriminalisiert** VT to decriminalize

entladen [ɛntˈlaːdn], *ptp* **entladen** IRREG **1** VT to unload; *Batterie etc* to discharge **2** VR (*Gewitter*) to break; (*Schusswaffe*) to go off; (*elektrische Spannung, Batterie etc*) to discharge; (*langsam*) to run down; (*fig: Emotion*) to vent itself

entlang [ɛntˈlaŋ] **1** PREP +ACC, +DAT or (*rare*) +GEN along; **den Fluss ~, ~ dem Fluss** or (*rare*) **des Flusses** along the river **2** ADV along; **am Bach ~** along (by the side of) the stream; **hier ~** this way

entlang- PREF along; **entlanggehen** VTI SEP IRREG AUX SEIN to walk along, to go along (*auch fig*); **am Haus ~** to walk along by the side of the house; **entlangschrammen** VI SEP AUX SEIN (*fig*) to scrape by; **haarscharf an etw** (*dat*) **~** to escape sth by the skin of one's teeth

entlarven [ɛntˈlarfn], *ptp* **entlarvt** VT (*fig*) *Spion, Dieb etc* to unmask; *Pläne, Betrug etc* to uncover; **sich ~** to reveal one's true colours (*Brit*) or colors (*US*); **sich als Schuft** *etc* **~** to reveal oneself to be a scoundrel *etc*

Entlarvung F -, -en exposure

entlassen [ɛntˈlasn], *ptp* **entlassen** VT IRREG (*aus* from) (= *gehen lassen, kündigen*) to dismiss; (*nach Streichungen*) to lay off; (*aus dem Krankenhaus*) to discharge; (*aus dem Gefängnis, aus Verpflichtungen*) to release; **aus der Schule ~ werden** to leave school; **jdn in den Ruhestand ~** to retire sb; **jdn aus der Verantwortung ~** to free sb from responsibility

Entlassung F -, -en dismissal; (*aus dem Krankenhaus, Gefängnis*) discharge; **um seine ~ einreichen** to tender one's resignation; **es gab 20 ~en** there were 20 redundancies (*esp Brit*) or lay-offs

entlasten [ɛntˈlastn], *ptp* **entlastet** VT *Achse, Telefonleitungen, Herz* to relieve the strain on; *Gewissen* (*Mil, Rail*) to relieve; *Verkehr* to ease; *Stadtzentrum* to relieve congestion in; (= *Arbeit abnehmen*) to take some of the load off; (*Jur*) *Angeklagten* (*völlig*) to exonerate; (*teilweise*) to support the case of; (*Comm*) *Vorstand* to approve the activities of; (*von Verpflichtungen, Schulden*) *jdn* to discharge; **jdn finanziell ~** to ease sb's financial burden

Entlastung F -, -en relief (*auch Mil, Rail etc*); (*von Achse etc, Herz*) relief of the strain (+*gen* on); (*Jur*) exoneration; (*Comm: von Vorstand*) approval; (*von Verpflichtungen etc*) release; **zu jds ~** (in order) to take some of the load off sb; **eine Aussage zur ~ des Angeklagten** a statement supporting the case of the defendant; **zu seiner ~ führte der Angeklagte an, dass ...** in his defence (*Brit*) or defense (*US*) the defendant stated that ...

Entlastungs-: Entlastungsmaterial NT (*Jur*) evidence for the defence (*Brit*) or defense (*US*); **Entlastungszeuge** M, **Entlastungszeugin** F (*Jur*) witness for the defence (*Brit*) or defense (*US*); **Entlastungszug** M relief train

Entlaubung F -, -en defoliation

Entlaubungsmittel NT defoliant

entlaufen [ɛntˈlaufn], *ptp* **entlaufen** VI IRREG AUX SEIN to run away (+*dat, von* from); **ein ~er Sklave/~es Kind** *etc* a runaway slave/child *etc*; **ein ~er Sträfling** an escaped convict; **ein ~er Hund** a lost or missing dog; **„Hund ~"** "dog missing"

entlausen [ɛntˈlauzn], *ptp* **entlaust** VT to delouse

entledigen [ɛntˈleːdɪgn], *ptp* **entledigt** VR (*form*) **sich jds/einer Sache ~** to rid oneself of sb/sth; **sich einer Pflicht** (*gen*)**/seiner Schulden ~** to discharge a duty/one's debts; **sich eines Komplizen ~** (*euph*) to dispose of an accomplice (*euph*); **sich seiner Kleidung ~** to remove one's clothes

entleeren [ɛntˈleːrən], *ptp* **entleert** VT to empty; *Darm* (*Sci*) *Glasglocke* to evacuate

Entleerung F emptying; (*von Darm, Glasglocke*) evacuation

entlegen [ɛntˈleːgn] ADJ out-of-the-way

Entlein [ˈɛntlain] NT -s, - duckling; **das hässliche ~** the Ugly Duckling

Entlobung F -, -en breaking off of one's engagement; **eine ~** a broken engagement

entlocken [ɛntˈlɔkn], *ptp* **entlockt** VT **jdm/einer Sache etw ~** to elicit sth from sb/sth

entlohnen [ɛntˈloːnən], *ptp* **entlohnt**, (*Sw*) **entlöhnen** [ɛntˈløːnən], *ptp* **entlöhnt** VT to pay; (*fig*) to reward

Entlohnung F -, -en (*Sw*) **Entlöhnung** F -, -en pay(ment); (*fig*) reward

entlüften [ɛntˈlʏftn], *ptp* **entlüftet** VT to ventilate; *Bremsen, Heizung* to bleed

Entlüftung F ventilation; (*von Bremsen, Heizung*) bleeding

entmachten [ɛntˈmaxtn], *ptp* **entmachtet** VT to deprive of power

Entmachtung F -, -en deprivation of power

entmannen [ɛntˈmanən], *ptp* **entmannt** VT to castrate; (*fig*) to emasculate

entmenschlichen [ɛntˈmɛnʃlɪçn], *ptp* **entmenschlicht** VT to dehumanize

entmenscht [ɛntˈmɛnʃt] ADJ bestial

entmilitarisieren [ɛntmilitariˈziːrən], *ptp* **entmilitarisiert** VT to demilitarize

Entmilitarisierung F -, -en demilitarization

entmündigen [ɛntˈmʏndɪgn], *ptp* **entmündigt** VT (*Jur*) to (legally) incapacitate; (*wegen Geisteskrankheit auch*) to certify; **das Fernsehen entmündigt die Zuschauer, wenn ...** television takes away the viewer's right to form an independent opinion when ...

Entmündigung F -, -en (legal) incapacitation; (*wegen Geisteskrankheit auch*) certification

entmutigen [ɛntˈmuːtɪgn], *ptp* **entmutigt** VT to discourage; **sich nicht ~ lassen** not to be discouraged

Entmutigung F -, -en discouragement

Entnahme [ɛntˈnaːmə] F -, -n (*form*) removal; (*von Blut*) extraction; (*von Geld*) withdrawal

entnazifizieren [ɛntnatsifiˈtsiːrən], *ptp* **entnazifiziert** VT to denazify

Entnazifizierung F -, -en denazification

entnehmen [ɛntˈneːmən], *ptp* **entnommen** [ɛntˈnɔmən] VT IRREG (*aus* +*dat*) to take (from); (*aus Kasse*) *Geld* to withdraw (from); (*fig:* = *erkennen, folgern*) to gather (from)

entnerven [ɛntˈnɛrfn], *ptp* **entnervt** VT to unnerve; **~d** unnerving; (= *nervtötend*) nerve-racking

entölen [ɛntˈløːlən], *ptp* **entölt** VT *Kakao* to extract the oil from

entpacken [ɛntˈpakn] VT, *ptp* **entpackt** (*Comput*) *Daten* to unpack

entpolitisieren [ɛntpolitiˈziːrən], *ptp* **entpolitisiert** VT to depoliticize

entpuppen [ɛntˈpʊpn], *ptp* **entpuppt** VR (*Schmetterling*) to emerge from its cocoon; **sich als Betrüger** *etc* **~** to turn out to be a cheat *etc*; **mal sehen, wie er sich entpuppt** we'll see how he turns out

entrahmen [ɛntˈraːmən], *ptp* **entrahmt** VT *Milch* to skim

enträtseln [ɛntˈrɛːtsln], *ptp* **enträtselt** VT to solve; *Sinn* to work out; *Schrift* to decipher

entrechten [ɛntˈrɛçtn], *ptp* **entrechtet** VT **jdn ~** to deprive sb of his rights; **die Entrechteten** those who have been deprived of their rights

Entrechtung F -, -en deprivation of rights; **die ~ des Parlaments** depriving parliament of its rights

entreißen [ɛntˈraisn], *ptp* **entrissen** [ɛntˈrɪsn] VT IRREG **jdm etw ~** *(lit, fig liter)* to snatch sth (away) from sb

entrichten [ɛntˈrɪçtn], *ptp* **entrichtet** VT *(form)* to pay

entringen [ɛntˈrɪŋən], *ptp* **entrungen** [ɛntˈrʊŋən] VT IRREG *(geh)* **jdm etw ~** to wrench sth from sb

entrinnen [ɛntˈrɪnən], *ptp* **entronnen** [ɛntˈrɔnən] VI IRREG AUX SEIN *(geh)* +DAT to escape from; *dem Tod ~* to escape; **es gibt kein Entrinnen** there is no escape

entrollen [ɛntˈrɔlən], *ptp* **entrollt** VT *Landkarte etc* to unroll; *Fahne, Segel* to unfurl

entrosten [ɛntˈrɔstn], *ptp* **entrostet** VT to derust

Entroster [ɛntˈrɔstɐ] M **-s, -**, **Entrostungsmittel** NT deruster

entrückt [ɛntˈrʏkt] ADJ *(geh)* *(= verzückt)* enraptured; *(= versunken)* lost in reverie

entrümpeln [ɛntˈrʏmpln], *ptp* **entrümpelt** VT to clear out; *(fig)* to tidy up

Entrümpelung [ɛntˈrʏmpəluŋ] F -, -en, **Entrümplung** [ɛntˈrʏmpluŋ] F -, -en clear-out; *(= das Entrümpeln)* clearing out; *(fig)* tidying up

entrüsten [ɛntˈrʏstn], *ptp* **entrüstet** 1 VT to outrage; *(= zornig machen)* to incense 2 VR **sich ~ über** *(+acc)* to be outraged at; *(= zornig werden)* to be incensed at

entrüstet [ɛntˈrʏstət] 1 ADJ outraged; *(= zornig)* incensed 2 ADV indignantly, outraged

Entrüstung F *(über +acc* at) indignation; *(= Zorn)* anger

entsaften [ɛntˈzaftn], *ptp* **entsaftet** VT to extract the juice from

Entsafter [ɛntˈzaftɐ] M **-s, -** juice extractor

entsalzen [ɛntˈzaltsn], *ptp* **entsalzt** VT IRREG to desalinate

Entsalzungsanlage F desalination plant

entschädigen [ɛntˈʃɛːdɪɡn], *ptp* **entschädigt** VT *(für* for) *(lit, fig)* to compensate; *(für Dienste etc)* to reward; *(esp mit Geld)* to remunerate; *(= Kosten erstatten)* to reimburse; **das Theaterstück entschädigte uns für das lange Warten** the play made up for the long wait

Entschädigung F -, -en compensation; *(für Dienste)* reward; *(mit Geld)* remuneration; *(= Kostenerstattung)* reimbursement

Entschädigungssumme F amount of compensation

entschärfen [ɛntˈʃɛrfn], *ptp* **entschärft** VT *Bombe etc* to defuse; *(fig) Kurve* to straighten out; *Krise, Lage* to defuse; *Argument* to neutralize; *Buch, Film* to tone down

Entscheid [ɛntˈʃait] M **-(e)s, -e** [-də] *(Sw, form)* = **Entscheidung**

entscheiden [ɛntˈʃaidn], *pret* **entschied** [ɛntˈʃiːt], *ptp* **entschieden** [ɛntˈʃiːdn] 1 VT to decide; **das Spiel/die Wahl ist entschieden/schon entschieden** the game/election has been decided/is already decided; **den Kampf/Krieg (um etw) für sich ~** to secure victory in the struggle/battle (for sth); **es ist noch nichts entschieden** nothing has been decided (as) yet; *siehe auch* **entschieden**

2 VI *(über +acc)* to decide (on); *(Jur auch)* to rule (on); **darüber habe ich nicht zu ~** that is not for me to decide

3 VR *(Mensch)* to decide; *(Angelegenheit)* to be decided; **sich für jdn/etw ~** to decide in favour *(Brit)* or favor *(US)* of sb/sth; **sich gegen jdn/etw ~** to decide against sb/sth; **jetzt wird es sich ~, wer der Schnellere ist** now we'll see who is the quicker

entscheidend 1 ADJ decisive; **die ~e Stimme** *(bei Wahlen etc)* the deciding vote; **der alles ~e Augenblick** the all-decisive moment; **das Entscheidende** the decisive factor 2 ADV *schlagen, schwächen* decisively; **~ zu etw beitragen** to be a crucial factor in sth

Entscheidung F decision; *(Jur auch)* ruling; *(der Geschworenen auch)* verdict; **Spiel um die ~** *(Sport)* deciding match; *(bei Gleichstand auch)* play-off; **wie ist die ~ ausgefallen?** which way did the decision go?; **es geht um die ~** it's going to decide things; **die Frage kommt heute zur ~** the question will be decided today

Entscheidungs-: Entscheidungsbefugnis F decision-making powers *pl*; **entscheidungsfreudig** ADJ decisive; **Entscheidungsfreudigkeit** F -, NO PL decisiveness; **Entscheidungshilfe** F aid to decision-making; **Entscheidungskampf** M decisive encounter; *(Sport)* deciding round/game *etc*; **Entscheidungsschlacht** F decisive battle; *(fig)* show-down *(inf)*; **entscheidungsschwach** ADJ indecisive; **Entscheidungsschwäche** F indecisiveness; **Entscheidungsspielraum** M room for manoeuvre *(Brit)* or

maneuver *(US)* in making a decision; **wir haben hierbei keinen ~** we don't have much choice in this; **Entscheidungsträger(in)** M(F) decision-maker; **entscheidungsunfähig** ADJ unable to make decisions; **Entscheidungsunfähigkeit** F inability to make decisions

entschied PRET *von* **entscheiden**

entschieden [ɛntˈʃiːdn] 1 PTP *von* **entscheiden** 2 ADJ **(a)** *(= entschlossen)* determined; *Befürworter* staunch; *Ablehnung* firm **(b)** NO PRED *(= eindeutig)* decided; **er ist ein ~er Könner in seinem Fach** he is unquestionably an expert in his subject 3 ADV **(a)** *(= strikt)* *ablehnen* firmly; *bekämpfen* resolutely; *von sich weisen, zurückweisen* staunchly **(b)** *(= eindeutig)* definitely; **das geht ~ zu weit** that's definitely going too far

Entschiedenheit F -, -en *(= Entschlossenheit)* determination; *(von Ablehnung)* firmness; **etw mit aller ~ dementieren** to deny sth categorically; **etw mit aller ~ ablehnen** to reject sth flatly

entschlacken [ɛntˈʃlakn], *ptp* **entschlackt** VT *(Metal)* to remove the slag from; *(Med) Körper* to purify

entschließen [ɛntˈʃliːsn], *pret* **entschloss** [ɛntˈʃlɔs], *ptp* **entschlossen** [ɛntˈʃlɔsn] VR to decide *(für, zu* on); **ich entschloss mich zum Kauf dieses Hauses** I decided to buy this house; **sich anders ~** to change one's mind; **sich zu nichts ~ können** to be unable to make up one's mind; **zu allem entschlossen sein** to be ready for anything; *siehe auch* **entschlossen**

Entschließung F resolution

entschloss PRET *von* **entschließen**

entschlossen [ɛntˈʃlɔsn] 1 PTP *von* **entschließen** 2 ADJ determined; **ich bin fest ~** I am absolutely determined; **er ist zum Schlimmsten ~** he will stop at nothing 3 ADV resolutely; **schnell und ~** fast and decisively; **kurz ~** without further ado

Entschlossenheit F -, NO PL determination

entschlüpfen [ɛntˈʃlʏpfn], *ptp* **entschlüpft** VI AUX SEIN to escape *(+dat* from); *(Küken)* to be hatched; *(fig: Wort etc)* to slip out *(+dat* from); **mir ist eine unüberlegte Bemerkung entschlüpft** I let slip an ill-considered remark

Entschluss M *(= Entscheidung)* decision; *(= Vorsatz)* resolution; **aus eigenem ~ handeln** to act on one's own initiative; **seinen ~ ändern** to change one's mind; **es ist mein fester ~ ...** it is my firm intention ...; **eine Frau von schnellen Entschlüssen sein** to be able to decide quickly

entschlüsseln [ɛntˈʃlʏsln], *ptp* **entschlüsselt** VT to decipher; *Funkspruch auch* to decode

Entschlüsselung F -, -en deciphering; *(von Funkspruch auch)* decoding

Entschluss-: entschlussfreudig ADJ decisive; **Entschlusskraft** F decisiveness

entschuldbar [ɛntˈʃʊltbaːɐ] ADJ excusable

entschuldigen [ɛntˈʃʊldɪɡn], *ptp* **entschuldigt** 1 VT to excuse; **etw mit etw ~** to excuse sth as due to sth; **das ist durch nichts zu ~!**, **das lässt sich nicht ~!** that is inexcusable!; **jdn bei jdm/einem Treffen ~** to make sb's excuses to sb/a meeting; **einen Schüler ~ lassen** *or* to ask for a pupil to be excused; **ich möchte meine Tochter für morgen ~** I would like to have my daughter excused for tomorrow; **ich bitte mich zu ~** I ask to be excused

2 VI **entschuldige/~ Sie (bitte)!** (do *or* please) excuse me!, sorry!; *(bei Bitte, Frage etc)* excuse me (please), pardon me *(US)*; **(na) ~ Sie/entschuldige mal!** excuse me!

3 VR **sich (bei jdm) (wegen or für etw) ~** *(= um Verzeihung bitten)* to apologize (to sb) (for sth); **sich (bei jdm) ~** *(= sich abmelden, sich rechtfertigen)* to excuse oneself; *(= sich bei Lehrer, Chef abmelden)* to ask (sb) to be excused; **sich (von jdm) ~ lassen** to send one's excuses *or* apologies (via sb); **sich mit Krankheit ~** to excuse oneself on account of illness

entschuldigend 1 ADJ apologetic 2 ADV apologetically

Entschuldigung F -, -en *(= Grund)* excuse; *(= Bitte um ~)* apology; *(Sch: = Brief)* note; **~!** excuse me!; *(= Verzeihung auch)* sorry!; **zu seiner ~ sagte er ...** he said in his defence *(Brit) or* defense *(US)* that ...; **ohne ~ fehlen** to be absent without an excuse; **(jdn) (wegen einer Sache) um ~ bitten** to apologize (to sb) (for sth); **ich bitte vielmals um ~(, dass ich mich verspätet habe)!** I do apologize (for being late)!

entschwefeln [ɛntˈʃveːfln], *ptp* **entschwefelt** VT to desulphurize

Entschwefelungsanlage F desulphurization plant

entschwinden [ɛntˈʃvɪndn], *ptp* **entschwunden** [ɛntˈʃvʊndn] VI IRREG AUX SEIN (*geh: lit, fig*) to vanish (*+dat* from, *in +acc* into)

entsenden [ɛntˈzɛndn], *ptp* **entsandt** *or* **entsendet** [ɛntˈzant, ɛntˈzɛndət] VT IRREG *or* REG *Abgeordnete etc* to send; *Boten auch* to dispatch

entsetzen [ɛntˈzɛtsn], *ptp* **entsetzt 🟦** VT (= *in Grauen versetzen*) to horrify **🟦** VR **sich über jdn/etw ~** to be horrified at *or* by sb/ sth; **sich vor etw** (*dat*) **~** to be horrified at sth; *siehe auch* **entsetzt**

Entsetzen [ɛntˈzɛtsn] NT **-s**, NO PL horror; (= *Erschrecken*) terror; **zu meinem größten ~ bemerkte ich, dass ...** to my horror I noticed that ...; **mit ~ sehen/hören, dass ...** to be horrified/ terrified to see/hear that ...

Entsetzensschrei M cry of horror

entsetzlich [ɛntˈzɛtslɪç] **🟦** ADJ dreadful **🟦** ADV **(a)** (= *schrecklich*) dreadfully; **~ aussehen** to look dreadful **(b)** (*inf:* = *sehr*) awfully; **~ viel (Geld)** an awful lot (of money) (*inf*)

entsetzt [ɛntˈzɛtst] **🟦** ADJ horrified (*über +acc* at, by) **🟦** ADV in horror; **jdn ~ anstarren** to give sb a horrified look; *siehe auch* **entsetzen**

entseuchen [ɛntˈzɔyçn], *ptp* **entseucht** VT (= *desinfizieren*) to disinfect; (= *dekontaminieren*) to decontaminate

Entseuchung F **-**, **-en** decontamination

entsichern [ɛntˈzɪçɐn], *ptp* **entsichert** VT **eine Pistole ~** to release the safety catch of a pistol; **eine entsicherte Pistole** a pistol with the safety catch off, a pistol with an unlocked safety catch (*esp US*)

entsinnen [ɛntˈzɪnən], *ptp* **entsonnen** [ɛntˈzɔnən] VR IRREG to remember (*einer Sache* (*gen*), *an etw* (*acc*) sth); **wenn ich mich recht entsinne** if my memory serves me correctly

entsorgen [ɛntˈzɔrgn], *ptp* **entsorgt** VT *Abfälle etc* to dispose of; *Ölplattform, Altautos* to break up; **eine Stadt ~** to dispose of a town's refuse and sewage

Entsorgung F **-**, **-en** waste disposal; **die ~ von Chemikalien** the disposal of chemicals

entspannen [ɛntˈʃpanən], *ptp* **entspannt 🟦** VT to relax; (*fig*) *Lage, Beziehungen* to ease (up) **🟦** VR to relax (*auch fig*); (= *ausruhen*) to rest; (*nach der Arbeit etc*) to unwind; (*Lage etc*) to ease

entspannt [ɛntˈʃpant] ADJ relaxed; **die Lage ist wieder etwas ~er** the situation is now less tense again

Entspanntheit F **-**, NO PL (*der Lage*) lack of tension (*+gen* in); **meine mangelnde ~** the fact that I wasn't relaxed

Entspannung F relaxation (*auch fig*); (*von Lage*) (Fin: an der Börse) easing(-up) (*von*); (*Pol*) easing of tension (*+gen* in), détente; **nach der Arbeit sehe ich zur ~ etwas fern** after work I watch television for a bit to help me unwind

Entspannungs-: **Entspannungspolitik** F policy of détente; **Entspannungsübungen** PL (*Med etc*) relaxation exercises *pl*

entspr. ABBR *von* **entsprechend**

entsprechen [ɛntˈʃprɛçn], *ptp* **entsprochen** [ɛntˈʃprɔxn] VI IRREG **+DAT** to correspond to; *der Wahrheit* to be in accordance with; *Anforderungen, Kriterien, Zweck* to fulfil (*Brit*), to fulfill (*US*); *einem Anlass* to be in keeping with; *Erwartungen* to live up to; *einer Beschreibung* to answer; *einer Bitte, einem Wunsch etc* to meet; **sich** *or* **einander ~** to correspond (with each other), to tally

entsprechend 🟦 ADJ corresponding; (= *zuständig*) relevant; (= *angemessen*) appropriate; **ein der Leistung ~es Gehalt** a salary commensurate with one's performance **🟦** ADV accordingly; (= *ähnlich, gleich*) correspondingly; **er wurde ~ bestraft** he was suitably punished; **etw ~ würdigen** to show suitable appreciation for sth **🟦** PREP **+DAT** in accordance with; (= *ähnlich, gleich*) corresponding to; **er wird seiner Leistung ~ bezahlt** he is paid according to output; **er hat sich den Erwartungen ~ entwickelt** he has progressed as we had hoped

Entsprechung F **-**, **-en** (= *Äquivalent*) equivalent; (= *Gegenstück*) counterpart; (= *Analogie*) parallel; (= *Übereinstimmung*) correspondence

entspringen [ɛntˈʃprɪŋən], *ptp* **entsprungen** [ɛntˈʃprʊŋən] VI IRREG AUX SEIN (*Fluss*) to rise; (= *sich herleiten von*) **+DAT** to arise from

Entstalinisierung [ɛntʃtaliniˈziːrʊŋ] F **-**, **-en** destalinization

entstammen [ɛntˈʃtamən], *ptp* **entstammt** VI AUX SEIN **+DAT** to come from

entstehen [ɛntˈʃteːən], *ptp* **entstanden** [ɛntˈʃtandn] VI IRREG AUX SEIN (= *ins Dasein treten*) to come into being; (= *seinen Ursprung haben*) to originate; (= *sich entwickeln*) to arise (*aus, durch* from); (= *verursacht werden*) to result (*aus, durch* from); (*Chem: Verbindungen*) to be produced (*aus* from, *durch* through, via); (= *geschrieben/gebaut etc werden*) to be written/built *etc*; **das Feuer war durch Nachlässigkeit entstanden** the fire was caused by negligence; **bei Entstehen eines Feuers** in the event of (a) fire; **wir wollen nicht den Eindruck ~ lassen, ...** we don't want to give (rise to) the impression that ...; **im Entstehen begriffen sein** to be emerging; **für ~den** *or* **entstandenen Schaden** for damages incurred

Entstehung F **-**, **-en** (= *das Werden*) genesis; (= *das Hervorkommen*) emergence; (= *Ursprung*) origin; (= *Bildung*) formation

entsteinen [ɛntˈʃtainən], *ptp* **entsteint** VT to stone

entstellen [ɛntˈʃtɛlən], *ptp* **entstellt** VT (= *verunstalten*) *Gesicht* to disfigure; (= *verzerren*) to distort; **etw entstellt wiedergeben** to distort sth

Entstickungsanlage [ɛntˈʃtıkʊŋʦ-] F denitrification plant

entstören [ɛntˈʃtøːrən], *ptp* **entstört** VT *Radio, Telefon* to free from interference; *Auto, Staubsauger etc* to fit a suppressor to

Entstörer M, **Entstörgerät** NT (*für Auto etc*) suppressor; (*für Radio, Telefon*) anti-interference device

Entstörungsdienst M, **Entstörungsstelle** F telephone maintenance service

enttabuisieren [ɛnttabuiˈziːrən], *ptp* **enttabuisiert** VT to free from taboos

Enttabuisierung F **-**, **-en** removal of taboos (*+gen* from)

enttarnen [ɛntˈtarnən], *ptp* **enttarnt** VT *Spion* to blow the cover of (*inf*); (*fig:* = *entlarven*) to expose; **er wurde enttarnt** (*Spion*) his cover was blown

Enttarnung F exposure

enttäuschen [ɛntˈtɔyʃn], *ptp* **enttäuscht 🟦** VT to disappoint; *Vertrauen* to betray; **enttäuscht sein über** (*+acc*)**/von** to be disappointed at/by *or* in; **sie ist im Leben oft enttäuscht worden** she has had many disappointments in life; **angenehm enttäuscht sein** (*hum*) to be pleasantly surprised **🟦** VI **unsere Mannschaft hat sehr enttäuscht** our team were very disappointing; **der neue Wagen hat enttäuscht** the new car is a disappointment

Enttäuschung F disappointment; **jdm eine ~ bereiten** to disappoint sb

entthronen [ɛntˈtroːnən], *ptp* **entthront** VT (*lit, fig*) to dethrone

entvölkern [ɛntˈfœlkɐn], *ptp* **entvölkert** VT to depopulate

entwaffnen [ɛntˈvafnən], *ptp* **entwaffnet** VT (*lit, fig*) to disarm

entwaffnend ADJ (*fig*) disarming

Entwaffnung F **-**, **-en** disarming; (*eines Landes*) disarmament

entwanzen [ɛntˈvantsn], *ptp* **entwanzt** VT to debug

entwarnen [ɛntˈvarnən], *ptp* **entwarnt** VI to sound the all-clear

Entwarnung F sounding of the all-clear; (= *Signal*) all-clear

entwässern [ɛntˈvɛsɐn], *ptp* **entwässert** VT *Grundstück, Moor, Keller* to drain; *Gewebe, Ödem, Körper* to dehydrate

Entwässerung F drainage; (*Chem*) dehydration

Entwässerungs-: **Entwässerungsanlage** F drainage system; **Entwässerungsgraben** M drainage ditch

entweder [ɛntˈveːdɐ] CONJ **~ ... oder ...** either ... or ...; **~ oder!** yes or no; **~ gleich oder gar nicht, ~ jetzt oder nie** it's now or never

entweichen [ɛntˈvaiçn], *ptp* **entwichen** [ɛntˈvıçn] VI IRREG AUX SEIN to escape (*+dat, aus* from)

entweihen [ɛntˈvaiən], *ptp* **entweiht** VT to violate (*auch fig*); (= *entheiligen*) to desecrate

entwenden [ɛntˈvɛndn], *ptp* **entwendet** VT (*form*) **jdm etw/etw aus etw ~** to steal sth from sb/sth

entwerfen [ɛntˈvɛrfn], *ptp* **entworfen** [ɛntˈvɔrfn] VT IRREG **(a)** (= *zeichnen, gestalten*) *Zeichnung etc* to sketch; *Muster, Modell etc* to design **(b)** (= *ausarbeiten*) *Gesetz, Vortrag, Schreiben etc* to draft; *Plan* to devise **(c)** (*fig*) (= *darstellen, darlegen*) *Bild* to depict; (= *in Umrissen darstellen*) to outline

entwerten [ɛnt'veːɐtn], *ptp* **entwertet** VT **(a)** (= *im Wert mindern*) to devalue **(b)** (= *ungültig machen*) to render invalid; *Münzen* to demonetize; *Briefmarke, Fahrschein* to cancel

Entwerter [ɛnt'veːɐtɐ] M **-s, -** (ticket-)cancelling (*Brit*) or (ticket-)canceling (*US*) machine

Entwertung F **(a)** (= *Wertminderung*) devaluation **(b)** (= *Ungültigmachung*) invalidation; (*von Briefmarke, Fahrschein*) cancellation

entwickeln [ɛnt'vɪkln], *ptp* **entwickelt** ◀ VT to develop (*auch Phot*); (*Phot*) *esp Diapositive* to process; (*Chem*) *Gas etc* to produce; *Mut, Energie* to show ◀ VR to develop (*zu* into); (*Chem: Gase etc*) to be produced; **das Projekt/der neue Angestellte entwickelt sich gut** the project/the new employee is coming along nicely; **sie hat sich ganz schön entwickelt** (*inf*) she's turned out really nicely

Entwickler [ɛnt'vɪklɐ] M **-s, -** (*Phot*) developer

Entwicklerbad NT (*Phot*) developing bath

Entwicklung F **-, -en** development; (= *Erzeugung*) (*Chem: von Gasen etc*) production; (*von Mut, Energie*) show; (*Phot*) developing; (*esp von Diapositiven*) processing; **das Flugzeug ist noch in der ~** the plane is still in the development stage; **Jugendliche, die noch in der ~ sind** young people who are still developing

Entwicklungs-: Entwicklungsalter NT adolescence; **Entwicklungsdienst** M voluntary service overseas (*Brit*), VSO (*Brit*), Peace Corps (*US*); **entwicklungsfähig** ADJ capable of development; **der Plan/die Idee ist durchaus ~** this plan/idea is definitely worth following up; **diese Stelle ist ~** this position has prospects; **Entwicklungshelfer(in)** M(F) VSO worker (*Brit*), Peace Corps worker (*US*); **Entwicklungshilfe** F foreign aid; **Entwicklungsjahre** PL formative years (*auch fig*); **Entwicklungsland** NT developing country; **entwicklungspolitisch** ADJ development aid policy *attr*; *Sprecher* on development aid policy; **Entwicklungsstadium** NT, **Entwicklungsstufe** F stage of development; (*der Menschheit etc*) evolutionary stage; **Entwicklungszeit** F period of development; (*Biol, Psych*) developmental period; (*Phot*) developing time

entwirren [ɛnt'vɪrən], *ptp* **entwirrt** VT (*lit, fig*) to untangle

entwischen [ɛnt'vɪʃn], *ptp* **entwischt** VI AUX SEIN (*inf*) to get away (+*dat, aus* from)

entwöhnen [ɛnt'vøːnən], *ptp* **entwöhnt** VT to wean (+*dat, von* from)

Entwöhnung F **-, -en** cure; (*von Säugling, Jungtier*) weaning

entwürdigen [ɛnt'vʏrdɪgn], *ptp* **entwürdigt** ◀ VT to degrade; (= *Schande bringen über*) to disgrace ◀ VR to degrade oneself

entwürdigend ADJ degrading

Entwürdigung F degradation; (= *Entehrung*) disgrace (+*gen* to)

Entwurf M **(a)** (= *Skizze, Abriss*) outline; (= *Design*) design; (*Archit, fig*) blueprint **(b)** (*von Plan, Gesetz etc*) (= *Vertragsentwurf, Konzept*) draft (version); (*einer Theorie auch*) outline; (*Parl: = Gesetzentwurf*) bill; **das Bild ist im ~ fertig** the sketch for the picture is finished; **die Doktorarbeit ist im ~ fertig** the framework for the PhD is finished

Entwurfsstadium NT **sich im ~ befinden** to be in the planning stage

entwurzeln [ɛnt'vʊrtsln], *ptp* **entwurzelt** VT (*lit, fig*) to uproot

entzaubern [ɛnt'tsaʊbɐn], *ptp* **entzaubert** VT **jdn/etw ~** to break the spell on sb/sth

entzerren [ɛnt'tsɛrən], *ptp* **entzerrt** VT to rectify

Entzerrung F rectification; **zeitliche ~** staggering

entziehen [ɛnt'tsiːən], *ptp* **entzogen** [ɛnt'tsoːgn] IRREG ◀ VT (+*dat* from) to withdraw; *Flüssigkeit* to draw; (*Chem*) to extract; **jdm Alkohol/Nikotin ~** to deprive sb of alcohol/nicotine; **jdm die Rente** *etc* **~** to stop sb's pension *etc*; **dem Redner das Wort ~** to ask the speaker to stop ◀ VR **sich jdm/einer Sache ~** to evade sb/sth; **sich seiner Verantwortung ~** to shirk one's responsibilities; **sich jds Verständnis/Kontrolle ~** to be beyond sb's understanding/control; **sich den** *or* **jds Blicken ~** to be hidden from sight

Entziehung F (*von Lizenz etc*) withdrawal; (*von Drogen etc*) (= *Wegnahme*) withdrawal; (= *Behandlung*) treatment for drug addiction; (*gegen Alkoholismus*) treatment for alcoholism

Entziehungskur F (*für Drogenabhängige*) cure for drug addiction; (*für Alkoholiker*) cure for alcoholism

entziffern [ɛnt'tsɪfɐn], *ptp* **entziffert** VT to decipher; *Geheimschrift, verschlüsselte Botschaft, DNS-Struktur* to decode; **ich kann den Namen nicht ~** I can't make out the name

Entzifferung F **-, -en** deciphering; (*von Funkspruch etc*) decoding

entzücken [ɛnt'tsʏkn], *ptp* **entzückt** VT to delight; **von jdm/über etw** (*acc*) **entzückt sein** to be delighted by sb/at sth

Entzücken [ɛnt'tsʏkn] NT **-s**, NO PL delight; **zu meinem (größten) ~** to my (great) delight; **in ~ geraten** to go into raptures; **jdn in (helles) ~ versetzen** to send sb into raptures

entzückend ADJ delightful; **das ist ja ~!** how delightful!

Entzug M, NO PL (*einer Lizenz etc*) withdrawal; (*Med*) (*von Drogen etc*) withdrawal; (= *Entziehungskur*) (*für Drogenabhängige*) cure for drug addiction; (*für Alkoholiker*) cure for alcoholism; **er ist auf ~** (*Med etc*) (*Drogenabhängiger*) he is being treated for drug addiction; (*Alkoholiker*) he is being dried out (*inf*); **kalter ~** (*sl: von Drogen*) cold turkey (*inf*)

Entzugserscheinung F, **Entzugssymptom** NT withdrawal symptom

entzünden [ɛnt'tsʏndn], *ptp* **entzündet** ◀ VT *Feuer* to light; (*fig*) *Streit etc* to spark off; *Hass* to inflame; *Fantasie, Begeisterung* to fire ◀ VR **(a)** (= *zu brennen anfangen*) to catch fire, to ignite (*esp Sci, Tech*); (*Streit*) to be sparked off; (*Hass*) to be inflamed; (*Fantasie, Begeisterung*) to be fired **(b)** (*Med*) to become inflamed; **entzündet** inflamed

entzündlich [ɛnt'tsʏntlɪç] ADJ *Gase, Brennstoff* inflammable; (*Med*) inflammatory; **~e Haut** skin which easily becomes inflamed

Entzündung F (*Med*) inflammation

Entzündungs- (*Med*): **entzündungshemmend** ADJ anti-inflammatory; **Entzündungshemmer** [-hɛmɐ] M **-s, -** antiphlogistic (*form*); **Entzündungsherd** M focus of inflammation

entzwei [ɛnt'tsvaɪ] ADJ PRED in two (pieces); (= *kaputt*) broken; (= *zerrissen*) torn

entzweibrechen VTI SEP IRREG (VI: AUX SEIN) to break in two; (= *zerbrechen*) to break

entzweien [ɛnt'tsvaɪən], *ptp* **entzweit** ◀ VT to turn against each other ◀ VR **sich (mit jdm) ~** to fall out (with sb)

entzwei-: entzweigehen VI SEP IRREG AUX SEIN to break (in two); **entzweireißen** VT SEP IRREG to tear in two; (= *zerreißen*) to tear to pieces; **entzweischlagen** VT SEP IRREG to strike in half; (= *zerschlagen*) to smash (to pieces); **entzweischneiden** VT SEP IRREG to cut in two; (= *zerschneiden*) to cut to pieces

Entzweiung F **-, -en** (*fig*) (= *Bruch*) split; (= *Streit*) quarrel

Enzephalogramm [ɛntsefalo'gram] NT, *pl* **-gramme** (*Med*) encephalogram

Enzian ['ɛntsiaːn] M **-s, -e** gentian; (= *Branntwein*) spirit distilled *from the roots of gentian*

Enzyklopädie [ɛntsyklopɛ'diː] F **-, -n** [-'diːən] encyclop(a)edia

enzyklopädisch [ɛntsyklo'pɛːdɪʃ] ADJ encyclop(a)edic

Enzym [ɛn'tsyːm] NT **-s, -e** enzyme

Epen PL *von* **Epos**

Epidemie [epide'miː] F **-, -n** [-'miːən] (*Med, fig*) epidemic

Epidemiologe [epidemio'loːgə] M **-n, -n**, **Epidemiologin** [-'loːgɪn] F **-, -nen** epidemiologist

epidemiologisch [epidemio'loːgɪʃ] ADJ epidemiological

epidemisch [epi'deːmɪʃ] ◀ ADJ (*Med, fig*) epidemic ◀ ADV **sich ~ ausbreiten** (*Med*) to spread as an epidemic; (*fig*) to spread like an epidemic

Epik ['eːpɪk] F **-**, NO PL epic poetry

Epiker ['eːpɪkɐ] M **-s, -**, **Epikerin** [-ərɪn] F **-, -nen** epic poet

Epilepsie [epilɛ'psiː] F **-, -n** [-'psiːən] epilepsy

Epileptiker [epi'lɛptikɐ] M **-s, -**, **Epileptikerin** [-ərɪn] F **-, -nen** epileptic

epileptisch [epi'lɛptɪʃ] ADJ epileptic

Epilog [epi'loːk] M **-s, -e** [-gə] epilogue

episch ['eːpɪʃ] ADJ (*lit, fig*) epic

Episode [epi'zoːdə] F **-, -n** episode

Epizentrum [epi'tsɛntrʊm] NT epicentre (*Brit*), epicenter (*US*)

epochal [epɔ'xaːl] ADJ epochal; (= *Epoche machend*) epoch-making

Epoche ['epɔxə] F **-, -n** epoch; **~ machen** to mark a new epoch; **~ machend** epoch-making

Epos ['eːpɔs] NT **-, Epen** ['eːpn] epic (poem)

Epoxydharz [epɔ'ksyːt-] NT epoxy resin

Eprouvette [epru'vɛt] F **-, -n** (Aus Chem) test tube

er [eːɐ] PERS PRON, gen **seiner**, dat **ihm**, acc **ihn** he; (von Dingen) it; (von Hund etc) it, he; (von Mond) it, she (poet); **wenn ich er wäre** if I were him; **er ist es** it's him; **er war es nicht, ich wars** it wasn't him, it was me; **sie ist größer als er** she is taller than he is or him

erachten [ɛɐ'laxtn], ptp **erachtet** VT (geh) **jdn/etw für** or **als etw ~** to consider sb/sth (to be) sth

Erachten [ɛɐ'laxtn] NT **-s**, NO PL **meines ~s, nach meinem ~** in my opinion

erarbeiten [ɛɐ'larbaitn], ptp **erarbeitet** VT **(a)** Vermögen etc to work for; Wissen etc to acquire **(b)** Entwurf etc to work out

Erbanlage F USU PL hereditary factor(s pl)

erbarmen [ɛɐ'barmən], ptp **erbarmt** ▓ VT **jdn ~** to arouse sb's pity; **es kann einen ~** it's pitiable; **er sieht zum Erbarmen aus** he's a pitiful sight; **das ist zum Erbarmen** it's pitiful ▓ VR +GEN to have pity (on) (auch hum inf); (= verzeihen, verschonen) to have mercy (on)

Erbarmen [ɛɐ'barmən] NT **-s**, NO PL (= Mitleid) pity (mit on); (= Gnade) mercy (mit on); **ohne ~** pitiless(ly); **kein ~ mit jdm kennen** to show sb no mercy

erbarmenswert ADJ pitiable

erbärmlich [ɛɐ'bɛrmlɪç] ▓ ADJ wretched; (inf: = furchtbar) Kälte terrible ▓ ADV sich verhalten abominably; (= sehr schlecht) singen appallingly; (inf: = furchtbar) frieren, wehtun terribly; **~ aussehen** to look terrible

Erbarmungs-: erbarmungslos (lit, fig) ▓ ADJ pitiless ▓ ADV pitilessly; **Erbarmungslosigkeit** F -, NO PL (lit, fig) pitilessness; **erbarmungswürdig** ADJ = **erbarmenswert**

erbauen [ɛɐ'bauən], ptp **erbaut** VT **(a)** (lit, fig: = errichten) to build **(b)** (fig: = seelisch bereichern) to uplift; **wir waren von der Nachricht nicht gerade erbaut** (inf) we weren't exactly delighted by the news; **der Chef ist von meinem Plan nicht besonders erbaut** (inf) the boss isn't particularly enthusiastic about my plan

Erbauer [ɛɐ'bauɐ] M **-s, -, Erbauerin** [-ərɪn] F **-, -nen** builder

erbaulich [ɛɐ'baulɪç] ADJ edifying (auch iro)

Erbe¹ ['ɛrbə] M **-n, -n** (lit, fig) heir (einer Person (gen) of or to sb, einer Sache (gen) to sth); **jdn zum** or **als ~n einsetzen** to appoint sb as one's heir

Erbe² NT **-s**, NO PL inheritance; (fig) heritage; (esp Unerwünschtes) legacy

erbeben [ɛɐ'beːbn], ptp **erbebt** VI AUX SEIN (geh: Erde, Mensch etc) to tremble

erben ['ɛrbn] VT (lit, fig) to inherit (von from); (inf: = geschenkt bekommen) to get

Erbengemeinschaft F community of heirs

erbetteln [ɛɐ'bɛtln], ptp **erbettelt** VT to get by begging; **die Kinder erbettelten sich die Erlaubnis, ...** the children managed to wheedle permission ...

erbeuten [ɛɐ'bɔytn], ptp **erbeutet** VT (Tier) to carry off; (Dieb) to get away with; (im Krieg) to capture

Erb-: Erbfaktor M (Biol) (hereditary) factor; **Erbfall** M (Jur) **im ~** in the case of inheritance; **Erbfolge** F (line of) succession

Erbgut NT, NO PL (Biol) genetic make-up

erbgut-: erbgutschädigend ADJ genetically harmful; **erbgutverändernd** ADJ Stoff causing genetic changes; **das hat eine ~e Wirkung** it causes genetic changes

Erbin ['ɛrbɪn] F **-, -nen** heiress; siehe auch **Erbe¹**

Erbinformation ['ɛrp-] F genetic information

erbitten [ɛɐ'bɪtn], ptp **erbeten** [ɛɐ'beːtn] VT IRREG to ask for; **sich ~/nicht ~ lassen** to be/not to be prevailed upon

erbittern [ɛɐ'bɪtɐn], ptp **erbittert** VT to incense

erbittert [ɛɐ'bɪtɐt] ▓ ADJ Widerstand, Gegner, Diskussion etc bitter ▓ ADV bitterly

Erbkrankheit ['ɛrp-] F hereditary disease

erblassen [ɛɐ'blasn], ptp **erblasst** VI AUX SEIN to (turn) pale; **vor Neid ~** to turn green with envy

Erblasser ['ɛrblasɐ] M **-s, -, Erblasserin** [-ərɪn] F **-, -nen** person who leaves an inheritance

erblich ['ɛrplɪç] ▓ ADJ hereditary ▓ ADV **er ist ~ belastet** (bei Eigenschaft) it's inherited; (bei Krankheit) it runs in the family; **etw ist ~ bedingt** sth is an inherited condition

erblicken [ɛɐ'blɪkn], ptp **erblickt** VT (geh) to see; (= erspähen) to spot; **in jdm/etw eine Gefahr** etc **~** to see sb/sth as a danger etc

erblinden [ɛɐ'blɪndn], ptp **erblindet** VI AUX SEIN to go blind

Erblindung F -, -en loss of sight

erblühen [ɛɐ'blyːən], ptp **erblüht** VI AUX SEIN (geh) to bloom; **zu voller Schönheit ~** (fig) to blossom out

Erb-: Erbmasse F estate; (Biol) genetic make-up; **Erbonkel** M (inf) rich uncle

erbosen [ɛɐ'boːzn], ptp **erbost** (geh) ▓ VT to infuriate; **erbost sein über** (+acc) to be infuriated at ▓ VR **sich ~ über** (+acc) to become furious or infuriated about

erbrechen [ɛɐ'brɛçn], ptp **erbrochen** [ɛɐ'brɔxn] VTIR IRREG **(sich)** (Med) to vomit; **etw bis zum Erbrechen tun** (fig) to do sth ad nauseam

erbringen [ɛɐ'brɪŋən], ptp **erbracht** [ɛɐ'braxt] VT IRREG to produce

Erbrochene(s) [ɛɐ'brɔxənə] NT, DECL AS ADJ, NO PL vomit

Erbschaft ['ɛrpʃaft] F **-, -en** inheritance; **eine ~ machen** or **antreten** to come into an inheritance; **die ~ des Faschismus** the legacy of fascism

Erbschaftssteuer F death duties pl, inheritance tax (Brit)

Erbse ['ɛrpsə] F **-, -n** pea; **gelbe** or **getrocknete ~n** dried peas

Erbsen-: erbsengroß ADJ the size of a pea; **Erbsenpüree** NT ≈ pease pudding (esp Brit); **Erbsensuppe** F pea soup; **Erbsenzähler** M **-s, -, Erbsenzählerin** F **-, -nen** (pej inf) bean-counter (pej inf); **Erbsenzählerei** [-tsɛːlə'rai] F -, NO PL (pej inf) bean-counting (pej inf)

Erb-: Erbstück NT heirloom; **Erbtante** F (inf) rich aunt; **Erbteil** NT or M (Jur) (portion of an/the) inheritance; **Erbverzicht** M renunciation of one's claim to an inheritance

Erdachse ['eːɐt-] F earth's axis

erdacht [ɛɐ'daxt] ADJ Geschichte made-up

Erd-: Erdanziehung F, NO PL gravitational pull of the earth; **Erdapfel** M (Aus, S Ger) potato; **Erdarbeiten** PL excavation(s pl); **Erdatmosphäre** F earth's atmosphere; **Erdbahn** F earth's orbit

Erdbeben NT earthquake

Erdbeben-: Erdbebengebiet NT earthquake area; **erdbebengefährdet** ADJ at risk from earthquakes; **Erdbebengürtel** M earthquake belt or zone; **Erdbebenherd** M seismic focus; **Erdbebenmesser** M **-s, -, Erdbebenmessgerät** NT seismograph; **erdbebensicher** ADJ Gebäude etc earthquake-proof; Gebiet not prone to earthquakes; **Erdbebenwarte** [-vartə] F **-, -n** seismological station

Erd-: Erdbeere F strawberry; **Erdbestattung** F burial; **Erdbewohner(in)** M(F) inhabitant of the earth; (gegenüber Marsbewohnern etc) terrestrial, earthling (hum)

Erdboden M ground; **etw dem ~ gleichmachen** to raze sth to the ground; **vom ~ verschwinden** to disappear off the face of the earth

Erde ['eːɐdə] F **-, -n (a)** (= Welt) earth, world; **auf der ganzen ~** all over the world; **niemand auf der ganzen ~** nobody in the whole world **(b)** (= Boden) ground; **unter der ~** underground; (fig) beneath the soil; **du wirst mich noch unter die ~ bringen** (inf) you'll be the death of me yet (inf); **über der ~** above ground; **mit beiden Beinen** or **Füßen (fest) auf der ~ stehen** (fig) to have both feet firmly on the ground **(c)** (= Erdreich, Bodenart) soil, earth (auch Chem); **~ zu ~** (Eccl) dust to dust; **seltene ~n** (Chem) rare earths **(d)** (Elec: = Erdung) earth, ground (US)

erden ['eːɐdn] VT (Elec) to earth, to ground (US)

erdenklich [ɛɐ'dɛŋklɪç] ADJ ATTR conceivable; **alles ~(e) Gute** all the very best; **sich** (dat) **alle** or **jede ~e Mühe geben** to take the greatest (possible) pains; **alles Erdenkliche tun** to do everything conceivable

Erd-: erdfarben [-farbn], **erdfarbig** ADJ earth-coloured (Brit), earth-colored (US); **erdfern** ADJ (Astron) far from the earth; **Erdferne** F (Astron) apogee; **Erdgas** NT natural gas; **Erdgeschichte** F geological history; **erdgeschichtlich** ADJ NO PRED geological; **Erdgeschoss** NT ground floor, first floor (US); **im ~** on the ground or first (US) floor; **Erdhörnchen** NT ground squirrel

erdichten [ɛɐˈdɪçtn̩], *ptp* **erdichtet** VT to invent; **das ist alles erdichtet und erlogen** it's all pure fabrication

erdig [ˈeːɐdɪç] ADJ earthy

Erd-: Erdinnere(s) [ˈeːɐtɪnərə] NT DECL AS ADJ bowels *pl* of the earth; **Erdklumpen** M clod of earth; **Erdkreis** M globe; **auf dem ganzen ~** all over the world; **Erdkunde** F geography; **erdkundlich** [ˈeːɐtkʊntlɪç] ADJ geographical; **Erdleitung** F (*Elec*) earth *or* ground (*US*) (connection); (= *Kabel*) underground wire; **Erdmännchen** NT (*Zool*) meerkat; **Erdnähe** F (*Astron*) perigee; **Erdnuss** F peanut; **Erdnussbutter** F peanut butter; **Erdoberfläche** F surface of the earth

Erdöl [ˈeːɐtøːl] NT (mineral) oil; **~ exportierend** oil-exporting

erdolchen [ɛɐˈdɔlçn̩], *ptp* **erdolcht** VT to stab (to death); **jdn mit Blicken ~** to look daggers at sb

Erdöl-: Erdölleitung F oil pipeline; **Erdölpreise** PL oil prices *pl*; **Erdölraffination** F petroleum refining; **Erdölverarbeitung** F processing of crude oil

Erd-: Erdpol M (*Geog*) (terrestrial) pole; **Erdreich** NT soil

erdreisten [ɛɐˈdraɪstn̩], *ptp* **erdreistet** VR **sich ~, etw zu tun** to have the audacity to do sth; **wie können Sie sich ~!** how dare you!

erdrosseln [ɛɐˈdrɔsln̩], *ptp* **erdrosselt** VT to strangle

Erdrosselung F strangulation

erdrücken [ɛɐˈdrʏkn̩], *ptp* **erdrückt** VT to crush (to death); (*fig:* = *überwältigen*) to overwhelm; **~de Übermacht** overwhelming superiority; **~des Beweismaterial** overwhelming evidence

Erd-: Erdrutsch M landslide; **politischer ~** political upheaval; (= *überwältigender Wahlsieg*) (political) landslide; **erdrutschartig** ADJ *Sieg* landslide *attr*; *Niederlage* devastating; **Erdrutschsieg** M landslide (victory); **Erdschicht** F layer (of the earth); **Erdstoß** M (seismic) shock; **Erdstrahlen** PL field lines *pl*; **Erdteil** M continent

erdulden [ɛɐˈdʊldn̩], *ptp* **erduldet** VT to suffer

Erd-: Erdumdrehung F rotation of the earth; **Erdumkreisung** F (*durch Satelliten*) orbit(ing) of the earth; **Erdumlaufbahn** F earth orbit; **Erdumrundung** F (*durch Satelliten*) orbit(ing) of the earth; **Erdumsegelung** F voyage around the world; **Erdumsegler(in)** M(F) round-the-world sailor

Erdung [ˈeːɐdʊŋ] F **-, -en** (*Elec*) earth(ing), ground(ing) (*US*)

Erd-: erdverbunden, erdverwachsen ADJ *Mensch, Volksstamm* close to the earth; **Erdwall** M earthwork

ereifern [ɛɐˈaɪfɐn], *ptp* **ereifert** VR to get excited (*über +acc* about)

ereignen [ɛɐˈaɪɡnən], *ptp* **ereignet** VR to occur

Ereignis [ɛɐˈaɪɡnɪs] NT **-ses, -se** event, occurrence; (= *Vorfall*) incident; (*besonderes*) occasion

ereignis-: ereignislos ADJ uneventful; **ereignisreich** ADJ eventful

Erektion [erɛkˈtsioːn] F **-, -en** (*Physiol*) erection

erfahren¹ [ɛɐˈfaːrən], *ptp* **erfahren** IRREG ■ VT (a) *Nachricht etc* to find out; (= *hören*) to hear (*von* about, of); **darf man Ihre Absichten ~?** might one inquire as to your intentions? (b) (= *erleben*) to experience; *Liebe, Verständnis* to receive; *Veränderungen etc* to undergo ☑ VI to hear (*von* about, of)

erfahren² [ɛɐˈfaːrən] ADJ experienced

Erfahrung F **-, -en** experience; (= *Übung auch*) practical knowledge; **aus (eigener) ~** from (one's own) experience; **nach meiner ~** in my experience; **~en sammeln** to gain experience; **etw in ~ bringen** to learn sth; **eine ~ machen** to have an experience; **seine ~en machen** to learn (things) the hard way; **jeder muss seine ~en selber machen** everyone has to learn by experience; **ich habe die ~ gemacht, dass ...** I have found that ...; **mit dieser neuen Maschine haben wir nur gute/schlechte ~en gemacht** we have found this new machine (to be) completely satisfactory/unsatisfactory; **ich habe mit der Ehe nur schlechte ~en gemacht** I've had a very bad experience of marriage (*esp Brit*), I've had very bad experience with marriage (*US*); **durch ~ wird man klug** (*Prov*) one learns by experience

Erfahrungs-: Erfahrungsaustausch M (*Pol*) exchange of experiences; **erfahrungsgemäß** ADV **~ ist es ...** experience shows ...

erfassen [ɛɐˈfasn̩], *ptp* **erfasst** VT (a) (= *mitreißen: Auto, Strömung*) to catch (b) (*Furcht, Verlangen etc*) to seize; **Angst erfasste sie** she was

seized by fear; **Mitleid erfasste sie** she was filled with compassion (c) (= *begreifen*) to grasp; **er hats endlich erfasst** he's caught on at last (d) (= *einbeziehen*) to include; (= *registrieren*) to record, to register; *Daten* to capture; **alle Fälle werden statistisch erfasst** statistics of all cases are being recorded; **das ist noch nicht statistisch erfasst worden** there are no statistics on it yet

Erfassung F registration, recording; (*von Daten*) capture; (= *Miteinbeziehung*) inclusion

erfinden [ɛɐˈfɪndn̩], *ptp* **erfunden** [ɛɐˈfʊndn̩] VT IRREG to invent; **das hat sie glatt erfunden** she made it all up; **frei erfunden** completely fictitious; **er hat die Arbeit auch nicht erfunden** (*inf*) he's not exactly crazy about work (*inf*)

Erfinder(in) M(F) inventor

Erfindergeist M inventive genius

erfinderisch [ɛɐˈfɪndərɪʃ] ADJ inventive

Erfindung F **-, -en** invention; **eine ~ machen** to invent something

Erfindungs-: Erfindungsgabe F inventiveness; **erfindungsreich** ADJ = **erfinderisch**; **Erfindungsreichtum** M ingenuity

Erfolg [ɛɐˈfɔlk] M **-(e)s, -e** [-ɡə] success; (= *Ergebnis, Folge*) result; (*Sport:* = *Sieg*) victory; **mit ~** successfully; **ohne ~** unsuccessfully; **viel ~!** good luck!; **~ haben** to be successful; **-(e) bei Frauen haben** to be successful with women; **keinen ~ haben** to be unsuccessful; **ohne ~ bleiben** *or* **sein** to be unsuccessful; **~ versprechend** promising; **ein voller ~** a great success

erfolgen [ɛɐˈfɔlɡn̩], *ptp* **erfolgt** VI AUX SEIN (*form*) (= *folgen*) to follow; (= *sich ergeben*) to result; (= *vollzogen werden*) to be carried out; (= *stattfinden*) to take place; (*Zahlung*) to be made; **nach erfolgter Zahlung** after payment has been made; **es erfolgte keine Antwort** no answer was forthcoming

Erfolg-: erfolglos ■ ADJ unsuccessful ☑ ADV unsuccessfully; **~ verlaufen** to be unsuccessful; **Erfolglosigkeit** F **-, NO PL** lack of success; **erfolgreich** ■ ADJ successful ☑ ADV successfully; **~ verlaufen** to be successful; **sich um etw ~ bewerben** to succeed in getting sth

Erfolgs-: Erfolgsaussicht F prospect of success; **Erfolgsautor(in)** M(F) successful author; **Erfolgserlebnis** NT feeling of success; **Erfolgskonto** NT (*Fin*) nominal account; **Erfolgskurs** M success; **auf ~ liegen** to be on course for success; **Erfolgsmeldung** F news *sing* of success; **endlich eine ~!** good news at last!; **Erfolgsrechnung** F (*Fin*) profit and loss account *or* statement (*US*), income statement; **außenwirtschaftliche ~** balance of payments; **hochgerechnete ~** extrapolated income statement; **zusammengefasste ~** earnings summary; **Erfolgsrezept** NT recipe for success; **Erfolgsroman** M successful novel; **Erfolgsserie** F string of successes

erfolgversprechend ADJ *siehe* **Erfolg**

erforderlich [ɛɐˈfɔrdəlɪç] ADJ necessary; **es ist dringend ~, dass ...** it is a matter of urgent necessity that ...; **etw ~ machen** to make sth necessary; **unbedingt ~** (absolutely) essential

erfordern [ɛɐˈfɔrdɐn], *ptp* **erfordert** VT to require

Erfordernis [ɛɐˈfɔrdɐnɪs] NT **-ses, -se** requirement

erforschen [ɛɐˈfɔrʃn̩], *ptp* **erforscht** VT *Land, Weltraum, Probleme* to explore; *Thema etc* to research; *Lage, Meinung, Wahrheit* to ascertain

Erforscher(in) M(F) (*eines Landes*) explorer; (*in Wissenschaft*) researcher

Erforschung F (*von Land, Weltraum etc*) exploration; (*von Problemen*) investigation (*+gen* into); (*wissenschaftlich*) research (*+gen* into); (*von Thema*) researching; (*von Lage, Meinung, Wahrheit*) ascertaining

erfragen [ɛɐˈfraːɡn̩], *ptp* **erfragt** VT *Weg* to ask; *Einzelheiten etc* to obtain; **Einzelheiten zu ~ bei ...** for details apply to ...

erfreuen [ɛɐˈfrɔyən], *ptp* **erfreut** VT to please; *Herz* to gladden; **er wollte damit die Menschen ~** he wanted to give people pleasure; **ja, sagte er erfreut** yes, he said delighted(ly); **über jdn/etw erfreut sein** to be pleased about sb/sth ☑ VR **sich einer Sache** (*gen*) **~** (*geh*) to enjoy sth; **sich an etw** (*dat*) **~** to enjoy sth

erfreulich [ɛɐˈfrɔylɪç] **1** ADJ pleasant; *Neuerung, Besserung etc* welcome; (= *befriedigend*) gratifying; **es ist wenig ~, dass wir ...** it's not very satisfactory that we ...; **es wäre ~, wenn die Regierung ...** it would be good if the government ...; **sehr ~!** very nice! **2** ADV fortunately; **Oma hat sich ~ wenig beklagt** it was pleasant how little granny complained

erfreulicherweise ADV happily; **wir haben ~ einmal ein Spiel gewonnen** I'm pleased to say that we've won a game at last

erfrieren [ɛɐˈfriːrən], *ptp* **erfroren** [ɛɐˈfroːrən] **1** VI IRREG AUX SEIN to freeze to death; (*Pflanzen*) to be killed by frost; **erfrorene Glieder** frostbitten limbs **2** VT **sich** (*dat*) **die Füße/Finger ~** to suffer frostbite in one's feet/fingers

Erfrierung F -, -en USU PL frostbite *no pl*; **Tod durch ~** death from exposure

erfrischen [ɛɐˈfrɪʃn], *ptp* **erfrischt** **1** VT to refresh **2** VI to be refreshing **3** VR to refresh oneself; (= *sich waschen*) to freshen up

erfrischend 1 ADJ (*lit, fig*) refreshing **2** ADV refreshingly; **~ wirken** to be refreshing

Erfrischung F -, -en refreshment

Erfrischungs-: **Erfrischungsgetränk** NT refreshment; **Erfrischungsraum** M cafeteria; **Erfrischungstuch** NT, *pl* **-tücher** refreshing towel

erfüllen [ɛɐˈfylən], *ptp* **erfüllt** **1** VT **(a)** *Raum etc* to fill; **Hass/Liebe/Ekel** *etc* **erfüllte ihn** he was filled with hate/love/disgust *etc*; **Freude erfüllte ihn** his heart was filled with joy; **es erfüllt mich mit Genugtuung, dass ...** it gives me great satisfaction to see that ...; **ein erfülltes Leben** a full life **(b)** (= *ausführen, einhalten*) to fulfil (*Brit*), to fulfill (*US*); *Soll* to achieve; *Formalitäten* to comply with; *Zweck, Funktion* to serve; **die Fee erfüllte ihm seinen Wunsch** the fairy granted him his wish; **erfüllst du mir einen Wunsch?** will you do something for me? **2** VR (*Wunsch, Voraussagung*) to be fulfilled

Erfüllung F fulfilment (*Brit*), fulfillment (*US*); (*von Erwartungen*) realization; (*eines Solls*) achievement; **in ~ gehen** to be fulfilled

Erfüllungsgehilfe M, **Erfüllungsgehilfin** F (*Jur*) ≈ agent

ergänzen [ɛɐˈgɛntsn], *ptp* **ergänzt** VT to supplement; (= *vervollständigen*) to complete; *Fehlendes* to supply; *Lager, Vorräte* to replenish; *Bericht* to add (sth) to; *Ausführungen* to amplify; *Worte, Summe* to add; *Gesetz, Gesetzentwurf* to amend; **seine Sammlung ~** to add to one's collection; **ergänzte Ausgabe** expanded edition; **einander** *or* **sich ~** to complement one another; **um das Team zu ~** to make up the numbers of the team; **-d hinzufügen** *or* **bemerken** to make an additional remark (*zu* to)

Ergänzung F -, -en **(a)** (= *das Ergänzen*) supplementing; (= *Vervollständigung*) completion; (*von Fehlendem*) supply(ing); (*eines Berichts*) addition (+*gen* to); (*von Summe*) addition; (*von Gesetz*) amendment; (*von Lager, Vorräten*) replenishment; **zur ~ meiner Sammlung** to add to my collection **(b)** (= *Zusatz: zu Buch etc*) supplement; (= *Hinzugefügtes*) (*Person*) addition; (*zu einem Gesetz*) amendment; (*Gram*) complement

Ergänzungs-: **Ergänzungsabgabe** F supplementary tax; **Ergänzungsband** M, *pl* **-bände** supplement(ary volume)

ergattern [ɛɐˈgatɐn], *ptp* **ergattert** VT (*inf*) to get hold of

ergeben[1] [ɛɐˈgeːbn], *ptp* **ergeben** IRREG **1** VT to yield; (= *zum Ergebnis haben*) to result in; (= *zeigen*) to reveal; *Betrag, Summe* to amount to **2** VR **(a)** (= *kapitulieren*) to surrender (+*dat* to); **sich in etw** (*acc*) **~** to submit to sth **(b)** (= *sich hingeben*) **sich einer Sache** (*dat*) **~** to give oneself up to sth; *der Schwermut* to sink into sth; *dem Dienst etc* to devote oneself to sth; **sich dem Suff** (*inf*) **~** to take to the bottle (*inf*) **(c)** (= *folgen*) to result (*aus* from); **daraus können sich Nachteile ~** this could turn out to be disadvantageous; **das eine ergibt sich aus dem anderen** the one (thing) follows from the other **(d)** (= *sich herausstellen*) to come to light; **es ergab sich, dass unsere Befürchtungen ...** it turned out that our fears ...

ergeben[2] [ɛɐˈgeːbn] ADJ (= *treu*) devoted; (= *demütig*) humble; (= *unterwürfig*) submissive; **einem Laster ~ sein** to be addicted to a vice

Ergebnis [ɛɐˈgeːpnɪs] NT **-ses, -se** result; **die Verhandlungen führten zu keinem ~** the negotiations led nowhere; **die Verhandlungen führten zu dem ~, dass ...** the negotiations led to the conclusion that ...; **zu einem ~ kommen** to come to a conclusion

ergebnislos 1 ADJ unsuccessful **2** ADV **~ bleiben/verlaufen** to come to nothing

Ergebnislosigkeit F -, NO PL lack of success

Ergebnisrechnung F profit and loss account *or* statement (*US*), income statement

ergehen [ɛɐˈgeːən], *ptp* **ergangen** [ɛɐˈgaŋən] IRREG **1** VI AUX SEIN **(a)** (*form*) (*an* +*acc* to) (= *erteilt, erlassen werden*) to go out; (*Einladung*) to be sent; **~ lassen** to issue; to send **(b)** (= *erdulden*) **etw über sich** (*acc*) **~ lassen** to let sth wash over one (*Brit*), to let sth roll off one's back (*US*); **sie ließ seine Zärtlichkeiten über sich** (*acc*) **~** she submitted to his intimacies **2** VI IMPERS AUX SEIN **es ist ihm schlecht/gut ergangen** he fared badly/well; **wie wird ihm schlecht ~** he will suffer; **wie ist es ihr in der Prüfung ergangen?** how did she fare in (*Brit*) *or* on (*US*) the exam? **3** VR (*fig*) **sich in etw** (*dat*) **~** to indulge in sth; **er erging sich in Schmähungen** he let out a stream of abuse; **sich (in langen Reden) über etw** (*acc*) **~** to hold forth at length on sth

ergiebig [ɛɐˈgiːbɪç] ADJ (*lit, fig*) productive; *Geschäft* lucrative; *Kupfervorkommen, Goldmine etc* high-yield *attr*, rich; (= *fruchtbar*) fertile; (= *sparsam im Verbrauch*) economical

Ergiebigkeit F -, NO PL (*lit, fig*) productiveness; (*von Geschäft*) profitability; (= *Fruchtbarkeit*) fertility; (= *Sparsamkeit im Verbrauch*) economy; **die ~ der Goldmine** the high yield of the gold mine

ergo [ˈɛrgo] CONJ therefore

Ergometer [ɛrgoˈmeːtɐ] NT ergometer

Ergonomie [ɛrgonoˈmiː] F -, NO PL ergonomics *sing*

ergonomisch [ɛrgoˈnoːmɪʃ] **1** ADJ ergonomic **2** ADV ergonomically

Ergotherapeut(in) [ɛrgoteraˈpɔyt(ɪn)] M(F) ergotherapist

Ergotherapie [ɛrgoteraˈpiː] F ergotherapy

ergötzen [ɛɐˈgœtsn], *ptp* **ergötzt** **1** VT to delight; **zum Ergötzen aller** to everyone's delight **2** VR **sich an etw** (*dat*) **~** to take delight in sth; (*schadenfroh auch, böswillig*) to gloat over sth

ergreifen [ɛɐˈgraifn], *ptp* **ergriffen** [ɛɐˈgrɪfn] VT IRREG **(a)** (= *packen*) to seize; (*Krankheit*) to overcome; **das Feuer ergriff den ganzen Wald** the fire engulfed the whole forest **(b)** (*fig*) *Gelegenheit, Macht* to seize; *Beruf* to take up; *Maßnahmen* to take; **er ergriff das Wort** he began to speak; (*Parl*) he took the floor **(c)** (*fig*) *jdn* (= *packen*) to seize; (= *bewegen*) to move; **von Furcht/Sehnsucht** *etc* **ergriffen werden** to be seized with fear/longing *etc*; **siehe auch ergriffen**

ergreifend ADJ (*fig*) touching (*auch iro*)

ergriffen [ɛɐˈgrɪfn] ADJ (*fig*) moved; **siehe auch ergreifen**

Ergriffenheit F -, NO PL emotion

ergründen [ɛɐˈgrʏndn], *ptp* **ergründet** VT *Sinn etc* to fathom; *Ursache, Motiv* to discover

Erguss M effusion; (= *Samenerguss*) ejaculation; (*fig*) outpouring

erhaben [ɛɐˈhaːbn] **1** ADJ **(a)** *Druck, Muster* embossed **(b)** (*fig*) *Gedanken, Stil* lofty; *Schönheit, Anblick* sublime; *Augenblick* solemn; *Herrscher* illustrious; **das Erhabene** the sublime **(c)** (= *überlegen*) superior; **er dünkt sich über alles/alle ~** thinks himself to be above it all/superior to everybody; **über etw** (*acc*) **~ (sein)** (to be) above sth **2** ADV **~ lächeln** to smile in a superior way; **~ tun** to act superior

Erhalt M, NO PL receipt; (= *das Erhalten*) preservation

erhalten [ɛɐˈhaltn], *ptp* **erhalten** IRREG **1** VT **(a)** (= *bekommen*) to get; *Resultat, Produkt, Genehmigung* to obtain; **(Betrag) dankend ~** (*form*) received with thanks (the sum of ...) **(b)** (= *bewahren*) *Gebäude, Natur* to preserve; *Gesundheit etc auch* to maintain; **jdn am Leben/bei guter Laune ~** to keep sb alive/in a good mood; **ich hoffe, dass du uns noch lange ~ bleibst** I hope you'll be with us for a long time yet; (= *nicht sterben*) I hope you'll have many more happy days; **erhalte dir deinen Frohsinn/Optimismus** stay cheerful/optimistic; **er hat sich** (*dat*) **seinen Frohsinn/Optimismus ~** he kept up his cheerfulness/optimism; **gut ~** well preserved (*auch hum inf*);

von der Altstadt sind nur noch ein paar Kirchen ~ of the old town only a few churches remain ▣ VR (*Brauch etc*) to be preserved, to remain; **sich frisch und gesund ~** to stay bright and healthy

erhältlich [ɛɐˈhɛltlɪç] ADJ available; **schwer ~** hard to come by

Erhaltung F **-, -en** (= *Bewahrung*) preservation

erhängen [ɛɐˈhɛŋən], *ptp* **erhängt** VT to hang; **Tod durch Erhängen** death by hanging; **sich ~** to hang oneself

erhärten [ɛɐˈhɛrtn], *ptp* **erhärtet** ▣ VT to harden; (*fig*) *Behauptung etc* to substantiate; *Verdacht* to harden ▣ VR (*fig: Verdacht*) to harden

erhaschen [ɛɐˈhaʃn], *ptp* **erhascht** VT to catch

erheben [ɛɐˈheːbn], *ptp* **erhoben** [ɛɐˈhoːbn] IRREG ▣ VT
(a) (= *hochheben*) to raise (*auch Math*); **seinen** *or* **den Blick ~** to look up; **etw zu einem Prinzip/einer Regel etc ~** to make sth into a principle/a rule *etc*
(b) *Gebühren* to charge; *Steuern* (= *einziehen*) to raise; (= *auferlegen*) to impose
(c) *Fakten, Daten* to ascertain
▣ VR to rise; (*Wind etc*) (*form: Frage etc*) to arise; (= *aufragen*) to rise (*über +dat* above); (= *sich auflehnen*) to rise (up) (in revolt); **sich über andere ~** to place oneself above others

erhebend ADJ elevating; (= *beeindruckend*) impressive; (= *erbaulich*) edifying

erheblich [ɛɐˈheːplɪç] ▣ ADJ (= *beträchtlich*) considerable; (= *wichtig*) important; (= *relevant*) relevant; *Verletzung* serious ▣ ADV (= *beträchtlich*) considerably; *beschädigen, verletzen* severely

Erhebung F **(a)** (= *Bodenerhebung*) elevation **(b)** (= *Aufstand*) uprising; (= *Meuterei*) mutiny **(c)** (*von Gebühren*) levying **(d)** (= *amtliche Ermittlung*) investigation; (= *Umfrage*) survey; **~en machen** *or* **anstellen über** (*+acc*) to make inquiries about *or* into (**e**) (= *das Erheben*) raising; **~ ins Quadrat** squaring; **~ in die dritte Potenz** cubing

erheitern [ɛɐˈhaitɐn], *ptp* **erheitert** ▣ VT to cheer (up); (= *belustigen*) to entertain ▣ VR to be amused (*über +acc* by); (*Gesicht*) to brighten

Erheiterung F **-, -en** amusement; **zur allgemeinen ~** to the general amusement

erhellen [ɛɐˈhɛlən], *ptp* **erhellt** ▣ VT to light up (*auch fig*); (*fig: = klären*) to elucidate; *Geheimnis* to shed light on ▣ VR (*lit, fig*) to brighten; (*plötzlich*) to light up

erhitzen [ɛɐˈhɪtsn], *ptp* **erhitzt** ▣ VT to heat (up) (*auf +acc* to); **die Gemüter ~** to inflame passions ▣ VR to get hot; (*fig: = sich erregen*) to become heated (*an +dat* over); (*Fantasie etc*) to be inflamed (*an +dat* at); **die Gemüter erhitzten sich** feelings were running high; **vom Tanzen erhitzt** hot from the dancing

erhoffen [ɛɐˈhɔfn], *ptp* **erhofft** VT to hope for; **sich** (*dat*) **etw ~** to hope for sth (*von* from); **was erhoffst du dir davon?** what do you hope to gain from it?

erhöhen [ɛɐˈhøːən], *ptp* **erhöht** ▣ VT to raise; *Zahl auch, Produktion, Kraft* to increase; *Wirkung, Schönheit* to heighten; *Spannung* to increase; (*Mus*) *Note* to sharpen; **etw um das Doppelte ~** increase sth by twice as much again; **erhöhte Temperatur haben** to have a temperature; **erhöhte Wachsamkeit/Anstrengungen** *etc* increased vigilance/efforts *etc* ▣ VR to rise, to increase

Erhöhung F **-, -en (a)** (= *das Erhöhen*) raising; (*von Zahl auch, von Preis, Miete, Produktion, Kraft*) increase; (*von Wirkung*) heightening; (*von Spannung*) intensification **(b)** (= *Lohnerhöhung*) rise (*Brit*), raise (*US*); (= *Preiserhöhung*) increase

Erhöhungszeichen NT (*Mus*) sharp (sign)

erholen [ɛɐˈhoːlən], *ptp* **erholt** VR to recover (*von* from); **sie hat sich von dem Schreck(en) noch nicht erholt** she hasn't got over the shock yet; **du siehst sehr erholt aus** you look very rested

erholsam [ɛɐˈhoːlzaːm] ADJ restful

Erholung F **-,** NO PL recovery; (= *Entspannung*) relaxation; **zur ~ an die See fahren** to go to the seaside in order to recover; **sie braucht dringend ~** she badly needs a break; **Urlaub ist zur ~ da** holidays (*esp Brit*) *or* vacations (*US*) are for relaxation; **gute ~!** have a good rest

Erholungs-: erholungsbedürftig ADJ in need of a rest; **Erholungsgebiet** NT recreation area; **Erholungspause** F break

erhören [ɛɐˈhøːrən], *ptp* **erhört** VT *Gebet etc* to hear; *Bitte, Liebhaber* to yield to

Eriesee [ˈeːriː-] M der **~** Lake Erie

erigiert [eriˈɡiːɐt] ADJ erect

Erika [ˈeːrika] F **-, Eriken** [-kn] (*Bot*) heather

erinnern [ɛɐˈɪnɐn], *ptp* **erinnert** ▣ VT **jdn an etw** (*acc*) **~** to remind sb of sth; **jdn daran ~, etw zu tun/dass ...** to remind sb to do sth/that ...
▣ VR **sich an jdn/etw ~** to remember sb/sth; **sich nur noch dunkel ~ an** (*+acc*) to have only a faint recollection of; **soweit** *or* **soviel ich mich ~ kann** as far as I remember
▣ VI **~ an** (*+acc*) to be reminiscent of; **sie erinnert sehr an ihre Mutter** she reminds one very much of her mother; **daran ~, dass ...** (= *erwähnen*) to point out that ...

Erinnerung F **-, -en** (*an +acc* of) memory; (*euph: = Mahnung*) reminder; (= *Andenken*) memento; **zur ~ an** (*+acc*) in memory of; (*an Ereignis*) in commemoration of; (*als Andenken*) as a memento of; **jdn/etw in guter/schlechter ~ haben** *or* **behalten** to have pleasant/unpleasant memories of sb/sth; **sich** (*dat*) **etw in die ~ zurückrufen** to call sth to mind; **wenn mich meine ~ nicht täuscht** if my memory doesn't deceive me **Erinnerungen** PL (= *Lebenserinnerungen*) reminiscences *pl*; (*Liter*) memoirs *pl*; **~en austauschen** to reminisce

Erinnerungs-: Erinnerungsstück NT keepsake (*an +acc* from); **Erinnerungsvermögen** NT, NO PL memory

Eritrea [eriˈtreːa] NT **-s** Eritrea

eritreisch [eriˈtreːɪʃ] ADJ Eritrean

erkalten [ɛɐˈkaltn], *ptp* **erkaltet** VI AUX SEIN (*lit, fig*) to cool (down *or* off), to go cold

erkälten [ɛɐˈkɛltn], *ptp* **erkältet** ▣ VR to catch a cold; (= *esp sich verkühlen*) to catch a chill; **sich stark** *or* **sehr/leicht erkältet haben** to have (caught) a bad/slight cold/chill ▣ VT **sich** (*dat*) **die Blase ~** to get a bladder infection

erkältet [ɛɐˈkɛltət] ADJ with a cold; (**stark**) **~ sein** to have (a) (bad) cold

Erkältung F **-, -en** cold; (*leicht*) chill

erkämpfen [ɛɐˈkɛmpfn], *ptp* **erkämpft** VT to win; **sich** (*dat*) **etw ~** to win sth; **hart erkämpft** hard-won; **er hat sich** (*dat*) **seine Position hart erkämpft** he fought hard for his position

erkennbar ADJ (= *wieder ~*) recognizable; (= *sichtbar*) visible; (= *wahrnehmbar, ersichtlich*) discernible

erkennen [ɛɐˈkɛnən], *ptp* **erkannt** [ɛɐˈkant] IRREG ▣ VT (= *wieder ~, anerkennen, einsehen*) to recognize (*an +dat* by); (= *wahrnehmen*) to see; **ich erkannte die Lage sofort** I immediately realized what the situation was; **kannst du ~, ob das da drüben X ist?** can you tell if that's X over there?; **jdn für schuldig ~** (*Jur*) to find sb guilty; (**jdm**) **etw zu ~ geben** to indicate sth (to sb); **jdm zu ~ geben, dass ...** to give sb to understand that ...; **sich zu ~ geben** to reveal oneself (*als* to be); **~ lassen** to show; **erkenne dich selbst!** know thyself!; **du bist erkannt!** I see what you're after
▣ VI **~ auf** (*+acc*) (*Jur*) *auf Freispruch* to grant; *auf Strafe* to impose; (*Sport*) *auf Freistoß etc* to award; **auf drei Jahre Haft ~** to impose a sentence of three years' imprisonment

erkenntlich [ɛɐˈkɛntlɪç] ADJ **sich (für etw) ~ zeigen** to show one's gratitude (for sth)

Erkenntnis [ɛɐˈkɛntnɪs] F (= *Wissen*) knowledge no pl; (= *das Erkennen*) recognition; (*Philos, Psych*) cognition no pl; (= *Einsicht*) insight; **zur ~ kommen** to see the light; **zu der ~ kommen** *or* **gelangen, dass ...** to come to the realization that ...

Erkennung F recognition

Erkennungs-: Erkennungsdienst M police records department; **erkennungsdienstlich** ADV **jdn ~ behandeln** to fingerprint and photograph sb; **Erkennungsmarke** F identity disc (*Brit*), identification tag (*US*); **Erkennungsmelodie** F signature tune

Erker [ˈɛrkɐ] M **-s, -** bay; (= *kleiner Vorbau*) oriel

Erker-: Erkerfenster NT bay window; oriel window; **Erkerzimmer** NT room with a bay window

erklärbar ADJ explicable, explainable; **leicht ~** easily explained; **schwer ~** hard to explain; **nicht ~** inexplicable

erklären [ɛɐˈklɛːrən], *ptp* **erklärt** ▣ VT **(a)** (= *erläutern*) to explain (*jdm etw* sth to sb); **ich kann mir nicht ~, warum ...** I can't understand why ...; **ich erkläre mir die Sache so: ...** the way I see it, ...

(b) (= *äußern, bekannt geben*) to declare (*als* to be); *Rücktritt* to announce; (*Politiker, Pressesprecher etc*) to say; **einem Staat den Krieg ~** to declare war on a country; **er erklärte ihr seine Liebe** he declared his love for her; **jdn für schuldig/tot/gesund** *etc* **~** to pronounce sb guilty/dead/healthy *etc* **2 VR (a)** (*Sache*) to be explained; **das erklärt sich daraus, dass ...** it can be explained by the fact that ...; **damit hat sich die Sache von selbst erklärt** the affair thereby explained itself; **das erklärt sich (von) selbst** that's self-explanatory **(b)** (*Mensch*) to declare oneself; **sich für/gegen jdn/etw ~** to declare oneself for/against sb/sth; *siehe auch* **erklärt 3 VI** to explain; **sie kann sehr gut ~** she's very good at explaining things

erklärend 1 ADJ explanatory; **einige ~e Worte** a few words of explanation **2** ADV **er fügte ~ hinzu ...** he added in explanation ...

erklärlich [ɛɐ̯ˈklɛːʁlɪç] ADJ **(a)** = **erklärbar (b)** (= *verständlich*) understandable; **ist Ihnen das ~?** can you find an explanation for that?; **mir ist einfach nicht ~, wie ...** I simply cannot understand how ...

erklärt [ɛɐ̯ˈklɛːɐ̯t] ADJ ATTR professed; *Favorit, Liebling* acknowledged; *siehe auch* **erklären**

Erklärung F **(a)** explanation **(b)** (= *Mitteilung, Bekanntgabe*) declaration; (*eines Politikers, Pressesprechers etc*) statement; **eine ~ (zu etw) abgeben** to make a statement (about *or* concerning sth)

erklecklich [ɛɐ̯ˈklɛklɪç] ADJ considerable

erklettern [ɛɐ̯ˈklɛtɐn], *ptp* **erklettert** VT to climb

erklimmen [ɛɐ̯ˈklɪmən], *pret* **erklomm** *or* **erklimmte** [ɛɐ̯ˈklɔm, ɛɐ̯ˈklɪmtə], *ptp* **erklommen** *or* **erklimmt** [ɛɐ̯ˈklɔmən, ɛɐ̯ˈklɪmt] VT (*geh*) to scale; (*fig*) *Spitze, höchste Stufe* to climb to

erklingen [ɛɐ̯ˈklɪŋən], *ptp* **erklungen** [ɛɐ̯ˈklʊŋən] VI IRREG AUX SEIN (*geh*) to ring out; **eine Harfe/ein Glöckchen/Stimmchen erklang** (the sound of) a harp/bell/voice was heard; **ein Lied ~ lassen** to burst (forth) into song; **die Gläser ~ lassen** to clink glasses

erkranken [ɛɐ̯ˈkraŋkn̩], *ptp* **erkrankt** VI AUX SEIN (= *krank werden*) to be taken ill (*Brit*) *or* sick, to get sick (*esp US*) (*an* +*dat* with); (*Organ, Pflanze, Tier*) to become diseased (*an* +*dat* with); **erkrankt sein** (= *krank sein*) to be ill/diseased; **an Krebs erkrankten Menschen** people with cancer; **die erkrankten Stellen** the diseased areas

Erkrankung F **-, -en** illness; (*von Organ, Pflanze, Tier*) disease

erkunden [ɛɐ̯ˈkʊndn̩], *ptp* **erkundet** VT (*esp Mil*) to reconnoitre (*Brit*), to reconnoiter (*US*); (= *feststellen*) to find out

erkundigen [ɛɐ̯ˈkʊndɪɡn̩], *ptp* **erkundigt** VR **sich (nach etw/über jdn) ~** to inquire (about sth/sb); **sich nach jdm ~** to ask after (*Brit*) *or* about sb; **sich bei jdm (nach etw) ~** to ask sb (about sth); **ich werde mich ~** I'll find out

Erkundigung F **-, -en** inquiry

Erkundung F **-, -en** (*Mil*) reconnaissance

Erlagschein [ɛɐ̯ˈlaːk-] M (*Aus*) giro transfer form

erlahmen [ɛɐ̯ˈlaːmən], *ptp* **erlahmt** VI AUX SEIN to tire; (*Kräfte, fig: Interesse, Eifer*) to flag

erlangen [ɛɐ̯ˈlaŋən], *ptp* **erlangt** VT to achieve

Erlangung F **-,** NO PL attainment

Erlass [ɛɐ̯ˈlas] M **-es, -e** *or* (*Aus*) **-e** [ˈlɛsə] **(a)** (= *Verfügung*) decree; (*der Regierung*) enactment **(b)** (= *das* **-en**) remission

erlassen [ɛɐ̯ˈlasn̩], *ptp* **erlassen** VT IRREG **(a)** *Verfügung* to pass; *Gesetz* to enact; *Embargo etc* to impose; *Dekret* to issue **(b)** *Strafe, Schulden etc* to remit; **jdm etw ~** *Schulden etc* to release sb from sth; *Gebühren* to waive sth for sb; **bitte ~ Sie es mir, darüber zu sprechen** please don't ask me to talk about that; **jdm die Strafarbeit ~** to let sb off a punishment

erlauben [ɛɐ̯ˈlaʊbn̩], *ptp* **erlaubt** VT **(a)** (= *gestatten*) to allow; **jdm etw ~** to allow sb (to do) sth; **es ist mir nicht erlaubt, das zu tun** I am not allowed to do that; **~ Sie?** (*form*), **Sie ~?** (*form*) may I?; **~ Sie, dass ich das Fenster öffne?** do you mind if I open the window?; **~ Sie, dass ich mich vorstelle** allow me to introduce myself; **~ Sie mal!** do you mind!; **soweit es meine Zeit/das Wetter erlaubt** (*form*) time/weather permitting **(b) sich** (*dat*) **etw ~** (= *gestatten, sich gönnen*) to allow oneself sth; (= *wagen*) to venture sth; (= *sich leisten*) to afford to do sth; **sich** (*dat*) **~, etw zu tun** (= *so frei sein*) to take the liberty of

doing sth; (= *sich leisten*) to afford to do sth; **darf ich mir ~ ...?** might I possibly ...?; **wenn ich mir die folgende Bemerkung ~ darf ...** if I might venture the following remark ...; **sich** (*dat*) **Frechheiten ~** to take liberties; **sich** (*dat*) **einen Scherz ~** to have a joke; **was die Jugend sich heutzutage alles erlaubt!** the things young people get up to nowadays!; **was ~ Sie sich (eigentlich)!** how dare you!

Erlaubnis [ɛɐ̯ˈlaʊpnɪs] F **-,** (*rare*) **-se** permission; (= *Schriftstück*) permit

erläutern [ɛɐ̯ˈlɔɪtɐn], *ptp* **erläutert** VT to explain; *Text* to comment on; **~d** explanatory; **~d fügte er hinzu** he added in explanation; **etw anhand von Beispielen ~** to illustrate sth with examples

Erläuterung F **-, -en** explanation; (*zu Text*) comment; **zur ~** in explanation

Erle [ˈɛʁlə] F **-, -n** alder

erleben [ɛɐ̯ˈleːbn̩], *ptp* **erlebt** VT to experience; (= *noch lebend erreichen*) to live to see; (= *durchmachen*) *schwere Zeiten, Sturm* to go through; *Aufstieg, Abenteuer, Enttäuschung, Erfolg* to have; *Misserfolg, Niederlage* to suffer; *Jahrhundertwende, erste Mondlandung* to see; *Schauspieler* to see (perform); **im Ausland habe ich viel erlebt** I had an eventful time abroad; **was haben Sie im Ausland erlebt?** what sort of experiences did you have abroad?; **Deutschland, wie ich es erlebt habe, war ...** I remember Germany as being ...; **wir haben wunderschöne Tage in Spanien erlebt** we had a lovely time in Spain; **etwas Angenehmes** *etc* **~** to have a pleasant *etc* experience; **sie hat schon viel Schlimmes erlebt** she's had a lot of bad times; **wir haben mit unseren Kindern viel Freude erlebt** our children have given us much pleasure; **ich habe es oft erlebt ...** I've often known *or* seen it happen ...; **ich möchte mal ~, dass du rechtzeitig kommst** I'd like to see you come on time; **das werde ich nicht mehr ~** I won't live to see that; **sie möchte mal etwas ~** she wants to have a good time; **er hat viel erlebt** he has been around (*inf*); **das muss man erlebt haben** you've got to have experienced it (for) yourself; **na, der kann was ~!** (*inf*) he's going to be (in) for it! (*inf*); **hat man so (et)was schon (mal) erlebt!** (*inf*) I've never heard anything like it!; **dass ich das noch ~ darf!** I never thought I'd see the day!

Erlebnis [ɛɐ̯ˈleːpnɪs] NT **-ses, -se** experience; (= *Abenteuer*) adventure

Erlebnis-: Erlebnisaufsatz M (*Sch*) essay based on personal experience; **Erlebnispark** M theme park; **erlebnisreich** ADJ eventful

erledigen [ɛɐ̯ˈleːdɪɡn̩], *ptp* **erledigt 1** VT **(a)** *Angelegenheit* to deal with; *Akte etc* to process; (= *ausführen*) *Auftrag* to carry out; (= *beenden*) *Arbeit* to finish off; *Sache* to settle; **Einkäufe ~** to do the shopping; **ich habe noch einiges in der Stadt zu ~** I've still got a few things to do in town; **die Sache/er ist für mich erledigt** as far as I'm concerned the matter's closed/I'm finished with him; **erledigt!** (*Stempel*) dealt with, processed; **das ist (damit) erledigt** that's settled; **wird erledigt!** will do! (*inf*); **zu ~** (*Vermerk auf Akten*) for attention; **schon erledigt!** I've already done it; (= *mache ich sofort*) consider it done **(b)** (*inf*) (= *ermüden*) to wear out; (= *ruinieren*) to finish; (= *töten*) to do in (*inf*); (= *k.o. schlagen*) to knock out **2 VR damit erledigt sich das Problem** that disposes of the problem; **das hat sich erledigt** that's all settled; **sich von selbst ~** to take care of itself

erledigt [ɛɐ̯ˈleːdɪçt] ADJ (*inf*) (= *erschöpft*) shattered (*Brit inf*), all in (*inf*); (= *ruiniert*) finished; **wenn jetzt die Bullen kommen, sind wir ~** if the cops come now, we've had it (*inf*)

Erledigung F **-, -en** (= *Ausführung*) execution; (= *Durchführung, Beendung*) completion; (*einer Sache, eines Geschäfts*) settlement; **ich habe noch einige ~en** I still have a few items of business to attend to; **einige ~en in der Stadt** a few things to do in town; **die ~ meiner Korrespondenz** dealing with my correspondence; **um rasche ~ wird gebeten** please give this your immediate attention; **in ~ Ihres Auftrages** (*form*) in execution of your order (*form*); **in ~ Ihrer Anfrage** (*form*) further to your inquiry

erlegen [ɛɐ̯ˈleːɡn̩], *ptp* **erlegt** VT **(a)** *Wild* to shoot **(b)** (*Aus, Sw*: = *bezahlen*) to pay

erleichtern [ɛɐ̯ˈlaɪçtɐn], *ptp* **erleichtert** VT (= *einfacher machen*) to make easier; (*fig*) *Last, Los* to lighten; (= *beruhigen, lindern*) to relieve; *Herz, Gewissen* to unburden; **jdm etw ~** to make sth easier for sb; **jdn um etw ~** (hum) to relieve sb of sth; **erleichtert aufatmen** to breathe a sigh of relief

Erleichterung F -, -en (= Beruhigung) relief

erleiden [ɛɐˈlaidn], ptp **erlitten** [ɛɐˈlɪtn] VT IRREG to suffer

erlernbar ADJ easily learned

erlernen [ɛɐˈlɛrnən], ptp **erlernt** VT to learn

erlesen [ɛɐˈleːzn] ADJ exquisite; **ein ~er Kreis** a select circle

erleuchten [ɛɐˈlɔʏçtn], ptp **erleuchtet** VT to light (up), to illuminate; (fig) to enlighten; **hell erleuchtet** brightly lit; **Stadt** brightly illuminated

Erleuchtung F -, -en (= Eingebung) inspiration

erliegen [ɛɐˈliːgn], ptp **erlegen** VI IRREG AUX SEIN +DAT (lit, fig) to succumb to; **einem Irrtum** to be the victim of; **zum Erliegen kommen/bringen** to come/bring to a standstill

erlischt [ɛɐˈlɪʃt] 3. PERS SING PRES von **erlöschen**

Erlös [ɛɐˈløːs] M -es, -e [-zə] proceeds pl

erlöschen [ɛɐˈlœʃn], pret **erlosch** [ɛɐˈlɔʃ], ptp **erloschen** [ɛɐˈlɔʃn] VI AUX SEIN (Feuer) to go out; (Gefühle, Interesse) to die; (Vulkan) to become extinct; (Leben) to come to an end; (Vertrag, Anspruch, Garantie, Mandat) to expire

erlösen [ɛɐˈløːzn], ptp **erlöst** VT (= retten) to save (aus, von from); (Rel) to redeem; (von Sünden, Qualen) to deliver (esp Bibl)

Erlöser [ɛɐˈløːze] M -s, -, **Erlöserin** [-ərɪn] F -, -nen (= Befreier) saviour (Brit), savior (US); **der ~** (Rel) the Redeemer

Erlösung F release; (= Erleichterung) relief; (Rel) redemption; **der Tod war für sie eine ~** death was a release for her

ermächtigt [ɛɐˈmɛçtɪçt] ADJ authorized

Ermächtigung [ɛɐˈmɛçtɪgʊŋ] F -, -en authorization

ermahnen [ɛɐˈmaːnən], ptp **ermahnt** VT to admonish; (warnend) to warn; (Jur) to caution; **muss ich dich immer erst ~?** do I always have to remind you first?

Ermahnung F admonition; (warnend) warning; (Jur) caution

Ermangelung [ɛɐˈmaŋəlʊŋ] F -, NO PL, **Ermanglung** [ɛɐˈmaŋlʊŋ] F -, NO PL (geh) **in ~** +gen because of the lack of; **in ~ eines Besseren** for lack of something better

ermäßigen [ɛɐˈmɛːsɪgn], ptp **ermäßigt** ⬛ VT to reduce ⬛ VR to be reduced

Ermäßigung F -, -en reduction; (= Steuerermäßigung) relief

ermessen [ɛɐˈmɛsn], ptp **ermessen** VT IRREG (= einschätzen) Größe, Weite, Wert to gauge; (= erfassen, begreifen können) to appreciate

Ermessen [ɛɐˈmɛsn] NT -s, NO PL (= Urteil) judgement; (= Gutdünken) discretion; **nach meinem ~** in my estimation; **nach menschlichem ~** as far as anyone can judge; **nach freiem ~** at one's discretion; **etw in jds ~** (acc) **stellen**, **etw jds ~** (dat) **anheim stellen** to leave sth to sb's discretion; **in jds ~** (dat) **liegen** or **stehen** to be within sb's discretion

Ermessens-: Ermessensfrage F matter of discretion; **Ermessensspielraum** M discretionary powers pl

ermitteln [ɛɐˈmɪtln], ptp **ermittelt** ⬛ VT to determine (auch Chem, Math), to ascertain; Person to trace; Tatsache, Identität to establish ⬛ VI to investigate; **gegen jdn ~** to investigate sb; **in einem Fall ~** to investigate a case

Ermittler(in) M(F) investigator; **verdeckter ~** undercover investigator

Ermittlung F -, -en (esp Jur) investigation; **~en anstellen** to make inquiries (über +acc about)

ermöglichen [ɛɐˈmøːklɪçn], ptp **ermöglicht** VT to facilitate; **jdm etw ~** to make sth possible for sb; **(nur) wenn Sie es ~ können** (form) (only) if you are able (to)

ermorden [ɛɐˈmɔrdn], ptp **ermordet** VT to murder; (esp aus politischen Gründen) to assassinate

Ermordung F -, -en murder; (esp politisch) assassination

ermüden [ɛɐˈmyːdn], ptp **ermüdet** ⬛ VT to tire ⬛ VI AUX SEIN to tire; (Tech) to fatigue

ermüdend ADJ tiring

Ermüdung F -, (rare) -en fatigue (auch Tech)

ermuntern [ɛɐˈmʊntɐn], ptp **ermuntert** VT (= ermutigen) to encourage (jdn zu etw sb to do sth); (= beleben, erfrischen) to liven up; (= aufmuntern) to cheer up

ermutigen [ɛɐˈmuːtɪgn], ptp **ermutigt** VT (= ermuntern) to encourage; (= Mut geben) to give courage

Ermutigung F -, -en encouragement

ernähren [ɛɐˈnɛːrən], ptp **ernährt** ⬛ VT to feed; (= unterhalten) to support; **schlecht ernährt** undernourished; **gut ernährt** well-nourished; **dieser Beruf ernährt seinen Mann** you can make a good living in this profession ⬛ VR to eat; **sich gesund ~** to have a healthy diet; **sich von etw ~** to live on sth; **sich selbst ~ müssen** to have to earn one's own living

Ernährer [ɛɐˈnɛːre] M -s, -, **Ernährerin** [-ərɪn] F -, -nen breadwinner

Ernährung F -, NO PL (= das Ernähren) feeding; (= Nahrung) food; (= Unterhalt) maintenance; **auf vernünftige ~ achten** to eat sensibly; **die ~ einer großen Familie** feeding a big family; **falsche/richtige/pflanzliche ~** the wrong/a proper/a vegetarian diet

Ernährungs- IN CPDS nutritional; **Ernährungsberater(in)** M(F) nutritional or dietary adviser; **Ernährungswissenschaft** F dietetics sing

ernennen [ɛɐˈnɛnən], ptp **ernannt** [ɛɐˈnant] VT IRREG to appoint; **jdn zu etw ~** to make sb sth

Ernennung F appointment (zu as)

erneuerbar ADJ renewable

erneuern [ɛɐˈnɔʏɐn], ptp **erneuert** VT to renew; Forderung, Kritik to reiterate; (= renovieren) to renovate; (= restaurieren) to restore; (= auswechseln) Öl to change; Maschinenteile to replace; **einen Vertrag ~** to renew a contract

Erneuerung F renewal; (= Renovierung) renovation; (= Restaurierung) restoration; (= Auswechslung) (von Öl) changing; (von Maschinenteil) replacement

Erneuerungsschein M (St Ex) renewal coupon

erneut [ɛɐˈnɔʏt] ⬛ ADJ ATTR renewed ⬛ ADV (once) again

erniedrigen [ɛɐˈniːdrɪgn], ptp **erniedrigt** ⬛ VT (= demütigen) to humiliate; (= herabsetzen) to degrade; (Mus) to flatten ⬛ VR to humble oneself; (pej) to demean oneself

Erniedrigung F -, -en humiliation; (= Herabsetzung) degradation; (Mus) flattening

Erniedrigungszeichen NT (Mus) flat (sign)

ernst [ɛrnst] ⬛ ADJ serious; (= eifrig, ernsthaft) Mensch, Gesinnung earnest; (= feierlich, elegisch) solemn; **~e Absichten haben** (inf) to have honourable (Brit) or honorable (US) intentions; **es ist nichts Ernstes** it's nothing serious; **~ bleiben** to remain serious; (= sich das Lachen verbeißen) to keep a straight face
⬛ ADV reden, zuhören earnestly; **es (mit jdm/etw) ~ meinen** to be serious (about sb/sth); **~ gemeint** serious; **jdn/etw ~ nehmen** to take sb/sth seriously; **es steht ~ um ihn** things look bad for him; (wegen Krankheit) he's in a bad way; **ich muss mal ganz ~ mit ihr reden** I have to have a serious talk with her

Ernst M -(e)s, NO PL seriousness; (= Dringlichkeit, Ernsthaftigkeit von Gesinnung) earnestness; **im ~** seriously; **allen ~es** quite seriously; **meinen Sie das allen ~es?, ist das Ihr ~?** are you (really) serious?; **das kann doch nicht dein ~ sein!** you can't be serious!; **es ist mir ~ damit** I'm serious about it; **mit etw ~ machen** to put sth into action; **mit einer Drohung ~ machen** to carry out a threat; **der ~ des Lebens** the serious side of life; **damit wird es jetzt ~** now it's serious

Ernst-: Ernstfall M emergency; **im ~** in case of emergency; **ernstgemeint** [-ɡəmaint] ADJ ATTR siehe **ernst**; **ernsthaft** ⬛ ADJ serious; (= eindringlich, eifrig) earnest ⬛ ADV seriously; **jdn ~ ermahnen/warnen** to give sb a serious warning

Ernsthaftigkeit ['ɛrnsthaftɪçkait] F -, NO PL seriousness; (= Eindringlichkeit, Eifrigkeit) earnestness; **ernstlich** ['ɛrnstlɪç] ⬛ ADJ serious; (attr: = eindringlich) earnest ⬛ ADV **~ besorgt um** seriously concerned about; **~ böse werden** to get really angry

Ernte ['ɛrntə] F -, -n (a) (= das Ernten) (von Getreide) harvest(ing); (von Kartoffeln) digging; (von Äpfeln etc) picking (b) (= Ertrag) harvest (an +dat of); (von Kartoffeln etc auch, von Äpfeln, fig) crop; **die ~ seines Fleißes** the fruits of his hard work

Ernte(dank)fest NT harvest festival

ernten ['ɛrntn] VT Getreide to harvest; Kartoffeln to dig; Äpfel, Erbsen to pick; (fig) Früchte, Lohn, Unfrieden to reap; Undank, Applaus, Spott to get

ernüchtern [ɛɐˈnʏçtɐn], ptp **ernüchtert** VT to sober up; (fig) to bring down to earth; **~d** sobering

Ernüchterung F -, -en sobering-up; (*fig*) disillusionment

Eroberer [ɛɐ'loːbərə] M **-s, -**, **Eroberin** [-ərɪn] F **-, -nen** conqueror

erobern [ɛɐ'loːbɐn], *ptp* **erobert** VT to conquer; *Festung, Stadt* to capture; (*fig*) *Sympathie etc, neue Märkte* to win; (*inf*: = *ergattern*) to get hold of; **im Sturm ~** (*Mil, fig*) to take by storm

Eroberung F -, -en (*lit, fig*) conquest; (*einer Festung, Stadt*) capture; **eine ~ machen** (*fig inf*) to make a conquest

eröffnen [ɛɐ'lœfnən], *ptp* **eröffnet** ▉ VT **(a)** (= *beginnen*) to open (*auch Fin, Mil etc*); *Konkursverfahren* to institute; **etw für eröffnet erklären** to declare sth open **(b)** (*hum, geh*) **jdm etw ~** to disclose sth to sb; **ich habe dir etwas zu ~** I have something to tell you ▉ VI (*Währungskurs*) to open (*mit* at)

Eröffnung F **(a)** (= *Beginn*) opening; (*von Konkursverfahren*) institution **(b)** (*humgeh*) disclosure; **jdm eine ~ machen** to disclose sth to sb; **ich habe dir eine ~ zu machen** I have something to tell you

Eröffnungsbilanz F (*Fin*) opening balance (sheet)

erogen [ero'geːn] ADJ erogenous

erörtern [ɛɐ'lœrtɐn], *ptp* **erörtert** VT to discuss (in detail)

Erosion [ero'zioːn] F **-, -en** (*Geol, Med*) erosion

Erotik [e'roːtɪk] F **-, NO PL** eroticism

erotisch [e'roːtɪʃ] ADJ erotic

Erpel ['ɛrpl] M **-s, -** drake

erpicht [ɛɐ'pɪçt] ADJ **auf etw** (*acc*) **~ sein** to be keen (*Brit*) *or* bent (*US*) on sth; **er ist nur auf Geld ~** he's only after money

erpressbar ADJ **~ sein** to be susceptible to blackmail; **sich ~ machen** to lay oneself open to blackmail

erpressen [ɛɐ'prɛsn], *ptp* **erpresst** VT *Geld etc* to extort (*von* from); *jdn* to blackmail; **die Kidnapper haben den Vater erpresst** the kidnappers tried to extort money from the father

Erpresser [ɛɐ'prɛsɐ] M **-s, -**, **Erpresserin** [-ərɪn] F **-, -nen** blackmailer; (*bei Entführung*) kidnapper

Erpresserbrief M blackmail letter

Erpressung F -, -en (*von Geld, Zugeständnissen*) extortion; (*eines Menschen*) blackmail; **die Kidnapper hatten keinen Erfolg mit ihrer ~** the kidnappers failed to get their ransom money

Erpressungsversuch M blackmail attempt; (*durch Gewaltandrohung*) attempt at obtaining money by menaces; (*bei Entführung*) attempt at getting a ransom

erproben [ɛɐ'proːbn], *ptp* **erprobt** VT to test

erprobt ADJ tried and tested; (= *zuverlässig*) reliable; (= *erfahren*) experienced

erquicklich [ɛɐ'kvɪklɪç] ADJ pleasant

erraten [ɛɐ'raːtn], *ptp* **erraten** VT IRREG to guess

erregbar ADJ excitable; (*sexuell*) easily aroused; (= *empfindlich*) sensitive; **schwer ~** not easily aroused

erregen [ɛɐ'reːgn], *ptp* **erregt** ▉ VT **(a)** (= *aufregen*) to excite; (*sexuell auch*) to arouse; (= *erzürnen*) to infuriate; **in der Debatte ging es erregt zu** the debate was quite heated; **erregt lief er hin und her** he paced back and forth in a state of agitation; **freudig erregt** excited **(b)** (= *hervorrufen, erzeugen*) to arouse; *Zorn* to provoke; *Aufsehen, öffentliches Ärgernis, Heiterkeit* to cause; *Aufmerksamkeit* to attract; *Zweifel* to raise ▉ VR to get excited (*über* +*acc* about); (= *sich ärgern*) to get annoyed (*über* +*acc* at)

Erreger [ɛɐ'reːgɐ] M **-s, -** (*Med*) cause; (= *Bazillus etc*) pathogene (*spec*)

Erregung F **(a)** NO PL (= *das Aufregen*) excitation; (*sexuell auch*) arousal; (= *das Erzürnen*) infuriating **(b)** NO PL (= *Erzeugung*) arousing; (*von Aufsehen, Heiterkeit*) causing; (*von Aufmerksamkeit*) attracting **(c)** (= *Zustand*) (*esp angenehm*) excitement; (*sexuell auch*) arousal; (= *Beunruhigung*) agitation; (= *Wut*) rage; **in ~ geraten** to get excited/aroused/agitated/into a rage; **jdn in ~ versetzen** to get sb excited/aroused/agitated

erreichbar ADJ reachable; (= *nicht weit*) within reach; (*Telec*) obtainable; *Glück, Ziel* attainable; **leicht ~** easily reached; within easy reach; easily attainable; **schwer ~ sein** (*Ort*) not to be very accessible; (*Mensch*) to be difficult to get hold of; (*Gegenstand*) to be difficult to reach; **zu Fuß ~** able to be reached on foot; (= *nicht weit*) within walking distance; **in**

~er Nähe near at hand (+*gen* to); **sind Sie morgen zu Hause ~?** can I get in touch with you at home tomorrow?

erreichen [ɛɐ'raiçn], *ptp* **erreicht** VT to reach; *Zug* to catch; *Absicht, Zweck* to achieve; (= *einholen*) to catch up with; **ein hohes Alter ~** to live to a ripe old age; **vom Bahnhof leicht zu ~** within easy reach of the station; **zu Fuß zu ~** able to be reached on foot; (= *nicht weit*) within walking distance; **wann kann ich Sie morgen ~?** when can I get in touch with you tomorrow?; **wir haben nichts erreicht** we achieved nothing; **bei ihm war nichts zu ~** you couldn't get anywhere with him

errichten [ɛɐ'rɪçtn], *ptp* **errichtet** VT to erect (*auch Math*), to put up; (*fig*: = *gründen*) to establish

erringen [ɛɐ'rɪŋən], *ptp* **errungen** [ɛɐ'rʊŋən] VT IRREG to gain; *den 3. Platz, Erfolg* to achieve; *Rekord* to set; **ein hart errungener Sieg** a hard-won victory

erröten [ɛɐ'røːtn], *ptp* **errötet** VI AUX SEIN (*über* +*acc* at) to flush; (*esp aus Verlegenheit, Scham*) to blush; (*Gesicht*) to go red; **jdn zum Erröten bringen** to make sb flush/blush

Errungenschaft [ɛɐ'rʊŋənʃaft] F **-, -en** achievement; (*inf*: = *Anschaffung*) acquisition

Ersatz [ɛɐ'zats] M, NO PL substitute (*auch Sport*); (*für Altes, Zerbrochenes, Mitarbeiter*) replacement; (*inf*: = *die ~spieler*) substitutes *pl*; (= *das Ersetzen*) replacement; (*durch Geld*) compensation; (*von Kosten*) reimbursement; **als ~ für jdn einspringen** to stand in for sb

Ersatz-: Ersatzbefriedigung F (*Psych*) vicarious satisfaction; **das Rauchen ist eine ~** smoking is a substitute; **Ersatzdienst** M (*Mil*) alternative service; **Ersatzkasse** F state health insurance scheme; **ersatzlos** ▉ ADJ **~e Streichung** (*von Stelle, Steuer, Regelung*) abolition; (*von Sendung, Veranstaltung*) cancellation ▉ ADV **etw ~ streichen** *Stelle, Steuer, Regelung* to abolish sth; *Sendung, Veranstaltung* to cancel sth; **Ersatzrad** NT (*Aut*) spare wheel; **Ersatzreifen** M (*Aut*) spare tyre (*Brit*) *or* tire (*US*); **Ersatzspieler(in)** M(F) (*Sport*) substitute; **Ersatzteil** NT spare (part); **Ersatzzeiten** PL (*Insur*) substitute qualifying periods *pl*

ersaufen [ɛɐ'zaufn], *ptp* **ersoffen** [ɛɐ'zɔfn] VI IRREG AUX SEIN (*inf*) (= *ertrinken*) to drown; (= *überschwemmt werden, Aut*) to be flooded

ersäufen [ɛɐ'zɔyfn], *ptp* **ersäuft** VT to drown

erschaffen [ɛɐ'ʃafn], *pret* **erschuf** [ɛɐ'ʃuːf], *ptp* **erschaffen** VT to create

Erschaffung F creation

erscheinen [ɛɐ'ʃainən], *ptp* **erschienen** [ɛɐ'ʃiːnən] VI IRREG AUX SEIN to appear; (= *vorkommen, wirken wie auch*) to seem (+*dat* to); (*Buch auch*) to come out; **es erscheint (mir) wünschenswert** it seems desirable (to me); **das Buch ist in** *or* **bei einem anderen Verlag erschienen** the book was published by another publisher

Erscheinen [ɛɐ'ʃainən] NT **-s, NO PL** appearance; (*von Geist auch*) apparition; (*von Buch auch*) publication; **um rechtzeitiges ~ wird gebeten** you are kindly requested to attend punctually; **er dankte den Besuchern für ihr (zahlreiches) ~** he thanked his (many) guests for coming; **mit seinem ~ hatte ich nicht mehr gerechnet** I no longer reckoned on his turning up

Erscheinung F -, -en **(a)** NO PL (= *das Erscheinen*) appearance; **in ~ treten** (*Merkmale*) to appear; (*Gefühle*) to show themselves; **sie tritt (persönlich) fast nie in ~** she hardly ever appears (in person) **(b)** (= *äußere ~*) appearance; (= *Krankheitserscheinung, Alterserscheinung*) symptom; (= *Zeichen*) sign; **es ist eine bekannte ~, dass ...** it is (a) well-known (phenomenon) that ... **(c)** (= *Gestalt*) figure; **seiner äußeren ~ nach** judging by his appearance **(d)** (= *Geistererscheinung*) apparition; (= *Traumbild*) vision

erschießen [ɛɐ'ʃiːsn], *ptp* **erschossen** [ɛɐ'ʃɔsn] IRREG ▉ VT to shoot (dead) ▉ VR to shoot oneself; *siehe auch* **erschossen**

Erschießung F -, -en shooting; (*Jur: als Todesstrafe*) execution; **er drohte mit ~ der Geiseln** he threatened to shoot the hostages; **Tod durch ~** (*Jur*) death by firing squad

Erschießungskommando NT firing squad

erschlaffen [ɛɐ'ʃlafn], *ptp* **erschlafft** VI AUX SEIN (= *ermüden*) to tire; (= *schlaff werden*) to go limp; (*Seil*) to slacken; (*Interesse, Eifer*) to wane

erschlagen[1] [ɛɐ'ʃla:gn], *ptp* **erschlagen** VT IRREG to kill; **vom Blitz ~ werden** to be struck (dead) by lightning

erschlagen[2] [ɛɐ'ʃla:gn] ADJ **~ sein** (*inf*) (= *todmüde*) to be worn out; (= *erstaunt*) to be flabbergasted (*inf*)

erschließen [ɛɐ'ʃli:sn], *ptp* **erschlossen** [ɛɐ'ʃlɔsn] VT IRREG **(a)** *Gebiet, Absatzmarkt, Baugelände* to develop; *Einnahmequelle* to find; *Rohstoffquellen, Bodenschätze* to tap; *Wählergruppen* to tap into; **erschlossen** *Gebiet* developed **(b)** (= *folgern*) to deduce (*aus* from); *Gedicht* to decipher

Erschließungskosten PL development costs *pl*

erschöpfen [ɛɐ'ʃœpfn], *ptp* **erschöpft** **1** VT to exhaust; **in erschöpftem Zustand** in a state of exhaustion **2** VR (*fig*) **sich in etw** (*dat*) **~** to amount to nothing more than sth; **darin erschöpft sich seine Bildung** that's the sum total of his education; **ein Schriftsteller, der sich erschöpft hat** an author who has expended his talent

erschöpfend **1** ADJ **(a)** (= *ermüdend*) exhausting **(b)** (= *ausführlich*) exhaustive **2** ADV exhaustively

Erschöpfung F **(a)** (= *völlige Ermüdung*) exhaustion; **bis zur ~ arbeiten** to work to the point of exhaustion **(b)** (*der Mittel, Vorräte etc*) exhaustion

Erschöpfungszustand M state of exhaustion *no pl*

erschossen [ɛɐ'ʃɔsn] ADJ (*inf*) **(völlig) ~ sein** to be dead beat (*Brit inf*), to be beat (*esp US inf*); *siehe auch* **erschießen**

erschrak PRET *von* **erschrecken 2**

erschrecken [ɛɐ'ʃrɛkn] **1** *pret* **erschreckte**, *ptp* **erschreckt** VT to frighten; (= *bestürzen, zusammenzucken lassen*) to startle **2** *pret* **erschreckte** *or* **erschrak** [ɛɐ'ʃrɛktə, ɛɐ'ʃra:k], *ptp* **erschreckt** *or* **erschrocken** [ɛɐ'ʃrɛkt, ɛɐ'ʃrɔkn] VIR (*vi: aux sein*) to be frightened (*vor +dat* by); (= *bestürzt sein*) to be startled; (= *zusammenzucken*) to jump; **ich bin erschrocken, wie schlecht er aussah** it gave me a shock to see how bad he looked; **sie erschrak bei dem Gedanken, dass ...** the thought that ... gave her a start; **sie erschrak bei dem Knall** the bang made her jump; **~ Sie nicht, wenn Sie ihn sehen, er ist sehr alt geworden** don't be alarmed when you see him, he's aged terribly; *siehe auch* **erschrocken**

erschreckend **1** ADJ alarming **2** ADV **~ aussehen** to look dreadful; **~ wenig Leute** alarmingly few people; **~ viele** an alarmingly large number

erschrickt [ɛɐ'ʃrɪkt] 3. PERS SING PRES *von* **erschrecken 2**

erschrocken [ɛɐ'ʃrɔkn] **1** PTP *von* **erschrecken 2** **2** ADJ frightened; (= *bestürzt*) startled **3** ADV **~ hochspringen/zusammenzucken** to jump, to (give a) start

erschuf PRET *von* **erschaffen**

erschüttern [ɛɐ'ʃʏtɐn], *ptp* **erschüttert** VT *Boden, Gebäude, Vertrauen, Glauben etc* to shake; (*fig*) *Glaubwürdigkeit* to cast doubt upon; (= *bewegen, Schock versetzen*) to shake severely; **jdn in seinem Glauben ~** to shake sb's faith; **seine Geschichte hat mich erschüttert** I was shattered by his story (*inf*); **über etw** (*acc*) **erschüttert sein** to be shattered by sth (*inf*); **mich kann nichts mehr ~** nothing surprises me any more; **ihn kann nichts ~** he always keeps his cool (*inf*)

erschütternd ADJ shattering (*inf*)

Erschütterung F **-, -en** (*des Bodens etc*) tremor; (*fig*) (*der Ruhe, Wirtschaftslage*) disruption; (*des Selbstvertrauens*) blow (*+gen* to); (= *seelische Ergriffenheit*) emotion; **ihr Tod löste allgemeine ~ aus** her death shocked everyone

erschweren [ɛɐ'ʃve:rən], *ptp* **erschwert** VT to make more difficult; **jdm etw ~** to make sth more difficult for sb; **es kommt noch ~d hinzu, dass ...** to compound matters, ...

erschwinglich [ɛɐ'ʃvɪŋlɪç] ADJ *Preise* within one's means; **das Haus ist für uns nicht ~** the house is not within our means

ersehen [ɛɐ'ze:ən], *ptp* **ersehen** VT IRREG (*form*) **etw aus etw ~** to see sth from sth

ersehnt [ɛɐ'ze:nt] ADJ longed-for; **heiß** *or* **lang ~** much-longed-for

ersetzbar ADJ replaceable; *Schaden* reparable

ersetzen [ɛɐ'zɛtsn], *ptp* **ersetzt** VT to replace (*auch Comput*)

ersichtlich [ɛɐ'zɪçtlɪç] ADJ obvious; **ohne ~en Grund** for no apparent reason; **hieraus ist klar ~, dass ...** it is obvious from this that ...

ersinnen [ɛɐ'zɪnən], *ptp* **ersonnen** [ɛɐ'zɔnən] VT IRREG to devise; (= *erfinden*) to invent

ersparen [ɛɐ'ʃpa:rən], *ptp* **erspart** **1** VT *Kosten, Zeit, Kummer etc* to save; **jdm/sich etw ~** to spare sb/oneself sth; **ich kann mir jeglichen Kommentar ~** I don't think I need to comment; **jdm eine Demütigung ~** to spare sb humiliation; **Sie können sich alles Weitere ~** you don't need to say any more; **ihr blieb auch nichts erspart** she was spared nothing; **das Ersparte** the savings *pl* **2** VR to be superfluous

Ersparnis [ɛɐ'ʃpa:ɐnɪs] F **-, -se** *or* (*Aus*) *nt* **-ses, -se** **(a)** NO PL (*an Zeit etc*) saving (*an +dat* of) **(b)** USU PL savings *pl*

ersprießlich [ɛɐ'ʃpri:slɪç] ADJ (= *förderlich*) beneficial; (= *nützlich*) fruitful; (= *angenehm*) pleasant

erst [e:ɐst] ADV **(a)** first; (= *anfänglich*) at first; **mach ~ (ein)mal die Arbeit fertig** finish your work first; **~ mal ist das gar nicht wahr ...** for one thing it's just not true ...; **wenn du das ~ einmal hinter dir hast** once you've got that behind you **(b)** (= *nicht mehr als, bloß*) only; (= *nicht früher als auch*) not until; **eben** *or* **gerade ~** just; **~ gestern** only yesterday; **~ jetzt** only just; **~ jetzt wissen wir ...** it is only now that we know ...; **~ morgen** not until *or* before tomorrow; **es ist ~ 6 Uhr** it is only 6 o'clock; **wir fahren ~ übermorgen/~ später** we're not going until the day after tomorrow/until later; **~ als** only when, not until; **~ wenn** only if *or* when, not until **(c)** (*emph: = gar, nun gar*) **da gings ~ richtig los** then it really got going; **was wird dann ~ passieren?** whatever will happen then?; **er ist schon ziemlich blöd, aber ~ sein Bruder!** he is fairly stupid, but you should see his brother!; **da fange ich ~ gar nicht an** I simply won't (bother to) begin; **jetzt ~ recht/recht nicht!** that just makes me all the more determined; **da tat er es ~ recht!** so he did it deliberately; **das macht es ~ recht schlimm** that makes it even worse **(d) wäre er doch ~ zurück!** if only he were back!; **diese Gerüchte darf man gar nicht ~ aufkommen lassen** these rumours (*Brit*) *or* rumors (*US*) mustn't even be allowed to start

erstarren [ɛɐ'ʃtarən], *ptp* **erstarrt** VI AUX SEIN (*Finger*) to grow stiff; (*Flüssigkeit*) to solidify; (*Gips, Zement etc*) to set; (*Blut, Fett etc*) to congeal; (*fig*) (*Blut*) to run cold; (*Lächeln*) to freeze; (*vor Schrecken, Entsetzen etc*) to be paralyzed (*vor +dat* with); **erstarrte Formen** fossilized forms

erstatten [ɛɐ'ʃtatn], *ptp* **erstattet** VT **(a)** *Unkosten* to refund **(b)** (*form*) **(Straf)anzeige gegen jdn ~** to report sb; **Meldung ~** to report; **Bericht ~** to (give a) report (*über +acc* on)

Erstattung F **-,** NO PL (*von Unkosten*) refund

erstaunen [ɛɐ'ʃtaunən], *ptp* **erstaunt** **1** VT to astonish; *siehe auch* **erstaunt** **2** VI (= *Erstaunen erregen*) to astonish (people); **seine Körperbeherrschung erstaunt immer wieder** his physical control never fails to amaze

Erstaunen [ɛɐ'ʃtaunən] NT astonishment; **jdn in ~ (ver)setzen** to astonish sb

erstaunlich [ɛɐ'ʃtaunlɪç] **1** ADJ astonishing **2** ADV astonishingly

erstaunt [ɛɐ'ʃtaunt] **1** ADJ astonished (*über +acc* about) **2** ADV in astonishment; **~ blicken** to look astonished; *siehe auch* **erstaunen**

Erst-: **Erstausgabe** F first edition; **erstbeste(r, s)** ['e:ɐst'bɛstə] ADJ ATTR *siehe* **erste(r, s)**

erstechen [ɛɐ'ʃtɛçn], *ptp* **erstochen** [ɛɐ'ʃtɔxn] VT IRREG to stab to death

erstehen [ɛɐ'ʃte:ən], *ptp* **erstanden** [ɛɐ'ʃtandn] IRREG **1** VT (*inf: = kaufen*) to buy **2** VI AUX SEIN (*form*) to arise

Erste-Hilfe-Leistung [e:ɐstə'hɪlfə-] F administering first aid

ersteigen [ɛɐ'ʃtaign], *ptp* **erstiegen** [ɛɐ'ʃti:gn] VT IRREG to climb; *Felswand auch, Stadtmauer* to scale

ersteigern [ɛɐ'ʃtaigɐn], *ptp* **ersteigert** VT to buy at an auction

Ersteinsatz ['e:ɐst-] M **~ (von Atomwaffen)** first strike

erstellen [ɛɐ'ʃtɛlən], *ptp* **erstellt** VT **(a)** (= *bauen*) to construct **(b)** (= *anfertigen*) *Liste etc* to draw up

erstemal ['e:ɐstəma:l] ADV *siehe* **erste(r, s)**

erstens ['e:ɐstns] ADV first(ly)

Erste(r) ['e:ɐstə(r)] MF DECL AS ADJ first; **die drei ~n** the first three; **der ~ in der Klasse** the top of the class; **der ~ des Monats** the first (day) of the month; **vom nächsten ~n an** as of the first of next month; **er kam als ~r** he was the first to come

erste(r, s) ['e:ɐstə] ADJ first; (*fig: = führend auch*) best, foremost; *Seite der Zeitung* front; **~r Stock, ~ Etage** first floor, second floor (*US*); **~r Klasse fahren** to travel first class; **das ~ Mal** the first time; **das tue ich das ~ Mal** I'm doing this for the first time; **zum ~n Mal** for the first time; **~ Güte** *or* **Qualität** top quality; **~ Hilfe** first aid; **die ~n drei** the first three (from each group); **~ Kontakte anknüpfen** to establish preliminary contacts; **am ~n** first; **an ~r Stelle** in the first place; **in ~r Linie** first and foremost; **nimm das ~ Beste!** take anything!; **er hat das erstbeste Auto gekauft** he bought the first car he saw; *siehe auch* **vierte(r, s)**

Erste(r)-Klasse- [ɛːˈɛstəˈklasə-, ɛːˈɛstəˈklasə-] (*Rail*) first class; **Erste(r)-Klasse-Abteil** NT first class compartment

Erste(s) [ˈeːɛstə(s)] MF DECL AS ADJ **das ~** the first thing; **als ~s** first of all; **fürs ~** for the time being; **zum ~n, zum Zweiten, zum Dritten** (*bei Auktionen*) going, going, gone!

ersticken [ɛɐˈʃtɪkn], *ptp* **erstickt** **1** VT **jdn** to suffocate; **Feuer** to smother; **Geräusche** to stifle; (*fig: = unterdrücken*) **Aufruhr etc** to suppress; **mit ersticker Stimme** in a choked voice **2** VI AUX SEIN to suffocate; (*Feuer*) to die; **an etw** (*dat*) **~** to be suffocated by sth; **an einer Gräte ~** to choke (to death) on a fish bone; **unsere Städte ~ im Verkehr** our cities are being choked by traffic; **in der Arbeit ~** (*inf*) to be up to one's neck in work (*inf*)

Erstickung F -, NO PL suffocation

Erst-: erstklassig **1** ADJ first-class **2** ADV **spielen** excellently; **~ schmecken** *or* **munden** to taste excellent; **das Auto fährt sich ~** that car drives like a dream; **Erstklassigkeit** F -, NO PL excellence; **Erstkommunion** F first communion

Erstlingswerk [ˈeːɛstlɪŋz-] NT first work

erstmalig [ˈeːɛstmaːlɪç] **1** ADJ first **2** ADV for the first time

erstmals [ˈeːɛstmals] ADV for the first time

erstreben [ɛɐˈʃtreːbn], *ptp* **erstrebt** VT to strive for

erstrebenswert ADJ desirable

erstrecken [ɛɐˈʃtrɛkn], *ptp* **erstreckt** VR to extend (*auf, über* +*acc* over); **sich auf jdn/etw ~** (*= betreffen*) to apply to sb/sth

Erst-: Erstschlag M (*mit Atomwaffen*) first strike; **Erstsemester** NT first-year student; **Erststimme** F first vote

---

ERSTSTIMME/ZWEITSTIMME

*For elections to the German Bundestag a fairly complex mixed system of voting operates. Each voter has two votes. The **Erststimme** is used to directly elect a representative in each of the 328 constituencies and accounts for half of the available seats. The **Zweitstimme** is cast for the Landesliste of a party. The number of party candidates sent to the Bundestag is in direct proportion to the result of the poll. The **Erststimme** and the **Zweitstimme** are cast independently of one another.* ▶ BUNDESTAG

---

erstunken [ɛɐˈʃtʊŋkn] ADJ **das ist ~ und erlogen** (*inf*) that's a pack of lies

ersuchen [ɛɐˈzuːxn], *ptp* **ersucht** VT (*form*) to request (*jdm um etw* sth of sb)

ertappen [ɛɐˈtapn], *ptp* **ertappt** VT to catch; **jdn/sich bei etw ~** to catch sb/oneself at sth; **ich habe ihn dabei ertappt** I caught him at it

erteilen [ɛɐˈtailən], *ptp* **erteilt** VT to give; **Lizenz** to issue; **jdm einen Verweis ~** to reproach sb; **Unterricht ~** to teach

Erteilung F giving; (*von Lizenz*) issuing; **für die ~ von Auskünften zuständig** responsible for giving information

ertönen [ɛɐˈtøːnən], *ptp* **ertönt** VI AUX SEIN (*geh*) to sound; **von etw ~** to resound with sth

Ertrag [ɛɐˈtraːk] M -(e)s, **-e** [-ˈtreːɡə] (*von Acker*) yield; (*= Ergebnis einer Arbeit*) return; (*= Einnahmen*) proceeds *pl*; **~ abwerfen** *or* **bringen** to bring in a return; **vom ~ seiner Bücher/seines Kapitals leben** to live on the proceeds from one's books/the return on one's capital

ertragen [ɛɐˈtraːɡn], *ptp* **ertragen** VT IRREG to bear; (*esp in Frage, Verneinung auch*) to stand; **das ist nicht mehr zu ~** it's unbearable; **wie erträgst du nur seine Launen?** how do you put up with his moods?

erträglich [ɛɐˈtreːklɪç] ADJ bearable; (*= leidlich*) tolerable

Ertragsfähigkeit F earning power; (*von Boden*) yield

ertränken [ɛɐˈtrɛŋkn], *ptp* **ertränkt** **1** VT to drown; **seinen Kummer** *or* **seine Sorgen im Alkohol ~** to drown one's sorrows **2** VR to drown oneself

erträumen [ɛɐˈtrɔymən], *ptp* **erträumt** VT to dream of; **das war alles nur erträumt** it was all in the mind; **sich** (*dat*) **etw ~** to dream of sth

ertrinken [ɛɐˈtrɪŋkn], *ptp* **ertrunken** [ɛɐˈtrʊŋkn] VI IRREG AUX SEIN to drown

Ertrinken [ɛɐˈtrɪŋkn] NT **-s**, NO PL drowning

erübrigen [ɛɐˈlyːbrɪɡn], *ptp* **erübrigt** **1** VT **Zeit, Geld** to spare **2** VR to be superfluous; **jedes weitere Wort erübrigt sich** there's nothing more to be said

Eruption [erʊpˈtsioːn] F -, **-en** eruption

erw. ABBR *von* **erweitert** extended

erwachen [ɛɐˈvaxn], *ptp* **erwacht** VI AUX SEIN to awake; (*aus Ohnmacht etc*) to come to (*aus* from); (*fig: Gefühle, Verdacht*) to be aroused; **von etw ~** to be awoken by sth; **ein böses Erwachen** (*fig*) a rude awakening

erwachsen [ɛɐˈvaksn], *ptp* **erwachsen** **1** VI IRREG AUX SEIN (*geh*) to arise; (*Vorteil, Kosten etc*) to result; **daraus erwuchsen ihm Unannehmlichkeiten** that caused him some trouble **2** ADJ grown-up, adult; **~ sein** (*Mensch*) to be grown-up *or* an adult

Erwachsenenbildung F adult education

Erwachsene(r) [ɛɐˈvaksənə] MF DECL AS ADJ adult

erwägen [ɛɐˈvɛːɡn], *ptp* **erwogen** [ɛɐˈvoːɡn] VT IRREG to consider

erwägenswert ADJ worth considering

Erwägung F -, **-en** consideration; **aus folgenden ~en (heraus)** for the following reasons; **etw in ~ ziehen** to consider sth

erwählen [ɛɐˈvɛːlən], *ptp* **erwählt** VT to choose

erwähnen [ɛɐˈvɛːnən], *ptp* **erwähnt** VT to mention

erwähnenswert ADJ worth mentioning

Erwähnung F -, **-en** mention (+*gen* of), reference (+*gen* to); **~ finden** (*form*) to be mentioned

erwärmen [ɛɐˈvɛrmən], *ptp* **erwärmt** **1** VT (*lit, fig*) to warm **2** VR to warm up; **sich für jdn/etw ~** (*fig*) to take to sb/sth; **ich kann mich für Goethe/Geometrie nicht ~** Goethe/geometry leaves me cold

Erwärmung F -, **-en** warming; **globale ~** global warming; **~ der Erdatmosphäre** warming of the earth's atmosphere

erwarten [ɛɐˈvartn], *ptp* **erwartet** VT **Gäste, Ereignis** to expect; **etw von jdm/etw ~** to expect sth from *or* of sb/sth; **ein Kind** *or* **Baby ~** to be expecting a child *or* baby; **das war zu ~** that was to be expected; **etw sehnsüchtig ~** to long for sth; **sie kann den Sommer kaum noch ~** she can hardly wait for the summer; **was mich da wohl erwartet?** I wonder what awaits me there; **es steht zu ~, dass ...** (*form*) it is to be expected that ...; **über Erwarten** beyond expectation

Erwartung F expectation; (*= Spannung, Ungeduld*) anticipation; **in ~ einer Sache** (*gen*) in anticipation of sth; **zu großen ~en berechtigen** to show great promise; **den ~en entsprechen** *or* **gerecht werden** to come up to expectations; (*= Voraussetzung erfüllen*) to meet the requirements; **hinter den ~en zurückbleiben** not to come up to expectations

erwartungsgemäß ADV as expected

erwecken [ɛɐˈvɛkn], *ptp* **erweckt** VT (*fig*) **Hoffnungen, Zweifel** to raise; **Erinnerungen** to bring back; **(bei jdm) den Eindruck ~, als ob ...** to give (sb) the impression that ...

erweichen [ɛɐˈvaiçn], *ptp* **erweicht** VT to soften; **jds Herz ~** to touch sb's heart; **sich (durch Bitten) nicht ~ lassen** to be unmoved (by entreaties)

erweisen [ɛɐˈvaizn], *ptp* **erwiesen** [ɛɐˈviːzn] IRREG **1** VT (a) (*= nachweisen*) to prove; **eine erwiesene Tatsache** a proven fact; **es ist noch nicht erwiesen** it has not been proved (*esp Brit*) *or* proven yet (b) (*= zuteil werden lassen*) to show; **jdm einen Gefallen/Dienst ~** to do sb a favour (*Brit*) *or* favor (*US*)/service; **jdm Achtung ~** to pay respect to sb; **jdm Gutes ~** to be good to sb; **wir danken für die erwiesene Anteilnahme** we thank you for the sympathy you have shown **2** VR **sich als etw ~** to prove to be sth; **sich jdm gegenüber dankbar ~** to show one's gratitude to sb; **es hat sich erwiesen, dass ...** it turned out that ...

erweiterbar ADJ (*auch Comput*) expandable

erweitern [ɛɐˈvaitɐn], *ptp* **erweitert** VTR to widen; **Absatzgebiet auch, Geschäft, Abteilung** to expand; (*Med*) to dilate; (*fig*) **Interessen, Kenntnisse, Horizont** to broaden; **Macht** to extend

Erweiterung F -, **-en** widening; (*von Absatzgebiet auch, von Geschäft, Abteilung*) expansion; (*Med*) dilation; (*fig*) (*von Interessen, Kenntnissen, Horizont*) broadening; (*von Macht*) extension

Erwerb [ɛɐˈvɛrp] M -(e)s, **-e** [-bə] (a) NO PL acquisition; (*= Kauf*) purchase; **beim ~ eines Autos** when buying a car (b) (*= Broterwerb, Beruf*) living; (*= Verdienst, Lohn*) earnings *pl*;

einem ~ nachgehen to follow a trade *or* (*akademisch*) profession

erwerben [ɛɐˈvɛrbn], *ptp* **erworben** [ɛɐˈvɔrbn] VT IRREG to acquire; *Achtung, Ehre, Vertrauen* to earn; *Titel, Pokal* to win; (*käuflich*) to purchase; **sich** (*dat*) **etw ~** to acquire sth; **er hat sich** (*dat*) **große Verdienste um die Firma erworben** he has done great service for the firm

Erwerbs-: erwerbsfähig ADJ (*form*) capable of gainful employment; **Erwerbsfähigkeit** F (*form*) ability to work; **erwerbslos** ADJ = **arbeitslos**; **erwerbstätig** ADJ (gainfully) employed; **Erwerbstätige(r)** MF DECL AS ADJ person in gainful employment; **Erwerbstätigkeit** F gainful employment; **erwerbsunfähig** ADJ (*form*) incapable of gainful employment; **Erwerbsunfähigkeit** F inability to work

Erwerbung F acquisition

erwidern [ɛɐˈviːdɐn], *ptp* **erwidert** VT **(a)** (= *antworten*) to reply (*auf +acc* to); (*schroff*) to retort; **darauf konnte er nichts ~** he had no answer to that; **auf meine Frage erwiderte sie, dass ...** in reply to my question, she said that ... **(b)** (= *entgegnen, entgelten*) to return

Erwiderung F **-, -en (a)** (= *Antwort*) reply; (*schroff*) retort; **in ~ Ihres Schreibens vom ...** (*form*) in reply to your letter of the ... **(b)** (= *Entgegnung*) return; (*von Gefühlen*) reciprocation; **ihre Liebe fand bei ihm keine ~** he did not return her love

erwiesenermaßen [ɛɐˈviːznɐˈmaːsn] ADV as has been proved (*esp Brit*) *or* proven; **der Angeklagte ist ~ schuldig** the accused has been proved (*esp Brit*) *or* proven guilty

erwirtschaften [ɛɐˈvɪrtʃaftn], *ptp* **erwirtschaftet** VT to make through good management; **Gewinne ~** to make profits

erwischen [ɛɐˈvɪʃn], *ptp* **erwischt** VT (*inf*) (= *erreichen, ertappen*) to catch; (= *ergattern*) to get (hold of); **jdn beim Stehlen ~** to catch sb stealing; **du darfst dich nicht ~ lassen** you mustn't get caught; **ihn hats erwischt!** (*verliebt*) he's got it bad (*inf*); (*krank*) he's got it; (*gestorben*) he's had it (*inf*)

erwünscht [ɛɐˈvʏnʃt] ADJ *Wirkung etc* desired; *Eigenschaft, Kenntnisse* desirable; (= *willkommen*) *Gelegenheit, Anwesenheit* welcome; **du bist hier nicht ~!** you're not welcome here!

erwürgen [ɛɐˈvʏrgn], *ptp* **erwürgt** VT to strangle

Erz [eːɐts, ɛrts] NT **-es, -e** ore; (= *Bronze*) bronze

erz-, Erz- IN CPDS **(a)** [eːɐts, ɛrts] (*Geol*) mineral **(b)** [ɛrts] (= *ausgemacht*) out-and-out; **sein Erzrivale** his arch-rival **(c)** [ɛrts] (*Rang bezeichnend*) arch-

erzählen [ɛɐˈtseːlən], *ptp* **erzählt** **1** VT **(a)** *Geschichte, Witz etc* to tell; **er hat seinen Traum/den Vorfall erzählt** he told (us *etc*) about his dream/the incident; **jdm etw ~** to tell sth to sb; **man erzählt sich, dass ...** people say that ...; **erzähl mal, was/wie ...** tell me/us what/how ...; **erzähl mal was** (*inf*) say something; **wem - Sie das!** (*inf*) you're telling me!; **das kannst du einem anderen ~** (*inf*) tell that to the marines (*inf*); **mir kannst du viel or nichts ~** (*inf*) don't give me that! (*inf*); **dem werd ich was ~!** (*inf*) I'll give him a piece of my mind (*inf*)
(b) (*Liter*) to narrate; **~de Dichtung** narrative fiction; **Grundformen des Erzählens** basic forms of narrative **2** VI **(a)** to tell (*von* about); **er kann gut ~** he's a good storyteller; **er hat die ganze Nacht erzählt** he told stories all night
(b) (*Liter*) to narrate

Erzählung F (*Liter*) story; (= *das Erzählen*) narration; (= *Bericht, Schilderung*) account; **in Form einer ~** in narrative form

Erz-: Erzbergbau M ore mining; **Erzbergwerk** NT ore mine; **Erzbischof** M archbishop; **erzbischöflich** ADJ ATTR archiepiscopal; **Erzbistum** NT archbishopric; **Erzengel** M archangel

erzeugen [ɛɐˈtsɔygn], *ptp* **erzeugt** VT (*Chem, Elec, Phys*) to generate; (*Comm*) *Produkt* to manufacture; *Wein, Butter etc* to produce; (*fig: = bewirken*) to cause; **der Autor versteht es, Spannung zu ~** the author knows how to create tension

Erzeuger [ɛɐˈtsɔygɐ] M **-s, -**, **Erzeugerin** F **-, -nen** (*Comm*) manufacturer; (*von Naturprodukten*) producer

Erzeuger-: Erzeugerland NT country of origin; **Erzeugerpreis** M manufacturer's price

Erzeugnis NT product; (*Agr*) produce *no indef art, no pl*; **deutsches ~** made in Germany

Erzeugung F (*Chem, Elec, Phys*) generation; (*von Waren*) manufacture; (*geistige, künstlerische*) creation

Erz-: erzfaul ADJ bone idle (*Brit inf*); **Erzfeind(in)** M(F) arch-enemy; **Erzgauner(in)** M(F) (*inf*) cunning rascal (*inf*)

Erz- [ˈeːɐts-, ˈɛrts-]: **Erzgebirge** NT Erzgebirge; **erzhaltig** ADJ ore-bearing

erziehbar ADJ *Kind* educable; *Tier* trainable; **schwer ~ Kind** difficult; *Hund* difficult to train; **ein Heim für schwer ~e Kinder** a home for problem children

erziehen [ɛɐˈtsiːən], *ptp* **erzogen** [ɛɐˈtsoːgn] VT IRREG *Kind* to bring up; *Tier, Körper, Gehör* to train; (= *ausbilden*) to educate; **ein Tier/ein Kind zur Sauberkeit etc ~** to train an animal/to bring up a child to be clean *etc*; **ein gut/schlecht erzogenes Kind** a well-brought-up/badly-brought-up child

Erzieher [ɛɐˈtsiːɐ] M **-s, -**, **Erzieherin** [-ərɪn] F **-, -nen** educator; (*in Kindergarten*) nursery school teacher; (= *Privatlehrer*) tutor; (= *Gouvernante*) governess

erzieherisch [ɛɐˈtsiːərɪʃ] **1** ADJ educational; **ein Vater mit wenig ~em Können** a father with little skill in bringing up children; **~e Maßnahmen ergreifen** to impose discipline; **verschiedene ~e Methoden** different ways of bringing up children **2** ADV **~ wertvoll** educationally valuable; **~ falsch** educationally unsound

Erziehung F, NO PL upbringing; (= *Ausbildung*) education; (= *das Erziehen*) bringing up; (*von Tieren, Körper, Gehör*) training; (= *Manieren*) (good) breeding; **die ~ zu(r) Höflichkeit** teaching (sb) good manners

Erziehungs-: Erziehungsberatung F educational guidance; **erziehungsberechtigt** ADJ having parental authority; **Erziehungsberechtigte(r)** [-bərɛçtɪçtə] MF DECL AS ADJ parent or (legal) guardian; **Erziehungsjahr** NT (*nach Geburt*) year off for bringing up one's child/children; (*im Rentenrecht*) year of credited contributions (for each child); **Erziehungsmethode** F educational method; **Erziehungsurlaub** M parental leave

erzielen [ɛɐˈtsiːlən], *ptp* **erzielt** VT *Erfolg, Ergebnis* to achieve; *Kompromiss, Einigung, Geschwindigkeit* to reach; *Gewinn* to make; *Preis* (*Mensch*) to secure; (*Gegenstand*) to fetch; (*Sport*) *Tor, Punkte* to score; *Rekord* to set; **was willst du damit ~?** what do you hope to achieve by that?

Erz-: erzkonservativ ADJ ultraconservative; **Erzlager** [ˈeːɐts-, ˈɛrts-] NT ore deposit; **Erzreaktionär(in)** M(F) ultrareactionary

erzürnen [ɛɐˈtsʏrnən], *ptp* **erzürnt** VT (*geh*) to anger

erzwingen [ɛɐˈtsvɪŋən], *ptp* **erzwungen** [ɛɐˈtsvʊŋən] VT IRREG to force; (*gerichtlich*) to enforce

es¹ [ɛs] PERS PRON, *gen* **seiner**, *dat* **ihm**, *acc* **es (a)** (*auf Dinge bezogen*) it; (*auf männliches Wesen bezogen*) (*nom*) he; (*acc*) him; (*auf weibliches Wesen bezogen*) (*nom*) she; (*acc*) her **(b)** (*auf Vorangehendes bezüglich*) **sie ist klug, er ist es auch** she is clever, so is he; **wer ist die Dame? – es ist meine Frau** who's the lady? – it's *or* she's my wife; **alle dachten, dass das ungerecht war, aber niemand sagte es** everyone thought it was unjust, but nobody said so **(c)** (*rein formales Subjekt*) **es ist kalt/8 Uhr/Sonntag** it's cold/8 o'clock/Sunday; **es friert mich** I am cold; **es freut mich, dass ...** I am pleased that ...; **es sei denn, dass ...** unless ... **(d)** (*rein formales Objekt*) **ich halte es für richtig, dass ...** I think it (is) right that ...; **ich hoffe es** I hope so; **ich habe es satt, zu** (+*infin*) I'm tired of (+*prp*) **(e)** (*bei unpersönlichem Gebrauch des Verbs*) **es gefällt mir** I like it; **es klopft** there's a knock (at the door); **es regnet** it's raining; **bei dem Licht liest es sich gut** this light is good for reading; **es darf geraucht werden** smoking is permitted **(f)** (*Einleitewort mit folgendem Subjekt*) **es geschah ein Unglück** there was an accident; **es gibt viel Arbeit** there's a lot of work; **es gibt viele Leute, die ...** there are a lot of people who ...; **es kamen viele Leute** a lot of people came; **es lebe der König!** long live the king!; **es meldete sich niemand** nobody replied; **es war einmal eine Königin** once upon a time there was a queen

es² NT **-, -** (*Mus*) E flat

Es NT **-, - (a)** (*Mus: Dur*) E flat **(b)** (*Psych*) id

Escape-Taste [ɛsˈkeːp] F (*Comput*) escape key

Esche [ˈɛʃə] F **-, -n** ash-tree; (= *Holz*) ash

Esel [ˈeːzl] M **-s, -** donkey; (*inf: = Dummkopf*) (silly) ass; **du alter ~!** you are an ass (*inf*); **ich ~!** silly (old) me!; **störrisch wie ein ~** as stubborn as a mule; **der ~ nennt sich selbst zuerst** (*prov*) it's rude to put yourself first; **wenn es dem ~ zu wohl wird, geht er aufs Eis (tanzen)** (*Prov*) complacency makes one *or* you reckless

Eselin [ˈeːzəlɪn] F **-, -nen** she-ass

Esels-: Eselsbrücke F (= *Gedächtnishilfe*) mnemonic; (*gereimt*) jingle; **Eselsohr** NT (*fig*) dog-ear; **ein Buch mit ~en** a dog-eared book

Eskalation [ɛskalaˈtsɪoːn] F **-, -en** escalation

eskalieren [ɛskaˈliːrən], *ptp* **eskaliert** VTI (*vi: aux sein*) to escalate

Eskapade [ɛskaˈpaːdə] F **-, -n** (*fig*) escapade

Eskimo [ˈɛskimo] M **-s, -s** Eskimo

Eskimofrau F Eskimo (woman)

Esoterik [ezoˈteːrɪk] F **-,** NO PL esotericism

Esoteriker [ezoˈteːrike] M **-s, -, Esoterikerin** [-ərɪn] F **-, -nen** esoteric

esoterisch [ezoˈteːrɪʃ] ADJ esoteric

Espe [ˈɛspə] F **-, -n** aspen

Espenlaub NT aspen leaves *pl*; **zittern wie ~** to shake like a leaf

Esperanto [ɛspeˈranto] NT **-s,** NO PL Esperanto

Espresso [ɛsˈpreso] M **-(s), -s** *or* **Espressi** [-si] espresso

Essay [ˈɛse, ɛˈseː] M *or* NT **-s, -s** (*Liter*) essay

essayistisch [ɛseˈɪstɪʃ] ADJ (*Liter*) *Roman* essayistic; **das ~e Werk Thomas Manns** the essays of Thomas Mann

Ess-: essbar ADJ edible; **habt ihr irgendetwas Essbares im Haus?** have you got anything to eat in the house?; **nicht ~** inedible; **Essecke** F eating area

essen [ˈɛsn], *pret* **aß** [aːs], *ptp* **gegessen** [ɡəˈɡɛsn] VTI to eat; **in dem Restaurant kann man gut ~** that's a good restaurant; **die Franzosen ~ gut** the French eat well; **da isst es sich gut** the food is good there; **warm/kalt ~** to have a hot/cold meal; **tüchtig** *or* **ordentlich ~** to eat well *or* properly; **sich satt ~** to eat one's fill; **sich krank ~** to overeat; **jdn arm ~** to eat sb out of house and home; **den Teller leer ~** to eat everything up; **~ Sie gern Äpfel?** do you like apples?; **wer hat davon gegessen?** who has been eating that?; **wer hat von meinem Teller gegessen?** who's been eating off my plate?; **gerade ~, beim Essen sein** to be in the middle of eating; **~ gehen** (*auswärts*) to eat out; **nach der Vorstellung gingen wir noch ~** after the performance we went for a meal; **das Thema ist schon lange/noch nicht gegessen** (*fig inf*) the subject is dead and buried/still alive; **selber ~ macht fett** (*prov*) it's not my problem

Essen [ˈɛsn] NT **-s, -** (= *Mahlzeit*) meal; (= *Nahrung*) food; (= *Küche*) cooking; (= *Mittagessen*) lunch; (= *Abendessen*) dinner; **das ~ kochen** *or* **machen** (*inf*) to cook the meal; **jdn zum ~ einladen** to invite sb for a meal; **(bitte) zum ~** lunch/dinner is ready; **~ auf Rädern** meals on wheels

Essen(s)-: Essen(s)ausgabe F serving of meals; (*Stelle*) serving counter; **ab 12.30 Uhr ist in der Kantine ~** meals are served in the canteen from 12.30; **Essen(s)marke** F meal voucher (*Brit*) *or* ticket (*US*); **Essen(s)zeit** F mealtime; **bei uns ist um 12.00 Uhr ~** we have lunch at 12; **die Kinder müssen abends zur ~ zu Hause sein** the children have to be at home in time for their evening meal

essentiell [ɛsɛnˈtsiɛl] ADJ = **essenziell**

Essenz [ɛˈsɛnts] F **-, -en** essence

essenziell [ɛsɛnˈtsiɛl] ADJ essential

Essig [ˈɛsɪç] M **-s, -e** [-ɡə] vinegar; **damit ist es ~** (*inf*) it's all off

Essiggurke F (pickled) gherkin

Ess-: Esskastanie F sweet chestnut; **Esskultur** F gastronomic culture; **Esslöffel** M (*für Suppe*) soup spoon; (*für Nachtisch*) dessert spoon; (*in Rezept*) tablespoon; **Essstäbchen** PL chopsticks *pl*; **Essstörung** F USU PL eating disorder; **Esstisch** M dining table; **Esswaren** PL food *sing*, provisions *pl*; **Esszimmer** NT dining room

Establishment [ɪsˈtɛblɪʃmənt] NT **-s, -s** (*Sociol, Press*) establishment

Este [ˈɛstə, ˈɛsta] M **-n, -n, Estin** [ˈeːstɪn, ˈɛstɪn] F **-, -nen** Est(h)onian

Ester [ˈɛstɐ] M **-s, -** (*Chem*) ester

Estland [ˈeːstlant, ˈɛst-] NT **-s** Est(h)onia

estländisch [ˈeːstlɛndɪʃ, ˈɛst-], **estnisch** [ˈeːstnɪʃ, ˈɛst-] ADJ Est(h)onian

Estragon [ˈɛstraɡɔn] M **-s,** NO PL tarragon

Eszett [ɛsˈtsɛt] NT **-, -** eszett, ß

etablieren [etaˈbliːrən], *ptp* **etabliert** VR to establish oneself

etabliert [etaˈbliːɐt] ADJ established; **er gehört jetzt zu den Etablierten** he is now part of the establishment

Etablissement [etablɪsəˈmãː] NT **-s, -s** establishment

Etage [eˈtaːʒə] F **-, -n** floor; **in** *or* **auf der 2. ~** on the 2nd *or* 3rd (*US*) floor

Etagen-: Etagenbad NT (*im Hotel*) shared bath; **Etagenbett** NT bunk bed; **Etagendusche** F (*im Hotel*) shared shower; **Etagenheizung** F heating system which covers one floor of a building; **Etagenwohnung** F apartment occupying the whole of one floor of a building

Etappe [eˈtapə] F **-, -n** stage

Etappen-: Etappensieg M (*Sport*) stage win; (*fig*) partial victory; **etappenweise 1** ADJ stage-by-stage **2** ADV stage by stage

Etat [eˈtaː] M **-s, -s** budget

Etat-: Etatjahr NT financial year; **etatmäßig 1** ADJ (*Admin*) budgetary **2** ADV **das Geld wurde ~ ausgegeben** the money was spent as budgeted; **nicht ~ erfasst** not in the budget; **Etatposten** M item in the budget

etc [ɛtˈtseːtera] ABBR *von* **et cetera** etc, et cetera

etc pp [ɛtˈtseːteraˈpeːpeː] ADV (*hum*) and so on and so forth

etepetete [eːtəpeˈteːtə] ADJ PRED (*inf*) fussy

Eternit® [eterˈniːt] M *or* NT **-s,** NO PL fibre (*Brit*) *or* fiber (*US*) cement

Ethik [ˈeːtɪk] F **-, -en** ethics *pl*; (= *Fach*) ethics *sing*

Ethik-: Ethikkommission F ethics committee; **Ethikunterricht** M (*Sch*) (teaching of) ethics

ethisch [ˈeːtɪʃ] ADJ ethical

ethnisch [ˈɛtnɪʃ] ADJ ethnic; **~e Säuberung** ethnic cleansing

Ethno- [ɛtno] IN CPDS ethno-

Ethnologe [ɛtnoˈloːɡə] M **-n, -n, Ethnologin** [-ˈloːɡɪn] F **-, -nen** ethnologist

Ethnologie [ɛtnoloˈɡiː] F **-, -n** [-ˈɡiːən] ethnology

Ethologie [etoloˈɡiː] F **-,** NO PL ethology

Ethos [ˈeːtɔs] NT **-,** NO PL ethos; (= *Berufsethos*) professional ethics *pl*

Etikett [etiˈkɛt] NT **-(e)s, -e** (*lit, fig*) label

Etikette [etiˈkɛtə] F **-, -n (a)** etiquette; **gegen die ~ (bei Hofe) verstoßen** to offend against (court) etiquette **(b)** (*Aus:* = *Etikett*) label

Etikettenschwindel M (*Pol*) juggling with names; **es ist reinster ~, wenn ...** it is just juggling with names if ...

etikettieren [etikɛˈtiːrən], *ptp* **etikettiert** VT (*lit, fig*) to label

etlichemal [ˈɛtlɪçaˈmaːl] ADV *siehe* **etliche(r, s)**

etliche(r, s) [ˈɛtlɪçə] INDEF PRON **(a)** SING ATTR quite a lot of; **nachdem ~ Zeit verstrichen war** after quite some time; **~ Mal** quite a few times **(b) etliche** PL quite a few **(c) etliches** SING (*substantivisch*) quite a lot; **um ~s älter als ich** quite a lot older than me

etruskisch [eˈtrʊskɪʃ] ADJ Etruscan

Etsch [ɛtʃ] F **-** Adige

Etüde [eˈtyːdə] F **-, -n** (*Mus*) étude

Etui [ɛtˈviː, eˈtyiː] NT **-s, -s** case

etwa [ˈɛtva] ADV **(a)** (= *ungefähr, annähernd*) about; **so ~, ~ so** more or less like this **(b)** (= *zum Beispiel*) for instance; **wenn man ~ behauptet, dass ...** for instance if one maintains that ... **(c)** (*entrüstet, erstaunt*) **hast du ~ schon wieder kein Geld dabei?** don't tell me you haven't got any money again!; **soll das ~ heißen, dass ...?** is that supposed to mean ...?; **willst du ~ schon gehen?** (surely) you don't want to go already! **(d)** (*zur Bestätigung*) **Sie kommen doch, oder ~ nicht?** you are coming, aren't you?; **das haben Sie wohl nicht mit Absicht gesagt, oder ~ doch?** surely you didn't say that on purpose; **sind Sie ~ nicht einverstanden?** do you mean to say that you don't agree?; **ist das ~ wahr?** (surely) it's not true!; **ist das ~ nicht wahr?** do you mean to say it's not true? **(e)** (*in Gegenüberstellung, einschränkend*) **nicht ~, dass ...** (it's) not that ...

etwaig [ˈɛtvaɪç, ɛtˈvaːɪç] ADJ ATTR possible; **~e Einwände/Unkosten** any objections/costs which might arise; **bei ~en Beschwerden/Schäden** *etc* in the event of (any) complaints/damage *etc*

etwas [ˈɛtvas] INDEF PRON **(a)** (*substantivisch*) something; (*fragend, bedingend auch, verneinend*) anything; (*unbestimmter Teil einer Menge*) some; any; **kannst du mir ~ (davon) leihen?** can you lend me some (of it)?; **~ anderes** something else; **das**

ist ~ (ganz) anderes that's something (quite) different; **er ist ~** (inf) he is somebody; **~ werden** (inf), **es zu ~ bringen** (inf) to get somewhere (inf); **aus ihm wird nie ~** (inf) he'll never become anything; **sie kann ~** she's good; **das ist immerhin ~** at least that's something; **hast du ~?** is (there) something wrong (with you)?; **sie hat ~ mit ihm** (inf) she's got something going on with him; **das ist sicher, wie nur ~** (inf) that's as sure as (sure) can be (inf); **da ist ~ (Richtiges) dran** there's something in that; **da ist ~ Wahres dran** there is some truth in that

(b) (adjektivisch) some; (fragend, bedingend auch) any; **~ Salz?** some salt?; **~ Nettes** something nice; **~ Schöneres habe ich noch nie gesehen** I have never seen anything more beautiful

(c) (adverbial) somewhat

Etwas ['ɛtvas] NT **-**, NO PL something; **das gewisse ~** that certain something; **ein winziges ~** a tiny little thing

Etymologie [etymolo'giː] F **-**, **-n** [-'giːən] etymology

etymologisch [etymo'loːgɪʃ] ADJ etymological

Et-Zeichen ['ɛt-] NT ampersand

EU [eː'luː] F - ABBR von **Europäische Union** EU

EU- [eː'luː-]: **EU-Beamte(r)** M DECL AS ADJ, **EU-Beamtin** F EU official; **EU-Behörde** F EU institution

euch [ɔʏç] PERS PRON DAT, ACC von **ihr** you; (dat auch) to/for you; (refl) yourselves; **ein Freund von ~** a friend of yours; **wascht ~!** wash yourselves; **setzt ~!** sit (yourselves (inf)) down!; **vertragt ~!** stop quarrelling (Brit) or quarreling (US)!

EU-einheitlich 🆒 ADJ standardized within the EU 🅱 ADV **etw ~ regeln** to regulate sth uniformly throughout the EU

euer ['ɔʏɐ] 🆒 POSS PRON (adjektivisch) your; **Euer** (Briefschluss) yours; **viele Grüße, ~ Hans** best wishes, yours, Hans; **das sind ~e** or **eure Bücher** those are your books; **ist das ~ Haus?** is that your house? 🅱 PERS PRON GEN von **ihr** (geh) wir werden ~ gedenken we will think of you; **~ beider gemeinsame Zukunft** your common future; **~ aller heimlicher Wunsch** the secret wish of all of you

euere(r, s) ['ɔʏɐɐ] POSS PRON = **eure(r, s)**

euert- ['ɔʏɐt] IN CPDS = **euret-**

EU-Erweiterung [eː'luː-] F enlargement of the EU

Eukalyptus [ɔʏka'lʏptʊs] M **-**, **Eukalypten** [-tn] (= Baum) eucalyptus (tree); (= Öl) eucalyptus oil

Eukalyptusbonbon M or NT eucalyptus sweet (Brit) or candy (US)

EU-Kommission F EU Commission

Eule ['ɔʏlə] F **-**, **-n** owl; **~n nach Athen tragen** (prov) to carry coals to Newcastle (Brit prov), to do something unnecessary

Eulenspiegel ['ɔʏlənʃpiːgl] M **Till ~** (lit) Till Eulenspiegel; **unser Sohn ist ein richtiger ~** (fig) our son is a real rascal (inf)

EU- [eː'luː-]: **EU-Ministerrat** M Council of Ministers; **EU-Mitgliedsland** NT EU member state; **EU-Norm** F EU standard

Eunuch [ɔʏ'nuːx] M **-en**, **-en** eunuch

Euphemismus [ɔʏfe'mɪsmʊs] M **-**, **Euphemismen** [-mən] euphemism

euphemistisch [ɔʏfe'mɪstɪʃ] 🆒 ADJ euphemistic 🅱 ADV euphemistically

Euphorie [ɔʏfo'riː] F **-**, **-n** [-'riːən] euphoria

euphorisch [ɔʏ'foːrɪʃ] ADJ euphoric

Euratom [ɔʏra'toːm] ABBR von **Europäische Atomgemeinschaft** European Atomic Community, Euratom

eure(r, s) ['ɔʏrə] POSS PRON **(a)** (substantivisch) yours; **der/die/das ~** or **Eure** (geh) yours; **tut ihr das ~** or **Eure** (geh) you do your bit (Brit) or part (US); **stets** or **immer der ~** or **Eure** (form) yours ever; **die ~n** or **Euren** (geh: = Familie) your family, your people; **ihr und die ~n** or **Euren** (geh) you and yours; **das ~** or **Eure** (geh: = Besitz) what is yours
(b) (adjektivisch) siehe **euer**

eurerseits ['ɔʏrɐ'zaɪts] ADV (= auf eurer Seite) for your part; (= von eurer Seite) from your part; **den Vorschlag habt ihr ~ gemacht** you made the suggestion yourselves

euresgleichen ['ɔʏrɐs'glaɪçn] PRON INV people like you; (pej auch) the likes of you

euretwegen ['ɔʏrɐt've:gn] ADV (= wegen euch) because of you; (= um euch) about you; (= für euch) on your behalf

euretwillen ['ɔʏrɐt'vɪlən] ADV **um ~** for your sake

Euro ['ɔʏro] M **-**, **-** (= Währung) euro

euro-, **Euro-** [ɔʏro] IN CPDS Euro-

Euro-: **Euroanlage** F investment on the Euromarket; **Euroanleihe** F eurocurrency loan; **Eurobond** M **-s**, **-s** Eurobond; **Eurocheque** ['ɔʏroʃɛk] M **-s**, **-s** Eurocheque (Brit), Eurocheck (US); **Euro-City-Zug** [-'sɪtɪ-] M European Inter-City train; **Eurogeldmarkt** M eurocurrency market; **Eurokapitalmarkt** M eurocapital or Eurobond market; **Eurokrat** [ɔʏro'kraːt] M **-en**, **-en**, **Eurokratin** [-'kraːtɪn] F **-**, **-nen** Eurocrat; **Eurokredit** M eurocredit; **Eurokreditmarkt** M eurocredit market; **Euroland** NT, NO PL (inf) Euroland (inf); **Euromarkt** M Euromarket

Europa [ɔʏ'roːpa] NT **-s** Europe

Europacup [-kap] M European cup

Europäer [ɔʏro'pɛːɐ] M **-s**, **-**, **Europäerin** [-ərɪn] F **-**, **-nen** European

europäisch [ɔʏro'pɛːɪʃ] ADJ European; **Europäischer Binnenmarkt** European Internal Market; **die Europäische Gemeinschaft** the European Community; **Europäischer Gerichtshof** European Court of Justice; **Europäische Kommission** European Commission; **Europäische Kulturhauptstadt** European City of Culture; **das Europäische Parlament** the European Parliament; **Europäische Union** European Union; **Europäisches Währungssystem** European Monetary System; **Europäische Währungsunion** European Monetary Union; **Europäische Wirtschaftsgemeinschaft** European Economic Community; **Europäischer Wirtschaftsraum** European Economic Area; **Europäische Zentralbank** European Central Bank

europäisieren [ɔʏropɛi'ziːrən], ptp **europäisiert** VT to Europeanize

Europa-: **Europameister(in)** M(F) (Sport) European champion; (= Team, Land) European champions pl; **Europameisterschaft** F European championship; **Europaparlament** NT European Parliament; **Europapass** M European passport; **Europapokal** M (Sport) European cup; **der Pokalsieger** (European) Cup-Winners' Cup; **Europarat** M Council of Europe; **Europawahlen** PL European elections pl; **europaweit** 🆒 ADJ Europe-wide 🅱 ADV throughout Europe

Euro-: **Europol** ['ɔʏropoːl] F **-**, NO PL Europol; **Euroscheck** M Eurocheque (Brit), Eurocheck (US); **Euroscheckkarte** F Eurocheque (Brit) or Eurocheck (US) card; **Eurostecker** M flat two-pinned plug; **Eurotunnel** M (= Kanaltunnel) Eurotunnel; **Eurovision** F, NO PL Eurovision; **Eurowährung** F eurocurrency; **Eurozeichen** NT euro symbol

EUSt. ABBR von **Einfuhrumsatzsteuer**

EU-Staat M EU country

Euter ['ɔʏtɐ] NT **-s**, **-** udder

Euthanasie [ɔʏtana'ziː] F **-**, NO PL euthanasia

e. V., E. V. ABBR von **eingetragener Verein**

ev. ABBR von **evangelisch**

Eva ['eːfa, 'eːva] F **-s** Eve; **sie ist eine echte ~** (hum) she is the archetypal woman

evakuieren [evaku'iːrən], ptp **evakuiert** VT to evacuate

Evakuierung F **-**, **-en** evacuation

evangelisch [evaŋ'geːlɪʃ] 🆒 ADJ Protestant 🅱 ADV **~ heiraten** to be married in the Protestant church; **~ beerdigt werden** to be buried as a Protestant; **~ beeinflusst** influenced by Protestantism; **seine Kinder ~ erziehen** to raise one's children as Protestants

Evangelist [evaŋge'lɪst] M **-en**, **-en**, **Evangelistin** [-'lɪstɪn] F **-**, **-nen** evangelist

Evangelium [evaŋ'geːliʊm] NT **-s**, **Evangelien** [-liən] Gospel; (fig) gospel

Eventualität [eventuali'tɛːt] F **-**, **-en** eventuality

Eventualverbindlichkeit F, **Eventualverpflichtung** F contingent liability

eventuell [even'tuɛl] 🆒 ADJ ATTR possible 🅱 ADV possibly; **~ rufe ich Sie später an** I may possibly call you later; **ich komme ~ ein bisschen später** I might (possibly) come a little later

> *Vorsicht!* **eventuell** *wird nicht mit dem englischen Wort* **eventual** *übersetzt.*

Evidenzbüro [evi'dɛnts-] NT (Aus) registry

ev.-luth. ABBR von **evangelisch-lutherisch** Lutheran Protestant

Evolution [evolu'tsioːn] F **-**, **-en** evolution

evolutionär [evolutsio'nɛ:ɐ], **evolutionistisch** [evolutsio'nɪstɪʃ] ADJ evolutionary

evtl. ABBR *von* **eventuell**

EWG [e:ve:'ge:] F - ABBR *von* **Europäische Wirtschaftsgemeinschaft** EEC

ewig ['e:vɪç] **1** ADJ eternal; *Eis, Schnee* perpetual; (*inf*) *Nörgelei etc* never-ending **2** ADV for ever; **auf ~** for ever; **das dauert ja ~ (und drei Tage** (*hum*)) it goes on for ever (and a day); **das dauert ja ~, bis ...** it'll take ages until ... (*inf*); **~ dankbar** eternally grateful; **ich habe Sie ~ lange nicht gesehen** (*inf*) I haven't seen you for absolutely ages

Ewiggestrige(r) ['e:vɪç'gestrɪgə] MF DECL AS ADJ person living in the past; (*gegen alles Neue*) stick-in-the-mud (*inf*)

Ewigkeit ['e:vɪçkaɪt] F -, -en eternity; (*inf*) ages; **bis in alle ~** for ever; **eine ~ or eine halbe ~** (*hum*) **dauern** (*inf*) to last an age; **es dauert eine ~ or eine halbe ~** (*hum*), **bis ...** (*inf*) it'll take absolutely ages until ... (*inf*); **ich habe sie seit ~en or einer ~ nicht gesehen** (*inf*) I haven't seen her for ages

EWR [e:ve:'ɛr] M - ABBR *von* **Europäischer Wirtschaftsraum** EEA

EWS [e:ve:'ɛs] NT - ABBR *von* **Europäisches Währungssystem** EMS

EWU [e:ve:'lu:] F - ABBR *von* **Europäische Währungsunion** EMU

ex [ɛks] ADV (*inf*) **(a)** (= *leer*) (**trink**) **ex!** down the hatch! (*esp Brit inf*); **etw (auf) ex trinken** to drink sth in one go *or* down in one **(b)** (*Schluss, vorbei*) (all) over; **ex und hopp** here today, gone tomorrow

Ex- IN CPDS ex-; **ihr Exmann** her ex-husband

exakt [ɛ'ksakt] **1** ADJ exact **2** ADV exactly; **~ arbeiten** to work accurately

Exaktheit F -, NO PL exactness

Examen [ɛ'ksa:mən] NT -s, - *or* **Examina** [-mɪna] exam; (*Univ*) final examinations *pl*; **~ machen** to do one's exams *or* finals; **das ~ mit Eins machen** to get top marks in an exam (*Brit*), to get the best grade in an exam (*US*); (*Univ*) ≈ to get a First (*Brit*), ≈ to get an A (*US*); **mündliches/schriftliches ~** oral/written examination

Exekution [ɛkseku'tsio:n] F -, -en execution; (*Aus:* = *Pfändung*) seizing

Exekutive [ɛkseku'ti:və] F -, -n, **Exekutivgewalt** F executive; (*Aus*) forces *pl* of law and order

Exempel [ɛ'ksɛmpl] NT -s, - (*geh*) example; **die Probe aufs ~ machen** to put it to the test

Exemplar [ɛksɛm'pla:ɐ] NT -s, -e specimen; (= *Buchexemplar, Zeitschriftenexemplar*) copy

exemplarisch [ɛksɛm'pla:rɪʃ] **1** ADJ exemplary; **das Urteil wurde ~ für alle folgenden Fälle** the verdict set a precedent for all subsequent cases **2** ADV **etw ~ durcharbeiten** to work through sth as an example; **jdn ~ bestrafen** to punish sb as an example (to others)

exerzieren [ɛksɛr'tsi:rən], *ptp* **exerziert** VTI to drill; (*fig*) to practise (*Brit*), to practice (*US*)

Exhibitionismus [ɛkshibitsio'nɪsmʊs] M -, NO PL exhibitionism

Exhibitionist [ɛkshibitsio'nɪst] M -en, -en, **Exhibitionistin** [-'nɪstɪn] F -, -nen exhibitionist

exhibitionistisch [ɛkshibitsio'nɪstɪʃ] ADJ exhibitionist

Exil [ɛ'ksi:l] NT -s, -e exile; **im (amerikanischen) ~ leben** to live in exile (in America); **ins ~ gehen** to go into exile

existent [ɛksɪs'tɛnt] ADJ (*geh*) existing

Existentialismus [ɛksɪstɛntsia'lɪsmʊs] M -, NO PL = **Existenzialismus**

existentiell [ɛksɪstɛn'tsiɛl] ADJ = **existenziell**

Existenz [ɛksɪs'tɛnts] F -, -en existence; (= *Lebensgrundlage, Auskommen*) livelihood; (*pej inf:* = *Person*) customer (*inf*); **eine gescheiterte or verkrachte ~** (*inf*) a failure; **sich eine (neue) ~ aufbauen** to make a (new) life for oneself

Existenz-: Existenzangst F (*Philos*) angst; (*wirtschaftlich*) fear for one's livelihood; **Existenzberechtigung** F right to exist; **hat die UNO noch eine ~?** can the UN still justify its existence?; **Existenzgründer(in)** M(F) (*Econ*) founder of a new business; **Existenzgrundlage** F basis of one's livelihood; **Existenzgründung** F establishing one's livelihood; (*Econ*) founding of a new business

Existenzialismus [ɛksɪstɛntsia'lɪsmʊs] M -, NO PL existentialism

Existenzialist [ɛksɪstɛntsia'lɪst] M -en, -en, **Existenzialistin** [-'lɪstɪn] F -, -nen existentialist

existenzialistisch [ɛksɪstɛntsia'lɪstɪʃ] ADJ existential(ist)

existenziell [ɛksɪstɛn'tsiɛl] ADJ (*geh*) existential; **das Problem der Umweltverschmutzung ist ~** the problem of environmental pollution is of vital significance; **von ~er Bedeutung** of vital significance

Existenzminimum NT subsistence level; (= *Lohn*) minimal living wage; **er verdient nicht einmal das ~** he does not even earn enough to live on

existieren [ɛksɪs'ti:rən], *ptp* **existiert** VI to exist

exkl. ABBR *von* **exklusive**

exklusiv [ɛksklu'zi:f] ADJ exclusive

Exklusivbericht M (*Press*) exclusive (report)

exklusive [ɛksklu'zi:və] **1** PREP +GEN excluding **2** ADV **Getränke ~** excluding drinks; **bis zum 20. ~** to the 20th exclusively

Exklusivität [ɛkskluzivi'tɛ:t] F -, NO PL exclusiveness

Exkurs [ɛks'kʊrs] M digression

Exkursion [ɛkskʊr'zio:n] F -, -en (study) trip

Exmatrikulation [ɛksmatrikula'tsio:n] F -, -en (*Univ*) being taken off the university register

exmatrikulieren [ɛksmatriku'li:rən], *ptp* **exmatrikuliert** VT (*Univ*) to take off the university register; **sich ~ lassen** to withdraw from the university register

exorzieren [ɛksɔr'tsi:rən], *ptp* **exorziert**, **exorzisieren** [ɛksɔrtsi'zi:rən], *ptp* **exorzisiert** VT to exorcize

Exorzist [ɛksɔr'tsɪst] M -en, -en, **Exorzistin** [-'tsɪstɪn] F -, -nen exorcist

Exot [ɛ'kso:t] M -en, -en, **Exote** [ɛ'kso:tə] M -n, -n, **Exotin** [ɛ'kso:tɪn] F -, -nen exotic animal/plant *etc*; (*Mensch*) exotic foreigner

exotisch [ɛ'kso:tɪʃ] ADJ exotic

expandieren [ɛkspan'di:rən], *ptp* **expandiert** VI to expand

Expansion [ɛkspan'zio:n] F -, -en (*Phys, Pol*) expansion

expansiv [ɛkspan'zi:f] ADJ *Politik* expansionist; *Wirtschaftszweige* expanding; *Gase* expansive

Expedient [ɛkspe'diɛnt] M -en, -en, **Expedientin** [-'diɛntɪn] F -, -nen (*Comm*) dispatch clerk

Expedition [ɛkspedi'tsio:n] F -, -en (= *Forschungsexpedition, Mil*) expedition

Experiment [ɛksperi'mɛnt] NT -(e)s, -e experiment; **~e machen** *or* **anstellen** to carry out experiments

Experimental- [ɛksperimɛn'ta:l] IN CPDS experimental; **Experimentalfilm** M experimental film

experimentell [ɛksperimɛn'tɛl] **1** ADJ experimental **2** ADV experimentally; **etw ~ nachweisen** to prove sth by experiment

experimentieren [ɛksperimɛn'ti:rən], *ptp* **experimentiert** VI to experiment (*mit* with)

Experte [ɛks'pɛrtə] M -n, -n, **Expertin** [-'pɛrtɪn] F -, -nen expert (*für* in)

Experten-: Expertenanhörung F specialist evidence; **Expertenkommission** F think tank; **Expertensystem** NT (*Comput*) expert system

Expertin F *siehe* **Experte**

Expertise [ɛksper'ti:zə] F -, -n (expert's) report

explodieren [ɛksplo'di:rən], *ptp* **explodiert** VI AUX SEIN (*lit, fig*) to explode

Explosion [ɛksplo'zio:n] F -, -en explosion; **etw zur ~ bringen** to detonate sth

Explosions-: explosionsartig **1** ADJ *Geräusch, Wirkung* explosive; *Wachstum, Zunahme* phenomenal **2** ADV explosively; **das Gerücht verbreitete sich ~** the rumour (*Brit*) *or* rumor (*US*) spread like wildfire; **Explosionsgefahr** F danger of explosion

explosiv [ɛksplo'zi:f] ADJ (*lit, fig*) explosive

Exponent[1] [ɛkspo'nɛnt] M -en, -en (*Math*) exponent

Exponent[2] [ɛkspo'nɛnt] M -en, -en, **Exponentin** [-'nɛntɪn] F -, -nen (*fig*) exponent

Exponential- [ɛkspone'ntsia:l-]: **Exponentialfunktion** F (*Math*) exponential function; **Exponentialgleichung** F (*Math*) exponential equation

Exponentin F *siehe* **Exponent**[2]

exponieren [ɛkspo'ni:rən], *ptp* **exponiert** **1** VT to expose; **an exponierter Stelle stehen** to be in an exposed position **2** VR (= *sich auffällig benehmen*) to behave boisterously; (*in der Politik*) to take a prominent stance; (*in Diskussion*) to make one's presence felt; **die Studenten wollen sich nicht mehr ~** the students are keeping a low profile

Export [eks'port] M **-(e)s, -e** export (*an +dat* of); (= *~waren*) exports *pl*

Export- IN CPDS export; **Exportabteilung** F export department; **Exportartikel** M export

Exporteur [ekspor'tø:ɐ] M **-s, -e, Exporteurin** [-'tø:rɪn] F **-, -nen** exporter

Export-: **Exportfinanzierung** F export financing; **Exportfinanzkredit** M (*Sw*) export (financing) credit; **Exportförderung** F measures *pl* to encourage exports; **Exportgeschäft** NT export business; **Exporthandel** M export business

exportieren *ptp* **exportiert** VTI to export

Export-: **Exportkauffrau** F, **Exportkaufmann** M exporter; **Exportkreditversicherung** F export credit guarantee *or* guaranty (*US*); **Exportüberschuss** M export surplus; **Exportware** F export; **Exportzoll** M export duty

Express- [eks'pres-]: **Expressbrief** M express letter; **Expressgut** NT express goods *pl*

Expressionismus [expresio'nɪsmʊs] M **-**, NO PL expressionism

Expressionist [expresio'nɪst] M **-en, -en, Expressionistin** [-'nɪstɪn] F **-, -nen** expressionist

expressionistisch [expresio'nɪstɪʃ] ADJ expressionist *no adv*, expressionistic

extern [eks'tern] ADJ external; *Fachleute auch* outside *attr*; **ein ~er Schüler** a day boy

exterritorial [eksterito'ria:l] ADJ extraterritorial

extra ['ekstra] **1** ADJ INV (*inf*) extra **2** ADV (e)specially; (= *gesondert*) separately; (= *zusätzlich*) extra; (*inf*: = *absichtlich*) on purpose; **etw ~ legen** to put sth in a separate place; **ich gebe Ihnen noch ein Exemplar ~** I'll give you an extra copy; **jetzt tu ichs ~!** (*inf*) just for that I will do it!

Extra ['ekstra] NT **-s, -s** extra

extrahieren [ekstra'hi:rən], *ptp* **extrahiert** VT to extract

Extrakt [eks'trakt] M (MED, PHARM AUCH NT) **-(e)s, -e** extract; (*von Buch etc*) synopsis

extraterrestrisch ADJ extraterrestrial

Extratour F (*fig inf*) special favour (*Brit*) *or* favor (*US*); **er will immer eine ~** he always wants something different

extravagant [ekstrava'gant] **1** ADJ extravagant **2** ADV extravagantly

Extravaganz [ekstrava'gants] F **-, -en** extravagance

extravertiert [ekstraver'ti:et] ADJ (*Psych*) extrovert

Extrawurst F **(a)** (*inf*: = *Sonderwunsch*) special favour (*Brit*) *or* favor (*US*); **jdm eine ~ braten** to make an exception for sb; **er will immer eine ~ (gebraten haben)** he always wants something different **(b)** (*Aus*: = *Lyoner*) type of pork or veal sausage

extrem [eks'tre:m] **1** ADJ extreme; *Belastung* excessive; **du bist immer so ~** you always go to extremes; **ist ja ~!** (*sl*) it's way out (*inf*) **2** ADV *kalt, rechts, primitiv* extremely; *sich verbessern, sich verschlechtern, sinken, steigen* radically; **ich habe mich ~ beeilt** I hurried as much as I could

Extrem [eks'tre:m] NT **-s, -e** extreme; **von einem ~ ins andere fallen** to go from one extreme to the other

Extremist [ekstre'mɪst] M **-en, -en, Extremistin** [-'mɪstɪn] F **-, -nen** extremist

extremistisch [ekstre'mɪstɪʃ] ADJ extremist

Extremität [ekstremi'tɛ:t] F **-, -en** extremity

Extremsport M extreme sport

extrovertiert [ekstrover'ti:et] ADJ = **extravertiert**

Ex-und-hopp- IN CPDS (*pej*) throwaway; **~-Mentalität** throwaway mentality

exzellent [ekstse'lent] (*geh*) **1** ADJ excellent **2** ADV **~ schmecken** to taste excellent; **~ speisen** to have an excellent meal; **sich ~ fühlen** to feel fantastic

exzentrisch [eks'tsentrɪʃ] ADJ (*Math, fig*) eccentric

exzerpieren [ekstser'pi:rən], *ptp* **exzerpiert** VT to select (*aus* from)

Exzerpt [eks'tserpt] NT **-(e)s, -e** excerpt

Exzess [eks'tses] M **-es, -e** excess; **bis zum ~** excessively; **etw bis zum ~ treiben** to take sth to excess

exzessiv [ekstse'si:f] ADJ excessive

Eyeliner ['ailainɐ] M **-s, -** eyeliner

EZB [e:tset'be:] F ABBR *von* **Europäische Zentralbank** ECB

Ff

F, f [εf] NT **-, -** F, f; **nach Schema F** (inf) in the usual way

F ABBR *von* **Fahrenheit, Farad**

f. ABBR *von* **folgende(r, s)**

Fa. ABBR *von* **Firma**

Fabel ['faːbl̩] F **-, -n** fable

Fabel-: fabelhaft 1 ADJ splendid; (*inf.* = *unglaublich groß*) fantastic **2** ADV splendidly; (*inf*: = *sehr, überaus*) fantastically; **Fabeltier** NT mythical creature; **der Fuchs als ~** the fox (as he appears) in fables; **Fabelwelt** F world of fantasy; **Fabelwesen** NT mythical creature

Fabrik [fa'briːk] F **-, -en** factory; (= *Papierfabrik*) mill; **in die ~ gehen** (inf) to work in a factory

> *Vorsicht!* **Fabrik** *wird nicht mit dem englischen Wort* **fabric** *übersetzt.*

Fabrikanlage F (manufacturing) plant; (= *Fabrikgelände*) factory premises *pl*

Fabrikant [fabri'kant] M **-en, -en**, **Fabrikantin** [-'kantɪn] F **-, -nen** (= *Fabrikbesitzer*) industrialist; (= *Hersteller*) manufacturer

Fabrikat [fabri'kaːt] NT **-(e)s, -e** (= *Marke*) make; (= *Produkt*) product; (= *Ausführung*) model

Fabrikation [fabrika'tsi̯oːn] F **-, -en** manufacture

Fabrikations-: Fabrikationsfehler M manufacturing fault; **Fabrikationsstätte** F manufacturing plant

Fabrik-: Fabrikgelände NT factory site; **Fabrikhalle** F factory building

Fabriks- IN CPDS (*Aus*) = **Fabrik-**

Fabrikverkauf M (= *Center*) factory outlet

fabrizieren [fabri'tsiːrən], *ptp* **fabriziert** VT (inf) *Möbelstück etc* to make; *geistiges Produkt* to produce; *Alibi, Lügengeschichte* to concoct

Facelifting ['feːslɪftɪŋ] NT **-s, -s** (*lit, fig*) face-lift

Facette [fa'sɛta] F **-, -n** facet

Facetten-: facettenartig 1 ADJ facet(t)ed **2** ADV *schleifen in* facets; **Facettenauge** NT compound eye

Fach [fax] NT **-(e)s, ⸚er** ['fɛçɐ] **(a)** compartment; (*in Schrank, Regal etc*) shelf; (*für Briefe etc*) pigeonhole **(b)** (= *Wissens-, Sachgebiet*) subject; (= *Gebiet*) field; (= *Handwerk*) trade; **ein Mann vom ~** an expert; **das ~ Medizin** *etc* medicine *etc* **(c)** (*Theat*) mode

-fach [fax] ADJ SUF (= *-mal*) times; **dreifach** three times; **für die dreifache Summe** for three times the amount; *siehe auch* **vierfach** *etc*

Fach-: Facharbeiter(in) M(F) skilled worker; **Facharzt** M, **Fachärztin** F specialist (*für in*); **fachärztlich** ADJ *Weiterbildung* specialist *attr*; *Untersuchung, Behandlung* by a specialist; **ein ~es Gutachten** a specialist's opinion; **Fachausbildung** F specialist training; **Fachausdruck** M technical term; **Fachbereich** M (= *Fachgebiet*) (special) field; (*Univ*) faculty; **fachbezogen** ADJ specifically related to one's/the subject; (= *fachlich beschränkt*) *Job, Weiterbildung, Kenntnisse* specialized; **Fachbuch** NT reference book; *wasserbautechnische Fachbücher* specialist books on hydraulic engineering; **Fachbuchhandlung** F specialist bookshop; **Fachbuchverlag** M specialist publishing company; **~ für Fremdsprachen** *etc* publisher of modern language *etc* books; **Fachchinesisch** NT, NO PL (inf) technical jargon

Fächer ['fɛçɐ] M **-s, -** fan; (*fig*) range

Fächer-: fächerartig 1 ADJ fanlike **2** ADV like a fan; **fächerförmig 2** ADV fan-shaped **2** ADV like a fan

fächern ['fɛçɐn] **1** VT to fan (out); (*fig*) to diversify; **gefächert** diverse; *Auswahl auch* varied; *Unterricht* diversified **2** VR to fan out

fächerübergreifend ADJ, ADV = **fachübergreifend**

Fach-: Fachfrau F expert; **fachfremd 1** ADJ *Mitarbeiter* with no background in the subject; *Lektüre, Aufgaben etc* unconnected (with the/one's subject) **2** ADV *siehe* **Fach (b)** outside one's own subject/field; **Fachgebiet** NT (special) field; **fachgemäß, fachgerecht 1** ADJ expert; *Ausbildung*

specialist *attr* **2** ADV expertly; **nicht ~** incompetently; **Fachgeschäft** NT specialist shop, specialty store (*US*); **Fachgruppe** F professional group; (*Univ*) study group; (= *Gruppe von Experten*) team of specialists; **Fachhandel** M specialist shops *pl*, specialty stores *pl* (*US*); **Fachhochschulabschluss** M diploma (*from higher education institution*); **Fachhochschule** F higher education institution

Fach-: Fachidiot(in) M(F) (inf) *person who can think of nothing but his/her subject*; **Fachjargon** M technical jargon; **Fachkenntnisse** PL specialized knowledge; **Fachkraft** F qualified employee; **Fachkreise** PL **in ~n** among experts; **fachkundig 1** ADJ informed; (= *erfahren*) with a knowledge of the subject; (= *fachmännisch*) proficient **2** ADV **jdn ~ beraten** to give sb informed advice; **~ betreut werden** to receive expert service; **fachkundlich** [-kʊntlɪç] ADJ **~er Unterricht** teaching of technical subjects; **Fachlehrer(in)** M(F) specialist subject teacher; **Fachleiter(in)** M(F) head of department

fachlich ['faxlɪç] **1** ADJ technical; *Ausbildung* specialist *attr*; *Spezialisierung* in one aspect of a/the subject; (= *beruflich*) professional **2** ADV **ein ~ ausgezeichneter Lehrer** a teacher who is academically excellent; **~ hervorragend sein** to be excellent in one's field; **sich ~ qualifizieren** to gain qualifications in one's field; **auf dem Laufenden bleiben** to keep up to date in one's subject

Fach-: Fachliteratur F specialist literature; **Fachmann** M, *pl* **-leute** *or* (*rare*) **-männer** expert; **fachmännisch** [-mɛnɪʃ] **1** ADJ expert **2** ADV expertly, expertly done; **Fachmesse** F trade fair; **Fachoberschule** F College of Further Education; **Fachrichtung** F subject area; **die ~ Mathematik** mathematics; **Fachschaft** ['faxʃaft] F **-, -en** (*Univ*) students *pl* of the/a department; **Fachschule** F technical college; **Fachschulreife** F entrance qualification for a technical college; **fachsimpeln** ['faxzɪmpl̩n] VI INSEP (inf) to talk shop; **Fachsprache** F technical terminology; **fachsprachlich 1** ADJ technical **2** ADV in technical terminology; **Fachstudium** NT *course of study at a technical college*; **fachübergreifend 1** ADJ *Problematik, Lernziel etc* inter-disciplinary **2** ADV across the disciplines; **Fachwelt** F experts *pl*; **Fachwerk** NT, NO PL half-timbering; **Fachwerkhaus** NT half-timbered house; **Fachwissen** NT (specialized) knowledge of the/one's subject; **Fachwort** NT, *pl* **-wörter** specialist term; **Fachwörterbuch** NT specialist dictionary; (*wissenschaftliches auch*) technical dictionary

Fackel ['fakl̩] F **-, -n** (*lit, fig*) torch

fackeln ['fakl̩n] VI (inf) to shillyshally; **nicht lange gefackelt!** no shillyshallying! (*esp Brit inf*)

Factoring ['fɛktərɪŋ] NT **-s**, NO PL (*Fin*) factoring

fad [faːt] ADJ PRED = **fade**

fade ['faːdə] ADJ **(a)** *Geschmack* insipid; *Essen auch* tasteless **(b)** (*fig*) = *langweilig*) dull **2** ADV **~ schmecken** to have not much of a taste

fädeln ['fɛːdl̩n] **1** VT to thread (*auf etw* (*acc*) onto sth) **2** VR **sich durch etw ~** to thread one's way through sth

Faden ['faːdn̩] M **-s, ⸚** ['fɛːdn̩] **(a)** (*lit, fig*) thread; (*an Marionetten*) string; (*Med*) stitch; **der rote ~** (*fig*) the leitmotif; **den ~ verlieren** (fig) to lose the thread; **er hält alle Fäden (fest) in der Hand** he holds the reins; **sein Leben hing an einem (dünnen** *or* **seidenen) ~** his life was hanging by a thread; **keinen guten ~ an jdm/etw lassen** (inf) to tear sb/sth to shreds (inf) **(b)** (= *Spinnenfaden etc*) thread; (= *Bohnenfaden*) string; **der**

Käse zieht Fäden the cheese has gone stringy; **die Bohnen haben Fäden** the beans are stringy

Faden-: fadenförmig ADJ thread-like; **Fadenkreuz** NT crosshair; **jdn/etw im ~ haben** to have sb/sth in one's sights; **ins ~ (+gen) geraten** to come into the firing line of; **Fadennudeln** PL vermicelli pl; **fadenscheinig** [-ʃainɪç] ADJ (lit) threadbare; (fig) Argument, Grund flimsy; Ausrede transparent; Trost poor; **Fadenwurm** M threadworm

Fadheit F -, -en (a) (von Essen) tastelessness (b) (fig: = Langeweile) dullness

Fading ['fɛːdɪŋ] NT -(s), NO PL (Rad) fading

fadisieren [fadi'ziːrən], ptp **fadisiert** VR (Aus) = **langweilen**

Fagott [fa'gɔt] NT -(e)s, -e bassoon

fähig ['fɛːɪç] ADJ (a) (= tüchtig) Mensch, Mitarbeiter etc capable; **sie ist ein ~er Kopf** she has an able mind (b) PRED (= befähigt, bereit) capable (zu, +gen of); (dazu) **~ sein, etw zu tun** to be capable of doing sth; **zu allem ~ sein** to be capable of anything

Fähigkeit F -, -en (= Begabung) ability; (= Tüchtigkeit auch) capability; (= praktisches Können) skill; **die ~ haben, etw zu tun** to be capable of doing sth; **eine Frau von großen ~en** a woman of great ability; **bei deinen ~en ...** with your talents ...

fahl [faːl] ADJ pale

Fahlheit F -, NO PL paleness

Fähnchen ['fɛːnçən] NT -s, - (a) DIM von Fahne (b) (= Wimpel) pennant (c) (inf, usu pej) flimsy dress

fahnden ['faːndn] VI to search (nach for)

Fahndung F -, -en search

Fahne ['faːnə] F -, -n (a) flag; **etw auf seine ~ schreiben** (fig) to take up the cause of sth; **mit fliegenden** or **wehenden ~n** with beat of drum and flourish of trumpets (liter), with flying colors (US); **mit fliegenden** or **wehenden ~n untergehen** to go down with all flags flying **(b)** (inf) **eine ~ haben** to reek of alcohol; **man konnte seine ~ schon aus drei Meter Entfernung riechen** you could smell the alcohol on his breath ten feet away **(c)** (Typ) galley (proof)

Fahnen-: Fahnenabzug M (Typ) galley (proof); **Fahnenmast** M flagpole; **Fahnenstange** F flagpole

Fähnlein ['fɛːnlain] NT -s, - (a) DIM von Fahne (b) (= kleine Gruppe) troop

Fahrausweis M (a) (Sw, form) ticket (b) (Sw) = **Führerschein**

Fahrbahn F roadway; (= Fahrspur) lane; **„Betreten der ~ verboten"** "pedestrians keep off the road"

Fahrbahn-: Fahrbahnmarkierung F road marking; **Fahrbahnverschmutzung** F dirt on the road

Fahr-: fahrbar ADJ Liege, Ständer etc on casters; Kran, Abschussrampe etc mobile; **~er Untersatz** (hum) wheels pl (hum); **Fahrbereitschaft** F (a) chauffeur-driven carpool; **~ haben** to be the driver on duty (b) (eines Fahrzeugs) good running order

Fähr-: Fährbetrieb M ferry service; **es herrschte reger ~** there were a lot of ferries running; **Fährboot** NT ferry (boat)

Fähre ['fɛːrə] F -, -n ferry

Fahreigenschaft F USU PL handling characteristic; **die ~en eines Wagens** the handling of a car; **der Wagen hat hervorragende ~en** the car handles excellently

---

fahren ['faːrən]

1 INTRANSITIVES VERB	**3** REFLEXIVES VERB
2 TRANSITIVES VERB	

pret **fuhr** [fuːɐ], ptp **gefahren** [gə'faːrən]

1 INTRANSITIVES VERB
(a) (= sich fortbewegen) AUX SEIN (Fahrzeug, Fahrgast) to go; (Autofahrer) to drive; (Zweiradfahrer) to ride; (Schiff) to sail; (Kran, Kamera, Rolltreppe etc) to move; **mit dem Auto/Zug fahren** to go by car/train; **mit dem Rad fahren** to cycle; **mit dem Aufzug fahren** to take the lift (Brit), to ride the elevator (US); **ich fuhr mit dem Fahrrad/Auto in die Stadt** I cycled/drove into town; **wollen wir fahren oder zu Fuß gehen?** shall we go by car or walk?; **links/rechts fahren** to drive on the left/right;

wie lange fährt man von hier nach Basel? how long does it take to get to Basle from here?; **wie fährt man von hier zum Bahnhof?** how do you get to the station from here?; **wie fährt man am schnellsten zum Bahnhof?** what is the quickest way to the station?; **zweiter Klasse fahren** to travel second class; **per Anhalter** or **Autostopp fahren** to hitch(hike); **gegen einen Baum fahren** to drive into a tree; **über den See fahren** to cross the lake; **die Lok fährt elektrisch/mit Dampf** the engine is powered by electricity/is steam-driven; **der Wagen fährt sehr ruhig** the car is very quiet

(b) (= losfahren) AUX SEIN (Verkehrsmittel, Fahrer, Mitfahrer) to go; **wann fährst du morgen nach Glasgow?** when are you leaving for Glasgow tomorrow?; **einen fahren lassen** (inf) to let off (inf); siehe auch **fahren lassen**

(c) (= verkehren) AUX SEIN **es fahren täglich zwei Fähren** there are two ferries a day; **fahren da keine Züge?** don't any trains go there?; **fahren Sie bis Walterplatz?** do you go as far as Walterplatz?; **der Bus fährt alle fünf Minuten** there's a bus every five minutes

(d) (= rasen, schießen) AUX SEIN **es fuhr ihm durch den Kopf, dass ...** the thought flashed through his mind that ...; **was ist (denn) in dich gefahren?** what's got into you?; **der Blitz fuhr in die Eiche** the lightning struck the oak

(e) (= zurechtkommen) AUX SEIN **(mit jdm) gut fahren** to get on well (with sb); **mit etw gut fahren** to be OK with sth (inf); **mit ihm sind wir gut/schlecht gefahren** we made a good/bad choice when we picked him; **mit der Billigreise nach Tunesien sind wir schlecht gefahren** the cheap trip to Tunisia turned out badly; **(bei etw) gut/schlecht fahren** to do well/badly (with sth)

(f) (= streichen) AUX SEIN or HABEN **er fuhr mit der Hand/einem Tuch über den Tisch** he ran his hand/a cloth over the table; **jdm/sich durchs Haar fahren** to run one's fingers through sb's/one's hair

2 TRANSITIVES VERB
(a) (= lenken) AUX HABEN Auto, Bus, Zug etc to drive; Fahrrad, Motorrad to ride; **schrottreif** or **zu Schrott fahren** (durch Unfall) to write off; (durch Verschleiß) to drive into the ground

(b) (= benutzen: Straße, Strecke etc) AUX SEIN to take; **welche Strecke fährt die Linie 59?** which way does the number 59 go?; **wir sind die Umleitung gefahren** we followed the diversion; **ich fahre lieber Autobahn** I prefer (driving on) motorways (Brit) or freeways (US)

(c) (= benutzen: Kraftstoff etc) AUX HABEN to use; Reifen to drive on

(d) (= befördern) AUX HABEN to take; (= hierher fahren) to bring; Personen to drive; **jemanden ins Krankenhaus fahren** to take sb to hospital; **wer hat Sie hierher ins Krankenhaus gefahren?** who brought you to the hospital?; **ich fahre dich nach Hause** I'll take you home

(e) (Geschwindigkeit) AUX SEIN to do; **in der Stadt darf man nur Tempo 50 fahren** in town the speed limit is 50 km/h

(f) (Sport) AUX HABEN or SEIN Rennen to take part in; Runde etc to do; Zeit, Rekord etc to clock up

(g) (Technik) AUX HABEN (= steuern, betreiben) to run; Überstunden to do; **eine Sonderschicht fahren** to put on an extra shift

3 REFLEXIVES VERB
✦**sich gut fahren mit diesem Wagen fährt es sich gut** it's good driving this car; **bei solchem Wetter/auf dieser Straße fährt es sich gut** it's good driving in that kind of weather/on this road; **der neue Wagen fährt sich gut** the new car is nice to drive

---

fahrend ADJ itinerant; Zug, Auto in motion; **ein unter panamaischer Flagge ~es Schiff** a ship sailing under a Panamanian flag

Fahrenheit ['faːrənhait] NO ART Fahrenheit

fahren lassen ptp **fahren lassen** or (rare) **fahren gelassen** VT IRREG (lit: = loslassen) to let go of; (fig) to abandon; siehe auch **fahren**

Fahrer ['faːrɐ] M -s, -, **Fahrerin** [-ərɪn] F -, -nen (a) driver (b) (Sport inf) (= Radfahrer) cyclist; (= Motorradfahrer) motorcyclist

Fahrerairbag M, **Fahrer-Airbag** M (Aut) driver airbag

Fahrerei [faːrə'rai] F -, -en driving

Fahrer-: Fahrerflucht F hit-and-run driving; **~ begehen** to fail to stop after causing an accident; **fahrerflüchtig** ADJ (form) hit-and-run attr; **~ sein** to have failed to stop after having caused an accident; **Fahrerhaus** NT (driver's) cab

Fahrerin F siehe Fahrer

Fahrerlaubnis F (form) driving licence (Brit), driver's license (US)

Fahrersitz M driver's seat

Fahrgast M passenger

Fahrgastraum M (von Auto) interior; (Rail etc) compartment

Fahr-: Fahrgelegenheit F transport no indef art, means of transport; **Fahrgemeinschaft** F carpool; **Fahrgestell** NT (Aut) chassis; (Aviat) undercarriage (esp Brit)

fahrig ['faːrɪç] ADJ nervous; (= unkonzentriert) distracted

Fahrigkeit F -, NO PL nervousness; (= Unkonzentriertheit) distractedness

Fahrkarte F ticket; (= Zeitfahrkarte, Streckenkarte) season ticket; (fig) passport (nach to)

Fahrkarten-: Fahrkartenautomat M ticket machine; **Fahrkartenkontrolle** F ticket inspection; **Fahrkartenschalter** M ticket office

Fahr-: Fahrkomfort M (motoring) comfort; **fahrlässig** ['faːrlɛsɪç] **1** ADJ negligent; (auch Jur) **2** ADV negligently; **~ handeln** to be guilty of negligence; **Fahrlässigkeit** F -, -en negligence (auch Jur); **Fahrlehrer(in)** M(F) driving instructor

Fährmann ['fɛːr-] M, pl **-männer** or **-leute** ferryman

Fahr-: Fahrplan M timetable (esp Brit), schedule (US); (fig) schedule; **Fahrplanauszug** M (Rail) timetable (esp Brit), schedule (US) (for a particular service); **fahrplanmäßig 1** ADJ scheduled attr, pred **2** ADV verkehren, ankommen on schedule; **es verlief alles ~** everything went according to schedule; **Fahrpraxis** F, NO PL driving experience no indef art; **Fahrpreis** M fare; **Fahrprüfung** F driving test

Fahrrad NT bike (inf)

Fahrrad-: Fahrradfahrer(in) M(F) cyclist; **Fahrradhelm** M cycle helmet; **Fahrradkurier(in)** M(F) cycle courier; **Fahrradrikscha** F trishaw; **Fahrradständer** M (bi)cycle stand; **Fahrradweg** M cycle path

Fahrrinne F (Naut) shipping channel

Fahrschein M ticket

Fahrschein-: Fahrscheinautomat M ticket machine; **Fahrscheinentwerter** M automatic ticket stamping machine (in buses/trams etc)

Fährschiff ['fɛːr-] NT ferry(boat)

Fahr-: Fahrschule F driving school; **Fahrschüler(in)** M(F) **(a)** (bei Fahrschule) learner (driver) (Brit), student (driver) (US) **(b)** pupil who has to travel some distance to and from school; **Fahrschullehrer(in)** M(F) driving instructor; **Fahrspur** F lane; **Fahrstil** M style of driving; **Fahrstreifen** M lane; **Fahrstuhl** M lift (Brit), elevator (US); **Fahrstuhlschacht** M lift (Brit) or elevator (US) shaft; **Fahrstunde** F driving lesson

Fahrt [faːrt] F -, -en **(a)** (= das Fahren) journey; „während der ~ nicht hinauslehnen" "do not lean out of the window while the train/bus etc is in motion"; **nach zwei Stunden ~** after travelling (Brit) or traveling (US) for two hours; (mit dem Auto auch) after two hours' drive **(b)** (= Fahrgeschwindigkeit) speed; **jdn in ~ bringen** to get sb going; **in ~ kommen** or **geraten/sein** to get/have got going **(c)** (= Reise) journey; **was kostet eine ~/eine einfache ~ nach London?** how much is it/is a one-way ticket or a single (Brit) to London?; **gute ~!** safe journey! **(d)** (= Ausflug, Wanderung) trip; **eine ~ machen** to go on a trip **(e)** (Naut) voyage; (= Überfahrt) crossing

fährt ['fɛːrt] 3. PERS SING PRES von fahren

Fahrtantritt M start of the journey

Fahrtdauer F time for the journey; **bei einer ~ von fünf Stunden** on a five-hour journey; **man muss für diese Strecke mit einer ~ von drei Stunden rechnen** you have to allow three hours for this stretch

Fährte ['fɛːrtə] F -, -n tracks pl; (= Witterung) scent; (= Spuren) trail; **auf der richtigen/falschen ~ sein** (fig) to be on the right/wrong track; **jdn auf eine falsche ~ locken** (fig) to put sb off the scent; **eine ~ verfolgen** (fig) to follow up (on) a lead; **eine falsche ~ verfolgen** (fig) to be on the wrong track

Fahrten-: Fahrtenbuch NT **(a)** (= Kontrollbuch) driver's log **(b)** (= Wandertagebuch) diary of a trip; **Fahrtenmesser** NT

sheath knife; **Fahrtenschreiber** M tachograph (Brit), trip recorder

Fahrtest M road test

Fahrt-: Fahrtkosten PL travelling (Brit) or traveling (US) expenses pl; **Fahrtrichtung** F direction of travel; (im Verkehr) direction of the traffic; **entgegen der ~** facing backwards; **in ~** facing the front; **die Züge in ~ Norden/Süden** etc the northbound/southbound etc trains; **die Autobahn ist in ~ Norden gesperrt** the northbound carriageway of the motorway is closed (Brit), the northbound lanes of the freeway are closed (US); **Fahrtrichtungsanzeiger** M (Aut) indicator (Brit), turn signal (US)

Fahr-: fahrtüchtig ADJ fit to drive; Wagen etc roadworthy; **Fahrtüchtigkeit** F fitness to drive; (von Wagen etc) roadworthiness

Fahrt-: Fahrtunterbrechung F break in the journey; **Fahrtwind** M airstream

Fahrverbot NT driving ban; **jdn mit ~ belegen** to ban sb from driving; **~ für Privatwagen** ban on private vehicles

Fährverkehr ['fɛːr-] M ferry traffic

Fahr-: Fahrwasser NT, NO PL **(a)** (Naut) shipping channel **(b)** (fig) **in jds ~** (acc) **geraten** to get in with sb; **in ein gefährliches ~ geraten** to get onto dangerous ground; **Fahrweise** F **seine ~** his driving; **Fahrwerk** NT (Aviat) undercarriage (esp Brit); (Aut) chassis

Fahrzeug NT, pl **-zeuge** vehicle; (= Luftfahrzeug) aircraft; (= Wasserfahrzeug) vessel

Fahrzeug-: Fahrzeugausstattung F vehicle accessories pl; **Fahrzeugbrief** M registration document; **Fahrzeughalter(in)** M(F) keeper of the vehicle; **Fahrzeugpapiere** PL vehicle documents pl; **Fahrzeugpark** M (form) fleet

Faible ['fɛːbl] NT -s, -s (geh) liking

fair [fɛːr] **1** ADJ fair (gegen to) **2** ADV fairly; **~ spielen** (Sport) to play fairly; (fig) to play fair

Fairness ['fɛːrnɛs] F -, NO PL fairness

Fäkalien [fɛˈkaːliən] PL faeces pl (Brit), feces pl (US)

Fakir ['faːkiːɐ] M -s, -e fakir

Fakt [fakt] NT or M -(e)s, -en fact; **~ ist, dass ...** the fact is that ...

faktisch ['faktɪʃ] **1** ADJ ATTR actual **2** ADV **(a)** in actual fact **(b)** (esp Aus inf: = praktisch) more or less

Faktor ['faktoːɐ] M -s, **Faktoren** [-ˈtoːrən] factor

Faktura [fakˈtuːra] F -, **Fakturen** [-rən] (Aus, dated) invoice

fakturieren [faktuˈriːrən], ptp **fakturiert** VT (Comm) to invoice

Fakturist [faktuˈrɪst] M -en, -en, **Fakturistin** [-ˈrɪstɪn] F -, -nen (Comm) **(a)** book-keeper **(b)** (Aus: = Rechnungsprüfer) invoice clerk

Fakultät [fakʊlˈtɛːt] F -, -en (Univ) faculty

fakultativ [fakʊltaˈtiːf] ADJ (geh) optional

Falke ['falkə] M -n, -n falcon; (fig) hawk

Falkland- ['falklant-, ˈfɔːklɛnt-]: **Falklandinseln** PL Falkland Islands pl; **Falklandkrieg** M Falklands War

Falkner ['falknɐ] M -s, -, **Falknerin** [-ərɪn] F -, -nen falconer

Fall¹ [fal] M -(e)s, **ˇe** ['fɛlə] **(a)** (= das Fallen) fall; (von Gardine etc) hang; (fig: von Menschen, Regierung) downfall; (von Plänen, Gesetz etc) failure; **im/beim ~ hat er ...** when/as he fell he ...; **zu ~ kommen** (lit geh) to fall; **über die Affäre ist er zu ~ gekommen** (fig) the affair was his downfall; **jdn zu ~ bringen** (lit geh) to trip up; (fig) Menschen to cause the downfall of; Regierung to bring down; Gesetz, Plan etc to thwart

Fall² M -(e)s, **ˇe** ['fɛlə] **(a)** (= Umstand) gesetzt den ~ assuming (that); **für den ~, dass ich ...** in case I ...; **für den ~ seines Todes, im ˇe meines Todes** in case I die; **für alle Fälle** just in case; **in jedem ~(e)** always; **in keinem ~(e)** never; **auf jeden ~** at any rate; **auf keinen ~** on no account; **auf alle Fälle** in any case; **für solche Fälle** for such occasions; **im äußersten ~(e)** if the worst comes to the worst; **im anderen ~(e)** if not; **im günstigsten/schlimmsten ~(e)** at best/worst; **im ˇe eines ˇes** if it comes to it; **wenn dieser ~ eintritt** if this should be the case **(b)** (= Sachverhalt, Jur, Med, Gram) case; **in diesem ~** in this case; **ein ~ von ...** a case of ...; **von ~ zu ~** from case to case; (hin und wieder) periodically; **in diesem ~(e) will ich noch einmal von einer Bestrafung absehen, aber ...** I won't punish you on this occasion, but ...; **jds ~ sein** (inf) to be sb's cup of tea (inf); **klarer ~!** (inf) you bet! (inf); **ein hoffnungsloser ~** a hopeless case; **der erste/zweite/dritte/vierte ~** the nominative/genitive/dative/accusative case

Fall-: Fallbeil NT guillotine; **Fallbrücke** F drawbridge; (= *Enterbrücke*) gangplank

Falle ['falə] F **-, -n (a)** (*lit, fig*) trap; **~n legen** to set traps; **in eine ~ geraten** *or* **gehen** (*lit*) to get caught in a trap; (*fig*) **to fall into a trap; jdm in die ~ gehen, in jds ~** (*acc*) **geraten** to walk *or* fall into sb's trap; **in der ~ sitzen** to be trapped; **jdn in eine ~ locken** (*fig*) to trick sb; **jdm eine ~ stellen** to set a trap for sb
(b) (*inf:* = *Bett*) bed; **in der ~ sein** *or* **liegen** to be in bed

fallen ['falən], *pret* **fiel** [fiːl], *ptp* **gefallen** [gə'falən] VI AUX SEIN
(a) (= *hinabfallen, umfallen*) to fall; (*Gegenstand, Wassermasse*) to drop; **etw ~ lassen** to drop sth; **über etw** (*acc*) **~** to trip over sth; **sich ~ lassen** to drop; (*fig*) to give up; **durch eine Prüfung** *etc* **~** to fail an exam *etc*; *siehe auch* **fallen lassen**
(b) (= *hängen: Vorhang, Kleid etc*) to hang; (= *reichen*) to come down (*bis auf +acc* to); **die Haare ~ ihr bis auf die Schultern/über die Augen/ins Gesicht/in die Stirn** her hair comes down to her shoulders/falls into her eyes/face/onto her forehead
(c) (= *abfallen, sinken*) to drop; (*Wasserstand, Preise, Fieber auch, Thermometer*) to go down; (*Fluss, Kurse, Wert, Aktien auch, Barometer*) to fall; (*Nachfrage, Ansehen*) to fall off; **im Kurs ~** to go down
(d) (= *im Krieg ums Leben kommen*) to fall; **gefallen** killed in action
(e) (= *erobert werden: Festung, Stadt etc*) to fall
(f) (*fig*) (*Gesetz, Passus etc*) to be dropped; (*Tabu, Brauch etc*) to disappear
(g) (*mit schneller Bewegung*) **jdm ins Lenkrad ~** to grab the steering wheel from sb; **die Tür fällt ins Schloss** the door clicks shut; **die Tür ins Schloss ~ lassen** to let the door shut
(h) (= *treffen: Wahl, Verdacht*) to fall (*auf +acc* (up)on); **das Licht fällt durch die Luke** the light comes in through the skylight; **das Los, das zu tun, fiel auf ihn** it fell to his lot to do that
(i) (= *stattfinden, sich ereignen: Weihnachten, Datum etc*) to fall (*auf +acc* on); (= *gehören*) to come (*unter +acc* under, *in +acc* within, under); **in eine Zeit ~** to belong to an era; **unter einen Begriff ~** to be part of a concept
(j) (= *zufallen: Erbschaft etc*) to go (*an +acc* to); **das Elsass fiel an Frankreich** Alsace fell to France; (*nach Verhandlungen*) Alsace went to France
(k) (*Entscheidung*) to be made; (*Urteil*) to be passed; (*Schuss*) to be fired; (*Sport: Tor*) to be scored
(l) (*Wort*) to be uttered; (*Name*) to be mentioned; (*Bemerkung*) to be made
(m) (= *sein*) **das fällt ihm leicht/schwer** he finds that easy/difficult

fällen ['fɛlən] VT **(a)** (= *umschlagen*) to fell **(b)** (*fig*) *Entscheidung* to make; *Urteil* to pass **(c)** (*Chem*) to precipitate **(d)** (*Math*) **das Lot ~** to drop a perpendicular

fallen lassen *ptp* **fallen lassen** *or* (*rare*) **fallen gelassen** VT IRREG
(a) (= *aufgeben*) *Plan, Mitarbeiter* to drop **(b)** (= *äußern*) *Bemerkung* to let drop; *siehe auch* **fallen**

Fallensteller [-ʃtɛlɐ] M **-s, -, Fallenstellerin** [-ərɪn] F **-, -nen** (*Hunt*) trapper

fallieren [fa'liːrən], *ptp* **falliert** VI (*Fin*) to go bankrupt

fällig ['fɛlɪç] ADJ due *pred*; (*Fin*) *Rechnung, Betrag etc auch* payable; *Wechsel* mature(d); **längst ~** long overdue; **die ~en Zinsen** the interest due; **~ werden** to become due; (*Wechsel*) to mature; **der Kerl ist ~** (*inf*) he's for it (*inf*)

Fälligkeit F **-, -en** (*Fin*) settlement date; (*von Wechseln*) maturity; **zahlbar bei ~** payable by settlement date; payable on maturity

Fälligkeitstag M, **Fälligkeitstermin** M settlement date; (*von Wechsel*) date of maturity

Fallobst ['faloːpst] NT windfalls *pl*

Fall-out [fɔːˈlaut] M **-s, -s, Fallout** M **-s, -s** fallout

Fall-: Fallreep [-reːp] NT **-(e)s, -e** (*Naut*) rope ladder; (= *Treppe*) gangway; **Fallrohr** NT drainpipe; **Fallrückzieher** M (*Ftbl*) overhead kick

falls [fals] CONJ (= *wenn*) if; (= *für den Fall, dass*) in case; **~ möglich** if possible; **gib mir deine Telefonnummer, ~ ich mich verspäten sollte** give me your phone number in case I'm late

Fallschirm M parachute; **mit dem ~ abspringen** to parachute; **mit dem ~ über Frankreich abspringen** to parachute out over France; (*in Kriegszeit*) to parachute into France; **etw mit dem ~ abwerfen** to drop sth by parachute

Fallschirm-: Fallschirmabsprung M parachute jump; **Fallschirmjäger(in)** M(F) (*Mil*) paratrooper; **die ~** (= *Einheit*) the paratroop(er)s; **Fallschirmspringen** NT parachuting; **Fallschirmspringer(in)** M(F) parachutist; **Fallschirmtruppe** F (*Mil*) paratroop(er)s *pl*

Fall-: Fallstrick M (*fig*) trap; **jdm ~e** *or* **einen ~ legen** to set a trap for sb (to walk into); **Fallstudie** F case study

fällt [fɛlt] 3. PERS SING PRES *von* **fallen**

Falltür F trapdoor

falsch [falʃ] **1** ADJ **(a)** (= *verkehrt, fehlerhaft*) wrong; (*in der Logik etc*) false; **richtig oder ~** right or wrong; **wahr oder ~** true or false; **wie mans macht, ist es ~** (*inf*) whatever I/you *etc* do it's bound to be wrong; **du machst dir völlig ~e Vorstellungen** you've got quite the wrong idea; **~er Alarm** (*lit, fig*) false alarm; **Sie sind hier ~** you're in the wrong place; **bei jdm an den Falschen geraten** *or* **kommen** to pick the wrong person in sb; **am ~en Ort** *or* **Platz sein** to have come to the wrong place; **im ~en Film sein** (*sl*) to be on another planet (*inf*)
(b) (= *unecht, nachgemacht*) *Zähne etc* false; (= *gefälscht*) *Pass etc* forged; *Geld* counterfeit; (= *betrügerisch*) bogus; **~er Zopf** hairpiece
(c) (= *unaufrichtig, unangebracht*) *Gefühl, Freund, Scham, Pathos etc* false; **ein ~er Hund** (*inf*), **eine ~e Schlange** (*inf*) a snake-in-the-grass; **ein ~es Spiel (mit jdm) treiben** to play (sb) false
2 ADV **(a)** (= *nicht richtig*) wrongly; **alles ~ machen** to do everything wrong; **jdn/etw (ganz) ~ verstehen** to (completely) misunderstand sb/sth; **~ verstandene Freundschaft** misinterpreted friendship; **jdn ~ informieren** to misinform sb; **die Uhr geht ~** the clock is wrong; **Kinder ~ erziehen** to bring children up badly; **~ spielen** (*Mus*) to play the wrong note/notes; (= *unrein*) to play off key; (*Cards*) to cheat; **~ liegen** to be wrong (*bei, in +dat* about, *mit* in); **~ verbunden sein** to have the wrong number
(b) (= *unaufrichtig*) falsely; **~ lachen** to give a false laugh

Falschaussage F (*Jur*) (*uneidliche*) ~ false statement

fälschen [ˈfɛlʃn] VT to forge; *Geld, Briefmarken auch* to counterfeit; *Geschichte, Tatsachen* (*Comm*) *Bücher* to falsify; **gefälscht** forged

Fälscher [ˈfɛlʃɐ] M **-s, -, Fälscherin** [-ərɪn] F **-, -nen** forger; (*von Geld, Briefmarken auch*) counterfeiter

Falsch-: Falschfahrer(in) M(F) ghost-driver (*esp US inf*), *person driving the wrong way on the motorway*; **Falschgeld** NT counterfeit money; **Falschheit** F **-, NO PL** falsity; (*von Menschen*) nastiness

fälschlich [ˈfɛlʃlɪç] **1** ADJ false **2** ADV wrongly, falsely

Falsch-: Falschmeldung F (*Press*) false report; **Falschmünzer** [-myntsɐ] M **-s, -, Falschmünzerin** [-ərɪn] F **-, -nen** forger; **Falschparker** [-parkɐ] M **-s, -, Falschparkerin** [-ərɪn] M **-, -nen** parking offender; **Falschspieler(in)** M(F) (*Cards*) cheat; (*professionell*) cardsharp(er)

Fälschung [ˈfɛlʃʊŋ] F **-, -en** forgery

fälschungssicher ADJ forgery-proof; *Fahrtenschreiber* tamper-proof

Falt-: faltbar ADJ foldable; (= *zusammenklappbar*) collapsible; *Stuhl, Tisch, Fahrrad* folding *attr*, collapsible; **Faltblatt** NT leaflet; **Faltboot** NT collapsible boat

Falte [ˈfaltə] F **-, -n (a)** (*in Stoff, Papier*) fold; (= *Knitterfalte, Bügelfalte*) crease **(b)** (*in Haut*) wrinkle; **strenge ~n** harsh lines; **die Stirn in ~n ziehen** *or* **legen** to knit one's brow **(c)** (*Geol*) fold

fälteln [ˈfɛltln] VT to pleat

falten [ˈfaltn] VTR to fold

Faltenrock M pleated skirt

Falter [ˈfaltɐ] M **-s, -** (= *Tagfalter*) butterfly; (= *Nachtfalter*) moth

faltig [ˈfaltɪç] ADJ (= *zerknittert*) creased; (= *in Falten gelegt*) hanging in folds; *Gesicht, Stirn, Haut* wrinkled

Falt-: Faltkalender M fold-out planner; **Faltkarte** F folding map; **Faltkarton** M collapsible box

Falz [falts] M **-es, -e** (= *Kniff, Faltlinie*) fold; (*zwischen Buchrücken und -deckel*) joint; (*Tech*) rabbet; (*zwischen Blechrändern*) join

Fam. ABBR *von* **Familie**

familiär [famiˈliːɐ] **1** ADJ **(a)** family attr **(b)** (= zwanglos) informal; (= freundschaftlich) close; (pej: = plump-vertraulich) familiar; **ein ~er Ausdruck** a colloquialism **2** ADV **mit jdm ~ verkehren** to be on close terms with sb; **da geht es so ~ zu** it's so informal there

> *Vorsicht!* **familiär** *wird im Allgemeinen nicht mit dem englischen Wort* **familiar** *übersetzt.*

Familie [faˈmiːliə] F **-, -n** family; **~ Müller** the Müller family; **~ Otto Francke** (als Anschrift) Mr & Mrs Otto Francke and family; **eine ~ gründen** to start a family; **~ haben** (inf) to have a family; **aus guter ~ sein** to come from a good family; **es liegt in der ~** it runs in the family; **zur ~ gehören** to be one of the family

Familien- IN CPDS family; **Familienangehörige(r)** MF DECL AS ADJ family member; **Familienbetrieb** M family business; **Familienfeier** F, **Familienfest** NT family party; **Familienkreis** M family circle; **die Trauung fand im engsten ~ statt** only the immediate family were present at the wedding; **Familienleben** NT family life; **Familienmitglied** NT member of the family; **Familienname** M surname, family name (US); **Familienoberhaupt** NT head of the family; **Familienpackung** F family(-size) pack; **Familienschmuck** M family jewels pl; **Familienstand** M marital status; **Familienvater** M father (of a family); **Familienverhältnisse** PL family background sing; **aus was für ~n kommt sie?** what is her family background?; **Familienvorstand** M (form) head of the family; **Familienzusammenführung** F (Pol) principle of allowing families to be united; **Familienzuwachs** M addition to the family

Fan [fɛn] M **-s, -s** fan; (Ftbl auch) supporter

Fanatiker [faˈnaːtikɐ] M **-s, -**, **Fanatikerin** [-ərɪn] F **-, -nen** fanatic

-fanatiker(in) M(F) SUF IN CPDS fanatic; **ein Fitnessfanatiker** a fitness fanatic

fanatisch [faˈnaːtɪʃ] **1** ADJ fanatical **2** ADV fanatically

fanatisiert [fanatiˈziːɐt] ADJ (geh) rabid

Fanatismus [fanaˈtɪsmʊs] M **-**, NO PL fanaticism

fand PRET von **finden**

Fanfare [fanˈfaːrə] F **-, -n** (Mus) fanfare

Fang [faŋ] M **-(e)s, ¨ e** [ˈfɛŋə] **(a)** NO PL (= das Fangen) hunting; (mit Fallen) trapping; (= Fischen) fishing; **zum ~ auslaufen** to go fishing **(b)** NO PL (= Beute) (lit, fig) catch; (Wild) bag; (fig: Gegenstände) haul; **einen guten ~ machen** to make a good catch/get a good bag/haul **(c)** USU PL (Hunt) (= Kralle) talon; (= Reißzahn) fang; **in den Fängen** +gen (fig) in the clutches of

Fangarm M (Zool) tentacle

fangen [ˈfaŋən], pret **fing** [fɪŋ], ptp **gefangen** [ɡəˈfaŋən] **1** VT to catch; (mit Fallen) to trap; **(sich dat) eine (Ohrfeige etc) ~** (inf) to catch it (Brit inf), to get one (US inf); siehe auch **gefangen 2** VI to catch; **Fangen spielen** to play tag **3** VR **(a)** (in einer Falle) to get caught **(b)** (= das Gleichgewicht wieder finden) to steady oneself; (beim Reden etc) to recover oneself; (Flugzeug) to straighten out; (seelisch) to get on an even keel again

Fänger [ˈfɛŋɐ] M **-s, -**, **Fängerin** [-ərɪn] F **-, -nen** (Sport) catcher

Fang-: **Fangflotte** F fishing fleet; **Fangfrage** F trick question; **Fanggründe** PL fishing grounds pl; **Fangleine** F **(a)** (Naut) hawser **(b)** (Aviat) arresting gear cable **(c)** (von Fallschirm) rigging line

Fangopackung [ˈfaŋɡo-] F fango pack

Fang-: **Fangquote** F (fishing) quota; **Fangschaltung** F (Telec) interception circuit; **Fangschiff** NT fishing boat; (mit Netzen) trawler; (= Walfangschiff) whaler; **Fangschuss** M (Hunt, fig) coup de grâce (with a gun)

fängt [fɛŋt] 3. PERS SING PRES von **fangen**

Fanklub [ˈfɛn-] M fan club

Fantasie¹ [fantaˈziː] F **-, -n** [-ˈziːən] **(a)** NO PL (= Einbildung) imagination; **eine schmutzige ~ haben** to have a dirty mind; **seiner ~ freien Lauf lassen** to give free rein to one's imagination **(b)** USU PL (= Trugbild, Vorstellung) fantasy

Fantasie² F **-, -n** (Mus) fantasia

Fantasie-: **fantasiearm** ADJ unimaginative; **fantasiebegabt** ADJ imaginative; **Fantasiegebilde** NT **(a)** (= fantastische Form) fantastic form **(b)** (= Einbildung) figment of the or one's imagination; **fantasielos** ADJ lacking in imagination;

Fantasielosigkeit F **-**, NO PL lack of imagination; **Fantasiepreis** M astronomical price (inf)

fantasieren [fantaˈziːrən], ptp **fantasiert 1** VI to fantasize (von about); (von Schlimmem) to have visions (von of); (Med) to be delirious; (Mus) to improvise **2** VT Geschichte to dream up; (Mus) to improvise; **was fantasierst du denn da?** (inf) what are you (going) on about? (inf); **er hat das alles fantasiert** that's all just (in) his imagination; **er fantasiert, dass die Welt untergeht** he has visions of the world coming to an end

fantasievoll 1 ADJ highly imaginative **2** ADV highly imaginatively; reden, antworten imaginatively

Fantast [fanˈtast] M **-en, -en**, **Fantastin** F **-, -nen** dreamer, visionary

fantastisch [fanˈtastɪʃ] **1** ADJ fantastic **2** ADV fantastically; **~ schmecken/aussehen** to taste/look fantastic; **~ klingen** to sound fantastic; **sie verdient ~** she earns a fantastic amount

Fantasyfilm [ˈfɛntəzi-] M fantasy film

FAQ [ɛflaˈkuː] F - (Comput) ABBR von **Frequently Asked Questions** FAQ

faradaysch [faraˈdeːʃ] ADJ **~er Käfig** Faraday cage

Farb- IN CPDS colour (Brit), color (US); **Farbaufnahme** F colo(u)r photo(graph); **Farbband** NT, pl -bänder (von Schreibmaschine) (typewriter) ribbon; **Farbbeutel** M paint bomb; **Farbbild** NT (Phot) colo(u)r photo(graph); **Farbdruck** M, pl -drucke colo(u)r print; **Farbdrucker** M colo(u)r printer

Farbe [ˈfarbə] F **-, -n (a)** (= Farbton, Tönung) colour (Brit), color (US); **~ bekommen** to catch the sun (inf); **~ verlieren** to go pale; **in ~** in colo(u)r; **etw in den dunkelsten** or **schwärzesten ~n schildern** or **ausmalen** to paint a black picture of sth; **etw in den glänzendsten ~n schildern** or **ausmalen** to paint a rosy picture of sth **(b)** (= Malerfarbe, Anstrichfarbe) paint; (für Farbbad) dye; (= Druckfarbe) ink **(c)** (Cards) suit; **~ bedienen** to follow suit; **~ bekennen** (fig) to lay one's cards on the table; (= klaren Standpunkt beziehen) to nail one's colo(u)rs to the mast

farbecht ADJ colourfast (Brit), colorfast (US)

Färbemittel NT dye

färben [ˈfɛrbn] **1** VT to colour (Brit), to color (US); Stoff, Haar to dye; siehe auch **gefärbt 2** VI (= abfärben) to run (inf) **3** VR to change colo(u)r; **ihre Wangen färbten sich leicht** she blushed slightly; **sich grün/blau** etc **~** to turn green/blue etc

Farben- IN CPDS colour (Brit), color (US); **farbenblind** ADJ colo(u)r-blind; **Farbenblindheit** F colo(u)r-blindness; **farbenfroh** ADJ colo(u)rful; **Farbenpracht** F blaze of colo(u)r; **in seiner ganzen ~** in all its glory; **farbenprächtig** ADJ gloriously colo(u)rful

Färber [ˈfɛrbɐ] M **-s, -**, **Färberin** [-ərɪn] F **-, -nen** dyer

Färberei [fɛrbəˈrai] F **-, -en (a)** (= Betrieb) dyeing works sing or pl **(b)** NO PL (= Verfahren) dyeing

Farb-: **Farbfernsehen** NT colo(u)r television; **Farbfernseher** M, **Farbfernsehgerät** NT colo(u)r television (set); **Farbfilm** M colo(u)r film; **Farbfilter** M (Phot) colo(u)r filter; **Farbfoto** NT colo(u)r photo(graph); **Farbfotografie** F (= Verfahren) colo(u)r photography; (= Bild) colo(u)r photo(graph); **Farbgebung** [-ɡeːbʊŋ] F **-, -en** colo(u)ring

farbig [ˈfarbɪç] **1** ADJ coloured (Brit), colored (US); Druck, Portkarte colour (Brit), color (US); (fig) Schilderung vivid **2** ADV (= in Farbe) anstreichen in a colo(u)r; (= anschaulich) schildern vividly; **~ fotografieren** to take colo(u)r photographs

färbig [ˈfɛrbɪç] ADJ (Aus) = **farbig**

Farbige(r) [ˈfarbɪɡə] MF DECL AS ADJ coloured (Brit) or colored (US) man/woman/person etc; **die ~n** colo(u)red people pl

Farb-: **Farbkasten** M paintbox; **Farbkissen** NT inkpad; **Farbkopierer** M colo(u)r copier; **farblich** [ˈfarplɪç] **1** ADJ colo(u)r attr **2** ADV **die Fotokopie ist ~ einwandfrei** the colo(u)rs in this photocopy are excellent; **zwei Sachen ~ aufeinander abstimmen** to match two things up for colo(u)r; **farblos** ADJ (lit, fig) colo(u)rless; **Farbmine** F colo(u)red-ink cartridge; **Farbstift** M colo(u)red pen; (= Buntstift) crayon, colo(u)red pencil; **Farbstoff** M (= Lebensmittelfarbstoff) (artificial) colo(u)ring; (= Hautfarbstoff) pigment; (für Textilien etc) dye; **Farbtafel** F colo(u)r plate; (= Tabelle) colo(u)r chart; **Farbton** M, pl -töne shade, hue; (= Tönung) tint

Färbung ['fɛrbʊŋ] F -, -en (= das Färben, Farbgebung) colouring (Brit), coloring (US); (= Tönung) tinge; (fig) slant

Farce ['farsə] F -, -n (a) (Theat, fig) farce (b) (Cook) stuffing

Farm [farm] F -, -en farm

Farmer ['farmɐ] M -s, -, **Farmerin** [-ərɪn] F -, -nen farmer

Farn [farn] M -(e)s, -e, **Farnkraut** NT fern; (= Adlerfarn) bracken

Färöer [fɛˈrøːɐ, ˈfɛːrøɐ] PL Faroes pl

Fasan [faˈzaːn] M -s, -e or -en pheasant

Fasche ['faʃə] F -, -n (Aus) bandage

faschen ['faʃən] VT (Aus) to bandage

faschieren [faˈʃiːrən], ptp **faschiert** VT (Aus Cook) to mince; **Faschiertes** mince; **faschiertes Laiberl** or **Laibchen** hamburger

Fasching ['faʃɪŋ] M -s, -e or -s Fasching

Faschings-: IN CPDS carnival; **Faschingsdienstag** M Shrove Tuesday; **Faschingszeit** F carnival period

Faschismus [faˈʃɪsmʊs] M -, NO PL fascism

Faschist [faˈʃɪst] M -en, -en, **Faschistin** [-ˈʃɪstɪn] F -, -nen fascist

faschistisch [faˈʃɪstɪʃ] ADJ fascist

faschistoid [faʃɪstoˈiːt] ADJ fascistic

faseln ['faːzln] (pej) 🟦 VI to drivel (inf) 🟦 VT **Blödsinn** ~ to talk drivel (inf); **das ist alles gefaselt** that's drivel (inf); **was hat er gefaselt?** what was he drivelling (Brit) or driveling (US) (on) about? (inf)

Faser ['faːzɐ] F -, -n fibre (Brit), fiber (US); **er hat keine trockene ~ am Leib** he's soaked through

faserig ['faːzərɪç] ADJ fibrous; Fleisch, Spargel auch stringy (pej); (= zerfasert) frayed

fasern ['faːzɐn] VI to fray

Fasnacht ['fasnaxt] F, NO PL = **Fastnacht**

fasrig ['faːzrɪç] ADJ = **faserig**

Fass [fas] NT -es, ⁀er ['fɛsə] barrel; (= kleines Bierfass) keg; (zum Gären, Einlegen) vat; (zum Buttern) (barrel) churn; (für Öl, Benzin, Chemikalien) drum; **vom** ~ on tap; Bier auch on draught (Brit) or draft (US); Sherry, Wein auch from the wood (esp Brit); **er trinkt nur Bier vom** ~ he only drinks draught (Brit) or draft (US) beer; **ein ~ ohne Boden** (fig) a bottomless pit; **das schlägt dem ~ den Boden aus** (inf) that beats everything!; **das brachte das ~ zum Überlaufen** (fig) that was the last straw (prov)

Fassade [faˈsaːdə] F -, -n (lit, fig) façade; (inf: = Gesicht) face; **das ist doch nur** ~ that's just a façade

Fass-: **fassbar** ['fasbaːɐ] ADJ comprehensible; **das ist doch nicht ~!** that's incomprehensible!; **Fassbier** NT draught (Brit) or draft (US) beer

Fässchen ['fɛsçən] NT -s, - DIM von **Fass** cask

fassen ['fasn] 🟦 VT (a) (= ergreifen) to take hold of; (hastig, kräftig) to grab; (= festnehmen) Einbrecher etc to apprehend (form); **jdn beim** or **am Arm** ~ to take/grab sb by the arm; **er fasste ihre Hand** he took her hand; **Schauder/Grauen/Entsetzen fasste ihn** he was seized with horror; **fass!** seize! (b) (fig) Beschluss, Entschluss to make; Mut to take; **Vertrauen zu jdm** ~ to come to trust sb; **den Vorsatz** ~, **etw zu tun** to make a resolution to do sth (c) (= begreifen) to grasp; **es ist nicht zu** ~ it's unbelievable; **ich fasse es nicht** I don't believe it (d) (= enthalten) to hold (e) (= aufnehmen) Essen to get; (Rail, Naut) Wasser, Kohlen to take on; **Essen ~!** come and get it! (f) (= einfassen) Edelsteine to set; Bild to frame; Quelle to surround; (fig: = ausdrücken) to express; **in Verse/Worte** ~ to put into verse/words; **neu** ~ Manuskript, Rede, Erzählung to revise; **etw weit/eng** ~ to interpret sth broadly/narrowly 🟦 VI (a) (= nicht abrutschen) to grip; (Zahnrad) to bite (b) (= greifen) **an/in etw** (acc) ~ to feel sth; (= berühren) to touch sth; **fass mal unter den Tisch** feel under the table; **sich** (dat) **an den Kopf** ~ (fig) to shake one's head in disbelief; **da fasst man sich** (dat) **an den Kopf** (inf) you wouldn't believe it, would you? 🟦 VR (= sich beherrschen) to compose oneself; **fass dich!** pull yourself together!; **sich in Geduld** ~ to be patient; **sich kurz** ~ to be brief; siehe auch **gefasst**

fässerweise ADV (= in großen Mengen) by the gallon; (= in Fässern) by the barrel

Fassette etc [faˈsɛtə] F -, -n = **Facette** etc

Fasson [faˈsõː] F -, -s (von Kleidung) style; (von Frisur) shape; **aus der ~ geraten** (lit) to go out of shape; **jeder soll nach seiner ~ selig werden** (prov) everyone has to find his own salvation

Fassung ['fasʊŋ] F -, -en (a) (von Juwelen) setting; (von Bild) frame; (Elec) holder (b) (= Bearbeitung, Wortlaut) version; **ein Buch in ungekürzter ~** the unabridged version of a book; **ein Film in deutscher ~** a film with German dubbing (c) NO PL (= Ruhe, Besonnenheit) composure; **die ~ bewahren** or **behalten** to maintain one's composure; **etw mit ~ tragen** to take sth calmly; **die ~ verlieren** to lose one's composure; **völlig außer ~ geraten** to lose all self-control; **jdn aus der ~ bringen** to throw sb (inf)

Fassungs-: **fassungslos** 🟦 ADJ stunned 🟦 ADV in bewilderment; **Fassungsvermögen** NT (lit, fig) capacity; **das übersteigt mein ~** that's beyond me

Fass-: **Fasswein** M wine from the wood; **fassweise** ADV by the barrel; (= in Fässern) in barrels

fast [fast] ADV almost; ~ **nie** hardly ever; ~ **nichts** hardly anything

> Vorsicht! **fast** wird nicht mit dem englischen Wort **fast** übersetzt.

fasten ['fastn] VI to fast

> Vorsicht! **fasten** wird nicht mit dem englischen Wort **to fasten** übersetzt.

Fastfood [fast'fuːd] NT -, NO PL, **Fast Food** NT -, NO PL fast food

Fastnacht ['fastnaxt] F, NO PL (= Fasching) Shrovetide carnival; (= Faschingsdienstag) Shrove Tuesday

FASTNACHT

Fastnacht is another word for **Karneval**. However, **Karneval** is celebrated in the Rhine area very differently from the way **Fastnacht** is celebrated in the Swabian-Alemannic region of Germany and in Switzerland. Here the period of celebration extends beyond Ash Wednesday; indeed **Fastnacht** in Basle does not even begin until after Ash Wednesday. The customs date back over 400 years and have their origin in ancient rites for the banishing of winter. Strict care is taken that only traditional costumes and wooden masks appear in the processions. Drums and bells are used to drive out the winter, while participants dressed as witches, goblins and other fantastic creatures play pranks on the spectators, sometimes even during the night or at the first light of dawn. ▶ KARNEVAL

Fastnachts-: **Fastnachtsnarr** M, **Fastnachtsnärrin** F disguised figure in Shrove Tuesday celebrations; **Fastnachtsumzug** M Shrove Tuesday procession

Fasttag M day of fasting

Faszination [fastsina'tsioːn] F -, -en fascination; ~ **ausstrahlen** to radiate charm

faszinieren [fastsi'niːrən], ptp **fasziniert** VTI to fascinate (an +dat about); ~**d** fascinating; **mich fasziniert der Gedanke, das zu tun** I'm very attracted by the idea of doing that

fatal [fa'taːl] ADJ (geh) (= verhängnisvoll) fatal; (= peinlich) embarrassing

Fata Morgana ['faːta mɔr'gaːna] F - -, - -s or Morganen [mɔr'gaːnən] (lit, fig) mirage

Fatsche ['fatʃə] F -, -n (Aus) bandage

Fatzke ['fatskə] M -n or -s, -n or -s (inf) stuck-up idiot

fauchen ['fauxn] VTI to hiss

faul [faul] ADJ (a) (= verfault) bad; Lebensmittel off pred (Brit), bad pred; Eier, Obst, Holz, Gesellschaftsordnung rotten; Geschmack, Geruch, Wasser foul; Zahn bad; Laub rotting (b) (= verdächtig) fishy (inf), suspicious; (Comm) Wechsel, Scheck dud (inf); Kredit bad; (= fadenscheinig) Ausrede flimsy; Kompromiss uneasy; Friede empty; (= dumm) Witz bad; **hier ist etwas** ~ (inf) there's something fishy here (inf); **etwas ist ~ daran** (inf), **an der Sache ist etwas** ~ (inf) there's something fishy about the whole business (inf); **etwas ist ~ im Staate Dänemark** (prov) there's something rotten in the State of Denmark (prov) (c) (= träge) lazy; **nicht** ~ (= reaktionsschnell) quick as you please

faulen ['faʊlən] VI AUX SEIN or HABEN to rot; (*Aas auch*) to putrefy; (*Zahn*) to decay; (*Lebensmittel*) to go bad

faulenzen ['faʊlɛntsn] VI to laze around

Faulheit F -, NO PL laziness; **er stinkt vor ~** (*inf*) he's a lazybones (*inf*)

faulig ['faʊlɪç] **1** ADJ going bad; *Wasser* stale; (*in Teich, See etc*) stagnating; *Geruch, Geschmack* foul **2** ADV **~ schmecken/ riechen** to taste/smell bad; (*Wasser*) to taste/smell foul

Fäulnis F ['fɔylnɪs] F -, NO PL rot; (*von Zahn*) decay; (*fig*) decadence; **~ erregend** putrefactive

Fäulniserreger M putrefier

Faul-: Faulpelz M (*inf*) lazybones *sing* (*inf*); **Faultier** NT sloth; (*inf: = Mensch*) lazybones *sing* (*inf*)

Fauna ['faʊna] F -, **Faunen** ['faʊnən] fauna

Faust [faʊst] F -, **Fäuste** ['fɔystə] fist; **die (Hand zur) ~ ballen** to clench one's fist; **jdm mit der ~ ins Gesicht schlagen** to punch sb in the face; **mit der ~ auf den Tisch schlagen** (*fig*) to take a hard line; **das passt wie die ~ aufs Auge** (*= passt nicht*) it's all wrong; (*Farbe*) it clashes horribly; (*= ist fehl am Platz*) it's completely out of place; (*= passt gut*) it's just the thing (*inf*); **auf eigene ~** (*fig*) on one's own initiative; *reisen, fahren* under one's own steam

Fäustchen ['fɔystçən] NT -s, - DIM *von* **Faust**; **sich** (*dat*) **ins ~ lachen** to laugh up (*Brit*) or in (*US*) one's sleeve; (*bei finanziellem Vorteil*) to laugh all the way to the bank (*inf*)

faustdick (*inf*) **1** ADJ **eine ~e Lüge** a whopping (great) lie (*inf*); **eine ~e Überraschung** a huge surprise **2** ADV **das ist ~ gelogen** that's a whopping lie (*inf*); **er hat es ~ hinter den Ohren** he's a sly one (*inf*); **~ auftragen** to lay it on thick (*inf*)

Fausthandschuh M mitt(en)

Fautfracht ['faʊt-] F dead freight, *sum paid by a charterer for part of ship not occupied by cargo*

Fauxpas [fo'pa] M -, - faux pas

favorisieren [favori'ziːrən], *ptp* **favorisiert** VT to favour (*Brit*), to favor (*US*); **die Wettbüros ~ X als Sieger** the betting shops have X to win; **favorisiert werden** to be favourite (*Brit*) or favorite (*US*)

Favorit [favo'riːt] M -**en, -en, Favoritin** [-'riːtɪn] F -, **-nen** favourite (*Brit*), favorite (*US*)

Fax [faks] NT -, **-e** fax

Faxanschluss M fax

faxen ['faksn] VT to fax

Faxen ['faksn] PL (*inf: = Alberei*) fooling around; **~ machen** to fool around; **die ~ dicke haben** to be fed up with all the nonsense

Fax-: Faxgerät NT fax machine; **Faxnummer** F fax number

Fazilität [fatsili'tɛːt] F -, **-en** (*Fin*) (credit *or* loan) facility

Fazit ['faːtsɪt] NT -s, -s *or* -e **das ~ der Untersuchungen war ...** on balance the result of the investigations was ...; **wenn wir aus diesen vier Jahren das ~ ziehen** if we take stock of these four years; **wenn ich das ~ ziehen müsste, würde ich sagen ...** on balance I would say ...

FCKW [ɛftseːkaːveː] M -s, -s ABBR *von* **Fluorchlorkohlenwasserstoff** CFC

FDP [ɛfdeː'peː] F - ABBR *von* **Freie Demokratische Partei**

Feature ['fiːtʃə] NT -s, -s (*Rad, TV*) feature programme (*Brit*) or program (*US*)

Feber ['feːbɐ] M -s, - (*Aus*) February; *siehe auch* **März**

Februar ['feːbruaːɐ] M -(s), -e February; *siehe auch* **März**

fechten ['fɛçtn], *pret* **focht** [fɔxt], *ptp* **gefochten** [gə'fɔxtn] **1** VI (*Sport*) to fence; (*geh: = kämpfen*) to fight; **das Fechten** fencing **2** VT **Degen/Florett ~** to fence with épées/foils

Fechter ['fɛçtɐ] M -s, -, **Fechterin** [-ərɪn] F -, **-nen** fencer

Fechtsport M fencing

Feder ['feːdɐ] F -, -**n (a)** (*= Vogelfeder*) feather; (*= Gänsefeder etc*) quill; (*= lange Hutfeder*) plume; **~n lassen müssen** (*inf*) not to escape unscathed; **jdn aus den ~n holen** (*inf*) to drag sb out

of bed (*inf*); **raus aus den ~n!** (*inf*) rise and shine! (*inf*) **(b)** (*= Schreibfeder*) quill; (*an ~halter*) nib **(c)** (*Tech*) spring

Feder-: Federball M (*= Ball*) shuttlecock, birdie (*US inf*); (*= Spiel*) badminton; **Federbein** NT (*Tech*) suspension strut; **Federbett** NT continental quilt; **federführend** ADJ *Behörde etc* in overall charge (*für* of); **Federführung** F **unter der ~** +*gen* under the overall control of; **die ~ haben** to be in charge; **Federgewicht** NT (*Sport*) featherweight (class); **Federhalter** M (*dip*) pen; (*= Füllfederhalter*) (fountain) pen; (*ohne Feder*) pen(holder); **federleicht** ADJ light as a feather; (*fig*) *Musik, Töne* floating; **Federlesen** NT -s, NO PL **nicht viel ~s mit jdm/ etw machen** to make short work of sb/sth; **ohne langes ~, ohne viel ~s** without any (further) ado; **Federmäppchen** NT, **Federmappe** F pencil case

federn ['feːdɐn] **1** VI **(a)** (*Eigenschaft*) to be springy **(b)** (*= hochfedern, zurückfedern*) to spring back; (*Fahrzeug*) to bounce (up and down); (*Springer, Turner: = hüpfen*) to bounce; **(in den Knien) ~** (*Sport*) to bend at the knees **2** VT to spring; *Auto, Räder* to fit with suspension; **ein Auto hydraulisch ~** to fit a car with hydraulic suspension; *siehe auch* **gefedert**

Federung ['feːdərʊŋ] F -, **-en** springs *pl*; (*Aut auch*) suspension

Feder-: Federvieh NT poultry; **Federweiße(r)** M DECL AS ADJ (*dial*) new wine

Fee [feː] F -, **-n** ['feːən] fairy

Feed-back ['fiːdbɛk] NT -s, -s, **Feedback** NT -s, -s feedback

Feeling ['fiːlɪŋ] NT (*inf*) -s, -s feeling (*für* for)

Fegefeuer ['feːgə-] NT **das ~** purgatory

fegen ['feːgn] **1** VT (*mit Besen*) to sweep; (*= auffegen*) to sweep up; (*Sw = wischen*) to wipe; (*mit Bürste*) to scrub **2** VI **(a)** (*= ausfegen*) to sweep (up) **(b)** AUX SEIN (*inf: = jagen*) to sweep

Fehde ['feːdə] F -, **-n** (*Hist*) feud; **mit jdm eine ~ ausfechten** to feud with sb; **mit jdm in ~ liegen** (*lit, fig*) to be feuding with sb

Fehdehandschuh M **jdm den ~ hinwerfen** (*lit, fig*) to throw down the gauntlet to sb

fehl [feːl] ADJ **~ am Platz(e)** out of place

Fehl-: Fehlanzeige F (*inf*) dead loss (*inf*); **~!** wrong!; **fehlbar** ADJ fallible; (*Sw*) guilty; **Fehlbesetzung** F miscasting; **eine ~** a piece of miscasting; **Fehlbestand** M deficiency; **Fehlbetrag** M (*form*) deficit; **Fehldiagnose** F wrong diagnosis; **Fehleinschätzung** F false estimation; (*der Lage*) misjudgement

fehlen ['feːlən] **1** VI **(a)** (*= mangeln*) to be lacking; (*= nicht vorhanden sein*) to be missing; (*in der Schule etc*) to be absent (*in* +*dat* from); (*= schmerzlich vermisst werden*) to be missed; **entschuldigt ~** to be absent; **unentschuldigt ~** (*Sch*) to play truant; **das Geld fehlt** there is no money; **etwas fehlt** there's something missing; **jdm fehlt etw** sb lacks sth; (*= wird schmerzlich vermisst*) sb misses sth; **mir ~ 20 Cent am Fahrgeld** I'm 20 cents short for my fare; **mir ~ die Worte** words fail me; **der/das hat mir gerade noch gefehlt!** (*inf*) he/that was all I needed (*iro*); **das durfte nicht ~** that had to happen **(b)** (*= los sein*) **was fehlt dir?** what's the matter (with you)?; **fehlt dir (et)was?** is something the matter with you?; **mir fehlt nichts** there's nothing the matter (with me); (*inf*) **dem Hund scheint etwas zu ~** there seems to be something wrong with the dog

2 VI IMPERS **es fehlt etw** *or* **an etw** (*dat*) there is a lack of sth; (*völlig*) there is no sth; **es ~ drei Messer** there are three knives missing; **es fehlt jdm an etw** (*dat*) sb lacks sth; **es an etw** (*dat*) **~ lassen** to be lacking in sth; **es fehlt hinten und vorn(e), es fehlt an allen Ecken und Enden** *or* **Kanten** we/they *etc* are short of everything; (*bei Kenntnissen*) he/she *etc* has a lot to learn; (*bei Klassenarbeit etc*) it's a long way from perfect; **wo fehlt es?** what's the trouble?; **es fehlte nicht viel und ich hätte ihn verprügelt** I almost hit him; **es fehlt(e) nur noch, dass wir sonntags arbeiten sollen** working Sundays is all we need (*iro*)

3 VT **weit gefehlt!** (*fig*) you're way out! (*inf*); (*ganz im Gegenteil*) far from it!

Fehl-: Fehlentscheidung F wrong decision; **Fehlfracht** F = **Fautfracht**

Fehler ['feːlɐ] M **-s, -** (a) (= *Irrtum, Unrichtigkeit*) mistake; (*Sport*) fault; **einen ~ machen** *or* **begehen** to make a mistake; **ihr ist ein ~ unterlaufen** she's made a mistake; **~!** (*Sport*) fault! (b) (= *Mangel*) fault; **jeder hat seine ~** we all have our faults; **das ist nicht mein ~** that's not my fault

Fehler-: Fehleranalyse F error analysis; **fehleranfällig** ADJ error-prone; **Fehleranfälligkeit** F proneness to errors; **Fehleranzeige** F (*Comput*) error message; **fehlerfrei** ADJ perfect; **Messung, Rechnung** correct; **~er Lauf/Sprung** (*Sport*) clear round/jump; **fehlerhaft** ADJ (*Mech, Tech*) faulty; **Ware** substandard; **Messung, Rechnung, Bescheide** incorrect; **Arbeit, Aussprache** poor; **Fehlerkode** M error code; **Fehlerkorrekturprogramm** NT (*Comput*) debugging program; **fehlerlos** ADJ = **fehlerfrei**; **Fehlermeldung** F (*Comput*) error message; **Fehlerquelle** F cause of the fault; (*in Statistik*) source of error; **Fehlerquote** F error rate

Fehl-: Fehlgeburt F miscarriage; **Fehlgriff** M mistake; **einen ~ tun** to make a mistake; **Fehlinvestition** F bad investment; **Fehlkonstruktion** F bad design; **der Stuhl ist eine ~** this chair is badly designed; **Fehlleistung** F slip, mistake; **freudsche ~** Freudian slip; **fehlplatziert** [-plasiːɐt] ADJ *Empörung etc* misplaced; **Fehlschlag** M (*fig*) failure; **fehlschlagen** VI SEP IRREG AUX SEIN to go wrong; (*Hoffnung*) to come to nothing; **Fehlschluss** M false conclusion; **Fehlstart** M false start; (*Space*) faulty launch; **Fehltritt** M (*geh*) false step; (*fig*) (= *Vergehen*) slip; (= *Affäre*) indiscretion; **Fehlurteil** NT miscarriage of justice; **Fehlzeiten** PL working hours *pl* lost; **Fehlzündung** F misfiring *no pl*; **eine ~** a backfire

Feier ['faiɐ] F **-, -n** celebration; (= *Party*) party; (= *Zeremonie*) ceremony; (= *Hochzeitsfeier*) reception; **zur ~ von etw** to celebrate sth; **zur ~ des Tages** in honour (*Brit*) *or* honor (*US*) of the occasion

Feierabend M (a) (= *Arbeitsschluss*) finishing time; (= *Geschäftsschluss*) closing time; **~ machen** to finish work; (*Geschäfte*) to close; **ich mache jetzt ~** I think I'll call it a day (*inf*); **um 16.00 Uhr ~ haben** to finish work at 4 o'clock; **~!** (*in Gaststätte*) time, please!; **nach ~** after work; **jetzt ist aber ~!** (*fig inf*) enough is enough; **damit ist jetzt ~** (*fig inf*) that's all over now (b) (= *Zeit nach Arbeitsschluss*) evening; **schönen ~!** have a nice evening!

feierlich ['faiɐlɪç] **1** ADJ (= *ernsthaft, würdig*) solemn; (= *festlich*) festive; (= *förmlich*) ceremonial; **das ist ja nicht mehr ~** (*inf*) that's beyond a joke (*inf*) **2** ADV solemnly; **einen Tag ~ begehen** to celebrate a day

Feierlichkeit F **-, -en** (a) (= *Ernsthaftigkeit, Würde*) solemnity; (= *Festlichkeit*) festiveness; (= *Förmlichkeit*) ceremony (b) USU PL (= *Veranstaltungen*) celebrations *pl*

feiern ['faiɐn] **1** VT (a) *Ereignis* to celebrate; *Party, Fest, Orgie* to hold; **das muss gefeiert werden!** that calls for a celebration (b) (= *umjubeln*) to fête; *siehe auch* **gefeiert 2** VI (= *eine Feier abhalten*) to celebrate; **die ganze Nacht ~** to make a night of it

Feiertag M holiday

feig [faik], **feige** ['faigə] **1** ADJ cowardly; **~ wie er war** like the coward he was **2** ADV in a cowardly way; **er zog sich ~ zurück** he retreated like a coward

Feige ['faigə] F **-, -n** fig

Feigen-: Feigenbaum M fig tree; **Feigenblatt** NT fig leaf; **ein ~ für etw** (*fig*) a front to hide sth; **als demokratisches ~** (*fig*) to give a veneer of democracy

Feigheit F **-,** NO PL cowardice

Feigling ['faiklɪŋ] M **-s, -e** coward

Feile ['failə] F **-, -n** file

feilen ['failən] VTI to file

feilschen ['failʃn] VI (*pej*) to haggle (*um* over)

fein [fain] **1** ADJ (a) (= *nicht grob*) fine; *Humor, Ironie* delicate; *Unterschiede* subtle; (*fig*: = *listig*) cunning (b) (= *erlesen*) excellent; *Geruch, Geschmack* delicate; *Gold, Silber* refined; *Mensch, Charakter* thoroughly nice; (= *prima*) great (*inf*); (*iro*) fine; **~!** great! (*inf*); (= *in Ordnung*) fine!; **das ist etwas Feines** that's really something (*inf*); **das ist nicht die ~e**

englische Art that's not the proper way to go about things; **vom Feinsten sein** to be first-rate; **italienisches Design vom Feinsten** Italian design at its finest (c) (= *scharf*) *Gehör, Gefühl* acute (d) (= *vornehm*) refined; **nicht ~ genug sein** not to be good enough; **dazu ist sie sich** (*dat*) **zu ~** that's beneath her **2** ADV (a) (= *nicht grob*) finely; **sie hat ein ~ geschnittenes Gesicht** she has fine features (b) (= *gut*) **~ säuberlich** (nice and) neat; **etw ~ machen** to do sth beautifully; **(he)raus sein** to be sitting pretty (c) (= *genau*) **etw ~ einstellen** to adjust sth precisely (d) (= *elegant*) **er hat sich ~ gemacht** he's dressed to kill (*inf*); **sie hat sich ~ gemacht** she's all dolled up (*inf*)

Feind [faint] M **-(e)s, -e** [-də], **Feindin** ['faindɪn] F **-, -nen** enemy; **sich** (*dat*) **jdn zum ~ machen** to make an enemy of sb; **sich** (*dat*) **~e schaffen** to make enemies; **er war ein ~ jeden Fortschritts** he was opposed to progress in any shape or form

-feind(in) M(F) SUF IN CPDS -hater; **eine Männerfeindin** a man-hater

Feind- IN CPDS enemy; **Feindbild** NT concept of an/the enemy

Feindin F *siehe* **Feind**

feindlich ['faintlɪç] **1** ADJ (a) (*Mil*: = *gegnerisch*) enemy; **im ~en Lager** (*lit, fig*) in the enemy camp (b) (= *feindselig*) hostile **2** ADV **jdm/einer Sache ~ gegenüberstehen** to be hostile to sb/sth

-feindlich ADJ SUF anti-; **deutschfeindlich** anti-German

Feindschaft ['faintʃaft] F **-, -en** hostility; **sich** (*dat*) **jds ~ zuziehen** to make an enemy of sb

feindselig **1** ADJ hostile **2** ADV hostilely; **jdn ~ ansehen** to give sb a hostile look

Feindseligkeit F **-, -en** hostility; **~en** hostilities

Fein-: feinfühlend, feinfühlig [-fyːlɪç] ADJ sensitive; (= *taktvoll*) tactful; **Feingefühl** NT, NO PL sensitivity; (= *Takt*) tact(fulness); **jds ~ verletzen** to hurt sb's feelings; **Feingehalt** M fineness; (*von Edelmetall*) assay(ed) value; **mit einem ~ von mindestens ...** assaying not less than ...; **vorgeschriebener ~** standard quality; **Feingehaltsstempel** M hallmark; **feingliederig** [-gliːdərɪç], **feingliedrig** [-gliːdrɪç] ADJ slender; **Feingold** NT refined gold

Feinheit F **-, -en** (a) (= *Zartheit*) fineness; **die ~ des britischen Humors** the delicate British humour (*Brit*) *or* humor (*US*) (b) (= *Erlesenheit*) excellence (c) (= *Schärfe*) keenness (d) (= *Vornehmheit*) refinement (e) **Feinheiten** PL niceties *pl*; (= *Nuancen*) subtleties *pl*; **das sind eben die ~en** it's the little things that make the difference

Fein-: Feinkost F delicacies *pl*; **„~"** "Delicatessen"; **Feinkostgeschäft** NT delicatessen; **feinmaschig** [-maʃɪç] ADJ with a fine mesh; *Strickwaren* finely knitted; **Feinmechanik** F precision engineering; **Feinschmecker** [-ʃmɛkɐ] M **-s, -**, **Feinschmeckerin** [-ərɪn] F **-, -nen** gourmet; (*fig*) connoisseur; **Feinsilber** NT refined silver; **feinsinnig** ADJ sensitive; *Unterscheidung* subtle; **Feinwäsche** F delicates *pl*; **Feinwaschmittel** NT mild(-action) detergent

feist [faist] ADJ fat

Feitel ['faitl] M **-s, -** (*Aus*) penknife

feixen ['faiksn] VI (*inf*) to smirk

Felchen ['fɛlçn] M **-s, -** whitefish

Feld [fɛlt] NT **-(e)s, -er** [-dɐ] (a) (= *offenes Gelände*) open country; **auf freiem ~** in the open country (b) (= *Acker*) field (c) (= *Flächenstück: auf Spielbrett*) square; (*an Zielscheibe*) ring; (*Her*) field (d) (*Sport*: = *Spielfeld, Gruppe*) field (e) (= *Kriegsschauplatz*) (battle)field; **gegen jdn/etw zu ~e ziehen** (*fig*) to crusade against sb/sth; **Argumente ins ~ führen** to bring arguments to bear; **das ~ räumen** (*fig*) to bow out (f) (*Ling, Min, Phys, Comput, fig*: = *Bereich*) field

Feld- IN CPDS field; **Feldarbeit** F (*Agr*) work in the fields; (*Sci, Sociol*) fieldwork; **Feldblume** F wild flower; **Feldflasche** F canteen (*Mil*), water bottle; **Feldforschung** F field work *or* research; **Feldhase** M European hare; **Feldherr(in)** M(F) commander; **Feldjäger(in)** M(F) ~ PL (*Mil*) military police; (*bei der Marine*) shore patrol; **Feldmaus** F field mouse; **Feldmesser** [-mɛsɐ] M **-s, -**, **Feldmesserin** [-ərɪn] F **-, -nen** (land) surveyor; **Feldpflanze** F agricultural crop; **Feldsalat** M lamb's lettuce; **Feldstecher** [-ʃtɛçɐ] M **-s, -** (pair of) binoculars; **Feldtheorie** F (*Ling, Phys, Psych*) field theory; **Feldversuch** M field test

Feld-Wald-und-Wiesen- IN CPDS (*inf*) run-of-the-mill; **ein ~ Thema** a run-of-the-mill subject

Feld-: Feldwebel ['feltve:bl] M **-s**, **-**, **Feldwebelin** [-bəlɪn] F **-**, **-nen** sergeant; (*fig inf*) sergeant-major (type); **Feldweg** M track across the fields; **Feldweibel** ['feltvaibl] M **-s**, **-**, **Feldweibelin** [-bəlɪn] F **-**, **-nen** (*Sw*) sergeant; **Feldzug** M (*old, fig*) campaign

Felge ['fɛlɡə] F **-**, **-n** (a) (*Tech*) (wheel) rim (b) (*Sport*) circle

Felgenbremse F calliper brake

Fell [fɛl] NT **-(e)s**, **-e** (a) fur; (*von Schaf, Lamm*) fleece; (*von toten Tieren*) skin; **ein gesundes ~** a healthy coat (b) (*fig inf*: = *Menschenhaut*) skin; **ein dickes ~ haben** to be thick-skinned; **jdm das ~ über die Ohren ziehen** to pull the wool over sb's eyes; **ihn** *or* **ihm juckt das ~** he's asking for a good hiding (c) (*von Trommel*) skin

Fell- IN CPDS fur; (*Schaffell- etc*) sheepskin *etc*; **eine ~mütze** a fur/sheepskin hat; **eine ~jacke** a fur/sheepskin jacket

Fels [fɛls] M **-en**, **-en** ['fɛlzn] rock; (= *Klippe*) cliff

Fels- IN CPDS *siehe auch* **Felsen-**: **Felsblock** M, *pl* **-blöcke** boulder; **Felsbrocken** M (lump of) rock

Felsen ['fɛlzn] M **-s**, **-** rock; (= *Klippe*) cliff

Felsen-: felsenfest 1 ADJ firm **2** ADV **~ überzeugt sein** to be absolutely convinced; **sich ~ auf jdn verlassen** to put one's complete trust in sb; **Felsenhöhle** F rock cave

felsig ['fɛlzɪç] ADJ rocky; (= *steil abfallend*) *Küste* cliff-lined

Fels-: Felsklippe F rocky cliff; (*im Meer*) stack; **Felsspalte** F crevice; **Felswand** F rock face

feminin [femi'ni:n] ADJ feminine

Femininum ['fe:mini:nʊm] NT **-s**, **Feminina** [-na] (*Gram*) feminine noun

Feminismus [femi'nɪsmʊs] M **-**, **Feminismen** [-mən] feminism

Feminist [femi'nɪst] M **-en**, **-en**, **Feministin** [-'nɪstɪn] F **-**, **-nen** feminist

feministisch [femi'nɪstɪʃ] **1** ADJ feminist **2** ADV **~ orientiert sein** to have feminist tendencies

Fenchel ['fɛnçl] M **-s**, NO PL fennel

Fender ['fɛndɐ] M **-s**, **-** fender

Feng-Shui [fɛŋ'fu:i] NT **-** Feng Shui

Fenster ['fɛnstɐ] NT **-s**, **-** window (*auch Comput, fig*); **weg vom ~** (*inf*) out of the game (*inf*), finished

Fenster- IN CPDS window; **Fensterbank** F, *pl* **-bänke**, **Fensterbrett** NT windowsill, window ledge; **Fensterbriefumschlag** M window envelope; **Fensterglas** NT window glass; (*in Brille*) plain glass; **Fensterheber** M (*Aut*) window winder (*Brit*) *or* raiser (*US*); (*elektronisch*) electric windows *pl*; **Fensterladen** M shutter; **Fensterleder** NT chamois *or* shammy (leather)

fensterln ['fɛnstɐln] VI (*S Ger, Aus*) to climb through one's sweetheart's bedroom window

Fenster-: fensterlos ADJ windowless; **Fensterplatz** M window seat; **Fensterputzer** [-pʊtsɐ] M **-s**, **-**, **Fensterputzerin** [-ərɪn] F **-**, **-nen** window cleaner; **Fensterrahmen** M window frame; **Fensterscheibe** F window pane; **Fenstersims** M window ledge, windowsill; **Fenstertechnik** F (*Comput*) windowing technique; **Fensterumschlag** M window envelope

Ferial- [fe'ria:l] IN CPDS (*Aus*) = **Ferien-**

Ferien ['fe:riən] PL holidays *pl* (*Brit*), vacation *sing* (*US*); (= *~reise*) holiday *sing* (*esp Brit*), vacation *sing* (*US*); (= *Parlamentsferien, Jur*) recess *sing*; **die großen ~** the summer holidays (*esp Brit*), the long vacation (*US, Univ*); **~ haben** to be on holiday (*esp Brit*) *or* vacation (*US*); **~ machen** to have *or* take a holiday (*esp Brit*) *or* vacation (*US*); **in die ~ gehen** *or* **fahren** to go on holiday (*esp Brit*) *or* vacation (*US*)

Ferien- IN CPDS holiday (*esp Brit*), vacation (*US*); **Feriendorf** NT holiday village; **Ferienhaus** NT holiday home; **Ferienwohnung** F holiday flat (*Brit*), vacation apartment (*US*); **Ferienzeit** F holiday period

Ferkel ['fɛrkl] NT **-s**, **-** piglet; (*fig*) (*unsauber*) pig, mucky pup (*Brit inf*); (*unanständig*) dirty pig (*inf*)

Ferment [fɛr'mɛnt] NT **-s**, **-e** enzyme

Fermentation [fɛrmɛnta'tsio:n] F **-**, **-en** fermentation

fermentieren [fɛrmɛn'ti:rən], *ptp* **fermentiert** VT to ferment

fern [fɛrn] **1** ADJ (a) (*räumlich*) distant, faraway; **~ von hier** far away from here; **von ~(e) betrachtet** seen from a distance; **der Ferne Osten** the Far East; **von ~(e) kennen** (*fig*) to know (only) slightly (b) (*zeitlich entfernt*) far-off; **~e Vergangenheit** (dim and) distant past; **in nicht (all)zu ~er Zeit** in the not-too-distant future; **der Tag ist nicht mehr ~, wo ...** the day is not far off when ... **2** PREP +GEN far (away) from

Fern-: fernab [fɛrn'lap] ADV far away; **~ gelegen** far away; **Fernabfrage** F (*Telec*) remote control; **Fernbedienung** F remote control; **fernbleiben** VI SEP IRREG AUX SEIN to stay away (+*dat, von* from); **Fernbleiben** NT **-s**, NO PL absence (*von* from); (= *Nichtteilnahme*) non-attendance; **Fernblick** M good view; **ein herrlicher ~** a splendid view for miles around

Ferne ['fɛrnə] F **-**, **-n** (a) (*räumlich*) distance; **in der ~** in the distance; **aus der ~** from a distance (b) (*zeitlich*) (= *Zukunft*) future; (= *Vergangenheit*) (distant) past; **in weiter ~ liegen** to be a long time off

ferner ['fɛrnɐ] **1** ADJ COMP *von* **fern** further; **für die ~e Zukunft** for the long term **2** ADV (a) further; **~ liefen ...** (*Sport*) also-rans ...; **unter ~ liefen rangieren** *or* **kommen** (*inf*) to be among the also-rans (b) (= *künftig*) in future; (**auch**) **~ etw machen** to continue to do sth

Fern-: Fernfahrer(in) M(F) long-distance lorry (*Brit*) *or* truck driver, trucker (*US*); **Fernfahrerlokal** NT transport café (*Brit*), truckstop (*US*); **Fernflug** M long-distance *or* long-haul flight; **Ferngespräch** NT trunk (*Brit*) *or* long-distance call; **ferngesteuert** [-gəʃtɔyɐt] remote-controlled; (*fig*) manipulated (*von* by); *siehe auch* **fernsteuern**; **Fernglas** NT (pair of) binoculars *pl*

fern halten VTR IRREG to keep away

Fern-: Fernheizung F district heating (*spec*); **Fernkopie** F (*Telec*) fax; **Fernkopierer** M fax (machine)

Fernlaster M long-distance lorry (*Brit*) *or* truck

Fernlast-: Fernlastverkehr M long-distance goods traffic; **Fernlastzug** M long-distance truck-trailer

Fern-: Fernlehrgang M correspondence course; **Fernleitung** F (a) (*Telec*) trunk (*Brit*) *or* long-distance line(s *pl*) (b) (= *Röhren*) pipeline; **Fernlicht** NT (*Aut*) full *or* high (*esp US*) beam; **mit ~ fahren, (das) ~ anhaben** to be *or* drive on full *or* high (*esp US*) beam; **fern liegen** VI IRREG (*fig*) (**jdm**) **~** to be far from sb's mind; **es liegt mir fern, das zu tun** far be it from me to do that; **nichts liegt** *or* **läge mir ferner** nothing could be further from my mind

Fernmelder [-mɛldɐ] M **-s**, **-** (*form*) telephone

Fernmelde-: Fernmeldesatellit M communications satellite; **Fernmeldetechnik** F telecommunications engineering; (= *Telefontechnik*) telephone engineering; **Fernmeldewesen** NT, NO PL telecommunications *sing*

Fern-: fernmündlich (*form*) **1** ADJ telephone *attr* **2** ADV by telephone; **Fernost** [fɛrn'lɔst] NO ART aus/in/nach **~** from/in/to the Far East; **Fernrakete** F long-range missile; **Fernreise** F long-haul journey; **Fernrohr** NT telescope; **Fernruf** M (*form*) telephone number; **~ 68190** Tel. 68190; **Fernschreiben** NT telex; **Fernschreiber** M teleprinter; (*Comm*) telex(-machine)

Fernseh- IN CPDS television, TV; **Fernsehansager(in)** M(F) television announcer; **Fernsehapparat** M television *or* TV set; **Fernsehdebatte** F televised debate

fernsehen VI SEP IRREG to watch television *or* TV

Fernsehen NT **-s**, NO PL television, TV, telly (*Brit inf*); **beim ~ arbeiten** to work *or* be in television; **vom ~ übertragen werden** to be televised; **im** *or* (*Sw*) **am ~** on television *etc*; **das ~ bringt etw** they're showing sth on television *etc*

Fernseher [-ze:ɐ] M **-s**, **-** (*inf*: = *Gerät*) television, TV, telly (*Brit inf*)

Fernseher [-ze:ɐ] M **-s**, **-**, **Fernseherin** [-ərɪn] F **-**, **-nen** (*inf*: = *Zuschauer*) (television) viewer

Fernseh-: Fernsehgebühr F television *or* TV licence fee (*Brit*); **Fernsehgerät** NT television *or* TV set; **Fernsehjournalist(in)** M(F) television *or* TV reporter; **Fernsehkamera** F television *or* TV camera; **wir haben Herrn Schmidt um die ~ gebeten** we've asked Herr Schmidt to speak to us; **Fernsehprogramm** NT (a) (= *Kanal*) channel, station (*US*) (b) (= *Sendung*) programme (*Brit*), program (*US*); (= *Sendefolge*) program(me)s *pl* (c) (= *Fernsehzeitschrift*) (television) program(me) guide, TV guide; **Fernsehpublikum** NT viewers *pl*, viewing public; **Fernsehsatellit** M TV satellite; **Fernsehsender** M television transmitter; **Fernsehsendung** F television programme (*Brit*) *or* program (*US*); **Fernsehspiel** NT television play; **Fernsehspot** M (a) (= *Werbespot*) TV ad(vertisement) (b) (= *Kurzfilm*) TV short; **Fernsehsprecher(in)** M(F) television announcer; **Fernsehteilnehmer(in)** M(F) (*form*) television viewer;

Fernsehturm M television tower; **Fernsehübertragung** F television broadcast; (*von außerhalb des Studios*) outside broadcast; **Fernsehwerbung** F television advertising; **Fernsehzeitschrift** F TV guide; **Fernsehzuschauer(in)** M(F) (television) viewer

Fernsicht F clear view; **(eine) gute ~ haben** to be able to see a long way

Fernsprech- IN CPDS (*form*) telephone; **siehe auch Telefon-**; **Fernsprechanschluss** M telephone; **15 Fernsprechanschlüsse haben** to have 15 lines

Fernsprecher M (*form*) (public) telephone

Fernsprech-: **Fernsprechgebühr** F telephone charges *pl*; **Fernsprechnetz** NT telephone system; **Fernsprechteilnehmer(in)** M(F) (*form*) telephone subscriber; **Fernsprechverkehr** M telephone traffic

Fern-: **fern stehen** VI IRREG **jdm/einer Sache ~** to have no connection with sb/sth; **ich stehe ihm ziemlich fern** I'm not on very close terms with him; **Fernsteuerung** F remote control; **~ haben** to be remote-controlled; **Fernstraße** F trunk *or* major road, highway (*US*); **Fernstudium** NT correspondence degree course (*with radio, TV etc*), ≈ Open University course (*Brit*)

──── FERNSTUDIUM ────

A **Fernstudium** is a university-level adult education course that does not require the student to attend a particular place of study. The best-known establishment for this type of correspondence course is the university at Hagen, which is a **Gesamthochschule**.

The expression **Fernstudium** is also used colloquially for any sort of teaching where the student does not attend regular classes. This is most commonly done by educational broadcasts on radio and television, which are developed by the broadcasting corporations in close cooperation with, amongst others, the **Deutsches Institut für Fernstudien in Tübingen**. ▶ GESAMTHOCHSCHULE

Fern-: **Ferntourismus** M long-haul tourism; **Fernuniversität** F ≈ Open University (*Brit*), ≈ correspondence school (*US*); **Fernverkehr** M (a) (*Transport*) long-distance traffic (b) (*Telec*) trunk (*Brit*) *or* long-distance traffic; **Fernwärme** F district heating (*spec*); **Fernweh** [-ve:] NT **-s**, NO PL wanderlust; **Fernziel** NT long-term goal

Ferse [ˈfɛrzə] F **-**, **-n** heel; **jdm (dicht) auf den ~n sein** *or* **folgen/bleiben** to be/stay hard *or* close on sb's heels

Fersenbein NT (*Anat*) heel bone

fertig [ˈfɛrtɪç] **1** ADJ (a) (= *abgeschlossen, vollendet*) finished; (= *ausgebildet*) qualified; (= *reif*) *Mensch, Charakter* mature; **mit der Ausbildung ~ sein** to have completed one's training (b) (= *zu Ende*) finished; **mit etw ~ sein, etw ~ haben** to have finished sth; **mit jdm ~ sein** (*fig*) to be finished with sb; **mit jdm/etw ~ werden** to cope with sb/sth; **du darfst nicht gehen, ~!** you're not going and that's that! (c) (= *bereit*) ready; **~ zur Abfahrt** ready to go *or* leave (d) (*inf*) (= *erschöpft*) shattered (*Brit inf*), all in (*inf*); (= *ruiniert*) finished; (= *erstaunt*) knocked for six (*Brit inf*) *or* for a loop (*US inf*); **mit den Nerven ~ sein** to be at the end of one's tether (*Brit*) *or* rope (*US*) **2** ADV **~ essen/lesen** to finish eating/reading; **etw ~ kaufen** to buy sth ready-made; **Essen to buy** sth ready-prepared; **~ ausgebildet** fully qualified

Fertig- IN CPDS finished; (*Build*) prefabricated; **Fertigbau** M (*Build*) **1** NO PL (= *Bauweise*) prefabricated building **2** *pl* **-bauten** (= *Gebäude*) prefabricated building, prefab; **fertig bekommen** VT IRREG to finish, to get finished; **fertig bringen** VT IRREG (a) (= *vollenden*) to get done (b) (= *imstande sein*) to manage; (*iro*) to be capable of; **ich habe es nicht fertig gebracht, ihr die Wahrheit zu sagen** I couldn't bring myself to tell her the truth; **er bringt das fertig** (*iro*) I wouldn't put it past him

fertigen [ˈfɛrtɪɡn] VT (*form*) to manufacture

Fertig-: **Fertiggericht** NT ready-to-serve meal; **Fertighaus** NT prefabricated house

Fertigkeit F **-**, **-en** skill; **wenig/eine große ~ in etw** (*dat*) **haben** not to be very/to be very skilled at *or* in sth

Fertig-: **fertig kriegen** VT (*inf*) = **fertig bringen**; **fertig machen** VT (a) (= *vollenden*) to finish (b) (= *bereit machen*) to get ready; **sich ~** to get ready (c) (*inf*) **jdn ~** (= *erledigen*) to do for sb; (= *ermüden*) to take it out of sb; (= *deprimieren*) to get sb

down; (= *abkanzeln*) to lay into sb (*inf*); **sich ~** to do oneself in; **Fertigprodukt** NT finished product; **fertig stellen** VT to complete; **Fertigstellung** F completion; **Fertigteil** NT finished part

Fertigung [ˈfɛrtɪɡʊŋ] F **-**, **-en** production

Fertigungs- IN CPDS production; **Fertigungskosten** PL production costs *pl*; **Fertigungslöhne** PL direct labour (*Brit*) *or* labor (*US*) costs *pl*

fesch [fɛʃ] ADJ (*S Ger, Aus: inf*) (= *modisch*) smart; (= *hübsch*) attractive; **das ist ~** that's great (*inf*); **sei ~!** (*Aus*) = *sei brav*) be good; (= *sei kein Frosch*) be a sport (*inf*)

Fessel [ˈfɛsl] F **-**, **-n** (a) (= *Bande*) (*lit, fig*) fetter, shackle; (= *Kette*) chain; **sich von den ~n befreien** to free oneself; **die ~n der Ehe/Liebe** the shackles of marriage/love (b) (*Anat*) (*von Huftieren*) pastern; (*von Menschen*) ankle

Fesselballon M captive balloon

fesseln [ˈfɛsln] VT (a) (*mit Tau etc*) to tie (up), to bind; (*mit Handschellen*) to handcuff; (*mit Ketten*) to chain (up); **jdn (an Händen und Füßen) ~** to tie/chain sb (hand and foot); **jdm die Hände auf dem Rücken ~** to tie sb's hands behind his back; **der Gefangene wurde gefesselt vorgeführt** the prisoner was brought in handcuffed/in chains; **jdn ans Bett ~** (*fig*) to confine sb to (his/her) bed; **jdn an jdn/sich ~** (*fig*) to bind sb to sb/oneself (b) (= *faszinieren*) to grip; *Aufmerksamkeit* to hold

fesselnd ADJ gripping

fest [fɛst] **1** ADJ (a) (= *hart*) solid; **~e Form** *or* **Gestalt annehmen** (*fig*) to take shape (b) (= *stabil*) solid; *Gewebe, Schuhe* tough, sturdy; (*Comm, Fin*) stable (c) (= *sicher, entschlossen*) firm; *Plan* firm, definite; *Stimme* steady; **eine ~e Meinung von etw haben** to have definite views on sth; **etw ist ~** (= *steht fest*) sth is definite (d) (= *kräftig*) firm; *Schlag* hard, heavy (e) (= *nicht locker*) tight; *Griff* firm; (*fig*) *Schlaf* sound (f) (= *ständig*) regular; *Freund(in)* steady; *Bindung, Stellung, Mitarbeiter* permanent; *Kosten, Tarif, Einkommen* fixed; *Redewendung* set; **in ~en Händen sein, sich in ~en Händen befinden** (*inf: Mädchen*) to be spoken for **2** ADV (a) (= *kräftig*) *anpacken, packen* firmly; *drücken, umarmen* tightly; (*inf: tüchtig, kräftig*) *helfen, arbeiten* with a will; **~ zuschlagen** to hit hard (b) (= *nicht locker*) *anziehen, zudrehen, verknoten, schließen* tight; **~ kochende Kartoffeln** waxy potatoes; **die Handbremse ~ anziehen** to put the handbrake on firmly; **er hat schon ~ geschlafen** he was sound asleep (c) (= *sicher*) *versprechen* faithfully; *zusagen* definitely; **sie sind an den Vertrag ~ gebunden** their contract is binding; **~ entschlossen sein** to be absolutely determined (d) (= *dauerhaft*) permanently; **Gehälter sind im Tarifvertrag ~ geregelt** salaries are set in the pay agreement; **~ befreundet sein** (*Freund und Freundin*) to be going steady; **jdn ~ anstellen** to employ sb as a regular member of staff; **~ angestellt** employed on a regular basis; **Geld ~ anlegen** to tie up money

Fest [fɛst] NT **-(e)s**, **-e** (a) (= *Feier*) celebration; (= *historische Begebenheit*) celebrations *pl*; (= *Party*) party; (= *Hochzeitsfest*) reception; (= *Kinderfest, Schützenfest*) carnival; **das war ein ~!** (*inf*) it was great fun; **man soll die ~e feiern, wie sie fallen** (*prov*) make hay while the sun shines (*prov*) (b) (= *kirchlicher Feiertag*) feast, festival; (= *Weihnachtsfest*) Christmas; **bewegliches/unbewegliches ~** movable/immovable feast; **frohes ~!** Merry *or* Happy (*esp Brit*) Christmas!

Fest-: **Festakt** M ceremony; **festangestellt** ADJ siehe **fest**; **Festangestellte(r)** MF DECL AS ADJ regular member of staff; **Festansprache** F address; **Festbeleuchtung** F festive lighting *or* lights *pl*; (*inf: im Haus*) blazing lights *pl*; **was soll denn diese ~?** (*inf*) why is the place lit up like a Christmas tree? (*inf*); **festbinden** VT SEP IRREG to tie up; **jdn/etw an etw** (*dat*) **~** to tie sb/sth to sth; **festdrehen** VT SEP to screw up tightly; **festdrücken** VT SEP to press in/down/together firmly

feste [ˈfɛstə] ADV (*inf*) = **fest**; **immer ~ druff!** let him/her *etc* have it! (*inf*)

Fest-: **Festessen** NT banquet; **festfahren** VR SEP IRREG (*fig*) to get bogged down; **festfressen** VR SEP IRREG to seize up; **Festgelage** NT banquet; **Festgeld** NT (*Fin*) time deposit; **festgewurzelt**

[-gəvʊrtslt] ADJ **wie** ~ rooted to the spot; **Festhalle** F festival hall

festhalten SEP IRREG **1** VT **(a)** (*mit den Händen*) to hold on to **(b)** (= *bemerken*) to stress, to emphasize **(c)** (= *inhaftieren*) to hold, to detain **(d)** (= *verewigen*) to record; *Atmosphäre etc* to capture; **etw schriftlich** ~ to record sth; **etw im Gedächtnis** ~ to bear sth firmly in mind **2** VI **an etw** (*dat*) ~ to hold *or* stick (*inf*) to sth **3** VR to hold on (*an* +*dat* -to) ~ to; **sich irgendwo** ~ to hold on to something; **halt dich fest!** (*lit*) hold tight!

festigen ['fɛstɪɡn] **1** VT to strengthen; *siehe auch* **gefestigt 2** VR to become stronger

Festiger ['fɛstɪɡɐ] M **-s, -** setting lotion

Festigkeit ['fɛstɪçkait] F -, NO PL (*von Material*) strength; (*fig*) steadfastness; (*von Meinung*) firmness; (*von Stimme*) steadiness; **die** ~ **seines Charakters** his strength of character

Festigung ['fɛstɪɡʊŋ] F -, -en strengthening

Festival ['fɛstɪval, 'festival] NT **-s, -s** festival

Fest-: festklammern SEP **1** VT to clip on (*an* +*dat* to); **Wäsche an** *or* **auf die Leine** ~ to peg washing on the line **2** VR to cling (*an* +*dat* to); **festklemmen** SEP **1** VT to wedge fast; (*mit Klammer, Klemme*) to clip; **festgeklemmt werden** (*aus Versehen*) to get stuck *or* jammed **2** VIR (*vi: aux sein*) to jam, to stick (fast); **Festkomma** NT (*auch Comput*) fixed point; **Festkörper** M (*Phys*) solid; **Festkörperphysik** F solid-state physics *sing*; **festkrallen** VR SEP (*Tier*) to dig one's claws in (*an* +*dat* -to); (*Mensch*) to dig one's nails in (*an* +*dat* -to); (*fig*) to cling (*an* +*dat* to); **Festland** NT (*nicht Insel*) mainland; (*nicht Meer*) dry land

festlegen SEP **1** VT **(a)** (= *festsetzen*) *Reihenfolge, Termin, Kurs etc* to fix (*auf* +*acc, bei* for); *Grenze auch* to establish; *Sprachgebrauch, Regelung, Arbeitszeiten* to lay down; **etw schriftlich/testamentarisch** ~ to stipulate sth in writing/in one's will **(b)** **jdn auf etw** (*acc*) ~**/darauf** ~, **etw zu tun** (= *festnageln*) to tie sb (down) to sth/to doing sth; (= *verpflichten*) to commit sb to sth/to doing sth **(c)** *Geld* to tie up **2** VR **(a)** (= *verbindlich sein*) to tie oneself down (*auf* +*acc* to); (= *sich verpflichten*) to commit oneself (*auf* +*acc* to) **(b)** (= *sich entschließen*) to decide (*auf* +*acc* on)

Festlegung F -, -en (= *Festsetzung*) fixing; (*von Grenze*) establishing; (*von Regelung, Arbeitszeiten*) laying-down

festlich ['fɛstlɪç] **1** ADJ festive; (= *feierlich*) solemn; (= *prächtig*) splendid, magnificent; **ein** ~**er Tag** a special day **2** ADV *geschmückt* festively; *gekleidet* formally; **etw** ~ **begehen** to celebrate sth

Fest-: festliegen VI SEP IRREG **(a)** (= *festgesetzt sein*) to have been fixed; (*Sprachgebrauch, Grenze*) to have been established **(b)** (*Fin: Geld*) to be tied up **(c)** (= *nicht weiterkönnen*) to be stuck; **festmachen** SEP **1** VT **(a)** (= *befestigen*) to fix on (*an* +*dat* -to); (= *festbinden*) to fasten (*an* +*dat* (on)to); (*Naut*) to moor **(b)** (= *vereinbaren*) to arrange; **ein Geschäft** ~ to clinch a deal **(c)** (= *beweisen, zeigen*) to demonstrate, to exemplify; **etw an etw/jdm** ~ (*fig*) to link sth to sth/sb **2** VI (*Naut*) to moor; **festnageln** VT SEP **(a)** *Gegenstand* to nail (down/up/on); **etw an/auf etw** (*dat*) ~ to nail sth to sth **(b)** (*fig inf*) **jdn** to tie down (*auf* +*acc* to); **Festnahme** [-naːmə] F -, -n arrest, apprehension; **festnehmen** VT SEP IRREG to arrest, to apprehend; **vorläufig** ~ to take into custody; **Sie sind festgenommen** you are under arrest; **Festnetz** NT (*Telec*) fixed-line network; **Festplatte** F (*Comput*) hard disk; **Festplattenlaufwerk** NT hard disk drive; **Festplatz** M festival ground; (*für Volksfest*) fairground; **Festpreis** M (*Comm*) fixed price; **Festpunkt** M (*auch Comput*) fixed point; **Festrede** F speech; **Festredner(in)** M(F) (main) speaker; **festschnallen** VTR SEP = **anschnallen**; **festschnüren** VT SEP = **festbinden**; **festschrauben** VT SEP to screw (in/on/down/up) tight; **festschreiben** VT SEP IRREG (*fig*) to establish; (*Jur*) to enact

festsetzen SEP **1** VT **(a)** (= *bestimmen*) *Preis, Rente, Grenze* to fix (*bei, auf* +*acc* at); *Arbeitszeiten* to lay down; **der Beginn der Veranstaltung wurde auf zwei Uhr festgesetzt** the event was scheduled to begin at 2 o'clock **(b)** (= *inhaftieren*) to detain **2** VR (*Staub, Schmutz*) to collect; (*Rost, Ungeziefer,*

unerwünschte Personen) to get a foothold; (*fig: Gedanke*) to take root

Festsetzung F -, -en **(a)** (*von Preis, Rente, Grenze*) fixing; (*von Ort, Termin*) arrangement; (*von Frist*) setting; (*von Arbeitszeiten*) laying-down **(b)** (= *Inhaftierung*) detention

festsitzen VI SEP IRREG **(a)** (= *klemmen, haften*) to be stuck; (*Schmutz*) to cling **(b)** (= *stecken geblieben sein*) to be stuck (*bei inf*); (*Naut*) to be aground

Festspiel NT (= *einzelnes Stück*) festival production; ~**e** PL (= *Veranstaltung*) festival *sing*

Festspielhaus NT festival theatre (*Brit*) *or* theater (*US*)

fest-: feststampfen VT SEP to pound down; **feststecken** SEP **1** VT to pin (*an* +*dat* (on)to, *in* +*dat* in) **2** VI (= *stecken geblieben sein*) to be stuck; **feststehen** VI SEP IRREG (= *sicher sein*) to be certain; (= *beschlossen sein*) to have been settled; (= *unveränderlich sein*) to be definite; **fest steht** *or* **eines steht fest, dass ...** one thing's (for) certain *or* sure and that is that ...; **so viel steht fest** this *or* so much is certain; **feststehend** ADJ ATTR (= *bestimmt, verbindlich*) definite; *Redewendung, Begriff, Reihenfolge* set; *Brauch* (well-)established; *Terminplan* fixed

feststellen VT SEP **(a)** (*Mech*) to lock (fast) **(b)** (= *ermitteln*) to ascertain, to find out; *Personalien, Sachverhalt, Datum, Ursache, Grund* to establish; *Schaden* to assess; *Krankheit* to diagnose; **einen Totalschaden an einem Wagen** ~ to assess a car as a total write-off **(c)** (= *erkennen*) to tell (*an* +*dat* from); *Fehler, Unterschied* to find, to detect; (= *bemerken*) to discover; (= *einsehen*) to realize; **wir mussten** ~, **dass wir uns geirrt hatten** we were forced to realize that we had made a mistake; **ich musste entsetzt/überrascht** *etc* ~, **dass ...** I was horrified/surprised *etc* to find that ... **(d)** (= *aussprechen*) to stress, to emphasize

Feststelltaste F (*von Tastatur*) caps lock

Feststellung F **(a)** (= *Ermittlung*) ascertainment; (*von Personalien, Sachverhalt, Datum, Ursache, Grund*) establishment; (*von Schaden*) assessment; (*von Krankheit*) diagnosis **(b)** (= *Erkenntnis*) conclusion **(c)** (= *Wahrnehmung*) observation; **die** ~ **machen, dass ...** to realize that ...; **wir mussten leider die** ~ **machen, dass ...** (*form*) it has come to our notice that ...; **ist das eine Frage oder eine** ~? is that a question or a statement (of fact)? **(d)** (= *Bemerkung*) remark, comment

Festtag M **(a)** (= *Ehrentag*) special *or* red-letter day **(b)** (= *Feiertag*) holiday, feast (day) (*Eccl*); **angenehme** ~**e!** Merry Christmas/Happy Easter *etc*!

Fest-: festtreten SEP IRREG **1** VT to tread down; (*in Teppich etc*) to tread in (*in* +*acc* -to) **2** VR to get trodden down/in; **das tritt sich fest!** (*hum inf*) don't worry, it's good for the carpet (*hum*); **Festübernahme** F (*Fin*) firm underwriting; **Festumzug** M procession

Festung ['fɛstʊŋ] F -, -en fortress

Fest-: Festveranstaltung F function; **festverzinslich** ADJ fixed-interest *attr*; **festwachsen** VI SEP IRREG AUX SEIN = **anwachsen**; **Festwertspeicher** M (*Comput*) read-only memory; **Festwiese** F festival ground; (*für Volksfest*) fairground; **Festzelt** NT carnival marquee; **festziehen** VT SEP IRREG to pull tight; *Schraube* to tighten (up); **Festzins** M fixed interest; **Festzinssatz** M fixed rate of interest; **Festzug** M carnival procession

Fete ['feːtə] F -, -n party; **eine** ~ **feiern** (*als Gastgeber*) to have *or* throw a party; (*als Gast*) to go to a party

Feten PL *von* **Fetus**

Fetischismus [fetɪ'ʃɪsmʊs] M -, NO PL fetishism

Fetischist [fetɪ'ʃɪst] M **-en, -en**, **Fetischistin** [-'ʃɪstɪn] F -, -nen fetishist

fett [fɛt] **1** ADJ **(a)** (= ~*haltig*) *Speisen, Kost* fatty; **ein** ~**er Bissen** *or* **Brocken** *or* **Happen** (*lit*) a juicy morsel; (*fig*) a lucrative deal **(b)** (= *dick*) fat; (*Typ*) *Überschrift, Schlagzeilen* bold **(c)** (= *üppig*) *Beute, Gewinn* fat; *Geschäft* lucrative; (*Aut*) *Gemisch etc* rich; ~**e Jahre** fat years **(d)** (*sl:* = *toll*) wicked (*sl*); **das ist voll** ~ that's really wicked (*sl*); ~**e Teile** (= *Busen*) tits *pl* (*sl*) **2** ADV **(a)** ~ **essen** to eat fatty food; ~ **kochen** to cook fatty food; (= *mit viel Fett*) to use a lot of fat

(b) (= *dick*) ~ **gedruckt** (*Typ*) in bold(face); **sich dick und ~ fressen** (*inf*) to stuff oneself (*inf*)

Fett [fɛt] NT **-(e)s, -e** fat; (*zum Schmieren*) grease; **tierische/ pflanzliche -e** animal/vegetable fats; ~ **ansetzen** to get fat; (*Tiere*) to fatten up; **in schwimmendem ~ backen** to deep-fry; **sein ~ bekommen** (*inf*) or **kriegen** (*inf*)/**weghaben** (*inf*) to get/ have what is coming to one (*inf*)

Fett-: fettarm 1 ADJ *Speisen* low-fat 2 ADV ~ **essen** to eat foods which are low in fat; ~ **kochen** to cook low-fat meals; **Fettauge** NT globule of fat; **Fettbauch** M paunch; (*inf*: = *fetter Mann*) fatso (*inf*); **Fettcreme** F skin cream with oil; **Fettdruck** M, NO PL (*Typ*) bold type

fetten [fɛtn] 1 VT to grease 2 VI to be greasy

Fett-: Fettfilm M greasy film; **Fettfleck** M grease spot, greasy mark; **fettfrei** 1 ADJ fat-free; *Milch* non-fat; *Kost* non-fatty; *Creme* non-greasy 2 ADV ~ **kochen** to cook fat-free meals; ~ **essen** to eat no fats; **fettgedruckt** ADJ ATTR *siehe* **fett**; **Fettgehalt** M fat content; **fetthaltig**, (*Aus*) **fetthältig** ADJ fatty

Fettheit F -, NO PL (*inf*: = *Dickheit*) fatness; (= *Fetthaltigkeit*) fattiness

fettig [ˈfɛtɪç] ADJ greasy

Fettigkeit F -, NO PL greasiness

Fett-: fettlos 1 ADJ fat-free 2 ADV **völlig ~ essen** to eat no fats at all; ~ **kochen** to cook fat-free meals; **Fettnäpfchen** [-nɛpfçən] NT **-s, -** (*inf*) **ins ~ treten** to put one's foot in it (*bei jdm* with sb); **Fettpolster** NT (*Anat*) (layer of) subcutaneous fat; (*hum inf*) padding *no pl*; ~ **haben** to be well-padded; **Fettpölsterchen** [-pœlstɐçən] NT **-s, -** padding *no pl*; **Fettpresse** F grease gun; **Fettschicht** F layer of fat; **Fettsucht** F, NO PL (*Med*) obesity; **fettsüchtig** ADJ (*Med*) obese; **fetttriefend** ADJ greasy; **Fettwanst** [-vanst] M **-(e)s, ⸚e** [-vɛnstə] (*pej*) potbelly; (= *Mensch*) paunchy man, fatso (*inf*)

Fetus [ˈfeːtʊs] M - *or* **-sses, -sse** *or* **Feten** [ˈfeːtn] foetus (*Brit*), fetus (*US*)

fetzen [ˈfɛtsn] 1 VI AUX SEIN (= *rasen*) to tear (*inf*) 2 VT to rip 3 VR (*inf*: = *sich streiten*) to quarrel viciously; **die beiden ~ sich den ganzen Tag** they are ripping into each other all day long (*inf*)

Fetzen [ˈfɛtsn] M **-s, -** (a) (*abgerissen*) shred; (= *Stofffetzen, Papierfetzen, Gesprächsfetzen*) scrap; (= *Kleidung*) rag; **etw in tausend ~ (zer)reißen** to tear sth into a thousand pieces; **..., dass die ~ fliegen** (*inf*) ... like crazy (*inf*) **(b)** (*Aus*: = *Scheuertuch*) rag

fetzig [ˈfɛtsɪç] ADJ (*dated sl*) wild, crazy (*inf*); *Rede* rousing

feucht [fɔyçt] ADJ damp; (= *schlüpfrig*) moist; (= *~heiß*) *Klima* humid; *Jahreszeit* wet, rainy; *Luftmassen* rain-bearing; *Hände* sweaty; *Tinte, Farbe* wet; **sie kriegte/hatte ~e Augen** her eyes moistened/were moist; **ein ~er Abend** (*hum*) a boozy (*inf*) or drunken evening; **eine ~e Aussprache haben** (*hum inf*) to splutter when one speaks; **das geht dich einen ~en Kehricht an** (*inf*) that's none of your goddamn business (*inf*); **~er Traum** (*inf*) wet dream

Feucht-: Feuchtbiotop NT damp biotope; **feuchtfröhlich** ADJ (*hum*) merry, convivial; **ein ~er Abend** an evening of convivial drinking; **Feuchtgebiet** NT marshland; **feuchtheiß** ADJ hot and damp, muggy

Feuchtigkeit [ˈfɔyçtɪçkaɪt] F -, NO PL (a) dampness; (= *Schlüpfrigkeit*) moistness; (*von Klima*) humidity; (*von Händen*) sweatiness (b) (= *Flüssigkeit*) moisture; (= *Luftfeuchtigkeit*) humidity

Feuchtigkeits-: Feuchtigkeitscreme F moisturizer, moisturizing cream; **Feuchtigkeitsgehalt** M, **Feuchtigkeitsgrad** M moisture level or content; **Feuchtigkeitsmesser** M **-s, -** hygrometer

feudal [fɔyˈdaːl] ADJ (a) (*Pol, Hist*) feudal (b) (*inf*: = *prächtig*) plush (*inf*); *Mahlzeit* slap-up *attr* (*Brit inf*), lavish

Feudal- IN CPDS feudal; **Feudalherrschaft** F feudalism

feudalistisch [fɔydaˈlɪstɪʃ] ADJ feudalistic

Feuer [ˈfɔyɐ] NT **-s, -** (a) (= *Brand, Flamme, Kaminfeuer, Herd*) fire; (= *olympisches ~*) flame; **am ~** by the fire; ~ **machen** to light a/ the fire; ~ **speien** to spew flames or fire; ~ **speiend** *Drache* fire-breathing; *Berg* spewing (forth) fire; ~! fire!; ~ **legen** to start a fire; **an etw** (*acc*)/**in etw** (*dat*) ~ **legen** to set fire to sth; ~ **fangen** to catch fire; **das brennt wie ~** (*fig*) that burns; **jdm ~ unterm Hintern** (*inf*) or **Arsch** (*sl*) **machen** to put a bomb under sb; **mit dem ~ spielen** (*fig*) to play with fire

(b) (= *Funkfeuer*) beacon; (*von Leuchtturm*) light **(c)** (*für Zigarette etc*) light; **haben Sie ~?** do you have a light?; **jdm ~ geben** to give sb a light **(d)** (= *Schwung*) passion; (*von Pferd*) mettle; ~ **haben** to be passionate/mettlesome; ~ **fangen** to be really taken (*bei* with); **bei jdm ~ fangen** to fall for sb; ~ **und Flamme sein** (*inf*) to be very enthusiastic (*für* about) **(e)** (= *Schießen*) fire; ~! fire!; ~ **frei!** open fire!; **das ~ einstellen** to cease firing

Feuer- IN CPDS fire; **Feueralarm** M fire alarm; **Feueranzünder** M firelighter; **feuerbeständig** ADJ fire-resistant; **Feuerbestattung** F cremation; **Feuereifer** M zeal; **mit ~ spielen/diskutieren** to play/discuss with zest; **feuerfest** ADJ fireproof; *Geschirr* heat-resistant; **Feuergefahr** F fire hazard or risk; **bei ~** in the event of fire; **feuergefährlich** ADJ (highly) (in)flammable or combustible; **Feuerholz** NT, NO PL firewood; **Feuerland** [ˈfɔyɐlant] NT **-s** Tierra del Fuego; **Feuerländer** [ˈfɔyɐlɛndɐ] M **-s, -**, **Feuerländerin** [-ərɪn] F **-, -nen** Fuegian; **Feuerleiter** F (*am Haus*) fire escape; (*bei Feuerwehrauto*) (fireman's) ladder; (*fahrbar*) turntable ladder; **Feuerlöschboot** NT fireboat; **Feuerlöscher** [-lœʃɐ] M **-s, -** fire extinguisher; **Feuermelder** [-mɛldɐ] M **-s, -** fire alarm; **er hat ein Gesicht wie ein ~(, so schön zum Reinschlagen)** (*sl*) he's got the kind of face that just makes you want to hit him

feuern [ˈfɔyɐn] 1 VI (a) (= *heizen*) **mit Öl/Gas ~** to have oil/gas heating; **mit Holz ~** to use wood for one's heating (b) (*Mil*) to fire 2 VT (a) *Ofen* to light; **Öl ~** to have oil heating; **Briketts ~** to use briquettes for one's heating (b) (*inf*) (= *werfen*) to fling (*inf*); (*Ftbl*) *Ball* to slam (*inf*) (c) (*inf*: = *entlassen*) to fire (*inf*), to sack (*inf*)

Feuer-: Feuerpause F break in the firing; (*vereinbart*) ceasefire; **Feuerqualle** F stinging jellyfish; **feuerrot** ADJ fiery red; *Haar auch* flaming; *Kleidung, Auto* scarlet; ~ **werden** (*vor Verlegenheit etc*) to turn crimson or scarlet; **Feuerschiff** NT lightship; **Feuerschlucker** [-ʃlʊkɐ] M **-s, -**, **Feuerschluckerin** [-ərɪn] F **-, -nen** fire-eater; **Feuerschneise** F fire break; **Feuerschutz** M (a) (= *Vorbeugung*) fire prevention (b) (*Mil*: = *Deckung*) covering fire; **feuerspeiend** ADJ ATTR *siehe* **Feuer; Feuerstein** M flint; **Feuerstelle** F campfire site; (= *Spuren eines Feuers*) burned spot, remains *pl* of a fire; (= *Herd*) fireplace; **Feuertreppe** F fire escape; **Feuertür** F fire door

Feuerung [ˈfɔyərʊŋ] F -, -en (a) (= *das Beheizen*) heating (b) (= *Brennstoff*) fuel (c) (= *Heizanlage*) heating system

Feuer-: Feuerwache F fire station; **Feuerwaffe** F firearm; **Feuerwasser** NT, NO PL (*inf*) firewater (*inf*); **Feuerwechsel** M exchange of fire

Feuerwehr F fire brigade (*Brit*), fire department (*US*); **fahren wie die ~** (*inf*) to drive like a bat out of hell (*inf*); ~ **spielen** (*fig*: = *Schlimmes verhindern*) to act as a troubleshooter

Feuerwehr-: Feuerwehrauto NT fire engine; **Feuerwehrfrau** F firewoman; **Feuerwehrmann** M, *pl* **-leute** or **-männer** fireman; **Feuerwehrschlauch** M fire hose; **Feuerwehrübung** F fire-fighting exercise

Feuer-: Feuerwerk NT fireworks *pl*; (*fig*) cavalcade; **Feuerwerkskörper** M firework; **Feuerzange** F fire tongs *pl*; **Feuerzangenbowle** F red wine punch

Feuerzeug NT, *pl* **-zeuge** (cigarette) lighter

Feuilleton [fœjəˈtõː, ˈfœjətõ] NT **-s, -s** (*Press*) (= *Zeitungsteil*) feature section; (= *Artikel*) feature (article)

feuilletonistisch [fœjətoˈnɪstɪʃ] ADJ **dieser Journalist ist ein ~es Talent** this journalist has a natural flair for writing feature articles; **dieser Aufsatz ist zu ~** (*pej*) this essay is too glib or facile

feurig [ˈfɔyrɪç] ADJ fiery

ff. ABBR *von* **folgende Seiten**

Fiaker [ˈfiakɐ] M **-s, -** (*Aus*) (a) (= *Kutsche*) (hackney) cab (b) (= *Kutscher*) cab driver, cabby (*inf*)

Fiasko ['fiasko] NT **-s, -s** (inf) fiasco; **mit seinem Buch erlebte er ein ~** his book was a complete flop (inf) or failure

Fiber ['fi:bɐ] F **-, -n** fibre (Brit), fiber (US)

Fiche [fi:ʃ] M or NT **-(s), -s (a)** (micro)fiche **(b)** (Sw: = Akte) file

ficht [fɪçt] 3. PERS SING PRES von **fechten**

Fichte ['fɪçtə] F **-, -n** (Bot) spruce

Fichten- IN CPDS spruce; **Fichtenzapfen** M spruce cone

Fick [fɪk] M **-s, -s** (vulg) fuck (vulg)

ficken ['fɪkn] VTI (vulg) to fuck (vulg); **mit jdm ~** to fuck sb (vulg)

Fickteufel M (vulg: = Penis) dick (sl), cock (sl)

Ficus ['fi:kʊs] M **-, Fici** ['fi:tsi] (= Zierpflanze) weeping fig

fidel [fi:'de:l] ADJ jolly, merry

Fidibus ['fi:dibʊs] M **- or -ses, - or -se** spill

Fidschiinseln ['fɪdʒi-] PL Fiji Islands pl

Fieber ['fi:bɐ] NT **-s,** (rare) **-** temperature; (sehr hoch, mit Fantasieren, = Krankheit) fever; **~ haben** to have a temperature; to be feverish; **40° ~ haben** to have a temperature of 40; **(jdm) das ~ messen** to take sb's temperature; **im ~ seiner Leidenschaft** in a fever of passion

Fieber-: **Fieberanfall** M bout of fever; **Fieberfantasien** PL feverish ravings pl; **fieberfrei** ADJ free of fever; **fieberhaft** **1** ADJ feverish **2** ADV feverishly

fieberig ['fi:bərɪç] ADJ feverish

Fieber-: **Fieberkurve** F temperature curve; **Fiebermesser** M **-s, -** (dated, Sw) thermometer

fiebern ['fi:bɐn] VI **(a)** (Kranker) to have a temperature; (schwer) to be feverish **(b)** (fig) **nach etw ~** to long feverishly for sth; **vor Ungeduld/Erregung** (dat) **~** to be in a fever of impatience/ excitement

Fieber-: **Fieberphantasien** PL = **Fieberfantasien;** **fiebersenkend** ADJ fever-reducing; **Fieberthermometer** NT (clinical) thermometer

fiebrig ['fi:brɪç] ADJ = **fieberig**

fiedeln ['fi:dln] VTI (humpej) to fiddle; **ein Liedchen ~** to play a song on the fiddle

fiel PRET von **fallen**

fiepen ['fi:pn] VI (Vogel) to cheep; (Hund, Mensch) to whimper

fies [fi:s] (inf) **1** ADJ nasty, horrible **2** ADV (= abstoßend, ekelhaft) nastily, horribly; (= gemein) in a nasty way; **~ aussehen** to look horrible; **~ riechen** to smell horrible; **benimm dich nicht so ~!** don't be so horrid!; (= ordinär) don't behave so horribly!

Fiesheit F **-, -en** USU PL (inf) mean trick

Fiesling ['fi:slɪŋ] M **-s, -e** (inf) (= abstoßender Mensch) slob (inf); (= gemeiner Mensch) bastard (sl)

Fifa ['fi:fa] F **-, FIFA** F **-** FIFA

fifty-fifty ['fɪftɪ'fɪftɪ] ADV (inf) fifty-fifty (inf); **~ machen** to go fifty-fifty (inf)

Figur [fi'gu:ɐ] F **-, -en (a)** (= Bildwerk, Abbildung) (Math, Sport, Mus) figure; (gedankenlos hingezeichnet) doodle **(b)** (= Gestalt, Persönlichkeit) figure; (= Körperform) (von Frauen) figure; (von Männern) physique; (inf: = Mensch) character; **auf seine ~ achten** to watch one's figure; **eine gute/schlechte/traurige ~ machen** or **abgeben** to cut a good/poor/sorry figure **(c)** (= Romanfigur, Filmfigur etc) character

figurativ [figura'ti:f] **1** ADJ figurative **2** ADV figuratively; (geh: = gegenständlich) representationally

Figürchen [fi'gy:ɐçən] NT **-s, -** DIM von **Figur**

Figurenlaufen NT **-s,** NO PL figure skating

figürlich [fi'gy:ɐlɪç] **1** ADJ **(a)** (= übertragen) figurative **(b)** (= figurmäßig) as regards the/her figure; (von Männern) as regards physique **(c)** (Art) figurative **2** ADV (= figurmäßig) in terms of the/one's figure; (= übertragen) figuratively

Fiktion [fɪk'tsio:n] F **-, -en** fiction

fiktiv [fɪk'ti:f] ADJ fictitious

Filet [fi'le:] NT **-s, -s** (Cook) fillet; (= Rinderfilet) fillet steak; (zum Braten) piece of sirloin or tenderloin (US)

filetieren [file'ti:rən] ptp **filetiert** VT to fillet

Filet-: **Filetsteak** NT fillet steak; **Filetstück** NT (Cook) piece of sirloin or tenderloin (US); (fig inf: = lohnendes Investitionsobjekt etc) prime investment choice

Filiale [fi'lia:lə] F **-, -n** branch

filigran [fili'gra:n] ADJ filigree

Filipina [fili'pi:na] F **-, -s** Filipina

Filipino[1] [fili'pi:no] M **-s, -s** Filipino

Filipino[2] [fili'pi:no] NT **-,** NO PL (Ling) Filipino, Tagalog

Film [fɪlm] M **-(e)s, -e (a)** (alle Bedeutungen) film; (= Spielfilm) film, movie (esp US), motion picture (US); (= Dokumentarfilm) documentary (film); **in einen ~ gehen** to go to and see a film, to go to a film; **da ist bei mir der ~ gerissen** (fig inf) I had a mental blackout (inf) **(b)** (= ~branche) films pl, movie business (esp US); **zum ~ gehen/kommen** to go/get or break into films or movies (esp US); **beim ~ arbeiten** or **sein** (inf) to work in films or in the movie business (esp US)

Film- IN CPDS film, movie (esp US); **Filmamateur(in)** M(F) home-movie enthusiast; **Filmbewertungsstelle** F ≈ board of film classification

Filmemacher(in) M(F) film-maker, movie-maker (esp US)

filmen ['fɪlmən] VTI to film

Filmerei [fɪlmə'rai] F **-, -en** (inf) filming

Film-: **Filmfestival** NT, **Filmfestspiele** PL film festival; **filmgerecht** **1** ADJ filmable **2** ADV **der Roman muss ~ bearbeitet werden** the novel will have to be adapted for the cinema; **Filmgeschäft** NT film industry, movie or motion-picture industry (esp US)

filmisch ['fɪlmɪʃ] **1** ADJ cinematic; **~es Porträt** film portrait; **eine ~e Dokumentation der Aufführung** a record on film of the production **2** ADV cinematically

Film-: **Filmkamera** F film or movie (esp US) camera; (= Schmalfilmkamera) cine camera (Brit), movie camera (esp US); **Filmkritik** F film or movie (esp US) criticism; (= Artikel) film or movie (esp US) review; (= Kritiker) film or movie (esp US) critics pl; **Filmkunst** F cinematic art; **Filmmaterial** NT film; **Filmmusik** F film music, movie soundtrack (esp US); **die originale ~** the original soundtrack; **Filmpreis** M film or movie (esp US) award; **Filmproduzent(in)** M(F) film or movie (esp US) producer; **Filmprojektor** M film or movie (esp US) projector; **Filmprüfstelle** F film censorship office; **Filmriss** M (lit) tear in a film; (fig inf) mental blackout (inf); **Filmrolle** F (= Spule) spool of film; (für Fotoapparat) roll of film; (= Part) film part or role, movie role (esp US); **Filmschaffende(r)** MF DECL AS ADJ film-maker, movie-maker (esp US); **Filmschauspieler** M film or movie (esp US) actor; **Filmschauspielerin** F film or movie (esp US) actress; **Filmstar** M filmstar, movie star (esp US); **Filmsternchen** NT starlet; **Filmstudio** NT film or movie (esp US) studio; **Filmverleih** M film or movie (esp US) distributors pl; **Filmvorführer(in)** M(F) projectionist; **Filmwelt** F film or movie (esp US) world

Filter ['fɪltɐ] NT or M **-s, -** filter; **eine Zigarette mit/ohne ~** a (filter-)tipped/plain cigarette

Filter-: **Filteranlage** F filter; **Filtereinsatz** M filter pad; **Filterkaffee** M filter or drip (US) coffee; **Filtermundstück** NT filter-tip

filtern ['fɪltɐn] VTI to filter

Filter-: **Filterpapier** NT filter paper; **Filterrückstand** M residue (after filtering); **Filterstaub** M filter dust; **Filtertüte** F filter bag

Filterung ['fɪltərʊŋ] F **-, -en** filtering

Filterzigarette F tipped or filter(-tipped) cigarette

Filtrat [fɪl'tra:t] NT **-(e)s, -e** filtrate

filtrieren [fɪl'tri:rən] ptp **filtriert** VT to filter

Filtrierung F **-, -en** filtering

Filz [fɪlts] M **-es, -e (a)** (Tex) felt; **grüner ~** green baize **(b)** (inf: = Bierdeckel) beer mat (esp Brit) or coaster (US) **(c)** (inf) (= Korruption) corruption; (Pol pej) sleaze (inf)

filzen ['fɪltsn] **1** VI (Tex) to felt, to go felty **2** VT (inf) (= durchsuchen) to search; (= berauben) to do over (inf)

Filzlaus F crab louse

Filzokratie [fɪltsokra'ti:] F **-, -n** [-'ti:ən] (Pol pej) web of patronage and nepotism, spoils system (US)

Filz-: **Filzpantoffel** M (carpet) slipper; **Filzschreiber, Filzstift** M felt(-tip) pen, felt-tip

Fimmel ['fɪml] M **-s, -** (inf) **(a)** (= Tick) mania; **er hat diesen ~ mit dem Unkrautjäten** he's got this thing about weeding (inf) **(b)** (= Spleen) obsession (mit about); **du hast wohl einen ~!** you're crazy (inf) or mad (inf)!

final [fi'na:l] ADJ final

Finale [fi'na:lə] NT **-s, -s or -** (Mus) finale; (Sport) final, finals pl

Finalsatz M final clause

Finanz [fi'nants] F -, NO PL financial world; **die hohe ~** the world of high finance; **Kreise der ~** financial circles

Finanz- IN CPDS financial; **Finanzakrobat(in)** M(F) (*pej inf*) financial juggler; **Finanzamt** NT tax office; **Finanzbeamte(r)** M DECL AS ADJ, **Finanzbeamtin** F tax official; **Finanzbehörde** F tax authority; **Finanzbuchhaltung** F financial accounting; **Finanzdienste** PL financial services *pl*

Finanzen [fi'nantsn] PL finances *pl*; **das übersteigt meine ~** that's beyond my means

Finanzer [fi'nantsə] M -s, -, **Finanzerin** [-ərɪn] F -, -nen (*Aus*: = *Zollbeamter*) customs officer *or* official

finanziell [finan'tsiel] ◼ ADJ financial ◼ ADV financially; **sich ~ an etw** (*dat*) **beteiligen** to take a (financial) stake in sth

finanzieren [finan'tsi:rən], *ptp* **finanziert** VT to finance, to fund; **frei ~** to finance privately; **ich kann ein neues Auto nicht ~** I can't afford a new car

Finanzierung F -, -en financing; **zur ~ von etw** to finance sth

Finanzierungs-: Finanzierungsdefizit NT budget deficit; **Finanzierungsgesellschaft** F finance company; **Finanzierungsloch** NT, **Finanzierungslücke** F financing gap; **Finanzierungsschätze** PL short-term gilts *pl* (*Brit*), Treasury bonds *pl* (*US*)

Finanz-: Finanzjahr NT financial year; **Finanzjongleur(in)** M(F) (*pej inf*) financial juggler; **finanzkräftig** ADJ financially strong; **Finanzmärkte** PL financial *or* finance markets *pl*; **Finanzminister(in)** M(F) ≈ Chancellor of the Exchequer (*Brit*), ≈ Treasury Secretary (*US*), finance minister; **Finanzministerium** NT Ministry of Finance, Treasury (*Brit*), Treasury Department (*US*); **Finanzpolitik** F financial policy; (= *Wissenschaft, Disziplin*) politics of finance; **finanzpolitisch** ◼ ADJ relating to financial policy ◼ ADV in terms of financial policy; **~ unklug** unwise as regards financial policy; **Finanzraum** M financial area; **integrierter ~** integrated financial area; **finanzschwach** ADJ financially weak; **Finanzspritze** F injection of capital; **ich brauche eine kleine ~** I could do with a little cash; **finanzstark** ADJ financially strong; **Finanzwechsel** M commercial paper; **Finanzwelt** F financial world; **Finanzwesen** NT, NO PL financial system; **ein Ausdruck aus dem ~** a financial term

finden ['fɪndn], *pret* **fand** [fant], *ptp* **gefunden** [gə'fʊndn] ◼ VT **(a)** (= *entdecken, vorfinden*) to find; **ich finde es nicht** I can't find it; **es ließ sich niemand ~** there was nobody to be found; **etwas an jdm ~** to see something in sb; **nichts dabei ~** to think nothing of it; *siehe auch* **gefunden**
(b) (*in Verbindung mit n siehe auch dort*) *Trost, Hilfe, Ruhe, Schlaf etc* to find; *Anklang, Zustimmung auch* to meet with; *Beifall* to meet *or* be met with; *Berücksichtigung, Beachtung* to receive; **Bestätigung ~** to be confirmed
(c) (= *ansehen, betrachten*) to think; **es kalt/warm/ganz erträglich** *etc* **~** to find it cold/warm/quite tolerable *etc*; **etw gut/zu teuer/eine Frechheit** *etc* **~** to think (that) sth is good/too expensive/a cheek *etc*; **jdn blöd/nett** *etc* **~** to think (that) sb is stupid/nice *etc*; **wie findest du das?** what do you think?; **wie finde ich das nun?** what do I think of (that)?
◼ VI (*lit, fig*: = *den Weg ~*) to find one's way; **er findet nicht nach Hause** (*lit*) he can't find his *or* the way home; (*fig*) he can't tear *or* drag himself away (*inf*); **zu sich selbst ~** to sort oneself out
◼ VTI (= *meinen*) to think; **~ Sie (das)?** do you think so?; **ich finde (das) nicht** I don't think so; **ich kann das** *or* **das kann ich nicht ~** I don't think so; **ich fände es besser, wenn ...** I think it would be better if ...
◼ VR **(a)** (= *zum Vorschein kommen*) to be found; **das wird sich (alles) ~** it will (all) turn up; (= *sich herausstellen*) it'll all come out (*inf*); **es fand sich niemand, der sich freiwillig gemeldet hätte** nobody volunteered
(b) (*Angelegenheit etc*: = *in Ordnung kommen*) to sort itself out; (*Mensch*: = *zu sich ~*) to sort oneself out
(c) (= *sich fügen*) **sich in etw** (*acc*) **~** to reconcile oneself to sth
(d) (= *sich treffen*) (*lit*) to find each other; (*fig*) to meet; **da haben sich aber zwei gefunden!** (*iro*) they'll make a fine pair

Finder ['fɪndə] M -s, -, **Finderin** [-ərɪn] F -, -nen finder
Finderlohn M reward for the finder
findig ['fɪndɪç] ADJ resourceful
Findling ['fɪntlɪŋ] M -s, -e (*Geol*) erratic (boulder)
Fineliner ['fainlainɐ] M -s, - (= *Stift*) fineliner
fing PRET *von* **fangen**

Finger ['fɪŋɐ] M -s, - finger; **der kleine ~** one's little finger, one's pinkie (*US, Scot*); **mit dem ~ auf jdn/etw zeigen** *or* **weisen** (*geh*) to point to sb/sth; **mit ~n auf jdn zeigen** (*fig*) to look askance at sb; **jdm eins auf die ~ geben** to give sb a rap across the knuckles; **zwei ~ breit** two fingers wide; **(nimm/lass die) ~ weg!** (get/keep your) hands off!; **sich** (*dat*) **nicht die ~ schmutzig machen** (*lit, fig*) not to get one's hands dirty; **das kann sich jeder an den (fünf** *or* **zehn) ~n abzählen** (*inf*) it sticks out a mile (to anybody) (*inf*); **jdm/etw in die ~ bekommen** *or* **kriegen** (*inf*) to get one's hands on sb/sth; **er hat überall seine ~ drin** (*inf*) he has a finger in every pie (*inf*); **wenn man ihm/dem Teufel den kleinen ~ gibt, (dann) nimmt er (gleich) die ganze Hand** (*prov*) give him an inch and he'll take a mile (*inf*); **lange ~ machen** (*hum inf*) to be light-fingered; **die ~ von jdm/etw lassen** (*inf*) to keep away from sb/sth; **sich** (*dat*) **bei** *or* **an etw** (*dat*) **die ~ verbrennen** to get one's fingers burned in sth; **jdm (scharf) auf die ~ sehen** to keep an eye *or* a close eye on sb; **sich** (*dat*) **etw aus den ~n saugen** to dream sth up; **sich** (*dat*) **die** *or* **alle ~ nach etw lecken** (*inf*) to be dying for sth (*inf*); **keinen ~ krumm machen** (*inf*) not to lift a finger (*inf*); **mich** *or* **mir juckt es in den ~n(, etw zu tun)** (*inf*) I'm itching to (do sth); **da hast du dich in den ~ geschnitten** (*inf*) you've made a big mistake; **er hat eine** *or* **zehn an jedem ~** he's got a woman for every day of the week; **jdn um den kleinen ~ wickeln** to twist sb (a)round one's little finger

Finger-: Fingerabdruck M fingerprint; **jds Fingerabdrücke nehmen** to take sb's fingerprints, to fingerprint sb; **genetischer ~** genetic fingerprint; **fingerbreit** ADJ the width of a finger; **Fingerbreit** M -, - finger's breadth, fingerbreadth; (*fig*) inch; **keinen ~ nachgeben** *or* **weichen** not to give an inch; **Fingerfarbe** F finger paint; **Fingergelenk** NT finger joint; **Fingerglied** NT phalanx (of the finger) (*form*); **Fingerhakeln** [-ha:kəln] NT -s, NO PL finger-wrestling; **Fingerhandschuh** M glove; **Fingerhut** M (*Sew*) thimble; **ein ~ (voll)** (*fig*) a thimbleful **(b)** (*Bot*) foxglove; **Fingerkuppe** F fingertip; **Fingerling** ['fɪŋɐlɪŋ] M -s, -e fingerstall

fingern ['fɪŋɐn] ◼ VI **an** *or* **mit etw** (*dat*) **~** to fiddle with sth; **nach etw ~** to fumble (around) for sth ◼ VT (= *manipulieren*) to fiddle (*inf*); (*inf*: = *bewerkstelligen*) *Projekt* to wangle (*inf*)

Finger-: Fingernagel M fingernail; **Fingernägel kauen** to bite one's (finger)nails; **Fingerring** M ring (for one's finger); **Fingerspitze** F fingertip, tip of one's finger; **das muss man in den ~n haben** you have to have a feel for it; **Fingerspitzengefühl** NT, NO PL (= *Einfühlungsgabe*) instinctive feel; (*im Umgang mit Menschen*) tact and sensitivity

fingieren [fɪŋ'gi:rən], *ptp* **fingiert** VT (= *vortäuschen*) to fake; (= *erdichten*) to fabricate

fingiert [fɪŋ'gi:ɐt] ADJ (= *vorgetäuscht*) bogus; (= *erfunden*) fictitious

Finish ['fɪnɪʃ] NT -s, -s **(a)** (= *Endverarbeitung*) finish; (= *Vorgang*) finishing **(b)** (*Sport*: = *Endspurt*) final spurt

finit [fi'ni:t] ADJ (*Gram*) finite

Fink [fɪŋk] M -en, -en finch

Finken ['fɪŋkn] M -s, - (*Sw*) slipper

Finne¹ ['fɪnə] F -, -n **(a)** (*Zool*: = *Stadium des Bandwurms*) bladder worm, cysticercus (*form*) **(b)** (= *Rückenflosse*) fin

Finne² M -n, -n Finn, Finnish man/boy

Finnin ['fɪnɪn] F -, -nen Finn, Finnish woman/girl

finnisch ['fɪnɪʃ] ADJ Finnish; **der Finnische Meerbusen** the Gulf of Finland

finnisch-ugrisch ['fɪnɪʃ'u:grɪʃ] ADJ = **finnougrisch**

Finnland ['fɪnlant] NT -s Finland

finnländisch ['fɪnlendɪʃ] ADJ Finnish

Finnmark ['fɪnmark] F, *pl* -mark (= *Währung*) Finnish mark, markka (*form*)

finnougrisch [fɪnoʊ'u:grɪʃ] ADJ Finno-Ugric, Finno-Ugrian

Finnwal ['fɪnva:l] M finback

finster ['fɪnstɐ] ◼ ADJ **(a)** (= *ohne Licht*) dark; *Zimmer, Wald, Nacht* dark (and gloomy); **im Finstern** in the dark; **im Finstern liegen** to be in darkness
(b) (= *dubios*) shady
(c) (= *mürrisch, düster*) grim; *Wolken* dark, black
(d) (*fig*: = *unaufgeklärt*) dark; **das ~(st)e Mittelalter** the Dark Ages *pl*
(e) (= *unheimlich*) sinister
◼ ADV **(a)** (= *mürrisch*) grimly; **es sieht ~ aus** (*fig*) things look

bleak; **jdn ~ ansehen** to give sb a black (*Brit*) *or* dirty look **(b)** (= *unheimlich*) **das alte Haus sah ziemlich ~ aus** the old house looked quite sinister

Finsternis ['finstɛnɪs] F **-, -se (a)** (= *Dunkelheit, Bibl* = *Hölle*) darkness **(b)** (*Astron*) eclipse

Firewall ['faiəwɔːl] F **-, -s** (*Comput*) firewall

Firlefanz ['fɪrləfants] M **-es,** NO PL (*inf*) **(a)** (= *Kram*) frippery **(b)** (= *Albernheit*) clowning *or* fooling around; **~ machen** to play the fool

firm [fɪrm] ADJ PRED **ich bin noch nicht ~** I don't really know it yet; **in einem Fachgebiet ~ sein** to have a sound knowledge of an area

Firma ['fɪrma] F **-, Firmen** ['fɪrmən] **(a)** company, firm; (= *Kleinbetrieb*) business; **die ~ Wahlster/Lexomat** Wahlster(s)/Lexomat **(b)** (= *Geschäfts- or Handelsname*) **eine ~ eintragen** to register a company name/the name of a business; **unter der ~ Smith** under the name of Smith; **unter eigener ~** under one's own name

Firmen-: Firmenaufdruck M company stamp; **firmeneigen** ADJ company *attr*; **~ sein** to belong to the company; **Firmeninhaber(in)** M(F) owner of the company; **firmenintern** ◼ ADJ within the company *attr; Weiterbildung, Berater auch* in-house *attr*; **~ sein** to be an internal company matter ◼ ADV **~ geregelt** decided within the company; **Firmenkopf** M company letterhead; **Firmenkundengeschäft** NT (*von Bank*) business with corporate customers; **Firmenlogo** NT company logo; **Firmenname** M company name; **Firmenregister** NT register of companies; **Firmenschild** NT company plaque; **Firmenstempel** M company stamp; **Firmenverzeichnis** NT trade directory; **Firmenwagen** M company car; **Firmenwert** M (*Comm*) goodwill; **Firmenzeichen** NT trademark

firmieren [fɪr'miːrən], *ptp* **firmiert** VI **als** *or* **mit ... ~** (*Comm, fig*) to trade under the name of ...

Firmung F **-, -en** (*Rel*) confirmation; **jdm die ~ erteilen** to confirm sb

Firmware ['fɜːemwɛːɐ, 'fœrm-] F (*Comput*) firmware

Firn [fɪrn] M **-(e)s, -e** névé, firn

firnig ['fɪrnɪç] ADJ *Schnee* névé *attr*

Firnis ['fɪrnɪs] M **-ses, -se** (= *Ölfirnis*) oil; (= *Lackfirnis*) varnish

firnissen ['fɪrnɪsn] VT (*mit Ölfirnis*) to oil; (*mit Lackfirnis*) to varnish

First [fɪrst] M **-(e)s, -e** (= *Dachfirst*) (roof) ridge

Fis [fɪs] NT **-, -, fis** [fɪs] NT **-, -** (*Mus*) F sharp; **in ~** in F sharp major/minor

Fisch [fɪʃ] M **-(e)s, -e (a)** (*Zool, Cook*) fish; **~e/drei ~e fangen** to catch fish/three fish(es); **~ verarbeitend** fish-processing; **ein großer** *or* **dicker ~** (*fig inf*) a big fish; **ein kleiner ~** one of the small fry; **ein (kalter) ~ sein** (*fig*) to be a cold fish; **munter** *or* **gesund sein wie ein ~ im Wasser** to be in fine fettle; **sich wohl fühlen wie ein ~ im Wasser** to be in one's element; **stumm wie ein ~ sein** (= *sich zu einem Thema nicht äußern*) to keep stumm (*inf*); **er war den ganzen Abend stumm wie ein ~** he didn't open his mouth all night (*inf*); **weder ~ noch Fleisch** neither fish nor fowl; **die ~e füttern** (*hum*) to be sick; **der ~ stinkt vom Kopf her** the problems are at the top **(b)** (*Astrol*) Pisces; **die ~e** (*Astron*) Pisces *sing*, the Fish *sing*; **ein ~ sein** to be Pisces *or* a Piscean

Fisch- IN CPDS fish; **Fischadler** M osprey; **fischarm** ADJ *Gewässer* low in fish; **Fischarmut** F scarcity of fish; **Fischbecken** NT fishpond; **Fischbein** NT, NO PL whalebone; **Fischbestand** M fish population; **Fischbude** F *stand selling fish and various snacks*, ≈ fish and chip stand (*Brit*); **Fischbulette** F fish cake; **Fischdampfer** M trawler

fischen ['fɪʃn] VTI (*lit, fig*) to fish; **mit (dem) Netz ~** to trawl; **(auf) Heringe ~** to fish for herring

Fischer ['fɪʃɐ] M **-s, -, Fischerin** [-ərɪn] F **-, -nen** fisherman/-woman

Fischer-: Fischerboot NT fishing boat; **Fischerdorf** NT fishing village

Fischerei [fɪʃə'rai] F **-, -en (a)** (= *das Fangen*) fishing **(b)** (= *~gewerbe*) fishing industry

Fischerei- IN CPDS fishing; **Fischereigrenze** F fishing limit; **Fischereihafen** M fishing port

Fischerin F **-, -nen** fisherwoman

Fischernetz NT fishing net

Fischfang M, NO PL **vom ~ leben** to live by fishing; **zum ~ auslaufen** to set off for the fishing grounds

Fischfang-: Fischfangflotte F fishing fleet; **Fischfanggebiet** NT fishing grounds *pl*

Fisch-: Fischfarm F fish farm; **Fischfilet** NT fish fillet; **Fischfrikadelle** F fishcake; **Fischfutter** NT fish food; **Fischgeschäft** NT fishmonger's (shop) (*Brit*), fish shop (*Brit*) *or* dealer (*US*); **Fischgräte** F fish bone; **Fischgrätenmuster** NT herringbone (pattern); **Fischhalle** F fish market hall; **Fischhändler(in)** M(F) fishmonger (*Brit*), fish dealer (*US*); (= *Großhändler*) fish merchant; **Fischkutter** M fishing cutter; **Fischmarkt** M fish market; **Fischmehl** NT fish meal; **Fischotter** M otter; **fischreich** ADJ *Gewässer* rich in fish; **Fischreichtum** M wealth of fish; **Fischreiher** M grey heron; **Fischrogen** M (hard) roe; **Fischschwarm** M shoal of fish; **Fischstäbchen** NT fish finger (*Brit*), fish stick (*US*); **Fischsterben** NT death of fish; **Fischtran** M train oil; **Fischtrawler** [-trɔːlɐ] M **-s, -** trawler; **fischverarbeitend** ADJ ATTR *siehe* Fisch; **Fischverarbeitung** F fish processing; **Fischwirtschaft** F fishing industry; **Fischzucht** F fish-farming; (*inf: auch* **Fischzuchtanstalt**) fish farm

Fisimatenten [fizima'tɛntn] PL (*inf*) (= *Ausflüchte*) excuses *pl*; (= *Umstände*) fuss; (= *Albernheiten*) nonsense

fiskalisch [fɪs'kaːlɪʃ] ADJ fiscal

Fiskus ['fɪskus] M **-, -se** *or* **Fisken** ['fɪskn] (= *Staatsvermögen*) treasury, exchequer (*Brit*); (*fig* = *Staat*) Treasury

Fisolen [fi'zoːlən] PL (*Aus*) green beans *pl*

Fissur [fɪ'suːɐ] F **-, -en** (*Anat*) fissure; (*Med*) crack

Fistelstimme F **(a)** (*Mus*) falsetto **(b)** (= *hohes Sprechstimmchen*) falsetto (voice)

fit [fɪt] ADJ fit; **sich ~ halten/machen** to keep/get fit

Fitness F **-,** NO PL physical fitness

Fitness-: Fitnesscenter NT, **Fitnessstudio** NT fitness centre (*Brit*) *or* center (*US*); **Fitnesstraining** NT fitness training

fitten ['fɪtn] VT (*Tech*) to fit

Fittich ['fɪtɪç] M **-(e)s, -e jdn unter seine ~e nehmen** (*hum*) to take sb under one's wing (*fig*)

fix [fɪks] ◼ ADJ **(a)** (*inf*) (= *flink*) quick; (= *intelligent*) quick, bright, smart; **in etw** (*dat*) **~ sein** to be quick at sth **(b)** (*inf*) **~ und fertig sein** (= *nervös*) to be at the end of one's tether (*Brit*) *or* rope (*US*); (= *erschöpft*) to be done in (*inf*), to be all in (*inf*); (*emotional, seelisch*) to be shattered; **jdn ~ und fertig machen** (= *nervös machen*) to drive sb mad (*Brit*) *or* crazy (*esp US*); (= *erschöpfen*) to wear sb out; (*emotional, seelisch*) to shatter sb; (*in Prüfung, Wettbewerb, Kampf etc*) to give sb a thrashing (*inf*); (= *ruinieren*) to do for sb (*inf*) **(c)** (= *feststehend*) fixed; **~e Idee** obsession, idée fixe ◼ ADV (*inf*: = *schnell*) quickly; **mach ~!** be quick!; **das geht ganz ~** that won't take long at all; **geht das nicht ~er?** does it have to take so long?

fixen ['fɪksn] VI **(a)** (*inf*: = *Drogen spritzen*) to fix (*inf*), to shoot (up) (*inf*) **(b)** (*St Ex*) to bear

Fixerstube F (*inf*) junkies' centre (*Brit*) *or* center (*US*) (*inf*)

Fixgeschäft NT (*Comm*) transaction for delivery by a fixed date; (*St Ex*) time bargain

Fixierbad [fɪ'ksiːɐ-] NT fixer

fixieren [fɪ'ksiːrən], *ptp* **fixiert** VT **(a)** (= *anstarren*) **jdn/etw (mit seinem Blick/seinen Augen) ~** to fix one's gaze/eyes on sb/sth **(b)** (= *festlegen*) to specify, to define; *Gehälter, Termin etc* to set (*auf +acc* for); (= *schriftlich niederlegen*) to record; **er ist zu stark auf seine Mutter fixiert** (*Psych*) he has a mother fixation **(c)** (= *haltbar machen*) to fix

Fixierung F **-, -en** (*Festlegung*) specification; (*von Gehältern, Terminen*) setting; (= *schriftliche Niederlegung*) recording; (*Psych*) fixation

Fixing ['fɪksɪŋ] NT **-s,** NO PL (*Fin*) fixing

Fix-: Fixkosten PL fixed costs *pl*; **Fixpunkt** M fixed point; **Fixstern** M fixed star

Fjord [fjɔrt] M **-(e)s, -e** [-də] fiord

FKK [ɛfka'kaː] NO ART **- ABBR** *von* Freikörperkultur; **~-Anhänger(in) sein** to be a nudist *or* naturist

FKK-Strand [ɛfka'kaː-] M nudist beach

flach [flax] ◼ ADJ **(a)** (= *eben, platt, niedrig*) flat; *Gebäude* low; *Abhang* gentle; *Boot* flat-bottomed; **die ~e Hand** the flat of one's hand; **auf dem ~en Land** in the middle of the country **(b)** (= *untief*) shallow **(c)** (= *nichts sagend*) flat; *Geschmack* insipid; (= *oberflächlich*) shallow **2** ADV ~ **atmen** to take shallow breaths; **sich ~ hinlegen** to lie down; ~ **liegen** to lie flat

Flach-: Flachbau M, *pl* -**bauten** low building; **Flachbauweise** F low style of building; **Flachbildschirm** M (*TV*) flat screen; **flachbrüstig** [-brʏstɪç] ADJ flat-chested; **Flachdach** NT flat roof

Fläche ['flɛçə] F -, -**n** area; (= *Oberfläche*) surface; (*von Würfel*) face; (= *Gelände, Landfläche/Wasserfläche*) expanse (of ground/water)

Flächen-: Flächenbrand M extensive fire; **sich zu einem ~ ausweiten** (*fig*) to spread to epidemic proportions; **flächendeckend** **1** ADJ extensive; **die ~e Versorgung der Bevölkerung mit Gas** an extensive gas supply for the population **2** ADV extensively, over a wide area; **wir müssen ~ arbeiten** we need blanket coverage; **Flächeninhalt** M area; **Flächenland** NT state (*as opposed to city state*); **Flächenmaß** NT unit of square measure; **Flächennutzung** F land utilization; **Flächenstaat** M state (*as opposed to city state*)

Flachheit F -, -**en** (a) (= *Plattheit*) flatness; (*von Gebäude*) lowness; (*von Abhang*) gentleness (b) (= *mangelnder Tiefgang*) flatness; (*von Geschmack*) insipidity; (= *Oberflächlichkeit*) shallowness

Flach-: Flachkopfschraube F countersunk (*Brit*) *or* flat-head (*US*) screw; **Flachland** NT lowland; (= *Tiefland*) plains *pl*; **Flachlandtiroler(in)** M(F) (*inf*) would-be mountain dweller; **flachlegen** SEP **1** VT (*sl*) *Frau* to lay (*sl*) **2** VR (*inf*) to lie down; **Flachmann** M, *pl* -**männer** (*inf*) hip flask

Flachs [flaks] M -**es**, NO PL (a) (*Bot, Tex*) flax (b) (*inf*: = *Neckerei, Witzelei*) kidding (*inf*); (= *Bemerkung*) joke; ~ **machen** to kid around (*inf*); **das war nur ~** I/he *etc* was only kidding (*inf*); **jetzt mal ganz ohne ~** joking *or* kidding (*inf*) apart

flachsen ['flaksn] VI (*inf*) to kid around (*inf*); **mit jdm ~** to kid sb (on) (*inf*)

flachsfarben ['flaksfarbn] ADJ flaxen

Flachzange F flat-nosed pliers *pl*

flackern ['flakɐn] VI (*lit, fig*) to flicker

Fladen ['flaːdn] M -**s**, - (a) (*Cook*) round flat dough-cake (b) (*inf*: = *Kuhfladen*) cowpat (*Brit*), cow dung

Fladenbrot NT unleavened bread; **ein ~** an unleavened loaf

Flagge ['flagə] F -, -**n** flag; **die belgische ~ führen** to fly the Belgian flag; **unter deutscher ~ fahren** to sail under a German flag

Flaggschiff ['flak-] NT (*lit, fig*) flagship

Flair [flɛːɐ] NT *or* (*rare*) M -**s**, NO PL (*geh*) atmosphere; (= *Nimbus*) aura; (*esp Sw*: = *Gespür*) flair

Flak [flak] F -, -(**s**) ABBR *von* Flug(zeug)abwehrkanone (a) anti-aircraft *or* ack-ack gun (b) (= *Einheit*) anti-aircraft *or* ack-ack unit

Flakon [fla'kõː] NT *or* M -**s**, -**s** bottle, flacon

flambieren [flam'biːrən], *ptp* **flambiert** VT (*Cook*) to flambé

Flame ['flaːmə] M -**n**, -**n** Fleming, Flemish man/boy

Flamin ['flaːmɪn] F -, -**nen**, **Flämin** ['flɛːmɪn] F -, -**nen** Fleming, Flemish woman/girl

Flamingo [fla'mɪŋɡo] M -**s**, -**s** flamingo

flämisch ['flɛːmɪʃ] ADJ Flemish

Flamme ['flamə] F -, -**n** (*lit, fig*) flame; **in ~n aufgehen** to go up in flames; **in** (*hellen*) ~**n stehen** to be ablaze; **etw auf kleiner ~ kochen** (*lit*) to cook sth on a low flame; (*fig*) to let sth ride; **etw auf großer ~ kochen** to cook sth fast

Flammen-: Flammenmeer NT sea of flames; **Flammenwerfer** M flame-thrower

Flandern ['flandɐn] NT -**s** Flanders *sing*

flandrisch ['flandrɪʃ] ADJ Flemish

Flanell [fla'nɛl] M -**s**, -**e** flannel

flanellen [fla'nɛlən] ADJ ATTR flannel

flanieren [fla'niːrən], *ptp* **flaniert** VI to stroll, to saunter

Flanke ['flaŋkə] F -, -**n** (a) (*Anat, Mil, Chess*) flank; (*von Bus, Lastzug etc*) side (b) (*Sport*) (*Turnen*) flank-vault; (*Ftbl*) cross; (= *Spielfeldseite*) wing

flankieren [flaŋ'kiːrən], *ptp* **flankiert** VT (*Mil, Chess, fig*) to flank; (*fig*: = *ergänzen*) to accompany; ~**de Maßnahmen** supporting measures

Flansch [flanʃ] M -(**e**)**s**, -**e** flange

flapsig ['flapsɪç] ADJ (*inf*) *Benehmen* cheeky (*Brit*), fresh (*US*); *Bemerkung* offhand

Fläschchen ['flɛʃçən] NT -**s**, - bottle

Flasche ['flaʃə] F -, -**n** (a) bottle; **mit der ~ aufziehen** to bottle-feed; **das Kind bekommt die ~** (*momentan*) the child is having its bottle; (*generell*) the child is bottle-fed; **eine ~ Wein/Bier** *etc* a bottle of wine/beer *etc*; **aus der ~ trinken** to drink (straight) out of *or* from the bottle; **zur ~ greifen** (*fig*) to take to the bottle (b) (*inf*: = *Versager*) complete loser (*inf*)

Flaschen-: Flaschenbatterie F array of bottles; **Flaschenbier** NT bottled beer; **Flaschengärung** F fermentation in the bottle; **flaschengrün** ADJ bottle-green; **Flaschenhals** M neck of a bottle; (*fig*) bottleneck; **Flaschenkind** NT bottle-fed baby; **Flaschennahrung** F baby milk; **Flaschenöffner** M bottle opener; **Flaschenpfand** NT deposit on bottles; **Flaschenpost** F message in a/the bottle; **mit der ~** in a bottle; **Flaschentomate** F plum tomato; **Flaschenwein** M bottled wine; **flaschenweise** ADV by the bottle; **Flaschenzug** M block and tackle

Flash [flɛʃ] M -**s**, -**s** (*Film*) flash; (= *Rückblende*) flashback; (*inf*) flash (*inf*)

Flatter- ['flatɐ]: **flatterhaft** ADJ fickle; **sie ist ziemlich ~** she's a bit of a butterfly; **Flatterhaftigkeit** ['flatɐhaftɪçkait] F -, NO PL fickleness

flatterig ['flatərɪç] ADJ fluttery; *Puls* fluttering

flattern ['flatɐn] VI AUX HABEN *or* (*bei Richtungsangabe*) AUX SEIN (*lit, fig*) to flutter; (= *mit den Flügeln schlagen*) to flap its wings; (*Fahne, Segel beim Sturm, Hose*) to flap; (*Haar*) to stream; (*Blick*) to flicker; (*Lenkung, Autorad*) to wobble; **ein Brief flatterte mir auf den Schreibtisch** a letter turned up on my desk

Flattersatz M (*Typ*) unjustified print

flau [flau] ADJ (a) *Brise, Wind* slack (b) *Geschmack* insipid; *Stimmung* flat (c) (= *übel*) queasy; (*vor Hunger*) faint; **mir ist ~** (**im Magen**) I feel queasy (d) (*Comm*) *Markt, Börse, Konjunktur* slack

Flauheit F -, NO PL (a) (*von Stimmung*) flatness (b) (= *Übelkeit*) queasiness; (*vor Hunger*) faintness (c) (*Comm*: *von Markt, Börse, Konjunktur*) slackness

Flaum [flaum] M -(**e**)**s**, NO PL (a) (= ~*federn, Härchen, auf Obst*) down (b) (*dial*: = *Schweinebauchfett*) lard

flaumig ['flaumɪç] ADJ downy; *Pullover, Schneedecke* fleecy; (*Aus*: = *flockig*) light and creamy

Flausch [flauʃ] M -(**e**)**s**, -**e** fleece

flauschig ['flauʃɪç] ADJ fleecy; (= *weich*) soft

Flausen ['flauzn] PL (*inf*) (= *Unsinn*) nonsense; (= *Illusionen*) fancy ideas *pl* (*inf*)

Flaute ['flautə] F -, -**n** (a) (*Met*) calm; **das Schiff geriet in eine ~** the ship was becalmed (b) (*fig*) (*Comm*) lull, slack period; (*der Leistung*) period of slackness

fläzen ['flɛːtsn] VR (*inf*) to sprawl (*in +acc* in)

Flechte ['flɛçtə] F -, -**n** (*Bot, Med*) lichen

flechten ['flɛçtn], *pret* **flocht** [flɔxt], *ptp* **geflochten** [ɡə'flɔxtn] VT *Haar* to plait (*Brit*), to braid (*esp US*); *Kranz, Korb, Matte* to weave; *Seil* to make; *Stuhl* to cane; **sich/jdm das Haar zu Zöpfen** *or* **in Zöpfe ~** to plait (*Brit*) *or* braid (*esp US*) one's/sb's hair

Fleck [flɛk] M -(**e**)**s**, -**e** *or* -**en** (a) (= *Schmutzfleck*) stain; **dieses Zeug macht ~en** this stuff stains (*in/auf etw acc*) sth); **einen ~ auf der** (**weißen**) **Weste haben** (*fig*) to have blotted one's copybook (b) (= *Farbfleck*) splotch; (*auf Arm etc*) blotch; (*auf Obst*) blemish; **ein grüner/gelber ~** a green/yellow *etc* patch; **weißer ~** white patch; (*auf Stirn von Pferd*) star, blaze; (*auf Landkarte*) blank area (c) (= *Stelle*) spot, place; **auf demselben ~** in the same place; **sich nicht vom ~ rühren** not to move *or* budge (*inf*); **nicht vom ~ kommen** not to get any further; **vom ~ weg** right away

Fleckchen ['flɛkçən] NT -**s**, - **ein schönes ~** (**Erde**) a lovely little spot

fleckenlos ADJ (*lit, fig*) spotless

Fleckentferner [-lɛntfɛrnɐ] M -**s**, -, **Fleckentfernungsmittel** NT stain-remover

Fleckerlteppich ['flɛkɐl-] M (*S Ger Aus*) rag rug

fleckig ['flɛkɪç] ADJ marked; *Obst* blemished; *Tierfell* speckled; *Gesichtshaut* blotchy

fleddern ['flɛdɐn] VT *Leichen* to rob

Fledermaus ['fleːdɐ-] F bat

Fleet [fleːt] NT -(e)s, -e (*N Ger*) canal

Flegel ['fleːgl] M -s, - (a) (= *Lümmel*) lout, yob (*Brit inf*); (= *Kind*) brat (*inf*) (b) (= *Dreschflegel*) flail

Flegelalter NT awkward adolescent phase

Flegel-: flegelhaft ▨ ADJ uncouth ▨ ADV *sich benehmen* uncouthly; **Flegelhaftigkeit** ['fleːglhaftɪçkait] F -, -en uncouthness; **Flegeljahre** PL awkward adolescent phase

flegeln ['fleːgln] VR to loll, to sprawl

flehen ['fleːən] VI (*geh*) to plead (*um* for, *zu* with)

flehentlich ['fleːəntlɪç] ▨ ADJ imploring, pleading; **eine ~e Bitte** an earnest plea ▨ ADV imploringly, pleadingly; **jdn ~ bitten** to plead with sb; **jdn ~ bitten, etw zu tun** to implore sb to do sth

Fleisch [flaiʃ] NT -(e)s, NO PL (a) (= *Gewebe, Muskelfleisch*) flesh; **nacktes ~** (*lit, fig hum*) bare flesh; **vom ~ fallen** to lose (a lot of) weight; **sich** (*dat or acc*) **ins eigene ~ schneiden** to cut off one's nose to spite one's face; **sein eigen ~ und Blut** (*geh*) his own flesh and blood; **jdm in ~ und Blut übergehen** to become second nature to sb (b) (= *Nahrungsmittel*) meat; (= *Fruchtfleisch*) flesh; **~fressende Pflanzen** carnivorous plants, carnivores; **~fressende Tiere** carnivores, carnivorous animals; **~verarbeitend** meat-processing

Fleisch- IN CPDS (*Cook*) meat; (*Anat*) flesh; **fleischarm** ADJ containing little meat; **~ sein** to contain little meat; **Fleischbeschau** F (a) meat inspection (b) (*hum inf*) cattle market (*inf*); **Fleischbrühe** F (= *Gericht*) bouillon; (= *Fond*) meat stock; **Fleischbrühwürfel** M (meat) stock cube

Fleischer ['flaiʃɐ] M -s, -, **Fleischerin** [-ərɪn] F -, -nen butcher; (*pej inf* = *Chirurg*) sawbones *sing* (*inf*)

Fleischerbeil NT meat cleaver

Fleischerei [flaiʃə'rai] F -, -en butcher's (shop) (*Brit*), butcher (shop) (*US*)

Fleischerin F *siehe* Fleischer

Fleisch-: Fleischesser(in) M(F) meat-eater; **Fleischextrakt** M beef extract; **fleischfarben** [-farbn], **fleischfarbig** ADJ flesh-coloured (*Brit*), flesh-colored (*US*); **Fleischfliege** F flesh-fly; **fleischfressend** ADJ *siehe* Fleisch; **Fleischhauer(in)** M(F) (*Aus*) butcher

fleischig ['flaiʃɪç] ADJ fleshy

Fleisch-: Fleischkäse M meat loaf; **Fleischkloß** M (a) meatball (b) (*pej inf*) mountain of flesh

fleischlich ['flaiʃlɪç] ADJ ATTR *Speisen, Kost* meat

Fleisch-: fleischlos ▨ ADJ (= *ohne Fleisch*) meatless; *Kost, Ernährung* vegetarian ▨ ADV **~ essen** to eat no meat; **~ kochen** to cook without meat; **Fleischsalat** M diced meat salad with mayonnaise; **Fleischspieß** M (*Cook*) meat skewer; **Fleischtomate** F beef tomato; **fleischverarbeitend** ADJ ATTR *siehe* Fleisch; **Fleischvergiftung** F food poisoning (*from meat*); **Fleischwolf** M mincer (*Brit*), meat grinder (*esp US*); **jdn durch den ~ drehen** to put sb through the mill; **Fleischwunde** F flesh wound; **Fleischwurst** F pork sausage

Fleiß [flais] M -(e)s, NO PL diligence; (= *eifriges Tätigsein*) industry; (= *Beharrlichkeit*) application; (*als Charaktereigenschaft*) industriousness; **mit ~ kann es jeder zu etwas bringen** anybody can succeed if they work hard; **er hat die Prüfung ausschließlich durch ~ geschafft** he passed the exam by sheer hard work; **mit ~** *bei der Sache sein* to work hard; **mit ~** (*S Ger*), **zu ~** (*N Ger*) (= *absichtlich*) deliberately, on purpose; **ohne ~ kein Preis** (*Prov*) no pain, no gain

fleißig ['flaisɪç] ▨ ADJ (a) (= *arbeitsam*) hard-working *no adv*, industrious; **~e Hände** busy hands; **Fleißiges Lieschen** (*Bot*) busy Lizzie (b) (= *Fleiß zeigend*) diligent, painstaking (c) (*inf*: = *unverdrossen*) keen ▨ ADV (a) (= *arbeitsam*) industriously, diligently; **~ studieren/arbeiten** to study/work hard (b) (*inf*: = *unverdrossen*) **trinken** quite a bit; *trainieren, Diät halten* like a good boy/girl

flektierbar ADJ (in)flectional (*form*); *Verb* conjugable; *Substantiv, Adjektiv* declinable

flektieren [flɛk'tiːrən], *ptp* **flektiert** VT to inflect (*form*); *Substantiv, Adjektiv* to decline; *Verb* to conjugate

flennen ['flɛnən] VI (*pej inf*) to blub(ber) (*inf*)

fletschen ['flɛtʃn] VT **die Zähne ~** to bare one's teeth

Fleurop® ['flɔyrɔp, 'floːrɔp, flɔy'roːp, fløˈroːp] F - Interflora®

flexibel [flɛ'ksiːbl] ▨ ADJ (*lit, fig*) flexible; *Holz, Kunststoff auch* pliable ▨ ADV flexibly

Flexibilisierung [flɛksibiliˈziːruŋ] F -, -en **~ der Arbeitszeit** transition to flexible working hours

Flexibilität [flɛksibiliˈtɛːt] F -, NO PL (*lit, fig*) flexibility

Flexion [flɛ'ksioːn] F -, -en (*Gram*) inflection

flicht [flɪçt] 3. PERS SING PRES *von* flechten

flicken ['flɪkn] VT to mend; (*mit Flicken*) to patch

Flicken ['flɪkn] M -s, - patch

Flickenteppich M rag rug

Flick-: Flickflack ['flɪkflak] M -s, -s (*Sport*) backflip; **Flickwäsche** F mending; **Flickwerk** NT **die Reform war reinstes ~** the reform had been carried out piecemeal; **Flickzeug** NT, *pl* **-zeuge** (*Sew*) sewing kit; (*für Reifen*) (puncture) repair kit

Flieder ['fliːdɐ] M -s, - lilac

fliederfarben [-farbn], **fliederfarbig** ADJ lilac

Fliege ['fliːgə] F -, -n (a) fly; **sie starben wie die ~n** they fell like flies; **er tut keiner ~ etwas zuleide** or **zu Leide** (*fig*), **er würde keiner ~ ein Bein ausreißen** (*fig*) he wouldn't hurt a fly; **zwei ~n mit einer Klappe schlagen** (*prov*) to kill two birds with one stone (*prov*); **die** or **'ne ~ machen** (*sl*) to beat it (*inf*) (b) (= *Schlips*) bow tie

fliegen ['fliːgn], *pret* **flog** [floːk], *ptp* **geflogen** [gə'floːgn] ▨ VI AUX SEIN (a) (*durch die Luft, mit Flugzeug*) to fly; (*Raumschiff, Raumfahrer*) to go, to travel (*form*) (b) (= *eilen*) to fly; **jdm/einander in die Arme ~** to fly into sb's/each other's arms; **jdm an den Hals ~** to hurl oneself at sb; **die Zeit fliegt** time flies; **auf jdn/etw ~** (*inf*) to be crazy about sb/sth (*inf*) (c) (*inf*: = *fallen*) to fall; **von der Leiter ~** to fall off the ladder; **durchs Examen ~** to fail or flunk (*inf*) one's exam (d) (*inf*: = *hinausgeworfen werden*) to be kicked out (*inf*) (*aus, von* of); **aus der Firma ~** to get the sack (*inf*); **von der Schule ~** to be chucked out of school (*inf*) (e) (= *geworfen werden*) to be thrown; **geflogen kommen** to come flying; **in den Papierkorb ~** to go into the wastepaper basket; **die Tür flog ins Schloss** the door flew shut; **ein Schuh flog ihm an den Kopf** he had a shoe flung at him; **aus der Kurve ~** to skid off the bend ▨ VT to fly ▨ VR **in dieser Maschine/nachts fliegt es sich angenehm** flying in this plane/at night is pleasant; **das Flugzeug fliegt sich leicht/schwer** this plane is easy/difficult to fly

fliegend ADJ ATTR *Fische, Untertasse, Start* flying; *Personal* flight; **~er Händler** travelling (*Brit*) or traveling (*US*) hawker; (*mit Lieferwagen*) mobile trader; **~er Teppich** flying carpet; **~e Hitze** hot flushes *pl* (*Brit*) or flashes *pl* (*US*)

Fliegen-: Fliegendreck M fly droppings *pl*; **Fliegenfänger** M (= *Klebestreifen*) flypaper; **Fliegenfenster** NT wire-mesh window; **Fliegengewicht** NT (*Sport, fig*) flyweight; **Fliegengitter** NT fly screen; **Fliegenklatsche** [-klatʃə] F -, -n fly swat; **Fliegenpilz** M fly agaric; **Fliegenrute** F fly rod

Flieger ['fliːgɐ] M -s, - (a) (= *Pilot*) airman; (*Mil: Rang*) aircraftman (*Brit*), airman basic (*US*) (b) (*inf*: = *Flugzeug*) plane (c) (= *Vogel*) flier

Flieger-: (Mil): Fliegerabwehr F air defence (*Brit*) or defense (*US*); **Fliegeralarm** M air-raid warning; **Fliegerangriff** M air raid

Fliegerei [fliːgəˈrai] F -, NO PL flying

Fliegerin ['fliːgərɪn] F -, -nen (= *Pilotin*) airwoman

fliegerisch ['fliːgərɪʃ] ADJ ATTR aeronautical

Fliegerjacke F bomber jacket

fliehen ['fliːən], *pret* **floh** [floː], *ptp* **geflohen** [gə'floːən] VI AUX SEIN to flee (*vor* +*dat* from); (= *entkommen*) to escape (*aus* from); **vor jdm/dem Krieg/der Polizei/einem Gewitter ~** to flee from sb/war/the police/before a storm; **aus dem Lande ~** to flee the country

fliehend ADJ *Kinn* receding; *Stirn* sloping

Fliehende(r) ['fliːəndə] MF DECL AS ADJ fugitive

Fliese ['fliːzə] F -, -n tile; **~n legen** to lay tiles; **etw mit ~n auslegen** to tile sth

fliesen ['fliːzn] VT to tile

Fließ-: Fließband NT, *pl* **-bänder** conveyor belt; (*als Einrichtung*) assembly or production line; **am ~ arbeiten** or **stehen** (*inf*) to work on the assembly or production line; **Fließbandfertigung** F belt production

fließen ['fliːsn], *pret* **floss** [flɔs], *ptp* **geflossen** [gə'flɔsn] VI AUX SEIN to flow; (*Fluss auch, Tränen*) to run; **es ist genug Blut geflossen** enough blood has been shed; **die Steuergelder**

flossen in dunkle Kanäle the taxes were diverted along rather dubious channels; **die Mittel für Jugendarbeit ~ immer spärlicher** less and less money is being made available for youth work; **Nachrichten ~ spärlich** the flow of news is minimal

fließend █1█ ADJ flowing; *Leitungswasser, Gewässer* running; *Verkehr* moving; *Rede, Vortrag, Sprache* fluent; *Grenze, Übergang* fluid **█2█** ADV *sprechen* fluently; **~ warm und kalt Wasser** running hot and cold water

Fließ-: Fließheck NT fastback; **Fließkomma** NT (*auch Comput*) floating point

Flimmer- ['flɪmə]: **flimmerfrei** ADJ (*Opt, Phot*) flicker-free; **Flimmerhärchen** NT cilium

flimmern ['flɪmən] VI to shimmer; (*Film, TV*) to flicker; **es flimmert mir vor den Augen** everything is swimming before my eyes

flink [flɪŋk] **█1█** ADJ (= *geschickt*) nimble; (= *schnell*) quick; *Mundwerk, Zunge* quick, ready **█2█** ADV *arbeiten, sich bewegen* quickly; *springen* nimbly; **ein bisschen ~!** (*inf*) get a move on! (*inf*); **mit etw ~ bei der Hand sein** to be quick (off the mark) with sth

Flinkheit F -, NO PL (= *Geschicktheit*) nimbleness; (= *Schnelligkeit*) quickness

Flinte ['flɪntə] F -, -n (= *Schrotflinte*) shotgun; **die ~ ins Korn werfen** (*fig*) to throw in the towel

Flipchart ['flɪptʃaːɐt] F flip chart

Flipper ['flɪpɐ] M -s, -, **Flipperautomat** M pinball machine

flippern ['flɪpɐn] **█1█** VT to flip **█2█** VI to play pinball

flippig ['flɪpɪç] (*inf*) **█1█** ADJ way-out (*inf*); **er ist ein ~er Typ** he's way-out (*inf*) **█2█** ADV way-out (*inf*)

flirren ['flɪrən] VI to whirr; (*Luft, Hitze*) to shimmer

Flirt [flɪrt, fløːɐt, flœrt] M -s, -s (= *Flirten*) flirtation

flirten ['flɪrtn, 'fløːɐtn, 'flœrtn] VI to flirt

Flitscherl ['flɪtʃɐl] NT -s, -(n) (*Aus pej inf*) slut

Flittchen ['flɪtçən] NT -s, - (*pej inf*) slut

Flitterwochen ['flɪtɐ-] PL honeymoon *sing*; **in die ~ fahren/in den ~ sein** to go/be on one's honeymoon

Flitzbogen ['flɪts-] M, **Flitzebogen** ['flɪtsə-] M bow and arrow; **ich bin gespannt wie ein ~** (*inf*) the suspense is killing me (*inf*); **gespannt wie ein ~ sein, ob ...** (*inf*) to be on tenterhooks waiting to see whether ...

Flitze ['flɪtsə] F **die ~ machen** (*sl: = verschwinden*) to bolt (*sl*)

flitzen ['flɪtsn] VI AUX SEIN (*inf*) (a) (= *sich schnell bewegen*) to dash (b) (= *nackt rennen*) to streak; (*das*) **Flitzen** streaking

floaten ['floːtn] VTI (*Fin*) to float; **~ (lassen)** to float

Floating ['floːtɪŋ] NT -s, -s (*Fin*) floating

flocht PRET *von* **flechten**

Flocke ['flɔkə] F -, -n flake; (= *Schaumflocke*) blob (of foam); (= *Staubflocke*) ball (of fluff)

flockig ['flɔkɪç] ADJ (*lit*) fluffy; (*fig*) lively

flog PRET *von* **fliegen**

floh PRET *von* **fliehen**

Floh [floː] M -(e)s, -̈e ['fløːə] (*Zool*) flea; **es ist leichter, einen Sack Flöhe zu hüten, als ...** I'd as soon jump in the lake as ...; **jdm einen ~ ins Ohr setzen** (*inf*) to put an idea in sb's head; **die Flöhe husten hören** (*inf*) to imagine things

Floh-: Flohhalsband NT flea collar; **Flohhüpfen** NT -s, NO PL tiddl(e)ywinks *sing, no art*; **Flohmarkt** M flea market; **Flohzirkus** M flea circus

Flop [flɔp] M -s, -s flop (*inf*)

Flora ['floːra] F -, **Floren** ['floːrən] flora

Florenz [floˈrents] NT -' *or* -ens Florence

Florett [floˈrɛt] NT -(e)s, -e (a) (= *Waffe*) foil; **~ fechten** to fence with a foil (b) (*auch* **Florettfechten**) foil-fencing

florieren [floˈriːrən], *ptp* **floriert** VI to flourish

Florist [floˈrɪst] M -en, -en, **Floristin** [-ˈrɪstɪn] F -, -nen florist

Floskel ['flɔskl] F -, -n set phrase; **eine höfliche/abgedroschene ~** a polite but meaningless/clichéd phrase

floskelhaft ADJ *Stil, Rede, Brief* cliché-ridden; *Phrasen, Ausdrucksweise* stereotyped

floss PRET *von* **fließen**

Floß [floːs] NT -es, -̈e ['fløːsə] raft

Flosse ['flɔsə] F -, -n (a) (*Zool* = *Fischflosse*) fin; (= *Walflosse, Robbenflosse*) flipper (b) (*Aviat, Naut*: = *Leitwerk*) fin (c) (= *Taucherflosse*) flipper

flößen ['fløːsn] VTI to raft

Flöte ['fløːtə] F -, -n (a) pipe; (= *Querflöte, Orgelflöte*) (*in Zusammensetzungen*) flute; (= *Blockflöte*) recorder; (= *Pikkoloflöte*) piccolo; (*des Pan*) pipes *pl*; (*dial*: = *Pfeife, Kesselflöte*) whistle; **die ~ or ~ spielen** *or* **blasen** to play the pipe *etc* (b) (= *Kelchglas*) flute glass

flöten ['fløːtn] **█1█** VT (*Mus*) to play on the flute; (*auf Blockflöte*) to play on the recorder **█2█** VI (*Mus*) to play the flute; (= *Blockflöte spielen*) to play the recorder **█3█** VTI (*Vogel, fig inf*) to warble

Flöten-: flöten gehen VI AUX SEIN (*inf*) to go to the dogs (*inf*); **Flötenkessel** M whistling kettle; **Flötenspieler(in)** M(F) piper; (*von Querflöte*) flautist; (*von Blockflöte*) recorder player; (*von Pikkoloflöte*) piccolo player; **Flötenton** M, *pl* **-töne** (a) (*lit*) sound of flutes/a flute (b) (*inf*) **jdm die Flötentöne beibringen** to teach sb what's what (*inf*)

Flötist [fløˈtɪst] M -en, -en, **Flötistin** [-ˈtɪstɪn] F -, -nen = **Flötenspieler(in)**

flott [flɔt] **█1█** ADJ (a) (= *zügig*) *Fahrt* quick; *Tempo, Geschäft* brisk; *Arbeiter, Bedienung* speedy (*inf*); *Tänzer* good; (= *flüssig*) *Stil, Artikel* racy (*inf*); (= *schwungvoll*) *Musik* lively; **den ~en Otto** *or* **Heinrich haben** (*hum inf*) to have the runs (*inf*) (b) (= *schick*) smart (c) PRED **~/wieder ~ werden** (*Schiff*) to be floated off/refloated; (*fig inf*: *Unternehmen*) to be/get back on its feet; **wieder ~ sein** (*Schiff*) to be afloat again; (*Mensch: finanziell*) to be in funds again; (*Unternehmen*) to be back on its feet **█2█** ADV (a) (= *zügig*) quickly, speedily; **ich komme ~ voran mit meiner Arbeit** I'm making speedy progress with my work; **aber ein bisschen ~!** and look lively! (b) (= *schick*) stylishly; **~ aussehen** to look stylish

Flotte ['flɔtə] F -, -n (*Naut, Aviat*) fleet

Flotten-: Flottenstützpunkt M naval base; **Flottenverband** M naval unit

Flöz [fløːts] NT -es, -e (*Min*) seam

Fluch [fluːx] M -(e)s, -̈e ['flyːçə] curse; **auf diesem Haus** there is a curse on this house; **das (eben) ist der ~ der bösen Tat** (*prov*) evil begets evil (*prov*)

fluchen ['fluːxn] VI to curse (and swear); **auf** *or* **über jdn/etw ~** to curse sb/sth

Flucht [flʊxt] F -, -en (a) (= *Fliehen*) flight (*vor* +*dat* from); (*geglückt*) escape, flight; **die ~ ergreifen** to take flight; (*erfolgreich auch*) to (make one's) escape; **auf der ~ sein** to be fleeing; (*Gesetzesbrecher*) to be on the run; **jdm zur ~ verhelfen** to help sb to escape; **auf der ~ erschossen werden** to be shot while attempting to escape; **die ~ nach vorn antreten** to take the bull by the horns; **die ~ in die Anonymität/die Krankheit antreten** to take refuge in anonymity/illness (b) (= *Häuserflucht*) row; (= *~linie*) alignment

Flucht-: fluchtartig █1█ ADJ hasty, hurried **█2█** ADV hastily, hurriedly; **Fluchtauto** NT escape car; (*von Gesetzesbrecher*) getaway car; **Fluchtburg** F refuge

flüchten ['flʏçtn] **█1█** VI (a) AUX SEIN (= *davonlaufen*) to flee (*vor* +*dat* from); (*erfolgreich*) to escape, to flee; **aus dem Land/Südafrika ~** to flee the country/from South Africa; **vor der Wirklichkeit ~** to escape reality; **sich in (den) Alkohol ~** to take refuge in alcohol; **sich in Ausreden ~** to resort to excuses (b) AUCH VR (*vi: aux sein*) (= *Schutz suchen*) to take refuge

Flucht-: Fluchtfahrzeug NT escape vehicle; (*von Gesetzesbrecher*) getaway vehicle; **Fluchtgefahr** F risk of escape, risk of an escape attempt; **Fluchtgeld** NT flight capital; **Fluchthelfer(in)** M(F) escape helper

flüchtig ['flʏçtɪç] **█1█** ADJ (a) (= *geflüchtet*) fugitive; **~ sein** to be still at large; **ein ~er Verbrecher** a criminal who hasn't been caught (b) (= *kurz*) fleeting, brief; *Gruß* brief (c) (= *oberflächlich*) cursory, sketchy **█2█** ADV (a) (= *kurz*) fleetingly, briefly; **~ erwähnen** to mention in passing (b) (= *oberflächlich*) cursorily, superficially; **etw ~ lesen** to skim through sth; **~ arbeiten** to work hurriedly; **jdn ~ kennen** to have met sb briefly

Flüchtigkeit F -, -en (a) (= Kürze) briefness, brevity (b) (= Oberflächlichkeit) sketchiness (c) (= Vergänglichkeit) fleeting nature

Flüchtigkeitsfehler M careless mistake

Fluchtkapital NT flight capital

Flüchtling ['flʏçtlɪŋ] M -s, -e refugee

Flüchtlings- IN CPDS refugee; **Flüchtlingshilfe** F aid to refugees; (inf: = Flüchtlingsorganisation) (refugee) relief agency; **Flüchtlingslager** NT refugee camp

Flug [fluːk] M -(e)s, -̈e ['flyːgə] (alle Bedeutungen) flight; (= Skiflug) jump; **im ~(e)** in the air; **einen ~ stornieren** to cancel a booking; **der ~ zum Mond** (= Fliegen) travel to the moon; (= spezifische Fahrt) the moon flight; **wie im ~(e)** (fig) in a flash

Flugabwehr F air defence (Brit) or defense (US)

Flugabwehr-: Flugabwehrkanone F anti-aircraft gun; **Flugabwehrrakete** F anti-aircraft missile

Flug-: Flugangel F fly rod; **Flugangst** F fear of flying; **Flugasche** F flying ashes pl; **Flugbegleiter(in)** M(F) flight attendant; **flugbereit** ADJ ready for takeoff; **Flugblatt** NT leaflet; (= Werbung auch) handbill; **Flugdatenschreiber** M flight recorder; **Flugdauer** F flying time; **Flugdrachen** M hang-glider

Flügel ['flyːgl] M -s, - (a) (Anat, Aviat) wing; **einem Vogel/jdm die ~ stutzen** or **beschneiden** to clip a bird's/sb's wings (b) (von Hubschrauber, Ventilator) blade; (= Windmühlenflügel) sail, vane (c) (= Altarflügel, Gebäudeflügel) wing; (= Fensterflügel) casement (form), side; (= Türflügel) door (of double doors), leaf (form); (= Lungenflügel) lung; (= Nasenflügel) nostril (d) (Pol, Mil, Sport) wing (e) (= Konzertflügel) grand piano, grand (inf); **auf dem ~ spielen** to play the piano; **am ~:** ... **at** or **on the piano:** ...

Flügel-: Flügelärmel M hanging sleeve; **flügelförmig** ADJ wing-shaped; **Flügelhorn** NT (Mus) flugelhorn; **Flügelkampf** M (Pol) factional dispute; **flügellahm** ADJ with injured wings/an injured wing; (fig) Industrie etc ailing; Mensch feeble; **~ sein** (lit) to have an injured wing/its wings injured; (fig: = mutlos) to be dejected or despondent; **einen Vogel ~ schießen** to wing a bird; **Flügelmutter** F, pl **-muttern** wing or butterfly nut; **Flügelschraube** F wing bolt; (= Flügelmutter) wing or butterfly nut; **Flügelspanne** F, **Flügelspannweite** F wing span; **Flügelstürmer** M (Sport) wing forward; **Flügeltür** F leaved door (form); (mit zwei Flügeln) double door; (= Verandatür) French window (Brit), French door (US)

Fluggast M (airline) passenger

Fluggast-: Fluggastkontrolle F airport security check; **Fluggastraum** M passenger cabin

flügge ['flʏgə] ADJ fully-fledged; (fig) Jugendlicher independent; **~ werden** (lit) to be able to fly; (fig) to leave the nest

Flug-: Fluggepäck NT baggage; **erlaubtes ~ 15 Kilo** baggage allowance 15 kilos; **Fluggesellschaft** F airline (company)

Flughafen M airport; (Mil) aerodrome (Brit), airdrome (US); **auf dem ~** at the airport

Flughafen-: Flughafenbus M airport bus; **Flughafengebühr** F airport charges pl; **Flughafengelände** NT airport grounds pl; **Flughafensteuer** F airport tax

Flug-: Flughöhe F flying height (auch Orn); (Aviat) altitude; **unsere** or **die ~ beträgt 10.000 Meter** we are flying at an altitude of 10,000 metres (Brit) or meters (US); **die ~ erreichen** to reach one's cruising altitude or flying height; **Flugkanzel** F cockpit; **Flugkapitän(in)** M(F) captain (of an/the aircraft); **Flugkilometer** M (air) kilometre (Brit) or kilometer (US); **Flugkörper** M flying object; **Fluglärm** M aircraft noise; **Fluglehrer(in)** M(F) flying instructor; **Fluglinie** F (a) (= Strecke) airway, air route (b) (= Fluggesellschaft) airline (company); **Fluglotse** M, **Fluglotsin** F air-traffic or flight controller; **Flugnummer** F flight number; **Flugobjekt** NT **ein unbekanntes ~** an unidentified flying object; **Flugpersonal** NT flight personnel pl; **Flugplan** M flight schedule; **Flugplatz** M airfield; (größer) airport; **Flugpreis** M air fare; **Flugrettungsdienst** M air rescue service; **Flugrichtung** F direction of flight; **die ~ ändern** to change one's flight course; **Flugroute** F air route

flugs [fluks] ADV without delay, speedily

Flug-: Flugsand M drifting sand; **Flugschanze** F (Sport) ski jump; **Flugschau** F air or flying display; **Flugschein** M

(a) pilot's licence (Brit) or license (US) (b) (= Flugticket) plane or air ticket; **Flugschneise** F flight path; **Flugschreiber** M flight recorder; **Flugschrift** F pamphlet; **Flugschüler(in)** M(F) trainee pilot; **Flugsicherheit** F air safety; **Flugsicherung** F air traffic control; **Flugsimulator** M flight simulator; **Flugsport** M flying, aviation; **Flugsteig** [-ʃtaik] M -(e)s, -e [-gə] gate; **Flugstunde** F (a) flying hour; **zehn ~n entfernt** ten hours away by air (b) (= Unterricht) flying lesson; **flugtauglich** ADJ Pilot fit to fly; Flugzeug airworthy; **Flugticket** NT plane ticket; **flugtüchtig** ADJ airworthy; **flugunfähig** ADJ unable to fly; Flugzeug (= nicht in Ordnung) not airworthy; **fluguntauglich** ADJ Pilot unfit to fly; Flugzeug not airworthy; **Flugunterbrechung** F stop; (mit Übernachtung auch) stopover; **fluguntüchtig** ADJ not airworthy; **Flugverbindung** F air connection; **es gibt auch eine ~** there are flights there too; **Flugverbot** NT flying ban; **nachts besteht ~ auf dem Flughafen** the airport is closed to air traffic at night; **ein ~ erlassen** to ground; (über bestimmten Gebieten) to ban from flying; **Flugverkehr** M air traffic; **Flugzeit** F flying time; **Flugzettel** M (Aus) leaflet; (= Werbung auch) handbill

Flugzeug NT, pl **-zeuge** aircraft, (aero)plane (Brit), (air)plane (US); (= Düsenflugzeug auch) jet; (= Segelflugzeug) glider; **im** or **mit dem** or **per ~** by air or plane; **ein ~ der Lufthansa** a Lufthansa plane/jet

Flugzeug- IN CPDS aircraft; **Flugzeugabsturz** M plane crash; **Flugzeugabwehr** F (Mil) air defence (Brit) or defense (US); **Flugzeugbau** M, NO PL aircraft construction no art; **Flugzeugbesatzung** F air crew, plane crew; **Flugzeugentführer(in)** M(F) (aircraft) hijacker, skyjacker; **Flugzeugentführung** F (aircraft) hijacking, skyjacking; **Flugzeughalle** F (aircraft) hangar; **Flugzeughypothek** F aircraft mortgage; **Flugzeugmodell** NT model plane; **Flugzeugpark** M fleet of aircraft; **Flugzeugrumpf** M fuselage; **Flugzeugträger** M aircraft carrier; **Flugzeugtyp** M model of aircraft; **Flugzeugunglück** NT plane crash

Flugziel NT destination

Fluktuation [fluktuaˈtsioːn] F -, -en fluctuation (+gen in)

fluktuieren [flukˈtuiːrən], ptp **fluktuiert** VI to fluctuate

Flunder ['flʊndɐ] F -, -n flounder

Flunkerei [flʊŋkəˈrai] F -, -en (inf) (a) NO PL (= Flunkern) storytelling (b) (= kleine Lüge) story

flunkern ['flʊŋkɐn] (inf) **1** VI to tell stories **2** VT to make up

Flunsch [flʊnʃ] M or F -(e)s, -e (inf) pout; **eine(n) ~ ziehen** or **machen** to pout

Fluor ['fluːoːɐ] NT -s, NO PL (abbr F) fluorine; (= ~verbindung) fluoride

Fluorchlorkohlenwasserstoff M chlorofluorocarbon

fluoreszieren [fluoresˈtsiːrən], ptp **fluoresziert** VI to be luminous

Fluorid [fluoˈriːt] NT -(e)s, -e [-də] (Chem) fluoride

Fluorit [fluoˈriːt] M -s, -e fluorspar, fluorite (US)

Fluorkohlenwasserstoff M fluorocarbon

Flur [fluːɐ] M -(e)s, -e corridor; (= Hausflur) hall

Vorsicht! **Flur** *wird nicht mit dem englischen Wort* **floor** *übersetzt.*

Flur-: Flurbereinigung F reparcelling of the agricultural land of a community; **Flurschaden** M damage to an agricultural area; (fig) damage

Fluse ['fluːzə] F -, -n bit of fluff; (= Wollfluse) bobble

Fluss [flʊs] M -es, -̈e ['flʏsə] (a) (= Gewässer) river; **am ~** by the river; Stadt on the river; **unten am ~** down by the river(side); **den ~ aufwärts/abwärts fahren** to go upstream or upriver/ downstream or downriver (b) (= kontinuierlicher Verlauf) flow; **etw kommt** or **gerät in ~** sth gets underway; (= sich verändern) sth moves into a state of flux; **im ~ sein** (= sich verändern) to be in a state of flux; (= im Gange sein) to be in progress

Fluss- IN CPDS river; **Flussaal** M common eel; **flussab(wärts)** [flʊsˈlap(vɛrts)] ADV downstream, downriver; **Flussarm** M arm of a/the river; **flussaufwärts** [flʊsˈlaufvɛrts] ADV upstream, upriver; **Flussbett** NT riverbed

Flüsschen ['flʏsçən] NT -s, - little river

Flussdiagramm NT flow chart or diagram

flüssig ['flʏsɪç] **1** ADJ **(a)** (= *nicht fest*) liquid; *Honig, Lack* runny; (= *geschmolzen*) *Glas, Metall* molten; *Butter* melted; **~ machen** to liquefy; *Glas, Metall, Wachs, Fett* to melt
(b) (= *fließend*) *Stil, Spiel* fluid; **den Verkehr ~ halten** to keep the traffic flowing
(c) (= *verfügbar*) *Geld* available; **~es Vermögen** liquid assets *pl*; **ich bin im Moment nicht ~** (*inf*) I'm out of funds at the moment; **wenn ich wieder ~ bin** when I'm in funds again
2 ADV **(a)** **~ ernährt werden** to be fed on liquids
(b) (= *fließend*) fluently; **~ lesen/schreiben/sprechen** to read/write/talk fluently
Flüssiggas NT liquid gas
Flüssigkeit F **-, -en (a)** (= *flüssiger Stoff*) liquid **(b)** NO PL (*von Metall, Glas, Wachs etc*) liquidity; (*von Geldern*) availability; (*von Stil*) fluidity
Flüssig-: Flüssigkristall M liquid crystal; **Flüssigkristallanzeige** F liquid-crystal display; **flüssig machen** VT to realize
Fluss-: Flusskrebs M crayfish (*Brit*), crawfish (*US*); **Flusslauf** M course of a/the river; **Flussmündung** F river mouth; (*von Gezeitenfluss*) estuary; **Flusspferd** NT hippopotamus; **Flussschiff** NT river boat; **Flussschifffahrt** F, NO PL river navigation; (= *Verkehr*) river traffic
flüstern ['flʏstən] VTI to whisper; (= *etwas lauter tuscheln*) to mutter; **sich ~d unterhalten** to talk in whispers; **das kann ich dir ~** (*inf*) take it from me (*inf*); **dem werde ich was ~** (*inf*) I'll tell him a thing or two (*inf*)
Flüster-: Flüsterpropaganda F underground rumours (*Brit*) or rumors (*US*) *pl*; **Flüstertüte** F (*hum inf*) megaphone
Flut [fluːt] F **-, -en (a)** (= *ansteigender Wasserstand*) incoming or flood tide; (= *angestiegener Wasserstand*) high tide; **es ist ~** the tide is coming in; it's high tide, the tide's in; **bei ~ baden** to swim when the tide is coming in/at high tide; **bei ~ einlaufen** to come in on the tide/at high tide; **die ~ geht zurück** the tide has turned or started to go out; *siehe* **Ebbe**
(b) USU PL (= *Wassermasse*) waters *pl*
(c) (*fig*: = *Menge*) flood
Flut-: Flutkatastrophe F flood disaster; **Flutkraftwerk** NT tidal power station; **Flutlicht** NT floodlight; **Flutlichtspiel** NT floodlit match
flutschen ['flʊtʃn̩] VI (*inf*) **(a)** AUX SEIN (*N Ger.* = *rutschen*) to slide **(b)** (= *funktionieren*) to go smoothly
Flutwelle F tidal wave
Fob-Klausel ['fɔp-] F fob clause
focht PRET *von* **fechten**
Fock [fɔk] F **-, -en** (*Naut*) foresail
Föderalismus [fødera'lɪsmʊs] M **-**, NO PL federalism
föderalistisch [fødera'lɪstɪʃ] ADJ federalist
Föderation [fødera'tsioːn] F **-, -en** federation
föderativ [fødera'tiːf] ADJ federal
föderieren [føde'riːrən], *ptp* **föderiert** VR to federate; **föderierte Staaten** federated states
fohlen ['foːlən] VI to foal
Fohlen ['foːlən] NT **-s, -** foal
Föhn [føːn] M **-(e)s, -e (a)** (= *Wind*) foehn, föhn; **wir haben ~** the foehn is blowing **(b)** (= *Haartrockner*) hairdryer
föhnen ['føːnən] VT to dry
Föhnfrisur F blow-dried hair
föhnig ['føːnɪç] ADJ foehn *attr*; **es ist ~** there's a foehn (wind)
Föhre ['føːrə] F **-, -n** Scots pine (tree)
Fokus ['foːkʊs] M **-, -se** focus
Folge ['fɔlɡə] F **-, -n (a)** (= *Reihenfolge*) order; (= *Aufeinanderfolge*) succession; (= *zusammengehörige Reihe*) (*Math*) sequence; (= *Lieferung einer Zeitschrift*) issue; (= *Fortsetzung*) instalment (*Brit*), installment (*US*); (*TV, Rad*) episode; (= *Serie*) series
(b) (= *Ergebnis*) consequence; (= *unmittelbare ~*) result; (= *Auswirkung*) effect; **als ~ davon** as a result (of that); **dies hatte zur ~, dass ...** the consequence or result of this was that ...; **dies hatte seine Entlassung zur ~** this resulted in his dismissal; **die ~n für den Tourismus** the effect on tourism; **für die ~n aufkommen** to take the consequences; **an den ~n eines Unfalls/einer Krankheit sterben** to die as a result of an accident/illness; **das wird ~n haben** that will have serious consequences; **ohne ~n bleiben** to have no consequences

(c) (*form*) **einem Befehl ~ leisten** to comply with an order; **einer Einladung** (*dat*) **~ leisten** to accept an invitation
Folge-: Folgeerscheinung F result, consequence; **Folgekosten** PL subsequent costs *pl*
folgen ['fɔlɡn̩] VI AUX SEIN **(a)** (= *kommen nach*) to follow (*jdm/einer Sache* sb/sth); **auf etw** (*acc*) **~** to follow sth, to come after sth; **auf jdn** (*im Rang*) **~** to come after sb (in rank); **~ Sie mir (bitte/unauffällig)!** come with me please; **es folgt nun** or **nun folgt ein Konzert** we now have a concert; **... dann ~ die Meldungen im Einzelnen ...** followed by the news in detail; **wie folgt** as follows
(b) (= *verstehen*) to follow (*jdm/einer Sache* sb/sth); **können Sie mir ~?** do you follow (me)?
(c) (= *gehorchen*) to do as or what one is told; **einem Befehl/einer Anordnung ~** to follow an order/instruction; **jdm ~** (*inf*) to do what sb tells one
(d) (= *hervorgehen*) to follow (*aus* from); **was folgt daraus für die Zukunft?** what are the consequences of this for the future?
folgend ADJ following; **Folgendes** the following; **im Folgenden** in the following; (*schriftlich auch*) below; **es handelt sich um Folgendes** it's like this; (*schriftlich*) it concerns the following
folgendermaßen ['fɔlɡndɐ'maːsn̩] ADV like this
Folgen-: folgenlos ADJ without consequences; (= *wirkungslos*) ineffective; **~ bleiben** not to have any consequences; to be ineffective; **das konnte nicht ~ bleiben** that was bound to have serious consequences/could not fail to be effective; **folgenschwer** ADJ serious; **die Maßnahme erwies sich als ~** the measure had serious consequences
Folge-: folgerichtig ADJ (logically) consistent; **das einzig Folgerichtige in dieser Situation** the only logical thing to do in this situation; **Folgerichtigkeit** F logical consistency
folgern ['fɔlɡɐn] **1** VT to conclude **2** VI to draw a (the) conclusion; **logisch ~ lernen** to learn to think logically
Folgerung ['fɔlɡərʊŋ] F **-, -en** conclusion; **daraus ergibt sich die ~, dass ...** from this it can be concluded that ...
Folgeschaden M consequential damages
folglich ['fɔlklɪç] ADV, CONJ consequently, therefore
folgsam ['fɔlkzaːm] ADJ obedient
Folie ['foːliə] F **-, -n** (= *Plastikfolie*) film; (*für Projektor*) transparency; (= *Metallfolie, Typ, Cook*) foil
Folklore [fɔlk'loːrə, 'fɔlkloːrə] F **-**, NO PL folklore; (= *Volksmusik*) folk music
folkloristisch [fɔlklo'rɪstɪʃ] ADJ folkloric; *Kleidung* ethnic; **~e Musik** folk music
Folter ['fɔltɐ] F **-, -n** (*lit, fig*) torture; **die ~ anwenden** to use torture; **jdn auf die ~ spannen** (*fig*) to keep sb on tenterhooks
Folterbank F, *pl* **-bänke** rack
Folterer ['fɔltərɐ] M **-s, -**, **Folterin** [-ərɪn] F **-, -nen** torturer
Folter-: Foltergerät NT, **Folterinstrument** NT instrument of torture; **Folterkammer** F, **Folterkeller** M torture chamber
foltern ['fɔltɐn] **1** VT to torture; **jdn ~ lassen** to have sb tortured **2** VI to use torture
Folterung ['fɔltərʊŋ] F **-, -en** torture
Folterwerkzeug NT instrument of torture
Fon¹ [foːn] NT **-s, -s = Phon**
Fon² [foːn] ABBR *von* **Telefon** Tel
Fön® [føːn] M **-(e)s, -e** hairdryer; *siehe auch* **Föhn**
Fonds [fõ] M **- (a)** (= *Geldreserve, fig geh*) fund; **keinen ~ für etw haben** to have no funds for sth **(b)** (*Fin*: = *Schuldverschreibung*) government bond
Fondue [fõ'dyː] NT **-s, -s** *or* F **-, -s** fondue
fönen ['føːnən] VT *siehe* **föhnen**
Fono- ['foːno-, fo:no-] = **Phono-**
Font [fɔnt] M **-s, -s** (*Comput*) font
Fontäne [fɔn'tɛːnə] F **-, -n** jet; (*geh*: = *Springbrunnen*) fountain
Fontanelle [fɔnta'nɛlə] F **-, -n** (*Anat*) fontanelle
foppen ['fɔpn̩] VT (*inf*) **jdn ~** to make a fool of sb; (= *necken*) to pull sb's leg (*inf*)
forcieren [fɔr'siːrən], *ptp* **forciert** VT to push; *Entwicklung auch, Tempo* to force; *Konsum, Produktion* to push or force up
forciert [fɔr'siːɐt] ADJ forced

Förder-: Förderanlage F conveyor; **Förderband** NT, *pl* -bänder conveyor belt

Förderer ['fœrdərə] M **-s**, -, **Förderin** [-ərɪn] F **-**, **-nen** sponsor; (= *Gönner*) patron

Förder-: Förderklasse F (*Sch*) special class; **Förderkorb** M mine cage; **Förderkurs** M (*Sch*) special classes *pl*; **Förderland** NT producing country; **Förderleistung** F output

förderlich ['fœrdəlɪç] ADJ beneficial (+*dat* to); **guten Beziehungen ~ sein** to be conducive to good relations; **ein der Weiterbildung ~er Kursus** a course which contributes to one's further education

Fördermittel PL aid *sing*

fordern ['fɔrdən] **1** VT **(a)** (= *verlangen*) to demand; *Preis* to ask; (*in Appell, Aufrufen etc* = *erfordern*) to call for **(b)** (*fig*: = *kosten*) *Menschenleben, Opfer* to claim **(c)** (*lit, fig*: = *herausfordern*) to challenge; **er ist noch nie im Leben richtig gefordert worden** he has never been faced with a real challenge **2** VI to make demands; **er fordert nur, ohne selbst zu geben** he demands everything as a right, without giving anything himself

fördern ['fœrdən] VT **(a)** (= *unterstützen*) to support; (= *propagieren*) to promote; (*finanziell*) *bestimmtes Projekt* to sponsor; *Nachwuchs, Künstler* to support; *jds Talent, Kunstverständnis, Neigung* to encourage, to foster; (= *voranbringen*) *Freundschaft, Frieden* to promote; *Verdauung* to aid; *Appetit* to stimulate; **jdn beruflich ~** to help sb in his career
(b) (= *steigern*) *Wachstum* to promote; *Umsatz, Absatz, Produktion, Verbrauch* to boost, to increase
(c) *Bodenschätze* to extract; *Kohle, Erz* to mine

Förder-: Förderplattform F (*Min*) production platform; **Förderquote** F (*Min*) production level; **Förderstufe** F (*Sch*) mixed ability class(es) *intended to foster the particular talents of each pupil*; **Förderturm** M (*Min*) winding tower; (*auf Bohrstelle*) derrick

Forderung ['fɔrdərʊŋ] F **-**, **-en (a)** (= *Verlangen*) demand (*nach* for); (= *Lohnforderung, Entschädigungsforderung etc*) claim (*nach* for); (*in Appell, Aufrufen etc*) call (*nach* for); **~ an jdn stellen** to make demands on sb; **hohe ~en an jdn stellen** to demand a lot of sb
(b) (*Comm*: = *Anspruch*) claim (*an* +*acc*, *gegen* on, against); **eine ~ einklagen** to sue for payment of a debt; **eine ~ eintreiben** *or* **einziehen** to collect a debt
(c) (= *Herausforderung*) challenge

Förderung ['fœrdərʊŋ] F **-**, **-en (a)** (= *Unterstützung*) support; (*finanziell*) sponsorship; (*von Nachwuchs, Künstler*) support; (*von Talent*) encouragement, fostering; (*von Verdauung*) aid (*gen* to); **Maßnahmen zur ~ des Fremdenverkehrs** measures to promote tourism **(b)** (*inf*: = *Förderungsbetrag*) grant **(c)** (= *Gewinnung*) extraction

Forderungsabtretung F (*Jur*) assignment of a claim

Förderungs-: Förderungsmaßnahme F supportive measure; **Förderungsmaßnahmen** PL assistance *sing*; **Förderungsmittel** PL aid *sing*; **Förderungsprogramm** NT aid programme (*Brit*) *or* program (*US*); **förderungswürdig** ADJ deserving support

Förderunterricht M special instruction

Forelle [fo'rɛlə] F **-**, **-n** trout

Foren PL *von* Forum

forensisch [fo'rɛnzɪʃ] ADJ forensic

Forfaitierung [fɔrfɛ'ti:rʊŋ] F **-**, **-en** (*Fin*) forfaiting, non-recourse financing

Form [fɔrm] F **-**, **-en (a)** form; (= *Gestalt, Umriss*) shape; **in ~ eines Dreiecks** in the shape of a triangle; **~ und Inhalt** form and content; **seine ~ verlieren, aus der ~ geraten** to lose its shape; **einer Sache** (*dat*) **~ (und Gestalt) geben** (*lit*) to shape sth; (*fig*) to give sth a coherent shape; **feste ~ annehmen** (*fig*) to take shape; **hässliche/gewalttätige ~en annehmen** (*fig*) to become ugly/violent; **(weibliche) ~en** feminine figure
(b) Formen PL (= *Umgangsformen*) manners *pl*; **die ~ wahren** to observe the proprieties; **der ~ wegen** *or* **halber, um der ~ zu genügen** as a matter of form; **in aller ~** formally
(c) (= *Kondition*) form; **in bester ~ sein** to be in great shape *or* on top form; **in ~ bleiben/kommen** to keep/get (oneself) fit *or* in condition; (*Sportler*) to keep/get in form; **außer ~** out of condition
(d) (= *Gießform*) mould (*Brit*), mold (*US*); (= *Kuchenform, Backform*) baking tin (*Brit*) *or* pan (*US*)

formal [fɔr'ma:l] **1** ADJ **(a)** formal **(b)** (= *äußerlich*) *Besitzer, Fehler, Grund* technical **2** ADV **(a)** formally **(b)** (= *äußerlich*) technically

Formaldehyd ['fɔrmaldehy:t, fɔrmalde'hy:t] M **-s**, NO PL formaldehyde

Formalie [fɔr'ma:liə] F **-**, **-n** USU PL formality

formalistisch [fɔrma'lɪstɪʃ] ADJ formalistic

Formalität [fɔrmali'tɛ:t] F **-**, **-en** formality

Format [fɔr'ma:t] NT **-(e)s**, **-e (a)** (= *Größenverhältnis*) size; (*von Zeitung, Papierbogen, Fotografie, Buch, Film*) format; **im ~ DIN A4** in A4 (format) **(b)** (= *Rang, Persönlichkeit*) stature **(c)** (*fig*: = *Niveau*) class (*inf*), quality; **internationales ~ haben** to be of international quality

formatieren [fɔrma'ti:rən], *ptp* **formatiert** VTI (*Comput*) to format

Formatierung F **-**, **-en** (*Comput*) formatting

Formatvorlage F (*Comput*) style

Form-: formbeständig ADJ **~ sein** to hold *or* retain its shape **(b)** (*Sport*) consistent in form; **Formblatt** NT form; **Formbrief** M form letter

Formel ['fɔrml] F **-**, **-n** formula; (*von Eid etc*) wording; (= *Floskel*) set phrase; **etw auf eine ~ bringen** to reduce sth to a formula

Formel-1-Rennen [fɔrml'1aɪns-] NT Formula-1 race

formell [fɔr'mɛl] **1** ADJ formal **2** ADV (= *offiziell*) formally, officially; **als Bürgermeister musste er den Vorfall ~ verurteilen** as mayor he had to deplore the incident as a matter of form

Formel-: Formelsammlung F (*Math*) formulary; **Formelsprache** F system of notation

formen ['fɔrmən] **1** VT to form, to shape; *Charakter auch, Eisen* to mould (*Brit*), to mold (*US*); *Wörter* to articulate; **schön geformte Glieder** beautifully shaped limbs; **der Krieg hat ihn geformt** the war shaped him *or* his character; **~de Kraft** formative power **2** VR (*lit*) to form *or* shape itself; (*fig*) to mature

Form-: Formfehler M irregularity; (*gesellschaftlich*) breach of etiquette; **Formgebung** [-ge:bʊŋ] F **-**, **-en** (*geh*) design; **formgerecht** ADJ (*lit, fig*) correct, proper

formieren [fɔr'mi:rən], *ptp* **formiert** VR to form up

-förmig [fœrmɪç] ADJ SUF -shaped; **sternförmig** star-shaped

Formkrise F (*esp Sport*) loss of form

förmlich ['fœrmlɪç] **1** ADJ **(a)** (= *formell*) formal **(b)** (= *regelrecht*) positive **2** ADV **(a)** (= *formell*) formally **(b)** (= *regelrecht*) positively; **ich hätte ~ weinen können** I really could have cried

Förmlichkeit F **-**, **-en (a)** NO PL (*von Benehmen*) formality **(b)** USU PL (= *Äußerlichkeit*) social convention; **bitte keine ~en!** please don't stand on ceremony

formlos ADJ **(a)** (= *ohne Form*) shapeless; *Vortrag, Aufsatz, Roman* unstructured **(b)** (= *zwanglos*) informal, casual **(c)** (*Admin*) *Antrag* unaccompanied by a form/any forms

Formlosigkeit F **-**, NO PL **(a)** (= *Gestaltlosigkeit*) shapelessness; (*von Vortrag, Aufsatz, Roman*) lack of structure **(b)** (= *Zwanglosigkeit*) informality, casualness

Form-: Formsache F matter of form; **formschön** ADJ elegant, elegantly proportioned; **Formschwäche** F poor form; **~n zeigen** to be on poor form; **Formtief** NT loss of form; **sich in einem ~ befinden** to be badly off form

Formular [fɔrmu'la:r] NT **-s**, **-e** form

formulieren [fɔrmu'li:rən], *ptp* **formuliert** VT to phrase, to formulate; **... wenn ich es mal so ~ darf** ... if I might put it like that

Formulierung F **-**, **-en** wording, formulation

Formung ['fɔrmʊŋ] F **-**, **-en (a)** NO PL (= *Formen*) forming, shaping; (*von Charakter, Eisen*) moulding (*Brit*), molding (*US*); (*von Wörtern*) articulation **(b)** (= *Form*) shape

formvollendet **1** ADJ perfect; *Vase etc* perfectly shaped; *Gedicht, Musikstück* perfectly structured **2** ADV **er verabschiedete/verneigte sich ~** he took his leave/bowed with perfect elegance

forsch [fɔrʃ] **1** ADJ brash **2** ADV brashly; **eine Sache ~ anpacken** to attack sth energetically

forschen ['fɔrʃn] **1** VI **(a)** (= *suchen*) to search (*nach* for) **(b)** (= *Forschung betreiben*) to research; **über etw** (*acc*) **~** to research into sth **2** VT (*Sw*) = **erforschen**

forschend 1 ADJ *Blick* searching **2** ADV searchingly; **etw ~ betrachten** to look at sth very closely; **jdn ~ ansehen** to give sb a searching look

Forscher ['fɔrʃe] M -s, -, **Forscherin** [-ərɪn] F -, -nen **(a)** (= *Wissenschaftler*) researcher; (*in Medizin, Naturwissenschaften*) research scientist **(b)** (= *Forschungsreisender*) explorer

Forschheit F -, -en brashness

Forschung ['fɔrʃʊŋ] F -, -en research *no pl*; **eingehende ~en** intensive research; **ältere/verschiedene ~en** older/various studies; **~en betreiben** to be engaged in research; **~ und Lehre** research and teaching; **~ und Entwicklung** research and development, R&D

Forschungs- IN CPDS research; **Forschungsaufgabe** F research assignment; (= *Forschungsauftrag eines Wissenschaftlers*) research duty; **Forschungsauftrag** M research assignment; **Forschungsgebiet** NT field of research; **ein/das ~ der Medizin** a/the field of medical research; **Forschungsinstitut** NT research institute; **Forschungsreise** F expedition; **Forschungsreisende(r)** MF DECL AS ADJ explorer; **Forschungssemester** NT sabbatical term; **Forschungsstation** F research station; **Forschungsstipendium** NT research fellowship; **Forschungstätigkeit** F research *no indef art*; **Forschungszentrum** NT research centre (*Brit*) *or* center (*US*)

Forst [fɔrst] M -(e)s, -e(n) forest

Forst-: Forstamt NT forestry office; **Forstbeamte(r)** M DECL AS ADJ, **Forstbeamtin** F forestry official

Förster ['fœrste] M -s, -, **Försterin** [-ərɪn] F -, -nen forest warden

Försterei [fœrstə'rai] F -, -en forest warden's lodge

Forst-: Forsthaus NT forester's lodge; **Forstrevier** NT forestry district; **Forstschaden** M forest damage *no pl*; **Forstschädling** M forest pest; **Forstwirt(in)** M(F) graduate in forestry; **Forstwirtschaft** F forestry

Forsythie [fɔr'zy:tsiə, (*Aus*) fɔr'zy:tiə] F -, -n forsythia

fort [fɔrt] ADV **(a)** (= *weg*) away; (= *verschwunden*) gone; **etw ist ~** sth has gone *or* disappeared; **es war plötzlich ~** it suddenly disappeared; **die Katze ist schon seit gestern ~** the cat has been missing since yesterday; **er ist ~** he has left *or* gone; (*dial:* = *ist nicht zu Hause*) he isn't here; **weit ~** far away, a long way away; **von zu Hause ~** away from home **(b)** (= *weiter*) on; **und so ~** and so on, and so forth; **das ging immer so weiter und so ~ und so ~** (*inf*) that went on and on and on; **in einem ~** incessantly

Fort [fo:ɐ] NT -s, -s fort

fort- PREF IN CPD VBS (= *weg*) away; (= *weiter*)

Fort-: Fortbestand M, NO PL continuance; (*von Staat, Institution*) continued existence; (*von Gattung etc*) survival; **fortbestehen** ptp **fortbestanden** VI SEP IRREG to continue; (*Staat, Institution*) to continue in existence; **fortbewegen** ptp **fortbewegt** SEP **1** VT to move away **2** VR to move; **Fortbewegung** F, NO PL locomotion; **Fortbewegungsmittel** NT means *sing* of locomotion; **fortbilden** VT SEP **jdn/sich ~** to continue sb's/one's education; **Fortbildung** F, NO PL further education; **berufliche ~** further vocational training; **Fortbildungskurs** M in-service training course; **fortbleiben** VI SEP IRREG AUX SEIN to stay away; **Fortbleiben** NT -s, NO PL absence; **Fortdauer** F continuation; **fortdauern** VI SEP to continue; **fortdauernd 1** ADJ continuing; (*in der Vergangenheit*) continued **2** ADV constantly, continuously; **fortfahren** SEP **1** VI **(a)** AUX SEIN (= *wegfahren*) to go away; (= *abfahren*) to leave, to go; (= *einen Ausflug machen*) to go out **(b)** AUX HABEN *or* SEIN (= *weitermachen*) to continue; **~, etw zu tun** to continue doing sth *or* to do sth; **in einer Tätigkeit ~** to continue with an activity; **ich fahre fort...** as I was about to say ... **2** VT (= *wegbringen*) to take away; *Wagen* to drive away; **Fortfall** M discontinuance; **fortfallen** VI SEP IRREG AUX SEIN to cease to exist; (= *nicht mehr zutreffend sein*) to cease to apply; (*Zuschuss etc*) to be discontinued; (= *abgeschafft werden*) to be abolished; **fortführen** VT SEP **(a)** (= *fortsetzen*) to continue, to carry on **(b)** (= *wegführen*) to take away; (*zu Fuß, fig*) to lead away; **Fortführung** F continuation; **Fortgang** M, NO PL (= *Verlauf*) progress; **seinen ~ nehmen** to progress; **fortgehen** VI SEP AUX SEIN **(a)** (= *weggehen*) to leave; **von zu Hause ~** to leave home; **geh fort!** go away!; **geh nicht fort!** don't go (away)! **(b)** (= *weitergehen*) to go on; **fortgeschritten** ADJ advanced; **zu ~er Stunde wurden sie fröhlich** as the night wore on they got quite merry; **er kam**

zu ~er Stunde he came at a late hour; **Fortgeschrittenenkurs** M advanced course; **Fortgeschrittene(r)** ['fɔrtgəʃrɪtnə] MF DECL AS ADJ advanced student; **fortgesetzt** ADJ continual, constant; *Betrug, Steuerhinterziehung, Handlung* repeated; *siehe auch* **fortsetzen**; **fortjagen** VT SEP *Menschen* to throw out (*aus, von* of); *Tier, Kinder* to chase out (*aus, von* of); **fortkönnen** VI SEP IRREG to be able to get away; **fortlassen** VT SEP IRREG **(a)** (= *weggehen lassen*) **jdn ~** to let sb go **(b)** (= *auslassen*) to leave out, to omit; **fortlaufen** VI SEP IRREG AUX SEIN to run away; **meine Freundin ist mir fortgelaufen** my girlfriend has (gone off) and left me; **fortlaufend 1** ADJ *Handlung* ongoing; *Erscheinen* serial *attr*; *Zahlungen* regular; (= *andauernd*) continual **2** ADV (= *andauernd*) continually; **~ nummeriert** *Geldscheine, Motoren* serially numbered; *Blätter, Seiten* consecutively numbered; **fortmüssen** VI SEP IRREG to have to go; **fortnehmen** VT SEP IRREG to take away (*jdm* from sb); **fortpflanzen** VR SEP to reproduce; (*Schall, Wellen, Licht*) to travel; (*Gerücht*) to spread

Fortpflanzung F, NO PL reproduction; (*von Pflanzen*) propagation

Fortpflanzungs-: fortpflanzungsfähig ADJ capable of reproduction; *Pflanze* capable of propagation; **Fortpflanzungsmedizin** F reproductive medicine; **Fortpflanzungsorgan** NT reproductive organ; **Fortpflanzungstrieb** M reproductive instinct; **fortpflanzungsunfähig** ADJ incapable of reproduction; *Pflanze* incapable of propagation

Fort-: forträumen VT SEP (*lit, fig*) to clear away; **fortreißen** VT SEP IRREG to snatch away; (*Menge, Flut, Strom*) to sweep *or* carry away; (*fig*) to carry away; **jdn/etw mit sich ~** (*lit*) to carry or sweep sb/sth along; **fortrennen** VI SEP IRREG AUX SEIN to race off *or* away; **Fortsatz** M (*Anat*) process; **fortschaffen** VT SEP to remove; **fortschicken** VT SEP to send away; *Brief etc* to send off; **fortschreiben** VT SEP IRREG **(a)** *Statistik etc* to extrapolate **(b)** (= *weiterführend aktualisieren*) *Programm etc* to continue; **Fortschreibung** F (*von Statistik*) extrapolation; (*von Programm*) continuation; **fortschreitend** ADJ progressive; *Alter, Wissenschaft* advancing

Fortschritt M advance; (*esp Pol*) progress *no pl*; **gute ~e machen** to make good progress; **~ erzielen** to make progress; **~e in der Medizin** advances in medicine; **das ist ein wesentlicher ~** that's a considerable step forward; **dem ~ dienen** to further progress

fortschrittlich ['fɔrtʃrɪtlɪç] **1** ADJ progressive **2** ADV progressively; **~ eingestellt sein** *or* **denken** to be progressive

Fortschrittlichkeit F -, NO PL progressiveness

Fortschritts-: fortschrittsfeindlich ADJ anti-progressive; **Fortschrittsfeindlichkeit** F anti-progressiveness; **Fortschrittsglaube** M belief in progress; **fortschrittsgläubig** ADJ **~ sein** to believe in progress; **das ~e 19. Jahrhundert** the 19th century with its belief in progress; **Fortschrittsgläubigkeit** F naïve belief in progress

fort-: fortsetzen SEP **1** VT to continue; **„wird fortgesetzt"** "to be continued"; *siehe auch* **fortgesetzt 2** VR (*zeitlich*) to continue; (*räumlich*) to extend

Fortsetzung ['fɔrtzɛtsʊŋ] F -, -en **(a)** NO PL (= *das Fortsetzen*) continuation; (*esp nach Unterbrechung*) resumption **(b)** (= *folgender Teil*) (*Rad, TV*) episode; (*eines Romans*) instalment (*Brit*), installment (*US*); **ein Film in drei ~en** a film in three parts; **„~ folgt"** "to be continued"

Fortsetzungs-: Fortsetzungsroman M serialized novel; **Fortsetzungsserie** F series

fort-: fortwährend 1 ADJ NO PRED constant, continual, incessant **2** ADV constantly, continually, incessantly; **fortwirken** VI SEP to continue to have an effect; **das wirkt noch bis heute fort** that still has an effect today; **das Gesehene wirkte noch lange in ihm fort** what he had seen affected him for a long time; **fortwollen** VI SEP to want to get away (*aus* from); **fortziehen** SEP IRREG **1** VT to pull away; (*mit großer Anstrengung*) to drag away; (*Strom, Strudel*) to carry away **2** VI AUX SEIN **(a)** (= *weiterziehen*) to move on; (*Vögel*) to migrate **(b)** (*von einem Ort*) to move away (*aus* from); (*aus einer Wohnung*) to move out (*aus* of)

Forum ['fo:rʊm] NT -s, Foren ['fo:rən] forum

Forumsdiskussion F, **Forumsgespräch** NT forum (discussion)

Forward ['fɔ:wəd, 'fo:rɛvart] M -(s), -s (*esp Aus Ftbl*) forward

fossil [fɔˈsiːl] ADJ ATTR fossil *attr*, fossilized; *Brennstoff, Energie* fossil *attr*

Fossil [fɔˈsiːl] NT **-s, -ien** [-liən] (*lit, fig*) fossil

Föten PL *von* **Fötus**

Foto [ˈfoːto] NT **-s, -s** photo(graph); **ein ~ machen** to take a photo(graph)

Foto- IN CPDS (*Sci*) photo; *siehe auch* **Photo-; Fotoalbum** NT photograph album; **Fotoapparat** M camera; **Fotoarbeiten** PL photographic work *sing*; **Fotoarchiv** NT photo archives *pl*; **Fotoartikel** PL photographic equipment *sing*; **Fotoatelier** NT (photographic) studio; **Foto-CD** [-tseːdeː] F Photo CD®; **Fotoecke** F corner; **Fotofinish** NT (*Sport*) photo finish

fotogen [fotoˈgeːn] ADJ photogenic

Fotograf [fotoˈgraːf] M **-en, -en, Fotografin** [-ˈgraːfɪn] F **-, -nen** photographer

> *Vorsicht!* **Fotograf** *wird nicht mit dem englischen Wort* **photograph** *übersetzt.*

Fotografie [fotograˈfiː] F **-, -n** [-ˈfiːən] photography; (= *Bild*) photo(graph)

fotografieren [fotograˈfiːrən] *ptp* **fotografiert** ▮ VT to photograph, to take a photo(graph) of; **sich ~ lassen** to have one's photo(graph) *or* picture taken ▮ VI to take photos *or* photographs

fotografisch [fotoˈgraːfɪʃ] ▮ ADJ photographic ▮ ADV photographically

Foto-: Fotokopie F photocopy; **fotokopieren** [fotoko'piːrən], *ptp* **fotokopiert** VT INSEP to photocopy; **Fotokopierer** M photocopier; **Fotolabor** NT photo lab; **Fotomodell** NT photographic model; **Fotomontage** F photomontage; **Fotoroman** M photo book; **Fototermin** M photo call

Fötus [ˈføːtʊs] M **-** *or* **-ses, Föten** *or* **-se** foetus (*Brit*), fetus (*US*)

Fotze [ˈfɔtsə] F **-, -n** (*vulg*) cunt (*vulg*)

foul [faul] ▮ ADJ (*Sport*) **das war aber ~** (*inf*) that was a foul ▮ ADV **~ spielen** to foul

Foul [faul] NT **-s, -s** (*Sport*) foul

Foulelfmeter [ˈfaul-] M (*Ftbl*) penalty (kick)

foulen [ˈfaulən] VTI (*Sport*) to foul; **es wurde viel gefoult** there was a lot of fouling

Foyer [foaˈjeː] NT **-s, -s** foyer; (*in Hotel auch*) lobby

FPÖ [ɛfpeːˈʔøː] F **-** ABBR *von* **Freiheitliche Partei Österreichs**

Fr. ABBR *von* **Frau**

Fracht [fraxt] F **-, -en (a)** (= *Ladung*) freight *no pl*; (*von Flugzeug, Schiff auch*) cargo; **etw per ~ schicken** to send sth freight, to freight sth **(b)** (= *~preis*) freight *no pl*, freightage *no pl*; (*bei Lastwagen*) carriage *no pl*; (= *~tarif*) freight/carriage rate

Frachtbrief M consignment note, waybill

Frachtbriefdoppel NT duplicate waybill

Frachter [ˈfraxtɐ] M **-s, -** freighter

Fracht-: Frachtflugzeug NT cargo *or* freight plane; **frachtfrei** ADJ, ADV carriage paid *or* free; **Frachtführer** M carrier; (*bei Straßentransport*) haulage contractor; **~ im Kombiverkehr** combined transport operator, CTO; **frei ~** free carrier; **Frachtgut** NT (ordinary) freight *no pl*; **etw als ~ schicken** to send sth (as ordinary) freight; **Frachtkosten** PL freight charges *pl*; **Frachtpostzentrum** NT parcel depot; **Frachtrate** F freight rate, carriage rate (*Brit*); **Frachtraum** M hold; (= *Ladefähigkeit*) cargo space; **Frachtschiff** NT cargo ship, freighter; **Frachtverkehr** M goods traffic; **Frachtvertrag** M contract of carriage; (= *Seefrachtvertrag*) (contract of) affreightment; **Frachtzentrum** NT (*für Gütertransport*) freight *or* goods depot (*esp Brit*); (*von Post*) parcel depot; **Frachtzettel** M consignment note, waybill; **Frachtzuschlag** M excess freight, freight surcharge

Frack [frak] M **-(e)s, -s** (*inf*) *or* **¨e** [ˈfrɛkə] tails *pl*, tail coat; **im ~** in tails

Frack-: Frackschoß M coat-tail; **Frackzwang** M requirement to wear tails; **„~" "tails", "white tie"**

Frage [ˈfraːgə] F **-, -n** question; **eine ~ zu etw** a question on sth; **jdm eine ~ stellen**, **an jdn eine ~ richten** to ask sb a question; **an jdn eine ~ haben** to have a question for sb; **gestatten Sie mir eine ~?** (*form*) might I ask a question?; **auf eine ~ mit Ja oder Nein antworten** to answer a question with a straight yes or no; **sind noch ~n?**, **hat jemand noch eine ~?** are there any further questions?; **auf eine dumme ~ (bekommt man) eine dumme Antwort** (*prov*) ask a silly question (get a silly answer) (*prov*); **das ist (doch sehr) die ~** that's (just *or* precisely) the question/problem; **das ist die große ~** that's the big question; **das ist gar keine ~, natürlich dürfen Sie heute freinehmen** you don't even need to ask, of course you can take today off; **das ist gar keine ~, das steht** *or* **ist außer ~** there's no question *or* doubt about it; **ohne ~** without question *or* doubt; **in ~ kommen** to be possible; (*Bewerber*) to be worth considering; **sollte er für diese Stelle in ~ kommen, ...** if he should be considered for this position ...; **in ~ kommende Möglichkeiten** possible opportunities; **für jdn/etw nicht in ~ kommen** to be out of the question for sb/sth; **das kommt (überhaupt) nicht in ~!** that's (quite) out of the question; **etw in ~ stellen** to question sth, to call sth into question; **eine ~ der Zeit/des Geldes** a question *or* matter of time/money; *siehe auch* **infrage**

-frage F SUF IN CPDS question of; (= *Problem auch*) problem of; **die Arbeitslosenfrage** the unemployment issue; **eine Zeit- und Kostenfrage** a question of time and money

Fragebogen M questionnaire; (= *Formular*) form

fragen [ˈfraːgn] ▮ VTI to ask; **nach** *or* **wegen** (*inf*) **jdm ~** to ask after sb; (*in Hotel etc*) to ask for sb; **ich fragte sie nach den Kindern** I asked her how the children were doing; **nach dem Weg/jds Namen/Alter ~** to ask the way/sb's name/age; **nach Arbeit/Post ~** to ask whether there is/was any work/mail; **nach den Ursachen ~** to inquire as to the causes; **nach den Folgen ~** to bother *or* care about the consequences; **er fragte nicht danach, ob ...** he didn't bother *or* care whether ...; **wegen etw ~** to ask about sth; **frag (mich/ihn) lieber nicht** you'd better not ask (me/him) that; **das frage ich dich!** I could ask you the same; **frag nicht so dumm!** don't ask silly questions; **du fragst zu viel** you ask too many questions; **da fragst du mich zu viel** (*inf*) I really couldn't say; **man wird ja wohl noch ~ dürfen** (*inf*) I was only asking (*inf*); **wenn ich (mal) ~ darf** if I may *or* might ask; **ohne lange zu ~** without asking a lot of questions; *siehe auch* **gefragt** ▮ VR to wonder; **das/da frage ich mich** I wonder; **das frage ich mich auch** that's just what I was wondering; **ja, das fragt man sich** yes, that's the question; **es fragt sich, ob ...** it's debatable *or* questionable whether *or* if ...; **da muss man sich ~, ob ...** you *or* one can't help wondering whether *or* if ...; **ich frage mich, wie/wo ...** I'd like to know how/where ...

fragend ▮ ADJ *Blick* questioning; (*Gram*) interrogative ▮ ADV **jdn ~ ansehen** to give sb a questioning look

Fragerei [fraːgəˈrai] F **-, -en** questions *pl*

Frage-: Fragesatz M (*Gram*) interrogative sentence; (= *Nebensatz*) interrogative clause; **Fragestellung** F formulation of a question; **das ist eine falsche ~** the question is wrongly formulated; **Fragestunde** F (*Parl*) question time *no art* (*Brit*); **Fragewort** NT, *pl* **-wörter** interrogative (particle); **Fragezeichen** NT question mark (*auch fig*); **hinter diese Behauptung muss man ein dickes** *or* **großes ~ setzen** (*fig*) this statement should be taken with a large pinch of salt

fraglich [ˈfraːklɪç] ADJ **(a)** (= *zweifelhaft*) uncertain; (= *fragwürdig*) doubtful, questionable; **eine ~e Sache** a moot point **(b)** (= *betreffend*) in question; *Angelegenheit* under discussion; **zu der ~en Zeit** at the time in question

fraglos ADV undoubtedly, unquestionably

Fragment [fraˈɡmɛnt] NT **-(e)s, -e** fragment

fragwürdig ADJ dubious

Fragwürdigkeit F **-, -en** dubious nature

Fraktion [frakˈtsioːn] F **-, -en (a)** (*Pol*) ≈ parliamentary *or* congressional (*US*) party; (*von mehreren Parteien*) ≈ coalition party; (= *Sondergruppe*) group, faction **(b)** (*Aus*: = *Ortsteil*) area **(c)** (*Chem*) fraction

> *Vorsicht!* **Fraktion** *wird im Allgemeinen nicht mit dem englischen Wort* **fraction** *übersetzt.*

Fraktions- IN CPDS (*Pol*) party; **Fraktionsführer(in)** M(F) party whip, floor leader (*US*); **fraktionslos** ADJ *Abgeordneter* independent; **Fraktionsmitglied** NT member of a parliamentary *etc* party; **Fraktionssitzung** F party meeting; **Fraktionssprecher(in)** M(F) party spokesperson; **Fraktionsvorsitzende(r)** MF DECL AS ADJ party whip, floor leader (*US*); **Fraktionszwang** M requirement to vote in accordance with party policy; **unter ~ stehen** to be under the whip

Franc [frã:] M **-, -s** franc

Franchise ['frɛntʃaiz] M **-**, NO PL franchise

Franchise- ['frɛntʃaiz-]: **Franchise-Geber(in)** M(F) franchisor; **Franchise-Nehmer(in)** M(F) franchisee

Franchising ['frɛntʃaizɪŋ] NT **-s**, NO PL franchising

Franke ['fraŋkə] M **-n, -n** (Geog) Franconian; (Hist) Frank

Franken¹ ['fraŋkn] NT **-s** Franconia

Franken² M **-s, -** (Schweizer) ~ (Swiss) franc

Frankfurt ['fraŋkfʊrt] NT **-s ~ (am Main)** Frankfurt (on the Main); **~ (Oder)** Frankfurt on the Oder

Frankfurter ['fraŋkfʊrtɐ] M **-s, -** (inf: = Würstchen) frankfurter

frankieren [fraŋ'ki:rən], ptp **frankiert** VT to stamp; (mit Maschine) to frank

Frankiermaschine F franking machine

Fränkin ['frɛŋkɪn] F **-, -nen** Franconian (woman)

fränkisch ['frɛŋkɪʃ] ADJ Franconian

Fränkler ['frɛŋklɐ] M **-s, -**, **Fränkli** ['frɛŋkli] NT **-s, -** (Sw inf) franc (piece)

franko ['fraŋko] ADV (Comm) carriage paid; (von Postsendungen) post-free (Brit), postpaid

Franko-: **frankokanadisch** ADJ French-Canadian; **frankophil** [fraŋko'fi:l] ADJ (geh) Francophile; **frankophob** [fraŋko'fo:p] ADJ (geh) Francophobe; **frankophon** [fraŋko'fo:n] ADJ francophone

Frankreich ['fraŋkraiç] NT **-s** France

Franse ['franzə] F **-, -n** (lose) (loose) thread; (von Haar) strand of hair; **~n** (= Pony) fringe (Brit), bangs pl (US)

fransen ['franzn] VI to fray (out)

fransig ['franzıç] ADJ (Sew) fringed no adv; Haar straggly no adv; (= ausgefasert) frayed no adv

Franz [frants] NT **-**, NO PL (Sch inf: = Französisch) French

Franzbranntwein M alcoholic liniment

Franzose [fran'tso:zə] M **-n, -n** (a) Frenchman/French boy; **er ist ~** he's French; **die ~n** the French (b) (= Werkzeug) monkey wrench

Französin [fran'tsø:zɪn] F **-, -nen** Frenchwoman/French girl; **sie ist ~** she's French

französisch [fran'tsø:zɪʃ] ADJ French; **die ~e Schweiz** French-speaking Switzerland; **die Französische Revolution** the French Revolution; **~es Bett** double bed; **~e Spielkarten** ordinary playing cards; **sich (auf) ~ empfehlen** to leave without saying goodbye; (= ohne zu zahlen) to leave without paying; (= sich unerlaubt entfernen) to take French leave; **es auf Französisch** or **~ machen** (inf) to have oral sex; siehe auch **deutsch**

frappant [fra'pant] (geh) **1** ADJ remarkable **2** ADV remarkably; **auf jdn ~ wirken** to astound sb

frappieren [fra'pi:rən], ptp **frappiert 1** VT (= verblüffen) to astound, to astonish **2** VI (Sache) to be astounding or astonishing

Fräse ['frɛ:zə] F **-, -n** (= Werkzeug) milling cutter; (für Holz) moulding (Brit) or molding (US) cutter; (= Bodenfräse) rotary hoe

fräsen ['frɛ:zn] VT to mill; Holz to mould (Brit), to mold (US)

Fräsmaschine F milling machine

fraß PRET von **fressen**

Fraß [fra:s] M **-es, -e** food; (pej inf) muck (inf) no indef art; **etw einem Tier zum ~ vorwerfen** to feed sth to an animal; **jdn den Kritikern zum ~ vorwerfen** to throw sb to the critics

fraternisieren [fraterni'zi:rən], ptp **fraternisiert** VI to fraternize

Fratz [frats] M **-es, -e** or (Aus) **-en, -en** (a) (pej) brat (b) (= schelmisches Mädchen) rascal

Fratze ['fratsə] F **-, -n** (a) grotesque face (b) (= Grimasse) grimace; (inf: = Gesicht) face; (fig: = Zerrbild) caricature; **jdm eine ~ schneiden** to pull or make a face at sb

frau [frau] INDEF PRON proposed feminist alternative to "man"; siehe **man**

Frau [frau] F **-, -en** (a) (= weiblicher Mensch) woman; **von ~ zu ~** woman to woman (b) (= Ehefrau) wife; **willst du meine ~ werden?** will you be my wife?; **jdn zur ~ haben** to be married to sb; **seine zukünftige ~** his bride-to-be; **seine geschiedene ~** his ex-wife (c) (= Anrede) madam; (mit Namen) Mrs; (für eine unverheiratete ~) Miss, Ms; **~ Doktor** doctor

Frauchen ['frauçən] NT **-s, -** DIM von **Frau** (inf: von Hund) mistress; **geh zum ~** go to your mistress

Frauen- IN CPDS women's; (einer bestimmten Frau) woman's; (Sport) ladies', women's; **Frauenarbeit** F (a) (= Arbeit für Frauen, von Frauen) women's labour (Brit) or labor (US); **das ist keine ~** that's no job for a woman; **niedrig bezahlte ~** badly paid jobs for women (b) (= Arbeit zugunsten der Frau) work among women; **in der ~ tätig sein** to be involved in work among women; **Frauenarzt** M, **Frauenärztin** F gynaecologist (Brit), gynecologist (US); **Frauenbeauftragte(r)** MF DECL AS ADJ (in Gewerkschaft etc) women's representative; (= Beamter) officer for women's issues; **Frauenberuf** M career for women; **Frauenbewegung** F women's (auch Hist) or feminist movement; **Frauenfeind** M misogynist; **frauenfeindlich** ADJ anti-women pred; Mensch, Verhalten auch misogynous; **Frauenfeindlichkeit** F misogyny; (im Berufsleben) discrimination against women; **Frauenfrage** F question of women's rights; **frauenfreundlich** ADJ pro-women pred; **Frauenfreundlichkeit** F positive attitude toward(s) women; **Frauengeschichte** F affair with a woman; **~n** (= Affären) womanizing; (= Erlebnisse) sexploits pl (hum inf), experiences pl with women; **Frauenhaar** NT (a) woman's hair (b) (Bot) maidenhair (fern); **Frauenhaus** NT (a) women's refuge (b) (Ethnologie) women's house; **Frauenheilkunde** F gynaecology (Brit), gynecology (US); **Frauenheld** M lady-killer; **Frauenkenner** M connoisseur of women; **Frauenkleider** PL women's clothes pl or clothing sing; **Frauenklinik** F gynaecological (Brit) or gynecological (US) clinic; **Frauenkrankheit** F, **Frauenleiden** NT gynaecological (Brit) or gynecological (US) disorder; **Facharzt für ~en und Geburtshilfe** gynaecologist (Brit) or gynecologist (US) and obstetrician; **Frauenpolitik** F feminist politics sing or pl; **Frauenquote** F quota for women; **Frauenrechtler** [-rɛçtlɐ] M **-s, -**, **Frauenrechtlerin** [-ərɪn] F **-, -nen** feminist; (in der heutigen Zeit auch) Women's Libber (inf); **Frauenschänder** [-ʃɛndɐ] M **-s, -** rapist; **Frauenschuh** M, NO PL (Bot) lady's slipper no pl; **Frauenüberschuss** M surplus of women; **Frauenwahlrecht** NT female suffrage no art; **Frauenzeitschrift** F women's magazine

Fräulein ['frɔylaɪn] NT **-s, -** or (inf) **-s** (dated) (a) (= unverheiratete weibliche Person) young lady (b) (= Anrede) Miss (c) (= weibliche Angestellte) young lady; (= Verkäuferin) assistant; (= Kellnerin) waitress; **~!** Miss!; (= Kellnerin auch) waitress!

fraulich ['frauliç] ADJ feminine; (= reif) womanly no adv

Freak ['fri:k] M **-s, -s** (inf) freak (inf)

freakig ['fri:kɪç] ADJ (inf) freaky (inf)

frech [frɛç] **1** ADJ (a) (= unverschämt) cheeky (esp Brit), fresh pred (esp US), impudent; Lüge bare-faced no adv; **~ werden** to get cheeky etc; **halt deinen ~en Mund!** (you) shut up and stop being cheeky etc; **~ wie Oskar** (inf) or **wie ein Spatz sein** (inf) to be a little monkey (b) (= herausfordernd) Kleidung, Texte etc saucy (inf) **2** ADV lachen impudently; anlügen brazenly; **jdm ~ kommen** to get cheeky with sb; **sich ~ benehmen** to be cheeky etc

Frechdachs M (inf) cheeky monkey (Brit), smart aleck

Frechheit F **-, -en** (a) NO PL (= Verhalten) impudence; **die ~ haben** or **besitzen, ... zu ...** to have the cheek (esp Brit) or impudence to ... (b) (= Äußerung, Handlung) bit of cheek (esp Brit) or impudence; **sich (dat) einige ~en erlauben** or **herausnehmen** to be a bit cheeky (esp Brit) or fresh (esp US); **solche ~en** what cheek (esp Brit) or impudence

Freeclimbing ['fri:klaimɪŋ] NT **-s** free climbing

Freesie ['fre:ziə] F **-, -n** freesia

Freeware ['fri:wɛ:ɐ] F **-, -s** (Comput) freeware

frei [frai]	
1 ADJEKTIV	**2** ADVERB

1 ADJEKTIV

(a) (= unbehindert) free; **frei von etw** free of sth; **sich von etw frei machen** to free oneself from sth; **die Straße frei machen** to clear the road; **der Film ist frei (für Jugendliche) ab 16 (Jahren)** this film is suitable for persons aged 16 years and over; **ich bin so frei** (form) may I?

✦frei + Substantiv

Siehe auch unter dem Eintrag für das jeweilige Substantiv.

freier Durchgang thoroughfare; **von Kiel nach Hamburg hatten wir freie Fahrt** we had a clear run from Kiel to Hamburg; **einem Zug freie Fahrt geben** to give a train the "go" signal; **auf freiem Fuß sein** to be free; **freie Hand haben** to have a free hand; **jdm freie Hand lassen** to give sb free rein; **aus freien Stücken** of one's own free will; **jdm zur freien Verfügung stehen** to be completely at sb's disposal; **aus freiem Willen** of one's own free will; **freier Zutritt** unrestricted access
(b) (= *unabhängig*) free; *Schriftsteller, Journalist etc* freelance; (= *nicht staatlich*) private

✦frei + Substantiv

Siehe auch unter dem Eintrag für das jeweilige Substantiv.

freier Beruf independent profession; **Freie Demokratische Partei** Free Democratic Party; **Freie Hansestadt Bremen** Free Hansa Town of Bremen; **Freie und Hansestadt Hamburg** Free Hansa Town of Hamburg; **freier Markt** free market; **freie Marktwirtschaft** free-market economy; **freier Mitarbeiter** freelancer; **freier Mitarbeiter sein** to be freelance; **als freier Mitarbeiter arbeiten** to work freelance; **die freie Wirtschaft** private enterprise; **in die freie Wirtschaft gehen** to go into the private sector
(c) (= *verfügbar*) *Mittel, Geld* available; *Zeit* free; **Herr Mayer ist jetzt frei** Mr Mayer is free now; **ich bin jetzt frei für ihn** I can see him now; (*am Telefon*) I can speak to him now
(d) (= *arbeitsfrei*) **morgen/Mittwoch ist frei** tomorrow/Wednesday is a holiday; *siehe auch* **freihaben, freinehmen**
(e) (= *unbesetzt*) *Zimmer, Toilette* vacant; *Taxi* for hire; **ist hier noch frei?, ist dieser Platz noch frei?** is this seat free?, is anyone sitting here?; **im Kino/Flugzeug waren noch zehn freie Plätze** in the cinema/plane there were still ten seats free; „**frei**" (*an Taxi*) "for hire"; (*an Toilettentür*) "vacant"; „**Zimmer frei**" "vacancies"; **haben Sie noch etwas frei?** (*in Hotel*) do you have any vacancies?; **bei HarperCollins sind einige Stellen frei** there are some vacancies at HarperCollins; **einen Platz frei machen** (= *aufstehen*) to vacate a seat; (= *leer räumen*) to clear a seat; **einen Platz für jdn frei lassen** to keep a seat for sb; **für etw Platz frei lassen/machen** to leave/make room for sth; **eine Wohnung frei machen** to vacate a flat (*Brit*) *or* an apartment; *siehe auch* **freimachen**
(f) (= *offen*) **unter freiem Himmel** in the open air; **auf freier Strecke** (*Rail*) between stations
(g) (= *kostenlos*) free; **Eintritt frei** admission free; **frei Schiff** free on board
(h) (= *unkonventionell*) *Sitten, Erziehung* liberal; **freie Liebe** free love
(i) (= *unbekleidet*) bare; **mit freiem Oberkörper** stripped to the waist

🔁 ADVERB
(a) (= *ungehindert*) freely; *sprechen* openly; **frei beweglich** free-moving; **frei erfunden** purely fictional; **er hat das frei erfunden** he made it up; **frei schalten und walten** to do what one wants; **frei definierbare Zeichen** (*Comput*) user-definable characters
✦frei (herum)laufen (*inf*) to be free; **der Verbrecher läuft immer noch frei herum** the criminal is still at large; **frei laufend** *Hunde, Katzen* feral; *Huhn* free-range; **Eier von frei laufenden Hühnern** free-range eggs
✦frei lebend *Wölfe, Mustangherden etc* living in the wild; *Katzen, Stadttauben* feral
✦frei stehen (*Haus*) to stand by itself; (*Sport*) to be free *or* not marked; **ein frei stehendes Gebäude** a free-standing building
✦frei nach based on; **frei nach Goethe** (*Zitat*) as Goethe didn't say
(b) (= *ungezwungen*) **sich frei und ungezwungen verhalten, frei und locker auftreten** to be easy-going; **sie benimmt sich etwas zu frei** she's rather free in her behaviour (*Brit*) *or* behavior (*US*); **frei atmen können** (= *erleichtert sein*) to be able to breathe easy
(c) (= *ohne Hilfsmittel*) unaided, without help; **das Kind kann frei stehen** the child can stand on its own; **frei schwimmen** to swim unaided; **frei sprechen** to speak without notes

Frei-: Freibad NT open-air (swimming) pool; **Freiballon** M free balloon; **freibekommen** ptp **freibekommen** VT SEP IRREG **(a)** (= *befreien*) **jdn ~** to get sb freed *or* released; **etw ~** to free sth **(b)** **einen Tag/eine Woche ~** to get a day/a week off; **Freiberufler** [-bəruːflɐ] M **-s, -**, **Freiberuflerin** [-ərɪn] F **-, -nen** freelancer; **freiberuflich 🔁** ADJ freelance **🔁** ADV **~ arbeiten** to work freelance; **~ tätig sein** to do freelance work, to freelance; **Freibetrag** M tax allowance; **freibleibend** ADJ subject to alteration

Freiburg [ˈfraɪbʊrk] NT **-s (a)** (*in Deutschland*) Freiburg **(b)** (*in der Schweiz: Kanton, Stadt*) Fribourg

Freie(r) [ˈfraɪə] MF DECL AS ADJ (*Hist*) freeman

Freier [ˈfraɪɐ] M **-s, - (a)** (*datedhum*) suitor **(b)** (*inf: von Dirne*) (prostitute's) client, john (*US inf*)

Freie(s) [ˈfraɪə] NT DECL AS ADJ **das ~** the open (air); **im ~n** in the open (air); **ins ~ gelangen** to get out; **im ~n übernachten** to sleep out in the open

Frei-: Freiexemplar NT free copy; **Freigabe** F release; (*von Preisen, Wechselkursen*) lifting of control (+gen on); (*von Straße, Strecke, Flugbahn*) opening; (*von Film*) passing; **Freigang** M, *pl* **-gänge** (*von Strafgefangenen*) day release; **~ bekommen** to be let out on parole; **während des ~s** while on parole; **Freigänger** [-ɡɛŋɐ] M **-s, -**, **Freigängerin** [-ərɪn] F **-, -nen** day release prisoner; **freigeben** SEP IRREG **🔁** VT to release (*an* +acc to); *Preise, Wechselkurse* to decontrol; *Straße, Strecke, Flugbahn* to open; *Film* to pass; **jdm den Weg ~** to let sb past *or* by **🔁** VI **jdm ~** to give sb a holiday (*Brit*), to give sb vacation (*US*); **jdm zwei Tage ~** to give sb two days off; **freigebig** [ˈfraɪgeːbɪç] ADJ generous; **Freigebigkeit** F **-**, NO PL generosity; **Freigehege** NT open-air *or* outdoor enclosure; **Freigeist** M freethinker; **Freigepäck** NT baggage allowance; **Freigrenze** F (*bei Steuer*) tax exemption limit; **freihaben** VI SEP IRREG to have a holiday (*Brit*), to have vacation (*US*); **ich habe heute/zwei Tage frei** I have today/two days off; **eine Stunde ~** (*Sch*) to have a free period; **die sechste Stunde ~** (*Sch*) to have the sixth period free; **er hat mittags eine Stunde frei** he has an hour free at midday; **Freihafen** M free port; **freihalten** SEP IRREG **🔁** VT **(a)** (= *nicht besetzen*) to keep free **(b)** (= *reservieren*) to keep **(c)** (= *jds Zeche begleichen*) to pay for; **sich von jdm ~ lassen** to let sb pay for one **🔁** VR **sich von etw ~** to avoid sth; *von Vorurteilen etc* to be free of sth; *von Verpflichtungen* to keep oneself free of sth; **Freihandelszone** F free trade area; **die kleine ~** EFTA, the European Free Trade Area; **freihändig** ADJ, ADV *Zeichnung* freehand; *Radfahren* (with) no hands; *Schießen* offhand (*spec*), without support

Freiheit [ˈfraɪhaɪt] F **-, -en** freedom *no pl*; **die ~** freedom; (= *persönliche ~ als politisches Ideal*) liberty; **~, Gleichheit, Brüderlichkeit** liberty, equality, fraternity; **persönliche ~** personal freedom; **in ~** (*dat*) **sein** to be free; (*Tier*) to be in the wild; **in ~ leben** (*Tier*) to live in the wild; **in ~ geboren** born free; **dichterische ~** poetic licence (*Brit*) *or* license (*US*); **alle ~en haben** to have all the freedom possible; **sich** (*dat*) **die ~ nehmen, etw zu tun** to take the liberty of doing sth; **sich** (*dat*) **zu viele ~en erlauben** to take too many liberties

freiheitlich [ˈfraɪhaɪtlɪç] **🔁** ADJ liberal; *Verfassung* based on the principle of liberty; *Demokratie* free; **die ~-demokratische Grundordnung** the free democratic constitutional structure **🔁** ADV *erziehen* liberally; **~ gesinnt** *or* **eingestellt** liberal

Freiheits-: Freiheitsberaubung F **-, -en** (*Jur*) wrongful deprivation of personal liberty; **Freiheitsbewegung** F liberation movement; **Freiheitsdrang** M, NO PL urge *or* desire for freedom; **Freiheitsentzug** M imprisonment; **freiheitsliebend** ADJ freedom-loving; **Freiheitsstatue** F Statue of Liberty; **Freiheitsstrafe** F prison sentence; **er erhielt eine ~ von zwei Jahren** he was given a two-year prison sentence

Frei-: freiheraus [ˈfraɪhəˈraʊs] ADV candidly, frankly; **Freikarte** F free *or* complimentary ticket; **freikaufen** VT SEP **jdn/sich ~** to buy sb's/one's freedom; **Freiklettern** NT **-s**, NO PL free climbing; **freikommen** VI SEP IRREG AUX SEIN (= *entkommen*) to get out (*aus* of); (= *befreit werden*) to be released *or* freed (*aus, von* from); **Freikörperkultur** F, NO PL nudism, naturism

Freiland-: Freilandei NT free-range egg; **Freilandgemüse** NT outdoor vegetables *pl*; **Freilandkultur** F outdoor cultivation; **Freilandversuch** M outdoor trial

Frei-: freilassen VT SEP IRREG to set free, to free; *Hund* to let off the lead (*esp Brit*) *or* leash; **Freilassung** F **-, -en** release; (*von Sklaven*) setting free; **freilaufend** ADJ *siehe* frei; **freilebend** ADJ *siehe* **frei**; **freilegen** VT SEP to expose; *Ruinen, Trümmer* to uncover; (*fig*) to lay bare

freilich [ˈfraɪlɪç] ADV (a) (= *allerdings*) admittedly; **es scheint ~ nicht leicht zu sein** admittedly it doesn't seem easy (b) (*esp S Ger.* = *natürlich*) of course

Freilicht- [ˈfraɪlɪçt] IN CPDS open-air; **Freilichtbühne** F open-air theatre (*Brit*) *or* theater (*US*)

Frei-: freimachen SEP ▣ VT to stamp; (*mit Frankiermaschine*) to frank; **einen Brief mit 56 Cent ~** to put stamps to the value of 56 cents on a letter; *siehe auch* **frei** ▣ VR (a) (= *freie Zeit einplanen*) to arrange to be free (b) (= *sich entkleiden*) to take one's clothes off; **Freimaurer** M Mason, Freemason; **freimaurerisch** [-maurərɪʃ] ADJ Masonic; **Freimaurerloge** F Masonic Lodge

Freimut M, NO PL frankness

freimütig [ˈfraɪmyːtɪç] ▣ ADJ frank ▣ ADV frankly

Frei-: freinehmen VT SEP IRREG **einen Tag ~** to take a day off; **freipressen** VT SEP **jdn ~** to obtain sb's release; **versuchen, jdn freizupressen** to demand sb's release; **Freiraum** M (*fig*) freedom *no art, no pl* (*zu* for); **die Universität ist kein gesellschaftlicher ~** university isn't a social vacuum; **freischaffend** ADJ ATTR freelance; **Freischaffende(r)** [-ʃafndə] MF DECL AS ADJ freelancer; **Freischärler** [-ʃɛːrlɐ] M **-s, -,** **Freischärlerin** [-ərɪn] F **-, -nen** guerrilla; **freischaufeln** VT SEP to clear, to dig clear; **Freischuss** M free shot; **freischwimmen** VR SEP IRREG (*Sport*) to pass a test by swimming *for 15 minutes*; (*fig*) to learn to stand on one's own two feet; **Freischwimmen** NT *15-minute swimming test*

FREISCHWIMMER

The **Freischwimmer** *badge is awarded to swimmers who can swim for 15 minutes without holding onto the side of the pool and dive from the lower diving board. Children without the* **Freischwimmer** *badge displayed on their trunks or swimsuit are not allowed to use the deep end of a public swimming pool unless supervised. The next level up is the* **Fahrtenschwimmer**, *which entails a 30-minute swimming test, beginning with a dive from the higher diving board.*

Frei-: freisetzen VT SEP to release; (*euph*) *Arbeitskräfte* to make redundant; (*vorübergehend*) to lay off; **Freisprechanlage** F hands-free (headset); (*im Auto*) hands-free (car kit); **freisprechen** VT SEP IRREG *Angeklagten, Beschuldigten* to acquit; **jdn von einer Schuld ~** (*Jur*) to find sb not guilty; **jdn von einem Verdacht ~** to clear sb of suspicion; **jdn wegen erwiesener Unschuld ~** to prove sb not guilty; **Freispruch** M acquittal; **es ergeht ~** the verdict is "not guilty"; **auf ~ plädieren** to plead not guilty; **Freistaat** M free state; **der ~ Bayern/Sachsen** the Free State of Bavaria/Saxony

---

FREISTAAT

During the Weimar Republic most Länder *were called* **Freistaat**, *although after the Second World War the majority chose other ways of describing themselves. Prior to re-unification only Bavaria kept the name* **Freistaat**, *as a sign of its independence within the federation. Today two of the new* Länder, *Saxony and Thuringia, also bear the title.*

Frei-: freistehen VI SEP IRREG (a) (= *überlassen sein*) **es steht jdm frei, etw zu tun** sb is free *or* at liberty to do sth; **das steht Ihnen völlig frei** that is completely up to you; **es steht Ihnen frei, ob …** it is up to you whether … (b) (= *leer stehen*) to stand empty; **freistellen** VT SEP (= *anheim stellen*) **jdm etw ~** to leave sth (up) to sb

Freistellungsauftrag M (*Fin*) notice of tax-exempt status

Freistil- IN CPDS freestyle;

Frei-: Freistoß M (*Ftbl*) free kick (*für* to, for); **Freistück** NT free copy; **Freistunde** F free hour; (*Sch*) free period

Freitag [ˈfraɪtaːk] M Friday; **der Schwarze ~** *the day of the Wall Street crash*; **ein schwarzer ~** a black day; *siehe auch* **Dienstag**

freitags [ˈfraɪtaːks] ADV on Fridays, on a Friday

Frei-: Freitreppe F (flight of) steps (+*gen* leading up to); **Freiumschlag** M stamped addressed envelope, s.a.e.; **Freiverkehr** M (*Fin*) over-the-counter trading; **im ~** over the counter; **Freiwild** NT (*fig*) fair game; **freiwillig** ▣ ADJ voluntary; (= *freigestellt*) *Versicherung, Unterricht* optional ▣ ADV voluntarily; **sich ~ melden** to volunteer (*zu, für* for); **sich ~ verpflichten** (*bei Militär*) to enlist; **Freiwillige(r)** [-vɪlɪɡə]

MF DECL AS ADJ volunteer; **Freiwurf** M free throw; **Freizeichen** NT (*Telec*) ringing tone

Freizeit F (a) (= *arbeitsfreie Zeit*) spare *or* leisure time (b) (= *Zusammenkunft*) weekend/holiday (*Brit*) *or* vacation (*US*) course; (*Eccl*) retreat

Freizeit-: Freizeitangebot NT leisure activity; **Freizeitausgleich** M time off in lieu (*Brit*), time off instead of pay (*US*); **Freizeitwert** M **München hat einen hohen ~** Munich has a lot to offer in the way of recreational and leisure facilities

Frei-: freizügig ▣ ADJ (a) (= *reichlich*) *Gebrauch, Anwendung* liberal (b) (*in moralischer Hinsicht*) permissive (c) (= *den Wohnort frei wählen können*) free to move ▣ ADV (a) (= *reichlich*) freely, liberally (b) (= *moralisch locker*) **sich ~ benehmen** to be loose; **~ gekleidet** provocatively dressed; **Freizügigkeit** [-tsyːɡɪçkaɪt] F **-,** NO PL (a) (= *Großzügigkeit*) liberality (b) (*in moralischer Hinsicht*) permissiveness (c) (= *Beweglichkeit: von Waren, freie Wahl des Wohnorts etc*) freedom of movement

fremd [frɛmt] ADJ (a) (= *andern gehörig*) someone else's; *Bank, Bibliothek, Firma* different; (*Comm, Fin, Pol*) outside *or* other; **ohne ~e Hilfe** without help from anyone else/outside; **ich schlafe nicht gern in ~en Betten** I don't like sleeping in strange beds; **~es Eigentum** someone else's property; **das ist nicht für ~e Ohren** that is not for other people to hear; **sich mit ~en Federn schmücken** to claim all the glory for oneself (b) (= *~ländisch*) foreign, alien (*esp Admin, Pol*) (c) (= *andersartig*) strange; *Planeten* other; *Welt* different (d) (= *unvertraut*) strange; **jdm ~ sein** (= *unbekannt*) to be unknown to sb; (= *unverständlich, nicht in jds Art*) to be alien to sb; **das ist eine mir ~e Seite seines Wesens** that is a side of his character which I haven't seen before; **ich bin hier/in London ~** I'm a stranger here/to London; **sich** *or* **einander** (*dat*) **~ werden** to grow apart; **sich ~ fühlen** to feel like a stranger; **~ tun** to be reserved

Fremd-: Fremdarbeiter(in) M(F) foreign worker; **fremdartig** ▣ ADJ strange; (= *exotisch*) exotic ▣ ADV **~ aussehen/klingen/anmuten** to look/sound/seem strange *etc*; **fremdbestimmt** ▣ ADJ heteronomous ▣ ADV **~ handeln** to act under orders

fremde(l)n [ˈfrɛmd(l)n] VI (*S Ger, Sw*) to be scared of strangers

Fremden-: fremdenfeindlich ADJ hostile to strangers; (= *ausländerfeindlich*) hostile to foreigners, xenophobic; **Fremdenfeindlichkeit** F xenophobia; **Fremdenführer** M guide(book); **Fremdenführer(in)** M(F) (tourist) guide; **Fremdenlegion** F Foreign Legion; **Fremdenverkehr** M tourism *no def art*

Fremde(r) [ˈfrɛmdə] MF DECL AS ADJ (= *Unbekannter, Ortsfremder*) stranger; (= *Ausländer*) foreigner; (*Admin, Pol*) alien; (= *Tourist*) visitor

Fremd-: Fremdfinanzierung F outside financing; **fremdgehen** VI SEP IRREG AUX SEIN (*inf*) to be unfaithful; **Fremdgelder** PL deposits and borrowed funds *pl*; **Fremdkapital** NT outside capital; **Fremdkörper** M foreign body; (*fig*) alien element; **sich als ~ fühlen** to feel out of place

Fremdsprache F foreign language; **eine Begabung für ~n** a gift for languages

Fremdsprachen-: Fremdsprachenkorrespondent(in) M(F), **Fremdsprachensekretär(in)** M(F) bilingual secretary; **Fremdsprachenunterricht** M language teaching

Fremd-: fremdsprachig ADJ in a foreign language; *Fähigkeiten* (foreign) language; **die ~e Bevölkerung** non-English/non-German *etc* speakers; **fremdsprachlich** ADJ foreign; **~er Unterricht** language teaching; **Fremdverschulden** NT third-party responsibility; **Fremdwährungskonto** NT foreign currency account; **Fremdwort** NT, *pl* **-wörter** borrowed *or* foreign word; **Rücksichtnahme ist für ihn ein ~** (*fig*) he's never heard of the word consideration

frenetisch [freˈneːtɪʃ] ▣ ADJ frenetic, frenzied; *Beifall* wild ▣ ADV wildly

frequentieren [frekvɛnˈtiːrən], *ptp* **frequentiert** VT (*geh*) to frequent

Frequenz [freˈkvɛnts] F **-, -en** (a) (= *Häufigkeit*) frequency (*auch Phys*); (*Med*) (pulse) rate (b) (= *Stärke*) numbers *pl*; (= *Verkehrsdichte*) volume of traffic

Frequenz- IN CPDS frequency; **Frequenzbereich** M (*Rad*) frequency range

Fressalien [frɛˈsaːliən] PL (*inf*) grub *sing* (*sl*)

Fresse [ˈfrɛsə] F **-, -n** (*vulg*) (= *Mund*) trap (*inf*), gob (*inf*); (= *Gesicht*) mug (*inf*); **die ~ halten** to shut one's trap *or* gob (*both inf*); **jdn** *or* **jdm in die ~ hauen**, **jdm die ~ polieren** to smash sb's face in (*inf*)

fressen [ˈfrɛsn], *pret* **fraß** [fraːs], *ptp* **gefressen** [gəˈfrɛsn] **1** VI (a) (= *essen*) to feed, to eat; (*sl: Menschen*) to eat; (*gierig*) to guzzle (*inf*); **jdm aus der Hand ~** (*lit, fig inf*) to eat out of sb's hand; **er isst nicht, er frisst (wie ein Schwein)** he eats like a pig (b) (= *zerstören*) to eat away (*an etw* (*dat*) sth)
2 VT (a) (= *verzehren*) (*Tier*) to eat; (= *sich ernähren von*) to feed *or* live on; (*sl: = gierig essen*) to guzzle (*inf*); **etwas zu ~** something to eat; **den Napf leer ~** (*Tiere*) to lick the bowl clean
(b) (*in Wendungen*) **Kilometer ~** to burn up the kilometres (*Brit*) *or* kilometers (*US*); **Löcher in etw** (*acc*) **~** (*lit*) to eat holes in sth; **ich habe dich zum Fressen gern** (*inf*) you're good enough to eat (*inf*); **ich fresse einen Besen** *or* **meinen Hut, wenn ...** (*inf*) I'll eat my hat if ...; **jdn/etw gefressen haben** (*inf*) to have had one's fill of sb/sth; **einen Narren** *or* **Affen an jdm/ etw gefressen haben** to dote on sb/sth
(c) (= *verbrauchen*) to eat *or* gobble up; *Zeit* to take up
3 VR (a) (= *sich bohren*) to eat one's way (*in +acc* into, *durch* through)
(b) **sich voll** *or* **satt ~** (*Tier*) to gorge itself; (*sl: Mensch*) to stuff oneself *or* one's face (*inf*)

Fressen NT **-s**, NO PL food; (*sl*) grub (*sl*); (*sl: = Schmaus*) blow-out (*inf*)

-fresser [frɛsə] M **-s, -**, **-fresserin** [-ərɪn] F **-, -nen** SUF IN CPDS (a) (= *Esser von etw*) eater (b) (= *Bekämpfer von jdm*) -basher (*inf*)

Fress-: Fressfeind M (*Zool*) predator; **Fressnapf** M feeding bowl; **Fresssack** M (*sl*) greedy guts (*Brit inf*), glutton

Frettchen [ˈfrɛtçən] NT **-s, -** ferret

Freude [ˈfrɔydə] F **-, -n** (a) NO PL pleasure; (*innig*) joy (*über +acc* at); (= *Erfreutheit*) delight (*über +acc* at); **~ an etw** (*dat*) **haben** to get *or* derive pleasure from sth; **er hat ~ an seinen Kindern** his children give him pleasure; **~ am Leben haben** to enjoy life; **vor ~** with joy; **der Garten ist seine ganze ~** the garden is his pride and joy; **daran hat er seine ~** that gives him pleasure; (*iro*) he thinks that's fun; **es ist eine (wahre** *or* **reine) ~, zu ...** it's a (real) pleasure to ...; **es war eine reine ~, das mit anzusehen** it was a joy to see; **es ist keine (reine) ~, das zu tun** (*iro*) it's not exactly fun doing that; **es ist mir eine ~, zu ...** it's a real pleasure for me to ...; **jdm ~ machen** to give sb pleasure; **er macht ihnen keine/wenig ~** he's no joy/not much of a joy to them; **es macht ihnen keine/wenig ~** they don't enjoy it (at all)/much; **jdm eine ~ machen** to make sb happy; **jdm eine ~ machen wollen** to want to do something to please sb; **zu meiner großen ~** to my great delight; **zu unserer größten ~ können wir Ihnen mitteilen ...** we are pleased to be able to inform you ...; **aus ~ an der Sache** for the love of it; **aus Spaß an der ~** (*inf*) for the fun *or* hell (*inf*) of it
(b) (= *Vergnügung*) joy; **die kleinen ~n des Lebens** the pleasures of life; **mit ~n** with pleasure; **da kommt ~ auf** this is where the fun starts

Freuden-: Freudenfest NT celebration; **Freudengeheul** NT, **Freudengeschrei** NT shrieks *pl* of joy; **Freudenhaus** NT (*datedhum*) house of pleasure; **Freudensprung** M joyful leap; **einen ~ machen** to jump for joy

freudestrahlend ADJ, ADV beaming with delight

freudig [ˈfrɔydɪç] **1** ADJ (a) (= *froh gestimmt*) joyful; (= *gern bereit*) willing; (= *begeistert*) enthusiastic; **jdn ~ stimmen** to raise sb's spirits (b) (= *beglückend*) happy; **eine ~e Nachricht** some good news; **ein ~es Ereignis** (*euph*) a happy event (*euph*) **2** ADV happily, joyfully; **einen Vorschlag ~ begrüßen** to greet a suggestion with delight; **~ überrascht sein** to be pleasantly surprised

freudsch [frɔytʃ] ADJ ATTR Freudian

freuen [ˈfrɔyən] **1** VR (a) (= *froh sein*) to be glad *or* pleased (*über +acc* about); **sich über ein Geschenk ~** to be pleased with a present; **sich sehr** *or* **riesig** (*inf*) **~** to be delighted (*über +acc* about); **sich an etw** (*dat*) **~** to get a lot of pleasure from sth; **sich für jdn ~** to be glad *or* pleased for sb; **sich seines Lebens ~** to enjoy life; **ich freue mich, Ihnen mitteilen zu können, ...** I'm pleased to be able to tell you ...
(b) **sich auf jdn/etw ~** to look forward to seeing sb/to sth; **sich zu früh ~** to get one's hopes up too soon

2 VT IMPERS to please; **es freut mich/ihn, dass ...** I'm/he's pleased *or* glad that ...; **das freut mich** I'm really pleased; **es freut mich sehr/es hat mich sehr gefreut, Ihre Bekanntschaft zu machen** (*form*) I'm pleased to meet/have met you

Freund [frɔynt] M **-(e)s, -e** [-də] (a) (= *Kamerad*) friend; **das habe ich ihm unter ~en gesagt** that was just between ourselves; **10 Euro unter ~en** 10 euros to a friend; **~ und Feind** friend and foe; **ein schöner ~** (*iro inf*) a fine friend (b) (= *Liebhaber*) boyfriend; (*esp älter*) gentleman-friend (c) (*fig*) (= *Anhänger*) lover; (= *Förderer*) friend; **ein ~ der Kunst** an art-lover, a lover/friend of art; **er ist kein ~ von vielen Worten** he's not one for talking much; **ich bin kein ~ von so etwas** I'm not one for that sort of thing

-freund(in) M(F) SUF IN CPDS (a) (= *Kamerad*) friend; **ein Schulfreund von mir** a schoolfriend of mine (b) (*fig*: = *Liebhaber*) lover of; **eine Musikfreundin** a music-lover, a lover of music

Freundchen [ˈfrɔyntçən] NT **-s, -** (*inf*) my friend (*iro*); **Freundchen, Freundchen!** watch it, mate (*Brit inf*) *or* my friend! (*iro*)

Freundeskreis M circle of friends; **etw im engsten ~ feiern** to celebrate sth with one's closest friends

Freundin [ˈfrɔyndɪn] F **-, -nen** (a) friend; (= *Liebhaberin*) girlfriend; (*esp älter*) lady-friend (b) (*fig*: = *Anhängerin, Förderin*) *siehe* **Freund** (c)

-freundin F SUF IN CPDS = **-freund(in)**

freundlich [ˈfrɔyntlɪç] **1** ADJ (a) (= *wohlgesinnt*) friendly *no adv*; **bitte recht ~!** say cheese! (*inf*), smile please!; **mit ~en Grüßen, mit ~em Gruß** (with) best wishes
(b) (= *liebenswürdig*) kind (*zu* to); **würden Sie bitte so ~ sein und das tun?** would you be so kind *or* good as to do that?; **das ist sehr ~ von Ihnen** that's very kind *or* good of you
(c) (= *ansprechend*) *Aussehen, Landschaft, Wetter etc* pleasant; *Zimmer, Einrichtung, Farben* cheerful; *Atmosphäre* friendly
2 ADV *bitten, fragen* nicely; **jdn ~ behandeln** to be friendly toward(s) sb

-freundlich ADJ SUF (a) (= *wohlgesinnt*) pro-; **eine israelfreundliche Politik** a pro-Israel policy (b) (= *liebend*) fond of; **er ist sehr kinderfreundlich** he is very fond of children (c) (= *geeignet*) -friendly; **umweltfreundlich** eco-friendly (d) (= *schonend*) kind to; **ein magenfreundlicher Kaffee** a coffee which is gentle on the stomach

freundlicherweise [ˈfrɔyntlɪçɐˈvaizə] ADV kindly

Freundlichkeit F **-, -en** (a) NO PL (= *Wohlgesonnenheit*) friendliness; (= *Liebenswürdigkeit*) kindness; (*von Aussehen, Landschaft, Wetter etc*) pleasantness; (*von Zimmer, Einrichtung, Farben*) cheerfulness; **würden Sie (wohl) die ~ haben, das zu tun?** would you be so kind *or* good as to do that? (b) (= *freundliche Handlung, Gefälligkeit*) kindness, favour (*Brit*), favor (*US*); (= *freundliche Bemerkung*) kind remark; **jdm ein paar ~en sagen** to say a few kind words to sb; (*iro*) to say a few choice words to sb

Freundschaft [ˈfrɔyntʃaft] F **-, -en** friendship; **mit jdm ~ schließen** to make *or* become friends with sb; **in aller ~** in all friendliness; **da hört die ~ auf** (*inf*) friendship doesn't go that far; **in Geldsachen hört die ~ auf** friendship doesn't extend to money matters

freundschaftlich [ˈfrɔyntʃaftlɪç] **1** ADJ friendly *no adv*; **~e Gefühle** feelings of friendship **2** ADV **jdm ~ verbunden sein** to be friends with sb; **mit jdm ~ verkehren** to be on friendly terms with sb; **jdm ~ gesinnt sein** to feel friendly toward(s) sb; **jdm ~ auf die Schulter klopfen** to give sb a friendly slap on the back

Freundschafts-: Freundschaftspreis M (special) price for a friend; **Freundschaftsspiel** NT (*Sport*) friendly game *or* match, friendly (*inf*)

Friede [ˈfriːdə] M **-ns, -n** (*old*) peace; **der ~ der Natur** the tranquillity of nature; **~ auf Erden** peace on earth; **~ sei mit euch** peace be with you; **~ seiner Asche** God rest his soul; **~, Freude, Eierkuchen** (*inf*) everything is rosy

Frieden [ˈfriːdn] M **-s, -** peace; (= *Vertrag*) peace treaty; **ein langer, ungestörter ~** a long period of uninterrupted peace; **im ~** in peacetime; **seit letztem Jahr herrscht in dieser Gegend ~** this region has been at peace since last year; **~ schließen** to make one's peace; (*Pol*) to conclude (*form*) *or* make peace; **der Westfälische ~** (*Hist*) the Peace of Westphalia; **sozialer ~** social harmony; **der häusliche ~** domestic harmony; **in ~ und**

Freundschaft or Eintracht leben to live in peace and harmony; **jdn in ~ lassen** to leave sb in peace; **um des lieben ~s willen** (*inf*) for the sake of peace and quiet; **ich traue dem ~ nicht** (*inf*) something (fishy) is going on (*inf*); **(er) ruhe in ~** rest in peace

Friedens- IN CPDS peace; **Friedensbewegung** F peace movement; **Friedensforschung** F peace studies *sing*; **Friedensnobelpreis** M Nobel peace prize; **Friedenspfeife** F peace pipe; **mit jdm die ~ rauchen** (*lit*) to smoke a peace pipe with sb; (*fig*) to make (one's) peace with sb; **Friedenspflicht** F (*Ind*) *obligation binding on employers and unions to avoid industrial action during wages negotiations*; **Friedensplan** M peace plan; **Friedenstaube** F dove of peace; **Friedensverhandlungen** PL peace negotiations *pl*; **Friedensvertrag** M peace treaty

friedfertig ['fri:tfɛrtɪç] ADJ *Mensch* peaceable; *Miteinander* peaceful; *Hund* placid

Friedhof ['fri:tho:f] M (= *Kirchhof*) graveyard; (= *Stadtfriedhof etc*) cemetery; **auf dem ~** in the graveyard/cemetery

friedlich ['fri:tlɪç] 🞩 ADJ peaceful; (= *friedfertig*) *Mensch* peaceable; **damit er endlich ~ ist** (*inf*) to keep him happy; **nun sei doch endlich ~!** (*fig inf*) give it a rest! (*inf*); **die ~e Nutzung der Kernenergie** the use of nuclear power for peaceful purposes 🞨 ADV (= *in Frieden*) peacefully; **~ sterben** or **einschlafen** (*euph*) to die peacefully; **jetzt kann ich ~ sterben** now I can die in peace

Friedrich ['fri:drɪç] M -s Frederick; **~ der Große** Frederick the Great; **seinen ~ Wilhelm unter etw** (*acc*) **setzen** (*inf*) to put one's signature to sth

frieren ['fri:rən], *pret* **fror** [fro:ɐ], *ptp* **gefroren** [gə'fro:rən] 🞩 VI **(a)** AUCH VT IMPERS (= *sich kalt fühlen*) to be cold; **ich friere, mich friert, es friert mich** (*geh*) I'm cold; **wie ein Schneider ~** (*inf*) to be frozen to the bone (*inf*); **mir** or **mich ~ die Zehen, mich friert es** or **ich friere an den Zehen** my toes are cold **(b)** AUX SEIN (= *gefrieren*) to freeze
🞨 VI IMPERS to freeze; **heute Nacht hat es gefroren** it was below freezing last night

Fries [fri:s] M **-es, -e** [-zə] (*Archit, Tex*) frieze

friesisch ['fri:zɪʃ] ADJ Fri(e)sian; *siehe auch* **deutsch**

Friesland ['fri:slant] NT -s Friesland

frigid [fri'gi:t], **frigide** [fri'gi:də] ADJ frigid

Frigidität [frigidi'tɛ:t] F -, NO PL frigidity

Frika(n)delle [frika(n)'dɛlə] F -, -n (*Cook*) rissole

Frisbee® ['frɪsbi] NT -, -s Frisbee®; **~ spielen** to play Frisbee®

Frisbeescheibe ['frɪsbi-] F Frisbee®

frisch [frɪʃ] 🞩 ADJ **(a)** (= *neu*) fresh; *Wäsche, Kleidung* clean; (= *feucht*) *Farbe, Fleck* wet; **~es Obst** fresh fruit; **~e Eier** new-laid (*Brit*) or freshly-laid eggs; **sich ~ machen** to freshen up; **mit ~en Kräften** with renewed vigour (*Brit*) or vigor (*US*); **~en Mut fassen** to gain new courage; **~e Luft schöpfen** to get some fresh air; **jdn an die ~e Luft setzen** (*inf*) to show sb the door; **jdn auf ~er Tat ertappen** to catch sb in the act
(b) (= *munter*) *Wesen, Art* bright, cheery; *Erzählung, Farbe* cheerful; (= *gesund*) *Aussehen, Gesichtsfarbe* fresh; *Mädchen* fresh-looking; **~ und munter sein** (*inf*) to be bright and lively **(c)** (= *kühl*) cool, chilly; **es weht ein ~er Wind** (*lit*) there's a fresh wind; (*fig*) the wind of change is blowing
🞨 ADV **(a)** (= *neu*) freshly; **~ von** or **aus etw** fresh from sth; **Bier ~ vom Fass** beer (straight) from the tap; **~ gestrichen** newly or freshly painted; (*auf Schild*) wet paint; **~ gebacken** (*inf*) *Ehepaar, Ehemann, Ehefrau* newly-wed; *Diplom-Ingenieur etc* newly-qualified; *Minister, Pressesprecher etc* newly-appointed; **~ gewaschen** clean; **das Bett ~ beziehen** to change the bed; **das ist mir noch ~ in Erinnerung** that is still fresh in my mind or memory
(b) (= *munter*) **immer ~ drauflos!** don't hold back!; **er redet/schreibt immer ~ drauflos** he just talks/writes away; **~ begonnen, halb gewonnen** (*prov*), **~ gewagt ist halb gewonnen** (*Prov*) a good start is half the battle

Frische ['frɪʃə] F -, NO PL (*von Wesen*) brightness, cheeriness; (*von Erzählung, Farbe*) cheerfulness; (= *gesundes Aussehen*) freshness; **in alter ~** (*inf*) as always

Frisch-: Frischei NT new-laid (*Brit*) or freshly-laid egg; **Frischfisch** M fresh fish; **Frischfleisch** NT fresh meat; **frischgebacken** [-gəbakn] ADJ *siehe* **frisch**; **Frischkäse** M cream cheese; **Frischluft** F fresh air; **Frischwurst** F sausage (*unsmoked,*

undried etc); **Frischzelle** F (*Med*) live cell; **Frischzellentherapie** F (*Med*) cellular or live-cell therapy

Friseur [fri'zø:ɐ] M **-s, -e** hairdresser; (= *Herrenfriseur auch*) barber; (= *Geschäft*) hairdresser's; barber's

Friseurin [fri'zø:rɪn] F -, **-nen** (female) hairdresser

Friseursalon [fri'zø:ɐ-] M hairdressing salon

Friseuse [fri'zø:zə] F -, **-n** (female) hairdresser

frisieren [fri'zi:rən], *ptp* **frisiert** 🞩 VT **(a)** (= *kämmen*) **jdn ~, jdm das Haar ~** to do sb's hair; (*nach dem Legen*) to comb sb's hair out; **eine modisch frisierte Dame** a lady with a fashionable hairdo **(b)** (*inf*: = *abändern*) *Abrechnung* to fiddle; *Bericht, Meldung* to doctor (*inf*); **die Bilanzen ~** to cook the books (*inf*) **(c)** (*inf*) *Auto, Motorrad, Motor* to soup up (*inf*) 🞨 VR to do one's hair

Frisör [fri'zø:ɐ] M **-s, -e, Frisöse** [-'zø:zə] F -, **-n** = **Friseur, Friseuse**

frisst [frɪst] 3. PERS SING PRES *von* **fressen**

Frist [frɪst] F -, **-en (a)** (= *Zeitraum*) period; (= *Kündigungsfrist*) period of notice; **eine ~ von vier Tagen/Wochen** *etc* four days/weeks *etc*; **eine ~ einhalten** to meet a deadline; (*bei Rechnung*) to pay within the period stipulated; **jds ~ verlängern, jdm die ~ verlängern** to give sb more time; **jds ~** or **jdm die ~ um zwei Tage verlängern** to give sb two more days; **innerhalb kürzester ~** without delay
(b) (= *Zeitpunkt*) deadline (*zu* for); (*bei Rechnung*) last date for payment **(c)** (= *Aufschub*) extension, period of grace; **jdm eine ~ von vier Tagen/Wochen geben** to give sb four days'/weeks' grace

fristen ['frɪstn] VT **sein Leben** or **Dasein ~** to eke out an existence

Fristenlösung F, **Fristenregelung** F *law allowing the termination of a pregnancy within the first three months*

Frist-: fristgerecht ADJ, ADV within the period stipulated; **jdm ~ kündigen** to fire sb with (proper) notice (*inf*); **~ kündigen** to give proper notice; **fristlos** ADJ, ADV without notice

Frisur [fri'zu:ɐ] F -, **-en** hairstyle

Friteuse [fri'tø:zə] F -, **-n** *siehe* **Fritteuse**

fritieren [fri'ti:rən], *ptp* **fritiert** VT *siehe* **frittieren**

Fritten ['frɪtn] PL (*inf*) chips *pl* (*Brit*), fries *pl* (*esp US inf*)

Frittenbude F (*inf*) chip shop (*Brit*), ≈ hotdog stand

Fritteuse [fri'tø:zə] F -, **-n** chip pan (*Brit*), deep-fat fryer

frittieren [fri'ti:rən], *ptp* **frittiert** VT to (deep-)fry

frivol [fri'vo:l] ADJ (= *leichtfertig*) frivolous; (= *anzüglich*) *Witz, Bemerkung* suggestive

Frivolität [frivoli'tɛ:t] F -, **-en (a)** NO PL (= *Leichtfertigkeit*) frivolity; (= *Anzüglichkeit: von Witz, Bemerkung*) suggestiveness **(b)** (= *Bemerkung*) risqué remark

Frl. ABBR *von* **Fräulein**

froh [fro:] ADJ happy; *Nachricht auch* good; (= *dankbar, erfreut*) glad, pleased, happy; **über etw** (*acc*) **~ sein** to be pleased with sth; (*darüber*) **~ sein, dass ...** to be glad or pleased that ...; **um etw ~ sein** to be grateful for sth; **~e Ostern!** Happy Easter!; **~e Weihnachten!** Happy (*esp Brit*) or Merry Christmas!; **die Frohe Botschaft** the Gospel

fröhlich ['frø:lɪç] 🞩 ADJ happy, cheerful; **~e Weihnachten!** Happy (*esp Brit*) or Merry Christmas!; **~es Treiben** gaiety 🞨 ADV (= *unbekümmert*) merrily

Fröhlichkeit F -, NO PL happiness; (= *fröhliches Wesen*) happy or cheerful nature; (= *gesellige Stimmung*) merriment

fromm [frɔm] ADJ, *comp* **~er** or **-er** ['frœmɐ], *superl* **~ste(r, s)** ['frœmstə] **(a)** (= *gläubig*) religious; *Christ* devout; *Werke* good; (= *scheinheilig*) pious, sanctimonious; **~e Sprüche** pious words **(b)** (*inf*) **eine ~e Lüge, ein ~er Betrug** self-deception; **das ist ja wohl nur ein ~er Wunsch** that's just a pipe dream

Frömmigkeit ['frœmɪçkaɪt] F -, NO PL (= *Gläubigkeit*) religiousness; (*von Christ*) devoutness

frönen ['frø:nən] VI +DAT (*geh*) to indulge in; *seiner Eitelkeit* to indulge

Fronleichnam [fro:n'laɪçna:m] M NO ART **-(e)s**, NO PL (the Feast of) Corpus Christi; **zu** or **an ~** at the Feast of Corpus Christi, on Corpus Christi

Front [frɔnt] F -, **-en (a)** (= *Vorderseite*) front; (= *Vorderansicht*) frontage; **die hintere ~** the back **(b)** (= *Kampflinie, -gebiet*) front **(c)** (*Met*) front **(d)** (= *Einheit*) ranks *pl*; (*in Namen*) front; **~ gegen jdn/etw machen** to make a stand against sb/sth

frontal [frɔn'taːl] **1** ADJ NO PRED *Angriff* frontal; *Zusammenstoß* head-on; *Position* at the front **2** ADV *angreifen* (*Mil*) from the front; (*fig*) head-on; *darstellen* front-on; *zusammenstoßen* head-on

Front-: Frontantrieb M (*Aut*) front-wheel drive; **Frontlader** [-laːdɐ] M **-s, -** front loader

fror PRET von **frieren**

Frosch [frɔʃ] M **-(e)s, ⁻e** ['frœʃə] frog; (= *Feuerwerkskörper*) (fire)cracker; **einen ~ in der Kehle** or **im Hals haben** (*inf*) to have a frog in one's throat; **sei kein ~!** (*inf*) be a sport!

Frosch-: Froschkönig M Frog Prince; **Froschlaich** M frogspawn; **Froschmann** M, *pl* **-männer** frogman; **Froschschenkel** M frog's leg

Frost [frɔst] M **-(e)s, ⁻e** ['frœstə] frost; **bei eisigem ~** in heavy frost; **~ (ab)bekommen** (*Hände, Ohren*) to get frostbitten; **~ vertragen (können)** to be able to stand the(e) frost

Frost-: frostanfällig ADJ susceptible to frost; **frostbeständig** ADJ frost-resistant; **Frostbeule** F chilblain

frösteln ['frœstln] **1** VI to shiver **2** VT IMPERS **es fröstelte mich** I shivered

frostig ['frɔstɪç] **1** ADJ (*lit, fig*) frosty; **ein ~er Hauch** an icy draught (*Brit*) or draft (*US*) **2** ADV **jdn ~ begrüßen/empfangen** to give sb a frosty greeting/reception; **~ klingen** to sound frosty; **jdn ~ abfertigen** to be very frosty to sb

Frost-: frostklar ADJ clear and frosty; **Frostschaden** M frost damage; **Frostschutz** M protection against frost; **Frostschutzmittel** NT (*Aut*) antifreeze

Frottee [frɔ'teː] NT or M **-s, -s** terry towelling (*Brit*), terry-cloth toweling (*US*)

Frottee-: Frotteehandtuch NT (terry) towel (*Brit*), terry-cloth towel (*US*); **Frotteetuch** NT, *pl* **-tücher** (terry) towel (*Brit*), terry-cloth towel (*US*)

frottieren [frɔ'tiːrən], *ptp* **frottiert** VT *Haut* to rub; **jdn, sich** to rub down

frotzeln ['frɔtsln] VTI (*inf*) to tease; **über jdn/etw ~** to make fun of sb/sth

Frucht [frʊxt] F **-, ⁻e** ['frʏçtə] (*Bot, fig*) fruit; (= *Embryo*) foetus (*Brit*), fetus (*US*); (*no pl*: = *Getreide*) crops *pl*; **Früchte** (= *Obst*) fruit *sing*; **Früchte tragen** (*lit, fig*) to bear fruit

fruchtbar ADJ (a) (*lit, fig*: = *fruchttragend, reiche Frucht bringend*) fertile (b) (*lit, fig*: = *viele Nachkommen zeugend, viel schaffend*) prolific; (*Bibl*) fruitful (c) (*fig*: = *nutzbringend*) fruitful

Fruchtbarkeit ['frʊxtbaːɐkait] F **-, NO PL** (a) (*lit, fig*: = *Zeugungsfähigkeit, Ergiebigkeit*) fertility (b) (*lit, fig*: = *viele Nachkommen zeugend, Schaffensreichtum*) prolificness (c) (*fig*: = *Nutzen*) fruitfulness

Frucht-: Fruchtbecher M fruit sundae; (*Bot*) cupule (*spec*), cup; **Fruchtblase** F amniotic sac

Früchtchen ['frʏçtçən] NT **-s, -** DIM von **Frucht** (*inf*) (= *Tunichtgut*) good-for-nothing; (= *Kind*) rascal (*inf*); **du bist mir ein sauberes** or **nettes ~** (*iro*) you're a right one (*inf*)

fruchten ['frʊxtn] VI to bear fruit; **nichts ~** to be fruitless

Früchtetee M fruit tea

fruchtig ['frʊxtɪç] ADJ fruity

Frucht-: Fruchtkapsel F (*Bot*) capsule; **fruchtlos** ADJ (*fig*) fruitless; **Fruchtsaft** M fruit juice; **Fruchtwasser** NT, NO PL (*Physiol*) amniotic fluid; **das ~ ist vorzeitig abgegangen** her waters broke early; **Fruchtwasseruntersuchung** F (*Med*) amniocentesis; **Fruchtzucker** M fructose

früh [fryː] **1** ADJ early; **am ~en Morgen** early in the morning, in the early morning; **in ~er Kindheit** in one's early childhood; **in ~ester Kindheit** very early in one's childhood; **der ~e Goethe** the young Goethe; **ein Werk des ~en Picasso** an early work by Picasso **2** ADV early; (= *in jungen Jahren*) young, at an early age; (*in Entwicklung*) early on; **von ~ auf** from an early age; **es ist noch ~ am Tag/im Jahr** it is still early in the day/year; **von ~ bis spät** from morning till night; **du hast dich nicht ~ genug angemeldet** you didn't apply early or soon enough; **zu ~ starten** to start too soon; **~ übt sich, was ein Meister werden will** (*Prov*) there's nothing like starting young **(b)** *Freitag/morgen* ~ Friday/tomorrow morning; **heute ~** this morning

Früh- IN CPDS early; **Frühaufsteher** [-laufʃteːɐ] M **-s, -, Frühaufsteherin** [-ərɪn] F **-, -nen** early riser, early bird (*inf*)

früher ['fryːɐ] COMP von **früh 1** ADJ **(a)** earlier; **in ~en Jahren/Zeiten** in the past; **in ~en Zeitaltern** in past ages **(b)** (= *ehemalig*) former; (= *vorherig*) *Besitzer, Wohnsitz* previous; **der Kontakt zu seinen ~en Freunden ist abgebrochen** he lost contact with his old friends **2** ADV **(a)** earlier; **~ gehts nicht** (= *kann nicht ~ gemacht werden*) it can't be done any earlier or sooner; (= *ich kann nicht ~ kommen*) I can't make it any earlier or sooner; **das hättest du ~ sagen müssen/wissen sollen** you should have said that before or sooner/known that before; **~ oder später** sooner or later
(b) (= *in jüngeren Jahren, in vergangenen Zeiten*) **Herr X, ~ Direktor eines Industriebetriebs** Herr X, formerly director of an industrial concern; **ich habe ihn ~ mal gekannt** I used to know him; **~ habe ich so etwas nie gemacht** I never used to do that kind of thing; **~ stand hier eine Kirche** there used to be a church here; **~ war alles besser/war das alles anders** things were better/different in the old days; **genau wie ~** just as it/he *etc* used to be; **Erzählungen von/Erinnerungen an ~** stories/memories of times gone by; **das habe ich noch von ~** I had it before; **ich kannte ihn von ~** I knew him before; **ich kenne ihn von ~** I've known him some time; **wir kennen uns noch von ~** we got to know each other some time ago; **meine Freunde von ~** my old friends

Früherkennung F (*Med*) early diagnosis

frühestens ['fryːəstns] ADV at the earliest; **wann kann das ~ fertig sein?** what is the earliest that can be ready?

früheste(r, s) ['fryːəstə] ADJ SUPERL von **früh**

Frühgeburt F premature birth; (= *Kind*) premature baby; **sie hatte/meine Tochter war eine ~** her baby/my daughter was premature or born prematurely

Frühjahr NT spring

Frühjahrs-: Frühjahrsmüdigkeit F springtime lethargy; **Frühjahrsputz** M spring-cleaning

Frühling ['fryːlɪŋ] M **-s, -e** spring; **es wird ~, der ~ kommt** spring is coming; **im ~** in spring; **seinen zweiten ~ erleben** to go through one's second adolescence

Frühlings- IN CPDS spring; **Frühlingsanfang** M first day of spring; **Frühlingsgefühle** PL (*hum inf*) **~ haben/bekommen** to be/get frisky (*hum inf*); **frühlingshaft 1** ADJ springlike **2** ADV **sich ~ kleiden** to dress in spring clothes; **es ist schon ~ warm** it's as warm as it is in spring; **Frühlingsrolle** F (*Cook*) spring roll; **Frühlingszwiebel** F spring onion (*Brit*), green onion (*US*)

Früh-: frühmorgens ADV early in the morning; **Frühnebel** M early morning mist; **frühpensionieren** *ptp* **frühpensioniert** VT INSEP **jdn ~** to give sb early retirement; **Frühpensionierung** F early retirement; **frühreif** ADJ precocious; (*körperlich*) mature at an early age; **Frührentner(in)** M(F) person who has retired early; **Frühschicht** F early shift; **Frühschoppen** [-ʃɔpn] M **-s, -** morning or (*mittags*) lunchtime drinking; **zum ~ gehen** to go for a morning/lunchtime drink

FRÜHSCHOPPEN

*A **Frühschoppen** is a social gathering in the morning, when friends sit together over a **Schoppen**. Depending on the region, this may be a glass of wine or a beer and schnapps. The custom of enjoying a **Frühschoppen** on Sundays between church and midday meal is still popular, particularly in rural areas.*

Frühstück NT **-s, -e** breakfast; (= *Frühstückspause*) morning or coffee break; **zweites ~** = elevenses (*Brit inf*), = midmorning snack; **was isst du zum ~?** what do you have for breakfast?; **die ganze Familie saß beim ~** the whole family were having breakfast

frühstücken ['fryːʃtʏkn] INSEP **1** VI to have breakfast, to breakfast **2** VT to breakfast on

Frühstücks-: Frühstücksbüfett NT breakfast buffet; **Frühstücksfernsehen** NT breakfast television; **Frühstückskartell** NT (*Econ sl*) gentlemen's agreement; **Frühstückspause** F morning or coffee break

Früh-: Frühwarnsystem NT early warning system; **frühzeitig 1** ADJ early; (= *vorzeitig auch*) premature **2** ADV early; (= *vorzeitig*) prematurely; (= *früh genug*) in good time, early

Frust [frʊst] M **-(e)s, NO PL** (*inf*) frustration *no art*; **das ist der totale ~, wenn ...** it's totally frustrating when ...

frusten ['frʊstn] VTI (*inf*) **von etw gefrustet sein** to be frustrated by sth; **das frustet** it's frustrating

Frustration [frʊstraˈtsioːn] F **-, -en** frustration

frustrieren [frʊsˈtriːrən], *ptp* **frustriert** VT to frustrate; (*inf*: = enttäuschen) to upset

FTP [ɛfteːˈpeː] NT **-s, -s** ABBR *von* **File Transfer Protocol** FTP

FU [ɛfˈluː] F - ABBR *von* **Freie Universität (Berlin)**

Fuchs [fʊks] M **-es, ⁀e** [ˈfʏksə] (**a**) (= *Tier*) fox; (*fig auch*) cunning devil (*inf*); **er ist ein alter** *or* **schlauer ~** (*inf*) he's a cunning old devil (*inf*) *or* fox (*inf*); **schlau wie ein ~** as cunning as a fox; **wo sich ~ und Hase** *or* **die Füchse gute Nacht sagen** (*hum*) in the middle of nowhere (**b**) (= *Pferd*) chestnut; (*mit hellerem Schwanz und Mähne*) sorrel

Fuchs-: Fuchsbandwurm M fox tapeworm; **Fuchsbau** M, *pl* **-baue** fox's den

fuchsen [ˈfʊksn] VT (*inf*) to annoy

Fuchsie [ˈfʊksiə] F **-, -n** (*Bot*) fuchsia

fuchsig [ˈfʊksɪç] ADJ (*inf*: = *wütend*) mad (*inf*)

Füchsin [ˈfʏksɪn] F **-, -nen** vixen

Fuchs-: Fuchsjagd F fox-hunting; (= *einzelne Jagd*) fox hunt; **Fuchspelz** M fox fur; **fuchsrot** ADJ *Fell* red; *Pferd* chestnut; *Haar* ginger; **Fuchsschwanz** M (**a**) fox's tail; (*Hunt*) (fox's) brush (**b**) (*Tech*: = *Säge*) handsaw; **fuchsteufelswild** ADJ (*inf*) hopping mad (*inf*)

Fuchtel [ˈfʊxtl̩] F **-, -n** (**a**) (*fig inf*: = *Knute*) control; **unter jds** (*dat*) **~** under sb's thumb (**b**) (*Aus, S Ger inf*: = *zänkische Frau*) shrew

fuchteln [ˈfʊxtl̩n] VI (*inf*) (**mit den Händen**) **~** to wave one's hands about (*inf*); **mit etw ~** to wave sth around; (*drohend*) to brandish sth

Fuffi [ˈfʊfi] M **-s, -s** (*hum inf*: = *Fünfzigeuroschein*) fifty (big ones *pl*) (*inf*)

Fuffziger [ˈfʊftsɪgɐ] M **-s, -** (*dial*) (= *Fünfzigeuroschein*) fifty-euro note (*Brit*) *or* bill (*US*); (= *Fünfzigcentstück*) fifty-cent piece; **er ist ein falscher ~** (*inf*) he's a real crook (*inf*)

Fug [fuːk] M (*geh*) **mit ~ und Recht** with complete justification; **etw mit ~ und Recht tun** to be completely justified in doing sth

Fuge [ˈfuːgə] F **-, -n** (**a**) joint; (= *Ritze*) gap, crack; **die Welt ist/ die Zeiten sind aus den ~n geraten** (*geh*) the world is/the times are out of joint (*liter*) (**b**) (*Mus*) fugue

fugen [ˈfuːgn̩] VT to joint

fügen [ˈfyːgn̩] **1** VT (**a**) (= *setzen, einfügen*) to put, to place; **Wort an Wort ~** to string words together (**b**) (*geh*: = *bewirken*) to ordain; (*Schicksal*) to decree; **der Zufall fügte es, dass ...** fate decreed that ... **2** VR (= *sich unterordnen*) to be obedient, to obey; **sich jdm/einer Sache** *or* **in etw** (*acc*) (*geh*) **~** to bow to sb/sth; *Anordnungen etc* to obey sth; **sich dem** *or* **in das Schicksal ~** to accept one's fate

fügsam [ˈfyːkzaːm] ADJ *Mensch, Tier* obedient

Fügung [ˈfyːgʊŋ] F **-, -en** (**a**) (= *Bestimmung*) chance, stroke of fate; **eine glückliche ~** a stroke of good fortune; **göttliche ~** divine providence; **eine ~ Gottes/des Schicksals** an act of divine providence/of fate; **eine seltsame ~ wollte es, dass er ...** by some strange chance he ... (**b**) (*Ling*: = *Wortgruppe*) construction

fühlbar ADJ (= *spürbar*) perceptible; (= *beträchtlich auch*) marked; **bald wird die Krise auch bei uns ~** the crisis will soon be felt here too

fühlen [ˈfyːlən] **1** VTI to feel; *Puls* to take; **Mitleid mit jdm ~** to feel sympathy for sb **2** VR to feel; **sich krank/beleidigt/ verantwortlich ~** to feel ill (*Brit*) *or* sick (*esp US*)/insulted/ responsible; **wie ~ Sie sich?** how are you feeling?, how do you feel?; **er fühlte sich als Held** he felt (like) a hero

Fühler [ˈfyːlɐ] M **-s, -** (*Zool*) feeler, antenna; (*von Schnecke*) horn; **seine ~ ausstrecken** (*fig inf*) to put out feelers (*nach* towards)

Fühlung [ˈfyːlʊŋ] F **-, -en** contact; **mit jdm in ~ bleiben/stehen** to remain *or* stay/be in contact *or* touch with sb

fuhr PRET *von* **fahren**

Fuhre [ˈfuːrə] F **-, -n** (= *Ladung*) load; (= *Taxieinsatz*) fare; **eine ~ Stroh** a (cart-)load of straw; **wir müssen die Leute in zwei ~n zum Bahnhof bringen** we'll have to take the people to the station in two loads

führen [ˈfyːrən] **1** VT (**a**) (= *geleiten*) to take; (= *vorangehen, -fahren*) to lead; **eine alte Dame über die Straße ~** to help an old lady across the road; **er führte uns durch das Schloss** he showed us (a)round the castle; **er führte uns durch Italien** he

was our guide in Italy; **eine Klasse zum Abitur ~** ≈ to see a class through to A-levels (*Brit*) *or* to their high school diploma (*US*); **jdn zum (Trau)altar ~** to lead sb to the altar (**b**) (= *leiten*) *Geschäft, Betrieb etc* to run; *Gruppe, Expedition etc* to lead, to head (**c**) (= *in eine Situation bringen*) to get (*inf*), to lead; (= *veranlassen zu kommen/gehen*) to bring/take; **der Hinweis führte die Polizei auf die Spur des Diebes** that tip put the police on the trail of the thief; **was führt Sie zu mir?** (*form*) what brings you to me?; **ein Land ins Chaos ~** to reduce a country to chaos (**d**) (= *registriert haben*) to have a record of; **wir ~ keinen Meier in unserer Kartei** we have no (record of a) Meier on our files (**e**) (= *handhaben*) *Pinsel, Bogen, Kamera etc* to wield; **den Löffel zum Mund/das Glas an die Lippen ~** to raise one's spoon to one's mouth/one's glass to one's lips (**f**) (= *entlangführen*) *Leitung, Draht* to carry (**g**) (*form*: = *steuern*) *Kraftfahrzeug* to drive; *Flugzeug* to fly; *Kran, Fahrstuhl* to operate; *Schiff* to sail (**h**) (= *transportieren*) to carry; (= *haben*) *Autokennzeichen, Wappen, Namen, Titel* to have; (= *selbst gebrauchen*) to use; **Geld/seine Papiere bei sich ~** (*form*) to carry money/one's papers on one's person; **der Fluss führt Hochwasser** the river is running high (**i**) (= *im Angebot haben*) to stock **2** VI (**a**) (= *in Führung liegen*) to lead; **die Mannschaft führt mit 10 Punkten Vorsprung** the team has a lead of *or* is leading by 10 points; **die Firma XY führt in Videorekordern** XY is the leading firm for video recorders (**b**) (= *verlaufen*) (*Straße*) to go; (*Kabel, Pipeline etc*) to run; (*Spur*) to lead; **die Brücke führt über die Elbe** the bridge spans the Elbe; **der Waldweg führt zu einem Gasthof** the forest path leads to an inn (**c**) (= *als Ergebnis haben*) **zu etw ~** to lead to sth, to result in sth; **das führt zu nichts** that will come to nothing; **wohin soll das alles nur ~?** where is it all leading (us)? **3** VR (*form*: = *sich benehmen*) to conduct oneself

führend ADJ leading *attr*; **die Amerikaner sind in der Leichtathletik ~** the Americans lead the world in athletics

Führer¹ [ˈfyːrɐ] M **-s, -** (= *Buch*) guide; **~ durch England** guide to England

Führer² [ˈfyːrɐ] M **-s, -**, **Führerin** [-ərɪn] F **-, -nen** (**a**) (= *Leiter*) leader; (= *Oberhaupt*) head; **der ~** (*Hist*) the Führer, the Fuehrer (**b**) (= *Fremdenführer, Bergführer*) guide (**c**) (*form*: = *Lenker*) driver; (*von Flugzeug*) pilot; (*von Kran, Fahrstuhl*) operator; (*von Schiff*) person in charge

Führer-: Führerhaus NT cab; (*von Kran auch*) cabin; **Führerschein** M (*für Auto*) driving licence (*Brit*), driver's license (*US*); (*für Motorboot*) motorboat licence (*Brit*) *or* license (*US*); **den ~ machen** (*Aut*) to learn to drive; (= *die Prüfung ablegen*) to take one's (driving) test; **jdm den ~ entziehen** to disqualify sb from driving; **ihm ist der ~ abgenommen worden** he's lost his licence (*Brit*) *or* license (*US*); **auf Probe** probationary driving licence (*Brit*) *or* driver's license (*US*)

Fuhrpark M fleet (of vehicles)

Führung [ˈfyːrʊŋ] F **-, -en** (**a**) NO PL guidance, direction; (*von Partei, Expedition etc*) leadership; (*Mil*) command; (*eines Unternehmens etc*) management (**b**) NO PL (= *die Führer*) leaders *pl*, leadership *sing*; (*Mil*) commanders *pl*; (*eines Unternehmens etc*) directors *pl* (**c**) (= *Besichtigung*) guided tour (*durch* of) (**d**) NO PL (= *Vorsprung*) lead; **die klare ~ haben** (*bei Wettkämpfen*) to have a clear lead; **in ~ gehen/liegen** to go into/be in the lead (**e**) (= *Betragen*) conduct; **wegen guter ~ vorzeitig aus der Haft entlassen werden** to be released from prison early for good behaviour (*Brit*) *or* behavior (*US*) (**f**) (*Mech*) guide, guideway (**g**) (*form*: = *Lenken*) **zur ~ eines Kraftfahrzeugs/ Wasserfahrzeugs/Flugzeugs berechtigt sein** to be licensed to drive a motor vehicle/be in charge of a vessel/fly an aircraft

Führungs-: Führungsanspruch M claims *pl* to leadership; **seinen ~ anmelden** to make a bid for the leadership; **Führungsaufgabe** F executive duty; **Führungskraft** F executive; **Führungsschiene** F guide rail; **führungsschwach** ADJ *Partei, Chef* weak; **Führungsschwäche** F weak leadership; **Führungsstärke** F strong leadership; **Führungsstil** M style of

leadership; (*Comm auch*) management style;
Führungszeugnis NT *siehe* **polizeilich**

Fuhr-: Fuhrunternehmen NT haulage business;
Fuhrunternehmer(in) M(F) haulier (*Brit*), haulage contractor;
Fuhrwerk NT wagon; (= *Pferdefuhrwerk*) horse and cart;
(= *Ochsenfuhrwerk*) oxcart; **Fuhrwesen** NT, NO PL cartage
business

Fülle ['fʏlə] F -, NO PL **(a)** (= *Körpermasse*) portliness
(b) (= *Stärke*) fullness; (*von Stimme, Klang auch*) richness; (*von
Haar*) body **(c)** (= *Menge*) wealth; **eine ~ von Fragen/
Eindrücken** *etc* a whole host of questions/impressions *etc*; **in
~** in abundance

füllen ['fʏlən] **1** VT to fill; (*Cook*) to stuff; **etw in Flaschen ~** to
bottle sth; **etw in Säcke ~** to put sth into sacks; *siehe auch*
gefüllt 2 VR (*Theater, Badewanne*) to fill up

Füller ['fʏlɐ] M -s, - (= *Füllfederhalter*) fountain pen

Füll-: Füllfederhalter M fountain pen; **Füllgewicht** NT
(a) (*Comm*) weight at time of packing; (*auf Dosen*) net
weight **(b)** (*von Waschmaschine*) maximum load, capacity

füllig ['fʏlɪç] ADJ *Mensch* portly; *Figur, Busen* generous; *Frisur*
bouffant *attr*

Füllung ['fʏlʊŋ] F -, -en filling; (= *Geflügelfüllung, Fleischfüllung,
Stofftierfüllung, Polsterfüllung*) stuffing; (*von Pralinen*) centre
(*Brit*), center (*US*)

Füllwort NT, *pl* -wörter filler (word)

Fummel ['fʊml] M -s, - (*inf*) rag; **im ~** (*sl*: = *in Frauenkleidung*) in
drag (*inf*)

Fummelkram M (*inf*) fiddly job (*inf*)

fummeln ['fʊmln] VI (*inf*) to fiddle; (= *hantieren*) to fumble;
(*erotisch*) to pet, to grope (*inf*); **an etw** (*dat*) *or* **mit etw ~** to
fiddle (about)/fumble around with sth

Fund [fʊnt] M -(e)s, -e [-də] find; (= *das Entdecken*) discovery;
einen ~ machen to make a find

Fundament [fʊnda'mɛnt] NT -(e)s, -e *lit, fig* foundation (*usu
pl*); **das ~ zu etw legen** (*fig*), **das ~ für etw schaffen** (*fig*) to lay
the foundations for sth

fundamental [fʊndamɛn'taːl] **1** ADJ fundamental **2** ADV
fundamentally

Fundamentalismus [fʊndamɛnta'lɪsmʊs] M -, NO PL
fundamentalism

Fundamentalist [fʊndamɛnta'lɪst] M -en, -en,
Fundamentalistin [-'lɪstɪn] F -, -nen fundamentalist

fundamentalistisch [fʊndamɛnta'lɪstɪʃ] ADJ fundamentalist

Fund-: Fundamt NT, **Fundbüro** NT lost property office (*Brit*), lost
and found (*US*); **Fundgrube** F (*fig*) treasure trove; **eine ~ des
Wissens** a treasury of knowledge

Fundi ['fʊndi] M -s, -s *or* F -, -s (*Pol inf*) fundamentalist (*of the
Green party*)

fundieren [fʊn'diːrən], *ptp* **fundiert** VT (*fig*) to back up

fundiert [fʊn'diːrt] ADJ sound; **schlecht ~** unsound

fündig ['fʏndɪç] ADJ (*Min*) *Sohle* rich; **~ werden** to make a strike;
(*fig*) to strike it lucky

Fundus ['fʊndʊs] M -, - (*lit, fig*) fund; (*Theat*) basic equipment

fünf [fʏnf] NUM five; **es ist ~ Minuten vor zwölf** (*lit*) it's five to
twelve; (*fig*) it's almost too late; **sie warteten bis ~ Minuten
vor zwölf** (*fig*) they waited till the eleventh hour; **seine ~
Sinne beieinander haben** *or* **beisammenhaben** to have all
one's wits about one; **seine ~ Sinne zusammennehmen** to
gather one's wits together; **~(e) gerade sein lassen** (*inf*) to
turn a blind eye; *siehe auch* **vier**

Fünf [fʏnf] F -, -en five; *siehe auch* **Vier**

Fünf- IN CPDS five; **Fünfcentstück** NT five-cent piece; **Fünfeck**
NT pentagon; **fünfeckig** ADJ pentagonal, five-cornered;
Fünfeuroschein M five-euro note (*Brit*) *or* bill (*US*); **fünffach**
['fʏnffax] ADJ fivefold; *siehe auch* **vierfach; fünffüßig** ADJ (*Poet*)
pentametrical; **~er Jambus** iambic pentameter;
Fünfganggetriebe NT five-speed gearbox;
Fünfgangschaltung F five-speed gears *pl*; **fünfhundert**
['fʏnfhʊndɐt] NUM five hundred; **Fünfjahresplan** M five-year
plan; **fünfjährig** ADJ *Frist, Plan, Amtszeit etc* five-year; *Kind* five-
year-old; **eine ~e Zeitspanne** a period of five years; *siehe auch*
vierjährig; Fünfkampf M (*Sport*) pentathlon

Fünfling ['fʏnflɪŋ] M -s, -e quintuplet

fünfmal ['fʏnfmaːl] ADV five times; *siehe auch* **viermal**

Fünfprozent- [fʏnfpro'tsɛnt-]: **Fünfprozenthürde** F (*Parl*) five-
percent hurdle; **Fünfprozentklausel** F five-percent rule

FÜNFPROZENTKLAUSEL

Electoral law in Germany contains a **Fünfprozentklausel**, *meaning
that only those parties that manage to poll at least 5% of the votes over
an entire electoral area may have a stake in the allocation of seats. This
rule was introduced after the Second World War to guard against the
fragmentation of parties, which was seen as one of the causes of the
collapse of the Weimar Republic.*

Fünf-: fünfseitig [-zaitɪç] ADJ (*Geometrie*) five-sided; *Brief* five-
page *attr*; **fünftägig** ADJ five-day *attr*; **fünftausend** ['fʏnf'tauznt]
NUM five thousand

Fünftel ['fʏnftl] NT -s, - fifth; *siehe auch* **Viertel**[1]

fünftens ['fʏnftns] ADV fifth(ly), in the fifth place

fünfte(r, s) ['fʏnftɐ] ADJ fifth; *siehe auch* **vierte(r, s)**

Fünf-: Fünfuhrtee M afternoon tea;
Fünfunddreißigstundenwoche F thirty-five-hour week;
fünfzehn ['fʏnftseːn] NUM fifteen

fünfzig ['fʏnftsɪç] NUM fifty; *siehe auch* **vierzig**

Fünfzigcentstück NT fifty-cent piece

Fünfziger ['fʏnftsɪɡɐ] M -s, - (*inf*) (= *Fünfzigeuroschein*) fifty-euro
note (*Brit*) *or* bill (*US*); (= *Fünfzigcentstück*) fifty-cent piece

Fünfzig-: Fünfzigeuroschein M fifty-euro note (*Brit*) *or* bill (*US*);
fünfzigjährig ADJ *Person* fifty-year-old *attr*; *Zeitspanne* fifty-
year; **er ist ~ verstorben** he died at (the age of) fifty

fungieren [fʊŋ'giːrən], *ptp* **fungiert** VI to function (*als* as a)

Funk [fʊŋk] M -s, NO PL radio; **über** *or* **per ~** by radio

-funk SUF IN CPDS programmes *pl* (*Brit*), programs *pl* (*US*);
Hausfrauenfunk program(me)s *pl* for housewives

Fünkchen ['fʏŋkçən] NT -s, - DIM *von* **Funke; ein ~ Wahrheit** a
grain of truth

Funke ['fʊŋkə] M -ns, -n **(a)** (*lit, fig*) spark; **~n sprühen** to spark,
to emit sparks; **~n sprühend** emitting sparks; (*fig*) *Diskussion*
lively; *Augen* flashing *attr*, fiery; **der zündende ~** (*fig*) the
vital spark; **arbeiten, dass die ~n fliegen** *or* **sprühen** (*inf*) to
work like crazy (*inf*) **(b)** (= *ein bisschen*) scrap; (*von Hoffnung*)
gleam, glimmer

funkeln ['fʊŋkln] VI to sparkle; (*Edelmetall*) (*Augen*) (*vor Freude*)
to twinkle; (*vor Zorn*) to glitter

funkelnagelneu ['fʊŋkl'naːɡl'nɔy] ADJ (*inf*) brand-new

funken ['fʊŋkn] **1** VT *Signal* to radio; **SOS ~** to send out an SOS
2 VI (= *senden*) to radio **3** VI IMPERS **endlich hat es bei ihm
gefunkt** (*inf*) it finally clicked (with him) (*inf*)

Funken ['fʊŋkn] M -s, - = **Funke**

Funkentstörung ['fʊŋkɛnt-] F suppression of interference

Funker ['fʊŋkɐ] M -s, -, **Funkerin** [-ərɪn] F -, -nen radio *or*
wireless operator

Funk-: Funkgerät NT **(a)** NO PL radio equipment
(b) (= *Sprechfunkgerät*) radio set, walkie-talkie; **Funkhaus** NT
broadcasting centre (*Brit*) *or* center (*US*); **Funkkontakt** M radio
contact; **Funkpeilung** F radio direction finding; **Funkruf** M
(a) radio call **(b)** (*Telec*) (radio) paging; **Funkrufdienst** M
(*Telec*) (radio) paging service; **Funksprechgerät** NT radio
telephone; (*tragbar*) walkie-talkie; **Funksprechverkehr** M
radiotelephony; **Funkspruch** M radio signal; (= *Mitteilung*)
radio message; **Funkstation** F radio station; **Funkstille** F radio
silence; (*fig*) silence; **Funkstreife** F police radio patrol;
Funkstreifenwagen M police radio patrol *or* squad car;
Funktelefon NT radio telephone

Funktion [fʊŋk'tsioːn] F -, -en (= *Zweck, Aufgabe*) (*Math*)
function; (*no pl*: = *Tätigkeit*) functioning; (= *Amt*) office;
(= *Stellung*) position; **in ~ treten** to come into operation;
(*Organ, Maschine etc*) to start to function; **in ~ sein** to be in
operation; (*Organ, Maschine etc*) to be functioning; **dieser
Bolzen hat die ~, den Apparat senkrecht zu halten** the
function of this bolt is to hold the machine upright

Funktionalität [fʊŋktsionali'tɛːt] F -, -en practicality

Funktionär [fʊŋktsio'nɛːɐ] M -s, -e, **Funktionärin** [-'nɛːrɪn] F -,
-nen functionary

funktionell [fʊŋktsio'nɛl] ADJ functional (*auch Med*), practical

funktionieren [fʊŋktsio'niːrən], *ptp* **funktioniert** VI to work;
(*Maschine etc auch*) to function; (*inf*: = *gehorchen*) to obey

Funktions-: Funktionsbild NT, NO PL job profile; **funktionsfähig** ADJ able to work; *Maschine etc auch* in working order; **Funktionsleiste** F (*Comput*) toolbar; **Funktionsstörung** F (*Med*) malfunction; **Funktionstaste** F (*Comput*) function key; **Funktionsverb** NT (*Ling*) empty verb

Funk-: Funkturm M radio tower; **Funkuhr** F radio-controlled clock; **Funkverbindung** F radio contact; **Funkverkehr** M radio communication *or* traffic

Funsel ['fɔnzl] F -, -n, **Funzel** ['fʊntsl] F -, -n (*inf*) dim light

für [fyːɐ̯] PREP +ACC **(a)** for; ~ **was ist denn dieses Werkzeug?** (*inf*) what is this tool (used) for?; **kann ich sonst noch etwas ~ Sie tun?** will there be anything else?; ~ **mich** for me; (= *meiner Ansicht nach*) in my opinion *or* view; ~ **zwei arbeiten** (*fig*) to do the work of two people; ~ **einen Deutschen ...** for a German ...; ~**s Erste** for the moment; ~**s nächste Mal** next time
(b) (*Zustimmung*) for, in favour (*Brit*) *or* favor (*US*) of; **sich ~ etw entscheiden** to decide in favo(u)r of sth; **was Sie da sagen, hat etwas ~ sich** there's something in what you're saying; **er hat was ~ sich** he's not a bad person; **das hat was ~ sich** it's not a bad thing
(c) (*Gegenleistung*) (in exchange) for; **das hat er ~ zehn Pfund gekauft** he bought it for ten pounds
(d) (*Ersatz*) for, instead of; ~ **jdn einspringen** to stand in for sb
(e) (*Aufeinanderfolge*) **Tag ~ Tag** day after day; **Schritt ~ Schritt** step by step
(f) (*in Verbindung mit vb, adj siehe auch dort*) **etw ~ sich behalten** to keep sth to oneself; ~ **etw bekannt sein** to be famous *or* known for sth; **ich halte sie ~ intelligent** I think she is intelligent
(g) was ~ *siehe* **was**

Für ['fyːɐ̯] NT **das ~ und Wider** the pros and cons *pl*

Fürbitte F (*Eccl, fig*) intercession

Furche ['fʊrçə] F -, -n (= *Ackerfurche, Gesichtsfalte*) furrow; (= *Wagenspur*) rut

Furcht [fʊrçt] F -, NO PL fear; **aus ~ vor jdm/etw** for fear of sb/sth; ~ **vor jdm/etw haben** *or* **empfinden** to fear sb/sth; **jdn in ~ versetzen**, **jdm ~ einflößen** to frighten *or* scare sb; ~ **einflößend**, ~ **erregend** terrifying; **ohne ~ und Tadel** without fear or reproach

furchtbar ADJ **❶** terrible, awful; **ich habe einen ~en Hunger** I'm terribly hungry (*inf*) **❷** ADV terribly (*inf*), awfully (*inf*); **wir haben ~ gelacht** we laughed ourselves silly (*inf*)

furchteinflößend ADJ *siehe* **Furcht**

fürchten ['fyrçtn] **❶** VT **jdn/etw ~** to be afraid of sb/sth, to fear sb/sth; **das Schlimmste ~** to fear the worst; **Gott ~** to fear God; *siehe auch* **gefürchtet**
❷ VR to be afraid (*vor* +*dat* of)
❸ VI **für** *or* **um jdn/jds Leben/etw ~** to fear for sb/sb's life/sth; **zum Fürchten aussehen** to look frightening *or* terrifying; **da kannst du das Fürchten lernen** that will scare you stiff (*inf*); **jdn das Fürchten lehren** to put the fear of God into sb

fürchterlich ['fyrçtəlɪç] ADJ, ADV = **furchtbar**

Furcht-: furchterregend ADJ *siehe* **Furcht**; **furchtlos** ADJ fearless; **Furchtlosigkeit** F -, NO PL fearlessness; **furchtsam** ['fʊrçtzaːm] ADJ timorous

füreinander [fyːɐ̯lai'nandɐ] ADV for each other, for one another

Furie ['fuːriə] F -, -n (*Myth*) fury; (*fig*) hellcat (*esp Brit*), termagant; **sie gingen wie ~n aufeinander los** they went for each other like wild things

furios [fu'rioːs] ADJ high-energy, dynamic

Furnier [fʊr'niːɐ̯] NT -s, -e veneer

furnieren [fʊr'niːrən] *ptp* **furniert** VT to veneer

Fürsorge F, NO PL **(a)** (= *Betreuung*) care; (= *Sozialfürsorge*) welfare **(b)** (*inf*: = *Sozialamt*) welfare (*inf*), welfare services *pl*; **der ~ zur Last fallen** to be a burden on the state **(c)** (*inf*: = *Sozialunterstützung*) social security (*Brit*), welfare (*US*); **von der ~ leben** to live on social security (*Brit*) *or* welfare (*US*)

fürsorgerisch ['fyːɐ̯zɔrgərɪʃ] **❶** ADJ welfare *attr* **❷** ADV **alte Menschen ~ betreuen** to look after the welfare of old people

Fürsorge-: Fürsorgesatz M rate of social security (benefit) (*Brit*), rate of welfare (*US*); **Fürsorgestaat** M welfare state

fürsorglich ['fyːɐ̯zɔrklɪç] **❶** ADJ caring; ~**e Pflege** attentive care **❷** ADV **jdn sehr ~ behandeln** to lavish care on sb

Fürsprache F recommendation; **für jdn ~ einlegen** to put in a word for sb (*inf*) (*bei* with); **auf ~ von jdm** on sb's recommendation

Fürsprecher(in) M(F) **(a)** advocate **(b)** (*Sw: = Rechtsanwalt*) barrister (*Brit*), lawyer

Fürst [fyrst] M -en, -en prince; (= *Herrscher*) ruler

Fürstentum ['fyrstntuːm] NT -s, -tümer [-tyːmɐ] principality; **das ~ Monaco/Liechtenstein** the principality of Monaco/Liechtenstein

Fürstin ['fyrstɪn] F -, -nen princess; (= *Herrscherin*) ruler

fürstlich ['fyrstlɪç] **❶** ADJ (*lit*) princely *no adv*; (*fig auch*) handsome **❷** ADV **jdn ~ bewirten** to entertain sb right royally; **jdn ~ belohnen** to reward sb handsomely; ~ **leben** to live like a king *or* lord

Furunkel [fu'rʊŋkl] NT *or* M -s, - boil

Fürwort NT, *pl* -wörter (*Gram*) pronoun

Furz [fʊrts] M -(e)s, ⸚e ['fyrtsə] (*inf*) fart (*inf*)

furzen ['fʊrtsn] VI (*inf*) to fart (*inf*)

Fusel ['fuːzl] M -s, - (*pej*) rotgut (*inf*), hooch (*esp US inf*)

Fusion [fu'zioːn] F -, -en amalgamation; (*von Unternehmen auch*) merger; (*von Atomkernen, Zellen*) fusion

fusionieren [fuzio'niːrən], *ptp* **fusioniert** VT to amalgamate; (*Unternehmen auch*) to merge

Fusionskontrolle F merger control

Fuß [fuːs] M -es, ⸚e ['fyːsə] **(a)** (= *Körperteil*) foot; (*S Ger, Aus: = Bein*) leg; **zu ~** on *or* by foot; **er ist gut/schlecht zu ~** he is steady/not so steady on his feet; **sich jdm zu Füßen werfen** to prostrate oneself before sb; **jdm zu Füßen fallen/liegen/sitzen** to fall/lie/sit at sb's feet; **jdm zu Füßen fallen** *or* **sinken** (*fig: Bittsteller*) to go down on one's knees before sb; **das Publikum lag/sank ihr zu Füßen** she had the audience at her feet; **über seine eigenen Füße stolpern** to trip over one's own feet; (*fig*) to get tied up in knots; **kalte Füße bekommen** (*lit, fig*), **sich** (*dat*) **kalte Füße holen** (*lit, fig*) to get cold feet; **so schnell/weit ihn seine Füße trugen** as fast/far as his legs would carry him; **bei ~!** heel!; **jdn mit Füßen treten** (*fig*) to walk all over sb; **etw mit Füßen treten** (*fig*) to treat sth with contempt; (**festen**) ~ **fassen** (*lit, fig*) to gain a foothold; (= *sich niederlassen*) to settle down; **auf eigenen Füßen stehen** (*fig*) to stand on one's own two feet; **jdn auf freien ~ setzen** to release sb, to set sb free; **jdn auf dem falschen ~ erwischen** (*fig*) to catch sb on the wrong foot; **mit einem ~ im Grab stehen** to have one foot in the grave
(b) (*von Gegenstand*) base; (= *Tisch-, Stuhlbein*) leg; (*von Schrank, Gebirge*) foot; **auf schwachen** *or* **tönernen Füßen stehen** to be built on sand
(c) (*Poet*) foot
(d) *pl* - (*Längenmaß*) foot; **12 ~ lang** 12 foot *or* feet long

Fuß-: Fußabdruck M footprint; **Fußabstreifer** [-lapʃtraifɐ] M -s, - footscraper; (= *Matte*) doormat

Fußball M **(a)** (*no pl*: = ~*spiel*) football (*esp Brit*), soccer **(b)** (= *Ball*) football (*esp Brit*), soccer ball

Fußballer [-balɐ] M -s, -, **Fußballerin** [-ərɪn] F -, -nen (*inf*) footballer (*esp Brit*), soccer player

Fußball-: Fußballmannschaft F football (*esp Brit*) *or* soccer team; **Fußballmeisterschaft** F football (*esp Brit*) *or* soccer league championship; **Fußballplatz** M football pitch (*esp Brit*), soccer field (*US*); **Fußballspieler(in)** M(F) football (*esp Brit*) *or* soccer player

Fußboden M floor

Fußboden-: Fußbodenbelag M floor covering; **Fußbodenheizung** F (under)floor heating

Fußbremse F foot brake

Fussel ['fʊsl] F -, -n *or* m -s, - fluff *no pl*; **ein(e) ~** a bit of fluff

fusselig ['fʊsəlɪç] ADJ (= *von Fusseln bedeckt*) covered with fluff; (= *fusselnd*) giving off fluff; (= *ausgefranst*) frayed; **sich** (*dat*) **den Mund ~ reden** (*inf*) to talk till one is blue in the face

fusseln ['fʊsln] VI to give off fluff

fußen ['fuːsn] VI to rest (*auf* +*dat* on)

Fuß-: Fußende NT (*von Bett*) foot; **Fußfessel** F ~**n** *pl* shackles *pl*; **elektronische ~** electronic tag

Fußgänger [-gɛŋɐ] M -s, -, **Fußgängerin** [-ərɪn] F -, -nen pedestrian

Fußgänger-: Fußgängerüberweg M pedestrian crossing (*Brit*), crosswalk (*US*); (*auch* **Fußgängerüberführung**) pedestrian bridge; **Fußgängerunterführung** F underpass, pedestrian subway (*Brit*); **Fußgängerzone** F pedestrian precinct *or* zone

Fußgelenk NT ankle

-füßig [fyːsɪç] ADJ SUF **(a)** -legged; **ein dreifüßiger Tisch** a three-legged table **(b)** (*Poet*) -foot; **fünffüßiger Jambus** iambic pentameter

fusslig ADJ = fusselig

Fuß-: Fußmarsch M walk; (*Mil*) march; **Fußmatte** F doormat; **Fußnote** F footnote; **Fußpflege** F chiropody; **zur ~ gehen** to go to the chiropodist; **Fußpfleger(in)** M(F) chiropodist; **Fußpilz** M (*Med*) athlete's foot; **Fußsohle** F sole of the foot; **Fußspur** F footprint; **Fußstapfen** M footprint; **in jds** (*acc*) **~ treten** (*fig*) to follow in sb's footsteps; **Fußstütze** F footrest; **Fußtritt** M (= *Geräusch*) footstep; (= *Spur auch*) footprint; (= *Stoß*) kick; **jdm einen ~ geben** *or* **versetzen** to kick sb; **einen ~ bekommen** (*fig*) to be kicked out (*inf*); **Fußweg** M **(a)** (= *Pfad*) footpath **(b)** (= *Entfernung*) **es sind nur 15 Minuten ~** it's only 15 minutes' walk; **Fußzeile** F (*Comput*) footer

Futon [ˈfuːtɔn] M -s, -s futon

Futter [ˈfʊtɐ] NT -s, - **(a)** NO PL (animal) food *or* feed; (*esp für Kühe, Pferde etc*) fodder; **gut im ~ sein** to be well-fed **(b)** (= *Auskleidung, Kleiderfutter*) lining

Futteral [fʊtəˈraːl] NT -s, -e case

futtern [ˈfʊtɐn] (*hum inf*) **1** VI to stuff oneself (*inf*) **2** VT to scoff (*Brit inf*), to scarf *or* chow (*US inf*)

füttern [ˈfʏtɐn] VT **(a)** *Tier, Kind, Kranke* to feed; **„Füttern verboten"** "do not feed the animals" **(b)** *Kleidungsstück* to line

Futter-: Futternapf M bowl; **Futterneid** M (*fig*) green-eyed monster (*hum*), jealousy; **Futterrübe** F *root vegetable used to feed animals*

Fütterung [ˈfʏtərʊŋ] F -, -en feeding; **die ~ der Nilpferde findet um 17.00 Uhr statt** feeding time for the hippos is 5 pm

Futur [fuˈtuːɐ] NT -(e)s, -e (*Gram*) future (tense)

Futures [ˈfjuːtʃɐs] PL (*St Ex*) futures pl

futuristisch [futuˈrɪstɪʃ] ADJ **(a)** (= *zukunftsweisend*) futuristic **(b)** (= *den Futurismus betreffend*) futurist

Futurologe [futuroˈloːɡə] M -n, -n, **Futurologin** [-ˈloːɡɪn] F -, -nen futurologist

Futurologie [futuroloˈɡiː] F -, NO PL futurology

futurologisch [futuroˈloːɡɪʃ] ADJ futurological

fuzeln [ˈfuːtsln] VI (*Aus*) to write small

Fuzzi [ˈfʊtsi] M -s, -s (*inf*) freak (*inf*)

Gg

G, g [geː] NT **-, -** G, g

g ABBR *von* **Gramm**

gab PRET *von* **geben**

Gabe [ˈgaːbə] F **-, -n** (= *Begabung*) gift; **die ~ haben, etw zu tun** to have a natural gift for doing sth

Gabel [ˈgaːbl] F **-, -n** fork; (= *Heugabel, Mistgabel*) pitchfork; (= *Deichsel*) shafts *pl*; (*Telec*) rest, cradle

gabeln [ˈgaːbln] VR to fork; *siehe auch* **gegabelt**

Gabelstapler [-ʃtaːplɐ] M **-s, -** fork-lift truck

Gabelung F **-, -en** fork

Gabentisch M table for Christmas or birthday presents

G8 F - G8

G8-Staat M G8 nation

gackern [ˈgakɐn] VI (*lit, fig*) to cackle

gaffen [ˈgafn] VI to gape (*nach* at)

Gaffer [ˈgafɐ] M **-s, -**, **Gafferin** [-ərɪn] F **-, -nen** gaper; **die neugierigen ~ bei einem Unfall** the nosy people standing staring at an accident

Gag [gɛ(ː)k] M **-s, -s** (= *Filmgag*) gag; (= *Werbegag*) gimmick; (= *Witz*) joke; (*inf*: = *Spaß*) laugh

gaga [ˈgaga] ADJ PRED INV (*inf*) gaga (*inf*)

Gage [ˈgaːʒə] F **-, -n** (*esp Theat*) fee; (= *regelmäßige ~*) salary

gähnen [ˈgɛːnən] VI (*lit, fig*) to yawn; **~de Leere** total emptiness; **im Kino herrschte ~de Leere** the cinema was (totally) deserted; **ein ~des Loch** a gaping hole; **ein Gähnen** a yawn; **das Gähnen unterdrücken** to stop oneself (from) yawning

GAL [geːʔaːˈʔɛl] F - ABBR *von* **Grün-Alternative Liste** electoral pact of Greens and alternative parties

Gala- [ˈgala, ˈgaːla] IN CPDS formal, evening; (*Mil*) full, ceremonial; (*Theat*) gala; **Galaabend** M gala evening; **Galaanzug** M formal *or* evening dress; (*Mil*) full *or* ceremonial dress; **Galaempfang** M formal reception

galaktisch [gaˈlaktɪʃ] ADJ galactic

Gala- [ˈgala, ˈgaːla]: **Galauniform** F (*Mil*) full dress uniform; **Galavorstellung** F (*Theat*) gala performance

Gäle [ˈgɛːlə] M **-n, -n**, **Gälin** [ˈgɛːlɪn] F **-, -nen** Gael

Galeere [gaˈleːrə] F **-, -n** galley

Galerie [galəˈriː] F **-, -n** (a) (= *Empore, Gang, Kunstgalerie, Mil, Naut*) gallery; **auf der ~** in the gallery (b) (= *Geschäftspassage*) arcade

Galgen [ˈgalgn] M **-s, -** gallows *pl*, gibbet; (*Film*) boom; (*Tech*) crossbeam; (= *Spiel*) hangman

Galgen-: **Galgenfrist** F reprieve; **jdm eine ~ geben** to give sb a reprieve; **Galgenhumor** M gallows humour (*Brit*) *or* humor (*US*); **sagte er mit ~** he said with a macabre sense of humo(u)r

Gälin F *siehe* **Gäle**

Galionsfigur F figurehead

gälisch [ˈgɛːlɪʃ] ADJ Gaelic

Galle [ˈgalə] F **-, -n** (*Anat*) (= *Organ*) gall bladder; (= *Flüssigkeit*) bile; (*Bot, Vet*) gall; (*fig*: = *Bosheit*) virulence; **bitter wie ~** bitter as gall; **seine ~ verspritzen** (*fig*) to pour out one's venom; **jdm kommt die ~ hoch** sb's blood begins to boil

Gallen- IN CPDS gall; **Gallenblase** F gall bladder; **Gallengang** M, *pl* **-gänge** bile duct; **Gallengrieß** M small gallstones *pl*; **Gallenkolik** F gallstone colic; **Gallenleiden** NT trouble with one's gall bladder; **Gallenstein** M gallstone

Gallien [ˈgaliən] NT **-s** Gaul

Gallier [ˈgaliɐ] M **-s, -**, **Gallierin** [-ərɪn] F **-, -nen** Gaul

gallisch [ˈgalɪʃ] ADJ Gallic

Gallone [gaˈloːnə] F **-, -n** gallon

Galopp [gaˈlɔp] M **-s, -s** *or* **-e** gallop; (= *Tanz*) galop; **im ~** (*lit*) at a gallop; (*fig*) at top speed; **langsamer ~** canter; **gestreckter/kurzer ~** full/checked gallop

galoppieren [galɔˈpiːrən], *ptp* **galoppiert** VI AUX HABEN *or* SEIN to gallop; **~de Inflation** galloping inflation

galt PRET *von* **gelten**

galvanisieren [galvaniˈziːrən], *ptp* **galvanisiert** VT to electroplate; (*mit Zink auch*) to galvanize

Gamasche [gaˈmaʃə] F **-, -n** gaiter; (= *kurze ~*) spat; (= *Wickelgamasche*) puttee

Gambe [ˈgambə] F **-, -n** viola da gamba

Gambia [ˈgambia] NT **-s** (the) Gambia

Gameboy® [ˈgeːmbɔy] M **-(s), -s** Gameboy®

Gameshow [ˈgeːmʃoː] F game show

Gamma [ˈgama] NT **-(s), -s** gamma

Gammastrahlen [ˈgama-] PL gamma rays *pl*

gammelig [ˈgaməlɪç] ADJ (*inf*) Lebensmittel, Auto old, ancient (*inf*); Kleidung tatty (*inf*); **das Fleisch ist ja schon ganz ~** the meat has already gone off (*Brit*) *or* bad

gammeln [ˈgamln] VI (*inf*) to loaf around (*inf*)

Gammler [ˈgamlɐ] M **-s, -**, **Gammlerin** [-ərɪn] F **-, -nen** long-haired layabout (*Brit*) *or* bum (*inf*)

Gams [gams] F **-, -(en)** [-zn] (*Aus, S Ger. Hunt*) chamois

Gämsbart M, **Gamsbart** M tuft of hair from a chamois worn as a hat decoration, shaving brush (*hum inf*)

Gämsbock M, **Gamsbock** M chamois buck

Gämse [ˈgɛmzə] F **-, -n** chamois

Gämsleder NT, **Gamsleder** NT chamois (leather)

gang [gaŋ] ADJ **~ und gäbe sein** to be quite usual

Gang¹ [gaŋ] M **-(e)s, ¨e** [ˈgɛŋə] **(a)** (*no pl*: = *~art*) walk, gait; (*eines Pferdes*) gait, pace; **einen leichten ~ haben** to be light on one's feet; **einen schnellen ~ haben** to be a fast walker; **jdn an seinem** *or* **am ~ erkennen** to recognize sb by the way he walks; **in aufrechtem ~** (*fig*) with one's head held high **(b)** (= *Besorgung*) errand; (= *Spaziergang*) walk; **einen ~ machen** *or* **tun** to go on an errand/for a walk; **einen ~ zum Anwalt/zur Bank machen** to pay a visit to one's lawyer/the bank; **einen schweren ~ tun** to do something difficult; **das war für ihn immer ein schwerer ~** it was always hard for him; **sein erster ~ war ...** the first thing he did was ...; **den ~ nach Canossa** *or* **Kanossa antreten** (*fig*) to eat humble pie; **der ~ nach Canossa** *or* **Kanossa** (*Hist*) the pilgrimage to Canossa; **der ~ an die Börse** flotation (on the stock exchange) **(c)** (*no pl*) (*Bewegung eines Motors*) running; (*einer Maschine*) running, operation; (= *Ablauf*) course; (*eines Dramas*) development; **der ~ der Ereignisse/der Dinge** the course of events/things; **seinen (gewohnten) ~ gehen** (*fig*) to run its usual course; **etw in ~ bringen** *or* **setzen** to get *or* set sth going; **etw in ~ halten** (*lit, fig*) to keep sth going; **in ~ kommen** to get going; **in ~ sein** to be going; (*fig*) to be under way; (= *los sein*) to be going on; **in vollem ~** in full swing; **es ist etwas im ~(e)** (*inf*) something's up (*inf*) **(d)** (= *Arbeitsgang*) operation; (*eines Essens*) course; (*Fechten, im Zweikampf*) bout; (*beim Rennen*) heat; **ein Essen von** *or* **mit vier Gängen** a four-course meal **(e)** (= *Verbindungsgang*) passage(way); (*Rail, in Gebäuden*) corridor; (= *Hausflur*) (*offen*) passage(way); (*hinter Eingangstür*) hallway; (*im oberen Stock*) landing; (*zwischen Sitzreihen, in Geschäft*) aisle; (*in einem Bergwerk*) tunnel, gallery; (= *Durchgang zwischen Häusern*) passage(way); (*Anat*) duct; (= *Gehörgang*) meatus; (*Tech*: *eines Gewindes*) thread **(f)** (*Mech*) gear; (*bei Fahrrad*) gear, speed; **den ersten ~ einschalten** *or* **einlegen** to engage first (gear); **auf** *or* **in den dritten ~ schalten** to change (*Brit*) *or* shift (*US*) into third (gear); **in die Gänge kommen** (*fig*) to get started *or* going

Gang² [gɛŋ] F **-, -s** gang

Gangart F walk, way of walking; (*von Pferd*) gait, pace; (= *Haltung*) carriage, bearing; (*fig*) stance; **Menschen haben eine aufrechte ~** humans walk upright; **eine leicht nach vorne gebeugte ~ haben** to walk with one's body bent slightly forward; **eine schnellere ~ vorlegen** to walk faster; **eine harte ~** (*fig*) a tough stance *or* line

gangbar ADJ (*lit*) Weg, Brücke etc passable; (*fig*) Lösung, Weg practicable; **nicht ~** impassable; impracticable

Gängelei [gɛŋəˈlai] F **-, -en** spoon-feeding; **warum wehrt er sich nicht gegen die ~ seiner Mutter/Frau?** why doesn't he fight against being tied to his mother's/wife's apron strings?

gängeln [ˈgɛŋln] VT (*fig*) jdn **~** to spoon-feed sb, to treat sb like a child; (*Mutter, Ehefrau*) to keep sb tied to one's apron strings

gängig ['gɛŋɪç] ADJ (= üblich) common; (= aktuell) current; Münze current; (= vertretbar) possible; **~e Praxis sein** to be common practice

Ganglien [gaŋ(g)liən] PL (Anat) ganglia pl

Gangschaltung F gears pl

Gangster ['gɛŋstɐ, 'gaŋstɐ] M **-s,** - gangster

Gangstermethoden ['gɛŋstɐ-, 'gaŋstɐ-] PL strong-arm tactics pl

Gangway ['gɛŋweː] F **-, -s** (Naut) gangway; (Aviat) steps pl

Ganove [ga'noːvə] M **-n, -n** (inf) crook; (hum: = listiger Kerl) sly old fox

Ganovin [ga'noːvɪn] F **-, -nen** (inf) crook

Gans [gans] F **-, ¬e** ['gɛnzə] goose; **wie die Gänse schnattern** to cackle away

Gans- IN CPDS (Aus) = **Gänse-**

Gänschen ['gɛnsçən] NT **-s,** - gosling; (fig inf) little goose (inf)

Gänse- IN CPDS goose; **Gänseblümchen** [-bly:mçən] NT **-s, -,** **Gänseblume** F daisy; **Gänsefüßchen** [-fy:sçən] PL (inf) inverted commas pl (Brit), quotation marks pl; **Gänsehaut** F (fig) goose pimples pl or flesh (Brit), goose bumps pl; **eine ~ bekommen or kriegen** (inf) to get goose pimples etc; **Gänseleberpastete** F pâté de foie gras, goose-liver pâté; **Gänsemarsch** M **im ~** in single or Indian file

Gänserich ['gɛnzərɪç] M **-s, -e, Ganser** ['ganzɐ] (Aus) M **-s, -** gander

ganz [gants] **1** ADJ **(a)** whole, entire; (= vollständig) complete; Wahrheit whole; **eine ~e Zahl** a whole number, an integer; **eine ~e Note** (Mus) a semibreve (Brit), a whole note (US); **eine ~e Pause** (Mus) a semibreve or whole note (US) rest; **die ~en Tassen/Kinder** (inf) all the cups/children; **~ England/ London** the whole of England/London (Brit), all (of) England/ London; **wir fuhren durch ~ England** we travelled (Brit) or traveled (US) all over England; **die ~e Zeit** all the time, the whole time; **eine ~e Menge** quite a lot; **sein ~es Geld** all his money; **sein ~es Vermögen** his entire or whole fortune; **seine ~e Kraft** all his strength; **sie ist seine ~e Freude** (inf) she's the apple of his eye (inf); **du hast mir den ~en Spaß verdorben** you've spoiled all my fun; **ein ~er Mann** a real man **(b)** Käse/eine Sammlung **~ or im Ganzen kaufen** to buy a whole cheese/a collection as a whole; **im (Großen und) Ganzen (genommen)** on the whole **(c)** (inf: = unbeschädigt) intact; **etw wieder ~ machen** to mend sth; **wieder ~ sein** to be mended **(d)** (inf: = nicht mehr als) all of; **ich verdiene im Monat ~e 2000 Euro** I earn all of 2000 euros a month; **noch ~e zehn Minuten** all of ten minutes

2 ADV (= völlig) quite; (= vollständig, ausnahmslos) completely; (= ziemlich, leidlich) quite; (= sehr) really; (= genau) exactly, just; **~ hinten/vorn** right at the back/front; **nicht ~** not quite; **~ gewiss!** most certainly, absolutely; **ein ~ gutes Buch** (= ziemlich) quite a good book; (= sehr gut) a very or really good book; **du hast ihn ~ fürchterlich beleidigt** you've really insulted him very badly; **ein ~ billiger Trick/ böser Kerl** a really cheap trick/evil character; **das ist mir ~ gleich** it's all the same or all one to me; **er hat ~ Recht** he's quite or absolutely right; **mit Ruß bedeckt** all or completely covered with soot; **allein** all alone; **du bist ja ~ nass** you're all wet; **~ wie Sie meinen** just as you think (best); **~ gleich wer** it doesn't matter who, no matter who; **eine Zeitschrift ~ lesen** to read a magazine right through; **das habe ich nicht ~ gelesen** I haven't read it all yet; **ein ~ ~ hoher Berg** a really really high mountain; **~ und gar** completely, utterly; **~ und gar nicht** not at all; **ein ~ klein wenig** just a little or tiny bit; **das mag ich ~ besonders gerne** I'm particularly or especially fond of that; **sie ist ~ die Mutter** she's just or exactly like her mother; **etw ~ oder gar nicht machen** to do sth properly or not at all

Gänze ['gɛntsə] F **-, NO PL** (form, Aus) entirety; **zur ~** in its entirety

Ganze(s) ['gantsə] NT DECL AS ADJ whole; (= alle Sachen zusammen) lot; (= ganzer Satz, ganze Ausrüstung) complete set; **etw als ~s sehen** to see sth as a whole; **das ~ kostet ...** altogether it costs ...; **das ~ alleine machen** to do it all on one's own; **das ist nichts ~s und nichts Halbes** that's neither one thing nor the other; **aufs ~ gehen** (inf) to go all out; **es geht ums ~** everything's at stake

Ganzheit F **-, (rare) -en** (= Einheit) unity; (= Vollständigkeit) entirety; **als ~** as an integral whole; **in seiner ~** in its entirety

ganzheitlich ['gantshaitlɪç] **1** ADJ (= umfassend einheitlich) integral; Lernen integrated; Medizin holistic **2** ADV **ein Problem ~ betrachten/darstellen** to view/present a problem in its entirety

Ganzheits-: Ganzheitsmedizin F holistic medicine; **Ganzheitsmethode** F look-and-say method

ganzjährig ADJ, ADV all (the) year round

gänzlich ['gɛntslɪç] ADV completely, totally

Ganz-: ganzseitig [-zaitɪç] ADJ full-page; **ganztägig** **1** ADJ all-day; Arbeit, Stelle full-time; **ein ~er Ausflug** a day trip **2** ADV **~ arbeiten** to work full-time; **sie ist jetzt ~ zu Hause** she's at home all day now; **das Schwimmbad ist ~ geöffnet** the swimming pool is open all day

ganztags ['gantsta:ks] ADV **arbeiten** full-time

Ganztags-: Ganztagsbeschäftigung F full-time occupation; **Ganztagsschule** F all-day school

gar [ga:ɐ] **1** ADV **(a)** (= überhaupt) at all; **~ keines** none at all or whatsoever; **~ kein Grund** no reason at all or whatsoever; **~ niemand** nobody at all or whatsoever; **~ nichts** nothing at all or whatsoever; **~ nicht schlecht** or übel not bad at all **(b)** (obs, Aus, S Ger: = sehr) really **2** ADJ Speise done pred, cooked

Garage [ga'ra:ʒə] F **-, -n** garage; (= Hochgarage, Tiefgarage) park (Brit), parking garage (US); **das Auto in einer ~ unterstellen** to garage one's car (Brit), to park one's car in a garage (esp US)

garagieren [gara'ʒi:rən], ptp **garagiert** VT (Aus, Sw) to park

Garant [ga'rant] M **-en, -en, Garantin** [-'rantɪn] F **-, -nen** guarantor

Garantie [garan'ti:] F **-, -n** [-'ti:ən] (lit, fig) guarantee; (auf Auto) warranty; **die Uhr hat ein Jahr ~** the watch is guaranteed for a year; **drei Jahre ~ auf etw** (acc) **gewähren** or **geben** to give a three-year guarantee/warranty on sth; **ich gebe dir meine ~ darauf** (fig inf) I guarantee (you) that; **unter ~** under guarantee/warranty; (fig: = garantiert) guaranteed

garantieren [garan'ti:rən], ptp **garantiert** **1** VT to guarantee (jdm etw sb sth); **er konnte mir nicht ~, dass ...** he couldn't give me any guarantee that ... **2** VI to give a guarantee; **für etw ~** to guarantee sth

garantiert [garan'ti:ɐt] ADV guaranteed; (inf) I bet (inf); **er kommt ~ nicht** I bet he won't come (inf)

Garantieschein M guarantee, certificate of guarantee (form); (für Auto) warranty

Garantin F siehe **Garant**

Garbe ['garbə] F **-, -n** (= Korngarbe) sheaf; (= Lichtgarbe) beam; (Mil: = Schussgarbe) burst of fire

Gärbottich ['gɛːɐ-] M fermenting vat

Garçonnière [garsɔ'nieːrə] F **-, -n** (Aus) one-room flat (Brit) or apartment, efficiency (US)

Garde ['gardə] F **-, -n** guard; **bei der ~** in the Guards; **die alte/ junge ~** (fig) the old/young guard

Garderobe [gardə'ro:bə] F **-, -n (a)** (= Kleiderbestand) wardrobe (Brit) **(b)** (= Kleiderablage) hall stand; (im Theater, Kino etc) cloakroom (Brit), checkroom (US); **seinen Mantel an der ~ abgeben** to leave one's coat in the cloakroom (Brit) or checkroom (US) **(c)** (Theat: = Umkleideraum) dressing room

Garderoben-: Garderobenfrau F cloakroom (Brit) or checkroom (US) attendant; **Garderobenmann** M, pl **-männer** cloakroom (Brit) or checkroom (US) attendant; **Garderobenmarke**, **Garderobenschein** M cloakroom (Brit) or checkroom (US) ticket; **Garderobenschrank** M hall cupboard; **Garderobenständer** M hat stand (Brit), hat tree (US)

Gardine [gar'di:nə] F **-, -n** curtain (Brit), drape (US); (= Scheibengardine) net (Brit) or café (US) curtain, curtain

Gardinen-: Gardinenpredigt F (inf) talking-to; **jdm eine ~ halten** to give sb a talking-to; **Gardinenstange** F curtain rail; (zum Ziehen) curtain rod

garen ['ga:rən] (Cook) VTI to cook; (auf kleiner Flamme) to simmer

gären ['gɛːrən], pret **gor** or **gärte**, ptp **gegoren** or **gegärt** **1** VI AUX HABEN or SEIN to ferment; (Hefe) to work; (fig: Gefühle etc) to seethe; **die Wut/das Unrecht gärte in ihm** he was seething with anger/a sense of injustice; **in ihm gärt es** he is in a state of inner turmoil **2** VT to ferment

Garette [ga'rɛtə] F **-, -n** (Sw: = Schubkarren) barrow

Garn [garn] NT -(e)s, -e (a) thread; (= *Häkelgarn*, fig: = *Seemannsgarn*) yarn; **ein ~ spinnen** (fig) to spin a yarn (b) (= *Netz*) net; **jdm ins ~ gehen** (fig) to fall into sb's trap

Garnele [gar'ne:lə] F -, -n (Zool) prawn; (= *Granat*) shrimp

garnieren [gar'ni:rən], *ptp* **garniert** VT *Kuchen, Kleid* to decorate; *Gericht* to garnish; (fig) *Reden etc* to garnish

Garnierung F -, -en (a) (= *das Garnieren*) decoration; (von *Gericht*, fig: von *Rede*) garnishing (b) (= *Material zur ~*) decoration; (von *Gericht*) garnish; **Zitate als ~ einer Rede** quotations to garnish a speech

Garnison [garni'zo:n] F -, -en (Mil) garrison

Garnitur [garni'tu:ɐ] F -, -en (a) (= *Satz*) set; (= *Unterwäsche*) set of (matching) underwear; **die erste ~** the pick of the bunch; **erste/zweite ~ sein, zur ersten/zweiten ~ gehören** to be first-rate or first-class/second-rate (b) (= *Besatz*) trimming

Gärstoff ['gɛ:ɐ-] M ferment

Garten ['gartn] M -s, ⸚ ['gɛrtn] garden; (= *Obstgarten*) orchard; **öffentlicher/botanischer/zoologischer ~/public/botanic(al)/zoological gardens** *pl*

Garten- IN CPDS garden; **Gartenarbeit** F gardening *no pl*; **Gartenbau** M, NO PL horticulture; **Gartengerät** NT gardening tool or implement; **Gartenhaus** NT summer house; (für *Geräte*) garden shed; (= *Hinterhaus*) back or rear building; **Gartenlokal** NT beer garden; (= *Restaurant*) garden café; **Gartenmöbel** PL garden furniture; **Gartenschere** F secateurs *pl* (Brit), pruning shears *pl*; (= *Heckenschere*) shears *pl*; **Gartenschlauch** M garden hose; **Gartenzwerg** M garden gnome

Gärtner ['gɛrtnɐ] M -s, -, **Gärtnerin** [-ərɪn] F -, -nen gardener

Gärtnerei [gɛrtnə'rai] F -, -en (a) (= *Baumschule*) (für *Setzlinge*) nursery; (für *Obst, Gemüse, Schnittblumen*) market garden (Brit), truck farm (US) (b) NO PL (= *Gartenarbeit*) gardening; (= *Gartenbau*) horticulture

gärtnern ['gɛrtnɐn] VI to garden

Gärung ['gɛ:rʊŋ] F -, -en fermentation; **in ~ kommen** to start fermenting

Gas [ga:s] NT -es, -e [-zə] gas; (Aut: = ~*pedal*) accelerator, gas pedal (esp US); **~ geben** (Aut) to accelerate; (auf höhere Touren bringen) to rev up; **mit ~ vergiften** to gas

Gas- IN CPDS gas; **Gasbehälter** M gas holder, gasometer; **Gasfeuerzeug** NT gas lighter; **Gasflasche** F bottle of gas, gas canister; **gasförmig** ADJ gaseous, gasiform; **Gashahn** M gas tap; **den ~ aufdrehen** (fig) to put one's head in the gas oven; **Gasheizung** F gas (central) heating; **Gasherd** M gas cooker; **Gaskammer** F gas chamber; **Gaskocher** M camping stove; **Gaskraftwerk** NT gas-fired power station; **Gaslaterne** F gas (street)lamp; **Gasleitung** F (= *Rohr*) gas pipe; (= *Hauptrohr*) gas main; **Gasmann** M, *pl* **-männer** gasman; **Gasmaske** F gas mask

Gasometer [gazo'me:tɐ] M gasometer

Gas-: **Gaspedal** NT (Aut) accelerator (pedal), gas pedal (esp US); **Gaspistole** F tear gas gun; **Gasrohr** NT gas pipe; (= *Hauptrohr*) gas main

Gässchen ['gɛsçən] NT -s, - alley(way)

Gasse ['gasə] F -, -n lane; (= *Durchgang*) alley(way); (S Ger, Aus: = *Stadtstraße*) street; (Rugby) line-out; **die schmalen ~n der Altstadt** the narrow streets and alleys of the old town; **eine ~ bilden** to clear a passage; (Rugby) to form a line-out; **eine ~ für jdn bilden** to make way or clear a path for sb; **sich** (dat) **eine ~ bahnen** to force one's way; **etw über die ~ verkaufen** (Aus) to sell sth to take away

Gassenjunge M, **Gassenmädchen** NT (pej) street urchin

Gassi ['gasi] ADV (inf) **~ gehen** to go walkies (Brit inf), to go for a walk; **mit einem Hund ~ gehen** to take a dog (for) walkies (Brit inf), to take a dog (out) for a walk

Gast [gast] M -es, ⸚e ['gɛstə] guest; (= *Besucher auch, Tourist*) visitor; (= *Gaststätte*) customer; (Theat) guest (star); (Univ: = ~*hörer*) observer, auditor (US); **Vorstellung vor geladenen Gästen** performance before an invited audience; **wir haben heute Abend Gäste** we're having company this evening; **bei jdm zu ~ sein** to be sb's guest(s); **in einem anderen Ort zu ~ sein** to visit another place

Gastarbeiter(in) M(F) immigrant or foreign worker

Gäste-: **Gästebett** NT spare or guest bed; **Gästebuch** NT visitors' book; **Gästehandtuch** NT guest towel; **Gästezimmer** NT guest or spare room

Gast-: **Gastfamilie** F host family; **gastfrei, gastfreundlich 1** ADJ hospitable **2** ADV hospitably; **Gastfreundlichkeit** F -, NO PL, **Gastfreundschaft** F -, NO PL hospitality; **gastgebend** ADJ ATTR *Land, Theater* host attr; *Mannschaft* home attr; **Gastgeber** M host; **Gastgeberin** F hostess; **Gastgeschenk** NT present (brought by a guest); **Gasthaus** NT, **Gasthof** M inn; **Gasthörer(in)** M(F) (Univ) observer, auditor (US)

gastieren [gas'ti:rən], *ptp* **gastiert** VI to guest

Gast-: **Gastland** NT host country; **gastlich** ['gastlɪç] **1** ADJ hospitable **2** ADV hospitably; **Gastlichkeit** F -, NO PL hospitality

gastrisch ['gastrɪʃ] ADJ (Med) gastric

Gastritis [gas'tri:tɪs] F -, **Gastritiden** [-'ti:dn] gastritis

Gastronom [gastro'no:m] M -en, -en, **Gastronomin** [-'no:mɪn] F -, -nen (= *Gastwirt*) restaurateur; (= *Koch*) cuisinier, cordon bleu cook (esp Brit)

Gastronomie [gastrono'mi:] F -, NO PL (form: = *Gaststättengewerbe*) catering trade; (geh: = *Kochkunst*) gastronomy

gastronomisch [gastro'no:mɪʃ] ADJ gastronomic

Gast-: **Gastspiel** NT (Theat) guest performance; (Sport) away match; **ein ~ geben** (lit) to give a guest performance; (fig inf) to make a fleeting or brief appearance; **Gastspielreise** F (Theat) tour; **auf ~** on tour; **Gaststätte** F (= *Restaurant*) restaurant; (= *Trinklokal*) pub (Brit), bar; **Gaststättengewerbe** NT catering trade; **Gaststube** F lounge

Gasturbine F gas turbine

Gast-: **Gastwirt** M (Besitzer) restaurant owner or proprietor; (Pächter) restaurant manager; (von *Kneipe*) landlord; **Gastwirtin** F (Besitzerin) restaurant owner or proprietress; (Pächterin) restaurant manageress; (von *Kneipe*) landlady; **Gastwirtschaft** F = **Gaststätte**

Gas-: **Gasuhr** F gas meter; **Gasverbrauch** M gas consumption; **Gasvergiftung** F gas poisoning; **Gasversorgung** F (= *System*) gas supply (+gen to); **Gaswerk** NT gasworks *sing or pl*; (= *Gasverwaltung*) gas board; **Gaswolke** F gas cloud; **Gaszähler** M gas meter

Gatte ['gatə] M -n, -n (form) husband, spouse (form); *siehe auch* **Gattin**

Gatter ['gatɐ] NT -s, - (= *Tür*) gate; (= *Zaun*) fence; (= *Rost*) grating, grid

Gattin ['gatɪn] F -, -nen (form) wife, spouse (form)

Gattung ['gatʊŋ] F -, -en (Biol) genus; (Liter, Mus, Art) genre; (fig: = *Sorte*) type, kind

Gattungs-: **Gattungsbegriff** M generic concept; **Gattungsname** M generic term

GAU [gau] M -(s) ABBR *von* **größter anzunehmender Unfall** MCA, maximum credible accident; (fig inf) worst-case scenario

Gaube ['gaubə] F -, -n dormer window

Gaudi ['gaudi] NT -s or (S Ger, Aus) f -, NO PL (inf) fun; **das war eine ~** that was great fun

Gaul [gaul] M -(e)s, **Gäule** ['gɔylə] (pej) nag, hack

Gaumen ['gaumən] M -s, - palate (auch fig), roof of the/one's mouth

Gaumen-: **Gaumenkitzel** M (inf) delight for the taste buds; **Gaumenlaut** M palatal (sound); **Gaumenzäpfchen** NT uvula

Gauner ['gaunɐ] M -s, - rogue, scoundrel; (= *Betrüger*) crook; (inf: = *gerissener Kerl*) cunning devil (inf); **kleine ~** (= *Kriminelle*) small-time crooks

Gaunerin ['gaunərɪn] F -, -nen rascal; (= *Betrügerin*) crook

Gazastreifen ['ga:za-] M Gaza Strip

Gaze ['ga:zə] F -, -n gauze

Gazelle [ga'tsɛlə] F -, -n gazelle

GB NT ABBR (a) *von* **Gigabyte** Gb (b) *von* **Großbritannien** GB

g-Druck ['ge:-] M, *pl* **-drücke** (Aviat) g-force

geartet [gə'la:ɐtət] ADJ **gutmütig ~ sein** to be good-natured; **freundlich ~ sein** to have a friendly nature; **er ist (eben) so ~(, dass ...)** it's (just) his nature (to ...); **so ~e Probleme** problems of this nature; **das Problem ist so ~, dass ...** the nature of the problem is such that ...

Geäst [gə'lɛst] NT -(e)s, NO PL branches *pl*

geb. ABBR *von* **geboren**

Gebäck [gə'bɛk] NT -(e)s, -e (= *Kekse*) biscuits *pl* (Brit), cookies *pl* (US); (= *süße Teilchen*) pastries *pl*; (= *rundes Hefegebäck*) buns *pl*; (= *Törtchen*) tarts *pl*; **allerlei (Kuchen und) ~** all kinds of cakes and pastries

gebacken PTP *von* **backen**

Gebälk [gə'bɛlk] NT **-(e)s, -e** timbers *pl*; (*Archit*: = *Verbindung zu Säulen*) entablature

geballt [gə'balt] **1** ADJ = *konzentriert*) *Energie, Kraft, Ladung* concentrated (*auch fig*); *Beschuss* massed; **eine ~e Ladung Salz** a pile of salt **2** ADV **es kommt alles ~ auf einmal** everything happens at once; **die Probleme treten jetzt ~ auf** the problems are piling up now; *siehe auch* **ballen**

gebar PRET *von* **gebären**

Gebärde [gə'bɛːɐdə] F **-, -n** gesture

gebärden [gə'bɛːɐdn], *ptp* **gebärdet** VR to behave

Gebärdendolmetscher(in) M(F) sign-language interpreter

Gebärdensprache F gestures *pl*; (= *Zeichensprache*) sign language; (*in Stummfilmen etc*) gesturing

Gebaren [gə'baːrən] NT **-s,** NO PL behaviour (*Brit*), behavior (*US*); (*Comm*: = *Geschäftsgebaren*) conduct

gebären [gə'bɛːrən], *pres* **gebärt** *or* (*geh*) **gebiert** [gə'biːɐt], *pret* **gebar** [gə'baːɐ], *ptp* **geboren** [gə'boːrən] **1** VT to give birth to; **geboren werden to be born; wo sind Sie geboren?** where were you born?; **aus der Not geborene Ideen** ideas stemming from necessity; *siehe auch* **geboren 2** VI to give birth

gebär- [gə'bɛːɐ-]: **gebärfähig** ADJ *Alter* child-bearing; *Frau* capable of bearing children; **gebärfreudig** ADJ *Frau* who has/ had given birth many times; *Tier* prolific; **ein ~es Becken haben** to have child-bearing hips

Gebärmutter F, *pl* **-mütter** (*Anat*) womb, uterus

Gebärmutter-: Gebärmutterhals M cervix; **Gebärmutterkrebs** M cervical cancer; **Gebärmuttermund** M mouth of the uterus

Gebarung F **-, -en** (*Aus Comm*: = *Geschäftsgebaren*) conduct

Gebarungs- (*Aus Comm*): **Gebarungsbericht** M financial report; **Gebarungsjahr** NT financial year; **Gebarungskontrolle** F audit

gebauchpinselt [gə'bauxpɪnzlt] ADJ (*hum inf*) **sich ~ fühlen** to feel flattered

Gebäude [gə'bɔydə] NT **-s, -** building; (= *Prachtgebäude*) edifice; (*fig*: = *Gefüge*) structure; (*von Ideen*) edifice; (*von Lügen*) web

Gebäude-: Gebäudekomplex M building complex; **Gebäudereinigung** F (= *das Reinigen*) commercial cleaning; (= *Firma*) cleaning contractors *pl*

gebaut [gə'baut] ADJ built; **gut ~ sein** to be well-built; **stark ~ sein** to have a broad frame; **... so, wie du ~ bist** (*inf*) ... a big man/woman like you; *siehe auch* **bauen**

---

geben ['geːbn]

| **1** TRANSITIVES VERB | **3** UNPERSÖNLICHES VERB |
| **2** INTRANSITIVES VERB | **4** REFLEXIVES VERB |

---

pret **gab** [gaːp], *ptp* **gegeben** [gə'geːbn]

1 TRANSITIVES VERB

(a) to give; (= *reichen*) to give, to pass; *Schatten, Kühle* to provide; *Karten* to deal; **gibs mir!** give it to me!, give me it!; **was darf ich Ihnen geben?** what can I get you?; **geben Sie mir bitte zwei Flaschen Bier** I'd like two bottles of beer, please; **ich gebe dir das Auto für 1000 Euro** (= *verkaufen*) I'll let you have the car for 1000 euros; **ich gebe dir das Auto für zwei Tage** (= *überlassen*) I'll let you have the car for two days; **sich** (*dat*) **(von jdm) etw geben lassen** to ask (sb) for sth; **geben Sie mir bitte Herrn Lang** (*Telec*) can I speak to Mr Lang please?; **ich gäbe viel darum, zu ...** I'd give a lot to ...; **jdm einen Tritt geben** to kick sb, to give sb a kick; (*fig inf*) to give sb the boot (*inf*); **gibs ihm (tüchtig)!** (*inf*) let him have it! (*inf*); **ein gutes Beispiel geben** to set a good example; **jdm etw zu verstehen geben** to make sth known to sb; **jdn/etw verloren geben** to give sb/sth up for lost; **das Buch hat mir viel gegeben** I got a lot out of the book; *siehe auch* **gegeben**

(b) (= *gewähren, verleihen*) to give; *Thema, Aufgabe, Problem* to set; **Taktgefühl ist ihm nicht gegeben** he's not over-endowed with tact; **es war ihm nicht gegeben, seine Eltern lebend wiederzusehen** he was not to see his parents alive again

(c) (= *schicken, übergeben*) to send; (*dial*: = *tun*) to put; **in die Post geben** to post (*Brit*), to mail (*esp US*); **ein Auto in Reparatur geben** to have a car repaired; **ein Kind in Pflege geben** to put a child in care; **Zucker über etw** (*acc*) **geben** (*dial*) to sprinkle sugar over sth; **Milch an den Teig geben** (*dial*) to add milk to the dough

(d) (= *ergeben, erzeugen*) to produce; **die Kuh gibt 25 Liter** the cow produces 25 litres (*Brit*) or liters (*US*); **2 + 2 gibt 4** 2 + 2 makes 4; **fünf Manuskriptseiten geben eine Druckseite** five pages of manuscript make one page of print; **Rotwein gibt Flecken** red wine leaves stains; **das gibt Ärger/Probleme** that will cause trouble/problems; **was wird das noch geben?** where will it end?

(e) (= *veranstalten*) *Konzert, Fest* to give; *Theaterstück etc* to do; **was wird heute im Theater gegeben?** what's on at the theatre (*Brit*) or theater (*US*) today?

(f) (= *unterrichten*) to teach; **er gibt Nachhilfeunterricht/ Tanzstunden** he does tutoring/gives dancing lessons

(g) (*andere Wendungen*)

✦**viel/nicht viel auf etw** (*acc*) **geben** to set great/little store by sth; **auf die Meinung der Lehrer brauchst du nichts zu geben** you needn't bother about what the teachers think; **ich gebe nicht viel auf seinen Rat** I don't think much of his advice

✦**etw von sich geben** *Laut, Worte, Flüche* to utter; *Meinung* to express; **was er gestern von sich gegeben hat, war völlig unverständlich** what he was going on about yesterday was completely incomprehensible

2 INTRANSITIVES VERB

(a) (*Cards*) to deal; **wer gibt?** whose turn is it to deal?

(b) (*Sport*) (= *Aufschlag haben*) to serve; **wer gibt?** whose turn is it to serve?

3 UNPERSÖNLICHES VERB

✦**es gibt** (+*sing*) there is; (+*pl*) there are; **gibt es einen Gott?** is there a God?; **heute gibts noch Regen** it's going to rain today; **es wird noch Ärger geben** there'll be trouble (yet); **darauf gibt es 10% Rabatt** you get 10% discount on it; **was gibts zum Mittagessen?** what's for lunch?; **freitags gibt es bei uns immer Fisch** we always have fish on Fridays; **wann gibts was zu essen? – es gibt gleich was** when are we going to get something to eat? – it's on its way; **es gibt gleich Mittagessen!** it's nearly time for lunch!; **jetzt gibt es keine Süßigkeiten mehr** (you're getting) no more sweets now; **was gibts?** what's the matter?, what is it?; **ein Mensch mit zwei Köpfen? das gibt es nicht!** a two-headed person? there's no such thing!; **das gibts doch nicht!** I don't believe it!; **das hat es ja noch nie gegeben!** it's unbelievable!; **so was gibts bei uns nicht!** (*inf*) that's just not on! (*inf*); **da gibts nichts** (*inf*) there's no two ways about it (*inf*); **was es nicht alles gibt!** it's a funny old world!; **gleich gibts was!** (*inf*) there's going to be trouble!

4 REFLEXIVES VERB

✦**sich geben**

(a) (= *nachlassen*) (*Regen*) to ease off; (*Schmerzen*) to ease; (*Leidenschaft, Begeisterung*) to cool; (*freches Benehmen*) to lessen

(b) (= *aufgeben, ergeben*) **sich gefangen geben** to give oneself up; **sich verloren geben** to give oneself up for lost

(c) (= *sich erledigen*) to sort itself out; (= *aufhören*) to stop; **das wird sich schon geben** it'll all work out

(d) (= *sich benehmen*) to behave; **sich als etw geben** to play sth; **sich freundlich geben** to be friendly; **sich von der besten Seite geben** to show one's best side; **nach außen gab er sich heiter** outwardly he seemed quite cheerful

---

Geber ['geːbɐ] M **-s, -**, **Geberin** [-ərɪn] F **-, -nen** giver; (*Cards*) dealer

Gebet [gə'beːt] NT **-(e)s, -e** prayer; **jdn ins ~ nehmen** (*fig*) to take sb to task; (*iro: bei Polizeiverhör etc*) to put the pressure on sb

Gebetbuch NT prayer book

gebeten PTP *von* **bitten**

gebeugt [gə'bɔykt] **1** ADJ **(a)** *Haltung* stooped; *Kopf* bowed; *Beine* bent; *Schultern* sloping **(b)** (*Gram*) *Verb, Substantiv* inflected **2** ADV **~ sitzen/stehen** to sit/stand hunched over; *siehe auch* **beugen**

Gebiet [gə'biːt] NT -(e)s, -e (a) area, region; (= *Fläche, Stadtgebiet*) area; (= *Staatsgebiet*) territory (b) (*fig: = Fach*) field; (= *Teilgebiet*) branch; **auf diesem ~** in this field

gebieten [gə'biːtn], *pret* gebot [gə'boːt], *ptp* geboten [gə'boːtn] (*geh*) ■ VT (= *verlangen*) to demand; (= *befehlen*) to command; **jdm etw ~** to command sb to do sth ■ VI (*geh:* = *verfügen*) **über etw** (*acc*) **~ über Geld etc** to have sth at one's disposal; **über Wissen etc** to have sth at one's command; *siehe auch* **geboten**

Gebiets-: Gebietsansässige(r) MF DECL AS ADJ resident; **Gebietsanspruch** M territorial claim; **Gebietskörperschaft** F regional administrative body; **gebietsweise** ADV (= *nach Gebieten*) locally; (= *in einzelnen Gebieten*) in some areas

Gebilde [gə'bɪldə] NT -s, - (= *Ding*) thing; (= *Gegenstand*) object; (= *Bauwerk*) construction; (= *Schöpfung*) creation; (= *Form*) shape; (*der Fantasie*) figment

gebildet [gə'bɪldət] ■ ADJ educated; (= *gelehrt*) learned; (= *kultiviert*) cultured; (= *belesen*) well-read ■ ADV **sich ~ unterhalten** to have a cultured conversation; *siehe auch* **bilden**

Gebimmel [gə'bɪml] NT -s, NO PL (*inf*) ting-a-ling (*inf*)

Gebinde [gə'bɪndə] NT -s, - (= *Blumengebinde*) arrangement; (= *Sträußchen*) posy; (= *Blumenkranz*) wreath

Gebirge [gə'bɪrgə] NT -s, - mountains *pl*, mountain range; **im/ins ~** in/into the mountains

gebirgig [gə'bɪrgɪç] ADJ mountainous

Gebirgs- IN CPDS mountain; **Gebirgsbach** M mountain stream; **Gebirgsjäger(in)** M(F) (*Mil*) mountain soldier; (*pl auch*) mountain troops *pl*; **Gebirgslandschaft** F (= *Gegend*) mountainous region; (= *Gemälde*) mountainscape; (= *Ausblick*) mountain scenery; **Gebirgsmassiv** NT massif; **Gebirgsrücken** M mountain ridge; **Gebirgsstock** M massif; **Gebirgszug** M mountain range

Gebiss [gə'bɪs] NT -es, -e (a) (= *die Zähne*) (set of) teeth *pl*; (= *künstliches ~*) dentures *pl* (b) (*am Pferdezaum*) bit

gebissen PTP *von* **beißen**

Gebläse [gə'blɛːzə] NT -s, - blower

geblasen PTP *von* **blasen**

geblichen PTP *von* **bleichen**

geblieben PTP *von* **bleiben**

Geblödel [gə'bløːdl] NT -s, NO PL (*inf*) nonsense; (*von Komiker*) patter; **die Unterhaltung artete in allgemeines ~ aus** the conversation degenerated into silliness

geblümt [gə'blyːmt], (*Aus*) **geblumt** [gə'bluːmt] ADJ flowered

Geblüt [gə'blyːt] NT -(e)s, NO PL (*geh*) (= *Abstammung*) descent; (*fig: = Blut*) blood; **von edlem ~** of noble blood

gebogen [gə'boːgn] PTP *von* **biegen**

geboren [gə'boːrən] ■ PTP *von* **gebären** ■ ADJ born; **er ist blind ~** he was born blind; **~er Engländer/Londoner sein** to be English/a Londoner by birth; **er ist der ~e Erfinder** he's a born inventor; **Hanna Schmidt ~e** *or* **geb. Müller** Hanna Schmidt, née Müller; **sie ist eine ~e Müller** she was born Müller

geborgen [gə'bɔrgn] ■ PTP *von* **bergen** ■ ADJ **sich ~ fühlen** to feel secure; **~ sein** to be secure

Geborgenheit F -, NO PL security

geborsten PTP *von* **bersten**

gebot PRET *von* **gebieten**

Gebot [gə'boːt] NT -(e)s, -e (a) (= *Gesetz*) law; (= *Regel, Vorschrift*) rule; (*Bibl*) commandment (b) (*geh: = Erfordernis*) requirement; **das ~ der Stunde** the needs of the moment; **Besonnenheit ist das ~ der Stunde** what is called for now is calm; **das ~ der Vernunft verlangt, dass ...** reason dictates that ... (c) (= *Verfügung*) command; **jdm zu ~e stehen** to be at sb's command *or* (*Geld etc*) disposal (d) (*Comm: bei Auktionen*) bid

geboten [gə'boːtn] ■ PTP *von* **gebieten, bieten** ■ ADJ (*geh*) (= *ratsam, angebracht*) advisable; (= *notwendig*) necessary; (= *dringend ~*) imperative; **bei aller ~en Achtung** with all due respect

Gebotsschild NT, *pl* -schilder sign giving orders

Gebr. ABBR *von* **Gebrüder** Bros

Gebrabbel [gə'brabl] NT -s, NO PL (*inf*) jabbering (*inf*)

gebracht PTP *von* **bringen**

gebrannt [gə'brant] ■ PTP *von* **brennen** ■ ADJ **~er Kalk** quicklime; **~e Mandeln** *pl* burnt (*Brit*) *or* baked (*US*) almonds *pl*; **~er Ton** fired clay; **~es Kind scheut das Feuer** (*Prov*) once bitten, twice shy (*Prov*)

gebraten PTP *von* **braten**

Gebrauch [gə'braux] M -(e)s, Gebräuche [gə'brɔyçə] (= *Benutzung*) (= *eines Wortes*) usage; (= *Anwendung*) application; (= *Brauch, Gepflogenheit*) custom; **falscher ~** misuse; (= *falsche Anwendung*) misapplication; **von etw ~ machen** to make use of sth; **in ~ sein** to be in use; **etw in ~ (*dat*) haben** to use sth; *Auto etc* to run sth; **zum äußeren/inneren ~** to be taken externally/internally

gebrauchen [gə'brauxn], *ptp* **gebraucht** VT (= *benutzen*) to use; (= *anwenden*) to apply; **sich zu etw ~ lassen** to be useful for sth; (= *missbrauchen*) to be used as sth; **nicht mehr zu ~ sein** to be useless; **er/das ist zu nichts zu ~** he's/that's absolutely useless; **das kann ich gut ~** I can really use that; **ich könnte ein neues Kleid/einen Whisky ~** I could use a new dress/a whisky; **Geld kann ich immer ~** money's always useful; *siehe auch* **gebraucht**

gebräuchlich [gə'brɔyçlɪç] ADJ (= *verbreitet*) common; (= *gewöhnlich*) usual, customary; (= *herkömmlich*) conventional; **nicht mehr ~** (*Ausdruck etc*) no longer used

Gebrauchs-: Gebrauchsanleitung F (*form*), **Gebrauchsanweisung** F (*für Arznei*) directions *pl*; (*für Geräte etc*) instructions *pl* (for use); **Gebrauchsartikel** M article for everyday use; (*pl: esp Comm*) basic consumer goods *pl*; **Gebrauchsgegenstand** M commodity; (= *Werkzeug, Küchengerät*) utensil; **Gebrauchsgut** NT USU PL consumer item; **Konsum- und Gebrauchsgüter** consumer and utility goods; **Gebrauchsmuster** NT registered pattern *or* design; **Gebrauchsmusterschutz** M protection of patterns and designs

gebraucht [gə'brauxt] ■ ADJ second-hand; *Auto auch, Verpackung* used ■ ADV **etw ~ kaufen** to buy sth second-hand; *siehe auch* **brauchen**

Gebrauchtwagen M used *or* second-hand car

gebräunt [gə'brɔynt] ADJ (= *braun gebrannt*) (sun-)tanned; *siehe auch* **bräunen**

Gebrechen [gə'brɛçn] NT -s, - (*geh*) affliction

gebrechlich [gə'brɛçlɪç] ADJ frail; (= *altersschwach*) infirm; (*fig: = unvollkommen*) weak

gebrochen [gə'brɔxn] ■ PTP *von* **brechen** ■ ADJ broken; **~e Zahl** (*Math*) fraction; **mit ~em Herzen, ~en Herzens** broken-hearted ■ ADV **~ Deutsch sprechen** to speak broken German

Gebrüder [gə'bryːdɐ] PL (*Comm*) Brothers *pl*; **~ Müller** Müller Brothers

Gebrüll [gə'brʏl] NT -(e)s, NO PL (*von Rind*) bellowing; (*von Esel*) braying; (*von Löwe*) roar; (*in Todesangst*) screaming; (*von Mensch*) yelling; **auf ihn mit ~!** (*inf*) go for him!

Gebrumm [gə'brʊm] NT -(e)s, NO PL, **Gebrumme** [gə'brʊmə] NT -s, NO PL buzzing; (*von Motor, von Bass, Singen*) droning; (*inf: = Gebrummel*) grumping (*inf*)

gebückt [gə'bʏkt] ■ ADJ **eine ~e Haltung** a stoop ■ ADV **~ gehen** to stoop; **~ stehen** to stand stooped; *siehe auch* **bücken**

Gebühr [gə'byːɐ] F -, -en (a) charge; (= *Postgebühr*) postage *no pl*; (= *Honorar, Beitrag*) fee; (= *Schulgebühr, Studiengebühr*) fees *pl*; (= *Vermittlungsgebühr*) commission; (= *Straßenbenutzungsgebühr*) toll; **~en erheben** to make a charge; **zu ermäßigter ~** at a reduced rate; **~ (be)zahlt Empfänger** postage to be paid by addressee; **die ~en für Rundfunk/Fernsehen werden erhöht** radio/television licences (*Brit*) are going up (b) (= *Angemessenheit*) **nach ~** suitably, properly; **über ~** excessively

gebühren [gə'byːrən], *ptp* **gebührt** (*geh*) ■ VI to be due (+*dat* to); **das gebührt ihm** (= *steht ihm zu*) it is his (just) due; (= *gehört sich für ihn*) it befits him ■ VR to be proper; **wie es sich gebührt** as is proper

gebührend ■ ADJ (= *verdient*) due; (= *angemessen*) suitable; (= *geziemend*) proper ■ ADV duly, suitably; **etw ~ feiern** to celebrate sth in a fitting manner; **etw ~ zu schätzen/würdigen wissen** to appreciate sth

Gebühren-: Gebühreneinheit F (*Telec*) (tariff) unit; **Gebührenerhöhung** F increase in charges; **gebührenfrei** ■ ADJ free of charge; *Brief, Paket* post-free (*Brit*), postpaid;

Telefonnummer Freefone® (*Brit*), toll-free (*US*) **2** ADV free of charge; **Gebührenordnung** F scale of charges; **gebührenpflichtig** [-pflɪçtɪç] **1** ADJ subject to a charge; *Autobahnbenutzung* subject to a toll; **~e Verwarnung** (*Jur*) fine; **~e Autobahn** toll road (*Brit*), turnpike (*US*) **2** ADV jdn ~ **verwarnen** to fine sb; **Gebührenzähler** M meter

gebunden [gəˈbʊndn] **1** PTP *von* **binden 2** ADJ tied (*an +acc* to); (*durch Verpflichtungen etc*) tied down; *Kapital* tied up; *Preise* controlled; (*Ling, Phys, Chem*) bound; *Buch* cased, hardback; *Wärme* latent; (*Mus*) legato; **vertraglich ~ sein** to be bound by contract; **anderweitig ~ sein** to be otherwise engaged

Geburt [gəˈbuːɐt] F **-, -en** (*lit, fig*) birth; (*fig* = *Produkt*) fruit, product; **von ~** by birth; **von ~ an** from birth; **bei der ~ sterben** (*Mutter*) to die in childbirth; (*Kind*) to die at birth; **das war eine schwere ~!** (*fig inf*) that took some doing (*inf*); **die Gnade der späten ~** the good fortune of being born too late (*and so free from association with the Nazi era*)

Geburten-: Geburtenkontrolle F, **Geburtenregelung** F birth control; **Geburtenrate** F birth rate; **geburtenschwach** ADJ *Jahrgang* with a low birthrate; **geburtenstark** ADJ *Jahrgang* with a high birthrate; **Geburtenzahlen** PL, **Geburtenziffer** F birthrate

gebürtig [gəˈbʏrtɪç] ADJ **~er Londoner sein, aus London ~ sein** to have been born in London

Geburts-: Geburtsanzeige F birth announcement; **Geburtsdatum** NT date of birth; **Geburtshaus** NT das ~ Kleists the house where Kleist was born; **Geburtshelfer(in)** M(F) (*Med* = *Arzt*) obstetrician; (= *Hebamme*) midwife; (*fig*) midwife; **Geburtsjahr** NT year of birth; **Geburtsort** M, *pl* **-orte** birthplace

Geburtstag M birthday; (*auf Formularen*) date of birth; **herzlichen Glückwunsch zum ~!** happy birthday!; **jdm zum ~ gratulieren** to wish sb (a) happy birthday; **heute habe ich ~** it's my birthday today

Geburtstags- IN CPDS birthday; **Geburtstagskind** NT birthday boy/girl

Geburtsurkunde F birth certificate

Gebüsch [gəˈbʏʃ] NT **-(e)s, -e** bushes *pl*; (= *Unterholz*) undergrowth, brush

Gecko [ˈgɛko] M **-s, -s** (*Zool*) gecko

gedacht [gəˈdaxt] **1** PTP *von* **denken, gedenken 2** ADJ *Linie, Größe, Fall* imaginary

Gedächtnis [gəˈdɛçtnɪs] NT **-ses, -se** memory; **etw aus dem ~ hersagen** to recite sth from memory; **das ist seinem ~ entfallen** it went out of his mind; **jdm im ~ bleiben** to stick in sb's mind; **im ~ bleiben** to be remembered; **etw im ~ behalten** to remember sth; **sich** (*dat*) **etw ins ~ zurückrufen** to call sth to mind; **wenn mich mein ~ nicht trügt** if my memory serves me right; **zum ~ der** *or* **an die Toten** in memory of the dead

Gedächtnis-: Gedächtnisfeier F commemoration; (*kirchliche*) memorial *or* commemorative service; **Gedächtnislücke** F gap in one's memory; (*Psych*) localized amnesia; **da habe ich eine ~** I just don't remember anything about it; **Gedächtnisschwund** M amnesia; **Gedächtnisverlust** M loss of memory

gedämpft [gəˈdɛmpft] ADJ **(a)** (= *vermindert*) *Geräusch* muffled; *Farben, Musikinstrument, Stimmung* muted; *Optimismus* cautious; *Licht, Freude* subdued; **mit ~er Stimme** in a low voice **(b)** (*Cook*) steamed; *siehe auch* **dämpfen**

Gedanke [gəˈdaŋkə] M **-ns, -n** thought (*über +acc* on, about); (= *Idee, Plan, Einfall*) idea; (= *Konzept*) concept; (= *Betrachtung*) reflection (*über +acc* on); **der bloße ~ an ...** the mere thought of ...; **da kam mir ein ~** then I had an idea; **in ~n vertieft** *or* **versunken/verloren sein** to be deep *or* sunk/lost in thought; **in ~n bin ich bei dir** my thoughts are with you; **jdn auf andere ~n bringen** to take sb's mind off things; **wo hat er nur seine ~n?** whatever is he thinking about?; **sich** (*dat*) **über etw** (*acc*) **~n machen** to think about sth; (= *sich sorgen*) to worry about sth; **man macht sich** (*dat*) **so seine ~n** (*inf*) I've got my ideas; **daran würde ich keinen ~n verschwenden** I wouldn't even give it a thought; **kein ~ (daran)!** (= *stimmt nicht*) not a bit of it! (*inf*); (= *kommt nicht infrage*) that's out of the question; **etw ganz in ~n** (*dat*) **tun** to do sth (quite) without thinking; **jds ~n lesen** to read sb's mind *or* thoughts; **ich kann doch nicht ~n lesen!** I'm not a mind-reader!; **auf einen ~n kommen** to have an idea; **wie kommen Sie auf den ~n?** what gives you that idea?; **auf dumme ~n kommen** (*inf*) to get up to mischief; **jdn auf den ~n bringen, etw zu tun** to give sb the idea of doing sth; **sich mit dem ~n tragen, etw zu tun** (*geh*), **mit dem ~n spielen, etw zu tun** to toy with the idea of doing sth; **der europäische/olympische ~** the European/Olympic idea

Gedanken-: Gedankenaustausch M (*Pol*) exchange of ideas; **gedankenlos** **1** ADJ (= *unüberlegt*) unthinking; (= *zerstreut*) absent-minded; (= *rücksichtslos*) thoughtless **2** ADV (= *unüberlegt*) unthinkingly; (= *rücksichtslos*) thoughtlessly; **etw ~ tun** to do sth without thinking; **Gedankenlosigkeit** F **-, -en** (*Unüberlegtheit*) lack of thought; (= *Zerstreutheit*) absent-mindedness; (= *Rücksichtslosigkeit*) thoughtlessness; **Gedankenstrich** M dash; **Gedankenübertragung** F telepathy

gedanklich [gəˈdaŋklɪç] **1** ADJ intellectual; (= *vorgestellt*) imaginary; **die große ~e Klarheit in seinem Werk** the great clarity of thought in his work **2** ADV intellectually

Gedeck [gəˈdɛk] NT **-(e)s, -e (a)** (= *Tischgedeck*) cover; **ein ~ auflegen** to lay (*Brit*) *or* set a place; **eine Tafel mit zehn ~en** a table laid (*Brit*) *or* set for ten (people) **(b)** (= *Menü*) set meal, table d'hôte **(c)** (*im Nachtklub*) cover charge

gedeckt [gəˈdɛkt] ADJ *Farben* muted; *Basar, Gang, Dach* covered; *Tisch* set *or* laid (*Brit*) for a meal; *siehe auch* **decken**

Gedeih [gəˈdai] M **auf ~ und Verderb** for better or (for) worse; **jdm auf ~ und Verderb ausgeliefert sein** to be completely and utterly at sb's mercy

gedeihen [gəˈdaiən], *pret* **gedieh** [gəˈdiː], *ptp* **gediehen** [gəˈdiːən] VI AUX SEIN to thrive; (*wirtschaftlich auch*) to prosper; (*geh* = *sich entwickeln*) to develop; (*fig* = *vorankommen*) to make progress

gedenken [gəˈdɛŋkn], *pret* **gedachte** [gəˈdaxtə], *ptp* **gedacht** [gəˈdaxt] VI IRREG +GEN **(a)** (*geh*) (= *denken an*) to remember; (= *erwähnen*) to recall; **in seiner Rede gedachte er der Toten** in his speech he remembered the dead **(b)** (= *feiern*) to commemorate **(c)** **~, etw zu tun** to propose to do sth

Gedenken [gəˈdɛŋkn] NT **-s**, NO PL memory (*an +acc* of); **zum** *or* **im ~ an jdn** in memory of sb

Gedenk-: Gedenkfeier F commemoration; **Gedenkminute** F minute's silence; **Gedenkstätte** F memorial; **Gedenkstunde** F hour of commemoration

Gedicht [gəˈdɪçt] NT **-(e)s, -e** poem; **die ~e Enzensbergers** Enzensberger's poetry *or* poems; **dieses Kleid/der Nachtisch ist ein ~** (*fig inf*) this dress/the dessert is sheer poetry

gediegen [gəˈdiːgn] ADJ **(a)** *Metall* pure, native (*Min*) **(b)** (*von guter Qualität*) high-quality; (= *geschmackvoll*) tasteful; (= *rechtschaffen*) upright; *Verarbeitung* solid; *Kenntnisse* sound **(c)** (*inf*. = *wunderlich*) peculiar

Gediegenheit F **-**, NO PL **(a)** (*von Metall*) purity **(b)** (= *gute Qualität*) high quality; (= *geschmackvolle Atmosphäre*) tastefulness; (= *Rechtschaffenheit*) uprightness; (*von Verarbeitung*) solidity; (*von Kenntnissen*) soundness

gedieh PRET *von* **gedeihen**

gediehen PTP *von* **gedeihen**

Gedöns [gəˈdøːns] NT **-es** [-zəs], NO PL (*dial, inf*) fuss

Gedränge [gəˈdrɛŋə] NT **-s**, NO PL (= *Menschenmenge*) crowd, crush; (= *Drängeln*) jostling; (*Sport*) bunching; (*Rugby*) scrum(mage); **vor der Theaterkasse herrschte ~** there was a big crowd at the ticket office; **ins ~ kommen** *or* **geraten** (*fig*) to get into a fix (*inf*)

Gedrängel [gəˈdrɛŋl] NT **-s**, NO PL (*inf*) (= *Menschenmenge*) crush; (= *Drängeln*) shoving (*inf*)

gedrängt [gəˈdrɛŋt] **1** ADJ packed; (*fig*) *Stil* terse; **~e Übersicht** synopsis **2** ADV **~ voll** packed full; **~ stehen** to be crowded together; *siehe auch* **drängen**

gedroschen PTP *von* **dreschen**

gedruckt [gəˈdrʊkt] ADJ printed; **lügen wie ~** (*inf*) to lie right, left and centre (*Brit inf*) *or* center (*US inf*); *siehe auch* **drucken**

gedrückt [gəˈdrʏkt] ADJ *Stimmung* depressed; *Schweigen* gloomy; **~er Stimmung sein** to feel depressed; *siehe auch* **drücken**

gedrungen [gəˈdrʊŋən] **1** PTP *von* **dringen 2** ADJ *Person, Gestalt* stocky; *Gebäude, Form* squat

geduckt [gəˈdʊkt] **1** ADJ *Haltung, Mensch* crouching; *Kopf* lowered **2** ADV **~ sitzen** to sit hunched up (*Brit*) *or* over (*US*); *siehe auch* **ducken**

Gedudel [gə'duːdl] NT **-s**, NO PL (inf) (von Klarinette etc) tootling; (von Dudelsack) droning, whining; (von Radio) noise

Geduld [gə'dʊlt] F **-**, NO PL patience; **mit jdm/etw ~ haben** to be patient with sb/sth; **sich mit ~ wappnen** to possess one's soul in patience; **mir geht die ~ aus, mir reißt die ~, ich verliere die ~** my patience is wearing thin; **jds ~ auf eine harte Probe stellen** to try sb's patience

gedulden [gə'dʊldn], ptp **geduldet** VR to be patient

geduldig [gə'dʊldɪç] **1** ADJ patient; **~ wie ein Lamm** meek as a lamb **2** ADV patiently

Gedulds-: Geduldsfaden M **jetzt reißt mir aber der ~!** (inf) I'm just about losing my patience; **Geduldsprobe** F trial of (one's) patience; **das war eine harte ~** it was enough to try anyone's patience

gedungen PTP von **dingen**

gedurft PTP von **dürfen**

geehrt [gə'leːɐt] ADJ honoured (Brit), honored (US); **sehr ~e Damen und Herren!** Ladies and Gentlemen!; **sehr ~er Herr Kurz!** dear Mr Kurz; **Sehr ~e Damen und Herren** (in Briefen) Dear Sir or Madam; siehe auch **ehren**

geeignet [gə'laignət] ADJ (= passend) suitable; (= richtig) right; **sie ist für diesen Posten nicht ~** she's not the right person for this job; **im ~en Augenblick** at the right moment; **er ist zu dieser Arbeit nicht ~** he's not suited to this work; **er wäre zum Lehrer gut/schlecht ~** he would/wouldn't make a good teacher; siehe auch **eignen**

Gefahr [gə'faːɐ] F **-**, **-en (a)** danger (für to, for); (= Bedrohung) threat (für to, for); **in ~ sein** or **schweben** to be in danger; (= bedroht) to be threatened; **in ~ geraten** to be under threat; **außer ~** (= nicht gefährdet) not in danger; (= nicht mehr gefährdet) out of danger; **sich ~en** or **einer ~ aussetzen** to put oneself in danger; **es besteht die ~, dass ...** there's a risk that ...; **er liebt die ~** he likes living dangerously; **wer sich in ~ begibt, kommt darin um** (Prov) if you play with fire, you must expect to get your fingers burned **(b)** (= Wagnis, Risiko) risk (für to, for); **auf eigene ~** at one's own risk or (stärker) peril; **auf die ~ hin, etw zu tun/dass jd etw tut** at the risk of doing sth/of sb doing sth; **~ laufen, etw zu tun** to run the risk of doing sth

gefährden [gə'fɛːɐdn], ptp **gefährdet** VT to endanger; (= bedrohen) to threaten; (= aufs Spiel setzen) to put at risk; **Versetzung** or **Vorrücken gefährdet** (Sch) comment on a school report indicating that the pupil may have to repeat a year

gefährdet [gə'fɛːɐdət] ADJ Tierart endangered; Ehe, Jugend, Bevölkerungsgruppe, Unternehmen, Gebiet at risk pred; **von Erdbeben ~** at risk from earthquakes; **Gefährdete** people at risk

Gefährdung F **-**, **-en (a)** (= das Gefährden) endangering; (= das Riskieren) risking **(b)** (= Gefahr) danger (+gen to)

gefahren PTP von **fahren**

Gefahren-: Gefahrenherd M danger area; **Gefahrenquelle** F source of danger; **Gefahrenzulage** F danger money

Gefahrgut NT hazardous materials pl

gefährlich [gə'fɛːɐlɪç] **1** ADJ dangerous **2** ADV dangerously

Gefährlichkeit F **-**, NO PL dangerousness

gefahrlos 1 ADJ safe; (= harmlos) harmless **2** ADV safely; (= harmlos) harmlessly

Gefährte [gə'fɛːɐtə] M **-n, -n**, **Gefährtin** [gə'fɛːɐtɪn] F **-**, **-nen** (geh) companion

Gefälle [gə'fɛlə] NT **-s**, **- (a)** (= Neigung) (von Fluss) drop, fall; (von Land, Straße) slope; (= Neigungsgrad) gradient; **das Gelände hat ein starkes ~** the land slopes down steeply; **ein ~ von 10%** a gradient of 10%; **starkes ~!** steep hill **(b)** (fig: = Unterschied) difference; **das Nord-Süd-~** the North-South divide

gefallen¹ [gə'falən], pret **gefiel** [gə'fiːl], ptp **gefallen** [gə'falən] VI to please (jdm sb); **es gefällt mir (gut)** I like it (very much or a lot); **es gefällt ihm, wie sie spricht** he likes the way she talks; **das gefällt mir gar nicht** I don't like it at all; **das könnte dir so ~!** (inf) no way! (inf); **das gefällt mir schon besser** (inf) that's more like it (inf); **er gefällt mir gar nicht** (inf: gesundheitlich) I don't like the look of him (inf); **sich** (dat) **etw ~ lassen** (= dulden) to put up with sth; **das lasse ich mir ~!** that's just the job (inf)

gefallen² [gə'falən] PTP von **fallen**, **gefallen¹**

Gefallen¹ [gə'falən] NT **-s**, NO PL (geh) pleasure; **an etw** (dat) **~ finden** to get pleasure from sth; **bei jdm ~ finden** to appeal to sb

Gefallen² M **-s**, **-** favour (Brit), favor (US); **jdn um einen ~ bitten** to ask sb a favo(u)r; **jdm einen ~ erweisen, jdm einen ~ tun** to do sb a favo(u)r; **tun Sie mir den ~ und schreiben Sie** would you do me a favo(u)r and write; **jdm etw zu ~ tun** (geh) to do sth to please sb

Gefallene(r) [gə'falənə] MF DECL AS ADJ soldier killed in action; **ein Denkmal für die ~n des Krieges** a memorial to those killed in the war

gefällig [gə'fɛlɪç] ADJ **(a)** (= hilfsbereit) obliging; **sich ~ zeigen** to show oneself willing to oblige; **jdm ~ sein** to oblige sb **(b)** (= ansprechend) pleasing; (= freundlich) pleasant **(c)** **Zigarette ~?** (form) would you care for a cigarette?; siehe auch **gefälligst**

Gefälligkeit F **(a)** (= Gefallen) favour (Brit), favor (US); **jdm eine ~ erweisen** to do sb a favo(u)r **(b)** NO PL (= gefälliges Wesen) pleasantness; (= Entgegenkommen) helpfulness; **etw aus ~ tun** to do sth out of the kindness of one's heart

gefälligst [gə'fɛlɪçst] ADV (inf) kindly; **sei ~ still!** kindly keep your mouth shut! (inf)

gefällt [gə'fɛlt] 3. PERS SING PRES von **gefallen¹**

gefangen [gə'faŋən] PTP von **fangen**

Gefangenen-: Gefangenenaustausch M exchange of prisoners; **Gefangenenhilfsorganisation** F prisoners' rights organization; **Gefangenenlager** NT prison camp

Gefangene(r) [gə'faŋənə] MF DECL AS ADJ captive; (= Sträfling, Kriegsgefangene, fig) prisoner; **keine ~n machen** (Mil) to take no prisoners (alive)

Gefangen-: gefangen halten VT IRREG to hold prisoner; Geiseln to hold; Tiere to keep in captivity; (fig) to captivate; **Gefangennahme** [-naːmə] F **-**, **-n** capture; (= Verhaftung) arrest; **bei der ~** on one's capture/arrest; **gefangen nehmen** VT IRREG to take captive; (= verhaften) to arrest; (Mil) to take prisoner; (fig) to captivate; **Gefangenschaft** [gə'faŋənʃaft] F **-**, NO PL captivity; **in ~ geraten** to be taken prisoner

Gefängnis [gə'fɛŋnɪs] NT **-ses**, **-se** prison, jail; (= ~strafe) imprisonment; **im ~ sein** or **sitzen** (inf) to be in prison; **ins ~ kommen** to be sent to prison; **zwei Jahre ~ bekommen** to get two years in prison; **auf Meineid steht ~** perjury is punishable by imprisonment

Gefängnis- IN CPDS prison; **Gefängnisdirektor(in)** M(F) prison governor, prison warden (esp US); **Gefängnishof** M prison yard; **Gefängnisstrafe** F prison sentence; **eine ~ von zehn Jahren** ten years' imprisonment; **er wurde zu einer ~ verurteilt** he was given a prison sentence; **Gefängniswärter(in)** M(F) warder (Brit), prison officer or guard

gefärbt [gə'fɛrpt] ADJ dyed; Lebensmittel artificially coloured (Brit) or colored (US); (fig) Aussprache tinged; Bericht biased; **konservativ ~ sein** to have a conservative bias; siehe auch **färben**

Gefasel [gə'faːzl] NT **-s**, NO PL (pej) drivel (inf)

Gefäß [gə'fɛːs] NT **-es**, **-e** vessel (auch Anat, Bot); (= Behälter) receptacle

gefasst [gə'fast] **1** ADJ (= ruhig) composed, calm; Stimme calm; Lächeln composed; **einen sehr ~en Eindruck machen** to appear cool, calm and collected; **auf etw** (acc) **~ sein** to be prepared for sth; **sich auf etw** (acc) **~ machen** to prepare oneself for sth; **er kann sich auf etwas ~ machen** (inf) I'll give him something to think about (inf) **2** ADV (= beherrscht) calmly; siehe auch **fassen**

Gefasstheit F **-**, NO PL composure, calm(ness)

Gefecht [gə'fɛçt] NT **-(e)s**, **-e** (lit, fig) battle; (Mil) engagement; (= Scharmützel) skirmish; **jdn/etw außer ~ setzen** (lit, fig) to put sb/sth out of action; **mit diesen Argumenten setzte er seinen Gegner außer ~** he shot down his opponent with these arguments; **Argumente ins ~ führen** to advance arguments; **im Eifer** or **in der Hitze des ~s** (fig) in the heat of the moment

Gefechts-: gefechtsbereit ADJ ready for battle; (= einsatzfähig) (fully) operational; **Gefechtskopf** M warhead; **Gefechtsstand** M command post

gefeiert [gə'faiɐt] ADJ celebrated; siehe auch **feiern**

Gefeilsche [gə'failʃə] NT **-s**, NO PL (inf) haggling

gefeit [gəˈfait] ADJ **gegen etw ~ sein** to be immune to sth; **niemand ist gegen den Tod ~** nobody is immortal; **dagegen ist keiner ~** that could happen to anyone

gefestigt [gəˈfɛstɪçt] ADJ established; *Charakter* steady; **sittlich ~ sein** to have a sense of moral responsibility; *siehe auch* **festigen**

Gefieder [gəˈfiːdɐ] NT **-s,** - plumage

gefiedert [gəˈfiːdɐt] ADJ feathered; *Blatt* pinnate

gefiel PRET *von* **gefallen**[1]

gefinkelt [gəˈfɪŋklt] ADJ (*esp Aus*) cunning

Geflacker [gəˈflakɐ] NT **-s,** NO PL flickering

Geflecht [gəˈflɛçt] NT **-(e)s, -e** (*lit, fig*) network; (= *Gewebe*) weave; (= *Rohrgeflecht*) wickerwork

gefleckt [gəˈflɛkt] ADJ spotted; *Blume, Vogel* speckled; *Haut* blotchy

Geflimmer [gəˈflɪmɐ] NT **-s,** NO PL shimmering; (*Film, TV*) flicker(ing); (*durch heiße Luft*) heat haze

geflissentlich [gəˈflɪsntlɪç] (*geh*) **1** ADJ deliberate, intentional; **zur ~en Beachtung** (*form*) for your attention **2** ADV deliberately, intentionally

geflochten PTP *von* **flechten**

geflogen PTP *von* **fliegen**

geflohen PTP *von* **fliehen**

geflossen PTP *von* **fließen**

Geflügel [gəˈflyːgl] NT **-s,** NO PL (*Zool*) (*Cook*) poultry *no pl*; (= *Vögel auch*) fowl

Geflügel- IN CPDS (*Cook*) chicken/turkey *etc*; (*allgemein*) poultry; **Geflügelfleisch** NT poultry; **Geflügelklein** NT **-s,** NO PL giblets *pl*; **Geflügelschere** F poultry shears *pl*

geflügelt [gəˈflyːglt] ADJ winged; **~e Worte** standard quotations

Geflügelzucht F poultry farming

Geflunker [gəˈflʊŋkɐ] NT **-s,** NO PL (*inf*) fibbing (*inf*); **das ist alles ~** it's all fibs (*inf*)

Geflüster [gəˈflʏstɐ] NT **-s,** NO PL whispering

gefochten PTP *von* **fechten**

Gefolge [gəˈfɔlgə] NT **-s,** - retinue, entourage; (= *Trauergefolge*) cortege; (*fig*) wake; **im ~** in the wake (+*gen* of)

Gefolgschaft [gəˈfɔlkʃaft] F **-, -en (a)** (= *die Anhänger*) following; (*Hist:* = *Gefolge*) entourage **(b)** (= *Treue*) allegiance (*auch Hist*)

Gefolgsmann M, *pl* **-leute** *or* **-männer, Gefolgsfrau** F follower; (*Hist*) liegeman/-woman

gefragt [gəˈfraːkt] ADJ *Waren, Sänger etc* in demand *pred*; *siehe auch* **fragen**

gefräßig [gəˈfrɛːsɪç] ADJ gluttonous; (*fig geh*) voracious; *Flammen, Feuer* all-enveloping; **~e Stille** (*hum*) the silence of people who enjoy their food

Gefräßigkeit F **-,** NO PL gluttony; (*fig geh*) voracity

Gefreite(r) [gəˈfraitə] MF DECL AS ADJ (*Mil*) lance corporal (*Brit*), private first class (*US*); (*Naut*) able seaman (*Brit*), seaman apprentice (*US*); (*Aviat*) leading aircraftman (*Brit*), airman first class (*US*)

gefressen [gəˈfrɛsn] PTP *von* **fressen**

Gefrett [gəˈfrɛt] NT **-s,** NO PL (*Aus*) worry

gefrieren *ptp* **gefroren** VI IRREG AUX SEIN (*lit, fig*) to freeze

Gefrier-: Gefrierfach NT freezer compartment, icebox (*esp US*); **Gefrierfleisch** NT frozen meat; **gefriergetrocknet** [-gətrɔknət] ADJ freeze-dried; **Gefrierkost** F frozen food; **Gefrierpunkt** M freezing point; (*von Thermometer*) zero; **auf dem ~ stehen** to be at freezing point/zero; **Gefrierschrank** M (upright) freezer; **Gefriertruhe** F freezer

gefroren PTP *von* **frieren, gefrieren**

Gefuchtel [gəˈfʊxtl] NT **-s,** NO PL gesticulating

Gefüge [gəˈfyːgə] NT **-s,** - (*lit, fig*) structure

gefügig [gəˈfyːgɪç] ADJ (= *willfährig*) submissive; (= *gehorsam*) obedient; **jdn ~ machen** to make sb bend to one's will

Gefühl [gəˈfyːl] NT **-(e)s, -e (a)** (= *Sinneswahrnehmung*) feeling; **etw im ~ haben** to have a feel for sth; **er hat kein ~ für heiß und kalt** he can't tell the difference between hot and cold **(b)** (= *seelische Empfindung, Ahnung*) feeling; (= *Emotionalität*) sentiment; **ich habe das ~, dass ...** I have the feeling that ...; **ich habe ein ~, als ob ...** I feel as though ...; **es geht gegen mein ~ ...** I don't like ...; **mein ~ täuscht mich nie** my instinct

is never wrong; **jds ~e erwidern** to return sb's affection; **jds ~e verletzen** to hurt sb's feelings; **er ist zu keinem menschlichen ~ fähig** he is incapable of (feeling) any human emotion; **~ und Verstand** emotion and reason; **das höchste der ~e** (*inf*) the ultimate **(c)** (= *Verständnis*) feeling; (= *Sinn*) sense; **ein ~ für Zahlen/Musik** a feeling for figures/music; **ein ~ für Gerechtigkeit/Proportionen/Rhythmus** a sense of justice/proportion/rhythm; **Tiere haben ein ~ dafür, wer sie mag** animals can sense who likes them; **einen Apparat mit ~ behandeln** to treat an appliance sensitively

gefühllos **1** ADJ (= *unempfindlich, hartherzig*) insensitive; (= *mitleidlos*) callous; *Glieder* numb **2** ADV coldly, callously; **sich ~ verhalten** to be cold

Gefühllosigkeit F **-, -en** (= *Unempfindlichkeit, Hartherzigkeit*) insensitivity; (= *Mitleidlosigkeit*) callousness; (*von Gliedern*) numbness

Gefühls-: gefühlsarm ADJ unemotional; **Gefühlsarmut** F lack of emotion *or* feeling; **Gefühlsausbruch** M emotional outburst; **gefühlsbedingt, gefühlsbestimmt** ADJ emotional; **gefühlsbetont** ADJ emotional; **Gefühlsduselei** [-duːzəˈlai] F **-, -en** (*pej*) mawkishness; **gefühlskalt** ADJ cold; **Gefühlskälte** F coldness; **Gefühlslage** F emotional state; **Gefühlsleben** NT emotional life; **gefühlsmäßig** **1** ADJ instinctive **2** ADV instinctively; **Gefühlsmensch** M emotional person; **Gefühlsnerv** M sensory nerve; **Gefühlssache** F matter of feeling; **Kochen ist zum großen Teil ~** cooking is largely something you have a feel for

gefühlvoll **1** ADJ **(a)** (= *empfindsam*) sensitive; (= *ausdrucksvoll*) expressive; *Volleystopp etc* delicate **(b)** (= *liebevoll*) loving **2** ADV with feeling; (= *ausdrucksvoll*) expressively

gefüllt [gəˈfʏlt] ADJ *Paprikaschoten etc* stuffed; *Brieftasche* full; **~e Pralinen** chocolates with soft centres (*Brit*), candies with soft centers (*US*); *siehe auch* **füllen**

Gefummel [gəˈfʊml] NT **-s,** NO PL (*inf*) fiddling (*inf*); (= *Hantieren*) fumbling (*inf*); (*erotisch*) groping (*inf*); **diese Arbeit ist ein furchtbares ~** this work is very tricky

gefunden [gəˈfʊndn] **1** PTP *von* **finden 2** ADJ **das war ein ~es Fressen für ihn** that was handing it to him on a plate

gefürchtet [gəˈfʏrçtət] ADJ dreaded *usu attr*; **~ sein** to be feared; *siehe auch* **fürchten**

gegabelt [gəˈgaːblt] ADJ forked; *siehe auch* **gabeln**

Gegacker [gəˈgakɐ] NT **-s,** NO PL (*li, fig*) cackle

gegangen PTP *von* **gehen**

gegeben [gəˈgeːbn] **1** PTP *von* **geben 2** ADJ **(a)** (= *bekannt*) given **(b)** (= *vorhanden*) given *attr*; *Bedingung, Voraussetzung* fulfilled *pred*; **bei den ~en Tatsachen/der ~en Situation** given these facts/this situation; **etw als ~ voraussetzen** to assume sth **(c)** (= *günstig*) **zu ~er Zeit** in due course

gegebenenfalls [gəˈgeːbnənˈfals] ADV should the situation arise; (= *wenn nötig*) if need be; (= *eventuell*) possibly; (*Admin*) if applicable

gegen [ˈgeːgn] PREP +ACC **(a)** (= *wider*) against; **X ~ Y** (*Sport, Jur*) X versus Y; **haben Sie ein Mittel ~ Schnupfen?** do you have anything for colds?; **etwas/nichts ~ jdn/etw haben** to have something/nothing against sb/sth; **10 ~ 1 wetten** to bet 10 to 1 **(b)** (= *in Richtung auf*) towards, toward (*US*); (= *nach*) to; (= *an*) against; **~ einen Baum rennen/prallen** to run/crash into a tree; **etw ~ das Licht halten** to hold sth (up) to the light **(c)** (= *ungefähr*) round about, around; (= *nicht mehr als*) getting on for; (= *nicht später als*) towards; **~ 5 Uhr** around 5 o'clock **(d)** (= *gegenüber*) towards, to; **sie ist immer fair ~ mich gewesen** she's always been fair to me **(e)** (= *im Austausch für*) for; **~ bar** for cash; **~ Bezahlung/Quittung** against payment/a receipt **(f)** (= *verglichen mit*) compared with

Gegen-: Gegenangebot NT counteroffer; **Gegenangriff** M (*Mil, fig*) counterattack; **Gegenanzeige** F (*Med*) contraindication; **Gegenbesuch** M return visit; **jdm einen ~ machen** to return sb's visit; **Gegenbeweis** M counterevidence *no indef art, no pl*; **den ~ zu etw erbringen** *or* **antreten** to produce evidence to counter sth; **bis zum ~ müssen wir ...** until we have evidence to the contrary we must ...

Gegend ['ge:gnt] F -, -en [-dn] area; (= *geografisches Gebiet, Körpergegend*) region; (= *Richtung*) direction; (*inf:* = *Nähe*) area; **eine schöne ~ Deutschlands** a beautiful part of Germany; **hier in der ~** (a)round here; **ungefähr in dieser ~** somewhere in this area; **die ganze ~ spricht davon** it's the talk of the neighbourhood (*Brit*) *or* neighborhood (*US*); **ein bisschen durch die ~ laufen** (*inf*) to have a stroll (a)round; **brüll nicht so durch die ~** (*inf*) don't scream your head off (*inf*)

Gegendarstellung F reply

gegeneinander [ge:gnlai'nandɐ] ADV against each other *or* one another; (= *zueinander*) to(wards) each other *or* one another; (= *im Austausch*) for each other *or* one another

Gegeneinander [ge:gnlai'nandɐ] NT -s, NO PL conflict

gegeneinander: gegeneinander prallen VI AUX SEIN to collide; **gegeneinander stellen** VT (*lit*) to put together; (*fig*) to compare; **gegeneinander stoßen** VI IRREG AUX SEIN to bump into each other; (= *kollidieren*) to collide

Gegen-: Gegenentwurf M alternative plan; **Gegenfahrbahn** F oncoming carriageway (*Brit*) *or* highway (*US*) *or* (= *Spur*) lane; **Gegenfrage** F counterquestion; **darf ich mit einer ~ antworten?** may I answer your question with another (of my own)?; **Gegengewicht** NT counterbalance (*auch fig*); **als (ausgleichendes) ~ zu etw wirken** (*lit, fig*) to counterbalance sth; **Gegengift** NT antidote (*gegen* to); **Gegengleis** NT opposite track; **gegenhalten** VI SEP (= *sich wehren*) to counter; (= *standhalten*) to stand one's ground; **Gegenkandidat(in)** M(F) rival candidate; **als ~ zu jdm aufgestellt werden** to be put up as a candidate against sb; **gegenläufig** ADJ (*Tech*) contrarotating; (*fig*) opposite; **Gegenleistung** F service in return; **als ~ für etw** in return for sth; **ich erwarte keine ~** I don't expect anything in return; **gegenlenken** VI SEP (*Aut*) to steer in the opposite direction; **gegenlesen** VTI SEP IRREG to countercheck; **Gegenlicht** NT **bei ~ Auto fahren** to drive with the light in one's eyes; **etw bei** *or* **im ~ aufnehmen** (*Phot*) to take a backlit photo(graph) of sth; **Gegenliebe** F requited love; (*fig:* = *Zustimmung*) approval; **sie fand keine ~** (*lit*) her love was not reciprocated; (*fig*) she met with no approval; **auf ~/wenig ~ stoßen** (*fig*) to be welcomed/hardly welcomed with open arms; **Gegenmaßnahme** F countermeasure; **~n zur Bekämpfung der Inflation** measures to counter inflation; **Gegenmittel** NT (*Med*) antidote (*gegen* to); **Gegenoffensive** F (*lit, fig*) counteroffensive; **Gegenpol** M counterpole; (*fig*) antithesis (*zu* of, to); **Gegenprobe** F crosscheck; **die ~ zu etw machen** to crosscheck sth; **Gegenrichtung** F opposite direction

Gegensatz M (= *konträrer ~*) contrast; (= *kontradiktorischer ~, Gegenteil*) opposite; (= *Unvereinbarkeit*) conflict; (= *Unterschied*) difference; **Gegensätze** (= *Meinungsverschiedenheiten*) differences pl; **im ~ zu** unlike, in contrast to; **Marx, im ~ zu ...** Marx, as against ...; **er, im ~ zu mir, ...** unlike me, he ...; **einen krassen ~ zu etw bilden** to contrast sharply with sth; **Gegensätze ziehen einander** *or* **sich an** (*prov*) opposites attract; **im ~ zu etw stehen** to conflict with sth; **Gegensätze ausgleichen** to even out differences; **unüberbrückbare Gegensätze** irreconcilable differences

gegensätzlich ['ge:gnzɛtslɪç] █ ADJ (= *konträr*) contrasting; (= *widersprüchlich*) opposing; (= *unterschiedlich*) different; (= *unvereinbar*) conflicting; **Schwarz und Weiß sind ~e Begriffe** black and white are opposites; **eine ~e Meinung** a conflicting view █ ADV **sie verhalten sich völlig ~** they behave in totally different ways; **~ veranlagt sein** to have contradictory characteristics

Gegensätzlichkeit F -, -en (+*gen* between) (= *Kontrast*) contrast; (= *Widersprüchlichkeit*) opposition; (= *Unterschiedlichkeit*) difference; (= *Unvereinbarkeit*) conflict; **die ~ dieser beiden Systeme** the contrast between these two systems; **bei aller ~ ...** in spite of all (the) differences ...

Gegen-: Gegenschlag M (*Mil*) reprisal; (*fig*) retaliation *no pl*; **einen ~ (gegen jdn) führen** to strike back (at sb); **zum ~ ausholen** to prepare to retaliate; **Gegenseite** F (*lit, fig*) other side; **gegenseitig** ['ge:gnzaitiç] █ ADJ mutual █ ADV each other, one another; **sich ~ bedingen** to be contingent (up)on one another *or* each other; **sich ~ ausschließen** to be mutually exclusive; **Gegenseitigkeit** F -, NO PL mutuality; **ein Abkommen/Vertrag auf ~** a reciprocal agreement/treaty; **Versicherung auf ~** mutual insurance; **das beruht auf ~** the

feeling is mutual; **Gegensprechanlage** F (two-way) intercom; (*Telec*) duplex (system)

Gegenstand M (= *Ding*) object, thing; (*Econ:* = *Artikel*) article; (= *Thema, Angelegenheit, Stoff*) subject; (*der Neugier, des Hasses etc*) (*Philos*) object; (*Aus:* = *Schulfach*) subject; **sie wurde mit einem stumpfen ~ erschlagen** she was killed by a blow from a blunt instrument; **~ des Gespötts** object of ridicule

gegenständlich ['ge:gnʃtɛntlɪç] ADJ concrete; (*Philos*) objective; (*Art*) representational; (= *anschaulich*) graphic(al); **die ~e Welt** the world of objects

gegenstandslos ADJ (= *überflüssig*) redundant, unnecessary; (= *grundlos*) unfounded; (= *hinfällig*) irrelevant; (*Art*) abstract; **bitte betrachten Sie dieses Schreiben als ~, falls ...** please disregard this notice if ...

Gegen-: gegensteuern VI SEP (*Aut*) to steer in the opposite direction; (*fig*) to take countermeasures; **Gegenstimme** F (*Parl*) vote against; **der Antrag wurde mit 250 Stimmen bei** *or* **und 30 ~n angenommen** the motion was carried by 250 votes to 30; **der Antrag wurde ohne ~n angenommen** the motion was carried unanimously; **Gegenstück** NT opposite; (= *passendes ~*) counterpart

Gegenteil NT, NO PL opposite (*von* of); (= *Umkehrung*) reverse (*von* of); **im ~!** on the contrary!; **ganz im ~** quite the reverse; **das ~ bewirken** to have the opposite effect; (*Mensch*) to achieve the exact opposite; **ins ~ umschlagen** to swing to the other extreme

gegenteilig █ ADJ *Ansicht, Wirkung, Erfahrung* opposite, contrary; **eine ~e Meinung** a contrary opinion; **~e Aussagen** contradictory statements; **~e Behauptungen** statements to the contrary; **ich habe nichts Gegenteiliges gehört** I've heard nothing to the contrary █ ADV **sich ~ entscheiden** to come to a different decision

gegenüber [ge:gn'y:bɐ] █ PREP +DAT (a) (*örtlich*) opposite; **er saß mir genau/schräg ~** he sat directly/diagonally opposite me

(b) (= *zu*) to; (= *in Bezug auf*) with regard to, as regards; (= *angesichts, vor*) in the face of; (= *im Vergleich zu*) compared with; **mir ~ hat er das nicht geäußert** he didn't say that to me; **allem Politischen ~ ist er misstrauisch** he's distrustful of anything political; **er ist allem Neuen ~ wenig aufgeschlossen** he's not very open-minded about anything new █ ADV opposite; **der Park ~** the park opposite; **die Leute von ~** (*inf*) the people opposite

Gegenüber [ge:gn'y:bɐ] NT -s, - (*bei Kampf*) opponent; (*bei Diskussion*) opposite number; **mein ~ im Zug/am Tisch** the person (sitting) opposite me in the train/at (the) table

gegenüber-: gegenüberliegen VI SEP IRREG +DAT to be opposite, to face; **sich** (*dat*) **~** to face each other; **gegenüberliegend** ADJ ATTR opposite; **das ~e Grundstück** the plot of land opposite; **gegenübersehen** VR SEP IRREG +DAT **sich einer Aufgabe ~** to be faced with a task; **gegenübersitzen** VI SEP IRREG +DAT to sit opposite; **gegenüberstehen** VI SEP IRREG +DAT to be opposite, to face; *jdm* to stand opposite; **jdm feindlich/freundlich/desinteressiert ~** to have a hostile/friendly/disinterested attitude toward(s) sb; **gegenüberstellen** VT SEP (= *konfrontieren mit*) to confront (+*dat* with); (*fig:* = *vergleichen*) to compare (+*dat* with); **Gegenüberstellung** F confrontation; (*fig:* = *Vergleich*) comparison

Gegen-: Gegenverkehr M oncoming traffic; **Gegenvorschlag** M counterproposal

Gegenwart F -, NO PL (a) (= *jetziger Augenblick*) present; (= *heutiges Zeitalter*) present (time *or* day); (*Gram*) present (tense); **die Literatur/Musik der ~** contemporary literature/music; **die Probleme der ~** the problems of today; **in der ~ stehen** (*Gram*) to be in the present (tense) (b) (= *Anwesenheit*) presence; **in ~** +*gen* in the presence of

gegenwärtig ['ge:gnvɛrtiç, ge:gn'vɛrtiç] █ ADJ (a) ATTR (= *jetzig*) present; **der ~e Preis** the current price (b) (*geh:* = *anwesend*) present *pred*; **es ist mir im Moment nicht ~** I can't recall it at the moment █ ADV (= *augenblicklich*) at present

Gegen-: Gegenwehr F resistance; **Gegenwert** M equivalent; **es wurden Waren im ~ von 8.000 Euro entwendet** goods to the value of *or* worth 8,000 euros were taken; **Gegenwind** M headwind; **wir hatten starken ~** there was a strong headwind; **Gegenwirkung** F counteraction; **diese Tabletten können eine ~ haben** these tablets can have the opposite effect; **gegenzeichnen** VT SEP to countersign; **Gegenzug** M (a) countermove; **im ~ zu etw** as a countermove to sth (b) (*Rail*) corresponding train in the other direction; (= *entgegenkommender Zug*) oncoming train

gegessen PTP *von* **essen**

geglichen PTP *von* **gleichen**

gegliedert [gə'gli:dət] ADJ jointed; (*fig*) structured; (= *organisiert*) organized; *siehe auch* **gliedern**

geglitten PTP *von* **gleiten**

geglommen PTP *von* **glimmen**

Gegner ['ge:gnɐ] M -s, -, **Gegnerin** [-ərɪn] F -, -nen opponent (*auch Sport*); (= *Rivale*) rival; (= *Feind*) enemy; **ein ~ der Todesstrafe sein** to be against capital punishment

gegnerisch ['ge:gnərɪʃ] ADJ ATTR opposing; (*Mil* = *feindlich*) enemy *attr*; *Übermacht* of the enemy; **das ~e Tor** the opponents' goal

gegolten PTP *von* **gelten**

gegoren PTP *von* **gären**

gegossen PTP *von* **gießen**

gegraben PTP *von* **graben**

gegriffen PTP *von* **greifen**

Gegröle [gə'grø:lə] NT -s, NO PL (*inf*) raucous bawling (*inf*)

Gehabe [gə'ha:bə] NT -s, NO PL (*inf*) affected behaviour (*Brit*) or behavior (*US*)

gehabt [gə'ha:pt] PTP *von* **haben**

Gehackte(s) [gə'haktə] NT DECL AS ADJ mince (*Brit*), ground meat (*US*)

Gehalt¹ [gə'halt] M -(e)s, -e (a) (= *Anteil*) content; **der ~ an Eiweiß/Kohlenhydraten** the protein/carbohydrate content (b) (*fig*) (= *Inhalt*) content; (= *Substanz*) substance

Gehalt² NT or (AUS) M -(e)s, ⸚er [gə'hɛltə] salary

gehalten [gə'haltn] ❶ PTP *von* **halten** ❷ ADJ **~ sein, etw zu tun** (*form*) to be required to do sth

Gehalts-: Gehaltsabrechnung F salary statement; **Gehaltsanspruch** M salary claim; **Gehaltsbescheinigung** F salary declaration; **Gehaltsempfänger(in)** M(F) salary-earner; **~ sein** to receive a salary; **die Firma hat 500 ~** the firm has 500 salaried staff; **Gehaltserhöhung** F salary increase; (*regelmäßig*) increment; **Gehaltsforderung** F salary claim; **Gehaltspfändung** F deduction of salary (at source); **Gehaltsverhandlung** F salary negotiations *pl*; **Gehaltsvorrückung** F -, -en (*Aus*) = **Gehaltserhöhung**; **Gehaltsvorstellung** F, **Gehaltswunsch** M salary requirement; **Gehaltszulage** F (= *Gehaltserhöhung*) salary increase; (*regelmäßige*) increment; (= *Extrazulage*) salary bonus

gehaltvoll ADJ *Speise* nourishing; *Wein* full-bodied; (*fig*) rich in content; **ein ~es Buch** a book which says a great deal

gehangen PTP *von* **hängen**

geharnischt [gə'ha:rnɪʃt] ADJ *Brief, Abfuhr etc* strong; *Antwort* sharp, sharply-worded

gehässig [gə'hɛsɪç] ❶ ADJ spiteful ❷ ADV spitefully; **~ von jdm reden** to say nasty things about sb

Gehässigkeit F -, -en spite(fulness); **~en** spiteful things; **jdm ~en sagen** to be spiteful to sb

gehauen PTP *von* **hauen**

gehäuft [gə'hɔyft] ❶ ADJ *Löffel* heaped; **das ~e Auftreten bestimmter Krankheiten** the frequent occurrence of certain diseases ❷ ADV in large numbers; **dieser Fehler tritt ~ auf** this error occurs more and more frequently; *siehe auch* **häufen**

Gehäuse [gə'hɔyzə] NT -s, - (a) (*von Gerät*) case; (= *Lautsprechergehäuse*) box; (= *großes Lautsprechergehäuse, Radiogehäuse*) cabinet (b) (= *Schneckengehäuse*) shell (c) (= *Obstgehäuse*) core

gehbehindert ['ge:bəhɪndɐt] ADJ unable to walk properly

Gehege [gə'he:gə] NT -s, - reserve; (*im Zoo*) enclosure; (= *Wildgehege*) preserve; **jdm ins ~ kommen** (*fig inf*) to get under sb's feet (*inf*); (= *ein Recht streitig machen*) to poach on sb's preserves

geheiligt [gə'hailɪçt] ADJ sacred; *Räume* sacrosanct; **sein ~es Mittagsschläfchen** (*inf*) his precious afternoon nap

geheim [gə'haim] ❶ ADJ secret; **seine ~sten Gefühle/Wünsche/Gedanken** his innermost feelings/wishes/thoughts; **streng ~** top secret; **~ bleiben** to remain (a) secret; **im Geheimen** in secret, secretly ❷ ADV secretly; **~ abstimmen** to vote by secret ballot

Geheim- IN CPDS secret; **Geheimdienst** M secret service; **Geheimfach** NT secret compartment; (= *Schublade*) secret drawer; **geheim halten** VT IRREG **etw (vor jdm) ~** to keep sth a secret (from sb); **Geheimhaltung** F, NO PL secrecy

Geheimnis [gə'haimnɪs] NT -ses, -se secret; (= *rätselhaftes ~*) mystery; **ein offenes ~** an open secret; **das ist das ganze ~** (*inf*) that's all there is to it; **aus etw ein/kein ~ machen** to make a big secret about sth/no secret of sth

Geheimnis-: Geheimniskrämerei [-krɛːmə'rai] F -, -en (*inf*) secretiveness; **Geheimnisträger(in)** M(F) bearer of secrets; **Geheimnisverrat** M ≈ offence under the Official Secrets Act (*Brit*), ≈ treason against the State (*US*); **geheimnisvoll** ADJ mysterious; **~ tun** to be mysterious; **mit etw ~ tun** to make a big mystery of sth

Geheim-: Geheimnummer F secret number (*auch Telec*); (= *Geheimzahl, PIN*) PIN (number); **Geheimpolizei** F secret police; **Geheimpolizist(in)** M(F) member of the secret police; **Geheimtür** F secret door; **Geheimzahl** F PIN (number)

geheißen PTP *von* **heißen**

gehemmt [gə'hɛmt] ❶ ADJ *Mensch* inhibited; *Benehmen* self-conscious ❷ ADV *sich benehmen* self-consciously; **~ sprechen** to have inhibitions in speaking; *siehe auch* **hemmen**

---

gehen ['ge:ən]

❶ INTRANSITIVES VERB	❸ UNPERSÖNLICHES VERB
❷ TRANSITIVES VERB	❹ REFLEXIVES VERB

pret **ging** [gɪŋ], *ptp* **gegangen** [gə'gaŋən] AUX SEIN

❶ INTRANSITIVES VERB

(a) to go; **gehen wir!** let's go!; **bitte gehen Sie!** (= *verlassen Sie das Zimmer*) please leave!; (*Vortritt gewährend*) **geh doch!** go on (then)!; **geh schon!** go on!; **er ist gegangen worden** (*hum inf*) he was given the push (*hum inf*); **er ist von uns gegangen** (*euph*) he has passed away

♦ **gehen + Infinitiv** **schwimmen/tanzen gehen** to go swimming/dancing; **spielen gehen** to go and play; **schlafen gehen** to go to bed

(b) (= *zu Fuß gehen*) to go, to walk; **das Kind lernt gehen** the baby is learning to walk; **am Stock/an Krücken** (*dat*) **gehen** to walk with a stick/with crutches; **wie lange geht man bis zum Bus?** how long a walk is it to the bus?; **er ging im Zimmer auf und ab** he walked up and down the room; **das Pferd geht (im Schritt)** the horse is walking; **das Pferd geht Trab** the horse is trotting

(c) (*mit Präposition*)

> *In Verbindung mit Präpositionen siehe auch unter dem Eintrag für die Präposition.*

♦ **gehen + an** **er ging an den Tisch** he went to the table; **gehen Sie (mir) nicht an meine Sachen!** don't touch my things!; **das Erbe ging an ihn** the inheritance went to him

♦ **gehen + auf** **sie gingen auf den Berg** they went up the mountain; **sie ging auf die Straße** she went out into the street; **auf die andere Seite gehen** to cross *or* go over to the other side; **das Fenster geht auf den Hof** the window overlooks the yard; **diese Tür geht auf den Balkon** this door leads onto the balcony; **das geht auf sein Konto** *or* **auf ihn** he's responsible for that; **das Bier geht auf mich** (*inf*) the beer's on me; **auf wen geht das Bier?** (*inf*) who's paying for the beer?

♦ **gehen + aus** **sie ging aus dem Zimmer** she went out of the room; **er ist wieder ohne Schirm aus dem Haus gegangen** he's gone out without his umbrella again; **jdm aus dem Licht/Weg gehen** to get out of sb's light/way

♦ **gehen + bis** **er ging bis zum Zaun** he went up to the fence; **er ging bis zur Straße** he went as far as the street; **das Wasser ging ihm bis zum Bauch** the water went up to his waist; **der Rock ging ihr bis zum Knöchel** the skirt went down to her ankles

♦ **gehen + gegen** **das geht gegen meine Prinzipien** *or* **meine Überzeugung** it's against my principles

♦ **gehen + in** **geh mal in die Küche** go into the kitchen; **in die Industrie/Politik gehen** to go into industry/politics; **in die Gewerkschaft/Partei gehen** to join the union/party; **wie viele**

Leute gehen in deinen Wagen? how many people can you get in your car?; **in diesem Saal gehen 300 Leute** this hall holds 300 people; **in diesen Krug geht ein ganzer Liter** this jug holds a whole litre (*Brit*) *or* liter (*US*); **3 geht in 9 dreimal** 3 into 9 goes 3; **das will mir nicht in den Kopf gehen** I just can't understand it; **in die tausende** *or* **Tausende gehen** to run into (the) thousands; **in sich** (*acc*) **gehen** to stop and think

✦**gehen + mit mit jdm gehen** to go with sb; (= *befreundet sein*) to go out with sb; **mit der Zeit gehen** to move with the times; **mit der Mode gehen** to follow fashion

✦**gehen + nach er ging nach München** he went to Munich; **diese Straße geht nach Hannover** this road goes to Hanover; **diese Tür geht nach draußen/nach nebenan** this door leads to the outside/into the next room; **wenn man nach seiner Aussage gehen kann** (= *urteilen*) if his statement is anything to go by; **man darf nicht nur nach dem Äußeren gehen** (= *urteilen*) you shouldn't go just by appearances

✦**gehen + über über die Straße gehen** to cross the road; **über die Brücke gehen** to go over the bridge; **die Brücke geht dort über den Fluss** the bridge crosses the river there; **die Reise geht über Dresden** we/they *etc* are going via Dresden; **sein Garten geht ihm über alles** his garden is the thing that means most to him; **nichts geht über** (+*acc*) **...** there's nothing to beat ...

✦**gehen + unter unter Menschen gehen** to mix with people; **jetzt ist er unter die Dichter gegangen** he's now joined the poetic fraternity

✦**gehen + zu zur Post gehen** to go to the post office; **zur Schule gehen** to go to school; **zu jdm gehen** to go to see sb; **zum Militär gehen** to join the army; **zum Theater gehen** to go on the stage; **zur Universität gehen** to go to university

(d) (= *sich bewegen*) **ich hörte, wie die Tür ging** I heard the door (go); **diese Tür/Schublade geht schwer** this door/drawer is very stiff; **heute geht ein scharfer Wind** there's a bitter wind today

(e) (= *ertönen*) (*Klingel, Glocke, Telefon*) to ring, to go; **wie geht das Lied/Gedicht?** how does the song/poem go?

(f) (= *funktionieren*) to work; (*Auto, Uhr*) to go; **dieses Programm geht nur, wenn man dieses Betriebssystem hat** this program only works if you've got this operating system; **die Uhr geht gut** the clock keeps good time; **die Uhr geht falsch/richtig** the clock is wrong/right; **so geht das, das geht so** this is the way to do it

(g) (= *florieren*) (*Geschäft*) to do well; (= *verkauft werden*) to sell; **wie gehen die Geschäfte?** how's business?

(h) (= *dauern*) to go on; **wie lange geht das denn noch?** how much longer is it going to go on?; **mein Kurs geht vom 2. bis 28. Juni** my course is from the 2nd to the 28th of June

(i) (= *aufgehen*) (*Hefeteig*) to rise

(j) (= *betreffen*) **der Artikel ging gegen ...** the article criticized ...; **das Buch ging um ...** the book was about ...; **die Wette geht um 100 Euro** the bet is for 100 euros; **mein Vorschlag geht dahin, dass ...** my suggestion is that ...

(k) (= *möglich, gut sein*) to be all right, to be OK (*inf*); **Montag geht** Monday's all right; **Montag, das geht gut** Monday's fine; **geht morgen? – ja, morgen geht gut** is tomorrow all right? – yes, tomorrow's fine; **das geht doch nicht** that's not on (*Brit*) *or* not OK (*inf*); **Dienstag geht auch nicht** (*inf*) Tuesday's no good either

(l) (*andere Redewendungen*) **(ach) geh (doch), das darf doch nicht wahr sein!** (*inf*) come on, that can't be true! (*inf*); **(ach) geh, so schlimm ist das nicht!** (*inf*) (oh) come on, it's not that bad!; **gehen Sie (mir) doch mit Ihren Ausreden!** (*inf*) I don't want any of your excuses!

✦**vor sich gehen** was geht hier vor sich? what's going on here?; **ich weiß nicht, wie das vor sich geht** I don't know the procedure

✦**so/zu weit gehen** to go so/too far

2 TRANSITIVES VERB **er ging eine Meile** he walked a mile; **ich gehe immer diesen Weg/diese Straße** I always go this way/along this road

3 UNPERSÖNLICHES VERB

(a) (= *ergehen*) **wie geht es Ihnen?** how are you?; (*zu Patient*) how are you feeling?; **wie gehts?** how are things?; (*bei Arbeit etc*) how's it going?; **wie gehts sonst?** (*inf*) how are things otherwise?; **wie gehts denn (so)? – es geht** (*inf*) how are things? – all right *or* not too bad (*inf*); **danke, es geht** (*inf*) all

right *or* not too bad (*inf*), thanks; **es geht ihm gut/schlecht** he's fine/not well; **es geht mir (wieder) besser** I'm better now; **sonst gehts dir gut?** (*iro*) are you sure you're feeling all right? (*iro*); **wie war denn die Prüfung? – ach, es ging ganz gut** how was the exam? – oh, it went quite well; **mir ist es genauso gegangen** (= *ich habe dasselbe erlebt*) it was just the same for me; (= *ich habe dasselbe empfunden*) I felt the same way; **lass es dir gut gehen** take care of yourself; **so geht es (eben)** (= *so ist das Leben*) that's how it goes

(b) (= *sich machen lassen, möglich sein*) **es geht** it is possible; (= *funktioniert*) it works; **solange es geht** as long as possible; **geht es?** (*ohne Hilfe*) can you manage?; **es geht nicht** (= *ist nicht möglich*) it's impossible; (= *kommt nicht in Frage*) it's not on; **es wird schon gehen** I'll/he'll *etc* manage; (= *wird sich machen lassen*) it'll be all right; **es geht eben nicht anders** there's no other way; **so geht es nicht** that's not the way to do it; (*entrüstet*) it just won't do; **morgen geht es nicht** tomorrow's no good

(c) (= *führen*) **dann geht es immer geradeaus** then it's straight on (*Brit*) *or* ahead; **dann ging es nach Süden/ins Gebirge** (= *gingen wir/sie etc*) then we/they *etc* set off for the south/the mountains; **wohin geht es diesmal in Urlaub?** where are you going on holiday (*Brit*) *or* vacation (*US*) this time?

(d) (*andere Wendungen*) **es geht ein starker Wind** there's a strong wind (blowing); **es geht das Gerücht** the rumour (*Brit*) *or* rumor (*US*) is going (a)round; **es geht auf 9 Uhr** it is approaching 9 o'clock

✦**es geht um** (= *betrifft*) **es geht um seinen Vertrag** it's about his contract; **worum gehts denn?** what's it about?; **worum geht es in diesem Film/bei eurem Streit?** what is this film/your argument about?; **es geht um Leben und Tod** it's a matter of life and death; **es geht um meinen Ruf** my reputation is at stake; **es geht ihm nur um eins** he's only interested in one thing; **darum geht es mir nicht** (= *habe ich nicht gemeint*) that's not my point; (= *spielt keine Rolle für mich*) that doesn't matter to me; **es geht bei diesem Geschäft um 5 Millionen** (= *sind im Spiel*) the deal involves 5 million; (= *stehen auf dem Spiel*) 5 million are at stake in the deal; **wenn es ums Schauspielern geht** when it comes to acting

✦**es geht nach jdm** it's up to sb; **wenn es nach mir ginge ...** if it were *or* was up to me ...; **es kann nicht immer alles nach dir gehen** you can't expect to have your own way all the time

4 REFLEXIVES VERB

✦**sich gehen es geht sich schlecht hier** it's not nice walking here; **in diesen Schuhen geht es sich bequem** these shoes are comfortable to walk in

Gehen NT **-s**, NO PL walking; (= *Abschied*) leaving; (*Sport*) walking; (= *Wettbewerb*) walk

gehen lassen ptp **gehen lassen** *or* (*rare*) **gehen gelassen** IRREG **1** VT (*inf*: = *in Ruhe lassen*) to leave alone **2** VR **(a)** (= *sich nicht beherrschen*) to lose control of oneself **(b)** (= *nachlässig sein*) to let oneself go

Geher ['ɡeːɐ] M **-s**, **-**, **Geherin** [-ərɪn] F **-**, **-nen** (*Sport*) walker

gehetzt [ɡəˈhɛtst] ADJ harassed; *siehe auch* **hetzen**

geheuer [ɡəˈhɔyɐ] ADJ **nicht ~** (= *beängstigend*) scary (*inf*); (= *spukhaft*) eerie, creepy (*inf*); (= *verdächtig*) dubious; (= *unwohl*) uneasy; **es ist mir nicht ganz ~** it is scary (*inf*); it is gives me the creeps (*inf*); it seems a bit dubious to me; I feel uneasy about it; **mir ist es hier nicht ~** (= *mir ist unheimlich*) this place gives me the creeps (*inf*); (= *mir ist unwohl*) I have an uneasy feeling about this place

Geheul [ɡəˈhɔyl] NT **-(e)s**, NO PL, **Geheule** [ɡəˈhɔylə] NT **-s**, NO PL howling

Gehgerät NT Zimmer® (*Brit*), walker (*US*)

Gehilfe [ɡəˈhɪlfə] M **-n**, **-n**, **Gehilfin** [-ˈhɪlfɪn] F **-**, **-nen (a)** (*dated*: = *Helfer*) assistant **(b)** (= *kaufmännischer ~*) trainee **(c)** (*Jur*) accomplice

Gehirn [ɡəˈhɪrn] NT **-(e)s**, **-e** brain; (= *Geist*) mind

Gehirn-: Gehirnblutung F brain haemorrhage (*Brit*) *or* hemorrhage (*US*); **Gehirnerschütterung** F concussion; **Gehirnschlag** M stroke; **Gehirnwäsche** F atrophy of the brain; **Gehirnwäsche** F brainwashing *no pl*; **jdn einer ~ unterziehen** to brainwash sb

gehoben [ɡəˈhoːbn] **1** PTP *von* **heben 2** ADJ *Sprache, Ausdrucksweise* elevated; (= *anspruchsvoll*) sophisticated;

Stellung senior; *Stimmung* elated; *Ansprüche* high; *Mittelschicht* upper; *Güter des* **~en Bedarfs** semi-luxuries; **~er Dienst** professional and executive levels of the civil service 🖫 ADV **sich ~ ausdrücken** to use elevated language

geholfen PTP *von* **helfen**

Gehör [ɡəˈhøːɐ̯] NT **-(e)s, -e (a)** (= *Hörvermögen*) hearing; (*Mus*) ear; **kein musikalisches ~ haben** to have no ear for music; **nach dem ~ singen/spielen** to sing/play by ear; **absolutes ~** perfect pitch **(b)** (*geh:* = *Anhörung*) **~ finden** to gain a hearing; **jdm ~/kein ~ schenken** to listen/not to listen to sb; **um ~ bitten** to request a hearing; **sich** (*dat*) **~ verschaffen** to obtain a hearing; (= *Aufmerksamkeit*) to gain attention

gehorchen [ɡəˈhɔrçn], ptp **gehorcht** VI to obey (*jdm* sb); (*Wagen, Maschine etc*) to respond (*jdm/einer Sache* to sb/sth); **seine Stimme gehorchte ihm nicht mehr** he lost control over his voice

gehören [ɡəˈhøːrən], ptp **gehört** 🖫 VI **(a) jdm ~** (= *jds Eigentum sein*) to belong to sb; **das gehört ihm** he owns the house; **ihr Herz gehört einem anderen** her heart belongs to another

(b) (= *den richtigen Platz haben*) to go; (*Mensch*) to belong; (= *gebühren*) to deserve; **das gehört nicht hierher** (*Gegenstand*) it doesn't go here; (*Vorschlag*) it is irrelevant here; **das Buch gehört ins Regal** the book goes on the bookshelves; **das gehört nicht zur Sache/zum Thema** that is off the point; **dieser Betrag gehört unter die Rubrik „Einnahmen"** this sum belongs under the heading "credits"; **er gehört ins Bett** he should be in bed

(c) ~ zu (= *zählen zu*) to be amongst, to be one of; (= *Bestandteil sein von*) to be part of; (= *Mitglied sein von*) to belong to; **es gehört zu seiner Arbeit/zu seinen Pflichten** it's part of his work/one of his duties; **zur Familie ~** to be one of the family; **zu diesem Kleid gehört ein blauer Hut** (= *ist Bestandteil von*) there is a blue hat to go with this dress; (= *würde dazu passen*) a blue hat would go with this dress; **zum Wild gehört einfach Rotwein** red wine is a must with venison

(d) ~ zu (= *Voraussetzung sein, nötig sein*) to be called for by; **zu dieser Arbeit gehört viel Konzentration** this work calls for a lot of concentration; **dazu gehört Mut** that takes courage; **dazu gehört nicht viel** it doesn't take much; **dazu gehört (schon) einiges** *or* **etwas** that takes some doing (*inf*); **dazu gehört mehr** there's more to it than that

🖪 VR to be (right and) proper; **das gehört sich einfach nicht** that's just not done; **wie es sich gehört** (= *wie es sich schickt*) as is (right and) proper; (= *wie es zünftig ist*) comme il faut; **benimm dich, wie es sich gehört!** behave yourself properly

gehörig [ɡəˈhøːrɪç] 🖫 ADJ **(a)** (*geh*) **jdm/zu etw ~** belonging to sb/sth; **zu etw ~ sein** to belong to sth; **nicht zur Sache ~** irrelevant; **alle nicht zum Thema ~en Vorschläge** all suggestions not relevant to the topic

(b) ATTR (= *gebührend*) proper

(c) (*inf:* = *beträchtlich, groß*) good attr; **eine ~e Achtung vor jdm haben** to have a healthy respect for sb; **eine ~e Tracht Prügel** a good thrashing

🖪 ADV (*inf:* = *ordentlich*) *ausschimpfen* severely; *verwarnen* sharply; **ich habs ihm ~ gegeben** (*inf*) I showed him what's what (*inf*); (*mit Worten*) I gave him a piece of my mind (*inf*); **jdn ~ verprügeln** to give sb a good beating; **ich habe mich in ihm ~ getäuscht** I was totally wrong about him; **da hast du dich ~ getäuscht!** you're badly mistaken

gehörlos ADJ (*form*) deaf; **~ sein** to have no hearing

Gehörlose(r) [ɡəˈhøːrloːzə] MF DECL AS ADJ (*form*) deaf person

Gehörnerv M auditory nerve

gehorsam [ɡəˈhoːrzaːm] 🖫 ADJ obedient 🖪 ADV obediently; **melde ~st** reporting, sir

Gehorsam [ɡəˈhoːrzaːm] M **-s**, NO PL obedience; **jdm den ~ verweigern** to refuse to obey sb

Gehör-: Gehörschutz M earmuffs pl; **Gehörsinn** M sense of hearing; **Gehörsturz** M (temporary) loss of hearing

Gehsteig [-ʃtaik] M **-(e)s, -e** [-ɡə] pavement (*Brit*), sidewalk (*US*)

Gehtnichtmehr [ˈɡeːtnɪçtmeːɐ̯] NT **trinken/tanzen bis zum ~** to drink/dance till one drops (*inf*); **sich bis zum ~ verschulden** to get up to one's ears in debt (*inf*)

Gehupe [ɡəˈhuːpə] NT **-s**, NO PL (*inf*) hooting, honking

Geh-: Gehversuch M **(a)** (*von Kind, nach Unfall, Verletzung*) attempt at walking; **erste ~e** first attempts at walking

(b) (*fig*) tentative step; **Gehwagen** M wheeled Zimmer® (*Brit*), walker (*US*); **Gehweg** M footpath

Geier [ˈɡaiɐ] M **-s, -** (*lit, fig*) vulture; **weiß der ~!** (*inf*) God knows!

Geige [ˈɡaiɡə] F **-, -n** violin, fiddle (*inf*); **die erste/zweite ~ spielen** (*lit*) to play first/second violin; (*fig*) to call the tune/play second fiddle

Geigen-: Geigenbauer M, pl **-**, **Geigenbauerin** F, pl **-nen** violin-maker; **Geigenbogen** M violin bow; **Geigenkasten** M violin case

Geiger [ˈɡaiɡɐ] M **-s, -**, **Geigerin** [-ərɪn] F **-, -nen** violinist, fiddler (*inf*); **erster ~** first violin

Geigerzähler M Geiger counter

geil [ɡail] 🖫 ADJ **(a)** horny; (*pej:* = *lüstern*) lecherous; **auf jdn ~ sein** to be lusting after sb **(b)** (*sl:* = *prima*) brilliant (*inf*), wicked (*sl*); **der Typ ist ~** he's a cool guy (*inf*) 🖪 ADV **(a)** (= *lüstern*) lecherously; **jdn ~ ansehen** to give sb a lecherous look **(b)** (*sl:* = *prima*) *spielen, tanzen* brilliantly; **~ aussehen** to look cool (*inf*)

Geilheit F **-**, NO PL horniness; (*pej:* = *Lüsternheit*) lecherousness

Geisel [ˈɡaizl̩] F **-, -n** hostage; **jdn als ~ nehmen** to take sb hostage; **~n stellen** to produce hostages

Geisel-: Geiseldrama NT hostage crisis; **Geiselhaft** F captivity (as a hostage); **Geiselnahme** [-naːmə] F **-, -n** hostage-taking; **Geiselnehmer(in)** M(F) hostage-taker

Geiß-: Geißblatt NT honeysuckle, woodbine; **Geißbock** M billy goat

geißeln [ˈɡaisl̩n] VT **(a)** (= *peitschen*) to whip **(b)** (*fig:* = *anprangern*) to castigate

Geist [ɡaist] M **-(e)s, -er (a)** NO PL (= *Denken, Vernunft*) mind; **~ und Materie** mind and matter

(b) (*Rel:* = *Seele, außerirdisches Wesen*) spirit; (= *Gespenst*) ghost; **~ und Körper** mind and body; **seinen ~ aufgeben** *or* **aushauchen** (*litero*) to give up the ghost; **der ~ ist willig, aber das Fleisch ist schwach** (*prov*) the spirit is willing, but the flesh is weak; **der Heilige ~** the Holy Ghost *or* Spirit; **gute/böse ~er** good/evil spirits; **von allen guten ~ern verlassen sein** (*inf*) to have taken leave of one's senses (*inf*); **jdm auf den ~ gehen** (*inf*) to get on sb's nerves (*inf*); **in dem Schloss gehen ~er um** the castle is haunted

(c) (*no pl:* = *Intellekt*) intellect, mind; (*fig:* = *Denker, Genie*) mind; **einen regen/lebhaften ~ haben** to have an active/lively mind; **die Rede zeugte nicht von großem ~** the speech was not particularly brilliant; **das geht über meinen ~** (*inf*) that's beyond me (*inf*); **hier scheiden sich die ~er** this is the parting of the ways; **sie sind verwandte ~er** they are kindred spirits; **kleine ~er** (*iro: ungebildet*) people of limited intellect; (*kleinmütig*) small-minded people

(d) NO PL (= *Wesen, Sinn, Gesinnung*) spirit; **in diesem Büro herrscht ein kollegialer ~** this office has a friendly atmosphere; **in seinem/ihrem ~** in his/her spirit; **in jds** (*dat*) **~ handeln** to act in the spirit of sb; **der ~ der Zeit/der russischen Sprache** the spirit of the times/of the Russian language; **daran zeigt sich, wes ~es Kind er ist** that (just) shows what kind of person he is

(e) NO PL (= *Vorstellung*) mind; **etw im ~(e) vor sich** (*dat*) **sehen** to see sth in one's mind's eye; **jdn als etw/als jdn einem Ort sehen** to see oneself as sth/as sb/in a place; **im ~e bin ich bei euch** I am with you in spirit

Geister-: Geisterbahn F ghost train; **Geisterbeschwörung** F **(a)** (= *Herbeirufung*) necromancy **(b)** (= *Austreibung*) exorcism; **Geisterfahrer(in)** M(F) (*inf*) ghost-driver (*US inf*), *person driving the wrong way on the motorway;* **Geistergeschichte** F ghost story

geistern [ˈɡaistɐn] VI AUX SEIN to wander like a ghost; **der Gedanke geisterte in seinem Hirn** *or* **durch sein Hirn** the thought haunted him

Geister-: Geisterstadt F ghost town; **Geisterstunde** F witching hour

Geistes-: geistesabwesend 🖫 ADJ absent-minded 🖪 ADV absent-mindedly; **~ blicken** to have an absent-minded look on one's face; **jdn ~ ansehen** to give sb an absent-minded look; **Geistesabwesenheit** F absent-mindedness; **Geistesblitz** M brainwave (*Brit*), brainstorm (*US*); **Geistesgegenwart** F presence of mind; **geistesgegenwärtig** 🖫 ADJ quick-witted 🖪 ADV quick-wittedly; **~ duckte er sich unter das Steuer** with great presence of mind he ducked below the steering wheel; **geistesgestört** ADJ mentally disturbed or (stärker) deranged; **du bist wohl ~!** (inf) are you out of your mind? (inf); **Geistesgestörtheit** F -, NO PL mental instability or (stärker) derangement; **Geistesgröße** F **(a)** NO PL (= Genialität) greatness of mind **(b)** (= genialer Mensch) great mind; **geisteskrank** ADJ mentally ill; **Geisteskranke(r)** MF DECL AS ADJ mentally ill person; **die ~n** the mentally ill; **Geisteskrankheit** F mental illness; (= Wahnsinn) insanity; **Geistesverfassung** F frame or state of mind; **Geisteswissenschaft** F arts subject; **die ~en** the arts; (als Studium) the humanities; **Geisteswissenschaftler(in)** M(F) arts scholar; (= Student) arts student; **geisteswissenschaftlich** 🔢 ADJ Fach, Studium, Fakultät arts attr 🔢 ADV **er ist mehr ~ orientiert** he is more orientated toward(s) the arts; **Geisteszustand** M mental condition; **jdn auf seinen ~ untersuchen** to give sb a psychiatric examination; **du musst dich mal auf deinen ~ untersuchen lassen** (inf) you need your head examined (inf)

Geistheiler [-hailɐ] M **-s**, -, **Geistheilerin** [-hailərɪn] F **-, -nen** faith healer

geistig ['gaistɪç] 🔢 ADJ **(a)** (= unkörperlich) Wesen, Liebe, Existenz spiritual; **~-moralische Erneuerung** spiritual and moral renewal; **~-seelisch** mental and spiritual **(b)** (= intellektuell) intellectual; (Psych) mental; **~e Nahrung** intellectual nourishment; **~er Diebstahl** plagiarism no pl; **~es Eigentum** intellectual property **(c)** (= imaginär) **jds ~es Auge** sb's mind's eye; **etw vor seinem ~en Auge sehen** to see sth in one's mind's eye 🔢 ADV (= intellektuell) intellectually; (Med) mentally; **~ nicht mehr folgen können** to be unable to understand more; **~ behindert/zurückgeblieben** mentally handicapped/retarded

geistlich ['gaistlɪç] ADJ spiritual; (= religiös) religious; (= kirchlich) ecclesiastical; Gewand clerical

Geistliche ['gaistlɪçə] F DECL AS ADJ woman priest; (von Freikirchen) woman minister

Geistliche(r) ['gaistlɪçə] M DECL AS ADJ clergyman; (= Priester) priest; (= Pastor, von Freikirchen) minister; (= Gefängnisgeistliche, Militärgeistliche etc) chaplain

Geist-: geistlos ADJ (= dumm) stupid; (= langweilig) dull; (= einfallslos) unimaginative; (= trivial) inane; **Geistlosigkeit** F **-, -en (a)** NO PL (= Dummheit) stupidity; (= Langweiligkeit) dullness; (= Einfallslosigkeit) unimaginativeness; (= Trivialität) inanity **(b)** (= geistlose Äußerung) inane remark; **geistreich** ADJ (= witzig) witty; (= klug) intelligent; (= einfallsreich) ingenious; Beschäftigung, Gespräch, Unterhaltung intellectually stimulating; (= schlagfertig) quick-witted; **das war sehr ~** (iro) that was bright (iro); **geisttötend** ADJ soul-destroying

Geiz [gaits] M **-es**, NO PL meanness (esp Brit), stinginess (inf)

geizen ['gaitsn] VI to be mean (esp Brit) or stingy (inf); (mit Worten, Zeit) to be sparing; **mit etw ~** to be mean etc with sth; **sie geizt nicht mit ihren Reizen** she doesn't mind showing what she's got

Geizhals M miser

geizig ['gaitsɪç] ADJ mean (esp Brit), stingy (inf)

Geizkragen M (inf) skinflint

Gejammer [gə'jamɐ] NT **-s**, NO PL moaning (and groaning)

Gejaule [gə'jaulə] NT **-s**, NO PL howling

Gejohle [gə'jo:lə] NT **-s**, NO PL howling; (von Betrunkenen etc) caterwauling

gekannt PTP von kennen

Gekeife [gə'kaifə] NT **-s**, NO PL nagging

Gekicher [gə'kɪçɐ] NT **-s**, NO PL giggling; (spöttisch) sniggering, snickering

Gekläff [gə'klɛf] NT **-(e)s**, NO PL yapping (auch fig pej)

Geklapper [gə'klapɐ] NT **-s**, NO PL clatter(ing)

Geklimper [gə'klɪmpɐ] NT **-s**, NO PL (inf) (= Klaviergeklimper) tinkling; (stümperhaft) plonking (inf); (= Banjogeklimper etc) twanging; (von Geld) jingling; (von Wimpern) fluttering

Geklirr [gə'klɪr] NT **-(e)s**, NO PL, **Geklirre** [gə'klɪrə] NT **-s**, NO PL clinking; (von Gläsern auch) tinkling; (von Fensterscheiben) rattling; (von Ketten etc) clanking; (von Waffen) clashing

geklungen PTP von klingen

Geknall [gə'knal] NT **-(e)s**, NO PL, **Geknalle** [gə'knalə] NT **-s**, NO PL banging; (von Pfropfen) popping; (von Peitsche) cracking; (bei Feuerwerk) banging

Geknatter [gə'knatɐ] NT **-s**, NO PL (von Motorrad) roaring; (von Maschinengewehr) chattering; (von Schüssen) rattling (out)

geknickt [gə'knɪkt] ADJ (inf) dejected; siehe auch knicken

Geknicktheit F -, NO PL (inf) dejection

gekniffen PTP von kneifen

gekommen PTP von kommen

gekonnt [gə'kɔnt] 🔢 PTP von können 🔢 ADJ masterly 🔢 ADV in a masterly fashion

Gekrächz [gə'krɛçts] NT **-es**, NO PL, **Gekrächze** [gə'krɛçtsə] NT **-s**, NO PL croaking

Gekrakel [gə'kra:kl] NT **-s**, NO PL (inf) scrawl, scribble

Gekreisch [gə'kraiʃ] NT **-(e)s**, NO PL, **Gekreische** [gə'kraiʃə] NT **-s**, NO PL screeching

Gekreuzigte(r) [gə'krɔytsɪçtə] MF DECL AS ADJ crucified (person); **Jesus der ~** Jesus the Crucified

Gekritzel [gə'krɪtsl] NT **-s**, NO PL **(a)** scribbling, scrawling; (= Männchenmalen) doodling **(b)** (= Gekritzeltes) scribble, scrawl; doodle

gekrochen PTP von kriechen

gekühlt [gə'ky:lt] 🔢 ADJ Getränke chilled; Räume air-conditioned 🔢 ADV **etw ~ servieren** to serve sth chilled; siehe auch kühlen

gekünstelt [gə'kynstlt] 🔢 ADJ artificial; Sprache, Benehmen auch affected 🔢 ADV affectedly; **er spricht sehr ~** his speech is very affected

Gel [ge:l] NT **-s**, **-e** gel

Gelaber [gə'la:bɐ] NT **-s**, NO PL, **Gelabere** [gə'la:bərə] NT **-s**, NO PL (inf) jabbering (inf), prattling (inf)

Gelächter [gə'lɛçtɐ] NT **-s**, - laughter; **in ~ ausbrechen** to burst into laughter; **sich dem ~ aussetzen** to make oneself a laughing stock

gelackmeiert [gə'lakmaiɐt] ADJ (inf) conned (inf); **~ sein, der Gelackmeierte sein** (= hintergangen worden sein) to have been conned (inf); (= dumm dastehen) to look like a complete fool

geladen [gə'la:dn] 🔢 PTP von laden[1], laden[2] 🔢 ADJ **(a)** loaded; (Phys, fig) Atmosphäre charged; (inf: = wütend) (hopping (inf)) mad; **mit Spannung ~** charged with tension **(b)** **~ haben** (inf) to be tanked up (inf)

Gelage [gə'la:gə] NT **-s**, - feast, banquet; (= Zechgelage) carouse

gelagert [gə'la:gɐt] ADJ **ähnlich ~** similar; **in anders/ähnlich/besonders ~en Fällen** in different/similar/exceptional cases; **anders ~** siehe auch lagern

gelähmt [gə'lɛ:mt] ADJ (lit, fig) paralysed; **er ist seit seinem Unfall ~** he's been paralysed since his accident; **er hat ~e Beine** his legs are paralysed; **er ist an beiden Beinen ~** he is paralysed in both legs; **vor Angst wie ~ sein** to be petrified

Gelände [gə'lɛndə] NT **-s**, - **(a)** (= Land) open country; (Mil: = Gebiet, Terrain) ground; **offenes ~** open country; **schwieriges ~** difficult terrain; **das ~ erkunden** (Mil) to reconnoitre (Brit), to reconnoiter (US) (= Gebiet) area **(c)** (= Fabrikgelände, Schulgelände etc) grounds pl; (= Baugelände) site; (= Ausstellungsgelände) exhibition centre (Brit) or center (US)

Gelände-: Geländefahrzeug NT cross-country vehicle; **geländegängig** ADJ Fahrzeug suitable for cross-country driving

Geländer [gə'lɛndɐ] NT **-s,** - railing(s pl); (= Treppengeländer) banister(s pl)

Gelände-: Geländerennen NT cross-country race; **Geländeritt** M cross-country riding; **ein ~** a cross-country ride; **für ~e ungeeignet** unsuitable for cross-country riding; **Geländewagen** M cross-country vehicle

gelang PRET von gelingen

gelangen [gə'laŋən], ptp **gelangt** VI AUX SEIN **an/auf etc etw** (acc)/**zu etw ~** (lit, fig) to reach sth; (fig: mit Mühe) to attain sth; (= erwerben) to acquire sth; **zum Ziel ~** to reach one's goal; **in jds Besitz** (acc) **~** to come into sb's possession; **in die richtigen/falschen Hände ~** to fall into the right/wrong hands; **zu Reichtum ~** to come into a fortune; (durch Arbeit) to make a or one's fortune; **zu Ruhm ~** to acquire fame; **zu einer Überzeugung ~** to become convinced; **an die Macht ~** to come to power

gelangweilt [gə'laŋvailt] 🔢 ADJ bored 🔢 ADV **die Zuschauer saßen ~ da** the audience sat there looking bored; **er hörte ihr ~ zu** he was bored listening to her; siehe auch langweilen

gelassen [gə'lasn] **1** PTP *von* **lassen 2** ADJ calm **3** ADV calmly; **~ blicken** to have a calm look on one's face; **sie blickte mich ~ an** she looked at me calmly

Gelassenheit F -, NO PL calmness

Gelatine [ʒela'tiːnə] F -, NO PL gelatine

gelaufen PTP *von* **laufen**

geläufig [gə'lɔyfɪç] ADJ (= *üblich*) common; (= *vertraut*) familiar; **eine ~e Redensart** a common saying; **das ist mir nicht ~** I'm not familiar with that

Geläufigkeit F -, NO PL (= *Häufigkeit*) frequency; (= *Leichtigkeit*) ease

gelaunt [gə'launt] ADJ PRED **gut ~** good-tempered; (*vorübergehend*) in a good mood; **schlecht ~** bad-tempered; (*vorübergehend*) in a bad mood; **wie ist er ~?** what sort of mood is he in?

Geläut [gə'lɔyt] NT **-(e)s**, NO PL, **Geläute** [gə'lɔytə] NT **-s**, NO PL chiming; (= *Läutwerk*) chime

gelb [gɛlp] ADJ yellow; (*bei Verkehrsampel*) amber; **die Blätter werden ~** the leaves are turning (yellow); **Gelbe Rübe** carrot; **~e Karte** (*Ftbl*) yellow card; **die Gelben Seiten** the Yellow Pages®; **die ~e Post** the postal service (*excluding telecommunications and banking services*); **~er Sack** yellow bag (*for the collection of recyclable packaging material*); **~ vor Neid** green with envy; **Löwenzahn blüht ~** the dandelion has a yellow flower

Gelb [gɛlp] NT **-s**, **-** *or* (*inf*) **-s** yellow; (*von Verkehrsampel*) amber; **die Ampel stand auf ~** the lights were (at) amber; **bei ~ stehen bleiben** to stop on amber

Gelbe(s) ['gɛlbə] NT DECL AS ADJ (*vom Ei*) yolk; **das ist nicht gerade das ~ vom Ei** (*inf*) it's not exactly brilliant

Gelbfieber NT yellow fever

gelblich ['gɛlplɪç] ADJ yellowish; *Gesichtsfarbe* sallow

Gelb-: Gelbsucht F jaundice; **gelbsüchtig** ADJ jaundiced; **er ist ~** he has jaundice

Geld [gɛlt] NT **-(e)s**, **-er** [-dɐ] **(a)** NO PL (= *Zahlungsmittel*) money; **bares ~** cash; **großes ~** notes *pl* (*Brit*), bills *pl* (*US*); **kleines ~** change; **aus etw ~ machen** to make money out of sth; **zu ~ machen** to sell off; *Aktien* to cash in; **(mit etw) ~ machen** (*inf*) to make money (from sth); **um ~ spielen** to play for money; **ins ~ gehen** (*inf*) *or* **laufen** (*inf*) to cost a pretty penny; **das kostet ein (wahnsinniges) ~** (*inf*) that costs a fortune; **etw für teures ~ kaufen** to pay a lot for sth; **ich stand ohne ~ da** I was left without a penny; **im ~ *or* im ~ schwimmen** (*inf*) to be rolling in it (*inf*); **er hat ~ wie Heu** (*inf*) he's got stacks of money (*inf*); **das ~ auf die Straße werfen** (*inf*) *or* **zum Fenster hinauswerfen** (*inf*) to spend money like water (*inf*); **da hast du dein ~ zum Fenster hinausgeworfen** (*inf*) that's money down the drain (*inf*); **mit ~ um sich werfen** *or* **schmeißen** (*inf*) to chuck one's money around (*inf*); **gutes ~ dem schlechten hinterherwerfen** *or* **nachwerfen** (*inf*) to throw good money after bad; **hinterm ~ her sein** (*inf*) to be a money-grubber (*Brit inf*), to be money-crazy (*US inf*); **sie/das ist nicht mit ~ zu bezahlen** (*inf*) this is priceless; **nicht für ~ und gute Worte** (*inf*) not for love nor money; **~ allein macht nicht glücklich(, aber es beruhigt)** (*prov*) money isn't everything(, but it helps) (*prov*); **~ oder Leben!** your money or your life!; **~ regiert die Welt** (*Prov*) money makes the world go round (*prov*)
(b) Gelder PL (= *summen*) money; **tägliche ~er** day-to-day loans *pl*; **staatliche/öffentliche ~er** state/public funds *pl*
(c) (*St Ex*: = *~kurs*) buying rate, bid price

Geld-: Geldangelegenheit F financial matter; **jds ~en** sb's financial affairs; **Geldanlage** F (financial) investment; **Geldausgabeautomat** M cash machine, ATM; **Geldautomat** M (*zum Geldabheben*) cash machine, ATM; (*zum Geldwechseln*) change machine; **Geldbeutel** M wallet, billfold (*US*); (*für Münzen*) purse (*Brit*), wallet (*US*); **tief in den ~ greifen** (*inf*) to dig deep (into one's pocket) (*inf*); **Geldbombe** F strongbox; **Geldbörse** F wallet, billfold (*US*); (*für Münzen*) purse (*Brit*), wallet (*US*); **Geldbote** M, **Geldbotin** F security guard; **Geldbuße** F (*Jur*) fine; **eine hohe ~** a heavy fine; **Gelddinge** PL financial matters *pl*; **Geldentwertung** F (= *Inflation*) currency depreciation; (= *Abwertung*) currency devaluation; **Gelderwerb** M **zum ~ arbeiten** to work to earn money; **etw zum ~ machen** to make money out of sth; **Geldfälschung** F counterfeiting; **Geldgeber(in)** M(F) financial backer; (*esp Rad*) (*TV*) sponsor; (*hum*: = *Arbeitgeber*)

employer; **Geldgeschäft** NT financial transaction; **Geldgeschenk** NT gift of money; **Geldgier** F avarice; **geldgierig** ADJ avaricious; **Geldhahn** M **(jdm) den ~ zudrehen** *or* **abdrehen** to cut off sb's money supply

geldig ['gɛldɪç] ADJ (*esp Aus*) moneyed

Geldkredit M money loan

geldlich ['gɛltlɪç] **1** ADJ financial **2** ADV financially

Geld-: Geldmarkt M money market; **Geldmarktpapiere** PL money market papers *pl*; **Geldmenge** F money supply; **Geldmittel** PL funds *pl*; **Geldnot** F (= *Geldmangel*) lack of money; (= *Geldschwierigkeiten*) financial difficulties *pl*; **Geldquelle** F source of income; **Geldsache** F money *or* financial matter; **in ~n hört die Gemütlichkeit auf** (*prov*) business is business (*prov*); **Geldschein** M banknote (*esp Brit*), bill (*US*); **Geldschrank** M safe; **Geldschwierigkeiten** PL financial difficulties *pl*; **Geldsorgen** PL financial *or* money worries *pl*; **~ haben**, **in ~ sein** to have financial *or* money worries; **Geldspende** F donation; **Geldspielautomat** M slot machine; **Geldstrafe** F fine; **jdn zu einer ~ verurteilen**, **jdn mit einer ~ belegen** to fine sb; **Geldstück** NT coin; **Geldumlauf** M circulation of money; **Geldverlegenheit** F financial embarrassment *no pl*; **in ~ sein** to be short of money; **jdm aus einer ~ helfen** to help sb out of his/her financial difficulties; **Geldverleiher** [-failɐ] M **-s**, **-**, **Geldverleiherin** [-ərɪn] F **-**, **-nen** moneylender; **Geldverschwendung** F waste of money; **Geldwaschanlage** F money-laundering outfit; **Geldwäsche** F money laundering; **Geldwechsel** M exchange of money; **beim ~ muss man eine Gebühr bezahlen** there is a charge for changing money; **„~"** "bureau de change" (*Brit*), exchange counter (*US*); **Geldwechselautomat** M change machine; **Geldwechsler** [-vɛkslɐ] M **-s**, **-**, **Geldwechslerin** [-ərɪn] F **-**, **-nen** moneychanger; **geldwert** ADJ **~er Vorteil** perk; **~e Leistung** payment in kind; **Geldwert** M cash value; (*Fin*: = *Kaufkraft*) (currency) value; **Geldzuwendungen** PL money *sing*; (= *Geldgeschenk*) gifts *pl* of money; (= *regelmäßiges Geldgeschenk*) allowance *sing*; **private ~ erhalten** to receive a private income

Gelee [ʒe'leː] M *or* NT **-s**, **-s** jelly

gelegen [gə'leːgn] **1** PTP *von* **liegen**
2 ADJ **(a)** (= *befindlich, liegend*) *Haus, Ort* situated; *Grundstück auch* located; **ein herrlich ~er Ort** a place in a magnificent area
(b) (= *passend*) opportune; **zu ~er Zeit** at a convenient time **(c)** PRED (= *wichtig*) **mir ist viel/nichts daran ~** it matters a great deal/doesn't matter to me
3 ADV **wenn ich nicht ~ komme, gehe ich gleich wieder** if it's not convenient, I'll go immediately; **du kommst mir gerade ~** you've come at just the right time; (*iro*) you do pick your time well; **es kommt mir sehr/nicht sehr ~** it comes just at the right/wrong time

Gelegenheit [gə'leːgnhait] F **-**, **-en (a)** (= *günstiger Umstand, Zeitpunkt*) opportunity; **bei ~** some time (or other); **bei passender ~** when the opportunity arises; **bei passender ~ werde ich ...** when I get the opportunity *or* chance I'll ...; **bei der ersten (besten)** ~ at the first opportunity; **(die) ~ haben** to get the opportunity *or* chance (*etw zu tun* to do sth)
(b) (= *Anlass*) occasion; **bei dieser ~** on this occasion

Gelegenheits-: Gelegenheitsarbeit F casual work *no pl*; **Gelegenheitsarbeiter(in)** M(F) casual labourer (*Brit*) *or* laborer (*US*); **Gelegenheitsgesellschaft** F ad hoc company; **Gelegenheitskauf** M bargain

gelegentlich [gə'leːgntlɪç] **1** ADJ ATTR occasional; **von ~en Ausnahmen abgesehen** except for the odd occasion **2** ADV (= *manchmal*) occasionally; (= *bei Gelegenheit*) some time (or other); **wenn Sie ~ dort sind** if you happen to be there; **lassen Sie ~ etwas von sich hören!** keep in touch

gelehrig [gə'leːrɪç] **1** ADJ quick and eager to learn **2** ADV **sich bei etw ~ anstellen** to be quick to grasp sth

gelehrt [gə'leːɐt] ADJ *Mensch* learned, erudite; (= *wissenschaftlich*) scholarly; *siehe auch* **lehren**

Gelehrte(r) [gə'leːɐtə] MF DECL AS ADJ scholar

Gelehrtheit F **-**, NO PL learning, erudition

Geleise [gə'laizə] NT **-s**, **-** (*geh, Aus*) = **Gleis**

Geleit [gə'lait] NT **-(e)s**, **-e** (*Hist*: = *Gefolge*) entourage; (= *Begleitung*) (*Mil, Naut*) escort; (= *Leichenzug*) cortege; **freies** *or* **sicheres ~** safe-conduct; **jdm das ~ geben** to escort sb; **„zum ~"** "preface"

Geleitschutz M escort; **jdm ~ gewähren** or **geben** to give sb an escort; (*persönlich*) to escort sb; **im ~ (von Polizeifahrzeugen)** under (police) escort

Gelenk [gə'lɛŋk] NT **-(e)s, -e** joint; (= *Handgelenk*) wrist; (= *Fußgelenk*) ankle; (= *Kettengelenk*) link; (= *Scharniergelenk*) hinge

Gelenk-: **Gelenkbus** M articulated bus; **Gelenkentzündung** F arthritis; **Gelenkfahrzeug** NT articulated vehicle

gelenkig [gə'lɛŋkıç] ADJ agile; (= *geschmeidig*) supple

Gelenkigkeit F -, NO PL agility; (= *Geschmeidigkeit*) suppleness

gelernt [gə'lɛrnt] ADJ trained; *Arbeiter* skilled; *siehe auch* **lernen**

gelesen PTP *von* **lesen**

geliebt ADJ dear; *siehe auch* **lieben**

Geliebte [gə'li:ptə] F DECL AS ADJ sweetheart; (= *Mätresse*) mistress

Geliebte(r) [gə'li:ptə] M DECL AS ADJ sweetheart; (= *Liebhaber*) lover

geliefert [gə'li:fət] ADJ **~ sein** (*inf*) to have had it (*inf*); **jetzt sind wir ~** that's the end (*inf*); *siehe auch* **liefern**

geliehen PTP *von* **leihen**

gelieren [ʒe'li:rən] *ptp* **geliert** VI to gel

Gelier- [ʒe'li:ɐ-]: **Geliermittel** NT gelling agent; **Gelierzucker** M preserving sugar

gelinde [gə'lındə] **1** ADJ (*inf*: = *heftig*) awful (*inf*); **da packte mich ~ Wut** I got pretty angry **2** ADV **~ gesagt** to put it mildly

gelingen [gə'lıŋən], *pret* **gelang** [gə'laŋ], *ptp* **gelungen** [gə'lʊŋən] VI AUX SEIN (= *glücken*) to succeed; (= *erfolgreich sein*) to be successful; **es gelang ihm, das zu tun** he succeeded in doing it; **es gelang ihm nicht, das zu tun** he failed to do it; **dem Häftling gelang die Flucht** the prisoner managed to escape; **dein Plan wird dir nicht ~** you won't succeed with your plan; **es will mir nicht ~** I can't seem to manage it; **es will mir nicht ~ ... zu ...** I can't seem to manage to ...; **das Bild ist ihr gut/schlecht gelungen** her picture turned out well/badly; *siehe auch* **gelungen**

Gelingen [gə'lıŋən] NT **-s**, NO PL (*geh*) (= *Glück*) success; (= *erfolgreiches Ergebnis*) successful outcome; **gutes ~ für Ihren Plan!** good luck with your plan!; **auf gutes ~!** to success!

gelitten PTP *von* **leiden**

gell, gelle ['gɛlə] INTERJ (*S Ger, Sw*) = **gelt**

gellen ['gɛlən] VI to shrill; (= *von lauten Tönen erfüllt sein*) to ring; **ein schriller Schrei gellte durch die Nacht** a shrill scream pierced the night

gellend ADJ piercing

geloben [gə'lo:bn], *ptp* **gelobt** VT (*geh*) to vow; **die Fürsten gelobten dem König Treue** the princes pledged their loyalty to the king; **ich habe mir gelobt, das Rauchen aufzugeben** I've vowed to give up smoking; **das Gelobte Land** (*Bibl*) the Promised Land

Gelöbnis [gə'lø:pnɪs] NT **-ses, -se** (*geh*) vow; **ein** or **das ~ ablegen** to take a vow

Gelöbnisfeier F swearing-in ceremony

gelogen PTP *von* **lügen**

Gelse ['gɛlzə] F -, **-n** (*Aus*) gnat, mosquito

gelt [gɛlt] INTERJ (*S Ger*) right; **morgen kommst du wieder, ~?** you'll be back tomorrow, won't you or right?; **~, du leihst mir 5 Euro?** you'll lend me 5 euros, won't you or right?; **es ist schön heute – ~?** it's nice today – isn't it just?

gelten ['gɛltn], *pret* **galt** [galt], *ptp* **gegolten** [gə'gɔltn] **1** VI
(**a**) (= *gültig sein*) to be valid; (*Gesetz*) to be in force; (*Preise*) to be effective; (*Münze*) to be legal tender; (= *erlaubt sein*) to be allowed; (= *zählen*) to count; **die Wette gilt!** the bet's on!; **was ich sage, gilt!** what I say goes!; **das gilt nicht!** that doesn't count!; (= *ist nicht erlaubt*) that's not allowed!; **das Gesetz gilt für alle** the law applies to everyone; **diese Karte gilt nur für eine Person** this ticket only admits one; *siehe auch* **geltend**
(**b**) +DAT (= *bestimmt sein für*) to be meant for
(**c**) +DAT (*geh*: = *sich beziehen auf*) to be for; **seine ganze Liebe galt der Musik** music was his only love
(**d**) (= *zutreffen*) to hold (good) for sb/sth, to go for sb/sth; **das gleiche gilt auch für ihn/von ihm** the same goes for him too/is true of him too
(**e**) **~ als** or **für** (*rare*) to be regarded as; **es gilt als sicher, dass ...** it seems certain that ...
(**f**) **~ lassen** to accept; **das lasse ich ~!** I accept that!; **für**

diesmal lasse ich es ~ I'll let it go this time
2 VTI IMPERS (*geh*) **es gilt, ... zu ...** it is necessary to ...; **jetzt gilt es, Mut zu zeigen/zusammenzuhalten** it is now a question of courage/of sticking together; **jetzt gilts!** this is it!
3 VT (= *wert sein*) to be worth; (= *zählen*) to count for; **was gilt die Wette?** what do you bet?

geltend ADJ ATTR *Preise, Tarife* current; *Gesetz, Regelung* in force; (= *vorherrschend*) *Meinung etc* prevailing; **~ machen** (*form*) to assert; **einen Einwand ~ machen** to raise an objection; **~es Recht** to be the law of the land

Geltung ['gɛltʊŋ] F -, **-en** (= *Gültigkeit*) validity; (*von Münzen*) currency; (= *Wert*) value, worth; (= *Einfluss*) influence; (= *Ansehen*) prestige; **an ~ verlieren** to lose prestige; **einer Sache** (*dat*) **~ verschaffen** to enforce sth; **sich** (*dat*) **~ verschaffen** to establish one's position; **etw zur ~ bringen** to show sth (off) to advantage; (*durch Kontrast*) to set sth off; **zur ~ kommen** to show to advantage; (*durch Kontrast*) to be set off; **in diesem Konzertsaal kommt die Musik voll zur ~** the music can be heard to its best advantage in this concert hall

Geltungs-: **Geltungsbedürfnis** NT, NO PL need for admiration; **geltungsbedürftig** ADJ desperate for admiration; **Geltungsbereich** M **der ~ einer Fahrkarte/eines Gesetzes** the area within which a ticket is valid/a law is operative; **Geltungsdauer** F (*einer Fahrkarte etc*) period of validity; **die ~ eines Vertrages/einer Genehmigung** the period during which a contract is in force/a licence (*Brit*) or license (*US*) is valid

Gelübde [gə'lʏpdə] NT **-s, -** (*Rel, geh*) vow

gelungen [gə'lʊŋən] **1** PTP *von* **gelingen 2** ADJ ATTR
(**a**) (= *geglückt*) successful; **ein gut ~er Braten** a roast that turned out very well; **eine nicht so recht ~e Überraschung** a surprise that didn't quite come off (**b**) (*inf*: = *drollig*) priceless (*inf*); **du bist mir ein ~er Bursche** you're priceless (*inf*)

Gelüst [gə'lʏst] NT **-(e)s, -e**, **Gelüste** [gə'lʏstə] NT **-s, -** (*geh*) desire; (= *Sucht*) craving (*auf* +acc, *nach* for)

GEMA ['ge:ma] F -, NO PL ABBR *von* **Gesellschaft für musikalische Aufführungs- und mechanische Vervielfältigungsrechte** musical copyright watchdog body

gemächlich [gə'mɛːçlıç] **1** ADJ leisurely; *Mensch* unhurried; **ein ~es Leben führen** to lead a quiet life **2** ADV *erledigen, frühstücken* leisurely; **er wanderte ~ durch die Wiesen** he took a leisurely stroll through the meadows; **ein ~ fließender Strom** a gently flowing river

gemacht [gə'maxt] ADJ made; **für etw ~ sein** to be made for sth; **ein ~er Mann sein** to be made; (**ist**) **~!** (*inf*) done! (*inf*); *siehe auch* **machen**

Gemächte [gə'mɛçtə] NT **-s, -** (*old, hum*) privates *pl* (*inf*)

Gemahl [gə'ma:l] M **-s, -e** (*geh*) (*form*) spouse (*old, form*), husband; (= *Prinzgemahl*) consort; **bitte grüßen Sie Ihren Herrn ~** please give my regards to your husband (*form*)

Gemahlin [gə'ma:lın] F -, **-nen** (*geh*) (*form*) spouse (*old, form*), wife; (*von König auch*) consort; **bitte empfehlen Sie mich Ihrer Frau ~** please give my regards to your wife (*form*)

Gemälde [gə'mɛːldə] NT **-s, -** painting

gemasert [gə'mazɐt] ADJ *Holz* grained

gemäß [gə'mɛːs] **1** PREP +DAT in accordance with; **~ den Bestimmungen** under the regulations; **~ § 209** under § 209 **2** ADJ appropriate (+dat to); **dieser Umgang ist seiner sozialen Stellung nicht ~** the company he is keeping does not befit his social position; **eine ihren Fähigkeiten ~e Arbeit** a job suited to her abilities

gemäßigt [gə'mɛːsıçt] ADJ moderate; *Klima, Zone* temperate; *Optimismus etc* qualified; *siehe auch* **mäßigen**

Gemäuer [gə'mɔyɐ] NT **-s, -** (*geh*) walls *pl*; (= *Ruine*) ruins *pl*

Gemauschel [gə'mauʃl] NT **-s**, NO PL (*pej inf*) scheming

Gemecker [gə'mɛkɐ] NT **-s**, NO PL, **Gemeckere** [gə'mɛkərə] NT **-s**, NO PL, **Gemeckre** [gə'mɛkrə] NT **-s**, NO PL (*von Ziegen*) bleating; (*inf*: = *Nörgelei*) bellyaching (*inf*); (= *meckerndes Lachen*) cackling

gemein [gə'main] **1** ADJ (**a**) PRED NO COMP (= *gemeinsam*) **etw ~ mit jdm/etw haben** to have sth in common with sb/sth; **nichts mit jdm ~ haben wollen** to want nothing to do with sb; **das ist beiden ~** it is common to both of them (**b**) ATTR NO COMP (*Biol, old*: = *üblich, verbreitet, öffentlich*) common; **~er Bruch** (*Math*) vulgar fraction; **das ~e Volk/Wohl** the common people/good (**c**) (= *niederträchtig, unverschämt*) mean; *Verräter, Lüge*

contemptible; **das war ~ von dir!** that was mean of you; **ein ~er Streich** a dirty trick
(d) (*inf.* = *unangenehm*) awful
2 ADV **(a)** (= *niederträchtig*) **behandeln** meanly; **betrügen, hintergehen** despicably; **er hat sie ~ im Stich gelassen** it was despicable how he abandoned her
(b) (*inf.* = *unangenehm*) awfully; **das hat ~ wehgetan** it hurt terribly

Gemeinde [gə'maɪndə] F **-, -n (a)** (= *Kommune*) municipality; (= *~bewohner auch*) community; (*inf.* = *~amt*) local authority **(b)** (= *Pfarrgemeinde*) parish; (*beim Gottesdienst*) congregation **(c)** (= *Anhängerschaft*) (*von Theater etc*) patrons *pl*; (*von Schriftsteller etc*) following

Gemeinde-: Gemeindeabgaben PL local taxes *pl*; **Gemeindeammann** M (*Sw*) **(a)** = **Gemeindevorsteher(in) (b)** (= *Gerichtsvollzieher*) bailiff; **Gemeindemitglied** NT (*Eccl*) parishioner; **Gemeindepräsident** M(F) (*Sw*) mayor; **Gemeinderat¹** M local council; **Gemeinderat²** M, **Gemeinderätin** F local councillor (*Brit*), councilman/-woman (*US*); **Gemeindeschwester** F district nurse; (*Eccl*) *nun now working in a parish as a nurse or social worker*; **Gemeindespital** NT (*Aus*) local hospital; **Gemeindevorsteher(in)** M(F) head of the local council; (= *Bürgermeister*) mayor; **Gemeindewahl** F local election

Gemein-: gemeingefährlich 1 ADJ dangerous to the public, constituting a public danger; **ein ~er Verbrecher** a dangerous criminal **2** ADV **~ handeln** to endanger public safety; **Gemeingut** NT, NO PL (*lit, fig*) common property; **Schumanns Lieder gehören zum ~ der Deutschen** Schumann's Lieder are part of the German heritage

Gemeinheit F **-, -en (a)** NO PL (= *Niedertracht, Unverschämtheit*) nastiness **(b)** (= *Tat*) dirty trick; (= *Behandlung*) nasty treatment *no pl*; (= *Worte*) mean thing; **das war eine ~** (= *Handlung*) that was a mean thing to do; (= *Bemerkung*) that was a mean thing to say **(c)** (*inf.* = *ärgerlicher Umstand*) (blasted (*Brit inf*)) nuisance

Gemein-: Gemeinkosten PL overheads *pl*; **gemeinnützig** ADJ of benefit to the public *pred*; (= *wohltätig*) charitable; **~er Verein** charitable organization; **Gemeinplatz** M commonplace

gemeinsam [gə'maɪnzaːm] **1** ADJ common; *Konto, Aktion, Ausflug, Nutzung* joint; *Freund* mutual; **sie haben vieles ~, ihnen ist vieles ~** they have a great deal in common; **unser ~es Leben** our life together; **der Gemeinsame Markt** the Common Market; **die ~e (europäische) Währung** the single (European) currency; **mit jdm ~e Sache machen** to make common cause with sb
2 ADV together; **etw ~ haben** to have sth in common; **es gehört den beiden ~** it belongs jointly to the two of them

Gemeinsamkeit F **-, -en** (= *gemeinsame Interessen, Eigenschaft etc*) common ground *no pl*; **die ~en zwischen ihnen sind sehr groß** they have a great deal in common

Gemeinschaft [gə'maɪnʃaft] F **-, -en** community; (= *Gruppe*) group; (= *Zusammensein*) company; **die ~ Unabhängiger Staaten** the Commonwealth of Independent States; **in ~ mit** jointly *or* together with

gemeinschaftlich [gə'maɪnʃaftlɪç] ADJ = **gemeinsam**

Gemeinschafts-: Gemeinschaftsantenne F block *or* party aerial (*Brit*) *or* antenna (*esp US*); **Gemeinschaftsarbeit** F teamwork; **das Buch ist eine ~ the book is a team effort**; (*von zwei Personen*) the book is a joint effort; **Gemeinschaftskonto** NT joint account; **Gemeinschaftskunde** F social studies *pl*; **Gemeinschaftspraxis** F joint practice; **Gemeinschaftsproduktion** F **(a)** (= *Gemeinschaftsarbeit*) teamwork **(b)** (*Rad, TV, Film*) co-production; **Gemeinschaftsunternehmen** NT (*Econ*) joint venture; **Gemeinschaftswerbung** F joint advertising *no pl*; **~ machen** to advertise jointly

Gemein-: Gemeinschuldner(in) M(F) adjudicated bankrupt, common debtor (*Scot*); **nicht entlasteter ~** undischarged debtor; **eine Forderung gegen den ~ haben** to have a claim in bankruptcy; **gemeinverständlich 1** ADJ generally comprehensible **2** ADV **sich ~ ausdrücken** to make oneself generally understood; **wissenschaftliche Probleme ~ darstellen** to present scientific problems in such a way that they can be generally understood; **Gemeinwerk** NT (*Sw*) voluntary work; **Gemeinwesen** NT community; (= *Staat*)

polity; **Gemeinwohl** NT public welfare; **das dient dem ~** it is in the public interest

Gemenge [gə'mɛŋə] NT **-s, - (a)** (= *Mischung*) mixture (*aus* of); (= *wirres Durcheinander*) jumble (*aus* of) **(b)** (= *Gewühl*) bustle; (= *Handgemenge*) scuffle

gemessen [gə'mɛsn] PTP *von* **messen**

Gemetzel [gə'mɛtsl] NT **-s, -** bloodbath

gemieden [gə'miːdn] PTP *von* **meiden**

Gemisch [gə'mɪʃ] NT **-(e)s, -e (a)** (*lit, fig*) mixture (*aus* of) **(b)** NO PL (= *Durcheinander*) jumble (*aus* of)

gemischt [gə'mɪʃt] ADJ mixed; **mit ~en Gefühlen** with mixed feelings; **~es Doppel** (*Sport*) mixed doubles *pl*; *siehe auch* **mischen**

gemocht PTP *von* **mögen**

gemolken PTP *von* **melken**

Gemotze [gə'mɔtsə] NT **-s**, NO PL (*inf*) moaning

Gemse ['gɛmzə] F **-, -n** *siehe* **Gämse**

Gemunkel [gə'mʊŋkl] NT **-s**, NO PL rumours *pl* (*Brit*), rumors *pl* (*US*)

Gemurmel [gə'mʊrml] NT **-s**, NO PL murmuring; **zustimmendes ~ ging durch den Saal** a murmur of approval ran through the hall

Gemüse [gə'myːzə] NT **-s,** (*rare*) - vegetables *pl*; **frisches ~** fresh vegetables; **ein ~** a vegetable; **junges ~** (*hum inf*) whippersnappers *pl* (*inf*)

Gemüse-: Gemüse(an)bau M, NO PL vegetable-growing; (*für den Handel*) market gardening (*Brit*), truck farming (*US*); **Gemüsebeilage** F vegetables *pl*; **~ nach Wunsch** a choice of vegetables; **Gemüseeintopf** M vegetable stew; **Gemüsegarten** M vegetable *or* kitchen garden; **quer durch den ~** (*hum inf*) a real assortment; **Gemüsehändler(in)** M(F) greengrocer (*esp Brit*), vegetable salesman/saleswoman (*US*); (= *Großhändler*) vegetable supplier; **Gemüsekonserve** F tinned (*Brit*) *or* canned vegetables *pl*; (*in Gläsern*) preserved vegetables *pl*; **Gemüseladen** M greengrocer's (shop) (*esp Brit*), produce shop (*US*); **Gemüsepflanze** F vegetable; **Gemüseplatte** F (*Cook*) **eine ~** assorted vegetables *pl*; **Gemüsesorte** F kind *or* type of vegetable; **Gemüsesuppe** F vegetable soup; **Gemüsezwiebel** F Spanish onion

gemusst PTP *von* **müssen**

gemustert [gə'mʊstɐt] ADJ patterned; *siehe auch* **mustern**

Gemüt [gə'myːt] NT **-(e)s, -er (a)** (= *Geist*) mind; (= *Charakter*) nature, disposition; (= *Seele*) soul; (= *Gefühl*) feeling; **viel ~ haben** to be very warm-hearted; **das denkst du (dir) so einfach in deinem kindlichen ~!** that's what you think in your innocence; **etwas fürs ~** (*hum*) something for the soul; (*Film, Buch etc*) something sentimental; **sich** (*dat*) **etw zu ~e führen** (*hum inf*) *Glas Wein, Speise, Buch etc* to indulge in sth; **das ist ihr aufs ~ geschlagen** that made her worry herself sick (*inf*)
(b) (*fig*: = *Mensch*) person; (*pl*) people; **sie ist ein ängstliches ~** she's a nervous soul; **die ~er erregen** to cause a stir; **wir müssen warten, bis sich die ~er beruhigt haben** we must wait until feelings have cooled down

gemütlich [gə'myːtlɪç] **1** ADJ **(a)** (= *bequem, behaglich*) comfortable; (= *freundlich*) friendly *no adv*; (= *zwanglos*) informal; *Schwatz, Beisammensein etc* cosy (*Brit*), cozy (*US*); **wir verbrachten einen ~en Abend** we spent a very pleasant evening
(b) *Mensch* pleasant; (= *leutselig*) friendly; (= *gelassen*) easy-going *no adv*
(c) (= *gemächlich*) leisurely
2 ADV **(a)** (= *behaglich*) leisurely; *einrichten* comfortably; **wir wollen das Wochenende ~ gestalten** we plan to have a leisurely weekend; **es sich/jdm ~ machen** to make oneself/sb comfortable
(b) (= *gemächlich*) leisurely; **er arbeitete ~ vor sich hin** he worked away at a leisurely pace

Gemütlichkeit F **-**, NO PL **(a)** (= *Bequemlichkeit, Behaglichkeit*) comfort; (*von Lokal, Wohnung*) comfortable ambience; (= *Freundlichkeit*) friendliness; (= *Zwanglosigkeit*) informality; (= *Intimität*) cosiness (*Brit*), coziness (*US*)
(b) (*von Mensch*) pleasantness; (= *Leutseligkeit*) friendliness; (= *Gelassenheit*) easy-going nature; **da hört doch die ~ auf!** (*inf*) that's going too far; **ein Prosit der ~!** happy days!
(c) (= *Gemächlichkeit*) leisureliness; **in aller ~** at one's leisure

Gemüts-: Gemütsart F disposition, nature; **Gemütsbewegung** F emotion; **bist du zu keiner ~ fähig?** can't you show some emotion?; **gemütskalt** ADJ cold; **gemütskrank** ADJ emotionally disturbed; **Gemütskrankheit** F emotional disorder; **Gemütslage** F mood; **je nach ~** as the mood takes me/him *etc*; **Gemütsmensch** M good-natured, phlegmatic person; **du bist vielleicht ein ~!** (*iro inf*) you're a fine one! (*inf*); (= *das ist unmöglich*) you'll be lucky! (*inf*); **Gemütsruhe** F calmness; (= *Phlegma*) placidness; **in aller ~** (*inf*) (as) cool as a cucumber (*inf*); (= *gemächlich*) at a leisurely pace; (= *aufreizend langsam*) as if there were all the time in the world; **deine ~ möchte ich haben!** (*iro*) I'd like to have your composure; **Gemütsverfassung** F, **Gemütszustand** M frame *or* state of mind

Gen [geːn] NT **-s, -e** gene

Gen- IN CPDS genetic; (= *genmanipuliert*) genetically modified *or* engineered

genannt PTP *von* **nennen**

genarbt [gəˈnarpt] ADJ *Leder* grained

genas PRET *von* **genesen**

genau [gəˈnau] **1** ADJ exact; **Genaueres** further details *pl*; **Genaueres weiß ich nicht** I don't know any more than that; **man weiß nichts Genaues über ihn** no-one knows anything definite about him
2 ADV **~!** (*inf*) exactly!, precisely!; **~ dasselbe** just *or* exactly the same; **~ in der Mitte** right in the middle; **~ das wollte ich sagen** that's just *or* exactly what I wanted to say; **etw ~ wissen** to know sth for certain; **etw ~ nehmen** to take sth seriously; **~ genommen** strictly speaking; **er nimmt es sehr/nicht sehr ~** he's very/not very particular (*mit etw* about sth); **einen Entschluss ~ überlegen** to consider a decision very carefully; **meine Uhr geht ~** my watch keeps accurate time; **es stimmt auf den Millimeter ~** it's right to the millimetre (*Brit*) *or* millimeter (*US*); **~este, aufs ~este** *or* **Genaueste** (right) down to the last (little) detail; **~ entgegengesetzt** diametrically opposed; **so ~ wollte ich es (nun auch wieder) nicht wissen!** (*iro*) you can spare me the details

Genauigkeit F **-,** NO PL (= *Exaktheit*) exactness; (= *Richtigkeit*) accuracy; (= *Präzision*) precision; (= *Sorgfalt*) meticulousness

genauso [gəˈnauzoː] ADV (*vor Adjektiv*) just as; (*allein stehend*) just *or* exactly the same

Genbank F, *pl* **-banken** gene bank

genehm [gəˈneːm] ADJ (*geh*) acceptable; **ist es so ~?** is that acceptable to you?; **wenn es ~ ist** if you are agreeable

genehmigen [gəˈneːmɪgn], *ptp* **genehmigt** VT to approve; (= *erlauben*) to sanction; (= *Lizenz erteilen*) to license; *Durchreise, Aufenthalt* to authorize; (= *zugestehen*) to grant; **wer kann mir die Teilnahme ~?** from whom do I get permission to take part?; **„genehmigt"** "approved"; (*inf*) permission granted (*hum*); **sich** (*dat*) **etw ~** to indulge in sth; (= *kaufen*) to splash out on sth; **sich** (*dat*) **einen ~** (*hum inf*) to have a little drink

Genehmigung F **-, -en** (= *Erlaubnis*) approval; (= *Lizenz*) licence (*Brit*), license (*US*); (*für Durchreise, Aufenthalt*) authorization; (= *Berechtigungsschein*) permit; **mit freundlicher ~ von** by kind permission of

geneigt [gəˈnaikt] ADJ (*geh*) *Zuhörer, Publikum* willing; *Aufmerksamkeit* kind; **~er Leser** gentle reader; **jdm/einer Sache ~ sein** to be well-disposed to sb/sth; **~ sein, etw zu tun** to be inclined to do sth; *siehe auch* **neigen**

Genera PL *von* **Genus**

General [genəˈraːl] M **-(e)s, -e** *or* **̈e** [-ˈreːlə], **Generalin** [-ˈraːlɪn] F **-, -nen** general

General-: Generalagentur F general agency; **Generalbevollmächtigte(r)** MF DECL AS ADJ plenipotentiary; (*Comm*) general representative; **Generalbundesanwalt** M, **Generalbundesanwältin** F Chief Federal Prosecutor; **Generaldirektion** F head office; **Generaldirektor(in)** M(F) chairman/-woman, president (*US*), CEO

Generalin F *siehe* **General**

generalisieren [genəraliˈziːrən], *ptp* **generalisiert** VI to generalize

General-: Generalkonsul(in) M(F) consul general; **Generalkonsulat** NT consulate general; **Generalprobe** F (*Theat*) (*fig*) dress rehearsal; (*Mus*) final rehearsal; **Generalsekretär(in)** M(F) secretary-general;

Generalstaatsanwalt M, **Generalstaatsanwältin** F *public prosecutor for a provincial court,* ≈ district attorney (*US*); **Generalstab** M general staff; **generalstabsmäßig 1** ADJ *Aktion* planned with military precision **2** ADV *planen, organisieren* with military precision; **Generalstreik** M general strike; **generalüberholen** *ptp* **generalüberholt** VT INFIN, PTP ONLY **etw ~** to give sth a general overhaul; **etw ~ lassen** to have sth generally overhauled; **Generalvertretung** F sole agency

Generation [genəraˈtsioːn] F **-, -en** generation; **ein technisches Gerät der ersten ~** a piece of first-generation technology; **~ X/@** generation X/@

Generationen-: Generationenkonflikt M generation gap; **Generationenvertrag** M (*Econ*) system whereby old people receive a pension from contributions being made by current working population

Generator [genəˈraːtoːɐ] M **-s, Generatoren** [-ˈtoːrən] generator

generell [genəˈrɛl] **1** ADJ general **2** ADV in general; (= *normalerweise*) normally

generieren [genəˈriːrən], *ptp* **generiert** VT (*Ling, geh*) to generate

Generikum [geˈneːrikʊm] NT **-s, Generika** [-ka] generic drug

genesen [gəˈneːzn], *pret* **genas** [gəˈnaːs], *ptp* **genesen** [gəˈneːzn] VI AUX SEIN (*geh*) to convalesce; (*fig*) to recuperate

Genesung [gəˈneːzʊŋ] F **-,** (*rare*) **-en** convalescence, recovery (*auch fig*); **auf dem Wege der ~** on the road to recovery

Genetik [geˈneːtɪk] F **-,** NO PL genetics *sing*

Genetiker [geˈneːtikɐ] M **-s, -, Genetikerin** [-ərɪn] F **-, -nen** geneticist

genetisch [geˈneːtɪʃ] **1** ADJ genetic; *Vater* biological **2** ADV genetically

Genezareth [geˈneːtsaret] **der See ~** the Sea of Galilee

Genf [gɛnf] NT **-s** Geneva

Genfer [ˈgɛnfɐ] ADJ ATTR Genevan; **der ~ See** Lake Geneva; **~ Konvention** Geneva Convention

Gen-: Genforscher(in) M(F) genetic researcher; **Genforschung** F genetic research

genial [geˈniaːl] ADJ brilliant; (= *erfinderisch*) ingenious; **ein ~er Mensch, ein Genialer** a genius; **ein ~es Werk** a work of genius; **das war eine ~e Idee** that idea was a stroke of genius

---

Vorsicht! **genial** *wird nicht mit dem englischen Wort* **genial** *übersetzt.*

Genialität [geniali̯ˈtɛːt] F **-,** NO PL (*von Künstler, Musiker etc*) genius; (*von Idee, Lösung etc*) brilliance; (= *Erfindungsreichtum*) ingenuity

Genick [gəˈnɪk] NT **-(e)s, -e** neck; **ein Schlag ins ~** a blow on the back of the neck; **sich** (*dat*) **das ~ brechen** to break one's neck; (*fig*) to kill oneself

Genick-: Genickschuss M shot in the neck; **Genickstarre** F stiffness of the neck; (*Med*) (cerebral) meningitis; **~ haben** (*inf*) to have a stiff neck

Genie¹ [ʒeˈniː] NT **-s, -s** genius

Genie² F **-, -s** (*Sw Mil*) engineer corps

genieren [ʒeˈniːrən], *ptp* **geniert** **1** VR to be embarrassed; **~ Sie sich nicht!** don't be shy!; **dabei geniere ich mich** I get embarrassed doing it; **ich geniere mich, das zu sagen** I don't like to say it; **er genierte sich (gar) nicht, das zu tun** it didn't bother him (at all) to do that **2** VT **jdn ~** (= *peinlich berühren*) to embarrass sb; (*olddial*: = *stören*) to disturb sb; **das geniert mich wenig!** that doesn't bother me

genießbar ADJ (= *essbar*) edible; (= *trinkbar*) drinkable; (*fig*: = *annehmbar*) acceptable; **er ist heute nicht ~** (*fig inf*) he is unbearable today

genießen [gəˈniːsn], *pret* **genoss** [gəˈnɔs], *ptp* **genossen** [gəˈnɔsn] VT **(a)** (*lit, fig*: = *sich erfreuen an*) to enjoy; **den Wein muss man ~** this is a wine to be savoured (*Brit*) *or* savored (*US*); **er ist heute nicht zu ~** (*inf*) he is unbearable today **(b)** (= *essen*) to eat; (= *trinken*) to drink; **das Essen ist kaum zu ~** the meal is scarcely edible; **der Wein ist kaum zu ~** the wine is scarcely drinkable

Genießer [gəˈniːsɐ] M **-s, -, Genießerin** [-ərɪn] F **-, -nen** connoisseur; (*des Lebens*) pleasure-lover; (= *Feinschmecker*) gourmet; **er ist ein stiller ~** he really knows how to enjoy life in his quiet way

genießerisch [gə'ni:sərɪʃ] **1** ADJ appreciative; **sein ~er Ausdruck** his expression of pleasure **2** ADV appreciatively; (= *mit Behagen*) pleasurably; (= *mit Genuss*) with relish

genital [geni'ta:l] ADJ genital

Genital- IN CPDS genital; **Genitalbereich** M genital area

Genitale [geni'ta:lə] NT **-s, Genitalien** [-liən] genital; **die Genitalien** the genitals *or* genitalia (*form*)

Genitiv ['ge:niti:f] M **-s, -e** [-və] (= *Fall*) genitive (case); (= *Form*) genitive (form); **im ~** in the genitive

Genitivobjekt NT genitive object

Gen-: **Genmais** M GM maize; **Genmanipulation** F genetic manipulation; **genmanipuliert** [-manɪpuli:et] ADJ genetically engineered *or* modified

Genom [ge'no:m] NT **-s, -e** genome

Genomanalyse F genome analysis

genommen PTP *von* nehmen

genoppt [gə'nɔpt] ADJ *Teppich, Stoff, Wolle* nubbly; *Gummi* pimpled

Genörgel [gə'nœrgl] NT **-s,** NO PL (*inf*) carping

genoss PRET *von* genießen

Genosse [gə'nɔsə] M **-n, -n, Genossin** [-'nɔsɪn] F **-, -nen** comrade; (*pej: = Kumpan*) pal (*inf*); **X und ~n** (*Jur*) X and others; (*pej*) X and co (*inf*)

genossen PTP *von* genießen

Genossen-: **Genossenschaft** [gə'nɔsnʃaft] F **-, -en** cooperative; **genossenschaftlich** [-ʃaftlɪç] **1** ADJ cooperative **2** ADV **~ organisiert** organized as a cooperative

Genossin F *siehe* Genosse

genötigt [gə'nø:tɪçt] ADJ **~ sein, etw zu tun** to be obliged to do sth; **sich ~ sehen, etw zu tun** to feel (oneself) obliged to do sth

Genozid [geno'tsi:t] M *or* NT **-(e)s, -e** *or* **-ien** [-də, -diən] (*geh*) genocide

Genre ['ʒãːrə] NT **-s, -s** genre

Gen-: **Gentechnik** F genetic engineering; **Gentechniker(in)** M(F) genetic engineer; **gentechnisch** **1** ADJ *Fortschritte etc* in genetic engineering **2** ADV *manipulieren, verändern* genetically; *produzieren, herstellen* by means of genetic engineering; **~ vermehren** to reproduce through genetic engineering; **~ veränderte Organismen** genetically manipulated organisms; **Gentechnologie** F genetic engineering; **gentechnologisch** **1** ADJ *Verfahren, Zeitalter* of genetic engineering **2** ADV **~ hergestellte Arzneimittel** drugs produced by means of genetic engineering; **Gentherapie** F gene therapy

genug [gə'nuːk] ADV enough; **~ davon** enough of that; **das ist wenig ~** that's precious little; **und damit noch nicht ~** and that's not all; **sag, wenns ~ ist!** (*beim Einschenken etc*) say when!; **(von etw) ~ haben** to have enough (of sth); (= *einer Sache überdrüssig sein*) to have had enough (of sth); **nicht ~, dass er sein ganzes Geld verspielt, außerdem ... er ...** not only does he gamble away all his money, he also ...; **Manns ~ sein, um zu ...** to be man enough to ...

Genüge [gə'ny:gə] F **-,** NO PL **zur ~ enough; etw zur ~ kennen** to know sth well enough; (*abwertender*) to know sth only too well

genügen [gə'ny:gn], *ptp* **genügt** VI **(a)** (= *ausreichen*) to be enough *or* sufficient (+*dat* for); **das genügt (mir)** that's enough *or* sufficient (for me); **dieses Haus genügt uns** we're happy with this house; **dieses Haus genügt für uns** this house is enough for us **(b)** +DAT **den Anforderungen** to satisfy; **jds Wünschen, Erwartungen** to fulfil (*Brit*), to fulfill (*US*)

genügend **1** ADJ **(a)** INV (= *ausreichend*) enough, sufficient **(b)** (= *befriedigend*) satisfactory **2** ADV (= *reichlich*) enough

genügsam [gə'ny:kza:m] **1** ADJ *Tier, Pflanze* undemanding; *Mensch auch* modest; **ein ~es Leben führen** to live modestly **2** ADV *leben* modestly; **sich ~ ernähren** to have a simple diet

Genügsamkeit F **-,** NO PL (*von Mensch*) undemanding nature; **die ~ einer Pflanze/eines Tieres** the modest requirements of a plant/an animal

Genugtuung [gə'nu:ktuʊŋ] F **-, (*rare*) -en** satisfaction (*über* +*acc* at); **ich hörte mit ~, dass ...** it gave me great satisfaction to hear that ...; **das hat mir ~ verschafft** that gave me a sense of satisfaction

Genus ['ge:nʊs, 'genʊs] NT **-, Genera** ['ge:nera, 'genera] (*Biol*) genus; (*Gram*) gender

Genuss [gə'nʊs] M **-es, ¨e** [gə'nʏsə] **(a)** NO PL (= *das Zusichnehmen*) consumption; (*von Drogen*) use; (*von Tabak*) smoking; **der ~ von Alkohol ist Kindern verboten** children are forbidden to consume alcohol (*form*); **der übermäßige ~ von Tabak** excessive smoking; **nach dem ~ der Pilze** after eating the mushrooms
(b) (= *Vergnügen*) pleasure; **etw mit ~ essen** to eat sth with relish; **den Wein hat er mit ~ getrunken** he really enjoyed the wine
(c) NO PL (= *Nutznießung*) **in den ~ von etw kommen** *von Vergünstigungen* to enjoy sth; *von Rente, Prämie etc* to be in receipt of sth

genüsslich [gə'nʏslɪç] **1** ADJ pleasurable **2** ADV with pleasure; **er grunzte ~** he grunted with obvious enjoyment; **er schmatzte ~** he smacked his lips with relish

Genuss-: **Genussmittel** NT *semi-luxury foods and tobacco*; **Genussschein** M (*Fin*) profit-participation certificate; **Genusssucht** F pursuit of pleasure; **genusssüchtig** ADJ pleasure-seeking

Geodreieck ['geo-] NT (*inf*) set square

Geograf [geo'gra:f] M **-en, -en, Geografin** [-'gra:fɪn] F **-, -nen** geographer

Geografie [geogra'fi:] F **-,** NO PL geography

geografisch [geo'gra:fɪʃ] ADJ NO PRED geographic(al)

Geologe [geo'lo:gə] M **-n, -n, Geologin** [-'lo:gɪn] F **-, -nen** geologist

Geologie [geolo'gi:] F **-,** NO PL geology

geologisch [geo'lo:gɪʃ] ADJ NO PRED geological

Geometrie [geome'tri:] F **-,** NO PL geometry

geometrisch [geo'me:trɪʃ] ADJ geometric

Geophysik F geophysics *sing*

geopolitisch ADJ NO PRED geopolitical

geordnet [gə'ɔrdnət] ADJ *Leben, Zustände* well-ordered; **in ~en Verhältnissen leben** to live a well-ordered life; **Kinder aus ~en Verhältnissen** children from well-ordered backgrounds; **~e Verhältnisse schaffen** to put things on an orderly basis; *siehe auch* **ordnen**

Georgien [ge'ɔrgiən] NT **-s** Georgia (*in Caucasia*)

georgisch ADJ Georgian

Geo-: **geostationär** ADJ geostationary; **Geowissenschaft** F earth science; **geozentrisch** [geo'tsentrɪʃ] ADJ geocentric

Gepäck [gə'pɛk] NT **-(e)s,** NO PL *no pl* (*Brit*), baggage *no pl*; **mit leichtem ~ reisen** to travel light

Gepäck-: **Gepäckabfertigung** F (= *Vorgang*) (*am Bahnhof*) luggage *etc* processing; (*am Flughafen*) checking-in of luggage *etc*; (= *Stelle*) (*am Bahnhof*) luggage *etc* office; (*am Flughafen*) luggage *etc* check-in; **Gepäckaufbewahrung** F (= *das Aufbewahren*) looking after left luggage *etc no art*; (*auch* **Gepäckaufbewahrungsstelle**) left-luggage office (*Brit*), baggage checkroom (*US*); **Gepäckausgabe** F (*auch* **Gepäckausgabestelle**) (*am Bahnhof*) (*zur Beförderung*) (out-counter of the) luggage *etc* office; (*zur Aufbewahrung*) (out-counter of the) left-luggage office (*Brit*) *or* baggage checkroom (*US*); (*am Flughafen*) luggage *etc* reclaim; **wir müssen noch zur ~** we still have to collect our luggage *etc*; **Gepäckband** NT, *pl* **-bänder** luggage *etc* conveyor belt; **Gepäcknetz** NT luggage *etc* rack

Gepäcks- (*Aus*) IN CPDS = **Gepäck-**

Gepäck-: **Gepäckschein** M luggage *etc* ticket; **Gepäckträger** M (*am Fahrrad*) carrier; **Gepäckträger(in)** M(F) porter (*Brit*), baggage handler (*Brit*) *or* carrier

Gepard ['ge:part] M **-s, -e** [-də] cheetah

gepfeffert [gə'pfɛfɐt] ADJ (*inf*) (= *hoch*) *Preise, Mieten* steep; (= *schwierig*) *Fragen, Prüfung* tough; (= *hart*) *Kritik* biting; **jdm eine ~e Ohrfeige geben** to clout sb (*inf*); *siehe auch* **pfeffern**

gepfiffen PTP *von* pfeifen

gepflegt [gə'pfle:kt] **1** ADJ **(a)** (= *nicht vernachlässigt*) well-looked-after; *Mensch, Äußeres, Hund* well-groomed; *siehe auch* **pflegen**
(b) (= *kultiviert, niveauvoll*) civilized; *Atmosphäre, Restaurant* sophisticated; *Ausdrucksweise, Gespräche, Sprache, Stil* cultured; *Umgangsformen* refined; (= *angenehm*) *Abend* pleasant
(c) (= *erstklassig*) *Speisen, Weine* excellent; (*inf:* = *von guter*

Qualität) decent; „**~e Küche**" "excellent cuisine"
2 ADV (= *kultiviert*) **sich ~ unterhalten** to have a civilized
conversation; **sich ~ ausdrücken** to have a cultured way of
speaking; **drück dich gefälligst ein bisschen ~er aus** don't be
so crude; **sehr ~ wohnen** to live in style; **so richtig ~ essen
gehen** (*inf*) to go to a really nice restaurant

Gepflogenheit [gə'pfloːgnhait] F **-, -en** (*geh*) (= *Gewohnheit*)
habit; (= *Verfahrensweise*) practice; (= *Brauch*) custom,
tradition

Geplänkel [gə'plɛŋkl] NT **-s,** - skirmish; (*fig*) squabble

Geplapper [gə'plapɐ] NT **-s,** NO PL babbling

Geplärr [gə'plɛr] NT **-(e)s,** NO PL, **Geplärre** [gə'plɛrə] NT **-s,** NO PL
bawling; (*von Radio*) blaring

Geplätscher [gə'plɛtʃɐ] NT **-s,** NO PL splashing; (*pej inf:*
= *Unterhaltung*) babbling

geplättet [gə'plɛtət] ADJ PRED (*inf*) floored (*inf*); **ich bin ganz ~**
(*inf*) I'm flabbergasted (*inf*); *siehe auch* **plätten**

Geplauder [gə'plaudɐ] NT **-s,** NO PL (*geh*) chatting

Gepolter [gə'pɔltɐ] NT **-s,** NO PL (= *Krach*) din; (*an Tür etc*)
banging; (*von Kutsche etc*) clattering

gepr. ABBR *von* **geprüft**

gepriesen PTP *von* **preisen**

gepunktet [gə'pʊŋktət] ADJ *Linie* dotted; *Stoff, Kleid* spotted;
(*regelmäßig*) polka-dot

Gequake [gə'kvaːkə] NT **-s,** NO PL croaking; (*pej inf:*
= *Geschwätz*) chatter

Gequäke [gə'kvɛːkə] NT **-s,** NO PL (*inf*) (*von Kind*) whining; (*von
Radio*) blaring

gequält [gə'kvɛːlt] ADJ *Lächeln* forced; *Miene, Ausdruck* pained;
Gesang, Stimme strained; *siehe auch* **quälen**

Gequassel [gə'kvasl] NT **-s,** NO PL (*pej inf*) chattering

Gequatsche [gə'kvatʃə] NT **-s,** NO PL (*pej inf*) gabbing (*inf*);
(= *Blödsinn*) twaddle (*inf*)

Gequieke [gə'kviːkə] NT **-s,** NO PL squealing

Gequietsche [gə'kviːtʃə] NT **-s,** NO PL squeaking; (*von Reifen,
Mensch*) squealing

gequollen PTP *von* **quellen**

gerade [gə'raːdə] **1** ADJ straight; *Zahl* even; (= *aufrecht*) *Haltung*
upright; (= *aufrichtig*) *Charakter* honest; *Mensch* upright;
(*fig*: = *aufrichtig*) *Charakter* honest; **eine ~ Körperhaltung haben** to hold oneself up straight; **das
~ Gegenteil** the exact opposite
2 ADV **(a)** (= *nicht krumm*) straight; **~ gewachsen sein** (*Baum*)
to be straight
(b) (= *im Augenblick, soeben*) just; **wenn Sie ~ Zeit haben** if
you have time just now; **wo Sie ~ da sind** just while you're
here; **er wollte ~ aufstehen** he was just about to get up; **der
Zug war ~ weg** the train had just gone; **~ erst** only just; **da wir
~ von Geld sprechen, ...** talking of money ...
(c) (= *knapp*) just; **~ so viel, dass er davon leben kann** just
enough for him to live on; **sie hat die Prüfung ~ so
bestanden** she just about passed the exam; **~ noch** only just;
~ noch zur rechten Zeit just in time; **das hat ~ noch gefehlt!**
(*iro*) that's all we wanted!
(d) (= *genau*) just; (= *direkt*) right; **~ heute hab ich an dich
gedacht** I was thinking of you just today; **~ deshalb** that's
just why; **~ umgekehrt, ~ das Gegenteil** just the opposite;
das ist es ja ~! that's just it!
(e) (= *speziell, besonders*) especially; **~, weil ...** just because ...;
~ du solltest dafür Verständnis haben you should be
particularly understanding; **sie ist nicht ~ eine Schönheit**
she's not exactly a beauty; **das war nicht ~ schön/interessant**
that wasn't exactly nice/interesting; **du kannst dich ~
beklagen** (*iro*) what are you complaining about?
(f) (= *ausgerechnet*) **warum ~ das?** why that of all things?;
warum ~ heute? why today of all days?; **warum ~ ich?** why me
of all people?; **warum ~ im Winter?** why in winter of all
times?; **warum ~ in Venedig?** why in Venice of all places?; **~
diesem Trottel musste ich begegnen** of all people I would
have to meet that idiot
(g) (*inf*: = *erst recht*) **nun ~!** you try and stop me now! (*inf*);
jetzt *or* **nun ~ nicht!** I'll be damned if I will! (*inf*)

Gerade [gə'raːdə] F **-n, -n (a)** (*Math*) straight line **(b)** (*Sport*)
(*von Renn-, Laufbahn*) straight; (*Boxen*) straight left/right

gerade-: **geradeaus** [gəraːdə'aus] ADV straight ahead; **gerade
biegen** VT IRREG to straighten out; **geradebiegen** VT SEP IRREG
(*fig inf*) to sort out; **geradeheraus** [gəraːdəhɛ'raus] (*inf*) **1** ADJ

PRED frank **2** ADV frankly; **~ gesagt** quite frankly; **gerade
machen** VT to straighten (out)

gerädert [gə'rɛːdɐt] ADJ (*inf*) **wie ~ sein, sich wie ~ fühlen** to be
or feel (absolutely) whacked (*inf*)

gerade-: **geradeso** [gəraːdə'zoː] ADV = **ebenso**; **geradestehen** VI
SEP IRREG AUX HABEN *or* SEIN **für jdn/etw ~** (*fig*) to be answerable
for sb/sth; **gerade(s)wegs** [gəraːdə(s)veːks] ADV straight; **~ auf
etw (***acc***) losgehen** (*fig*) to get straight down to sth; **geradezu**
[gəraːdə'tsuː, gəraːdə'tsuː] ADV **(a)** (= *beinahe*) virtually;
(= *wirklich, durchaus*) really; **das ist doch ~ Selbstmord** that's
nothing short of suicide; **das ist ja ~ lächerlich!** that is
absolutely ridiculous! **(b)** (= *ohne Umschweife*) frankly; **~ aufs
Ziel zusteuern** (*fig*) to go straight to the point

geradlinig [-liːnɪç] **1** ADJ straight; *Entwicklung etc* linear; (*fig:*
= *aufrichtig*) straight **2** ADV **~ denken/handeln** to be straight;
~ verlaufen to run in a straight line

gerammelt [gə'ramlt] ADV **~ voll** (*inf*) chock-a-block (*inf*); *siehe
auch* **rammeln**

Gerangel [gə'raŋl] NT **-s,** NO PL (= *Balgerei*) scrapping; (*fig:*
= *zäher Kampf*) wrangling; **ein kurzes ~ der beiden Spieler** a
short scrap between the two players; **das ~ um die
Sonderangebote** the tussle over the bargains

Geranie [ge'raːniə] F **-, -n** geranium

gerann PRET *von* **gerinnen**

gerannt PTP *von* **rennen**

Geraschel [gə'raʃl] NT **-s,** NO PL rustle, rustling

Gerassel [gə'rasl] NT **-s,** NO PL rattle, rattling

gerät [gə'rɛːt] 3. PERS SING PRES *von* **geraten**[1]

Gerät [gə'rɛːt] NT **-(e)s, -e** piece of equipment; (= *Vorrichtung*)
device; (= *Apparat*) gadget; (= *landwirtschaftliches ~*)
implement; (= *elektrisches ~*) appliance; (= *Radiogerät,
Fernsehgerät, Telefon*) set; (= *Messgerät*) instrument;
(= *Küchengerät*) utensil; (= *Werkzeug, Gartengerät*) tool;
(= *Turngerät*) piece of apparatus; (*inf*: = *Penis*) tool (*sl*)

geraten[1] [gə'raːtn], *pret* **geriet** [gə'riːt], *ptp* **geraten** [gə'raːtn] VI
AUX SEIN **(a)** (= *zufällig gelangen*) to get (*in* +*acc* into); **an jdn ~**
(= *jdn kennen lernen*) to come across sb; (= *jdn bekommen*) to
find sb; **an etw** (*acc*) **~** to come by sth; **an einen Ort ~** to come
to a place; **an den Richtigen/Falschen ~** to come to the right/
wrong person; **unter ein Fahrzeug ~** to fall under a vehicle;
mit der Hand in eine Maschine ~ to get one's hand caught in
a machine; **in Gefangenschaft ~** to be taken prisoner; **das
Schiff ist in einen Sturm ~** the boat got caught in a storm; **in
Bewegung ~** to begin to move; **ins Stocken ~** to come to a
halt; **ins Schleudern ~** to go into a skid; **in Brand ~** to catch
fire; **in Angst/Begeisterung/Schwierigkeiten ~** to get scared/
enthusiastic/into difficulties; **in Vergessenheit ~** to sink into
oblivion; **auf krumme Wege** *or* **die schiefe Bahn ~** to stray
from the straight and narrow; **aus der Fassung/der Form ~** to
lose one's composure/one's shape; **außer sich ~ (***vor etw dat***)**
to be beside oneself (with sth)
(b) (= *sich entwickeln, gelingen, ausfallen*) to turn out; **ihm
gerät einfach alles** everything he does turns out well; **der
Junge/Kaktus ist gut ~** the boy/cactus turned out well; **nach
jdm ~** to take after sb

geraten[2] PTP *von* **raten, geraten**[1]

Geräte-: **Geräteschuppen** M tool shed; **Geräteturnen** NT
apparatus gymnastics *no pl*

Geratewohl NT **aufs ~** on the off-chance; (*aussuchen,
auswählen etc*) at random; **wir schlugen aufs ~ diesen Weg ein**
we decided to trust to luck and come this way

Gerätschaften PL (= *Ausrüstung*) equipment *sing*;
(= *Werkzeug*) tools *pl*

Geräucherte(s) [gə'rɔyçətə] NT, NO PL DECL AS ADJ smoked meat
(*especially bacon and ham*)

geraum [gə'raum] ADJ ATTR **vor ~er Zeit** some time ago; **seit ~er
Zeit** for some time; **es dauerte eine ~e Weile** it took some
time

geräumig [gə'rɔymɪç] ADJ spacious, roomy

Geräusch [gə'rɔyʃ] NT **-(e)s, -e** sound; (*esp unangenehm*) noise;
mit einem dumpfen ~ with a dull thud

Geräusch-: **geräuscharm** ADJ quiet; **geräuschempfindlich** ADJ
sensitive to noise; (*Tech*) sound-sensitive; **geräuschlos 1** ADJ
silent **2** ADV silently, without a sound; **Geräuschlosigkeit** F
-, NO PL quietness, noiselessness; **Geräuschpegel** M sound
level; **geräuschvoll 1** ADJ (= *laut*) loud; (= *lärmend*) noisy

☒ ADV (= *laut*) loudly; (= *lärmend*) noisily; **weniger ~** with less noise

Geräusper [gəˈrɔyspɐ] NT **-s**, NO PL throat-clearing

gerben [ˈgɛrbn] VT to tan; **vom Wetter gegerbte Haut** weather-beaten skin

Gerbera [ˈgɛrbəra] F **-**, **-(s)** (*Bot*) gerbera

Gerberei [gɛrbəˈrai] F **-**, **-en (a)** NO PL (= *Gerben*) tanning **(b)** (= *Werkstatt*) tannery

gerecht [gəˈrɛçt] **☒** ADJ **(a)** (= *rechtgemäß, verdient*) just; (= *unparteiisch auch*) fair; **~ gegen jdn sein** to be fair *or* just to sb; **~er Lohn für alle Arbeiter!** fair wages for all workers!; **seinen ~en Lohn bekommen** (*fig*) to get one's just deserts; **die Gerechten** the just **(b)** (= *berechtigt*) just, legitimate; **~er Zorn** righteous anger; **sich für eine ~e Sache einsetzen** to fight for a just cause **(c) jdm/einer Sache ~ werden** to do justice to sb/sth; **Bedingungen, Erwartungen** to fulfil (*Brit*) *or* fulfill (*US*) sth **☒** ADV (= *rechtgemäß*) justly

-gerecht ADJ SUF suitable for; **behindertengerecht** suitable for disabled people

gerechterweise [gəˈrɛçtɐˈvaizə] ADV to be fair

gerechtfertigt [gəˈrɛçtfɛrtɪçt] ADJ justified

Gerechtigkeit [gəˈrɛçtɪçkait] F **-**, NO PL justice; (= *das Gerechtsein*) justness; (= *Unparteilichkeit*) fairness; **die ~ nahm ihren Lauf** justice took its course; **jdm/einer Sache ~ widerfahren lassen** to be just to sb/sth; (*fig*) to do justice to sb/sth

Gerede [gəˈreːdə] NT **-s**, NO PL talk; (= *Klatsch*) gossip(ing); **ins ~ kommen** *or* **geraten** to get oneself talked about; **jdn ins ~ bringen** to get sb talked about; **kümmere dich nicht um das ~ der Leute** don't worry about what people say

geregelt [gəˈreːglt] ADJ **Arbeit(szeiten), Mahlzeiten** regular; **Leben** well-ordered; **~er Katalysator** computer-controlled *or* feedback catalytic converter; *siehe auch* **regeln**

gereizt [gəˈraitst] **☒** ADJ (= *verärgert*) irritated; (= *reizbar*) irritable, touchy; (= *nervös*) edgy; **im Zimmer herrschte ~e Stimmung** there was a strained atmosphere in the room **☒** ADV (= *verärgert*) irritably; *siehe auch* **reizen**

Gereiztheit F **-**, NO PL (= *Verärgertheit*) irritation; (= *Reizbarkeit*) irritability, touchiness; (= *Nervosität*) edginess; **die ~ der Atmosphäre** the strained atmosphere

Geriatrie [geriaˈtriː] F **-**, NO PL geriatrics *sing*

geriatrisch [geˈriaːtrɪʃ] ADJ geriatric

Gericht[1] [gəˈrɪçt] NT **-(e)s**, **-e** (= *Speise*) dish; **leckere ~e** delicious meals

Gericht[2] NT **-(e)s**, **-e (a)** (= *Behörde*) court (of justice); (= *Gebäude*) court(house), law courts *pl*; (= *die Richter*) court, bench; **Hohes ~!** My Lord! (*Brit*), Your Honor! (*US*); **vor ~ erscheinen/aussagen** to appear/testify in court; **vor ~ stehen** to stand trial; **jdn/einen Fall vor ~ bringen** to take sb/a case to court; **mit etw vor ~ gehen** to take legal action about sth **(b) das Jüngste** *or* **Letzte ~** the Last Judgement; **über jdn/etw ~ halten** to pronounce judgement on sb/sth; **über jdn zu ~ sitzen** (*fig*) to sit in judgement on sb; **mit jdm (scharf) ins ~ gehen** (*fig*) to judge sb harshly

gerichtlich [gəˈrɪçtlɪç] **☒** ADJ ATTR judicial; **Bestimmung, Entscheidung etc** court; **Medizin, Psychologie** forensic; **Verhandlung** legal; **~e Schritte gegen jdn einleiten** to initiate legal proceedings against sb; **laut ~em Beschluss** according to the decision of a/the court; **ein ~es Nachspiel** a court sequel; **ein ~es Nachspiel haben** to finish up in court; **eine Sache ~** *or* **auf ~em Weg klären** to settle a matter in court *or* by litigation **☒** ADV **anerkannt** by a court; **durchsetzbar** legally; **klären** in court; **jdn ~ belangen** (= *strafrechtlich*) to prosecute sb; (= *zivilrechtlich*) to bring legal proceedings against sb; **~ gegen jdn vorgehen** to take legal action against sb; **jdm etw ~ untersagen lassen** to get an injunction against sb doing sth; **~ vereidigter Dolmetscher** court-appointed interpreter; **~ angeordnet** ordered by the courts

Gerichtsbarkeit [gəˈrɪçtsbaːrkait] F **-**, **-en** jurisdiction

Gerichts-: Gerichtsbeschluss M court decision; **Gerichtsentscheid** M, **Gerichtsentscheidung** F court decision; **Gerichtsferien** PL court vacation, recess; **Gerichtshof** M court (of justice), law court; **Oberster ~ Supreme Court** (of Justice); **der hohe ~** the high court;

Gerichtskasse F **den Betrag von 200 Euro an die ~ zahlen** to pay the court 200 euros; **Gerichtskosten** PL court costs *pl*; **jdn zum Tragen der ~ verurteilen** (*form*), **jdm die ~ auferlegen** (*form*) to order sb to pay costs; **Gerichtsmedizin** F forensic medicine; **Gerichtsmediziner(in)** M(F) forensic doctor; **gerichtsmedizinisch** **☒** ADJ forensic medical *attr* **☒** ADV **die Leiche wurde ~ untersucht** the body was examined by an expert in forensic medicine; **Gerichtssaal** M courtroom; **Gerichtsschreiber(in)** M(F) clerk of the court (*Brit*), registrar (*US*); **Gerichtsstand** M (*form*) court of jurisdiction; **Gerichtstermin** M date of a/the trial; (*für Zivilsachen*) date of a/the hearing; **einen ~ ansetzen** to fix a date for a/the trial/hearing; **Gerichtsverfahren** NT court *or* legal proceedings *pl*; **ein ~ gegen jdn einleiten** to institute legal proceedings against sb; **er wurde ohne ordentliches ~ verurteilt** he was sentenced without a proper trial; **Gerichtsverhandlung** F trial; (*zivil*) hearing; **Gerichtsvollzieher** [-fɔltsiːɐ] M **-s**, **-**, **Gerichtsvollzieherin** [-ərɪn] F **-**, **-nen** bailiff; **Gerichtsweg** M **auf dem ~** through the courts

gerieben [gəˈriːbn] PTP *von* **reiben**

geriet PRET *von* **geraten**[1]

gering [gəˈrɪŋ] **☒** ADJ **(a)** (= *niedrig, nicht sehr groß*) low; **Menge, Vorrat, Betrag, Entfernung** small; **Wert** little *attr*; (= *kurz*) **Zeit, Entfernung** short; **mit ~en Ausnahmen** with few exceptions; **seine Leistung erhielt eine zu ~e Bewertung** his achievement wasn't rated highly enough **(b)** (= *unbedeutend, unerheblich*) slight; **Chance** *auch* slim; **Bedeutung, Rolle** minor; **das ist meine ~ste Sorge** that's the least of my worries; **die Kosten sind nicht ~** the costs are not inconsiderable; **nicht das Geringste** nothing at all; **nicht im Geringsten** not in the least *or* slightest; **das Geringste** the least thing **(c)** (= *unzulänglich*) **Qualität, Kenntnisse** poor; (= *abschätzig*) **Meinung** low **☒** ADV **(a)** (= *wenig*) **~ gerechnet** at a conservative estimate **(b)** (= *abschätzig*) **~ von jdm sprechen** to speak badly of sb; **~ von jdm denken** to have a low opinion of sb

gering achten VT = **gering schätzen**

geringelt [gəˈrɪŋlt] ADJ **Muster** ringed; **Socken** hooped; *siehe auch* **ringeln**

Gering-: geringfügig [-fyːgɪç] **☒** ADJ (= *unwichtig*) insignificant; **Verbesserung, Unterschied** slight; **Vergehen, Verletzung** minor; **Einzelheiten** minor, trivial; **Betrag** small; **~e Beschäftigung** part-time employment; **~ Beschäftigte** *pl* ≈ part-time workers *pl* **☒** ADV slightly; **Geringfügigkeit** F **-**, **-en (a)** (*Jur*) **ein Verfahren wegen ~ einstellen** to dismiss a case because of the trifling nature of the offence (*Brit*) *or* offense (*US*) **(b)** (*von Betrag*) insignificance **(c)** (= *Kleinigkeit*) little thing, trifle; **gering schätzen** VT (= *verachten*) **Menschen, Leistung** to think little of; **Erfolg, Reichtum, menschliches Leben** to place little value on; (= *missachten*) **Gefahr, Folgen** to disregard; **eine Tugend, die man nicht ~ sollte** a virtue not to be despised; **geringschätzig** [-ʃɛtsɪç] **☒** ADJ contemptuous **☒** ADV contemptuously; **Geringschätzung** F, NO PL (= *Ablehnung*) disdain; (*von Bemerkung*) disparagement (*für, +gen* of); (= *schlechte Meinung*) low opinion (*für, +gen* of); (*für Erfolg, Reichtum, menschliches Leben*) low regard (*für, +gen* for)

gerinnen [gəˈrɪnən], pret **gerann** [gəˈran], ptp **geronnen** [gəˈrɔnən] VI AUX SEIN to coagulate; (*Blut auch*) to clot; (*Milch auch*) to curdle; **mir gerann (vor Schreck) das Blut in den Adern** (*fig*) my blood ran cold

Gerinnsel [gəˈrɪnzl] NT **-s**, **-** (= *Blutgerinnsel*) clot

Gerinnung F **-**, **-en** coagulation

Gerippe [gəˈrɪpə] NT **-s**, **-** skeleton; (*von Schiff, Flugzeug auch, von Schirm, Gebäude*) frame; (*fig* = *Grundplan*) framework; **er ist nur noch ein ~** he's nothing but skin and bones

gerippt [gəˈrɪpt] ADJ ribbed *no adv*; **Säule** fluted *no adv*; **~e Sohlen** grip soles

gerissen [gəˈrɪsn] **☒** PTP *von* **reißen** **☒** ADJ cunning

Gerissenheit F **-**, NO PL cunning

geritten PTP *von* **reiten**

Germ [gɛrm] M *or* F **-**, NO PL (*Aus*) baker's yeast

Germane [gɛrˈmaːnə] M **-n**, **-n**, **Germanin** [-ˈmaːnɪn] F **-**, **-nen** Teuton; **die alten ~n** the Teutons

germanisch [gɛrˈmaːnɪʃ] ADJ Germanic; **~es Seminar** Institute of Germanic Studies

germanisieren [gɛrmaniˈziːrən], *ptp* **germanisiert** VT to Germanize

Germanismus [gɛrmaˈnɪsmʊs] M -, **Germanismen** [-mən] (*Ling*) Germanism

Germanist [gɛrmaˈnɪst] M -en, -en, **Germanistin** [-ˈnɪstɪn] F -, -nen Germanist

Germanistik [gɛrmaˈnɪstɪk] F -, NO PL German (studies *pl*); ~ studieren to do German studies, to study German

germanistisch [gɛrmaˈnɪstɪʃ] ADJ German; *Zeitschrift* on German studies

germanophil [gɛrmanoˈfiːl] ADJ Germanophile

Germanophilie [gɛrmanofiˈliː] F -, NO PL Germanophilia

germanophob [gɛrmanoˈfoːp] ADJ Germanophobe

Germanophobie [gɛrmanofoˈbiː] F Germanophobia

gern [gɛrn], **gerne** [ˈgɛrnə] ADV, *comp* **lieber**, *superl* **am liebsten** (a) (= *freudig*) with pleasure; (= *bereitwillig*) with pleasure, willingly; (**aber**) ~! of course!; **ja, ~!** (yes) please; **kommst du mit?** – **ja, ~** – are you coming too? – oh yes, I'd like to; **darf ich das?** – **ja, ~** can I do that? – (yes,) of course; ~ **geschehen!** you're welcome! (*esp US*), not at all!; „**Witwer, 61, sucht Partnerin, ~ älter/mit Kindern**" "widower, aged 61, seeks partner, age not important/children not a problem"; **etw ~ tun** to like doing sth *or* to do sth (*esp US*); **etw ~ essen/trinken** to like sth; **sie isst am liebsten Spargel** asparagus is her favourite (*Brit*) *or* favorite (*US*) food; **das tue ich für mein Leben ~** I adore doing that; **etw ~ sehen** to like sth; **das sähe ich ~** I would welcome it; **das wird nicht ~ gesehen** that's frowned (up)on; **ein ~ gesehener Gast** a welcome visitor; **das glaube ich ~** I can well believe it; **das würde ich zu ~ tun** I'd really love to do that; **ich bin ~ dazu bereit** I'm quite willing to do it; **jdn/etw ~ haben** *or* **mögen** to like sb/sth, to be fond of sb/ sth; **das kannst du ~ haben** you're welcome to it; **er hat es ~, wenn man ihm schmeichelt** he likes being flattered; **ich hätte** *or* **möchte ~ ...** I would like ...; **ich hätte ~ Herrn Kurtz gesprochen** could I speak to Mr Kurtz?; **wie hätten Sie es (denn) ~?** how would you like it?; **du kannst/er kann mich mal ~ haben!** (*inf*) (you can)/(he can) go to hell! (*inf*), screw you/ him (*sl*)
(b) (= *gewöhnlich*, *oft*) **etw ~ tun** to tend to do sth; **morgens lässt er sich ~ viel Zeit** he likes to leave himself a lot of time in the mornings

Gernegroß [ˈgɛrnəgroːs] M -, -e (*hum*) **er war schon immer ein kleiner ~** he always did like to act big (*inf*)

Geröchel [gəˈrœçl] NT -s, NO PL groans *pl*; (*von Sterbenden*) (death) rattle

gerochen PTP *von* **riechen**

Geröll [gəˈrœl] NT -(e)s, -e detritus *no pl*; (*im Gebirge auch*) scree *no pl*; (*größeres*) boulders *pl*

geronnen PTP *von* **rinnen**, **gerinnen**

Geröstete [gəˈrœstətə, gəˈrøːstətə] PL DECL AS ADJ (*S Ger, Aus: Cook*) sauté potatoes *pl*

Gerste [ˈgɛrstə] F -, -n barley

Gersten- IN CPDS barley; **Gerstenkorn** NT, *pl* -körner (a) barleycorn (b) (*Med*) stye

Gerte [ˈgɛrtə] F -, -n switch

gertenschlank ADJ slim and willowy

Geruch [gəˈrʊx] M -(e)s, -e [gəˈrʏçə] (a) smell, odour (*Brit*), odor (*US*) (*nach* of); (*unangenehm*) stench (*nach* of); (= *Duft*) fragrance, perfume (*nach* of); (*von Kuchen etc*) aroma (*nach* of); **der starke ~ nach Alkohol/Knoblauch** the reek of alcohol/ garlic (b) NO PL (= *Geruchssinn*) sense of smell

Geruch-: **geruchlos** ADJ odourless (*Brit*), odorless (*US*); (= *duftlos*) scentless; **Geruchlosigkeit** F -, NO PL lack of smell

Geruchs-: **Geruchsbelästigung** F **das ist eine ~** the smell is a real nuisance; **Geruchsnerv** M olfactory nerve; **Geruchsorgan** NT olfactory organ; **Geruchssinn** M, NO PL sense of smell

Gerücht [gəˈrʏçt] NT -(e)s, -e rumour (*Brit*), rumor (*US*); **es geht das ~, dass ...** there's a rumo(u)r (going a)round that ...; **das halte ich für ein ~** (*inf*) I have my doubts about that

Gerüchteküche F (*inf*) gossip factory (*inf*); **die Pressestelle ist eine wahre ~** the press office is filled with rumour-mongers (*Brit*) *or* rumor-mongers (*US*)

geruchtilgend ADJ deodorizing *no adv*

Geruckel [gəˈrʊkl] NT -s, NO PL jerking, jolting

gerufen PTP *von* **rufen**

geruhsam [gəˈruːzaːm] **1** ADJ peaceful; *Spaziergang etc* leisurely **2** ADV leisurely; ~ **essen** to eat in peace (and quiet)

Geruhsamkeit F -, NO PL peacefulness; (*von Spaziergang etc*) leisureliness

Gerumpel [gəˈrʊmpl] NT -s, NO PL rumbling

Gerümpel [gəˈrʏmpl] NT -s, NO PL junk

Gerundium [geˈrʊndiʊm] NT -s, **Gerundien** [-diːən] gerund

Gerundiv [gerʊnˈdiːf] NT -s, -e [-və] gerundive

gerungen PTP *von* **ringen**

Gerüst [gəˈrʏst] NT -(e)s, -e scaffolding *no pl*; (= *Gestell*) trestle; (*fig*: = *Gerippe*) framework (*zu* of)

Gerüst-: **Gerüstbau** M, NO PL erection of scaffolding; „**W. Friedrich GmbH, ~**" "W. Friedrich Ltd, Scaffolders"; **Gerüstbauer** M, *pl* -, **Gerüstbauerin** F scaffolder

Gerüttel [gəˈrʏtl] NT -s, NO PL shaking (about); (*im Zug, Wagen etc*) jolting (about)

gerüttelt [gəˈrʏtlt] **1** ADJ **ein ~es Maß von** *or* **an etw** (*dat*) a fair amount of sth; **er besitzt ein ~es Maß (an) Unverschämtheit** he has more than his fair share of impudence **2** ADV ~ **voll** jam-packed (*inf*)

gesalzen [gəˈzaltsn] **1** PTP *von* **salzen 2** ADJ (*fig inf*) *Preis, Rechnung* steep; *Witz* spicy

gesammelt [gəˈzamlt] ADJ *Aufmerksamkeit, Kraft* collective; *Werke* collected; *siehe auch* **sammeln**

gesamt [gəˈzamt] ADJ ATTR whole, entire; **die ~en Lehrkräfte** all the teachers; **im Gesamten** in all; **die ~en Kosten** the total costs

Gesamt-: **Gesamtausgabe** F complete edition; **Gesamtbetrag** M total (amount); **Gesamtbetriebsrat** M general *or* central works council; **Gesamteindruck** M general impression; **Gesamteinkommen** NT total income; **Gesamtergebnis** NT overall result; **Gesamtertrag** M total yield; **Gesamtfläche** F total area; **Gesamtgewicht** NT total weight; (*eines LKWs etc auch*) laden weight

Gesamtheit F -, NO PL totality; **die ~ der ...** all the ...; (= *die Summe*) the totality of ...; **die ~ (der Bevölkerung)** the population (as a whole); **die ~ der Studenten/Arbeiter** all the students/workers; **in seiner ~** in its entirety; **das Volk in seiner ~** the nation as a whole

gesamtheitlich **1** ADJ overall **2** ADV as a whole

Gesamthochschule F ≈ polytechnic (*Brit*), ≈ college

GESAMTHOCHSCHULE

A **Gesamthochschule** *is an institution of higher education which combines* Hochschulen *and* Fachhochschulen *and provides a wider choice of subjects. Within each subject area a range of courses are available that vary in emphasis and length and which lead to different final qualifications, depending on the student's objectives. In addition, it is easier to change between subjects at a* **Gesamthochschule** *than it is at a conventional university.* ▶ FACHHOCHSCHULE

Gesamt-: **Gesamtkatalog** M central catalogue (*Brit*) *or* catalog (*US*); **Gesamtkosten** PL total costs *pl*; **Gesamtkunstwerk** NT (*bei Wagner*) synthesis of the arts; (= *Show, Happening*) multimedia performance *or* show; **Gesamtnote** F (*Sch*) overall mark (*Brit*) *or* grade (*US*); **Gesamtrendite** F compound yield; **Gesamtschau** F synopsis (*über* +acc of); **gesamtschuldnerisch** **1** ADJ **-e Haftung** joint and several liability **2** ADV ~ **bürgen für** to guarantee jointly and severally for; ~ **haften** to be jointly and severally liable; **Gesamtschule** F comprehensive school

---

GESAMTSCHULE

The **Gesamtschulen**, *created during the educational reforms of the 1970s, were intended to replace the traditional three-way division of schools into* Hauptschule, Realschule *and* Gymnasium *with a single system. Pupils have the chance to learn a subject at a level appropriate to them: for example, if their lack of ability at mathematics has meant they cannot go to a* Gymnasium, *they may still study, say, languages to a high level at the* **Gesamtschule**. *In addition, pupils who may not initially have been considered suitable to take their* Abitur *can still have the opportunity to take it.* ▶ ABITUR, GYMNASIUM, HAUPTSCHULE, REALSCHULE

Gesamt-: **Gesamtsumme** F total amount; **Gesamtübersicht** F general survey (*über* +acc of); **Gesamtwerk** NT complete works *pl*; **Gesamtwert** M total value; **im ~ von ...** totalling (*Brit*) *or* totaling (*US*) ... in value; **Gesamtwertung** F (*Sport*) overall placings *pl*; **er liegt in der ~ vorn** he has the overall lead; **Gesamtwirtschaft** F national economy; **gesamtwirtschaftlich** 🞰 ADJ national economic *attr* 🞲 ADV **~ nicht vertretbar** not justifiable from the point of view of the national economy; **Gesamtzahl** F total number; **eine ~ von 8.000 Punkten** a total of 8,000 points

gesandt PTP *von* senden[1]

Gesandte(r) [gəˈzantə] M DECL AS ADJ, **Gesandtin** [gəˈzantɪn] F **-, -nen** envoy, legate; (*inf*: = *Botschafter*) ambassador; **päpstlicher ~r** (papal) nuncio

Gesandtschaft F **-, -en** legation; (*inf*: = *Botschaft*) embassy; (= *päpstliche ~*) nunciature

Gesang [gəˈzaŋ] M **-(e)s, -̈e** [gəˈzɛŋə] (a) (= *Lied, Vogelgesang*) song (b) NO PL (= *das Singen*) singing

Gesang-: Gesangbuch NT (*Eccl*) hymnbook; **das richtige/ falsche ~ haben** (*inf*) to belong to the right/wrong denomination; **Gesanglehrer(in)** M(F) singing teacher

gesanglich [gəˈzaŋlɪç] ADJ vocal; *Begabung* for singing

Gesangs- IN CPDS (*Aus*) = **Gesang-**

Gesäß [gəˈzɛːs] NT **-es, -e** seat, bottom

Gesäß-: Gesäßbacke F buttock, cheek; **Gesäßmuskel** M gluteal muscle (*spec*); **Gesäßtasche** F back pocket

gesch. ABBR *von* **geschieden** divorced

Geschädigte(r) [gəˈʃɛːdɪçtə] MF DECL AS ADJ victim

geschaffen PTP *von* schaffen[1]

Geschäft [gəˈʃɛft] NT **-(e)s, -e** (= *Gewerbe, Handel*) business *no pl*; (= *Geschäftsabschluss*) (business) deal *or* transaction; **~ ist ~** business is business; **wie geht das ~?, wie gehen die ~e?** how's business?; **mit jdm ins ~ kommen** to do business with sb; **mit jdm ~e machen** to do business with sb; **im ~ sein** to be in business; **für jdn die ~e führen** to act for sb; (*im Gewerbe, Handel*) to run the business for sb; **ein ~ tätigen** to do a deal; **ein gutes/schlechtes ~ machen** to make a good/bad deal; **dabei hat er ein ~ gemacht** he made a profit by it; **~e mit etw machen** to make money out of sth (b) (= *Aufgabe*) duty; **seinen ~en nachgehen** to go about one's business (c) (= *Firma*) business; (= *Laden*) shop (*Brit*), store; (*inf*: = *Büro*) office; **ich gehe um 8 Uhr ins ~** I go to work *or* to the office at 8.00; **im ~** at work, in the office; (= *im Laden*) in the shop (d) (*baby-talk*: = *Notdurft*) **kleines/großes ~** little/big job (*baby-talk*)

Geschäfte-: Geschäftemacher(in) M(F) (*pej*) profiteer; **Geschäftemacherei** [-maxəˈraɪ] F **-, -en** (*pej*) profiteering *no indef art*

geschäftig [gəˈʃɛftɪç] 🞰 ADJ (= *betriebsam*) busy; **~es Treiben, ~es Hin und Her** hustle and bustle 🞲 ADV busily; **~ hin und her laufen** to bustle (a)round (busily); **~ tun, sich ~ geben** to try to look busy

Geschäftigkeit F **-,** NO PL busyness; (= *geschäftiges Treiben*) (hustle and) bustle; **eine enorme ~ entfalten** *or* **an den Tag legen** to get incredibly busy

geschäftlich [gəˈʃɛftlɪç] 🞰 ADJ business *attr*; (= *sachlich*) *Ton* businesslike; **ich habe mit ihm etwas Geschäftliches zu besprechen** I have some business to discuss with him 🞲 ADV (= *in Geschäften*) on business; (= *wegen Geschäften*) because of business; (= *gesehen*) from a business point of view; **sie hat morgen ~ in Berlin zu tun** she has to be in Berlin on business tomorrow; **~ verhindert** prevented by business; **~ verreist** away on business; **~ mit jdm verkehren** to have business dealings with sb

Geschäfts-: Geschäftsabschluss M business deal; **Geschäftsauto** NT company car; **Geschäftsbedingungen** PL terms *pl* of business; **Geschäftsbereich** M (*Parl*) responsibilities *pl*; **Minister ohne ~** minister without portfolio; **Geschäftsbericht** M report; (*einer Gesellschaft*) company report; **Geschäftsbeziehungen** PL business connections *pl* (*zu* with); **Geschäftsbrief** M business letter; **geschäftsfähig** ADJ (a) (*Jur*) capable of contracting (*form*), competent (*form*); **voll/beschränkt ~ sein** to have complete/ limited competence (b) *Firma, System* able to function; **Geschäftsfähigkeit** F (a) (*Jur*) (legal) competence (b) (*von Firma, System*) ability to function; **Geschäftsfrau** F businesswoman; **Geschäftsfreund(in)** M(F) business associate; **geschäftsführend** ADJ ATTR executive;

(= *stellvertretend*) acting; *Regierung* caretaker; **Geschäftsführer(in)** M(F) (*von Laden*) manager/manageress; (*von Unternehmen*) managing director, CEO; (*von Verein*) secretary; (*von Partei*) whip; **Geschäftsführung** F management; **mit der ~ beauftragt** (*abbr* **m.d.G.b.**) in charge of administration; **Geschäftsgebaren** NT business methods *pl*; **Geschäftsinhaber(in)** M(F) owner (of a business); (*von Laden, Restaurant*) proprietor/proprietress; **Geschäftsinteresse** NT business interest; **Geschäftsjahr** NT financial year; **Geschäftskosten** PL business expenses *pl*; **das geht alles auf ~** it's all on expenses; **Geschäftslage** F (a) (= *Wirtschaftslage*) business situation (b) **in erstklassiger ~** in a good business location; **Geschäftsleitung** F management; **Geschäftsliste** F (*Sw*) = **Tagesordnung**; **Geschäftsmann** M, *pl* **-leute** businessman; **geschäftsmäßig** 🞰 ADJ businesslike 🞲 ADV **klingen** businesslike; *erledigen, gekleidet sein* in a businesslike manner; **Geschäftsmethoden** PL business methods *pl*; **Geschäftsordnung** F standing orders *pl*; **zur ~!** point of order!; **eine Frage zur ~** a question on a point of order; **Geschäftspartner(in)** M(F) business partner; (= *Geschäftsfreund*) business associate; **Geschäftsreise** F business trip; **auf ~ sein** to be on a business trip; **geschäftsschädigend** ADJ bad for business; **~es Verhalten** = **Geschäftsschädigung**; **Geschäftsschädigung** F **-, -en** conduct *no art* injurious to the interests of the company (*form*); **Geschäftsschluss** M close of business; (*von Läden*) closing time; **nach ~** out of office *or* working hours/after closing time; **Geschäftssitz** M place of business; **Geschäftsstelle** F offices *pl*; **Geschäftsstraße** F shopping street; **Geschäftsstunden** PL office *or* working hours *pl*; (*von Läden*) (shop (*esp Brit*) *or* store) opening hours *pl*; **„~“** "hours of opening"; **geschäftstüchtig** ADJ business-minded; **geschäftsunfähig** ADJ (*Jur*) not capable of contracting (*form*), (legally) incompetent (*form*); **Geschäftsunfähigkeit** F (*Jur*) (legal) incompetence; **Geschäftsverbindung** F business connection; **in ~ mit jdm stehen** to have business connections with sb; **Geschäftsverkehr** M (a) business *no art*; **in regem ~ mit einer Firma stehen** to do a considerable amount of business with a firm (b) (= *Straßenverkehr*) business traffic; **Geschäftsvolumen** NT volume of trade; **Geschäftszeiten** PL business hours *pl*; (*von Büros*) office hours *pl*; **während der üblichen ~** during normal business/ office hours

geschah PRET *von* **geschehen**

gescheckt [gəˈʃɛkt] ADJ spotted; *Pferd* skewbald, pinto (*US*)

geschehen [gəˈʃeːən] *pret* **geschah** [gəˈʃaː], *ptp* **geschehen** [gəˈʃeːən] VI AUX SEIN to happen (*jdm* to sb); (= *ausgeführt werden*) to be done; (*Verbrechen*) to be committed; **ihr Selbstmord geschah aus Verzweiflung** her despair led her to commit suicide; **es ist nun einmal ~** what's done is done; **es wird ihm nichts ~** nothing will happen to him; **das geschieht ihm (ganz) recht** it serves him right; **ihm ist ein Unrecht ~** he has been wronged; **ihm ist ein Missgeschick ~** he had a mishap; **er wusste nicht, wie ihm geschah** he didn't know what was going on; **was soll mit ihm/damit ~?** what is to be done with him/it?; **als er sie sah, war es um ihn ~** he was lost the moment he set eyes on her; **da war es um meine Seelenruhe ~** that was an end to my peace of mind; **es kann ~, dass ...** it could happen that ...; **und so geschah es, dass ...** and so it happened *or* came about that ...; **es muss etwas ~** something must be done; **so ~ am ...** such was the case on ...

Geschehen [gəˈʃeːən] NT **-s,** (*rare*) - events *pl*

gescheit [gəˈʃaɪt] ADJ (a) clever; *Mensch, Idee* bright; (= *vernünftig*) sensible; **du bist wohl nicht recht ~?** you must be out of your mind; **sei ~!** be sensible; **es wäre ~ ...** it would be wiser ...; **jetzt bin ich so ~ wie vorher** I'm none the wiser now (b) (*S Ger*: = *tüchtig, ordentlich*) proper, good; **wie ~** (*Aus inf*) good *or* crazy (*inf*)

Geschenk [gəˈʃɛŋk] NT **-(e)s, -e** present, gift; (= *Schenkung*) gift; **jdm ein ~ machen** to give sb a present; **jdm etw zum ~ machen** to give sb sth (as a present); **ein ~ seiner Mutter** a present from his mother; **das war ein ~ des Himmels** it was a godsend; **kleine ~e erhalten die Freundschaft** (*prov*) little presents keep a friendship alive

Geschenk- IN CPDS gift; **Geschenkartikel** M gift; **Geschenkpackung** F gift pack *or* box; (*von Pralinen*) gift box; **Geschenkpapier** NT wrapping paper; **etw in ~ einwickeln** to giftwrap sth

Geschenks- [gəˈʃɛŋks] (*Aus*) IN CPDS = **Geschenk-**

Geschichte [gəˈʃɪçtə] F **-, -n (a)** NO PL (= *Historie*) history; **~ des Altertums/der Neuzeit, Alte/Neue ~** ancient/modern history; **~ machen** to make history; **das ist längst ~** that's past history **(b)** (= *Erzählung, Lügengeschichte*) story; (= *Kurzgeschichte*) short story; **das sind alles bloß ~n** that's all just made up; **~n erzählen** to tell stories **(c)** (*inf*: = *Angelegenheit, Sache*) affair, business *no pl*; (= *Liebesaffäre*) affair; **das sind alte ~n** that's old hat (*inf*); **alte ~n wieder aufwärmen** to rake up the past; **die ganze ~** the whole business; **eine schöne ~!** (*iro*) a fine how-do-you-do! (*inf*); **das sind ja nette ~n!** (*iro*) this is a fine thing; **mach keine ~n!** don't be silly! (*inf*); (= *Dummheiten*) don't do anything silly!

geschichtlich [gəˈʃɪçtlɪç] **1** ADJ (= *historisch*) historical; (= *bedeutungsvoll*) historic **2** ADV historically; **~ bedeutsam** historic; **etw ~ betrachten** to consider sth from the historical point of view; **~ belegt** or **nachgewiesen sein** to be a historical fact

Geschichts-: Geschichtsatlas M historical atlas; **Geschichtsfälschung** F falsification of history; **Geschichtsforscher(in)** M(F) historian; **Geschichtsforschung** F historical research; **Geschichtskenntnis** F knowledge of history *no pl*, historical knowledge *no pl*; **Geschichtsklitterung** [-klɪtərʊŋ] F **-, -en** historical misrepresentation; **geschichtslos** ADJ *Land, Stadt* with no history; *Zeit* with no historical records; *Volk* with no sense of history; **Geschichtsschreiber(in)** M(F) historian; **Geschichtsschreibung** F historiography; **Geschichtswissenschaft** F (science of) history; **Geschichtszahl** F (historical) date

Geschick¹ [gəˈʃɪk] NT **-(e)s, -e** (*geh*) (= *Schicksal*) fate; (= *politische etc Entwicklung, Situation*) fortune; **ein gütiges ~** providence; **ein schlimmes/schweres/trauriges ~** a sad fate

Geschick² NT **-s,** NO PL (= *~lichkeit*) skill

Geschicklichkeit [gəˈʃɪklɪçkaɪt] F **-,** NO PL skill, skilfulness (*Brit*), skillfulness (*US*); (= *Beweglichkeit*) agility; **für** or **zu etw ~ haben** or **zeigen** to be clever at sth

geschickt [gəˈʃɪkt] **1** ADJ **(a)** skilful (*Brit*), skillful (*US*); (= *beweglich*) agile **(b)** (*S Ger*) = **praktisch 2** ADV (= *clever*) cleverly; **~ agieren** to be clever

Geschicktheit F **-,** NO PL = **Geschicklichkeit**

geschieden [gəˈʃiːdn] **1** PTP *von* **scheiden 2** ADJ divorced; **eine ~e Frau** a divorced woman, a divorcee; **Uta Schwarz, ~e Böhme** Uta Schwarz, former married name Böhme; **von dem Moment an waren wir (zwei) ~e Leute** (*inf*) after that it was the parting of the ways for us (*inf*)

geschienen PTP *von* **scheinen**

Geschimpfe [gəˈʃɪmpfə] NT **-s,** NO PL (*inf*) cursing; (*tadelnd*) scolding

Geschirr [gəˈʃɪr] NT **-(e)s, -e (a)** NO PL (= *Haushaltsgefäße*) crockery (*Brit*), tableware; (= *Küchengeschirr*) pots and pans *pl*, kitchenware; (= *Teller etc*) china; (*zu einem Mahlzeit benutzt*) dishes *pl*; (= *Service*) **~ (ab)spülen** to wash up **(b)** (= *Service*) (*dinner/tea etc*) service; (= *Glasgeschirr*) set of glasses; (= *feuerfestes ~*) set of ovenware **(c)** (*von Zugtieren*) harness

Geschirr-: Geschirraufzug M dumb waiter; **Geschirrschrank** M china cupboard (*Brit*) or cabinet (*US*); **Geschirrspülen** NT **-s,** NO PL washing-up; **Geschirrspülmaschine** F dishwasher; **Geschirrspülmittel** NT washing-up liquid (*Brit*), dishwashing liquid (*US*); **Geschirrtuch** NT, *pl* **-tücher** tea towel (*Brit*), dishtowel (*US*)

Geschiss [gəˈʃɪs] NT **-es,** NO PL (*inf*) fuss and bother

geschissen PTP *von* **scheißen**

geschlafen PTP *von* **schlafen**

geschlagen PTP *von* **schlagen**

Geschlecht [gəˈʃlɛçt] NT **-(e)s, -er** sex; (*Gram*) gender; **Jugendliche beiderlei ~s** young people of both sexes; **das andere ~** the opposite sex; **das schwache/schöne/starke ~** the weaker/fair/stronger sex

Geschlechtertrennung F segregation of the sexes

geschlechtlich [gəˈʃlɛçtlɪç] **1** ADJ sexual **2** ADV **mit jdm ~ verkehren** to have sexual intercourse with sb; **sich ~ vermehren** (*Biol*) to reproduce sexually

Geschlechts-: Geschlechtsakt M sex(ual) act; **Geschlechtschromosom** NT sex chromosome;

Geschlechtsgenosse M, **Geschlechtsgenossin** F person of the same sex; **jds ~n** those or people of the same sex as sb; **Geschlechtshormon** NT sex hormone; **geschlechtskrank** ADJ suffering from a sexually transmitted disease; **ein Geschlechtskranker** a person with a sexually transmitted disease; **Geschlechtskrankheit** F sexually transmitted disease; **Geschlechtsleben** NT sex life; **geschlechtslos** ADJ asexual (*auch Biol*), sexless; **Geschlechtsmerkmal** NT sex(ual) characteristic; **Geschlechtsorgan** NT sex(ual) organ; **geschlechtsreif** ADJ sexually mature; **geschlechtsspezifisch** ADJ (*Sociol*) sex-specific; **Geschlechtsteil** NT genitals *pl*; **Geschlechtsumwandlung** F sex change; **Geschlechtsverkehr** M sexual intercourse

geschlichen PTP *von* **schleichen**

geschliffen [gəˈʃlɪfn] **1** PTP *von* **schleifen²** **2** ADJ *Manieren, Ausdrucksweise* polished

geschlossen [gəˈʃlɔsn] **2** ADJ closed; (= *vereint*) united, unified; **in sich** (*dat*) **~** self-contained; *Mensch, Charakter* well-rounded; *Buch, Handlung* well-knit; *Systeme, Produktionskreisläufe* closed; **es war eine ~e Wolkendecke vorhanden** the sky was completely overcast; **ein ~es Ganzes** a unified whole; **~e Gesellschaft** closed society; (= *Fest*) private party **3** ADV **~ für etw sein/stimmen** to be/vote unanimously in favour (*Brit*) or favor (*US*) of sth; **~ hinter jdm stehen** to stand solidly behind sb; **wir gingen ~ mit der ganzen Klasse ins Kino** the whole class went to the cinema en masse; **dieser Vokal wird ~ ausgesprochen** this vowel has closed articulation

Geschlossenheit F **-,** NO PL unity

Geschluchze [gəˈʃlʊxtsə] NT **-s,** NO PL sobbing

geschlungen PTP *von* **schlingen¹, schlingen²**

Geschlürfe [gəˈʃlʏrfə] NT **-s,** NO PL (*inf*) slurping

Geschmack [gəˈʃmak] M **-(e)s, "-e** or (*hum, inf*) **"er** [gəˈʃmɛkə, gəˈʃmɛkɐ] (*lit, fig*) taste; (*no pl*: = *Geschmackssinn*) sense of taste; **je nach ~** to one's own taste; **Salz (je) nach ~ hinzufügen** add salt to taste; **an etw** (*dat*) **~ finden** to acquire a taste for sth; **auf den ~ kommen** to acquire a taste for it; **einen guten ~ haben** (*Essen*) to taste good; **sie hat einen guten ~** (*fig*) she has good taste; **für meinen ~** for my taste; **das ist nicht mein/nach meinem ~** that's not my/to my taste; **die Geschmäcker sind verschieden** tastes differ; **über ~ lässt sich (nicht) streiten** (*prov*) there's no accounting for taste(s) (*prov*)

geschmacklich [gəˈʃmaklɪç] **1** ADJ (*lit, fig*) as regards taste; **ausgezeichnete ~e Qualitäten** (*form*) exquisite taste **2** ADV **besser/hervorragend/Spitzenklasse sein** to taste better/fantastic/excellent; **etw ~ verbessern** to improve the taste of sth

geschmacklos ADJ (*lit, fig*) tasteless

Geschmacklosigkeit F **-, -en (a)** NO PL (*lit, fig*) tastelessness, lack of taste **(b)** (= *Beispiel der ~*) example of bad taste; (= *Bemerkung*) remark in bad taste; **das ist eine ~!** that is the most appalling bad taste!

Geschmacks-: Geschmacksfrage F question of (good) taste; **Geschmacksnerv** M taste bud; **Geschmacksrichtung** F taste; **in sieben neuen ~en** in seven new flavours (*Brit*) or flavors (*US*); **Geschmackssache** F matter of taste; **das ist ~** it's (all) a matter of taste; **Geschmackssinn** M, NO PL sense of taste; **Geschmacksverirrung** F **unter ~ leiden** (*iro*) to have no taste; **der Hut ist eine ~** that hat is an aberration

geschmackvoll **1** ADJ tasteful; **~e Kleider tragen** to dress tastefully; **das war eine nicht sehr ~e Bemerkung** that remark was not in very good taste **2** ADV tastefully

geschmeidig [gəˈʃmaɪdɪç] **1** ADJ **(a)** *Leder, Haut, Bewegung* supple; *Fell* sleek; (= *weich*) *Handtuch, Haar* soft; (= *anschmiegsam*) soft and clinging **(b)** (*fig*) (= *anpassungsfähig*) flexible; (= *wendig*) adroit **2** ADV (= *wendig*) smoothly, supply; (*in Bezug auf Tanzen*) lithely

Geschmeidigkeit F **-,** NO PL **(a)** (*von Leder, Haut, Bewegung*) suppleness; (*von Fell*) sleekness; (= *Weichheit*: *von Handtuch, Haar*) softness; (= *Anschmiegsamkeit*) clinging softness **(b)** (*fig*) (= *Anpassungsfähigkeit*) flexibility; (= *Wendigkeit*) adroitness

Geschmier [gəˈʃmiːr] NT **-(e)s,** NO PL, **Geschmiere** [gəˈʃmiːrə] NT **-s,** NO PL (*inf*) mess; (= *Handschrift*) scrawl; (= *Geschriebenes*) scribble; (= *schlechtes Bild*) daub

geschmissen PTP *von* **schmeißen**

geschmolzen PTP *von* **schmelzen**

Geschmorte(s) [gəˈʃmoːɐtə] NT DECL AS ADJ (Cook) braised meat

Geschnatter [gəˈʃnatɐ] NT **-s**, NO PL (lit) cackle, cackling; (fig) jabber, jabbering

Geschnetzelte(s) [gəˈʃnɛtsltə] NT DECL AS ADJ (esp Sw Cook) meat cut into strips stewed to produce a thick sauce

geschniegelt [gəˈʃniːɡlt] ADJ (pej) flashy; ~ **und gebügelt** or **gestriegelt** spruced up

geschnitten PTP von **schneiden**

geschnoben PTP von **schnauben**

Geschnüffel [gəˈʃnʏfl] NT **-s**, NO PL sniffing; (fig) nosing or sniffing around

geschoben PTP von **schieben**

gescholten PTP von **schelten**

Geschöpf [gəˈʃœpf] NT **-(e)s**, **-e** (= Geschaffenes) creation; (= Lebewesen) creature

geschoren PTP von **scheren**[1]

Geschoss[1] [gəˈʃɔs] NT **-es**, **-e**, **Geschoß**[1] [gəˈʃoːs] (Aus, S Ger) NT **-es**, **-e** projectile (form); (= Wurfgeschoss, Rakete etc auch) missile

Geschoss[2] NT **-es**, **-e**, **Geschoß**[2] (Aus, S Ger) NT **-es**, **-e** (= Stockwerk) floor, storey (Brit), story (US); **im ersten ~** on the first (Brit) or second (US) floor

Geschossbahn F trajectory

geschossen PTP von **schießen**

-geschossig [gəˈʃɔsɪç], (Aus, S Ger) **-geschoßig** [gəˈʃoːsɪç] ADJ SUF -storeyed (Brit), -storied (US); **mehrgeschossig** multistorey etc

Geschrei [gəˈʃraɪ] NT **-s**, NO PL shouts pl, shouting; (von Verletzten, Babys, Popfans) screams pl, screaming; (= schrilles ~) shrieks pl, shrieking; (fig: = Aufhebens) fuss; **viel ~ um etw machen** to make a big fuss about sth

Geschreibsel [gəˈʃraɪpsl] NT **-s**, NO PL (inf) scribble; (fig: = Schreiberei) scribblings pl

geschrieben PTP von **schreiben**

geschrieen, geschrien PTP von **schreien**

geschritten PTP von **schreiten**

geschunden PTP von **schinden**

Geschütz [gəˈʃʏts] NT **-es**, **-e** gun; **schweres ~** heavy artillery; **eine Kanone ist ein ~** a cannon is a piece of artillery; **ein ~ auffahren** to bring up a gun; **schweres** or **grobes ~ auffahren** (fig) to bring up one's big guns

geschützt [gəˈʃʏtst] ADJ Winkel, Ecke sheltered; Pflanze, Tier protected; siehe auch **schützen**

Geschwader [gəˈʃvaːdɐ] NT **-s**, **-** squadron

Geschwafel [gəˈʃvaːfl] NT **-s**, NO PL (inf) waffle (Brit inf), blather (inf)

Geschwalle [gəˈʃvalə] NT **-s**, NO PL (pej inf) waffle (Brit inf), blather (inf)

Geschwätz [gəˈʃvɛts] NT **-es**, NO PL (pej) prattle; (= Klatsch) gossip

Geschwatze [gəˈʃvatsə] NT **-s**, NO PL, (S Ger) **Geschwätze** [gəˈʃvɛtsə] NT **-s**, NO PL (inf) chattering

geschwätzig [gəˈʃvɛtsɪç] ADJ garrulous; (= klatschsüchtig) gossipy

Geschwätzigkeit F **-**, NO PL garrulousness; (= Klatschsucht) constant gossiping

geschweift [gəˈʃvaɪft] ADJ (a) curved; **~e Klammer** (Typ) curly bracket; siehe auch **schweifen** (b) Stern with a tail

geschweige [gəˈʃvaɪɡə] CONJ ~ (**denn**) let alone, never mind

geschwiegen PTP von **schweigen**

Geschwindigkeit [gəˈʃvɪndɪçkaɪt] F **-, -en** speed; (Phys: von Masse) velocity; **mit einer ~ von ...** at a speed of ...; **mit höchster ~** at top speed; **mit rasender ~ fahren** to belt along (inf); **an ~ zunehmen** to gather speed; (Phys: Masse) to gain momentum

Geschwindigkeits-: **Geschwindigkeitsbegrenzung** F **-, -en**, **Geschwindigkeitsbeschränkung** F speed limit; **gegen die ~ verstoßen** to exceed the speed limit; **Geschwindigkeitsüberschreitung** [-ly:bɐʃraɪtʊŋ] F **-, -en**, **Geschwindigkeitsübertretung** F speeding

Geschwister[1] [gəˈʃvɪstɐ] PL brothers and sisters pl, siblings pl; **wir sind drei ~** there are three of us in my or our family; **haben Sie noch ~?** do you have any brothers or sisters?

Geschwister[2] NT **-s**, **-** (form, Sw) sibling (form)

Geschwisterchen [gəˈʃvɪstɐçən] NT **-s**, **-** little brother/sister

geschwisterlich [gəˈʃvɪstɐlɪç] **1** ADJ brotherly/sisterly **2** ADV in a brotherly/sisterly way

geschwollen [gəˈʃvɔlən] **1** PTP von **schwellen 2** ADJ (pej) pompous **3** ADV (pej) pompously

geschwommen PTP von **schwimmen**

geschworen [gəˈʃvoːrən] PTP von **schwören**

Geschworenen-: **Geschworenenbank** F, pl **-bänke** jury box; (= die Geschworenen) jury; **Geschworenengericht** NT = Schwurgericht; **Geschworenenliste** F panel

Geschworene(r) [gəˈʃvoːrənə] MF DECL AS ADJ juror; **die ~n** the jury sing or pl

Geschwulst [gəˈʃvʊlst] F **-, ̈-e** [gəˈʃvʏlstə] growth

geschwunden PTP von **schwinden**

geschwungen [gəˈʃvʊŋən] **1** PTP von **schwingen 2** ADJ curved; **eine kühn ~e Nase** an aquiline nose; **~e Klammer** (Typ) curly bracket

Geschwür [gəˈʃvyːɐ] NT **-s**, **-e** ulcer; (= Furunkel) boil; (fig) running sore

gesegnet [gəˈzeːɡnət] ADJ (geh) **mit etw ~ sein** to be blessed with sth; **im ~en Alter von 84 Jahren** at the ripe old age of 84; **einen ~en Schlaf haben** to be a sound sleeper; **einen ~en Appetit haben** to have a healthy appetite; siehe auch **segnen**

gesehen PTP von **sehen**

Geselchte(s) [gəˈzɛlçtə] NT DECL AS ADJ (S Ger, Aus) salted and smoked meat

Geselle [gəˈzɛlə] M **-n**, **-n** (= Handwerksgeselle) journeyman

gesellen [gəˈzɛlən], ptp **gesellt** VR **sich zu jdm ~** to join sb; **dazu gesellte sich noch, dass ...** (geh) in addition to this was the fact that ...

Gesellen-: **Gesellenbrief** M journeyman's certificate; **Gesellenjahre** PL years pl as a journeyman; **Gesellenprüfung** F examination to become a journeyman; **Gesellenstück** NT journeyman's piece; **Gesellenzeit** F period as a journeyman

gesellig [gəˈzɛlɪç] **1** ADJ sociable; Tier gregarious; Verkehr social; **der Mensch ist ein ~es Tier** man is a social animal; **~es Beisammensein** social gathering **2** ADV **sie saßen ~ bei einer Flasche Wein zusammen** they were sitting together enjoying a bottle of wine

Geselligkeit F **-, -en (a)** NO PL sociability, conviviality; (von Tieren) gregariousness; (= geselliges Leben) social intercourse; **die ~ lieben** to be sociable **(b)** (= Veranstaltung) social gathering

Gesellin [gəˈzɛlɪn] F **-, -nen** (= Handwerksgesellin) journeyman

Gesellschaft [gəˈzɛlʃaft] F **-, -en (a)** (Sociol, fig: = Oberschicht) society; **die ~ verändern** to change society; **eine Dame der ~** a society lady
(b) (= Vereinigung) society; (Comm) company; **~ des bürgerlichen Rechts** private company or corporation (US); **~ mit beschränkter Haftung** limited company (Brit) or corporation (US)
(c) (= Abendgesellschaft) reception, party; (= Gäste) guests pl, party; **eine erlesene ~ hatte sich eingefunden** a select group of people had gathered
(d) (= Umgang, Begleitung) company; **zur ~ to be sociable; in schlechte ~ geraten** to get into bad company; **da befindest du dich in guter ~** then you're in good company; **jdm ~ leisten** to keep sb company
(e) (= Kreis von Menschen) group of people; (pej) bunch (inf); **diese Familie/Abteilung ist eine komische ~** that family/department are an odd bunch (inf); **wir waren eine bunte ~** we were a mixed bunch

Gesellschafter [gəˈzɛlʃaftɐ] M **-s**, **-**, **Gesellschafterin** [-ərɪn] F **-, -nen** (Comm) (= Teilhaber) shareholder; (= Partner) partner; **stiller ~** sleeping (Brit) or silent (US) partner

gesellschaftlich [gəˈzɛlʃaftlɪç] **1** ADJ social **2** ADV **er ist ~ erledigt** he's ruined socially; **sich ~ unmöglich machen** or **daneben benehmen** to disgrace oneself socially

Gesellschafts-: **Gesellschaftsanteil** M (Comm) share of the business; **Gesellschaftsanzug** M formal dress; **gesellschaftsfähig** ADJ socially acceptable; **Gesellschaftsform** F social system; **Gesellschaftskapital** NT (Comm) company's capital; **gesellschaftskritisch** **1** ADJ critical of society; **die ~e Funktion einer Zeitung** the function of a newspaper as a critic of society **2** ADV **sich ~ äußern** to be critical of society; **~ denken** to have a critical attitude toward(s) society; **Gesellschaftsordnung** F social system; **Gesellschaftsraum** M function room; **Gesellschaftsschicht** F social stratum; **Gesellschaftsspiel** NT party game; **Gesellschaftssystem** NT social system; **Gesellschaftstanz** M ballroom dance; **Gesellschaftsvertrag** M (*Philos*) social contract; (*Comm*) partnership agreement

gesessen PTP *von* **sitzen**

Gesetz [gə'zɛts] NT **-es, -e** (*Jur*, = *Naturgesetz, Prinzip*) law; (= ~*buch*) statute book; (*Parl*: = *Vorlage*) bill; (*nach Verabschiedung*) act; (= *Satzung, Regel*) rule; **das Copyrightgesetz** the Copyright Act; (**zum**) = **werden** to become law; **auf Grund des ~es, nach dem ~** under the law (*über +acc* on); **vor dem ~** in (the eyes of the) law; **im Sinne des ~es** within the meaning of the act; **das ~ der Schwerkraft** the law of gravity; **das ~ des Dschungels** the law of the jungle; **das erste** *or* **oberste ~ (der Wirtschaft** *etc***)** the golden rule (of industry *etc*); **ein ungeschriebenes ~** an unwritten rule

Gesetz-: Gesetzblatt NT law gazette; **Gesetzbuch** NT statute book; **Bürgerliches ~** Civil Code; **Gesetzentwurf** M (draft) bill

Gesetzes-: Gesetzesbrecher(in) M(F) law-breaker; **Gesetzeshüter(in)** M(F) (*iro*) guardian of the law; **Gesetzesinitiative** F legislative initiative; (*Sw*: = *Volksbegehren*) petition for a referendum; **Gesetzeskraft** F the force of law; **~ erlangen** to become law; **~ haben** to be law; **Gesetzeslücke** F legal loophole; **gesetzestreu** ADJ *Person* law-abiding; *Verhalten* in accordance with the law; **Gesetzestreue** F seine ~ **wurde angezweifelt** it was questioned how law-abiding he was; **Gesetzesübertretung** F infringement of a/the law; **Gesetzesvorlage** F (draft) bill; **gesetzeswidrig ■** ADJ illegal; (*unrechtmäßig*) unlawful **②** ADV illegally; (= *unrechtmäßig*) unlawfully; **Gesetzeswidrigkeit** F **(a)** NO PL illegality; (= *Unrechtmäßigkeit*) unlawfulness **(b)** PL (= *gesetzeswidrige Handlungen*) illegal acts *pl*

Gesetz-: gesetzgebend ADJ ATTR legislative; **die ~e Gewalt** the legislature; **Gesetzgeber** M legislative body; **Gesetzgebung** [-geːbʊŋ] F **-, -en** legislation *no pl*

gesetzlich [gə'zɛtslɪç] **■** ADJ *Verpflichtung, Bestimmungen, Vertreter, Zahlungsmittel* legal; *Feiertag, Rücklage, Zinsen, Regelungen* statutory; (= *rechtmäßig*) lawful; **~e Krankenversicherung** statutory health insurance **②** ADV legally; (= *durch Gesetze auch*) by law; (= *rechtmäßig*) lawfully

Gesetzlichkeit F **-**, NO PL **(a)** (= *Regel*) law **(b)** (= *das Gesetzlichsein*) legality; (= *Rechtmäßigkeit*) lawfulness; (= *Rechtsordnung*) law

Gesetz-: gesetzlos ADJ lawless; **gesetzmäßig ■** ADJ **(a)** (= *gesetzlich*) legal; (= *rechtmäßig*) lawful **(b)** (= *einem Naturgesetz folgend*) following a set pattern **②** ADV **(a)** (= *dem Gesetz entsprechend*) legally **(b)** (= *regelmäßig*) **~ ablaufen** to follow a set pattern

gesetzt [gə'zɛtst] **■** ADJ (= *reif*) sedate, sober; **ein Herr im ~en Alter** a man of mature years; *siehe auch* **setzen ②** CONJ **~ den Fall, ...** assuming (that) ...

Gesetztheit F **-**, NO PL (= *Reife*) sedateness

Geseufze [gə'zɔyftsə] NT **-s**, NO PL sighing

ges. gesch. ABBR *von* **gesetzlich geschützt** reg'd

gesichert [gə'zɪçɐt] ADJ *Einkommen, Existenz* secure; *Fakten, Erkenntnisse* definite; **~es Gewehr** gun with the safety catch on; *siehe auch* **sichern**

Gesicht [gə'zɪçt] NT **-(e)s, -er (a)** face; **ein ~ machen** *or* **ziehen** (*inf*) to make *or* pull a face; **ein intelligentes/trauriges/böses/wütendes ~ machen** to look intelligent/sad/cross/angry; **ein langes ~ machen** to make a long face; **was machst du denn heute für ein ~?** what's up with you today?; **jdm ein ~ schneiden** (*inf*) to make a face at sb; **jdm ins ~ sehen** to look sb in the face; **den Tatsachen ins ~ sehen** to face facts; **jdm etw ins ~ sagen** to tell sb sth to his face; **mir schien die Sonne ins ~** the sun was (shining) in my eyes; **es stand ihr im** *or* **ins ~ geschrieben** it was written all over her face; **sein wahres ~ zeigen** to show (oneself in) one's true colours (*Brit*) *or* colors (*US*); **das sieht man ihm am ~ an** you can tell (that) from his face; **jdm wie aus dem ~ geschnitten sein** to be the spitting image of sb; **das** *or* **sein ~ verlieren** to lose face; **das ~ wahren** *or* **retten** to save face

(b) (*fig*: = *Aussehen*) appearance; **ein anderes/freundlicheres ~ bekommen** to look quite different/more friendly; **die Sache bekommt ein anderes ~** the matter takes on a different complexion; **das gibt der Sache ein neues ~** that puts a different complexion on the matter *or* on things

(c) NO PL (*old*: = *Sehvermögen*) sight; **das zweite ~** second sight; **etw aus dem ~ verlieren** (*lit, fig*) to lose sight of sth; **jdn/etw zu ~ bekommen** to set eyes on sb/sth

Gesichts-: Gesichtsausdruck M (facial) expression; **Gesichtscreme** F face cream; **Gesichtsfarbe** F complexion; **Gesichtshaut** F facial skin; **Gesichtskontrolle** F face check (*carried out by bouncers*); **Gesichtslähmung** F facial paralysis; **gesichtslos** ADJ (*fig*) faceless; **Gesichtsmaske** F face mask; (*eines Chirurgen*) mask; **Gesichtsmilch** F face lotion; **Gesichtsmuskel** M facial muscle; **Gesichtsnerv** M facial nerve; **Gesichtspackung** F face pack; **Gesichtspartie** F part of the/one's face; **Gesichtspflege** F care of one's face; **Gesichtspunkt** M (= *Betrachtungsweise*) point of view, standpoint; (= *Einzelheit*) point; **Gesichtsrose** F (*Med*) facial erysipelas (*spec*); **Gesichtsverlust** M loss of face; **Gesichtswasser** NT, *pl* **-wässer** face lotion; **Gesichtszüge** PL features *pl*

Gesims [gə'zɪms] NT **-es, -e** [-zə] ledge

Gesindel [gə'zɪndl] NT **-s**, NO PL (*pej*) riffraff *pl*

gesinnt [gə'zɪnt] ADJ USU PRED **jdm gut/günstig/übel ~ sein** to be well/favourably (*Brit*) *or* favorably (*US*)/ill disposed to(wards) sb; **jdm freundlich/feindlich ~ sein** to be friendly/hostile to(wards) sb; **sozial/fortschrittlich ~ sein** to be socially/progressively minded; **er ist anders ~ als wir** his views are different from ours; **die so ~en Mitglieder** the members holding this view

Gesinnung [gə'zɪnʊŋ] F **-, -en** (= *Charakter*) cast of mind; (= *Ansichten*) views *pl*; (= *Einstellung*) fundamental attitude; (= *Denkart*) way of thinking; (*einer Gruppe*) ethos; **eine liberale ~** liberal-mindedness; **eine edle ~** noble-mindedness; **anständige ~** decency; **seiner ~ treu bleiben** to remain loyal to one's basic convictions; **wegen seiner ~ verfolgt werden** to be persecuted because of one's views; **seine wahre ~ zeigen** to show (oneself in) one's true colours (*Brit*) *or* colors (*US*)

Gesinnungs-: Gesinnungsfreund(in) M(F), **Gesinnungsgenosse** M, **Gesinnungsgenossin** F like-minded person; **Herr Klein und seine Gesinnungsgenossen von der Opposition** Mr Klein and people from the Opposition who share his views; **gesinnungslos** (*pej*) **■** ADJ unprincipled **②** ADV **sich ~ verhalten** to behave in an unprincipled manner

gesittet [gə'zɪtət] **■** ADJ **(a)** (= *wohlerzogen*) well-mannered **(b)** (= *zivilisiert, kultiviert*) civilized **②** ADV **die Kinder benahmen sich sehr ~** the children were very well-mannered; **die Demonstration lief ~ ab** it was an orderly demonstration

Gesocks [gə'zɔks] NT **-es**, NO PL (*pej inf*) riffraff *pl*

Gesöff [gə'zœf] NT **-(e)s, -e** (*inf*) muck (*inf*)

gesoffen PTP *von* **saufen**

gesogen PTP *von* **saugen**

gesondert [gə'zɔndɐt] **■** ADJ separate **②** ADV separately; **~ berücksichtigt werden** to receive special consideration

gesonnen [gə'zɔnən] **■** PTP *von* **sinnen ②** ADJ **(a) ~ sein, etw zu tun** to be of a mind to do sth **(b)** (*incorrect*) = **gesinnt**

gesotten [gə'zɔtn] **■** PTP *von* **sieden ②** ADJ (*dial*) boiled; **Gesottenes** boiled meat

gespalten [gə'ʃpaltn] **■** PTP *von* **spalten ②** ADJ *Bewusstsein* split; *Lippe, Rachen* cleft; *Huf* cloven; *Zunge* forked; *Gesellschaft, Nation, Konjunktur* divided; **mit ~er Zunge reden** (*old*) (*liter*) to talk falsely; (*esp in Indianergeschichten*) to talk with forked tongue; **bei dieser Frage sind die Meinungen ~** opinions are divided on this question

Gespann [gə'ʃpan] NT **-(e)s, -e (a)** (= *Zugtiere*) team; (= *zwei Ochsen*) yoke **(b)** (= *Ochsengespann*) oxcart; (= *Pferdegespann*) horse and cart; (*zur Personenbeförderung*) horse and carriage; (*fig inf*: = *Paar*) pair; **ein gutes ~ abgeben** to make a good team

gespannt [gə'ʃpant] **■** ADJ **(a)** *Seil, Schnur* taut **(b)** (*fig*) *Lage* tense; *Beziehungen auch* strained; **seine Nerven waren aufs Äußerste** *or* **äußerste ~** his nerves were at breaking point **(c)** (= *neugierig*) curious; (= *begierig*) eager; *Aufmerksamkeit* close; **ich bin ~, wie er darauf reagiert** I wonder how he'll react to that; **ich bin sehr ~, was ich zu Weihnachten bekomme** I'm dying to know what I'm getting for Christmas; **ich bin schon sehr auf diesen Film ~** I'm dying to see this film; **ich bin ~ wie ein Regenschirm** (*hum inf*) *or*

Flitzbogen (*hum inf*) I'm dying to know/see/find out; **da bin ich aber ~!** I'm looking forward to that; (*iro*) (oh really?) that I'd like to see!
2 ADV intently; **~ zuhören/zusehen** to be engrossed with what's going on; **~ in seinem Buch lesen** to be engrossed in one's book; *siehe auch* **spannen**

Gespanntheit F -, NO PL **(a)** (*von Seil, Schnur*) tension **(b)** (*fig*) (*von Lage*) tension; (*von Beziehungen auch*) strain **(c)** (= *Neugierde*) eager anticipation; **es herrscht große ~** everyone is on tenterhooks (*esp Brit*) *or* on pins and needles (*US*)

Gespenst [gə'ʃpɛnst] NT -(e)s, -er ghost; (*fig:* = *Gefahr*) spectre (*Brit*), specter (*US*); **~er sehen** (*fig inf*) to imagine things

Gespenster-: Gespenstergeschichte F ghost story; **gespensterhaft 1** ADJ ghostly *no adv*; (*fig*) eerie, eery **2** ADV eerily; **er sah ~ bleich aus** he was deathly pale; **~ wirken/aussehen** to seem/look eerie; **Gespensterstunde** F witching hour

gespenstisch [gə'ʃpɛnstɪʃ] ADJ, ADV **(a)** = **gespensterhaft (b)** (*fig:* = *bizarr, unheimlich*) eerie, eery; **es ist ~ ruhig** there is an eerie calm

gespieen PTP *von* **speien**

gespielt [gə'ʃpiːlt] ADJ feigned; **mit ~em Interesse** with a pretence (*Brit*) *or* pretense (*US*) of being interested; *siehe auch* **spielen**

gespien PTP *von* **speien**

gespiesen (*hum*) PTP *von* **speisen**

gesponnen PTP *von* **spinnen**

gespornt [gə'ʃpɔrnt] ADJ *siehe* **gestiefelt**

Gespött [gə'ʃpœt] NT -(e)s, NO PL mockery; (= *Gegenstand des Spotts*) laughing stock; **jdn/sich zum ~ der Leute machen** to make sb/oneself a laughing stock; **zum ~ werden** to become a laughing stock

Gespräch [gə'ʃprɛːç] NT -(e)s, -e **(a)** (= *Unterhaltung*) conversation; (= *Diskussion*) discussion; (= *Dialog*) dialogue (*Brit*), dialog (*US*); **-e** (*Pol*) talks; **ich habe ein sehr interessantes ~ mit ihm geführt** I had a very interesting conversation with him; **ein ~ unter vier Augen** a confidential *or* private talk; **ein ~ unter Freunden** a conversation between friends; **das ~ auf etw** (*acc*) **bringen** to steer the conversation *etc* (a)round to sth; **im ~ sein** (*lit*) to be being talked about; (*in der Schwebe*) to be under discussion; **mit jdm ins ~ kommen** to get into conversation with sb; (*fig*) to establish a dialogue (*Brit*) *or* dialog (*US*) with sb
(b) (= *Gesprächsstoff*) **das ~ des Tages** the topic of the hour; **das ~ der Stadt** the talk of the town; **zum ~ werden** to become a talking point
(c) (*Telec:* = *Anruf*) (telephone) call; **wir haben in unserem gestrigen ~ vereinbart, dass ...** we agreed in our telephone conversation yesterday that ...; **ein ~ für dich** a call for you; **stundenlange ~e führen** to be on the telephone for hours

gesprächig [gə'ʃprɛːçɪç] ADJ talkative; (= *mitteilsam*) communicative; **jdn ~ machen** to make sb talk

Gesprächigkeit F -, NO PL talkativeness; (= *Mitteilsamkeit*) communicativeness

Gesprächs-: Gesprächsbereitschaft F (*esp Pol*) readiness to talk; **Gesprächsdauer** F **(a)** (*Telec*) call time **(b)** **nach vierstündiger ~** after four hours of talks; **Gesprächseinheit** F (*Telec*) unit; **Gesprächsgebühr** F (*Telec*) charge for a/the call; **Gesprächsgegenstand** M topic; **der Skandal ist ~ Nummer eins** the scandal is the number one topic; **Gesprächspartner(in)** M(F) interlocutor (*form*); **~ bei der Diskussion sind die Herren X, Y und Z** taking part in the discussion are Mr X, Mr Y and Mr Z; **mein ~ bei den Verhandlungen** my opposite number at the talks; **er ist nicht gerade ein anregender ~** he's not exactly an exciting conversationalist; **wer war dein ~?** who did you talk with?; **mein ~ heute Abend ist ...** with me this evening is ...; **Gesprächsstoff** M topics *pl*; (= *Diskussionsstoff*) topics to discuss; **Gesprächsteilnehmer(in)** M(F) participant in a/the discussion; (*Fernsehserien etc*) panellist (*Brit*), panelist (*US*); **Gesprächsthema** NT = **Gesprächsgegenstand**; **Gesprächsumleitung** F (*Telec*) call routing system; **gesprächsweise** ADV in conversation

gespreizt [gə'ʃpraitst] (*fig*) **1** ADJ affected **2** ADV affectedly; *siehe auch* **spreizen**

gesprenkelt [gə'ʃprɛŋklt] ADJ speckled; **schwarz ~** speckled with black; *siehe auch* **sprenkeln**

Gespritzte(r) [gə'ʃprɪtstə] M DECL AS ADJ (*S Ger, Aus*) spritzer

gesprochen PTP *von* **sprechen**

gesprossen PTP *von* **sprießen**

gesprungen PTP *von* **springen**

Gespür [gə'ʃpyːɐ] NT -s, NO PL feel(ing)

gest. ABBR *von* **gestorben**

Gestagen [gɛsta'geːn] NT -s, -e (*Med*) gestagen

Gestalt [gə'ʃtalt] F -, -en **(a)** (*lit, fig*) (*= Umriss auch*) shape; **in ~ von** (*fig*) in the form of; **(feste) ~ annehmen** *or* **gewinnen** to take shape; **einer Sache** (*dat*) **~ geben** *or* **verleihen** to shape sth **(b)** (= *Wuchs*) build **(c)** (= *Person, Persönlichkeit, Traumgestalt*) figure; (*in Literaturwerken auch, pej:* = *Mensch*) character

gestalten [gə'ʃtaltn], *ptp* **gestaltet 1** VT *Text, Wohnung* to lay out; *Programm, Abend, Layout* to arrange; *Arbeitsplatz, Benutzeroberfläche, Arbeitszeit, Freizeit, Abend* to organize; *Schaufenster* to dress; *Zukunft, Beziehung, Gesellschaft, Politik* to shape; **etw rationeller/effizienter/flexibler ~** to make sth more rational/efficient/flexible; **ich gestalte mein Leben so, wie ich will** I organize my life the way I want to; **die Gastgeber haben den Abend sehr lebendig gestaltet** our hosts laid on a very lively evening; **einen Stoff literarisch ~** to give literary form to one's material
2 VR (= *werden*) to become; (= *sich entwickeln*) to turn (*zu* into); **sich schwierig ~** (*Verhandlungen etc*) to run into difficulties; **sich zu einem Erfolg ~** to turn out to be a success

Gestalter [gə'ʃtaltɐ] M -s, -, **Gestalterin** [-ərɪn] F -, -nen creator; (*Tech: rare*) designer

gestalterisch [gə'ʃtaltərɪʃ] ADJ creative

Gestaltung F -, -en (= *das Gestalten*) shaping, forming (*zu* into); (*von Wohnung*) layout; (*von Abend, Programm*) arrangement; (*von Schaufenster*) dressing; (*von Freizeit*) structuring; **wir bemühen uns um eine möglichst interessante ~ des Sprachunterrichts** we are trying to structure our language-teaching as interestingly as possible

Gestammel [gə'ʃtaml] NT -s, NO PL stammering

gestand PRET *von* **gestehen**

gestanden 1 PTP *von* **stehen**, **gestehen 2** ADJ ATTR *Seefahrer, Fachmann etc* experienced; **ein ~er Mann, ein ~es Mannsbild** a mature and experienced man

geständig [gə'ʃtɛndɪç] ADJ **~ sein** to have confessed; **ein ~er Mörder** a murderer who confessed

Geständnis [gə'ʃtɛntnɪs] NT -ses, -se confession; **ein ~ ablegen** to make a confession; **jdm ein ~ machen** to make a confession to sb

Gestänge [gə'ʃtɛŋə] NT -s, - (*von Gerüst*) bars *pl*, struts *pl*; (*von Maschine*) linkage

Gestank [gə'ʃtaŋk] M -(e)s, NO PL stink

Gestänker [gə'ʃtɛŋkɐ] NT -s, NO PL (*inf*) stirring (*inf*)

Gestapo [ge'staːpo, gə'ʃtaːpo] F -, NO PL Gestapo

gestatten [gə'ʃtatn], *ptp* **gestattet 1** VT to allow; (= *einwilligen in*) to consent to; **jdm etw ~** to allow sb sth; **~ Sie eine Frage?** may I ask you something *or* a question?; **sich** (*dat*) **~, etw zu tun** (*geh*) to take the liberty of doing sth; **sich** (*dat*) **etw ~** to permit oneself sth; **wenn ich mir eine Frage/Bemerkung ~ darf ...** (*geh*) if I might be permitted a question/comment ...; **wenn es die Umstände ~ ...** (*geh*) circumstances permitting ...
2 VI **~ Sie?(, darf ich ...)**, **~ Sie, dass ich ...?** may I ...?, would you mind if I ...?; **wenn Sie ~ ...** with your permission ...

Geste ['gɛstə, 'geːstə] F -, -n (*lit, fig*) gesture

Gesteck [gə'ʃtɛk] NT -(e)s, -e flower arrangement

gestehen [gə'ʃteːən], *pret* **gestand** [gə'ʃtant], *ptp* **gestanden** [gə'ʃtandn] VTI to confess (*jdm etw* sth to sb); **offen gestanden ...** to be frank ...

Gestehungskosten [gə'ʃteːʊŋs-] PL, **Gestehungspreis** M (*Comm*) production costs *pl*

Gestein [gə'ʃtain] NT -(e)s, -e rock(s *pl*); (= *Schicht*) rock stratum

Gesteins-: Gesteinsart F type of rock; **Gesteinsbrocken** M rock; **Gesteinskunde** F petrography

Gestell [gə'ʃtɛl] NT -(e)s, -e stand; (= *Regal*) shelf; (= *Ablage*) rack; (= *Rahmen, Bettgestell, Brillengestell, Tischgestell*) frame;

(*auf Böcken*) trestle; (= *Wäschegestell*) clothes dryer; (*aus Holz*) clotheshorse; (*figinf*: = *Beine*) pins *pl* (*inf*)

gestelzt [gə'ʃteltst] **1** ADJ stilted **2** ADV reden, sich ausdrücken stiltedly

gestern ['gɛstɐn] ADV yesterday; ~ **Abend** (*früh*) yesterday evening; (*spät*) last night; **die Zeitung von** ~ yesterday's paper; **Ansichten von** ~ outdated views; **er ist nicht von** ~ (*inf*) he wasn't born yesterday; ~ **vor acht Tagen** a week (ago) yesterday, yesterday week; ~ **in acht Tagen** a week (from) yesterday

gestiefelt [gə'ʃtiːflt] ADJ wearing boots; **der Gestiefelte Kater** Puss-in-Boots; ~ **und gespornt** (*fig inf*) ready for the off (*Brit inf*)

gestiegen PTP *von* **steigen**

Gestik ['gɛstɪk, 'geːstɪk] F -, NO PL gestures *pl*

gestikulieren [gɛstiku'liːrən], *ptp* **gestikuliert** VI to gesticulate

gestimmt [gə'ʃtɪmt] ADJ froh/düster ~ in a cheerful/sombre (*Brit*) or somber (*US*) mood; *siehe auch* **stimmen**

Gestirn [gə'ʃtɪrn] NT -(e)s, -e heavenly body

gestisch ['gɛstɪʃ, 'geːstɪʃ] **1** ADJ gestural **2** ADV etw ~ und mimisch zum Ausdruck bringen to express sth using gestures and mime

Gestöber [gə'ʃtøːbɐ] NT -s, - (*leicht*) snow flurry; (*stark*) snowstorm

gestochen [gə'ʃtɔxn] **1** PTP *von* **stechen** **2** ADJ Handschrift, Zeichnung clear, neat **3** ADV ~ scharfe Fotos needle-sharp photographs; **wie** ~ **schreiben** to write clearly

gestohlen [gə'ʃtoːlən] **1** PTP *von* **stehlen** **2** ADJ der/das kann mir ~ bleiben (*inf*) he/it can go hang (*inf*)

Gestöhn [gə'ʃtøːn] NT -(e)s, NO PL, **Gestöhne** [gə'ʃtøːnə] NT -s, NO PL moaning, groaning

gestorben PTP *von* **sterben**

gestört [gə'ʃtøːɐt] ADJ disturbed; Rundfunkempfang poor; **seelisch/geistig** ~ **sein** to be (psychologically/mentally) disturbed; **Kinder aus** ~**en Familien** children from problem families; *siehe auch* **stören**

gestoßen PTP *von* **stoßen**

Gestotter [gə'ʃtɔtɐ] NT -s, NO PL stuttering, stammering

gestreift [gə'ʃtraɪft] ADJ striped; **eine rot-grün** ~**e Bluse** a red and green striped blouse; *siehe auch* **streifen**

gestrichen [gə'ʃtrɪçn] **1** PTP *von* **streichen** **2** ADJ (= *genau voll*) **ein** ~**es Maß** a level measure; **ein** ~**er Teelöffel voll** a level teaspoon(ful) **3** ADV ~ **voll** level; (= *sehr voll*) full to the brim; **er hat die Hosen** ~ **voll** (*inf*) he's wetting himself (*inf*); **ich habe die Nase** ~ **voll** (*inf*) I'm fed up (to the back teeth with it) (*inf*)

gestriegelt [gə'ʃtriːɡlt] ADJ ~ **und gebügelt** dressed up to the nines; *siehe auch* **striegeln**

gestrig ['gɛstrɪç] ADJ ATTR yesterday's; **unser** ~**es Gespräch** our conversation (of) yesterday; **unser** ~**es Schreiben** our letter of yesterday; **am** ~**en Tage** (*geh*) yesterday

gestritten PTP *von* **streiten**

Gestrüpp [gə'ʃtrʏp] NT -(e)s, -e undergrowth; (*fig*) jungle

gestuft [gə'ʃtuːft] ADJ (= *in Stufen*) terraced; Haarschnitt layered; (*fig*) = *abgestuft*) graded; (*zeitlich*) staggered; *siehe auch* **stufen**

Gestühl [gə'ʃtyːl] NT -(e)s, -e seating

gestunken PTP *von* **stinken**

Gestüt [gə'ʃtyːt] NT -(e)s, -e stud

Gesuch [gə'zuːx] NT -(e)s, -e petition (*auf +acc, um* for); (= *Antrag*) application (*auf +acc, um* for)

gesucht [gə'zuːxt] ADJ (= *begehrt*) sought after; **sehr** ~ (very) much sought after; **Ingenieure sind** ~**e Arbeitskräfte** engineers are much sought after; *siehe auch* **suchen**

Gesülze [gə'zʏltsə] NT -s, NO PL (*inf*) claptrap (*inf*)

gesund [gə'zʊnt] **1** ADJ, *comp* -**er** *or* ⁼**er** [gə'zʏndɐ], *superl* -**este(r, s**) *or* ⁼**este(r, s**) [gə'zʏndəsta] (*allgemein*) healthy; (= *arbeits-, leistungsfähig*) fit; **frisch und** ~, ~ **und munter**, ~ **wie ein Fisch (im Wasser)** (as) sound as a bell; **ich fühle mich nicht ganz** ~ I don't feel very well; **sonst bist du** ~? (*iro inf*) are you feeling all right? (*iro*); **wieder** ~ **werden** to get better; **Äpfel sind** ~ apples are good for you; **bleib (schön)** ~! look after yourself **2** ADV, *comp* ⁼**er** *or* -**er**, *superl* am ⁼**esten** *or* -**esten** ~ **leben** to have a healthy lifestyle; **sich** ~ **ernähren** to have a healthy

diet; ~ **essen** to eat healthily; **jdn** ~ **pflegen** to nurse sb back to health; *siehe auch* **gesundschreiben**

Gesunde(r) [gə'zʊndə] MF DECL AS ADJ healthy person

Gesundheit F -, NO PL (= *Wohlbefinden*) health; (= *gesunder Zustand, Zuträglichkeit*) healthiness; (= *Arbeits-, Leistungsfähigkeit*) fitness; **bei guter** ~ in good health; **bei bester** ~ in the best of health; ~! bless you; **auf Ihre** ~! your (very good) health; **eine robuste/zarte** ~ **haben** to have a robust/delicate constitution

gesundheitlich [gə'zʊnthaitlɪç] **1** ADJ ~**e Schäden** damage to one's health; **sein** ~**er Zustand** (the state of) his health; **aus** ~**en Gründen** for health reasons **2** ADV ~ **geht es mir nicht besonders** my health is not particularly good; **wie geht es Ihnen** ~? how is your health?; **sie ist** ~ **angeschlagen** she is in poor health

Gesundheits-: **Gesundheitsamt** NT public health department; **Gesundheitsapostel** M (*iro*) health freak (*inf*); **Gesundheitsdienst** M health service; **Gesundheitsfanatiker(in)** M(F) health freak (*inf*); **Gesundheitsfarm** F health farm; **gesundheitshalber** ADV for health reasons; **gesundheitsschädigend**, **gesundheitsschädlich** ADJ unhealthy; **Gesundheitswesen** NT, NO PL health service; **Gesundheitszeugnis** NT certificate of health; **Gesundheitszustand** M, NO PL state of health

gesund-: **gesundschreiben** VT SEP IRREG **jdn** ~ to certify sb (as) fit; **gesundschrumpfen** SEP **1** VT (*fig*) to streamline **2** VR to be streamlined; **gesundstoßen** VR SEP IRREG (*sl*) to line one's pockets (*inf*)

gesungen PTP *von* **singen**

gesunken PTP *von* **sinken**

getan [gə'taːn] **1** PTP *von* **tun** **2** ADJ nach ~**er Arbeit** when the day's work is done

Getier [gə'tiːɐ] NT -s, NO PL (**a**) (= *Tiere, esp Insekten*) creatures *pl* (**b**) (*einzelnes*) creature

getigert [gə'tiːgɐt] ADJ (*mit Streifen*) striped; (*mit Flecken*) piebald; ~**e Katze** tabby (cat)

getönt [gə'tøːnt] ADJ Glas, Scheibe, Brille tinted; *siehe auch* **tönen²**

Getöse [gə'tøːzə] NT -s, NO PL din; (*von Auto, Beifall etc*) roar; **mit** ~ with a din *etc*

getragen [gə'traːgn] PTP *von* **tragen**

Geträller [gə'trɛlɐ] NT -s, NO PL trilling

Getrampel [gə'trampl] NT -s, NO PL (= *Beifallsgetrampel, Protestgetrampel*) stamping

Getränk [gə'trɛŋk] NT -(e)s, -e drink; **er gibt viel für** ~**e aus** he spends a lot on drink

Getränke-: **Getränkeautomat** M drinks (*Brit*) *or* beverage (*US*) machine; **Getränkekarte** F (*in Café*) list of beverages; (*in Restaurant*) wine list; **Getränkemarkt** M drinks cash-and-carry (*Brit*), beverage store (*US*)

Getrappel [gə'trapl] NT -s, NO PL patter; (= *Hufgetrappel*) clop

getrauen [gə'trauən], *ptp* **getraut** VR to dare; **getraust du dich** *or* **dir** (*inf*) **das?** do you dare do that?

Getreide [gə'traɪdə] NT -s, - grain; **in diesem Klima wächst kein** ~ grain doesn't grow in this climate; **das** ~ **steht gut** the grain crop is doing well

Getreide-: **Getreide(an)bau** M, NO PL cultivation of grain *or* cereals; **Getreideart** F cereal; **Getreideflocke** F USU PL cereal; **Getreidemühle** F (= *Müllereibetrieb, Gerät*) flour mill; **Getreidesilo** NT *or* M, **Getreidespeicher** M silo

getrennt [gə'trɛnt] **1** ADJ separate; **sie führten** ~**e Kasse** they each paid for themselves **2** ADV ~ **wohnen** not to live together; ~ **leben** to live apart; ~ **schlafen** not to sleep together; *siehe auch* **trennen**

Getrenntschreibung F writing as two/three *etc* words; **zu beachten ist die** ~ **von „wie viel"** remember that "wie viel" is written as two (separate) words

getreten PTP *von* **treten**

getreu [gə'trɔʏ] **1** ADJ (= *genau, entsprechend*) faithful, true *no adv* **2** PREP +DAT true to

Getriebe [gə'triːbə] NT -s, - (**a**) (*Tech*) gears *pl*; (= ~*kasten*) gearbox; (= *Antrieb*) drive (**b**) (= *lebhaftes Treiben*) bustle

Getriebe- IN CPDS (*Tech*) gear

getrieben PTP *von* **treiben**

Getriebe-: Getriebeöl NT gear(box) oil; **Getriebeschaden** M gearbox trouble *no indef art*

getroffen PTP *von* **treffen**

getrogen PTP *von* **trügen**

Getrommel [gə'trɔml] NT **-s**, NO PL drumming

getrost [gə'tro:st] **1** ADJ confident; **du kannst ~ sein, sei ~** rest assured, never fear **2** ADV **(a)** (= *vertrauensvoll*) confidently; **~ sterben** to die in peace **(b)** (= *bedenkenlos*) **wenn er frech ist, darfst du ihm ~ eine runterhauen** if he's naughty, feel free to hit him; **du kannst dich ~ auf ihn verlassen** you need have no fears about relying on him; **man kann ~ behaupten/annehmen, dass ...** one need have no hesitation in *or* about asserting/assuming that ...

getrübt [gə'try:pt] ADJ **ein ~es Verhältnis zu jdm haben** to have an unhappy relationship with sb; *siehe auch* **trüben**

getrunken PTP *von* **trinken**

Getto ['geto] NT **-s**, **-s** ghetto

Getue [gə'tu:ə] NT **-s**, NO PL (*pej*) to-do (*inf*); (= *geheuchelte Höflichkeit*) affectation; **ein ~ machen** to make a to-do (*inf*); (= *überhöflich sein, sich wichtig machen*) to put on airs

Getuschel [gə'tʊʃl] NT **-s**, NO PL whispering

geübt [gə'ly:pt] ADJ *Auge, Ohr, Griff* practised (*Brit*), practiced (*US*); *Fahrer, Segler etc* proficient; **~ sein** to be experienced; **im Schreiben/Reden ~ sein** to be a proficient writer/talker; *siehe auch* **üben**

GEW [ge:le:'ve:] F - ABBR *von* **Gewerkschaft Erziehung und Wissenschaft** ≈ NUT (*Brit*), teachers' union

Gewächs [gə'vɛks] NT **-es**, **-e (a)** (= *Pflanze*) plant **(b)** (*Med*) growth

gewachsen [gə'vaksn] **1** PTP *von* **wachsen¹ 2** ADJ **(a)** (= *von allein entstanden*) evolved **(b)** **jdm ~ sein** to be a match for sb; **einer Sache** (*dat*) **~ sein** to be up to sth; **er ist seinem Bruder (an Stärke/Intelligenz) durchaus ~** he is his brother's equal in strength/intelligence

Gewächshaus NT greenhouse; (= *Treibhaus*) hothouse

gewagt [gə'va:kt] ADJ **(a)** (= *kühn*) daring; (= *gefährlich*) risky **(b)** (= *anzüglich*) risqué; *siehe auch* **wagen**

gewählt [gə've:lt] **1** ADJ *Sprache* elegant **2** ADV **sich ~ ausdrücken** to express oneself elegantly; *siehe auch* **wählen**

Gewähltheit F -, NO PL elegance

Gewähr [gə've:ɐ] F -, NO PL guarantee; **jdm ~ dafür geben, dass ...** to guarantee (sb *or* to sb) that ...; **keine ~ für etw bieten** to offer no guarantee for sth; **die ~ für jds Zahlungsfähigkeit übernehmen** to guarantee sb's ability to pay; **die Angabe erfolgt ohne ~** this information is supplied without liability; **„ohne ~"** (*auf Fahrplan, Preisliste*) "subject to change"; (*bei Lottozahlen, statistischen Angaben*) "no liability assumed"; **für etw ~ leisten** to guarantee sth

gewähren [gə've:rən] *ptp* **gewährt** VT to grant; *Rabatt, Vorteile, Sicherheit, Trost, Schutz* to give; **jdm Unterstützung ~** to provide sb with support; **jdn ~ lassen** (*geh*) not to stop sb

gewährleisten [gə've:ɐlaistn] *ptp* **gewährleistet** VT INSEP (= *sicherstellen*) to ensure (*jdm etw* sb sth); (= *garantieren*) to guarantee (*jdm etw* sb sth)

Gewährleistungsanspruch M warranty claim

Gewahrsam [gə'va:ɐza:m] M **-s**, NO PL **(a)** (= *Verwahrung*) safekeeping; **etw in ~ nehmen/haben** to take sth into/have sth in safekeeping; **etw (bei jdm) in ~ geben** to hand sth over (to sb) for safekeeping **(b)** (= *Haft*) custody

Gewährung F, NO PL granting; (*von Rabatt, Vorteilen*) giving; (*von Sicherheit, Schutz*) affording

Gewalt [gə'valt] F **-, -en (a)** (= *Machtbefugnis, Macht, Herrschaft*) power; **die ausübende** *or* **vollziehende/gesetzgebende/richterliche ~** the executive/legislature/judiciary; **elterliche ~** parental authority; **jdn/etw in seine ~ bringen** to bring sb/sth under one's control; **jdn in seiner ~ haben** to have sb in one's power; **sich in der ~ haben** to have oneself under control; **in jds ~** (*dat*) **sein** *or* **stehen** to be in sb's power; **die ~ über etw** (*acc*) **verlieren** to lose control of sth; **~ über Leben und Tod (haben)** (to have) power over life and death **(b)** NO PL (= *Zwang*) force; (= *~tätigkeit*) violence; **~ anwenden** to use force; **höhere ~** acts/an act of God; **nackte ~** brute force; **mit ~** by force; **mit aller ~** (*inf*) for all one is worth **(c)** NO PL (= *Heftigkeit, Wucht*) force

Gewalt-: Gewaltakt M act of violence; **Gewaltanwendung** F use of force; **gewaltbereit** ADJ ready to use violence;

Gewaltbereitschaft F propensity to violence; **Gewalteinwirkung** F violence

Gewaltenteilung F, **Gewaltentrennung** F separation of powers

gewaltig [gə'valtɪç] **1** ADJ **(a)** (= *heftig*) *Sturm etc* violent **(b)** (= *groß, riesig*) colossal; *Anblick* tremendous; *Stimme, Töne* powerful; (*inf*: = *sehr groß*) colossal (*inf*); *Summe* huge **(c)** (*geh*: = *mächtig*) powerful; **die Gewaltigen der Erde** the mighty rulers of the world **2** ADV (*inf*: = *sehr*) enormously; **sich ~ irren** to be very much mistaken; **du musst dich ~ ändern** you'll have to change one hell of a lot (*inf*)

Gewalt-: gewaltlos 1 ADJ non-violent **2** ADV (= *ohne Zwang*) without force; (= *ohne Gewaltanwendung*) without violence; **Gewaltlosigkeit** F -, NO PL non-violence; **gewaltsam** [gə'valtza:m] **1** ADJ forcible; *Tod, Auseinandersetzung, Aufstand* violent **2** ADV forcibly, by force; **Gewalttat** F act of violence; **Gewalttäter(in)** M(F) violent criminal; **gewalttätig** ADJ violent; **Gewalttätigkeit** F (*no pl*: = *Brutalität*) violence; (= *Handlung*) act of violence; **Gewaltverbrechen** NT crime of violence; **gewaltverherrlichend** ADJ glorifying violence *pred*; **Gewaltverzicht** M non-aggression; **Gewaltvideo** NT violent video, video nasty (*Brit*)

Gewand [gə'vant] NT **-(e)s**, **-̈er** [gə'vɛndə] (*geh*: = *Kleidungsstück*) garment; (*weites, langes*) robe, gown; (*fig*: = *Maske*) guise; **ein altes Buch in neuem ~** an old book with a new look

gewandt [gə'vant] **1** PTP *von* **wenden 2** ADJ skilful (*Brit*), skillful (*US*); (*körperlich*) nimble; (= *geschickt*) deft; *Auftreten, Redner, Stil* elegant **3** ADV elegantly

Gewandtheit F -, NO PL skilfulness (*Brit*), skillfulness (*US*); (*von Körper*) nimbleness; (= *Geschicktheit*) deftness; (*von Stil*) elegance

gewann PRET *von* **gewinnen**

Gewäsch [gə'vɛʃ] NT **-(e)s**, NO PL (*pej inf*) claptrap (*inf*)

gewaschen PTP *von* **waschen**

Gewässer [gə'vɛsɐ] NT **-s**, - stretch of water; **~ pl** inshore waters *pl*; **ein fließendes/stehendes ~** a stretch of running/standing water

Gewebe [gə've:bə] NT **-s**, - (= *Stoff*) fabric, material; (= *~art*) weave; (*Biol*) tissue; (*fig*) web

Gewebeprobe F (*Med*) tissue sample

Gewehr [gə've:ɐ] NT **-(e)s**, **-e** (= *Flinte*) rifle; (= *Schrotbüchse*) shotgun

Gewehr-: Gewehrlauf M (*von Flinte*) rifle barrel; (*von Schrotbüchse*) barrel of a shotgun; **Gewehrmündung** F (*von Flinte/Schrotbüchse*) muzzle (of a rifle/shotgun)

Geweih [gə'vai] NT **-(e)s**, **-e** antlers *pl*; **das ~** the antlers; **ein ~** a set of antlers

Gewerbe [gə'vɛrbə] NT **-s**, - **(a)** trade; **Handel und ~** trade and industry; **das älteste ~ der Welt** (*hum*) the oldest profession in the world (*hum*); **ein ~ (be)treiben** *or* **ausüben** to practise (*Brit*) *or* practice (*US*) a trade **(b)** (*Sw*: = *Bauerngehöft*) farm

Gewerbe-: Gewerbeanmeldung F, **Gewerbeanzeige** F registration (*of a trade or business*); **Gewerbeaufsicht** F ≈ health and safety control; **Gewerbeaufsichtsamt** NT ≈ factory inspectorate (*Brit*); **Gewerbebetrieb** M commercial enterprise; **Gewerbefläche** F commercial space; **Gewerbegebiet** NT industrial area; (*eigens angelegt*) trading estate (*esp Brit*); **Gewerbemüll** M commercial waste; **Gewerbeschein** M trading licence (*Brit*) *or* license (*US*); **Gewerbesteuer** F trade tax; **Gewerbetreibende(r)** [-traibndə] MF DECL AS ADJ trader

gewerblich [gə'vɛrplɪç] **1** ADJ commercial; *Lehrling, Genossenschaft* trade *attr*; (= *industriell*) industrial; **die ~en Berufe** the trades **2** ADV **diese Räume dürfen nicht ~ genutzt werden** these rooms are not to be used for commercial purposes

gewerbsmäßig 1 ADJ professional; **der ~e Vertrieb von etw** selling sth as a business; **~e Unzucht** (*form*) prostitution **2** ADV professionally, for gain

Gewerkschaft [gə'vɛrkʃaft] F **-, -en** (trade *or* trades *or* labor (*US*)) union

Gewerkschafter [gə'vɛrkʃaftɐ] M **-s**, -, **Gewerkschafterin** [-ərɪn] F **-, -nen**, **Gewerkschaftler** [gə'vɛrkʃaftlɐ] M **-s**, -, **Gewerkschaftlerin** [-ərɪn] F **-, -nen** trade *or* labor (*US*) unionist

gewerkschaftlich [gə'vɛrkʃaftlɪç] **1** ADJ (trade or labor (US)) union attr; **~er Vertrauensmann** (im Betrieb) shop steward (esp Brit) **2** ADV **wir haben uns ~ organisiert** we organized ourselves into a union; **~ organisierter Arbeiter** union member; **~ tätig sein** to be active in the union

Gewerkschafts- IN CPDS (trade or labor (US)) union; **Gewerkschaftsbeiträge** PL union dues pl; **Gewerkschaftsbund** M, pl **-bünde** federation of trade or labor (US) unions, ≈ Trades Union Congress (Brit), ≈ Federation of Labor (US); **gewerkschaftseigen** ADJ owned by a (trade or labor (US)) union; **Gewerkschaftsführer(in)** M(F) (trade or labor (US)) union leader; **Gewerkschaftsvorsitzende(r)** MF DECL AS ADJ (trade or labor (US)) union president

gewesen [gə've:zn] **1** PTP von **sein¹** **2** ADJ ATTR former

gewichen PTP von **weichen²**

Gewicht [gə'vɪçt] NT **-(e)s, -e** weight; **dieser Stein hat ein großes ~** this rock is very heavy; **dieser Stein hat ein ~ von 100 kg** this rock weighs 100 kg; **er hat sein ~ gehalten** he has stayed the same weight; **er brachte zu viel ~ auf die Waage** he weighed in too heavy; **spezifisches ~** specific gravity; **~ haben** (lit) to be heavy; (fig) to carry weight; **ins ~ fallen** to be crucial; **nicht ins ~ fallen** to be of no consequence; **auf etw** (acc) **~ legen, einer Sache** (dat) **~ beilegen or beimessen** to set (great) store by sth

Gewicht-: Gewichtheben NT **-s,** NO PL (Sport) weightlifting; **Gewichtheber** [-he:bɐ] M **-s, -, Gewichtheberin** [-ərɪn] F **-, -nen** weightlifter

gewichtig [gə'vɪçtɪç] ADJ (fig) (= wichtig) weighty; (= einflussreich) influential

Gewichts-: Gewichtsabnahme F loss of weight; **Gewichtsangabe** F indication of weight; **die Hersteller von Fleischwaren sind zur ~ verpflichtet** the manufacturers of meat products are obliged to show the weight; **Gewichtsklasse** F (Sport) weight (category); **Gewichtsverlagerung** F shifting of weight; (fig) shift of or in emphasis; **Gewichtsverlust** M weight loss; **Gewichtszunahme** F increase in weight

gewieft [gə'vi:ft] ADJ (inf) crafty (in +dat at)

Gewieher [gə'vi:ɐ] NT **-s,** NO PL whinnying; (fig) braying

gewiesen PTP von **weisen**

gewillt [gə'vɪlt] ADJ **~ sein, etw zu tun** to be willing to do sth; (= entschlossen) to be determined to do sth

Gewimmel [gə'vɪml] NT **-s,** NO PL swarm; (= Menge) crush

Gewimmer [gə'vɪmɐ] NT **-s,** NO PL whimpering

Gewinde [gə'vɪndə] NT **-s, -** (Tech) thread

Gewindegang M, pl **-gänge** pitch (of screw thread)

Gewinn [gə'vɪn] M **-(e)s, -e (a)** (= Ertrag) profit; **~ abwerfen or bringen** to make a profit; **~ bringend** profitable; **etw mit ~ verkaufen** to sell sth at a profit; siehe auch **gewinnbringend** **(b)** (= Preis, Treffer) prize; (bei Wetten, Glücksspiel) winnings pl; **einen großen ~ machen** to win a lot **(c)** NO PL (fig: = Vorteil) gain; **das ist ein großer ~ (für mich)** I have gained a lot from this; **ein ~ für die Abteilung** a valuable addition to the department

Gewinn-: Gewinnabführung F profit transfer; (aus dem Ausland) repatriation of profits; **Gewinnabführungsvertrag** M profit transfer agreement; **Gewinnanteil** M (Comm) dividend; **Gewinnausschüttung** F **-, -en** prize draw; **Gewinnbeteiligung** F **(a)** (Ind) (= Prinzip) profit-sharing; (= Summe) (profit-sharing) bonus **(b)** (= Dividende) dividend; **gewinnbringend** **1** ADJ (lit, fig) profitable **2** ADV profitably; **~ wirtschaften** to make a profit

gewinnen [gə'vɪnən], pret **gewann** [gə'van], ptp **gewonnen** [gə'vɔnən] **1** VT **(a)** (= siegen in) to win; (= erwerben, bekommen) to gain, to win; Preis, jds Herz to win; **jdn (für etw) ~** to win sb over (to sth); **Zeit ~** to gain time; **was ist damit gewonnen?** what good is that?; **wie gewonnen, so zerronnen** (Prov) easy come easy go (prov) **(b)** (als Profit) to make (a profit of) **(c)** (= erzeugen) to produce, to obtain; Erze etc to mine, to extract; (aus Altmaterial) to reclaim **2** VI **(a)** (= Sieger sein) to win (bei, in +dat at) **(b)** (= profitieren) to gain; (= sich verbessern) to gain something; **an Bedeutung ~** to gain (in) importance; **an Höhe ~** to gain height; **an Geschwindigkeit ~** to pick up or gain speed

gewinnend ADJ (fig) winning, winsome

Gewinner [gə'vɪnɐ] M **-s, -, Gewinnerin** [-ərɪn] F **-, -nen** winner

Gewinnerstraße F (inf) **auf der ~ sein** to be on the way to victory

Gewinn-: Gewinnerwartung F anticipated profit; **Gewinnerzielungsabsicht** F (Comm) profit motive; **Gewinnmaximierung** F maximization of profit(s); **Gewinnrücklage** F revenue reserve; **satzungsmäßige ~n** statutory revenue reserves; **Gewinnspanne** F profit margin; **Gewinnspiel** NT competition; (TV) game show; **Gewinn- und Verlustrechnung** F profit and loss account (Brit), income statement (US)

Gewinnung [gə'vɪnʊŋ] F **-,** (rare) **-en** (von Kohle, Öl) extraction; (von Energie, Plutonium) production

Gewinn-: Gewinnverteilung F profit distribution; **Gewinnvortrag** M retained profits pl; **~ aus dem Vorjahr** profit brought forward; **Gewinnwarnung** F (Comm) profit warning; **Gewinnzahl** F winning number

Gewinsel [gə'vɪnzl] NT **-s,** NO PL (lit, fig) whining

Gewirr [gə'vɪr] NT **-(e)s,** NO PL tangle; (fig: = Durcheinander) jumble; (von Paragrafen, Klauseln, Stimmen) confusion; (von Gassen) maze

Gewisper [gə'vɪspɐ] NT **-s,** NO PL whispering

gewiss [gə'vɪs] **1** ADJ **(a)** (= sicher) certain (+gen of); **ich bin dessen ~** (geh) I'm certain of it; **darüber weiß man noch nichts Gewisses** nothing certain is known as yet **(b)** ATTR certain; **ein ~er Herr Müller** a certain Herr Müller; **in ~em Maße** to some or a certain extent; **in ~em Sinne** in a (certain) sense **2** ADV (geh) certainly; **Sie denken ~, dass ...** no doubt you think that ...; **ich weiß es ganz ~** I'm certain of it; **eins ist (ganz) ~** one thing is certain; **eins weiß ich (ganz) ~** there's one thing I know for certain; **(ja) ~!** certainly, sure (esp US); **(aber) ~ (doch)!** (but) of course

Gewissen [gə'vɪsn] NT **-s,** NO PL conscience; **ein schlechtes ~** a guilty conscience; **jdn/etw auf dem ~ haben** to have sb/sth on one's conscience; **jdm ins ~ reden** to have a serious talk with sb; **jdm ins ~ reden, etw zu tun** to get sb to do sth

Gewissens-: gewissenhaft **1** ADJ conscientious **2** ADV conscientiously; **gewissenlos** **1** ADJ unscrupulous; (= verantwortungslos) irresponsible; **~ sein** to have no conscience **2** ADV unscrupulously; **sich unmenschlich und ~ verhalten** to behave inhumanly and immorally

Gewissens-: Gewissensbisse PL pangs pl of conscience; **mach dir deswegen keine ~!** there's nothing for you to feel guilty about; **~ bekommen** to get a guilty conscience; **ohne ~** without feeling guilty; **Gewissensentscheidung** F question of conscience; **Gewissensfrage** F matter of conscience; **Gewissenskonflikt** M moral conflict

gewissermaßen [gə'vɪsɐ'ma:sn] ADV (= sozusagen) so to speak; (= auf gewisse Weise) in a way

Gewissheit F **-, -en** certainty; **mit ~** with certainty; **wissen for certain**

Gewitter [gə'vɪtɐ] NT **-s, -** thunderstorm; (fig) storm

Gewitterfront F (Met) storm front

gewitterig [gə'vɪtərɪç] **1** ADJ thundery **2** ADV **~ schwül** thundery (and oppressive)

gewittern [gə'vɪtɐn], ptp **gewittert** VI IMPERS **es gewittert** it's thundering

Gewitter-: Gewitterschauer M thundery shower; **Gewitterwolke** F thundercloud; (fig inf) storm cloud

gewittrig [gə'vɪtrɪç] ADJ, ADV = **gewitterig**

Gewitzel [gə'vɪtsl] NT **-s,** NO PL joking, jokes pl

gewitzt [gə'vɪtst] ADJ crafty, cunning

gewoben PTP von **weben**

gewogen¹ [gə'vo:gn] PTP von **wiegen²**

gewogen² ADJ (geh) well-disposed (+dat towards)

Gewogenheit F **-,** NO PL (geh) favourable (Brit) or favorable (US) attitude

gewöhnen [gə'vø:nən], ptp **gewöhnt** **1** VT **jdn an etw** (acc) **~** to accustom sb to sth; **einen Hund an Sauberkeit ~** to house-train a dog; **Sie werden sich noch daran ~ müssen, dass ...** you'll have to get used to the fact that ...; **an jdn/etw gewöhnt sein, jdn/etw gewöhnt sein** (inf) to be used to sb/sth; **daran gewöhnt sein, etw zu tun** to be used to doing sth; **das**

bin ich gewöhnt I'm used to it

2 VR sich an jdn/etw ~ to get used to sb/sth; **sich daran ~, etw zu tun** to get used to doing sth

Gewohnheit [gə'voːnhait] F -, -en habit; **aus (lauter) ~** from (sheer) force of habit; **die ~ haben, etw zu tun** to have a habit of doing sth; **das ist ihr zur ~ geworden** it's become a habit with her; **sich** (dat) **etw zur ~ machen** to make a habit of sth

Gewohnheits-: gewohnheitsgemäß, gewohnheitsmäßig **1** ADJ habitual **2** ATTR (= ohne nachzudenken) automatically; **Gewohnheitsmensch** M creature of habit; **Gewohnheitssache** F question of habit; **Gewohnheitsverbrecher(in)** M(F) habitual criminal

gewöhnlich [gə'voːnlıç] **1** ADJ **(a)** (= allgemein, üblich) usual; (= normal) normal; (= durchschnittlich) ordinary; (= alltäglich) everyday; **ein ~er Sterblicher** an ordinary mortal **(b)** (pej: = ordinär) common **2** ADV normally; **wie ~** as usual; **sie zieht sich immer so ~ an** she always wears such plain clothes

gewohnt [gə'voːnt] ADJ usual; **etw ~ sein** to be used to sth

Gewöhnung [gə'vøːnʊŋ] F, NO PL (= das Sichgewöhnen) habituation (an +acc to); (= das Angewöhnen) training (an +acc in); (= Sucht) habit, addiction; **die ~ an den Kindergarten kann bei einigen Kindern ziemlich lange dauern** it can take a fairly long time for some children to get used to kindergarten

Gewölbe [gə'vœlbə] NT -s, - vault

gewölbt [gə'vœlpt] ADJ Stirn domed; Himmel, Decke, Dach vaulted; siehe auch **wölben**

gewollt [gə'vɔlt] ADJ **(a)** (= gekünstelt) forced **(b)** (= erwünscht) desired; siehe auch **wollen**[2]

gewonnen PTP von **gewinnen**

geworben PTP von **werben**

geworden PTP von **werden**

geworfen PTP von **werfen**

gewrungen PTP von **wringen**

Gewühl [gə'vyːl] NT -(e)s, NO PL **(a)** (pej: = das Wühlen) (in Kisten, Schubladen etc) rummaging around; (im Schlamm etc) wallowing about **(b)** (= Gedränge) crowd, throng; (= Verkehrsgewühl) chaos, snarl-up (Brit inf)

gewunden [gə'vʊndn] **1** PTP von **winden**[1] **2** ADJ Weg, Fluss etc winding; Erklärung tortuous

gewunken (dial) PTP von **winken**

Gewürz [gə'vʏrts] NT -es, -e spice; (= Kräutersorte) herb; (= Pfeffer, Salz) condiment

Gewürz-: Gewürzbord NT spice rack; **Gewürzgurke** F pickled gherkin; **Gewürzkraut** NT potherb; **Gewürzmischung** F mixed herbs pl; (= Gewürzsalz) herbal salt; **Gewürznelke** F clove; **Gewürzpaprika** M paprika; **Gewürzregal** NT spice rack; **Gewürzständer** M cruet (set)

gewusst PTP von **wissen**

Geysir ['gaizır] M -s, -e geyser

gez. ABBR von **gezeichnet**

gezackt [gə'tsakt] ADJ Fels jagged; Hahnenkamm toothed; Blatt serrated; siehe auch **zacken**

gezahnt [gə'tsaːnt], **gezähnt** [gə'tsɛːnt] ADJ (auch Bot) serrated; (Tech) cogged; Briefmarke perforated

Gezappel [gə'tsapl] NT -s, NO PL (inf) wriggling

gezeichnet [gə'tsaiçnət] ADJ marked; **vom Tode ~ sein, ein vom Tode Gezeichneter sein** to have the mark of death on one; **sein Gesicht war von Krankheit ~** one could see from his face how ill he was; siehe auch **zeichnen**

Gezeiten [gə'tsaitn] PL tides pl

Gezeiten-: Gezeitenkraftwerk NT tidal power plant; **Gezeitenstrom** M tidal current; **Gezeitentafel** F table of (the) tides; **Gezeitenwechsel** M turn of the tide

Gezerre [gə'tsɛrə] NT -s, NO PL tugging

Gezeter [gə'tseːtɐ] NT -s, NO PL (inf) (lit) nagging; (fig) clamour (Brit), clamor (US)

gezielt [gə'tsiːlt] **1** ADJ purposeful; Schuss well-aimed; Frage, Maßnahme, Forschung etc specific; Werbung selective; Hilfe well-directed; Indiskretion deliberate **2** ADV vorgehen, ansetzen directly; forschen, planen, helfen specifically; werben selectively; **~ schießen** to shoot to kill; **er hat sehr ~ gefragt** he asked very specific questions; siehe auch **zielen**

geziemend ADJ proper

geziert [gə'tsiːɐt] **1** ADJ affected **2** ADV affectedly; siehe auch **zieren**

gezogen PTP von **ziehen**

Gezwitscher [gə'tsvɪtʃɐ] NT -s, NO PL chirruping

gezwungen [gə'tsvʊŋən] **1** PTP von **zwingen** **2** ADJ (= nicht entspannt) forced; Atmosphäre strained; Stil, Benehmen stiff **3** ADV stiffly; **~ lachen** to give a forced or strained laugh; **~ wirken** to seem strained

gezwungenermaßen [gə'tsvʊŋənɐ'maːsn] ADV of necessity; **etw ~ tun** to be forced to do sth

ggf. ABBR von **gegebenenfalls**

Ghana ['gaːna] NT -s Ghana

ghanaisch ['gaːnaiʃ] ADJ Ghanaian

Ghetto ['geto] NT -s, -s ghetto

Ghostwriter ['goːstraitɐ] M -s, -, **Ghostwriterin** [-ərın] F -, -nen ghostwriter; **er ist der ~ des Premiers** he ghosts for the PM

gibt [giːpt] 3. PERS SING PRES von **geben**

Gicht [gıçt] F -, -en, NO PL (Med, Bot) gout

Giebel ['giːbl] M -s, - gable

Giebel-: Giebeldach NT gabled roof; **Giebelseite** F gable end; **Giebelzimmer** NT attic room

Gier [giːɐ] F -, NO PL greed (nach for)

gierig ['giːrıç] **1** ADJ greedy; (nach Geld) avaricious; (= lüstern) lustful; **~ nach etw sein** to be greedy for sth; (sexuell) to lust for sth **2** ADV greedily

Gießbach M (mountain) torrent

gießen ['giːsn], pret **goss** [gɔs], ptp **gegossen** [gə'gɔsn] **1** VT **(a)** Flüssigkeit to pour; (= verschütten) to spill; Pflanzen, Garten etc to water; **gieß das Glas nicht so voll!** don't fill the glass so full! **(b)** Glas to found (zu in/into); Metall auch to cast (zu in/to) **2** VI IMPERS to pour; **es gießt in Strömen** or **wie aus Eimern** it's pouring down

Gießerei [giːsə'rai] F -, -en **(a)** NO PL (= Gießen) casting, founding **(b)** (= Werkstatt) foundry

Gieß-: Gießform F mould (Brit), mold (US); **Gießkanne** F watering can; **Gießkannenprinzip** NT (inf) principle of indiscriminate all-round (Brit) or all-around (US) distribution

Gift [gıft] NT -(e)s, -e (lit, fig) poison; (= Bakteriengift) toxin; (= Schlangengift, fig: = Bosheit) venom; **das ist (wie) ~ für ihn** (inf) that is very bad for him; **darauf kannst du ~ nehmen** (inf) you can bet your life on that (inf); **sein ~ verspritzen** to be venomous; **~ und Galle spucken** (inf) or **speien** to be fuming

Vorsicht! Gift wird nicht mit dem englischen Wort gift übersetzt.

giften ['gıftn] VI (inf) to be nasty (gegen about)

Gift-: Giftfracht F, NO PL toxic cargo; **giftfrei** ADJ non-toxic; **Giftgas** NT poison gas; **giftgrün** ADJ bilious green

giftig ['gıftıç] **1** ADJ **(a)** (= Gift enthaltend) poisonous; Stoff, Chemikalien etc auch toxic **(b)** (fig: = boshaft, hasserfüllt) venomous; (= zornig) vitriolic **(c)** (= grell) bilious **2** ADV **(a)** (= böse) venomously **(b)** (= grell) **etw ist ~ grün/gelb** sth is a bilious green/yellow

Giftigkeit F, NO PL **(a)** poisonous nature; (von Stoff, Chemikalien etc auch) toxicity **(b)** (fig) (= Boshaftigkeit) venom; (= Zornigkeit) vitriol

Gift-: Giftküche F devil's workshop; **Giftmord** M poisoning; **Giftmörder(in)** M(F) poisoner; **Giftmüll** M toxic waste; **Giftpilz** M poisonous toadstool; **Giftschlange** F poisonous snake; **Giftschrank** M poison cabinet; **Giftstoff** M poisonous substance; **Giftzahn** M fang; **Giftzwerg** M (inf) spiteful little devil (inf)

Gigabyte ['giga-] NT (Comput) gigabyte

Gigant [gi'gant] M -en, -en, **Gigantin** [-'gantın] F -, -en giant; (Myth) Titan

gigantisch [gi'gantıʃ] ADJ gigantic

Gigantomanie [gigantoma'niː] F, NO PL (geh) love of things big

Gigawatt ['giga-] NT (Elec) gigawatt

Gigerl ['giːgɐl] M or NT -s, -(n) (Aus inf) dandy

Gigolo ['ʒiːgolo, 'ʒigolo] M -s, -s gigolo

Gilde ['gıldə] F -, -n guild

Gildehaus NT guildhall

Gilet [ʒi'leː] NT -s, -s (Aus, Sw) waistcoat (Brit), vest (US)

gilt [gɪlt] 3. PERS SING PRES *von* **gelten**

Gimpel ['gɪmpl] M **-s, -** (*Orn*) bullfinch

Gin [dʒɪn] M **-s, -s** gin; **~ Tonic** gin and tonic

ging PRET *von* **gehen**

Ginseng ['gɪnzɛŋ, 'ʒɪnzɛŋ] M **-s, -s** (*Bot*) ginseng

Ginster ['gɪnstɐ] M **-s, -** (*Bot*) broom; (= *Stechginster*) gorse

Gipfel ['gɪpfl] M **-s, -** (**a**) (= *Bergspitze*) peak; (= *höchster Punkt eines Berges*) summit (**b**) (*fig*: = *Höhepunkt*) height; (*der Vollkommenheit*) epitome; **das ist der ~!** (*inf*) that's the limit (**c**) (= *~konferenz*) summit (**d**) (*Sw*: = *Croissant*) croissant

Gipfel-: Gipfelgespräch NT (*Pol*) summit talks *pl*; **Gipfelkonferenz** F (*Pol*) summit conference; **Gipfelkreuz** NT cross on the summit of a/the mountain

gipfeln ['gɪpfln] VI to culminate (*in +dat* in)

Gipfel-: Gipfelpunkt M (*lit*) zenith; (*fig*) high point; **Gipfeltreffen** NT (*Pol*) summit (meeting)

Gips [gɪps] M **-es, -e** (**a**) plaster; (= *gebrannter ~*) (*Art*) plaster (of Paris); (*Chem*) gypsum (**b**) (= *~verband*) plaster

Gips- IN CPDS plaster; **Gipsabdruck** M, **Gipsabguss** M plaster cast; **Gipsbein** NT (*inf*) leg in a cast

gipsen ['gɪpsn] VT to plaster; *Arm, Bein* to put in a cast

Gipser ['gɪpsɐ] M **-s, -**, **Gipserin** [-ərɪn] F **-, -nen** plasterer

gipsern ['gɪpsɐn] ADJ ATTR plaster

Gips-: Gipsfigur F plaster (of Paris) figure; **Gipsverband** M (*Med*) plaster cast

Giraffe [gi'rafə] F **-, -n** giraffe

Girant [ʒi'rant] M **-en, -en**, **Girantin** [-'rantɪn] F **-, -nen** endorser, indorser

Girat [ʒi'raːt] M **-en, -en**, **Giratin** [-'raːtɪn] F **-, -nen** endorsee, indorsee

Giri ['ʒiːri] (*Aus*) PL *von* **Giro**

Girlande [gɪr'landə] F **-, -n** garland (*aus* of)

Girlie ['gøːɐli, 'gœrli] NT **-s, -s** (*inf*) girlie (*inf*)

Girlitz ['gɪrlɪts] M **-es, -e** (*Orn*) serin (finch)

Giro ['ʒiːro] NT **-s, -s** *or* (*Aus*) **Giri** ['ʒiːri] (*Fin*) (bank) giro; (= *Indossament*) endorsement; **durch ~** by giro

Giro-: Girokonto NT current account; **Giroverkehr** M giro system; (= *Girogeschäft*) giro transfer (business); **Girozentrale** F clearing house

gis [gɪs] NT **-, -**, **Gis** NT **-, -** (*Mus*) G sharp

Gischt [gɪʃt] M **-(e)s, -e** *or* f **-, -en** spray

Gitarre [gi'tarə] F **-, -n** guitar

Gitarrist [gita'rɪst] M **-en, -en**, **Gitarristin** [-'rɪstɪn] F **-, -nen** guitarist

Gitter ['gɪtɐ] NT **-s, -** bars *pl*; (*engstäbig, vor Türen, Schaufenstern*) grille; (*in Fußboden, Straßendecke*) grid, grating; (*für Gewächse etc*) lattice, trellis; (= *feines Drahtgitter*) (wire-)mesh; (*Phys, Chem*: = *Kristallgitter*) lattice; (*Elec, Geog*) grid; **hinter ~n** (*fig inf*) behind bars

Gitter-: Gitterbett NT cot (*Brit*), crib (*US*); **Gitterelektrode** F (*Elec*) grid (electrode); **Gitterfenster** NT barred window; **Gitternetz** NT (*Geog*) grid; **Gitterrost** M grid, grating; **Gitterstab** M bar

Gk F **-**, NO PL ABBR *von* **Gemeinschaftskunde** (*Sch inf*) social studies *pl*

Glace ['glaːsə] F **-, -n** (*Sw*) ice (cream)

Glacéhandschuh M, **Glacéehandschuh** M kid glove; **jdn mit ~en anfassen** (*fig*) to handle sb with kid gloves

Glacéleder NT, **Glacéeleder** NT glacé leather

Gladiator [gla'diaːtoːɐ] M **-s, Gladiatoren** [-'toːrən] gladiator

Gladiole [gla'dioːlə] F **-, -n** (*Bot*) gladiolus

Glamour ['glɛmɐ] M *or* NT **-s**, NO PL (*Press sl*) glamour (*Brit*), glamor (*US*)

glamourös [glamu'røːs] ADJ glamorous

Glanz [glants] M **-es**, NO PL gleam; (= *Funkeln*) sparkle, glitter; (*von Augen*) sparkle; (*von Haaren, Seide, Perlen*) sheen; (*von Farbe*) gloss; (*fig*) (*der Schönheit, Jugend*) radiance; (*von Ruhm, Erfolg*) glory; (= *Gepränge, Pracht*) splendour (*Brit*), splendor (*US*); **mit ~ und Gloria** (*iro inf*) in grand style; **eine Prüfung mit ~ bestehen** (*inf*) to pass an exam with flying colours (*Brit*) *or* colors (*US*)

Glanzabzug M (*Phot*) glossy print

glänzen ['glɛntsn] VI (*lit, fig*) to shine; (= *glitzern*) to glisten; (= *funkeln*) to sparkle; (*Hosenboden, Ellbogen, Nase*) to be shiny; **vor jdm ~ wollen** to want to shine in front of sb

glänzend ■ ADJ shining; (= *strahlend*) radiant; (= *blendend*) dazzling; (= *glitzernd*) glistening; (= *funkelnd*) sparkling, glittering; *Papier* glossy, shiny; *Stoff, Nase, Hosenboden, Ellbogen* shiny; (*fig*) brilliant; *Aussehen, Fest* dazzling; (= *erstklassig*) marvellous (*Brit*), marvelous (*US*); **~ in Form** (*inf*) in splendid form ② ADV (= *sehr gut*) brilliantly; **wir haben uns ~ amüsiert** we had a great time (*inf*); **mir geht es ~** I'm just fine

Glanz-: Glanzlack M gloss (paint); **Glanzleistung** F brilliant achievement; **eine wissenschaftliche ~** a brilliant scientific achievement; **Glanzlicht** NT (*Art, fig*) highlight; **glanzlos** ADJ (*lit, fig*) dull; *Lack, Oberfläche* matt; **Glanzpapier** NT glossy paper; **Glanzstück** NT pièce de résistance; **glanzvoll** ADJ (*fig*) brilliant; (= *prachtvoll*) glittering; **Glanzzeit** F heyday; **seine ~ ist vorüber** he has had his day

Glarus ['glaːros] NT - Glarus

Glas [glaːs] NT **-es, ⸚er** ['glɛːzə] *or* (*als Maßangabe*) **-** (= *Stoff, Gefäß*) glass; (= *Konservenglas*) jar; **buntes** *or* **farbiges** *or* **gefärbtes ~** coloured (*Brit*) *or* colored (*US*) glass; (*von Fenstern*) stained glass; **„Vorsicht ~!"** "glass – handle with care"; **ein ~ Milch** a glass of milk; **zu tief ins ~ gucken** (*inf*) *or* **schauen** (*inf*), **ein ~ über den Durst trinken** (*inf*) to have one too many; **unter ~** behind glass; (*Gewächs*) under glass (**b**) (= *Brillenglas*) lens *sing*

Glas- IN CPDS glass; **Glasballon** M carboy; **Glasbaustein** M glass block; **Glasbläser(in)** M(F) glass-blower; **Glasbläserei** [-blɛːzə'rai] F **-, -en** (**a**) NO PL (= *Handwerk*) glass-blowing (**b**) (= *Werkstatt*) glassworks *sing or pl*

Gläschen ['glɛːsçən] NT **-s, -** DIM *von* **Glas** (= *Getränk*) little drink; **darauf müssen wir ein ~ trinken** we must drink to that

Glascontainer M bottle bank

Glaser ['glaːzɐ] M **-s, -**, **Glaserin** [-ərɪn] F **-, -nen** glazier

Glaserei [glaːzə'rai] F **-, -en** (**a**) NO PL (= *Handwerk*) glazing (**b**) (= *Werkstatt*) glazier's workshop

gläsern ['glɛːzɐn] ADJ glass; (*fig*: = *durchschaubar*) transparent; *Verwaltung* open; **der ~e Bürger** the citizen under the eye of Big Brother

Glasfabrik F glassworks *sing or pl*

Glasfaser F fibreglass (*Brit*), fiberglass (*US*)

Glasfaser-: Glasfaserkabel NT optical fibre (*Brit*) *or* fiber (*US*) cable; **glasfaserverstärkt** [-fɛɐʃtɛrkt] ADJ fibreglass-reinforced (*Brit*), fiberglass-reinforced (*US*)

Glas-: Glasfiber F glass fibre (*Brit*) *or* fiber (*US*); **Glasfiberstab** M (*Sport*) glass fibre (*Brit*) *or* fiber (*US*) pole; **Glasgeschirr** NT glassware; **Glasglocke** F glass cover *or* dome; **Glashaus** NT greenhouse; (*in botanischen Gärten etc*) glasshouse; **wer (selbst) im ~ sitzt, soll nicht mit Steinen werfen** (*Prov*) people who live in glass houses shouldn't throw stones (*Prov*)

glasieren [gla'ziːrən], *ptp* **glasiert** VT to glaze; *Kuchen* to ice (*Brit*), to frost (*esp US*)

glasig ['glaːzɪç] ADJ *Blick* glassy; (*Cook*) *Kartoffeln* waxy; *Speck, Zwiebeln* transparent

Glas-: glasklar ADJ (*lit*) clear as glass; (*fig*) crystal-clear; **Glaskugel** F glass ball; (= *Murmel*) marble; **Glasmalerei** F glass painting; **Glasnudel** F fine Chinese noodle; **Glasperle** F glass bead; **Glasplatte** F glass top; **Glasscheibe** F sheet of glass; (*von Fenster*) pane of glass; **Glasscherbe** F fragment of glass; **~n** broken glass; **Glasschneider** M glass cutter; **Glasschrank** M glass-fronted cupboard; **Glassplitter** M splinter of glass

Glasur [gla'zuːɐ] F **-, -en** glaze; (*Metal*) enamel; (= *Zuckerguss*) icing (*Brit*), frosting (*esp US*)

glatt [glat] ■ ADJ, *comp* **-er** *or* **⸚er** ['glɛtə], *superl* **-este(r, s)** *or* **⸚este(r, s)** ['glɛtəstə] (**a**) (= *eben*) smooth; *Haar* straight; (*Med*) *Bruch* clean; *Stoff* (= *faltenlos*) uncreased; (*Aus*) *Mehl* finely ground (**b**) (= *schlüpfrig*) slippery (**c**) (*fig*) *Landung, Ablauf* smooth; **eine ~e Eins** (*Sch*) a straight A (**d**) ATTR (*inf*: = *klar, eindeutig*) outright; **das kostet ~e 1.000 Euro** it costs a good 1,000 euros (**e**) (*pej*: = *allzu gewandt*) smooth ② ADV, *comp* **-er** *or* **⸚er**, *superl* **am -esten** *or* **⸚esten** (**a**) (= *eben*) bügeln, hobeln, walzen (till) smooth; *polieren* highly; *rühren*

till smooth; ~ **rasieren** to shave; ~ **rasiert** *Mann, Kinn* clean-shaven; *Beine* shaved; ~ **stricken** to knit garter stitch; *siehe auch* **glatt kämmen** *etc*
(b) (= *problemlos*) smoothly; *siehe auch* **glatt gehen**
(c) (*inf:* = *einfach*) completely; *leugnen, ablehnen* flatly; *vergessen* clean; **das ist doch ~ gelogen** that's a downright lie; **die Rechnung ist ~ aufgegangen** the sum works out exactly

Glätte ['glɛtə] F -, NO PL **(a)** (= *Ebenheit*) smoothness; (*von Haar*) sleekness **(b)** (= *Schlüpfrigkeit*) slipperiness **(c)** (= *Politur*) polish **(d)** (*fig*) (*des Auftretens*) smoothness; (*des Stils*) polish

Glatteis NT ice; „**Vorsicht ~!**" "danger, black ice"; **sich auf ~ begeben** (*fig*), **aufs ~ geraten** (*fig*) to skate on thin ice; **jdn aufs ~ führen** (*fig*) to take sb for a ride

Glatteisbildung F formation of black ice

Glätteisen ['glɛt-] NT (*Sw*) iron

Glatteisgefahr F danger of black ice

glätten ['glɛtn] **1** VT (= *glatt machen*) to smooth out; (= *glatt streichen*) *Haar, Tuch* to smooth; (*esp Sw:* = *bügeln*) to iron; (*fig:* = *stilistisch ~*) to polish up **2** VR to smooth out; (*Wellen, Meer, fig*) to subside

glatt-: **glatt gehen** VI IRREG AUX SEIN to go smoothly; **glatt kämmen** VT to comb straight; **glatt machen** VT (= *glatt streichen*) to smooth out; *Haare* to smooth (down); (*mit Kamm*) to comb straight; **glatt schleifen** VT IRREG to rub smooth; *Linsen, Diamanten etc* to grind smooth; **glattstellen** VT SEP (*Fin*) to settle; (*St Ex*) to even up; **eine Position ~** to close a position; **glatt streichen** VT IRREG to smooth out; *Haare* to smooth (down); **glattweg** ['glatvɛk] ADV (*inf*) simply, just like that (*inf*); **das ist ~ erlogen** that's a blatant lie

Glatze ['glatsə] F -, -n **(a)** bald head; **eine ~ bekommen/haben** to go/be bald; **sich** (*dat*) **eine ~ schneiden lassen** to have one's head shaved **(b)** (*inf:* = *Skinhead*) skin (*inf*)

Glatz-: **Glatzkopf** M bald head; (*inf:* = *Mann mit Glatze*) baldie (*inf*); **glatzköpfig** ADJ bald(-headed)

Glaube ['glaubə] M -ns, NO PL faith (*an* +*acc* in); (= *Überzeugung, Meinung*) belief (*an* +*acc* in); **im guten** *or* **in gutem ~n** in good faith; **(bei jdm) ~n finden** to be believed (by sb); **den ~n an jdn/etw verlieren** to lose faith in sb/sth; **jdm ~n schenken** to believe sb; **jdn in dem ~n (be)lassen, dass ...** to let sb believe that ...; **lass ihn bei seinem ~n!** let him keep his illusions

glauben ['glaubn] VTI to believe (*an* +*acc* in); (= *meinen, annehmen, vermuten*) to think; **jdm ~** to believe sb; **das glaube ich dir gerne/nicht** I quite/don't believe you; **ich glaube kein Wort davon** I don't believe a word of it; **jdm (etw) aufs Wort ~** to take sb's word (for sth); **d(a)ran ~ müssen** (*inf:* = *sterben*) to cop it (*Brit inf*), to bite the dust (*US inf*); **das glaubst du doch selbst nicht!** you can't be serious; **wers glaubt, wird selig** (*iro*) a likely story (*iro*); **wer hätte das je geglaubt!** who would have thought it?; **ich glaubte ihn zu kennen, doch ...** I thought I knew him, but ...; **er glaubte sich unbeobachtet** he thought nobody was watching him; **es ist nicht** *or* **kaum zu ~** it's unbelievable; **ich glaube, ja** I think so; **ich glaube, nein** I don't think so

Glauben ['glaubn] M -s, NO PL = **Glaube**

Glaubens-: **Glaubensbekenntnis** NT creed; **Glaubensgemeinschaft** F religious sect; (*christliche auch*) denomination

Glaubersalz ['glaubɐ-] NT (*Chem*) Glauber('s) salt

glaubhaft **1** ADJ credible; (= *einleuchtend*) plausible; **(jdm) etw (überzeugend) ~ machen** to substantiate sth (to sb) **2** ADV credibly

Glaubhaftigkeit ['glauphaftɪçkait] F -, NO PL credibility; (= *Evidenz*) plausibility

gläubig ['glɔybɪç] **1** ADJ *Katholik etc* devout; (= *vertrauensvoll*) trusting **2** ADV ~ **hörten sie meiner Geschichte zu** they listened to and believed my story

Gläubige(r) ['glɔybɪgə] MF DECL AS ADJ believer; **die ~n** the faithful

Gläubiger ['glɔybɪgɐ] M -s, -, **Gläubigerin** ['glɔybɪgərɪn] F -, -nen (*Comm*) creditor

glaubwürdig **1** ADJ *Mensch, Beweise* credible; **~e Quellen** reliable sources **2** ADV credibly; **sich ~ verhalten** to be reliable *or* credible

Glaubwürdigkeit F -, NO PL credibility

Glaukom [glau'ko:m] NT -s, -e (*Med*) glaucoma

gleich [glaiç]	
1 ADJEKTIV	**2** ADVERB

1 ADJEKTIV

(a) (= *identisch, ähnlich*) same; **das gleiche, aber nicht dasselbe Auto** a similar car, but not the same one; **der/die/das gleiche ... wie** the same ... as; **ich fahre den gleichen Wagen wie Sie** I drive the same car as you; **das kommt** *or* **läuft aufs Gleiche hinaus** it amounts to the same thing; **es ist genau das Gleiche** it's exactly the same; **es waren die Gleichen, die ...** it was the same ones who ...; **ihr Männer seid doch alle gleich!** you men are all the same!; **es ist mir (alles** *or* **ganz) gleich** it's all the same to me; **Gleich und Gleich gesellt sich gern** (*Prov*) birds of a feather flock together (*Prov*); **Gleiches mit Gleichem vergelten** to pay sb back in kind; **ganz gleich wer/was** *etc* no matter who/what *etc*
(b) (= *gleichwertig, gleichberechtigt*) equal; **zu gleichen Teilen** in equal parts; **zwei mal zwei (ist) gleich vier** two twos are four; **jdm (an etw** *dat*) **gleich sein** to be sb's equal (in sth); **alle Menschen sind gleich, nur einige sind gleicher** (*hum*) all men are equal, but some are more equal than others

2 ADVERB

(a) (= *ohne Unterschied*) equally; (= *auf gleiche Weise*) alike, the same; **der Lehrer behandelt alle Kinder gleich** the teacher treats all the children equally; **gleich gekleidet** dressed alike; **sie sind gleich groß/alt/schwer** they are the same size/age/weight

◆**gleich bleibend** *Kurs* constant; *Temperatur* (*von Wetter*) steady; (*in Brutkasten etc*) constant; **gleich bleibend sein** to remain the same; (*Temperatur*) (*von Wetter*) to remain steady; (*in Brutkasten etc*) to remain constant; **mehr Urlaub bei gleich bleibendem Gehalt** more holidays (*esp Brit*) *or* vacation (*US*) with the same pay; **gleich bleibend gute Qualität** consistent(ly) good quality

◆**gleich geartet** of the same kind; (= *ähnlich*) similar

◆**gleich gesinnt** *or* **denkend** like-minded

◆**gleich lautend** identical; **gleich lautende Abschrift** duplicate (copy); **gleich lautende Wörter** homophones; (= *gleich buchstabiert*) homonyms
(b) (*räumlich*) right, just; **gleich hinter dem Haus** just behind the house
(c) (*zeitlich*) (= *sofort*) immediately; (= *bald*) in a minute; **ich komme gleich** I'm just coming; **ich komme gleich wieder** I'll be right back; **du kriegst gleich eine Ohrfeige** you'll get a slap in a minute; **es muss nicht gleich sein** there's no hurry; **es ist gleich drei Uhr** it's almost three o'clock; **das mache ich gleich heute** I'll do that today; **gleich zu** *or* **am Anfang** right at the beginning; **gleich danach** straight afterwards; **ich werde ihn gleich morgen besuchen** I'll go and see him tomorrow; **habe ich es nicht gleich gesagt?** what did I tell you?; **das habe ich mir gleich gedacht** I thought that straight away; **warum nicht gleich so?** why didn't you say/do that in the first place?; **na komm schon! – gleich!** come along! – I'm just coming!; **wann machst du das? – gleich!** when are you going to do it? – right away; **gleich als** *or* **nachdem er ...** as soon as he ...; **so wirkt das Bild gleich ganz anders**, the picture has changed completely; **wenn das stimmt, kann ichs ja gleich aufgeben** if that's true I might as well give up right now; **deswegen brauchst du nicht gleich zu weinen** there's no need to start crying because of that; **er ging gleich in die Küche/vor Gericht** he went straight to the kitchen/to court; **sie hat sich gleich zwei Hüte gekauft** she went and bought TWO hats; **bis gleich!** see you later!
(d) (*in Fragesätzen*) again; **wie war doch gleich die Nummer/Ihr Name?** what was the number/your name again?

Gleich-: **gleichaltrig** ADJ (of) the same age; **die beiden sind ~** they are both the same age; **Gleichaltrige** people/children (of) the same age; **gleichartig** **1** ADJ of the same kind (+*dat* as); (= *ähnlich*) similar (+*dat* to) **2** ADV in the same way; similarly; **gleichauf** ['glaiç'lauf] ADV (*esp Sport*) equal; **gleichbedeutend** ADJ synonymous (*mit* with); (= *so gut wie*) tantamount (*mit* to); **Gleichbehandlungsgrundsatz** M principle of equal treatment; **gleichberechtigt** ADJ with equal *or* the same rights; *Partner, Möglichkeiten, Dialog* equal; **~ sein** to have equal rights; **Gleichberechtigung** F equal rights *sing or pl*, equality (+*gen* for); **gleich bleiben** VI IRREG AUX SEIN to stay the same; **sich** (*dat*) **~** (*Mensch*) to stay the same; **das bleibt sich gleich** it doesn't matter; **gleichbleibend** ADJ *siehe* **gleich**

gleichen ['glaiçn], *pret* **glich** [glɪç], *ptp* **geglichen** [gə'glɪçn] VI jdm/einer Sache **~** to be like sb/sth; **sich ~** to be alike; **jdm an Erfahrung/Schönheit ~** to equal sb in experience/beauty

gleichermaßen ['glaiçɐ'maːsn] ADV, **gleicherweise** ['glaiçɐ'vaizə] ADV equally; **~ ... und ...** both ... and ...

Gleich-: **gleichfalls** ADV (= *ebenfalls*) likewise; (= *auch*) also; (= *zur gleichen Zeit*) at the same time; **danke ~!** thank you, (and) the same to you; **gleichfarbig** ADJ (of) the same colour (*Brit*) *or* color (*US*); **gleichförmig** ADJ (= *einheitlich, fig:* = *eintönig*) uniform (*auch Phys*); **Gleichförmigkeit** ['glaiçfœrmɪçkait] F -, NO PL uniformity (*auch Phys*); **gleichgeartet** ADJ *siehe* **gleich**; **gleichgesinnt** ADJ *siehe* **gleich**; **gleichgestellt** ADJ equal (+*dat* to, with), on a par (+*dat* with); **er spricht nur mit Gleichgestellten** he only speaks to his equals; **rechtlich ~** equal in law; *siehe auch* **gleichstellen**

Gleichgewicht NT, NO PL (*lit*) balance, equilibrium (*auch Phys, Chem*); (*fig*) (= *Stabilität*) balance; (= *seelisches ~*) equilibrium; **im ~** (*lit*) balanced, in equilibrium; **das ~ verlieren, aus dem ~ kommen** to lose one's balance *or* equilibrium (*auch fig*); **jdn aus dem ~ bringen** to throw sb off balance; **das ~ zwischen ...** (*dat*) **und ... halten** to maintain a proper balance between ... and ...; **diese Dinge müssen sich** (*dat*) **das ~ halten** (*fig*) these things should balance each other out; **das ~ der Kräfte** the balance of power

Gleichgewichts-: **Gleichgewichtsorgan** NT organ of equilibrium; **Gleichgewichtssinn** M sense of balance; **Gleichgewichtsstörung** F impaired balance

gleichgültig ADJ indifferent (*gegenüber, gegen* to, towards); (= *uninteressiert*) apathetic (*gegenüber, gegen* towards); (= *unwesentlich*) unimportant; **das ist mir ~** it's a matter of (complete) indifference to me; **Politik ist ihm ~** he doesn't care about politics; **~, was er tut** no matter what he does; **es ist mir ~, was er tut** I don't care what he does; **er war ihr nicht ~ geblieben** he had not remained indifferent to him

Gleichgültigkeit F indifference (*gegenüber, gegen* to, towards); (= *Desinteresse*) apathy (*gegenüber, gegen* towards)

Gleichheit F -, **-en** (a) NO PL (= *gleiche Stellung*) equality; (= *Identität*) identity; (= *Übereinstimmung*) correspondence; (*Ind*) parity (b) (= *Ähnlichkeit*) similarity

Gleichheitszeichen NT (*Math*) equals sign

Gleich-: **Gleichklang** M (*fig*) harmony; **gleichkommen** VI SEP IRREG AUX SEIN +DAT (a) (= *die gleiche Leistung etc erreichen*) to equal (*an* +*dat* for, in), to match (*an* +*dat* for, in) (b) (= *gleichbedeutend sein mit*) to amount to; **gleichlautend** ADJ *siehe* **gleich**; **Gleichmacherei** [-maxə'rai] F -, **-en** (*pej*) levelling down (*Brit pej*), leveling down (*US pej*); **gleichmäßig** ❶ ADJ regular; *Proportionen* symmetrical ❷ ADV (a) (= *regelmäßig*) regularly; **er ist immer ~ freundlich** he is always consistently friendly (b) *in gleicher Stärke, Größe, Anzahl* evenly; **die Farbe ~ auftragen** apply the paint evenly; **Gleichmäßigkeit** F regularity; (*von Proportionen*) symmetry; **mit** *or* **in schöner ~** (*iro*) with monotonous regularity; **gleichnamig** [-naːmɪç] ADJ of the same name; (*Math*) with a common denominator; **Brüche ~ machen** to reduce fractions to a common denominator

Gleichnis ['glaiçnɪs] NT -**ses**, -**se** (*Liter*) simile; (= *Allegorie*) allegory; (*Bibl*) parable

Gleich-: **gleichrangig** [-ranɪç] ADJ *Beamte etc* equal in rank (*mit* to); *Straßen etc* of the same grade (*mit* as); *Probleme, Regelungen etc* equally important; **Gleichrichter** M (*Elec*) rectifier

gleichsam ['glaiçzaːm] ADV (*geh*) as it were

Gleich-: **gleichschalten** SEP (*Pol, NS: pej*) ❶ VT to force into line ❷ VR to conform; **gleichschenklig** [-ʃeŋklɪç], **gleichschenklig** [-ʃeŋklɪç] ADJ *Dreieck* isosceles; **Gleichschritt** M, NO PL (*Mil*) marching in step; **im ~** (*lit, fig*) in step; **im ~, marsch!** forward march!; **gleichsehen** VI SEP IRREG jdm/einer Sache **~** to look like sb/sth; **gleichseitig** [-zaitɪç] ADJ *Dreieck* equilateral; **gleichsetzen** VT SEP (= *als dasselbe ansehen*) to equate (*mit* with); (= *als gleichwertig ansehen*) to treat as

equivalent (*mit* to); **Gleichstand** M, NO PL (a) (*Sport*) **den ~ erzielen** to draw level; **beim ~ von 1:1** with the scores level (*Brit*) *or* equal at 1 all (b) (*Pol*) equal stage of development; **gleichstellen** VT SEP (a) (*rechtlich etc*) to treat as equal; *siehe auch* **gleichgestellt** (b) = **gleichsetzen**; **Gleichstellung** F (*rechtlich etc*) equality (+*gen* of, for), equal status (+*gen* of, for); **Gleichstellungsbeauftragte(r)** MF DECL AS ADJ equal rights representative; **Gleichstrom** M (*Elec*) direct current, DC; **gleichtun** VT IMPERS SEP IRREG **es jdm ~** to equal sb

Gleichung ['glaiçʊŋ] F -, **-en** equation

Gleich-: **gleichwertig** [-veːrtɪç] ADJ of the same value; *Leistung, Qualität* equal (+*dat* to); *Gegner* evenly matched; *Partner* equal; (*Chem*) equivalent; **Gleichwertigkeit** F, NO PL equal value; (*von Leistung, Qualität*) equality; (*Chem*) equivalence; **gleichwinkelig, gleichwinklig** ADJ (*Geometrie*) with (all) angles equal; **gleichzeitig** ❶ ADJ simultaneous ❷ ADV at the same time; **Gleichzeitigkeit** ['glaiçzaitɪçkait] F -, NO PL simultaneity

Gleis [glais] NT -**es**, -**e** [-zə] (*Rail*) line, track, rails *pl*; (= *einzelne Schiene*) rail; (= *Bahnsteig*) platform; (*fig*) rut; **~ 6** platform *or* track (*US*) 6; **„Überschreiten der ~e verboten"** "passengers must not cross the line (*Brit*) *or* tracks"; **aus dem ~ kommen** (*fig*) to go off the rails (*Brit inf*), to get off the track (*US inf*); **wieder im richtigen ~ sein** (*fig*) to be back on track

Gleis-: **Gleisanlagen** PL railway (*Brit*) *or* railroad (*US*) lines *pl*; **Gleisarbeiten** PL line *or* track repairs *pl*; **Gleisbau** M, NO PL railway (*Brit*) *or* railroad (*US*) construction; **Gleisbaustelle** F place where work is being done on the line; **überall auf der Strecke waren ~n** work was being done all along the line

-gleisig [glaizɪç] ADJ SUF (*lit, fig*) -track; **eingleisig** single-track; **mehrgleisig** multi-track; **eine eingleisige Denkweise** a narrow-minded way of thinking

gleiten ['glaitn], *pret* **glitt** [glɪt], *ptp* **geglitten** [gə'glɪtn] VI (a) AUX SEIN (*Vogel, Flugzeug, Tänzer, Boot, Skier, Schlange*) to glide; (*Blick*) to pass; (*Hand*) to slide; **ein Lächeln glitt über ihr Gesicht** a smile flickered across her face; **sein Auge über etw** (*acc*) **~ lassen** to cast an eye over sth; **die Finger über etw** (*acc*) **~ lassen** to slide one's fingers over *or* across sth (b) AUX SEIN (= *rutschen*) to slide; (*Auto*) to skid; (= *entgleiten: Gegenstand*) to slip; (*geh:* = *ausrutschen*) to slip; **zu Boden ~** to slip to the ground; (*auf den Fußboden*) to slip to the floor; **ins Gleiten kommen** to start to slide *or* slip (c) (*Ind inf:* = *gleitende Arbeitszeit haben*) to have flex(i)time

gleitend ADJ **~e Löhne** *or* **Lohnskala** sliding wage scale; **~e Arbeitszeit** flex(i)time; **~er Übergang** gradual transition

Gleit-: **Gleitflug** M glide; **im ~ niedergehen** to glide down; **Gleitflugzeug** NT glider; **Gleitklausel** F (*Comm*) escalator clause; **Gleitkomma** NT floating point; **Gleitmittel** NT (*Med*) lubricant; **Gleitschirm** M paraglider; **Gleitschirmfliegen** NT -**s**, NO PL paragliding; **Gleitsichtbrille** F varifocals *pl*; **Gleitzeit** F flex(i)time

Gletscher ['glɛtʃɐ] M -**s**, - glacier

Gletscher-: **gletscherartig** ADJ glacial; **Gletscherbrand** M glacial sunburn; **Gletscherbrille** F sunglasses *pl*; **Gletscherforschung** F glaciology; **Gletscherkunde** F glaciology; **Gletscherskifahren** NT glacier skiing; **Gletscherspalte** F crevasse

Glibber ['glɪbɐ] M -**s**, NO PL (*inf*) slime

glibberig ['glɪbərɪç] ADJ (*inf*) slimy

glich PRET *von* **gleichen**

Glied [gliːt] NT -(**e**)**s**, -**er** [-də] (a) (= *Körperteil*) limb; (= *Fingerglied, Zehenglied*) joint; **an allen ~ern zittern** to be shaking all over; **der Schreck fuhr ihm in alle ~er** the shock made him shake all over; **der Schreck sitzt** *or* **steckt ihr noch in den ~ern** she is still shaking with (*Brit*) *or* from (*esp US*) the shock (b) (= *Penis*) penis, organ (c) (= *Kettenglied, fig*) link (d) (= *Teil*) section (e) (= *Mitglied*) member; (*Mil etc*) rank; (*Bibl*) generation; (*Math*) term

gliedern ['gliːdɐn] ❶ VT (a) (= *ordnen*) to structure (b) (= *unterteilen*) to (sub)divide (*in* +*acc* into); *siehe auch* **gegliedert** ❷ VR (= *zerfallen in*) **sich ~ in** (+*acc*) to (sub)divide into; (= *bestehen aus*) to consist of

Glieder-: Gliederreißen NT **-s**, NO PL, **Gliederschmerz** M rheumatic pains pl; **Gliedersatz** M (Ling) period; **Gliederschwere** F heaviness in one's limbs

Gliederung ['gli:dərʊŋ] F **-, -en (a)** (= das Gliedern) structuring; (= das Unterteilen) subdivision **(b)** (= Aufbau) structure; (= Unterteilung, von Organisation) subdivision

Glied-: Gliedmaßen PL limbs pl; **Gliedsatz** M (Ling) subordinate clause; **Gliedstaat** M member or constituent state

glimmen ['glɪmən], pret **glomm** or (rare) **glimmte** [glɔm, 'glɪmtə], ptp **geglommen** or (rare) **geglimmt** [gə'glɔmən, gə'glɪmt] VI to glow

Glimmer ['glɪmɐ] M **-s, -** (Min) mica

glimmern ['glɪmɐn] VI to glimmer

glimpflich ['glɪmpflɪç] **1** ADJ (= mild) mild, light; Unfall minor; Verletzungen slight; Folgen negligible; **wegen des ~en Ausgangs des Unfalls** because the accident wasn't too serious; **einen ~en Ausgang nehmen** to pass off without serious consequences **2** ADV bestrafen mildly; **~ davonkommen** to get off lightly; **mit jdm ~ umgehen** or **verfahren** to treat sb leniently; mit Gefangenem to treat sb humanely; **~ abgehen** or **ablaufen** or **verlaufen** to pass (off) without serious consequences; **die Sache ist für sie ~ abgegangen** or **verlaufen** they got off lightly

glitschig ['glɪtʃɪç] ADJ (inf) slippy (inf)

glitt PRET von **gleiten**

Glitzer- ['glɪtsɐ] IN CPDS glitzy (inf)

glitzern ['glɪtsɐn] VI to glitter; (Stern auch) to twinkle

global [glo'ba:l] **1** ADJ **(a)** (= weltweit) global; **~e Erwärmung** global warming **(b)** (= ungefähr, pauschal) general **2** ADV **(a)** (= weltweit) world-wide; **~ verbreitet** global **(b)** (= pauschal) jdm etw **~ erläutern** to give sb a general idea of sth; **~ gerechnet** in round figures

globalisieren [globali'zi:rən], ptp **globalisiert** VT to globalize

Globalisierung F **-**, NO PL globalization

Global-: Globalrendite F compound yield; **Globalzession** F blanket assignment

Globen PL von **Globus**

Globetrotter ['glo:bətrɔtɐ, 'glo:ptrɔtɐ] M **-s, -**, **Globetrotterin** [-ərɪn] F **-, -nen** globetrotter

Globus ['glo:bʊs] M **-** or **-ses**, **Globen** or **-se** globe

Glöckchen ['glœkçən] NT **-s, -** (little) bell

Glocke ['glɔkə] F **-, -n (a)** (auch Blüte) bell; (= Käseglocke etc) cover; (= Taucherglocke) (diving) bell; **nach den ~n von Big Ben** after the chimes from Big Ben; **etw an die große ~ hängen** (inf) to shout sth from the rooftops; **über der Stadt wölbte sich eine dichte ~ von Rauch** a thick pall of smoke hung over the city **(b)** (sl: = Hoden) **Glocken** PL balls pl

Glocken-: Glockenblume F bellflower, campanula; **glockenförmig** ADJ bell-shaped; **Glockengeläut** NT, **Glockengeläute** NT (peal of) bells pl; **Glockengießerei** F bellfoundry; **glockenhell** ADJ (geh) bell-like; Stimme auch as clear as a bell; **Glockenklang** M (peal of) bells pl; **Glockenläuten** NT **-s**, NO PL (peal of) bells pl; **Glockenrock** M flared skirt; **Glockenschlag** M stroke (of a/the bell); (von Uhr auch) chime; **es ist mit dem ~ 6 Uhr** on the stroke it will be 6 o'clock; **auf den** or **mit dem ~** on the stroke of eight/nine etc; (= genau pünktlich) on the dot; **Glockenspiel** NT (in Turm) carillon; (automatisch auch) chimes pl; (= Instrument) glockenspiel; **Glockenturm** M belfry; **Glockenzeichen** NT ring of a/the bell; **auf ein ~ erschien der Butler** a ring on the bell summoned the butler; **Glockenzug** M (= Glockenstrang) bell rope; (= Klingelschnur) bell pull

Glöckner ['glœknɐ] M **-s, -**, **Glöcknerin** [-ərɪn] F **-, -nen** bell-ringer; „**Der ~ von Notre-Dame**" "The Hunchback of Notre Dame"

glomm PRET von **glimmen**

glorifizieren [glorifi'tsi:rən], ptp **glorifiziert** VT to glorify

glorios [glo'rio:s] ADJ (oft iro) glorious

glorreich ['glo:raɪç] **1** ADJ glorious **2** ADV zurückkehren, herrschen victoriously; **~ siegen** to have a glorious victory; **seine Laufbahn ~ beenden** to bring one's career to a glorious conclusion

Gloss [glɔs] NT **-, -** gloss

Glossar [glɔ'sa:ɐ] NT **-s, -e** glossary

Glotz-: Glotzauge NT **(a)** (usu pl: inf) goggle eye (inf); **~n machen** to gawp **(b)** (Med) exophthalmia (spec); **glotzäugig** [-ɔʏgɪç] ADJ, ADV (inf) goggle-eyed (inf)

Glotze ['glɔtsə] F **-, -n** (inf) **(a)** (= Fernseher) gogglebox (Brit inf), boob tube (US inf) **(b)** (= Bildschirm) screen

glotzen ['glɔtsn] VI (pej inf) to gawp (auf +acc at)

Glubschauge ['glʊpʃ-] NT (inf) = **Glotzauge (a)**

Glück [glʏk] NT **-(e)s**, (rare) **-e (a)** luck; **ein seltenes ~** a funny stroke of luck; **~/kein ~ haben** to be lucky/unlucky; **~ gehabt!** that was lucky; **auf gut ~** (aufs Geratewohl) on the off chance; (= unvorbereitet) trusting to luck; (= wahllos) at random; **~!** how lucky!; **ein ~, dass ...** it is/was lucky that ...; **es ist ein wahres ~, dass ...** it's really lucky that ...; **du hast ~ im Unglück gehabt** it could have been a great deal worse (for you); **viel ~ (bei ...)!** good luck (with ...)!; **~ bei Frauen haben** to be successful with women; **jdm ~ für etw wünschen** to wish sb luck for sth; **jdm ~ wünschen zu ...** to congratulate sb on ...; **jdm zum neuen Jahr/zum Geburtstag ~ wünschen** to wish sb (a) Happy New Year/happy birthday; **zum ~** luckily; **das ist dein ~!** that's lucky for you!; **mehr ~ als Verstand haben** to have more luck than brains; **sie weiß noch nichts von ihrem ~** (iro) she doesn't know anything about it yet; **damit wirst du bei ihr kein ~ haben** that won't work with her; **~ bringend** lucky; **sein ~ machen** to make one's fortune; **sein ~ probieren** or **versuchen** to try one's luck; **er kann von ~ reden** or **sagen, dass ...** he can count himself lucky that ...; **~ muss der Mensch haben** (inf) my/your etc luck is in; **das hat mir gerade noch zu meinem ~ gefehlt!** (iro) that was all I wanted; **man kann niemanden zu seinem ~ zwingen** (prov) you can lead a horse to water but you can't make him drink (Prov); **jeder ist seines ~es Schmied** (Prov) life is what you make it (prov) **(b)** (= Freude) happiness; **eheliches ~** marital bliss; **er ist ihr ganzes ~** he is her whole life; **~ und Glas, wie leicht bricht das!** (Prov) happiness is such a fragile thing

Glucke ['glʊkə] F **-, -n** (= Bruthenne) broody hen; (mit Jungen) mother hen; **wie eine ~** like a mother hen

glücken ['glʏkn] VI AUX SEIN to be a success; **ihm glückt alles/nichts** everything/nothing he does is a success; **geglückt** Feier, Experiment, Aktion successful; Wahl lucky; Überraschung real; **dieses Bild/die Torte ist dir gut geglückt** your picture/cake has turned out very well; **endlich ist es ihm geglückt** at last he managed it; **es wollte nicht ~** it wouldn't go right

gluckern ['glʊkɐn] VI to glug

glücklich ['glʏklɪç] **1** ADJ **(a)** (= erfolgreich, vom Glück begünstigt) lucky; (= vorteilhaft, treffend, erfreulich) happy; **~e Reise!** bon voyage!; **er kann sich ~ schätzen(, dass ...)** he can count himself lucky (that ...); **wer ist der/die Glückliche?** who is the lucky man/woman/girl etc? **(b)** (= froh, selig) happy; **ein ~es Ende, ein ~er Ausgang** a happy ending; **~ machen** to bring happiness; **jdn ~ machen** to make sb happy **2** ADV **(a)** (= mit Glück) by or through luck; (= vorteilhaft, treffend, erfreulich) happily; **~ zurückkommen** (= in Sicherheit) to come back safely **(b)** (= froh, selig) happily

glücklicherweise [glʏklɪçɐ'vaɪzə] ADV luckily

glücklos ADJ hapless

Glücks-: Glücksbringer [-brɪŋɐ] M **-s, -** lucky charm; **Glücksfall** M stroke of luck; **durch einen ~** by a lucky chance; **Glücksgefühl** NT feeling of happiness; **Glückskind** NT child of Fortune; **Glücksklee** M four-leaf(ed) clover; **Glückspfennig** M lucky penny, (shiny) pfennig piece supposed to bring luck; **Glückspilz** M lucky devil (inf); **Glückssache** F das ist ~ it's a matter of luck; **ich hab gedacht ... — Denken ist ~** (inf) I thought ... — you thought?; **Glücksschwein** NT, **Glücksschweinchen** [-fvaɪnçən] NT **-s, -** pig as a symbol of good luck; **Glücksspiel** NT game of chance; **Glücksspieler(in)** M(F) gambler; **Glückssträhne** F lucky streak; **eine ~ haben** to be on a lucky streak

glückstrahlend ADJ beaming with happiness

Glücks-: Glückstreffer M stroke of luck; (beim Schießen, Ftbl) fluke (inf); **Glückszahl** F lucky number

Glückwunsch M congratulations pl (zu on); **herzlichen ~!** congratulations; **herzlichen ~ zum Geburtstag!** happy

birthday; **Glückwünsche zur bestandenen Prüfung**
congratulations on passing your examination

Glückwunsch-: Glückwunschkarte F greetings card;
Glückwunschschreiben NT letter of congratulations;
Glückwunschtelegramm NT greetings telegram

Glühbirne F (electric) light bulb

glühen [ˈglyːən] VI to glow; **vor Fieber/Scham ~** to be flushed
with fever/shame

glühend ▪ ADJ glowing; (= heiß ~) Metall red-hot; Hitze
blazing; (fig: = leidenschaftlich) ardent; Hass burning; Wangen
flushed ▪ ADV lieben madly; **~ heiß** scorching; **jdn ~
beneiden** to be consumed by envy for sb; **jdn ~ verehren** to
worship sb

Glüh-: Glühlampe F (form) electric light bulb; **Glühwein** M
mulled wine, glogg (US); **Glühwürmchen** [-vyrmçən] NT glow-
worm; (fliegend) firefly

Glukose [gluˈkoːzə] F -, -n glucose

Glut [gluːt] F -, -en (= glühende Masse, Kohle) embers pl;
(= Tabaksglut) burning ash; (= Hitze) heat

Gluthitze F sweltering heat

Glykol [glyˈkoːl] NT -s, -e glycol

Glyzerin [glytseˈriːn] NT -s, NO PL (Chem) glycerin(e)

Glyzinie [glyˈtsiːniə] F -, -n wisteria

GmbH [geːʔɛmbeːˈhaː] F -, -s ABBR von **Gesellschaft mit
beschränkter Haftung** Ltd

Gnade [ˈgnaːdə] F -, -n (= Barmherzigkeit) mercy; (= heilig
machende ~) grace; (= Gunst) favour (Brit), favor (US);
(= Verzeihung) pardon; **um ~ bitten** to ask for mercy; **jds ~
finden, bei jdm** or **vor jdm** or **vor jds Augen** (dat) **~ finden** to
find favo(u)r with sb or in sb's eyes; **~ vor** or **für Recht
ergehen lassen** to temper justice with mercy; **ohne ~**
without mercy; **~!** mercy!; **die ~ haben, etw zu tun** (iro) to
graciously consent to do sth

Gnaden-: Gnadenbrot NT, NO PL **jdm das ~ geben** to keep sb
in his/her old age; **einem Pferd das ~ geben** to put a horse
out to grass; **Gnadenfrist** F (temporary) reprieve; **eine ~ von
24 Stunden** a 24 hour(s') reprieve, 24 hours' grace;
Gnadengesuch NT plea for clemency; **gnadenlos** ▪ ADJ
merciless; ▪ ADV mercilessly; **Gnadenschuss** M coup de grâce
(by shooting)

gnädig [ˈgnɛːdɪç] ▪ ADJ (= barmherzig) merciful; (= gunstvoll,
herablassend) gracious; Strafe lenient; **~e Frau** (form) madam,
ma'am; **sei doch so ~ und mach mal Platz!** (iro) would you be
so good as to make some room?
▪ ADV (= milde) urteilen leniently; zensieren generously;
(= herablassend) lächeln, nicken graciously; **~ davonkommen** to
get off lightly; **es ~ machen** to be lenient; **machen wirs ~ mit
dem Hausputz** let's take it easy with the cleaning

Gneis [gnais] M -es, -e [-zə] (Geol) gneiss

Gnom [gnoːm] M -en, -en gnome

Gnu [gnuː] NT -s, -s (Zool) gnu

Goal [goːl] NT -s, -s (Aus, Sw: Sport) goal

Goal- [ˈgoːl-] (Aus, Sw): **Goalgetter** [-gɛtɐ] M -s, -, **Goalgetterin**
[-ərɪn] F -, -nen scorer; **Goalkeeper** [-kiːpɐ] M -s, -,
Goalkeeperin [-ərɪn] F -, -nen, **Goalmann** M, pl -männer
goalkeeper

Gobelin [gobəˈlɛ̃ː] M -s, -s tapestry, Gobelin

Gockel [ˈgɔkl] M -s, - (esp S Ger, baby talk) cock; (fig) old goat
(inf)

Goderl [ˈgoːdɐl] NT -s, -n **jdm das ~ kratzen** (Aus inf) to butter
sb up (inf)

Go-go-Girl [ˈgoːgogœrl] NT -s, -s go-go dancer

Gokart [ˈgoːkaːɐt] M -(s), -s go-cart

Golanhöhen PL, **Golan-Höhen** PL Golan Heights pl

Gold [gɔlt] NT -(e)s [-dəs], NO PL (inf (abbr **Au**) (lit, fig) gold; **nicht mit
~ zu bezahlen** or **aufzuwiegen sein** to be worth one's weight
in gold; **er hat ein Herz aus ~** he has a heart of gold; **zehnmal
olympisches ~ holen** to win ten golds in the Olympics; **es ist
nicht alles ~, was glänzt** (Prov) all that glitters is not gold
(Prov)

Gold- IN CPDS gold; (von Farbe, Zool) golden; **Goldader** F vein
of gold; **Goldammer** [-amɐ] F -, -n yellowhammer; **Goldamsel**
F gold(en) oriole; **Goldbarren** M gold ingot; **Goldbarsch** M
(= Rotbarsch) redfish; **Golddeckung** F (Fin)

gold backing; **golddurchwirkt** [-dʊrçvɪrkt] ADJ shot with gold
thread

golden [ˈgɔldn] ▪ ADJ ATTR (lit, fig) golden; (= aus Gold) gold;
~er Humor irrepressible sense of humour (Brit) or humor (US);
~e Worte wise words; **die ~e Mitte** or **den ~en Mittelweg
wählen** to strike a happy medium; **sich** (dat) **eine ~e Nase
verdienen** to make a mint; **~e Hochzeit** golden wedding
(anniversary); **~er Schnitt** (Math, Art) golden section; **das
Goldene Buch** the visitors' book; **das Goldene Vlies** (Myth)
the Golden Fleece; **das Goldene Kalb** (Bibl) the golden calf;
der Tanz ums Goldene Kalb (fig) the worship of Mammon
(fig)
▪ ADV like gold; **~ schimmern** to shimmer like gold

Gold-: Goldfaden M gold thread; **goldfarben** [-farbn],
goldfarbig ADJ golden, gold-coloured (Brit), gold-colored (US);
Goldfeder F gold nib; **Goldfieber** NT (fig) gold fever;
Goldfisch M goldfish; **goldgefasst** ADJ Brille gold-rimmed;
Edelstein set in gold; **goldgelb** ADJ golden brown;
Goldgewicht NT gold weight; **Goldgräber** [-grɛːbɐ] M -s, -,
Goldgräberin [-ərɪn] F -, -nen gold-digger;
Goldgräberstimmung F gold-rush mood; **Goldgrube** F (lit, fig)
gold mine; **goldhaltig**, (Aus) **goldhältig** ADJ gold-bearing;
Goldhamster M (golden) hamster

goldig [ˈgɔldɪç] ADJ (fig inf: = allerliebst) sweet; **du bist vielleicht
~!** (iro) the ideas you get!

Gold-: Goldklausel F gold clause; **Goldklumpen** M gold
nugget; **Goldkredit** M gold credit; **Goldküste** F (Geog) Gold
Coast; **Goldlack** M (a) (Bot) wallflower (b) (= Glanzlack) gold
lacquer

Goldmedaille F gold medal

Goldmedaillengewinner(in) M(F) gold medallist (Brit) or
medalist (US)

Gold-: Goldmine F gold mine; **Goldmünze** F gold coin;
Goldparität F (Fin) gold parity; **Goldpreis** M gold price;
Goldrahmen M gilt frame; **Goldrand** M gold edge; **mit ~** with
a gold edge; **Goldrausch** M gold fever; **Goldregen** M (Bot)
laburnum; **goldreich** ADJ rich in gold; **Goldreserve** F (Fin)
gold reserves pl; **goldrichtig** (inf) ▪ ADJ absolutely right;
Mensch all right (inf) ▪ ADV exactly right; **sich verhalten,
machen** too perfectly; **du liegst (damit) ~** you're absolutely
right (there); **sie hat ~ gehandelt** what she did was
absolutely right; **Goldschatz** M golden treasure; (von Geld)
hoard of gold; (Kosewort) treasure

Goldschmied(in) M(F) goldsmith

Goldschmiede-: Goldschmiedearbeit F (= Gegenstand)
worked gold article; **Goldschmiedehandwerk** NT,
Goldschmiedekunst F gold work

Gold-: Goldschnitt M, NO PL gilt edging; **Goldstück** NT piece
of gold; (= Münze) gold coin; (fig inf) treasure; **Goldsuche** F
search for gold; **Goldsucher(in)** M(F) gold-hunter; **Goldtopas**
M yellow topaz; **Goldvorkommen** NT -s, - gold deposit;
Goldwaage F gold balance; **jedes Wort** or **alles auf die ~ legen**
(= sich vorsichtig ausdrücken) to weigh one's words;
(= überempfindlich sein) to be hypersensitive; **Goldwährung** F
gold standard; **eine ~ a currency on the gold standard;
Goldwäscher M -s, -, **Goldwäscherin** [-ərɪn] F -, -nen
gold panner; **Goldwert** M, NO PL value in gold; (= Wert des
Goldes) value of gold; **Goldzahn** M gold tooth

Golf¹ [gɔlf] M -(e)s, -e (= Meerbusen) gulf; **der ~ von Biskaya** the
Bay of Biscay; **der (Persische) ~** the (Persian) Gulf

Golf² NT -s, NO PL (Sport) golf

Golf- IN CPDS (Sport) golf; (Geog, Pol) Gulf

Golfer [ˈgɔlfɐ] M -s, -, **Golferin** [-ərɪn] F -, -nen (inf) golfer

Golf-: Golfkrieg M Gulf War; **Golfplatz** M golf course;
Golfschläger M golf club; **Golfspiel** NT das ~ golf;
Golfspieler(in) M(F) golfer; **Golfstaaten** PL die ~ the Gulf
States pl; **Golfstrom** M, NO PL (Geog) Gulf Stream; **Golftasche**
F golf bag; **Golfwagen** M caddie cart

Gondel [ˈgɔndl] F -, -n gondola

Gondel-: Gondelbahn F cable railway; **Gondelführer(in)** M(F)
gondolier

gondeln [ˈgɔndln] VI AUX SEIN (inf) (= reisen) to travel (a)round;
(= herumfahren) to drive (a)round; **nach Schönefeld und
zurück ~** to travel to Schönefeld and back; **durch die Welt ~**
to go globetrotting (inf)

Gondoliere [gɔndoˈliːərə] M -, Gondolieri [-ri] gondolier

Gong [gɔŋ] M **-s, -s** gong; (*bei Boxkampf etc*) bell
Gongschlag M stroke of the gong
gönnen ['gœnən] VT **jdm etw ~** not to (be)grudge sb sth; (= *zuteil werden lassen*) to grant sb sth; **jdm etw nicht ~** to (be)grudge sb sth; not to grant sb sth; **sich** (*dat*) **etw ~** to allow oneself sth; **er gönnte mir keinen Blick** he didn't spare me a single glance; **ich gönne ihm diesen Erfolg/seine Frau von ganzem Herzen** I'm delighted for him that he's had this success/that he has such a nice wife; **das sei ihm gegönnt** I don't (be)grudge him that; **man gönnt sich ja sonst nichts** (*hum inf*) you've got to spoil yourself sometimes
Gönner ['gœnɐ] M **-s, -**, **Gönnerin** [-ərɪn] F **-, -nen** patron; (*Frau auch*) patroness
Gönner-: gönnerhaft (*pej*) **◨** ADJ patronizing **◩** ADV patronizingly; **~ tun, sich ~ geben** to play the big benefactor; **Gönnermiene** F (*pej*) patronizing air
Gonorrhö [gɔnɔˈrøː] F **-, -en** [-ˈrøːən], **Gonorrhöe** [gɔnɔˈrøː] F **-, -n** [-ˈrøːən] (*Med*) gonorrhoea (*Brit*), gonorrhea (*US*)
gor PRET *von* **gären**
Gör [gøːɐ] NT **-(e)s, -en** (*inf:* = *kleines Kind*) kid (*inf*); (= *Mädchen*) little miss
Göre ['gøːrə] F **-, -n** (= *kleines Mädchen*) little miss; (= *kleines Kind*) kid (*inf*)
Gore-Tex® ['goːrətɛks] NT **-, NO PL** Gore-Tex®
Gorilla [goˈrɪla] M **-s, -s** gorilla
goss PRET *von* **gießen**
Gosse ['gɔsə] F **-, -n** gutter; **in der ~ enden** *or* **landen** to end up in the gutter; **jdn aus der ~ holen** *or* **ziehen** to pull sb out of the gutter
Gote ['goːtə] M **-n, -n**, **Gotin** ['goːtɪn] F **-, -nen** Goth
Göteborg ['gøːtəbɔrk] NT **-s** Gothenburg
Gotik ['goːtɪk] F **-, NO PL** (*Art*) Gothic (style); (= *gotische Epoche*) Gothic period
Gotin F *siehe* **Gote**
gotisch ['goːtɪʃ] ADJ Gothic
Gott [gɔt] M **-es, ¨er** ['gœtɐ] (a) god; (*als Name*) God; **~ der Herr** the Lord God; **~ (der) Vater** God the Father; **der liebe ~** the good Lord; **er ist ihr ~** she worships him like a god; **bei ~ schwören** to swear by Almighty God
(b) (*in Wendungen*) **den lieben ~ einen guten** *or* **frommen Mann sein lassen** (*inf*) to take things as they come; **er ist wohl (ganz und gar) von ~** *or* **von den Göttern verlassen** (*inf*) he's (quite) taken leave of his senses; **wie ~ ihn geschaffen hat** (*hum inf*) as naked as the day (that) he was born; **ein Anblick** *or* **Bild für die Götter** (*hum inf*) a sight for sore eyes; **das wissen die Götter** (*inf*) God (only) knows; **er hat ~ weiß was erzählt** (*inf*) he said God knows what (*inf*); **ich bin weiß ~ nicht prüde, aber ...** God knows I'm no prude but ...; **~ und die Welt** (*fig*) everybody; **über ~ und die Welt reden** (*fig*) to talk about anything and everything; **im Namen ~es** in the name of God; **dann mach es eben in ~es Namen** just do it then; **leider ~es** unfortunately; **~es Mühlen mahlen langsam** (*hum*) the mills of God grind slowly (but they grind exceeding fine); **ein Leben wie ~ in Frankreich führen, wie ~ in Frankreich leben** (*inf*) to be in the lap of luxury
(c) (*in Ausrufen*) **grüß ~!** (*esp S Ger, Aus*) hello, good morning/afternoon/evening; **~ hab ihn selig!** God have mercy on his soul; **ach (du lieber) ~!** (*inf*) oh Lord! (*inf*); **mein ~!, ach ~!** (my) God!; (*als Leerformel in Antworten*) (oh) well; **großer ~!** good Lord!; **um ~es willen!** for God's sake!; **~ sei Dank!** thank God!
gottergeben ◨ ADJ (= *demütig*) meek; (= *fromm*) pious **◩** ADV meekly
Götter-: Göttersage F myth about the gods/a god; **Götterspeise** F (*Myth*) food of the gods; (*Cook*) jelly (*Brit*), Jell-O® (*US*); **Göttertrank** [-traŋk] M **-(e)s, -tränke** [-trɛŋkə] (*Myth*) drink of the gods
Gottes-: Gottesanbeterin [-anbeːtərɪn] F **-, -nen** (*Zool*) praying mantis; **Gottesdienst** M (*Eccl*) service; **zum ~ gehen** to go to church; **gottesfürchtig** ADJ God-fearing; **Gotteshaus** NT place of worship; **Gotteskrieger(in)** M(F) religious terrorist; **Gotteslästerer** [-lɛstərɐ] M **-s, -**, **Gotteslästerin** [-ərɪn] F **-, -nen** blasphemer; **gotteslästerlich ◨** ADJ blasphemous **◩** ADV blasphemously; **Gotteslästerung** F **-, -en** blasphemy

Gottheit F **-, -en (a)** NO PL (= *Göttlichkeit*) divinity, godhood, godship; **die ~** (= *Gott*) the Godhead **(b)** (= *esp heidnische Göttergestalt*) deity
Göttin ['gœtɪn] F **-, -nen** goddess
göttlich ['gœtlɪç] **◨** ADJ (*lit, fig*) divine **◩** ADV **wir haben uns ~ amüsiert** (= *lustig gemacht*) we were terribly amused; (= *gut unterhalten*) we had a wonderful time
Gott-: gottlob [gɔtˈloːp] INTERJ thank God; **gottlos** ADJ godless; (= *verwerflich*) ungodly
Gotts-: gotterbärmlich (*inf*) **◨** ADJ godawful (*inf*) **◩** ADV dreadfully; **Gottsöberste(r)** ['gɔtsløːbɛstə] M DECL AS ADJ (*Aus iro*) his lordship (*iro*); **die ~n** the noble lords
Gott-: Gottvater M, NO PL God the Father; **gottverdammt, gottverflucht** ADJ ATTR (*inf*) goddamn(ed) (*inf*); **gottverlassen ◨** ADJ godforsaken **◩** ADV **~ allein** utterly alone; **Gottvertrauen** NT faith in God; **dein ~ möchte ich haben!** I wish I had your faith
Götze ['gœtsə] M **-n, -n** (*lit, fig*) idol
Götzen-: Götzenbild NT idol, graven image (*Bibl*); **Götzendiener(in)** M(F) idolater/idolatress; (*fig*) worshipper; **Götzendienst** M, **Götzenglaube** M, **Götzenverehrung** F idolatry
Götzzitat NT **das ~** ≈ the V-sign (*Brit*), ≈ the finger (*US*)
Gouvernante [guvɐˈnantə] F **-, -n** governess; (*pej*) schoolmarm
gouvernantenhaft ADJ schoolmarmish
Gouvernement [guvɐnəˈmãː] NT **-s, -s (a)** (*Hist*) (= *Regierung*) government; (= *Verwaltung*) administration **(b)** province
Gouverneur [guvɐˈnøːɐ] M **-s, -e**, **Gouverneurin** [-ˈnøːrɪn] F **-, -nen** governor
GPS¹ [geːpeːˈʔɛs] F - ABBR *von* **Grüne Partei der Schweiz** Swiss Green Party
GPS² NT - ABBR *von* **Global Positioning System** GPS
Grab [graːp] NT **-(e)s, ¨er** ['grɛːbɐ] grave; (= *Gruft*) tomb; (*fig:* = *Untergang*) end; **das Heilige ~** the Holy Sepulchre (*Brit*) *or* Sepulcher (*US*); **jdn zu ~e tragen** to bear sb to his grave; **ein Geheimnis mit ins ~ nehmen** to take a secret with one to the grave; **(bis) über das ~ hinaus** beyond the grave; **verschwiegen wie ein** *or* **das ~** (as) silent as the grave; **er würde sich im ~ umdrehen, wenn ...** he would turn in his grave if ...; **du bringst mich noch ins ~** *or* **an den Rand des ~es!** you'll be the death of me yet (*inf*); **mit einem Bein** *or* **Fuß im ~e stehen** (*fig*) to have one foot in the grave; **sich** (*dat*) **selbst sein** *or* **sich** (*dat*) **sein eigenes ~ graben** *or* **schaufeln** (*fig*) to dig one's own grave
Grabbeigabe F (*Archeol*) burial object
Grabbeltisch ['grabl-] M (*inf*) cheap goods counter
graben ['graːbn] VT, *pret* **grub** [gruːp], *ptp* **gegraben** [gəˈgraːbn] **◨** VT (*in Erde etc*) to dig
◩ VI (*auch Archeol*) to dig; **nach Gold/Erz ~** to dig for gold/ore; **in etw** (*dat*) **~** (*fig:* *in Archiven, Quellen, jds Vergangenheit*) to dig around in sth
◪ VR **sich in etw** (*acc*) **~** (*Zähne, Krallen*) to sink into sth; **der Fluss hat sich in den Fels gegraben** the river has eaten its way into the rock; **sich durch etw ~** to dig one's way through sth
Graben ['graːbn] M **-s, ¨** ['grɛːbn] ditch; (= *trockener ~*) (*Mil*) trench; (*Sport*) ditch; (*Sport:* = *Wassergraben*) water jump; (= *Burggraben*) moat; (*Geol*) rift (valley)
Grabenkampf M, **Grabenkrieg** M (*Mil*) trench warfare *no pl, no indef art*
Gräber PL *von* **Grab**
Gräber-: Gräberfeld NT cemetery; **Gräberfund** M grave find
Grab-: Grabfund M grave find; **Grabgeläute** NT **(a)** (death) knell (b) ~ **Grabgesang**; **Grabgesang** M **(a)** funeral hymn **(b)** (*fig*) **der ~ einer Sache** (*gen*) **sein** to sound the death knell for sth; **Grabgewölbe** NT vault; (*von Kirche, Dom*) crypt; **Grabinschrift** F epitaph, inscription (*on gravestone etc*); **Grabkammer** F burial chamber; **Grabkreuz** NT (cross-shaped) gravestone; **Grabmal** NT, *pl* **-mäler** *or* (*geh*) **-male** monument; (= *Grabstein*) gravestone; **das ~ des Unbekannten Soldaten** the tomb of the Unknown Warrior; **Grabschändung** F defilement of graves
grabschen ['grapʃn] VTI = **grapschen**
Grabstein M gravestone
gräbt [grɛːpt] 3. PERS SING PRES *von* **graben**
Grabung F **-, -en** (*Archeol*) excavation

Gracht [ɡraxt] F -, -en canal

grad [ɡraːt] (inf) = **gerade**

Grad [ɡraːt] M -(e)s, -e [-də] (Sci, Univ, fig) degree; (Mil) rank; (Typ: = Schriftgrad) size; **unterm 32. ~ nördlicher Breite** latitude 32 degrees north; **4 ~ Kälte** 4 degrees below freezing point; **4 ~ Wärme** 4 degrees above freezing point; **20 ~ Fahrenheit/Celsius** 20 (degrees) Fahrenheit/centigrade; **null ~** zero; **in ~e einteilen** to calibrate; **ein Verwandter zweiten/ dritten ~es** a relative once/twice removed; **Vetter zweiten ~es** second cousin; **Verbrennungen ersten/zweiten ~es** (Med) first-/second-degree burns; **in einem** or **bis zu einem gewissen ~(e)** up to a certain point; **in hohem ~(e)** to a great extent; **im höchsten ~(e)** extremely

grad- = **gerade-**

Gradation [ɡradaˈtsioːn] F -, -en gradation

grade [ˈɡraːdə] (inf) = **gerade**

Gradeinteilung F calibration

graduell [ɡraˈduɛl] **1** ADJ (= allmählich) gradual; (= gering) slight **2** ADV (= geringfügig) slightly; (= allmählich) gradually

graduieren [ɡraduˈiːrən], ptp **graduiert 1** VT (a) (= in Grade einteilen) to calibrate (b) (Univ) to confer a degree upon; **graduierter Ingenieur** engineering graduate **2** VI (Univ) to graduate

Graduierte(r) [ɡraduˈiːrtə] MF DECL AS ADJ graduate

Grad-: Gradunterschied M difference of degree; **gradweise** ADJ, ADV by degrees

Graf [ɡraːf] M -en, -en count; (britischer ~) earl; **~ Koks** or **Rotz** (inf) His Highness (hum inf)

Graffiti [ɡraˈfiːti] NT -s, -s graffiti

Graffiti-Sprayer(in) M(F) graffiti sprayer

Graffito [ɡraˈfiːto] M or NT -(s), **Graffiti** [-ˈfiːti] (Art) graffito

Grafik [ˈɡraːfɪk] F -, -en (a) NO PL (Art) graphic arts pl; (= Technik) graphics sing; (= Entwurf) design (b) (Art: = Darstellung) graphic; (= Druck) print; (= Schaubild) illustration; (= technisches Schaubild) diagram

Grafik-: Grafikbildschirm M (Comput) graphics screen; **Grafikdrucker** M graphics printer

Grafiker [ˈɡraːfɪkə] M -s, -, **Grafikerin** [-ərɪn] F -, -nen graphic artist; (= Illustrator) illustrator; (= Gestalter) (graphic) designer

Grafik- (Comput): grafikfähig ADJ **~ sein** to be able to do graphics; **Grafikfähigkeit** F graphics capability; **Grafikkarte** F graphics card; **Grafikmodus** M graphics mode; **Grafikmöglichkeit** F graphics facility; **Grafikprogramm** NT graphics program

Gräfin [ˈɡrɛːfɪn] F -, -nen countess

grafisch [ˈɡraːfɪʃ] **1** ADJ graphic; (= schematisch) diagrammatic; **~es Gewerbe** graphic trades pl **2** ADV graphically; **eine Funktion ~ darstellen** (Math) to show a function on a graph

Grafit etc [ɡraˈfiːt] M -s, -e = **Graphit** etc

gräflich [ˈɡrɛːflɪç] ADJ count's/earl's; **das ~e Schloss** the count's/earl's castle

Grafologe [ɡrafoˈloːɡə] M -n, -n, **Grafologin** [-ˈloːɡɪn] F -, -nen graphologist

Grafologie [ɡrafoloˈɡiː] F -, NO PL graphology

Grafschaft [ˈɡraːfʃaft] F -, -en land of a count; earldom; (Admin) county

Gral [ɡraːl] M -s, NO PL (Liter) **der (Heilige) ~** the (Holy) Grail

Grals- IN CPDS of the (Holy) Grail; **Gralshüter(in)** M(F) (lit) keeper of the (Holy) Grail; (fig) guardian

Gram [ɡraːm] M -(e)s, NO PL (geh) grief, sorrow

grämen [ˈɡrɛːmən] **1** VR **sich über jdn/etw ~** to grieve over sb/ sth; **sich zu Tode ~** to die of grief **2** VT to grieve

gramerfüllt [-lɛɐfʏlt] ADJ (geh) grief-stricken

grämlich [ˈɡrɛːmlɪç] ADJ morose

Gramm [ɡram] NT -s, -e or (nach Zahlenangabe) - gram(me); **100 ~ Mehl** 100 gram(me)s of flour

Grammatik [ɡraˈmatɪk] F -, -en grammar

grammatikalisch [ɡramatiˈkaːlɪʃ] **1** ADJ grammatical **2** ADV grammatically

Grammatikregel F grammatical rule

grammatisch [ɡraˈmatɪʃ] **1** ADJ grammatical **2** ADV grammatically

Grammofon [ɡramoˈfoːn] NT -s, -e, **Grammophon®** NT -s, -e (dated) gramophone (dated)

gram- [ɡram-] (Med): **gramnegativ** ADJ Gram-negative; **grampositiv** ADJ Gram-positive

gramvoll ADJ (geh) grief-stricken, sorrowful

Granat [ɡraˈnaːt] M -(e)s, -e or (Aus) -en (a) (Miner) garnet (b) (N Ger: = Garnele) shrimp

Granatapfel M pomegranate

Granate [ɡraˈnaːtə] F -, -n (Mil) (= Geschoss) shell; (= Handgranate) grenade

Grand [ɡrɑ̃ː] M -s, -s (Cards) grand; **~ ouvert** open grand; **~ Hand** grand solo

Grandezza [ɡranˈdɛtsa] F -, NO PL grandeur

grandios [ɡranˈdioːs] **1** ADJ magnificent; (hum) fantastic (inf) **2** ADV (= hervorragend) magnificently; **sich ~ amüsieren** to have a magnificent or fantastic time; **sich ~ erholen** to make a splendid recovery

Grand Prix [ɡrɑ̃ˈpriː] M -, - - Grand Prix

Granit [ɡraˈniːt] M -s, -e granite; **auf ~ beißen (bei …)** to bang one's head against a brick wall (with …)

Granne [ˈɡranə] F -, -n (= Ährenborste) awn, beard

grantig [ˈɡrantɪç] (inf) **1** ADJ grumpy **2** ADV grumpily

Granulat [ɡranuˈlaːt] NT -(e)s, -e granules pl

granulieren [ɡranuˈliːrən], ptp **granuliert** VTI to granulate

Grapefruit [ˈɡreːpfruːt] F -, -s grapefruit

Graphik [ˈɡraːfɪk] F -, -en = **Grafik**

graphisch [ˈɡraːfɪʃ] ADJ, ADV = **grafisch**

Graphit [ɡraˈfiːt] M -s, -e graphite

Graphit-: graphitgrau ADJ dark grey (Brit) or gray (US); **Graphitstift** M lead pencil

Graphologe [ɡrafoˈloːɡə] M -n, -n, **Graphologin** [-ˈloːɡɪn] F -, -nen graphologist

Graphologie [ɡrafoloˈɡiː] F -, NO PL graphology

grapschen [ˈɡrapʃn], **grapsen** [ˈɡrapsn] (inf) **1** VT **sich** (dat) **etw ~** to grab sth **2** VI (a) **nach etw ~** to make a grab at sth (b) (= fummeln) to grope (inf)

Grapscher [ˈɡrapʃɐ] M -s, - (inf: = Person) groper (inf)

Gras [ɡraːs] NT -es, ⁻er [ˈɡrɛːzə] grass; **ins ~ beißen** (inf) to bite the dust (inf); **das ~ wachsen hören** to be highly perceptive; (= zu viel hineindeuten) to read too much into things; **über etw** (acc) **~ wachsen lassen** (fig) to let the dust settle on sth; **wo er zuschlägt, wächst kein ~ mehr** (inf) he packs quite a punch; **wo er hinlangt, da wächst kein ~ mehr** once he gets his hands on something you'll never recognize it any more

Gras- IN CPDS grass; **grasbedeckt, grasbewachsen** [-bəvaksn] ADJ grassy; **Grasbüschel** NT tuft of grass

grasen [ˈɡraːzn] VI to graze

Gras-: Grasfläche F grassland; (= Rasen) patch of grass; **Grasfresser** M herbivore; **grasgrün** ADJ grass-green; **Grashalm** M blade of grass; **Grashüpfer** M (inf) grasshopper

grasig [ˈɡraːzɪç] ADJ grassy

Grassamen M grass seed

grassieren [ɡraˈsiːrən], ptp **grassiert** VI to be rife

grässlich [ˈɡrɛslɪç] **1** ADJ (a) hideous (b) (= intensiv, unangenehm) dreadful; **Mensch** horrible **2** ADV (a) (= schrecklich) horribly (b) (inf: = äußerst) dreadfully

Grat [ɡraːt] M -(e)s, -e (= Berggrat) ridge; (Tech) burr; (Archit) hip (of roof); (fig) (dividing) line, border

Gräte [ˈɡrɛːtə] F -, -n (fish) bone

Gratifikation [ɡratifikaˈtsioːn] F -, -en bonus

gratinieren [ɡratiˈniːrən], ptp **gratiniert** VT (Cook) to brown (the top of); **gratinierte Zwiebelsuppe** onion soup au gratin

gratis [ˈɡraːtɪs] ADV free; (Comm) free (of charge)

Gratis- IN CPDS free; **Gratisaktie** F bonus share; **Gratisprobe** F free sample

Grätsche [ˈɡrɛːtʃə] F -, -n (Sport) straddle

grätschen [ˈɡrɛːtʃn] **1** VI AUX SEIN to do a straddle (vault) **2** VT **Beine** to straddle

Grätschsprung M straddle vault

Gratulant [ɡratuˈlant] M -en, -en, **Gratulantin** [-ˈlantɪn] F -, -nen well-wisher; **er war der erste ~** he was the first to offer his congratulations

Gratulation [gratula'tsio:n] F -, -en congratulations *pl*; **zur ~ bei jdm erscheinen** to call on sb to congratulate him/her

gratulieren [gratu'li:rən], *ptp* **gratuliert** VI **jdm (zu einer Sache) ~** to congratulate sb (on sth); **jdm zum Geburtstag ~** to wish sb many happy returns (of the day); **(ich) gratuliere!** congratulations!; **Sie können sich** (*dat*) **~, dass alles gut gegangen ist** you can count yourself lucky that everything went off all right

Gratwanderung F (*lit*) ridge walk; (*fig*) tightrope walk

grau [grau] **1** ADJ grey (*Brit*), gray (*US*); (= *trostlos*) gloomy; **~e Haare bekommen, ~ werden** (*inf*) to go grey (*Brit*) or gray (*US*); **der Himmel** *or* **es sieht ~ in ~ aus** the sky *or* it is looking very grey (*Brit*) or gray (*US*); **er malte die Lage ~ in ~** (*fig*) he painted a gloomy picture of the situation; **~e Eminenz** éminence grise; **der ~e Markt** (*Comm*) the grey (*Brit*) or gray (*US*) market; **die (kleinen) ~en Zellen** (*hum*) the little grey (*Brit*) or gray (*US*) cells; **die ~e Substanz** (*Anat*) the grey (*Brit*) or gray (*US*) matter; **der ~e Alltag** the daily grind; **~ ist alle Theorie** (*prov*) theory is no use without practice **2** ADV (= *mit ~er Farbe*) **anstreichen, färben** grey (*Brit*), gray (*US*), **tapezieren** *auch*, **einrichten, sich kleiden** in grey (*Brit*) or gray (*US*); **~ gestreift** grey-striped (*Brit*), gray-striped (*US*); **~ meliert** flecked with grey (*Brit*) or gray (*US*); **Haar** *auch* greying (*Brit*), graying (*US*)

Grau [grau] NT -s, - *or* (*inf*) -s grey (*Brit*), gray (*US*); (*fig*) dullness

Graubrot NT bread made from more than one kind of flour

Graubünden [grau'byndn] NT -s (*Geog*) the Grisons

Graubündner [grau'byndnɐ] M -s, -, **Graubündnerin** [-ərɪn] F -, -nen inhabitant of the Grisons

Gräuel ['grɔyəl] M -s, - (a) NO PL (= *Grauen, Abscheu*) horror; **~ vor etw** (*dat*) **haben** to have a horror of sth (b) (= *~tat*) atrocity (c) (= *Gegenstand des Abscheus*) abomination; **sie/er/ es ist mir ein ~** I loathe her/him/it; **es ist mir ~, das zu tun** I loathe doing that

Gräuel-: **Gräuelgeschichte** F, **Gräuelmärchen** NT horror story; **Gräuelmeldung** F, **Gräuelnachricht** F report of an atrocity/ atrocities; **Gräueltat** F atrocity

grauen¹ ['grauən] VI (*geh*: *Tag*) to dawn; **es begann zu ~** dawn began to break

grauen² VI IMPERS **mir graut vor etw** (*dat*), **es graut mir vor etw** (*dat*) I dread sth; **mir graut vor ihm** I'm terrified of him

Grauen ['grauən] NT -s, NO PL horror (*vor +dat* of); **mich überlief ein ~** I shuddered with horror; **~ erregend** atrocious

grauenhaft, grauenvoll **1** ADJ atrocious; *Schmerz* terrible; (*inf*) *Durcheinander* horrendous **2** ADV atrociously; **~ aussehen** to look ghastly; **die Wohnung war ~ durcheinander** the apartment was in a horrendous mess

Grau-: **Graugans** F grey(lag) (*Brit*) or gray(lag) (*US*) goose; **graugestreift** ADJ *siehe* **grau**; **grauhaarig** ADJ grey-haired (*Brit*), gray-haired (*US*)

graulich¹ ['graulɪç], **gräulich¹** ['grɔylɪç] ADJ = **grässlich**

graulich², gräulich² ADJ (= *Farbe*) greyish (*Brit*), grayish (*US*)

Graumarkt M grey (*Brit*) or gray (*US*) market

graumeliert ADJ ATTR *siehe* **grau**

Graupe ['graupə] F -, -n grain of pearl barley; **~n** pearl barley *sing*

Graupel ['graupl] F -, -n (small) hailstone; **~n** soft hail *sing*

graupelig ['graupəlɪç] ADJ *Schauer* of soft hail; **~er Schnee** snow mixed with fine hail; **~er Hagel** soft hail

grauplig ['grauplɪç] ADJ = **graupelig**

Graus [graus] M -es [-zas], NO PL horror; **es war ein ~ zu sehen, wie …** it was terrible to see how …; **es ist ein ~ mit ihm!** he's impossible!

grausam ['grauza:m] **1** ADJ (a) (= *gefühllos, roh*) cruel (*gegen, zu* to) (b) (*inf*) terrible **2** ADV (a) (= *auf schreckliche Weise*) cruelly; **~ ums Leben kommen** to die a cruel death; **sich ~ für etw rächen** to take a (a) cruel revenge for sth (b) (*inf*: = *furchtbar*) terribly

Grausamkeit F -, -en (a) NO PL cruelty (b) (= *grausame Tat*) (act of) cruelty; (*stärker*) atrocity

grausen ['grauzn] VI IMPERS **mir graust vor** *or* **es graust mir vor der Prüfung** I am dreading the exam

Grausen ['grauzn] NT -s, NO PL (a) = **Grauen** (b) (*inf*) **da kann man das große** *or* **kalte ~ kriegen** it's enough to give you the creeps (*inf*)

grausig ['grauzɪç] ADJ, ADV = **grauenhaft**

Grau-: **Grauspecht** M grey-headed (*Brit*) or gray-headed (*US*) woodpecker; **Graustufe** F shade of grey (*Brit*) or gray (*US*); **Grauton** M, *pl* **-töne** grey colour (*Brit*), gray color (*US*); **Grauwal** M grey (*Brit*) or gray (*US*) whale; **Grauzone** F (*fig*) grey (*Brit*) or gray (*US*) area

Graveur [gra'vø:ɐ] M -s, -e, **Graveurin** [-'vø:rɪn] F -, -nen engraver

Gravier- [gra'vi:ɐ-]: **Gravieranstalt** F engraving establishment; **Gravierarbeit** F engraving

gravieren [gra'vi:rən], *ptp* **graviert** VT to engrave

gravierend ADJ serious

Gravier-: **Graviermaschine** F engraving machine; **Graviernadel** F graver, burin

Gravierung [gra'vi:rʊŋ] F -, -en engraving

Gravis ['gra:vɪs] M -, - (*Gram*) grave accent

Gravitation [gravita'tsio:n] F -, NO PL gravitational pull

gravitieren [gravi'ti:rən], *ptp* **gravitiert** VI (*Phys, fig*) to gravitate (*zu* towards)

Gravur [gra'vu:ɐ] F -, -en, **Gravüre** [gra'vy:rə] F -, -n engraving

Grazie ['gra:tsiə] F -, -n (a) (*Myth*) Grace; (*hum*) beauty, belle (b) NO PL (= *Liebreiz*) grace(fulness)

grazil [gra'tsi:l] **1** ADJ delicate **2** ADV **~ gebaut sein** to have a delicate figure

graziös [gra'tsiø:s] **1** ADJ graceful; (= *lieblich*) charming **2** ADV gracefully

Greencard ['gri:nka:ɐd] F -, -s green card

Greenwich-Zeit ['grɪnɪdʒ-, -ɪtʃ-] F, **Greenwicher Zeit** ['grɪnɪdʒɐ-] F (**die**) **~** GMT, Greenwich Mean Time

Greif [graif] M -(e)s *or* -en, -e(n) (*Myth*) (**Vogel**) **~** griffin

Greif-: **Greifarm** M claw arm; **greifbar** ADJ (= *konkret*) tangible; (= *erreichbar, erhältlich*) available; **~e Gestalt** *or* **~e Formen annehmen** to take on (a) tangible form; **~ nahe, in ~er Nähe** within reach

greifen ['graifn], *pret* **griff** [grɪf], *ptp* **gegriffen** [gə'grɪfn] **1** VT (a) (= *nehmen, packen*) to take hold of; (= *grapschen*) to seize, to grab; *Akkord* to strike; **eine Oktave ~** to stretch an octave; **diese Zahl ist zu hoch/zu niedrig gegriffen** (*fig*) this figure is too high/low; **zum Greifen nahe sein** (*Sieg*) to be within reach; (*Folgerung*) to be obvious (*to anyone*); **aus dem Leben gegriffen** taken from life (b) (= *fangen*) to catch; **sich** (*dat*) **jdn/etw ~** to grab sb/sth; **den werde ich mir mal ~** (*inf*) I'm going to tell him a thing or two (*inf*) **2** VI (a) (= *fassen*) **hinter sich** (*acc*) **~** to reach behind one; **um sich ~** to spread; **unter etw** (*acc*) **~** to reach under sth; **in etw** (*acc*) **~** to put one's hand into sth; **nach einer Sache ~** to reach for sth; (*um zu halten*) to clutch *or* (*hastig*) grab at sth; **an etw** (*acc*) **~** to take hold of sth; (= *berühren*) to touch sth; **zu etw ~** *zu Pistole* to reach for sth; *zu Methoden, Mitteln* to turn to sth; **zur Flasche ~** to take to the bottle; **tief in die Tasche ~** (*fig*) to dig deep in one's pocket(s); **in die Saiten/Tasten ~** to strike up a tune; **nach den Sternen ~** to reach for the stars; **nach dem rettenden Strohhalm ~** to clutch at a straw; **zum Äußersten ~** to resort to extremes; **nach der Macht ~** to try to seize power (b) (= *nicht rutschen, einrasten*) to grip; (*fig*) (= *wirksam werden*) to take effect; (= *zum Ziel/Erfolg führen*) to achieve its ends; (= *zutreffen*) (*Gesetz, Vorschrift*) to apply; (*Vergleich, Unterscheidung*) to hold; **zu kurz ~** to fall short

Greifer ['graifɐ] M -s, - (*Tech*) grab

Greif-: **Greiftrupp** M riot squad; **Greifvogel** M bird of prey

Greis [grais] M -es, -e [-zə] old man

Greisen-: **Greisenalter** NT extreme old age; **greisenhaft** ADJ very old, aged *attr*; (*von jüngeren Menschen*) *Gesicht, Ansicht, Aussehen* aged *attr*; **das ~e Verhalten dieser Kinder** the way these children behave like old people; **Greisenhaftigkeit** ['graiznhaftɪçkait] F -, NO PL **sie zeigt keine Anzeichen von ~** she shows no signs of old age; **verfrühte ~** premature ageing; **die ~ dieser Kindergesichter** the little old men's faces of these children

Greisin ['graizɪn] F -, -nen old lady

grell [grɛl] **1** ADJ *Stimme, Schrei, Ton* shrill; *Licht, Sonne* dazzling; *Farbe* garish; *Kleidung, Mode* loud, flashy **2** ADV (= *sehr hell*) *scheinen* brightly; (= *schrill*) shrilly; (= *auffallend*) garishly; ~ **beleuchtet** or **erleuchtet** dazzlingly bright; ~ **leuchten** to be garish; ~ **klingen/tönen** to sound shrill

grellbunt ADJ gaudily coloured (Brit) or colored (US); *Farbe* gaudy

Gremium ['gre:miʊm] NT **-s, Gremien** ['gre:miən] body; (= *Ausschuss*) committee

Grenz- IN CPDS border, frontier; **Grenzabfertigung** F border clearance; **Grenzbegradigung** F straightening of the border/ a border/borders; **Grenzbereich** M border zone; (fig) limits pl; **im ~ liegen** (fig) to lie at the limits; **Grenzbewohner(in)** M(F) inhabitant of the/a border zone; (esp in unwegsamen Gebieten) frontiersman/-woman

Grenze ['grentsə] F **-, -n** border; (= *Landesgrenze auch*) frontier; (= *Stadtgrenze*) (zwischen Grundstücken) boundary; (fig: zwischen Begriffen) dividing line; (fig: = äußerstes Maß, Schranke) limits pl; **die ~ zwischen Spanien und Frankreich** the Spanish-French border; **die ~ zu Österreich** the Austrian border; **über die ~ gehen/fahren** to cross the border; **(bis) zur äußersten ~ gehen** (fig) to go as far as one can; **jdm ~n setzen** to lay down limits for sb; **einer Sache** (dat) **~n setzen** or **stecken** to set a limit or limits to sth; **keine ~n kennen** (fig) to know no bounds; **seine ~n kennen** to know one's limitations; **seiner Großzügigkeit sind keine ~n gesetzt** there is no limit to his generosity; **hart an der ~ des Möglichen** bordering on the limits of what is possible; **jdn in seine ~n verweisen** (fig) to put sb in his place; **sich in ~n halten** (fig) to be limited; **die ~n des Möglichen** the bounds of possibility; **die oberste/unterste ~** (fig) the upper/lower limit; **an ~n stoßen** (fig) to come up against limiting factors; **alles hat seine ~n** there is a limit or there are limits to everything

grenzen ['grentsn] VI **an etw** (acc) ~ (lit) to border (on) sth; (fig) to border on sth

Grenzen-: grenzenlos ■ ADJ (lit, fig) boundless ■ ADV boundlessly; (fig) immensely; **Grenzenlosigkeit** F **-,** NO PL boundlessness; (fig) immensity

Grenz-: Grenzfall M borderline case; **Grenzfluss** M river forming a/the border or frontier; **Grenzgänger** [-gɛŋə] M **-s, -,** **Grenzgängerin** [-ərɪn] F **-, -nen** (= *Arbeiter*) international commuter (across a local border); (= *heimlicher ~*) illegal border crosser; **Grenzgebiet** NT border zone; (fig) border(ing) area; **Grenzkonflikt** M border dispute; **Grenzlinie** F border line; (Sport) line; **grenznah** ADJ close to the border; **Grenzposten** M border guard; **Grenzschutz** M **(a)** NO PL protection of the border(s) **(b)** (= *Truppen*) border guard(s); **Grenzsituation** F borderline situation; **Grenzstadt** F border town; **Grenzstreitigkeit** F boundary dispute; (Pol) border dispute; **Grenzübergang** M **(a)** (= *Stelle*) border crossing(-point) **(b)** (= *Grenzübertritt*) crossing of the border; **grenzüberschreitend** ADJ ATTR (Comm, Jur) cross-border; **Grenzübertritt** M crossing of the border; **Grenzverkehr** M border traffic; **kleiner ~** regular border traffic; **Grenzverlauf** M boundary line (between countries); **Grenzwache** F border guard; **Grenzwacht** F (Sw) border guard; **Grenzwert** M limit; **Grenzzwischenfall** M border incident

Gretchenfrage ['gre:tçən-] F (fig) crunch question (inf)

Greuel ['grɔyəl] M **-s, -** siehe **Gräuel**

greulich ['grɔylɪç] ADJ, ADV siehe **gräulich**[1]

Greyerzer ['graiɛtsə] M **-s, - ~** (Käse) Gruyère

Griebe ['gri:bə] F **-, -n ≈** crackling no indef art, no pl (Brit), ≈ cracklings pl (US)

Griebenschmalz NT ≈ dripping with crackling etc

Grieche ['gri:çə] M **-n, -n, Griechin** ['gri:çɪn] F **-, -nen** Greek

Griechenland ['gri:çnlant] NT **-s** Greece

Griechin F **-, -nen** Greek (woman/girl)

griechisch ['gri:çɪʃ] ADJ Greek; **~-orthodox** Greek Orthodox; **~-römisch** Graeco-Roman, Greco-Roman (esp US); siehe auch **deutsch**

Griesgram ['gri:sgra:m] M **-(e)s, -e** grouch (inf)

griesgrämig ['gri:sgrɛːmɪç] ■ ADJ grumpy ■ ADV grumpily; **~ aussehen** to look grumpy; **er guckte ~ in die Gegend** he looked around with a grumpy expression on his face

Grieß [gri:s] M **-es, -e (a)** semolina; (= *Reisgrieß*) ground rice **(b)** (= *Kies*) gravel (auch Med)

Grieß-: Grießbrei M semolina; **Grießkloß** M, **Grießklößchen** [-klø:sçən] NT **-, -** semolina dumpling

griff PRET von **greifen**

Griff [grɪf] M **-(e)s, -e (a)** (= *das Greifen*) **der ~ an etw** (acc) taking hold of sth; (= *Berührung*) touching sth; **der ~ nach etw** reaching for sth; **einen ~ in die Kasse tun** to put one's hand in the till; **der ~ nach der Droge/der Flasche** taking to drugs/the bottle; **der ~ nach der Macht** the bid for power; **das ist ein ~ nach den Sternen** that's just reaching for the stars **(b)** (= *Handgriff*) grip, grasp; (beim Ringen, Judo, Bergsteigen) hold; (beim Turnen) grip; (Mus: = *Fingerstellung*) fingering; (inf: = *Akkord*) chord; **mit festem ~** firmly; **jdn/etw im ~ haben** (fig) to have sth/sb under control; **ein falscher ~** (fig) a false move; **jdn/etw in den ~ bekommen** (fig) to gain control of sb/ sth; (geistig) to get a grasp of sth; **(mit jdm/etw) einen guten** or **glücklichen ~ tun** to make a wise choice (with sb/sth); **etw mit einem ~ tun** (fig) to do sth in a flash **(c)** (= *Stiel, Knauf*) handle; (= *Pistolengriff*) butt; (= *Schwertgriff*) hilt; (an Saiteninstrumenten) neck

Griff-: griffbereit ADJ handy; **etw ~ halten** to keep sth handy; **Griffbrett** NT (Mus) fingerboard

Griffel ['grɪfl] M **-s, -** slate pencil; (Bot) style

Griffelkasten M pencil case

griffig ['grɪfɪç] ■ ADJ Boden, Fahrbahn etc that has a good grip; Rad, Sohle, Profil that grips well; Gewebe firm; (fig) Ausdruck handy; Slogan pithy; Formulierung, Theorie concise; (Aus) Mehl coarse-grained; **etw auf eine ~e Formel bringen** to break sth down into a simple phrase ■ ADV (= *eingängig*) pithily

Griffigkeit F **-,** NO PL grip; (von Slogan) pithiness

Griffloch NT finger hole

Grill [grɪl] M **-s, -s** grill; (Aut: = *Kühlergrill*) grille

Grille ['grɪlə] F **-, -n** (Zool) cricket

grillen ['grɪlən] ■ VT to grill ■ VR **sich ~ (lassen)** (inf) to roast (inf)

Grill- (Cook): **Grillfest** NT barbecue party; **Grillgericht** NT grill; **Grillplatz** M barbecue area; **Grillrestaurant** NT, **Grillroom** [-ruːm] M **-s, -s, Grillstube** F grillroom

Grimasse [gri'masə] F **-, -n** grimace; **~n schneiden** or **ziehen** or **machen** to grimace; **sein Gesicht zu einer ~ verziehen** to twist one's face into a grimace

Grimassenschneider(in) M(F) face-puller

Grimmdarm M colon

Grimmen ['grɪmən] NT **-s,** NO PL (S Ger) griping pains pl

grimmig ['grɪmɪç] ■ ADJ **(a)** (= *zornig*) furious; Gegner fierce; Miene, Humor grim **(b)** (= *sehr groß, heftig*) Kälte, Spott etc severe ■ ADV furiously, grimly; **~ lächeln** to smile grimly

Grind [grɪnt] M **-(e)s, -e** [-də] scab

grinsen ['grɪnzn] VI to grin

Grinsen NT **-s,** NO PL grin

grippal [grɪ'pa:l] ADJ (Med) influenzal; **~er Infekt** influenza infection

Grippe ['grɪpə] F **-, -n** flu; (= *Erkältung*) cold

Grippe- IN CPDS flu; **Grippe(schutz)impfung** F influenza vaccination; **Grippewelle** F wave of flu

Grips [grɪps] M **-es, -e** (inf) brains pl (inf); **nun strengt mal euren ~ an** use your common sense

Grislibär ['grɪsli-] M, **Grizzlybär** ['grɪsli-] M grizzly (bear)

grob [gro:p] ■ ADJ, comp **ër** ['grø:bə], superl **ste(r, s)** ['grø:pstə] **(a)** (= *nicht fein*) coarse; Arbeit dirty attr **(b)** (= *ungefähr*) rough; **in ~en Umrissen** roughly **(c)** (= *schlimm, groß*) gross (auch Jur); **den gröbsten Schmutz habe ich schon weggeputzt** I have already cleaned off the worst of the dirt; **ein ~er Fehler** a bad mistake; **wir sind aus dem Gröbsten heraus** we're out of the woods (now); **~e Fahrlässigkeit** gross negligence **(d)** (= *brutal, derb*) rough; (fig: = *derb*) coarse; Antwort rude; (= *unhöflich*) ill-mannered; **~ gegen jdn werden** to become offensive (towards sb) ■ ADV, comp **ër**, superl **am ~sten (a)** (= *nicht fein*) coarsely **(b)** (= *ungefähr*) **~ geschätzt/gemessen/gerechnet** approximately, roughly; **etw ~ umreißen/skizzieren** to give a rough idea of sth **(c)** (= *schlimm*) **~ fahrlässig handeln** to commit an act of gross negligence **(d)** (= *brutal*) roughly; (= *unhöflich*) rudely; (= *barsch*) curtly; **~ mit jdm umspringen** to rough sb up; **jdm ~ kommen** (inf) to get coarse with sb

grob-, Grob- IN CPDS coarse

Grobe(s) ['gro:bə] NT DECL AS ADJ (fig) dirty work; **ein Mann fürs ~** (inf) a man who does the dirty work

grobfaserig, grobfasrig ADJ coarse-fibred (Brit), coarse-fibered (US)

Grobheit F **-, -en (a)** (= Beschimpfung, Ausdrucksweise) foul language no pl **(b)** (= Manieren) bad manners pl **(c)** (von Material) coarseness

Grobian ['gro:bia:n] M **-(e)s, -e** brute

Grob-: grobmaschig [-maʃɪç] **1** ADJ large-meshed; (= grob gestrickt) loose-knit attr **2** ADV coarsely; **grobschlächtig** [-ʃlɛçtɪç] ADJ coarse; Mensch heavily built; (fig) unrefined

Grog [grɔk] M **-s, -s** grog

groggy ['grɔgi] ADJ PRED (Boxen) groggy; (inf: = erschöpft) all-in (inf)

grölen ['grø:lən] VTI (pej) to bawl; **~de Stimme/Menge** raucous voice/crowd; **~d durch die Straßen ziehen** to roam rowdily through the streets

Grölerei [grø:lə'rai] F **-, -en** (pej) bawling no pl

Groll [grɔl] M **-(e)s, -en** (= Zorn) anger; (= Erbitterung) resentment; **einen ~ gegen jdn hegen** to harbour (Brit) or harbor (US) a grudge against sb

grollen ['grɔlən] VI (geh) **(a)** (= dröhnen) to rumble **(b)** (= böse sein) (jdm) **~ to** be annoyed (with sb); **(mit) seinem Schicksal ~ to** bemoan one's fate

Grönland ['grø:nlant] NT **-s** Greenland

Grönländer ['grø:nlɛndɐ] M **-s, -, Grönländerin** [-ərɪn] F **-, -nen** Greenlander

grönländisch ['grø:nlɛndɪʃ] ADJ Greenland attr

Grönlandwal M bowhead (whale)

Gros [gro:] NT **-, -** [gro:s] (= Mehrzahl) major part; siehe auch **en gros**

Groschen ['grɔʃn] M **-s, - (a)** (Aus) groschen; (in Polen = grosz) grosz; (Hist) groschen **(b)** (Hist inf: = 10 Pfennig) 10-pfennig piece; (fig) penny, cent (US); **der ~ ist gefallen** (hum inf) the penny has dropped (inf)

---

groß [gro:s]

1 ADJEKTIV	**2** ADVERB

1 ADJEKTIV, comp **⁻er** ['grø:sə], superl **⁻te(r, s)** ['grø:stə]
(a) big; Fläche, Raum, Haus, Hände big, large; Höhe, Breite great; Größe, Tube, Dose, Packung etc large; (Typ) Buchstabe capital; **ein ganz großes Haus/Buch** a great big house/book; **die Wiese ist 10 Hektar groß** the field measures 10 hectares; **ein 2 Hektar großes Grundstück** a 2-hectare piece of land; **ein großes Bier, ein Großes** (inf) ≈ a pint (of beer) (Brit), a big beer; **großes Geld** notes pl (Brit), bills pl (US); **ich habe nur großes Geld** I haven't any change on me; **im Großen und Ganzen (gesehen)** by and large

(b) (= hoch, hoch gewachsen) tall; **wie groß bist du?** how tall are you?; **er ist 1,80 Meter groß** he is 1.80 metres (Brit) or meters (US) tall; **du bist groß geworden** you've grown

(c) (= älter) Bruder, Schwester big; **unsere Große** our eldest (daughter); (von zweien) our elder daughter; **unser Großer** our eldest (son); (von zweien) our elder son; **Groß und Klein** young and old (alike); **mit etw groß geworden sein** to have grown up with sth; **die Großen** (= Erwachsene) the grown-ups; (= ältere Kinder) the older children

(d) (zeitlich) Verzögerung, Rede big, long; **die große Pause** (Sch) the long or lunch break; **die großen Ferien** the summer holidays (Brit) or holiday (US)

(e) (= beträchtlich, wichtig, bedeutend) great; Gewinn, Ereignis big; Katastrophe, Schreck terrible; Summe large; Geschwindigkeit high; **er hat Großes geleistet** he has achieved great things; **im Kleinen wie im Großen** whether the scale be large or small; **eine große Dummheit machen** to do something very stupid; **großen Durst haben** to be very thirsty; **er ist kein großer Esser** (inf) he's not a big eater; **eine der größeren Firmen** one of the major companies; **das große Ganze** the broader view; **großer Lärm** a lot of noise; **großen Hunger haben** to be very hungry; **ich habe große Lust zu verreisen** I'd really like to go away (on holiday (Brit) or vacation (US)); **sie hatte große Lust, sich zu verkleiden** she really wanted to get dressed up; **ich habe keine große Lust I**

don't particularly want to; **große Mode sein** to be all the rage (inf); **ich bin kein großer Redner** (inf) I'm no great speaker; **ich bin kein großer Opernfreund** (inf) I'm not a great opera lover; **im größten Regen/Schneesturm** in the midst of a downpour/snowstorm; **jds große Stunde** sb's big moment; **eine größere Summe** a biggish sum; **er ist kein großer Trinker** (inf) he's not a big drinker; **große Worte** big words; **große Worte machen** to use grand words

(f) (= großartig, bewundernswert) (iro) great

(g) (in Eigennamen) Great; **der Große Ozean** the Pacific; **Alfred/Friedrich der Große** Alfred/Frederick the Great

2 ADVERB, comp **⁻er**, superl **am ⁻ten**
(a) (= nicht klein) **groß gewachsen** tall; **groß gemustert** with a large print; **groß kariert** large-check(ed); **groß machen** (baby talk) to do number two (baby talk); **groß daherreden** (inf) to talk big (inf); siehe **großschreiben**

(b) (= in großem Ausmaß) **groß einkaufen gehen** to go on a spending spree; **groß ausgehen** to go out somewhere expensive; **groß feiern** to have a big celebration; **groß aufgemacht** elaborately dressed; **groß angelegt** large-scale; **groß und breit** (fig inf) at great length

(c) (= besonders) **jdn groß anblicken** to give sb a hard stare; **groß in Mode sein** to be all the rage (inf); **was ist das schon groß?** (inf) big deal! (inf); **was ist da schon groß machen/sagen?** (inf) what can you do/say?; **ich habe mich nie groß um Politik gekümmert** (inf) I've never been a great one for politics (inf); **ich kümmere mich nicht groß darum** (inf) I don't take much notice; **ganz groß rauskommen** (inf) to make the big time (inf)

Groß- PREF (vor Namen von Ballungsräumen) Greater; **~~Berlin** Greater Berlin

Groß-: Großabnehmer(in) M(F) (Comm) bulk purchaser; **Großaktionär(in)** M(F) major shareholder; **Großanlass** M (Sw) = Großveranstaltung; **großartig 1** ADJ wonderful; Erfolg tremendous; **er hat Großartiges geleistet** he has achieved great things; **eine ~e Frau** a wonderful woman **2** ADV wonderfully; **ha, ~** (iro) wonderful!; **~ tun** (pej) to give oneself airs; **Großartigkeit** F **-, -en** magnificence; **Großaufnahme** F (Phot, Film) close-up; **Großbaustelle** F construction site; **Großbetrieb** M large concern; (Agr) big farm; **Großbezüger** [-bətsy:gɐ] M **-s, -, Großbezügerin** [-ərɪn] F **-, -nen** (Sw) bulk purchaser; **Großbildschirm** M large screen; **Großbrand** M major or big fire; **Großbritannien** [gro:sbri'taniən] NT (Great) Britain; **großbritannisch** [gro:sbri'taniʃ] ADJ (Great) British; **Großbuchstabe** M capital (letter), upper case letter; **Großbuchstabe** M capital (letter), upper case letter (Typ); **Großdruck** M (Sociol) upper classes pl; **Großdruck** M, NO PL large print; **ein Buch im ~** a large-print book

Größe ['grø:sə] F **-, -n (a)** (= Format, Maßeinheit) size; **nach der ~** according to size; **er trägt** or **hat ~ 48** he takes or is size 48 **(b)** NO PL (= Höhe, Körpergröße) height; (= Flächeninhalt) size, area; (= Dimension) size, dimensions pl; (Math, Phys) quantity; (Astron) magnitude; **nach der ~** according to height/size; **eine unbekannte ~** (lit, fig) an unknown quantity **(c)** NO PL (= Ausmaß) extent; (= Bedeutsamkeit) significance **(d)** NO PL (= Erhabenheit) greatness **(e)** (= bedeutender Mensch) important figure

Groß-: Großeinkauf M bulk purchase, bulk purchasing no indef art, no pl; **Großeinsatz** M **~ der Feuerwehr/Polizei** etc large-scale operation by the fire brigade/police etc; **der ~ von Truppen** the large-scale deployment of troops; **großelterlich** ADJ ATTR of one's grandparents; **im ~en Haus wohnen** to live in one's grandparents' house; **Großeltern** PL grandparents pl; **Großenkel** M great-grandchild; (= Junge) great-grandson; **Großenkelin** F great-granddaughter

Größenordnung F scale; (= Größe) magnitude; (Math) order (of magnitude); **ich denke an anderen ~en** I think on a different scale

großenteils ['gro:sn'tails] ADV mostly; **er macht seine Arbeit ~ selbstständig** he does his work mostly on his own

Größen-: Größenunterschied M (im Format) difference in size; (in der Höhe, im Wuchs) difference in height; (in der Bedeutung) difference in importance; **Größenverhältnis** NT proportions pl (+gen between); (= Maßstab) scale; **im ~ 1:100** on the scale 1:100; **etw im richtigen ~ sehen** to see sth in perspective; **Größenwahn(sinn)** M megalomania;

größenwahnsinnig ADJ *Mensch, Bauten etc* megalomaniac(al); **er ist ~** he is a megalomaniac

größer COMP *von* **groß**

Groß-: **Großfahndung** F large-scale manhunt; **Großfamilie** F extended family; **Großflughafen** M major airport; **Großformat** NT large size; **großformatig** [-fɔrmaːtɪç] ADJ large-size; *Bücher, Fotos auch* large-format; **großgewachsen** ADJ *siehe* **groß**; **Großgrundbesitz** M large-scale land-holding; **Großgrundbesitzer(in)** M(F) big landowner

Großhandel M wholesale trade; **etw im ~ kaufen** to buy sth wholesale

Großhandels- IN CPDS wholesale; **Großhandelskauffrau** F, **Großhandelskaufmann** M wholesaler; **Großhandelspreis** M wholesale price

Groß-: **Großhändler(in)** M(F) wholesaler; (*inf*: = *Großhandlung*) wholesaler's; **Großhandlung** F wholesale business; **großherzig** ADJ generous, magnanimous; **~e Motive** the best of motives; **Großhirn** NT cerebrum; **Großhirnrinde** F cerebral cortex

Grossist [grɔˈsɪst] M **-en, -en**, **Grossistin** [-ˈsɪstɪn] F **-, -nen** wholesaler; (*inf*: = *Großhandlung*) wholesaler's

Groß-: **Großkapitalist(in)** M(F) big capitalist; **was, du willst 50 Euro? ich bin doch kein ~!** what - you want 50 euros? I'm not made of money! (*inf*); **großkariert** ADJ *siehe* **groß**; **Großkatze** F big cat; **Großkaufmann** M wholesale merchant; **Großkind** NT (*Sw*) grandchild; **Großkopfe(r)te(r)** [ˈgroːskɔpfətə, -kəpfetə] MF DECL AS ADJ (*Aus, S Ger: pej*) bigwig (*inf*); **Großkotz** [ˈgroːskɔts] M **-es, -e** (*pej inf*) swank (*inf*); **großkotzig** [ˈgroːskɔtsɪç] (*pej inf*) **1** ADJ swanky (*inf*) **2** ADV swankily (*inf*), pretentiously; **~ auftreten** to be pretentious; **Großkraftwerk** NT large power plant; **Großküche** F canteen kitchen; **Großkunde** M, **Großkundin** F (*Comm*) major client; **Großkundgebung** F mass rally

Großmacht F (*Pol*) great power

Großmachtstellung F great-power status

Groß-: **Großmarkt** M hypermarket (*Brit*), large supermarket; **großmaschig** [-maʃɪç] ADJ, ADV = **grobmaschig**; **Großmast** M mainmast; **Großmaul** NT (*pej inf*) bigmouth (*inf*); **großmäulig** [-mɔylɪç] (*pej inf*) **1** ADJ big-mouthed *attr* (*inf*); *Erklärungen, Worte* boastful **2** ADV boastfully; **~ verkünden, dass ...** to brag that ...; **Großmut** F **-**, NO PL magnanimity; **großmütig** [-myːtɪç] **1** ADJ magnanimous **2** ADV magnanimously; **Großmutter** F grandmother; **das kannst du deiner ~ erzählen!** (*inf*) you can tell that one to the marines (*Brit inf*), pull the other one (*inf*); **großmütterlich** ADJ ATTR (a) (= *von der Großmutter*) of one's grandmother; **im ~en Haus wohnen** to live in one's grandmother's house; **das ~e Erbe** one's inheritance from one's grandmother (b) (= *in der Art einer Großmutter*) grandmotherly; **großmütterlicherseits** ADV on one's grandmother's side; **Großneffe** M great-nephew; **Großnichte** F great-niece; **Großonkel** M great-uncle; **großporig** ADJ large-pored; **Großprojekt** NT large-scale project; **Großputz** M **-es, -e** ≈ spring-cleaning; **Großrat** M, **Großrätin** F (*Sw*) member of a/the Cantonal parliament

Großraum M (*einer Stadt*) **der ~ München** the Munich area

Großraum-: **Großraumabteil** NT (*Rail*) open-plan carriage (*Brit*) *or* car (*US*); **Großraumbüro** NT open-plan office; **Großraumflugzeug** NT large-capacity aircraft

Groß-: **großräumig** [-rɔymɪç] **1** ADJ (a) (= *mit großen Räumen*) with large rooms; **~ sein** to have large rooms (b) (= *mit viel Platz, geräumig*) roomy (c) (= *über große Flächen*) extensive (d) (= *im großen Umkreis*) **~es Umfahren eines Gebietes** making a large detour (a)round an area **2** ADV **ein Gebiet ~ absperren** to cordon off a large area; **Ortskundige sollten den Bereich ~ umfahren** local drivers should find an alternative route well away from the area; **Großraumwagen** M (*von Straßenbahn*) articulated tram (*esp Brit*) *or* streetcar (*US*); (*Rail*) open-plan carriage (*Brit*) *or* car (*US*); **Großrechner** M mainframe (computer); **Großreinemachen** [-raɪnəmaxn] NT **-s**, NO PL ≈ spring-cleaning; **groß schreiben** VT IRREG **groß geschrieben werden** (*fig inf*) to be stressed; **großschreiben** VT SEP IRREG **im Wort ~** to write a word with a capital in capitals; **Großschreibung** F capitalization; **Großsegel** NT (*Naut*) mainsail; **großsprecherisch** [-ʃprɛçərɪʃ] ADJ (*pej*) boastful; **großspurig** [-ʃpuːrɪç] (*pej*) **1** ADJ flashy (*inf*) **2** ADV **etw ~ erklären** to make a show of saying sth; **~ reden** to speak flamboyantly; **sich ~ benehmen** to be flashy

Großstadt F city

Großstadtbevölkerung F city population

Großstädter(in) M(F) city dweller

großstädtisch **1** ADJ big-city *attr* **2** ADV **München wirkt ~er als Bonn** Munich has more of a big-city feel to it than Bonn

Großstadt- IN CPDS city; **Großstadtmensch** M city dweller; **der ~** urban man, city dwellers *pl*

Groß-: **Großtante** F great-aunt; **Großtat** F great feat; **eine medizinische ~** a great medical feat; **großtechnisch** **1** ADJ large-scale **2** ADV **Kernkraft ~ erzeugen** to produce nuclear power on a large scale

Großteil M large part; **zum ~** in the main; **zu einem ~** for the most part

großteils [ˈgroːstails], **größtenteils** [ˈgrøːstnˈtails] ADV in the main

größte(r, s) SUPERL *von* **groß**

größtmöglich ADJ ATTR greatest possible

Groß-: **großtun** SEP IRREG (*pej*) **1** VI to show off **2** VR **sich mit etw ~** to boast about sth; **Großvater** M grandfather; **großväterlich** ADJ (a) (= *vom Großvater*) of one's grandfather; **er hat den ~en Betrieb übernommen** he has taken over his grandfather's business; **das ~e Erbe** one's inheritance from one's grandfather (b) (= *in der Art eines Großvaters*) grandfatherly; **großväterlicherseits** ADV on one's grandfather's side; **Großveranstaltung** F big event; (= *Großkundgebung*) mass rally; **eine sportliche ~** a big sporting event; **Großverdiener(in)** M(F) big earner; **Großwetterlage** F general weather situation; **die politische ~** the general political climate; **Großwild** NT big game; **großziehen** VT SEP IRREG to raise; *Tier* to rear; **großzügig** **1** ADJ generous; (= *weiträumig*) spacious; *Plan* ambitious **2** ADV generously; (= *spendabel*) magnanimously; (= *weiträumig*) spaciously; **~ gerechnet** at a generous estimate; **Großzügigkeit** [-tsyːgɪçkait] F **-**, NO PL generosity; (= *Weiträumigkeit*) spaciousness; (*von Plan*) (large) scale, ambitiousness

grotesk [groˈtɛsk] **1** ADJ grotesque **2** ADV grotesquely; **~ wirken/aussehen** to look grotesque

groteskerweise [groˈtɛskəˈvaizə] ADV ironically enough

Grotte [ˈgrɔtə] F **-, -n** (a) (= *Höhle*) grotto (b) (*sl*: = *Vagina*) pussy (*sl*)

Grottenolm [-ɔlm] M **-s, -e** (*Zool*) olm (*spec*)

Groupie [ˈgruːpi] NT **-s, -s** groupie

grub PRET *von* **graben**

Grübchen [ˈgryːpçən] NT **-s, -** dimple

Grube [ˈgruːbə] F **-, -n** pit; (*klein*) hole; (*Min*) mine; **wer andern eine ~ gräbt(, fällt selbst hinein)** (*Prov*) you can easily fall into your own trap

Grübelei [gryːbəˈlai] F **-, -en** brooding *no pl*

grübeln [ˈgryːbln] VI to brood (*über +acc* about, over)

Grübler [ˈgryːblɐ] M **-s, -**, **Grüblerin** [-ərɪn] F **-, -nen** brooder

grüblerisch [ˈgryːblərɪʃ] ADJ pensive

grüezi [ˈgryːɛtsi] INTERJ (*Sw*) hello, hi (*inf*), good morning/afternoon/evening

Gruft [grʊft] F **-, ⸚e** [ˈgrʏftə] tomb, vault; (*in Kirchen*) crypt

Grufti [ˈgrʊfti] M **-s, -s** (a) (*inf*: = *älterer Mensch*) old fogey (*inf*) (b) (*sl*: = *Okkultist*) ≈ goth

grummeln [ˈgrʊmln] VI to rumble; (*inf*: = *brummeln*) to mumble

grün [gryːn] **1** ADJ (*alle Bedeutungen*) green; (*Pol auch*) ecological; **~e Heringe** fresh herrings; **Aal ~** (*Cook*) (dish of) fresh eel (*with parsley sauce*); **~er Salat** lettuce; **die Grüne Insel** the Emerald Isle; **ein ~er Junge** (*inf*) a greenhorn (*inf*); **~es Licht (für etw) geben/haben** (*fig*) to give/have got the green light (for sth); **komm an meine ~e Seite!** (*inf*) come and sit up close to me; **am ~en Tisch, vom ~en Tisch aus** from a bureaucratic ivory tower; **über die ~e Grenze fahren/kommen** (*inf*) to cross the border illegally (*in a wood etc*); **~e Minna** (*inf*) Black Maria (*Brit inf*), paddy wagon (*US inf*); **die ~e Tonne** container for recyclable waste; **wir haben ~e Weihnachten gehabt** we didn't have a white Christmas; **~e Welle** phased traffic lights; **~e Welle bei 60 km/h** traffic lights phased for 60 kmph; **~ im Gesicht werden** to go green (about the gills (*inf*)); **auf keinen ~en Zweig kommen** (*fig inf*) to get nowhere; **die beiden sind sich gar nicht ~** (*inf*) there's no love lost between them; **er ist dir nicht ~** (*inf*) you're not in his good books (*inf*)

2 ADV (= *in ~er Farbe) gekleidet* (in) green; (= *mit ~er Farbe) streichen, anmalen* green; *umranden, unterstreichen* in green; **sich ~ und blau** *or* **gelb ärgern** (*inf*) to be furious; **jdn ~ und blau** *or* **gelb schlagen** (*inf*) to beat sb black and blue

Grün [gryːn] NT **-s, -** *or* (*inf*) **-s** green; (= *~flächen*) green spaces *pl*; (*Golf*) green; **die Ampel steht auf ~** the light is (at (*Brit*)) green; **das ist dasselbe in ~** (*inf*) it's (one and) the same (thing)

Grün- IN CPDS green; **Grünalge** F green alga; **grünalternativ** ADJ (*Pol*) green alternative; **Grünanlage** F green space; **grünäugig** [-ɔygɪç] ADJ green-eyed

Grund [grʊnt] M **-(e)s, ⁀e** ['grʏndə] **(a)** NO PL (= *Erdboden*) ground; **~ und Boden** land; **in ~ und Boden** (*fig*) *sich blamieren, schämen* utterly; *verdammen* outright **(b)** (*Aus*) (= *Bauplatz*) (building) plot; (= *~stück*) grounds *pl*, land *no indef art, no pl* **(c)** NO PL (*von Gefäßen, Becken etc*) bottom; (= *Meeresgrund*) (sea)bed; **ein Schiff auf ~ setzen** to scuttle a ship **(d)** NO PL (*lit, fig:* = *Fundament*) foundation(s *pl*); (= *das Innerste*) depths *pl*; **von ~ auf** *or* **aus** completely; *ändern* fundamentally; *neu gebaut, geplant* from scratch; **ein von ~ auf aufrechter Mensch** a thoroughly honest fellow; **den ~ zu etw legen** (*lit, fig*) to lay the foundations of *or* for sth; **einer Sache** (*dat*) **auf den ~ gehen** (*fig*) to get to the bottom of sth; **im ~e seines Herzens** in one's heart of hearts; **im ~e (genommen)** basically **(e)** (= *Ursache, Veranlassung, Ausrede*) reason; **aus gesundheitlichen** *etc* **Gründen** for health *etc* reasons; **aus dem einfachen ~e, dass ...** for the simple reason that ...; **ohne ~** without reason; **einen ~ zum Feiern haben** to have good cause for (a) celebration; **du hast keinen ~ zum Klagen** you have no cause for complaint; **jdm ~ (zu etw) geben** to give sb good reason (for sth); **aus diesem ~** for this reason; **aus guten Gründen, mit gutem ~** with good reason; **aus welchem ~(e)?** for what reason?; **aus Gründen** *+gen* for reasons of; **auf ~ =** → **aufgrund; zu ~e =** → **zugrunde**

Grund-: **grundanständig** ADJ thoroughly decent; **Grundanstrich** M first coat; **Grundbegriff** M basic concept; **Grundbesitz** M land; (= *das Besitzen*) ownership of land; **Grundbesitzer(in)** M(F) landowner; **Grundbuch** NT land register; **Grundbuchauszug** M extract from the land charges register, certificate of title (*US*); **Grunddienstbarkeit** F easement, real servitude; **grundehrlich** ADJ thoroughly honest

gründen ['grʏndn] **1** VT to found; *Argument etc* to base (*auf +acc* on); *Heim, Geschäft* to set up; **gegründet 1857** founded in 1857; **eine Familie ~** to get married (and have a family) **2** VR **sich auf etw** (*acc*) **~** to be based on sth

Gründer ['grʏndɐ] M **-s, -, Gründerin** [-ərɪn] F **-, -nen** founder

Gründerjahre PL (*Hist*) *years of rapid industrial expansion in Germany (from 1871)*

Grund-: **Grunderwerb** M acquisition of land; **Grunderwerb(s)steuer** F tax on land acquisition; **grundfalsch** ADJ utterly wrong; **Grundfarbe** F primary colour (*Brit*) *or* color (*US*); (= *Grundierfarbe*) ground colour (*Brit*) *or* color (*US*); **Grundfläche** F (*Math*) base; **Grundform** F basic form (*auch Gram*); **Grundfreibetrag** M tax-free allowance; **Grundgebühr** F basic charge; **Grundgedanke** M basic idea;

Grundgesetz NT **(a)** (= *Grundprinzip*) basic law **(b) das ~** the (German) Constitution

Grundhandelsgewerbe NT basic commercial business

grundieren [grʊnˈdiːrən], *ptp* **grundiert** VT to undercoat; (*Art*) to ground

Grundierfarbe F, **Grundierschicht** F undercoat

Grundierung F **-, -en (a)** NO PL (= *das Grundieren*) undercoating; (*Art*) grounding **(b)** (= *Farbe, Fläche*) undercoat; (*Art*) ground

Grund-: **Grundkurs** M (*Sch, Univ*) basic course; **Grundlage** F basis; **auf der ~ von** *or* *+gen* on the basis of; **die ~n einer Wissenschaft** the fundamental principles of a science; **die ~n eines Lehrfachs** the rudiments of a subject; **jeder ~ entbehren** to be completely unfounded; **Grundlagenforschung** F pure research; **Grundlast** F (*Tech*) constant load; **Grundlastkapazität** F (*Tech*) constant load capacity; **grundlegend 1** ADJ fundamental (*für* to); *Werk, Textbuch* standard **2** ADV fundamentally; **sich zu etw ~ äußern** to make a statement of fundamental importance on sth

gründlich ['grʏntlɪç] **1** ADJ thorough; *Arbeit* painstaking **2** ADV thoroughly; (*inf:* = *sehr auch*) really; **jdm ~ die Meinung sagen** to give sb a real piece of one's mind; **da haben Sie sich ~ getäuscht** you're completely mistaken there

Gründlichkeit F **-,** NO PL thoroughness

Grund-: **Grundlinie** F (*Math, Sport*) baseline; **Grundlinienspiel** NT baseline game; **Grundlohn** M basic pay; **grundlos 1** ADJ (*fig:* = *unbegründet*) unfounded; **~es Lachen** laughter for no reason (at all) **2** ADV (*fig*) without reason; **Grundmauer** F foundation wall; **bis auf die ~n niederbrennen** to be gutted; **Grundnahrungsmittel** NT basic food(stuff)

Gründonnerstag [gryːnˈdɔnɛstaːk] M Maundy Thursday

Grund-: **Grundpfeiler** M (*Archit*) supporting pier; (*fig*) cornerstone, keystone; **Grundrechenart** F, **Grundrechnungsart** F basic arithmetical operation; **Grundriss** M (*von Gebäude*) ground *or* floor plan; (*Math*) base; (= *Abriss*) outline, sketch; **„~ der chinesischen Grammatik"** "Outlines of Chinese Grammar"

Grundsatz M principle; **aus ~** on principle; **ein Mann mit** *or* **von Grundsätzen** a man of principle

Grundsatz-: **Grundsatzdebatte** F, **Grundsatzdiskussion** F debate on (general) principles; **Grundsatzentscheidung** F decision of general principle

grundsätzlich ['grʊntzɛtslɪç] **1** ADJ fundamental; *Verbot* absolute; *Möglichkeit* in principle; *Frage* of principle **2** ADV (= *allgemein, im Prinzip*) in principle; (= *aus Prinzip*) on principle; (= *immer*) always; (= *völlig*) absolutely; **sich zu etw ~ äußern** to make a statement of principle on sth; **ihre Meinungen sind ~ verschieden** their views are fundamentally different; **das erlaube ich Ihnen ~ nicht** I will most definitely not permit that; **das ist ~ verboten** it is absolutely forbidden; **das ist ~ möglich** it is possible in principle; **er hat ~ kein Interesse für so etwas** he has absolutely no interest in that sort of thing

Grund-: **Grundschrift** F (*Typ*) base type; **Grundschuld** F mortgage; **Grundschule** F primary (*Brit*) *or* elementary school;

Grundschüler(in) M(F) primary (*Brit*) or elementary(-school) pupil

Grund-: Grundstein M (*lit, fig*) foundation stone; **den ~ zu etw legen** (*lit*) to lay the foundation stone of sth; (*fig*) to lay the foundations of or for sth; **Grundsteinlegung** [-le:gɔŋ] F -, -en laying of the foundation stone; **Grundsteuer** F (local) property tax

Grundstück NT plot (of land); (*bebaut*) property; (= *Anwesen*) estate

Grundstücks-: Grundstückspreis M land price; **Grundstücksspekulation** F property speculation

Grund-: Grundstudium NT (*Univ*) basic course; **Grundstufe** F (a) first stage; (*Sch*) ≈ junior (*Brit*) or grade (*US*) school (b) (*Gram*) positive (degree)

Gründung F -, -en founding; (*von Heim, Geschäft*) setting up; **die ~ einer Familie** getting married (and having a family)

Grund-: grundverkehrt ADJ completely wrong; **grundverschieden** ADJ totally different; **Grundwasser** NT, NO PL ground water; **Grundwasserspiegel** M water table; **Grundwehrdienst** M national (*Brit*) or selective (*US*) service; **Grundwort** NT, *pl* **-wörter** (*Gram*) root; **Grundzug** M essential feature; **"Grundzüge der Geometrie"** "Basic Geometry"

Grüne(r) [ˈgryːnə] MF DECL AS ADJ (*Pol*) Green

Grüne(s) [ˈgryːnə] NT DECL AS ADJ (= *Farbe*) green; (*als Ausschmückung*) greenery; (= *Gemüse*) greens *pl*; (= *Grünfutter*) green stuff; **ins ~ fahren** to go to the country

Grün-: Grünfink M greenfinch; **Grünfläche** F green space; **Grünfutter** NT green fodder; (*inf*: = *Salat*) salad; (*inf*: = *Gemüse*) greens *pl* (*inf*); **Grüngürtel** M green belt; **Grünkohl** M (curly) kale; **grünlich** [ˈgryːnlɪç] ADJ greenish; **Grünpflanze** F non-flowering or foliage plant; **Grünschnabel** M (*inf*) (little) whippersnapper (*inf*); (= *Neuling*) greenhorn (*inf*); **sei still, du ~!** be quiet, you little know-all! (*Brit inf*) or know-it-all (*US inf*); **Grünspan** M, NO PL verdigris; **Grünspecht** M green woodpecker; **Grünstreifen** M central reservation (*Brit*), median (strip) (*US, Austral*); (*am Straßenrand*) grass verge

grunzen [ˈgrʊntsn] VTI to grunt

Grünzeug NT, NO PL greens *pl*

Grüppchen [ˈgrʏpçən] NT -s, - (*usu pej*) little group

Gruppe [ˈgrʊpə] F -, -n group (*auch Math*); (*von Pfadfindern*) section; (= *Klasse, Kategorie*) class; **~n (zu je fünf/sechs) bilden** to make groups (of five/six)

Gruppen- IN CPDS group; **Gruppenakkord** M group piecework; **im ~** under a collective piece rate scheme; **Gruppenarbeit** F teamwork; **Gruppenführer(in)** M(F) group leader; (*Mil*) squad leader; **Gruppenreise** F group travel *no pl*; **Gruppensex** M group sex; **gruppenspezifisch** ADJ group-specific; **Gruppentherapie** F group therapy; **Gruppenunterricht** M group learning; **gruppenweise** ADV in groups

gruppieren [grʊˈpiːrən], *ptp* **gruppiert** **1** VT to group **2** VR to form a group/groups

Gruppierung F -, -en (a) NO PL grouping (b) (= *Konstellation*) grouping; (= *Gruppe*) group; (*Pol*) faction

Grusel-: Gruselfilm M horror film; **Gruselgeschichte** F horror story

gruselig [ˈgruːzəlɪç] ADJ horrifying; *Geschichte, Film* spine-chilling

Gruselmärchen NT horror story

gruseln [ˈgruːzln] **1** VTI IMPERS **mich** or **mir gruselt auf Friedhöfen** cemeteries give me the creeps; **hier kann man das Gruseln lernen** this will teach you the meaning of fear **2** VR **hier würde ich mich ~** a place like this would give me the creeps; **sie gruselt sich vor Schlangen** snakes give her the creeps

Gruß [gruːs] M -es, ⸚e [ˈgryːsə] (a) greeting; (= ~geste, *Mil*) salute; **zum ~** in greeting
(b) (*als Zeichen der Verbundenheit*) **viele Grüße** best wishes (*an* +*acc* to); **bestell Renate bitte viele Grüße von mir** please give Renate my regards; **schick mir einen ~ aus Paris** drop me a line from Paris; **sag ihm einen schönen ~** say hello to him (from me); **einen (schönen) ~ an Ihre Gattin!** my regards to your wife
(c) (*als Briefformel*) **mit bestem ~, mit besten Grüßen** yours; **mit brüderlichem/sozialistischem ~** (*Pol*) yours fraternally; **mit freundlichen Grüßen** or **freundlichem ~** (*bei Anrede Mr/Mrs/Miss X*) Yours sincerely, Yours truly (*esp US*); (*bei Anrede Sir(s)/Madam*) Yours faithfully, Yours truly (*esp US*)

grüßen [ˈgryːsn] **1** VT (a) (= *guten Tag sagen zu*) to greet; (*Mil*) to salute; **grüßt er dich auch nicht?** doesn't he say hello to you either?; **grüß dich!** (*inf*) hi! (*inf*)
(b) (= *Grüße übermitteln*) **Otto lässt dich (schön) ~** Otto sends his regards; **ich soll Sie von ihm ~** he sends his regards *etc*; **grüß mir deine Mutter!, grüß deine Mutter von mir!** give my regards to your mother; **und grüß mir Wien/den Goldenen Löwen** and say hello to Vienna/the Golden Lion for me **2** VI to say hello; (*Mil*) to salute; **Otto lässt ~** Otto sends his regards

Gruß-: Grußformel F form of greeting; (*am Briefanfang*) salutation; (*am Briefende*) complimentary close; **grußlos** ADV without a word of greeting; (*beim Abschied*) without saying goodbye; **Grußtelegramm** NT greetings telegram; (*Pol*) goodwill telegram

Grütze [ˈgrʏtsə] F -, -n (a) groats *pl*; (= *Brei*) gruel; **rote ~** *type of red fruit jelly* (b) NO PL (*inf*: = *Verstand*) brains *pl* (*inf*); **der hat ~ im Kopf** (*inf*) he's got brains (*inf*)

Gschaftlhuber [ˈkʃaftlhuːbɐ] M -s, -, **Gschaftlhuberin** [-ərɪn] F -, -nen (*S Ger, Aus*: *inf*) busybody

gschamig [ˈkʃaːmɪç] ADJ (*Aus inf*) bashful

Gspusi [ˈkʃpuːzi] NT -s, -s (*S Ger, Aus*: *inf*) (a) (= *Liebschaft*) affair (b) (= *Liebste(r)*) darling

GT-Wagen [geːˈteː-] M (*Aut*) GT (model)

Guatemala [guateˈmaːla] NT -s Guatemala

guatemaltekisch [guatemalˈteːkɪʃ] ADJ Guatemalan

Guave [ˈguaːvə] F -, -en guava

Guayana [guaˈjaːna] NT -s Guiana; (= *ehem. Brit.-~*) Guyana

guayanisch [guaˈjaːnɪʃ] ADJ *siehe* **Guayana** Guianese/Guyanese

gucken [ˈgʊkn] **1** VI (= *sehen*) to look (*zu* at); (= *hervorschauen*) to peep (*aus* out of); **lass mal ~!** let's have a look **2** VT (*inf*) **Fernsehen ~** to watch television

Guckloch NT peephole

Guerilla[1] [geˈrɪlja] F -, -s (a) (= ~*krieg*) guerilla war (b) (= ~*einheit*) guerilla unit

Guerilla[2] M -(s), -s (= ~*kämpfer*) guerilla

Guerilla-: [geˈrɪlja] IN CPDS guerilla; **Guerillakrieg** M guerilla war

Guerillero [gerɪlˈjeːro] M -s, -s, **Guerillera** [gerɪlˈjeːra] F -, -s guerilla fighter

Guernsey [ˈgøːɐnzi] NT -s Guernsey

Gugelhupf [ˈguːglhʊpf] M -s, -e (*S Ger, Aus*), **Gugelhopf** [ˈguːglhɔpf] M -s, -e (*Sw*) (*Cook*) gugelhupf

Guillotine [gɪljoˈtiːnə, gijoˈtiːnə] F -, -n guillotine

guillotinieren [gɪljotiˈniːrən, gijo-], *ptp* **guillotiniert** VT to guillotine

Guinea [giˈneːa] NT -s (*Geog*) Guinea

guineisch [giˈneːɪʃ] ADJ Guinean

Gulasch ['gu:laʃ, 'gʊlaʃ] NT or M **-(e)s, -e** or **-s** goulash

Gulaschsuppe F goulash soup

Gulden ['gʊldn] M **-s, -** (*Hist*) florin; (= *niederländischer ~*) g(u)ilder

Gülle ['gʏlə] F **-**, NO PL (*S Ger*, *Sw*) liquid manure

Gully ['gʊli] M or NT **-s, -s** drain

gültig ['gʏltɪç] ADJ valid; **nach den ~en Bestimmungen** according to current regulations; **nach dem bis Mai noch ~en Gesetz** according to the law in force until May; **ab wann ist der Fahrplan ~?** when does the timetable come into effect or force?; **~ werden** to become valid; (*Gesetz, Vertrag*) to come into force

Gültigkeit F **-**, NO PL validity; (*von Gesetz*) legal force

Gummi ['gʊmi] NT or M **-s, -s** (= *Material*) rubber; (= *~arabikum*) gum; (= *Radiergummi*) rubber, eraser; (= *~band*) rubber band; (*in Kleidung etc*) elastic; (*inf*: = *Kondom*) rubber (*esp US inf*), Durex®

Gummi- IN CPDS rubber; **gummiartig** ◨ ADJ rubbery ◩ ADV like rubber; **Gummiband** NT, *pl* **-bänder** rubber band; (*in Kleidung*) elastic; **Gummibärchen** [-bɛːɐçən] NT **-s, -** ≈ jelly baby (*Brit*), gummi bear; **Gummibaum** M rubber plant; **Gummiboot** NT rubber dinghy

Gummierung F **-**, **-en** (a) (= *Verfahren*) gumming **(b)** (= *gummierte Fläche*) gum

Gummi-: **Gummihose** F, **Gummihöschen** [-høːsçən] NT plastic pants *pl*; **Gummiknüppel** M rubber truncheon; **Gummiparagraf** M (*inf*) ambiguous clause; **Gummireifen** M rubber tyre (*Brit*) or tire (*US*); **Gummistiefel** M rubber boot, wellington (boot) (*Brit*); (*bis zu den Oberschenkeln*) wader; **Gummistrumpf** M elastic stocking; **Gummizelle** F padded cell; **Gummizug** M (piece of) elastic

Gunst [gʊnst] F **-**, NO PL favour (*Brit*), favor (*US*); (*des Schicksals etc*) benevolence; **zu meinen/deinen ~en** in my/your favo(u)r; **jdm eine ~ erweisen** (*geh*) to do sb a kindness; **jdm die ~ erweisen, etw zu tun** (*geh*) to be so gracious as to do sth for sb; **zu ~en = zugunsten**

günstig ['gʏnstɪç] ◨ ADJ favourable (*Brit*), favorable (*US*); (*zeitlich, bei Reisen etc*) convenient; *Angebot, Preis etc* reasonable; **bei ~er Witterung** weather permitting; **im ~sten Fall(e)** with luck; **mit Geschäften und Erholungsmöglichkeiten in ~er Lage** convenient for shops and recreational facilities ◩ ADV *kaufen, verkaufen* for a good price; *einkaufen, beziehen* at a good price; **jdm etw ~er geben** to give sb sth at a discount; **jdm/einer Sache ~ gesinnt sein** (*geh*) to be favourably (*Brit*) or favorably (*US*) disposed toward(s) sb/sth; **es trifft sich ~, dass …** it's very lucky that …; **die Stadt liegt ~** (**für**) the town is well situated (for); **„Fernseher ~ abzugeben"** "television for sale: bargain price"

günstigstenfalls ADV at the very best

Günstling ['gʏnstlɪŋ] M **-s, -e** (*pej*) favourite (*Brit*), favorite (*US*)

Gurgel ['gʊrɡl] F **-**, **-n** throat; (= *Schlund*) gullet; **jdm die ~ zudrücken** or **abdrücken** or **abschnüren** or **zuschnüren** (*lit, fig*) to strangle sb; **dann springt** or **geht sie mir an die ~!** (*inf*) she'll kill me (*inf*)

Gurgelmittel NT gargle

gurgeln ['gʊrɡln] VI (a) (= *den Rachen spülen*) to gargle **(b)** (*Wasser, Laut*) to gurgle

Gürkchen ['gʏrkçən] NT **-s, -** mini gherkin (*Brit*), baby gherkin pickle (*US*)

Gurke ['gʊrkə] F **-**, **-n** (a) cucumber; (= *Essiggurke*) gherkin; **saure ~n** pickled gherkins **(b)** (*sl*: = *Schrottauto*) banger (*Brit inf*), jalopy (*inf*)

Gurken-: **Gurkenhobel** M slicer; **Gurkensalat** M cucumber salad

gurren ['gʊrən] VI (*lit, fig*) to coo

Gurt [gʊrt] M **-(e)s, -e** (= *Gürtel, Sicherheitsgurt, Ladestreifen*) belt; (= *Riemen*) strap

Gürtel ['gʏrtl] M **-s, -** (= *Gurt, Zone*) belt; (= *Absperrkette*) cordon; **den ~ enger schnallen** (*lit, fig*) to tighten one's belt

Gürtel-: **Gürtellinie** F waist; **ein Schlag unter die ~** (*lit*) a blow below the belt; **das war ein Schlag unter die ~** (*fig*) that really was (hitting) below the belt; **Gürtelreifen** M radial (tyre (*Brit*) or tire (*US*)); **Gürtelrose** F (*Med*) shingles *sing or pl*; **Gürteltier** NT armadillo

Gurt-: **Gurtmuffel** M (*inf*) person who refuses to wear a seat belt; **Gurtpflicht** F, NO PL **es besteht ~** the wearing of seat belts is compulsory; **Gurtstraffer** [-ʃtrafɐ] M **-s, -** (*Aut*) seat-belt tensioner

GUS [ɡʊs] F **-** ABBR *von* **Gemeinschaft Unabhängiger Staaten** CIS

Guss [ɡʊs] M **-es, ⸚e** ['ɡʏsə] (a) (*Metal*) (*no pl*: = *das Gießen*) casting; (= *~stück*) cast; (**wie**) **aus einem ~** (*fig*) a unified whole **(b)** (= *Strahl*) stream; (*inf*: = *Regenguss*) downpour; **kalte Güsse** (*Med*) cold affusions **(c)** (= *Zuckerguss*) icing, frosting (*esp US*); (*durchsichtig*) glaze

Guss-: **Gusseisen** NT cast iron; **gusseisern** ADJ cast-iron; **Gussform** F mould (*Brit*), mold (*US*)

gut [ɡuːt] ◨ ADJ, *comp* **besser** ['bɛsɐ], *superl* **beste(r, s)** ['bɛstə] good; **das ist ~ gegen** or **für** (*inf*) **Husten** it's good for coughs; **wozu ist das ~?** (*inf*) what's that for?; **sie ist immer für eine Überraschung ~** (*inf*) she's always good for a surprise; **das war Pech, aber wer weiß, wozu es ~ ist** it was bad luck, but it's an ill wind (that blows nobody any good) (*Brit prov*), it was bad luck, but every cloud has a silver lining (*prov*); **sei so ~ (und) gib mir das** would you mind giving me that; **würden Sie so ~ sein und …** would you be good enough to …; **dafür ist er sich zu ~** he wouldn't stoop to that sort of thing; **sind die Bilder/ die Brötchen ~ geworden?** did the pictures/rolls turn out all right?; **ist dein Magen wieder ~?** is your stomach better again?; **es wird alles wieder ~!** everything will be all right; **wie ~, dass …** it's good that …; **~, dass du das endlich einsiehst** it's a good job (that) you realize it at last; **so was ist immer ~** that's always useful; **ich will es damit ~ sein lassen** I'll leave it at that; **lass mal ~ sein!** (= *ist genug*) that's enough; (= *ist erledigt*) just leave it; **jetzt ist aber ~!** (*inf*) that's enough; **das ist ja alles ~ und schön, aber …** that's all very well but …; **~e Besserung!** get well soon; **auf ~e Freundschaft!** here's to us!; **auf ~es Gelingen!** here's to success!; **~!** good; (= *in Ordnung*) (all) right, OK; **schon ~!** (it's) all right; **also** or **nun ~!** all right then; **~ und schön** (*inf*) fair enough; **du bist ~!** (*inf*) you're a fine one!

◩ ADV, *comp* **besser**, *superl* **am besten** well; **~ schmecken/ riechen** to taste/smell good; **es ~ haben** to have a good time of it, to have it good (*esp US*); **unser Volk hat es noch nie so ~ gehabt** our people have never had it so good; **er hat es in seiner Jugend nicht ~ gehabt** he had a hard time (of it) when he was young; **du hast es ~!** you've got it made; **das kann ~ sein** that may well be; **so ~ wie nichts** next to nothing; **so ~ wie nicht** hardly; **so ~ wie verloren** as good as lost; **es dauert ~(e) drei Stunden** it lasts a good three hours; **nehmen Sie ~ ein Pfund Mehl** take a good pound of flour; **~ aussehend** good-looking; **~ betucht** (*inf*) well-off (*inf*); **~ bezahlt** *Person, Job* highly-paid; **~ dotiert** *Job* well-paid; *Vertrag* lucrative; **~ gehend** flourishing; **~ gelaunt** cheerful; **~ gemeint** well-meaning, well-meant; **~ sitzend** well-fitting; **~ verdienend** with a good salary; **das ist aber ~ gewogen/eingeschenkt!** that's a generous measure; **~ und gern** easily; **(das hast du) ~ gemacht!** well done!; **machs ~!** (*inf*) cheers! (*Brit*); (*stärker*) take care; **pass ~ auf!** be very careful

Gut [ɡuːt] NT **-(e)s, ⸚er** ['ɡyːtɐ] (a) (= *Eigentum*) property; (*lit, fig*: = *Besitztum*) possession; **irdische Güter** worldly goods; **geistige Güter** intellectual wealth; **bewegliche Güter** movables; **unbewegliche Güter** immovables **(b)** (= *Ware, Frachtgut*) item; **Güter** goods; (= *Frachtgut*) freight *sing*, goods (*esp Brit*) **(c)** (= *Landgut*) estate

Gut-: **Gutachten** ['ɡuːtlaxtn] NT **-s, -** report; **Gutachter** ['ɡuːtlaxtɐ] M **-s, -**, **Gutachterin** F **-**, **-nen** expert; (*Jur: in Prozess*) expert witness; **gutartig** ADJ *Kind, Hund etc* good-natured; *Geschwulst, Geschwür* benign; **Gutartigkeit** F, NO PL (*von Kind, Tier etc*) good nature; (*von Geschwulst*) benignity; **gutaussehend** ADJ *siehe* **gut**; **gutbürgerlich** ADJ solid middle-class; *Küche* good plain; **Gutdünken** ['ɡuːtdʏŋkn] NT **-s**, NO PL discretion; **nach (eigenem) ~** as one sees fit

Güte ['ɡyːtə] F **-**, NO PL (a) (= *Herzensgüte, Freundlichkeit*) goodness; **ein Vorschlag zur ~** a suggestion; **in ~** amicably; **meine ~, ist der dumm!** (*inf*) my goodness, is he stupid! (*inf*); **ach du liebe** or **meine ~!** (*inf*) oh my goodness! **(b)** (*einer Ware*) quality; **ein Reinfall erster ~** (*inf*) a first-class flop

Gütegrad M, **Güteklasse** F (*Comm*) grade

Gutenacht-: **Gutenachtgeschichte** [ɡuːtəˈnaxt-] F bedtime story; **Gutenachtkuss** [ɡuːtəˈnaxt-] M goodnight kiss

Güter-: **Güterabfertigung** F (a) NO PL dispatch of freight or goods (*esp Brit*) **(b)** (= *Abfertigungsstelle*) freight or goods (*esp*

Brit) office; **Güterbahnhof** M freight depot; **Güterdepot** NT goods depot; **Güterfernverkehr** M long-distance haulage; **Gütergemeinschaft** F (*Jur*) community of property; **in ~ leben** to have community of property; **Güternahverkehr** M short-distance haulage (*up to 50 km*); **Gütertrennung** F (*Jur*) separation of property; **in ~ leben** to have separation of property; **Güterverkehr** M freight traffic; **Güterwagen** M (*Rail*) freight car; **Güterzug** M freight train

Gute(s) ['guːtə] NT DECL AS ADJ **~s tun** to do good; **es hat alles sein ~s** (*prov*) every cloud has a silver lining (*Prov*); **alles ~!** all the best!; **man hört über sie nur ~s** you hear so many good things about her; **jdm (viel) ~s tun** to be (very) good to sb; **des ~n zu viel tun** to overdo things; **das ist des ~n zu viel** that is too much of a good thing; **das ~ daran** the good thing about it; **das ~ im Menschen** the good in man; **im ~n wie im Bösen** for better or for worse; **im ~n** *sich trennen* amicably; **ich sage es dir im ~n** I want to give you a friendly piece of advice

Gut-: gut gehen IRREG AUX SEIN **1** VI IMPERS **es geht ihm gut** he is doing well; (= *er ist gesund*) he is well; **sonst gehts dir gut?** (*iro*) are you feeling all right? **2** VI to go (off) well; **das ist noch einmal gut gegangen** it turned out all right; **wenn es gut geht** with luck; **das konnte ja nicht ~** it was bound to go wrong; **wenn das man gut geht!** (*N Ger*) that's asking for trouble; **hoffentlich geht es mit den beiden gut!** (*inf*) I hope things will work out for the two of them; **gutgehend** ADJ ATTR *siehe* **gut**; **gutgläubig** ADJ trusting; (= *vertrauensselig auch*) credulous; **guthaben** ['guːthaːbn] VT SEP IRREG **etw ~** to be owed sth (*bei* by); **Guthaben** ['guːthaːbn] NT **-s, -** (*Fin*: = *Bankguthaben*) credit; **auf meinem Konto ist** *or* **habe ich ein ~ von 500 Euro** my account is 500 euros in credit; **gutheißen** ['guːthaisn] VT SEP IRREG to approve of; (= *genehmigen*) to approve; **gutherzig** ADJ kind-hearted

gütig ['gyːtɪç] ADJ kind; (= *edelmütig*) generous

gütlich ['gyːtlɪç] **1** ADJ amicable **2** ADV amicably; **sich ~ einigen** to come to an amicable agreement; **sich an etw** (*dat*) **~ tun** to use sth freely

Gut-: gutmachen VT SEP **(a)** *Fehler* to put right; *Schaden* to make good; **das kann ich ja gar nicht wieder ~!** (*fig*) how on earth can I ever repay you! **(b)** (= *gewinnen*) to make (*bei* out of, on); **gutmütig** ['guːtmyːtɪç] ADJ good-natured; **Gutmütigkeit** F **-**, NO PL good nature; **jds ~ ausnützen** to presume upon sb's good nature

Gutsbesitzer(in) M(F) lord/lady of the manor; (*als Klasse*) landowner

Gut-: Gutschein M voucher; (*für Umtausch*) credit note; **gutschreiben** ['guːtʃraibn] VT SEP IRREG to credit (+*dat* to); **Gutschrift** F **(a)** NO PL (= *Vorgang*) crediting **(b)** (= *Bescheinigung*) credit note; (= *Betrag*) credit (item)

Gutschriftsanzeige F (*von Bank*) credit advice; (*bei zurückgenommener Ware*) credit note, credit receipt (*US*)

Guts-: Gutsherr M squire; **Gutsherrin** F lady of the manor; **Gutshof** M estate; **Gutsverwalter(in)** M(F) steward

gut tun VI IRREG **jdm ~** to do sb good; **das tut gut** that's good; **o, wie gut das tut!** oh, that's good

guttural [gutuˈraːl] ADJ guttural

Gut-: gutunterrichtet ADJ ATTR *siehe* **unterrichtet**; **gutwillig** ADJ willing; (= *entgegenkommend*) obliging; (= *wohlwollend*) well-meaning

GuV ABBR *von* **Gewinn- und Verlustrechnung**

Guyana [guˈjaːna] NT **-s** Guiana; (= *ehem. Brit.~~*) Guyana

guyanisch [guˈjaːnɪʃ] ADJ *siehe* **Guyana** Guianese/Guyanese

gymnasial [gymnaˈziaːl] ADJ ATTR ≈ at grammar schools (*Brit*), ≈ at high schools (*US*); **die ~e Oberstufe** ≈ the sixth form (*Brit*), ≈ the twelfth grade (*US*)

Gymnasiast [gymnaˈziast] M **-en, -en**, **Gymnasiastin** [-ˈziastɪn] F **-, -nen** ≈ grammar school pupil (*Brit*), ≈ high school student (*US*)

Gymnasium [gymˈnaːziʊm] NT **-s, Gymnasien** [-ziən] (*Sch*) ≈ grammar school (*Brit*), ≈ high school (*US*)

Vorsicht! **Gymnasium** *wird nicht mit dem englischen Wort* **gymnasium** *übersetzt.*

GYMNASIUM

A **Gymnasium** is a secondary school which pupils attend for nine years and which leads to the Abitur. The final two years at a **Gymnasium** (two and a half in some Länder) are known as the Kollegstufe. The curriculum varies according to the type of school: in a **humanistisches Gymnasium** Latin and Greek are taught; in a **neusprachliches Gymnasium** English, Latin and French or other lingua franca are taught; and in a **mathematisch-naturwissenschaftliches Gymnasium** the emphasis is on the sciences. A **Gymnasium** may offer several of these curricula, which pupils must choose from when they reach a certain class, usually the seventh or ninth.

Since nowadays many students who have taken their Abitur do not necessarily continue studying but undertake a period of training instead, new types of **Gymnasien** (for example Wirtschaftsgymnasien) have been created with an emphasis on practical work. ▶ ABITUR, KOLLEGSTUFE

Gymnastik [gymˈnastɪk] F **-**, NO PL keep-fit exercises *pl*; (= *Turnen*) gymnastics *sing*; **~ machen** to do keep-fit (exercises)/gymnastics

Gymnastikanzug M leotard

Gynäkologe [gynɛkoˈloːgə] M **-n, -n**, **Gynäkologin** [-ˈloːgɪn] F **-, -nen** gynaecologist (*Brit*), gynecologist (*US*), gyno (*esp US inf*)

Gynäkologie [gynɛkoloˈgiː] F **-**, NO PL gynaecology (*Brit*), gynecology (*US*)

gynäkologisch [gynɛkoˈloːgɪʃ] **1** ADJ gynaecological (*Brit*), gynecological (*US*) **2** ADV **sich ~ untersuchen lassen** to have a gyn(a)ecological examination; **~ betreuen/behandeln** to give/administer gyn(a)ecological treatment

Gyros ['gyːros] NT **-**, NO PL ≈ doner kebab

Hh

H, h [haː] NT **-,** - H, h; (*Mus*) B

h ABBR *von* **hora(e)** (= *Stunde*) hr; **120 km/h** 120 km/h *or* kmph

ha¹ ABBR *von* **Hektar** hectare

ha² [haː] INTERJ ha; (*triumphierend*) aha; (*überrascht, erstaunt, verärgert*) oh; (*verächtlich*) huh

hä [hɛ, hɛː] INTERJ what

Haag [haːk] M **-s der ~, Den ~** The Hague

Haager [haːgɐ] ADJ ATTR Hague; **~ Konventionen** Hague Conventions; **~ Schiedshof** International Court of Justice in The Hague

Haar [haːɐ] NT **-(e)s, -e** (a) hair; **sich** (*dat*) **die ~e** *or* **das ~ schneiden lassen** to get one's hair cut
(b) (*in Wendungen*) **~e auf den Zähnen haben** to be a tough customer (*Brit*) *or* cookie (*esp US*); **jdm kein ~ krümmen** not to harm a hair on sb's head; **darüber lass dir keine grauen ~e wachsen** don't worry your head about it; **er findet immer ein ~ in der Suppe** he always finds something to quibble about; **sie gleichen sich** (*dat*) **aufs ~** they are the spitting image of each other; **das ist an den ~en herbeigezogen** that's rather far-fetched; **an jdm/etw kein** *or* **nicht ein gutes ~ lassen** to pull sb/sth to pieces; **sich** (*dat*) **in die ~e geraten** *or* **kriegen** (*inf*) to quarrel; **um kein ~ besser** not a bit better; **um ein** *or* **ums ~** very nearly; **er hat mich um ein ~ getroffen** he just missed me by a hair's breadth

haaren [haːrən] VI (*Tier*) to moult (*Brit*), to molt (*US*); (*Pelz etc*) to shed (hair); (*Teppich*) to shed VR (*Tier*) to moult (*Brit*), to molt (*US*)

Haaresbreite [haːrəsbraitə] F INV (**nur**) **um ~** very nearly; **verfehlen** by a hair's breadth

Haar-: Haarfarbe F hair colour (*Brit*) *or* color (*US*); **Haarfestiger** M (hair) setting lotion; **Haargel** NT hair gel; **haargenau** ADJ exact; *Übereinstimmung* total ADV exactly; **die Beschreibung trifft ~ auf ihn zu** the description fits him exactly; **jdm etw ~ erklären** to explain sth to sb in great detail; **das trifft ~ zu** that is absolutely right

haarig [haːrɪç] ADJ hairy; (*inf*) (= *heikel, gefährlich*) hairy (*inf*); (= *schwierig*) nasty

Haar-: Haarklammer F (= *Klemme*) hairgrip (*Brit*), bobby pin (*US*); (= *Spange*) hair slide (*Brit*), barrette (*US*); **haarklein** (*inf*) ADJ *Beschreibung* detailed ADV in great detail; **Haarlack** M hair lacquer; **Haarnadelkurve** F hairpin bend; **Haarpflege** F hair care; **zur ~** (for caring) for one's hair; **Haarriss** M hairline crack; **haarscharf** ADJ *Beschreibung, Wiedergabe* exact; *Unterschied* very fine; *Beobachtung* very close ADV *treffen* exactly; *danebentreffen, vorbeitreffen* barely; *folgern, schließen* precisely; **die Kugel ging ~ daneben** the bullet missed by a hair's breadth; **Haarschleife** F hair ribbon; **Haarschnitt** M haircut; **Haarspalter** [-ʃpaltɐ] M **-s, -, Haarspalterin** [-ərɪn] F **-, -nen** pedant; **Haarspalterei** [-ʃpaltəˈrai] F **-, -en** splitting hairs *no indef art, no pl*; **eine solche ~** hairsplitting like that; **haarspalterisch** [-ʃpaltərɪʃ] ADJ hairsplitting; *Unterschied* minute; **Haarspange** F hair slide (*Brit*), barrette (*US*); **Haarspitze** F end (of a hair); **gespaltene ~n** split ends; **Haarspliss** M split ends *pl*; **Haarspray** NT *or* M hairspray; **Haarspülung** F (hair) conditioner; **haarsträubend** [-ʃtrɔybnt] ADJ hair-raising; (= *empörend*) shocking; (= *unglaublich*) *Frechheit* incredible ADV *brutal* hair-raisingly; *schlecht* painfully; *obszön* terribly; *frech* incredibly; *sich benehmen* shockingly; **Haarteil** NT hairpiece; **Haartönung** F tinting; **Haartrockner** [-trɔknɐ] M **-s, -** hairdryer; **Haarwäsche** F washing one's hair *no art*; **eine regelmäßige ~** washing one's hair regularly; **Haarwaschmittel** NT shampoo; **Haarwirbel** M cowlick; (*am Hinterkopf*) crown; **Haarwuchs** M growth of hair; **einen kräftigen ~ haben** to have a full head of hair; **einen spärlichen ~ haben** to have a thin head of hair

Hab [haːp] NT **~ und Gut** possessions, worldly goods *all pl*

Habe [haːbə] F **-, NO PL** (*geh*) belongings *pl*

haben [haːbn̩]

1 HILFSVERB	**3** UNPERSÖNLICHES VERB
2 TRANSITIVES VERB	**4** REFLEXIVES VERB

pres **hat** [hat], *pret* **hatte** [hatə], *ptp* **gehabt** [gəˈhaːpt]

1 HILFSVERB

ich habe/hatte gerufen I have/had called, I've/I'd called; **er will sie gesehen haben** he says (that) he saw her; **du hättest den Brief früher schreiben können** you could have written the letter earlier

2 TRANSITIVES VERB

In Verbindung mit Substantiv siehe auch Eintrag für das jeweilige Substantiv.

*Im Präsens wird im britischen Englisch oft **have got** verwendet.*

(a) (= *besitzen*) to have; **wir haben ein Haus/Auto** we've got a house/car; **ich hatte viele Bücher** I had a lot of books; **er hat eine Brille** he's got glasses; **was man hat, das hat man** (*inf*) what you've got, you've got; **wer hat, der hat** some people have everything; **die habens** (**ja**) (*inf*) they can afford it
(b) (= *als Eigenschaft aufweisen*) **sie hatte blaue Augen/lange Beine** she had blue eyes/long legs; **er hat eine große Nase/abstehende Ohren** he's got a big nose/sticking-out ears; **man hat wieder lange Haare** long hair is in fashion again
(c) (= *bekommen, erhalten*) to have; *Note* to get; **was möchten Sie haben?** what would you like?; **da hast du 10 Euro/das Buch** there's 10 euros/the book; **wie hätten Sie es gern?** how would you like it?; **woher hast du denn das?** where did you get that from?; **Schule/Unterricht haben** to have school/lessons; **in der ersten Stunde haben wir Englisch** (*inf*) we have English first lesson; **was hast du diesmal in Englisch?** what did you get in English this time?; **gute Schulnoten haben** to get good marks (*Brit*) *or* grades (*US*); **was haben wir heute für ein Wetter?** what's the weather like today?; **heute haben wir 10°** it's 10° today; **wie viel Uhr haben wir?** what's the time?; **was für ein Datum haben wir heute?, den Wievielten haben wir heute?** what's today's date?
(d) (= *verfügen über*) *Zeit, Muße, Beziehungen, Erfahrung* to have; **Zeit haben, etw zu tun** to have the time to do sth; **ich habe jetzt keine Zeit** I haven't got time now; **die Sache hat Zeit** it's not urgent; **mit Computern habe ich keine Erfahrung** I've got no experience of computers
(e) (= *zeitweise ergriffen, bedrückt sein von*) to have; **Durst haben** to be thirsty; **Hunger haben** to be hungry; **Grippe/Masern haben** to have flu/measles; **Husten haben** to have a cough; **Fieber haben** to have a temperature; **Peter hat Windpocken** Peter's got chicken pox; **Angst haben** to be afraid; **gute/schlechte Laune haben** to be in a good/bad mood; **Sorgen haben** to be worried; **was hat er denn?** what's the matter with him?; **hast du was?** is something the matter?; **ich habe nichts** I'm all right
(f) (= *sich zusammensetzen aus*) **ein Meter hat 100 cm** there are 100 cm in a metre (*Brit*) *or* meter (*US*); **ein Euro hat 100 Cent** there are 100 cents in a euro; **unser Haus hat 4 Etagen** our house has 4 storeys (*Brit*) *or* stories (*US*)
(g) (*mit Präposition*)

*Für **haben** in Verbindung mit Präpositionen siehe auch unter dem Eintrag für die Präposition.*

♦**haben + an** **sie werden schon merken, was sie an ihr haben** they'll see what an asset she is; **jd/etw hat eine nette Art an sich** (*dat*) there is something nice about sb/sth; **das hat er/sie/es so an sich** (*dat*) that's just the way he/she/it is; **es am Herzen/Magen/an der Leber haben** (*inf*) to have heart/stomach/liver trouble

◆ haben + für sich das hat etwas für sich there's something to be said for that

◆ haben + gegen etwas gegen jdn/etw haben to have something against sb/sth; jdn/etw gegen sich haben to have sb/sth against one

◆ haben + in es in den Beinen haben (*inf:* = *leiden*) to have trouble with one's legs

◆ haben + in sich das hat es in sich (*inf*) (= *schwierig*) that's a tough one; (= *alkoholreich*) that's strong; (= *reichhaltig*) that's rich

◆ haben + mit etwas mit jdm haben (*euph*) to have a thing with sb (*inf*); was hat es mit seiner Frage auf sich? what is his question actually about?

◆ haben + von etwas von etw haben (*inf*) to get something out of sth; das hast du jetzt davon! now see what's happened!; das hat er von seinem Leichtsinn that's what comes of his foolishness; die blonden Haare hat sie von ihrem Vater she gets her blonde hair from her father; mehr/weniger von etw haben (*inf*) to get more/less out of *or* from sth; da habe ich dann mehr davon that way I get more out of it; nichts davon/ von etw haben to get nothing out of it/sth; sie hat viel von ihrem Vater/wenig von ihrer Mutter she's very like her father/ not at all like her mother

◆ haben + vor sich wissen Sie eigentlich, wen Sie vor sich (*dat*) haben? do you actually realize who you're talking to?

(h) (*in anderen Verbindungen*)

◆ es haben + Adjektiv es gut/schön/bequem haben to have it good/nice/easy; sie hat es warm in ihrem Zimmer it's warm in her room; wir haben es noch weit bis nach Hause it's still a long way home; es schlecht haben to have a bad time; er hat es nicht leicht mit ihr he has a hard time with her

◆ haben + zu + Infinitiv (= *verfügen über, müssen*) to have to; nichts mehr zu essen haben to have nothing left to eat; ich habe zu tun I'm busy; ich habe nichts zu tun I have nothing to do; du hast zu gehorchen you have to obey; ich habe nicht zu fragen I'm not to ask questions

◆ zu haben sein etw ist zu haben (= *erhältlich*) sth is to be had; jd ist zu haben (= *nicht verheiratet*) sb is single; (*sexuell*) sb is available; für etw zu haben sein to be ready for sth; er ist nicht dafür zu haben (= *nicht interessiert*) he's not keen on it (*Brit*), he's not interested in it; (= *möchte nicht beteiligt sein*) he won't have anything to do with it

(I) (*andere Wendungen*) ich habs! (*inf*) I've got it!; wie gehabt as before; ich kann das nicht haben! (*inf*) I can't stand it!

◼ UNPERSÖNLICHES VERB

◆ es hat (*dial:* = *es gibt*) (*bei Objekt im Singular*) there is; (*bei Objekt im Plural*) there are; es hat noch Kaffee there's still some coffee left; damit hat es noch Zeit it can wait

◆ es hat sich (*inf*) und damit hat es sich and that's that

◼ REFLEXIVES VERB

◆ sich haben

(a) (= *sich anstellen*) (*inf*) to make a fuss

(b) (= *erledigt sein*) die Sache hat sich that's done

Haben ['ha:bn] NT **-s**, NO PL credit; im ~ stehen to be on the credit side

Habenichts ['ha:bənɪçts] M **-(es)**, **-e** have-not

Haben-: **Habensaldo** NT credit balance; **Habenseite** F credit side; **Habenzinsen** PL interest *sing* on credit

Haberer ['ha:bərə] M **-s**, - (*Aus inf*) guy (*inf*)

Hab-: **Habgier** F greed; **habgierig** ADJ greedy

Habicht ['ha:bɪçt] M **-s**, **-e** hawk; (= *Hühnerhabicht*) goshawk

Habilitation [habilita'tsio:n] F **-**, **-en** (a) (= *Festakt*) ceremony at which sb receives his/her qualification as a professor

(b) (= *Lehrberechtigung*) postdoctoral lecturing qualification

Habitat [habi'ta:t] NT **-s**, **-e** (*Zool*) habitat

Habseligkeiten ['ha:pze:lɪçkaɪtn] PL belongings *pl*

hacke ['hakə] ADJ (*sl:* = *betrunken*) plastered (*inf*)

Hacke¹ ['hakə] F **-**, **-n** (a) (*dial:* = *Ferse, am Strumpf*) heel

(b) (*dial, Mil:* = *Absatz*) heel; die **-n zusammenschlagen** *or* **zusammenklappen** (*Mil*) to click one's heels

Hacke² F **-**, **-n** (a) (= *Pickel*) pickaxe (*Brit*), pickax (*US*); (= *Gartenhacke*) hoe **(b)** (*Aus*) hatchet

Hackebeil NT chopper

hackedicht ADJ (*sl:* = *betrunken*) plastered (*inf*)

hacken ['hakn] **◼** VT **(a)** (= *zerkleinern*) to chop; (*im Fleischwolf*) to mince (*Brit*), to grind (*US*) **(b)** Garten, Erdreich to hoe **(c)** (*mit spitzem Gegenstand*) Loch to hack; (*Vogel*) to peck **◼** VI **(a)** (*mit dem Schnabel*) to peck; (*mit spitzem Gegenstand*) to hack; nach jdm/etw ~ to peck at sth **(b)** (*im Garten etc*) to hoe **(c)** (*Comput*) to hack (*in* +acc into)

Hacken ['hakn] M **-s**, - (= *Ferse*) heel

Hacker ['hakɐ] M **-s**, -, **Hackerin** [-ərɪn] F **-**, **-nen** (*Comput*) hacker

hackevoll ADJ (*inf*), **hackezu** ADJ (*sl:* = *betrunken*) plastered (*inf*)

Hack-: **Hackfleisch** NT mince (*Brit*), ground meat (*US*); jdn zu *or* aus jdm ~ machen (*inf*) to make mincemeat of sb (*inf*); (= *verprügeln*) to beat sb up; **Hackordnung** F (*lit, fig*) pecking order

Hafen ['ha:fn] M **-s**, **-̈** ['hɛ:fn] harbour (*Brit*), harbor (*US*); (= *Handelshafen, für große Schiffe*) port; (= *Jachthafen*) marina; (= *~anlagen*) docks *pl*; im ~ der Ehe landen to get married

Häfen ['hɛ:fn] M **-s**, - (*Aus*) **(a)** (sauce)pan **(b)** (*inf:* = *Gefängnis*) jug (*inf*)

Hafen- IN CPDS harbour (*Brit*), harbor (*US*); (*bei Handelshafen, für große Schiffe*) port; **Hafenanlagen** PL docks *pl*; **Hafenarbeiter(in)** M(F) dockworker; **Hafenrundfahrt** F (boat-)trip round the harbo(u)r; **Hafenstadt** F port

Hafer ['ha:fɐ] M **-s**, - oats *pl*; ihn sticht der ~ (*inf*) he's feeling his oats (*inf*)

Hafer-: **Haferbrei** M porridge; **Haferflocken** PL rolled oats *pl*; **Haferschleim** M gruel

Haft [haft] F **-**, NO PL (*vor dem Prozess*) custody; (= *~strafe*) imprisonment; (= *~zeit*) prison sentence; (*politisch*) detention; sich in ~ befinden to be in custody/prison/ detention; eine ~ absitzen (*inf*) to do time (*inf*); in ~ sitzen to be held in custody/prison/detention; in ~ nehmen to take into custody

-haft ADJ SUF **(a)** (= *-artig*) -like; -ish; -ly; kindhaft childlike; jungenhaft boyish; frauenhaft womanly; riesenhaft gigantic **(b)** (*auf Eigenschaft bezüglich*) -ly; -ive; lebhaft lively; schwatzhaft talkative **(c)** (*in Verbableitungen*) -ing; wohnhaft residing **(d)** (*Möglichkeit bezeichnend*) -ible, -able; glaubhaft credible

Haft-: **Haftanstalt** F detention centre (*Brit*) *or* center (*US*); **haftbar** ADJ legally responsible; (*für etw*) (legally) liable; jdn für etw ~ machen to make sb liable for sth; **Haftbarkeit** ['haftba:ɐkaɪt] F **-**, NO PL (*für jdn*) (legal) responsibility; (*für etw*) (legal) liability; **Haftbefehl** M warrant; einen ~ gegen jdn ausstellen to issue a warrant for sb's arrest

haften¹ ['haftn] VI (*Jur*) für jdn ~ to be (legally) responsible for sb; für etw ~ to be (legally) liable for sth; (jdm) für jdn/etw ~ (= *verantwortlich sein*) to be responsible (to sb) for sb/sth; die Versicherung hat für den Schaden nicht gehaftet the insurance company did not accept liability (for the damage); für Garderobe kann nicht gehaftet werden all articles are left at owner's risk

haften² VI **(a)** (= *kleben*) to stick (*an* +dat to); (*Klebstoff auch, Reifen*) (*Phys*) to adhere; (= *sich festsetzen:* Rauch, Schmutz, Geruch) to cling (*an* +dat to); an jdm ~ (*fig: Makel etc*) to stick to sb **(b)** (*Eindruck, Erinnerung*) to stick (in one's mind); (*Blick*) to become fixed; an etw (*dat*) ~ (= *hängen*) to be fixed on sth

haften bleiben VI IRREG AUX SEIN to stick (*an or auf* +dat to); (= *sich festsetzen:* Rauch, Schmutz, Geruch) to cling; (*Klebstoff*) to stick, to adhere; (*Phys*) to adhere; (*Eindruck, Gelerntes*) to stick

Häftling ['heftlɪŋ] M **-s**, **-e** prisoner

Haft-: **Haftnotiz** F Post-it®; **Haftpflicht** F **(a)** (= *Schadenersatz- pflicht*) (legal) liability; (*für Personen*) (legal) responsibility; die ~ der Versicherung erstreckt sich nicht auf Glas und Silber the insurance does not cover glass and silver **(b)** (*inf:* = *~versicherung*) personal *or* public (*US*) liability insurance; (*für Auto*) ≈ third party insurance; ich bin in keiner ~ I don't have any personal liability insurance *etc*; **haftpflichtig** [-pflɪçtɪç] ADJ liable; **haftpflichtversichert** [-fɛɐzɪçɐt] ADJ ~ sein to have personal *or* public (*US*) liability insurance; (*Autofahrer*) ≈ to have third-party insurance; **Haftpflichtversicherung** F personal *or* public (*US*) liability insurance *no indef art*; *(von Autofahrer)* ≈ third-party insurance; **Haftstrafe** F prison sentence

Haftung ['haftʊŋ] F **-, -en (a)** *(Jur)* (legal) liability; *(für Personen)* (legal) responsibility; **für Ihre Garderobe übernehmen wir keine ~** articles are left at owner's risk **(b)** *(Tech, Phys, von Reifen)* adhesion

Hafturlaub M parole

Hagebutte ['haːɡəbʊtə] F **-, -n** rose hip; *(inf: = Heckenrose)* dog rose

Hagel ['haːɡl] M **-s**, NO PL **(a)** hail; *(= ~schauer)* hailstorm **(b)** *(von Steinen, Geschossen)* hail; *(von Vorwürfen, Drohungen, Anschuldigungen)* stream; *(von Schimpfworten)* stream, torrent

Hagelkorn NT, *pl* **-körner** hailstone

hageln ['haːɡln] **1** VI IMPERS **es hagelt** it's hailing **2** VI **etw hagelt auf jdn/etw** *(Schläge, Geschosse, Steine)* sth rains down on sb/sth; *(Vorwürfe, Schimpfworte)* sb is showered with sth **3** VT IMPERS *(lit)* to hail (down); **es hagelte etw** *(fig)* sth rained down; *Vorwürfe, Schimpfworte* there was a shower of sth

hager ['haːɡɐ] ADJ gaunt

Häher ['hɛːɐ] M **-s, -** jay

Hahn [haːn] M **-(e)s, ⸚e** ['hɛːnə] **(a)** *(= männlicher Vogel)* cock; *(jünger)* cockerel; *(= Wetterhahn)* weathercock; **~ im Korb sein** *(= Mann unter Frauen)* to be cock of the walk; **danach kräht kein ~ mehr** *(inf)* no one cares two hoots about that any more *(inf)* **(b)** *pl auch* **-en** *(Tech)* tap, faucet *(US)* **(c)** *(= Abzug)* trigger

Hähnchen ['hɛːnçən] NT **-s, -** chicken; *(= junger Hahn)* cockerel

Hahnenfuß M *(Bot)* buttercup

Hai [hai] M **-(e)s, -e**, **Haifisch** M *(lit, fig)* shark

Haifischflossensuppe F shark's-fin soup

Haiti [haˈiːti] NT **-s** Haiti

haitisch [haˈiːtɪʃ] ADJ Haitian

Häkchen ['hɛːkçən] NT **-s, - (a)** *(Sew)* (small) hook **(b)** *(= Zeichen)* tick *(Brit)*, check *(US)*; *(auf Buchstaben)* accent

Häkelarbeit F crochet (work) *no indef art*; *(= Gegenstand)* piece of crochet (work)

häkeln ['hɛːkln] VTI to crochet

Häkelnadel F crochet hook

haken ['haːkn] **1** VI **es hakt** *(fig)* there are sticking points; **es hakt bei jdm** *(inf: = versteht nicht)* sb is stuck **2** VT **(a)** *(= befestigen)* to hook *(an +acc* to) **(b)** *(= einhängen, um etw legen)* to hook (*in +acc* in, *um* around)

Haken ['haːkn] M **-s, - (a)** hook; *(aus Holz auch)* peg; **~ und Öse** hook and eye **(b)** *(inf: = Schwierigkeit)* snag; **die Sache hat einen ~** there's a snag; **ein Angebot ohne ~ und Ösen** an offer with no strings attached **(c)** *(Boxen)* hook **(d)** = **Häkchen (b)**

Haken-: Hakenkralle F pinch hook; **Hakenkreuz** NT swastika; **Hakennase** F hooked nose

halb [halp] **1** ADJ **(a)** *(Bruchteil)* half; *Lehrauftrag etc* part-time; **ein Kuchen/Meter** *etc* half a cake/metre *(Brit)* or meter *(US) etc*; **eine ~e Stunde** half an hour; **alle ~e Stunde** every half hour; **ein ~es Jahr** six months *pl*; **auf ~er Höhe** at half the normal height; *(zum Gipfel)* halfway up; **auf ~em Wege, auf ~er Strecke** *(lit)* halfway; *(fig)* halfway through; **zum ~en Preis** (at) half price; **den Apfel nur ~ essen** to eat only half the apple **(b)** *(Mus)* **eine ~e Note** a minim *(Brit)*, a half-note *(US)*; **ein ~er Ton** a semitone; **~e Pause** minim *(Brit)* or half-note *(US)* rest **(c)** INV *(Uhrzeit)* **~ zehn** half past nine; **fünf Minuten vor/nach ~ zwei** twenty-five (minutes) past one/to two; **es schlägt ~** it's striking the half hour; **um drei Minuten nach ~** at three minutes past the half hour; **um fünf Minuten nach ~** at twenty-five to **(d)** INV, NO ART *(bei geografischen Namen)* **~ Deutschland/London** half of Germany/London **(e)** *(= teilweise, stückhaft)* **Maßnahmen** half; *Reformen* partial; **~e Arbeit leisten** to do a bad job; **die ~e Wahrheit** part of the truth; **nichts Halbes und nichts Ganzes** neither one thing nor the other; **mit ~em Ohr** with half an ear; **keine ~en Sachen machen** not to do things by halves **(f)** *(inf: = große Anzahl, großer Teil)* **die ~e Stadt/Welt/Arbeit** half the town/world/work; **(noch) ein ~es Kind sein** to be hardly more than a child

2 ADV **(a)** *(= zur Hälfte)* half; **~ gar** half-cooked; *(fig)* **Idee** half-baked; **~ links** *(Sport)* spielen (at) inside left; *(im Theater)* sitzen left of centre *(Brit)* or center *(US)*; **~ links abbiegen** to fork left;

~ rechts *(Sport)* spielen (at) inside right; *(im Theater)* sitzen right of centre *(Brit)* or center *(US)*; **~ rechts abbiegen** to fork right; **~ voll** half-filled; *Behälter auch* half-full; **die Zeit ist ~ vorbei** half the time has already gone

(b) *(= nicht ganz, teilweise)* half; **~ fest** *Zustand, Materie* semi-solid; *Gelee* half-set; **~ offen** half-open; **~ reif** half-ripe; **~ verdaut** *(lit, fig)* half-digested; **in ~ wachem Zustand** half awake; **~ so gut** half as good; **das ist ~ so schlimm** it's not as bad as all that; *(Zukünftiges)* that won't be too bad; **etw nur ~ machen** to only half-do sth *(inf)*

(c) *(= fast vollständig)* almost; **blind, roh** half; **~ fertig** half-finished; *(Ind)* semi-finished; *(fig)* immature; **ich war schon ~ fertig** I was almost finished; **~ nackt** half-naked; *Arm* half-covered; **~ tot** *(lit)* half dead; **wir haben uns ~ totgelacht** we almost died laughing

(d) **~ lachend, ~ weinend** half laughing, half crying; **~ Mensch, ~ Pferd** half man, half horse

(e) **mit jdm ~-e-~e machen** *(inf)* to go 50/50 with sb

Halb-: halbamtlich ADJ semi-official; **halbautomatisch** ADJ semi-automatic; **halbbitter** ADJ *Schokolade* semi-sweet; **Halbblut** NT *(= Mensch)* half-caste; *(= Tier)* crossbreed; **Halbblüter** [-blyːtɐ] M **-s, -** crossbreed; **Halbbruder** M half-brother

Halbe ['halbə] F DECL AS ADJ *(esp S Ger)* = **Halbe(r)**

Halbedelstein M semi-precious stone

Halbe(r) ['halbə] M DECL AS ADJ half a litre *(Brit)* or liter *(US)* (of beer)

-halber ADV SUF *(= wegen)* on account of; *(= um ... willen)* for the sake of; **gesundheitshalber** for medical reasons; **vorsichtshalber** to be on the safe side

Halb-: halbfertig ADJ ATTR *siehe* **halb**; **halbfett 1** ADJ **(a)** *(Typ)* secondary bold **(b)** *Lebensmittel* medium-fat **2** ADV *(Typ)* in secondary bold; **Halbfinale** NT semi-final; **Halbgeschwister** PL half brothers and sisters *pl*; **Halbgott** M *(Myth, fig)* demigod; **Halbgötter in Weiß** *(iro)* doctors; **halbherzig 1** ADJ half-hearted **2** ADV half-heartedly

halbieren [halˈbiːrən] *ptp* **halbiert** VT to halve; *(Geometrie)* to bisect; *(= in zwei schneiden)* to cut in half; **eine Zahl ~** to divide a number by two

Halbinsel F peninsula

Halbjahr NT half-year *(auch Comm)*, six months; **im ersten/zweiten ~** in the first/last six months of the year

Halbjahres-: Halbjahresbilanz F half-yearly figures *pl*; **Halbjahreszeugnis** NT *(Sch)* half-yearly report

Halb-: halbjährig ADJ ATTR *Kind* six-month-old; *Lehrgang etc* six-month; *Kündigung* six months; **halbjährlich 1** ADJ yearly *(auch Comm)*, six-monthly; **in ~em Wechsel** changing every six months **2** ADV every six months; **Halbjude** M, **Halbjüdin** F half Jew; **~ sein** to be half Jewish; **Halbkanton** M sub-canton; **Halbkonsonant** M semi-consonant; **Halbkreis** M semicircle; **Halbkugel** F hemisphere; **nordliche/südliche ~** northern/southern hemisphere; **halblang** ADJ *Kleid, Rock* mid-calf length; *Haar* chin-length; **nun mach mal ~!** *(inf)* now wait a minute!; **Halbleiter** M *(Phys)* semiconductor; **halbmast** ['halpmast] ADV at half-mast; **(eine Flagge) ~ hissen** to hoist a flag to half-mast; **~ flaggen** to fly flags/a flag at half-mast; **Halbmesser** M **-s, -** radius; **Halbmond** M half-moon; *(= Symbol)* crescent; **bei ~** when there is a half-moon; **wir haben ~** there's a half-moon; **halbmondförmig** ADJ crescent-shaped; **halbnackt** ADJ ATTR *siehe* **halb**; **Halbpension** F half-board; **Halbschatten** M half shadow; *(Astron)* penumbra; **Halbschlaf** M light sleep; **im ~ sein** to be half asleep; **Halbschuh** M shoe; **Halbschwester** F half-sister; **halbseiden** ADJ *(lit)* fifty per cent *(Brit)* or percent *(US)* silk; *(fig)* *Dame* fast; *Aussehen* flashy; *(= zweifelhaft, undurchsichtig)* dubious; **~es Milieu, ~e Kreise** the demimonde; **halbseitig** [-zaitɪç] **1** ADJ *Anzeige etc* half-page; *(Med)* *Kopfschmerzen* in one side of one's head; **~e Lähmung** one-sided paralysis **2** ADV **~ gelähmt** paralyzed on one side; **Halbstarke(r)** M DECL AS ADJ young hooligan; **halbstündig** [-ʃtʏndɪç] ADJ ATTR half an hour attr, lasting half an hour; **halbstündlich 1** ADJ half-hourly **2** ADV every half an hour, half-hourly

halbtags ['halptaːks] ADV *(= morgens)* in the mornings; *(= nachmittags)* in the afternoons; *(in Bezug auf Angestellte auch)* part-time

Halbtags-: Halbtagsarbeit F, **Halbtagsbeschäftigung** F half-day job; (*von Angestellten auch*) part-time job; **Halbtagskraft** F worker employed for half-days only; **Halbtagsschule** F half-day school

Halb-: Halbton M, *pl* **-töne** (*Mus*) semitone; (*Art, Phot*) halftone; **halbtrocken** ADJ *Wein* medium-dry; **Halbvokal** M semivowel; **halbvoll** ADJ ATTR *siehe* **halb**; **Halbwahrheit** F half-truth; **Halbwaise** F *person who has lost one parent*; **er/sie ist ~** he/she has lost one of his/her parents; **halbwegs** ['halp've:ks] ADV partly; *gut, adäquat* reasonably; *annehmbar* halfway; **wenn es dir wieder ~ gut geht** when you're feeling a bit better; **Halbwelt** F demimonde; **Halbweltergewicht** NT light-welterweight; **Halbwert(s)zeit** F (*Phys*) half-life; **Halbwissen** NT (*pej*) superficial knowledge; **halbwöchentlich** ❶ ADJ twice-weekly ❷ ADV twice weekly; **Halbzeit** F (*Sport*) (= *Hälfte*) half; (= *Pause*) half-time

Halde ['haldə] F **-, -n** (= *Abfallhalde*) mound; (*Min*: = *Abbauhalde*) slag heap; (*fig*) mountain; **etw auf ~ legen** *Ware, Vorräte* to stockpile sth; *Pläne etc* to shelve sth

half PRET *von* **helfen**

Hälfte ['hɛlftə] F **-, -n** (a) half; **die ~ der Kinder war abwesend** half the children were absent; **die ~ einer Sache** (*gen*) *or* **von etw** half (of) sth; **Rentner zahlen die ~** pensioners pay half price; **um die ~ mehr** half as much again; **um die ~ zu viel** too much by half; **um die ~ steigen** to increase by half; **um die ~ kleiner** half as small *or* big; **um die ~ größer** half as big again; **es ist zur ~ fertig/voll** it is half finished/full; **die Beiträge werden je zur ~ vom Arbeitgeber und Arbeitnehmer bezahlt** the employer and employee each pay half (of) the contribution; **meine bessere ~** (*hum inf*) my better half (*hum inf*)
(b) (= *Mitte*: *von Fläche*) middle; **auf der ~ des Weges** halfway

Halfter¹ ['halftə] M *or* NT **-s, -** (*für Tiere*) halter

Halfter² F **-, -n** *or* nt **-s, -** (= *Pistolenhalfter*) holster

halftern ['halftən] VT to put a halter on

Hall [hal] M **-(e)s, -e** echo

Halle ['halə] F **-, -n** hall; (= *Hotelhalle*) lobby; (= *Werkshalle, Fabrikhalle*) shed; (= *Sporthalle*) (sports) hall, gym(nasium); (= *Tennishalle*) covered tennis court(s *pl*); (= *Schwimmhalle*) indoor swimming pool; (= *Flugzeughalle*) hangar; **in der ~** (*im Gegensatz zu draußen*) inside, indoors

halleluja [hale'lu:ja] INTERJ halleluja(h)

hallen ['halən] VI to echo (*auch fig*)

Hallen- IN CPDS (*Sport*) indoor; **Hallenbad** NT indoor swimming pool; **Hallenfußball** M indoor football (*esp Brit*) *or* soccer

Hallig ['halɪç] F **-, -en** [-gn] *a small island off the west coast of Schleswig-Holstein*

hallo [ha'lo:, 'halo] INTERJ hello

Halluzination [halutsina'tsio:n] F **-, -en** hallucination; **ich leide wohl an ~en** (*fig*) I must be seeing things

halluzinieren [halutsi'ni:rən], *ptp* **halluziniert** VI to hallucinate

Halm [halm] M **-(e)s, -e** (= *Grashalm*) blade of grass; (= *Strohhalm, zum Trinken*) straw

Halogen [halo'ge:n] NT **-s, -e** halogen

Halogen-: Halogenbirne F halogen bulb; **Halogen(glüh)lampe** F halogen lamp; **Halogenlicht** NT halogen light; **Halogenscheinwerfer** M halogen headlamp

Hals [hals] M **-es, ¨e** ['hɛlzə] (a) (*von außen gesehen*) neck; **sich** (*dat*) **nach jdm/etw den ~ verrenken** (*inf*) to crane one's neck to see sb/sth; **jdm um den ~ fallen** to fling one's arms (a)round sb's neck; **sich jdm an den ~ werfen** (*fig inf*) to throw oneself at sb; **sich** (*dat*) **den ~ brechen** (*inf*) to break one's neck; **etw kostet jdn den ~** (*inf*), **etw bricht jdm den ~** (*inf*) sth will cost sb his/her neck; **über Kopf abreisen/den Koffer packen** to leave/pack one's case in a rush; **ihr steht das Wasser bis zum ~** (*fig*) she is up to her neck in it (*inf*); **bis über den ~** (*fig inf*) up to one's ears; **jdn auf dem *or* am ~ haben** (*inf*) to be saddled with sb (*inf*); **jdm jdn/etw vom ~e schaffen** (*inf*) to get sb/sth off sb's back (*inf*)
(b) (= *Kehle, Rachen*) throat; **sie hat es am *or* im ~** (*inf*) she has a sore throat; **aus vollem ~(e)** at the top of one's voice; **aus vollem ~(e) lachen** to roar with laughter; **es hängt *or* wächst mir zum ~ heraus** (*inf*) I'm sick and tired of it; **sie hat es in den falschen *or* verkehrten ~ bekommen** (*inf*) (= *sich verschlucken*) it went down the wrong way; (= *falsch verstehen*) she took it

---

wrongly; **er kann den ~ nicht voll (genug) kriegen** (*fig inf*) he is never satisfied
(c) (= *Flaschenhals, Geigenhals, Säulenhals*) (*von Knochen*) neck; (= *Notenhals*) stem; (= *Gebärmutterhals*) cervix

Hals-: Halsausschnitt M neck(line); **Halsband** NT, *pl* **-bänder** (= *Hundehalsband*) collar; (= *Schmuck*) necklace; **halsbrecherisch** ['halsbrɛçərɪʃ] ❶ ADJ dangerous; *Tempo* breakneck ❷ ADV *herumturnen, klettern* recklessly; **~ schnell/rasant/wild** at breakneck pace; *fahren* at breakneck speed; **Halsentzündung** F sore throat; **Halskette** F (= *Schmuck*) necklace; (*für Hund*) chain; **Halskrause** F (*Fashion*) (*Zool*) ruff; (*Med*) cervical collar; **Hals-Nasen-Ohren-Arzt** M, **Hals-Nasen-Ohren-Ärztin** F ear, nose and throat specialist; **Halsschlagader** F carotid (artery); **Halsschmerzen** PL sore throat *sing*; **halsstarrig** [-ʃtarɪç] ADJ obstinate; **Halstuch** NT, *pl* **-tücher** scarf; **Hals- und Beinbruch** INTERJ good luck; **Halsweh** [-ve:] NT **-s**, NO PL sore throat

halt¹ [halt] INTERJ stop; (*Mil*) halt

halt² ADV (*dial*) (a) *siehe* **eben 2(d)** (b) (*Aus*) **und so ~** and so on *or* forth

Halt [halt] M **-(e)s, -e** (a) (*für Füße, Hände, Festigkeit*) hold; (*lit, fig*: = *Stütze*) support; (*fig*: = *innerer ~*) security *no art*; **jdm/einer Sache ~ geben** to support sb/sth; **dem Haar ~ geben** to give hold to one's hair; **keinen ~ haben** to have no hold/support; **ohne inneren ~** insecure
(b) (*geh*: = *Anhalten*) stop; **ohne ~** non-stop; **~ machen** to stop; **vor nichts ~ machen** (*fig*) to stop at nothing; **vor niemandem ~ machen** (*fig*) to spare no-one

hält [hɛlt] 3. PERS SING PRES *von* **halten**

haltbar ADJ (a) (= *nicht leicht verderblich*) **~ sein** (*Lebensmittel*) to keep (well); **~e Lebensmittel** food which keeps (well); **das ist sechs Monate ~** that will keep for six months; **etw ~ machen** to preserve sth; **~ bis 6.11.** use by 6 Nov; **nur begrenzt ~** perishable
(b) (= *widerstandsfähig*) durable; *Stoff, Kleider* hard-wearing; *Beziehung, Ehe* long-lasting
(c) *Behauptung, Theorie, Annahme, Position, Rang, Platz* tenable; *Zustand, Lage* tolerable; **diese Position ist nicht mehr ~** this position can't be maintained any longer
(d) PRED *Festung* defensible; **die Stadt ist nicht mehr ~** the town can't be held any longer
(e) (*Sport*) *Ball, Wurf* stoppable

Haltbarkeit ['haltba:ɐkait] F **-**, NO PL (a) (*von Lebensmitteln*) **eine längere ~ haben** to keep longer; **Lebensmittel von kurzer ~** perishable food; **die begrenzte ~ von Fleisch** the perishability of meat (b) (= *Widerstandsfähigkeit*) durability (c) (*von Behauptung, Theorie, Annahme*) tenability

Haltbarkeits-: Haltbarkeitsdatum NT best-before date, use-by date; **Haltbarkeitsdauer** F *length of time for which food may be kept*; **eine kurze/lange ~ haben** to be/not to be perishable

Haltegriff M (a) handle; (*in Bus*) strap; (*an Badewanne*) handrail (b) (*Sport*) hold

halten ['haltn]	
❶ TRANSITIVES VERB	❸ REFLEXIVES VERB
❷ INTRANSITIVES VERB	

pret **hielt** [hi:lt], *ptp* **gehalten** [gə'haltn]

❶ TRANSITIVES VERB
(a) (= *festhalten*) to hold; **jdm etw halten** to hold sth for sb; **sich** (*dat*) **den Kopf/Bauch halten** to hold one's head/stomach
(b) (= *in eine bestimmte Position bringen*) **etw gegen das Licht halten** to hold sth up to the light; **den Arm in die Höhe halten** to hold one's arm up; **einen Fuß/einen Zeh ins Wasser halten** to put a foot/a toe in the water
(c) (= *tragen*) **die drei Pfeiler halten die Brücke** the three piers support the bridge; **meinst du, der kleine Nagel hält das schwere Ölbild?** do you think this small nail will take the weight of the heavy oil painting?; **nur zwei morsche Bretter hielten den Balkon noch** there were only two rotten boards holding the balcony up
(d) (= *zurückhalten, aufhalten*) to hold; (*Sport*) to save; **die Wärme/Feuchtigkeit halten** to retain heat/moisture; **er kann den Urin *or* das Wasser nicht halten** he's incontinent; **ich**

konnte ihn/es gerade noch halten I just managed to grab hold of him/it; **haltet den Dieb!** stop thief!; **sie ist nicht zu halten** (fig) there's no holding her back; **es hält mich hier nichts mehr** there's nothing to keep me here any more; **es hält dich niemand** nobody's stopping you
(e) (= behalten) Festung, Rekord to hold; Position to hold (on to); **den Schnabel** or **Mund halten** (inf) to keep one's mouth shut (inf)
(f) (= unterhalten, besitzen) Chauffeur, Lehrer to employ; Haustier to keep; Auto to run; **sich** (dat) **eine Geliebte halten** to keep a mistress; **sich** (dat) **eine Perserkatze/einen Hausfreund halten** to have a Persian cat/a live-in lover
(g) (= einhalten, erfüllen) to keep; **ein Versprechen halten** to keep a promise; **man muss halten, was man verspricht** a promise is a promise; **der Film hält nicht, was er/der Titel verspricht** the film doesn't live up to expectations/its title
(h) (= beibehalten, aufrechterhalten) Niveau to keep up; Tempo, Disziplin, Temperatur to maintain; Kurs to keep to; **die Balance** or **das Gleichgewicht halten** to keep one's balance; **den Ton halten** to stay in tune; **die These lässt sich nicht länger halten** or **ist nicht länger zu halten** this hypothesis is no longer tenable; **Kontakt halten** to keep in touch; **(mit jdm) Verbindung halten** to keep in touch (with sb); **Abstand halten!** keep your distance!; **etw sauber halten** to keep sth clean; **viel Sport hält jung/schlank** doing a lot of sport keeps you young/slim; **wenn es neblig ist sollten Sie den Abstand immer so groß wie möglich halten** if it's foggy you should always stay as far as possible from the car in front
(i) (= behandeln) to treat; **er hält seine Kinder sehr streng** he's very strict with his children
(j) (= handhaben, verfahren mit) **das kannst du (so) halten, wie du willst** that's entirely up to you

◆**es mit etw/jdm halten wie hältst du es mit Ihrer Steuererklärung?** how do you deal with your tax return?; **wie hältst dus mit der Religion?** what's your attitude toward(s) religion?; **wir halten es mit den Abrechnungen anders** we deal with invoices in a different way; **er hält es nicht so sehr mit der Sauberkeit** he's not over-concerned about cleanliness; **es mehr** or **lieber mit jdm/etw halten** to prefer sb/sth
(k) (= gestalten) **ein in Brauntönen gehaltener Raum** a room done in different shades of brown; **sie beschloss das Zimmer in Grün zu halten** she decided to do the room in green; **das Mobiliar ist in einem hellen Holz gehalten** the furniture is made of a light wood
(l) (= veranstalten, abhalten) Fest, Pressekonferenz to give; Rede to make; Gottesdienst, Zwiesprache to hold; Wache to keep; **Selbstgespräche halten** to talk to oneself; **Unterricht halten** to teach; **Mittagsschlaf halten** to have an afternoon nap; **Winterschlaf halten** to hibernate
(m) (= einschätzen, denken)

◆**jdn/etw für etw halten** to think sb/sth sth; **ich habe das Bild für ein Original gehalten** I thought the picture was an original; **etw für angebracht/schön halten** to think sth appropriate/beautiful; **ich habe ihn (irrtümlich) für seinen Bruder gehalten** I (mis)took him for his brother; **wofür halten Sie mich?** what do you take me for?; **das halte ich nicht für möglich** I don't think that is possible

◆**etw von jdm/etw halten** to think sth of sb/sth; **nicht viel von jdm/etw halten** not to think much of sb/sth; **nicht viel vom Beten/Sparen halten** not to be a great one for praying/saving (inf); **ich halte nichts davon, das zu tun** I'm not in favour (Brit) or favor (US) of (doing) that

◆**etwas/viel auf etw** (acc) **halten** to consider sth important/very important; **der Chef hält viel auf Pünktlichkeit** the boss attaches a lot of importance to punctuality
(n) siehe **gehalten**

2 INTRANSITIVES VERB
(a) (= festhalten) to hold; (= haften bleiben) to stick; (Sport) to make a save; **kannst du mal einen Moment halten?** can you just hold that (for) a moment?
(b) (= bestehen bleiben, haltbar sein) to last; (Konserven) to keep; (Frisur) (Comm: Preise) to hold; (Stoff) to be hard-wearing; **Rosen halten länger, wenn ...** roses last longer if ...; **dieser Stoff hält lange** this material is hard-wearing
(c) (= stehen bleiben, anhalten) to stop; **zum Halten bringen** to bring to a standstill

◆**halt mal** (= Moment mal) hang on (inf)
(d) (andere Redewendungen)

◆**auf sich** (acc) **halten** (= auf sein Äußeres achten) to take a pride in oneself; (= selbstbewusst sein) to be self-confident
◆**an sich** (acc) **halten** (= sich beherrschen) to control oneself
◆**zu jdm halten** (= beistehen, treu sein) to stand by sb; (= favorisieren) to support sb

3 REFLEXIVES VERB
◆**sich halten**
(a) (= sich festhalten) to hold on (an +dat to); **er konnte sich gerade noch am Halteriemen halten** he just managed to grab hold of the strap; **er konnte sich auf dem wilden Mustang nur drei Sekunden halten** he could only stay on the wild mustang three seconds
(b) (= eine bestimmte Körperhaltung haben) to carry oneself; **sich (im Gleichgewicht) halten** to keep one's balance; **sich auf den Beinen halten** to stay on one's feet; **sich (nach) links halten** to keep (to the) left; **sich nach Westen halten** to keep going westwards; **der Autofahrer hielt sich ganz rechts** the driver kept to the right; **ich halte mich an die alte Methode** I'll stick to the old method; **sich an ein Versprechen halten** to keep a promise; **sich an die Tatsachen/den Text halten** to keep to the facts/text
(c) (= sich nicht verändern) (Lebensmittel, Blumen) to keep; (Wetter) to last; (Geruch, Rauch) to linger; (Preise) to hold; (Brauch, Sitte) to continue
(d) (= seine Position behaupten) to hold on; (in Kampf) to hold out; **das Geschäft kann sich in dieser Straße nicht halten** the shop can't continue to stay open in this street

◆**sich gut halten** (in Prüfung, Spiel etc) to do well
(e) (= sich beherrschen) to control oneself; **sich nicht halten können** to be unable to control oneself
(f) (andere Wendungen)

◆**sich halten an** (+acc) **sich an jdn halten** (= sich wenden an) to ask sb; (= sich richten nach) to follow sb; (= sich gut stellen mit) to keep in with sb; **ich halte mich lieber an den Wein** I'd rather stick to wine

◆**sich halten für er hält sich für einen Spezialisten/für besonders klug** he thinks he's a specialist/very clever

Halter¹ [ˈhaltɐ] M **-s, -** (a) (= Halterung) holder
(b) (= Sockenhalter) garter; (= Strumpfhalter, Hüfthalter) suspender (Brit) or garter (US) belt
Halter² [ˈhaltɐ] M **-s, -**, **Halterin** [-ərɪn] F **-, -nen** (Jur: von Kraftfahrzeug, Tier) owner
Halteriemen M strap
halterlos ADJ **~e Strümpfe** hold-ups (Brit), stockings not requiring a garter belt (US)
Halterung [ˈhaltərʊŋ] F **-, -en** mounting; (für Regal etc) support
Halte-: Halteschild NT, pl **-schilder** stop sign; **Haltestelle** F stop; **Halteverbot** NT (absolutes or uneingeschränktes) ~ no stopping; (= Stelle) no-stopping zone; **eingeschränktes** ~ no waiting; (= Stelle) no-waiting zone; **hier ist** ~ there's no stopping here; **im** ~ **stehen** to have parked in a no-stopping zone; **Halteverbot(s)schild** NT, pl **-schilder** no-stopping sign
-haltig [haltɪç], (Aus) **-hältig** [hɛltɪç] ADJ SUF containing; **stark alkoholhaltig** with a high alcohol content
Halt-: haltlos ADJ (= schwach) insecure; (= hemmungslos) unrestrained; (= unbegründet) groundless; **Haltlosigkeit** F **-**, NO PL (= Schwäche) lack of security; (= Hemmungslosigkeit) lack of inhibitions; (= Unbegründetheit) groundlessness; **haltmachen** VI SEP siehe **Halt**
Haltung [ˈhaltʊŋ] F **-, -en** (a) (= Körperhaltung) posture; (= Stellung) position; (esp Sport) (= typische Stellung) stance; (bei der Ausführung) style; ~ **annehmen** (esp Mil) to stand to attention **(b)** (= Auftreten) manner; (= Einstellung) attitude; **in majestätischer/würdiger** ~ with majestic/dignified bearing **(c)** NO PL (= Beherrschtheit) composure; ~ **bewahren** to keep one's composure **(d)** NO PL (von Tieren, Fahrzeugen) keeping
Halunke [haˈlʊŋkə] M **-n, -n** scoundrel; (hum) rascal
hämatologisch [hɛmatoˈloːɡɪʃ] ADJ haematological (Brit), hematological (US)
Hämatom [hɛmaˈtoːm] NT **-s, -e** haematoma (Brit), hematoma (US)
Hamburg [ˈhambʊrk] NT **-s** Hamburg
Hamburger [ˈhambʊrɡɐ] M **-s, -** (Cook) hamburger

hamburgisch [ˈhamburgɪʃ] ADJ Hamburg *attr*

Häme [ˈhɛːmə] F -, NO PL *(rare)* malice

hämisch [ˈhɛːmɪʃ] **1** ADJ malicious **2** ADV maliciously; **er hat sich ~ gefreut** he gloated

Hammel [ˈhaml] M **-s**, - *or (rare)* = [ˈhɛml] **(a)** *(Zool)* wether **(b)** NO PL *(Cook)* mutton

Hammel-: Hammelfleisch NT mutton; **Hammelherde** F herd of wethers; *(pej inf)* flock of sheep; **Hammelkeule** F *(Cook)* leg of mutton

Hammer [ˈhamɐ] M **-s**, = [ˈhɛmɐ] *(auch Anat)* hammer; (= *Holzhammer*) mallet; **~ und Sichel** hammer and sickle; **unter den ~ kommen** to come under the hammer; **das ist ein ~!** *(inf: = unerhört)* that's absurd!

hämmern [ˈhɛmɐn] **1** VI *(mit Hammer, Gegenstand)* to hammer; *(mit den Fäusten etc)* *(Puls, Herz, Blut)* to pound; *(Maschine, Motor)* to make a hammering sound **2** VT to hammer; *(Blech, Metallgefäße, Schmuck etc)* to beat; **jdm etw ins Bewusstsein ~** *(inf)* to hammer sth into sb's head *(inf)* **3** VI IMPERS **es hämmert** there's a sound of hammering

Hammer-: Hammerwerfen NT **-s**, NO PL *(Sport)* hammer(-throwing); **Hammerwerfer(in)** M(F) *(Sport)* hammer-thrower

Hammondorgel [ˈhamənd-] F electric organ

Hämoglobin [hɛmoglo'biːn] NT **-s**, NO PL haemoglobin *(Brit)*, hemoglobin *(US)*

Hämophilie [hɛmofi'liː] F -, -n [-'liːən] haemophilia *(Brit)*, hemophilia *(US)*

Hämorrhoiden [hɛmɔro'iːdən] PL, **Hämorriden** [hɛmɔr'iːdən] PL piles *pl*, haemorrhoids *pl (Brit)*, hemorrhoids *pl (US)*

Hampelei [hampə'lai] F -, -en *(pej inf)* (continual) fidgeting *no pl*

Hampelmann M, *pl* -männer jumping jack; **er ist nur ein ~** *(inf)* he just lets people walk all over him; **jdn zu einem ~ machen** *(inf)* to walk all over sb

hampeln [ˈhampln] VI to jump about; (= *zappeln*) to fidget

Hamster [ˈhamstɐ] M **-s**, - hamster

Hamsterer [ˈhamstərə] M **-s**, -, **Hamsterin** [-ərɪn] F -, -nen *(inf)* hoarder

Hamsterkauf M panic buying *no pl*; **Hamsterkäufe machen** to buy in order to hoard; *(bei Knappheit)* to panic-buy

hamstern [ˈhamstɐn] VTI (= *ansammeln*) to hoard; *(bei Hamsterfahrt)* to forage; (= *Hamsterkäufe machen*) to panic-buy

Hand [hant]

gen **Hand**, *pl* **Hände** [ˈhɛndə]

SUBSTANTIV (F)
(a) *(allgemein)* hand *(auch Mus, Cards)*; **jdm die Hand geben** *or* **reichen** *(geh)* to give sb one's hand; **in die Hände klatschen** to clap one's hands; **Hände hoch!** (put your) hands up!; **Hand aufs Herz** hand on heart; **eine Hand breit** ≈ six inches wide; **zwei Hände breit** ≈ a foot wide

◆**eine Hand voll** *(lit, fig)* a handful

(b) *(Sport)* NO PL *(inf: = Handspiel)* handball; **Hand machen** to handle the ball

(c) *(mit Adjektiv)*

Siehe auch unter dem Eintrag für das jeweilige Adjektiv.

ein Auto aus erster Hand a car which has had one previous owner; **etw aus erster Hand wissen** to have first-hand knowledge of sth; **in festen Händen sein** *(fig)* to be spoken for; **mit der flachen Hand** with the palm of one's hand; **bei etw eine glückliche Hand haben** to be lucky with sth; **in guten Händen sein** to be in good hands; **mit leeren Händen** empty-handed; **letzte Hand an etw** *(acc)* **legen** to put the finishing touches to sth; **linker Hand, zur linken Hand** on the left-hand side; **aus** *or* **von privater Hand** privately; **„aus privater Hand abzugeben"** "private sale"; **rechter Hand, zur rechten Hand** on *or* to the right(-hand side); **eine sichere Hand** *(lit)* a steady hand; *(fig)* a sure hand; **in sicheren Händen sein** to be in safe hands; **eine starke Hand** *(fig)* a firm hand; **das Geld mit vollen Händen ausgeben** to spend money hand over fist *(inf)*; **hinter**

vorgehaltener Hand on the quiet; **aus zweiter Hand** second hand

(d) *(mit Präposition)*

Siehe auch unter dem Eintrag für die jeweilige Präposition.

◆**an + Hand** **er hatte seine kleine Tochter an der Hand** he had his little daughter by the hand; **er hat jemanden an der Hand, der mir meine Küche streichen könnte** he knows of somebody who could paint my kitchen for me; **jdn an die Hand nehmen** to take sb by the hand; **jdm an die Hand gehen** to lend sb a (helping) hand; **an Hand von** *or* +*gen* = **anhand**

◆**auf + Hand/Händen** **auf der Hand** *(Cards)* in one's hand; **das liegt auf der Hand** *(inf)* that's obvious; **jdn auf Händen tragen** to cherish sb

◆**aus + Hand** **aus der Hand zeichnen, entwerfen etc** freehand; **jdm etw aus der Hand nehmen** to take sth from sb *(auch fig)*; **jdm aus der Hand fressen** *(lit, fig)* to eat out of sb's hand; **etw aus der Hand geben** to let sth out of one's hands; **etw aus der Hand legen** to put sth aside

◆**bei + Hand** **jdn bei der Hand nehmen** to take sb by the hand; **etw bei der Hand haben** to have sth to hand; *Ausrede, Erklärung* to have sth ready; **mit etw schnell** *or* **gleich bei der Hand sein** *(inf)* to be ready with sth

◆**in + Hand/Hände(n)** **Hand in Hand** hand in hand; **jdm/einer Sache in die Hände arbeiten** to play into sb's hands/the hands of sth; **etw in der Hand haben** to have sth; **ich habe diese Entscheidung nicht in der Hand** the decision is out of my hands; **etw gegen jdn in der Hand haben** to have sth on sb; **diese Gebiete sind zurzeit in serbischer Hand** these areas are in Serbian hands at the moment; **dieser Laden ist schon seit Jahren in türkischer Hand** this shop has been owned by Turks for years; **der Badestrand ist im Juli immer fest in deutscher Hand** in July this beach is always taken over by Germans; **in jds Hände** *(acc)* **übergehen** to pass to sb *or* into sb's hands; **sich in der Hand haben** to have a grip on oneself; **etw liegt** *or* **ist in jds Hand** *(dat)* sth is in sb's hands; **etw in die Hand nehmen** to pick sth up; *(fig)* to take sth in hand; **jdm etw in die Hand** *or* **Hände spielen** to pass sth on to sb

◆**mit + Hand/Händen** **mit der Hand** (= *in Handarbeit*) by hand; **(bei etw) mit Hand anlegen** to lend a hand (with sth); **das ist mit Händen zu greifen** *(fig)* that's obvious; **sich mit Händen und Füßen gegen etw wehren** to fight sth tooth and nail

◆**um + Hand** **um jds Hand bitten** *or* **anhalten** to ask for sb's hand (in marriage)

◆**unter + Hand/Händen** **unter der Hand** *(fig)* on the quiet; **jdm unter der Hand** *or* **den Händen wegsterben** to die while under sb's care

◆**von + Hand/Händen** **von Hand geschrieben** handwritten; **von Hand genäht** hand-sewn; **von Hand zu Hand gehen** to pass from hand to hand; **die Arbeit ging ihr leicht von der Hand** she found the work easy; **die Arbeit ging ihr flott** *or* **schnell von der Hand** she sailed through the work; **etw lässt sich nicht von der Hand weisen, etw ist nicht von der Hand zu weisen** sth is undeniable; **von der Hand in den Mund leben** to live from hand to mouth

◆**zu + Hand/Händen** **zur Hand sein** to be at hand; **etw zur Hand haben** to have sth to hand; *Ausrede, Erklärung* to have sth ready; **jdm zur Hand gehen** to lend sb a (helping) hand; **zu jds Händen, zu Händen von jdm** for the attention of sb

(e) *(mit Verb)*

Siehe auch unter dem Eintrag für das jeweilige Verb.

die *or* **seine Hand aufhalten** *or* **hinhalten** *(fig inf)* to hold out one's hand (for money); **darauf gaben sie sich die Hand** they shook hands on it; **man konnte die Hand nicht vor (den) Augen sehen** you couldn't see your hand in front of your face; **eine Hand wäscht die andere** you scratch my back, I'll scratch yours; **ich wasche meine Hände in Unschuld** I wash my hands of it *or* of the matter; **die Hände überm Kopf zusammenschlagen** to throw up one's hands in horror

◆**Hand + haben** **die Hand auf etw** *(dat)* **haben** to keep a tight rein on sth; **alle Hände voll zu tun haben** to have one's hands full; **Hand und Fuß haben** to make sense; **diese Ausrede hat weder Hand noch Fuß** this excuse doesn't stand up

✦**Hand/Hände + legen die Hände in den Schoß legen** (*fig*) to sit back and do nothing; **seine** *or* **die Hand für jdn ins Feuer legen** to vouch for sb

✦**Hand + reichen sich** *or* **einander die Hand fürs Leben reichen** to tie the knot; **sich** *or* **einander** (*geh*) **die Hand reichen können** (*fig*) to be tarred with the same brush; **da können wir uns die Hand reichen** snap! (*inf*)

Handarbeit F **(a)** work done by hand; (*Gegenstand*) handmade article; **etw in ~ herstellen** to produce sth by hand **(b)** (= *Nähen, Sticken etc, als Schulfach*) needlework *no pl*; **diese Tischdecke ist ~** this tablecloth is handmade; **eine ~ aus dem 18. Jahrhundert** a piece of needlework from the 18th century **(c)** (*kunsthandwerklich*) handicraft *no pl*; **eine ~** a piece of handicraft work

Handarbeiten NT -s, NO PL (*Sch*) needlework

Hand-: Handball M **(a)** (= *Ball*) handball **(b)** NO PL (*inf auch nt*) (= *Spiel*) handball; **Handballer** [-balɐ] M **-s, -**, **Handballerin** [-ərɪn] F **-, -nen** handball player; **Handballspiel** NT **(a)** (= *Spiel*) game of handball **(b)** (= *Disziplin*) handball *no def art*; **Handballspieler(in)** M(F) handball player; **handbedient** [-bədiːnt] ADJ hand-operated; **Handbesen** M hand brush; **Handbetrieb** M hand operation; **für** *or* **mit ~** hand-operated; **Handbewegung** F sweep of the hand; (= *Geste, Zeichen*) gesture; **Handbohrer** M gimlet; **Handbohrmaschine** F (hand) drill; **Handbremse** F handbrake (*Brit*), parking brake (*US*); **Handbuch** NT handbook; (*technisch*) manual

Händchen [ˈhɛntçən] NT **-s, -** DIM *von* **Hand** little hand; **~ halten** (*inf*) to hold hands; **~ haltend** holding hands; **~ haltend gehen/sitzen** to walk/sit hand in hand; **für etw ein ~ haben** (*inf*) to have a knack for sth; (= *gut können*) to be good at sth; **~ geben** to shake hands

Händedruck M, *pl* -drücke handshake

Handel¹ [ˈhandl] M **-s**, NO PL **(a)** (= *das Handeln*) trade; (*esp mit illegaler Ware*) traffic; **~ mit etw/einem Land** trade in sth/with a country **(b)** (= *Warenverkehr*) trade; (= *Warenmarkt*) market; **im ~ sein** to be on the market; **etw in den ~ bringen** to put sth on the market; **etw aus dem ~ ziehen** to take sth off the market; **(mit jdm) ~ (be)treiben** to trade (with sb); **~ treibend** trading **(c)** (= *Abmachung, Geschäft*) deal **(d)** (= *Wirtschaftszweig*) commerce

Handel² [ˈhandl] M **-s, ⸗** [ˈhɛndl] USU PL quarrel

handelbar ADJ (*Fin*) negotiable

Handelfmeter M penalty for a handball

handeln [ˈhandln] 🔟 VI **(a)** (= *Handel treiben*) to trade; **er handelt mit Gemüse** he's in the vegetable trade; **er handelt mit Drogen** he traffics in drugs; **er handelt in Gebrauchtwagen** he's in the second-hand car trade **(b)** (= *feilschen*) to haggle (*um* over); (*fig: = verhandeln*) to negotiate (*um* about); **ich lasse schon mit mir ~** I'm open to persuasion; (*in Bezug auf Preis*) I'm open to offers **(c)** (= *tätig werden, agieren, sich verhalten*) to act **(d)** (= *zum Thema haben*) **von etw ~** (*acc*) ~ to deal with sth 🔢 VR IMPERS **(a)** **es handelt sich bei diesen so genannten UFOs um optische Täuschungen** these so-called UFOs are optical illusions; **es handelt sich hier/dabei um ein Verbrechen** it's a crime we are dealing with here/there; **bei dem Festgenommenen handelt es sich um X** the person arrested is X **(b)** (= *betreffen*) **sich um etw ~** to be about sth **(c)** (= *um etw gehen, auf etw ankommen*) **sich um etw ~** to be a question of sth; **es handelt sich nur ums Überleben** it's simply a question of survival 🔢 VT **(a)** (= *verkaufen*) to sell (*für* at, for); (*an der Börse*) to quote (*mit* at) **(b)** (*Preis etc* = *hinaufhandeln*) to push up; (= *herunterhandeln*) to bring down **(c)** (*fig*) **er wird als der neue Außenminister gehandelt** (= *ist im Gespräch*) he is being talked about for the position of foreign minister

Handeln NT -s, NO PL **(a)** (= *Feilschen*) bargaining, haggling **(b)** (= *das Handeltreiben*) trading; **das ~ mit Antiquitäten** trading in antiques **(c)** (= *Verhalten*) behaviour (*Brit*), behavior (*US*) **(d)** (= *das Tätigwerden*) action

Handels-: Handelsabkommen NT trade agreement; **Handelsartikel** M commodity; **Handelsbank** F, *pl* -banken merchant bank; **Handelsbezeichnung** F trade name; **Handelsbeziehungen** PL trade relations *pl*; **Handelsbilanz** F balance of trade; **aktive/passive ~** balance of trade surplus/deficit; **Handelsdefizit** NT trade deficit; **handelseinig** ADJ PRED **~ werden/sein** to agree terms; **Handelsembargo** NT trade embargo; **Handelsfirma** F (commercial) firm; **Handelsflotte** F merchant fleet; **Handelsgericht** NT commercial court; **Handelsgesellschaft** F commercial company; **Handelsgesetz** NT commercial law; **Handelsgut** NT commodity; **Handelshafen** M trading port; **Handelskammer** F chamber of commerce; **Handelsklasse** F grade; **Heringe der ~ 1** grade 1 herring; **Handelslehrer(in)** M(F) teacher of commercial subjects; **Handelsmarine** F merchant navy; **Handelsmarke** F trade name; **Handelsname** M trade name; **Handelsniederlassung** F branch (of a trading organization); **Handelspartner(in)** M(F) trading partner; **Handelsplatz** M trading centre (*Brit*) *or* center (*US*); **Handelspolitik** F trade policy; **Handelsrealschule** F (*esp Sw*) commercial school *or* college; **Handelsrecht** NT commercial law *no def art, no pl*; **handelsrechtlich** 🔟 ADJ of commercial law 🔢 ADV according to commercial law; **Handelsregister** NT register of companies; **Handelsreisende(r)** MF DECL AS ADJ commercial traveller (*Brit*) *or* traveler (*US*); **Handelsschiff** NT trading ship; **Handelsschifffahrt** F merchant shipping *no def art*; **Handelsschranke** F USU PL trade barrier; **Handelsschule** F commercial school *or* college; **Handelsspanne** F profit margin; **Handelsstraße** F (*Hist*) trade route; **handelsüblich** ADJ usual (in the trade *or* in commerce); *Produkt, Ware* standard; **etw zu den ~en Preisen kaufen** to buy sth at normal (trade) prices; **Handelsunternehmen** NT commercial enterprise; **Handelsverkehr** M trade; **Handelsvertreter(in)** M(F) commercial traveller (*Brit*) *or* traveler (*US*); **Handelsvertretung** F trade mission; **Handelsware** F commodity; **keine ~** no commercial value; **Handelswaren** PL commodities *pl*, merchandise *sing*; **Handelswechsel** M trade bill; **Handelswesen** NT, NO PL commerce *no def art*; **Handelszentrum** NT trading centre (*Brit*) *or* center (*US*); **Handelszweig** M branch

handeltreibend ADJ ATTR *siehe* **Handel**

Handeltreibende(r) [-traibndə] MF DECL AS ADJ trader

Hände-: händeringend [ˈhɛndərɪŋənt] ADV wringing one's hands; (*fig*) *um etw bitten* imploringly; **~ nach etw suchen** to search desperately for sth; **Händeschütteln** NT -s, NO PL handshaking; **Händetrockner** [-trɔknɐ] M **-s, -** hand drier

Hand-: Handfeger M [-feːgɐ] **-s, -** hand brush; **Handfessel** F **(a)** manacle; **etw als ~ benutzen** to tie sb's hands together with sth **(b)** (= *Handschelle*) handcuff; **handfest** ADJ **(a)** *Essen* substantial **(b)** (*fig*) *Schlägerei* violent; *Skandal* huge; *Vorschlag, Argument* well-founded; *Beweis* solid; *Lüge, Betrug* flagrant, blatant; **Handfeuerwaffe** F handgun; **Handfläche** F palm (of the/one's hand); **Handfunkgerät** NT walkie-talkie; **handgearbeitet** ADJ handmade; *Stickerei etc* handworked; **Handgelenk** NT wrist; **aus dem ~** (*fig inf*) (= *ohne Mühe*) effortlessly; (= *improvisiert*) off the cuff; **etw aus dem ~ schütteln** (*fig inf*) to do sth effortlessly; **handgemacht** ADJ handmade; **handgemein** ADJ **(mit jdm) ~ werden** to come to blows (with sb); **Handgemenge** NT scuffle; **handgenäht** [-gənɛːt] ADJ hand-sewn; **Handgepäck** NT hand luggage *no pl or* baggage *no pl*; **handgeschrieben** ADJ handwritten; **handgestrickt** [-gəʃtrɪkt] ADJ hand-knitted; (*fig*) homespun; *Lösung* homegrown; **Handgranate** F hand grenade; **handgreiflich** [ˈhantgraiflɪç] 🔟 ADJ *Streit, Auseinandersetzung* violent; **~ werden** to become violent 🔢 ADV **etw ~ vor Augen führen** to demonstrate sth clearly; **Handgreiflichkeit** F **-, -en** USU PL violence *no pl*; **Handgriff** M **(a)** (= *Bewegung*) movement; (*im Haushalt*) chore; **keinen ~ tun** not to lift a finger; **mit einem ~ öffnen** with one flick of the wrist; (= *schnell*) in no time; **mit ein paar ~en** in next to no time **(b)** (= *Gegenstand*) handle; **handgroß** ADJ hand-sized; **handhabbar** ADJ manageable; **leicht/schwer ~** easy/difficult to manage; **Handhabe** [ˈhanthaːbə] F (*fig*) **ich habe gegen ihn keine ~** I have no hold on him; **etw als ~ (gegen jdn) benutzen** to use sth as a lever (against sb); **handhaben** VT INSEP to handle; *Maschine auch* to operate; *Gesetz* to implement; **Handhabung** [ˈhanthaːbʊŋ] F **-, -en** handling; (*von Maschine auch*) operation; (*von Gesetz*) implementation; **Handhebel** M hand-operated lever

Handheld-PC [ˈhɛnthɛlt-] M handheld PC

-händig [hɛndɪç] ADJ SUF -handed; **linkshändig** left-handed

Handikap [ˈhɛndikɛp] NT **-s, -s** (*Sport, fig*) handicap

handikapen [ˈhɛndikɛpn] VT INSEP to handicap

händisch ['hɛndɪʃ] ADJ (Aus) manual

Hand-: Handkarren M handcart; **Handkoffer** M (small) suitcase; **Handkurbel** F hand crank; (Aut) starting handle; **Handkuss** M kiss on the hand; **mit ~** (fig inf) with pleasure; **zum ~ kommen** (Aus fig) to come off worse; **Handlanger** ['hantlaŋɐ] M **-s, -** odd-job man; (fig) (= Untergeordneter) dogsbody (Brit inf), drudge (US); (pej: = Gehilfe) henchman; **Handlangerin** ['hantlaŋərɪn] F **-, -nen** (lit) odd-job woman; (fig) (= Untergeordnete) dogsbody (Brit inf), drudge (US); (pej: = Gehilfin) henchman

Händler ['hɛndlɐ] M **-s, -**, **Händlerin** [-ərɪn] F **-, -nen** trader; (= Autohändler) dealer; (= Ladenbesitzer) shopkeeper (Brit), store owner (US); (= Fischhändler) fishmonger (Brit), fish dealer (US); (= Fleischhändler) butcher; (= Gemüsehändler) greengrocer (Brit), produce dealer (US); **ambulanter** or **fliegender ~** street trader

Händler-: Händlerpreis M trade price; **Händlerrabatt** M trade discount

Hand-: Handlesekunst F (die) ~ palmistry; **Handleser(in)** M(F) palm reader; **Handleuchte** F inspection lamp

handlich ['hantlɪç] ADJ **(a)** Gerät, Format, Form handy; Gepäckstück manageable; Auto manoeuvrable (Brit), maneuverable (US) **(b)** (Sw: = behände) handy **(c)** (Sw: = mit der Hand) with one's hand(s)

Hand-: Handlinie F line (in the palm of the hand); **Handliniendeutung** F (die) ~ palmistry

Handlung ['handlʊŋ] F **-, -en** action; (= Tat, Akt) act; (= Handlungsablauf) plot; **der Ort der ~** the scene of the action

Handlungs-: Handlungsablauf M plot; **Handlungsbedarf** M need for action; **Handlungsbevollmächtigte(r)** MF DECL AS ADJ authorized agent; **handlungsfähig** ADJ Regierung, Bündnis capable of acting; (Jur) authorized to act; **eine ~e Mehrheit** a working majority; **Handlungsreisende(r)** MF DECL AS ADJ (Comm) commercial traveller (Brit) pr traveler (US), rep; **Handlungsspielraum** M scope (of action); **handlungsunfähig** ADJ Regierung, Bündnis incapable of acting; (Jur) without power to act; **Handlungsvollmacht** F proxy; **Handlungsweise** F conduct no pl

Hand-: Handmehr ['hantmeːɐ] NT **-s**, NO PL (Sw) show of hands; **Handpflege** F care of one's hands; **Handpuppe** F glove (Brit) or hand (US) puppet; **Handreichung** ['hantraiçʊŋ] F **-, -en** **(a)** (= Hilfe) helping hand no pl **(b)** (= Instruktion, Empfehlung) recommendation **(c)** (= Handzettel) handout; **Handrücken** M back of the/one's hand; **Handschelle** F USU PL handcuff; **jdm ~n anlegen** to handcuff sb; **in ~n** in handcuffs; **Handschlag** M **(a)** (= Händedruck) handshake; **mit** or **durch** or **per ~** with a handshake; **ein Geschäft durch ~ abschließen** to shake on a deal; **goldener ~** (fig inf) golden handshake (inf) **(b) keinen ~ tun** not to do a stroke (of work); **Handschreiben** NT handwritten letter; **Handschrift** F **(a)** handwriting; (fig) (trade)mark; **etw trägt/verrät jds ~** (fig) sth bears sb's (trade)mark; **eine kräftige/gute ~ haben** or **schreiben** (fig inf) to be a hard/good hitter **(b)** (= Text) manuscript; **Handschriftendeutung** F (die) ~ the study of handwriting, graphology; **handschriftlich** ADJ handwritten ADV korrigieren, einfügen by hand; sich bewerben in writing; **einen Brief ~ beantworten** to answer a letter by hand

Handschuh M (= Fingerhandschuh) glove; (= Fausthandschuh) mitten, mitt (inf)

Handschuhfach NT, **Handschuhkasten** M (Aut) glove compartment

Hand-: handsigniert [-zɪgniːɐt] ADJ signed; **Handspiel** NT, NO PL **(a)** (Sport) handball **(b)** (Cards) (finishing a game by) playing all one's hand at once; **Handstand** M (Sport) handstand; **Handstandüberschlag** M (Sport) handspring; **Handstreich** M in or durch einen ~ in a surprise coup; (Mil) by surprise; **handstreichartig** ADJ sudden and unexpected ADV suddenly and unexpectedly; **Handtasche** F handbag (Brit), purse (US); **Handtaschenraub** M bag-snatching

Handtuch NT, pl **-tücher** towel; (= Geschirrhandtuch) tea towel (Brit), dish towel (US); (= Papierhandtuch) paper towel; **das ~ werfen** to throw in the towel

Hand-: Handumdrehen NT (fig) **im ~** in the twinkling of an eye; **handverlesen** ADJ Obst etc hand-graded; (fig) Gesellschaft etc hand-picked; **Handvoll** ['hantfɔl] F **-, -** siehe Hand; **Handwagen** M handcart; **Handwaschbecken** NT wash-hand

basin; **Handwäsche** F washing by hand; (= Wäschestücke) hand wash

Handwerk NT trade; (= Kunsthandwerk) craft; (fig: = Tätigkeit) business; **das ~ des Bäckers** the baking trade; **das ~ des Schneiders/Schreiners** the trade of tailor/joiner; **das ~ des Töpfers** the potter's craft; **der Krieg ist das einzige ~, das er versteht** or **beherrscht** war is the only business he knows anything about; **sein ~ verstehen** or **beherrschen** (fig) to know one's job; **jdm ins ~ pfuschen** (fig) to tread on sb's toes; **jdm das ~ legen** (fig) to put a stop to sb's game (inf) or to sb

Handwerker ['hantvɛrkɐ] M **-s, -** tradesman, (skilled) manual worker; (= Kunsthandwerker) craftsman; **wir haben seit Wochen die ~ im Haus** we've had workmen or tradesmen in the house for weeks

Handwerkerin ['hantvɛrkərɪn] F **-, -nen** tradeswoman, (skilled) manual worker; (= Kunsthandwerkerin) craftswoman

Handwerkerschaft ['hantvɛrkəʃaft] F **-**, NO PL trade sing or pl

handwerklich ['hantvɛrklɪç] ADJ siehe Handwerker(in) Ausbildung as a manual worker/craftsman/craftswoman; (fig) technical; **~er Beruf** skilled trade; **die ~e Ausführung des Möbelstücks** the craftsmanship of the piece of furniture; **~es Können** craftsmanship; **~e Fähigkeiten** manual skills; **~e Tätigkeit** skilled manual job ADV **das ist ~ eine Katastrophe** this is a disgraceful piece of work; **~ begabt sein** to be good with one's hands; **eine ~ ausgezeichnete Leistung** a masterpiece of craftsmanship; **~ ist der Fotograf perfekt** technically the photographer is perfect

Handwerks-: Handwerksberuf M skilled trade; **Handwerksbetrieb** M workshop; **Handwerkskammer** F trade corporation; **Handwerksmeister(in)** M(F) master craftsman/-woman; **Handwerkszeug** NT, NO PL tools pl; (fig) tools pl of the trade, equipment

Handy ['hɛndi] NT **-s, -s** (Telec) mobile (phone), cell(ular) phone (US)

Vorsicht! **Handy** *wird nicht mit dem englischen Wort* **handy** *übersetzt.*

Handzeichen NT signal; (bei Abstimmung) show of hands; **durch ~** by a show of hands

hanebüchen ['haːnəbyːçn] ADJ (geh) outrageous

Hanf [hanf] M **-(e)s**, NO PL hemp

Hang [haŋ] M **-(e)s, ⁻e** ['hɛŋə] **(a)** (= Abhang) slope **(b)** NO PL (= Neigung) tendency

Hangar ['haŋgaːɐ, haŋˈgaːɐ] M **-s, -s** hangar

Hänge-: Hängebauch M drooping belly (inf); **Hängebrücke** F suspension bridge; **Hängebrust** F, **Hängebusen** M (pej) sagging breasts pl

hangeln ['haŋln] VIR (vi: aux sein or haben) **er hangelte sich am Fels hinunter** he let himself down the cliff hand over hand; **er hangelte sich über den Abgrund** he crossed the chasm hand over hand

Hänge-: Hängemappe F suspension file; **Hängematte** F hammock

hängen ['hɛŋən]	
1 INTRANSITIVES VERB	**3** REFLEXIVES VERB
2 TRANSITIVES VERB	

1 INTRANSITIVES VERB, pret **hing** [hɪŋ], ptp **gehangen** [gəˈhaŋən] **(a)** (= herunterhängen, befestigt sein, gehenkt werden) to hang; (Wohnwagen etc, Lautsprecher, Telefonapparat etc) to be connected (up) (an +dat to); **die Vorhänge hängen schief** the curtains don't hang straight; **die Gardinen hängen schon** the curtains are already up; **ihre Haare hängen bis auf die Schultern** her hair comes down to her shoulders; **die Haare hängen ihr ins Gesicht** her hair falls over her face; **das Bild hängt an der Wand/am Nagel** the picture is hanging on the wall/from a nail; **das Bild hängt schief** the picture is (hanging) crooked; **der Patient hängt an der künstlichen Niere/am Tropf** the patient is on the kidney machine/on the drip; **sie hing ihm am Hals** she hung (a)round his neck; **sie hing ihm an der Schulter** she clung to his shoulder; **mit hängenden Schultern** with drooping shoulders; **die Blumen**

ließen die Köpfe hängen the flowers drooped; **den Kopf hängen lassen** (fig) to be downcast; **eine Gefahr/ein Fluch hängt über uns** danger/a curse is hanging over us; **eine unerträgliche Spannung hing im Raum** there was unbearable tension in the room

(b) (= festhängen) to be caught (an +dat on); (= kleben) to be stuck (an +dat to); **mit dem Ärmel an einem Dorn hängen** to have one's sleeve caught on a thorn; **ihre Blicke** or **Augen hingen an dem Sänger** her eyes were fixed on the singer; **sie hing am Mund** or **an den Lippen des Redners** she hung on the speaker's every word; **daran hängt viel Arbeit** there's a lot of work involved in that

(c) (= sich aufhalten) (inf) to hang around (inf); **sie hängt ständig in Diskos** she hangs around discos; **er hängt den ganzen Tag vor dem Fernseher** he sits in front of the television all day

(d) (= behangen sein)

✦**hängen voller** or **voll** to be full of; **der Baum hängt voller Früchte** the tree is laden down with fruit

(e) (= sich neigen) to lean; **der Wagen hängt (stark) nach rechts** the car leans (badly) to the right; **häng nicht so auf dem Stuhl** (inf) don't slouch on your chair like that

(f) (Chess) **die Partie hängt** the game has been held over or adjourned; **der Springer hängt** the knight is vulnerable

(g) (gefühlsmäßig)

✦**an jdm/etw hängen** (= lieben) to love sb/sth; (inf: = abhängen von) to depend on sb/sth; **ich hänge am Leben/an meinem Beruf** I love life/my job; **es hängt an ihm/an unserer Abstimmung, ob ...** it depends on him/on our vote whether ...

2 TRANSITIVES VERB, pret **hängte** or **hing**, ptp **gehängt** or **gehangen**

(a) (= aufhängen, henken) to hang; **am nächsten Tag wurde er gehängt** they hanged him the next day; **er hängte den Telefonhörer in die Gabel** he replaced the receiver

✦**hängen an** (+acc) (= anschließen) to connect to; (= befestigen) Wohnwagen etc to hitch up to; **das Bild an die Wand hängen** to hang the picture on the wall; **eine Notiz ans schwarze Brett hängen** to put a note on the notice board (Brit) or bulletin board (US)

(b) (= hängen lassen) to dangle; **die Füße ins Wasser hängen** to dangle one's feet in the water

3 REFLEXIVES VERB

✦**sich hängen** pret **hängte**, ptp **gehängt**

✦**sich an etw** (acc) **hängen** (= sich festhalten) to hang on to sth; (= festsetzen) to stick to sth; (= sich gefühlmäßig binden) to be fixated on sth; **er hängte sich an den untersten Ast** he hung onto the lowest branch; **er hängte sich ihr an den Hals/Arm/Rockzipfel** he hung on to her neck/arm/coat-tails; **er hängte sich ans Telefon** or **an die Strippe** (inf) he got on the phone; **sich an ein Fahrzeug hängen** (= dicht verfolgen) to be in hot pursuit of a vehicle

✦**sich an jdn hängen** (= anschließen) to tag on to sb (inf); (= gefühlmäßig binden) to become attached to sb; (= verfolgen) to go after sb

✦**sich in etw** (acc) **hängen** (sl) (= sich engagieren) to be involved in sth

Hängen NT -s, NO PL **Tod durch ~** death by hanging; **mit ~ und Würgen** (inf) by the skin of one's teeth

hängen bleiben VI IRREG AUX SEIN **(a)** (= sich verfangen) to get caught (an +dat on)

(b) (Sport) (= zurückbleiben) to get left behind; (= nicht durch-, weiterkommen) not to get through; **der Aufschlag blieb im Netz hängen** the ball didn't get past the net; **die Mannschaft blieb schon in der ersten Runde hängen** the team didn't get past the first round

(c) (Sch inf: = nicht versetzt werden) to stay down

(d) (= sich aufhalten) to stay on; **bei einer Nebensächlichkeit ~ to** get sidetracked

(e) (= sich festsetzen, haften bleiben) to get stuck (in, an +dat on); (Blick, Augen) to rest (an +dat on); **es bleibt ja doch alles an mir hängen** (fig inf) in the end it's all down to me anyhow (inf); **der Verdacht ist an ihm hängen geblieben** suspicion rested on him; **vom Lateinunterricht ist bei ihm nicht viel hängen geblieben** (fig inf) not much of his Latin stuck (inf)

hängen lassen ptp **hängen lassen** or (rare) **gelassen** IRREG **1** VT **(a)** (= vergessen) to leave behind **(b)** (inf: = im Stich lassen) to let down **2** VR to let oneself go; **lass dich nicht so hängen!** don't let yourself go like this!

Hänge-: Hängeohr NT lop ear; **Hängepartie** F (Chess) adjourned game; (fig) stalemate

Hänger ['hɛŋɐ] M -s, - **(a)** (= Anhänger) trailer **(b)** (= Hängekleid) loose dress; (= Mantel) loose(-fitting) coat **(c)** (inf: im Text) **einen ~ haben** to go blank **(d)** (inf) = **Durchhänger**

Hangerl ['haŋɐl] NT -s, -(n) (Aus) **(a)** (= Lätzchen) bib **(b)** (= Geschirrhandtuch) tea towel (Brit), dish towel (US)

Hängeschrank M wall cupboard

Hanglage F sloping site; **in ~** situated on a slope

hängt [hɛŋt] 3. PERS SING PRES von **hängen**

Hannover [ha'noːfɐ] NT -s Hanover

Hannoveraner[1] [hanovə'raːnɐ] M -s, - (= Pferd) Hanoverian (horse)

Hannoveraner[2] [hanovə'raːnɐ] M -s, -, **Hannoveranerin** [-ərɪn] F -, **-nen** Hanoverian

hannoversch [ha'noːfɐʃ] ADJ Hanoverian

Hans [hans] M -' or **-ens** [-zns] **~ Guckindieluft** Johnny Head-in-the-Air; (fig) lucky dog (inf)

Hansa ['hanza] F -, NO PL (Hist) Hanseatic League, Hansa, Hanse

Hansaplast® [hanza'plast, 'hanza-] NT -(e)s, NO PL Elastoplast® (Brit), Band-Aid® (esp US)

Hänschen ['hɛnsçən] NT -s, - DIM von Hans; **was ~ nicht lernt, lernt Hans nimmermehr** (Prov) ≈ you can't teach an old dog new tricks (Prov)

Hansdampf [hans'dampf, 'hans-] M -(e)s, **-e** Jack-of-all-trades (and master of none); **er ist ein ~ in allen Gassen** he knows everybody and everything

Hanse ['hanzə] F -, NO PL (Hist) Hanseatic League

Hanseat [hanze'aːt] M **-en, -en**, **Hanseatin** [hanze'aːtɪn] F -, **-nen** citizen of a Hansa town; (Hist) Hanseatic merchant

hanseatisch [hanze'aːtɪʃ] ADJ Hanseatic

Hansel ['hanzl] M -s, -, **Hänsel** ['hɛnzl] M -s, - (dial: = Trottel) dolt; **Hänsel und Gretel** Hansel and Gretel; **ein paar ~** (dial: = wenige) a few

Hänselei [hɛnzə'lai] F -, **-en** teasing no pl

hänseln ['hɛnzln] VT to tease

Hanse-: Hansestadt F Hansa or Hanseatic town; **hansestädtisch** ADJ Hanseatic

*In the Middle Ages the **Hanse** (Hanseatic League) was a powerful alliance of independent trading centres on the Baltic and North Sea coasts. Its aim was to represent and protect the common commercial interests of its members. From the time of the Thirty Years' War up to the present the Hanseatic tradition has been continued by Lübeck, Hamburg and Bremen in particular. Bremen and Hamburg are both independent Länder with the titles **Freie Hansestadt Bremen** and **Freie Hansestadt Hamburg** respectively. Since re-unification other cities - Stralsund, Wismar, Greifswald and Rostock - have re-adopted the title of **Hansestadt**.*

Hanswurst [hans'vʊrst, 'hans-] M -(e)s, -e or (hum) ⁼e clown

Hantel ['hantl] F -, **-n** (Sport) dumbbell

hantieren [han'tiːrən] ptp **hantiert** VI **(a)** (= arbeiten) to be busy **(b)** (= umgehen mit) **mit etw ~** to handle sth **(c)** (= herumhantieren) to tinker about (an +dat with, on)

hapern ['haːpɐn] VI IMPERS (inf) **es hapert an etw** (dat) (= fehlt) there is a shortage of sth; **es hapert bei jdm mit etw** (= fehlt) sb is short of sth; **es hapert (bei jdm) mit etw** (= klappt nicht) sb has a problem with sth; **mit der Grammatik hapert es bei ihm** he's poor at grammar

Häppchen ['hɛpçən] NT -s, - DIM von Happen morsel; (= Appetithappen) titbit (Brit), tidbit (US)

häppchenweise ADV (inf: lit, fig) bit by bit

Happen ['hapn] M -s, - (inf) mouthful; (= kleine Mahlzeit) bite

Happening ['hɛpənɪŋ] NT -s, -s (Theat) happening; (Art) action painting

happig ['hapɪç] ADJ (inf) steep (inf)

happy ['hɛpi] ADJ INV (inf) happy

Happy-End ['hɛpi'ɛnt] NT -s, -s, **Happyend** NT -s, -s happy ending

Harass ['haras] M **-es, -e, Harasse** ['harasə] F **-, -n** (*Aus, Sw*: = *Kasten, Kiste*) crate

Härchen ['hɛːɐçən] NT **-s, -** DIM *von* **Haar** little hair

Hardliner ['haːɐdlaɪnɐ] M **-s, -, Hardlinerin** [-ərɪn] F **-, -nen** (*Pol*) hardliner

Hardthöhe F Hardthöhe (*German Ministry of Defence*)

Hardware ['haːɐdwɛːɐ] F **-, -s** (*Comput*) hardware

Harem ['haːrɛm] M **-s, -s** (*auch hum inf*) harem

Harfe ['harfə] F **-, -n** harp

Harfenist [harfə'nɪst] M **-en, -en, Harfenistin** [-'nɪstɪn] F **-, -nen** harpist

Harke ['harkə] F **-, -n** (*esp N Ger*) rake; **jdm zeigen, was eine ~ ist** (*fig inf*) to show sb what's what (*inf*)

harken ['harkn] VTI (*esp N Ger*) to rake

harmlos 🗎 ADJ (= *ungefährlich*) harmless; *Berg, Piste, Kurve* easy; (= *unschuldig, gutartig, naiv*) innocent 🗎 ADV (= *ungefährlich*) harmlessly; (= *unschuldig*) innocently

Harmlosigkeit F **-,** NO PL (= *Ungefährlichkeit*) harmlessness; (= *Unschuld, Naivität*) innocence

Harmonie [harmo'niː] F **-, -n** [-'niːən] (*Mus, fig*) harmony

harmonieren [harmo'niːrən], *ptp* **harmoniert** VI to harmonize

Harmonika [har'moːnika] F **-, -s** *or* **Harmoniken** harmonica; (= *Mundharmonika auch*) mouth organ; (= *Ziehharmonika*) accordion

harmonisch [har'moːnɪʃ] 🗎 ADJ (*Mus, Math*) harmonic; (= *wohlklingend, fig*) harmonious 🗎 ADV harmoniously; **~ klingende Akkorde** harmonious chords; **~ komponiert sein** to be a harmonious composition; **~ verlaufen** to be harmonious; **sie leben ~ zusammen** they live together in harmony

harmonisieren [harmoni'ziːrən], *ptp* **harmonisiert** VT *Musik, Steuern* to harmonize; (*fig*) to coordinate

Harmonisierung F **-, -en** (*von Musik, Steuern*) harmonization; (*fig*) coordination

Harn [harn] M **-(e)s, -e** urine; **~ lassen** to urinate

Harn-: Harnblase F bladder; **Harndrang** M (*form*) urge to urinate

Harnisch ['harnɪʃ] M **-(e)s, -e** armour (*Brit*), armor (*US*); **in ~ sein** (*fig*) to be up in arms; **jdn in ~ bringen** (*fig*) to get sb up in arms

Harn-: Harnlassen NT **-s,** NO PL (*form*) urination; **Harnleiter** M ureter; **Harnröhre** F urethra; **harntreibend** ADJ (*form*) diuretic; **Harnwege** PL (*Anat*) urinary tract *sing*

Harpune [har'puːnə] F **-, -n** harpoon

Harpunier [harpu'niːɐ] M **-s, -e, Harpunierin** [-'niːrɪn] F **-, -nen** harpooner

harpunieren [harpu'niːrən], *ptp* **harpuniert** VTI to harpoon

harsch [harʃ] ADJ (a) (= *barsch*) harsh (b) (= *verharscht*) *Schnee* frozen

hart [hart] 🗎 ADJ, *comp* **⁼er** ['hɛrtə], *superl* **⁼este(r, s)** ['hɛrtəstə] (a) (= *nicht weich, nicht sanft*) hard; *Wind* strong; *Ei* hard-boiled; **~ werden** to get hard; **Eier ~ kochen** to hard-boil eggs; **er hat einen ~en Schädel** *or* **Kopf** (*fig*) he's pig-headed; **ein ~es Herz haben** (*fig*) to be hard-hearted

(b) (= *scharf*) *Konturen, Kontrast, Formen* sharp; (*Phot*) *Negativ* sharp; (*Gesichts)züge, Konsonant* hard; *Licht, Klang, Ton, Aussprache, Akzent* harsh

(c) (= *rau*) *Spiel, Gegner* rough; (*fig*) *Getränke* strong; *Droge* hard; *Porno* hard-core; *Kriminalfilm etc, Western* tough

(d) (= *widerstandsfähig, robust*) tough; **gelobt sei, was ~ macht** (*prov, usu iro*) treat 'em rough, make 'em tough! (*inf*); **er ist ~ im Nehmen** he's tough

(e) (= *stabil, sicher*) *Währung, Devisen* stable; **in ~en Dollars** in hard dollars

(f) (= *streng, gnadenlos, kompromisslos*) hard; *Wort* strong; *Strafe, Urteil, Kritik* severe; *Maßnahmen, Gesetze, Politik, Kurs* tough; *Auseinandersetzung* violent; **er ist durch eine ~e Schule gegangen** (*fig*) it's not been easy for him; **~ bleiben** to stand firm; **~ mit jdm sein** to be hard on sb; **es geht ~ auf ~** it's a tough fight

(g) (= *schwer zu ertragen*) *Los, Schicksal, Tatsache* hard, cruel; *Verlust* cruel; *Wirklichkeit, Wahrheit* harsh; *Arbeit, Leben, Zeiten* hard, tough; **oh, das war ~!** (*inf: Witz etc*) oh, that was painful!; **das Härteste** (*sl:* = *Zumutung*) a real bummer (*inf*) *or* pisser (*Brit sl*)

🗎 ADV, *comp* **⁼er**, *superl* **am ⁼esten** (a) (= *nicht weich*) hard; **er**

schläft gerne ~ he likes sleeping on a hard surface/bed; **~ gefroren** frozen solid *pred;* **~ gekocht** *Ei* hard-boiled; **~ geworden** hard

(b) (= *scharf*) kontrastiert sharply; **~ klingen** (*Sprache*) to sound hard; (*Bemerkung*) to sound harsh; **er spricht manche Laute zu ~ aus** he pronounces some sounds too hard

(c) (= *heftig, rau*) roughly; *fallen, aufprallen, zuschlagen* hard; **er lässt die Kupplung immer so ~ kommen** he always lets the clutch out so roughly; **~ bedrängt** hard-pressed; **~ bedrängt sein** to be put under pressure; **jdn ~ anfahren** to bite sb's head off (*inf*); **jdm ~ zusetzen** to give sb a hard time; **etw trifft jdn ~** (*lit, fig*) sth hits sb hard; **~ diskutieren** to have a vigorous discussion; **~ spielen** (*Sport*) to play rough

(d) (= *streng*) severely; **~ durchgreifen** to take tough action; **jdn ~ anfassen** to be hard on sb; **man muss sie ~ anfassen** you have to keep them in line

(e) (= *mühevoll*) hard; **~ arbeiten** to work hard; **es kommt mich ~ an** I find it hard

(f) (= *nahe*) close (*an* +*dat* to); **das ist ~ an der Grenze der Legalität/des Zumutbaren** that's on the very limits of legality/of what's reasonable; **das ist ~ an der Grenze zum Kriminellen/zum Kitsch** that's very close to being criminal/kitsch; **~ am Wind (segeln)** (*Naut*) (to sail) close to the wind

Härte ['hɛrtə] F **-, -n** (a) hardness; (*von Matratze*) firmness; (*von Aufprall, Ruck*) violence; (= ~*grad*) degree (of hardness)

(b) NO PL (= *Schärfe*) (*von Konturen, Kontrast, Formen*) sharpness; (*von Gesichtszügen*) hardness; (*von Licht, Klang, Akzent*) harshness

(c) (= *Rauheit: von Spiel, Gegner*) roughness *no pl*

(d) NO PL (= *Stabilität: von Währung, Devisen*) stability

(e) NO PL (= *Strenge*) hardness; (*von Worten*) harshness; (*von Strafe, Urteil, Kritik*) severity; (*von Maßnahmen, Gesetz, Politik*) toughness; (*von Auseinandersetzung*) violence; **mit großer ~ diskutieren** to have a very heated discussion

(f) (= *Belastung*) (*von Schicksal, Verlust*) cruelty; (*von Wahrheit*) harshness; **soziale ~n** social hardships; (= *Fälle*) cases of social hardship; **das ist die ~** (*sl:* = *Zumutung*) that's a bit much (*inf*)

härten ['hɛrtn] VT to harden; *Stahl auch* to temper

härter COMP *von* **hart**

Härter ['hɛrtɐ] M **-s, -** (*Tech*) hardener, hardening agent

Härteskala F scale of hardness, Mohs scale

härteste(r, s) SUPERL *von* **hart**

Härtetest M endurance test; (*fig*) acid test

Hart-: Hartfaserplatte F hardboard, fiberboard (*US*); **hartgefroren** ADJ ATTR *siehe* **hart; hartgesotten** ADJ **(a)** (*fig*) hard-boiled **(b)** (*Aus*) *siehe* **hart; Hartgummi** M or NT hard rubber; **hartherzig** ADJ hard-hearted; **Hartherzigkeit** [-hɛrtsɪçkaɪt] F **-,** NO PL hard-heartedness; **Hartholz** NT hardwood; **hartnäckig** ['hartnɛkɪç] 🗎 ADJ stubborn; *Lügner, Husten* persistent; (= *beharrlich*) persistent 🗎 ADV (= *beharrlich*) persistently; (= *stur*) stubbornly; **Hartnäckigkeit** F **-,** NO PL stubbornness; (= *Beharrlichkeit*) doggedness; **Hartschalenkoffer** M hard-sided case; **Hartweizengrieß** M semolina; **Hartwurst** F salami-type sausage

Harz¹ [haːɐts] NT **-es, -e** resin

Harz² M **-es** (*Geog*) Harz Mountains *pl*

harzartig ADJ resin-like, resinous, resinoid

harzen ['haːɐtsn] 🗎 VT *Wein* to treat with resin 🗎 VI (*Baum, Holz*) to secrete resin

Harzer ['haːɐtsɐ] ADJ (*Geog*) Harz; **~ Roller** (*Zool*) roller canary; (*Cook*) (roll-shaped) Harz cheese

harzhaltig ADJ *Holz* resinous

harzig ['haːɐtsɪç] ADJ (a) *Holz, Geruch, Geschmack, Wein* resinous (b) (*Sw fig:* = *zähflüssig*) slow-moving

Hasardspiel [ha'zart-] NT game of chance; (*fig geh*) gamble; **glatte Fahrbahnen machen das Autofahren zum ~** slippery roads make driving hazardous

Hasch [haʃ] NT **-s,** NO PL (*inf*) hash (*inf*)

Haschee [ha'ʃeː] NT **-s, -s** (*Cook*) hash

haschen VI (*inf*) to smoke (hash) (*inf*)

Häschen ['hɛːsçən] NT **-s, -** (a) DIM *von* **Hase** young hare (b) (*inf:* = *Kaninchen, Playboyhäschen*) bunny (*inf*) (c) (= *Kosename*) sweetheart

Hascherl ['haʃɐl] NT **-s, -(n)** (*Aus inf*) poor soul

Haschisch [ˈhaʃɪʃ] NT or M **-(s)**, NO PL hashish

Haschmich [ˈhaʃmɪç] M **-s**, NO PL (inf) **einen ~ haben** to have a screw loose (inf)

Hase [ˈhaːzə] M **-n, -n** hare; (männlich auch) buck; (dial: = Kaninchen, Osterhase, in Märchen) rabbit; **falscher ~** (Cook) meat loaf; **wissen/sehen, wie der ~ läuft** (fig inf) to know/see which way the wind blows; **alter ~** (fig inf) old hand; **da liegt der ~ im Pfeffer** (inf) that's the crux of the matter; **mein Name ist ~ (, ich weiß von nichts)** I don't know anything about anything

Hasel- [ˈhaːzl]: **Haselnuss** F hazelnut; **Haselstrauch** M hazelbush

Hasen-: **Hasenpfeffer** M (Cook) ≈ jugged hare; **hasenrein** ADJ **jd/etw ist nicht (ganz) ~** (inf) sb/sth is not (quite) above board; **Hasenscharte** F (Med) harelip

Häsin [ˈhɛːzɪn] F **-, -nen** female hare

Hass [has] M **-es**, NO PL (a) hatred (auf +acc, gegen of); **Liebe und ~** love and hate; **sich** (dat) **jds ~ zuziehen, jds ~ auf sich** (acc) **ziehen** to incur sb's hatred (b) (inf: = Wut, Ärger) **wenn ich so was sehe, könnt ich einen ~ kriegen** (inf) when I see something like that I could get really angry; **einen ~ (auf jdn) schieben** (inf) or **haben** (inf) to be really sore (with sb) (inf)

hassen [ˈhasn] ① VT to hate; **etw ~ wie die Pest** (inf) to detest sth ② VI to hate

hassenswert ADJ hateful

hässlich [ˈhɛslɪç] ① ADJ (a) (= scheußlich) ugly; **~ wie die Nacht** or **die Sünde** (as) ugly as sin (b) (= gemein, unerfreulich) nasty ② ADV (a) (= gemein) **sich ~ benehmen** to be nasty; **~ über jdn sprechen** to say nasty things about sb (b) (= häßlich schön) hideously; **~ zugerichtet sein** to be in a hideous state; **~ grün/braun/gelb** a hideous green/brown/yellow

Hässlichkeit F **-, -en** (a) NO PL (= Scheußlichkeit) ugliness (b) (= Gemeinheit, Unfreundlichkeit) nastiness (c) (Bemerkung) nasty remark

Hassliebe F love-hate relationship (für with)

hast [hast] 2. PERS SING PRES von **haben**

Hast [hast] F **-**, NO PL haste; **voller ~** in great haste; **mit einer solchen ~** in such haste; **nur keine (jüdische) ~!** not so fast!

haste [ˈhastə] (inf) CONTR von **hast du; ~ was, biste was** (prov) money brings status

hasten [ˈhastn] VI AUX SEIN (geh) to hasten (form)

hastig [ˈhastɪç] ① ADJ hasty ② ADV hastily; **nicht so ~!** not so fast!; **er schlang sein Essen ~ hinunter** he gobbled down his food

hat [hat] 3. PERS SING PRES von **haben**

hätscheln [ˈhɛtʃln] VT (= zu weich behandeln) to pamper; Industrie, Firma to give preferential treatment to

hatschi [haˈtʃiː, ˈhatʃi] INTERJ atishoo (Brit), achoo; **~ machen** (baby-talk) to sneeze

hatte PRET von **haben**

Hattrick [ˈhɛtrɪk] M (Sport) hat-trick; (fig) masterstroke

Haube [ˈhaubə] F **-, -n** (a) (= Kopfbedeckung) bonnet; (Aus, S Ger: = Mütze) (woollen) cap; (von Krankenschwester etc) cap; **jdn unter die ~ bringen** (hum) to marry sb off; **unter der ~ sein** (hum) to be married; **unter die ~ kommen** (hum) to get married (b) (bei Vögeln) crest (c) (allgemein: = Bedeckung) cover; (= Trockenhaube) (hair) dryer, drying hood (US); (für Kaffee-, Teekanne) cosy (Brit), cozy (US); (= Motorhaube) bonnet (Brit), hood (US)

Haubitze [hauˈbɪtsə] F **-, -n** howitzer

Hauch [haux] M **-(e)s, -e** (a) (geh: = Atem) breath; (= Luftzug) breeze (b) (von Duft) smell; **ein ~ von Frühling** (poet) a breath of spring (c) (= Flair) aura, air (d) (= Andeutung, Anflug) hint

hauchdünn ① ADJ extremely thin; Scheiben, Schokoladentäfelchen wafer-thin; Strümpfe, Strumpfhose sheer; (fig) Mehrheit extremely narrow; Sieg extremely close ② ADV **das Make-up ~ auftragen** to apply a thin layer of foundation; **etw ~ schneiden** to cut sth wafer-thin

hauchen [ˈhauxn] VTI to breathe; **gegen/auf etw** (acc) **~** to breathe on sth; **er hauchte mir den Zigarettenrauch ins Gesicht** he blew cigarette smoke in(to) my face

Haue [ˈhauə] F **-, -n** (a) (S Ger, Sw, Aus) (= Pickel) pickaxe (Brit), pickax (US); (= Gartenhacke) hoe (b) NO PL (inf: = Prügel) (good) hiding (inf); **~ kriegen** to get a good hiding (inf)

hauen [ˈhauən], pret **haute** [ˈhautə], ptp **gehauen** or (dial) **gehaut** [ɡəˈhauən, ɡəˈhaut] ① VT (a) pret auch **hieb** [hiːp] (inf: = schlagen) to hit; **er haute den Stein in zwei Teile** he smashed the stone in two; **hau(t) ihn!** let him have it! (inf) (b) (= meißeln) Statue, Figur to carve; Stufen, Loch to cut (c) (inf: = stoßen) jdn, Gegenstand to shove (inf); Körperteil to bang (an +acc on, against); **das haut einen vom Stuhl** or **aus den Latschen** or **aus dem Anzug** it really knocks you sideways (inf) (d) (inf) (= werfen) to chuck (inf); Farbe to slap (inf) (auf +acc on); **er hat ihm eine 6 ins Zeugnis gehauen** he slammed a 6 on his report (Brit) or report card (US) (inf) (e) (dial) (= fällen) Baum to chop (down); (= zerhacken) Holz, Fleisch to chop (up) ② VI (a) pret auch **hieb** [hiːp] (inf: = schlagen) to hit; **jdm auf die Schulter ~** to slap sb on the shoulder; **hau doch nicht so (auf die Tasten)** don't thump like that (b) (inf: = prügeln) **nicht ~, Papi!** don't hit me, daddy!; **er haut immer gleich** he's quick to lash out (c) pret **hieb** [hiːp] (geh: mit Waffe) to lash out; **er hieb mit dem Degen (auf seinen Gegner)** he made a thrust (at his opponent) with his dagger (d) AUX SEIN (inf: = stoßen) to bang; **er ist mit dem Fuß gegen einen spitzen Stein gehauen** he banged his foot against a sharp stone ③ VR (inf) (a) (= sich prügeln) to scrap (b) (= sich setzen, legen) to fling oneself

Hauer [ˈhauɐ] M **-s, -** (Zool) tusk

Häufchen [ˈhɔyfçən] NT **-s, -** DIM von **Haufen** small heap; **ein ~ Unglück** a picture of misery

Haufen [ˈhaufn] M **-s, -** (a) heap; **jdn/ein Tier über den ~ rennen/fahren** etc (inf) to knock sb/an animal down; **jdn/ein Tier über den ~ schießen** (inf) or **knallen** (inf) to shoot sb/an animal down; **etw** (acc) **über den ~ werfen** (inf) or **schmeißen** (inf) (= verwerfen) to throw or chuck (inf) sth out; (= durchkreuzen) to mess sth up (inf); **der Hund hat da einen ~ gemacht** the dog has made a mess there (inf); **so viele Dummköpfe/so viel Geld habe ich noch nie auf einem ~ gesehen** (inf) I've never seen so many fools/so much money in one place before (b) (inf: = große Menge) load (inf); **ein ~ Unsinn** a load of (old) rubbish (inf); **ein ~ Zeit** loads of time (inf); **ich hab noch einen ~ zu tun** I still have loads to do (inf); **in ~** by the ton (inf); **er hat einen ganzen ~ Freunde** he has a whole load of friends (inf) (c) (= Schar) crowd; (von Vögeln) flock; (= Sternenhaufen) cluster of stars

häufen [ˈhɔyfn] ① VT to pile up; (= sammeln) to accumulate; siehe auch **gehäuft** ② VR (lit, fig: = sich ansammeln) to mount up; (= zahlreicher werden: Unfälle, Fehler, Fachausdrücke etc) to occur increasingly often; **es darf sich nur nicht ~** just as long as they don't happen too often

haufenweise ADV (a) (= in Haufen) in heaps (b) (inf: = in großer Zahl, Menge) heaps of (inf); **etw ~ haben** to have heaps of sth (inf)

häufig [ˈhɔyfɪç] ① ADJ frequent ② ADV often

Häufigkeit F **-, -en** frequency; (= räumliche Verbreitung) commonness

Häufung [ˈhɔyfʊŋ] F **-, -en** (a) (fig: = das Anhäufen) accumulation (b) (das Sichhäufen) increasing number; **in ähnlicher ~** in similar numbers

Haupt [haupt] NT **-(e)s, Häupter** [ˈhɔyptɐ] (a) (geh: = Kopf) head; **eine Reform an ~ und Gliedern** a total reform (b) (= zentrale Figur) head

Haupt- IN CPDS main, principal; **Hauptaktion** F siehe **Haupt- und Staatsaktion**; **Hauptaktionär(in)** M(F) main shareholder; **Hauptakzent** M (a) (Ling) primary accent or stress (b) (fig) main emphasis; **Hauptaltar** M high altar; **hauptamtlich** ① ADJ full-time; **~e Tätigkeit** full-time office ② ADV (on a) full-time (basis); **~ tätig sein** to work full-time; **Hauptanschluss** M (Telec) main extension; **nur einen ~ haben** to have a phone without extensions; **Hauptarbeit** F main (part of the) work; **Hauptausgang** M main exit; **Hauptbahnhof** M main station; **hauptberuflich** ① ADJ Lehrer, Gärtner etc full-time; **~e Tätigkeit** main occupation ② ADV full-time; **~ tätig sein** to be employed full-time; **er ist ~ bei dieser Firma tätig** (= voll angestellt) he is employed full-time by this firm; (im Gegensatz zu Nebenerwerb) his main employment is at this firm; **Hauptbeschäftigung** F main occupation; **Hauptbetrieb**

M **(a)** (= *Zentralbetrieb*) headquarters *sing or pl*
(b) (= *geschäftigste Zeit*) peak period; (= *Hauptverkehrszeit*) rush hour; **Hauptbuch** NT (*Comm*) ledger; **Hauptdarsteller** M leading man; **Hauptdarstellerin** F leading lady; **Haupteingang** M main entrance

Häuptelsalat M (*Aus*) lettuce

Haupt-: Hauptfach NT (*Sch, Univ*) main subject, major (*US*); **etw im ~ studieren** to study sth as one's main subject, to major in sth (*US*); **Hauptfeld** NT (*bei Rennen*) (main) pack; **Hauptfigur** F central figure; **Hauptfilm** M main film; **Hauptgegenstand** M **(a)** main topic **(b)** (*Aus Sch*) = Hauptfach; **Hauptgericht** NT main course

Hauptgeschäft NT (= *Zentrale*) head office

Hauptgeschäfts-: Hauptgeschäftsstelle F head office, headquarters *sing or pl*; **Hauptgeschäftsstraße** F main shopping street; **Hauptgeschäftszeit** F peak (shopping) period

Haupt-: Hauptgewicht NT (*lit*) major part of the weight; (*fig*) main emphasis; **Hauptgewinn** M first prize; **Haupthahn** M mains cock, mains tap (*Brit*); **Hauptlast** F main load, major part of the load; (*fig*) main burden; **Hauptleitung** F mains *pl*

Häuptling [ˈhɔyptlɪŋ] M **-s, -e** chief(tain); (*esp von Dorf*) headman; (*figinf*: = *Boss*) chief (*inf*)

Haupt-: Hauptmahlzeit F main meal; **Hauptmenü** NT (*Comput*) main menu; **Hauptmieter(in)** M(F) main tenant; **Hauptmotiv** NT **(a)** (= *Beweggrund*) primary *or* main motive **(b)** (*Art, Liter, Mus*) main *or* principal motif; **Hauptnahrungsmittel** NT staple food; **Hauptnenner** M (*Math, fig*) common denominator; **Hauptperson** F (*lit, fig*) central figure; **Hauptpost** F (*inf*), **Hauptpostamt** NT main post office; **Hauptprobe** F final rehearsal; (= *Kostümprobe*) dress rehearsal; **Hauptprozessor** M (*Comput*) main processor; **Hauptquartier** NT (*Mil, fig*) headquarters *sing or pl*; **Hauptrechnungsart** F (*Math*) basic arithmetical operation; **Hauptreisezeit** F peak travelling (*Brit*) *or* traveling (*US*) time(s-*pl*); **Hauptrolle** F (*Film, Theat*) leading role, lead; **die ~ spielen** (*fig*) to be all-important; (= *wichtigste Person sein*) to play the main role; **Hauptsache** F main thing; (*in Brief, Rede etc*) main point; **in der ~** in the main; **~, es klappt/du bist glücklich** the main thing is that it comes off/you're happy; **hauptsächlich** ◨ ADV mainly ◪ ADJ main; **Hauptsaison** F peak season; **~ haben** to have its/their peak season; **Hauptsatz** M **(a)** (*Gram*) (*übergeordnet*) main clause; (*allein stehend*) sentence **(b)** (*Mus*) first subject; **Hauptschiff** NT (*Archit*) nave; **Hauptschlagader** F aorta; **Hauptschulabschluss** M **den ~ haben** ≈ to have completed secondary school *or* junior high (school) (*US*); **Hauptschule** F ≈ secondary school, ≈ junior high (school) (*US*); **Hauptschüler(in)** M(F) ≈ secondary school *or* junior high (school) (*US*) pupil

A **Hauptschule** caters for the last five years (or three years after an *Orientierungsstufe*) of the compulsory nine years at school in Germany. Subsequently pupils can add on a tenth continuation year and, if their marks are good enough, obtain a **qualifizierter Hauptschulabschluss**, known colloquially as a **Quali**, which gives them a better chance in the job market and also entitles them to attend a **Fachoberschule**.

In Austria a **Hauptschule** covers school years five to eight and also offers opportunities for young people who wish to go on to higher education. In Switzerland compulsory schooling is covered by a **Volksschule**. ▶ ORIENTIERUNGSSTUFE

Haupt-: Hauptsegel NT mainsail; **Hauptseminar** NT (*Univ*) seminar for advanced students; **Hauptsicherung** F (*Elec*) main fuse; **Hauptspeicher** M (*Comput*) main memory; **Hauptstadt** F capital (city); **Hauptstädter(in)** M(F) metropolitan; **hauptstädtisch** ADJ metropolitan; **Hauptstraße** F (= *Durchgangsstraße*) main road; (*im Stadtzentrum etc*) main street; **Haupttton** M, *pl* **-töne** (*Ling*) primary stress; (*Mus*) principal note; **Haupttreffer** M top prize, jackpot (*inf*); **den ~ machen** (*inf*) to hit the jackpot (*inf*); **Haupttribüne** F main stand; (*Sport auch*) grandstand; **Haupt- und Staatsaktion** F **aus etw eine ~ machen** to make a great issue of sth

Hauptverkehr M peak(-hour) traffic; (= *Verkehrsteilnehmer*) bulk of the traffic

Hauptverkehrs-: Hauptverkehrsader F main highway (*US*), arterial route; **Hauptverkehrsstraße** F (*in Stadt*) main street; (= *Durchgangsstraße*) main thoroughfare; (*zwischen Städten*) main highway, trunk road (*Brit*); **Hauptverkehrszeit** F peak traffic times *pl*; (*in Stadt, bei Pendlern auch*) rush hour

Haupt-: Hauptversammlung F general meeting; **Hauptwäsche** F, **Hauptwaschgang** M main wash; **Hauptwohnsitz** M main place of residence; **Hauptwort** NT, *pl* **-wörter** (*Gram*) noun; **Hauptzeuge** M, **Hauptzeugin** F principal witness; **Hauptzollamt** NT main customs office

hau ruck [ˈhau ˈrʊk] INTERJ heave-ho

Hauruckverfahren NT **etw im ~ tun** to do sth in a great hurry

Haus [haus]

gen **Haus**, pl **Häuser** [ˈhɔyzɐ]

SUBSTANTIV (NT)
(a) (= *Gebäude*) house; (*auch Astrol: von Schnecke*) shell; **lass uns ins Haus gehen** let's go inside *or* into the house; **mit jdm Haus an Haus wohnen** to live next door to sb; **Haus der Jugend** youth centre (*Brit*) *or* center (*US*)
(b) (= *Zuhause, Heim*) home; **Haus und Hof** *or* **Herd verlassen** to leave house and home; **Haus und Hof verlieren** to lose the roof over one's head; **etw ins Haus liefern** to deliver sth to the door; **wir liefern frei Haus** we offer free delivery; **jdm das Haus verbieten** not to allow sb in the house; **aus dem Haus sein** to be away from home; **außer Haus essen** to eat out; **im Hause meiner Schwester** at my sister's (house); **ein Fernsehgerät kommt mir nicht ins Haus!** I won't have a television set in the house!; **ins Haus stehen** (*fig*) to be on the way; **jdm steht etw ins Haus** (*fig*) sb is facing sth; **Haus halten** = haushalten
✦**nach Hause** *or* (*Aus, Sw*) **nachhause** (*lit, fig*) home; **jdn nach Hause bringen** to take sb home
✦**zu Hause** *or* (*Aus, Sw*) **zuhause** at home; **Borussia hat zu Hause 3:1 gewonnen** Borussia have won 3-1 at home; **bei jdm zu Hause** in sb's house; **bei uns zu Hause** at home; **heute bin ich für niemanden zu Hause** I'm not at home to anybody today; **irgendwo zu Hause sein** (*Mensch, Tier*) to live somewhere; (= *sich heimisch fühlen*) to feel at home somewhere; **dieser Brauch ist in Polen zu Hause** this custom comes from Poland; **in etw** (*dat*) **zu Hause sein** (*fig*) to be at home in sth; **sich wie zu Hause fühlen** to feel at home; **fühl dich wie zu Hause!** make yourself at home!
(c) (= *Unternehmen*) House (*form*); **das Haus Siemens** (*geh*) the House of Siemens; **„Haus Talblick"** "Talblick (House)"; **das erste Haus am Platze** (*geh*) (= *Hotel*) the best hotel in town; (= *Kaufhaus*) the best store in town; **er ist nicht im Hause** (= *in der Firma*) he's not in; **in unserem Hause dulden wir keine Drogen/keinen Alkohol** (= *in unserer Firma*) we do not allow drugs/alcohol on the premises
(d) (= *Bewohnerschaft eines Hauses*) household; **der Herr des Hauses** (*form*) the head of the household; **ein Freund des Hauses** a friend of the family; **die Dame/Tochter etc des Hauses** (*form*) the lady/daughter *etc* of the house
(e) (= *Herkunft*) (*geh*) **aus gutem/bürgerlichem Haus(e)** from a good/middle-class family; **aus adligem Haus(e)** of noble birth; **von Hause aus** (= *ursprünglich*) originally; (= *von Natur aus*) naturally
(f) (= *Dynastie*) House; **das Haus Windsor** the House of Windsor; **das Haus Habsburg** the Hapsburg dynasty; **aus dem Haus Davids** of the House of David
(g) (= *Theater*) theatre (*Brit*), theater (*US*); (= *Saal, Publikum*) house; **das große/kleine Haus** the main/small theatre (*Brit*) *or* theater (*US*); **vor vollem Haus spielen** to play to a full house
(h) (*Parl*) House; **Hohes Haus!** (*form*) ≈ honourable (*Brit*) *or* honorable (*US*) members (of the House)!; **dieses hohe Haus ...** the *or* this House ...

Haus-: Hausantenne F roof aerial (*Brit*) *or* antenna (*US*); **Hausapotheke** F medicine cupboard; **Hausarbeit** F **(a)** housework *no pl* **(b)** (*Sch*) homework *no indef art, no pl*, piece of homework, assignment (*esp US*); **Hausarrest** M (*im Internat*) detention; (*Jur*) house arrest; **~ haben** to be in detention/under house arrest; **Fritz kann nicht zum Spielen rauskommen, er hat ~** Fritz can't come out to play - he's grounded *or* being kept in; **Hausarzt** M, **Hausärztin** F GP; (*von*

Heim, Anstalt) resident doctor; **Hausaufgabe** F (*Sch*) homework *sing, no indef art*; **seine ~n machen** (*auch fig*) to do one's homework; **hausbacken** ['hausbakn] ADJ (*fig*) homespun, homely (*US*); *Kleidung* unadventurous; **Hausbank** F, *pl* **-banken** bank; **Hausbau** M, NO PL (= *das Bauen*) building of a/the house; **Hausbesetzer** [-bəzetsɐ] M **-s, -,** **Hausbesetzerin** [-ərɪn] F **-, -nen** squatter; **Hausbesetzung** F squatting; (*Einzug*) moving into a squat; **Hausbesitzer** M house-owner; (= *Hauswirt*) landlord; **Hausbesitzerin** F house-owner; (= *Hauswirtin*) landlady; **Hausbesorger** [-bəzɔrgɐ] M **-s, -, Hausbesorgerin** [-ərɪn] F **-, -nen** (*Aus*) caretaker, janitor; **Hausbesuch** M home visit; **Hausbewohner(in)** M(F) (house) occupant; **Hausboot** NT houseboat

Häuschen ['hɔʏsçən] NT **-s, -** (a) DIM *von* Haus (b) (*fig inf*) **ganz aus dem ~ sein vor ...** to be out of one's mind with ... (*inf*); **ganz aus dem ~ geraten** to go berserk (*inf*) (c) (*euph inf*: = *Toilette*) smallest room (*Brit hum inf*), bathroom (*US*)

Haus-: Hausdetektiv(in) M(F) house detective; (*von Kaufhaus*) store detective; **Hausdurchsuchung** F (*Aus*) = **Haussuchung**; **Hauseigentümer(in)** M(F) homeowner

hausen ['hauzn] VI (a) (= *wohnen*) to live (b) (= *wüten*) (**übel** *or* **schlimm**) **~** to wreak havoc; **schrecklich ~** to wreak the most dreadful havoc; **wie die Wandalen ~** to act like vandals (c) (*Sw, S Ger*: = *sparsam sein*) to be economical

Häuser-: Häuserflucht F row of houses; **Häuserreihe** F row of houses; (*aneinander gebaut*) terrace; **Häuserschlucht** F **die ~en New Yorks** the urban jungle of New York

Haus-: Hausflur M (entrance) hall, hallway; **Hausfrau** F (a) housewife; (= *Gastgeberin*) hostess (b) (*Aus, S Ger*: = *Hauswirtin*) landlady; **hausfraulich** ADJ housewifely; **hausgemacht** ADJ home-made; (*fig*) *Problem etc* of one's own making; **Hausfreund** M (a) (= *Freund der Familie*) friend of the family (b) (*euph inf*) man friend; **Hausfreundin** F (= *Freundin der Familie*) friend of the family; **Hausfriedensbruch** M (*Jur*) trespass (*in sb's house*); **Hausgemeinschaft** F household (community); **mit jdm in ~ leben** to live together with sb (in the same household)

Haushalt ['haushalt] M **-(e)s, -e** (a) (= *Hausgemeinschaft*) household; (= *Haushaltsführung*) housekeeping; **Geräte für den ~** household utensils; **den ~ führen** to run the household; **jdm den ~ führen** to keep house for sb (b) (*fig: Biol etc*) balance (c) (= *Etat*) budget

Haushalt- IN CPDS = **Haushalts-**

haushalten ['haushaltn] VI SEP IRREG (a) (= *sparsam wirtschaften*) to be economical; **mit etw ~ mit Geld, Zeit** to be economical with sth (b) (= *den Haushalt führen*) to keep house

Haushälter ['haushɛltɐ] M **-s, -, Haushälterin** [-ərɪn] F **-, -nen, Haushalter(in)** M(F) housekeeper

Haushalts- IN CPDS household; (*Pol*) budget; **Haushaltsartikel** M household item; **Haushaltsdefizit** NT (*Pol*) budget deficit; **Haushaltsfragen** PL (*Pol*) budgetary questions *pl*; **Haushaltsführung** F housekeeping; **doppelte ~** running two homes; **Haushaltsgeld** NT housekeeping money; **Haushaltshilfe** F domestic *or* home help; **Haushaltsjahr** NT (*Pol, Econ*) financial year; **Haushaltskasse** F household budget; **Haushaltsloch** NT budget deficit; **das ~ stopfen** to cure current budget shortfalls; **Haushaltspackung** F family pack; **Haushaltsplan** M (*Pol*) budget; **Haushaltswaren** PL household goods *pl*

Haushaltungsvorstand M (*form*) head of the household

Haus-: Hausherr M (a) head of the household; (= *Gastgeber, Sport*) host (b) (*Jur*) householder (c) (*Aus, S Ger*) (= *Hausbesitzer*) house-owner; (= *Hauswirt*) landlord; **Hausherrin** F (a) lady of the house; (= *Gastgeberin*) hostess (b) (*Aus, S Ger*: = *Hausbesitzerin*) house-owner; (= *Hauswirtin*) landlady; **haushoch** ADJ (as) high as a house/houses; (*fig*) *Sieg* crushing; **der haushohe Favorit** the hot favourite (*Brit inf*) *or* favorite (*US inf*) ADV high (in the sky); **jdn ~ schlagen** to give sb a thrashing (*inf*); **~ gewinnen** to win hands down; **jdm ~ überlegen sein** to be head and shoulders above sb

hausieren [hau'ziːrən] *ptp* **hausiert** VI to hawk (*mit etw* sth); **mit etw ~ gehen** (*fig*) *mit Plänen etc* to hawk sth about; *mit Gerüchten* to peddle sth; **„Hausieren verboten"** "no hawkers *or* peddlers"

Hausierer [hau'ziːrɐ] M **-s, -, Hausiererin** [-ərɪn] F **-, -nen** hawker, peddler

Hausis ['hauzɪz] PL (*inf*: = *Hausaufgaben*) homework

Haus-: Hauskatze F domestic cat; **Hauskauf** M house-buying *no art*, house purchase

häuslich ['hɔʏslɪç] **1** ADJ domestic; *Pflege* home *attr*; (= *der Familie gehörend*) family *attr*; (= *an häuslichen Dingen interessiert*) domesticated; (= *das Zuhause liebend*) home-loving; **der ~e Herd** the family home **2** ADV **sich ~ niederlassen** to make oneself at home; **sich ~ einrichten** to settle in

Häuslichkeit F **-,** NO PL domesticity

Hausmacher-: Hausmacherart F **Wurst** *etc* **nach ~** home-made-style sausage *etc*; **Hausmacherkost** F home cooking

Haus-: Hausmann M, *pl* **-männer** (= *den Haushalt versorgender Mann*) househusband; **Hausmannskost** F plain cooking *or* fare; (*fig*) plain fare; **Hausmeister** M caretaker; **Hausmitteilung** F internal memo; **Hausmittel** NT household remedy; **Hausmüll** M domestic refuse; **Hausnummer** F house number; **Hausordnung** F house rules *pl or* regulations *pl*; **Hausputz** M house cleaning; **Hausrat** M, NO PL household equipment; **Hausratversicherung** F (household) contents insurance; **Haussammlung** F house-to-house *or* door-to-door collection; **Hausschlüssel** M front-door key; **Hausschuh** M slipper

Hausse ['(h)oːs(ə)] F **-, -n** (*Econ*: = *Aufschwung*) boom (*an +dat* in); (*St Ex*: = *Kurssteigerung*) bull market; **~ haben** (*St Ex*) to rise on the Stock Exchange; **wenn man ~ hat, ...** (*St Ex*) when there's a bull market ...; **auf ~ spekulieren** (*St Ex*) to bull

Haussegen M **bei ihnen hängt der ~ schief** (*hum*) they're a bit short on domestic bliss (*inf*)

Hausse- ['(h)oːs(ə)-]: **Haussemarkt** M bull market; **Hausseposition** F long *or* bull position; **Haussespekulation** F (*St Ex*) bull speculation

Haussier [(h)oːˈsieː] M **-s, -s** (*St Ex*) bull

Haus-: Hausstand M household; **einen ~ gründen** to set up house; **Haussuchung** [-zuːxʊŋ] F **-, -en** (*in einem Haus*) house search; (*in mehreren Häusern*) house-to-house search; **Haussuchungsbefehl** M search warrant; **Haustier** NT domestic animal; (*aus Liebhaberei gehalten*) pet; **Haustür** F front door; **gleich vor der ~** (*fig inf*) on one's doorstep; **Hausverbot** NT ban on entering the house; **jdm ~ erteilen** to ban sb from the house; **Hausverwalter(in)** M(F) (house) supervisor; **Hausverwaltung** F property management; **Hauswart** [-vart] M **-(e)s, -e, Hauswartin** F **-, -nen** caretaker, janitor; **Hauswirt** M landlord; **Hauswirtin** F landlady

Hauswirtschaft F (a) (= *Haushaltsführung*) housekeeping (b) (*Sch*) home economics *sing*

hauswirtschaftlich ADJ domestic; **ein ~er Kurs** a course on home economics; **~ interessiert** interested in domestic matters

Hauswirtschafts-: Hauswirtschaftslehre F (*Sch*) home economics *sing*; **Hauswirtschaftsschule** F school of home economics

Haus-: Hauswurfsendung F (house-to-house) circular; **Hauszelt** NT frame tent

Haut [haut] F **-, Häute** ['hɔʏtə] skin; (*dick, esp von größerem Tier*) hide; (= *geschälte Schale von Obst etc*) peel; (*inf*: = *Mensch*) sort (*inf*); **nass bis auf die ~** soaked to the skin; **nur ~ und Knochen sein** to be nothing but skin and bone(s); **mit ~ und Haar(en)** (*inf*) completely; **er ist ihr mit ~ und Haar(en) verfallen** (*inf*) he's head over heels in love with her; **in seiner ~ möchte ich nicht stecken** I wouldn't like to be in his shoes; **er fühlt sich nicht wohl in seiner ~** (*inf*), **ihm ist nicht wohl in seiner ~** (*inf*) (= *unglücklich, unzufrieden*) he's (feeling) rather unsettled; (= *unbehaglich*) he feels uneasy; **er kann nicht aus seiner ~ heraus** (*inf*) he can't change the way he is; **auf der faulen ~ liegen** (*inf*), **sich auf die faule ~ legen** (*inf*) to sit back and do nothing

Haut- IN CPDS skin; **Hautabschürfung** F graze; **Hautarzt** M, **Hautärztin** F dermatologist; **Hautausschlag** M (skin) rash

Häutchen ['hɔʏtçən] NT **-s, -** DIM *von* Haut (*auf Flüssigkeit*) skin; (*Anat, Bot*) membrane; (*an Fingernägeln*) cuticle

haute PRET *von* hauen

häuten ['hɔʏtn] **1** VT *Tiere* to skin **2** VR (*Tier*) to shed its skin; (*Schlange auch*) to slough (its skin)

hauteng ADJ skintight

Hautevolee [(h)oːtvoˈleː] F **-,** NO PL upper crust

Haut-: Hautfarbe F skin colour (*Brit*) *or* color (*US*); **nur, weil er eine andere ~ hat** just because his skin is a different colo(u)r; **hautfarben** [-farbn] ADJ flesh-coloured (*Brit*), flesh-colored (*US*)

-häutig [hɔytɪç] ADJ SUF -skinned; **dunkelhäutig** dark-skinned

Haut-: Hautjucken NT -s, NO PL itching; **eine Creme gegen ~** a cream for skin irritations; **Hautklinik** F dermatology clinic; **hautnah** 🔢 ADJ (a) (*Anat*) close to the skin (b) (= *sehr eng*, *Sport*) (very) close (c) (*fig inf*: = *wirklichkeitsnah*) Kontakt (very) close; *Problem* that affects us/him *etc* directly; *Darstellung*, *Schilderung* deeply affecting 🔢 ADV (a) (= *eng*) **~ in Kontakt mit jdm/etw kommen** to come into (very) close contact with sb/sth (b) (*inf*: = *direkt*) *darstellen, schildern* realistically; **etw ~ erleben** to experience sth at close quarters; **Hautpflege** F skin care; **Hautpilz** M (*Med*) fungal skin infection; **hautschonend** ADJ kind to the skin; **Hauttransplantation** F (= *Operation*) skin graft; (= *Verfahren*) skin grafting

Havarie [hava'ri:] F -, -n [-'ri:ən] (= *Unfall*) accident; (= *Schaden*) damage *no indef art, no pl*

havarieren [hava'ri:rən], *ptp* **havariert** VI (a) (*Schiff*) to be damaged (b) (*Aus: Fahrzeug*) to crash

Hawaii [ha'vaii, ha'vai] NT **-s** Hawaii

Hawaiianer [havai'ia:nɐ] M **-s, -, Hawaiianerin** [-ərɪn] F -, -nen Hawaiian

Hawaiigitarre [ha'vaii-, ha'vai-] F Hawaiian guitar

hawaiisch [ha'vaiiʃ] ADJ Hawaiian

Haxe ['haksə] F -, -n (*Cook*) leg (joint); (*S Ger inf* = *Fuß*) foot; (= *Bein*) leg; **„~n abkratzen!"** (*hum inf*) "wipe your feet!"

Hbf ABBR *von* **Hauptbahnhof**

H-Bombe ['ha:-] F H-bomb

h. c. [ha:'tse:] ABBR *von* **honoris causa**

HD-Diskette [ha:'de:-] F (*Comput*) HD diskette

he [he:] INTERJ hey; (*fragend*) eh

Headhunter ['hɛdhantɐ] M **-s, -, Headhunterin** [-ərɪn] F -, -nen head-hunter

Hearing ['hi:ərɪŋ] NT **-(s), -s** hearing

heavy ['hɛvi] ADJ PRED (*sl*: = *schwierig*) heavy (*inf*); **das war einfach zu ~ für sie** (*Erlebnis etc*) it was simply too much for her to take

Hebamme ['he:plamə, 'he:bamə] F -, -n midwife

Hebebühne F hydraulic ramp

Hebel ['he:bl] M **-s, -** (a) (*Phys*) (= *Griff*) lever; (*fig*) leverage; **alle ~ in Bewegung setzen** (*inf*) to move heaven and earth; **am längeren ~ sitzen** (*inf*) to have the whip hand (b) (*Sport*: = *-griff*) lever hold

heben ['he:bn], *pret* **hob** [ho:p], *ptp* **gehoben** [gə'ho:bn] 🔢 VT (a) (= *nach oben bewegen*) to lift; *Augenbraue, Kamera, Fernglas* to raise; **einen ~ gehen** (*inf*) to go for a drink; **er hebt gern einen** (*inf*) he likes a drink; *siehe auch* **gehoben** (b) (= *nach oben befördern, hochheben*) to lift; *Wrack* to raise; *Schatz* to dig up; (*Sport*) *Gewicht* to lift; **jdn auf die Schultern ~** to lift sb onto one's shoulders (c) (= *verbessern*) *Selbstbewusstsein, Effekt* to heighten; *Ertrag, Geschäft* to increase; *Stimmung, Wohlstand* to improve; *Niveau* to raise; *jds Ansehen* to boost; **jds Stimmung ~** to cheer sb up (d) (*S Ger*: = *halten*) to hold 🔢 VR (a) (= *sich nach oben bewegen*) to rise; (*Nebel, Deckel*) to lift; **sich ~ und senken** (*Schiff*) to rise and fall; (*Busen*) to heave; **da hob sich seine Stimmung** that cheered him up (b) (*S Ger*: = *sich halten*) to hold on (*an +dat* to) 🔢 VI (a) (*Sport*) to do weightlifting (b) (*S Ger*: = *haltbar sein*) to hold; (*Nahrungsmittel*) to keep

Heber ['he:bɐ] M **-s, -** (a) (*Chem*) pipette (b) (*Tech*) (hydraulic) jack

Hebesatz M (*Fin*) rate of assessment

hebräisch [he'brɛ:ıʃ] ADJ Hebrew

Hebung ['he:bʊŋ] F -, -en (a) (*von Schatz, Wrack etc*) recovery, raising (b) (*Geol*) elevation (c) NO PL (*fig*: = *Verbesserung*) improvement; (*von Effekt, Selbstbewusstsein*) heightening; (*von Lebensstandard, Niveau*) rise; **seine Fröhlichkeit trug zur ~ der gedrückten Stimmung bei** his cheerfulness helped to relieve the subdued mood (d) (*Poet*) stressed syllable

hecheln ['hɛçln] 🔢 VT *Flachs, Hanf* to hatchel 🔢 VI (a) (*inf*: = *lästern*) to gossip (b) (= *keuchen*) to pant

Hecht [hɛçt] M **-(e)s, -e** (*Zool*) pike; (*inf*: = *Bursche*) guy (*inf*); **er ist (wie) ein ~ im Karpfenteich** (*fig*) (= *sehr aktiv*) he certainly shakes people up; (= *sorgt für Unruhe*) he's a stirrer (*inf*)

hechten ['hɛçtn] VI AUX SEIN (*inf*) to dive; (*beim Schwimmen*) to do a racing dive; (*beim Turnen*) to do a forward dive

Heck [hɛk] NT **-(e)s, -e** *pl auch* **-s** (*Naut*) stern; (*Aviat*) tail; (*Aut*) rear

Heckantrieb M (*Aut*) rear-wheel drive

Hecke ['hɛkə] F -, -n hedge; (*am Wegrand*) hedgerow

Hecken-: Heckenrose F dog rose; **Heckenschere** F hedge clippers *pl*; **Heckenschütze** M, **Heckenschützin** F sniper

Heck-: Heckklappe F (*Aut*) tailgate; **hecklastig** [-lastıç] ADJ tail-heavy; **Heckmotor** M (*Aut*) rear engine; **mit ~** rear-engined

Heckscheibe F (*Aut*) rear windscreen (*Brit*) *or* windshield (*US*)

Heckscheiben-: Heckscheibenheizung F rear windscreen (*Brit*) *or* windshield (*US*) heater; **Heckscheibenwischer** M rear windscreen (*Brit*) *or* windshield (*US*) wiper

Heck-: Hecktür F (*Aut*) tailgate; (*von Lieferwagen*) rear doors *pl*; **Hecktürmodell** NT hatchback (car)

heda ['he:da] INTERJ hey there

Hedgegeschäft ['hɛdʒ-] NT, **Hedging** ['hɛdʒɪŋ] NT **-s, -s** hedging

Hedonismus [hedo'nısmʊs] M **-**, NO PL hedonism

Heer [he:ɐ] NT **-(e)s, -e** (*lit, fig*) army

Hefe ['he:fə] F -, -n yeast

Hefe-: Hefegebäck NT yeast-risen pastry; **Hefekranz** M ≈ savarin; **Hefekuchen** M yeast cake; **Hefepilz** M yeast plant; **Hefeteig** M yeast dough

Heft¹ NT **-(e)s, -e** (a) (= *Schreibheft*) exercise book (b) (= *Zeitschrift*) magazine; (= *Comicheft*) comic; (= *Nummer*) issue; **„National Geographic 1998, ~ 3"** "National Geographic 1998, No 3"

Heft² [hɛft] NT **-(e)s, -e** (*von Werkzeug, Messer*) handle; (*von Dolch, Schwert*) hilt; **das ~ in der Hand haben** (*fig*) to hold the reins; **das ~ in der Hand behalten** (*fig*) to remain in control; **das ~ aus der Hand geben** (*fig*) to hand over control; **jdm das ~ aus der Hand nehmen** (*fig*) to seize control from sb

Heftchen ['hɛftçən] NT **-s, -** (a) DIM *von* **Heft** (b) (*pej*) (= *billiger Roman*) cheap novel; (= *schlechte Zeitschrift, Comicheftchen*) rag (*pej inf*) (c) (= *Fahrkartenheftchen, Eintrittskartenheftchen*) book(let) of tickets; (= *Briefmarkenheftchen*) book of stamps

heften ['hɛftn] 🔢 VT (a) (= *nähen*) *Saum, Naht* to tack (up); *Buch* to sew; (= *klammern*) to clip (*an +acc* to); (*mit Heftmaschine*) to staple (*an +acc* to) (b) (= *befestigen*) to pin, to fix; **den Blick** *or* **die Augen auf jdn/ etw ~** to fix one's eyes on sb/sth 🔢 VR (a) (*Blick, Augen*) **sich auf jdn/etw ~** to fix onto sb/sth (b) **sich an jdn ~** to latch on to sb; **sich an jds Spur** *or* **Fährte ~** to follow sb's trail; **sich an jds Fersen** *or* **Sohlen ~** (*fig*) (= *jdn verfolgen*) to dog sb's heels; (*bei Rennen etc*) to stick to sb's heels

Hefter ['hɛftɐ] M **-s, -** (a) (loose-leaf) file (b) (= *Heftapparat*) stapler

Heftfaden M, **Heftgarn** NT tacking thread

heftig ['hɛftıç] 🔢 ADJ (a) (= *stark, gewaltig*) violent; *Kopfschmerzen, Fieber, Frost, Erkältung* severe; *Schmerz, Abneigung* intense; *Liebe, Leidenschaft* burning *no adv*, intense; *Widerstand* vehement; *Weinen* bitter; *Lachen* uproarious; *Atmen, Regen* heavy; *Kontroverse, Kampf, Wind* fierce; **ein ~er Regenguss** a downpour (b) (= *jähzornig, ungehalten*) *Mensch* violent(-tempered); *Ton* fierce; *Worte* violent; **~ werden** to fly into a passion (c) (*sl*: = *sehr gut*) wicked (*sl*); **das ist ganz schön ~** (*sl*: = *unangenehm*) that's a bummer (*sl*) *or* a pisser (*Brit sl*) 🔢 ADV *regnen, schneien, zuschlagen* hard; *verprügeln, kritisieren* severely; *schütteln, rühren* vigorously; *nicken* emphatically; *zittern* badly; *dementieren, schimpfen* vehemently; *verliebt* passionately; **es stürmt/gewittert ~** there is a violent storm/ thunderstorm; **sich ~ streiten** to have a violent argument; **der Regen schlug ~ gegen die Scheiben** the rain pounded against the windows; **sie knallte die Tür ~ ins Schloss** she slammed the door (shut)

Heftigkeit F, NO PL (= *Stärke, Gewalt*) violence; (*von Kopfschmerzen, Frost*) severity; (*von Schmerz, Liebe, Abneigung*) intensity; (*von Widerstand*) vehemence; (*von Kampf, Wind*) ferocity; (*von Regen*) heaviness

Heft-: Heftklammer F staple; **Heftmaschine** F stapler; **Heftpflaster** NT (sticking) plaster, adhesive tape (US); **Heftstich** M tacking stitch; **Heftzwecke** F drawing pin (Brit), thumb tack (US)

hegen ['heːgn] VT **(a)** (= pflegen) to care for; jdn ~ und pflegen to lavish care and attention on sb **(b)** Hass, Groll, Verdacht to harbour (Brit), to harbor (US); Misstrauen, Achtung, Abneigung to feel; Zweifel to entertain; Hoffnung, Wunsch to cherish; Plan, Unternehmen to foster; **ich hege den starken Verdacht, dass ...** I have a strong suspicion that ...; **ich hege schon lange den Plan auszuwandern** for a long time I've been contemplating emigrating

Hehl [heːl] NT or M **kein** or **keinen ~ aus etw machen** to make no secret of sth

Hehler ['heːlɐ] M **-s, -**, **Hehlerin** [-ərɪn] F **-, -nen** receiver (of stolen goods); **der ~ ist schlimmer als der Stehler** (Prov) it is worse to condone a crime than to commit it

Hehlerei [heːləˈrai] F **-, -en** receiving (stolen goods)

Heide¹ ['haidə] F **-, -n (a)** moor; (= ~land) moorland **(b)** (= ~kraut) heather

Heide² ['haidə] M **-n, -n**, **Heidin** ['haidɪn] F **-, -nen** heathen; (= Nichtjude) Gentile

Heide-: Heidekraut NT heather; **Heideland** NT moorland

Heidelbeere F bilberry, blueberry (esp US)

Heiden-: Heidenangst F **eine ~ vor etw** (dat) **haben** (inf) to be scared stiff of sth (inf); **Heidenarbeit** F (inf) real slog (inf); **Heidenlärm** M (inf) unholy din (inf); **Heidenspaß** M (inf) terrific fun; **einen ~ haben** to have a whale of a time (inf); **das macht ihm einen ~** he finds it terrific fun

Heidin F siehe **Heide²**

heidnisch ['haidnɪʃ] **1** ADJ heathen; (auf Götterkult bezüglich) pagan **2** ADV like a heathen; **~ leben** to live a heathen life

Heidschnucke ['haitʃnʊkə] F **-, -n** German moorland sheep

heikel ['haikl] ADJ **(a)** (= schwierig, gefährlich) tricky **(b)** (dial) Mensch particular (in Bezug auf +acc about); (in Bezug aufs Essen) fussy **(c)** (dial) Stoff, Farbe difficult

heil [hail] **1** ADJ **(a)** (= unverletzt) Mensch unhurt; Glieder unbroken; Haut undamaged; **wieder ~ sein/werden** (= wieder gesund) to be/get better again; (Wunde) to have healed/to heal up; (Knochen) to have mended/to mend; **~ machen** (inf) (= reibar) to make better; (= reparieren) to fix; **mit ~en Gliedern** or **~ am Ziel ankommen** to reach the finish without breaking any bones; **mit ~er Haut davonkommen** to escape unscathed **(b)** (inf: = ganz) intact; **die Uhr ist wieder ~** the clock's back in working order; **die ~e Welt** an ideal world (without problems, uncertainties etc) **2** ADV (= unverletzt) all in one piece; **~ nach Hause kommen** to get home safe and sound; **etw ~ überstehen** Unfall to come through sth without a scratch; Prüfung to get through sth

Heil [hail] **1** NT **-s**, NO PL **(a)** (= Wohlergehen) wellbeing; **sein ~ bei jdm versuchen** (inf) to try one's luck with sb; **jdm ~ und Segen wünschen** to wish sb every blessing **(b)** (Eccl, fig) salvation; **sein ~ in etw** (dat) **suchen** to seek one's salvation in sth; **sein ~ in der Flucht suchen** to flee for one's life **2** INTERJ **~!** hail! (old); **~ dem König!** long live or God save the King!; **~ Hitler!** (NS) heil Hitler!; **Berg/Ski/Petri ~!** good climbing/skiing/fishing!

Heiland ['hailant] M **-(e)s, -e** [-də] Saviour (Brit), Savior (US)

Heil-: Heilanstalt F nursing home; (für Sucht- oder Geisteskranke) home; **~ für Geisteskranke** mental home; **Heilbad** NT (= Bad) medicinal bath; (= Ort) spa; **heilbar** ADJ curable

Heilbutt M halibut

heilen ['hailən] **1** VI AUX SEIN (Wunde, Bruch) to heal (up); (Entzündung) to clear up **2** VT Kranke, Krankheiten to cure; Wunde to heal; (Rel) to heal; **jdn von etw ~** (lit, fig) to cure sb of sth; **von jdm/etw geheilt sein** (fig) to have got over sb/sth

heilig ['hailɪç] ADJ **(a)** holy; (bei Namen von Heiligen) Saint; (pej) holier-than-thou; **jdm ~ sein** (lit, fig) to be sacred to sb; **die ~e Veronika** Saint Veronica; **der ~e Augustinus** Saint Augustine; **Heiliger Abend** Christmas Eve; **die Heilige Jungfrau** the Blessed Virgin; **Heilige Maria** Holy Mary; **der Heilige Geist/Vater/Stuhl** the Holy Spirit/Father/See; **die Heiligen Drei Könige** the Three Kings or Wise Men; **das**

Heilige Land the Holy Land; **die Heilige Schrift** the Holy Scriptures pl; **das Heilige Römische Reich** the Holy Roman Empire; **das Heiligste** (lit, fig) the holy of holies **(b)** (fig: = ernst) Eid, Pflicht, Recht sacred; Eifer, Zorn righteous; **~e Kuh** sacred cow; **es ist mein ~er Ernst** I am deadly serious **(c)** (inf: = groß) incredible (inf); **von einer ~en Angst gepackt werden** to be scared out of one's wits **(d)** (inf: in Ausrufen) **(ach du) ~er Bimbam** or **Strohsack!, ~es Kanonenrohr!** holy smoke! (inf)

Heiligabend [hailɪçˈlaːbnt] M Christmas Eve

Heiligabend is the evening of December 24th and is the time for *Bescherung*, when people exchange presents. According to tradition, the presents are brought - especially in Protestant areas - by the *Christkind*, a mythical figure somewhere between an angel and the baby Jesus. Around midnight candle-lit *Christmetten* take place. These are festive Christmas services in celebration of Jesus' birth. A traditional meal - commonly goose, turkey or carp - is eaten on Christmas Day.

Heiligenschein M halo; **jdn mit einem ~ umgeben** (fig) to put sb on a pedestal; **sich mit einem ~ umgeben** (fig) to be holier-than-thou

Heilige(r) ['hailɪgə] MF DECL AS ADJ (lit, fig) saint

Heilig-: Heiligkeit F **-**, NO PL holiness; (= Geweihtheit, Geheiligtheit auch, von Eigentum) sacredness; **heilig sprechen** VT IRREG to canonize; **Heiligsprechung** F **-, -en** canonization; **Heiligtum** ['hailɪçtuːm] NT **-s, -tümer** [-tyːmɐ] (= Stätte) shrine; (= Gegenstand) (holy) relic; **Schändung eines ~s** sacrilege; **jds ~ sein** (inf) (Zimmer) to be sb's sanctum; (Gegenstand etc) to be sacrosanct (to sb)

Heil-: Heilklima NT healthy climate; **Heilkraft** F healing power; **heilkräftig** ADJ Pflanze, Tee medicinal; Wirkung curative; **ein ~es Mittel** a curative; **Heilkraut** NT USU PL medicinal herb; **Heilkundige(r)** [-kʊndɪgə] MF DECL AS ADJ person skilled in the art of healing; **heillos 1** ADJ unholy (inf); Schreck terrible, frightful **2** ADV **sich ~ verirren** to get hopelessly lost; **~ verschuldet sein** to be up to one's ears in debt; **die Partei war ~ zerstritten** the party was hopelessly divided; **Heilmethode** F cure; **Heilmittel** NT (lit, fig) remedy; (= Medikament) medicine; **Heilpflanze** F medicinal plant; **Heilpraktiker(in)** M(F) non-medical practitioner; **heilsam** ['hailzaːm] ADJ (fig: = förderlich) salutary

Heilsarmee F Salvation Army

Heilung ['hailʊŋ] F **-, (rare) -en** (= das Heilen) (von Wunde) healing; (von Krankheit, Kranken) curing; (Rel) healing; (= das Gesundwerden) cure

heim [haim] ADV home; **~, bitte** let's go home

Heim [haim] NT **-(e)s, -e** (= Zuhause, Anstalt) home; (= Obdachlosenheim, für Lehrlinge) hostel; (= Studentenwohnheim) hall of residence, dormitory (US); (von Sportverein) clubhouse; (= Freizeitheim) recreation centre (Brit) or center (US)

Heim- IN CPDS home; **Heimarbeit** F (Ind) homework no indef art, outwork no indef art; **etw in ~ herstellen lassen** to have sth produced by homeworkers; **Heimarbeitsplatz** M **die Zahl der Heimarbeitsplätze nimmt zu** more and more people work from home

Heimat ['haimaːt] F **-, -en** home

Heimat- IN CPDS home; **Heimatanschrift** F home address; **Heimatdichter(in)** M(F) regional writer; **Heimatkunde** F (Sch) local history; **heimatkundlich** [-kʊntlɪç] local history attr; **Heimatland** NT native country; **heimatlich** ['haimaːtlɪç] **1** ADJ native; Bräuche, Dialekt local; Gefühle, Wehmut nostalgic; Klänge of home; **die ~en Berge** the mountains of (one's) home; **~er Boden** native soil **2** ADV **das mutet mich ~ an, das kommt mir ~ vor, das berührt mich ~** that reminds me of home; **heimatlos** ADJ homeless; **Heimatlose(r)** ['haimaːtloːzə] MF DECL AS ADJ homeless person; **die ~n** the homeless; **Heimatmuseum** NT museum of local history; **Heimatschriftsteller(in)** M(F) regional writer; **Heimatvertriebene(r)** MF DECL AS ADJ displaced person, expellee (esp from eastern regions of the German Empire at the end of World War II)

Heim-: heimbegleiten ptp **heimbegleitet** VT SEP jdn ~ to take sb home; **heimbringen** VT SEP IRREG (= nach Hause bringen) to bring home; (= heimbegleiten) to take home

Heimchen ['haimçən] NT **-s, -** (*Zool*) house cricket; **~ (am Herd)** (*pej*: = *Hausfrau*) housewife

heimdürfen VI SEP IRREG **darf ich/sie heim?** may I/she go home?

heimelig ['haiməlıç] ADJ cosy (*Brit*), cozy (*US*)

Heim-: heimfahren VTI SEP IRREG (VI:AUX SEIN) to drive home; **Heimfahrt** F journey home; (*Naut*) voyage home; **heimfinden** VI SEP IRREG to find one's way home; **heimgehen** SEP IRREG AUX SEIN **1** VI to go home; (*euph geh*) to pass away *or* on **2** VI IMPERS **es geht heim** we're going home

heimisch ['haimɪʃ] ADJ **(a)** (= *einheimisch*: *Zoo, Bot*) indigenous (*in* +acc to); (= *national*) domestic; (= *ortsansässig*) local; (= *regional*) regional; *Rohstoffe, Gewässer, Landschaft* native; **etw ~ machen** to introduce sth (*in* +*dat* to) **(b)** (= *vertraut*) familiar; **sich ~ fühlen** to feel at home; **in einer Sprache** *etc* **~ sein** to be at home in a language *etc*; **~ werden** to settle in (*an, in* +*dat* to)

Heim-: Heimkehr ['haimke:ɐ] F **-**, NO PL homecoming; **heimkehren** VI SEP AUX SEIN to return home (*aus* from); **heimkommen** VI SEP IRREG AUX SEIN to come home; **heimkönnen** VI SEP IRREG to be able to go home; **Heimleiter(in)** M(F) *siehe* **Heim** head of a/the home/hostel; **Heimleitung** F *siehe* **Heim** person(s) in charge of a/the home/ hostel

heimlich ['haimlıç] **1** ADJ (= *geheim, verborgen*) secret; *Benehmen* secretive; *Bewegungen* furtive **2** ADV secretly; *lachen* inwardly; **er blickte sie ~ an** he stole a glance at her; **sich ~ entfernen** to steal away; **~, still und leise** (*inf*) quietly, on the quiet

Heimlichkeit F **-, -en** secrecy; (= *Geheimnis*) secret

Heimlich-: Heimlichtuer [-tu:ɐ] M **-s, -**, **Heimlichtuerin** [-ərın] F **-, -nen** secretive person; **Heimlichtuerei** F secretiveness; **heimlich tun** VI IRREG to be secretive (*mit* about)

Heim-: heimmüssen VI SEP IRREG to have to go home; **Heimreise** F journey home; (*Naut*) voyage home; **heimreisen** VI SEP AUX SEIN to travel home; **heimschicken** VT SEP to send home; **Heimspiel** NT (*Sport*) home match *or* game

heimsuchen ['haimzu:xn] VT SEP to strike; (*für längere Zeit*) to plague; (*Feind*) to attack; (*Gespenst*) to haunt; (*Krankheit, Albträume, Vorstellungen*) to afflict; (*Schicksal*) to overtake; (*inf*: = *besuchen*) to descend on (*inf*); **von Dürre heimgesucht** drought-stricken; **vom Streik heimgesucht** strike-torn; **von Krieg heimgesucht** war-torn

Heimtrainer M exercise machine; (= *Trimmrad*) exercise bike

heimtrauen VR SEP to dare to go home

Heimtücke F, NO PL (= *Hinterlist*) insidiousness; (= *Boshaftigkeit*) maliciousness; (*von Mensch*) treachery; (*von Krankheit*) insidiousness; (*Jur*) malice; (= *Gefährlichkeit*) treacherous nature

heimtückisch **1** ADJ (= *hinterlistig*) insidious; (= *boshaft*) malicious; *Krankheit* insidious; (= *gefährlich*) *Glatteis, Maschine* treacherous **2** ADV *überfallen, verraten* treacherously

Heim-: Heimvorteil M (*Sport, fig*) home advantage; **heimwärts** ['haimvɛrts] ADV (= *nach Hause zu*) home; (= *auf dem Heimweg*) on the way home; **~ ziehen/gehen** to go homewards; **Heimweg** M way home *or* back **~ machen** to set out for home; **Heimweh** [-ve:] NT **-s**, NO PL homesickness *no art*; **~ haben/bekommen** to be/become homesick (*nach* for); **heimwehkrank** ADJ homesick; **Heimwerker** [-vɛrkɐ] M **-s, -**, **Heimwerkerin** [-ərın] F **-, -nen** do-it-yourself *or* DIY enthusiast; **Heimwerkerbedarf** M DIY products *pl*; **heimwollen** VI SEP to want to go home; **heimzahlen** VT SEP **jdm etw ~** to pay sb back for sth

Heini ['haini] M **-s, -s** (*inf*) guy (*inf*); (= *Dummkopf*) fool

Heinzelmännchen ['haintslmɛnçən] NT brownie

Heirat ['hairɑ:t] F **-, -en** marriage; (= *Feier*) wedding

heiraten ['hairɑ:tn] **1** VT to marry **2** VR to get married **3** VI to get married; **~ müssen** (*euph*) to have to get married; **„wir ~"** "we are getting married"; **„geheiratet haben ..."** ≈ "marriages"

Heirats-: Heiratsantrag M proposal (of marriage); **jdm einen ~ machen** to propose to sb; **Heiratsschwindler(in)** M(F) *person who makes a marriage proposal under false pretences*; **Heiratsurkunde** F marriage certificate

heiser **1** ADJ hoarse; (= *dunkel klingend*) husky; *Laut* croaky **2** ADV **~ reden** to talk hoarsely; **sich ~ schreien/reden** to shout/talk oneself hoarse

Heiserkeit F **-**, NO PL hoarseness

heiß **1** ADJ **(a)** hot; *Zone* torrid; **jdm ist/wird ~** sb is/is getting hot; **sie hat einen ~en Kopf** (*wegen Fieber*) she has a burning forehead; **etw ~ machen** to heat sth up; **~e Tränen weinen** to cry one's heart out; **heiß!** (*inf*: = *fast gefunden*) you're hot **(b)** (= *heftig*) heated; *Begierde, Liebe, Wunsch* burning; **~en Dank** very many thanks **(c)** (= *aufreizend*) *Musik, Sachen, Bilder* hot; (*inf*: = *sexuell erregt*) hot, horny (*inf*); **~e Höschen** hot pants; **jdn ~ machen** (*inf*) to turn sb on (*inf*) **(d)** (= *gefährlich*) hot; *Gegend, Thema* hotly-disputed; **ein ~es Eisen** a hot potato; **ein ~es Eisen anfassen** (*inf*) to grasp the nettle **(e)** ATTR (*inf*) *Favorit, Tip, Maschine* hot; **ein ~er Ofen** a motorbike; **~er Draht** hotline; **~e Spur** firm lead **(f)** PRED (*inf*: = *brünstig*) **~ sein** to be on heat **2** ADV **(a)** (= *nicht kalt*) **~ waschen** to wash with hot water; **etw ~ trinken** to drink sth hot; **~ baden** to have a hot bath; **~ duschen** to take a hot shower; **es überläuft mich ~ und kalt** I feel hot and cold all over; **es wird nichts so ~ gegessen, wie es gekocht wird** (*prov*) things are never as bad as they seem **(b)** (= *heftig*) **sich** (*dat*) **etw ~ wünschen** to be dying to have sth; **~ ersehnt** much longed for; **~ geliebt** dearly beloved; **eine ~ geführte Diskussion** a passionate discussion; **es ging ~ her** things got heated; **~ umkämpft** fiercely fought over; *Markt* fiercely contested; **~ umstritten** *Frage* hotly debated; *Künstler etc* highly controversial; **jdn/etw ~ und innig lieben** to love sb/sth madly

heißen ['haisn], *pret* **hieß** [hi:s], *ptp* **geheißen** [gə'haisn] **1** VT **(a)** (= *nennen*) to call; **das heiße ich klug vorgehen!** that's what I call being clever; **jdn einen Lügner** *etc* **~** to call sb a liar *etc*; **oder wie heißt man das?** (*inf*) or what do you call it? **(b)** (*geh*: = *auffordern*) to bid (*form*); **jdn etw tun ~** to bid sb do sth (*form*); **jdn willkommen ~** to bid sb welcome **2** VI **(a)** (= *den Namen haben, bezeichnet werden*) to be called (*Brit*) *or* named; (= *als Titel haben*) to be titled; **wie ~ Sie/heißt die Straße?** what are you/is the street called?, what's your name/the name of the street?; **ich heiße Müller** I'm called *or* my name is Müller; **sie heißt jetzt anders** she has a different name now; **nach jdm ~** to be called after (*Brit*) *or* for (*US*) sb; **wie heißt das?** what is that called?; **eigentlich heißt es richtig X** actually the correct word is X; **... und wie sie alle ~ ...** and the rest of them; **... so wahr ich Franz-Josef heiße** (*als Bekräftigung*) ... as sure as I'm standing here; **... dann will ich Fridolin ~** ... then I'm a Dutchman (*Brit*) *or* a monkey's uncle **(b)** (= *bestimmte Bedeutung haben*) to mean; **was heißt „gut" auf Englisch?** what is the English (word) for "gut"?; **soll** *or* **will ~** (*am Satzanfang*) in other words; **ich weiß, was es heißt, allein zu sein** I know what it means to be alone **(c)** **das heißt** that is; (= *in anderen Worten*) that is to say **3** VI IMPERS **(a)** **es heißt, dass ...** (= *es geht die Rede*) they say that ...; **es soll nicht ~, dass ...** never let it be said that ... **(b)** (= *zu lesen sein*) **in der Bibel/im Gesetz/in seinem Brief heißt es, dass ...** the Bible/the law/his letter says that ...; **es heißt hier ...** it says here ... **(c)** (= *nötig sein*) **es heißt, etw zu tun** you/we/he *etc* must do sth; **nun heißt es handeln** now it's time to act

Heiß-: heißgeliebt ADJ *siehe* **heiß**; **Heißhunger** M ravenous appetite; **etw mit ~ essen** to eat sth ravenously; **etw mit wahrem ~ verschlingen** (*fig*) to really devour sth; **heißhungrig** **1** ADJ ravenous **2** ADV ravenously; **heißlaufen** VI SEP IRREG AUX SEIN (*Motor, Auto, Maschinenteil*) to overheat; (*Telefonleitungen, -drähte*) to buzz; **Heißluft** F hot air; *Kochen* **mit ~** fan-assisted cooking; **Heißluftherd** M fan-assisted oven; **heißumkämpft** [-lʊmkɛmpft] ADJ ATTR *siehe* **heiß**

heiter ['haitɐ] ADJ (= *fröhlich*) cheerful; (= *ausgeglichen*) serene; (= *amüsant*) *Geschichte* amusing; (= *leicht betrunken*) merry; (= *hell, klar*) bright; *Wetter* fine; (*Met*) fair; **~ werden** to become cheerful; (*Gesicht*) to brighten; (*Wetter*) to brighten up; **das kann ja ~ werden!** (*iro*) that sounds great (*iro*); **aus ~em Himmel** (*fig*) out of the blue

Heiterkeit F **-**, NO PL (= *Fröhlichkeit*) cheerfulness; (= *Ausgeglichenheit*) serenity; (= *Helligkeit, Klarheit*) (*von Himmel, Tag*) clearness; (= *heitere Stimmung*) merriment;

(= *Belustigung*) amusement; **allgemeine ~ hervorrufen** to cause general amusement

heizen ['haitsn] **1** VI (= *die Heizung anhaben*) to have the/one's heating on; (= *Wärme abgeben*) to give off heat; **mit Holz/ Strom** *etc* **~** to use wood/electricity *etc* for heating; **ab November wird geheizt** the heating is put on in November **2** VT (= *warm machen*) to heat; (= *verbrennen*) to burn; **den Ofen heize ich nur mit Holz** I only burn wood in the stove

Heiz-: Heizkessel M boiler; **Heizkörper** M (= *Gerät*) heater; (*von Zentralheizung*) radiator; (= *Element*) heating element; **Heizkosten** PL heating costs *pl*; **Heizkraft** F heating power; **Heizkraftwerk** NT thermal power station; **Heizlüfter** [-lyftɐ] M **-s, -** fan heater; **Heizöl** NT fuel oil; **Heizstrahler** M electric (wall) heater

Heizung ['haitsʊŋ] F **-, -en** heating

Heizwert M calorific value

Hektar [hɛk'taːɐ, 'hɛktaːɐ] NT or M **-s, -e** hectare

Hektik ['hɛktɪk] F **-, NO PL** (= *Hast*) hectic rush; (*von Großstadt etc*) hustle and bustle; (*von Leben etc*) hectic pace; **sie isst/ arbeitet mit einer solchen ~** she eats/works at such a hectic pace; **nur keine ~** take it easy

hektisch ['hɛktɪʃ] **1** ADJ (*auch dated Med*) hectic; *Mensch auch, Arbeiten* frantic **2** ADV hectically; **es geht ~ zu** things are hectic; **ich lebe zurzeit ~** my life is very hectic just now; **nur mal nicht so ~** take it easy

Hekto-: Hektoliter [hɛkto'liːtɐ, 'hɛkto-] M or NT hectolitre (*Brit*), hectoliter (*US*); **Hektowatt** [hɛkto'vat, 'hɛkto-] NT hectowatt

Helanca® [he'laŋka] NT **-, NO PL** stretch fabric

helau [he'lau] INTERJ *greeting used at Carnival time*

Held [hɛlt] M **-en, -en** [-dn] hero; **kein ~ in etw** (*dat*) **sein** not to be very brave about sth; (*in Schulfach etc*) to be no great shakes at sth (*inf*)

Helden-: heldenhaft 1 ADJ heroic **2** ADV heroically; **Heldenmut** M heroic courage; **Heldentat** F heroic deed; **Heldentum** ['hɛldntuːm] NT **-s, NO PL** heroism

Heldin ['hɛldɪn] F **-, -nen** heroine; *siehe auch* **Held**

helfen ['hɛlfn] *pret* **half** [half], *ptp* **geholfen** [gə'hɔlfn] VI
(a) (= *Beistand geben*) to help (*jdm* sb); **jdm bei etw ~** to help sb with sth; **er half ihr aus dem Mantel/einer Verlegenheit** he helped her off with her coat/out of a difficulty; **ihm/dir ist nicht zu ~** he is/you are beyond help; **ich kann mir nicht ~, ich muss es tun** I can't help doing it; **ich werd dir/ihm (schon) ~!** I'll give you/him what for (*inf*); **ich werde dir ~, die Tapeten zu beschmieren** I'll teach you to mess up the wallpaper (*inf*); **er weiß sich** (*dat*) **zu ~** he is very resourceful; **man muss sich** (*dat*) **nur zu ~ wissen** (*prov*) you just have to use your head; **er weiß sich** (*dat*) **nicht mehr zu ~** he is at his wits' end; **hilf dir selbst, dann** *or* **so hilft dir Gott** (*Prov*) God helps those who help themselves (*Prov*)
(b) AUCH VI IMPERS (= *dienen, nützen*) to help; **es hilft nichts** it's no use; **da hilft alles nichts ...** there's nothing for it ...; **das hilft mir wenig, damit ist mir nicht geholfen** that's not much help to me; **das hat mir schon viel geholfen** that has been a great help to me; **was hilfts?** what's the use?
(c) (= *heilsam sein*) to help; (= *heilen: auch Arzt*) to cure; **diese Arznei hilft gegen** *or* **bei Kopfweh** this medicine helps to relieve headaches; **jetzt kann nur noch eine Operation ~** only an operation will help now

Helfer ['hɛlfɐ] M **-s, -**, **Helferin** [-ərɪn] F **-, -nen** helper; (= *Mitarbeiter*) assistant; (*von Verbrecher*) accomplice; (*inf*: = *Gerät*) help; **~ in Steuersachen** tax adviser; **ein ~ in der Not** a friend in need

Helfershelfer(in) M(F) accomplice; (*Jur*: *vor/nach begangener Tat*) accessory before/after the fact

Helgoland ['hɛlgolant] NT **-s** Heligoland

Helikopter [heli'kɔptɐ] M **-s, -** helicopter

Helikopter-Skiing [-skiːɪŋ] NT **-s, NO PL**, **Helikopterskiing** NT **-s, NO PL** helicopter skiing

Helium ['heːliʊm] NT **-s, NO PL** (*abbr* **He**) helium

hell [hɛl] **1** ADJ **(a)** (*optisch*) light; *Licht, Beleuchtung, Himmel* bright; *Farbe* light, pale; *Kleidungsstück* light-coloured (*Brit*), light-colored (*US*); *Haar, Teint* fair; (*fig*) *Zukunft* bright; **es wird ~** it's getting light; **~ bleiben** to stay light; **am ~en Tage** in broad daylight; **in ~en Flammen** in flames; **~es Bier** ≈ lager (*esp Brit*)
(b) (*akustisch*) *Laut, Ton, Stimme* high(-pitched); *Gelächter*

ringing
(c) (*inf*: = *klug*) *Junge* bright; (= *geistig klar*) *Augenblicke* lucid; **er ist ein ~er Kopf, er hat einen ~en Kopf** he has brains; *siehe auch* **helle**
(d) ATTR (= *stark, groß*) great; *Verwunderung etc* utter; *Verzweiflung, Unsinn* sheer, utter; *Neid* pure; **in ~en Scharen** in great numbers; **seine ~e Freude an etw** (*dat*) **haben** to find great joy in sth
2 ADV **(a)** (= *licht*) brightly; **~ leuchtend** brightly shining; *Farbe* bright; *Kleid* brightly coloured (*Brit*) *or* colored (*US*)
(b) (= *hoch*) **~ klingen** to sound high(-pitched); **~ tönen** to have a high-pitched ring
(c) (= *sehr*) absolutely; **von etw ~ begeistert/entzückt sein** to be very enthusiastic/quite delighted about sth

hell- IN CPDS (*esp auf Farben bezüglich*) light; **hellauf** ['hɛl'lauf] ADV completely; **~ begeistert sein** to be wildly enthusiastic; **hellblau** ADJ light blue; **hellblond** ADJ very fair, blonde

helle ['hɛlə] ADJ PRED (*inf*) bright

Hellebarde [hɛlə'bardə] F **-, -n** (*Hist*) halberd

Heller ['hɛlɐ] M **-s, -** (*Hist*) heller; **das ist keinen (roten** *or* **lumpigen)** *or* **nicht einen ~ wert** that isn't worth a brass farthing (*Brit*), that's worth nothing; **er besitzt keinen (roten** *or* **lumpigen) ~** he doesn't have a penny to his name (*esp Brit*); **auf ~ und Pfennig, bis auf den letzten ~** (down) to the penny (*esp Brit*); **stimmen** down to the last detail

Helle(s) ['hɛlə] NT DECL AS ADJ (= *Bier*) ≈ lager (*esp Brit*)

hell-: hellhäutig ADJ fair-skinned; (*von Rasse auch*) pale-skinned; **hellhörig** ADJ keen (*Brit*) *or* quick (*US*) of hearing; (*Archit*) poorly soundproofed; **~ sein** (*fig*: *Mensch*) to have sharp ears; **als er das sagte, wurde ich ~** when he said that I pricked up my ears; **jdn ~ machen** to make sb prick up their ears

hellicht ADJ *siehe* **helllicht**

Helligkeit F **-, NO PL** lightness; (*von Licht, Beleuchtung, Himmel*) brightness; (*von Haar, Teint, Haut*) fairness; (= *helles Licht*) light; (*Phys, Astron*) luminosity

Helligkeitsregler M brightness control

helllicht ['hɛllɪçt] ADJ **am ~en Tage** in broad daylight

Hell-: Hellraumprojektor M (*Sw*) overhead projector; **hellrot** ADJ bright red; **hellsehen** VI INFIN ONLY **~ können** to be clairvoyant; **Hellseher** [-zeːɐ] M **-s, -**, **Hellseherin** [-ərɪn] F **-, -nen** (*lit, fig*) clairvoyant; **hellseherisch** ADJ ATTR clairvoyant; **hellwach** ADJ (*lit*) wide-awake; (*fig*) alert; **Hellwerden** NT **-s, NO PL** daybreak

Helm [hɛlm] M **-(e)s, -e** helmet

Helm-: Helmpflicht F **es besteht ~** the wearing of crash helmets is compulsory; **Helmschmuck** M crest

Hemd [hɛmt] NT **-(e)s, -en** [-dn] (= *Oberhemd*) shirt; (= *Unterhemd*) vest (*Brit*), undershirt (*US*); **etw wie das** *or* **sein ~ wechseln** (*fig*) to change sth with monotonous regularity; **jdn bis aufs ~ ausziehen** (*fig inf*) to fleece sb (*inf*); **sich** (*dat*) **(wegen etw) ins ~ machen** (*sl*) to get all worked up (about sth) (*inf*)

Hemds-: Hemdsärmel M shirtsleeve; **in ~n** in one's shirtsleeves; **hemdsärmelig** ADJ shirt-sleeved; (*fig inf*) down-to-earth; *Ausdrucksweise, Empfang, Einstellung* casual

Hemisphäre [hemi'sfɛːrə] F hemisphere

hemmen ['hɛmən] VT *Entwicklung, Fortschritt* to hinder; *Lauf der Geschehnisse etc* to check; (= *verlangsamen*) to slow down; *Maschine, Rad* to check; *Wasserlauf* to stem; (*Med*) *Blut* to staunch; (*Psych*) to inhibit; *siehe auch* **gehemmt**

Hemm-: Hemmschuh M brake shoe; (*fig*) hindrance (*für* to); **jdm einen ~ in den Weg legen** (*fig*) to obstruct sb; **Hemmschwelle** F inhibition level

Hemmung ['hɛmʊŋ] F **-, -en (a)** (*Psych*) inhibition; (= *Bedenken*) scruple; **keine ~en kennen** to have no inhibitions; **nur keine ~en!** don't feel inhibited **(b)** (*von Entwicklung, Fortschritt*) hindering; (= *Verlangsamung*) slowing down

Hemmungs-: hemmungslos 1 ADJ (= *rückhaltlos*) unrestrained; (= *skrupellos*) unscrupulous **2** ADV *brüllen, schreien, jubeln, weinen* without restraint; *sich hingeben, genießen* wantonly; *foltern, töten* without conscience; **jdn ~ machen** to remove sb's inhibitions; **Hemmungslosigkeit** F **-, -en** (= *Rückhaltlosigkeit*) lack *no pl* of restraint; (= *Skrupellosigkeit*) unscrupulousness *no pl*

Hendl ['hɛndl] NT **-s, -(n)** (*Aus*) chicken

Hengst [hɛŋst] M -(e)s, -e stallion; (= Kamelhengst, Eselhengst) male; (sl: = Mann) stud (inf)

Henkel ['hɛŋkl] M -s, - handle

Henker ['hɛŋkɐ] M -s, - hangman; (= Scharfrichter) executioner

Henna ['hɛna] F - or nt -(s), NO PL henna

Henne ['hɛnə] F -, -n hen

Hepatitis [hepa'tiːtɪs] F -, **Hepatitiden** [-ti'tiːdn] hepatitis

her [heːɐ] ADV siehe auch herkommen, hermüssen, her sein etc
(a) (räumlich) von der Kirche/Frankreich/dem Meer ~ from the church/France/the sea; ~ zu mir! come here (to me); um mich ~ (all) around me; von weit ~ from a long way off or away
(b) (in Aufforderung) Bier/Essen ~! bring (me/us) some beer/food (here); ~ mit dem Geld! hand over your money!; ~ damit! give me that; immer ~ damit! let's have it/them (then)
(c) (von etwas aus gesehen) von der Idee/Form ~ as for the idea/form; vom finanziellen Standpunkt ~ from the financial point of view
(d) (zeitlich) ich kenne ihn von früher ~ I know him from before; von der Schule/meiner Kindheit ~ since school/my childhood; von der letzten Saison ~ from last season

herab [hɛ'rap] ADV down; den Hügel/die Treppe ~ down the hill/stairs; von oben ~ (down) from above

herab- PREF siehe auch herunter-, runter- down; **herabblicken** VI SEP (lit, fig) to look down (auf +acc on); **herabhängen** VI SEP IRREG to hang down; langes ~des Haar long, flowing hair; **herablassen** SEP IRREG **1** VT to let down **2** VR (lit, fig) to lower oneself; sich zu etw ~ to deign to do sth; sich auf jds Ebene (acc) ~ to descend to sb's level; **herablassend 1** ADJ condescending; Verachtung haughty **2** ADV condescendingly; sich ~ benehmen to be condescending; **herabmindern** VT SEP (= schlecht machen) to belittle; (= bagatelisieren) to minimize; (= reduzieren) to reduce; **herabsehen** VI SEP IRREG (lit, fig) to look down (auf +acc on); **herabsetzen** VT SEP to reduce; Niveau to lower; Leistungen, Fähigkeiten, jdn to belittle; zu stark herabgesetzten Preisen at greatly reduced prices; **Herabsetzung** [-zɛtsʊŋ] F -, -en reduction; (von Niveau) lowering; (von Leistungen, Fähigkeiten) belittling; (= Kränkung) slight; **herabsteigen** VI SEP IRREG AUX SEIN to descend; **herabstürzen** SEP **1** VT to push off (von etw sth) **2** VI AUX SEIN to fall off (von etw sth); (Felsbrocken) to fall down (von from); (geh: Wasserfall) to cascade down **3** VR to jump off (von etw sth); **herabwürdigen** SEP **1** VT to belittle **2** VR to degrade oneself

Heraldik [he'raldɪk] F -, NO PL heraldry

heran [hɛ'ran] ADV rechts/links ~! over to the right/left; immer or nur ~! come on (then)!; bis an etw (acc) ~ close to sth, right by sth; (mit Bewegungsverb) right up to sth

heran- PREF siehe auch ran-: **heranbilden** VT SEP to train (up); (in der Schule) to educate; **heranfahren** VTI SEP IRREG AUX SEIN to drive or (mit Fahrrad) ride up (an +acc to); **heranführen** SEP **1** VT jdn to lead up; jdn an etw (acc) ~ (lit) to lead/bring sb up to sth; (fig) (an Frage, Problem) to lead or bring sb to sth; (Lehrer etc) to introduce sb to sth **2** VI an etw (acc) ~ (lit, fig) to lead to sth; **herankommen** VI SEP IRREG AUX SEIN
(a) (räumlich, zeitlich) to approach (an etw (acc) sth); das lasse ich mal an mich ~ (fig inf) I'll cross that bridge when I come to it (prov); er lässt alle Probleme an sich ~ he always adopts a wait-and-see attitude (b) (= erreichen) an den Chef/Motor kommt man nicht heran you can't get hold of the boss/get at or to the engine (c) (= sich messen können mit) an jdn/etw ~ to be up to the standard of sb/sth; er kommt nicht an seinen Vater heran he's not a patch on (Brit) or a match for (US) his father (d) (= grenzen an) an etw (acc) ~ to verge on sth; **heranmachen** VR SEP (inf) sich an etw (acc) ~ to get down to sth; sich an jdn ~ to approach sb; an Mädchen to chat sb up (esp Brit inf), to flirt with sb; **herannahen** VI SEP AUX SEIN (geh) to approach; **heranreichen** VI SEP AUX SEIN an jdn/etw ~ (lit) (Mensch) to reach sb/sth; (Weg, Gelände etc) to reach (up to) sth; (fig: = sich messen können mit) to come near sb/sth; **heranreifen** VI SEP AUX SEIN (Obst) to ripen; (fig) (Jugendliche) to mature; (Plan, Entschluss, Idee) to mature, to ripen; zur Frau/zum Mann/zum Erwachsenen ~ to mature into a woman/a man/an adult; **heranrücken** VI SEP AUX SEIN (= sich nähern) to approach (an etw (acc) sth); (= dicht aufrücken) to move nearer (an +acc to); er rückte mit seinem Stuhl heran he drew his chair nearer; **heranschleichen** VIR SEP IRREG (vi: aux sein) to creep up (an etw (acc) to sth, an jdn on sb); **herantasten** VR SEP (lit) to feel one's way over (an +acc to); (fig) to feel one's way; sich

an eine Frage ~ to approach a matter cautiously; **herantreten** VI SEP IRREG AUX SEIN (lit) to move up (an +acc to); näher ~ to move nearer; bitte treten Sie näher heran! this way!; an jdn ~ (fig) to confront sb; mit etw an jdn ~ (= sich wenden an) to approach sb with sth; **heranwachsen** VI SEP IRREG AUX SEIN (geh) to grow; (Kind) to grow up; (fig: Probleme, Konkurrenz) to grow up (jdm around sb); die ~de Generation the up-and-coming generation; **Heranwachsende(r)** MF DECL AS ADJ (Jur) adolescent; **heranziehen** SEP IRREG **1** VT (a) (= näher bringen) to pull over, to draw near (an +acc to); (= zu Hilfe holen) to call in; Literatur to consult; jdn zur Unterstützung ~ to enlist sb's support (c) (= einsetzen) Arbeitskräfte, Kapital to bring in (d) (= geltend machen) Recht, Paragrafen, Quelle, Zitat to bring into play (e) (= aufziehen) Tier, Kind to raise; Pflanze to cultivate; jdn zu etw ~ to bring sb up to be sth; sich (dat) Revolutionäre/Jasager ~ (pej) to make revolutionaries/yes men for oneself **2** VI AUX SEIN to approach; (Mil) to advance

herauf [hɛ'rauf] **1** ADV up; vom Tal ~ up from the valley; von unten ~ up from below **2** PREP +ACC up; den Fluss/den Berg/die Treppe ~ up the river/mountain/stairs

herauf- PREF siehe auch rauf- up; **heraufbeschwören** ptp **heraufbeschworen** VT SEP IRREG (a) (= wachrufen) to evoke (b) (= herbeiführen) to cause; **heraufbringen** VT SEP IRREG to bring up; **heraufdürfen** VI SEP IRREG (inf) to be allowed up; **heraufkommen** VI SEP IRREG AUX SEIN to come up; (auf Boot, Kutsche) to climb aboard; (Mond, Geräusch, Nebel, Wolke) to rise; (Gewitter) to approach; **heraufllassen** VT SEP IRREG to allow (to come) up; **heraufreichen** SEP **1** VT to hand up **2** VI to reach; der Baum reicht bis zum Fenster herauf the tree comes up to the window; **heraufsetzen** SEP VT Preise etc to increase; **heraufsteigen** VI SEP IRREG AUX SEIN (= heraufklettern) to climb up; (Dampf, Rauch) to rise; (Erinnerungen) to well up (in jdm in sb); **heraufziehen** SEP IRREG **1** VT to pull up **2** VI AUX SEIN (a) (Gewitter, Unheil etc) to approach (b) (= nach oben umziehen) to move up

heraus [hɛ'raus] ADV siehe auch herauskommen, heraus sein etc out; ~ da! (inf) get out of there!; da ~? out of there?; ~ aus den Federn! (inf) rise and shine! (inf); ~ mit ihm (inf) get him out!; ~ damit! (inf) (= gib her) hand it over!; (= ~ mit der Sprache!) out with it! (inf); zum Fenster ~ out of the window; nach vorn ~ wohnen to live at the front; aus einem Gefühl der Verlassenheit ~ out of a feeling of forlornness

heraus- PREF siehe auch raus- out; **herausarbeiten** SEP VT (aus Stein, Holz) to carve (aus out of); (fig) to bring out; **herausbekommen** ptp **herausbekommen** VT SEP IRREG (a) Fleck, Nagel etc to get out (aus of) (b) Täter, Ursache, Geheimnis to find out (aus jdm from sb); Lösung, Aufgabe to work out (c) Wechselgeld to get back; Sie bekommen noch 1 Euro heraus you still have 1 euro change to come; **herausboxen** VT SEP (inf) jdn to bail out (inf); **herausbringen** VT SEP IRREG (a) (lit) to bring out (aus of) (b) (inf: = entfernen, ermitteln) = herausbekommen (c) (auf den Markt bringen) to bring out; jdn/etw ganz groß ~ to launch sb/sth in a big way; die Affäre wurde in allen Zeitungen groß herausgebracht the affair made a big splash in the papers (d) (= hervorbringen) Worte to utter; aus ihm war kein Wort herauszubringen they couldn't get a (single) word out of him; **herausdrehen** VT SEP Birne, Schraube to unscrew (aus from); **herausfahren** SEP IRREG **1** VI AUX SEIN (a) (aus of) to come out; (Zug) to pull out; (Radfahrer) to ride out (b) (= schnell herauskommen) to leap out; (= entweichen) to come out; (Wort etc) to slip out **2** VT (a) (aus of) Zug, Auto to drive out; Fahrrad to ride out (b) (Sport) eine gute or schnelle Zeit/den Vorsprung ~ to make good time/the lead; einen Sieg ~ to drive to victory; (bei Rad-/Motorradrennen) to ride to victory; verlorene Minuten ~ to make up for lost time; **herausfiltern** VT SEP to filter out (aus of); **herausfinden** SEP IRREG **1** VT to find out **2** VIR to find one's way out (aus of); **herausfischen** VT SEP (inf) to fish out (inf) (aus of); sich (dat) etw ~ to pick sth out (for oneself); sich immer das Beste aus allem ~ always to take the best of everything

Herausforderer [hɛ'rausfɔrdərɐ] M -s, -, **Herausforderin** [-ərɪn] F -, -nen challenger

herausfordern [hɛ'rausfɔrdɐn] SEP **1** VT (esp Sport) to challenge (zu to); (= provozieren) to provoke (zu etw to do sth); Kritik, Protest to invite; Gefahr to court; Unglück to invite; das

Schicksal ~ to tempt fate **2** VI **zu etw** ~ (= *provozieren*) to invite sth

herausfordernd **1** ADJ provocative; *Reden, Haltung, Blick* challenging **2** ADV (= *aggressiv, sexuell*) provocatively; (= *lockend*) invitingly; **jdn** ~ **ansehen** to give sb a provocative look

Herausforderung F challenge; (= *Provokation*) provocation

Herausgabe F **(a)** (= *Rückgabe*) return; (*von Personen*) handing over **(b)** (*von Buch etc*) publication

herausgeben SEP IRREG **1** VT **(a)** (= *zurückgeben*) to return, to hand back; *Gefangene etc* to hand over **(b)** (= *veröffentlichen, erlassen*) to issue; *Buch, Zeitung* to publish; (= *bearbeiten*) to edit **(c)** (= *Wechselgeld geben*) *Betrag* to give in *or* as change; **wie viel hat er dir herausgegeben?** how much change *or* what change did he give you (back)?; **2 Euro/zu wenig** ~ to give 2 euros change/too little change **(d)** (= *herausreichen*) to hand *or* pass out (*aus*) **2** VI (= *Wechselgeld geben*) to give change (*auf +acc* for); **er hat vergessen, mir herauszugeben** he's forgotten to give me my change; **können Sie (mir)** ~? can you give me change?; **falsch** ~ to give the wrong change

Herausgeber(in) M(F) (= *Verleger*) publisher; (= *Redakteur*) editor

heraus-: herausgehen VI SEP IRREG AUX SEIN (*aus* of) to go out; (*Fleck, Korken etc*) to come out; **aus sich** ~ (*fig*) to come out of one's shell (*fig*); **heraushaben** VT SEP IRREG (*inf*) **(a)** (= *entfernt haben*) to have got out (*aus* of); **ich will ihn aus der Firma** ~ I want him out of the firm **(b)** (= *begriffen haben*) to have got (*inf*); (= *gelöst haben*) to have solved; *Geheimnis* to have found out; **jetzt hat er die Handhabung der Maschine heraus** he's got the hang of the machine now (*inf*); **heraushalten** SEP IRREG **1** VT **(a)** (*lit*) *Hand, Gegenstand* to put *or* stick out (*aus* of) **(b)** (= *fernhalten, nicht verwickeln*) to keep out **2** VR to keep out of it; **sich aus etw** ~ to keep out of sth; **herausholen** VT SEP **(a)** (*lit*) to get out (*aus* of) **(b)** *Bedingungen, Vorteil* to gain; *günstiges Ergebnis, hohe Umsätze, Vorsprung, gute Zeit, Sieg* to achieve; *Gewinn* to make; *Herstellungskosten* to recoup; **etw aus etw** ~ to get sth from sth; **alles aus sich** ~ to get the best from oneself; **das Letzte aus sich** ~ to give one's all **(c)** (= *herauspauken*) to get off the hook (*inf*); **mein Anwalt wird mich da** ~ my solicitor will get me off the hook (*inf*)); **heraushören** VT SEP (= *wahrnehmen*) to hear; (= *fühlen*) to sense (*aus* in)

herauskommen VI SEP IRREG AUX SEIN **(a)** (= *nicht innen bleiben*) to come out (*aus* of); **ich bin schon seit Tagen aus den Kleidern/dem Haus nicht herausgekommen** I haven't had these clothes off/I haven't been out of the house in days; **sie kommt zu wenig heraus** (*inf*) she doesn't go *or* get out enough; **aus sich** ~ to come out of one's shell; **er kam aus dem Staunen/der Verwunderung nicht heraus** he couldn't get over his astonishment/amazement; **er kam aus dem Lachen nicht heraus** he couldn't stop laughing **(b)** (*aus bestimmter Lage*) to get out (*aus* of); **aus seinen Schwierigkeiten/Sorgen** ~ to get over one's difficulties/ worries **(c)** (= *auf den Markt kommen, bekannt werden, sichtbar werden*) to come out; (*Gesetz*) to come into force; (*Fleck*) to appear; (= *zur Geltung kommen, hörbar werden*) to come over; **ganz groß** ~ (*inf*) to make a big splash (*inf*) **(d)** (= *geäußert werden*) to come out; **mit der Sprache** ~ to come out with it (*inf*) **(e)** (= *Resultat haben*) **bei etw** ~ to come out of sth; **und was soll dabei** ~? and what is that supposed to achieve?; **bei dieser Rechenaufgabe kommt 10 heraus** this sum comes to 10; **es kommt nichts dabei heraus, da kommt nichts bei heraus** (*inf*) it doesn't get us anywhere; **dabei wird nichts Gutes** ~ no good will come of it; **es kommt auf eins** *or* **auf dasselbe** *or* **aufs Gleiche heraus** it comes (down) to the same thing **(f)** (*inf*: = *aus der Übung kommen*) to get out of practice **(g)** (*Cards*) to lead; **wer kommt heraus?** whose lead is it?

heraus-: herauskriegen VT SEP (*inf*) = **herausbekommen**; **herauskristallisieren** *ptp* **herauskristallisiert** **1** VT (*Chem*) to crystallize (*aus* out of); (*fig*) *Fakten, Essenz, Punkte* to extract (*aus* from) **2** VR (*Chem*) to crystallize (out); (*fig*) to crystallize; **herauslassen** VT SEP IRREG to let out (*aus* of); **herauslesen** VT SEP IRREG (= *erkennen*) to gather (*aus* from); **was die Kritiker aus seinem Roman alles** ~ **wollen** the things

the critics try to read into his novel; **herauslocken** VT SEP (*aus* of) to entice out; **etw aus jdm** ~ to get sth out of sb; **jdn aus seiner Reserve** ~ to draw sb out of his shell; **herausmachen** SEP (*inf*) **1** VT (*aus* of) to take out; *Fleck* to get out **2** VR (= *sich gut entwickeln*) to come on (well); (*finanziell*) to do well; **sie hat sich prächtig herausgemacht** she has really blossomed; **herausmüssen** VI SEP IRREG (*inf*) **(a)** (= *entfernt werden müssen*) to have to come out **(b)** (= *aufstehen müssen*) to have to get up **(c)** (= *gesagt werden müssen*) to have to come out; **herausnehmbar** ADJ removable; **herausnehmen** VT SEP IRREG **(a)** (= *entfernen*) to take out (*aus* of); (*inf*) *Zahn* to pull out; *Kind* (*aus der Schule etc*) to take away (*aus* from); **sich** (*dat*) **die Mandeln** ~ **lassen** to have one's tonsils out; **den Gang** ~ (*Aut*) to put the car into neutral **(b)** (*inf*: = *sich erlauben*) **es sich** (*dat*) ~**, etw zu tun** to have the nerve to do sth (*inf*); **sich** (*dat*) **Freiheiten** ~ to take liberties; **Sie nehmen sich zu viel heraus** you're going too far; **herausragen** VI SEP = **hervorragen**; **herausreden** VR SEP to talk one's way out of it (*inf*); **herausreißen** VT SEP IRREG **(a)** (*lit*) (*aus* of) to tear out; *Zahn, Baum* to pull out; **jdn aus etw** ~ *aus Umgebung* to tear sb away from sth; *aus Arbeit, Spiel, Unterhaltung* to drag sb away from sth; *aus Schlaf, Träumerei* to startle sb out of sth; *aus Lethargie, Sorgen* to shake sb out of sth **(b)** (*inf*: *aus Schwierigkeiten*) **jdn** ~ to get sb out of it (*inf*) **(c)** (*inf*: = *wieder gutmachen*) to save; **herausrücken** **1** VT (*inf*: = *hergeben*) *Geld* to cough up (*inf*); *Beute, Gegenstand* to hand over **2** VI AUX SEIN **(a)** (= *hergeben*) **mit etw** ~ *mit Geld* to cough sth up (*inf*); *mit Beute* to hand sth over **(b)** (= *aussprechen*) **mit etw** ~ to come out with sth; **mit der Sprache** ~ to come out with it; **herausrutschen** VI SEP AUX SEIN (*lit, fig*) to slip out (*aus* of); **das ist mir nur so herausgerutscht** it just slipped out somehow; **herausschinden** VT SEP IRREG (*inf*) = **herausschlagen** (b); **herausschlagen** VT SEP IRREG **(a)** (*lit*) to knock out (*aus* of) **(b)** (*inf*: = *erreichen*) *Geld* to make; *Erlaubnis, Verzögerung, Gewinn, Vorteil* to get; *Zeit* to gain; **herausschmecken** SEP **1** VT to taste **2** VI to be prominent (over the other flavours (*Brit*) *or* flavors (*US*)); **herausschneiden** VT SEP IRREG to cut out (*aus* of); **herausschreien** VT SEP IRREG to shout out

heraus sein VI IRREG AUX SEIN (*inf*) to be out; (= *bekannt sein*) to be known; (= *entschieden sein*) to have been decided *or* to be settled; (*Worte*) to have come out; **aus der Schule** ~ to have left school; **aus dem Gröbsten** *or* **Ärgsten** *or* **Schlimmsten** ~ to have got past the worst (part); (*bei Krise, Krankheit*) to be over the worst

heraußen [heˈrausn] ADV (*S Ger, Aus*) out here

heraus-: herausspringen VI SEP IRREG AUX SEIN (*aus* of) **(a)** (*lit*) to jump out **(b)** (= *sich lösen*) to come out; **aus dem Gleis** ~ to jump the rails **(c)** (*inf*) **dabei springt ein fetter Gewinn heraus** there is a handsome profit in it; **dabei springt nichts heraus** there's nothing to be got out of it; **was springt für mich dabei heraus?** what's in it for me?; **herausstellen** SEP **1** VT **(a)** (*lit*) to put outside; (*Sport*) to send off **(b)** (*fig*: = *hervorheben*) to emphasize; *jdn* to give prominence to **2** VR (*Unschuld, Wahrheit*) to come to light; **sich als falsch/wahr/richtig/ begründet** ~ to prove (to be) wrong/true/correct/well-founded; **es stellte sich heraus, dass ...** it emerged that ...; **es wird sich** ~**, wer Recht hat/was getan werden muss** we shall see who is right/what must be done; **das muss sich erst** ~ that remains to be seen; **herausstrecken** VT SEP to stick out (*zu, aus* of); **heraussuchen** VT SEP to pick out; **herauswachsen** VI SEP IRREG AUX SEIN to grow out (*aus* of); **herauswagen** VR SEP to dare to come out (*aus* of); **herauswinden** VT SEP IRREG (*fig*) to wriggle out of it; **sich aus etw** ~ to wriggle out of sth; **herauswirtschaften** VT SEP to make (*aus* out of); **herauswollen** VI SEP to want to get out (*aus* of); **er wollte nicht mit der Sprache heraus** (*inf*) he didn't want to come out with it (*inf*)

herb [hɛrp] **1** ADJ **(a)** *Geruch* sharp; *Geschmack* sharp, tangy; *Parfüm* tangy; *Wein* dry **(b)** *Enttäuschung, Verlust, Niederlage* bitter; *Erwachen* rude; *Erkenntnis, Wahrheit* cruel **(c)** (= *streng*) *Züge, Gesicht* severe, harsh; *Art, Wesen, Charakter, Mensch* dour; *Schönheit* severe **(d)** *Worte, Kritik* harsh **2** ADV ~ **riechen** *or* **duften** to smell tangy; ~ **schmecken** to taste tangy; (*Wein*) to taste dry

Herbarium [hɛrˈbaːriʊm] NT **-s, Herbarien** herbarium, herbary

herbei [hɛrˈbai] ADV (*geh*) come (here)

herbei-: herbeibringen VT SEP IRREG *jdn, Gegenstand* to bring over; *Indizien, Beweise* to provide; *Sachverständige* to bring in; **herbeiführen** VT SEP **(a)** (= *bewirken*) to bring about;

(= *verursachen*) to cause; **den Tod** *etc* ~ (*Med*) to cause death *etc* (*form*) **(b)** (*an einen Ort*) to bring; **herbeilaufen** VI SEP IRREG AUX SEIN to come running up; **herbeireden** VT SEP **etw** ~ to bring sth about by talking about it; **Probleme** ~ to create problems by talking about them; **herbeischaffen** VT SEP to bring; *Geld* to get; *Beweise* to produce; **herbeisehnen** VT SEP to long for; **herbeiströmen** VI SEP AUX SEIN (*geh*) to come in (their) crowds

herbekommen *ptp* **herbekommen** VT SEP IRREG (*inf*) to get

Herberge ['hɛrbɛrgə] F **-, -n (a)** NO PL (= *Unterkunft*) lodging *no indef art*; (*fig*) refuge **(b)** (= *Jugendherberge*) (youth) hostel

Herbergs-: Herbergseltern PL (youth hostel) wardens *pl*; **Herbergsmutter** F, *pl* -**mütter**, **Herbergsvater** M (youth hostel) warden

herbestellen *ptp* **herbestellt** VT SEP to ask to come

Herbheit F **-,** NO PL **(a)** (*von Geruch*) sharpness; (*von Parfüm*) tanginess; (*von Geschmack*) sharpness, tanginess; (*von Wein*) dryness **(b)** (*von Enttäuschung, Verlust*) bitterness **(c)** (= *Strenge*) (*von Gesicht, Zügen*) severity, harshness; (*von Art, Wesen, Charakter, Mensch*) dourness; **die** ~ **dieser Wahrheit/Erkenntnis** the cruel truth/realization **(d)** (*von Worten, Kritik*) harshness

Herbizid [hɛrbi'tsiːt] NT **-(e)s, -e** [-də] herbicide

herbringen VT SEP IRREG to bring (here); **bring mir das Buch her** bring me the book (over); *siehe auch* **hergebracht**

Herbst [hɛrpst] M **-(e)s, -e** autumn, fall (*US*); **im** ~ in autumn, in the fall (*US*); **auch der** ~ **hat noch schöne Tage** (*prov*) you're never too old

Herbst- IN CPDS autumn, fall (*US*); **Herbstanfang** M beginning of autumn *or* fall (*US*); **Herbstaster** F Michaelmas daisy; **Herbstferien** PL autumn holiday(s *pl*) (*esp Brit*) *or* vacation (*US*); (*Sch*) autumn half-term holiday(s *pl*) (*esp Brit*) *or* vacation (*US*); **herbstlich** ['hɛrpstlɪç] ADJ autumn *attr*; (= *wie im Herbst auch*) autumnal; **das Wetter wird schon** ~ autumn *or* fall (*US*) is in the air; **das Wetter ist schon** ~ it's already autumn *or* fall (*US*) weather **②** ADV ~ **kühles Wetter** cool autumn *or* fall (*US*) weather; ~ **gefärbtes Laub** leaves in autumnal colours (*Brit*) *or* fall colors (*US*); **Herbst-Tagundnachtgleiche** F DECL AS ADJ autumnal equinox; **Herbstzeitlose** ['hɛrpstsaitloːzə] F DECL AS ADJ meadow saffron

Herd [heːrt] M **-(e)s, -e** [-də] **(a)** (= *Küchenherd*) cooker, stove; (= *Kohleherd*) range; (*fig*: = *Heim*) home; **eigener** ~ **ist Goldes wert** (*Prov*) there's no place like home (*Prov*) **(b)** (*Med*) focus; (*Geol*: *von Erdbeben*) epicentre (*Brit*), epicenter (*US*); (*fig*: *von Rebellion etc*) seat

Herde ['heːrdə] F **-, -n** (*lit*) herd; (*von Schafen, fig geh*: = *Gemeinde*) flock

Herden-: Herdeninstinkt M (*lit, fig pej*) herd instinct; **Herdentier** NT gregarious animal; **Herdentrieb** M (*lit, fig pej*) herd instinct

Herdplatte F (*von Elektroherd*) hotplate; (*von Kohleherd*) (top) plate

herein [hɛ'rain] ADV in; **herein!** come in!, come! (*form*); **nur** ~**!** do come in!; **immer** ~**!** come along in!; **hier** ~**!** in here!; **von (dr)außen** ~ from outside

herein- PREF *siehe auch* **rein-** in; **hereinbekommen** *ptp* **hereinbekommen** VT SEP IRREG (*inf*) *Waren* to get in; *Radiosender* to get; *Unkosten etc* to recover; **hereinbitten** VT SEP IRREG to ask (to come) in; **hereinbrechen** VI SEP IRREG AUX SEIN **(a)** (*Wasser, Flut*) to gush in; **über jdn/etw** ~ (*lit, fig*) to descend upon sb/sth **(b)** (*Gewitter*) to break; (*Krieg, Pest*) to break out; **das Unglück brach über ihn herein** misfortune overtook him; **hereinbringen** VT SEP IRREG **(a)** (= *nach innen bringen*) to bring in **(b)** (*inf*: = *wettmachen*) *Geldverlust* to make good; *Zeit-, Produktionsverluste* to make up for; *Unkosten* to get back; **hereindürfen** VI SEP IRREG (*inf*) to be allowed in; **darf ich herein?** may I come in?; **hereinfahren** VTI SEP IRREG (*vi: aux sein*) to drive in; (*mit Fahrrad*) to ride in; **hereinfallen** VI SEP IRREG AUX SEIN **(a)** (= *nach innen fallen*) to fall in in (*in +acc* -to) **(b)** (*inf*) (= *sich täuschen lassen*) to fall for it (*inf*); (= *betrogen werden*) to be had (*inf*); **auf jdn/etw** ~ to be taken in by sb/sth; **mit jdm/etw** ~ to have a bad deal with sb/sth; **hereinführen** VT SEP to show in; **hereinholen** VT SEP to bring in (*in +acc* -to); **hereinkommen** VI SEP IRREG AUX SEIN to come in (*in +acc* -to); **wie ist er hereingekommen?** how did he get in?; **ins Haus** ~ to come in; **hereinkriegen** VT SEP (*inf*) = **hereinbekommen**; **hereinlassen** VT SEP IRREG to let in (*in +acc* -to); **hereinlegen** VT

SEP **(a)** (= *nach innen legen*) to lay (down) **(b)** (*inf*) **jdn** ~ (= *betrügen*) to take sb for a ride (*inf*); (= *anführen*) to take sb in; **hereinplatzen** VI SEP AUX SEIN (*inf*) to burst in (*in +acc* to); **bei jdm** ~ to burst in on sb; **hereinregnen** VI IMPERS SEP **es regnet herein** the rain is coming in; **hereinrufen** VT SEP IRREG to call in; **hereinschneien** SEP **①** VI IMPERS **es schneit herein** the snow's coming in **②** VI AUX SEIN (*inf*) to drop in (*inf*); **hereinsehen** VI SEP IRREG to look in (*inf*); **hereinspazieren** *ptp* **hereinspaziert** VI SEP AUX SEIN to breeze in (*in +acc* -to); **hereinspaziert!** come right in!; **hereinstecken** VT SEP (*inf*) to put in; **hereinströmen** VI SEP AUX SEIN to pour in (*in +acc* -to); **hereinwagen** VR SEP to dare to come in (*in +acc* -to); **hereinwollen** VI SEP (*inf*) to want to come in

Her-: herfahren SEP IRREG **①** VI AUX SEIN to come *or* get here; **hinter/vor jdm/etw** ~ to drive *or* (*mit Rad*) ride (along) behind/ in front of *or* ahead of sb/sth; **der Detektiv fuhr hinter dem Auto her** the detective followed the car **②** VT to drive here; **Herfahrt** F journey here; **auf der** ~ on the way here; **herfallen** VI SEP IRREG AUX SEIN **über jdn** ~ to attack sb; (= *kritisieren*) to pull sb to pieces; **über etw** (*acc*) ~ to descend upon sth; *über Geschenke, Essbares etc* to pounce upon sth; **herfinden** VI SEP IRREG to find one's way here

herg. ABBR *von* **hergestellt** mfd

Hergang M, *pl* (*rare*) -**gänge** (*von Schlacht*) course; **schildern Sie mir den genauen** ~ **dieses Vorfalls** tell me exactly what happened; **der** ~ **des Unfalls** the way the accident happened

her-: hergeben SEP IRREG **①** VT (= *weggeben*) to give away; (= *überreichen, aushändigen*) to hand over; (= *zurückgeben*) to give back; **gib das her!** give me that; **viel/einiges** ~ (*inf*: = *erbringen*) to be a lot of use/of some use; **wenig** ~ (*inf*) not to be much use; **das Thema gibt viel/nichts her** there's a lot/ nothing to this topic; **was die Beine hergaben** as fast as one's legs would carry one; **was die Lunge/Stimme hergab** at the top of one's voice; **seinen Namen für etw** ~ to lend one's name to sth **②** VR **sich zu** *or* **für etw** ~ to be (a) party to sth; **dazu gebe ich mich nicht her** I won't have anything to do with it; **eine Schauspielerin, die sich für solche Filme hergibt** an actress who allows herself to be involved in such films; **hergebracht** ADJ (= *traditionell*) traditional; **in** ~**er Weise** as is/ was traditional; *siehe auch* **herbringen**; **hergehen** SEP IRREG AUX SEIN **①** **hinter/vor/neben jdm** ~ to walk (along) behind/ in front of *or* ahead of/beside sb; ~ **und etw tun** (= *einfach tun*) just to (go and) do sth **②** VI IMPERS (*inf*) (= *zugehen*) **es ging heiß her** things got heated (*inf*); **hier geht es hoch her** there's plenty going on here; **hergehören** *ptp* **hergehört** VI SEP to belong here; **herhaben** VT SEP IRREG (*inf*) **wo hat er das her?** where did he get that from?; **herhalten** SEP IRREG **①** VT to hold out **②** VI to suffer (for it); **für etw** ~ to pay for sth; **sie muss als Sündenbock** ~ she is the scapegoat; **als Entschuldigung für etw** ~ to be used as an excuse for sth; **herholen** VT SEP (*inf*) to fetch; ~ **lassen** to send for; **weit hergeholt sein** (*fig*) to be far-fetched; **herhören** VI SEP (*inf*) to listen; **alle** *or* **alles mal** ~**!** everybody listen (to me)

Hering ['heːrɪŋ] M **-s, -e (a)** herring; **dünn wie ein** ~ as thin as a rake (*Brit*) *or* rail (*US*) **(b)** (= *Zeltpflock*) (tent) peg **(c)** (*fig inf*: = *schwächlicher Mensch*) weakling

herinnen [hɛ'rɪnən] ADV (*S Ger, Aus*) = **drinnen**

her-: herkommen VI SEP IRREG AUX SEIN to come here; (= *sich nähern*) to come; (= *herstammen*) to come from; **komm her!** come here!; **von jdm/etw** ~ (= *stammen*) to come from sb/sth; **ich weiß nicht, wo das herkommt** (*was der Grund ist*) I don't know why it is; **herkömmlich** ['heːrkœmlɪç] ADJ conventional

Herkunft ['heːrkʊnft] F **-,** ⸚**e** [-kʏnftə] origin; (*soziale*) background; **er ist britischer** ~ (*gen*), **er ist seiner** ~ **nach Brite** he is of British descent

Herkunfts-: Herkunftsbezeichnung F (*Comm*) designation of origin; **Herkunftsland** NT (*Comm*) country of origin

her-: herlaufen VI SEP IRREG AUX SEIN to come running; **hinter** (*lit, fig*)**/vor/neben jdm** ~ to run after/ahead of/beside sb; **herleiten** SEP **①** VT (= *ableiten, folgern*) to derive (*aus* from) **②** VR **sich von etw** ~ to be derived from sth; **herlocken** VT SEP to lure

hermachen SEP (*inf*) **①** VR **sich über etw** (*acc*) ~ **über** *Arbeit, Buch, Essen* to get stuck into sth (*inf*); *über Eigentum, Gegenstände* to pounce (up)on sth; **sich über jdn** ~ to lay into sb (*inf*) **②** VT **viel** ~ to look impressive; **wenig** ~ not to look very impressive; **nichts** ~ not to be up to much (*inf*)

Hermesbürgschaft [ˈhɛrmɛs-] F government export credit guarantee

hermetisch [hɛrˈmeːtɪʃ] **1** ADJ (lit, fig) hermetic **2** ADV ~ **abgeriegelt** completely sealed off

hermüssen VI SEP IRREG (inf) (a) **das muss her** I/we have to have it (b) (= kommen müssen) to have to come (here); **hinter jdm ~** to have to go after sb

hernehmen VT SEP IRREG (= beschaffen) to get; **wo soll ich das ~?** where am I supposed to get that from?

heroben [hɛˈroːbn] ADV (Aus, S Ger) up here

Heroin [heroˈiːn] NT -s, NO PL heroin

Heroin-: **heroinabhängig** ADJ addicted to heroin; **Heroinabhängige(r)** MF DECL AS ADJ heroin addict; **heroinsüchtig** ADJ addicted to heroin; **Heroinsüchtige(r)** MF DECL AS ADJ heroin addict

heroisch [heˈroːɪʃ] (geh) **1** ADJ heroic **2** ADV heroically

Herpes [ˈhɛrpɛs] M -, NO PL (Med) herpes

Herr [hɛr] M -(e)n, -en (a) (= Gebieter) lord, master; (= Herrscher) lord, ruler (über +acc of); **mein ~ und Gebieter** my lord and master; **die ~en der Schöpfung** (hum: = Männer) the gentlemen; **sein eigener ~ sein** to be one's own master; **~ einer Sache** (gen) **sein/werden** (= bewältigen) to have/get sth under control; **~ der Lage** or **Situation sein/bleiben** to be/ remain master of the situation; **nicht mehr ~ seiner Sinne sein** not to be in control of oneself any more; **man kann nicht** or **niemand kann zwei ~en dienen** (prov) no man can serve two masters (prov); **wie der ~, so Gescherr!** (Prov) like master, like man! (prov)
(b) (= Gott, Christus) Lord; **er ist ein großer Schwindler/Esser** etc **vor dem ~n** (hum inf) what a great fibber/eater etc he is
(c) (= feiner ~, Mann) gentleman; **„~en"** (= Toilette) "gents", "men"
(d) (vor Eigennamen) Mr; (vor Titeln) usu not translated; (in Anrede ohne Namen) sir; **(mein) ~!** sir!; **der ~ wünscht?** what can I do for you, sir?; **~ Dr./Doktor/Professor Schmidt** Dr/ Doctor/Professor Schmidt; **~ Doktor** doctor; **~ Professor** professor; **~ Präsident/Vorsitzender** Mr President/Chairman; **der ~ Präsident/Vorsitzende** the President/Chairman; **lieber** or **sehr geehrter** or **sehr verehrter** (form) **~ Bell** (in Brief) Dear Mr Bell; **an den ~n Abgeordneten C. Schmidt** C. Schmidt, MP; **werte ~en, sehr geehrte ~en** (in Brief) Dear Sirs (Brit), to whom it may concern (US)
(e) (allgemein gesehen: = Tanzpartner, Begleiter) gentleman; (auf eine bestimmte Dame bezogen) partner; (bei Cocktailparty, Theaterbesuch etc) (gentleman) companion
(f) (Sport) **4x100m-Staffel der ~en** men's 4 x 100m relay

Herrchen [ˈhɛrçən] NT -s, -, DIM von Herr (inf: von Hund) master; **geh zum ~** go to your master

Herreise F journey here; **auf der ~ von Köln** on the journey from Cologne

Herren- IN CPDS men's; (auf einzelnes Exemplar bezüglich) man's; **Herrenausstatter** [-ˈlaʊsʃtatɐ] M -s, -, **Herrenausstatterin** [-ərɪn] F -, -nen gents' outfitter; **Herrenbegleitung** F ~ **erwünscht** please bring a gentleman or (bei Ball) partner; **in ~** in the company of a gentleman; **Herrendoppel** NT (Tennis etc) men's doubles sing; **Herreneinzel** NT (Tennis etc) men's singles sing; **Herrenfriseur(in)** M(F) men's hairdresser, barber; **herrenlos** ADJ abandoned; Hund etc stray; **Herrenmangel** M shortage of men; **Herrensattel** M (man's) saddle; **im ~ reiten** to ride astride; **Herrenschneider(in)** M(F) gentlemen's tailor; **Herrenschnitt** M (= Frisur) haircut like a man's; **Herrentoilette** F men's toilet or restroom (US), gents sing

Herrgotts-: **Herrgottsfrühe** F **in aller ~** (inf) at the crack of dawn; **Herrgottswinkel** M (S Ger, Aus) corner of a room with a crucifix

herrichten VT SEP (a) (= vorbereiten) to get ready (+dat, für for); Bett to make; Tisch to set (b) (= instand setzen, ausbessern) to do up (inf)

Herrin [ˈhɛrɪn] F -, -nen (Hist: = Herrscherin) female ruler

herrisch [ˈhɛrɪʃ] **1** ADJ imperious **2** ADV imperiously; auffordern peremptorily

herrlich [ˈhɛrlɪç] **1** ADJ marvellous (Brit), marvelous (US); Kleid gorgeous, lovely; **das ist ja ~** (iro) that's great **2** ADV **du bist so ~ doof/naiv** (iro) you are so wonderfully stupid/naïve; **wir haben uns ~ amüsiert** we had a marvel(l)ous time; **~ schmecken** or **munden** to taste absolutely delicious

Herrlichkeit F -, -en (a) NO PL (= Schönheit, Pracht) magnificence; **Pracht und ~** pomp and circumstance; (von Natur) glory; **aus und vorbei mit der ~** here we go again (b) USU PL (= prächtiger Gegenstand) treasure

Herrschaft [ˈhɛrʃaft] F -, -en (a) NO PL (= Macht) power; (= Staatsgewalt) rule; **unter der ~** under the rule (+gen, von of); **während der ~** (+gen) in the reign of
(b) NO PL (= Gewalt, Kontrolle) control
(c) **die ~en** (= Damen und Herren) the ladies and gentlemen; **ältere ~en** (iro: = alte Leute) old folks; **was wünschen die ~en?** what can I get you?; (von Butler) you rang?; **(meine) ~en!** ladies and gentlemen!
(d) (inf: Ausruf) **~ (noch mal)** hang it (all) (inf)

herrschaftlich [ˈhɛrʃaftlɪç] ADJ of a person of high standing; (= vornehm) grand; **die ~e Kutsche** his lordship's coach

herrschen [ˈhɛrʃn] **1** VI (a) (= Macht, Gewalt haben) to rule; (König) to reign; (fig) (Mensch) to dominate; (Geld) to hold sway
(b) (= vorherrschen) (Angst, Ungewissheit, Zweifel) to prevail; (Verkehr, Ruhe, Betriebsamkeit) to be prevalent; (Nebel, Regen, Kälte) to be predominant; (Krankheit, Not) to be rampant; (Meinung, Ansicht) to predominate; **überall herrschte Freude/ Terror** there was joy/terror everywhere; **im Zimmer herrschte bedrückende Stille** it was oppressively quiet in the room; **hier herrscht Ordnung** things are orderly (a)round here; **hier herrscht ein anderer Ton** the atmosphere is different here; **hier ~ ja Zustände!** things are in a pretty state around here! **2** VI IMPERS **es herrscht schlechtes Wetter** the weather is bad; **es herrschte Schweigen** silence reigned; **es herrscht Ungewissheit darüber, ob ...** there is uncertainty about whether ...

herrschend ADJ Partei, Klasse ruling; König reigning; Bedingungen, Verhältnisse, Meinungen prevailing; Mode current; **die Herrschenden** the rulers, those in power

Herrscher [ˈhɛrʃɐ] M -s, -, **Herrscherin** [-ərɪn] F -, -nen (über +acc of) ruler; (= König/Königin auch) sovereign

Herrschsucht F, NO PL domineeringness

herrschsüchtig ADJ domineering

her-: **herrühren** VI SEP **von etw ~** to be due to sth; **hersagen** VT SEP to recite; **herschaffen** VT SEP (inf) = herbeischaffen; **herschenken** VT SEP (inf: = verschenken) to give away; **herschicken** VT SEP to send; **jdn hinter jdm ~** to send sb after sb; **hersehen** VT SEP IRREG (= hierher sehen) to look here; **zu jdm ~** to look in sb's direction; **hinter jdm/etw ~** to follow sb/sth with one's eyes; **her sein** VI IRREG AUX SEIN (a) (zeitlich) **das ist schon 5 Jahre her** that was 5 years ago; **es ist kaum ein Jahr her, dass ...** it's hardly a year since ...; **wie lange ist es her?** how long ago was it? (b) (= herstammen) to come from; **mit jdm/etw ist es nicht weit her** (inf) sb/sth is not up to much (inf) (c) **hinter jdm/etw ~** to be after sb/sth; **dahinter ~, dass jd etw tut** to be on to sb to do sth; **herspionieren** ptp **herspioniert** VI SEP **hinter jdm ~** to spy on sb; **herstammen** VI SEP (a) (= abstammen) to come from (b) (= herrühren) **von etw ~** to stem from sth

herstellen VT SEP (a) (= erzeugen) to produce; (esp industriell) to manufacture; **von Hand ~** to make by hand; **in Deutschland hergestellt** made in Germany
(b) (= zustande bringen) to establish; (Telec) Verbindung to make; Stromkreis to complete
(c) (gesundheitlich) jdn to restore to health; Gesundheit to restore; **er ist wieder ganz hergestellt** he has quite recovered
(d) (an bestimmten Platz) to put or place here; **sich (zu jdm) ~** to come over (to sb); **etw zu jdm ~** to put sth by sb

Hersteller [ˈheːʃtɛlɐ] M -s, -, **Herstellerin** [-ərɪn] F -, -nen (= Produzent) manufacturer; (in Verlag) production manager

Herstellung F (a) (= Erzeugung) production; (esp industriell) manufacture (b) (= das Zustandebringen) establishment (c) (von Gesundheit) restoration (d) (= Abteilung in Verlag) production department

Herstellungs-: **Herstellungskosten** PL manufacturing costs pl; **Herstellungsland** NT country of manufacture; **Herstellungsverfahren** NT manufacturing method

hertrauen VR SEP to dare to come here

Hertz [hɛrts] NT -, - (Phys, Rad) hertz

herüben [hɛˈryːbn] ADV (S Ger, Aus) over here

herüber [hɛˈryːbɐ] ADV over here; (über Fluss, Straße, Grenze etc) across; **~ und hinüber** to and fro; **da ~** over/across there

herüber- PREF *siehe auch* **rüber-** over; (*über Fluss, Straße, Grenze etc*) across; **herüberbringen** VT SEP IRREG *siehe* **herüber** to bring over/across (*über etw* (*acc*) sth); **herüberdürfen** VI SEP IRREG *siehe* **herüber** to be allowed (to come) over/across; **herübergeben** VT SEP IRREG to pass (*über +acc* over); **herüberholen** VT SEP to fetch; *jdn* to fetch over; **herüberkommen** VI SEP IRREG AUX SEIN *siehe* **herüber** to come over/across (*über etw* (*acc*) sth); (*inf: zu Nachbarn*) to pop round (*Brit inf*), to call round; **wie sind die Leute (über die Mauer/den Fluss) herübergekommen?** how did the people get over (the wall)/across (the river)?; **herüberlassen** VT SEP IRREG *siehe* **herüber** to allow (to come) over/across (*über etw* (*acc*) sth); (*aus Land*) to allow (to come) out; **herüberreichen** SEP **1** VT to pass (*über +acc* over) **2** VI to reach across (*über etw* (*acc*) sth); **herüberretten** VT SEP **etw in die Gegenwart ~** to preserve sth; **herübersehen** VI SEP IRREG *siehe* **herüber** to look over (*über etw* (*acc*) sth); **zu jdm ~** to look over/across to sb; **herüberwerfen** VT SEP IRREG *siehe* **herüber** to throw over/across (*über etw* (*acc*) sth); **herüberwollen** VI SEP IRREG *siehe* **herüber** to want to come over/across (*über etw* (*acc*) sth); **herüberziehen** SEP IRREG *siehe* **herüber** (*über etw* (*acc*) sth) **1** VT to pull over/across; (*fig*) to win over **2** VI AUX SEIN (*Truppen, Wolken*) to move over/across; (= *umziehen*) to move

herum [hɛˈrʊm] ADV (a) (*örtlich richtungsangebend*) **um ... ~** (a)round; **links/rechts ~** (a)round to the left/right; **hier/dort ~** (a)round here/there; **oben ~** (*über Gegenstand, Berg*) over the top; (*in Bezug auf Körper*) (a)round the top; **sie ist oben ~ ziemlich füllig** she's quite well endowed (*hum*); **unten ~** (*unter Gegenstand*) underneath; (*um Berg, in Bezug auf Körper*) (a)round the bottom; **oben/unten ~ fahren** to take the top/ lower road; **wasch dich auch unten ~** (*euph*) don't forget to wash down below; **immer um etw ~** (a)round and (a)round sth

(b) (= *kreisförmig angeordnet, in der Nähe*) **um ... ~** around; **alle um mich ~ wussten, dass ...** everyone (a)round me knew that ...

(c) (= *ungefähr*) **um ... ~** (*Mengenangabe*) about, around; (*Zeitangabe*) (at) about *or* around; *siehe auch* **herum sein**

herum- PREF *siehe auch* **umher-**, **rum-** (a)round; **herumalbern** VI SEP (*inf*) to fool around; **herumärgern** VR SEP (*inf*) **sich mit jdm/ etw ~** to keep struggling with sb/sth; **herumbasteln** VI SEP (*inf*) to mess around (*inf*) (*an +dat* with); **herumbekommen** *ptp* **herumbekommen** VT SEP IRREG (*inf*) *jdn* to talk round (*esp Brit*) *or* around (*esp US*); **etw ~** to (manage to) get sth round (*um etw* sth); **herumbringen** VT SEP IRREG (*inf*) *Zeit* to get through; **herumbrüllen** VI SEP to yell; **herumdoktern** [hɛˈrʊmdɔktɐn] VI SEP (*inf*) **an jdm/einer Krankheit/einer Wunde ~** to try to cure sb/ an illness/to heal a wound (*unsuccessfully, using many different treatments*); **an etw** (*dat*) **~** (*fig*) to fiddle around with sth; **herumdrehen** SEP **1** VT *Schlüssel* to turn; (= *wenden*) *Decke, Tuch, Braten etc* to turn (over) **2** VR to turn (a)round; (*im Liegen*) to turn over **3** VI (*inf*) **an etw** (*dat*) **~** to fiddle around with sth; **herumdrucksen** VI SEP (*inf*) to hum and haw (*inf*); **herumerzählen** *ptp* **herumerzählt** VT SEP **etw bei jdm ~** to tell sb about sth; **erzähl das nicht herum** don't spread that (a)round; **herumfahren** SEP IRREG **1** VI AUX SEIN (a) (= *umherfahren*) to go *or* (*mit Auto*) drive (a)round; **in der Stadt ~** to go/drive (a)round the town (*um etw ~* so or (*mit Auto*) drive *or* (*mit Schiff*) sail (a)round (c) (= *sich rasch umdrehen*) to turn (a)round quickly **2** VT to drive (a)round; **herumflegeln** VI SEP to loll around; **herumfliegen** VI SEP IRREG **1** VI AUX SEIN to fly (a)round (*um jdn/etw* sb/sth); (*inf:* = *herumliegen*) to be kicking around (*inf*) **2** VT *jdn* to fly (a)round; **herumfuchteln** VI SEP (*inf*) (**mit den Händen**) **~** to wave one's hands around (*Brit*); **mit einer Pistole ~** to wave a pistol around; **herumführen** SEP **1** VT (a) *jdn, Tier* to lead (a)round (*um etw* sth); (*bei Besichtigung*) to show (a)round; **jdn in einer Stadt/im Haus ~** to show sb (a)round a town/the house (b) (= *leiten, dirigieren*) **jdn/etw um etw ~** to direct sb/ sth (a)round sth (c) (= *bauen*) **etw um etw ~** to build sth (a)round sth **2** VI **um etw ~** to go (a)round sth; **herumfummeln** VI SEP (*inf*) (*an +dat* with) to fiddle around; (*an Auto*) to mess around; (= *basteln*) to tinker (around); **herumgehen** VI SEP IRREG AUX SEIN (*inf*) (a) (= *um etw ~*) to walk (a)round (*um etw* sth) (b) (= *umhergehen*) to wander (a)round (*in etw* (*dat*) sth); **es ging ihm im Kopf herum** it went round and round in his head (c) (= *von einem zum andern gehen: Mensch*) to go (a)round; (= *herumgereicht werden*) to be passed (a)round; (= *weitererzählt werden*) to go (a)round (*in*

etw (*dat*) sth); **etw ~ lassen** to circulate sth (d) (*zeitlich:* = *vorbeigehen*) to pass; **herumhaben** VT SEP IRREG (*inf*) *Zeit* to have finished; **herumhacken** VI SEP (*fig inf*) **auf jdm ~** to pick on sb (*inf*); **herumhängen** VI SEP IRREG (*inf*) (a) (= *sich lümmeln*) to loll around (b) (= *ständig zu finden sein*) to hang out (*inf*); **herumirren** VI SEP AUX SEIN to wander (a)round; **herumkommandieren** *ptp* **herumkommandiert** SEP (*inf*) **1** VT to order about **2** VI to give orders; **herumkommen** VI SEP IRREG AUX SEIN (*inf*) (a) (= *um eine Ecke etc*) to come (a)round (*um etw* sth) (b) (= *herumgehen, herumfahren etc können*) to get (a)round (*um etw* sth); **mit den Armen um etw ~** to be able to get one's arms (a)round sth (c) (= *vermeiden können*) **um etw ~** to get out of sth; **wir kommen um die Tatsache nicht herum, dass ...** we cannot get away from the fact that ... (d) (= *reisen*) to get (a)round (*in etw* (*dat*) sth); **herumkriegen** VT SEP (*inf*) = **herumbekommen**; **herumkritisieren** *ptp* **herumkritisiert**, **herumkritteln** [-krɪtln] VI SEP to find fault (*an +dat* with); **herumlaborieren** [-labo'riːrən], *ptp* **herumlaboriert** VI SEP (*inf*) **an etw** (*dat*) **~** to try to get rid of sth; **herumlaufen** VI SEP IRREG AUX SEIN (*inf*) (= *um etw ~*) to run (a)round (*um etw* sth); (= *umherlaufen*) to run (a)round; **so kannst du doch nicht ~** (*fig inf*) you can't go (a)round (looking) like that; **herumliegen** VI SEP IRREG (*inf*) to lie (a)round (*um etw* sth); **herumlümmeln** VIR SEP (*inf*) to loll around; **herumlungern** VI SEP AUX HABEN or SEIN (*inf*) to hang around; **herummachen** SEP (*inf*) **1** VI (a) (= *sich überlegen*) to consider (b) (= *sich beschäftigen*) **an jdm ~** to fuss about sb; **an etw** (*dat*) **~** to mess around with sth; **mit jdm ~** to mess around with sb (c) (= *herumfingern*) **an etw** (*dat*) **~** to pick at sth; **an den Haaren ~** to fiddle with sth (d) (= *herumnörgeln*) **an jdm/etw ~** to go on at sb/about sth (*inf*) **2** VT to put (a)round (*um etw* sth); **herumnörgeln** VI SEP **an jdm/etw ~** to find fault with sb/ sth; **herumquälen** VR SEP (*inf*) to struggle; (*mit Problemen*) to worry oneself sick (*mit* over) (*inf*); **sich mit Rheuma ~** to be plagued by rheumatism; **herumraten** VI SEP IRREG (*inf*) to guess; **herumrätseln** VI SEP **an etw** (*dat*) **~** to (try to) figure sth out; **er rätselte herum** he tried to figure it out; **herumreden** VI SEP (*inf*) (= *belangloses Zeug reden*) to talk away; **um etw ~** (= *ausweichend*) to talk around sth; **herumreichen** VT SEP (a) (= *herumgeben*) to pass (a)round; (*fig inf*) *Besucher* to show off (b) (= *lang genug sein*) to reach (a)round (*um etw* sth); **herumreisen** VI SEP AUX SEIN to travel (a)round; **herumreiten** VI SEP IRREG (*fig inf*) **auf jdm/etw ~** to keep on at sb/about sth; **herumrennen** VI SEP IRREG AUX SEIN (*inf*) to run (a)round (*um etw* sth); **herumschlagen** VI SEP IRREG (*inf*) **sich mit jdm ~** to fight with sb; (*fig*) to fight a running battle with sb; **sich mit etw ~** (*fig*) to keep struggling with sth; **herumschleppen** VT SEP (*inf*) *Sachen* to lug (a)round (*inf*); *jdn* to drag (a)round (*inf*); **etw mit sich ~** *Kummer, Sorge, Problem* to be troubled by sth; **herumschnüffeln** VI SEP (*inf*) to sniff (a)round (*in etw* (*dat*) sth); (*fig*) to snoop (a)round (*in +dat* in); **herumschreien** VI SEP IRREG (*inf*) to shout out loud; **herum sein** VI IRREG AUX SEIN (*inf*) (a) (= *vorüber sein*) to be past (b) (*Gerücht, Neuigkeit*) to have got (a)round (c) (= *in jds Nähe sein*) **um jdn ~** to be around sb; **herumsitzen** VI SEP IRREG AUX HABEN or SEIN to sit (a)round (*um jdn/etw* sb/sth); **herumspielen** VI SEP (*inf*) **mit etw ~** to play around with sth; **an etw** (*dat*) **~** to fiddle around with sth; **herumsprechen** VR SEP IRREG to get (a)round; **es dürfte sich herumgesprochen haben, dass ...** it has probably got out that ...; **herumstehen** VI SEP IRREG AUX HABEN or SEIN (a) (*Sachen*) to be lying around; **der Sessel steht blöd herum** the chair is in a stupid place (b) (*Menschen*) to stand (a)round (*um jdn/etw* sb/sth); **herumstöbern** VI SEP (a) (= *suchen*) to rummage around (b) (= *herumschnüffeln*) to snoop (a)round; **herumstochern** VI SEP (*inf*) to poke around; **im Essen ~** to pick at one's food; **in den Zähnen ~** to pick one's teeth; **herumstreiten** VR SEP IRREG to squabble; **herumstreunen**, **herumstrolchen** VI SEP AUX SEIN (*inf*) to prowl (a)round; **herumtoben** VI SEP (*inf*) (a) AUCH AUX SEIN (= *umherlaufen*) to romp (a)round (*Brit*) (b) (= *schimpfen*) to shout and scream; **herumtrampeln** VI SEP AUX SEIN (*inf*) to trample (*auf +dat* on); **jdm auf den Nerven ~**, **auf jds Nerven** *dat* **~** to get on sb's nerves; **auf jdm ~** (*fig*) to get at sb; **herumtreiben** VR SEP IRREG (*inf*) (= *herumziehen in* (*inf*); (*in schlechter Gesellschaft*) to hang (a)round in bad company; **die treibt sich mal wieder irgendwo in Spanien herum** she's off roaming around in Spain again (*inf*)

Herumtreiber(in) M(F) (*pej*) **(a)** (= *Mensch ohne feste Arbeit, Wohnsitz*) tramp **(b)** (*inf*) (= *Streuner*) vagabond; (*liederlich*) good-for-nothing; (= *Frau*) tramp (*inf*)

herum-: herumwerfen SEP IRREG **1** VT **(a)** (= *achtlos werfen*) to throw around (*in etw* (*dat*) *sth*) **(b)** *Kopf* to turn (quickly); *Steuer, Hebel* to throw around **2** VR to roll over; **sich (im Bett) ~** to toss and turn (in bed) **3** VI (*inf*) **mit Bemerkungen/Geld** *etc* ~ to throw remarks/one's money *etc* around; **herumzappen** VI SEP (*TV inf*) to zap around (*inf*); **herumzeigen** VT SEP to show (a)round; **herumziehen** VI SEP IRREG AUX SEIN (= *von Ort zu Ort ziehen*) to move around; (*inf*: = *sich herumtreiben in*) to go around (*in etw* (*dat*) *sth*); **in der Welt ~** to roam the world; **mit jdm ~** (*inf*) to go around with sb; **herumziehend** ADJ ATTR *Händler* itinerant; *Musikant, Schauspieler* wandering; **herumzigeunern** *ptp* **herumzigeunert** VI SEP AUX SEIN (*pej*) to (a)round (*in etw* (*dat*) *sth*)

herunten [heˈrʊntn] ADV (*S Ger, Aus*) down here

herunter [heˈrʊntɐ] **1** ADV down; **~!** get down!; **~ mit euch** get down; **~ mit ihm** get him down; **~ damit** get it down; (*in Bezug auf Kleider*) take it off; **da/hier ~** down there/here; **den Hut ~, ~ mit dem Hut** take your hat off; **vom Berg ~** down the mountain; **bis ins Tal ~** down into the valley; *siehe auch* **herunter sein** *etc* **2** PREP +ACC (*nachgestellt*) down

herunter- PREF *siehe auch* **runter-, herab-** down; **herunterbekommen** *ptp* **herunterbekommen** VT SEP IRREG = **herunterkriegen**; **herunterbrennen** VI SEP IRREG **(a)** (*Sonne*) to scorch down **(b)** AUX SEIN (*Haus, Feuer, Kerze etc*) to burn down; **herunterbringen** VT SEP IRREG **(a)** (= *nach unten bringen*) to bring down **(b)** (*inf*) = **herunterkriegen**; **herunterdrücken** VT SEP *Hebel, Pedal* to press down; *Preise* to force down; *Niveau* to lower; **herunterfahren** SEP IRREG **1** VI AUX SEIN to go down; **heruntergefahren kommen** to come down **2** VT to bring down; (*Comput*) to shut down; **herunterfallen** VI SEP IRREG AUX SEIN to fall down; **von etw ~** to fall off sth; **ihm fiel die Kinnlade herunter** his jaw dropped; **heruntergeben** VT SEP IRREG to hand down; **heruntergehen** VI SEP IRREG AUX SEIN to go down; (*Flugzeug*) to descend; **von etw ~** (*inf*) to get off sth; **auf etw** (*acc*) **~** (*Preise*) to go down to sth; (*Geschwindigkeit*) to slow down; **mit den Preisen ~** to lower one's prices; **heruntergekommen** ADJ *Haus* dilapidated; *Stadt* run-down; *Mensch* down-at-heel; **herunterhandeln** VT SEP (*inf*) *Preis, Gebühren* to beat down; **etw um 20 Euro ~** to get 20 euros knocked off (*inf*) **(auf etw** *acc*) ~ to knock sb down to sth); **herunterhauen** VT SEP IRREG (*inf*) **(a)** **jdm eine ~** to slap sb on the side of the head **(b)** (= *schnell machen*) to dash *or* knock off (*inf*); **herunterholen** VT SEP to fetch down; (*inf*) *Vogel, Flugzeug* to bring down; **herunterklappen** VT SEP to turn down; *Sitz* to fold down; *Deckel* to close; **herunterkommen** VI SEP IRREG AUX SEIN **(a)** (= *nach unten kommen*) to come down; (*inf*: = *herunterkönnen*) to get down **(b)** (*fig inf*: = *verfallen*) (*Stadt, Firma*) to go downhill; (*Wirtschaft*) to go to rack and ruin; (*gesundheitlich*) to become run-down; **er ist so weit heruntergekommen, dass ...** (*sittlich*) he has sunk so low that ...; *siehe* **heruntergekommen (c)** (*fig inf*: = *wegkommen: von schlechten Noten etc*) to get over (*von etw* sth); **von Drogen/vom Alkohol ~** to kick the habit (*inf*); **herunterkönnen** VI SEP IRREG to be able to get down; **herunterkriegen** VT SEP (*inf*) **(a)** (= *herunterholen, schlucken können*) to get down; (= *abmachen können*) to get off **(b)** (= *abnehmen*) to lose; **herunterkurbeln** VT SEP *Fensterscheibe* to wind down; **herunterladen** VT SEP IRREG (*Comput*) to download (*auf* +*acc* onto); **herunterlassen** SEP IRREG **1** VT (= *abseilen*) to lower; *Hose* to take down; **sie lässt mich nicht herunter** (*inf*) she won't let me down **2** VR (*an Seil*) to lower oneself; **herunterleiern** [heˈrʊntlaiɐn] VT SEP (*inf*) to reel off; **heruntermachen** VT SEP (*inf*) **(a)** (= *schlecht machen*) to run down **(b)** (= *zurechtweisen*) to tell off **(c)** (= *abmachen*) to take down; *Schminke, Farbe, Dreck* to take off; **herunterputzen** VT SEP (*inf*) **jdn ~** to give sb an earful (*inf*); **herunterreichen** SEP IRREG **1** VT to pass down **2** VI to reach down; **herunterschalten** VI SEP IRREG (*Aut*) to change *or* shift (*US*) down (*in* +*acc* into); **herunterschrauben** VT SEP (*fig*) *Ansprüche, Niveau* to lower; **heruntersehen** VI SEP IRREG **(a)** (*von oben*) to look down **(b)** (*fig*: = *mustern*) **an jdm ~** to look sb up and down **(c)** (*fig*: = *geringschätzig behandeln*) **auf jdn ~** to look down on sb; **herunter sein** VI SEP IRREG AUX SEIN (*inf*) **(a)** (*von oben*) to be down **(b)** (= *abgeschnitten sein*) to be (cut) off **(c)** (*Fieber, Preise*) to be down; **wenn die 5 Kilo Übergewicht herunter sind**

when I/you *etc* have lost those 5 kilos excess weight **(d)** (*inf*) **mit den Nerven ~** to be at the end of one's tether (*Brit*) *or* rope (*US*); **mit der Gesundheit ~** to be run-down; **herunterspielen** VT SEP (*inf*: = *verharmlosen*) to play down; **herunterwirtschaften** VT SEP (*inf*) to bring to the brink of ruin; **herunterwollen** VI SEP (*inf*) to want to get down; **herunterziehen** SEP IRREG **1** VT (= *nach unter ziehen*) to pull down; (= *ausziehen*) to pull off; **etw von etw ~** to pull sth off sth **2** VI AUX SEIN to move down

hervor [hɛɐˈfoːɐ] ADV **aus etw ~** out of sth; **hinter dem Tisch ~** out from behind the table

hervor-: hervorbringen VT SEP IRREG **(a)** (= *entstehen lassen*) to produce; *Worte* to utter **(b)** (= *verursachen*) *Unheil, Böses* to create; **hervorgehen** VI SEP IRREG AUX SEIN **(a)** (= *sich ergeben*) to follow; **daraus geht hervor, dass ...** from this it follows that ... **(b)** (= *etwas überstehen*) to emerge; **als Sieger ~** to emerge victorious; **aus etw ~** to come out of sth; **hervorheben** VT SEP IRREG to emphasize; **hervorholen** VT SEP to bring out; **hervorkommen** VI SEP IRREG AUX SEIN to come out (*hinter* +*dat* from behind); **hervorlocken** VT SEP to entice out (*aus* from, *hinter* +*dat* from behind); **hervorragen** VI SEP **(a)** (*Felsen, Stein etc*) to jut out; (*Nase*) to protrude **(b)** (*fig*: = *sich auszeichnen*) to stand out; **hervorragend 1** ADJ **(a)** (*fig*: = *ausgezeichnet*) excellent; **er hat Hervorragendes geleistet** his achievement was outstanding **(b)** (*lit*: = *vorstehend*) projecting; *esp Körperteil* protruding **2** ADV (= *ausgezeichnet*) very well; **etw ~ beschreiben/interpretieren** to give an excellent description/interpretation of sth; **~ kochen** to be an excellent cook; **~ schmecken** to taste exquisite; **hervorrufen** VT SEP IRREG **(a)** (= *rufen*) **jdn ~** to call (to) sb to come out; (*Theat etc*) to call for sb **(b)** (= *bewirken*) to cause; *Bewunderung* to arouse; *Eindruck* to create; **hervorsehen** VI SEP IRREG (*Unterrock*) to show; (*Mensch*) to look out; **hinter etw** (*dat*) **~** (*Mensch*) to look out from behind sth; (*Mond, Sterne*) to shine out from behind sth; **hervorsprudeln** VI SEP AUX SEIN to gush out; **hervorstechen** VI SEP IRREG AUX SEIN (*lit, fig*) to stand out; **hervorstechend** ADJ striking; **hervorstehen** VI SEP IRREG AUX SEIN (*Spitze*) to jut out; (*Nase, Ohren etc*) to stick out; **hervortun** VR SEP IRREG to distinguish oneself; (*inf*: = *sich wichtig tun*) to show off (*mit etw* sth); **hervorziehen** VT SEP IRREG to pull out (*unter* +*dat* from under); **etw aus/zwischen etw** (*dat*) **~** to pull sth out of/from among sth

Her-: herwagen VR SEP IRREG to dare to come; **herwärts** [ˈheːɐvɛrts] ADV on the way here; **Herweg** M, NO PL way here; **auf dem ~ on** the way here

Herz [hɛrts]

gen **Herzens**, *pl* **Herzen**

SUBSTANTIV (NT)
heart; (= *Spielkartenfarbe*) hearts *pl*; **Operation/Eingriff am offenen Herzen** open-heart surgery; **sein Herz schlägt sehr schnell** he has a very high heart rate; **mir schlug das Herz bis zum Hals** my heart was pounding; **sein Herz schlug höher** his heart leapt; **die Herzen höher schlagen lassen** to touch people's hearts; **komm an mein Herz** come into my arms; **ein Herz auf das i malen** to draw a heart on (top of) the i; **Herz ist Trumpf** hearts are trumps; **das Parlament befindet sich im Herzen der Stadt** the parliament is in the heart of the city; **im Grund seines/meines Herzens** in his/my heart of hearts; **ein Herz und eine Seele sein** to be the best of friends

✦Adjektiv + Herz **mit ganzem Herzen** wholeheartedly; **er ist mit ganzem Herzen bei der Arbeit** he is putting his heart and soul into his work; **jdm von ganzem Herzen danken** to thank sb with all one's heart; **ein goldenes Herz** a heart of gold; **ein gutes Herz haben** (*fig*) to have a good heart; **schweren Herzens** with a heavy heart; **jdm das Herz schwer machen** to grieve sb; **aus tiefstem Herzen** from the bottom of one's heart

✦Präposition + Herz

Die in Verbindung mit **Herz** *verwendeten Präpositionen sind alphabetisch angeordnet.*

es liegt mir am Herzen I am very concerned about it; **es liegt mir sehr am Herzen, dass der Spielplatz gebaut wird** it's very important to me that the playground be built; **dieser Hund ist mir ans Herz gewachsen** I have become attached to this dog; **jdm etw ans Herz legen** to entrust sth to sb's care; **ich lege es dir ans Herz, das zu tun** I would ask you particularly to do that; **etw auf dem Herzen haben** to have sth on one's mind; **jdn auf Herz und Nieren prüfen** to examine sb very thoroughly; **er hat sie in sein Herz geschlossen** he has grown fond of her; **ein Mann nach meinem Herzen** a man after my own heart; **ohne Herz** heartless; **es wurde ihr leichter ums Herz** she felt relieved; **ich weiß, wie es dir ums Herz ist** I know how you feel; **von Herzen** with all one's heart; **etw von Herzen gern tun** to love doing sth; **jdn von Herzen gern haben** to love sb dearly; **von Herzen kommend** heartfelt; **eine schwere Last** or **eine Zentnerlast fiel ihr vom Herzen** she felt a weight lifted from her mind; **sich** (*dat*) **etw vom Herzen reden** to get sth off one's chest; **sich** (*dat*) **etw zu Herzen nehmen** to take sth to heart

✦Verb + Herz

Die in Verbindung mit **Herz** *verwendeten Verben sind alphabetisch angeordnet (siehe auch* **Präposition + Herz**).

alles, was das Herz begehrt everything one's heart desires; **mir blutet das Herz, mein Herz blutet** (*auch iro*) my heart bleeds; **jds Herz brechen** to break sb's heart; **alle Herzen im Sturm erobern** to capture people's hearts; **gib deinem Herzen einen Stoß!** go on!; **hast du denn (gar) kein Herz?** how can you be so heartless?; **haben Sie doch ein Herz!** have a heart!; **ein Herz für jdn/etw haben** to be fond of sb/sth; **er hat das Herz auf dem** or **am rechten Fleck** his heart is in the right place; **sein Herz an jdn/etw hängen** to commit oneself heart and soul to sb/sth; **jds Herz hängt an jdm/etw** sb is committed heart and soul to sb/sth; **an Geld** sb is preoccupied with sth; **seinem Herzen Luft machen** to give vent to one's feelings; **das Herz auf der Zunge tragen** to speak one's mind; **es zerreißt mir das Herz** it breaks my heart

Herz-: Herzanfall M heart attack; **Herzass** NT ace of hearts; **Herzattacke** F heart attack
herzaubern VT SEP to produce out of thin air
Herz-: Herzbeschwerden PL heart trouble *sing*; **Herzbube** M jack of hearts
Herzchen ['hɛrtsçən] NT **-s, -** little heart; (*inf*: *Kosewort*) (little) darling
Herz-: Herzchirurg(in) M(F) heart surgeon; **Herzdame** F (*Cards*) queen of hearts
herzeigen VT SEP to show; **zeig (mal) her!** let's see; **das kann man ~** that's worth showing off
Herzens-: Herzensbrecher(in) M(F) (*fig inf*) heartbreaker; **herzensgut** ADJ good-hearted; **Herzensgüte** F good-heartedness; **Herzenslust** F **nach ~** to one's heart's content; **Herzenswunsch** M dearest wish
Herz-: herzerfrischend ADJ refreshing; **herzergreifend** ADJ heart-rending; **herzerweichend** [-ɛɐvaiçnt] **1** ADJ heart-rending **2** ADV heart-rendingly; **Herzfehler** M heart defect; **Herzflattern** NT **-s,** NO PL palpitations *pl* (of the heart); **Herzflimmern** NT **-s,** NO PL heart flutter; (= *Kammerflimmern*) (ventricular) fibrillation; **herzförmig** ADJ heart-shaped; **Herzgegend** F, NO PL cardiac region; **Herzgeräusche** PL heartbeats *pl*
herzhaft ADJ **(a)** (= *kräftig*) hearty; *Händedruck, Griff* firm; *Geschmack* strong **(b)** (= *nahrhaft*) *Essen* substantial **2** ADV **~ gähnen** to yawn loudly; **alle griffen ~ zu** everyone got stuck in (*inf*); **das schmeckt ~** that's good honest fare; **jdn ~ küssen** to give sb a big fat kiss; **~ lachen** to laugh hard
herzziehen SEP IRREG **1** VT to draw closer; **jdn/etw hinter sich** (*dat*) **~** to pull sb/sth (along) behind one **2** VI AUX SEIN **(a)** (= *herankommen*) to approach; **hinter/neben/vor jdm ~** to march along behind/beside/in front of sb **(b)** (= *umziehen*) to move here **(c)** AUCH AUX HABEN **über jdn/etw ~** (*inf*) to knock sb/sth (*inf*)
herzig ['hɛrtsɪç] ADJ sweet
Herz-: Herzinfarkt M heart attack; **Herzkammer** F ventricle; **Herzklappe** F cardiac valve; **Herzklappenfehler** M valvular heart defect; **Herzklopfen** NT **-s,** NO PL **ich hatte/bekam ~** my heart was/started pounding; (*durch Kaffee*) I had/got palpitations; **mit ~** with a pounding heart; **herzkrank** ADJ

suffering from a heart condition; **~ sein/werden** to have/get a heart condition; **Herzkranzgefäß** NT USU PL coronary (blood) vessel; **herzleidend** ADJ with a heart condition
herzlich ['hɛrtslɪç] **1** ADJ *Empfang, Freundschaft, Atmosphäre* warm; *Wesen, Mensch* warm(-hearted); *Lachen* hearty; *Bitte* sincere; **~e Grüße an Ihre Frau** kind(est) regards to your wife; **mit ~en Grüßen** kind regards; **~en Dank!** many thanks; **~es Beileid!** you have my sincere sympathy; **zu jdm ~ sein** to be kind to sb
2 ADV (= *freundlich*) warmly; *sich bedanken, Glück wünschen* sincerely; (= *ziemlich*) *langweilig, uninteressant* totally; **jdm ~ gratulieren** to congratulate and wish sb all the best; **~ schlecht** pretty awful; **~ wenig** precious little; **~ gern!** with the greatest of pleasure!; **ich würde ~ gern einmal wieder die Stätten meiner Kindheit besuchen** I should so much like to visit my childhood haunts again
Herzlichkeit F -, NO PL (*von Empfang, Freundschaft*) warmth; (*von Wesen, Mensch*) warm(-hearted)ness
Herz-: Herzlinie F heart line; **herzlos** ADJ heartless; **Herzlosigkeit** F -, NO PL heartlessness *no pl*; **Herz-Lungen-Maschine** F heart-lung machine; **Herzmittel** NT cardiac drug
Herzog ['hɛrtso:k] M **-s, ⸚e** or (*rare*) **-e** ['hɛrsø:gə, -tso:gə] duke
Herzogin ['hɛrtso:gɪn] F **-, -nen** duchess
herzoglich ['hɛrtso:klɪç] ADJ ATTR ducal
Herzogtum ['hɛrtso:ktu:m] NT **-s, -tümer** [-ty:mɐ] duchy
Herz-: Herzrhythmus M heart rhythm; **Herzrhythmusstörung** F palpitations *pl*; **Herzschlag** M **(a)** (*einzelner*) heartbeat **(b)** (= *Herztätigkeit*) heart rate **(c)** (= *Herzstillstand*) heart failure *no indef art, no pl*; **Herzschrittmacher** M pacemaker; **Herzschwäche** F a weak heart; **wegen einer vorübergehenden ~** because my/his *etc* heart faltered for a moment; **an ~ leiden** to have a weak heart; **Herzstich** M USU PL stabbing pain in the chest; **Herzstillstand** M cardiac arrest; **Herzstück** NT (*fig geh*) heart; **Herztätigkeit** F cardiac activity
herzu- [hɛɐ'tsu] IN CPDS = **herbei-**
herzzerreißend **1** ADJ heartbreaking **2** ADV **~ weinen** to weep distressingly
Hesse ['hɛsə] M **-n, -n,** **Hessin** ['hɛsɪn] F **-, -nen** Hessian
Hessen ['hɛsn] NT **-s** Hesse
hessisch ['hɛsɪʃ] ADJ Hessian
Hete ['he:tə] M **-n, -n** or *f* **-, -n** USU PL (*pej sl*: = *Heterosexuelle(r)*) hetty (*sl*)
hetero ['he:tero, 'hɛtero, he'te:ro] ADJ PRED (*inf*) hetero (*inf*), straight (*inf*)
Hetero-: heterogen [hetero'ge:n] ADJ (*geh*) heterogeneous; **Heterosexualität** [hetero-] F heterosexuality; **heterosexuell** [hetero-] ADJ heterosexual; **Heterosexuelle(r)** [heteroze'ksuɛlə] MF DECL AS ADJ heterosexual
hethitisch [he'ti:tɪʃ] ADJ Hittite
Hetz [hɛts] F **-,** (*rare*) **-en** (*Aus inf*) laugh (*inf*); **aus** or **zur ~** for a laugh
Hetz- (*pej*) IN CPDS inflammatory
Hetze ['hɛtsə] F **-, -n (a)** NO PL (= *Hast*) (mad) rush **(b)** NO PL (*pej*: = *Aufreizung*) rabble-rousing propaganda
hetzen ['hɛtsn] **1** VT **(a)** (*lit, fig*: = *jagen*) to hound; **die Hunde auf jdn/etw ~** to set the dogs on(to) sb/sth **(b)** (*inf*: = *antreiben*) to rush **2** VI **(a)** (= *sich beeilen*) to rush; **hetz nicht so** don't be in such a rush **(b)** AUX SEIN (= *eilen*) to tear; **ich bin ganz schön gehetzt, um ...** I rushed like mad to ... (*inf*) **(c)** (*pej*: = *Hass schüren*) to agitate; (*inf*: = *lästern*) to say malicious things; **gegen jdn/etw ~** to stir up hatred against sb/sth; **zum Krieg ~** to agitate for war; **gegen Minderheiten ~** to stir up hatred against minorities; **bei jdm gegen jdn ~** to try to turn sb against sb; *siehe auch* **gehetzt**
Hetzerei [hɛtsə'rai] F **-, -en (a)** NO PL (= *Hast*) (mad) rush **(b)** (= *das Hassschüren*) rabble-rousing; **~ zum Krieg** warmongering
Hetz-: hetzhalber ADV (*Aus inf*) for a laugh (*inf*); **Hetzjagd** F **(a)** (*lit, fig*) hounding (*auf +acc* of) **(b)** (*fig*: = *Hast*) rush; **es war die reinste ~** it was one mad rush; **Hetzkampagne** F malicious campaign
Heu [hɔy] NT **-(e)s,** NO PL hay
Heuchelei [hɔyçə'lai] F **-, -en** hypocrisy; **spar dir deine ~en** cut out the hypocrisy

heucheln [ˈhɔʏçl̩n] **1** VI to be a hypocrite **2** VT *Zuneigung, Mitleid etc* to feign

Heuchler [ˈhɔʏçlɐ] M **-s, -**, **Heuchlerin** [-ərɪn] F **-, -nen** hypocrite

heuchlerisch [ˈhɔʏçlərɪʃ] ADJ hypocritical

heuer [ˈhɔʏɐ] ADV (*S Ger, Aus, Sw*) this year

Heuer [ˈhɔʏɐ] F **-, -n** (*Naut*) pay

heuern [ˈhɔʏɐn] VT to hire

Heuervertrag M contract of employment (*of seaman*)

Heulboje F (*Naut*) whistling buoy

heulen [ˈhɔʏlən] VI **(a)** (*inf:* = *weinen*) to bawl (*inf*), to wail; (*vor Schmerz*) to scream; (*vor Wut*) to howl; **ich hätte ~ können** I could have cried; **es ist einfach zum Heulen** it's enough to make you weep **(b)** (*Flugzeug, Motor*) to roar; (*Wind, Tiere*) to howl; (*Sirene*) to wail

Heulerei [hɔʏləˈraɪ] F **-, -en** (*inf*) constant bawling (*inf*)

Heul- (*inf*): **Heulkrampf** M fit of blubbering (*inf*); **Heulpeter** [ˈhɔʏlpeːtɐ] M **-s, -**, **Heulsuse** [ˈhɔʏlzuːzə] F **-, -n** crybaby (*inf*)

heurig [ˈhɔʏrɪç] ADJ ATTR (*S Ger, Aus*) this year's

Heurige(r) [ˈhɔʏrɪɡə] M DECL AS ADJ (*esp Aus*) new wine

HEURIGER

*Heuriger is the name given in Austria to wine from the most recent harvest, drunk from Martinmas (November 11th) onwards. Bars where the wine is drunk are also called **Heurige**. The **Heurige** bars in the area around Vienna are especially well known.*

Heu-: **Heuschnupfen** M hay fever; **Heuschrecke** [ˈhɔʏʃrɛkə] F **-, -n** grasshopper; (*in heißen Ländern*) locust

heute [ˈhɔʏtə], **heut** [hɔʏt] (*inf*) ADV **(a)** (= *an diesem Tag*) today; **~ Morgen** this morning; **~ Abend** this evening, tonight; **~ früh** this morning; **~ Nacht** tonight; „~ geschlossen" "closed today"; **~ noch** (= *heutzutage*) still ... today, even today; **ich muss ~ noch zur Bank** I must go to the bank today; **bis ~** (= *bisher,* = *immer noch*) to this day; **bis ~ nicht** (= *noch nicht*) not ... to this day; **von ~ ab** *or* **an, ab ~** from today (on); **~ in einer Woche** a week today, today week; **~ vor acht Tagen** a week ago today; **~ in einem Jahr** a year from today; **Milch/die Zeitung von ~** today's milk/paper; **lieber ~ als morgen** the sooner the better; **etw von ~ auf morgen verschieben** to put sth off until tomorrow; **von ~ auf morgen** (*fig:* = *rasch, plötzlich*) overnight **(b)** (= *in der gegenwärtigen Zeit*) nowadays, today; **das Heute** the present, today; **das Italien/der Mensch von ~** present-day *or* contemporary Italy/man; **der Bauer/die Frau/die Stadt von ~** today's farmers/women/towns; **die Jugend von ~** the young people of today

heutig [ˈhɔʏtɪç] ADJ ATTR today's; (= *gegenwärtig*) contemporary; **der ~e Tag** today; **am ~en Abend** this evening; **anlässlich Ihres ~en Geburtstags** to mark your birthday today; **unser ~es Schreiben** (*Comm*) our letter of today('s date); **bis zum ~en Tage** to date, to this day; **aus ~er Sicht** from today's standpoint

heutzutage [ˈhɔʏtsutaːɡə] ADV nowadays

Hexa- [hɛksa] IN CPDS hexa-; **hexadezimal** [hɛksadetsiˈmaːl] ADJ (*Comput*) hexadecimal, hex; **Hexaeder** [hɛksaˈeːdɐ] NT **-s, -** hexahedron; **Hexagon** [hɛksaˈɡoːn] NT **-s, -e** hexagon; **hexagonal** [hɛksaɡoˈnaːl] ADJ hexagonal; **Hexagramm** [hɛksaˈɡram] NT, *pl* **-gramme** hexagram; **Hexameter** [hɛˈksaːmetɐ] M hexameter

Hexe [ˈhɛksə] F **-, -n** witch; (*inf:* = *altes Weib*) old hag; **diese kleine ~!** that little minx!

hexen [ˈhɛksn̩] VI to practise (*Brit*) *or* practice (*US*) witchcraft; **er kann ~** he knows (how to work) black magic; **ich kann doch nicht ~** (*inf*) I can't work miracles

Hexen-: **Hexenhaus** NT enchanted house; **Hexenhäuschen** [-hɔʏsçən] NT gingerbread house; **Hexenjagd** F (*Hist, fig*) witch-hunt; **Hexenkessel** M (*fig*) pandemonium *no art*; **Hexenmeister** M sorcerer; **Hexenprozess** M witch trial; **Hexenschuss** M (*Med*) lumbago; **Hexenverbrennung** F burning of a witch/witches; **Hexenverfolgung** F witch-hunt

Hexerei [hɛksəˈraɪ] F **-, -en** witchcraft *no pl*, sorcery, witchery *no pl*; (*von Zaubertricks*) magic *no pl*

HG F **-** ABBR *von* **Handelsgesellschaft**

hg. ABBR *von* **herausgegeben** ed.

HGB [haːɡeːˈbeː] NT **-** ABBR *von* **Handelsgesetzbuch**

hibbelig [ˈhɪbəlɪç] ADJ (*dial*) jittery

Hibiskus [hiˈbɪskʊs] M **-, Hibisken** [-kn̩] hibiscus

Hickhack [ˈhɪkhak] M *or* NT **-s, -s** squabbling *no pl*

hieb (*geh*) PRET *von* **hauen**

Hieb [hiːp] M **-(e)s, -e** [-bə] **(a)** (= *Schlag*) stroke, blow; (= *Fausthieb*) blow; (= *Peitschenhieb*) lash, crack; (*Fechten*) cut; **auf einen ~** (*inf*) in one go **(b)** (= *~wunde*) gash **(c) Hiebe** PL (*dated:* = *Prügel*) hiding **(d)** (*fig*) dig, cutting remark; **der ~ saß** that (dig) struck home

Hieb-: **hiebfest** ADJ **hieb- und stichfest** (*fig*) watertight; **Hiebwaffe** F cutting weapon

hielt PRET *von* **halten**

hier [hiːɐ] ADV **(a)** (*räumlich*) here; **das Haus ~** this house; **dieser ~** this one (here); **~ und da** here and there; **Herr Direktor ~, Herr Direktor da** (*iro*) yes sir, yes sir, three bags full, sir; **~ draußen/drinnen** out/in here; **~ entlang** along here; **~ herum** (a)round here; **~ hinein** in here; **~ oben/unten** up/down here; **er ist von ~** he comes from (a)round here; **er ist nicht von ~** he's a stranger here; **Tag Klaus, ~ (spricht) Hans** (*Telec*) hello, Klaus, Hans here; **~ spricht Dr. Müller** (*Telec*) this is Dr Müller (speaking); **von ~ ab** from here (on *or* onwards); **von ~ aus** from here; **das Hier und Heute** (*geh*) the here and now; **er ist ein bisschen ~** (*inf*) he's got a screw loose (*inf*); **~ zu Lande** = **hierzulande** **(b)** (*zeitlich*) now; **~ und da** (every) now and then; **von ~ ab** *or* **an** from now on **(c)** (*fig*) here; **das steht mir bis ~** (*inf*) I've had it up to here (with it) (*inf*); **~ versagte ihm die Stimme** here *or* at this point his voice failed him

hieran [hiˈran, hiˈran, (*emph*) ˈhiːran] ADV **(a)** (*lit*) here **(b)** (*fig*) **wenn ich ~ denke** when I think of *or* about this; **er erinnert sich ~** he remembers this; **~ erkenne ich es** I recognize it by this; **~ kann es keinen Zweifel geben** there can be no doubt about that

Hierarchie [hierarˈçiː] F **-, -n** [-ˈçiːən] hierarchy

hierarchisch [hieˈrarçɪʃ] **1** ADJ hierarchic(al) **2** ADV hierarchically; *aufbauen, gliedern* with a hierarchical structure

hier-: **hierauf** [ˈhiːˈrauf, hiˈrauf, (*emph*) ˈhiːrauf] ADV **(a)** (*lit*) (on) here, on this **(b)** (*fig*) on this; (= *daraufhin*) hereupon; **er setzte sich, und ~ ...** he sat down and then ...; **hieraufhin** [ˈhiːˈraufhɪn, hiˈraufhɪn, (*emph*) ˈhiːraufhɪn] ADV hereupon; **und ~ ...** and then ...; **hieraus** [ˈhiːˈraus, hiˈraus, (*emph*) ˈhiːraus] ADV **(a)** (*lit*) out of this, from here; **~ ist das Geld gestohlen worden** the money was stolen from here **(b)** (*fig*) from this; **~ folgt, dass ...**, **~ geht hervor, dass ...** from this it follows that ...; **hier behalten** VT IRREG **jdn/etw ~** to keep sb/sth here; **hierbei** [ˈhiːˈbai, hiˈbai, (*emph*) ˈhiːbai] ADV **(a)** (*lit:* = *währenddessen*) doing this **(b)** (*fig*) (= *bei dieser Gelegenheit*) on this occasion; (= *in diesem Zusammenhang*) in this connection; **hier bleiben** VI IRREG AUX SEIN to stay here; **hier geblieben!** stop!; **hierdurch** [ˈhiːˈdʊrç, hiˈdʊrç, (*emph*) ˈhiːdʊrç] ADV **(a)** (*lit*) through here **(b)** (*fig*) through this; **~ teilen wir Ihnen mit, dass ...** we hereby inform you that ...; **hierein** [ˈhiːˈrain, hiˈrain, (*emph*) ˈhiːrain] ADV (*lit*) in(to) this, in here; **hierfür** [ˈhiːˈfyːɐ, hiˈfyːɐ, (*emph*) ˈhiːfyːɐ] ADV for this; **hiergegen** [ˈhiːˈɡeːɡn̩, hiˈɡeːɡn̩, (*emph*) ˈhiːɡeːɡn̩] ADV (*lit, fig*) against this; **hierher** [ˈhiːˈheːɐ, hiˈheːɐ, (*emph*) ˈhiːheːɐ] ADV here; **(komm) ~!** come here; **bis ~** (*örtlich*) up to here; (*zeitlich*) up to now; **mir stehts bis ~** (*inf*) I'm fed up to here (*inf*); **hierherauf** [ˈhiːheˈrauf, hiːheˈrauf, (*emph*) ˈhiːheːrauf] ADV up here; **bis ~** up to here

hierher: **hierher bringen** VT IRREG to bring (over) here; **hierher fahren** IRREG **1** VI AUX SEIN to come here **2** VT *etw* to drive here; *jdn* to drive (here); **hierher gehören** VI to belong here; (*fig:* = *relevant sein*) to be relevant; **diese ~de Bemerkungen** irrelevant remarks; **hierher laufen** VI IRREG AUX SEIN to run here; **hierher gelaufen kommen** to come running up; **hierher legen** **1** VT to lay (down) here **2** VR to lie (down) here; **hierher locken** VT to entice here; **hierher setzen** **1** VT to put here **2** VR to sit (down) here; **hierher stellen** **1** VT to put here **2** VR to stand here

hierherum [ˈhiːheˈrʊm, hiːheˈrʊm, (*emph*) ˈhiːheːrʊm] ADV (a)round here; (= *in diese Richtung*) this way (a)round; (*inf:* = *ungefähr hier*) (a)round here (somewhere)

hier-: **hierhin** [ˈhiːɐˈhɪn, hiːɐˈhɪn, (*emph*) ˈhiːɐhɪn] ADV here; **~ und dorthin** here and there; **bis ~** up to here; **hierhinaus** [ˈhiːɐhiˈnaus, hiːɐhiˈnaus, (*emph*) ˈhiːɐhinaus] ADV out here;

hierhinein ['hiːɛhˈnain, hiːɛhˈnain, (emph)] 'hiːɛhˈnain] ADV in here; **hierin** ['hiˈrɪn, hiˈrɪn, (emph)] 'hiˈrɪn] ADV (lit, fig) in this; **hier lassen** VT IRREG to leave here; **hiermit** ['hiːɛ'mɪt, hiːɛ'mɪt, (emph) 'hiˈɛmɪt] ADV with this; ~ **ist der Fall erledigt** this settles the matter; ~ **bin ich einverstanden** I agree to this; ~ **erkläre ich ...** (form) I hereby declare ... (form); ~ **bestätigen wir den Eingang Ihres Briefes** we herewith acknowledge receipt of your letter; ~ **wird bescheinigt, dass ...** this is to certify that ...

Hieroglyphe [hieroˈglyːfə] F **-, -n** hieroglyph(ic); (fig hum) hieroglyphic

hier-: hier sein VI IRREG AUX SEIN to be here; **Hiersein** NT während meines ~s during my stay; **was ist der Zweck seines ~s?** what is the purpose of his being here?; **hierüber** ['hiˈryːbɐ, hiˈryːbɐ, (emph) 'hiˈryːbɐ] ADV (a) (lit) over this or here; (= oberhalb dieser Stelle) over it (b) (fig) about this; ~ **ärgere ich mich** this makes me angry; **hierum** ['hiˈrʊm, hiˈrʊm, (emph) 'hiˈrʊm] ADV (a) (lit) (a)round this or here (b) (fig) about this; ~ **handelt es sich nicht** this isn't the issue; **hierunter** ['hiˈrʊntɐ, hiˈrʊntɐ, (emph) 'hiˈrʊntɐ] ADV (a) (lit) under this or here (b) (fig) by this or that; (= in dieser Kategorie) among these; ~ **fallen auch die Sonntage** this includes Sundays; **hiervon** ['hiˈɛfɔn, hiˈɛfɔn, (emph) 'hiˈɛfɔn] ADV (a) (lit) (örtlich) from here or this; (= von diesem etc) from this; (= aus diesem Material) out of this (b) ~ **habe ich nichts gewusst** I knew nothing about this; ~ **abgesehen** apart from this; ~ **kannst du nichts haben** you can't have any of this; **hierzu** ['hiːɛ'tsuː, hiˈɛtsuː, (emph) 'hiˈɛtsu] ADV (a) (= dafür) for this; (= dazu) with this (b) (= außerdem) in addition to this (c) (= zu diesem Punkt) about this; ~ **gehören auch die Katzen** this also includes the cats; **vgl. ~ S. 370** cf p 370; **hierzulande** ['hiˈɛtsuˈlandə, (emph) 'hiˈɛtsulandə], **hier zu Lande** ADV in these parts

hiesig ['hiːzɪç] ADJ ATTR local; **die ~en Verhältnisse** local conditions; **meine ~en Verwandten** my relatives here; **er ist kein Hiesiger** he is not a local

hieß PRET von **heißen**

hieven ['hiːfn, 'hiːvn] VT (esp Naut) to heave

Hi-Fi-Anlage ['haifi-] F hi-fi system

high [hai] ADJ PRED (inf) high (inf)

Highlife ['hailaif] NT **-s**, NO PL high life; ~ **machen** (inf) to live it up (inf)

Highlight ['hailait] NT **-s, -s** highlight

Hightech [hai'tɛk] NT -, NO PL high tech

Hightech- [hai'tɛk] IN CPDS high-tech; **Hightechunternehmen** NT high-tech company

hihi [hi'hiː] INTERJ heehee

hilf [hɪlf] IMPER SING von **helfen**

Hilfe ['hɪlfə] F **-, -n (a)** NO PL help; (finanzielle) aid, assistance; (für Notleidende) relief; **zu ~! help!; um ~ rufen/schreien** to call/shout for help; **jdm zu ~ kommen** to come to sb's aid; **jdm ~ leisten** to help sb; ~ **suchend** Mensch seeking help; Blick imploring; **die ~ Suchenden** those seeking help; **sich ~ suchend umsehen** or **umblicken** to look (a)round for help; **ohne ~** without help; (= selbstständig) unaided; **etw zu ~ nehmen** to use sth; **ohne fremde ~ gehen** to walk unaided; **mit ~** = mithilfe

(b) (= Hilfsmittel, ~stellung) aid; (= Haushaltshilfe) (domestic) help; **du bist mir eine schöne ~!** (iro) a fine help YOU are (to me)! (iro)

(c) (Comput) help; **Online-~** on-line help

Hilfe-: hilfebedürftig ADJ = hilfsbedürftig; **Hilfefunktion** F (Comput) help function; **Hilfeleistung** F assistance; **unterlassene ~** (Jur) denial of assistance; **Hilferuf** M call for help; **Hilfestellung** F (Sport, fig) support; **jdm ~ geben** to give sb support; (fig auch) to back sb up; **hilfesuchend** ADJ, ADV siehe Hilfe

Hilf-: hilflos [1] ADJ helpless [2] ADV helplessly; **meinen, stammeln** uncertainly; **einer Sache** (dat) ~ **ausgeliefert sein** to be completely at the mercy of sth; **Hilflosigkeit** F -, NO PL helplessness; **hilfreich** ADJ helpful, useful; **eine ~e Hand** a helping hand

Hilfs-: Hilfsaktion F relief action; **Hilfsarbeiter(in)** M(F) labourer (Brit), laborer (US); (in Fabrik) unskilled worker; **hilfsbedürftig** ADJ in need of help; (= Not leidend) needy, in need pred; **die Hilfsbedürftigen** the needy, those in need; **hilfsbereit** ADJ helpful, ready to help pred; **Hilfsdienst** M emergency service; (bei Katastrophenfall) (emergency) relief service; **Hilfsfonds** M relief fund; **Hilfskraft** F assistant;

(= Aushilfe) temporary worker; **wissenschaftliche/fachliche ~** research/technical assistant; **Hilfsmittel** NT aid; **Hilfsorganisation** F relief organization; **Hilfsprogramm** NT **(a)** (zur Hungerhilfe etc) relief programme (Brit) or program (US) **(b)** (Comput) utility program; **Hilfssheriff** [-ʃɛrɪf] M **-s, -s** deputy sheriff; **Hilfsstoffe** PL consumables pl; **Hilfsverb** NT auxiliary or helping (US) verb; **Hilfswerk** NT relief organization; **Hilfszeitwort** NT auxiliary or helping (US) verb

hilft [hɪlft] 3. PERS SING PRES von **helfen**

Himalaja [hiˈmaːlaja, himaˈlaːja] M **-(s) der ~** the Himalayas pl

Himbeere ['hɪmbeːrə] F raspberry

Himbeer-: Himbeergeist M, NO PL (white) raspberry brandy; **Himbeerstrauch** M raspberry bush

Himmel ['hɪml] M **-s**, (poet) **- (a)** sky; **am ~** in the sky; **unter dem ~ Spaniens, unter spanischem ~** under a Spanish sky; **zwischen ~ und Erde** in midair; **jdn/etw in den ~ (er)heben** or **loben** or **rühmen** to praise sb/sth to the skies; **gute Lehrer fallen nicht vom ~** good teachers don't grow on trees **(b)** (Rel: = ~reich) heaven; **im ~** in heaven; **in den ~ kommen** to go to heaven; **der ~ auf Erden** heaven on earth; **(das) weiß der ~!** (inf) God (only) knows; **das schreit zum ~** it's a scandal; **es stinkt zum ~** (inf) it stinks to high heaven (inf); **(ach) du lieber ~!** (inf) good Heavens!; **um(s) ~s willen** (inf) for Heaven's sake (inf); ~ **und Hölle** (= Kinderspiel) hopscotch; ~ **und Hölle** or **Erde in Bewegung setzen** to move heaven and earth **(c)** (= Betthimmel etc) canopy; (im Auto) roof

Himmel-: himmelangst ['hɪml'aŋst] ADJ PRED **mir wurde ~** I was scared to death; **Himmelbett** NT four-poster (bed); **himmelblau** ADJ sky-blue; **Himmeldonnerwetter** ['hɪml'dɔnɐvɛtɐ] INTERJ (inf) damn it (inf); ~ **noch (ein)mal!** damn and blast it! (inf)

Himmelfahrt F **(a)** (Rel) **Christi ~** the Ascension of Christ; **Mariä ~** the Assumption of the Virgin Mary **(b)** (no art: = Feiertag) Ascension Day

Himmelfahrt (Ascension Day) is a public holiday in Germany and celebrates the Ascension of Christ into heaven forty days after Easter. It is also popularly called Vatertag (Father's Day) or Männertag: fathers, like mothers on Mother's Day, receive a small present from their children. Men often take advantage of the opportunity to leave their wives and children at home on this day and go out drinking with their friends.

Himmelfahrts-: Himmelfahrtskommando NT (Mil inf) suicide squad or (= Unternehmung) mission; **Himmelfahrtsnase** F (hum inf) turned-up nose

Himmel-: himmelhoch [1] ADJ sky-high [2] ADV high into the sky; ~ **jauchzend, zu Tode betrübt** up one minute and down the next; **himmelschreiend** ADJ Unrecht scandalous; Unkenntnis, Verhältnisse appalling; Unsinn utter attr; Schande crying attr

Himmels-: Himmelskörper M heavenly body; **Himmelsrichtung** F direction; **die vier ~en** the four points of the compass

himmel-: himmelweit (fig inf) [1] ADJ tremendous, fantastic (inf); **zwischen uns besteht ein ~er Unterschied** there's a world of difference between us [2] ADV ~ **voneinander entfernt** (fig), ~ **verschieden** (fig) poles apart; **sich ~ unterscheiden** to be worlds apart from each other; **wir sind noch ~ davon entfernt** we're still nowhere near it

himmlisch ['hɪmlɪʃ] [1] ADJ heavenly; **eine ~e Fügung** divine providence [2] ADV (= wunderbar) schmecken heavenly; warm, bequem wonderfully; ~ **passen** to fit perfectly; ~ **singen** to sing exquisitely; ~ **schön** just heavenly

hin [hɪn] ADV **(a)** (räumlich) **bis zum Haus ~** up to the house; **geh doch ~ zu ihr!** go to her; **nach Süden/Stuttgart ~** towards (Brit) or toward (US) the south/Stuttgart; **die Wüste erstreckt sich über 2000 km ~** the desert stretches for 2000 km; **nach außen ~** (fig) outwardly; **das Boot glitt über die Wellen ~** the boat glided along over the waves; ~ **fahre ich mit dem Zug, zurück ...** on the way out I'll take the train, coming back ...; **die Fähre geht heute Abend nur noch (zur Insel) ~** the ferry's only making the outward trip (to the island) this evening; **zur anderen Seite ~ sind es 2 km** it's 2 kms to the other side; **bis zu diesem Punkt ~** up to this point; **dreht euch/seht mal**

alle zur Tafel ~ face the/look at the blackboard
(b) (*als Teil eines Wortpaares*) **~ und her** (*räumlich*) to and fro;
(= **~ und zurück**) there and back; **etw ~ und her überlegen** to
weigh sth up; **etw ~ und her diskutieren** to discuss sth over
and over; **das Hin und Her** the comings and goings *pl*; **nach
langem Hin und Her** eventually; **Regen/Skandal ~, Regen/
Skandal her** rain/scandal or no rain/scandal; **Mörder/Sohn ~,
Mörder/Sohn her** murderer/son or not; **~ und zurück** there
and back; **eine Fahrkarte ~ und zurück** a return (ticket), a
round trip ticket (*esp US*); **einmal London ~ und zurück** a
return *or* round trip ticket (*esp US*) to London; **~ und zurück?
– nein, nur ~ bitte** return *or* round trip ticket (*esp US*) ? – no,
just a single (*Brit*) *or* one way please; **der Flug von X nach Y ~
und zurück kostet ...** the return flight *or* round trip ticket (*esp
US*) from X to Y costs ...; **~ und wieder** (every) now and then
(c) (*zeitlich*) **es sind nur noch drei Tage ~** it's only three days
(from) now; **bis zu den Wahlen sind es noch drei Wochen ~**
it's (still) three weeks till the elections; **bis dahin ist es noch
lange ~** it's a long time till then; **noch weit ~** a long way off;
über die Jahre ~ over the years; **die Kälte zog sich bis in den
Juni ~** the cold lasted up until (and during) June
(d) (*fig*) **auf meine Bitte/meinen Vorschlag ~** at my request/
suggestion; **auf meinen Brief/Anruf ~** on account of my letter/
phone call; **auf die Gefahr ~, ... zu werden** at the risk of
being ...; **auf sein Versprechen ~** on the basis of his promise;
auf seinen Rat ~ on his advice; **etw auf etw** (*acc*) **~
untersuchen/prüfen** to inspect/check sth for sth; **etw auf etw**
(*acc*) **~ planen/anlegen** to plan/design sth with sth in mind;
vor sich *acc* **~ sprechen** *etc* to talk *etc* to oneself; **vor sich** *acc*
~ stieren to stare straight ahead; **vor sich** *acc* **~ dösen** to doze
(e) (*inf: als trennbarer Bestandteil von Adverbien*) **da will ich
nicht ~** I don't want to go (there); **wo geht ihr ~?** where are
you going?
(f) (*elliptisch*) **nichts wie ~** (*inf*) let's go (then)!; **wo ist es/sie ~?**
where has it/she gone?; *siehe auch* **hin sein**

hinab [hɪˈnap] ADV, PREF = **hinunter**

hinarbeiten VI SEP **auf etw** (*acc*) **~ auf ein Ziel** to work toward(s)
sth; *auf eine Prüfung* to work for sth

hinauf [hɪˈnaʊf] ADV up; **den Berg/die Straße/den Fluss ~** up the
mountain/street/river; **die Treppe ~** up the stairs, upstairs;
dort ~ up there; **bis ~ zu** up to

hinauf- PREF *siehe auch* **herauf-, rauf-** up; **hinaufarbeiten** VR SEP
(*lit, fig*) to work one's way up; **hinaufbegleiten** *ptp*
hinaufbegleitet VT SEP to take up(stairs); **hinaufblicken** VI SEP
to look up; **hinaufbringen** VT SEP IRREG to take up;
hinauffahren SEP IRREG 🔢 VI AUX SEIN to go up 🔢 VT to take up;
hinaufführen VTI SEP to lead up; **hinaufgehen** VI SEP IRREG AUX
SEIN to go up; **mit dem Preis ~** to put up the price;
hinaufklettern VI SEP AUX SEIN to climb up; **auf einen Baum ~**
to climb up a tree; **hinaufkommen** VI SEP IRREG AUX SEIN to
come up; (= *schaffen*) to (manage to) get up; **hinaufreichen**
SEP 🔢 VI to reach up 🔢 VT to hand up; **hinaufschicken** VT SEP
to send up; **hinaufschrauben** VT SEP to screw up; (*fig*) *Preise* to
put up; *Produktion, Forderungen* to step up; **hinaufsehen** VI SEP
IRREG to look up; **hinaufsteigen** VI SEP AUX SEIN to climb
up; **hinaufziehen** SEP IRREG 🔢 VT to pull up 🔢 VI AUX SEIN to
move up 🔢 VR to pull oneself up; **sich an einem Seil ~** to pull
oneself up with a rope

hinaus [hɪˈnaʊs] ADV **(a)** (*räumlich*) ~ **(mit dir!)** (get) out!;
über (+*acc*) **~** beyond, over; **aus dem** *or* **zum Fenster ~** out of
the window; **hier/dort ~** this/that way out; **nach hinten/vorn
~ wohnen** to live towards (*Brit*) *or* toward (*US*) *or* facing the
back/the front
(b) (*zeitlich*) **auf Jahre/Monate ~** for years/months to come;
bis weit über die siebzig ~ until well over *or* past seventy; **wir
werden damit über Mittwoch ~ beschäftigt sein** we'll be busy
with that until after Wednesday
(c) (*fig*) **über** (+*acc*) **~** over and above; **darüber ~** over and
above this; *siehe auch* **hinaus sein, hinauswollen** *etc*

hinaus- PREF *siehe auch* **heraus-, raus-:** **hinausbefördern** *ptp*
hinausbefördert VT SEP *jdn* to chuck out (*inf*) (*aus* of);
hinausbegleiten *ptp* **hinausbegleitet** VT SEP to see out (*aus* of);
hinausbeugen VR SEP to lean out; **sich zum Fenster ~**
to lean out of the window; **hinausbringen** VT SEP IRREG to take
out (*aus* of); **hinausbugsieren** *ptp* **hinausbugsiert** VT SEP (*inf*)
jdn to steer out (*aus* of); **hinausdürfen** VI SEP IRREG to be
allowed (to go) out (*aus* of); **darf ich hinaus?** may I go out?;
hinausekeln VT SEP (*inf*) to drive out (*aus* of); **hinausfahren** SEP

IRREG 🔢 VI AUX SEIN **(a) aus etw ~** to go out of sth **(b)** (= *reisen*)
to go out; **aufs Meer ~** to sail out across the sea 🔢 VT *Wagen*
to drive out (*aus* of); **hinausfinden** VI SEP IRREG to find the way
out (*aus* of); **hinausfliegen** SEP IRREG 🔢 VI AUX SEIN (*aus* of)
(a) (= *fortfliegen*) to fly out; (*inf:* = *hinausfallen*) to go flying
out (*inf*) **(b)** (*inf:* = *hinausgeworfen werden*) to get kicked out
(*inf*) 🔢 VT to fly out (*aus* of); **hinausführen** SEP 🔢 VI **(a)** (= *nach
draußen führen*) to lead out (*aus* of); (= *weiter führen als*)
über etw (*acc*) **~** (*lit, fig*) to go beyond sth 🔢 VT to lead out
(*aus* of); (*Weg, Reise*) to take (*über* +*acc* beyond); **hinausgehen**
SEP IRREG AUX SEIN 🔢 VI **(a)** (= *nach draußen gehen*) to go
out(side) **(b) auf etw** (*acc*) **~** (*Tür, Zimmer*) to open onto sth;
das Fenster geht nach Osten hinaus the window faces east;
das Fenster geht zum Hof hinaus the window looks out onto
the courtyard; **zu** *or* **nach etw ~** (*Straße, Weg*) to go out to sth
(c) (*fig:* = *überschreiten*) **über etw** (*acc*) **~** to go beyond sth;
das geht über meine Kräfte hinaus it's too much for me to
cope with; **über seine Befugnisse ~** to overstep one's
authority 🔢 VI IMPERS **wo geht es hinaus?** where's the way
out?; **hinaushalten** VT SEP IRREG to hold out; **den Kopf zum
Fenster ~** to stick one's head out of the window; **hinausjagen**
SEP (*aus* of) 🔢 VT (*lit*) to drive out 🔢 VI AUX SEIN to bolt out;
hinauskommen VI SEP IRREG AUX SEIN **(a)** (= *nach außen
kommen*) to come out(side); **ich bin den ganzen Tag noch
nicht hinausgekommen** I haven't been out(side) yet today; **zu
jdm aufs Land ~** to come out to see sb in the country **(b) über
etw** (*acc*) **~** to go beyond sth; (*fig*) to get beyond sth **(c)** (*fig:*
= *hinauslaufen*) **das kommt auf dasselbe** *or* **auf eins** *or* **aufs
Gleiche hinaus** it comes down to the same thing;
hinauskomplimentieren [hɪˈnaʊskɔmplimɛntiːrən], *ptp*
hinauskomplimentiert VT SEP (*hum*) to usher out (*aus* of);
hinauslassen VT SEP IRREG (*aus* of) to leave out;
(= *hinausbegleiten*) to show out; **hinauslaufen** VI SEP IRREG AUX
SEIN (*aus* of) **(a)** (*lit*) to run out **(b)** (*fig*) **auf etw** (*acc*) **~** to
amount to sth; **es läuft auf dasselbe** *or* **auf eins** *or* **aufs
Gleiche hinaus** it comes to the same thing; **wo(rauf) soll das
~?** how's it all going to end?; **hinauslehnen** VR SEP to lean out
(*aus* of); **sich zum Fenster ~** to lean out of the window;
hinausmüssen VI SEP IRREG to have to go out (*aus* of);
hinausposaunen *ptp* **hinausposaunt** VT SEP (*inf*) to broadcast
(*inf*); **hinausschaffen** VT SEP to take out (*aus* of);
hinausschicken VT SEP to send out (*aus* of); **hinausschieben**
VT SEP IRREG **(a)** *Gegenstand* to push out (*aus* of) **(b)** (*fig*) to
put off; **hinausschmeißen** VT SEP IRREG (*inf*) to kick out (*inf*)
(*aus* of); **Hinausschmiss** M (*inf*) man drohte ihm mit **~ (aus dem
Restaurant)** they threatened to kick him out (of the
restaurant) (*inf*); **das war ein regelrechter ~** he/she *etc* was
simply kicked out (*inf*); **hinausschreien** VT SEP IRREG 🔢 VI to
shout out (*aus* of); **zum Fenster ~** to shout out of the window
🔢 VT (*geh*) *Schmerz, Hass* to proclaim (*geh*); **hinaus sein** VI
IRREG AUX SEIN **(a)** (*lit inf:* = *hinausgegangen sein*) to be out, to
have gone out **(b)** (*fig:* = *hinter sich haben*) **über etw** (*acc*) **~** to
be past sth; **hinaussteigen** VI SEP IRREG AUX SEIN to climb out
(*aus* of); **zum Fenster ~** to climb out of the window;
hinausstellen VT SEP to put *or* take out(side); *Sportler* to send
off; **hinausströmen** VI SEP AUX SEIN to pour out (*aus* of);
hinausstürmen VI SEP AUX SEIN to storm out (*aus* of);
hinausstürzen SEP (*aus* of) 🔢 VI AUX SEIN **(a)** (= *hinausfallen*) to
fall out **(b)** (= *hinauseilen*) to rush out 🔢 VR to throw oneself
out 🔢 VT to throw out; **hinauswachsen** VI SEP IRREG AUX SEIN
über etw (*acc*) **~** (*lit*) to grow taller than sth; (*fig:* durch
zunehmende Reife, Fortschritte etc) to outgrow sth; **er wuchs
über sich selbst hinaus** he surpassed himself; **hinauswagen** VR
SEP to venture out (*aus* of); **hinauswerfen** VT SEP IRREG (*aus* of)
(a) (= *nach außen werfen, wegwerfen*) to throw out; **einen
Blick ~** to glance out(side); **das ist hinausgeworfenes Geld** it's
money down the drain **(b)** (*inf:* = *entfernen*) to chuck out
(*inf*); **hinauswollen** VI SEP IRREG to want to go *or* get out (*aus* of);
worauf willst du hinaus? (*fig*) what are you getting at?; **hoch
~** to aim high; **hinausziehen** SEP IRREG 🔢 VT **(a)** (= *nach
draußen ziehen*) to pull out (*aus* of) **(b)** (*fig*) *Verhandlungen etc*
to protract; *Urlaub etc* to prolong 🔢 VI AUX SEIN to go out (*aus*
of); **in die Welt ~** to go out into the world; **aufs Land/vor die
Stadt ~** to move out into the country/out of town; **den
Dampf/Rauch ~ lassen** to let the steam/smoke out 🔢 VR
(*Verhandlungen etc*) to drag on; (*Abfahrt etc*) to be delayed
🔢 VT IMPERS **es zog ihn hinaus in die weite Welt** he felt the
urge to go out into the big wide world; **bei diesem schönen
Wetter zieht's mich hinaus** I want to be out-of-doors with the

weather like this; **hinauszögern** SEP **1** VT to delay **2** VR to be delayed

hin-: hinbekommen ptp **hinbekommen** VT SEP IRREG (inf) = **hinkriegen; hinbeordern** ptp **hinbeordert** VT SEP to summon; **hinbestellen** ptp **hinbestellt** VT SEP to tell to go/come; **hinbiegen** VT SEP IRREG (fig inf) (= in Ordnung bringen) to arrange; (= deichseln) to wangle (inf); Text, Wortlaut to twist; **die Sache** or **das werden wir schon ~** we'll sort it out somehow; **hinblättern** VT SEP (inf) to fork out (inf); **Hinblick** M **im** or **in ~ auf** (+acc) (= angesichts) in view of; (= mit Bezug auf) with regard to; **im ~ darauf, dass ...** in view of the fact that ...; **hinbringen** VT SEP IRREG **(a)** jdn, etw to take there **(b)** (fig) Zeit to spend; (in Muße) to while away **(c)** = **hinkriegen; hindenken** VI SEP IRREG **wo denkst du hin?** whatever are you thinking of!

hinderlich ['hɪndəlɪç] ADJ **~ sein** to be in the way; **einer Sache** (dat) **~ sein** to be a hindrance to sth; **eher ~ als nützlich sein** to be more of a hindrance than a help; **jdm ~ sein** to get in sb's way

hindern ['hɪndɐn] **1** VT **(a)** Fortschritte, Wachstum to impede; jdn to hinder (bei in) **(b)** (= abhalten von) to prevent (an +dat from), to stop; **ja bitte, ich will Sie nicht ~** please do, I won't stand in your way **2** VI (= stören) to be a hindrance (bei to)

Hindernis ['hɪndɐnɪs] NT **-ses, -se (a)** (lit, fig) obstacle; (= Erschwernis, Behinderung) hindrance; **gesetzliches ~** (form) legal impediment; **jdm ~se in den Weg legen** (fig) to put obstacles in sb's path or way; **eine Reise mit ~sen** a journey full of hitches **(b)** (Sport: = Hürde) hurdle; (beim Pferderennen) fence, jump; (Golf) hazard

Hindernisrennen NT steeplechase

Hinderung F **-, -en (a)** (= Behinderung) hindrance; **ohne ~** without let or hindrance (Jur) **(b)** (= Störung) obstruction

Hinderungsgrund M obstacle; **etw als ~ angeben** to give sth as an excuse

hindeuten VI SEP to point (auf +acc, zu at); **es deutet alles darauf hin, dass ...** everything indicates that ...

Hindi ['hɪndi] NT - Hindi

Hindu ['hɪndu] M **-(s), -(s)** Hindu

Hinduismus [hɪndu'ɪsmʊs] M **-, NO PL** Hinduism

hinduistisch [hɪndu'ɪstɪʃ] **1** ADJ Hindu **2** ADV **~ denken** to have Hindu beliefs; **~ beeinflusst** influenced by Hinduism; **~ erzogen werden** to be brought up (as) a Hindu

hindurch [hɪn'dʊrç] ADV **(a)** (räumlich) through; **dort ~** through there; **mitten ~** straight through; **quer ~** straight across; **durch den Wald ~** through the wood **(b)** (zeitlich) through(out); **das ganze Jahr ~** throughout the year; **die ganze Zeit ~** all the time; **Jahre ~** for years (and years); **den ganzen Tag ~** all day (long); **durch etw ~** through sth

hindürfen VI SEP IRREG to be allowed to go (zu to)

hinein [hɪ'naɪn] ADV **(a)** (räumlich) in; **da ~** in there; **nur ~!** (inf) go right in!; **~ mit dir!** (inf) in you go!; **in etw** (acc) **~** into sth; **bis in etw** (acc) **~** right inside sth; **mitten ~ in etw** (acc) right into the middle of sth; **leg es oben/unten ~** put it in the top/bottom **(b)** (zeitlich) into; **bis tief in die Nacht ~** far into the night

hinein- PREF siehe auch **ein-, herein-, rein-** in; **hineinbekommen** ptp **hineinbekommen** VT SEP IRREG (inf) to get in (in +acc -to); **hineinbringen** VT SEP IRREG **(a)** (= hineintragen) to take in (in +acc -to) **(b)** (inf: = hineinbekommen) to get in (in +acc -to); **hineinbugsieren** ptp **hineinbugsiert** VT SEP (inf) to manoeuvre (Brit) or maneuver (US) in (in +acc -to); **hineindenken** VR SEP IRREG **sich in ein Problem ~** to think oneself into a problem; **sich in jdn ~** to put oneself in sb's position; **hineindrängen** SEP (in +acc -to) **1** VT to push in **2** VIR (vi: aux sein) to push one's way in; **hineinfallen** VI SEP IRREG AUX SEIN to fall in (in +acc -to); **hineinfressen** VT SEP IRREG (inf) **etw in sich** (acc) **~** (lit) to wolf sth (down) (inf); (fig) Kummer etc to suppress sth; **hineingehen** VI SEP IRREG AUX SEIN (= hineinpassen) to go in (in +acc -to); **in den Bus gehen 50 Leute hinein** the bus holds 50 people; **hineingeraten** ptp **hineingeraten** VI SEP IRREG AUX SEIN **in etw** (acc) **~** to get into sth; **hineingucken** VI SEP (inf) (in Zimmer, Kiste) to look in (in +acc -to); (in Buch) to take a look in (in etw (acc) sth); **hineinklettern** VI SEP AUX SEIN to climb in (in +acc -to); **hineinknien** VR SEP (fig inf) **sich in etw** (acc) **~** to get into sth (inf); **hineinkommen** VI SEP IRREG AUX SEIN (in +acc -to) **(a)** (= betreten) to come in **(b)** (lit, fig: = hineingelangen können) to get in; **nach 21 Uhr kommt man nicht (mehr) hinein**

you can't get in after 9 o'clock **(c)** = **hineingeraten; hineinkomplimentieren** [hɪ'naɪnkɔmplimenti:rən], ptp **hineinkomplimentiert** VT SEP to usher in (in +acc -to); **hineinkriegen** VT SEP (inf) to get in (in +acc -to); **hineinlachen** VI SEP **in sich** acc **~** to laugh to oneself; **hineinlassen** VT SEP IRREG to let in (in +acc -to); **hineinlegen** VT SEP **(a)** (lit, fig) Gefühl etc to put in (in +acc -to) **(b)** (= hineindeuten) **etw in jds Worte** acc **~** to put sth in sb's mouth; **hineinmanövrieren** ptp **hineinmanövriert** VT SEP to manoeuvre (Brit) or maneuver (US) in (in +acc -to); **hineinpassen** VI SEP **in etw** (acc) **~** to fit into sth; (fig) to fit in with sth; **hineinpfuschen** VI SEP (inf) **jdm in seine Arbeit/Angelegenheiten ~** to meddle in sb's work/affairs; **hineinplatzen** VI SEP AUX SEIN (fig inf) to burst in (in +acc -to); **hineinprojizieren** ptp **hineinprojiziert** VT SEP to project (in +acc into); **sich in jdn ~** to project one's ideas/feelings etc into or onto sb; **hineinpumpen** VT SEP to pump in (in +acc -to); **hineinreden** VI SEP (lit: = unterbrechen) to interrupt (jdm sb); **jdm ~** (fig: = sich einmischen) to meddle in sb's affairs; **jdm in seine Angelegenheiten/Entscheidungen/in alles ~** to meddle in sb's affairs/decision-making/in all sb's affairs; **hineinregnen** VI IMPERS SEP **es regnet (ins Zimmer) hinein** (the) rain is coming in(to) the room; **hineinschaffen** VT SEP to bring/take in (in +acc -to); **hineinschlagen** VT SEP IRREG (in +acc -to) Nagel to knock in; Eier to break in; Krallen to sink in; **ein Loch ins Eis ~** to knock a hole in the ice; **hineinschleichen** VR SEP IRREG (vi: aux sein) to creep in (in +acc -to); **hineinschliddern** [-ʃlɪdɐn] VI SEP AUX SEIN **in etw** (acc) **~** to get mixed up with sth; **hineinschlingen** VT SEP IRREG **etw (gierig) in sich** (acc) **~** to devour sth (greedily); **hineinschlittern** VI SEP AUX SEIN (inf) = **hineinschliddern; hineinschlüpfen** VI SEP AUX SEIN to slip in (in +acc -to); **hineinschmuggeln** VT SEP to smuggle in (in +acc -to); **hineinschreiben** VT SEP IRREG to write in (in etw (acc) sth); **hineinschütten** VT SEP to pour in (in +acc -to); **etw in sich** acc **~** (inf) to knock sth back (inf); **hineinsehen** VI SEP IRREG to look in; **ins Zimmer/Fenster ~** to look into the room/in at the window; **sich** (dat) **in etw** acc **~ lassen** to keep sth to oneself; **hineinspielen** VI SEP (= beeinflussen) to have a part to play (in +acc in); **in etw** (acc) **~** (= grenzen an) to verge on sth; **da spielen noch andere Gesichtspunkte hinein** other factors enter into it; **hineinsprechen** VI SEP **ins Mikrofon ~** to speak into the microphone; **hineinstecken** VT SEP to put in (in +acc -to); **Geld/Arbeit** etc **in etw** (acc) **~** to put money/some work etc into sth; **hineinsteigern** VR SEP to get worked up; **sich in seine Wut/Hysterie/seinen Ärger ~** to work oneself up into a rage/hysterics/a temper; **sich in seinen Kummer ~** to let oneself be completely taken up with one's worries; **sich in seinen Schmerz ~** to let the pain take one over completely; **sie hat sich in die Vorstellung hineingesteigert, dass ...** she has managed to convince herself that ...; **sich in eine Rolle ~** to become completely caught up in a role; **hineinstopfen** VT SEP to stuff in (in +acc -to); **Essen in sich** (acc) **~** to stuff oneself (with food) (inf); **hineinströmen** VI SEP AUX SEIN to flood in (in +acc -to); (geh: Menschenmassen) to pour in (in +acc -to); **hineinstürzen** SEP **1** VI AUX SEIN to rush in (in +acc -to); (= hineineilen) to rush in (in +acc -to); **zur Tür ~** to rush in through the door **2** VT to throw in (in +acc -to) **3** VR to plunge in (in +acc -to); **sich in die Arbeit ~** to throw oneself into one's work; **sich ins Vergnügen ~** to plunge in and start enjoying oneself; **hineintreiben** VT SEP IRREG to drive in (in +acc -to); **jdn in etw** (acc) **~** (fig) to force sb into sth; **hineintun** VT SEP IRREG to put in (in +acc -to); **einen Blick in etw** (acc) **~** to take a look in sth; (ins Buch etc) to take a look at sth; **hineinversetzen** ptp **hineinversetzt** VR SEP **sich in jdn** or **in jds Lage ~** to put oneself in sb's position; **sich in eine Rolle ~** to empathize with a part; **hineinwagen** VR SEP to venture in (in +acc -to); **hineinwerfen** VT SEP IRREG to throw in (in +acc -to); **den Ball durchs Fenster ~** to throw the ball in through the window; **hineinwollen** VI SEP (inf) to want to go in (in +acc -to); **das will mir nicht in den Kopf hinein** I just can't understand it; **hineinziehen** SEP IRREG **1** VT to pull in (in +acc -to); **jdn in eine Angelegenheit/einen Streit ~** to drag sb into an affair/a quarrel **2** VI (in +acc -to) to go in; (in ein Haus) to move in; **hineinzwängen** SEP (in +acc -to) **1** VT to force in **2** VR to squeeze (oneself) in

hin-: hinfahren SEP IRREG **1** VI AUX SEIN to go there; **mit der Hand über etw** (acc) **~** to run one's hand over sth **2** VT to drive there; **Hinfahrt** F journey there; (Naut) voyage out; (Rail) outward journey; **auf der ~** on the way there *etc*; **hinfallen** VI SEP IRREG AUX SEIN to fall (down)

hinfällig ADJ **(a)** *Mensch* frail **(b)** (*fig*: = *ungültig*) invalid; **etw ~ machen** to render sth invalid

hin-: **hinfinden** VI SEP IRREG (*inf*) to find one's way there; **hinfläzen, hinflegeln** VR SEP (*inf*) to loll around; **hinfliegen** VI SEP IRREG AUX SEIN to fly there; (*inf*: = *hinfallen*) to fall flat on one's face (*inf*); **der Ball flog über die Köpfe hin** the ball flew over their heads; **Hinflug** M outward flight; **hinführen** ◼1 VT to lead there; **jdn zu etw ~** (*fig*) to lead sb to sth ◼2 VI to lead there; **wo soll das ~?** (*fig*) where is this leading to?

hing PRET *von* hängen

Hingabe F, NO PL (*fig*) (= *Begeisterung*) dedication; (= *Selbstlosigkeit*) devotion; (= *völliges Aufgehen*) (self-)abandon; **mit ~ tanzen/singen** *etc* to dance/sing *etc* with abandon

hingeben SEP IRREG ◼1 VT to give up; *Leben* to sacrifice ◼2 VR **sich einer Sache** (*dat*) **~ der Arbeit** to devote oneself to sth; *dem Laster, Genuss, der Verzweiflung* to abandon oneself to sth; **sich Hoffnungen ~** to cherish hopes; **sich einer Illusion ~** to labour (*Brit*) *or* labor (*US*) under an illusion; **sie gab sich ihm hin** she gave herself to him

hingebungsvoll ◼1 ADJ (= *selbstlos*) devoted; (= *begeistert*) abandoned ◼2 ADV (= *selbstlos*) devotedly; (= *begeistert*) with abandon; *lauschen* raptly

hingegen [hɪnˈgeːgn] CONJ (*geh*) however

hin-: **hingegossen** [ˈhɪngəɡɔsn] ADJ (*fig inf*) **sie lag/saß wie ~ auf dem Bett** she had draped herself artistically on the bed; **hingehen** VI SEP IRREG AUX SEIN **(a)** (= *dorthin gehen*) to go (there); **gehst du auch hin?** are you going too?; **wo gehst du hin?** where are you going?; **wo geht es hier hin?** where does this go? **(b)** (*Zeit*) to pass **(c)** (*fig*: = *tragbar sein*) **das geht gerade noch hin** that will just about do; **diesmal mag es noch ~** I'll let it go this once; **(jdm) etw ~ lassen** to let sb get away with sth; **hingehören** ptp **hingehört** VI SEP to belong; **wo gehört das hin?** where does this belong?; **hingerissen** ◼1 ADJ enraptured; **hin- und hergerissen sein** to be torn (*zwischen* between); **ich bin ganz hin- und hergerissen** (*iro*) absolutely fantastic! (*iro*) ◼2 ADV with rapt attention; *siehe auch* **hinreißen**; **Hingucker** [-ɡʊkɐ] M **-s, -** (*inf*: = *Sache*) eye-catcher (*inf*); **hinhaben** VT SEP IRREG (*inf*) **wo willst du dies ~?** where do you want this (to go)?; **hinhalten** VT SEP IRREG **(a)** (= *entgegenstrecken*) to hold out (*jdm* to sb) **(b)** (*fig*) *jdn* to put off

Hinhaltetaktik F delaying tactics *pl*

hinhauen SEP IRREG (*inf*) ◼1 VT **(a)** (= *nachlässig machen*) to knock off (*inf*) **(b)** (= *hinwerfen*) to slam down ◼2 VI **(a)** (= *zuschlagen*) to hit hard; **(mit der Faust) ~** to thump *or* clobber (*inf*) it/sth (with one's fist) **(b)** (= *gut gehen*) **es hat hingehauen** I/we *etc* just managed it; **das wird schon ~** it will be OK (*inf*) **(c)** (= *klappen, in Ordnung sein*) to work; **ich habe das so lange geübt, bis es hinhaute** I practised (*Brit*) *or* practiced (*US*) it till I could do it ◼3 VR (*inf*: = *sich schlafen legen*) to crash out (*inf*) ◼4 VI IMPERS **es hat ihn hingehauen** he fell over

hinhören VI SEP to listen

Hinkebein [ˈhɪŋkəbain] NT, **Hinkefuß** [ˈhɪŋkəfuːs] M (*inf*: = *verletztes Bein*) gammy leg (*inf*)

Hinkelstein [ˈhɪŋkl-] M (*inf*) menhir

hinken [ˈhɪŋkn] VI **(a)** (= *gehbehindert sein*) to limp; **mit** *or* **auf dem rechten Bein ~** to have a limp in one's right leg **(b)** AUX SEIN (= *sich fortbewegen*) to limp **(c)** (*fig*) *Beispiel* to be inappropriate; (*Vergleich*) to be misleading; (*Vers, Reim*) to be clumsy

hin-: **hinklotzen** VT SEP (*inf*) *Hochhäuser etc* to throw up; **hinknallen** SEP (*inf*) ◼1 VT to slam down ◼2 VI AUX SEIN to fall flat; **hinknien** VIR SEP (*vi: aux sein*) to kneel (down); **hinkommen** VI SEP IRREG AUX SEIN **(a)** (= *an einen Ort ~*) **(da) ~** to get there; **nach X ~** to get to X; **kommst du mit mir hin?** are you coming too?; **wie komme ich zu dir hin?** how do I get to your place? **(b)** (= *an bestimmten Platz gehören*) to go; **wo ist das Buch hingekommen?** where has the book gone?; **wo kämen wir denn hin, wenn ...** (*inf*) where would we be if ... **(c)** (*inf*: = *in Ordnung kommen*) **das kommt schon noch hin** that will turn out OK (*inf*) **(d)** (*inf*: = *auskommen*) to manage; **wir**

kommen (damit) hin we will manage **(e)** (*inf*: = *ausreichen, stimmen*) to be right; **hinkriegen** VT SEP (*inf*) **(a)** (= *fertig bringen*) to manage; **das hast du gut hingekriegt** you've made a nice job of it; **wie kriegt sie das bloß immer hin?** I don't know how she does it **(b)** (= *in Ordnung bringen*) to mend, to fix; (*gesundheitlich*) to cure; **Hinkunft** F (*Aus*) **in ~** in (the) future; **hinkünftig** (*Aus*) ◼1 ADJ future ◼2 ADV in (the) future; **hinlangen** VI SEP (*inf*) **(a)** (= *zupacken*) to grab him/her/it *etc*; (= *ziehen/schieben*) to pull/push hard; (*dial*: = *anfassen*) to touch; (= *zuschlagen*) to take a (good) swipe (*inf*); (= *sich bedienen*) to help oneself to a lot; (= *viel Geld verlangen*) to overcharge **(b)** (= *ausreichen*) to do; (*Geld*) to stretch; **hinlänglich** [ˈhɪnlɛŋlɪç] ◼1 ADJ (= *ausreichend*) adequate; **keine ~e Anzahl** an insufficient number ◼2 ADV (= *ausreichend*) adequately; (= *zu Genüge*) sufficiently; **~ bekannt sein** to be common knowledge; **hinlaufen** VI SEP IRREG AUX SEIN **(a)** (= *zu bestimmter Stelle laufen*) to run there; (= *vorbei-, entlang-, dahinlaufen*) to run; (*inf*: *zu Veranstaltung, Amt, Rechtsanwalt etc*) to rush **(b)** (*dial inf*: = *nicht fahren*) to walk; **hinlegen** ◼1 VT **(a)** (= *hintun*) to put down; *Zettel* to leave (*jdm* for sb); (= *flach legen*) *Verletzten etc* to lay down; (*ins Bett, zum Schlafen*) to put to bed; (*inf*: = *bezahlen müssen*) to fork out (*inf*) **(b)** (*inf*: = *glänzend darbieten*) to perform; *Rede, Vortrag* to give effortlessly and brilliantly; **er hat einen tollen Stepptanz hingelegt** he did a neat bit of tap-dancing ◼2 VR to lie down; **hinlegen!** (*Mil*) down!; **sich lang ~, sich der Länge nach ~** (*inf*) to fall flat; **da legst du dich (lang) hin!** (*inf*) it's unbelievable

hinmachen SEP (*inf*) ◼1 VT **(a)** (= *anbringen*) to put on; *Bild* to put up **(b)** (= *kaputtmachen*) to ruin ◼2 VI (= *Notdurft verrichten*) to do one's/its *etc* business (*euph*)

Hin-: **hinmüssen** VI SEP IRREG to have to go; **hinnehmen** VT SEP IRREG **(a)** (= *ertragen*) to take; *Beleidigung* to swallow; **etw als selbstverständlich ~** to take sth for granted **(b)** (*inf*: = *mitnehmen*) to take; **hinreichend** ◼1 ADJ (= *ausreichend*) adequate; (= *genug*) sufficient; (= *reichlich*) ample; **keine ~en Beweise** insufficient evidence ◼2 ADV *lange, oft* enough; *aufklären, informieren* adequately; **es ist noch ~ Zeit** there is ample time; **Hinreise** F outward journey; (*mit Schiff*) outward voyage; **Hin- und Rückreise** journey there and back; **auf der ~** on the way there; **hinreißen** VT SEP IRREG (*fig*) **(a)** (= *begeistern*) to thrill; *siehe auch* **hingerissen** **(b)** (= *überwältigen*) **jdn zu etw ~** to force sb into sth; **die Zuschauer zu Beifallsstürmen ~** to elicit thunderous applause from the audience; **sich ~ lassen** to let oneself be carried away; **hinreißend** ◼1 ADJ fantastic; *Landschaft, Anblick* enchanting; *Schönheit, Mensch* captivating; *Redner* fantastic ◼2 ADV (= *schön*) **aussehen** to look quite enchanting; **~ (schön) Klavier spielen** to play the piano quite enchantingly; **hinrichten** VT SEP to execute; **jdn durch den Strang ~** to hang sb; **jdn durch den elektrischen Stuhl ~** to execute sb on the electric chair

Hinrichtung F execution

hin-: **hinsagen** VT SEP to say without thinking; **hinschaffen** VT SEP to get there; **hinschicken** VT SEP to send; **hinschmeißen** VT SEP IRREG (*inf*) (= *hinwerfen*) to fling down (*inf*); (*fig*: = *aufgeben*) *Arbeit etc* to chuck in (*inf*); **hinschreiben** SEP IRREG ◼1 VT to write; (= *flüchtig niederschreiben*) to scribble down (*inf*); *Aufsatz* to dash off ◼2 VI (*inf*) to write (there); **hinsehen** VI SEP IRREG to look; **ich kann (gar) nicht ~** I can't bear to look; **bei genauerem Hinsehen** on looking more carefully

hin sein VI IRREG AUX SEIN (*inf*) **(a)** (= *kaputt sein*) to have had it; **hin ist hin** what's done is done **(b)** (= *erschöpft sein*) to be exhausted **(c)** (= *verloren sein*) to be lost; (*Ruhe*) to have disappeared; (= *ruiniert sein*) to be in ruins **(d)** (= *tot sein*) to have kicked the bucket (*inf*) **(e)** (= *begeistert sein*) **(von etw) hin (und weg) sein** to be mad about sth; *siehe auch* **hin**

hinsetzen SEP ◼1 VT to put *or* set down; *jdn* to seat, to put; *Kind* to sit down ◼2 VR **(a)** (*lit*) to sit down; **sich gerade ~** to sit up straight **(b)** (*inf*: = *sich bemühen*) to buckle down to it

Hinsicht F, NO PL **in dieser ~** in this respect; **in mancher** *or* **gewisser ~** in some respects; **in jeder ~** in every respect; **in finanzieller ~** financially; **in wirtschaftlicher ~** economically; **in beruflicher ~** with regard to my/his *etc* job; **in ~ auf** (+*acc*) (= *bezüglich*) with regard to; (= *in Anbetracht*) in view of

hinsichtlich [ˈhɪnzɪçtlɪç] PREP +GEN (= *bezüglich*) with regard to; (= *in Anbetracht*) in view of

hin-: **Hinspiel** NT (*Sport*) first leg; **hinstarren** VI SEP to stare; **hinstellen** SEP ◼1 VT **(a)** (= *niederstellen*) to put down; (*an*

bestimmte Stelle) to put; (*inf*) *Gebäude* to put up
(b) (= *auslegen*) *Vorfall, Angelegenheit, Sachlage* to describe; **jdn/etw als jdn/etw ~** (= *bezeichnen*) to make sb/sth out to be sb/sth **2** VR to stand; (*Fahrer*) to park; **sich gerade ~** to stand up straight; **sich vor jdn** *or* **jdm ~** to stand in front of sb; **sie hat sich vor mich/ihn hingestellt** she came and stood in front of me/went and stood in front of him; **sich als etw ~** (*fig*) to make oneself out to be sth; **hinstrecken** VT SEP *Hand, Gegenstand* to hold out

hintanstellen [hɪntˈʔanˌ] VT SEP (= *zurückstellen*) to put last; (= *vernachlässigen*) to neglect

hinten [ˈhɪntn̩] ADV **(a)** behind; **von ~** from the back; (*bei Menschen auch*) from behind; **nach ~** to the back; **von weit ~** from the very back; **~ im Buch/in der Schlange** at the back of the book/queue (*Brit*) *or* line (*US*); **~ auf der Liste** at the end of the list; **sich ~ anstellen** to join the end of the queue (*Brit*) *or* line (*US*); **~ im Bild** in the back of the picture; **nach ~ laufen** to run to the back; **von ~ anfangen** to begin from the end; **das Alphabet von ~ aufsagen** to say the alphabet backwards; **etw ~ anfügen** to add sth at the end
(b) (= *am rückwärtigen Ende, auf der Rückseite*) at the back; (*Naut*) aft; (= *am Gesäß*) on one's behind; **von ~** from behind; **~ im Auto/Bus** in the back of the car/bus; **der Blinker ~** the rear indicator (*esp Brit*) *or* blinker (*US*); **das Buch ist ~ schmutzig** the back (cover) of the book is dirty; **ein nach ~ gelegenes Zimmer** a room facing the back; **ein Blick nach ~** a look behind; **~ und vorn nichts haben** (*inf*) to be as flat as a pancake (*esp Brit inf*) *or* board (*US inf*); **nach ~** to the back; **fallen, ziehen** backwards; **etw von ~ und vorn betrachten** (*fig*) to consider sth from all angles
(c) (= *weit entfernt*) **das Auto da ~** the car back there; **sie waren ziemlich weit ~** they were quite far back
(d) (*fig*) **~ und vorn** *betrügen* left, right and centre (*Brit*) *or* center (*US*); *bedienen* hand and foot; *verwöhnen* rotten (*inf*); **das stimmt ~ und vorn nicht, das stimmt weder ~ noch vorn** that is absolutely untrue; **das reicht** *or* **langt ~ und vorn nicht** *or* **weder ~ noch vorn** that's nowhere near enough; **dann heißt es Frau Schmidt ~ und Frau Schmidt vorn** then it's Mrs Schmidt this and Mrs Schmidt that; **ich weiß nicht mehr, wo ~ und vorn ist** I don't know whether I'm coming or going

hinten-: hintendran [ˈhɪntnˈdran] ADV (*inf*) (= *am hinteren Ende*) at the back; (*fig*: = *im Hintertreffen*) behind; **hintenherum** [ˈhɪntnhɛˈrʊm] ADV **(a)** (= *von der hinteren Seite*) from the back; **kommen Sie ~** come (a)round the back **(b)** (*fig inf*) (= *auf Umwegen*) in a roundabout way; (= *illegal*) under the counter; **hintenüber** [ˈhɪntnˈlyːbɐ] ADV backwards

hinter [ˈhɪntɐ] PREP +DAT *or* (*mit Bewegungsverben*) +ACC
(a) (*räumlich*) behind; **~ jdm/etw her** behind sb/sth; **~ etw** (*acc*) **kommen** (*fig*: = *herausfinden*) to get to the bottom of sth; **~ die Wahrheit kommen** to get to the truth; **sich ~ jdn stellen** (*lit*) to stand behind sb; (*fig*) to support sb; **~ jdm/etw stehen** (*lit, fig*) to be behind sb/sth; **jdn ~ sich** (*dat*) **haben** (*lit, fig*) to have sb behind one; **jdn weit ~ sich** (*dat*) **lassen** to leave sb far behind; **~ etw** (*dat*) **stecken, sich ~ etw** (*dat*) **verbergen** to be behind sth; **~ seinen Reden steckt nicht viel** there's not much in his speeches
(b) +DAT (= *nach*) after; **vier Kilometer ~ Glasgow/~ der Grenze** four kilometres (*Brit*) *or* kilometers (*US*) outside Glasgow/beyond the border; **~ diesem Satz steht ein Fragezeichen** there is a question mark at the end of this sentence
(c) +DAT (*in Rangfolge*) after; (*in Bedeutung*) behind
(d) **etw ~ sich** (*dat*) **haben** (= *zurückgelegt haben*) to have got through sth; *Strecke* to have covered sth; *Land* to have left sth; (= *überstanden haben*) to have got sth over (and done) with; *Krankheit, Zeit* to have been through sth; *anstrengende Tage* to have had sth; *Studium* to have completed sth; **sie hat viel ~ sich** she has been through a lot; **das Schlimmste haben wir ~ uns** we are over the worst; **etw ~ sich** (*acc*) **bringen** to get sth over (and done) with; *Strecke* to cover sth; *Arbeit* to get sth done; **das liegt ~ ihr** that is behind her; **sich ~ etw** (*acc*) **machen** to get down to sth
(e) (*inf*) = **dahinter**

Hinter-: Hinterachse F rear axle; **Hinterausgang** M back exit; **Hinterbänkler** [-bɛŋklɐ] M **-s, -**, **Hinterbänklerin** [-ərɪn] F **-, -nen** (*Pol pej*) backbencher; **Hinterbein** NT hind leg; **sich auf die ~e stellen** *or* **setzen** (*lit*) to rear up (on one's hind legs); (*fig inf*) (= *sich widersetzen*) to kick up a fuss (*inf*); (= *sich anstrengen*) to pull one's socks up (*inf*)

hintere ADJ = **hintere(r, s)**

hintereinander [hɪntɐlaɪˈnandɐ] ADV (*räumlich*) one behind the other; (= *in Reihenfolge, nicht gleichzeitig, ohne Unterbrechung*) one after the other; **~ hereinkommen** to come in one by one; **dicht ~** (*räumlich*) close behind one another; (*zeitlich*) close on one another; **zwei Tage ~** two days running; **dreimal ~** three times in a row; **etw ~ tun** (= *nicht gleichzeitig*) to do sth one after the other; (= *der Reihe nach*) to do sth in turn; (= *ohne Unterbrechung*) to do sth in one go

hintereinander-: hintereinanderher ADV behind one another; **hintereinander schalten** VT (*Elec*) to connect in series; **hintereinanderweg** [hɪntɐlaɪnandɐˈvɛk] ADV (*zeitlich*) running; (= *nacheinander*) one after the other

Hintereingang M rear entrance

hintere(r, s) [ˈhɪntərə] ADJ back; (*von Tier, Gebäude, Zug auch*) rear; **der/die/das Hintere** the one at the back; **das ~ Ende des Saals** the back of the room; **die Hinteren** those at the back; **am ~n Ende** at the far end; *siehe auch* **hinterste(r, s)**

Hinter-: hinterfragen *ptp* **hinterfragt** VT INSEP to question; **etw kritisch ~** to examine sth critically; **Hintergedanke** M ulterior motive; **ohne ~n** without any ulterior motive(s); **hintergehen** *ptp* **hintergangen** VT INSEP IRREG to deceive

Hintergrund M (*von Bild, Raum*) background; (*von Bühne, Saal*) back; (*fig*: = *verborgene Zusammenhänge*) background *no pl* (+*gen* to); **im ~** in the background; **vor dem ~** (*lit, fig*) against the background; **im ~ bleiben/stehen** (*lit, fig*) to stay/be in the background; **in den ~ treten** *or* **rücken** (*fig*) to be pushed into the background

hintergründig [ˈhɪntɐɡrʏndɪç] **1** ADJ cryptic **2** ADV cryptically

Hintergrund-: Hintergrundinformation F USU PL background information *no pl* (*über* +*acc* about, on); **Hintergrundprogramm** NT (*Comput*) background program

Hinter-: Hinterhalt M **(a)** ambush; **jdn aus dem ~ überfallen** to ambush sb; **im ~ lauern** *or* **liegen** to lie in wait *or* (*esp Mil*) ambush **(b)** (*inf*) **etw im ~ haben** to have sth in reserve; **ohne ~** unreservedly; **hinterhältig** [ˈhɪntɐhɛltɪç] **1** ADJ devious **2** ADV in an underhand way, deviously; **Hinterhältigkeit** F **-, -en** deviousness; (= *Handlung*) devious act; **Hinterhaus** NT *part of a tenement house accessible only through a courtyard and thus considered inferior*

hinterher [hɪntɐˈheːɐ, ˈhɪntɐheːɐ] ADV (*räumlich*) behind; (*zeitlich*) afterwards

hinterher-: hinterherfahren VI SEP IRREG AUX SEIN to drive behind (*jdm* sb); **hinterherhinken** VI SEP AUX SEIN to limp behind (*jdm* sb); (*fig*) to lag behind (*hinter etw* (*dat*) sth, *mit* with, in); **hinterherlaufen** VI SEP IRREG AUX SEIN to run behind (*jdm* sb); **jdm ~** (*fig inf*) to run after sb; **hinterherschicken** VT SEP to send on (*jdm* to sb); **jdn ~** to send after (*jdm* sb); **hinterher sein** VI IRREG AUX SEIN (*inf*) (*lit*: = *verfolgen*) to be after (*jdm* sb); (*fig*: = *zurückgeblieben sein*) to lag behind (*jdm* sb); **~, dass ...** to see to it that ...

Hinter-: Hinterhof M back yard; (*zwischen Vorder- und Hinterhaus*) courtyard; **Hinterkopf** M back of one's head; **etw im ~ haben/behalten** (*inf*) to have/keep sth in the back of one's mind; **Hinterlage** F (*Sw*) security; **Hinterland** NT hinterland; (*Ind*) back-up area; **hinterlassen** *ptp* **hinterlassen** VT INSEP IRREG to leave; (*testamentarisch auch*) to bequeath (*jdm etw* so sth, sth to sb); **~e Werke/Schriften** posthumous works; **hinterlegen** *ptp* **hinterlegt** VT INSEP **(a)** (= *verwahren lassen*) to deposit **(b)** (= *als Pfand ~*) to leave; **Hinterlegung** [hɪntɐˈleːɡʊŋ] F **-, -en** deposit

Hinterlist F **(a)** (= *Tücke*) craftiness; (= *Verrat*) treachery **(b)** (= *Trick, List*) ruse

hinterlistig **1** ADJ (= *tückisch*) crafty; (= *verräterisch*) treacherous; (= *betrügerisch*) deceitful **2** ADV (= *tückisch*) cunningly; (= *betrügerisch*) deceitfully

Hintermann M, *pl* **-männer (a)** person behind; (= *Auto*) car behind; **mein ~** the person/car behind me **(b)** (*inf*) (= *Gewährsmann*) contact; **die Hintermänner des Skandals** the men behind the scandal

Hintern [ˈhɪntɐn] M **-s, -** (*inf*) backside (*inf*); **jdm den ~ versohlen** to tan sb's hide; **ein paar auf den ~ bekommen** to get one's bottom smacked (*inf*); **den ~ voll bekommen** to get one's bottom smacked (*inf*); **sich ~ setzen** (= *hinfallen*) to fall on one's bottom *etc*; (= *eifrig arbeiten*) to buckle down to work; **jdm in den ~ kriechen** to suck up to sb; **ich könnte mir** *or* **mich in den ~ beißen** I could kick myself

Hinter-: Hinterrad NT rear wheel; **Hinterradantrieb** M rear wheel drive; **hinterrücks** ['hɪntɐryks] ADV from behind; (*fig:* = *heimtückisch*) behind sb's back; *ermorden* treacherously

Hinterseite F back; (*von Münze*) reverse side

hinterste(r, s) ['hɪntəstə] ADJ SUPERL *von* **hintere(r, s)** very back; (= *entlegenste*) remotest; **die Hintersten** those at the very back; **das ~ Ende** the very end *or* (*von Saal*) back; **das Hinterste zuvorderst kehren** (*inf*) to turn everything upside down

Hinter-: Hinterteil NT **(a)** (*inf*) backside (*inf*); (*von Tier*) hindquarters *pl* **(b)** AUCH M (= *hintere Teil*) back part; **Hintertreffen** NT **im ~ sein** to be at a disadvantage; **ins ~ geraten** *or* **kommen** to fall behind; **hintertreiben** *ptp* **hintertrieben** VT INSEP IRREG (*fig*) to foil; *Gesetz* to block; **Hintertreppe** F back stairs *pl*; **Hintertupfingen** ['hɪntɐ'tʊpfɪŋən] NT **-s**, NO PL (*inf*) the back of beyond (*esp Brit*), the middle of nowhere; **Hintertür** F, (*Aus*) **Hintertürl** [-tyːɐl] NT **-s, -n** back door; (*fig inf:* = *Ausweg, Umweg*) loophole; **durch die ~** (*fig*) through the back door; **sich** (*dat*) **eine ~** *or* **ein ~chen offen halten** *or* **offen lassen** (*fig*) to leave oneself a way out *or* a loophole; **hinterziehen** *ptp* **hinterzogen** VT INSEP IRREG *Steuern* to evade; *Material* to appropriate; **Hinterziehung** F (*von Steuern*) evasion; (*von Material*) appropriation; **Hinterzimmer** NT back room

hin-: hintreten VI SEP IRREG **(a)** AUX SEIN **vor jdn ~** to go up to sb; **vor Gott ~** to step before sb; **zu jdm/etw ~** to step over to sb/sth **(b)** (= *mit Fuß stoßen*) to kick; **hintun** VT SEP IRREG (*inf*) to put; **ich weiß nicht, wo ich ihn ~ soll** (*fig*) I can't (quite) place him

hinüber [hɪ'nyːbɐ] ADV over; (*über Grenze, Straße, Fluss auch*) across; **da ~** over there; **~ und herüber** back and forth; **quer ~** right across; *siehe auch* **hinüber sein**

hinüber- PREF *siehe auch* **herüber-**, **rüber-: hinüberbefördern** *ptp* **hinüberbefördert** VT SEP to transport across (*über etw* (*acc*) sth); **hinüberbringen** VT SEP IRREG to take across (*über etw* (*acc*) sth); **hinüberdämmern** VI SEP AUX SEIN (= *einschlafen*) to doze off; (= *sterben*) to pass away in one's sleep; **hinüberfahren** SEP IRREG ◼ VT (*über etw* (*acc*) sth) *jdn* to take across; *Auto* to drive across ◼ VI AUX SEIN to travel across; **nach Frankreich ~** to go across to France; **über den Fluss ~** to cross the river; **hinüberführen** SEP ◼ VT *jdn* (*über die Straße/dort/in das andere Zimmer*) ~ to take sb across the street)/over (there)/ over (into the other room) ◼ VI (= *verlaufen: Straße, Brücke*) to go across (*über etw* (*acc*) sth); **hinübergehen** VI SEP IRREG AUX SEIN (= *hingehen*) to go across; (*zu anderem Haus, zu jdm*) to go over (*über etw* (*acc*) sth); **hinüberhelfen** VI SEP IRREG **jdm ~** to help sb across (*über etw* (*acc*) sth); (*fig: über Schwierigkeiten*) to help sb out (*über* +*acc* of); **hinüberlassen** VT SEP IRREG to let across; (*über Kreuzung, Brücke auch, zu Besuch*) to let over (*über etw* (*acc*) sth); **hinüberreichen** SEP ◼ VT to pass across; (*über Zaun etc*) to pass over (*jdm* to sb, *über etw* (*acc*) sth) ◼ VI to reach across (*über etw* (*acc*) sth); (*fig*) to extend (*in* +*acc* into); **hinüberretten** SEP ◼ VT to bring to safety; (*fig*) *Humor, Tradition* to keep alive; **etw in die Gegenwart ~** to keep sth alive ◼ VR (*über Grenze*) to reach safety; **hinüberschicken** VT SEP to send across *or* (*zu Besuch*) over (*über etw* (*acc*) sth); **hinüberschwimmen** VI SEP IRREG AUX SEIN to swim across (*über etw* (*acc*) sth); **hinüber sein** VI IRREG AUX SEIN (*inf*) **(a)** (= *verdorben sein*) to be off; (= *kaputt, unbrauchbar, tot sein*) to have had it (*inf*); (= *ruiniert sein: Firma, Politiker*) to be done for (*inf*) **(b)** (= *betrunken sein*) to be well away (*inf*); (= *betäubt sein*) to be (knocked) out (*inf*); **hinüberwechseln** VI SEP AUX HABEN *or* SEIN to change over (*zu, in* +*acc* to); **zu einer anderen Partei ~** to go over to another party

hin und her *siehe* **hin**

Hinundhergerede NT (*inf*) **das ewige ~** this continual carrying-on (*inf*)

Hin- und Rück-: Hin- und Rückfahrt F return journey; **Hin- und Rückflug** M return flight; **Hin- und Rückweg** M round trip

hinunter [hɪ'nʊntɐ] ◼ ADV down; **bis ~ zu** down to; **ins Tal ~** down into the valley; **dort** *or* **da ~** down there; **~ mit ihm!** down with him; **~ mit der Arznei** get this medicine down ◼ PREP +ACC (*nachgestellt*) down

hinunter- PREF *siehe auch* **herunter-**, **runter-** down; **hinunterbringen** VT SEP IRREG to take down; (*inf:* = *schlucken können*) to be able to get down; **hinunterfahren** SEP IRREG ◼ VI AUX SEIN to go down ◼ VT *jdn* to take down; *Fahrzeug* to drive down; **hinunterfließen** VI SEP IRREG AUX SEIN to flow down;

hinuntergehen VI SEP IRREG AUX SEIN to go down; (*Flugzeug*) to descend (*auf* +*acc* to); **hinunterkippen** VT SEP to tip down; (*inf*) *Getränke* to knock back (*inf*); **hinunterklettern** VI SEP AUX SEIN to climb down; **hinunterlassen** VT SEP IRREG to lower; **er lässt mich nicht hinunter** (*inf*) he won't let me get down; **hinunterlaufen** VI SEP IRREG AUX SEIN to run down; **es lief ihm eiskalt den Rücken hinunter** a shiver ran down his spine; **hinunterschalten** VI SEP (*Aut*) to change *or* shift (*US*) down; **hinunterschlingen** VT SEP IRREG (*inf*) to gulp down; *Essen* to gobble down; **hinunterschlucken** VT SEP to swallow (down); (*fig*) *Beleidigung* to swallow; *Kritik* to take; *Ärger, Tränen* to choke back; **hinuntersehen** VI SEP IRREG to look down; **hinunterspülen** VT SEP **(a)** (*in Toilette, Ausguss*) to flush away; **etw die Toilette/den Ausguss ~** to flush sth down the toilet/ drain **(b)** *Essen, Tablette* to wash down; (*fig*) *Ärger* to soothe; **hinunterstürzen** SEP ◼ VI AUX SEIN **(a)** (= *hinunterfallen*) to tumble down **(b)** (= *eilig hinunterlaufen*) to rush down ◼ VT *jdn* to throw down; *Getränk* to gulp down ◼ VR to throw oneself down; **hinunterwerfen** VT SEP IRREG to throw down; (*inf: fallen lassen*) to drop; **einen Blick ~** to glance down; **hinunterwürgen** VT SEP *Essen etc* to choke down; (*fig*) *Wut, Tränen* to choke back

hinwagen VR SEP to dare to go there

hinwärts ['hɪnvɛrts] ADV on the way there; **die Strecke ~** the way there

hinweg [hɪn'vɛk] ADV **(a)** **über jdn/etw ~** over sb *or* sb's head/ sth **(b)** (*zeitlich*) **über eine Zeit ~** over a period of time; **über zwei Jahre ~** over (a period of) two years

Hinweg M way there; **auf dem ~** on the way there

hinweg- PREF *siehe auch* **weg-** away; **hinweggehen** VI SEP IRREG AUX SEIN **über etw** (*acc*) ~ to pass over sth; **hinweghelfen** VI SEP IRREG (*fig*) **jdm über etw** (*acc*) ~ to help sb get over sth; **hinwegkommen** VI SEP IRREG AUX SEIN (*fig*) **über etw** (*acc*) ~ (= *überstehen, verwinden*) to get over sth; **ich komme nicht darüber hinweg, dass ...** (*inf*) I can't get over the fact that ...; **hinwegsehen** VI SEP IRREG **über jdn/etw ~** (*lit*) to see over sb *or* sb's head/sth; (*fig*) (= *ignorieren*) to ignore sb/sth; (= *unbeachtet lassen*) to overlook sb/sth; **darüber ~, dass ...** to overlook the fact that ...; **hinwegsetzen** VR SEP (*fig*) **sich über etw** (*acc*) ~ (= *nicht beachten*) to disregard sth; (= *überwinden*) to overcome sth; **hinwegtäuschen** VT SEP *jdn* **über etw** (*acc*) ~ to mislead sb about sth; **darüber ~, dass ...** to hide the fact that ...; **sich nicht darüber ~ lassen, dass ...** not to blind oneself to the fact that ...

Hinweis ['hɪnvais] M **-es, -e** [-zə] **(a)** (= *Rat*) piece of advice; (= *Bemerkung*) comment; (*amtlich*) notice; **darf ich mir den ~ erlauben, dass ...** may I point out that ...; **~e für den Benutzer** notes for the user **(b)** (= *Verweis*) reference; **unter ~ auf** (+*acc*) with reference to **(c)** (= *Anhaltspunkt, Anzeichen*) indication; (*esp von Polizei*) clue

hinweisen SEP IRREG ◼ VT **jdn auf etw** (*acc*) ~ to point sth out to sb ◼ VI **auf jdn/etw ~** to point to sb/sth; (= *verweisen*) to refer to sb/sth; **darauf ~, dass ...** to point out that ...; (*nachdrücklich*) to stress that ...; (= *anzeigen*) to indicate that ...

hinweisend ADJ (*Gram*) demonstrative

Hinweisschild NT, *pl* **-schilder**, **Hinweistafel** F sign

hin-: hinwerfen SEP IRREG ◼ VT **(a)** (= *wegwerfen, zu Boden werfen*) to throw down; (= *fallen lassen*) to drop; **jdm etw ~** to throw sth to sb **(b)** (= *flüchtig machen*) *Bemerkung* to drop casually; *Wort* to say casually; *Zeilen, Roman, Zeichnung* to dash off; **eine hingeworfene Bemerkung** a casual remark **(c)** (*inf:* = *aufgeben*) *Arbeit, Stelle* to give up ◼ VR to throw oneself down; **hinwirken** VI SEP **auf etw** (*acc*) ~ to work toward(s) sth; **kannst du (nicht) (bei ihm) darauf ~, dass er mich empfängt?** couldn't you use your influence to get him to see me?; **hinwollen** VI SEP (*inf*) to want to go

Hinz [hɪnts] M **~ und Kunz** (*inf*) every Tom, Dick and Harry; **von ~ zu Kunz** from pillar to post (*Brit*), from one place to another

hin-: hinziehen SEP IRREG ◼ VT **(a)** (= *zu sich ziehen*) to draw (*zu* towards); (*fig:* = *anziehen*) to attract (*zu* to) **(b)** (*fig:* = *in die Länge ziehen*) to draw out ◼ VI AUX SEIN **(a)** (= *sich in bestimmte Richtung bewegen*) to move (*über* +*acc* across, *zu* towards) **(b)** (= *umziehen*) to move there ◼ VR **(a)** (= *lange dauern*) to drag on; (= *sich verzögern*) to be delayed **(b)** (= *sich erstrecken*) to stretch; **hinzielen** VI SEP **auf etw** (*acc*) ~ to aim at sth; (*Pläne etc*) to be aimed at sth; (*Bemerkung*) to refer to sth

hinzu [hɪnˈtsuː] ADV (= überdies) besides; ~ **kommt noch, dass ich ...** moreover I ...

hinzu-: hinzufügen VT SEP to add (+dat to); (= beilegen) to enclose; **hinzukommen** VI SEP IRREG AUX SEIN (= zusätzlich eintreten) to ensue; (= beigefügt werden) to be added; **zu etw ~** to be added to sth; **es kommt noch hinzu, dass ...** there is also the fact that ...; **kommt sonst noch etwas hinzu?** will there be anything else?; **hinzutun** VT SEP IRREG (inf) to add; **hinzuzählen** VT SEP to add; **hinzuziehen** VT SEP IRREG to consult

Hiobsbotschaft F bad tidings pl

hip [hɪp] ADJ (sl) hip (inf)

Hippie [ˈhɪpi] M **-s, -s** hippie

hippokratisch [hɪpoˈkraːtɪʃ] ADJ Hippocratic

Hirn [hɪrn] NT **-(e)s, -e (a)** (Anat) brain **(b)** (inf) (= Kopf) head; (= Verstand) brains pl, mind; **sich** (dat) **das ~ zermartern** to rack one's brain(s); **diese Idee ist doch nicht deinem ~ entsprungen?** that's not your brainwave, is it? **(c)** (Cook) brains pl

Hirn- siehe auch **Gehirn-: Hirngespinst** [-gəʃpɪnst] NT **-(e)s, -e** fantasy; **Hirnhaut** F (Anat) meninges pl; **Hirnhautentzündung** F (Med) meningitis; **hirnlos** ADJ brainless; **hirnrissig** ADJ hare-brained; **Hirntod** M (Med) brain death; **hirntot** ADJ braindead; **Hirntumor** M brain tumour (Brit) or tumor (US); **hirnverbrannt** [-vɛɐbrant] ADJ hare-brained; **Hirnwindung** F (Anat) convolution of the brain

Hirsch [hɪrʃ] M **-es, -e** (= Paarhufer) deer; (= Rothirsch) red deer; (= männlicher Rothirsch) stag; (Cook) venison

Hirsch-: Hirschjagd F stag hunting; (einzelne Jagd) stag hunt; **Hirschkäfer** M stag beetle; **Hirschkalb** NT (male) fawn; **Hirschkeule** F haunch of venison; **Hirschkuh** F hind; **Hirschleder** NT buckskin; **hirschledern** ADJ buckskin; **Hirschlederne** [-leːdənə] F DECL AS ADJ (esp Aus) buckskin breeches pl

Hirse [ˈhɪrzə] F **-, -n** millet

Hirt [hɪrt] M **-en, -en** (dated) herdsman; (= Schafhirt) shepherd; siehe auch **Hirtin**

Hirtin [ˈhɪrtɪn] F **-, -nen** herdswoman; (= Schafhirtin) shepherdess; siehe auch **Hirt**

Hisb Allah [hɪsˈbɔlaː] F **-**, NO PL, **Hisbollah** [hɪsˈbɔla] F **-**, NO PL Hizbollah

Hispanistik [hɪspaˈnɪstɪk] F **-**, NO PL Spanish (language and literature)

hissen [ˈhɪsn] VT to hoist

Histamin [hɪstaˈmiːn] NT **-s**, NO PL histamine

Historiker [hɪsˈtoːrikɐ] M **-s, -**, **Historikerin** [-ərɪn] F **-, -nen** historian

historisch [hɪsˈtoːrɪʃ] **1** ADJ historical; (= geschichtlich bedeutsam) Gestalt, Ereignis, Gebäude historic **2** ADV historically; **das ist ~ belegt** there is historical evidence for this; **~ denken** to think in historical terms; **~ betrachtet** considered from a historical perspective

Hit [hɪt] M **-s, -s** (Mus, Comput, fig inf) hit

Hitler-: Hitlergruß M Hitler salute; **Hitlerjugend** F Hitler Youth (organization); **Hitlerjunge** M member of the Hitler Youth; **Hitlerzeit** F Hitler era

Hit-: Hitliste F charts pl; **Hitparade** F hit parade

Hitze [ˈhɪtsə] F **-, -n (a)** heat; (= ~welle) heat wave; **~ abweisend** heat-repellent; **die fliegende ~ bekommen** (Med) to get hot flushes (Brit) or flashes (US); (inf) **bei starker/mittlerer/mäßiger ~ backen** (Cook) bake in a hot/medium/moderate oven **(b)** (fig) passion; **in ~ geraten** to get heated; **leicht in ~ geraten** to get worked up easily; **in der ~ des Gefecht(e)s** (fig) in the heat of the moment

Hitze-: hitzeabweisend ADJ siehe Hitze; **hitzebeständig** ADJ heat-resistant; **Hitzebläschen** [-blɛːsçən] PL heat rash sing; **hitzeempfindlich** ADJ sensitive to heat; **hitzefrei** ADJ **~ haben** to have time off from school on account of excessively hot weather; **Hitze(schutz)schild** M, pl **-schilde** heat shield; **Hitzewallung** F USU PL (Med) hot flush (Brit) or flash (US); **Hitzewelle** F heat wave

hitzig [ˈhɪtsɪç] **1** ADJ (= aufbrausend) Mensch hot-headed; Antwort, Reaktion, Atmosphäre, Debatte heated; (= leidenschaftlich) passionate; Blut hot; **~ werden** (Mensch) to flare up; (Debatte) to grow heated; **nicht so ~!** don't get so excited!, hold your horses! (inf) **2** ADV (= heftig) heatedly;

eine Debatte ~ **führen** to lead a heated debate; **es ging ~ zu** things got heated

Hitzschlag M (Med) heatstroke

HIV [haːliːˈfau] NT **-(s),** (rare) **-(s)** ABBR von **Human Immunodeficiency Virus** HIV

HIV- [haːliːfau] IN CPDS HIV-; **HIV-infiziert** [haːliːˈfau-] ADJ HIV-infected; **HIV-negativ** ADJ HIV-negative; **HIV-positiv** ADJ HIV-positive; **HIV-Virus** [haːliːˈfau-] NT HIV-virus

Hiwi [ˈhiːvi] M **-s, -s (a)** ABBR von **Hilfswillige(r) (b)** (Univ sl) helper **(c)** (pej inf: = Hilfskraft) dogsbody (Brit inf), drudge (US)

Hj. ABBR von **Halbjahr**

hl. ABBR von **heilig**

H-Milch [ˈhaː-] F long-life milk

HNO-Arzt [haːlɛnˈloː-] M, **HNO-Ärztin** F ENT specialist

hob PRET von **heben**

Hobby [ˈhɔbi] NT **-s, -s** hobby

Hobby-: Hobbyfotograf(in) M(F) amateur photographer; **Hobbyraum** M workroom

Hobel [ˈhoːbl] M **-s, -** (Tech) plane; (Cook) slicer

Hobelbank F, pl **-bänke** carpenter's or joiner's bench

hobeln [ˈhoːbln] VT **(a)** AUCH VI (Tech) to plane (an etw (dat) sth); (= glätten) Brett to plane down; **wo gehobelt wird, da fallen Späne** (Prov) you can't make an omelette without breaking eggs (Prov) **(b)** (Cook) to slice

Hobelspan M, (Aus) **Hobelscharte** F shaving

---

hoch [hoːx]

1 ADJEKTIV	**2** ADVERB

1 ADJEKTIV, attr hohe(r, s) [ˈhoːə], comp höher [ˈhøːɐ], superl =ste(r, s) [ˈhøːçstə]

(a) (längenmäßig) high; Wuchs, Baum, Mast tall; Leiter tall, long; **ein hohes, geräumiges Zimmer** a spacious room with a high ceiling; **der Schnee lag/das Wasser stand zwei Fuß hoch** the snow/water was feet deep; **das ist mir zu hoch** (fig inf) that's (well) above (esp Brit) or over my head

(b) (mengenmäßig) Preis, Verdienst, Temperatur, Druck etc high; Betrag, Summe large; Strafe, Gewicht heavy; Schaden extensive; Lotteriegewinn big; Profit high, big; **die britische Armee musste hohe Verluste hinnehmen** the British Army suffered heavy losses; **in hohem Maße verdächtig** highly suspicious; **in hohem Maße gefährdet** in grave danger; **mit hoher Wahrscheinlichkeit** in all probability

(c) (Alter) great, advanced; **ein hohes Alter erreichen** to live to a great or an advanced age

(d) (Mus) high; **das hohe C** top C

(e) (= bedeutend) high; Ehre, Bedeutung, Genuss, Gut, Glück great; Fest, Besuch, Feiertag, Jubiläum important; Offizier high-ranking; **er/sie ist hoher** or **der hohe Favorit** he/she is the hot favourite (Brit) or favorite (US); **ein hohes Tier** (fig inf) a big fish (inf); **hohe Persönlichkeiten aus Politik und Wirtschaft** important or top (inf) politicians and businesspeople; **das hohe Haus** (Parl) the House

(f) (feste Wendungen) **der hohe Norden** the far North; **es ist hohe Zeit** (geh) it's high time; siehe auch **höchste(r, s)**

2 ADVERB, comp höher, superl am =sten

(a) (= oben) high; **hoch oben** high up; **hoch am Himmel** high in the sky; (Flugzeug, Vogel) high up in the sky; **10.000 Fuß hoch fliegen** to fly at a height of 10,000 feet; **zwei Treppen hoch wohnen** to live two floors up; **die See geht hoch** the sea is running high; **wie hoch steht das Thermometer?** what's the temperature?; **wie hoch kalkulieren Sie seine Chancen?** how would you rate his chances?

(b) (= nach oben) up; **er sah zu uns hoch** (inf) he looked up to us; **hoch emporragend** towering (up); **hoch werfen** to throw high; **hoch gewachsen** tall; **ein hoch aufgeschossener Mann** a very tall man; **den Kopf hoch tragen** to hold one's head high; **die Nase hoch tragen** (inf) to be stuck-up (inf)

(c) (Mus) high; **die Sopranistin sang etwas zu hoch** the soprano sang a bit sharp

(d) (Math) **7 hoch 3** 7 to the power of 3

(e) (= sehr) begabt, angesehen, beansprucht, entwickelt, industrialisiert highly; zufrieden, erfreut very; **hoch beglückt** highly delighted

(f) (= *mit viel Geld*) bezahlt, dotiert highly; *besteuert* heavily
(g) (*im übertragenen Sinn*)

◆**hoch + Adjektiv**

Die in Verbindung mit **hoch** *verwendeten Adjektive sind alphabetisch angeordnet.*

hoch auflösend (*Comput, TV*) high-resolution; **er ist hoch betagt** he has reached a great *or* an advanced age; **hoch empfindlich** (*Tech*) *Material, Gerät, Instrumente* highly sensitive; *Film* fast; *Stoff* very delicate; **hoch gespannt** *Erwartungen* extreme; **hoch gesteckt** (*fig*) *Ziele* ambitious; *Ansprüche, Erwartungen* considerable; **hoch gestellte Persönlichkeiten aus Politik und Wirtschaft** important *or* top (*inf*) politicians and businesspeople; **hoch konzentriert** *Säure* highly concentrated; **hoch qualifiziert** highly qualified; *Arbeitsplätze* for the highly qualified; **hoch stehend** (*gesellschaftlich*) of high standing; (*kulturell*) highly advanced; (*geistig*) highly intellectual; (*entwicklungsmäßig, qualitativ*) superior; **hoch verzinslich** high interest-bearing; **sie sind uns als Gäste hoch willkommen** we are delighted to welcome them as our guests

◆**hoch + Verb**

Die in Verbindung mit **hoch** *verwendeten Verben sind alphabetisch angeordnet.*

das rechne ich ihm hoch an (I think) that is very much to his credit; **zu hoch einschätzen** to overestimate; **hoch favorisiert sein** to be the hot favourite (*Brit*) *or* favorite (*US*); **hoch gewinnen** to win handsomely; **hoch hinauswollen** to be ambitious; **wie hoch kommt das?** how much is that?; **wenn es hoch kommt** (*inf*) at (the) most; **hoch schätzen** (*zahlenmäßig*) to estimate generously; (= *verehren*) to respect highly; **zu hoch schätzen** to overestimate; **hoch geschätzt** *Mensch* highly esteemed; *Organisation, Preis* highly prestigious; **in Japan ist dieses Gericht eine hoch geschätzte Delikatesse** in Japan, this dish is considered a great delicacy; **hoch setzen** *or* **spielen** to play for high stakes; **hoch verlieren** to lose heavily; **hoch verschuldet** deep in debt; **dieses Gemälde ist hoch versichert** this picture is heavily insured; **hoch wetten** to place high bets; *siehe auch* **hoch achten, hoch fliegen** *etc* **(h)** (*andere Wendungen*) **die Polizei rückte an, 50 Mann hoch** (*inf*) the police arrived, 50 strong; **hoch!** cheers!; **die Menge rief hoch!** the crowd cheered

◆**hoch in** hoch in den Bergen high in the mountains; **hoch in der Luft** high in the air; **hoch in den Siebzigern** in one's late seventies

◆**hoch und heilig** hoch und heilig versprechen to promise faithfully

Hoch [hoːx] NT **-s, -s (a)** (= *Ruf*) **ein** (dreifaches) **~ für** *or* **auf jdn ausbringen** to give three cheers for sb; **ein ~ dem Brautpaar** a toast to the bride and groom **(b)** (*Met, fig*) high

Hoch-: hoch achten VT to respect highly; **Hochachtung** F deep respect; **jdm seine ~ für seine Leistung zollen** to be full of admiration for sb's achievement; **bei aller ~ vor jdm/etw** with (the greatest) respect for sb/sth; **meine ~!** well done!; **mit vorzüglicher ~** (*form: Briefschluss*) yours faithfully (*Brit*), sincerely yours (*US*); **hochachtungsvoll** ADV (*Briefschluss*) (*bei Anrede mit Sir/Madam*) yours faithfully (*Brit*), sincerely yours (*US*); (*bei Anrede mit Namen*) yours sincerely (*Brit*), sincerely yours (*US*); **Hochadel** M high nobility; **hochaktiv** ADJ *Atommüll etc* high-level; **hochaktuell** ADJ highly topical; **Hochaltar** M high altar; **hochanständig** ADJ very decent; **hocharbeiten** VR SEP to work one's way up; **hochauflösend** ADJ *siehe* hoch; **Hochbahn** F elevated railway (*Brit*) *or* railroad (*US*), el (*US inf*); **Hochbau** M, NO PL structural engineering; *siehe auch* **Hoch- und Tiefbau**; **hochbegabt** ADJ ATTR *siehe* hoch; **Hochbegabtenförderung** F bursary (*Brit*) *or* scholarship for gifted students; **Hochbegabte(r)** MF DECL AS ADJ gifted person *or* child; **hochbeinig** ADJ long-legged; *Auto* high on the road; **hochbekommen** ptp **hochbekommen** VT SEP IRREG *Stein, Motorhaube etc* to (manage to) lift *or* get up; *Reißverschluss* to (manage to) get *or* do up; **er bekommt keinen hoch** (*inf: Erektion*) he can't get it up (*inf*); **hochbetagt** ADJ aged *attr*, advanced in years; **Hochbetrieb** M (*in Geschäft, Fabrik etc*) peak period; (*im Verkehr*) rush hour; (= *Hochsaison*)

high season; **~ haben** to be at one's/its busiest; **hochblicken** VI SEP to look up; **hochbringen** VT SEP IRREG (*inf*) **(a)** (= *nach oben bringen*) to bring *or* take up **(b)** (*inf*: = *hochheben, hochdrücken können*) to (manage to) get up; **einen/keinen ~** (*inf*) to be able/not to be able to get it up (*inf*); **Hochburg** F (*fig*) stronghold; **hochdeutsch** ADJ standard *or* High German; **Hochdeutsch(e)** NT standard *or* High German; *siehe auch* **Deutsch(e)**; **hochdienen** VR SEP to work one's way up; **hochdotiert** [-dotiːɐt] ADJ ATTR *siehe* hoch; **hochdrehen** VT SEP *Fenster* to wind up; *Motor* to rev

Hochdruck M **(a)** NO PL (*Met*) high pressure **(b)** NO PL (*Typ*: = *Verfahren*) surface *or* relief printing **(c)** *pl* **-drucke** (*Typ*: = *Gedrucktes*) relief print **(d)** NO PL (*Phys*) high pressure **(e)** NO PL (*Med*) high blood pressure **(f)** NO PL (*fig*) **mit ~ arbeiten** to work at full stretch

Hochdruckgebiet NT (*Met*) high-pressure area

Hoch-: Hochebene F plateau; **hochempfindlich** ADJ *siehe* hoch; **Hochenergie-Laser** M high-energy laser; **hochentwickelt** [-ɛntvɪklt] ADJ ATTR *siehe* hoch; **hochexplosiv** ADJ (*lit, fig*) highly explosive; **hochfahren** SEP IRREG **1** VI AUX SEIN **(a)** (= *nach oben fahren*) to go up; (*in Auto*) to drive *or* go up **(b)** (*erschreckt*) to start (up); **aus dem Schlaf ~** to wake up with a start **2** VT to take up; (*in Auto auch*) to drive up; (*Comput, Tech*) to start up; (*fig*) *Produktion* to increase; **hochfahrend** ADJ **(a)** (= *überheblich*) arrogant **(b)** = **hochfliegend**; **Hochfinanz** F high finance; **Hochfläche** F plateau; **hochfliegen** VI IRREG AUX SEIN to fly up; (= *in die Luft geschleudert werden*) to be thrown up; **hochfliegend** ADJ *Pläne, Ideen etc* ambitious; (= *übertrieben*) high-flown; **Hochform** F top form; **Hochformat** NT vertical format; **Hochfrequenz** F (*Elec*) high frequency; **Hochgarage** F multistorey car park (*Brit*), multistory parking garage (*US*); **Hochgebirge** NT high mountains *pl*; **hoch gehen** VI IRREG AUX SEIN (= *sich nach oben bewegen*) to rise; (*Preise*) to go up, to rise; (*Wellen*) to surge; **hochgehen** VI SEP IRREG AUX SEIN **(a)** (*inf*: = *hinaufgehen*) to go up **(b)** (*inf*: = *explodieren*) to blow up; (*Bombe*) to go off; **etw ~ lassen** to blow sth up **(c)** (*inf*: = *wütend werden*) to go through the roof **(d)** (*inf*: = *gefasst werden*) to get nabbed (*inf*); **jdn ~ lassen** to bust sb (*inf*); **hochgeistig** ADJ highly intellectual; *Lektüre, Mensch auch* highbrow *no adv*; **Hochgenuss** M special treat; (= *großes Vergnügen*) great pleasure; **jdm ein ~ sein** to be a real treat for sb; **hochgerüstet** [-gərʏstət] ADJ *Land* with a full military arsenal; *Technik, System* highly sophisticated; **eine ~e Supermacht** a military superpower; **hochgeschätzt** ADJ ATTR *siehe* hoch; **hochgeschlossen** ADJ *Kleid etc* high-necked

Hochgeschwindigkeits- IN CPDS high-speed; **Hochgeschwindigkeitszug** M high-speed train

hoch-: hochgespannt ADJ *siehe* hoch; **hochgesteckt** [-gəʃtɛkt] ADJ *siehe* hoch; **hochgestellt** [-gəʃtɛlt] ADJ ATTR *Ziffer* superscript, superior; *siehe auch* hoch; **hochgestochen** ADJ (*pej inf*) highbrow; *Reden* highfaluting; *Stil* pompous; (= *eingebildet*) stuck-up (*inf*); **hochgewachsen** ADJ *siehe* hoch; **hochgezüchtet** [-gətsʏçtət] ADJ (*usu pej*) *Motor* souped-up (*inf*); *Geräte* fancy; *Tiere, Pflanzen* overbred; *System, Wohlfahrtsstaat etc* over-developed

Hochglanz M high polish *or* shine; (*Phot*) gloss

Hochglanz- IN CPDS glossy; **Hochglanzabzug** M (*Phot*) glossy print; **Hochglanzpapier** NT high gloss paper

Hoch-: hochgradig [-graːdɪç] **1** ADJ NO PRED extreme; (*inf*) *Unsinn etc* absolute, utter **2** ADV extremely; **hochhackig** [-hakɪç] ADJ *Schuhe* high-heeled; **hochhalten** VT SEP IRREG **(a)** (= *in die Höhe halten*) to hold up **(b)** (= *in Ehren halten*) to uphold; **Hochhaus** NT high-rise building; (= *Wolkenkratzer*) sky-scraper; **hochheben** VT SEP IRREG *Hand, Arm* to lift, to raise; *Kind, Last* to lift up; **durch Hochheben der Hände abstimmen** to vote by (a) show of hands; **hochinteressant** ADJ very *or* most interesting; **hochjubeln** VT SEP (*inf*) *Künstler, Film, Politiker etc* to hype (up) (*inf*); **hochkämmen** VT SEP *Haar* to put up; **hochkant** ['hoːxkant] ADV **(a)** (*lit*) on end; **~ stellen** to put on end **(b)** (*fig inf: auch* hochkantig) **~ hinauswerfen/hinausfliegen** to chuck/be chucked out (*inf*); **hochkarätig 1** ADJ *Diamanten, Gold* high-carat **(b)** (*fig*) top-class **2** ADV **ein ~ besetzter Film** a film with a top-class cast; **hochklappbar** ADJ *Tisch, Stuhl* folding; *Sitz* tip-up; **hochklappen** VT SEP *Tisch, Stuhl* to fold up; *Sitz* to tip up; *Kühlerhaube, Deckel* to lift (up); *Mantelkragen* to turn up; **hochkochen** SEP **1** VT *Thema* to stir up **2** VI AUX SEIN

(*Emotionen*) to run high; **hochkommen** VI SEP IRREG AUX SEIN **(a)** (*inf.* = *hinauf-, heraufkommen*) to come up **(b)** (*inf*) **das Essen ist ihm hochgekommen** he threw up (his meal) (*inf*); **es kommt mir hoch** it makes me sick **(c)** (= *aufstehen können*) (to manage to) get up **(d)** (*inf: beruflich, gesellschaftlich*) to come up in the world; **niemanden (neben sich** *dat*) ~ **lassen** not to tolerate competition; **Hochkonjunktur** F boom; **hochkönnen** VI SEP IRREG (*inf*) (= *aufstehen können*) to be able to get up; (= *hinaufsteigen können*) to be able to get up (*auf etw* (*acc*) onto sth, *auf Berg* the mountain); **hochkonzentriert** ADJ *Mensch* very focused; *Gesichtsausdruck* of great concentration; *siehe auch* **hoch**; **hochkrempeln** VT SEP to roll up; **hochkriegen** VT SEP (*inf*) = **hochbekommen**; **hochkurbeln** VT SEP *Fenster* to wind up; **hochladen** VT SEP IRREG (*Comput*) to upload; **Hochland** NT highland; **das schottische ~** the Scottish Highlands *pl*; **Hochlandkaffee** M high-grown coffee; **hochleben** VI SEP jdn ~ **lassen** to give three cheers for sb; **er lebe hoch!** three cheers (for him)!; **hoch lebe der König!** long live the King!

Hochleistung F first-class performance

Hochleistungs- IN CPDS high-performance; **Hochleistungssport** M top-class sport; **Hochleistungssportler(in)** M(F) top athlete

Hoch-: Hochlohnland NT country with high wage costs; **hochmodern** [-modɛrn] ◼ ADJ very modern ◼ ADV in a very modern way; **Hochmoor** NT moor; **Hochmut** M arrogance; ~ **kommt vor dem Fall** (*Prov*) pride comes before a fall (*Prov*); **hochmütig** [ˈhoːxmyːtɪç] ADJ arrogant; **hochnäsig** [ˈhoːxnɛːzɪç] (*inf*) ◼ ADJ snooty (*inf*) ◼ ADV snootily (*inf*); **Hochnebel** M (low) stratus; **hochnehmen** VT SEP IRREG **(a)** (= *heben*) to lift; *Kind, Hund* to pick *or* lift up **(b)** (*inf:* = *necken*) jdn ~ to pull sb's leg **(c)** (*inf:* = *verhaften*) to pick up (*inf*); **Hochofen** M blast furnace; **hochpäppeln** VT SEP (*inf*) *Tier, Kind, Kranken* to feed up; (*fig*) to nurse back to health; **Hochplateau** NT plateau; **hochpreisig** [-praizɪç] ADJ high-priced; **Hochpreispolitik** F policy of high pricing; **hochprozentig** ADJ *alkoholische Getränke* high-proof; *Lösung* highly concentrated; *Gewinnzuwächse, Rabatte* high-percentage; *Wertpapiere* high-interest; **hochqualifiziert** ADJ ATTR *siehe* **hoch**; **hochragen** VI SEP AUX SEIN *or* HABEN (*Bäume*) to rise (up); (*Berge, Türme, Häuser*) to tower (up); **hochrechnen** SEP ◼ VT to project ◼ VI to make a projection; **Hochrechnung** F projection; **Hochrelief** NT high relief; **hochrot** ADJ bright red; **mit ~em Gesicht** with one's face as red as a beetroot (*Brit*) *or* beet (*US*); **Hochruf** M cheer; **hochrutschen** VI SEP AUX SEIN (*Kleidungsstück*) to ride up; (*inf:* = *aufrücken*) to move up; **Hochsaison** F high season; **hochschätzen** VT SEP *siehe* **hoch**; **hochschaukeln** SEP ◼ VT *Problem, Angelegenheit* to blow up ◼ VR to work oneself up; **hochschlagen** SEP IRREG ◼ VT *Kragen* to turn up ◼ VI AUX SEIN (*Wellen*) to surge up; (*Flammen*) to leap up; **hochschnellen** VI SEP AUX SEIN to leap up; **hoch schrauben** VT (*lit*) to raise; (*fig*) *Preise* to force up; *Erwartungen* to raise; *Forderungen, Ansprüche* to increase

Hochschul-: Hochschulabschluss M degree; **mit ~** with a degree; **Hochschulabsolvent(in)** M(F) graduate; **Hochschul(aus)bildung** F (= *Ausbildung*) college training; (*an Universität*) university training; (= *Bildung*) university education

Hochschule F college; (= *Universität*) university; **Technische ~** technical college, college of technology

Hochschüler(in) M(F) student

Hochschul-: Hochschullehrer(in) M(F) *siehe* **Hochschule** college/university teacher, lecturer (*Brit*); **Hochschulpolitik** F higher education policy; **Hochschulreform** F university reform; **Hochschulreife** F *academic standard required for university entrance;* **er hat (die) ~** ≈ he's got his A-levels (*Brit*), ≈ he's graduated from high school (*US*)

hochschwanger ADJ well advanced in pregnancy

Hochsee F high sea; **auf ~** on the high seas

Hochsee-: Hochseefischerei F deep-sea fishing; **Hochseeschifffahrt** F deep-sea shipping; **hochseetüchtig** ADJ ocean-going

Hoch-: hochsehen VI SEP IRREG to look up; **hochsensibel** ADJ highly sensitive; **Hochsicherheitsgefängnis** NT high-security prison; **Hochsicherheitstrakt** M high-security wing; **Hochsitz** M (*Hunt*) (raised) hide; **Hochsommer** M height of the summer; (= *Zeitabschnitt*) midsummer *no art*; **hochsommerlich** ADJ very summery

Hochspannung F (*Elec*) high voltage, high tension; (*fig*) high tension; „**Vorsicht ~**" "danger - high voltage"

Hochspannungs-: Hochspannungsleitung F high-tension line; **Hochspannungsmast** M pylon

Hoch-: Hochsprache F standard language; **hochspringen** VI SEP IRREG AUX SEIN **(a)** (*inf:* = *aufspringen*) to jump up (*an jdm* on sb); **auf etw** (*acc*) ~ to jump (up) on sth **(b)** (*inf:* = *schnell hinauflaufen*) to run up; **Hochspringer(in)** M(F) high jumper; **Hochsprung** M (= *Disziplin*) high jump; (= *Sprung*) jump

höchst [høːçst] ◼ ADJ *siehe* **höchste(r, s)** ◼ ADV (= *überaus*) extremely, most

Höchstalter [høːçst-] NT maximum age

Hoch-: Hochstapelei [hoːxʃtaːpəˈlai] F (= *Jur*) fraud; (*einzelner Fall*) swindle; (*fig:* = *Aufschneiderei*) boasting *no pl*; **hochstapeln** [ˈhoːxʃtaːpln] VI SEP to be fraudulent; (*fig*) to put one over (*inf*); **Hochstapler** [ˈhoːxʃtaːple] M **-s, -**, **Hochstaplerin** [-ərɪn] F **-, -nen** confidence trickster; (*Mann auch*) con man (*inf*); (*fig*) fraud

Höchst- [høːçst-]: **Höchstbeitrag** M maximum contribution; **Höchstbetrag** M maximum amount; **Höchstbetragshypothek** F maximum (amount) mortgage; **Höchstbietende(r)** [-biːtndə] MF DECL AS ADJ highest bidder

höchste ADJ = **höchste(r, s)**

Höchste = **Höchste(s)**

hoch-: hochstecken VT SEP to pin up; **hochstehend** ADJ **(a)** *siehe* **hoch (b)** *Kragen* turned-up; **hochstellen** VT SEP **(a)** (*an höhere Stelle*) *Stühle etc* to put up; (*außer Reichweite*) to put *or* place high up; *siehe auch* **hoch**, **hochgestellt (b)** *Kragen* to turn up; **Hochstelltaste** F (*Comput*) shift key

höchstenfalls [ˈhøːçstnfals] ADV at (the) most

höchstens [ˈhøːçstns] ADV **(a)** (= *nicht mehr, länger als*) not more than; (= *bestenfalls*) at the most, at best **(b)** (= *außer*) except

höchste(r, s) [ˈhøːçstə] ◼ ADJ SUPERL *von* **hoch (a)** (*räumliche Ausdehnung*) highest; *Wuchs, Zimmer, Baum, Mast* tallest; *Leiter* longest

(b) *Preis, Verdienst, Temperatur, Druck etc* highest; *Betrag, Summe* largest; *Strafe, Gewicht* heaviest; *Profit* highest, biggest; *Lotteriegewinn* biggest; *Verlust* most severe; *Schaden* most expensive; (= *maximal*) *Verdienst, Temperatur, Geschwindigkeit etc* maximum *attr*; **im ~n Grade/Maße** extremely; **im ~n Fall(e)** at the most

(c) (*im Rang*) highest; *Ehre* greatest; *Fest* most important; *Offizier* highest-ranking; **die ~ Instanz** the supreme court of appeal

(d) ATTR (*qualitativ, äußerst*) *Lebensstandard, Ansprüche* highest; *Bedeutung, Genuss, Glück, Gut, Freude* greatest; *Not, Gefahr, Wichtigkeit* utmost, greatest; *Konzentration* extreme

(e) *Alter* greatest; (*Mus*) highest

(f) (*in Wendungen*) ~ **Zeit** *or* **Eisenbahn** (*inf*) high time; **aufs Höchste** *or* ~ **erfreut** *etc* highly *or* greatly *or* tremendously (*inf*) pleased *etc*; **das ist das Höchste, was ich bezahlen/tun kann** that is the most I can pay/do

◼ ADV **am ~n (a)** (= *in größter Höhe*) highest; **mittags steht die Sonne am ~n** the sun is highest at noon

(b) (= *in größtem Ausmaß*) *verehren, schätzen* most (of all); *versichern, begabt* most; *besteuert, verlieren* (the) most heavily; *verschuldet* (the) most deeply; **in der Rangordnung am ~n stehen** to be the highest up in the hierarchy; **er ist am ~n qualifiziert** he is the most (highly) qualified; **am ~n stehen** (*Kurse, Temperatur*) to be at its highest

Höchste(s) [ˈhøːçstə] NT DECL AS ADJ (*fig*) highest good

Höchst- [ˈhøːçst-]: **Höchstfall** M **im ~** (= *nicht mehr, länger als*) not more than; (= *bestenfalls*) at the most, at best; **Höchstform** F (*Sport*) top form; **Höchstgebot** NT highest bid; **Höchstgeschwindigkeit** F top *or* maximum speed; **zulässige ~** speed limit; **Höchstgrenze** F upper limit; **Höchstleistung** F best performance; (*bei Produktion*) maximum output; **Höchstmaß** NT maximum amount (*an +dat* of); **höchstpersönlich** [ˈhøːçstperˈzøːnlɪç] ADV personally; **es ist der Prinz ~** it's the prince in person; **Höchstpreis** M top *or* maximum price; **Höchststand** M highest level; **Höchststrafe** F maximum penalty; **höchstwahrscheinlich** [ˈhøːçstvaːrˈʃainlɪç] ADV most probably *or* likely; **Höchstwert** M maximum value

hochstylen VT SEP to give style to; (*pej*) *Person* to hype (up) (*inf*); *Laden etc* to tart up (*Brit inf*), to dress up (*esp US*); **ein hochgestyltes Produkt** a stylish product

höchstzulässig ADJ ATTR maximum (permissible)

Hoch-: Hochtechnologie F high technology; **Hochtemperaturreaktor** M high temperature reactor; **Hochtour** F **auf ~en laufen/arbeiten** (*Maschinen*) to run at full speed; (*fig: Mensch, Fabrik etc*) to run/work at full steam; **etw auf ~en bringen** *Motor* to rev sth up to full speed; *Maschine, Produktion, Kampagne* to get sth into full swing; **jdn auf ~en bringen** (*inf*) to get sb really going (*inf*); **hochtrabend** (*pej*) **1** ADJ pompous **2** ADV pompously; **hoch treiben** VT IRREG **(a)** (= *hinauftreiben*) to drive up **(b)** (*fig*) *Preise, Löhne, Kosten* to force up; **Hoch- und Tiefbau** M, NO PL structural and civil engineering; **hochverehrt** ADJ ATTR highly respected or esteemed; (*in Brief*) esteemed (*old*); **~er Herr Vorsitzender ...** Mr Chairman ...; **~er Herr Präsident!** Mr President, Sir!; (*in Brief*) Dear Sir; **Hochverrat** M high treason; **hochverzinslich** ADJ *siehe* **hoch**; **Hochwasser** NT, *pl* **-wasser (a)** (= *Höchststand von Flut*) high tide **(b)** (= *überhoher Wasserstand in Flüssen, Seen*) high water; (= *Überschwemmung*) flood; **~ haben** (*Fluss*) to be in flood; **hochwerfen** VT SEP IRREG to throw up; **hochwertig** [-veːɐtɪç] ADJ high-quality; *Nahrungsmittel* highly nutritious; *Stahl* high-grade; (*Chem*) high-valency *attr*; **Hochwild** NT big game (*including bigger game birds*); **hochwillkommen** ADJ ATTR most or very welcome; **Hochzahl** F exponent

Hochzeit[1] [ˈhɔxtsait] F **-, -en** wedding; (= *Eheschließung auch*) marriage; **etw zur ~ geschenkt bekommen/schenken** to get/ give sth as a wedding present; **grüne ~** wedding day; **silberne/goldene/diamantene ~** silver/golden/diamond wedding (anniversary); **man kann nicht auf zwei ~en tanzen** (*prov*) you can't have your cake and eat it (*prov*)

Hochzeit[2] [ˈhoːxtsait] F **-, -en** (= *Blütezeit*) golden age

Hochzeits- IN CPDS wedding; **Hochzeitsanzeige** F wedding announcement; **Hochzeitsfeier** F wedding celebration; (= *Empfang*) reception, wedding breakfast; **Hochzeitskleid** NT wedding dress; **Hochzeitsnacht** F wedding night; **Hochzeitsreise** F honeymoon; **wohin geht die ~?** where are you going on (your) honeymoon?; **Hochzeitstag** M wedding day; (= *Jahrestag*) wedding anniversary

Hoch-: hochziehen SEP IRREG **1** VT **(a)** *Gegenstand* to pull up; *Fahne* to run up; *Augenbrauen* to raise; **die Maschine ~** (*Aviat*) to put the aircraft into a steep climb **(b)** (*inf*: = *bauen*) to throw up (*inf*) **2** VR to pull oneself up; **sich an etw** (*dat*) **~** to climb up sth; (*fig inf*) to get a kick out of sth (*inf*); **Hochzinspolitik** F (*Econ*) high interest rate policy

Hocke [ˈhɔkə] F **-, -n** squatting position; (= *Übung*) squat; (*beim Turnen*) squat vault; (*beim Skilaufen*) crouch; **in die ~ gehen** to squat (down)

hocken [ˈhɔkn̩] VI (*S Ger: aux sein*) **(a)** (= *in der Hocke sitzen*) to squat, to crouch **(b)** (*inf*: = *sitzen*) to sit **(c)** (*pej inf*) to sit around **(d)** AUX SEIN (*Sport*) **übers Pferd ~** to squat-vault over the horse

Hocker [ˈhɔkɐ] M **-s, -** (= *Stuhl*) stool; **jdn vom ~ reißen** or **hauen** (*fig inf*) to bowl sb over (*inf*)

Höcker [ˈhœkɐ] M **-s, - (a)** (*von Kamel*) (*inf*: = *Buckel*) hump; (*auf Schnabel*) knob **(b)** (= *Erhebung*) bump; (*in Gelände*) hump; (= *kleiner Hügel*) hummock

Hockergrab NT seated burial

Hockey [ˈhɔki, ˈhɔkɛ] NT **-s**, NO PL hockey (*Brit*), field hockey (*US*)

Hockey-: Hockeyball M (field (*US*)) hockey ball; **Hockeyschläger** M (field (*US*)) hockey stick; **Hockeyspieler(in)** M(F) (field (*US*)) hockey player

Hode [ˈhoːdə] M **-n, -n** or *f* **-, -n, Hoden** [ˈhoːdn̩] M **-s, -** testicle

Hodensack M scrotum

Hof [hoːf] M **-(e)s, ⸚e** [ˈhøːfə] **(a)** (= *Platz*) yard; (= *Innenhof*) courtyard; (= *Schulhof*) playground; (= *Kasernenhof*) square **(b)** (= *Bauernhof*) farm; (= *Gebäudekomplex*) farm(yard) **(c)** (= *Fürstenhof*) court; **bei** or **am ~e** at court; **am ~e Ludwig XIV.** at the court of Louis XIV; **~ halten** (*lit, fig*) to hold court **(d)** (*um Sonne, Mond*) halo

hoffen [ˈhɔfn̩] **1** VI to hope; **auf Gott ~** to trust in God; **auf jdn ~** to set one's hopes on sb; **auf etw** (*acc*) **~** to hope for sth; **sie hofften auf ihre Verbündeten** (*auf Erscheinen*) they were waiting for their allies; (*auf Hilfe*) they set their hopes on their allies; **ich will nicht ~, dass er das macht** I hope he doesn't do that

2 VT to hope for; **~ wir das Beste!** let's hope for the best!; **es ist zu ~** it is to be hoped; **ich hoffe es** I hope so; **das will ich** (*doch wohl*) **~** I should (jolly well (*Brit inf*)) hope so; **das wollen wir ~** let's hope so

hoffentlich [ˈhɔfn̩tlɪç] ADV hopefully; **hoffentlich!** I hope so; **~ nicht** I/we hope not; **~ ist das bald vorbei** hopefully it will be over soon; **du bist mir doch ~ nicht böse** I hope (that) you're not angry with me

Hoffnung [ˈhɔfnʊŋ] F **-, -en** hope; (*auf Gott*) trust (*auf* +acc in); **sich** (*dat*) **~en machen** to have hopes; **sich** (*dat*) **keine ~en machen** not to hold out any hopes; **er macht sich ~en bei ihr** (*inf*) he thinks his chances with her are quite good; **mach dir keine ~(en)!** I wouldn't even think about it; **jdm ~en machen** to raise sb's hopes; **jdm ~en machen, dass ...** to lead sb to hope that ...; **jdm auf etw** (*acc*) **~en machen** to lead sb to expect sth; **jdm keine ~en machen** not to hold out any hopes for sb; **die ~ aufgeben/verlieren** to abandon/lose hope; **in der ~, bald von Ihnen zu hören** hoping to hear from you soon; **zu schönen** or **zu den schönsten ~en berechtigen** to give rise to great hopes; **~ auf etw** (*acc*) **haben** to have hopes of getting sth

Hoffnungs-: hoffnungslos **1** ADJ hopeless **2** ADV hopelessly; **Hoffnungslosigkeit** F **-**, NO PL hopelessness; (= *Verzweiflung*) despair; **Hoffnungsschimmer** M glimmer of hope; **Hoffnungsträger(in)** M(F) person on whom hopes are pinned; **er war der ~ der Partei** he carried the hopes of the party

Hof-: Hofgang M, *pl* **-gänge** yard exercise; **Hofhund** M watchdog; **Hofknicks** M court or formal curtsey (*Brit*) or curtsy (*US*)

höflich [ˈhøːflɪç] **1** ADJ polite; (= *zuvorkommend*) courteous **2** ADV politely; **ich bitte Sie ~** I (would) respectfully ask you; **wir teilen Ihnen ~(st) mit** we would like to inform you

Höflichkeit F **-, -en (a)** NO PL politeness; (= *Zuvorkommenheit*) courteousness **(b)** (= *höfliche Bemerkung*) compliment; **jdm ~en sagen** to compliment sb

Höflichkeits-: Höflichkeitsbesuch M courtesy visit; **Höflichkeitsfloskel** F (*pej*), **Höflichkeitsformel** F polite phrase; **höflichkeitshalber** ADV out of courtesy

Hoflieferant(in) M(F) purveyor to the court

Höfling [ˈhøːflɪŋ] M **-s, -e** courtier

Hof-: Hofnarr M (*Hist*) court jester; **Hoftor** NT yard gate

hohe ADJ *siehe* **hoch**

Höhe [ˈhøːə] F **-, -n (a)** (= *Ausdehnung nach oben*) height; (= *Flughöhe, Berghöhe, über Meeresspiegel*) height, altitude; (*Astron*) (*Math*) altitude; (*von Schnee, Wasser*) depth; **in die/ der ~** (up) into/in the air; **aus der ~** from above; **an ~ gewinnen** (*Aviat*) to gain height, to climb; **in einer ~ von** at a height/an altitude of; **in die ~ gehen/treiben** (*fig: Preise etc*) to go up/force up **(b)** (= *Anhöhe*) hill; (= *Gipfel*) top, summit; (*fig*: = *~punkt, Blütezeit etc*) height; **auf der ~ sein** (*fig inf*) (*leistungsfähig*) to be at one's best; (*gesund*) to be (as) fit as a fiddle; **sich nicht auf der ~ fühlen, nicht auf der ~ sein** (*leistungsfähig*) to feel below par; (*gesundheitlich*) not to be up to scratch; **die ~n und Tiefen des Lebens** the ups and downs of life; **das ist doch die ~!** (*fig inf*) that's the limit! **(c)** (= *Ausmaß, Größe*) level; (*von Summe, Gewinn, Verlust, Gewicht, Geldstrafe*) size, amount; (*von Wert, Druck*) amount; (*von Einkommen*) size; (*von Schaden*) extent; **ein Zuwachs/ Betrag in ~ von** an increase/amount of; **Zinsen in ~ von** interest at the rate of; **bis zu einer ~ von** up to a maximum of **(d)** (= *Tonhöhe*) (*Mus: von Stimme*) pitch; (*Rad*) treble *no pl*; **die ~n einstellen** (*Rad*) to adjust the treble **(e)** (*Naut, Geog*: = *Breitenlage*) latitude; **auf der ~ von** at the level of; **auf der ~ von Dover** (*Naut*) off Dover; **auf gleicher ~** level with each other

Hoheit [ˈhoːhait] F **-, -en (a)** NO PL (= *Staatshoheit*) sovereignty (*über* +acc over) **(b)** (= *Mitglied einer fürstlichen Familie*) member of a/the royal family; (*als Anrede*) Highness

hoheitlich [ˈhoːhaitlɪç] ADJ (*von Staatsgewalt ausgehend*) sovereign; (*von einem Fürsten*) *Gemächer* royal; *Auftreten, Geste* majestic

Hoheits-: Hoheitsabzeichen NT nationality marking; **Hoheitsgebiet** NT sovereign territory; **Hoheitsgewalt** F (national) jurisdiction; **Hoheitsgewässer** PL territorial waters *pl*

Höhen-: Höhenangabe F altitude reading; (*auf Karte*) altitude mark; **Höhenangst** F fear of heights; **Höhenflosse** F (*Aviat*)

tailplane; **höhengleich** ◨ ADJ level ◩ ADV on a level; **Höhenkrankheit** F (*Med*) altitude sickness; **Höhenlage** F altitude; **Höhenleitwerk** NT (*Aviat*) elevators *pl*; **Höhenlinie** F contour (line); **Höhenmarke** F benchmark; **Höhenmesser** M **-s, -** (*Aviat*) altimeter; **Höhenmessung** F **(a)** (*Aviat*) measuring altitude **(b)** (*Tech*) levelling (*Brit*), leveling (*US*); **Höhenruder** NT (*Aviat*) elevator; **Höhensonne** F (= *Lampe*) sunray lamp; (= *Behandlung*) sunray treatment; **Höhenunterschied** M difference in altitude; **höhenverstellbar** ADJ height-adjustable; **Höhenzug** M mountain range

Höhepunkt M highest point; (*von Abend, Tag, Leben*) high spot; (*von Veranstaltung*) highlight; (*von Karriere*) (*des Ruhms, der Macht, des Glücks etc*) height, peak; (*von Entwicklung*) peak; (*von Kurve*) vertex; (*eines Stücks, = Orgasmus*) climax; **auf den ~ bringen** to bring to a climax; **den ~ erreichen** to reach a *or* its/one's climax; (*Krankheit*) to reach *or* come to a crisis; **den ~ überschreiten** to pass the peak

höher [ˈhøːɐ] ◨ ADJ COMP *von* **hoch** (*lit, fig*) higher; *Macht* superior; *Klasse* upper; *Auflage* bigger; (*Comput*) *Programmiersprache* high-level; **~e Schule** secondary school, high school (*esp US*); **~e Gewalt** an act of God; **in ~em Maße** to a greater extent; **~er Blödsinn** (*iro*) utter nonsense; **in ~en Regionen** *or* **Sphären schweben** to have one's head in the clouds; **sich zu Höherem berufen fühlen** to feel (oneself) called to higher things
◩ ADV **(a)** (= *weiter nach oben*) *wachsen, steigen, fliegen* higher; **~ liegen** to be higher up; **~ liegend** higher; **ihre Herzen schlugen ~** their hearts beat faster
(b) (= *mit ~em Wert*) *bewertet, versichert* more highly; **sich ~ versichern** to increase one's insurance (cover); **~ gestellt** higher, more senior; **~ stehend** higher

hohe(r, s) ADJ *siehe* **hoch**

höher-: **höhergestellt** ADJ ATTR *siehe* **höher**; **höher schrauben** VT (*fig*) to increase; *Preise* to force *or* push up; **höher stufen** VT *Person* to upgrade

hohl [hoːl] ◨ ADJ (*lit, fig*) hollow; *Geschwätz etc* empty; *Blick* empty, vacant; **ein ~es Kreuz** a hollow back; **in der ~en Hand** in the hollow of one's hand; **aus der ~en Hand trinken** to drink with cupped hands; **~e Gasse** narrow pass *or* defile ◩ ADV **~ klingen** to sound hollow; **~ scheinen** to appear *or* seem hollow

Höhle [ˈhøːlə] F **-, -n** cave; (*in Baum*) hole; (= *Tierbehausung*) cave, den; (= *Augenhöhle*) socket; (*fig* = *schlechte Wohnung*) hovel

Höhlen- IN CPDS cave; **Höhlenbär** M cave-bear; **Höhlenbewohner(in)** M(F) cave dweller, troglodyte; (*männlich auch*) caveman; **Höhlenforscher(in)** M(F) cave explorer; (*unter der Erde auch*) potholer; **Höhlenforschung** F, **Höhlenkunde** F speleology; **Höhlenmalerei** F cave painting; **Höhlenmensch** M caveman; **Höhlentier** NT cave-animal

Hohl-: **Hohlheit** F, NO PL (*lit, fig* = *Leere*) hollowness; (*von Geschwätz*) emptiness; **Hohlkörper** M hollow body; **Hohlkreuz** NT (*Med*) hollow back; **Hohlmaß** NT measure of capacity; **Hohlraum** M hollow space; (*Build auch*) cavity; **Hohlraumversiegelung** F **-, -en** (*Aut*) cavity seal

Höhlung [ˈhøːlʊŋ] F **-, -en** hollow

Hohn [hoːn] M **-(e)s**, NO PL scorn, derision; **jdn mit ~ und Spott überschütten** to heap *or* pour scorn on sb; **nur ~ und Spott ernten** to get nothing but scorn and derision; **ein ~ auf etw** (*acc*) a mockery of sth; **das ist der reine** *or* **reinste ~** it's an utter mockery

höhnen [ˈhøːnən] ◨ VT (*geh*) *jdn* to mock ◩ VI to jeer, to sneer (*über* +*acc* at)

Hohngelächter NT scornful *or* derisive laughter

höhnisch [ˈhøːnɪʃ] ◨ ADJ scornful, sneering ◩ ADV scornfully; **~ grinsen** to sneer; **jdn ~ verspotten** to jeer at sb

hoi [hɔy] INTERJ (*Sw*) hello

Hokuspokus [hoːkʊsˈpoːkʊs] M **-**, NO PL (= *Zauberformel*) hey presto; (= *Zauberstück*) (conjuring) trick(s *pl*); (*fig*) (= *Täuschung*) hocus-pocus (*inf*); (= *Drumherum*) fuss; **die veranstalten immer einen ~** they always make such a fuss

Holding [ˈhoːldɪŋ] F **-, -s**, **Holdinggesellschaft** F (*Comm*) holding company

holen [ˈhoːlən] VT **(a)** (= *gehen*) to fetch, to get; (= *herunternehmen*) to get *or* take down; (= *herausnehmen*) to get *or* take out; **Luft** *or* **Atem ~** to draw breath; **jdn aus dem Bett ~** to get sb out of bed; **das Kind musste geholt werden** the baby had to be pulled out; **jdn ~ lassen** to send for sb; **einen Moment, ich lasse ihn schnell ans Telefon ~** just a moment, I'll have someone fetch *or* get him to the phone; **der Professor hat seinen Assistenten an die neue Uni geholt** the professor brought his assistant to the new university **(b)** (= *abholen*) to fetch, to pick up; *Verbrecher, Patienten* to take away **(c)** (= *kaufen*) to get, to pick up (*inf*) **(d)** (= *sich zuziehen*) *Krankheit* to catch, to get; *elektrischen Schlag* to get; **sich** (*dat*) **Schläge ~** to get a beating; **sonst wirst du dir etwas ~** or you'll catch something; **sich** (*dat*) **eine Erkältung/den Tod** (*inf*) **~** to catch a cold/one's death (*inf*) **(e)** (= *bekommen, erwerben, gewinnen*) to get; **sich** (*dat*) **etw ~** to get (oneself) sth; **dabei ist nichts zu ~** (*inf*) there's nothing in it; **bei ihm ist nichts zu ~** (*inf*) you *etc* won't get anything out of him **(f)** (*Naut*) *Anker* to raise; *Segel, Taue* to take in

Holland [ˈhɔlant] NT **-s** Holland, the Netherlands *pl*

Holländer [ˈhɔlɛndɐ] M **-s, -** (= *Mensch*) Dutchman; **die ~** the Dutch (people); **er ist ~** he is Dutch *or* a Dutchman

Holländerin [ˈhɔlɛndərɪn] F **-, -nen** Dutchwoman, Dutch girl; *siehe auch* **Holländer**

holländisch [ˈhɔlɛndɪʃ] ADJ Dutch

Hölle [ˈhœlə] F **-**, (*rare*) **-n** hell; **in der ~** in hell; **die ~ auf Erden** hell on earth; **zur ~ mit ...** to hell with ...; (*inf*) **zur ~ kommen** to go to hell; **ich werde ihm die ~ heiß machen** (*inf*) I'll give him hell (*inf*); **er machte ihr das Leben zur ~** he made her life (a) hell (*inf*); **es war die (reinste) ~** (*inf*) it was (pure) hell (*inf*); **die ~ ist los** (*inf*) all hell has broken loose (*inf*)

Höllen- IN CPDS (= *der Hölle*) of hell, infernal; (*inf.* = *groß*) hellish (*inf*), infernal (*inf*); **Höllenangst** F (*inf*) terrible fear; **eine ~ haben** to be scared stiff (*inf*); **Höllenstein** M (*Chem*) silver nitrate, lunar caustic

höllisch [ˈhœlɪʃ] ◨ ADJ **(a)** ATTR (= *die Hölle betreffend*) infernal, of hell **(b)** (*inf.* = *außerordentlich*) dreadful, hellish (*inf*); **eine ~e Angst haben** to be scared stiff (*inf*) ◩ ADV (*inf*) like hell (*inf*), hellishly (*inf*); **~ fluchen** to swear like a trooper; **die Prüfung war ~ schwer** the exam was hellish(ly) difficult (*inf*)

Hollywoodschaukel [ˈhɔliwʊd-] F swing hammock

Holm [hɔlm] M **-(e)s, -e (a)** (*von Barren*) bar; (*von Geländer*) rail; (*von Leiter*) side rail **(b)** (= *Axtholm*) shaft, handle

Holocaust [ˈhoːlokaust, holoˈkaust, ˌhɔlakɔːst] M **-(s), -(s)** holocaust

Holocaust- [ˈhoːlokaust, holoˈkaust, ˌhɔlakɔːst] IN CPDS holocaust; **Holocaust-Gedenkstätte** F holocaust memorial

Holografie [holograˈfiː] F **-, -n** [-ˈfiːən] holography

Hologramm [holoˈgram] NT, *pl* **-gramme** hologram

holperig [ˈhɔlpərɪç] ◨ ADJ **(a)** *Weg, Pflaster* bumpy **(b)** *Rede, Verse* stumbling ◩ ADV **~ lesen** to read jerkily

holpern [ˈhɔlpɐn] VI to bump, to jolt; **~de Verse** stumbling verse

holprig [ˈhɔlprɪç] ADJ = **holperig**

Holunder [hoˈlʊndɐ] M **-s, -** elder; (= *Früchte*) elderberries *pl*

Holz [hɔlts] NT **-es, ~er** [ˈhœltsə] wood; (*esp zum Bauen, Schreinern*) timber, lumber (*esp US*); **ein ~** a piece of wood; a piece of timber *or* lumber (*esp US*); (= *~art*) a wood; **flüssiges ~** (*Tech*) plastic wood; **aus ~** made of wood, wooden; **~ fällen** to fell trees; **~ sägen** (*lit*) to saw wood; (*inf.* = *schnarchen*) to snore, to saw wood (*US inf*); **~ verarbeitend** wood-processing; **aus einem anderen ~ (geschnitzt) sein** (*fig*) to be cast in a different mould (*Brit*) *or* mold (*US*); **aus grobem ~ geschnitzt sein** (*fig*) to be insensitive; **aus hartem** *or* **härterem ~ geschnitzt sein** (*fig*) to be made of stern *or* sterner stuff; **aus demselben ~ geschnitzt sein** (*fig*) to be cast in the same mould (*Brit*) *or* mold (*US*); **~ vor der Hütte** *or* **Tür haben** (*inf*) to be well-stacked (*inf*); **Holz!** (*Tennis etc*) wood!

Holz- IN CPDS wood; (= *aus ~ auch*) wooden; (*Build, Comm etc*) timber, lumber (*esp US*); **Holzapfel** M crab apple; **Holzarbeiter(in)** M(F) woodworker; (*im Wald*) woodcutter, lumberjack (*esp US*); **holzarm** ADJ *Gegend* sparsely wooded; *Papier* with (a) low wood content; **Holzauge** NT **~ sei wachsam** (*inf*) be careful; **Holzbearbeitung** F woodworking; (*im Sägewerk*) timber processing; **Holzbein** NT wooden leg; **Holzbläser(in)** M(F) woodwind player; **Holzblasinstrument** NT woodwind instrument; **Holzbock** M **(a)** (= *Stützgestell*) wooden stand *or* trestle **(b)** (= *Insekt*) wood tick, dog tick;

Holzboden M (= *Fußboden*) wooden floor; **Holzbohrer** M (*Tech*) wood drill

Hölzchen ['hœltsçən] NT **-s, -** small piece of wood; (= *Streichholz*) match

Holzerei [hɔltsə'rai] F **-, -en** (*inf*) (= *Rauferei*) roughhouse (*inf*); (*Ftbl auch*) rough game *or* match

hölzern ['hœltsɐn] 🔢 ADJ (*lit, fig*) wooden 🔢 ADV (*fig*) woodenly, stiffly

Holz-: Holzfällen NT **-s,** NO PL tree-felling; **Holzfäller** M **-s, -, Holzfällerin** [-ərɪn] F **-, -nen** woodcutter, lumberjack (*esp US*); **Holzfaser** F wood fibre (*Brit*) *or* fiber (*US*); **Holzfaserplatte** F (wood) fibreboard (*Brit*) *or* fiberboard (*US*); **Holzfäule** [-fɔylə] F **-,** NO PL wood rot; **holzfrei** ADJ *Papier* wood-free; **Holzhacken** NT **-s,** NO PL cutting *or* chopping wood; **holzhaltig** ADJ *Papier* woody; **Holzhammer** M mallet; **jdm etw mit dem ~ beibringen** to hammer sth into sb (*inf*); **Holzhammermethode** F (*inf*) sledgehammer method (*inf*); **Holzhaus** NT wooden *or* timber house

holzig ['hɔltsɪç] ADJ woody

Holz-: Holzkitt M plastic wood; **Holzklotz** M block of wood, log; (= *Spielzeug*) wooden brick; **Holzkohle** F charcoal; **Holzkopf** M (*fig inf*) blockhead (*inf*); **Holzpantine** [-pantiːnə] F **-, -n, Holzpantoffel** M clog; **Holzschädling** M wood pest; **Holzscheit** NT piece of (fire)wood, log; **Holzschneider(in)** M(F) wood engraver; **Holzschnitt** M wood engraving; **holzschnittartig** (*fig*) 🔢 ADJ simplistic 🔢 ADV simplistically; **Holzschnitzer(in)** M(F) wood carver; **Holzschnitzerei** F (art *or* craft of) wood carving; **Holzschuh** M wooden shoe, clog; **Holzschutzmittel** NT wood preservative; **Holzschwamm** M dry rot; **Holzspan** M chip (of wood); (*beim Hobeln*) wood shaving; **Holzstich** M wood engraving; **Holzstoß** M pile of wood; **Holztäfelung** F wood(en) panelling (*Brit*) *or* paneling (*US*); **holzverarbeitend** ADJ ATTR *siehe* Holz; **Holzverarbeitung** F wood-processing; **Holzverschlag** M (a) (= *Schuppen*) wooden shed (b) (= *Verpackung*) wooden crate; **Holzwaren** PL wooden articles *pl*; **Holzweg** M logging-path; **auf dem ~ sein** (*fig inf*) to be on the wrong track (*inf*); **wenn du meinst, ich gebe dir das, dann bist du auf dem ~** if you think I'm going to give it to you, you've got another think (*Brit*) *or* thought (*US*) coming (*inf*); **Holzwirtschaft** F timber *or* lumber (*esp US*) industry; **Holzwolle** F wood-wool; **Holzwurm** M woodworm

Home- ['hoːm-]: **Homebanking** ['hoːmbɛŋkɪŋ] NT **-,** NO PL home banking; **Homepage** ['hoːmpeːdʒ] F **-,** (*Comput: im Internet*) home page; **Homesitter** ['hoːmzɪtɐ] M **-s, -, Homesitterin** [-ərɪn] F **-, -nen** housesitter

Hommage [ɔ'maːʒ] F **-, -n** homage

homo-, Homo- IN CPDS homo; **Homoehe** F (*inf*) gay marriage; **homogen** [homo'geːn] ADJ homogeneous; **homogenisieren** [homogeni'ziːrən], *ptp* **homogenisiert** VT to homogenize; **Homogenität** [homogeni'tɛːt] F **-,** NO PL homogeneity; **Homograf** [homo'graːf] NT **-s, -e** (*Ling*) homograph; **homonym** [homo'nyːm] ADJ homonymous; **Homonym** [homo'nyːm] NT **-(e)s, -e** homonym

Homöopath [homøo'paːt] M **-en, -en, Homöopathin** [-'paːtɪn] F **-, -nen** homoeopath

Homöopathie [homøopa'tiː] F **-,** NO PL homoeopathy

homöopathisch [homøo'paːtɪʃ] ADJ homoeopathic

Homo-: homophon [homo'foːn], **homofon** ADJ (*Mus*) homophonic; (*Ling*) homophonous; **Homophon** [homo'foːn] NT **-s, -e, Homofon** NT **-s, -e** (*Ling*) homophone; **Homosexualität** [homozɛksualiˈtɛːt] F homosexuality; **homosexuell** [homozɛˈksuɛl] ADJ homosexual; **Homosexuelle(r)** MF DECL AS ADJ homosexual

Hongkong ['hɔŋkɔŋ] NT **-s** Hong Kong

Honig ['hoːnɪç] M **-s,** NO PL honey; **türkischer ~** halva(h), ≈ nougat; **sie schmierte ihm ~ ums Maul** *or* **um den Bart** (*fig inf*) she buttered him up (*inf*); **~ aus etw saugen** (*fig inf*) to capitalize on sth

Honig-: Honigbiene F honeybee; **honigfarben** [-farbn] ADJ honey-coloured (*Brit*), honey-colored (*US*); **honiggelb** ADJ honey-yellow; **Honigklee** M (*Bot*) melitot; **Honigkuchen** M honey cake; **Honigkuchenpferd** NT **grinsen wie ein ~** (*inf*) to grin like a Cheshire cat; **Honiglecken** NT **-s,** NO PL (*fig*) **das ist kein ~** it's no picnic; **Honigmelone** F honeydew melon; **honigsüß** 🔢 ADJ as sweet as honey; (*fig*) *Worte, Ton* honeyed; *Lächeln* sickly sweet 🔢 ADV **er lächelte ~** he smiled a sickly

sweet smile; **Honigtau** M (*pflanzlich, tierisch*) honeydew; **Honigwabe** F honeycomb

Honorar [hono'raːɐ] NT **-s, -e** fee; (= *Autorenhonorar*) royalty

Honorar-: Honorarabrechnung F statement of account; (*von Schriftsteller*) royalties account; **honorarfrei** ADJ free of charge; **Honorarkonsul(in)** M(F) honorary consul

Honoratioren [honora'tsioːrən] PL dignitaries *pl*

honorieren [hono'riːrən], *ptp* **honoriert** VT (a) (= *bezahlen*) to pay; (*Fin*) *Wechsel, Scheck* to honour (*Brit*), to honor (*US*), to meet; **jdm etw ~** to remunerate sb for sth (b) (= *würdigen wissen*) *Vorschläge* to acknowledge; (= *belohnen*) *Bemühungen* to reward

Honorierung F **-, -en** (*einer Rechnung*) payment (of a fee); (= *Bezahlung*) remuneration; (*Comm: von Wechsel, Scheck*) acceptance

honoris causa [ho'noːrɪs 'kauza] ADV **Dr. ~** honorary doctor

Hopfen ['hɔpfn] M **-s, -** (*Bot*) hop; (*beim Brauen*) hops *pl*; **bei *or* an ihm ist ~ und Malz verloren** (*inf*) he's a hopeless case

Hopfen- IN CPDS hop; **Hopfendarre** [-darə] F **-, -n** hop drier *or* kiln; **Hopfenstange** F hop-pole

hopp [hɔp] INTERJ quick; **bei ihr muss alles ~ ~ gehen** she insists on doing everything double-quick (*inf*); **mach mal ein bisschen ~!** (*inf*) chop, chop! (*inf*); **~e -e Reiter machen** (*baby-talk*) to ride a cock-horse (*on sb's knee*) (*Brit*), to ride the horsy (*US*)

hoppeln ['hɔpln] VI AUX SEIN (*Hase*) to lollop

hoppla ['hɔpla] INTERJ whoops, oops; **~, jetzt komm ich!** look out, here I come!

hops ADJ PRED (*inf*) **~ sein** (= *verloren*) to be lost; (*Geld*) to be down the drain (*inf*); (= *entzwei*) to be broken *or* kaputt (*inf*); *siehe auch* hopsgehen, hopsnehmen

hopsa ['hɔpsa] INTERJ = hoppla

hopsala ['hɔpsala] INTERJ upsadaisy

hopsasa ['hɔpsasa] INTERJ up we go

hopsen ['hɔpsn] VI AUX SEIN (*inf*) (= *hüpfen*) to hop; (= *springen*) to jump

hopsgehen VI SEP IRREG AUX SEIN (*inf*: = *verloren gehen*) to get lost; (*inf*: = *entzweigehen*) to get broken; (*inf*: = *sterben*) to croak (*inf*)

hopsnehmen VT SEP IRREG **jdn ~** (*inf*: = *verhaften*) to nab sb (*inf*)

Hör-: hörbar ADJ audible; **Hörbereich** M (*des Ohrs*) hearing range; (*eines Senders*) transmission area; **Hörbrille** F hearing-aid glasses *pl or* spectacles *pl*; **Hörbuch** NT talking book

horchen ['hɔrçn] VI to listen (+*dat, auf +acc* to); (*heimlich*) to eavesdrop

Horcher ['hɔrçɐ] M **-s, -, Horcherin** [-ərɪn] F **-, -nen** eavesdropper; **der ~ an der Wand hört seine eigne Schand** (*Prov*) eavesdroppers never hear any good about themselves

Horde ['hɔrdə] F **-, -n** (*lit, fig*) horde

hordenweise ['hɔrdnvaizə] ADV in hordes

hören ['høːrən] VTI (a) (= *wahrnehmen*) to hear; (= *zuhören*) to listen; **ich höre dich nicht** I can't hear you; **er hat an der Wand gehört** he was listening at the wall; **schwer ~** to be hard of hearing; **du hörst wohl schwer *or* schlecht!** (*inf*) you must be deaf!; **hört, hört!** (*Zustimmung*) hear! hear!; (*Missfallen*) come, come!; **etw an etw** (*dat*) **~** to hear sth from sth; **das lässt sich ~** (*fig*) that doesn't sound bad; **das lässt sich schon eher ~** (*inf*) that sounds (a bit) more like it; **das werde ich noch lange ~ müssen** *or* **zu ~ bekommen** I shall never hear the end *or* last of it; **ich will gar nichts ~!** I don't want to hear it; **er hört sich gern reden** he likes the sound of his own voice; **hör mal!, ~ Sie mal!** listen; **na ~ Sie mal!** wait a minute!
(b) (= *anhören*) to listen to; *Berichte, Sänger* to hear; (*Rad:* = *empfangen*) to get; **ich will auch gehört werden** I want to be heard too; **bei wem ~ Sie in diesem Semester?** whose lectures are you going to this term?; **eine französische Vorlesung bei Professor X ~** to go to a French lecture by Professor X
(c) (= *sich nach etw richten*) to listen, to pay attention; (*dial:* = *gehorchen*) to obey, to listen; **auf jdn/etw ~** to listen to *or* heed sb/sth; **wer nicht ~ will, muss fühlen** (*Prov*) what did I tell you?; **der Hund hört auf den Namen Tobias** the dog answers to the name of Tobias
(d) (= *erfahren*) to hear; **von etw ~** to hear about *or* of sth; **von jdm ~** (= *Nachricht bekommen*) to hear from sb; **Sie werden noch von mir ~** *or* **zu ~ kriegen** (*inf*: = *Drohung*) you'll be hearing from me; **nie gehört!** (*inf*) never heard of him/it *etc*;

etwas/nichts von sich ~ lassen to get/not to get in touch; **lassen Sie von sich ~** keep in touch; **ich lasse von mir ~** I'll be in touch; **man höre und staune!** would you believe it!; **so etwas** or **das habe ich ja noch nie gehört!** I've never heard anything like it (in all my life)!; **er wollte nichts** or **von nichts gehört haben** he pretended not to have heard anything about it; **ich will davon** or **von der Sache nichts gehört haben** I don't want to know anything about it; **ich will mal nichts gehört haben** (inf) I haven't heard a thing, right? (inf)

Hören NT **-s**, NO PL hearing; (= *Radiohören*) listening; **das ~ von Musik** listening to music; **es verging ihm ~ und Sehen** he didn't know whether he was coming or going (inf); **er fuhr so schnell, dass mir ~ und Sehen verging** he drove so fast I almost passed out

Hörensagen NT vom **~** from or by hearsay

hörenswert ADJ **~ sein** to be worth hearing, to be worth listening

Hörer[1] ['hø:rɐ] M **-s, -** (*Telec*) receiver; (= *Kopfhörer*) headphone, earphone

Hörer[2] ['hø:rɐ] M **-s, -**, **Hörerin** [-ərɪn] F **-, -nen** (*Rad*) listener; (*Univ*) student (attending lectures); **sich als ~ einschreiben** to enrol (*Brit*) or enroll (*US*) for a lecture course

Hörerschaft ['hø:rɐʃaft] F **-,** (*rare*) **-en** (*Rad*) listeners pl, audience; (*Univ*) number of students (attending a lecture)

Hör-: Hörfolge F (*Rad*) radio series; (= *Geschichte in Fortsetzungen*) radio serial; **Hörfunk** M sound radio; **Hörgerät** NT, **Hörhilfe** F hearing aid; **Hörgrenze** F auditory threshold; **hörig** ADJ dependent (+dat on); (*Hist*) in bondage; **jdm (sexuell) ~ sein** to be (sexually) dependent on sb; **er ist ihr ~** she has sexual power over him

Horizont [hori'tsɔnt] M **-(e)s, -e** (*lit, fig*) horizon; **am ~** on the horizon; **das geht über meinen ~** (*fig*) that is beyond me; **er hat einen begrenzten** or **beschränkten ~** he has limited horizons

horizontal [horitsɔn'ta:l] **1** ADJ horizontal; **das ~e Gewerbe** (*inf*) the oldest profession in the world (inf) **2** ADV horizontally

Horizontale [horitsɔn'ta:lə] F **-(n), -n** (*Math*) horizontal (line)

Hormon [hɔr'mo:n] NT **-s, -e** hormone

hormonal [hɔrmo'na:l], **hormonell** [hɔrmo'nɛl] **1** ADJ hormone attr, hormonal **2** ADV behandeln, beeinflussen with hormones; *beeinflusst, gesteuert* by hormones; **~ bedingt sein** to be caused by hormones; (*Störung*) to be caused by a hormonal imbalance

Hormon-: Hormonbehandlung F hormone treatment; **Hormoncocktail** M hormone cocktail; **Hormondrüse** F endocrine gland; **Hormonhaushalt** M hormone or hormonal balance

Hörmuschel F (*Telec*) earpiece

Horn [hɔrn] NT **-(e)s, ̈er** ['hœrnə] **(a)** (*von Tieren*) (= *Trinkhorn*) horn; (*fig inf*: = *Beule*) bump, lump; **jdn mit den Hörnern aufspießen** to gore sb; **sich** (*dat*) **die Hörner ablaufen** or **abschleifen** or **abstoßen** (inf) to sow one's wild oats; **jdm Hörner aufsetzen** (inf) to cuckold sb; **das ~ von Afrika** (*Geog*) the Horn of Africa
(b) (*Mus*) horn; (*Mil*) bugle; **ins gleiche ~ blasen** or **stoßen** or **tuten** to chime in
(c) (*bei Schnecke*) horn, feeler

Horn-: hornartig ADJ horn-like; **Hornberger Schießen** ['hɔrnbergə] NT **wie das ~ ausgehen** or **enden** to come to nothing; **Hornbläser(in)** M(F) (*Mus*) horn player; **Hornbrille** F horn-rimmed glasses pl

Hörnchen ['hœrnçən] NT **-s, - (a)** (= *kleines Horn*) little horn **(b)** (= *Gebäck*) croissant **(c)** (*Zool*) squirrel; (= *Backenhörnchen*) chipmunk, ground squirrel; (= *Flughörnchen*) flying squirrel

Hörnerv M auditory nerve

Horn-: Hornhaut F callus; (*des Auges*) cornea; **Hornhautentzündung** F (*Med*) inflammation of the cornea; **Hornhauttrübung** F (*Med*) corneal opacity

Hornisse [hɔr'nɪsə] F **-, -n** hornet

Hornissennest NT hornet's nest

Hornist [hɔr'nɪst] M **-en, -en**, **Hornistin** [-'nɪstɪn] F **-, -nen** horn player; (*Mil*) bugler

Horoskop [horo'sko:p] NT **-s, -e** horoscope; **jdm das ~ stellen** to cast sb's horoscope

horrend [hɔ'rɛnt] **1** ADJ horrendous **2** ADV *teuer* horrendously

Hörrohr NT **(a)** ear trumpet **(b)** (*Med*) stethoscope

Horror ['hɔrɔr] M **-s**, NO PL horror (*vor* +dat of)

Horror- IN CPDS horror; **Horrorfilm** M horror film; **Horrorszene** F horrific scene; **Horrortrip** M (*inf*) horror trip (inf)

Hör-: Hörsaal M (*Univ*) lecture theatre (*Brit*) or theater (*US*); **Hörschwelle** F auditory threshold; **Hörspiel** NT (*Rad*) radio play

Horst [hɔrst] M **-(e)s, -e (a)** (= *Nest*) nest; (= *Adlerhorst*) eyrie **(b)** (= *Fliegerhorst*) military airfield

Hörsturz M hearing loss

horten ['hɔrtn] VT to hoard; *Rohstoffe etc* to stockpile

Hortensie [hɔr'tɛnziə] F **-, -n** hydrangea

Hörweite F hearing range; **in/außer ~** within/out of hearing or earshot

Höschen ['hø:sçən] NT **-s, - (a)** (= *Kinderhose*) (pair of) trousers pl (*esp Brit*) or pants pl (*esp US*); (= *Strampelhöschen*) (pair of) rompers pl; **kurze(s) ~** (pair of) shorts pl **(b)** (= *Unterhose*) (pair of) panties pl; (*für Kinder*) (pair of) underpants (*Brit*)

Hose ['ho:zə] F **-, -n** trousers pl (*esp Brit*), pants pl (*esp US*); (= *Unterhose*) underpants pl, pants pl (*Brit*); **ich brauche eine neue ~** I need a new pair of trousers *etc*; **die ~n anhaben** (*fig inf*) to wear the trousers (*Brit*) or pants (inf); **das Herz fiel** or **rutschte ihr in die ~** (*inf*) her heart was in her mouth; **die ~n voll haben** (*lit*) to have dirtied oneself; (*fig inf*) to be scared shitless (*sl*); **sich** (*dat*) **in die ~n machen** (*lit*) to dirty oneself; (*fig inf*) to shit oneself (*sl*); **in die ~ gehen** (*inf*) to be a complete flop (inf); **tote ~** (*inf*) nothing doing (inf)

Vorsicht! **Hose** *wird nicht mit dem englischen Wort* **hose** *übersetzt.*

Hosen-: Hosenanzug M trouser suit (*Brit*), pantsuit (*US*); **Hosenaufschlag** M turn-up (*Brit*), cuff (*US*); **Hosenbandorden** M Order of the Garter; **Hosenbein** NT trouser (*esp Brit*) or pant (*esp US*) leg; **Hosenboden** M seat of (trousers (*esp Brit*) or pants (*esp US*)); **sich auf den ~ setzen** (*inf*) (= *arbeiten*) to get stuck in (inf); (= *still sitzen*) to sit down and stay sitting down; **Hosenbügel** M trouser (*esp Brit*) or pant (*esp US*) hanger; **Hosenbund** M, pl **-bünde** waistband; **Hosenlatz** M (= *Verschluss*) flies pl, fly; (*von Latzhose*) bib; **Hosenrock** M culottes pl; **Hosenscheißer(in)** M(F) **(a)** (*inf*: = *Kind*) mucky pup (*Brit inf*), pig (inf) **(b)** (*sl*: = *Feigling*) chicken (inf); (= *Junge*) scaredy-pants (*inf*); **Hosenschlitz** M flies pl, fly; **Hosenspanner** M trouser (*esp Brit*) or pant (*esp US*) hanger; **Hosentasche** F trouser (*esp Brit*), pant(s) or trousers pocket (*US*); **Hosenträger** PL (pair of) braces pl (*Brit*) or suspenders pl (*US*)

Hospitant [hɔspi'tant] M **-en, -en**, **Hospitantin** [-'tantɪn] F **-, -nen** (*Univ*) someone sitting in on lectures or (*Sch*) classes, auditor (*US*)

hospitieren [hɔspi'ti:rən], *ptp* **hospitiert** VI (*Univ*) to sit in on lectures or (*Sch*) classes (*bei jdm* with sb)

Hospiz [hɔs'pi:ts] NT **-es, -e** hospice; (= *christliches ~*) private hotel under religious management

Host [ho:st] M **-s, -s** (*Comput*) host

Hostess ['hɔstɛs, hɔs'tɛs] F **-, -en** hostess

Hostrechner [ho:st-] M host computer

Hostie ['hɔstiə] F **-, -n** (*Eccl*) host, consecrated wafer

Hotdog ['hɔtdɔk] NT or M **-s, -s, Hot Dog** NT or M **-s, -s** (*Cook*) hot dog

Hotel [ho'tɛl] NT **-s, -s** hotel

Hotelboy M bellboy (*US*), bellhop (*US*)

Hotelfach NT, NO PL hotel management

Hotelfach-: Hotelfachfrau F hotel manageress; **Hotelfachmann** M hotel manager; **Hotelfachschule** F college of hotel management

Hotel-: Hotelführer M hotel guide; **Hotelnachweis** M hotel register; **Hotelportier** M hotel porter; **Hotel- und Gaststättengewerbe** NT catering or hotel and restaurant trade; **Hotelverzeichnis** NT hotel register

Hotkey ['hɔtki:] M **-s, -s** (*Comput*) hot key

Hotline ['hɔtlain] F **-, -s** helpline; **eine ~ einrichten** to set up a helpline

Hottentotte [hɔtn'tɔtə] M **-n, -n**, **Hottentottin** [-'tɔtɪn] F **-, -nen** Hottentot

Hptst. ABBR *von* **Hauptstadt**

Hr. ABBR *von* **Herr** Mr

Hrn. ABBR *von* **Herrn**

hrsg. ABBR *von* **herausgegeben** edited, ed.

Hrsg. ABBR *von* **Herausgeber** ed.

HTML [haːteːˈɛmˈʔɛl] ABBR *von* **Hyper Text Markup Language** HTML

hü [hyː] INTERJ (= *vorwärts*) gee up; (= *nach links*) wo hi; **einmal sagt er hü, einmal hott** (*inf*) first he says one thing and then another

Hub [huːp] M **-(e)s, ⁼e** [ˈhyːbə] (*Tech*) (a) (*bei Maschinen*: = *Kolbenhub*) (piston) stroke (b) (*bei Kränen*: = *Leistung*) lifting *or* hoisting capacity

Hubbel [ˈhʊbl] M **-s, -** (*inf*) bump

hüben [ˈhyːbn] ADV over here, (on) this side; **~ und** *or* **wie drüben** on both sides

Hubraum M (*Aut*) cubic capacity

hübsch [hypʃ] **1** ADJ (a) (= *gut aussehend*) pretty; (= *reizvoll*) *Ausflug, Geschenk* lovely, delightful; (*inf*: = *nett*) lovely, nice; **sich ~ machen** to make oneself look pretty; **ihr (beiden) Hübschen** (*inf*) you two
(b) (*iro inf*: = *unangenehm*) fine, nice; **eine ~e Geschichte/ Bescherung** a pretty kettle of fish; **das kann ja ~ werden** that'll be just great
(c) (*inf*: = *beträchtlich*) tidy, pretty; **ein ~es Vermögen** a pretty penny (*inf*); **ein ~es Sümmchen** a tidy sum
2 ADV (a) (= *nett*) einrichten, dekorieren, gestalten, sich kleiden nicely; **~ aussehen** to look pretty
(b) (= *ziemlich*) pretty; *fluchen, dazulernen, reinlegen* really; **ganz ~ viel bezahlen** to pay quite a bit
(c) (*inf*: = *wie es sein soll*) **~ artig/leise** nice and good/quiet; **das werde ich ~ bleiben lassen** I'm going to leave well alone; **das wirst du ~ bleiben lassen!** don't you dare; **sei ~ artig!** be a good boy/girl

Hubschrauber [ˈhuːpʃraʊbɐ] M **-s, -** helicopter

Hubschrauberlandeplatz M heliport

Hucke [ˈhʊkə] F **-, -n** (*inf*) **jdm die ~ voll hauen** to give sb a good thrashing (*inf*); **die ~ voll kriegen** to get a thrashing (*inf*); **jdm die ~ voll lügen** to tell sb a pack of lies

huckepack [ˈhʊkəpak] ADV piggy-back (*auch Comput*), pick-a-back; **ein Kind ~ nehmen/tragen** to give a child a piggy-back (ride)

Huckepack- [ˈhʊkəpak-]: **Huckepackverfahren** NT (*Space, Rail*) piggy-back system; (*Chem*) piggy-back process; **Huckepackverkehr** M (*Rail*) piggy-back transport (*US*), motorail service; **im ~** by motorail

hudeln [ˈhuːdln] VI (*esp S Ger, Aus: inf*) to work sloppily

hudlig [ˈhuːdlɪç] (*esp S Ger, Aus: inf*) **1** ADJ sloppy (*inf*) **2** ADV sloppily

Huf [huːf] M **-(e)s, -e** hoof; **einem Pferd die ~e beschlagen** to shoe a horse

Huf-: **Hufeisen** NT horseshoe; **hufeisenförmig 1** ADJ horseshoe-shaped **2** ADV in the shape of a horseshoe; **Huflattich** M **-s, -e** (*Bot*) coltsfoot; **Hufnagel** M horseshoe nail; **Hufschmied(in)** M(F) blacksmith

Hüftbein NT hipbone

Hüfte [ˈhyftə] F **-, -n** hip; (*von Tieren*) haunch; **die Arme in die ~n stützen** to put one's hands on one's hips

Hüft-: **Hüftgegend** F hip region; **Hüftgelenk** NT hip joint; **Hüftgürtel** M, **Hüfthalter** M girdle; **hüfthoch 1** ADJ *Pflanzen etc* waist-high; *Wasser etc* waist-deep; **hüfthohe Gummistiefel** rubber waders **2** ADV **wir standen ~ im Farnkraut/Schlamm** we stood up to the waist in ferns/mud

Hüftier NT hoofed animal

Hüft-: **Hüftknochen** M hipbone; **Hüftleiden** NT hip trouble

Hügel [ˈhyːgl] M **-s, -** hill; (= *Grab-, Erdhaufen*) mound; **ein kleiner ~** a hillock

Hügel-: **Hügelbeet** NT raised bed; **Hügelgrab** NT (*Archeol*) barrow

hügelig [ˈhyːgəlɪç] ADJ hilly

Hugenotte [hugəˈnɔtə] M **-n, -n**, **Hugenottin** [-ˈnɔtɪn] F **-, -nen** Huguenot

Huhn [huːn] NT **-(e)s, ⁼er** [ˈhyːnɐ] (a) chicken (*auch Cook*); (= *Henne*) hen, chicken; (*Gattung*) fowl; **mit den Hühnern aufstehen** (*inf*) to get up with the lark; **mit den Hühnern zu**

Bett gehen (*inf*) to go to bed early; **da lachen ja die Hühner** (*inf*) what a joke (b) (*fig inf*) **du krankes ~** you poor old thing; **ein verrücktes** *or* **komisches** *or* **ulkiges ~** a strange *or* odd character; **ein dummes ~** a silly goose

Hühnchen [ˈhyːnçən] NT **-s, -** (young) chicken, pullet; (= *Brathühnchen*) (roast) chicken; **mit jdm ein ~ zu rupfen haben** (*inf*) to have a bone to pick with sb (*inf*)

Hühner-: **Hühnerauge** NT (*Med*) corn; **Hühnerbouillon** F, **Hühnerbrühe** F (*clear*) chicken broth; **Hühnerbrust** F (*Cook*) chicken breast; (*Med inf*) pigeon breast (*Brit*), chicken breast (*US*); **eine ~ haben** (*sl*: = *flacher Busen*) to be as flat as a pancake (*esp Brit inf*) *or* a board (*US inf*); **Hühnerei** [-laɪ] NT hen's egg; **Hühnerfrikassee** [-frikaseː] NT **-s, -s** chicken fricassee; **Hühnerfutter** NT chicken feed; **Hühnerklein** [-klaɪn] NT **-s**, NO PL (*Cook*) chicken trimmings *pl*; **Hühnerstall** M henhouse, chicken coop; **Hühnerzucht** F chicken breeding *or* farming

hui [huɪ] INTERJ whoosh; **~, das war aber schnell!** wow, that was quick!; **außen ~, innen pfui** (*prov inf*) he/she/it is fine on the outside, but inside it's a different story (*inf*)

Hula-Hoop-Reifen [huːlaˈhup-] M Hula Hoop®

Hülle [ˈhʏlə] F **-, -n** (a) cover; (*für Ausweiskarten etc*) holder, case; (= *Cellophanhülle*) wrapping; **die ~n fallen lassen** to peel *or* strip off; **die sterbliche ~** the mortal remains *pl* (b) **in ~ und Fülle** in abundance; **Äpfel/Whisky/Frauen/Sorgen** *etc* **in ~ und Fülle** apples/whisky/women/worries *etc* galore; **es gab alles in ~ und Fülle** there was an abundance of everything

hüllen [ˈhʏlən] VT (*geh*) to wrap; **in Dunkel gehüllt** shrouded in darkness; **in Wolken gehüllt** enveloped in clouds; **sich (über etw** *acc*) **in Schweigen ~** to remain silent (on *or* about sth)

Hüllwort NT, *pl* **-wörter** (*Ling*) euphemism

Hülse [ˈhʏlzə] F **-, -n** (a) (= *Schale*) hull, husk; (= *Schote*) pod (b) (= *Etui, Kapsel*) case; (*für Film*) cartridge; (*von Geschoss*) case; (*von Patronen*) (cartridge) case

Hülsenfrucht F USU PL peas and beans *pl*, pulse (*form*)

human [huˈmaːn] **1** ADJ humane **2** ADV humanely; **die Abschiebung ~er gestalten** to carry out deportations in a more humane way

Humanismus [humaˈnɪsmʊs] M **-**, NO PL humanism; (*Hist*) Humanism

Humanist [humaˈnɪst] M **-en, -en**, **Humanistin** [-ˈnɪstɪn] F **-, -nen** humanist; (*Hist*) Humanist; (= *Altsprachler*) classicist

humanistisch [humaˈnɪstɪʃ] **1** ADJ humanist(ic); (*Hist*) Humanist; (= *altsprachlich*) classical; **~e Bildung** classical education; **~es Gymnasium** *secondary school with bias on Latin and Greek*, ≈ grammar school (*Brit*) **2** ADV **jdn ~ bilden** to provide sb with a humanistic *or* classical education; **~ gebildet** educated in the classics *or* humanities; **~ erzogen werden** to receive a humanistic *or* classical education

humanitär [humaniˈtɛːɐ] ADJ humanitarian

Humanität [humaniˈtɛːt] F **-**, NO PL humaneness, humanity; (*als Bildungsideal*) humanitarianism

Humanitätsduselei [-duːzəlaɪ] F **-, -en** (*pej*) sentimental humanitarianism

Humanmedizin F (human) medicine

Humbug [ˈhʊmbʊk] M **-s**, NO PL (*inf*) humbug (*inf*)

Hummel [ˈhʊml] F **-, -n** bumblebee

Hummer [ˈhʊmɐ] M **-s, -** lobster

Hummer-: **Hummerkrabben** PL king prawns *pl*; **Hummerreuse** F lobster pot; **Hummerschere** F lobster claw

Humor [huˈmoːɐ] M **-s**, (*rare*) **-e** humour (*Brit*), humor (*US*); (= *Sinn f-*) sense of humo(u)r; **er hat keinen (Sinn f-) ~** he has no sense of humo(u)r; **sie nahm die Bemerkung mit ~ auf** she took the remark in good humo(u)r; **er verliert nie den ~** he never loses his sense of humo(u)r; **da hat selbst sie den ~ verloren** even she didn't think it funny any more; **~ ist, wenn man trotzdem lacht** (*prov*) having a sense of humo(u)r means looking on the bright side

Humorist [humoˈrɪst] M **-en, -en**, **Humoristin** [-ˈrɪstɪn] F **-, -nen** humorist; (= *Komiker*) comedian

humoristisch [humoˈrɪstɪʃ] ADJ humorous; **er ist** *or* **hat ein großes ~es Talent** he is a very amusing person

Humor-: **humorlos 1** ADJ humourless (*Brit*), humorless (*US*) **2** ADV humourlessly (*Brit*), humorlessly (*US*); **sich ~ verhalten** to have no sense of humour (*Brit*) *or* humor (*US*); **er hat recht ~ auf unsere Scherze reagiert** he didn't find our jokes funny at all; **Humorlosigkeit** F **-**, NO PL humourlessness (*Brit*),

humorlessness (US); **mit der für sie typischen** ~ with her usual lack of humour (Brit) or humor (US); **humorvoll** 🔒 ADJ humorous, amusing 🔒 ADV humorously, amusingly; ~ **über etw** (acc) **hinweggehen** to make light of sth; **er kann sehr ~ erzählen** he is a very amusing talker

humpeln ['hʊmpln] VI **(a)** AUX SEIN to hobble **(b)** (inf: = ständig hinken) to limp

Humpen ['hʊmpn] M **-s, -** tankard, mug; (aus Ton) stein

Humusboden M, **Humuserde** F humus soil

Hund [hʊnt] M **-(e)s, -e** [-də] dog; (esp Jagdhund) hound; (inf: = Schurke) swine (inf); **junger ~** puppy, pup; **die Familie der ~e** the dog or canine family; **~e, die (viel) bellen, beißen nicht** (Prov) empty vessels make most noise (Prov); **getroffene ~e bellen** (inf) if the cap fits, wear it; **wie ~ und Katze leben** to live like cat and dog; **damit kann man keinen ~ hinterm Ofen hervorlocken** (inf) that's not going to tempt anybody; **er ist bekannt wie ein bunter ~** (inf) everybody knows him; **da wird der ~ in der Pfanne verrückt** (inf) it's enough to drive you crazy (inf); **da liegt der ~ begraben** (inf) (so) that's what is/was behind it all; (Haken, Problem etc) that's the problem; **er ist ein armer ~** he's a poor soul; **auf den ~ kommen** (inf) to go to the dogs (inf); **vor die ~e gehen** (inf) to go to the dogs (inf); (= sterben) to die; (= getötet werden) to be killed; **du blöder ~** (inf) you stupid bastard (sl); **du gemeiner ~** (inf) you rotten bastard (sl); **du schlauer** or **gerissener ~** (inf) you crafty devil (inf); **kein ~** (inf) not a (damn (inf)) soul; **schlafende ~e soll man nicht wecken** (prov) let sleeping dogs lie (Prov)

Hündchen ['hʏntçən] NT **-s, -** DIM von **Hund** little dog; (= junger Hund) puppy

Hunde-: **Hundeart** F breed (of dog); **Hundebiss** M dog bite; **hundeelend** ADJ (inf) **mir ist ~** I feel lousy (inf); **Hundeführer(in)** M(F) dog handler; **Hundefutter** NT dog food; **Hundehalsband** NT dog collar; **Hundehalter(in)** M(F) (form) dog owner; **Hundehaltung** F owning a dog/dogs; **Hundehütte** F (lit, fig) (dog) kennel; **Hundekot** M dog dirt (Brit) or mess (inf); **Hundekuchen** M dog biscuit; **Hundeleben** NT (inf) dog's life (inf); **Hundeleine** F dog lead (Brit) or leash; **Hundeliebhaber(in)** M(F) dog lover; **Hundemarke** F dog licence (Brit) or license (US) disc, dog tag (US); (hum inf: = Erkennungsmarke) identity disc, dog tag (US inf); **hundemüde** ADJ PRED, ADV (inf) dog-tired; **Hunderasse** F breed (of dog)

hundert ['hʊndɛt] NUM a or one hundred; **einige ~** or **Hundert Menschen** a few hundred people; **einer unter ~** one in a hundred

Hundert¹ ['hʊndɛt] F **-, -en** (= Zahl) hundred

Hundert² NT **-s, -e** hundred; **es geht in die ~e** or **hunderte** it runs into the hundreds; **~e** or **hunderte von Menschen** hundreds of people; **einer unter ~en** or **hunderten** one out of hundreds; **zehn vom ~** ten per cent (Brit) or percent (US); **zu ~en** or **hunderten** by the hundred

hunderteins ['hʊndɛt'|ains] NUM a or one hundred and one

Hunderter ['hʊndɛtɐ] M **-s, -** **(a)** (von Zahl) (the) hundred **(b)** (= Geldschein) hundred(-euro/-pound/-dollar etc) note (Brit) or bill (US)

hunderterlei ['hʊndɛtɐ'lai] ADJ INV a hundred and one

Hundert-: **Hunderteuroschein** M hundred-euro note (Brit) or bill (US); **hundertfach** 🔒 ADJ hundredfold; **die ~e Menge** a hundred times the amount 🔒 ADV a hundred times; **jdm etw ~ zurückgeben** (fig) to repay sb a hundred times over for sth; **hundertfünfzigprozentig** (iro) 🔒 ADJ fanatical; **er ist ein Hundertfünfzigprozentiger** he's a fanatic 🔒 ADV **sich/etw ~ beweisen** to prove oneself/sth twice over; **Hundertjahrfeier** F centenary, centennial (US); **hundertjährig** ADJ ATTR (one-)hundred-year-old; **das Ergebnis einer ~en Entwicklung/Arbeit** the result of a hundred years of development/work; **Hundertjährige(r)** [-jɛːrɪgə] MF DECL AS ADJ centenarian; **hundertmal** ADV a hundred times; **Hundertmeterlauf** M (Sport) **der/ein ~** the/a 100 metres (Brit) or meters (US) sing; **hundertprozentig** 🔒 ADJ (a or one) hundred per cent (Brit) or percent (US); **Alkohol** pure; **ein ~er Konservativer** etc an out-and-out conservative etc 🔒 ADV a or one hundred per cent (Brit) or percent (US); **Sie haben ~ Recht** you're absolutely right; **das weiß ich ~** that's a fact; **ich werde ihn ~ im Krankenhaus besuchen** I'll definitely visit him in hospital; **~?** (inf) are you absolutely sure?

Hundertstel ['hʊndɛtstl] NT **-s, -** hundredth

hundertste(r, s) ['hʊndɛtstə] ADJ hundredth; **vom Hundertsten ins Tausendste kommen** (fig) to get carried away

Hundert-: **hunderttausend** NUM a or one hundred thousand; **~e** or **Hunderttausende von Menschen** hundreds of thousands of people; **hundertundeins** ['hʊndɛtʊnt'|ains] NUM a or one hundred and one; **hundertweise** ADV by the hundred, in hundreds

Hunde-: **Hundesalon** M dog parlour (Brit) or parlor (US); **Hundescheiße** F (inf) dog shit (sl), dog mess (inf); **Hundeschlitten** M dog sled(ge) or sleigh; **Hundeschnauze** F nose, snout; **kalt wie eine ~** (fig inf) cold(-blooded); **Hundestaffel** F dog branch; **Hundesteuer** F dog licence (Brit) or license (US) fee; **Hundezwinger** M (dog) compound; (städtisch) dog pound

Hündin ['hʏndɪn] F **-, -nen** bitch

hündisch ['hʏndɪʃ] ADJ (fig) sycophantic; **~e Ergebenheit** dog-like devotion

Hunds-: **hundsgemein** ['hʊntsgə'main] (inf) 🔒 ADJ shabby; (= schwierig) fiendishly difficult; **Schmerz** etc terrible; **er kann ~ werden** he can get really nasty 🔒 ADV **es tut ~ weh** it hurts like hell (inf); **Hundstage** ['hʊnts-] PL dog days pl

Hüne ['hyːnə] M **-n, -n** giant

Hunger ['hʊŋɐ] M **-s**, NO PL (lit, fig) hunger (nach for); (= Hungersnot) famine; (nach fernen Ländern, Sonne etc) yearning; (nach Literatur) appetite; ~ **bekommen/haben** to get/be hungry; **ich habe keinen richtigen ~** I'm not really hungry; ~ **auf etw** (acc) **haben** to feel like (eating) sth; **den ~ bekämpfen** to combat hunger; ~ **leiden** (geh) to go hungry, to starve; **~s** (liter) or **vor ~ sterben** to starve to death; **ich sterbe vor ~** (inf) I'm starving (inf); ~ **ist der beste Koch** (Prov) hunger is the best cook (Prov)

Hunger-: **Hungergefühl** NT hungry feeling; **Hungerkur** F starvation diet; **Hungerland** NT famine-stricken country; **Hungerlohn** M starvation wages pl; (fig auch) pittance

hungern ['hʊŋɐn] 🔒 VI **(a)** (= Hunger leiden) to go hungry, to starve; **jdn ~ lassen** to let sb go hungry; (zur Strafe auch) to make sb starve **(b)** (= fasten) to go without food 🔒 VT IMPERS (geh) **mich hungert** I am or feel hungry; **ihn hungert nach Macht** he is hungry for power 🔒 VR **sich zu Tode ~** to starve oneself to death; **sich schlank ~** to go on a starvation diet

hungernd ADJ NO COMP hungry, starving

Hungerödem NT (Med) famine oedema (spec)

Hungersnot F famine

Hunger-: **Hungerstreik** M hunger strike; **Hungertuch** NT **am ~ nagen** (fig) to be starving

hungrig ['hʊŋrɪç] ADJ (lit, fig) hungry (nach for); ~ **nach etw** or **auf etw** (acc) **sein** to feel like (eating) sth; ~ **nach Literatur** hungry for good literature

Hunne ['hʊnə] M **-n -n**, **Hunnin** ['hʊnɪn] F **-, -nen** (Hist) Hun

Hunni ['hʊni] M **-s, -s** (hum inf: = Hunderteuroschein) hundred (inf)

Hupe ['huːpə] F **-, -n** horn; **auf die ~ drücken** to sound the horn

hupen ['huːpn] VI to sound or hoot the horn; **„hupen"** "sound your horn"

Hüpfburg ['hʏpf-] F bouncy castle®

hüpfen ['hʏpfn] VI AUX SEIN to hop; (Lämmer, Zicklein etc) to gambol; (Ball) to bounce; **vor Freude ~** to jump for joy; **sein Herz hüpfte vor Freude** his heart leapt for joy; **Hüpfen spielen** to play (at) hopscotch

Hup- ['huːp-]: **Hupkonzert** NT (inf) chorus of horns; **Hupton** M, pl **-töne** sound of a horn; **Hupzeichen** NT (Aut) hoot; **„~ geben"** "sound your horn"

Hürde ['hʏrdə] F **-, -n (a)** (Sport, fig) hurdle; **eine ~ nehmen** to clear a hurdle **(b)** (= Viehzaun) fold, pen

Hure ['huːrə] F **-, -n** whore

huren ['huːrən] VI (inf) to whore

Huren-: **Hurenbock** M (vulg) whoremonger; **Hurensohn** M (vulg) bastard (sl), son of a bitch (sl)

hurra [hʊ'raː, 'hʊra] INTERJ hurray, hurrah

Hurra [hʊ'raː, 'hʊra] NT **-s, -s** cheers pl; **ein dreifaches ~** three cheers

Hurra-: **Hurrageschrei** NT cheering; **Hurraruf** M cheer

Hurrikan ['hʊrikan, 'harɪkən] M **-s, -e** or (bei engl. Aussprache) **-s** hurricane

husch [huʃ] INTERJ **(a)** (*aufscheuchend*) shoo **(b)** (*antreibend*) come on **(c)** (= *schnell*) quick; **er macht seine Arbeit immer ~ ~** (*inf*) he always whizzes through his work (*inf*); **und ~, weg war er** and whoosh! he was gone

huschen [ˈhuʃn] VI AUX SEIN to dart; (*Mäuse etc auch*) to scurry; (*Lächeln*) to flash, to flit; (*Licht*) to flash

Husky [ˈhaski] M **-s, -s** husky

hüsteln [ˈhyːstln] VI to cough slightly; **er hüstelte nur spöttisch** he just cleared his throat sarcastically

husten [ˈhuːstn] 🚹 VI to cough; **auf etw** (*acc*) **~** (*inf*) not to give a damn for sth (*inf*) 🚺 VT to cough; **Blut to cough (up)**; **denen werde ich was** *or* **eins ~** (*inf*) I'll tell them where they can get off (*inf*)

Husten [ˈhuːstn] M **-s**, NO PL cough; **~ haben** to have a cough

Husten-: Hustenanfall M coughing fit; **Hustenbonbon** M *or* NT cough sweet (*Brit*) *or* drop; **Hustenmittel** NT cough medicine; **Hustenreiz** M tickle in the throat; **seinen ~ unterdrücken** to suppress the urge to cough; **Hustensaft** M cough syrup *or* mixture; **hustenstillend** 🚹 ADJ cough-relieving 🚺 ADV **das wirkt ~** it relieves coughing; **Hustentee** M *tea which is good for coughs*

Hut¹ [huːt] M **-(e)s, ⸚e** [ˈhyːtə] hat; (*von Pilz*) cap; **den ~ aufsetzen/abnehmen/lüften** (*geh*) to put on/take off/raise one's hat; **vor jdm den ~ abnehmen** *or* **ziehen** (*fig*) to take off one's hat to sb; **~ ab!** I take my hat off to him/you *etc*; **~ ab vor solcher Leistung!** I take my hat off to you/that; **das kannst du dir an den ~ stecken!** (*inf*) you can keep it (*inf*); **unter einen ~ bringen** *or* **kriegen** (*inf*) to reconcile; *Verpflichtungen, Termine* to fit in; **den** *or* **seinen ~ nehmen (müssen)** (*inf*) to (have to) go; **das ist doch ein alter ~!** (*inf*) that's old hat! (*inf*); **eins auf den ~ kriegen** (*inf*) to get an earful (*inf*); **damit/mit ihm habe ich nichts am ~** (*inf*) I don't want to have anything to do with that/him

Hut² F **-**, NO PL **(a)** (*geh*) keeping; **unter** *or* **in meiner ~** in my keeping; (*Kinder*) in my care **(b) auf der ~ sein** to be on one's guard (*vor +dat* against)

Hütchen [ˈhyːtçən] NT **-s, -** DIM *von* **Hut¹** little hat

Hütchenspiel NT thimblerig

hüten [ˈhyːtn] 🚹 VT to look after, to mind; (*geh*) *Geheimnisse, Briefe, Gegenstände* to keep; **das Bett/Haus ~** to stay in bed/indoors 🚺 VR to (be on one's) guard (*vor +dat* against); **ich werde mich ~!** not likely!; **du wirst dich schwer ~!** you'll do nothing of the kind!; **ich werde mich ~, ihm das zu erzählen** there's no chance of me telling him that; **sich ~, etw zu tun** to take care not to do sth; **~ Sie sich vor ihm** be on your guard against him

Hüter [ˈhyːtɐ] M **-s, -, Hüterin** [-ərɪn] F **-, -nen** guardian, custodian; (= *Viehhüter*) herdsman; **die ~ der Ordnung** (*hum*) the custodians of the law

Hut-: Hutmacher(in) M(F) hat maker; (*von Damenhüten auch*) milliner; **Hutschachtel** F hatbox

Hutsche [ˈhʊtʃə] F **-, -n** (*Aus*) swing

hutschen [ˈhʊtʃn] (*Aus*) 🚹 VI = **schaukeln** 🚺 VR (*inf*) to go away

Hütte [ˈhʏtə] F **-, -n (a)** hut; (*hum*: = *Haus*) humble abode; (= *Jagdhütte*) (hunting) lodge; (= *Holzhütte, Blockhütte*) cabin; (= *Schutzhütte*) hut, bothy (*Scot*); (= *Hundehütte*) kennel **(b)** (*Tech*) (= *Hüttenwerk*) iron and steel works *pl or sing*; (= *Glashütte*) glassworks *pl or sing*

Hütten-: Hüttenindustrie F iron and steel industry; **Hüttenkäse** M cottage cheese; **Hüttenkunde** F metallurgy; **Hüttenschuh** M slipper-sock; **Hüttenwesen** NT, NO PL iron and steel industry; **Hüttenzauber** M après-ski party

Hutzel- [ˈhʊtsl] F **-, -n** (*S Ger*) dried pear

Hutzelbrot NT (*S Ger*) fruit bread; **ein ~ a fruit loaf**

hutzelig [ˈhʊtsəlɪç] ADJ *Obst* dried; *Mensch* wizened

Hutzel-: Hutzelmännchen NT, **Hutzelmännlein** NT gnome; **Hutzelweiblein** NT (*inf*) wizened old woman

hutzlig [ˈhʊtslɪç] ADJ = **hutzelig**

HwG [haːveːˈgeː] (*Admin sl*) ABBR *von* **häufig wechselnder Geschlechtsverkehr** frequent changing of sexual partners

Hyäne [ˈhyɛːnə] F **-, -n** hyena; (*fig*) wildcat

Hyazinthe [hyaˈtsɪntə] F **-, -n** hyacinth

hybrid [hyˈbriːt] ADJ (*Biol, Ling*) hybrid

Hybridantrieb [hyˈbriːt-] M hybrid drive

Hydrant [hyˈdrant] M **-en, -en** hydrant

Hydrat [hyˈdraːt] NT **-(e)s, -e** hydrate

Hydraulik [hyˈdraʊlɪk] F **-**, NO PL hydraulics *sing*; (= *Antrieb, Anlage*) hydraulics *pl*

hydraulisch [hyˈdraʊlɪʃ] 🚹 ADJ hydraulic 🚺 ADV hydraulically

hydrieren [hyˈdriːrən], *ptp* **hydriert** VT (*Chem*) to hydrogenate

Hydro- [hydro-]: **Hydrokultur** [hydro-, ˈhyːdro-] F (*Bot*) hydroponics *sing*; **Hydrolyse** [hydroˈlyːzə] F **-, -n** (*Chem*) hydrolysis; **Hydrotherapie** F (*Med*) hydrotherapy

Hygiene [hyˈɡieːnə] F **-**, NO PL hygiene

Hygienepapier NT (toilet) tissue

hygienisch [hyˈɡieːnɪʃ] 🚹 ADJ hygienic 🚺 ADV hygienically

Hygro- [hygro-]: **Hygrometer** [hygroˈmeːtɐ] NT **-s, -** (*Met*) hygrometer; **Hygroskop** [hygroˈskoːp] NT **-s, -e** (*Met*) hygroscope

Hymne [ˈhʏmnə] F **-, -n** hymn; (= *Nationalhymne*) (national) anthem

hyperaktiv [hypɛlakˈtiːf] ADJ hyperactive

Hyperbel [hyˈpɛrbl] F **-, -n** (*Math*) hyperbola; (*Rhetorik*) hyperbole

hyperkorrekt [hy-pɛ-] ADJ hypercorrect

hyperkritisch [hypɛ-, ˈhyːpɛ-] ADJ hypercritical

Hyperlink [ˈhaɪpɐlɪŋk] M *or* NT **-s, -s** (*Comput*) hyperlink

Hypermedium [haɪpɛ-] NT **-s, -medien** [-diən] (*Comput*) hypermedium

hypermodern [hy-pɛ-] (*inf*) 🚹 ADJ ultramodern 🚺 ADV in an ultramodern way

hypersensibel [hypɛ-] ADJ hypersensitive

Hypertext [ˈhaɪpɛ-] M, NO PL (*Comput*) hypertext

Hypnose [hʏpˈnoːzə] F **-, -n** hypnosis; **unter ~ stehen** to be under hypnosis; **jdn in ~ versetzen** to put sb under hypnosis

hypnotisch [hʏpˈnoːtɪʃ] ADJ hypnotic

Hypnotiseur [hʏpnotiˈzøːɐ] M **-s, -e, Hypnotiseurin** [-zøːrɪn] F **-, -nen** hypnotist

hypnotisieren [hʏpnotiˈziːrən], *ptp* **hypnotisiert** VT to hypnotize

Hypochonder [hypoˈxɔndɐ, hypo-] M **-s, -** hypochondriac

Hypophyse [hypoˈfyːzə] F **-, -n** (*Anat*) hypophysis (*spec*), pituitary gland

Hypotenuse [hypoteˈnuːzə] F **-, -n** (*Math*) hypotenuse

Hypothek [hypoˈteːk] F **-, -en** mortgage; (*fig*) (= *Belastung*) burden of guilt; (= *Handikap*) handicap; **eine ~ aufnehmen** to raise a mortgage; **etw mit einer ~ belasten** to mortgage sth

Hypothekaranlagen [hypoteˈkaːr-] PL mortgage investments *pl*

hypothekarisch [hypoteˈkaːrɪʃ] 🚹 ADJ **~er Gläubiger** mortgagee; **~er Kredit** mortgage credit; **~e Sicherheit** mortgage security 🚺 ADV **das Haus ist ~ belastet** the house is mortgaged

Hypotheken-: Hypothekenbank F, *pl* **-banken** *bank specializing in mortgages*; **Hypothekenbrief** M mortgage deed *or* certificate; **Hypothekendarlehen** NT mortgage (loan); **hypothekenfrei** ADJ unmortgaged; **Hypothekengläubiger(in)** M(F) mortgagee; **Hypothekenpfandbrief** M mortgage bond; **Hypothekenschuld** F mortgage debt; **Hypothekenschuldner(in)** M(F) mortgagor, mortgager; **Hypothekenzinsen** PL mortgage interest

Hypothese [hypoˈteːzə] F hypothesis

hypothetisch [hypoˈteːtɪʃ] 🚹 ADJ hypothetical 🚺 ADV hypothetically

Hysterie [hʏsteˈriː] F **-, -n** [-ˈriːən] hysteria

hysterisch [hʏsˈteːrɪʃ] 🚹 ADJ hysterical; **einen ~en Anfall bekommen** (*fig*) to go into *or* have hysterics 🚺 ADV hysterically

Ii

I, i [iː] NT I, i; **der Punkt** *or* **das Tüpfelchen auf dem i** (*lit*) the dot on the i; (*fig*) the final touch

i [iː] INTERJ (*inf*) ugh (*inf*); **i wo!** not a bit of it! (*inf*)

i. A. ABBR *von* **im Auftrag** pp

IAEA [iːlaːleːˈlaː] F - ABBR *von* **Internationale Atomenergie-Agentur** IAEA

iah [ˈiˈaː, iˈaː] INTERJ heehaw

iahen [ˈiˈaːən, iˈaːən], *ptp* **iaht** VI to heehaw (*inf*)

Iambus [ˈiambʊs] M -, **Iamben** [-bn] (*Poet*) iamb(us)

iberisch [iˈbeːrɪʃ] ADJ Iberian; **die Iberische Halbinsel** the Iberian Peninsula

Iberoamerika [iˈbeːroˌameːrika] NT Ibero-America

ibidem [iˈbiːdɛm, ˈiːbidɛm] ADV ibid

IC [iːˈtseː] M **-(s), -s** ABBR *von* **Intercityzug**

IC- [iːˈtseː] IN CPDS intercity; **IC-Betreuer(in)** M(F) intercity steward

ICE [iːtseːˈleː] M **-(s), -s** ABBR *von* **Intercityexpresszug**

ich [ɪç] PERS PRON, *gen* **meiner**, *dat* **mir**, *acc* **mich** I; **immer ~!** (it's) always me!; **immer ~ soll an allem schuld sein** it's always my fault; **~ Idiot!** what an idiot I am!; **und ~ Idiot habe es gemacht** and idiot that I am, I did it; **ihr könnt ja hingehen, aber ~ nicht!** you're welcome to go, but I won't; **wer hat den Schlüssel? – ~ nicht!** who's got the key? – not me!; **~ selbst** I myself; **könnte ~ bitte den Chef sprechen? – das bin ~ (selbst)** could I speak to the boss? – I am the boss *or* that's me; **~ (selbst) war es** it was me *or* I (*form*); **wer hat gerufen? – ~!** who called? – (it was) me, I did!; **~ bins!** it's me!

Ich [ɪç] NT **-(s), -(s)** self; (*Psych*) ego; **mein anderes *or* zweites ~** (= *selbst*) my other self; (= *andere Person*) my alter ego

Ich-: **ichbezogen** ADJ self-centred (*Brit*), self-centered (*US*); **Icherzähler** [ˈɪçɛɐtseːlɐ] M **-s, -**, **Icherzählerin** [-ərɪn] F -, **-nen** first-person narrator; **Icherzählung** F first-person narrative; **Ichform** F first person; **Ichlaut** M (*Phon*) ch sound as in ich, palatal fricative

IC-Zuschlag [iːˈtseː-] M intercity supplement

ideal [ideˈaːl] **1** ADJ ideal **2** ADV ideally; **da wohnt ihr ~** where you live is ideally located

Ideal [ideˈaːl] NT **-s, -e** ideal

Ideal- IN CPDS ideal; **Idealbild** NT ideal

idealerweise [ideˈaleˈvaizə] ADV ideally

Ideal-: **Idealfall** M ideal case; **im ~** ideally; **Idealgewicht** NT ideal weight

idealisieren [idealiˈziːrən], *ptp* **idealisiert** VT to idealize

Idealismus [ideaˈlɪsmʊs] M -, NO PL idealism

Idealist [ideaˈlɪst] M **-en, -en**, **Idealistin** [-ˈlɪstɪn] F -, **-nen** idealist

idealistisch [ideaˈlɪstɪʃ] ADJ idealistic

Ideal-: **Idealvorstellung** F ideal; **Idealzustand** M ideal state of affairs

Idee [iˈdeː] F -, **-n** [iˈdeːən] **(a)** (= *Einfall, Philos*) idea; **die ~ zu etw** the idea for sth; **wie kommst du denn auf DIE ~?** whatever gave you that idea?; **ich kam auf die ~, sie zu fragen** I hit on the idea of asking her; **jdn auf die ~ bringen, etw zu tun** to give sb the idea of doing sth; **jdn auf andere ~n bringen** to make sb think about something else; **~n müsste man haben!** what it is to have ideas!
(b) (= *ein wenig*) shade, trifle; **eine ~ Salz** a hint of salt; **keine ~ besser** not a whit better

ideell [ideˈɛl] ADJ ideational (*form, Philos*); *Wert, Anteil, Gesichtspunkt, Ziele* non-material; *Bedürfnisse, Unterstützung* spiritual

Identifikation [identifikaˈtsioːn] F -, **-en** identification

Identifikationsfigur F role model

identifizieren [identifiˈtsiːrən], *ptp* **identifiziert** **1** VT to identify **2** VR **sich ~ mit** to identify (oneself) with

Identifizierung F -, **-en** identification

identisch [iˈdɛntɪʃ] ADJ identical (*mit* with)

Identität [identiˈtɛːt] F -, **-en** identity

Identitäts-: **Identitätskrise** F identity crisis; **Identitätsnachweis** M proof of identity

Ideologe [ideoˈloːgə] M **-n, -n**, **Ideologin** [-ˈloːgɪn] F -, **-nen** ideologist

Ideologie [ideoloˈgiː] F -, **-n** [-ˈgiːən] ideology

ideologisch [ideoˈloːgɪʃ] **1** ADJ ideological **2** ADV ideologically

ideologisieren [ideologiˈziːrən], *ptp* **ideologisiert** VT to ideologize

Idiom [iˈdioːm] NT **-s, -e** idiom

Idiomatik [idioˈmaːtɪk] F -, NO PL idiomaticalness; (= *Redewendungen*) idioms *pl*

idiomatisch [idioˈmaːtɪʃ] **1** ADJ idiomatic **2** ADV idiomatically; **~ völlig einwandfreie/richtige Übersetzungen** perfect/correct idiomatic translations

Idiot [iˈdioːt] M **-en, -en**, **Idiotin** [iˈdioːtɪn] F -, **-nen** idiot

Idioten-: **Idiotenhügel** M (*hum inf*) nursery *or* beginners' slope; **idiotensicher** (*inf*) **1** ADJ foolproof **2** ADV **~ gestaltet** *or* **konzipiert sein** to be designed to be foolproof; **~ zu bedienen** extremely simple to operate

Idiotie [idioˈtiː] F -, **-n** [-ˈtiːən] idiocy; (*inf*) lunacy

Idiotin F *siehe* **Idiot**

idiotisch [iˈdioːtɪʃ] ADJ idiotic

Idol [iˈdoːl] NT **-s, -e** idol

idyllisch [iˈdʏlɪʃ] **1** ADJ idyllic **2** ADV idyllically; **hier wohnt ihr wirklich ~** it's really idyllic where you live

IG [iːˈgeː] F -, **-s** ABBR *von* **Industriegewerkschaft** ≈ TU (*Brit*)

Igel [ˈiːgl] M **-s, -** (*Zool*) hedgehog

igitt(igitt) [iˈgɪt(iˈgɪt)] INTERJ (*inf*) ugh! (*inf*)

Iglu [ˈiːglu] M *or* NT **-s, -s** igloo

Ignoranz [ɪgnoˈrants] F -, NO PL ignorance

ignorieren [ɪgnoˈriːrən], *ptp* **ignoriert** VT to ignore

IHK [iːhaːˈkaː] F -, **-s** ABBR *von* **Industrie- und Handelskammer**

ihm [iːm] PERS PRON DAT *von* **er, es** (*bei Personen*) to him; (*bei Tieren und Dingen*) to it; (*nach Präpositionen*) him; **ich gab es ~** I gave it (to) him; **ich gab ~ den Brief** I gave him the letter, I gave the letter to him; **es war ~, als ob er träumte** he felt as though he were dreaming; **es ist ~ nicht gut** he doesn't feel well; **sie schnitt ~ die Haare** she cut his hair (for him); **ein Freund von ~** a friend of his, one of his friends; **wir gingen zu ~** (= *haben ihn aufgesucht*) we went to see him; (= *mit zu ihm nach Hause*) we went to his place (*inf*); **ich habe ~ das gemacht** I did it for him

ihn [iːn] PERS PRON ACC *von* **er** him; (*bei Tieren und Dingen*) it

ihnen [ˈiːnən] PERS PRON DAT *von* **sie** to them; (*nach Präpositionen*) them; *siehe auch* **ihm**

Ihnen [ˈiːnən] PERS PRON DAT *von* **Sie** to you; (*nach Präpositionen*) you; *siehe auch* **ihm**

ihr [iːɐ] **1** PERS PRON **(a)** *gen* **euer**, *dat* **euch**, *acc* **euch** 2. PERS PL NOM you **(b)** DAT *von* **sie** (*bei Personen*) to her; (*bei Tieren und Dingen*) to it; (*nach Präpositionen*) her/it; *siehe auch* **ihm** **2** POSS PRON **(a)** (*einer Person*) her; (*eines Tiers, Dinges, Abstraktum*) its **(b)** (*von mehreren*) their

Ihr [iːɐ] POSS PRON SING AND PL your; **~ Franz Müller** (*Briefschluss*) yours, Franz Müller

ihrer [ˈiːrɐ] PERS PRON (*geh*) **(a)** GEN *von* **sie** (*bei Personen*) of her; **wir werden ~ gedenken** we will remember her **(b)** GEN *von* **sie** of them; **es waren ~ zehn** there were ten of them; **wir werden ~ gedenken** we will remember them

Ihrer [ˈiːrɐ] PERS PRON GEN *von* **Sie** (*geh*) of you; **wir werden ~ gedenken** we will remember you

ihre(r, s) [ˈiːrə] POSS PRON (*substantivisch*) **(a)** (*einer Person*) hers; (*eines Tiers*) its; **der/die/das ~** *or* **Ihre** (*geh*) hers/its; **sie tat das ~** *or* **Ihre** (*geh*) she did her part; **Ihre Majestät** Her Majesty; **sie und die ~n** *or* **Ihren** (*geh*: = *Familie*) she and hers; **das ~** *or* **Ihre**

(geh: = *Besitz*) what is hers
 (b) (*von mehreren*) theirs; **der/die/das ~ or Ihre** (*geh*) theirs; **sie taten das ~ or Ihre** (*geh*) they did their part

Ihre(r, s) ['iːrə] POSS PRON SING AND PL (*substantivisch*) yours; **der/die/das ~** (*geh*) yours; **schöne Grüße an Sie und die ~n** (*geh*) best wishes to you and your family; **tun Sie das ~** (*geh*) you do your bit

ihrerseits ['iːrɐ'zaits] ADV (*bei einer Person*) for her part; (*bei mehreren*) for their part; (*von ihrer Seite*) on her/their part

Ihrerseits ['iːrɐ'zaits] ADV for your part; (*von Ihrer Seite*) on your part

ihresgleichen ['iːrəs'glaiçn] PRON INV (*von einer Person*) people like her; (*von mehreren*) people like them; (*von Dingen*) others like it; **eine Frechheit, die ~ sucht!** incredible impudence!

Ihresgleichen ['iːrəs'glaiçn] PRON INV people like you

ihretwegen ['iːrət've:gn], **ihretwillen** ['iːrət'vilən] ADV (*bei Personen*) (= *wegen ihr/ihnen*) (*sing*) because of her; (*pl*) because of them; (= *um sie*) about her/them; (= *für sie*) on her/their behalf; (*bei Dingen und Tieren*) (*sing*) because of it; (*pl*) because of them; **sie sagte, ~ könnten wir gehen** she said that, as far as she was concerned, we could go

Ihretwegen ['iːrət've:gn], **Ihretwillen** ['iːrət'vilən] ADV because of you; (= *um Sie*) about you; (= *für Sie*) on your behalf

Ikone [i'koːnə] F **-, -n** (*auch fig*) icon

illegal [ile'gaːl, 'il-] **1** ADJ illegal **2** ADV illegally; **sich ~ betätigen** to engage in illegal activities

Illegalität [ilegali'tɛːt, 'il-] F **-, -en** illegality

illegitim [ilegi'tiːm, 'il-] ADJ illegitimate

illiquid [ili'kviːt, 'il-] ADJ (*Comm*) illiquid

Illusion [ilu'zioːn] F **-, -en** illusion; **jdm alle ~en nehmen** or **rauben** to rob sb of all his/her *etc* illusions; **sich** (*dat*) **~en machen** to delude oneself; **darüber macht er sich keine ~en** he doesn't have any illusions about it; **sich der ~ hingeben, dass ...** to be under the illusion that ...

illusionslos ADJ **ein ~er Mensch** a person with no illusions; **sein** to have no illusions

illusorisch [ilu'zoːrɪʃ] ADJ illusory; **es ist völlig ~, zu glauben ...** it's a complete illusion to believe ...

Illustration [ilʊstra'tsioːn] F **-, -en** illustration; **zur ~ von etw** as an illustration of sth

illustrativ [ilʊstra'tiːf] **1** ADJ **(a)** (*mit Anschauungsmaterial*) illustrated **(b)** (= *anschaulich*) illustrative **2** ADV **(a)** (= *mit Anschauungsmaterial*) with illustrations; **etw ~ aufzeigen** to show sth with illustrations **(b)** (= *anschaulich*) vividly; **er hat sehr ~ geschildert, wie ...** he described very vividly how ...

Illustrator [ilʊs'traːtoːɐ] M **-s, Illustratoren** [-'toːrən], **Illustratorin** [-'toːrɪn] F **-, -nen** illustrator

illustrieren [ilʊs'triːrən], *ptp* **illustriert** VT to illustrate (*jdm etw* sth for sb)

Illustrierte [ilʊs'triːətə] F DECL AS ADJ magazine

Iltis ['iltis] M **-ses, -se** polecat

im [im] PREP CONTR *von* **in dem (a)** (*räumlich*) in the; **im zweiten Stock** on the second floor; **im Theater** at the theatre (*Brit*) or theater (*US*); **die Beleuchtung im Theater** the lighting in the theatre (*Brit*) or theater (*US*); **im Bett** in bed; **im „Faust"** in "Faust"
 (b) (*zeitlich*) in the; **im Mai** in May; **im Jahre 1866** in (the year) 1866; **im Alter von 91 Jahren** at the age of 91; **im letzten/nächsten Jahr** last/next year; **im letzten Jahr des Krieges** in the last year of the war
 (c) +SUPERL **nicht im Geringsten** not in the slightest
 (d) (*als Verlaufsform*) **im Kommen/Gehen** *etc* **sein** to be coming/going *etc*; **etw im Liegen/Stehen** *etc* **tun** to do sth lying down/standing up *etc*
 (e) **im Trab/Laufschritt** *etc* at a trot/run *etc*

IM [iː'ɛm] M **-s, -s** ABBR *von* **inoffizieller Mitarbeiter (der Stasi)** (Stasi) collaborator

Image ['imitʃ] NT **-(s), -s** image

imaginär [imagi'nɛːɐ] ADJ imaginary

Imbiss ['imbis] M **-es, -e** snack

Imbiss-: Imbisshalle F snack bar; **Imbissstand** M ≈ hot-dog stand; **Imbissstube** F café; (*in Kaufhaus etc*) cafeteria

Imitation [imita'tsioːn] F **-, -en** imitation

imitieren [imi'tiːrən], *ptp* **imitiert** VT to imitate; **imitierter Schmuck** imitation jewellery (*Brit*) or jewelry (*US*)

Imker ['imkɐ] M **-s, -, Imkerin** [-ərɪn] F **-, -nen** beekeeper

Imkerei [imkə'rai] F **-, NO PL** beekeeping

immateriell [imate'riɛl, 'im-] ADJ *Vermögenswerte* immaterial

Immatrikulation [imatrikula'tsioːn] F **-, -en** matriculation (*form*)

immatrikulieren [imatriku'liːrən], *ptp* **immatrikuliert** **1** VT to register (*at university*) (*an* +*dat* at) **2** VR to matriculate (*form*)

immens ['imɛns] **1** ADJ immense, huge, enormous **2** ADV immensely; **~ groß sein** to be huge

immer ['imɐ] ADV **(a)** (= *häufig, ständig*) always; **schon ~** always; **auf** or **für ~** for ever, for always; **~ diese Aufregung/Nörgelei** this continual excitement/grumbling; **~ diese Probleme!** all these problems!; **~ diese Studenten** these wretched students (*inf*); **~, wenn ...** whenever ..., every time that ...; **~ mal** (*inf*) from time to time; **geradeaus gehen** to keep going straight on; **~ langsam voran!** (*inf*), **(nur) ~ schön langsam!** (*inf*) take your time (about it); **~ (schön) mit der Ruhe** (*inf*) take it easy; **(nur) ~ her damit!** (*inf*) (just) hand it over!; **noch ~, ~ noch** still; **~ noch nicht** still not (yet); **~ wieder** again and again; **etw ~ wieder tun** to keep on doing sth; **wie ~** as usual
 (b) +COMP **~ besser** better and better; **~ häufiger** more and more often; **~ mehr** more and more; **es nimmt ~ mehr zu** it keeps on increasing; **~ größer werdende Schulden** constantly increasing debts; **nicht ~, aber ~ öfter** not always, but more and more often
 (c) wer (auch) whoever; **wie (auch)** however; **wann (auch) ~** whenever; **wo (auch) ~** wherever; **was (auch) ~** whatever
 (d) (*inf: = jeweils*) **gib mir ~ drei Bücher auf einmal** give me three books at a time; **stellt euch in einer Reihe auf, ~ zwei zusammen** line up in twos; **~ am dritten Tag** every third day

immer-: immergrün ['imɐgryːn] ADJ ATTR (*lit, fig*) evergreen; **Immergrün** ['imɐgryːn] NT **-s, -e** evergreen; **immerhin** ['imɐ'hɪn] ADV all the same, anyhow, at any rate; (= *wenigstens*) at least; (= *schließlich*) after all

Immigrant [imi'grant] M **-en, -en, Immigrantin** [-'grantɪn] F **-, -nen** immigrant

Immigration [imigra'tsioːn] F **-, -en** immigration

immigrieren [imi'griːrən], *ptp* **immigriert** VI AUX SEIN to immigrate

Immission [imi'sioːn] F (*Jur*) effect on nearby property of gases, smoke, noise, smells etc

Immissions-: Immissionsschutz M air pollution control; **Immissionsschutzgesetz** NT air pollution laws *pl*

immobil [imo'biːl, 'im-] ADJ immoveable

Immobilie [imo'biːliə] F **-, -n (a) eine ~** a property **(b) Immobilien** PL real estate *sing*; (*in Zeitungsannoncen*) property *sing*

Immobilien-: Immobilienfonds M (*Fin*) real estate fund; **Immobilienhändler(in)** M(F), **Immobilienmakler(in)** M(F) (real) estate agent (*Brit*), realtor (*US*)

immun [i'muːn] ADJ immune (*gegen* to)

Immun- [i'muːn-] IN CPDS (*Med*) immune; **Immunabwehr** F (*Med*) immune defence (*Brit*) or defense (*US*)

immunisieren [imuni'ziːrən], *ptp* **immunisiert** VT (*form*) to immunize (*gegen* against)

Immunität [imuni'tɛːt] F **-, (rare) -en** immunity

Immunologe [ɪmuno'loːgə] M **-n, -n, Immunologin** [-'loːgɪn] F **-, -nen** immunologist

immunologisch [ɪmuno'loːgɪʃ] ADJ immunological

Immun-: Immunschwäche F immunodeficiency; **Immunschwächekrankheit** F immune deficiency disease *or* syndrome; **Immunsystem** NT immune system

Imperativ ['ɪmperatiːf] M **-s, -e** [-və] (*Gram*) imperative (form); (*Philos*) imperative

imperativisch [ɪmpera'tiːvɪʃ] ADJ (*Gram*) imperative

Imperfekt ['ɪmperfɛkt] NT (*Gram*) imperfect (tense)

Imperialismus [ɪmperia'lɪsmʊs] M **-, NO PL** imperialism

imperialistisch [ɪmperia'lɪstɪʃ] ADJ imperialistic

Imperium [ɪm'peːriʊm] NT **-s, Imperien** [-riən] (= *Gebiet*) empire; (= *Herrschaft*) imperium

impfen ['ɪmpfn] VT to vaccinate

Impfling ['ɪmpflɪŋ] M **-s, -e** *person who has just been or is to be vaccinated*

Impf-: Impfpass M vaccination card; **Impfpflicht** F compulsory vaccination; **Impfpistole** F vaccination gun; **Impfschaden** M vaccine damage; **Impfschein** M certificate of vaccination; **Impfschutz** M protection given by vaccination; **Impfstoff** M vaccine, serum

Impfung F **-, -en** vaccination

Implantat [ɪmplan'taːt] NT **-(e)s, -e** implant

Implantation [ɪmplanta'tsioːn] F **-, -en** (*Med*) implantation

implementieren [ɪmplemen'tiːrən], *ptp* **implementiert** VT (*geh*) to implement

implizieren [ɪmpli'tsiːrən], *ptp* **impliziert** VT to imply

implizit [ɪmpli'tsiːt], **implizite** [ɪm'pliːtsite] ADV (*geh*) by implication

implodieren [ɪmplo'diːrən], *ptp* **implodiert** VI AUX SEIN to implode

Implosion [ɪmplo'zioːn] F **-, -en** implosion

imponieren [ɪmpo'niːrən], *ptp* **imponiert** VI to impress (*jdm* sb)

imponierend ADJ impressive

Imponiergehabe NT (*Zool*) display pattern; (*fig pej*) exhibitionism

Import [ɪm'pɔrt] M **-(e)s, -e** (= *Handel, Ware*) import; **der ~ sollte den Export nicht übersteigen** imports should not exceed exports; **der ~ von Obst und Gemüse** the import *or* importation of fruit and vegetables; **der Salat ist holländischer ~** the lettuce was imported from Holland

Import- IN CPDS import; **Importabgabe** F import duty *or* tariff; **Importbeschränkung** F import quota

Importeur [ɪmpɔr'tøːɐ] M **-s, -e, Importeurin** [-'tøːrɪn] F **-, -nen** importer

importieren [ɪmpɔr'tiːrən], *ptp* **importiert** VT (*auch Comput*) to import

Import-: Importland NT importing country; **Importlizenz** F import licence (*Brit*) *or* license (*US*); **Importzoll** M import duty *or* tariff

imposant [ɪmpo'zant] ADJ *Gebäude, Kunstwerk, Figur* imposing; *Leistung* impressive; *Stimme* commanding

impotent ['ɪmpotɛnt, ɪmpo'tɛnt] ADJ impotent

Impotenz ['ɪmpotɛnts, ɪmpo'tɛnts] F **-, NO PL** impotence

imprägnieren [ɪmprɛ'gniːrən], *ptp* **imprägniert** VT to impregnate; (= *wasserdicht machen*) to (water)proof

Imprägnierung F **-, -en** impregnation; (*von Geweben*) (water)proofing; (*nach der Reinigung*) reproofing

Impresario [ɪmpre'zaːrio] M **-s, -s** *or* **Impresari** [-ri] impresario

Impression [ɪmprɛ'sioːn] F impression (*über +acc* of)

Impressionismus [ɪmprɛsio'nɪsmʊs] M **-, NO PL** impressionism

Impressionist [ɪmprɛsio'nɪst] M **-en, -en, Impressionistin** [-'nɪstɪn] F **-, -nen** impressionist

impressionistisch [ɪmprɛsio'nɪstɪʃ] ADJ impressionistic

Impressum [ɪm'prɛsʊm] NT **-s, Impressen** [-sn] imprint; (*von Zeitung*) masthead

Improvisation [ɪmproviza'tsioːn] F **-, -en** improvisation

improvisieren [ɪmprovi'ziːrən], *ptp* **improvisiert** VTI to improvise

Impuls [ɪm'pʊls] M **-es, -e** impulse; **etw aus einem ~ heraus tun** to do sth on impulse; **einer Sache** (*dat*) **neue ~e geben** to give sth new impetus; **äußere ~e veranlassten ihn dazu** external factors made him do it

impulsiv [ɪmpʊl'ziːf] **1** ADJ impulsive **2** ADV impulsively

Impulsivität [ɪmpʊlzivi'tɛːt] F **-, NO PL** impulsiveness

imstande [ɪm'ʃtandə] ADJ PRED **~ sein, etw zu tun** (= *fähig*) to be capable of doing sth; (= *in der Lage*) to be in a position to do sth; **er ist zu allem ~** he's capable of anything; **er ist ~ und erzählt es meiner Mutter** he's (quite) capable of telling my mother

in [ɪn] **1** PREP *siehe auch* **im, ins** (a) (*räumlich*) (*wo?* +*dat*) in; (*innen*) in(side); (*wohin?* +*acc*) in, into; **sind Sie schon in Deutschland gewesen?** have you ever been to Germany?; **in der Schweiz** in Switzerland; **in die Schweiz** to Switzerland; **in die Schule/Kirche gehen** to go to school/church; **er ist in der Schule/Kirche** he's at *or* in school/church; **er ging ins Konzert** he went to the concert
(b) (*zeitlich: wann?* +*dat*) in; **in diesem Jahr** (*laufendes Jahr*) this year; (*jenes Jahr*) (in) that year; **heute/morgen in acht Tagen/zwei Wochen** a week/two weeks today/tomorrow; **bis ins 18. Jahrhundert** into the 18th century; **vom 16. bis ins 18. Jahrhundert** from the 16th to the 18th century
(c) (*räumlich*) **in Englisch steht er sehr schwach** he's very weak in English; **das ist in Englisch** it's in English; **ins Englische übersetzen** to translate into English; **er macht jetzt in Gebrauchtwagen** (*inf*) he's in the second-hand car business now; **sie hat es in sich** (*dat*) (*inf*) she's quite a girl; **der Text/die Rechenarbeit hat es in sich** (*dat*) (*inf*) the text/the arithmetic test is a tough one; **dieser Whisky hat es in sich** (*dat*) (*inf*) this whisky has quite a kick (*inf*)
2 ADJ PRED (*inf*) **in sein** to be in (*inf*)

inadäquat ADJ inadequate

inaktiv ADJ inactive; *Mitglied* non-active

inakzeptabel ADJ unacceptable

Inanspruchnahme [ɪn'ʔanʃprʊxnaːmə] F **-, -n** (*form*)
(a) (= *Beanspruchung*) demands *pl*, claims *pl* (+*gen* on); **im Falle einer ~ von Arbeitslosenunterstützung** where unemployment benefit has been sought (*form*); **bei ~ des Versicherungsschutzes entfällt der Rabatt** the discount is forfeited should an insurance claim be submitted (b) (*von Einrichtungen, Verkehrssystem etc*) utilization; **wegen zu geringer ~** as a result of under-utilization

inbegr. ABBR *von* **inbegriffen**

Inbegriff ['ɪnbəgrɪf] M, **NO PL** perfect example; (*der Schönheit, Güte, des Bösen etc*) epitome, embodiment; **sie war der ~ der Schönheit/Tugend** she was beauty/virtue personified

inbegriffen ['ɪnbəgrɪfn] ADJ PRED included; **die Mehrwertsteuer ist im Preis ~** the price is inclusive of VAT

Inbetriebnahme [ɪnbə'triːpnaːmə] F **-, -n** commissioning; (*von Gebäude, U-Bahn etc*) inauguration; **die ~ des Geräts erfolgt in zwei Wochen** the appliance will be put into operation in two weeks

Inbrunst ['ɪnbrʊnst] F, **NO PL** fervour (*Brit*), fervor (*US*)

inbrünstig ['ɪnbrʊnstɪç] **1** ADJ fervent, ardent **2** ADV fervently, ardently

Inbusschlüssel® ['ɪnbʊs-] M (*Tech*) Allen key®

Incoterm ['ɪŋkotɛrm] M **-s, -s** ABBR *von* **International Commercial Term** Incoterm

Indanthren® [ɪndan'treːn] NT **-s, -e** colourfast dye

Indefinitpronomen [ɪndefi'niːt-, 'ɪndefiniːt-] NT indefinite pronoun

indem [ɪn'deːm] CONJ (a) (= *während der ganzen Zeit*) while; (= *in dem Augenblick*) as; **~ er sich hinsetzte, sagte er ...** sitting down, he said ... (b) (= *dadurch, dass*) **~ man etw macht** by doing sth

Inder ['ɪndɐ] M **-s, -, Inderin** [-ərɪn] F **-, -nen** Indian

indes [ɪn'dɛs], **indessen** [ɪn'dɛsn] ADV (a) (*zeitlich*) meanwhile, (in the) meantime (b) (*adversativ*) however

Index ['ɪndɛks] M **-(es), -e** *or* **Indizes** ['ɪnditseːs] index (*auch Comput*); (*Eccl*) Index

indexieren [ɪndɛ'ksiːrən], *ptp* **indexiert** VTI (*Comput*) to index

Indexklausel F (= *Wertsicherungsklausel*) index clause; (= *Gleitklausel*) escalator clause

Indianer [ɪn'diaːnɐ] M **-s, -, Indianerin** [-ərɪn] F **-, -nen** American Indian, Native American; (*in Western*) (Red) Indian

indianisch [ɪn'diaːnɪʃ] ADJ American Indian, Native American; (*in Western*) (Red) Indian

Indianistik [ɪndia'nɪstɪk] F **-, NO PL** American Indian studies *pl*, Native American studies *pl*

Indien ['ɪndiən] NT **-s** India

Indikation [ɪndika'tsio:n] F **-**, **-en** (*Med*) indication; **ethische/ medizinische/soziale** ~ ethical/medical/social grounds for the termination of pregnancy

Indikativ ['ɪndikati:f] M **-s, -e** [-və] (*Gram*) indicative

Indikator [ɪndi'ka:to:ɐ] M **-s, Indikatoren** [-'to:rən] indicator

Indio ['ɪndio] M **-s, -s** (Central/South American) Indian

indirekt ['ɪndirɛkt, ɪndi'rɛkt] ◼ ADJ indirect; **~e Rede** indirect or reported speech ◼ ADV indirectly; **~ beleuchtet sein** to have indirect lighting

indisch ['ɪndɪʃ] ADJ Indian; **der Indische Ozean** the Indian Ocean

indiskret [ɪndɪs'kre:t, 'ɪn-] ◼ ADJ indiscreet ◼ ADV indiscreetly

Indiskretion [ɪndɪskre'tsio:n, 'ɪn-] F indiscretion

indiskutabel [ɪndɪsku'ta:bl, 'ɪn-] ADJ out of the question; (= *sehr schlecht*) indescribably bad

Individualismus [ɪndividua'lɪsmʊs] M **-**, NO PL individualism

Individualist [ɪndividua'lɪst] M **-en, -en**, **Individualistin** [-'lɪstɪn] F **-**, **-nen** individualist

Individualität [ɪndividuali'tɛ:t] F **-**, **-en** (a) NO PL individuality (b) (= *Charakterzüge*) individual characteristic

Individualverkehr [ɪndivi'dua:l-] M (*Mot*) private transport

individuell [ɪndivi'duɛl] ◼ ADJ individual ◼ ADV individually; **etw ~ gestalten** to give sth a personal note; **es ist ~ verschieden** it differs from person to person

Individuum [ɪndi'vi:duʊm] NT **-s, Individuen** [-duən] individual

Indiz [ɪn'di:ts] NT **-es, -ien** [-tsiən] (a) (*Jur*) clue; (*als Beweismittel*) piece of circumstantial evidence; **alles beruht nur auf ~ien** everything rests only on circumstantial evidence (b) (= *Anzeichen*) sign (*für* of)

Indizes PL von **Index**

Indizienbeweis M circumstantial evidence *no pl*

indizieren [ɪndi'tsi:rən], *ptp* **indiziert** VT (*Med*) to indicate; (*Eccl*) to put on the Index; (*Comput*) to index

Indochina ['ɪndo'çi:na] NT Indochina

indogermanisch ['ɪndogɛr'ma:nɪʃ] ADJ Indo-European

Indonesien [ɪndo'ne:ziən] NT **-s** Indonesia

indonesisch [ɪndo'ne:zɪʃ] ADJ Indonesian

indossieren [ɪndɔ'si:rən], *ptp* **indossiert** VT (*Comm*) to endorse

Induktion [ɪndʊk'tsio:n] F **-**, **-en** induction

induktiv [ɪndʊk'ti:f, 'ɪn-] ADJ inductive

industrialisieren [ɪndʊstriali'zi:rən], *ptp* **industrialisiert** VT to industrialize

Industrialisierung F **-**, **-en** industrialization

Industrie [ɪndʊs'tri:] F **-**, **-n** [-'tri:ən] industry; **in der ~ arbeiten** to work in industry

Industrie- IN CPDS industrial; **Industrieabfälle** PL industrial waste; **Industrieanlage** F industrial plant or works pl; **Industrieerzeugnis** NT industrial product; **Industriegebiet** NT industrial area; **Industriegelände** NT industrial site; **Industriegewerkschaft** F industrial union; **~ Druck und Papier** printers' union; **Industriekauffrau** F, **Industriekaufmann** M industrial clerk; **Industrieland** NT industrialized country; **Industrielandschaft** F industrial landscape

industriell [ɪndʊstri'ɛl] ◼ ADJ industrial ◼ ADV industrially

Industrielle(r) [ɪndʊstri'ɛlə] MF DECL AS ADJ industrialist

Industrie-: **Industriemüll** M industrial waste; **Industrienation** F industrial nation; **Industrieroboter** M industrial robot; **Industriestadt** F industrial town; **Industrie- und Handelskammer** F chamber of commerce; **Industriezweig** M branch of industry

ineffektiv [ɪnlɛfɛk'ti:f, 'ɪn-] ◼ ADJ ineffective, ineffectual; (= *unproduktiv auch*) inefficient ◼ ADV ineffectively; (= *unproduktiv auch*) inefficiently

Ineffektivität [ɪnlɛfɛktivi'tɛ:t, 'ɪn-] F ineffectiveness, ineffectualness; (= *Unproduktivität auch*) inefficiency

ineffizient ['ɪnlɛfitsiɛnt] ADJ inefficient

ineinander [ɪnlai'nandɐ] ADV *sein, liegen etc* in(side) one another or each other; *legen, hängen etc* into one another or each other; **~ übergehen** to merge (into one another or each other); **sich ~ verlieben** to fall in love (with each other)

ineinander: **ineinander fließen** VI IRREG AUX SEIN to merge; **ineinander greifen** VI IRREG (*lit*) to interlock; (*Zahnräder,*

Zinken auch) to mesh; (*fig: Ereignisse, Ressorts etc*) to overlap; **ineinander passen** VI to fit together; **ineinander schieben** VTR IRREG to telescope; **sich ~ lassen** to be telescopic

Infanterie [ɪnfantə'ri:, 'ɪn-] F **-**, **-n** [-'ri:ən] infantry

infantil [ɪnfan'ti:l] ADJ infantile

Infarkt [ɪn'farkt] M **-(e)s, -e** (*Med*) infarct (*spec*); (= *Herzinfarkt*) coronary (thrombosis)

Infekt [ɪn'fɛkt] M **-(e)s, -e**, **Infektion** [ɪnfɛk'tsio:n] F **-**, **-en** infection

Infektions-: **Infektionsgefahr** F danger of infection; **Infektionsherd** M focus of infection; **Infektionskrankheit** F infectious disease

infektiös [ɪnfɛk'tsiø:s] ADJ infectious

Inferno [ɪn'fɛrno] NT **-s**, NO PL (*lit, fig*) inferno

infinit [ɪnfi'ni:t, 'ɪn-] ADJ (*Gram*) non-finite

infinitesimal [ɪnfinitezi'ma:l] ADJ (*Math*) infinitesimal

Infinitiv ['ɪnfiniti:f] M **-s, -e** [-və] infinitive

Infinitiv-: **Infinitivkonstruktion** F infinitive construction; **Infinitivsatz** M infinitive clause

infizieren [ɪnfi'tsi:rən], *ptp* **infiziert** ◼ VT to infect ◼ VR to get infected (*bei* by)

in flagranti [ɪn fla'granti] ADV in the act

Inflation [ɪnfla'tsio:n] F **-**, **-en** inflation

inflationär [ɪnflatsio'nɛ:ɐ] ◼ ADJ inflationary; (*fig*) over-extensive ◼ ADV **sich ~ entwickeln** to develop in an inflationary way

Inflations-: **Inflationsangst** F fear of inflation; **inflationshemmend** ◼ ADJ anti-inflationary ◼ ADV **~ wirken** to be anti-inflationary; **Inflationsrate** F rate of inflation

inflexibel [ɪnflɛ'ksi:bl, 'ɪn-] ADJ (*lit, fig*) inflexible

Inflexibilität [ɪnflɛksibili'tɛ:t, 'ɪn-] F (*lit, fig*) inflexibility

Info ['ɪnfo] F **-**, **-s** (*inf*) (a) (= *Information*) info (*inf*) (b) (*Sch inf*: = *Informatik*) computer studies *pl*

infolge [ɪn'fɔlgə] PREP +GEN or VON as a result of

infolgedessen [ɪnfɔlgə'dɛsn] ADV consequently, as a result

Informatik [ɪnfɔr'ma:tɪk] F **-**, NO PL informatics *sing*; (= *Schulfach*) computer studies *pl*

Informatiker [ɪnfɔr'ma:tikɐ] M **-s, -**, **Informatikerin** [-ərɪn] F **-**, **-nen** computer or information scientist

Information [ɪnfɔrma'tsio:n] F (a) information *no pl* (*über* +acc about, on); **eine ~** (a piece of) information; **~en weitergeben** to pass on information; **zu Ihrer ~** for your information (b) (= *Stelle*) information desk

informationell [ɪnfɔrmatsio'nɛl] ADJ informational; **~e Selbstbestimmung** control over one's personal data

Informations-: **Informationsaustausch** M exchange of information; **Informationsdefizit** NT lack of information; **Informationsgesellschaft** F information society; **Informationsmaterial** NT information; **Informationsstand** M (a) information stand (b) NO PL (= *Wissensstand*) level of information; **Informationstechnik** F information technology; **Informationsvorsprung** M **einen ~ haben** to be better informed

informativ [ɪnfɔrma'ti:f] ◼ ADJ informative ◼ ADV informatively; **~ berichten** to give an informative report

informatorisch [ɪnfɔrma'to:rɪʃ] ADJ informational

informell [ɪnfɔr'mɛl, 'ɪn-] ◼ ADJ informal ◼ ADV informally

informieren [ɪnfɔr'mi:rən], *ptp* **informiert** ◼ VT to inform (*über* +acc, von about, of); **da bist du falsch** or **nicht richtig informiert** you've been misinformed; **jdn nur unvollständig/ einseitig ~** to give sb only part of/one side of the information; **informierte Kreise** informed circles ◼ VR to find out, to inform oneself (*über* +acc about); **sich ständig über etw** (*acc*) **~** to keep oneself informed about sth

Infostand ['ɪnfo-] M (*inf*) information stand

Infotainment [ɪnfo'te:nmənt] NT **-s**, NO PL infotainment

Info-Telefon ['ɪnfo-] NT, **Infotelefon** NT information line

infrage [ɪn'fra:gə], **in Frage** ADV **~ kommen** to be possible; **~ kommend** possible; *Bewerber* worth considering; **sollte er für diese Stelle ~ kommen, ...** if he should be considered for this position ...; **für jdn/etw nicht ~ kommen** to be out of the question for sb/sth; **das kommt (überhaupt) nicht ~!** that's (quite) out of the question!; **etw ~ stellen** to question sth, to call sth into question

Infra- ['ɪnfra-]: **infrarot** ADJ infrared; **Infraschall** M infrasonic waves *pl*; **Infrastruktur** F infrastructure

Infusion [ɪnfu'zio:n] F infusion

Ing. ABBR *von* **Ingenieur**

Ingenieur [ɪnʒe'niø:ɐ] M **-s, -e**, **Ingenieurin** [-'niø:rɪn] F **-, -nen** engineer

Ingenieur-: **Ingenieurbüro** [ɪnʒe'niø:ɐ-] NT engineer's office; **Ingenieurschule** [ɪnʒe'niø:ɐ-] F school of engineering

Ingwer ['ɪŋvɐ] M **-s, -** ginger

Inh. **(a)** ABBR *von* **Inhaber** prop. **(b)** ABBR *von* **Inhalt**

Inhaber ['ɪnha:bɐ] M **-s, -**, **Inhaberin** [-ərɪn] F **-, -nen** owner; (*von Konto, Aktie, Lizenz, Patent, Rekord, Orden*) holder; (*von Scheck, Pass*) bearer

Inhaber-: **Inhaberaktie** F bearer share, bearer stock (*US*); **Inhaberobligation** F bearer security

inhaftieren [ɪnhaf'ti:rən], *ptp* **inhaftiert** VT to take into custody

Inhaftierung F **-, -en** (= *das Inhaftieren*) arrest; (= *Haft*) imprisonment

inhalieren [ɪnha'li:rən], *ptp* **inhaliert** VTI (*Med inf*) to inhale

Inhalt M **(a)** (*von Behälter, Paket*) contents *pl* **(b)** (*von Buch, Brief, Begriff*) content, contents *pl*; (*des Lebens*) meaning; **über ~e diskutieren** to discuss the real issues; **ein Brief des ~s, dass ...** (*form*) a letter to the effect that ... **(c)** (*Math*) (= *Flächeninhalt*) area; (= *Rauminhalt*) volume; **der ~ der Flasche beträgt zwei Liter** the bottle holds two litres (*Brit*) or liters (*US*)

inhaltlich ['ɪnhaltlɪç] ADJ, ADV as regards content

Inhalts-: **Inhaltsangabe** F summary; **inhaltslos** ADJ empty; *Buch, Vortrag* lacking in content; **Inhaltsübersicht** F summary of the contents; **Inhaltsverzeichnis** NT list or table of contents; **„~"** "contents"

inhuman [ɪnhu'ma:n, 'ɪn-] **1** ADJ inhuman; (= *unbarmherzig*) inhumane **2** ADV inhumanly

initialisieren [ɪnitsiali'zi:rən], *ptp* **initialisiert** VT (*Comput*) to initialize

Initialisierung F **-, -en** (*Comput*) initialization

initiativ [initsia'ti:f] ADJ **~ werden** to take the initiative

Initiative [initsia'ti:və] F **-, -n** **(a)** initiative; **aus eigener ~** on one's own initiative; **die ~ ergreifen** to take the initiative; **auf jds ~** (*acc*) **hin** on sb's initiative **(b)** (*Sw Pol*) petition for a referendum

Injektion [ɪnjɛk'tsio:n] F **-, -en** injection

Injektionsspritze F hypodermic (syringe)

injizieren [ɪnji'tsi:rən], *ptp* **injiziert** VT (*form*) to inject (*jdm etw sb with sth*)

Inka ['ɪŋka] M **-(s), -s** Inca

Inkasso [ɪn'kaso] NT **-s, -s** or (*Aus*) **Inkassi** [-si] (*Fin*) collection

Inkasso-: **Inkassobüro** NT (*Fin*) collection agency; **Inkassostelle** F (*Fin*) collection point

Inkaufnahme [ɪn'kaufna:mə] F **-, NO PL** (*form*) acceptance; **unter ~ finanzieller Verluste** accepting the inevitable financial losses

inkl. ABBR *von* **inklusive**

inklusive [ɪnklu'zi:və] **1** PREP +GEN inclusive of; **~ Heizung** inclusive of or including heating **2** ADV inclusive

inkognito [ɪn'kɔgnito] ADV incognito

inkompatibel [ɪnkɔmpa'ti:bl, 'ɪn-] ADJ incompatible

Inkompatibilität F incompatibility

inkompetent [ɪnkɔmpe'tɛnt, 'ɪn-] ADJ incompetent

Inkompetenz [ɪnkɔmpe'tɛnts, 'ɪn-] F incompetence

inkonsequent [ɪnkɔnze'kvɛnt, 'ɪn-] **1** ADJ inconsistent **2** ADV inconsistently

Inkonsequenz [ɪnkɔnze'kvɛnts, 'ɪn-] F inconsistency

inkorrekt [ɪnkɔ'rɛkt, 'ɪn-] **1** ADJ incorrect **2** ADV incorrectly; *gekleidet* inappropriately

In-Kraft-Treten [ɪn'krafttre:tn] NT **-s, NO PL** coming into effect or force; **das ~ von etw verhindern** to prevent sth from coming into effect or force; **bei ~ von etw** when sth comes/came *etc* into effect or force

Inkubationszeit F incubation period

Inkulanz [ɪnku'lants, 'ɪn-] F disobligingness

Inland NT, NO PL **(a)** (*als Staatsgebiet*) home; **im ~ hergestellte Waren** home-produced goods; **im In- und Ausland** at home and abroad; **die Gebühren für einen Brief im ~** domestic letter rates **(b)** (= *Inneres eines Landes*) inland; **im ~** inland; **ins ~ ziehen** to move inland

Inland- IN CPDS (*Comm*) home, domestic; (*Geog*) inland; **Inlandeis** NT ice sheet; **Inlandflug** M domestic or internal flight

inländisch ['ɪnlɛndɪʃ] ADJ domestic; (*Geog*) inland

Inlands-: **Inlandsfrachtkosten** PL domestic freight charges *pl*; **Inlandsmarkt** M home or domestic market; **Inlandsporto** NT inland postage; **Inlandstransport** M domestic transport; **Inlandsverkehr** M domestic traffic; (= *Handel*) home trade; **Briefe im ~** domestic letters

Inlaut M **im ~ vorkommen** to occur in (word) medial position

inliegend ADJ, ADV (*Aus form*) enclosed

Inline-Skater ['ɪnlainske:tɐ] M **-s, -**, **Inlineskater** M **-s, -**, **Inline-Skaterin** [-ərɪn] F **-, -nen**, **Inlineskaterin** F **-, -nen** rollerblader

Inline-Skates ['ɪnlainske:ts] PL, **Inlineskates** PL Rollerblades® *pl*

inmitten [ɪn'mɪtn] **1** PREP +GEN in the middle or midst of **2** ADV **~ von** amongst, surrounded by

innehaben ['ɪnəha:bn] VT SEP IRREG (*form*) to hold

innehalten ['ɪnəhaltn] SEP IRREG VI to pause; **er hielt im Sprechen inne** he stopped speaking in mid-flow

innen ['ɪnən] ADV inside; (= *auf der Innenseite*) on the inside; (= *im Haus*) indoors, inside; **nach ~** inwards; **tief ~ tut es doch weh** deep down inside it really hurts; **die Tür geht nach ~ auf** the door opens inwards; **von ~** from (the) inside; **wie sieht das Haus von ~ aus?** what does the house look like inside?

Innen-: **Innenantenne** F indoor aerial (*Brit*) or antenna (*US*); **Innenarchitekt(in)** M(F) interior designer; **Innenarchitektur** F interior design; **Innenaufnahme** F indoor photo(graph); (*Film*) indoor shot or take; **Innenausstattung** F interior décor *no pl*; (= *das Ausstatten*) interior decoration and furnishing; (*von Auto*) interior fittings *pl* (*Brit*) or fixtures *pl*; **Innenbahn** F (*Sport*) inside lane; **Innenbeleuchtung** F interior lighting; **Innendienst** M office duty; **im ~ sein** to work in the office; **~ machen** or **haben** to be on office duty; **innendrin** ['ɪnən'drɪn] ADV (*inf*) inside; **Inneneinrichtung** F (interior) furnishings *pl*; (= *das Einrichten*) interior furnishing *no pl*; **Innenfinanzierung** F internal financing; **Innenfläche** F **(a)** (= *innere Fläche*) inside; (*der Hand*) palm **(b)** (= *Flächeninhalt*) internal surface area; **Innenhof** M inner courtyard; (*bei Universitäten, Klöstern*) quadrangle, quad (*inf*); **Innenleben** NT, NO PL **(a)** (*inf: seelisch*) inner life; **sein ~ offenbaren** to reveal one's innermost thoughts or feelings **(b)** (*inf: körperlich*) insides *pl*; **Innenleuchte** F (*Aut*) courtesy or interior light; **Innenminister(in)** M(F) minister of the interior; (*in GB*) Home Secretary; (*in den USA*) Secretary of the Interior; **Innenministerium** NT ministry of the interior; (*in GB*) Home Office; (*in den USA*) Department of the Interior; **Innenpolitik** F domestic policy; (= *innere Angelegenheiten*) home or domestic affairs *pl*; **innenpolitisch** **1** ADJ domestic, internal; *Sprecher* on domestic policy; **auf ~em Gebiet** in the field of home affairs **2** ADV **~ gesehen** from the point of view of domestic policy; **~ unverantwortlich/bedenklich** irresponsible/questionable as far as domestic policy is concerned; **~ hat die Regierung versagt** the government has failed with its domestic policy; **Innenraum** M **(a)** **Innenräume** inner rooms *pl* **(b)** NO PL room inside; (*von Wagen*) interior; **mit großem ~** with a lot of room inside; (*Wagen auch*) with a large interior; **Innenseite** F inside; **die ~ von etw nach außen kehren** to turn sth inside out; **Innenspiegel** M (*Aut*) interior mirror; **Innenstadt** F town centre (*Brit*) or center (*US*); (*einer Großstadt*) city centre (*Brit*) or center (*US*); **Innentasche** F inside pocket; **Innentemperatur** F inside temperature; (*in einem Gebäude*) indoor temperature

inner- ['ɪnɐ-]: **innerbetrieblich** **1** ADJ in-house **2** ADV in-house, within the company or corporation; **das wird ~ geregelt werden** that will be settled in-house; **innerdeutsch** ADJ **der ~e Handel** the domestic German trade; **die ~e Grenze** (*Hist*) the inner-German border

Innereien [ɪnə'raiən] PL innards *pl*; (*von Geflügel auch*) giblets *pl*

innere(r, s) ['ɪnərə] ADJ inner; (= *im Körper befindlich, inländisch*) internal; **Facharzt für ~ Krankheiten** internist; **das ~ Ohr** the inner ear; **die ~n Angelegenheiten eines Landes** the home or domestic affairs of a country; **~r Monolog** (*Liter*) interior monologue; **im innersten Herzen** in one's heart of hearts;

eine ~ Uhr (*inf*) an internal clock; **~ Werte** *pl* inner worth *no pl*; **vor meinem ~n Auge** in my mind's eye

Innere(s) ['ɪnərə] NT DECL AS ADJ **(a)** inside; (*von Kirche, Wagen, Schloss*) interior; (= *Mitte*) middle, centre (*Brit*), center (*US*); **Minister des Inner(e)n** minister of the interior; (*in GB*) Home Secretary; (*in den USA*) Secretary of the Interior; **das ~ nach außen kehren** to turn something inside out; **ins ~ des Landes** into the heart of the country **(b)** (*fig*: = *Gemüt, Geist*) heart; **ich wusste, was in seinem ~n vorging** I knew what was going on inside him; **im tiefsten ~n** in one's heart of hearts

innerhalb ['ɪnɛhalp] 🔢 PREP +GEN **(a)** (*örtlich*) inside, within; **~ dieser Regelung** within this ruling **(b)** (*zeitlich*) within 🔢 ADV inside; (*eines Landes*) inland; **weiter ~** further in

innerlich ['ɪnɛlɪç] 🔢 ADJ **(a)** (= *körperlich*) internal **(b)** (= *geistig, seelisch*) inward, inner *no adv*; *Gedicht, Mensch* inward; *Hemmung* inner 🔢 ADV **(a)** (= *im Körper*) internally **(b)** (= *gemütsmäßig*) inwardly, inside; **~ gefestigt sein** to have inner strength; **jdm ~ verbunden sein** to have very deep feelings for sb; **~ lachen** to laugh inwardly *or* to oneself

inner-: innerparteilich 🔢 ADJ within the party; **eine ~e Diskussion** a party discussion 🔢 ADV (with)in the party; **innerstaatlich** ADJ domestic, internal

innerste(r, s) ['ɪnɛstə] ADJ SUPERL *von* **innere(r, s)** innermost, inmost

Innerste(s) ['ɪnɛstə] NT DECL AS ADJ (*lit*) innermost part, heart; (*fig*) heart; **tief im ~n liebte sie ihn** in her heart of hearts she loved him; **bis ins ~ getroffen** deeply hurt

innert ['ɪnɛt] PREP +GEN *or* DAT (*Aus, Sw*) within, in, inside (of)

innewerden ['ɪnə-] VI SEP IRREG AUX SEIN (**sich** *dat*) **einer Sache** (*gen*) **~** to become aware of sth

innewohnen ['ɪnə-] VI SEP +DAT to be inherent in

innig ['ɪnɪç] 🔢 ADJ **(a)** *Glückwünsche, Grüße, Beileid* heartfelt; *Freundschaft, Kontakte, Beziehung* intimate; **mein ~ster Wunsch** my dearest wish **(b)** (*Chem*) *Verbindung* intimate 🔢 ADV deeply, profoundly; **etw aufs ~ste** *or* **Innigste erhoffen/wünschen** to hope/wish for sth most fervently; **jdn ~ lieben** to love sb dearly

Innovation [ɪnova'tsioːn] F -, **-en** innovation

innovativ [ɪnova'tiːf] 🔢 ADJ innovative 🔢 ADV innovatively; **~ tätig sein** to do innovative work

Innung ['ɪnʊŋ] F -, **-en** (trade) guild

inoffiziell [ɪnɔfi'tsiɛl, 'ɪn-] 🔢 ADJ unofficial 🔢 ADV unofficially

inoperabel [ɪnlopɛr'raːbl, 'ɪn-] ADJ (*Med*) inoperable

inopportun [ɪnlɔpɔr'tuːn, 'ɪn-] ADJ inopportune

in petto [ɪn 'pɛto] *siehe* **petto**

in puncto [ɪn 'pʊŋkto] *siehe* **punkto**

Input ['ɪnpʊt] M *or* NT -s, **-s** input

Inquisition [ɪnkvizi'tsioːn] F -, **-en** Inquisition

Inquisitor [ɪnkvi'ziːtoːe] M -s, **Inquisitoren** [-'toːrən] inquisitor

inquisitorisch [ɪnkvizi'toːrɪʃ] 🔢 ADJ inquisitorial 🔢 ADV inquisitorially

ins [ɪns] CONTR *von* **in das**; **~ Rollen/Rutschen geraten** *or* **kommen** to start rolling/sliding

Insasse ['ɪnsasə] M **-n, -n, Insassin** ['ɪnsasɪn] F -, **-nen** (*von Fahrzeug*) passenger; (*von Anstalt*) inmate

insbesondere [ɪnsbə'zɔndərə] ADV particularly, in particular

Inschrift F inscription

Insekt [ɪn'zɛkt] NT **-(e)s, -en** insect

Insekten-: Insektenbekämpfung F insect control; **Insektenbekämpfungsmittel** NT insecticide; **Insektenfresser** M insect eater, insectivore (*form*); **Insektengift** NT insecticide; **Insektenkunde** F entomology; **Insektenschutzmittel** NT insect repellent; **Insektenstich** M (*von Ameisen, Mücken, Flöhen*) insect bite; (*von Bienen, Wespen*) (insect) sting

Insektizid [ɪnzɛkti'tsiːt] NT **-s, -e** [-də] (*form*) insecticide

Insel ['ɪnzl] F -, **-n** (*lit, fig*) island; **die Britischen ~n** the British Isles; **die ~ Man** the Isle of Man; **reif für die ~ sein** (*inf*) to be ready to get away from it all

Inselbewohner(in) M(F) islander

Inselchen ['ɪnzlçən] NT -s, little island

Insel-: Inselgruppe F group of islands; **Insellage** F island position; **Großbritannien, infolge seiner ~ ...** Great Britain, because it is an island ...; **inselreich** ADJ with a lot of islands;

Inselstaat M island state; **Inselvolk** NT island nation *or* race *or* people; **Inselwelt** F island world; **die ~ Mittelamerikas** the world of the Central American islands

Inserat [ɪnze'raːt] NT **-(e)s, -e** advertisement

Inserent [ɪnze'rɛnt] M **-en, -en, Inserentin** [-'rɛntɪn] F -, **-nen** advertiser

inserieren [ɪnze'riːrən], *ptp* **inseriert** VTI to advertise

insgeheim [ɪnsgə'haim, 'ɪns-] ADV secretly

insgesamt [ɪnsgə'zamt, 'ɪns-] ADV (= *alles zusammen*) altogether; (= *im Großen und Ganzen*) all in all; **die Kosten belaufen sich auf ~ 1.000 Euro** the costs amount to a total of 1,000 euros; **ein Verdienst von ~ 2.000 Euro** earnings totalling (*Brit*) *or* totaling (*US*) 2,000 euros

Insider ['ɪnsaidɐ] M **-s, -, Insiderin** [-ərɪn] F -, **-nen** insider; **der Witz war nur für ~ verständlich** that was an in-joke (*Brit*) *or* inside joke (*esp US*); **~ der Jazzszene** those in on the jazz scene

Insider- ['ɪnsaidɐ-]: **Insidergeschäft** NT insider deal; **Insiderhandel** M insider trading

insistieren [ɪnzɪs'tiːrən], *ptp* **insistiert** VI (*geh*) to insist (*auf* +*dat* on)

inskünftig ['ɪnskʏnftɪç] ADJ, ADV (*Sw*) = **zukünftig**

insofern [ɪnzo'fɛrn, m'zo:fɛrn, 'ɪn-] 🔢 ADV in this respect; **~ als** in so far as 🔢 [ɪnzo'fɛrn, m'zo:fɛrn, 'ɪn-] CONJ (= *wenn*) if

insolvent [ɪnzɔl'vɛnt, 'ɪn-] ADJ (*Comm*) insolvent

Insolvenz [ɪnzɔl'vɛnts, 'ɪn-] F -, **-en** (*Comm*) insolvency

insoweit [ɪn'zo:vait, ɪnzo'vait, 'ɪn-] ADV, CONJ = **insofern**

in spe [ɪn 'spe:] ADJ (*inf*) to be

Inspektion [ɪnspɛk'tsioːn] F -, **-en** inspection; (*Aut*) service; **ich habe mein Auto zur ~ gebracht** I've taken my car in for a service

Inspektionsreise F tour of inspection

Inspektor [ɪn'spɛktoːe] M **-s, Inspektoren** [-'toːrən], **Inspektorin** [-'toːrɪn] F -, **-nen** inspector; (= *Verwalter, Aufseher*) superintendent

Inspiration [ɪnspira'tsioːn] F -, **-en** inspiration

inspirieren [ɪnspi'riːrən], *ptp* **inspiriert** VT to inspire; **sich von etw ~ lassen** to get one's inspiration from sth

inspizieren [ɪnspi'tsiːrən], *ptp* **inspiziert** VT to inspect

instabil [ɪnsta'biːl, 'ɪn-] ADJ unstable

Instabilität F instability

Installateur [ɪnstala'tø:e] M **-s, -e, Installateurin** [-'tø:rɪn] F -, **-nen** plumber; (= *Elektroinstallateur*) electrician; (= *Gasinstallateur*) gas fitter

Installation [ɪnstala'tsioːn] F -, **-en (a)** (*no pl*: = *das Installieren*) installation; (*Tech*) installation, fitting **(b)** (= *Anlage*) installation; (*in Bauten*) fittings *pl*; (= *Wasserinstallation*) plumbing *no pl*

installieren [ɪnsta'liːrən], *ptp* **installiert** 🔢 VT to install (*auch fig, Comput*), to put in 🔢 VR to install oneself

instand [ɪn'ʃtant] ADJ in good condition; (= *funktionsfähig*) in working order; **etw ~ halten** to maintain sth; **etw ~ setzen** to get sth into good condition/into working order

Instand- [ɪn'ʃtant-]: **Instandhaltung** F maintenance; **Instandhaltungskosten** PL maintenance costs *pl*; **Instandsetzung** [ɪn'ʃtantzɛtsʊŋ] F -, **-en** (*von Gerät*) overhaul; (*von Gebäude*) restoration; (= *Reparatur*) repair

Instanz [ɪn'stants] F -, **-en (a)** (= *Behörde*) authority **(b)** (*Jur*) court; (= *Verhandlungsstadium*) (court) case; **Verhandlung in erster/letzter ~** first/final court case; **Berufung in erster/ zweiter ~** first/second appeal; **ein Urteil letzter ~** (*lit, fig*) a final judgement; **er ging durch alle ~en** he went through all the courts

Instinkt [ɪn'stɪŋkt] M **-(e)s, -e** (*lit, fig*) instinct; **aus ~** instinctively

instinktiv [ɪnstɪŋk'tiːf] 🔢 ADJ instinctive 🔢 ADV instinctively

Institut [ɪnsti'tuːt] NT **-(e)s, -e** institute

Institution [ɪnstitu'tsioːn] F -, **-en** institution

institutionell [ɪnstitutsio'nɛl] ADJ institutional

instruieren [ɪnstru'iːrən], *ptp* **instruiert** VT to instruct; (*über Unternehmen, Plan etc*) to brief

Instruktion [ɪnstrʊk'tsioːn] F -, **-en** instruction; **laut ~** according to instructions

Instrument [ɪnstru'mɛnt] NT **-(e)s, -e** instrument

instrumental [ɪnstrumɛn'taːl] (*Mus*) **1** ADJ instrumental **2** ADV jdn ~ **begleiten** to provide the instrumental accompaniment for sb; ~ **musizieren** to play musical instruments

instrumentalisieren [ɪnstrumɛntali'ziːrən], *ptp* **instrumentalisiert** VT (a) (*Mus*) to arrange for instruments (b) *Theorie, Plan etc* to harness; (= *ausnutzen*) to exploit

Instrumenten-: Instrumentenbrett NT instrument panel; **Instrumentenflug** M instrument flight; **Instrumententafel** F control panel

Insuffizienz ['ɪnzʊfitsiɛnts] F -, -en (*Med, geh*) insufficiency

Insulaner [ɪnzu'laːnɐ] M -s, -, **Insulanerin** [-ərɪn] F -, -en (*usu hum*) islander

Insulin [ɪnzu'liːn] NT -s, NO PL insulin

Insulin- IN CPDS insulin; **Insulinschock** M insulin *or* hypoglycaemic (*Brit spec*) *or* hypoglycemic (*US spec*) shock; **Insulinstoß** M insulin boost

inszenatorisch [ɪnstsena'toːrɪʃ] ADJ directing *attr*, directorial; *Anforderungen* directorial; **eine ~e Glanzleistung** a brilliant piece of directing *or* (*fig*) stage management

inszenieren [ɪnstse'niːrən], *ptp* **inszeniert** VT (a) (*Theat*) to direct; (*Rad, TV*) to produce (b) (*fig*) to stage-manage; **einen Streit ~** to start an argument

Inszenierung F -, -en production; **ein Stück in neuer ~ aufführen** to put on a new production of a play

intakt [ɪn'takt] ADJ intact

Intaktheit F -, NO PL intactness

integer [ɪn'teːgɐ] (*geh*) **1** ADJ ~ **sein** to be full of integrity; **ein integrer Mensch** a person of integrity **2** ADV **sich ~ verhalten** to behave with integrity

integral [ɪnte'graːl] ADJ ATTR integral

Integral [ɪnte'graːl] NT -s, -e integral

Integral-: Integralhelm M full-face helmet; **Integralrechnung** F integral calculus

Integration [ɪntegra'tsioːn] F -, -en integration

Integrations-: Integrationsfigur F unifying figure; **Integrationsklasse** F (*Sch*) integrated class

Integrationsklassen are classes designed to enable physically and mentally disabled children and young people to attend a conventional school instead of a special school. This is regarded as having benefits for both the disabled and able-bodied children.

integrierbar ADJ integrable (*auch Math*)

integrieren [ɪnte'griːrən], *ptp* **integriert** VT to integrate (*auch Math*); **integrierte Gesamtschule** ≈ comprehensive (school) (*Brit*), ≈ high school (*US*)

Integrität [ɪntegri'tɛːt] F -, NO PL (*geh*) integrity

Intellekt [ɪnte'lɛkt] M -(e)s, NO PL intellect

intellektuell [ɪntelɛk'tuɛl] ADJ intellectual

Intellektuelle(r) [ɪntelɛk'tuɛlə] MF DECL AS ADJ intellectual

intelligent [ɪnteli'gɛnt] **1** ADJ intelligent **2** ADV cleverly, ingeniously; *sich verhalten* intelligently; ~ **ausgedacht** well thought out

Intelligenz [ɪnteli'gɛnts] F -, -en intelligence; (= *Personengruppe*) intelligentsia *pl*; **künstliche ~** artificial intelligence

Intelligenzbestie F (*pej inf*) egghead (*inf*)

Intelligenz-: Intelligenzquotient M intelligence quotient, IQ; **Intelligenztest** M intelligence test; **einen ~ mit jdm machen** to test sb's IQ

Intendant [ɪnten'dant] M -en, -en, **Intendantin** [-'dantɪn] F -, -nen director; (*Theat*) theatre (*Brit*) *or* theater (*US*) manager

Intendanz [ɪnten'dants] F -, -en (= *Amt*) directorship; (= *Büro*) director's office; (*Theat*) theatre (*Brit*) *or* theater (*US*) manager's office

intendieren [ɪnten'diːrən], *ptp* **intendiert** VT (*geh*) to intend

Intensität [ɪntenzi'tɛːt] F -, (*rare*) -en intensity

intensiv [ɪnten'ziːf] **1** ADJ intensive; *Beziehungen* deep, very close; *Farbe, Gefühl, Geruch, Geschmack, Blick* intense **2** ADV jdn ~ **beobachten** to watch sb intently; (*Polizei*) to put sb under close surveillance; **sich ~ bemühen** to try hard; ~ **bestrebt sein** to make an intense effort; ~ **duftend** with an intense scent; ~ **nach etw schmecken** to taste strongly of sth

intensivieren [ɪntenzi'viːrən], *ptp* **intensiviert** VT to intensify

Intensivierung F -, -en intensification

Intensiv-: Intensivkurs M intensive course; **Intensivstation** F intensive care unit

Intention [ɪnten'tsioːn] F -, -en intention, intent

inter- [ɪntɐ], **Inter-** IN CPDS inter-; **Interaktion** F interaction; **interaktiv** **1** ADJ interactive **2** ADV interactively; ~ **gestaltet** designed for interactive use; **Interbanksatz** M interbank rate

Intercity [ɪntɐ'sɪti] M -(s), -s intercity (train)

Intercity-: Intercityexpress M high-speed intercity (train); **Intercityzug** M intercity (train)

interessant [ɪntɐe'sant] **1** ADJ interesting; **zu diesem Preis ist das nicht ~ für uns** (*Comm*) we are not interested at that price; **das ist ja ~!** (that's) very interesting!; **sich ~ machen** to attract attention (to oneself); **sich bei jdm ~ machen** to attract sb's attention **2** ADV **sich ~ anhören**, ~ **klingen** to sound interesting; **sich ~ lesen** to be interesting; **diese Autorin schreibt sehr ~** this author's writing is very interesting; ~ **erzählen** to tell interesting stories

interessanterweise [ɪntɐe'santɐ'vaizə] ADV interestingly enough

Interesse [ɪntɐ'esə] NT -s, -n interest; ~ **an jdm/etw** *or* **für jdn/ etw haben** to be interested in sb/sth; **im ~ +*gen*** in the interests of; **es liegt in Ihrem eigenen ~** it's in your own interest(s); **die ~n eines Staates wahrnehmen** to look after the interests of a state

Interesse-: interessehalber ADV out of interest; **interesselos** ADJ indifferent

Interessen-: Interessenbereich M, **Interessengebiet** NT field of interest; **das gehört nicht zu meinem ~** that isn't one of my interests; **Interessengemeinschaft** F (a) community of interests; (= *Menschen*) group of people sharing interests (b) (*Econ*) syndicate; **Interessensphäre** F (*Pol*) sphere of influence

Interessent [ɪntɐe'sɛnt] M -en, -en, **Interessentin** [-'sɛntɪn] F -, -nen interested person *or* party (form); (= *Bewerber auch*) applicant; (*Comm*: = *Kauflustiger auch*) prospective customer; ~**en werden gebeten …** those interested are requested …

Interessentenkreis M market

interessieren [ɪntɐe'siːrən], *ptp* **interessiert** **1** VT to interest (*für, an +dat* in); **das interessiert mich (gar) nicht!** I'm not (the least *or* slightest bit) interested; **das hat dich nicht zu ~!** that's none of your business! **2** VR to be interested (*für* in)

interessiert [ɪntɐe'siːɐt] **1** ADJ interested (*an +dat* in); **vielseitig ~ sein** to have a wide range of interests; **politisch ~** interested in politics; **ein ~er Mensch** a person with a number of interests **2** ADV with interest; **sich ~ zeigen** to act interested; **sich an etw** (*dat*) ~ **zeigen** to show an interest in sth

Interface ['ɪntɐfeːs] NT -, -s (*Comput*) interface

Interferenz [ɪntɐfe'rɛnts] F -, -en (*Phys, Ling*) interference *no pl*

Interferon [ɪntɐfe'roːn] NT -s, -e interferon

Interims- ['ɪntɐɪms-] IN CPDS interim; **Interimsabkommen** NT interim agreement; **Interimsdividende** F interim dividend; **Interimskonto** NT suspense account; **Interimsregierung** F caretaker *or* provisional government; **Interimsschein** M (*Fin*) scrip

Interjektion [ɪntɐjɛk'tsioːn] F -, -en interjection

Inter-: interkontinental [ɪntɐkɔntinen'taːl] ADJ intercontinental; **Interkontinentalrakete** [ɪntɐkɔntinen'taːl-] F intercontinental missile

Intermezzo [ɪntɐ'mɛtso] NT -s, -s *or* **Intermezzi** [-tsi] (*Mus*) intermezzo; (*fig auch*) interlude; (*ärgerlich*) contretemps *sing*

intermittierend [ɪntɐmɪ'tiːrənt] ADJ intermittent

intern [ɪn'tɛrn] **1** ADJ internal; ~**er Schüler** boarder; **diese Maßnahmen müssen vorläufig ~ bleiben** for the time being these measures must be kept private **2** ADV internally

-intern ADJ SUF **schulinterne/ausschussinterne Angelegenheiten** internal school/committee matters; **etw schulintern regeln** to settle sth internally within the school/schools

Internat [ɪntɐ'naːt] NT -(e)s, -e boarding school

international [ɪntɐnatsio'naːl] **1** ADJ international **2** ADV internationally; ~ **von Interesse** of international interest; ~

operierende Organisationen international organizations; ~ **kochen** to cook foreign dishes

Internationale [ɪntɛnatsioˈnaːlə] F **-, -n** Internationale

internationalisieren [ɪntɛnatsionaliˈziːrən], *ptp* **internationalisiert** VT to internationalize

Internatsschüler(in) M(F) boarder

Internet [ˈɪntɛnet] NT **-,** NO PL (*Comput*) Internet; **Anschluss ans ~ haben** to be connected to the Internet; **im ~ surfen** to surf the Internet

Internet-: Internetbenutzer(in) M(F) Internet user; **Internetbroker** M Internet broker; **Internetbrowser** M Internet browser; **Internetcafé** NT Internet café; **Internethandel** M Internet trading, e-commerce; **Internetknoten** M point of presence, pop; **Internetnutzer(in)** M(F) Internet user; **Internetprovider** M Internet provider; **Internetseite** F web page; **Internetzugriff** M Internet access

internieren [ɪntɛˈniːrən], *ptp* **interniert** VT to intern

Internierung F **-, -en** internment

Internierungslager NT internment camp

Internist [ɪntɛˈnɪst] M **-en, -en**, **Internistin** [-ˈnɪstɪn] F **-, -nen** internist

Interpol [ˈɪntɛpoːl] F - Interpol

Interpret [ɪntɛˈpreːt] M **-en, -en**, **Interpretin** [-ˈpreːtɪn] F **-, -nen** interpreter (*of music, art etc*); **Lieder verschiedener ~en** songs by various singers

Interpretation [ɪntɛpretaˈtsioːn] F **-, -en** interpretation; (*eines Liedes auch*) version

interpretieren [ɪntɛpreˈtiːrən], *ptp* **interpretiert** VT to interpret; **etw falsch ~** to misinterpret sth

Interpretin F *siehe* **Interpret**

Interpunktion F punctuation

Interrailkarte [ˈɪntɛre:l-] F inter-rail ticket

Interregio [ɪntɛˈreːgio] M **-s, -s**, **Interregiozug** M *fast train running at regular intervals*

Interrogativ-: Interrogativpronomen [ɪntɛrogaˈtiːf-] NT interrogative pronoun; **Interrogativsatz** [ɪntɛrogaˈtiːf-] M interrogative clause

interstellar [ɪntɛsteˈlaːɐ] ADJ interstellar

Intervall [ɪntɛˈval] NT **-s, -e** interval (*auch Mus*)

Intervallschaltung F interval switch

intervenieren [ɪntɛveˈniːrən], *ptp* **interveniert** VI to intervene

Intervention [ɪntɛvenˈtsioːn] F **-, -en** intervention

Interview [ˈɪntɛvjuː, ɪntɛˈvjuː] NT **-s, -s** interview

interviewen [ɪntɛˈvjuːən, ˈɪntɛ-], *ptp* **interviewt** VT to interview (*jdn zu etw* sb about sth)

Intifada [ɪntiˈfaːda] F **-,** NO PL intifada

intim [ɪnˈtiːm] ADJ intimate; **ein ~er Kenner von etw sein** to have an intimate knowledge of sth

Intimbereich M **(a)** (*Anat*) genital area **(b)** (*fig*) = **Intimsphäre**

Intimität [ɪntimiˈtɛːt] F **-, -en** intimacy; **bitte keine ~en!** please don't go into intimate details; **zwischen den beiden kam es zu ~en** they became intimate with each other; **~en austauschen** to kiss and pet

Intim-: Intimpartner(in) M(F) (*form*) sexual partner; **Intimschmuck** M body jewellery (*Brit*) *or* jewelry (*US*); **Intimsphäre** F private life; **jds ~ verletzen** to invade sb's privacy; **diese Frage greift in die ~ ein** that question is an invasion of my/your *etc* privacy; **Intimverkehr** M intimacy; **~ mit jdm haben** to be intimate with sb

intolerant [ɪntoleˈrant, ˈɪn-] ADJ intolerant (*einer Sache gegenüber* of sth, *jdm gegenüber* of *or* towards sb) ADV intolerantly; **in solchen Dingen zeigt er sich absolut ~** he is completely intolerant about such things

Intoleranz [ɪntoleˈrants, ˈɪn-] F intolerance

Intranet [ˈɪntranet] NT **-s, -s** (*Comput*) Intranet

intransitiv ADJ intransitive ADV intransitively

intravenös [ɪntraveˈnøːs] ADJ intravenous ADV intravenously

Intrigant [ɪntriˈgant] M **-en, -en**, **Intrigantin** [-ˈgantɪn] F **-, -nen** schemer

Intrige [ɪnˈtriːgə] F **-, -n** scheme

intrigieren [ɪntriˈgiːrən], *ptp* **intrigiert** VI to intrigue, to scheme

introvertiert [ɪntrovɛrˈtiːɐt] ADJ introverted

Introvertiertheit F **-,** NO PL introversion

Intuition [ɪntuiˈtsioːn] F **-, -en** intuition

intuitiv [ɪntuiˈtiːf] ADJ intuitive ADV intuitively

intus [ˈɪntʊs] ADJ (*inf*) **etw ~ haben** (= *wissen*) to get *or* have got (*Brit*) sth into one's head (*inf*); *Essen, Alkohol* to have sth down (*inf*) *or* inside one (*inf*); **er hat schon etwas** *or* **einiges ~** he's had a few

Invalide [ɪnvaˈliːdə] M **-n, -n**, **Invalidin** [-ˈliːdɪn] F **-, -nen** disabled person, invalid; **er ist ~** he's disabled, he's an invalid

Invalidin F *siehe* **Invalide**

Invalidität [ɪnvalidiˈtɛːt] F **-,** NO PL disability

invariabel [ɪnvaˈriaːbl, ˈɪn-] ADJ invariable

Invariante F **-, -n** (*Math*) invariant, invariable

Invasion [ɪnvaˈzioːn] F **-, -en** (*lit, fig*) invasion

Inventar [ɪnvɛnˈtaːɐ] NT **-s, -e (a)** (= *Verzeichnis*) inventory; (*Comm*) assets and liabilities *pl*; **das ~ aufnehmen** to do the inventory; **etw ins ~ aufnehmen** to put sth on the inventory **(b)** (= *Einrichtung*) fittings *pl* (*Brit*), equipment; (= *Maschinen*) equipment *no pl*, plant *no pl*; **er gehört schon zum ~** (*fig*) he's part of the furniture

Inventur [ɪnvɛnˈtuːɐ] F **-, -en** stocktaking; **~ machen** to stocktake

Inversion [ɪnvɛrˈzioːn] F **-, -en** (*Gram*) inversion

Inversionswetterlage F inverted atmospheric conditions *pl*

investieren [ɪnvɛsˈtiːrən], *ptp* **investiert** VT (*Comm*) to invest; **Gefühle in jdn ~** (*inf*) to become (emotionally) involved with sb VI to invest

Investition [ɪnvɛstiˈtsioːn] F **-, -en** investment

Investitions- IN CPDS investment; **Investitionsgut** NT USU PL item of capital expenditure; **Investitionsgüter** capital goods *pl*; **Investitionsgüterindustrie** F capital goods industry; **Investitionshilfe** F investment aid; **Investitionskredit** M capital investment loan; **Investitionsrechnung** F investment arithmetic, capital budgeting computation

Investment [ɪnˈvɛstmənt] NT **-s, -s** investment

Investment-: Investmentbanking [-bɛŋkɪŋ] NT **-s,** NO PL investment banking; **Investmentfonds** M investment fund; **Investmentgesellschaft** F investment trust; **Investmentpapier** NT, **Investmentzertifikat** NT investment fund certificate; **Investmentplan** M investment programme (*Brit*) *or* program (*US*)

Investor [ɪnˈvɛstoːɐ] M **-s, -en**, **Investorin** [-toːrɪn] F **-, -nen** investor

In-vitro-Fertilisation [ɪnˈviːtrofɛrtilizatsioːn] F **-, -en** in vitro fertilization

inwendig [ˈɪnvɛndɪç] ADV (*inf*) **jdn/etw in- und auswendig kennen** to know sb/sth inside out

inwiefern [ɪnviˈfɛrn], **inwieweit** [ɪnviˈvait] ADV (*im Satz*) to what extent; (*allein stehend*) in what way

Inzahlungnahme [ɪnˈtsaːlʊŋnaːmə] F **-, -n** (*Comm*) **die ~ von etw** the acceptance of sth in part payment *or* as a trade-in; **bei ~ des alten Wagens** when the old car is traded in

Inzest [ɪnˈtsɛst] M **-(e)s, -e** incest *no pl*

inzestuös [ɪntsɛstuˈøːs] ADJ incestuous ADV **er lebte jahrelang ~ mit seiner Tochter** he lived for years in an incestuous relationship with his daughter

Inzucht F inbreeding

inzwischen [ɪnˈtsvɪʃn] ADV (in the) meantime, meanwhile; **ich gehe ~ zur Bank** I'll go to the bank in the meantime; **er hat sich ~ verändert** he's changed since (then); **sie ist ~ 18 geworden** she's now 18

IOK [iːloːˈkaː] NT **-s** ABBR *von* **Internationales Olympisches Komitee** IOC

Ion [ioːn, ˈiːɔn] NT **-s, -en** [ˈioːnən] ion

I-Punkt [ˈiː-] M dot on the i

IQ [iːˈkuː] M **-s, -s** ABBR *von* **Intelligenzquotient** IQ

i. R. [iːˈɛr] ABBR *von* **im Ruhestand** retd

Irak [iˈraːk, ˈiːrak] M **-s (der) ~** Iraq

irakisch [iˈraːkɪʃ] ADJ Iraqi

Iran [iˈraːn] M **-s (der) ~** Iran

iranisch [iˈraːnɪʃ] ADJ Iranian

irdisch [ˈɪrdɪʃ] ADJ earthly *no adv*; **den Weg alles Irdischen gehen** to go the way of all flesh

Ire [ˈiːrə] M **-n, -n** Irishman; Irish boy; **die ~n** the Irish; **er ist ~** he's Irish; *siehe auch* **Irin**

irgend [ˈɪrgnt] **1** ADV at all; **wenn ~ möglich, wenn es ~ geht** if it's at all possible; **was ich ~ kann ...** whatever I can ...; **so sanft wie ~ möglich** as gently as possible; **so lange ich ~ kann** as long as I possibly can **2** MIT INDEF PRON **~ so ein Tier** some animal; **ein Fuchs oder ~ so ein Tier** a fox or some such animal; *siehe auch* **irgendetwas, irgendjemand**

irgendein [ˈɪrgntˈlain] INDEF PRON some; *(fragend, verneinend, bedingend)* any; **ich will nicht ~ Buch** I don't want just any *(old (inf))* book; **haben Sie noch ~en Wunsch?** is there anything else you would like?; **das kann ~ anderer machen** somebody else can do it

irgendeine(r, s) [ˈɪrgntˈlainə] INDEF PRON *(nominal) (bei Personen)* somebody, someone; *(bei Dingen)* something; *(fragend, verneinend, bedingend)* anybody; anything; **welchen wollen Sie? – ~n** which one do you want? – any one

irgendeinmal [ˈɪrgntlainˈmaːl] ADV some time or other, sometime; *(fragend, bedingend)* ever

irgendetwas [ˈɪrgntˈletvas] INDEF PRON something; *(fragend, verneinend, bedingend)* anything; **was zieh ich an? – ~** what shall I wear? – anything *or* any old thing *(inf)*

irgendjemand [ˈɪrgntˈjeːmant] INDEF PRON somebody; *(fragend, verneinend, bedingend)* anybody; **ich bin nicht ~** I'm not just anybody

irgendwann [ˈɪrgntˈvan] ADV some time; **~ einmal** some time; *(fragend, bedingend)* ever

irgendwas [ˈɪrgntˈvas] INDEF PRON *(inf)* something; *(fragend, verneinend, bedingend)* anything; **was soll ich sagen? – ~** what shall I say? – anything *or* any old thing *(inf)*

irgendwelche(r, s) [ˈɪrgntˈvɛlçə] INDEF PRON some; *(fragend, verneinend, bedingend, = jede beliebige)* any; **sind noch ~ Reste da?** is there anything left?

irgendwer [ˈɪrgntˈveːɐ] INDEF PRON *(inf)* somebody; *(fragend, verneinend, bedingend)* anybody; **ich bin nicht ~** I'm not just anybody

irgendwie [ˈɪrgntˈviː] ADV somehow (or other); **ist es ~ möglich?** is it at all possible?; **kannst du dir das ~ vorstellen?** can you possibly imagine it?; **ich hab das ~ schon mal gesehen** I've just got a feeling I've seen it before

irgendwo [ˈɪrgntˈvoː] ADV somewhere (or other), someplace *(esp US inf)*; *(fragend, verneinend, bedingend)* anywhere, any place *(esp US inf)*

irgendwoher [ˈɪrgntvoˈheːɐ] ADV from somewhere (or other), from someplace *(esp US inf)*; *(fragend, verneinend, bedingend)* from anywhere *or* any place *(esp US inf)*

irgendwohin [ˈɪrgntvoˈhɪn] ADV somewhere (or other), someplace *(esp US inf)*; *(fragend, verneinend, bedingend)* anywhere, any place *(esp US inf)*

Iridium [iˈriːdiʊm] NT **-s**, NO PL *(abbr* **Ir)** iridium

Irin [ˈiːrɪn] F **-, -nen** Irishwoman; Irish girl; **sie ist ~** she is Irish; *siehe auch* **Ire**

Iris [ˈiːrɪs] F **-,** *or (Opt auch)* **Iriden** [iˈriːdn] iris

irisch [ˈiːrɪʃ] ADJ Irish; **~-römisches Bad** Turkish bath; **Irische See** Irish Sea

Irland [ˈɪrlant] NT **-s** Ireland; (= *Republik ~)* Eire

irländisch [ˈɪrlɛndɪʃ] ADJ Irish

Ironie [iroˈniː] F **-,** *(rare)* **-n** [-ˈniːən] irony

ironisch [iˈroːnɪʃ] **1** ADJ ironic, ironical **2** ADV ironically

irr [ɪr] ADJ, ADV = **irre**

irrational [ɪratsioˈnaːl, ˈɪr-] **1** ADJ irrational *(auch Math)* **2** ADV irrationally

Irrationalität [ɪratsionaliˈtɛːt, ˈɪr-] F irrationality

irre [ˈɪrə] **1** ADJ **(a)** (= *geistesgestört)* mad; **~s Zeug reden** *(fig)* to say crazy things **(b)** (= *verwirrt)* confused **(c)** *(dated inf)* Party, Hut wild *(inf)* **2** ADV **(a)** (= *verrückt)* insanely; **wie ~** *(fig inf)* like crazy *(inf)* **(b)** *(dated inf)* **er war ~ angezogen** he was wearing wild clothes *(inf)*; **~ gut** brilliant *(inf)* **(c)** *(dated inf: = sehr)* incredibly

Irre [ˈɪrə] F **-,** NO PL **jdn in die ~ führen** *(lit, fig)* to lead sb astray

irreal [ˈɪreaːl, ɪreˈaːl] ADJ unreal

Irre-: irreführen VT SEP to mislead; **sich ~ lassen** to be misled; **irreführend** **1** ADJ misleading **2** ADV **sie hat sich ~ ausgedrückt** the way she said it was very misleading; **die Strecke ist ~ ausgeschildert** the signs are very misleading; **Irreführung** F misleading

irregulär [ɪreguˈlɛːɐ, ˈɪr-] ADJ *(auch Mil)* irregular

Irregularität [ɪregulariˈtɛːt, ˈɪr-] F **-, -en** irregularity

irrelevant [ɪreleˈvant, ˈɪr-] ADJ irrelevant *(für* for, to)

Irrelevanz [ɪreleˈvants, ˈɪr-] F irrelevance *(für* for, to)

irremachen VT SEP to confuse, to muddle

irren [ˈɪrən] **1** VI **(a)** (= *sich täuschen)* to be mistaken *or* wrong; **Irren ist menschlich** *(Prov)* to err is human **(b)** AUX SEIN (= *umherschweifen)* to wander **2** VR to be mistaken *or* wrong; **jeder kann sich mal ~** everyone makes mistakes; **sich in jdm/ etw ~** to be mistaken in *or* about sb/about sth, to be wrong about sb/sth; **wenn ich mich nicht irre ...** if I'm not mistaken ...

irreparabel [ɪrepaˈraːbl, ˈɪr-] **1** ADJ irreparable **2** ADV *beschädigen* irreparably; **das Organ ist ~ geschädigt** the organ has suffered irreversible damage

Irre(r) [ˈɪrə] MF DECL AS ADJ lunatic; *(fig auch)* madman/-woman; **ein armer ~r** *(hum inf)* a poor fool

irrereden VI SEP to talk dementedly

Irresein NT insanity; **manisch-depressives ~** manic depression

irreversibel [ɪreverˈziːbl, ˈɪr-] ADJ irreversible

Irr-: Irrfahrt F wandering; **Irrgarten** M maze, labyrinth

irrig [ˈɪrɪç] ADJ incorrect

irrigerweise [ˈɪrɪgəˈvaizə] ADV wrongly

irritieren [ɪriˈtiːrən], *ptp* **irritiert** VT (= *verwirren)* to confuse; (= *ärgern)* to irritate

Irrsinn M, NO PL madness; **das ist ja ~!** *(inf)* that's (sheer *or* absolute) madness!

irrsinnig **1** ADJ crazy, insane; *(inf: = stark)* terrific; **wie ein Irrsinniger** like a madman; **ein ~er Verkehr** a terrific amount of traffic **2** ADV *(inf)* (= *äußerst)* incredibly; **sich freuen** so much; **das Kind schrie wie ~** the child yelled like crazy *(inf)*; **~ viel** a hell of a lot *(inf)*; **~ viele Leute** *(inf)* a tremendous number of people

Irrsinns- IN CPDS *(inf)* terrific; **Irrsinnshitze** F *(inf)* **da ist eine ~** the heat there is absolutely incredible; **Irrsinnstat** F insanity

Irrtum [ˈɪrtuːm] M **-s, -tümer** [-tyːmɐ] mistake; **ein ~ von ihm** a mistake on his part; **im ~ sein, sich im ~ befinden** to be wrong; **Irrtum! wrong!**; **~ vorbehalten!** *(Comm)* errors excepted; **einen ~ zugeben** to admit to (having made) a mistake

irrtümlich [ˈɪrtyːmlɪç] **1** ADJ ATTR erroneous **2** ADV erroneously; (= *aus Versehen)* by mistake

irrtümlicherweise [ˈɪrtyːmlɪçɐˈvaizə] ADV erroneously; (= *aus Versehen)* by mistake

Irrweg M **(a)** (= *Irrfahrt)* wandering **(b)** *(fig)* **auf dem ~ sein** to be on the wrong track; **zu studieren erwies sich für ihn als ~** going to university turned out to be a mistake for him; **auf ~e geraten** to go astray

ISBN [iːɛsbeːˈlɛn] F **-, -s** ABBR **(a)** *von* **Internationale Standard-Buchnummer** ISBN **(b)** *(Comput) von* **Industrial Standard Business Network** ISBN

Ischias [ˈɪʃias, ˈɪsçias] M or NT **-,** NO PL sciatica

Ischiasnerv M sciatic nerve

ISDN [iːɛsdeːˈlɛn] ABBR *von* **Integrated Services Digital Network** *(Telec)* ISDN

ISDN-Netz [iːɛsdeːˈlɛn-] NT *(Telec)* ISDN network

Islam [ɪsˈlaːm, ˈɪslam] M **-s**, NO PL Islam

islamisch [ɪsˈlaːmɪʃ] **1** ADJ Islamic **2** ADV **~ heiraten** to have a Muslim wedding; (= *beeinflusst* influenced by Islam; **seine Kinder ~ erziehen** to raise one's children as Muslims

Islamisierung [ɪslamiˈziːrʊŋ] F **-, -en** Islamization

Island [ˈiːslant] NT **-s** Iceland

Isländer [ˈiːslɛndɐ] M **-s, -, Isländerin** [-ərɪn] F **-, -nen** Icelander

isländisch [ˈiːslɛndɪʃ] ADJ Icelandic

Iso-Drink [ˈiːzo-] M, **Isodrink** M isotonic drink

Isolation [izolaˈtsioːn] F **-, -en (a)** (= *das Absondern)* isolation; (= *Einzelhaft)* solitary confinement **(b)** *(Elec, gegen Lärm, Kälte etc)* insulation

Isolationsfolter F *(pej)*, **Isolationshaft** F solitary confinement

Isolator [izoˈlaːtoːɐ] M **-s, Isolatoren** [-ˈtoːrən] insulator

Isolier- [izoˈliːɐ-]: **Isolierband** NT, *pl* **-bänder** insulating tape, friction tape *(US)*; **Isolierbox** F *(für Imbiss, Getränke etc)* cooler (box)

isolieren [izo'li:rən], *ptp* **isoliert** ◨ VT **(a)** (= *absondern*) to isolate; **jdn isoliert halten** to keep sb in isolation; *Häftling* to keep sb in solitary confinement; **völlig isoliert leben** to live in complete isolation; **ein Problem isoliert betrachten** to look at a problem in isolation **(b)** *elektrische Leitungen, Häuser, Fenster* to insulate ◩ VR to isolate oneself

Isolier-: **Isolierfenster** NT double-glazed window; **Isolierkanne** F Thermos® flask, vacuum flask; **Isoliermaterial** NT insulating material; **Isolierstation** F isolation ward

Isoliertheit [izo'li:ethait] F -, -en isolatedness

Isolierung F -, -en = Isolation

Isomatte ['i:zo-] F foam mattress

isotonisch [izo'to:nɪʃ] ADJ isotonic

Israel ['ɪsrae:l, 'ɪsrael] NT -s Israel

Israeli¹ [ɪsra'e:li] M -(s), -(s) Israeli

Israeli² [ɪsra'e:li] F -, -(s), **Israelin** [ɪsra'e:lɪn] F -, -nen Israeli

israelisch [ɪsra'e:lɪʃ] ADJ Israeli

Israelit [ɪsrae'li:t] M -en, -en, **Israelitin** [-'li:tɪn] F -, -nen Israelite

israelitisch [ɪsrae'li:tɪʃ] ADJ Israelite

isst [ɪst] 3. PERS SING PRES *von* **essen**

ist [ɪst] 3. PERS SING PRES *von* **sein¹**

Ist-: **Istbestand** ['ɪst-] M (= *Geld*) cash in hand; (= *Waren*) actual stock; **Istkosten** PL actual costs *pl*

IT [ai'ti:] F - ABBR *von* **Informationstechnologie** IT

Italien [i'ta:liən] NT -s Italy

italienisch [ita'lie:nɪʃ] ADJ Italian; **die ~e Schweiz** Italian-speaking Switzerland

Italowestern ['i:talo-, i'ta:lo-] M spaghetti western

i-Tüpfelchen ['i:-] NT dot (on the/an i); **bis aufs ~** (*fig*) (right) down to the last (little) detail

i. V. [i:'fau] ABBR *von* **in Vertretung, im Vorjahr, in Vorbereitung**

IWF [i:ve:'lɛf] M - ABBR *von* **Internationaler Währungsfonds** IMF

Jj

J, j [jɔt, (*Aus*) je:] NT J, j

ja [ja:] ADV **(a)** (*zustimmend*) yes; (*bei Trauung*) I do; **ich glaube ja** (yes,) I think so; **Ja und Amen** *or* **ja und amen zu etw sagen** (*inf*) to agree (slavishly) with sth; **wenn ja** if so
(b) (*fragend*) really?; **ich habe gekündigt – ja?** I've quit – really?; **ja, bitte?** yes?
(c) (*feststellend*) **aber ja!** but of course; **ach ja!** oh yes; **nun ja** oh well; **kann ich reinkommen? – ja bitte** can I come in? – yes, do; **ja doch** *or* **freilich** *or* **gewiss** yes, of course; **ja so!** I see
(d) (*unbedingt*) **komm ja pünktlich!** be punctual; **sei ja vorsichtig!** be careful; **vergessen Sie es JA nicht!** don't forget, whatever you do!; **tu das JA nicht, ich warne dich!** just don't do that, I'm warning you
(e) (*einräumend, schließlich*) **es ist ja noch früh** it's still early (after all); **sie ist ja erst fünf** (after all) she's only five; **es ist ja nicht so schlimm** it's not really as bad as all that; **das ist ja richtig, aber ...** that's (certainly) right, but ...; **ich kann es ja mal versuchen, aber ...** I could always try it, but ...
(f) (*als Steigerung*) even; **das ist gut, ja sogar sehr gut** it's good, in fact it's very good
(g) (*feststellend*) **da kommt er ja** there he is; **das ist es ja** that's just it; **ja, was haben wir denn hier?** well, what have we here?; **das sag ich ja!** that's just what I say; **das wissen wir ja alle** we all know that (anyway); **Sie wissen ja, dass ...** as you know ...; **Sie wissen ja, wie das so ist** you know how it is(, don't you?)
(h) (*verstärkend, = wirklich*) just; **das ist ja fürchterlich** that's (just) terrible
(i) (*= aber*) **ja, sagen Sie mal** now look here; **ja, was du nicht sagst!** you don't say!
(j) (*vergewissernd*) right?; **du rufst mich doch an, ja?** you'll give me a call, won't you?

Ja [ja:] NT **-s, -(s)** yes; **mit Ja antworten/stimmen** to answer/vote yes; **ein Ja zum Kind/Frieden** a vote in favour (*Brit*) *or* favor (*US*) of children/peace; **das Ja vor dem Traualtar sprechen** to say "I do" at the altar

Jacht [jaxt] F **-, -en** yacht

Jäckchen ['jɛkçən] NT **-s, - (a)** DIM *von* **Jacke** little jacket
(b) (*= Babyjäckchen*) matinée jacket (*Brit*), knitted cardigan

Jacke ['jakə] F **-, -n** jacket, coat (*esp US*); (*= Wolljacke*) cardigan; **das ist ~ wie Hose** (*inf*) it's six of one and half a dozen of the other (*inf*); **wem die ~ passt ...** (*fig inf*) if the cap (*Brit*) *or* shoe (*US*) fits ...

Jacketkrone ['dʒɛkɪt-] F jacket crown

Jackett [ʒa'kɛt] NT **-s, -s** jacket, coat (*esp US*)

Jackpot ['dʒɛkpɔt] M **-s, -s** (*im Lotto etc*) rollover jackpot; **den ~ knacken** to hit the jackpot

Jade ['ja:də] M *or* F **-, NO PL** jade

Jagd [ja:kt] F **-, -en** [-dn] **(a)** hunt; (*= das Jagen*) hunting; (*fig: = Verfolgung*) chase (*nach* after); (*= Wettlauf*) race; **die ~ auf Rotwild/Fasanen** deerhunting/pheasant-hunting; **auf der ~ (nach etw) sein** to be hunting (for sth); **auf die ~ (nach etw) gehen** (*lit, fig*) to go hunting (for sth); **auf jdn/etw ~ machen** (*lit, fig*) to hunt for sb/sth; **die ~ nach Geld/Glück** the pursuit of money/fortune **(b)** (*= ~revier*) preserve, shoot

Jagd-: jagdbar ADJ **... sind ~ ...** may be hunted; **Jagdgebiet** NT hunting ground; **Jagdgewehr** NT hunting rifle; **Jagdgöttin** F goddess of hunting; **Jagdgründe** PL **in die ewigen ~ eingehen** to go to the happy hunting grounds; **Jagdhaus** NT hunting lodge; **Jagdhorn** NT hunting horn; **Jagdhund** M hunting dog; **Jagdhütte** F hunting lodge; **Jagdrevier** NT shoot; (*von Indianern etc*) preserve; **Jagdschein** M hunting licence (*Brit*) *or* license (*US*); **einen ~ haben** (*hum*) to be certified (*inf*); **Jagdschloss** NT hunting lodge; **Jagdverbot** NT ban on hunting; (*als Strafe*) ban from hunting; **Jagdwesen** NT, NO PL hunting; **Jagdwild** NT game; **Jagdzeit** F hunting *or* shooting season

jagen ['ja:ɡn] **1** VT **(a)** *Tier, Menschen* to hunt
(b) (*= hetzen*) to chase; (*= treiben*) *Wild* to drive; **jdn in die Flucht ~** to put sb to flight; **jdn aus dem Bett ~** to chase sb out of bed; **jdn aus dem Haus ~** to drive sb out of the house; **jdm eine Spritze in den Arm ~** (*inf*) to stick a needle in sb's arm; **ein Unglück jagte das andere** one misfortune

followed hard on (the heels of) the other; **mit diesem Essen kannst du mich ~** (*inf*) I wouldn't eat this if you paid me
(c) (*= erlegen*) to bag
2 VI **(a)** (*= auf die Jagd gehen*) to hunt
(b) AUX SEIN (*= rasen*) to race; **nach etw ~** to chase after sth; **in ~der Eile** in great haste

Jäger ['jɛ:ɡɐ] M **-s, - (a)** hunter, huntsman; **~ und Sammler** hunters and gatherers **(b)** (*Mil*) (*= Gebirgsjäger*) rifleman; (*= Jagdflieger*) fighter pilot **(c)** (*= Jagdflugzeug*) fighter (plane)

Jägerei [jɛɡə'rai] F **-, NO PL** hunting

Jägerin ['jɛ:ɡərɪn] F **-, -nen** huntress, huntswoman; *siehe auch* **Jäger (a, b)**

Jäger-: Jägerlatein NT (*inf*) hunters' yarns *pl*; **jdm ~ auftischen** to tell sb tall stories about one's hunting exploits; **Jägerschnitzel** NT *veal or pork cutlet with mushrooms and peppers*

Jaguar ['ja:ɡua:ɐ] M **-s, -e** jaguar

jäh [jɛ:], **jähe** ['jɛ:ə] (*geh*) **1** ADJ **(a)** (*= plötzlich*) sudden
(b) (*= steil*) sheer **2** ADV **(a)** (*= plötzlich*) suddenly; *enden, wechseln, sich bewegen* abruptly **(b)** (*= steil*) steeply

Jahr [ja:ɐ] NT **-(e)s, -e (a)** year; **ein halbes ~** six months *sing or pl*; **ein drei viertel ~** nine months *sing or pl*; **anderthalb ~e** one and a half years *sing*, eighteen months *sing or pl*; **zwei ~e Garantie** a two-year guarantee; **im ~(e) 1066** in (the year) 1066; **die sechziger ~e** the sixties *sing or pl*; **alle ~e** every year; **alle ~e wieder** year after year; **auf ~e hinaus** for years ahead; **auf ~ und Tag** to the very day; **pro ~** a year; **das Buch des ~es** the book of the year; **noch nach ~en** years later; **nach ~ und Tag** after (many) years; **vor ~ und Tag** (many) years ago; **seit ~ und Tag** for years; **mit den ~en** over the years; **zwischen den ~en** (*inf*) between Christmas and New Year; **(freiwilliges) soziales/ökologisches ~** year of voluntary work in the social services/environmental sector
(b) (*= Alter, Lebensjahr*) **er ist zehn ~e (alt)** he is ten years old; **mit dreißig ~en** at the age of thirty; **Personen über 18 ~e/ unter 18 ~en** people over/under (the age of) 18; **in die ~e kommen** (*inf*) to be getting on (in years); **man sieht ihm seine ~e nicht an** his age doesn't show; **in den besten ~en sein** *or* **stehen** to be in the prime of one's life; **mit den ~en** as one gets older

jahraus [ja:ɐ'laus] ADV **~, jahrein** year in, year out

Jahrbuch NT yearbook; (*= Ausgabe einer Sammlung etc*) annual; (*= Kalender*) almanac

Jährchen ['jɛ:ɐçən] NT **-s, -** (*hum inf*) year

jahrelang [ja:ɐ'ralaŋ] **1** ADJ ATTR years of **2** ADV for years; **und dann dauerte es noch ~, bevor ...** and then it took years until ...

jähren ['jɛ:rən] VR **heute jährt sich der Tag, dass ...** *or* **an dem ...** it's a year ago today that ...

Jahres- IN CPDS annual, yearly; **Jahresabschluss** M **(a)** (*Comm*) annual accounts *pl* **(b)** (*= Jahresende*) end of the year; **Jahresarbeitszeit** F working year; **meine ~ beträgt 1500 Stunden** I work 1500 hours per year; **Jahresbeginn** M beginning of the year; **Jahresbeitrag** M annual subscription; **Jahresbericht** M annual report; **Jahresbilanz** F (*Comm*) annual balance sheet; **Jahreseinkommen** M net annual income; **Jahresende** NT end of the year; **Jahresfeier** F anniversary; (*= Feierlichkeiten*) anniversary celebrations *pl*; **Jahresgehalt** NT annual salary; **Jahreshauptversammlung** F (*Comm*) annual general meeting, AGM; **Jahreskarte** F annual season ticket; **Jahresnetzkarte** F annual season ticket; **Jahresring** M (*eines Baumes*) annual ring; **Jahrestag** M anniversary; **Jahresüberschuss** M net income for the year; **Jahresurlaub** M annual holiday (*esp Brit*) *or* vacation (*US*), annual leave; **Jahreswagen** M one-year-old car; **Jahreswechsel** M, **Jahreswende** F new year; **Jahreswirtschaftsbericht** M annual economic report; **Jahreszahl** F date, year; **Jahreszeit** F season; **für die ~ zu kalt** cold for the time of year

Jahrgang M, *pl* **-gänge (a)** (*Sch, Univ*) year; **er ist ~ 1980** he was born in 1980; **die Jahrgänge 1980-83** the 1980-83 age group; **er ist mein ~, wir sind ein ~** we were born in the same year; (*als Schulabgänger etc*) we were in the same year **(b)** (*= alle Zeitschriften etc von einem Jahr*) year's issues *pl*; (*einer*

Fachzeitschrift) volume; **Nr. 20,** ~ **31** No. 20, 31st year; **Spiegel,** ~ **2002** Spiegel of the year 2002 **(c)** (*von Wein*) vintage

Jahrhundert [jaːɐ̯ˈhʊndɐt] NT century; **das ~ der Aufklärung** the Age of Enlightenment; ~**e haben die Menschen …** for centuries men have …

jahrhunderte- [jaːɐ̯ˈhʊndɐtə-]: **jahrhundertealt** ADJ centuries-old; **jahrhundertelang** 🔢 ADJ centuries of 🔢 ADV for centuries

Jahrhundert-: Jahrhundertfeier F centenary; (= *Feierlichkeiten*) centenary celebrations *pl*; **Jahrhundertwende** F turn of the century

-jährig [jɛːrɪç] ADJ SUF **(a)** (= … *Jahre alt*) -year-old; **ein Fünfjähriger** a five-year-old **(b)** (= *Jahre dauernd*) years of; **nach elfjährigen Verhandlungen** after eleven years of negotiations; **nach dreijähriger Verspätung** after a three-year delay **(c)** (*Ordinalzahl*) **das 70-jährige Jubiläum** the 70th anniversary; **das zehnjährige Bestehen von etw** the tenth anniversary of sth

jährlich [jɛːrlɪç] 🔢 ADJ annual, yearly 🔢 ADV every year; (*Comm*) per annum; **einmal/zweimal ~** once/twice a year

Jahr-: Jahrmarkt M (fun-)fair; **Jahrmillionen** [jaːɐ̯mɪˈlioːnən] PL millions of years; **Jahrtausend** [jaːɐ̯ˈtauznt] NT millennium; **in unserem ~** in our millennium; ~**e** thousands of years; **Jahrtausendfeier** [jaːɐ̯ˈtauznt-] F millennium; (= *Feierlichkeiten*) millennium celebrations *pl*; **Jahrtausendwende** F millennium; **Jahrzehnt** [jaːɐ̯ˈtseːnt] NT -(e)s, -e decade

Jähzorn M violent temper; (*plötzlicher Ausbruch*) violent outburst; **im ~** in a violent temper

jähzornig ADJ irascible; (= *erregt*) furious; **er ist manchmal so ~, dass …** he sometimes becomes so furious that …

Jakobsmuschel F scallop

Jalousie [ʒaluˈziː] F -, -n [-ziːən] venetian blind

Jamaika [jaˈmaika] NT -s Jamaica

jamaikanisch [jamaiˈkaːnɪʃ] ADJ Jamaican

Jambus [ˈjambʊs] M -, **Jamben** [-bn] (*Poet*) iamb(us)

Jammer [ˈjamɐ] M -s, NO PL **(a)** (= *Elend*) misery; **es ist ein ~, diesen Verfall mit ansehen zu müssen** it is heartbreaking to have to watch this decay; **es wäre ein ~, wenn …** (*inf*) it would be a crying shame if … (*inf*) **(b)** (= *Klage*) wailing

Jammer-: Jammergeschrei NT (*inf*) wailing; **Jammergestalt** F wretched figure; **Jammerlappen** M (*sl*) wet (*inf*)

jämmerlich [ˈjɛmɐlɪç] 🔢 ADJ pitiful; (*inf*) Erklärung, Bericht, Entschuldigung *etc* pathetic (*inf*); Feigling terrible 🔢 ADV sterben *etc* pitifully; versagen miserably; (*inf.* = *sehr*) terribly (*inf*); (*inf.* = *schlecht*) pathetically

jammern [ˈjamɐn] VI to wail (*über +acc* over); **nach jdm/etw ~** to whine for sb/sth; **der Gefangene jammerte um Wasser** the prisoner begged pitifully for water

jammerschade ADJ **es ist ~** (*inf*) it's a terrible pity

Janker [ˈjaŋkɐ] M -s, - (*S Ger, Aus*) Tyrolean jacket; (= *Strickjacke*) cardigan

Jänner [ˈjɛnɐ] M -s, - (*Aus, Sw*) January

Januar [ˈjanuaːɐ̯] M -(s), -e January; *siehe auch* **März**

Japan [ˈjaːpan] NT -s Japan

japanisch [jaˈpaːnɪʃ] ADJ Japanese

Japanologie [japanoloˈgiː] F -, NO PL Japanese studies

japsen VI (*inf*) to pant

Jargon [ʒarˈgõː] M -s, -s jargon

Jasager [ˈjaːzaːgɐ] M -s, - yes man

Jasagerin [ˈjaːzaːgərɪn] F -, -nen yes woman

Jasmin [jasˈmiːn] M -s, -e jasmine

Jastimme [ˈjaː-] F vote in favour (*Brit*) or favor (*US*) (of)

jäten [ˈjɛːtn] VTI to weed

Jauche [ˈjauxə] F -, NO PL liquid manure; (= *Abwasser*) sewage; **das stinkt wie ~** it stinks to high heaven

Jauchegrube F cesspool; (*Agr*) liquid manure pit

jauchzen [ˈjauxtsn] VI (*geh*) to rejoice (*liter*); (*Publikum*) to cheer; (*Kinder*) to shout and cheer

Jauchzer [ˈjauxtsɐ] M -s, - jubilant cheer *or* shout; **sie stieß einen lauten, begeisterten ~ aus** she gave a loud yippee (*inf*)

jaulen [ˈjaulən] VI (*lit, fig*) to howl

Jause [ˈjauzə] F -, -n (*Aus*) break (for a snack); (= *Proviant*) snack; **eine ~ halten** *or* **machen** to stop for a snack

jausen [ˈjauzn] VI (*Aus*) to stop for a snack; (*auf Arbeit*) to have a tea (*Brit*) *or* coffee (*esp US*) break

Java [ˈjaːva] NT -s Java

javanisch [jaˈvaːnɪʃ] ADJ Javanese

jawohl [jaˈvoːl] ADV, **jawoll** [jaˈvɔl] (*huminf*) ADV yes; (*Mil*) yes, sir; (*Naut*) aye, aye, sir; **stimmt das wirklich? ‒ ~** is that really right? ‒ yes, it is

Jawort [ˈjaː-] NT, *pl* **-worte** **jdm das ~ geben** to say yes to sb; (*bei Trauung*) to say "I do"; **sich** *or* **einander das ~ geben** to get married

Jazz [dʒɛs, jats] M -, NO PL jazz

Jazzer [ˈdʒɛsɐ, ˈjatsɐ] M -s, -, **Jazzerin** [-ərɪn] F -, -nen (*inf*) jazz musician

Jazzkeller [ˈdʒɛs-, ˈjats-] M jazz club

je¹ [jeː] 🔢 ADV **(a)** (= *jemals*) ever **(b)** (= *jeweils*) every, each; **für je drei Stück zahlst du einen Euro** you pay one euro for (every) three; **je zwei Schüler aus jeder Klasse** two children from each class; **ich gebe euch je zwei Äpfel** I'll give you two apples each 🔢 PREP +ACC (= *pro*) per; **je Person zwei Stück** two per person; **je zehn Exemplare ein Freiexemplar** one free copy for every ten copies 🔢 CONJ **(a) je eher, desto** *or* **umso besser** the sooner the better; **je länger, je lieber** the longer the better **(b) je nach** according to, depending on; **je nach Wunsch** just as one wishes; **je nachdem** it all depends; **je nachdem, wie gut man arbeitet …** depending on how well you work …

je² INTERJ **ach** *or* **o je!** oh dear!

Jeans [dʒiːnz] PL jeans *pl*

Jeans- [ˈdʒiːnz-] IN CPDS denim; **Jeansanzug** M denim suit; **Jeansstoff** M denim

jedenfalls [ˈjeːdnˈfals] ADV in any case; (= *zumindest*) at least; **er sagte nichts über den Mord, ~ nichts Neues** he said nothing about the murder, or at least nothing new

jede(r, s) [ˈjeːdə] INDEF PRON **(a)** (*adjektivisch*) (= *einzeln*) each; (*esp von zweien*) either; (= *jeder von allen*) every; (= *jeder beliebige*) any; **ohne ~ Anstrengung/Vorstellung** *etc* without any effort/idea *etc*, with no effort/idea *etc*; ~**s Mal** every time; ~**s Mal, wenn sie …** every time she …, whenever she …; ~**s Mal ist es so(, dass …)** it happens every time (that …); **fern von ~r Kultur** far from all civilization **(b)** (*substantivisch*) (= *einzeln*) each (one); (= *jeder von allen*) everyone; (= *jeder Beliebige*) anyone; ~ **von uns** each (one)/every one/any one of us; ~ **von uns beiden** each (one) of us; ~**r Zweite** every other *or* second one; ~**r für sich** everyone for himself; ~**r/‒/‒s für sich ist ganz nett, aber beide zusammen …** each one alone is quite nice, but together …; **das kann ~r** anyone can do that; **das kann nicht ~r** not everyone can do that; **er spricht nicht mit ~m** he doesn't speak to just anybody

jedermann [ˈjeːdɐman] INDEF PRON everyone, everybody; (= *jeder Beliebige auch*) anyone, anybody; **Jedermann** (*Theat*) Everyman; **das ist nicht ~s Sache** it's not everyone's cup of tea (*inf*)

jederzeit [ˈjeːdɐtsait] ADV at any time; **du kannst ~ kommen** you can come any time (you like)

jedesmal [ˈjeːdəsˈmaːl] ADV *siehe* **jede(r, s)**

jedoch [jeˈdɔx] CONJ, ADV however

Jeep® [dʒiːp] M -s, -s Jeep®

jegliche(r, s) [ˈjeːklɪçə] INDEF PRON (*adjektivisch*) any; (*substantivisch*) each (one)

jeher [jeːˈheːɐ̯, ˈjeːˈheːɐ̯] ADV **von** *or* **seit ~** always; **das ist schon seit ~ so** it has always been like that

Jehova [jeˈhoːva] M -s Jehovah; **die Zeugen ~s** Jehovah's Witnesses

jein [jain] ADV (*hum*) yes and no

Jelängerjelieber [jeˈlɛŋɐjeˈliːbɐ] NT -s, - honeysuckle

jemals [ˈjeːmaːls] ADV ever

jemand [ˈjeːmant] INDEF PRON somebody; (*bei Fragen, bedingenden Sätzen auch, Negation*) anybody; **ohne ~en zu fragen** without asking anybody; ~ **Fremdes** a stranger; ~ **Neues** somebody new; ~ **anders** somebody else

Jenaer Glas® [ˈjeːnaɐ̯] NT Pyrex®

jene(r, s) [ˈjeːnə] DEM PRON (*geh*) **(a)** (*adjektivisch*) that; (*pl*) those; (= *der Vorherige, die Vorherigen*) the former; **in ~r Zeit** at that time, in those times **(b)** (*substantivisch*) that one; (*pl*) those (ones); (= *der Vorherige, die Vorherigen*) the former; **von diesem und ~m sprechen** to talk about this and that

jenseitig ['jɛːnzaitɪç, 'jɛn-] ADJ ATTR opposite, other; **die ~en Vororte** the suburbs on the other side

jenseits ['jɛːnzaits, 'jɛn-] **1** PREP +GEN on the other side of; **2 km ~ der Grenze** 2 kms beyond the border **2** ADV **~ von** on the other side of; **~ von Gut und Böse** beyond good and evil

Jenseits ['jɛːnzaits, 'jɛn-] NT -, NO PL hereafter, next world; **jdn ins ~ befördern** (*inf*) to send sb to kingdom come (*inf*)

Jersey ['dʒœːrzi] NT -s (*Geog*) Jersey

Jesus ['jeːzʊs] M, *gen* **Jesu**, *dat* - *or* **Jesu** ['jeːzu], *acc* - *or* **Jesum** ['jeːzʊm] Jesus; **~ Christus** Jesus Christ

Jet [dʒɛt] M -(s), -s (*inf*) jet

Jetlag ['jʒɛtlɛg] M -s, -s jetlag; **unter ~ leiden** to suffer from jetlag

Jeton [ʒa'tõː] M -s, -s chip

Jetset ['dʒɛtsɛt] M -s, (*rare*) -s (*inf*) jet set

jetten ['dʒɛtn] VI AUX SEIN (*inf*) to jet (*inf*)

jetzig ['jɛtsɪç] ADJ ATTR present *attr*, current; **in der ~en Zeit** in present times; **im ~en Augenblick** at the present moment (in time)

jetzt [jɛtst] ADV now; **bis ~** so far; **ich bin ~ (schon) fünf Tage hier** I have been here five days now; **gleich ~, ~ gleich** right now; **schon ~** already; **~ schon?** already?; **~ noch?** (what) now?; **das ist noch ~ der Fall** it's still the case today; **~ oder nie!** (it's) now or never!; **habe ich ~ das Bügeleisen herausgezogen?** now did I unplug the iron?

Jetzt [jɛtst] NT -, NO PL (*geh*) present

jew. ABBR *von* **jeweils**

jeweilig ['jeːvailɪç] ADJ ATTR respective; (= *vorherrschend*) *Verhältnisse, Bedingungen* prevailing; **die ~e Regierung** the government of the day

jeweils ['jeːvails] ADV at a time, at any one time; (= *jedes Mal*) each time; (= *jeder Einzelne*) each; **~ am Monatsletzten** on the last day of each month; **die ~ betroffenen Landesregierungen müssen ...** each of the governments concerned must ...; **die ~ Größten aus einer Gruppe** the biggest from each group

Jg. ABBR *von* **Jahrgang**

JH ABBR *von* **Jugendherberge** YH

Jh. ABBR *von* **Jahrhundert**

jiddisch ['jɪdɪʃ] ADJ Yiddish

Job [dʒɔp] M -s, -s (*inf*) job

jobben ['dʒɔbn] VI (*inf*) to work

Jobkiller M (*inf*) job killer

Jobsharing [-ʃɛːrɪŋ] NT -s, NO PL job sharing

Joch [jɔx] NT -(e)s, -e (*lit, fig*) yoke; (= *Bergjoch*) ridge

Jochbein NT cheekbone

Jockei ['dʒɔke, 'dʒɔkai] M -s, -s, **Jockey** ['dʒɔki] M -s, -s jockey

Jod [joːt] NT -(e)s [-dəs], NO PL (*abbr* J) iodine

jodeln ['joːdln] VTI to yodel

jodhaltig ADJ containing iodine

jodiert [jo'diːɐt] ADJ **~es Speisesalz** iodized table salt

Joga ['joːga] M *or* NT -(s), NO PL yoga

Jogasitz M, NO PL lotus position

joggen ['dʒɔgn] VI AUX HABEN *or* (*bei Richtungsangabe*) SEIN to jog

Jogger ['dʒɔgɐ] M -s, -, **Joggerin** [-ərɪn] F -, -nen jogger

Jogging ['dʒɔgɪŋ] NT -, NO PL jogging

Jogging- IN CPDS jogging; **Jogginganzug** M jogging suit

Joghurt ['joːgʊrt] M *or* NT -(s), -(s) yog(h)urt

Joghurtbereiter [-bəraitɐ] M -s, -s yog(h)urt maker

Jogurt ['joːgʊrt] M *or* NT -(s), -(s) *siehe* **Joghurt**

Johannis-: Johannisbeere F **Rote ~** redcurrant; **Schwarze ~** blackcurrant; **Johannisbeerstrauch** M (*roter*) redcurrant bush; (*schwarzer*) blackcurrant bush; **Johanniskraut** NT, NO PL St. John's wort

Johanniter [joha'niːtɐ] M -s, - Knight of St. John of Jerusalem; **~ Unfallhilfe** St. John's Ambulance (Brigade)

johlen ['joːlən] VI to howl

Joint [dʒɔynt] M -s, -s (*inf*) joint (*inf*)

Jointventure [dʒɔynt 'vɛntʃə] NT -s, -s, **Joint Venture** NT - -s, - -s (*Comm*) joint venture

Jojo [jo'jo, 'joːjoː] NT -s, -s yo-yo

Jojo-Effekt M yo-yo effect

Joker ['joːke, 'dʒoːke] M -s, - (*Cards*) joker; (*fig*) trump card

Jongleur [ʒõˈgløːɐ, ʒõˈløːɐ] M -s, -e, **Jongleurin** [-ˈgløːrɪn, -ˈløːrɪn] F -, -nen juggler

jonglieren [ʒõˈgliːrən, ʒõˈliːrən], *ptp* **jongliert** VI (*lit, fig*) to juggle

Jordanien [jɔrˈdaːniən] NT -s Jordan

jordanisch [jɔrˈdaːnɪʃ] ADJ Jordanian

Jot [jɔt] NT -, - (the letter) J/j

Joule [dʒuːl] NT -(s), - (*abbr* J) joule

Journal [ʒʊrˈnaːl] NT -s, -e (*Comm*) daybook

Journaldienst M (*Aus*) = **Bereitschaftsdienst**

Journalismus [ʒʊrnaˈlɪsmʊs] M -, NO PL journalism

Journalist [ʒʊrnaˈlɪst] M -en, -en, **Journalistin** [-ˈlɪstɪn] F -, -nen journalist

Journalistik [ʒʊrnaˈlɪstɪk] F -, NO PL journalism

journalistisch [ʒʊrnaˈlɪstɪʃ] **1** ADJ journalistic **2** ADV **~ arbeiten** to work as a journalist; **jdn ~ ausbilden** to train sb to be a journalist; **etw ~ aufbereiten** to edit sth for journalistic purposes; **~ geschrieben** written in a journalistic style

jovial [joˈviaːl] **1** ADJ jovial **2** ADV jovially

Jovialität [joviali'tɛːt] F -, NO PL joviality

Joystick ['dʒɔystɪk] M -s, -s (*Comput*) joystick

jr. ABBR *von* **junior** jnr, jr

Jubel ['juːbl] M -s, NO PL (*von Volk, Menge etc*) jubilation; (= *~rufe auch*) cheering; **~, Trubel, Heiterkeit** laughter and merriment

jubeln ['juːbln] VI to cheer; **jubelt nicht zu früh** don't start celebrating too early

Jubilar [jubiˈlaːɐ] M -s, -e, **Jubilarin** [-ˈlaːrɪn] F -, -nen person celebrating an anniversary

Jubiläum [jubiˈlɛːʊm] NT -s, **Jubiläen** [-ˈlɛːən] jubilee; (= *Jahrestag*) anniversary

Jubiläums- IN CPDS jubilee; **Jubiläumsjahr** NT jubilee year

juchzen ['jʊxtsn] VI to shriek with delight

jucken ['jʊkn] **1** VTI to itch; **es juckt mich am Rücken, der Rücken juckt mir** *or* **mich** my back itches; **der Stoff juckt mich** this material makes me itch; **es juckt mich, das zu tun** (*inf*) I'm itching to do it (*inf*); **ihn juckt das Geld dabei** (*inf*) he finds the money attractive; **das juckt mich doch nicht** (*inf*) I don't care; **lass ~** (*sl*) let your hair down (*inf*) **2** VR (= *kratzen*) to scratch

Juck-: Juckpulver NT itching powder; **Juckreiz** M itching; **einen ~ in der Nase haben** to have an itch in one's nose

Jude ['juːdə] M -n, -n Jew; **er ist ~** he is a Jew; *siehe auch* **Jüdin**

Juden-: judenfeindlich **1** ADJ anti-Semitic **2** ADV **sich ~ verhalten** to be anti-Semitic; **sich ~ äußern** to make anti-Semitic remarks; **Judenheit** F -, NO PL Jewry; **Judenstern** M star of David; **Judentum** ['juːdntuːm] NT -s, NO PL **(a)** (= *Judaismus*) Judaism **(b)** (= *Gesamtheit der Juden*) Jews *pl* **(c)** (= *jüdisches Wesen*) Jewishness; **Judenverfolgung** F persecution of (the) Jews

Jüdin ['jyːdɪn] F -, -nen Jew, Jewish woman

jüdisch ['jyːdɪʃ] **1** ADJ Jewish **2** ADV **~ heiraten** to have a Jewish wedding; **~ beeinflusst** influenced by Judaism; **seine Kinder ~ erziehen** to raise one's children as Jews

Judo[1] ['juːdo] M -s, -s *or* f -, -s (*Pol inf*) Young Democrat

Judo[2] NT -s, NO PL judo

Jugend ['juːgnt] F -, NO PL youth; (*Sport*) youth team; **frühe ~** adolescence; **früheste ~** early adolescence; **von ~ an** *or* **auf** from one's youth; **die heutige ~, die ~ von heute** young people *or* the youth of today; **die weibliche/männliche ~** young women/men; **Haus der ~** youth centre (*Brit*) *or* center (*US*)

Jugend-: Jugendalter NT adolescence; **Jugendamt** NT youth welfare department; **Jugendarbeit** F, NO PL **(a)** (= *Arbeit Jugendlicher*) youth employment **(b)** (= *Jugendfürsorge*) youth work; **Jugendarbeitslosigkeit** F youth unemployment; **Jugendarrest** M (*Jur*) detention; **Jugendbuch** NT book for young people; **jugendfrei** ADJ suitable for young people; *Film* U(-certificate) (*Brit*), G (*US*); **Jugendfreund(in)** M(F) friend of one's youth; **Jugendfürsorge**

F youth welfare; (*für Schulkinder*) child guidance;
jugendgefährdend ADJ liable to corrupt the young;
Jugendgericht NT juvenile court

Jugendherberge F youth hostel

Jugendherbergs-: Jugendherbergsausweis M youth
hostelling card (*Brit*), youth hostel ID (*US*), YHA card (*Brit*);
Jugendherbergsmutter F, **Jugendherbergsvater** M youth
hostel warden

Jugend-: Jugendhilfe F (*Admin*) help for young people;
Jugendirresein NT (*Med*) juvenile schizophrenia;
Jugendjahre PL days *pl* of one's youth; **Jugendkriminalität** F
juvenile delinquency

jugendlich ['juːɡntlɪç] 🟫 ADJ (= *jung*) young; (= *von Jugend, jung
wirkend*) youthful; **~e Banden** gangs of youths; **ein ~er Täter**
a young offender; **~er Leichtsinn** youthful frivolity; **das sagst
du so in deinem ~en Leichtsinn** (*hum*) I admire your
confidence 🟫 ADV youthfully; **sich ~ geben** to appear
youthful; **~ wirken** to seem youthful; **er kleidet sich immer
sehr ~** he always wears very youthful clothes

Jugendliche(r) ['juːɡntlɪçə] MF DECL AS ADJ adolescent;
(*männlich auch*) youth

Jugendlichkeit F -, NO PL youthfulness

Jugend-: Jugendliebe F (a) young love (b) (= *Geliebter*) love
of one's youth; **Jugendmannschaft** F youth team;
Jugendpflege F youth welfare; **Jugendpfleger(in)** M(F) youth
(welfare) worker; **Jugendpsychologie** F adolescent
psychology; **Jugendrecht** NT law relating to young persons;
Jugendrichter(in) M(F) (*Jur*) magistrate (*in a juvenile court*);
Jugendschutz M protection of children and young people;
Jugendstil M, NO PL (*Art*) Art Nouveau; **Jugendstrafanstalt** F
(*form*) young offenders' institution (*Brit*), juvenile correction
institution *or* facility (*US*); **Jugendstrafe** F detention *no art* in
a young offenders' (*Brit*) *or* juvenile correction (*US*)
institution; **Jugendstreich** M youthful exploit; **Jugendsünde**
F youthful misdeed; **Jugendtraum** M youthful dream;
Jugendverband M youth organization; **Jugendweihe** F (*Rel*)
initiation; (*in Eastern Germany*) ceremony in which 14-year-olds
are given adult social status; **Jugendzeit** F youth, younger
days *pl*; **Jugendzentrum** NT youth centre (*Brit*) or center (*US*)

Jugoslawe [jugo'slaːvə] M -n, -n, **Jugoslawin** [-'slaːvɪn] F -, -nen
Yugoslav

Jugoslawien [jugo'slaːviən] NT -s Yugoslavia

jugoslawisch [jugo'slaːvɪʃ] ADJ Yugoslav(ian)

Julei [juːˈlai, 'juːlai] M -(s), -s (*esp Comm*) July

Juli[1] ['juːli] M -(s), -s July; *siehe auch* **März**

Juli[2] M -s, -s *or* f -, -s (*Pol inf*) Young Liberal

Jumbo ['jumbo] M -s, -s, **Jumbojet** ['jumbodʒɛt] M jumbo (jet)

jun. ABBR *von* junior jun

jung [jʊŋ] 🟫 ADJ, *comp* **⁺er** ['jʏŋə], *superl* **⁺ste(r, s)** ['jʏŋstə] (*lit, fig*)
young; *Aktien* new; **Jung und Alt** (both) young and old; **von
~ auf** from one's youth; **wie ein ~er Gott** divinely; **er sieht
aus wie ein ~er Gott** he looks divine (*inf*); *siehe auch* **jünger,
jüngste(r, s)**
🟫 ADV, *comp* **⁺er**, *superl* **am ⁺sten ~ aussehen** to look young; **~
heiraten/sterben** to marry/die young; **jünger heiraten** to
marry earlier; **sie starb jünger als ihr Mann** she died before her
husband; **~ gefreit, nie gereut** (*Prov*) if you marry young you
won't regret it; **so ~ kommen wir nicht mehr zusammen** (*hum*)
you're only young once

Jung- IN CPDS young; **Jungakademiker(in)** M(F) graduate;
Jungbürger(in) M(F) junior citizen

Jungchen ['jʊŋçən] NT -s, - (*inf*) lad (*inf*)

Jungdemokrat(in) M(F) Young Democrat

Junge ['jʊŋə] M -n, -n *or* (*dated inf*) -ns *or* (*inf*) Jungs [jʊŋs] boy;
(= *Laufjunge*) errand boy; (*Cards*) jack; **Junge, Junge!** (*inf*) boy
oh boy (*inf*); **sie ist ein richtiger ~** she's a real tomboy; **alter ~**
(*inf*) my old pal (*inf*); **mein lieber ~!** my dear boy; (*in Brief*) my
dear son; **ein schwerer ~** (*inf*) a (big-time) crook (*inf*)

jungen ['jʊŋən] VI to have young

Jungen-: jungenhaft ADJ boyish; **sie ist ein ~es Mädchen** she's
a bit of a tomboy; **Jungenschule** F boys' school;
Jungenstreich M boyish prank

Junge(r) MF DECL AS ADJ (*inf*) der/die ~ Mr/Miss X junior, the
young Mr/Miss X; **die ~n** the young ones

jünger ['jʏŋə] 🟫 ADJ (a) COMP *von* jung younger; **Holbein der
Jüngere** Holbein the Younger (b) *Geschichte, Entwicklung etc*

recent; **die ~e Steinzeit** the New Stone Age 🟫 ADV **sie sieht ~
aus, als sie ist** she looks younger than she is, she doesn't
look her age; *siehe auch* **jung**

Jünger ['jʏŋə] M -s, - (*Bibl, fig*) disciple

Jüngerin ['jʏŋərɪn] F -, -nen (*fig*) disciple

Junge(s) NT DECL AS ADJ (*Zool*) young one; (*von Hund*)
pup(py); (*von Katze*) kitten; (*von Wolf, Löwe, Bär*) cub; (*von
Vogel*) young bird; **die ~n** the young

Jungfer ['jʊŋfə] F -, -n **eine alte ~** an old maid

Jungfern-: Jungfernfahrt F maiden voyage; **Jungfernflug** M
maiden flight; **Jungfernhäutchen** NT (*Anat*) hymen (*Anat*);
Jungferninseln PL Virgin Islands *pl*; **Jungfernschaft**
['jʊŋfənʃaft] F -, NO PL virginity

Jungfilmer(in) M(F) young film maker; **die deutschen ~** the
young German film makers

Jungfrau F virgin; (*Astron, Astrol*) Virgo *no art*; **ich bin ~** I am a
virgin; (*Astrol*) I am (a) Virgo; **die ~ von Orléans** Joan of Arc,
the Maid of Orleans; **dazu bin ich gekommen wie die ~ zum
Kind(e)** it just fell into my hands

jungfräulich ['jʊŋfrɔylɪç] ADJ virgin

Jungfräulichkeit F -, NO PL (*von Mädchen, Schnee*) virginity

Junggeselle M bachelor

Junggesellen-: Junggesellenbude F (*inf*) bachelor pad (*inf*);
Junggesellendasein NT, **Junggesellenleben** NT bachelor's
life; **Junggesellentum** ['jʊŋɡəzɛləntuːm] NT -s, NO PL
bachelorhood; **Junggesellenwohnung** F bachelor apartment;
Junggesellenzeit F bachelor days *pl*

Junggesellin F single woman

Junglehrer(in) M(F) student teacher

Jüngling ['jʏŋlɪŋ] M -s, -e (*literhum*) youth

Jungsozialist(in) M(F) Young Socialist

jüngste(r, s) ['jʏŋstə] ADJ (a) SUPERL *von* jung youngest
(b) *Werk, Schöpfung, Ereignis* latest, (most) recent; *Zeit,
Vergangenheit* recent; **in der ~n Zeit** recently; **ein Ausdruck
aus der ~n Zeit** a recent expression; **das Jüngste Gericht** the
Last Judgement; **der Jüngste Tag** Doomsday, the Day of
Judgement; **man merkt, dass er/sie nicht mehr der/die Jüngste
ist** you can tell that he/she is not as young as he/she used to
be; **sie ist auch nicht mehr die Jüngste** she's no (spring)
chicken (*inf*)

Jung-: Jungtier NT young animal; **Jungverheiratete(r)**
[-fɛɐhairatətə] MF DECL AS ADJ newly-wed; **Jungvieh** NT young
cattle *pl*; **Jungwähler(in)** M(F) young voter

Juni ['juːni] M -(s), -s June; *siehe auch* **März**

junior ['juːnioːɐ] ADJ *Franz Schulz ~* Franz Schulz, Junior

Junior ['juːnioːɐ] M -s, Junioren [juː'nioːrən] (a) (*usu hum*: = *Sohn*)
junior; **wie gehts dem ~?** how's junior? (b) (*auch Juniorchef*)
son of the boss; **kann ich mal den ~(chef) sprechen?** can I
speak to Mr X junior? (c) USU PL (*Sport*) junior

Juniorin [juː'nioːrɪn] F -, -nen (*Sport*) junior

Juniorpass M (*Rail*) ≈ young person's railcard (*Brit*), ≈ youth
railroad pass (*US*)

Junkfood ['dʒaŋkfuːd] NT -s, -s, **Junk Food** NT -s, -s (*inf*) junk
food

Junkie ['dʒaŋki] M -s, -s (*inf*) junkie (*inf*)

Junkmail ['dʒaŋkmeːl] F junk mail

Juno ['juːno] M -(s), -s (*esp Comm*) June

Junta ['xʊnta, 'jʊnta] F -, Junten [-tn] (*Pol*) junta

Jupe [ʒyːp] M -s, -s (*Sw*) skirt

jur. ABBR *von* juristisch

Jura[1] ['juːra] M -s, NO PL (*Geol, Geog*) Jura (Mountains) *pl*; **der
Kanton ~** the Canton of Jura

Jura[2] NO ART (*Univ*) law

jurassisch [juːˈrasɪʃ] ADJ (*Geol*) Jurassic; (= *aus Kanton Jura*) of the
Canton of Jura

Jurist [juːˈrɪst] M -en, -en, **Juristin** [-ˈrɪstɪn] F -, -nen jurist;
(= *Student*) law student

Juristendeutsch NT, **Juristensprache** F, NO PL legalese (*pej*),
legal jargon

juristisch [juːˈrɪstɪʃ] 🟫 ADJ legal; *Studium auch* law *attr*; **die ~e
Fakultät** the Faculty of Law; **eine ~e Person** a legal entity
🟫 ADV legally; **~ denken** to think in legal terms; **etw ~
betrachten** to consider the legal aspects of sth; **etw ~
bewerten** to assess sth from a legal point of view

Juror ['ju:ro:ɐ] M **-s, Juroren** [-'ro:rən], **Jurorin** [-'ro:rɪn] F **-, -nen** member of the jury

Jury [ʒyˈri:, 'ʒy:ri] F **-, -s** jury *sing or pl*

Jus [ʒy:] F or M or NT **-**, NO PL **(a)** (= *Bratensaft*) gravy; (*geliert*) dripping **(b)** (*Sw:* = *Fruchtsaft*) juice

Juso ['ju:zo] M **-s, -s** *or f* **-, -s** ABBR *von* **Jungsozialist** Young Socialist

justieren [jʊsˈti:rən], *ptp* **justiert** VT to adjust; (*Typ, Comput*) to justify

Justierschraube F (*Tech*) adjusting screw

Justierung F **-, -en** adjustment; (*Typ, Comput*) justification

just in time [dʒʌstinˈtaim] ADV (*Ind*) just in time

Just-in-time- [dʒʌstinˈtaim-] IN CPDS (*Ind*) just-in-time

Justitia [jʊsˈti:tsia] F **-s** Justice; (*fig*) the law

Justiz [jʊsˈti:ts] F **-**, NO PL (*als Prinzip*) justice; (*als Institution*) judiciary; (= *die Gerichte*) courts *pl*

Justiz-: Justizbeamte(r) M DECL AS ADJ, **Justizbeamtin** F judicial officer; **Justizbehörde** F legal authority; **Justizirrtum** M miscarriage of justice, judicial error (*esp US*);
Justizminister(in) M(F) minister of justice, justice minister; **Justizministerium** NT ministry of justice, ≈ Department of Justice (*US*); **Justizvollzugsanstalt** F (*form*) place of detention

Jütland ['jy:tlant] NT **-s** (*Geog*) Jutland

Juwel[1] [juˈve:l] M or NT **-s, -en** jewel; **~en** (= *Schmuck*) jewellery (*Brit*), jewelry (*US*)

Juwel[2] NT **-s, -e** (*fig*) jewel, gem

Juwelier [juveˈli:ɐ] M **-s, -e, Juwelierin** [-'li:rɪn] F **-, -nen** jeweller (*Brit*), jeweler (*US*); (= *Geschäft*) jewel(l)er's (shop)

Jux [jʊks] M **-es, -e** (*inf*) etw aus **~ tun/sagen** to do/say sth as a joke; **etw aus lauter ~ und Tollerei tun** to do sth out of sheer high spirits; **sich** (*dat*) **einen ~ aus etw machen** to make a joke (out) of sth

juxen ['jʊksn] VI (*inf*) to joke

jwd [jɔtveˈde:] ADV (*hum*) in the back of beyond (*Brit*), in the middle of nowhere; (= *weit entfernt*) miles out (*inf*)

Kk

K, k [kaː] NT -, - K, k

Kabarett [kabaˈrɛt, ˈkabarɛt, -re] NT -s, -e or -s cabaret; (= *Darbietung*) cabaret (show); **ein politisches ~** a satirical political revue

Kabarettist [kabarɛˈtɪst] M -en, -en, **Kabarettistin** [-ˈtɪstɪn] F -, -nen cabaret artist

kabarettistisch [kabarɛˈtɪstɪʃ] ADJ cabaret attr; (politisch-satirisch) political revue attr

kabbeln [ˈkabln] VIR (inf) to bicker

Kabel [ˈkaːbl] NT -s, - (Elec) wire; (= *Telefonkabel*) cord; (= *Strom- oder Telegrafenleitung, Drahtseil*) cable

Kabel-: Kabelanschluss M (TV) cable connection; **~bekommen** to get cable (TV); **Kabelbaum** M (Elec) harness; **Kabelfernsehen** NT cable television

Kabeljau [ˈkaːbljau] M -s, -e or -s cod

Kabine [kaˈbiːnə] F -, -n (= *Umkleidekabine, Anprobierkabine, Duschkabine*) cubicle; (Naut, Aviat, von Kran) cabin; (= *Vorführkabine*) projection room; (= *Seilbahnkabine*) car

Kabinenpersonal NT (Aviat) cabin crew

Kabinett[1] [kabiˈnɛt] NT -s, -e **(a)** (Pol) cabinet **(b)** (für Kunstsammlungen) (= *Raum*) gallery; (= *Schrank*) cabinet

Kabinett[2] M -s, -e (Wein) high-quality German white wine

Kabinetts-: Kabinettsbeschluss M cabinet decision; **Kabinettsumbildung** F cabinet reshuffle

Kabis [ˈkaːbɪs] M -, NO PL (Sw) = **Kohl**

Kabrio [ˈkaːbrio] NT -(s), -s (inf) convertible

Kabriolett [kabrioˈlɛt, (Aus, S Ger) kabrioˈleː] NT -s, -s **(a)** (Aut) convertible **(b)** (Hist) cabriolet

Kachel [ˈkaxl] F -, -n (glazed) tile; **etw mit ~n auslegen** to tile sth

kacheln [ˈkaxln] VT to tile

Kachelofen M tiled stove

kackbraun ADJ (sl) dirty brown

Kacke [ˈkakə] F -, NO PL (sl) **(a)** (vulg) crap (sl), shit (sl); **dann ist aber die ~ am Dampfen** (sl) then the shit really will hit the fan (sl) **(b)** (sl: = *Mist*) crap (inf); **so 'ne ~** shit (sl)

kacken [ˈkakn] VI (vulg) to crap (sl)

kackig [ˈkakɪç] ADJ (sl) Farbe shitty (inf)

Kadaver [kaˈdaːve] M -s, - carcass

Kader [ˈkaːdɐ] M -s, - (Mil, Pol) cadre; (Sport) squad; (= *Fachleute*) group of specialists; (= *Fachmann*) specialist; (Sw: = *Vorgesetzte*) management

Kaderschmiede F, NO PL (pej) élite school

Kadmium [ˈkatmiʊm] NT -s, NO PL CD cadmium

Käfer [ˈkɛːfɐ] M -s, - beetle (auch inf: VW)

Kaff [kaf] NT -s, -s or -e (inf) dump (inf)

Kaffee [ˈkafe, kaˈfeː] M -s, -s **(a)** coffee; **zwei ~, bitte!** two coffees, please; **~ kochen** to make coffee; **das ist kalter ~** (inf) that's old hat (inf) **(b)** NO PL (= *Nachmittagskaffee*) ≈ (afternoon) tea (Brit); **~ und Kuchen** coffee and cakes, ≈ afternoon tea (Brit)

Kaffee-: Kaffeebohne F coffee bean; **Kaffeefahrt** F day trip; (= *Verkaufsfahrt*) promotional trip (during which passengers are served coffee and offered goods to buy); **Kaffeefilter** M coffee filter; (inf. = *Filterpapier*) filter (paper); **Kaffeegeschirr** NT coffee set; **Kaffeehaus** NT café; **Kaffeekanne** F coffeepot; **Kaffeeklatsch** M, NO PL (inf), **Kaffeekränzchen** NT coffee klatsch (US), ≈ coffee morning (Brit); **ich treffe mich mit meinen Freundinnen zu einem ~** I'm meeting some friends for a chat over a (cup of) coffee or tea; **Kaffeelöffel** M coffee spoon; **Kaffeemaschine** F coffee machine; **Kaffeemühle** F coffee grinder; **Kaffeepause** F coffee break; **Kaffeesatz** M coffee grounds pl; **aus dem ~ wahrsagen or lesen** to read (the) tea leaves; **Kaffeeservice** [-zɛrviːs] NT coffee set; **Kaffeestrauch** M coffee tree; **Kaffeetasse** F coffee cup; **Kaffeewärmer** [-vɛrmɐ] M -s, - cosy (Brit) or cozy (US) (for coffeepot)

Käfig [ˈkɛːfɪç] M -s, -e [-gə] cage; **sie sitzt in einem goldenen ~** (fig) she is just a bird in a gilded cage

kahl [kaːl] ADJ Mensch, Kopf bald; (= ~ *geschoren*) shaved; Vogel bald; Wand, Raum, Pflanze, Baum bare; Landschaft, Berge barren; **eine ~e Stelle** a bald patch; **~ werden** (Mensch) to go bald; (Baum) to lose its leaves

Kahl-: Kahlfraß M defoliation; **kahl fressen** VT IRREG to strip bare; Ernte to destroy completely; **Kahlheit** F -, NO PL (von Mensch, Kopf, Vogel) baldness; (von Wand, Raum, Pflanze, Baum) bareness; (von Landschaft, Berg) barrenness; **Kahlkopf** M bald head; (= *Mensch*) bald person; **ein ~ sein** to be bald; **kahlköpfig** ADJ baldheaded; **kahl scheren** VT IRREG Schafe to shear; Hecken to cut right back; **jdn ~** to shave sb's head; **Kahlschlag** M **(a)** (= *abgeholzte Fläche*) clearing **(b)** (= *Tätigkeit*) deforestation **(c)** (inf) **(Aktion) ~** (= *Entlassungen*) axing; (= *Abriss*) demolition

Kahn [kaːn] M -(e)s, ⁻e [ˈkɛːnə] **(a)** (small) boat; (= *Stechkahn*) punt; **~ fahren** to go boating/punting **(b)** (= *Lastschiff*) barge; **ein alter ~** (inf) an old tub (inf)

Kai [kai] M -s, -e or -s quay

Kaigebühren PL, **Kaigeld** NT dock dues pl

Kaiman [ˈkaiman] M -s, -e (Zool) cayman

Kairo [ˈkairo] NT -s Cairo

Kaiser [ˈkaizɐ] M -s, - emperor; **der deutsche ~** the Kaiser; **des ~s neue Kleider** (fig) the emperor's new clothes; **wo nichts ist, hat der ~ sein Recht verloren** (Prov) you can't get blood from a stone; **das ist ein Streit um des ~s Bart** that's just splitting hairs; siehe auch **Kaiserin**

Kaiser-: Kaiseradler M imperial eagle; **Kaiserhaus** NT imperial family

Kaiserin [ˈkaizərɪn] F -, -nen empress; siehe auch **Kaiser**

kaiserlich [ˈkaizɐlɪç] ADJ imperial; **Seine Kaiserliche Majestät/Hoheit** His Imperial Majesty/Highness

kaiserlich-königlich [ˈkaizɐlɪçˈkøːnɪklɪç] ADJ imperial and royal (pertaining to the Dual Monarchy of Austro-Hungary)

Kaiser-: Kaiserpfalz F imperial palace; **Kaiserreich** NT empire; **Kaiserschmarren, Kaiserschmarrn** [-ʃmarn] M -s, - (Aus) sugared, cut-up pancake with raisins; **Kaiserschnitt** M Caesarean (section)

Kaisertum [ˈkaizɐtuːm] NT -s, **Kaisertümer** [-tyːmɐ] **(a)** (= *Regierungsform, Reich*) Empire **(b)** (= *Amt*) emperorship

Kajak [ˈkajak] M or NT -s, -s kayak

Kajal [kaˈjaːl] M -, NO PL kohl

Kajalstift M kohl eye pencil

Kajüte [kaˈjyːtə] F -, -n cabin; (größer auch) stateroom

Kakadu [ˈkakadu] M -s, -s cockatoo

Kakao [kaˈkaːo, kaˈkau] M -s, -s cocoa; **jdn durch den ~ ziehen** (inf) (= *veralbern*) to make fun of sb; (= *boshaft reden*) to run sb down (Brit), to put sb down

Kakao-: Kakaobohne F cocoa bean; **Kakaopulver** NT cocoa powder; **Kakaostrauch** M cacao palm

Kakerlak [ˈkakɐlak] M -s or -en, -en cockroach

Kaki [ˈkaːki] F -, -s kaki

Kaktee [kakˈteː] F -, -n [-ˈteːən], **Kaktus** [ˈkaktʊs] M -, **Kakteen** [-ˈteːən] or (inf) -se cactus

Kalabrien [kaˈlaːbriən] NT -s Calabria

Kalauer [ˈkaːlauɐ] M -s, - corny joke; (= *Wortspiel*) corny pun; (= *alter Witz*) old chestnut

kalauern [ˈkaːlauɐn] VI (inf) to joke; (= *Wortspiele machen*) to pun

Kalb [kalp] NT -(e)s, ⁻er [ˈkɛlbɐ] calf; (von Rehwild auch) fawn

kalben [ˈkalbn] VI (Kuh, Gletscher) to calve

Kalb-: Kalbfell NT = **Kalbsfell**; **Kalbfleisch** NT veal

Kalbs-: Kalbsbraten M roast veal; **Kalbsfell** NT (= *Fell*) calfskin; **Kalbshachse** [-haksə] F -, -n, **Kalbshaxe** F (Cook) knuckle of veal; **Kalbskeule** F leg of veal; **Kalbsleber** F calves' liver; **Kalbsleder** NT calfskin; **Kalbsschnitzel** NT veal cutlet

Kaldaune [kalˈdaunə] F -, -n entrails pl

Kalebasse [kaleˈbasə] F -, -n calabash

Kaleidoskop [kalaido'skoːp] NT -s, -e kaleidoscope

Kalender [kaˈlɛndɐ] M -s, - calendar; (= *Taschenkalender, Terminkalender*) diary; **etw im ~ rot anstreichen** to make sth a red-letter day

Kalender-: Kalenderjahr NT calendar year; **Kalendermonat** M calendar month; **Kalenderspruch** M calendar motto

Kali ['ka:li] NT **-s, -s** potash

Kaliber [ka'li:bɐ] NT **-s, -** (*lit, fig*) calibre (*Brit*), caliber (*US*); (*zum Messen*) calibrator

Kalif [ka'li:f] M **-en, -en** caliph

Kalifornien [kali'fɔrniən] NT **-s** California

kalifornisch [kali'fɔrnɪʃ] ADJ Californian

kalihaltig ADJ containing potassium

Kalium ['ka:liom] NT **-s**, NO PL (*abbr* **K**) potassium

Kalk [kalk] M **-(e)s, -e** lime; (*zum Tünchen*) whitewash; (*Anat*) calcium; **gebrannter ~** quicklime; **gelöschter ~** slaked lime; **bei ihm rieselt schon der ~** (*inf*) he's losing his marbles (*inf*)

Kalk-: kalkartig ADJ chalky; **Kalkboden** M chalky soil

kalken ['kalkn] VT **(a)** (= *tünchen*) to whitewash **(b)** (*Agr*) to lime

Kalk-: Kalkerde F chalky soil; **Kalkgrube** F lime pit; **kalkhaltig** ADJ *Boden* chalky; *Wasser* hard; **Kalkmangel** M (*Med*) calcium deficiency; (*von Boden*) lime deficiency; **Kalkstein** M limestone

Kalkül [kal'ky:l] M or NT **-s, -e (a)** (*geh*) calculation *usu pl* **(b)** (*Math*) calculus

Kalkulation [kalkula'tsio:n] F **-, -en** calculation; (= *Kostenberechnung*) costing

kalkulatorisch [kalkula'to:rɪʃ] **■** ADJ arithmetical; (*Fin*) *Kosten* imputed; **-e Methoden** methods of calculation **②** ADV **das ist ~ einwandfrei, aber ...** the figures are perfect, but ...

kalkulierbar ADJ calculable

kalkulieren [kalku'li:rən] *ptp* **kalkuliert** VT to calculate

Kalorie [kalo'ri:] F **-, -n** [-'ri:ən] calorie

Kalorien-: kalorienarm **■** ADJ low-calorie **②** ADV **sich ~ ernähren** to have a low-calorie diet; **~ essen** to eat low-calorie food; **Kalorienbombe** F (*inf*) **das ist eine echte ~** it's got about sixty million calories (*inf*); **kalorienreduziert** [-redutsi:ɐt] ADJ *Mahlzeit* reduced-calorie; **-e Kost** reduced calorie food; **kalorienreich** **■** ADJ high-calorie **②** ADV **~ essen** to eat high-calorie food; **sich ~ ernähren** to have a high-calorie diet

kalt [kalt] **■** ADJ, *comp* **=er** ['kɛltɐ], *superl* **=este(r, s)** ['kɛltəstə] cold; **mir ist/wird ~** I am/I'm getting cold; **im Kalten** in the cold; **~e Platte** plate *of cold meats, cheeses, salad etc*; **jdm die ~e Schulter zeigen** to give sb the cold shoulder; **den Sprung ins ~e Wasser wagen** (*fig*) to jump in at the deep end; **~es Grausen** or **Entsetzen überkam mich** my blood ran cold; **der Kalte Krieg** the Cold War

② ADV, *comp* **=er**, *superl* **am =esten ~ schlafen** to sleep in an unheated room; **~ baden/duschen** to have a cold bath/to take a cold shower; **etw ~ waschen** to wash sth in cold water; **abends essen wir ~** we eat a cold meal in the evening; **etw ~ stellen** to put sth to chill; **etw ~ lagern** to store sth cold; **die Wohnung kostet ~ 800 Euro** the flat (*Brit*) *or* apartment costs 800 euros without heating; **da kann ich nur ~ lächeln** (*inf*) that makes me laugh; **~ lächelnd** (*iro*) cool as you please; **es überlief** *or* **überrieselte ihn ~** cold shivers ran through him; **jdn ~ erwischen** to shock sb; *siehe auch* **kaltstellen**

Kalt-: kalt bleiben VI IRREG AUX SEIN (*fig*) to remain unmoved; **Kaltblut** NT carthorse; **Kaltblüter** [-bly:tɐ] M **-s, -** (*Zool*) cold-blooded animal; **kaltblütig** [-bly:tɪç] **■** ADJ **(a)** (*fig*) *Mensch, Mord* cold-blooded; (= *gelassen*) cool **(b)** (*Zool*) cold-blooded **②** ADV cold-bloodedly; **Kaltblütigkeit** F **-**, NO PL (*fig*) (*von Mensch, Verbrechen*) cold-bloodedness; (= *Gelassenheit*) cool(ness)

Kälte ['kɛltə] F **-**, NO PL **(a)** (*von Wetter, Material etc*) cold; (= *~periode*) cold spell; **die ~ des Stahls/Steins etc** the coldness of the steel/stone *etc*; **fünf Grad ~** five degrees below freezing; **bei dieser ~** in this cold; **hier ist eine solche ~, dass ...** it is so cold here that ... **(b)** (*fig*) coldness, coolness

Kälte-: kältebeständig ADJ cold-resistant; **Kälteeinbruch** M cold spell; **kälteempfindlich** ADJ sensitive to cold; **Kältegrad** M degree of frost; **Kältesturz** M cold spell; **Kältetechnik** F refrigeration technology; **Kältetod** M **den ~ sterben** to freeze to death; **kälteunempfindlich** ADJ insensitive to cold; **Kältewelle** F cold spell

Kalt-: Kaltfront F (*Met*) cold front; **kaltgepresst** [-gəprest] ADJ *Öl* cold-pressed; **kaltherzig** ADJ cold-hearted; **Kaltherzigkeit** [-hɛrtsɪçkaɪt] F **-**, NO PL cold-heartedness; **kaltlächelnd** ADV *siehe*

kalt; kalt lassen VT IRREG (*fig*) **jdn ~** to leave sb cold; **Kaltluft** F (*Met*) cold air; **Kaltluftfront** F (*Met*) cold front; **kaltmachen** VT SEP (*sl*) to do in (*inf*); **Kaltmiete** F rent exclusive of heating; **Kaltschale** F (*Cook*) *cold sweet soup*; **kaltschnäuzig** [-ʃnɔytsɪç] (*inf*) **■** ADJ (= *gefühllos*) callous; (= *unverschämt*) insolent; *Kritiker* sarcastic **②** ADV (= *gefühllos*) callously; (= *unverschämt*) insolently; **~ sagte sie ...** as cool as you please she said ...; **Kaltschweißen** VT **-s**, NO PL cold weld; **Kaltstart** M (*Aut, Comput*) cold start; **Kaltstartautomatik** F automatic choke; **kaltstellen** VT SEP (*inf*) **jdn** to demote; *siehe auch* **kalt**

Kalvinismus [kalvi'nɪsmʊs] M **-**, NO PL Calvinism

Kalvinist [kalvi'nɪst] M **-en, -en, Kalvinistin** [-'nɪstɪn] F **-, -nen** Calvinist

kalvinistisch [kalvi'nɪstɪʃ] ADJ Calvinist(ic)

Kalzium ['kaltsiom] NT **-s**, NO PL (*abbr* **Ca**) calcium

kam PRET *von* **kommen**

Kambodscha [kam'bɔdʒa] NT **-s** Cambodia

kambodschanisch [kambɔ'dʒa:nɪʃ] ADJ Cambodian

Kamel [ka'me:l] NT **-(e)s, -e (a)** camel **(b)** (*inf*) clown (*inf*); **ich ~!** silly me!

Kamelie [ka'me:liə] F **-, -n** camellia

Kamelle [ka'mɛlə] F **-, -n** USU PL (*inf*) **das sind doch alte** *or* **olle ~n** that's old hat (*inf*); **sie hat nichts als alte** *or* **olle ~n erzählt** she just said the same old things

Kamera ['kamɐa, 'ka:mərə] F **-, -s** camera

Kamerad [kamə'ra:t] M **-en, -en** [-dn], **Kameradin** [-'ra:dɪn] F **-, -nen** (*Mil etc*) comrade; (= *Gefährte, Lebenskamerad*) companion

Kameraderie [kamərade'ri:] F **-**, NO PL (*pej*) bonhomie

Kameradschaft [kamə'ra:tʃaft] F **-, -en** camaraderie

kameradschaftlich [kamə'ra:tʃaftlɪç] **■** ADJ comradely; **eine ~e Ehe** a companionate marriage **②** ADV **rein ~ zusammenleben** to live together purely as friends; **sich ~ verhalten** to act loyally; **~ miteinander umgehen** to be very friendly to each other

Kamera-: Kameraeinstellung F shot; **Kamerafahrt** F camera movement; **Kamerafrau** F camerawoman; **Kameraführung** F camera work; **Kameramann** M, *pl* **-männer** cameraman; **Kameraschwenk** M pan

Kamerun ['kamərun] NT **-s** the Cameroons *pl*

Kamikaze [kami'ka:tsə, kami'ka:zə] M **-, -** kamikaze

Kamikaze-: IN CPDS kamikaze; **Kamikazeflieger(in)** M(F) kamikaze pilot

Kamille [ka'mɪlə] F **-, -n** camomile

Kamillentee M camomile tea

Kamin [ka'mi:n] M or (DIAL) NT **-s, -e (a)** (= *Schornstein, Felskamin*) chimney; (= *Abzugsschacht*) flue; **etw in den ~ schreiben** to write sth off **(b)** (= *offene Feuerstelle*) fireplace; **wir saßen am** *or* **vor dem ~** we sat by *or* in front of the fire

Kamin-: Kamingarnitur F fireside companion set; **Kaminkehrer** [-ke:rə] M **-s, -, Kaminkehrerin** [-ərɪn] F **-, -nen** (*dial*) chimney sweep; **Kaminsims** M or NT mantelpiece

Kamm [kam] M **-(e)s, =e** ['kɛmə] **(a)** (*für Haar, = Webekamm, von Tieren*) comb; **alle/alles über einen ~ scheren** (*fig*) to lump everyone/everything together **(b)** (*Cook*) (*Hammelfleisch*) (middle) neck; (*Schweinefleisch*) shoulder; (*Rindfleisch*) neck **(c)** (= *Gebirgskamm, Wellenkamm*) crest

kämmen ['kɛmən] **■** VT to comb **②** VR to comb one's hair

Kammer ['kamɐ] F **-, -n (a)** (*allgemein*) (*Parl*) chamber; (= *Ärztekammer, Anwaltskammer*) professional association; (= *Herzkammer*) ventricle; **erste/zweite ~** Upper/Lower House **(b)** (= *Zimmer*) (small) room; (*dial:* = *Schlafzimmer*) bedroom

Kammer-: Kammerdiener M valet; **Kammerjäger(in)** M(F) (= *Schädlingsbekämpfer*) pest controller (*Brit*), exterminator (*US*); (= *Leibjäger*) (head) gamekeeper

Kämmerlein ['kɛmɐlaɪn] NT **-s, -** chamber; **im stillen ~** in private

Kammer-: Kammermusik F chamber music; **Kammerton** M, NO PL concert pitch; **Kammerzofe** F chambermaid

Kamm-: Kammgarn NT worsted; **Kammmuschel** F scallop; **Kammrad** NT cogwheel

Kampagne [kam'panjə] F **-, -n** campaign

Kampf [kampf] M **-(e)s, =e** ['kɛmpfə] fight (*um* for); (*Mil:* = *Gefecht*) battle; (*Mil:* = *Feindbegegnung*) engagement; (= *Boxkampf*) fight; **jdm/einer Sache den ~ ansagen** (*fig*) to declare war on sb/sth; **den ~ (gegen jdn/etw) aufnehmen** to commence battle (against sb/sth); (*fig*) to take up the fight (against sb/sth); **den ~/die Kämpfe einstellen** to stop fighting; **auf in den ~!** (*hum*) once more unto the breach! (*hum*); **er ist im ~ gefallen** he fell in action; **der ~ ums Dasein** the struggle for existence; **der ~ der Geschlechter** *or* **zwischen den Geschlechtern** the battle of the sexes; **der ~ um die Macht** the battle for power; **ein ~ auf Leben und Tod** a fight to the death; **innere Kämpfe** inner conflicts

Kampf-: Kampfabstimmung F vote; **es kam zur ~** they put it to the vote; **Kampfansage** F declaration of war; (*Sport*) announcement; **Kampfeinsatz** M combat mission

kämpfen ['kɛmpfn̩] **1** VI to fight (*um, für* for); **gegen etw ~** to fight (against) sth; **mit dem Tode ~** to fight for one's life; **mit den Tränen ~** to fight back one's tears; **gegen die Wellen ~** to battle against the waves; **ich hatte mit schweren Problemen zu ~** I had difficult problems to contend with; **ich habe lange mit mir ~ müssen, ehe ...** I had a long battle with myself before ... **2** VT (*usu fig*) *Kampf* to fight

Kampfer ['kampfɐ] M **-s**, NO PL camphor

Kämpfer ['kɛmpfɐ] M **-s**, -, **Kämpferin** [-ərɪn] F **-**, **-nen** fighter; (= *Krieger auch*) warrior

kämpferisch ['kɛmpfərɪʃ] **1** ADJ aggressive; *Spiel auch* attacking **2** ADV aggressively; **sich ~ einsetzen** to fight hard; **sich ~ bewähren** to fight well

Kampf-: Kampfflugzeug NT fighter (plane); **Kampfgas** NT poison gas; **Kampfgeist** M, NO PL fighting spirit; **Kampfhandlung** F USU PL clash *usu pl*; **Kampfhubschrauber** M helicopter gunship; **Kampfhund** M fighting dog; **kampflos 1** ADJ peaceful; *Sieg* uncontested **2** ADV peacefully, without a fight; **sich ~ ergeben, ~ aufgeben** to surrender without a fight; **kampflustig** ADJ belligerent; **Kampfplatz** M battlefield; (*Sport*) arena; **Kampfpreis** M **(a)** (*in Wettkampf*) prize **(b)** (*Comm*) cut-throat price; **Kampfrichter(in)** M(F) (*Sport*) referee; (*Tennis*) umpire; (*Schwimmen, Skilaufen*) judge; **Kampfsport** M martial art; **Kampfstoff** M weapon; **Kampftrinker(in)** M(F) (*sl*) pisshead (*inf*); **kampfunfähig** ADJ (*Mil*) unfit for action; *Boxer* unfit to fight; **einen Panzer/ein Schiff ~ machen** to put a tank/ship out of action; **Kampfunfähigkeit** F (*Mil*) unfitness for action; (*von Boxer*) unfitness to fight; **Kampfwagen** M chariot

kampieren [kam'pi:rən], *ptp* **kampiert** VI to camp (out); **im Wohnzimmer ~** (*inf*) to doss down (*Brit*) *or* camp out (*US*) in the sitting room (*inf*)

Kanada ['kanada] NT **-s** Canada

Kanadier [ka'na:diɐ] M **-s**, - **(a)** Canadian **(b)** (*Sport*) Canadian canoe

Kanadierin [ka'na:diərɪn] F **-**, **-nen** Canadian (woman/girl)

kanadisch [ka'na:dɪʃ] ADJ Canadian

Kanake [ka'na:kə] M **-n**, -**n**, **Kanakin** [-'na:kɪn] F **-**, **-nen** (= *Südseeinsulaner*) Kanaka; (*pej sl*: = *Ausländer, Südländer*) wop (*pej*), dago (*pej*)

Kanal [ka'na:l] M **-s**, **Kanäle** [ka'nɛ:lə] **(a)** (= *Schifffahrtsweg*) canal; (= *Wasserlauf*) channel; (*zur Bewässerung*) ditch; (*zur Entwässerung*) drain; (*für Abwässer*) sewer; **der (Ärmel)kanal** the (English) Channel **(b)** (*Rad, TV, fig*: = *Weg*) channel

Kanal-: Kanalarbeiter(in) M(F) **(a)** sewerage worker **(b)** PL (*Pol fig*) pressure group; **Kanaldeckel** M drain cover

Kanalisation [kanaliza'tsio:n] F **-**, **-en (a)** (*für Abwässer*) sewerage system; (= *das Kanalisieren*) sewerage installation **(b)** (= *Begradigung eines Flusslaufes*) canalization

kanalisieren [kanali'zi:rən], *ptp* **kanalisiert** VT *Fluss* to canalize; (*fig*) *Energie, Emotionen, Informationen* to channel; *Gebiet* to install sewers in

Kanaltunnel M Channel Tunnel

Kanaren [ka'na:rən] PL (*form*) Canaries *pl*

Kanarienvogel [ka'na:riən-] M canary

Kanarische Inseln [ka'na:rɪʃə] PL Canary Islands *pl*

Kandare [kan'da:rə] F **-**, **-n** (curb) bit; **jdn an die ~ nehmen** (*fig*) to take sb in hand

Kandidat [kandi'da:t] M **-en**, **-en**, **Kandidatin** [-'da:tɪn] F **-**, **-nen** candidate; (*bei Bewerbung auch*) applicant; **jdn als ~en aufstellen** to nominate sb

Kandidatur [kandida'tu:ɐ] F **-**, **-en** candidacy

kandidieren [kandi'di:rən], *ptp* **kandidiert** VI (*Pol*) to stand, to run (*für* for); **für das Amt des Präsidenten ~** to run for president

kandiert [kan'di:ɐt] ADJ *Frucht* candied

Kandis(zucker) ['kandɪs-] M **-**, NO PL rock candy

Känguru ['kɛŋguru] NT **-s**, -**s**, **Känguruh** NT **-s**, -**s** kangaroo

Kaninchen [ka'ni:nçən] NT **-s**, - rabbit; **sich wie ~ vermehren** (*inf*) to breed like rabbits

Kaninchen-: Kaninchenbau M, *pl* **-baue** rabbit warren; **Kaninchenstall** M rabbit hutch

Kanister [ka'nɪstɐ] M **-s**, - can; (= *Blechkanister*) jerry can

kann [kan] 3. PERS SING PRES *von* **können**

Kännchen ['kɛnçən] NT **-s**, - (*für Milch*) jug; (*für Kaffee*) pot; **ein ~ Kaffee** a pot of coffee

Kanne ['kanə] F **-**, **-n** can; (= *Teekanne, Kaffeekanne*) pot; (= *Milchkanne*) churn; (= *Gießkanne*) watering can; **sich** (*dat*) **die ~ geben** (*sl*: = *sich betrinken*) to get plastered (*inf*)

Kannibale [kani'ba:lə] M **-n**, -**n**, **Kannibalin** [-'ba:lɪn] F **-**, **-nen** cannibal

kannibalisch [kani'ba:lɪʃ] ADJ cannibalistic; (= *brutal*) rough

Kannibalismus [kaniba'lɪsmʊs] M **-**, NO PL cannibalism

kannte PRET *von* **kennen**

Kanon ['ka:nɔn] M **-s**, -**s** canon

Kanone [ka'no:nə] F **-**, **-n (a)** gun; (*Hist*) cannon; (*sl*: = *Pistole*) shooter (*inf*); **mit ~n auf Spatzen schießen** (*inf*) to take a sledgehammer to crack a nut **(b)** (*fig inf*: = *Könner*) ace (*inf*) **(c)** (*inf*) **das ist unter aller ~** that defies description

Kanossa [ka'nɔsa] NT **-s** (*fig*) humiliation

Kanossagang M, *pl* **-gänge einen ~ machen** *or* **antreten müssen** to eat humble pie

Kante ['kantə] F **-**, **-n** (*eines Gegenstandes, einer Fläche*) edge; (= *Rand, Borte*) border; (= *Webkante*) selvage; **Geld auf die hohe ~ legen** (*inf*) to put money away; **Geld auf den hohen ~ haben** (*inf*) to have (some) money put away

Kanten ['kantn̩] M **-s**, - (*N Ger*) crust

kantig ['kantɪç] ADJ *Holz* edged; *Gesicht* angular; *Charakter* awkward

Kantine [kan'ti:nə] F **-**, **-n** canteen

Kanton [kan'to:n] M **-s**, **-e** canton

Switzerland is a democratic federal state made up of individual states called cantons. There are 26 cantons, of which six are so-called demi-cantons formed by splitting single cantons in two. The cantons are autonomous within the limits set by the Federal Constitution. They are thus responsible for the organization of their own government by means of a cantonal constitution. The result is that state authorities differ from canton to canton both in name and structure.

kantonal [kanto'na:l] **1** ADJ cantonal **2** ADV **~ anerkannt** recognized *or* accepted throughout the canton; **~ finanziert** financed by the canton; **~ geregelt** regulated by the cantons *or* at cantonal level; **~ unterschiedliche Praxis** practices that differ from one canton to the other

Kantonist [kanto'nɪst] M **-en**, **-en ein unsicherer ~ sein** to be unreliable

Kanu ['ka:nu] NT **-s**, -**s** canoe

Kanüle [ka'ny:lə] F **-**, **-n** (*Med*) cannula

Kanzel ['kantsl̩] F **-**, **-n (a)** pulpit; **von der ~ herab** from the pulpit **(b)** (*Aviat*) cockpit

Kanzlei [kants'lai] F **-**, **-en (a)** (= *Dienststelle*) office; (= *Büro eines Rechtsanwalts, Notars etc*) chambers *pl* **(b)** (*Hist, Pol*) chancellery

Kanzler ['kantslɐ] M **-s**, -, **Kanzlerin** [-ərɪn] F **-**, **-nen (a)** (= *Regierungschef*) chancellor **(b)** (= *diplomatischer Beamter*) chancellor, chief secretary **(c)** (*Univ*) vice chancellor

Kanzler-: Kanzleramt NT (= *Gebäude*) chancellory; (= *Posten*) chancellorship; **Kanzleramtschef(in)** M(F) head of the chancellory; **Kanzlerbonus** M advantage of being the chancellor in power

Kanzlerin F *siehe* **Kanzler**

Kanzlerkandidat(in) M(F) candidate for the position of chancellor

Kap [kap] NT **-s, -s** cape; **~ der Guten Hoffnung** Cape of Good Hope; **~ Hoorn** Cape Horn

Kapazität [kapatsi'tɛːt] F **-, -en** capacity; (fig: = *Experte*) expert

Kapelle [ka'pɛlə] F **-, -n (a)** (= *kleine Kirche etc*) chapel **(b)** (*Mus*) orchestra

Kaper ['kaːpɐ] F **-, -n** (*Bot, Cook*) caper

kapern ['kaːpɐn] VT (*Naut*) *Schiff* to seize; (*fig inf*) *Ding* to commandeer (*inf*); *jdn* to grab; (= *mit Beschlag belegen*) to collar (*inf*)

Kaperschiff NT privateer

kapieren [ka'piːrən], *ptp* **kapiert** (*inf*) 1 VT to get (*inf*) 2 VI to get it (*inf*); **kapiert?** got it? (*inf*); **er hat schnell kapiert** he caught on quick (*inf*)

kapital [kapi'taːl] ADJ **(a)** (*Hunt*) *Hirsch* royal; **einen ~en Bock schießen** (*fig*) to make a real bloomer (*Brit inf*) or blooper (*US inf*) **(b)** (= *grundlegend*) *Missverständnis etc* major

Kapital [kapi'taːl] NT **-s, -e** or **-ien** [-liən] **(a)** (*Fin*) capital *no pl*; (= *angelegtes* ~) capital investments *pl*; **er ist mit 35% am ~ dieser Firma beteiligt** he has a 35% stake in this firm **(b)** (*fig*) asset; **aus etw ~ schlagen** (*pej: lit, fig*) to make capital out of sth; (*fig auch*) to capitalize on sth

Kapital-: Kapitalanlage F capital investment; **Kapitalanleger(in)** M(F) capital investor; **Kapitalbeteiligung** F equity interest; **Kapitaldecke** F capital resources *pl*; **Kapitaleinlage** F capital contribution; **Kapitalerhöhung** F capital increase; **Kapitalertrag(s)steuer** F capital gains tax; **Kapitalflussrechnung** F cash flow statement; **Kapitalherabsetzung** F capital decrease; **eine ~ vornehmen** to write down the capital

kapitalisieren [kapitali'ziːrən], *ptp* **kapitalisiert** VT to capitalize

Kapitalisierung F **-, -en** capitalization

Kapitalismus [kapita'lɪsmʊs] M **-**, NO PL capitalism

Kapitalist [kapita'lɪst] M **-en, -en, Kapitalistin** [-'lɪstɪn] F **-, -nen** capitalist

kapitalistisch [kapita'lɪstɪʃ] ADJ capitalist

Kapital-: Kapitalkonto NT equity account; **kapitalkräftig** ADJ financially strong; **~ sein** to have plenty of capital; **Kapitallebensversicherung** F endowment insurance; **Kapitalmarkt** M capital market; **Kapitalverbrechen** NT serious crime; (*mit Todesstrafe*) capital crime; **Kapitalverkehr** M capital transactions *pl*; **freier ~** (*in der EU*) free movement of capital; **~ mit dem Ausland** external capital transactions *pl*

Kapitän [kapi'tɛːn] M **-s, -e, Kapitänin** [-'tɛːnɪn] F **-, -nen** (*Naut, Mil, Aviat, Sport*) captain; (*esp auf kleinerem Schiff*) skipper (*inf*); **~ zur See** (*Mil*) captain

Kapitel [ka'pɪtl] NT **-s, -** chapter; **das ist ein anderes ~** that's another story; **das ist ein ~ für sich** that's a story all to itself

Kapitell [kapi'tɛl] NT **-s, -e** capital

Kapitulation [kapitula'tsioːn] F **-, -en** (*lit, fig*) capitulation (*vor +dat* to, in the face of); **bedingungslose ~** unconditional surrender

kapitulieren [kapitu'liːrən], *ptp* **kapituliert** VI (= *sich ergeben*) to surrender; (*fig:* = *aufgeben*) to give up (*vor +dat* in the face of)

Kaplan [ka'plaːn] M **-s, Kapläne** [ka'plɛːnə] (*in Pfarrei*) curate; (*mit besonderen Aufgaben*) chaplain

Kaposi [ka'poːzi] NT **-(s), -s, Kaposisarkom** NT (*Med*) Kaposi's sarcoma

Kappe ['kapə] F **-, -n** cap; (= *Fliegerkappe, Motorradmütze*) helmet; (= *Narrenmütze*) jester's cap; (*von Jude*) skullcap; **eine ~ aus Schnee** a snowcap; **das nehme ich auf meine ~** (*fig inf*) I'll take the responsibility for that; **das geht auf meine ~** (*inf*) (= *ich bezahle*) that's on me; (= *ich übernehme die Verantwortung*) that's my responsibility

kappen ['kapn] VT (*Naut*) *Tau, Leine* to cut; *Ast* to cut back; (*Med*) *Mandeln* to clip (off); (*fig inf*) *Finanzmittel* to cut (back)

Kappes ['kapəs] M **-, -** (*dial: = Kohl*) cabbage; **~ reden** (*inf*) to talk (a load of) rubbish or baloney (*inf*)

Käppi ['kɛpi] NT **-s, -s** cap

Kapriole [kapri'oːlə] F **-, -n** capriole; (*fig*) caper

Kapsel ['kapsl] F **-, -n** (= *Etui*) container; (*Anat, Bot, Pharm, Space etc*) capsule; (= *einer Flasche*) cap; (= *Sprengkapsel*) detonator

Kapselheber M bottle-opener

kaputt [ka'pʊt] ADJ (*inf*) broken; *esp Maschine, Glühbirne etc* kaput (*inf*); (= *erschöpft*) *Mensch* shattered (*Brit inf*); *Ehe* broken; *Beziehungen, Gesundheit* ruined; *Nerven* shattered;

Firma bust *pred* (*inf*); **das alte Auto/ihre Ehe ist ~** (= *irreparabel*) the old car/her marriage has had it (*inf*); **irgendetwas muss an deinem Auto ~ sein** something must be wrong with your car; **der Fernseher ist ~** (*zeitweilig*) the TV is on the blink (*inf*); **mein ~es Bein** my bad leg; (*gebrochen*) my broken leg; **mein ~es Auge** my bad eye (*inf*); **meine Jacke ist ~** (= *nicht mehr tragbar*) my jacket has had it (*inf*); (= *zerrissen*) my jacket is torn; (*am Saum*) my jacket is coming apart; **die ~e Welt** this mess of a world; **ein ~er Typ** a wreck (*inf*)

kaputt-: kaputtfahren VT SEP IRREG (*inf*) (= *überfahren*) to run over; *Auto* to run into the ground; (*durch Unfall*) to smash (up); **kaputtgehen** VI SEP IRREG AUX SEIN (*inf*) to break; (*esp Maschine, Glühbirne*) to go kaput (*inf*); (*Ehe*) to break up (*an +dat* because of); (*Beziehungen, Gesundheit, Nerven*) to be ruined; (*Firma*) to go bust (*inf*); (*Waschmaschine, Auto*) to break down; (*Kleidung*) to come to pieces; (= *zerrissen werden*) to tear; (*Blumen*) to die off; **in dem Büro/an diesem Job gehe ich noch kaputt** this office/job will be the death of me (*inf*); **kaputtkriegen** VT SEP (*inf*) *Zerbrechliches* to break; *Auto* to ruin; *jdn* to wear out; **das Auto/der Hans ist nicht kaputtzukriegen** this car/Hans just goes on for ever; **kaputtlachen** VR SEP (*inf*) to die laughing (*inf*); **ich lach mich kaputt!** what a laugh!; **kaputtmachen** SEP (*inf*) 1 VT to ruin; *Zerbrechliches* to break, to smash; *Brücke, Sandburg* to knock down; (= *erschöpfen*) *jdn* to wear out; **diese ewigen Sorgen machen mich kaputt** these never-ending worries will be the death of me (*inf*) 2 VR (= *sich überanstrengen*) to wear oneself out

Kapuze [ka'puːtsə] F **-, -n** hood; (= *Mönchskapuze*) cowl

Karabiner [kara'biːnɐ] M **-s, -** **(a)** (= *Gewehr*) carbine **(b)** (*auch* **Karabinerhaken**) karabiner

Karacho [ka'raxo] NT **-s**, NO PL **mit** or **im ~** (*inf*) at full tilt; **er rannte/fuhr mit ~ gegen die Wand** he ran/drove smack into the wall (*inf*)

Karaffe [ka'rafə] F **-, -n** carafe; (*mit Stöpsel*) decanter

Karambolage [karambo'laːʒə] F **-, -n** (*Aut*) collision; (*Billard*) cannon

Karamell [kara'mɛl] M **-s**, NO PL caramel *no pl*

Karamelle [kara'mɛlə] F **-, -n** caramel (toffee)

Karaoke [kara'oːke] NT **-**, NO PL karaoke

Karat [ka'raːt] NT **-(e)s, -e** or (*bei Zahlenangabe*) **-** (*Measure*) carat

Karate NT **-(s)**, NO PL karate

-karäter [karɛːtɐ] M SUF IN CPDS **-s, - Zehnkaräter** ten-carat stone; (= *Diamant*) ten-carat diamond

-karätig [karɛːtɪç] ADJ SUF (*inf*) **zehnkarätig** ten-carat

Karawane [kara'vaːnə] F **-, -n** caravan

Kardan- [kar'daːn-]: **Kardangelenk** NT universal joint; **Kardantunnel** M transmission tunnel; **Kardanwelle** F prop(eller) shaft

Kardinal [kardi'naːl] M **-s, Kardinäle** [-'nɛːlə] **(a)** (*Eccl*) cardinal **(b)** (*Orn*) cardinal (bird)

Kardinal-: Kardinalfehler M cardinal error; **Kardinalzahl** F cardinal (number)

Kardiogramm [kardio'gram] NT, *pl* **-gramme** cardiogram

Kardiologe [kardio'loːgə] M **-n, -n, Kardiologin** [-'loːgɪn] F **-, -nen** cardiologist

kardiologisch [kardio'loːgɪʃ] ADJ cardiological

Karenz- [ka'rɛnts-]: **Karenztag** M unpaid day of sick leave; **Karenzzeit** F waiting period

Karfiol [kar'fioːl] M **-s**, NO PL (*Aus*) cauliflower

Karfreitag [kaːɐ'fraitaːk] M Good Friday

karg [kark] 1 ADJ **(a)** (= *spärlich*) meagre (*Brit*), meager (*US*); *Boden* barren

(b) (= *geizig*) mean, sparing

2 ADV **(a)** (= *spärlich*) **~ ausgestattet sein** (*Mensch*) to have few possessions; **seine Bibliothek ist noch ziemlich ~ ausgestattet** there aren't many books in his library yet; **~ möbliert** sparsely furnished; **~ leben** to lead a meagre (*Brit*) or meager (*US*) existence

(b) (= *knapp*) **~ ausfallen/bemessen sein** to be meagre (*Brit*) or meager (*US*); **etw ~ bemessen** to be stingy with sth (*inf*); **die Portionen sind sehr ~ bemessen** they are very stingy with the helpings (*inf*)

Kargheit ['karkhait] F **-**, NO PL meagreness (*Brit*), meagerness (*US*); (*von Möblierung*) sparseness; (*von Boden*) barrenness

kärglich [ˈkɛrklɪç] **1** ADJ meagre (*Brit*), meager (*US*), sparse; *Mahl* frugal; **unter ~en Bedingungen leben** to live in impoverished conditions **2** ADV **sie leben ~** they lead a meagre (*Brit*) *or* meager (*US*) existence

Kargo [ˈkargo] M **-s, -s** cargo

Karibik [kaˈriːbɪk] F **- die ~** the Caribbean

karibisch [kaˈriːbɪʃ] ADJ Caribbean; **das Karibische Meer** the Caribbean Sea; **die Karibischen Inseln** the Caribbean Islands

kariert [kaˈriːʀt] **1** ADJ *Stoff, Muster* checked, checkered (*esp US*); *Papier* squared **2** ADV (*inf*) **red nicht so ~!** don't talk such rubbish; **~ gucken** to look puzzled

Karies [ˈkaːries] F **-, NO PL** caries

Karikatur [karikaˈtuːɐ] F **-, -en** caricature

Karikaturist [karikatuˈrɪst] M **-en, -en, Karikaturistin** [-ˈrɪstɪn] F **-, -nen** cartoonist; (= *Personenzeichner auch*) caricaturist

karikieren [kariˈkiːrən], *ptp* **karikiert** VT to caricature

kariös [kaˈriøːs] ADJ *Zahn* decayed

karitativ [karitaˈtiːf] **1** ADJ charitable **2** ADV **sich ~ betätigen, ~ tätig sein** to do charitable work

Karl [karl] M **-s** Charles; **~ der Große** Charlemagne

Karma [ˈkarma] NT **-s, NO PL** karma

Karneval [ˈkarnəval] M **-s, -e** *or* **-s** carnival

KARNEVAL

Karneval *is the period of celebration between Epiphany and Ash Wednesday, also colloquially known as the **fünfte Jahreszeit** (fifth season). Celebrations take a variety of forms: there are meetings at which humorous speeches are made and carnival songs are sung; masked balls for young and old; and on the so-called **tolle Tage** (literally, "crazy days") normal life in many regions is turned completely upside down. During the **tolle Tage** power is symbolically assumed in many towns by a carnival prince and princess. This is especially so in Rheinland, where **Karneval** has been celebrated in its present form since 1823. **Rosenmontag** is generally a holiday in this region, allowing people to watch the processions and join in the celebrations. In Southern Germany and Austria the carnival period is called **Fasching** and the processions take place on the Tuesday before Ash Wednesday.*
▶ FASTNACHT, ROSENMONTAG

Karnevalszug M carnival procession

Kärnten [ˈkɛrntn] NT **-s** Carinthia

Karo [ˈkaːro] NT **-s, -s (a)** (= *Quadrat*) square; (*auf der Spitze stehend*) diamond; (*Muster*) check; (*diagonal*) diamond **(b)** (*Cards: einzelne Karte*) diamond NO PL (= *Spielkartenfarbe*) diamonds *pl*

Karomuster NT checked *or* checkered (*esp US*) pattern

Karosse [kaˈrɔsə] F **-, -n** (= *Prachtkutsche*) (state) coach; (*fig:* = *großes Auto*) limousine

Karosserie [karɔsəˈriː] F **-, -n** [-ˈriːən] bodywork

Karotte [kaˈrɔtə] F **-, -n** carrot

Karpaten [karˈpaːtn] PL Carpathian Mountains *pl*

Karpfen [ˈkarpfn] M **-s, -** carp

Karpfenteich M carp pond

Karre [ˈkarə] F **-, -n (a)** = **Karren (b)** (*inf:* = *klappriges Auto*) (old) crate (*inf*)

Karree [kaˈreː] NT **-s, -s (a)** (= *Viereck*) rectangle; (= *Rhombus*) rhombus; (= *Quadrat, Formation: esp Mil*) square **(b)** (= *Häuserblock*) block; **einmal ums ~ gehen** to walk round the block **(c)** (*esp Aus: Cook*) loin

karren [ˈkarən] VT to cart; **jdn ~** (*inf: mit Auto*) to drive sb

Karren [ˈkarən] M **-s, - (a)** (= *Wagen*) cart; (*esp für Garten, Baustelle*) (wheel)barrow; (*für Gepäck etc*) trolley; **ein ~ voll Obst** a cartload of fruit **(b)** (*fig inf*) **jdm an den ~ fahren** *or* **pinkeln** to take sb to task; **jdn in den Dreck fahren** to get things in a mess; **der ~ ist hoffnungslos verfahren, der ~ steckt im Dreck** we/they *etc* are really in a mess; **den ~ aus dem Dreck ziehen, den ~ wieder flottmachen** to get things sorted out

Karrette [kaˈretə] F **-, -n** (*Sw: = Schubkarre*) (hand)cart

Karriere [kaˈrieːrə] F **-, -n** (= *Laufbahn*) career; **~ machen** to make a career for oneself

Karriere-: Karrierefrau F career woman; **karrieregeil** ADJ (*pej*) career-mad; **Karriereknick** M **es kam zu einem ~** his/her career took a downturn; **Karrieremacher(in)** M(F) careerist; **karrieresüchtig** ADJ career-driven

Karsamstag [kaːrˈzamstaːk] M Easter Saturday

karstig [ˈkarstɪç] ADJ karstic

Karte [ˈkartə] F **-, -n (a)** (*auch Comput*) card **(b)** (= *Fahrkarte, Eintrittskarte*) ticket; (= *Einladungskarte*) invitation (card); (= *Bezugsschein*) coupon; (= *Essenskarte*) luncheon voucher, meal ticket (*US*); (= *Mitgliedskarte*) (membership) card **(c)** (= *Landkarte*) map; (= *Seekarte*) chart **(d)** (= *Speisekarte*) menu; (= *Weinkarte*) wine list; **nach der ~** à la carte **(e)** (= *Spielkarte*) (playing) card; **jdm die ~n lesen** to tell sb's fortune from the cards; **du solltest deine ~n aufdecken** (*fig*) you ought to put your cards on the table; **alles auf eine ~ setzen** (*lit*) to stake everything on one card; (*fig*) to stake everything on one chance; (= *andere Möglichkeiten ausschließen*) to put all one's eggs in one basket (*prov*); **du hast auf die falsche ~ gesetzt** (*fig*) you backed the wrong horse; **schlechte/gute ~n haben** to have a bad/good hand; (*fig*) to be in a difficult/strong position

Kartei [karˈtai] F **-, -en** card index

Kartei-: Karteikarte F index card; **Karteikasten** M file-card box; **Karteileiche** F (*inf*) sleeping member; **die meisten Mitglieder sind bloß ~n** most of the members are just names on the files; **Karteischrank** M filing cabinet

Kartell [karˈtɛl] NT **-s, -e (a)** (*Comm*) cartel **(b)** (= *Interessenvereinigung*) alliance; (*pej*) cartel

Kartell-: Kartellamt NT, **Kartellbehörde** F ≈ Monopolies and Mergers Commission (*Brit*), anti-trust commission (*esp US*); **Kartellrecht** NT (= *Kartellgesetz*) monopolies *or* (*esp US*) anti-trust law; (= *Kartellgesetzgebung*) legislation against monopolies, anti-trust legislation (*esp US*)

Karten-: Kartenhaus NT **(a)** house of cards; **wie ein ~ zusammenstürzen** *or* **in sich zusammenfallen** to collapse like a house of cards **(b)** (*Naut*) chart room; **Karteninhaber(in)** M(F) cardholder; **Kartenlesen** NT **-s, NO PL (a)** (*von Landkarten etc*) mapreading **(b)** (= *Wahrsagen*) fortune-telling (*using cards*), reading the cards; **Kartenspiel** NT **(a)** (= *das Spielen*) cardplaying; (= *ein Spiel*) card game; **beim ~** when playing cards **(b)** (= *Karten*) pack (of cards); **Kartentelefon** NT cardphone; **Kartenvorverkauf** M advance sale of tickets; (= *Stelle*) advance booking office

Kartoffel [karˈtɔfl] F **-, -n** potato; **rin in die ~n, raus aus den ~n** (*inf*) first it's one thing, then (it's) another; **etw/jdn fallen lassen wie eine heiße ~** (*inf*) to drop sth/sb like a hot potato

Kartoffel- IN CPDS potato; **Kartoffelbrei** M mashed potatoes *pl*; **Kartoffelchips** PL potato crisps (*Brit*), potato chips *pl* (*US*); **Kartoffelpuffer** M *fried grated potato cakes*; **Kartoffelpüree** NT mashed potatoes *pl*; **Kartoffelsalat** M potato salad; **Kartoffelschäler** [-ˌʃɛːlɐ] M **-s, -** potato peeler

kartografisch [kartoˈgraːfɪʃ] **1** ADJ cartographic(al) **2** ADV **diese Gegend ist noch nicht besonders gut ~ erfasst** this area hasn't been mapped very well yet

Karton [karˈtɔŋ, karˈtõ, karˈtoːn] M **-s, -s (a)** (= *steifes Papier, Pappe*) cardboard; **ein ~** a piece of cardboard **(b)** (= *Schachtel*) cardboard box

Kartonage [kartoˈnaːʒə] F **-, -n** (= *Verpackung*) cardboard packaging

kartonieren [kartoˈniːrən], *ptp* **kartoniert** VT *Bücher* to bind in board; **kartoniert** paperback

Kartusche [karˈtʊʃə] F **-, -n** (= *Behälter*) cartridge

Karussell [karʊˈsɛl] NT **-s, -s** *or* **-e** merry-go-round, carousel; **~ fahren** to have a ride on the merry-go-round *etc*

Karwoche [ˈkaːrɛ-] F (*Eccl*) Holy Week

karzinogen [kartsinoˈgeːn] (*Med*) **1** ADJ carcinogenic **2** ADV **~ wirken** to act as a carcinogen

Karzinom [kartsiˈnoːm] NT **-s, -e** (*Med*) carcinoma, malignant growth

Kasachstan [kazaxsˈtaːn] NT **-s** Kazakhstan

kaschieren [kaˈʃiːrən], *ptp* **kaschiert** VT **(a)** (*fig:* = *überdecken*) to conceal **(b)** *Bucheinband* to laminate

Kaschmir[1] [ˈkaʃmiːɐ] M **-s** (*Geog*) Kashmir

Kaschmir[2] M **-s, -e** (*Tex*) cashmere

Käse [ˈkɛːzə] M **-s, - (a)** cheese **(b)** (*inf:* = *Unsinn*) twaddle (*inf*)

Käse- IN CPDS cheese; **Käseblatt** NT, **Käseblättchen** [-ˌblɛtçən] NT **-s, -** (*inf*) local rag (*inf*); **Käsebrot** NT bread and cheese; **Käsebrötchen** NT cheese roll; **Käseecke** F cheese triangle;

Käsefondue NT cheese fondue; **Käsegebäck** NT cheese savouries pl (Brit) or savories pl (US); **Käsekuchen** M cheesecake

Käserei [kɛːzə'raɪ] F **-, -en (a)** (= Betrieb) cheese dairy **(b)** NO PL (= Käseherstellung) cheese-making

Kaserne [ka'zɛrnə] F **-, -n** barracks pl

Käse-: Käsestange F cheese straw (Brit), cheese stick (US); **käseweiß** ADJ (inf) white (as a ghost)

käsig ['kɛːzɪç] ADJ **(a)** (fig inf) Gesicht, Haut pasty; (vor Schreck) pale **(b)** (lit) cheesy

Kasino [ka'ziːno] NT **-s, -s (a)** (= Spielbank) casino **(b)** (= Offizierskasino) (officers') mess; (= Speiseraum) dining room

Kaskoversicherung ['kasko-] F (Aut) (= Teilkaskoversicherung) ≈ third party, fire and theft insurance; (= Vollkaskoversicherung) fully comprehensive insurance; (Naut) hull insurance

Kasper ['kaspɐ] M **-s, -**,(Aus, S Ger) **Kasperl** ['kaspɐl] M or NT **-s, -(n)**, (S Ger) **Kasperle** ['kaspɐlə] M or NT **-s, - (a)** (im Puppenspiel) Punch (esp Brit) **(b)** (inf) clown (inf)

Kasperle-: Kasperlefigur F Punch glove (Brit) or hand (US) puppet; **Kasperletheater** NT Punch and Judy (show) (esp Brit), puppet show; (= Gestell) Punch and Judy theatre (esp Brit), puppet theater (US)

kaspern ['kaspɐn] VI (inf) to clown around (inf)

Kaspisches Meer ['kaspɪʃəs] NT Caspian Sea

Kassa ['kasa] F **-, Kassen** ['kasn] (esp Aus) = **Kasse (a)**

Kassa- (esp Aus): **Kassageschäft** NT (Comm) cash transaction; (St Ex) spot transaction; **Kassakurs** M spot rate; **Kassamarkt** M spot market

Kasse ['kasə] F **-, -n (a)** (= Zahlstelle) cash desk (Brit) or point, cash register (US); (= Zahlraum) cashier's office; (Theat etc) box office; (in Bank) bank counter; (in Supermarkt) checkout; **an der ~** (in Geschäft) at the desk (esp Brit), at the (checkout) counter (esp US) **(b)** (= Geldkasten) cash box; (in Läden) cash register; (= Geldmittel) coffers pl; (bei Spielen) kitty; (in einer Spielbank) bank; **die ~n klingeln** the money is really rolling in **(c)** (= Bargeld) cash; **ein Verkauf per ~** (form) a cash sale; **netto ~ net payment; gegen ~** for cash; **bei ~ sein** (inf) to be in the money (inf); **knapp bei ~ sein** (inf) to be short of cash; **gut/ schlecht bei ~ sein** (inf) to be well-off/badly-off; **~ machen** to check one's finances; (in Geschäft) to cash up (Brit), to count up the earnings (US); **zur ~ bitten** to ask for money; **jdn zur ~ bitten** to ask sb to pay up **(d)** (inf: = Sparkasse) (savings) bank **(e)** = Krankenkasse

Kasseler ['kasələ] NT **-s, -** lightly smoked pork loin

Kassen-: Kassenabschluss M cashing up; **~ machen** to cash up (Brit), to count up the earnings (US); **Kassenarzt** M, **Kassenärztin** F doctor who treats members of medical insurance schemes; ≈ National Health general practitioner (Brit); **Kassenbeleg** M sales receipt or check (US); **Kassenbestand** M cash balance, cash in hand; **Kassenbon** M sales slip; **Kassenbrille** F (pej inf) NHS specs pl (Brit inf), standard-issue glasses pl; **Kassenpatient(in)** M(F) patient belonging to medical insurance scheme, ≈ National Health patient (Brit); **Kassenprüfung** F audit; **Kassenschlager** M (Theat etc) box-office hit; (Ware) big seller; **Kassenstand** M (Comm) cash in till (Brit) or register (US); **Kassenstunden** PL hours pl of business (of cashier's office etc); **Kassensturz** M (Comm) cashing up (Brit), counting up the earnings (US); **~ machen** to check one's finances; (Comm) to cash up (Brit), to count up the earnings (US); **Kassenwart** [-vart] M **-s, -e**, **Kassenwartin** [-vartɪn] F **-, -nen** treasurer; **Kassenzettel** M sales slip

Kassette [ka'sɛtə] F **-, -n (a)** (= Kästchen) case **(b)** (für Bücher) slipcase; (= Bücher in ~) set, pack (Comm); (= Geschenkkassette) gift case/set; (für Schallplatten) box; set; (= Tonbandkassette, Filmbehälter) cassette; (= Aufbewahrungskassette) container; (für Film) can **(c)** (Archit) coffer

Kassetten-: Kassettendeck NT cassette deck; **Kassettenrekorder** M cassette recorder

kassieren [ka'siːrən] ptp **kassiert** VT **(a)** Gelder etc to collect (up); (inf) Abfindung, Finderlohn to pick up (inf) **(b)** (inf: = wegnehmen) to take away **(c)** (inf: = verhaften) to nab (inf) VI (= abrechnen) to take the money; **bei jdm ~** to collect money from sb; **Sie haben bei mir schon kassiert** I've paid already; **darf ich ~, bitte?** would you like to pay now?

Kassierer [ka'siːrɐ] M **-s, -**, **Kassiererin** [-ərɪn] F **-, -nen** cashier; (= Bankkassierer) clerk; (= Einnehmer) collector; (eines Klubs) treasurer

Kastanie [kas'taːniə] F **-, -n** chestnut; (= Rosskastanie) (horse) chestnut; (= Edelkastanie) (sweet) chestnut; (Holz) chestnut (wood)

Kästchen ['kɛstçən] NT **-s, - (a)** (= kleiner Kasten) small box; (für Schmuck) casket **(b)** (auf kariertem Papier) square

Kaste ['kastə] F **-, -n** caste

Kasten ['kastn] M **-s, ≈** ['kɛstn] **(a)** box; (= Kiste) crate; (= Truhe) chest; (Aus: = Schrank) cupboard; (N Ger: = Schublade) drawer; (= Briefkasten) postbox (Brit), letter box (Brit), mailbox (US); (= Schaukasten) display case; (= Brotkasten) breadbin (Brit), breadbox (US); (Sport: = Gerät) box **(b)** (inf) (= alter Wagen, Flugzeug) crate (inf); (= altes großes Haus) barn (of a place) (inf); (= Radio, Fernsehapparat etc) box (inf) **(c)** (inf: = großer, breiter Mann) heavyweight (inf) **(d)** (inf) **sie hat viel auf dem ~** she's brainy (inf) **(e)** (inf: = Fußballtor) goal

Kasten-: Kastenform F (Cook) (square) baking tin (Brit) or pan (US); **Kastenwagen** M (Aut) truck, panel truck (US); (auf Bauernhof) box cart

Kastilien [kas'tiːliən] NT **-s** Castile

Kastration [kastra'tsioːn] F **-, -en** castration; **chemische ~** chemical castration

kastrieren [kas'triːrən], ptp **kastriert** VT (lit, fig) to castrate

Kasus ['kaːzus] M **- -** ['kaːzuːs] (Gram) case

Kat [kat] M **-s, -s** (Aut) ABBR von Katalysator cat

Katalanien [kata'laːniən] NT **-s** Catalonia

katalanisch [kata'laːnɪʃ] ADJ Catalan

Katalog [kata'loːk] M **-(e)s, -e** [-gə] catalogue (Brit), catalog (US)

katalogisieren [katalogi'ziːrən], ptp **katalogisiert** VT to catalogue (Brit), to catalog (US)

Katalonien [kata'loːniən] NT **-s** Catalonia

Katalysator [kataly'zaːtoːɐ] M **-s, Katalysatoren** [-'toːrən] (lit, fig) catalyst; (Aut) catalytic converter

Katalysator-: Katalysatorauto NT car fitted with a catalytic converter; **Katalysator-Modell** NT model with a catalytic converter

Katalyse [kata'lyːzə] F **-, -n** (Chem) catalysis

katalytisch [kata'lyːtɪʃ] ADJ catalytic

Katamaran [katama'raːn] M **-s, -e** catamaran

Katapult [kata'pʊlt] NT or M **-(e)s, -e** catapult

katapultieren [katapʊl'tiːrən], ptp **katapultiert** VT to catapult; VR to catapult oneself; (Pilot) to eject

Katarr [ka'tar] M **-s, -e**, **Katarrh** M **-s, -e** catarrh

Katasteramt NT land registry

katastrophal [katastro'faːl] ADJ disastrous; **der Mangel an Brot ist ~ geworden** the bread shortage has become catastrophic ADV geschwächt, unterernährt, zugerichtet disastrously; **sich ~ auswirken** to have catastrophic effects; **das Zimmer sieht ja ~ aus** the room looks absolutely disastrous

Katastrophe [katas'troːfə] F **-, -n** disaster; (Theat, Liter) catastrophe, (tragic) dénouement; **der ist eine ~** (inf) he's a real disaster (area) (inf)

Katastrophen-: Katastrophenabwehr F disaster prevention; **Katastrophenalarm** M emergency alert; **Katastropheneinsatz** M duty or use in case of disaster; **für den ~** for use in case of disaster; **Katastrophengebiet** NT disaster area; **Katastrophenschutz** M disaster control; (im Voraus) disaster prevention

Kategorie [katego'riː] F **-, -n** [-'riːən] category; **er gehört auch zur ~ derer, die ...** he's the sort or type who ...

kategorisch [kate'goːrɪʃ] ADJ categorical; Ablehnung auch flat; **der ~e Imperativ** the categorical imperative ADV categorically; **ich weigerte mich ~** I refused outright; **... erklärte er ~** ... he declared emphatically

kategorisieren [kategori'ziːrən], ptp **kategorisiert** VT to categorize

Kater ['kaːtɐ] M **-s, - (a)** tom(cat) **(b)** (nach Alkoholgenuss) hangover

Katerstimmung F depression

kath. ABBR *von* **katholisch**

Kathedrale [kate'dra:lə] F **-, -n** cathedral

Katheter [ka'te:tɐ] M **-s, -** (*Med*) catheter

Kathode [ka'to:də] F **-, -n** (*Phys*) cathode

Katholik [kato'li:k] M **-en, -en, Katholikin** [-'li:kɪn] F **-, -nen** (Roman) Catholic

katholisch [ka'to:lɪʃ] **1** ADJ (Roman) Catholic; **sie ist streng ~** she's a strict Catholic **2** ADV **~ denken** to have Catholic views; **~ heiraten** to have a Catholic wedding; **~ beerdigt werden** to have a Catholic burial; **~ beeinflusst** influenced by Catholicism; **seine Kinder ~ erziehen** to raise one's children (as) Catholics

Katholizismus [katoli'tsɪsmʊs] M **-,** NO PL (Roman) Catholicism

Kat-Modell NT (*Aut*) ABBR *von* **Katalysator-Modell**

katzbuckeln [ˈkatsbʊkln] VI (*pej inf*) to grovel

Kätzchen [ˈkɛtsçən] NT **-s, -** (a) (= *junge Katze*) (*inf*: = *Mädchen*) kitten; (= *Katze*) pussy (*inf*) (b) (*Bot*) catkin

Katze [ˈkatsə] F **-, -n** cat; **meine Arbeit war für die Katz** (*fig*) my work was a waste of time; **Katz und Maus mit jdm spielen** to play cat and mouse with sb; **wie die ~ um den heißen Brei herumschleichen** to beat about the bush; **die ~ im Sack kaufen** to buy a pig in a poke (*prov*); **die ~ lässt das Mausen nicht** (*Prov*) the leopard cannot change its spots (*Prov*); **bei Nacht sind alle ~n grau** all cats are grey (*Brit*) *or* gray (*US*) at night; **wenn die ~ aus dem Haus ist, tanzen die Mäuse (auf dem Tisch)** (*Prov*) when the cat's away the mice will play (*Prov*)

Katzen-: Katzenauge NT (a) (= *Straßenmarkierung*) Catseye®; (= *Rückstrahler*) reflector (b) (*Min*) cat's-eye; **Katzenbuckel** M arched back (of a cat); **einen ~ machen** to arch one's back; **Katzenjammer** M (*inf*) (a) (= *Kater*) hangover (b) (= *jämmerliche Stimmung*) depression, the blues *pl* (*inf*); **Katzensprung** M (*inf*) stone's throw; **Katzenstreu** F cat litter; **Katzentisch** M (*hum*) children's table; **die Kinder essen am ~** the children are eating at their own table; **Katzentür** F cat flap

Katz-und-Maus-Spiel NT cat-and-mouse game

Kauderwelsch [ˈkaudɐvɛlʃ] NT **-(s),** NO PL (*pej*) (= *Fach- oder Geheimsprache*) jargon; (= *Gemisch aus mehreren Sprachen/Dialekten*) hotchpotch (*Brit*) *or* mishmash of different languages/dialects; (= *unverständliche Sprache*) gibberish

kauen [ˈkauən] **1** VT to chew; **Nägel** to bite; **Wein** to taste **2** VI to chew; **an etw** (*dat*) **~** to chew (on) sth; **an den Nägeln ~** to bite one's nails; **das Kauen** chewing

kauern [ˈkauɐn] VIR (*vi auch aux sein*) to crouch (down); (*ängstlich*) to cower; (*Schutz suchend*) to be huddled (up)

Kauf [kauf] M **-(e)s, Käufe** [ˈkɔyfə] buying *no pl*, purchase (*esp form*), purchasing *no pl* (*esp form*); (= *das Gekaufte*) buy; **das war ein günstiger ~** that was a good buy; **diese Käufe haben sich gelohnt** it was worth buying these; **ein ~ auf Kredit** a credit purchase; **etw zum ~ anbieten** to offer sth for sale; **einen ~ abschließen** *or* **tätigen** (*form*) to complete a purchase; **etw in ~ nehmen** (*fig*) to accept sth

kaufen [ˈkaufn] **1** VT (a) (*auch sich* (*dat*) *kaufen*) to buy, to purchase (*esp form*); **diese Zigaretten werden viel gekauft** we sell a lot of these cigarettes; **diese Zigaretten werden nicht gekauft** nobody buys these cigarettes; **dafür kann ich mir nichts ~** (*iro*), **was kann man sich** (*dat*) **dafür (schon) ~** (*iro*) what use is that to me! (b) (= *bestechen*) jdn to bribe; **Spiel** to fix; **Stimmen** to buy; **der Sieg war gekauft** it was fixed (c) **sich** (*dat*) **jdn ~** (*inf*) to give sb a piece of one's mind (*inf*); (*tätlich*) to fix sb (*inf*) **2** VI to buy; (= *Einkäufe machen*) to shop; **auf dem Markt kauft man billiger** it is cheaper to shop at the market; **das Kaufen** buying

Käufer [ˈkɔyfɐ] M **-s, -, Käuferin** [-ərɪn] F **-, -nen** buyer; (= *Kunde*) customer

Käufermarkt M buyer's market

Kauf-: Kauffrau F businesswoman; **Kaufhaus** NT department store; **Kaufhausdetektiv(in)** M(F) store detective; **Kaufkraft** F (*von Geld*) purchasing power; (*vom Käufer*) spending power; **Kunden mit ~** customers with money to spend; **kaufkräftig** ADJ **eine ~e Währung** a currency with good purchasing power; **~e Kunden** customers with money to spend; **ein ~er Markt** a market with strong purchasing power

Kaufkraft-: Kaufkraftindex M purchasing power index; **Kaufkraftlenkung** F control of (consumer) spending; **Kaufkraftschwund** M drop in purchasing power; **Kaufkraftüberhang** M excess (consumer) spending power; **Kaufkraftverlust** M loss of purchasing power; **Kaufladen** M (= *Spielzeug*) toy shop; **Kaufleute** PL *von* **Kaufmann**

käuflich [ˈkɔyflɪç] **1** ADJ (a) (= *zu kaufen*) for sale; **etwas, was nicht ~ ist** something which cannot be bought (b) (*fig*) venal; **~e Liebe** (*geh*) prostitution; **Freundschaft ist nicht ~** friendship cannot be bought (c) (*fig*: = *bestechlich*) venal; **~ sein** to be easily bought; **ich bin nicht ~** you cannot buy me! **2** ADV **etw ~ erwerben** (*form*) to purchase sth

Kaufmann M, *pl* **-leute** (a) (= *Geschäftsmann*) businessman; (= *Händler*) trader; (= *Tabakkaufmann, Gewürzkaufmann, Wollkaufmann etc*) merchant; **gelernter ~** person with qualifications in business (b) (= *Einzelhandelskaufmann*) small shopkeeper, grocer; **zum ~ gehen** to go to the grocer's

kaufmännisch [-mɛnɪʃ] **1** ADJ commercial; **~er Angestellter** office worker; **~e Buchführung** commercial book-keeping; **er wollte einen ~en Beruf ergreifen** he wanted to make a career in business; **er übt einen ~en Beruf aus** he is in business; **Fachschule für ~e Berufe** business school; **alles Kaufmännische** everything to do with business **2** ADV **sie ist ~ tätig** she is a businesswoman; **~ denken** to think in business terms; **nicht sehr ~ gedacht** not very businesslike

Kauf-: Kaufoption F (*St Ex*) call option; (*Comm*) option to buy; **Kaufpreis** M purchase price; **Kaufrausch** M spending spree; **im ~ sein** to be on a spending spree; **Kaufsucht** F compulsive shopping; **ihre ~** her shopping addiction; **kaufsüchtig** ADJ addicted to shopping; **~ sein** to be a shopaholic (*inf*); **Kaufvertrag** M bill of sale; **Kaufzwang** M obligation to buy; **kein/ohne ~** no/without obligation

Kaugummi M or NT chewing gum

kaukasisch [kau'ka:zɪʃ] ADJ Caucasian

Kaukasus [ˈkaukazʊs] M **- der ~** (the) Caucasus

Kaulquappe [ˈkaul-] F tadpole

kaum [kaum] **1** ADV (a) (= *noch nicht einmal*) hardly, scarcely; **er verdient ~ 1000 Euro** he earns barely 1000 euros; **das kostet ~ 200 Euro** it doesn't even cost 200 euros; **man braucht ~ 10 Liter** you'll need less than 10 litres (*Brit*) *or* liters (*US*); **~ jemand/jemals** hardly anyone/ever; **es ist ~ zu glauben, wie ...** it's hardly believable *or* to be believed how ...; **ich hatte ~ noch damit gerechnet, dass ...** I hardly thought that ... any more (b) (= *wahrscheinlich nicht*) hardly; **kaum!** hardly; **wohl ~, ich glaube ~** I hardly think so **2** CONJ hardly, scarcely; **~ dass wir das Meer erreicht hatten ...** no sooner had we reached the sea than ...; **~ gerufen, eilte der Diener herbei** no sooner summoned, the servant hurried in

Kaurimuschel [ˈkauri-] F cowrie shell

kausal [kau'za:l] **1** ADJ causal; **~ für etw sein** to be the cause of sth **2** ADV causally

Kausalität [kauzali'tɛ:t] F **-, -en** causality

Kausal-: Kausalsatz M causal clause; **Kausalzusammenhang** M causal connection

Kautabak M chewing tobacco

Kaution [kau'tsio:n] F **-, -en** (a) (*Jur*) bail; **~ stellen** to stand bail; **er stellte 1000 Euro ~** he put up 1000 euros (as) bail; **gegen ~** on bail; **jdn gegen ~ freilassen** to release sb on bail; **jdn gegen ~ freibekommen** to bail sb out (b) (*Comm*) security (c) (*für Miete*) deposit; **zwei Monatsmieten ~** two months' deposit

Kautschuk [ˈkautʃʊk] M **-s, -e** (India) rubber

Kauwerkzeuge PL masticatory organs *pl*

Kauz [kauts] M **-es, Käuze** [ˈkɔytsə] (a) screech owl (b) (= *Sonderling*) odd fellow; **ein komischer ~** an odd bird; **ein wunderlicher alter ~** a strange old bird

Käuzchen [ˈkɔytsçən] NT **-s,** DIM *von* **Kauz**

kauzig [ˈkautsɪç] **1** ADJ odd **2** ADV oddly

Kavalier [kava'li:ɐ] M **-s, -e** (= *galanter Mann*) gentleman; **der ~ genießt und schweigt** one does not boast about one's conquests

Kavaliersdelikt NT trivial offence (*Brit*) *or* offense (*US*)

Kavalier(s)start M (*Aut*) racing start

Kavallerie [kavalə'riː] F **-, -n** [-'riːən] (*Mil*) cavalry

Kaventsmann [ka'vɛnts-] M, *pl* **-männer** (*N Ger inf*) whopper (*inf*)

Kaviar ['kaːviar] M **-s, -e** caviar

KB [kaː'beː] NT **-(s), -(s)**, **KByte** ['kaːbait] NT **-(s), -(s)** ABBR *von* **Kilobyte** k, kbyte

kcal ABBR *von* **Kilokalorie**

Kebab [ke'baːp, ke'bap] M **-(s), -s** kebab

keck [kɛk] **1** ADJ **(a)** (= *frech*) cheeky (*Brit*), fresh (*US*) **(b)** (= *flott*) *Mädchen* pert; *Kleidungsstück* jaunty **2** ADV cheekily (*Brit*), saucily; **sie trug den Hut ~ auf einem Ohr** she wore her hat at a jaunty angle over one ear

Keckheit F **-, -en** (= *Frechheit*) cheekiness (*Brit*), impudence

Keeper ['kiːpɐ] M **-s, -**, **Keeperin** ['kiːpərɪn] F **-, -nen** (*Aus Sport*) (goal)keeper

Keepsmiling [kiːp'smailɪŋ] NT **-(s)**, NO PL fixed smile

Kefir ['keːfɪr, 'keːfiːr] M **-s**, NO PL kefir (*a milk product similar to yoghurt, of Turkish origin*)

Kegel ['keːgl] M **-s, -** (a) (= *Spielfigur*) skittle; (*bei Bowling*) pin **(b)** (*Geometrie*) cone; (= *Bergkegel*) peak **(c)** (= *Lichtkegel, Scheinwerferkegel*) beam (of light)

Kegel-: Kegelbahn F (bowling) lane; (= *Anlage*) skittle alley; (*automatisch*) bowling alley; **kegelförmig 1** ADJ conical **2** ADV conically; **Kegelkugel** F bowl

kegeln ['keːgln] VI to play skittles; (*bei Bowling*) to play bowls

Kehle ['keːlə] F **-, -n** (a) (= *Gurgel*) throat; **das ist ihm in die falsche ~ gekommen, er hat das in die falsche ~ bekommen** (*lit*) it went down the wrong way; (*fig*) he took it the wrong way; **aus voller ~** at the top of one's voice **(b)** (= *ausgerundeter Winkel*) moulding (*Brit*), molding (*US*); (= *Rille*) groove

Kehlkopf M larynx

Kehlkopf-: Kehlkopfentzündung F, **Kehlkopfkatarr(h)** M laryngitis; **Kehlkopfkrebs** M cancer of the throat; **Kehlkopfmikrofon** NT throat microphone

Kehllaut M guttural (sound)

Kehlung ['keːlʊŋ] F **-, -en** (*Archit*) groove, flute

Kehlverschlusslaut M (*Phon*) glottal stop

Kehr-: Kehraus ['keːrʔaus] M **-**, NO PL last dance; (*fig*: = *Abschiedsfeier*) farewell celebration; **Kehrbesen** M broom; **Kehrblech** NT (*S Ger*) shovel

Kehre ['keːrə] F **-, -n** (a) (sharp) bend; (= *Haarnadelkurve*) hairpin bend **(b)** (= *Turnübung*) rear vault

kehren[1] ['keːrən] **1** VT (a) (= *drehen*) to turn; **in sich** (*acc*) **gekehrt** (= *versunken*) pensive; (= *verschlossen*) introspective **(b)** (= *kümmern*) to bother; **was kehrt mich das?** what do I care about that?; **das kehrt mich einen Dreck!** (*inf*) I don't give a damn about that! (*inf*) **2** VR (a) (= *sich drehen*) to turn; **eines Tages wird sich sein Hochmut gegen ihn ~** one day his arrogance will rebound against him **(b)** (= *sich kümmern*) **er kehrt sich nicht daran, was die Leute sagen** he doesn't care what people say **3** VI to turn (round); (*Wind*) to turn

kehren[2] VTI (*esp S Ger*: = *fegen*) to sweep

Kehricht ['keːrɪçt] M *or* NT **-s**, NO PL (a) (*old, form*) sweepings *pl* **(b)** (*Sw*: = *Müll*) rubbish (*Brit*), trash (*US*)

Kehrichtsack M (*Sw*) rubbish bag

Kehrichtverbrennungsanlage F (*Sw*) incineration plant

Kehr-: Kehrmaschine F (= *Straßenkehrmaschine*) road-sweeper; (= *Teppichkehrmaschine*) carpet-sweeper; **Kehrplatz** M (*Sw*) turning area; **Kehrreim** M chorus; **Kehrschaufel** F shovel; **Kehrseite** F (*von Münze*) reverse; (*fig*: = *Nachteil*) drawback; (*fig*: = *Schattenseite*) other side; **die ~ der Medaille** the other side of the coin

Kehrt-: kehrtmachen VI SEP to turn round; (= *zurückgehen*) to turn back; (*Mil*) to about-turn; **Kehrtwendung** F about-turn

keifen ['kaifn] VI to bicker

Keil [kail] M **-(e)s, -e** wedge (*auch Mil*); (= *Faustkeil*) hand-axe (*Brit*), hand-ax (*US*); **einen ~ zwischen zwei Freunde treiben** (*fig*) to drive a wedge between two friends

Keilabsatz M wedge heel

Keile ['kailə] PL (*inf*) thrashing; **~ bekommen** *or* **kriegen** *or* **beziehen** to get *or* to be given a thrashing; **dahinten gibts gleich ~** there's going to be a fight over there

keilen ['kailən] **1** VT (a) (*mit Keil*) to wedge **(b)** (*dated sl*: = *anwerben*) *Mitglieder* to rope in (*inf*) **2** VR (*dial inf*: = *sich prügeln*) to fight

Keiler ['kailɐ] M **-s, -** wild boar

Keilerei [kailə'rai] F **-, -en** (*inf*) punch-up (*inf*)

Keil-: keilförmig ADJ wedge-shaped **2** ADV **sich ~ zuspitzen** to form a wedge; (*Turmspitze*) to form a point; **Keilhose** F, **Keilhosen** PL ski pants *pl*; **Keilkissen** NT, (*Aus*) **Keilpolster** NT wedge-shaped pillow (*used as a headrest*); **Keilriemen** M drive belt; (*Aut*) fan belt; **Keilschrift** F cuneiform script

Keim [kaim] M **-(e)s, -e** (a) (= *kleiner Trieb*) shoot **(b)** (= *Embryo*) (*fig*) embryo, germ; (= *Krankheitskeim*) germ; **im ~e** (*fig*) in embryonic form; **etw im ~ ersticken** to nip sth in the bud **(c)** (*fig*: *des Hasses, der Liebe etc*) seed *usu pl*; **den ~ zu etw legen** to sow the seeds of sth

keimen ['kaimən] VI (a) (*Saat*) to germinate; (*Pflanzen*) to put out shoots; (*Knollen*) to sprout **(b)** (*Verdacht*) to be aroused; (*Hoffnung*) to stir (*in one's breast* (*liter*)

Keim-: keimfrei ADJ germ-free, free of germs *pred*; (*Med, auch fig*) sterile; **~ machen** to sterilize; **Keimling** ['kaimlɪŋ] M **-s, -e** (a) (= *Embryo*) embryo **(b)** (= *Keimpflanze*) shoot; **keimtötend** ADJ germicidal; **~es Mittel** germicide

Keimung ['kaimʊŋ] F **-, -en** germination

Keimzelle F germ cell; (*fig*) nucleus

kein [kain], **keine** ['kainə], **kein** INDEF PRON (a) (*adjektivisch*) no; (*mit sing n*) no, not a; (*mit pl n, bei Sammelbegriffen, bei Abstrakten*) no, not any; **hast du ~ Gefühl?** haven't you got (*esp Brit*) *or* don't you have any feeling?; **ich sehe da ~en Unterschied** I don't see any difference; **sie hatte ~e Chance** she didn't have a *or* any chance; **er ist ~ Lehrer** he's no teacher; (= *~ guter auch*) he's no teacher; **~e Widerrede/Ahnung!** no arguing/idea!; **~e schlechte Idee** not a bad idea; **~e Lust!** don't want to; **~e Angst!** don't worry; **das ist ~e Antwort auf unsere Frage** that's not an *or* the answer to our question; **~ bisschen** not a bit; **ich habe ~ bisschen Lust/Zeit** I've absolutely no desire to/time; **~ anderer als er ...** only he ..., no-one else but he ...; **das habe ich ~em anderen als dir gesagt** I haven't told anybody else apart from you; **~ Einziger** (= *niemand*) not a single one *or* person; **~ einziges Mal** not a single time; **in ~ster Weise** (*strictly incorrect*) not in the least **(b)** (= *nicht einmal*) less than; **~e Stunde/drei Monate** less than an hour/three months; **~e 5 Euro** under 5 euros

keine(r, s) ['kainə] INDEF PRON (*substantivisch*) (= *niemand*) nobody (*auch subj*), no-one (*auch subj*), not anybody, not anyone; (*von Gegenstand*) not one, none; (*bei Abstraktum*) none; (*obj*) not any, none; (*von Gegenständen, bei Abstrakta*) none; (*obj*) not any, none; **es war ~d da** there was nobody *etc* there, there wasn't anybody *etc* there; (*Gegenstand*) there wasn't one there; **es waren ~ da** (*Gegenstände*) there weren't any there; **ich habe ~s** I haven't got one; **von diesen Platten ist ~ ...** none of these records is ...; **haben Sie Avocados? – nein, leider haben wir ~** do you have any avocados? – no, I'm afraid we haven't (any); **~r von uns/von uns beiden** none/neither of us; (*betont*) not one of us; **er hat ~n von beiden angetroffen** he didn't meet either of them, he met neither of them; **~s der (beiden) Kinder/Bücher** neither of the children/books; **~s der sechs Kinder/Bücher** none of the six children/books; (*betont*) not one of the six children/books

keinerlei [ˈkainɐˈlai] ADJ ATTR INV no ... what(so)ever *or* at all; **dafür gibt es ~ Beweise** there is no proof of it what(so)ever

keinesfalls [ˈkainəsˈfals] ADV under no circumstances, not ... under any circumstances; **das bedeutet jedoch ~, dass ...** however, in no way does this mean that ...

keineswegs [ˈkainəsˈveːks] ADV not at all; (*als Antwort*) not in the least; **ich fühle mich ~ schuldig** I do not feel in the least guilty

keinmal [ˈkainmaːl] ADV never once, not once; **ich bin ihr noch ~ begegnet** I've never met her

keins [kains] = **keines**

Keks [keːks] M **-es, -e** *or* (*Aus*) nt **-, -** biscuit (*Brit*), cookie (*US*); **jdm auf den ~ gehen** (*inf*) to get on sb's nerves

Kelch [kɛlç] M **-(e)s, -e (a)** (= *Trinkglas*) goblet; (*Eccl*) chalice; **dieser ~ ist noch einmal an mir vorübergegangen** I have been spared again **(b)** (*Bot*) calyx

Kelchglas NT goblet

Kelle [ˈkɛlə] F **-, -n (a)** (= *Suppenkelle etc*) ladle; (= *Schaumlöffel*) straining spoon **(b)** (= *Maurerkelle*) trowel **(c)** (= *Signalstab*) signalling (*Brit*) *or* signaling (*US*) disc

Keller [ˈkɛlɐ] M **-s, -** cellar; (= *Geschoss*) basement; (= *Esslokal*) (cellar) restaurant; (= *Kneipe*) (cellar) bar; **im ~ sein** (*fig*) to be at rock-bottom; **in den ~ rutschen** *or* **fallen** (*fig*) to reach rock-bottom

Kellerassel F woodlouse

Kellerei [kɛləˈrai] F **-, -en** (= *Weinkellerei*) wine producer's; (= *Sektkellerei*) champagne producer's; (= *Lagerraum*) cellar(s *pl*)

Keller-: Kellergeschoss NT basement; **Kellergewölbe** NT vaulted cellar roof; (= *Keller*) cellars *pl*; (= *Verlies*) dungeon; **Kellerkneipe** F (*inf*), **Kellerlokal** NT cellar bar; **Kellermeister(in)** M(F) vintner; (*in Kloster*) cellarer; **Kellerwohnung** F basement flat (*Brit*) *or* apartment

Kellner [ˈkɛlnɐ] M **-s, -** waiter

Kellnerin [ˈkɛlnərɪn] F **-, -nen** waitress

kellnern [ˈkɛlnɐn] VI (*inf*) to work as a waiter/waitress, to wait on tables (*US*)

Kelte [ˈkɛltə] M **-n, -n**, **Keltin** [ˈkɛltɪn] F **-, -nen** Celt

Kelter [ˈkɛltɐ] F **-, -n** winepress; (= *Obstkelter*) press

keltern [ˈkɛltɐn] VT *Trauben, Wein* to press

keltisch [ˈkɛltɪʃ] ADJ Celtic

Kenia [ˈkeːnia] NT **-s** Kenya

kenianisch [keˈniaːnɪʃ] ADJ Kenyan

kennen [ˈkɛnən], *pret* **kannte** [ˈkantə], *ptp* **gekannt** [gəˈkant] VT to know; **er kennt das Leben** he knows about life; **er kennt den Hunger nicht** he doesn't know what hunger is; **er kennt keine Müdigkeit** he never gets tired; **so was ~ wir hier nicht!** we don't have that sort of thing here; **jdn als etw ~** to know sb to be sth; **~ Sie sich schon?** do you know each other (already)?; **~ Sie den (schon)?** (*Witz*) have you heard this one?; **das ~ wir (schon)** (*iro*) we know all about that; **kennst du mich noch?** do you remember me?; **wie ich ihn kenne ...** if I know him (at all) ...; **du kennst dich doch!** you know what you're like; **so kenne ich dich ja (noch) gar nicht!** I've never known you like this before; **da kennst du mich aber schlecht** that just shows how little you know me; **da kennt er gar nichts** (*inf*) (= *hat keine Hemmungen*) he has no scruples whatsoever; (= *ihm ist alles egal*) he doesn't give a damn (*inf*)

kennen lernen VT to get to know; (= *zum ersten Mal treffen*) to meet; **sich ~** to get to know each other; to meet each other; **jdn/einen näher ~** to get to know sb/sth better; **ich freue mich, Sie kennen zu lernen** (*form*) (I am) pleased to meet you; **ich habe ihn als einen zuverlässigen Mitarbeiter kennen gelernt** I came to know him as a reliable colleague; **der soll** *or* **wird mich noch ~** (*inf*) he'll have me to reckon with (*inf*); **bei näherem Kennenlernen erwies er sich als ...** on closer acquaintance he proved to be ...

Kenner [ˈkɛnɐ] M **-s, -**, **Kennerin** [-ərɪn] F **-, -nen** **(a)** (= *Sachverständiger*) expert (*von, +gen* on *or* in), authority (*von, +gen* on); **~ der internen Vorgänge** those who know about the internal procedures **(b)** (= *Weinkenner etc*) connoisseur

Kennerblick M expert's eye

kennerhaft 🔳 ADJ like a connoisseur; **mit ~em Blick/Griff** with the eye/touch of an expert 🔳 ADV expertly; *lächeln, nicken* knowingly

Kennermiene F connoisseur's expression; **mit ~ betrachtete er ...** he looked at ... like a connoisseur; **er versuchte, eine ~ aufzusetzen** he tried to look like a connoisseur; (*bei Erklärung etc*) he tried to look knowledgeable

kenntlich [ˈkɛntlɪç] ADJ (= *zu erkennen*) recognizable (*an +dat* by); (= *deutlich*) clear; **etw ~ machen** to identify sth (clearly); **etw für jdn ~ machen** to make sth clear to sb; **bei Dunkelheit gut ~ sein** to be easily distinguishable in the dark

Kenntnis [ˈkɛntnɪs] F **-, -se (a)** (= *Wissen*) knowledge *no pl*; **über ~se von etw verfügen** to know about sth; **gute ~se in Mathematik haben** to have a good knowledge of mathematics **(b)** NO PL (*form*) **etw zur ~ nehmen, von etw ~ nehmen** to note sth; **ich nehme zur ~, dass ...** I note that ...; **zur ~** (*auf Mitteilung*) for your information; **jdn von etw in ~ setzen** to inform sb about sth; **von etw ~ erhalten** to learn about sth; **das entzieht sich meiner ~** I have no knowledge of it

Kenntnisnahme [-naːmə] F **-,** NO PL (*form*) **zur ~ an ...** for the attention of ...; **nach ~** after perusal (*form*)

-kenntnisse [kɛntnɪsə] PL SUF IN CPDS knowledge of ...; **Sprach-/Englischkenntnisse** knowledge of languages/English

Kenntnisstand M, NO PL **nach dem neuesten ~** according to the latest information

Kennung [ˈkɛnʊŋ] F **-, -en** (*Telec*) call sign; (*von Leuchtfeuern*) signal; (*Comput*) password

Kennwort NT, *pl* **-wörter** (= *Chiffre*) codename; (= *Losungswort*) password, codeword; (*Comm*) reference

Kennzeichen NT **(a)** (*Aut*) number plate (*Brit*), license plate (*US*); (*Aviat*) markings *pl*; **amtliches** *or* **polizeiliches ~** registration number (*Brit*), license number (*US*) **(b)** (= *Markierung*) mark; (*bei Tier*) marking(s *pl*); (*in Personenbeschreibung*) **unveränderliche ~** distinguishing marks; **besondere ~** particular characteristics **(c)** (= *Eigenart, Charakteristikum*) (typical) characteristic (*für, +gen* of); (*für Qualität*) hallmark; (= *Erkennungszeichen*) mark, sign; **als ~ eine Nelke im Knopfloch vereinbaren** to agree on a carnation in one's buttonhole as a means of identification

kennzeichnen VT INSEP **(a)** (= *markieren*) to mark; (*durch Etikett*) to label; *Weg etc* to signpost **(b)** (= *charakterisieren*) to characterize; **jdn als etw ~** to show sb to be sth

Kennziffer F (code) number; (*Math*) characteristic; (*Comm*) reference number; (*bei Zeitungsinserat*) box number

kentern [ˈkɛntɐn] VI AUX SEIN (*Schiff*) to capsize

Keramik [keˈraːmɪk] F **-, -en (a)** NO PL (*Art*) ceramics *pl*; (*als Gebrauchsgegenstände*) pottery; (= *Arbeitszweig*) ceramics *sing* **(b)** (= *Kunstgegenstand*) ceramic; (= *Gebrauchsgegenstand*) piece of pottery; **~en** ceramics/pottery

keramisch [keˈraːmɪʃ] ADJ ceramic; *Gebrauchsgegenstand auch* pottery

Kerbe [ˈkɛrbə] F **-, -n** notch; (*kleiner*) nick; **in die gleiche** *or* **dieselbe ~ hauen** *or* **schlagen** (*fig inf*) to take the same line

Kerbel [ˈkɛrbl] M **-s,** NO PL chervil

kerben [ˈkɛrbn] VT *Holz* to cut *or* carve a notch/notches in; *Inschrift, Namen* to carve

Kerbholz NT (*fig inf*) **etwas auf dem ~ haben** to have done something wrong; **er hat so manches auf dem ~** he has quite a record

Kerbtier NT insect

Kerker [ˈkɛrkɐ] M **-s, - (a)** (*Hist, geh*) dungeon (*esp Hist*), prison; (= *Strafe*) imprisonment **(b)** (*Aus*) = **Zuchthaus**

Kerl [kɛrl] M **-s, -e** *or* **-s** (*inf*) guy (*inf*); (*pej*) character; (= *Mädchen*) girl; **du gemeiner ~!** you mean thing (*inf*); **ein ganzer** *or* **richtiger ~** a real man; **er ist nicht ~ genug dazu** he is not man enough to do that

Kern [kɛrn] M **-(e)s, -e** (*von Obst*) pip; (*von Steinobst*) stone; (= *Nusskern*) kernel; (*Phys, Biol*) nucleus; (*fig*) (*von Problem, Sache*) heart; (*von Gruppe*) core; **jede Legende hat einen wahren ~** at the heart of every legend there is a core of truth; **in ihr steckt ein guter ~** there's some good in her somewhere; **der harte ~** (*fig*) the hard core

Kern- IN CPDS (= *Nuklear-*) nuclear; **Kernarbeitszeit** F core time; **Kernbrennstoff** M nuclear fuel; **Kernenergie** F nuclear energy; **Kernfach** NT (*Sch*) core subject; **Kernfamilie** F (*Sociol*) nuclear family; **Kernforscher(in)** M(F) nuclear scientist; **Kernforschung** F nuclear research; **Kernforschungszentrum** NT nuclear research centre (*Brit*) *or* center (*US*); **Kernfrage** F central issue; **Kernfusion** F nuclear fusion; **Kerngebiet** NT heartland; **Kerngedanke** M central idea; **Kerngehäuse** NT core; **kerngesund** ADJ completely fit; (fig) Staatshaushalt, Firma, Land very healthy

kernig ['kɛrnɪç] **1** ADJ **(a)** (fig) Ausspruch pithy; (= urwüchsig) earthy; (= kraftvoll) robust; (sl: = gut) great (inf) **(b)** (lit) Frucht full of pips **2** ADV pithily

Kernkraft F -, NO PL nuclear power

Kernkraft- IN CPDS nuclear power; **Kernkraftbefürworter(in)** M(F) supporter of nuclear power; **Kernkraftgegner(in)** M(F) opponent of nuclear power; **Kernkraftwerk** NT nuclear power station

Kern-: **kernlos** ADJ seedless; **Kernobst** NT pomes pl (spec); **Kernphysik** F nuclear physics sing; **Kernphysiker(in)** M(F) nuclear physicist; **Kernplasma** NT nucleoplasm; **Kernpunkt** M central point; **Kernreaktion** F nuclear reaction; **Kernreaktor** M nuclear reactor; **Kernsatz** M key sentence, key phrase; (Ling) kernel sentence; (Satzform) simple sentence; **Kernschatten** M complete shadow; (Astron) umbra; **Kernschmelze** F meltdown; **Kernseife** F washing soap; **Kernspaltung** F nuclear fission; **die erste ~** the first splitting of the atom; **Kernspin-Tomograf** ['kɛrnspɪn-] M MRI scanner; **Kernspin-Tomografie** F magnetic resonance imaging; **Kernstück** NT (fig) centrepiece (Brit), centerpiece (US); (von Theorie etc) crucial part; (von Roman etc) crucial passage; **Kerntechnik** F nuclear technology; **kerntechnisch** ADJ ~e Anlage nuclear plant; ~e Entwicklung development of nuclear technology; **Kernteilchen** NT nuclear particle; **Kernteilung** F (Biol) nuclear division; **Kernunterricht** M (Sch) core curriculum; **Kernverschmelzung** F (Phys) nuclear fusion; (Biol) cell union

Kernwaffe F nuclear weapon

Kernwaffen-: **kernwaffenfrei** ADJ nuclear-free; **Kernwaffensperrvertrag** M Nuclear Nonproliferation Treaty; **Kernwaffenversuch** M nuclear (weapons) test

Kernzeit F core time

Kerosin [kero'ziːn] NT -s, -e kerosene

Kerze ['kɛrtsə] F -, -n **(a)** (= Wachskerze, Blüte der Kastanie) candle **(b)** (Aut) plug **(c)** (Turnen) shoulder-stand **(d)** (Ftbl) skyer

Kerzen-: **kerzengerade** ADJ (lit) perfectly straight; (fig) Mensch (as) straight as a die (Brit) or an arrow (US); **Kerzenhalter** M candlestick; (am Weihnachtsbaum, auf Kuchen etc) candle holder; **Kerzenleuchter** M candlestick; **Kerzenlicht** NT, NO PL candlelight; **Kerzenschlüssel** M (spark) plug spanner (Brit), (spark) plug wrench (US)

Kescher ['kɛʃɐ] M -s, - fishing net; (= Hamen) landing net

kess [kɛs] **1** ADJ (= flott) saucy; Kleid, Hut etc jaunty; (= vorwitzig) cheeky (Brit), fresh (US); (= frech) impudent; **eine ~e Lippe riskieren** to be cheeky (Brit) or fresh (US) **2** ADV saucily

Kessel ['kɛsl] M -s, - **(a)** (= Teekessel) kettle; (= Waschkessel) copper; (= Kochkessel) pot; (für offenes Feuer) cauldron; (esp in Brauerei) vat; (= Dampfkessel) boiler; (= Behälter für Flüssigkeiten etc) tank **(b)** (= Mulde) basin; (Hunt) semi-circular ring of hunters; (Mil) encircled area

Kessel-: **Kesselpauke** F kettle drum; **Kesselstein** M scale; **Kesseltreiben** NT (Hunt) hunt using a circle of beaters; (fig: in Zeitung etc) witch-hunt

Ketchup ['kɛtʃap] M or NT -(s), -s siehe **Ketschup**

Ketschup ['kɛtʃap] M or NT -(s), -s ketchup

Kette ['kɛtə] F -, -n (lit, fig) chain; (von Kettenfahrzeug) chain track; (fig) (von Menschen, Fahrzeugen) line; (von Unfällen, Erfahrungen etc) string; **jdn an die ~ legen** (fig) to keep sb on a tight leash; **eine ~ von Ereignissen** a chain of events

ketten ['kɛtn] VT to chain (an +acc to); jdn an sich (acc) ~ (fig) to bind sb to oneself; **sich an jdn/etw ~** (fig) to tie oneself to sb/sth

Ketten-: **Kettenbrief** M chain letter; **Kettenfahrzeug** NT tracked vehicle; **Kettenglied** NT (chain-)link; **Kettenhemd** NT (Hist) coat of (chain) mail; **Kettenkarussell** NT merry-go-round (with gondolas or seats suspended on chains); **Kettenraucher(in)** M(F) chain-smoker; **Kettenreaktion** F chain reaction; **Kettensäge** F chain saw; **Kettenschaltung** F dérailleur gear

Ketzer ['kɛtsɐ] M -s, -, **Ketzerin** [-ərɪn] F -, -nen (Eccl, fig) heretic

Ketzerei [kɛtsə'raɪ] F -, NO PL heresy

ketzerisch ['kɛtsərɪʃ] **1** ADJ (Eccl, fig) heretical **2** ADV heretically; **~ klingen** to sound like heresy

keuchen ['kɔʏçn] VI **(a)** (= schwer atmen) to pant; (Asthmatiker etc) to wheeze; **mit ~dem Atem** panting; wheezing **(b)** AUX SEIN (= sich fortbewegen) to puff

Keuchhusten M whooping cough

Keule ['kɔʏlə] F -, -n club; (Sport) (Indian) club; (Cook) leg; (von Wild) leg; **chemische ~** (bei Polizeieinsatz) Chemical Mace®; **die chemische ~ einsetzen** (Agr: zur Insektenvernichtung etc) to use chemical agents

keusch [kɔʏʃ] **1** ADJ chaste **2** ADV chastely

Keuschheit F -, NO PL chastity

Keuschheitsgürtel M chastity belt

Keyboard ['kiːbɔːɐd] NT -s, -s (Mus) keyboard; **sie spielt ~** she plays keyboards

Keyboardspieler(in) ['kiːbɔːɐd-] M(F) (Mus) keyboards player

kfm. ABBR von **kaufmännisch**

Kfz [kaːɛf'tsɛt] NT -(s), -(s) (form) ABBR von **Kraftfahrzeug** motor vehicle

Kfz- IN CPDS = **Kraftfahrzeug-**

kg ABBR von **Kilogramm** kg

KG [kaː'geː] F -, -s ABBR von **Kommanditgesellschaft** ≈ limited partnership

KGaA ABBR von **Kommanditgesellschaft auf Aktien**

KGB [kageː'beː] M -(s), NO PL (Hist) KGB

khaki ['kaːki] ADJ INV khaki

KHz, kHz ABBR von **Kilohertz** kHz

Kibbuz [kɪ'buːts] M -, **Kibbuzim** or -e [kibu'tsiːm] kibbutz

Kicherei [kɪçə'raɪ] F -, -en giggling

Kichererbse F chickpea

kichern ['kɪçɐn] VI to giggle

Kick [kɪk] M -(s), -s (inf: = Stoß) kick; (sl: = Spiel) kick-about; (fig inf: = Nervenkitzel) kick (inf)

Kickboard® ['kɪkbɔːɐt] NT -s, -s micro-scooter

Kickboxen NT kick boxing

kicken ['kɪkn] (Ftbl inf) **1** VT to kick **2** VI to play football (Brit) or soccer; (= den Ball ~) to kick; **für eine Mannschaft ~** to play for a team

Kicker ['kɪkɐ] M -s, -, **Kickerin** [-ərɪn] F -, -nen (Ftbl inf) player

Kickstarter M (bei Motorrad) kick-starter

Kid [kɪt] NT -s, -s USU PL (inf: = Jugendlicher) kid (inf)

kidnappen ['kɪtnɛpn] VT INSEP to kidnap

Kidnapper ['kɪtnɛpɐ] M -s, -, **Kidnapperin** [-ərɪn] F -, -nen kidnapper

Kidnapping ['kɪtnɛpɪŋ] NT -s, -s kidnapping

Kiebitz ['kiːbɪts] M -es, -e (Orn) lapwing; (Cards inf) kibitzer

Kiefer¹ ['kiːfɐ] F -, -n pine (tree); (= Holz) pine(wood)

Kiefer² M -s, - jaw; (= ~knochen) jawbone

Kiefer-: **Kieferbruch** M broken or fractured jaw; **Kieferchirurg(in)** M(F) oral surgeon; **Kieferhöhle** F (Anat) maxillary sinus

Kiefernzapfen M pine cone

Kiefer-: **Kieferorthopäde** M, **Kieferorthopädin** F orthodontist; **Kieferorthopädie** F orthodontics sing

Kieker ['kiːkɐ] M -s, - **jdn auf dem ~ haben** (inf) to have it in for sb (inf)

Kiel [kiːl] M -(e)s, -e **(a)** (= Schiffskiel) keel; **ein Schiff auf ~ legen** to lay down a ship **(b)** (= Federkiel) quill

Kiel-: **kielholen** VT INSEP (Naut) **(a)** Schiff to careen **(b)** Matrosen to keelhaul; **Kielwasser** NT wake; **in jds ~** (dat) **segeln** or **schwimmen** (fig) to follow in sb's wake

Kieme ['kiːmə] F -, -n gill

Kies [kiːs] M **-es, -e** gravel; (*am Strand*) shingle

Kiesel [ˈkiːzl] M **-s,** - pebble

Kiesel-: **Kieselerde** F silica; **Kieselsäure** F (*Chem*) silicic acid; (= *Siliziumdioxyd*) silica; **Kieselstein** M pebble; **Kieselstrand** M pebble beach

Kiesgrube F gravel pit

Kiez [kiːts] M **-es, -e** (*dial*) **(a)** (= *Stadtgegend*) district **(b)** (*inf*: = *Bordellgegend*) red-light district

kiffen [ˈkɪfn] VI (*inf*) to smoke pot (*inf*)

Kiffer [ˈkɪfɐ] M **-s,** -, **Kifferin** [-ərɪn] F **-, -nen** (*inf*) pot-smoker (*inf*)

kikeriki [kikəriˈkiː] INTERJ cock-a-doodle-doo

Kilbi [ˈkɪlbi] F **-, Kilbenen** [ˈkɪlbənən] (*Sw*) fair

killen [ˈkɪlən] (*sl*) **1** VT to bump off (*inf*); (*esp mit Auftrag*) to hit (*inf*) **2** VI to kill

Killer [ˈkɪlɐ] M **-s,** -, **Killerin** [-ərɪn] F **-, -nen** (*inf*) killer; (*gedungener*) hit man/woman

Killer- IN CPDS killer; **Killerinstinkt** M (*inf*) killer instinct; **Killerzelle** F (*Physiol*) killer cell

Kilo [ˈkiːlo] NT **-s, -s** *or* (*bei Zahlenangabe*) - kilo

Kilo- [kiːlo] IN CPDS kilo-; **Kilobyte** NT kilobyte; **Kilogramm** [kiloˈgram] NT kilogram(me); **Kilohertz** [kiloˈhɛrts, ˈkilo-] NT kilohertz; **Kilojoule** NT kilojoule; **Kilokalorie** F kilocalorie

Kilometer [kiloˈmeːtɐ] M kilometre (*Brit*), kilometer (*US*); (*inf*: = *Stundenkilometer*) k (*inf*); **wir konnten nur 80 ~ fahren** we could only do 80

Kilometer-: **Kilometergeld** NT mileage (allowance); **kilometerlang** **1** ADJ miles long; **~e Strände** miles and miles of beaches; **ein ~er Stau** a traffic jam several miles/kilometres (*Brit*) *or* kilometers (*US*) long **2** ADV for miles (and miles); **Kilometerpauschale** F mileage allowance (against tax); **Kilometerstand** M mileage; **kilometerweit** **1** ADJ miles long; **in ~er Entfernung** miles away in the distance **2** ADV for miles (and miles); **Kilometerzähler** M mileage indicator

Kilo-: **Kilowatt** [kiloˈvat, ˈkilo-] NT kilowatt; **Kilowattstunde** F kilowatt hour

Kimme [ˈkɪmə] F **-, -n (a)** (*von Gewehr*) back sight **(b)** (*inf*: = *Gesäßfalte*) cleft between the buttocks

Kimono [ˈkiːmono, kiˈmoːno, ˈkɪmono] M **-s, -s** kimono

Kind [kɪnt] NT **-(e)s, -er** [-dɐ] child, kid (*inf*); (= *Kleinkind*) baby; (*esp Psych, Med*) infant; **ein ~ erwarten** to be expecting a baby; **ein ~ bekommen** *or* **kriegen** to have a baby; **von ~ an** *or* **auf hat er ...** since he was a child he has ...; **ein ~ seiner Zeit sein** to be a child of one's times; **sie ist kein ~ von Traurigkeit** (*hum*) she enjoys life; **er ist ein großes ~** he's a big baby; **sich freuen wie ein ~** to be as pleased as Punch; **er kann sich wie ein ~ freuen** he takes a childlike pleasure in (simple) things; **das weiß doch jedes ~!** any five-year-old would tell you that!; **da kommt das ~ im Manne durch** all men are boys at heart; **wie sag ichs meinem ~e?** (*hum*) I don't know how to put it; (*bei Aufklärung*) what to tell your children; **das ist nichts für kleine ~er** (*fig inf*) that's not for your young ears/eyes; **aus ~ern werden Leute** (*prov*) children grow up quickly, don't they?; **er und Narren** *or* **Betrunkene sagen die Wahrheit** (*fig*) children and fools speak the truth; **mit ~ und Kegel** (*hum inf*) with the whole family; **das ~ mit dem Bade ausschütten** (*prov*) to throw out the baby with the bathwater (*prov*); **los, ~er!** let's go, kids!; **hört mal alle her, ~er!** listen, kids; **~er, ~er!** dear, dear!

Kindchen [ˈkɪntçən] NT **-s,** - DIM *von* **Kind** child; (*zu Erwachsenen*) kid(do) (*inf*)

Kindel [ˈkɪndl] NT **-s, -(n)** (*dial*) DIM *von* **Kind** kiddy

Kinder-: **Kinderarbeit** F child labour (*Brit*) *or* labor (*US*); **Kinderarzt** M, **Kinderärztin** F paediatrician (*Brit*), pediatrician (*US*); **Kinderbeihilfe** F (*Aus*) *benefit paid for having children*; **Kinderbekleidung** F children's wear; **Kinderbett** NT cot; **Kinderbuch** NT children's book

Kinderchen [ˈkɪndɐçən] PL children *pl*

Kinderdorf NT children's village

Kinderei [kɪndɐˈrai] F **-, -en** childishness *no pl*; **~en** childishness

Kinder-: **Kindererziehung** F bringing up of children; (*durch Schule*) education of children; **sie versteht nichts von ~** she knows nothing about bringing up/educating children;

Kinderfahrkarte F child's ticket; **Kinderfahrrad** NT child's bicycle; **kinderfeindlich** **1** ADJ anti-child; *Architektur, Planung* not catering for children; **~e Steuerpolitik** tax policies which penalize having children; **eine ~e Gesellschaft** a society hostile to children **2** ADV without regard to children; **sich ~ verhalten** to be hostile to children; **Kinderfeindlichkeit** F hostility to children; (*von Architektur*) failure to cater for children; **Kinderfernsehen** NT children's television; **Kinderfest** NT children's party *or* (*von Stadt etc*) fête; **Kinderfreibetrag** M child allowance; **kinderfreundlich** **1** ADJ *Mensch* fond of children; *Gesellschaft* child-orientated; *Möbel, Architektur etc* child-friendly; **eine ~e Steuerpolitik** a tax policy which encourages one to have children **2** ADV with children in mind; **sich ~ verhalten** to be tolerant of children; **sich ~ geben** to show a fondness for children; (*heucheln*) to pretend to be fond of children; **Kinderfreundlichkeit** F (*von Mensch*) fondness for children; (*von Möbeln, Architektur etc*) child-friendliness; **der Autor beklagt die mangelnde ~ in Deutschland** the author laments the fact that German society is not child-orientated; **Kindergarten** M ≈ nursery school, ≈ kindergarten

Kinder-: **Kindergärtner(in)** M(F) ≈ nursery-school teacher; **Kindergeld** NT *benefit paid for having children*; **Kindergesicht** NT baby face; **Kinderheilkunde** F paediatrics *sing* (*Brit*), pediatrics *sing* (*US*); **Facharzt für ~** paediatrician (*Brit*), pediatrician (*US*); **Kinderheim** NT children's home; **Kinderhort** [-hɔrt] M **-(e)s, -e** day-nursery (*Brit*), daycare centre (*Brit*) *or* center (*US*); **Kinderkleidung** F children's clothes *pl*; **Kinderkram** M (*inf*) kids' stuff (*inf*); **Kinderkrankenhaus** NT children's hospital; **Kinderkrankheit** F childhood illness; (*fig*) teething troubles *pl*; **Kinderkrippe** F day-nursery (*Brit*), daycare centre (*Brit*) *or* center (*US*); **kinderleicht** **1** ADJ dead easy (*inf*); **es ist ~** it's kid's stuff (*inf*) **2** ADV easily

Kinderlein [ˈkɪndɐlain] PL children *pl*

Kinder-: **kinderlieb** ADJ fond of children; **Kinderlied** NT nursery rhyme; **kinderlos** ADJ childless; **Kindermädchen** F nanny; **Kindermärchen** NT (children's) fairy tale; **Kindermord** M child murder; (*Jur*) infanticide; **der bethlehemitische ~** (*Bibl*), **der ~ zu Bethlehem** (*Bibl*) the massacre of the innocents; **Kinderpfleger** M paediatric (*Brit*) *or* pediatric (*US*) nurse; **Kinderpflegerin** F paediatric (*Brit*) *or* pediatric (*US*) nurse; (= *Kindermädchen*) nanny; **Kinderpopo** M (*inf*) baby's bottom (*inf*); **glatt wie ein ~** smooth as a baby's bottom (*inf*); **Kinderpornografie** F child pornography; **Kinderprostitution** F child prostitution; **Kinderraub** M baby-snatching; (= *Entführung*) kidnapping (of a child/children); **kinderreich** ADJ with many children; *Familie* large; **Kinderreichtum** M an abundance of children; **der ~ Kenias** the abundance of children in Kenya; **Kinderreim** M nursery rhyme; **Kinderreisebett** NT travel cot; **Kinderschar** F swarm of children; **Kinderschuh** M child's shoe; **~e sind teuer** children's shoes are dear; **etw steckt noch in den ~en** (*fig*) sth is still in its infancy; **Kinderschutz** M protection of children; **Kinderschutzbund** M, *pl* **-bünde** child protection agency, ≈ NSPCC (*Brit*); **Kinderschwester** F paediatric (*Brit*) *or* pediatric (*US*) nurse; **kindersicher** **1** ADJ childproof **2** ADV *aufbewahren* out of reach of children; **die Autotür lässt sich ~ verschließen** the car door has a child lock; **die Flasche lässt sich ~ verschließen** the bottle has a childproof cap; **Kindersicherung** F (*Aut*) child lock; (*an Flasche*) childproof cap; **Kindersitz** M child's seat; (*im Auto*) child seat; **Kinderspiel** NT children's game; (*fig*) child's play *no art*; **Kinderspielplatz** M children's playground; **Kinderspielzeug** NT (children's) toys *pl*; **Kinderstation** F children's ward; **Kindersterblichkeit** F infant mortality; **Kinderstreich** M childish prank; **Kinderstube** F (*fig*) upbringing; **Kinderstuhl** M child's chair; (= *Hochstuhl*) high chair; **Kindertagesheim**

NT, **Kindertagesstätte** F day nursery (*Brit*), daycare centre (*Brit*) or center (*US*);

Kindertagesstätten, or *KiTas* for short, are daycare centres for children whose parents are in full-time employment. They range from crèches for babies to playgroups for children between the ages of one and three and day centres for children of school age.

Kinder-: Kinderteller M (*in Restaurant*) children's portion; **Kindervers** M nursery rhyme; **Kinderwagen** M pram (*Brit*), baby carriage (*US*); (= *Sportwagen*) pushchair (*Brit*), (baby-)stroller (*esp US*); **Kinderzimmer** NT child's/children's room; (*esp für Kleinkinder*) nursery; **Kinderzulage** F, **Kinderzuschlag** M child benefit (*Brit*), *benefit paid for having children*

Kindes-: Kindesalter NT childhood; **im ~** at an early age; **Kindesaussetzung** F abandoning of children; **~en** cases of children being abandoned; **Kindesbeine** PL **von ~n** from childhood; **Kindesentführung** F kidnapping (of a child/children); **Kindesentziehung** F (*Jur*) child abduction; **Kindesmisshandlung** F child abuse; **Kindestötung** F (*Jur: von eigenem Säugling*) infanticide; **Kindesverwechslung** F confusion of children's identity

Kind-: Kindfrau F Lolita; **kindgemäß** ◼ ADJ suitable for children/a child ◼ ADV appropriately for children/a child; **kindhaft** ADJ childlike

Kindheit F **-, -en** childhood; (= *früheste ~*) infancy

Kindheits-: Kindheitserinnerung F childhood memory; **Kindheitstraum** M childhood dream

Kindi ['kɪndi] M **-s, -** (*inf*: = *Kindergarten*) nursery

kindisch ['kɪndɪʃ] (*pej*) ◼ ADJ childish ◼ ADV childishly; **sich ~ über etw** (*acc*) **freuen** to be as pleased as Punch about sth; **er kann sich ~ freuen** he takes a childlike pleasure in (simple) things

kindlich ['kɪndlɪç] ◼ ADJ childlike ◼ ADV like a child; **~ wirken** to be childlike

Kindlichkeit F **-,** NO PL childlikeness

Kinds- IN CPDS *siehe auch* **Kindes-: Kindskopf** M (*inf*) big kid (*inf*); **sei kein ~** don't be so childish; **Kindslage** F (*Med*) presentation of the foetus (*Brit*) or fetus (*US*); **Kindstod** M **plötzlicher ~** cot death (*Brit*), crib death (*US*)

Kinetik [ki'ne:tɪk] F **-,** NO PL kinetics *sing*

kinetisch [ki'ne:tɪʃ] ADJ kinetic

King [kɪŋ] M **-(s), -s** (*inf*) king

Kinkerlitzchen ['kɪŋkɛlɪtsçən] PL (*inf*) knick-knacks *pl* (*inf*)

Kinn [kɪn] NT **-(e)s, -e** chin

Kinn-: Kinnhaken M hook to the chin; **Kinnlade** [-la:də] F **-, -n** jaw(-bone)

Kino ['ki:no] NT **-s, -s** cinema; **ins ~ gehen** to go to the cinema

Kino- IN CPDS cinema, movie (*esp US*); **Kinocenter** [-sɛntɐ] NT **-s, -** cinema complex; **Kinogänger** [-gɛŋɐ] M **-s, -**, **Kinogängerin** [-ərɪn] F **-, -nen** cinemagoer (*Brit*), moviegoer (*US*); **Kinohit** M blockbuster

Kiosk ['ki:ɔsk, kiɔsk] M **-(e)s, -e** kiosk

Kipa ['kɪpa] F **-, -s** kippa

Kippe ['kɪpə] F **-, -n (a)** (*Sport*) spring **(b) auf der ~ stehen** (*Gegenstand*) to be balanced precariously; **sie steht auf der ~** (*fig*) it's touch and go with her; **es steht auf der ~, ob ...** (*fig*) it's touch and go whether ...; **zwei Schüler stehen auf der ~** two pupils might have to repeat the year **(c)** (*inf*) (= *Zigarettenstummel*) cigarette stub; (= *Zigarette*) fag (*Brit inf*), butt (*US inf*) **(d)** (= *Müllkippe, Min*) tip

kippen ['kɪpn] ◼ VT **(a)** *Behälter, Fenster* to tilt; *Ladefläche, Tisch* to tip (up); (= *umstoßen*) *Urteil* to overturn; *Regierung, Minister* to topple; **einen ~** (*inf*: = *trinken*) to have a drink; **ein paar** or **einen hinter die Binde** or **hinter den Latz ~** (*inf*) to have a couple (*inf*)
(b) (*mit Ortsangabe:* = *schütten*) to tip
◼ VI AUX SEIN to tip over; (*esp höhere Gegenstände*) to topple (over); (*Fahrzeug, Schiff*) to overturn; (*Mensch*) to topple; (*Wechselkurse, Gewinne*) to plummet; **aus den Latschen** or **Pantinen ~** (*fig inf*) (= *überrascht sein*) to fall through the floor (*inf*); (= *ohnmächtig werden*) to pass out

Kippfenster NT tilt window

Kipp-: Kipplore F tipper wagon; **Kippschalter** M toggle switch

Kirche ['kɪrçə] F **-, -n** (= *Gebäude, Organisation*) church; (= *bestimmte Glaubensgemeinschaft*) Church; (= *Gottesdienst*) church *no art*; **zur ~ gehen** to go to church; **die ~ im Dorf lassen** (*fig*) not to get carried away

Kirchen- IN CPDS church; **Kirchenaustritt** M leaving the Church *no art*; **~e** (cases of) people leaving the Church; **Kirchenbank** F, *pl* **-bänke** (church) pew; **Kirchenbesuch** M church-going; **Kirchenchor** M church choir; **Kirchendiener(in)** M(F) sexton; **Kirchenglocke** F church bell; **Kirchenlicht** NT **kein (großes) ~ sein** (*fig inf*) to be not very bright; **Kirchenlied** NT hymn; **Kirchenmaus** F **arm wie eine ~** poor as a church mouse; **Kirchenschiff** NT (= *Längsschiff*) nave; (= *Querschiff*) transept; **Kirchenspaltung** F schism; **Kirchensteuer** F church tax; **Kirchentag** M Church congress

kirchlich ['kɪrçlɪç] ◼ ADJ church *attr*; *Zustimmung, Missbilligung* by the church; *Gebot, Gericht* ecclesiastical; *Land, Mensch* religious; *Recht* canon ◼ ADV **sich ~ trauen lassen** to get married in church; **~ bestattet werden** to have a Christian funeral

Kirchturm M church steeple

Kirchturmspitze F church spire

Kirchweih [-vai] F **-, -en** fair

The **Kirchweih** - also called *Kirmes* or *Kerwe* in some regions and *Chilbi* or *Kilbi* in Switzerland - is a celebration that takes place every year in villages, districts or small towns in commemoration of the consecration of the local church. There are all sorts of different rural customs associated with the **Kirchweih**, but common to them all is a fair lasting several days.

Kirgisien [kɪr'gi:ziən] NT **-s** Kirghizia

kirgisisch [kɪr'gi:zɪʃ] ADJ Kirghiz

Kirgistan ['kɪrgɪsta:n] NT **-s**, **Kirgisistan** [kɪr'gi:zɪsta:n] NT **-s** Kirghizia

Kirmes ['kɪrmɛs, 'kɪrmɐs] F **-, -sen** (*dial*) fair

Kirsche ['kɪrʃə] F **-, -n** cherry; (= *Holz*) cherry(wood); **mit ihm ist nicht gut ~n essen** (*fig*) it's best not to tangle with him

Kirsch-: Kirschkern M cherry stone; **Kirschlikör** M cherry brandy; **kirschrot** ADJ cherry(-red); **Kirschtomate** F cherry tomato; **Kirschtorte** F cherry gateau (*Brit*) or cake (*US*); **Schwarzwälder ~** Black Forest gateau (*Brit*) or cake (*US*); **Kirschwasser** NT kirsch

Kissen ['kɪsn] NT **-s, -** cushion; (= *Kopfkissen*) pillow; (= *Stempelkissen, an Heftpflaster*) pad

Kissen-: Kissenbezug M cushion cover; (*von Kopfkissen*) pillow case; **Kissenschlacht** F pillow fight

Kiste ['kɪstə] F **-, -n (a)** (= *Behälter*) box; (*für Wein etc*) case; (= *Lattenkiste*) crate; (= *Truhe*) chest; (*sl*: = *Bett*) sack (*inf*); **(mit jdm) in die ~ springen** (*sl*: = *ins Bett gehen*) to jump into the sack (with sb) (*inf*)
(b) (*inf*) (= *Auto, Flugzeug*) crate (*inf*); (= *Schiff*) tub (*inf*); (= *Fernsehen*) box (*inf*); (= *Computer*) computer
(c) (*inf*) (= *Angelegenheit*) affair; (= *Beziehungskiste*) relationship; **fertig ist die ~!** that's that (done)!

Kitsch [kɪtʃ] M **-es**, NO PL kitsch

kitschig ['kɪtʃɪç] ◼ ADJ kitschy ◼ ADV in a kitschy way

Kitt [kɪt] M **-(e)s, -e** (= *Fensterkitt*) putty; (*für Porzellan, Stein etc*) cement; (*fig*) bond

Kittchen ['kɪtçən] NT **-s, -** (*inf*) clink (*inf*)

Kittel ['kɪtl] M **-s, - (a)** (= *Arbeitskittel*) overall; (*von Arzt, Laborant etc*) (white) coat **(b)** (= *blusenartiges Kleidungsstück*) smock **(c)** (*Aus*: = *Damenrock*) skirt

kitten ['kɪtn] VT to cement; *Fenster* to putty; (= *füllen*) to fill; (*fig*) to patch up

Kitz [kɪts] NT **-es, -e** (= *Rehkitz*) fawn; (= *Ziegenkitz, Gämsenkitz*) kid

Kitzel ['kɪtsl] M **-s, -** tickle; (= *~gefühl*) tickling feeling; (*fig*) thrill

kitzelig ['kɪtsəlɪç] ADJ (*lit, fig*) ticklish

kitzeln ['kɪtsln] ◼ VT (*lit, fig*) to tickle; **sie kitzelt der Reiz des Neuen** she cannot resist the challenge of something new ◼ VI to tickle ◼ VT IMPERS **es kitzelt mich** I've got a tickle; **es kitzelt mich, das zu tun** I'm itching to do it

Kitzler ['kɪtslɐ] M **-s, -** (*Anat*) clitoris

kitzlig ['kɪtslɪç] ADJ (*lit, fig*) ticklish

Kiwi[1] ['kiːvi] F **-, -s** (= *Frucht*) kiwi

Kiwi[2] M **-s, -s** (*Orn*) kiwi; (*inf:* = *Neuseeländer*) Kiwi

KKW [kaːkaːˈveː] NT **-s, -s** ABBR *von* Kernkraftwerk

Klacks [klaks] M **-es, -e** (*inf*) **(a)** (= *Geräusch*) splosh **(b)** (*von Kartoffelbrei, Sahne etc*) dollop (*inf*) **(c)** (*fig*) **das ist ein ~** (= *einfach*) that's a piece of cake (*inf*); (= *wenig*) that's nothing (*inf*); **500 Euro sind für ihn ein ~** 500 euros is peanuts to him (*inf*)

Kladderadatsch [kladəraˈdatʃ] M **-(e)s, -e** (*inf*) **(a)** (*Geräusch*) crash-bang-wallop (*inf*) **(b)** (*fig*) (= *Kram, Durcheinander*) mess; (= *Streit*) bust-up (*inf*); (= *Skandal*) scandal; **da haben wir den ~!** what a mess!

klaffen ['klafn] VI to gape; **zwischen uns beiden klafft ein Abgrund** (*fig*) we are poles apart

kläffen ['klɛfn] VI (*pejfig*) to yap

Klage ['klaːgə] F **-, -n (a)** (= *Beschwerde*) complaint; **(bei jdm) über jdn/etw ~ führen** to lodge a complaint (with sb) about sb/sth; **~n (über jdn/etw) vorbringen** to make complaints (about sb/sth); **Grund zu ~n** *or* **zur ~** reason for complaint; **dass mir keine ~n kommen!** (*inf*) don't let me hear any complaints
(b) (= *Äußerung von Schmerz*) complaint; (= *Äußerung von Trauer*) lament(ation) (*um, über +acc* for); (= *~laut*) plaintive cry
(c) (*Jur*) (*im Zivilrecht*) action; (*im Strafrecht*) charge; (= *Scheidungsklage*) petition; (= *~schrift, Wortlaut*) charge; **eine ~ gegen jdn einreichen** *or* **erheben** to institute proceedings against sb; **eine ~ abweisen** to reject a charge; **eine ~ auf etw** (*acc*) an action for sth

Klage-: Klagelaut M plaintive cry; (*schmerzerfüllt*) cry of pain; **Klagelied** NT lament; **ein ~ über jdn/etw anstimmen** (*fig*) to complain about sb/sth; **Klagemauer** F **die ~** the Wailing Wall

klagen ['klaːgn] VI **(a)** (= *jammern*) to moan; (*Tiere*) to cry **(b)** (= *trauern, Trauer äußern*) to lament (*um jdn/etw* sb/sth), to wail **(c)** (= *sich beklagen*) to complain; **über etw** (*acc*) **~ to** complain about sth; **über Rückenschmerzen/Schlaflosigkeit ~** to complain of backache/insomnia; **ohne zu ~** without complaining; **ich kann nicht ~** (*inf*) mustn't grumble (*inf*) **(d)** (*Jur*) to sue (*auf +acc* for)
2 VT **(a) jdm sein Leid/seine Not/seinen Kummer ~** to pour out one's sorrow/distress/grief to sb **(b)** (*Aus*) = **verklagen**

Kläger ['klɛːgɐ] M **-s, -**, **Klägerin** [-ərɪn] F **-, -nen** (*Jur*) (*im Zivilrecht*) plaintiff; (*im Strafrecht auch*) prosecuting party; (*in Scheidungssachen*) petitioner; **wo kein ~ ist, ist auch kein Richter** (*Prov*) well, if no-one complains ...

Klage-: Klageschrift F (*Jur*) charge; (*bei Scheidung*) petition; **Klageweib** NT wailer

kläglich ['klɛːklɪç] **1** ADJ pitiful; *Leistung auch, Einwand, Niederlage* pathetic; *Rest* miserable; *Verhalten* despicable **2** ADV *fehlschlagen, scheitern, misslingen* miserably; *miauen, blöken, wimmern, betteln* pitifully; **~ versagen** to fail miserably

klaglos ADV (= *ohne Klagen*) uncomplainingly; **etw ~ hinnehmen** (*ohne zu klagen*) to accept sth without complaint; (*ohne zu widersprechen*) to accept sth without objection

Klamauk [klaˈmaʊk] M **-s**, NO PL (*inf*) (= *Alberei*) horseplay; (*im Theater etc*) slapstick; **~ machen** (= *albern*) to fool about

klamm [klam] ADJ **(a)** = *steif vor Kälte*) numb **(b)** (= *feucht*) damp **(c)** (*inf: finanziell*) hard up (*inf*)

Klamm [klam] F **-, -en** gorge

Klammer ['klamɐ] F **-, -n (a)** (= *Wäscheklammer*) peg; (= *Hosenklammer*) clip; (= *Büroklammer*) paperclip; (= *Heftklammer*) staple
(b) (= *Haarklammer*) (hair)grip
(c) (*Med*) (= *Wundklammer*) clip; (= *Zahnklammer*) brace
(d) (*in Text, Math,* = *~ausdruck*) bracket; (*Mus*) brace; **~ auf/zu** open/close brackets; **in ~n** in brackets; **runde/eckige/spitze ~n** round/square/pointed brackets; **geschweifte** *or* **geschwungene ~n** braces; **eine ~ auflösen** (*Math*) to eliminate the brackets

Klammeraffe M **(a)** (*Zool*) spider monkey; **er ist ein richtiger ~** (*fig inf*) he's always clinging on to you **(b)** (*Typ inf*) at-sign, "@"

klammern ['klamɐn] **1** VT (*an +acc* to) *Wäsche* to peg; *Papier etc* to staple; (*Tech*) to clamp; (*Med*) *Wunde* to clip; *Zähne* to brace **2** VR **sich an jdn/etw ~** (*lit, fig*) to cling to sb/sth **3** VI (*Sport*) to clinch

klammheimlich (*inf*) **1** ADJ clandestine; **eine ~e Freude empfinden** to be secretly delighted **2** ADV on the quiet; **~ aus dem Haus gehen** to sneak out of the house

Klamotte [klaˈmɔtə] F **-, -n (a)** (*inf*) (= *Kleider*) **Klamotten** PL gear sing (*inf*) **(b)** (*pej:* = *Theaterstück, Film*) rubbishy old play/film *etc*; **das ist doch eine alte ~** (*inf*), **das sind doch alte ~n** (*inf*) that's old hat (*inf*)

klang PRET *von* klingen

Klang [klaŋ] M **-(e)s, ¨e** ['klɛŋə] sound; (= *Tonqualität*) tone; (= *Melodie*) tune; **der ~ von Glocken** the chiming of bells; **der ~ von Glöckchen** the tinkling of small bells; **der ~ von Gläsern** the clinking of glasses; **Klänge** *pl* (= *Musik*) sounds; **der Name hat einen guten ~** the name has a good ring to it; (= *guten Ruf*) the name has a good reputation

Klang-: Klangeffekt M sound effect; **Klangfarbe** F tone colour (*Brit*) *or* color (*US*); **Klangkörper** M (*von Musikinstrument*) body; (= *Orchester*) orchestra

klanglich ['klaŋlɪç] **1** ADJ *Qualität* tonal; **~e Unterschiede** differences in sound; (*von Tonqualität*) tonal difference **2** ADV tonally; **~ gut sein** (*Musik, Lied, Gedicht, Stimme*) to sound good; (*Instrument, Gerät*) to have a good sound; **~ ähnlich** similar as far as tone is concerned

Klang-: klanglos ADJ toneless; *siehe* sang- und klanglos; **klangtreu** ADJ *Wiedergabe* faithful; *Empfänger* high-fidelity; *Ton* true; **~ sein** to have high fidelity; **Klangtreue** F fidelity; **klangvoll** ADJ *Stimme, Sprache* sonorous; *Wiedergabe* full; *Melodie* tuneful; (*fig*) *Titel, Name* fine-sounding

Klappe ['klapə] F **-, -n (a)** flap; (*an Lastwagen*) tailgate; (*seitlich*) side-gate; (*an Kombiwagen*) back; (*von Tisch*) leaf; (*von Ofen*) shutter; (= *Klappdeckel*) (hinged) lid; (*an Oboe etc*) key; (= *Falltür*) trapdoor; (*Film*) clapperboard
(b) (= *Schulterklappe*) strap; (= *Hosenklappe, an Tasche*) flap; (= *Augenklappe*) patch; (*von Visier*) shutter
(c) (= *Fliegenklappe*) (fly) swat
(d) (= *Herzklappe*) valve
(e) (*inf:* = *Mund*) trap (*inf*); **die ~ halten** to shut one's trap (*inf*); **eine große ~ haben** to have a big mouth (*inf*)
(f) (*Aus Telec*) extension
(g) (*sl: von Homosexuellen*) cottage (*sl*)

klappen ['klapn] **1** VT **etw nach oben/unten ~** *Sitz, Bett* to fold sth up/down; *Kragen* to turn sth up/down; *Deckel* to raise/lower sth; **etw nach vorn/hinten ~** *Sitz* to tip sth forward/back; *Deckel* to lift sth forward/back **2** VI (*fig inf*) (= *gelingen*) to work; (= *gut gehen*) to work (out); (*Aufführung, Abend*) to go smoothly; **wenn das mal klappt** if that works out; **hat es mit den Karten/dem Job geklappt?** did you get the tickets/job OK (*inf*)?; **mit dem Flug hat alles geklappt** the flight went all right

Klapper ['klapɐ] F **-, -n** rattle

klapperig ['klapərɪç] ADJ = **klapprig**

klappern ['klapɐn] VI (= *Geräusch machen*) to clatter; (*Klapperschlange, Fenster, Baby*) to rattle; (*Lider*) to bat; **er klapperte vor Kälte/Angst mit den Zähnen** his teeth were chattering with cold/fear; **Klappern gehört zum Handwerk** (*prov*) making a big noise is part of the business

klappernd ADJ clattering; *Auto* rattling; *Zähne* chattering

Klapper-: Klapperschlange F (*Zool*) rattlesnake; (*fig*) rattletrap; **Klapperstorch** M (*baby-talk*) stork; **er glaubt noch immer an den ~** he still believes in the stork

Klapp-: Klappfahrrad NT folding bicycle; **Klappmesser** NT flick knife (*Brit*), switchblade (*US*)

klapprig ['klaprɪç] ADJ rickety; (*fig inf*) *Mensch* shaky

Klapp-: Klappsitz M folding seat; **Klappstuhl** M folding chair; **Klappverdeck** NT folding hood

Klaps [klaps] M **-es, -e (a)** (*inf*) **einen ~ haben** to have a screw loose (*inf*) **(b)** (= *Schlag*) smack

Klapsmühle F (*pej inf*), **Klapse** ['klapsə] F **-, -n** (*pej inf*) nut house (*inf*)

klar [klaːɐ] **1** ADJ clear; (= *fertig*) ready; **~ zum Gefecht** *or* **Einsatz** (*Mil*) ready for action; **~ zum Start** (*Sport*) ready (for the start); **~ Schiff machen** (*lit, fig, Naut*) to clear the decks; **ein ~er Fall** (*inf*) sure thing (*inf*); **ein ~er Fall von ...** (*inf*) a clear case of ...; **das ist doch ~!** (inf) of course; **alles ~?** everything all right or OK? (inf); **jetzt ist** or **wird mir alles ~!** now I understand; **einen ~en Augenblick haben** to have a lucid moment; **geistig ~ sein, bei ~em Verstand sein** to be in full possession of one's faculties; **~ wie Kloßbrühe** or **dicke Tinte** (inf) clear as mud (inf); **sich** (dat) **über etw** (acc) **im Klaren sein** to be aware of sth; **sich** (dat) **darüber im Klaren sein, dass ...** to realize that ...; **mit jdm ins Klare kommen** to straighten things out with sb

2 ADV clearly; **~ denkend** clear-thinking; **immer ~er hervortreten** to become more and more apparent; **habe ich mich ~ genug ausgedrückt?** have I made myself perfectly clear?; **na ~!** (inf) of course!; **etw ~ und deutlich sagen** to spell sth out; **jdm etw ~ und deutlich sagen** to tell sb sth straight (inf); **~ auf der Hand liegen** to be perfectly obvious

Klar [klaːɐ] NT **-(e)s, -(e)** (Aus: = Eiweiß) (egg) white

Kläranlage F sewage plant; (von Fabrik) purification plant

klären ['klɛːrən] **1** VT to clear; Wasser, Luft to purify; Abwasser to treat; Bier, Wein to fine; Fall, Sachlage to clarify; Frage to settle **2** VI (Sport) to clear (the ball) **3** VR (Wasser, Himmel) to clear; (Wetter) to clear up; (Meinungen, Sachlage) to become clear; (Streitpunkte) to be clarified; (Frage) to be settled

Klare(r) ['klaːrə] M DECL AS ADJ (inf) schnapps

klargehen VI SEP IRREG AUX SEIN (inf) to be OK (inf); **ist es mit dem Examen klargegangen?** did the exam go OK? (inf)

Klärgrube F cesspit

Klarheit F **-, -en** clarity; (= geistige ~) lucidity; **sich** (dat) **~ über etw** (acc) **verschaffen** to get clear about sth; **über Sachlage** to clarify sth; **darüber besteht (völlige) ~** that is (completely) clear; **alle ~en (restlos) beseitigt!** (hum) (it's as) clear as mud! (inf)

Klarinette [klari'nɛtə] F **-, -n** clarinet

Klarinettist [klarine'tɪst] M **-en, -en, Klarinettistin** [-'tɪstɪn] F **-, -nen** clarinettist

Klar-: klarkommen VI SEP IRREG AUX SEIN (inf) to manage; **mit jdm/etw ~** to be able to cope with sb/sth; **Klarlack** M clear varnish; **klarmachen** SEP **3** VT to make clear; Schiff to get ready; Flugzeug to clear; **jdm etw ~** to make sth clear to sb; **sich** (dat) **etw ~** to realize sth; **sich** (dat) **die Unterschiede ~** to get the differences clear in one's own mind **2** VI (Naut) to get ready

Klärschlamm M sludge

Klarsicht- ['klaːzɪçt] IN CPDS transparent; **Klarsichtfolie** F clear film; **Klarsichthülle** F clear plastic folder; **Klarsichtpackung** F see-through pack

Klar-: klarspülen VTI SEP to rinse; **klarstellen** VT SEP (= klären) to clear up; (= klarmachen) to make clear; **ich möchte ~, dass ...** I would like to make it clear that ...; **Klarstellung** F clarification; **Klartext** M uncoded text; **im ~** in clear; (fig inf) in plain English; **wir sollten endlich ~ reden** (fig inf) let's not beat about the bush anymore (inf); **mit jdm ~ reden** (fig inf) to give sb a piece of one's mind

Klärung ['klɛːrʊŋ] F **-, -en** purification; (fig) clarification

klar werden IRREG AUX SEIN VI **jdm wird etw klar** sth becomes clear to sb; **ist dir das noch immer nicht klar geworden?** do you still not understand?; **sich** (dat) **(über etw** acc**) ~** to get (sth) clear in one's mind

klasse ['klasə] (inf) **1** ADJ great (inf) **2** ADV brilliantly

Klasse ['klasə] F **-, -n (a)** class; (= Spielklasse) league; (= Güteklasse) grade; (= Führerscheinklasse, Gewinnklasse) category; **ein Fahrschein zweiter ~** a second-class ticket; **das ist (große) ~!** (inf) that's great! (inf) **(b)** (Sch) class, form; (= Raum) classroom

Klasse- IN CPDS (inf) top-class; **eine ~mannschaft** a top-class team; **Petra ist eine ~frau** Petra is a great woman; (= gut aussehend) Petra is a gorgeous woman

Klassen-: Klassenarbeit F (written) class test; **Klassenausflug** M field trip; **Klassenbeste(r)** MF DECL AS ADJ best pupil (in the class); **wer ist ~(r)?** who is top of the class?; **Klassenbewusstsein** NT class consciousness; **Klassenbuch** NT (class-)register; **Klassendurchschnitt** M class average; **Klassenfeind(in)** M(F) (Pol) class enemy; **Klassenkamerad(in)** M(F) classmate; **Klassenkampf** M class struggle; **Klassenlehrer(in)** M(F), **Klassenleiter(in)** M(F) class teacher; **klassenlos** ADJ Gesellschaft classless; Krankenhaus one-class; **Klassenspiegel** M (Sch) seating plan of the class;

Klassensprecher(in) M(F) (Sch) class representative, ≈ form captain (Brit); **Klassenstärke** F (Sch) size of a/the class/the classes; **Klassentreffen** NT (Sch) class reunion; **Klassenunterschied** M class difference; **klassenweise 1** ADJ by class **2** ADV sitzen, sich aufstellen in classes; erscheinen as a class; **Klassenziel** NT (Sch) required standard; **das ~ nicht erreichen** not to reach the required standard; (fig) not to make the grade; **Klassenzimmer** NT classroom

klassifizieren [klasifi'tsiːrən], ptp **klassifiziert** VT to classify; **~d** classificatory

Klassifizierung F **-, -en** classification

-klassig [klasɪç] ADJ SUF -class; **erst-/zweitklassig** first-/second-class

Klassik ['klasɪk] F **-,** NO PL classical period; (inf: = klassische Musik/Literatur) classical music/literature

Klassiker ['klasɪkɐ] M **-s, -, Klassikerin** [-ərɪn] F **-, -nen** classic; **ein ~ des Jazz** a jazz classic; **die antiken ~** the classics

klassisch ['klasɪʃ] **1** ADJ **(a)** (= die Klassik betreffend, antik, traditionell) classical **(b)** (= typisch, vorbildlich, zeitlos, iro inf: = prächtig) classic **2** ADV classically

Klassizismus [klasi'tsɪsmʊs] M **-,** NO PL classicism

klassizistisch [klasi'tsɪstɪʃ] ADJ classical

-klässler [klɛslɐ] M **-s, -, -klässlerin** [-ərɪn] F **-, -nen** IN CPDS (Sch) -former

Klatsch [klatʃ] M **-(e)s, -e (a)** (Geräusch) splash; (bei Schlag, Aufprall) smack **(b)** NO PL (pej inf: = Tratsch) gossip

Klatschbase F (pej inf) (tratschend) gossip; (redselig) chatterbox (inf)

klatschen ['klatʃn] **1** VI **(a)** (= Geräusch machen) to clap; **in die Hände ~** to clap one's hands **(b)** (= einen Klaps geben) to slap; **jdm auf die Schenkel/sich** (dat) **gegen die Stirn ~** to slap sb's thighs/one's forehead **(c)** AUX SEIN (= aufschlagen) (harte Gegenstände) to go smack; (Flüssigkeiten) to splash; **der Regen klatschte gegen die Fenster** the rain beat against the windows **(d)** (pej inf: = tratschen) to gossip **2** VT **(a)** (= geräuschvoll schlagen) to clap; Takt to clap out; **jdm Beifall ~** to applaud sb **(b)** (= knallen) to smack; (= werfen) to throw; Fliegen to swat

Klatschen NT **-s,** NO PL **(a)** (= Beifallklatschen) applause **(b)** (inf: = Tratschen) gossiping

Klatsch-: Klatschkolumnist [-kolʊmnɪst] M **-en, -en, Klatschkolumnistin** [-nɪstɪn] F **-, -nen** (inf) gossip columnist; **Klatschmohn** M (corn) poppy; **klatschnass** ADJ (inf) sopping wet (inf); **Klatschspalte** F (Press inf) gossip column

Klaue ['klauə] F **-, -n** claw; (= Huf) hoof; (pej inf) (= Hand) talons pl (pej inf); (= Schrift) scrawl (pej); **in den ~n der Verbrecher** etc in the clutches of the criminals etc

klauen ['klauən] (inf) **1** VT to pinch (inf) (jdm etw sth from sb) **2** VI to steal

Klauenseuche F siehe Maul- und Klauenseuche

Klausel ['klauzl] F **-, -n** clause; (= Vorbehalt) proviso; (= Bedingung) condition

Klaustrophobie [klaustrofo'biː] F **-, -n** [-'biːən] (Psych) claustrophobia

Klausur [klau'zuːɐ] F **-, -en (a)** (Univ auch Klausurarbeit) exam **(b)** NO PL (= Abgeschlossenheit) seclusion; **eine Arbeit unter** or **in ~ schreiben** to write an essay under examination conditions

Klaviatur [klavia'tuːɐ] F **-, -en** keyboard

Klavier [kla'viːɐ] NT **-s, -e** piano; **~ spielen** to play the piano

Klavier- IN CPDS piano; **Klavierbegleitung** F piano accompaniment; **Klavierhocker** M piano stool; **Klavierkonzert** NT (= Musik) piano concerto; (= Vorstellung) piano recital; **Klavierspieler(in)** M(F) pianist; **Klavierstimmer** [-ʃtɪmɐ] M **-s, -, Klavierstimmerin** [-ərɪn] F **-, -nen** piano tuner

Klebe-: Klebeband NT, pl **-bänder** adhesive tape; **Klebebindung** F (Typ) adhesive binding

kleben ['kleːbn] **1** VI (= festkleben) to stick; **an etw** (dat) **~** (lit) to stick to sth; **am Vordermann ~** (Aut inf) to tailgate the person in front; **an seinen Händen klebt Blut** (fig) he has blood on his hands; **klebt nicht so am Text** don't stick so close to the text **2** VT to stick; Film, Tonband to splice; **jdm eine ~** (inf) to belt sb (one) (inf)

Kleb-: Klebfläche F surface to be stuck; **Klebfolie** F adhesive film

klebrig ['kleːbrɪç] ADJ sticky; *Farbe* tacky; (= *klebfähig*) adhesive

Kleb-: **Klebstoff** M adhesive; **Klebstreifen** M adhesive tape; (*zum Befeuchten*) gummed tape

Klebung ['kleːbʊŋ] F -, -en bond

kleckern ['klɛkɐn] **1** VT to spill **2** VI (a) (= *Kleckse machen*) to make a mess (b) (= *tropfen*) to spill (c) (*inf*: = *stückchenweise arbeiten*) to fiddle around; **nicht ~, sondern klotzen** (*inf*) to do things in a big way (*inf*)

kleckerweise ['klɛkɐvaɪzə] ADV in dribs and drabs

Klecks [klɛks] M **-es, -e** (= *Tintenklecks*) (ink)blot; (= *Farbklecks*) blob; (= *Fleck*) stain

klecksen ['klɛksn] VI to make blots/a blot

Klee [kleː] M **-s**, NO PL clover; **jdn/etw über den grünen ~ loben** to praise sb/sth to the skies

Kleeblatt NT cloverleaf; (*Mot*) cloverleaf (intersection); (*fig*: = *Menschen*) threesome; **vierblättriges ~** four-leaf clover; **das irische ~** the (Irish) shamrock

Kleid [klaɪt] NT **-(e)s, -er** [-də] (a) (= *Damenkleid*) dress; **ein zweiteiliges ~** a two-piece (suit) (b) (= *Kleidung*) **Kleider** PL clothes *pl*, clothing *sing* (*esp Comm*); **warme ~er mitbringen** to bring warm clothes; **~er machen Leute** (*Prov*) fine feathers make fine birds (*Prov*)

kleiden ['klaɪdn] **1** VR to dress; **gut/schlecht gekleidet sein** to be well/badly dressed; **weiß/schwarz gekleidet** dressed in white/black **2** VT (*geh*) (a) (= *mit Kleidern versehen*) to clothe, to dress; (*fig*) *Gedanken, Ideen* to couch; **etw in schöne Worte ~** to dress sth up in fancy words (b) (= *jdm stehen*) **jdn ~** to suit sb

Kleider-: **Kleiderbügel** M coat hanger; **Kleiderbürste** F clothes brush; **Kleiderhaken** M coat hook; **Kleiderkasten** M (*Aus, Sw*) wardrobe (*esp Brit*), closet (*US*); **Kleiderordnung** F dress regulations *pl*; **Kleiderschrank** M (a) wardrobe (b) (*inf*: *Mensch*) great hulk (of a man) (*inf*)

Kleidung ['klaɪdʊŋ] F -, NO PL clothes *pl*, clothing (*esp Comm*); **warme ~** warm clothes; **für jds (Nahrung und) ~ sorgen** to (feed and) clothe sb

Kleidungsstück NT garment; **~e** *pl* clothes *pl*; **ein warmes ~ mitnehmen** to bring something warm (to wear)

Kleie ['klaɪə] F -, NO PL bran

klein [klaɪn] **1** ADJ (a) (= *nicht groß*) little, small; *Finger* little; *Format, Gehalt, Rente, Zahl, (Hand)schrift, Buchstabe* small; (*Mus*) *Terz* minor; **die kleinen Antillen** *etc* the lesser Antilles *etc*; **Klein Paris** little Paris; **der Kleine Bär** *or* **Wagen** the Little Bear, Ursa Minor; **haben Sie es nicht ~er?** do you not have anything smaller?; **ein ~ bisschen** *or* **wenig** a little (bit); **ein ~ bisschen** *or* **wenig Salat** a little (bit of) salad; **ein ~es Bier, ein Kleines** (*inf*) a small beer, ≈ half a pint (*Brit*); **~es Geld** small change; **Klein Roland** little Roland; **hallo, ~er Mann!** hello, little man; **ein schönes ~es Auto** a nice little car; **er fährt ein ~es Auto** he drives a small car; **eine ~, hübsche Wohnung** a small, pretty apartment; **eine hübsche ~e Wohnung** a nice little apartment; **mein ~er Bruder** my little brother; **als ich (noch) ~ war** when I was little; **sich ~ machen** (= *sich bücken*) to bend down low; (= *sich zusammenrollen*) to curl up tight; **macht euch ein bisschen ~er!** squeeze up closer; **den mach ich SO ~ (mit Hut)!** (*hum*) I'll make him look THAT big; **~ aber oho** (*inf*) small but impressive; **ganz ~ (und hässlich) werden** (*inf*) to look humiliated *or* deflated; **im Kleinen** in miniature; **bis ins Kleinste** right down to the smallest detail; **von ~ an** *or* **auf** (= *von Kindheit an*) from his childhood; **~e Kinder ~e Sorgen, große Kinder große Sorgen** (*prov*) bigger children just mean bigger problems

(b) (= *kurz*) *Wuchs, Schritt* little, small, short; *Weile, Pause, Vortrag* short; **~ für sein Alter** small for his age; **er ist ~er als sein Bruder** he's smaller than his brother; **einen Kopf ~er als jd sein** to be a head shorter than sb

(c) (= *geringfügig*) little, slight; *Betrag, Summe* small; **beim ~sten Schreck** at the slightest shock; **das ~ere Übel** the lesser evil; **ein paar ~ere Fehler** a few minor mistakes

(d) (= *unbedeutend*) petty (*pej*); *Leute* ordinary; **er ist ein ~er Geist** he is small-minded; **der ~e Mann** the man in the street; **ein ~er Ganove** a petty crook; **sein Vater war (ein) ~er Beamter** his father was a minor civil servant

2 ADV (a) (= *in kleiner Schrift*) small; **er schreibt sehr ~** he writes very small; **~ gedruckt** in small print; **~ gemustert** small-patterned; **~ kariert** *Stoff* finely checked; *siehe auch* **kleinkariert, kleinschreiben**

(b) (*auf kleine Hitze*) **etw ~ stellen** *or* **drehen** to put sth on a low heat; **etw ~er stellen** *or* **drehen** to turn sth down

(c) (*in Wendungen*) **~ anfangen** to start off in a small way; **~ beigeben** (*inf*) to give in; **~ geraten sein** (*Gegenstand*) to have come out a little (too) small; (*Mensch*) to be a bit small; **etw ~ halten** *Anzahl, Kosten* to keep sth down; *Party, Feier* to keep sth small

Klein-: **Kleinaktionär(in)** M(F) small shareholder; **Kleinanzeige** F classified advertisement; **Kleinasien** NT Asia Minor; **Kleinauto** NT small car; **kleinbekommen** VT SEP IRREG = **kleinkriegen**; **Kleinbetrieb** M small business; **bäuerlicher ~** smallholding; **handwerklicher ~** (small) workshop; **industrieller ~** small factory; **Klein- und Mittelbetriebe** small and medium(-sized) enterprises *pl*; **Kleinbildkamera** F 35mm camera; **Kleinbuchstabe** M small letter; **Kleinbürger(in)** M(F) petty bourgeois; **kleinbürgerlich** ADJ lower middle-class; **er reagierte typisch ~** his reaction was typically lower middle-class; **Kleinbürgertum** NT (*Sociol*) lower middle class, petty bourgeoisie; **Kleinbus** M minibus

Kleineleutemilieu NT world of ordinary people

Kleine(r) ['klaɪnə] MF DECL AS ADJ (a) little one *or* child; (= *Junge*) little boy; (= *Mädchen*) little girl; (= *Säugling*) baby; **unser ~r** (= *Jüngster*) our youngest (child); **die lieben ~n** (*iro*) the dear little things; **eine hübsche ~** a pretty little girl *or* thing; **die Katze mit ihren ~n** the cat with its kittens *or* babies (*inf*)

(b) (*inf*: *auch* **Kleines**: = *Schatz, Liebling*) baby (*inf*); **na ~/~r!** (*zu einem Kind*) hello little girl/boy!; **na ~r!** (*Prostituierte zu einem Passanten*) hello, love (*esp Brit*)

Kleine(s) ['klaɪnə] NT DECL AS ADJ **etwas ~s** (*inf*) a little baby

Klein-: **Kleinfamilie** F (*Sociol*) nuclear family; **kleingedruckt** ADJ ATTR *siehe* **klein**; **Kleingedruckte(s)** [-gədrʊktə] NT DECL AS ADJ small print; **Kleingeist** M (*pej*) small-minded person; **Kleingeld** NT (small) change; **das nötige ~ haben** (*fig*) to have the necessary wherewithal (*inf*); **kleingemustert** ADJ *siehe* **klein**; **kleingewachsen** ADJ short; *Baum* small; **Kleingewerbe** NT small business; **klein hacken** VT to chop up small; **Kleinheit** F -, -en smallness; **Kleinhirn** NT (*Anat*) cerebellum; **Kleinholz** NT, NO PL firewood; **~ aus jdm machen** (*inf*) to make mincemeat out of sb (*inf*)

Kleinigkeit ['klaɪnɪçkaɪt] F -, -en (a) little *or* small thing; (= *Bagatelle*) trifle; (= *Einzelheit*) minor detail; **ich habe noch ein paar ~en in der Stadt zu erledigen** I still have a few little things to attend to in town; **es war nur eine ~ zu reparieren** there was only something minor to be repaired; **die Reparatur/Prüfung war eine ~** the repair job/exam was no trouble at all; **eine ~ essen** to have a bite to eat; **jdm eine ~ schenken/bezahlen** to give/pay sb a little something; **die ~ von 1.000 Euro** (*iro*) the small matter of 1,000 euros; **wegen** *or* **bei jeder ~** for the slightest reason; **sich um jede ~ selbst kümmern müssen** to have to take care of every little detail personally; **das war doch (nur) eine ~!** it was nothing; **das ist doch eine ~!** that isn't (asking) much; **das ist für mich keine ~** that is no small matter for me; **wir haben noch ein paar ~en geändert** we've made one or two small changes; **sich nicht mit ~en abgeben** *or* **befassen** not to bother over details

(b) (= *ein bisschen*) **eine ~** a little (bit); **das wird eine ~ dauern** it will take a little while

Klein-: **kleinkariert 1** ADJ (*fig*) small-time (*inf*); **~ sein** (*fig*) to be small-minded **2** ADV *reagieren* narrow-mindedly; **~ denken** to think small; **~ handeln, sich ~ verhalten** to be narrow-minded; *siehe auch* **klein; Kleinkind** NT small child, toddler (*inf*); **Kleinkram** M (*inf*) odds and ends *pl*; (= *kleinere Arbeiten*) odd jobs *pl*; (= *Trivialitäten*) trivialities *pl*

kleinkriegen VT SEP (a) (*lit*) *Holz* to chop (up) (b) (*inf*: = *kaputtmachen*) to smash (c) (*inf*) (= *gefügig machen*) to bring into line (*inf*); (= *unterkriegen, mürbe machen*) to get down; (*körperlich*) to tire out; **er ist einfach nicht kleinzukriegen** he just won't be beaten; **unser altes Auto ist einfach nicht kleinzukriegen** our old car just goes on for ever

Kleinkunst F cabaret

Kleinkunstbühne F cabaret

kleinlaut 1 ADJ subdued, meek; **dann wurde er ganz ~** it took the wind out of his sails **2** ADV *fragen* meekly; **etw ~ zugeben** to admit sth shamefacedly; **~ um Verzeihung bitten** to apologize rather sheepishly

kleinlich ['klaınlıç] **1** ADJ petty; (= *knauserig*) mean (*esp Brit*), stingy (*inf*); (= *engstirnig*) narrow-minded **2** ADV (= *knauserig*) stingily; (= *engstirnig*) narrow-mindedly

klein machen VT **(a)** (= *zerkleinern*) to chop up **(b)** (*inf*) *Geld* (= *wechseln*) to change; (= *ausgeben*) to blow (*inf*) **(c)** (*inf*: = *erniedrigen*) **jdn ~** to make sb look small

Klein-: klein schneiden VT IRREG to cut up small; **klein schreiben** VT IRREG (*fig*) to set little store by; **klein geschrieben werden** to count for (very) little; **kleinschreiben** VT SEP IRREG (*mit kleinem Anfangsbuchstaben*) to write without a capital; **ein Wort ~** to write a word without a capital; **Kleinschreibung** F use of small initial letters; **Kleinstadt** F small town; **kleinstädtisch** ADJ provincial (*pej*)

kleinstmöglich ADJ smallest possible

Kleinstwagen M (*Aut*) minicar

Klein-: Kleintier NT small animal; **Kleintierpraxis** F small animal (veterinary) practice; **Kleinvieh** NT **~ macht auch Mist** (*prov*) every little helps; **Kleinwagen** M small car; **kleinweis** ['klaınvais] ADV (*Aus*) gradually; **kleinwüchsig** [-vy:ksıç] ADJ (*geh*) small; **Kleinwüchsigkeit** F (*Med*) restricted growth

Kleister ['klaıstɐ] M **-s, -** (= *Klebstoff*) paste

kleistern ['klaıstɐn] VT (= *kleben*) to paste

Klematis [kle'ma:tıs, 'kle:matıs] F **-, -** (*Bot*) clematis

Klementine [klemen'ti:nə] F **-, -n** clementine

Klemmbrett NT clipboard

Klemme ['klɛmə] F **-, -n (a)** (= *Haarklemme, für Papiere etc*) clip; (*Elec*) crocodile clip; (*Med*) clamp **(b)** (*fig inf*) **in der ~ sitzen** *or* **sein** to be in a jam (*inf*); **jdm aus der ~ helfen** to help sb out of a jam (*inf*)

klemmen ['klɛmən] **1** VT *Draht etc* to clamp; (*in Spalt*) to stick, to wedge; **sich** (*dat*) **den Finger in etw** (*dat*) **~** to catch one's finger in sth; **sich** (*dat*) **etw unter den Arm ~** to stick sth under one's arm **2** VR to catch oneself (*in +dat* in); **sich hinter etw** (*acc*) **~** (*inf*) to get stuck into sth (*inf*); **sich hinter jdn ~** (*inf*) to get on to sb **3** VI (*Tür, Schloss etc*) to stick

Klempner ['klɛmpnɐ] M **-s, -, Klempnerin** [-ərın] F **-, -nen** plumber

Klempnerei [klɛmpnə'raı] F **-, -en (a)** NO PL plumbing **(b)** (= *Werkstatt*) plumber's workshop

klempnern ['klɛmpnɐn] VI to do plumbing

Kleopatra [kle'o:patra] F **-s** Cleopatra

Kleptomane [klɛpto'ma:nə] M **-n, -n, Kleptomanin** [-'ma:nın] F **-, -nen** kleptomaniac

Kleptomanie [klɛptoma'ni:] F **-,** NO PL kleptomania

Klettband ['klɛtbant] NT, *pl* **-bänder** Velcro® (strip)

Klette ['klɛtə] F **-, -n** (*Bot*) burdock; (= *Blütenkopf*) bur(r); (*pej*: = *lästiger Mensch*) nuisance; **sich wie eine ~ an jdn hängen** to cling to sb like a limpet

Kletter-: Kletteraffe M (*inf*) **er ist ein richtiger ~** he can climb like a monkey; **Kletterbaum** M climbing tree

Kletterer ['klɛtərɐ] M **-s, -, Kletterin** [-ərın] F **-, -nen** climber

Klettergerüst NT climbing frame

klettern ['klɛtɐn] VI AUX SEIN to climb; (*mühsam*) to clamber; **auf Bäume ~** to climb trees

Kletter-: Kletterpflanze F climbing plant; **Kletterrose** F climbing rose

Klettverschluss ['klɛt-] M Velcro® fastener

Klick [klık] M **-s, -s** (*Comput*) click

klicken ['klıkn] VI to click

Klient [kli'ɛnt] M **-en, -en, Klientin** [-'ɛntın] F **-, -nen** client

Klientel [klien'te:l] F **-, -en** clients *pl*

Kliff [klıf] NT **-(e)s, -e** cliff

Kliffküste F cliffs *pl*

Klima ['kli:ma] NT **-s, -s** *or* **Klimate** [kli'ma:tə] (*lit, fig*) climate; (*fig auch*) atmosphere

Klima-: Klimaänderung F climatic change; **Klimaanlage** F air conditioning (system); **mit ~** air-conditioned; **Klimaforscher(in)** M(F) climatologist; **Klimakatastrophe** F climatic disaster; **Klimakunde** F climatology

Klimaschutz M climate protection

Klimaschutz-: Klimaschutzabkommen NT agreement on climate change; **Klimaschutzprogramm** NT climate protection programme

klimatisch [kli'ma:tıʃ] **1** ADJ NO PRED climatic **2** ADV **~ günstige Verhältnisse** a favourable (*Brit*) *or* favorable (*US*) climate; **ein ~ ungünstiger Ort** a location with an unfavourable (*Brit*) *or* unfavorable (*US*) climate; **eine ~ angenehme Gegend** an area with a pleasant climate; **~ bedingt sein** (*Wachstum*) to be dependent on the climate; (*Krankheit*) to be caused by climatic conditions

klimatisieren [klimati'zi:rən], *ptp* **klimatisiert** VT to air-condition

Klimawechsel M (*lit, fig*) change in the climate

Klimbim [klım'bım] M **-s,** NO PL (*inf*) odds and ends *pl*; (= *Umstände*) fuss (and bother)

Klimmzug M (*Sport*) pull-up; **geistige Klimmzüge machen** (*fig*) to do mental acrobatics

klimpern ['klımpɐn] VI to tinkle; (= *stümperhaft ~*) to plonk away (*inf*); (*auf Banjo*) to twang; **mit Geld ~** to jingle coins; **mit den Wimpern ~** (*inf*) to flutter one's eyelashes

Klinge ['klıŋə] F **-, -n** blade

Klingel ['klıŋl] F **-, -n** bell

Klingelbeutel M collection bag

klingeln ['klıŋln] VI to ring (*nach* for); **es hat schon zum ersten/ zweiten/dritten Mal geklingelt** (*in Konzert, Theater*) the three-/two-/one-minute bell has already gone; **es hat schon geklingelt** (*in Schule*) the bell has already gone; **es hat geklingelt** (*Telefon*) the phone just rang; (*an Tür*) somebody just rang the doorbell; **es klingelt an der Tür** (*als Bühnenanweisung*) there is a ring at the door; **Klingeln** ringing

klingen ['klıŋən], *pret* **klang** [klaŋ], *ptp* **geklungen** [gə'klʊŋən] VI to sound; (*Glocke, Ohr*) to ring; (*Glas*) to clink; (*Metall*) to clang; **nach etw ~** to sound like sth; **die Gläser ~ lassen** to clink glasses; **die Glocke klingt dumpf/hell** the bell has a dull/ clear ring

Klinik ['kli:nık] F **-, -en** clinic; (= *Universitätsklinik*) (university) hospital

Klinikum ['kli:nikʊm] NT **-s, Klinika** *or* **Kliniken** [-ka, -kn] (*Univ*) **(a)** medical centre (*Brit*) *or* center (*US*) **(b)** (= *Ausbildung*) internship

klinisch ['kli:nıʃ] **1** ADJ clinical; **~er Blick** cold glance **2** ADV clinically; **~ tot** clinically dead

Klinke ['klıŋkə] F **-, -n** (= *Türklinke*) (door) handle; **~n putzen** (*inf*) to go from door to door; (*um Ware zu verkaufen*) to sell from door to door; **die Interessenten geben sich** (*dat*) **die ~ in die Hand** there's a constant stream of interested parties

Klinkenputzer [-pʊtsɐ] M **-s, -, Klinkenputzerin** [-ərın] F **-, -nen** (*inf*) = *Hausierer*) hawker; (= *Vertreter*) door-to-door salesman/saleswoman

Klinker ['klıŋkɐ] M **-s, -** **(a)** (= *Ziegelstein*) clinker brick **(b)** (*Naut*) clinker

klipp [klıp] ADV **~ und klar** clearly, plainly; (= *offen*) frankly

Klipp [klıp] M **-s, -s** clip

Klippe ['klıpə] F **-, -n** (= *Felsklippe*) cliff; (*im Meer*) rock; (*fig*) hurdle; **~n umschiffen** (*lit, fig*) to negotiate obstacles

Klippen-: Klippenküste F rocky coast; **klippenreich** ADJ rocky

Klips [klıps] M **-es, -e** = **Clip**

klirren ['klırən] VI to clink; (*Glas auch*) to tinkle; (*Fensterscheiben*) to rattle; (*Waffen*) to clash; (*Ketten, Sporen*) to jangle; (*Lautsprecher, Mikrofon*) to crackle; (*Eis*) to crunch; **~de Kälte** crisp cold

Klirrfaktor M distortion (factor)

Klischee [kli'ʃe:] NT **-s, -s** (*Typ*) plate; (*fig*: = *Ausdruck, Phrase*) cliché

Klischee-: klischeehaft **1** ADJ (*fig*) stereotyped **2** ADV stereotypically; **Klischeevorstellung** F cliché, stereotype

Klitoris ['kli:torıs] F **-, -** *or* **Klitorides** [kli'to:ride:s] clitoris

Klitsche ['klıtʃə] F **-, -n** (*pej inf*) (*Theat*) small-time theatre (*Brit*) *or* theater (*US*); (= *Kleinbetrieb*) tiny outfit (*inf*)

klitschig ['klıtʃıç] ADJ (*dial*) doughy

klitschnass ADJ (*inf*) drenched

klitzeklein ['klıtsə'klaın] **1** ADJ (*inf*) tiny **2** ADV **schneiden, schreiben, kopieren** very small

Klo [klo:] NT **-s, -s** (*inf*) loo (*Brit inf*), john (*US inf*); **aufs ~ gehen** to go to the loo (*Brit inf*) *or* john (*US inf*)

klobig ['klo:bıç] **1** ADJ hefty (*inf*), bulky; *Mensch* hulking great (*inf*); *Schuhe* clumpy; *Benehmen* boorish; *Hände* massive, hefty (*inf*) **2** ADV *aussehen* bulky; *bauen, sich abheben* massively; ~ **wirken** (*Gebäude*) to look big and clumsy; (*Schuhe*) to seem clumpy

Klo-: **Klobürste** F (*inf*) toilet brush; **Klofrau** F, **Klomann** M, *pl* -**männer** (*inf*) toilet attendant

Klon [klo:n] M -**s**, -**e** clone

klonen ['klo:nən] VTI to clone

Klonen NT -**s**, NO PL cloning

klönen ['klø:nən] VI (*inf*) to (have a) chat

Klönschnack M (*N Ger inf*) chat

Klopapier NT (*inf*) toilet *or* loo (*Brit inf*) paper

Klöpfel ['klœpfl] M -**s**, - (= *Holzhammer*) square mallet; (= *Steinmetzwerkzeug*) stonemason's maul

klopfen ['klɔpfn] **1** VT to knock; *Fleisch, Teppich* to beat; *Steine* to knock down; **den Takt ~** to beat time **2** VI to knock; (*leicht auch*) to tap; (*Herz*) to beat; (*vor Aufregung, Anstrengung*) to pound; (*Puls, Schläfe*) to throb; (*Specht*) to tap; **sie klopften wiederholt heftig an die Tür** they kept pounding away at the door; **es klopft** (*Theat*) there is a knock at the door; **es hat geklopft** there's someone knocking at the door; **„bitte laut ~"** "please knock loudly"; **jdm auf die Schulter ~** to tap sb on the shoulder; **jdm auf den Rücken/den Hintern ~** to pat sb on the back/the bottom; **jdm auf die Finger ~** (*lit, fig*) to give sb a rap on the knuckles

Klopfer ['klɔpfɐ] M -**s**, - (= *Türklopfer*) (door) knocker; (= *Fleischklopfer*) (meat) mallet; (= *Teppichklopfer*) carpet beater

Klöppel ['klœpl] M -**s**, - (= *Glockenklöppel*) clapper; (= *Spitzenklöppel*) bobbin; (= *Trommelklöppel*) stick

Klöppelarbeit F pillow lace

klöppeln ['klœpln] VI to make (pillow) lace; **eine Tischdecke ~** to make a lace tablecloth

Klops [klɔps] M -**es**, -**e** (*Cook*) meatball; (*dated inf*: = *schwerer Fehler*) howler (*inf*)

Klosett [klo'zɛt] NT -**s**, -**e** *or* -**s** toilet

Klosett-: **Klosettbrille** F toilet seat; **Klosettbürste** F toilet brush; **Klosettdeckel** M toilet seat lid; **Klosettfrau** F, **Klosettmann** M, *pl* -**männer** toilet attendant; **Klosettpapier** NT toilet paper

Kloß [klo:s] M -**es**, -**e** ['klø:sə] dumpling; (= *Fleischkloß*) meatball; (= *Bulette*) rissole; **einen ~ im Hals haben** (*fig*) to have a lump in one's throat

Kloster ['klo:stɐ] NT -**s**, -̈ ['klø:stɐ] cloister; (= *Mönchskloster auch*) monastery; (= *Nonnenkloster auch*) convent; **ins ~ gehen** to enter a monastery/convent

klösterlich ['klø:stɐlɪç] ADJ *Leben* monastic/convent; *Stille, Abgeschiedenheit* cloistered

Klöten ['klø:tn] PL (*sl*) balls *pl* (*sl*)

Klotz [klɔts] M -**es**, -̈**e** ['klœtsə] *or* (*inf*) -**er** ['klœtsɐ] (= *Holzklotz*) block (of wood); (*pej*: = *Betonklotz*) concrete block; (*inf*: = *Person*) great lump (*inf*); **sich** (*dat*) **einen ~ ans Bein binden** (*inf*) to tie a millstone around one's neck; **jdm ein ~ am Bein sein** to be a hindrance to sb; **schlafen wie ein ~** (*inf*) to sleep like a log

Klötzchen ['klœtsçən] NT -**s**, - (building) block

klotzen ['klɔtsn] **1** VT (*inf*) *Hochhäuser in die Stadt* ~ to throw up skyscrapers in the town **2** VI (*sl*) (= *hart arbeiten*) to slog (away) (*inf*)

klotzig ['klɔtsɪç] (*inf*) **1** ADJ huge **2** ADV (**a**) *werben* like crazy (*inf*); ~ **verdienen/absahnen** to rake it in (*inf*) (**b**) (= *klobig*) massively; ~ **wirken** to seem bulky

Klub [klʊb] M -**s**, -**s** club

Klub-: **Klubhaus** NT clubhouse; **Klubjacke** F blazer; **Klubsessel** M club chair

Kluft [klʊft] F -, -̈**e** ['klʏftə] (**a**) (= *Erdspalte*) cleft; (*zwischen Felsenrändern*) ravine; (*in Bergen*) crevasse; (= *Abgrund*) chasm (**b**) (*fig*) gulf, gap; **in der Partei tat sich eine tiefe ~ auf** a deep rift opened up in the party (**c**) NO PL (= *Uniform, Kleidung*) uniform; (*inf*: = *Kleidung*) gear (*inf*)

klug [klu:k] **1** ADJ, *comp* -̈**er** ['kly:gɐ], *superl* -̈**ste(r, s)** ['kly:ksta] clever; *Augen* intelligent; (= *vernünftig*) *Entscheidung, Rat* wise, sound; *Überlegung* prudent; **es wird am klügsten sein, wenn ...** it would be most sensible if ...; **es wäre politisch/geschäftlich ~ ...** it would make good political/business sense ...; **ein ~er Kopf** a capable person; **ein ~er Kopf, der Kleine** he's a bright boy; **ich werde daraus nicht ~, da soll einer draus ~ werden** I

cannot make head or tail (*Brit*) *or* heads or tails (*US*) of it; **aus ihm werde ich nicht ~** I can't make him out; **im Nachhinein ist man immer klüger** one learns by experience; **~e Reden halten** *or* **führen** (*iro*) to make fine-sounding speeches; **~e Bemerkungen/Ratschläge** (*iro*) clever *or* helpful remarks/ advice (*iro*); **wenn du ~ bist, haust du sofort ab** if you're smart you'll beat it (*inf*); **wer war denn so ~ ...** (*iro*) who was the clever one ...; **so ~ bin ich auch** (*iro*) you don't say!; **nun bin ich genauso ~ wie zuvor** *or* **vorher** I am still none the wiser; **der Klügere gibt nach** (*Prov*) discretion is the better part of valour (*Brit*) *or* valor (*US*) (*Prov*) **2** ADV, *comp* -̈**er**, *superl* **am ~sten ~ reden** *or* **tun kann jeder ...** anyone can talk ...

klugerweise ['klu:gɐvaizə] ADV (very) wisely

Klugheit F -, NO PL cleverness; (= *Vernünftigkeit: von Entscheidung, Rat*) wisdom, soundness; (= *Geschicktheit: von Antwort, Geschäftsmann*) shrewdness; **aus ~** (very) wisely; **deine ~en kannst du dir sparen** (*iro*) you can save your clever remarks

Klug-: **klugscheißen** VI SEP IRREG (*inf*) to shoot one's mouth off (*inf*); **Klugscheißer(in)** M(F) (*inf*) smart aleck (*inf*), smart-ass (*esp US sl*)

klumpen ['klʊmpn] VI (*Sauce*) to go lumpy

Klumpen ['klʊmpn] M -**s**, - lump; (= *Erdklumpen auch*) clod; (= *Goldklumpen*) nugget; (= *Blutklumpen*) clot; ~ **bilden** (*Mehl etc*) to go lumpy; (*Blut*) to clot

Klump-: **Klumpfuß** M club foot; **klumpfüßig** ADJ club-footed

klumpig ['klʊmpɪç] ADJ lumpy

Klüngel ['klʏŋl] M -**s**, - (*inf*: = *Clique*) clique

Klüngelwirtschaft F (*inf*) nepotism *no pl*

Klunker ['klʊŋkɐ] M -**s**, - (*inf*) (= *Edelstein*) rock (*inf*); (= *großer Modeschmuck*) chunky jewellery (*Brit*) *or* jewelry (*US*)

Klüver ['kly:vɐ] M -**s**, - (*Naut*) jib

Klüverbaum M (*Naut*) jib boom

km ABBR *von* **Kilometer** km

KMB ABBR *von* **Klein- und Mittelbetriebe**

km/h ABBR *von* **Kilometer pro Stunde** kph

KMU ABBR *von* **kleine und mittlere Unternehmen**

knabbern ['knabɐn] VTI to nibble; **etwas zum Knabbern holen** to get something to nibble on (*inf*); **nichts zu ~ haben** (*inf*) to have nothing to eat; **daran wirst du noch zu ~ haben** (*fig inf*) it will really give you something to think about

Knabe ['kna:bə] M -**n**, -**n** (*liter*) boy, lad (*esp Brit inf*); **na alter ~!** (*inf*) well old boy (*inf*)

Knaben-: **Knabenchor** M boys' choir; **knabenhaft** ADJ boyish; **Knabenkraut** NT (wild) orchid

Knäckebrot ['knɛkə-] NT crispbread

knacken ['knakn] **1** VT (**a**) *Nüsse* to crack; *Läuse* to crush (**b**) (*inf*) *Auto* to break into; *Geldschrank* to crack (**c**) (*fig inf*: = *bezwingen*) *Rätsel, Kode, Organisation* to crack; *Tabu* to break **2** VI (**a**) (= *brechen*) to crack, to snap; (*Glas etc*) to crack; (*Dielen, Stuhl*) to creak; (*Holz*: = *knistern*) to crackle; **mit den Fingern ~** to crack one's fingers; **die Leitung knackt** (*Tel*) the line is crackly; **es knackt im Gebälk** the beams are creaking; **an etw** (*dat*) **zu ~ haben** (*inf*) to have sth to think about; (= *darüber hinwegkommen*) to have a rough time getting over sth; **an dieser Aufgabe hatte ich ganz schön zu ~** (*inf*) I really had to sweat over this exercise (**b**) (*inf*: = *schlafen*) to sleep

Knacker ['knakɐ] M -**s**, - (**a**) = **Knackwurst** (**b**) (*pej inf*) **alter ~** old fog(e)y (*inf*)

Knacki ['knaki] M -**s**, -**s** (*inf*: = *Knastbruder*) jailbird (*inf*); (*sl*: = *alter Mann*) old guy (*inf*)

knackig ['knakɪç] **1** ADJ crisp; *Apfel auch, Salat, Gemüse* crunchy; (*inf*) *Mädchen* tasty (*inf*); *Figur, Rock, Hose* sexy **2** ADV (**a**) (= *mit Schwung*) ~ **rangehen** (*bei Arbeit*) to get a move on (*inf*); (*beim anderen Geschlecht*) to move in fast (*inf*) (**b**) (= *ordentlich*) ~ **braun sein** to have a fantastic tan

Knack-: **Knacklaut** M glottal stop; **Knackpunkt** M (*inf*) crunch (*inf*)

Knacks [knaks] M -**es**, -**e** (**a**) (= *Sprung, Geräusch*) crack (**b**) (*inf*: = *Schaden*) **das Radio/der Fernseher hat einen ~** there is something wrong with the radio/television; **die Ehe der beiden hat schon lange einen ~** their marriage has been breaking up for a long time; **er hat einen ~ weg** he's a bit screwy (*inf*); (*gesundheitlich*) his health isn't so good

Knackwurst F *type of frankfurter, the skin of which makes a cracking sound when bitten*

Knall [knal] M **-(e)s, -e** bang; (*mit Peitsche*) crack; (*bei Tür*) slam; (*von Korken*) pop; **der ~ eines Schusses** a shot; **~ auf Fall** (*inf*) all of a sudden; **jdn ~ auf Fall entlassen** (*inf*) to dismiss sb completely out of the blue (*inf*); **einen ~ haben** (*inf*) to be crazy (*inf*)

Knall-: Knallbonbon NT (Christmas) cracker; **knallbunt** ADJ (*inf*) brightly coloured (*Brit*) *or* colored (*US*)

knallen ['knalən] ◼ VI (a) (= *krachen*) to bang; (= *explodieren*) to explode; (*Schuss*) to ring out; (*Feuerwerk*) to (go) bang; (*Korken*) to (go) pop; (*Peitsche*) to crack; (*Tür etc*) to slam; (*aux sein:* = *auftreffen*) to bang; **mit der Tür ~** to slam the door; **die Korken ~ lassen** (*fig*) to pop a cork; **draußen knallte es** there was a shot/were shots outside; **sei nicht so frech, sonst knallts** (*inf:* = *es gibt Prügel*) don't be so cheeky (*Brit*) *or* fresh (*US*), *or* there'll be trouble; **der Fahrer ist gegen die Windschutzscheibe geknallt** the driver hit the windscreen (*Brit*) *or* windshield (*US*)
(b) (*inf: Sonne*) to beat down
◼ VT to bang; *Tür, Buch auch* to slam; *Peitsche* to crack; **den Hörer auf die Gabel ~** (*inf*) to slam down the receiver; **jdm eine ~** (*inf*) to belt sb (one) (*inf*); **jdm ein paar vor den Latz ~** (*inf*) to belt sb (one) (*inf*)

Knall-: knalleng ADJ (*inf*) skintight; **Knallerbse** F toy torpedo

Knallerei [knalə'rai] F **-, -en** (*inf*) (= *Schießerei*) shooting; (*Feuerwerk*) banging of fireworks

Knall-: knallgelb ADJ (*inf*) bright yellow; **knallgrün** ADJ (*inf*) bright green; **knallhart** (*inf*) ◼ ADJ *Film* brutal; *Porno* hardcore; *Job, Geschäft, Wettbewerb* really tough; *Truppen, Mensch* as hard as nails; *Schuss, Schlag* really hard; *Methode* brutal; *Forderung* uncompromising ◼ ADV brutally; **~ verhandeln** to drive a hard bargain; **knallheiß** ADJ (*inf*) boiling hot; **Knallhitze** F (*inf*) blazing heat

knallig ['knaliç] (*inf*) ◼ ADJ *Farben* loud ◼ ADV **~ gelb** gaudy yellow; **~ bunt** gaudy

Knall-: Knallkopf M (*inf*), **Knallkopp** [-kɔp] M **-s, -köppe** [-kœpə] (*inf*) fathead (*inf*); **Knallkörper** M firecracker; **knallrot** ADJ (*inf*) bright red; *Gesicht* as red as a beetroot (*Brit inf*) *or* beet (*US inf*)

knapp [knap] ◼ ADJ (a) *Vorräte, Arbeitsstellen, Geld* scarce; *Taschengeld* meagre (*Brit*), meager (*US*); *Gehalt* low; **mein Geld ist ~** I'm short of money; **mein Geld wird ~** I am running out of money; **~ mit (dem) Geld sein** (*inf*) to be short of money
(b) (= *gerade noch ausreichend*) *Zeit, Geld, Miete* just enough; *Mehrheit, Sieg* narrow; *Kleidungsstück etc* (= *eng*) tight; (= *kurz*) short; *Bikini* scanty
(c) (= *nicht ganz*) almost; **ein ~es Pfund Mehl** just under a pound of flour; **seit einem ~en** *or* **~ einem Jahr wohne ich hier** I have been living here for almost a year
(d) (= *kurz und präzis*) *Stil, Worte* concise; *Geste* terse; (= *lakonisch*) *Antwort* pithy
(e) (= *gerade so eben*) just; **mit ~er Not** only just
◼ ADV **(a)** (= *nicht reichlich*) rechnen, kalkulieren conservatively; *bemessen* too closely; **mein Geld/meine Zeit ist ~ bemessen** I am short of money/time; **ihr Vater hat ihr das Taschengeld ~ bemessen** her father was stingy with her pocket money (*inf*)
(b) (= *haarscharf*) **wir haben ~ verloren/gewonnen** we only just lost/won; **der Rock endete ~ über dem Knie** the skirt came to just above the knee; **es war ~ daneben** it was a near miss; **~ vorbei ist auch daneben** (*inf*) a miss is as good as a mile (*prov*); **aber nicht zu ~** (*inf*) and how!
(c) (= *nicht ganz*) not quite; **~ zwei Wochen** not quite two weeks

knapp halten VT IRREG **jdn ~** to keep sb short (*mit of*)

Knappheit F **-, NO PL** shortage; (*fig: des Ausdrucks*) conciseness; **wegen der ~ der uns zur Verfügung stehenden Zeit** because of the shortness of the time at our disposal

knapsen ['knapsn] VI (*inf*) to scrimp (*mit, an +dat* on); **an etw** (*dat*) **zu ~ haben** to have a rough time getting over sth

Knarre ['knarə] F **-, -n** (*sl:* = *Gewehr*) shooter (*inf*)

knarren ['knarən] VI to creak; **eine ~de Stimme** a grating voice

Knast M **-(e)s, ⸚e** *or* **-e** ['knɛstə] (*inf*) clink (*inf*), can (*US sl*); **in den ~ wandern** to be put behind bars

Knatsch [knaːtʃ] M **-es, NO PL** (*inf*) trouble; **das gibt ~** that means trouble

knatschig ['knaːtʃiç] ADJ (*inf*) (= *verärgert*) miffed (*inf*); (= *schlecht gelaunt*) grumpy (*inf*)

knattern ['knatɐn] VI (*Motorrad*) to roar; (*Maschinengewehr*) to rattle; (*Schüsse*) to rattle out; (*Fahne im Wind*) to flap

Knäuel ['knɔyəl] M *or* NT **-s, -** ball; (*wirres*) tangle; (*fig:* = *Durcheinander*) muddle; (*von Menschen*) group

Knauf [knauf] M **-(e)s, Knäufe** ['knɔyfə] (= *Türknauf*) knob; (*von Schwert*) pommel

Knauser ['knauzɐ] M **-s, -, Knauserin** [-ərɪn] F **-, -nen** (*inf*) scrooge (*inf*)

Knauserei [knauzə'rai] F **-, NO PL** (*inf*) meanness (*esp Brit*)

knauserig ['knauzərɪç] ADJ (*inf*) mean (*esp Brit*)

Knauserin F **-, -nen** *siehe* Knauser

knausern ['knauzɐn] VI (*inf*) to be mean (*esp Brit*) (*mit* with)

Knaus-Ogino-Methode ['knausloˈgiːnoː-] F (*Med*) rhythm method

knausrig ADJ (*inf*) mean (*esp Brit*)

Knausrigkeit F **-, NO PL** (*inf*) meanness (*esp Brit*)

knautschen ['knautʃn] VTI (*inf*) to crumple (up)

Knebel ['kneːbl] M **-s, -** (= *Mundknebel*) gag; (= *Paketknebel*) (wooden) handle; (*an Mänteln*) toggle

knebeln ['kneːbln] VT *jdn, Presse* to gag

Knebelvertrag M oppressive contract; **jdn durch einen ~ binden** to screw sb down with a tight contract (*inf*)

Knecht [knɛçt] M **-(e)s, -e (a)** servant; (*beim Bauern*) farm worker; (= *Stallknecht*) stableboy; **~ Ruprecht** *helper to St Nicholas (Santa Claus)* **(b)** (*fig:* = *Sklave*) slave (+*gen* to)

Knechtschaft ['knɛçtʃaft] F **-, -en** slavery

kneifen ['knaifn] *pret* **kniff** [knɪf], *ptp* **gekniffen** [gə'knɪfn] ◼ VT to pinch; **jdn** *or* **jdm in den Arm ~** to pinch sb's arm ◼ VI **(a)** (= *zwicken*) to pinch; **die Bluse kneift** the blouse is too tight **(b)** (*inf*) (= *ausweichen*) to back out (*vor +dat* of)

Kneifzange F pliers *pl*; (*kleine*) pincers *pl*; **eine ~** (a pair of) pliers/pincers

Kneipe ['knaipə] F **-, -n** (*inf:* = *Lokal*) pub (*Brit*), bar

Kneipenbummel M pub crawl (*Brit*), bar hop (*US*)

kneippen ['knaipn] VI to undergo a Kneipp cure

Kneippkur F Kneipp cure (*type of hydropathic treatment combined with diet, rest etc*)

Knesset(h) ['knɛsɛt] F **-, NO PL** Knesset

Knete ['kneːtə] F **-, NO PL** (*dated sl:* = *Geld*) dough (*inf*)

kneten ['kneːtn] VT *Teig* to knead; *Plastilin, Ton* to work; *Figuren* to model; (= *formen*) to form; *Muskeln, Rücken* to knead

Knet-: Knetgummi M *or* NT Plasticine®; **Knetmasse** F modelling (*Brit*) *or* modeling (*US*) clay

Knick [knɪk] M **-(e)s, -e** *or* **-s (a)** (= *leichter Sprung*) crack **(b)** (= *Kniff, Falte*) crease; (= *Eselsohr*) dog-ear; (= *Biegung*) (sharp) bend; (*bei Draht, auf Oberfläche*) kink; **einen ~ machen** to bend sharply **(c)** (*fig: in Karriere etc*) downturn

knicken ['knɪkn] ◼ VI AUX SEIN to snap ◼ VT to snap; *Papier* to fold; **„nicht ~!"** "do not bend *or* fold"; *siehe auch* **geknickt**

Knicker ['knɪkɐ] M **-s, -, Knickerin** [-ərɪn] F **-, -nen** (*inf*) scrooge (*inf*)

Knickerbocker ['knɪkɛbɔkɐ] PL plus fours *pl*

knickerig ['knɪkərɪç] ADJ (*inf*) stingy (*inf*)

Knickerigkeit F **-, NO PL** (*inf*) stinginess (*inf*)

Knickerin F **-, -nen** *siehe* **Knicker**

Knicks [knɪks] M **-es, -e** bob; (*tiefer*) curts(e)y; **einen ~ machen** to curts(e)y (*vor +dat* to)

knicksen ['knɪksn] VI to curts(e)y (*vor +dat* to)

Knie [kniː] NT **-s, - (a)** knee; **auf ~n** on one's knees, on bended knee; **(vor jdm) auf die ~ fallen** *or* **in die ~ sinken** to fall on *or* drop to one's knees (before sb); **sich vor jdm auf die ~ werfen** to throw oneself on one's knees in front of sb; **jdn auf ~n bitten** to go down on bended knees to sb (and beg); **in die ~ gehen** to kneel; (*fig*) to be brought to one's knees; **jdn in** *or* **auf die ~ zwingen** (*esp fig*) to bring sb to his/her knees; **jdn übers ~ legen** (*inf*) to put sb across one's knee; **etw übers ~ brechen** (*fig*) to rush (at) sth
(b) (= *Flussknie*) sharp bend; (*in Rohr, Tech:* = *Winkelstück*) elbow

Knie-: Kniebeuge F (Sport) knee bend; **in die ~ gehen** to bend one's knees; **Kniebundhose** F knee breeches pl; **Kniefall** M genuflection (form); **einen ~ vor jdm tun** (geh) or **machen** (lit, fig) to kneel before sb; (fig auch) to bow before sb; **kniefällig** ADV on one's knees, on bended knee; **Kniegelenk** NT knee joint; **Kniekehle** F back of the knee

knien [kni:n, 'kni:ən] **1** VI to kneel; **im Knien** on one's knees, kneeling **2** VR to kneel (down); **sich in die Arbeit ~** (fig) to get down to one's work

Knie-: Kniescheibe F kneecap; **Knieschnackler** [-ʃnaklɐ] M **-s, -** (dial inf) wobbly knees pl; **Knieschützer** [-ʃvtsɐ] M **-s, -** kneeguard; **Kniestrumpf** M knee sock; **knietief** ADJ knee-deep

kniff PRET von **kneifen**

Kniff [knɪf] M **-(e)s, -e (a)** (inf) trick; **den ~ bei etw heraushaben** to have the knack of sth (inf); **es ist ein ~ dabei** there is a (special) knack to it (inf) **(b)** (= Falte) crease, fold **(c)** (= Kneifen) pinch

kniffelig ['knɪfəlɪç], **knifflig** ['knɪflɪç] ADJ (inf) fiddly; (= heikel) tricky

Knigge ['knɪgə] M **-(s), -** etiquette manual

Knilch [knɪlç] M **-s, -e** (pej inf) clown (inf)

knipsen ['knɪpsn] **1** VT **(a)** Fahrschein to punch **(b)** (Phot inf) to snap (inf) **2** VI **(a)** (Phot inf) to take pictures **(b)** (= klicken) to click; **mit den Fingern ~** to snap one's fingers

Knirps [knɪrps] M **-es, -e (a)** (= Junge) whippersnapper; (pej) squirt **(b) Knirps®** folding or telescopic umbrella

knirschen ['knɪrʃn] VI to crunch; (Getriebe) to grind; **mit den Zähnen ~** to grind one's teeth

knistern ['knɪstɐn] VI (Feuer) to crackle; (Papier, Seide) to rustle; **mit Papier** etc **~** to rustle paper etc; **es knistert im Gebälk** (fig) there is trouble brewing

knitter-: knitterarm ADJ crease-resistant; **knitterfrei** ADJ Stoff, Kleid non-crease

knittern ['knɪtɐn] VTI to crease

Knobelbecher M **(a)** dice cup **(b)** (Mil sl) army boot

knobeln ['kno:bln] VI **(a)** (= würfeln) to play dice; (um eine Entscheidung) to toss for it (inf) **(b)** (= nachdenken) to puzzle (an +dat over)

Knoblauch ['kno:plaux, 'kno:blaux, 'knɔplaux, 'knɔblaux] M, NO PL garlic

Knoblauch-: Knoblauchbrot NT garlic bread; **Knoblauchpresse** F garlic press; **Knoblauchzehe** F clove of garlic

Knöchel ['knœçl] M **-s, -** (= Fußknöchel) ankle; (= Fingerknöchel) knuckle

Knochen ['knɔxn] M **-s, -** bone; **Fleisch mit/ohne ~** meat on/off the bone; **die Wunde geht bis auf den ~** the wound has penetrated to the bone; **mir tun alle ~ weh** (inf) every bone in my body is aching; **er ist bis auf die ~ abgemagert** he is just (a bag of) skin and bones; **brich dir nicht die ~!** (inf) don't break your neck!; **dem breche ich alle ~ einzeln** (inf) I'll break every bone in his body; **ihr steckt** or **sitzt die Angst in den ~** (inf) she's scared stiff (inf); **die Angst ist ihr in die ~ gefahren** it gave her a real fright; **der Schreck fuhr ihr in die ~** she was paralyzed with shock; **nass bis auf die ~** (inf) soaked to the skin; **kein Mark** or **keinen Mumm in den ~ haben** (inf) to have no guts (inf)

Knochen-: Knochenarbeit F hard graft (inf); **Knochenbau** M, NO PL bone structure; **Knochenbruch** M fracture; **Knochengerüst** NT skeleton; **knochenhart** (inf) **1** ADJ rock-hard; (fig) Job, Kerl really tough **2** ADV vorgehen ruthlessly; trainieren, fordern, verhandeln rigorously; **Knochenhaut** F periosteum (spec); **Knochenmark** NT bone marrow; **Knochenmehl** NT bone meal; **knochentrocken** (inf) **1** ADJ bone-dry (inf); (fig) Humor etc very dry **2** ADV very dryly

knöchern ['knœçɐn] ADJ bone attr, of bone; (inf) Mensch, Körperbau bony; (pej inf: = nicht anpassungsfähig) set in one's ways

knochig ['knɔxɪç] ADJ bony

Knock-down [nɔk'daun] M **-(s), -s**, **Knockdown** M **-(s), -s** knockdown

Knock-out [nɔk'laut] M **-(s), -s**, **Knockout** M **-(s), -s** knockout

Knödel ['knø:dl] M **-s, -** dumpling

Knöllchen ['knœlçən] NT **-s, - (a)** DIM von **Knolle (b)** (inf: = Strafzettel) (parking) ticket

Knolle ['knɔlə] F **-, -n** (Bot) nodule, tubercule; (von Kartoffel, Dahlie) tuber; (= Kartoffel) potato; (inf: = Nase) conk (Brit inf), honker (US inf)

Knollen ['knɔlən] M **-s, -** (= Klumpen) lump

Knollenblätterpilz M amanita; **grüner ~** deadly amanita; **weißer ~** destroying angel

Knopf [knɔpf] M **-(e)s, ⸚e** ['knœpfə] **(a)** (an Kleidungsstück etc) button **(b)** (an Gerät, elektrischer Anlage etc) (push) button; (an Akkordeon) button **(c)** (an Tür, Stock) knob; (= Sattelknopf, Degenknopf) pommel

knöpfen ['knœpfn], (Aus inf) **knöpfeln** ['knœpfln] VT to button (up); **einen Kragen auf ein Kleid ~** to button a collar to a dress; **ein Kleid zum Knöpfen** a dress that buttons up

Knopf-: Knopfloch NT buttonhole; **Knopfzelle** F round cell battery

Knorpel ['knɔrpl] M **-s, -** (Anat) (Zool) cartilage; (Cook) gristle

knorpelig ['knɔrpəlɪç] ADJ (Anat) cartilaginous; Fleisch gristly

Knorren ['knɔrən] M **-s, -** (im Holz) knot; (an Weide) burl; (= Baumstumpf) (tree) stump

knorrig ['knɔrɪç] ADJ Baum gnarled; Holz, Klotz knotty

Knospe ['knɔspə] F **-, -n** bud; **~n ansetzen** or **treiben** to bud

Knötchen ['knø:tçən] NT **-s, -** DIM von **Knoten**

knoten ['kno:tn] VT Seil etc to (tie into a) knot

Knoten ['kno:tn] M **-s, - (a)** knot; (Med) (= Geschwulst) lump; (= Gichtknoten) tophus (spec); (Phys, Bot, Math, Astron) node; (fig: = Verwicklung) plot; **sich** (dat) **einen ~ ins Taschentuch machen** (inf) to tie a knot in one's handkerchief **(b)** (Naut) knot **(c)** (= Haarknoten) bun **(d)** = **Knotenpunkt**

Knotenpunkt M (Mot) (road) junction; (Rail) junction; (fig) centre (Brit), center (US)

Knöterich ['knø:tərɪç] M **-s, -e** knotgrass

knotig ['kno:tɪç] ADJ knotty, full of knots; Äste, Finger, Hände gnarled; Geschwulst nodular

Know-how ['no:hau, no:'hau] NT **-s**, NO PL know-how

Knubbel ['knʊbl] M **-s, -** (inf) lump

knuddeln ['knʊdln] VT (dial) to kiss and cuddle

knüllen ['knʏlən] VT to crumple

Knüller ['knʏlɐ] M **-s, -** (inf) sensation; (Press) scoop

knüpfen ['knʏpfn] **1** VT Knoten to tie; Band to knot, to tie (up); Teppich to knot; Netz to mesh; Freundschaft to form; **jdn an den nächsten Baum/den Galgen ~** (inf) to string sb up (inf); **etw an etw** (acc) **~** (lit) to tie sth to sth; (fig) Bedingungen to attach sth to sth; Hoffnungen to pin sth on sth; **große Erwartungen an etw** (acc) **~** to have great expectations of sth; **Kontakte ~** (zu or mit) to establish contact (with) **2** VR **sich an etw** (acc) **~** to be linked to sth; **an diese Bemerkung knüpften sich einige Fragen** this remark raised several questions; **an diese Zeit ~ sich für mich viele Erinnerungen** I have many memories of this time

Knüppel ['knʏpl] M **-s, - (a)** (= Stock) stick; (= Waffe) cudgel, club; (= Polizeiknüppel) truncheon; **Politik des großen ~s** big stick policy; **jdm (einen) ~ zwischen die Beine werfen** (fig) to put a spoke in sb's wheel (Brit) **(b)** (Aviat) joystick; (Aut) gear stick (Brit), gearshift (US)

knüppeln ['knʏpln] VI to use one's truncheon **2** VT to club; (Polizei) to use one's truncheon on

Knüppelschaltung F (Aut) floor-mounted gear change (Brit), floor shift (US)

knurren ['knʊrən] **1** VI (Hund etc) to growl; (wütend) to snarl; (Magen) to rumble; (fig: = sich beklagen) to groan (über +acc about) **2** VTI (= mürrisch sagen) to growl

Knurren NT **-s**, NO PL (von Hund) growl(ing); (wütend) snarl(ing); (von Magen) rumble, rumbling; (= Klagen) moan(ing)

knurrig ['knʊrɪç] ADJ grumpy; Angestellte etc disgruntled

Knusperhäuschen [-hɔysçən] NT gingerbread house

knuspern ['knʊspɐn] VTI to crunch; **etwas zum Knuspern** something to nibble; **an etw** (dat) **~** to crunch away at sth

knusprig ['knʊsprɪç] **1** ADJ crisp; (fig) Mädchen scrumptious (inf) **2** ADV gebacken, gebraten crisply; **~ braun** Hähnchen crispy brown; Mensch with a super tan; **etw ~ grillen** to grill sth until it is crispy

knutschen ['knu:tʃn] (inf) **1** VT to smooch with (inf) **2** VIR to smooch (inf)

Knutschfleck M (inf) lovebite (inf)

k. o. [kaːˈloː] ADJ PRED (*Sport*) knocked out; (*fig inf*) whacked (*inf*); **jdn ~ schlagen** to knock sb out

K. o. [kaːˈloː] M **-(s), -s** knockout, K.O.; **Sieg durch ~** victory by a knockout

Koala [koˈaːla] M **-s, -s**, **Koalabär** M koala (bear)

koalieren [kolaˈliːrən], *ptp* **koaliert** VI (*esp Pol*) to form a coalition (*mit* with)

Koalition [kolaliˈtsioːn] F **-, -en** (*esp Pol*) coalition; **kleine/große ~** little/grand coalition

Koalitions- IN CPDS coalition; **Koalitionsabsprache** F coalition agreement; **Koalitionsfreiheit** F freedom to form a coalition; **Koalitionsgespräch** NT coalition talks *pl*; **Koalitionspartner(in)** M(F) coalition partner

koaxial [kolaˈksiaːl] ADJ (*Tech*) coaxial

Kobalt [ˈkoːbalt] NT **-s**, NO PL (*abbr* **Co**) cobalt

kobaltblau ADJ cobalt blue

Kobold [ˈkoːbɔlt] M **-(e)s, -e** [-də] goblin

Kobra [ˈkoːbra] F **-, -s** cobra

Koch[1] [kɔx] M **-s, ⸚e** [ˈkœça], **Köchin** [ˈkœçɪn] F **-, -nen** cook; (*von Restaurant etc*) chef; **viele Köche verderben den Brei** (*Prov*) too many cooks spoil the broth (*Prov*)

Koch[2] NT **-s**, NO PL (*Aus*) (= *Apfelmus etc*) purée; (= *Griesbrei etc*) pudding

Koch-: Kochbuch NT cookery book; **kochecht** ADJ (*Tex*) *Farbe* fast at 100°; *Wäsche etc* suitable for boiling; **Kochecke** F kitchen area

köcheln [ˈkœçln] VI (*lit, fig*) to simmer

Köchelverzeichnis [ˈkœçl-] NT (*Mus*) Köchel index; **~ 25** Köchel *or* K. (number) 25

kochen [ˈkɔxn] **1** VI (a) (*Flüssigkeit, Speise*) to boil; **etw langsam** *or* **auf kleiner Flamme ~ lassen** to let sth simmer (over a low heat); **etw zum Kochen bringen** to bring sth to the boil; **jdn zum Kochen bringen** (*fig inf*) to make sb's blood boil; **der Kühler/das Auto kocht** (*inf*) the cooling system/car is overheating; **er kochte vor Wut** (*inf*) he was boiling with rage **(b)** (= *Speisen zubereiten*) to cook; (= *als Koch fungieren*) to do the cooking; (= *als Koch arbeiten*) to work as a cook; **er kocht gut** he's a good cook; **er kocht pikant** his cooking is (always) highly seasoned **2** VT **(a)** *Flüssigkeit, Teer, Nahrungsmittel, Wäsche* to boil; **etw langsam** *or* **auf kleiner Flamme ~** to simmer sth over a low heat **(b)** (= *zubereiten*) *Essen* to cook; *Kaffee, Tee, Kakao* to make; **etw gar/weich ~** to cook sth through/until (it is) soft; **Eier weich/hart ~** to soft-boil/hard-boil eggs **3** VI IMPERS (= *am Kochen sein*) to be boiling; **es kocht in ihr** she is boiling with rage; **im Stadion kochte es wie in einem Hexenkessel** the atmosphere in the stadium was electric

kochend 1 ADJ (*lit, fig*) boiling **2** ADV **~ heiß sein** to be boiling hot; (*Suppe etc*) to be piping hot

Kocher [ˈkɔxɐ] M **-s, -** (= *Herd*) cooker; (= *Campingkocher*) (Primus®) stove; (= *Wasserkocher*) ≈ (electric) kettle

Köcher [ˈkœçɐ] M **-s, -** (*für Pfeile*) quiver

Koch-: Kochfeld NT ceramic hob; **kochfest** ADJ (*Tex*) = kochecht; **Kochgelegenheit** F cooking facilities *pl*; **Kochgeschirr** NT (*esp Mil*) mess tin (*Mil*); **Kochherd** M cooker

Köchin F *siehe* Koch[1]

Koch-: Kochkunst F culinary art; **seine ~** *or* **Kochkünste** his cooking (ability); **Kochlöffel** M cooking spoon; **Kochnische** F kitchenette; **Kochplatte F (a)** (= *Herdplatte*) hotplate **(b)** (= *Kocher*) cooker; **Kochrezept** NT recipe; **Kochsalz** NT common salt; (*Chem auch*) sodium chloride; (*Cook*) cooking salt; **Kochschinken** M boiled ham; **Kochtopf** M (*cooking*) pot; (*mit Stiel*) saucepan; **Kochwäsche** F washing that can be boiled

Kode [koːt, ˈkoːdə] M **-s, -s** code

Kodein [kodeˈiːn] NT **-s**, NO PL codeine

Köder [ˈkøːdɐ] M **-s, -** bait; (*fig auch*) lure

ködern [ˈkøːdɐn] VT (*lit*) to lure; (*fig*) to tempt; **jdn zu ~ versuchen** to woo sb; **jdn für etw ~** to rope sb into sth (*inf*); **sich von jdm/etw nicht ~ lassen** not to be tempted by sb/sth; **sie köderte ihn mit ihrem Geld** she lured him with her money

Kodex [ˈkoːdɛks] M **-** *or* **-es, -e** *or* **Kodices** *or* **Kodizes** [ˈkoːditseːs] codex; (*fig*) (moral) code

kodieren [koˈdiːrən], *ptp* **kodiert** VT to (en)code

Kodierung F **-, -en** (en)coding

Koedukation [ˈkoːledukatsioːn, koleduˈkatsioːn] F **-**, NO PL coeducation

Koeffizient [koɛfiˈtsiɛnt] M **-en, -en** coefficient

Koexistenz [ˈkoːlɛksɪstɛnts, koˈlɛksɪsˈtɛnts] F, NO PL coexistence

Koffein [kɔfeˈiːn] NT **-s**, NO PL caffeine

koffeinfrei ADJ decaffeinated

Koffer [ˈkɔfɐ] M **-s, -** (suit)case; (= *Überseekoffer, Schrankkoffer*) trunk; (= *Arztkoffer*) bag; (*für Schreibmaschine, Kosmetika etc*) (carrying) case; **die ~ packen** (*lit, fig*) to pack one's bags; **aus dem ~ leben** to live out of a suitcase

Koffer-: Kofferanhänger M luggage label; **Kofferkuli** M (luggage) trolley (*Brit*), cart (*US*); **Kofferradio** NT portable radio; **Kofferraum** M (*Aut*) boot (*Brit*), trunk (*US*); (= *Volumen*) luggage space

Kognak [ˈkɔnjak] M **-s, -s** *or* **-e** brandy

Kohabitation [kohabitaˈtsioːn] F **-, -en** (*form*) cohabitation

Kohl [koːl] M **-(e)s, -e (a)** (*cabbage*); **das macht den ~ auch nicht fett** (*inf*) that's not much help **(b)** (*inf:* = *Unsinn*) nonsense

Kohldampf M, NO PL (*inf*) **~ haben** *or* **schieben** to be starving

Kohle [ˈkoːlə] F **-, -n (a)** (= *Brennstoff*) coal; (= *Stück ~*) (lump of) coal; **glühende ~n** (*lit*) (glowing) embers; **glühende** *or* **feurige ~n auf jds Haupt** (*acc*) **sammeln** (*geh*) to heap coals of fire on sb's head; **(wie) auf (glühenden** *or* **heißen) ~n sitzen** to be like a cat on a hot tin roof; **die ~n aus dem Feuer holen** (*fig*) to pull the chestnuts out of the fire **(b)** (= *Verkohltes, Holzkohle*) charcoal; **(tierische** *or* **medizinische) ~** animal charcoal **(c)** (*Art:* = *~stift*) (stick of) charcoal **(d)** (*Tech*) carbon **(e)** (*inf:* = *Geld*) dough (*inf*); **die ~ stimmt** the money's right; **gut** *or* **fett ~ machen** (*sl:* = *gut verdienen*) to make a lot of money

Kohle-: Kohlefilter M charcoal filter; **Kohlehydrat** NT carbohydrate; **Kohlekraftwerk** NT coal-fired power station

Kohlen- IN CPDS coal; **Kohlenbergbau** M coal-mining; **Kohlenbergwerk** NT coal mine; **Kohlendioxid** NT carbon dioxide; **Kohlenheizung** F coal heating; (= *Anlage*) coal heating system; **Kohlenherd** M range; **Kohlenmonoxid** NT carbon monoxide; **Kohlenofen** M (coal-burning) stove; **Kohlenpott** M (*infml:* = *Ruhrgebiet*) Ruhr (basin *or* valley); **Kohlenrevier** NT coal-mining area; **Kohlensäure F (a)** (*Chem*) carbonic acid **(b)** (*in Getränken*) fizz (*inf*); **kohlensäurehaltig** ADJ *Getränke* carbonated

Kohlenstoff M (*abbr* **C**) carbon

Kohlenstoff-Datierung [-datiːrʊŋ] F **-, -en** (radio)carbon dating

Kohlen-: Kohlenwasserstoff M hydrocarbon; **Kohlenzange** F (pair of) fire tongs *pl*; **Kohlenzeche** F coal mine

Kohle-: Kohlepapier NT carbon paper; **Kohlepfennig** M, NO PL *special tax paid on electricity to subsidize the coal industry*; **Kohlestab** M (*Tech*) carbon rod; **Kohlestift** M (*Art*) piece of charcoal; **Kohletablette** F (*Med*) charcoal tablet; **Kohlezeichnung** F charcoal drawing

Kohl-: Kohlkopf M cabbage; **Kohlmeise** F great tit; **kohl(pech)rabenschwarz** ADJ **(a)** *Haar* jet black; *Nacht* pitch-black **(b)** (*inf:* = *sehr schmutzig*) as black as coal; **Kohlrabi** [koːlˈraːbi] M **-(s), -** kohlrabi; **Kohlrübe** F (*Bot*) swede (*Brit*), rutabaga (*US*); **Kohlsalat** M coleslaw; **kohlschwarz** ADJ *Haare, Augen* jet black; *Gesicht, Hände* black as coal; **Kohlsprosse** F (*Aus*) (Brussels) sprout; **Kohlweißling** [-vaislɪŋ] M **-s, -e** cabbage white (butterfly)

Koitus [ˈkoːitʊs] M **-, -se** *or* **-** [ˈkoːituːs] (*esp Med*) coitus

Koje [ˈkoːjə] F **-, -n (a)** (*esp Naut*) bunk, berth; (*inf:* = *Bett*) bed; **sich in die ~ hauen** (*inf*) to hit the sack (*inf*) **(b)** (= *Ausstellungskoje*) stand

Kojote [koˈjoːtə] M **-n, -n** coyote

Kokain [kokaˈiːn] NT **-s**, NO PL cocaine

kokainsüchtig ADJ addicted to cocaine; **ein Kokainsüchtiger** a cocaine addict

kokett [koˈkɛt] **1** ADJ coquettish **2** ADV coquettishly

Koketterie [kokɛtəˈriː] F **-, -n** [-ˈriːən] coquetry

kokettieren [kɔkɛ'tiːrən], *ptp* **kokettiert** VI to flirt; **mit seinem Alter ~** to play upon one's age; **mit einem Gedanken/System** *etc* **~** to toy with an idea/method *etc*

Kokon [ko'kɔ̃] M **-s, -s** (*Zool*) cocoon

Kokos¹ ['koːkɔs] F **-, -** (= *Palme*) coconut palm

Kokos² NT **-,** NO PL coconut

Kokos- IN CPDS coconut; **Kokosfett** NT coconut oil; **Kokosflocken** PL desiccated coconut; **Kokosläufer** M coconut matting; **Kokosmilch** F coconut milk; **Kokosnuss** F coconut; **Kokospalme** F coconut palm *or* tree; **Kokosraspeln** PL desiccated coconut

Koks¹ [koːks] M **-es, -e** coke

Koks² M *or* NT **-es,** NO PL (*inf* = *Kokain*) coke (*inf*)

koksen ['koːksn] VI (*inf* = *Kokain nehmen*) to take coke (*inf*)

Kokser ['koːksɐ] M **-s, -, Kokserin** [-ərɪn] F **-, -nen** (*inf*) coke addict (*inf*)

Kola ['koːla] F **-,** NO PL (*Nuss*) cola *or* kola nut

Kolben ['kɔlbn] M **-s, -** (a) (= *dickes Ende, Gewehrkolben*) butt; (*Tech*: = *Motorkolben, Pumpenkolben*) piston; (*Chem*: = *Destillierkolben*) retort; (*von Glühlampe*) bulb; (*von Lötapparat*) bit (b) (*Bot*) spadix; (= *Maiskolben*) cob

Kolben-: Kolbenfresser M (*inf*) piston seizure; (**den**) **~ haben** to have piston seizure; **Kolbenhub** M (*von Pumpe*) plunger stroke; (*Aut*) piston stroke; **Kolbenring** M piston ring

Kolchos ['kɔlçɔs] M *or* NT **-,** **Kolchose** [-'çoːzə], **Kolchose** [kɔl'çoːzə] F **-, -n** collective farm

Kolibakterien ['koːli-] PL E.coli *pl*

Kolibri ['koːlibri] M **-s, -s** humming bird

Kolik ['koːlɪk] F **-, -en** colic

Kolkrabe ['kɔlk-] M raven

kollabieren [kɔla'biːrən], *ptp* **kollabiert** VI AUX SEIN (*Med, fig*) to collapse

Kollaborateur [kɔlabora'tøːɐ] M **-s, -e, Kollaborateurin** [-'tøːrɪn] F **-, -nen** (*Pol*) collaborator

Kollaboration [kɔlabora'tsioːn] F **-, -en** collaboration

kollaborieren *ptp* **kollaboriert** VI to collaborate

Kollage [kɔ'laːʒə] F **-, -n** = **Collage**

Kollaps [kɔlaps, kɔ'laps] M **-es, -e** (*Med, fig*) collapse; **einen ~ erleiden** to collapse

Kollateralschaden M collateral damage *no pl*

Kolleg [kɔ'leːk] NT **-s, -s** *or* **-ien** [-giən] (a) (*Univ*) (= *Vorlesung*) lecture; (= *Vorlesungsreihe*) (course of) lectures *pl* (b) (*Sch*) college (c) (*Eccl*) theological college

Kollege [kɔ'leːgə] M **-n, -n, Kollegin** [-'leːgɪn] F **-, -nen** colleague; (*Arbeiter auch*) workmate; **seine ~n in der Ärzteschaft** his fellow doctors; **~ kommt gleich!** somebody will be with you right away; **Herr ~!** Mr X; **der (Herr) ~ (Müller)** (*Parl*) the honourable (*Brit*) *or* honorable (*US*) member

kollegial [kɔle'giaːl] **1** ADJ **das war nicht sehr ~ von ihm** that wasn't what you would expect from a colleague; **mit ~en Grüßen** ≈ yours sincerely (*Brit*), sincerely yours (*US*) **2** ADV loyally; **sich ~ verhalten** to be a good colleague; **~ eingestellt sein** to be co-operative

Kollegialität [kɔlegiali'tɛːt] F **-,** NO PL loyalty (to one's colleagues)

Kollegin F *siehe* **Kollege**

Kollegium [kɔ'leːgiʊm] NT **-s, Kollegien** [-giən] (a) (= *Lehrerkollegium etc*) staff; (= *Ausschuss*) working party (b) = **Kolleg**

KOLLEGSTUFE

The **Kollegstufe**, or reformierte gymnasiale Oberstufe, refers to the final two school years in a **Gymnasium** (two and a half years in some Länder). Pupils have the opportunity to choose which subjects to study, thereby taking account of their abilities and interests, and to follow courses for one semester only. This system, introduced in the 1970s, is designed to prepare pupils for university. ▶ GYMNASIUM

Kollektion [kɔlɛk'tsioːn] F **-, -en** collection; (= *Sortiment*) range; **~ (an Mustern)** (set of) samples

kollektiv [kɔlɛk'tiːf] **1** ADJ collective **2** ADV collectively

Kollektiv [kɔlɛk'tiːf] NT **-s, -e** [-və] collective

Kollektor [kɔ'lɛktoːɐ] M **-s, Kollektoren** [-'toːrən] (*Elec*) collector; (= *Sonnenkollektor*) solar collector

Koller ['kɔlɐ] M **-s, -** (*inf*) (= *Anfall*) funny mood; (= *Wutanfall*) rage; (= *Tropenkoller*) tropical madness; **seinen ~ bekommen/haben** to get into/to be in one of one's funny moods; **einen ~ haben/bekommen** to be in/fly into a rage

kollidieren [kɔli'diːrən], *ptp* **kollidiert** VI (*geh*) (a) AUX SEIN (*Fahrzeuge*) to collide (b) AUX SEIN *or* HABEN (*fig*) to clash; **miteinander ~** to clash; **er ist mit dem Gesetz kollidiert** he has collided with the law

Kollier [kɔ'lieː] NT **-s, -s** necklet

Kollision [kɔli'zioːn] F **-, -en** (*geh*) (= *Zusammenstoß*) collision; (= *Streit*) conflict, clash; (*von Terminen*) clash

Kollisionskurs M (*Naut, Aviat*) collision course; **auf ~ gehen, einen ~ ansteuern** (*fig*) to be heading for trouble

Kollo ['kɔlo] NT **-s, Kolli** ['kɔli] package

Kolloquium [kɔ'loːkviʊm, kɔ'lɔkviʊm] NT **-s, Kolloquien** [-kviən] colloquium; (*Aus Univ*: = *Prüfung*) examination

Köln [kœln] NT **-s** Cologne

Kölner ['kœlnɐ] ADJ ATTR Cologne; **der ~ Dom** Cologne Cathedral

kölnisch ['kœlnɪʃ] ADJ Cologne *attr*; **er spricht Kölnisch** he speaks (the) Cologne dialect

Kölnischwasser NT, NO PL, **kölnisch Wasser** NT, NO PL eau de Cologne

Koloniakübel [ko'loːnia-] M (*Aus*) dustbin (*Brit*), trash can (*US*)

Kolonial- [kolo'niaːl] IN CPDS colonial; **Kolonialherrschaft** F colonial rule

Kolonialismus [kolonia'lɪsmʊs] M **-,** NO PL colonialism

Kolonial-: Kolonialmacht F colonial power; **Kolonialstil** M Colonial (style); **Kolonialzeit** F colonial times *pl*; **ein Relikt aus der ~** a relic of the colonial past

Koloniawagen [ko'loːnia-] M (*Aus*) refuse truck

Kolonie [kolo'niː] F **-, -n** [-'niːən] (*alle Bedeutungen*) colony; (= *Ferienkolonie*) camp

Kolonisation [koloniza'tsioːn] F **-,** NO PL (a) (= *Erschließung: von Gebiet*) settlement (b) (= *Kolonisieren: von Land*) colonization

kolonisieren [koloni'ziːrən], *ptp* **kolonisiert** VT (a) (= *erschließen*) *Gebiet* to settle in (b) (= *zur Kolonie machen*) *Land* to colonize

Kolonne [ko'lɔnə] F **-, -n** column; (= *Autoschlange*) (*fig*: = *Menge*) queue (*Brit*), line; (*zur Begleitung esp Mil*) convoy; (= *Arbeitskolonne*) gang; „**Achtung ~!**" "convoy"; **~ fahren** to drive in (a) convoy

Koloratur [kolora'tuːɐ] F **-, -en** coloratura

kolorieren [kolo'riːrən], *ptp* **koloriert** VT to colour (*Brit*), to color (*US*)

Kolorit [kolo'riːt] NT **-(e)s, -e** (*Art*) colouring (*Brit*), coloring (*US*); (*Mus*) (tone) colour (*Brit*) *or* color (*US*); (*Liter, fig*) atmosphere

Koloss [ko'lɔs] M **-es, -e** colossus

kolossal [kolo'saːl] **1** ADJ *Gebäude, Figur* colossal; *Glück, Gefühl* tremendous; *Dummheit* crass **2** ADV (*inf*) tremendously, enormously; **sich ~ verschätzen** to make a colossal mistake

Kolossal-: Kolossalfilm M epic film; **Kolossalgemälde** NT (*inf*) spectacular painting; **Kolossalschinken** M (*pej geh*) spectacular

Kolosseum [kolɔ'seːʊm] NT **-s,** NO PL **das ~** the Colosseum

kolportieren [kɔlpɔr'tiːrən], *ptp* **kolportiert** VT to spread; **die Zeitung kolportierte, dass ...** the paper spread the story that ...

kölsch [kœlʃ] ADJ = **kölnisch**

Kölsch [kœlʃ] NT **-, -** (a) (= *Bier*) ≈ (strong) lager (b) (= *Dialekt*) **er spricht ~** he speaks (the) Cologne dialect

kolumbianisch [kolʊm'biaːnɪʃ] ADJ Colombian

Kolumbien [ko'lʊmbiən] NT **-s** Colombia

kolumbisch [ko'lʊmbɪʃ] ADJ Colombian

Kolumbus [ko'lʊmbʊs] M **-'** **Christoph ~** Christopher Columbus

Kolumne [ko'lʊmnə] F **-, -n** (*Typ, Press*) column

Kolumnentitel M (*Typ*) headline, running head

Koma ['koːma] NT **-s, -s** *or* **-ta** [-ta] (*Med*) coma; **im ~ liegen** to be in a coma; **ins ~ fallen** to go into a coma

Kombi ['kɔmbi] M **-s, -s** (*Aut*) estate (car) (*Brit*), station wagon (*esp US*)

Kombikarte F (= *Fahr- und Eintrittskarte*) combined ticket (*for travel and admission*)

Kombination [kɔmbinaˈtsioːn] F **-, -en (a)** (= *Verbindung, Zusammenstellung, Zahlenkombination*) combination; (*Sport*: = *Zusammenspiel*) concerted move, (piece of) teamwork; **alpine/nordische ~** (*Ski*) Alpine/Nordic combination **(b)** (= *Schlussfolgerung*) deduction; (= *Vermutung*) conjecture **(c)** (= *Kleidung*) suit, ensemble; (= *Hemdhose*) combinations *pl*; (= *Arbeitsanzug*) overalls *pl*; (= *Fliegerkombination*) flying suit

Kombinations-: Kombinationsgabe F powers *pl* of deduction; **Kombinationsschloss** NT combination lock

kombinieren [kɔmbiˈniːrən], *ptp* **kombiniert** ⓘ VT to combine; **Möbel zum Kombinieren** unit furniture; **zum beliebigen Kombinieren** to mix and match ⓘ VI (= *folgern*) to deduce; (= *vermuten*) to suppose; **gut ~ können** to be good at deducing *or* deduction; **ich kombiniere: ...** I conclude: ...; **du hast richtig kombiniert** your conclusion is right

Kombi-: Kombiwagen M estate (car) (*Brit*), station wagon (*esp US*); **Kombizange** F combination pliers *pl*

Kombüse [kɔmˈbyːzə] F **-, -n** (*Naut*) galley

Komet [koˈmeːt] M **-en, -en** comet; (*fig*) meteor

kometenhaft ADJ (*fig*) *Aufstieg, Karriere* meteoric; *Aufschwung* rapid

Komfort [kɔmˈfoːɐ] M **-s**, NO PL (*von Hotel etc*) luxury; (*von Möbel etc*) comfort; (*von Auto*) luxury features *pl*; (*von Gerät*) extras *pl*; (*von Wohnung*) amenities *pl*, mod cons *pl* (*Brit inf*); **ein Auto mit allem ~** a luxury car

-komfort M SUF IN CPDS comfort; **Fahrkomfort** (motoring) comfort; **ein Fernsehgerät mit großem Bedienungskomfort** a television set with easy-to-use controls

komfortabel [kɔmfɔrˈtaːbl] ⓘ ADJ (= *mit Komfort ausgestattet*) luxurious, luxury *attr*; *Haus, Wohnung* well-appointed; (= *bequem*) *Sessel, Bett* comfortable; (= *praktisch*) *Bedienung* convenient ⓘ ADV (= *bequem*) comfortably; (= *mit viel Komfort*) luxuriously

Komik [ˈkoːmɪk] F **-**, NO PL (= *das Komische*) comic; (= *komische Wirkung*) comic effect; (= *lustiges Element*: *von Situation*) comic element

Komiker [ˈkoːmɪkɐ] M **-s, -, Komikerin** [-ərɪn] F **-, -nen** comedian; (*fig auch*) joker (*inf*); **Sie ~** you must be joking

komisch [ˈkoːmɪʃ] ⓘ ADJ **(a)** (= *spaßhaft, ulkig*) funny; (*Theat*) *Rolle, Person, Oper* comic; **das Komische daran** the funny thing about it
(b) (= *seltsam, verdächtig*) funny; **~, dass ich das übersehen habe** it's funny that I should have missed that; **mir ist/wird so ~** (*inf*) I feel funny; **er war so ~ zu mir** he acted so strangely towards (*Brit*) *or* toward (*US*) me
ⓘ ADV strangely; *riechen, schmecken, sich fühlen* strange; **jdm ~ vorkommen** to seem strange to sb

komischerweise [ˈkoːmɪʃəˈvaɪzə] ADV funnily enough

Komitee [komiˈteː] NT **-s, -s** committee

Komma [ˈkɔma] NT **-s, -s** *or* **-ta** [-ta] comma; (*Math*) decimal point; **fünf/null ~ drei** five/nought point three

Kommandant [kɔmanˈdant] M **-en, -en, Kommandantin** [-ˈdantɪn] F **-, -nen** (*Mil*) commanding officer; (*von Festung auch*) commander; (*Naut*) captain; (*von Stadt*) commandant

Kommandeur [kɔmanˈdøːɐ] M **-s, -e, Kommandeurin** [-ˈdøːrɪn] F **-, -nen** commander

kommandieren [kɔmanˈdiːrən], *ptp* **kommandiert** ⓘ VT **(a)** (= *befehligen*) to command **(b)** (= *befehlen*) **jdn an einen Ort ~** to order sb to a place; **ich kommandierte ihn zu mir** I ordered him to appear before me; **sich von jdm ~ lassen** to let oneself be ordered about by sb ⓘ VI **(a)** (= *Befehlsgewalt haben*) to be in command; **~der General/Offizier** commanding general/officer **(b)** (= *Befehle geben*) to command; **er kommandiert gern** he likes ordering people about

Kommanditgesellschaft [kɔmanˈdiːt-] F (*Comm*) ≈ limited partnership

Kommanditist [kɔmandiˈtɪst] M **-en, -en, Kommanditistin** [-ˈtɪstɪn] F **-, -nen** ≈ limited partner

Kommando [kɔˈmando] NT **-s, -s** command; **auf ~ schreit ihr alle ...** (up)on the command (you) all shout ...; **ich mache nichts auf ~** I don't do things to order *or* on command; **wie auf ~ stehen bleiben** to stand still as if by command; **der Hund gehorcht auf ~** the dog obeys on command; **das ~**

haben *or* führen/übernehmen to be in *or* have/take command (*über +acc* of); **wer hat das ~?** who is in command?

Kommando-: Kommandobrücke F (*Naut*) bridge; **Kommandokapsel** F (*Space*) command module; **Kommandoraum** M control room

---

kommen [ˈkɔmən]

ⓘ INTRANSITIVES VERB	ⓘ TRANSITIVES VERB
ⓘ UNPERSÖNLICHES VERB	

pret **kam** [kaːm], *ptp* **gekommen** [gəˈkɔmən] AUX SEIN

ⓘ INTRANSITIVES VERB
(a) (*allgemein*) to come; **ich komme (schon)** I'm (just) coming; **er wird gleich kommen** he'll be here right away; **da kommt er ja!** here he comes!; **ich habe zwei Stunden gewartet, aber sie kam und kam nicht** I waited two hours but she just didn't come; **wann soll der Zug kommen?** when's the train due?; **der Mai ist gekommen** May is here; **ich glaube, es kommt ein Unwetter** I think there's some bad weather on the way; **er schießt auf alles, was ihm vor die Flinte kommt** he shoots at everything he gets in his sights; **da kann** *or* **könnte ja jeder kommen und sagen ...** anybody could come along and say ...; **wann kommt Ihr Baby?** when's your baby due?; **das Baby kam zu früh/an Heiligabend** the baby arrived early/on Christmas Eve; **komm ich heut nicht, komm ich morgen** (*prov*) you'll see me when you see me; **kommt Zeit, kommt Rat** (*Prov*) things have a way of working themselves out; **wer zuerst kommt, mahlt zuerst** (*Prov*) first come first served (*prov*)

✦**(nach Hause) kommen** (= *ankommen*) to get home; (= *zurückkehren*) to come home; **bitte komm nach Hause!** please come home!; **von der Arbeit kommen** to get home from work; **zum Essen kommen** to come home for lunch/dinner *etc*

✦**komm!** come on!; **komm, sag schon** come on, tell me; **ach komm!** come on!

✦**komm, komm!** come on!; **komm, komm, wir müssen uns beeilen!** come on, we must hurry!; **komm, komm, werd nicht frech!** now now, don't be cheeky (*Brit*) *or* fresh (*US*)!
(b) (= *aufgenommen werden*) to go; **ins Gefängnis kommen** to go to prison; **ins Altersheim/Krankenhaus kommen** to go into an old people's home (*esp Brit*) *or* senior citizens' home (*US*)/into hospital; **in die** *or* **zur Schule kommen** to start school
(c) (= *hingehören*) to go; **das Buch kommt ins oberste Fach** the book goes on the top shelf; **das kommt unter „Sonstiges"** that comes under "miscellaneous"; **da kommt ein Deckel drauf** it has to have a lid on it
(d) (= *erscheinen, folgen*) to come; (*Zähne*) to come (through); **das Lied kommt als Nächstes** that song is next; **ich komme zuerst an die Reihe** I'm first; **bohren, bis Öl/Grundwasser kommt** to bore until one strikes oil/finds water; **pass auf, ob hier eine Tankstelle kommt** watch out for a filling station; **jetzt muss bald die Grenze/Hannover kommen** we should soon be at the border/in Hanover; **das Schlimmste kommt noch** the worst is yet to come; **warte, das kommt noch** wait, that comes later; **jetzt kommts!** wait for it! (*inf*); **wie sie (gerade) kommen** just as they come
(e) (= *gelangen, erreichen können*) to get; (= *mit Hand etc erreichen können*) to reach; **ich komme zurzeit nicht an die frische Luft** I never get out into the fresh air; **durch den Zoll/die Prüfung kommen** to get through customs/the exam; **ich komme mit meiner Hand bis an die Decke** I can touch the ceiling with my hand; **in das Alter kommen, wo ...** to reach the age when ...
(f) (= *aufgeführt oder gesendet werden*) (*TV, Rad, Theat etc*) to be on; **was kommt im Fernsehen?** what's on TV?; **Kobra 13, bitte kommen!** come in Kobra 13!
(g) (= *geschehen, sich zutragen*) to happen; **egal, was kommt** whatever happens; **komme, was da wolle** come what may; **seine Hochzeit kam für alle überraschend** his wedding came as a surprise to everyone; **das musste ja so kommen, so musste es ja kommen** it had to happen

✦**davon** *oder* **daher kommen** daher kommt es, dass ... that's why ...; **das kommt davon, dass ...** that's because ...; **das kommt davon** *or* **daher, dass es so viel geregnet hat** it's

because of all the rain we've had; **das kommt davon, wenn man nicht zuhört** that comes from not listening; **das kommt davon!** see what happens?
(h) (= *geraten*) **ins Wackeln kommen** to start shaking; **in Bewegung kommen** to start moving; **ins Erzählen kommen** to start telling a story; **zum Stehen** or **Stillstand kommen** to come to a halt or standstill
(i) (= *sich entwickeln*) (*Samen, Pflanzen*) to come on; **der Schnittlauch kommt schön** the chives are coming on well
(j) (*inf*) (= *einen Orgasmus haben*) to come (*sl*)
(k) (*mit Dativ*)

> *Wenn* **kommen** *mit dem Dativ und einem Substantiv oder Adjektiv verwendet wird, siehe auch unter dem Eintrag für das entsprechende Substantiv oder Adjektiv.*

ihm kamen Zweifel he started to have doubts; **jdm kommen die Tränen** tears come to sb's eyes; **mir kommen die Tränen!** you're going to make me cry!; **mir kommt ein Gedanke** or **eine Idee** I've just had a thought; **es kommt mir gerade, dass …** it has just occurred to me that …; **das Wort/sein Name kommt mir im Moment nicht** the word/his name escapes me for the moment; **du kommst mir gerade recht** (*iro*) you're just what I need; **das kommt mir gerade recht** that's just fine; **jdm frech kommen** to be cheeky (*Brit*) or fresh (*US*) to sb; **jdm dumm kommen** to act stupid; **komm mir nur nicht so!** don't take that attitude with me!; **wie kommst du mir denn?** what kind of attitude is that?
(l) (*mit Verb*)

> *Wenn* **kommen** *mit einem Verb verbunden ist, siehe auch unter dem Eintrag für das jeweilige Verb.*

der kleine Johannes kam angelaufen little Johannes came running up to me/us; **da kommt ein Vogel geflogen** there's a bird; **ich komme dann zu dir gefahren** I'll drive over to your place then; **kommt essen!** come and eat!; **jdn besuchen kommen** to come and see sb; **auf dem Sessel/neben jdm zu sitzen kommen** to get to sit in the armchair/next to sb; **jdn kommen sehen** to see sb coming; **ich habe es ja kommen sehen** I saw it coming

✦**jdn kommen lassen** to send for sb
✦**etw kommen lassen** *Mahlzeit, Taxi* to order sth; **die Kupplung kommen lassen** to let the clutch in
(m) (*mit Präposition*)

> *Wenn* **kommen** *mit einer Präposition verwendet wird, siehe auch unter dem Eintrag für die entsprechende Präposition.*

✦**an etw** (*acc*) **kommen** (= *sich verschaffen*) to get hold of sth; **ich bin mit der Hand an die Kochplatte gekommen** I touched the hotplate
✦**auf etw** (*acc*) **kommen** (= *kosten, sich belaufen, sprechen über*) to come to; (= *sich erinnern, sich ausdenken*) to think of; **und dann kamen wir auf das leidige Thema Überstunden** then we came onto the vexed question of overtime; **auf eine Idee** or **einen Gedanken kommen** to get an idea; **wie kommst du darauf?** what makes you think that?; **darauf bin ich nicht gekommen** I didn't think of that; **der Wagen kommt in 16 Sekunden auf 100 km/h** the car reaches 100 km/h in 16 seconds; **auf jeden Haushalt kommen 100 Liter Wasser pro Tag** each household gets 100 litres (*Brit*) or liters (*US*) of water per day; **das kommt auf die Rechnung/auf mein Konto** that goes onto the bill/into my account; **ich komme im Moment nicht auf seinen Namen** his name escapes me for the moment; **auf ihn/darauf lasse ich nichts kommen** (*inf*) I won't hear a word against him/it
✦**hinter etw** (*acc*) **kommen** (= *herausfinden*) to find sth out, to find out sth
✦**mit etw/jdm kommen** **da kommt sie mit ihrem kleinen Bruder** here she comes with her little brother; **mit einer Frage/einem Anliegen kommen** to have a question/a request; **komm mir nicht wieder damit!** don't start that all over again!; **komm (mir) bloß nicht mit DER Entschuldigung** don't come to me with THAT excuse!; **damit kann ich ihm nicht kommen** (*mit Entschuldigung*) I can't give him that; (*mit Bitte*) I can't ask him that; **komm mir nicht schon wieder mit deinem Vater!** don't start going on about your father again!

✦**um etw kommen** (= *verlieren*) *um Geld, Besitz, Leben* to lose sth; *um Essen, Schlaf* to go without sth
✦**zu etw kommen** (= *Zeit finden für*) to get round to sth; (= *erhalten*) to come by sth; *zu Ehre* to receive sth; (= *erben*) to come into sth; **wie komme ich zu der Ehre?** to what do I owe this honour (*Brit*) or honor (*US*)?; **zu einem Entschluss/einer Einigung kommen** to come to a conclusion/an agreement
✦**zu nichts kommen** (*zeitlich*) not to get (a)round to anything; (= *erreichen*) to achieve nothing
✦**zu sich kommen** (= *Bewusstsein wiedererlangen*) to come round; (= *aufwachen*) to come to one's senses; (= *sich fassen*) to get over it; (= *sich finden*) to find oneself

2 UNPERSÖNLICHES VERB
(a) **es kommen jetzt die Clowns** and now the clowns; **es kommen jetzt die Nachrichten** and now the news
(b) (*im übertragenen Sinn*) **es ist weit gekommen!** it has come to that!; **es kommt noch einmal so weit** or **dahin, dass …** it will get to the point where …; **so weit kommt es (noch)** that'll be the day (*inf*); **ich wusste, dass es so kommen würde** I knew that would happen; **wie kommt es, dass du …?** how come you …? (*inf*); **dazu kam es gar nicht mehr** it didn't come to that; **es kam zum Streit** there was a quarrel; **es kam eins zum anderen** one thing led to another; **und so kam es, dass …** and that is how it came about that …; **es kam, wie es kommen musste** the inevitable happened; **es kommt immer anders, als man denkt** (*prov*), **erstens kommt es anders und zweitens als man denkt** (*hum inf*) things never turn out the way you expect

3 TRANSITIVES VERB (*inf*: = *kosten*) to cost; **das kommt mich auf die Dauer teurer** that'll cost me more in the long term

Kọmmen NT -s, NO PL coming; **ein einziges ~ und Gehen** a constant coming and going; **etw ist im ~** sth is on the way in; **jd ist im ~** sb is on his/her way up

kommend ADJ *Jahr, Woche, Generation* coming; *Ereignisse, Mode* future; **(am) ~en Montag** next Monday; **in den ~en Jahren** in the years to come; **der ~e Meister** the future champion; **er ist der ~e Mann in der Partei** he is the rising star in the party

Kommentar [kɔmɛnˈtaːɐ] M -s, -e (= *Bemerkung, Stellungnahme*) comment; (*Press, Jur, Liter*) commentary; **jeden (weiteren) ~ ablehnen** to decline to comment (further); **kein ~!** no comment

Kommentator [kɔmɛnˈtaːtoːɐ] M -s, **Kommentatoren** [-ˈtoːrən], **Kommentatorin** [-ˈtoːrɪn] F -, -nen commentator

kommentieren [kɔmɛnˈtiːrən] *ptp* **kommentiert** VT (= *Press etc*) to comment on; (*Jur, Liter*) to write a commentary on; **kommentierte Ausgabe** (*Liter*) annotated edition

kommerziell [kɔmɛrˈtsi̯ɛl] **1** ADJ commercial **2** ADV commercially

Kommilitone [kɔmiliˈtoːnə] M -n, -n, **Kommilitonin** [-ˈtoːnɪn] F -, -nen fellow student

Kommissar [kɔmɪˈsaːɐ] M -s, -e, **Kommissarin** [-ˈsaːrɪn] F -, -nen, (*esp Aus*) **Kommissär** [kɔmɪˈsɛːɐ] M -s, -e, **Kommissärin** [-ˈsɛːrɪn] F -, -nen (*Admin*) commissioner; (= *Polizeikommissar*) inspector; (*ranghöher*) (police) superintendent

Kommissariat [kɔmɪsaˈri̯aːt] NT -(e)s, -e (a) (*Admin*) (= *Amt*) commissionership; (= *Dienststelle, Amtsbereich*) commissioner's department (b) (*Polizei*) (= *Amt*) office of inspector; office of superintendent; (= *Dienststelle, Amtsbereich*) superintendent's department; (*Aus*: = *Polizeidienststelle*) police station

Kommissarin F, **Kommissärin** F *siehe* **Kommissar**

kommissarisch [kɔmɪˈsaːrɪʃ] **1** ADJ temporary **2** ADV temporarily

Kommission [kɔmɪˈsi̯oːn] F -, -en (a) (= *Ausschuss*) committee; (*zur Untersuchung*) commission (b) (*Comm*) commission; **etw in ~ geben** to give sth (to a dealer) for sale on commission; **etw in ~ nehmen/haben** to take/have sth on commission

kommissjonsweise ADJ, ADV (*Comm*) on commission

Kommittent [kɔmɪˈtɛnt] M -en, -en, **Kommittentin** [-ˈtɛntɪn] F -, -nen (*im Kommissionsgeschäft*) principal; (*im Überseehandel*) consignor, sender; **~ und Kommissionär** principal and commission agent

Kommode [kɔ'moːdə] F -, -n chest of drawers; (hohe) tallboy, highboy (US)

kommunal [kɔmu'naːl] **1** ADJ local; (= städtisch auch) municipal; ~es Wahlrecht right to vote in local elections **2** ADV locally; (= städtisch auch) municipally

Kommunal-: Kommunalabgaben PL local rates and taxes pl; **Kommunalpolitik** F local government politics sing or pl; **Kommunalverwaltung** F local government; **Kommunalwahlen** PL local (government) elections pl

Kommune [kɔ'muːnə] F -, -n (a) local authority district **(b)** (= Wohngemeinschaft) commune

Kommunikation [kɔmunika'tsioːn] F -, -en communication; **die ~ ist unmöglich geworden** communication has become impossible

Kommunikations-: Kommunikationsmittel NT means sing of communication; **Kommunikationsschwierigkeiten** PL communication difficulties pl

kommunikativ [kɔmunika'tiːf] ADJ communicative

Kommunikee [kɔmuni'keː] NT -s, -s communiqué

Kommunion [kɔmu'nioːn] F -, -en (Eccl) (Holy) Communion; (= Erstkommunion) first Communion

Kommuniqué [kɔmyni'keː, kɔmuni'keː] NT -s, -s communiqué

Kommunismus [kɔmu'nɪsmʊs] M -, NO PL communism

Kommunist [kɔmu'nɪst] M -en, -en, **Kommunistin** [-'nɪstɪn] F -, -nen Communist

kommunistisch [kɔmu'nɪstɪʃ] ADJ communist

kommunizieren [kɔmuni'tsiːrən], ptp **kommuniziert** VI **(a)** (= in Kommunikation sein) to communicate; ~de Röhren (Phys) communicating tubes **(b)** (Eccl) to receive (Holy) Communion

Komödiant [komø'diant] M -en, -en, **Komödiantin** [-'diantɪn] F -, -nen **(a)** (old) actor/actress, player (old) **(b)** (fig) play-actor

komödiantisch [komø'diantɪʃ] **1** ADJ (= schauspielerisch) acting; (pej) histrionic **2** ADV comically

Komödie [ko'møːdiə] F -, -n comedy; (fig) (= heiteres Ereignis) farce; (= Täuschung) play-acting; **die Stuttgarter ~** the Stuttgart Comedy Theatre (Brit) or Theater (US); **~ spielen** (fig) to put on an act

Kompagnon [kɔmpa'jõː, 'kɔmpanjõ] M -s, -s (Comm) partner, associate; (iro) pal (inf)

kompakt [kɔm'pakt] **1** ADJ compact; (inf: = gedrungen) Mensch stocky **2** ADV compactly

Kompakt-: Kompaktkamera F compact camera; **Kompaktwagen** M (Aut) small family car, subcompact (US)

Kompanie [kɔmpa'niː] F -, -n [-'niːən] (Mil) company

Kompaniechef(in) M(F), **Kompanieführer(in)** M(F) (Mil) company commander

Komparativ ['kɔmparatiːf] M -s, -e [-və] (Gram) comparative

Komparse [kɔm'parzə] M -n, -n, **Komparsin** [-'parzɪn] F -, -nen (Film) extra; (Theat) supernumerary; **er war nur ein ~** he only had a walk-on part

Kompass ['kɔmpas] M -es, -e compass; **nach dem ~** by the compass

Kompassnadel F compass needle

kompatibel [kɔmpa'tiːbl] ADJ (liter, Tech) compatible

Kompatibilität [kɔmpatibili'tɛːt] F -, -en (liter, Tech) compatibility

Kompensation [kɔmpenza'tsioːn] F -, -en compensation

kompensieren [kɔmpen'ziːrən], ptp **kompensiert** VT to compensate for

kompetent [kɔmpe'tent] **1** ADJ competent **2** ADV competently; **jdm ~ Auskunft geben** to inform sb knowledgeably

Kompetenz [kɔmpe'tents] F -, -en **(a)** (area of) competence; (eines Gerichts) jurisdiction; **da hat er ganz eindeutig seine ~en überschritten** he has quite clearly exceeded his authority here; **das fällt in die ~ dieses Amtes** that's the responsibility of this office; **seine mangelnde ~ in dieser Frage** his lack of competence in this issue **(b)** (Ling) competence

Kompetenz-: Kompetenzbereich M area of competence; **Kompetenzgerangel** NT bickering over responsibilities; **Kompetenzstreitigkeiten** PL dispute over respective areas of responsibility

komplementär [kɔmplemen'tɛːɐ] ADJ complementary

Komplementär [kɔmplemen'tɛːɐ] M -s, -e, **Komplementärin** [-'tɛːrɪn] F -, -nen fully liable partner in a limited partnership

Komplementärfarbe F complementary colour (Brit) or color (US)

komplett [kɔm'plet] **1** ADJ complete; **ein ~es Frühstück** a full breakfast; **ein ~es Menü** a (full) three course meal **2** ADV completely

komplex [kɔm'pleks] **1** ADJ complex **2** ADV complexly; **die Situation stellt sich ~ dar** the situation appears to be complex; **~ aufgebaut** complex in structure

Komplex [kɔm'pleks] M -es, -e **(a)** (= Gebäudekomplex) complex; (= Fragen-/Themenkomplex) set of questions/issues **(b)** (Psych) complex; **er steckt voller ~e** he has so many complexes

Komplexität [kɔmpleksi'tɛːt] F -, NO PL complexity

Komplikation [kɔmplika'tsioːn] F -, -en complication

Kompliment [kɔmpli'ment] NT -(e)s, -e compliment; **jdm ~e machen** to compliment sb (wegen on); **mein ~!** my compliments!

Komplize [kɔm'pliːtsə] M -n, -n, **Komplizin** [-'pliːtsɪn] F -, -nen accomplice

komplizieren [kɔmpli'tsiːrən], ptp **kompliziert** VT to complicate

kompliziert [kɔmpli'tsiːɐt] **1** ADJ complicated; (Med) Bruch compound **2** ADV in a complicated way

Kompliziertheit F -, NO PL complexity

Komplizin F siehe **Komplize**

Komponente [kɔmpo'nentə] F -, -n component

komponieren [kɔmpo'niːrən], ptp **komponiert** VTI to compose

Komponist [kɔmpo'nɪst] M -en, -en, **Komponistin** [-'nɪstɪn] F -, -nen composer

Komposita PL von **Kompositum**

Komposition [kɔmpozi'tsioːn] F -, -en composition

Kompositum [kɔm'poːzitʊm] NT -s, **Komposita** [-ta] (Gram, Pharm) compound

Kompost [kɔm'pɔst, 'kɔmpɔst] M -(e)s, -e compost

Kompostieranlage F composting facility

kompostieren [kɔmpɔs'tiːrən], ptp **kompostiert** **1** VT to compost **2** VI to make compost

Kompott [kɔm'pɔt] NT -(e)s, -e stewed fruit, compote

Kompression [kɔmpre'sioːn] F -, -en (Tech) compression

Kompressionsprogramm NT (Comput) compression program

Kompressor [kɔm'presoːɐ] M -s, **Kompressoren** [-'soːrən] compressor

komprimieren [kɔmpri'miːrən], ptp **komprimiert** VT to compress; (fig) to condense

Kompromiss [kɔmpro'mɪs] M -es, -e compromise; **einen ~ schließen** to (make a) compromise; **sie sind zu keinem ~ bereit** they are not willing to compromise

Kompromiss-: kompromissbereit ADJ willing to compromise; **Kompromissbereitschaft** F willingness to compromise; **kompromisslos** ADJ uncompromising; **Kompromisslosigkeit** F -, NO PL (von Mensch) uncompromising attitude; (von Haltung, Politik) uncompromising nature; **Kompromisslösung** F compromise solution

Kondensation [kɔndenza'tsioːn] F -, -en (Chem, Phys) condensation

kondensieren [kɔnden'ziːrən], ptp **kondensiert** VTI (vi: aux haben or sein) (lit, fig) to condense

Kondens- [kɔn'dens-]: **Kondensmilch** F evaporated milk; **Kondensstreifen** M (Aviat) vapour (Brit) or vapor (US) trail; **Kondenswasser** NT condensation

Kondition [kɔndi'tsioːn] F -, -en (auch Comm) condition; (= Durchhaltevermögen) stamina; **wie ist seine ~?** what sort of condition is he in?; **er hat überhaupt keine ~** he is completely unfit; (fig) he has absolutely no stamina; **zu den üblichen ~en** (Comm) under the usual terms

Konditionalsatz M conditional clause

konditionieren [kɔnditsio'niːrən], ptp **konditioniert** VT (Biol, Psych) to condition

Konditions-: Konditionsschwäche F lack no pl of fitness; **Konditionstraining** NT fitness training

Konditor [kɔn'diːtoːɐ] M **-s, Konditoren** [-'toːrən], **Konditorin** [-'toːrɪn] F **-, -nen** pastry cook (*Brit*), confectioner (*US*)

Konditorei F **-, -en** cake shop (*Brit*), confectioner's shop (*US*); (*mit Café*) café

Kondolenz- [kɔndo'lɛnts-] IN CPDS of condolence; **Kondolenzbuch** NT book of condolence

kondolieren [kɔndo'liːrən], *ptp* **kondoliert** VI (**jdm**) ~ to offer one's condolences (to sb); **schriftlich** ~ to write a letter of condolence

Kondom [kɔn'doːm] M or NT **-s, -e** condom

Kondukteur [kɔndʊk'tøːɐ] M **-s, -e** (*Aus, Sw*) conductor

Kondukteurin [kɔndʊk'tøːrɪn] F **-, -nen** (*Aus, Sw*) conductress

Konfektion [kɔnfɛk'tsioːn] F **-, -en** (= *Herstellung*) manufacture of ready-to-wear clothing (*Brit*); (= *Industrie*) clothing industry; (= *Bekleidung*) ready-to-wear clothes *pl or* clothing (*Brit*)

Konfektions- IN CPDS ready-to-wear; **Konfektionsgröße** F (*clothing*) size; **welche ~ haben Sie?** what size are you?; **Konfektionsware** F ready-to-wear clothing

Konferenz [kɔnfe'rɛnts] F **-, -en** conference; (= *Besprechung*) meeting; (= *Ausschuss*) committee

Konferenz- IN CPDS conference; **Konferenzschaltung** F (*Telec*) conference circuit; (*Rad, TV*) (television/radio) linkup; **Konferenzteilnehmer(in)** M(F) *siehe* **Konferenz** person attending a conference/meeting; **Konferenzzimmer** NT conference room

Konfession [kɔnfe'sioːn] F **-, -en** (*religious*) denomination; **welche ~ haben Sie?** what denomination are you?

Vorsicht! **Konfession** *wird nicht mit dem englischen Wort* **confession** *übersetzt.*

konfessionell [kɔnfɛsio'nɛl] **1** ADJ denominational **2** ADV ~ **gebundene Schulen** schools which are affiliated with a specific denomination

Konfessions-: konfessionslos ADJ nondenominational; **Konfessionsschule** F denominational school

Konfetti [kɔn'fɛti] NT **-s**, NO PL confetti

Konfiguration [kɔnfɪgura'tsioːn] F **-, -en** configuration

konfigurieren [kɔnfɪgu'riːrən], *ptp* **konfiguriert** VT *Computer, Software* to configure

Konfirmand [kɔnfɪr'mant] M **-en, -en** [-dn], **Konfirmandin** [-'mandɪn] F **-, -nen** (*Eccl*) confirmand

Konfirmandenblase F (*inf*) weak bladder

Konfirmation [kɔnfɪrma'tsioːn] F **-, -en** (*Eccl*) confirmation

konfirmieren [kɔnfɪr'miːrən], *ptp* **konfirmiert** VT (*Eccl*) to confirm

Konfiserie [kõfizə'riː] F **-, -n** [-'riːən] (*Sw*) (a) (= *Konditorei*) cake shop (*Brit*), confectioner's (shop) (*US*); (*mit Café*) café (b) (= *Konfekt*) confectionery

konfiszieren [kɔnfɪs'tsiːrən], *ptp* **konfisziert** VT to confiscate

Konfitüre [kɔnfi'tyːrə] F **-, -n** jam

Konflikt [kɔn'flɪkt] M **-s, -e** conflict; **mit etw in ~ geraten** to come into conflict with sth; **kommst du da nicht mit deinem Gewissen in ~?** how can you reconcile that with your conscience?

konform [kɔn'fɔrm] **1** ADJ *Ansichten etc* concurring; **in etw** (*dat*) ~ **sein** to agree on sth **2** ADV **mit jdm/etw ~ gehen** to agree with sb/sth (*in +dat* about)

-konform ADJ SUF in conformity with; **CSU-konforme Kandidaten** candidates adhering to the CSU line

Konformismus [kɔnfɔr'mɪsmʊs] M **-**, NO PL conformism

konformistisch [kɔnfɔr'mɪstɪʃ] **1** ADJ conformist, conforming **2** ADV ~ **eingestellt sein** to tend to conform with everything; **sich ~ verhalten** to be a conformist

Konfrontation [kɔnfrɔnta'tsioːn] F **-, -en** confrontation

Konfrontationskurs M **auf ~ gehen**, ~ **steuern** to be heading for a confrontation

konfrontieren [kɔnfrɔn'tiːrən], *ptp* **konfrontiert** VT to confront (*mit* with); **zwei Parteien ~** to bring two parties face to face

konfus [kɔn'fuːs] **1** ADJ confused **2** ADV confusedly; ~ **klingen** to sound confused; **ein ~ geschriebener Bericht** a report written in a confused style

Konfusion F **-, -en** confusion

Konglomerat [kɔnglome'raːt, kɔŋ-] NT **-(e)s, -e** (a) (*Geol*) conglomerate (b) (= *Ansammlung*) conglomeration

Kongo ['kɔŋgo] M **-(s)** (a) (*auch* **Demokratische Republik ~**) (Democratic Republic of the) Congo; (*auch* **~-Brazzaville**) (People's Republic of the) Congo (b) (= *Fluss*) Congo

Kongolese [kɔŋgo'leːzə] M **-n, -n**, **Kongolesin** [-'leːzɪn] F **-, -nen** Congolese

kongolesisch [kɔŋgo'leːzɪʃ] ADJ Congolese

Kongress [kɔn'grɛs, kɔŋ-] M **-es, -e** (a) (*Pol*) congress; (*fachlich*) convention; **der Wiener ~** the Congress of Vienna (b) (*in USA*) Congress

kongruent [kɔngru'ɛnt, kɔŋ-] ADJ (*Math*) congruent; (*Gram*) concordant; (*geh*) *Ansichten* concurring

K.-o.-Niederlage [kaː'loː-] F KO defeat

König ['køːnɪç] M **-s, -e** [-gə] king; **die Heiligen Drei ~e** The Three Kings *or* Magi; **der ~ der Tiere** the king of the beasts; **der ~ der Lüfte** the lord of the skies; **der Kunde ist ~** the customer is always right

Königin ['køːnɪgɪn] F **-, -nen** (*auch Zool*) queen

Königin-: Königinmutter F, *pl* **-mütter** queen mother; **Königinpastete** F vol-au-vent

königlich ['køːnɪklɪç] **1** ADJ royal; *Geschenk, Gehalt* princely; **Seine/Ihre Königliche Hoheit** His/Her Royal Highness **2** ADV (a) (*inf:* = *köstlich, ungeheuer*) **sich ~ freuen** to be as pleased as Punch (*inf*); **sich ~ amüsieren** to have the time of one's life (*inf*) (b) (= *fürstlich*) *bewirten* like royalty; *belohnen* richly

Königreich NT kingdom

Königtum ['køːnɪçtuːm] NT **-s, -tümer** [-tyːmɐ] (a) NO PL kingship (b) (= *Reich*) kingdom

konisch ['koːnɪʃ] **1** ADJ conical **2** ADV conically

Konjugation [kɔnjuga'tsioːn] F **-, -en** conjugation

konjugieren [kɔnju'giːrən], *ptp* **konjugiert** VT to conjugate

Konjunktion [kɔnjʊŋk'tsioːn] F **-, -en** (*Astron, Gram*) conjunction

Konjunktiv ['kɔnjʊŋktiːf] M **-s, -e** [-və] (*Gram*) subjunctive

konjunktivisch ['kɔnjʊŋkti:vɪʃ] ADJ subjunctive

Konjunktur [kɔnjʊŋk'tuːɐ] F **-, -en** economic situation, economy; (= *Hochkonjunktur*) boom; **steigende/fallende** *or* **rückläufige ~** upward/downward economic trend

Konjunktur-: konjunkturabhängig ADJ dependent on economic factors; **Konjunkturabschwung** M economic downturn; **Konjunkturaufschwung** M economic upturn; **konjunkturbedingt** ADJ influenced by *or* due to economic factors

konjunkturell [kɔnjʊŋktu'rɛl] **1** ADJ economic; *Arbeitslosigkeit* due to economic factors **2** ADV economically; ~ **bedingt** caused by economic factors

Konjunktur-: Konjunkturprognose F economic forecast; **Konjunkturrückgang** M slowdown in the economy; **Konjunkturschwäche** F weakness in the economy; **Konjunkturzyklus** M business cycle, trade cycle (*Brit*)

konkav [kɔn'kaːf, kɔŋ-] **1** ADJ concave **2** ADV concavely

konkret [kɔn'kreːt, kɔŋ-] **1** ADJ concrete; **ich kann dir nichts Konkretes sagen** I can't tell you anything concrete **2** ADV **drück dich ~er aus** would you put that in rather more concrete terms; **ich kann mir ~ vorstellen, wie ...** I can very clearly imagine how ...; **ich kann es dir noch nicht ~ sagen** I can't tell you definitely

Konkurrent [kɔnkʊ'rɛnt, kɔŋ-] M **-en, -en**, **Konkurrentin** [-'rɛntɪn] F **-, -nen** rival; (*Comm auch*) competitor

Konkurrenz [kɔnkʊ'rɛnts, kɔŋ-] F **-, -en** (= *Wettbewerb*) competition; (= *~betrieb*) competitors *pl*; (= *Gesamtheit der Konkurrenten*) competition; **jdm ~ machen** (*Comm*) (*fig*) to compete with sb; (*Comm auch*) to be in competition with sb; **zur ~ (über)gehen** to go over to the competition

Konkurrenz-: konkurrenzfähig ADJ competitive; **Konkurrenzkampf** M competition; **konkurrenzlos** **1** ADJ without competition **2** ADV ~ **billig** undoubtedly the cheapest

konkurrieren [kɔnkʊ'riːrən, kɔŋ-], *ptp* **konkurriert** VI to compete; (*Comm auch*) to be in competition

Konkurs [kɔn'kʊrs, kɔŋ-] M **-es, -e** bankruptcy; **in ~ gehen** to go bankrupt; ~ **machen** (*inf*) to go bust (*inf*)

Konkurs-: Konkursmasse F bankrupt's estate; **Konkursverfahren** NT bankruptcy proceedings *pl*;

Konkursverwalter(in) M(F) receiver; (von Gläubigern bevollmächtigt) trustee

können ['kœnən], pret **konnte** ['kɔntə], ptp **gekonnt** or (bei modal aux vb) **können** [gə'kɔnt, 'kœnən] VTI, MODAL AUX VB
(a) (= vermögen) to be able to; **ich kann es/das machen** I can do it, I am able to do it; **ich kann es/das nicht machen** I cannot or can't do it, I am not able to do it; **ich habe es sehen ~** I could see it, I was able to see it; **es ist furchtbar, nicht schlafen zu ~** it's terrible not to be able to sleep, he was able to do it; **morgen kann ich nicht** I can't (manage) tomorrow; **das hättest du gleich sagen ~** you could have said that straight away; **das hätte ich dir gleich sagen ~** I could have told you that straight away; **ich kann nicht mehr** I can't go on; (ertragen) I can't take any more; (essen) I can't manage any more; **kannst du noch?** can you go on?; (essen) can you manage some more?; **mir kann keiner!** (inf) it's not my problem; **ich habe das alles schriftlich, mir kann keiner!** (inf) I've got it all in writing, they can't touch me; **so schnell er konnte** as fast as he could or was able to; **~ vor Lachen!** (inf) I wish I could
(b) (= beherrschen) Sprache to (be able to) speak; Schach to be able to play; Klavier spielen, lesen, schwimmen, Ski laufen etc to be able to, to know how to; **was ~ Sie?** what can you do?; **was du alles kannst!** the things you can do!; **sie kann was** she's very capable; **unser Chef kann nichts** our boss is useless; **er kann gut Englisch** he speaks English well; **er kann kein Französisch** he doesn't speak French; **er kann/er kann nicht schwimmen** he can/can't swim; siehe auch **gekonnt**
(c) (= dürfen) to be allowed to; **kann ich jetzt gehen?** can I go now?; **könnte ich ...?** could I ...?; **er kann sich nicht beklagen** he can't complain; **man kann wohl sagen, dass ...** one could well say that ...; **du kannst mich (gern haben)!** (inf) get lost! (inf); **er kann mich (mal)** (inf) he can go to hell (inf)
(d) (= möglich sein) **Sie könnten Recht haben** you could or might or may be right; **er kann jeden Augenblick kommen** he could or might or may come any minute; **das kann nur er gewesen sein** it can only have been him; **das kann nicht sein** that can't be true; **es kann sein, dass er dabei war** he could or might or may have been there; **es kann nicht sein, dass er dabei war** he couldn't or can't possibly have been there; **kann sein** maybe, could be
(e) (mit Partikel) **für etw ~** to be to blame for sth; **ich kann nichts dafür** it's not my fault

Können NT -s, NO PL ability, skill

Könner ['kœnɐ] M -s, -, **Könnerin** [-ərɪn] F -, -nen expert

konnte PRET von **können**

Konsekutivsatz M consecutive clause

Konsens [kɔn'zɛns] M -es, -e [-zə] agreement

konsequent [kɔnze'kvɛnt] **1** ADJ consistent **2** ADV sich weigern, einhalten, befolgen strictly; ablehnen emphatically; verfechten, eintreten für rigorously; behandeln, argumentieren, verbieten consistently; **~ handeln** to be consistent; **er hat ~ "Nein" gesagt** he stuck to his answer of "no"; **wir werden ~ durchgreifen** we will take rigorous action

Konsequenz [kɔnze'kvɛnts] F -, -en consequence; **die ~en tragen** to take the consequences; (aus etw) **die ~en ziehen** to come to the obvious conclusion; **ich werde meine ~en ziehen** there's only one thing for me to do

konservativ [kɔnzerva'ti:f, 'kɔnzervati:f] **1** ADJ conservative; (Brit Pol) Conservative, Tory **2** ADV conservatively; **das ist ~ gerechnet** that's a conservative estimate

Konservative(r) [kɔnzerva'ti:və] MF DECL AS ADJ conservative; (Brit Pol) Conservative, Tory

Konservatorium [kɔnzerva'to:riʊm] NT -s, **Konservatorien** [-riən] conservatory

Konserve [kɔn'zervə] F -, -n preserved food; (in Dosen) tinned (Brit) or canned food; (= Konservendose) tin (Brit), can; (Med: = Blutkonserve etc) stored blood etc; blood bottle; (Rad, TV) prerecorded material; (= Tonkonserve) recorded music

Konservenbüchse F, **Konservendose** F tin (Brit), can

konservieren [kɔnzer'vi:rən], ptp **konserviert** VT to preserve, to conserve; Leichen to preserve; Auto to wax

Konservierung F -, NO PL preservation, conservation; (der Umwelt) conservation; (von Leichen) preservation

konsistent [kɔnzɪs'tɛnt] **1** ADJ (a) (fest) Masse solid (b) Politik, Antwort (Comput) Daten, Oberfläche consistent **2** ADV durchführen, behaupten consistently

Konsistenz [kɔnzɪs'tɛnts] F -, -en consistency; (von Gewebe) texture

konsolidieren [kɔnzoli'di:rən], ptp **konsolidiert** **1** VT (also Fin, Econ) to consolidate **2** VR to consolidate

Konsolidierung F -, -en consolidation

Konsonant [kɔnzo'nant] M -en, -en consonant

Konsorten [kɔn'zɔrtn] PL (pej inf) gang (inf); **X und ~** X and his gang (inf)

Konsortialkredit [kɔnzɔr'tsia:l-] M syndicated loan

Konsortium [kɔn'zɔrtsiʊm] NT -s, **Konsortien** [-tsiən] (Comm) consortium

konspirativ [kɔnspira'ti:f] ADJ conspiratorial; **~er Treff** meeting place (for terrorists etc); **~e Wohnung** safe house

konstant [kɔn'stant] **1** ADJ constant **2** ADV gut, schlecht, niedrig, hoch consistently

Konstante [kɔn'stantə] F -(n), -n constant

Konstanz ['kɔnstants] NT (Geog) - Constance

Konstellation [kɔnstela'tsio:n] F -, -en (a) constellation (b) (fig) line-up; (von Umständen, Faktoren etc) combination; **diese wirtschaftliche/politische ~** this economic/political situation; **die ~ in dem Gremium** the make-up of the committee

Konstitution [kɔnstitu'tsio:n] F -, -en constitution

konstitutionell [kɔnstitutsio'nɛl] **1** ADJ constitutional **2** ADV (a) (Pol: = verfassungsmäßig) constitutionally (b) (Med: = körperlich) **er war ~ im Vorteil** he had a better constitution; **für etw ~ anfällig sein** to be intrinsically susceptible to sth

konstruieren [kɔnstru'i:rən], ptp **konstruiert** VT to construct (auch Math, Gram); **ein konstruierter Fall** a hypothetical case; **der Satz klingt sehr konstruiert** the sentence sounds very artificial

Konstrukteur [kɔnstrʊk'tø:ɐ] M -s, -e, **Konstrukteurin** [-'tø:rɪn] F -, -nen designer

Konstruktion [kɔnstrʊk'tsio:n] F -, -en construction

Konstruktions-: Konstruktionsbüro NT drawing office; **Konstruktionsfehler** M (im Entwurf) design fault; (im Aufbau) structural defect

konstruktiv [kɔnstrʊk'ti:f] **1** ADJ constructive **2** ADV constructively

Konsul ['kɔnzʊl] M -s, -n, **Konsulin** [-lɪn] F -, -nen consul

Konsulargebühren PL consular fees pl

konsularisch [kɔnzu'la:rɪʃ] ADJ consular

Konsulat [kɔnzu'la:t] NT -(e)s, -e consulate

Konsulatsfaktura F consular invoice

konsultieren [kɔnzʊl'ti:rən], ptp **konsultiert** VT (form) to consult

Konsum [kɔn'zu:m] M -s, NO PL (= Verbrauch) consumption

Konsumartikel [kɔn'zu:m-] M consumer item; **~ pl** consumer goods pl

Konsument [kɔnzu'mɛnt] M -en, -en, **Konsumentin** [-'mɛntɪn] F -, -nen consumer

Konsum-: Konsumgesellschaft F consumer society; **Konsumgut** NT USU PL consumer item; **Konsumgüter** pl consumer goods pl; **Konsumgüterindustrie** F consumer goods industry; **Konsumkredit** M personal loan

Kontakt [kɔn'takt] M -(e)s, -e contact (auch Elec); **~e** pl (Aut) contact breakers pl; **mit jdm/etw in ~ kommen** to come into contact with sb/sth; **mit jdm ~ bekommen, zu jdm ~ finden** to get to know sb; **mit jdm ~ aufnehmen** to get in contact or touch with sb; **mit jdm in ~ stehen** to be in contact or touch with sb; **keinen ~ mehr haben, den ~ verloren haben** to have lost contact or touch

Kontakt-: Kontaktadresse F accommodation address; **er hinterließ eine ~** he left behind an address where he could be contacted; **Kontaktanzeige** F personal ad; **Kontaktanzeigen** PL personal column; **Kontaktarm** ADJ **er ist ~** he lacks contact with other people; **Kontaktarmut** F lack of human contact; **Kontaktbildschirm** M touch-sensitive screen; **Kontaktfrau** F (= Agentin) contact; **Kontaktlinse** F contact lens; **Kontaktmangel** M lack of contact; **Kontaktmann** M, pl -**männer** (= Agent) contact; **Kontaktperson** F contact

Kontamination [kɔntamina'tsio:n] F -, -en (auch Kerntechnik) contamination; (Gram) blend(ing)

kontaminieren [kɔntamiˈniːrən], *ptp* **kontaminiert** VI to contaminate; (*Gram*) to blend

Konten PL *von* **Konto**

Konten-: **Kontenklasse** F class of accounts; **Kontenrahmen** M chart of accounts

Konter- [ˈkɔntɐ-] IN CPDS (*Sport*) counter-; **Konteradmiral(in)** M(F) rear admiral; **Konterangriff** M counterattack

kontern [ˈkɔntɐn] **1** VT *Angriff, Vorwurf* to counter **2** VI to counter; (*Sport*) to counterattack

Konter-: **Konterrevolution** F counter-revolution; **Konterschlag** M (*Sport*) (*fig*) counterattack; (*Boxen*) counterpunch

Kontext [ˈkɔntɛkst] M context

Konti PL *von* **Konto**

Kontinent [ˈkɔntinɛnt, kɔntiˈnɛnt] M **-(e)s, -e** continent

kontinental [kɔntinɛnˈtaːl] ADJ continental

Kontinental-: **Kontinentaleuropa** NT the Continent; **Kontinentalklima** NT continental climate; **Kontinentalsockel** M continental shelf

Kontingent [kɔntɪŋˈɡɛnt] NT **-(e)s, -e** (*Mil:* = *Truppenkontingent*) contingent; (*Comm*) quota, share; (= *Zuteilung*) allocation

kontinuierlich [kɔntinuˈiːrlɪç] **1** ADJ continuous **2** ADV continuously

Kontinuität [kɔntinuiˈtɛːt] F **-**, NO PL continuity

Konto [ˈkɔnto] NT **-s**, **Konten** *or* **Konti** [ˈkɔntn, ˈkɔnti] account; **auf meinem/mein ~** in my/into my account; **das geht auf mein ~** (*inf*) (= *ich bin schuldig*) I am to blame for this

Konto-: **Kontoauszug** M (bank) statement; **Kontoauszugsdrucker** M *bank statement machine*; **Kontobewegung** F transaction; **kontoführend** ADJ *Bank* where an account is held; **Kontoführung** F running of an account; **Kontoführungsgebühr** F bank charge; **Kontoinhaber(in)** M(F) account holder; **Kontokorrent** [ˈkɔntokɔˈrɛnt] NT **-s, -e**, **Kontokorrentkonto** NT current account, cheque account (*Brit*), checking account (*US*); **Kontokorrentkredit** M overdraft (facility); **Kontonummer** F account number; **Kontostand** M balance

kontra [ˈkɔntra] PREP +ACC against; (*Jur*) versus

Kontra [ˈkɔntra] NT **-s, -s** (*Cards*) double; **~ geben** (*Cards*) to double; **jdm ~ geben** (*fig*) to contradict sb

Kontrabass M double bass

Kontrahent [kɔntraˈhɛnt] M **-en, -en**, **Kontrahentin** [-ˈhɛntɪn] F **-, -nen** (= *Vertragsschließender*) contracting party; (= *Gegner*) adversary

Kontraindikation [kɔntra-, ˈkɔntra-] F (*Med*) contraindication

Kontra-: **kontraproduktiv** ADJ counterproductive; **Kontrapunkt** M (*Mus*) counterpoint

Kontrast [kɔnˈtrast] M **-(e)s, -e** contrast

Kontrast-: **kontrastarm** ADJ **~ sein** to be lacking in contrast; (*Programm, Landschaft*) to be monotonous; **Kontrastbrei** M (*Med*) barium meal

kontrastieren [kɔntrasˈtiːrən], *ptp* **kontrastiert** VI to contrast

Kontrast-: **Kontrastmittel** NT (*Med*) contrast medium; **Kontrastprogramm** NT alternative programme (*Brit*) *or* program (*US*); **Kontrastregler** M contrast (control); **kontrastreich** ADJ **~ sein** to be full of contrast

Kontrollabschnitt M (*Comm*) counterfoil, stub

Kontrolllampe F *siehe* **Kontrolllampe**

Kontrolle [kɔnˈtrɔlə] F **-, -n (a)** (= *Beherrschung, Regulierung*) control; **über jdn/etw die ~ verlieren** to lose control of sb/sth; **jdn/etw unter ~ haben/halten** to have/keep sb/sth under control; **der Brand geriet außer ~** the fire got out of control **(b)** (= *Nachprüfung*) check (+gen on); (= *Aufsicht*) supervision; (= *Schutz*) safeguard; (= *Passkontrolle*) passport control; (= *Zollkontrolle*) customs examination; **jdn/etw einer ~ unterziehen** to check sb/sth; **zur ~ haben wir noch einmal alles nachgerechnet** we went over all the figures again to check; **~n durchführen** to carry out checks; **die ~n an der Grenze wurden verschärft** the border controls were tightened; **die ~ von Lebensmitteln** the inspection of foodstuffs **(c)** (= *Stelle*) (*für Überprüfung, Verkehr*) checkpoint; (= *Passkontrolle*) passport control; (= *Zollkontrolle*) customs; (*vor Fabrik*) gatehouse; (*an der Grenze*) border post; (*in Bibliothek etc*) checkout desk

(d) (= *Person*) inspector; (= *Pass-/Zollkontrolle*) passport/customs officer; (*in Fabrik*) security officer; (= *Polizist*) (*im Verkehr*) traffic police; (*an der Grenze*) frontier guard; (*in Bibliotheken etc*) person at the checkout desk

Kontrolleur [kɔntrɔˈløːɐ] M **-s, -e**, **Kontrolleurin** [-ˈløːrɪn] F **-, -nen** inspector

kontrollierbar ADJ controllable; *Behauptung* verifiable

kontrollieren [kɔntrɔˈliːrən], *ptp* **kontrolliert** VT **(a)** (= *regulieren, beherrschen*) to control **(b)** (= *nachprüfen, überwachen*) to check; (= *Aufsicht haben über*) to supervise; **die Qualität der Waren muss streng kontrolliert werden** a strict check must be kept on the quality of the goods; **jdn/etw nach etw *or* auf etw** (*acc*) **~** to check sb/sth for sth; **Gemüse aus kontrolliert biologischem Anbau** organically grown vegetables; **kontrollierte Drogenabgabe** medical prescription of narcotics; **staatlich kontrolliert** state-controlled

Kontroll-: **Kontrolllampe** F pilot lamp; (*Aut: für Ölstand*) warning light; **Kontrollpunkt** M checkpoint; **Kontrollstelle** F checkpoint; **Kontrollsystem** NT control system; **Kontrollturm** M control tower; **Kontrollzentrum** NT control centre (*Brit*) *or* center (*US*); (*Space also*) mission control

kontrovers [kɔntroˈvɛrs] **1** ADJ controversial **2** ADV **(etw) ~ diskutieren** to have a controversial discussion (about sth)

Kontroverse [kɔntroˈvɛrzə] F **-, -n** controversy

Kontur [kɔnˈtuːɐ] F **-, -en** outline, contour; **~en annehmen** to take shape

Konturenstift M liner

Konvektor [kɔnˈvɛktɔr] **-s, Konvektoren** [-ˈtoːrən] M convector (heater)

Konvention [kɔnvɛnˈtsioːn] F **-, -en (a)** (= *Herkommen*) convention; **sich über die ~en hinwegsetzen** to ignore (social) conventions **(b)** (*im Völkerrecht*) convention

Konventionalstrafe [kɔnvɛntsioˈnaːl-] F penalty (for breach of contract)

konventionell [kɔnvɛntsioˈnɛl] **1** ADJ conventional **2** ADV conventionally

konvergent [kɔnvɛrˈɡɛnt] ADJ convergent

Konvergenz [kɔnvɛrˈɡɛnts] F **-, -en** convergence

Konversation [kɔnvɛrzaˈtsioːn] F **-, -en** conversation; **~ machen** to make conversation

Konversationslexikon NT encyclopaedia (*Brit*), encyclopedia (*US*)

Konversion [kɔnvɛrˈzioːn] F **-, -en** conversion

Konverter [kɔnˈvɛrtɐ] M **-s, -** converter

konvertieren [kɔnvɛrˈtiːrən], *ptp* **konvertiert** **1** VT to convert (*in +acc* to) **2** VI AUX HABEN *or* SEIN to be converted

konvex [kɔnˈvɛks] **1** ADJ convex **2** ADV convexly

Konvoi [ˈkɔnvɔy, kɔnˈvɔy] M **-s, -s** convoy; **im ~ fahren** to drive in convoy

Konzentrat [kɔntsɛnˈtraːt] NT **-(e)s, -e** concentrate

Konzentration [kɔntsɛntraˈtsioːn] F **-, -en** concentration (*auf +acc* on)

Konzentrations-: **Konzentrationsfähigkeit** F powers *pl* of concentration; **Konzentrationslager** NT concentration camp; **Konzentrationsschwäche** F weak *or* poor concentration

konzentrieren [kɔntsɛnˈtriːrən], *ptp* **konzentriert** **1** VT to concentrate (*auf +acc* on); *Truppen auch* to mass **2** VR to concentrate (*auf +acc* on); (*Untersuchung, Arbeit etc*) to be concentrated (*auf +acc* on)

konzentriert [kɔntsɛnˈtriːt] **1** ADJ **(a)** (*Chem*) concentrated **(b)** **mit ~er Aufmerksamkeit** with all one's concentration **2** ADV *arbeiten, zuhören* intently; *nachdenken, spielen* intensely; *rechnen* carefully

konzentrisch [kɔnˈtsɛntrɪʃ] (*Math, Mil*) **1** ADJ concentric **2** ADV concentrically

Konzept [kɔnˈtsɛpt] NT **-(e)s, -e** (= *Rohentwurf*) draft; (= *Plan, Programm*) plan; (= *Begriff, Vorstellung*) concept; **jdn aus dem ~ bringen** to put sb off (*esp Brit*); (*inf: aus dem Gleichgewicht*) to upset sb; **aus dem ~ geraten** to lose one's thread; **das passt mir nicht ins ~** that doesn't fit in with my plans; (= *gefällt mir nicht*) I don't like the idea; **jdm das ~ verderben** to spoil sb's plans

Konzeptpapier NT rough paper

Konzern [kɔn'tsɛrn] M **-s, -e** combine; **die ~e haben zu viel Macht** the big companies have too much power

Konzert [kɔn'tsɛrt] NT **-(e)s, -e** concert; (= *Komposition*) concerto

konzertiert [kɔntsɛr'tiːɐt] ADJ **~e Aktion** (*Fin, Pol*) concerted action

Konzession [kɔntsɛ'sioːn] F **-, -en (a)** (= *Gewerbeerlaubnis*) concession, licence (*Brit*), license (*US*) **(b)** (= *Zugeständnis*) concession (*an +acc* to)

Konzessionär [kɔntsɛsioˈnɛːɐ] M **-s, -e**, **Konzessionärin** [-'nɛːrɪn] F **-, -nen** concessionaire, licensee

Konzessivsatz M (*Gram*) concessive clause

Konzil [kɔn'tsiːl] NT **-s, -e** *or* **-ien** [-liən] (*Eccl, Univ*) council

konzipieren [kɔntsi'piːrən], *ptp* **konzipiert** ◻ VT to conceive ◻ VI (*Med*) to conceive

Kooperation [koʔopera'tsioːn] F **-, -en** cooperation

kooperativ [koʔopera'tiːf] ◻ ADJ cooperative ◻ ADV cooperatively

Kooperative [koʔopera'tiːvə] F **-, -n** (*Econ*) cooperative

kooperieren [koʔope'riːrən], *ptp* **kooperiert** VI to cooperate

Koordinate [koʔɔrdi'naːtə] F **-, -n** (*Math*) coordinate

Koordinaten- (*Math*): **Koordinatenachse** F coordinate axis; **Koordinatenkreuz** NT, **Koordinatensystem** NT coordinate system

Koordination [koʔɔrdina'tsioːn] F **-, -en** coordination

Koordinator [koʔɔrdi'naːtoːɐ] M **-s, Koordinatoren** [-'toːrən], **Koordinatorin** [-'toːrɪn] F **-, -nen** coordinator

koordinieren [koʔɔrdi'niːrən], *ptp* **koordiniert** VT to coordinate

koordinierend ADJ (*auch Gram*) coordinating

Kopenhagen [ko:pn'ha:gn] NT **-s** Copenhagen

Kopf [kɔpf]

gen **Kopf(e)s**, *pl* **Köpfe** ['kœpfə]

SUBSTANTIV (M) **-(e)s, ⁼e** ['kœpfə]
(a) (*allgemein*) head; (= *Zeitungskopf*) head; (= *Nachrichtenüberschrift*) heading; (= *Briefkopf*) (letter)head; (= *Sprengkopf, Gefechtskopf*) warhead; (= *Sinn*) head, mind; (= *Denker*) thinker; (= *leitende Persönlichkeit*) leader; (= *Bandenführer*) brains *sing*; **Salatkopf** head of lettuce; **Kohlkopf** head of cabbage; **Kopf oder Zahl?** heads or tails!; **Kopf hoch!** chin up!; **von Kopf bis Fuß** from head to foot; **einen schweren** *or* **dicken** (*inf*) **Kopf haben** to feel groggy; (*von Alkohol*) to have a hangover; **ein kluger/findiger Kopf** an intelligent/ ingenious person; **er ist ein fähiger Kopf** he's a very capable person; **die besten Köpfe** the best brains; **seinen eigenen Kopf haben** (*inf*) to have a mind of one's own
(b) (*mit Präposition*)

✦**an + Kopf** Kopf an Kopf shoulder to shoulder; (*Sport, Pferderennen*) neck and neck; **jdm etw an den Kopf werfen** *or* **schmeißen** (*inf*) to chuck sth at sb (*inf*); **jdm Beschimpfungen** *or* **Beleidigungen an den Kopf werfen** to hurl insults at sb; **sich** (*dat*) **an den Kopf fassen** *or* **schlagen** (*verständnislos*) to be left speechless

✦**auf + Kopf** auf dem Kopf stehen to stand on one's head; **er hat bei seiner Sauftour sein ganzes Gehalt auf den Kopf gehauen** (*inf*) he blew all his wages on his drinking spree; **jdm auf den Kopf spucken können** (*inf*) to tower above sb; **sie ist nicht auf den Kopf gefallen** she's no fool; **etw auf den Kopf stellen** to turn sth upside down; **du kannst dich auf den Kopf stellen, du wirst ihn nicht umstimmen** (*inf*) you can talk till you're blue in the face, you won't get him to change his mind (*inf*); **jdm etw auf den Kopf zusagen** to tell sb sth to his/ her face; **auf jds Kopf** (*acc*) **20.000 Euro aussetzen** to put 20,000 euros on sb's head

✦**aus dem Kopf** der Gedanke will mir nicht aus dem Kopf I can't get the thought out of my head; **sich** (*dat*) **etw aus dem Kopf schlagen** to put sth out of one's mind

✦**durch den Kopf** sich (*dat*) etw durch den Kopf gehen lassen to think about sth

✦**im Kopf** in one's head; **etw im Kopf haben** to have sth in one's head; **was man nicht im Kopf hat, muss man in den Beinen haben** (*inf*) you'd forget your/I'd forget my *etc* head if it wasn't screwed on (*inf*); **nichts als Tanzen/Fußball im Kopf**

haben to think of nothing but dancing/football; **andere Dinge im Kopf haben** to have other things on one's mind; **der Gedanke geht mir im Kopf herum** I can't get the thought out of my head; **etw im Kopf rechnen** to work sth out in one's head; **er ist nicht ganz richtig** *or* **klar im Kopf** (*inf*) he is not quite right in the head (*inf*); **das hältst du** *or* **hält man ja im Kopf nicht aus!** (*inf*) it's absolutely incredible! (*inf*)

✦**in den Kopf** mir ist neulich in den Kopf gekommen, dass ... the other day it crossed my mind that ...; **es will mir nicht in den Kopf** I can't figure it out; **sie hat es sich** (*dat*) **in den Kopf gesetzt, das zu tun** she's dead set on doing it

✦**mit + Kopf** mit bloßem Kopf bareheaded; **mit besoffenem Kopf** (*inf*) drunk out of one's mind (*inf*); **mit dem Kopf durch die Wand wollen** (*inf*) to be hell-bent on getting one's own way(, regardless)

✦**nach + Kopf** es muss ja nicht immer alles nach deinem Kopf gehen you can't have things your own way all the time

✦**pro Kopf** also 20 Euro, das gibt dann 5 Euro pro Kopf so 20 euros, that means 5 euros each; **das Einkommen pro Kopf** the per capita income

✦**über + Kopf** jdm über den Kopf wachsen (*lit*) to outgrow sb; (*fig*) (*Sorgen etc*) to be more than sb can cope with; (*Konkurrent etc*) to outstrip sb; **das könnt ihr nicht einfach über ihren Kopf hinweg entscheiden** you can't just decide without consulting her

✦**vor den Kopf** ich war wie vor den Kopf geschlagen I was dumbfounded; **musst du den Chef immer so vor den Kopf stoßen?** must you always antagonize the boss?

✦**zu Kopf(e)** (jdm) zu Kopf(e) steigen to go to sb's head
(c) (*mit Verb*)

Die in Verbindung mit **Kopf** *verwendeten Verben sind alphabetisch angeordnet (siehe auch unter dem Eintrag für das jeweilige Verb).*

er wird uns nicht gleich den Kopf abschlagen *or* abreißen he won't kill us; **einen kühlen Kopf behalten** *or* **bewahren** to keep a cool head; **seinen Kopf durchsetzen** to get one's own way; **den Kopf hängen lassen** (*fig*) to be despondent; **den Kopf für jdn/etw hinhalten** (*inf*) to take the rap for sb/sth (*inf*); **jdn den Kopf kosten** (*fig*) to cost sb his job; **das hat ihn den Kopf gekostet** (*fig*) that was the end of the road for him; **sich** (*dat*) **einen/keinen Kopf um** *or* **über etw** (*acc*) **machen** to think/not think about sth; **mach dir keinen Kopf!** (*inf*: = *keine Sorgen*) don't worry yourself (*inf*); **jdn einen Kopf kürzer machen** (*inf*) to chop sb's head off; **für etw Kopf und Kragen riskieren** to risk one's neck for sth; **es werden Köpfe rollen** heads will roll; **Kopf stehen** (*lit*) to stand on one's head; (*fig*) (*vor Aufregung*) to be in a state of excitement; (*vor Empörung*) to be in a (state of) turmoil; (*durcheinander sein: Haus etc*) to be upside down; **ich weiß schon gar nicht mehr** *or* **kaum mehr, wo mir der Kopf steht** I don't know if I'm coming or going; **jdm den Kopf verdrehen** to turn sb's head; **den Kopf nicht verlieren** not to lose one's head; **Kopf und Kragen wagen** (*inf*) (*körperlich*) to risk life and limb; (*beruflich etc*) to risk one's neck; **jdm den Kopf waschen** (*lit*) to wash sb's hair; (*fig inf*) to give sb a telling-off; **sich** (*dat*) **über etw** (*acc*) **den Kopf zerbrechen** to rack one's brains over sth; **die Köpfe zusammenstecken** to go into a huddle (*inf*)

Kopf-: **Kopf-an-Kopf-Rennen** NT neck-and-neck race; **Kopfbahnhof** M terminal (station); **Kopfball** M (*Ftbl*) header; **Kopfbedeckung** F headgear; **als ~ trug er ...** on his head he wore ...; **ohne ~** without a hat

Köpfchen ['kœpfçən] NT **-s, -** DIM *von* **Kopf** little head; (*fig hum*) brains *pl*; **~, ~!** clever stuff!; **~ haben** to be brainy (*inf*); **du bist aber ein kluges ~** (*iro*) clever *or* smart cookie, eh! (*inf*)

köpfen ['kœpfn] ◻ VT **(a)** jdn to behead; (*hum*) Flasche Wein to crack (open); **ein Ei ~** to cut the top off an egg **(b)** (*Ftbl*) to head ◻ VI **(a)** (*als Todesstrafe*) das Köpfen beheading **(b)** (*Ftbl*) **ins Tor ~** to head the ball in

Kopf-: **Kopfende** NT head; **Kopfgeburt** F (*fig*) intellectual creation; **Kopfgeld** NT bounty (*on sb's head*); **Kopfgeldjäger** M bounty hunter; **Kopfhaut** F scalp; **Kopfhörer** M headphone

-köpfig [kœpfɪç] ADJ SUF -headed; **eine fünfköpfige Familie** a family of five

Kopf-: Kopfjäger(in) M(F) head-hunter; **Kopfkissen** NT pillow; **Kopfkissenbezug** M pillow case *or* slip; **kopflastig** [-lastıç] ADJ (*lit, fig*) top-heavy; *Flugzeug* nose-heavy; **Kopflaus** F head louse; **kopflos** ■ ADJ (*fig*) in a panic; (*lit*) headless; ~ **werden** to lose one's head ■ ADV ~ **handeln** to lose one's head; ~ **reagieren** to lose one's head; ~ **durch die Gegend laufen** to run about like a headless chicken (*Brit*), to run around like a chicken with its head cut off (*US*); **Kopflosigkeit** F -, NO PL (= *Panik*) panic; **Kopfprämie** F reward; **kopfrechnen** VI INFIN ONLY to do mental arithmetic; **Kopfrechnen** NT mental arithmetic; **Kopfsalat** M lettuce; **kopfscheu** ADJ timid, shy; **jdn ~ machen** to intimidate sb; **Kopfschmerzen** PL headache; ~ **haben** to have a headache; **sich** (*dat*) **über** *or* **um etw** (*acc*) *or* **wegen etw ~ machen** (*fig*) to worry about sth; **Kopfschmerztablette** F headache tablet; **Kopfschuss** M shot in the head; **Kopfschütteln** NT -s, NO PL shaking the head; **mit einem ~** with a shake of one's head; **kopfschüttelnd** ADJ, ADV shaking one's head; **Kopfschutz** M protection for the head; (= *Kopfschützer*) headguard; **Kopfsprung** M dive; **einen ~ machen** to dive (headfirst); **Kopfstand** M headstand; **einen ~ machen** to stand on one's head; **kopfstehen** VI SEP IRREG AUX SEIN *siehe* Kopf; **Kopfsteinpflaster** NT cobblestones *pl*; **eine Gasse mit ~** a cobbled street; **Kopfstütze** F headrest; (*Aut*) head restraint; **Kopftuch** NT, *pl* **-tücher** (head)scarf; **kopfüber** ADV (*lit, fig*) headfirst; **Kopfverletzung** F head injury; **Kopfweh** [-ve:] NT -s, NO PL headache; ~ **haben** to have a headache; **Kopfwunde** F head wound; **Kopfzeile** F (*Comput*) header; **Kopfzerbrechen** NT -s, NO PL **jdm ~ machen** to be a headache for sb (*inf*); **sich** (*dat*) **über etw** (*acc*) ~ **machen** to worry about sth

Kopie [ko'pi:, (*Aus*) 'ko:piə] F -, **-n** [-'pi:ən, (*Aus*) -piən] copy; (= *Ablichtung*) photocopy; (*Phot*) print; (*fig*) carbon copy

Kopier-: Kopierapparat M photocopier; **Kopierbefehl** M (*Comput*) copy command

kopieren [ko'pi:rən], *ptp* **kopiert** ■ VT to copy; (= *nachahmen*) to imitate; (= *ablichten*) to photocopy; (= *durchpausen*) to trace; (*Phot*) *Film* to print; **eine Datei auf die Festplatte ~** to copy a file onto the hard disk; **oft kopiert, nie erreicht** often imitated but never equalled (*Brit*) *or* equaled (*US*) ■ VI to copy; (= *fotokopieren*) to photocopy

Kopierer [ko'pi:rɐ] M -s, - copier

Kopier-: Kopierfunktion F (*Comput*) copy function; **Kopiergerät** NT photocopier; **kopiergeschützt** ADJ (*Comput, HiFi*) copy-protected; **Kopierschutz** M (*Comput, HiFi*) copy protection; **mit ~** copy-protected; **Kopierstift** M indelible pencil

Kopilot(in) ['ko:-] M(F) copilot

Koppel¹ [kɔpl] NT -s, - *or* (*Aus*) f -, **-n** (*Mil*) belt

Koppel² F -, **-n** (a) (= *Weide*) paddock; **auf** *or* **in der ~** in the paddock (b) (= *Hundekoppel*) pack; (= *Pferdekoppel*) string

Koppelgeschäft NT tie-in deal

koppeln ['kɔpln] VT (a) (= *zusammenbinden*) to tie together (b) (= *verbinden*) to couple (*etw an etw acc* sth to sth); *zwei Dinge* to couple together; *Raumschiffe* to link up; (*fig*) to couple; (*als Bedingung*) to tie; *Ziele, Zwecke* to combine; **einen Vertrag mit einer Klausel ~** to attach a clause to a contract (c) (*Elec*) to couple

Koppelung ['kɔpəluŋ] F -, **-en** (a) (*Elec*) coupling (b) (= *Verbindung*) (*lit*) coupling; (*fig, von Raumschiffen*) linkup

Koppelungsmanöver NT (*Space*) docking manoeuvre (*Brit*) *or* maneuver (*US*); **ein ~ durchführen** to link up

Kopplung ['kɔpluŋ] F = Koppelung

Koproduktion ['ko:-] F coproduction

Koproduzent(in) ['ko:-] M(F) coproducer

kopulieren [kopu'li:rən], *ptp* **kopuliert** VI (= *koitieren*) to copulate

kor PRET *von* küren

Koralle [ko'ralə] F -, **-n** coral

Korallen-: Korallenbank F, *pl* **-bänke** coral reef; **Korallenriff** NT coral reef; **korallenrot** ADJ coral(-red); **Korallentiere** PL coral

Koran [ko'ra:n, 'ko:ra(:)n] M -s, NO PL Koran

Koranschule F Koranic school

Korb [kɔrp] M -(e)s, **-e** ['kœrbə] (a) basket (*auch Econ, Fin*); (= *Bienenkorb*) hive; (= *Förderkorb*) cage; **ein ~ Äpfel** a basket of apples (b) (= ~*geflecht*) wicker; **ein Sessel aus ~ a**

wicker(work) *or* a basket(work) chair (c) (*inf*: = *Abweisung*) refusal; **einen ~ bekommen/kriegen, sich** (*dat*) **einen ~ holen** to be turned down; **jdm einen ~ geben** to turn sb down

Korb-: Korbball M basketball; **Korbblütler** [-bly:tlɐ] M -s, - (*Bot*) composite (flower)

Körbchen ['kœrpçən] NT -s, - (a) DIM *von* **Korb** (*von Hund*) basket (b) (*von Büstenhalter*) cup

Korb-: Korbflasche F demijohn; **Korbmacher(in)** M(F) basket maker; **Korbmöbel** PL wicker(work) *or* basket(work) furniture; **Korbsessel** M wicker(work) *or* basket(work) chair; **Korbwaren** PL wickerwork *or* basketwork (articles *pl*)

Kord [kɔrt] M -(e)s, **-e** [-də] (*Tex*) cord, corduroy

Kordel ['kɔrdl] F -, **-n** cord

Kordilleren [kɔrdıl'je:rən] PL (*Geog*) Cordilleras *pl*

Korea [ko're:a] NT -s Korea

Koreaner [kore'a:nɐ] M -s, -, **Koreanerin** [-ərın] F -, **-nen** Korean

koreanisch [kore'a:nıʃ] ADJ Korean

Korfu ['kɔrfu, kɔr'fu:] NT -s Corfu

Koriander [ko'riandɐ] M -s, NO PL coriander

Korinthe [ko'rıntə] F -, **-n** currant

Korinthenkacker [-kakɐ] M -s, -, **Korinthenkackerin** [-ərın] F -, **-nen** (*inf*) fusspot (*Brit inf*), fussbudget (*US inf*)

Kork [kɔrk] M -(e)s, **-e** (*Bot*) (= *Korken*) cork; (*aus Plastik*) stopper

Korkeiche F cork oak *or* tree

Korken ['kɔrkn] M -s, - cork; (*aus Plastik*) stopper

Korkenzieher [-tsi:ɐ] M -s, - corkscrew

korkig ['kɔrkıç] ■ ADJ corky ■ ADV ~ **schmecken** (*Wein*) to be corked

Kormoran [kɔrmo'ra:n] M -s, **-e** cormorant

Korn¹ [kɔrn] NT -(e)s, **-er** ['kœrnɐ] (a) (= *Samenkorn*) seed, grain; (= *Pfefferkorn*) corn; (= *Salzkorn, Sandkorn, Tech, Phot, Typ*) grain; (= *Hagelkorn*) stone; (= *Staubkorn*) speck (b) NO PL (= *Getreide*) grain, corn (*Brit*); **das ~ steht gut** the grain *or* corn (*Brit*) looks promising

Korn² M -(e)s, - *or* **-s** (= ~*branntwein*) corn schnapps

Korn³ NT -(e)s, **-e** (*am Gewehr*) front sight, bead; **jdn/etw aufs ~ nehmen** (*lit*) to draw a bead on sb/sth; **jdn aufs ~ nehmen** (*fig*) to start keeping tabs on sb

Kornblume F cornflower

Körnchen ['kœrnçən] NT -s, - DIM *von* **Korn¹** small grain, granule; **ein ~ Wahrheit** a grain of truth

Körner-: Körnerfresser M (*Zool*) grain-eating bird; **Körnerfresser(in)** M(F) (*inf*) health food freak (*inf*); **Körnerfutter** NT grain *or* corn (*Brit*) (for animal feeding)

körnig ['kœrnıç] ADJ granular, grainy

-körnig ADJ SUF -grained; **grob-/feinkörnig** coarse-/fine-grained

Kornkammer F (*lit, fig*) granary

Korona [ko'ro:na] F -, **Koronen** [-nən] corona; (*inf*) crowd (*inf*)

Koronar- [koro'na:ɐ-] (*Med*) IN CPDS coronary; **Koronararterie** F coronary artery

Körper ['kœrpɐ] M -s, - (*alle Bedeutungen*) body; ~ **und Geist** mind and body; **am ganzen ~ beben** *or* **zittern/frieren** to tremble/to be cold all over

Körper-: Körperbau M, NO PL physique, build; **körperbehindert** [-bəhındɐt] ADJ physically handicapped; **Körperbehinderte(r)** MF DECL AS ADJ physically handicapped person; **die ~n** the physically handicapped; **körpereigen** ADJ occurring naturally in the body; **Körpergeruch** M body odour (*Brit*) *or* odor (*US*), BO (*inf*); **Körpergewicht** NT weight; **Körpergröße** F height; **Körperhaltung** F posture, bearing

körperlich ['kœrpɐlıç] ■ ADJ physical; (= *stofflich*) material; ~**e Arbeit** manual work; ~**e Züchtigung** corporal punishment ■ ADV physically

Körper-: Körperlotion F body lotion; **Körpermaße** PL measurements *pl*; **Körperöffnung** F (*Anat*) orifice of the body; **Körperpflege** F personal hygiene

Körperschaft ['kœrpɐʃaft] F -, **-en** corporation, (corporate) body; **gesetzgebende ~** legislative body

Körperschaft(s)steuer F corporation tax

Körper-: Körperschwäche F physical weakness; **Körpersprache** F body language; **Körperteil** M part of the body; **Körpertemperatur** F body temperature;

Körperverletzung F (*Jur*) physical injury; **fahrlässige ~** physical injury resulting from negligence

Korporal [kɔrpo'raːl] M **-s, -e** *or* **Korporäle** [-'rɛːlə], **Korporalin** [-'raːlɪn] F **-, -nen** corporal

Korps [koːɐ] NT **-, -** [koːɐ(s), koːɐs] (*Mil*) corps

korpulent [kɔrpu'lɛnt] ADJ corpulent

Korpus¹ ['kɔrpʊs] M **-, -se** (*Art*) body of Christ; (*hum inf*: = *Körper*) body

Korpus² NT **-, Korpora** ['kɔrpora] (*Ling*) corpus

korrekt [kɔ'rɛkt] **1** ADJ **(a)** (= *richtig, anständig*) correct; *Frage* civil; **politisch ~** politically correct **(b)** (*sl*: = *toll*) wicked (*sl*) **2** ADV correctly; *gekleidet* appropriately; *darstellen* accurately

korrekterweise [kɔ'rɛktɐ'vaizə] ADV to be correct

Korrektheit F **-,** NO PL correctness; **politische ~** political correctness

Korrektor [kɔ'rɛktoːɐ] M **-s, Korrektoren** [-'toːrən], **Korrektorin** [-'toːrɪn] F **-, -nen** (*Typ*) proofreader

Korrektur [kɔrɛk'tuːɐ] F **-, -en** correction; (*Typ*) (= *Vorgang*) proofreading; (= *Verbesserung*) proof correction; (= *~fahne*) proof; **~ lesen** to proofread (*bei etw* sth)

Korrektur-: Korrekturfahne F galley (proof); **Korrekturflüssigkeit** F correction fluid, White-Out® (*US*); **Korrekturspeicher** M correction memory; **Korrekturtaste** F correction key; **Korrekturzeichen** NT proofreader's mark

Korrespondent [kɔrɛspɔn'dɛnt] M **-en, -en, Korrespondentin** [-'dɛntɪn] F **-, -nen** correspondent

Korrespondenz [kɔrɛspɔn'dɛnts] F **-, -en** correspondence

Korrespondenzbank F, *pl* **-banken** correspondent bank

korrespondieren [kɔrɛspɔn'diːrən], *ptp* **korrespondiert** VI **(a)** (*in Briefwechsel stehen*) to correspond **(b)** (= *entsprechen*) to correspond (*mit* to, with)

Korridor ['kɔridoːɐ] M **-s, -e** (= *auch Luftkorridor etc*) corridor; (= *Flur*) hall

korrigierbar ADJ able to be corrected; **ein nicht so leicht ~er Sprachfehler** a speech defect which is not so easy to correct

korrigieren [kɔri'giːrən], *ptp* **korrigiert** VT (= *berichtigen*) to correct; *Aufsätze etc auch* to mark; *Meinung, Einstellung* to change; **nach oben/unten ~** to adjust upwards/downwards

korrodieren [kɔro'diːrən], *ptp* **korrodiert** VTI (*vi: aux sein*) to corrode

Korrosion [kɔro'zioːn] F **-, -en** corrosion

Korrosions-: korrosionsbeständig, korrosionsfest ADJ corrosion-resistant; **korrosionsfrei** ADJ noncorroding; **Korrosionsschutz** M corrosion prevention

korrupt [kɔ'rʊpt] **1** ADJ corrupt **2** ADV *handeln* corruptly; **als ~ gelten** to be considered corrupt

Korruptheit F **-,** NO PL corruptness

Korruption [kɔrʊp'tsioːn] F **-,** NO PL corruption

Korse ['kɔrzə] M **-n, -n, Korsin** ['kɔrzɪn] F **-, -nen** Corsican

Korsett [kɔr'zɛt] NT **-s, -s** *or* **-e** corset

Korsika ['kɔrzika] NT **-s** Corsica

Korsin F *siehe* **Korse**

korsisch ['kɔrzɪʃ] ADJ Corsican

Korso ['kɔrso] M **-s, -s** (= *Umzug*) parade, procession

Kortison [kɔrti'zoːn] NT **-s, -e** (*Med*) cortisone

Koryphäe [kory'fɛːə] F **-, -n** genius; (*auf einem Gebiet*) eminent authority

Kosak [ko'zak] M **-en, -en** Cossack

koscher ['koːʃɐ] **1** ADJ (*Rel, fig inf*) kosher **2** ADV **(a)** **~ kochen/schlachten** to cook/slaughter according to kosher requirements **(b)** (*fig inf*) **dabei ist es nicht ganz ~ zugegangen** that wasn't quite kosher (*inf*)

K.-o.-Schlag [kaː'oː-] M knockout blow; **durch ~ siegen** to win by a knockout

Kose- ['koːzə-]: **Kosename** M pet name; **Kosewort** NT, *pl* **-wörter** *or* **-worte** term of endearment

K.-o.-Sieg [kaː'oː-] M knockout victory

Kosinus ['koːzinʊs] M (*Math*) cosine

Kosmetik [kɔs'meːtɪk] F **-,** NO PL beauty culture; (= *Kosmetika, fig*) cosmetics *pl*; **eine Reform, die sich nicht nur auf ~ beschränkt** a reform which is not merely cosmetic

Kosmetiker [kɔs'meːtɪkɐ] M **-s, -, Kosmetikerin** [-ərɪn] F **-, -nen** beautician, cosmetician

Kosmetik-: Kosmetikkoffer M vanity case; **Kosmetiktuch** NT, *pl* **-tücher** paper tissue

kosmetisch [kɔs'meːtɪʃ] **1** ADJ cosmetic; **ein ~es Mittel** a cosmetic **2** ADV *behandeln* cosmetically

kosmisch ['kɔsmɪʃ] ADJ cosmic; **~ beeinflusst werden** to be influenced by the stars

Kosmo- [kɔsmo-]: **Kosmonaut** [kɔsmo'naut] M **-en, -en, Kosmonautin** [-'nautɪn] F **-, -nen** cosmonaut; **Kosmopolit** [kɔsmopo'liːt] M **-en, -en, Kosmopolitin** [-'liːtɪn] F **-, -nen** cosmopolitan; **kosmopolitisch** [kɔsmopo'liːtɪʃ] ADJ cosmopolitan

Kosmos ['kɔsmɔs] M **-,** NO PL cosmos

Kosovo ['kɔsovo] M **-s** (*Geog*) (**der**) **~** Kosovo

Kosovo-Albaner(in) M(F) Kosovo Albanian

Kost [kɔst] F **-,** NO PL **(a)** (= *Nahrung, Essen*) fare; **vegetarische/fleischlose ~** vegetarian/meatless diet; **geistige ~** (*fig*) intellectual fare; **leichte/schwere ~** (*fig*) easy/heavy going **(b)** (**freie**) **~ und Logis** *or* **Wohnung** (free) board and lodging

kostbar **1** ADJ (= *wertvoll*) valuable, precious; (= *luxuriös*) luxurious, sumptuous **2** ADV sumptuously; **sich kleiden** luxuriously

Kostbarkeit ['kɔstbaːɐkait] F **-, -en** (= *Gegenstand*) precious object; (= *Leckerbissen*) delicacy

kosten¹ ['kɔstn] **1** VT **(a)** (*lit, fig*) to cost; **was kostet das?** how much *or* what does it cost?; **was soll das ~?** what's it going to cost?; **das kostet nicht die Welt** it doesn't cost the earth; **koste es, was es wolle** whatever the cost; **das/die lasse ich mich etwas ~** I don't mind spending a bit of money on it/them; **jdn sein Leben/den Sieg ~** to cost sb his life/the victory **(b)** (= *in Anspruch nehmen*) *Zeit, Geduld etc* to take **2** VI to cost; **das kostet** (*inf*) it costs a bit

kosten² ['kɔstn] **1** VT (= *probieren*) to taste **2** VI to taste; **willst du mal ~?** would you like a taste?; **von etw ~** to taste *or* try sth

Kosten ['kɔstn] PL cost(s); (*Jur*) costs *pl*; (= *Unkosten*) expenses *pl*; **die ~ tragen** to bear the cost(s *pl*); **auf ~ von** *or* **+gen** (*fig*) at the expense of; **auf seine ~ kommen** to cover one's expenses; (*fig*) to get one's money's worth; **~ spielen keine Rolle** money's no object; **~ sparend** cost-saving; **etw ~ sparend herstellen** to produce sth at low cost; **~ sparender arbeiten** to reduce costs

Kosten-: Kostenart F type of cost; **Kostenbremse** F (*inf*) **auf die ~ treten, die ~ anziehen** to curb costs; **Kostendämpfung** F **-, -en** curbing cost expansion; **kostendeckend 1** ADJ **~e Preise** prices that cover one's costs **2** ADV cost-effectively; **~ arbeiten** to cover one's costs; **~ wirtschaften** to avoid a deficit; **Kostendeckung** F cost-effectiveness; **kostengünstig 1** ADJ economical **2** ADV *arbeiten, produzieren* economically; **kostenintensiv** ADJ (*Econ*) cost-intensive; **kostenlos** ADJ, ADV free (of charge); **Kosten-Nutzen-Analyse** F, **Kosten-Nutzen-Rechnung** F cost-benefit analysis; **kostenpflichtig** [-pflɪçtɪç] **1** ADJ liable to pay costs **2** ADV **eine Klage ~ abweisen** to dismiss a case with costs; **~ verwarnt werden** to be fined; **~ verurteilt werden** to have to pay costs; **ein Kfz ~ abschleppen** to tow away a car at the owner's expense; **Kostenplanung** F costing; **Kostenpunkt** M cost question; **~?** (*inf*) what'll it cost?; **~: 100 Euro** (*inf*) cost, 100 euros; **Kostenrechnung** F calculation of costs; **Kostensatz** M rate; **kostensparend** ADJ *siehe* **Kosten; Kostenstelle** F cost centre (*Brit*) *or* center (*US*); **Kostenträger(in)** M(F) (**der**) **~ sein** to bear the cost; **Kostenvoranschlag** M (costs) estimate

köstlich ['kœstlɪç] **1** ADJ **(a)** *Wein, Speise* exquisite; *Luft* magnificent **(b)** (= *amüsant*) priceless; **du bist ja ~** you're priceless **2** ADV **(a)** (= *gut*) *schmecken* delicious **(b)** **sich ~ amüsieren/unterhalten** to have a great time

Köstlichkeit F **-, -en (a)** (= *köstliche Sache*) treat; **eine kulinarische ~** a culinary delicacy **(b)** NO PL (*von Speise, Getränk*) **ein Wein von einmaliger ~** a uniquely exquisite wine

Kost-: Kostprobe F (*von Wein, Käse etc*) taste; (*fig*) sample; **kostspielig** [-ʃpiːlɪç] ADJ costly

Kostüm [kɔs'tyːm] NT **-s, -e (a)** (*Theat*: = *Tracht*) costume **(b)** (= *Maskenkostüm*) fancy dress **(c)** (= *Damenkostüm*) suit

Kostüm-: Kostümball M fancy-dress ball; **Kostümbildner** [-bɪltnɐ] M **-s, -, Kostümbildnerin** [-ərɪn] F **-, -nen** costume designer

kostümieren [kɔsty'miːrən], *ptp* **kostümiert** VR to dress up

Kostüm-: Kostümprobe F (*Theat*) dress rehearsal; **Kostümverleih** M (theatrical) costume agency

Kot [koːt] M **-(e)s**, NO PL (*form*) excrement

Kotangens [ˈkoː-] M (*Math*) cotangent

Kotelett [ˈkɔtlet, kɔtˈlet] NT **-(e)s, -s** *or (rare)* **-e** chop

Kotelette [kotəˈletə] F **-, -n** USU PL sideburn

Köter [ˈkøːtɐ] M **-s, -** (*pej*) damn dog (*inf*)

Kotflügel M (*Aut*) wing

Kotzbrocken M (*inf*) mean bastard (*Brit sl*), son of a bitch (*esp US sl*)

Kotze [ˈkɔtsə] F **-**, NO PL (*vulg*) puke (*sl*); **da kommt einem die ~ hoch** it makes you want to puke (*sl*)

kotzen [ˈkɔtsn̩] VI (*sl*) to throw up (*inf*), to puke (*sl*); **das ist zum Kotzen** it makes you sick; **du bist zum Kotzen** you make me sick; **da kann man das große Kotzen kriegen** it makes you want to puke (*sl*)

kotzübel ADJ (*inf*) **mir ist ~** I feel like throwing up (*inf*)

KP [kaːˈpeː] F **-, -s** ABBR *von* **Kommunistische Partei**

Krabbe [ˈkrabə] F **-, -n** (*Zool*) (*klein*) shrimp; (*größer*) prawn

krabbeln [ˈkrabl̩n] VI AUX SEIN to crawl

Krabbencocktail M prawn cocktail

Krach [krax] M **-(e)s, ⁻e** [ˈkrɛçə] (a) NO PL (= *Lärm*) noise, din; (= *Schlag*) crash; **~ machen** to make a noise or din (b) (*inf:* = *Zank, Streit*) row (*inf*) (*um* about); **mit jdm ~ haben** to have a row with sb (*inf*); **mit jdm ~ kriegen** to have a row with sb (*inf*); **~ schlagen** to make a fuss (c) (= *Börsenkrach*) crash

krachen [ˈkraxn̩] ❶ VI (a) (= *Lärm machen*) to crash; (*Holz*) to creak; (*Schuss*) to ring out; (*Donner*) to crash; **~d fallen** *etc* to fall *etc* with a crash; **..., dass es nur so krachte** (*lit*) ... with a crash; (*fig*) ... with a vengeance; **sonst kracht's!** (*inf*) or **there'll be trouble; gleich kracht's** (*inf*) there's going to be trouble; **es hat gekracht** (*inf: Zusammenstoß*) there's been a crash

(b) AUX SEIN (*inf*) (= *aufplatzen*) to split; (= *brechen*) to break; (*Eis*) to crack

(c) AUX SEIN (*inf:* = *aufprallen*) to crash

❷ VR (*inf*) to have a row (*inf*)

Kracher [ˈkraxɐ] M **-s, -** banger (*Brit*), firecracker (*US*)

Krachmacher(in) M(F) (*lit*) noisy person; (*fig*) troublemaker

krächzen [ˈkrɛçtsn̩] VI to croak; (*Vogel*) to caw; **eine ~de Stimme** a croaky voice

Krächzen NT **-s**, NO PL croak(ing); (*von Vogel*) caw(ing)

Kräcker [ˈkrɛkɐ] M **-s, -** (*Cook*) cracker

kraft [kraft] PREP +GEN (*form*) by virtue of; (= *mittels*) by use of; **~ meines Amtes** by virtue of my office

Kraft [kraft] F **-, ⁻e** [ˈkrɛftə] (a) (*körperlich, sittlich*) strength *no pl*; (*geistig, schöpferisch*) powers *pl*; (*militärisch, wirtschaftlich*) strength; (*von Prosa, Stimme*) power; (= *Energie*) energy, energies *pl*; **die Kräfte (mit jdm) messen** to try one's strength (against sb); (*fig*) to pit oneself against sb; **mit frischer ~** with renewed strength; **mit letzter ~** with one's last ounce of strength; **mit vereinten Kräften werden wir ...** if we join forces we will ...; **das geht über meine Kräfte, das übersteigt meine Kräfte** it's too much for me; **ich bin am Ende meiner ~** I can't take any more; **mit aller** or **voller ~** with all one's might; **er will mit aller ~ durchsetzen, dass ...** he will do his utmost to ensure that ...; **aus eigener ~** by oneself; **nach (besten) Kräften** to the best of one's ability; **er tat, was in seinen Kräften stand** he did everything (with)in his power; **wieder bei Kräften sein** to have (got) one's strength back; **wieder zu Kräften kommen** to regain one's strength

(b) (*Phys: einer Reaktion etc*) force; (*der Sonne etc*) strength, power; **die treibende ~** (*fig*) the driving force; **das Gleichgewicht der Kräfte** (*Pol*) the balance of power

(c) (*usu pl: in Wirtschaft, Politik etc*) force

(d) NO PL (*Jur:* = *Geltung*) force; **in ~ sein/treten/setzen** to be in/come into/bring into force; **außer ~ sein** to be no longer in force; **außer ~ treten** to cease to be in force; **außer ~ setzen** to annul

(e) NO PL (*Naut:* = *Geschwindigkeit*) force; **halbe/volle ~ voraus!** half/full speed ahead

(f) (= *Arbeitskraft*) employee, worker; (= *Haushaltskraft*) domestic help; (= *Lehrkraft*) teacher

Kraft-: Kraftakt M strongman act; (*fig*) show of strength; **Kraftanstrengung** F exertion; **Kraftausdruck** M, *pl* **-ausdrücke**

swearword; **Kraftausdrücke** strong language; **Kraftbrühe** F beef tea

Kräfte-: Kräftespiel NT power play; **Kräfteverhältnis** NT (*Pol*) balance of power; (*von Mannschaften etc*) relative strength

Kraftfahrer(in) M(F) (*form*) driver

Kraftfahrzeug NT motor vehicle

Kraftfahrzeug-: Kraftfahrzeugbrief M (vehicle) registration document; **Kraftfahrzeugkennzeichen** NT (vehicle) registration; **Kraftfahrzeugmechaniker(in)** M(F) motor mechanic; **Kraftfahrzeugschein** M (vehicle) registration document; **Kraftfahrzeugsteuer** F motor vehicle tax, road tax (*Brit*); **Kraftfahrzeugversicherung** F car insurance

kräftig [ˈkrɛftɪç] ❶ ADJ strong; *Pflanze* healthy; *Schlag* hard; *Händedruck* firm; *Fluch* violent; *Suppe, Essen* nourishing; (= *groß*) *Portion, Preiserhöhung* big; *Beifall* loud; **einen ~en Schluck nehmen** to take a good swig; **eine ~e Tracht Prügel** a good beating

❷ ADV (a) *gebaut* strongly, powerfully; *zuschlagen, treten, pressen, drücken, blasen* hard; *klatschen* loudly; *lachen, mitsingen* heartily; *fluchen, niesen* violently; **etw ~ schütteln/polieren/umrühren** to give sth a good shake/polish/stir; **jdn ~ verprügeln** to give sb a thorough beating; **~ essen** to eat well; **~ trinken** to drink a lot; **husten Sie mal ~** have a good cough; **sich für etw ~ einsetzen** to support sth strongly

(b) (*zur Verstärkung*) really; **die Preise sind ~ gestiegen** prices have really gone up; **sich ~ ausweinen** to have a good cry; **sich ~ ärgern** to get really annoyed

kräftigen [ˈkrɛftɪɡn̩] VT (*geh*) *Körper, Muskeln* to strengthen; **jdn ~** to build up sb's strength; (*Luft, Bad etc*) to invigorate sb; (*Essen, Mittel etc*) to fortify sb

kraftlos ❶ ADJ (= *schwach*) weak; (= *schlaff*) limp; (= *machtlos*) powerless; (*Jur*) invalid ❷ ADV weakly; **~ sank er zurück** he fell feebly back

Kraftlosigkeit F **-**, NO PL weakness

Kraft-: Kraftmensch M strongman; **Kraftpaket** NT (= *Mensch*) powerhouse; (= *Auto, Maschine*) powerful machine; **Kraftprobe** F test of strength; (*zwischen zwei Gruppen, Menschen*) trial of strength; **Kraftprotz** M (*inf*) muscle man (*inf*); **Kraftrad** NT motorcycle, motorbike; **Kraftraum** M power training gym; **Kraftsport** M sport(s *pl*) involving strength; **Kraftsportler(in)** M(F) power athlete; **Kraftstoff** M fuel; **kraftstrotzend** ADJ vigorous; (= *muskulös*) with bulging muscles; **ein ~es Baby** a big strong bouncing baby; **Krafttraining** NT power training; **Kraftverkehr** M motor traffic; **Kraftverschwendung** F waste of energy; **kraftvoll** ❶ ADJ (*geh*) *Stimme* powerful ❷ ADV powerfully; **bei etw ~ zubeißen können** to be able to sink one's teeth into sth; **Kraftwagen** M motor vehicle; **Kraftwerk** NT power station

Kragen [ˈkraːɡn̩] M **-s, -** *or* (*S Ger, Sw auch*) ⁻ [ˈkrɛːɡn̩] collar; **jdn am** *or* **beim ~ packen** to grab sb by the collar; (*fig inf*) to collar sb; **mir platzte der ~** (*inf*) I blew my top (*inf*); **jetzt platzt mir aber der ~!** this is the last straw!; **jetzt gehts ihm an den ~** (*inf*) he's (in) for it now (*inf*)

Kragenweite F (*lit*) collar size; **eine ~ zu groß für jdn sein** (*fig inf*) to be too much for sb (to handle); **das ist nicht meine ~** (*fig inf*) that's not my cup of tea (*inf*)

Krähe [ˈkrɛːə] F **-, -n** crow; **eine ~ hackt der anderen kein Auge aus** (*Prov*) birds of a feather stick or flock together (*Prov*)

krähen [ˈkrɛːən] VI to crow

Krakau [ˈkraːkau] NT **-s** Cracow

Krakauer [ˈkraːkauɐ] F **-, -** (*Cook*) spicy smoked sausage with garlic

Krake [ˈkraːkə] M **-n, -n** octopus; (*Myth*) Kraken

krakeelen [kraˈkeːlən], *ptp* **krakeelt** VI (*inf*) to make a racket (*inf*)

Krakel [ˈkraːkl̩] M **-s, -** (*inf*) scrawl, scribble

Krakelei [kraːkəˈlai] F **-, -en** (*inf*) scrawl, scribble

krakelig [ˈkraːkəlɪç] ❶ ADJ scrawly ❷ ADV **~ schreiben** to scrawl, to scribble; **~ unterschreiben** to scrawl one's signature; **meine Kinder malen** ~ my children do scribbly drawings

Kralle [ˈkralə] F **-, -n** claw; (= *Parkkralle*) wheel clamp (*Brit*), Denver boot (*US*); **jdn/etw in seinen ~n haben** (*fig inf*) to have sb/sth in one's clutches; **jdn aus den ~n des Todes retten** to rescue sb from the jaws of death; (**bar**) **auf die ~** (*inf*) (cash) on the nail (*Brit inf*) or on the barrelhead (*US inf*)

krallen [ˈkralən] VR **sich an jdn/etw ~** (*lit, fig*) to cling to sb/sth; (*Tier*) to dig its claws into sb/sth; **sich in etw** (*acc*) **~** to sink its claws into sth; (*mit Fingern*) to dig one's fingers into sth

Kram [kra:m] M **-(e)s**, NO PL (inf) (= Gerümpel) junk; (= Zeug) stuff (inf); (= Angelegenheit) business; **den ~ satt haben/ hinschmeißen** to be fed up with/to chuck the whole business (inf); **das passt mir nicht in den ~** it's a confounded nuisance; **mach doch deinen ~ allein!** do it yourself!

kramen ['kra:mən] 🔳 VI (a) (= wühlen) to rummage about (in +dat in, nach for) (b) (Sw inf) to do a bit of shopping 🔳 VT **etw aus etw ~** to fish sth out of sth

Kramladen M (pej inf) tatty little shop (inf); (= Trödelladen) junk shop

Krampf [krampf] M **-(e)s**, **ᴸe** ['krempfə] (a) (= Zustand) cramp; (= Verkrampfung, Zuckung) spasm; (wiederholt) convulsion(s pl); (= Anfall, Lachkrampf) fit; **einen ~ haben/bekommen** to have/get (a) cramp (b) NO PL (inf) (= Getue) palaver (inf); (= Unsinn) nonsense (c) (esp Sw inf: = krampfhaftes Tun, Bemühen) strain

Krampf-: **Krampfader** F varicose vein; **krampfartig** 🔳 ADJ convulsive 🔳 ADV convulsively

krampfen ['krampfn] 🔳 VT Finger, Hand to clench (um etw around sth) 🔳 VR **sich um etw ~** to clench sth 🔳 VI (Sw inf: = hart arbeiten) to slave away (inf)

Krampfer ['krampfɐ] M **-s**, -, **Krampferin** [-ərɪn] F **-**, **-nen** (sl) hard worker

Krampf-: **krampfhaft** 🔳 ADJ Zuckung convulsive; (inf: = angestrengt, verzweifelt) desperate; Lachen forced 🔳 ADV **sich ~ bemühen** to try desperately hard; **~ nachdenken** to rack one's brains; **sich ~ an etw** (dat) **festhalten** (lit, fig inf) to cling desperately to sth; **krampflösend** ADJ antispasmodic (spec)

Kran [kra:n] M **-(e)s**, **ᴸe** ['kre:nə] or **-e** (a) (dial: = Hahn) tap (esp Brit), faucet (US)

Kranich ['kra:nɪç] M **-s**, **-e** (Orn) crane

krank [kraŋk] 🔳 ADJ, comp **ᴸer** ['krɛŋkɐ], superl **ᴸste(r, s)** ['krɛŋkstə] (a) (= nicht gesund) ill usu pred, sick (auch fig); (= leidend) invalid; Pflanze, Organ diseased; Zahn, Bein bad; Wirtschaft, Firma ailing; **~ werden** to fall ill or sick; **schwer ~** seriously ill; **vor Aufregung/Angst ~** sick with excitement/fear; **vor Heimweh ~** homesick; **du bist wohl ~!** (inf iro) there must be something wrong with you!
(b) (sl: = verrückt) off one's head (inf) 🔳 ADV, comp **ᴸer**, superl **am ᴸsten sich ~ stellen** to pretend to be ill or sick; **das macht/du machst mich ~!** (inf) it gets/you get on my nerves! (inf)

kränkeln ['krɛŋkln] VI to be ailing (auch Wirtschaft, Firma), to be in poor health

kranken ['kraŋkn] VI to suffer (an +dat from); **das krankt daran, dass ...** (fig) it suffers from the fact that ...

kränken ['krɛŋkn] VT jdn ~ to hurt sb('s feelings); **sie war sehr gekränkt** she was very hurt; **es kränkt mich, dass ...** it hurts me that ...; **jdn in seiner Ehre ~** to offend sb's pride; **~d** hurtful

Kranken-: **Krankenakte** F medical file; **Krankenbesuch** M visit (to a sick person); (von Arzt) (sick) call; **Krankenbett** NT sickbed; **Krankengeld** NT sickness benefit; (von Firma) sick pay; **Krankengymnast** [-ɡʏmnast] M **-en**, **-en**, **Krankengymnastin** [-ɡʏmnastɪn] F **-**, **-nen** physiotherapist; **Krankengymnastik** F physiotherapy

Krankenhaus NT hospital; **ins ~ gehen** (als Patient) to go into (the US) hospital

Krankenhaus- IN CPDS hospital; **Krankenhausaufenthalt** M stay in hospital; **Krankenhauskosten** PL hospital charges pl; **krankenhausreif** ADJ in need of hospital treatment; **jdn ~ schlagen** to beat the hell out of sb (inf)

Kranken-: **Krankenkasse** F (= Versicherung) medical insurance; (= Gesellschaft) medical insurance company; **ich bin in einer privaten ~** I have private medical insurance; **er ist in keiner ~** he has no medical insurance; **Krankenpflege** F nursing; **Krankenpfleger** M orderly; (von Schwestern-ausbildung) male nurse; **Krankenpflegeschüler(in)** M(F) student nurse; **Krankenschein** M medical insurance record card; **Krankenschwester** F nurse; **Krankenstand** M (a) (von Firma) level of sickness (b) **im ~ sein** to be sick or ill; **Krankenversicherung** F medical insurance; **soziale/private ~** state or national/private health insurance; **Krankenversicherungsausweis** M health insurance card, medical card (Brit); **Krankenwagen** M ambulance

Kranke(r) ['kraŋkə] MF DECL AS ADJ invalid; (= Patient) patient; **die ~n** the sick

krankfeiern VI SEP (inf) to take a sickie (inf); **das Krankfeiern ist ein großes Problem** absenteeism is a great problem; **geh doch heute nicht ins Büro, feier doch krank** don't go in to the office today, say you're not feeling well

krankhaft 🔳 ADJ (a) Stelle, Zelle diseased; Vergrößerung, Zustand morbid; Aussehen sickly; **die Untersuchungen haben keinen ~en Befund ergeben** the examinations revealed no sign(s) of disease; **~er Befund der Leber** diseased liver; **~e Veränderung** affection (b) (seelisch) pathological 🔳 ADV (a) (Med) abnormally; **sich ~ verändern** to show pathological changes (b) (auf seelische Zustände bezogen) pathologically

Krankheit F **-**, **-en** (lit, fig) illness; (eine bestimmte ~ wie Krebs, Masern etc auch) disease; (von Pflanzen) disease; **wegen ~** due to illness; **(eine) ~ vorschützen**, **eine ~ vortäuschen** to pretend to be ill; **von einer ~ befallen werden** to catch an illness/a disease; (Pflanze, Organ) to become diseased; **nach langer/schwerer ~** after a long/serious illness; **während/seit meiner ~** during/since my illness; **das soll ein Auto sein? das ist eine ~!** (fig inf) call that a car? that's just an apology for one!

Krankheits-: **Krankheitsbild** NT symptoms pl; **Krankheitserreger** M pathogen; **krankheitshalber** ADV due to illness

kranklachen VR (inf) to kill oneself (laughing) (inf)

kränklich ['krɛŋklɪç] ADJ sickly

Krank-: **krankmachen** VI SEP (inf) = krankfeiern; **krankmelden** VR SEP to let sb/one's boss etc know that one is sick or ill; (telefonisch) to phone in sick; (esp Mil) to report sick; **sie hat sich krankgemeldet** she is off sick; **Krankmeldung** F notification of illness; **krankschreiben** VT SEP IRREG jdn ~ to give sb a medical certificate; (esp Mil) to put sb on the sick list; **er ist schon seit einem halben Jahr krankgeschrieben** he's been off sick for six months

Kränkung ['krɛŋkʊŋ] F **-**, **-en** insult; **etw als ~ empfinden** to take offence (Brit) or offense (US) at sth

Kranz [krants] M **-es**, **ᴸe** ['krɛntsə] (a) wreath (b) (= kreisförmig Angeordnetes) ring, circle (c) (Tech: = Radkranz) rim (d) (dial Cook) ring

Kränzchen ['krɛntsçən] NT **-s**, - (fig: = Kaffeekränzchen) coffee circle

Krapfen ['krapfn] M **-s**, - (dial Cook) ≈ doughnut (Brit), ≈ donut (US)

krass [kras] 🔳 ADJ (a) (= auffallend) glaring; Dissonanz jarring; Unterschied extreme; (= extrem) Fall, Haltung, Lage extreme; Materialist, Unkenntnis crass; Egoist, Ungerechtigkeit, Lüge blatant; Außenseiter rank; (= unverblümt) Schilderung, Worte, Stil stark; **etw ~ finden** (inf) to find sth gross (b) (sl: = unmöglich) gross (inf); **das ist echt ~** that's a real bummer (inf) (c) (sl: = toll) wicked (sl) 🔳 ADV **sich ausdrücken** crudely; schildern garishly; widersprechen completely; kontrastieren sharply; **sich ~ von etw abheben** to contrast sharply with sth; **um es ~ zu sagen, ~ gesagt** to put it bluntly

Krater ['kra:tɐ] M **-s**, - crater

Kratz-: **Kratzbürste** F wire brush; (inf) prickly character; **kratzbürstig** [-bʏrstɪç] ADJ (inf) prickly

kratzen ['kratsn] 🔳 VT (a) (mit Nägeln, Werkzeug) to scratch; (= abkratzen) to scrape (von off); **es kratzt (mich) im Hals** my throat feels rough (b) (inf: = stören) to bother; **das kratzt mich nicht** (inf), **das soll or kann mich nicht ~** (inf) I couldn't care less (about that); **das braucht dich (doch) nicht (zu) ~** it's nothing to do with you 🔳 VI to scratch; **es kratzt (mir) im Hals** my throat feels rough; **an etw** (dat) **~** (fig) to scratch away at sth; **diese Sache hat an seinem guten Ruf gekratzt** this business has tarnished his reputation 🔳 VR to scratch oneself

Kratzer ['kratsɐ] M **-s**, - (= Schramme) scratch

kratzig ['kratsɪç] ADJ (inf) scratchy (inf)

Kratzwunde F scratch

Kraul [kraul] NT **-(s)**, NO PL (Schwimmen) crawl; **(im) ~ schwimmen** to do the crawl

kraulen[1] ['kraulən] AUX HABEN or SEIN (*Schwimmen*) ▮ VI to do the crawl ▮ VT **er hat** *or* **ist die Strecke gekrault** he swam the stretch front crawl; **er hat** *or* **ist 100 m gekrault** he did a 100m crawl

kraulen[2] VT to fondle; **jdn am Kinn ~** to tickle sb under the chin

kraus [kraus] ADJ crinkly; *Haar, Kopf* frizzy; *Stirn* wrinkled; (*fig*: = *verworren*) muddled, confused; **die Stirn ~ ziehen** to knit one's brow; (*missbilligend*) to frown; **die Nase ~ ziehen** to screw up one's nose

Krause ['krauzə] F **-, -n** (a) (= *Halskrause*) ruff; (*an Ärmeln etc*) ruffle, frill (b) (*inf*) (*von Haar, Kopf*) frizziness; (= *Frisur*) frizzy hair; **im Regen bekomme ich eine ~** my hair goes frizzy in the rain

kräuseln ['krɔyzln] ▮ VT *Haar* to make frizzy; (*Sew*) to gather; (*Tex*) to crimp; *Stirn* to knit; *Nase* to screw up; *Wasseroberfläche* to ruffle ▮ VR (*Haare*) to go frizzy; (*Stirn, Nase*) to wrinkle up; **gekräuselte Haare** frizzy hair

Krauskopf M frizzy head; (= *Frisur*) frizzy hair/hairstyle; (= *Mensch*) curly-head

Kraut [kraut] NT **-(e)s, Kräuter** ['krɔytɐ] (a) (*Pflanze*: = *esp Heilkraut, Würzkraut*) herb; **dagegen ist kein ~ gewachsen** (*fig*) there is no remedy for that
(b) NO PL (= *grüne Teile von Pflanzen*) foliage; (*von Gemüse*) tops *pl*; (= *Spargelkraut*) asparagus leaves *pl*; **wie ~ und Rüben durcheinander liegen** (*inf*) to lie (around) all over the place (*inf*); **ins ~ schießen** (*lit*) to go to seed; (*fig*) to get out of control
(c) NO PL (= *Rotkraut, Weißkraut*) cabbage; (= *Sauerkraut*) sauerkraut
(d) (*pej*: = *Tabak*) tobacco

Kräuter-: Kräuterbutter F herb butter; **Kräuterlikör** M herbal liqueur; **Kräutertee** M herb(al) tea

Krautsalat M ≈ coleslaw

Krawall [kra'val] M **-s, -e** (a) (= *Aufruhr*) riot; (*inf*) (= *Rauferei*) brawl; (= *Lärm*) racket (*inf*); **~ machen** (*inf*) to make a racket (*inf*); (= *randalieren*) to go on the rampage; (*auch* **Krawall schlagen**: = *sich beschweren*) to kick up a fuss

Krawallbruder M, **Krawallmacher(in)** M(F) (*inf*) hooligan; (= *Krakeeler*) rowdy (*inf*)

Krawatte [kra'vatə] F **-, -n** tie, necktie (*esp US*)

kraxeln ['kraksln] VI AUX SEIN (*S Ger*) to clamber (up)

Kreation [krea'tsio:n] F **-, -en** (*Fashion etc*) creation

kreativ [krea'ti:f] ▮ ADJ creative ▮ ADV creatively; **~ veranlagt** creatively inclined; **~ begabt** creative

Kreativität [kreativi'tɛ:t] F **-,** NO PL creativity

Kreatur [krea'tu:ɐ] F **-, -en** (a) (*lit, fig, pej*) creature (b) NO PL (= *alle Lebewesen*) creation; **die ~** all creation

Krebs [kre:ps] M **-es, -e** (a) (= *Taschenkrebs, Einsiedlerkrebs*) crab; (= *Flusskrebs*) crayfish, crawfish (*US*); **rot wie ein ~** red as a lobster (b) (*Gattung*) crustacean; (= *Hummer, Krabbe etc*) crayfish, crawfish (*US*) (c) (*Astrol*) Cancer; **der ~** (*Astron*) Cancer (d) (*Med*) cancer; (*Bot*) canker; **~ erregend** *or* **auslösend** carcinogenic

krebsen ['kre:psn] VI (*inf*: = *sich abmühen*) to struggle; (*Umsatz, Industrie*) to languish; **in den Umfragen krebst die Partei bei 6 Prozent** the party is languishing at 6 per cent in the polls

Krebs-: krebsfördernd ▮ ADJ cancer-inducing; **eine ~e Wirkung haben** to increase the risk of cancer ▮ ADV **~ wirken** to increase the risk of (getting) cancer; **Krebsforschung** F cancer research; **Krebsgeschwulst** F (*Med*) cancer, cancerous growth; **Krebsgeschwür** NT (*Med*) cancerous ulcer; (*fig*) cancer; **Krebsklinik** F cancer clinic; **krebskrank** ADJ suffering from cancer; **~ sein** to have cancer; **Krebskranke(r)** MF DECL AS ADJ cancer victim; (= *Patient*) cancer patient; **Krebskrankheit** F cancer; **krebsrot** ADJ red as a lobster; **Krebstiere** PL crustaceans *pl*, crustacea *pl*; **Krebsvorsorge** F, **Krebsvorsorgeuntersuchung** F cancer checkup

Kredit[1] [kre'di:t] M **-(e)s, -e** credit; **auf ~** on credit; **er hat bei uns/der Bank ~** his credit is good with us/the bank; **in seiner Stammkneipe hat er ~** he gets credit at his local pub (*Brit inf*) *or* bar; **~ haben** (*fig*) to have standing

Kredit[2] ['kre:dit] NT **-s, -s** (= *Habenseite*) credit (side)

Kredit- [kre'di:t-]: **Kreditanstalt** F credit institution; **Kreditaufnahme** F borrowing; **sich zu einer ~ entschließen** to decide to obtain a loan; **Kreditauskunft** F credit

information; (= *Anfrage*) credit inquiry; **Kreditbrief** M letter of credit; **kreditfähig** ADJ creditworthy; **Kreditgeber(in)** M(F) creditor; **Kreditgenossenschaft** F credit cooperative, credit union (*US*); **Kredithai** M (*inf*) loan shark (*inf*)

kreditieren [kredi'ti:rən], *ptp* **kreditiert** VT **jdm einen Betrag ~, jdn für einen Betrag ~** to advance sb an amount, to credit sb with an amount

Kredit- [kre'di:t-]: **Kreditinstitut** NT bank; **Kreditkarte** F credit card; **Kreditlimit** NT credit limit; **Kreditnehmer(in)** M(F) borrower

Kreditor ['kredito:ɐ] M **-s, Kreditoren** [-'to:rən], **Kreditorin** [-'to:rɪn] F **-, -nen** creditor

Kredit- [kre'di:t-]: **Kreditplafond** M credit ceiling; **Kreditpolitik** F lending policy; **Kreditrahmen** M credit range; **den ~ ausschöpfen/sprengen** to use up/exceed the credit range; **Kreditschutzverein** M credit bureau; **Kreditvereinbarung** F credit arrangement; **Allgemeine ~en** General Arrangements to Borrow, GAB; **Kreditversicherung** F credit insurance; **~ bei Auslandsgeschäften** export credit insurance; **Kreditwesengesetz** NT banking act; **kreditwürdig** ADJ creditworthy; **Kreditwürdigkeit** F creditworthiness

Kreide ['kraidə] F **-, -n** chalk; **eine ~** a piece of chalk; **bei jdm (tief) in der ~ sein** *or* **stehen** to be (deep) in debt to sb

Kreide- [kraid-]: **kreidebleich** ADJ (as) white as a sheet; **Kreidefelsen** M chalk cliff; **kreidehaltig** ADJ chalky; **kreideweiß** ADJ = **kreidebleich**; **Kreidezeichnung** F chalk drawing

kreieren [kre'i:rən], *ptp* **kreiert** VT to create

Kreis [krais] M **-es, -e** [-zə] (a) circle; **einen ~ beschreiben** *or* **schlagen** *or* **ziehen** to describe a circle; **einen ~ um jdn bilden** *or* **schließen** to form a circle around sb; **im ~ (gehen/sitzen)** (to go (a)round/sit) in a circle; **(weite) ~e ziehen** (*fig*) to have (wide) repercussions; **sich im ~ bewegen** *or* **drehen** (*lit*) to turn (a)round in a circle; (*fig*) to go (a)round in circles; **mir dreht sich alles im ~e** everything's going (a)round and (a)round; **der ~ schließt sich** (*fig*) we *etc* come full circle; **störe meine ~e nicht!** (*fig*) leave me in peace!
(b) (*Elec*: = *Stromkreis*) circuit
(c) (= *Stadtkreis, Landkreis*) district; **~ Leipzig** Leipzig District, the District of Leipzig
(d) (*fig: von Menschen*) circle; **der ~ seiner Leser** his readers *pl*; **weite ~e der Bevölkerung** wide sections of the population; **im ~e von Freunden/seiner Familie** with friends/his family; **eine Feier im engen** *or* **kleinen ~** a celebration for a few close friends and relatives; **in seinen/ihren** *etc* **~en** in the circles in which he/she *etc* moves; **das kommt (auch) in den besten ~en vor** that happens even in the best of circles

kreischen ['kraiʃn] VI to screech

Kreisdiagramm NT pie chart

Kreisel ['kraizl] M **-s, -** (*Tech*) gyroscope; (= *Spielzeug*) (spinning) top; (*inf: im Verkehr*) roundabout (*Brit*), traffic circle (*US*), rotary (*US*); **den ~ schlagen** to spin the top

kreisen ['kraizn] VI AUX SEIN or HABEN to circle (*um* (a)round, *über +dat* over); (*um eine Achse*) to revolve (*um* around); (*Satellit, Planet*) to orbit (*um etw* sth); (*Blut, Öl etc*) to circulate (*in +dat* through); (*fig: Gedanken, Wünsche, Gespräch*) to revolve (*um* around); **die Arme ~ lassen** to swing one's arms around (in a circle); **den Becher ~ lassen** to hand the cup (a)round

Kreis-: kreisförmig ▮ ADJ circular ▮ ADV **sich ~ bewegen** to move in a circle; **~ angelegt** arranged in a circle; **sich ~ aufstellen** to form a circle; **kreisfrei** ADJ **~e Stadt** town which is an administrative district in its own right; **Kreisinhalt** M area of a/the circle

Kreislauf M (= *Blutkreislauf, Ölkreislauf, von Geld*) circulation; (*der Natur, des Wassers*) cycle

Kreislauf-: Kreislaufkollaps M circulatory collapse; **Kreislaufstörungen** PL circulatory trouble *sing*

Kreis-: kreisrund ADJ (perfectly) circular; **Kreissäge** F circular saw; (*inf*: = *Hut*) boater

Kreißsaal M delivery room

Kreis-: Kreisstadt F district town, ≈ county town (*Brit*); **Kreisumfang** M circumference (of a/the circle); **Kreisverkehr** M roundabout (*Brit*) *or* rotary (*US*) traffic; (= *Kreisel*) roundabout (*Brit*), traffic circle (*US*), rotary (*US*); **dort gibt es viel ~** there are a lot of roundabouts *etc* there; **Kreiswehrersatzamt** NT district recruiting office

Krematorium [krema'to:riʊm] NT **-s, Krematorien** [-riən] crematorium

kremig ['kre:mɪç] **1** ADJ creamy **2** ADV *rühren, schlagen* until creamy; **~ schmecken** to taste creamy

Kreml ['kre:ml, 'krɛml] M **-s der** ~ the Kremlin

Krempe ['krɛmpə] F **-, -n** (= *Hutkrempe*) brim

Krempel ['krɛmpl] M **-s**, NO PL (*inf*) (= *Sachen*) stuff (*inf*); (= *wertloses Zeug*) junk; **ich werfe den ganzen ~ hin** I'm chucking the whole lot in (*inf*); **dann kannst du deinen ~ allein machen** then you can (damn well (*inf*)) do it yourself

krempeln ['krɛmpln] VT *siehe* **hochkrempeln, umkrempeln** *etc*

Kren [kre:n] M **-s**, NO PL (*Aus*) horseradish

krepieren [kre'pi:rən], *ptp* **krepiert** VI AUX SEIN **(a)** (= *platzen*) to explode **(b)** (*inf*) (= *sterben*) to croak (it) (*inf*); (= *elend sterben*) to die a wretched death; **das Tier ist ihm krepiert** the animal died on him (*inf*)

Krepp [krɛp] M **-s, -e** *or* **-s** crepe

Krepppapier NT crepe paper

Kreppsohle F crepe sole

Kresse ['krɛsə] F **-**, NO PL cress

Kreta ['kre:ta] NT **-s** Crete

Kreter ['kre:tɐ] M **-s, -, Kreterin** [-ərɪn] F **-, -nen** Cretan

kretisch ['kre:tɪʃ] ADJ Cretan

kreucht [krɔyçt] (*obspoet*) 3 PERS SING *von* **kriechen; alles was da ~ und fleucht** all living creatures

kreuz [krɔyts] ADV **~ und quer** all over; **~ und quer durch die Gegend fahren** to travel *or* (*im Auto*) drive all over the place

Kreuz [krɔyts] NT **-es, -e (a)** cross; (*als Anhänger etc*) crucifix; **das ~ des Südens** (*Astron*) the Southern Cross; **jdn ans ~ schlagen** *or* **nageln** to nail sb to the cross; **ein ~ schlagen** *or* **machen** to make the sign of the cross; **zwei Gegenstände über ~ legen** to put two objects crosswise one on top of the other; **es ist ein *or* ich habe mein ~ mit ihm/damit** he's/it's an awful problem; **ich mache drei ~e, wenn er geht** (*inf*) it'll be such a relief when he has gone **(b)** (*Anat*) small of the back; (*von Tier*) back; **ich habe Schmerzen im ~** I've got a backache; **ich habs im ~** (*inf*) I have back trouble **(c)** (*Archit*: = *Fensterkreuz*) mullion and transom **(d)** (*Mus*) sharp **(e)** (= *Autobahnkreuz*) intersection **(f)** (*Cards*) (= *Farbe*) clubs *pl*; (= *Karte*) club; **die ~dame** the Queen of Clubs

Kreuzblütler [-bly:tlɐ] M **-s, -** cruciferous plant

kreuzen ['krɔytsn] **1** VT to cross (*auch Biol*) **2** VR to cross; (*Meinungen, Interessen*) to clash; (*Biol*) to interbreed; **die Briefe haben sich gekreuzt** the letters crossed in the post (*Brit*) *or* mail **3** VI AUX HABEN *or* SEIN (*Naut*) to cruise; (= *Zickzack fahren*) to tack

Kreuzer ['krɔytsɐ] M **-s, -** (*Naut*) cruiser

Kreuz-: Kreuzfahrer M (*Hist*) crusader; **Kreuzfahrt** F **(a)** (*Naut*) cruise; **eine ~ machen** to go on a cruise **(b)** (*Hist*) crusade; **Kreuzfeuer** NT (*Mil, fig*) crossfire; **im ~ (der Kritik) stehen** (*fig*) to be under fire (from all sides); **ins ~ (der Kritik) geraten** (*fig*) to come under fire (from all sides); **kreuzförmig** ADJ cross-shaped **2** ADV in the shape of a cross; **etw ~ anordnen** to arrange sth crosswise; **Kreuzgang** M, *pl* **-gänge** cloister; **Kreuzgelenk** NT (*Tech*) universal joint; **Kreuzgewölbe** NT (*Archit*) cross *or* groin vault

kreuzigen ['krɔytsɪgn] VT to crucify

Kreuzigung ['krɔytsɪgʊŋ] F **-, -en** crucifixion

Kreuz-: Kreuzotter F (*Zool*) adder, viper; **Kreuzschlitzschraube** F Phillips® screw; **Kreuzschlitzschraubenzieher** M Phillips® screwdriver; **Kreuzschlüssel** M wheel brace; **Kreuzschmerzen** PL backache *sing*; **Kreuzstich** M (*Sew*) cross-stitch

Kreuzung ['krɔytsʊŋ] F **-, -en (a)** (= *Straßenkreuzung*) crossroads *sing* **(b)** (= *das Kreuzen*) crossing **(c)** (= *Rasse*) hybrid; (= *Tiere*) cross, crossbreed

Kreuz-: Kreuzverhör NT cross-examination; **jdn ins ~ nehmen** to cross-examine sb; **Kreuzweg** M (= *Wegkreuzung, fig*) crossroads *sing*; **kreuzweise** ADV crosswise; **du kannst mich ~!** (*inf*) (you can) get stuffed! (*Brit inf*), you can kiss my ass! (*US sl*); **Kreuzworträtsel** NT crossword puzzle; **Kreuzzug** M (*lit, fig*) crusade

Krevette [kre'vɛtə] F **-, -n** shrimp

kribbelig ['krɪbəlɪç] ADJ edgy (*inf*); (= *kribbelnd*) tingly (*inf*)

kribbeln ['krɪbln] **1** VT (= *kitzeln*) to tickle; (= *jucken*) to make itch **2** VI (= *jucken*) to itch; (= *prickeln*) to tingle; **auf der Haut ~** to cause a prickling sensation; (*angenehm*) to make the skin tingle; **es kribbelt mir im Fuß** (*lit*) I have pins and needles in my foot; **es kribbelt mir in den Fingern, etw zu tun** (*inf*) I'm itching to do sth; **ein Kribbeln im Bauch haben** to have a feeling of anticipation in one's stomach

Kricket ['krɪkət] NT **-s, -s** (*Sport*) cricket

kriechen ['kri:çn], *pret* **kroch** [krɔx], *ptp* **gekrochen** [gə'krɔxn] VI AUX SEIN to creep (*auch Pflanze, Tech*), to crawl (*auch Schlange*); (= *langsam fahren*) to crawl (along); (*fig: Zeit*) to creep by; (*fig: = unterwürfig sein*) to grovel (*vor +dat* before), to crawl (*vor +dat* to); **aus dem Ei ~** to hatch (out); **auf allen vieren ~** to crawl on all fours; **unter die Bettdecke ~** to slip under the covers; **die Kälte kroch mir in die Knochen** the cold seeped into my bones

kriecherisch ['kri:çərɪʃ] (*inf*) **1** ADJ grovelling (*Brit*), groveling (*US*) **2** ADV **sich ~ benehmen/verhalten** to grovel

Kriech-: Kriechgang M, NO PL crawling gear; **Kriechspur** F crawler lane; **Kriechtier** NT (*Zool*) reptile

Krieg [kri:k] M **-(e)s, -e** [-gə] war; (= *Art der Kriegsführung*) warfare; **~ anfangen mit** to start a war with; **einer Partei** *etc* **den ~ erklären** (*fig*) to declare war on a party *etc*; **~ führen (mit** *or* **gegen)** to wage war (on); **~ führend** warring; **in ~ und Frieden** in war and in peace; **im ~(e)** in war; (*als Soldat*) away fighting; **im ~ sein** *or* **stehen (mit), ~ haben (mit), sich im ~ befinden (mit)** to be at war (with)

kriegen ['kri:gn] VT (*inf*) to get; *Zug, Bus, Schnupfen, Weglaufenden auch* to catch; *Junge, ein Kind* to have; **sie kriegt ein Kind** she's going to have a baby; **eine Glatze ~** to go bald; **es mit jdm zu tun ~** to be in trouble with sb; **wenn ich dich kriege!** just (you) wait till I catch you!; **sie ~ sich** (*in Kitschroman*) boy gets girl; **dann kriege ich zu viel** then it gets too much for me; **wenn du nicht sofort aufhörst, kriegst du ein paar!** (*inf*) if you don't stop that right now, I'll belt you! (*inf*); **jdn dazu ~, etw zu tun** to get sb to do sth; **etw gemacht ~** to get sth done

Krieger ['kri:gɐ] M **-s, -, Kriegerin** [-ərɪn] F **-, -nen** warrior; (= *Indianerkrieger*) brave; **ein müder ~ sein** (*fig inf*) to have no go left in one

Kriegerdenkmal NT war memorial

kriegerisch ['kri:gərɪʃ] **1** ADJ warlike *no adv*; *Haltung auch* belligerent; *Einsatz* military; **eine ~e Auseinandersetzung** military conflict **2** ADV *auftreten, eingestellt sein* belligerently; **sich ~ auseinander setzen** to engage in military conflict

Krieg-: kriegführend ADJ *siehe* **Krieg; Kriegführung** F warfare *no art*; (*eines Feldherrn*) conduct of the war

Kriegs-: Kriegsausbruch M outbreak of war; **es kam zum ~** war broke out; **kriegsbedingt** ADJ caused by (the) war; **Kriegsbeginn** M start of the war; **Kriegsbeil** NT tomahawk; **das ~ begraben** (*fig*) to bury the hatchet; **das ~ ausgraben** (*fig*) to start a fight; **Kriegsbemalung** F (*lithum*) war paint; **Kriegsbeschädigte(r)** MF DECL AS ADJ war-disabled person; **die ~n** the war disabled; **Kriegsdienst** M (*oldform*) military service; **den ~ verweigern** to be a conscientious objector; **Kriegsende** NT end of the war; **Kriegserklärung** F declaration of war; **Kriegsfall** M (eventuality of war); **dann träte der ~ ein** then war would break out; **Kriegsfuß** M (*inf*) **mit jdm auf ~ stehen** to be at odds with sb; **Kriegsgebiet** NT war zone; **Kriegsgefahr** F danger of war; **Kriegsgefangene(r)** MF DECL AS ADJ prisoner of war, P.O.W.; **Kriegsgefangenschaft** F captivity; **in ~ sein** to be a prisoner of war; **aus der ~ kommen** to return from captivity; **Kriegsgegner(in)** M(F) **(a)** opponent of a/the war; (= *Pazifist*) pacifist **(b)** (= *Gegner im Krieg*) wartime enemy; **Kriegsgerät** NT military equipment; **Kriegsgericht** NT (wartime) court martial; **jdn vor ein ~ stellen** to court-martial sb; **Kriegsherr(in)** M(F) warlord; *oberster ~* (*Hist*) commander-in-chief; **Kriegsjahr** NT year of war; **die ~e** the war years; **im ~ 1945** (during the war) in 1945; **im dritten ~** in the third year of the war; **Kriegskamerad(in)** M(F) fellow soldier; **kriegsmüde** ADJ war-weary; **Kriegsopfer** NT war victim; **Kriegsrat** M council of war; **~ halten** (*fig*) to have a pow-wow (*inf*); **Kriegsrecht** NT conventions of war *pl*; (*Mil*) martial law; **Kriegsschauplatz** M theatre (*Brit*) *or* theater (*US*) of war; **Kriegsschiff** NT warship;

Kriegsspiel NT war game; **Kriegsspielzeug** NT war toy; **Kriegsstärke** F war establishment; **die Armee auf ~ bringen** to make the army ready for war; **Kriegsteilnehmer** M combatant; (= *Staat*) combatant nation; (= *ehemaliger Soldat*) ex-serviceman; **Kriegstreiber** M **-s, -**, **Kriegstreiberin** F **-, -nen** (*pej*) warmonger; **Kriegsverbrechen** NT war crime; **Kriegsverbrecher(in)** M(F) war criminal; **Kriegsversehrte(r)** MF DECL AS ADJ war-disabled person; **die Kriegsversehrten** the war-disabled; **Kriegszeit** F wartime; **in ~en** in times of war; **sie erzählten von ihrer ~** they told about their wartime experiences; **Kriegszustand** M state of war; **im ~** at war

Krill [krɪl] M **-(s)**, NO PL (*Biol*) krill

Krim [krɪm] F **- die ~** the Crimea

Krimi ['kriːmi] M **-s, -s** (*inf*) (crime) thriller; (*rätselhaft*) whodunnit (*inf*); (= *Buch: mit Detektiv als Held*) detective novel

Kriminal- [krimi'naːl-]: **Kriminalbeamte(r)** M DECL AS ADJ, **Kriminalbeamtin** F detective; **Kriminalfilm** M crime film, crime movie (*esp US*); (*rätselhaft*) murder mystery

kriminalisieren [kriminali'ziːrən], *ptp* **kriminalisiert** VT to criminalize

Kriminalist [krimina'lɪst] M **-en, -en**, **Kriminalistin** [-'lɪstɪn] F **-, -nen** criminologist

Kriminalistik [krimina'lɪstɪk] F **-**, NO PL criminology

kriminalistisch [krimina'lɪstɪʃ] ▣ ADJ criminological; **~er Spürsinn besitzen** to have a nose for solving crimes ▣ ADV **~ begabt sein** to have a talent for solving crimes

Kriminalität [kriminali'tɛːt] F **-**, NO PL crime; (= *Ziffer*) crime rate; **organisierte ~** organized crime

Kriminal-: **Kriminalkommissar(in)** M(F) detective superintendent; **Kriminalpolizei** F criminal investigation department; **Kriminalpolizist(in)** M(F) detective; **Kriminalroman** M *siehe* **Krimi** (crime) thriller; detective novel; murder mystery

kriminell [krimi'nɛl] ▣ ADJ (*lit, fig inf*) criminal; **~ werden** to become a criminal; **~e Energie** criminal resolve ▣ ADV **(a)** (= *fahrlässig*) criminally **(b)** (*inf*: = *gefährlich*) glatt, schlüpfrig, schnell dangerously

Kriminelle(r) [krimi'nɛlə] MF DECL AS ADJ criminal

Krimskrams ['krɪmskrams] M **-es**, NO PL (*inf*) odds and ends *pl*

Kringel ['krɪŋl] M **-s, -** (*der Schrift*) squiggle; (*Cook*: = *Zuckerkringel etc*) ring

kringelig ['krɪŋəlɪç] ADJ crinkly; **sich ~ lachen** (*inf*) to laugh oneself silly (*inf*)

kringeln ['krɪŋln] VR to go frizzy; **sich ~ vor Lachen** (*inf*) to kill oneself laughing (*inf*)

Kripo ['kriːpo, 'krɪpo] F **-, -s** (*inf*) ABBR *von* **Kriminalpolizei**; **die ~** the cops *pl* (*inf*)

Kripo- IN CPDS (*inf*) police; **Kripobeamte(r)** M DECL AS ADJ, **Kripobeamtin** F police detective

Krippe ['krɪpə] F **-, -n (a)** (= *Futterkrippe*) (hay)rack **(b)** (= *Kinderkrippe, Weihnachtskrippe*) crib; (*Bibl*) crib, manger **(c)** (= *Kinderhort*) crèche (*Brit*), daycare centre (*Brit*) *or* center (*US*)

Krippentod M cot death (*Brit*), crib death (*US*)

Krise ['kriːzə] F **-, -n** crisis; **er hatte eine schwere ~** he was going through a difficult crisis; **die ~ kriegen** (*inf*) to go crazy (*inf*)

kriseln ['kriːzln] VI IMPERS (*inf*) **es kriselt** trouble is brewing

Krisen-: **krisenanfällig** ADJ crisis-prone; **krisenfest** ▣ ADJ stable ▣ ADV **Geld ~ in Grundbesitz anlegen** to invest money in property to secure it against economic crises; **Krisenfestigkeit** F stability (in the face of a crisis); **Krisengebiet** NT crisis area; **Krisenherd** M flash point, trouble spot; **Krisenmanagement** NT crisis management; **krisensicher** ▣ ADJ stable ▣ ADV **Geld ~ in Grundbesitz anlegen** to invest money in property to secure it against economic crises; **Krisensitzung** F emergency session; **Krisenstab** M (special) action committee

Kristall¹ [krɪs'tal] M **-s, -e** crystal; **~e bilden** to form crystals

Kristall² NT **-s**, NO PL (= *~glas*) crystal (glass); (= *~waren*) crystalware

kristallen [krɪs'talən] ADJ (made of) crystal; *Stimme* crystal-clear

Kristalleuchter M *siehe* **Kristallleuchter**

Kristallglas NT crystal glass

kristallisieren [krɪstali'ziːrən], *ptp* **kristallisiert** VIR (*lit, fig*) to crystallize

Kristall-: **kristallklar** ADJ crystal-clear; **Kristallleuchter** M crystal chandelier

Kriterium [kri'teːriʊm] NT **-s, Kriterien** [-riən] criterion

Kritik [kri'tiːk] F **-, -en (a)** NO PL criticism (*an +dat* of); **an jdm/etw ~ üben** to criticize sb/sth; **Gesellschafts-/Literaturkritik** social/literary criticism; **unter aller** *or* **jeder ~ sein** (*inf*) to be beneath contempt **(b)** (= *Rezensieren*) criticism; (= *Rezension*) review; **der Film bekam schlechte ~en** the film got bad reviews **(c)** NO PL (= *Urteilsfähigkeit*) discrimination; **ohne jede ~** uncritically

Kritiker ['kriːtikɐ] M **-s, -**, **Kritikerin** [-ərɪn] F **-, -nen** critic

Kritik-: **kritikfähig** ADJ able to criticize; **Kritikfähigkeit** F critical faculty; **kritiklos** ▣ ADJ uncritical ▣ ADV uncritically; **etw ~ hinnehmen** to accept sth without criticism

kritisch ['kriːtɪʃ] ▣ ADJ (*alle Bedeutungen*) critical ▣ ADV kommentieren, bewerten, sich äußern critically; **~ eingestellt sein** to be critical; **sich jdm gegenüber ~ verhalten** to be critical of sb; **die Lage ~ beurteilen** to make a critical appraisal of the situation; **jdm/einer Sache ~ gegenüberstehen** to be critical of sb/sth

kritisieren [kriti'ziːrən], *ptp* **kritisiert** VTI to criticize

Kritzelei [krɪtsə'lai] F **-, -en** scribble; (= *das Kritzeln*) scribbling; (= *Männchenmalen etc*) doodle; doodling; (*an Wänden*) graffiti

kritzeln ['krɪtsln] VTI to scribble, to scrawl; (= *Männchen malen etc*) to doodle

Kroate [kro'aːtə] M **-n, -n**, **Kroatin** [-'aːtɪn] F **-, -nen** Croat, Croatian

Kroatien [kro'aːtsiən] NT **-s** Croatia

kroatisch [kro'aːtɪʃ] ADJ Croat, Croatian

kroch PRET *von* **kriechen**

Krokant [kro'kant] M **-s**, NO PL (*Cook*) cracknel

Krokette [kro'kɛtə] F **-, -n** (*Cook*) croquette

Krokodil [kroko'diːl] NT **-s, -e** crocodile

Krokodilleder NT crocodile skin

Krokodilstränen PL crocodile tears *pl*

Krokus ['kroːkʊs] M **-, -** *or* **-se** crocus

Krone ['kroːnə] F **-, -n (a)** crown **(b)** (= *Mauerkrone*) coping; (= *Schaumkrone*) cap, crest; (= *Zahnkrone*) crown; (= *Baumkrone*) top; **die ~ der Schöpfung** the pride of creation; **die ~ des Ganzen war, dass ...** (*fig*) (but) what capped it all was that ...; **das setzt doch allem die ~ auf** (*inf*) that beats everything; **einen in der ~ haben** (*inf*) to be tipsy; **dabei fällt dir keine Perle** *or* **kein Stein** *or* **Zacken aus der ~** (*inf*) it won't hurt you **(c)** (= *Währungseinheit*) (*in Tschechien, Slowakei*) crown; (*in Dänemark, Norwegen*) krone; (*in Schweden, Island*) krona

krönen ['krøːnən] VT (*lit, fig*) to crown; **jdn zum König ~** to crown sb king; **von Erfolg gekrönt sein/werden** to be crowned with success; **gekrönte Häupter** crowned heads; **damit wurde ihre glänzende Laufbahn gekrönt** this was the crowning achievement of her career; **der ~de Abschluss** the culmination

Kronenkorken M crown cap

Kron- ['kroːn-]: **Kronerbe** M heir to the crown; **Kronerbin** F heiress to the crown; **Kronkolonie** F crown colony; **Kronkorken** M crown cap; **Kronleuchter** M chandelier; **Kronprinz** M crown prince; (*in Großbritannien auch*) Prince of Wales; (*fig*) heir apparent; **Kronprinzessin** F crown princess; (*fig*) heir apparent

Krönung ['krøːnʊŋ] F **-, -en** coronation; (*fig*) culmination; (*von Veranstaltung*) high point; (*Archit*) coping stone

Kronzeuge ['kroːn-] M, **Kronzeugin** F (*Jur*) person who gives *or* turns King's/Queen's evidence (*Brit*) *or* State's evidence (*US*); (= *Hauptzeuge*) principal witness; (*fig*) main authority; **~ sein**, **~ auftreten** to turn King's/Queen's evidence (*Brit*) *or* State's evidence (*US*); to appear as principal witness

Kropf [krɔpf] M **-(e)s, ~e** ['krœpfə] **(a)** (*von Vogel*) crop **(b)** (*Med*) goitre (*Brit*), goiter (*US*); **überflüssig wie ein ~** totally superfluous

kross [krɔs] (*N Ger*) ▣ ADJ crisp ▣ ADV backen, braten until crisp

Kröte ['krøːtə] F **-, -n (a)** (*Zool*) toad; **eine ~ schlucken** (*fig inf*) to bite the bullet **(b)** (*inf*) **Kröten** PL pennies (*inf*); **die paar ~n** the few pounds

Krücke ['krʏkə] F **-, -n (a)** crutch; (*fig*) prop; **auf** *or* **an ~n** (*dat*) **gehen** to walk on crutches **(b)** (*inf*) (= *Nichtskönner*) dead loss (*inf*); (= *altes Fahrrad*) unfashionable bike (*inf*)

Krug [kruːk] M **-(e)s, ¨e** ['kryːgə] (= *Milchkrug etc*) jug; (= *Bierkrug*) (beer) mug; (= *Maßkrug*) litre (*Brit*) *or* liter (*US*) mug; **der ~ geht so lange zum Brunnen, bis er bricht** (*Prov*) one day you/they *etc* will come unstuck (*inf*)

Krümel ['kryːml] M **-s, -** (= *Brotkrümel etc*) crumb

krümelig ['kryːməlɪç] ADJ crumbly

krümeln ['kryːmln] VTI to crumble; (*beim Essen*) to make crumbs

krumm [krʊm] **1** ADJ **(a)** crooked; (= *hakenförmig*) hooked; *Beine* bandy; *Rücken* hunched; **etw ~ biegen** to bend sth; **~ und schief** askew; **sich ~ und schief lachen** (*inf*) to fall about laughing (*inf*); **einen ~en Rücken machen** to stoop; (*fig*) bow and scrape **(b)** (*inf*: = *unehrlich*) crooked (*inf*); **~er Hund** (*pej*) crooked swine; **ein ~es Ding drehen** (*sl*) to do something crooked; **etw auf die ~e Tour versuchen** to try to wangle sth (*inf*) **2** ADV (= *nicht gerade*) **~ stehen/sitzen** to slouch; **~ gehen** to walk with a stoop; **~ wachsen** to grow crooked; **~ gewachsen** crooked; **keinen Finger ~ machen** (*inf*) not to lift a finger

krummbeinig ADJ bow-legged

krümmen ['krʏmən] **1** VT to bend; **die Katze krümmte den Buckel** the cat arched its back; **gekrümmte Oberfläche** curved surface **2** VR to bend; (*Fluss*) to wind; (*Straße*) to curve; (*Wurm*) to writhe; (*Mensch*) to double up; **sich vor Schmerzen** (*dat*) **~** to double up with pain

Krumm-: krummlachen VR SEP (*inf*) to double up with laughter; **krumm nehmen** VT IRREG (*inf*) (*jdm*) **etw ~** to take offence (*Brit*) *or* offense (*US*) at sth; **Krummschwert** NT scimitar

Krümmung ['krʏmʊŋ] F **-, -en (a)** (= *das Krümmen*) bending **(b)** (= *Biegung*) (*von Weg, Fluss*) turn; (*Math, Med, von Fläche*) curvature; (*Opt: von Linse*) curve, curvature, figure

Krüppel ['krʏpl] M **-s, -** cripple; **zum ~ werden** to be crippled; **jdn zum ~ machen** to cripple sb; **jdn zum ~ schlagen** to (beat and) cripple sb

Kruste ['krʊstə] F **-, -n** crust; (*von Schweinebraten*) crackling; (*von Braten*) crisped outside

krustig ['krʊstɪç] ADJ crusty; *Topf etc* encrusted

Krux [krʊks] F **-, NO PL** = **Crux**

Kruzifix ['kruːtsifɪks, krutsɪˈfɪks] NT **-es, -e** crucifix

kryokonservieren [kryokɔnzɛrˈviːrən], *ptp* **kryokonserviert** VT to preserve cryogenically

Krypta ['krʏpta] F **-, Krypten** ['krʏptn] crypt

kryptisch ['krʏptɪʃ] ADJ *Bemerkung* cryptic; **sich ~ ausdrücken** to express oneself cryptically

Krypto- [krʏpto], **krypto-** IN CPDS crypto-; **Kryptogramm** NT, *pl* **-gramme** cryptogram

Krypton ['krʏptɔn, krʏpˈtoːn] NT **-s, NO PL** (*abbr* **Kr**) krypton

Kuba ['kuːba] NT **-s** Cuba

Kubaner [kuˈbaːnɐ] M **-s, -, Kubanerin** [-ərɪn] F **-, -nen** Cuban

kubanisch [kuˈbaːnɪʃ] ADJ Cuban

Kübel ['kyːbl] M **-s, -** bucket; (*für Pflanzen*) tub; **es regnet (wie) aus** *or* **mit ~n** it's bucketing down (*Brit*), it's coming down in buckets (*US*)

Kubik [kuˈbiːk] NT **-, -** (*Aut inf*: = *Hubraum*) cc

Kubik-: Kubikmeter M *or* NT cubic metre (*Brit*) *or* meter (*US*); **Kubikwurzel** F cube root; **Kubikzahl** F cube number; **Kubikzentimeter** M *or* NT cubic centimetre (*Brit*) *or* centimeter (*US*)

kubisch ['kuːbɪʃ] ADJ cubic(al); *Gleichung* cubic; *Lampen* cube-shaped

Kubismus [kuˈbɪsmʊs] M **-, NO PL** (*Art*) cubism

kubistisch [kuˈbɪstɪʃ] ADJ (*Art*) cubist(ic)

Küche ['kʏçə] F **-, -n (a)** kitchen; (*klein*) kitchenette **(b)** (= *Kochkunst*) **gutbürgerliche ~** good home cooking; **chinesische ~** Chinese cooking **(c)** (= *Speisen*) dishes *pl*, food; **warme/kalte ~** hot/cold food

Kuchen ['kuːxn] M **-s, -** cake; (*mit Obst gedeckt*) (fruit) flan

Kuchenblech NT baking sheet

Küchenchef(in) M(F) chef

Kuchen-: Kuchenform F cake tin (*Brit*) *or* pan (*US*); **Kuchengabel** F pastry fork

Küchen-: Küchengerät NT kitchen utensil; (*kollektiv*) kitchen utensils *pl*; (*elektrisch*) kitchen appliance; **Küchenherd** M cooker (*Brit*), range (*US*); **Küchenhilfe** F kitchen help; **Küchenmaschine** F food processor; **Küchenmesser** NT kitchen knife; **Küchenpersonal** NT kitchen staff; **Küchenrolle** F kitchen roll; **Küchenschabe** F (*Zool*) cockroach

Kuchenteig M cake mixture; (= *Hefeteig*) dough

Küchen-: Küchentuch NT, *pl* **-tücher** kitchen towel; **Küchenwaage** F kitchen scales *pl*

Kücken ['kʏkn] NT **-s, -** (*Aus*) = **Küken**

kuckuck ['kʊkʊk] INTERJ cuckoo

Kuckuck ['kʊkʊk] M **-s, -e (a)** cuckoo **(b)** (*inf*: = *Siegel des Gerichtsvollziehers*) bailiff's seal (for distraint of goods) **(c)** (*euph inf*: = *Teufel*) devil; **zum ~ (noch mal)!** hell's bells! (*inf*); **hols der ~!** botheration! (*dated inf*); **geh zum ~, scher dich zum ~** go to blazes (*inf*); **(das) weiß der ~** heaven (only) knows (*inf*)

Kuckucks-: Kuckucksei NT cuckoo's egg; **man hat uns ein ~ untergeschoben** (*inf*) we've been left holding the baby (*inf*); **jdm ein ~ ins Nest legen** (*inf*) to foist something on sb; **Kuckucksuhr** F cuckoo clock

Kuddelmuddel ['kʊdlmʊdl] M *or* NT **-s, NO PL** (*inf*) muddle

Kufe ['kuːfə] F **-, -n (a)** (*von Schlitten, Schlittschuh etc*) runner; (*von Flugzeug*) skid **(b)** (= *Holzbottich*) tub

Küfer ['kyːfɐ] M **-s, -** cellarman; (*S Ger.* = *Böttcher*) cooper

Kugel ['kuːgl] F **-, -n (a)** ball; (*geometrische Figur*) sphere; (= *Erdkugel*) globe; (= *Kegelkugel*) bowl; (= *Gewehrkugel*) bullet; (*für Luftgewehr*) pellet; (= *Kanonenkugel*) (cannon)ball; (*Sport:* = *Stoßkugel*) shot; (= *Christbaumkugel*) glitter ball; **sich** (*dat*) **eine ~ durch den Kopf jagen** *or* **schießen** to blow one's brains out; **ich geb mir die ~** (*sl*: = *erschieße mich*) I'll shoot myself (*inf*); **eine ruhige ~ schieben** (*inf*) to have a cushy number (*inf*); (*aus Faulheit*) to swing the lead (*Brit inf*), to play hookey (*US inf*) **(b)** (= *Gelenkkugel*) head (of a bone)

Kugel-: Kugelblitz M (*Met*) ball lightning; **Kugelfang** M butt; **die Leibwächter sollen als ~ dienen** the bodyguards are meant to act as a bullet-screen; **Kugelfisch** M globefish, puffer; **kugelförmig 1** ADJ spherical **2** ADV spherically; **Kugelgelenk** NT (*Anat, Tech*) ball-and-socket joint; **Kugelhagel** M hail of bullets; **Kugelkopf** M golf ball; **Kugelkopfschreibmaschine** F golf-ball typewriter; **Kugellager** NT ball bearing

kugeln ['kuːgln] **1** VI AUX SEIN (= *rollen, fallen*) to roll **2** VR to roll (around); **sich (vor Lachen) ~** (*inf*) to double up (laughing); **ich könnte mich ~** (*inf*) it's screamingly funny (*inf*)

Kugel-: kugelrund ADJ as round as a ball; (*inf*) *Mensch* barrel-shaped (*inf*); **Kugelschreiber** M ballpoint (pen), Biro® (*Brit*); **Kugelschreibermine** F refill (for a ballpoint pen); **kugelsicher** ADJ bullet-proof; **Kugelstoßen** NT **-s, NO PL** shot-putting; **Sieger im ~** winner in the shot(-put); **Kugelstoßer** [-ʃtoːsɐ] M **-s, -, Kugelstoßerin** [-ərɪn] F **-, -nen** shot-putter

Kuh [kuː] F **-, ¨e** ['kyːə] cow; (*pej inf*: = *Mädchen, Frau*) cow (*inf*); **die ~ vom Eis bringen** (*fig inf*) to save the situation; **heilige ~** (*lit, fig*) sacred cow

Kuh-: Kuhdorf NT (*pej inf*) one-horse town (*inf*); **Kuhfladen** M cowpat; **Kuhglocke** F cowbell; **Kuhhandel** M (*pej inf*) horse-trading *no pl* (*inf*); **ein ~** a bit of horse-trading (*inf*); **Kuhhaut** F cowhide; **das geht auf keine ~** (*inf*) that is absolutely staggering

kühl [kyːl] **1** ADJ (*lit, fig*) cool; (= *abweisend*) cold; **mir wird etwas ~** I'm getting rather chilly; **abends wurde es ~** in the evenings it got cool; **ein ~er Kopf** (*fig*) a cool-headed person; **einen ~en Kopf bewahren** to keep a cool head; **ein ~er Rechner** a cool, calculating person **2** ADV coolly; **etw ~ lagern** to store sth in a cool place; **„~ servieren"** "serve chilled"

Kühl-: Kühlanlage F refrigeration plant; **Kühlbecken** NT (*für Brennelemente*) cooling pond; **Kühlbox** F cooler

Kuhle ['kuːlə] F **-, -n** (*N Ger*) hollow; (= *Grube*) pit

Kühle ['kyːlə] F **-, NO PL** (*lit*) cool(ness); (*fig*) coolness; (= *Abweisung*) coldness

kühlen ['ky:lən] **1** VT to cool; *(auf Eis)* to chill; *siehe auch* **gekühlt 2** VI to be cooling

Kühler ['ky:le] M **-s, -** *(Tech)* cooler; *(Aut)* radiator; *(inf:* = *~haube)* bonnet *(Brit)*, hood *(US)*; *(= Sektkühler)* ice bucket

Kühler-: Kühlerfigur F *(Aut)* radiator mascot *(Brit)*, hood ornament *(US)*; **Kühlerhaube** F *(Aut)* bonnet *(Brit)*, hood *(US)*

Kühl-: Kühlfach NT freezer compartment *(Brit)*, deep freeze; **Kühlmittel** NT *(Tech)* coolant; **Kühlraum** M cold storage room; **Kühlschrank** M fridge *(Brit)*, refrigerator; **Kühltasche** F cold bag; **Kühltruhe** F (chest) freezer; *(in Lebensmittelgeschäft)* freezer (cabinet); **Kühlturm** M *(Tech)* cooling tower

Kühlung ['ky:lʊŋ] F **-,** NO PL *(= das Kühlen)* cooling; *(= Kühle)* coolness; **zur ~ des Motors** to cool the engine; **der Wind brachte etwas ~** the wind cooled things down a little; **auch bei ~ nur begrenzt haltbar** perishable even when kept in cold storage

Kühl-: Kühlwagen M *(Rail)* cold storage wagon; *(= Lastwagen)* cold storage truck; **Kühlwasser** NT coolant; *(Aut)* radiator water

Kuh-: Kuhmilch F cow's milk; **Kuhmist** M cow dung

kühn [ky:n] **1** ADJ *(lit, fig)* bold; **das übertrifft meine ~sten Erwartungen** it's beyond my wildest dreams **2** ADV *(lit, fig)* boldly

Kühnheit F **-, -en** (a) NO PL boldness (b) *(Handlung)* bold act

Kuh-: Kuhscheiße F *(inf)* cowshit *(sl)*; **Kuhstall** M cowshed; **Kuhweide** F pasture

k. u. k. ['ka:lʊnt'ka:] ABBR *von* **kaiserlich und königlich** imperial and royal

Küken ['ky:kn] NT **-s, -** *(= Huhn)* chick; *(inf)* = *junges Mädchen)* young goose *(inf)*; *(= Nesthäkchen)* baby of the family *(inf)*; *(= jüngste Person)* baby

Kukuruz ['kʊkʊrʊts, 'ku:kurʊts] M **-(es)**, NO PL *(Aus)* maize, corn

kulant [ku'lant] **1** ADJ accommodating; *Bedingungen* fair **2** ADV accommodatingly

Kulanz [ku'lants] F **-,** NO PL **auf** *or* **aus ~** as a courtesy; **kann ich auf Ihre ~ zählen?** I wonder if you could oblige me in this

Kuli ['ku:li] M **-s, -s** (a) *(= Lastträger)* coolie; *(fig)* slave (b) *(inf:* = *Kugelschreiber)* ballpoint (pen), Biro® *(Brit)*

kulinarisch [kuli'na:rɪʃ] ADJ culinary

Kulisse [ku'lɪsə] F **-, -n** scenery *no pl*; *(= Teilstück)* flat; *(hinten auf Bühne)* backdrop; *(an den Seiten)* wing; *(fig:* = *Hintergrund)* backdrop; *(St Ex)* unofficial market; **vor der ~ der Schweizer Alpen** against the backdrop of the Swiss Alps; **hinter den ~n** *(fig)* behind the scenes; **die ~ für etw bilden** *(lit, fig)* to provide the backdrop for *or* to sth

Kulleraugen PL *(inf)* big wide eyes *pl*

kullern ['kʊlɐn] VTI *(vi: aux sein)* *(inf)* to roll

Kult [kʊlt] M **-(e)s, -e** cult; *(= Verehrung)* worship; **einen ~ mit jdm/etw treiben** to make a cult out of sb/sth; **mit denen wird jetzt so ein ~ getrieben** they have become such cult figures

Kult- IN CPDS cult-; **Kultbuch** NT cult book; **Kultfigur** F cult figure; **Kultfilm** M cult film

kultivieren [kʊlti'vi:rən], *ptp* **kultiviert** VT *(lit, fig)* to cultivate

kultiviert [kʊlti'vi:ɐt] **1** ADJ cultivated, refined **2** ADV *speisen, sich einrichten* stylishly; *sich ausdrücken* in a refined manner; **könnt ihr euch nicht etwas ~er unterhalten?** couldn't you make your language just a little more refined?; **wenn Sie ~ reisen wollen** if you want to travel in style

Kultiviertheit F **-,** NO PL refinement

Kult-: Kultstätte F place of worship; **Kultsymbol** NT ritual symbol

Kultur [kʊl'tu:ɐ] F **-, -en** (a) *(no pl:* = *Kunst und Wissenschaft)* culture; **ein Volk von hoher ~** a highly cultured *or* civilized people; **er hat keine ~** he is uncultured; **politische ~** political culture (b) *(= Lebensform)* civilization; **dort leben verschiedene ~en harmonisch zusammen** different cultures live harmoniously together there (c) *(= Bakterienkultur, Pilzkultur etc)* culture (d) *(= Bestand angebauter Pflanzen)* plantation

Kultur-: Kulturabkommen NT cultural agreement; **Kulturarbeit** F cultural activities *pl*; **Kulturaustausch** M cultural exchange; **Kulturbanause** M, **Kulturbanausin** F *(inf)* philistine; **Kulturbetrieb** M *(inf)* culture industry; **Kulturbeutel** M sponge *or* toilet bag *(Brit)*, washbag; **Kulturdenkmal** NT cultural monument

kulturell [kʊltu'rɛl] **1** ADJ cultural **2** ADV culturally

Kultur-: Kulturerbe NT cultural heritage; **Kulturgeschichte** F history of civilization; **kulturgeschichtlich** ADJ historico-cultural; **Kulturgut** NT cultural possessions *pl*; **Kulturhauptstadt** F cultural capital; **~ Europas, Europäische ~** European City of Culture; **Kulturhoheit** F independence in matters of education and culture; **Kulturkreis** M culture group *or* area; **Kulturkritik** F critique of (our) culture; **kulturlos** ADJ lacking culture; **Kulturpessimismus** M despair of civilization; **Kulturpflanze** F cultivated plant; **Kulturpolitik** F cultural and educational policy; **Kulturpolitiker(in)** M(F) *politician who concerns himself mainly with cultural and educational policies*; **kulturpolitisch** ADJ politico-cultural; **~e Fragen** matters with both a cultural and a political aspect; **Kulturrevolution** F cultural revolution; **Kulturschaffende(r)** [-ʃafndə] MF DECL AS ADJ creative artist; **Kulturschale** F Petri dish; **Kulturschock** M culture shock; **Kultursprache** F language of the civilized world; **Kulturstätte** F place of cultural interest; **Kulturteil** M *(von Zeitung)* arts section; **Kulturträger(in)** M(F) vehicle of civilization; **Kulturvolk** NT civilized people *sing*

Kultus- ['kʊltʊs-]: **Kultusminister(in)** M(F) minister of education and the arts; **Kultusministerium** NT ministry of education and the arts

Kümmel ['kʏml] M **-s, -** (a) NO PL *(= Gewürz)* caraway (seed) (b) *(inf:* = *Schnaps)* kümmel

Kummer ['kʊmɐ] M **-s,** NO PL *(= Gram, Betrübtheit)* sorrow; *(= Unannehmlichkeit, Ärger)* problems *pl*; **hast du ~?** is something wrong?; **aus** *or* **vor ~ sterben** to die of sorrow; **er fand vor ~ keinen Schlaf mehr** such was his sorrow that he was unable to sleep; **jdm ~ machen** *or* **bereiten** to cause sb worry; **zu jds ~** to sb's dismay; **wenn das dein einziger ~ ist** if that's your only problem; **wir sind (an) ~ gewöhnt** *(inf)* it happens all the time

Kummerkasten M *(inf: in Zeitung, Zeitschrift)* agony column *(Brit)*, advice column

Kummerkastenonkel M *(inf)* agony uncle *(Brit inf)*, advice columnist

Kummerkastentante F *(inf)* agony aunt *(Brit inf)*, advice columnist

kümmerlich ['kʏmɐlɪç] **1** ADJ (a) *(= karg, armselig)* miserable; *Lohn, Mahlzeit* paltry; *Aufsatz* scanty (b) *(= schwächlich)* puny; *Vegetation, Baum* stunted **2** ADV *leben, wachsen, sich entwickeln* poorly; **sich ~ ernähren** to live on a meagre *(Brit)* *or* meager *(US)* diet

kümmern **1** VT to concern; **was kümmert mich die Firma?** what do I care about the firm?; **was kümmert Sie das?** what business is that of yours?; **was kümmert mich das?** what's that to me? **2** VR **sich um jdn/etw ~** to look after sb/sth; **sich darum ~, dass ...** to see to it that ...; **aber darum kümmert sich im Stadtrat ja keiner** but nobody on the council does anything about it; **kümmere dich nicht um Sachen, die dich nichts angehen** don't worry about things that don't concern you; **kümmere dich gefälligst um deine eigenen Angelegenheiten!** mind your own business!; **er kümmert sich nicht darum, was die Leute denken** he doesn't care (about) what people think

Kummerspeck M *(inf)* flab caused by overeating because of emotional problems; **sie hat ganz schön ~ angesetzt** she's been putting on weight through comfort eating

Kumpel ['kʊmpl] M **-s, -** *or* *(inf)* **-s** *or* *(Aus)* **-n** (a) *(Min:* = *Bergmann)* miner (b) *(inf:* = *Arbeitskollege, Kamerad)* pal *(inf)*

kumulativ [kumula'ti:f] **1** ADJ cumulative **2** ADV cumulatively

Kumulus ['ku:mulʊs] M **-, Kumuli** ['ku:muli], **Kumuluswolke** F cumulus (cloud)

kündbar ADJ *Vertrag* terminable; *Anleihe* redeemable; **Beamte sind nicht ohne weiteres ~** civil servants cannot be dismissed just like that; **die Mitgliedschaft ist sehr schwer ~** it is very difficult to cancel one's membership

Kunde[1] ['kʊndə] F **-,** NO PL *(geh)* news *sing*

Kunde[2] ['kʊndə] M **-n, -n**, **Kundin** [-dɪn] F **-, -nen** customer; *(pej inf)* customer *(inf)*

-kunde ['kʊndə] F SUF IN CPDS study of; **Denkmalskunde** study of historical monuments; **Erdkunde** geography; **Pflanzenkunde** botany

Kunden-: Kundendienst M customer service; *(= Abteilung)* service department; **Kundenfang** M *(pej)* touting for

customers; **auf ~ sein** to be touting for customers;
Kundenkarte F (von Firma, Organisation) charge card; (von
Kaufhaus etc) (department (US)) store card; (von Bank) bank
card; **Kundenkreditkarte** F charge or store card; **Kundenkreis**
M customers pl, clientele; **Kundennummer** F customer
number

Kundgebung ['kʊntɡeːbʊŋ] F **-, -en (a)** (Pol) rally
(b) (= Bekanntgabe) declaration

kundig ['kʊndɪç] ADJ (geh) knowledgeable; (= sachkundig)
expert; **einer Sache** (gen) **~ sein** to have a knowledge of sth;
sich ~ machen to inform oneself

-kundig ADJ SUF with a good knowledge of; **fachkundig** with a
good knowledge of the subject; **gesetzkundig** well-versed in
the law

kündigen ['kʏndɪɡn̩] **1** VT Stellung to hand in one's notice for;
Abonnement, Mitgliedschaft, Kredite to cancel; Vertrag to
terminate; Tarife to discontinue; Hypothek (Bank) to foreclose
(on); (Hausbesitzer) to terminate; (Aus) Person to dismiss; **jdm
die Wohnung ~, jdn aus einer Wohnung ~** (Aus) to give sb
notice to quit his/her flat (Brit) or to vacate his/her
apartment (US); **ich habe meine Wohnung gekündigt** I've
given in my notice for my flat (Brit) or apartment; **die
Stellung ~** to hand in one's notice; **jdm die Stellung ~** to give
sb his/her notice; **jdm die Freundschaft ~** to break off a
friendship with sb
2 VI (Arbeitnehmer) to hand in one's notice; (Mieter) to give
in one's notice; **jdm ~** (Arbeitgeber) to give sb his/her notice;
(Arbeitnehmer) to hand in one's notice to sb; (Vermieter) to
give sb notice to quit (Brit) or to vacate his apartment (US);
(Mieter) to give in one's notice to sb; **zum 1. April ~** to hand
in one's notice for April 1st; (Mieter) to give in one's notice
for April 1st; (bei Mitgliedschaft) to cancel one's membership
as of April 1st; **bei jdm/einer Firma ~** to hand in one's notice
to sb/a firm

Kündigung ['kʏndɪɡʊŋ] F **-, -en (a)** (= Mitteilung) (von Vermieter)
notice to quit (Brit) or to vacate one's apartment (US); (von
Mieter) notice; (von Stellung) notice; (von Vertrag)
termination; (von Hypothek) notice of foreclosure; (von
Anleihe) notice of withdrawal; (von Mitgliedschaft,
Abonnement) (letter of) cancellation
(b) (= das Kündigen) (von Mieter, Vermieter) giving notice; (von
Arbeitgeber) dismissal; (von Arbeitnehmer) handing in one's
notice; (von Vertrag) termination; (von Hypothek) foreclosure;
(von Anleihe) withdrawal; (von Tarifen) discontinuation; (von
Mitgliedschaft, Abonnement) cancellation; **ich drohte (dem
Chef) mit der ~** I threatened to hand in my notice (to my
boss); **ihm wurde gestern die ~ ausgesprochen** he was given
his notice yesterday; **Vertrag mit vierteljährlicher ~** contract
with three months' notice on either side; **vierteljährliche ~
haben** to have (to give) three months' notice

Kündigungs-: Kündigungsfrist F period of notice;
Kündigungsgrund M grounds pl for giving notice;
Kündigungsschutz M protection against wrongful dismissal

Kundin F siehe **Kunde²**

Kundmachung ['kʊntmaxʊŋ] F **-, -en** (Aus, Sw, S Ger) =
Bekanntmachung

Kundschaft ['kʊntʃaft] F **-, -en (a)** customers pl; **es ist ~ im
Geschäft** there are customers in the shop **(b)** (= Erkundung)
reconnaissance

kundschaften ['kʊntʃaftn̩] VI INSEP (Mil) to reconnoitre (Brit), to
reconnoiter (US)

Kundschafter ['kʊntʃaftɐ] M **-s, -, Kundschafterin** [-ərɪn] F **-,
-nen** spy; (Mil) scout

kundtun ['kʊnttuːn] VT SEP IRREG (geh) to make known

künftig ['kʏnftɪç] **1** ADJ future; **das ~e Leben** the next life;
meine ~e Frau my wife-to-be **2** ADV in future

Kungelei [kʊŋə'lai] F **-, -en** (inf) scheming

kungeln ['kʊŋln̩] VI (inf) to scheme; **mit denen hat er viel
gekungelt** he did a lot of wheeling and dealing with them

Kunst [kʊnst] F **-, ̈e** ['kʏnstə] **(a)** art; **die schönen Künste** fine art
sing, the fine arts
(b) (= Können, Fertigkeit) art, skill; **mit seiner ~ am** or **zu Ende
sein** to be at one's wits' end; **die ~ besteht darin, ...** the art is
in ...; **ärztliche ~** medical skill
(c) (= ~stück) trick; **das ist keine ~!** it's like taking candy
from a baby (inf); (= ein Kinderspiel) it's a piece of cake (inf);
so einfach ist das, das ist die ganze ~ it's that easy, that's all

there is to it
(d) (inf) **das ist eine brotlose ~** there's no money in that; **was
macht die ~?** how are things?

Kunst- IN CPDS (Art) art; (= künstlich) artificial; **Kunstakademie**
F art college; **Kunstbanause** M, **Kunstbanausin** F (pej)
philistine; **Kunstdruck** M, pl **-drucke** art print; **Kunstdünger**
M chemical fertilizer; **Kunsterzieher(in)** M(F) art teacher;
Kunsterziehung F (Sch) art; **Kunstfaser** F synthetic fibre (Brit)
or fiber (US); **Kunstfehler** M professional error; (weniger ernst)
slip; **wegen eines ärztlichen ~s** because of medical
malpractice; **kunstfertig** (geh) **1** ADJ skilful (Brit), skillful (US)
2 ADV skilfully (Brit), skillfully (US); **Kunstflug** M aerobatics
sing, stunt flying; **ein ~** a piece of stunt flying;
Kunstfreund(in) M(F) art lover; **Kunstgegenstand** M objet
d'art; (Gemälde) work of art; **kunstgemäß, kunstgerecht**
1 ADJ (= fachmännisch) proficient **2** ADV proficiently;
Kunstgeschichte F history of art; **Kunstgewerbe** NT arts and
crafts pl; **ein Fachgeschäft für ~** an arts and crafts shop;
kunstgewerblich ADJ **~e Gegenstände** craft objects; **~er Zweig**
arts and crafts department; **Kunstgriff** M trick; **Kunstherz** NT
artificial heart; **Kunsthochschule** F art college;
Kunstkritiker(in) M(F) art critic; **Kunstleder** NT imitation
leather

Künstler ['kʏnstlɐ] M **-s, -, Künstlerin** [-ərɪn] F **-, -nen (a)** artist;
(= Unterhaltungskünstler) artiste; **bildender ~** visual artist
(b) (= Könner) genius (in +dat at)

künstlerisch ['kʏnstlərɪʃ] **1** ADJ artistic **2** ADV artistically; **~
wertvoll** of artistic value

Künstler-: Künstlername M pseudonym; **Künstlerpech** NT
(inf) hard luck

künstlich ['kʏnstlɪç] **1** ADJ artificial; Zähne, Wimpern,
Fingernägel false; Faserstoffe synthetic; Diamanten fake (inf);
~e Intelligenz artificial intelligence **2** ADV **(a)** fertigen,
herstellen artificially **(b)** (mit Apparaten) **jdn ~ ernähren** (Med)
to feed sb artificially **(c)** (inf: = übertrieben) **sich ~ aufregen** to
get all worked up (inf) about nothing

Kunst-: Kunstsammlung F art collection; **Kunstschätze** PL art
treasures pl; **Kunstschwimmen** NT exhibition swimming;
Kunstseide F artificial silk; **Kunstsprache** F artificial
language; **Kunstspringen** NT diving

Kunststoff M man-made material

Kunststoff-: kunststoffbeschichtet ADJ synthetic-coated;
Kunststoffflasche F plastic bottle

Kunst-: Kunststück NT trick; **~!** (iro) hardly surprising!; **das ist
kein ~** (fig) there's nothing to it; (= keine große Leistung) that's
nothing to write home about; **Kunsttischler(in)** M(F) cabinet-
maker; **Kunstturnen** NT gymnastics sing; **kunstvoll 1** ADJ
artistic; (= kompliziert) elaborate **2** ADV elaborately;
Kunstwerk NT work of art

kunterbunt ['kʊntɐbʊnt] **1** ADJ Sammlung, Gruppe etc motley
attr; Programm varied; Leben chequered (Brit), checkered (US)
2 ADV chaotically; **eine ~ zusammengewürfelte Gruppe** a
motley assortment; **~ durcheinander** all jumbled up

Kunz [kʊnts] M siehe **Hinz**

Kupfer ['kʊpfɐ] NT **-s**, NO PL (abbr Cu) copper

Kupfer- IN CPDS copper; **Kupferblech** NT sheet copper;
Kupferdraht M copper wire; **Kupfergeld** NT coppers pl;
kupferhaltig ADJ containing copper; **kupferrot** ADJ copper-
red; **Kupferstecher** [-ʃtɛçɐ] M **-s, -, Kupferstecherin** [-ərɪn] F **-,
-nen** copper(plate) engraver; **Kupferstich** M copperplate
(engraving); (Kunst) copper(plate) engraving

Kupon [ku'põː] M **-s, -s** coupon; siehe auch **Coupon**

Kuponbogen M (Fin) coupon sheet

Kuppe ['kʊpə] F **-, -n** (= Bergkuppe) (rounded) hilltop; (von
Straße) hump; (= Fingerkuppe) tip

Kuppel ['kʊpl̩] F **-, -n** dome

Kuppelei [kʊpə'lai] F **-,** NO PL (Jur) procuring

kuppeln ['kʊpl̩n] **1** VT **(a) = koppeln (b)** (Tech) to couple **2** VI
(a) (Aut) to operate the clutch **(b)** (inf: = Paare
zusammenführen) to match-make

Kuppler ['kʊplɐ] M **-s, -, Kupplerin** [-ərɪn] F **-, -nen** matchmaker
(+gen for); (Jur) procurer/procuress

Kupplung ['kʊplʊŋ] F **-, -en (a)** (Tech) coupling; (Aut etc)
clutch; **die ~ (durch)treten** to disengage the clutch; **die ~
kommen lassen** (Aut) to let the clutch up **(b)** (= das Koppeln)
coupling

Kupplungs- IN CPDS (*Aut*) clutch; **Kupplungspedal** NT clutch pedal; **Kupplungsseil** NT, **Kupplungszug** M clutch cable

Kur [kuːɐ] F **-, -en** (*in Badeort*) (health) cure; (= *Haarkur etc*) treatment *no pl*; (= *Schlankheitskur, Diätkur*) diet; **in** *or* **zur ~ fahren** to go to a spa; **jdn zur ~ schicken** to send sb to a spa; **eine ~ machen** to take a cure; (= *Schlankheitskur*) to diet

Kür [kyːɐ] F **-, -en** (*Sport*) free section; **eine ~ laufen** to do the free skating; **eine ~ tanzen/turnen** to do the free section

Kurant [ku'rant] M **-en, -en**, **Kurantin** [-'rantɪn] F **-, -nen** (*Sw*) = **Kurgast**

Kur-: **Kuraufenthalt** M stay at a spa; **Kurbad** NT spa

Kurbel ['kʊrbl] F **-, -n** crank; (*an Fenstern, Rollläden etc*) winder

kurbeln VTI to turn; (*inf*: = *filmen*) to film; **wenn du daran kurbelst ...** if you turn it ...

Kurbelwelle F crankshaft

Kürbis ['kʏrbɪs] M **-ses, -se** pumpkin

Kürbisflasche F gourd

Kurde ['kʊrdə] M **-n, -n**, **Kurdin** [-dɪn] F **-, -nen** Kurd

Kurdistan ['kʊrdɪstaːn, ˌkʊrdɪstan] NT **-s** Kurdistan

kuren ['kuːrən] VI (*Sw*) (*inf*) to take a cure; (*in Mineralbad*) to take the waters

küren ['kyːrən], *pret* **kürte** *or* (*rare*) **kor** ['kyːɐta, koːɐ], *ptp* **gekürt** *or* **gekoren** [gə'kyːɐt, gə'koːrən] VT (*oldgeh*) to choose, to elect (*zu* as)

Kur-: **Kurgast** M (*Patient*) patient at a spa; (*Tourist*) visitor to a spa; **Kurhaus** NT assembly rooms *pl* (at a spa)

Kurie ['kuːriə] F **-, NO PL** (*Eccl*) Curia

Kurier [ku'riːɐ] M **-s, -e**, **Kurierin** [-'riːrɪn] F **-, -nen** courier; (*Hist*) messenger

Kurierdienst M courier service

kurieren [ku'riːrən], *ptp* **kuriert** VT (*lit, fig*) to cure (*von* of); **von dieser Stadt/Idee/ihm bin ich kuriert** I've had enough of this town/this idea/him

kurios [ku'rioːs] **1** ADJ (= *merkwürdig*) strange, curious **2** ADV strangely, curiously

Kuriosität [kurioziˈtɛːt] F **-, -en (a)** (*Gegenstand*) curio(sity) **(b)** (= *Eigenart*) peculiarity

Kurkuma ['kʊrkuma] F **-, Kurkumen** [-'kuːmən] turmeric

Kurort M spa

KURORT

*A **Kurort** is an area specializing in natural health remedies such as springs, mud and salt water. When patients are sent by their doctors to a **Kurort**, the insurance companies pay most of the cost. **Kurorte** also levy a **Kurtaxe** on every visitor. This is a special charge to help cover the cost of the many recreational and leisure facilities available in the resort.*

Kur-: **Kurpackung** F (*für Haare*) hair repair kit; **Kurpfuscher(in)** M(F) (*pej inf*) quack (doctor)

Kurs [kʊrs] M **-es, -e** [-zə] **(a)** (*Naut, Aviat*) (*fig*) course; (*Pol*: = *Richtung*) line; **den ~ halten** to hold (the) course; **vom ~ abkommen** to deviate from one's/its course; (= *nehmen auf* (+*acc*) to set course for; **~ haben auf** (+*acc*) to be heading for; **harter/weicher ~** (*Pol*) hard/soft line; **den ~ ändern** (*lit, fig*) to change (one's) course; **den ~ beibehalten** (*lit, fig*) to stick to (one's) course; **jdn/etw wieder auf ~ bringen** (*fig*) to bring sb/sth back on course

(b) (*Fin*) (= *Wechselkurs*) exchange rate; (= *Börsenkurs, Aktienkurs*) price; (= *Marktpreis*) market value; **zum ~ von** at the rate of; **der amtliche ~ des Dollars** the official dollar exchange rate; **hoch im ~ stehen** (*Aktien*) to be high; (*fig*) to be popular (*bei* with)

(c) (= *Lehrgang*) course (*in* +*dat, für* in)

Kurs-: **Kursänderung** F (*lit, fig*) change of course; **Kursbericht** M (*Fin*) stock market report; **Kursbuch** NT (*Rail*) (railway) timetable

Kurschatten M **-s, -** (*hum inf*) lady/gentleman friend (*met during a stay at a spa*); **sie war zuerst nur sein ~** he first met her at a spa

Kurs-: **Kurseinbuße** F decrease in value; **das Pfund hat weitere ~n hinnehmen müssen** the pound suffered further losses (on the exchange market); **Kursgewinn** M profit (on the stock exchange *or* (*bei Wechsel*) foreign exchange market); **der jüngste ~ des Pfundes** the recent increase in the value of the pound

kursieren [kʊr'ziːrən], *ptp* **kursiert** VI AUX HABEN *or* SEIN to circulate

Kursindex M (*St Ex*) stock exchange index

kursiv [kʊr'ziːf] **1** ADJ italic; **Anmerkungen sind ~** notes are in italics **2** ADV in italics

Kursive [kʊr'ziːvə] F **-, -n**, **Kursivschrift** F italics *pl*; **in ~ gesetzt** printed in italics

Kurs-: **Kurskorrektur** F (*lit, fig*) course correction; (*St Ex*) corrective price adjustment; **Kursleiter(in)** M(F) course tutor (*esp Brit*); **Kursnotierung** F quotation

kursorisch [kʊr'zoːrɪʃ] **1** ADJ cursory **2** ADV **etw ~ lesen/ überfliegen** to skim through sth

Kurs-: **Kursrisiko** NT market risk; **Kursrückgang** M fall in prices; **Kursschwankung** F fluctuation in exchange rates; (*St Ex*) fluctuation in market rates; **Kurssystem** NT (*Sch, Univ*) course system; **Kursverlust** M (*Fin*) loss (on the stock exchange *or* foreign exchange market); **das Pfund musste ~e hinnehmen** the pound suffered losses on the foreign exchange market; **Kurswagen** M (*Rail*) through coach

Kurtaxe F visitors' tax (at spa)

Kurve ['kʊrvə, 'kʊrfə] F **-, -n** (*Math, inf*: = *Körperrundung*) curve; (= *Biegung, Straßenkurve*) bend; (*an Kreuzung*) corner; (*von Geschoss*) trajectory; (*statistisch, = Fieberkurve etc*) graph; **die Straße macht eine ~** the road bends; **die ~ kratzen** (*inf*) to scrape through (*inf*); (= *schnell weggehen*) to make tracks (*inf*); **die ~ kriegen** (*inf*) (*mit Auto etc*) to make the corner; (*fig*) to make it

kurvenreich ADJ *Straße, Strecke* winding; (*inf*) *Frau* curvaceous; **„~e Strecke"** "(series of) bends"

kurvig ['kʊrvɪç] **1** ADJ winding **2** ADV **die Straße verläuft sehr ~** the street bends sharply

kurz [kʊrts] **1** ADJ, *comp* **=er** ['kʏrtsɐ], *superl* **=este(r, s)** ['kʏrtsəsta] short; *Blick, Folge* quick; (= *klein und stämmig*) stocky; **etw kürzer machen** to make sth shorter; **ich will es ~ machen** I'll make it brief; **~e Hosen** short trousers; (= *Shorts*) shorts; **den Kürzeren ziehen** (*fig inf*) to come off worst; **in** *or* **mit ein paar ~en Worten** in a few brief words

2 ADV, *comp* **=er**, *superl* **am =esten (a)** X **hat ~ abgespielt** (*Sport*) X's pass was short; **(zu) ~ schießen/werfen** *etc* to shoot/throw *etc* (too) short; **die Hundeleine ~ halten** to keep the dog on a short lead (*Brit*) *or* line (*US*); **eine Sache ~ abtun** to dismiss sth out of hand; **zu ~ kommen** to come off badly; **~ entschlossen** without a moment's hesitation; **~ gesagt** in a nutshell; **sich ~ fassen** to be brief; **~ gefasst** concise; **~ geschnitten** cropped; **~ und bündig** concisely, tersely (*pej*); **~ und gut** in a word; **~ und schmerzlos** (*inf*) short and sweet; **jdn ~ und klein hauen** *or* **schlagen** to beat sb up; **etw ~ und klein hauen** *or* **schlagen** to smash sth to pieces

(b) (= *für eine kurze Zeit*) briefly; **ich bleibe nur ~** I'll only stay for a short while; **darf ich mal ~ stören?** could I just interrupt for a moment?; **ich muss mal ~ weg** I'll just have to go for a moment; **darf ich mal ~ fragen ...?** could I just quickly ask ...?

(c) (*zeitlich, räumlich*: = *nicht lang, nicht weit*) shortly; **~ bevor/ nachdem** shortly before/after; **er hat den Wagen erst seit ~em** he's only had the car for a short while; **seit ~em gibt es Bier in der Kantine** recently there's been beer in the canteen; **über ~ oder lang** sooner or later; **(bis) vor ~em** (until) recently; **~ nacheinander** shortly after each other

Kurz-: **Kurzarbeit** F short time; **kurzarbeiten** VI SEP to be on short time; **Kurzarbeiter(in)** M(F) short-time worker; **Kurzarbeitergeld** NT short-time allowance; **kurzärmelig, kurzärmlig** ADJ short-sleeved; **kurzatmig** ADJ (*Med*) short of breath; (*fig*) short-winded

Kürze ['kʏrtsə] F **-, -n**, NO PL shortness; (*fig*) (= *Bündigkeit*) brevity, conciseness; **in ~** (= *bald*) shortly; **in aller ~** very briefly; **in der ~ liegt die Würze** (*Prov*) brevity is the soul of wit

Kürzel ['kʏrtsl] NT **-s, -** (= *stenografisches Zeichen*) shorthand symbol; (*Ling*: = *Kurzwort*) contraction; (= *Abkürzung*) abbreviation

kürzen ['kʏrtsn] VT *Kleid, Rede etc* to shorten; *Buch auch* to abridge; (*Math*) *Bruch* to cancel (down); *Gehalt, Etat, Ausgaben, Produktion* to cut (back)

Kurze(r)[1] ['kʏrtsə] M DECL AS ADJ (*inf*) **(a)** (= *Schnaps*) short **(b)** (= *Kurzschluss*) short (circuit)

Kurze(r)[2] MF DECL AS ADJ (*inf*: = *Kind*) kid (*inf*)

kurzerhand ['kʊrtsɐ'hant] ADV without further ado; *entlassen* on the spot; **etw ~ ablehnen** to reject sth out of hand

Kurz-: Kurzform F shortened form (*von, zu* of, for); **kurzfristig** [-frɪstɪç] **1** ADJ short-term; *Wettervorhersage* short-range **2** ADV (= *auf kurze Sicht*) for the short term; (= *für kurze Zeit*) for a short time; **~ seine Pläne ändern** to change one's plans at short notice; **~ gesehen** looked at in the short term; **Kurzgeschichte** F short story; **Kurzhaardackel** M short-haired dachshund; **kurzhaarig** ADJ short-haired; **kurz halten** VT IRREG **jdn ~** to keep sb short

kürzlich ['kʏrtslɪç] **1** ADV recently; **erst** *or* **gerade ~** only *or* just recently **2** ADJ recent

Kurz-: Kurzmeldung F newsflash; **Kurznachrichten** PL the news headlines *pl*; **Kurzparker** [-parkɐ] M **-s, -** „nur für ~" "short-stay (*Brit*) *or* short-term parking only"; **Kurzparkzone** F short-stay (*Brit*) *or* short-term parking zone; **kurzschließen** SEP IRREG **1** VT to short-circuit **2** VR (= *in Verbindung treten*) to get in contact (*mit* with); **Kurzschluss** M **(a)** (*Elec*) short circuit; **einen ~ haben** to be short-circuited; **einen ~ bekommen** to short-circuit **(b)** (*fig: auch* **Kurzschlusshandlung**) rash action; **das war ein ~** *or* **eine ~handlung** something just went snap; **Kurzschlussreaktion** F knee-jerk reaction; **kurzsichtig** [-zɪçtɪç] (*lit, fig*) **1** ADJ short-sighted **2** ADV short-sightedly; **Kurzsichtigkeit** F~, NO PL (*lit, fig*) short-sightedness

Kurzstrecken-: Kurzstreckenflugzeug NT short-haul aircraft; **Kurzstreckenrakete** F short-range missile

Kürzung ['kʏrtsʊŋ] F **-, -en** shortening; (*eines Berichts, Buchs etc*) abridgement; (*von Gehältern, von Etat, der Produktion*) cut (+*gen* in)

Kurzurlaub M short holiday (*esp Brit*) *or* vacation (*US*); (*Mil*) short leave

Kurzwahl- (*Telec*): **Kurzwahlspeicher** M speed-dial number memory; **Kurzwahltaste** F speed-dial button

Kurzwaren PL haberdashery (*Brit*), notions *pl* (*US*)

Kurzwelle F (*Rad*) short wave

Kurzzeit- IN CPDS short-term; **Kurzzeitgedächtnis** NT short-term memory; **Kurzzeitmesser** M **-s, -** timer; **Kurzzeitspeicher** M short-term memory

kuschelig ['kʊʃəlɪç] (*inf*) **1** ADJ cosy (*Brit*), cozy (*US*) **2** ADV **~ weich** soft and cosy (*Brit*) *or* cozy (*US*); **~ warm** snug and warm

kuscheln ['kʊʃln] **1** VI to cuddle (*mit* with) **2** VR **sich an jdn ~** to snuggle up to sb; **sich in etw** (*acc*) **~** to snuggle up in sth

Kuschel-: Kuschelrock M (*Mus inf*) soft rock; **Kuschelsex** M loving sex; **wir machen nur ~** we just cuddle up together in bed; **Kuscheltier** NT cuddly toy

kuschen ['kʊʃn] VI (*Hund etc*) to get down; (*fig*) to knuckle under

Kusine [ku'ziːnə] F **-, -n** (female) cousin

Kuss [kʊs] M **-es, ⁼e** ['kʏsə] kiss

Küsschen ['kʏsçən] NT **-s, -** little kiss; **gib ~** give us a kiss

kussecht ADJ *Lippenstift* kiss-proof

küssen ['kʏsn] **1** VTI to kiss; **jdm die Hand ~** to kiss sb's hand **2** VR to kiss (each other)

Küste ['kʏstə] F **-, -n** coast; (= *Ufer*) shore

Küsten- IN CPDS coastal; **Küstengebiet** NT coastal area; **Küstengewässer** PL, **Küstenmeer** NT coastal waters *pl*; **Küstenschifffahrt** F coastal shipping; **Küstenwacht** F coastguard

Kutsche ['kʊtʃə] F **-, -n** coach; (*inf*: = *Auto*) jalopy (*inf*)

Kutscher ['kʊtʃɐ] M **-s, -** coachman, driver

Kutscherin ['kʊtʃərɪn] F **-, -nen** driver

kutschieren [kʊ'tʃiːrən], *ptp* **kutschiert** **1** VI AUX SEIN to drive; **durch die Gegend ~** (*inf*) to drive around **2** VT to drive; **jdn im Auto durch die Gegend ~** to drive sb around

Kutte ['kʊtə] F **-, -n** habit

Kuttel ['kʊtl] F **-, -n** USU PL (*S Ger, Aus, Sw*) entrails *pl*

Kutter ['kʊtɐ] M **-s, -** (*Naut*) cutter

Kuvert [ku've:ɐ, ku've:ɐ, ku'vert] NT **-s, -s** *or* (*bei dt. Aussprache*) **-(e)s, -e** (= *Briefkuvert*) envelope

Kuwait [ku'vait, 'ku:vait] NT **-s** Kuwait

Kuwaiter [ku'vaitɐ, 'ku:vaitɐ] M **-s, -**, **Kuwaiterin** [-ərɪn] F **-, -nen** Kuwaiti

Kuwaiti [ku'vaiti] M **-s, -s** Kuwaiti

kuwaitisch [ku'vaitɪʃ, 'ku:vaitʃ] ADJ Kuwaiti

Kux [kʊks] M **-es, -e** (*St Ex*) mining share *or* stock

kW ABBR *von* **Kilowatt**

KWG ABBR *von* **Kreditwesengesetz**

kWh ABBR = **Kilowattstunde**

Kybernetik [kybɛr'ne:tɪk] F **-,** NO PL cybernetics *sing*

kybernetisch [kybɛr'ne:tɪʃ] ADJ cybernetic

kyrillisch [ky'rɪlɪʃ] ADJ Cyrillic

KZ [ka:'tsɛt] NT **-s, -s** ABBR *von* **Konzentrationslager**

LI

L, I [ɛl] NT -, - L, l

I ABBR *von* Liter

labern ['laːbɐn] (*inf*) **1** VI to prattle (on *or* away) (*inf*) **2** VT to talk; **was laberst du denn da?** what are you prattling on about? (*inf*)

Labial(laut) [laˈbiaːl-] M -s, -e labial

labil [laˈbiːl] **1** ADJ unstable; *Gesundheit* delicate; *Kreislauf* poor; *Patient* frail; (*psychisch*) *Mensch* with no strength of character; *Charakter* weak **2** ADV **die Situation wird als ~ eingeschätzt** the situation is considered to be unstable; **jdn als psychisch ~ einstufen** to consider sb emotionally unstable

Labilität [labiliˈtɛːt] F -, NO PL instability; (*von Patient*) frailness; **wegen der ~ seiner Gesundheit** because of his unstable state of health; **die ~ seines Kreislaufs/Charakters** his poor circulation/weak character

Labor [laˈboːɐ] NT -s, -s *or* -e laboratory

Laborant [laboˈrant] M -en, -en, **Laborantin** [-ˈrantɪn] F -, -nen lab(oratory) technician

Laborwerte PL laboratory results *pl*

Labskaus ['lapskaus] NT -, NO PL (*N Ger*) stew made of meat, fish and mashed potato

Labyrinth [labyˈrɪnt] NT -(e)s, -e labyrinth

Lachanfall M laughing fit

Lache¹ ['laxə, 'laːxə] F -, -n (= *Pfütze*) puddle

Lache² ['laxə] F -, -n (*inf*) laugh

lächeln ['lɛçln] VI to smile; **verlegen/freundlich ~** to give an embarrassed/a friendly smile

Lächeln NT -s, NO PL smile

lachen ['laxn] **1** VI to laugh (*über +acc* at); **jdn zum Lachen bringen, jdn ~ machen** to make sb laugh; **zum Lachen sein** (= *lustig*) to be hilarious; (= *lächerlich*) to be laughable; **mir ist nicht zum Lachen (zumute)** I'm in no laughing mood; **dass ich nicht lache!** (*inf*) don't make me laugh! (*inf*); **du hast gut ~!** it's all right for you to laugh! (*inf*); **gezwungen/verlegen/ herzlich ~** to give a forced/an embarrassed/a hearty laugh; **wer zuletzt lacht, lacht am besten** (*Prov*) he who laughs last, laughs longest (*Prov*); **die Sonne** *or* **der Himmel lacht** the sun is shining brightly; **ihm lachte das Glück/der Erfolg** fortune/success smiled on him

2 VT **da gibt es gar nichts zu ~** that's nothing to laugh about; **was gibt es denn da zu ~?** what's so funny about that?; **er hat bei seiner Frau nichts zu ~** (*inf*) he has a hard time of it with his wife; **das wäre doch gelacht** it would be ridiculous; **sich scheckig ~** (*inf*), **sich** (*dat*) **einen Ast** *or* **Bruch ~** (*inf*) to kill oneself (*inf*); **sich** (*dat*) **eins (ins Fäustchen) ~** (*inf*) to have a little snigger

Lachen NT -s, NO PL laughter; (= *Art des Lachens*) laugh; **vor ~ schreien** to shriek with laughter; **dir wird das ~ schon noch vergehen!** you'll soon be laughing on the other side of your face (*Brit*) *or* out of the other side of your mouth (*US*)

Lacherfolg M **ein ~ sein, einen ~ haben** *or* **erzielen** to make everybody laugh

lächerlich ['lɛçɐlɪç] **1** ADJ **(a)** ridiculous; (= *komisch*) comical; **jdn/etw ~ machen** to make sb/sth look silly (*vor jdm* in front of sb); **jdn/sich ~ machen** to make a fool of sb/oneself (*vor jdm* in front of sb); **etw ins Lächerliche ziehen** to make fun of sth **(b)** (= *geringfügig*) *Kleinigkeit, Anlass* trivial; *Preis* ridiculously low **2** ADV ridiculously

Lächerlichkeit F -, -en **(a)** NO PL absurdity; **die ~ seiner Bemerkung/ihrer Verkleidung** his ridiculous comment/her ridiculous get-up (*inf*); **jdn der ~ preisgeben** to make a laughing stock of sb **(b)** (= *Geringfügigkeit*) triviality

Lach-: **Lachgas** NT laughing gas; **lachhaft** ADJ ridiculous; **Lachnummer** F (*inf*: = *Witz, Mensch*) joke (*inf*)

Lachs [laks] M -es, -e salmon

Lachs-: **lachsfarben** [-farbn], **lachsfarbig** ADJ salmon pink; **Lachsforelle** F salmon *or* sea trout; **Lachsschinken** M smoked, rolled fillet of ham

Lack [lak] M -(e)s, -e varnish; (= *Autolack*) paint; (*für ~arbeiten*) lacquer

Lack-: **Lackaffe** M (*pej inf*) flash Harry (*Brit inf*), real flashy dude (*US inf*); **Lackarbeit** F lacquerwork; **Lackfarbe** F gloss paint

Lackierarbeiten PL (*von Möbeln etc*) varnishing; (*von Autos*) spraying

lackieren [laˈkiːrən], *ptp* **lackiert** VTI *Holz* to varnish; *Fingernägel auch* to paint; *Auto* to spray

Lackiererei [lakiːrəˈrai] F -, -en **(a)** (= *Autolackiererei*) paint shop; (= *Möbellackiererei*) varnisher's **(b)** (*Handwerk*) lacquerwork

Lackierung F -, -en **(a)** (= *das Lackieren*) (*von Autos*) spraying; (*von Möbeln*) varnishing **(b)** (= *der Lack*) (*von Auto*) paintwork; (= *Holzlackierung*) varnish; (*für Lackarbeiten*) lacquer

Lackierwerkstatt F, **Lackierwerkstätte** F (*für Autos*) paint shop; (*für Möbel*) varnisher's

Lackleder NT patent leather

Lackmuspapier ['lakmʊs-] NT litmus paper

ladbar ADJ (*Comput*) loadable

Lade-: **Ladefläche** F load area; **Ladegerät** NT battery charger; **Ladegewicht** NT load capacity; **Ladehemmung** F **das Gewehr hat ~** the gun is jammed; **er hatte plötzlich ~** (*inf*) he had a sudden mental block; **Ladeliste** F loading list; (*von Schiff, Flugzeug*) manifest

laden¹ ['laːdn], *pret* **lud** [luːt], *ptp* **geladen** [gəˈlaːdn] **1** VT **(a)** (= *beladen*) to load; **das Schiff hat Autos geladen** the ship has a cargo of cars; **der Lkw hat zu viel geladen** the lorry is overloaded; **Verantwortung/Schulden auf sich** (*acc*) **~** to saddle oneself with responsibility/debts; **eine schwere Schuld auf sich** (*acc*) **~** to place oneself under a heavy burden of guilt; *siehe auch* **geladen** **(b)** *Schusswaffe* to load; (= *wieder aufladen*) *Batterie, Akku* to recharge; (*Phys*) to charge **(c)** (*Comput*) to load **2** VI **(a)** (*auch Comput*) to load (up) **(b)** (*Phys*) to charge

laden² *pret* **lud** [luːt], *ptp* **geladen** [gəˈlaːdn] VT **(a)** (*liter*: = *einladen*) to invite; **nur für geladene Gäste** by invitation only **(b)** (*form*: *vor Gericht*) to summon

Laden¹ ['laːdn] M -s, ⸚ ['lɛːdn] (= *Geschäft*) shop (*esp Brit*), store (*US*); (*inf*: = *Betrieb, Unternehmung*) outfit (*inf*); **der ~ läuft** (*inf*) business is good; **es wird eine Zeit dauern, bis der ~ läuft** (*inf*) it will be some time before the business gets going; **den ~ schmeißen** (*inf*) to run the show; (= *zurechtkommen*) to manage; **den (ganzen) ~ hinschmeißen** (*inf*) to chuck the whole thing in (*inf*)

Laden² M -s, ⸚ *or* - (= *Fensterladen*) shutter

Laden-: **Ladendieb(in)** M(F) shoplifter; **Ladendiebstahl** M shoplifting; **Ladenhüter** M non-seller; **Ladenkette** F chain of shops (*esp Brit*) *or* stores; **Ladenpreis** M shop *or* store (*US*) price

Ladenschluss M **nach/vor ~** after/before the shops (*esp Brit*) *or* stores (*US*) shut; **um fünf Uhr ist ~** the shops (*esp Brit*) *or* stores (*US*) shut at five o'clock

Ladenschluss-: **Ladenschlussgesetz** NT law governing the hours of trading; **Ladenschlusszeit** F (shop (*esp Brit*) *or* store (*US*)) closing time

Ladentisch M shop counter; **über den/unter dem ~** over/under the counter

Lade-: **Ladeplatz** M loading bay; **Laderampe** F loading ramp; **Laderaum** M load room; (*Aviat, Naut*) hold; **Ladeschein** M bill of lading

lädieren [lɛˈdiːrən], *ptp* **lädiert** VT *Kunstwerk, Briefmarke* to damage; *Körperteil* to injure; **lädiert sein/aussehen** (*hum*) to be/look the worse for wear; **sein lädiertes Image** his tarnished image

lädt [lɛːt] 3. PERS SING PRES *von* **laden**

Ladung ['laːdʊŋ] F -, -en **(a)** load; (*von Schnee, Steinen, Unflätigkeiten etc*) whole load (*inf*); (*von Sprengstoff*) charge; **eine geballte ~ Schnee/Dreck** (*inf*) a handful of snow/mud; **eine geballte ~ von Schimpfwörtern** a whole torrent of abuse **(b)** (= *Vorladung*) summons *sing*

Ladungsverzeichnis NT = **Ladeliste**

lag PRET *von* **liegen**

Lage ['laːgə] F **-, -n (a)** (= *geografische* ~) situation; **in günstiger ~** well-situated; **eine gute/ruhige ~ haben** to be in a good/quiet location; **in höheren ~n Schneefall** snow on higher ground
(b) (= *Art des Liegens*) position
(c) (= *Situation*) situation; **in der ~ sein, etw zu tun** (*befähigt sein*) to be able to do sth; **dazu bin ich nicht in der ~** I'm not in a position to do that; **in der glücklichen/beneidenswerten ~ sein, etw zu tun** to be in the happy/enviable position of doing sth; **nach ~ der Dinge** as things stand; **die ~ der Dinge erfordert es, dass ...** the situation requires that ...
(d) (= *Schicht*) layer
(e) (*Mus*) (= *Stimmlage*) register; (= *Tonlage*) pitch; (*auf Instrument*) position
(f) (= *Runde*) round

Lage-: Lagebericht M report; (*Mil*) situation report; **Lagebesprechung** F discussion of the situation; **eine ~ abhalten** to discuss the situation

Lager ['laːgɐ] NT **-s, - (a)** (= *Unterkunft*) camp; **sein ~ aufschlagen** to set up camp
(b) (*fig*) (= *Partei*) camp; (*von Staaten*) bloc; **ins andere ~ überwechseln** to change camps
(c) *pl auch* **Läger** ['lɛːgɐ] (= *Vorratsraum*) store(room); (*von Laden*) stockroom; (= *~halle*) warehouse; (= *Vorrat*) stock; **am ~ sein** to be in stock; **etw auf ~ legen** (*Comm*) to store sth; **etw auf ~ haben** to have sth in stock; (*fig*) *Witz etc* to have sth on tap (*inf*)
(d) (*Tech*) bearing
(e) (*Geol*) bed; (= *~stätte*) deposit

Lager-: Lagerempfangsschein M warehouse receipt; **Lagerfeuer** NT campfire; **Lagergebühr** F, **Lagergeld** NT storage charge; **Lagerhalle** F warehouse; **Lagerhaus** NT warehouse; **Lagerleben** NT camp life; **Lagerleiter(in)** M(F) camp commander; (*in Ferienlager etc*) camp leader

lagern ['laːgɐn] **1** VT **(a)** (= *aufbewahren*) to store; **kühl ~!** keep in a cool place
(b) (= *hinlegen*) *jdn* to lay down; *Bein etc* to rest; **den Kopf/einen Kranken weich ~** to rest one's head/lay an invalid on something soft; **das Bein hoch ~** to put one's leg up; *siehe auch* **gelagert**
2 VI **(a)** (*Vorräte, Waren, Abfall etc*) to be stored
(b) (= *liegen*) to lie; **vor der Küste lagert Erdöl** there are deposits of oil lying off the coast
(c) (*Truppen etc*) to camp, to be encamped

Lager-: Lagerraum M storeroom; (*in Geschäft*) stockroom; **Lagerstätte** F (*Geol*) deposit

Lagerung ['laːgərʊŋ] F **-, -en** storage

Lageskizze F sketch-map

lahm [laːm] **1** ADJ **(a)** (= *gelähmt*) *Bein, Mensch, Tier* lame; (*inf*: = *steif*) stiff; **er ist auf dem linken Bein ~** he is lame in his left leg **(b)** (*inf*: = *langsam, langweilig*) dreary; *Ausrede, Entschuldigung* lame; *Geschäftsgang* slow; **eine ~e Ente sein** (*inf*) to have no zip (*inf*) **2** ADV (*inf*) (= *langsam*) slowly; (= *wenig überzeugend*) lamely

lahmen ['laːmən] VI to be lame (*auf +dat* in)

lähmen ['lɛːmən] VT to paralyze; *Verhandlungen, Verkehr* to hold up; **er ist durch einen Unfall gelähmt** he was paralyzed in an accident; *siehe auch* **gelähmt**

lahm legen VT *Verkehr, Produktion, Flughafen* to bring to a standstill; *Industrie auch, Stromversorgung* to paralyze

Lähmung ['lɛːmʊŋ] F **-, -en** (*lit*) paralysis; (*fig*) immobilization

Laib [laip] M **-(e)s, -e** [-bə] (*esp S Ger*) loaf

Laich [laiç] M **-(e)s, -e** spawn

laichen ['laiçn] VI to spawn

Laie ['laiə] M **-n, -n** (*lit, fig*) layman, layperson; **er ist ein ökonomischer ~** he is no expert in economics; **~n** the lay public; **die ~n** *pl* (*Eccl*) the laity

Laien-: Laiendarsteller(in) M(F) amateur actor/actress; **laienhaft 1** ADJ *Arbeit* amateurish; *Urteil, Meinung* lay *attr* **2** ADV *spielen* amateurishly; **etw ~ ausdrücken** to put sth in simple terms; **etw ~ übersetzen** to do an amateurish translation of sth

Laisser-faire [lɛseˈfɛːr] NT **-,** NO PL (*Econ, fig*) laissez-faire

Lakai [laˈkai] M **-en, -en** (*lit, fig*) lackey

Lake ['laːkə] F **-, -n** brine

Laken ['laːkn] NT **-s, -** sheet

lakonisch [laˈkoːnɪʃ] **1** ADJ laconic **2** ADV laconically

Lakritz [laˈkrɪts] M **-es, -e** (*dial*), **Lakritze** [laˈkrɪtsə] F **-, -n** liquorice (*Brit*), licorice

lala ['laˈla] ADV (*inf*) **so ~** so-so (*inf*)

lallen ['lalən] VTI to babble; (*Betrunkener*) to mumble

Lama¹ ['laːma] NT **-s, -s** (*Zool*) llama

Lama² M **-(s), -s** (*Rel*) lama

Lamelle [laˈmɛlə] F **-, -n (a)** (*Biol*) lamella **(b)** (*Tech*) commutator bar; (*von Jalousien*) slat

Lametta [laˈmɛta] NT **-s,** NO PL lametta; (*hum:* = *Orden*) gongs *pl* (*inf*)

laminieren [lamiˈniːrən], *ptp* **laminiert** VT (*Tex*) to draw; (*Typ*) to laminate

Lamm [lam] NT **-(e)s, ⸚er** ['lɛmɐ] lamb

Lamm-: Lammfell NT lambskin; **Lammfleisch** NT lamb; **lammfromm 1** ADJ *Gesicht, Miene* innocent; **~ sein** to be like a (little) lamb **2** ADV like a little lamb/little lambs; **Lammwolle** F lambswool

Lampe ['lampə] F **-, -n** light; (= *Öllampe, Stehlampe, Tischlampe*) lamp; (= *Glühlampe*) bulb

Lampen-: Lampenfieber NT stage fright; **Lampenschirm** M lampshade

Lampion [lamˈpiõː, lamˈpiɔŋ] M **-s, -s** Chinese lantern

LAN [lan] NT **-s, -s** (*Comput*) LAN

lancieren [lãˈsiːrən], *ptp* **lanciert** VT *Produkt, Künstler, Initiative* to launch; *Meldung, Nachricht* to put out; **jdn/etw in etw** (*acc*) **~** to get sb/sth into sth

Land [lant] NT **-(e)s, ⸚er** ['lɛndɐ] **(a)** (= *Gelände, Festland*) land; (= *Landschaft*) country, landscape; **ein Stück ~** a plot of land; **an ~ gehen** to go ashore; **jdn an ~ setzen** to put sb ashore; **an ~ schwimmen** to swim to the shore; **~ sehen** (*lit*) to sight land; **endlich können wir ~ sehen/sehe ich ~** (*fig*) at last we/I can see the light at the end of the tunnel; **etw an ~ ziehen** to pull sth ashore; **einen Fisch an ~ ziehen** to land a fish; **einen Millionär/einen Auftrag an ~ ziehen** (*inf*) to land a millionaire/an order; **~ in Sicht!** land submerged!; **bei uns/euch zu ~e** back home, in our/your country
(b) (= *ländliches Gebiet*) country; **aufs ~** (in)to the country; **auf dem ~** in the country; **vom ~(e)** from the country
(c) (= *Staat*) country; (= *Bundesland*) (*in BRD*) Land, state; (*in Österreich*) province; **das ~ Hessen** the state of Hesse; **das ~ Tirol** the province of Tyrol; **~ und Leute kennen lernen** to get to know the country and the inhabitants; **das ~ der unbegrenzten Möglichkeiten** the land of limitless opportunity; **das ~ der aufgehenden Sonne** the land of the rising sun; **aus aller Herren Länder(n)** from all over the world

Land-: Landammann M (*Sw*) *highest official in a Swiss canton*; **Landbesitz** M landholding; **~ haben** to be a landowner; **Landbesitzer(in)** M(F) landowner; **Landbevölkerung** F rural population

Lande-: Landeanflug M approach; **Landebahn** F runway; **Landebrücke** F jetty; **Landeerlaubnis** F permission to land; **Landefähre** F (*Space*) landing module; **Landeklappe** F landing flap

landen ['landn] **1** VI AUX SEIN to land; (*inf*) (= *enden*) to land up; (= *Eindruck machen*) to get somewhere; **weich ~** to make a soft landing; **alle anonymen Briefe ~ sofort im Papierkorb** all anonymous letters go straight into the wastepaper basket **2** VT (*lit, fig*) to land

Landenge F isthmus

Lande-: **Landepiste** F landing strip; **Landeplatz** M (*für Flugzeuge*) place to land; (*ausgebaut*) landing strip; (*für Schiffe*) landing place

Ländereien [lɛndə'raiən] PL estates *pl*

Länder-: **Länderfinanzausgleich** M, NO PL balancing of federal budgets; **Länderkampf** M (*Sport*) international contest; (= *Länderspiel*) international (match); **Länderrisiko** NT (*Fin*) country *or* sovereign risk; **Länderspiel** NT international (match)

Landes-: **Landesbank** F, *pl* **-banken** regional bank; **Landesebene** F **auf ~** at state level; **landeseigen** ADJ *siehe* **Land** (c) owned by the country/state/province; **Landesgericht** NT district court; **Landesgrenze** F (*von Staat*) national boundary; (*von Bundesland*) state *or* (*Aus*) provincial boundary; **Landeshauptmann** M (*Aus*) head of the government of a province; **Landeshauptstadt** F capital of a Land; (*Aus*) capital of a province; **Landesinnere(s)** NT DECL AS ADJ interior; **Landeskunde** F knowledge of the/a country; (*Univ*) regional and cultural studies *pl*; **landeskundig** ADJ **~er Reiseleiter** courier who knows the country; **landeskundlich** [-kʊntlɪç] **1** ADJ *Kenntnisse, Aspekte* of a/the country's geography and culture **2** ADV in geography and culture; **Landesliste** F (*Parl*) *regional list of parliamentary candidates for election to Federal parliament*; **Landesregierung** F government of a Land; (*Aus*) provincial government; **Landessprache** F national language; **der ~ unkundig sein** not to know the language

Landesteg M landing stage

Landes-: **Landesteil** M region; **landesüblich** ADJ customary; **das ist dort ~** that's the custom there; **Landesverrat** M treason; **Landesversicherungsanstalt** F regional pensions office (*for waged employees*)

Landeverbot NT refusal of landing permission; **~ erhalten** to be refused permission to land

Land-: **Landflucht** F migration from the land; **Landfrau** F countrywoman; **Landfriedensbruch** M (*Jur*) breach of the peace; **Landgericht** NT district court; **landgestützt** [-gəʃtʏtst] ADJ *Raketen* land-based; **Landgut** NT estate; **Landhaus** NT country house; **Landjäger** M (= *Wurst*) *pressed smoked sausage*; **Landkarte** F map; **Landklima** NT continental climate; **Landkreis** M administrative district; **Landkrieg** M land warfare; **Luft- und ~** war in the air and on the ground; **See- und ~** war at sea and on land; **landläufig** **1** ADJ popular; **entgegen ~er** *or* **der ~en Meinung** contrary to popular opinion **2** ADV commonly

Ländle ['lɛntlə] NT **-s**, NO PL **das ~** (*inf*) Baden-Württemberg

Landleben NT country life

ländlich ['lɛntlɪç] **1** ADJ rural; *Tracht* country *attr*; *Tanz* country *attr*, folk *attr*; *Idylle* pastoral; *Stille, Frieden* of the countryside, rural **2** ADV **eine ~ geprägte Region** a rural area; **eine ~ wirkende Stadt** a town which gives a rural impression

Land-: **Landluft** F country air; **Landmaschinen** PL agricultural machinery *sing*; **Landmine** F land mine; **Landplage** F plague; (*fig inf*) pest; **Landrat**[1] M (*Sw*) *cantonal parliament*; **Landrat**[2] M, **Landrätin** F (*Ger*) *head of the administration of a Landkreis*; **Landratte** F (*hum*) landlubber; **Landregen** M steady rain

Landschaft ['lantʃaft] F **-, -en** scenery *no pl*; (= *ländliche Gegend*) countryside; (*Gemälde, fig*) landscape; **eine öde ~** a barren landscape; **die ~ um London** the countryside around London; **die ~en Italiens** the types of countryside in Italy; **in der ~ herumstehen** (*inf*) to stand around; **da stand einsam ein Hochhaus in der ~** (*herum*) (*inf*) there was one solitary skyscraper to be seen; **die politische ~** the political scene

landschaftlich ['lantʃaftlɪç] **1** ADJ *Schönheiten etc* scenic; *Besonderheiten* regional **2** ADV *abwechslungsreich, eintönig* scenically; **diese Gegend ist ~ ausgesprochen reizvoll** the scenery in this area is particularly delightful; **das ist ~ unterschiedlich** it differs from one part of the country to another

Landschafts-: **Landschaftsform** F land form; **Landschaftsgärtner(in)** M(F) landscape gardener;

Landschaftsschutz M protection of the countryside; **Landschaftsschutzgebiet** NT nature reserve

Landschulheim NT = Schullandheim

Lands-: **Landsmann** M, *pl* **-leute** compatriot; **Landsmännin** [-mɛnɪn] F **-, -nen** compatriot

Land-: **Landstraße** F country road; (= *Straße zweiter Ordnung*) secondary *or* B (*Brit*) road; (*im Gegensatz zur Autobahn*) ordinary road; **Landstreicher** [-ʃtraiçɐ] M **-s**, **-**, **Landstreicherin** [-ərɪn] F **-, -nen** (*pej*) tramp; **Landstreicherei** [lantʃtraiçəˈrai] F **-**, NO PL vagrancy; **Landstreitkräfte** PL land forces *pl*; **Landtag** M Landtag (*state parliament*); **Landtagswahlen** PL (*West*) German regional elections *pl*

Landung ['landʊŋ] F **-, -en** landing; **zur ~ gezwungen werden** to be forced to land

Landungs-: **Landungsboot** NT landing craft; **Landungsbrücke** F jetty; **Landungssteg** M landing stage

Land-: **Landurlaub** M shore leave; **Landvermesser** [-fɛmɛsɐ] M **-s**, **-**, **Landvermesserin** [-ərɪn] F **-, -nen** land surveyor; **Landvermessung** F land surveying; **Landvolk** NT country people *pl*; **Landweg** M **auf dem ~** by land; **Landwein** M homegrown wine; **Landwirt(in)** M(F) farmer

Landwirtschaft F agriculture; (*Betrieb*) farm; (= *Landwirte*) farmers *pl*; **~ betreiben** to farm; **Land- und Forstwirtschaft** agriculture and forestry

landwirtschaftlich **1** ADJ agricultural; **~e Geräte** agricultural implements **2** ADV *tätig sein* agriculturally; *geprägt sein* by agriculture; **~ genutzt** used for agricultural purposes

Landwirtschafts- IN CPDS agricultural;

Landzunge F spit (of land), promontory

lang [laŋ] **1** ADJ, *comp* **ᴱer** ['lɛŋɐ], *superl* **ᴱste(r, s)** ['lɛŋstɐ] **(a)** long; **das ist seit ~em geplant** that has been planned (for) a long time; **das war seit ~em geplant** it was planned a long time ago; **vor ~er Zeit** a long time ago; **in nicht allzu ~er Zeit** in the not too distant future; **hier wird mir der Tag** *or* **die Zeit nicht ~** I won't get bored here; **etw länger machen** to make sth longer; **er machte ein ~es Gesicht** his face fell; **man sah überall nur ~e Gesichter** you saw nothing but long faces; **etw von ~er Hand vorbereiten** to prepare sth carefully **(b)** (*inf: = groß gewachsen*) *Mensch* tall; **eine ~e Latte sein, ein ~er Lulatsch sein, ein ~es Elend** *or* **Ende sein** to be a (real) beanpole (*inf*) **2** ADV, *comp* **ᴱer**, *superl* **am ᴱsten der ~ erwartete Regen** the long-awaited rain; **der ~ ersehnte Tag/Urlaub** the longed-for day/holiday (*esp Brit*) *or* vacation (*US*); **~ anhaltender Beifall** prolonged applause; **~ gehegt** *Wunsch* long-cherished; **~ gestreckt** long; **nur einen Augenblick ~** only for a moment; **zwei Stunden ~** for two hours; **mein ganzes Leben ~** all my life; **~ und breit** at great length; *siehe auch* **lange, entlang**

lang-: **langärmelig** ADJ long-sleeved; **langatmig** [-laːtmɪç] **1** ADJ long-winded **2** ADV in a long-winded way; **er schreibt ~** his style of writing is long-winded; **langbeinig** ADJ long-legged

lange ['laŋə], (*S Ger*, **lang** *Aus*) ADV, *comp* **ᴱer** ['lɛŋə], *superl* **am längsten** ['lɛŋstn] **(a)** (*zeitlich*) a long time; (*in Fragen, Negativsätzen*) long; **die Sitzung hat heute ~/nicht ~ gedauert** the meeting went on (for) a long time/didn't go on (for) long today; **wie ~ lernst du schon Deutsch/bist du schon hier?** how long have you been learning German (for)/been here (for)?; **es ist noch gar nicht ~ her, dass ...** it's not long since we ...; **er wird es nicht mehr ~ machen** (*inf*) he won't last long; **bis Weihnachten ist es ja noch ~ hin** it's still a long time till Christmas; **je länger, je lieber** the more the better; (*zeitlich*) the longer the better **(b)** (*inf: = längst*) **noch ~ nicht** not by any means; **~ nicht so ...** nowhere near as ...; **er verdient ~ nicht so viel** he doesn't earn nearly as much; **wenn er das schafft, kannst du das schon ~** if he can do it, you can do it easily

Länge ['lɛŋə] F **-, -n (a)** (*zeitlich, räumlich*) length; (*inf: von Mensch*) height; **eine ~ von 10 Metern haben** to be 10 metres (*Brit*) *or* meters (*US*) long; **ein Seil von 10 Meter ~** a rope 10 metres (*Brit*) *or* meters (*US*) long; **ein Vortrag von einer Stunde ~** an hour-long lecture; **eine Fahrt von einer Stunde ~** an hour's journey; **etw der ~ nach falten** to fold sth lengthways; **der ~ nach hinfallen** to fall flat; **in die ~ schießen** *or* **wachsen** to shoot up; **etw in die ~ ziehen** to drag sth out (*inf*); **sich in die ~ ziehen** to go on and on; **einen Artikel in seiner vollen ~ abdrucken** to print an article in its entirety **(b)** (*Sport*) length; **mit einer ~ gewinnen** to win by a length;

(jdm/einer Sache) um ~n voraus sein (*fig*) to be streets ahead (of sb/sth)

(c) (*Geog*) longitude; **der Ort liegt auf** *or* **unter 20 Grad östlicher ~** the town has a longitude of 20 degrees east

(d) (*in Buch*) long-drawn-out passage; (*in Film*) long-drawn-out scene

langen ['laŋən] (*dial inf*) **①** VI **(a)** (= *sich erstrecken, greifen*) to reach (*nach* for, *in* +*acc* in, into); **bis an etw** (*acc*) **~** to reach sth

(b) (= *fassen*) to touch (*an etw* (*acc*)) sth

(c) (= *ausreichen*) to be enough; (= *auskommen*) to get by; **mir** *or* **für mich langt es** I've had enough; **das Geld langt nicht** there isn't enough money; **jetzt langts mir aber!** I've had just about enough!

② VT (= *reichen*) **jdm etw ~** to give sb sth; **jdm eine ~** to give sb a clip on the ear (*inf*)

Längen-: **Längengrad** M degree of longitude; (*auch* **Längenkreis**) meridian; **Längenmaß** NT measure of length

länger COMP *von* **lang, lange**

längerfristig [-frɪstɪç] **①** ADJ longer-term **②** ADV in the longer term; *planen* for the longer term

langersehnt ADJ ATTR *siehe* **lang**

Langeweile ['laŋəvailə, laŋə'vailə] F, *gen - or* **Langenweile** ['laŋənvailə], *dat - or* **Langerweile** ['laŋɐvailə] NO PL boredom; **~ haben** to be bored

Lang-: **langfristig** [-frɪstɪç] **①** ADJ long-term **②** ADV in the long term; *planen* for the long term; **langgehen** SEP IRREG, AUX SEIN **①** VI **(a)** (*Weg etc*) **wo gehts hier lang?** where does this (road *etc*) go? **(b)** **sie weiß, wo es langgeht** she knows what's what; **hier bestimme ich, wo es langgeht** I decide what's what here **②** VT to go along; **langgestreckt** ADJ *siehe* **lang**; **langhaarig** ADJ long-haired; **Langhaarige(r)** [-haːrɪgə] MF DECL AS ADJ long-haired man/woman *etc*; **so ein ~r** some long-haired type; **langjährig** **①** ADJ *Freundschaft, Bekannter, Gewohnheit* long-standing; *Erfahrung, Verhandlungen, Recherchen* many years of; *Mitarbeiter* of many years' standing **②** ADV for many years; **Langlauf** M (*Ski*) cross-country (skiing); **Langläufer(in)** M(F) (*Ski*) cross-country skier; **Langlaufski** M cross-country ski; **langlebig** [-leːbɪç] ADJ long-lived; *Gerücht* persistent; *Mensch, Tier* long-lived; **~ sein** to last a long time; to be persistent; to live to an old age; **Langlebigkeit** F -, NO PL (*von Stoff, Waren*) durability; (*von Gerücht*) persistence; (*von Mensch, Tier*) longevity

länglich ['lɛŋlɪç] ADJ oblong

Lang-: **Langmut** ['laŋmuːt] F -, NO PL forbearance; **langmütig** ['laŋmyːtɪç] ADJ forbearing

längs [lɛŋs] **①** ADV lengthways; **~ gestreift** *Stoff* with lengthways stripes **②** PREP +GEN along; **die Bäume ~ des Flusses** the trees along (the banks of) the river

Längsachse F longitudinal axis

langsam ['laŋzaːm] **①** ADJ slow

② ADV **(a)** slowly; **geh/fahr/sprich ~er!** slow down!, walk/drive/speak (a bit) more slowly; **~, ~!, immer schön ~!** (*inf*) (take it) easy!; **~, aber sicher** slowly but surely

(b) (= *allmählich, endlich*) **es wird ~ Zeit, dass ...** it's high time that ...; **~ müsstest du das aber wissen** it's about time you knew that; **ich muss jetzt ~ gehen** I must be getting on my way; **kannst du dich ~ mal entscheiden?** could you start making up your mind?; **~ (aber sicher) reicht es mir** I've just about had enough

Langsamkeit F -, NO PL slowness

langsam treten VI IRREG (*inf*) to go easy (*inf*)

Langschläfer [-ʃlɛːfɐ] M -s, -, **Langschläferin** [-ərɪn] F -, -nen late-riser

Längs-: **Längsfaden** M warp; **längsgestreift** ADJ *siehe* **längs**

Langspielplatte F long-playing record

Längs-: **Längsrichtung** F longitudinal direction; **in ~ zu etw verlaufen** to run longitudinally along sth; **längsschiffs** ['lɛŋsʃɪfs] ADV broadside on; **Längsschnitt** M longitudinal section; **Längsseite** F long side; (*Naut*) broadside; **Längsstreifen** PL lengthways stripes *pl*

längst [lɛŋst] ADV **(a)** (= *seit langem, schon lange*) for a long time; (= *vor langer Zeit*) a long time ago; **als wir ankamen, war der Zug ~ weg** when we arrived the train had long since gone **(b)** *siehe* **lange**

längstens ['lɛŋstns] ADV **(a)** (= *höchstens*) at the most **(b)** (= *spätestens*) at the latest

längste(r, s) ['lɛŋstə] SUPERL *von* **lang**

Langstrecken-: **Langstreckenflug** M long-distance flight; **Langstreckenflugzeug** NT long-range aircraft; **Langstreckenrakete** F long-range missile; **Langstreckenwaffe** F long-range weapon

Längswand F long wall

Languste [laŋ'gʊstə] F -, -n crayfish, crawfish (*US*)

langweilen ['laŋvailən] INSEP **①** VT to bore **②** VI to be boring **③** VR to be bored; **sich tödlich** *or* **zu Tode ~** to be bored to death; *siehe auch* **gelangweilt**

langweilig ['laŋvailɪç] **①** ADJ **(a)** boring **(b)** (*inf*: = *langsam*) slow **②** ADV boringly

Langweiligkeit F -, NO PL **aufgrund der ~ ihres Unterrichts/des Buches** because her teaching/the book is so boring

Lang-: **Langwelle** F long wave; **langwierig** ['laŋviːrɪç] **①** ADJ long **②** ADV over a long period; **eine ~ verlaufende Krankheit** a long-term illness; **~ über etw** (*acc*) **beraten** to have lengthy discussions about sth

Langzeit- ['laŋtsait] IN CPDS long-term; **Langzeitarbeitslose(r)** MF DECL AS ADJ **ein ~r** someone who is long-term unemployed; **die ~n** the long-term unemployed; **Langzeitgedächtnis** NT long-term memory; **Langzeitstudie** F long-range study; **Langzeitwirkung** F long-term effect

Lanolin [lano'liːn] NT -s, NO PL lanolin

Lanze ['lantsə] F -, -n (= *Waffe*) lance; (*zum Werfen*) spear

Laos ['laːɔs] NT -' Laos

laotisch [la'oːtɪʃ] ADJ Laotian

lapidar [lapi'daːɐ] **①** ADJ succinct **②** ADV succinctly

Lappalie [la'paːliə] F -, -n trifle

Lappen ['lapn] M -s, - **(a)** (= *Stück Stoff*) cloth; (= *Waschlappen*) face cloth (*Brit*), washcloth (*US*)

(b) (*inf*: = *Geldschein*) note, bill (*US*); **die paar ~** ≈ a couple of quid (*Brit inf*) *or* dollars (*US*)

(c) (*sl*: = *Führerschein*) licence (*Brit*), license (*US*)

(d) (*inf*) **jdm durch die ~ gehen** to slip through sb's fingers; **die Sendung ist mir durch die ~ gegangen** I missed the programme (*Brit*) *or* program (*US*)

läppern ['lɛpɐn] VR IMPERS (*inf*) **es läppert sich** it (all) mounts up

läppisch ['lɛpɪʃ] **①** ADJ silly; **wegen ~en zwei Euro macht er so ein Theater** (*inf*) he makes such a fuss about a mere two euros **②** ADV **sich verhalten** foolishly

Lappland ['laplant] NT -s Lapland

lappländisch ['laplɛndɪʃ] ADJ Lapp

Lapsus ['lapsʊs] M -, - ['lapsuːs] mistake; (*gesellschaftlich, diplomatisch*) faux pas

Laptop ['lɛptɔp] M -s, -s (*Comput*) laptop

Lärche ['lɛrçə] F -, -n larch

Lärm [lɛrm] M -(e)s, NO PL noise; (= *Aufsehen*) fuss; **~ schlagen** (*lit*) to raise the alarm; (*fig*) to kick up a fuss; **„Viel ~ um nichts"** "Much Ado about Nothing"; **viel ~ um nichts machen** to make a lot of fuss about nothing; **viel ~ um jdn/etw machen** to make a big fuss about sb/sth

Lärm-: **Lärmbekämpfung** F noise abatement; **Lärmbelästigung** F noise pollution; **sie beschwerten sich wegen der unzumutbaren ~** they complained about the unacceptable noise level

lärmen ['lɛrmən] VI to make a noise; **~d** noisy

lärmig ['lɛrmɪç] ADJ (*esp Sw*) noisy

Lärmschutz M noise prevention

Lärmschutz-: **Lärmschutzmaßnahmen** PL noise prevention measures *pl*; **Lärmschutzwall** M, **Lärmschutzwand** F sound barrier

Larve ['larfə] F -, -n (= *Tierlarve*) larva

las PRET *von* **lesen**

Lasagne [la'zanjə] PL lasagne *sing*

lasch [laʃ] (*inf*) **①** ADJ **(a)** *Erziehung, Gesetz, Kontrolle, Polizei, Eltern* lax; *Vorgehen* feeble; (= *schlaff*) *Bewegungen* feeble; *Händedruck* limp **(c)** *Speisen* insipid **②** ADV **(a)** (= *nicht streng*) in a lax way; *vorgehen* feebly **(b)** (= *schlaff*) *bewegen* feebly; **die Hände drücken** limply

Lasche ['laʃə] F -, -n (= *Schlaufe*) loop; (= *Schuhlasche*) tongue; (*als Schmuck, Verschluss*) tab, flap; (*Tech*) splicing plate

Laschheit F -, NO PL **(a)** (*von Erziehung, Gesetz, Kontrolle etc*) laxity; (*von Vorgehen*) feebleness **(b)** (= *Schlaffheit*) feebleness; (*von Händedruck*) limpness

Laser ['le:zɐ] M **-s, -** laser

Laser- ['le:zɐ-] IN CPDS laser; **Laserchirurgie** F laser surgery; **Laserdrucker** M (*Typ*) laser (printer); **Laserkanone** F laser gun; **Laserpistole** F laser gun; (*bei Geschwindigkeitskontrollen*) radar gun; **Laserstrahl** M laser beam; **Lasertechnik** F, NO PL laser technology; **Laserwaffe** F laser weapon

lasieren [la'zi:rən], *ptp* **lasiert** VT *Bild, Holz* to varnish; *Glas* to glaze

---

lassen ['lasn]

1 MODALVERB	**3** INTRANSITIVES VERB
2 TRANSITIVES VERB	**4** REFLEXIVES VERB

pret **ließ** [li:s], *ptp* **gelassen** [gə'lasn]

1 MODALVERB, *ptp* **lassen**

Die Übersetzung hängt oft vom Vollverb ab, siehe auch dort.

(a) (= *veranlassen*) **etw tun lassen** to have sth done; **ich muss mich mal untersuchen lassen** I'll have to have a checkup; **sich** (*dat*) **einen Zahn ziehen lassen** to have a tooth out; **jdm mitteilen lassen, dass ...** to let sb know that ...; **jdm ausrichten lassen, dass ...** to leave a message for sb that ...; **er lässt Ihnen mitteilen, dass ...** he wants you to know that ...; **jdn rufen** *or* **kommen lassen** to send for sb; **sich** (*dat*) **etw kommen lassen** to have sth delivered

(b) (= *zulassen*)

Bei absichtlichen Handlungen wird **lassen** *mit* **to let** *übersetzt, bei versehentlichen Handlungen mit* **to leave**.

die Bohnen fünf Minuten kochen lassen let the beans boil for five minutes; **warum hast du das Licht brennen lassen?** why did you leave the light on?; **Wasser in die Badewanne laufen lassen** to run water into the bath; **sich** (*dat*) **einen Bart/die Haare wachsen lassen** to grow a beard/one's hair; **jdn warten lassen** to keep sb waiting; **den Tee ziehen lassen** to let the tea draw (*Brit*) *or* steep (*US*); **etw kochen lassen** to boil sth

(c) (= *erlauben*) to let; **jdn etw sehen/hören lassen** to let sb see/hear sth; **er hat sich nicht überreden lassen** he couldn't be persuaded; **ich lasse mich nicht belügen/zwingen** I won't be lied to/coerced; **ich lasse gern mit mir handeln** I'm quite willing to negotiate; **lass mich machen!** let me do it!; **lass das sein!** don't (do it)!; (= *hör auf*) stop it!

(d) (= *Möglichkeit bieten*) **das Fenster lässt sich leicht öffnen** the window opens easily; **das Fenster lässt sich nicht öffnen** (*grundsätzlich nicht*) the window doesn't open; (*momentan nicht*) the window won't open; **das Wort lässt sich schwer/nicht übersetzen** the word is hard to translate/can't be translated; **das lässt sich machen** that can be done; **es lässt sich essen/trinken** it's edible/drinkable; **hier lässt es sich bequem sitzen** it's nice sitting here; **das lässt sich nicht mehr ändern** it's too late to do anything about it now; **daraus lässt sich schließen** *or* **folgern, dass ...** one can conclude from this that ...

(e) (*im Imperativ*) **lass uns gehen!** let's go!; **lass es dir gut gehen!** take care of yourself!; **lass dir das gesagt sein!** let me tell you this!; **lass ihn nur kommen!** just let him come!; **lasset uns beten** let us pray

2 TRANSITIVES VERB

(a) (= *unterlassen*) to stop; (= *momentan aufhören*) to leave; **lass das!** don't do it!; (= *hör auf*) stop that!; **lass das Jammern** stop your moaning; **lass diese Bemerkungen!** that's enough of that kind of remark!; **lassen wir das!** let's leave it!; **er kann das Rauchen/Trinken nicht lassen** he can't stop smoking/drinking; **tu was du nicht lassen kannst!** if you must, you must!

✦es lassen er kann es nicht lassen! he will keep on doing it!; **er hat es versucht, aber er kann es nicht lassen** he's tried, but he can't help it *or* himself; **dann lassen wir es eben** let's drop the whole idea; **wenn du nicht willst, dann lass es doch** if you

don't want to, then don't; **ich habe es dann doch gelassen** in the end I didn't

(b) (= *zurücklassen, loslassen*) to leave; **jdn allein lassen** to leave sb alone; **lass mich (los)!** let me go!; **lass mich (in Ruhe)!** leave me alone!

(c) (= *überlassen*) **jdm etw lassen** to let sb have sth; (= *behalten lassen*) to let sb keep sth; **das muss man ihr lassen** (= *zugestehen*) you've got to give her that

(d) (= *hineinlassen, hinauslassen*) to let (in +*acc* into, *aus* out of); **einen (Furz) lassen** (*inf*) to let off (*inf*)

(e) (= *belassen*) to leave; **etw lassen, wie es ist** to leave sth (just) as it is

3 INTRANSITIVES VERB

✦von jdm/etw lassen (= *ablassen*) to give sb/sth up

✦lass mal lass mal, ich mach das schon leave it, I'll do it; **lass mal, ich zahle das schon** no, that's all right, I'll pay

4 REFLEXIVES VERB

✦sich lassen sich vor Freude nicht zu lassen wissen *or* **nicht lassen können** to be beside oneself with joy

---

lässig ['lɛsɪç] **1** ADJ (= *ungezwungen*) casual; (= *nachlässig*) careless; (*inf*: = *gekonnt*) cool (*inf*) **2** ADV (= *ungezwungen*) casually; (= *nachlässig*) carelessly; (*inf*: = *leicht*) easily; **das hat er ganz ~ hingekriegt** pretty cool, the way he did that (*inf*)

Lässigkeit F -, NO PL (= *Ungezwungenheit*) casualness; (= *Nachlässigkeit*) carelessness; (*inf*: = *Gekonntheit*) coolness (*inf*)

Lasso ['laso] M *or* NT **-s, -s** lasso

lässt [lɛst] 3. PERS SING PRES *von* **lassen**

Last [last] F **-, -en (a)** load; (= *Traglast*) load, burden; (*lit, fig*: = *Gewicht*) weight; **Aufzug nur für ~en** goods lift **(b)** (*fig*: = *Bürde*) burden; **jdm zur ~ fallen/werden** to be/become a burden on sb; **die ~ des Amtes** the weight of office; **damit war uns eine schwere ~ vom Herzen** *or* **von der Seele genommen** that took a load off our minds; **jdm etw zur ~ legen** to accuse sb of sth; **der neuerliche Überfall geht zulasten** *or* **zu ~en der Rebellen** the rebels are being held responsible for the recent attack; **das geht zulasten** *or* **zu ~en der Sicherheit im Lande** that is detrimental to national security **(c) Lasten** PL (= *Kosten*) costs; (*des Steuerzahlers*) charges; **zu jds ~en gehen** to be chargeable to sb

lasten ['lastn] VI to weigh heavily (*auf* +*dat* on); **eine schwere Sorge hat auf ihr gelastet** a terrible worry weighed her down; **auf dem Haus lastet noch eine Hypothek** the house is still encumbered (with a mortgage) (*form*); **auf ihm lastet die ganze Verantwortung** all the responsibility rests on him

Lasten-: Lastenaufzug M hoist; **lastenfrei** ADJ *Grundstück* unencumbered; **Lastentaxi** NT *van plus driver to rent*

Laster¹ ['lastɐ] M **-s, -** (*inf*: = *Lastwagen*) truck

Laster² NT **-s, -** (= *Untugend*) vice

lasterhaft 1 ADJ depraved **2** ADV **~ leben** to lead a depraved life

lästerlich ['lɛstɐlɪç] ADJ malicious; (= *gotteslästerlich*) blasphemous; **~e Bemerkung** gibe (*über* +*acc* at)

lästern ['lɛstɐn] VI to bitch (*inf*); **über jdn/etw ~** to bitch about sb/sth (*inf*); **wir haben gerade über dich gelästert** (*hum*) we were just talking about you

Lastex® ['lasteks] NT **-,** NO PL stretch fabric

Lastfahrzeug NT goods vehicle

lästig ['lɛstɪç] ADJ tiresome; *Husten, Kopfschuppen etc* troublesome; **wie ~!** what a nuisance!; **jdm ~ sein** to bother sb; **jdm ~ fallen** to be a nuisance to sb; **jdm ~ werden** to become a nuisance (to sb); (= *zum Ärgernis werden*) to get annoying (to sb); **etw als ~ empfinden** to think sth is annoying

Last-: Lastkahn M barge; **Lastkraftwagen** M (*form*) heavy goods vehicle

Last-Minute- [la:st'mɪnɪt-]: **Last-Minute-Flug** M standby flight; **Last-Minute-Reise** F late availability holiday (*esp Brit*) *or* vacation (*US*); **Last-Minute-Ticket** NT standby ticket

Last-: Lastschiff NT freighter; **Lastschrift** F debit; (*Eintrag*) debit entry; **Lastschriftverfahren** NT direct debit; **Lasttier** NT beast

of burden; **Lastwagen** M truck; **Lastwagenfahrer(in)** M(F)
truck driver; **Lastzug** M truck-trailer (*US*), juggernaut (*Brit inf*)

Lasur [laˈzuːɐ] F **-, -en** (*auf Holz, Bild*) varnish; (*auf Glas, Email*)
glaze

Latein [laˈtain] NT **-s** Latin; **mit seinem ~ am Ende sein** to be
stumped (*inf*)

Latein-: **Lateinamerika** NT Latin America;
Lateinamerikaner(in) M(F) Latin American;
lateinamerikanisch ADJ Latin-American

lateinisch [laˈtainɪʃ] ADJ Latin

latent [laˈtɛnt] **1** ADJ latent; *Selbstmörder* potential **2** ADV
latently; **~ vorhanden sein** to be latent

Laterne [laˈtɛrnə] F **-, -n** (= *Leuchte*) (*Archit*) lantern;
(= *Straßenlaterne*) streetlight

Laternenpfahl M lamppost

Latex [ˈlaːtɛks] M **-, Latizes** [ˈlaːtitseːs] latex

Latinum [laˈtiːnʊm] NT **-s**, NO PL **kleines/großes ~** basic/
advanced Latin exam

latschen [ˈlaːtʃn̩] VI AUX SEIN (*inf*) to wander; (*durch die Stadt etc*)
to traipse; (*schlurfend*) to slouch along

Latschen [ˈlaːtʃn̩] M **-s, -** (*inf*) (= *Hausschuh*) slipper; (*pej*:
= *Schuh*) worn-out shoe

Latschenkiefer F mountain pine

Latte [ˈlatə] F **-, -n** (a) (= *schmales Brett*) slat (b) (*Sport*) bar; (*Ftbl*)
(cross)bar (c) (*inf*: = *Liste*) **eine (ganze) ~ von Wünschen/
Vorstrafen** a whole string of things that he *etc* wants/of
previous convictions (d) (*sl*) **eine ~ haben** to have a hard-on
(*sl*)

Latten-: **Lattenrost** M duckboards *pl*; (*in Bett*) slatted frame;
Lattenschuss M (*Ftbl*) shot against the bar; **Lattenzaun** M
wooden fence

Latz [lats] M **-es, ˹e** [ˈlɛtsə] *or* (*Aus*) **-e** (*bei Kleidung* = *Lätzchen*)
bib; (= *Hosenlatz*) (front) flap; **jdm eins vor den ~ knallen** (*inf*)
or **ballern** (*inf*) to sock sb one (*inf*)

Lätzchen [ˈlɛtsçan] NT **-s, -** bib

Latzhose F (pair of) dungarees *pl* (*Brit*) *or* overalls *pl* (*US*)

lau [lau] **1** ADJ (a) (= *mild*) *Wind, Abend* mild (b) (= *~warm*)
tepid; (*fig*) lukewarm **2** ADV (a) (= *mild*) *wehen* gently
(b) (*fig*) *empfangen, behandeln* half-heartedly

Laub [laup] NT **-(e)s** [-bəs], NO PL leaves *pl*

Laubbaum M deciduous tree

Laube [ˈlaubə] F **-, -n** (a) (= *Gartenhäuschen*) summerhouse
(b) (= *Gang*) arbour (*Brit*), arbor (*US*), pergola; (= *Arkade*)
arcade

Laub-: **Laubfrosch** M (European) tree frog; **Laubhölzer** PL
deciduous trees *pl*; **Laubsäge** F fret saw; **Laubsägearbeit** F
fretwork; **Laubwald** M deciduous wood *or* (*größer*) forest

Lauch [laux] M **-(e)s, -e** allium (*form*); (*esp S Ger*: = *Porree*) leek

Lauchzwiebel F spring onion (*Brit*), scallion (*US*)

Lauer [ˈlauɐ] F **-**, NO PL **auf der ~ sein** *or* **liegen** to lie in wait; **sich
auf die ~ legen** to settle down to lie in wait

lauern [ˈlauɐn] VI (*lit, fig*) to lurk, to lie in wait (*auf +acc* for);
(*inf*) to wait (*auf +acc* for); **ein ~der Blick** a furtive glance

Lauf [lauf] M **-(e)s, Läufe** [ˈlɔyfə] (a) (= *schneller Schritt*) run;
(*Sport*: = *Wettlauf, -fahrt*) race; (= *Durchgang*) run, heat
(b) (= *Verlauf*) course; **im ~e der Jahre** in the course of the
years; **im ~e der Zeit** in the course of time; **einer Entwicklung**
(*dat*) **freien ~ lassen** to allow a development to take its (own)
course; **seiner Fantasie freien ~ lassen** to give free rein to
one's imagination; **sie ließ ihren Gefühlen freien ~** she gave
way to her feelings; **seinen ~ nehmen** to take its course; **den
Dingen ihren ~ lassen** to let things take their course; **das ist
der ~ der Dinge** *or* **der Welt** that's the way things go
(c) (= *Gang, Arbeit*) running, operation; (*Comput*) run
(d) (= *Flusslauf, auch Astron*) course; **der obere/untere ~ der
Donau** the upper/lower reaches of the Danube
(e) (= *Gewehrlauf*) barrel; **ein Tier vor den ~ bekommen** to get
an animal in one's sights

Lauf-: **Laufbahn** F career; **Laufband** NT, *pl* **-bänder**
(= *Förderband*) conveyor belt; (*in Flughafen etc*) travelator
(*Brit*), moving sidewalk (*US*); (= *Sportgerät*) treadmill

laufen [ˈlaufn̩] *pret* **lief** [liːf], *ptp* **gelaufen** [gəˈlaufn̩] **1** VI AUX SEIN
(a) (= *rennen*) to run; **lauf doch!** get a move on! (*inf*)
(b) (*inf*) (= *gehen*) to go; **er läuft dauernd ins Kino/auf die
Polizei** he's always off to the cinema/always running to the

police
(c) (= *zu Fuß gehen*) to walk; **das Kind läuft schon** the child
can already walk; **das Laufen lernen** to learn to walk; **er läuft
sehr unsicher** he's very unsteady on his feet
(d) (= *fließen*) to run; (= *schmelzen: Käse, Butter*) to melt;
Wasser in einen Eimer/die Badewanne ~ lassen to run water
into a bucket/the bath
(e) (= *undicht sein*) (*Gefäß, Wasserhahn*) to leak; (*Wunde*) to
weep; **seine Nase läuft, ihm läuft die Nase** his nose is running
(f) (= *in Betrieb sein*) to run; (*Uhr*) to go; (*Gerät, Maschine*)
(= *eingeschaltet sein*) to be on; (= *funktionieren*) to work
(g) (*Comput*) to run; **ein Programm ~ lassen** to run a program
(h) (*fig*: = *im Gange sein*) (*Prozess, Verhandlung*) to go on;
(*Bewerbung, Antrag*) to be under consideration; (= *gezeigt
werden*) (*Film, Stück*) to be on; **der Film lief schon, als wir
ankamen** the film had already started when we arrived; **etw
läuft gut/schlecht** sth is going well/badly; **die Sache/das
Geschäft läuft jetzt** it/the shop is going well now; **sehen wir
die Sache läuft** to see how things go; **alles/die Dinge ~ lassen**
to let everything/things slide; **die Sache ist gelaufen** (*inf*) it's
in the bag (*inf*)
(i) (= *bezeichnet werden*) **das Auto läuft unter meinem Namen**
or **auf meinen Namen** the car is in my name; **das Konto läuft
unter der Nummer ...** the number of the account is ...; **das
läuft unter „Sonderausgaben"** that comes under "special
expenses"
(j) (= *sich bewegen*) to run; **auf Grund ~** to run aground; **es
lief mir eiskalt über den Rücken** a chill ran up my spine
(k) (= *verlaufen*) (*Fluss etc*) to run; (*Weg*) to go
2 VT (a) AUX HABEN *or* SEIN (*Sport*) *Rekordzeit* to run; *Rekord* to
set; **Rennen ~** to run (in races); **Ski ~** to ski; **Schlittschuh ~** to
skate; **Rollschuh ~** to roller-skate
(b) AUX SEIN (= *zu Fuß gehen*) to walk; (*schnell*) to run
(c) **sich** (*dat*) **eine Blase ~** to give oneself a blister
3 VR **sich warm ~** to warm up; **sich müde ~** to tire oneself out;
in den Schuhen läuft es sich gut/schlecht these shoes are
good/bad for walking/running in

laufend **1** ADJ ATTR (= *ständig*) *Arbeiten, Ausgaben* regular;
Kredit outstanding; (= *regelmäßig*) *Wartung* routine; *Monat,
Jahr, Konto* (*form*) current; **30 Euro der ~e Meter** 30 eurosper
metre (*Brit*) *or* meter (*US*); **~e Nummer** serial number; (*von
Konto*) number; **auf dem Laufenden bleiben/sein** to keep
(oneself)/be up-to-date *or* informed; **jdn auf dem Laufenden
halten** to keep sb up-to-date *or* informed; **mit etw auf dem
Laufenden sein** to be up-to-date on sth
2 ADV continually

laufen lassen *ptp* **laufen lassen** *or* (*rare*) **laufen gelassen** VT
IRREG (*inf*) **jdn ~** to let sb go

Läufer¹ [ˈlɔyfɐ] M **-s, -** (a) (*Chess*) bishop (b) (*Teppich*) rug;
(= *Treppenläufer, Tischläufer*) runner

Läufer² [ˈlɔyfɐ] M **-s, -, Läuferin** [-ərɪn] F **-, -nen** (*Sport*) runner;
(= *Hürdenläufer*) hurdler; (*Ftbl*) halfback; **rechter/linker ~** (*Ftbl*)
right/left half

Lauferei [laufəˈrai] F **-, -en** (*inf*) running about *no pl*

Lauf-: **lauffähig** ADJ (*Comput*) **das Programm ist unter Windows
~** the program can be run under Windows; **Lauffeuer** NT **sich
wie ein ~ verbreiten** to spread like wildfire

läufig [ˈlɔyfɪç] ADJ in heat

Lauf-: **Laufkundschaft** F occasional customers *pl*; **Laufmasche**
F ladder (*Brit*), run; **Laufpass** M **jdm den ~ geben** (*inf*) to give
sb his marching orders (*inf*); **Laufrichtung** F (*Mech*) direction
of travel; **Laufschritt** M trot; (*Mil*) double-quick; **im ~** (*Mil*) at
the double; **er näherte sich im ~** he came trotting up;
Laufschuh M (*inf*) walking shoe; **Laufstall** M playpen; (*für
Tiere*) pen; **Laufsteg** M catwalk

läuft [lɔyft] 3. PERS SING PRES *von* **laufen**

Lauf-: **Laufwerk** NT running gear; (*Comput*) drive; **Laufzeit** F
(a) (*von Wechsel, Vertrag*) term; (*von Kredit*) period (b) (*von
Maschine*) (operational) life; (= *Betriebszeit*)
running time (c) (*von Brief, Postsendung*) delivery time
(d) (*Comput: von Programm*) run-time (e) (*Sport*) time

Lauge [ˈlaugə] F **-, -n** (*Chem*) lye; (= *Seifenlauge*) soapy water;
(= *Salzlauge*) salt solution

Laugenbrezel F pretzel stick

Lauheit [ˈlauhait] F **-**, NO PL (*von Wind, Abend*) mildness; (*von
Haltung*) half-heartedness

Laune ['launə] F -, -n (a) (= *Stimmung*) mood; **(je) nach (Lust und)** ~ just as the mood takes one; **gute/schlechte ~ haben**, **(bei** *or* **in) guter/schlechter ~ sein** to be in a good/bad mood; **was hat er für ~?** what sort of (a) mood is he in?; ~ **machen** to be fun **(b)** (= *Grille, Einfall*) whim; **eine ~ der Natur** a whim of nature; **etw aus einer ~ heraus tun** to do sth on a whim

launenhaft ADJ moody; (= *unberechenbar*) capricious; *Wetter* changeable ADV moodily; (= *unberechenbar*) capriciously

launisch ['launɪʃ] ADJ, ADV = **launenhaft**

Laus [laus] F -, **Läuse** ['lɔyzə] louse; (= *Blattlaus*) greenfly; **ihm ist (wohl) eine ~ über die Leber gelaufen** *or* **gekrochen** (*inf*) something's eating at him (*inf*)

Lauschangriff M bugging operation (*gegen* on)

lauschen ['lauʃn] VI (a) (*geh*) to listen (+*dat, auf* +*acc* to) **(b)** (= *heimlich zuhören*) to eavesdrop

Lausebengel M (*inf*), **Lausejunge** M (*inf*) little devil (*inf*); (*wohlwollend*) rascal

lausen ['lauzn] VT to delouse; **ich glaub, mich laust der Affe!** (*inf*) well I'll be blowed! (*Brit inf*)

lausig ['lauzɪç] (*inf*) ADJ lousy (*inf*); *Kälte* freezing ADV awfully; (*vor Adjektiv auch*) damn(ed) (*inf*)

laut¹ [laut] ADJ (a) (= *nicht leise*) loud **(b)** (= *lärmend, voll Lärm*) noisy; (= *auffällig, aufdringlich*) *Mensch* loudmouthed; *Farbe etc* loud; **er wird immer gleich/ wird niemals** ~ he always/never gets obstreperous **(c)** (= *hörbar*) out loud *pred, adv*, aloud *pred, adv*; ~ **werden** (= *bekannt*) to become known; **etw** ~ **werden lassen** to make sth known

ADV loudly; ~**er sprechen** to speak louder, to speak up; **etw** ~**(er) stellen** to turn sth up (loud); ~ **auflachen** to laugh out loud; ~ **nachdenken** to think aloud; **das kannst du aber** ~ **sagen** (*fig inf*) you can say that again

laut² PREP +GEN *or* DAT (*geh*) according to

Laut [laut] M -(e)s, -e sound; **heimatliche** ~**e** sounds of home; **keinen** ~ **von sich geben** not to make a sound

lauten ['lautn] VI to be; (*Rede, Argumentation*) to go; (*Schriftstück*) to read, to go; (= *sich belaufen*) to amount (*auf* +*acc* to); **dieser Erlass lautet wörtlich ...** the exact text of this decree is ...; **auf den Namen ...** ~ (*Pass*) to be in the name of ...; (*Scheck*) to be payable to ...; **die Anklage lautet auf Mord** the charge is (one of) murder

läuten ['lɔytn] VTI (a) (*Glocke, Mensch*) to ring; (*Wecker*) to go (off); **es hat geläutet** the bell rang; **(nach) jdm** ~ to ring for sb **(b)** **er hat davon (etwas)** ~ **hören** (*inf*) he has heard something about it

lauter¹ ['laute] ADJ INV (= *nur*) nothing but; ~ **Unsinn/Freude** *etc* pure nonsense/joy *etc*; **vor** ~ **Rauch/Autos kann man nichts sehen** you can't see anything for all the smoke/cars; **das sind** ~ **Idioten** they are nothing but idiots

lauter² ADJ (*geh: = aufrichtig*) honourable (*Brit*), honorable (*US*); *Wahrheit* honest; ~**er Wettbewerb** fair competition

Laut-: **lauthals** ['lauthals] ADV at the top of one's voice; **Lautlehre** F phonetics *sing*, phonology; **lautlich** ['lautlɪç] ADJ phonetic ADV phonetically; **lautlos** ADJ silent ADV silently; **Lautmalerei** F onomatopoeia; **lautmalerisch** ADJ onomatopoeic; **Lautschrift** F phonetics *pl*; (*System auch*) phonetic alphabet

Lautsprecher M (loud)speaker; **über** ~ over the loudspeaker(s)

Lautsprecher-: **Lautsprecheranlage** F öffentliche ~ PA system; **Lautsprecherbox** F speaker

Laut-: **lautstark** ADJ loud; (*Rad, TV etc*) high-volume; *Partei, Protest* vociferous ADV loudly; *protestieren auch* vociferously; **Lautstärke** F (a) loudness; (*von Protest etc*) vociferousness **(b)** (*Rad, TV etc*) volume; **Lautstärkeregler** M (*Rad, TV*) volume control; **Lautverschiebung** F sound shift

lauwarm ADJ slightly warm; *Flüssigkeit* lukewarm; (*fig*) lukewarm ADV (*fig*) half-heartedly

Lava ['la:va] F -, **Laven** ['la:vn] lava

Lavabo ['la:vabo] NT -(s), -s (*Sw*) washbasin

Lavendel [la'vɛndl] M -s, - lavender

Lawine [la'vi:nə] F -, -n (*lit, fig*) avalanche

Lawinen-: **lawinenartig** ADJ like an avalanche ADV like an avalanche; ~ **anwachsen** to snowball; **Lawinengefahr** F

danger of avalanches; **lawinensicher** ADJ *Ort* secure from avalanches ADV *gebaut* to withstand avalanches

lax [laks] ADJ lax ADV laxly

Laxheit F -, NO PL laxity

Lay-out ['le:laut] NT -s, -s, **Layout** NT -s, -s layout

Layouter ['le:laute] M -s, -, **Layouterin** [-ərɪn] F -, -nen designer

Lazarett [latsa'rɛt] NT -(e)s, -e (*Mil*) (*in Kaserne etc*) sickbay; (*selbstständiges Krankenhaus*) hospital

LCD- [eltse:'de:] IN CPDS LCD; **LCD-Anzeige** F LCD display

Leadsänger(in) ['li:d-] M(F) lead singer

leasen ['li:zn] VT (*Comm*) to lease

Leasing ['li:zɪŋ] NT -s, -s (*Comm*) leasing

Leasing- ['li:zɪŋ-]: **Leasinggeber(in)** M(F) lessor; **Leasingnehmer(in)** M(F) lessee; **Leasing-Vertrag** M lease

leben ['le:bn] VI to live; (= *am Leben sein*) to be alive; (= *weiterleben*) to live on; **er lebt noch** he is still alive; **er lebt nicht mehr** he is no longer alive; **er hat nicht lange gelebt** he didn't live (for) long; **von etw** ~ to live on sth; **es lebe** *or* **lang lebe der König!** long live the King!; **wie geht es dir? – man lebt (so)** (*inf*) how are you? – surviving; **lebst du noch?** (*hum inf*) are you still in the land of the living? (*hum*); **genug zu** ~ **haben** to have enough to live on; ~ **und** ~ **lassen** to live and let live; **einsam/christlich/gesund** ~ to live a lonely/ Christian/healthy life; **allein/glücklich** ~ to live alone/ happily; **für etw** ~, **einer Sache** (*dat*) ~ (*geh*) to live for sth; **hier lebt es sich gut, hier lässt es sich (gut)** ~ it's a good life here

VT to live; **jeder muss sein eigenes Leben** ~ we've all got our own lives to live

Leben ['le:bn] NT -s, - (a) life; **das** ~ life; **am** ~ **sein/bleiben** to be/stay alive; **das** ~ **vor/hinter sich** (*dat*) **haben** to have one's life ahead of/behind one; **solange ich am** ~ **bin** as long as I live; **jdm das** ~ **retten** to save sb's life; **es geht um** ~ **und Tod**, **es ist eine Sache auf** ~ **und Tod** it's a matter of life and death; **mit dem** ~ **davonkommen** to escape with one's life; **mit dem** ~ **spielen, sein** ~ **aufs Spiel setzen** to dice with death; **mit dem** ~ **abschließen** to prepare for death; **seinem** ~ **ein Ende machen** *or* **bereiten** to put an end to one's life; **einer Sache** (*dat*) **zu neuem** ~ **verhelfen** to breathe new life into sth; **etw ins** ~ **rufen** to bring sth into being; **seines** ~**s nicht mehr sicher sein** to fear for one's life; **ums** ~ **kommen** to die; **jdn am** ~ **lassen** to spare sb's life; **um sein** ~ **laufen** *or* **rennen** to run for one's life; **sich** (*dat*) **das** ~ **nehmen** to take one's (own) life; **der Mann/die Frau meines** ~**s** my ideal man/woman; **etw für sein** ~ **gern tun** to love doing sth; **etw für sein** ~ **gern essen/ trinken** to love sth; **jdn künstlich am** ~ **erhalten** to keep sb alive artificially; **er hat es nie leicht gehabt im** ~ he has never had an easy life; **ein** ~ **lang** one's whole life (long); **zum ersten Mal** *or* **das erste Mal im** ~ for the first time in one's life; **ich habe noch nie im** ~ *or* **in meinem** ~ **geraucht** I have never smoked (in) all my life; **nie im** ~! never!; **ein Roman, den das** ~ **schrieb** a novel of real life; **ein Film nach dem** ~ a film from real life; **das** ~ **geht weiter** life goes on; **so ist das** ~ **(eben)** that's life

(b) (= *Betriebsamkeit*) life; **auf dem Markt herrscht reges** ~ the market is a hive of activity; ~ **in etw** (*acc*) **bringen** (*inf*) to liven sth up

lebend ADJ live *attr*, alive *pred*; *Wesen, Seele, Beispiel, Sprache* living; **„Vorsicht, ~e Tiere"** "attention, live animals"; **die Lebenden** the living ADV alive; ~ **gebärend** viviparous

Lebend-: **Lebendgeburt** F live birth; **Lebendgewicht** NT live weight

lebendig [le'bɛndɪç] ADJ (a) (= *nicht tot*) live *attr*, alive *pred*; *Wesen* living; ~**e Junge** live young; ~**e Junge gebären** to bear one's young live; **jdn bei ~em Leibe verbrennen, jdn ~en Leibes verbrennen** (*liter*) to burn sb alive; **er nimmts von den Lebendigen** (*hum inf*) he'll have the shirt off your back (*inf*) **(b)** (*fig: = lebhaft*) lively *no adv*; *Darstellung, Bild, Erinnerung* vivid; *Glaube* fervent

ADV (a) (= *lebend*) alive; **er ist dort ~ begraben** (*fig inf*) it's a living death for him there **(b)** (*fig: = lebhaft*) vividly

Lebendigkeit F - liveliness

Lebens-: **Lebensabend** M old age; **Lebensalter** NT age; **ein hohes** ~ **erreichen** to have a long life; (*Mensch auch*) to reach a ripe old age (*inf*); **Lebensarbeitszeit** F working life; **Lebensart** F, NO PL (a) (= *Lebensweise*) way of life

(b) (= *Manieren*) manners *pl*; (= *Stil*) style; **eine feine ~ haben** to have exquisite manners/style; **eine kultivierte ~ haben** to be cultivated; **Lebensauffassung** F attitude to life; **Lebensaufgabe** F life's work; **lebensbedrohend, lebensbedrohlich** ⬛ ADJ life-threatening ⬛ ADV *krank, verletzt* critically; **Lebensberechtigung** F right to exist; **Lebensdauer** F life(span); (*von Maschine*) life; **Lebensende** NT end (of sb's/one's life); **sie lebte bis an ihr ~ in Armut** she lived in poverty till the day she died; **lebenserhaltend** ADJ life-preserving; *Geräte* life-support *attr*; **Lebenserinnerungen** PL memoirs *pl*; **Lebenserwartung** F life expectancy; **lebensfähig** ADJ viable; **Lebensfähigkeit** F viability; **Lebensform** F (*Biol*) life form; (= *Form menschlichen Zusammenlebens*) way of life; **lebensfremd** ADJ out of touch with life; **Lebensfreude** F joie de vivre; **lebensfroh** ADJ merry; **Lebensführung** F lifestyle; **Lebensgefahr** F (mortal) danger; „**~!**" "danger!"; **es besteht (akute) ~** there is danger (to life); **er ist *or* schwebt in (akuter) ~** his life is in danger; (*Patient*) he is in a critical condition; **außer ~ sein** to be out of danger; **lebensgefährlich** ⬛ ADJ highly dangerous; *Krankheit, Verletzung* critical ⬛ ADV critically; (*inf*) *glatt, schnell* dangerously; **Lebensgefährte** M, **Lebensgefährtin** F partner; **Lebensgemeinschaft** F long-term relationship; **eingetragene ~** registered partnership; **lebensgroß** ADJ, ADV life-size; **Lebensgröße** F life-size; **eine Figur in ~** a life-size figure; **etw in ~ malen** to paint sth life-size; **da stand er in voller ~** (*hum*) there he was (as) large as life (and twice as ugly) (*inf*)

Lebenshaltung F **(a)** (= *Unterhaltskosten*) cost of living **(b)** (= *Lebensführung*) lifestyle

Lebenshaltungs-: Lebenshaltungsindex M cost-of-living index; **Lebenshaltungskosten** PL cost of living *sing*

Lebens-: Lebensinhalt M purpose in life; **etw zu seinem ~ machen** to devote oneself to sth; **das ist sein ganzer ~** his whole life revolves (a)round it; (*inf*); **Lebensjahr** NT year of (one's) life; **in seinem fünften ~** in the fifth year of his life; **nach Vollendung des 18. ~es** on attaining the age of 18; **Lebenslage** F situation; **in jeder ~** in any situation; **lebenslänglich** ⬛ ADJ *Rente, Strafe* for life; *Gefangenschaft auch* life *attr*; **ein Lebenslänglicher** (*inf*) a lifer (*inf*); **sie hat „~"** *or* **Lebenslänglich bekommen** (*inf*) she got life (*inf*) ⬛ ADV for life; **~ im Zuchthaus** *or* **hinter Gittern sitzen** (*inf*) to be inside for life (*inf*); **Lebenslauf** M life; (*bei Bewerbungen*) curriculum vitae (*Brit*), résumé (*US*); **Lebenslinie** F lifeline; **Lebenslüge** F sham existence; **mit einer ~ leben** to live a lie; **Lebenslust** F zest for life; **lebenslustig** ADJ in love with life

Lebensmittel PL food *sing*

Lebensmittel-: Lebensmittelchemie F food chemistry; **lebensmittelgerecht** ⬛ ADJ suitable for putting food in ⬛ ADV *verpacken* suitably for food; **Lebensmittelgeschäft** NT grocer's (shop); **Lebensmittelvergiftung** F food poisoning

Lebens-: lebensmüde ADJ weary of life; **ein Lebensmüder** a potential suicide; **ich bin doch nicht ~!** (*inf*: = *verrückt*) I'm not completely mad! (*inf*); **lebensnotwendig** ADJ essential; *Organ, Sauerstoff etc* vital (for life); **Lebensnotwendigkeit** F necessity of life; **Lebenspartner(in)** M(F) long-term partner; **Lebenspartnerschaft** F long-term relationship; **eingetragene ~** registered partnership; **Lebenspartnerschaftsgesetz** NT *law governing registered partnerships for lesbians and gay men*; **Lebensqualität** F quality of life; **Lebensraum** M (*Pol*) lebensraum; (*Biol*) habitat; **Lebensretter(in)** M(F) rescuer; **du bist mein ~** you've saved my life; **Lebensstandard** M standard of living; **Lebensumstände** PL circumstances *pl*; **damals waren die ~ schwierig** conditions made life difficult in those days; **lebensunfähig** ADJ *Lebewesen, System* nonviable; **Lebensunterhalt** M **(a)** **seinen ~ verdienen** to earn one's living; **seinen ~ bestreiten** to make one's living; **sie verdient den ~ für die Familie** she is the breadwinner of the family; **für jds ~ sorgen** to support sb; **etw zu seinem ~ tun** to do sth for a living **(b)** (= *Unterhaltskosten*) cost of living; **lebensverlängernd** ADJ *Maßnahme* life-prolonging; **Lebensversicherung** F life insurance; **eine ~ abschließen** to take out a life insurance policy; **Lebenswandel** M way of life; **einen einwandfreien/zweifelhaften** *etc* **~ führen** to lead an irreproachable/a dubious *etc* life; **Lebensweise** F way of life; **lebenswert** ADJ worth living; **lebenswichtig** ADJ essential; *Organ, Bedürfnisse, Entscheidung* vital; *Nährstoffe* essential; **Lebenswille** M will to live; **Lebenszeichen** NT sign of life; **kein ~ mehr von sich geben** to show no sign(s) of life;

Lebenszeit F life(time); **auf ~** for life; **Beamter auf ~** permanent (*Brit*) *or* tenured (*US*) civil servant; **Mitglied auf ~** life member

Leber [ˈleːbɐ] F **-, -n** liver; **ich habe es mit der ~ zu tun** (*inf*), **ich habe es an der ~** (*inf*) I've got liver trouble; **frei** *or* **frisch von der ~ weg reden** (*inf*) to speak out

Leber-: Leberfleck M mole; (*Hautfärbung*) liver spot; **Leberkäse** M, NO PL ≈ meat loaf; **Leberknödel** M liver dumpling; **leberkrank** ADJ suffering from a liver disorder; **Leberkrebs** M cancer of the liver; **Leberleiden** NT liver disorder; **Leberpastete** F liver pâté; **Lebertran** M cod-liver oil; **Leberwert** M liver function reading; **Leberwurst** F liver sausage

Lebewesen NT living thing; **kleinste ~** microorganisms

lebhaft ⬛ ADJ **(a)** (= *voll Leben, rege*) lively *no adv*; *Gespräch, Streit* animated; (*Comm*) *Geschäfte, Verkehr, Nachfrage* brisk **(b)** *Erinnerung, Eindruck, Vorstellungsvermögen* vivid; *Fantasie, Muster, Interesse, Beifall* lively; *Farbe* bright ⬛ ADV **(a)** (= *rege*) *reagieren, strampeln* strongly; **~ diskutieren** to have a lively discussion; **es geht ~ zu** it is lively; **das Geschäft geht ~** business is brisk; **die Börse schloss ~** business was brisk on the Stock Exchange at the close of the day **(b)** (= *deutlich*) vividly; **ich kann mir ~ vorstellen, dass ...** I can (very) well imagine that ... **(c)** (= *intensiv*) intensely; **eine ~ geführte Debatte** a lively debate; **~ bedauern** to regret deeply

Lebhaftigkeit [ˈleːphaftɪçkaɪt] F **-**, NO PL liveliness; (*Comm: von Geschäften*) briskness; (= *Deutlichkeit: von Erinnerung, Eindruck*) vividness; (*von Farbe*) brightness

Lebkuchen M gingerbread

Leb-: leblos ADJ lifeless; *Pracht* empty; **~er Gegenstand** inanimate object; **Leblosigkeit** F **-**, NO PL lifelessness; **Lebzeiten** PL **zu jds ~** in sb's lifetime; (= *Zeit*) in sb's day

lechzen [ˈlɛçtsn̩] VI to pant; **nach etw ~** to thirst for sth

leck [lɛk] ADJ leaky; **~ sein** to leak

Leck [lɛk] NT **-(e)s, -s** leak

lecken¹ [ˈlɛkn̩] VI (= *undicht sein*) to leak

lecken² VTI to lick; **an jdm/etw ~** to lick sb/sth

lecker [ˈlɛkɐ] ⬛ ADJ *Speisen* delicious; (*inf*) *Mädchen* lovely ⬛ ADV *zubereitet* deliciously; **~ schmecken/aussehen** to taste/look delicious

Leckerbissen M **(a)** (*Speise*) delicacy, titbit (*Brit*), tidbit (*US*) **(b)** (*fig*) gem

Leckermaul NT, **Leckermäulchen** [-mɔʏlçən] NT **-s, -** (*inf*) **ein ~ sein** to have a sweet tooth

led. ABBR *von* **ledig**

Leder [ˈleːdɐ] NT **-s, -** **(a)** leather; (= *Fensterleder*) chamois; (= *Wildleder*) suede; **in ~ gebunden** leather-bound; **zäh wie ~** as tough as old boots (*Brit inf*), as tough as shoe leather (*US*) **(b)** (*inf*: = *Fußball*) ball; **am ~ bleiben** to stick with the ball

Leder- IN CPDS leather; **lederartig** ADJ *Stoff* leatherlike; **Ledergarnitur** F leather-upholstered suite; **Lederhose** F leather trousers *pl* (*esp Brit*) *or* pants *pl* (*esp US*); (*aus Wildleder*) suede trousers *pl* (*esp Brit*) *or* pants *pl* (*esp US*); (*kurz*) lederhosen *pl*; (*von Tracht*) leather shorts *pl*; (*Bundhose*) leather breeches *pl*

*Contrary to popular belief outside the country, **Lederhose** is not the traditional costume for the whole of Germany. Only in Bavaria and Austria are leather knee-breeches and the **Gamsbart** hat the traditional male costume. The women in these areas wear a **Dirndl**: a dress with a bodice and apron. Other parts of Germany have different costumes – for example, in the Black Forest the traditional costume for women includes a wide black hat with three large red bobbles on top.*

Leder-: Lederjacke F leather jacket; (*aus Wildleder*) suede jacket; **Ledermantel** M leather coat; (*aus Wildleder*) suede coat

ledern [ˈleːdɐn] ADJ **(a)** (= *aus Leder*) leather **(b)** (= *zäh*) *Fleisch, Haut* leathery

ledig [ˈleːdɪç] ADJ **(a)** (= *unverheiratet*) single; (*inf*) *Mutter* unmarried; (*S Ger*) *Kind* illegitimate **(b)** (*geh*: = *unabhängig*) free; (*los und*) **~ sein** to be footloose and fancy free

Ledige(r) [ˈleːdɪɡə] MF DECL AS ADJ single person

lediglich [ˈleːdɪklɪç] ADV merely

leer [leːɐ] **1** ADJ empty; *Blätter, Seite auch* blank; *Gesichtsausdruck, Blick* blank; **eine ~e Stelle** an empty space; **vor einem ~en Haus** *or* **vor ~en Bänken spielen** (*Theat*) to play to an empty house; **ins Leere starren/treten** to stare/step into space; **ins Leere laufen** (*fig*) to come to nothing; **mit ~en Händen** (*fig*) empty-handed

2 ADV **eine Zeile ~ lassen** to leave a line (blank); **etw ~ machen** to empty sth; **den Teller ~ essen** to eat everything on the plate; **(wie) ~ gefegt Straßen, Stadt** *etc* deserted; **etw ~ trinken** to empty sth; **~ stehen** to stand empty; **~ stehend** empty; *siehe auch* **leer laufen**

Leere [ˈleːrə] F -, NO PL (*lit, fig*) emptiness

leeren [ˈleːrən] **1** VT to empty **2** VR to empty

Leer-: leergefegt [-gəfeːkt] ADJ (*fig*) *siehe* **leer**; **Leergewicht** NT unladen weight; (*von Behälter*) empty weight; **Leergut** NT empties *pl*; **Leerlauf** M **(a)** (*Aut*) neutral; (*von Fahrrad*) freewheel; **im ~ fahren** to coast; **das Auto ist im ~** the engine is in neutral; (= *stehend mit laufendem Motor*) the engine is idling **(b)** (*fig*) slack; **leer laufen** VI IRREG AUX SEIN **(a)** (*Fass etc*) to run dry; **~ lassen** to empty **(b)** (*Motor*) to idle; (*Maschine*) to run idle; (*Betrieb etc*) to be idle; **leerstehend** ADJ *siehe* **leer**; **Leertaste** F (*von Tastatur*) space-bar

Leerung [ˈleːrʊŋ] F -, -en emptying; **die ~ der Mülltonnen erfolgt wöchentlich** the dustbins (*Brit*) *or* garbage cans (*US*) are emptied once a week; **nächste ~ 18 Uhr** (*an Briefkasten*) next collection (*Brit*) *or* pickup (*US*) 6 p.m.

legal [leˈɡaːl] **1** ADJ legal **2** ADV legally

legalisieren [leɡaliˈziːrən], *ptp* **legalisiert** VT to legalize

Legalität [leɡaliˈtɛːt] F -, NO PL legality; **(etwas) außerhalb der ~** (*euph*) (slightly) outside the law

Legasthenie [leɡasteˈniː] F -, -n [-ˈniːən] dyslexia

Legastheniker [leɡasˈteːnikɐ] M -s, -, **Legasthenikerin** [-ərɪn] F -, -nen dyslexic

Lege-: Legebatterie F hen battery; **Legehenne** F laying hen

legen [ˈleːɡn̩] **1** VT **(a)** (= *lagern*) to lay down; (*mit adv*) to lay; *Flasche etc* to lay on its side **(b)** (*mit Raumangabe*) to put; **etw beiseite ~** to put sth aside *or* (*weglegen*) away; **etw in Essig** *etc* **~** to preserve sth in vinegar *etc*; **ein Tier an die Kette ~** to chain an animal (up) **(c)** (*mit Angabe des Zustandes*) **etw in Falten ~** to fold sth; **er legte die Stirn in Falten** he frowned; **eine Stadt in Schutt und Asche ~** to reduce a town to rubble **(d)** (= *verlegen*) to lay; *Bomben* to plant; **Feuer** *or* **einen Brand ~** to start a fire **2** VTI (*Huhn*) to lay **3** VR **(a)** (= *hinlegen*) to lie down (*auf +acc* on); **sich ins** *or* (*geh*) **zu Bett ~** to go to bed; **sich in die Sonne ~** to lie in the sun **(b)** (*mit Ortsangabe: Nebel, Rauch*) to settle (*auf +acc* on); **sich auf die Seite ~** to lie on one's side; **sich in die Kurve ~** to lean into the corner **(c)** (= *abnehmen*) (*Lärm*) to die down; (*Sturm, Wind auch, Kälte*) to let up; (*Rauch, Nebel*) to clear; (*Zorn, Begeisterung, Arroganz, Nervosität*) to wear off; (*Anfangsschwierigkeiten*) to sort themselves out

legendär [leɡɛnˈdɛːɐ] ADJ legendary; **er/das ist schon fast ~** he/it has already become almost legendary

Legende [leˈɡɛndə] F -, -n (*alle Bedeutungen*) legend

leger [leˈʒeːɐ, leˈʒɛːɐ] **1** ADJ *Kleidung, Benehmen, Ausdrucksweise* casual; *Sitz* comfortable; *Typ* casual, informal; *Atmosphäre* relaxed **2** ADV casually; *sich ausdrücken* informally; **etw sitzt ~** sth is comfortable

Leggings [ˈlɛɡɪŋs] PL, **Leggins** [ˈlɛɡɪns] PL leggings *pl*

legieren [leˈɡiːrən], *ptp* **legiert** VT **(a)** *Metall* to alloy **(b)** (*Cook*) *Suppe etc* to thicken

Legierung [leˈɡiːrʊŋ] F -, -en alloy; (*Verfahren*) alloying

Legion [leˈɡioːn] F -, -en legion

Legionär [leɡioˈnɛːɐ] M -s, -e legionary, legionnaire

Legislative [leɡɪslaˈtiːvə] F -, -n legislature

Legislaturperiode F parliamentary term (*Brit*), legislative period (*US*)

legitim [leɡiˈtiːm] **1** ADJ legitimate; **deine Vorwürfe erscheinen mir ~** I think your accusations are justified **2** ADV legitimately

Legitimation [leɡitimaˈtsioːn] F -, -en identification; (= *Berechtigung*) authorization

legitimieren [leɡitiˈmiːrən], *ptp* **legitimiert** **1** VT *Beziehung, Kind* to legitimize; (= *berechtigen*) to entitle; (= *berechtigt erscheinen lassen*) to justify; (= *Erlaubnis geben*) to authorize; **die demokratisch legitimierte Regierung** the democratically elected government **2** VR to show (proof of) authorization; (= *sich ausweisen*) to identify oneself

Leguan [leˈɡuaːn, ˈleːɡuaːn] M -s, -e iguana

Lehm [leːm] M -(e)s, -e loam; (= *Ton*) clay

lehmig [ˈleːmɪç] ADJ loamy; (= *tonartig*) claylike

Lehne [ˈleːnə] F -, -n (= *Armlehne*) arm(rest); (= *Rückenlehne*) back (rest)

lehnen [ˈleːnən] **1** VT to lean (*an +acc* against) **2** VI to be leaning (*an +dat* against) **3** VR to lean (*an +acc* against, *auf +acc* on)

Lehn-: Lehnstuhl M easy chair; **Lehnwort** NT, *pl* **-wörter** (*Ling*) loan word

Lehramt NT **das ~** the teaching profession; (= *Lehrerposten*) teaching post (*esp Brit*) *or* position; **ein ~ ausüben** to hold a teaching post (*esp Brit*) *or* position; **Prüfung für das höhere ~** examination for secondary school teachers

Lehr-: lehrbar ADJ teachable; **Lehrbrief** M (= *Zeugnis*) apprenticeship certificate; **Lehrbuch** NT textbook

Lehre [ˈleːrə] F -, -n **(a)** (= *das Lehren*) teaching **(b)** (*von Christus, Buddha, Marx etc*) teachings *pl*; (= *Lehrmeinung*) doctrine; (*von Galilei, Kant, Freud etc*) theory; (*von Erdaufbau, Leben etc*) science; **die christliche ~** Christian doctrine/teaching **(c)** (= *negative Erfahrung*) lesson; (*einer Fabel*) moral; **jdm eine ~ erteilen** to teach sb a lesson; **seine ~(n) aus etw ziehen** to learn a lesson from sth; **lass dir das eine ~ sein** let that be a lesson to you! **(d)** (= *Berufslehre*) apprenticeship; (*in nicht handwerklichem Beruf*) training; **eine ~ machen** to train; (*in Handwerk*) to do an apprenticeship; **bei jdm die ~ (durch)machen, bei jdm in die ~ gehen** to serve one's apprenticeship with sb; **sie machte eine ~ als** *or* **zur Bürokauffrau** she trained as an office administrator

LEHRE

Lehre is the name for vocational training in trade and industry. It is strictly regulated and usually lasts three years, although those who have their Abitur are often allowed to reduce this by one year. The trainees, so-called Auszubildende or Azubis for short, work in a company and become familiar with all the different areas of their future profession. In addition, they receive instruction at a vocational college for two days a week or in blocks of seminars. At the end of the training period they take their Gesellenprüfung ▶ ABITUR

lehren [ˈleːrən] VTI to teach; (*Univ auch*) to lecture (*ein Fach* in a subject); **jdn** *or* **jdm** (*inf*) **lesen ~** to teach sb to read *etc*; **die Zukunft wird es ~** time (alone) will tell; **ich werde dich ~, so frech zu antworten!** I'll teach you to answer back! (*inf*); *siehe auch* **gelehrt**

Lehrer [ˈleːrɐ] M -s, -, **Lehrerin** [-ərɪn] F -, -nen teacher; (= *Fluglehrer, Fahrlehrer etc*) instructor/instructress; **er ist ~** he's a (school)teacher; **~(in) für Philosophie/Naturwissenschaften** teacher of philosophy/science; (*in der Schule*) philosophy/science teacher

Lehrer-: Lehrerausbildung F teacher training; **Lehrerkollegium** NT (teaching) staff; **in diesem ~** amongst the teaching staff of this school; **Lehrerkonferenz** F (*Sch*) staff meeting; **Lehrerschaft** [ˈleːrɐʃaft] F -, -en (*form*) (teaching) staff; **Lehrerzimmer** NT staff (*esp Brit*) *or* teachers' room

Lehr-: Lehrfach NT subject; **Lehrgang** M, *pl* **-gänge** course (*für* in); **Lehrherr(in)** M(F) master (of an apprentice); **Lehrjahr** NT year as an apprentice; **~e sind keine Herrenjahre** (*Prov*) life's not easy at the bottom; **Lehrkörper** M (*form*) teaching staff; **Lehrkraft** F (*form*) teacher

Lehrling [ˈleːrlɪŋ] M -s, -e apprentice; (*in nicht handwerklichem Beruf*) trainee

Lehr-: Lehrmeister(in) M(F) master; **Lehrmittel** NT teaching aid; (*pl auch*) teaching materials *pl*; **Lehrplan** M (teaching) curriculum; (*für ein Schuljahr*) syllabus; **lehrreich** ADJ (= *informativ*) instructive; *Erfahrung* educational; **Lehrsatz** M (*Math, Philos*) theorem; (*Eccl*) dogma; **Lehrstelle** F position for an apprentice; (*in nicht handwerklichem Beruf*) position for a trainee; (*aus Sicht des Auszubildenden*) position as an apprentice/a trainee; **wir haben zwei ~n zu vergeben** we have vacancies for two apprentices/trainees; **Lehrstoff** M subject; (*eines Jahres*) syllabus; **Lehrstuhl** M (*Univ*) chair (*für* of); **jdn auf einen ~ berufen** to offer sb a chair; **Lehrtochter** F (*Sw*) apprentice; (*in nicht handwerklichem Beruf*) trainee; **Lehrvertrag** M indentures *pl*; (*in nicht handwerklichem Beruf*) contract as a trainee; **Lehrzeit** F apprenticeship

Leib [laip] M **-(e)s, -er** [-bə] (= *Körper*) body; **mit ~ und Seele** heart and soul; *wünschen* with all one's heart; **mit ~ und Seele singen** to sing one's heart out; **mit ~ und Seele dabei sein** to put one's heart and soul into it; **etw am eigenen ~(e) erfahren** *or* (**ver**)**spüren** to experience sth for oneself; **der hat vielleicht einen Ton am ~!** (*inf*) talk about rude!; **am ganzen ~(e) zittern/frieren/schwitzen** to be shaking/freezing/sweating all over; **sich** (*dat*) **jdn/etw vom ~e halten** to keep sb/sth at bay; **halt ihn mir vom ~** keep him away from me; **bleib mir damit vom ~e!** (*inf*) stop pestering me with it (*inf*)

leiben ['laibn] VI **wie er leibt und lebt** to a T (*inf*)

Leibes-: Leibeserziehung F physical education; **Leibeskraft** F **aus Leibeskräften schreien** *etc* to shout *etc* with all one's might (and main); **Leibesübung** F (physical) exercise; **~en** (*Schulfach*) physical education *no pl*

leibhaft ADJ (*rare*) = **leibhaftig**

leibhaftig [laip'haftɪç, 'laiphaftɪç] 🟦 ADJ personified; **die ~e Güte** *etc* goodness *etc* personified; (**wie**) **der ~e Teufel, (wie) der Leibhaftige** (as) the devil himself 🟨 ADV in person

leiblich ['laiplɪç] ADJ (**a**) (= *körperlich*) physical, bodily; **die ~en Genüsse** the pleasures of the flesh; **für das ~e Wohl sorgen** to take care of our/their *etc* bodily needs (**b**) *Mutter, Vater* natural; *Kind* by birth; *Bruder, Schwester* full; *Verwandte* blood; (*emph*: = *eigen*) (very) own

Leib-: Leibwache F bodyguard; **Leibwächter(in)** M(F) bodyguard

Leiche ['laiçə] F **-, -n** corpse; (*inf*: = *Bierleiche, Schnapsleiche*) drunken body (*inf*); **wie eine Leiche or wandelnde ~ aussehen** to look like death (warmed up (*Brit inf*) *or* over (*US inf*)); **er geht über ~n** (*inf*) he'd stop at nothing; **nur über meine ~!** (*inf*) over my dead body!; **eine ~ im Keller haben** (*fig*) to have a skeleton in the cupboard (*Brit*) *or* closet

Leichen-: Leichenbeschauer [-bəʃauɐ] M **-s, -**, **Leichenbeschauerin** [-ərɪn] F **-, -nen** doctor conducting a postmortem; **leichenblass** ADJ deathly pale; **Leichenfledderei** [-fledərai] F **-, -en** robbing of dead people; **das ist die reinste ~** (*fig*) what vultures!; **Leichenhalle** F, **Leichenhaus** NT mortuary; **Leichenschau** F postmortem (examination); **Leichenschauhaus** NT morgue; **Leichenstarre** F rigor mortis *no art*; **Leichenwagen** M hearse

Leichnam ['laiçnaːm] M **-s, -e** (*form*) body

leicht [laiçt] 🟦 ADJ (**a**) (= *nicht schwer, nicht ernst*) (*Mil*) light; (= *aus ~em Material*) *Koffer, Kleidung* lightweight; **mit ~er Hand** lightly; (*fig*) effortlessly; **jdn um einiges ~er machen** to relieve sb of some of his money

(**b**) (= *schwach, geringfügig, nicht wichtig*) slight; *Regen, Wind, Frost, Schläge, Schlaf, Berührung, Atmen* light; (*Jur*) *Diebstahl, Vergehen etc* petty

(**c**) (*ohne Schwierigkeiten, einfach*) easy; **mit dem werden wir (ein) ~es Spiel haben** he'll be no problem; **keinen ~en Stand haben** not to have an easy time (of it) (*bei, mit* with); **nichts ~er als das!** nothing (could be) easier *or* simpler

(**d**) (= *moralisch locker*) *Lebenswandel* loose; **~es Mädchen** floozy (*inf*)

🟨 ADV (**a**) (= *einfach*) easily; **es sich** (*dat*) (**bei etw**) **~ machen** not to make much of an effort (with sth); **sie hat es immer ~ gehabt (im Leben)** she's always had it easy; **man hats nicht ~** (*inf*) it's a hard life; **das ist or geht ganz ~** it's quite easy; **die Aufgabe ist ~ zu lösen** *or* **lässt sich ~ lösen** the exercise is easy to do; **~ zu beantworten/verstehen** easy to answer/understand; **~ begreifen** to understand quickly; **~ verdaulich** easily digestible; **das ist ~er gesagt als getan** that's easier said than done; **du hast ~ reden** it's all very well for you; *siehe auch* **leicht machen** *etc*

(**b**) (= *schnell, unversehens*) easily; **er wird ~ böse/ist ~ beleidigt** *etc* he is quick to get angry/take offence (*Brit*) *or* offense (*US*) *etc*; **~ zerbrechlich** very fragile; **~ verderblich** highly perishable; **man kann einen Fehler ~ übersehen** it's easy to miss a mistake; **das ist ~ möglich** that's quite possible; **~ entzündlich** *Brennstoff etc* highly (in)flammable; **entzündliche Haut** skin which easily becomes inflamed; **das**

passiert mir so ~ nicht wieder I won't let that happen again in a hurry (*inf*); **das passiert mir so ~ nicht wieder, dass ich dir Geld borge** I won't lend you money again in a hurry (*inf*)

(**c**) (= *geringfügig, nicht schwer*) *geweht* finely; *bewaffnet* not heavily; **das Haus ist ~ gebaut** the house is built of light materials; **ein zu ~ gebautes Haus/Auto** a flimsily built house/car; **~ bekleidet sein** to be scantily clad; **~ gekleidet sein** to be (dressed) in light clothes

(**d**) (= *schwach*) *regnen* not hard; **es hat ~ gefroren** there was a light frost; **~ gewürzt/gesalzen** lightly seasoned/salted; **zu ~ gewürzt/gesalzen** not seasoned/salted enough

(**e**) (= *nicht ernsthaft*) slightly

Leicht-: Leichtathlet(in) M(F) (track and field) athlete; **Leichtathletik** F (track and field) athletics *sing*; **leichtentzündlich** ADJ ATTR *siehe* **leicht; leicht fallen** VI IRREG AUX SEIN to be easy (*jdm* for sb); **Sprachen sind mir schon immer leicht gefallen** I've always found languages easy; **leichtfertig** 🟦 ADJ thoughtless; (*moralisch*) of easy virtue 🟨 ADV thoughtlessly; **~ handeln** to act without thinking; **etw ~ aufs Spiel setzen** to risk sth without giving it a thought; **Leichtgewicht** NT (*Sport, fig*) lightweight; **Weltmeister im ~** world lightweight champion; **leichtgläubig** ADJ credulous; (= *leicht zu täuschen*) gullible; **Leichtgläubigkeit** F credulity; (= *Arglosigkeit*) gullibility

Leichtheit F **-**, NO PL lightness; (= *Geringfügigkeit*) slightness; (= *Einfachheit: von Aufgabe etc*) easiness

leichthin ['laiçthin] ADV lightly

Leichtigkeit ['laiçtɪçkait] F **-**, NO PL (**a**) (= *Mühelosigkeit*) ease; **mit ~** with no trouble (at all) (**b**) (= *Unbekümmertheit*) light-heartedness

Leicht-: leichtlebig [-leːbɪç] ADJ happy-go-lucky; **leicht machen** VT (*jdm*) **etw ~** to make sth easy (for sb); **sich** (*dat*) **etw ~, sich** (*dat*) **es mit etw ~** (= *es sich bequem machen*) to make things easy for oneself with sth; (= *nicht gewissenhaft sein*) to take it easy with sth; (= *vereinfachen*) to oversimplify sth; **Leichtmetall** NT light metal; **leicht nehmen** VT IRREG **etw ~** (= *nicht ernsthaft behandeln*) to take sth lightly; (= *sich keine Sorgen machen*) not to worry about sth; **das Leben ~** not to take things too seriously; **das Leben nicht ~** to take everything too seriously

Leichtsinn M (= *unvorsichtige Haltung*) foolishness; (= *Unbesorgtheit, Sorglosigkeit*) thoughtlessness; **sträflicher ~** criminal negligence; **unverzeihlicher ~** unforgivable stupidity; **das ist (ein) ~** that's foolish *or* silly; **so ein ~!** how silly (can you get)!

leichtsinnig 🟦 ADJ foolish; (= *unüberlegt*) thoughtless 🟨 ADV *handeln, mit etw umgehen* thoughtlessly; **~ schnell fahren** to drive recklessly; **~ mit etw umgehen** to be careless with sth

Leichtsinnsfehler M careless mistake

Leicht-: leichtverdaulich ADJ ATTR *siehe* **leicht; Leichtverletzte(r)** MF DECL AS ADJ **die ~n** the slightly injured; **Leichtverwundete(r)** MF DECL AS ADJ slightly wounded soldier/man *etc*; **die ~n** the walking wounded; **Leichtwasserreaktor** M light water reactor

leid [lait] ADJ PRED (= *überdrüssig*) **jdn/etw ~ sein** to be tired of sb/sth

Leid [lait] NT **-(e)s** [-dəs], NO PL (**a**) (= *Kummer, Sorge*) sorrow, grief *no indef art*; (= *Unglück*) misfortune; (= *Böses, Schaden*) harm; **viel ~ erfahren/ertragen (müssen)** to suffer/have to suffer a great deal; **es soll dir kein ~ zugefügt werden** *or* **geschehen** no harm will come to you; **sich** (*dat*) **ein ~ antun** (*liter*) to injure oneself; **jdm sein ~ klagen** to tell sb one's troubles; **zu ~e** = **zuleide**

(**b**) **etw tut jdm ~** sb is sorry about *or* for sth; **tut mir ~!** (I'm) sorry!; **es tut mir ~, dass ich so spät gekommen bin** I'm sorry for coming so late; **es tut uns ~, Ihnen mitteilen zu müssen ...** we regret to have to inform you ...; **er/sie tut mir ~** I'm sorry for him/her, I pity him/her; **es kann einem ~ tun, wenn ...** you can't help feeling sorry when ...; **das wird dir noch ~ tun** you'll be sorry

(**c**) (*Sw*: = *Begräbnis*) funeral

(**d**) (*Sw*: = *Trauerkleidung*) mourning

leiden ['laidn] *pret* **litt** [lɪt], *ptp* **gelitten** [gə'lɪtn] 🟦 VT (**a**) (= *ertragen müssen*) to suffer; **viel zu ~ haben** to have a great deal to bear (**b**) **jdn/etw ~ können** to like sb/sth 🟨 VI to suffer (*an +dat, unter +dat* from); **die Farbe hat durch die**

grelle Sonne sehr gelitten the harsh sun hasn't done the paint any good; *siehe auch* **leidend**

Leiden ['laidn] NT **-s, - (a)** suffering; **das sind (nun mal) die Freuden und ~ des Lebens!** ah, the trials and tribulations of life! **(b)** (= *Krankheit*) illness; (= *Beschwerden*) complaint; **das ist ja eben das ~!** (*inf*) that's just the trouble

-leiden NT SUF IN CPDS complaint; **Augen-/Leberleiden** eye/liver complaint

leidend ADJ (= *kränklich*) ailing; (*inf*) *Miene* long-suffering; **~ aussehen** to look ill

Leidenschaft ['laidnʃaft] F **-, -en** passion; **etw mit ~ tun** to do sth with passionate enthusiasm; **ich koche mit großer ~** cooking is a great passion of mine

leidenschaftlich ['laidnʃaftlıç] **1** ADJ passionate **2** ADV passionately; **etw ~ gern tun** to be mad about doing sth (*inf*)

leidenschaftslos **1** ADJ dispassionate **2** ADV dispassionately

Leidens-: **leidensfähig** ADJ **wir sind nicht unbegrenzt ~** we do not have an unlimited capacity for suffering; **Leidensgefährte** M, **Leidensgefährtin** F fellow-sufferer

leider ['laidɐ] ADV unfortunately; **ich kann ~ nicht kommen** unfortunately I can't come

leidgeprüft [-gəpry:ft] ADJ sorely afflicted

leidig ['laidıç] ADJ ATTR tiresome; **wenn bloß das ~e Geld nicht wäre** if only we didn't have to worry about money

leidlich ['laitlıç] **1** ADJ reasonable **2** ADV reasonably; **wie gehts? – danke, ~!** how are you? – not too bad, thanks; **sie ist noch so ~ davongekommen** she didn't come out of it too badly

Leidtragende(r) ['laittragndə] MF DECL AS ADJ **(a)** (= *Hinterbliebener eines Verstorbenen*) **ein ~r** a bereaved man; **eine ~** a bereaved woman; **die ~n** the bereaved **(b)** (= *Benachteiligter*) **der/die ~** the one to suffer

Leidwesen ['laitve:zn] NT **zu jds ~** (much) to sb's disappointment

Leier ['laiɐ] F **-, -n** (*Mus*) lyre; (= *Drehleier*) hurdy-gurdy

Leierkasten M barrel organ

Leierkastenfrau F, **Leierkastenmann** M, *pl* **-männer** organ-grinder

Leih-: **Leiharbeit** F, NO PL subcontracted work; **Leiharbeiter(in)** M(F) subcontracted worker; **Leihauto** NT hire(d) car (*Brit*), rental (car) (*US*); **Leihbibliothek** F, **Leihbücherei** F lending library

Leihe ['laiə] F **-, -n** (= *das Verleihen*) lending; (= *das Vermieten*) hiring; (= *das Verpfänden*) pawning

leihen ['laiən], *pret* **lieh** [li:], *ptp* **geliehen** [gə'li:ən] VT to lend; *Sachen auch* to loan; (= *entleihen*) to borrow; (= *mieten, ausleihen*) to hire

Leih-: **Leihgabe** F loan; **Leihgebühr** F hire *or* rental charge; (*für Buch*) lending charge; **Leihhaus** NT pawnshop; **Leihmutter** F, *pl* **-mütter** surrogate mother; **Leihstimme** F (*Pol*) tactical vote; **Leihwagen** M hire(d) car (*Brit*), rental (car) (*US*); **leihweise** ADV on loan

Leim [laim] M **-(e)s, -e** glue; **jdm auf den ~ gehen** *or* **kriechen** (*inf*) to be taken in by sb; **aus dem ~ gehen** (*inf*) (*Sache*) to fall apart; (*Mensch*) to lose one's figure

leimen ['laimən] VT (= *zusammenkleben*) to glue (together); **jdn ~** (*inf*) to take sb for a ride (*inf*); **der Geleimte** the mug (*inf*)

Lein [lain] M **-(e)s, -e** flax

Leine ['lainə] F **-, -n** cord; (= *Tau, Zeltleine*) rope; (= *Schnur*) string; (= *Angelleine, Wäscheleine*) (*Naut*) line; (= *Hundeleine*) leash; **~n los!** cast off!

leinen ['lainən] ADJ linen; (*grob*) canvas; *Bucheinband* cloth

Leinen ['lainən] NT **-s, -** linen; (*grob, segeltuchartig*) canvas; (*als Bucheinband*) cloth

Leinenschlafsack M sheet sleeping bag

Lein-: **Leinsamen** M linseed; **Leintuch** NT, *pl* **-tücher** (*S Ger, Aus, Sw*) sheet; **Leinwand** F **-**, NO PL canvas; (*für Dias*) screen

leise ['laizə] **1** ADJ **(a)** quiet; *Stimme, Schritt, Klopfen* soft; *Radio* low; (*aus der Ferne*) faint; **auf ~n Sohlen** treading softly; **... sagte er mit ~r Stimme** ... he said in a low voice **(b)** (= *gering, schwach*) slight; *Schlaf, Regen, Berührung* light; *Wind, Wellenschlag* light, gentle; **nicht die ~ste Ahnung haben** not to have the slightest idea; **ich habe nicht die ~ste Veranlassung, ...** there isn't the slightest reason why I ... **(c)** (= *sanft, zart*) gentle; *Musik* soft

2 ADV (= *nicht laut*) quietly; **~r singen** to sing more quietly; **ein ~ geführtes Gespräch** a quiet talk; **das Radio (etwas) ~r stellen** to turn the radio down (slightly); **sprich doch ~r!** keep your voice down a bit

Leiste ['laistə] F **-, -n (a)** (= *Holzleiste etc*) strip (of wood *etc*); (= *Zierleiste*) trim; (= *Umrandung*) border; (*zur Bilderaufhängung, zur Führung von Arbeitsstücken etc*) rail; (= *Scheuerleiste*) skirting (board) (*Brit*), baseboard (*US*) **(b)** (*Anat*) groin

leisten ['laistn] VT **(a)** (= *erringen, erreichen*) to achieve; *Arbeit, Überstunden* to do; (*Maschine*) to manage; (= *ableisten*) *Wehrdienst etc* to complete; **etwas/viel/nichts ~** (*Mensch*) (= *arbeiten*) to do something/a lot/nothing; (= *vollbringen*) to achieve something/a great deal/nothing; (*Maschine*) to be quite good/very good/no good at all; (*Auto, Motor etc*) to be quite powerful/very powerful/to have no power; **der Motor des Autos leistet 150 PS** the car has a 150-hp engine; **Großartiges/Erstaunliches/Überragendes** *etc* **~** to do something really great/amazing/excellent *etc*; **gute/ganze Arbeit ~** to do a good/thorough job; **in meiner Position muss ich schon etwas ~** in my position I have to do my work and do it well; **er hat immer das Gefühl, nichts zu ~** he always has the feeling that he isn't doing a good job; **seine Arbeit ~** to do one's work well **(b)** (*in festen Verbindungen mit ~ siehe auch dort*) **jdm Hilfe ~** to give sb some help; **jdm gute Dienste ~** (*Gegenstand*) to serve sb well; (*Mensch*) to be useful to sb; **Zahlungen ~** to make payments **(c)** (= *sich erlauben*) **sich** (*dat*) **etw ~** to allow oneself sth; (= *sich gönnen*) to treat oneself to sth; (= *kaufen*) to buy sth; **sich** (*dat*) **etw ~ können** (*finanziell*) to be able to afford sth; **sich** (*dat*) **eine Frechheit/Frechheiten ~** to be cheeky (*Brit*) *or* impudent; **da hast du dir ja was (Schönes** *or* **Nettes) geleistet** (*iro*) you've really done it now; **er hat sich tolle Sachen/Streiche geleistet** he got up to the craziest things/pranks

Leisten-: **Leistenbruch** M (*Med*) hernia; **Leistengegend** F groin

Leistung ['laistʊŋ] F **-, -en (a)** (= *Geleistetes*) performance; (*großartige, gute*) (*Sociol*) achievement; (= *Ergebnis*) result(s); (= *geleistete Arbeit*) work *no pl*; **eine große ~ vollbringen** to achieve a great success; **das ist eine ~!** that's quite an achievement; **das ist keine besondere ~** that's nothing special; **nach ~ bezahlt werden** to be paid on results; **das liegt weit unter der üblichen ~** that is well below the usual standard; **die ~en sind besser geworden** the levels of performance have improved; **seine schulischen/sportlichen ~en haben nachgelassen** his school work/athletic ability has deteriorated; **eine ~ der Technik** a feat of engineering; **schwache ~!** that's not very good **(b)** (= *Leistungsfähigkeit*) capacity (*auch Comput*); (*von Motor, Energiequelle*) power; (*von Fabrik, Firma*) potential output **(c)** (*Jur*) (= *Übernahme einer Verpflichtung*) obligation; (= *Zahlung*) payment; **die ~en des Reiseveranstalters** what the travel company offers **(d)** (= *Aufwendungen: einer Versicherung, Krankenkasse, sozial*) benefit; (= *Dienstleistung*) service; (= *Zahlungsleistung*) payment

Leistungs-: **Leistungsabfall** M (*in Bezug auf Qualität*) drop in performance; (*in Bezug auf Quantität*) drop in productivity; **Leistungsdruck** M, NO PL pressure (to do well); **Leistungsfach** NT (*Sch*) special subject; **leistungsfähig** ADJ (= *konkurrenzfähig*) competitive; (= *produktiv*) efficient, productive; *Motor* powerful; *Maschine* productive; (*Fin*) solvent; *Mensch* able; *Arbeiter* efficient; *Organ, Verdauungssystem etc* functioning properly; **leistungsfördernd** **1** ADJ conducive to efficiency; (*in Schule, Universität etc*) conducive to learning; *Substanz* performance-enhancing **2** ADV to improve performance; **Leistungsgesellschaft** F meritocracy, achievement-orientated society (*pej*); **Leistungsgrenze** F upper limit; **Leistungskontrolle** F (*Sch, Univ*) assessment; (*in der Fabrik*) productivity check; **zur ~** (in order) to assess progress/check productivity; **Leistungskurs** M *advanced course in specialist subjects*

Leistungskurse are the two specialist subjects chosen by pupils in the upper classes of a Gymnasium, during the Kollegstufe. Six hours a week are devoted to each of these subjects, allowing more time for special projects and the pupils' own work. Those taking the Abitur have to write a Facharbeit – similar to a short university seminar paper – in one of the subjects. Together with examinations in both specialist subjects, this makes up a third of the overall mark for the Abitur.

In a Gesamtschule, Leistungskurse are more advanced courses
▶ ABITUR, GESAMTSCHULE, GYMNASIUM, KOLLEGSTUFE

Leistungs-: leistungsorientiert ADJ *Gesellschaft* competitive; *Lohn* performance-related; **Leistungsort** M (*Fin*) place of performance; **Leistungsprämie** F productivity bonus; **Leistungsprinzip** NT achievement principle; **Leistungsprüfung** F (*Sch*) achievement test; (*Tech*) performance test; **Leistungssport** M competitive sport; **Leistungssteigerung** F *siehe* Leistung increase in performance/achievement *etc*; **Leistungsstörungen** PL (*Jur*) defective performance; **Leistungsstufe** F (*Sch*) special subject class; **Leistungstest** M (*Sch*) achievement test; (*Tech*) performance test; **Leistungsvermögen** NT capabilities *pl*; **Leistungszulage** F, **Leistungszuschlag** M productivity bonus

Leit- ['lait-]: **Leitartikel** M leader (*Brit*), editorial; **Leitartikler** [-'arti:klɐ, -'artiklɐ] M **-s, -**, **Leitartiklerin** [-ərɪn] F **-, -nen** leader writer (*Brit*), editorial writer; **Leitbild** NT model

leiten ['laitn] VT (**a**) (= *in bestimmte Richtung lenken*) to lead; (*fig*) *Leser, Schüler etc* to guide; *Verkehr* to route; *Gas, Wasser* to conduct; (= *umleiten*) to divert; **etw an die zuständige Stelle ~** to pass sth on to the proper authority; **sich von jdm/etw ~ lassen** (*lit, fig*) to (let oneself) be guided by sb/sth; *von Vorstellung, Idee, Emotion* to be governed by sth; **das Öl wird (durch Rohre) zum Hafen geleitet** the oil is piped to the port (**b**) (= *verantwortlich sein für*) to be in charge of; *Expedition, Partei, Regierung, Bewegung, Sitzung, Duskussion, Verhandlungen* to lead; (*als Vorsitzender*) to chair; *Theater, Orchester, Theatergruppe etc* to run (**c**) (*Phys*) *Wärme, Strom, Licht* to conduct; (**etw**) **gut/schlecht ~** to be a good/bad conductor (of sth)

leitend ADJ leading; *Gedanke, Idee* central; *Stellung, Position* managerial; *Ingenieur, Beamter* in charge; (*Phys*) conductive; **nicht ~** (*Phys*) nonconductive; **~e(r) Angestellte(r)** executive; **die ~e Hand** (*fig*) the guiding hand

Leiter[1] ['laitɐ] F **-, -** (*lit, fig*) ladder; (= *Stehleiter*) steps *pl*

Leiter[2] M **-s, -** (**a**) leader; (*von Hotel, Restaurant, Geschäft*) manager; (= *Abteilungsleiter*) (*in Firma*) head; (*von Schule*) head (*esp Brit*), principal (*esp US*); (*von Orchester, Chor, Theatergruppe etc*) director; **kaufmännischer/künstlerischer ~** sales/artistic director; *siehe auch* **Leiterin** (**b**) (*Phys*) conductor

Leiterbahn F (*Comput*) strip conductor

Leiterin ['laitərɪn] F **-, -nen** leader; (*von Hotel, Restaurant*) manager; (*von Geschäft*) manageress; (= *Abteilungsleiterin*) (*in Firma*) head; (*von Schule*) head (*esp Brit*), principal (*esp US*); (*von Orchester, Chor, Theatergruppe etc*) director; **kaufmännische/künstlerische ~** sales/artistic director

Leiter-: Leiterplatte F (*Comput*) circuit board; **Leiterwagen** M handcart

Leit-: Leitfaden M (*fig*) main connecting thread *or* theme; (*Fachbuch*) introduction; (= *Gebrauchsanleitung*) manual; **leitfähig** ADJ (*Phys*) conductive; **Leithammel** M bellwether; (*fig inf*) leader; **Leitidee** F central idea; **Leitlinie** F (*im Verkehr*) broken (white) line; (*fig*) broad outline; (= *Bestimmung*) guideline; (*Math*) directrix; **Leitmotiv** NT (*Mus, Liter, fig*) leitmotif; **Leitplanke** F crash barrier; **Leitspruch** M motto

Leitung ['laitʊŋ] F **-, -en** (**a**) NO PL (= *das Leiten*) leading; (= *Regierung, Führung*) conducting; (*von Verkehr*) routing; (*von Gas, Wasser*) conducting (**b**) NO PL (*von Menschen, Organisationen*) running; (*von Partei, Regierung*) leadership; (*von Betrieb*) management; (*von Schule*) headship (*esp Brit*), principalship (*US*); **die ~ einer Sache** (*gen*) **haben** to be in charge of sth; **unter der ~ von jdm** (*Mus*) conducted by sb; **die ~ des Gesprächs hat Horst Bauer** Horst Bauer is leading the discussion (**c**) (= *die Leitenden*) leaders *pl*; (*eines Betriebes etc*)

management *sing or pl*; (*einer Schule*) head teachers *pl* (**d**) (*für Gas, Wasser, Elektrizität etc bis zum Haus*) main; (*für Gas, Wasser im Haus*) pipe; (*für Elektrizität im Haus*) wire; (*dicker*) cable; (= *Überlandleitung für Elektrizität*) line; (= *Telefonleitung*) (= *Draht*) wire; (*dicker*) cable; (= *Verbindung*) line; **eine lange ~ haben** (*hum inf*) to be slow on the uptake; **bei dir steht wohl jemand** *or* **du stehst wohl auf der ~** (*hum inf*) you're slow on the uptake

Leitungs-: Leitungsmast M (*Elec*) (electricity) pylon; **Leitungsnetz** NT (*Elec*) (electricity) grid; (*für Wasser, Gas*) mains system; (*Telec*) (telephone) network; **Leitungsrohr** NT main; (*im Haus*) (supply) pipe; **Leitungswasser** NT tap water

Leit-: Leitwährung F reserve currency; **Leitwerk** NT (*Aviat*) tail unit

Leitzins M base rate

Leitzins-: Leitzinserhöhung F increase in the base rate; **Leitzinssatz** M bank rate

Leitz-Ordner® ['laits-] M lever-arch file

Lektion [lɛk'tsio:n] F **-, -en** lesson; **jdm eine ~ erteilen** (*fig*) to teach sb a lesson

Lektor ['lɛkto:ɐ] M **-s, Lektoren** [-'to:rən], **Lektorin** [-'to:rɪn] F **-, -nen** (*Univ*) foreign language assistant; (= *Verlagslektor*) editor

Lektüre [lɛk'ty:rə] F **-, -n** (*no pl*: = *das Lesen*) reading; (= *Lesestoff*) reading matter

Vorsicht! **Lektüre** *wird nicht mit dem englischen Wort* **lecture** *übersetzt.*

Lemming ['lɛmɪŋ] M **-s, -e** lemming

Lende ['lɛndə] F **-, -n** (*Anat, Cook*) loin

Lenden-: Lendengegend F lumbar region; **Lendenschurz** M loincloth; **Lendenstück** NT piece of loin; **Lendenwirbel** M lumbar vertebra

Leninismus [leni'nɪsmʊs] M **-,** NO PL Leninism

leninistisch [leni'nɪstɪʃ] ADJ Leninist

lenken ['lɛŋkn] 🚹 VT (**a**) (= *führen, leiten*) to direct; (*fig*: = *beeinflussen*) *Sprache, Presse etc* to influence; *Kind* to guide; **staatlich gelenkte Medien** state-controlled media (**b**) (= *steuern*) *Auto, Flugzeug, Schiff etc* to steer; *Pferde* to drive; **sich leicht ~ lassen** to be easy to steer/drive (**c**) (*fig*) *Schritte, Gedanken, seine Aufmerksamkeit, Blick* to direct (*auf +acc* to); *jds Aufmerksamkeit, Blicke* to draw (*auf +acc* to); *Verdacht* to throw (*auf +acc* onto); *Gespräch* to steer; *Schicksal* to guide; **das Gespräch in eine andere Richtung ~** to steer the conversation in another direction; **die Geschicke des Landes/der Partei ~** to control the future of the country/party 🚩 VI (= *steuern*) to steer

Lenkrad NT (steering) wheel

Lenkrad- (*Aut*): **Lenkradschaltung** F column(-mounted) (gear) change (*Brit*) *or* shift (*US*); **Lenkradschloss** NT steering (wheel) lock; **Lenkradsperre** F steering wheel lock

Lenksäule F steering column

Lenkstange F (*von Fahrrad etc*) handlebars *pl*

Lenkung ['lɛŋkʊŋ] F **-, -en** (**a**) (= *das Lenken*) direction; (*fig*: = *Beeinflussung*) influencing; (= *das Steuern*) steering (**b**) (*Tech*: = *Lenkeinrichtung*) steering

Lenz [lɛnts] M **-es, -e** (*liter*: = *Frühling*) spring(time); **sie zählt 20 ~e** (*hum*) she has seen 20 summers (*liter, hum*)

Leopard [leo'part] M **-en, -en** [-dn] leopard

Leopardin [leo'pardɪn] F **-, -nen** leopardess

Lepra ['le:pra] F **-,** NO PL leprosy

lepros [le'pro:s], **leprös** [le'prø:s] ADJ leprous

Lerche ['lɛrçə] F **-, -n** lark

Lern-: lernbar ADJ learnable; **lernbehindert** [-bəhɪndɐt] ADJ with learning difficulties; **Lernbehinderte(r)** MF DECL AS ADJ child/person *etc* with learning difficulties; **Lerneifer** M eagerness to learn

lernen ['lɛrnən] 🚹 VT (**a**) (= *Fertigkeit erwerben in*) to learn; **lesen/schwimmen** *etc* **~** to learn to read/swim *etc*; **etw von/bei jdm ~** to learn sth from sb; **jdn lieben/schätzen ~** to come to love/appreciate sb; **er lernts nie** he never learns; **er wirds nie ~** he'll never learn (**b**) *Beruf* to learn; *Bäcker, Schlosser etc* to train as; **er hat zwei Jahre gelernt** he trained for two years; (*in Handwerk*) he did a two-year apprenticeship; **das will gelernt sein** it's a question of practice; **gelernt ist gelernt** (*Prov*) once you've learned something ...; *siehe auch* **gelernt**

2 VI **(a)** (= *Kenntnisse erwerben*) to learn; (= *arbeiten*) to study; (= *Schulaufgaben machen*) to do (one's) homework; **die Mutter lernte drei Stunden mit ihm** his mother spent three hours helping him with his homework; **von ihm kannst du noch (was) ~!** he could teach you a thing or two **(b)** (= *sich in der Ausbildung befinden*) to go to school; (*in Universität*) to study; (*in Beruf*) to train **3** VR **der Text/die Rolle lernt sich leicht/schwer/schnell** the text/part is easy/hard to learn/doesn't take long to learn

Lerner ['lɛrnɐ] M **-s, -**, **Lernerin** [-ərɪn] F **-, -nen** learner

Lern-: Lernmittel PL schoolbooks and equipment *pl*; **Lernmittelfreiheit** F free provision of schoolbooks and equipment; **Lernprogramm** NT (*Comput*) (*für Software*) tutorial program; (*didaktisches Programm*) learning program; **Lernprozess** M learning process; **Lernschwester** F student nurse

Les-: Lesart F (*lit, fig*) version; **lesbar 1** ADJ **(a)** (= *leserlich*) legible; (*Comput*) readable **(b)** (= *verständlich*) *Buch* readable **2** ADV **(a)** (= *leserlich*) legibly; **gut ~ angebracht** very visible **(b)** (= *verständlich*) readably

Lesbe ['lɛsbə] F **-, -n** (*inf*) lesbian

Lesbierin ['lɛsbiərɪn] F **-, -nen** lesbian

lesbisch ['lɛsbɪʃ] ADJ lesbian

Lese ['le:zə] F **-, -n** (= *Ernte*) harvest; (= *Weinart*) vintage; (= *Beerenlese*) picking

Lese-: Lesebrille F reading glasses *pl*; **Lesebuch** NT reader; **Lesegerät** NT (*Comput*) reading device, reader; **Lesekopf** M (*Comput*) read head

lesen¹ ['le:zn], *pret* **las** [la:s], *ptp* **gelesen** [gə'le:zn] **1** VTI **(a)** (*Geschriebenes*) to read (*auch Comput*); (*Eccl*) *Messe* to say; **hier/in der Zeitung steht** *or* **ist zu ~, dass ...** it says here/in the paper that ...; **die Schrift ist kaum zu ~** the writing is scarcely legible **(b)** (= *deuten*) *Gedanken* to read; **jdm (sein Schicksal) aus der Hand ~** to read sb's palm; **in den Sternen ~** to see in the stars; **aus ihren Zeilen habe ich einen Vorwurf/eine gewisse Unsicherheit gelesen** I could tell from what she had written that she was reproaching me/felt a certain amount of uncertainty; **etw in jds Augen/Miene** (*dat*) **~** to see sth in sb's eyes/from sb's manner **(c)** (*Univ*) to lecture **2** VR (*Buch, Bericht etc*) to read; **bei diesem Licht liest es sich nicht gut** this light isn't good for reading (in)

lesen² *pret* **las** [la:s], *ptp* **gelesen** [gə'le:zn] VT **(a)** (= *sammeln*) *Trauben, Beeren* to pick; (*nach der Ernte*) *Ähren* to glean **(b)** (= *verlesen*) *Erbsen, Linsen etc* to sort

lesenswert ADJ worth reading

Leser ['le:zɐ] M **-s, -**, **Leserin** [-ərɪn] F **-, -nen** reader

Leserbrief M (reader's) letter; **einen ~ an eine Zeitung schreiben** to write a letter to a newspaper; **„~e"** "letters to the editor"

Leserin F *siehe* **Leser**

Leser-: leserlich ['le:zɛlɪç] **1** ADJ legible **2** ADV legibly; **Leserschaft** ['le:zɐʃaft] F **-, -en** readership

Lese-: Lesesaal M reading room; **Lesespeicher** M (*Comput*) read-only memory, ROM; **Lesestift** M (*für Barcodes*) bar code scanner; **Lesestoff** M reading material; **ich brauche noch ~** I need something to read; **Lesezeichen** NT bookmark(er)

Lesung ['le:zʊŋ] F **-, -en** (= *Dichterlesung*) (*Parl*) reading; (*Eccl auch*) lesson

Lethargie [letar'gi:] F **-, -n** [-'gi:ən] (*Med, fig*) lethargy

Lette ['lɛtə] M **-n, -n**, **Lettin** ['lɛtɪn] F **-, -nen** Lett, Latvian

lettisch ['lɛtɪʃ] ADJ Lettish, Latvian

Lettland ['lɛtlant] NT **-s** Latvia

Letzt [lɛtst] F **zu guter ~** in the end

letztemal ADV *siehe* **letzte(r, s)**

letztendlich ['lɛtst'ɛntlɪç] ADV at (long) last; (= *letzten Endes*) at the end of the day

letztens ['lɛtstns] ADV recently; **erst ~, ~ erst** only recently

Letzte(r) ['lɛtstə] MF DECL AS ADJ **der ~ seines Stammes** the last of his line; **der ~ des Monats** the last (day) of the month; **der/ die ~ in der Klasse sein** to be at the bottom of the class; **~(r) werden** to be last; **als ~(r) (an)kommen/(weg)gehen/fertig sein** to be the last to arrive/leave/finish; **er wäre der ~, dem ich ...**

he would be the last person I'd ...; **den ~n beißen die Hunde** (*Prov*) (the) devil take the hindmost (*prov*)

letzte(r, s) ['lɛtstə] ADJ **(a)** (*örtlich, zeitlich*) last; (= *endgültig, allerletzte*) final, last; (= *restlich*) last (remaining); **auf dem ~n Platz** *or* **an ~r Stelle liegen** to be (lying) last; **mein ~s Geld** the last of my money; **das ~ Mal** (the) last time; **zum ~n Mal** (for) the last time; **in ~r Zeit** recently; **jdm die ~ Ehre erweisen, jdm das ~ Geleit geben** to pay one's last respects to sb; **der ~ Wille** the last will and testament **(b)** (= *neueste*) *Mode, Nachricht, Neuigkeit etc* latest **(c)** (= *schlechtester*) most terrible; **das ist der ~ Schund** *or* **Dreck** that's absolute trash; **er ist der ~ Mensch** (*inf*) he's a terrible person; **jdn wie den ~n Dreck/Sklaven** *etc* **behandeln** to treat sb like dirt/a slave *etc*

letztere(r, s) ['lɛtstərə] ADJ the latter

Letzte(s) ['lɛtstə] NT DECL AS ADJ **(a)** (= *Äußerste*) last thing; **sein ~s (her)geben** to give one's all; **das ist ja das ~!** (*inf*) that really is the limit **(b)** **zum Dritten und zum ~n** (*bei Auktion*) for the (third and) last time of asking; **bis aufs ~** completely, totally; **bis ins ~** (right) down to the last detail; **bis zum ~n** to the utmost; **am** *or* **zum ~n** last; **fürs ~** lastly

Letzt-: letztlich ['lɛtstlɪç] ADV in the end; **das ist ~ egal** it comes down to the same thing in the end; **letztmals** ['lɛtstma:ls] ADV for the last time; **letztmöglich** ADJ ATTR last possible; **Letztnummernspeicher** M last number redial

Leucht-: Leuchtanzeige F illuminated display; **Leuchtdiode** F light-emitting diode; **Leuchtdiodenanzeige** F LED display

Leuchte ['lɔʏçtə] F **-, -n** (= *Leuchtkörper*) light; (*inf: Mensch*) genius

leuchten ['lɔʏçtn] VI **(a)** (*Licht*) to shine; (*Flammen, Feuer, Lava, Zifferblatt*) to glow; (= *aufleuchten*) to flash **(b)** (*Mensch*) **mit einer Lampe in/auf etw** (*acc*) **~** to shine a lamp into/onto sth; **musst du mir direkt in die Augen ~?** do you have to shine that thing straight into my eyes?; **kannst du (mir) nicht mal ~?** can you shine the lamp *or* (*mit Taschenlampe*) the torch (*Brit*) *or* flashlight (for me)?

leuchtend 1 ADJ (*lit, fig*) shining; *Farbe* bright; **etw in den ~sten Farben schildern/preisen** to paint sth/speak of sth in glowing colours (*Brit*) *or* colors (*US*); **ein ~es Vorbild** a shining example **2** ADV *rot, gelb* bright; **der Nachthimmel war ~ hell** the night sky was brightly lit

Leuchter ['lɔʏçtɐ] M **-s, -** (= *Kerzenleuchter*) candlestick; (= *Armleuchter*) candelabra; (= *Kronleuchter*) chandelier; (= *Wandleuchter*) sconce

Leucht-: Leuchtfarbe F fluorescent colour (*Brit*) *or* color (*US*); (= *Anstrichfarbe*) fluorescent paint; **Leuchtfeuer** NT navigational light; **Leuchtkugel** F flare; **Leuchtpistole** F flare pistol; **Leuchtrakete** F signal rocket; **Leuchtreklame** F neon sign; **Leuchtschrift** F neon writing; **eine ~** a neon sign; **Leuchtstift** M highlighter; **Leuchtturm** M lighthouse

leugnen ['lɔʏgnən] **1** VT to deny; **~, etw getan zu haben** to deny having done sth; **es ist nicht zu ~, dass ...** it cannot be denied that ...; **der Angeklagte leugnete die Tat** the defendant denied the offence (*Brit*) *or* offense (*US*); (*vor Gericht*) the defendant pleaded not guilty **2** VI to deny everything

Leukämie [lɔʏkɛ'mi:] F **-, -n** [-'mi:ən] leukaemia (*Brit*), leukemia (*US*)

Leukoplast® [lɔʏko'plast] NT **-(e)s, -e** Elastoplast® (*Brit*), Bandaid® (*US*)

Leumund ['lɔʏmʊnt] M **-(e)s** [-dəs], NO PL reputation, name

Leumundszeugnis NT character reference

Leute ['lɔʏtə] PL **(a)** people *pl*; **alle ~** everybody; **vor allen ~n** in front of everybody; **kleine ~** (*fig*) ordinary people; **was sollen denn die ~ davon denken?** what will people think?; **kommt, ~!** come on folks; **es ist nicht wie bei armen ~n** (*hum inf*) we're not on the breadline yet (*hum inf*); **ich kenne meine ~!** (*inf*) I know them/him *etc*; **etw unter die ~ bringen** (*inf*) *Gerücht, Geschichte* to spread sth around; *Geld* to spend sth; **unter die ~ kommen** (*inf*) (*Mensch*) to meet people **(b)** (= *Mannschaft, Arbeiter etc*) **der Offizier ließ seine ~ antreten** the officer ordered his men to fall in; **dafür brauchen wir mehr ~** we need more people *or* (*Personal*) staff for that

Leutnant ['lɔʏtnant] M **-s, -s** *or* **-e** (second) lieutenant; (*bei der Luftwaffe*) pilot officer (*Brit*), second lieutenant (*US*); **~ zur See**

sublieutenant (*Brit*), lieutenant junior grade (*US*); **jawohl, Herr ~!** yes, sir; (*Naut*) aye aye, sir

Leviten [le'vi:tn] PL **jdm die ~ lesen** (*inf*) to haul sb over the coals

Lexikograf [lɛksiko'graːf] M **-en, -en, Lexikografin** [-'graːfɪn] F **-, -nen** lexicographer

lexikografisch [lɛksiko'graːfɪʃ] **1** ADJ lexicographic(al) **2** ADV lexicographically

Lexikon ['lɛksikɔn] NT **-s, Lexika** [-ka] encyclopedia; (= *Wörterbuch*) dictionary, lexicon

lfd. ABBR *von* **laufend**

Liane ['liaːnə] F **-, -n** liana

Libanese [liba'neːzə] M **-n, -n, Libanesin** [-'neːzɪn] F **-, -nen** Lebanese

libanesisch [liba'neːzɪʃ] ADJ Lebanese

Libanon ['liːbanɔn] M **-(s) der** ~ (*Land*) the Lebanon; (*Gebirge*) the Lebanon Mountains *pl*

Libelle [li'bɛlə] F **-, -n** (*Zool*) dragonfly; (*in Wasserwaage*) spirit level

liberal [libe'raːl] **1** ADJ liberal **2** ADV liberally; ~ **eingestellt sein** to be liberal

Liberale(r) [libe'raːlə] MF DECL AS ADJ (*Pol*) Liberal

liberalisieren [liberali'ziːrən], *ptp* **liberalisiert** VT to liberalize

Libero ['liːbero] M **-s, -s** (*Ftbl*) sweeper

Libretto [li'brɛto] NT **-s, -s** *or* **Libretti** [-ti] libretto

Libyen ['liːbyən] NT **-s** Libya

Libyer ['liːbyɐ] M **-s, -, Libyerin** [-ərɪn] F **-, -nen** Libyan

libysch ['liːbyʃ] **1** ADJ Libyan

licht [lɪçt] ADJ **(a)** (= *hell*) light; **einen ~en Augenblick** *or* **Moment haben** to have a lucid moment **(b)** *Wald, Haar* sparse; **eine ~e Stelle im Wald** a sparsely-wooded spot in the forest **(c)** (*Tech*) **~e Höhe** headroom; **~e Weite** (internal) width; **~er Durchmesser** internal diameter

Licht [lɪçt] NT **-(e)s, -er** *or* (*rare*) **-e (a)** NO PL light; **~ machen** (= *anschalten*) to switch *or* put on a light; (= *anzünden*) to light a candle/lantern *etc*; **ich möchte es noch bei ~ fertig bekommen** I'd like to get it finished while it's still light; **in der ganzen Stadt fiel das ~ aus** all the lights in the town went out; **hier gehen bald die ~er aus** (*fig*) we're about to hit troubled waters; **etw gegen das ~ halten** to hold sth up to the light; **gegen das ~ fotografieren** to take a photograph into the light; **bei ~e besehen** *or* **betrachtet** (*lit*) in the daylight; (*fig*) in the cold light of day; **~ und Schatten** light and shade (*auch Art*); **wo ~ ist, ist auch Schatten** (*Prov*) there's no joy without sorrow (*prov*); **das ~ der Welt erblicken** (*geh*) to (first) see the light of day; **das ~ scheuen** (*lit*) to shun the light (of day); **~ am Ende des Tunnels sehen** (*fig*) to see a light at the end of the tunnel

(b) (*fig*) light; (= *Könner*) genius; **~ in eine (dunkle) Sache bringen** to shed some light on a matter; **im ~ unserer Erfahrungen** in the light of our experiences; **etw ans ~ bringen/zerren** to bring/drag sth out into the open; **ans ~ kommen** to come to light; **jdn hinters ~ führen** to pull the wool over sb's eyes; **mir geht ein ~ auf(, warum ...)** now I see (why ...); **ein schiefes/schlechtes** *or* **kein gutes ~ auf jdn/etw werfen** to show sb/sth in the wrong/a bad light; **das wirft ein bezeichnendes ~ auf seinen Charakter** that shows him for what he really is; **etw ins rechte ~ rücken** *or* **setzen** to show sth in a favourable (*Brit*) *or* favorable (*US*) light; (= *richtig stellen*) to show sth in its true light

(c) (= *~quelle*) light; (= *Kerze*) candle; **die ~er der Großstadt** the bright lights of the big city

Licht-: lichtbeständig ADJ lightproof; *Farben, Stoff* non-fade; **Lichtbild** NT (= *Dia*) slide; (*form*: = *Foto*) photograph; **Lichtbildervortrag** M illustrated lecture; **Lichtblick** M (*fig*) ray of hope; **Lichtbündel** NT pencil (of rays); **lichtdurchlässig** ADJ pervious to light; *Stoff* that lets the light through; **lichtecht** ADJ non-fade; **Lichtechtheit** F non-fade properties *pl*; **Lichteffekt** M lighting effect; **Lichteinfall** M incidence of light; **Lichteinwirkung** F action of light; **lichtempfindlich** ADJ sensitive to light; **Lichtempfindlichkeit** F sensitivity to light; (*Phot*) film speed

lichten¹ ['lɪçtn] **1** VT *Wald* to thin (out) **2** VR (*Reihen, Wald, Dickicht, Haare*) to thin (out); (*Nebel, Wolken, Dunkel*) to lift; (*Bestände*) to go down

lichten² VT *Anker* to weigh

Lichter-: Lichterkette F (*an Weihnachtsbaum*) fairy lights *pl*; (*von Menschen*) *long line of demonstrators carrying lights*; **lichterloh** ['lɪçtɐ'loː] ADV **~ brennen** (*lit*) to be ablaze; (*fig: Herz*) to be aflame

Licht-: Lichtgeschwindigkeit F the speed of light; **Lichtgestalt** F (*fig*) shining light; **Lichtgriffel** M (*Comput*) light pen; **Lichthupe** F (*Aut*) flash (of the headlights); **jdn durch ~ warnen** to warn sb by flashing one's lights; **Lichtjahr** NT light year; **~e entfernt sein** (*fig*) to be light years away (*von* from); **jdm um ~e voraus sein** to be light years ahead of sb; **lichtlos** ADJ dark; **ein ~es Zimmer** a room which doesn't get any light; **Lichtmangel** M lack of light; **Lichtmaschine** F (*für Gleichstrom*) dynamo; (*für Drehstrom*) alternator; **Lichtquelle** F source of light; **Lichtschacht** M air shaft; **Lichtschalter** M light switch; **Lichtschein** M gleam of light; **lichtscheu** ADJ averse to light; (*fig*) *Gesindel* shady; **Lichtschranke** F photoelectric barrier

Lichtschutz-: Lichtschutzfaktor M protection factor; **Lichtschutzfilter** M light filter

Licht-: Lichtsignal NT light signal; **Lichtstärke** F (*Opt*) luminous intensity; (*Phot*) speed; **Lichtstift** M (*Comput*) light pen; **Lichtstrahl** M ray of light; (*fig*) ray of sunshine; **lichtundurchlässig** ADJ opaque

Lichtung ['lɪçtʊŋ] F **-, -en** clearing

Licht-: Lichtverhältnisse PL lighting conditions *pl*; **Lichtverschmutzung** F light pollution

Lid [liːt] NT **-(e)s, -er** [-də] eyelid

Lid-: Lidschatten M eye shadow; **Lidschlag** M blink; **Lidstrich** M eyeliner

lieb [liːp] **1** ADJ **(a)** (= *liebenswürdig, hilfsbereit*) kind; (= *nett, reizend*) nice; (= *niedlich*) *Kerl(chen), Ding* sweet; (= *artig*) *Kind, Schulklasse* good; **(es sendet dir) (viele) ~e Grüße deine Silvia** love Silvia; **~e Grüße an deine Eltern** give my best wishes to your parents; **würdest du (bitte) so ~ sein und das Fenster aufmachen** *or* **das Fenster aufzumachen?, sei bitte so ~ und mache das Fenster auf** would you do me a favour (*Brit*) *or* favor (*US*) and open the window?; **bei jdm ~ Kind sein** (*pej*) to be sb's pet; **sich bei jdm ~ Kind machen** (*pej*) to suck up to sb (*inf*)

(b) *Gast, Besuch* (= *angenehm*) pleasant; (= *willkommen*) welcome

(c) (= *angenehm*) **etw ist jdm ~** sb likes sth; **es wäre mir ~, wenn ...** I'd like it if ...; **es ist mir ~, dass ...** I'm glad that ...; **es wäre ihm ~er** he would prefer it; *siehe auch* **lieber, liebste(r, s)**

(d) (= *geliebt, geschätzt*) dear, beloved (*iro, form*); (*in Briefanrede*) dear; **~e Monika, das geht doch nicht** (my) dear Monika, that's just not on; **der ~e Gott** the Good Lord; **~er Gott** (*Anrede*) dear God *or* Lord; **(mein) Liebes** (my) love; **er ist mir ~ und wert** *or* **teuer** he's very dear to me; **~ geworden** well-loved; *Klischee* much-loved; **eine mir ~ gewordene Gewohnheit** a habit of which I've grown very fond; **den ~en langen Tag** (*inf*) the whole livelong day; **das ~e Geld!** the money, the money!; **(ach) du ~er Himmel/~er Gott/~e Güte/ ~e Zeit/~es Lieschen** *or* **Lottchen/~es bisschen** (*inf*) good heavens *or* Lord!

(e) **~ste(r, s)** favourite (*Brit*), favorite (*US*); **sie ist mir die Liebste von allen** she is my favo(u)rite

2 ADV **(a)** (= *liebenswürdig*) danken, grüßen sweetly, nicely; **jdm ~ schreiben** to write a sweet letter to sb; **sich ~ um jdn kümmern** to be very kind to sb; **er hat mir wirklich ~ geholfen** it was really sweet the way he helped me; **jdn ~ behalten** to stay fond of sb

(b) (= *artig*) nicely; **geh jetzt ~ nach Hause** be a sweetie, go home

liebäugeln ['liːpɔygln] VI INSEP **mit etw ~** to have one's eye on sth; **mit einem neuen Auto ~** to be toying with the idea of getting a new car; **mit dem Gedanken ~, etw zu tun** to be toying with the idea of doing sth

Liebe ['liːbə] F **-, -n (a)** love (*zu jdm, für jdn* for *or* of sb, *zu etw* of sth); **die große ~** the real thing (*inf*); **Heirat aus ~** love match; **etw mit viel ~ tun** to do sth with loving care; **bei aller ~** with the best will in the world; **in ~** with love; **~ macht blind** (*Prov*) love is blind (*Prov*); **wo die ~ hinfällt!** love is a funny thing

(b) (= *Sex*) sex; **eine Nacht der ~** a night of love; **sie/er ist gut in der ~** (*inf*) she/he is good at making love

(c) (*inf*: = *Gefälligkeit*) favour (*Brit*), favor (*US*)

(d) (= *Geliebte(r)*) love, darling; **sie ist eine alte ~ von mir** she is an old flame of mine

Liebelei [liːbəˈlai] F **-, -en** (*inf*) flirtation, affair

lieben [ˈliːbn] ▯ VT to love; (*als Liebesakt*) to make love (*jdn* to sb); **etw nicht ~** not to like sth; **das liebe ich (gerade)!** marvellous (*Brit*) *or* marvelous (*US*), isn't it? (*iro*); **sich** *or* **einander ~** to love one another *or* each other; (*euph*) to make love; *siehe auch* **geliebt** ▯ VI to love; **etw ~d gern tun** to love to do sth

lieben lernen VT to come to love

liebenswert ADJ lovable

liebenswürdig ▯ ADJ kind; (= *liebenswert*) charming ▯ ADV kindly

liebenswürdigerweise [ˈliːbnsvʏrdɪɡəˈvaizə] ADV kindly

Liebenswürdigkeit F **-, -en (a)** (= *Höflichkeit*) politeness; (= *Freundlichkeit*) kindness; **würden Sie die ~ haben, das zu tun** *or* **und das tun?** (*form*) would you be kind enough to do that? **(b)** (*iro*: = *giftige Bemerkung*) charming remark (*iro*)

lieber [ˈliːbɐ] ▯ ADJ COMP *von* **lieb**
▯ ADV COMP *von* **gern (a)** (= *vorzugsweise*) rather, sooner; **das tue ich ~** (*im Augenblick*) I would *or* I'd rather do that; (*grundsätzlich auch*) I prefer doing that; **ich trinke ~ Wein als Bier** I prefer wine to beer; **(das möchte ich) ~ nicht!** I would *or* I'd rather not
(b) (= *besser, vernünftigerweise*) better; **bleibe ~ im Bett** you had *or* you'd better stay in bed; **ich hätte ~ nachgeben sollen** I would have done better *or* I'd have done better to have given in; **sollen wir gehen? – ~ nicht!** should we go? – better not; **nichts ~ als das** there's nothing I'd rather do/have *etc*

Liebe(r) [ˈliːbə] MF DECL AS ADJ dear; **meine ~n** my dears

Liebes- IN CPDS love; **Liebesabenteuer** NT amorous adventure; **Liebesbeziehung** F (sexual) relationship; **Liebesbrief** M love letter; **Liebesdienst** M labour (*Brit*) *or* labor (*US*) of love; (*fig*: = *Gefallen*) favour (*Brit*), favor (*US*); **Liebesentzug** M, NO PL withdrawal of affection; **Liebeserklärung** F declaration of love; **jdm eine ~ machen** to declare one's love to sb; **Liebesfilm** M love film; **Liebesgeschichte** F **(a)** (*Liter*) love story **(b)** (*inf*: = *Liebschaft*) love affair; **Liebesheirat** F love match; **Liebeskummer** M lovesickness; **~ haben** to be lovesick; **vor ~ konnte sie nicht mehr essen** she was so lovesick that she couldn't eat; **Liebesleben** NT love life; **Liebesmüh** F **das ist vergebliche** *or* **verlorene ~** that is futile; **Liebespaar** NT lovers *pl*; **Liebesroman** M romantic novel; **Liebesschatulle** F (*hum sl*: = *Vagina*) love hole (*sl*); **Liebestöter** [-tøːtɐ] PL (*hum*) passion killers *pl* (*esp Brit hum*)

liebevoll ▯ ADJ loving; *Umarmung* affectionate ▯ ADV lovingly; *umarmen* affectionately; **er wurde von allen ihn ~ Blacky** he was affectionately known to all as Blacky

lieb-: **lieb gewinnen** VT IRREG to grow fond of; **liebgeworden** ADJ ATTR *siehe* **lieb**; **lieb haben** VT IRREG to love; (*weniger stark*) to be (very) fond of

Liebhaber [-haːbɐ] M **-s, -**, **Liebhaberin** [-ərɪn] F **-, -nen (a)** lover **(b)** (= *Interessent, Freund*) enthusiast; (= *Sammler*) collector; **ein ~ von etw** a lover of sth; **das ist nur etwas für ~** it's an acquired taste; **das ist ein Wein/Auto für ~** that is a wine/car for connoisseurs

Liebhaberei [-haːbəˈrai] F **-, -en** (*fig*: = *Steckenpferd, Hobby*) hobby; **etw aus ~ tun** to do sth as a hobby

Liebhaberwert M collector's value

lieblich [ˈliːplɪç] ▯ ADJ lovely, delightful; *Duft, Geschmack, Wein* sweet ▯ ADV *singen* delightfully; **~ klingen** to sound delightful; **~ aussehen** to look lovely; **~ duften/schmecken** to smell/taste sweet

Liebling [ˈliːplɪŋ] M **-s, -e** darling; (= *bevorzugter Mensch*) favourite (*Brit*), favorite (*US*)

Lieblings- IN CPDS favourite (*Brit*), favorite (*US*); **mein ~gericht** my favo(u)rite meal

lieb-: **lieblos** ▯ ADJ *Ehemann, Eltern* unloving; *Bemerkung, Behandlung* unkind; *Benehmen* inconsiderate ▯ ADV unkindly; (= *ohne Sorgfalt*) carelessly; **~ gekocht/zubereitet** *etc* cooked/prepared *etc* any old way (*inf*); **Lieblosigkeit** F **-, -en (a)** NO PL (= *liebloser Charakter*) (*von Ehemann, Eltern*) unloving nature; (*von Bemerkung, Behandlung*) unkindness; (*von Benehmen*) inconsiderateness **(b)** (*Äußerung*) unkind remark; (*Tat*) unkind act; **Liebschaft** [ˈliːpʃaft] F **-, -en** affair

liebsten [ˈliːpstn] ADV **am ~** *siehe* **liebste(r, s)**

Liebste(r) [ˈliːpstə] MF DECL AS ADJ sweetheart

liebste(r, s) [ˈliːpstə] ▯ ADJ SUPERL *von* **lieb** ▯ ADV SUPERL *von* **gern**; **am ~n** best; **am ~n hätte ich ...** what I'd like most would be (to have) ...; **am ~n lese ich Kriminalromane/esse ich scharfe Speisen/gehe ich ins Kino** best of all I like detective novels/spicy food/going to the cinema; **am ~n hätte ich ihm eine geklebt!** (*inf*) I could have belted him (*inf*); **das würde ich am ~n tun** that's what I'd like to do best

Liechtenstein [ˈlɪçtnʃtain] NT **-s** Liechtenstein

liechtensteinisch [ˈlɪçtnʃtainɪʃ] ADJ Liechtenstein

Lied [liːt] NT **-(e)s, -er** [-dɐ] song; (= *Kirchenlied*) hymn; (= *Weihnachtslied*) carol; (*Mus*) lied (*spec*); **das Ende vom ~** (*fig inf*) the upshot (of all this); **das ist dann immer das Ende vom ~** it always ends like that; **es ist immer dasselbe** *or* **das alte** *or* **gleiche ~** (*inf*) it's always the same old story (*inf*); **davon kann ich ein ~ singen, davon weiß ich ein ~ zu singen** I could tell you a thing or two about that (*inf*)

Lieder-: **Liederabend** M evening of songs; (*von Sänger*) song recital; **Liederbuch** NT *siehe* **Lied** songbook; hymn book; book of carols

liederlich [ˈliːdɐlɪç] ▯ ADJ (= *schlampig*) slovenly *attr, pred*; (= *unmoralisch*) *Leben, Mann* dissolute; *Frau, Mädchen* loose ▯ ADV (= *schlampig*) sloppily; (= *unmoralisch*) dissolutely

Liedermacher(in) M(F) singer-songwriter

lief PRET *von* **laufen**

Lieferant [liːfəˈrant] M **-en, -en**, **Lieferantin** [-ˈrantɪn] F **-, -nen** supplier; (= *Auslieferer*) deliveryman/-woman

Lieferantenkredit M supplier's credit

Liefer-: **lieferbar** ADJ (= *vorrätig*) available; (= *zustellbar*) deliverable (*rare*); **die Ware ist sofort ~** the article can be supplied/delivered at once; **Lieferbedingungen** PL terms *pl* of supply *or* (*für Zustellung*) delivery; **Lieferfirma** F supplier; (= *Zusteller*) delivery firm; **Lieferfrist** F delivery period; **die ~ einhalten** to meet the delivery date

liefern [ˈliːfɐn] ▯ VT **(a)** *Waren* to supply; (= *zustellen*) to deliver (*an* +*acc* to); **jdm etw ~** to supply sb with sth/deliver sth to sb
(b) (= *zur Verfügung stellen*) to supply; *Beweise, Gesprächsstoff, Informationen, Sensationen* to provide; *Ertrag* to yield; (= *hervorbringen*) *Ergebnis* to produce; (*inf*: = *stellen*) to provide; **jdm eine Schlacht/ein Wortgefecht ~** to do battle/verbal battle with sb; **sie lieferten sich eine regelrechte Schlacht** they had a real battle; (*Sport*) they put up a real fight; **jdm einen Vorwand ~** to give sb an excuse; *siehe auch* **geliefert**
▯ VI to supply; (= *zustellen*) to deliver; **wir ~ nicht ins Ausland/nach Frankreich** we don't supply the foreign market/(to) France

Liefer-: **Lieferort** M place *or* point of delivery; **Lieferschein** M delivery note; **Liefertermin** M delivery date

Lieferung [ˈliːfərʊŋ] F **-, -en** (= *Versand, Versandgut*) delivery; (= *Versorgung*) supply; **bei ~ zu bezahlen** payable on delivery; **Zahlung bis 14 Tage nach ~** account payable within 14 days of delivery

Lieferungs-: **Lieferungsort** M place *or* point of delivery; **Lieferungsverzug** M delay in delivery

Liefer-: **Liefervertrag** M contract of sale; **ein ~ über 5.000 Autos** a contract to supply *or* (*für Zustellung*) deliver 5,000 cars; **Lieferverzug** M delay in delivery; **Lieferwagen** M delivery van *or* truck (*US*); (*offen*) pick-up; **Lieferzeit** F delivery period, lead time (*Comm*)

Liege [ˈliːɡə] F **-, -n** couch; (= *Campingliege*) camp bed (*Brit*), cot (*US*); (*für Garten*) lounger (*Brit*), lounge chair (*US*)

---

liegen [ˈliːɡn]

pret **lag** [laːɡ], *ptp* **gelegen** [ɡəˈleːɡn] AUX HABEN *or* (*S Ger*) SEIN

INTRANSITIVES VERB

siehe auch **liegen bleiben, liegen lassen, gelegen**.

(a) (= *flach liegen: Mensch*) to lie; (*inf*: = *krank sein*) to be laid up (*inf*); **ich liege lieber hart** I prefer (to sleep on) a hard mattress; **in diesem Bett liegt es sich** or **liegt man hart/weich** this bed is hard/soft; **im Bett/Krankenhaus liegen** to be in bed/hospital; **das lange Liegen** (*von Patient etc*) being in bed a long time; **in diesem Grab liegen meine Eltern** my parents are in this grave; **auf welchem Friedhof liegt dein Vater?** which cemetery is your father buried in?

(b) (= *flach liegen: Gegenstand*) to lie; (*Flasche etc*) to lie on its side; (*Schnee*) to lie; (*Hitze, Nebel*) to hang; **auf dem Boden haben sie teure Teppiche liegen** they have expensive carpets on the floor; **die Stadt lag in dichtem Nebel** thick fog hung over the town; **der Schnee bleibt nicht liegen** the snow isn't lying (*esp Brit*) or sticking (*US*); **der Kopf muss hoch/tief liegen** the head must be higher/lower than the rest of the body; **etw liegen lassen** to leave sth (there); **in der Kurve liegen** (*Auto*) to hold the corner; (*Rennfahrer*) to corner; **der Wagen liegt gut auf der Straße** the car holds the road well

(c) (= *sich befinden*) to be; **das Schiff liegt am Kai** the ship is (tied up) alongside the quay; **das Schiff liegt vor Anker** the ship is lying at anchor; **die Betonung liegt auf der zweiten Silbe** the stress is on the second syllable; **die Preise liegen zwischen 60 und 80 Euro** the prices are between 60 and 80 euros; **seine Fähigkeiten liegen auf einem anderen Gebiet** his abilities lie in a different direction; **so, wie die Dinge jetzt liegen** as things stand at the moment; **damit liegst du (gold)richtig** (*inf*) you're (dead (*inf*)) right there; **bei mir liegen Sie richtig (damit)** (*inf*) you've come to the right person (for that)

(d) (= *eine bestimmte Lage, einen bestimmten Rang haben*) to be; (*Haus, Stadt etc*) to be (situated or located); **verstreut liegen** to be scattered; **nach Süden/der Straße liegen** to face south/the road; **einen Ort links/rechts liegen lassen** to pass by a place; **auf den hintersten Plätzen/in Führung/an der Spitze liegen** to be at the bottom/in the lead/right out in front

(e) (= *lasten*) **auf dieser Familie scheint ein Fluch zu liegen** there seems to be a curse on this family; **die Verantwortung/Schuld dafür liegt bei ihm** the responsibility/blame for that lies with him; **die Entscheidung liegt beim Volk/bei Ihnen** the decision rests with the people/with you; **das liegt ganz bei dir** that is completely up to you

(f) (= *geeignet sein, passen*) **das liegt mir/ihm nicht** it doesn't suit me/him; (*Beruf*) it doesn't appeal to me/him; (*jds Art*) I don't/he doesn't like it; (*Mathematik etc*) I have/he has no aptitude for it; **diese Rolle liegt ihr** this part is perfect for her

(g) (*Redewendungen*)

✦**liegen an es liegt mir viel daran** (= *ist mir wichtig*) that matters a lot to me; **es liegt mir wenig/nichts daran** that doesn't matter much/at all to me; **es liegt mir viel an ihm/an meinem Beruf** he/my job is very important to me; **was liegt (dir) schon daran?** what does it matter (to you)?; **an jdm/etw liegen** (= *als Grund haben*) to be because of sb/sth; **woran liegt es?** why is that?; **das liegt daran, dass ...** that is because...; **an mir soll es nicht liegen!** I'll go along with that; **an mir soll es nicht liegen, dass** or **wenn die Sache schief geht** it won't be my fault if things go wrong

liegen bleiben VI IRREG AUX SEIN **(a)** (= *nicht aufstehen*) to remain lying (down); (**im Bett**) ~ to stay in bed; **er blieb bewusstlos auf dem Boden liegen** he lay unconscious on the floor; **bleib liegen!** don't get up!

(b) (= *vergessen werden*) to get left behind

(c) (= *nicht verkauft werden*) not to sell

(d) (= *nicht ausgeführt werden*) not to get done

(e) (= *auf einer Stelle bleiben*) to lie around; (*Schnee*) to lie (*esp Brit*), to stick (*US*)

(f) (*Auto*) to conk out (*inf*)

liegend ADV **(a)** (= *flach*) ~ **aufbewahren** to store flat; *Flasche etc* to store on its side **(b)** (= *im Liegen*) while lying down

liegen lassen *ptp* **liegen lassen** or (*rare*) **liegen gelassen** VT IRREG (= *nicht erledigen*) to leave; (= *vergessen*) to leave (behind); (= *herumliegen lassen*) to leave lying around; **sie hat alles liegen gelassen, um dem Kind zu helfen** she dropped everything to (go and) help the child

Liege-: Liegeplatz M place to lie; (*auf Schiff, in Zug etc*) berth; (= *Ankerplatz*) moorings *pl*; (*von großem Schiff*) berth; **Liegesitz** M reclining seat; (*auf Boot*) couchette; **Liegestuhl** M (*mit Holzgestell*) deck chair; (*mit Metallgestell*) lounger (*Brit*), lounge chair (*US*); **Liegestütz** [-ʃtʏts] M **-es, -e** (*Sport*) press-up

(*Brit*), push-up (*US*); **Liegewagen** M (*Rail*) couchette coach (*Brit*) or car (*esp US*)

lieh PRET *von* **leihen**

lies [liːs] IMPER SING *von* **lesen**

ließ PRET *von* **lassen**

liest [liːst] 3. PERS SING PRES *von* **lesen**

Lift [lɪft] M **-(e)s, -e** or **-s** (= *Personenlift*) lift (*Brit*), elevator (*esp US*); (= *Güterlift*) lift (*Brit*), hoist; (= *Skilift*) ski lift

liften ['lɪftn] VT to lift; **sich** (*dat*) **das Gesicht ~ lassen** to have a face-lift

Liga ['liːga] F **-, Ligen** [-gn] league

light [lait] ADJ PRED INV **(a)** light; **Limo ~** diet lemonade, low-calorie lemonade **(b)** (*iro*: = *seicht*) lightweight

Light- [lait] IN CPDS light, lite; (= *kalorienarm auch*) low-calorie, diet *attr*

Likör [li'køːɐ] M **-s, -e** liqueur

lila ['liːla] ADJ INV purple

Lilie ['liːliə] F **-, -n** lily

Liliput- ['liːliput] IN CPDS miniature; **eine ~eisenbahn** a miniature railway; **im ~format** in miniature

Liliputaner [liliputa'neːɐ] M **-s, -, Liliputanerin** [-ərɪn] F **-, -nen** midget

Limette [li'mɛtə] F **-, -n** sweet lime

Limit ['lɪmɪt] NT **-s, -s** or **-e** limit; (*Fin*) ceiling

limitieren [limi'tiːrən], *ptp* **limitiert** VT (*form*) to limit; (*Fin*) to put a ceiling on

Limo ['lɪmo, 'liːmo] F **-, -s** (*inf*) = **Limonade**

Limonade [limo'naːdə] F **-, -n** lemonade; (*in weiterem Sinn*) soft drink

Limone [li'moːnə] F **-, -n** lime

Linde ['lɪndə] F **-, -n** (= *Baum*) linden or lime (tree); (= *Holz*) limewood

Lindenblütentee M lime blossom tea

lindern ['lɪndɐn] VT to ease

Linderung ['lɪndəruŋ] F **-, -en** easing

lindgrün ADJ lime green

Lineal [line'aːl] NT **-s, -e** ruler

linear [line'aːɐ] **1** ADJ linear; **~e Abschreibung** (*Fin*) straight-line depreciation **2** ADV linearly

Linguist [lɪŋ'ɡuɪst] M **-en, -en, Linguistin** [-'ɡuɪstɪn] F **-, -nen** linguist

Linguistik [lɪŋ'ɡuɪstɪk] F **-, NO PL** linguistics *sing*

linguistisch [lɪŋ'ɡuɪstɪʃ] **1** ADJ linguistic **2** ADV linguistically; **~ interessiert** interested in linguistics

Linie ['liːniə] F **-, -n (a)** line (*auch Sport, Pol, Naut*); (= *Umriss*) (out)line; **ein Schreibblock mit ~n** a ruled (*esp Brit*) or lined notepad; **sich in einer ~ aufstellen** to line up; **auf der gleichen ~** along the same lines; **einer Sache** (*dat*) **fehlt die klare ~** there's no clear line to sth; **auf der ganzen ~** (*fig*) all along the line; **auf ~ bleiben** (*fig*) to toe the line; **sie hat ein Gesicht mit klaren/verschwommenen ~n** she has clear-cut/ill-defined features; **auf die (schlanke) ~ achten** to watch one's figure; **in erster/zweiter ~ kommen** (*fig*) to come first/second; **in erster ~ muss die Arbeitslosigkeit bekämpft werden** the fight against unemployment must come first

(b) (*Mil*) (= *Stellung*) line; (= *Formation*) rank

(c) (= *Verkehrsverbindung, -strecke*) route; (= *Buslinie, Eisenbahnlinie*) line, route; **fahren Sie mit der ~ 2** take the (number) 2; **auf einer ~ verkehren** to work a route; **die ~ Köln-Bonn** the Cologne-Bonn line

Linien-: Linienblatt NT ruled (*esp Brit*) or lined sheet (*placed under writing paper*); **Linienbus** M public service bus; **Liniendienst** M regular service; (*Aviat*) scheduled service; **Linienflug** M scheduled flight; **Linienrichter** M (*Sport*) linesman; (*Tennis*) line judge; **Linienrichterin** F (*Sport*) lineswoman; (*Tennis*) line judge; **Linienschiff** NT regular service ship; **Linienverkehr** M regular traffic; (*Aviat*) scheduled traffic

linieren [li'niːrən], *ptp* **liniert, liniieren** [lini'iːrən], *ptp* **liniiert** VT to rule (*esp Brit*) or draw lines on; **lini(i)ert** lined

link [lɪŋk] (*inf*) **1** ADJ *Typ* underhanded, double-crossing; *Masche, Tour* dirty; **ein ganz ~er Hund** (*pej*) a nasty piece of work (*pej inf*); **ein ganz ~es Ding drehen** to get up to a bit of no good (*inf*) **2** ADV **sich jdm gegenüber ~ verhalten** to mess

(*Brit*) *or* jerk (*esp US*) sb around (*inf*); **komm mir nicht so ~** stop messing (*Brit*) *or* jerking (*esp US*) me around (*inf*)

Link [lɪŋk] M **-s, -s** (*Comput*) link

Linke ['lɪŋkə] F DECL AS ADJ **(a)** (*Hand*) left hand; (*Seite*) left(-hand) side; (*Boxen*) left; **zur ~n (des Königs) saß ...** to the left (of the king) sat ... **(b)** (*Pol*) **die ~** the Left

linken ['lɪŋkn] VT (*inf*: = *hereinlegen*) to con (*inf*)

Linke(r) ['lɪŋkə] MF DECL AS ADJ (*Pol*) left-winger

linke(r, s) ['lɪŋkə] ADJ ATTR left; *Rand, Spur etc* left(-hand); (*Pol*) left-wing; **die ~ Seite** the left(-hand) side; (*von Stoff*) the wrong side; **auf der ~n Seite** on the left-hand side, on the left; **~r Hand, zur ~n Hand** on the *or* one's left; **~ Masche** (*Stricken*) purl (stitch); **eine ~ Masche stricken** to purl one; **zwei ~ Hände haben** (*inf*) to have two left hands (*inf*); **er ist heute mit dem ~n Bein** *or* **Fuß zuerst aufgestanden** (*inf*) he got out of bed on the wrong side this morning (*inf*)

links [lɪŋks] ❶ ADV **(a)** on the left; *schauen, abbiegen* (to the) left; **nach ~** (to the) left; **von ~** from the left; **~ von etw** (to the *or* on the) left of sth; **~ von jdm** to *or* on sb's left; **sich ~ halten** to keep to the left; **weiter ~** further to the left; **sich ~ einordnen** to move into the left-hand lane; **jdn ~ liegen lassen** (*fig inf*) to ignore sb; **weder ~ noch rechts schauen** (*lit*) to look neither left nor right; (*fig*) not to let oneself be distracted; **~ stehen** *or* **sein** (*Pol*) to be on the left; **mit ~** (*inf*) just like that; **das mache ich mit ~** (*inf*) I can do that with my eyes shut (*inf*)
(b) (= *verkehrt*) bügeln on the wrong side; *tragen* wrong side out; **~ stricken** to purl; **eine (Masche) ~, drei (Maschen) rechts** purl one, knit three
❷ PREP +GEN on *or* to the left of

Links-: Linksabbieger [-lapbiːɡɐ] M **-s, -, Linksabbiegerin** [-ərɪn] F **-, -nen** motorist/cyclist/car *etc* turning left; **Linksabbiegerspur** F left-hand turn-off lane; **Linksaußen** [-'lausn] M **-, -** (*Ftbl*) outside left; (*Pol*) extreme left-winger; **linksbündig** ❶ ADJ (*Typ*) ranged left ❷ ADV flush left; **Linksextremist(in)** M(F) left-wing extremist; **Linkshänder** [-hɛndɐ] M **-s, -, Linkshänderin** [-ərɪn] F **-, -nen** left-hander, left-handed person; **~ sein** to be left-handed; **linkshändig** ADJ, ADV left-handed; **Linkskurve** F left-hand bend; **linkslastig** [-lastɪç] ADJ (*lit*) *Boot* listing to the left; *Auto* down at the left; (*fig*) leaning to the left; **linksradikal** ❶ ADJ (*Pol*) radically left-wing; **die Linksradikalen** the left-wing radicals ❷ ADV **~ eingestellt sein** to be a left-wing radical; **~ klingen** to sound radically left-wing; **linksrheinisch** ADJ, ADV to *or* on the left of the Rhine; **Linksruck** M, **Linksrutsch** M (*Pol*) shift to the left; **linksseitig** [-zaitɪç] ADJ, ADV on the left(-hand) side; **~ gelähmt** paralyzed on the left side; **~ blind** blind in the left eye; **Linksverkehr** M, NO PL driving on the left *no def art*; **in Großbritannien ist ~** they drive on the left in Britain; **im ~ muss man ...** when driving on the left one must ...

Linoleum [li'noːleʊm] NT **-s**, NO PL linoleum, lino

Linolschnitt [li'noːl-] M (*Art*) linocut

Linse ['lɪnzə] F **-, -n (a)** (*Bot, Cook*) lentil **(b)** (*Opt*) lens

Lipgloss ['lɪpɡlɔs] NT **-, -** lip gloss

Lippe ['lɪpə] F **-, -n** lip; (*Bot auch*) labium; **eine (große** *or* **dicke) ~ riskieren** (*inf*) to be brazen; **das bringe ich nicht über die ~n** I can't bring myself to say it; **es wird** *or* **soll kein Wort über meine ~n kommen** not a word shall pass my lips; **er brachte kein Wort über die ~n** he couldn't say a word; **von den ~n lesen** to read lips

Lippen-: Lippenbalsam M lip balm; **Lippenbekenntnis** NT lip service; **Lippenpflegestift** M lip salve (stick) (*Brit*), chapstick®; **Lippenstift** M lipstick

liquid [li'kviːt] ADJ = **liquide**

Liquidation [likvidaˈtsi̯oːn] F **-, -en** (*form*) **(a)** (= *Auflösung*) liquidation; **in ~ treten** to go into liquidation **(b)** (= *Rechnung*) account

Liquidator [likvi'daːtoːɐ] M **-s, Liquidatoren** [-'toːrən], **Liquidatorin** [-'toːrɪn] F **-, -nen** (*Fin*) liquidator

liquide [li'kviːdə] ADJ (*Econ*) *Geld, Mittel* liquid; *Firma, Geschäftsmann* solvent; **ich bin nicht ~** (*inf*) I'm out of funds (*inf*)

liquidieren [likvi'diːrən], *ptp* **liquidiert** VT **(a)** *Geschäft* to put into liquidation; *Betrag* to charge **(b)** *Firma* to liquidate; *jdn* to eliminate

Liquidität [likvidiˈtɛːt] F **-**, NO PL (*Econ*) liquidity

lismen ['lɪsmən] VTI (*Sw*) to knit

lispeln ['lɪspln] VTI to lisp; (= *flüstern*) to whisper

Lissabon ['lɪsabɔn, lɪsaˈbɔn] NT **-s** Lisbon

List [lɪst] F **-, -en** (= *Täuschung*) cunning; (= *trickreicher Plan*) ruse; **mit ~ und Tücke** (*inf*) with a lot of coaxing

Liste ['lɪstə] F **-, -n** (= *Aufstellung*) list; (= *Wählerliste*) register; (*von Parteien*) (party) list (*of candidates under the proportional representation system*)

Listen-: Listenplatz M (*Pol*) place on the party list (*of candidates under the proportional representation system*); **Listenpreis** M list price

listig ['lɪstɪç] ❶ ADJ cunning ❷ ADV cunningly

Litauen ['liːtauən, 'lɪtauən] NT **-s** Lithuania

Litauer ['liːtauɐ, 'lɪtauɐ] M **-s, -, Litauerin** [-ərɪn] F **-, -nen** Lithuanian

litauisch ['liːtauiʃ, 'lɪtauiʃ] ADJ Lithuanian

Liter ['liːtɐ, 'lɪtɐ] M *or* NT **-s, -** litre (*Brit*), liter (*US*)

literarisch [litɐˈraːrɪʃ] ❶ ADJ literary ❷ ADV **~ gebildet/informiert sein** to be knowledgeable in literature; **~ interessiert** interested in literature

Literatur [litɐraˈtuːɐ] F **-, -en** literature

Literatur-: Literaturgeschichte F history of literature; **Literaturkritik** F literary criticism; (= *Kritikerschaft*) literary critics *pl*; **Literaturkritiker(in)** M(F) literary critic; **Literaturverzeichnis** NT bibliography; **Literaturwissenschaft** F literary studies *pl*; **vergleichende ~** comparative literature; **Literaturwissenschaftler(in)** M(F) literature specialist

Liter-: Literflasche F litre (*Brit*) *or* liter (*US*) bottle; **Litermaß** NT litre (*Brit*) *or* liter (*US*) measure; **literweise** ADV (*lit*) by the litre (*Brit*) *or* liter (*US*); (*fig*) by the gallon

Litfaßsäule ['lɪtfas-] F advertisement pillar

Lithografie [litografiː] F **-, -n** [-'fiːən] **(a)** (*Verfahren*) lithography **(b)** (*Druck*) lithograph

Litschi ['lɪtʃi] F **-, -s** lychee, litchi

litt PTP *von* **leiden**

Liturgie [litʊrˈɡiː] F **-, -n** [-'ɡiːən] liturgy

liturgisch [li'tʊrɡɪʃ] ADJ liturgical

Litze ['lɪtsə] F **-, -n** braid; (*Elec*) flex

live [laif] ADJ PRED, ADV *Rad, TV* live; **wir konnten ~ dabei sein** we were able to see everything live

Lizenz [li'tsɛnts] F **-, -en** licence (*Brit*), license (*US*); **etw in ~ herstellen** to manufacture sth under licence (*Brit*) *or* license (*US*)

Lizenz-: Lizenzausgabe F licensed edition; **Lizenzgeber(in)** M(F) licenser; (*Behörde*) licensing authority; **Lizenzgebühr** F licence (*Brit*) *or* license (*US*) fee; (*im Verlagswesen*) royalty; **Lizenzinhaber(in)** M(F) licensee; **Lizenznehmer(in)** M(F) licensee; **Lizenzspieler(in)** M(F) (*Ftbl*) professional player

Lkw M, **LKW** ['ɛlkaːveː, ɛlkaːˈveː] M **-(s), -(s)** ABBR *von* **Lastkraftwagen**

Lob [loːp] NT **-(e)s** [-bəs], NO PL praise; (= *Belobigung*) commendation; **(viel) ~ für etw bekommen** to be (highly) praised for sth; **(über jdn/etw) des ~es voll sein** (*geh*) to be full of praise for sb/sth; **den Schülern wurde für ihre hervorragenden Leistungen ein ~ erteilt** the pupils were commended for their outstanding achievements

Lobby ['lɔbi] F **-, -s** lobby

Lobbyist [lɔbiˈɪst] M **-en, -en, Lobbyistin** [-'ɪstɪn] F **-, -nen** lobbyist

loben ['loːbn] VT to praise; **sein neues Werk wurde allgemein sehr gelobt** his new work was universally acclaimed; **jdn/etw ~d erwähnen** to commend sb/sth; **das lob ich mir** that's what I like to see/hear *etc*

lobenswert ❶ ADJ laudable ❷ ADV laudably

Lobhudelei [loːphuːdəˈlai] F **-, -en** (*pej*) gushing

löblich ['løːplɪç] ADJ (*also iro*) commendable; **die ~e Ausnahme sein** to be the notable exception

Lob-: Loblied NT song of praise; **ein ~ auf jdn/etw anstimmen** *or* **singen** (*fig*) to sing sb's praises/the praises of sth; **Lobrede** F eulogy; **eine ~ auf jdn halten** (*lit*) to make a speech in sb's honour (*Brit*) *or* honor (*US*); (*fig*) to eulogize sb

Local-Bus ['loːkəlbas] M (*Comput*) local bus

Loch [lɔx] NT **-(e)s, ⸚er** ['lœçɐ] (= Öffnung, Lücke, Defizit) hole; (in Reifen) puncture; (= Luftloch) gap; (Billard) pocket; (fig inf: = elende Wohnung, Raum) dump (inf); (inf: = Kneipe) dive (inf); (inf: = Gefängnis) clink (inf); **sich** (dat) **ein ~ in den Kopf/ins Knie** etc **schlagen** to cut one's head/knee etc open; **jdm ein ~** or **Löcher in den Bauch fragen** (inf) to pester sb to death (with all one's questions) (inf); **ein ~** or **Löcher in die Luft gucken** or **starren** (inf) to gaze into thin air; **ein großes ~ in jds (Geld)beutel** (acc) or **Tasche** (acc) **reißen** (inf) to make a big hole in sb's pocket

lochen ['lɔxn] VT to punch holes/a hole in; (= perforieren) to perforate; Fahrkarte to punch

Locher ['lɔxɐ] M **-s, -** (= Gerät) punch

löcherig ['lœçərɪç] ADJ (lit, fig) full of holes

löchern ['lœçɐn] VT (inf) to pester (to death) with questions (inf)

Lochkarte F punch card

löchrig ['lœçrɪç] ADJ = **löcherig**

Lochstreifen M (punched) paper tape

Lochung ['lɔxʊŋ] F **-, -en** punching; (= Perforation) perforation

Lochzange F punch

Locke ['lɔkə] F **-, -n** (Haar) curl; **~n haben** to have curly hair

locken[1] ['lɔkn] VTR Haar to curl; **gelockt** Haar curly; Mensch curly-haired

locken[2] VT **(a)** Tier to lure; **die Henne lockte ihre Küken** the hen called to its chicks **(b)** jdn to tempt; (mit Ortsangabe) to lure; **das Angebot lockt mich sehr** I'm very tempted by the offer

lockend ADJ tempting

Locken-: Lockenkopf M curly hairstyle; (Mensch) curly-head; **Lockenstab** M (electric) curling tongs pl (Brit), (electric) curling iron (US); **Lockenwickel** M, **Lockenwickler** [-vɪklɐ] M **-s, -** (hair) curler

locker ['lɔkɐ] **1** ADJ (lit, fig) loose; Kuchen, Schaum light; (= nicht gespannt) slack; Haltung, Sitzweise, Muskulatur relaxed; (inf: = liberal, unkompliziert) laid-back (inf); **~ werden** (lit) (fig) to get loose; (Muskeln, Mensch) to loosen up; (Seil) to go slack; (Verhältnis) to become more relaxed; (Kuchen) to be light; **eine ~e Hand haben** (fig: = schnell zuschlagen) to be quick to hit out; **ein ~er Vogel** (inf) a bit of a lad (inf) **2** ADV **(a)** (= nicht stramm) loosely; etw **~ machen** to loosen sth; Seil etc to slacken sth; etw **~ lassen** to slacken sth off; Bremse to let sth off; **~ sitzen** (Ziegel, Schraube etc) to be loose; **bei ihm sitzt das Geld ~** he is free with his money; **bei ihm sitzt die Hand ziemlich ~** she's quick to lash out (inf); **bei ihm sitzt der Revolver ~** he's trigger-happy; **bei ihm sitzt das Messer ~** he'd pull a knife at the slightest excuse **(b)** (= nicht verkrampft) laufen loosely; schreiben naturally; etw **~ sehen** to be relaxed about sth; **jdn ~ machen** to relax sb; **~ sitzen** (Mensch) to relax; **~ drauf sein** (inf) to be laid-back (inf) **(c)** (= oberflächlich) kennen, bekannt sein casually **(d)** (inf: = leicht) easily; **vom Hocker** (sl) just like that (inf); **das mache ich ganz ~** I can do it just like that (inf)

locker-flockig ADJ laid-back (inf)

Lockerheit F **-, NO PL** looseness; (von Kuchen etc) lightness; (von Seil etc) slackness; (= Entspanntheit) relaxed state; **etw in aller ~ tun** to do sth in a relaxed way

locker-: lockerlassen VI SEP IRREG (inf) **nicht ~** not to let up; **lockermachen** VT SEP (inf) Geld to shell out (inf)

lockern ['lɔkɐn] **1** VT **(a)** (= locker machen) to loosen; Boden to break up; Griff to relax; Seil to slacken; (lit, fig) Zügel to slacken **(b)** (= entspannen) Arme, Beine, Muskeln to loosen up; (fig) Vorschriften, Atmosphäre to relax **2** VR to work itself loose; (Moral) to become lax; (Sport) to loosen up; (zum Warmwerden) to warm up; (Verkrampfung, Spannung) to ease off; (Atmosphäre, Beziehungen, Mensch) to become more relaxed

lockig ['lɔkɪç] ADJ Haar curly; Mensch curly-headed

Lockung ['lɔkʊŋ] F **-, -en** lure; (= Versuchung) temptation

Lockvogel M decoy (bird); (fig) decoy

Lockvogelangebot NT inducement

Loden ['loːdn] M **-s, -** loden (cloth)

Lodenmantel M loden (coat)

Löffel ['lœfl] M **-s, -** **(a)** (als Besteck) spoon; (als Maßangabe) spoonful; (von Bagger) bucket; **den ~ abgeben** (inf) to kick the bucket (inf) **(b)** (Hunt) ear; (inf: von Mensch) ear, lug (Brit

inf); **jdm ein paar hinter die ~ hauen** (inf), **jdm eins hinter die ~ geben** (inf) to give sb a clip (a)round the ear; **ein paar hinter die ~ kriegen** (inf) to get a clip (a)round the ear

Löffelbagger M excavator

löffeln ['lœfln] VT to spoon; (mit der Kelle) to ladle

Loft [lɔft] NT **-s, -s** (Build) luxury attic flat (Brit) or apartment

log[1] PRET von **lügen**

log[2] ABBR von **Logarithmus**

Log [lɔk] NT **-s, -e** [-gə] (Naut) log

Logarithmentafel F log table

Logarithmus [loga'rɪtmʊs] **-, Logarithmen** [-mən] M logarithm, log

Logbuch NT log(book)

Loge ['loːʒə] F **-, -n** **(a)** (Theat) box **(b)** (= Freimaurerloge) lodge **(c)** (= Pförtnerloge) lodge

Logik ['loːgɪk] F **-, NO PL** logic; **in der ~** in logic; **du hast vielleicht eine ~!** your logic is a bit quaint

logisch ['loːgɪʃ] **1** ADJ logical; (inf: = selbstverständlich) natural; **gehst du auch hin? – ~** are you going too? – of course **2** ADV logically; **~ denken** to think logically; **~ folgern** to come to a logical conclusion

logischerweise ['loːgɪʃɐ'vaizə] ADV logically

Logistik [lo'gɪstɪk] F **-, NO PL** **(a)** (Mil, Econ) logistics sing **(b)** (Math) logic

logistisch [lo'gɪstɪʃ] **1** ADJ logistic **2** ADV logistically

Logo ['loːgo] NT **-(s), -s** (= Firmenlogo) logo

Logopäde [logo'pɛːdə] M **-n, -n**, **Logopädin** [-'pɛːdɪn] F **-, -nen** speech therapist

Logopädie [logopɛ'diː] F **-, NO PL** speech therapy

Lohn [loːn] M **-(e)s, ⸚e** ['løːnə] **(a)** (= Arbeitsentgelt) wage(s pl), pay no pl, no indef art; **wie viel ~ bekommst du?** how much do you get (paid)?; **2% mehr ~ verlangen** to demand a 2% pay rise (Brit) or pay raise (US) **(b)** (fig) (= Belohnung/Vergeltung) reward; (= Strafe) punishment; **als** or **zum ~ für ...** as a reward/punishment for ...; **sein verdienter ~** one's just reward; **das ist nun der ~ für meine Mühe!** (iro), **das ist ein schlechter ~ für all die Mühe** that's (all) the thanks I get for my trouble

Lohn-: Lohnabbau M reduction of earnings; **lohnabhängig** ADJ Arbeiter wage-earning; Leistungen, Rente wage-linked; **Lohnabhängige(r)** MF DECL AS ADJ wage earner; **Lohnabrechnung** F wages slip (Brit), pay slip; **Lohnarbeit** F labour (Brit), labor (US); **Lohnauftrag** M etw im **~ herstellen** or **fertigen** to manufacture sth under a contracting-out agreement; **Lohnausgleich** M wage adjustment; **bei vollem ~** with full pay; **Lohnbuchhalter(in)** M(F) wages clerk (Brit), pay clerk; **Lohnbuchhaltung** F wages accounting; (= Büro) wages office (Brit), pay(roll) office; **Lohnempfänger(in)** M(F) wage earner

lohnen ['loːnən] **1** VIR to be worth it or worthwhile; **es lohnt (sich), etw zu tun** it is worth(while) doing; **die Mühe lohnt sich** it is worth the effort; **der Film lohnt sich wirklich** the film is really worth seeing; **das lohnt sich nicht für mich** it's not worth my while **2** VT **(a)** (= es wert sein) to be worth; **das Ergebnis lohnt die Mühe** the result makes all the effort worthwhile **(b)** (= danken) jdm etw **~** to reward sb for sth; **er hat mir meine Hilfe mit Undank gelohnt** he repaid my help with ingratitude

löhnen ['løːnən] VTI (inf) to shell out (inf)

lohnend ADJ rewarding; (= nutzbringend) worthwhile; (= einträglich) profitable; (= sehens-/hörenswert) worth seeing/hearing

lohnenswert ADJ worthwhile

Lohn-: Lohnerhöhung F (wage or pay) rise (Brit), (wage or pay) raise (US); **Lohnforderung** F wage demand or claim; **Lohnfortzahlung** F continued payment of wages; **Lohngefälle** NT pay differential; **Lohngruppe** F wage group; **Lohnliste** F payroll; **Lohnnebenkosten** PL additional wage costs pl (Brit) or labor costs pl (US); **Lohnpolitik** F pay policy; **Lohnrunde** F pay round

Lohnsteuer F income tax (paid on earned income)

Lohnsteuer-: Lohnsteuerjahresausgleich M annual adjustment of income tax; **beim letzten ~ habe ich 500 Euro**

zurückbekommen at the end of the last tax year I got back 500 euros; **Lohnsteuerkarte** F (income) tax card

Lohn-: Lohnstreifen M pay slip; **Lohnstückkosten** PL (*Comm*) unit wage costs *pl* (*Brit*) *or* labor costs *pl* (*US*); **Lohntüte** F pay packet

Loipe ['lɔypə] F **-, -n** cross-country ski run

Lok [lɔk] F **-, -s** ABBR *von* **Lokomotive** engine

lokal [lo'kaːl] **1** ADJ **(a)** (= *örtlich*) local; **~es Rechnernetz** (*Comput*) local area network **(b)** (*Gram*) of place **2** ADV locally; **jdn ~ betäuben** to give sb a local anaesthetic (*Brit*) *or* anesthetic (*US*); **ein ~ wirkendes Schmerzmittel** a local painkiller

Lokal [lo'kaːl] NT **-s, -e (a)** (= *Gaststätte*) pub (*esp Brit*), bar; (*esp auf dem Land*) inn (*esp Brit*), restaurant (*esp US*); (= *Restaurant*) restaurant **(b)** (= *Versammlungsraum*) meeting place

Lokale(s) [lo'kaːlə] NT DECL AS ADJ local news *sing*

lokalisieren [lokali'ziːrən], *ptp* **lokalisiert** VT **(a)** (= *Ort feststellen*) to locate **(b)** (*Med*) to localize; (*auf einen Ort*) to limit (*auf +acc* to)

Lokalität [lokali'tɛːt] F **-, -en** (= *örtliche Beschaffenheit*) locality; (= *Raum*) facilities *pl*; **sich mit den ~en auskennen** to know the district

Lokal-: Lokalkolorit NT local colour (*Brit*) *or* color (*US*); **Lokalnachrichten** PL local news *sing*; **Lokalpatriotismus** M local patriotism; **Lokalsatz** M (*Gram*) (adverbial) clause of place; **Lokalteil** M local section; **Lokaltermin** M (*Jur*) visit to the scene of the crime; **Lokalverbot** NT ban; **~ haben** to be barred from a pub (*esp Brit*) *or* bar

Lokführer(in) M(F) engine driver

Loko- ['loːko-] (*St Ex*) **: Lokogeschäft** NT spot deal; **Lokokauf** M spot purchase; **Lokokurs** M spot price; **Lokomarkt** M spot market

Lokomotive [lokomo'tiːvə, lokomi'tiːfə] F **-, -n** locomotive, (railway) engine

Loko- ['loːko-] (*St Ex*) **: Lokopreis** M spot price; **Lokowaren** PL spot commodities *pl*, spots *pl*

Lombard ['lɔmbart] M *or* NT **-(e)s, -e** [-də] (*Fin*) loan on security

Lombard-: Lombardgeschäft NT loan on security; **Lombardkredit** [-kre'diːt] M collateral loan; **Lombardsatz** M rate for loans on security

London ['lɔndɔn] NT **-s** London

Londoner ['lɔndɔnɐ] ADJ ATTR London

Look [lʊk] M **-s, -s** (*Mode*) look

Looping ['luːpɪŋ] M *or* NT **-s, -s** (*Aviat*) looping the loop; **einen ~ machen** to loop the loop

Lorbeer ['lɔrbeːɐ] M **-s, -en (a)** (*lit: Gewächs*) laurel; (*als Gewürz*) bay leaf; (= *~kranz*) laurel wreath **(b)** (*fig: = Erfolg*) **Lorbeeren** PL laurels *pl*; **sich auf seinen ~en ausruhen** (*inf*) to rest on one's laurels; **damit kannst du keine ~en ernten** that's no great achievement

Lorbeer-: Lorbeerbaum M laurel (tree); **Lorbeerblatt** NT bay leaf; **Lorbeerkranz** M laurel wreath

Lore ['loːrə] F **-, -n** (*Rail*) truck; (= *Kipplore*) tipper

Lorokonto ['loːro-] NT loro account

los [loːs] **1** ADJ PRED **(a)** (= *nicht befestigt*) loose; **der Hund ist von der Leine ~** the dog is off the leash **(b)** (= *frei*) **jdn/etw ~ sein** (*inf*) to be rid of sb/sth; **ich bin mein ganzes Geld ~** (*inf*) I'm cleaned out (*inf*) **(c)** (*inf*) **etwas ist ~/es ist nichts ~** (= *geschieht*) there's something/nothing going on; (= *nicht in/in Ordnung*) there's something/nothing wrong; **mit jdm/etw ist nichts (mehr) ~** (*inf*) sb/sth isn't up to much (any more); **was ist denn hier/da ~?** what's going on here/there (then)?; **was ist ~?** what's up?; **wo ist denn hier was ~?** where's the action here (*inf*)?; **als mein Vater das hörte, da war was ~!** when my father heard

about it all hell broke loose (*inf*) **2** ADV **(a)** (*Aufforderung*) **~!** come on!; (= *geh/lauf schon*) get going!; **nun aber ~!** let's get going; (*zu andern*) get going (*inf*); **nichts wie ~!** let's get going; **auf die Plätze *or* Achtung, fertig, ~** on your marks, get set, go!, ready, steady, go! **(b)** (= *weg*) **wir wollen früh ~** we want to leave early

Los [loːs] NT **-es, -e** [-zə] **(a)** (*für Entscheidung*) lot; (*in der Lotterie, auf Jahrmarkt etc*) ticket; **das große ~ gewinnen** *or* **ziehen** (*lit, fig*) to hit the jackpot; **etw durch das ~ entscheiden** *or* **bestimmen** *or* **ermitteln** to decide sth by drawing lots **(b)** NO PL (= *Schicksal*) lot

-los ADJ SUF -less; **vater-/mutterlos** father-/motherless; **richtungslos** without direction

lösbar ADJ soluble

los-: losbinden VT SEP IRREG to untie (*von* from); **losbrechen** SEP IRREG **1** VT to break off **2** VI AUX SEIN (*Gelächter etc*) to break out; (*Sturm, Gewitter*) to break

Lösch-: Löscharbeit F USU PL firefighting operations *pl*; **Löschblatt** NT sheet of blotting paper

löschen ['lœʃn] **1** VT **(a)** *Feuer, Brand, Flammen, Kerze* to put out; *Licht* to turn out *or* off; *Kalk* to slake; *Durst* to quench; *Schrift (an Tafel), Tonband etc* to erase; *Tafel* to wipe; *Schuld* to cancel; *Eintragung, Zeile* to delete; *Konto* to close; *Firma, Name* to strike (*Brit*) *or* cross off; *Tinte* to blot; (*Comput*) *Speicher, Bildschirm* to clear; *Festplatte* to wipe; *Daten, Information* to delete **(b)** (*Naut*) *Ladung* to unload **2** VI **(a)** (*Feuerwehr etc*) to put out a/the fire **(b)** (= *aufsaugen*) to blot **(c)** (*Naut*) to unload

Lösch-: Löschfahrzeug NT fire engine; **Löschflugzeug** NT firefighting plane; **Löschmannschaft** F team of firefighters; **Löschpapier** NT (piece of) blotting paper; **Löschschaum** M extinguishant foam; **Löschtaste** F (*Comput*) delete key

Löschung ['lœʃʊŋ] F **-, -en (a)** (*von Schuld, Hypothek*) paying off; (*von Eintragung*) deletion; (*von Konto*) closing; (*von Firma, Namen*) striking (*Brit*) *or* crossing off; (*Comput: von Daten*) deletion **(b)** (*Naut: von Ladung*) unloading

lose ['loːzə] **1** ADJ (*lit, fig*) loose; (= *nicht gespannt*) *Seil* slack; **etw ~ verkaufen** to sell sth loose **2** ADV loosely; **~ sitzen** to be loose

Lösegeld NT ransom (money)

losen ['loːzn] VI to draw lots (*um* for); **wir ~, wer ...** we'll draw lots to decide who ...

lösen ['løːzn] **1** VT **(a)** (= *losmachen, abtrennen, entfernen*) to remove (*von* from); *Knoten, Fesseln, Gürtel, Haare* to undo; *Arme* to unfold; *Hände* to unclasp; *Handbremse* to let off; *Husten, Krampf* to ease; *Muskeln* to loosen up; (*lit, fig: = lockern*) to loosen **(b)** (= *klären, Lösung finden für*) *Aufgabe, Problem* to solve; *Konflikt, Schwierigkeiten* to resolve **(c)** (= *annullieren*) *Vertrag* to cancel; *Verlobung* to break off; *Verbindung, Verhältnis* to sever; *Ehe* to dissolve **(d)** (= *zergehen lassen*) to dissolve (*auch Chem*) **(e)** (= *kaufen*) *Karte* to buy **2** VR **(a)** (= *sich losmachen*) to detach oneself (*von* from); (= *sich ablösen*) to come off (*von etw* sth); (*Knoten, Haare*) to come undone; (*Schuss*) to go off; (*Husten, Krampf, Spannung*) to ease; (*Schleim, Schmutz*) to loosen; (*Atmosphäre*) to relax; (*Muskeln*) to loosen up; (*lit, fig: = sich lockern*) to (be)come loose; (*Lawine*) to break away; **sich von jdm ~** to break away from sb (*auch Sport*); **sich von etw ~** *von Verpflichtungen* to free oneself of sth; *von Vorstellung, Vorurteilen, Gedanken* to rid oneself of sth; *von Partnern, Vaterland, Vergangenheit* to break with sth **(b)** (= *sich aufklären*) to be solved; **sich von selbst ~** to solve itself **(c)** (= *zergehen*) to dissolve (*in +dat* in) (*auch Chem*); **die Tablette löst sich gut/schlecht** the tablet dissolves easily/doesn't dissolve easily

Loser ['luːzɐ] M **-s, -** (*inf: = Verlierer*) loser

los-: losfahren VI SEP IRREG AUX SEIN (= *abfahren*) to set off; (*Fahrzeug*) to move off; (*Auto*) to drive off; **losgehen** VI SEP IRREG AUX SEIN **(a)** (= *weggehen*) to set off; (*Schuss, Bombe etc*) to go off; (**mit dem Messer) auf jdn ~** to go for sb (with a knife) **(b)** (*inf: = anfangen*) to start; (*Geschrei der Menge*) to go up; **gleich gehts los** it's just about to start; (*bei Streit*) any minute now; **jetzt gehts los!** here we go!; (*Vorstellung*) it's starting!; (*Rennen*) they're off!; **gehts bald los?** will it start soon?; (*Reise etc*) are we off soon?; **jetzt gehts aber los!** (*inf*) you're kidding! (*inf*); (*bei Frechheit*) do you mind!; **loshaben** VT SEP IRREG (*inf*) **etwas/nichts ~** to be pretty clever (*inf*)/pretty stupid (*inf*)

-losigkeit SUF **-, -en** -lessness; **Hoffnungslosigkeit** hopelessness

los-: loskaufen SEP █ VT to buy out; *Entführten* to ransom █ VR to buy oneself out (*aus* of); **loslachen** VI SEP to burst out laughing; **loslassen** VT SEP IRREG (a) (= *nicht mehr festhalten*) to let go of; (*fig*: = *nicht fesseln*) *Mensch* to let go; **der Gedanke/ die Frage** *etc* **lässt mich nicht mehr los** I can't get the thought/problem *etc* out of my mind (b) *jdn* (*auf jdn*) **~** (*fig inf*) to let sb loose (on sb); **die Hunde auf jdn ~** to put *or* set the dogs on(to) sb; **wehe, wenn sie losgelassen ...** (*hum inf*) once let them off the leash ...; **loslaufen** VI SEP IRREG AUX SEIN (= *zu laufen anfangen*) to start to run; **loslegen** VI SEP (*inf*) to get going; (*mit Schimpfen*) to let rip (*inf*)

löslich ['løːslɪç] ADJ soluble; **leicht/schwer ~** readily/not readily soluble; **~er Kaffee** instant coffee

los-: losmachen SEP █ VT (= *befreien*) to free; (= *losbinden*) to untie; *Handbremse* to let off; *jdn* **von einer Kette ~** to unchain sb █ VI (*Naut*) to cast off █ VR to get away (*von* from); **der Hund hat sich losgemacht** the dog has got loose; **losmüssen** VI SEP IRREG (*inf*) to have to go

Losnummer F ticket number

los-: losreißen VR SEP IRREG **sich (von etw) ~** (*Hund etc*) to break loose (from sth); (*fig*) to tear oneself away (from sth); **losrennen** VI SEP IRREG AUX SEIN (*inf*) to run off; (= *anfangen zu laufen*) to start to run

Löss [lœs] M **-es, -e**, **Löß** [løːs] M **-es, -e** (*Geol*) loess

los-: losschicken VT SEP to send off; **losschießen** VI SEP IRREG (= *zu schießen anfangen*) to open fire; **schieß los!** (*fig inf*) fire away! (*inf*); **losschrauben** VT SEP to unscrew; **losstürzen** VI SEP AUX SEIN to rush off; **auf jdn/etw ~** to pounce on sb/sth

Lösung ['løːzʊŋ] F **-, -en** (a) solution (+*gen* to); (= *das Lösen*) solution (+*gen* of); (*eines Konfliktes, von Schwierigkeiten*) resolving; **zur ~ dieser Schwierigkeiten** to resolve these problems (b) (= *Annullierung*) (*eines Vertrages*) cancellation; (*von Beziehungen, einer Verlobung*) breaking off; (*einer Verbindung, eines Verhältnisses*) severance; (*einer Ehe*) dissolving (c) (*Chem*) solution

Lösungsmittel NT solvent

loswerden VT SEP IRREG AUX SEIN to get rid of; *Gedanken* to get out of one's mind; *Geld* (*beim Spiel etc*), *Hab und Gut* to lose; *Geld* (= *ausgeben*) to spend

Lot [loːt] NT **-(e)s, -e** (a) (= *Senkblei*) plumb line; (*Naut*) sounding line; **im ~ sein** to be in plumb (b) (*Math*) perpendicular; **die Sache ist wieder im ~** things have been straightened out; **die Sache wieder ins (rechte) ~ bringen** to put things right

Lötapparat M soldering appliance

löten ['løːtn] VTI to solder

Lothringen ['loːtrɪŋən] NT **-s** Lorraine

lothringisch ['loːtrɪŋɪʃ] ADJ of Lorraine, Lorrainese

Lotion [loˈtsioːn] F **-, -en** lotion

Löt-: Lötkolben M soldering iron; **Lötlampe** F blowlamp; **Lötmetall** NT solder

Lotse ['loːtsə] M **-n, -n**, **Lotsin** F **-, -nen** (*Naut*) pilot; (= *Fluglotse*) air-traffic *or* flight controller; (*Aut*) navigator; (*fig*) guide

lotsen ['loːtsn] VT to guide; *Schiff auch* to pilot; **jdn irgendwohin ~** (*inf*) to drag sb somewhere (*inf*)

Lotsin F *siehe* **Lotse**

Lotterie [lɔtəˈriː] F **-, -n** [-ˈriːən] lottery; (= *Tombola*) raffle

Lotterie-: Lotteriegewinn M *siehe* **Lotterie** lottery/raffle prize *or* (*Geld*) winnings *pl*; **Lotterielos** NT *siehe* **Lotterie** lottery/raffle ticket

Lotterleben ['lɔtɐ-] NT (*inf*) dissolute life

Lotto ['lɔto] NT **-s, -s** lottery, ≈ National Lottery (*Brit*); (**im**) **~ spielen** to do (*Brit*) *or* play the lottery; **du hast wohl im ~ gewonnen** you must have won the lottery

Lotto-: Lottogeschäft NT, **Lottoladen** M (*inf*) lottery agency; **Lottogewinn** M lottery win; (*Geld*) lottery winnings *pl*;

Lottoschein M lottery coupon; **Lottozahlen** PL winning lottery numbers *pl*

Lötung ['løːtʊŋ] F **-, -en** (= *das Löten*) soldering; (= *Lötstelle*) soldered joint

Lötzinn M solder

Low-Budget- [loʊˈbadʒət] IN CPDS low-budget;

Löwe ['løːvə] M **-n, -n** lion; **der ~** (*Astron*) Leo, the Lion; (*Astrol*) Leo; **im Zeichen des ~n geboren sein** to be born under the (sign of) Leo; **~ sein** to be (a) Leo; **sich in die Höhle des ~n begeben** (*inf*) to go into the lion's den

Löwen-: Löwenanteil M (*inf*) lion's share; **Löwenmähne** F (*lit*) lion's mane; (*fig*) flowing mane; **Löwenmaul** NT, **Löwenmäulchen** [-mɔylçən] NT **-s, -** snapdragon, antirrhinum; **Löwenzahn** M dandelion

Löwin ['løːvɪn] F **-, -nen** lioness

loyal [loaˈjaːl] █ ADJ loyal █ ADV loyally; **sich jdm gegenüber ~ verhalten** to be loyal to(wards) sb

Loyalität [loajaliˈtɛːt] F **-, -en** loyalty (*jdm gegenüber* to sb)

LP [ɛlˈpeː] F **-, -s** LP

LSD [ɛlɛsˈdeː] NT **-(s)** LSD

lt. ABBR *von* laut²

Luchs [lʊks] M **-es, -e** lynx; **Augen wie ein ~ haben** (*inf*) to have eyes like a hawk

Lücke ['lʏkə] F **-, -n** (*lit, fig*) gap; (*zwischen Wörtern auch, auf Formularen etc*) space; (= *Ungereimtheit, Unvollständigkeit etc*) hole; (= *Gesetzeslücke*) loophole; (*in Versorgung*) break; **~ (im Wissen) haben** to have gaps in one's knowledge; **sein Tod hinterließ eine schmerzliche ~** (*geh*) his death has left a void in our lives

Lücken-: Lückenbüßer [-byːsɐ] M **-s, -**, **Lückenbüßerin** [-ərɪn] F **-, -nen** (*inf*) stopgap; **~ spielen** to be used as a stopgap; **lückenhaft** █ ADJ full of gaps; *Versorgung* deficient; *Gesetz, Alibi* full of holes; **sein Wissen ist sehr ~** there are great gaps in his knowledge █ ADV **sich erinnern** vaguely; *informieren, zusammenstellen* sketchily; *ausbilden, versorgen* deficiently; **lückenlos** █ ADJ complete; *Kontrolle auch, Überwachung* thorough; *Kenntnisse* perfect; (*Mil*) *Abwehr* perfect; *Aufklärung* full █ ADV completely; **Lückentest** M (*Sch*) completion test (*Brit*), fill-in-the-gaps test

lud PRET *von* laden

Luder ['luːdɐ] NT **-s, -** (*inf*) minx; **armes/dummes ~** poor/stupid creature; **so ein ordinäres ~!** what a common little hussy!

Luft [lʊft] F **-, (liter) ~e** ['lʏftə] (a) air *no pl*; **im Zimmer ist schlechte ~** it is stuffy in the room; **dicke ~** (*inf*) a bad atmosphere; **an** *or* **in die/der (frischen) ~** in the fresh air; **(frische) ~ schnappen** (*inf*) *or* **schöpfen** (*geh*) to get some fresh air; **die ~ ist rein** (*inf*) the coast is clear; **aus der ~** from the air; **die ~ ist raus** (*fig inf*) the fizz has gone; **jdn an die (frische) ~ setzen** (*inf*) to show sb the door; **in die ~ fliegen** (*inf*) to explode; **etw in die ~ jagen** (*inf*) *or* **sprengen** to blow sth up; **leicht** *or* **schnell in die ~ gehen** (*fig*) to be quick to blow one's top (*inf*); **er geht gleich in die ~** (*fig*) he's about to blow his top; **es liegt ein Gewitter in der ~** there's a storm brewing; **es liegt etwas in der ~** there's something in the air; **das kann sich doch nicht in ~ aufgelöst haben** it can't have vanished into thin air; **in der ~ hängen** (*Sache*) to be (very much) up in the air; (*Mensch*) to be left dangling; **die Behauptung ist aus der ~ gegriffen** this statement is (a) pure invention; **vor Freude in die ~ springen** to jump for joy; **von ~ und Liebe/von ~ leben** to live on love/air; **jdn wie ~ behandeln** to treat sb as though he/she just didn't exist; **er ist ~ für mich** I'm not speaking to him

(b) (= *Atem*) breath; **der Kragen schnürt mir die ~ ab** this collar is choking me; **nach ~ schnappen** to gasp for breath; **die ~ anhalten** (*lit*) to hold one's breath; **nun halt mal die ~ an!** (*inf*: = *rede nicht*) hold your tongue!; (= *übertreibe nicht*) come on! (*inf*); **keine ~ mehr kriegen** not to be able to breathe; **tief ~ holen** (*lit, fig*) to take a deep breath; **mir blieb vor Schreck/Schmerz die ~ weg** I was breathless with shock/pain

(c) (= *Wind*) breeze; **sich** (*dat*) **~ machen** (*fig*), **seinem Herzen ~ machen** (*fig*) to get everything off one's chest; **seinem Ärger/Zorn** *etc* **~ machen** to give vent to one's annoyance/anger *etc*

(d) (*fig*: = *Spielraum, Platz*) space, room

Luft-: Luftabwehr F (*Mil*) anti-aircraft defence (*Brit*) *or* defense (*US*); **Luftabwehrrakete** F anti-aircraft missile; **Luftangriff** M air raid (*auf* +*acc* on); **einen ~ auf eine Stadt fliegen** to carry out an air raid on a town; **Luftaufnahme** F aerial photo(graph); **Luftballon** M balloon; **Luftbelastung** F, NO PL atmospheric pollution; **Luftbild** NT aerial picture; **Luftblase** F air bubble; **Luftbrücke** F airlift; **über eine ~** by airlift

Lüftchen ['lʏftçən] NT **-s,** - breeze

Luft-: luftdicht ▮ ADJ airtight *no adv* ▮ ADV **die Ware ist ~ verpackt** the article is in airtight packaging; **ein ~ verschlossener Behälter** an airtight container; **Luftdruck** M, NO PL air pressure

lüften ['lʏftn] ▮ VT **(a)** *Raum, Kleidung, Bett* to air; (*ständig, systematisch*) to ventilate **(b)** (= *hochheben*) *Hut, Schleier* to raise; **das Geheimnis war gelüftet** the secret was out ▮ VI (= *Luft hereinlassen*) to let some air in

Luft-: Luftfahrt F aeronautics *sing*; (*mit Flugzeugen*) aviation *no art*; **Luftfeuchtigkeit** F (atmospheric) humidity; **Luftfilter** or M air filter; **Luftflotte** F air fleet; **Luftfracht** F air freight; **Luftfrachtbrief** M air consignment note (*Brit*); **Luftfrachtgebühren** PL air freight (charges) *pl*; **luftgekühlt** ADJ air-cooled; **luftgestützt** [-gəʃtʏtst] ADJ *Flugkörper* air-launched; **luftgetrocknet** [-gətrɔknət] ADJ air-dried; **Luftgewehr** NT air rifle, air gun

luftig ['lʊftɪç] ▮ ADJ *Zimmer* airy; *Plätzchen* breezy; *Kleidung* light ▮ ADV **~ gekleidet** lightly dressed

Luft-: Luftkampf M air battle; **Luftkissen** NT air cushion; (*von ~boot*) cushion of air; **Luftkissenboot** NT, **Luftkissenfahrzeug** NT hovercraft; **Luftkrieg** M aerial warfare; **Luftkühlung** F air-cooling; **Luftkurort** M (climatic) health resort; **Luftlandetruppe** F airborne troops *pl*; **luftleer** ADJ **(völlig) ~ sein** to be a vacuum; **~er Raum** vacuum; **etw im ~en Raum diskutieren** (*fig*) to discuss sth in a vacuum *or* in the abstract; **Luftlinie F 200 km** *etc* ~ 200 km *etc* as the crow flies; **Luftloch** NT air hole; (*Aviat*) air pocket; **Luftmatratze** F air bed (*Brit*), Lilo® (*Brit*), air mattress (*esp US*); **Luftpirat(in)** M(F) (aircraft) hijacker, skyjacker (*esp US*); **Luftpost** F airmail; **mit ~** by airmail; **Luftpumpe** F pneumatic pump; (*für Fahrrad*) (bicycle) pump; **Luftraum** M airspace; **Luftreinhaltung** F prevention of air pollution; **Luftrettungsdienst** M air rescue service; **Luftröhre** F (*Anat*) windpipe, trachea; **Luftröhrenschnitt** M tracheotomy; **Luftschacht** M ventilation shaft; **Luftschiff** NT airship; **Luftschlacht** F air battle; **die ~ um England** the Battle of Britain; **Luftschlange** F (paper) streamer; **Luftschloss** NT (*fig*) castle in the air

Luftschutz M anti-aircraft defence (*Brit*) *or* defense (*US*)

Luftschutz-: Luftschutzbunker M, **Luftschutzkeller** M, **Luftschutzraum** M air-raid shelter; **Luftschutzübung** F air-raid drill

Luft-: Luftspiegelung F mirage; **Luftsprung** M jump in the air; **vor Freude einen ~** *or* **Luftsprünge machen** to jump for joy; **Luftstreitkräfte** PL air force *sing*; **Luftstrom** M stream of air; **Luftstützpunkt** M air base; **Luft- und Raumfahrttechnik** F aerospace technology

Lüftung ['lʏftʊŋ] F **-, -en** airing; (*ständig, systematisch*) ventilation

Lüftungsschacht M ventilation shaft

Luft-: Luftveränderung F change of air; **Luftverkehr** M air traffic; **Luftverpestung** [-EN (*pej*)]; **Luftverschmutzung** F air pollution; **Luftwaffe** F (*Mil*) air force; **die (deutsche) ~** the Luftwaffe; **Luftwaffenstützpunkt** M air-force base; **Luftweg** M (= *Flugweg*) air route; (= *Atemweg*) respiratory tract; **etw auf dem ~ befördern** to transport sth by air; **Luftzug** M (mild) breeze; (*in Gebäude*) draught (*Brit*), draft (*US*)

Lug [luːk] M **~ und Trug** lies *pl* (and deception)

Lüge ['lyːgə] F **-, -n** lie, falsehood; **jdn der ~ überführen** to catch sb (out) lying; **das ist alles ~** that's all lies; **jdn/etw ~n strafen** to give the lie to sb/sth; **~n haben kurze Beine** (*prov*) truth will out (*esp Brit prov*)

lügen ['lyːgn], *pret* **log** [loːk], *ptp* **gelogen** [gə'loːgn] ▮ VI to lie; **wie gedruckt ~** (*inf*) to lie like mad (*inf*); **wer einmal lügt, dem glaubt man nicht, und wenn er auch die Wahrheit spricht** (*Prov*) remember the boy who cried "wolf" (*prov*) ▮ VT **das ist gelogen!** that's a lie!

Lügen-: Lügendetektor M lie detector; **Lügengebäude** NT, **Lügengespinst** [-gəʃpɪnst] NT **-(e)s, -e** (*geh*) tissue *or* web of lies; **Lügengeschichte** F pack of lies; **lügenhaft** ADJ *Erzählung* made-up; **seine ~en Geschichten** his tall stories; **Lügenmärchen** NT tall story

Lügner ['lyːgnɐ] M **-s,** -, **Lügnerin** [-ərɪn] F **-, -nen** liar

lügnerisch ['lyːgnərɪʃ] ADJ *Mensch, Worte* untruthful

Luke ['luːkə] F **-, -n** hatch; (= *Dachluke*) skylight

lukrativ [lukra'tiːf] ▮ ADJ lucrative ▮ ADV lucratively

Lulatsch ['luːla(ː)tʃ] M **-(es), -e** (*hum inf*) *langer* ~ beanpole (*inf*)

Lümmel ['lʏml] M **-s, -** (a) (*pej*) oaf; **du ~, du** you rogue you **(b)** (*hum inf*: = *Penis*) willie (*Brit inf*), weenie (*US inf*)

lümmelhaft (*pej*) ▮ ADJ ill-mannered ▮ ADV ill-manneredly

lümmeln ['lʏmln] VR (*inf*) to sprawl; (= *sich hinlümmeln*) to flop down

Lump [lʊmp] M **-en, -en** (*pej*) rogue

lumpen ['lʊmpn] VT (*inf*) **sich nicht ~ lassen** to splash out (*inf*)

Lumpen ['lʊmpn] M **-s, -** (a) rag (pl) (*S Ger*: = *Lappen*) cloth

Lumpen-: Lumpenpack NT (*pej inf*) riffraff *pl* (*pej*); **Lumpensammler** M (a) (= *Lumpenhändler*) rag-and-bone man **(b)** (*hum:* = *Bus/Bahn/Zug*) last bus/tram/train

lumpig ['lʊmpɪç] ▮ ADJ (a) *Kleidung* ragged, tattered **(b)** *Gesinnung, Tat* shabby **(c)** ATTR (*inf*: = *geringfügig*) measly (*inf*) ▮ ADV (a) (= *zerlumpt*) raggedly; **~ aussehen** to look tattered; **~ herumlaufen** to go around in rags **(b)** (= *gemein*) shabbily

Lunch [lantʃ] M **-(es)** *or* **-s, -e(s)** *or* **-s** lunch, luncheon (*form*)

Lunchpaket ['lantʃ-] NT lunch packet

Lüneburger Heide ['lyːnəbʊrgɐ] F Lüneburg Heath

Lunge ['lʊŋə] F **-, -n** lungs *pl*; (= *Lungenflügel*) lung; **(auf) ~ rauchen** to inhale; **sich** (*dat*) **die ~ aus dem Hals** *or* **Leib schreien** (*inf*) to yell till one is blue in the face (*inf*); **die (grünen) ~n einer Großstadt** the lungs of a city

Lungen-: Lungenbraten M (*Aus*) loin roast (*Brit*), porterhouse (steak); **Lungenentzündung** F pneumonia; **Lungenflügel** M lung; **lungenkrank** ADJ **~ sein** to have a lung disease; **Lungenkranke(r)** MF DECL AS ADJ person suffering from a lung disease; **Lungenkrebs** M lung cancer; **Lungenzug** M deep drag (*inf*)

lungern ['lʊŋɐn] VI (*inf*) to loaf *or* hang around

Lunte ['lʊntə] F **-, -n** (*Hist*) fuse; **~ riechen** (= *Verdacht schöpfen*) to smell a rat (*inf*); (= *Gefahr wittern*) to sense danger

Lupe ['luːpə] F **-, -n** magnifying glass; **jdn/etw unter die ~ nehmen** (*inf*) (= *beobachten*) to keep a close eye on sb/sth; (= *prüfen*) to examine sb/sth closely

Lupine [lu'piːnə] F **-, -n** lupin

Lurch [lʊrç] M **-(e)s, -e** amphibian

Lusche ['lʊʃə] F **-, -n** (*Cards*) low card; (*fig*) cipher

Lust [lʊst] F **-, ⁻e** ['lʏstə] (a) NO PL (= *Freude*) pleasure, joy; **er hat die ~ daran verloren, die ~ daran ist ihm vergangen** he has lost all interest in it; **da kann einem die (ganze)** *or* **alle ~ vergehen, da vergeht einem die ganze ~** (*inf*) you feel like giving up; **jdm die ~ an etw** (*dat*) **nehmen** to take all the fun out of sth for sb; **sie ging mit/ ohne ~ an die Arbeit** she set to work enthusiastically/ without enthusiasm
(b) NO PL (= *Neigung*) inclination; **zu etw ~ (und Liebe) haben** to feel like sth; **ich habe keine ~, das zu tun** I don't really want to do that; (= *bin nicht dazu aufgelegt*) I don't feel like doing that; **ich habe ~, das zu tun** I'd like to do that; (= *bin dazu aufgelegt*) I feel like doing that; **ich habe jetzt keine ~** I'm not in the mood just now; **ich hätte ~ dazu** I'd like to; **hast du ~?** how about it?; **auf etw** (*acc*) **~ haben** to feel like sth; **jdm ~ zu etw** *or* **auf etw** (*acc*) **machen** to put sb in the mood for sth; **mach, wie du ~ hast** (*inf*) do as you like; **~ kriegen, etw zu tun** to feel like doing sth; **ich habe nicht übel ~, ... zu ...** I've a good mind to ...; **ganz** *or* **je nach ~ und Laune** (*inf*) just depending on how I/you *etc* feel
(c) (= *sinnliche Begierde*) desire; **~ haben** to feel desire; **er/sie hat ~** (*inf*) he's/she's in the mood (*inf*)

Lustauster F (*hum sl*: = *Vagina*) love hole (*sl*)

lustbetont ADJ pleasure-orientated; *Beziehung, Mensch* sensual

Lüsterklemme ['lʏstɐ-] F (*Elec*) connector

lüstern ['lʏstɐn] ▮ ADJ lascivious; **nach etw ~ sein** to lust after sth ▮ ADV lasciviously

Lüsternheit F **-**, NO PL lasciviousness

Lustgewinn M pleasure

Lusthöhle F (*hum sl*: = *Vagina*) love hole (*sl*)

lustig ['lʊstɪç] ▮ ADJ (= *munter*) merry; (= *humorvoll*) funny, amusing; **es wurde ~** things got quite merry; **das ist ja ~!** (*iro*),

das finde ich aber ~! (*iro*) (that's) very amusing (*iro*); **das kann ja ~ werden!** (*iro*) that's going to be fun (*iro*); **sich über jdn/ etw ~ machen** to make fun of sb/sth
2 ADV **(a)** (= *fröhlich*) **sich ~ unterhalten** to have a lot of fun; **auf ihren Partys geht es ~ zu** her parties are always a lot of fun
(b) (= *humorvoll*) amusingly
(c) (*inf*: = *unbekümmert*) happily
Lustigkeit F -, NO PL (= *Munterkeit*) merriness (*dated*); (*von Mensch*) joviality; (*von Geschichte*) funniness
Lüstling ['lʏstlɪŋ] M -s, -e lecher
Lust-: lustlos 1 ADJ unenthusiastic; (*Fin*) *Börse* slack **2** ADV unenthusiastically; **Lustlosigkeit** F -, NO PL lack of enthusiasm; (*Fin: von Börse*) slackness; **Lustmolch** M (*hum inf*) sex maniac (*inf*); (*bewundernd*) sexpot (*inf*); **Lustmörder(in)** M(F) sex killer; **Lustobjekt** NT sex object; **Lustprinzip** NT (*Psych*) pleasure principle; **Lustspiel** NT comedy; **Lustverlust** M, NO PL **unter ~ leiden** to have lost one's zest for life; **lustvoll 1** ADJ full of relish **2** ADV with relish
luth. ABBR *von* **lutherisch**
lutherisch ['lʊtərɪʃ], **luthersch** ['lʊtɐʃ] ADJ Lutheran
lutschen ['lʊtʃn] VTI to suck (*an etw* (*dat*)) sth)
Lutscher ['lʊtʃɐ] M -s, - lollipop
Lutschtablette F (*Med*) lozenge
Lüttich ['lʏtɪç] NT -s Liège
Luxemburg ['lʊksmbʊrk] NT -s Luxembourg

luxemburgisch ['lʊksmbʊrgɪʃ] ADJ Luxembourgian
luxuriös [lʊksu'riøːs] **1** ADJ luxurious; **ein ~es Leben** a life of luxury **2** ADV luxuriously; **~ Urlaub machen** to take a luxurious holiday (*esp Brit*) or vacation (*US*)
Luxus ['lʊksʊs] M -, NO PL luxury; (*pej*: = *Verschwendung, Überfluss*) extravagance; **den ~ lieben** to love luxury; **ich leiste mir den ~ und ...** I'll treat myself to the luxury of ...
Luxus- IN CPDS luxury; **Luxusausführung** F de luxe model; **Luxusdampfer** M luxury cruise ship; **Luxushotel** NT luxury hotel
Luzern [lu'tsɛrn] NT -s Lucerne
LVA [ɛlfau'laː] F -, -s ABBR *von* **Landesversicherungsanstalt**
Lychee ['lɪtʃi] F -, -s lychee, litchi
Lymphdrüse ['lʏmf-] F lymph(atic) gland
Lymphe ['lʏmfə] F -, -n lymph
Lymphknoten ['lʏmf-] M lymph node
Lymphozyt [lʏmfo'tsyːt] M -en, -en lymphocyte
lynchen ['lʏnçn, 'lɪnçn] VT (*lit*) to lynch; (*fig*) to kill
Lynch- ['lʏnç-]: **Lynchjustiz** F lynch law; **Lynchmord** M lynching
Lyrik ['lyːrɪk] F -, NO PL lyric poetry *or* verse
Lyriker ['lyːrikɐ] M -s, -, **Lyrikerin** [-ərɪn] F -, -nen lyric poet
lyrisch ['lyːrɪʃ] **1** ADJ (*lit, fig*) lyrical; *Dichtung, Dichter* lyric **2** ADV lyrically
LZB [ɛltsɛt'beː] F -, -s ABBR *von* **Landeszentralbank**

Mm

M, m [ɛm] NT **-, -** M, m

m ABBR *von* **Meter**

MA. ABBR *von* **Mittelalter**

Maas [maːs] F - Meuse, Maas

Maastricht-Vertrag [maːsˈtrɪçt] M Maastricht Treaty

Machart F make; (= *Muster*) design; (*lit, fig* = *Stil*) style

machbar ADJ feasible

Machbarkeitsstudie F feasibility study

Mache [ˈmaxə] F **-, -n** (*inf*) **(a)** (= *Technik*) structure **(b)** (= *Vortäuschung*) sham; **reine** *or* **pure ~ sein** to be (a) sham **(c) etw in der ~ haben** (*inf*) to be working on sth; **in der ~ sein** (*inf*) to be in the making; **der Film war noch in der ~** (*inf*) the film was still being made; **jdn in die ~ nehmen** (*sl*) to have a go at sb (*inf*)

---

machen [ˈmaxn]

| **1** TRANSITIVES VERB | **3** REFLEXIVES VERB |
| **2** INTRANSITIVES VERB | |

---

1 TRANSITIVES VERB

Wenn **machen** *sich auf eine nicht näher gekennzeichnete Aktivität bezieht oder stellvertretend für ein anderes Verb steht, wird es in den meisten Fällen mit* **to do** *übersetzt.*

(a) (= *tun*) to do; **die Hausarbeit/den Garten machen** to do the housework/the garden; **ich mache dir das schon** I'll do that for you; **ich mache das schon** (= *bringe das in Ordnung*) I'll see to that; (= *erledige das*) I'll do that; **gut, wird gemacht** right, will do (*inf*); **wie mans macht, ists verkehrt** whatever you do is wrong; **was habe ich nur falsch gemacht?** what have I done wrong?; **er macht, was er will** he does what he likes; **soll ich ihn nach seinem Gehalt fragen? – so etwas macht man nicht!** shall I ask how much he earns? – you don't ask that (question)!; **das lässt sich machen/nicht machen** that can/can't be done; **(da ist) nichts zu machen** (= *geht nicht*) (there's) nothing to be done; (= *kommt nicht infrage*) nothing doing; **ich kann da auch nichts machen** I can't do anything about it either; **ich mache es wohl am besten so, dass ich etwas früher komme** I would do best to come a bit earlier; **das lässt er nicht mit sich machen** he won't stand for that; *siehe auch* **gemacht**

✦**was macht jd/etw?** **was machst du da?** what are you doing (there)?; **was hast du denn nun wieder gemacht?** what have you done now?; **was macht die Arbeit?** how's the work going?; **was macht dein Bruder (beruflich)?** what does your brother do (for a living)?; **was macht dein Bruder?** (= *wie geht es ihm?*) how's your brother doing?

✦**es machen machs kurz!** make it short!; **machs gut!** all the best!; **er wirds nicht mehr lange machen** (*inf*) he won't last long; **mit mir kann mans ja machen!** (*inf*) the things I put up with! (*inf*)

(b) (= *anfertigen, zubereiten*) to make; **Bier wird aus Gerste gemacht** beer is made from barley; **aus Holz gemacht** made of wood; **sich/jdm etw machen lassen** to have sth made for oneself/sb; **er ist für den Beruf wie gemacht** he's made for the job

(c) (= *verursachen, bewirken*) Schwierigkeiten, Arbeit to make (*jdm* for sb); Mühe, Schmerzen to cause (*jdm* for sb); **jdm Angst/Sorgen/Freude machen** to make sb afraid/worried/happy; **jdm Hoffnung/Mut/Kopfschmerzen machen** to give sb hope/courage/a headache; **das macht Hunger** that makes you hungry; **das macht die Kälte** it's the cold that does that; **machen, dass etw geschieht** to make sth happen; **mach, dass er gesund wird!** make him better!; **(viel) von sich reden machen** to be much talked about

(d) (= *hervorbringen*) Laut, Geräusch to make; **mäh/miau machen** to baa/miaow; **brumm machen** to go "brumm"

(e) (= *bilden*) Kreuzzeichen, Kreis to make; **die Straße macht einen Knick** the road bends

(f) (*machen + Substantiv*)

Siehe auch unter dem Eintrag für das jeweilige Substantiv.

einen Ausflug machen to go on an outing; **Bilder machen** to take photos; **ein Diplom machen** to do a diploma; **Halt machen** to call a halt; **einen Handstand machen** to do a handstand; **einen Kopfsprung machen** to dive (headfirst); **einen Kurs machen** (= *teilnehmen*) to do a course; **eine Party machen** to have a party; **Pause machen** to have a break; **eine Prüfung machen** to do (*esp Brit*) *or* take an exam; **Punkte machen** to get points; **ein Spiel machen** to play a game

(g) (*machen + Adjektiv*)

Siehe auch unter dem Eintrag für das jeweilige Adjektiv.

 to make; **jdn nervös/unglücklich machen** to make sb nervous/unhappy; **etw größer/kleiner machen** to make sth bigger/smaller; **etw sauber/schmutzig machen** to get sth clean/dirty; **etw leer machen** to empty sth; **etw kürzer machen** to shorten sth; **jdn alt/jung machen** (= *aussehen lassen*) to make sb look old/young; **machs dir doch bequem/gemütlich** make yourself comfortable/at home; **er macht es sich** (*dat*) **nicht leicht** he doesn't make it easy for himself

(h) (= *ergeben*) (*inf*) to make; Summe, Preis to be; **drei und fünf macht** *or* **machen acht** three and five makes eight; **was** *or* **wie viel macht sechs geteilt durch zwei?** what is six divided by two?; **was** *or* **wie viel macht das (alles zusammen)?** how much is that altogether?

(l) (= *spielen*) (*inf, Theat*) to play; Dolmetscher, Schiedsrichter etc to be; **den Ghostwriter für jdn machen** to be sb's ghostwriter

(j) (= *Notdurft verrichten*) (*inf*) **einen Haufen** *or* **sein Geschäft machen** (*euph*: Hund) to do its business (*euph*)

(k) (= *ordnen, reparieren, säubern*) to do; **die Küche muss mal wieder gemacht werden** (= *gereinigt, gestrichen*) the kitchen needs doing again; **das Auto machen lassen** to have the car seen to; **das Bett machen** to make the bed

(l) (*andere Wendungen*)

✦**machen + aus** etw aus jdm/etw machen (= *verwandeln in*) to turn sb/sth into sth; (= *darstellen, interpretieren als*) to make sth of sb/sth; **etwas aus sich machen** to make something of oneself

✦**machen + zu** jdn/etw zu etw machen (= *verwandeln in*) to turn sb/sth into sth; **jdn zum Wortführer/Sklaven/zu seiner Frau machen** to make sb spokesman/a slave/one's wife; **jdm etw zur Hölle/Qual machen** to make sth hell/a misery for sb

✦**nichts/etwas machen** (= *ausmachen, schaden*) **macht nichts!** it doesn't matter!; **macht das was?** does that matter?; **das macht mir nichts!** that doesn't matter to me!; **der Regen/die Kälte macht mir nichts** I don't mind the rain/cold; **die Kälte macht dem Motor nichts** the cold doesn't hurt the engine

✦**sich etw machen** sich (*dat*) **viel aus jdm/etw machen** to like sb/sth; **sich** (*dat*) **wenig aus jdm/etw machen** not to be very keen on (*esp Brit*) *or* thrilled with (*esp US*) sb/sth; **sich** (*dat*) **nichts aus etw machen** (= *keinen Wert legen auf*) not to be very keen on (*esp Brit*) *or* thrilled with (*esp US*) sth; (= *sich nicht ärgern*) not to let sth bother one; **mach dir nichts draus!** don't let it bother you!; **sich** (*dat*) **einen schönen Abend/ein paar gemütliche Stunden machen** to have a nice evening/a few pleasant hours; **sich** (*dat*) **jdn zum Freund/Feind machen** to make sb one's friend/enemy; **sich** (*dat*) **etw zur Aufgabe/zum Grundsatz machen** to make sth one's job/a principle

2 INTRANSITIVES VERB

(a) (= *tun*) **lass ihn nur machen** (= *hindre ihn nicht*) just let him do it; (= *verlass dich auf ihn*) just leave it to him; **lass mich mal machen** let me do it; (= *ich bringe das in Ordnung*) let me see to that

(b) (*machen + Adjektiv*) **das macht müde/gesund/schlank** that makes you tired/healthy/slim; **das Kleid macht alt/schlank** that dress makes you look old/slim

(c) (= *sich beeilen*) (*inf*) to get a move on (*inf*); **ich mach ja schon!** I'm being as quick as I can!; **sie machten, dass sie nach**

Hause kamen they hurried home; **mach, dass du hier wegkommst** or **verschwindest!** (you just) get out of here! **(d)** (= *Notdurft verrichten*) (*inf*) to go to the toilet; (*Hund etc*) to do its business (*euph*); **ins Bett machen** to wet the bed; **groß/klein machen** (*baby-talk*) to do a poo/wee (*baby-talk*) **(e)** (*Redewendungen*)

✦**machen auf etw** (*acc*) (*inf*) **jetzt macht sie auf große Dame** she's playing the grand lady now; **sie macht auf verständnisvoll/gebildet** she's doing her understanding/ cultured bit (*inf*); **jetzt macht sie auf beleidigt** now she's acting insulted (*esp US*) or the injured innocent (*Brit*); **er macht auf Schau** he's out for effect (*inf*)

✦**machen in etw** (*dat*) (*inf: beruflich*) to be in sth; **er macht in Politik** he's in politics

❸ REFLEXIVES VERB

✦**sich machen**
(a) (= *sich entwickeln*) to come on
(b) (= *aussehen*) to look; **der Schal macht sich sehr hübsch zu dem Kleid** the scarf looks very pretty with that dress
(c) (*andere Wendungen*) **sich an etw** (*acc*) **machen** to get down to sth; **sich auf den Weg machen** to get going; **sich zum Fürsprecher/Anwalt machen** to make oneself spokesman/ advocate; **sich verständlich machen** to make oneself understood; **sie will sich doch nur wichtig machen** she's trying to make herself seem important; **sich bei jdm beliebt/ verhasst machen** (*inf*) to make oneself popular with/hated by sb

Machenschaften ['maxnʃaftn] PL wheelings and dealings *pl*, machinations *pl*

Macher ['maxɐ] M **-s, -**, **Macherin** [-ərɪn] F **-, -nen** (*inf*) man/ woman of action

-macher(in) M(F) SUF IN CPDS -maker; **Kleider-/Möbelmacher(in)** clothes/furniture-maker

Macho ['matʃo] M **-s, -s** macho (*inf*)

Macht [maxt] F **-, ⁻e** ['mɛçtə] **(a)** NO PL (= *Einfluss, Kraft*) power; (= *Stärke*) might, power; **die ~ die Gewohnheit/Verhältnisse/ des Schicksals** the force of habit/circumstance(s)/destiny; **alles, was in unserer ~ steht, alles in unserer ~ Stehende** everything (with)in our power; **mit ~** with a vengeance; **mit aller ~** with all one's might
(b) NO PL (= *Herrschaft, Befehlsgewalt*) power; **die ~ ergreifen/ erringen** to seize/gain power; **an die ~ gelangen** (*form*) or **kommen** to come to power; **jdn an die ~ bringen** to bring sb to power; **an der ~ sein/bleiben** to be/remain in power; **die ~ übernehmen** to assume power
(c) (= *außerirdische Kraft, Großmacht*) power

Macht-: Machtanspruch M claim to power; **Machtbereich** M sphere of control; **Machtblock** M, *pl* **-blöcke** power bloc; **Machtergreifung** F **-, -en** seizure of power; **Machthaber** [-ha:bɐ] M **-s, -**, **Machthaberin** [-ərɪn] F **-, -nen** ruler; (*pej*) dictator; **die ~ in Ruritanien** the rulers of Ruritania

mächtig ['mɛçtɪç] **❶** ADJ **(a)** (= *einflussreich*) powerful; **die Mächtigen (dieser Erde)** the powerful (of this world)
(b) (= *sehr groß*) mighty; *Körper* massive; *Essen* heavy; (*inf: = enorm*) *Hunger, Durst, Glück* terrific (*inf*); **~e Angst** or **einen ~en Bammel haben** (*inf*) to be scared stiff (*inf*)
❷ ADV (*inf: = sehr*) terrifically (*inf*); *schneien, brüllen, sich beeilen* like mad (*inf*); **sich ~ anstrengen** to make a terrific effort (*inf*); **da hast du dich ~ getäuscht** you've made a big mistake there; **darüber hat sie sich ~ geärgert** she got really angry about it

Mächtigkeit F **-**, NO PL powerfulness; (*von Felsen, Körper*) massiveness

Macht-: Machtkampf M power struggle; **machtlos** ADJ powerless; (= *hilflos*) helpless; **gegen diese Argumente war ich ~** I was powerless against these arguments; **Machtlosigkeit** F **-**, NO PL powerlessness; (= *Hilflosigkeit*) helplessness; **Machtposition** F position of power; **Machtprobe** F trial of strength; **Machtübernahme** F takeover (*durch* by); **Machtverhältnisse** PL balance *sing* of power; **machtvoll ❶** ADJ powerful **❷** ADV powerfully; *eingreifen* decisively; **Machtwechsel** M changeover of power; **Machtwort** NT, *pl* **-worte** word (*+gen* from); **ein ~ sprechen** to exercise one's authority

Machwerk NT (*pej*) sorry effort; **das ist ein ~ des Teufels** that is the work of the devil

Macke ['makə] F **-, -n** (*inf*) **(a)** (= *Tick, Knall*) quirk; **eine ~ haben** (*inf*) to be cracked (*inf*) **(b)** (= *Fehler, Schadstelle*) fault

MAD [ɛmla:'de:] M - ABBR *von* **Militärischer Abschirmdienst** ≈ MI5 (*Brit*), ≈ CIA (*US*)

Madagaskar [mada'gaska:r] NT **-s** Madagascar; (*Pol: heutzutage*) Malagasy Republic

Mädchen ['mɛːtçən] NT **-s, -** girl; (= *Tochter auch*) daughter; (= *Dienstmädchen*) maid; **ein ~ für alles** (*inf*) a dogsbody (*Brit inf*), a gofer; (*im Haushalt auch*) a maid-of-all-work

Mädchen-: mädchenhaft ❶ ADJ girlish **❷** ADV *sich bewegen, aussehen* like a (young) girl; *kichern auch* girlishly (*pej*); **sich ~ kleiden** to dress like a girl; **Mädchenhandel** M white slave trade; **Mädchenhändler(in)** M(F) white-slaver; **Mädchenname** M **(a)** (*Vorname*) girl's name; **~n** girls' names **(b)** (*von verheirateter Frau*) maiden name; **Mädchenschule** F girls' school

Made ['ma:də] F **-, -n** maggot; **wie die ~ im Speck leben** (*inf*) to live in clover

Mädel ['mɛːdl] NT **-s, -(s)** (*dial*), **Madel** ['ma:dl] NT **-s, -n** (*Aus*) lass (*dial*), girl; *siehe auch* **Mädchen**

Madenwurm M threadworm

madig ['ma:dɪç] ADJ maggoty; *Obst auch* worm-eaten; **jdn/etw ~ machen** (*inf*) to run sb/sth down; **jdm etw ~ machen** (*inf*) to put sb off sth

Madl ['ma:dl] NT **-s, -n** (*Aus*), **Mädle** ['mɛːdlə] NT **-s, -** (*S Ger*) lass (*dial*), girl; *siehe auch* **Mädchen**

Madrid [ma'drɪt] NT **-s** Madrid

Madrider [ma'drɪdɐ] ADJ ATTR Madrid

Mafia ['mafia] F, **Maffia** ['mafia] F **-**, NO PL Mafia

Mafia-Boss M, **Maffia-Boss** M Mafia boss

mafios [ma'fio:s] ADJ Mafia *attr*; *Zustände* Mafia-like

Mafioso [ma'fio:zo] M **-**, **Mafiosi** [-zi] mafioso

mag [ma:k] 3. PERS SING PRES *von* **mögen**

Magazin [maga'tsi:n] NT **-s, -e (a)** (= *Lager*) storeroom; (*esp für Sprengstoff, Waffen*) (*old: = Speicher*) magazine; (= *Bibliotheksmagazin*) stockroom **(b)** (*am Gewehr*) magazine **(c)** (= *Zeitschrift*) magazine; (*TV, Rad*) magazine programme (*Brit*), news magazine (show) (*US*)

Magd [ma:kt] F **-, ⁻e** ['mɛːkdə] (*old*) (= *Dienstmagd*) maid; (= *Landarbeiterin*) farm girl; (= *Kuhmagd*) milkmaid

Magen ['ma:gn] M **-s, ⁻** ['mɛːgn] or **-** stomach, tummy (*inf*); **mit leerem ~, auf nüchternen ~** on an empty stomach; **(die) Liebe geht durch den ~** (*Prov*) the way to a man's heart is through his stomach (*prov*); **etw liegt jdm (schwer** or **wie Blei** or **bleiern) im ~** (*inf*) sth lies heavily on sb's stomach; (*fig*) sth preys on sb's mind; **jdm auf den ~ schlagen** (*inf*) to upset sb's stomach; (*fig*) to upset sb; **sich** (*dat*) **den ~ verderben** or **verkorksen** (*inf*) to get an upset stomach

Magen-: Magenbeschwerden PL stomach or tummy (*inf*) trouble *sing*; **Magenbitter** M bitters *pl*; **Magen-Darm-Katarr(h)** M gastroenteritis; **Magen-Darm-Trakt** M gastrointestinal tract; **Magengegend** F stomach region; **Magengeschwür** NT stomach ulcer; **Magengrube** F pit of the stomach; **ein Schlag in die ~** a blow in the solar plexus; **Magenknurren** NT **-s**, NO PL stomach rumbles *pl*; **Magenkrampf** M stomach cramp; **Magenkrebs** M cancer of the stomach; **Magenleiden** NT stomach disorder; **Magensaft** M gastric juice; **Magensäure** F gastric acid; **Magenschleimhaut** F stomach lining; **Magenschleimhautentzündung** F gastritis; **Magenschmerzen** PL stomachache *sing*; **Magenverstimmung** F upset stomach, stomach upset; **Magenweh** [-ve:] NT **-s**, NO PL = **Magenschmerzen**

mager ['ma:gɐ] **❶** ADJ **(a)** (= *fettarm*) *Fleisch* lean; *Kost* low-fat **(b)** (= *dünn*) thin, skinny (*inf*); (= *abgemagert*) emaciated; (*Typ*) *Druck* roman **(c)** (= *dürftig*) meagre (*Brit*), meager (*US*); (*Tech*) *Mischung* weak; *Ergebnis* poor
❷ ADV **(a)** (= *fettarm*) **~ essen** to be on a low-fat diet; **~ kochen** to cook low-fat meals
(b) (= *dürftig*) meagrely (*Brit*), meagerly (*US*); **~ ausfallen** to be meagre (*Brit*) or meager (*US*)

Magerkeit F **-**, NO PL **(a)** (= *Fettarmut*) (*von Fleisch*) leanness; (*von Kost*) low fat content **(b)** (*von Mensch*) thinness; (= *Abgemagertheit*) emaciation

Mager-: Magermilch F skimmed milk; **Magerquark** [-kvark] M low-fat cottage cheese (US) or curd cheese; **Magersucht** F (Med) anorexia; **magersüchtig** ADJ anorexic

magisch ['maːgɪʃ] **1** ADJ magic(al); Quadrat, (Tech) Auge, (Econ) Dreieck, (Phys) Zahlen magic **2** ADV magically; **von jdm/etw ~ angezogen werden** to be attracted to sb/sth as if by magic

Magister [ma'gɪstɐ] M **-s, - ~ (Artium)** (Univ) M.A., Master of Arts; **~ (Pharmaciae)** (Aus) MSc or Master of Science in pharmacology

Magma ['magma] NT **-s, Magmen** [-mən] (Geol) magma

magna cum laude ['magna 'kʊm 'laudə] ADV (Univ) magna cum laude

Magnesium [ma'gneːziʊm] NT **-s,** NO PL (abbr **Mg**) magnesium

Magnet [ma'gneːt] M **-s** or **-en, -e(n)** (lit, fig) magnet

Magnet- IN CPDS magnetic; **Magnetbahn** F magnetic railway; **Magnetband** NT, pl **-bänder** magnetic tape

magnetisch [ma'gneːtɪʃ] **1** ADJ (lit, fig) magnetic; **eine ~e Anziehungskraft auf jdn ausüben** (fig) to have a magnetic attraction for sb **2** ADV magnetically; **von etw ~ angezogen werden** (fig) to be drawn to sth like a magnet

Magnetismus [magne'tɪsmʊs] M **-,** NO PL magnetism

Magnet-: Magnetkarte F magnetic card; **Magnetkartenleser** M magnetic card reader; **Magnetnadel** F magnetic needle; **Magnetpol** M magnetic pole; **Magnetschalter** M (Aut) solenoid switch; **Magnetschwebebahn** F magnetic levitation railway; **Magnetspule** F coil; **Magnetstreifen** M magnetic strip; **Magnetstreifenkarte** F magnetic strip card; **Magnetzündung** F (Aut) magneto ignition

Magnolie [mag'noːliə] F **-, -n** magnolia

Magnumflasche ['magnʊm-] F magnum (bottle)

mäh [mɛː] INTERJ baa

Mahagoni [maha'goːni] NT **-s,** NO PL mahogany

Maharadscha [maha'raːdʒa] M **-s, -s** maharaja(h)

Maharani [maha'raːni] F **-, -s** maharani

Mähdrescher M combine (harvester)

mähen¹ ['mɛːən] **1** VT Gras to cut; Getreide to reap; Rasen to mow **2** VI to reap; (= Rasen ~) to mow

mähen² VI (Schaf) to bleat

Mahl [maːl] NT **-(e)s, -e** or **¬er** ['mɛːlə] (liter) meal, repast (form); (= Gastmahl) banquet

mahlen ['maːlən], pret **mahlte** ['maːltə], ptp **gemahlen** [gə'maːlən] **1** VT to grind **2** VI to grind; (Räder) to spin

Mahlzeit F meal; **~!** (inf) greeting used around mealtimes; (= guten Appetit) enjoy your meal; **(prost) ~!** (iro inf) that's just great (inf)

Mähmaschine F mower; (= Getreidemähmaschine) reaper

Mahnbescheid M, **Mahnbrief** M reminder

Mähne ['mɛːnə] F **-, -n** (lit, fig) mane

mahnen ['maːnən] **1** VT **(a)** (= erinnern) to remind (wegen, an +acc of); (warnend, missbilligend) to admonish (wegen, an +acc on account of); Schuldner to send a reminder to; **jdn schriftlich/brieflich ~** to remind sb in writing/by letter **(b)** (= auffordern) **jdn zur Eile/Geduld/Ruhe** etc **~** to urge or (warnend, missbilligend) admonish sb to hurry/be patient/be quiet etc **2** VI **(a)** (wegen Schulden etc) to send a reminder **(b)** **zur Eile/Geduld/Vorsicht ~** to urge haste/patience/caution

Mahn-: Mahnmal NT memorial; **Mahnschreiben** NT reminder

Mahnung ['maːnʊŋ] F **-, -en (a)** (= Ermahnung) exhortation; (warnend, missbilligend) admonition **(b)** (geh: = warnende Erinnerung) reminder; **zur ~ an** (+acc) in memory of **(c)** (= Mahnbrief) reminder

Mahnverfahren NT collection proceedings pl

Mähren ['mɛːrən] NT **-s** Moravia

mährisch ['mɛːrɪʃ] ADJ Moravian

Mai [mai] M **-(e)s** or **-** or (poet) **-en, -e** May; **der Erste ~** May Day; **wie einst im ~** (as if) in the first flush of youth; siehe auch **März**

Mai- IN CPDS May; (Pol) May Day; **Maibaum** M maypole; **Maifeiertag** M (form) May Day no art; **Maiglöckchen** NT lily of the valley; **Maikäfer** M cockchafer; **Maikundgebung** F May Day rally

Mail [meːl] F **-, -s** (Comput) e-mail

Mailand ['mailant] NT **-s** Milan

Mailbox ['meːlbɔks] F (Comput) mailbox

mailen ['meːln] VTI (Comput) to e-mail

Mailing ['meːlɪŋ, 'meːlɪŋ] NT **-s, -s** mailing; **ein ~ an alle Kunden durchführen** to send a mailing to all customers

Main [main] M **-s** Main

Mais [mais] M **-es,** NO PL maize, (Indian) corn (esp US)

Maische ['maiʃə] F **-, -n** (= Biermaische) mash; (= Weinmaische) must; (= Schnapsmaische) wort

Mais-: Maisflocken PL cornflakes pl; **maisgelb** ADJ corn-coloured (Brit), corn-colored (US); **Maiskolben** M corn cob; (Gericht) corn on the cob; **Maismehl** NT maize or corn (esp US) meal

Maisonette [mɛzo'nɛt] F **-, -n, Maisonette-Wohnung** F maisonette

Maisstärke F cornflour (Brit), cornstarch (US)

Majestät [majɛs'tɛːt] F **-, -en** (Titel) Majesty; **Seine/Ihre/Eure** or **Euer ~** His/Her/Your Majesty

majestätisch [majɛs'tɛːtɪʃ] **1** ADJ majestic **2** ADV majestically

Majo ['maːjo] F **-, -s** (inf: = Majonäse) mayo (inf)

Majonäse [majo'nɛːzə] F **-, -n** mayonnaise

Major [ma'joːɐ] M **-s, -e, Majorin** [ma'joːrɪn] F **-, -nen** (Mil) major; (in Luftwaffe) squadron leader (Brit), major (US)

Majoran ['majoraːn, 'majoran] M **-s, -e** marjoram

Majorin F siehe **Major**

Majorität [majori'tɛːt] F **-, -en** majority

Majorz [ma'jɔrts] M **-es,** NO PL (Sw) first-past-the-post system; (= Mehrheit) majority

makaber [ma'kaːbɐ] ADJ macabre; Witz, Geschichte sick

Makedonien [make'doːniən] NT **-s** Macedonia

makedonisch [make'doːnɪʃ] ADJ Macedonian

Makel ['maːkl] M **-s, - (a)** (= Schandfleck) stigma; **ohne ~** without a stain on one's reputation; (Rel) unblemished; **ein ~ auf seiner blütenreinen Weste** a stain on his reputation **(b)** (= Fehler) blemish; (von Charakter) flaw; (bei Waren) flaw, defect

Mäkelei [mɛkə'lai] F **-, -en** carping no pl (an +dat, über +acc about, over)

makellos **1** ADJ Reinheit, Frische spotless; Charakter, Lebenswandel, Gesinnung unimpeachable; Figur, Haut, Frisur perfect; Kleidung, Haare immaculate; Alibi watertight; Vortrag, Spiel, Englisch, Deutsch flawless; Klang (von Instrument) perfect **2** ADV rein spotlessly; **~ gekleidet sein** to be impeccably dressed; **~ weiß** spotless white

mäkeln ['mɛːkln] VI (inf) (= nörgeln) to carp (an +dat at); (= zu wählerisch sein) to be finicky (inf) (an +dat about, over)

Make-up [meːk'ʔap] NT **-s, -s** make-up; (flüssig) liquid make-up

Makkaroni [maka'roːni] PL macaroni sing

Makler ['maːklɐ] M **-s, -, Maklerin** [-ərɪn] F **-, -nen** broker; (= Grundstücksmakler) estate agent (Brit), real-estate agent (US)

Maklergebühr F brokerage

Makrele [ma'kreːlə] F **-, -n** mackerel

Makro ['makro] NT **-s, -s** (Comput) macro

Makro-, makro- [makro] IN CPDS macro-; **Makrobefehl** M (Comput) macro command; **makrobiotisch** [-'bioːtɪʃ] **1** ADJ macrobiotic **2** ADV **sich ~ ernähren** to be on a macrobiotic diet; **Makrokosmos** M macrocosm

Makulatur [makula'tuːɐ] F **-, -en** (Typ) wastepaper; (fig pej) rubbish (Brit), trash (esp US); **~ reden** (inf) to talk nonsense

makulieren [maku'liːrən], ptp **makuliert** VT to pulp

mal¹ [maːl] ADV (Math) times; (bei Maßangaben) by; **zwei ~ zwei** (Math) two times two

mal² ADV (inf) = **einmal**

-mal ADV SUF times; **drei-/fünfmal** three/five times

Mal¹ [maːl] NT **-(e)s, -e** or (poet) **¬er** ['mɛːlə] **(a)** (= Fleck) mark **(b)** (Sport) (Schlagball) base; (Rugby) posts pl; (= feld) touch

Mal² NT **-(e)s, -e** time; **das eine ~** once; **erinnerst du dich an das eine ~ in Düsseldorf?** do you remember that time in Düsseldorf?; **nur das eine ~** just (the) once; **(nur) dieses eine ~** (just) this once; **das eine oder andere ~** now and then or again; **ein/kein einziges ~** once/not once; **ein für alle ~(e)** once and for all; **voriges** or **das vorige ~** the time before; **das soundsovielte** or **x-te ~** (inf) the umpteenth (inf or nth) time; **als ich letztes** or **das letzte ~ in London war** (the) last time I was in London; **beim ersten ~(e)** the first time; **beim zweiten/ letzten** *etc* **~** the second/last *etc* time; **zum ersten/letzten** *etc* **~** for the first/last *etc* time; **zu verschiedenen ~en** at various times; **zu wiederholten ~en** time and again; **von ~ zu ~** each *or* every time; **für dieses ~** for now; **mit einem ~(e)** all at once

Malaie [ma'laɪə] M **-n, -n, Malaiin** [ma'laɪɪn] F **-, -nen** Malay

malaiisch [ma'laɪɪʃ] ADJ Malayan, Malay *attr*

Malaria [ma'laːria] F **-**, NO PL malaria

Malaysia [ma'laɪzia] NT **-s** Malaysia

malaysisch [ma'laɪzɪʃ] ADJ Malaysian

Malbuch NT colouring (*Brit*) *or* coloring (*US*) book

Malediven [male'diːvn] PL Maldives *pl*, Maldive Islands *pl*

malen ['maːlən] **1** VTI (*mit Pinsel und Farbe*) to paint; (= *zeichnen*) to draw; **sich/jdn ~ lassen** to have one's/sb's portrait painted; **etw rosig/schwarz** *etc* **~** (*fig*) to paint a rosy/black *etc* picture of sth; **er hat während des Vortrags (Männchen) gemalt** he was doodling during the talk; **er malt (als Beruf)** he's an artist **2** VR (= *Selbstbildnis machen*) to paint a self-portrait

Maler ['maːlɐ] M **-s, -, Malerin** [-ərɪn] F **-, -nen** painter; (= *Kunstmaler auch*) artist

Malerei [maːlə'raɪ] F **-, -en (a)** (*no pl*: = *Malkunst*) art **(b)** (= *Bild*) painting; (= *Zeichnung*) drawing

Malerfarbe F paint

Malerin F *siehe* **Maler**

malerisch ['maːlərɪʃ] **1** ADJ **(a)** (= *bildnerisch*) in painting; *Talent, Können* as a painter **(b)** (= *pittoresk*) picturesque **2** ADV picturesquely

Malheur [ma'løːɐ] NT **-s, -s** *or* **-e** mishap; **ihm ist ein kleines ~ passiert** (*inf*) he's had a little accident

Mali ['maːli] NT **-s** Mali

Malkasten M paintbox

Mallorca [ma'jɔrka, ma'lɔrka] NT **-s** Majorca, Mallorca

mallorquinisch [maljɔr'kiːnɪʃ] ADJ Majorcan

malnehmen VTI SEP IRREG to multiply (*mit* by)

Maloche [ma'lɔxa, ma'loːxə] F **-**, NO PL (*inf*) hard work; **auf ~ sein** to be working hard; **du musst zur ~** you've got to go to work

malochen [ma'lɔxn, ma'loːxn], *ptp* **malocht** VI (*inf*) to work hard

Malstift M crayon

Malta ['malta] NT **-s** Malta

Malteser [mal'teːzɐ] M **-s, -, Malteserin** [-'teːzərɪn] F **-, -nen** Maltese

maltesisch [mal'teːzɪʃ] ADJ Maltese

Maltose [mal'toːzə] F **-**, NO PL maltose

malträtieren [maltrɛ'tiːrən], *ptp* **malträtiert** VT to ill-treat, to maltreat

Malus ['maːlʊs] M **-ses, -** [-lu:s] *or* **-se** (*Insur*) supplementary (high-risk) premium; (*Univ*) minus point

Malve ['malvə] F **-, -n** (*Bot*) mallow; (= *Stockrose*) hollyhock

malvenfarben [-farbn], **malvenfarbig** ADJ mauve

Malvinen [mal'viːnən] PL Falklands *pl*

Malz [malts] NT **-es**, NO PL malt

Malz-: Malzbier NT malt beer, ≈ stout (*Brit*); **Malzbonbon** NT *or* M malt lozenge

Malzeichen NT multiplication sign

Mama ['mamaː] F **-s, -s** (*inf*) mummy (*Brit*), mommy (*US*)

Mama- ['mama-]: **Mamakind** NT (*pej*) mummy's (*Brit*) *or* mommy's (*US*) boy/girl; **Mamasöhnchen** NT **-s, -** (*pej*) mummy's (*Brit*) *or* mommy's (*US*) darling

Mami ['mami] F **-s, -s** (*inf*) mummy (*Brit*), mommy (*US*)

Mammografie [mamogra'fiː] F **-, -n** [-'fiːən] mammography

Mammut ['mamʊt, 'mamuːt] NT **-s, -s** *or* **-e** mammoth

Mammut- IN CPDS (*lit, fig*) mammoth; (= *lange dauernd*) marathon; **Mammutbaum** M sequoia, giant redwood; **Mammutprozess** M marathon trial

mampfen ['mampfn] VTI (*inf*) to munch; **ich brauche was zu ~** I want something to eat

man [man] INDEF PRON, *dat* **einem**, *acc* **einen (a)** you, one; (= *ich*) one; (= *wir*) we; **~ kann nie wissen** you *or* one can never tell; **das tut ~ nicht** that's not done; **~ wird doch wohl noch fragen dürfen** there's no law against asking; **~ wende sich an ...** apply to ...

(b) (= *jemand*) somebody, someone; **~ hat mir erklärt, dass ...**

it was explained to me that ...; **~ hat festgestellt, dass ...** it has been established that ...

(c) (= *die Leute*) they *pl*, people *pl*; **früher glaubte ~, dass ...** people used to believe that ...; **~ will die alten Häuser niederreißen** they want to pull down the old houses; **diese Hemden trägt ~ nicht mehr** people don't wear these shirts any more; **~ hat öfters versucht, ...** many attempts have been made ...

Management ['mɛnɛdʒmənt] NT **-s, -s** management

Management-Buy-out ['mɛnɛdʒməntbaiaut] NT **-s, -s** (*Ind*) management buyout

managen ['mɛnɛdʒn] VT (*inf*) to manage

Manager ['mɛnɛdʒɐ] M **-s, -, Managerin** [-ərɪn] F **-, -nen** manager

manch [manç] INDEF PRON **(a)** INV (*in Zusammensetzung mit ein, eine(r, s), substantiviertem Adjektiv und (geh) Substantiv*) many a; **~ eine(r)**, **~ ein Mensch** many a person; **~ einem kann man nie Vernunft beibringen** you can never teach sense to some people; **~ anderer** many another; **~ Schönes** (*geh*) many a beautiful thing

(b) (*adjektivisch*) **~e(r, s)** quite a few +*pl*, many a +*sing*; (*pl*: = *einige*) some +*pl*; **~er, der ...** a person who ...; **~e hundert Euro** several hundreds of euros; **~es Schöne** quite a few beautiful things

(c) (*substantivisch*) **~e(r)** a good many people *pl*; (*pl*: = *einige*) some (people); **~er lernts nie** some people never learn; **~es** (= *vieles*) quite a few things *pl*; (= *einiges*) some things *pl*; **in ~em hat er Recht** he's right about a lot of/some things

mancherlei ['mançɐ'laɪ] ADJ INV (*adjektivisch mit pl n*) various, a number of; (*substantivisch*) various things *pl*, a number of things

manchmal ['mançmaːl] ADV sometimes

Mandant [man'dant] M **-en, -en, Mandantin** [-'dantɪn] F **-, -nen** (*Jur*) client

Mandarine [manda'riːnə] F **-, -n** mandarin (orange), tangerine

Mandat [man'daːt] NT **-(e)s, -e (a)** (= *Auftrag, Vollmacht*) mandate (*auch Pol*) (+*gen* from); (*von Anwalt*) brief; (*Parl*: = *Abgeordnetensitz*) seat; **sein ~ niederlegen** (*Parl*) to resign one's seat **(b)** (= *Gebiet*) mandated territory, mandate

Mandel ['mandl] F **-, -n (a)** almond **(b)** (*Anat*) tonsil

Mandel-: Mandelbaum M almond tree; **Mandelentzündung** F tonsillitis

Mandoline [mando'liːnə] F **-, -n** mandolin

Mandrill [man'drɪl] M **-s, -e** (*Zool*) mandrill

Mandschurei [mandʒu'rai, mantʃu'rai] F **- die ~** Manchuria

Manege [ma'neːʒə] F **-, -n** ring, arena

Mangan [maŋ'gaːn] NT **-s**, NO PL (*abbr* **Mn**) manganese

-mangel M SUF IN CPDS shortage of ...; (*Med*) ... deficiency; **Ärztemangel** shortage of doctors; **Vitaminmangel** vitamin deficiency

Mangel¹ ['maŋəl] F **-, -n** mangle; (= *Heißmangel*) rotary iron; **durch die ~ drehen** to put through the mangle; (*fig inf*) to put through it (*inf*); *Prüfling etc* to put through the mill; **jdn in die ~ nehmen/in der ~ haben** (*fig inf*) to give sb a going-over (*inf*)

Mangel² M **-s, -̈** (= *Fehler*) fault; (= *Unzulänglichkeit*) shortcoming; (= *Charaktermangel*) flaw

(b) NO PL (= *das Fehlen*) lack (*an* +*dat* of); (= *Knappheit*) shortage (*an* +*dat* of); (*Med*) deficiency (*an* +*dat* of); **aus ~ or wegen ~s an** (+*dat*) due to a lack of; **wegen ~s an Beweisen** for lack of evidence; **~ an Vitamin C** vitamin C deficiency; **~ an etw** (*dat*) **haben** to lack sth

Mängelbericht M list of faults

Mängelerscheinung F (*Med*) deficiency symptom; **eine ~ sein** (*fig*) to be in short supply (*bei* with)

mangelfrei, mängelfrei ADJ free of faults

mangelhaft **1** ADJ (= *unzulänglich, schlecht*) poor; *Informationen, Interesse* insufficient; (= *fehlerhaft*) *Sprachkenntnisse, Ware* faulty; (*Schulnote*) poor **2** ADV poorly; **er spricht nur ~ Englisch** he doesn't speak English very well

Mängelhaftung F (*Jur*) liability for faults

Mangelkrankheit F deficiency disease

mangeln¹ ['maŋln] VT *Wäsche* to (put through the) mangle; (= *heiß ~*) to iron

mangeln² **1** VI IMPERS **es mangelt an etw** (*dat*) there is a lack of sth; (= *unzureichend vorhanden auch*) there is a shortage of sth; **er ließ es an nichts ~** he made sure that nothing was lacking; **es mangelt jdm an etw** (*dat*) sb lacks sth; **~des Selbstvertrauen/Verständnis** *etc* a lack of self-confidence/ understanding *etc*; **wegen ~der Aufmerksamkeit** through not paying attention; **das Kino wurde wegen ~der Sicherheit geschlossen** the cinema was closed because of inadequate safety precautions

2 VI **etw mangelt jdm/einer Sache** sb/sth lacks sth

mangels ['maŋls] PREP +GEN (*form*) for lack of

Mangelware F scarce commodity; **~ sein** (*fig*) to be a rare thing; (*Ärzte, gute Lehrer etc*) not to grow on trees

Mango ['maŋgo] F **-, -s** *or* **-nen** [-ˈgoːnən] (*auch* **Mangopflaume**) mango

Mangobaum M mango tree

Mangold ['maŋgɔlt] M **-(e)s, -e** [-də] mangel(wurzel)

Mangrove [maŋˈgroːvə] F **-, -n** mangrove

Manie [maˈniː] F **-, -n** [-ˈniːən] mania

Manier [maˈniːɐ] F **-, -en (a)** NO PL (= *Art und Weise*) manner; (*eines Künstlers etc*) style **(b) Manieren** PL (= *Umgangsformen*) manners; **was sind das für ~en?** (*inf*) that's no way to behave

manierlich [maˈniːɐlɪç] **1** ADJ **(a)** *Kind* well-mannered; *Benehmen* good **(b)** (*inf*: = *einigermaßen gut*) reasonable; *Aussehen, Frisur, Kleidung* respectable **2** ADV *essen* politely; *sich benehmen* properly; *sich kleiden* respectably

Manifest [maniˈfɛst] NT **-(e)s, -e** manifesto

Manifestation [manifɛstaˈtsioːn] F **-, -en** manifestation; (*Sw*: = *Kundgebung*) demonstration

manifestieren [manifɛsˈtiːrən], *ptp* **manifestiert** (*geh*) **1** VT to demonstrate, to manifest **2** VI (*Sw*) to demonstrate **3** VR to manifest oneself

Maniküre [maniˈkyːrə] F **-, -n (a)** (= *Handpflege*) manicure **(b)** (= *Handpflegerin*) manicurist

maniküren [maniˈkyːrən], *ptp* **manikürt** VT to manicure

Manipulation [manipulaˈtsioːn] F **-, -en** manipulation; (= *Trick*) manoeuvre (*Brit*), maneuver (*US*)

manipulierbar ADJ manipulable; **leicht ~** easily manipulated; **schwer ~** difficult to manipulate

manipulieren [manipuˈliːrən], *ptp* **manipuliert** VT to manipulate

manisch ['maːnɪʃ] ADJ manic; **~-depressiv, ~-melancholisch** manic-depressive

Manko ['maŋko] NT **-s, -s (a)** (*Comm*: = *Fehlbetrag*) deficit; **~ haben** (*inf*) *or* **machen** (*inf*) to be short (*inf*); **~ machen** (*inf*: *bei Verkauf*) to make a loss **(b)** (*fig*: = *Nachteil*) shortcoming

Mann [man] M **-(e)s, ̈er** ['mɛnɐ] **(a)** man; **der böse** *or* **schwarze ~** the bogeyman; **ein feiner ~** a (perfect) gentleman; **der erste ~ sein** (*fig*) to be in charge; **der ~ im Mond(e)** the man in the moon; **ein ~ von Wort** a man of his word; **drei ~ hoch** (*inf*) three of them together; **wie ein ~** as one man; **auf den ~ dressiert sein** to be trained to go for people; **etw an den ~ bringen** (*inf*) to get rid of sth; **seinen ~ stehen** to hold one's own; (= *auf eigenen Füßen stehen*) to stand on one's own two feet; **einen kleinen ~ im Ohr haben** (*hum*) to be crazy (*inf*); **und ein ~, ein Wort, er hats auch gemacht** and, as good as his word, he did it; **~ gegen ~** man against man; **pro ~** per head; **ein Gespräch unter Männern** *or* **von ~ zu ~** a man-to-man talk; *siehe auch* **Mannen**

(b) (= *Ehemann*) husband; **~ und Frau werden** to become man and wife

(c) *pl* **Leute** (= *Besatzungsmitglied*) man; **20 ~** 20 hands *or* men; **mit ~ und Maus untergehen** to go down with all hands; (*Passagierschiff*) to go down with no survivors

(d) *pl* **Leute** (= *Teilnehmer, Sport, Cards*) man

(e) (*inf*: *als Interjektion*) (my) God (*inf*); **~, das kannst du doch nicht machen!** hey, you can't do that!; **mach schnell, ~!** hurry up, man!; **~, oh ~!** oh boy! (*inf*); **(mein) lieber ~!** my God! (*inf*)

Männchen ['mɛnçən] NT **-s, -** DIM *von* **Mann (a)** little man; (= *Zwerg*) man(n)ikin; **~ malen** ≈ to doodle **(b)** (*Biol*) male; (= *Vogelmännchen*) male, cock **(c)** **~ machen** (*Tier*) to sit up on its hind legs; (*Hund*) to (sit up and) beg

Mannen ['manən] PL (*Hist*: = *Gefolgsleute*) men *pl*

Mannequin [manəˈkɛ̃ː, ˈmanəkɛ̃] NT **-s, -s** (fashion) model

Männer PL *von* **Mann**

Männer- IN CPDS men's; (= *eines bestimmten Mannes*) man's; **Männerberuf** M male profession; **Männerfang** M **auf ~ ausgehen/sein** to go/be looking for a man/men; (*zwecks Heirat*) to go/be husband-hunting; **Männerfreundschaft** F friendship between men; **er hat immer ~en vorgezogen** he

has always preferred friendship(s) with other men; **Männergeschichte** F affair with a man; (= *Erlebnisse*) sexploits *pl* (*hum inf*); **Männerhaus** NT men's house; **Männermagazin** NT magazine for men; **männermordend** ADJ man-eating; **Männersache** F (*Angelegenheit*) man's business; (*Arbeit*) job for a man; **~n** men's affairs; **Fußball war früher ~** football used to be a male preserve; **Männerüberschuss** M surplus of men

Mannesalter NT manhood *no art*; **im besten ~ sein** to be in one's prime

mannigfach ['manɪçfax] ADJ ATTR manifold

mannigfaltig ['manɪçfaltɪç] ADJ diverse

Mannjahr NT (*Ind*) man-year

Männlein ['mɛnlain] NT **-s, -** DIM *von* **Mann** little man; (= *Zwerg*) man(n)ikin; **~ und Weiblein** (*hum inf*) boys and girls

männlich ['mɛnlɪç] **1** ADJ **(a)** male; *Reim, Wort* masculine **(b)** (*fig*: = *mannhaft*) *Stärke, Mut, Entschluss, Wesen, Stimme* manly; *Auftreten* masculine; *Frau* mannish **2** ADV **~ dominiert** male-dominated; **~ geprägt** masculine

Männlichkeit F **-,** NO PL (*fig*) manliness; (*von Auftreten*) masculinity; (*von Frau*) mannishness

Mannloch NT (*Tech*) manhole

Mannschaft ['manʃaft] F **-, -en** (*Sport, fig*) team; (*Naut, Aviat*) crew; **~(en)** (*Mil*) men *pl*

Mannschafts- IN CPDS (*Sport*) team; **Mannschaftsaufstellung** F team line-up; (*das Aufstellen*) selection of the team; **Mannschaftsgeist** M team spirit; **Mannschaftskampf** M (*Sport*) team event; **Mannschaftsraum** M (*Sport*) team quarters *pl*; (*Mil*) men's quarters *pl*; (*Naut*) crew's quarters *pl*; (= *Umkleideraum*) changing rooms *pl*; **Mannschaftssieger** M (*Sport*) winning team

Manns- ['mans-]: **mannshoch** ADJ as high as a man; **der Schnee liegt ~** the snow is six feet deep; **mannstoll** ADJ man-mad (*esp Brit inf*)

Mannweib NT (*pej*) mannish woman

Manometer [manoˈmeːtɐ] NT **-s, -** (*Tech*) pressure gauge; **~!** (*inf*) wow! (*inf*)

Manöver [maˈnøːvɐ] NT **-s, -** (*lit, fig*) manoeuvre (*Brit*), maneuver (*US*)

Manöver-: Manövergelände NT exercise area; (*ständig*) ranges *pl*; **Manöverkritik** F (*fig*) postmortem; **Manöverschaden** M damage resulting from military manoeuvres (*Brit*) *or* maneuvers (*US*)

manövrieren [manøˈvriːrən], *ptp* **manövriert** VTI (*lit, fig*) to manoeuvre (*Brit*), to maneuver (*US*)

Manövrier-: manövrierfähig ADJ manoeuvrable (*Brit*), maneuverable (*US*); (*fig*) flexible; **manövrierunfähig** ADJ disabled

Mansarde [manˈzardə] F **-, -n** garret; (*Boden*) attic

Manschette [manˈʃɛtə] F **-, -n (a)** (= *Ärmelaufschlag*) cuff; (*zur Blutdruckmessung*) blood pressure cuff **(b)** (= *Umhüllung*) frill **(c)** **~n haben** (*inf*) to be scared stupid (*inf*)

Manschettenknopf M cufflink

Mantel ['mantl] M **-s, ̈** ['mɛntl] **(a)** coat; (= *Umhang*) cloak **(b)** (*Tech*) (= *Rohrmantel*) jacket; (= *Geschossmantel*) casing; (= *Reifenmantel*) outer tyre (*Brit*) *or* tire (*US*) **(c)** (*fig*) cloak; **etw mit dem ~ der christlichen Nächstenliebe zudecken** to forgive and forget sth

Mantel- IN CPDS (*Tex*) coat; **Mantelpavian** M sacred *or* hamadryas baboon; **Manteltarifvertrag** M (*Ind*) general agreement on conditions of employment; **Mantel-und-Degen-Film** M swashbuckling film

Mantra ['mantra] NT **-(s), -s** mantra

mantschen ['mantʃn] VI (*inf*) to mess around (*inf*)

manuell [maˈnuɛl] **1** ADJ manual **2** ADV manually

Manuskript [manuˈskrɪpt] NT **-(e)s, -e** manuscript; (*Rad, Film, TV*) script

Maoismus [maoˈɪsmʊs] M **-,** NO PL Maoism

maoistisch [maoˈɪstɪʃ] **1** ADJ Maoist **2** ADV **~ gesinnt** Maoist

Maori ['mauri, maˈoːri] M **-(s), -(s)** *or* f **-, -(s)** Maori

Mappe ['mapə] F -, -n (= *Aktenhefter*) file; (= *Aktentasche*) briefcase; (= *Schulmappe*) (school) bag; (= *Federmappe, Bleistiftmappe*) pencil case

Vorsicht! **Mappe** *wird nicht mit dem englischen Wort* **map** *übersetzt.*

Marabu ['ma:rabu] M -s, -s (*Orn*) marabou
Maracuja [mara'ku:ja] F -, -s passion fruit
Marathon[1] ['ma:ratɔn, 'maratɔn] M -s, -s marathon
Marathon[2] NT -s, -s (*fig*) marathon
Marathon- IN CPDS marathon; **Marathonlauf** M marathon; **Marathonläufer(in)** M(F) marathon runner
Märchen ['mɛːɐçən] NT -s, - fairy tale; (*inf*) tall story
Märchen- IN CPDS fairy-tale; **Märchenbuch** NT book of fairy tales; **Märchenerzähler(in)** M(F) teller of fairy tales; (*fig*) storyteller; **märchenhaft** ADJ fairy-tale *attr*, fabulous; (*fig*) fabulous ADV *reich* fabulously; *singen, malen* beautifully; ~ schön incredibly beautiful; **Märchenland** NT fairyland; **Märchenprinz** M Prince Charming; (*fig auch*) fairy-tale prince; **Märchenprinzessin** F (*fig*) fairy-tale princess
Marder ['mardɐ] M -s, - marten
Margarine [marga'ri:nə, (*Aus*) -'ri:n] F -, -n margarine
Marge ['marʒə] F -, -n (*Comm*) margin
Margerite [marga'ri:tə] F -, -n daisy
marginal [margi'na:l] ADJ marginal ADV marginally; *betreffen, interessieren* slightly
Maria [ma'ri:a] F -s Mary; **die Mutter ~** the Virgin Mary
Mariä [ma'ri:ɛ] F: **Mariä Empfängnis** F the Immaculate Conception; **Mariä Himmelfahrt** F Assumption
Marien- [ma'ri:ən-]: **Marienaltar** M Lady altar; **Marienkäfer** M ladybird (*Brit*), ladybug (*US*); **Marienverehrung** F adoration of the Virgin Mary
Marihuana [mari'hua:na] NT -s, NO PL marijuana
Marille [ma'rilə] F -, -n (*Aus*) apricot
Marinade [mari'na:də] F -, -n (a) (*Cook*) marinade; (= *Soße*) mayonnaise-based sauce (b) **Marinaden** PL (= *Fischkonserven*) canned *or* tinned (*Brit*) fish
Marine [ma'ri:nə] F -, -n navy
Marine- IN CPDS naval; **marineblau** ADJ navy-blue
marinieren [mari'ni:rən], *ptp* **mariniert** VT *Fisch, Fleisch* to marinate; **marinierter Hering** pickled herring
Marionette [mario'nɛtə] F -, -n marionette; (*fig*) puppet
Marionetten- IN CPDS puppet; **Marionettenregierung** F puppet government; **Marionettenspieler(in)** M(F) puppeteer; **Marionettentheater** NT puppet theatre (*Brit*) *or* theater (*US*)
maritim [mari'ti:m] ADJ maritime
Mark[1] [mark] NT -(e)s, NO PL (= *Knochenmark*) marrow; (*Bot*: = *Gewebemark*) medulla; (= *Fruchtfleisch*) purée; **bis ins** ~ (*fig*) to the core; **jdn bis ins ~ treffen** (*fig*) to cut sb to the quick; **es geht mir durch ~ und Bein** (*inf*) it goes right through me
Mark[2] F -, - *or* (*hum*) ⁼er ['mɛrkɐ] (*Hist*) mark; **Deutsche ~** Deutschmark
markant [mar'kant] ADJ (= *ausgeprägt*) clear-cut; *Schriftzüge* clearly defined; (= *hervorstechend*) *Kinn etc* prominent; (= *auffallend*) *Erscheinung, Persönlichkeit* striking ADV (= *auffallend*) strikingly; **sich ~ unterscheiden** to be strikingly different
Marke ['markə] F -, -n (a) (*bei Lebens- und Genussmitteln*) brand; (*bei Industriegütern*) make; **du bist (vielleicht) eine ~!** (*inf*) you're a right one (*inf*)
(b) (= *Briefmarke*) stamp; (= *Essensmarke*) voucher; (= *Rabattmarke*) (trading) stamp; (= *Lebensmittelmarke*) coupon
(c) (= *Erkennungsmarke*) disc; (= *Hundemarke*) dog licence disc (*Brit*), dog tag (*US*); (= *Garderobenmarke*) cloakroom counter; (*Zettel*) cloakroom ticket *or* check (*US*); (= *Polizeimarke*) badge; (= *Spielmarke*) chip
(d) (= *Rekordmarke*) record; (= *Wasserstandsmarke*) watermark; (= *Stand, Niveau*) level
Marken-: **Markenartikel** M proprietary article; **Markenbutter** F nonblended butter, best quality butter; **Markenerzeugnis** NT, **Markenfabrikat** NT proprietary article; **Markenname** M brand *or* proprietary name; **Markenpiraterie** F brand name piracy; **Markenschutz** M protection of trademarks;

Markenware F proprietary goods *pl*; **Markenzeichen** NT (*lit, fig*) trademark
Marker ['markɐ] M -s, -(s) (= *Markierstift*) highlighter
Marketing ['markətɪŋ] NT -s, NO PL marketing
markieren [mar'ki:rən], *ptp* **markiert** VT (*lit, fig*) (*Sport*) to mark; (*Comput auch*) to highlight; (*inf*: = *vortäuschen*) to play; **den starken Mann ~** to play the strong man; **den Dummen** *or* **Dusseligen ~** (*inf*) to act dumb VI (*inf*: = *so tun, als ob*) to put it on (*inf*); **markier doch nicht!** stop putting it on (*inf*)
Markierstift M highlighter
Markierung F -, -en marking; (= *Zeichen*) mark
markig ['markɪç] ADJ *Spruch, Worte* pithy; (*iro*: = *großsprecherisch*) bombastic ADV (*iro*: = *großsprecherisch*) bombastically; **sich ~ ausdrücken** to be fond of strong expressions
Markise [mar'ki:zə] F -, -n awning
Mark-: **Markknochen** M (*Cook*) marrowbone; **Markstück** NT (*Hist*) (one-)mark piece
Markt [markt] M -(e)s, ⁼e ['mɛrktə] (a) market; (= *Jahrmarkt*) fair; **dienstags/jede Woche einmal ist** ~ *or* **wird ~ abgehalten** there is a market every Tuesday/week
(b) (*Comm*) market; (= *Warenverkehr*) trade; **auf dem** *or* **am ~** on the market; **auf den ~ bringen** to put on the market; **auf den ~ kommen** *or* **gebracht werden** to come on the market
(c) (= ~*platz*) marketplace; (= *in the marketplace*); **am ~ wohnen** to live on the marketplace
Markt- IN CPDS market; **Marktanteil** M market share; **Marktbeobachtung** F market study *or* survey; **Marktbericht** M (*Fin*) stock market report; **Marktbude** F market stall; **marktfähig** ADJ *Produkt, Unternehmen* marketable; **Marktfahrer(in)** M(F) (*Aus*) (travelling (*Brit*) *or* traveling (*US*)) market trader; **Marktform** F market form; **Marktforscher(in)** M(F) market researcher; **Marktforschung** F market research; **Marktfrau** F (woman) stallholder; **Marktführer(in)** M(F) market leader; **marktgängig** ADJ (= *marktfähig*) marketable; (= *marktüblich*) current; **Markthalle** F covered market; **Marktlage** F state of the market; **Marktnische** F (market) niche; **Marktplatz** M market square; **am/auf dem ~** on/in the marketplace; **marktreif** ADJ *Produkt* ready for the market; **Marktreife** F **ein Produkt zur ~ entwickeln** to develop a product into a marketable commodity; **Marktschreier(in)** M(F) barker; **marktschreierisch** [-ʃraɪərɪʃ] ADJ loud and vociferous; (*fig*) blatant ADV loudly and vociferously; (*fig*) blatantly; **Marktstand** M market stall; **Marktstudie** F market survey; **marktüblich** ADJ *Preis, Konditionen* current; **zu ~en Konditionen** at usual market terms; **Marktwirtschaft** F market economy; **marktwirtschaftlich** ADJ ATTR market-economy *attr* ADV ~ **orientiert** market-economy-based; ~ **organisiert** with a market-based economy; ~ **arbeiten** to work economically
Marmelade [marmə'la:də] F -, -n jam (*Brit*), jelly (*US*); (= *Orangenmarmelade*) marmalade
Marmor ['marmo:ɐ] M -s, -e marble
Marmor- IN CPDS marble; **Marmorbruch** M marble quarry
marmorieren [marmo'ri:rən], *ptp* **marmoriert** VT to marble
Marmorkuchen M marble cake
marmorn ['marmɔrn, 'marmo:ɐn] ADJ marble
marode [ma'ro:də] ADJ washed-out (*inf*); *Gebäude, Anlagen* ramshackle; *Wirtschaft etc* ailing
Marokkaner [marɔ'ka:nɐ] M -s, -, **Marokkanerin** [-ərɪn] F -, -nen Moroccan
marokkanisch [marɔ'ka:nɪʃ] ADJ Moroccan
Marokko [ma'rɔko] NT -s Morocco
Marotte [ma'rɔtə] F -, -n quirk
Mars [mars] M -, NO PL (*Myth, Astron*) Mars
Marsbewohner(in) M(F) Martian
marsch [marʃ] INTERJ (a) (*Mil*) march (b) (*inf*) off with you; ~ **ins Bett!** off to bed with you at the double! (*inf*)
Marsch [marʃ] M -(e)s, ⁼e ['mɛrʃə] (= *auch ~musik*) march; (= *Wanderung*) hike; **einen ~ machen** to go on a march/hike; **sich in ~ setzen** to move off; **jdm den ~ blasen** (*inf*) to give sb a rocket (*inf*)
Marsch-: **Marschbefehl** M (*Mil*) (*für Truppen*) marching orders *pl*; (*für Einzelnen*) travel orders *pl*; **marschbereit** ADJ ready to move; **Marschflugkörper** M cruise missile; **Marschgepäck** NT pack

marschieren [mar'ʃiːrən], *ptp* **marschiert** VI AUX SEIN to march; (*fig*) to march off

Marsch-: Marschland NT marsh(land); **Marschmusik** F military marches *pl*; **Marschrichtung** F, **Marschroute** F (*lit*) route of march; (*fig*) line of approach; **Marschverpflegung** F rations *pl*; (*Mil*) field rations *pl*

Marshallplan ['marʃal-] M (*Pol*) Marshall Plan

Marsmensch M Martian

Marterl ['martel] NT **-s, -n** (*S Ger, Aus*) wayside shrine with a crucifix

Marterpfahl M stake

martialisch [mar'tsiaːlɪʃ] (*geh*) 🔳 ADJ martial 🔳 ADV *brüllen, aussehen* in a warlike manner

Martinshorn NT (*von Polizei und Feuerwehr*) siren; **mit ~** with its siren blaring

Märtyrer ['mertyrɐ] M **-s, -**, **Märtyrerin** [-ərɪn] F **-, -nen** (*Eccl, fig*) martyr; **sich als ~ aufspielen** (*pej*) to make a martyr of oneself

Martyrium [mar'tyːriʊm] NT **-s, Martyrien** [-riən] martyrdom; (*fig*) ordeal

Marxismus [mar'ksɪsmʊs] M **-**, NO PL Marxism

Marxismus-Leninismus M Marxism-Leninism

Marxist [mar'ksɪst] M **-en, -en**, **Marxistin** [-'ksɪstɪn] F **-, -nen** Marxist

marxistisch [mar'ksɪstɪʃ] 🔳 ADJ Marxist 🔳 ADV *klingen etc* Marxist; **~ gesinnte Kreise** Marxist groups; **seine Lehre ist ~ beeinflusst** he is influenced by (the teachings of) Marx

marxsch [marksʃ] ADJ ATTR Marxian

März [merts] M **-(es)** *or* (*poet*) **-en, -e** March; **im ~** in March; **im Monat ~** in the month of March; **heute ist der zweite ~** today is March the second *or* March second (*US*); (*geschrieben*) today is 2nd March *or* March 2nd; **Berlin, den 4. ~ 2001** (*in Brief*) Berlin, March 4th, 2001, Berlin, 4th March 2001; **am Mittwoch, dem** *or* **den 4. ~** on Wednesday the 4th of March; **am ersten ~ fahren wir nach ...** on the first of March we are going to ...; **in diesem ~** this March; **im Laufe des ~** during March; **der ~ war sehr warm** March was very warm; **Anfang/ Ende/Mitte ~** at the beginning/at the end/in the middle of March

Märzenbecher M (*Bot*) snowflake

Marzipan [martsi'paːn, 'martsipaːn] NT **-s, -e** marzipan

Masche ['maʃə] F **-, -n (a)** (= *Strickmasche, Häkelmasche*) stitch; (*von Netz*) hole; (*von Kettenhemd*) link; **die ~n eines Netzes** the mesh *sing* of a net; **rechte/linke ~n** (*beim Stricken*) plain/ purl stitches; **jdm durch die ~n schlüpfen** to slip through sb's net; **durch die ~n des Gesetzes schlüpfen** to slip through a loophole in the law
(b) (*inf* = *Trick*) trick; (= *Eigenart*) fad; **die ~ raushaben** to know how to do it; **er versucht es immer noch auf die alte ~** he's still trying the same old trick; **das ist seine neueste ~, das ist die neueste ~ von ihm** that's his latest (fad *or* craze)

Maschen-: Maschendraht M wire netting; **Maschendrahtzaun** M wire-netting fence

Maschin- [ma'ʃiːn] (*Aus*) IN CPDS = **Maschine(n)-**

Maschine [ma'ʃiːnə] F **-, -n** machine; (= *Motor*) engine; (= *Flugzeug*) plane; (= *Schreibmaschine*) typewriter; (*inf*: = *Motorrad*) bike; **etw in der ~ waschen** to machine-wash sth; **etw auf** *or* **mit der ~ schreiben, etw in die ~ tippen** *or* **schreiben** to type sth; **~ schreiben** to type; **sie schreibt ~** she types

maschinegeschrieben ADJ typewritten

maschinell [maʃi'nɛl] 🔳 ADJ *Herstellung, Bearbeitung* mechanical, machine *attr*; *Anlage, Übersetzung* machine *attr*; **~e Ausstattung** machines *pl* 🔳 ADV mechanically; **die Produktion erfolgt weitgehend ~** production is predominantly mechanized

Maschinen-: Maschinenbau M mechanical engineering; **Maschinenbauer** M, *pl* **-**, **Maschinenbauerin** F, *pl* **-nen** mechanical engineer; **Maschinendefekt** M mechanical fault; **Maschinenfabrik** F engineering works *sing or pl*; **maschinengeschrieben** ADJ typewritten; **Maschinengewehr** NT machine gun; **mit ~(en) beschießen** to machine-gun; **Maschinenlaufzeit** F machine running time; **maschinenlesbar** ADJ machine-readable; **Maschinenöl** NT lubricating oil; **Maschinenpark** M plant; **Maschinenpistole** F submachine gun; **Maschinenraum** M plant room; (*Naut*) engine room; **Maschinenschaden** M mechanical fault; (*Aviat*

etc) engine fault; **Maschinenschlosser(in)** M(F) machine fitter; **Maschinenschrift** F typescript; **in ~** typed; **maschinenschriftlich** ADJ typewritten *no adv*; **Maschinenstürmer** M (*Hist, fig*) Luddite; **Maschinenstürmerei** [-ʃtyrməˈrai] F **-**, NO PL Luddism; **Maschinenteil** NT machine part; **Maschinenwärter(in)** M(F) machine minder

Maschinist [maʃi'nɪst] M **-en, -en**, **Maschinistin** [-'nɪstɪn] F **-, -nen** (= *Schiffsmaschinist*) engineer; (= *Eisenbahnmaschinist*) engine driver, engineer (*US*)

Maser ['maːze] F **-, -n** vein; **Holz mit feinen ~n** wood with a fine grain

maserig ['maːzərɪç] ADJ grained

Masern ['maːzɐn] PL measles *sing*; **die ~ haben** to have (the) measles

Maserung ['maːzərʊŋ] F **-, -en** grain

Maske ['maskə] F **-, -n (a)** (*lit, fig*) mask; **die ~ abnehmen** *or* **ablegen** to take off one's mask; (*fig*) to let fall one's mask; **die ~ fallen lassen** *or* **abwerfen** (*fig*) to throw off one's mask; **jdm die ~ herunterreißen** *or* **vom Gesicht reißen** (*fig*) to unmask sb **(b)** (*Theat*: = *Aufmachung*) make-up; **~ machen** to make up

Masken-: Maskenball M masked ball; **Maskenbildner** [-bɪltnɐ] M **-s, -**, **Maskenbildnerin** [-ərɪn] F **-, -nen** make-up artist

Maskerade [maskə'raːdə] F **-, -n** costume

maskieren [mas'kiːrən], *ptp* **maskiert** 🔳 VT **(a)** (= *verkleiden*) to dress up; (= *unkenntlich machen*) to disguise **(b)** (= *verbergen*) to mask, to disguise 🔳 VR to dress up; (= *sich unkenntlich machen*) to disguise oneself

maskiert [mas'kiːɐt] ADJ masked

Maskierung F **-, -en (a)** (= *das Verkleiden*) dressing up; (= *Sich-Unkenntlichmachen*) disguising oneself **(b)** (= *Verkleidung*) fancy-dress costume; (*von Spion etc*) disguise **(c)** (= *Verhüllung*) masking

Maskottchen [mas'kɔtçən] NT **-s, -** (lucky) mascot

maskulin [masku'liːn] ADJ masculine

Maskulinum ['maskuliːnʊm] NT **-s, Maskulina** [-na] masculine noun

Masochismus [mazɔ'xɪsmʊs] M **-**, NO PL masochism

Masochist [mazɔ'xɪst] M **-en, -en**, **Masochistin** [-'xɪstɪn] F **-, -nen** masochist

masochistisch [mazɔ'xɪstɪʃ] 🔳 ADJ masochistic 🔳 ADV **~ veranlagt sein** to have masochistic inclinations

maß PRET *von* **messen**

Maß[1] [maːs] NT **-es, -e (a)** (= *~einheit*) measure (*für* of); (= *Zollstock*) rule; (= *Bandmaß*) tape measure; **~ und Gewichte** weights and measures; **das ~ aller Dinge** (*fig*) the measure of all things; **das richtige** *or* **rechte ~ halten** (*fig*) to strike the right balance; **mit zweierlei** *or* **verschiedenem ~ messen** (*fig*) to operate a double standard; **das ~ ist voll** (*fig*) enough's enough; **und, um das ~ voll zu machen ...** (*fig*) and to cap it all ... (*esp Brit*), and to top it all off ... (*esp US*); **in reichem ~(e)** abundantly; **in reichem ~(e) vorhanden sein** to be abundant; (*Energie, Zeit etc*) to be plentiful
(b) (= *Abmessung*) measurement; **sich** (*dat*) **etw nach ~ anfertigen lassen** to have sth made to measure; **~ nehmen** to measure up; **bei jdm ~ nehmen** to take sb's measurements; **Schuhe/Hemden nach ~** shoes/shirts made to measure, custom-made shoes/shirts
(c) (= *Ausmaß*) extent; **ein solches/gewisses ~ an** *or* **von ...** such a degree/a certain degree of ...; **in hohem ~(e)** to a high degree; **in solchem ~(e) dass ..., in einem ~(e), dass ...** to such an extent that ...; **in nicht geringem ~(e)** in no small measure; **in geringem ~(e)** to a small extent; **in vollem ~(e)** fully; **in besonderem ~e** especially; **in höchstem ~e** extremely
(d) (= *Mäßigung*) moderation; **~ halten** to be moderate; **in** *or* **mit ~en** in moderation; **ohne ~ und Ziel** immoderately

Maß[2] F **-, -** (*S Ger, Aus*) litre (*Brit*) *or* liter (*US*) (tankard) of beer; **zwei ~ Bier** two litres (*Brit*) *or* liters (*US*) of beer

Massage [ma'saːʒə] F **-, -n** massage

Massage-: Massagesalon M (*euph*) massage parlour (*Brit*) *or* parlor (*US*); **Massagestab** M vibrator

Massaker [ma'saːkɐ] NT **-s, -** massacre

Maß-: Maßangabe F measurement; (*bei Hohlmaßen*) volume *no pl*; **Maßanzug** M made-to-measure *or* custom-made suit; **Maßarbeit** F (*inf*) **das war ~** that was a neat bit of work

Masse [ˈmasə] F **-, -n (a)** (= *Stoff*) mass; (*Cook*) mixture
(b) (= *große Menge*) heaps *pl* (*inf*); (*von Besuchern etc*) host; **die (breite) ~ der Bevölkerung** the bulk of the population; **eine ganze ~** (*inf*) a lot; **sie kamen in wahren ~n** they came in droves; **die ~ muss es bringen** (*Comm*) the profit only comes with quantity
(c) (= *Menschenmenge*) crowd; **in der ~ untertauchen** to disappear into the crowd
(d) (= *Bevölkerungsmasse*) masses *pl* (*auch pej*); **die namenlose** *or* **graue** *or* **breite ~** the masses *pl*
(e) (= *Konkursmasse*) assets *pl*; (= *Erbmasse*) estate
(f) (*Phys*) mass
Maßeinheit F unit of measurement
Massekabel NT ground cable
Massen- IN CPDS mass; **Massenabsatz** M bulk selling; **das ist kein Artikel für den ~** that isn't intended for the mass market; **Massenandrang** M crush; **Massenarbeitslosigkeit** F mass unemployment; **Massenartikel** M mass-produced article; **Massenaufgebot** NT large body; **in einem ~ erscheinen** to turn up in force; **Massenauflauf** M, NO PL crowds *pl* of people; **es gab einen ~ am Unfallort** huge crowds of people gathered at the scene of the accident; **Massenentlassung** F mass redundancy; **Massenfabrikation** F, **Massenfertigung** F mass production; **Massengrab** NT mass grave; **Massengüter** PL bulk goods *pl*; **massenhaft** 1 ADJ on a huge scale; **~ Fanbriefe/Sekt** *etc* (*inf*) masses of fan letters/champagne *etc* (*inf*) 2 ADV on a huge scale; **kommen, erscheinen, eingehen, austreten** in droves; **Massenherstellung** F mass production; **Massenkarambolage** F pile-up (*inf*); **Massenmedien** PL mass media *pl*; **Massenmord** M mass murder; **Massenmörder(in)** M(F) mass murderer; **Massenproduktion** F mass production; **Massensterben** NT mass of deaths; **Massentierhaltung** F intensive livestock farming
Massenvernichtung F mass extermination
Massenvernichtungs-: Massenvernichtungslager NT extermination camp; **Massenvernichtungsmittel** PL means *sing* of mass extermination; **Massenvernichtungswaffe** F weapon of mass destruction
Massen-: Massenversammlung F mass meeting; **Massenwahn** M mass hysteria; **Massenware** F mass-produced article
Masseur [maˈsøːɐ] M **-s, -e** masseur
Masseurin [maˈsøːrɪn] F **-, -nen** (*Berufsbezeichnung*) masseuse
Masseuse [maˈsøːzə] F **-, -n** (*in Eros-Center etc*) masseuse
maßgebend 1 ADJ (= *ausschlaggebend*) *Einfluss* decisive; *Meinung, Ansicht, Text* definitive; *Fachmann* authoritative; (= *wichtig*) *Persönlichkeit* leading; (= *zuständig*) competent; **das Verhalten des Chefs ist ~ für die Mitarbeiter** the boss's behaviour (*Brit*) *or* behavior (*US*) sets the standard for his employees; **das ist hier nicht ~** that doesn't weigh here 2 ADV **sie hat ~ dazu beigetragen** she made a significant contribution to it
maßgeblich 1 ADJ (= *entscheidend*) *Einfluss* decisive; *Faktor* deciding; (= *führend*) *Person, Firma, Rolle* leading; *Beteiligung* substantial; **~en Anteil an etw** (*dat*) **haben** to make a major contribution to sth 2 ADV decisively; **~ an etw** (*dat*) **beteiligt sein** to play a substantial role in sth
maßgeschneidert [-ɡəʃnaɪdɐt] ADJ *Anzug* made-to-measure, custom-made; (*fig*) *Lösung, Produkte* tailor-made
Maßhalteappell M appeal for moderation
maßhalten M SEP IRREG *siehe* **Maß¹**
massieren¹ [maˈsiːrən], *ptp* **massiert** 1 VT *Körper, Haut* to massage 2 VI to give (a) massage
massieren² *ptp* **massiert** 1 VT *Truppen* to mass 2 VR to amass; (*Truppen*) to mass
massig [ˈmasɪç] 1 ADJ massive, huge 2 ADV (*inf*) **~ Arbeit/Geld** *etc* masses of work/money *etc* (*inf*)
mäßig [ˈmɛːsɪç] 1 ADJ **(a)** (= *bescheiden*) moderate
(b) (= *unterdurchschnittlich*) *Leistung, Schulnote etc* mediocre; *Begabung, Beifall, Erfolg* moderate; *Gesundheit* middling 2 ADV **(a)** (= *nicht viel*) moderately; **etw ~ tun** to do sth in moderation; **~ essen** to eat with moderation; **~, aber regelmäßig** in moderation but regularly **(b)** (= *nicht besonders*) moderately; *groß* reasonably; **sich nur ~ anstrengen** not to make much of an effort

-mäßig ADJ, ADV SUF **(a)** (*in einer bestimmten Art*) -like; **geschäftsmäßiges Verhalten** businesslike behaviour (*Brit*) *or* behavior (*US*) **(b)** (*bezüglich einer Sache*) -wise; **geldmäßig haben wir Probleme** we are having problems moneywise
mäßigen [ˈmɛːsɪɡn] 1 VT (= *mildern*) *Anforderungen* to moderate; *Zorn, Ungeduld* to curb; **sein Tempo ~** to slow down; *siehe auch* **gemäßigt** 2 VR (*im Essen, Trinken, Temperament*) to restrain oneself; **sich im Ton ~** to moderate one's tone
Mäßigkeit F **-,** NO PL **(a)** (*beim Essen, Trinken*) moderation; (*von Forderungen, Preisen etc*) moderateness **(b)** (= *Mittelmäßigkeit*) mediocrity; (*von Begabung, Beifall*) moderateness
Mäßigung F **-,** NO PL restraint
massiv [maˈsiːf] 1 ADJ **(a)** (= *pur, nicht hohl, stabil*) solid **(b)** (= *heftig*) *Beleidigung* gross; *Drohung, Kritik* serious; *Anschuldigung* severe; *Protest, Forderung, Unterstützung* strong; **~ werden** to turn nasty 2 ADV **(a)** (= *wuchtig*) *gebaut* massively **(b)** (= *heftig*) severely; *protestieren, fördern, unterstützen* strongly; **jdm ~ drohen** to issue a serious threat to sb **(c)** (= *stark*) *zunehmen, verstärken* greatly; *erhöhen* massively; *steigen* strongly; *einschränken, behindern* severely; **sich ~ verschlechtern** to deteriorate sharply
Massiv [maˈsiːf] NT **-s, -e** [-və] (*Geol*) massif
Maßkrug M litre (*Brit*) *or* liter (*US*) beer mug; (= *Steinkrug*) stein
maßlos 1 ADJ extreme; *Mensch* (*in Forderungen etc auch, im Essen etc*) immoderate; **er war ~ in seiner Wut/Freude** *etc* his rage/joy *etc* knew no bounds 2 ADV (= *äußerst*) extremely; *übertreiben* grossly; **es ist alles ~ traurig** (*inf*) it's all very sad; **er raucht/trinkt ~** he smokes/drinks to excess
Maßlosigkeit F **-, -en** extremeness; (= *Übermäßigkeit*) excessiveness; (= *Grenzenlosigkeit*) boundlessness; (*im Essen etc*) lack of moderation; **die ~ seiner Forderungen** his excessive demands
Maßnahme [-naːmə] F **-, -n** measure; **~n gegen jdn/etw treffen** *or* **ergreifen** to take measures against sb/sth; **sich zu ~n gezwungen sehen** to be forced to take action
Maßschneider(in) M(F) bespoke *or* custom (*US*) tailor
Maßstab M **(a)** (= *Lineal*) ruler; (= *Zollstock*) rule **(b)** (= *Kartenmaßstab, Modell, Ausmaß*) scale; **die Karte hat einen kleinen/großen ~** it's a small-scale/large-scale map; **im ~ 1:1000** on a scale of 1:1000; **im ~ 1:25000 gezeichnet** drawn to a scale of 1:25000; **etw in verkleinertem ~ darstellen** to scale sth down; **Klimaverschiebungen im großen ~** large-scale climate changes **(c)** (*fig*: = *Richtlinie, Kriterium*) standard; **für jdn als** *or* **zum ~ dienen, für jdn einen ~ abgeben** to serve as a model for sb; **sich** (*dat*) **jdn/etw zum** *or* **als ~ nehmen** to take sb/sth as a yardstick; **das ist für mich kein ~** I don't take that as my yardstick
maßstab(s)gerecht, maßstab(s)getreu ADJ, ADV (true) to scale; **eine ~e Karte** an accurate scale map
maßvoll 1 ADJ moderate 2 ADV moderately
Mast¹ [mast] M **-(e)s, -en** *or* **-e** (*Naut, Rad, TV*) mast; (= *Stange*) pole; (*Elec*) pylon
Mast² F **-, -en** (= *das Mästen*) fattening; (= *Futter*) feed; (= *Schweinemast*) mast
Mast-: Mastbaum M mast; **Mastdarm** M rectum
mästen [ˈmɛstn] 1 VT to fatten 2 VR (*inf*) to stuff (*inf*) oneself
Masturbation [mastʊrbaˈtsioːn] F **-, -en** masturbation
masturbieren [mastʊrˈbiːrən], *ptp* **masturbiert** VTI to masturbate
Match [mɛtʃ] NT *or* M **-(e)s, -e(s)** match
Matchball [mɛtʃ-] M (*Tennis*) match point
Material [mateˈriaːl] NT **-s, -ien** [-liən] material; (= *Baumaterial, Utensilien, Gerät*) materials *pl*; (= *Beweismaterial, Belastungsmaterial*) evidence
Material-: Materialermüdung F (*von Metall*) metal fatigue; **Materialfehler** M material defect
Materialismus [materiaˈlɪsmʊs] M **-,** NO PL materialism
Materialist [materiaˈlɪst] M **-en, -en, Materialistin** [-ˈlɪstɪn] F **-, -nen** materialist
materialistisch [materiaˈlɪstɪʃ] 1 ADJ materialist(ic); (*pej*) materialistic 2 ADV materialistically

Material-: **Materialkosten** PL cost of materials *sing*; **Materialprüfung** F testing of materials; **Materialsammlung** F collection of material

Materie [ma'te:riə] F **-, -n (a)** NO PL (*Phys, Philos*) matter *no art* **(b)** (= *Stoff, Thema*) subject matter *no indef art*; **die ~ beherrschen** to know one's stuff

materiell [mate'riel] **1** ADJ material; (= *gewinnsüchtig*) materialistic **2** ADV **(a)** (= *finanziell*) financially; (*pej*: = *materialistisch*) materialistically; **~ eingestellt sein** (*pej*) to be materialistic **(b)** (= *das Material betreffend*) materially; **die Behörde war ~ und personell umfangreich ausgestattet** the authority was fully provided for with resources and staff

Mathe ['matə] F **-**, NO PL (*Sch inf*) maths *sing* (*Brit inf*), math (*US inf*)

Mathematik [matema'ti:k] F **-**, NO PL mathematics *sing no art*

Mathematiker [mate'ma:tikɐ] M **-s, -**, **Mathematikerin** [-ərɪn] F **-, -nen** mathematician

mathematisch [mate'ma:tɪʃ] **1** ADJ mathematical **2** ADV mathematically

Matjes ['matjəs] M **-, -**, **Matjeshering** M young herring

Matratze [ma'tratsə] F **-, -n** mattress

matriarchalisch [matriar'ça:lɪʃ] **1** ADJ matriarchal **2** ADV **eine ~ orientierte Bewegung** a matriarchal movement; **sie regiert die Familie ~** she rules the family like a matriarch

Matrix ['ma:trɪks] F **-**, **Matrizen** *or* **Matrizes** [ma'trɪtsn, ma'tri:tse:s] (*Math, Med, Biol*) matrix

Matrixdrucker M dot-matrix (printer)

Matrose [ma'tro:zə] M **-n, -n**, **Matrosin** [-'tro:zɪn] F sailor; (*als Rang*) ordinary seaman

Matrosen- IN CPDS sailor; **Matrosenanzug** M sailor suit; **Matrosenmütze** F sailor's cap

Matrosin F *siehe* **Matrose**

Matsch [matʃ] M **-(e)s**, NO PL (*inf*) (= *breiige Masse*) mush; (= *Schlamm*) mud; (= *Schneematsch*) slush; **~ aus jdm machen** (*sl*) to beat sb to a pulp (*inf*)

Matschbirne F (*inf*) bad head (*inf*)

matschig ['matʃɪç] ADJ (*inf*) (= *breiig*) *Obst* mushy; (= *schlammig*) *Straße, Weg* muddy; *Schnee* slushy

matt [mat] **1** ADJ **(a)** (= *schwach*) *Kranker* weak; *Glieder* weary; **sich ~ fühlen** to have no energy **(b)** (= *glanzlos*) *Augen, Metall, Farbe* dull; (= *nicht glänzend*) *Farbe, Papier, Foto* mat(t); (= *trübe*) *Licht* dim; *Glühbirne* pearl; *Spiegel* cloudy **(c)** (*fig*) *Entschuldigung, Widerspruch, Entgegnung* feeble; *Echo* faint; (*St Ex*: = *flau*) slack **(d)** (*Chess*) (check)mate; **jdn ~ setzen** to checkmate sb (*auch fig*), to mate sb **2** ADV **(a)** (= *schwach*) weakly **(b)** (= *nicht hell*) dimly; **~ glänzend** dull **(c)** (= *ohne Nachdruck*) lamely

Matt [mat] NT **-s, -s** (*Chess*) (check)mate

Matte¹ ['matə] F **-, -n** mat; **auf der ~ stehen** (*inf*: = *bereit sein*) to be there and ready for action; **du musst um sechs bei mir auf der ~ stehen** you must be at my place at six; **jdn auf die ~ legen** (= *niederschlagen*) to floor sb

Matte² F **-, -n** (*liter*: *Sw, Aus*) alpine meadow

Mattheit F **-**, NO PL **(a)** (= *Schwäche*) weakness; (*von Gliedern*) weariness; (= *Energielosigkeit*) lack of energy **(b)** (= *Glanzlosigkeit*: *von Augen, Farbe*) dullness; (= *Trübheit*: *von Licht*) dimness

mattieren [ma'ti:rən], *ptp* **mattiert** VT to give a mat(t) finish to; **mattiert sein** to have a mat(t) finish

Mattlack M dull *or* mat(t) lacquer

Mattscheibe F **(a)** (*Phot*) focus(s)ing screen; (*inf*: = *Fernseher*) telly (*Brit inf*), tube (*US inf*) **(b)** (*inf*) **eine ~ haben/kriegen** (= *dumm sein*) to be soft/go soft in the head (*inf*); (= *nicht klar denken können*) to have/get a mental block; **als ich das gesagt habe, muss ich wohl eine ~ gehabt haben** I can't have been really with it when I said that (*inf*)

Matur [ma'tu:ɐ] NT **-s**, NO PL, **Maturum** [ma'tu:rʊm] NT **-s**, NO PL (*old*), **Matura** [ma'tu:ra] F **-**, NO PL (*Aus, Sw*) *siehe* **Abitur**

Maturand [matu'rant] M **-en, -en** [-dn], **Maturandin** [-'randɪn] F **-, -nen** (*old, Sw*), **Maturant** [matu'rant] M **-en, -en** [-tn], **Maturantin** [-'rantɪn] F **-, -nen** (*Aus*) *siehe* **Abiturient(in)**

maturieren [matu'ri:rən], *ptp* **maturiert** VI (*Aus*: = *Abitur machen*) to take one's school-leaving exam (*Brit*), to graduate (from high school) (*US*)

Maturität [maturi'te:t] F **-**, NO PL (*Sw*: = *Hochschulreife*) matriculation exam(ination) (*Brit*), high school diploma (*US*)

Mätzchen ['mɛtsçən] NT **-s, -** (*inf*) antic; **~ machen** to fool around (*inf*); **mach keine ~, schmeiß die Pistole weg!** don't try anything funny, just drop the gun!

Mauer ['mauɐ] F **-, -n** (*lit, fig*) wall; **die (Berliner) ~** (*Hist*) the (Berlin) Wall; **gegen eine ~ des Schweigens anrennen** (*fig*) to run up against a wall of silence

Mauerblümchen [-bly:mçən] NT **-s, -** (*fig inf*) (*beim Tanzen*) wallflower; (= *schüchternes Mädchen*) shy young thing

mauern ['mauɐn] **1** VI **(a)** (= *Maurerarbeit machen*) to build, to lay bricks **(b)** (*Cards*) to hold back; (*Ftbl slfig*) to stonewall **2** VT to build; **der Beckenrand muss gemauert werden** the edge of the pool must be bedded in mortar

Mauer-: **Mauerschütze** M *East German border guard who shot people fleeing west*; **Mauerschwalbe** F, **Mauersegler** M swift; **Mauerspeis** [-ʃpais] M **-es**, NO PL (*esp S Ger*: = *Mörtel*) mortar; **Mauervorsprung** M projection on a/the wall; **Mauerwerk** NT **(a)** (= *Steinmauer*) stonework; (= *Ziegelmauer*) brickwork; **ein mittelalterliches ~** a medieval stone structure **(b)** (= *die Mauern*) walls *pl*

Maul [maul] NT **-(e)s**, **Mäuler** ['mɔylɐ] mouth; (*von Löwe etc, von Zange*) jaws *pl*; (*inf*: *von Menschen*) gob (*Brit inf*), trap (*esp US sl*); (*von Schraubenschlüssel*) head; **ein böses** *or* **ungewaschenes** *or* **gottloses ~** (*inf*) an evil tongue; **ein großes ~ haben** (*inf*) to be a bigmouth (*inf*); **(hungrige) Mäuler stopfen** (*inf*) to feed (hungry) mouths; **darüber werden sich die Leute das ~ zerreißen** (*inf*) that will start people's tongues wagging; **dem Volk** *or* **den Leuten aufs ~ schauen** (*inf*) to listen to what people really say; **halt's ~!** (*vulg*), **~ halten!** (*vulg*) shut your face (*sl*); **halt dein ungewaschenes ~** (*sl*) keep your dirty mouth shut (*inf*)

Maul-: **Maulbeerbaum** M mulberry (tree); **Maulbeere** F mulberry

maulen ['maulən] VI (*inf*) to moan

Maul-: **Maulesel** M mule; **maulfaul** ADJ (*inf*) uncommunicative; **Maulheld(in)** M(F) (*pej*) show-off; **Maulkorb** M (*lit, fig*) muzzle; **einem Hund/jdm einen ~ umhängen** to muzzle a dog/sb; **Maultaschen** PL (*Cook*) pasta squares *pl*; **Maultier** NT mule; **Maul- und Klauenseuche** F (*Vet*) foot-and-mouth disease (*Brit*), hoof-and-mouth disease (*US*)

Maulwurf ['maulvʊrf] M **-(e)s**, **Maulwürfe** [-vʏrfə] (*auch fig*) mole

Maulwurfshaufen M, **Maulwurfshügel** M molehill

Maurer ['maurɐ] M **-s, -**, **Maurerin** [-ərɪn] F **-, -nen** bricklayer; **pünktlich wie die ~** (*hum*) super-punctual

Maurer-: **Maurerarbeit** F bricklaying (work) *no pl*; **Maurerhandwerk** NT bricklaying

Maurerin F *siehe* **Maurer**

Maurerkelle F (bricklayer's) trowel

Mauretanien [maure'ta:niən] NT **-s** Mauritania

mauretanisch [maure'ta:nɪʃ] ADJ Mauritanian

Mauritius [mau'ri:tsiʊs] NT **-'** Mauritius

Maus [maus] F **-**, **Mäuse** ['mɔyzə] mouse (*auch Comput*); **weiße ~** (*fig inf*) traffic cop (*inf*); **weiße Mäuse sehen** (*fig inf*) to see pink elephants (*inf*); **da beißt die ~ keinen Faden ab** (*inf*: = *nicht zu ändern*) there's no changing that; **eine graue ~** (*fig inf*) a mouse (*inf*)

Mauschelei [mauʃə'lai] F **-, -en** (*inf*: = *Korruption*) swindle; **das war bestimmt ~** it was definitely a swindle

mauscheln ['mauʃln] VTI (= *manipulieren*) to fiddle (*inf*)

Mäuschen ['mɔysçən] NT **-s, - (a)** little mouse **(b)** (*fig*) sweetheart (*inf*)

mäuschenstill ['mɔysçən'ʃtɪl] **1** ADJ dead quiet; (= *reglos*) stock-still **2** ADV quiet as a mouse

Mäusebussard M (common) buzzard

Mausefalle F mousetrap

Mauseloch NT mousehole; **sich in ein ~ verkriechen** (*fig*) to crawl into a hole in the ground

mausen ['mauzn] VI to catch mice; **diese Katze maust gut** the cat is a good mouser

Mauser ['mauzɐ] F **-**, NO PL (*Orn*) moult (*Brit*), molt (*US*); **in der ~ sein** to be moulting (*Brit*) *or* molting (*US*)

mausern ['mauzɐn] VR **(a)** (*Orn*) to moult (*Brit*), to molt (*US*) **(b)** (*inf*) to blossom out (*inf*)

mausetot ['mauzə'to:t] ADJ (*inf*) stone-dead

mausgesteuert [-gəʃtɔyɐt] ADJ (*Comput*) mouse-driven

mausig ['mauzɪç] ADJ **sich ~ machen** (*inf*) to get uppity (*inf*)

Maus-: Mausklick M (*Comput*) mouse click; **etw per ~ steuern/ aktivieren** to control/activate sth by clicking the mouse; **Mausmatte** F (*Comput*) mouse pad; **Maussteuerung** F (*Comput*) mouse control; **Mauszeiger** M (*Comput*) mouse pointer

Maut [maut] F **-, -en** toll

Maut-: Mautgebühr F toll (charge); **Mautschranke** F toll barrier (*Brit*), turnpike (*US*); **Mautstelle** F tollgate; **Mautstraße** F toll road, turnpike (*US*)

max. ABBR *von* **maximal**

maxi ['maksi] ADJ PRED (*Fashion*) maxi; **Maxi tragen** to wear maxi skirts/dresses

Maxi- ['maksi-] IN CPDS **(a)** maxi- **(b)** (= *Riesen-*) giant-sized; **eine ~flasche** a giant-sized bottle **(c)** (*Fashion*) (really) long; **ein ~kleid** a long dress

maximal [maksi'ma:l] **1** ADJ maximum **2** ADV (= *höchstens*) at most; **bis zu ~ £ 100** up to a maximum of £100

Maximal- [maksi'ma:l] IN CPDS maximum;

Maxime [ma'ksi:mə] F **-, -n** (*Liter, Philos*) maxim

maximieren [maksi'mi:rən], *ptp* **maximiert** VT (*Econ, Comput*) to maximize

Maximierung F **-, -en** (*Econ*) maximization

Maximum ['maksimʊm] NT **-s, Maxima** [-ma] maximum (*an +dat* of)

Mayonnaise [majɔ'nɛ:zə] F **-, -n** mayonnaise

Mazedonien [matse'do:niən] NT **-s** Macedonia

Mäzen [mɛ'tse:n] M **-s, -e**, **Mäzenin** [-'tse:nɪn] F **-, -nen** patron

MB [ɛm'be:] ABBR *von* **Megabyte** Mb

MByte, Mbyte ['ɛmbait] ABBR *von* **Megabyte** mbyte

MdB M, **M. d. B.** [ɛm'de:'be:] M **-s, -e** ABBR *von* **Mitglied des Bundestages** Member of the Bundestag

MdE [ɛm'de:'e:] M **-s, -s**, **MdEP** [ɛm'de:'e:'pe:] M **-s, -s** ABBR *von* **Mitglied des Europäischen Parlaments** MEP

MdL M, **M. d. L.** [ɛm'de:'lɛl] M **-s, -s** ABBR *von* **Mitglied des Landtages** Member of the Landtag

MDR [ɛm'de:'lɛr] M **-** ABBR *von* **Mitteldeutscher Rundfunk**

m. E. ABBR *von* **meines Erachtens** in my opinion

Mechanik [me'ça:nɪk] F **-, NO PL** (*Phys*) mechanics *sing*

Mechaniker [me'ça:nikɐ] M **-s, -**, **Mechanikerin** [-ərɪn] F **-, -nen** mechanic

mechanisch [me'ça:nɪʃ] **1** ADJ (*alle Bedeutungen*) mechanical **2** ADV mechanically

mechanisieren [meçani'zi:rən], *ptp* **mechanisiert** VT to mechanize

Mechanisierung F **-, -en** mechanization

Mechanismus [meça'nɪsmʊs] M **-, Mechanismen** [-mən] mechanism; (= *Methode, Arbeitsablauf*) machinery

Meckerei [mɛkə'rai] F **-, -en** (*inf*) grumbling

Meckerer ['mɛkərɐ] M **-s, -**, **Meckerin** [-ərɪn] F (*inf*) grumbler

meckern ['mɛkɐn] VI (*Ziege*) to bleat; (*inf: Mensch*) to moan; **über jdn/etw** (*acc*) **~** (*inf*) to moan about sb/sth

Mecklenburg-Vorpommern ['me:klənbʊrkfo:ɐpɔmən, 'mɛklənbʊrk-] NT Mecklenburg-West Pomerania

Medaille [me'daljə] F **-, -n** (= *Gedenkmünze*) medallion; (*bei Wettbewerben*) medal

Medaillon [medal'jöː] NT **-s, -s** **(a)** (= *Bildchen*) medallion; (= *Schmuckkapsel*) locket **(b)** (*Cook*) médaillon

medial [me'dia:l] **1** ADJ (= *die Medien betreffend*) media *attr* **2** ADV **wir leben in einer ~ vernetzten Welt** we live in a world interconnected through the media; **ein Ereignis ~ ausschlachten** to exploit an event in the media

Mediathek [media'te:k] F **-, -en** multimedia centre (*Brit*) or center (*US*)

Medien ['me:diən] PL media *pl*

Medien-: Medienberater(in) M(F) press adviser; **Medienereignis** NT media event; **Mediengesellschaft** F media society; **Medienkonzern** M media group; **Medienlandschaft** F, **NO PL** media landscape; **Medienpolitik** F (mass) media policy; **Medienpräsenz** F, **NO PL** media presence; **Medienreferent(in)** M(F) press officer; **Medienrummel** M media excitement; **Medienverbund** M **etw im ~ lernen** to learn sth using the multimedia system; **medienwirksam** **1** ADJ **eine ~e Kampagne** a campaign geared toward(s) the media **2** ADV **etw ~ präsentieren** to gear sth toward(s) the media

Medikament [medika'mɛnt] NT **-(e)s, -e** medicine

Medikamenten-: medikamentenabhängig ADJ **~ sein** to be addicted to medical drugs; **Medikamentenmissbrauch** M drug abuse; **Medikamentensucht** F, **NO PL** drug dependency

medikamentös [medikamen'tø:s] **1** ADJ medicinal **2** ADV medicinally

Medio ['me:dio] M **-(s), -s** (*Comm*) mid-month

Mediothek [medio'te:k] F **-, -en** multimedia centre (*Brit*) or center (*US*)

Meditation [medita'tsio:n] F **-, -en** meditation

mediterran [medite'ra:n] ADJ Mediterranean

meditieren [medi'ti:rən], *ptp* **meditiert** VI to meditate

Medium ['me:diʊm] NT **-s, Medien** [-diən] medium

Medizin [medi'tsi:n] F **-, -en** medicine

Medizinball M (*Sport*) medicine ball

Mediziner [medi'tsi:nɐ] M **-s, -**, **Medizinerin** [-ərɪn] F **-, -nen** doctor; (*Univ*) medic (*inf*)

medizinisch [medi'tsi:nɪʃ] **1** ADJ **(a)** (= *ärztlich*) medical; **~e Fakultät** faculty of medicine; **~-technische Assistentin**, **~-technischer Assistent** medical technician **(b)** (= *heilend*) *Kräuter, Bäder* medicinal; *Shampoo* medicated **2** ADV medically; **sich ~ beraten lassen** to get medical advice; **jdn ~ behandeln** to treat sb (medically); **~ beobachtet werden** to be under (medical) observation; **~ wirksame Kräuter** medicinal herbs

Medizinmann M, *pl* **-männer** medicine man

Meduse [me'du:zə] F **-, -n** **(a)** (*Myth*) Medusa **(b)** (*Zool*) medusa (*spec*), jellyfish

Meer [me:ɐ] NT **-(e)s, -e** (*auch fig*) sea; (= *Weltmeer*) ocean; **am ~(e)** by the sea; **ans ~ fahren** to go to the sea(side); **über dem ~** above sea level

Meer-: Meerbusen M gulf, bay; **Bottnischer ~** Gulf of Bothnia; **Meerenge** F straits *pl*, strait

Meeres-: Meeresalgen PL seaweed, marine algae *pl* (*spec*); **Meeresbiologe** M, **Meeresbiologin** F marine biologist; **Meeresboden** M seabed; **Meeresfauna** F marine fauna; **Meeresfisch** M saltwater fish; **Meeresflora** F marine flora; **Meeresforschung** F oceanography; **Meeresfrüchte** PL seafood *sing*; **Meereshöhe** F sea level; **Meeresklima** NT maritime climate; **Meereskunde** F oceanography; **meereskundlich** [-kʊntlɪç] ADJ oceanographic(al); **Meeresschildkröte** F turtle; **Meeresspiegel** M sea level; **über/unter dem ~** above/below sea level; **Meeresströmung** F ocean current; **Meeresufer** NT coast

Meer-: meergrün ADJ sea-green; **Meerjungfer** F, **Meerjungfrau** F mermaid; **Meerkatze** F long-tailed monkey; **Meerrettich** M horseradish; **Meersalz** NT sea salt; **Meerschaumpfeife** F meerschaum (pipe); **Meerschweinchen** [-ʃvaincən] NT **-s, -** guinea pig

Meerwasser NT sea water

Meerwasser-: Meerwasseraufbereitung F treatment of sea water; **Meerwasserentsalzung** F desalination of sea water; **Meerwasserentsalzungsanlage** F desalination plant

Meeting ['mi:tɪŋ] NT **-s, -s** meeting

Mega-, mega- ['me:ga] IN CPDS **(a)** (*eine Million*) mega- **(b)** (*inf*: = *Super-*) mega- (*inf*); **Megabit** NT megabit; **Megabit-Chip** M megabit chip; **Megabyte** [-'bait] NT megabyte; **Megafon** [mega'fo:n] NT **-s, -e** = **Megaphon**; **megageil** ADJ (*sl*) mega (*inf*); **Megahertz** NT megahertz; **mega-out** ADJ (*inf*) totally out; **Megaphon** [mega'fo:n] NT **-s, -e** megaphone; **Megastar** M (*inf*) megastar; **Megatonne** F megaton; **Megawatt** NT **-s, -** megawatt

Mehl [me:l] NT **-(e)s, -e** flour; (*gröber*) meal; (= *Pulver, Zementmehl*) powder

mehlig ['me:lɪç] **1** ADJ *Äpfel, Kartoffeln* mealy **2** ADV **~ schmecken** to taste mealy; **~ kochend** mealy

Mehl-: Mehlschwitze F (*Cook*) roux; **Mehlspeise** F **(a)** (= *Gericht*) flummery **(b)** (*Aus*) (= *Nachspeise*) dessert; (= *Kuchen*) pastry; **Mehltau** M (*Bot*) mildew

mehr [meːɐ] **1** INDEF PRON INV COMP *von* **viel, sehr** more; **zu ~ hat es nicht gelangt** *or* **gereicht** that was all I/you *etc* could manage; **ist das alles, ~ kostet das nicht?** is that all it costs?; **mit ~ oder weniger Erfolg** with a greater or lesser degree of success

2 ADV **(a)** (= *in höherem Maße*) more; **immer ~** more and more; **~ oder weniger** *or* **minder** (*geh*) more or less; **würden Sie das gerne tun? – ja, nichts ~ als das** would you like to? – there's nothing I'd rather do

(b) (+*neg*: = *sonst, länger*) **ich habe kein Geld ~** I haven't *or* I don't have any more money; **du bist doch kein Kind ~!** you're no longer a child!; **es hat sich keiner ~ beworben** nobody else has applied; **es besteht keine Hoffnung ~** there's no hope left; **kein Wort ~!** not another word!; **es war niemand ~ da** there was no-one left; **daran erinnert sich niemand ~** nobody can remember that any more; **wenn niemand ~ einsteigt, ...** if nobody else gets in ...; **nicht ~** not any longer, no longer; **nicht ~ lange** not much longer; **er lebt nicht ~** he is dead; **das darf nicht ~ vorkommen** that must not happen again; **nichts ~** nothing more; **nie ~** never again

Mehr [meːɐ] NT **-**, NO PL **(a)** (*esp Sw*: = *Mehrheit*) majority **(b)** (= *Zuwachs*) increase; **mit einem ~ an Mühe** with more effort

Mehr-: **Mehrarbeit** F extra work; **Mehraufwand** M additional expenditure; **Mehrausgabe** F additional expense(s *pl*); **mehrbändig** ADJ in several volumes; **Mehrbedarf** M greater need (*an* +*dat* of, for); (*Comm*) increased demand (*an* +*dat* for); **Mehrbelastung** F excess load; (*fig*) additional burden; **Mehrbereichsöl** NT (*Aut*) multigrade oil; **mehrdeutig** [-dɔytɪç] **1** ADJ ambiguous **2** ADV ambiguously; **Mehrdeutigkeit** F **-, -en** ambiguity; **mehrdimensional 1** ADJ multi-dimensional **2** ADV *darstellen* multi-dimensionally; **eine ~ arbeitendes Programm** a multi-dimensional program; **Mehreinnahme** F additional revenue

mehrere [ˈmeːrərə] INDEF PRON several

mehreres [ˈmeːrərəs] INDEF PRON several things *pl*

mehrerlei [ˈmeːrɐˈlai] INDEF PRON INV **(a)** (*substantivisch*) several things *pl* **(b)** (*adjektivisch*) several kinds of

mehrfach [ˈmeːrfax] **1** ADJ multiple; (= *zahlreich*) numerous; (= *wiederholt*) repeated; **ein ~er Millionär** a multimillionaire; **der ~e Meister im Weitsprung** the man who has been the long jump champion several times; **die Unterlagen in ~er Ausfertigung einsenden** to send in several copies of the documents **2** ADV (= *öfter*) many times; (= *wiederholt*) repeatedly

Mehrfache(s) [ˈmeːrfaxə] NT DECL AS ADJ **das ~** *or* **ein ~s des Kostenvoranschlags** several times the estimated cost; **verdient er wirklich mehr? – ja, das ~** *or* **ein ~s** does he earn more? – yes, several times as much

Mehrfach-: **Mehrfachstecker** M (*Elec*) multiple adaptor; **Mehrfachtäter(in)** M(F) multiple offender

Mehr-: **Mehrfahrtenkarte** F multi-journey ticket; **Mehrfamilienhaus** NT house for several families; **mehrfarbig** ADJ multicoloured (*Brit*), multicolored (*US*)

Mehrheit F **-, -en (a)** NO PL (= *größerer Teil*) majority (*with sing or pl vb*); **weitaus in der ~** decidedly in the majority **(b)** (= *Stimmenmehrheit*) majority; **die absolute/einfache** *or* **relative ~** an absolute/a simple *or* relative majority; **die ~ haben** *or* **besitzen/gewinnen** *or* **erringen** to have/win *or* gain a majority; **mit zwei Stimmen ~** with a majority of two (votes)

mehrheitlich [-haitlɪç] ADV **wir sind ~ der Ansicht, dass ...** the majority of us think(s) that ...; **der Stadtrat hat ~ beschlossen ...** the town council has reached a majority decision ...; **an einer Gesellschaft ~ beteiligt sein** to be the majority shareholder in a company

Mehrheits-: **Mehrheitsbeschluss** M, **Mehrheitsentscheidung** F majority decision; **Mehrheitsbeteiligung** F (*Fin*) majority interest *or* holding; **mehrheitsfähig** ADJ capable of winning a majority; **Mehrheitswahl** F first-past-the-post election; **Mehrheitswahlrecht** NT first-past-the-post system

Mehr-: **mehrjährig** ADJ ATTR of several years; **~e Klinikerfahrung** several years of clinical experience; **Mehrkampf** M (*Sport*) multidiscipline event; **Mehrkosten** PL additional costs *pl*; (*in Hotel etc*) additional expenses *pl*; **mehrmalig** [ˈmeːrmaːlɪç] ADJ ATTR repeated; **mehrmals** [ˈmeːrmaːls] ADV several times; **Mehrparteiensystem** NT multiparty system

Mehrplatz- [ˈmeːrplats] IN CPDS (*Comput*) multi-user; **mehrplatzfähig** ADJ (*Comput*) capable of supporting multi-user operation; **Mehrplatzrechner** M (*Comput*) multi-user system

Mehr-: **mehrsilbig** ADJ polysyllabic; **mehrsprachig 1** ADJ *Person, Wörterbuch* multilingual; *Brief, Fragebogen etc* in several languages **2** ADV in several languages; **~ aufwachsen** to grow up multilingual; **mehrstimmig 1** ADJ (*Mus*) for several voices; **~es Lied** part-song **2** ADV *spielen* in more than one voice; **~ singen** to sing in harmony; **mehrstöckig 1** ADJ multistorey (*Brit*), multistory (*US*) **2** ADV **~ bauen** to build multistorey (*Brit*) *or* multistory (*US*) buildings; **mehrstufig** ADJ multistage; **mehrstündig** [-ʃtʏndɪç] ADJ ATTR *Verhandlungen* lasting several hours; **mit ~er Verspätung eintreffen** to arrive several hours late; **mehrtägig** ADJ ATTR *Konferenz* lasting several days; **nach ~er Abwesenheit** after several days' absence; **mehrteilig** ADJ in several parts; **Mehrverbrauch** M additional consumption

Mehrweg- [ˈmeːrveːk-] IN CPDS reusable; **Mehrwegflasche** F returnable bottle; **Mehrwegsystem** NT (bottle *or* packaging) return system; **Mehrwegverpackung** F reusable packaging

Mehr-: **Mehrwert** M (*Econ*) added value; **Mehrwertsteuer** F value added tax; **mehrwöchig** [-vœçɪç] ADJ ATTR lasting several weeks; *Abwesenheit* of several weeks; **Mehrzahl** F, NO PL **(a)** (*Gram*) plural **(b)** (= *Mehrheit*) majority

Mehrzweck- [ˈmeːrtsvɛk-] IN CPDS multipurpose; **Mehrzweckhalle** F multipurpose room

meiden [ˈmaidn], *pret* **mied** [miːt], *ptp* **gemieden** [ɡəˈmiːdn] VT to avoid

Meile [ˈmailə] F **-, -n** mile

Meilen-: **meilenlang 1** ADJ mile-long **2** ADV for miles; **Meilenstein** M (*lit, fig*) milestone; **meilenweit 1** ADJ of many miles; **~e Sandstrände** miles and miles of sandy beaches **2** ADV for miles; **~ auseinander/entfernt** (*lit, fig*) miles apart/away

Meiler [ˈmailɐ] M **-s, -** (= *Kohlenmeiler*) charcoal kiln; (= *Atommeiler*) (atomic) pile

mein [main] POSS PRON (*adjektivisch*) my; **~ verdammtes Auto** (*inf*) this damn car of mine (*inf*)

Meineid [ˈmainlait] M perjury *no indef art*; **einen ~ leisten** *or* **ablegen** to perjure oneself

meineidig [ˈmainlaidɪç] ADJ perjured

Meineidige(r) [ˈmainlaidɪɡə] MF DECL AS ADJ perjurer

meinen [ˈmainən] **1** VI (= *denken, glauben*) to think; **ich würde/man möchte ~** I/one would think; **wie ~ Sie?** I beg your pardon?; **ich meine nur so** (*inf*) it was just a thought; **wie Sie ~!** as you wish; **wenn du meinst!** if you like

2 VT **(a)** (= *der Ansicht sein*) to think; **was ~ Sie dazu?** what do you think *or* say?; **~ Sie das im Ernst?** are you serious about that?; **das will ich ~!** I quite agree!; **das sollte man ~!** one would think so

(b) (= *sagen wollen, beabsichtigen, abzielen auf*) to mean; (*inf*: = *sagen*) to say; **was ~ Sie damit?, wie ~ Sie das?** what do you mean?; (*drohend*) (just) what do you mean by that?; **damit bin ich gemeint** that's meant for me; **so war es nicht gemeint** it wasn't meant like that; **sie meint es gut** she means well; **sie meint es nicht böse** she means no harm; **die Sonne hat es aber heute wieder gut (mit uns) gemeint!** the sun's done its best for us again today

meiner [ˈmainɐ] PERS PRON GEN *von* **ich** of me

meine(r, s) [ˈmainə] POSS PRON (*substantivisch*) mine; **der/die/das Meine** (*geh*) mine; **ich tu das Meine** (*geh*) I'll do my bit; **das Meine** (*geh*: = *Besitz*) what is mine; **die Meinen** (*geh*: = *Familie*) my people, my family

meinerseits [ˈmainɐzaits] ADV as far as I'm concerned; **ich ~** I personally; **Vorschläge/Einwände ~** suggestions/objections from me; **ganz ~!** the pleasure's (all) mine

meines-: **meinesgleichen** [ˈmainəsˈɡlaiçn] PRON INV (= *meiner Art*) people like me *or* myself; (= *gleichrangig*) my own kind

meinet-: **meinetwegen** [ˈmainətˈveːɡn] ADV **(a)** (= *wegen mir*) because of me; (= *mir zuliebe*) for my sake; (= *um mich*) about me; (= *für mich*) on my behalf **(b)** (= *von mir aus*) as far as I'm concerned; **~!** if you like; **wenn Ihr das tun wollt, ~, aber ...** if you want to do that, fair enough (*inf*), but ...; **meinetwillen** [ˈmainətˈvilən] ADV **um ~** (= *mir zuliebe*) for my sake; (= *wegen mir*) on my account

meins [mains] POSS PRON mine

Meinung ['mainʊŋ] F -, -en opinion; (= *Urteil*) judgement; **eine vorgefasste ~** a preconceived idea; **nach meiner ~, meiner ~ nach** in my opinion; **ich bin der ~, dass ...** I'm of the opinion that ...; **eine/keine hohe ~ von jdm/etw haben** to think/not to think highly of sb/sth; **einer ~ sein** to share the same opinion; **geteilter ~ sein** to have different opinions; **ganz meine ~!** I completely agree!; **das ist auch meine ~!** that's just what I think; **jdm** (*kräftig or vernünftig*) **die ~ sagen** (*inf*) to give sb a piece of one's mind (*inf*)

> *Vorsicht!* **Meinung** *wird nicht mit dem englischen Wort* **meaning** *übersetzt.*

Meinungs-: Meinungsaustausch M exchange of views (*über +acc* on, about); **Meinungsforscher(in)** M(F) (opinion) pollster; **Meinungsforschung** F (public) opinion polling; **Meinungsforschungsinstitut** NT opinion research institute; **Meinungsfreiheit** F freedom of speech; **Meinungsumfrage** F (public) opinion poll; **Meinungsverschiedenheit** F difference of opinion

Meise ['maizə] F -, -n titmouse; **eine ~ haben** (*inf*) to be crazy (*inf*)

Meißel ['maisl] M -s, - chisel

meißeln ['maisln] VTI to chisel

meist [maist] ADV = **meistens**

meistbietend ADJ highest bidding; **Meistbietender** highest bidder; **~ or an den Meistbietenden versteigern** to sell to the highest bidder

meisten ['maistn] **am ~** ADV (**a**) SUPERL *von* **viel** the most (**b**) SUPERL *von* **sehr** most of all; **am ~ bekannt** best known

meistens ['maistns] ADV mostly; (= *zum größten Teil*) for the most part

Meister ['maistɐ] M -s, - (**a**) (= *Handwerksmeister*) master (craftsman); (*in Laden*) boss (*inf*); (*in Fabrik*) foreman; (*Sport*) champion; (*Mannschaft*) champions *pl*; **seinen ~ machen** to take one's master craftsman's diploma (**b**) (= *Lehrmeister, Künstler*) master (*auch fig*); **es ist noch kein ~ vom Himmel gefallen** (*Prov*) no-one is born a master

meiste(r, s) ['maistə] INDEF PRON SUPERL *von* **viel** (**a**) (*adjektivisch*) **die ~n Leute** most people; **die ~n Leute, die ...** most of the people who ...; **du hast die ~ Zeit** you have (the) most time (**b**) (*substantivisch*) **die ~n** most people; **die ~n (von ihnen)** most (of them); **das ~** most of it; **du hast das ~ you** have (the) most

Meister- IN CPDS master; **Meisterbrief** M master craftsman's diploma; **meisterhaft** 1 ADJ masterly 2 ADV brilliantly; **er versteht es ~ zu lügen** he is brilliant at lying

Meisterin ['maistərɪn] F -, -nen (= *Handwerksmeisterin*) master craftswoman; (= *Frau von Handwerksmeister*) master craftsman's wife; (*in Fabrik*) forewoman; (*Sport*) champion

Meisterleistung F masterly performance; (*iro*) brilliant achievement

meistern ['maistɐn] VT to master; **Schwierigkeiten** to overcome; **sein Leben ~** to come to grips with one's life

Meisterprüfung F examination for master craftsman's diploma

Meisterschaft ['maistɐʃaft] F -, -en (**a**) (*Sport*) championship; (*Veranstaltung*) championships *pl* (**b**) NO PL (= *Können*) mastery

Meisterschaftsspiel NT (*Sport*) league match

Meister-: Meisterstück NT (*von Handwerker*) work done to qualify as master craftsman; (*fig*) masterpiece; (= *geniale Tat*) master stroke; **Meistertitel** M (*im Handwerk*) title of master craftsman; (*Sport*) championship title; **Meisterwerk** NT masterpiece

Meist-: Meistgebot NT highest bid; **meistgefragt** ADJ ATTR most in demand; **meistgekauft** [-gəkauft] ADJ ATTR best-selling; **meistgelesen** ADJ ATTR most widely read

Mekka ['mɛka] NT -s (*Geog, fig*) Mecca

Melancholie [melaŋko'li:] F -, -n [-'li:ən] melancholy

melancholisch [melaŋ'ko:lɪʃ] 1 ADJ melancholy 2 ADV **sagen** in a melancholy voice; **sie sann ~ vor sich hin** she was thinking melancholy thoughts

Melange [me'lã:ʒə] F -, -n (*Aus*: = *Milchkaffee*) coffee with milk

Melanom [mela'no:m] NT -s -e (*Med*) melanoma

Melasse [me'lasə] F -, -n molasses

Melde-: Meldeamt NT, **Meldebüro** (*inf*) NT registration office; **Meldebehörde** F registration authorities *pl*; **Meldefrist** F registration period

melden ['mɛldn] 1 VT (**a**) (= *anzeigen, berichten*) **eine Geburt/Änderungen (der Behörde** *dat*) **~** to notify the authorities of a birth/changes; **wie soeben gemeldet wird** (*Rad, TV*) according to reports just coming in; **das wird gemeldet!** (*Sch*) I'll tell on you (*Sch inf*); **(bei jdm) nichts zu ~ haben** (*inf*) to have no say
(**b**) (= *ankündigen*) to announce; **wen darf ich ~?** who(m) shall I say (is here)?
2 VR (**a**) (= *antreten*) to report (*zu* for); **sich zum Dienst ~** to report for work; **sich freiwillig ~** to volunteer; **sich zu or für etw ~** (*esp Mil*) to volunteer for sth; (*für Arbeitsplatz*) to apply for sth; (*für Lehrgang*) to enrol (*Brit*) or enroll (*US*) for sth; **sich auf eine Anzeige ~** to answer an advertisement; **sich arbeitslos ~** to register as unemployed, to sign on; *siehe auch* **krankmelden**
(**b**) (*fig*: = *sich ankündigen*) to announce one's presence; (*Sport*) (*zur Prüfung*) to enter (one's name) (*zu* for); (*durch Handaufheben*) to put one's hand up; (*Rad, TV*) to come on the air
(**c**) (*esp Telec*: = *antworten*) to answer; **bitte ~!** (*Telec*) come in, please; **es meldet sich niemand** there's no answer
(**d**) (= *von sich hören lassen*) to get in touch (*bei* with); **melde dich wieder** keep in touch; **seitdem hat er sich nicht mehr gemeldet** he hasn't been heard of since; **wenn du was brauchst, melde dich** if you need anything give (me) a shout (*inf*)

Melde-: Meldepflicht F (**a**) (*beim Ordnungsamt*) compulsory registration (*when moving house*); **polizeiliche ~** obligation to register with the police (**b**) **~ des Arztes** the doctor's obligation to notify the authorities (*of people with certain contagious diseases*); **meldepflichtig** [-pflɪçtɪç] ADJ (**a**) *Mensch* obliged to register (**b**) *Krankheit* notifiable; *Unfall, Schadensfall* that must be reported

MELDEPFLICHT

A **Meldepflicht** *is a regulation requiring an individual to notify the authorities of certain things such as a change of address or a birth. Everyone who takes up residence in Germany is obliged to register with the* **Einwohnermeldeamt** *within a week (three days in Austria). If you move to a different address, you must first of all inform the authorities in your previous place of residence. In Switzerland regulations vary from canton to canton.*

Meldung ['mɛldʊŋ] F -, -en (**a**) (= *Mitteilung*) announcement (**b**) (*Press, Rad, TV*) report (*über +acc* on, about); **~en in Kürze** news headlines *pl*; **~en vom Sport** sports news *sing* (**c**) (*dienstlich, bei Polizei*) report; (**eine**) **~ machen** to make a report (**d**) (*Sport*: = *Examensmeldung*) entry; **seine ~ zurückziehen** to withdraw (**e**) (*Comput*) message

meliert [me'li:ɐt] ADJ *Haar* greying (*Brit*), graying (*US*), streaked with grey (*Brit*) or gray (*US*); *Wolle* flecked

melken ['mɛlkn] *pres* **melkt** [mɛlkt], *pret* **melkte** ['mɛlktə], *ptp* **gemolken** [gə'mɔlkn] 1 VT (**a**) *Kuh, Ziege etc* to milk; **frisch gemolkene Milch** milk fresh from the cow (**b**) (*fig inf*) to fleece (*inf*) 2 VI to milk

Melodie [melo'di:] F -, -n [-'di:ən] melody; (= *Weise auch*) tune; **nach der ~ von ...** to the tune of ...

melodiös [melo'diø:s] (*geh*) 1 ADJ melodious 2 ADV melodiously; **~ klingen** to sound melodious

melodisch [me'lo:dɪʃ] 1 ADJ melodic 2 ADV **~ klingen** to sound melodic

melodramatisch [melodra'ma:tɪʃ] 1 ADJ melodramatic (*auch fig*) 2 ADV melodramatically; **~ klingen** to sound melodramatic

Melone [me'lo:nə] F -, -n (**a**) melon (**b**) (*Hut*) bowler (*Brit*), derby (*US*)

Membran [mɛm'bra:n] F -, -en, **Membrane** [mɛm'bra:nə] F -, -n (**a**) (*Anat*) membrane (**b**) (*Phys, Tech*) diaphragm

Memme ['mɛmə] F -, -n (*inf*) sissy (*inf*)

memmenhaft (*inf*) 1 ADJ lily-livered (*inf*), yellow-bellied (*inf*) 2 ADV like a yellow-belly (*inf*)

Memo ['me:mo] NT -s, -s memo

Memoiren [me'moa:rən] PL memoirs *pl*

Menge ['mɛŋə] F **-, -n (a)** (= *Quantum*) quantity; **in ~n zu** in quantities of
(b) (*inf*) (= *große Anzahl*) load (*inf*); (= *Haufen*) pile (*inf*); **eine ~** a lot, lots (*inf*); **eine ~ Zeit/Häuser** a lot of time/houses; **jede ~ loads** *pl* (*inf*); **wir haben jede ~ getrunken** we drank a hell of a lot (*inf*); **eine ganze ~** quite a lot; **sie bildet sich eine ~ auf ihre Schönheit ein** she's incredibly conceited about her looks
(c) (= *Menschenmenge*) crowd; (*geh*) (= *Masse*) mass; (= *das Volk*) people; (*pej*: = *Pöbel*) mob; **in der ~ untertauchen** to disappear into the crowd
(d) (*Math*) set
mengen ['mɛŋən] **1** VT (*geh*) to mix (*unter +acc* with) **2** VR to mingle (*unter +acc* with)
Mengen-: Mengenangabe F quantity; **Mengenlehre** F (*Math*) set theory; **mengenmäßig 1** ADJ quantitative **2** ADV as far as quantity is concerned; **Mengenrabatt** M bulk discount
Menhir ['mɛnhiːɐ] M **-s, -e** (*Archeol*) standing stone
Meniskus [me'nɪskʊs] M **-, Menisken** [-kn] meniscus
Mensa ['mɛnza] F **-, Mensen** [-zn] (*Univ*) canteen, refectory (*Brit*)
Mensaessen NT (*Univ*) (= *Mahlzeit*) college meal; (= *Kost*) college food
Mensch[1] [mɛnʃ] M **-en, -en (a)** (= *Person*) person, man/ woman; **von ~ zu ~** man-to-man/woman-to-woman; **es war kein ~ da** there was nobody there; **als ~** as a person; **des ~en Wille ist sein Himmelreich** (*Prov*) do what you want if it makes you happy (*inf*); **das konnte kein ~ ahnen!** no-one (on earth) could have foreseen that!; **viel unter den ~en kommen** to get around (a lot); **man muss die ~en nehmen, wie sie sind** you have to take people as they are; **Aktion ~** *charity for people with disabilities*
(b) (*als Gattung*) **der ~** man; **die ~en** man *sing*, human beings *pl*; **~ bleiben** (*inf*) to stay human; **ich bin auch nur ein ~!** I'm only human; **wie die ersten** or **letzten ~en** (*inf*) like animals; **~ und Tier** man and beast; **alle ~en müssen sterben** we are all mortal
(c) (= *die Menschheit*) **die ~en** mankind, man; **alle ~en** everyone; **so sind die ~en** that's human nature
(d) (*inf*: *als Interjektion*) hey; **~, das habe ich ganz vergessen** damn, I completely forgot (*inf*); **~, da habe ich mich aber getäuscht** boy, was I wrong! (*inf*); **~, habe ich mich beeilt/ geärgert!** boy, did I rush/was I angry! (*inf*); **~ Meier!** gosh! (*dated inf*)
Mensch[2] NT **-(e)s, -er** (*sl*) cow (*inf*); (*gemein*) bitch (*sl*)
Mensch ärgere dich nicht [mɛnʃ 'ɛrɡərə dɪç nɪçt] NT **- - - -,** NO PL (= *Spiel*) ludo (*Brit*), aggravation (*US*)
Menschen- IN CPDS human; **Menschenaffe** M ape; **menschenähnlich** ADJ manlike, like a human being/human beings; **Menschenansammlung** F gathering (of people); **Menschenauflauf** M crowd (of people); **menschenfeindlich** ADJ *Mensch* misanthropic; *Landschaft etc* inhospitable; *Politik, Gesellschaft* inhumane; **Menschenfresser(in)** M(F) **(a)** (*inf*) (= *Kannibale*) cannibal; (= *Raubtier*) man-eater; **ich bin doch kein ~!** I won't eat you! **(b)** (*Myth*) ogre; **menschenfreundlich 1** ADJ *Mensch* philanthropic, benevolent; *Gegend* hospitable; *Politik, Gesellschaft* humane; **diese Affenart ist nicht sehr ~** this species of ape does not like humans **2** ADV **sich ~ geben** to like to give the impression of being a philanthropist; **Menschenführung** F leadership; **Menschengedenken** NT **der kälteste Winter seit ~** the coldest winter in living memory; **Menschenhand** F human hand; **von ~ geschaffen** fashioned by the hand of man; **das liegt nicht in ~** that is beyond man's control; **Menschenhandel** M slave trade; (*Jur*) trafficking (in human beings); **Menschenjagd** F manhunting; **eine ~** a manhunt; **Menschenkenner(in)** M(F) judge of character; **Menschenkenntnis** F, NO PL knowledge of human nature; **~ haben** to know human nature; **Menschenkette** F human chain; **Menschenleben** NT human life; **ein ~ lang** a whole lifetime; **~ waren nicht zu beklagen** there was no loss of life; **Verluste an ~** loss of human life; **das Unglück hat zwei ~ gefordert** the accident claimed two lives; **menschenleer** ADJ deserted; **Menschenliebe** F (= *Nächstenliebe*) love of mankind or humanity; **aus reiner ~** from the sheer goodness of one's heart; **Menschenmaterial** NT manpower; **Menschenmenge** F crowd (of people); **menschenmöglich** ADJ humanly possible; **das Menschenmögliche tun** to do all that is humanly possible; **Menschenrecht** NT human right; **die Allgemeine**

Erklärung or **Deklaration der ~e** the Universal Declaration of Human Rights; **Menschenrechtsverletzung** F violation of human rights
Menschen-: menschenscheu ADJ afraid of people; **Menschenschinder** [-ʃɪndɐ] M **-s, -, Menschenschinderin** [-ərɪn] F **-, -nen** slave-driver; **Menschenseele** F human soul; **keine ~** (*fig*) not a (living) soul
Menschenskind INTERJ heavens above
Menschen-: menschenunmöglich ADJ absolutely impossible; **menschenunwürdig 1** ADJ beneath human dignity; *Behandlung* inhumane; *Behausung* unfit for human habitation **2** ADV *behandeln* inhumanely; *hausen, unterbringen* under inhuman conditions; **menschenverachtend 1** ADJ inhuman **2** ADV inhumanely; **Menschenverstand** M human understanding *no art*; **gesunder ~** common sense; **Menschenwürde** F human dignity *no art*; **menschenwürdig 1** ADJ *Behandlung* humane; *Leben, Tod* dignified; *Lebensbedingungen* fit for human beings; *Unterkunft* fit for human habitation **2** ADV *behandeln* humanely; *unterbringen, wohnen* in decent conditions; **~ leben** to live in conditions fit for human beings
Menschheit F **-,** NO PL **die ~** mankind, humanity; **Verbrechen gegen die** or **an der ~** crimes against humanity
menschlich ['mɛnʃlɪç] **1** ADJ **(a)** (= *human*) human; *Behandlung etc* humane **2** ADV **(a)** (= *human*) humanely **(b)** (*inf*: = *zivilisiert*) decently; **(einigermaßen) ~ aussehen** (*inf*) to look more or less human **(c)** (= *als Mensch*) personally, as a person; **sie ist mir ~ sympathisch** I like her as a person
Menschlichkeit F **-,** NO PL humanity *no art*; **aus reiner ~** on purely humanitarian grounds; **Verbrechen gegen die ~** crimes against humanity
Menstruation [mɛnstrua'tsioːn] F **-, -en** menstruation
menstruieren [mɛnstru'iːrən], *ptp* **menstruiert** VI to menstruate
mental [mɛn'taːl] **1** ADJ mental **2** ADV mentally
Mentalität [mɛntali'tɛːt] F **-, -en** mentality
Menthol [mɛn'toːl] NT **-s, -e** menthol
Menü [me'nyː] NT **-s, -s (a)** (= *Tagesmenü*) set meal, table d'hôte (*form*); **des Tages** (set) meal of the day (*Brit*), (daily) special **(b)** (*Comput*) menu
Menü- IN CPDS (*Comput*) menu; **Menüanzeige** F menu display; **Menübefehl** M (*Comput*) menu command; **Menüführung** F menu-driven operation; **menügesteuert** [-ɡəʃtɔyɐt] ADJ menu-driven; **Menüleiste** F menu strip; **Menüsteuerung** F menu-driven operation; **Menüzeile** F menu line
Merchandising ['mœːrtʃəndaɪzɪŋ] NT **-s,** NO PL merchandising
Merk-: merkbar 1 ADJ (*= wahrnehmbar*) noticeable **(b)** (= *im Gedächtnis zu behalten*) retainable; **leicht/schwer ~** easy/difficult to remember **2** ADV noticeably; **Merkblatt** NT leaflet
merken ['mɛrkn] VT **(a)** (= *wahrnehmen, entdecken*) to notice; (= *spüren*) to feel; (= *erkennen*) to realize; **ich merke nichts!** I can't feel anything!; **davon habe ich nichts gemerkt** I didn't notice anything; **jdn etw ~ lassen** to make sb feel sth; **hat er dich etwas ~ lassen?** did you notice anything in the way he behaved?; **woran hast du das gemerkt?** how could you tell that?; **wie soll ich das ~?** how am I supposed to tell (that)?; **du merkst auch alles!** (*iro*) nothing escapes you, does it?; **das merkt jeder/keiner!** everyone/no-one will notice!; **das ist kaum zu ~, davon merkt man kaum etwas** it's hardly noticeable; **das ist zu ~** you can tell
(b) (= *im Gedächtnis behalten*) to remember; **merke: ...** NB or note: ...; **sich** (*dat*) **jdn/etw ~** to remember sb/sth; **sich** (*dat*) **eine Autonummer ~** to make a (mental) note of a licence (*Brit*) or license (*US*) number; **das werde ich mir ~!, ich werde mir ~!** (*inf*) I won't forget that; **das hat er sich gemerkt** he's taken it to heart; **merk dir das!** mark my words!
(c) (= *im Auge behalten*) **sich** (*dat*) **etw ~** to remember sth; **diesen Schriftsteller wird man sich** (*dat*) **~ müssen** this author is someone to take note of
merklich ['mɛrklɪç] **1** ADJ noticeable **2** ADV noticeably; **kaum ~** almost imperceptibly
Merkmal ['mɛrkmaːl] NT **-s, -e** characteristic; (*Biol, Zool*) distinctive mark; „**besondere ~e ...**" "distinguishing marks ..."
Merk- (*Sch*): **Merksatz** M mnemonic (sentence); **Merkspruch** M mnemonic (*form*)

Merkur [mɛrˈkuːɐ] M **-s**, NO PL (*Myth, Astron*) Mercury

Merk-: **merkwürdig** [ˈmɛrkvʏrdɪç] ▊ ADJ strange ▨ ADV strangely; **~ riechen** to have a strange smell; **er hat sich ganz ~ verändert** he has undergone a curious change; **merkwürdigerweise** [ˈmɛrkvʏrdɪgəˈvaizə] ADV strangely enough; **Merkwürdigkeit** F **-, -en (a)** NO PL (= *Seltsamkeit*) strangeness **(b)** (= *Eigentümlichkeit*) peculiarity

meschugge [meˈʃʊgə] ADJ (*inf*) nuts (*inf*)

Mess-: **Messband** NT, *pl* **-bänder** tape measure; **messbar** ▊ ADJ measurable ▨ ADV measurably; **Messbecher** M (*Cook*) measuring jug; **Messdaten** PL readings *pl*

Messe¹ [ˈmɛsə] F **-, -n** (*Eccl, Mus*) mass

Messe² F **-, -n** (trade) fair; **auf der ~** at the fair

Messe³ F **-, -n** (*Naut, Mil*) mess

Messe- IN CPDS fair; **Messeangebot** NT fair exhibits *pl*; **Messegast** M fair visitor; **Messegelände** NT exhibition centre (*Brit*) or center (*US*); **Messehalle** F fair pavilion

messen [ˈmɛsn], *pret* **maß** [maːs], *ptp* **gemessen** [gəˈmɛsn] ▊ VT to measure; *Verlauf* to time; (= *abschätzen*) *Entfernung etc* to judge; **jds Blutdruck/Temperatur ~** (*Arzt*) to take sb's blood pressure/temperature; (*Instrument*) to measure sb's blood pressure/temperature; **er misst 1,90 m** he is 1.90 m tall; **seine Kräfte/Fähigkeiten mit jdm ~** to match one's strength/skills against sb's; **seine Kräfte/Fähigkeiten an etw** (*dat*) **~** to test one's strength/skills on sth; **etw an etw** (*dat*) **~** (= *vergleichen*) to compare sth with sth ▨ VI to measure ▣ VR **sich mit jdm ~** (*geh: im Wettkampf*) to compete with sb; (*in geistigem Wettstreit*) to pit oneself against sb; **sich mit jdm/etw nicht ~ können** to be no match for sb/sth

Messer [ˈmɛsɐ] NT **-s, -** knife; **unters ~ kommen** (*Med inf*) to go under the knife; **jdm das ~ an die Kehle setzen** (*lit, fig*) to hold a knife to sb's throat; **damit würden wir ihn ans ~ liefern** (*fig*) that would be putting his head on the block; **jdn der Mafia ans ~ liefern** to rat on sb to the Mafia (*sl*); **ins (offene) ~ laufen** to walk straight into the trap; **ein Kampf/sich bekämpfen bis aufs ~** (*fig*) a fight/to fight to the finish; **auf des ~s Schneide stehen** (*fig*) to be on a razor's edge; **es steht auf des ~s Schneide, ob …** it's touch and go whether …

Messer- IN CPDS knife; **Messerheld(in)** M(F) (*inf*) knifer (*inf*); **messerscharf** ▊ ADJ (*lit, fig*) razor-sharp; *Folgerung* clear-cut ▨ ADV *argumentieren* shrewdly; **~ schließen** (*iro*) to conclude shrewdly (*iro*); **Messerschneide** F knife edge; **Messerwerfer(in)** M(F) knife-thrower

Messe-: **Messestadt** F (town with an) exhibition centre (*Brit*) or center (*US*); **Messestand** M stand (at the/a fair)

Mess-: **Messfühler** M probe; (*Met*) gauge; **Messgerät** NT **(a)** (*für Öl, Druck etc*) measuring instrument **(b)** (*Eccl*) Mass requisites *pl*

Messing [ˈmɛsɪŋ] NT **-s**, NO PL brass

Messing- IN CPDS brass; **Messingblech** NT sheet brass; **Messingschild** NT, *pl* **-schilder** brass plate

Mess-: **Messinstrument** NT gauge; **Messlatte** F measuring stick; (*fig*: = *Maßstab*) threshold; **die ~ hoch legen** (*fig*) to set a high standard; **Messstab** M (*Aut*: = *Ölmessstab etc*) dipstick; **Messtechnik** F measurement technology; **Messtischblatt** NT ordnance survey map

Messung [ˈmɛsʊŋ] F **-, -en (a)** (= *das Messen*) measuring; (= *das Ablesen*) reading; (*von Blutdruck*) taking; (*Tech*: = *das Anzeigen*) gauging **(b)** (= *Messergebnis*) measurement; (= *Ableseergebnis*) reading

Messwert M measurement; (= *Ableseergebnis*) reading

Metall [meˈtal] NT **-s, -e** metal; **~ verarbeitend** metal-processing *attr*, metal-working *attr*

Metall- IN CPDS metal-; **Metallarbeiter(in)** M(F) metalworker; **metallartig** ▊ ADJ metallic ▨ ADV metallically; **~ aussehen** to look metallic; **sich ~ anfühlen** to feel like metal; **Metallbearbeitung** F metalworking

metallen [meˈtalən] ▊ ADJ metal; (*geh*) *Klang, Stimme* metallic ▨ ADV *glänzen* metallically; **~ klingen** to sound tinny

Metall-: **Metallermüdung** F metal fatigue; **metallhaltig** ADJ metalliferous

metallic [meˈtalɪk] ADJ metallic; **~-blau** metallic blue

Metallic- [meˈtalɪk] IN CPDS metallic; **Metalliclack** M metallic paint

Metallurgie [metalʊrˈgiː] F **-**, NO PL metallurgy

Metall-: **metallverarbeitend** ADJ *siehe* **Metall**; **Metallverarbeitung** F metal processing

Metamorphose [metamɔrˈfoːzə] F **-, -n** metamorphosis

Metapher [meˈtafɐ] F **-, -n** metaphor

metaphorisch [metaˈfoːrɪʃ] ▊ ADJ metaphoric(al) ▨ ADV metaphorically

Metastase [metaˈstaːzə] F **-, -n** metastasis

Meteor [meteˈoːɐ, ˈmeteoːɐ] M or NT **-s, -e** [-ˈoːrə] meteor

Meteorit [meteoˈriːt] M **-en, -en** meteorite

Meteorologe [meteoroˈloːgə] M **-n, -n**, **Meteorologin** [-ˈloːgɪn] F **-, -nen** meteorologist; (*im Wetterdienst*) weather forecaster

Meteorologie [meteoroloˈgiː] F **-**, NO PL meteorology

meteorologisch [meteoroˈloːgɪʃ] ▊ ADJ meteorological ▨ ADV meteorologically; **sich ~ auswirken** to have a meteorological effect

Meter [ˈmeːtɐ] M or NT **-s, -** metre (*Brit*), meter (*US*); **in/auf 500 ~(n) Höhe** at a height of 500 metres (*Brit*) or meters (*US*); **nach ~n** by the metre (*Brit*) or meter (*US*)

Meter-: **meterhoch** ▊ ADJ *Wellen, Mauer, Pflanze* metres (*Brit*) or meters (*US*) high; *Schnee* metres (*Brit*) or meters (*US*) deep ▨ ADV **der Schnee lag ~** the snow was very deep; **die Akten türmten sich ~ auf seinem Schreibtisch** the files were piled three feet high on his desk; **meterlang** ADJ metres (*Brit*) or meters (*US*) long; **~e Lochstreifen** yards and yards of punch tape; **Metermaß** NT **(a)** (= *Bandmaß*) tape measure **(b)** (= *Stab*) (metre (*Brit*) or meter (*US*)) rule; **Meterware** F (*Tex*) piece goods; **meterweise** ADV by the metre (*Brit*) or meter (*US*)

Methadon [metaˈdoːn] NT **-s**, NO PL methadone

Methan [meˈtaːn] NT **-s**, NO PL, **Methangas** NT methane

Methode [meˈtoːdə] F **-, -n (a)** method; **etw mit ~ machen** to do sth methodically; **das hat ~** (*inf*) there's (a) method behind it **(b) Methoden** PL (= *Sitten*) behaviour (*Brit*), behavior (*US*); **was sind denn das für ~n?** what sort of way is that to behave?

methodisch [meˈtoːdɪʃ] ▊ ADJ methodical ▨ ADV methodically

Methodist [metoˈdɪst] M **-en, -en**, **Methodistin** [-ˈdɪstɪn] F **-, -nen** Methodist

methodistisch [metoˈdɪstɪʃ] ADJ Methodist

Methusalem [meˈtuːzalɛm] M **-s** Methuselah

Methylalkohol [meˈtyːl-] M methyl alcohol

Metrik [ˈmeːtrɪk] F **-, -en** (*Poet, Mus*) metrics *sing*

metrisch [ˈmeːtrɪʃ] ▊ ADJ (*Sci*) *Maß* metric; (*Poet, Mus auch*) metrical ▨ ADV in metres (*Brit*) or meters (*US*)

Metro [ˈmeːtro, ˈmetro] F **-, -s** metro

Metronom [metroˈnoːm] NT **-s, -e** (*Mus*) metronome

Metropole [metroˈpoːlə] F **-, -n (a)** (= *größte Stadt*) metropolis **(b)** (= *Zentrum*) centre (*Brit*), center (*US*)

Mettwurst [ˈmɛt-] F **-, -¨e** (smoked) pork/beef sausage

Metzelei [mɛtsəˈlai] F **-, -en** butchery

metzeln [ˈmɛtsln] VT to slaughter

Metzger [ˈmɛtsgɐ] M **-s, -**, **Metzgerin** [-ərɪn] F **-, -nen** butcher

Metzger- IN CPDS *siehe* **Fleischer-**

Metzgerei [mɛtsgəˈrai] F **-, -en** butcher's (shop)

Meuchel- [ˈmɔyçl-]: **Meuchelmord** M (treacherous) murder; **Meuchelmörder(in)** M(F) (treacherous) assassin

Meute [ˈmɔytə] F **-, -n** pack (of hounds); (*fig pej*) mob

Meuterei [mɔytəˈrai] F **-, -en** mutiny

meutern [ˈmɔytɐn] VI to mutiny; **die ~den Soldaten** the mutinous soldiers

Mexikaner [mɛksiˈkaːnɐ] M **-s, -**, **Mexikanerin** [-ərɪn] F **-, -nen** Mexican

mexikanisch [mɛksiˈkaːnɪʃ] ADJ Mexican

Mexiko [ˈmɛksiko] NT **-s** Mexico; **~ City**, **~-Stadt** Mexico City

MEZ ABBR *von* **mitteleuropäische Zeit**

MfG ABBR *von* **Mit freundlichen Grüßen**

MG [ɛmˈgeː] NT **-(s), -(s)** ABBR *von* **Maschinengewehr**

MHz ABBR *von* **Megahertz**

miau [miˈau] INTERJ miaow (*Brit*), meow

miauen [miˈauən], *ptp* **miaut** VI to meow

mich [mɪç] ▊ PERS PRON ACC *von* **ich** me ▨ REFLEXIVE PRON myself; **ich fühle ~ wohl** I feel fine

Michel [ˈmɪçl] M **-s der deutsche ~** (*fig*) the plain honest German

mickerig ['mɪkərɪç], **mickrig** ['mɪkrɪç] (*inf*) **1** ADJ pathetic; *altes Männchen* puny **2** ADV pathetically

midi ['mɪdɪ] ADJ PRED (*Fashion*) midi; **Midi tragen** to wear mid-length skirts/dresses

mied PRET *von* **meiden**

Mieder-: **Miederhöschen** [-hø:sçən] NT panty girdle; **Miederwaren** PL corsetry *sing*

Mief [mi:f] M **-s**, NO PL (*inf*) fug; (*muffig*) stale air; (= *Gestank*) stink; **der ~ der Provinz/des Kleinbürgertums** (*fig*) the oppressive claustrophobic atmosphere of the provinces/petty bourgeoisie

miefen ['mi:fn] VI (*inf*) to stink; **hier mieft es** there's a smell in here; (*muffig*) the air in here is so stale

Miene ['mi:nə] F **-, -n** (= *Gesichtsausdruck*) expression; **eine finstere ~ machen** to look grim; **gute ~ zum bösen Spiel machen** to grin and bear it

mies [mi:s] (*inf*) **1** ADJ rotten (*inf*); *Qualität* poor; **in den Miesen sein** (*inf*) to be in the red **2** ADV badly; **er hat sich ihr gegenüber ~ verhalten** he was rotten to her (*inf*)

Miesepeter ['mi:zəpe:tɐ] M **-s, -** (*inf*) grouch (*inf*)

miesepeterig ['mi:zəpe:tərɪç], **miesepetrig** ['mi:zəpe:trɪç] ADJ (*inf*) grouchy (*inf*)

mies machen VT (*inf*) to run down

Miesmacher(in) M(F) (*inf*) killjoy

Miesmuschel F mussel

Mietauto NT hire(d) car

Miete ['mi:tə] F **-, -n** (*für Wohnung*) rent; (*für Gegenstände*) rental; (*für Dienstleistungen*) charge; **rückständige ~** (rent) arrears; **zur ~ wohnen** to live in rented accommodation; **das ist die halbe ~** (*fig inf*) that's half the battle

mieten ['mi:tn] VT to rent; *Boot, Auto* to rent, to hire (*esp Brit*)

Mieter ['mi:tɐ] M **-s, -**, **Mieterin** [-ərɪn] F **-, -nen** tenant; (= *Untermieter*) lodger

Mieterhöhung F rent increase

Mieter-: **Mieterschaft** ['mi:tɐʃaft] F **-, -en** tenants *pl*; **Mieterschutz** M rent control; **Mieterschutzgesetz** NT Rent Act

Miet-: **mietfrei** ADJ, ADV rent-free; **Mietrückstände** PL rent arrears *pl*

Miets-: **Mietshaus** NT block of (rented) flats (*Brit*), apartment house (*US*); **Mietskaserne** F (*pej*) tenement house

Miet-: **Mietspiegel** M rent level; **Mietverhältnis** NT tenancy; **Mietvertrag** M lease; (*von Auto*) rental agreement; **Mietwagen** M hire(d) car (*Brit*), rental (car) (*US*); **Mietwohnung** F rented flat (*Brit*) *or* apartment

Mieze ['mi:tsə] F **-, -n** (*inf*) (a) (= *Katze*) pussy(-cat) (*inf*) (b) (= *Mädchen*) chick (*inf*)

Migräne [mi'grɛ:nə] F **-**, NO PL migraine

Migration [migra'tsio:n] F **-, -en** migration

Mikado [mi'ka:do] NT **-s, -s** (= *Spiel*) pick-a-stick

Mikro ['mi:kro] NT **-s, -s** (*inf*) ABBR *von* **Mikrofon** mike (*inf*)

Mikrobe [mi'kro:bə] F **-, -n** microbe

Mikro- IN CPDS micro-(*inf*); **Mikrochip** M microchip; **Mikroelektronik** F microelectronics *sing*; **Mikrofiche** ['mi:krofi:ʃ] M *or* NT **-s, -s** microfiche

Mikrofon [mikro'fo:n, 'mi:krofo:n] NT **-s, -e** microphone

Mikrogramm NT microgram(me)

Mikrokosmos M microcosm

Mikrometer NT micron; (*Gerät*) micrometer

Mikrophon [mikro'fo:n, 'mi:krofo:n] NT **-s, -e** microphone

Mikro-: **Mikroprozessor** M microprocessor; **Mikroroller** M micro-scooter; **Mikrosender** M microtransmitter

Mikroskop [mikro'sko:p] NT **-s, -e** microscope

mikroskopisch [mikro'sko:pɪʃ] **1** ADJ microscopic **2** ADV microscopically; **etw ~ untersuchen** to examine sth under the microscope; **~ klein** (*fig*) microscopically small

Mikrowelle F microwave

Mikrowellenherd M microwave (oven)

Milbe ['mɪlbə] F **-, -n** mite

Milch [mɪlç] F **-**, NO PL (*alle Bedeutungen*) milk; (= *Fischsamen*) milt

Milch- IN CPDS milk; **milchartig** ADJ milky; **Milchbar** F milk bar; (*sl*: = *Busen*) tits *pl* (*sl*); **Milchbrötchen** NT roll made with milk and sugar; **Milchdrüse** F mammary gland; **Milcheiweiß** NT

lactoprotein; **Milchflasche** F milk bottle; **Milchgebiss** NT milk teeth *pl*; **Milchgeschäft** NT dairy; **Milchglas** NT frosted glass

milchig ['mɪlçɪç] **1** ADJ milky **2** ADV **~ trüb** opaque; **~ blau** pale blue; **~ bleich** milk-white

Milch-: **Milchkaffee** M milky coffee; **Milchkanne** F milk can; (*größer*) (milk) churn; **Milchkuh** F milk cow; (*fig inf*) source of easy income; **Milchladen** M dairy; **Milchmädchenrechnung** F (*inf*) naïve fallacy; **Milchmixgetränk** NT milk shake; **Milchprodukt** NT milk product; **Milchpulver** NT powdered milk; **Milchreis** M round-grain rice; (*als Gericht*) rice pudding; **Milchsee** M (*in der EU*) milk lake; **Milchspeise** F milk-based food; **Milchstraße** F Milky Way; **Milchstraßensystem** NT Milky Way system *or* galaxy; **Milchtüte** F milk carton; **Milchzahn** M milk tooth

mild [mɪlt], **milde** ['mɪldə] **1** ADJ (a) *Wetter, Abend, Luft, Käse, Zigarette* mild; *Speisen* light
(b) (= *nachsichtig, barmherzig*) lenient; *Worte* mild; **eine ~e Gabe** alms *pl*
2 ADV (a) (= *sanft*) mildly, gently
(b) (= *nachsichtig*) leniently; **jdn ~ stimmen** to put sb in a generous mood; **~e gesagt** *or* **ausgedrückt** to put it mildly
(c) (= *nicht stark*) *gewürzt* mildly; **~ schmecken** to taste mild; **die Seife riecht ~** the soap is mildly scented

Milde ['mɪldə] F **-**, NO PL (a) (= *Sanftheit, Lindheit*) mildness (b) (= *Nachsichtigkeit, Barmherzigkeit*) leniency; **~ walten lassen** to be lenient

mildern ['mɪldɐn] **1** VT (*geh*) *Schmerz* to soothe; *Kälte* to alleviate; *Angst* to calm; *Strafe, Urteil* to mitigate; *Gegensätze, Schärfe, Konflikt, Problem, Härte, Druck* to reduce; *Ausdrucksweise, Zorn* to moderate; *Sanktionen* to relax; *Folgen* to make less severe; **~de Umstände** (*Jur*) mitigating circumstances **2** VR (*Wetter*) to become milder; (*Gegensätze*) to become less crass; (*Zorn*) to abate; (*Schmerz*) to ease

Milieu [mi'liø:] NT **-s, -s** (= *Umwelt*) environment; (= *Lokalkolorit*) atmosphere; (= *Verbrechermilieu*) underworld; (*von Prostitution*) world of prostitutes

Milieu- [mi'liø:-]: **milieugeschädigt** [-gəʃe:dɪçt], **milieugestört** ADJ maladjusted (*due to adverse social factors*); **Milieuschaden** M effects *pl* of adverse social factors

militant [mili'tant] **1** ADJ militant **2** ADV **~ kommunistisch/antikommunistisch sein** to be a militant communist/anticommunist

Militanz [mili'tants] F **-**, NO PL militancy

Militär[1] [mili'tɛ:ɐ] NT **-s**, NO PL military *pl*; **beim ~ sein** (*inf*) to be in the forces; **zum ~ einberufen werden** to be called up (*Brit*) *or* drafted (*US*); **zum ~ müssen** (*inf*) to have to join the army; **zum ~ gehen** to join the army

Militär[2] M **-s, -s** (army) officer

Militär- IN CPDS military; **Militärarzt** M, **Militärärztin** F army doctor; (= *Offizier*) medical officer; **Militärdienst** M military service; **(seinen) ~ ableisten** to do national service; **Militärgericht** NT military court

militärisch [mili'tɛ:rɪʃ] **1** ADJ military; **mit allen ~en Ehren** with full military honours (*Brit*) *or* honors (*US*); **einen Konflikt mit ~en Mitteln lösen** to resolve a conflict with the use of troops **2** ADV militarily; **~ grüßen** to salute; **es geht dort streng ~ zu** it's very regimented there

Militarismus [milita'rɪsmʊs] M **-**, NO PL militarism

militaristisch [milita'rɪstɪʃ] ADJ militaristic

Military ['mɪlɪtəri] F **-, -s** (*Sport*) three-day event

Militärzeit F army days *pl*

Miliz [mi'li:ts] F **-, -en** militia

milkt [mɪlkt] (*old*) 3. PERS SING PRES *von* **melken**

Mille ['mɪlə] F **-, -** (*inf*) grand (*inf*); **5 ~** 5 grand (*inf*)

Millennium [mɪ'lɛniʊm] NT **-s, Millennien** [-niən] (*geh*) millennium

Milliardär [mɪliar'dɛ:ɐ] M **-s, -e**, **Milliardärin** [-'dɛ:rɪn] F **-, -nen** billionaire

Milliarde [mɪ'liardə] F **-, -n** thousand millions (*Brit*), billion (*US*)

milliardstel [mɪ'liartstl] ADJ thousand millionth (*Brit*), billionth (*US*)

Milliardstel [mɪ'liartstl] NT **-s, -** thousand millionth part (*Brit*), billionth part (*US*)

milliardste(r, s) [mɪ'liartstə] ADJ thousand millionth (*Brit*), billionth (*US*)

Milli- ['mɪlɪ] IN CPDS milli-; **Millibar** NT millibar; **Milligramm** NT milligram(me); **Milliliter** M millilitre (Brit), milliliter (US); **Millimeter** M or NT millimetre (Brit), millimeter (US); **millimetergenau** ⚡ ADJ Berechnung, Planung extremely precise ⚡ ADV to the millimetre (Brit) or millimeter (US); **Millimeterpapier** NT graph paper

Million [mɪ'lioːn] F -, -en million; **eine ~ Londoner ist** or **sind unterwegs** a million Londoners are on their way; **zwei ~en** two millions; **zwei ~en Einwohner** two million inhabitants; **~en begeisterter Zuschauer** or **von begeisterten Zuschauern** millions of enthusiastic viewers; **~en Mal** a million times

Millionär [mɪlio'nɛːɐ] M -s, -e millionaire; **vom Tellerwäscher zum ~** from rags to riches; **es zum ~ bringen** to make a million

Millionärin [mɪlio'nɛːrɪn] F -, -nen millionairess

Millionen-: Millionenauflage F million copies pl; millions of copies pl; **Millionenauftrag** M contract worth millions; **millionenfach** ⚡ ADJ millionfold; **der ~e Mord an den Juden** the murder of millions of Jews ⚡ ADV a million times; **Millionengeschäft** NT multi-million-pound/dollar etc industry; **ein ~ abschließen** to conclude a (business) deal worth millions; **Millionenschaden** M damage no pl running into millions; **Millionenstadt** F town with over a million inhabitants

millionstel [mɪ'lioːnstl] ADJ millionth

Millionstel [mɪ'lioːnstl] NT -s, - millionth part

millionste(r, s) [mɪ'lioːnstə] ADJ millionth

Milz [mɪlts] F -, -en spleen

Milzbrand M (Med, Vet) anthrax

mimen ['miːmən] VT **er mimt den Unschuldigen** (inf) he's acting innocent or the innocent (Brit); **er mimt den Kranken** (inf) he's pretending to be sick

Mimik ['miːmɪk] F -, NO PL facial expression; **etw durch ~ ausdrücken** to express sth facially

Mimikry ['mɪmɪkri] F -, NO PL (Zool, fig) mimicry

mimisch ['miːmɪʃ] ⚡ ADJ mimic ⚡ ADV darstellen using mime; **sich verständigen, zum Ausdruck bringen** by using mime

Mimose [mi'moːzə] F -, -n mimosa; **empfindlich wie eine ~ sein** to be oversensitive

mimosenhaft ⚡ ADJ (fig) oversensitive ⚡ ADV (fig) reagieren oversensitively

min. ABBR von minimal

Min., min. ABBR von Minute(n)

Minarett [mina'rɛt] NT -s, -e or -s minaret

minder ['mɪndɐ] ADV less; **mehr oder ~** more or less; **nicht ~ wichtig als** no less important than

Minder-: minderbegabt ADJ less gifted; **minderbegütert** [-bəɡyːtɐt] ADJ less well-off; **Mindereinnahmen** PL decrease sing in receipts

mindere(r, s) ADJ ATTR lesser; Güte, Qualität inferior

Minderheit F -, -en minority

Minderheits-: Minderheitsbeteiligung F minority interest; **Minderheitsregierung** F minority government

Minder-: minderjährig [-jɛːrɪç] ADJ who is (still) a minor; **Minderjährige(r)** [-jɛːrɪɡə] MF DECL AS ADJ minor; **Minderjährigkeit** [-jɛːrɪçkait] F -, NO PL minority

mindern ['mɪndɐn] ⚡ VT Ansehen to diminish; Rechte to erode; Freude, Vergnügen to lessen; Risiko, Chancen to reduce ⚡ VR (Ansehen, Wert, Qualität) to diminish; (Freude, Vergnügen) to lessen

Minderung ['mɪndəʀʊŋ] F -, -en (= Herabsetzung) diminishing no indef art; (von Wert, Qualität) reduction (+gen in); (von Rechten) erosion; (von Freude, Vergnügen) lessening

minderwertig [-veːɐtɪç] ADJ inferior

Minderwertigkeit F inferiority; **die ~ der Qualität** the low quality

Minderwertigkeitskomplex M inferiority complex

Minderzahl F minority; **in der ~ sein** to be in the minority

Mindest- ['mɪndəst] IN CPDS minimum; **Mindestabstand** M minimum distance; **Mindestalter** NT minimum age; **Mindestbetrag** M minimum amount; **Waren für einen ~ von 100 Euro** goods to a minimum value of 100 euros

mindestens ['mɪndəstns] ADV at least

mindeste(r, s) ['mɪndəstə] SUPERL von wenig ⚡ ADJ ATTR least, slightest; **nicht die ~ Angst** not the slightest trace of fear; **das**

Mindeste the (very) least; **das wäre das Mindeste gewesen** that's the least he/she etc could have done ⚡ ADV **zum Mindesten** at least; **nicht im Mindesten** not in the least; **das bezweifle ich nicht im Mindesten** I don't doubt that at all

Mindest-: Mindestgebot NT (bei Auktionen) reserve price; **Mindestgeschwindigkeit** F minimum speed; **Mindesthaltbarkeitsdatum** NT best-before date; **Mindestlohn** M minimum wage; **Mindestmaß** NT minimum; **Mindestreserve** F (Fin) minimum reserves pl; **Mindestwert** M minimum value; **im ~ von** to a minimum value of; **Mindestzinssatz** M minimum lending rate

Mine ['miːnə] F -, -n **(a)** (Min, Mil) mine **(b)** (= Bleistiftmine) lead; (= Kugelschreibermine, Filzstiftmine) reservoir; (austauschbar) refill; **die ~ ist leer/läuft aus** (von Kugelschreiber) the pen has run out/is leaking; (von Filzstift) the felt-tip has run out/is leaking; **eine neue ~** a refill; (für Bleistift) a new lead

Minen-: Minenfeld NT (Mil) minefield; **Minenleger** [-leːɡɐ] M -s, - (Mil, Naut) minelayer; **Minensuchboot** NT, **Minensucher** M (inf) minesweeper

Mineral [mine'raːl] NT -s, -e or -ien [-liən] mineral

Mineral-: Mineralbad NT mineral bath; (= Ort) spa; (= Schwimmbad) swimming pool fed from a mineral spring; **Mineralbrunnen** M mineral spring

mineralisch [mine'raːlɪʃ] ADJ mineral

Mineralogie [mineralo'ɡiː] F -, NO PL mineralogy

mineralogisch [minera'loːɡɪʃ] ADJ mineralogical

Mineral-: Mineralöl NT (mineral) oil; **Mineralölgesellschaft** F oil company; **Mineralölsteuer** F tax on oil; **Mineralquelle** F mineral spring; **Mineralwasser** NT mineral water

mini ['mɪni] ADJ INV (Fashion) mini; **Mini tragen** to wear a mini

Mini ['mɪni] M -s, -s (inf: = ~rock) mini

Mini- IN CPDS mini-; **Mini-Anlage** F mini hi-fi

Miniatur [minia'tuːɐ] F -, -en (Art) miniature

Miniatur- IN CPDS miniature; **Miniaturausgabe** F miniature version; (Buch) miniature edition

Mini-: Minibar F (im Hotel etc) minibar; **Minibikini** M scanty bikini; **Minibus** M minibus; **Minidisk, Minidisc** F -, -s (= Tonträger) Minidisc®; (Comput) minidisk; **Minigolf** NT crazy golf (Brit), putt-putt golf (US)

minimal [mini'maːl] ⚡ ADJ Unterschied, Aufwand minimal; Verlust, Verbesserung, Steigerung marginal; Gewinn, Chance very small; Preise, Benzinverbrauch, Gehalt very low; **mit ~er Anstrengung** with a minimum of effort ⚡ ADV (= wenigstens) at least; (= geringfügig) minimally

Minimal- IN CPDS minimum; **minimal-invasiv** [-ɪnva'ziːf] ADJ minimally invasive; **~e Chirurgie** minimally invasive surgery

minimieren [mini'miːrən] ptp **minimiert** VT (Econ, Comput) to minimize

Minimierung F -, -en minimization

Minimum ['miːnimʊm] NT -s, **Minima** [-ma] minimum (an +dat of)

Mini-: Minipille F minipill; **Minirock** M miniskirt

Minister [mi'nɪstɐ] M -s, -, **Ministerin** [-ərɪn] F -, -nen (Pol) minister (Brit) (für of), secretary (für for)

Ministeramt NT ministerial office

ministeriell [ministe'riɛl] ADJ ATTR ministerial

Ministerin F siehe Minister

Ministerium [minɪs'teːrium] NT -s, **Ministerien** [-riən] ministry (Brit), department

Minister-: Ministerkonferenz F conference of ministers; **Ministerpräsident(in)** M(F) prime minister; (eines Bundeslandes) leader of a Federal German state; **Ministerrat** M council of ministers; (von EG) Council of Ministers; **Ministersessel** M ministerial post (esp Brit) or position

Ministrant [minɪs'trant] M -en, -en, **Ministrantin** [-'trantɪn] F -, -nen (Eccl) server

Minna ['mɪna] F -, NO PL (fig inf) maid; **jdn zur ~ machen** (inf) to tear a strip off sb (Brit inf)

Minne- ['mɪnə-]: **Minnesang** M minnesong; **Minnesänger** M, **Minnesinger** M -s, - minnesinger

minus ['miːnʊs] ⚡ PREP +GEN minus ⚡ ADV minus; **~ 10 Grad, 10 Grad ~** minus 10 degrees; **~ machen** (inf) to make a loss

Minus ['miːnʊs] NT -, - **(a)** (= Fehlbetrag) deficit; (auf Konto) overdraft; (fig: = Nachteil) bad point; (in Beruf etc) disadvantage **(b)** (= ~zeichen) minus (sign)

Minus-: Minuspol M negative pole; **Minustemperatur** F temperature below freezing; **Minuszeichen** NT minus sign

Minute [mi'nu:tə] F **-, -n** minute; **es ist 10 Uhr und 21 ~n** (*form*) it is 21 minutes past 10 o'clock; **auf die ~** (**genau** *or* **pünktlich**) (right) on the dot; **in letzter ~** at the last minute

Minuten-: minutenlang 𝟙 ADJ ATTR several minutes of; **~es Schweigen** several minutes' silence 𝟚 ADV for several minutes; **Minutenzeiger** M minute hand

Minze ['mɪntsə] F **-, -n** (*Bot*) mint

Mio. ABBR *von* **Million(en)** m

mir [mi:ɐ] PERS PRON DAT *von* **ich** to me; (*nach Präpositionen*) me; **ein Freund von ~** a friend of mine; **von ~ aus!** (*inf*) I don't mind; **~ nichts, dir nichts** (*inf*: *unhöflich*) without so much as a by-your-leave; **es war ~ nichts, dir nichts weg** the next thing I knew it had gone; **wie du ~, so ich dir** (*prov*) tit for tat (*inf*); (*als Drohung*) I'll get my own back (on you); **dass ihr ~ nicht an die Bücher geht!** (*inf*) don't you touch those books!; **du bist ~ vielleicht einer!** (*inf*) you're a right one, you are! (*inf*); *siehe auch* **ihm**

Mirabelle [mira'bɛlə] F **-, -n** mirabelle

Misch-: Mischarbeitsplatz M (*Comput*) mixed work station; **Mischbatterie** F mixer tap; **Mischbrot** NT *bread made from more than one kind of flour*

mischen ['mɪʃn] 𝟙 VT to mix; *Tabak-, Tee-, Kaffeesorten auch* to blend; **die Karten neu ~** (*lit, fig*) to reshuffle the pack; *siehe auch* **gemischt** 𝟚 VR (= *sich vermengen*) to mix; **sich unter jdn/etw ~** to mix with sb/sth; **sich in etw** (*acc*) **~** to meddle in sth; **sich in das Gespräch ~** to butt into the conversation 𝟛 VI (*Cards*) to shuffle; **wer mischt?** whose turn is it to shuffle?

Misch-: Mischfinanzierung F mixed financing; **Mischform** F mixture; **Mischgewebe** NT mixed fibres (*Brit*) *or* fibers (*US*) pl

Mischling ['mɪʃlɪŋ] M **-s, -e (a)** (*Mensch*) mixed race person **(b)** (*Zool*) half-breed

Misch-: Mischmasch ['mɪʃmaʃ] M **-(e)s, -e** (*inf*) mishmash (*aus* of); **Mischmaschine** F cement-mixer; **Mischpult** NT (*Rad, TV*) mixing desk; (*von Band*) sound mixer

Mischung ['mɪʃʊŋ] F **-, -en (a)** (= *das Mischen*) mixing; (*von Tee-, Kaffee-, Tabaksorten*) blending **(b)** (*lit, fig*: = *Gemischtes*) mixture (*auch Chem*); (*von Tee etc*) blend

Mischungsverhältnis NT ratio (of a mixture)

Mischwald M mixed (deciduous and coniferous) woodland

miserabel [mizə'raːbl] (*inf*) 𝟙 ADJ lousy (*inf*); *Gesundheit* miserable; *Gefühl* ghastly; *Benehmen* dreadful; *Qualität* poor; *Ruf* terrible; (= *gemein*) *Kerl etc* nasty 𝟚 ADV dreadfully; **~ schmecken** to taste lousy (*inf*); **man isst dort ~** the food there is just lousy (*inf*); **~ riechen** to smell horrible; **er hat ~ abgeschnitten** he got lousy marks (*Brit inf*) *or* grades (*US inf*)

Misere [mi'ze:rə] F **-, -n** (*von Leuten, Wirtschaft etc*) plight; (*von Hunger, Krieg etc*) misery; **jdn aus einer ~ herausholen** to get sb out of trouble; **es ist eine ~, wie/dass ...** it is dreadful how/that ...

miss IMPER SING *von* **messen**

missachten [mɪs'laxtn, 'mɪs-], *ptp* **missachtet** VT INSEP **(a)** (= *ignorieren*) *Warnung, Ratschlag* to ignore; *Gesetz, Verbot* to flout **(b)** (= *gering schätzen*) *jdn* to despise; *Hilfe, Angebot* to disdain

Missachtung F **(a)** (= *Ignorieren*) disregard (*gen* for); (*von Gesetz, Verbot*) flouting (*gen* of) **(b)** (= *Geringschätzung*) disrespect (+*gen* for); disdain (+*gen* of, for)

Missbildung F deformity

missbilligen [mɪs'bɪlɪgn], *ptp* **missbilligt** VT INSEP to disapprove of

missbilligend 𝟙 ADJ disapproving 𝟚 ADV disapprovingly

Missbrauch ['mɪsbraux] M abuse; (= *falsche Anwendung*) misuse; (*von Notbremse, Feuerlöscher, Kreditkarte*) improper use; **vor ~ wird gewarnt** use only as directed; (*an Notbremse etc*) do not misuse

missbrauchen [mɪs'brauxn], *ptp* **missbraucht** VT INSEP *Vertrauen* to abuse; (*geh*: = *vergewaltigen*) to assault; **jdn für *or* zu etw ~** to use sb for sth; **etw für politische Zwecke ~** to abuse sth for political purposes; **sexuell missbraucht** sexually abused

missbräuchlich ['mɪsbrɔʏçlɪç] 𝟙 ADJ incorrect; (= *unerlaubt*) improper 𝟚 ADV incorrectly; (= *unerlaubterweise*) improperly

missen ['mɪsn] VT (*geh*) to do without; *Erfahrung* to miss

Misserfolg M failure; (*Theat, Buch etc auch*) flop

Missernte F crop failure

missfallen [mɪs'falən], *ptp* **missfallen** VI INSEP IRREG +DAT to displease; **es missfällt mir, wie er ...** I dislike the way he ...

Missfallen NT **-s**, NO PL displeasure (*über* +*acc* at)

Missfallens-: Missfallensäußerung F expression of disapproval; **Missfallensbekundung** F **-, -nen**, **Missfallenskundgebung** F demonstration of disapproval

missgebildet ['mɪsɡəbɪldət] ADJ deformed

Missgeburt F deformed person/animal; (*fig inf*) failure; **du ~!** (*sl*) you psycho! (*pej sl*)

Missgeschick NT mishap; (= *Pech, Unglück*) misfortune; **ein kleines ~** a slight mishap

missglücken [mɪs'ɡlʏkn], *ptp* **missglückt** VI INSEP AUX SEIN to fail; **das ist ihr missglückt** she failed; **der Kuchen ist (mir) missglückt** the cake didn't turn out; **ihm missglückt alles** everything he does goes wrong; **ein missglückter Versuch** an unsuccessful attempt

missgönnen [mɪs'ɡœnən], *ptp* **missgönnt** VT INSEP **jdm etw ~** to (be)grudge sb sth

Missgriff M mistake

Missgunst F enviousness (*gegenüber* of)

missgünstig 𝟙 ADJ envious (*auf* +*acc* of) 𝟚 ADV enviously

misshandeln [mɪs'handln], *ptp* **misshandelt** VT INSEP to ill-treat

Misshandlung F ill-treatment; (= *Kindesmisshandlung*) cruelty (to children)

Mission [mɪ'sioːn] F **-, -en** (*Eccl, Pol, fig*) mission; (= *diplomatische Vertretung*) legation, mission (*US*); (= *Gruppe*) delegation

Missionar [mɪsio'naːɐ] M **-s, -e, Missionarin** [-'naːrɪn] F **-, -nen** (*Aus*) **Missionär** [mɪsio'nɛːɐ] M **-s, -e, Missionärin** [-'nɛːrɪn] F **-, -nen** missionary

missionarisch [mɪsio'naːrɪʃ] 𝟙 ADJ missionary 𝟚 ADV with missionary zeal

missionieren [mɪsio'niːrən], *ptp* **missioniert** 𝟙 VI (*litfig*) to proselytize 𝟚 VT *Land, Mensch* to (work to) convert; (*fig*) to convert

Missklang M discord (*auch Mus*); (= *Misston*) discordant note; **ein ~** (*fig*) a note of discord

Misskredit [-kre'diːt] M, NO PL discredit; **jdn/etw in ~ bringen** to discredit sb/sth

misslang PRET *von* **misslingen**

misslich ['mɪslɪç] ADJ (*geh*) *Lage* awkward; *Umstand auch, Verzögerung* unfortunate; **das ist ja eine ~e Sache** that is a bit awkward/unfortunate

missliebig ['mɪsliːbɪç] ADJ unpopular; **politisch ~e Personen** people who have fallen out of favour (*Brit*) *or* favor (*US*) with the government

misslingen [mɪs'lɪŋən], *pret* **misslang** [mɪs'laŋ], *ptp* **misslungen** [mɪs'lʊŋən] VI INSEP AUX SEIN = **missglücken**

Misslingen NT **-s**, NO PL failure

misslungen PTP *von* **misslingen**

Missmanagement NT mismanagement

missraten¹ [mɪs'raːtn], *ptp* **missraten** VI INSEP IRREG AUX SEIN to go wrong; (*Kind*) to become wayward; **der Kuchen ist (mir) ~** the cake didn't turn out

missraten² [mɪs'raːtn] ADJ *Kind* wayward; **der ~e Kuchen** the cake which went wrong

Missstand M disgrace no pl; (*allgemeiner Zustand*) deplorable state of affairs no pl; (= *Ungerechtigkeit*) abuse; (= *Mangel*) defect; **einen ~/Missstände beseitigen** to remedy something which is wrong/things which are wrong; **Missstände in der Regierung/im Management anprangern** to denounce misgovernment/mismanagement

Missstimmung F **(a)** (= *Uneinigkeit*) discord; **eine ~** a note of discord **(b)** (= *Missmut*) ill feeling no indef art

misst [mɪst] 3. PERS SING PRES *von* **messen**

misstrauen [mɪs'trauən], *ptp* **misstraut** VI INSEP +DAT to mistrust

Misstrauen NT **-s**, NO PL mistrust, distrust (*gegenüber* of); (*esp einer Sache, Handlung gegenüber*) suspiciousness (*gegenüber* of); **~ gegen jdn/etw haben**, **jdm/einer Sache ~ entgegenbringen** to mistrust sb/sth; to be suspicious of sth

Misstrauens- (Parl): **Misstrauensantrag** M motion of no confidence; **Misstrauensvotum** NT vote of no confidence

misstrauisch ['mɪstrauɪʃ] ❶ ADJ mistrustful; (= argwöhnisch) suspicious ❷ ADV sceptically (Brit), skeptically (US)

Missverhältnis NT discrepancy; (in Proportionen) imbalance; **seine Leistung steht im ~ zu seiner Bezahlung** there is a discrepancy between the work he does and his salary

missverständlich ['mɪsfɛɐ̯ʃtɛntlɪç] ❶ ADJ unclear; **~e Ausdrücke** expressions which could be misunderstood ❷ ADV unclearly; **ich habe mich ~ ausgedrückt** I didn't express myself clearly

Missverständnis NT misunderstanding; (= falsche Vorstellung) misconception

missverstehen ['mɪsfɛɐ̯ʃteːən], ptp **missverstanden** VT INSEP IRREG to misunderstand; **Sie dürfen mich nicht ~** please do not misunderstand me; **in nicht misszuverstehender Weise** unequivocally

Misswahl F beauty contest

Misswirtschaft F maladministration

Mist [mɪst] M **-es**, NO PL (a) (= Tierkot) droppings pl; (= Pferdemist, Kuhmist etc) dung; (= Dünger) manure; **das ist nicht auf seinem ~ gewachsen** (inf) he didn't think that up himself
(b) (inf) (= Unsinn, Schund) rubbish (esp Brit); **~!** blast! (inf); **so ein ~!** what a darned or blasted nuisance (inf); **was soll der ~?** what's all this nonsense?; **da hat er ~ gemacht** or **gebaut** he really messed that up (inf); **~ verzapfen** (= dummes Zeug reden) to talk nonsense; **mach keinen ~!** don't be a fool!

> *Vorsicht!* **Mist** *wird nicht mit dem englischen Wort* **mist** *übersetzt.*

Mistel ['mɪstl] F **-, -n** mistletoe no pl

Mist-: **Mistgabel** F pitchfork (used for shifting manure); **Misthaufen** M manure heap; **Mistkäfer** M dung beetle; **Mistkerl** M (inf) dirty or rotten pig (inf); **Miststück** NT (inf), **Mistvieh** NT (inf) (= Mann) bastard (sl); (= Frau auch) bitch (sl); **Mistwetter** NT (inf) lousy weather

mit [mɪt] ❶ PREP +DAT (a) with; **ein Topf ~ Suppe** a pot of soup; **ein Kleid ~ Jacke** a dress and jacket; **wie wärs ~ einem Bier?** (inf) how about a beer?
(b) (= ~ Hilfe von) with; **~ der Bahn/dem Bus/dem Auto** by train/bus/car; **ich fahre ~ meinem eigenen Auto zur Arbeit** I drive to work in my own car; **~ der Post** by post (Brit) or mail; **~ Gewalt** by force; **~ Bleistift/Tinte/dem Kugelschreiber schreiben** to write in pencil/ink/ballpoint; **~ dem nächsten Flugzeug/Bus kommen** to come on the next plane/bus
(c) (zeitlich) **~ achtzehn Jahren** at (the age of) eighteen; **~ einem Mal** all of a sudden; **~ der Zeit** in time
(d) (bei Maß-, Mengenangaben) **~ 1 Sekunde Vorsprung gewinnen** to win by 1 second; **etw ~ 50.000 Euro versichern** to insure sth for 50,000 euros; **~ 80 km/h** at 80 km/h; **~ 4:2 gewinnen** to win 4-2
(e) (= einschließlich) including
(f) (Begleitumstand, Art und Weise, Eigenschaft) with; **du ~ deinen dummen Ideen** (inf) you and your stupid ideas; **~ Muße** (at one's) leisure; **~ lauter Stimme** in a loud voice; **~ Verlust** at a loss
(g) (= betreffend) **was ist ~ ihr los?** what's the matter with her?; **wie geht** or **steht es ~ deiner Arbeit?** how is your work going?; **~ meiner Reise wird es nichts** my trip is off
❷ ADV **er war ~ dabei** he went or came too; **er ist ~ der Beste der Gruppe/Mannschaft** he is one of the best in the group/the team; **das gehört ~ dazu** that's part and parcel of it; **etw ~ in Betracht ziehen** to consider sth as well

Mitarbeit F cooperation; (= Teilnahme) participation (auch Sch); **~ bei** or **an etw** (dat) work on sth; **unter ~ von** in collaboration with

mitarbeiten VI SEP (= mithelfen) to cooperate (bei on); (bei Projekt etc) to collaborate; **an** or **bei etw ~** to work on sth; **im Unterricht ~** to take an active part in lessons; **seine Frau arbeitet mit** (inf) his wife works too

Mitarbeiter(in) M(F) (= Betriebsangehöriger) employee; (= Kollege) colleague; (an Projekt etc) collaborator; **die ~ an diesem Projekt/bei dieser Firma** those who work on this project/for this firm; **freier ~** freelance; **inoffizieller ~** (DDR: von Stasi) unofficial collaborator

Mitarbeiterstab M staff

mitbekommen ptp **mitbekommen** VT SEP IRREG (a) **etw ~** to get sth (b) (inf) (= verstehen) to get (inf); (= bemerken) to realize; **hast du das noch nicht ~?** (= erfahren) you mean you didn't know that?

mitbenutzen ptp **mitbenutzt**, (esp S Ger, Aus, Sw) **mitbenützen** ptp **mitbenützt** VT SEP to share (the use of)

Mitbenutzung F, (esp S Ger, Aus, Sw) **Mitbenützung** F **-, -en** joint use

Mitbesitzer(in) M(F) co-owner

mitbestimmen ptp **mitbestimmt** SEP ❶ VI to have a say (bei in); **~d sein** or **wirken** to have an influence (bei, für on) ❷ VT to have an influence on

Mitbestimmung F co-determination, participation (bei in); **~ der Arbeiter** or **am Arbeitsplatz** worker participation

Mitbestimmungsrecht NT right of participation (in decision-making etc)

Mitbewerber(in) M(F) (fellow) competitor; (für Stelle) (fellow) applicant

Mitbewohner(in) M(F) (fellow) occupant; **die ~ in unserem Haus** the other occupants of the house

mitbringen VT SEP IRREG (a) Geschenk etc to bring; Freund, Begleiter to bring along; (beim Zurückkommen) to bring back; **jdm etw ~** to bring sth for sb; **jdm etw von** or **aus der Stadt ~** to bring (sb) sth back from town; **jdm etw vom Bäcker ~** to get (sb) sth from the baker's; **was sollen wir der Gastgeberin ~?** what should we take to our hostess?; **die richtige Einstellung ~** to have the right attitude; **bring gute Laune mit** come ready to enjoy yourself; **Sie haben schönes Wetter mitgebracht!** lovely weather you've brought with you!
(b) Mitgift, Kinder, Kapital to bring with one; **etw in die Ehe ~** to have sth when one gets married
(c) (fig) Befähigung, Voraussetzung etc to have

Mitbringsel ['mɪtbrɪŋzl] NT **-s, -** (Geschenk) small present; (Andenken) souvenir

Mitbürger(in) M(F) fellow citizen; **meine Stuttgarter ~** my fellow citizens from Stuttgart; (in Anrede) fellow citizens of Stuttgart; **die älteren ~** senior citizens

mitdenken VI SEP IRREG to follow sb's train of thought/line of argument; (= Ideen einbringen) to make a contribution; **du denkst ja mit!** good thinking; **denk mal mit** help me/us etc think

mitdürfen VI SEP IRREG **wir durften nicht mit** we weren't allowed to go along

miteinander [mɪtlaɪ'nandɐ] ADV with each other; (= gemeinsam) together; **alle ~!** all together; **wir haben lange ~ geredet** we had a long talk; **sie reden nicht mehr ~** they are not talking (to each other) any more

Miteinander [mɪtlaɪ'nandɐ] NT **-s**, NO PL cooperation

mitempfinden ptp **mitempfunden** SEP IRREG ❶ VT to feel too, to share ❷ VI **mit jdm ~** to feel for sb, to sympathize with sb

miterleben ptp **miterlebt** VT SEP to experience; Krieg auch to live through; (im Fernsehen) to watch

mitessen SEP IRREG ❶ VT Schale etc to eat as well; Mahlzeit to share ❷ VI (bei jdm) **~** to eat with sb; **willst du nicht ~?** why don't you have something to eat too?

Mitesser [-ɛsɐ] M **-s, -** blackhead

mitfahren VI SEP IRREG AUX SEIN to go (with sb); **sie fährt mit** she is going too; (mit mir/uns zusammen) she is going with me/us; (mit jdm) **~** to go with sb; (= mitgenommen werden) to get a lift or ride (esp US) with sb; **jdn ~ lassen** to allow sb to go; (= jdn mitnehmen) to give sb a lift or ride (esp US); **kann ich (mit Ihnen) ~?** can you give me a lift or a ride (esp US)?; **er fährt jeden Morgen mit mir im Auto mit** I give him a lift or ride (esp US) in my car every morning; **wie viel Leute können bei dir ~?** how many people can you take (with you)?

Mitfahrer(in) M(F) fellow passenger; (vom Fahrer aus gesehen) passenger

Mitfahrerzentrale F agency for arranging lifts or rides (esp US)

Mitfahrgelegenheit F lift

mitfühlen VI SEP **mit jdm ~** to feel for sb

mitfühlend ❶ ADJ sympathetic ❷ ADV sympathetically

mitführen VT SEP Papiere, Ware, Waffen etc to carry (with one); (Fluss) to carry along

mitgeben VT SEP IRREG jdm etw ~ to give sb sth to take with them; *Rat, Erziehung* to give sb sth; **das gebe ich dir noch mit** take that (with you) too

Mitgefühl NT sympathy

mitgehen VI SEP IRREG AUX SEIN **(a)** (= *mit anderen gehen*) to go too; **mit jdm ~** to go with sb; **gehen Sie mit?** are you going (too)?; **er ging bis 50.000 Euro mit** (*bei Auktion*) he went with the bidding until it reached 50,000 euros; **mit der Mode ~** to keep up with fashion **(b)** (*fig: Publikum etc*) to respond (favourably (*Brit*) *or* favorably (*US*)) (*mit* to) **(c)** (*inf*) **etw ~ lassen** to steal sth

Mitgift ['mɪtɡɪft] F **-, -en** dowry

Mitgiftjäger M (*inf*) dowry-hunter (*Brit*), fortune-hunter

Mitgliederversammlung F general meeting

Mitglieds-: Mitgliedsausweis M membership card; **Mitgliedsbeitrag** M membership fee, membership dues *pl*

Mitgliedschaft ['mɪtɡliːtʃaft] F **-, -en** membership

Mitgliedsstaat M member state

mithaben VT SEP IRREG etw ~ to have sth (with one); **hast du alles mit?** have you got everything?

mithalten VI SEP IRREG (= *sich beteiligen*) to join in (*mit* with); (= *bei Leistung, Tempo etc nachkommen*) (*mit* with) to keep up; (*bei Versteigerung*) to stay in the bidding; **bei einer Diskussion ~ können** to be able to hold one's own in a discussion; **er kann so erstklassig Englisch, da kann keiner ~** he speaks such excellent English, no-one can touch him (*inf*)

mithelfen VI SEP IRREG to help; **hilf doch ein bisschen mit** give us a hand

mithilfe, mit Hilfe [mɪt'hɪlfə] PREP +GEN with the help (+*gen* of)

Mithilfe F assistance, aid; **unter ~ der Kollegen** with the aid of colleagues

mithören SEP **1** VT to listen to (too); *Gespräch* to overhear; (*heimlich*) to listen in on; *Vorlesung* to attend; **ich habe alles mitgehört** I heard everything **2** VI IMPERS **es hört jd mit** sb is listening

Mitinhaber(in) M(F) (*von Haus etc*) joint owner; (*von Firma auch*) joint proprietor

Mitkämpfer(in) M(F) (*im Krieg*) comrade-in-arms; (*Sport*) (= *Teamkollege*) team-mate; (= *Partner*) partner

mitkommen VI SEP IRREG AUX SEIN **(a)** (= *mit anderen kommen*) to come along (*mit* with); (*Sendung, Brief etc*) to come; **kommst du auch mit?** are you coming too?; **ich kann nicht ~** I can't come; **komm doch mit!** come with us/me *etc*!; **bis zum Bahnhof ~** to come as far as the station; **ich bin gerade noch mit dem Zug mitgekommen** I just caught the train **(b)** (*inf*) (= *mithalten*) to keep up; (= *verstehen*) to follow; **da komme ich nicht mit** that's beyond me; **sie kommt in der Schule/in Französisch gut mit** she is getting on well at school/with French

mitkönnen VI SEP IRREG (*inf*) **(a)** (= *mitkommen können*) to be able to come (*mit* with); (= *mitgehen können*) to be able to go (*mit* with) **(b)** (*usu neg*) (= *verstehen*) to be able to follow

mitkriegen VT SEP (*inf*) = **mitbekommen**

Mitläufer(in) M(F) (*Pol, pej*) fellow traveller (*Brit*) *or* traveler (*US*)

Mitlaut M consonant

Mitleid NT, NO PL pity (*mit* for); (= *Mitgefühl*) sympathy (*mit* with, for); **~ erregend** pitiful

Mitleidenschaft F jdn/etw in ~ ziehen to affect sb/sth (detrimentally)

mitleidig ['mɪtlaɪdɪç] **1** ADJ pitying; (= *mitfühlend*) sympathetic; *Mensch* compassionate **2** ADV pityingly; (= *mitfühlend*) compassionately

mitlesen VTI SEP IRREG to read too; *Text* to follow; **etw (mit jdm) ~** to read sth at the same time (as sb)

mitmachen VTI SEP **(a)** (= *teilnehmen*) *Spiel, Singen etc* to join in; *Reise, Expedition, Ausflug* to go on; *Kurs* to do; *Mode* to follow; *Wettbewerb* to take part in; **(bei) etw ~** to join in sth; **er macht alles mit** he always joins in (all the fun); **da mache ich nicht mit** (= *ohne mich*) count me out!; **meine Augen/meine Beine machen nicht mehr mit** my eyes/legs are giving up; **wenn das Wetter mitmacht** if the weather cooperates **(b)** (*inf*: = *einverstanden sein*) **da kann ich nicht ~** I can't go along with that; **das mache ich nicht mehr mit** I've had quite enough (of that); **ich mache das nicht mehr lange mit** I won't take that much longer

(c) (= *erleben*) to live through; (= *erleiden*) to go through; **sie hat viel mitgemacht** she has been through a lot in her time

Mitmensch M fellow man *or* creature

mitmischen VI SEP (*inf*) (= *sich beteiligen*) to be involved (*in* +*dat, bei* in)

mitmüssen VI SEP IRREG (= *mitkommen müssen*) to have to come too; (= *mitgehen müssen*) to have to go too

Mitnahme [-naːmə] F **-**, NO PL **(jdm) die ~ von etw empfehlen** to recommend sb to take sth with them

mitnehmen VT SEP IRREG **(a)** (= *mit sich nehmen*) to take (with one); (= *ausleihen*) to borrow; (= *kaufen*) to take; **jdn (im Auto) ~** to give sb a lift *or* ride (*esp US*); **einmal Pommes frites zum Mitnehmen** a bag of chips to take away (*Brit*), French fries to go (*US*); **Gewinne ~** (*St Ex*) to take profits **(b)** (= *erschöpfen*) *jdn* to exhaust; (= *beschädigen*) to be bad for; **mitgenommen aussehen** to look the worse for wear **(c)** (*inf*) *Sehenswürdigkeit, Veranstaltung* to take in

mitrechnen VT SEP to count; *Betrag* to count in; **Feiertage nicht mitgerechnet** excluding public holidays

mitreden SEP **1** VI (= *Meinung äußern*) to join in (*bei etw* sth); (= *mitbestimmen*) to have a say (*bei* in); **da kann er nicht ~** he wouldn't know anything about that; **da kann ich ~** I should know; **sie will überall ~** (*inf*) she always has to have her say **2** VT **da möchte ich auch ein Wörtchen ~** I'd like to have some say (in this) too; **Sie haben hier nichts mitzureden** this is none of your concern

Mitreisende(r) MF DECL AS ADJ fellow passenger

mitreißen VT SEP IRREG (*Fluss, Lawine*) to sweep away; (*Fahrzeug*) to carry along; **sich ~ lassen** (*fig*) to allow oneself to be carried away; **der Schauspieler/seine Rede hat alle mitgerissen** everyone was carried away by the actor's performance/his speech

mitreißend 1 ADJ *Rhythmus, Enthusiasmus* infectious; *Reden, Musik* rousing; *Film, Fußballspiel* thrilling **2** ADV *vortragen* infectiously; **er redete ~** he gave a rousing speech

mitsamt [mɪt'zamt] PREP +DAT together with

mitschicken VT SEP (*in Brief etc*) to enclose

mitschleifen VT SEP to drag along

mitschneiden VT SEP IRREG to record

Mitschnitt M recording

mitschreiben VI SEP IRREG to take notes

Mitschuld F share of the blame (*an* +*dat* for); (*an einem Verbrechen*) complicity (*an* +*dat* in); **ihn trifft eine ~** a share of the blame falls on him; (*an Verbrechen*) he is implicated (*an* +*dat* in)

mitschuldig ADJ (*an Verbrechen*) implicated (*an* +*dat* in); (*an Unfall*) partly responsible (*an* +*dat* for); **sich ~ machen** to incur (some) blame (*an* +*dat* for); (*an Verbrechen*) to become implicated (*an* +*dat* in)

Mitschuldige(r) MF DECL AS ADJ accomplice; (= *Helfershelfer*) accessory

Mitschüler(in) M(F) school-friend; (*in derselben Klasse*) classmate

mitsingen SEP IRREG **1** VT to join in (singing) **2** VI to join in the singing; **in einer Oper/einem Chor etc ~** to sing in an opera/choir *etc*

mitspielen VI SEP **(a)** (= *auch spielen*) to play too; (*in Mannschaft etc*) to play (*bei* in); **in einem Film/bei einem Theaterstück ~** to be in a film/play; **bei einem Orchester ~** to play in an orchestra; **wer spielt mit?** who wants to play?; (*in Mannschaft*) who's playing?; (*Theat etc*) who's in it? **(b)** (*fig inf*) (= *mitmachen*) to play along (*inf*); (= *sich beteiligen*) to be involved in; **wenn das Wetter mitspielt** if the weather's OK (*inf*) **(c)** (*Gründe, Motive*) to play a part (*bei* in) **(d)** (= *Schaden zufügen*) **er hat ihr übel *or* schlimm *or* hart mitgespielt** he has treated her badly; **das Leben hat ihr übel *etc* mitgespielt** she has had a hard life

Mitspieler(in) M(F) (*Sport*) player; (*Theat*) member of the cast; **seine ~** (*Sport*) his team-mates; (*Theat*) the other members of the cast

Mitsprache F a say

Mitspracherecht NT right to a say in a matter; **jdm ein ~ einräumen *or* gewähren** to allow *or* grant sb a say (*bei* in)

mitsprechen SEP IRREG VI to join in; **bei etw ~** to join in sth; (= *mitbestimmen*) to have a say in sth

Mittag ['mɪtaːk] M -(e)s, -e (a) midday; **gegen** ~ around midday; **über** ~ at midday, at lunchtime(s); **am** ~ at midday, at lunchtime; **jeden** ~ every day at midday, every lunchtime; **jeden ~ gegen halb eins** every day at half past twelve; **gestern/heute/morgen** ~ at midday yesterday/today/tomorrow; **Dienstag** ~ Tuesday (at) midday, Tuesday lunchtime; **zu** ~ **essen** to have lunch or dinner; **etwas Warmes zu** ~ **essen** to have a cooked lunch (Brit) or warm lunch (US)

(b) (inf: Pause) lunch hour, lunch-break; ~ **machen/haben** to take/have one's lunch hour or lunch-break; **sie macht gerade** ~ she's at lunch

Mittagessen NT lunch; **sie saßen beim** ~ they were having lunch

mittäglich 1 ADJ ATTR midday, lunchtime; Schläfchen afternoon **2** ADV at lunchtimes

mittags ADV at lunchtime; **die Deutschen essen** ~ **warm** the Germans have a hot meal at midday; ~ **(um) 12 Uhr, (um) 12 Uhr** ~ at 12 noon, at 12 o'clock midday; **sonnabends** ~ Saturday lunchtime

Mittags-: Mittagshitze F midday heat; **Mittagspause** F lunch hour; ~ **machen/haben** to take/have one's lunch hour; (Geschäft etc) to close at lunchtime; **Mittagsschlaf** M afternoon nap; **Mittagstisch** M dinner table; **am** ~ **sitzen** to be sitting (at the table) having lunch; **Mittagszeit** F lunchtime; **während** or **in der** ~ at lunchtime; **um die** ~ around midday or lunchtime

Mittäter(in) M(F) accomplice

Mittäterschaft F complicity

Mittdreißiger ['mɪtdraɪsɪɡɐ] M -s, -, **Mittdreißigerin** [-ərɪn] F -, -nen man/woman in his/her mid-thirties

Mitte ['mɪtə] F -, -n (a) (= Mittelpunkt, mittlerer Teil) middle; (von Kreis, Kugel, Stadt, Sport) centre (Brit), center (US); **ein Buch bis zur** ~ **lesen** to read half of a book; ~ **August** in the middle of August; ~ **des Jahres/des Monats** halfway through the year/month; ~ **der siebziger Jahre** in the mid-seventies; **er ist** ~ **vierzig** or **der Vierziger** he's in his mid-forties; **die goldene** ~ the golden mean; **in der** ~ in the middle; (zwischen zwei Menschen) in between (them/us etc); (zwischen Ortschaften) halfway

(b) (Pol) centre (Brit), center (US); **die linke/rechte** ~ centre-left/-right (Brit), center-left/-right (US); **in der** ~ **stehen** to be moderate; **in der** ~ **zwischen** midway between; **rechts/links von der** ~ right/left of centre (Brit) or center (US)

(c) (von Gruppe, Gesellschaft) **einer aus unserer** ~ one of us; **ich bin gern in eurer** ~ I like being with you; **in unserer** ~ in our midst

mitteilen SEP **1** VT **jdm etw** ~ to tell sb sth; (= benachrichtigen) to inform sb of sth; (= bekannt geben) to announce sth to sb **2** VR (= kommunizieren) to communicate (jdm with sb); **er kann sich gut/schlecht** ~ he finds it easy/difficult to communicate

mitteilsam ['mɪttaɪlzaːm] ADJ communicative; (pej) garrulous

Mitteilung F (= Bekanntgabe) announcement; (= Benachrichtigung) notification; (Comm, Admin) communication; (an Mitarbeiter etc) memo; (von Korrespondenten, Reporter etc) report; **eine** ~ **bekommen, dass ...** to hear that ...

Mitteilungsbedürfnis NT need to talk to other people

Mittel ['mɪtl] NT -s, - (a) (Math: = Durchschnitt) average; **im** ~ on average; **arithmetisches/geometrisches** ~ arithmetical/geometrical mean

(b) (= ~ zum Zweck, Transportmittel etc) means sing; (= Maßnahme, Methode) way; (= Werbemittel, Propagandamittel, zur Verkehrsbeeinflussung) device; (= Lehrmittel) aid; ~ **und Wege finden** to find ways and means; ~ **zum Zweck** a means to an end; **als letztes** or **äußerstes** ~ as a last resort; **zu anderen** ~**n greifen, andere** ~ **anwenden** to use other means or methods; **ihm ist jedes** ~ **recht** he will do anything (to achieve his ends); **ihm war jedes** ~ **recht, dazu war ihm jedes** ~ **recht** he did not care how he did it; **etw mit allen** ~**n verhindern/bekämpfen** to do one's utmost to prevent/oppose sth; **etw mit allen** ~**n versuchen** to try one's utmost to do sth; **sie hat mit allen** ~**n gekämpft, um ...** she fought tooth and nail to ...

(c) PL (= Geldmittel) resources pl; (= Medikament) (kosmetisch) preparation; (= Medizin) medicine; (= Putzmittel) cleaning

---

agent; (= Fleckenmittel) stain remover; (= Waschmittel) detergent; (= Haarwaschmittel) shampoo; **welches** ~ **nimmst du?** what do you use?; (Med: = einnehmen) what do you take?; **ein** ~ **zum Einreiben** something to be rubbed in; **das ist ein** ~ **gegen meine Erkältung/Schuppen** that is for my cold/dandruff; ~ **zum Putzen** cleaning stuff; **sich** (dat) **ein** ~ **(gegen Kopfschmerzen/Husten etc) verschreiben lassen** to get the doctor to prescribe something (for headaches/a cough etc); **welches** ~ **hat der Arzt dir verschrieben?** what did the doctor give you?; **es gibt kein** ~ **gegen Schnupfen** there is no cure for the common cold; **das beste** ~ **für** or **gegen etw** the best cure for sth

Mittel-: mittelaktiv ADJ Atommüll etc intermediate-level; **Mittelalter** NT Middle Ages pl; **da herrschen Zustände wie im** ~! (inf) it is positively medieval there; **mittelalterlich** [-laltɐlɪç] **1** ADJ medieval **2** ADV **eine** ~ **anmutende Stadt** a medieval-looking town; ~ **geprägt sein** to show a medieval influence; **Mittelamerika** NT Central America (and the Caribbean); **mittelamerikanisch** ADJ Central American; **mittelbar 1** ADJ indirect (auch Jur); Schaden consequential **2** ADV indirectly; **Mitteldeutschland** NT Germany east of the Harz Mountains excluding Pomerania etc; **Mittelding** NT (= Mischung) cross (zwischen +dat, aus between); **Mitteleuropa** NT Central Europe; **Mitteleuropäer(in)** M(F) Central European; **mitteleuropäisch** ADJ Central European; ~**e Zeit** Central European Time; **Mittelfeld** NT (Sport) midfield; **Mittelfinger** M middle finger; **mittelfristig** [-frɪstɪç] **1** ADJ Finanzplanung, Kredite medium-term; Voraussage medium-range **2** ADV in the medium term; **Mittelgebirge** NT low mountain range; **Mittelgewicht** NT middleweight; **mittelgroß** ADJ medium-sized; **Mittelklasse** F (a) (Comm) middle of the market; **ein Wagen der** ~ a mid-range car **(b)** (Sociol) middle classes pl; **Mittelklassewagen** M mid-range car; **Mittellinie** F centre (Brit) or center (US) line; **Mittelmaß** NT mediocrity no art; **das (gesunde)** ~ the happy medium; ~ **sein** to be average; **seine Leistungen bewegen sich im** ~, **seine Leistungen gehen nicht über das** ~ **hinaus** his performance is mediocre; **mittelmäßig 1** ADJ mediocre **2** ADV indifferently; begabt, gebildet moderately; ausgestattet modestly; **wie gefällt es dir hier?** – **so** ~ how do you like it here? – so-so (inf); **Mittelmäßigkeit** F mediocrity

Mittelmeer NT Mediterranean (Sea)

Mittelmeer- IN CPDS Mediterranean; **Mittelmeerraum** M Mediterranean (region), Med (inf)

Mittel-: Mittelohrentzündung F, **Mittelohrvereiterung** F inflammation of the middle ear; **mittelprächtig** (hum inf) **1** ADJ reasonable; (= ziemlich schlecht) pretty awful (inf) **2** ADV not bad; **sich** ~ **fühlen** to feel not too bad; **Mittelpunkt** M (Math) (räumlich) centre (Brit), center (US); (fig: visuell) focal point; **er muss immer** ~ **sein** or **im** ~ **stehen** he always has to be the centre (Brit) or center (US) of attention; **er steht im** ~ **des Interesses** he is the centre (Brit) or center (US) of attention

mittels ['mɪtls] PREP +GEN or DAT (geh) by means of

Mittel-: Mittelscheitel M centre parting (Brit), center part (US); **Mittelschicht** F (Sociol) middle class; **Mittelschule** F (a) (inf: = Realschule) ≈ secondary modern school (dated Brit), ≈ junior high (US) **(b)** (Sw, Aus: = Oberschule) secondary school, high school (US)

Mittelsmann M, pl -männer or -leute, **Mittelsperson** F intermediary

Mittel-: Mittelstand M middle classes pl; **mittelständisch** [-ʃtɛndɪʃ] ADJ middle-class; Betrieb medium-sized; **Mittelstreifen** M central reservation (Brit), median (strip) (US); **Mittelstück** NT middle part; (von Braten etc) middle; **Mittelstufe** F (Sch) middle school (Brit), junior high (US); **Mittelstürmer(in)** M(F) (Sport) centre-forward (Brit), center-forward (US); **Mittelteil** M or NT middle section; **Mittelweg** M middle course; **der goldene** ~ the happy medium; **einen** ~ **gehen** or **einschlagen** to steer a middle course; **einen** ~ **suchen** to try to find a happy medium; **Mittelwelle** F (Rad) medium wave(band); **Mittelwert** M mean

mitten ['mɪtn] ADV ~ **an etw** (dat)/**auf etw** (dat)/**in etw** (dat)/**bei etw** (right) in the middle of sth; ~ **aus etw** (right) from the middle of sth; ~ **durch etw** (right) through the middle of sth; ~ **darin/darein** (right) in the middle of it; ~ **darunter** (räumlich) right under it/them; (= dabei) right amongst it/them; ~ **in der Luft/im Atlantik** in mid-air/mid-Atlantic; ~ **ins Gesicht** right in the face; **es ist noch** ~ **in der Nacht** it's still the middle of the night; **~ im Leben** in the middle of life; **~ in** or **bei der Arbeit** in the middle of working; **~ unter uns** (right) in our midst; **der Stock brach ~ entzwei** the stick broke clean in two

mitten-: mittendrin [mɪtn'drɪn] ADV (right) in the middle of it; **~ in der Stadt/der Arbeit** (right) in the middle of the town/one's work; **~, etw zu tun** (right) in the middle of doing sth; **mittendurch** [mɪtn'dʊrç] ADV (right) through the middle

Mitternacht F midnight no art

mitternächtig [-nɛçtɪç], **mitternächtlich** ADJ ATTR midnight; **zu ~er Stunde** (geh) at the midnight hour

Mitternachtssonne F midnight sun

Mittfünfziger ['mɪtfʏnftsɪgɐ] M **-s, -**, **Mittfünfzigerin** [-ərɪn] F **-, -nen** man/woman in his/her mid-fifties

Mittler ['mɪtlɐ] M **-s, -**, **Mittlerin** [-ərɪn] F **-, -nen** mediator; (liter. Ideen, Sprache etc) medium

mittlere(r, s) ['mɪtlərə] ADJ ATTR **(a)** (= dazwischenliegend) middle; **der/die/das ~** the middle one; **der Mittlere Osten** the Middle East

(b) (= den Mittelwert bildend) medium; (= mittelschwer) Kursus, Aufgabe intermediate; (= durchschnittlich) average; (Math) mean; (= von mittlerer Größe) Betrieb medium-sized; **von ~m Wert** of medium value; **~n Alters** middle-aged; **~ Reife** (Sch) first public examination in secondary school, ≈ O-levels (Brit)

MITTLERE REIFE

mittlere Reife is the term still generally used for the intermediate school certificate. This is normally gained after successful completion of the six years (four in many Länder) in a Realschule. All pupils who complete their tenth year at a Gymnasium also automatically receive their mittlere Reife. If pupils from a Realschule achieve good examination results, they can move up to the eleventh year of a Gymnasium and try for the Abitur. The mittlere Reife entitles a pupil to attend a Fachoberschule and take the Fachabitur there after two years ▶ ABITUR, GYMNASIUM, REALSCHULE

---

mittlerweile ['mɪtlɐ'vaɪlə] ADV in the meantime

mittrinken VI SEP IRREG to have a drink with us/them etc

Mitt-: Mittsechziger ['mɪtzɛçtsɪgɐ] M **-s, -**, **Mittsechzigerin** [-ərɪn] F **-, -nen** man/woman in his/her mid-sixties; **Mittsiebziger** ['mɪtzi:ptsɪgɐ] M **-s, -**, **Mittsiebzigerin** [-ərɪn] F **-, -nen** man/woman in his/her mid-seventies; **Mittsommer** ['mɪtzɔmɐ] M midsummer; **Mittsommernacht** F Midsummer's Night

mittun VI SEP IRREG (inf) to join in

Mitt-: Mittvierziger ['mɪtfɪrtsɪgɐ] M **-s, -**, **Mittvierzigerin** [-ərɪn] F **-, -nen** man/woman in his/her mid-forties; **Mittwoch** ['mɪtvɔx] M **-s, -e** Wednesday; siehe auch Dienstag; **mittwochs** ['mɪtvɔxs] ADV on Wednesdays; siehe auch dienstags; **Mittzwanziger** ['mɪttsvantsɪgɐ] M **-s, -**, **Mittzwanzigerin** [-ərɪn] F **-, -nen** man/woman in his/her mid-twenties

mitunter [mɪt'ʊntɐ] ADV from time to time

mitverantwortlich ADJ jointly responsible pred

Mitverantwortung F share of the responsibility; **~ haben** to have a share of the responsibility; **die** or **jede ~ ablehnen** to abnegate (all) responsibility

mitverdienen ptp **mitverdient** VI SEP to (go out to) work as well

mitwirken VI SEP to play a part (an +dat, bei in); (= beteiligt sein) to be involved (an +dat, bei in); (Schriftsteller, Regisseur etc) to collaborate (an +dat, bei on); (= mitspielen) (Schauspieler, Diskussionsteilnehmer) to take part (an +dat, bei in); (in Film) to appear (an +dat in); (in Chor, Orchester etc) to perform (in +dat in, an +dat, bei in); **ohne sein Mitwirken wäre das unmöglich gewesen** it would have been impossible without his involvement

Mitwirkende(r) [-vɪrkndə] MF DECL AS ADJ participant (an +dat, bei in); (= Mitspieler) performer (an +dat, bei in); (= Schauspieler) actor (an +dat, bei in); **die ~n** (Theat) the cast pl

Mitwirkung F (= Beteiligung, Mitarbeit) involvement (an +dat, bei in); (= Zusammenarbeit) cooperation (an +dat, bei in); (an Buch, Film) collaboration (an +dat, bei on); (= Teilnahme) (an Diskussion, Projekt) participation (an +dat, bei in); (von Schauspieler) appearance (an +dat, bei in); (von Tänzer, Orchester, Chor) performance (an +dat, bei in); **unter ~ von** with the assistance of

Mitwisser [-vɪsɐ] M **-s, -**, **Mitwisserin** [-ərɪn] F **-, -nen** (Jur) accessory (+gen to); **~ sein** to know about it; **~ einer Sache** (gen) **sein** to know about sth; **jdn zum ~ machen** to tell sb (all) about it; (Jur) to make sb an accessory

Mitwohnzentrale F agency for arranging shared accommodation

mitwollen VI SEP (= mitgehen wollen) to want to go along; (= mitkommen wollen) to want to come along

mitzählen VTI SEP to count; Betrag to count in

mixen ['mɪksn] VT to mix

Mixer¹ ['mɪksɐ] M **-s, -** (= Küchenmixer) blender; (= Rührmaschine) mixer

Mixer² ['mɪksɐ] M **-s, -**, **Mixerin** [-ərɪn] F **-, -nen (a)** (= Barmixer) cocktail waiter/waitress **(b)** (Film, Rad, TV) mixer

Mixtur [mɪks'tu:ɐ] F **-, -en** (Pharm, Mus, fig) mixture

ml ABBR von **Milliliter** millilitre (Brit), milliliter (US)

mm ABBR von **Millimeter** millimetre (Brit), millimeter (US)

Mnemo- [mnemo-]: **Mnemotechnik** F mnemonics sing; **mnemotechnisch** 🕮 ADJ mnemonic 🕮 ADV mnemonically

Mob [mɔp] M **-s**, NO PL (pej) mob

mobben ['mɔbn] VT to bully (at work)

Mobbing ['mɔbɪŋ] NT **-s**, NO PL workplace bullying

Möbel ['mø:bl] NT **-s, -** (= ~stück) piece of furniture; **~ pl** furniture sing

Möbel- IN CPDS furniture; **Möbelpacker** [-pakɐ] M **-s, -**, **Möbelpackerin** [-ərɪn] F **-, -nen** furniture packer; **Möbelschreiner(in)** M(F) cabinet-maker; **Möbelspedition** F removal firm (Brit), moving company (US); **Möbelstück** NT piece of furniture; **Möbelwagen** M removal van (Brit), moving van (US)

mobil [mo'bi:l] 🕮 ADJ **(a)** mobile; (Comm, Jur) Vermögen, Kapital movable; (= mitnehmbar) Drucker portable; **~es Vermögen** movables pl; **~ machen** (Mil) to mobilize **(b)** (inf: = flink, munter) lively; **jdn ~ machen** to liven sb up 🕮 ADV **mit jdm ~ telefonieren** to call sb on one's mobile (phone)

Mobile ['mo:bilə] NT **-s, -s** mobile

Mobilfunk M cellular radio

Mobilfunknetz NT cellular network

Mobiliar [mobi'lia:ɐ] NT **-s**, NO PL furnishings pl

mobilisieren [mobili'zi:rən], ptp **mobilisiert** VT (Mil) (fig) to mobilize; (Comm) Kapital to make liquid

Mobilität [mobili'tɛ:t] F **-**, NO PL mobility

Mobil-: Mobilmachung [mo'bi:lmaxʊŋ] F **-, -en** (Mil) mobilization; **Mobiltelefon** NT mobile phone

möblieren [mø'bli:rən], ptp **möbliert** VT to furnish; **neu ~** to refurnish; **möbliert wohnen** to live in furnished accommodation

mochte PRET von **mögen**

Möchtegern- ['mœçtəgɐn-] IN CPDS (iro) would-be; **ein ~-Schauspieler** a would-be actor

modal [mo'da:l] ADJ (Gram) modal

Modalität [modali'tɛ:t] F **-, -en** USU PL (von Plan, Vertrag etc) arrangement; (von Verfahren, Arbeit) procedure

Modal- (Gram): **Modalsatz** M (adverbial) clause of manner; **Modalverb** NT modal verb

Mode ['mo:də] F **-, -n** fashion; (= Sitte) custom; **~ sein** to be fashionable; (Sitte) to be the custom; **das ist jetzt ~** that's the latest fashion; **in ~/aus der ~ kommen** to come into/go out of fashion; **die ~** or **alle ~n mitmachen, mit** or **nach der ~ gehen, sich nach der ~ richten** to keep up with the latest fashions

---

Vorsicht! **Mode** *wird nicht mit dem englischen Wort* **mode** *übersetzt.*

Mode-: Modearzt M, **Modeärztin** F fashionable doctor; **Modeausdruck** M, pl **-ausdrücke** in-phrase; (Wort) in-word, buzz word; **modebewusst** ADJ fashion-conscious; **Modedesigner(in)** M(F) fashion designer; **Modehaus** NT fashion house; **Modeheft** NT, **Modejournal** NT fashion magazine; **Modekrankheit** F fashionable complaint

Model ['mɔdl] NT **-s, -s** (Fashion) model

Modell [mo'dɛl] NT **-s, -e** model; **zu etw ~ stehen** to be the model for sth; **jdm ~ stehen/sitzen** to sit for sb

Modell-: Modelleisenbahn F model railway (*esp Brit*) *or* railroad (*US*); (*als Spielzeug*) train set; **Modellflugzeug** NT model aeroplane (*Brit*) *or* airplane (*US*)

modellieren [modɛ'liːrən], *ptp* **modelliert** VTI to model

modeln ['mɔdln] VI (*Fashion*) to model

Modem ['moːdɛm] NT **-s, -e** modem

Modenschau F fashion show

Moderation [modera'tsioːn] F **-, -en** (*Rad, TV*) presentation; **die ~ heute Abend hat: ...** tonight's presenter is ...

Moderator [mode'raːtoːɐ] M **-s, Moderatoren** [-'toːrən], **Moderatorin** [-'toːrɪn] F **-, -nen** presenter

moderieren [mode'riːrən], *ptp* **moderiert** VTI (*Rad, TV*) to present

moderig ['moːdərɪç] **1** ADJ *Geruch* musty **2** ADV **~ riechen** to smell musty; **~ schmecken** to taste mouldy (*Brit*) *or* moldy (*US*)

modern¹ ['moːdɐn] VI AUX SEIN *or* HABEN to rot

modern² [mo'dɛrn] **1** ADJ modern *no adv*; (= *modisch*) fashionable; *Politik, Ansichten, Eltern, Lehrer* progressive; **~ sein** (*Kleidung, Möbel*) to be fashionable; **~ werden** to come into fashion; **der ~e Mensch** modern man **2** ADV *bauen, ausstatten* in a modern style; *sich kleiden* fashionably; *denken* open-mindedly; **~ wohnen** to live in modern housing; **~ eingestellt sein** to be modern

modernisieren [modɛrni'ziːrən], *ptp* **modernisiert** **1** VT to modernize **2** VI to get up to date

Mode-: Modesache F **das ist reine ~** it's just the fashion; **Modesalon** M fashion house; **Modeschau** F fashion show; **Modeschmuck** M costume jewellery (*Brit*) *or* jewelry (*US*); **Modeschöpfer, Modeschöpferin** M(F) fashion designer; **Modewort** NT, *pl* **-wörter** in-word, buzz word; **Modezeichner(in)** M(F) fashion illustrator; **Modezeitschrift** F fashion magazine

Modi PL *von* **Modus**

Modifikation [modifika'tsioːn] F **-, -en** modification

modifizieren [modifi'tsiːrən], *ptp* **modifiziert** VT to modify

modisch ['moːdɪʃ] **1** ADJ stylish **2** ADV fashionably, stylishly

Modistin [mo'dɪstɪn] F **-, -nen** milliner

modrig ['moːdrɪç] ADJ, ADV = **moderig**

Modul [mo'duːl] NT **-s, -e** (*Comput*) module

modular [modu'laːɐ] **1** ADJ modular **2** ADV of modules

Modulation [modula'tsioːn] F **-, -en** modulation

Modus ['moːdʊs, 'mɔdʊs] M **-, Modi** ['moːdi, 'mɔdi] (a) way; **~ Vivendi** (*geh*) modus vivendi (b) (*Gram*) mood (c) (*Comput*) mode

Mofa ['moːfa] NT **-s, -s** small moped

Mogelei [moːgə'lai] F **-, -en** cheating *no pl*

mogeln ['moːgln] VI to cheat

Mogelpackung F misleading packaging; (*fig*) sham; **den Wählern eine ~ verkaufen** (*fig*) to sell the electorate false promises

mögen ['møːgn], *pret* **mochte** ['mɔxtə], *ptp* **gemocht** [gə'mɔxt] **1** VT to like; **sie mag das (gern)** she (really) likes that; **was möchten Sie, bitte?** what would you like?; **was can I do for you?**; **~ Sie eine Praline/etwas Wein?** (*form*) would you like a chocolate/some wine?; **nein danke, ich möchte lieber Tee** no thank you, I would prefer tea *or* would rather have tea **2** VI (a) (= *etw tun ~*) to like to; **ich mag nicht mehr** I've had enough; (= *bin am Ende*) I can't take any more; **kommen Sie mit?** – **ich möchte gern, aber ...** are you coming too? – I'd like to, but ... (b) (= *gehen/fahren wollen*) to want to go; **ich möchte lieber in die Stadt** I would prefer to go into town **3** *ptp* **mögen** MODAL AUX VB (a) (*im Konjunktiv: Wunsch*) to like to +*infin*; **möchten Sie etwas essen?** would you like something to eat?; **wir möchten (gern) etwas trinken** we would like something to drink; **hier möchte ich nicht wohnen** (= *würde nicht gern*) I wouldn't like to live here; (= *will nicht*) I don't want to live here; **ich möchte dazu nichts sagen** I don't want to say anything about that; **ich hätte gern dabei sein ~** I would like to have been there; **das möchte ich auch wissen** I'd like to know that too (b) (*im Konjunktiv: einschränkend*) **man möchte meinen, dass ...** you would think that ...; **ich möchte fast sagen ...** I would almost say ...

(c) (*geh: Einräumung*) **es mag wohl sein, dass er Recht hat, aber ...** he may well be right, but ...; **was sie auch sagen mag** whatever she says; **mag kommen was da will** come what may; **mag es schneien, so viel es will** it can snow as much as it likes **(d)** (*Vermutung*) **es mochten etwa fünf Stunden vergangen sein** about five hours must have passed; **sie mag/mochte etwa zwanzig sein** she must be/have been about twenty; **was mag das wohl heißen?** what might that mean? **(e)** (= *wollen*) to want; **sie mag nicht bleiben** she doesn't want to stay **(f)** (*Aufforderung, indirekte Rede*) **(sagen Sie ihm,) er möchte zu mir kommen** would you tell him to come and see me; **Sie möchten zu Hause anrufen** you should call home

Mogler ['moːglɐ] M **-s, -**, **Moglerin** [-ərɪn] F **-, -nen** cheat

möglich ['møːklɪç] ADJ (a) possible; **alles Mögliche** everything you can think of; **alles Mögliche tun** to do everything possible; **er tat sein Möglichstes** he did his utmost; **aus allen ~en Richtungen** from all directions; **er hat allen ~en Blödsinn gemacht** he did all sorts of stupid things; **so viel/bald wie ~** as much/soon as possible; **das ist doch nicht ~!** that's impossible; **nicht ~!** never!; **das wäre woanders nicht ~** that couldn't happen anywhere else; **ist denn so was ~?** would you credit it? (*inf*); **im Bereich** *or* **Rahmen des Möglichen** within the realms of possibility **(b)** (*attr* = *eventuell*) *Kunden, Interessenten, Nachfolger* potential, possible; **alle ~en Fälle** every eventuality; **alles Mögliche bedenken** to consider everything

möglicherweise ['møːklɪçɐ'vaizə] ADV possibly; **~ kommt er morgen** he might (possibly) come tomorrow

Möglichkeit F **-, -en (a)** possibility; **es besteht die ~, dass ...** there is a possibility that ...; **nach ~** if possible; **ist denn das die ~?** (*inf*), **ist es die ~!** (*inf*) it's impossible! **(b)** (= *Aussicht*) chance; (= *Gelegenheit*) opportunity; **die ~ haben, etw zu tun** to have the chance/opportunity to do sth *or* of doing sth; **er hatte keine andere ~** he had no other choice; **das Land der unbegrenzten ~en** the land of unlimited opportunity **(c)** USU PL (= *Fähigkeiten*) capabilities; **der Mietpreis übersteigt meine finanziellen ~en** the rent is beyond my means

möglichst ['møːklɪçst] ADV **~ genau/schnell/oft** as accurately/quickly/often as possible; **in ~ kurzer Zeit** as quickly as possible

Mohair [mo'heːɐ] M **-s, -e**, **Mohär** [mo'heːɐ] M **-s, -e** (*Tex*) mohair

Mohammedaner [mohame'daːnɐ] M **-s, -**, **Mohammedanerin** [-ərɪn] F **-, -nen** Mohammedan (*dated*)

mohammedanisch [mohame'daːnɪʃ] **1** ADJ Mohammedan (*dated*) **2** ADV *erziehen* as a Mohammedan (*dated*); *aufwachsen* Mohammedan (*dated*)

Mohikaner [mohi'kaːnɐ] M **-s, -**, **Mohikanerin** [-ərɪn] F **-, -nen** Mohican; **der letzte ~** (*fig*) the very last one

Mohn [moːn] M **-(e)s, -e** poppy; (= *~samen*) poppy seed

Mohn- IN CPDS poppy; (*Cook*) (poppy-)seed; **Mohnblume** F poppy

Mohr [moːɐ] M **-en, -en**, **Mohrin** [-rɪn] F **-, -nen** (*old*) (*blacka*)moor (*old*); **der ~ hat seine Schuldigkeit getan, der ~ kann gehen** (*prov*) as soon as you've served your purpose they've no further interest in you

Möhre ['møːrə] F **-, -n** carrot

Mohrenkopf M *small chocolate-covered cream cake*; (= *Negerkuss*) chocolate marshmallow with biscuit base

Mohrrübe F carrot

moin [mɔyn] INTERJ (*N Ger inf*) **~(, ~)!** morning (*inf*); (= *hallo*) hi (*inf*)

Mokick ['moːkɪk] NT **-s, -s** moped with a kick-starter

mokieren [mo'kiːrən], *ptp* **mokiert** VR to sneer (*über* +*acc* at)

Molch [mɔlç] M **-(e)s, -e** salamander; (= *Wassermolch*) newt

Moldau ['mɔldau] F - (*Fluss*) Vltava

Moldawien [mɔl'daːviən] NT **-s** Moldavia

Molekül [mole'kyːl] NT **-s, -e** molecule

molekular [moleku'laːɐ] ADJ molecular

Molkerei [mɔlkə'rai] F **-, -en** dairy

Molkerei-: Molkereibutter F blended butter; **Molkereiprodukt** NT dairy product

Moll [mɔl] NT **-, -** (*Mus*) minor (key); **a-~** A minor; **a-~-Tonleiter** scale of A minor

mollig [ˈmɔlɪç] (*inf*) 🔢 ADJ **(a)** cosy (*Brit*), cozy (*US*); (= *warm, behaglich*) snug **(b)** (= *rundlich*) plump 🔢 ADV ~ **warm** warm and cosy (*Brit*) or cozy (*US*)

Moll-: **Molltonart** F minor key; **Molltonleiter** F minor scale

Molotowcocktail [ˈmoːlotɔf-] M Molotov cocktail

Molukken [moˈlʊkn] PL (*Geog*) Moluccas *pl*

Moment[1] [moˈmɛnt] M **-(e)s, -e** moment; **einen ~ lang** for a moment; **jeden ~** any time or minute; **einen ~, bitte** one moment please; **kleinen ~!** just a second!; **~ mal!** just a minute!; **im ~** at the moment; **im ersten ~** for a moment

Moment[2] NT **-(e)s, -e (a)** (= *Bestandteil*) element **(b)** (= *Umstand*) fact; (= *Faktor*) factor **(c)** (*Phys*) moment; (= *Kraftwirkung*) momentum

momentan [momɛnˈtaːn] 🔢 ADJ **(a)** (= *vorübergehend*) momentary **(b)** (= *augenblicklich*) present *attr* 🔢 ADV **(a)** (= *vorübergehend*) for a moment **(b)** (= *augenblicklich*) at the moment

Monaco [ˈmoːnako, moˈnako] NT **-s** Monaco

Monarch [moˈnarç] M **-en, -en**, **Monarchin** [-ˈnarçɪn] F **-, -nen** monarch

Monarchie [monarˈçiː] F **-, -n** [-ˈçiːən] monarchy

monarchistisch [monarˈçɪstɪʃ] 🔢 ADJ pro-monarchist 🔢 ADV **eine ~ orientierte Partei** a pro-monarchist party

Monat [ˈmoːnat] M **-(e)s, -e** month; **der ~ Mai** the month of May; **sie ist im sechsten ~ (schwanger)** she's in the sixth month; **was verdient er im ~?** how much does he earn a month?; **am 12. dieses ~s** or **des laufenden ~s** on the 12th (of this month); **auf ~e hinaus** months ahead; **jdn zu drei ~en (Haft) verurteilen** to sentence sb to three months' imprisonment; **von ~ zu ~** month by month

monatelang 🔢 ADJ ATTR **Verhandlungen, Kämpfe** which go on for months; **seine ~e Abwesenheit** his months of absence; **nach ~em Warten** after waiting for months; **mit ~er Verspätung** months late 🔢 ADV for months

-monatig [moːnatɪç] ADJ SUF **-month**; **ein dreimonatiger Urlaub** a three-month holiday (*esp Brit*) or vacation (*US*)

monatlich [ˈmoːnatlɪç] 🔢 ADJ monthly 🔢 ADV every month; **er zahlt ~ 500 Euro** he pays 500 euros a month

-monatlich ADJ SUF **zwei-/dreimonatlich** every two/three months; **allmonatlich** every month

Monats-: **Monatsanfang** M beginning of the month; **Monatseinkommen** NT monthly income; **Monatsende** NT end of the month; **Monatsgehalt** NT monthly salary; **ein ~** one month's salary; **Monatskarte** F monthly season ticket; **Monatslohn** M monthly wage; **~ bekommen** to be paid monthly; **Monatsmitte** F middle of the month; **Monatsrate** F monthly instalment (*Brit*) or installment (*US*)

monat(s)weise ADJ, ADV monthly

Mönch [mœnç] M **-(e)s, -e** monk

Mond [moːnt] M **-(e)s, -e** [-də] moon; **auf** or **hinter dem ~ leben** (*inf*) to be behind the times; **du lebst wohl auf dem ~!** (*inf*) where have you been?; **deine Armbanduhr geht nach dem ~** (*inf*) your watch is way out (*inf*)

mondän [mɔnˈdɛːn] ADJ chic

Mond-: **Mondaufgang** M moonrise; **Mondauto** NT moon buggy; **Mondbahn** F moon's orbit; (*Space*) lunar orbit; **Mondfähre** F (*Space*) lunar module; **Mondfinsternis** F eclipse of the moon, lunar eclipse; **mondhell** 🔢 ADJ moonlit 🔢 ADV **~ erleuchtet** lit by the moon, moonlit; **Mondjahr** NT lunar year; **Mondlandefähre** F (*Space*) lunar module; **Mondlandung** F moon landing; **Mondlicht** NT moonlight; **Mondphasen** PL phases *pl* of the moon; **Mondpreis** M (*inf*) astronomical price (*inf*); **Mondschein** M moonlight; **Mondsichel** F crescent moon; **Mondsonde** F (*Space*) lunar probe; **Mondumlaufbahn** F (*Space*) lunar orbit; **Monduntergang** F moonset

Monegasse [moneˈgasə] M **-n, -n**, **Monegassin** [-ˈgasɪn] F **-, -nen** Monegasque

monegassisch [moneˈgasɪʃ] ADJ Monegasque

monetär [moneˈtɛːɐ] 🔢 ADJ monetary 🔢 ADV **ihre Politik ist ~ geprägt** her policy is monetary; **eine ~ orientierte Denkweise** monetary thinking

Monetarismus [monetaˈrɪsmʊs] M **-**, NO PL (*Econ*) monetarism

Mongole [mɔnˈgoːlə] M **-n, -n**, **Mongolin** [-ˈgoːlɪn] F **-, -nen** Mongolian

Mongolei [mɔŋɡoˈlai] F **- die ~** Mongolia; **die Innere/Äußere ~** Inner/Outer Mongolia

mongolisch [mɔŋˈgoːlɪʃ] ADJ Mongolian

Mongolismus [mɔŋɡoˈlɪsmʊs] M **-**, NO PL (*Med*) mongolism

mongoloid [mɔŋɡoloˈiːt] ADJ Mongol; (*Med*) mongoloid

monieren [moˈniːrən], *ptp* **moniert** VT to complain about; **sie hat moniert, dass …** she complained that …

Monitor [ˈmoːnitoːɐ] M **-s, -e** or **Monitoren** [-ˈtoːrən] (*TV, Phys*) monitor

Mono-, **mono-** [ˈmoːno, ˈmono] IN CPDS mono-; **monochrom** [monoˈkroːm] ADJ monochrome; **monogam** [monoˈɡaːm] 🔢 ADJ monogamous 🔢 ADV **leben** monogamously; **Monogamie** [monoɡaˈmiː] F **-**, NO PL monogamy; **Monogramm** [monoˈɡram] NT, *pl* **-gramme** monogram

Monokel [moˈnɔkl] NT **-s, -** monocle

Monolog [monoˈloːk] M **-(e)s, -e** [-ɡə] (*Liter*) (*fig*) monologue; (= *Selbstgespräch*) soliloquy; **einen ~ halten** (*fig*) to hold a monologue

Monopol [monoˈpoːl] NT **-s, -e** monopoly (*auf +acc, für* on)

Monopol- IN CPDS monopoly; **Monopolbildung** F monopolization *no pl*

monopolisieren [monopoliˈziːrən], *ptp* **monopolisiert** VT (*lit, fig*) to monopolize

Monopolist [monopoˈlɪst] M **-en, -en**, **Monopolistin** [-ˈlɪstɪn] F **-, -nen** monopolist

Monopol-: **Monopolkommission** F monopolies commission; **Monopolstellung** F monopoly

Monopoly® [moˈnoːpoli] NT **-**, NO PL Monopoly®

monoton [monoˈtoːn] 🔢 ADJ monotonous 🔢 ADV monotonously

Monoxid [ˈmoːnɔksiːt, ˈmɔnɔksiːt, monoˈksiːt] NT monoxide

Monster [ˈmɔnstɐ] NT **-s, -** (*inf*) = **Monstrum**

Monster- IN CPDS (*usu pej*) mammoth; **Monsterfilm** M mammoth (film) production

Monstren PL *von* **Monstrum**

Monstrosität [mɔnstroziˈtɛːt] F **-, -en** monstrosity; (= *riesige Größe*) monstrous size; (= *Ungeheuer*) monster

Monstrum [ˈmɔnstrʊm] NT **-s, Monstren** [-trən] (= *Ungeheuer*) monster; (*fig*: = *Missbildung*) monstrosity; (*inf*: = *schweres Möbel*) hulking great piece of furniture (*inf*)

Monsun [mɔnˈzuːn] M **-s, -e** monsoon

Montag [ˈmoːntaːk] M Monday; *siehe auch* **Dienstag**

Montage [mɔnˈtaːʒə] F **-, -n (a)** (*Tech*) (= *Aufstellung*) installation; (*von Gerüst*) erection; (= *Zusammenbau*) assembly; (*Typ*) stripping; **auf ~ (dat) sein** to be away on a job **(b)** (*Art, Liter*) montage; (*Film*) editing

Montage-: **Montageband** NT, *pl* **-bänder** assembly line; **Montagehalle** F assembly shop; **Montagewerk** NT assembly plant

montags [ˈmoːntaːks] ADV on Mondays; *siehe auch* **dienstags**

Montagsauto M (*hum*) problem car

Monteur [mɔnˈtøːɐ] M **-s, -e**, **Monteurin** [-ˈtøːrɪn] F **-, -nen** (*Tech*) fitter; (= *Heizungsmonteur, Fernmeldemonteur, Elektromonteur*) engineer

montieren [mɔnˈtiːrən], *ptp* **montiert** VT **(a)** (*Tech*) to install; (= *zusammenbauen*) to assemble; (= *befestigen*) **Bauteil** to fit (*auf +acc, an +acc* to); **Dachantenne** to put up; (= *aufstellen*) **Gerüst** to erect; **etw an die Wand ~** to fix sth to the wall **(b)** (*Art, Film, Liter*) **Einzelteile** to create a montage from; **aus etw montiert sein** to be a montage of sth

Monument [monuˈmɛnt] NT **-(e)s, -e** monument

monumental [monumɛnˈtaːl] 🔢 ADJ monumental 🔢 ADV monumentally

Monumental- [monumɛnˈtaːl] IN CPDS monumental;

Moonboots [ˈmuːnbuːts] PL moon boots *pl*

Moor [moːɐ] NT **-(e)s, -e** bog; (= *Hochmoor*) moor

Moor-: **Moorbad** NT mud bath; **Moorboden** M marshy soil; **Moorhuhn** NT grouse

moorig [ˈmoːrɪç] ADJ boggy

Moos [moːs] NT **-es, -e** moss

Mop [mɔp] M **-s, -s** *siehe* **Mopp**

Moped [ˈmoːpet, ˈmoːpeːt] NT **-s, -s** moped

Mopedfahrer(in) M(F) moped rider

Mopp [mɔp] M **-s, -s** mop

Mops [mɔps] M **-es, ⸚e** ['mœpsə] **(a)** (*Hund*) pug (dog) **(b)** (= *Dickwanst*) roly-poly (*inf*) **(c) Möpse** PL (*sl*: = *Busen*) tits *pl* (*sl*)

Moral [mo'ra:l] F -, NO PL **(a)** (= *Sittlichkeit*) morals *pl*; **die ~ sinkt/ steigt** moral standards are declining/rising; **die bürgerliche/ sozialistische ~** bourgeois/socialist morality; **eine doppelte ~** double standards *pl*, a double standard; **~ predigen** to moralize (*jdm* to sb) **(b)** (= *Lehre, Nutzanwendung*) moral; **und die ~ von der Geschicht':** ... and the moral of this story is ... **(c)** (= *Ethik*) ethics *pl* **(d)** (= *Disziplin*: *von Volk, Soldaten*) morale

moralisch [mo'ra:lɪʃ] ADJ moral; **das war eine ~e Ohrfeige für die Regierung** that was one in the eye (*Brit*) *or* that was a black eye (*US*) for the government (*inf*); **einen** *or* **seinen Moralischen haben** (*inf*) to have (a fit of) the blues (*inf*) ADV *bedenklich, verpflichtet* morally; **ein ~ hoch stehender Mensch** a person of high moral standing

Moralist [mora'lɪst] M **-en, -en, Moralistin** [-'lɪstɪn] F -, **-nen** moralist

moralistisch [mora'lɪstɪʃ] ADJ moralistic

Moral-: Moralkodex M moral code; **Moralpredigt** F sermon; **~en halten** to moralize; **jdm eine ~ halten** to give sb a sermon

Moräne [mo're:nə] F -, **-n** (*Geol*) moraine

Morast [mo'rast] M **-(e)s, -e** *or* **Moräste** [mo'restə] (*lit, fig*) mire

morastig [mo'rastɪç] ADJ marshy; (= *schlammig*) muddy

Moratorium [mora'to:riʊm] NT **-s, Moratorien** [-riən] moratorium

morbid [mɔr'bi:t] ADJ (*Med*) morbid; (*fig geh*) degenerate

Morbus-Down-Syndrom ['mɔrbʊs'daun-] NT Down's syndrome

Morchel ['mɔrçl] F -, **-n** (*Bot*) morel

Mord [mɔrt] M **-(e)s, -e** [-də] murder, homicide (*US*) (*an +dat* of); (*an Politiker etc*) assassination (*an +dat* of); **politischer ~** political killing; **das ist ja ~!** (*inf*) it's (sheer) murder! (*inf*); **dann gibt es ~ und Totschlag** (*inf*) all hell will break out (*inf*)

Mörder ['mœrdɐ] M **-s, -, Mörderin** [-ərɪn] F -, **-nen** murderer (*auch Jur*), killer; (= *Attentäter*) assassin

---

Vorsicht! **Mörder** *wird nicht mit dem englischen Wort* **murder** *übersetzt.*

---

mörderisch ['mœrdərɪʃ] ADJ (*lit*) *Anschlag* murderous; (*fig*) (= *schrecklich*) dreadful; *Preise* iniquitous; *Konkurrenzkampf* cutthroat ADV (*inf*) (= *entsetzlich*) dreadfully; *stinken* like hell (*inf*); *wehtun* like crazy (*inf*)

Mord-: Mordfall M murder *or* homicide (*US*) (case); **der ~ Dr. Praun** the Dr Praun murder *or* homicide (*US*) (case); **Mordinstrument** NT murder weapon; **Mordkommission** F murder squad, homicide squad (*US*)

Mords- ['mɔrts] IN CPDS (*inf*) incredible, terrible; (= *toll, prima*) hell of a (*inf*); **Mordsding** NT (*inf*) whopper (*inf*); **Mordsgeld** NT (*inf*) fantastic amount of money; **Mordskerl** M (*inf*) **(a)** (= *verwegener Mensch*) hell of a guy (*inf*) **(b)** (= *starker Mann*) enormous guy (*inf*); **Mordskrach** M (*inf*) hell of a din (*inf*); (= *Streit*) hell of a row (*inf*); **mordsmäßig** (*inf*) ADJ incredible; **ich habe einen ~en Hunger** I could eat a horse (*inf*) ADV (= *sehr*) incredibly; (= *furchtbar*) dreadfully; **Mordswut** F (*inf*) terrible temper; **eine ~ im Bauch haben** to be in a hell of a temper (*inf*)

Mord-: Mordverdacht M suspicion of murder; **unter ~** (*dat*) **stehen** to be suspected of murder; **Mordwaffe** F murder weapon

morgen ['mɔrgn] ADV tomorrow; **~ früh/Mittag/Abend** tomorrow morning/lunchtime/evening; **~ in acht Tagen** tomorrow week, a week (from) tomorrow; **~ um diese** *or* **dieselbe Zeit** this time tomorrow; **bis ~/~ früh!** see you tomorrow/in the morning; **~, ~, nur nicht heute, sagen alle faulen Leute** (*Prov*) tomorrow never comes (*Prov*); **~ ist auch (noch) ein Tag!** (*Prov*) tomorrow is another day (*prov*)

Morgen[1] ['mɔrgn] M **-s, -** (= *Tagesanfang*) morning; **am ~, des ~s** (*geh*) in the morning; **gestern ~** yesterday morning; **heute ~** this morning; **bis in den ~ (hinein)** into the early hours; **den ganzen ~** the whole morning; **es wird ~** day is breaking; **guten ~!** good morning; **~!** (*inf*) morning, hi (*inf*)

Morgen[2] M **-s, -** (*Measure*) ≈ acre

Morgen- IN CPDS morning; **Morgendämmerung** F dawn, daybreak; **in der ~** at first light

morgendlich ['mɔrgntlɪç] ADJ morning *attr*; (= *frühmorgendlich*) early morning *attr*; **die ~e Stille** the quiet of the early morning ADV **es war ~ kühl** *or* **frisch** it was cool as it often is in the morning

Morgen-: Morgenessen NT (*Sw*: = *Frühstück*) breakfast; **Morgenfrühe** [-fry:ə] F -, NO PL early morning; **sie brachen in aller ~ auf** they left at (the) break of dawn; **Morgengrauen** [-grauən] NT **-s, -** dawn; **im** *or* **beim ~** in the first light of dawn; **Morgenlatte** (*sl*) early-morning hard-on (*sl*); **Morgenmantel** M dressing gown; **Morgenmuffel** M (*inf*) **sie ist ein schrecklicher ~** she's terribly grumpy in the mornings (*inf*); **Morgenrock** M housecoat; **Morgenrot** NT **-s**, NO PL, **Morgenröte** F -, **-n** sunrise; (*fig*) dawn(ing)

morgens ['mɔrgns] ADV in the morning; **(um) drei Uhr ~, ~ (um) drei Uhr** at three o'clock in the morning; **~ und abends** morning and evening; (*fig*: = *dauernd*) morning, noon and night; **von ~ bis mittags** in the morning; **von ~ bis abends** from morning to night

Morgen-: Morgenstunde F morning hour; **zu früher ~** early in the morning; **bis in die frühen ~n** into the early hours; **Morgenstund(e) hat Gold im Mund(e)** (*Prov*) the early bird catches the worm (*Prov*)

morgig ['mɔrgɪç] ADJ ATTR tomorrow's; **der ~e Tag** tomorrow; **sein ~er Besuch** his visit tomorrow

Mormone [mɔr'mo:nə] M **-n, -n, Mormonin** [-'mo:nɪn] F -, **-nen** Mormon

Morphem [mɔr'fe:m] NT **-s, -e** morpheme

Morphium ['mɔrfiʊm] NT **-s**, NO PL morphine

morphiumsüchtig ADJ addicted to morphine

Morphologie [mɔrfolo'gi:] F -, NO PL morphology

morphologisch [mɔrfo'lo:gɪʃ] ADJ morphological

morsch [mɔrʃ] ADJ (*lit, fig*) rotten; *Knochen* brittle

Morse- ['mɔrzə-]: **Morsealphabet** NT Morse (code); **im ~** in Morse (code); **Morseapparat** M Morse telegraph

morsen ['mɔrzn] VI to send a message in Morse (code) VT to send in Morse (code)

Mörser ['mœrzɐ] M **-s, -** mortar (*auch Mil*)

Morsezeichen ['mɔrzə-] NT Morse signal

Mörtel ['mœrtl] M **-s, -** (*zum Mauern*) mortar; (= *Putz*) stucco

Mosaik [moza'i:k] NT **-s, -e(n)** (*lit, fig*) mosaic

Mosambik [mozam'bɪk, -'bi:k] NT **-s** Mozambique

Moschee [mɔ'ʃe:] F -, **-n** [-'ʃe:ən] mosque

Moschus ['mɔʃʊs] M -, NO PL musk

Möse ['mø:zə] F -, **-n** (*vulg*) cunt (*vulg*)

Mosel[1] ['mo:zl] F - (*Geog*) Moselle

Mosel[2] M **-s, -, Moselwein** M Moselle (wine)

mosern ['mo:zɐn] VI (*inf*) to gripe (*inf*)

Moses ['mo:zəs, 'mo:zɛs] M **-'** *or* (*liter*) **Mosis** ['mo:zɪs] Moses; **bin ich ~?** (*hum inf*) don't ask me

Moskau ['mɔskau] NT **-s** Moscow

Moskauer[1] ['mɔskauɐ] ADJ ATTR Moscow *attr*

Moskauer[2] ['mɔskauɐ] M **-s, -, Moskauerin** [-ərɪn] F -, **-nen** Muscovite

Moskito [mɔs'ki:to] M **-s, -s** mosquito

Moskitonetz NT mosquito net

Moslem ['mɔslɛm] M **-s, -s, Moslemin** [mɔs'le:mɪn] F -, **-nen** Moslem

moslemisch [mɔs'le:mɪʃ] ADJ ATTR Moslem ADV *erziehen* as a Moslem; *aufwachsen* Moslem

Moslime [mɔs'li:mə] F -, **-n** Moslem

Most [mɔst] M **-(e)s**, NO PL **(a)** (unfermented) fruit juice; (*für Wein*) must **(b)** (*S Ger, Sw*: = *Apfelmost*) cider

Motel [mo'tɛl] NT **-s, -s** motel

Motion [mo'tsio:n] F -, **-en** (*Sw*: = *Antrag*) motion

Motiv [mo'ti:f] NT **-s, -e** [-və] **(a)** (*Psych, Jur, fig*) motive; **das ~ einer Tat** the motive for a deed; **aus welchem ~ heraus?** for what motive? **(b)** (*Art, Liter*) subject; (= *Leitmotiv, Topos, Mus*) motif

Motivation [motiva'tsio:n] F -, **-en** motivation

motivieren [moti'vi:rən] *ptp* **motiviert** VT **(a)** *Mitarbeiter* (= *anregen*) to motivate; **politisch motiviert** politically motivated **(b)** (= *begründen*) **etw (jdm gegenüber) ~** to give (sb) reasons for sth; (*rechtfertigend*) to justify sth (to sb); *Verhalten, Abwesenheit* to account for sth (to sb)

Motor ['mo:tɔr, mo'to:ɐ] M **-s, -en** [-'to:rən] motor; (*von Fahrzeug*) engine; (*fig*) driving force (+*gen* in)

Motor-: **Motorblock** M, *pl* **-blöcke** engine block; **Motorboot** NT motorboat

Motorenöl NT engine oil

Motorhaube F bonnet (*Brit*), hood (*US*)

-motorig [moto:rɪç] ADJ SUF -engined; **einmotorig** single-engined; **zweimotorig** twin-engined

Motorik [mo'to:rɪk] F **-**, NO PL (*Physiol*) motor activity; (= *Lehre*) study of motor activity

motorisch [mo'to:rɪʃ] **1** ADJ (*Physiol*) *Nerv, Störung* motor *attr* **2** ADV **sie ist ~ gestört** she suffers from an impairment of the motor nerves

motorisieren [motori'zi:rən], *ptp* **motorisiert** VT to motorize; **sich ~** to get motorized; **motorisiertes Zweirad** motorized bike

Motorrad ['mo:tɔrra:t, mo'to:ɐra:t] NT motorbike; **fahren Sie (ein) ~?** do you ride a motorbike?

Motorrad-: **Motorradfahrer(in)** M(F) motorcyclist; **Motorradsport** M motorcycle racing

Motor-: **Motorroller** M (motor) scooter; **Motorsäge** F power saw; **Motorschaden** M engine trouble *no pl*

Motte ['mɔtə] F **-, -n** moth; **von ~n zerfressen** moth-eaten; **du kriegst die ~!** (*inf*) blow me! (*inf*)

Motten-: **Mottenkiste** F (*fig*) **etw aus der ~ hervorholen** to dig sth out; **aus der ~ des 19. Jahrhunderts stammen** (*inf*) to be a relic of the 19th century; **Mottenkugel** F mothball; **Mottenpulver** NT moth powder; **mottenzerfressen** ADJ moth-eaten

Motto ['mɔto] NT **-s, -s** (= *Wahlspruch*) motto; **unter dem ~ ... stehen** to have ... as *or* one's motto

motzen ['mɔtsn] VI (*inf*) to beef (*inf*)

Mountainbike ['mauntɪnbaɪk] NT **-s, -s** mountain bike

Möwe ['mø:və] F **-, -n** seagull

MP F **-, -s** (a) [ɛm'pe:] ABBR *von* **Militärpolizei** Military Police (b) [ɛm'pi:] ABBR *von* **Maschinenpistole**

MP3 [ɛmpe'drai] NT **-** (*Comput*) MP3

Mrd. ABBR *von* **Milliarde**

MS [ɛm'ɛs] ABBR *von* **multiple Sklerose** MS

MS-: **MS-krank** ADJ suffering from MS; **MS-Kranke(r)** MF DECL AS ADJ MS sufferer

MTA[1] [ɛmte:'la:] M **-s, -s** ABBR *von* **medizinisch-technischer Assistent**

MTA[2] [ɛmte:'la:] F **-, -s** ABBR *von* **medizinisch-technische Assistentin**

Mücke ['mʏkə] F **-, -n** (= *Insekt*) mosquito, midge (*Brit*); **aus einer ~ einen Elefanten machen** (*inf*) to make a mountain out of a molehill

Mucken ['mʊkn] PL (*inf*) moods *pl*; (**seine**) **~ haben** to be moody; (*Sache*) to be temperamental; **jdm die ~ austreiben** to sort sb out (*inf*)

Mückenstich M mosquito bite, midge bite (*Brit*)

Mucks [mʊks] M **-es, -e** (*inf*) sound; **einen/keinen ~ sagen** to make/not to make a sound; (*widersprechend*) to say/not to say a word; **ohne einen ~** (= *widerspruchslos*) without a murmur

mucksmäuschenstill [-mɔysçən-] ADJ, ADV (*inf*) (as) quiet as a mouse

müde ['my:də] **1** ADJ tired; **einer Sache** (*gen*) **~ werden** to tire of sth; **einer Sache** (*gen*) **~ sein** to be tired of sth; **ich bin es ~, das zu tun** I'm tired of doing that; **keine ~ Mark** (*inf*) not a single penny
2 ADV (a) (= *erschöpft*) **sich ~ reden/kämpfen** to tire oneself out talking/fighting; **sich ~ laufen** to tire oneself out running about
(b) (= *gelangweilt*) **~ lächeln** to give a weary smile; **~ lächelnd** with a weary smile; **~ abwinken** to make a weary gesture (with one's hand)

-müde ADJ SUF tired of ...; **amtsmüde** tired of office; **kampfmüde** tired of fighting

Müdigkeit ['my:dɪçkaɪt] F **-**, NO PL (= *Schlafbedürfnis*) tiredness; (= *Schläfrigkeit*) sleepiness; **vor ~** (*dat*) **umfallen** to drop from

exhaustion; **nur keine ~ vorschützen!** (*inf*) don't (you) tell me you're tired

Müesli ['my:esli] NT **-s, -s** (*Sw*) muesli

Muffe ['mʊfə] F **-, -n** (a) (*Tech*) sleeve (b) (*inf*) **~ kriegen/haben** to be scared stiff (*inf*)

-muffel M **-s, -** SUF IN CPDS (*inf*) **ein Mode-/Computermuffel sein** to have no time for fashion/computers; **er ist ein fürchterlicher Krawattenmuffel** he hates wearing ties

muffelig ['mʊfəlɪç] (*inf*) **1** ADJ grumpy **2** ADV grumpily; **~ aussehen** to look grumpy

Muffensausen ['mʊfnzauzn] NT (*inf*) **~ kriegen/haben** to get/be scared stiff (*inf*)

muffig ['mʊfɪç] **1** ADJ (a) *Geruch, Zimmer* musty; (*fig*) *Tradition, Institution* stuffy (b) (*inf*) *Gesicht* grumpy **2** ADV (a) *riechen* musty (b) (*inf*: = *lustlos*) grumpily; **~ dreinsehen** to look grumpy

Mugge ['mʊgə] F **-, -n** ABBR *von* **musikalisches Gelegenheitsgeschäft** (*inf*) gig (*inf*)

muh [mu:] INTERJ moo

Mühe ['my:ə] F **-, -n** trouble; **nur mit ~** only just; **mit Müh und Not** (*inf*) with great difficulty; **alle/viel ~ haben** to have a tremendous amount of/a great deal of trouble (*etw zu tun* doing sth); **das ist mit einigen ~n** *or* **einiger ~ verbunden** that involves considerable effort; **mit jdm/etw seine ~ haben** to have a great deal of trouble with sb/sth; **es ist der** (*gen*) *or* **die ~ wert, es lohnt die ~** it's worth the trouble (*etw zu tun* of doing sth); **sich** (*dat*) **etwas/mehr/keine ~ geben** to take some/more/no trouble; **er hat sich** (*dat*) **große ~ gegeben** he has taken a lot of trouble; **gib dir keine ~!** (= *sei still*) save your breath; (= *hör auf*) don't bother; **sich** (*dat*) **die ~ machen, etw zu tun** to take the trouble to do sth; **sie hatte sich die ~ umsonst gemacht** her efforts were wasted; **jdm ~ machen** to give sb some trouble; **wenn es Ihnen keine ~ macht** if it isn't too much trouble; **es hat viel ~ gekostet** it took a great deal of trouble; **verlorene ~** a waste of effort

mühelos **1** ADJ effortless **2** ADV effortlessly

muhen ['mu:ən] VI to moo

Mühle ['my:lə] F **-, -n** (a) mill; (= *Kaffeemühle*) grinder (b) (*fig*) (= *Routine*) treadmill; (= *Bürokratie*) wheels *pl* of bureaucracy; **die ~n der Justiz mahlen langsam** the wheels of justice grind slowly (c) (= *~spiel*) nine men's morris (*esp Brit*)

Mühlen- IN CPDS = **Mühl-**

Mühlespiel NT **das ~** nine men's morris (*esp Brit*)

Mühl- ['my:l] IN CPDS mill; **Mühlrad** NT millwheel; **Mühlstein** M millstone

mühsam ['my:za:m] **1** ADJ arduous; **ein ~es Geschäft sein** to be a painstaking business **2** ADV with difficulty; **~ verdientes Geld** hard-earned money

Mukoviszidose [mukovɪstsi'do:zə] F **-**, NO PL (*Med*) mucoviscidosis (*spec*)

Mulatte [mu'latə] M **-n, -n, Mulattin** [-'latɪn] F **-, -nen** mulatto

Mulde ['mʊldə] F **-, -n** (a) (= *Geländesenkung*) hollow (b) (= *Trog*) trough (c) (*für Bauschutt*) skip

Mull [mʊl] M **-(e)s, -e** (a) (= *Torfmull*) garden peat (b) (= *Gewebe*) muslin; (*Med*) gauze

Müll [mʏl] M **-(e)s**, NO PL rubbish, garbage (*esp US*); (= *Industriemüll*) waste; (*inf*: = *Unsinn*) trash (*inf*); **etw in den ~ werfen** to throw sth out; „**~ abladen verboten**" "dumping prohibited"

Müll-: **Müllabfuhr** F (= *Müllabholung*) refuse *or* garbage (*US*) collection; (= *Stadtreinigung*) refuse *etc* collection department; **Müllabladeplatz** M dump

Mullah ['mʊla] M **-s, -s** Mullah

Mullbinde F gauze bandage

Müll-: **Müllcontainer** M rubbish skip, dumpster (*US*); **Mülldeponie** F waste disposal site (*form*), sanitary (land)fill (*US form*); **Mülleimer** M rubbish bin (*Brit*), garbage can (*US*); **Müllheizkraftwerk** NT *power station using refuse-derived fuel*; **Müllkippe** F rubbish *or* garbage (*US*) dump; **Müllmann** M, *pl* **-männer** *or* **-leute** (*inf*) dustman (*Brit*), garbage man (*US*); **Müllschlucker** M refuse chute; **Müllsortieranlage** F refuse sorting plant; **Müllsortierung** F **-**, NO PL sorting of waste; **Mülltonne** F dustbin (*Brit*), trash can (*US*); **Mülltourismus** M, NO PL *shipment of waste to other countries*; **Mülltüte** F bin liner (*Brit*), trash-can liner (*US*); **Müllverbrennungsanlage** F incinerating plant; **Müllverwertung** F refuse utilization; **Müllwagen** M dust-cart (*Brit*), garbage truck (*US*)

Mullwindel F gauze nappy (*Brit*) *or* diaper (*US*)

mulmig ['mʊlmɪç] ADJ (*inf*: = *bedenklich*) uncomfortable; **es wird ~ things** are getting (a bit) uncomfortable; **ich hatte ein ~es Gefühl im Magen, mir war ~ zumute** *or* **zu Mute** (*lit*) I felt queasy; (*fig*) I had butterflies (in my tummy) (*inf*)

Multi ['mʊlti] M **-s, -s** (*inf*) multinational (organization)

Multi-, multi- ['mʊlti] IN CPDS multi-; **multifunktional** ADJ multi-function(al); **multikulturell** ADJ multicultural; **multilateral** **1** ADJ multilateral **2** ADV multilaterally

Multimedia [mʊlti'meːdia] PL multimedia *pl*

Multimedia- IN CPDS multimedia; **multimediafähig** ADJ PC capable of multimedia

Multi-: multimedial [mʊltime'diaːl] **1** ADJ multimedia *attr*; **das ~e Zeitalter** the age of multimedia **2** ADV **eine ~ geprägte Welt** a world dominated by multimedia; **der Computer kann ~ genutzt werden** the computer is equipped for multimedia use; **Multimillionär(in)** M(F) multimillionaire; **multinational** **1** ADJ multinational **2** ADV multinationally

multipel [mʊl'tiːpl] ADJ multiple; **multiple Sklerose** multiple sclerosis

Multiple-choice-Verfahren ['mʌltɪpl'tʃɔɪs-] NT, **Multiplechoiceverfahren** NT multiple choice (method)

Multiplex-Kino NT, **Multiplexkino** ['mʊltɪpleks-] NT multiplex (cinema)

Multiplikation [mʊltiplika'tsioːn] F **-, -en** multiplication

Multiplikationszeichen NT multiplication sign

multiplizieren [mʊltipli'tsiːrən], *ptp* **multipliziert** **1** VT (*lit, fig*) to multiply (*mit* by) **2** VR (*fig*) to multiply

Multitalent NT all-rounder (*Brit*), multi-talent (*US*)

Mumie ['muːmiə] F **-, -n** mummy

mumifizieren [mumifi'tsiːrən], *ptp* **mumifiziert** VT to mummify

Mumm [mʊm] M **-s,** NO PL (*inf*) (a) (= *Kraft*) strength (b) (= *Mut*) guts *pl* (*inf*)

mümmeln ['mʏmln] VI to nibble

Mumps [mʊmps] M *or* (INF) F **-,** NO PL (the) mumps *sing*

München ['mʏnçən] NT **-s** Munich

Münchener ['mʏnçənə] ADJ ATTR Munich; **das ~ Abkommen** (*Hist*) the Munich Agreement

Mund [mʊnt] M **-(e)s,** ⁻**er** *or* (*rare*) **-e** *or* ⁻**e** ['mʏndə, -də, 'mʏndə] mouth; (*inf*: = ~*werk*) tongue; **etw in den ~ nehmen** to put sth in one's mouth; **dieses Wort nehme ich nicht in den ~** I never use that word; **den ~ aufmachen** *or* **auftun** (*lit, fig*) to open one's mouth; (*fig*: = *seine Meinung sagen*) to speak up; **jdm den ~ verbieten** to order sb to be quiet; **halt den ~!** shut up! (*inf*); **er kann den ~ einfach nicht halten** (*inf*) he can't keep his big mouth shut (*inf*); **jdm über den ~ fahren** to cut sb short; **jdm den ~ stopfen** (*inf*) to shut sb up (*inf*); **Sie haben mir das in den ~ gelegt** you're putting words into my mouth; **in aller ~e sein** to be on everyone's lips; **wie aus einem ~e** with one voice; **von ~ zu ~ gehen** to be passed on from person to person; **Sie nehmen mir das Wort aus dem ~(e)** you've taken the (very) words out of my mouth; **jdm nach dem ~(e) reden** (*inf*) to say what sb wants to hear; **sie ist nicht auf den ~ gefallen** (*inf*) she's never at a loss for words; **den ~ (zu/reichlich) voll nehmen** (*inf*) to talk (too/pretty) big (*inf*)

Mundart F dialect; **~ sprechen** to speak dialect

mundartlich ['mʊntaːɐtlɪç] **1** ADJ dialect(al) **2** ADV in dialect; **das Wort wird ~ gebraucht** it's a dialect word

Mund-: Mundatmung F oral breathing; **Munddusche** F water jet

Mündel ['mʏndl] NT *or* (JUR) M **-s,** - ward

mündelsicher (*St Ex*) **1** ADJ ≈ gilt-edged *no adv* **2** ADV **anlegen** in secure gilt-edged investments

münden ['mʏndn] VI AUX SEIN *or* HABEN (*Bach, Fluss*) to flow (*in* +*acc* into); (*Straße, Gang*) to lead (*in* +*acc*, *auf* +*acc* into); (*fig*: *Fragen, Probleme*) to lead (*in* +*acc* or +*dat* to); **die B 3 mündet bei Celle in die B 1** the B3 joins the B1 at Celle

Mund-: mundfaul ADJ (*inf*) too lazy to say much; **sei doch nicht so ~!** make an effort and say something!; **Mundgeruch** M bad breath; **Mundharmonika** F mouth organ

mündig ['mʏndɪç] ADJ of age; (*fig*) mature; **~ werden** to come of age; **der ~e Bürger** the politically mature citizen

mündlich ['mʏntlɪç] **1** ADJ verbal; *Prüfung, Leistung* oral; **~e Verhandlung** (*Jur*) hearing; **das Mündliche** (*inf: Sch, Univ*) the oral; (*bei Doktorprüfung etc*) the oral, the viva (voce) (*Brit*) **2** ADV **testen** orally; *informieren, besprechen* personally; **jdn ~ prüfen** to submit sb to an oral examination; **etw ~ abmachen** to have a verbal agreement on sth; **etw ~ überliefern** to pass sth on by word of mouth; **alles andere** *or* **Weitere ~!** I'll tell you the rest when I see you

Mund-: Mundorgel F cheng; **Mundpflege** F oral hygiene *no art*; **Mundpropaganda** F verbal propaganda; **Mundschutz** M mask (over one's mouth); **Mundstück** NT (*von Pfeife, Blasinstrument*) mouthpiece; (*von Zigarette*) tip; **ohne ~** untipped; **mundtot** ADJ (*inf*) **jdn ~ machen** to silence sb

Mündung ['mʏndʊŋ] F **-, -en** (*von Fluss, Rohr*) mouth; (= *Trichtermündung*) estuary; (*von Straße*) end; (= *Gewehrmündung, Kanonenmündung*) muzzle; **die ~ des Missouri in den Mississippi** the confluence of the Missouri and the Mississippi; **die ~ der Straße auf die B 11** the point where the road joins the B11

Mund-: Mundverkehr M oral intercourse; **Mundwasser** NT mouthwash; **Mundwerk** NT (*inf*) **ein gutes** *or* **flinkes ~ haben** to be a fast talker (*inf*); **ein böses ~ haben** to have a vicious tongue (in one's head); **ein freches ~ haben** to be cheeky (*Brit*) *or* fresh (*US*); **ein loses** *or* **lockeres ~ haben** to have a big mouth (*inf*); **ein großes ~ haben** to talk big (*inf*); **Mund-zu-Mund-Beatmung** F mouth-to-mouth resuscitation

Munition [muni'tsioːn] F **-, -en** ammunition; (*Mil*: *als Sammelbegriff*) munitions *pl*

munkeln ['mʊŋkln] VTI **man munkelt** *or* **es wird gemunkelt, dass …** it's rumoured (*Brit*) *or* rumored (*US*) that …; **man munkelt allerlei, allerlei wird gemunkelt** you hear all kinds of rumours (*Brit*) *or* rumors (*US*); **im Dunkeln ist gut ~** darkness is the friend of thieves/lovers

Mun-Sekte ['muːn-] F Moonies *pl*

Münster ['mʏnstɐ] NT **-s,** - minster, cathedral

munter ['mʊntɐ] **1** ADJ (a) (= *lebhaft*) lively *no adv*; *Farben* bright; (= *fröhlich*) cheerful; **~ werden** to liven up; **~ und vergnügt** bright and cheery (b) (= *wach*) awake; (= *aufgestanden*) up and about; **jdn wieder ~ machen** to wake sb up (again) **2** ADV (= *unbekümmert*) blithely; **drauflosreden** to prattle away merrily; **sie redete ~ weiter** she just kept on talking regardless

Munterkeit F **-,** NO PL (= *Lebhaftigkeit*) liveliness; (*von Farben*) brightness; (= *Fröhlichkeit*) cheerfulness

Muntermacher M (*Med inf*) pick-me-up (*inf*)

Münz-: Münzanstalt F mint; **Münzautomat** M slot machine

Münze ['mʏntsə] F **-, -n** (a) (= *Geldstück*) coin; **jdm etw mit** *or* **in gleicher ~ heimzahlen** (*fig*) to pay sb back in his own coin for sth (b) (= *Münzanstalt*) mint

Münzeinwurf M (coin) slot

münzen ['mʏntsn] VT to mint; **das war auf ihn gemünzt** (*fig*) that was aimed at him

Münz-: Münzfernsprecher M (*form*) pay phone; **Münzkunde** F numismatics *sing*; **Münzspielautomat** M, **Münzspielgerät** NT (*form*) slot machine; **Münztankstelle** F coin-operated petrol (*Brit*) *or* gas (*US*) station; **Münztelefon** NT pay phone; **Münzwechsler** [-vɛkslɐ] M **-s,** - change machine

mürbe ['mʏrbə], (*esp Aus, S Ger*) **mürb** [mʏrp] ADJ (a) crumbly; (= *zerbröckelnd*) crumbling; *Stoff, Gewebe* worn through; *Holz* rotten (b) *Fleisch* tender; (= *abgehangen*) well-hung; *Obst* soft; **~ klopfen** to tenderize (c) (*fig*: = *zermürbt*) **jdn ~ machen** to wear sb down; **~ werden/sein** to be worn down; **jdn ~ kriegen** to break sb

Mürbeteig M short(-crust) pastry

Murks [mʊrks] M **-es,** NO PL (*inf*) **~ machen** *or* **bauen** to bungle things (*inf*); **das ist ~!** that's a botch-up (*inf*)

Murmel ['mʊrml] F **-, -n** marble

murmeln ['mʊrmln] VTI to murmur; (*undeutlich*) to mumble; (= *brummeln*) to mutter; **etw vor sich** (*acc*) **hin ~** to mutter sth to oneself

Murmeltier NT marmot

murren ['mʊrən] VI to grumble (*über* +*acc* about)

mürrisch ['mʏrɪʃ] **1** ADJ (= *abweisend*) sullen; (= *schlecht gelaunt*) grumpy **2** ADV (= *abweisend*) sullenly; (= *schlecht gelaunt*) grumpily

Mus [muːs] NT or M **-es, -e** mush; (= *Apfelmus, Kartoffelmus*) puree; (= *Pflaumenmus*) jam (*Brit*), jelly (*US*)

Muschel ['mʊʃl] F **-, -n** (a) mussel (*auch Cook*); (*Schale*) shell (b) (= *Ohrmuschel*) external ear (c) (*Telec*) (= *Sprechmuschel*) mouthpiece; (= *Hörmuschel*) ear piece

Muschi ['mʊʃi] F **-, -s** (*inf*) pussy (*sl*)

Muse ['muːzə] F **-, -n** (*Myth*) Muse

Museum [mu'zeːʊm] NT **-s, Museen** [-'zeːən] museum

Musical ['mjuːzikl] NT **-s, -s** musical

Musicbox ['mjuːzik-] F jukebox

Musik [mu'ziːk] F **-, -en** (a) music; **die ~ lieben** to love music; **~ machen** to play some music; **das ist ~ in meinen Ohren** (*fig*) that's music to my ears (b) (= ~*kapelle*) band; **hier ist** *or* **spielt die ~!** (*fig inf*) this is where it's at (*inf*)

musikalisch [muzi'kaːlɪʃ] **1** ADJ musical **2** ADV begabt musically; **jdn ~ ausbilden** to give sb a musical training

Musikalität [muzikali'tɛːt] F **-,** NO PL musicality

Musikantenknochen [muzi'kantn-] M funny bone, crazy bone (*US*)

Musik-: Musikautomat M (= *Musikbox*) jukebox; **Musikbegleitung** F musical accompaniment; **unter ~** accompanied by music; **Musikberieselung** F (*inf*) constant background music; **Musikbox** F jukebox

Musiker ['muːzikɐ] M **-s, -, Musikerin** [-ərɪn] F **-, -nen** musician

Musik-: Musikhochschule F college of music; **Musikinstrument** NT musical instrument; **Musikkapelle** F band; **Musikkassette** F music cassette; **Musikliebhaber(in)** M(F) music-lover; **Musiksaal** M music room; **Musikschule** F music school; **Musiksendung** F music programme (*Brit*) *or* program (*US*); **Musikstück** NT piece of music; **Musikstunde** F music lesson; **Musikunterricht** M music lessons *pl*; (*Sch*) music

musisch ['muːzɪʃ] **1** ADJ Fächer, Gymnasium (fine) arts *attr*; Begabung for the arts; Erziehung in the (fine) arts; Veranlagung, Mensch artistic **2** ADV **begabt/interessiert** gifted/interested in the (fine) arts; **~ veranlagt** artistically inclined

musizieren [muzi'tsiːrən], *ptp* **musiziert** VI to play a musical instrument; **sie saßen auf dem Marktplatz und musizierten** they sat in the market place playing their instruments

Muskat [mʊs'kaːt, 'mʊskat] M **-(e)s, -e** nutmeg

Muskatblüte F mace

Muskateller(wein) [mʊska'tɛlɐ-] M **-s, -** muscatel

Muskatnuss F nutmeg

Muskel ['mʊskl] M **-s, -n** muscle; **(viele) ~n haben** to be muscular; **seine ~n spielen lassen** (*lit, fig*) to flex one's muscles

Muskel-: Muskelkater M aching muscles *pl*; **~ haben** to be stiff; **er hatte (einen) ~ in den Beinen** his legs were stiff; **Muskelkraft** F physical strength; **Muskelkrampf** M muscle cramp *no indef art*; **Muskelriss** M torn muscle; **sich** (*dat*) **einen ~ zuziehen** to tear a muscle; **Muskelschwund** M muscular atrophy; **Muskelzerrung** F pulled muscle

Muskulatur [mʊskula'tuːɐ] F **-, -en** muscular system

muskulös [mʊsku'løːs] **1** ADJ muscular **2** ADV **~ gebaut sein** to have a muscular build

Müsli ['myːsli] NT **-(s), -s** muesli

Muslim ['mʊslɪm] M **-s, -s** Moslem

Muslime [mʊs'liːmə] F **-, -n** Moslem

muss [mʊs] 3. PERS SONG PRES *von* müssen

Muss [mʊs] NT **-,** NO PL **es ist ein/kein ~** it's/it's not a must

Muße ['muːsə] F **-,** NO PL leisure; **dafür fehlt mir die ~** I don't have the time or leisure

Mussehe F (*inf*) shotgun wedding (*inf*)

müssen ['mʏsn] **1** MODAL AUX VB, *pret* **musste** ['mʊstə], *ptp* **müssen** (a) (*Zwang*) to have to; (*Notwendigkeit*) to need to; **ich muss** (*Zwang*) I have to, I must *only pres*; (*Notwendigkeit auch*) I need to; **muss er?** does he have to?; **er sagte, er müsse bald gehen** he said he would have to go soon; **ich hätte es sonst allein tun ~** otherwise I would have had to do it alone; **ich muss jetzt gehen** *or* **weg** (*inf*) I must be going now; **wir ~ Ihnen leider mitteilen, dass ...** we regret to (have to) inform you (that) ...; **muss das (denn) sein?** is that (really) necessary?; **das musste (ja so) kommen** that had to happen; **das muss man sich** (*dat*) **mal vorstellen!** (just) imagine that!;

jetzt muss ich dir mal was sagen now let me tell you something; **was habe ich da hören ~?** what's this I hear? (b) (= *sollen*) **das müsste ich/müsstest du eigentlich wissen** I/you ought to know that, I/you should know that (c) (*Vermutung, Wahrscheinlichkeit*) **es muss geregnet haben** it must have rained; **es muss nicht wahr sein** it needn't be true; **es müssten zehntausend Zuschauer im Stadion gewesen sein** there must have been ten thousand spectators in the stadium; **er müsste schon da sein** he should be there by now; **so muss es gewesen sein** that's how it must have been; **was muss bloß in ihm vorgehen?** what goes on in his mind? (d) (*Wunsch*) **(viel) Geld müsste man haben!** if only I were rich!; **man müsste noch mal von vorn anfangen können!** if only one could begin again!; **man müsste noch mal zwanzig sein!** oh, to be twenty again!

2 VI, *pret* **musste** ['mʊstə], *ptp* **gemusst** [gə'mʊst] (a) (= *weggehen, -fahren ~*) to have to go (b) (*inf*: = *austreten ~*) **ich muss mal** I need to go to the loo (*Brit inf*) *or* bathroom (*esp US*) (c) (= *gezwungen sein*) to have to; **hast du gewollt? – nein, gemusst** did you want to? – no, I had to; **kein Mensch muss ~** (*hum*) there's no such thing as `must'

Mussheirat F (*inf*) shotgun wedding (*inf*)

müßig ['myːsɪç] **1** ADJ (= *untätig*) idle; Leben, Tage, Stunden of leisure; (= *überflüssig, unnütz*) futile **2** ADV (= *untätig*) idly

Müßigkeit F **-,** NO PL (= *Überflüssigkeit*) futility

musste PRET *von* müssen

Mustang ['mʊstaŋ] M **-s, -s** mustang

Muster ['mʊstɐ] NT **-s, -** (a) (= *Vorlage, Dessin*) pattern; (*für Brief, Bewerbung etc*) specimen; **die Parade läuft immer nach demselben ~ ab** the parade always takes the same form (b) (= *Probestück*) sample; (*Buch, Korrekturfahne etc*) specimen; **~ ohne Wert** sample of no commercial value (c) (*fig*: = *Vorbild*) model (*an* +*dat* of); (= *Verhaltensmuster*) pattern

Muster-: IN CPDS model; **Musterbeispiel** NT classic example; **Musterbuch** NT pattern book; **Musterexemplar** NT fine specimen; **ein ~ von einer Frau** a model wife; **ein ~ von einem Idioten** a perfect idiot; **mustergültig** **1** ADJ exemplary **2** ADV **sich ~ benehmen** to be a model of good behaviour (*Brit*) *or* behavior (*US*); **Musterknabe** M (*iro*) paragon; **Musterkoffer** M sample case

mustern ['mʊstɐn] VT (a) (= *betrachten*) to scrutinize; **jdn kühl/ skeptisch ~** to survey sb coolly/sceptically (*Brit*) *or* skeptically (*US*); **jdn von oben bis unten ~** *or* **von Kopf bis Fuß ~** to look sb up and down (b) (*Mil*: = *inspizieren*) to inspect (c) (*Mil*: *für Wehrdienst*) **jdn ~** to give sb his/her medical (d) (*Tex*) *siehe* gemustert

Muster-: Musterpackung F sample pack; (= *Attrappe*) display pack; **Musterprozess** M test case; **Musterschüler(in)** M(F) model pupil; (*fig*) star pupil

Musterung F **-, -en** (a) (= *Muster*) pattern (b) (*Mil*) (*von Truppen*) inspection; (*von Rekruten*) medical examination for military service (c) (*durch Blicke*) scrutiny

Mut [muːt] M **-(e)s,** NO PL courage (*zu* +*dat* for); (= *Zuversicht*) heart; **(wieder) ~ fassen** to pluck up courage (again); **~ haben** to have (a lot of) courage; **keinen ~ haben** not to have any courage; **mit frischem ~** with new heart; **nur ~!** cheer up!; **den ~ verlieren** to lose heart; **~ bekommen** to gain confidence; **wieder ~ bekommen** to take heart; **jdm ~ zusprechen** *or* **machen** to encourage sb; **sich gegenseitig ~ machen** to keep each other's spirits up; **das gab ihr wieder neuen ~** that gave her new heart; **mit dem ~ der Verzweiflung** with the courage born of desperation; **der ~ zum Leben** the will to live; **zu ~e** = zumute

Mutant [mu'tant] M **-en, -en, Mutante** [mu'tantə] F **-, -n** (*Biol*) mutant; **du ~!** (*sl*) you psycho! (*pej sl*)

Mutation [muta'tsioːn] F **-, -en** mutation

mutieren [mu'tiːrən], *ptp* **mutiert** VI (= *sich ˈerblich ändern*) to mutate

mutig ['muːtɪç] **1** ADJ courageous **2** ADV courageously

mutmaßen ['muːtmaːsn] VTI INSEP (= *vermuten*) to conjecture; **es wurde viel über seine Abwesenheit gemutmaßt** there was a lot of conjecture as to the reason for his absence

mutmaßlich ['muːtmaːslɪç] **1** ADJ ATTR Vater presumed; Täter, Terrorist suspected **2** ADV **~ soll er der Vater sein** he is presumed to be the father

Mutmaßung ['muːtmaːsʊŋ] F -, -en conjecture

Mutprobe F test of courage

Mutter¹ ['mʊtɐ] F -, ⸗ ['mʏtɐ] mother; **sie ist ~ von drei Kindern** she's a mother of three; **wie bei ~n** (*dial*) just like (at) home; (*Essen*) just like mother makes; **die ~ aller ...** (*fig*) the mother of all ...

Mutter² F -, -n (*Tech*) nut

Mutterberatungsstelle F child welfare clinic

Mütterchen ['mʏtɐçən] NT -s, - **(a)** (= *Mutter*) mummy (*Brit inf*), mommy (*US inf*) **(b)** (= *alte Frau*) grandma **(c)** **~ Russland** Mother Russia

Müttergenesungs-: **Müttergenesungsheim** NT *rest centre for mothers, especially of large families;* **Müttergenesungswerk** NT *organization providing rest for mothers*

Mutter-: **Muttergesellschaft** F (*Comm*) parent company; **Mutterinstinkt** M maternal instinct; **Mutterkuchen** M (*Anat*) placenta; **Mutterland** NT mother country

Mütterlein ['mʏtɐlain] NT -s, - = **Mütterchen**

mütterlich ['mʏtɐlɪç] **1** ADJ **(a)** maternal; **die ~en Pflichten** one's duties as a mother **(b)** (= *liebevoll besorgt*) motherly *no adv* **2** ADV like a mother; **jdn ~ umsorgen** to mother sb

mütterlicherseits ADV on his/her *etc* mother's side; **sein Großvater ~** his maternal grandfather

Mutter-: **Mutterliebe** F motherly love; **Muttermal** NT, *pl* **-male** birthmark; **Muttermilch** F mother's milk; **etw mit der ~ einsaugen** (*fig*) to learn sth from the cradle; **Muttermord** M matricide; **Muttermund** M (*Anat*) cervix; **Mutterplatine** F (*Comput*) motherboard

Mutterschaft ['mʊtɐʃaft] F -, NO PL motherhood; (*nach Entbindung*) maternity

Mutterschafts-: **Mutterschaftsgeld** NT maternity pay (*esp Brit*); **Mutterschaftshilfe** F maternity benefit (*esp Brit*); **Mutterschaftsurlaub** M maternity leave

Mutter-: **Mutterschiff** NT (*Space*) mother ship; **Mutterschutz** M legal protection of expectant and nursing mothers; **Mutterschwein** NT sow; **mutterseelenallein** ADJ, ADV all alone; **Muttersöhnchen** [-zøːnçən] NT -s, - (*pej*) mummy's boy (*Brit*), mommy's boy (*US*); **Muttersprache** F native language, mother tongue; **Muttersprachler** [-ʃpraːxlɐ] M -s, -; **Muttersprachlerin** [-ərɪn] F -, -nen native speaker; **muttersprachlich** ADJ native-language *attr*; **~er Unterricht für Ausländer** language lessons for foreigners in their mother tongue; **Muttertag** M Mother's Day; **Muttertier** NT mother (animal); (= *Zuchttier*) brood animal

Mutti ['mʊti] F -, -s (*inf*) mummy (*Brit inf*), mommy (*US inf*)

mutwillig ['muːtvɪlɪç] **1** ADJ **(a)** (*geh* = *übermütig*) mischievous **(b)** (= *böswillig*) malicious **2** ADV zerstören *etc* wilfully

Mütze ['mʏtsə] F -, -n cap; (= *Pudelmütze, Pelzmütze*) hat; **was or eins auf die ~ kriegen** (*inf*) to get a telling-off (*inf*); (= *verprügelt werden*) to get bashed (*inf*)

Mützenschirm M peak

MW ABBR *von* Megawatt

MwSt., MWSt. ABBR *von* Mehrwertsteuer VAT

Myanmar [myˈanmaːɐ] NT -s Myanmar

Myom [myˈoːm] NT -s, -e (*Med*) myoma

mysteriös [mysteˈriøːs] **1** ADJ mysterious **2** ADV mysteriously

Mystik ['mʏstɪk] F -, NO PL mysticism *no art*

mystisch ['mʏstɪʃ] ADJ mystic(al); (*fig* = *geheimnisvoll*) mysterious

Mythen PL *von* Mythos

mythisch ['myːtɪʃ] ADJ mythical

Mythologie [mytoloˈgiː] F -, -n [-ˈgiːən] mythology

mythologisch [mytoˈloːgɪʃ] ADJ mythologic(al)

Mythos ['myːtɔs] M -, Mythen ['myːtn] (*lit, fig*) myth; **sie war zeitlebens von einem ~ umgeben** she was a legend in her time

Nn

N, n [ɛn] NT -, - N, n; **n-te** nth

N ABBR *von* **Norden**

'n [n] (*inf*) ABBR *von* **ein, einen**

na [na] INTERJ (*inf*) **(a)** (*Frage, Anrede, Resignation, Erleichterung, Zweifel*) well; (*Aufforderung*) then; **na, kommst du mit?** well, are you coming?; **na du?** hey, you!; **na ja** well; **na gut, na schön** all right; **na also!, na eben!** (well), there you are (then)!; **na, endlich!** about time!; **na und ob!** you bet! (*inf*); **na, wenn das mal klappt!** well, if it comes off **(b)** (*Beschwichtigung*) come (on) (now) **(c)** (*Ermahnung*) now; (*Zurückweisung*) well; **na (na)!** now, now!; **na warte!** just you wait!; **na so was** *or* **so etwas!** well, I never!; **na und?** so what?; **na ich danke!** no thank you!; **na, wirds bald?** come on, aren't you ready yet?

Nabel ['naːbl] M **-s, -** (*Anat*) navel; **der ~ der Welt** (*fig*) the hub of the universe

Nabel-: Nabelschau F **~ betreiben** to be bound up in oneself; **Nabelschnur** F, **Nabelstrang** M (*Anat*) umbilical cord

nach [naːx] **▓** PREP +DAT **(a)** (*örtlich*) to; **ich nahm den Zug ~ Mailand** (= *bis*) I took the train to Milan; (= *in Richtung*) I took the Milan train; **er ist schon ~ London abgefahren** he has already left for London; **~ Osten** eastward(s); **~ Westen** westward(s); **~ links/rechts** (to the) left/right; **von links ~ rechts** from (the) left to (the) right; **~ jeder Richtung, ~ allen Richtungen** (*lit*) in all directions; (*fig*) on all sides; **~ hinten/ vorn** to the back/front; (*in Wagen/Zug etc auch*) to the rear/ front; **~ ... zu** towards ... (*Brit*), toward ... (*US*); **~ Norden zu** *or* **hin** to(wards) the north **(b)** (*in Verbindung mit vb siehe auch dort*) **~ jdm/etw suchen** to look for sb/sth; **sich ~ etw sehnen** to long for sth; **~ etw schmecken/riechen** to taste/smell of sth **(c)** (*zeitlich*) after; **fünf (Minuten) ~ drei** five (minutes) past *or* after (*US*) three; **~ Christi Geburt, ~ unserer Zeitrechnung** AD, anno Domini (*form*); **~ zehn Minuten war sie wieder da** she was back ten minutes later; **was wird man ~ zehn Jahren über ihn sagen?** what will people be saying about him in ten years' time?; **~ Empfang** *or* **Erhalt** *or* **Eingang** on receipt; **~ allem, was geschehen ist** after all that has happened **(d)** (*Reihenfolge*) after; **die dritte Straße ~ dem Rathaus** the third road after the town hall; **ich komme ~ Ihnen!** I'm after you; **(bitte) ~ Ihnen!** after you!; **~ „mit" steht der Dativ** "mit" takes the dative **(e)** (= *laut, entsprechend*) according to; (= *im Einklang mit*) in accordance with; **~ Artikel 142c** under article 142c; **manche Arbeiter werden ~ Zeit, andere ~ Leistung bezahlt** some workers are paid by the hour, others according to productivity; **etw ~ Gewicht kaufen** to buy sth by weight; **die Uhr ~ dem Radio stellen** to put a clock right by the radio; **seinem Wesen** *or* **seiner Natur ~ ist er sehr sanft** he's very gentle by nature; **seiner Veranlagung ~ hätte er Musiker werden sollen** with his temperament he should have been a musician; **ihrer Sprache ~ (zu urteilen)** judging by her language; **~ allem, was ich gehört habe** from what I've heard; **~ allem, was ich weiß** as far as I know; **Knödel ~ schwäbischer Art** Swabian dumplings **(f)** (= *angelehnt an*) after; **~ einem Gedicht von Schiller** after a poem by Schiller; **er wurde ~ seinem Großvater genannt** he was named after (*Brit*) or for (*US*) his grandfather **▓** ADV (*zeitlich*) **~ und ~** little by little; **~ wie vor** still

nachahmen ['naːxlaːmən] VT SEP to imitate; (= *karikieren*) to take off (*Brit*); (= *kopieren*) to copy

Nachahmer ['naːxlaːmɐ] M **-s, -, Nachahmerin** [-ərɪn] F **-, -nen** imitator; (*eines großen Vorbilds*) emulator; (*pej: Art, Liter*) copyist

Nachahmung ['naːxlaːmʊŋ] F **-, -en (a)** (= *das Imitieren*) imitation; (= *das Karikieren*) taking off (*Brit*); (= *das Kopieren*) copying; **etw zur ~ anraten** *or* **empfehlen** to recommend sth as an example **(b)** (= *die Imitation*) imitation; (= *Karikatur*) takeoff (*Brit*), impression; (= *Kopie*) copy

Nachahmungstäter(in) M(F) copy-cat criminal

Nachbar ['naxbaːɐ] M **-n** *or* **-s, -n, Nachbarin** [-rɪn] F **-, -nen** neighbour (*Brit*), neighbor (*US*); **Herr X war beim Konzert mein**

~ Mr X sat next to me at the concert; ~s Garten the next-door garden; **die lieben ~n** (*iro*) the neighbo(u)rs

Nachbar-: Nachbardorf NT neighbouring (*Brit*) *or* neighboring (*US*) village; **Nachbarhaus** NT house next door; **in unserem ~, bei uns im ~** in the house next door (to us)

Nachbarin F *siehe* **Nachbar**

Nachbarland NT neighbouring (*Brit*) *or* neighboring (*US*) country

nachbarlich ['naxbaːɐlɪç] ADJ (= *freundlich*) neighbourly *no adv* (*Brit*), neighborly *no adv* (*US*); (= *benachbart*) neighbo(u)ring *no adv*; **~e Freundlichkeit** neighbo(u)rliness

Nachbarschaft ['naxbaːɐʃaft] F **-, NO PL** (= *Gegend*) neighbourhood (*Brit*), neighborhood (*US*); (= *Nachbarn*) neighbo(u)rs *pl*; (= *Nähe*) vicinity; **gute ~ halten** *or* **pflegen** to keep on good terms with the neighbo(u)rs

Nachbeben NT aftershock

nachbehandeln *ptp* **nachbehandelt** VT SEP (*Med*) **jdn/etw ~** to give sb/sth follow-up treatment

Nachbehandlung F (*Med*) follow-up treatment *no indef art*

nachbereiten *ptp* **nachbereitet** VT SEP (*Sch*) to assess afterwards

nachbessern SEP **▓** VT Lackierung to retouch; Gesetz, Vertrag to amend; Angebot to improve **▓** VI to make improvements

Nachbesserung F **-, -en** (*von Gesetz, Beschluss*) amendment; **~en vornehmen/fordern** to make/demand improvements

nachbestellen *ptp* **nachbestellt** VT SEP to order some more; (*Comm*) to reorder; (*nachträglich*) to put in a late order for

Nachbestellung F repeat order (*gen* for); (= *nachträgliche Bestellung*) late order (*gen* for)

nachbeten VT SEP (*inf*) to repeat parrot-fashion

nachbezahlen *ptp* **nachbezahlt** SEP **▓** VT to pay; (*später*) to pay later; Steuern ~ to pay back-tax **▓** VI to pay the rest

Nachbildung F copy; (*exakt*) reproduction

nachblicken VI SEP = **nachsehen**

nachdatieren *ptp* **nachdatiert** VT SEP to postdate

nachdem [naːx'deːm] CONJ **(a)** (*zeitlich*) after **(b)** (*modal*) *siehe* **je (c)** (*S Ger*: = *da, weil*) since

nachdenken VI SEP IRREG to think (*über* +*acc* about); **darüber darf man gar nicht ~** it doesn't bear thinking about; **laut ~** to think out loud; **denk mal gut** *or* **scharf nach!** think carefully!

Nachdenken NT thought; **nach langem ~** after (giving the matter) considerable thought; **gib mir ein bisschen Zeit zum ~** give me a bit of time to think (about it)

nachdenklich ['naːxdɛŋklɪç] ADJ Mensch, Miene thoughtful; Geschichte, Worte thought-provoking; **jdn ~ stimmen** *or* **machen** to set sb thinking; **~ gestimmt sein** to be in a thoughtful mood

Nachdruck M, *pl* **-drucke (a)** NO PL (= *Betonung*) stress; (= *Tatkraft*) vigour (*Brit*), vigor (*US*); **einer Sache** (*dat*) **~ verleihen** to lend weight to sth; **besonderen ~ darauf legen, dass ...** to put special emphasis on the fact that ...; **mit ~** vigorously; **etw mit ~ betreiben** to pursue sth with vigo(u)r; **etw mit ~ sagen** to say sth emphatically **(b)** (= *das Nachdrucken*) reprinting; (= *das Nachgedruckte*) reprint

nachdrucken VT SEP to reprint

nachdrücklich ['naːxdrʏklɪç] **▓** ADJ emphatic **▓** ADV firmly; **jdm ~ raten, etw zu tun** to advise sb strongly to do sth; **jdn ~ warnen** to give sb a firm warning

Nachdurst M (*nach Alkoholgenuss*) dehydration; **~ haben** to be dehydrated

nacheifern VI SEP **jdm/einer Sache ~** to emulate sb/sth

nacheinander [naːxlaɪ'nandɐ] ADV one after another; **zweimal ~** twice in a row; **kurz/unmittelbar ~** shortly/immediately after each other

nachempfinden *ptp* **nachempfunden** VT SEP IRREG Stimmung to feel; Text, Musik to relate to; (= *nachvollziehen*) to understand; **ich kann (Ihnen) Ihre Entrüstung ~** I can understand how horrified you must be; **das kann ich ihr ~** I can understand how she feels

nacherzählen *ptp* **nacherzählt** VT SEP to retell

Nacherzählung F retelling; (Sch) (story) reproduction
nachfahren VI SEP IRREG AUX SEIN to follow (on); **jdm ~** to follow sb
nachfassen SEP 🔲 VI (a) (= nachgreifen) to get a firmer grip; (= noch einmal zufassen) to regain one's grip (b) (inf: = nachforschen) to probe a bit deeper (c) (inf: = Essen ~) to have a second helping 🔲 VT (inf: = nachholen) to have a second helping of; **Essen ~** to have a second helping
nachfeiern VTI SEP (= später feiern) to celebrate later
Nachfolge F, NO PL succession; **jds ~ antreten** to succeed sb
Nachfolge- IN CPDS follow-up; **Nachfolgemodell** NT (von Produkt, Auto) successor (+gen to)
nachfolgen VI SEP AUX SEIN (= hinterherkommen) to follow (on); **jdm ~** to follow sb; **jdm im Amt ~** to succeed sb in office
nachfolgend ADJ following; **wie im Nachfolgenden ausgeführt** as detailed below; **Nachfolgendes, das Nachfolgende** the following
Nachfolgeorganisation F successor organization
Nachfolger ['naːxfɔlɡɐ] M **-s, -, Nachfolgerin** [-ərɪn] F **-, -nen** (im Amt etc) successor; **Friedrich Reißnagel ~** successors to Friedrich Reißnagel
nachfordern VT SEP to put in another demand for
Nachforderung F subsequent demand
nachforschen VI SEP to try to find out; (polizeilich etc) to carry out an investigation (+dat into); (amtlich etc) to make inquiries (+dat into)
Nachforschung F enquiry; (polizeilich etc) investigation; **~en anstellen** to make inquiries
Nachfrage F (a) (Comm) demand (nach, in +dat for); **danach besteht eine rege/keine ~** there is a great/no demand for it (b) (= Erkundigung) inquiry; **danke der ~** (form) thank you for your concern; (inf) nice of you to ask
Nachfragemonopol NT buyer's monopoly
nachfragen VI SEP to ask, to inquire
nachfühlen VT SEP = nachempfinden
nachfüllen VT SEP leeres Glas etc to refill; halbleeres Glas, Batterie etc to top up (Brit) or off (US); **Öl ~** to top up (Brit) or off (US) with oil
Nachfüllpack M, **Nachfüllpackung** F refill pack; **etw im ~ kaufen** to buy the refill pack of sth
nachgeben SEP IRREG 🔲 VI (a) (Boden, Untergrund) to give way (+dat to); (= federn) to give; (fig) (Mensch) to give in (+dat to) (b) (Comm: Preise, Kurse) to drop 🔲 VT (= noch mehr geben) **darf ich Ihnen noch etwas Gemüse ~?** may I give you a few more vegetables?
Nachgebühr F excess (postage)
nachgehen VI SEP IRREG AUX SEIN (a) +DAT (= hinterhergehen) to follow; **jdm ~** to go after (b) (Uhr) to be slow (c) +DAT (= ausüben) Beruf to practise (Brit), to practice (US); Studium, Vergnügungen, Interesse etc to pursue; Geschäften to go about; **welcher Tätigkeit gehen Sie nach?** what is your occupation?; **seiner Arbeit ~** to do one's job (d) +DAT (= erforschen) to investigate (e) +DAT (= zu denken geben) to haunt
nachgelassen ADJ Werke, Briefe, Papiere posthumously published; siehe auch **nachlassen**
nachgemacht ADJ Gold, Leder etc imitation; Geld counterfeit; siehe auch **nachmachen**
Nachgeschmack M (lit, fig) aftertaste; **einen üblen ~ hinterlassen** (fig) to leave a bad taste in the mouth
nachgiebig ['naːxɡiːbɪç] 🔲 ADJ (a) Material pliable; Boden soft (b) (fig) Mensch, Haltung soft; (= entgegenkommend) accommodating; **jdn ~ machen** to soften sb up 🔲 ADV **sie behandelt die Kinder zu ~** she's too soft with the children
Nachgiebigkeit F **-, NO PL (a)** (von Material) pliability; (von Boden) softness (b) (fig) (von Mensch, Haltung) softness; (= Entgegenkommen) compliance; **~ zeigen** to be accommodating; **es darf keine ~ gegenüber Schulschwänzern geben** we must stand firm against truancy
nachgrübeln VI SEP to think (über +acc about); (= sich Gedanken machen) to ponder (über +acc on)
nachgucken VTI SEP = nachsehen
nachhaken VI SEP (inf) to dig deeper; **bei jdm ~** to pump sb (inf)
Nachhall M reverberation; (= Nachklang) echo

nachhallen VI SEP to reverberate
nachhaltig ['naːxhaltɪç] 🔲 ADJ lasting; Wachstum auch, Widerstand sustained; **~e Nutzung** (von Energie, Rohstoffen etc) sustainable use 🔲 ADV (a) (= mit langer Wirkung) with lasting effect; **ihre Gesundheit hat sich ~ gebessert** there has been a lasting improvement in her health; **sich ~ verschlechtern** to continue to deteriorate; **etw ~ beeinflussen** to have a profound effect on sth (b) (= ökologisch bewusst) with a view to sustainability
Nachhaltigkeit F **-, NO PL** sustainability
nachhause [naːx'hauzə] ADV (Aus, Sw) home
Nachhauseweg M way home
nachhelfen VI SEP IRREG to help; **jdm ~** to help sb; **sie hat ihrer Schönheit etwas nachgeholfen** she has given nature a helping hand; **er hat dem Glück ein bisschen nachgeholfen** he engineered himself a little luck; **jds Gedächtnis** (dat) **~ to** jog sb's memory
nachher [naːx'heːɐ, 'naːx-] ADV (a) (= danach) afterwards; (= später) later; **bis ~** see you later! (b) (inf: = möglicherweise) **~ stimmt das gar nicht** (it) could be that's not true at all
Nachhilfe F help, assistance; (Sch) private coaching or tuition or tutoring (US)
Nachhilfe-: Nachhilfelehrer(in) M(F) private tutor; **Nachhilfestunde** F private lesson; **Nachhilfeunterricht** M private tuition or tutoring (US)
Nachhinein ['naːxhɪnaɪn] ADV **im ~** afterwards; (rückblickend) in retrospect
Nachholbedarf M **einen ~ an etw** (dat) **haben** to have a lot to catch up on in the way of sth
nachholen VT SEP (a) (= aufholen) Versäumtes to make up; **den Schulabschluss ~** to sit one's school exams as an adult (b) **jdn ~** (= nachkommen lassen) to get sb to join one
nachjagen VI SEP AUX SEIN +DAT to chase (after)
Nachkalkulation F (actual) cost determination
nachkaufen VT SEP to buy later; **kann man diese Knöpfe auch ~?** is it possible to buy replacements for these buttons?
nachklingen VI SEP IRREG AUX SEIN (Ton, Echo) to go on sounding; (Worte, Erinnerung) to linger; **die Melodie klang noch lange in mir nach** the tune stayed in my head for some time
Nachkomme ['naːxkɔmə] M **-n, -n** descendant; **ohne ~n** without issue (form)
nachkommen VI SEP IRREG AUX SEIN (a) (= später kommen) to come (on) later; **jdm ~** to follow sb; **wir kommen gleich nach** we'll follow in just a couple of minutes; **Sie können Ihre Familie/Ihr Gepäck ~ lassen** you can let your family join you later/have your luggage or baggage sent on (after) (b) (= mitkommen, Schritt halten) to keep up (c) +DAT (= erfüllen) seiner Pflicht to carry out; einer Anordnung, Forderung, einem Wunsch to comply with
Nachkriegs- ['naːxkriːks-] IN CPDS post-war; **Nachkriegsdeutschland** NT post-war Germany
nachladen VTI SEP IRREG to reload
Nachlass ['naːxlas] M **-es, -e** or **-lässe** [-lɛsə] **(a)** (= Preisnachlass) discount (auf +acc on) **(b)** (= Erbschaft) estate; **Gedichte aus dem ~** unpublished poems
nachlassen SEP IRREG 🔲 VT Preis, Summe to reduce; **10% vom Preis ~** to give a 10% discount; siehe auch **nachgelassen** 🔲 VI to decrease; (Regen, Sturm, Nasenbluten, Hitze) to ease off; (Leistung, Geschäfte) to drop off; (Preise) to fall; **nicht ~!** keep it up!; **bei der Suche nach etw nicht ~** not to let up in the search for sth; **er hat in letzter Zeit sehr nachgelassen** he hasn't been nearly as good recently; **er hat in or mit seinem Eifer sehr nachgelassen** he's lost a lot of his enthusiasm; **sobald die Kälte nachlässt** as soon as it gets a bit warmer
nachlässig ['naːxlɛsɪç] 🔲 ADJ careless; (= unachtsam) thoughtless 🔲 ADV carelessly; (= unachtsam) thoughtlessly
Nachlässigkeit F **-, -en** carelessness; (= Unachtsamkeit) thoughtlessness
nachlaufen VI SEP IRREG AUX SEIN +DAT **jdm/einer Sache ~** to run after sb/sth; **den Mädchen ~** to chase girls
Nachlese F second harvest; (= Ährennachlese) gleaning; (Ertrag) gleanings pl
nachlesen VT SEP IRREG (in einem Buch) to read; (= nachschlagen) to look up; (= nachprüfen) to check up; **man**

kann das in der Bibel ~ it says so in the Bible; **das kannst du bei Goethe ~** you can find it in Goethe

nachliefern SEP ■ VT (= *später liefern*) to deliver at a later date; (= *zuzüglich liefern*) to make a further delivery of; (*inf:* = *später abgeben*) *Unterlagen* to hand in later; (*fig*) *Begründung etc* to give later; **könnten Sie noch 25 Stück ~?** could you deliver another 25? ■ VI to make further deliveries

Nachlieferung F delivery; **wir warten auf die ~** we're waiting for the rest to be delivered

nachlösen SEP ■ VI to pay on the train; (*zur Weiterfahrt*) to pay the extra ■ VT *Fahrkarte* to buy on the train; (*zur Weiterfahrt*) to buy another

nachm. ABBR *von* **nachmittags** p.m.

nachmachen VT SEP **(a)** (= *nachahmen*) to copy; (= *nachäffen*) to mimic; **sie macht mir alles nach** she copies everything I do; **das mach mir mal einer nach!, das macht mir so schnell keiner nach!, das soll erst mal einer ~!** I'd like to see anyone else do that!
(b) (= *fälschen*) to forge; (= *imitieren*) to copy; *siehe auch* **nachgemacht**
(c) (*inf:* = *nachholen*) to make up; **er hat das Abitur in der Abendschule nachgemacht** ≈ he did A levels at night school (*Brit*), ≈ he completed his high school diploma at night school (*US*)

Nachmieter(in) M(F) next tenant; **unser ~** the tenant after us; **wir müssen einen ~ finden** we have to find someone to take over the apartment *etc*

Nachmittag ['naːxmɪtaːk] M afternoon; **am ~** in the afternoon; **gestern/morgen/Dienstag/heute ~** yesterday/tomorrow/Tuesday/this afternoon; **am heutigen ~** this afternoon; **am ~ des 14. Oktober** on the afternoon of October 14th; **vom ~ an** from about two o'clock; **bis zum ~** till the afternoon

nachmittäglich ['naːxmɪtɛːɡlɪç] ■ ADJ NO PRED afternoon *attr* ■ ADV in the afternoon; **die ~ stattfindenden Kurse** the afternoon courses

nachmittags ['naːxmɪtaːks] ADV in the afternoon; (= *jeden Nachmittag*) in the afternoon(s); **von ~ an** from about two o'clock; **Dienstag** *or* **dienstags ~** every Tuesday afternoon; **er isst immer erst ~** he never eats till (the) afternoon

Nachnahme ['naːxnaːmə] F **-, -n** cash *or* collect (*US*) on delivery, COD; (*inf:* = *~sendung*) COD package; **etw als** *or* **per ~ schicken** to send sth COD

Nachname M surname; **wie heißt du mit ~n?** what is your surname?

nachplappern VT SEP to repeat parrot-fashion

Nachporto NT excess (postage)

nachprüfbar ■ ADJ verifiable; **die Ergebnisse sind jederzeit ~** the results can be verified at any time ■ ADV (= *nachweislich*) *wahr, falsch* demonstrably; **was er sagte, war ~ wahr** what he said could be proved (*Brit*) *or* proven to be true

nachprüfen SEP ■ VT **(a)** *Aussagen, Tatsachen* to verify **(b)** *Kandidaten* (= *nochmals prüfen*) to re-examine; (= *später prüfen*) to examine at a later date ■ VI to check

Nachprüfung F **(a)** (*von Aussagen, Tatsachen*) check (+*gen* on); **bei der ~ der Meldungen** when the reports were checked **(b)** (= *nochmalige Prüfung*) re-examination; (*Termin*) resit

nachrechnen VTI SEP to check; **rechne noch einmal nach!** you'd better do your sums again

Nachrede F **üble ~** (*Jur*) defamation of character

nachreichen VT SEP to hand in later

nachreisen VI SEP AUX SEIN **jdm ~** to follow sb

nachrennen VI SEP IRREG AUX SEIN (*inf*) = **nachlaufen**

Nachricht ['naːxrɪçt] F **-, -en** (= *Mitteilung, Botschaft*) message; (= *Meldung*) (piece of) news *sing*; **eine ~** a message; some news *sing*, a piece of news *sing*; **die ~en** the news *sing* (*auch Rad, TV*); **~en aus Politik und Kultur** news from the world of politics and culture; **„Sie hören ~en"** "this *or* here is the news"; **das sind aber schlechte ~en** that's bad news; **die letzte ~ von ihm kam aus Indien** the last news of him was from India; **~ erhalten, dass ...** to receive (the) news that ...; **wir geben Ihnen ~** we'll let you know

Nachrichten-: **Nachrichtenagentur** F news agency; **Nachrichtendienst** M **(a)** (*Rad, TV*) news service **(b)** (*Pol, Mil*) intelligence (service); **nachrichtendienstlich** ■ ADJ *Erkenntnisse, Tätigkeit, Mittel etc* intelligence *attr*; *Vorschriften etc* intelligence service *attr* ■ ADV **~ erfasst sein** to be on the

files of the intelligence service; **~ beobachtet werden** to be under surveillance; **Nachrichtenmagazin** NT news magazine; **Nachrichtensperre** F news blackout; **Nachrichtensprecher(in)** M(F) newsreader; **Nachrichtentechnik** F telecommunications *sing*

nachrücken VI SEP AUX SEIN to move up; (*auf Stelle, Posten*) to succeed (*auf* +*acc* to); (*Mil*) to advance

Nachrücker ['naːxrʏkɐ] M **-s, -**, **Nachrückerin** [-ərɪn] F **-, -nen** successor

Nachruf M obituary

nachrufen VTI SEP IRREG +DAT to shout after

nachrüsten SEP ■ VI (*Mil*) to deploy new arms; (= *modernisieren*) to modernize ■ VT *Kraftwerk etc* to modernize; **ein Auto mit einem Airbag/einen Computer mit einer Soundkarte ~** to fit a car with an air bag/a computer with a sound card

Nachrüstung F **(a)** (*Mil*) deployment of new arms; (= *Modernisierung*) arms modernization **(b)** (*Tech*) (*von Kraftwerk etc*) modernization; (*von Auto etc*) refit

nachsagen VT SEP **(a)** (= *wiederholen*) to repeat; **jdm alles ~** to repeat everything sb says **(b)** (= *behaupten*) **jdm etw ~** to attribute sth to sb; **jdm Schlechtes ~** to speak ill of sb; **man kann ihr nichts ~** you can't say anything against her; **ihm wird nachgesagt, dass ...** it's said that he ...; **das lasse ich mir nicht ~!** I'm not having that said of me!

Nachsaison F off season

nachsalzen SEP IRREG ■ VT to add more salt to ■ VI to add more salt

nachschauen VTI SEP (*esp dial*) = **nachsehen**

nachschenken VTI SEP **jdm etw ~** to top sb up (*Brit*) *or* off (*US*) with sth; **darf ich (dir) noch etwas Wein ~?** can I give you a little more wine?

nachschicken VT SEP to forward

nachschießen VT SEP IRREG (*inf*) *Geld* to add (to it)

nachschlagen SEP IRREG ■ VT *Stelle, Zitat, Wort* to look up ■ VI **(a)** AUX SEIN (= *ähneln*) **jdm ~** to take after sb **(b)** (*in Lexikon*) to look

Nachschlagewerk NT reference book

Nachschlüssel M duplicate key; (= *Dietrich*) skeleton key

nachschmeißen VT SEP IRREG (*inf*) **jdm etw ~** to fling sth after sb (*Brit*) *or* at sb's back (*US*); **das ist ja nachgeschmissen!** it's a real bargain

nachschnüffeln VI SEP (*inf*) **jdm ~** to spy on sb

Nachschrift F (= *Protokoll*) transcript; (= *Zugefügtes*) (*abbr* **NS**) postscript, PS

Nachschub M (*Mil*) supplies *pl* (*an* +*dat* of); (*Material*) reinforcements *pl*

nachschütten VT SEP *Kies, Sand* to pour in (some) more; *Kohlen* to put on (some) more; (*inf:* = *nachgießen*) to pour (some) more

nachschwatzen, (*S Ger, Aus*) **nachschwätzen** VT SEP (*inf*) = **nachplappern**

nachsehen SEP IRREG ■ VI **(a)** **jdm/einer Sache ~** to follow sb/sth with one's eyes; (= *hinterherschauen*) to gaze after sb/sth **(b)** (= *gucken*) to look and see; (= *nachschlagen*) to (have a) look; **in der Schublade ~** to (have a) look in the drawer ■ VT **(a)** to (have a) look at; (= *prüfen*) to check; *Schulaufgaben etc* (= *durchsehen*) to read through, to check; (= *nachschlagen*) to look up **(b)** (= *verzeihen*) **jdm etw ~** to forgive sb (for) sth

Nachsehen NT **das ~ haben** to be left standing; (= *keine Chance haben*) not to get anywhere; (= *nichts bekommen*) to be left empty-handed

Nachsendeantrag M *application to have one's mail forwarded*

nachsenden VT SEP IRREG to forward

Nachsicht ['naːxzɪçt] F **-, NO PL** (= *Milde*) leniency; (= *Geduld*) forbearance; **er wurde ohne ~ bestraft** he was punished without mercy; **er kennt keine ~** he knows no mercy; **~ üben** to be lenient/forbearing; **mit jdm/etw ~/keine ~ haben** to make allowances/no allowances for sb/sth; **jdn um ~ bitten** to ask sb to be lenient/forbearing

nachsichtig ['naːxzɪçtɪç], **nachsichtsvoll** ■ ADJ (= *milde*) lenient; (= *geduldig*) forbearing (*gegen, mit* with) ■ ADV leniently; **~ mit jdm umgehen** to be understanding with sb; **jdn ~ behandeln** to be lenient with sb

Nachsichtwechsel M after-sight bill

Nachsilbe F suffix

nachsitzen VI SEP IRREG (*Sch*) ~ **(müssen)** to be kept in; **jdn ~ lassen** to keep sb in

Nachsommer M Indian summer

Nachsorge F (*Med*) aftercare

Nachsorgeklinik F aftercare clinic

Nachspann ['naːxʃpan] M **-s, -e** credits *pl*

Nachspeise F dessert; **als ~** for dessert

Nachspiel NT (*Theat*) epilogue (*Brit*), epilog (*US*); (*Mus*) closing section; (*fig*) sequel; **das geht nicht ohne ~ ab** that's bound to have repercussions; **das wird noch ein (unangenehmes) ~ haben** that will have (unpleasant) consequences; **ein gerichtliches ~ haben** to have legal repercussions

nachspielen SEP ▨ VT to play ▨ VI (*Sport*) to play stoppage time (*Brit*) *or* overtime (*US*); (*wegen Verletzungen*) to play injury time (*Brit*) *or* injury time (*US*); **der Schiedsrichter ließ ~** the referee allowed stoppage time/injury time (*Brit*), the referee allowed (injury) overtime (*US*)

nachspionieren *ptp* **nachspioniert** VI SEP (*inf*) **jdm ~** to spy on sb

nachsprechen VT SEP IRREG to repeat; **jdm etw ~** to repeat sth after sb

nachspülen VTI SEP to rinse; **ein Bier zum Nachspülen** (*inf*) a beer to wash it down

nächstbeste(r, s) ['nɛːçstˈbəstə] ADJ ATTR **der ~ Zug/Job** the first train/job that comes along; **der/die/das Nächstbeste ... the** first ... I/you *etc* see

nachstehen VI SEP IRREG **keinem ~** to be second to none (*in +dat* in); **jdm in nichts ~** to be sb's equal in every way; **jdm an Intelligenz** (*dat*) **nicht ~** to be every bit as intelligent as sb

nachstehend ▨ ADJ ATTR *Bemerkung, Ausführungen* following; **im Nachstehenden** below, in the following; **das ~e Adjektiv** the adjective which follows the noun ▨ ADV (= *weiter unten*) below

nachstellen SEP ▨ VT (a) (*Gram*) **nachgestellt** postpositive; **im Französischen wird das Adjektiv (dem Substantiv) nachgestellt** in French the adjective is put after the noun (b) (*Tech*) (= *neu einstellen*) to adjust (c) **einen Vorfall/den Unfallhergang ~** to reconstruct an incident/the accident; **eine Szene ~** to recreate a scene ▨ VI **jdm ~** to follow sb; (= *aufdringlich umwerben*) to pester sb; **einem Tier ~** to hunt an animal

Nächstenliebe F brotherly love; (= *Barmherzigkeit*) compassion; **~ üben** to love one's neighbour (*Brit*) *or* neighbor (*US*) as oneself

nächstens ['nɛːçstns] ADV (= *das nächste Mal*) (the) next time; (= *bald einmal*) some time soon

Nächste(r) ['nɛːçstə] MF DECL AS ADJ (a) next one; **der ~, bitte** next please (b) (*fig*: = *Mitmensch*) neighbour (*Brit*), neighbor (*US*); **jeder ist sich selbst der ~** (*Prov*) charity begins at home (*Prov*); **du sollst deinen ~n lieben wie dich selbst** (*Bibl*) (thou shalt) love thy neighbo(u)r as thyself

nächste(r, s) ['nɛːçstə] ADJ SUPERL *von* **nah(e)** (a) (= *nächstgelegen*) nearest; **ist dies der ~ Weg zum Bahnhof?** is this the quickest way to the station?; **in ~r Nähe** in the immediate vicinity; **in ~r Entfernung** not far away; **aus ~r Entfernung** *or* **Nähe** from close by; **sehen, betrachten** at close quarters; **schießen** at close range (b) (= *unmittelbar folgend*) next; **im ~n Haus** next door (c) (*zeitlich*) next; **~s Mal** next time; **bis zum ~n Mal!** till the next time!; **Dienstag ~r Woche** Tuesday next week; **am ~n Morgen/Tag(e)** (the) next morning/day; **bei ~r** *or* **bei der ~n Gelegenheit** at the earliest opportunity; **in ~r Zukunft** in the near future; **in den ~n Jahren** in the next few years; **in ~r Zeit** some time soon (d) *Angehörige, Freunde etc* closest; **die ~n Verwandten** the immediate family; **der ~ Angehörige** the next of kin (e) (*in Adverbialkonstruktionen*) **am ~n** closest; (*räumlich auch*) nearest

Nächste(s) ['nɛːçstə] NT DECL AS ADJ **das ~** the next thing; (= *das erste*) the first thing; **als ~s** next/first

nächst-: **nächstgelegen** ADJ ATTR nearest; **nächsthöher** ['nɛːçstˈhøːə] ADJ ATTR one higher; **die ~e Klasse** one class higher; **nächstliegend** ['nɛːçstˈliːgnt] ADJ ATTR (*lit*) nearest; (*fig*)

most obvious; **das Nächstliegende** the most obvious thing (to do)

nachsuchen VI SEP (a) (= *suchen*) to look; **such mal nach, ob ...** (have a) look and see if ... (b) (*form*: = *beantragen*) **um etw ~** to request sth (*bei jdm* of sb)

Nacht [naxt] F **-, ⁓e** ['nɛçtə] (*lit, fig*) night; **es wird/ist/war ~** it's getting/it is/it was dark; **heute ~** tonight; (= *letzte ~*) last night; **Dienstag ~** (on) Tuesday night; **12 Uhr ~** (*Aus*) midnight; **in der** *or* **bei ~** at night; **in der ~ vom 12. zum 13. April** during the night of April 12th to 13th; **in der ~ auf** *or* **zum Dienstag** during Monday night; **diese ~** tonight; **bis tief in die ~ arbeiten, bis in die späte ~ arbeiten** to work late into the night; **über ~** (*lit, fig*) overnight; **über ~ bleiben** to stay the night; **sich** (*dat*) **die ~ um die Ohren schlagen** (*inf*) to make a night of it; **die ~ zum Tage machen** to stay up all night (working *etc*); **eines ~s** one night; **letzte** *or* **vergangene ~** last night; **ganze Nächte** for nights (on end); **die ganze ~ (lang)** all night long; **vier Nächte lang** for four nights; **gute ~!** good night!; **na, dann gute ~!** (*inf*) what a prospect!; **bei ~ und Nebel** (*inf*) at dead of night

Nacht- IN CPDS night; **Nachtarbeit** F night-work; **Nachtasyl** NT night shelter; **nachtblind** ADJ nightblind; **Nachtblindheit** F night blindness; **Nachtbus** M night bus; **Nachtdienst** M (*von Person*) night duty; (*von Apotheke*) all-night service; **~ haben** (*Person*) to be on night duty; (*Apotheke*) to be open all night

Nachteil ['naːxtail] M **-(e)s, -e** disadvantage; **~e von** *or* **durch etw haben** to lose by sth; **im ~ sein, sich im ~ befinden** to be at a disadvantage (*jdm gegenüber* with sb); **daraus entstanden** *or* **erwuchsen ihm ~e** this brought its disadvantages for him; **der ~, allein zu leben** the disadvantage of living alone; **er hat sich zu seinem ~ verändert** he has changed for the worse; **das soll nicht Ihr ~ sein** you won't lose by it; **zu jds ~** to sb's disadvantage/detriment

nachteilig ['naːxtailiç] ▨ ADJ (= *ungünstig*) disadvantageous; (= *schädlich*) detrimental; **es ist nichts Nachteiliges über ihn bekannt** nothing unfavourable (*Brit*) *or* unfavorable (*US*) is known about him ▨ ADV *behandeln* unfavourably (*Brit*), unfavorably (*US*); **er hat sich sehr ~ über mich geäußert** he spoke very unfavo(u)rably about me; **sich ~ auf etw** (*acc*) **auswirken** to have a detrimental effect on sth

nächtelang ['nɛçtəlaŋ] ADV for nights (on end)

Nacht-: **Nachtessen** NT (*S Ger, Aus*) supper; **Nachteule** F (*fig inf*) night owl; **Nachtfalter** M moth; **Nachtflug** M night flight; **Nachtflugverbot** NT ban on night flights; **Nachthemd** NT (*für Damen*) nightdress; (*für Herren*) nightshirt

Nachtigall ['naxtɪgal] F **-, -en** nightingale; **~, ick hör dir trapsen** (*dial hum*) I see it all now

Nachtisch M dessert

Nacht-: **Nachtklub** M night club; **Nachtleben** NT night life

nächtlich ['nɛçtlɪç] ADJ ATTR (= *jede Nacht*) nightly; (= *in der Nacht*) night; **die ~e Stadt** the town at night; **zu ~er Stunde** at a late hour; **~e Ausgangssperre** night-time curfew; **~e Ruhestörung** (*Jur*) breach of the peace during the night

Nacht-: **Nachtlokal** NT night club; **Nachtmensch** M night person; **Nachtportier** M night porter; **Nachtquartier** NT **ein ~ aufschlagen** to bed down (for the night)

Nachtrag ['naːxtraːk] M **-(e)s, Nachträge** [-trɛːgə] postscript; (*zu einem Buch*) supplement

nachtragen VT SEP IRREG (a) (= *hinterhertragen*) **jdm etw ~** (*lit*) to take sth after sb; (*fig*) to hold sth against sb (b) (= *hinzufügen*) to add; *Summe* to enter up

nachtragend ADJ unforgiving; **er war nicht ~** he didn't bear a grudge

nachträglich ['naːxtrɛːklɪç] ▨ ADJ (= *zusätzlich*) additional; (= *später*) later; (= *verspätet*) belated; (= *nach dem Tod*) posthumous ▨ ADV (= *zusätzlich*) additionally; (= *später*) later; (= *verspätet*) belatedly; (= *nach dem Tod*) posthumously

Nachtrags- IN CPDS supplementary; **Nachtragshaushalt** M (*Pol*) supplementary budget

nachtrauern VI SEP +DAT to mourn

Nachtruhe F night's rest; (*in Anstalten*) lights-out

nachts [naxts] ADV at night; **dienstags ~** (on) Tuesday nights

Nacht-: **Nachtschalter** M night desk; **Nachtschattengewächs** NT (*Bot*) solanum (*spec*); **Nachtschicht** F night shift; **~ haben** to be on night shift *or* on nights; **nachtschlafend** ADJ **bei** *or*

zu ~er Zeit or **Stunde** in the middle of the night; **Nachtschwärmer(in)** M(F) (hum) night owl; **Nachtschwester** F night nurse; **Nachtsichtgerät** NT night vision aid; **Nachtspeicherofen** M storage heater

nachtsüber [ˈnaxtslyːbɐ] ADV by night

Nacht-: Nachttarif M (bei Verkehrsmitteln) night fares pl; (bei Strom etc) off-peak rate; **Nachttier** NT nocturnal animal; **Nachttisch** M bedside table; **Nachttopf** M chamber pot; **Nachttresor** M night safe (Brit), night depository (US); **Nacht-und-Nebel-Aktion** F cloak-and-dagger operation; **Nachtvogel** M nocturnal bird; **Nachtwache** F night watch; (im Krankenhaus) night duty; **bei einem Kranken ~ halten** to sit with a patient through the night; **~ haben** to be on night duty; **Nachtwächter(in)** M(F) (in Betrieben etc) night watchman; (inf) dope (inf); **Nachtzeit** F night-time

Nachuntersuchung F (= weitere Untersuchung) further examination; (= spätere Untersuchung) check-up

nachvollziehbar ADJ comprehensible

nachvollziehen ptp **nachvollzogen** VT SEP IRREG to understand

nachwachsen VI SEP IRREG AUX SEIN to grow again; **die neue Generation, die jetzt nachwächst** the young generation who are now taking their place in society

nachwachsend ADJ Rohstoff renewable; Generation up-and-coming, younger

Nachwahl F (Pol) ≈ by-election

Nachwehen PL after-pains pl; (fig) painful aftermath sing

nachweinen VI SEP +DAT to mourn; **dieser Sache weine ich nicht nach** or **keine Träne nach** I won't shed any tears over that

Nachweis [ˈnaːxvais] M **-es, -e** (= Beweis) proof (+gen, für, über +acc of); (= Zeugnis) certificate; (= Zahlungsnachweis) proof of payment (über +acc of); **als** or **zum ~** as proof; **den ~ für etw erbringen** or **führen** or **liefern** to furnish proof of sth

nachweisbar 🔢 ADJ (= beweisbar) provable; Fehler, Irrtum demonstrable; (Tech, Chem) detectable; **dem Angeklagten ist keinerlei Schuld ~** it cannot be proved that the accused is in any way guilty 🔢 ADV **im war ~ 500 Kilometer entfernt** it can be proved that I was 500 kilometres (Brit) or kilometers (US) away; **Radioaktivität ist ~ vorhanden** radioactivity is present in detectable amounts

nachweisen [ˈnaːxvaizn] VT SEP IRREG (= beweisen, aufzeigen) to prove; (Tech, Med) to detect; **die Polizei konnte ihm nichts ~** the police could not prove anything against him; **dem Angeklagten konnte seine Schuld nicht nachgewiesen werden** the accused's guilt could not be proved (Brit) or proven

nachweislich [ˈnaːxvaislɪç] 🔢 ADJ provable; Fehler, Irrtum demonstrable 🔢 ADV falsch demonstrably; **er war ~ in London** it can be proved (Brit) or proven that he was in London

Nachwelt F **die ~** posterity

nachwerfen VT SEP IRREG **jdm etw ~** (lit) to throw sth at sb; **das ist nachgeworfen** (inf) that's a gift

nachwinken VI SEP **jdm ~** to wave (goodbye) to sb

nachwirken VI SEP to continue to have an effect

Nachwirkung F aftereffect; (fig) consequence

Nachwort NT, pl **-worte** epilogue (Brit), epilog (US)

Nachwuchs M (a) (fig: = junge Kräfte) young people pl; **es mangelt an ~** there's a lack of young blood; **der wissenschaftliche ~** the new generation of academics (b) (hum: = Nachkommen) offspring pl

nachzahlen VTI SEP to pay extra; (= später zahlen) to pay later; **20 Euro ~** to pay 20 euros extra

nachzählen VTI SEP to check

Nachzahlung F (nachträglich) back-payment; (zusätzlich) additional payment

nachzeichnen VT SEP Linie, Umriss to go over; (fig: = wiedergeben) to reproduce

nachziehen SEP IRREG 🔢 VT (a) (= hinterherziehen) etw ~ to pull sth behind one; **das rechte Bein ~** to drag one's right leg (b) Linie, Umriss to go over; Lippen to paint in; Augenbrauen to pencil in (c) Schraube, Seil to tighten (up) 🔢 VI (a) AUX SEIN +DAT (= folgen) to follow (b) (Schach etc) to make the next move; (inf: = gleichtun) to follow suit

Nachzügler [ˈnaːxtsyːklɐ] M **-s, -**, **Nachzüglerin** [-ərɪn] F **-, -nen** latecomer, late arrival (auch fig)

Nackedei [ˈnakədai] M **-(e)s, -e** or **-s** (hum inf) naked body or person; (Kind) little bare monkey (hum inf)

Nacken [ˈnakn] M **-s, -** (nape of the) neck; **jdm den ~ steifen** to back sb up; **jdn im ~ haben** (inf) to have sb after one; **jdm im ~ sitzen** (inf) to breathe down sb's neck; **ihm sitzt die Furcht im ~** he's frightened out of his wits (inf)

Nacken-: Nackenhaar NT hair at the nape of the neck; **Nackenrolle** F bolster; **Nackenstarre** F stiffness of the neck; **~ kriegen** to get a stiff neck

nackig [ˈnakɪç], (Aus) (**nackert** [ˈnakɐt] inf) 🔢 ADJ bare 🔢 ADV in the nude

nackt [nakt] 🔢 ADJ (a) Mensch naked, nude (esp Art); Arm, Kinn, Haut etc bare; neugeborenes Tier naked; **einem ~en Mann in die Tasche greifen** (fig inf) to look for money where there is none (b) Erde, Wand bare (c) (fig) (= unverblümt) naked; Wirklichkeit stark; Tatsachen, Zahlen bare; **das ~e Leben retten** to escape with one's life 🔢 ADV baden, schlafen in the nude; tanzen, herumlaufen auch naked; **er stand ganz ~ da** he was standing there stark naked (Brit inf)

Nackt-: Nacktbaden NT **-s**, NO PL nude bathing; **Nacktbadestrand** M nudist beach

Nackte(r) [ˈnaktə] MF DECL AS ADJ nude

Nackt-: Nacktheit F **-**, NO PL nakedness; (von Mensch auch) nudity; (= Kahlheit) bareness; **Nacktkultur** F nudism; **Nacktschnecke** F slug

Nadel [ˈnaːdl] F **-, -n** (a) needle; (von Plattenspieler) stylus; (= Stecknadel) (Comput: von Drucker) pin; (= Häkelnadel) hook; (inf: = Spritze) needle; **etw mit heißer ~ nähen** (fig inf) to cobble sth together quickly (inf); **nach einer ~ im Heuhaufen suchen** (fig) to look for a needle in a haystack; **an der ~ hängen** (inf) to be hooked on heroin (b) (= Haarnadel, Hutnadel, Krawattennadel) pin (c) (= Blattnadel, Eisnadel, Kristallnadel) needle

Nadel-: Nadelbaum M conifer; **Nadeldrucker** M dot-matrix printer

nadeln [ˈnaːdln] VI (Baum) to shed (its needles)

Nadel-: Nadelöhr NT eye of a needle; (fig) narrow passage; **Nadelstich** M prick; (beim Nähen, Med) stitch; **jdm ~e versetzen** (fig) to needle sb; **eine Politik der ~e** a policy of pinpricks; **Nadelstreifen** PL pinstripes pl; **Nadelstreifenanzug** M pinstripe(d) suit; **Nadelwald** M coniferous forest

Nagel [ˈnaːgl] M **-s, ̈** [ˈnɛːgl] nail (auch Anat); (= Zwecke) tack; (aus Holz) peg; (an Schuhen) hobnail, stud; (Med) pin; **sich (dat) etw unter den ~ reißen** or **ritzen** (inf) to swipe sth (inf); **etw an den ~ hängen** (fig) to chuck sth in (inf); **den ~ auf den Kopf treffen** (fig) to hit the nail on the head; **Nägel mit Köpfen machen** (inf) to do the job properly

Nagel-: Nagelbürste F nailbrush; **Nagelfeile** F nailfile; **Nagelhaut** F cuticle

Nägelkauen NT **-s**, NO PL nail-biting

Nagel-: Nagelknipser [-knɪpsɐ] M **-s, -** nail clippers pl; **Nagellack** M nail varnish; **Nagellackentferner** [-lɛntfɛrnɐ] M **-s, -** nail varnish remover

nageln [ˈnaːgln] VT to nail (an +acc, auf +acc on)to)

Nagel-: nagelneu ADJ (inf) brand new; **Nagelpflege** F nail care; **~ machen** to give oneself a manicure; **Nagelprobe** F (fig) acid test; **Nagelschere** F (pair of) nail scissors pl

nagen [ˈnaːgn] 🔢 VI (lit, fig) to gnaw (an +dat at); (= knabbern) to nibble (an +dat at); (Rost, Wasser) to eat (an +dat into) 🔢 VT to gnaw

nagend ADJ Hunger gnawing; Zweifel, Gewissen nagging

Nager [ˈnaːgɐ] M **-s, -**, **Nagetier** NT rodent

nah [naː] ADJ, ADV = **nahe**

Nahaufnahme F (Phot) close-up

nahe [ˈnaːə] 🔢 ADJ, comp **näher** [ˈnɛːɐ], superl **nächste(r, s)** [ˈnɛːçstə] (a) (örtlich) near pred, close pred, nearby; **der Nahe Osten** the Middle East; **von ~m** at close quarters; **jdm nah sein** to be near (to) sb; **Rettung** or **Hilfe ist nah** help is at hand (b) (zeitlich) near (c) (= eng) Freund, Beziehung etc close; **~ Verwandte** close relatives 🔢 ADV, comp **näher**, superl **am nächsten** (a) (örtlich) near, close; **~ an** near to; **nah(e) bei** close to; **nah beieinander** close together; **nah liegend** nearby; **~ liegend** Gedanke, Lösung which suggests itself; *Verdacht, Vermutung* natural; **aus ~ liegenden Gründen** for obvious reasons; **~ vor** right in front of; **von nah und fern** from near and far; **jdm zu nah(e) treten** (*fig*) to offend sb; **jdm/einer Sache zu nah(e) kommen** to get too close to sb/sth

(b) (*zeitlich*) **Weihnachten steht nah(e) bevor** Christmas is just (a)round the corner; **nah(e) bevorstehend** approaching **(c)** (= *eng*) closely; **nah verwandt** closely-related **ϐ** PREP +DAT near (to), close to; **der Ohnmacht/dem Wahnsinn** *etc* **nah(e) sein** to be on the verge of fainting/madness *etc*

Nähe [ˈnɛːə] F -, NO PL **(a)** (*örtlich*) (= *Nahesein*) nearness, closeness; (= *Umgebung, Nachbarschaft*) vicinity, neighbourhood (*Brit*), neighborhood (*US*); **in meiner ~** near me; **in der ~ des Gebäudes** near the building; **in unmittelbarer ~** (+*gen*) right next to; **aus der ~** from close to **(b)** (*zeitlich*) closeness **(c)** (*emotional etc*) closeness

nahe bringen VT IRREG +DAT (*fig*) **jdm etw ~** to bring sth home to sb

nahe gehen VI IRREG AUX SEIN +DAT (*fig*) to upset

nahe kommen VI IRREG AUX SEIN +DAT (*fig*) **jdm ~** (= *vertraut werden*) to get on close terms with sb; **jdm/einer Sache ~** (= *fast gleichen*) to come close to sb/sth; **sich** *or* **einander ~** to become close; **das kommt der Wahrheit schon eher nahe** that is getting nearer the truth

nahe legen VT (*fig*) **jdm etw ~** to suggest sth to sb; **jdm ~, etw zu tun** to advise sb to do sth

nahe liegen VI IRREG (*fig: Idee, Frage, Lösung*) to suggest itself; **die Vermutung/die Annahme/der Verdacht liegt nahe, dass ...** it seems reasonable to suppose/assume/suspect that ...

naheliegend ADJ *siehe* **nahe**

nähen [ˈnɛːən] **ϐ** VT to sew; *Kleid* to make; *Wunde, Verletzten* to stitch (up); **er musste genäht werden** he had to have stitches **ϐ** VI to sew

näher [ˈnɛːɐ] COMP *von* **nah(e)** **ϐ** ADJ **(a)** (*örtlich*) closer; **jdm/einer Sache ~** closer to sb/sth; **dieser Weg ist ~** this road is shorter; **die ~e Umgebung** the immediate vicinity **(b)** (*zeitlich*) closer, sooner *pred* **(c)** (= *genauer*) *Auskünfte, Einzelheiten* further *attr* **ϐ** ADV **(a)** (*örtlich, zeitlich*) closer; **~ kommen** *or* **rücken** to approach; **bitte treten Sie ~** just step up! **(b)** (= *genauer*) more closely; *besprechen, erklären, ausführen* in more detail; **ich habe mir das Bild ~ angesehen** I had a closer look at the picture; **sich mit etw ~ befassen** *or* **beschäftigen** to go into sth; **jdn/etw ~ kennen lernen** to get to know sb/sth better; **ich kenne ihn nicht ~** I don't know him well; **der Sache** (*dat*) **~ kommen** to be nearer the mark

Nähere(s) [ˈnɛːərə] NT DECL AS ADJ details *pl*; (*über Stellenangebot etc*) further details *pl*; **alles ~** all details; **~s erfahren Sie von ...** further details from ...

Naherholungsgebiet NT recreational area (*close to a town*)

näher kommen VI IRREG AUX SEIN (*fig*) **jdm ~** to get closer to sb; **sie sind sich** *or* **einander näher gekommen** they've become closer

nähern [ˈnɛːɐn] VR **sich (jdm/einer Sache) ~** to approach (sb/sth); **der Abend näherte sich seinem Ende** the evening was drawing to a close

nahe stehen VI IRREG +DAT (*fig*) to be close to; (*Pol*) to sympathize with; **sich ~** to be close

nahezu [ˈnaːəˈtsuː] ADV nearly

Nähfaden M, **Nähgarn** NT (sewing) thread

Nahkampf M (*Mil*) close combat

Nähkästchen NT, **Nähkasten** M sewing box; **aus dem Nähkästchen plaudern** (*inf*) to give away private details

nahm PRET *von* **nehmen**

Näh-: **Nähmaschine** F sewing machine; **Nähnadel** F needle

Nahost [naːˈɔst] M **in/aus ~** in/from the Middle East

nahöstlich [naːˈœstlɪç] ADJ ATTR Middle East(ern)

Nährboden M (*lit*) fertile soil; (*für Bakterien*) culture medium; (*fig*) breeding-ground

nähren [ˈnɛːrən] (*geh*) **ϐ** VT to feed; (*fig*) (= *steigern*) to increase; *Hoffnung* to build up; (= *haben*) *Hoffnungen, Zweifel, Verdacht* to nurture; **er sieht gut genährt aus** he looks well-fed **ϐ** VR to feed oneself; (*Tiere*) to feed; **sich von** *or* **mit etw ~** to live on sth

nahrhaft ADJ *Kost* nourishing; **ein ~es Essen** a square meal

Nähr-: **Nährlösung** F nutrient solution; **Nährstoff** M USU PL nutrient

Nahrung [ˈnaːrʊŋ] F -, NO PL food; **flüssige ~** liquids *pl*; **feste ~** solids *pl*; **geistige ~** intellectual stimulation; **keine ~ zu sich nehmen** to take no nourishment; **einer Sache** (*dat*) **(neue) ~ geben** to help to nourish sth

Nahrungs-: **Nahrungskette** F (*Biol*) food chain; **Nahrungsmittel** NT food(stuff); **Nahrungssuche** F search for food

Nährwert M nutritional value; **hat das einen praktischen ~?** (*inf*) does that have any practical value?; **das hat doch keinen (praktischen) ~** (*inf*) it's pretty pointless

Naht [naːt] F -, **ⁱe** [ˈnɛːtə] seam; (*Tech auch*) join; (*Med*) stitches *pl*; (*Anat*) suture; **aus allen Nähten platzen** to be bursting at the seams

nahtlos **ϐ** ADJ (*lit*) *Teil, Anzug* seamless; (*fig*) *Übergang* smooth; *Bräune* perfect **ϐ** ADV **die Diskussion schloss (sich) ~ an den Vortrag an** the discussion followed on smoothly from the lecture; **sich ~ in etw** (*acc*) **einfügen** to fit right in with sth; **~ braun** tanned all over

Nahtoderfahrung F, **Nahtoderlebnis** NT near-death experience

Nahverkehr M local traffic; **der öffentliche ~** local public transport; **im ~** on local journeys

Nahverkehrs-: **Nahverkehrsmittel** PL means *pl* of local transport; **Nahverkehrszug** M local train

Nähzeug NT, *pl* **-zeuge** sewing kit

Nahziel NT immediate aim

naiv [naˈiːf] **ϐ** ADJ naive **ϐ** ADV naively; **sich ~ geben** to give the impression of being naive

Naivität [naiviˈtɛːt] F -, NO PL naivety

Name [ˈnaːmə] M **-ns, -n**, **Namen** [ˈnaːmən] M **-s, -** (= *Benennung*) name; (*fig:* = *Ruf*) name, reputation; **mit ~n, des ~ns** (*geh*) by the name of; **dem ~n nach** by name; **dem ~n nach müsste sie Schottin sein** judging by her name she must be Scottish; **auf jds ~n** (*acc*) in sb's name; **er nannte seinen ~n** he gave his name; **ich möchte keine ~n nennen, aber ...** I don't want to mention any names but ...; **wie war doch gleich Ihr ~?** what was the name?; **dazu gebe ich meinen ~n nicht her** I won't lend my name to that; **der ~ tut nichts zur Sache** his/my *etc* name's irrelevant; **einen ~n haben** (*fig*) to have a name; **sich** (*dat*) **(mit etw) einen ~n machen** to make a name for oneself (with sth); **die Sache beim ~n nennen** (*fig*) to call a spade a spade; **im ~n** (+*gen*) on behalf of; **im ~n des Volkes** in the name of the people; **im ~n des Gesetzes** in the name of the law

namens [ˈnaːməns] **ϐ** ADV (= *mit Namen*) by the name of, called **ϐ** PREP +GEN (*form:* = *im Auftrag*) in the name of

Namens- IN CPDS name; **Namensaktie** F (*St Ex*) registered share; **Namensnennung** F naming names; **auf ~ wollen wir doch verzichten** we don't need to name names; **Namenspapier** NT (*Fin*) registered security; **Namensschild** NT, *pl* **-schilder** nameplate; **Namensschwester** F namesake; **Namenstag** M Saint's day; **Namensvetter** M namesake; **Namenszeichen** NT initials *pl*

namentlich [ˈnaːməntlɪç] **ϐ** ADV by name; **wir bitten, von einer ~en Aufführung der Spender abzusehen** we would request that you refrain from naming the donors; **~e Abstimmung** roll call vote; **~er Aufruf** roll call **ϐ** ADV **(a)** (= *insbesondere*) (e)specially **(b)** (= *mit Namen*) by name; **es wurde ~ abgestimmt** there was a roll call vote

namhaft ADJ **(a)** (= *bekannt*) famous; **~ machen** (*form*) to identify **(b)** (= *beträchtlich*) considerable

Namibia [naˈmiːbia] NT **-s** Namibia

Namibier [naˈmiːbiɐ] M **-s, -**, **Namibierin** [-ərɪn] F **-, -nen** Namibian

namibisch [naˈmiːbɪʃ] ADJ Namibian

nämlich [ˈnɛːmlɪç] ADV **(a)** (= *und zwar*) namely; (*geschrieben*) viz; (= *genauer gesagt*) to be exact **(b)** (= *denn*) since; **..., es ist ~ sehr regnerisch** ... since it's very rainy

nannte PRET *von* **nennen**

Nano- [ˈnaːno-]: **Nanogramm** NT nanogram; **Nanometer** M or NT nanometer; **Nanosekunde** F nanosecond; **Nanotechnologie** F nanotechnology

nanu [naˈnuː] INTERJ well I never; **~, wer ist das denn?** hello (hello), who's this?

Napf [napf] M **-(e)s, ˸e** ['nɛpfə] bowl

Nappa(leder) ['napa-] NT **-(s), -s** nappa leather

Narbe ['narbə] F **-, -n** (*lit, fig*) scar; (= *Pockennarbe*) pock(mark); **eine ~ hinterlassen** to leave a scar

narbig ['narbɪç] ADJ scarred

Narkose [nar'koːzə] F **-, -n** anaesthesia (*Brit*), anesthesia (*US*); **jdm eine ~ geben** to put sb under anaesthetic (*Brit*) or anesthetic (*US*); **ohne ~** without an(a)esthetic; **unter ~** under an(a)esthetic; **aus der ~ aufwachen** to come out of the an(a)esthetic

Narkosearzt M, **Narkoseärztin** F anaesthetist (*Brit*), anesthesiologist (*US*)

narkotisch [nar'koːtɪʃ] **1** ADJ narcotic; *Düfte* overpowering **2** ADV *duften* overpoweringly; **der süße Geruch wirkte ~ auf uns** the sweet smell had a druglike effect on us

narkotisieren [narkoti'ziːrən], *ptp* **narkotisiert** VT (*lit, fig*) to drug

Narr [nar] M **-en, -en**, **Närrin** ['nɛrɪn] F **-, -nen** fool; (= *Teilnehmer am Karneval*) carnival reveller (*Brit*) or reveler (*US*); **jdn zum ~en haben** or **halten** to make a fool of sb

Narren-: **Narrenfreiheit** F freedom to do whatever one wants; **sie hat bei ihm ~** he gives her a) free rein; **Narrenhaus** NT madhouse; **Narrenkappe** F jester's cap; **narrensicher** ADJ, ADV foolproof

Narrheit F **-, -en (a)** NO PL folly **(b)** (= *Streich*) prank; (= *dumme Tat*) stupid thing to do

Närrin F *siehe* **Narr**

närrisch ['nɛrɪʃ] **1** ADJ foolish; (= *verrückt*) mad; **die ~en Tage** *Fasching* and the period leading up to it; **das ~e Treiben** *Fasching* celebrations; **sich wie ~ gebärden** to act crazy; **ganz ~ auf jdn/etw sein** (*inf*) to be crazy about sb/sth (*inf*) **2** ADV foolishly; **es ~ treiben** to go wild; **sie hüpfte ganz ~ durchs Haus** she was bouncing around the house like crazy (*inf*)

Narzisse [nar'tsɪsə] F **-, -n** narcissus

Narzissmus [nar'tsɪsmʊs] M **-**, NO PL narcissism

narzisstisch [nar'tsɪstɪʃ] ADJ narcissistic

NASA F **-**, **Nasa** ['naːza] F **-** NASA

nasal [na'zaːl] **1** ADJ nasal; **~er Ton** nasal twang **2** ADV nasally; **~ klingen** to sound nasal

Nasallaut M nasal (sound)

naschen ['naʃn] **1** VI to eat sweet things; (= *heimlich kosten*) to pinch (*Brit*) or snitch (*esp US*) a bit (*inf*); **darf ich mal ~?** can I try a bit?; **an etw** (*dat*) **~** to pinch (*Brit*) or snitch (*esp US*) a bit of sth (*inf*); (= *anknabbern*) to (have a) nibble at sth **2** VT to nibble; **sie nascht gern Süßigkeiten** she has a sweet tooth; **hast du was zum Naschen?** have you got something for my sweet tooth?

Nasch-: **naschhaft** ADJ fond of sweet things; **die Kinder sind so ~** the children are always nibbling at things; **sei nicht so ~** you and your sweet tooth; **Naschhaftigkeit** ['naʃhaftɪçkaɪt] F **-**, NO PL constant snacking; **Naschkatze** F (*inf*) guzzler (*inf*); **ich bin halt so eine alte ~** I've got such a sweet tooth

Nase ['naːzə] F **-, -n** (*Organ, Sinn, fig*) nose; **mir blutet die ~, meine ~ blutet** my nose is bleeding; **jdm die ~ putzen** to wipe sb's nose; **sich** (*dat*) **die ~ putzen** (= *sich schnäuzen*) to blow one's nose; **pro ~** (*hum*) per head; **es liegt vor deiner ~** (*inf*) it's right in front of your nose; **(immer) der ~ nachgehen** (*inf*) to follow one's nose; **eine gute ~ für etw haben** (*inf*) to have a good nose for sth; **die richtige ~ für etw haben** (*inf*) to have a nose for sth; **fass dich an deine eigene ~!** (*inf*) you can (*iro*) or can't talk!; **jdm etw/die Würmer aus der ~ ziehen** (*inf*) to drag sth/it all out of sb; **jdm etw unter die ~ reiben** (*inf*) to rub sb's nose in sth (*inf*); **die ~ rümpfen** to turn up one's nose (*über +acc* at); **jdm auf der ~ herumtanzen** (*inf*) to act up with sb (*inf*); **seine ~ gefällt mir nicht** (*inf*) I don't like his face; **ihm wurde ein Neuer vor die ~ gesetzt** (*inf*) they put a new man over him; **ich sah es ihm an der ~ an** (*inf*) I could see it written all over his face (*inf*); **jdm etw vor der ~ wegschnappen** (*inf*) just to beat sb to sth; **der Zug fuhr ihm vor der ~ weg** (*inf*) he missed the train by seconds; **die ~ voll haben** (*inf*) to be fed up (*inf*); **die ~ von jdm/etw voll haben** (*inf*) to be fed up to the back teeth with sb/sth (*Brit inf*); **jdn an der ~ herumführen** to give sb the runaround (*inf*); (*als Scherz*) to pull sb's leg; **jdm etw auf die ~ binden** (*inf*) to tell sb all about sth; **er steckt**

seine ~ in alles (hinein) (*inf*) he sticks his nose into everything; **die ~ vorn haben** (*inf*) to be ahead by a nose

naselang ADV **alle ~** all the time

näseln ['nɛːzln] VI to speak through one's nose

näselnd **1** ADJ *Stimme, Ton* nasal **2** ADV nasally; **~ sprechen** to talk through one's nose

Nasen-: **Nasenbär** M coati; **Nasenbluten** NT **-s**, NO PL **~ haben** to have a nosebleed; **häufiges ~** frequent nosebleeds; **Nasenflügel** M side of the nose; **seine ~ fingen an zu zittern** his nose began to twitch; **Nasenhöhle** F nasal cavity; **Nasenloch** NT nostril; **Nasenschleimhaut** F mucous membrane (of the nose); **Nasenspitze** F tip of the/sb's nose; **ich seh es dir an der ~ an** I can see it written all over your face; **Nasenspray** M or NT nasal spray; **Nasentropfen** PL nose drops *pl*

Nase-: **Naserümpfen** NT **-s**, NO PL wrinkling (up) or screwing up (*Brit*) one's nose; **auf etw** (*acc*) **mit ~ reagieren** to turn one's nose up at sth; **naseweis** ['naːzəvais] **1** ADJ cheeky (*Brit*), fresh (*US*); (= *vorlaut*) forward; (= *neugierig*) nosy (*inf*) **2** ADV (= *frech*) impudently; (= *vorlaut*) precociously; (= *neugierig*) nosily; **Naseweis** ['naːzəvais] M **-es, -e** (= *Vorlauter*) precocious brat; (= *Neugieriger*) nosy parker (*Brit inf*), curious George (*US inf*)

Nashorn ['naːshɔrn] NT rhinoceros

-nasig [naːzɪç] ADJ SUF -nosed; **plattnasig** flat-nosed

nass [nas] **1** ADJ, *comp* **nasser** or **nässer** ['nɛsə], *superl* **nasseste(r, s)** or **nässeste(r, s)** wet; **etw ~ machen** to make sth wet; (*für bestimmten Zweck*) to wet sth; *Bügelwäsche* to dampen sth; **durch und durch ~** wet through; **wie ein ~er Sack** (*inf*) like a wet rag (*inf*) **2** ADV, *comp* **nasser** or **nässer**, *superl* **am nassesten** or **nässesten** *Staub wischen* with a damp cloth; **den Boden ~ wischen** to mop the floor

Nässe ['nɛsə] F **-**, NO PL wetness; **in der ~ stehen** to stand in the wet; **„vor ~ schützen"** "keep dry"; **vor ~ triefen** to be dripping wet

nässen ['nɛsn] VI (*Wunde*) to weep

Nass-: **nasskalt** ADJ cold and damp; **Nassrasur** F **die ~** wet shaving; **eine ~** a wet shave; **Nass-Trocken-Rasierer** [-raziːre] M **-s, -** wet/dry shaver; **Nasszelle** F wet cell

Nation [na'tsioːn] F **-, -en** nation

national [natsio'naːl] **1** ADJ national; (= *patriotisch*) nationalist, nationalistic (*usu pej*) **2** ADV (= *auf nationaler Ebene*) nationwide; *regeln* nationally; (= *patriotisch*) nationalistically; **~ eingestellt sein, ~ denken** to be nationalist or nationalistic (*usu pej*)

National- [natsio'naːl] IN CPDS national; **Nationalcharakter** M national character; **Nationalchina** NT Nationalist China; **nationalchinesisch** ADJ Chinese Nationalist; **Nationalelf** F national (football) team; **die italienische ~** the Italian (national) team; **er hat dreimal in der ~ gespielt** he's been capped three times; **Nationalfarben** PL national colours *pl* (*Brit*) or colors *pl* (*US*); **Nationalfeiertag** M national holiday; **Nationalgericht** NT national dish; **Nationalheld** M national hero; **Nationalheldin** F national heroine; **Nationalhymne** F national anthem

Nationalismus [natsiona'lɪsmʊs] M **-**, NO PL nationalism

Nationalist [natsiona'lɪst] M **-en, -en**, **Nationalistin** [-'lɪstɪn] F **-, -nen** nationalist

nationalistisch [natsiona'lɪstɪʃ] **1** ADJ nationalist, nationalistic (*usu pej*) **2** ADV nationalistically

Nationalität [natsionali'tɛːt] F **-, -en** nationality

Nationalitätskennzeichen NT nationality sticker or (*aus Metall*) plate

National-: **Nationalmannschaft** F national team; **er spielt in der schottischen ~** he plays for Scotland; **die Fußball-~** the national football team; **Nationalpark** M national park; **Nationalrat**[1] M (*Gremium*) (*Sw*) National Council; (*Aus*) National Assembly; **Nationalrat**[2] M, **Nationalrätin** F (*Sw*) member of the National Council, ≈ MP; (*Aus*) deputy of the National Assembly, ≈ MP

National-: Nationalsozialismus M National Socialism; **Nationalsozialist(in)** M(F) National Socialist; **nationalsozialistisch** 🔟 ADJ National Socialist 🔢 ADV ~ **denken** to be a follower of National Socialism; **Nationalspieler(in)** M(F) international (footballer *etc*); **Nationalstraße** F (*Aus, Sw*) national highway; **Nationaltracht** F national dress

NATO F -, **Nato** ['na:to] F - **die** ~ NATO

Natrium ['na:triʊm] NT -s, NO PL (*abbr* Na) sodium

Natron ['na:trɔn] NT -s, NO PL bicarbonate of soda; **kohlensaures** ~ sodium carbonate

Natter ['natɐ] F -, -n adder; (*fig*) snake

natur [na'tu:ɐ] ADJ INV (*Cook*) **Schnitzel/Fisch** ~ *cutlet/fish not cooked in breadcrumbs*

Natur [na'tu:ɐ] F -, -en (a) NO PL (= *Kosmos, Schöpfungsordnung*) nature; **die Giraffe ist ein Meisterwerk der** ~ the giraffe is one of Nature's masterpieces; **wie sich dieses Tier in der freien** ~ **verhält** how this animal behaves in the wild
(b) NO PL (= *freies Land*) countryside; **in der freien** ~ in the open countryside
(c) NO PL (= ~*zustand*) nature; **sie sind von** ~ **so gewachsen** they grew that way naturally; **ich bin von** ~ **(aus) schüchtern** I am shy by nature; **sein Haar ist von** ~ **aus blond** his hair is naturally blond; **zurück zur** ~! back to nature; **nach der** ~ **zeichnen/malen** to draw/paint from nature
(d) (= *Beschaffenheit, Wesensart*) nature; (*Mensch*) type; **die menschliche** ~ human nature; **es liegt in der** ~ **der Sache** *or* **der Dinge** it is in the nature of things; **das geht gegen meine** ~ it goes against the grain; **das entspricht nicht meiner** ~, **das ist meiner** ~ **zuwider** it's not in my nature; **eine Frage allgemeiner** ~ a question of a general nature; **das ist ihm zur zweiten** ~ **geworden** it's become second nature to him

Naturalien [natu'ra:liən] PL natural produce; **in** ~ **bezahlen** to pay in kind; **Handel mit** ~ barter(ing) with goods

naturalisieren [naturali'zi:rən], *ptp* **naturalisiert** VT (a) (*Jur*) to naturalize (b) (*Biol, Zool*) **naturalisiert werden, sich** ~ to be naturalized, to naturalize

naturalistisch [natura'lɪstɪʃ] 🔟 ADJ naturalistic 🔢 ADV naturalistically

Naturallohn M payment in kind

Natur-: Naturapostel M (*hum*) health fiend (*inf*); **naturbelassen** ADJ *Lebensmittel, Material* natural; **Naturdenkmal** NT natural monument

Naturell [natu'rɛl] NT -s, -e temperament

Natur-: Naturereignis NT (impressive) natural phenomenon; **Naturerzeugnis** NT natural product; **Naturfarbe** F (a) natural colour (*Brit*) *or* color (*US*) (b) (*auch* **Naturfarbstoff**) natural dye; **naturfarben** [-farbn] ADJ natural-coloured (*Brit*), natural-colored (*US*); **Naturfaser** F natural fibre (*Brit*) *or* fiber (*US*); **Naturfreund(in)** M(F) nature-lover; **Naturgas** NT (*S Ger, Sw*) natural gas; **naturgegeben** ADJ (*lit*) natural; (*fig auch*) normal; **naturgemäß** 🔟 ADJ **-e Waldwirtschaft** natural forestry methods 🔢 ADV naturally; **Naturgesetz** NT law of nature; **naturgetreu** 🔟 ADJ *Darstellung* lifelike; (= *in Lebensgröße*) life-size 🔢 ADV realistically; **etw** ~ **wiedergeben** to reproduce sth true to life; **Naturheilkunde** F nature healing; **Naturheilverfahren** NT natural cure; **Naturkatastrophe** F natural disaster; **Naturlandschaft** F natural landscape; **Naturlehrpfad** M nature trail

natürlich [na'ty:ɐlɪç] 🔟 ADJ (*alle Bedeutungen*) natural; **in seiner ~en Größe** life-size; **eines ~en Todes sterben** to die of natural causes; **~e Person** (*Jur*) natural person; **~e Zahl** natural number; **es geht nicht mit ~en Dingen zu** there's something

---

odd going on; **~e Auslese** (*Biol*) natural selection 🔢 ADV (a) naturally; **die Krankheit verlief ganz** ~ the illness took its natural course
(b) (= *selbstverständlich*) naturally; **~!** naturally!, of course!

natürlicherweise [na'ty:ɐlɪçɐ'vaizə] ADV naturally

Natürlichkeit F -, NO PL naturalness

Natur-: Naturpark M ≈ national park; **Naturprodukt** NT natural product; **~e** *pl* natural produce *sing*; **naturrein** ADJ natural; **Naturschätze** PL natural resources *pl*; **Naturschutz** M conservation; **unter (strengem)** ~ **stehen** (*Pflanze, Tier*) to be a protected species; **dieses Gebiet steht unter** ~ this is a conservation area; **etw unter** ~ **stellen** to classify sth as a protected species; **Naturschutzgebiet** NT conservation area; **Naturschutzpark** M ≈ national park; **Naturseide** F natural silk; **Naturtalent** NT (*Person*) naturally talented person; (*Begabung*) natural talent; **sie ist ein** ~ she is a natural; **naturtrüb** ADJ *Saft, Bier* (naturally) cloudy; **naturverbunden** ADJ nature-loving; **Naturvolk** NT primitive people

Natur-: Naturwissenschaft F natural sciences *pl*; (*Zweig*) natural science; **Naturwissenschaftler(in)** M(F) (natural) scientist; **naturwissenschaftlich** 🔟 ADJ scientific 🔢 ADV scientifically; ~ **forschen/arbeiten** to do scientific research/work; ~ **interessiert sein** to be interested in science; **Naturzustand** M natural state

nautisch ['nautɪʃ] ADJ navigational; *Instrumente auch, Ausbildung, Ausdruck* nautical; **~e Meile** nautical *or* sea mile

Navigation [naviga'tsio:n] F -, NO PL navigation

Navigations-: Navigationsfehler M navigational error; **Navigationsraum** M chartroom; **Navigationssystem** NT navigation system

Navigator [navi'ga:to:ɐ] F -s, **Navigatoren** [-'to:rən], **Navigatorin** [-'to:rɪn] F -, -nen (*Aviat*) navigator

navigieren [navi'gi:rən], *ptp* **navigiert** VTI to navigate

Nazi ['na:tsi] M -s, -s Nazi

Nazismus [na'tsɪsmʊs] M -, **Nazismen** [-mən] (*pej*: = *Nationalsozialismus*) Nazism

nazistisch [na'tsɪstɪʃ] (*pej*) 🔟 ADJ Nazi 🔢 ADV ~ **orientierte Kreise** Nazi groups; ~ **angehaucht sein** to be a Nazi sympathizer; ~ **anmutende Parolen** Nazi-sounding slogans

NB [ɛn'be:] ABBR *von* nota bene NB

n. Br. ABBR *von* nördlicher Breite

NC [ɛn'tse:] M -(s), -(s) (*Univ*) ABBR *von* Numerus clausus

NC-Fach NT (*Univ*) subject with restricted entry

n. Chr. ABBR *von* nach Christus AD

ne [ne:] ADV (*inf*) = nee

'ne [nə] (*inf*) ABBR *von* eine

Neandertaler [ne'andɛta:lɐ] M -s, - Neanderthal man

Neapel [ne'a:pl] NT -s Naples

Nebel ['ne:bl] M -s, - mist; (*dichter*) fog; (*mit Abgasen*) smog; (*Mil: künstlich*) smoke; (*Astron*) nebula; (*fig*) mist, haze; **bei (dichtem)** ~ in thick mist/fog

Nebel-: Nebelauflösung F nach ~ after the fog has lifted; **Nebelbank** F, *pl* -bänke fog bank; **Nebelbildung** F fog; **stellenweise** ~ foggy patches

nebelhaft ADJ (*fig*) vague

Nebelhorn NT (*Naut*) foghorn

nebelig ['ne:bəlɪç] ADJ misty; (*bei dichterem Nebel*) foggy

Nebel-: Nebelleuchte F (*Aut*) rear fog light; **Nebelscheinwerfer** M (*Aut*) fog lamp; **Nebelschlussleuchte** F (*Aut*) rear fog light; **Nebelschwaden** M USU PL waft of mist; **Nebelwerfer** M (*Mil*) multiple rocket launcher

neben ['ne:bn] PREP (a) (*örtlich*: +*dat or* (*mit Bewegungsverben*) +*acc*) beside, next to; **er fuhr** ~ **dem Zug her** he kept level with the train; **er ging** ~ **ihr** he walked beside her
(b) (= *außer*: +*dat*) apart from, aside from (*esp US*); ~ **anderen Dingen** along with *or* amongst other things (c) (= *verglichen mit*: +*dat*) compared with

Neben-: Nebenaltar M side altar; **nebenamtlich** 🔟 ADJ *Tätigkeit* secondary 🔢 ADV as a second job; **er unterrichtet** ~ he also works as a teacher

nebenan [ne:bn'lan] ADV next door; **die Tür** ~ the next door

Neben-: Nebenarm M (*von Fluss*) branch; **Nebenausgabe** F incidental expense; **Nebenausgang** M side exit

nebenbei [ne:bn'bai] ADV (a) (= *gleichzeitig*) at the same time; **etw** ~ **machen** to do sth on the side (b) (= *außerdem*) in addition; **die ~ entstandenen Kosten** the additional expenses **(c)** (= *beiläufig*) incidentally; **~ bemerkt** *or* **gesagt** by the way; **das mache ich so ~** (*inf*) that's just a sideline; (= *kein Problem*) I'll do that without any problem (*Brit inf*)

Neben-: Nebenberuf M second job, sideline; **er ist im ~ Nachtwächter** he has a second job as a night watchman; **nebenberuflich** 1 ADJ extra 2 ADV as a second job; **er verdient ~ mehr als hauptberuflich** he earns more from his second job than he does from his main job; **Nebenbuhler(in)** M(F) rival; **Nebendarsteller** M supporting actor; **die ~** the supporting cast *sing*; **Nebendarstellerin** F supporting actress

nebeneinander [neːbnlaɪˈnandɐ] ADV **(a)** (*räumlich*) side by side; (*bei Rennen*) neck and neck; **drei ~, zu dritt ~** three abreast **(b)** (*zeitlich*) simultaneously

nebeneinanderher ADV side by side; **sie leben nur noch ~** (*Ehepaar etc*) they're just two people living in the same house

nebeneinander-: nebeneinander schalten VT SEP (*Elec*) to put in parallel; **nebeneinander sitzen** VI SEP IRREG **~** (*S Ger: aux sein*) to sit side by side; **nebeneinander stellen** VT SEP to place *or* put side by side; (*fig:* = *vergleichen*) to compare

Neben-: Nebeneingang M side entrance; **Nebeneinkünfte** PL, **Nebeneinnahmen** PL additional income; **Nebenerscheinung** F concomitant; (*von Krankheit*) secondary symptom; (*von Medikament*) side effect; (*von Tourismus etc*) knock-on effect; **Nebenfach** NT (*Sch, Univ*) subsidiary (subject), minor (*US*); **Nebenfluss** M tributary; **Nebengebäude** NT (= *Zusatzgebäude*) annex, outbuilding, (= *Nachbargebäude*) neighbouring (*Brit*) *or* neighboring (*US*) building; **Nebengeräusch** NT (*Rad, Telec*) interference; **Nebengleis** NT (*Rail*) siding, sidetrack (*US*); **Nebenhaus** NT house next door

nebenher [neːbnˈheːɐ] ADV **(a)** (= *zusätzlich*) in addition **(b)** (= *gleichzeitig*) at the same time

nebenher- [neːbnˈheːɐ] PREF alongside, beside it/him *etc*; **~laufen** to run alongside

Neben-: Nebenhöhle F (*Physiol*) sinus (of the nose); **Nebenhöhlenentzündung** F (*Med*) sinusitis; **Nebenkosten** PL additional costs *pl*

nebenordnen VT SEP INFIN AND PTP ONLY (*Gram*) to coordinate

Neben-: Nebenprodukt NT by-product; **Nebenraum** M (*benachbart*) adjoining room; (*weniger wichtig*) side room; **Nebenrolle** F supporting role; (*fig*) minor role; **eine ~ spielen** (*lit, fig*) to play a supporting role; **das spielt für mich nur eine ~** that's only of minor concern to me; **Nebensache** F minor matter; **das ist (für mich) ~** that's not the point (as far as I'm concerned); **die schönste ~ der Welt** the greatest trivial pursuit in the world; **nebensächlich** ADJ minor, trivial; **etw als ~ abtun** to dismiss sth as irrelevant; **Nebensächliches** minor matters *pl*; **es ist doch völlig ~, wann er kommt** it doesn't matter a bit when he comes; **Nebensaison** F low season; **Nebensatz** M (*Gram*) subordinate clause; **Nebenstelle** F (*Telec*) extension; (*Comm*) branch; (*Post*) sub-post office; **Nebenstellenanlage** F (*Telec*) private branch exchange; **Nebenstraße** F (*in der Stadt*) side street; (= *Landstraße*) minor road; **Nebenstrecke** F (*Rail*) local line; (*Aut*) minor road; **Nebenverdienst** M secondary income; **Nebenwinkel** M (*Math*) adjacent angle; **Nebenwirkung** F side effect; **Nebenzimmer** NT (= *benachbarter Raum*) next room; (= *Nebengelass*) side room

neblig [ˈneːblɪç] ADJ = **nebelig**

nebulos [nebuˈloːs], **nebulös** [nebuˈløːs] 1 ADJ vague; **er redete so ~es Zeug** he was so vague 2 ADV vaguely

Necessaire [neseˈsɛːɐ] NT **-s, -s** (= *Kulturbeutel*) toilet bag (*Brit*), washbag (*US*); (*zur Nagelpflege*) manicure case; (= *Nähzeug*) sewing bag

necken [ˈnɛkn] 1 VT to tease; **jdn mit jdm/etw ~** to tease sb about sb/sth 2 VR **sich** *or* **einander ~, sich mit jdm ~** to tease each other; **was sich liebt, das neckt sich** (*Prov*) teasing is a sign of affection

neckisch [ˈnɛkɪʃ] 1 ADJ (= *scherzhaft*) teasing; *Einfall, Melodie* amusing; *Unterhaltung* bantering; (*inf:* = *kokett, kess*) *Kleid, Frisur* coquettish; *Spielchen* mischievous 2 ADV (= *scherzhaft*) teasingly; (= *kokett*) coquettishly

nee [neː] ADV (*inf*) no, nope (*inf*); **~, so was!** no, really!

Neffe [ˈnɛfə] M **-n, -n** nephew

Negation [negaˈtsioːn] F **-, -en** negation

negativ [ˈneːgatiːf, negaˈtiːf] 1 ADJ negative 2 ADV **(a)** (= *ablehnend*) *antworten* negatively; **sich ~ zu etw stellen** to adopt a negative attitude toward(s) sth; **ich beurteile seine Arbeit sehr ~** I have a very negative view of his work; **die Untersuchung verlief ~** the examination proved negative; **die Antwort/Beurteilung fiel ~er aus als erwartet** the answer/assessment was less favourable (*Brit*) *or* favorable (*US*) than expected; **zu etw ~ eingestellt sein** to have reservations about sth; **alles ~ sehen** to be pessimistic **(b)** (= *ungünstig*) **sich ~ auf etw** (*acc*) **auswirken** to be detrimental to sth; **die Umsatzentwicklung wird ~ eingeschätzt** the prognosis for turnover is negative **(c)** (*Elec*) **etw ~ (auf)laden** to put a negative charge on sth

Negativ [ˈneːgatiːf, negaˈtiːf] NT **-s, -e** [-və] (*Phot*) negative

Neger [ˈneːgɐ] M **-s, -** (*usu pej*) Negro (*pej*); **angeben wie zehn nackte ~** (*inf*) to shoot one's big mouth off (*inf*)

Negerin [ˈneːgərɪn] F **-, -nen** (*usu pej*) Negro woman (*pej*)

Negerkuss M chocolate marshmallow with biscuit base

negieren [neˈgiːrən], *ptp* **negiert** VT (= *verneinen*) *Satz* to negate; (= *bestreiten*) *Tatsache, Behauptung* to deny

Negligé [negliˈʒeː] NT **-s, -s**, **Negligee** NT **-s, -s** negligee

Negoziation [negotsiaˈtsioːn] F **-, -en**, **Negoziierung** [negotsiˈiːrʊŋ] F **-, -en** (*Fin*) negotiation

nehmen [ˈneːmən], *pret* **nahm** [naːm], *ptp* **genommen** [gəˈnɔmən] VTI (= *ergreifen*) to take; *Schmerz* to take away; (= *versperren*) *Blick, Sicht* to block; (= *benutzen*) *Bürste, Zutaten, Farbe* to use; (= *berechnen*) to charge; (= *behandeln*) to handle; (= *auswählen*) *Essen, Menü* to have; **etw in die Hand ~** (*lit*) to pick sth up; (*fig*) to take sth in hand; **etw an sich** (*acc*) **~** (= *aufbewahren*) to take care *or* charge of sth; (= *sich aneignen*) to take sth (for oneself); **jdm etw ~** to take sth (away) from sb; **um ihm die Angst zu ~** to stop him being afraid; **ihm sind seine Illusionen genommen worden** his illusions were shattered; **er ließ es sich** (*dat*) **nicht ~, mich persönlich hinauszubegleiten** he insisted on showing me out himself; **diesen Erfolg lasse ich mir nicht ~** I won't be robbed of this success; **woher ~ und nicht stehlen?** (*inf*) where on earth am I going to find any/one *etc*?; **sie ~ sich** (*dat*) **nichts** (*inf*) one's as good as the other; **sich** (*dat*) **vom Brot/Fleisch ~** to help oneself to bread/meat; **~ Sie sich doch bitte!** please help yourself; **man nehme ...** (*Cook*) take ...; **sich** (*dat*) **etw ~** to take sth; **sich** (*dat*) **einen Anwalt/eine Hilfe ~** to get a lawyer/some help; **wie viel ~ Sie dafür?** how much will you take for it?; **jdn zu sich ~** to take sb in; **etw ~, wie es kommt** to take sth as it comes; **jdn ~, wie er ist** to take sb as he is; **etw auf sich** (*acc*) **~** to take sth upon oneself; **etw zu sich ~** to take sth; **der Patient hat nichts zu sich ~ können** the patient has been unable to take nourishment; **wie mans nimmt** (*inf*) depending on your point of view; **wissen, wie man jdn ~ muss** *or* **soll** to know how to take sb

Nehmer [ˈneːmɐ] M **-s, -**, **Nehmerin** [-ərɪn] F **-, -nen** **(a)** recipient **(b)** (= *Käufer*) taker

Neid [naɪt] M **-(e)s** [-dəs], NO PL envy (*auf +acc* of); **aus ~** out of envy; **der ~ der Besitzlosen** (*inf*) sour grapes (*inf*); **nur kein ~!** don't be envious!; **grün (und gelb) vor ~** (*inf*) green with envy; **das muss ihm der ~ lassen** (*inf*) you have to say that much for him; **jds** (*acc*) **or bei jdm ~ erregen** *or* **(er)wecken** to make sb envious; **vor ~ platzen** (*inf*) *or* **vergehen** to die of envy

neiden [ˈnaɪdn] VT **jdm etw ~** to envy sb (for) sth

Neid-: neiderfüllt [-ɛɐfʏlt] 1 ADJ *Blick* filled with envy 2 ADV enviously; **Neidhammel** M (*inf*) envious person; **der alte/du alter ~!** he's/you're just jealous

neidisch [ˈnaɪdɪʃ], (*S Ger, Aus*) **neidig** [ˈnaɪdɪç] 1 ADJ jealous, envious; **auf jdn/etw ~ sein** to be jealous of sb/sth 2 ADV enviously

neidlos 1 ADJ ungrudging, without envy 2 ADV graciously; **das gebe ich ~ zu** I'm willing to admit it graciously

Neige [ˈnaɪgə] F **-, -n (a)** (= *Überrest*) remains *pl*; **etw bis zur ~ auskosten** (= *genießen*) to savour (*Brit*) *or* savor (*US*) sth to the full; **etw bis zur bitteren ~ auskosten** *or* **kennen lernen** to suffer sth to the full **(b)** NO PL (*geh:* = *Ende*) **zur ~ gehen** to draw to an end; **die Vorräte gehen zur ~** the provisions are fast becoming exhausted

neigen [ˈnaɪgn] 1 VT (= *beugen*) *Kopf, Körper* to bend; (*zum Gruß*) to bow; (= *kippen*) *Behälter, Glas* to tip 2 VR to bend; (*Ebene*) to slope; (*Gebäude etc*) to lean;

(= *kippen*) to tip (up); (*Schiff*) to list; **sich nach vorne/nach hinten/zur Seite ~** (*Mensch*) to lean forward/backwards/to one side; **mit seitwärts geneigtem Kopf** with his/her head held to one side

3 VI **zu etw ~** to tend toward(s) sth; (= *für etw anfällig sein*) to be susceptible to sth; **zu der Ansicht** or **Annahme ~, dass ...** to tend toward(s) the view that ...; *siehe auch* **geneigt**

Neigung ['naɪɡʊŋ] F **-, -en (a)** (= *das Neigen*) inclination; (= *Gefälle*) incline; (*esp Rail*) gradient (*Brit*), grade (*US*); (= *Schräglage*) tilt; (*von Schiff*) list **(b)** (= *Tendenz*) (*Med*: = *Anfälligkeit*) proneness, tendency; (= *Hingezogensein, Veranlagung*) leaning *usu pl*; (= *Hang, Lust*) inclination; **etw aus ~ tun** to do sth by inclination **(c)** (= *Zuneigung*) affection; **jds ~ erwidern** to return sb's affection

nein [naɪn] ADV no; (*Überraschung*) no; **kommt er? – ~!** is he coming? – no(, he isn't); **da sage ich nicht Nein** I wouldn't say no to that; **~, ~ und nochmals ~** for the last time, no!; **Hunderte, ~ Tausende, hunderte, ~ tausende** hundreds, no thousands; **~, so was!** well I never!; **~, doch!** no!; **o ~!, aber ~!** certainly not!; **~, dass du dich auch mal wieder sehen lässt!** fancy seeing you again; **~ wie nett, dass du mich mal besuchst!** well, how nice of you to visit me

Nein [naɪn] NT **-s**, NO PL no; **bei seinem ~ bleiben** to stick to one's refusal; **mit Ja oder ~ stimmen** to vote yes or no; (*Parl auch*) to vote yea or aye (*Brit*) or nay

Nektar ['nɛktar] M **-s**, NO PL nectar

Nektarine [nɛkta'riːnə] F **-, -n** nectarine

Nelke ['nɛlkə] F **-, -n (a)** pink; (*gefüllt*) carnation **(b)** (*Gewürz*) clove

nennbar ADJ specifiable; **Gefühl, Phänomen, Gedanke etc** nam(e)able; **nicht ~** unspecifiable; unnam(e)able

Nennbetrag M (*Comm*) = **Nennwert**

nennen ['nɛnən], *pret* **nannte** ['nantə], *ptp* **genannt** [ɡə'nant] **3** VT **(a)** (= *bezeichnen*) to call; (= *einen bestimmten Namen geben*) to name, to call; **jdn nach jdm ~** to name sb after (*Brit*) or for (*US*) sb; **Friedrich II., genannt „der Große"** Frederick II, known as Frederick the Great; **das nennst du schön?** you call that beautiful?

(b) (= *angeben, aufzählen*) to name; *Beispiel, Grund, Details* to give; **die genannten Namen** the names mentioned; **können Sie mir einen guten Anwalt ~?** could you give me the name of a good lawyer?

(c) (= *erwähnen*) to mention; **das (weiter oben) Genannte** the above; **das genannte Schloss** the above-mentioned castle **2** VR to call oneself; **und so was nennt sich Liebe/modern** (*inf*) and they call that love/modern; **und so was (wie er) nennt sich modern/Dichter** (*inf*) and he calls himself modern/a poet

nennenswert **3** ADJ considerable, not inconsiderable; **nicht ~** not worth mentioning; **nichts Nennenswertes** nothing worth mentioning; **die Demonstration verlief ohne ~e Zwischenfälle** the demonstration went off without major incident **2** ADV significantly

Nenner ['nɛnɐ] M **-s, -** (*Math*) denominator; **kleinster gemeinsamer ~** (*lit, fig*) lowest common denominator; **etw auf einen (gemeinsamen) ~ bringen** (*lit, fig*) to reduce sth to a common denominator

Nennung ['nɛnʊŋ] F **-, -en** (= *das Nennen*) naming; (*Sport*) entry

Nennwert M (*Fin*) nominal value; **zum ~** at par; **über/unter dem ~** above/below par; **eine Aktie im** or **zum ~ von 50 Euro** a share with a nominal value of 50 euros

neo-, Neo- [neo] IN CPDS neo-

Neologismus [neolo'ɡɪsmʊs] M **-, Neologismen** [-mən] neologism

Neon ['neːɔn] NT **-s**, NO PL (*abbr* **Ne**) neon

Neo-: **Neonazi** ['neːona:tsi] M neo-Nazi; **Neonazismus** [neona'tsɪsmʊs, 'neːo-] M neo-Nazism

Neon-: **Neonlicht** NT neon light; **Neonreklame** F neon sign; **Neonröhre** F neon tube

Neoprenanzug [neo'preːn-] M wet suit

Nepal ['neːpal, ne'pa:l] NT **-s** Nepal

nepalesisch [nepa'leːzɪʃ] ADJ Nepalese

Nepp [nɛp] M **-s**, NO PL (*inf*) **so ein ~!, das ist ja ~!** it's a rip-off! (*inf*)

neppen ['nɛpn] VT (*inf*) to rip off (*inf*)

Nepplokal NT (*inf*) clip joint (*inf*)

Neptun [nɛp'tuːn] M **-s** Neptune

Nerv [nɛrf] M **-s** or **-en, -en** nerve; (*Bot auch*) vein; **(leicht) die ~en verlieren** to lose one's nerve easily; **er hat trotz allem die ~en behalten** or **nicht verloren** in spite of everything he kept his cool (*inf*); (*die Selbstbeherrschung nicht verloren*) in spite of everything he didn't lose control; **die ~en sind (mit) ihm durchgegangen** he lost his cool (*inf*); **sie kennt** or **hat keine ~en** she doesn't get nervous; **der hat (vielleicht) ~en!** (*inf*) he's got a nerve! (*inf*); **er hat ~en wie Drahtseile** or **Stricke** he has nerves of steel; **es geht** or **fällt mir auf die ~en** (*inf*) it gets on my nerves; **jdm den (letzten) ~ töten** or **rauben** (*inf*) to get on sb's nerves; **den ~ haben, etw zu tun** to have the nerve to do sth; **das kostet ~en** it's a strain on the nerves; **~en zeigen** to show nerves

nerven ['nɛrfn] (*inf*) **3** VT **jdn (mit etw) ~** to get on sb's nerves (with sth); **genervt sein** (= *nervös sein*) to be worked up; (= *gereizt sein*) to be irritated **2** VI **das nervt** it gets on your nerves; **du nervst!** (*inf*) you're bugging me! (*inf*)

Nerven- ['nɛrfn-]: **Nervenarzt** M, **Nervenärztin** F neurologist; **nervenaufreibend** **3** ADJ nerve-racking **2** ADV **die Klasse ist ~ laut** the noise of the class plays on the nerves; **Nervenbelastung** F strain on the nerves; **Nervenbündel** NT fascicle; (*fig inf*) bag of nerves (*inf*); **Nervengas** NT (*Mil*) nerve gas; **Nervengift** NT neurotoxin; **Nervenheilanstalt** F psychiatric hospital; **Nervenheilkunde** F neurology; **Nervenkitzel** M (*fig*) thrill; **etw als einen äußersten ~ empfinden** to get a big thrill out of sth; **Nervenklinik** F psychiatric clinic; **Nervenkostüm** NT (*hum*) **ein starkes/schwaches ~ haben** to have strong/weak nerves; **nervenkrank** ADJ (*geistig*) mentally ill; (*körperlich*) suffering from a nervous disease; **Nervenkrieg** M (*fig*) war of nerves; **Nervenprobe** F trial; **Nervensache** F (*inf*) question of nerves; **reine ~!** it's all a question of nerves; **Nervensäge** F (*inf*) pain (in the neck) (*inf*); **Nervenschmerz** M neuralgia *no pl*; **Nervensystem** NT nervous system; **Nervenzentrum** NT (*Physiol, fig*) nerve centre (*Brit*) or center (*US*); **Nervenzusammenbruch** M nervous breakdown

nervig ['nɛrfɪç, 'nɛrvɪç] ADJ (*inf*: = *irritierend*) irritating; **Mensch, wie ~!** God, how irritating!; **der ist vielleicht ~** he gets on your nerves

nervlich ['nɛrflɪç] **3** ADJ *Belastung, Anspannung* nervous; **der ~e Zustand des Patienten** the state of the patient's nerves; **ein ~es Wrack** a nervous wreck **2** ADV **er ist ~ erschöpft** he suffers from nervous exhaustion; **~ bedingt** nervous; **~ angespannt sein** to be suffering from nervous exhaustion; **~ überlastet** or **überanstrengt sein** to be under a great deal of stress

nervös [nɛr'vøːs] **3** ADJ nervous; **jdn ~ machen** to make sb nervous; (= *ärgern*) to get on sb's nerves **2** ADV nervously; **die Krankheit ist rein ~ bedingt** the illness is purely nervous in origin

Nervosität [nɛrvozi'tɛːt] F **-**, NO PL nervousness; (*Stimmung*) tension

nervtötend ['nɛrf-] (*inf*) **3** ADJ nerve-racking; *Arbeit* soul-destroying **2** ADV irritatingly

Nerz [nɛrts] M **-es, -e** mink

Nessel ['nɛsl] F **-, -n (a)** (*Bot*) nettle; **sich in die ~n setzen** (*inf*) to put oneself in a spot (*inf*) **(b) Nesseln** PL (= *Quaddeln*) nettle rash

Nessel-: **Nesselausschlag** M, **Nesselfieber** NT nettle rash; **Nesselschlafsack** M sheet sleeping bag

Nessessär NT **-s, -s** *siehe* **Necessaire**

Nest [nɛst] NT **-(e)s, -er (a)** (= *Brutstätte*) nest **(b)** (*fig*: = *Schlupfwinkel*) hideout; **ein ~ von Dieben** a den of thieves **(c)** (*fig*: = *Heim*) nest; **sein eigenes ~ beschmutzen** to foul one's own nest; **sich ins gemachte** or **warme ~ setzen** (*inf*) (*durch Heirat*) to marry (into) money; (*beruflich*) to move straight into a good job; **da hat er sich ins gemachte** or **warme ~ gesetzt** (*inf*) he's got it made (*inf*) **(d)** (*fig inf*: = *Bett*) bed; **raus aus dem ~!** rise and shine! (*inf*) **(e)** (*pej inf*: *Ort*) (*schäbig*) dump (*inf*); (*klein*) little place

Nest-: **Nestbeschmutzer** [-bəʃmʊtsɐ] M **-s, -**, **Nestbeschmutzerin** [-ərɪn] F **-, -nen** (*pej*) denigrator of one's family/country; **Nestbeschmutzung** F (*pej*) denigration of one's family/country

nesteln ['nɛstln] VI **an etw** (*dat*) **~** to fumble (around) with sth

Nest-: Nesthäkchen NT baby of the family; **Nestwärme** F (fig) happy home life

Netikette, Netiquette [nɛtiˈkɛtə] F - (Comput) netiquette

Net-Surfer(in) [ˈnɛt-] M(F) (inf) Net-surfer (inf)

nett [nɛt] 🔟 ADJ nice; **eine ~e Stange Geld kosten** (inf) to cost a pretty penny (inf); **sei so ~ und räum auf!** would you mind clearing up?; **Oma war so ~ und hat schon abgewaschen** Grandma very kindly washed the dishes; **~, dass Sie gekommen sind!** nice of you to come; **was Netteres ist dir wohl nicht eingefallen?** (iro) you do say/do some nice things 🔢 ADV nicely, nice; **wir haben uns ~ unterhalten** we had a nice chat; **hier werden die Gäste ~ bedient** the waiters are very friendly here; **~ aussehen** to be nice-looking; **die Geschenk war ~ gemeint** the gift was well-meant; **sie plaudert ~** she's nice to talk to

netterweise [ˈnɛtɐˈvaizə] ADV kindly

Nettigkeit [ˈnɛtɪçkait] F -, -en (a) NO PL (= nette Art) kindness (b) **Nettigkeiten** PL (= nette Worte) kind words, nice things

netto [ˈnɛto] ADV (Comm) net; **ich verdiene ~ £ 1500** or **£ 1500 ~ im Monat** I earn £1500 net a month

Netto- IN CPDS net; **Nettogewicht** NT net weight; **Nettoinvestition** F net investment; **Nettokreditaufnahme** [-kreˈdiːt-] F net borrowing; **Nettolohn** M take-home pay; **Nettopreis** M net price; **Nettosozialprodukt** NT net national product; **Nettozins** M net interest

Netz [nɛts] NT -es, -e (a) net; (= Spinnennetz) web; (= Einkaufsnetz) string bag; (= Gepäcknetz) (luggage) rack; (fig: von Lügen, Heuchelei) web; (= Maschenwerk) netting; **ans ~ gehen** (Sport) to go up to the net; **ins ~ gehen** (Ftbl) to go into the (back of the) net; (Tennis) to hit the net; **ins ~ schlagen** to play into the net; **~!** (Sport) let!; **jdm ins ~ gehen** (fig) to fall into sb's trap; **jdm durchs ~ gehen** (fig) to give sb the slip (b) (= System) network; (= Stromnetz) mains sing or pl; (= Überlandnetz) (national) grid; (Comput) network; **das soziale ~** the social security net; **ans ~ gehen** (Kraftwerk) to be connected to the grid; **Strom geht ins ~** the grid is supplied with electricity; **das Kraftwerk musste vom ~ genommen werden** the power station had to be shut down (c) (= Internet) **das ~** the Net; **im ~ surfen** (inf) to surf the Net (inf); **etw ins ~ stellen** to put sth on the Net

Netz-: Netzanbieter [-ˈanbiːtə] M -s, - (Telec) network provider; (Comput) Internet (service) provider; **Netzanschluss** M (Elec) mains connection; **Netzball** M (Tennis etc) net ball; **Netzbetreiber** M (Telec) network operator; (Comput) Internet operator; **Netzcomputer** M network computer; **Netzgerät** NT mains receiver

Netzhaut F retina

Netzhaut-: Netzhautablösung F detachment of the retina; **Netzhautentzündung** F retinitis

Netz-: Netzkarte F (Rail) unlimited travel ticket; **Netznutzer(in)** M(F) Net user; **Netzspannung** F mains voltage; **Netzstrümpfe** PL fishnet stockings pl; **Netzsurfer(in)** M(F) (inf) Net-surfer (inf); **Netzteil** NT mains adaptor

Netzwerk NT (Elec, Comput, fig) network

Netzwerk- (Comput): **Netzwerkkarte** F network card; **Netzwerkserver** M network server; **Netzwerktreiber** M network driver

Netzzugang M (Comput, Telec) network access; (zum Internet) Net access

neu [nɔy] 🔟 ADJ new; (= frisch gewaschen) Hemd, Socken clean; Wein young; **jdm zum ~en Jahr Glück wünschen** to wish sb (a) Happy New Year; **~eren Datums** of (more) recent date; **die ~(e)ste Mode** the latest fashion; **der ~(e)ste Tanz** the latest dance; **die ~esten Nachrichten** the latest news; **die ~eren Sprachen** modern languages; **ein ganz ~er Wagen** a brand-new car; **das ist mir ~!** that's new(s) to me; **mir ist die Sache ~** this is all new to me; **schlechte Laune ist mir ~ an ihm** it's something new for me to see him in a bad mood; **eine ~e Bearbeitung** a revised edition; (von Oper etc) a new version; **Geschichte der ~eren Zeit** recent history; **in ~erer Zeit** in modern times; **erst in ~erer Zeit** only recently; **seit ~(e)stem** recently; **seit ~(e)stem gibt es ...** since recently there has been ...; **aufs Neue** (geh) afresh, anew; **auf ein Neues!** (als Toast) (here's) to the New Year!; (Aufmunterung) let's try again; **der/die Neue** the newcomer; **die Neuen** the newcomers; **was ist das Neue an dem Buch?** what's new about the book?; **das Neu(e)ste in der Mode/auf dem Gebiet**

der Weltraumforschung the latest in fashion/in the field of space research; **weißt du schon das Neu(e)ste?** have you heard the latest (news)?; **was gibts Neues?** (inf) what's new?; **das Neu(e)ste vom Tage** the latest news; **das Neu(e)ste vom Neuen** the very latest (things); **von ~em** (= von vorn) afresh; (= wieder) again 🔢 ADV (a) (= von vorn) **~ anfangen** to start all over (again); **~ beginnen** to start again from scratch; **Vorhänge/ein Kleid ~ anfertigen lassen** to have new curtains/a new dress made; **sich/jdn ~ einkleiden** to buy oneself/sb a new set of clothes; **etw ~ anschaffen** to buy sth new; **~ bauen** to build a new house; **~ geschaffen** newly created (b) (= zusätzlich) **~ hinzukommen zu etw** to join sth; **Mitarbeiter ~ einstellen** to hire new employees; **Tierarten ~ entdecken** to discover new species of animals (c) (= erneut) **etw ~ auflegen** to publish a new edition of sth; **~ drucken** to reprint; **~ bearbeiten** to revise; **ein Zimmer ~ einrichten** to refurnish a room; **frei werdende Stellen werden nicht ~ besetzt** vacant positions will not be filled; **ich hatte das Buch verloren und musste es ~ kaufen** I lost the book and had to buy another copy; **~ eröffnet** (= wieder eröffnet) reopened; **~ ordnen** to reorganize; **die Rollen ~ besetzen** to recast the roles (d) (= seit kurzer Zeit) **ich habe mir das ganz ~ gekauft** I just bought it; **~ gebacken** fresh-baked; (fig) newly-fledged; **das Buch ist ~ erschienen** the book is a recent publication; **er ist ~ hinzugekommen** he's joined (him/them) recently; **~ gewählt** newly elected; **hier ist im Supermarkt ~ entstanden/gebaut worden** a supermarket has just been opened/built here; **~ eröffnet** newly-opened; **wir sind ~ hierher gezogen** we have just moved here; **der Schüler ist ganz ~ in unserer Klasse** the pupil is new in our class; **~ vermählt** newly married

Neu-: Neuankömmling M newcomer; **neuapostolisch** [ˈnɔyapɔsˈtoːlɪʃ] 🔟 ADJ New Apostolic 🔢 ADV **jdn ~ erziehen** to raise sb as a member of the New Apostolic Church

neuartig ADJ new; **ein ~es Wörterbuch** a new type of dictionary; **es ist ganz ~** it is of a completely new type

Neuartigkeit [ˈnɔyartɪçkait] F -, -en novelty

Neubau M, pl -bauten new house/building

Neubau-: Neubaugebiet NT development area; **Neubausiedlung** F new housing estate; **Neubauwohnung** F newly-built apartment

Neu-: Neubearbeitung F revised edition; (von Oper etc) new version; (= das Neubearbeiten) revision; **Neubeginn** M new beginning(s pl); **Neu-Delhi** [nɔyˈdeːli] NT -s New Delhi; **neudeutsch** (iro, pej) 🔟 ADJ new German 🔢 ADV in the new German manner; **sprechen** in new German

Neuenburg [ˈnɔyənburk] NT -s (Kanton) Neuchâtel

Neu-: Neuengland NT New England; **neuenglisch** ADJ (a) modern English (b) (= zu Neuengland gehörend) New England attr; **Neuentdeckung** F rediscovery; (Mensch) new discovery; (Ort) newly discovered place; **Neuentwicklung** F new development

neuerdings [ˈnɔyɐˈdɪŋs] ADV recently

Neu-: neueröffnet [-ˈerlœfnət] ADJ ATTR siehe neu; **Neueröffnung** F (new) opening; (= Wiedereröffnung) reopening; **es gab zwei ~en** two new shops (Brit) or stores opened; **Neuerscheinung** F (Buch) new or recent publication; (CD) new release; (= Neuheit) new or recent phenomenon

Neuerung [ˈnɔyərʊŋ] F -, -en innovation; (= Reform) reform

neuestens [ˈnɔyəstns] ADV lately

Neu-: Neufundland [ˈnɔyˈfʊntlant] NT -s Newfoundland; **Neufundländer[1]** [ˈnɔyˈfʊntlɛndɐ] M -s, - (Hund) Newfoundland (dog); **Neufundländer[2]** [ˈnɔyˈfʊntlɛndɐ] M -s, -, **Neufundländerin** [-ərɪn] F -, -nen Newfoundlander; **neufundländisch** [ˈnɔyˈfʊntlɛndɪʃ] ADJ Newfoundland; **neugeboren** ADJ newborn; **sich wie ~ fühlen** to feel (like) a new man/woman; **Neugeborene(s)** [-ˈgəboːrənə] NT DECL AS ADJ newborn child; **neugeschaffen** ADJ ATTR siehe neu; **neugewählt** [-ˈgəvɛːlt] ADJ ATTR siehe neu

Neugier [ˈnɔygiːɐ] F -, NO PL, **Neugierde** [ˈnɔygiːɐdə] F -, NO PL curiosity (auf +acc about)

neugierig [ˈnɔygiːrɪç] 🔟 ADJ curious (auf +acc about); (pej) nosy (inf); (= gespannt) curious to know; Blick, Fragen inquisitive; **ein Neugieriger** an inquisitive person; (pej auch) a nos(e)y parker (*Brit inf*), a curious George (*US inf*); **jdn ~ machen** to excite *or* arouse sb's curiosity; **ich bin ~, ob** I wonder if; **da bin ich aber ~!** I can hardly wait (*inf*) **2** ADV full of curiosity; **etw ~ untersuchen** to study sth curiously; (*Tier*) to examine sth inquisitively; **er fragt zu ~** he's too curious

Neu-: Neugliederung F reorganization, restructuring; **Neugotik** F Gothic revival; **neugotisch** ADJ neo-Gothic; **neugriechisch** ADJ Modern Greek; **Neuguinea** [nɔygiˈneːa] NT New Guinea

Neuheit ['nɔyhait] F **-, -en** (a) NO PL (= *das Neusein*) novelty; **es wird bald den Reiz der ~ verlieren** the novelty will soon wear off (b) (= *neue Sache*) innovation, new thing/idea; **dieses Gerät ist eine ~ auf dem Markt** this item is new on the market

neuhochdeutsch ADJ New High German

Neuigkeit ['nɔyɪçkait] F **-, -en** (a) (piece of) news; **die ~en** the news *sing* (b) (= *das Neusein*) novelty

Neuinszenierung F new production

Neujahr ['nɔyjaːɐ, nɔyˈjaːɐ] NT New Year; **an ~** on New Year's Day; **jdm zu(m) ~ gratulieren** to wish sb a Happy New Year; **~ begehen** *or* **feiern** to celebrate the New Year; **Pros(i)t ~!** (here's) to the New Year!

Neujahrs-: Neujahrsabend M New Year's Eve, Hogmanay (*Scot*); **Neujahrstag** M New Year's Day

Neu-: Neukaledonien [nɔykaleˈdoːniən] NT **-s** New Caledonia; **neukaledonisch** [nɔykaleˈdoːnɪʃ] ADJ New Caledonian; **Neuland** NT, NO PL virgin land; (*fig*) new ground; **~ betreten** *or* **beschreiten** to break new ground; **er betrat wissenschaftliches/geistiges ~** he broke new ground in science/intellectually

neulich ['nɔylɪç] ADV recently; **~ Abend** *or* **abends** the other evening

Neuling ['nɔylɪŋ] M **-s, -e** newcomer; (*pej auch*) beginner

neumodisch (*pej*) **1** ADJ new-fangled (*pej*) **2** ADV **sich ~ anziehen** to dress in the latest fashions; **~ einrichten** to be furnished according to the latest style; **sich ~ ausdrücken** to use new-fangled words

Neumond M new moon; **bei ~** at new moon; **heute ist ~** there's a new moon today

neun [nɔyn] NUM nine; **alle ~(e)!** (*beim Kegeln*) strike!; **er warf alle ~(e)** he got a strike; *siehe auch* **vier**

Neun [nɔyn] F **-, -en** nine; **ach du grüne ~e!** (*inf*) well I'm blowed (*Brit inf*) *or* I'll be damned!; *siehe auch* **Vier**

Neun-: neunhundert ['nɔynhʊndɐt] NUM nine hundred; **neunmal** ['nɔynmaːl] ADV nine times; *siehe auch* **viermal**; **neuntausend** ['nɔyntauznt] NUM nine thousand

Neuntel ['nɔyntl] NT **-s, -** ninth; *siehe auch* **Viertel[1]**

neuntens ['nɔyntns] ADV ninth(ly), in the ninth place

neunte(r, s) ['nɔyntə] ADJ ninth; *siehe auch* **vierte(r, s)**

neunzehn ['nɔyntseːn] NUM nineteen

neunzehnte(r, s) ['nɔyntseːntə] ADJ nineteenth; *siehe auch* **vierte(r, s)**

neunzig ['nɔyntsɪç] NUM ninety; *siehe auch* **vierzig**

Neunziger ['nɔyntsɪgɐ] M **-s, -, Neunzigerin** [-ərɪn] F **-, -nen** (*Mensch*) ninety-year-old; *siehe auch* **Vierziger[2]**

neunzigste(r, s) ['nɔyntsɪçstə] ADJ ninetieth; *siehe* **vierte(r, s)**

Neu-: Neuordnung F reorganization; (= *Reform*) reform; **Neuphilologe** M, **Neuphilologin** F modern linguist; **Neuphilologie** F modern languages *sing or pl*

Neuralgie [nɔyralˈgiː] F **-, -n** [-ˈgiːən] neuralgia

neuralgisch [nɔyˈralgɪʃ] ADJ neuralgic; **ein ~er Punkt** a trouble area

Neu-: Neuregelung F revision; **eine ~ des Verkehrs** a new traffic management scheme; **neureich** ADJ nouveau riche

Neuritis [nɔyˈriːtɪs] F **-, Neuritiden** [-riˈtiːdn] neuritis

Neuro- [nɔyro] IN CPDS neuro; **Neurochirurgie** F neurosurgery; **Neurodermitis** [nɔyrodɛrˈmiːtɪs] F **-, Neurodermitiden** [-miˈtiːdn] (*Med*) neurodermatitis; **Neurologe** [nɔyroˈloːgə] M **-n, -n, Neurologin** [-ˈloːgɪn] F **-, -nen** neurologist; **Neurologie** [nɔyroloˈgiː] F **-** [-ˈgiːən] neurology; **neurologisch** [nɔyroˈloːgɪʃ] **1** ADJ neurological **2** ADV neurologically; **~erkrankt sein** to have a neurological disease

Neuron ['nɔyrɔn] NT **-s, -e(n)** [-ˈroːnə(n)] neuron

Neurose [nɔyˈroːzə] F **-, -n** neurosis

Neurotiker [nɔyˈroːtikɐ] M **-s, -, Neurotikerin** [-ərɪn] F **-, -nen** neurotic

neurotisch [nɔyˈroːtɪʃ] **1** ADJ neurotic **2** ADV neurotically; **~ klingen** to sound neurotic; **dein Misstrauen wirkt ~** you are neurotically suspicious

Neurotransmitter [-transmɪtɐ] M **-s, -** (*Med*) neurotransmitter

Neu-: Neusatz M (*Typ*) new setting; **Neuschnee** M fresh snow; **über Nacht gab es bis zu 37 Zentimeter ~** up to 37 cm of fresh snow fell overnight; **Neuseeland** [nɔyˈzeːlant] NT **-s** New Zealand; **Neuseeländer** [nɔyˈzeːlɛndə] M **-s, -, Neuseeländerin** [-ərɪn] F **-, -nen** New Zealander; **neuseeländisch** [nɔyˈzeːlɛndɪʃ] ADJ New Zealand; **neusprachlich** ADJ modern language *attr*; **~er Zweig** (*Sch*) modern language side; **~es Gymnasium** ≈ grammar school (*Brit*), ≈ high school (*esp US, Scot*) (*stressing modern languages*)

Neustart M (*Comput*) restart, reboot

neustens ['nɔystns] ADV **= neuestens**

neutral [nɔyˈtraːl] **1** ADJ neutral **2** ADV neutrally

neutralisieren [nɔytraliˈziːrən], *ptp* **neutralisiert** VT to neutralize

Neutralität [nɔytraliˈtɛːt] F **-, NO PL** neutrality

Neutron ['nɔytrɔn] NT **-s, -en** [-ˈtroːnən] neutron

Neutronen- IN CPDS neutron; **Neutronenbombe** F neutron bomb

Neutrum ['nɔytrʊm] NT **-s, Neutra** *or* **Neutren** [-tra, -trən] (*Gram, fig*) neuter; **ein ~** (*Gram*) a neuter noun

Neu-: Neuveranlagung F (*Fin*) reassessment; **neuvermählt** [-fɛɐmɛːlt] ADJ *siehe* **neu; Neuvermählte(r)** [-fɛɐmɛːltə] MF DECL AS ADJ **die ~n** the newly-weds; **Neuverschuldung** F new borrowings *pl*; **Neuwagen** M new car; **Neuwert** M value when new; **neuwertig** ADJ as new; **Neuzeit** F modern era, modern times *pl*; **Literatur/Gesellschaft der ~** modern literature/society; **neuzeitlich** ADJ modern; **Neuzugang** M new entry

New Age ['njuː 'eːdʒ] NT **-, NO PL** new age

Newcomer ['njuːkamɐ] M **-(s), -** newcomer

Newsgroup ['njuːzgruːp] F **-, -s** (*Comput*) news group

New York ['njuːˈjɔːk] NT **-s** New York

nicht [nɪçt] ADV (a) (*Verneinung*) not; **~ leitend** non-conducting; **~ rostend** rustproof; **Stahl** stainless; **~ amtlich** unofficial; **~ öffentlich** = **nichtöffentlich; er raucht ~** (*augenblicklich*) he isn't smoking; (*gewöhnlich*) he doesn't smoke; **alle lachten, nur er ~** everybody laughed except him; **ich kann das ~ — ich auch ~** I can't do it — neither *or* nor can I; **~ mehr** *or* **länger** not any longer; **~ mehr als** no *or* not more than; **~ mehr und ~ weniger als** no more and no less than; **~ heute und ~ morgen** neither today nor tomorrow; **~ (ein)mal** not even

(b) (*Bitte, Gebot, Verbot*) **~ berühren!** do not touch; (*gesprochen*) don't touch; **~ rauchen!** no smoking; **~! don't!,** no!; **tus ~!** don't do it!; **~ doch!** stop it!, don't!; **bitte ~!** please don't; **nur das ~!** anything but that!; **nun wein mal ~ gleich!** now don't start crying

(c) (*rhetorisch*) **er kommt, ~ (wahr)?** he's coming, isn't he *or* is he not (*esp Brit*)?; **er kommt ~, ~ wahr?** he isn't coming, is he?; **ich darf kommen, ~ (wahr)?** I can come, can't I?; **jetzt wollen wir Schluss machen, ~?** let's leave it now, OK?

(d) (*doppelte Verneinung*) **~ uninteressant/unschön** *etc* not uninteresting/unattractive *etc*

(e) (*Verwunderung, Resignation etc*) **was die Kinder ~ alles wissen!** the things children know about!; **was ich ~ alles durchmachen muss!** the things I have to go through!

Nicht-, nicht- [nɪçt] PREF non-; **nichtamtlich** ADJ unofficial; **Nichtangriffspakt** M non-aggression pact; **Nichtbeachtung** F, **Nichtbefolgung** F non-observance; **Nichtbezahlung** F non-payment

Nichte ['nɪçtə] F **-, -n** niece

Nicht-: nichtehelich ADJ (*Jur*) *Kinder, Abstammung* illegitimate; *Mutter, Vater* unmarried; **in ~er Lebensgemeinschaft leben** to cohabit; **Kinder aus ~en Beziehungen** children born outside wedlock (*form*); **Nichteinmischung** F (*Pol*) non-intervention; **Nichtgefallen** NT **bei ~ (zurück)** if not satisfied (return)

nichtig ['nɪçtɪç] ADJ (a) (*Jur*. = *ungültig*) invalid; **etw für ~ erklären** to declare sth invalid; *Ehe auch* to annul sth (b) (= *unbedeutend*) trifling; *Versuch* vain; *Drohung* empty

Nichtigkeit F **-, -en** (a) (*Jur*. = *Ungültigkeit*) invalidity (b) USU PL (= *Kleinigkeit*) trifle

Nicht-: nichtleitend ADJ (*Elec*) *siehe* **nicht; Nichtmetall** NT nonmetal; **nichtöffentlich** ADJ ATTR not open to the public, private; **~e Sitzung/Konferenz** meeting/conference in camera (*Jur*) *or* behind closed doors; **Nichtraucher(in)** M(F) non-smoker; **ich bin ~** I don't smoke; **„~"** (*Rail*) "no smoking" (*Brit*), "non-smoking car" (*US*); (*Aviat*) "non-smoking seats"; **Nichtraucherabteil** NT no-smoking compartment; **Nichtraucherzone** F no-smoking area; **nichtrostend** ADJ ATTR *siehe* **nicht**

nichts [nɪçts] INDEF PRON INV nothing; (*fragend, bedingend auch*) not ... anything; **ich weiß ~** I know nothing, I don't know anything; **~ als** nothing but; **~ anderes als** not ... anything but *or* except; **~ da!** (*inf*) (= *weg da*) no you don't!; (= *ausgeschlossen*) nothing doing (*inf*); **~ ahnend** (*adjektivisch*) unsuspecting; (*adverbial*) unsuspectingly; **~ sagend** meaningless; *Vergnügen* frivolous; *Mensch* insignificant; *antworten* non-committally; **~ zu danken!** don't mention it; **für** *or* **um ~** for nothing; **das ist ~ für mich** that's not my thing (*inf*); **für ~ und wieder ~** (*inf*) for damn all (*inf*); **~ zu machen** nothing doing (*inf*); **~ mehr** nothing more, not ... anything more; **ich weiß ~ Näheres** *or* **Genaues** I don't know any details; **das war wohl ~** (*inf*) that's not much good; **~ wie raus/ rein/hin** *etc* (*inf*) let's get out/in/over there *etc* (on the double); **ich mag** *or* **will ~ mehr davon hören** I don't want to hear any more about it; **er ist zu ~ nutze** *or* **zu gebrauchen** he's useless

Nichts[1] [nɪçts] NT **-, **, NO PL (*Philos*) nothingness; (= *Leere*) emptiness; (= *Kleinigkeit*) trifle; **etw aus dem ~ erschaffen** to create sth out of nothing *or* the void; **vor dem ~ stehen** to be left with nothing

Nichts[2] NT **-es, -e** (= *Mensch*) nobody

nichtsahnend ADJ *siehe* **nichts**

Nichtschwimmer(in) M(F) non-swimmer

Nichtschwimmerbecken NT pool for non-swimmers

nichtsdestotrotz [nɪçtsdɛstoˈtrɔts] ADV nonetheless

Nichtsesshafte(r) [ˈnɪçtzɛshaftə] MF DECL AS ADJ (*form*) person of no fixed abode (*form*)

Nichts-: Nichtskönner(in) M(F) washout (*inf*); **er ist ein ~** he's (worse than) useless; **Nichtsnutz** [ˈnɪçtsnʊts] M **-es, -e** good-for-nothing; **nichtsnutzig** [ˈnɪçtsnʊtsɪç] ADJ useless; (= *unartig*) good-for-nothing; **nichtssagend** ADJ *siehe* **nichts; Nichtstun** [ˈnɪçtstuːn] NT idleness; (= *Muße*) leisure; **das süße ~** idle bliss

Nicht-: Nichtveranlagungsbescheid M (*Fin*) non-assessment declaration; **Nichtveranlagungsbescheinigung** F (*Fin*) non-assessment note; **Nichtverbreitung** F (*von Kernwaffen etc*) non-proliferation; **Nichtwähler(in)** M(F) non-voter; **Nichtwissen** NT ignorance (*um* about); **sich mit ~ entschuldigen** to plead ignorance; **Nichtzutreffende(s)** [-tsuːtrɛfndə] NT DECL AS ADJ (**etwas**) **~s** something incorrect; **~s (bitte) streichen!** (please) delete as applicable

Nickel [ˈnɪkl] NT **-s, ** NO PL (*abbr* **Ni**) nickel

Nickelbrille F metal-rimmed glasses *pl*

nicken [ˈnɪkn] VI (a) (*lit, fig*) to nod; **mit dem Kopf ~** to nod one's head; **ein leichtes Nicken** a slight nod (b) (*inf*: = *schlummern*) to snooze (*inf*)

Nickerchen [ˈnɪkɐçən] NT **-s, ** - (*inf*) snooze (*inf*)

Nicki [ˈnɪki] M **-s, -s** velour(s) pullover

nie [niː] ADV never; **~ im Leben** never ever; **machst du das? ~ ~ im Leben!** will you do it? – not on your life; **~ und nimmer** never ever; **~ wieder** *or* **mehr** never again

nieder [ˈniːdɐ] **1** ADJ ATTR (a) *Triebe, Instinkt, Motiv* low, base; *Arbeit* menial
(b) (= *primitiv*) *Kulturstufe* low, primitive; *Entwicklungsstufe* low, early
(c) (= *weniger bedeutend*) lower; *Geburt, Herkunft* lowly; *Volk* common
(d) (*esp S Ger.* = *niedrig*) low; **die ~e Jagd** small game hunting **2** ADV down; **die Waffen ~!** lay down your arms; **auf und ~** up and down; **das Auf und Nieder** (*lit*) the bobbing up and down; (*fig*) the ups and (the) downs *pl*; **mit dem Kaiser!** down with the Kaiser!

Nieder-, nieder- [ˈniːdɐ] PREF (*Geog*) Lower, lower; **~bayern** Lower Bavaria; **niederbrennen** VTI SEP IRREG (*vi: aux sein*) to burn down; **niederdeutsch** ADJ (a) (*Geog*) North German (b) (*Ling*) Low German; **niederdrücken** VT SEP (a) (*lit*) to press down (b) (= *bedrücken*) *jdn* ~ to depress sb; **Niederfrequenz** F low frequency; (*Akustik*) audio frequency; **niedergehen** VI

SEP IRREG AUX SEIN to descend; (*Bomben, Regen, Giftstoff, Komet*) to fall; (*Vorhang*) to fall; (*Gewitter*) to break (*auch fig*); **niedergeschlagen 1** ADJ dejected **2** ADV dejectedly; *siehe auch* **niederschlagen; niederknüppeln** VT SEP to club down; **Niederlage** F **(a)** (*Mil, Sport, fig*) defeat (*gegen* by) **(b)** (= *Lager*) warehouse, store **(c)** (= *Filiale*) branch (office)

Niederlande [ˈniːdəlandə] PL **die ~** the Netherlands *sing or pl*
Niederländer [ˈniːdəlɛndɐ] M **-s, ** - Dutchman; **die ~** the Dutch
Niederländerin [ˈniːdəlɛndərɪn] F **-, -nen** Dutchwoman
niederländisch [ˈniːdəlɛndɪʃ] ADJ Dutch, Netherlands

niederlassen VR SEP IRREG **(a)** (= *sich setzen*) to sit down; (= *sich niederlegen*) to lie down; (*Vögel*) to land **(b)** (= *Wohnsitz nehmen*) to settle (*down*); (*in Amtsitz*) to take up official residence **(c)** (= *Praxis, Geschäft eröffnen*) to set up in business; **sich als Arzt/Rechtsanwalt ~** to set up (a practice) as a doctor/lawyer

Niederlassung [-lasʊŋ] F **-, -en (a)** NO PL (= *das Niederlassen*) settling, settlement; (*eines Arztes etc*) establishment **(b)** (= *Siedlung*) settlement **(c)** (*Comm*) registered office; (= *Zweigstelle*) branch

Niederlassungsbewilligung F (*Sw*) residence permit

niederlegen SEP **1** VT **(a)** (= *hinlegen*) to lay *or* put down; *Kranz, Blumen* to lay; *Waffen* to lay down **(b)** (= *aufgeben*) *Dienst, Amt, Mandat* to resign (from); *Krone, Führung* to renounce; **die Arbeit ~** (= *aufhören*) to stop work(ing); (= *streiken*) to down tools **(c)** (= *schriftlich festlegen*) to write down **2** VR to lie down

Niederlegung [-leːgʊŋ] F **-, -en (a)** (*von Kranz*) laying; (*von Waffen*) laying down **(b)** (*von Amt, Dienst, Mandat*) resignation (from); (*von Kommando*) resignation (of); (*der Krone*) abdication; **~ der Arbeit** walkout

Nieder-: niedermachen VT SEP **(a)** (= *töten*) to massacre **(b)** (*fig*: = *heftig kritisieren*) to run down; **Niederösterreich** NT Lower Austria; **Niederrhein** M Lower Rhine; **niederrheinisch** ADJ lower Rhine; **Niedersachsen** NT Lower Saxony; **niedersächsisch** ADJ of Lower Saxony

Niederschlag M **(a)** (*Met*) precipitation (*form*); (*Chem*) precipitate; (= *Bodensatz*) sediment, dregs *pl*; (*fig*: = *Ausdruck*) expression; **radioaktiver ~** (radioactive) fallout; **für morgen sind heftige Niederschläge gemeldet** tomorrow there will be heavy rain/hail/snow **(b)** (*Boxen*) knockdown blow; (*über 10 Sekunden*) knockout, KO

niederschlagen SEP IRREG **1** VT *jdn* to knock down; *Aufstand, Revolte* to suppress; *Augen, Blick* to lower; *siehe auch* **niedergeschlagen 2** VR (*Flüssigkeit*) to condense; (*Bodensatz*) to settle; (*Chem*) to precipitate; (*Met*) to fall; **die Untersuchung schlug sich in einer Reform nieder** the investigation resulted in a reform; **sich in etw** (*dat*) **~** (*Erfahrungen, Vorfälle etc*) to find expression in sth; *in Statistik* to be reflected in sth

Nieder-: niederschmetternd ADJ shattering; **niederschreiben** VT SEP IRREG to write down; **Niederschrift** F (= *das Niederschreiben*) writing down; (= *Niedergeschriebenes*) notes *pl*; (= *Protokoll*) (*einer Sitzung*) minutes *pl*; (*Jur*) record; **Niederspannung** F (*Elec*) low voltage; **niederstechen** VT SEP IRREG to stab; **niedertourig** [-tuːrɪç] **1** ADJ *Motor, Maschine* low-revving **2** ADV **~ fahren** to drive with low revs; **Niedertracht** [ˈniːdɛtraxt] F **-, ** NO PL despicableness; (*als Rache*) malice; (= *niederträchtige Tat*) despicable act; **niederträchtig** [ˈniːdɛtrɛçtɪç] **1** ADJ despicable; (= *rachsüchtig*) malicious **2** ADV despicably; *verleumden, verraten* maliciously; **Niederträchtigkeit** F **-, -en (a)** NO PL = **Niedertracht (b)** (*Tat*) despicable behaviour *no pl* (*Brit*) *or* behavior *no pl* (*US*); (*rachsüchtig*) malicious behaviour *no pl* (*Brit*) *or* behavior *no pl* (*US*); **das ist eine ~** that's despicable; **niedertrampeln** VT SEP to trample underfoot

Niederung [ˈniːdərʊŋ] F **-, -en** (= *Senke*) depression; (= *Mündungsgebiet*) flats *pl*; (*sumpfig*) marsh; **die ~en des Alltags** the down side of everyday life; **in solche ~en begebe ich mich nicht** (*fig*) I will not sink to such depths

niederwerfen SEP IRREG **1** VT to throw down; *Aufstand* to suppress **2** VR to throw oneself down

Niederwild NT small game

niedlich [ˈniːtlɪç] **1** ADJ cute **2** ADV sweetly; **~ aussehen** to look sweet; **sie hat das Lied ~ gesungen** she sang that song sweetly; **das Kätzchen lag so ~ auf meinem Bett** the kitten looked so sweet lying on my bed

niedrig ['niːdrɪç] ■ low; *Stand, Herkunft, Geburt* low(ly) ■ ADV low; *etw* ~**er berechnen** to charge less for sth; *etw zu* ~ **veranschlagen** to underestimate sth; *etw* ~ **einstufen** to give sth a low classification; **jdn gehaltsmäßig ~er einstufen** to pay sb a lower salary; **ich schätze seine Chancen sehr ~ ein** I don't think much of his chances; ~ **denken** to think base thoughts; **von jdm ~ denken, jdn ~ einschätzen** to have a low opinion of sb

Niedrigenergiehaus NT low-energy house

Niedrigkeit F -, NO PL **(a)** lowness; **die ~ der Häuser** the low-built style of the houses **(b)** *(von Gedanken, Beweggründen)* baseness

Niedriglohnland NT low-wage country

Niedrig-: Niedrigstrahlung F low-level radiation; **Niedrigwasser** NT, *pl* **-wasser** *(Naut)* low tide

niemals ['niːmaːls] ADV never

niemand ['niːmant] INDEF PRON nobody; **es war ~ zu Hause** there was nobody at home, there wasn't anybody at home; ~ **anders** *or* **anderer** *(S Ger)* **kam** nobody else came; **herein kam ~ anders** *or* **anderer** *(S Ger)* **als der Kanzler selbst** in came none other than the Chancellor himself; ~ **Fremdes** no strangers; **er hat es ~(em) gesagt** he hasn't told anyone, he has told no-one

Niemand ['niːmant] M -s, NO PL **er ist ein ~** he's a nobody

Niemandsland NT no-man's-land

Niere ['niːrə] F -, -n kidney; **künstliche ~** kidney machine; **es geht mir an die ~n** *(inf)* it gets me down *(inf)*

Nieren- IN CPDS *(Anat)* renal; **Nierenbecken** NT pelvis of the kidney; **Nierenbeckenentzündung** F pyelitis *(spec)*; **Nierenentzündung** F nephritis *(spec)*; **nierenförmig** ADJ kidney-shaped; **Nierenkrankheit** F, **Nierenleiden** NT kidney disease; **Nierenschale** F kidney dish; **Nierenschützer** [-ʃʏtsə] M -s, - kidney belt; **Nierenstein** M kidney stone; **Nierensteinzertrümmerer** [-tseɐtrʏmərə] M -s, - lithotripter *(spec)*; **Nierentasche** F bum bag *(Brit)*, fanny pack *(US)*; **Nierentisch** M kidney-shaped table

nieseln ['niːzln] VI IMPERS to drizzle

Nieselregen M drizzle

niesen ['niːzn] VI to sneeze

Niet [niːt] M -(e)s, -e *(spec)*, **Niete** ['niːtə] F -, -n rivet; *(auf Kleidung)* stud

Niete F -, -n (= *Los)* blank; *(inf: = Mensch)* dead loss *(inf)*

nieten ['niːtn] VT to rivet

Nietenhose F (pair of) studded jeans *pl*

niet- und nagelfest ['niːtlʊnt 'naːɡlfɛst] ADJ *(inf)* nailed *or* screwed down

Niger¹ ['niːɡɐ] M -s (= *Fluss)* Niger

Niger² NT -s (= *Staat)* Niger

Nigeria [niˈɡeːria] NT -s Nigeria

nigerianisch [niɡeriˈaːnɪʃ] ADJ Nigerian

nigrisch ['niːɡrɪʃ] ADJ Nigerian

Nihilismus [nihiˈlɪsmʊs] M -, NO PL nihilism

Nihilist [nihiˈlɪst] M -en, -en, **Nihilistin** [-ˈlɪstɪn] F -, -nen nihilist

nihilistisch [nihiˈlɪstɪʃ] ADJ nihilistic

Nikkei-Index ['nɪkei-] M -, NO PL *(St Ex)* Nikkei Index

Nikolaus ['nɪkolaus, 'niːkolaus] M **(a)** *(= Name)* Nicholas **(b)** -, -e *or (hum inf)* **Nikoläuse** [-lɔyzə] St Nicholas; (= *~tag)* St Nicholas' Day

NIKOLAUS

Nikolaus (known as Samichlaus in Switzerland) is a saint, usually represented as wearing a tall hat, long gown and white bushy beard, who traditionally brings gifts for children on December 6th. He either places his presents in boots left outside the front door the night before, or he arrives in person. In many regions he is accompanied by Knecht Ruprecht or, particularly in Austria, by Krampus, who beats naughty children with a birch or carries them off in a sack. Increasingly, Nikolaus is presented as a benevolent character similar to the English and American Santa Claus.

Nikotin [nikoˈtiːn] NT -s, NO PL nicotine

Nikotin-: nikotinarm ADJ low-nicotine; **nikotinfrei** ADJ nicotine-free; **Nikotinpflaster** NT nicotine patch

Nil [niːl] M -s Nile

Nilpferd NT hippopotamus

nimm [nɪm] IMPER SING *von* **nehmen**

nimmermüde ['nɪmɐˈmyːdə] ADJ ATTR tireless

nimmersatt ['nɪmɐzat] ADJ insatiable

Nimmersatt ['nɪmɐzat] M -(e)s, -e glutton; **ein ~ sein** to be insatiable

Nimmerwiedersehen NT *(inf)* **auf ~!** I never want to see you again; **auf ~ verschwinden** to disappear never to be seen again

nimmt [nɪmt] 3. PERS SING PRES *von* **nehmen**

Nippel ['nɪpl] M -s, - **(a)** *(Tech)* nipple **(b)** *(inf: = Brustwarze)* nipple

nippen ['nɪpn] VTI to nip *(an +dat* at); *(an Glas etc)* to sip from; **am** *or* **vom Wein ~** to sip (at) the wine

Nippes ['nɪpəs] PL, **Nippsachen** ['nɪp-] PL ornaments *pl*, knick-knacks *pl*

Nippon ['nɪpɔn] NT -s Japan

nirgends ['nɪrɡnts] ADV nowhere, not ... anywhere; **ihm gefällt es ~** he doesn't like it anywhere; ~ **sonst** nowhere else; **das sieht man fast ~ mehr** you hardly see that any more

nirgendwo ['nɪrɡntˈvoː] ADV = **nirgends**

nirgendwohin ['nɪrɡntvoˈhɪn] ADV nowhere, not ... anywhere

Nische ['niːʃə] F -, -n niche; (= *Kochnische etc)* recess; *(fig)* niche

nisten ['nɪstn] VI to nest

Nist-: Nistkasten M nest(ing) box; **Nistplatz** M nesting place

Nitrat [niˈtraːt] NT -(e)s, -e nitrate

nitrieren [niˈtriːrən], *ptp* **nitriert** VT to nitrate

Nitro- ['nitro] IN CPDS nitro; **Nitroglyzerin** NT nitroglycerine; **Nitrolack** M nitrocellulose paint; **Nitroverdünnung** F cellulose thinner

Niveau [niˈvoː] NT -s, -s *(lit, fig)* level; **auf gleichem ~ liegen** to be on the same level; **auf hohem/niedrigem ~ liegen** *(fig)* to be at a high/low level; **intelligenzmäßig steht er auf dem ~ eines Dreijährigen** he has the mental age of a three-year-old; **diese Schule hat ein hohes ~** this school has high standards; **unter ~** below par; **unter meinem ~** beneath me; **~/kein/wenig ~ haben** to be of a high/low/fairly low standard; *(Mensch)* to be cultured/not at all/not very cultured; **ein Hotel mit ~** a hotel with class

nivellieren [nivɛˈliːrən], *ptp* **nivelliert** ■ VT *(lit, fig)* to level off ■ VI *(Surv)* to level

nix [nɪks] INDEF PRON *(inf)* = **nichts**

Nixe ['nɪksə] F -, -n water nymph; *(mit Fischschwanz)* mermaid; *(hum: = Badenixe)* bathing belle

Nizza ['nɪtsa] NT -s Nice

NN ABBR *von* **Normalnull**

NO ABBR *von* **Nordosten**

nobel ['noːbl] ■ ADJ (= *edelmütig)* noble; *(inf)* (= *großzügig)* lavish; (= *kostspielig)* extravagant; (= *elegant)* posh *(inf)* ■ ADV (= *edelmütig)* nobly; (= *großzügig)* generously; ~ **wohnen** to live in posh surroundings; **das war ~ gedacht** that was a noble thought; ~ **geht die Welt zugrunde** *(iro)* there's nothing like going out in style

Nobelpreis [noˈbɛl-] M Nobel prize

Nobelpreisträger(in) M(F) Nobel prizewinner

noch [nɔx] ■ ADV **(a)** (= *weiterhin, bis jetzt, wie zuvor)* still; ~ **nicht** not yet; **immer ~, ~ immer** still; **er dachte ~ lange an sie** it was a long time before he stopped thinking of her; ~ **nie** never; **ich gehe kaum ~ aus** I hardly go out any more; **ich möchte gerne ~ bleiben** I'd like to stay on longer **(b)** (= *irgendwann)* some time, one day; **das kann ~ passieren** that might still happen; **er wird ~ kommen** he'll come (yet) **(c)** (= *eben, nicht später als)* **das muss ~ vor Dienstag fertig sein** it has to be ready by Tuesday; **ich habe ihn ~ vor zwei Tagen gesehen** I saw him only two days ago; **er ist ~ am selben Tag gestorben** he died the very same day; **ich tue das ~ heute** *or* **heute ~** I'll do it today; ~ **im 18. Jahrhundert** as late as the 18th century; **gerade ~** (only) just; ~ **keine drei Tage** not three days **(d)** *(einschränkend)* (only) just; *(gerade)* ~ **gut genug** (only) just good enough **(e)** (= *außerdem, zusätzlich)* **wer war ~ da?** who else was there?; **(gibt es)** ~ **etwas?** (is there) anything else?; ~ **etwas Fleisch** some more meat; ~ **einer** another (one); ~ **ein Bier** another beer; ~ **einmal** *or* **mal** (once) again, once more; **und es regnete auch ~** *or* ~ **dazu** and on top of that it was raining;

dumm und ~ dazu frech stupid and impudent with it (*inf*); **ich gebe Ihnen ~ zwei dazu** I'll give you two extra; **~ ein Wort!** (not) another word!
(f) (*bei Vergleichen*) even, still; **das ist ~ viel wichtiger als ...** that is far more important still than ...; **(und) seien sie auch ~ so klein** however small they may be; **und wenn du auch ~ so bittest ...** however much you ask ...
(g) (*inf*) **wir fanden Fehler ~ und nöcher** (*hum inf*) we found tons (*inf*) of mistakes; **Geld ~ und nöcher** (*hum inf*) heaps and heaps of money (*inf*); **ich kann Ihnen Beispiele ~ und nöcher geben** I can give you any number of examples
2 CONJ (*weder ... noch ...*) nor; **nicht X, ~ Y, ~ Z** not X nor Y nor Z

nochmalig ['nɔxmaːlɪç] ADJ ATTR renewed; **eine ~e Überprüfung** another check

nochmals ['nɔxmaːls] ADV again

Nockenwelle ['nɔkn-] F camshaft

No-Future-Generation F no-future generation

NOK [enloː'kaː] NT **-s** ABBR *von* **Nationales Olympisches Komitee**

nölen ['nøːlən] VI (*inf*) to moan

Nomade [noˈmaːdə] M **-n, -n**, **Nomadin** [noˈmaːdɪn] F **-, -nen** (*lit, fig*) nomad

Nomaden- IN CPDS nomadic; **Nomadentum** [noˈmaːdntuːm] NT **-s**, NO PL nomadism

Nomadin F **-, -nen** (*lit, fig*) nomad

nomadisch [noˈmaːdɪʃ] **1** ADJ nomadic **2** ADV **~ leben** to live a nomadic lifestyle

Nomen ['noːmən] NT **-s, Nomina** ['noːmina] (*Gram*) noun; **nomen est omen** (*geh*) true to your/his *etc* name

nominal [nomiˈnaːl] (*Econ*) **1** ADJ nominal **2** ADV nominally

Nominal- IN CPDS (*Gram, Fin*) nominal; **Nominalstil** M nominal style; **Nominalverzinsung** F nominal yield; **Nominalwert** M (*Fin*) nominal value; **Nominalzins** M (*Fin*) nominal interest rate

Nominativ ['nominatiːf] M **-s, -e** [-və] nominative

nominell [nomiˈnɛl] ADJ, ADV in name only

nominieren [nomiˈniːrən], *ptp* **nominiert** VT to nominate

nonkonformistisch **1** ADJ nonconformist **2** ADV **sich ~ verhalten** to act unconventionally

Nonne ['nɔnə] F **-, -n** nun

Nonnenkloster NT convent

Nonsens ['nɔnzɛns] M **-(es)**, NO PL nonsense

nonstop [nɔn'ʃtɔp, -'stɔp] ADV non-stop

Non-Stop-, Nonstop- IN CPDS non-stop; **Nonstopbetrieb** M **im ~** non-stop

Noppe ['nɔpə] F **-, -n** (= *Gumminoppe*) nipple, knob; (*von Tischtennisschläger, Gummisohle auch*) pimple; (= *Knoten*) burl; (= *Schlinge*) loop

Nord-, nord- IN CPDS (*in Ländernamen*) (*politisch*) North; (*geografisch auch*) the North of ..., Northern; **Nordafrika** NT North Africa; **Nordamerika** NT North America; **Nordatlantik** M North Atlantic; **Nordatlantikpakt** M North Atlantic Treaty; **nordatlantisch** ADJ North Atlantic; **~es Verteidigungsbündnis, ~e Allianz** NATO Alliance; **norddeutsch** ADJ North German; **die ~e Tiefebene** the North German lowlands *pl*; **die Norddeutschen** the North Germans; **Norddeutschland** NT North(ern) Germany

Norden ['nɔrdn] M **-s**, NO PL north; (*von Land*) North; **aus dem ~, von ~ (her)** from the north; **gegen** *or* **gen** (*liter*) *or* **nach ~** north(wards), to the north; **der Balkon liegt nach ~** the balcony faces north(wards); **nach ~ hin** to the north; **im ~ der Stadt/des Landes** in the north of the town/country; **im/aus dem hohen ~** in/from the far north; **weiter** *or* **höher im ~** further north; **im Münchner ~** on the north side of Munich; **im ~ Frankreichs** in the north of France

Nord-: Nordengland NT the North of England; **nordfriesisch** ADJ North Frisian; **Nordhalbkugel** F northern hemisphere; **nordirisch** ADJ Northern Irish; **Nordirland** NT Northern Ireland

nordisch ['nɔrdɪʃ] ADJ *Wälder* northern; *Völker, Sprache, Mythologie* Nordic; (*Ski*) nordic; **~e Kombination** (*Ski*) nordic combined

Nord-: Nordkap NT North Cape; **Nordkorea** NT North Korea

nördlich ['nœrtlɪç] **1** ADJ northern; *Kurs, Wind, Richtung* northerly; **der ~e Polarkreis** the Arctic Circle; **der ~e**

Wendekreis the Tropic of Cancer; **52 Grad ~er Breite** 52 degrees north **2** ADV (to the) north; **~ von Köln (gelegen)** north of Cologne; **es liegt ~er** *or* **weiter ~** it is further (to the) north **3** PREP +GEN (to the) north of

Nordlicht NT northern lights *pl*, aurora borealis; (*fig hum*: *Mensch*) Northerner

Nordost- IN CPDS north-east; (*bei Namen*) North-East; **~england** North-East England

Nordosten M north-east; (*von Land*) North East; **aus** *or* **von ~** from the north-east; **nach ~** to the north-east, north-east(wards); **im ~ Brasiliens** in the North East of Brazil

nordöstlich **1** ADJ *Gegend* north-eastern; *Wind* north(erly) **2** ADV (to the) north-east; **~ von ...** north-east of ... **3** PREP +GEN (to the) north-east of

Nord-Ostsee-Kanal M Kiel Canal

Nordpol M North Pole

Nordpolar-: Nordpolargebiet NT Arctic (Zone); **Nordpolarmeer** NT Arctic Ocean

Nordrhein-Westfalen ['nɔrtrainvɛst'faːlən] NT North Rhine-Westphalia

nordrhein-westfälisch ['nɔrtrainvɛst'fɛːlɪʃ] ADJ North Rhine-Westphalian

Nord-: Nordsee ['nɔrtzeː] F North Sea; **Nordstaaten** PL (*Hist*) northern states *pl*, Union; **Nord-Süd-Gefälle** ['nɔrt'zyːt-] NT north-south divide; **Nordwand** F (*von Berg*) north face

nordwärts ['nɔrtvɛrts] ADV north(wards); **der Wind dreht ~** the wind is moving round to the north

Nordwest- IN CPDS north-west; (*bei Namen*) North-West; **~england** North-West England

Nordwesten M north-west; (*von Land*) North West; **aus** *or* **von ~** from the north-west; **nach ~** to the north-west, north-west(wards); **im ~ Englands** in the North West of England

nordwestlich **1** ADJ *Gegend* north-western; *Wind* north(erly) **2** ADV (to the) north-west; **~ von** (to the) north-west of **3** PREP +GEN (to the) north-west of

Nordwind M north wind

Nörgelei [nœrgəˈlai] F **-, -en** moaning; (= *Krittelei*) nit-picking (*inf*)

nörgeln ['nœrgln] VI to moan; (= *kritteln*) to niggle (*an +dat, über +acc* about); **er hat immer an allem zu ~** he always finds something to moan about

Norm [nɔrm] F **-, -en** **(a)** norm; (= *Größenvorschrift*) standard (specification); **als ~ gelten, die ~ sein** to be (considered) normal **(b)** (= *Leistungssoll*) quota; **die ~ erfüllen/erreichen** to achieve one's quota

normal [nɔrˈmaːl] **1** ADJ normal; *Format, Maß, Gewicht* standard; **bist du noch ~?** (*inf*) have you gone mad? **2** ADV normally; **er ist ~ groß** his height is normal; **~ aussehen/riechen** to look/smell normal; **benimm dich ganz ~** act naturally; **benimm dich doch mal ~!** act like a normal human being, can't you?

Normal- [nɔrˈmaːl] IN CPDS **(a)** (= *üblich*) normal **(b)** (= *genormt*) standard; **Normalbenzin** NT regular (petrol (*Brit*) *or* gas (*US*))

normalerweise [nɔrˈmaːleˈvaizə] ADV normally

Normal-: Normalfall M normal case; **im ~** normally, usually; **das ist der ~** that is the norm; **Normalgewicht** NT normal weight; (*genormt*) standard weight

normalisieren [nɔrmaliˈziːrən], *ptp* **normalisiert** **1** VT to normalize **2** VR to get back to normal

Normalität [nɔrmaliˈtɛːt] F **-, -en** normality

Normal-: Normalnull NT **-s**, NO PL (*abbr* **NN**) ≈ sea level; **Normalverbraucher(in)** M(F) average consumer; **(geistiger) ~** (*inf*) middlebrow; **Otto ~** (*inf*) the man in the street; **Normalzustand** M normal state; (= *normale Verhältnisse*) normal conditions *pl*; (*Chem, Phys*) natural state

Normandie [nɔrmanˈdiː, nɔrmaˈdiː] F - Normandy

Normanne [nɔrˈmanə] M **-n, -n**, **Normannin** [-ˈmanɪn] F **-, -nen** Norman

normannisch [nɔrˈmanɪʃ] ADJ Norman

normativ [nɔrmaˈtiːf] ADJ normative

Normblatt NT standard specifications sheet

normen ['nɔrmən] VT to standardize

normwidrig ADJ deviant; (*Tech*) non-standard

Norwegen ['nɔrveːgn] NT **-s** Norway

Norweger [ˈnɔrveˌgə] M **-s, -**, **Norwegerin** [-ərɪn] F **-, -nen** Norwegian

norwegisch [ˈnɔrveˌgɪʃ] ADJ Norwegian

Nostalgie [nɔstalˈgiː] F **-, NO PL** nostalgia

nostalgisch [nɔsˈtalgɪʃ] **1** ADJ nostalgic **2** ADV nostalgically; ~ **anmutende Bilder** nostalgic pictures

Nostro- [ˈnɔstro:] (*Fin*): **Nostrogeschäft** NT nostro transaction; **Nostrokonto** NT nostro account

Not [noːt] F **-, ⁻e** [ˈnøːtə] **(a)** NO PL (= *Mangel, Elend*) need(iness), poverty; **hier herrscht große ~** there is great poverty here; **aus ~** out of poverty; **~ leiden** to suffer deprivation; **~ leidend** *Bevölkerung, Land* impoverished; *Unternehmen, Wirtschaft* ailing; (*Comm*) *Wechsel, Wertpapier* dishonoured (*Brit*), dishonored (*US*); *Kredit* unsecured; **jds ~** (*acc*) **lindern** to improve sb's lot; **~ macht erfinderisch** (*Prov*) necessity is the mother of invention (*Prov*); **in der ~ frisst der Teufel Fliegen** (*Prov*), **in der ~ schmeckt jedes Brot** (*Prov*) beggars can't be choosers (*prov*)

(b) (= *Bedrängnis*) distress *no pl*, affliction; (= *Problem*) problem; **in seiner ~** in his hour of need; **in unserer ~ blieb uns nichts anderes übrig** in this emergency we had no choice; **in ~ sein** to be in distress; **in ~ geraten** to get into serious difficulties; **wenn ~ am Mann ist** if the need arises; (= *im ~fall*) in an emergency; **der Retter in der ~** the knight in shining armour (*Brit*) *or* armor (*US*); **in höchster ~ sein, sich in höchster ~ befinden** to be in dire straits; **in Ängsten und Nöten schweben** to be in fear and trembling

(c) NO PL (= *Sorge, Mühe*) difficulty; **er hat seine liebe ~ mit ihr/damit** he really has problems with her/it; **die Eltern hatten ~, ihre fünf Kinder zu ernähren** the parents had difficulty in feeding their five children

(d) (= *Zwang, Notwendigkeit*) necessity; **der ~ gehorchend** bowing to necessity; **etw nicht ohne ~ tun** not to do sth without having to; **ohne ~** without good cause; **zur ~** if necessary; (= *gerade noch*) just about; **aus der ~ eine Tugend machen** to make a virtue (out) of necessity; **~ tun** *or* **sein** to be necessary

Notar [noˈtaːɐ] M **-s, -e**, **Notarin** [-ˈtaːrɪn] F **-, -nen** notary public

Notariat [notaˈriaːt] NT **-(e)s, -e** notary's office

notariell [notaˈriɛl] (*Jur*) **1** ADJ notarial **2** ADV **~ beglaubigt** legally certified; **~ beurkunden** to notarize

Not-: Notarzt M, **Notärztin** F emergency doctor; **Notarztwagen** M emergency doctor's car; **Notaufnahme** F casualty (unit) (*Brit*), emergency room (*US*); **Notaufnahmelager** NT reception centre (*Brit*) *or* center (*US*); **Notausgang** M emergency exit; **Notbehelf** M stopgap (measure); **Notbremse** F emergency brake; **die ~ ziehen** (*lit*) to pull the emergency brake; (*fig*) to put the brakes on; **Notbremsung** F emergency stop; **Notdienst** M **~ haben** (*Apotheke*) to be open 24 hours; (*Arzt, Elektriker etc*) to be on call

notdürftig [ˈnoːtdʏrftɪç] **1** ADJ (= *kaum ausreichend*) meagre (*Brit*), meager (*US*), poor; (= *behelfsmäßig*) makeshift *no adv*; *Kleidung* scanty **2** ADV *bekleidet* scantily; *reparieren* in a makeshift way; **versorgen** poorly; **wir konnten uns mit den Einheimischen ~ verständigen** we could just about communicate with the natives; **damit Sie sich wenigstens ~ verständigen können** so that you can at least communicate to some extent

Note [ˈnoːtə] F **-, -n (a)** (*Mus, Pol*) note

(b) Noten PL music; **~n lesen** to read music; **nach ~n spielen/singen** to play/sing from music

(c) (*Sch, Sport*) mark

(d) (= *Banknote*) (bank)note, bill (*US*)

(e) NO PL (= *Eigenart*) (*in Bezug auf Gespräch, Brief etc*) note; (*in Bezug auf Beziehungen, Atmosphäre*) tone, character; (*in Bezug auf Einrichtung, Kleidung*) touch; **das ist meine persönliche ~** that's my trademark; **ein Parfüm mit einer herben ~** a perfume with something tangy about it

Notebook [ˈnoːtbʊk] M OR NT **-s, -s** notebook (computer)

Noten-: Notenbank F, *pl* **-banken** issuing bank; **Notenbankgeld** NT central bank money; **Notenblatt** NT sheet of music; **Notenheft** NT (*mit Noten*) book of music; (*ohne Noten*) manuscript book; **Notenschlüssel** M clef; **Notenständer** M music stand

Notfall M emergency; **für den ~ nehme ich einen Schirm mit** I'll take an umbrella (just) in case; **im ~** if necessary; **bei einem**

~ in case of emergency; **im äußersten ~** in an extreme emergency; **er ist ein ~** (*Kranker*) he is an emergency case

notfalls [ˈnoːtfals] ADV if necessary

notgedrungen [ˈnoːtgədrʊŋən] **1** ADJ enforced **2** ADV of necessity; **ich muss mich ~ dazu bereit erklären** I'm forced to agree

notieren [noˈtiːrən], *ptp* **notiert 1** VTI **(a)** (= *Notizen machen*) to note down; (*schnell*) to jot down; (= *bemerken*) to note; **ich notiere (mir) den Namen** I'll make a note of the name **(b)** (= *vormerken*) *Auftrag* to note, to book; **zu welchem Termin waren Sie notiert?** what time was your appointment?; **jdn (für etw) ~** to put sb's name down (for sth) **(c)** (*St Ex*: = *festlegen*) to quote (*mit at*) **2** VI (*St Ex*: = *wert sein*) to be quoted (*auf +acc* at)

Notierung F **-, -en (a)** (*Comm*) note **(b)** (*St Ex*) quotation **(c)** (*Mus*) notation

Notifikation [notifikaˈtsioːn] F **-, -en** (*Fin*) notification

nötig [ˈnøːtɪç] **1** ADJ necessary; **ist das unbedingt ~?** is that absolutely necessary?; **die ~en Unkosten** the unavoidable costs; **wenn ~** if necessary; **etw ~ haben** to need sth; **etw bitter ~ haben** to need sth badly; **er hat das natürlich nicht ~** (*iro*) but, of course, he's different; **ich habe es nicht ~, mich von dir anschreien zu lassen** I don't need to let you shout at me; **die habens gerade ~** (*inf*) that's the last thing they need; **du hast es gerade ~, so zu reden** (*inf*) you can *or* can't talk (*inf*); **das habe ich nicht ~!** I don't need that; **das Nötige** the necessary; **das Nötigste** the (bare) necessities; **alles zum Bergsteigen unbedingt Nötige** everything necessary for mountaineering **2** ADV (= *dringend*) etwas **~ brauchen** to need something urgently; **ich muss mal ~** (*inf*) I'm dying to go (*inf*)

Nötigung [ˈnøːtɪgʊŋ] F **-, -en** (= *Zwang*) compulsion; (*Jur*) coercion; **sexuelle ~** sexual assault

Notiz [noˈtiːts] F **-, -en (a)** (= *Vermerk*) note; (= *Zeitungsnotiz*) item; **sich** (*dat*) **~en machen** to make notes **(b) ~ nehmen von** to take notice of; **keine ~ nehmen von** to ignore; **kaum ~ nehmen von** to hardly take any notice of

Notiz-: Notizblock M, *pl* **-blöcke** notepad; **Notizbuch** NT notebook; **Notizzettel** M piece of paper; **er hinterließ mir einen ~ mit seiner Adresse** he left me a note of his address on a piece of paper

Not-: Notkühlsystem NT emergency cooling system; **Notlage** F crisis; (= *Elend*) plight; **in ~n** in an emergency; **jds ~** (*acc*) **ausnutzen** to exploit sb's situation; **sich in einer (finanziellen etc) ~ befinden** to find oneself in serious (financial *etc*) difficulties

notlanden [ˈnoːtlandn], *pret* **notlandete**, *ptp* **notgelandet** [ˈnoːtgəlandət] VI AUX SEIN to make an emergency landing

Notlandung F emergency landing

notleidend ADJ *siehe* **Not**

Not-: Notleine F emergency cord; **Notlösung** F compromise solution; (*provisorisch*) temporary solution; **Notlüge** F white lie

notorisch [noˈtoːrɪʃ] **1** ADJ **(a)** (= *gewohnheitsmäßig*) habitual **(b)** (= *allbekannt*) notorious **2** ADV notoriously

Not-: Notrad NT (*Aut*) spare wheel; **Notruf** M (*Telec*) (*Gespräch*) emergency call; (*Nummer*) emergency number; **Notrufsäule** F emergency telephone; **Notrutsche** F (*Aviat*) escape chute

notschlachten [ˈnoːtʃlaxtn], *pret* **notschlachtete**, *ptp* **notgeschlachtet** [ˈnoːtgəʃlaxtət] VT to put down

Notstand M crisis; (*Pol*) state of emergency; (*Jur*) emergency; **den ~ ausrufen** to declare a state of emergency; **einen ~ beheben** to end a crisis; **einen ~ abwenden** to avert a crisis/an emergency

Notstands-: Notstandsgebiet NT (*wirtschaftlich*) deprived area; (*bei Katastrophen*) disaster area; **Notstandsgesetze** PL (*Pol*) emergency laws *pl*

Notstromaggregat NT emergency power generator

Notwehr [ˈnoːtveːɐ] F, NO PL self-defence (*Brit*), self-defense (*US*); **in** *or* **aus ~** in self-defence (*Brit*) *or* self-defense (*US*)

notwendig [ˈnoːtvɛndɪç, noːtˈvɛndɪç] **1** ADJ necessary; (= *unvermeidlich auch*) inevitable; **ich habe alles Notwendige erledigt** I've done everything (that's) necessary; **das Notwendigste** the (bare) necessities; **sich auf das Notwendigste beschränken** to stick to essentials **2** ADV necessarily; **eine rationale Denkweise ist ~ geboten** rational thinking is strongly recommended; **~ brauchen** to need urgently

Notwendigkeit F -, -en necessity

Notzucht F (*Jur*) rape; **~ begehen** *or* **verüben** to commit rape (*an +dat* on)

Nougat ['nu:gat] M *or* NT **-s, -s** nougat

Novelle [no'vɛlə] F **-, -n** (a) novella (b) (*Pol*) amendment

novellieren [novɛ'li:rən], *ptp* **novelliert** VT (*Pol*) to amend

novellistisch [novɛ'lɪstɪʃ] **1** ADJ novella-like **2** ADV **den Stoff ~ behandeln** to use the material for a novella; **eine ~ erzählte Geschichte** a novella-like story

November [no'vɛmbɐ] M **-(s),** - November; *siehe auch* **März**

novemberlich [no'vɛmbɐlɪç] ADJ November-like

Novize [no'vi:tsə] M **-n, -n,** F **-, -n, Novizin** [-'vi:tsɪn] F **-, -nen** novice

NPD [ɛnpe:'de:] F - ABBR *von* **Nationaldemokratische Partei Deutschlands**

Nr. ABBR *von* **Numero, Nummer** No.

NS (a) ABBR *von* **Nachschrift** PS (b) ABBR *von* **nationalsozialistisch**

NSP [ɛnɛs'pe:] NT - ABBR *von* **Nettosozialprodukt**

N. T. ABBR *von* **Neues Testament** NT

Nu [nu:] M **im Nu** in no time

Nuance ['nyã:sə] F **-, -n** (= *kleiner Unterschied*) nuance; (= *Kleinigkeit*) shade; **um eine ~ zu laut** a shade too loud; **sie unterscheiden sich nur in ~n voneinander** they differ only very slightly

nuancieren [nyã'si:rən], *ptp* **nuanciert** VT to nuance

nüchtern ['nʏçtɐn] **1** ADJ (a) (*ohne Essen*) **der Patient muss ~ sein** the patient must have an empty stomach; **eine Medizin ~ einnehmen** to take a medicine on an empty stomach; **mit ~em/auf ~en Magen** with/on an empty stomach (b) (= *nicht betrunken*) sober; **wieder ~ werden** to sober up (c) (= *sachlich, vernünftig*) down-to-earth *no adv*, rational; *Zahlen, Tatsachen* bare, plain **2** ADV (= *sachlich*) unemotionally

Nüchternheit F -, NO PL (a) **überzeugen Sie sich von der ~ des Patienten** make sure that the patient's stomach is empty (b) (= *unbetrunkener Zustand*) soberness (c) (= *Sachlichkeit, Vernünftigkeit*) rationality

nuckeln ['nʊkln] VI (*inf*) (*Mensch*) to suck (*an +dat* at); (*Tier*) to suckle (*an +dat* from); **am Daumen ~** to suck one's thumb

Nudel ['nu:dl] F **-, -n** USU PL (a) (*als Beilage*) pasta *no pl*; (*als Suppeneinlage, chinesische*) noodle; (= *Fadennudel*) vermicelli *pl* (b) (*inf: Mensch*) (*dick*) dumpling (*inf*); (*komisch*) character

Nudist [nu'dɪst] M **-en, -en, Nudistin** [-'dɪstɪn] F **-, -nen** nudist

Nugat ['nu:gat] M *or* NT **-s, -s** nougat

nuklear [nukle'a:ɐ] **1** ADJ ATTR nuclear **2** ADV with nuclear weapons

Nuklear- [nukle'a:ɐ] IN CPDS nuclear; **Nuklearschlag** M nuclear strike

Nukleinsäure F nucleic acid

null [nʊl] NUM zero; (*inf:* = *kein*) zero (*inf*); (*Telec*) O (*Brit*), zero; (*Sport*) nil; (*Tennis*) love; **~ Komma eins** (nought) point one; **es ist ~ Uhr zehn** it's ten past twelve *or* midnight; **zwei Minuten ~ Sekunden** (*bei Zeitansagen*) two minutes precisely; (*bei Rennen*) two minutes dead; **~ Fehler** zero (*inf*) mistakes; **es steht ~ zu ~** there's no score; **das Spiel wurde ~ zu ~ beendet** the game was a goalless (*Brit*) *or* no-score draw; **eins zu ~** one-nil; **~ und nichtig** (*Jur*) null and void; **~ Ahnung haben** to have absolutely no idea; **Temperaturen unter ~** sub-zero temperatures; **gleich ~ sein** to be absolutely nil *or* zero; **in ~ Komma nichts** (*inf*) in less than no time; **von ~ auf hundert in 20 Sekunden** (*Aut*) ≈ from nought (*esp Brit*) *or* zero to sixty in 20 seconds; **bei ~ anfangen** to start from scratch; **die Stunde ~** the new starting point

Null [nʊl] F **-, -en** (a) (*Zahl*) nought, naught (*US*), zero; (= *Gefrierpunkt*) zero; **die ~** zero (b) (*inf: Mensch*) dead loss (*inf*)

nullachtfünfzehn [nʊlaxt'fʏnftse:n], **nullachtfuffzehn** [nʊlaxt'fʊftse:n] (*inf*) **1** ADJ INV run-of-the-mill (*inf*) **2** ADV in a run-of-the-mill way

Null-Bock- ['nʊl'bɔk] (*inf*) IN CPDS apathetic; **die ~-Generation** *generation characterized by complete apathy*

Null-: Nulldiät F starvation diet; **Nullkuponanleihe** F zero coupon bond; **Nullleiter** M (*Elec*) earth (wire) (*Brit*), ground

(wire) (*US*); **Nullmeridian** M Greenwich Meridian; **Nullnummer** F (*von Zeitung etc*) pilot; **Nullpunkt** M zero; **die Stimmung sank unter den ~** the atmosphere froze; **auf den ~ sinken, den ~ erreichen** to hit rock-bottom; **Nullrunde** F **in diesem Jahr gab es eine ~ für Beamte** there has been no pay increase this year for civil servants; **ich bin gegen eine ~ bei den Renten** I am in favour (*Brit*) *or* favor (*US*) of an increase in pensions; **Nullsummenspiel** NT zero-sum game; **Nulltarif** M (*für Verkehrsmittel*) free travel; (= *freier Eintritt*) free admission; **zum ~** (*hum*) free of charge

Numeri PL *von* **Numerus**

numerieren [nume'ri:rən], *ptp* **numeriert** VT *siehe* **nummerieren**

numerisch [nu'me:rɪʃ] **1** ADJ numeric(al) **2** ADV numerically; **~ überlegen/unterlegen sein** to be superior/inferior in number

Numerus ['nu:merʊs, 'nʊmerʊs] M **-, Numeri** [-ri] (*Gram*) number; **~ clausus** (*Univ*) restricted entry; **sozialer ~ clausus** *restricted access to higher education on basis of financial means*

*The **Numerus clausus**, or NC for short, controls admissions to certain over-subscribed university courses such as medicine, information technology and architecture. The main admission criterion is the mark obtained in the **Abitur**. Places are allocated by the **Zentralstelle für die Vergabe von Studienplätzen**, or ZVS* ▶ ABITUR

Nummer ['nʊmɐ] F **-, -n** (*Math, von Zeitschrift, in Varieté*) number; (= *Größe*) size; (*inf: Mensch*) character; (*inf:* = *Koitus*) screw (*sl*); (*mit Prostituierter*) trick (*inf*); **nur eine ~ unter vielen sein** (*fig*) to be a cog (in the machine); **er hat** *or* **schiebt eine ruhige ~** (*inf*) he's onto a cushy number (*inf*); **auf ~ Sicher gehen** (*inf*) to play (it) safe; **Gesprächsthema ~ eins** the number one talking point; **eine ~ abziehen** (*inf*) to put on an act; **eine ~ machen** *or* **schieben** (*inf*) to have it off; **dieses Geschäft ist eine ~/ein paar ~n zu groß für ihn** this business is out of/well out of his league

nummerieren [nʊme'ri:rən], *ptp* **nummeriert** VT to number

Nummerierung F -, -en numbering

Nummern-: Nummernblock M (*Comput: auf Tastatur*) numeric keypad; **Nummernkonto** NT (*Fin*) numbered account; **Nummernschild** NT (*Aut*) number plate (*Brit*), license plate (*US*); **Nummernspeicher** M (*Telec*) memory

nun [nu:n] ADV (a) (= *jetzt*) now; **~ endlich** (now) at last; **was ~?** what now?
(b) (= *danach*) then; **~ erst ging er** only then did he go **(c) ich bin ~ eben dumm** I'm just stupid, that's all; **er will ~ mal nicht** he simply doesn't want to; **~, wenns unbedingt sein muss** well, if I/you *etc* really must; **das ist ~ (ein)mal so** that's just the way things are; **~ ja** well yes; **~ gut** (well) all right; **~, meinetwegen** well, as far as I'm concerned; **~ gerade erst!**, **~ erst recht!** just for that (I'll do it)!; **~ taten wirs erst recht nicht** just because they/he/she *etc* said/did that, we didn't do it
(d) (*Folge*) now; **das hast du ~ davon!** (it) serves you right
(e) (*Aufforderung*) come on
(f) (*bei Fragen*) well; **~?** well?
(g) (*beschwichtigend*) come on; **~, ~!** (*warnend*) come on now; (*tröstend*) there, there

nur [nu:ɐ] ADV (a) (*einschränkend*) only; **alle, ~ ich nicht** everyone except me; **~ schade, dass ...** it's just a pity that ...; **~ dass ...** it's just that ..., only ...; **der Kranke isst fast ~ noch Obst** the sick man eats virtually nothing but fruit these days; **nicht ~ ..., sondern auch** not only ... but also; **alles, ~ das nicht!** anything but that!; **warum möchtest du das denn wissen? – ach, ~ so!** why do you want to know? – oh just because; **ich hab das ~ so gesagt** I was just talking; **warum hast du das gemacht? – ~ so** why did you do that? – I just did
(b) (*verstärkend*) just; **wie schnell er ~ redet** doesn't he speak fast!; **dass es ~ so krachte** making a terrible din *or* racket
(c) (*mit Fragepronomen*) -ever, on earth (*inf*); **was/wer/wie** *etc* **~?** but what/who/how *etc*?; **was hat er ~?** what on earth (*inf*) is the matter with him?; **wie kannst du ~ (so etwas sagen)?** how could you (say such a thing)?; **sie bekommt alles, was sie ~ will** she gets whatever she wants
(d) (*Wunsch, Bedingung*) **wenn er ~ (erst) käme** if only he would come; **es wird klappen, wenn er ~ nicht die Nerven verliert** it will be all right as long as he doesn't lose his nerve *inf*

(e) (*mit Negationen*) just, ... whatever you do
(f) (*Aufforderung*) just; **geh ~!** just go; **~ zu!** go on; **sieh ~** just look; **~ her damit!** (*inf*) let's have it; **sagen Sie es ~**, **Sie brauchen es ~ zu sagen** just say (the word); **er soll ~ lachen!** let him laugh
(g) **~ mehr** (*dial: esp Aus*) only ... left

Nürnberg ['nʏrnberk] NT **-s** Nuremberg; **jdm etw mit dem ~er Trichter beibringen** (*inf*) to drum sth into sb; **die ~er Prozesse** the Nuremberg (war) trials

nuscheln ['nʊʃln] VTI (*inf*) to mutter

Nuss [nʊs] F **-, ⁻e** ['nʏsə] **(a)** nut; **eine harte ~ zu knacken haben** (*fig*) to have a tough nut to crack **(b)** (*inf: Mensch*) jerk (*inf*); **eine taube ~** a dead loss (*inf*); **eine doofe ~** a stupid clown (*inf*)

Nuss-: Nussbaum M (*Baum*) walnut tree; (*Holz*) walnut; **Nussknacker** M nutcracker

Nüster ['nyːstɐ] F **-, -n** nostril

Nut [nuːt] F **-, -en** (*spec*), **Nute** ['nuːtə] F **-, -n** groove; (*zur Einfügung*) rabbet; (= *Keilnut*) keyway; **~ und Feder** tongue and groove; **~ und Zapfen** mortise and tenon

Nutte ['nʊtə] F **-, -n** (*inf*) tart (*inf*)

Nut- und Federbrett NT tongue and groove board

nutz [nʊts] ADJ (*S Ger, Aus*) = **nütze**

nutzbar ADJ *Rohstoffe, Gebäude, Wasserstraßen* us(e)able; *Boden* productive; *Bodenschätze* exploitable; **~e Fläche** (*in Gebäude*) us(e)able floor space; **landwirtschaftlich ~e Fläche** agriculturally productive land; **~ machen** to make us(e)able; *Sonnenenergie* to harness; *Sümpfe* to reclaim; *Bodenschätze* to exploit

nutzbringend ◼ ADJ profitable ◼ ADV profitably; **etw ~ anwenden** to use sth profitably

nütze ['nʏtsə] ADJ PRED **zu etw ~ sein** to be useful for sth; **zu nichts ~ sein** to be no use for anything

nutzen ['nʊtsn] ◼ VI to be of use, to be useful (*jdm zu etw* to sb for sth); **die Ermahnungen haben genutzt/nichts genutzt** the warnings had the desired effect/didn't do any good; **es nutzt nichts** it's no use; **alle Anstrengungen haben nichts genutzt** all our efforts were useless; **da nutzt alles nichts** there's nothing to be done; **das nutzt (mir/dir) nichts** that won't help (me/you); **das nutzt niemandem** that's of no use to anybody; **es nutzt wenig** it isn't much use
◼ VT to make use of, to use; *Gelegenheit* to take advantage of; *Bodenschätze, Energien* to use

Nutzen ['nʊtsn] M **-s, -** **(a)** use; (= *Nützlichkeit*) usefulness; **zum ~ der Öffentlichkeit** for the benefit of the public; **jdm von ~ sein** to be useful to sb **(b)** (= *Vorteil*) advantage, benefit; (= *Gewinn*) profit; **jdm ~ bringen** (*Vorteil*) to be of advantage to sb; (*Gewinn*) to bring sb profit; **von etw ~ haben** to gain by sth; **aus etw ~ ziehen** to reap the benefits of sth

nützen ['nʏtsn] VTI = **nutzen**

Nutzer ['nʊtsɐ] M **-s, -**, **Nutzerin** [-ərɪn] F **-, -nen** user

Nutz-: Nutzfahrzeug NT farm vehicle; military vehicle *etc*; (*Comm*) commercial vehicle; **Nutzfläche** F us(e)able floor space; **(landwirtschaftliche) ~** (*Agr*) (agriculturally) productive land; **Nutzholz** NT (utilizable) timber; **Nutzlast** F payload

nützlich ['nʏtslɪç] ADJ useful; **sich ~ machen** to make oneself useful

nutzlos ◼ ADJ **(a)** useless; (= *unergiebig, vergeblich*) futile *attr*, in vain *pred* **(b)** (= *unnötig*) needless ◼ ADV **(a)** (= *ohne Nutzen*) uselessly; **ich fühle mich ~** I feel useless **(b)** (= *unnötig*) futilely; **er hat seine Zeit ~ mit Spielen zugebracht** he wasted his time playing; **sein Leben ~ aufs Spiel setzen** to risk one's life needlessly

Nutzlosigkeit F **-**, NO PL uselessness; (= *Uneinträglichkeit, Vergeblichkeit*) futility

Nutznießer ['nʊtsniːsɐ] M **-s, -**, **Nutznießerin** [-ərɪn] F **-, -nen** beneficiary; (*Jur*) usufructuary

Nutzung ['nʊtsʊŋ] F **-, -en** (= *Gebrauch*) use; (= *das Ausnutzen*) exploitation; (*von Ressourcen, Technologie*) use; (*Jur: Ertrag*) benefit; **jdm etw zur ~ überlassen** to give sb the use of sth

NW ABBR *von* **Nordwesten** NW

Nylon® ['naɪlɔn] NT **-(s)**, NO PL nylon

Nymphchen ['nʏmfçən] NT **-s, -** nymphet

Nymphe ['nʏmfə] F **-, -n** (*Myth*) nymph; (*fig*) sylph; (*Zool*) nymph(a); **die ~n** (*Anat*) the nymphae *pl*

Nymphomanin [nʏmfo'maːnɪn] F **-, -nen** nymphomaniac

O, o [oː] NT **-, -** O, o

o INTERJ oh; **O Gott!** O God!

O ABBR *von* **Osten**

Oase [oˈaːzə] F **-, -n** oasis; *(fig)* haven

ob [ɔp] CONJ **(a)** *(indirekte Frage)* if, whether; **wir gehen spazieren, ob es regnet oder nicht** we're going for a walk whether it rains or not; **ob reich, ob arm** whether rich or poor; **ob er (wohl) morgen kommt?** I wonder if he'll come tomorrow?; **ob ich keine Angst gehabt hätte, fragte er** hadn't I been afraid, he asked; **er hat gefragt, ob dus geklaut hast – ob ich was?** *(inf)* he asked if you swiped it – if I what? *(inf)*; **ob Sie mir wohl mal helfen können?** could you possibly help me?
(b) *(verstärkend)* **und ob** *(inf)* you bet *(inf)*
(c) *(vergleichend)* **als ob** as if; **(so) tun als ob** *(inf)* to pretend; **tu nicht so als ob!** stop pretending!

OB [oːˈbeː] M **-s, -s** ABBR *von* **Oberbürgermeister**

o. B. ABBR *von* **ohne Befund**

Obacht [ˈoːbaxt] F **-,** NO PL *(esp S Ger)* **(aber) ~!** watch out!; **~ geben auf** (+*acc*) (= *aufmerken*) to pay attention to; (= *bewachen*) to keep an eye on; **du musst ~ geben, dass du keine Fehler machst** you must be careful not to make any mistakes

ÖBB ABBR *von* **Österreichische Bundesbahnen**

Obdach [ˈɔpdax] NT, NO PL *(geh)* shelter; **kein ~ haben** to be homeless; *(vorübergehend)* to have no shelter; **Menschen ohne ~** homeless people

obdachlos ADJ homeless; **~ werden** to be made homeless

Obdachlosenasyl NT, **Obdachlosenheim** NT hostel for the homeless

Obdachlose(r) [ˈɔpdaxloːzə] MF DECL AS ADJ homeless person; **die ~n** the homeless

Obdachlosigkeit F **-,** NO PL homelessness

Obduktion [ɔpdukˈtsioːn] F **-, -en** postmortem (examination)

obduzieren [ɔpduˈtsiːrən], *ptp* **obduziert** VT to carry out a postmortem on

O-Beine [ˈoː-] PL *(inf)* bow legs *pl*

o-beinig [ˈoː-], **O-beinig** ADJ bow-legged

Obelisk [obaˈlɪsk] M **-en, -en** obelisk

oben [ˈoːbn] ADV **(a)** (= *am oberen Ende*) at the top; (= *an der Oberfläche*) on the surface; *(im Hause)* upstairs; (= *in der Höhe*) up; **~ und unten (von etw) verwechseln** to get sth upside down; **wir möchten lieber ~ wohnen** we'd rather live high(er) up; **möchten Sie lieber ~ schlafen?** *(im oberen Bett)* would you like the top bunk?; **wir wohnen rechts ~** *or* **~ rechts** we live on the top floor to the right; **~ rechts** *or* **rechts ~ (in der Ecke)** in the top right-hand corner; **der ist ~ nicht ganz richtig** *(inf)* he's not quite right up top *(inf)*; **~ ohne gehen** *or* **tragen** *(inf)* to be topless; **ganz ~** right at the top; **hier/dort ~** up here/there; **die ganze Sache steht mir bis hier ~** *(inf)* I'm sick to death of the whole thing *(inf)*; **bis ~ (hin)** to the top; **hoch ~** high (up) above; **beim Festessen saß er weiter ~ an der Tafel** at the banquet he sat nearer the top of the table; **~ auf dem Berg/der Leiter/dem Dach** on top of the mountain/ladder/roof; **~ am Himmel** up in the sky; **im Himmel** up in heaven; **~ im Norden** up (in the) north; **~ herum** (a)round the top; *(von Frau)* up top; *(von Jacke)* (a)round the chest; **nach ~** up, upwards; *(im Hause)* upstairs; **der Fahrstuhl fährt nach ~** the lift *(Brit)* or elevator *(US)* is going up; **der Weg nach ~** *(fig)* the road to the top; **nach ~ zu** *or* **hin** towards *(Brit)* or toward *(US)* the top; **von ~ (her)** down; *(im Hause)* down(stairs); **ich komme gerade von ~** *(am Berg)* I've just come from the top; *(im Hause)* I've just been upstairs; **von ~ bis unten** from top to bottom; *(von Mensch)* from top to toe; **jdn von ~ bis unten mustern** to look sb up and down; **jdn von ~ herab behandeln** to be condescending to sb; **weiter ~** further up
(b) *(inf: = die Vorgesetzten)* **die da ~** the powers that be *(inf)*; **das wird ~ entschieden** that's decided higher up; **etw nach ~ (weiter)melden/weitergeben** to report sth/to pass sth on to a superior; **der Befehl kommt von ~** it's orders from above
(c) (= *vorher*) above; **siehe ~** see above; **~ erwähnt** *attr* above-

mentioned; **wie ~ erwähnt** as mentioned above; **der weiter ~ erwähnte Fall** the case referred to before *or* above

Oben-ohne- IN CPDS topless; **Oben-ohne-Bedienung** F topless waitress service

Ober [ˈoːbɐ] M **-s, -** (= *Kellner*) waiter; **Herr ~!** waiter!

ober- [ˈoːbɐ], **Ober-** IN CPDS *(Geog)* Upper; *(im Rang)* senior; *(inf: = besonders)* really; **Oberarm** M upper arm; **Oberaufsicht** F supervision; **die ~ haben** *or* **führen** to be in *or* have overall control *(über +acc* of); **unter (der) ~** (+*gen*) under the supervision (of); **Oberbefehl** M *(Mil)* supreme command; **Oberbegriff** M generic term; **Oberbürgermeister** M Lord Mayor; **Oberbürgermeisterin** F mayoress; **Oberdeck** NT upper deck

obere(r, s) [ˈoːbərə] ADJ ATTR *Ende, Stockwerke, (Schul)klassen* upper, top; *Flusslauf* upper; **die Oberen** *(inf)* the top brass *(inf)*; **die ~n Zehntausend** *(inf)* high society; *siehe* **oberste(r, s)**

Oberfläche F surface *(auch fig)*; *(Tech, Math)* surface area; *(Comput)* (user) interface; **an der ~ schwimmen** to float; **das Buch bleibt an der ~** *(fig)* the book doesn't go very deep

oberflächlich [-flɛçlɪç] **1** ADJ superficial; **~e Verletzung** surface wound; **bei ~er Betrachtung** at a quick glance; **er ist sehr ~ in seiner Arbeit** his work is very superficial; **nach ~er Schätzung** at a rough estimate
2 ADV superficially; **sie arbeitet ~** she doesn't do her work thoroughly; **etw ~ lesen** to skim through sth; **jdn (nur) ~ kennen** to know sb (only) slightly; **etw (nur) ~ kennen** to have (only) a superficial knowledge of sth; **sich ~ unterhalten** to have a superficial conversation; **~ leben** to lead a superficial life

Ober-: Obergeschoss NT upper floor; *(bei zwei Stockwerken)* top floor; **im zweiten ~** on the second *(Brit)* or third *(US)* floor; **Obergrenze** F upper limit; **oberhalb** [ˈoːbɐhalp] **1** PREP +GEN above **2** ADV above; **~ von Basel** above Basel; **weiter ~** further up; **Oberhand** F *(fig)* upper hand; **die ~ über jdn/etw gewinnen** to gain the upper hand over sb/sth, to get the better of sb/sth; **Oberhaupt** NT (= *Repräsentant*) head; (= *Anführer*) leader; **Oberhaus** NT *(Pol)* upper house; *(in GB)* House of Lords; **Oberhemd** NT shirt

Oberin F **-, -nen (a)** *(im Krankenhaus)* matron **(b)** *(Eccl)* Mother Superior

Ober-: oberirdisch ADJ, ADV above ground; **Oberkellner** M head waiter; **Oberkellnerin** F head waitress; **Oberkiefer** M upper jaw; **Oberkommando** NT (= *Oberbefehl*) Supreme Command; (= *Befehlsstab*) headquarters *pl*; **Oberkörper** M upper part of the body; **mit bloßem** *or* **freiem** *or* **nacktem ~** stripped to the waist; **den ~ freimachen** to strip to the waist; **Oberland** NT, NO PL *(Geog)* uplands *pl*; **das Berner ~** the Bernese Oberland; **Oberlandesgericht** NT *provincial high court and court of appeal*; **Oberlauf** M upper reaches *pl*; **Oberleder** NT (leather) uppers *pl*; **Oberleitung** F **(a)** (= *Führung*) direction; **die ~ eines Projekts haben** to be in overall charge of a project **(b)** *(Elec)* overhead cable; **Oberlippe** F upper lip; **Oberösterreich** NT Upper Austria; **Oberpriester** M high priest; **Oberpriesterin** F high priestess; **oberrheinisch** ADJ upper Rhine; **die Oberrheinische Tiefebene** the Upper Rhine Valley; **im Oberrheinischen** along *or* around the upper Rhine

Obers [ˈoːbɐs] NT **-,** NO PL *(Aus)* cream

Oberschenkel M thigh

Oberschenkel-: Oberschenkelbruch M broken thighbone; **Oberschenkelhals** M head of the thighbone; **Oberschenkelknochen** M thighbone, femur

Ober-: Oberschicht F top layer; *(Sociol)* upper strata (of society) *pl*; **oberschlau** *(inf)* **1** ADJ really clever **2** ADV really cleverly; **Oberschule** F (= *weiterführende Schule*) secondary school; **Oberschulrat** M, **Oberschulrätin** F school inspector; **Oberschwester** F senior nursing officer; **Oberseite** F top (side)

Oberst [ˈoːbɐst] M **-en, -e(n) (a)** *(Heer)* colonel **(b)** *(Luftwaffe)* group captain *(Brit)*, colonel *(US)*

Oberstaatsanwalt M, **Oberstaatsanwältin** F public prosecutor, procurator fiscal *(Scot)*, district attorney *(US)*

oberste(r, s) [ˈoːbəstə] ADJ **(a)** (= ganz oben) Stockwerk, Schicht uppermost, very top; **das Oberste zuunterst kehren** to turn everything upside down **(b)** Gebot, Gesetz, Prinzip supreme; Dienstgrad highest, most senior; **die ~n Kreise der Gesellschaft** the upper echelons of society; **Oberstes Gericht, Oberster Gerichtshof** supreme court; (in GB) High Court (of Justice); (in USA) Supreme Court

Ober-: Oberstufe F upper school; (Univ) advanced level; **Oberteil** NT or M upper part, top; **Obertrottel** M (inf) first-class idiot; **Obervolta** [oːbɐˈvɔlta] NT **-s** Upper Volta; **Oberwasser** NT (fig inf) **~ haben** to feel better; **sobald sein älterer Bruder dabei ist, hat er (wieder) ~** he feels much braver when his elder brother is around; **wieder ~ gewinnen** or **bekommen** to be in a better position; **Oberweite** F bust measurement; **sie hat ~ 94** ≈ she has a 38-inch bust; **die hat eine ganz schöne ~!** she's very well-endowed

obgleich [ɔpˈglaiç] CONJ although

Obhut [ˈɔphuːt] F **-**, NO PL (geh) (= Aufsicht) care; (= Verwahrung) keeping; **jdn/etw jds ~** (dat) anvertrauen to put sb/sth in sb's care; **jdn in ~ nehmen** to take care of sb; **unter jds ~** (dat) **sein** to be in sb's care

obige(r, s) [ˈoːbɪgə] ADJ ATTR above

Objekt [ɔpˈjɛkt] NT **-(e)s, -e** (auch Gram) object; (Comm: = Grundstück etc) property; (Phot) subject

objektiv [ɔpjɛkˈtiːf] **1** ADJ objective **2** ADV objectively; **~ Stellung nehmen** to take an objective stance; **~ gesehen** or **betrachtet ist das falsch** seen objectively this is wrong

Objektiv [ɔpjɛkˈtiːf] NT **-s, -e** [-və] (object) lens

objektivieren [ɔpjɛktiˈviːrən], ptp **objektiviert** VT Problem, Aussage to treat objectively

Objektivität [ɔpjɛktiviˈtɛːt] F **-**, NO PL objectivity; **sich um größte ~ bemühen** to try to be as objective as possible

Objekt-: Objektsatz M (Gram) object clause; **Objektschutz** M protection of property; **Objektträger** M slide

Oblate [oˈblaːtə] F **-, -n** wafer; (Eccl) host

obligat [obliˈgaːt] ADJ obligatory

Obligation [obligaˈtsioːn] F **-, -en** (auch Fin) obligation

obligatorisch [obligaˈtoːrɪʃ] ADJ obligatory; Fächer, Vorlesung compulsory; Qualifikationen necessary

Obligo [ˈoːbligo, ˈɔbligo] NT **-s, -s (a)** (Fin) guarantee; **ohne ~** without recourse **(b)** (= Verpflichtung) obligation

Oboe [oˈboːə] F **-, -n** oboe

Oboist [oboˈɪst] M **-en, -en**, **Oboistin** [-ˈɪstɪn] F **-, -nen** oboist

Obolus [ˈoːbolus] M **-, -se** contribution

Obrigkeit [ˈoːbrɪçkait] F **-, -en (a)** (als Begriff, Konzept) authority **(b)** (= Behörden) **die ~** the authorities pl

Observatorium [ɔpzɛrvaˈtoːriʊm] NT **-s, Observatorien** [-riən] observatory

observieren [ɔpzɛrˈviːrən], ptp **observiert** VT (form) to observe; **er ist schon einige Monate observiert worden** he has been under surveillance for several months

obsessiv [ɔpzɛˈsiːf] **1** ADJ obsessive **2** ADV obsessively

obskur [ɔpsˈkuːɐ] **1** ADJ (= fragwürdig, zweifelhaft) obscure; (= verdächtig) suspect **2** ADV obscurely; **~ aussehen/erscheinen** to look/seem obscure

obsolet [ɔpzoˈleːt] ADJ obsolete

Obst [oːpst] NT **-(e)s**, NO PL fruit

Obst-: Obstbau M, NO PL fruit-growing; **Obstbaum** M fruit tree; **Obstgarten** M orchard; **Obstkuchen** M fruit flan; (gedeckt) fruit tart

Obstler [ˈoːpstlɐ] M **-s, -** (dial) fruit schnapps

Obstruktion [ɔpstrʊkˈtsioːn] F **-, -en** obstruction; **~ betreiben** to obstruct, to block

Obst-: Obstsaft M fruit juice; **Obsttorte** F fruit flan; (gedeckt) fruit tart; **Obstwasser** NT, pl **-wässer** fruit schnapps

obszön [ɔpsˈtsøːn] **1** ADJ obscene **2** ADV obscenely; **~ klingen** to sound obscene

Obszönität [ɔpstsøniˈtɛːt] F **-, -en** obscenity

obwohl [ɔpˈvoːl] CONJ although

Ochs [ɔks] M **-en, -en**, **Ochse** [ˈɔksə] M **-n, -n (a)** ox; (junger Ochse) bullock; **~ am Spieß** roast ox; **er stand da wie der ~ vorm** or **am Berg** or **vorm (neuen) Scheunentor** (inf) he stood there like a cow at a five-barred gate (inf) **(b)** (inf: = Dummkopf) dope (inf)

Ochsenschwanzsuppe [ˈɔksn-] F oxtail soup

Öchsle [ˈœkslə] NT **-s, -** measure of alcohol content of drink according to its specific gravity

Ocker [ˈɔkɐ] M or NT **-s, -** ochre (Brit), ocher (US)

ockerbraun, ockergelb ADJ ochre (Brit), ocher (US)

öd [øːt] ADJ = **öde**

od. ABBR von **oder**

öde [ˈøːdə] ADJ **(a)** (= verlassen) Stadt, Strand deserted; (= unbewohnt) desolate; (= unbebaut) waste; **öd und leer** dreary and desolate **(b)** (fig: = fade) dull; Dasein dreary; (inf: = langweilig) grim (inf)

oder [ˈoːdɐ] CONJ or; **~ aber** or else; **~ auch** or even; **entweder ... ~** either ... or; **~ so** (am Satzende) or something; **~ so ähnlich** or something like that; **so wars doch, ~ (etwa) nicht?** that was what happened, wasn't it it?; **du kommst doch, ~?** you're coming, aren't you?; **der Mörder hat sein Opfer nie vorher gesehen, ~ doch?** the murderer had never seen his victim before, or had he?; **damit war der Fall erledigt, ~ doch nicht?** with that the case was closed, or perhaps not?; **~ soll ich lieber mitkommen?** maybe I should come along?; **lassen wir es so, ~?** let's leave it at that, OK?

Oder [ˈoːdɐ] F **-** Oder

Oder-Konto NT joint account, account which can be operated by any of the account holders independently

Ödipuskomplex [ˈøːdipus-] M Oedipus complex

OECD-Land [oːleːtseːˈdeː-] NT OECD member country

OEZ ABBR von **Osteuropäische Zeit**

Ofen [ˈoːfn] M **-s, ̈** [ˈøːfn] **(a)** (= Heizofen) heater; (= Kohleofen) stove; (= Heizungsofen) boiler; (= Kachelofen) tiled stove; **hinter dem ~ hocken** to be a stay-at-home; **jdn hinter dem ~ hervorlocken** to tempt sb; **jetzt ist der ~ aus** (inf) that's it (inf) **(b)** (= Herd, Backofen) oven **(c)** (Tech) furnace; (= Brennofen) kiln; (= Trockenofen) drying oven; (= Hochofen) blast furnace; (= Schmelzofen) smelting furnace; (= Müllverbrennungsofen) incinerator **(d)** (inf: = Motorrad) **ein heißer ~** a fast bike (inf)

Off [ɔf] NT **-**, NO PL (TV, Theat) offstage; **aus dem ~** offstage; **eine Stimme aus dem ~** a voice off

offen [ˈɔfn] **1** ADJ **(a)** open; Bein ulcerated; Flamme, Licht naked; Haare loose; Rechnung outstanding; **ein ~er Brief** an open letter; **er geht mit ~em Hemd** he is wearing an open-neck shirt; **der Laden hat bis 10 Uhr ~** the shop (esp Brit) or store is open until 10 o'clock; **die Teilnahme ist für alle ~** anyone can take part; **~er Wein** wine by the carafe/glass; **auf ~er Strecke** (Straße) on the open road; (Rail) between stations; **wir hielten auf ~er Strecke** we stopped in the middle of nowhere; **auf ~er Straße** in the middle of the street; (Landstraße) on the open road; **Beifall auf ~er Szene** spontaneous applause; **mit ~em Munde dastehen** (fig) to stand gaping; **Tag der ~en Tür** open day; **ein ~es Haus haben** or **führen** to keep open house; **überall ~e Türen finden** (fig) to find a warm welcome everywhere; **im ~es Wort mit jdm reden** to have a frank talk with sb; **Haus der ~en Tür** open house; **~e Handelsgesellschaft** general partnership **(b)** (= frei) Stelle vacant; **~e Stellen** vacancies **2** ADV openly; (= freimütig) candidly; (= deutlich) clearly; **die Karten ~ auf den Tisch legen** to lay one's cards on the table; **etw ~ aussprechen** to say sth out loud; **etw ~ einräumen** to be perfectly willing to admit sth; **~ gestanden** or **gesagt** quite honestly; **seine Meinung ~ sagen** to speak one's mind; **sag mir ganz ~ deine Meinung** tell me your honest opinion; **die Probleme treten ~ zutage** the problems can be clearly identified; **wir sollten den Konflikt ~ austragen** we should bring the matter out in the open; **die Haare ~ tragen** to wear one's hair loose or down; **Wein ~ verkaufen** to sell wine on draught (Brit) or draft (US); (glasweise) to sell wine by the glass

offenbar 1 ADJ obvious; **sein Zögern machte ~, dass ...** it showed from the way he hesitated that ...; **~ werden** to become obvious **2** ADV (= vermutlich) apparently; **er hat ~ den Zug verpasst** he must have missed the train; **da haben Sie sich ~ geirrt** you seem to have made a mistake

Offenbarung [ɔfnˈbaːrʊŋ] F **-, -en** revelation

Offenbarungseid M (Jur) oath of disclosure; **den ~ leisten** (lit) to swear an oath of disclosure; (fig) to admit defeat; **mit diesem Programm hat die Partei ihren ~ geleistet** with this programme (Brit) or program (US) the party has revealed its political bankruptcy

offen-: offen bleiben VI IRREG AUX SEIN to remain open; **alle offen gebliebenen Probleme** all remaining problems; **offen halten** VT IRREG to keep open

Offenheit F -, NO PL (*gegenüber* about) openness, candour (*Brit*), candor (*US*); **schonungslose ~** brutal frankness; **in aller** *or* **schöner ~** quite openly

offen-: offenkundig ■ ADJ obvious; *Beweise* clear ② ADV blatantly; **offen lassen** VT IRREG to leave open; **offen legen** VT to disclose; **Offenlegung** [-le:gʊŋ] F -, -en disclosure; **Offenmarktpolitik** F (*Fin*) free market policy; **offensichtlich** [ɔfn̩zɪçtlɪç, ɔfn̩ˈzɪçtlɪç] ■ ADJ obvious ② ADV obviously

offensiv ■ ADJ offensive ② ADV offensively; *verkaufen* aggressively; **es wurde ~ geworben** the advertising campaign was aggressive

Offensive F -, -n offensive; **in die ~ gehen** to take the offensive

offen stehen VI IRREG (*S Ger: auch aux sein*) (a) (*Tür, Fenster*) to be open; (*Knopf*) to be undone
(b) (*Comm: Rechnung, Betrag*) to be outstanding
(c) **jdm ~** (*fig: = zugänglich sein*) to be open to sb; **uns stehen zwei Möglichkeiten offen** there are two possibilities open to us; **dir stehen noch alle Möglichkeiten offen** you still have plenty of options; **die (ganze) Welt steht ihm offen** he has the (whole) world at his feet; **es steht ihr offen, sich uns anzuschließen** she's free to join us

öffentlich ■ ADJ public; **im ~en Leben stehen** to be in public life; **die ~e Meinung/Moral** public opinion/morality; **die ~e Ordnung** law and order; **~es Recht** (*Jur*) public law; **Anstalt/ Körperschaft des ~en Rechts** public institution/corporation; **~e Schule** state school, public school (*US*); **der ~e Dienst** the civil service ② ADV publicly; **sich ~ äußern** to voice one's opinion in public; **etw ~ bekannt machen** to make sth public

Öffentlichkeit F -, NO PL (a) (= *Zugänglichkeit*) **der Verteidiger bestand auf der ~ der Verhandlung** the defence (*Brit*) *or* defense (*US*) counsel insisted that the trial take place in public; **~ der Rechtsprechung** administration of justice in open court; **die ~ einer Versammlung herstellen** to make a meeting public
(b) (= *Allgemeinheit*) (general) public; **die ~ scheuen** to shun publicity; **in** *or* **vor aller ~** in public; **unter Ausschluss der ~** in secret *or* private; (*Jur*) in camera; **als er das erste Mal vor die ~ trat** when he made his first public appearance; **mit etw an** *or* **vor die ~ treten** *or* **gehen, etw vor die ~ bringen** to bring sth to public attention; **etw der ~ zugänglich machen** to open sth to the public; **im Licht der ~ stehen** to be in the public eye

Öffentlichkeits-: Öffentlichkeitsarbeit F public relations work; **öffentlichkeitswirksam** ■ ADJ **~ sein** to be good publicity ② ADV **wir müssen besonders ~ werben** we need particularly effective publicity

öffentlich-rechtlich [ˈœfntlɪçˈrɛçtlɪç] ADJ ATTR (under) public law; **~er Rundfunk/~es Fernsehen** ≈ public-service broadcasting

Offerte [ɔˈfɛːrtə] F -, -n (*Comm*) offer

offiziell [ɔfiˈtsiɛl] ■ ADJ official; *Einladung, Besuch auch* formal; **wie von ~er Seite verlautet** according to official sources; **auf dem Empfang ging es schrecklich ~ zu** the reception was extremely formal ② ADV officially

Offizier [ɔfiˈtsiːɐ] M -s, -e, **Offizierin** [-tsiːrɪn] F -, -nen officer

offline [ˈɔflaɪn] ADV (*Comput*) off line

Offlinebetrieb [ˈɔflaɪn-] M (*Comput*) off-line mode

öffnen [ˈœfnən] VT to open; **jdm den Blick für etw ~** to open sb's eyes to sth; **das Museum wird um 10 geöffnet** the museum opens at 10; **eine Datei ~** (*Comput*) to open a file ② VI to open; **es hat geklingelt, könnten Sie mal ~?** that was the doorbell, would you answer it?; **der Nachtportier öffnete mir** the night porter opened the door for me ③ VR (*Tür, Blume, Augen*) to open; (= *weiter werden*) to open out; **sich jdm ~** to confide in sb

Öffner [ˈœfnɐ] M -s, - opener

Öffnung [ˈœfnʊŋ] F -, -en (a) NO PL (= *das Öffnen*) opening; (*von Partei, Bewegung*) opening up; **~ der Leiche** postmortem
(b) (= *offene Stelle*) opening

Öffnungs-: Öffnungspolitik F policy of openness; **Öffnungszeiten** PL hours *pl* of business

Offsetdruck [ˈɔfset-] M, *pl* **-drucke** offset (printing)

oft [ɔft] ADV, *comp* **~er** [ˈœftə], (*rare*) *superl* **am ~esten** [ˈœftəstn̩] (= *häufig*) often; (= *in kurzen Abständen*) frequently; **schon so**

~, ~ genug often enough; **wie ~ warst du schon in Deutschland?** how often *or* how many times have you been to Germany?; **des Öfteren** quite often; **je öfter ...** the more often ...

öfter(s) [ˈœftɐ(s)] ADV (every) once in a while; (= *wiederholt*) from time to time; **öfter mal was Neues** (*inf*) variety is the spice of life (*prov*)

oh [oː] INTERJ = **o**

OHG [oːhaːˈɡeː] F -, -s ABBR *von* **offene Handelsgesellschaft**

ohne [ˈoːnə] ■ PREP +ACC without; **~ (die) Vororte hat die Stadt 100.000 Einwohner** excluding *or* not including the suburbs, the city has 100,000 inhabitants; **~ mich!** count me out!; **er ist nicht ~** (*inf*) he's not bad (*inf*); **die Sache ist (gar) nicht (so) ~** (*inf*) (= *interessant*) it's not bad; (= *schwierig*) it's not that easy (*inf*); **~ Mehrwertsteuer** excluding VAT; **ich hätte das ~ weiteres getan** I'd have done it without a second thought; **so etwas kann man ~ weiteres sagen** it's quite all right to say that; **so etwas kann man in feiner Gesellschaft nicht ~ weiteres sagen** you can't say that sort of thing in polite society; **ich würde ~ weiteres sagen, dass ...** I would not hesitate to say that ...; **er hat den Brief ~ weiteres unterschrieben** he signed the letter just like that; **das Darlehen ist ~ weiteres bewilligt worden** the loan was granted without any problem; **ihm können Sie ~ weiteres vertrauen** you can trust him implicitly; **das lässt sich ~ weiteres arrangieren** that can easily be arranged ② CONJ **~ zu zögern** without hesitating; **~ dass ich ihn darum gebeten hätte, kam er mich besuchen** he came to see me without me inviting him

ohne-: ohneeinander [ˈoːnəlaɪˈnandɐ] ADV without one another; **ohnegleichen** [ˈoːnəˈɡlaɪçn̩] ADJ INV unparalleled; **seine Frechheit ist ~** I've never known anybody have such a nerve; **er singt ~** as a singer he's in a class by himself; **ohnehin** [ˈoːnəˈhɪn] ADV anyway; **wir sind ~ zu viel Leute** there are too many of us already; **es ist ~ schon spät** it's late enough as it is

Ohnmacht [ˈoːnmaxt] F -, -en (a) (*Med*) faint; **in ~ fallen** to faint; **aus der ~ erwachen** to recover consciousness
(b) (= *Machtlosigkeit*) powerlessness

ohnmächtig [ˈoːnmɛçtɪç] ■ ADJ (a) (= *bewusstlos*) unconscious; **~ werden** to faint (b) (= *machtlos*) powerless; **~e Wut, ~er Zorn** impotent rage ② ADV (= *hilflos*) helplessly; **einer Sache** (*dat*) **~ gegenüberstehen** to be helpless *or* powerless in the face of sth; **~ zusehen** to look on helplessly

oho [oˈhoː] INTERJ oho; *siehe* **klein**

Ohr [oːɐ] NT -(e)s, -en ear; **seine ~en sind nicht mehr so gut** his hearing isn't too good any more; **auf einem ~ taub sein** to be deaf in one ear; **auf dem ~ bin ich taub** (*fig*) nothing doing (*inf*); **auf taube/offene ~en stoßen** to fall on deaf/ sympathetic ears; **bei jdm ein aufmerksames/geneigtes/ offenes ~ finden** to find sb a ready/willing/sympathetic listener; **ein offenes ~ für jdn/etw haben** to be ready to listen to sb/sth; **ein scharfes** *or* **feines ~ haben** to have a good ear; **die ~en steif halten** (*inf*) to keep one's chin up; **die ~en anlegen** to put its ears back; **mach** *or* **sperr die ~en auf!** (*inf*) clean out your ears (*inf*); **mir klingen die ~en** my ears are burning; **jdm die ~en voll jammern** (*inf*) to keep (going) on at sb; **ganz ~ sein** (*hum*) to be all ears; **sich aufs ~ legen** *or* **hauen** (*inf*) to turn in (*inf*); **sitzt er auf seinen ~en?** (*inf*) is he deaf or something?; **jdn bei den ~en nehmen, jdm die ~en lang ziehen** (*inf*) to tweak sb's ear(s); **diese Nachricht war nicht für fremde ~en bestimmt** this piece of news was not meant for other ears; **jdm eins** *or* **ein paar hinter die ~en geben** (*inf*) to give sb a smack on the ear; **ein paar** *or* **eins hinter die ~en kriegen** (*inf*) to get a smack on the ear; **jdm etw um die ~en hauen** (*inf*) *or* **schlagen** (*inf*) to hit sb over the head with sth; **schreib es dir hinter die ~en** (*inf*) has that sunk in? (*inf*); **noch nass** *or* **feucht** *or* **nicht trocken hinter den ~en sein** to be still wet behind the ears; **jdm etw ins ~ sagen** to whisper sth in sb's ear; **du hast wohl Dreck** *or* **Watte in den ~en!** (*inf*) are you deaf or something?; **ich habe seine Worte noch deutlich im ~** his words are still ringing in my ears; **jdm (mit etw) in den ~en liegen** to badger sb (about sth); **jdn übers ~ hauen** (*inf*) to take sb for a ride (*inf*); **bis über die** *or* **beide ~en verliebt sein** to be head over heels in love; **bis über die** *or* **beide ~en verschuldet sein** to be up to one's ears *or* eyes (*Brit*) in debt; **viel um die ~en haben** (*inf*) to have a lot on (one's plate) (*inf*); **es ist mir**

zu ~en gekommen it has come to my ears (*form*); **dein Wort in Gottes ~** God willing

Öhr [øːɐ] NT **-(e)s, -e** eye

Ohren-: **Ohrenarzt** M, **Ohrenärztin** F ear specialist; **ohrenbetäubend** ❶ ADJ (*fig*) deafening ❷ ADV **~ laut** deafeningly loud; **Ohrensausen** NT **-s**, NO PL (*Med*) buzzing in one's ears; **Ohrenschmalz** NT earwax; **Ohrenschmaus** M **das Konzert war ein richtiger ~** the concert was a real delight to hear; **moderne Musik ist oft kein ~** modern music is often far from easy on the ear; **Ohrenschmerzen** PL earache; **Ohrenschützer** PL earmuffs *pl*; **Ohrenstöpsel** M earplug; **Ohrenzeuge** M, **Ohrenzeugin** F earwitness

Ohrfeige [ˈoːɐfaɪɡə] F **-, -n** slap (*on or round* (*Brit*) the face); (*als Strafe*) smack on the ear; **jdm eine ~ geben** *or* **verabreichen** *or* **verpassen** (*inf*) to slap sb's face; **eine ~ bekommen** to get a slap round (*Brit*) *or* in (*US*) the face

ohrfeigen [ˈoːɐfaɪɡn̩] VT INSEP **jdn ~** to slap *or* hit sb; (*als Strafe*) to give sb a smack on the ear; **ich könnte mich selbst ~, dass ich das gemacht habe** I could kick myself for doing it

Ohr-: **Ohrläppchen** NT (ear)lobe; **Ohrmuschel** F (outer) ear

Ohropax® [ˈoːropaks, oːroˈpaks] NT **-,** - earplugs *pl*

Ohr-: **Ohrring** M earring; **Ohrstecker** M stud earring; **Ohrwurm** M (*Zool*) earwig; **der Schlager ist ein richtiger ~** (*inf*) that's a really catchy record (*inf*)

oje [oˈjeː], **ojemine** [oˈjeːmine] INTERJ oh dear

okay [oˈkeː] INTERJ okay

Okkupation [ɔkupaˈtsi̯oːn] F **-, -en** occupation

Öko [ˈøːko] M **-s, -s** (*inf*: = *Umweltschützer*) Green

Öko- IN CPDS eco-, ecological; **Öko-Audit** [-ˈaudɪt] M *or* NT **-s, -s** green *or* environmental audit; **Ökobauer** M **-n, -n**, **Ökobäuerin** F **-, -nen** (*inf*) ecologically-minded farmer; **Ökokrise** F ecological crisis; **Ökoladen** M wholefood shop

Ökologe [økoˈloːɡə] M **-n, -n**, **Ökologin** [-ˈloːɡɪn] F **-, -nen** ecologist

Ökologie [økoloˈɡiː] F **-**, NO PL ecology

ökologisch [økoˈloːɡɪʃ] ❶ ADJ ecological, environmental ❷ ADV ecologically; **anbauen, aufziehen** organically; **~ wirtschaftende Betriebe** companies saving on natural resources

Ökonometrie [økonomeˈtriː] F **-**, NO PL econometrics *sing*

Ökonomie [økonoˈmiː] F **-, -n** (a) NO PL (= *Wirtschaftlichkeit*) economy (b) (= *Wirtschaft*) economy (c) NO PL (= *Wirtschaftswissenschaft*) economics *sing*; **politische ~ studieren** to study political economy

ökonomisch [økoˈnoːmɪʃ] ❶ ADJ economic (a) (= *sparsam*) economic(al) ❷ ADV economically; **~ mit etw umgehen** to be sparing with sth; **etw ~ einsetzen** to use sth sparingly; **~ wirtschaften** to be economical

Öko-: **Ökopapier** NT recycled paper; **Ökopartei** F ecology party; **Ökosphäre** F ecosphere; **Ökosystem** NT ecosystem

Oktaeder [ɔktaˈeːdɐ] NT **-s,** - octahedron

Oktanzahl [ɔkˈtaːn-] F octane number

Oktave [ɔkˈtaːvə] F **-, -n** octave

Oktober [ɔkˈtoːbɐ] M **-(s),** - October; *siehe auch* **März**

Oktoberfest NT Munich beer festival

OKTOBERFEST

*The beer festival known as the **Oktoberfest** takes place annually in Munich from the middle of September until the first weekend in October. Beer tents representing Munich's breweries are set up on the **Wies'n**, a large festival site in the city. In the tents local people and tourists sit at long wooden tables and drink a particularly strong festival beer served only in one-litre mugs. Pretzels and various kinds of sausage are available, and people sing along with the brass bands that are often in attendance.*

ökumenisch [økuˈmeːnɪʃ] ❶ ADJ ecumenical ❷ ADV **~ denken** to be ecumenically minded; **~ getraut werden** *to be married by a priest and a minister together*

Öl [øːl] NT **-(e)s, -e** oil; **ätherische Öle** (*Chem*) essential oils; **in Öl malen** to paint in oils; **Öl auf die Wogen gießen** (*prov*) to pour oil on troubled waters; **Öl ins Feuer gießen** (*prov*) to add fuel to the fire (*prov*); **solche Schmeicheleien gehen ihm runter wie Öl** (*inf*) he laps up compliments like that

Öl-: **Ölabscheider** [-lapʃaɪdɐ] M **-s,** - oil separator; **Ölbaum** M olive tree; **Ölberg** M Mount of Olives; **Ölbild** NT oil painting

Oldie [ˈoːldi] M **-s, -s** (*inf*: = *Schlager*) (golden) oldie (*inf*)

Oldtimer [ˈoːldtaɪmɐ] M **-s,** - (a) (= *Auto*) veteran car; (*Rail*) historic train; (*Aviat*) veteran plane (b) (*Sport*) veteran

ölen [ˈøːlən] VT to oil; **wie geölt** (*inf*) like clockwork (*inf*)

Öl-: **Ölexportland** NT oil-exporting country; **Ölfarbe** F oil-based paint; (*Art*) oil (paint *or* colour (*Brit*) *or* color (*US*)); **mit ~n malen** to paint in oils; **Ölfeld** NT oil field; **Ölfilm** M film of oil; **Ölförderland** NT oil-producing country; **Ölgemälde** NT oil painting; **Ölheizung** F oil-fired central heating

ölig [ˈøːlɪç] ADJ oily; (*fig auch*) greasy

oliv [oˈliːf] ADJ PRED olive(-green); **ein Kleid in Oliv** an olive-green dress

Olive [oˈliːvə] F **-, -n** olive

Oliven-: **Olivenbaum** M olive tree; **olivenfarben** [-farbn̩], **olivenfarbig** ADJ ATTR olive-green; **Olivenhain** M olive grove; **Olivenöl** NT olive oil

olivgrün ADJ olive-green

Öl-: **Ölkanal** M oil duct; **Ölkanne** F, **Ölkännchen** NT oil can; **Ölkonzern** M oil company; **Ölkrise** F oil crisis; **Öllache** [-ˈlaxə, -ˈlaːxə] F patch of oil; **Öllieferant(in)** M(F) oil producer; **Ölmalerei** F oil painting; **Ölmessstab** M (*Aut*) dipstick; **Ölmühle** F oil mill; **Ölofen** M oil heater; **Ölpest** F oil pollution; **Ölplattform** F oil rig; **Ölquelle** F oil well; **Ölsardine** F sardine; **sechs Leute im Auto, da sitzt ihr ja wie die ~n** (*inf*) with six people in the car, you must be crammed in like sardines (*inf*); **Ölscheich** M (*pej*) oil sheik; **Ölschicht** F layer of oil; **Ölstand** M oil level; **Ölstandsanzeiger** M oil pressure gauge; **Ölteppich** M oil slick; **Ölverbrauch** M oil consumption; **Ölvorkommen** NT oil deposit; **Ölwanne** F (*Aut*) sump (*Brit*), oil pan (*US*); **Ölwechsel** M oil change; **den ~ machen** to change the oil

Olymp [oˈlʏmp] M **-s (a)** (*Berg*) Mount Olympus; **die Götter des ~** the gods of Mount Olympus **(b)** (*Theat*) **der ~** the gods

Olympiade [olʏmˈpi̯aːdə] F **-, -n** (= *Olympische Spiele*) Olympic Games *pl*

Olympia-: **Olympiasieger(in)** M(F) Olympic champion; **Olympiastadion** NT Olympic stadium; **Olympiateilnehmer(in)** M(F) participant in the Olympic Games

olympisch [oˈlʏmpɪʃ] ADJ **(a)** (= *den Olymp betreffend*) Olympian (*auch fig*) **(b)** (= *die Olympiade betreffend*) Olympic; **die Olympischen Spiele** the Olympic Games

Ölzeug NT oilskins *pl*

Oma [ˈoːma] F **-, -s** (*inf*) granny (*inf*); **die alte ~ da drüben** the old dear over there *inf*

Oman [oˈmaːn] NT **-s** Oman

omanisch [oˈmaːnɪʃ] ADJ Omani

Ombudsfrau [ˈɔmbʊts-] F ombudswoman

Ombudsmann [ˈɔmbʊts-] M, *pl* **-männer** ombudsman

Omelett [ɔm(ə)ˈlɛt] NT **-(e)s, -e** *or* **-s**, **Omelette** [ɔm(ə)ˈlɛt] F **-, -n** omelette

Omen [ˈoːmən] NT **-s,** - *or* **Omina** [ˈoːmina] omen

Omnibus [ˈɔmnibʊs] M bus; (*im Überlandverkehr*) bus, coach (*Brit*)

OmU ABBR *von* **Original(fassung) mit Untertiteln**

onanieren [onaˈniːrən] *ptp* **onaniert** VI to masturbate

Onkel [ˈɔŋkl̩] M **-s,** - (a) uncle; **~ Sam** (= *USA*) Uncle Sam **(b)** (*Kindersprache*: = *erwachsener Mann*) uncle; **sag dem guten Tag!** say hello to the nice man!; **der ~ Doktor** the nice doctor

Onkologe [ɔŋkoˈloːɡə] M **-n, -n**, **Onkologin** [-ˈloːɡɪn] F **-, -nen** oncologist

Onkologie [ɔŋkoloˈɡiː] F **-**, NO PL (*Med*) oncology

online [ˈɔnlaɪn] ADJ PRED (*Comput*) on line; **~ arbeiten** to work on line

Online- [ˈɔnlaɪn] IN CPDS (*Comput*) on-line; **Online-Anbieter** M on-line (service) provider; **Onlinebanking** [-bɛŋkɪŋ] NT **-s** on-line *or* Internet banking; **Onlinebetrieb** M on-line mode; **Onlinedienst** M on-line service; **Onlineservice** [-zɐˈviːs, -zœrvɪs] M on-line service

onomatopoetisch [onomatopoˈeːtɪʃ] (*form*) ❶ ADJ onomatopoeic ❷ ADV onomatopoeically

OP [oːˈpeː] M **-s, -s** ABBR *von* **Operationssaal**

Opa [ˈoːpa] M **-s, -s** (inf) grandpa (inf); (fig) old grandpa (inf)
opak [oˈpaːk] ADJ opaque
Opal [oˈpaːl] M **-s, -e** opal
OPEC [ˈoːpɛk] F **- die ~** OPEC; **~-Länder** OPEC countries pl
Oper [ˈoːpɐ] F **-, -n** opera; (Ensemble) Opera; **an die** or **zur ~ gehen** to become an opera singer
Operateur [opəraˈtøːɐ] M **-s, -e**, **Operateurin** [-ˈtøːrɪn] F **-, -nen** (Med) surgeon
Operation [opəraˈtsioːn] F **-, -en** operation
Operations-: Operationssaal M operating theatre (Brit) or room (US); **Operationsschwester** F theatre sister (Brit), operating room nurse (US)
operativ [opəraˈtiːf] ⬛ ADJ (Med) operative, surgical; (Mil, Econ) strategic, operational ⬛ ADV (a) (Med) surgically; **eine Geschwulst ~ entfernen** to remove a growth surgically (b) (Mil) strategically (c) (Econ) **das Unternehmen steckt ~ in den roten Zahlen** the company is operating in the red; **unser Betrieb ist auch in den USA ~ tätig** our company also has operations in the USA
Operator [ˈɔpəreːtɐ, opəraˈtoːɐ] M **-s, -s**, or (bei dt. Aussprache) **Operatoren** [-ˈtoːrən], **Operatorin** [-ˈtoːrɪn] F **-, -nen** (computer) operator
Operette [opəˈrɛtə] F **-, -n** operetta
operieren [opəˈriːrən], ptp **operiert** ⬛ VT Patienten, Krebs, Magen to operate on; **jdn am Magen ~** to operate on sb's stomach ⬛ VI to operate; **sich ~ lassen** to have an operation; **ambulant ~** to operate on an out-patient basis; **wir müssen in den Verhandlungen sehr vorsichtig ~** we must tread very carefully in the negotiations; **ein weltweit ~des Unternehmen** a worldwide business
Opern-: Opernglas NT opera glasses pl; **Opernhaus** NT opera house; **Opernsänger(in)** M(F) opera singer; **Operntext** M libretto
Opfer [ˈɔpfɐ] NT **-s, - (a)** (= ~gabe) sacrifice (auch fig); **zum** or **als ~ as** a sacrifice; **sie brachten ein ~ aus Wein und Wasser dar** they made an offering of water and wine; **jdm etw zum ~ bringen, jdm etw als ~ darbringen** to offer sth as a sacrifice to sb; **für ihre Kinder scheut sie keine ~** for her children she considers no sacrifice too great; **ein ~ bringen** to make a sacrifice (b) (= Geschädigte) victim; **jdm/einer Sache zum ~ fallen** to be (the) victim of sb/sth; **sie fiel seinem Charme zum ~** she fell victim to his charm; **ein ~ einer Sache** (gen) **werden** to fall victim to sth; **das Erdbeben forderte viele ~** the earthquake claimed many victims
opfern [ˈɔpfɐn] ⬛ VT (a) (= als Opfer darbringen) to sacrifice; Feldfrüchte etc to offer (up) (b) (fig: = aufgeben) to give up ⬛ VI to make a sacrifice ⬛ VR (a) **sich für etw ~** (= hingeben) to devote one's life to sth; **sich** or **sein Leben für jdn/etw ~** to sacrifice oneself or one's life for sb/sth (b) (inf: = sich bereit erklären) to be a martyr (inf); **wer opfert sich und isst die Reste auf?** (inf) who's going to be a martyr and eat up the leftovers? (inf)
Opium [ˈoːpiʊm] NT **-s**, NO PL opium
Opium-: Opiumhöhle F opium den; **Opiumraucher(in)** M(F) opium smoker
Opponent [ɔpoˈnɛnt] M **-en, -en**, **Opponentin** [-ˈnɛntɪn] F **-, -nen** opponent
opponieren [ɔpoˈniːrən], ptp **opponiert** VI to oppose (gegen jdn/etw sb/sth), to offer opposition (gegen to)
opportun [ɔpɔrˈtuːn] ADJ (geh) opportune
Opportunismus [ɔpɔrtuˈnɪsmʊs] M **-**, NO PL opportunism
Opportunist [ɔpɔrtuˈnɪst] M **-en, -en**, **Opportunistin** [-ˈnɪstɪn] F **-, -nen** opportunist
opportunistisch [ɔpɔrtuˈnɪstɪʃ] ⬛ ADJ opportunistic, opportunist ⬛ ADV opportunistically; **~ handeln** to act in an opportunist fashion
Opposition [ɔpoziˈtsioːn] F **-, -en** opposition (auch Pol, Astron); **etw aus (lauter) ~ tun** to do sth out of (sheer) contrariness; **in ~ zu etw stehen** to stand in opposition to sth; **in die ~ gehen** (Pol) to go into opposition
oppositionell [ɔpozitsioˈnɛl] ADJ opposition
OP-Schwester [oːˈpeː-] F ABBR von Operationsschwester

optieren [ɔpˈtiːrən], ptp **optiert** VI (form: auch Pol) **~ für** to opt for
Optik [ˈɔptɪk] F **-, -en (a)** NO PL (Phys) optics (b) (= Linsensystem) lens system; **du hast wohl einen Knick in der ~!** (inf) can't you see straight? (inf) (c) (= Sicht, Sehweise) point of view; **das ist eine Frage der ~** (fig) it depends on your point of view; **in** or **aus seiner ~** in his eyes (d) (= Mode, Aussehen) look; (= Schein) appearances pl; **das ist nur hier wegen der ~** it's just here because it looks good; **etw in die rechte ~ bringen** to put sth into the right perspective
Optiker [ˈɔptikɐ] M **-s, -**, **Optikerin** [-ərɪn] F **-, -nen** optician
optimal [ɔptiˈmaːl] ⬛ ADJ optimal, optimum attr ⬛ ADV perfectly; **etw ~ nutzen** to put sth to the best possible use
optimieren [ɔptiˈmiːrən], ptp **optimiert** VT to optimize
Optimierung F **-, -en** optimization
Optimismus [ɔptiˈmɪsmʊs] M **-**, NO PL optimism
Optimist [ɔptiˈmɪst] M **-en, -en**, **Optimistin** [-ˈmɪstɪn] F **-, -nen** optimist
optimistisch [ɔptiˈmɪstɪʃ] ⬛ ADJ optimistic ⬛ ADV optimistically; **etw ~ sehen** or **einschätzen** to be optimistic about sth
Option [ɔpˈtsioːn] F **-, -en (a)** (= Wahl) option (für in favour of) (b) (= Anrecht) option (auf +acc on)
Optionenbörse F options exchange or market
Options-: Optionsanleihe F optional bond; **Optionsfrist** F option period; **Optionspreis** M option price; **Optionsrecht** NT option right; **Optionsschein** M warrant
optisch [ˈɔptɪʃ] ⬛ ADJ visual; Gesetze, Instrumente optical; **~e Täuschung** optical illusion ⬛ ADV (a) (= vom Eindruck her) optically, visually; **dieser Bezirk unterscheidet sich schon rein ~ von ...** the very appearance of this area distinguishes it from ... (b) (= mit ~en Mitteln) optically
Orakel [oˈraːkl̩] NT **-s, -** oracle
oral [oˈraːl] ⬛ ADJ oral ⬛ ADV orally; **~ mit jdm verkehren** to have oral sex with sb
orange [oˈrãːʒə] ADJ INV orange; **ein ~** or **~ner Rock** an orange skirt
Orange¹ [oˈrãːʒə] F **-, -n** (Frucht) orange
Orange² NT **-, -** or (inf) **-s** orange
Orangeade [orãˈʒaːdə] F **-, -n** orangeade (esp Brit), orange juice
Orangeat [orãˈʒaːt] NT **-s, -e** candied (orange) peel
Orangenmarmelade [oˈrãːʒən-] F orange marmalade
Orang-Utan [ˈoːraŋ-ˈluːtan] M **-s, -s** orang-utan
ORB [oːˈleːbeː] M **-** ABBR von Ostdeutscher Rundfunk Brandenburg
Orchester [ɔrˈkɛstɐ, (old) ɔrˈçɛstɐ] NT **-s, -** orchestra
Orchestergraben M orchestra pit
Orchidee [ɔrçiˈdeː(ə)] F **-, -n** [-ˈdeːən] orchid
Orden [ˈɔrdn̩] M **-s, - (a)** (Gemeinschaft) (holy) order (b) (= Ehrenzeichen) decoration; (Mil) medal; **jdm einen ~ (für etw) verleihen** to decorate sb (for sth); **einen ~ bekommen** to be decorated
ordentlich [ˈɔrdntlɪç] ⬛ ADJ (a) Mensch, Zimmer tidy (b) (= ordnungsgemäß) **~es Gericht** court of law; **~es Mitglied** full member; **~er Professor** (full) professor (c) (= anständig) respectable (d) (inf: = tüchtig) **ein ~es Frühstück** a proper breakfast; **eine ~e Tracht Prügel** a proper hiding (inf) (e) (inf: = richtig) real (f) (= annehmbar, ganz gut) Preis, Leistung reasonable ⬛ ADV (a) (= geordnet) neatly; **hier geht es ~ zu** we do things by the book here; **bei ihr sieht es immer ~ aus** her house always looks neat and tidy (b) (= ordnungsgemäß) anmelden, abmelden, regeln correctly; studieren, lernen seriously; **~ arbeiten** to be a thorough and precise worker (c) (= anständig) sich kleiden, sich benehmen appropriately; hinlegen, aufhängen properly (d) (inf: = tüchtig) **~ essen** to eat (really) well; **nicht ~ essen** not to eat properly; **~ trinken** to drink a lot; **ihr habt sicher Hunger, greift ~ zu** you're sure to be hungry, dig in (inf); **alle haben ~ zugelangt** everyone got stuck in (inf); **jdn ~ verprügeln** to give sb a real beating; **sich ~ vertun** to be way off (inf); **es hat ~ geregnet** it really rained; **~ Geld verdienen**

to make a pile of money (*inf*)
(e) (= *annehmbar*) ganz *or* recht ~ quite well

Order [ˈɔːdɐ] F **-, -s** *or* **-n** (*also Comm*) order; **~ erhalten** *or* **bekommen, etw zu tun** to receive orders to do sth

ordern [ˈɔːdɐn] VT (*Comm*) to order

Ordinalzahl [ɔrdiˈnaːl-] F ordinal number

ordinär [ɔrdiˈnɛːɐ] **1** ADJ **(a)** (= *gemein, unfein*) vulgar **(b)** (= *alltäglich*) ordinary **2** ADV vulgarly; **~ aussehen** to look like a tart (*Brit inf*) *or* tramp (*US inf*)

> *Vorsicht!* **ordinär** *wird im Allgemeinen nicht mit dem englischen Wort* **ordinary** *übersetzt.*

Ordinate [ɔrdiˈnaːtə] F **-, -n** ordinate
Ordinatenachse F axis of ordinates
ordnen [ˈɔːdnən] VT *Gedanken, Ideen, Material, Sektor, Markt* to organize; *Sammlung* to sort out; *Akten, Finanzen, Hinterlassenschaft, Privatleben* to put in order; (= *sortieren*) to order; (*Comput*) to sort; **neu ~** *Struktur, Verhältnisse* to reorganize; *Kleidung, Haar* to straighten up; **das Steuerrecht wird neu geordnet** tax law is being reformed; *siehe auch* **geordnet**
Ordner¹ [ˈɔːdnɐ] M **-s, -** (= *Aktenordner*) file
Ordner² [ˈɔːdnɐ] M **-s, -**, **Ordnerin** [-ərɪn] F **-, -nen** steward
Ordnung [ˈɔːdnʊŋ] F **-, -en (a)** (= *das Ordnen*) ordering; **bei der ~ der Papiere** when putting the papers in order **(b)** (= *geordneter Zustand*) order; **~ halten** to keep things tidy; **~ schaffen, für ~ sorgen** to put things in order; **Sie müssen mehr für ~ in Ihrer Klasse sorgen** you'll have to keep more discipline in your class; **auf ~ halten** *or* **sehen** to be tidy; **etw in ~ halten** to keep sth in order; **etw in ~ bringen** (= *reparieren*) to fix sth; (= *herrichten*) to put sth in order; (= *bereinigen*) to clear sth up; **ich finde es (ganz) in ~, dass ...** I think it quite right that ...; **(das ist) in ~!** (*inf*) (that's) OK (*inf*) !; **geht in ~** (*inf*) sure (*inf*); **Ihre Bestellung geht in ~** we'll see to your order; **der ist in ~** (*inf*) he's OK (*inf*); **da ist etwas nicht in ~** there's something wrong there; **die Maschine ist (wieder) in ~** the machine's fixed *or* in order (again); **das kommt schon wieder in ~** (*inf*) that will soon sort itself out; **es ist alles in bester** *or* **schönster ~** everything's fine; **jetzt ist die/seine Welt wieder in ~** all is right with the/his world again; **jdn zur ~ rufen** to call sb to order; **jdn zur ~ anhalten** to tell sb to be tidy; **jdn zur ~ erziehen** to teach sb tidy habits; **~ muss sein!** we must have order!; **hier** *or* **bei uns herrscht ~** we like to have a little order around here; **hier herrscht ja eine schöne ~** (*iro*) this is a nice mess **(c)** (= *Gesetzmäßigkeit*) routine; **alles muss (bei ihm) seine ~ haben** (*räumlich*) he has to have everything in its proper place; (*zeitlich*) he does everything according to a fixed schedule; **das Kind braucht seine ~** the child needs a routine **(d)** (= *Vorschrift*) rules *pl*; **ich frage nur der ~ halber** I'm only asking as a matter of form **(e)** (= *Rang, auch Biol*) order; **Straße erster ~** first-class road; **das war ein Skandal erster ~** (*inf*) that was a scandal of first order

Ordnungs-: Ordnungsamt NT ≈ town clerk's office; **Ordnungsgeld** NT = Ordnungsstrafe; **ordnungsgemäß 1** ADJ according to the regulations, proper; **ich werde mich selbst um die ~e Abwicklung Ihrer Bestellung kümmern** I will see to it myself that your order is correctly dealt with **2** ADV correctly; **ordnungshalber** ADV as a matter of form; **Ordnungshüter(in)** M(F) (*hum*) custodian of the law (*hum*); **Ordnungsstrafe** F fine; **jdn mit einer ~ belegen** to fine sb; **ordnungswidrig 1** ADJ irregular; *Parken, Verhalten* (*im Straßenverkehr*) illegal **2** ADV *parken* illegally; **~ handeln** to go against rules; (*ungesetzlich*) to act illegally; **Ordnungswidrigkeit** F infringement; **Ordnungszahl** F **(a)** (*Math*) ordinal number **(b)** (*Phys*) atomic number

Organ [ɔrˈgaːn] NT **-s, -e (a)** (*Med, Biol*) organ **(b)** (*inf*: = *Stimme*) voice **(c)** (= *Behörde, Einrichtung, Zeitschrift*) organ; **die ausführenden ~e** the executors; **wir sind nur ausführendes ~** we are only responsible for implementing orders; **beratendes ~** advisory body

Organ-: Organbank F, *pl* **-banken** (*Med*) organ bank; **Organentnahme** F (*Med*) organ removal; **Organgesellschaft** F dependent company; **Organhandel** M trade in transplant organs

Organigramm [ɔrganiˈgram] NT **-s, -e** organization chart
Organisation [ɔrganizaˈtsi̯oːn] F **-, -en** organization
Organisator [ɔrganiˈzaːtoːɐ] M **-s, Organisatoren** [-ˈtoːrən], **Organisatorin** [-ˈtoːrɪn] F **-, -nen** organizer
organisatorisch [ɔrganizaˈtoːrɪʃ] **1** ADJ *Schwierigkeiten, Maßnahmen* organizational; **eine ~e Höchstleistung** a masterpiece of organization; **er ist ein ~es Talent** he has a talent for organization **2** ADV organizationally; **~ hatte einiges nicht geklappt** the organization left something to be desired; **dazu brauchen wir einen ~ versierten Menschen** we need someone with good organizational skills
organisch [ɔrˈgaːnɪʃ] **1** ADJ organic; *Erkrankung, Leiden* physical **2** ADV **(a)** (*Med*) organically, physically; *gesund* physically **(b)** (= *sinnvoll*) **sich ~ einfügen** to blend in (*in +acc* with, into)
organisieren [ɔrganiˈziːrən], *ptp* **organisiert 1** VTI (= *veranstalten, aufbauen*) to organize; **er kann ausgezeichnet ~** he's excellent at organizing; **etw neu ~** to reorganize sth **2** VR to organize
organisiert [ɔrganiˈziːɐt] ADJ organized; **die ~e Kriminalität** organized crime
Organismus [ɔrgaˈnɪsmʊs] M **-, Organismen** [-mən] organism
Organizer [ˈɔːgənaizɐ] M **-s -** (*Comput*) Personal Digital Assistant, PDA
Organ-: Organkredit M corporate loan; **Organspende** F organ donation; **Organspender(in)** M(F) donor (*of an organ*); **Organspenderausweis** M donor card; **Organverpflanzung** F transplant(ation) (*of organs*)
Orgasmus [ɔrˈgasmʊs] M **-, Orgasmen** [-mən] orgasm
Orgel [ˈɔrgl] F **-, -n** (*Mus*) organ
Orgelpfeife F organ pipe; **die Kinder standen da wie die ~n** (*hum*) the children were standing in order of height
Orgie [ˈɔrgi̯ə] F **-, -n** orgy; **~n feiern** (*lit*) to have orgies; (*fig*) to go wild; (*Phantasie etc*) to run riot
Orient [ˈoːriɛnt, oˈriɛnt] M **-s, NO PL (a)** (*liter*: = *der Osten*) Orient; **vom ~ zum Okzident** from east to west **(b)** (= *arabische Welt*) ≈ Middle East; **der Vordere ~** the Near East; **der Alte ~** the ancient Orient
Orientale [oriɛnˈtaːlə] M **-n, -n**, **Orientalin** [-ˈtaːlɪn] F **-, -nen** person from the Middle East
orientalisch [oriɛnˈtaːlɪʃ] ADJ Middle Eastern
Orientalistik [oriɛntaˈlɪstɪk] F **-, NO PL** ≈ Middle Eastern and oriental studies *pl*
orientieren [oriɛnˈtiːrən], *ptp* **orientiert 1** VT **(a)** (= *unterrichten*) **jdn ~** to put sb in the picture (*über +acc* about); **unsere Broschüre orientiert Sie über unsere Sonderangebote** our brochure gives you information about our special offers; **darüber ist er gut/falsch/nicht orientiert** he is well/wrongly/not informed on *or* about that **(b)** (= *ausrichten*: *lit, fig*) to orientate (*nach, auf +acc* to, towards); **am Text orientierte Illustrationen** text-related illustrations; **links orientiert sein** to tend to the left **2** VI (= *informieren*) to give information **3** VR **(a)** (= *sich unterrichten*) to inform oneself (*über +acc* about, on) **(b)** (= *sich zurechtfinden*) to orientate oneself (*an +dat, nach* by); **in einer fremden Stadt kann ich mich gar nicht ~** I just can't find my way around in a strange city **(c)** (= *sich einstellen*) to adapt (oneself) (*an +dat, auf +acc* to) **(d)** (= *sich ausrichten*) to be orientated (*nach, an +dat* towards); **sich nach Norden/links ~** to bear north/left
Orientierung F **-, -en (a)** (= *Unterrichtung*) information; **zu Ihrer ~** for your information **(b)** (= *das Zurechtfinden*) orientation; **die ~ verlieren** to lose one's bearings **(c)** (= *das Ausrichten*) orientation (*an +dat* according to, *auf +acc* towards) **(d)** (= *Ausrichtung*) orientation (*an +dat* towards, *auf +acc* to)
Orientierungssinn M, **NO PL** sense of direction
Orientteppich M Oriental carpet; (= *Brücke*) Oriental rug
Orig. ABBR *von* **Original**
original [origiˈnaːl] **1** ADJ original **2** ADV **~ Meißener Porzellan** genuine Meissen porcelain; **Jeans ~ aus (den) USA** original American jeans; **~ verpackt sein** to be in the original packaging
Original [origiˈnaːl] NT **-s, -e (a)** original **(b)** (*Mensch*) character
Originalfassung F original (version); **in ~** in the original; **in der englischen ~** in the original English

Originalität [originali'tɛːt] F -, NO PL **(a)** (= *Echtheit*) authenticity **(b)** (= *Urtümlichkeit*) originality

Original-: Originalton M, *pl* **-töne** original soundtrack; **(im) ~ Schröder** (*fig*) in Schröder's own words; **Originalverpackung** F original packaging

originell [origi'nɛl] **1** ADJ (= *selbstständig*) *Idee, Argumentation, Interpretation* original; (= *neu*) novel; (= *geistreich*) witty; **sie ist ein ~er Kopf** she's got an original mind **2** ADV originally; (= *witzig*) wittily; **das hat er sich** (*dat*) **sehr ~ ausgedacht** that's a very original idea of his

Orkan [ɔr'kaːn] M **-(e)s, -e (a)** hurricane **(b)** (*fig*) storm; **ein ~ der Entrüstung brach los** a storm of indignation broke out

Orkan-: orkanartig ADJ *Wind* gale-force; **Orkanstärke** F hurricane force

Ornament [ɔrna'mɛnt] NT **-(e)s, -e** decoration, ornament; **eine Vase mit figürlichen ~en** a vase decorated with figures; **etw mit ~en versehen** to put ornaments on/in sth

ornamental [ɔrnamɛn'taːl] **1** ADJ ornamental **2** ADV ornamentally

Ornithologe [ɔrnito'loːgə] M **-n, -n**, **Ornithologin** [-'loːgɪn] F **-, -nen** ornithologist

Ort¹ [ɔrt] M **-(e)s, -e (a)** (= *Platz, Stelle*) place; **~ des Treffens** meeting place; **~ der Handlung** (*Theat*) scene of the action; **an den ~ der Tat** *or* **des Verbrechens zurückkehren** to return to the scene of the crime; **am angegebenen ~** in the place quoted; **ohne ~ und Jahr** without indication of place and date of publication; **an ~ und Stelle** on the spot; **an ~ und Stelle ankommen** to arrive (at one's destination); **das ist höheren ~(e)s entschieden worden** (*humform*) the decision came from above; **höheren ~(e)s ist das bemerkt worden** (*humform*) it's been noticed in high places
(b) (= *Ortschaft*) place; (= *Dorf*) village; (= *Stadt*) town; **~e über 100.000 Einwohner** places with more than 100,000 inhabitants; **er ist im ganzen ~ bekannt** the whole village/town *etc* knows him; **am ~ in the place; das beste Hotel am ~** the best hotel in town; **wir haben keinen Arzt am ~** we have no resident doctor; **mitten im ~** in the centre (*Brit*) *or* center (*US*) (of the place/town); **der nächste ~** the next village/town *etc*; **von ~ zu ~** from place to place

Ort² M **-(e)s, ̈-er** [ˈœrtɐ] **(a)** position (*auch Astron*); (*Math*) locus **(b)** (*Min*) coal face; **vor ~** at the (coal) face; (*fig*) on the spot

Örtchen [ˈœrtçən] NT **-s, -** (= *kleiner Ort*) small place; **das (stille** *or* **gewisse) ~** (*inf*) the smallest room (*inf*)

orten [ˈɔrtn] VT to locate

orthodox [ɔrto'dɔks] **1** ADJ (*lit, fig*) orthodox **2** ADV **(a)** (*Rel*) **leben** to lead an orthodox life; **~ heiraten** to be married in the Eastern Orthodox Church; (*jüdisch*) to be married in an orthodox Jewish ceremony **(b)** (= *starr*) **denken** conventionally; **~ an etw** (*dat*) **festhalten** to stick rigidly to sth

Orthografie [ɔrtogra'fiː] F **-, -n** [-'fiːən] orthography

orthografisch [ɔrto'graːfɪʃ] **1** ADJ orthographic(al) **2** ADV orthographically; **ein ~ schwieriges Wort** a hard word to spell; **er schreibt nicht immer ~ richtig** his spelling is not always correct

Orthopäde [ɔrto'pɛːdə] M **-n, -n**, **Orthopädin** [-'pɛːdɪn] F **-, -nen** orthopaedic (*Brit*) *or* orthopedic (*US*) specialist

orthopädisch [ɔrto'pɛːdɪʃ] ADJ orthopaedic (*Brit*), orthopedic (*US*)

örtlich [ˈœrtlɪç] **1** ADJ local **2** ADV locally; **das ist ~ verschieden** it varies from place to place; **der Konflikt war ~ begrenzt** the conflict was limited to one area; **jdn/etw ~ betäuben** to give sb/sth a local anaesthetic (*Brit*) *or* anesthetic (*US*)

Örtlichkeit F **-, -en** locality; **sich mit der ~/den ~en vertraut machen** to get to know the place; **er ist mit den ~en gut vertraut** he knows his way about; **die ~en** (*euph*) the cloakroom (*euph*)

Ortsangabe F place of publication; (*bei Anschriften*) (name of) the) town; (= *Standortangabe*) (name of) location; (*Theat:* = *Szenenbeschreibung*) location; **ohne ~** no place of publication indicated

Ortschaft [ˈɔrtʃaft] F **-, -en** village; (*größer*) town; **geschlossene ~** built-up area

Orts-: ortsfremd ADJ non-local; **ich bin hier ~** I'm a stranger here; **ein Ortsfremder** a stranger; **Ortsgespräch** NT (*Telec*) local call; **Ortskrankenkasse** F **Allgemeine ~** compulsory

medical insurance scheme; **ortskundig** ADJ **nehmen Sie sich einen ~en Führer** get a guide who knows his way around; **ein Ortskundiger** somebody who knows his way around; **Ortsmitte** F centre (*Brit*), center (*US*); **Ortsname** M place name; **Ortsnetz** NT (*Telec*) local (telephone) exchange area; (*Elec*) local grid; **Ortsschild** NT place name sign; **Ortssinn** M sense of direction; **Ortstarif** M (*bei Briefen*) local postal charge; (*Telec*) charge for local phone call; **ortsüblich** ADJ local; **~e Mieten** standard local rents; **das ist hier ~** it is usual here; **Ortsverkehr** M local traffic; **selbst im ~ hat der Brief noch drei Tage gebraucht** even a local letter took three days; **Gebühren im ~** (*Telec*) charges for local (phone) calls; (*von Briefen*) local postage rates; **Ortszeit** F local time

Ortung [ˈɔrtʊŋ] F **-, -en** locating

O-Saft [ˈoː-] M (*inf*) orange juice, O-J (*US inf*)

Öse [ˈøːzə] F **-, -n** loop; (*an Kleidung*) eye; *siehe* **Haken**

Oslo [ˈɔslo] NT **-s** Oslo

osmanisch [ɔs'maːnɪʃ] ADJ Ottoman

Osmose [ɔs'moːzə] F **-, NO PL** osmosis

Ossi [ˈɔsi] M **-s, -s** (*inf*) East German

Ost-, ost- IN CPDS (*bei Ländern, Erdteilen*) (*als politische Einheit*) East; (*geografisch auch*) Eastern, the East of …; (*bei Städten, Inseln*) East; **Ostalgie** [ɔstal'giː] F *nostalgia for the former GDR*; **Ostblock** M, NO PL (*Hist*) Eastern bloc; **ostdeutsch** ADJ East German; **Ostdeutschland** NT (*Geog*) East(ern) Germany

Osten [ˈɔstn] M **-s**, NO PL **(a)** east; (*von Land*) East; **der Ferne ~** the Far East; **der Nahe** *or* **Mittlere ~** the Middle East; **aus dem ~, von ~ her** from the east; **gegen** *or* **gen** (*liter*) *or* **nach ~** east(wards), to the east; **nach ~ (hin)** to the east; **im ~ der Stadt/des Landes** in the east of the town/country; **weiter im ~** further east; **im ~ Frankreichs** in the east of France **(b)** (*Pol*) **der ~** (= *Ostdeutschland*) East Germany; (*dated:* = *Ostblock*) the East

Osteoporose [ɔsteopo'roːzə] F **-, NO PL** (*Med*) osteoporosis

Oster- [ˈoːstə-]: **Osterei** NT Easter egg; **Osterfest** NT Easter; **das jüdische ~** the Jewish Feast of the Passover; **Osterglocke** F daffodil; **Osterhase** M Easter bunny; **Osterinsel** F Easter Island

österlich [ˈøːstəlɪç] ADJ Easter

Oster- [ˈoːstə-]: **Ostermarsch** M Easter peace march; **Ostermontag** [ˈoːstəˈmoːntaːk] M Easter Monday

Ostern [ˈoːstən] NT **-, -** Easter; **frohe** *or* **fröhliche ~!** Happy Easter!; **an ~** on Easter Day; **zu** *or* **an ~** at Easter; (**zu** *or* **über) ~ fahren wir weg** we're going away at Easter; **das ist ein Gefühl wie Weihnachten und ~ (zusammen)** it's like having Christmas and Easter rolled into one

Österreich [ˈøːstəraɪç] NT **-s** Austria; **~-Ungarn** (*Hist*) Austria-Hungary

Österreicher [ˈøːstəraɪçə] M **-s, -**, **Österreicherin** [-ərɪn] F **-, -nen** Austrian; **er ist ~** he's (an) Austrian

österreichisch [ˈøːstəraɪçɪʃ] ADJ Austrian; **~-ungarisch** (*Hist*) Austro-Hungarian; **das Österreichische** (*Ling*) Austrian

Ostersonntag [ˈoːstəˈzɔntaːk] M Easter Sunday

Osterweiterung [ˈɔst-] F (*von Nato, EU*) eastward expansion

Osterwoche [ˈoːstə-] F Easter week

Ost- [ɔst-]: **Osteuropa** NT East(ern) Europe; **osteuropäisch** ADJ East(ern) European; **Ostfriese** [-'friːzə] M, **Ostfriesin** [-'friːzɪn] F East Frisian; **ostfriesisch** ADJ East Frisian; **Ostfriesische Inseln** PL East Frisian Islands *pl*; **Ostfriesland** NT [-'friːslant] **-s** East Frisia

östlich [ˈœstlɪç] **1** ADJ *Richtung, Winde* easterly; *Gebiete* eastern; **30° ~er Länge** 30° (longitude) east **2** ADV **~ von Hamburg/des Rheins** (to the) east of Hamburg/of the Rhine **3** PREP +GEN (to the) east of

Ostpreuße M, **Ostpreußin** F East Prussian

Ostpreußen NT East Prussia

ostpreußisch ADJ East Prussian

Östrogen [œstro'ge:n] NT **-s, -e** oestrogen (*Brit*), estrogen (*US*)

Ost- [ɔst-]: **Ostsee** ['ɔstze:] F **die ~** the Baltic (Sea); **Ostverträge** PL (*Pol*) *political, social and economic agreements made between West Germany and some Eastern bloc countries in the early 1970s*; **ostwärts** [-vɛrts] ADV eastwards; **Ost-West-Achse** F East-West link; **Ostwind** M east wind

OSZE [o:ɛstset'le:] F ABBR *von* **Organisation für Sicherheit und Zusammenarbeit in Europa** OSCE

Oszillograf [ɔstsɪlo'gra:f] M **-en, -en** oscillograph

O-Ton [o:-] M, *pl* **-Töne** ABBR *von* **Originalton**

Otter[1] [ɔte] M **-s, -** otter

Otter[2] F **-, -n** viper

ÖTV [ø:te:'fau] F - ABBR *von* **Gewerkschaft Öffentliche Dienste, Transport und Verkehr** ≈ TGWU (*Brit*), ≈ TWU (*US*)

out [aut] ADJ PRED *Mode etc* out

outen ['autn] (*inf*) **1** VT (*als Homosexuellen*) to out (*inf*); (*als Trinker, Spitzel etc*) to expose **2** VR (*als Homosexueller*) to come out (*inf*); **er outete sich als Schwuler** he came out (*inf*)

Outfit ['autfɪt] NT **-(s), -s** outfit

Outing ['autɪŋ] NT **-s** (*inf: als Homosexueller*) outing (*inf*); **er hat Angst vor dem ~** (*geoutet zu werden*) he's afraid of being outed (*inf*); (*sich zu outen*) he's afraid of coming out (*inf*)

Output ['autput] M *OR* NT **-s, -s** (*Comput, Ind*) output

Outsourcing ['autsɔ:rsɪŋ] NT **-s**, NO PL outsourcing

Ouvertüre [uver'ty:rə] F **-, -n** overture

oval [o'va:l] ADJ oval

Ovation [ova'tsio:n] F **-, -en** ovation (*für jdn/etw* for sb/sth); **stehende ~en** standing ovations

Overall ['o:vərɔ:l] M **-s, -s** overalls *pl*

Overhead- ['o:vehed-]: **Overheadfolie** F transparency; **Overheadprojektor** M overhead projector

Overkill ['o:vekɪl] M **-(s)** overkill

Ovolacto-Vegetabile(r) [ovo'laktovegeta'bi:lə] MF DECL AS ADJ ovo-lacto-vegetarian

ÖVP [ø:fau'pe:] F - ABBR *von* **Österreichische Volkspartei**

Ovulation [ovula'tsio:n] F **-, -en** ovulation

Oxid [ɔ'ksi:t] NT **-(e)s, -e**, **Oxyd** [ɔ'ksy:t] NT **-(e)s, -e** [-də] oxide

Oxidation [ɔksida'tsio:n] F **-, -en**, **Oxydation** [ɔksyda'tsio:n] F **-, -en** oxidation

oxidieren [ɔksi'di:rən], *ptp* **oxidiert**, **oxydieren** [ɔksy'di:rən], *ptp* **oxydiert** VTI (*vi: aux sein or haben*) to oxidize

Ozean ['o:tsea:n, otse'a:n] M **-s, -e** ocean

ozeanisch [otse'a:nɪʃ] ADJ *Flora, Klima* oceanic; *Sprachen, Kunst* Oceanic

Ozeanografie [otseanogra'fi:] F **-**, NO PL oceanography

Ozelot ['o:tselɔt, 'ɔtselɔt] M **-s, -e** ocelot

Ozon [o'tso:n] NT or (INF) M **-s**, NO PL ozone

Ozon-, ozon- IN CPDS ozone; **Ozonalarm** M ozone warning; **Ozonhülle** F ozone layer; **Ozonloch** NT hole in the ozone layer; **Ozonschicht** F ozone layer; **Ozonschild** M, NO PL ozone shield; **Ozonwert** M ozone level

Pp

P, p [pe:] NT **-,** - P, p

paar [paːɐ] ADJ INV **ein ~** a few; (= *zwei oder drei auch*) a couple of; **ein ~ Mal(e)** a few times; (= *zwei- oder dreimal auch*) a couple of times; **schreiben Sie mir ein ~ Zeilen** drop me a line; **du kriegst ein ~!** (*inf*) I'll land you one! (*Brit inf*), I'll kick your butt (*US inf*)

Paar [paːɐ] NT **-s, -e** pair; (= *Mann und Frau auch*) couple; **ein ~ Schuhe** a pair of shoes; **ein ~ Würstchen** two sausages; **ein ungleiches ~** an odd pair; (*Menschen auch*) an odd couple; **das sind zwei ~ Stiefel** *or* **Schuhe** (*fig*) they are two completely different things

paaren [ˈpaːrən] VR (*Tiere*) to mate; (*Chem*) to be paired; (*fig*) to be combined

Paarhufer [-huːfɐ] M (*Zool*) cloven-hoofed animal

paarig [ˈpaːrɪç] ADJ in pairs; **~e Blätter** paired leaves

Paarlauf M, **Paarlaufen** NT pairs *pl*

paarmal [ˈpaːɐmaːl] ADV *siehe* **paar**

Paarung [ˈpaːrʊŋ] F **-, -en (a)** (*Sport*) (*fig liter*) combination; (*Sport*: = *Gegnerschaft*) match **(b)** (= *Kopulation*) mating

paarweise ADV in pairs

Pacht [paxt] F **-, -en** lease; (*Entgelt*) rent; **etw in** *or* **zur ~ haben** to have sth on lease

pachten [ˈpaxtn] VT to lease; **du hast das Sofa doch nicht für dich gepachtet** (*inf*) don't hog the sofa (*inf*); **er tat so, als hätte er die Weisheit für sich (allein) gepachtet** (*inf*) he behaved as though he was the only clever person around

Pächter [ˈpɛçtɐ] M **-s, -**, **Pächterin** [-ərɪn] F **-, -nen** tenant, leaseholder

Pack¹ [pak] M **-(e)s, -e** *or* **⸚e** [ˈpɛkə] (*von Zeitungen, Büchern, Wäsche*) stack; (*zusammengeschnürt*) bundle

Pack² NT **-s**, NO PL (*pej*) rabble *pl* (*pej*)

Päckchen [ˈpɛkçən] NT **-s, -** package; (*Post*) small packet; (= *Packung*) packet, pack; **ein ~ Zigaretten** a packet *or* pack (*esp US*) of cigarettes; **ein ~ Spielkarten** a pack of (playing) cards; **jeder hat sein ~ zu tragen** (*fig inf*) we all have our cross to bear

Packeis NT pack ice

packen [ˈpakn] **1** VT **(a)** *Koffer* to pack; *Paket* to make up; (= *verstauen*) to stow (away); **Sachen in ein Paket ~** to make things up into a parcel; **etw ins Paket ~** to pack sth into the parcel; **jdn ins Bett ~** (*inf*) to tuck sb up (in bed) **(b)** (= *fassen*) to grab (hold of); (*Gefühle*) to seize; **von der Leidenschaft gepackt** in the grip of passion; **jdn bei der Ehre ~** to appeal to sb's sense of honour (*Brit*) *or* honor (*US*); **den hat es aber ganz schön gepackt** (*inf*) he's got it bad (*inf*) **(c)** (*fig*: = *mitreißen*) to grip **(d)** (*inf*: = *schaffen*) to manage; **hast du die Prüfung gepackt?** did you (manage to) get through the exam?; **du packst das schon** (*inf*) you'll manage it OK **2** VI **(a)** (= *den Koffer ~*) to pack **(b)** (*fig*: = *mitreißen*) to thrill **(c)** (*Comput*: = *komprimieren*) to compress **3** VR (*inf*: = *abhauen*) to clear out (*inf*)

Packen [ˈpakn] M **-s, -** heap, stack; (*zusammengeschnürt*) bundle

Pack-: Packesel M packmule; (*fig*) packhorse; **Packmaterial** NT packing material; **Packpapier** NT brown paper; **Packraum** M packing room; **Packtasche** F saddlebag; **Packtier** NT pack animal

Packung [ˈpakʊŋ] F **-, -en (a)** (= *Schachtel*) packet; (*von Pralinen*) box; **eine ~ Zigaretten** a packet *or* pack (*esp US*) of cigarettes **(b)** (*Med*) compress; (*Kosmetik*) face pack

Packungsbeilage F (*bei Medikamenten*) enclosed instructions *pl* for use

Pädagoge [pɛdaˈgoːgə] M **-n, -n**, **Pädagogin** [-ˈgoːgɪn] F **-, -nen** educationalist

Pädagogik [pɛdaˈgoːgɪk] F **-**, NO PL educational theory

pädagogisch [pɛdaˈgoːgɪʃ] **1** ADJ educational; **~e Hochschule** college of education; **seine ~en Fähigkeiten** his teaching ability; **das ist nicht sehr ~** that's not a very educationally sound thing to do **2** ADV educationally; **~ falsch** wrong from an educational point of view; **das Spielzeug ist ~ wertvoll** it is an educational toy

Paddel [ˈpadl] NT **-s, -** paddle

Paddelboot NT canoe

paddeln [ˈpadln] VI AUX SEIN *or* HABEN to paddle; (*als Sport*) to canoe; (= *schwimmen*) to dog-paddle

Paddler [ˈpadlɐ] M **-s, -**, **Paddlerin** [-ərɪn] F **-, -nen** canoeist

Pädiatrie [pɛdiaˈtriː] F **-**, NO PL paediatrics *sing* (*Brit*), pediatrics *sing* (*US*)

pädiatrisch [pɛˈdiaːtrɪʃ] ADJ paediatric (*Brit*), pediatric (*US*)

Pädophile(r) [pɛdoˈfiːlə] MF DECL AS ADJ paedophile (*Brit*), pedophile (*US*)

paffen [ˈpafn] (*inf*) **1** VI **(a)** (= *heftig rauchen*) to puff away **(b)** (= *nicht inhalieren*) to puff; **du paffst ja bloß!** you're just puffing at it! **2** VT to puff (away) at

Page [ˈpaːʒə] M **-n, -n** (*Hist*) page; (= *Hotelpage*) bellboy, bellhop (*US*)

Pagenkopf M page-boy (hairstyle *or* haircut)

Pager [ˈpeːdʒɐ] M **-s, -** (*Telec*) pager

Paillette [paiˈjɛtə] F **-, -n** sequin

Paket [paˈkeːt] NT **-s, -e** (= *Bündel*) pile; (*zusammengeschnürt*) bundle; (= *Packung*) packet; (*Post*) parcel; (*fig*: *von Angeboten, Gesetzesvorschlägen*) package; (= *Aktienpaket*) dossier; (*Comput*) package

Paket-: Paketbombe F parcel bomb; **Paketkarte** F dispatch form; **Paketpost** F parcel post; **Paketschalter** M parcels counter

Pakistan [ˈpaːkɪstaːn] NT **-s** Pakistan

Pakistaner [pakɪsˈtaːnɐ] M **-s, -**, **Pakistanerin** [-ərɪn] F **-, -nen**, **Pakistani** [pakɪsˈtaːni] M **-(s), -(s)** *or* f **-, -s** Pakistani

pakistanisch [pakɪsˈtaːnɪʃ] ADJ Pakistani

Pakt [pakt] M **-(e)s, -e** pact; **einen ~ (ab)schließen (mit)** to make a pact (with); **einem ~ beitreten** to enter into an agreement

Paläo-, paläo- [palɛo] PREF palaeo- (*Brit*), paleo- (*US*)

Palast [paˈlast] M **-(e)s, Paläste** [paˈlɛstə] (*lit, fig*) palace

Palästina [palɛsˈtiːna] NT **-s** Palestine

Palästinenser [palɛstiˈnɛnzɐ] M **-s, -**, **Palästinenserin** [-ərɪn] F **-, -nen** Palestinian

Palästinenser-: Palästinenserstaat M Palestinian state; **Palästinensertuch** NT, *pl* **-tücher** keffiyeh (*esp Brit*), kaffiyeh

palästinensisch [palɛstiˈnɛnzɪʃ], **palästinisch** [palɛˈstiːnɪʃ] ADJ Palestinian

palatal [palaˈtaːl] ADJ palatal

Palatschinke [palaˈtʃɪŋkə] F **-, -n** (*Aus*) stuffed pancake

Palaver [paˈlaːvɐ] NT **-s, -** (*lit, fig inf*) palaver (*inf*)

Palette [paˈlɛtə] F **-, -n (a)** (*Malerei*) palette; (*fig*) range **(b)** (= *Stapelplatte*) pallet

paletti [paˈlɛti] ADV (*inf*) OK (*inf*)

Palisander M **-s, -**, **Palisanderholz** NT jacaranda

Palme [ˈpalmə] F **-, -n** palm; **jdn auf die ~ bringen** (*inf*) to make sb see red (*inf*); **unter ~n** under (the) palm trees

Palm-: Palmkätzchen NT pussy willow; **Palmlilie** F yucca

Palm-PC [ˈpaːm-] M palmtop

Palmsonntag M Palm Sunday

Palmtop [ˈpaːmtɔp] M **-s, -s** palmtop

Pampa [ˈpampa] F **-, -s** pampas *pl*

Pampasgras [ˈpampas-] NT pampas grass

Pampe [ˈpampə] F **-**, NO PL (*pej*) mush (*inf*)

Pampelmuse [pampl̩ˈmuːzə] F **-, -n** grapefruit

Pampers® [ˈpɛmpɐs] PL (disposable) nappies *pl* (*Brit*) *or* diapers *pl* (*US*)

pampig [ˈpampɪç] (*inf*) **1** ADJ **(a)** (= *breiig*) gooey (*inf*); *Kartoffeln* soggy **(b)** (= *frech*) stroppy (*Brit inf*), bad-tempered **2** ADV (= *frech*) **jdm ~ antworten** to talk back to sb; **jdm ~ kommen** to be stroppy (*Brit inf*) *or* bad-tempered with sb

pan- [pan] PREF pan-; **~afrikanisch** pan-African; **~amerikanisch** pan-American

Panama [ˈpanama, ˈpaˌnama] NT **-s, -s** Panama

Panamakanal M, NO PL Panama Canal

panaschieren [pana'ʃiːrən], *ptp* **panaschiert** VI (*Pol*) to split one's ticket

Panda ['panda] M **-s, -s** panda

Paneel [pa'neːl] NT **-s, -e** (*form*) (*einzeln*) panel; (= *Täfelung*) panelling (*Brit*), paneling (*US*)

Panflöte ['paːn-] F panpipes *pl*, Pan's pipes *pl*

päng [pɛŋ] INTERJ bang

panieren [pa'niːrən], *ptp* **paniert** VT to bread

Paniermehl NT breadcrumbs *pl*

Panik ['paːnɪk] F **-, -en** panic; **(eine) ~ brach aus** *or* **breitete sich aus** panic broke out *or* spread; **in ~ ausbrechen** *or* **geraten** to panic; **jdn in ~ versetzen** to throw sb into a state of panic; **von ~ ergriffen** panic-stricken; **nur keine ~!** don't panic!

Panik-: **Panikkauf** M (*Comm*) panic buying; **Panikmache** F (*inf*) panicmongering (*Brit*), inciting panic; **Panikstimmung** F state of panic

panisch ['paːnɪʃ] **1** ADJ NO PRED panic-stricken; **~e Angst** terror; **sie hat ~e Angst vor Schlangen** she's terrified of snakes; **er hatte eine ~e Angst zu ertrinken** he was terrified of drowning; **~er Schrecken** panic **2** ADV in panic, frantically; **~ reagieren** to panic; **sich ~ fürchten (vor)** to be terrified (by)

Panne ['panə] F **-, -n (a)** (= *technische Störung*) hitch (*inf*), breakdown; (= *Reifenpanne*) puncture, flat (tyre (*Brit*) *or* tire (*US*)); **ich hatte eine ~ mit dem Fahrrad, mein Fahrrad hatte eine ~** I had some trouble with my bike; (*Reifenpanne*) I had a puncture flat; **ich hatte eine ~ mit dem Auto, mein Auto hatte eine ~** my car broke down; **mit der neuen Maschine passieren dauernd ~n** the new machine keeps breaking down
(b) (*fig inf*) slip (*bei etw* with sth); **mit jdm/etw eine ~ erleben** to have (a bit of) trouble with sb/sth; **uns ist eine ~ passiert** we've slipped up; **da ist eine ~ passiert mit dem Brief** something has gone wrong with the letter

Pannen-: **Pannendienst** M, **Pannenhilfe** F breakdown service; **Pannenkoffer** M emergency toolkit; **Pannenkurs** M car maintenance course

Panorama [pano'raːma] NT **-s, Panoramen** [-mən] panorama

panschen ['panʃn] **1** VT to adulterate; (= *verdünnen*) to water down **2** VI (*inf*) to splash (about)

Panscher ['panʃɐ] M **-s, -, Panscherin** [-ərɪn] F **-, -nen** (*pej inf*) adulterator

Panscherei [panʃə'raɪ] F **-, -en (a)** (= *Vermischen*) adulteration; (*mit Wasser*) watering down **(b)** (*inf.* = *Herumspritzen*) splashing (about)

Pansen ['panzn] M **-s, -** (*Zool*) rumen

Panter ['pantɐ] M **-s, -** = **Panther**

Pantheismus [pante'ɪsmʊs] M **-, NO PL** pantheism

Panther ['pantɐ] M **-s, -** panther

Pantoffel [pan'tɔfl] M **-s, -n** slipper; **unterm ~ stehen** (*inf*) to be henpecked (*inf*); **unter den ~ kommen** *or* **geraten** (*inf*) to become henpecked (*inf*)

Pantöffelchen [pan'tœflçən] NT **-s, -** slipper

Pantolette [panto'lɛtə] F **-, -n** slip-on (shoe)

Pantomime[1] [panto'miːmə] F **-, -n** mime

Pantomime[2] [panto'miːmə] M **-n, -n, Pantomimin** [-'miːmɪn] F **-, -nen** mime

pantomimisch [panto'miːmɪʃ] **1** ADJ *Darstellung* in mime **2** ADV in mime

pantschen ['pantʃn] VTI = **panschen**

Panzer ['pantsɐ] M **-s, - (a)** (*Mil*) tank
(b) (*Hist.* = *Rüstung*) armour *no indef art* (*Brit*), armor *no indef art* (*US*), suit of armo(u)r
(c) (= *Panzerung*) armour (*Brit*) *or* armor (*US*) plating
(d) (*von Schildkröte, Insekt*) shell; (= *dicke Haut*) armour (*Brit*), armor (*US*)
(e) (*fig*) shield; **sich mit einem ~ (gegen etw) umgeben** to harden oneself (against sth); **sich mit einem ~ aus etw umgeben** to put up a defensive barrier of sth; **ein ~ der Gleichgültigkeit** a wall of indifference

Panzer-: **Panzerabwehr** F anti-tank defence (*Brit*) *or* defense (*US*); (*Truppe*) anti-tank unit; **Panzerfaust** F bazooka; **Panzerglas** NT bulletproof glass; **Panzerhemd** NT coat of mail

panzern ['pantsɐn] VT to armour-plate (*Brit*), to armor-plate (*US*); **gepanzerte Fahrzeuge** armoured (*Brit*) *or* armored (*US*) vehicles; **gepanzerte Tiere** shell-bearing animals

Panzer-: **Panzerschrank** M safe; **Panzersperre** F anti-tank obstacle

Papa ['papa] M **-s, -s** (*inf*) daddy (*inf*)

Papagei [papa'gaɪ, 'papagaɪ] M **-s, -en** parrot; **er plappert alles wie ein ~ nach** he repeats everything parrot fashion

Papageienkrankheit F (*Med*) parrot fever

Papageientaucher M puffin

Paparazzo [papa'ratso] M **-s, Paparazzi** [-tsi] (*inf*) paparazzo

Papaya [pa'paːja] F **-, -s** papaya

Papeterie ['papetəri:] F **-, -n** [-riːən] (*Sw*) stationer's

Papi ['papi] M **-s, -s** (*inf*) daddy (*inf*), pappy (*US inf*)

Papier [pa'piːɐ] NT **-s, -e (a)** NO PL (*Material*) paper; **ein Blatt ~** a sheet of paper; **~ verarbeitend** *Industrie* paper-processing; **etw zu ~ bringen** to put sth down on paper; **~ ist geduldig** (*Prov*) you can write what you like; **das Abkommen ist das ~ nicht wert, auf dem es gedruckt ist** the agreement isn't worth the paper it's written on
(b) (= *politisches Dokument, Schriftstück*) paper
(c) **Papiere** PL (identity) papers *pl*; (= *Urkunden*) documents *pl*; **er hatte keine ~e bei sich** he had no means of identification on him; **seine ~e bekommen** (= *entlassen werden*) to get one's cards
(d) (*Fin.* = *Wertpapier*) security

Papiereinzug M paper feed

Papier-: **Papierfabrik** F paper mill; **Papierfetzen** M scrap of paper; **Papierformat** NT paper size; **Papiergeld** NT paper money; **Papierkorb** M (waste)paper basket; **Papierkram** M (*inf*) bumf (*Brit inf*), stuff (to read) (*inf*); **Papierkrieg** M (*inf*) **vor lauter ~ kommen wir nicht zur Forschung** there's so much paperwork we can't get on with our research; **erst nach einem langen ~** after going through a lot of red tape; **einen ~ (mit jdm) führen** to go through a lot of red tape (with sb); **Papiermaché** [papie:ma'fe:] NT **-s, -s** papier-mâché; **Papierschlange** F streamer; **Papierserviette** F paper serviette (*esp Brit*) *or* napkin; **Papierstau** M paper jam; **Papiertaschentuch** NT paper hankie, tissue; **Papiertiger** M (*fig*) paper tiger; **Papiertonne** F paper recycling bin; **papierverarbeitend** ADJ ATTR *siehe* Papier; **Papiervorschub** M paper feed; **Papierwaren** PL stationery *no pl*; **Papierwarengeschäft** NT, **Papierwarenhandlung** F stationer's (shop); **Papierzufuhr** F (*von Drucker*) paper tray

papp [pap] ADJ (*inf*) **ich kann nicht mehr ~ sagen** I'm about to go pop (*inf*)

Papp-: **Pappband** [-bant] M, *pl* **-bände** (*Einband*) pasteboard; (*Buch*) hardback; **Pappbecher** M paper cup; **Pappdeckel** M (thin) cardboard

Pappe ['papə] F **-, -n** (= *Pappdeckel*) cardboard; (= *Dachpappe*) roofing felt; **dieser linke Haken war nicht von ~** (*inf*) that was a mean left hook

Pappeinband M pasteboard

Pappel ['papl] F **-, -n** poplar

päppeln ['pɛpln] VT (*inf*) to nourish

pappen ['papn] **1** VT to stick (*an +acc, auf +acc* on) **2** VI (*inf*) (= *klebrig sein*) to be sticky; (*Schnee*) to pack; **das Hemd pappt an mir** my shirt is sticking to me

Pappenheimer [-haɪmɐ] PL **ich kenne meine ~** (*inf*) I know you lot/that lot (inside out) (*inf*)

papperlapapp [papɐla'pap] INTERJ (*inf*) rubbish (*Brit inf*)

pappig ['papɪç] ADJ (*inf*) sticky; *Brot* doughy

Papp-: **Pappkarton** M (= *Schachtel*) cardboard box; (*Material*) cardboard; **Pappmaché** ['papmaʃe:] NT **-s, -s, Pappmaschee** NT **-s, -s** papier-mâché; **Pappnase** F false nose; **Pappschachtel** F cardboard box; **Pappschnee** M wet snow; **Pappteller** M paper plate

Paprika ['paprika, 'pa:prika] M **-s, -(s)** (*no pl*: = *Gewürz*) paprika; (= *~schote*) pepper; (*Sw*: = *Peperoni*) chilli (*Brit*), chili

Paprikaschote F pepper; (= *rote ~*) pepper, pimento (*US*); **gefüllte ~n** stuffed peppers

Papst [pa:pst] M **-(e)s, ~e** ['pe:pstə] pope; (*fig*) high priest

Päpstin ['pe:pstɪn] F **-, -nen** popess; (*fig*) high priestess

päpstlich ['pe:pstlɪç] ADJ papal; (*fig pej*) pontifical; **~er als der Papst sein** to be more Catholic than the Pope

Papua ['pa:pua, pa'pu:a] M **-(s), -(s)** *or* f **-, -s** Papuan

Papua-Neuguinea ['pa:puanɔʏgi'ne:a] NT **-s** Papua New Guinea

papuanisch [papu'a:nɪʃ] ADJ Papuan

Papyrus [pa'py:rʊs] M -, **Papyri** [-ri] papyrus
Papyrusrolle F papyrus (scroll)
Parabel [pa'ra:bl] F -, -n (a) (*Liter*) parable (b) (*Math*) parabola
Parabolantenne F satellite dish
parabolisch [para'bo:lɪʃ] ADJ (a) (*Liter*) parabolic; **eine ~e Erzählung** a parable (b) (*Math*) parabolic
Parabolspiegel M parabolic reflector
Parade [pa'ra:də] F -, -n (a) parade (*auch Mil*); **die ~ abnehmen** to take the salute (b) (*Sport*) (*Fechten, Boxen*) parry; (*Ballspiele*) save; (*Reiten*) check; **jdm in die ~ fahren** (*fig*) to cut sb off short
Paradebeispiel NT prime example
Paradefall M prime example
Paradeiser [para'daizɐ] M -s, - (*Aus*) tomato
Paradies [para'di:s] NT -es, -e [-zə] (*lit, fig*) paradise; **hier ist es so schön wie im ~** it's like paradise here; **das ~ auf Erden** heaven on earth
paradiesisch [para'di:zɪʃ] **1** ADJ (*fig*) heavenly; **dort herrschen ~e Zustände für Autofahrer** it's heaven for car drivers there **2** ADV *leer* blissfully; *schön* incredibly; **hier ist es ~ ruhig** it's incredibly peaceful here; **sich ~ wohl fühlen** to be blissfully happy
Paradiesvogel M bird of paradise; (*fig inf*) exotic creature
Paradigma [para'dɪgma] NT -s, **Paradigmen** [-mən] paradigm
paradigmatisch [paradɪ'gma:tɪʃ] ADJ paradigmatic
paradox [para'dɔks] **1** ADJ paradoxical **2** ADV paradoxically
Paradox [para'dɔks] NT -es, -e paradox
Paraffin [para'fi:n] NT -s, -e (*Chem*) (= *Paraffinöl*) (liquid) paraffin; (= *Paraffinwachs*) paraffin wax
Paraglider M -s, - (= *Schirm*) paraglider
Paragliding ['pa:raglaidɪŋ] NT -s, NO PL paragliding
Paragraf [para'gra:f] M -en, -en (*Jur*) section; (= *Abschnitt*) paragraph

Paragraf 218 of the criminal code concerns abortion. Since abortion is a highly controversial issue, Paragraf 218 has become a byword for the entire abortion debate. In Germany abortion is legal up to the third month of pregnancy, provided the pregnant woman has undergone thorough counselling.

parallel [para'le:l] **1** ADJ parallel (*auch Comput*) **2** ADV parallel; **~ schalten** (*Elec*) to connect in parallel
Parallelcomputer [para'le:l-] M parallel computer
Parallele [para'le:lə] F -, -n (*lit*) parallel (line); (*fig*) parallel; **eine ~/~n zu etw ziehen** (*lit*) to draw a line/lines parallel to sth; (*fig*) to draw a parallel/parallels to sth
Parallelität [paraleli'tɛ:t] F -, -en parallelism
Parallelklasse F parallel class
Parallelogramm [paralelo'gram] NT -s, -e parallelogram
Parallel- [para'le:l-]: **Parallelrechner** M (*Comput*) parallel computer; **Parallelschaltung** F parallel connection; **Parallelschwung** M (*Ski*) parallel turn
Paralympics [para'lɪmpɪks] PL Paralympics *pl*
Paralytiker [para'ly:tikɐ] M -s, -, **Paralytikerin** [-ərɪn] F -, -nen (*Med*) paralytic
paralytisch [para'ly:tɪʃ] ADJ paralytic
Parameter [pa'ra:metɐ] M -s, - parameter
paramilitärisch ['pa:ra-] ADJ paramilitary
Paranoia [para'nɔya] F -, NO PL paranoia
paranoid [parano'i:t] ADJ paranoid
Paranoiker [para'nɔikɐ] M -s, -, **Paranoikerin** [-ərɪn] F -, -nen paranoiac
Paranuss [para-] F (*Bot*) Brazil nut
paraphieren [para'fi:rən], *ptp* **paraphiert** VT (*Pol*) to initial
Parapsychologie ['pa:ra-] F parapsychology
Parasit [para'zi:t] M -en, -en (*Biol, fig*) parasite
parasitär [parazi'tɛ:rə], **parasitisch** [para'zi:tɪʃ] **1** ADJ (*Biol, fig*) parasitic(al) **2** ADV **~ leben** to live parasitically
parat [pa'ra:t] ADJ *Antwort, Beispiel etc* ready; *Werkzeug etc* handy; **halte dich ~** be ready; **er hatte immer eine Ausrede ~** he always had an excuse ready; **seine stets ~e Ausrede** his ever-ready excuse

Pärchen ['pɛ:eçən] NT -s, - (courting) couple; **ihr seid mir so ein ~!** (*iro*) you're a fine pair!
pärchenweise ADV in pairs
Parcours [par'ku:ɐ] M -, - [-'ku:ɐ(s), -'ku:ɐs] (*Reiten*) showjumping course; (*Sportart*) showjumping; (= *Rennstrecke, Hindernisstrecke*) course
pardon [par'dɔ̃:] INTERJ sorry
Pardon [par'dɔ̃:] M *or* NT -s, NO PL (a) pardon; **jdn um ~ bitten** to ask sb's pardon (b) (*inf*) **kein ~ kennen** to be ruthless
Parenthese [parɛn'te:zə] F parenthesis; **in ~** in parenthesis; **etw in ~ setzen** to put sth in parentheses
Parfum [par'fœ̃] NT -s, -s, **Parfüm** [par'fy:m] NT -s, -e *or* -s perfume
Parfümerie [parfymə'ri:] F -, -n [-'ri:ən] perfumery
parfümieren [parfy'mi:rən], *ptp* **parfümiert 1** VT to perfume **2** VR to put perfume on
pari ['pa:ri] ADV (*Fin*) par; **al ~, zu ~** at par (value); **über ~** above par; **unter ~** below par
parieren [pa'ri:rən], *ptp* **pariert 1** VT (a) (*Fechten*) (*fig*) to parry; (*Ftbl*) to deflect (b) (*Reiten*) to rein in **2** VI to obey; **aufs Wort ~** to jump to it
Parikurs ['pa:ri-] M (*Fin*) par of exchange
Paris [pa'ri:s] NT -' Paris
Pariser M -s, - (a) Parisian (b) (*inf*: = *Kondom*) French letter (*inf*)
Pariserin [pa'ri:zərɪn] F -, -nen Parisienne
Parität [pari'tɛ:t] F -, -en (*auch Comput*) parity
paritätisch [pari'tɛ:tɪʃ] **1** ADJ equal; **~e Mitbestimmung** equal representation **2** ADV equally; **eine Kommission ~ besetzen** to provide equal representation on a committee
Park [park] M -s, -s park; (*von Schloss*) grounds *pl*
Parka ['parka] M -(s), -s *or* f -, -s parka
Park-and-ride-System ['pa:kənd'raid-] NT park and ride system
Park-: Parkanlage F park; **Parkbahn** F (*Space*) parking orbit; **Parkbank** F, *pl* -bänke park bench; **Parkbucht** F parking bay; **Parkdeck** NT parking level
parken ['parkn] VTI (*auch Comput*) to park; **ein ~des Auto** a parked car; **„Parken verboten!"** "No Parking"
Parkett [par'kɛt] NT -s, -e (a) (= *Fußboden*) parquet (flooring); **ein Zimmer mit ~ auslegen** to lay parquet (flooring) in a room; **sich auf jedem ~ bewegen können** (*fig*) to be able to move in any society; **auf dem internationalen ~** in international circles; **sich auf glattem ~ bewegen** (*fig*) to be skating on thin ice
(b) (= *Tanzfläche*) (dance) floor; **eine tolle Nummer aufs ~ legen** (*inf*) to put on a great show
(c) (*Theat*) stalls *pl*, parquet (*US*)
(d) (*St Ex*) trading floor; **auf dem ~** on the trading floor
Parkett(fuß)boden M parquet floor
Park-: Parkgebühr F parking fee; **Parkhaus** NT multi-storey (*Brit*) *or* multi-story (*US*) car park
parkieren [par'ki:rən], *ptp* **parkiert** VTI (*Sw*) = **parken**
Parkingmeter ['parkɪŋ-] M (*Sw*) parking meter
Parkinsonkranke(r) ['pa:ɐkɪnzən-] MF DECL AS ADJ person suffering from Parkinson's disease
parkinsonsche Krankheit ['pa:ɐkɪnzənʃə-] F Parkinson's disease
Park-: Parkkralle F wheel clamp (*Brit*), Denver boot (*US*); **Parkleitsystem** NT parking guidance system; **Parklicht** NT parking light; **Parklücke** F parking space; **Parkmöglichkeit** F parking facility; **Parkplatz** M car park, parking lot (*esp US*); (*für Einzelwagen*) (parking) space (*Brit*) *or* spot (*US*); **bewachter/ unbewachter ~** car park with/without an attendant; **Parkplatznot** F shortage of parking spaces; **Parkscheibe** F parking disc; **Parkschein** M car-parking ticket; **Parkscheinautomat** M (*Mot*) ticket machine (*for parking*); **Parkstudium** NT (*Univ*) interim course of study (*while waiting for a place*); **Parksünder(in)** M(F) parking offender (*Brit*), illegal parker; **Parkuhr** F parking meter; **Parkverbot** NT parking ban; **hier ist ~** you're not allowed to park here; **im ~ stehen** to be parked illegally; **Parkwächter(in)** M(F) (*auf Parkplatz*) car-park attendant; (*von Anlagen*) park keeper
Parlament [parla'mɛnt] NT -(e)s, -e parliament; **das ~ auflösen** to dissolve parliament; **jdn ins ~ wählen** to elect sb to

parliament; **im ~ vertreten sein** to be represented in parliament

Parlamentarier [parlamɛnˈtaːriɐ] M **-s, -**, **Parlamentarierin** [-ɪərɪn] F **-, -nen** parliamentarian

parlamentarisch [parlamɛnˈtaːrɪʃ] **1** ADJ parliamentary; **~er Geschäftsführer** ≈ party whip; **der Parlamentarische Rat** the Parliamentary Council **2** ADV **~ regieren** to govern by a parliament; **~ vertreten sein** to be represented in parliament

Parlaments-: **Parlamentsausschuss** M parliamentary committee; **Parlamentsbeschluss** M vote of parliament; **Parlamentsferien** PL recess; **in die ~ gehen** to go into recess; **Parlamentsmitglied** NT member of parliament; (*in GB*) Member of Parliament, MP; (*in USA*) Congressman; **Parlamentswahl** F USU PL parliamentary election(s *pl*)

Parmaschinken [ˈparma-] M Parma ham

Parmesan(käse) [parmeˈzaːn-] M **-s**, NO PL Parmesan (cheese)

Parodie [paroˈdiː] F **-, -n** [-ˈdiːən] parody (*auf +acc* on, *zu* of)

parodieren [paroˈdiːrən], *ptp* **parodiert** VT to parody

parodistisch [paroˈdɪstɪʃ] ADJ parodistic (*liter*); **~e Sendung** parody; **er hat ~e Fähigkeiten** he's good at taking people off

Parodontose [parodɔnˈtoːzə] F **-, -n** periodontosis (*spec*)

Parole [paˈroːlə] F **-, -n (a)** (*Mil*) password **(b)** (*fig*: = *Wahlspruch*) motto; (*Pol*) slogan

Paroli [paˈroːli] NT **jdm ~ bieten** (*geh*) to defy sb

Parsing [ˈpaːsɪŋ] NT **-s** (*Comput*) parsing

Part [part] M **-s, -e (a)** (= *Anteil*) share **(b)** (*Theat, Mus*) part

Partei [parˈtai] F **-, -en (a)** (*Pol*) party; **bei** *or* **in der ~** in the party; **die ~ wechseln** to change parties **(b)** (*Jur*) party; **meine ~** my client **(c)** (*fig*) **~ sein** to be biased (*Brit*) *or* biassed; **jds ~** (*acc*) **ergreifen**, **für jdn ~ ergreifen** *or* **nehmen** to take sb's side; **gegen jdn ~ ergreifen** *or* **nehmen** to take sides against sb; **ein Richter sollte über den ~en stehen** a judge should be impartial **(d)** (*im Mietshaus*) tenant

Partei-: **Parteiabzeichen** NT party badge; **Parteianhänger(in)** M(F) party supporter; **Parteibuch** NT party membership book; **das richtige/falsche ~ haben** to belong to the right/wrong party; **das ~ ab-** *or* **zurückgeben** to leave the party; **Parteichef(in)** M(F) party leader

Parteienfinanzierung F party financing

Partei-: **Parteifreund(in)** M(F) fellow party member; **Parteiführer(in)** M(F) party leader; **Parteiführung** F leadership of a party; (*Vorstand*) party leaders *pl*; **Parteigenosse** M, **Parteigenossin** F party member; **parteiintern** **1** ADJ internal party *attr*; **~e Kritik** criticism from within the party **2** ADV within the party

parteiisch [parˈtaiɪʃ] **1** ADJ biased (*Brit*), biassed **2** ADV **~ urteilen** to be biased (in one's judgement)

parteilich [parˈtailɪç] **1** ADJ party *attr* **2** ADV **~ organisiert sein** to belong to a (political) party; **Maßnahmen, die nicht ~ gebunden sind** measures which are independent of party politics; **ein ~ ungebundener Kandidat** an independent candidate

Parteilichkeit F **-**, NO PL partiality

Parteilinie F party line; **auf die ~ einschwenken** to toe the party line

parteilos ADJ *Abgeordneter, Kandidat* independent; **der Journalist war ~** the journalist wasn't aligned with any party

Parteilose(r) [parˈtailoːzə] MF DECL AS ADJ independent

Partei-: **Parteimitglied** NT party member; **Parteinahme** [-naːmə] F **-, -n** partisanship; **parteipolitisch** **1** ADJ party political **2** ADV as far as party politics go; **dieser Schritt ist ~ geboten** party politics demand this step; **Parteiprogramm** NT (party) manifesto, (party) program (*US*); **Parteispende** F party donation; **Parteispendenaffäre** F party donations scandal; **Parteitag** M party conference *or* convention (*esp US*); **Parteivolk** NT grass roots *pl* of the party; **Parteivorsitzende(r)** MF DECL AS ADJ party leader; **Parteivorstand** M party executive; **Parteizugehörigkeit** F party membership; **was hat er für eine ~?** what party does he belong to?

parterre [parˈtɛr] ADV on the ground (*esp Brit*) *or* first (*US*) floor

Parterre [parˈtɛr(ə)] NT **-s, -s** (*von Gebäude*) ground floor (*esp Brit*), first floor (*US*)

Partie [parˈtiː] F **-, -n** [-ˈtiːən] **(a)** (= *Teil, Ausschnitt*) part **(b)** (*Theat, Mus*) part **(c)** (*Sport*) game; (*Fechten*) round; **eine ~ Schach spielen** to play a game of chess; **die ~ verloren geben** (*lit, fig*) to give the game up as lost; **eine gute/schlechte ~ liefern** to give a good/bad performance **(d)** (*Comm*) lot **(e)** (*inf*) catch (*inf*); **eine gute ~ (für jdn) sein** to be a good catch (for sb) (*inf*); **eine gute ~ machen** to marry (into) money **(f)** **mit von der ~ sein** to be in on it; **da bin ich mit von der ~** count me in **(g)** (*Aus*: = *Arbeitergruppe*) gang

partiell [parˈtsiɛl] **1** ADJ partial **2** ADV partially; **~ differenzieren** (*Math*) to form a partial derivative

partienweise [parˈtiːənvaizə] ADV (*Comm*) in lots

Partikel [parˈtiːkl, parˈtɪkl] F **-, -n** (*Gram, Phys*) particle

Partisan [partiˈzaːn] M **-s** *or* **-en, -en**, **Partisanin** [-ˈzaːnɪn] F **-, -nen** partisan

Partitur [partiˈtuːɐ] F **-, -en** [-ˈtuːrən] (*Mus*) score

Partizip [partiˈtsiːp] NT **-s, -ien** [-piən] (*Gram*) participle; **~ I** *or* **Präsens** present participle; **~ II** *or* **Perfekt** past participle

Partizipation [partitsipaˈtsioːn] F **-, -en** participation (*an +dat* in)

Partizipationsgeschäft NT (*Comm*) transaction conducted by several parties

Partizipialkonstruktion [partitsiˈpiaːl-] F participial construction

partizipieren [partitsiˈpiːrən], *ptp* **partizipiert** VI to participate (*an +dat* in)

Partner [ˈpartnɐ] M **-s, -**, **Partnerin** [-ərɪn] F **-, -nen** partner; (*Film*) co-star; **als jds ~ spielen** (*in Film*) to play opposite sb; (*Sport*) to be sb's partner

Partnerschaft [ˈpartnɐʃaft] F **-, -en** partnership; (= *Städtepartnerschaft*) twinning

partnerschaftlich [ˈpartnɐʃaftlɪç] **1** ADJ **~es Verhältnis** (relationship based on) partnership; **~e Zusammenarbeit** working together as partners; **in gutem ~em Einvernehmen** in a spirit of partnership **2** ADV **~ zusammenarbeiten** to work in partnership; **~ zusammenleben** to live together as equal partners; **das haben wir ~ gelöst** we solved it together

Partner-: **Partnerstadt** F twin town (*Brit*), sister city (*US*); **Partnertausch** M **(a)** (*Tanz, Tennis*) change of partners **(b)** (*sexuell*) partner-swopping

Party [ˈpaːɐti] F **-, -s** party; **eine ~ geben** *or* **veranstalten** to give *or* have a party; **bei** *or* **auf einer ~** at a party; **auf eine** *or* **zu einer ~ gehen** to go to a party

Partyservice [-zøːɐvɪs, -zœrvɪs] M party catering service

Parzelle [parˈtsɛlə] F **-, -n** plot

Pasch [paʃ] M **-(e)s, -e** *or* **=e** [ˈpɛʃə] (*beim Würfelspiel*) doublets *pl*

Pascha [ˈpaʃa] M **-s, -s** pasha; **wie ein ~** like Lord Muck (*Brit*) *or* His Highness (*inf*)

Pass [pas] M **-es, =e** [ˈpɛsə] **(a)** passport **(b)** (*im Gebirge etc*) pass **(c)** (*Ballspiele*) pass **(d)** (*Reitsport*) amble

passabel [paˈsaːbl] **1** ADJ passable **2** ADV reasonably well; **schmecken** passable; **aussehen** presentable; **mir gehts ganz ~** I'm all right

Passage [paˈsaːʒə] F **-, -n** passage; (= *Ladenstraße*) arcade

Passagier [pasaˈʒiːɐ] M **-s, -e**, **Passagierin** [-ˈʒiːrɪn] F **-, -nen** passenger; **ein blinder ~** a stowaway

Passagier-: **Passagierdampfer** M passenger steamer; **Passagierflugzeug** NT passenger aircraft, airliner; **Passagierliste** F passenger list

Passah [ˈpasa] **-s**, NO PL, **Passahfest** NT (Feast of the) Passover

Passamt NT passport office

Passant [paˈsant] M **-en, -en**, **Passantin** [-ˈsantɪn] F **-, -nen** passer-by

Passat [paˈsaːt] M **-s, -e**, **Passatwind** M trade wind

Passbild NT passport photo(graph)

passé [paˈseː], **passee** ADJ PRED passé; **diese Mode ist längst ~** this fashion went out long ago; **die Sache ist längst ~** that's all in the past

passen¹ [ˈpasn] VI **(a)** (= *die richtige Größe, Form haben*) to fit **(b)** (= *harmonieren*) **zu etw ~** to go with sth; (*im Ton*) to match sth; **zu jdm ~** (*Mensch*) to suit sb; **zueinander ~** to go together;

das passt zu ihm, so etwas zu sagen that's just like him to say that; **es passt nicht zu dir, Bier zu trinken** you don't look right drinking beer; **diese Einstellung passt gut zu ihm** that attitude is just like him; **diese Einstellung passt nicht mehr in die heutige Zeit** this attitude is not acceptable nowadays; **so ein formeller Ausdruck passt nicht in diesen Satz** such a formal expression is all wrong in this sentence; **Streiks ~ nicht in die konjunkturelle Landschaft** strike action is inappropriate in the current economic situation; **das Rot passt da nicht** the red is all wrong there; **das Bild passt besser in das andere Zimmer** the picture would go better in the other room; **ins Bild ~** to fit the picture

(c) (= *genehm sein*) to suit; **er passt mir (einfach) nicht** I (just) don't like him; **Sonntag passt uns nicht/gut** Sunday is no good for us/suits us fine; **das passt mir gar nicht** (= *ungelegen*) that doesn't suit me at all; (= *gefällt mir nicht*) I don't like that at all; **das passt mir gar nicht, dass du schon gehst** I don't want you to go now; **wenns dem Chef passt ...** if it suits the boss ...; **das könnte dir so ~!** (*inf*) you'd like that, wouldn't you?; **ihre Raucherei passt mir schon lange nicht** this smoking of hers has been annoying me for a long time

passen² VI (*Cards, fig*) to pass; **(ich) passe!** (I) pass!

passend ADJ **(a)** (*in Größe, Form*) gut/schlecht ~ well-/ill-fitting; **er trägt kaum mal einen ~en Anzug** he hardly ever wears a suit that fits; **ein ~er Schlüssel (zu diesem Schloss)** a key that fits (this lock)

(b) (*in Farbe, Stil*) matching; **etwas dazu Passendes** something that goes with it, something to match; **ich muss jetzt dazu ~e Schuhe kaufen** now I must buy some matching shoes

(c) (= *genehm*) *Zeit, Termin* convenient; **er kam zu jeder ~en und unpassenden Zeit** he came at any time, no matter how inconvenient

(d) (= *angemessen*) *Bemerkung, Benehmen, Kleidung* suitable, appropriate, fitting; *Wort* right, proper; **sie trägt zu jeder Gelegenheit einen ~en Hut** she always wears a hat to suit *or* match the occasion; **bei jeder ~en und unpassenden Gelegenheit** at every opportunity, whether appropriate or not

(e) *Geld* exact

2 ADV **(a)** **etw ~ machen** *Kleidung* to alter sth; *Brett etc* to fit sth; **etw ~ kürzen** to shorten sth to fit

(b) (= *abgezählt*) **den Fahrpreis ~ bereithalten** to have the exact fare ready; **haben Sie es ~?** have you got the right money?

Pass-: **Passform** F fit; **eine gute ~ haben** to be a good fit; **Passfoto** NT passport photo(graph)

passierbar ADJ *Brücke, Grenze* passable; *Fluss, Kanal, Pass* negotiable

passieren [pa'si:rən], *ptp* **passiert** **1** VI AUX SEIN **(a)** (= *sich ereignen*) to happen (*mit* to); **ihm ist etwas Schreckliches passiert** something terrible has happened to him; **ihm ist beim Bergsteigen etwas passiert** he had an accident while mountaineering; **beim Sturz ist ihm erstaunlicherweise nichts passiert** miraculously he wasn't hurt in the fall; **was ist denn passiert?** what's the matter?; **es wird dir schon nichts ~** nothing is going to happen to you; **es ist ein Unfall passiert** there has been an accident; **das kann auch nur mir ~!** that could only happen to me!; **dass mir das ja nicht mehr** *or* **nicht noch mal passiert!** see that it doesn't happen again!; **so was ist mir noch nie passiert!** that's never happened to me before!; (*empört*) I've never known anything like it!

(b) (= *durchgehen*) to pass; (*Gesetz*) to be passed; **jdn ungehindert ~ lassen** to let sb pass

2 VT **(a)** (= *vorbeigehen an*) to pass; **die Grenze ~** to cross (over); **die Zensur ~** to be passed by the censor; **das Parlament ~** (*Gesetz*) to be passed by parliament

(b) (*Cook*) to strain

Passier-: **Passierschein** M pass; **Passierschlag** M (*Tennis*) passing shot

Passion [pa'sio:n] F **-, -en** passion; (*religiös*) Passion; **er ist Jäger aus ~** he has a passion for hunting

passioniert [pasio'ni:ɐt] ADJ enthusiastic

Passionsfrucht F passion fruit

passiv ['pasi:f, pa'si:f] **1** ADJ passive; **~e Bestechung** corruption *no pl*; **~es Mitglied** non-active member; **~es Rauchen** passive smoking; **~e Handelsbilanz** (*Comm*) adverse trade balance **2** ADV passively; **sich ~ verhalten** to be passive

Passiv ['pasi:f] NT **-s, -e** [-və] (*Gram*) passive (voice)

Passiva [pa'si:va] PL, **Passiven** [-vn] PL (*Comm*) liabilities *pl*

Passivität [pasivi'tɛ:t] F **-, NO PL** passivity

Passiv-: **Passivposten** M (*Comm*) debit entry; **Passivrauchen** NT passive smoking; **Passivsaldo** M (*Comm*) debit account; **Passivseite** F (*Comm*) debit side

Pass-: **Passkontrolle** F passport control; **~!** (your) passports please!; **Passstraße** F (mountain) pass

Passus ['pasus] M **-, -** ['pasu:s] passage

Passwort NT, *pl* **-wörter** (*Comput*) password

Passwortschutz M password protection

Paste ['pastə] F **-, -n**, **Pasta** ['pasta] F **-, Pasten** ['pastn] paste

Pastell [pas'tɛl] NT **-s, -e** pastel

Pastell-: **Pastellfarbe** F pastel (crayon); (*Farbton*) pastel (shade); **pastellfarben** [-farbn] **1** ADJ pastel(-coloured) (*Brit*), pastel(-colored) (*US*) **2** ADV in pastel colours (*Brit*) *or* colors (*US*), in pastels; **Pastellmaler(in)** M(F) pastellist (*Brit*), pastelist (*US*); **Pastellmalerei** F drawing in pastels; **Pastellstift** M pastel (crayon); **Pastellton** M, *pl* **-töne** pastel shade

Pastetchen [pas'te:tçən] NT **-s, -** vol-au-vent

Pastete [pas'te:tə] F **-, -n (a)** (= *Schüsselpastete*) pie; (= *Pastetchen*) vol-au-vent; (*ungefüllt*) vol-au-vent case **(b)** (= *Leberpastete etc*) pâté

pasteurisieren [pastøri'zi:rən], *ptp* **pasteurisiert** VT to pasteurize

Pastille [pas'tɪlə] F **-, -n** pastille

Pastor ['pasto:ɐ, pas'to:ɐ] M **-s, Pastoren** [-'to:rən], **Pastorin** [-'to:rɪn] F **-, -nen** *siehe* **Pfarrer**

Patchwork ['pɛtʃwɔːɐk, -wœrk] NT **-s, NO PL** (*Tex, fig*) patchwork

Pate ['pa:tə] M **-n, -n** (= *Taufzeuge*) godfather; (= *Mafiaboss*) godfather; (= *Firmzeuge*) sponsor; **bei etw ~ gestanden haben** (*fig*) to be the force behind sth

Paten-: **Patenkind** NT godchild; **Patenonkel** M godfather; **Patenschaft** ['pa:tnʃaft] F **-, -en** godparenthood; sponsorship; **die ~ für** *or* **über jdn/etw übernehmen** (*fig*) to take on the responsibility for sb/sth; **Patensohn** M godson; **Patenstadt** F twin(ned) town (*Brit*), sister city (*US*)

patent [pa'tɛnt] ADJ ingenious; **ein ~er Kerl** a great guy/girl (*inf*); **sie ist eine ~e Frau** she's a tremendous woman

Patent [pa'tɛnt] NT **-(e)s, -e (a)** (= *Erfindung, Urkunde*) patent (*für etw* for sth, *auf etw* on sth); **etw als** *or* **zum ~ anmelden**, **ein ~ auf** *or* **für etw anmelden** to apply for a patent on *or* for sth; **„(zum) ~ angemeldet"** "patent pending" **(b)** (= *Ernennungsurkunde*) commission **(c)** (*Sw*) permit **(d)** (*inf.* = *Mechanismus*) apparatus; **der Haken, so ein blödes ~** this hook, the stupid thing

Patentamt NT Patent Office

Patentante F godmother

patentierbar ADJ patentable

patentieren [patɛn'ti:rən], *ptp* **patentiert** VT to patent; **sich** (*dat*) **etw ~ lassen** to have sth patented

Patentlösung F (*fig*) easy answer; **bei der Kindererziehung gibt es keine ~** there's no instant recipe for success in bringing up children

Patentochter F goddaughter

Patent-: **Patentrezept** NT (*fig*) = **Patentlösung**; **Patentschutz** M protection by (letters) patent

Pater ['pa:tɐ] M **-s, -** *or* **Patres** ['patre:s] (*Eccl*) Father

pathetisch [pa'te:tɪʃ] **1** ADJ emotional; *Beschreibung auch* dramatic **2** ADV dramatically; **das war zu ~ gespielt** it was overacted

Pathologe [pato'lo:gə] M **-n, -n**, **Pathologin** [-'lo:gɪn] F **-, -nen** pathologist

Pathologie [patolo'gi:] F **-, -n** [-'gi:ən] pathology

pathologisch [pato'lo:gɪʃ] (*Med, fig*) **1** ADJ pathological **2** ADV pathologically

Pathos ['pa:tɔs] NT **-, NO PL** emotiveness; **ein Gedicht mit/ohne ~ vortragen** to recite a poem with great drama/without drama; **die Rede enthielt zu viel falsches ~** the speech contained too much false emotionalism; **mit viel ~ in der Stimme** in a voice charged with emotion

Patience [pa'siã:s] F **-, -n** patience *no pl*; **~n legen** to play patience; **eine ~ legen** to play (a game of) patience

Patient [paˈtsiɛnt] M **-en, -en, Patientin** [-ˈtsiɛntɪn] F **-, -nen** patient; **ich bin ~ von** or **bei Dr X** I'm Dr X's patient; **~en mit Lungenentzündung** pneumonia patients

Patin [ˈpaːtɪn] F **-, -nen** godmother; (= *Firmpatin*) sponsor

Patina [ˈpaːtina] F **-, NO PL** (*lit, fig*) patina; **~ ansetzen** (*lit*) to patinate; (*fig*) to take on a hallowed air of tradition

Patres PL *von* **Pater**

patriarchalisch [patriarˈçaːlɪʃ] (*lit, fig*) **1** ADJ patriarchal **2** ADV patriarchally; **er regiert ~** his rule is patriarchal

Patriarchat [patriarˈçaːt] NT **-(e)s, -e** patriarchy

Patriot [patriˈoːt] M **-en, -en, Patriotin** [-ˈoːtɪn] F **-, -nen** patriot

patriotisch [patriˈoːtɪʃ] **1** ADJ patriotic **2** ADV *reden, sich verhalten, denken* patriotically; **~ klingen** to sound patriotic

Patriotismus [patrioˈtɪsmʊs] M **-, NO PL** patriotism

Patrone [paˈtroːnə] F **-, -n** (*Film, Mil, von Füller, von Drucker*) cartridge; (*Tex*) point paper design

Patrouille [paˈtrʊljə] F **-, -n** patrol; (**auf**) **~ gehen** to patrol

patrouillieren [patrʊlˈjiːrən], *ptp* **patrouilliert** VI to patrol

Patsche [ˈpatʃə] F **-, -n** (*inf*) **(a)** (= *Hand*) paw (*inf*) **(b)** (= *Matsch*) mud; (= *Schneematsch*) slush; (*fig*) jam (*inf*); **in der ~ sitzen** or **stecken** to be in a jam (*inf*); **jdm aus der ~ helfen, jdn aus der ~ ziehen** to get sb out of a jam (*inf*); **jdn in der ~ (sitzen) lassen** to leave sb in the lurch **(c)** (= *Feuerpatsche*) beater; (= *Fliegenpatsche*) swat

patschen [ˈpatʃn] VI **(a)** (*mit Flüssigkeit*) to splash; **das Baby patschte mit der Hand in die Suppe** the baby went splat with his hand in the soup **(b)** (*inf: mit Hand, Fuß*) **das Baby patschte auf den Tisch/an die Möbel** the baby smacked the table/the furniture; **die Kinder ~ mit den Händen** the children clap their hands (together); **er patschte ihr auf die Schulter** he patted her on the shoulder

patschnass [ˈpatʃˈnas] ADJ (*inf*) soaking wet; **draußen ist es ~!** it's soaking wet outside

patt [pat] ADJ PRED, ADV (*Chess, fig*) in stalemate

Patt [pat] NT **-s, -s** (*lit, fig*) stalemate

Pattsituation F (*lit, fig*) stalemate

patzen [ˈpatsn] VI (*inf*) to slip up; **der Pianist hat gepatzt** the pianist fluffed a passage; **der Schauspieler hat gepatzt** the actor fluffed his lines

Patzen [ˈpatsn] M **-s, -** (*Aus*) blotch

Patzer [ˈpatsɐ] M **-s, -** (*inf: = Fehler*) slip; **mir ist ein ~ unterlaufen** I made a slip

patzig [ˈpatsɪç] (*inf*) **1** ADJ snotty (*inf*) **2** ADV **jdm ~ kommen** to be snotty to sb (*inf*)

Pauke [ˈpaʊkə] F **-, -n** (*Mus*) kettledrum; **mit ~n und Trompeten durchfallen** (*inf*) to fail miserably; **auf die ~ hauen** (*inf*) (= *angeben*) to brag; (= *feiern*) to paint the town red

pauken [ˈpaʊkn] **1** VI **(a)** (*inf: = Pauke spielen*) to drum **(b)** (*inf: = lernen*) to swot (*Brit inf*), to cram (*inf*); **meine Mutter hat immer mit mir gepaukt** my mother always helped me with my cramming (*inf*) **2** VT to study up on (*US*); **Englisch ~** to study up on (*US*) English

Pauken-: Paukenschlag M drum beat; **wie ein ~** (*fig*) like a thunderbolt; **Paukenschlägel** M drumstick; **Paukenspieler(in)** M(F) drummer

Pauker [ˈpaʊkɐ] M **-s, -, Paukerin** [-ərɪn] F **-, -nen** **(a)** (*inf: = Paukenspieler*) timpanist **(b)** (*Sch inf: = Lehrer*) teacher; **da geht unser ~** there's sir (*Brit inf*), there's the teach (*US inf*)

Paukerei [paʊkəˈraɪ] F **-, -en** (*Sch inf*) swotting (*Brit inf*), cramming (*inf*); **ich hab diese ~ satt** I'm fed up with school

Paukist [paʊˈkɪst] M **-en, -en, Paukistin** [-ˈkɪstɪn] F **-en, -en** timpanist

pausbäckig [ˈpaʊsbɛkɪç] ADJ chubby-cheeked

pauschal [paʊˈʃaːl] **1** ADJ **(a)** (= *vorläufig geschätzt*) estimated; (= *einheitlich*) flat-rate *attr only* **(b)** (*fig*) *Behauptung, Kritik, Urteil* sweeping **2** ADV **(a)** (= *nicht spezifiziert*) at a flat rate; **ich schätze die Baukosten ~ auf etwa eine halbe Million Euro** I'd estimate the overall building costs to be half a million euros; **die Werkstatt berechnet ~ pro Inspektion 200 Euro** the garage has a flat rate of 200 euros per service; **die Einkommensteuer kann ~ festgesetzt werden** income tax can be set at a flat rate; **die Gebühren werden ~ bezahlt** the charges are paid in a lump sum; **die Kosten verstehen sich ~** the costs are fixed;

alle bekommen ~ £ 20 pro Woche mehr there will be an across-the-board increase of £20 a week **(b)** (= *nicht differenziert*) *abwerten* categorically; **so ~ kann man das nicht sagen** that's much too sweeping a statement; **ein Volk ~ verurteilen** to condemn a people wholesale

Pauschale [paʊˈʃaːlə] F **-, -n** (= *Einheitspreis*) flat rate; (= *vorläufig geschätzter Betrag*) estimated amount

Pauschalgebühr F (= *Einheitsgebühr*) flat rate (charge); (= *vorläufig geschätzter Betrag*) estimated charge

pauschalieren [paʊʃaˈliːrən], *ptp* **pauschaliert** VT to estimate at a flat rate

Pauschal-: Pauschalpreis M (= *Einheitspreis*) flat rate; (= *vorläufig geschätzter Betrag*) estimated price; (= *Inklusivpreis*) inclusive price; **Pauschalreise** F package holiday (*esp Brit*) or tour; **Pauschalsumme** F lump sum; **Pauschaltarif** M flat rate; **Pauschalurteil** NT sweeping statement

Pauschbetrag [ˈpaʊʃ-] M flat rate

Pause F **-, -n** **(a)** (= *Unterbrechung*) break; (= *Rast*) rest; (= *das Innehalten*) pause; (*Theat*) interval; (*Sch*) break, recess (*US*); (*Pol*) recess; **(eine) ~ machen, eine ~ einlegen** (= *sich entspannen*) to have a break; (= *rasten*) to rest; (= *innehalten*) to pause; **du hast jetzt mal ~!** (*inf*) now, you keep quiet!; **nach einer langen ~ sagte er ...** after a long silence he said ...; **immer wieder entstanden ~n in der Unterhaltung** the conversation was full of gaps; **ohne ~ arbeiten** to work nonstop; **die große ~** (*Sch*) (the) break (*Brit*), recess (*US*); (*in Grundschule*) playtime; **zur ~ stand es 3:1** (*Ftbl*) it was 3-1 at half-time **(b)** (*Mus*) rest; **eine halbe/ganze ~** a minim (*Brit*) or half-note (*US*)/semibreve (*Brit*) or whole-note (*US*) rest

pausen [ˈpaʊzn] VT to trace

Pausen-: Pausenbrot NT something to eat at break; **Pausenfüller** M stopgap; **Pausenhof** M playground, schoolyard; **pausenlos** **1** ADJ NO PRED nonstop **2** ADV continuously; **er arbeitet ~** he works nonstop; **Pausenstand** M half-time score

pausieren [paʊˈziːrən], *ptp* **pausiert** VI to (take a) break; **der Torwart musste wegen einer Verletzung ~** the goalkeeper had to rest up because of injury

Pavian [ˈpaːviaːn] M **-s, -e** baboon

Pavillon [ˈpavɪljõ] M **-s, -s** pavilion

Pay-TV [ˈpeːtiːviː] NT **-s, NO PL** pay TV

Pazifik [paˈtsiːfɪk, ˈpaːtsifɪk] M **-s** Pacific

pazifisch [paˈtsiːfɪʃ] ADJ Pacific; **der Pazifische Ozean** the Pacific (Ocean); **der (asiatisch-)pazifische Raum** the Pacific Rim

Pazifismus [patsiˈfɪsmʊs] M **-, NO PL** pacifism

Pazifist [patsiˈfɪst] M **-en, -en, Pazifistin** [-ˈfɪstɪn] F **-, -nen** pacifist

pazifistisch [patsiˈfɪstɪʃ] **1** ADJ pacifist **2** ADV **~ eingestellt sein** to be a pacifist; **sich ~ geben** to give the impression of being a pacifist

PC [peːˈtseː] M **-s, -s** ABBR *von* **Personalcomputer** PC

PDS [peːdeːˈʔɛs] F ABBR *von* **Partei des Demokratischen Sozialismus**

PDS

The PDS (Partei des Demokratischen Sozialismus) emerged in 1989/90 from the Sozialistische Einheitspartei Deutschlands (SED), which was the official ruling party of the former East Germany. The PDS champions people's rights in the new Länder and aims to establish itself as a left-wing socialist party throughout Germany.

Pech [pɛç] NT **-(e)s, -e (a)** (*Stoff*) pitch; **die beiden halten zusammen wie ~ und Schwefel** (*inf*) the two are as thick as thieves (*Brit*) or inseparable **(b)** NO PL (*inf: = Missgeschick*) bad luck; **bei etw ~ haben** to be unlucky in or with sth; **~ gehabt!** tough! (*inf*); **sie ist vom ~ verfolgt** bad luck follows her around; **so ein ~!** just my/our *etc* luck!; **~ im Spiel, Glück in der Liebe** (*prov*) unlucky at cards, lucky in love (*prov*)

Pech-: pech(raben)schwarz ADJ (*inf*) pitch-black; *Haar* jet-black; **Pechsträhne** F (*inf*) run of bad luck; **Pechvogel** M (*inf*) unlucky person

Pedal [pe'da:l] NT **-s, -e** pedal; **(fest) in die ~e treten** to pedal (hard)

Pedant [pe'dant] M **-en, -en, Pedantin** [-'dantɪn] F **-, -nen** pedant

Pedanterie [pedantə'ri:] F **-, -n** [-'ri:ən] pedantry

pedantisch [pe'dantɪʃ] **1** ADJ pedantic **2** ADV pedantically

Peddigrohr ['pedɪç-] NT cane

Peeling ['pi:lɪŋ] NT **-s, -s** peeling

Peepshow ['pi:pʃo:] F peep show

Pegel ['pe:gl] M **-s, -** (*in Flüssen, Kanälen, Meer*) water depth gauge; (*Elec*) level recorder

Pegelstand M water level

peilen ['pailən] VT *Wassertiefe* to sound; *U-Boot, Sender, Standort* to get a fix on; *Richtung* to plot; (= *entdecken*) to detect; **die Lage ~** (*inf*) to see how the land lies; **über den Daumen ~** (*inf*) to guess roughly; **über den Daumen gepeilt** (*inf*) at a rough estimate; **es ~** (*sl*: = *durchblicken*) to get it (*inf*)

peinigen ['painɪgn] VT to torture; (*fig*) to torment; **jdn bis aufs Blut ~** to torture sb till he bleeds; (*fig*) to torment sb mercilessly

peinlich ['painlɪç] **1** ADJ **(a)** (= *unangenehm*) (painfully) embarrassing; *Überraschung* nasty; **ich habe das ~e Gefühl, dass ...** I have a terrible feeling that ...; **es war ihm ~(, dass ...)** he was embarrassed (because ...); **es ist mir sehr ~, aber ich muss es Ihnen einmal sagen** I don't know how to put it, but you really ought to know; **es ist mir sehr ~, aber die Arbeit ist immer noch nicht fertig** I'm really sorry but the work still isn't finished; **das ist mir ja so ~** I feel awful about it; **es war so schlecht, dass es schon ~ war** (*inf*) it was so bad it was (really) painful (*inf*)
(b) (= *gewissenhaft*) meticulous; *Sparsamkeit* careful; **in seinem Zimmer/auf seinem Schreibtisch herrschte ~e** *or* **~ste Ordnung** his room/his desk was meticulously tidy
2 ADV **(a)** (= *unangenehm*) **~ berührt sein** (*hum*) to be profoundly shocked (*iro*); **~ wirken** to be embarrassing **(b)** (= *gründlich*) painstakingly; *sauber* meticulously; **der Koffer wurde ~ genau untersucht** the case was gone through very thoroughly; **er vermied es ~st, davon zu sprechen** he was at pains not to talk about it

Peinlichkeit F **-, -en** (= *Unangenehmheit*) awkwardness; **die ~ seines Benehmens** his embarrassing behaviour (*Brit*) or behavior (*US*); **diese ~en auf der Bühne** these embarrassing scenes on stage

Peitsche ['paitʃə] F **-, -n** whip

peitschen ['paitʃn] VTI to whip; (*fig*) to lash

pejorativ [pejora'ti:f] **1** ADJ pejorative **2** ADV pejoratively

Pekinese [peki'ne:zə] M **-n, -n** pekinese

Peking ['pe:kɪŋ] NT **-s** Peking, Beijing

Pekingoper F Peking Opera

Pelikan ['pe:lika:n, peli'ka:n] M **-s, -e** pelican

Pelle ['pelə] F **-, -n** (*inf*) skin; (*abgeschält*) peel; **der Chef sitzt mir auf der ~** (*inf*) I've got the boss on my back (*inf*); **er geht mir nicht von der ~** (*inf*) he won't stop pestering me

pellen ['pelən] (*inf*) **1** VT *Kartoffeln, Wurst* to skin, to peel; *Ei* to take the shell off **2** VR (*Mensch, Körperhaut*) to peel

Pellkartoffeln PL potatoes *pl* boiled in their jackets

Pelz [pelts] M **-es, -e** fur

pelzig ['peltsɪç] ADJ furry; *Zunge* furred(-over), furry

Pelz-: Pelzimitation F imitation fur; **Pelztierfarm** F fur farm; **Pelztierzucht** F fur farming; **Pelzwaren** PL furs *pl*

Pendant [pã'dã:] NT **-s, -s** counterpart

Pendel ['pendl] NT **-s, -** pendulum

pendeln ['pendln] VI **(a)** (= *schwingen*) to swing (to and fro); **er ließ die Beine ~** he let his legs dangle; **der DAX pendelte um die 3000-Marke** the DAX index fluctuated around the 3000 level **(b)** AUX SEIN (= *hin und her fahren*) (*Zug, Fähre etc*) to shuttle; (*Mensch*) to commute; (*fig*) to vacillate

Pendel-: Pendeltür F swing door; **Pendelverkehr** M shuttle service; (= *Berufsverkehr*) commuter traffic

Pendler ['pendlɐ] M **-s, -, Pendlerin** [-ərɪn] F **-, -nen** commuter

Pendolino [pendo'li:no] M **-s, -s** (*Rail*) tilting train

penetrant [pene'trant] **1** ADJ **(a)** *Gestank, Geschmack* penetrating, overpowering
(b) (*fig*: = *aufdringlich*) insistent; **seine Selbstsicherheit ist schon ~** his self-confidence is overpowering; **ein ~er Kerl** a nuisance
2 ADV **(a)** (= *stark*) **das Parfüm riecht ~** the perfume is overpowering; **das schmeckt ~ nach Knoblauch** you can't taste anything for garlic
(b) (= *aufdringlich*) **jdn ~ nach etw ausfragen** to ask sb insistent questions about sth; **er ist mir ~ auf die Pelle gerückt** he just wouldn't take no for an answer

Penetranz [pene'trants] F **-, NO PL** (*von Geruch, Geschmack*) pungency; (*fig*: = *Aufdringlichkeit*) pushiness

Penetration [penetra'tsio:n] F **-, -en** penetration

penetrieren [pene'tri:rən], *ptp* **penetriert** VT to penetrate

peng [pɛŋ] INTERJ bang

penibel [pe'ni:bl] **1** ADJ **(a)** (= *gründlich, genau*) precise **(b)** (*dial*: = *peinlich*) painful **2** ADV *sauber* meticulously; **ein ~ ordentliches Zimmer** an immaculately clean and tidy room; **mein Mann rechnet mir jeden Pfennig ~ vor** my husband knows exactly where every penny I spend goes; **er macht seine Buchführung äußerst ~** he is very meticulous about his bookkeeping

Penis ['pe:nɪs] M **-, -se** *or* **Penes** ['pe:ne:s] penis

Penizillin [penitsɪ'li:n] NT **-s, -e** penicillin

Pennbruder ['pen-] M (*inf*) tramp

Penne¹ ['penə] F **-, -n** (*Sch inf*) school

Penne² ['penə] PL (= *Nudeln*) penne *sing*

pennen ['penən] VI (*inf*) (= *schlafen*) to sleep; (= *dösen*) to be half-asleep; **der Meier pennt schon wieder im Unterricht** Meier's having a little nap again during the lesson; **du bist dran, penn nicht!** it's your turn, wake up!

Penner ['penɐ] M **-s, -, Pennerin** [-ərɪn] F **-, -nen** (*inf*) **(a)** tramp, bum (*inf*) **(b)** (= *verschlafener Mensch*) sleepyhead (*inf*) **(c)** (= *Blödmann*) plonker (*inf*)

Pension [pã'zio:n, pã'sio:n, pen'zio:n] F **-, -en (a)** (= *Fremdenheim*) guesthouse **(b)** NO PL (= *Verpflegung, Kostgeld*) board; **halbe/ volle ~** half/full board; **die ~ pro Tag macht 80 Euro** half/full board is 130 euros a day **(c)** (= *Ruhegehalt*) pension **(d)** NO PL (= *Ruhestand*) retirement; **in ~ gehen** to retire; **in ~ sein** to be retired; **jdn in ~ schicken** to retire sb

Pensionär [pãzio'nɛ:ɐ, pãsio'nɛ:ɐ, penzio'nɛ:ɐ] M **-s, -e, Pensionärin** [-'nɛ:rɪn] F **-, -nen** (*Pension beziehend*) pensioner; (*im Ruhestand befindlich*) retired person

pensionieren [pãzio'ni:rən, pãsio'ni:rən, pensio'ni:rən], *ptp* **pensioniert** VT to pension off; **sich ~ lassen** to retire; **sich vorzeitig ~ lassen** to take early retirement

Pensions-: Pensionsalter NT retirement age; **Pensionsanspruch** M right to a pension; **pensionsberechtigt** ADJ entitled to a pension; **Pensionsgast** M paying guest; **Pensionsgeschäft** NT repurchase agreement, repo

Pensum ['penzʊm] NT **-s, Pensa** *or* **Pensen** [-za, -sn] workload; (*Sch*) curriculum; (= *Trainingspensum*) programme (*Brit*), program (*US*); **tägliches ~** daily quota; **er hat sein ~ nicht geschafft** he didn't achieve his target

Penthouse ['penthaʊs] NT **-, -s** penthouse (apartment)

Pentium® ['pentsɪʊm] M **-(s), -s** (*Comput*) Pentium® PC; (*Chip*) Pentium® chip

Pentium-Prozessor® M Pentium® processor

Pentop ['pentɔp] M **-s, -s** (*Comput*) pentop

Pep [pep] M **-(s), NO PL** (*inf*) pep (*inf*), life; **das Kleid hat ~** that dress has style

Peperoni [pepe'ro:ni] PL chillies *pl* (*Brit*), chilies *pl*; (*Sw*: = *Paprika*) pepper

peppig ['pepɪç] (*inf*) **1** ADJ *Musik, Show* lively; *Kleidung* jolly **2** ADV **die Band spielte ~** the band played lively music; **sie war ~ zurechtgemacht** she was really dolled up (*inf*)

per [per] PREP **(a)** (= *mittels, durch*) by; **~ Adresse** (*Comm*) care of, c/o; **mit jdm ~ du sein** (*inf*) to be on first-name terms with sb; **~ procura** (*Comm*) per procura; **~ Saldo** (*Fin*) net; **~ pedes** (*hum*) on foot; **~ se** per se; **~ definitionem** by definition **(b)** (*Comm*: = *gegen*) against **(c)** (*Comm, Econ*: = *bis, am*) by **(d)** (*Comm*: = *pro*) per; **~ annum** per annum

perfekt [per'fekt] **1** ADJ **(a)** (= *vollkommen*) perfect **(b)** PRED (= *abgemacht*) settled; **etw ~ machen** to settle sth; **die Sache ~ machen** to clinch the deal; **der Vertrag ist ~** the contract is all settled; **damit war die Niederlage ~** total defeat was then inevitable **2** ADV (= *sehr gut*) perfectly; **~ kochen** to be a perfect cook; **~ Englisch sprechen** to speak perfect English

Perfekt ['pɛrfɛkt] NT **-s, -e** perfect (tense)
Perfektion [pɛrfɛk'tsioːn] F **-**, NO PL perfection; **etw (bis) zur ~ entwickeln** *Produkt* to hone sth; *Betrugsmanöver, Ausreden etc* to get sth down to a fine art
perfektionieren [pɛrfɛktsio'niːrən], *ptp* **perfektioniert** VT to perfect
Perfektionismus [pɛrfɛktsio'nɪsmʊs] M **-**, NO PL perfectionism
Perfektionist [pɛrfɛktsio'nɪst] M **-en, -en, Perfektionistin** [-'nɪstɪn] F **-, -nen** perfectionist
perfektionistisch [pɛrfɛktsio'nɪstɪʃ] **1** ADJ perfectionist **2** ADV **du musst nicht alles so ~ machen** you don't have to be such a perfectionist
perforieren [pɛrfo'riːrən], *ptp* **perforiert** VT to perforate
Pergament [pɛrga'mɛnt] NT **-(e)s, -e (a)** (= *präparierte Tierhaut*) parchment **(b)** (= *Handschrift*) parchment **(c)** (= *~papier*) greaseproof paper
Pergola ['pɛrgola] F **-**, **Pergolen** [-lən] arbour (*Brit*), arbor (*US*)
Periode [pe'rioːdə] F **-, -n** period (*auch Physiol*); (*Math*) repetend; (*Elec*) cycle; **0,33 ~ 0.33** recurring; **ihre ~ ist ausgeblieben** she didn't get her period; **~n pro Sekunde** cycles per second
Periodensystem NT periodic system; (*Tafel*) periodic table
periodisch [pe'rioːdɪʃ] **1** ADJ periodic(al); (= *regelmäßig*) regular; (*Phys*) periodic; **~er Dezimalbruch** recurring fraction **2** ADV periodically
Peripherie [perife'riː] F **-, -n** [-'riːən] periphery; (*von Kreis*) circumference; (*von Stadt*) outskirts *pl*; (*von Computer*) periphery
Peripheriegerät NT peripheral
Periskop [peri'skoːp] NT **-s, -e** periscope
Perle ['pɛrlə] F **-, -n** pearl; (= *Glasperle, Wasserperle, Schweißperle*) bead; **~n vor die Säue werfen** (*prov*) to cast pearls before swine (*prov*)
perlen ['pɛrlən] VI (= *sprudeln*) to bubble; (*Champagner*) to fizz; (= *fallen, rollen*) to trickle; **der Schweiß perlte ihm von/auf der Stirn** beads of sweat were running down/stood out on his forehead; **Wasser perlt auf eine Fettschicht** water forms into droplets on a greasy surface
Perlen-: Perlenkette F, **Perlenkollier** NT string of pearls; **Perlentaucher(in)** M(F) pearl diver
Perl-: Perlhuhn NT guinea fowl; **Perlmutt** ['pɛrlmʊt, pɛrl'mʊt] NT **-s**, NO PL, **Perlmutter** ['pɛrlmʊtɐ, pɛrl'mʊtɐ] F **-** *no pl or* NT **-s**, NO PL mother-of-pearl
Perlon® ['pɛrlɔn] NT **-s**, NO PL ≈ nylon
Perl-: Perlwein M sparkling wine; **Perlzwiebel** F cocktail onion
Permafrostboden M permafrost
permanent [pɛrma'nɛnt] **1** ADJ permanent **2** ADV constantly
permeabel [pɛrme'aːbl] ADJ permeable
permissiv [pɛrmɪ'siːf] ADJ permissive
Permissivität [pɛrmɪsivi'tɛːt] F **-**, NO PL permissiveness
Perpetuum mobile [pɛr'peːtuʊm 'moːbilə] NT **-, -, -(s)** perpetual motion machine
perplex [pɛr'plɛks] ADJ dumbfounded
Perron [pɛ'rɔː] M **-s, -s** (*old, Sw, Aus*) platform
Perser¹ ['pɛrzɐ] M **-s, -** (*inf*) (= *Teppich*) Persian carpet; (= *Brücke*) Persian rug
Perser² ['pɛrzɐ] M **-s, -, Perserin** [-ərɪn] F **-, -nen** Persian
Persianer [pɛr'ziaːnɐ] M **-s, -** Persian lamb
Persien [pɛr'ziaːn] NT **-s** Persia
Persilschein [pɛr'ziːl-] M (*Hist*) denazification certificate; (*hum inf*) clean bill of health (*inf*); **jdm einen ~ ausstellen** (*hum inf*) to absolve sb of all responsibility
persisch [pɛrzɪʃ] ADJ Persian; **Persischer Golf** Persian Gulf
Person [pɛr'zoːn] F **-, -en** person; (*Liter, Theat*) character; **~en** people; **eine aus 6 ~en bestehende Familie** a family of 6; **ein Vier-~en-Haushalt** a four-person household; **pro ~** per person; **die eigene ~** oneself; **was seine (eigene) ~ betrifft** as for himself; **ich für meine ~ ...** I for my part ...; **er ist Vorsitzender und Schatzmeister in einer ~** he's the chairman and treasurer rolled into one; **jdn zur ~ vernehmen** (*Jur*) to question sb concerning his identity; **Angaben zur ~ machen** to give one's personal details; **natürliche/juristische ~** (*Jur*) natural/juristic *or* artificial person; **sie ist die Geduld in ~** she's patience personified; **es geht um die ~ des Kanzlers,**

nicht um das Amt it concerns the chancellor as a person, not the office; **lassen wir seine ~ aus dem Spiel** let's leave personalities out of it; **wir müssen die ~ von der Sache trennen** we must keep the personal and the factual aspects separate; **die ~en der Handlung** the characters (in the action); (*Theat auch*) the dramatis personae; **das Verb steht in der ersten ~ Plural** the verb is in the first person plural
Personal [pɛrzo'naːl] NT **-s**, NO PL personnel; **fliegendes ~** aircrew; **ungenügend/ausreichend mit ~ versehen sein** to be understaffed/adequately staffed
Personal-: Personalabbau M, NO PL staff cuts *pl*; **Personalabteilung** F personnel (department); **Personalausweis** M identity card; **Personalbestand** M number of staff; **Personalchef(in)** M(F) personnel manager; **Personalcomputer** M personal computer; **Personalgesellschaft** F unlimited company
personalisieren [pɛrzonali'ziːrən], *ptp* **personalisiert** VTI to personalize
Personal-: Personalkosten PL personnel costs *pl*; **Personalkredit** M personal *or* consumer credit; **Personalleiter(in)** M(F) personnel manager; **Personalpolitik** F personnel policy; **Personalpronomen** NT personal pronoun; **Personalunion** F personal union; **er ist Kanzler und Parteivorsitzender in ~** he is at the same time Prime Minister and party chairman
Persönchen [pɛr'zøːnçən] NT **-s, -** (*inf*) little lady (*inf*)
personell [pɛrzo'nɛl] **1** ADJ staff *attr*, personnel *attr*; **Konsequenzen** for staff **2** ADV **die Abteilung wird ~ aufgestockt** more staff will be taken on in the department; **~ unzureichend/zu großzügig ausgestattet sein** to be understaffed/overstaffed; **die Verzögerungen der Produktion sind ~ bedingt** the delays in production are caused by staff problems
Personen-: Personenaufzug M (passenger) lift (*Brit*), elevator (*US*); **Personenbeschreibung** F (personal) description; **personenbezogen** ADJ *Daten, Informationen* personal; **Personenfernverkehr** M (*esp Rail*) long-distance passenger services *pl*; **Personengedächtnis** NT memory for faces; **Personengesellschaft** F partnership; **Personenkreis** M group of people; **Personennahverkehr** M local passenger services *pl*; **öffentlicher ~** local public transport; **Personenschaden** M injury to persons; **ein Unfall mit/ohne ~** an accident in which people were injured/in which nobody was injured; **es gab keine ~** no-one was injured; **Personenschutz** M personal security; **Personenstand** M marital status; **Personenverkehr** M passenger services *pl*; **Personenwaage** F scales *pl*; **Personenwagen** M (*Aut*) car, automobile (*US*); **Personenzug** M (*Gegensatz: Schnellzug*) slow train; (*Gegensatz: Güterzug*) passenger train
personifizieren [pɛrzonifi'tsiːrən], *ptp* **personifiziert** VT to personify; **er läuft herum wie das personifizierte schlechte Gewissen** he's going around with guilt written all over his face
Personifizierung F **-, -en** personification
persönlich [pɛr'zøːnlɪç] **1** ADJ personal; *Atmosphäre, Umgangsformen* friendly; **~es Fürwort** personal pronoun; **~ werden** to get personal **2** ADV personally; (*auf Briefen*) private (and confidential); **etw ~ meinen/nehmen** *or* **auffassen** to mean/take sth personally; **er interessiert sich ~ für seine Leute** he takes a personal interest in his people
Persönlichkeit F **-, -en (a)** NO PL (= *Charakter*) personality; (*von Hotel, Einrichtung*) character **(b)** (= *bedeutender Mensch*) personality; **er ist eine ~** he's quite a personality; **~en des öffentlichen Lebens** public figures
Persönlichkeitswahl F *electoral system in which a vote is cast for a candidate rather than a party*; **diese Wahl war eine reine ~** (*inf*) this election boiled down to a question of the candidates' personalities
Perspektive [pɛrspɛk'tiːvə] F **-, -n** (*Art, Opt*) perspective; (= *Blickpunkt*) angle; (= *Gesichtspunkt*) point of view; (*fig*: = *Zukunftsausblick*) prospects *pl*; **das eröffnet ganz neue ~n für uns** that opens new horizons for us; **für etw keine ~ sehen** to see no future for sth
perspektivisch [pɛrspɛk'tiːvɪʃ] **1** ADJ **(a)** perspective *attr*; **die Zeichnung ist nicht ~** the drawing is not in perspective; **~e Verkürzung** foreshortening **(b)** (= *auf die Zukunft gerichtet*) prospective **2** ADV in perspective; **~ verkürzt** foreshortened;

dieses Bild ist ~ verzerrt the perspective in this picture is distorted

perspektivlos ADJ without prospects

Perspektivlosigkeit F -, NO PL lack of prospects

Peru [peˈruː] NT **-s** Peru

peruanisch [peˈruaːnɪʃ] ADJ Peruvian

Perücke [peˈrʏkə] F -, **-n** wig

pervers [perˈvɛrs] **1** ADJ perverted; **ein ~er Mensch** a pervert **2** ADV perversely; **~ veranlagt sein** to be a pervert

Perversion [perverˈzioːn] F -, **-en** perversion

Perversität [perverziˈtɛːt] F -, **-en** perversion

pervertieren [perverˈtiːrən], *ptp* **pervertiert 1** VT to pervert **2** VI AUX SEIN to become perverted

Pessar [pɛˈsaːɐ] NT **-s, -e** pessary; (*zur Empfängnisverhütung*) diaphragm

Pessimismus [pesiˈmɪsmʊs] M -, NO PL pessimism

Pessimist [pesiˈmɪst] M **-en, -en**, **Pessimistin** [-ˈmɪstɪn] F -, **-nen** pessimist

pessimistisch [pesiˈmɪstɪʃ] **1** ADJ pessimistic **2** ADV pessimistically; **~ eingestellt sein** to be pessimistic

Pest [pɛst] F -, NO PL (*Hist*, *Med*) plague; (*fig*) plague; **jdn/etw wie die ~ hassen** (*inf*) to loathe (and detest) sb/sth; **jdn wie die ~ meiden** (*inf*) to avoid sb like the plague! **wie die ~ stinken** (*inf*) to stink to high heaven (*inf*); **jdm die ~ an den Hals wünschen** (*inf*) to wish sb would drop dead (*inf*)

Pestizid [pɛstiˈtsiːt] NT **-(e)s, -e** [-də] pesticide

PET [pɛt] NT ABBR *von* **Polyethylenterephthalat** PET, polyethylene terephthalate

Petersilie [peteˈziːliə] F -, **-n** parsley

Peterwagen [ˈpeːtɐ-] M (*inf*) police *or* patrol car

PET-Flasche [ˈpɛt-] F PET bottle

Petition [petiˈtsioːn] F -, **-en** petition

Petrischale [ˈpeːtri-] F Petri dish

Petro-: Petrochemie [petroçeˈmiː, ˈpeːtro-] F petrochemistry; **petrochemisch** ADJ petrochemical; **Petrodollar** M petrodollar

Petroleum [peˈtroːleʊm] NT **-s**, NO PL paraffin (oil) (*Brit*), kerosene (*esp US*)

Petroleumlampe F paraffin (*Brit*) *or* kerosene (*esp US*) lamp

Petting [ˈpɛtɪŋ] NT **-s, -s** petting

petto [ˈpɛto] ADV **etw in ~ haben** (*inf*) to have sth up one's sleeve (*inf*)

Petze [ˈpɛtsə] F -, **-n** (*Sch inf*) snitch (*Sch inf*)

petzen [ˈpɛtsn] (*inf*) **1** VT **der petzt alles** he always tells; **er hat gepetzt, dass ...** he (went and) told that ...; **er hats dem Lehrer gepetzt** he told the teacher **2** VI to tell (tales) (*bei* to)

Petzer [ˈpɛtsɐ] M **-s, -**, **Petzerin** [-ərɪn] F -, **-nen** (*Sch inf*) snitch (*Sch inf*)

peu à peu [pø a ˈpø] ADV (*inf*) little by little

Pf (*Hist*) ABBR *von* **Pfennig**

Pfad [pfaːt] M **-(e)s, -e** [-də] (*auch Comput*) path; **neue ~e in der Medizin** new directions in medicine

Pfadfinder M, **Pfader** [ˈpfaːdɐ] M **-s, -** (*Sw*) (Boy) Scout; **er ist bei den Pfadern** he's in the (Boy) Scouts

Pfadfinderin F, **Pfaderin** [-ərɪn] F -, **-nen** (*Sw*) Girl Guide (*Brit*), Girl Scout (*US*)

Pfahl [pfaːl] M **-s, ⸚e** [ˈpfɛːlə] post; (= *Brückenpfahl*) pile; (= *Marterpfahl*) stake

Pfahl-: Pfahlbau M, *pl* **-bauten (a)** NO PL (*Bauweise*) building on stilts; **im ~** on stilts **(b)** (*Haus*) house built on stilts; **Pfahldorf** NT pile village

Pfalz [pfalts] F -, **-en (a)** NO PL (= *Rheinpfalz*) Rhineland *or* Lower Palatinate **(b)** NO PL (= *Oberpfalz*) Upper Palatinate **(c)** (*Hist*) (= *Burg*) palace; (= *Gebiet eines Pfalzgrafen*) palatinate

Pfälzer [ˈpfɛltsɐ] ADJ ATTR Palatine

pfälzisch [ˈpfɛltsɪʃ] ADJ Palatine

Pfand [pfant] NT **-(e)s, ⸚er** [ˈpfɛndɐ] security; (*beim Pfänderspiel*) forfeit; (= *Verpackungspfand, Nutzungspfand*) deposit; (*fig*) pledge; **ich gebe mein Wort als ~** I pledge my word; **etw gegen ~ leihen** to lend sth against a security; *Fahrrad, Schlittschuh etc* to hire (*Brit*) *or* rent (*US*) sth out in return for a deposit; **auf dem Glas ist ~** there's a deposit on the glass; **auf der Flasche sind 50 Cent ~** there's 50 cents (back) on the bottle (*inf*); **ein ~ einlösen** to redeem a pledge; **etw als ~ behalten** to keep sth as (a) security

pfändbar ADJ (*Jur*) distrainable (*form*); **der Fernseher ist nicht ~** the bailiffs can't take the television

Pfandbrief M (*von Bank, Regierung*) bond

pfänden [ˈpfɛndn] VT (*Jur*) to impound; *Konto, Lohn, Gehalt* to seize; **jdn ~** to impound some of sb's possessions; **jdn ~ lassen** to get the bailiffs onto sb

Pfänderspiel NT (game of) forfeits

Pfand-: Pfandflasche F returnable bottle; **Pfandhaus** NT pawnshop; **Pfandleihe** F **(a)** (*das Leihen*) pawnbroking **(b)** (= *Pfandhaus*) pawnshop; **Pfandleiher** [-laiɐ] M **-s, -**, **Pfandleiherin** [-ərɪn] F -, **-nen** pawnbroker; **Pfandschein** M pawn ticket

Pfändung [ˈpfɛndʊŋ] F -, **-en** seizure

Pfanne [ˈpfanə] F -, **-n** (*Cook*) pan; (*Anat*) socket; (= *Gießpfanne*) ladle; **jdn in die ~ hauen** (*inf*) to do the dirty on sb (*inf*); (= *vernichtend schlagen*) to wipe the floor with sb (*inf*); **etwas auf der ~ haben** (*inf: geistig*) to have it up there (*inf*)

Pfannengericht NT (*Cook*) fry-up

Pfannkuchen M (= *Eierpfannkuchen*) pancake; (= *Berliner*) (jam) doughnut (*Brit*) *or* donut (*US*)

Pfarrei [pfaˈrai] F -, **-en** (= *Gemeinde*) parish; (= *Amtsräume*) priest's office

Pfarrer [ˈpfarɐ] M **-s, -**, **Pfarrerin** [-ərɪn] F -, **-nen** (*katholisch, evangelisch*) parish priest; (*anglikanisch auch*) vicar; (*von Freikirchen*) minister; (= *Gefängnispfarrer, Militärpfarrer etc*) chaplain, padre; **als nächster wird Herr ~ Schmidt sprechen** the Reverend Michael Schmidt is going to speak next

Pfarr-: Pfarrgemeinde F parish; **Pfarrhaus** NT (*anglikanisch*) vicarage; (*methodistisch*) (*Scot*) manse; (*katholisch*) presbytery; **Pfarrkirche** F parish church

Pfau [pfau] M **-(e)s** *or* **-en, -en** peacock

Pfauenauge NT (= *Tagpfauenauge*) peacock butterfly; (= *Nachtpfauenauge*) peacock moth

Pfeffer [ˈpfɛfɐ] M **-s, -** pepper; **~ und Salz** (*lit*) salt and pepper; (*Stoffmuster*) pepper-and-salt; **er kann hingehen** *or* **bleiben, wo der ~ wächst!** (*inf*) he can go to hell (*inf*); **sie hat ~ im Hintern** (*inf*) *or* **Arsch** (*sl*) she's a lot of get-up-and-go (*inf*)

pfefferig [ˈpfɛfərɪç] ADJ peppery

Pfeffer-: Pfefferkorn NT, *pl* **-körner** peppercorn; **Pfefferkuchen** M gingerbread

Pfefferminz [ˈpfɛfɐmɪnts, -ˈmɪnts] NT **-es, -(e)**, **Pfefferminzbonbon** NT *or* M peppermint

Pfefferminze [ˈpfɛfɐmɪntsə, -ˈmɪntsə] F -, NO PL peppermint

Pfeffermühle F pepper mill

pfeffern [ˈpfɛfɐn] VT **(a)** (*Cook*) to season with pepper; (*fig*) to pepper; *siehe auch* **gepfeffert (b)** (*inf*) (= *heftig werfen*) to fling; **jdm eine ~** to clout sb one (*Brit inf*)

pfeffrig [ˈpfɛfrɪç] ADJ = **pfefferig**

Pfeife [ˈpfaifə] F -, **-n (a)** whistle; (= *Querpfeife*) fife (*esp Mil*), piccolo; (= *Bootsmannspfeife, Orgelpfeife*) pipe; **nach jds ~ tanzen** to dance to sb's tune **(b)** (*zum Rauchen*) pipe; **~ rauchen** (= *Pfeifenraucher sein*) to smoke a pipe **(c)** (*inf: = Versager*) wash-out (*inf*)

pfeifen [ˈpfaifn], *pret* **pfiff** [pfɪf], *ptp* **gepfiffen** [ɡəˈpfɪfn] **1** VI to whistle (**+*dat* for); (*auf einer Trillerpfeife*) to blow one's whistle; (*Mus: = auf einer Pfeife spielen*) to pipe; (*Wind*) to whistle; (*Radio*) to whine; **aus** *or* **auf dem letzten Loch ~** (*inf*) (= *erschöpft sein*) to be on one's last legs (*inf*); (*finanziell*) to be broke (*inf*); **ich pfeife darauf!** (*inf*) I couldn't care less; **ich pfeife auf seine Meinung** (*inf*) I couldn't care less about what he thinks; **~der Atem** wheezing **2** VT to whistle; (*Mus*) to pipe; (*Sport inf*) *Spiel* to ref (*inf*); *Abseits, Foul* to give; **das ~ ja schon die Spatzen von den Dächern** that's common knowledge

Pfeifer [ˈpfaifɐ] M **-s, -**, **Pfeiferin** [-ərɪn] F -, **-nen** piper

Pfeif-: Pfeifkessel M whistling kettle; **Pfeifkonzert** NT barrage *or* hail of catcalls *or* whistles

Pfeil [pfail] M **-s, -e** arrow; (*bei Armbrust auch*) bolt; (= *Wurfpfeil*) dart; **~ und Bogen** bow and arrow; **alle seine ~e verschossen haben** (*fig*) to have shot one's bolt; **Amors ~** Cupid's arrow; **der grüne ~** (*Mot*) the filter (arrow)

Pfeiler [ˈpfailɐ] M **-s, -** (*lit, fig*) pillar; (*von Hängebrücke*) pylon; (= *Stützpfeiler*) buttress

Pfeil-: pfeilförmig ◆1 ADJ V-shaped ◆2 ADV ~ angeordnet arranged in a V; **pfeilgerade** ◆1 ADJ as straight as a die; **eine ~ Linie** a dead straight line ◆2 ADV **sie kam ~ auf uns zu** she headed straight for us; **Pfeilgift** NT arrow poison; **Pfeilköcher** M quiver; **Pfeilspitze** F arrowhead; **Pfeiltaste** F (*Comput*) arrow key

Pfennig ['pfɛnɪç] M **-s, -e** [-gə] *or (nach Zahlenangabe)* **-** (*Hist*) pfennig, *one hundredth of a mark;* **er hat keinen ~ (Geld)** he hasn't got a penny to his name; **es ist keinen ~ wert** (*fig*) it's not worth a thing *or* a red cent (*US*); **für seine Chancen gebe ich keinen ~** I don't give much for his chances (*inf*); **auf den ~ sehen** (*fig*) to watch every penny; **mit dem** *or* **jedem ~ rechnen müssen** (*fig*) to have to watch every penny; **wer den ~ nicht ehrt, ist des Talers nicht wert** (*Prov*) ≈ take care of the pennies, and the pounds will take care of themselves (*Brit Prov*), ≈ a penny saved is a penny earned (*US*)

Pfennig-: Pfennigabsatz M stiletto heel; **Pfennigfuchser** [-fʊksɐ] M **-s, -**, **Pfennigfuchserin** [-ərɪn] F **-, -nen** (*inf*) miser (*inf*)

Pferch [pfɛrç] M **-es, -e** fold

pferchen ['pfɛrçn] VT to cram

Pferd [pfeːɐt] NT **-(e)s, -e** [-də] (*Tier, Turngerät*) horse; (*Chess*) knight; **zu ~(e)** on horseback; **aufs falsche/richtige ~ setzen** (*lit, fig*) to back the wrong/right horse; **wie ein ~ arbeiten** *or* **schuften** (*inf*) to work like a Trojan; **keine zehn ~e brächten mich dahin** (*inf*) wild horses couldn't drag me there; **mit ihm kann man ~e stehlen** (*inf*) he's a great sport (*inf*); **er ist unser bestes ~ im Stall** he's our best man; **ich glaub, mich tritt ein ~** (*inf*) blow me down (*dated inf*)

Pferde-: Pferdeapfel M piece of horse dung; **Pferdeäpfel** horse droppings *pl;* **Pferdebremse** F horsefly; **Pferdedroschke** F hackney cab; **Pferdefliege** F horsefly; **Pferdefuhrwerk** NT horse and cart; **Pferdegebiss** NT horsey teeth; **Pferdehaar** NT horsehair; **Pferdeknecht** M groom; **Pferdekoppel** F paddock; **Pferderennbahn** F race course; **Pferderennen** NT (*Sportart*) (horse) racing; (*einzelnes Rennen*) (horse) race; **Pferdeschlachter(in)** M(F) butcher; **Pferdeschlachterei** F slaughterhouse; **Pferdeschlitten** M horse-drawn sleigh; **Pferdeschwanz** M horse's tail; (*Frisur*) ponytail; **Pferdesport** M equestrian sport; **Pferdestall** M stable; **Pferdestärke** F horse power *no pl,* hp *abbr;* **Pferdezucht** F horse breeding; (= *Gestüt*) stud farm; **Pferdezüchter(in)** M(F) horse breeder

pfiff PRET *von* **pfeifen**

Pfiff [pfɪf] M **-s, -e** (a) whistle; (*Theat auch*) catcall (b) (= *Reiz*) style; **der Soße fehlt noch der letzte ~** the sauce still needs that extra something; **einem Kleid den richtigen ~ geben** to give a dress real style; **eine Inneneinrichtung mit ~** a stylish interior

Pfifferling ['pfɪfɐlɪŋ] M **-s, -e** chanterelle; **er kümmert sich keinen ~ um seine Kinder** (*inf*) he couldn't care less about his children; **keinen ~ wert** (*inf*) not worth a thing

pfiffig ['pfɪfɪç] ◆1 ADJ smart, cute; *Idee* smart ◆2 ADV cleverly

Pfiffigkeit F **-,** NO PL sharpness; (*von Idee*) cleverness

Pfingsten ['pfɪŋstn] NT **-, -** Whitsun (*Brit*), Pentecost

Pfingst-: Pfingstmontag M Whit Monday (*Brit*), Pentecost Monday (*US*); **Pfingstrose** F peony; **Pfingstsonntag** M Whit Sunday (*Brit*), Pentecost; **Pfingstwoche** F Whit week (*Brit*), the week of the Pentecost holiday (*US*)

Pfirsich ['pfɪrzɪç] M **-s, -e** peach

Pfirsich-: Pfirsichbaum M peach tree; **Pfirsichblüte** F peach blossom; **pfirsichfarben** [-farbn] ADJ peach(-coloured) (*Brit*), peach(-colored) (*US*)

Pflanze ['pflantsə] F **-, -n (a)** (= *Gewächs*) plant; **~n fressend** herbivorous (b) (*inf: Mensch*) **er/sie ist eine komische** *or* **seltsame ~** he/she is a strange fish (*inf*)

pflanzen ['pflantsn] VT to plant

Pflanzen-: Pflanzenfarbstoff M vegetable dye; **Pflanzenfaser** F plant fibre (*Brit*) *or* fiber (*US*); **Pflanzenfett** NT vegetable fat; **pflanzenfressend** ADJ ATTR *siehe* Pflanze; **Pflanzenfresser** M herbivore; **Pflanzenkunde** F, **Pflanzenlehre** F, NO PL botany; **Pflanzenmargarine** F vegetable margarine; **Pflanzenöl** NT vegetable oil; **Pflanzenschutzmittel** NT pesticide

pflanzlich ['pflantslɪç] ◆1 ADJ *Fette, Nahrung* vegetable *attr; Zellen, Organismen* plant *attr* ◆2 ADV **sich rein ~ ernähren** to eat no animal products; (*Tier*) to be a herbivore

Pflanzung ['pflantsʊŋ] F **-, -en** (= *das Pflanzen*) planting; (= *Plantage*) plantation

Pflaster ['pflastɐ] NT **-s, - (a)** (= *Heftpflaster*) (sticking) plaster (*Brit*), adhesive tape (*US*); (*fig*: = *Entschädigung*) sop (*auf +acc* to) (b) (= *Straßenpflaster*) (road) surface; (= *Kopfsteinpflaster*) cobbles *pl;* **~ treten** (*inf*) to trudge the streets; **ein gefährliches** *or* **heißes ~** (*inf*) a dangerous place; **ein teures ~** (*inf*) a pricey place (*inf*)

pflastern ['pflastɐn] VT *Straße, Hof* to surface; (*mit Kopfsteinpflaster*) to cobble; (*mit Steinplatten*) to pave; **eine Straße neu ~** to resurface a road; **ihre Filmkarriere war mit unzähligen Misserfolgen gepflastert** her film career was made up of a series of failures

Pflasterstein M (= *Kopfstein*) cobble(stone); (= *Steinplatte*) paving stone

Pflaume ['pflaumə] F **-, -n (a)** plum; **getrocknete ~** prune (b) (*inf: Mensch*) dope (*inf*) (c) (*sl:* = *Vagina*) cunt (*vulg*)

Pflege ['pfleːgə] F **-,** NO PL care; (*von Kranken auch*) nursing; (*von Beziehungen, Künsten*) cultivation; (*von Maschinen, Gebäuden*) maintenance; **jdn/etw in ~ nehmen** to look after sb/sth; **jdn/etw in ~ geben** to have sb/sth looked after; **ein Kind in ~ nehmen** (*dauernd*) to foster a child; **ein Kind in ~ geben** to have a child fostered; (*stundenweise*) to have a child looked after; (*Behörde*) to foster a child out (*zu jdm* with sb); **die ~ von jdm/etw übernehmen** to look after sb/sth; **der Garten/Kranke braucht viel ~** the garden/sick man needs a lot of care and attention; **häusliche ~** care in the home

Pflege-: pflegebedürftig ADJ in need of care (and attention); **wenn alte Leute ~ werden** when old people start to need looking after; **Pflegeberuf** M caring profession; **Pflegedienst** M home nursing service; **Pflegeeltern** PL foster parents *pl;* **Pflegefall** M case for nursing; **sie ist ein ~** she needs constant care; **Pflegegeld** NT (*für Pflegekinder*) boarding-out allowance; (*für Kranke*) attendance allowance; **Pflegeheim** NT nursing home; **Pflegekind** NT foster child; **Pflegekosten** PL nursing fees *pl;* **Pflegekostenversicherung** F private nursing insurance; **pflegeleicht** ADJ easy-care; **Pflegemittel** NT (= *Kosmetikum*) cosmetic care product; (*Aut*) cleaning product; **Pflegemutter** F, *pl* **-mütter** foster mother

pflegen ['pfleːgn] ◆1 VT to look after; *Kranke auch* to nurse; *Beziehungen, Kunst, Freundschaft* to cultivate; *Maschinen, Gebäude, Denkmäler* to maintain; **etw regelmäßig ~** to attend to sth regularly; **eine Creme, die die Haut pflegt** a cream which is good for the skin; *siehe auch* **gepflegt** ◆2 VI (= *gewöhnlich tun*) to be in the habit (*zu* of); **sie pflegte zu sagen** she used to say; **wie es so zu gehen pflegt** as usually happens; **wie man zu sagen pflegt** as they say ◆3 VR (a) (= *sein Äußeres ~*) to care about one's appearance (b) (= *sich schonen*) to take it easy (*inf*)

Pflege-: Pflegepersonal NT nursing staff; **Pflegeprodukt** NT care product; **~e für die Haut/das Auto** skin/car care products

Pfleger ['pfleːgɐ] M **-s, -** (*im Krankenhaus*) orderly; (*voll qualifiziert*) (male) nurse

Pflegerin ['pfleːgərɪn] F **-, -nen** nurse

Pflege-: Pflegesatz M hospital and nursing charges *pl;* **Pflegeserie** F (= *Kosmetika*) line of cosmetic products; **Pflegesohn** M foster son; **Pflegestation** F nursing ward; **Pflegetochter** F foster daughter; **Pflegevater** M foster father; **Pflegeversicherung** F nursing care insurance

PFLEGEVERSICHERUNG

*Pflegeversicherung was introduced in Germany in 1995 and is compulsory for members of state and private health insurance schemes. It covers the costs associated with long-term nursing care, for example in the case of old age or severe disability. The **Pflegeversicherung** also pays a certain amount to those who have to care for relatives at home and covers their social security contributions. **Pflegeversicherung** costs are borne jointly by employee and employer.*

pfleglich ['pfleːklɪç] ◆1 ADJ careful ◆2 ADV *behandeln, umgehen* carefully, with care

Pflicht [pflɪçt] F **-, -en (a)** (= *Verpflichtung*) duty (*zu* to); **Rechte und ~en** rights and responsibilities; **jdn in die ~ nehmen** to remind sb of his duty; **die ~ ruft** duty calls; **ich habe es mir zur ~ gemacht** I've taken it upon myself; **ich tue nur meine ~** I'm only doing my duty; **das ist ~** you have to do that, it's compulsory; **es ist seine (verdammte** *inf*) **~ und Schuldig-**

keit(**, das zu tun)** he damn well ought to (do it) (*inf*)
(b) (*Sport*) compulsory section
Pflicht-: Pflichtbesuch M duty visit; **pflichtbewusst** ADJ
conscientious; **Pflichtbewusstsein** NT sense of duty
Pflichtenheft NT (*für Geräte*) specification
Pflicht-: Pflichterfüllung F fulfilment (*Brit*) *or* fulfillment (*US*)
of one's duty; **Pflichtfach** NT compulsory subject;
Pflichtgefühl NT sense of duty; **pflichtgemäß** ⬛ ADJ dutiful;
~es Ermessen proper discretion ⬛ ADV dutifully; **ich teile
Ihnen ~ mit** it is my duty to inform you; **etw ~ tun müssen** to
be required to do sth; **Pflichtlektüre** F compulsory reading;
(*Sch auch*) set book(*s pl*); **Pflichtübung** F compulsory
exercise; **pflichtvergessen** ADJ neglectful of one's duty;
Pflichtvergessenheit F neglect of duty; **pflichtversichert**
[-fɛɐzɪçət] ADJ compulsorily insured; **Pflichtversicherte(r)** MF
DECL AS ADJ compulsorily insured person;
Pflichtversicherung F compulsory insurance;
Pflichtverteidiger(in) M(F) *counsel for the defence appointed by
the court and paid from the legal aid fund;* **pflichtwidrig** ⬛ ADJ
~es Verhalten failure to carry out one's duty ⬛ ADV **er hat
sich ~ verhalten** he failed to carry out his duty
Pflock [pflɔk] M **-(e)s, ⁺e** ['pflœkə] peg; (*für Tiere*) stake
pflücken ['pflʏkn] VT to pick; (= *sammeln*) to pick
Pflücker ['pflʏkɐ] M **-s, -**, **Pflückerin** [-ərɪn] F **-, -nen** picker
Pflücksalat M picking salad, *lettuce that is picked a few leaves
at a time*
Pflug [pfluːk] M **-es, ⁺e** ['pflyːgə] plough (*Brit*), plow (*US*);
(= *Schneepflug*) snowplough (*Brit*), snowplow (*US*)
pflügen ['pflyːgn] VTI (*lit, fig*) to plough (*Brit*), to plow (*US*)
Pfortader F portal vein
Pforte ['pfɔrtə] F **-, -n** (= *Tor*) gate; (*Geog*) gap; **die Messe öffnet
am Sonntag ihre ~n** the (trade) fair opens its doors on
Sunday; **Nepal, die ~ zum Himalaya** Nepal, the gateway to the
Himalayas
Pförtner¹ ['pfœrtnɐ] M **-s, -** (*Anat*) pylorus
Pförtner² ['pfœrtnɐ] M **-s, -**, **Pförtnerin** [-ərɪn] F **-, -nen** porter;
(*von Fabrik*) gateman/-woman; (*von Wohnhaus, Behörde*)
doorman/-woman
Pförtnerloge F porter's office; (*in Fabrik*) gatehouse; (*in
Wohnhaus, Büro*) doorman's office
Pfosten ['pfɔstn] M **-s, -** post; (= *senkrechter Balken*) upright;
(= *Fensterpfosten*) (window) jamb; (= *Türpfosten*) doorpost;
(= *Stütze*) support; (*Ftbl*) (goal)post
Pfötchen ['pføːtçən] NT **-s, -** DIM *von* Pfote little paw; **~ geben**
(*fig inf*) to shake hands; **(gib) ~!** (*zu Hund*) give me a paw!
Pfote ['pfoːtə] F **-, -n (a)** paw **(b)** (*inf:* = *Hand*) paw (*inf*); **sich**
(*dat*) **die ~n verbrennen** (*inf*) to burn one's fingers; **seine ~n
überall drin haben** (*fig inf*) to have a finger in every pie (*inf*)
Pfropf [pfrɔpf] M **-(e)s, -e** *or* ⁺e ['pfrœpfə] (= *Stöpsel*) stopper;
(= *Kork, Sektpfropf*) cork; (= *Wattepfropf etc*) plug; (*von Fass,
Korbflasche*) bung; (*Med:* = *Blutpfropf*) (blood) clot;
(*verstopfend*) blockage
pfropfen ['pfrɔpfn] VT **(a)** *Pflanzen* to graft **(b)** (= *verschließen*)
Flasche to bung, to stop up **(c)** (*inf:* = *hineinzwängen*) to cram;
er pfropfte den Korken in die Flasche he shoved the cork in
the bottle; **gepfropft voll** jam-packed (*inf*)
Pfropfen ['pfrɔpfn] M **-s, -** = Pfropf
pfui [pfui] INTERJ (*Ekel*) ugh; (*Missbilligung*) tut tut; (*zu Hunden*)
oy; (*Buhruf*) boo; **fass das nicht an, das ist ~** (*inf*) don't touch
it, it's dirty; **~ Teufel** *or* **Deibel** *or* **Spinne** (*all inf*) ugh; **~
schäme dich** shame on you!; **da kann ich nur ~** *or* **Pfui sagen**
it's simply disgraceful
Pfund [pfʊnt] NT **-(e)s, -e** [-də] *or* (*nach Zahlenangabe*) **-
(a)** (= *Gewicht*) (*in Deutschland*) 500 grams; (*in Großbritannien*)
pound; **drei ~ Äpfel** three pounds of apples; **er bewegte
seine ~e mit Mühe** he moved his great bulk with effort;
überflüssige ~e abspecken to shed surplus pounds
(b) (= *Währungseinheit*) pound; (= *irisches ~*) punt;
(= *türkisches ~*) lira; **in ~** in pounds; **zwanzig ~ Sterling** twenty
pounds sterling
Pfund- IN CPDS pound; **Pfundbetrag** M amount in pounds
-pfünder [pfʏndɐ] M **-s, -** IN CPDS -pounder; **ein Fünfpfünder**
(*Fisch*) a five-pounder
-pfündig [pfʏndɪç] ADJ SUF weighing ... pounds
Pfunds- IN CPDS (*inf*) great (*inf*); **Pfundskerl** M (*inf*) great guy
(*inf*)

pfundweise ADV by the pound
Pfusch [pfʊʃ] M **-(e)s**, NO PL (*inf*) = Pfuscherei
pfuschen ['pfʊʃn] VI **(a)** (= *schlecht arbeiten*) to bungle; (= *einen
Fehler machen*) to slip up; **jdm ins Handwerk ~** to meddle in
sb's affairs **(b)** (*Sch*) to cheat **(c)** (*Aus:* = *schwarzarbeiten*) to
(do) work on the side (*esp Brit inf*)
Pfuscher ['pfʊʃɐ] M **-s, -** (*inf*), **Pfuscherin** [-ərɪn] F **-, -nen** (*inf*)
bungler
Pfuscherei [pfʊʃəˈrai] F **-, -en** (= *das Pfuschen*) bungling *no pl*;
(= *gepfuschte Arbeit*) botch-up (*inf*)
Pfütze ['pfʏtsə] F **-, -n** puddle
PH [peːˈhaː] F **-, -s** ABBR *von* pädagogische Hochschule
phallisch ['falɪʃ] ADJ phallic
Phallus ['falʊs] M **-, -se** *or* Phalli *or* Phallen ['fali, 'falən] phallus
Phallussymbol NT phallic symbol
Phänomen [fɛnoˈmeːn] NT **-s, -e** phenomenon
phänomenal [fɛnomeˈnaːl] ⬛ ADJ phenomenal ⬛ ADV
phenomenally (well); **~ aussehen** to look phenomenal
Phantasie [fantaˈziː] F **-, -n** [-'ziːən] = Fantasie
phantastisch [fanˈtastɪʃ] ADJ, ADV = fantastisch
Phantom [fanˈtoːm] NT **-s, -e** (= *Trugbild*) phantom; **einem ~
nachjagen** (*fig*) to tilt at windmills
Phantom-: Phantombild NT Identikit® (picture), Photofit®
(picture); **Phantomschmerz** M phantom limb pain
Pharao ['faːrao] M **-s, Pharaonen** [faraˈoːnən] Pharaoh
Pharaonen- IN CPDS of the Pharaohs; **~gräber** tombs of the
Pharaohs
Pharisäer [fariˈzɛːɐ] M **-s, -** pharisee
pharisäerhaft ADJ pharisaic(al)
Pharisäertum [fariˈzɛːɐtuːm] NT **-s**, NO PL (*fig*) self-righteousness
pharm. ABBR *von* pharmazeutisch
Pharma- ['farma-]: **Pharmahersteller(in)** M(F) drug
manufacturer; **Pharmaindustrie** F pharmaceuticals industry
Pharmakologe [farmakoˈloːgə] M **-n, -n**, **Pharmakologin**
[-'loːgɪn] F **-, -nen** pharmacologist
pharmakologisch [farmakoˈloːgɪʃ] ⬛ ADJ pharmacological
⬛ ADV pharmacologically
Pharma- ['farma-]: **Pharmaprodukt** NT pharmaceutical
product; **Pharmaproduzent(in)** M(F) pharmaceuticals
producer; **Pharmaunternehmen** NT pharmaceuticals
company
Pharmazeut [farmaˈtsɔyt] M **-en, -en**, **Pharmazeutin** [-'tsɔytɪn] F
-, -nen pharmacist, druggist (*US*)
pharmazeutisch [farmaˈtsɔytɪʃ] ⬛ ADJ pharmaceutical;
~-technische Assistentin, **~-technischer Assistent**
pharmaceutical assistant ⬛ ADV pharmaceutically
Phase ['faːzə] F **-, -n** phase
-phasig [faːzɪç] ADJ SUF -phase; **dreiphasig** three-phase
Pheromon [feroˈmoːn] NT **-s, -e** pheromone
Philatelist [filateˈlɪst] M **-en, -en**, **Philatelistin** [-'lɪstɪn] F **-, -nen**
philatelist
Philharmonie [fɪlharmoˈniː:, fiːlharmoˈniː:] F **-, -n** [-'niːən]
(= *Orchester*) philharmonic (orchestra); (= *Konzertsaal*)
philharmonic hall
Philharmoniker [fɪlharˈmoːnikɐ, fiːlharˈmoːnikɐ] M **-s, -**,
Philharmonikerin [-ərɪn] F **-, -nen** (= *Musiker*) member of a
philharmonic orchestra
Philippinen [fɪlɪˈpiːnən] PL Philippines *pl*
philippinisch [fɪlɪˈpiːnɪʃ] ADJ Filipino
Philologe [filoˈloːgə] M **-n, -n**, **Philologin** [-'loːgɪn] F **-, -nen**
philologist
Philologie [filoloˈgiː] F **-**, NO PL philology
philologisch [filoˈloːgɪʃ] ⬛ ADJ philological ⬛ ADV
philologically; **~ gesehen** from a philological point of view
Philosoph [filoˈzoːf] M **-en, -en**, **Philosophin** [-'zoːfɪn] F **-, -nen**
philosopher
Philosophie [filozoˈfiː] F **-, -n** [-'fiːən] philosophy
philosophieren [filozoˈfiːrən] ptp **philosophiert** VI to
philosophize (*über +acc* about)
philosophisch [filoˈzoːfɪʃ] ⬛ ADJ philosophical ⬛ ADV
philosophically
Phlegma ['flɛgma] NT **-s**, NO PL apathy

Phlegmatiker [fleˈgmaːtikɐ] M **-s**, **-**, **Phlegmatikerin** [-ərɪn] F **-**, **-nen** apathetic person

phlegmatisch [fleˈgmaːtɪʃ] **1** ADJ apathetic **2** ADV apathetically; **~ veranlagt sein** to be apathetic (by nature)

Phobie [foˈbiː] F **-**, **-n** [-ˈbiːən] phobia (*vor* +*dat* about)

Phon [foːn] NT **-s**, **-s** phon

Phonem [foˈneːm] NT **-s**, **-e** phoneme

Phonetik [foˈneːtɪk] F **-**, NO PL phonetics *sing*

Phonetiker [foˈneːtikɐ] M **-s**, **-**, **Phonetikerin** [-ərɪn] F **-**, **-nen** phonetician

phonetisch [foˈneːtɪʃ] **1** ADJ phonetic; **~e Schrift** phonetic transcription **2** ADV **etw ~ (um)schreiben** to write *or* transcribe sth phonetically

Phönix [ˈføːnɪks] M **-(es)**, **-e** phoenix; **wie ein ~ aus der Asche steigen** to rise like a phoenix from the ashes

Phonotypist [fonotyˈpɪst] M **-en**, **-en**, **Phonotypistin** [-ˈpɪstɪn] F **-**, **-nen** audiotypist

Phon- [foːn-]: **phonstark** ADJ *Lautsprecher* powerful; *Lärm* loud; **Phonstärke** F decibel

Phosphat [fɔsˈfaːt] NT **-(e)s**, **-e** phosphate

phosphat-: **phosphatfrei** ADJ phosphate-free; **phosphathaltig** ADJ containing phosphates

Phosphor [ˈfɔsfɔɐ] M **-s**, NO PL (*abbr* **P**) phosphorus

phosphoreszieren [fɔsforesˈtsiːrən] *ptp* **phosphoresziert** VI to phosphoresce

Photo [ˈfoːto] NT **-s**, **-s** = **Foto**

Photo- IN CPDS photo; *siehe auch* **Foto-**; **photoelektrisch** ADJ photoelectric; **Photosynthese** [fotozynˈteːzə, ˈfoːtozynteːzə] F **-**, NO PL (*Phys*) photosynthesis; **Photovoltaik** [fotovɔlˈtaːɪk] F **-**, NO PL (*Phys*) photovoltaics *sing*; **photovoltaisch** [-vɔlˈtaːɪʃ] ADJ photovoltaic; **Photozelle** F photoelectric cell

Phrase [ˈfraːzə] F **-**, **-n** phrase; (*pej*) empty phrase; **abgedroschene ~** cliché, hackneyed phrase (*Brit*); **das sind alles nur ~n** that's just (so many) words; **~n dreschen** (*inf*) to churn out one cliché after another

Phrasen-: **Phrasendrescher(in)** M(F) (*pej*) windbag (*inf*); **Phrasendrescherei** [-dreʃəˈraɪ] F **-**, **-en** (*pej*) phrasemongering; (= *Geschwafel*) hot air

Phraseologie [frazeoloˈgiː] F **-**, **-n** [-ˈgiːən] phraseology; (*Buch*) dictionary of idioms

phraseologisch [frazeoˈloːgɪʃ] ADJ phraseological; **~es Wörterbuch** dictionary of idioms

pH-Wert [peːˈhaː-] M pH value

Physik [fyˈziːk] F **-**, NO PL physics *sing*

physikalisch [fyziˈkaːlɪʃ] **1** ADJ physical; **~e Experimente durchführen** to carry out physics experiments; **~e Therapie** physical therapy **2** ADV physically; **das ist ~ nicht erklärbar** that can't be explained by physics

Physiker [ˈfyːzikɐ] M **-s**, **-**, **Physikerin** [-ərɪn] F **-**, **-nen** physicist; (*Student auch*) physics student

Physiksaal M physics lab

Physikum [ˈfyːzikom] NT **-s**, NO PL (*Univ*) preliminary examination in medicine

physiologisch [fyzioˈloːgɪʃ] **1** ADJ physiological **2** ADV physiologically

Physiotherapeut(in) [fyzioteraˈpɔyt] M(F) physiotherapist

Physiotherapie [fyzioteraˈpiː] F physiotherapy

physisch [ˈfyːzɪʃ] **1** ADJ physical **2** ADV physically

Pi [piː] NT **-(s)**, **-s** pi; **etw Pi mal Daumen machen** (*inf*) to do sth off the top of one's head

Pianist [piaˈnɪst] M **-en**, **-en**, **Pianistin** [-ˈnɪstɪn] F **-**, **-nen** pianist

piano ADV (*Mus*) piano

picheln [ˈpɪçln] VI (*inf*) to booze (*inf*)

Pickel [ˈpɪkl] M **-s**, **-** (a) spot (b) (= *Spitzhacke*) pick(axe) (*Brit*), pick(ax) (*US*); (= *Eispickel*) ice axe (*Brit*), ice ax (*US*)

Vorsicht! **Pickel** *wird nicht mit dem englischen Wort* **pickle** *übersetzt.*

pickelig [ˈpɪkəlɪç] ADJ spotty

picken [ˈpɪkn] VTI to peck (*nach* at)

picklig [ˈpɪklɪç] ADJ spotty

Picknick [ˈpɪknɪk] NT **-s**, **-s** *or* **-e** picnic; **zum ~ fahren** to go for a picnic; **~ machen** to have a picnic

picknicken [ˈpɪknɪkn] VI to (have a) picnic

Picogramm [pikoˈgram] NT, *pl* **-gramme** *or (nach Zahlenangabe)* **- picogramme** (*Brit*), picogram (*US*)

PID [peːliːˈdeː] F **-** ABBR *von* **Präimplantationsdiagnostik** pre-implantation diagnosis, PID

pieken [ˈpiːkn] VTI (*inf*) to prick; **es hat nur ein bisschen gepiekt** it was just a bit of a prick

piekfein [ˈpiːkˈfain] (*inf*) **1** ADJ posh (*inf*) **2** ADV **~ eingerichtet sein** to have classy furnishings; **~ angezogen sein** to look snazzy (*inf*); **~ speisen** to have a really posh meal (*inf*)

pieksen [ˈpiːksn] VTI = **pieken**

piep [piːp] INTERJ tweet(-tweet), chirp(-chirp), cheep(-cheep); (*von Armbanduhr, Telefon*) beep(-beep)

Piep [piːp] M **-s**, **-e** (= *geräusch*) peep, beep; (*inf*) **er sagt keinen ~** *or* **gibt keinen ~ von sich** he doesn't say a (single) word; **keinen ~ mehr machen** to have had it (*inf*); **er traute sich nicht mal, ~ zu sagen** *or* **machen** (*inf*) he wouldn't have dared to say boo to a goose (*inf*)

piepe [ˈpiːpə], **piepegal** [ˈpiːpleˈgaːl] ADJ PRED (*inf*) all one (*inf*)

piepen [ˈpiːpn] VI (*Vogel*) to cheep; (*Maus*) to squeak; (*Funkgerät etc*) to bleep; **bei dir piepts wohl!** (*inf*) are you off your head rocker? (*inf*); **es war zum Piepen!** (*inf*) it was a scream! (*inf*)

piepsen [ˈpiːpsn] VI = **piepen**

Piepser [ˈpiːpsɐ] M **-s**, **-** (*inf*) (a) = **Piep** (b) (*Telec*) bleeper

Pier [piːɐ] M **-s**, **-s** *or* **-e**, *or* f **-**, **-s** jetty

piercen [ˈpiːɐsn] VT to pierce; **sich** (*dat*) **die Zunge ~ lassen** to get one's tongue pierced

Piercing [ˈpiːɐsɪŋ] NT **-s**, **-s** (a) NO PL body piercing (b) (*Körperschmuck*) piece of body jewellery (*Brit*) *or* jewelry (*US*); **~s aus Gold** gold body jewellery (*Brit*) *or* jewelry (*US*)

piesacken [ˈpiːzakn] VT (*inf*: = *quälen*) to torment; (= *belästigen*) to pester

Pietät [pieˈtɛːt] F **-**, NO PL (= *Ehrfurcht vor den Toten*) reverence *no pl*; (= *Achtung*) respect (*gegenüber jdm/etw, vor etw* (*dat*)) for sb/sth)

pietätlos [piˈtɛːtloːs] **1** ADJ irreverent; (= *ohne Achtung*) lacking in respect **2** ADV irreverently; **~ über Tote sprechen** to speak disrespectfully of the dead

Pietätlosigkeit F **-**, **-en** irreverence; (*Tat*) impiety; **das ist eine ~ sondergleichen!** that shows a complete lack of reverence!

Pietismus [pieˈtɪsmʊs] M **-**, NO PL Pietism

pietistisch [pieˈtɪstɪʃ] ADJ pietistic

Pigment [pɪˈgment] NT **-(e)s**, **-e** pigment

Pigmentation [pɪgmɛntaˈtsioːn] F **-**, **-en** pigmentation

Pigmentfleck M pigmentation mark

Pik[1] [piːk] M (*inf*) **einen ~ auf jdn haben** to have something against sb

Pik[2] NT **-s**, **-** (*Cards*) (*no pl: Farbe*) spades *pl*; (= *~karte*) spade; **dastehen wie ~-sieben** (*inf*) to look completely bewildered

pikant [piˈkant] **1** ADJ piquant; (*fig*) piquantly; **~ gewürzt** well-seasoned; **~ schmecken** to taste piquant

Pike [ˈpiːkə] F **-**, **-n** pike; **von der ~ auf dienen** (*fig*) to rise from the ranks; **etw von der ~ auf lernen** (*fig*) to learn sth starting from the bottom

pikfein [ˈpiːkˈfain] ADJ, ADV = **piekfein**

pikiert [piˈkiːɐt] (*inf*) **1** ADJ put out; **sie machte ein ~es Gesicht** she looked put out **2** ADV **~ reagieren** to be put out *or* peeved (*inf*); **~ das Gesicht verziehen** to look peeved (*inf*)

Pikkolo [ˈpɪkolo] M **-s**, **-s** (a) (*fig*: = *kleine Ausgabe*) mini-version; (*auch* **Pikkoloflasche**) quarter bottle of champagne (b) (*Mus*: *auch* **Pikkoloflöte**) piccolo

Piktogramm [pɪktoˈgram] NT, *pl* **-gramme** pictogram

Pilger [ˈpɪlgɐ] M **-s**, **-**, **Pilgerin** [-ərɪn] F **-**, **-nen** pilgrim

Pilgerfahrt F pilgrimage

pilgern [ˈpɪlgɐn] VI AUX SEIN to make a pilgrimage; (*inf*: = *gehen*) to make one's way

Pille [ˈpɪlə] F **-**, **-n** pill; (= *Antibabypille*) pill; **die ~ danach** the morning-after pill; **die ~ für den Mann** the male pill; **eine ~ (ein)nehmen** *or* **schlucken** to take a pill; **sie nimmt die ~** she's on the pill; **das war eine bittere ~ für ihn** (*fig*) that was a bitter pill for him (to swallow)

Pilot [piˈloːt] M **-en**, **-en**, **Pilotin** [-ˈloːtɪn] F **-**, **-nen** pilot

Pilot-: **Pilotanlage** F pilot plant; **Pilotballon** M pilot balloon; **Pilotfilm** M pilot film

Pilotin F -, -nen pilot

Pilotprojekt NT pilot scheme

Pils [pɪls] NT -, -, **Pilsener** ['pɪlzənɐ] NT -s, -, **Pilsner** ['pɪlznɐ] NT -s, - Pils

Pilz [pɪlts] M -es, -e (a) fungus; (giftig) toadstool; (essbar) mushroom; (= Mikropilz) mould (Brit), mold (US); (= Atompilz) mushroom cloud; ~e sammeln, in die ~e gehen (inf) to go mushroom-picking; wie ~e aus der Erde or aus dem Boden schießen or sprießen to spring up like mushrooms (b) (= Hautpilz) fungal skin infection

Pilz-: **Pilzkrankheit** F fungal disease; **Pilzkunde** F, NO PL mycology; **pilztötend** ADJ fungicidal; **Pilzvergiftung** F fungus poisoning

Pimmel ['pɪml] M -s, - (inf: = Penis) willie (inf)

pimpern ['pɪmpɐn] VI (inf) to do it (inf)

PIN [pɪn] F ABBR von persönliche Identifikationsnummer PIN; ~-Nummer PIN number

Pin [pɪn] M -s, -s (a) (Comput: von Stecker) pin (b) (= Anstecknadel) badge

pingelig ['pɪŋəlɪç] ADJ (inf) finicky (inf)

Pingpong ['pɪŋpɔŋ] NT -s, -s (inf) ping-pong

Pinguin ['pɪŋguiːn] M -s, -e penguin

Pinie ['piːniə] F -, -n pine

pink [pɪŋk] ADJ shocking pink

Pinkel ['pɪŋkl] M -s, - (inf) ein feiner or vornehmer ~ a swell, His Highness (inf)

pinkeln ['pɪŋkln] VI (inf) to pee (inf)

Pinkelpause F (inf) toilet break; der Bus hielt zu einer ~ the bus made a toilet stop

Pinne ['pɪnə] F -, -n (a) (inf: = Stift) pin (b) (für Kompassnadel) pivot (c) (= Ruderpinne) tiller

Pinnwand [pɪn-] F (notice) board

Pinsel ['pɪnzl] M -s, - (a) brush (b) (inf) ein eingebildeter ~ a jumped-up (Brit) or hopped-up (US) so-and-so (inf)

pinseln ['pɪnzln] VTI (inf: = streichen) to paint (auch Med); (pej: = malen) to daub; (inf: = schreiben) to pen

Pinte ['pɪntə] F -, -n (inf: = Lokal) bar

Pin-up-Girl [pɪn'lap-] NT pin-up (girl)

Pinzette [pɪn'tsɛtə] F -, -n (pair of) tweezers pl

Pionier [pio'niːɐ] M -s, -e, **Pionierin** [-'niːərɪn] F -, -nen (a) (Mil) sapper (b) (fig) pioneer

Pioniergeist M, NO PL pioneering spirit

Pipeline ['paɪplaɪn] F -, -s pipeline

Pipette [pi'pɛtə] F -, -n pipette

Pipi [pi'pi:] NT or M -s, -s (baby-talk) wee(-wee) (baby-talk); ~ machen to do a wee(-wee)

Pipi-: **Pipifax** ['piːpifaks] NT or M -, NO PL (inf) nonsense; **Pipimädchen** ['piːpi-] NT (pej) bimbo (inf)

Piranha [pi'ranja] M -(s), -s piranha

Pirat [pi'raːt] M -en, -en, **Piratin** [-'raːtɪn] F -, -nen (lit, fig) pirate; (= Luftpirat) hijacker

Piraten-: **Piratenschiff** NT pirate ship; **Piratensender** M pirate radio station

Piraterie [piratə'riː] F -, -n [-'riːən] (lit, fig) piracy

Piratin F siehe Pirat

Pirouette [pi'ruɛtə] F -, -n pirouette

Pirsch [pɪrʃ] F -, NO PL stalk; auf (die) ~ gehen to go stalking

Pisse ['pɪsə] F -, NO PL (vulg) piss (sl)

pissen ['pɪsn] VI (vulg) to (take a) piss (sl); (sl: = regnen) to pour down (inf)

Pissnelke F (sl) nerd (inf)

Pistazie [pɪs'taːtsiə] F -, -n pistachio

Piste ['pɪstə] F -, -n (Ski) piste; (= Rennbahn) track; (Aviat) runway; (behelfsmäßig) landing strip; (im Zirkus) barrier

Pisten-: **Pistenraupe** F piste caterpillar; **Pistensau** F (Ski sl), **Pistenschreck** M (Ski inf) hooligan on the piste

Pistole [pɪs'toːlə] F -, -n pistol; jdn mit vorgehaltener ~ (zu etw) zwingen to force sb (to do sth) at gunpoint; jdm die ~ auf die Brust setzen (fig) to hold a pistol to sb's head; wie aus der ~ geschossen (fig) like a shot (inf)

Pit-Bull-Terrier ['pɪtbʊl-] M pit bull terrier

pitschenass ['pɪtʃə'nas], **pitschnass** ['pɪtʃ'nas] (inf) ADJ soaking (wet)

pittoresk [pɪto'rɛsk] 1 ADJ picturesque 2 ADV picturesquely; ~ aussehen to look picturesque

Pixel ['pɪksl] NT -s, -s (Comput) pixel

Pizza ['pɪtsa] F -, -s or **Pizzen** ['pɪtsn] pizza

Pizzabäcker(in) M(F) pizza chef

Pizzeria [pɪtsə'riːa] F -, -s or **Pizzerien** [-'riːən] pizzeria

Pkw ['peːkaːveː, peːka'veː] M -s, -s ABBR von Personenkraftwagen car

Placebo [pla'tseːbo] NT -s, -s placebo

Placebo-Effekt M (lit, fig) placebo effect

Plackerei [plakə'raɪ] F -, -en (inf) grind (inf)

plädieren [plɛ'diːrən] ptp **plädiert** VI (Jur, fig) to plead (für, auf +acc for)

Plädoyer [plɛdoa'jeː] NT -s, -s (Jur) summation (US), summing up; (fig) plea

Plage ['plaːgə] F -, -n (a) plague (b) (fig: = Mühe) nuisance; (= Plackerei) (hard) grind (inf); sie hat ihre ~ mit ihm he's a trial for her

Plagegeist M nuisance

plagen ['plaːgn] 1 VT to plague; (mit Bitten und Fragen auch) to pester; dich plagt doch was, heraus mit der Sprache something's worrying you, out with it; ein geplagter Mann a harassed man 2 VR (a) (= leiden) to be troubled (mit by) (b) (= sich abrackern) to slave away (inf); (= sich Mühe geben) to go to a lot of trouble (mit over, with)

Plagiat [pla'giaːt] NT -(e)s, -e (= geistiger Diebstahl) plagiarism (b) (Buch, Film etc) book/film etc resulting from plagiarism; (= nachgebildeter Markenartikel) counterfeit product; dieses Buch ist ein ~ this book is plagiarism

plagiieren [plagi'iːrən] ptp **plagiiert** VTI to plagiarize

Plakafarbe® ['plaka-] F poster paint

Plakat [pla'kaːt] NT -(e)s, -e (an Litfaßsäulen etc) poster; (aus Pappe) placard

plakatieren [plaka'tiːrən] ptp **plakatiert** VT to placard; (fig) to broadcast

plakativ [plaka'tiːf] 1 ADJ Wirkung, Farben striking; Sprüche pithy; Gehabe showy 2 ADV ~ formuliert catchy; etw ~ formulieren to express sth in a catchy phrase; ~ wirkende Lieder catchy songs

Plakat-: **Plakatsäule** F advertisement pillar; **Plakatträger(in)** M(F) man/woman carrying a sandwich board; **Plakatwerbung** F poster advertising

Plakette [pla'kɛtə] F -, -n (= Abzeichen) badge; (Münze) commemorative coin; (an Wänden) plaque

plan [plaːn] ADJ flat; Ebene, Fläche plane attr

Plan[1] [plaːn] M -(e)s, ⸚e ['plɛːnə] (a) plan; den ~ fassen, etw zu tun to plan to do sth; wir haben den ~, ... we're planning to ...; Pläne machen or schmieden to make plans (b) (= Stadtplan) (street) map; (= Grundriss, Bauplan) plan; (= Zeittafel) schedule; (= Wirtschaftsplan) economic plan

Plan[2] M -(e)s, ⸚e [plɛːnə] (obs: = ebene Fläche) plain; auf dem ~ erscheinen, auf den ~ treten (fig) to arrive or come on the scene; jdn auf den ~ rufen (fig) to bring sb into the arena

Plane ['plaːnə] F -, -n tarpaulin; (von LKW) hood; (= Schutzdach) canopy

planen ['plaːnən] VTI to plan

Planerfüllung F realization of a/the plan

Planet [pla'neːt] M -en, -en planet

planetarisch [plane'taːrɪʃ] ADJ planetary

Planetarium [plane'taːriom] NT -s, **Planetarien** [-riən] planetarium

planieren [pla'niːrən] ptp **planiert** VT Boden to level (off); Werkstück to planish

Planierraupe F bulldozer

Planke ['plaŋkə] F -, -n plank; (= Leitplanke) crash barrier

plänkeln ['plɛŋkln] VI (fig) to squabble

Plankosten PL budgeted costs pl, standard cost

Plankostenrechnung F standard or marginal costing

Plankton ['plaŋktɔn] NT -s, NO PL plankton

planlos 1 ADJ unmethodical; (= ziellos) random 2 ADV umherirren, durchstreifen aimlessly; vorgehen without any clear direction; *durchsuchen* haphazardly; **etw ~ durchblättern** to flick aimlessly through sth

Planlosigkeit F -, NO PL lack of planning

planmäßig ❶ ADJ (= *wie geplant*) as planned; (= *pünktlich*) on schedule; (= *methodisch*) methodical; **~e Ankunft/Abfahrt** scheduled time of arrival/departure ❷ ADV
(a) (= *systematisch*) systematically (b) (= *fahrplanmäßig*) on schedule; **~ kommt der Zug um 7 Uhr an** the train is scheduled to arrive at 7 o'clock

Planschbecken NT paddling pool (*Brit*), wading pool (*US*)

planschen ['planʃn] VI to splash around

Plan-: Plansoll NT output target; **Planstelle** F post

Plantage [plan'ta:ʒə] F -, -n plantation

Planung ['pla:nʊŋ] F -, -en planning; **diese Straße ist noch in ~** this road is still being planned; **schon in der ~** at the planning stage

Plan-: Planwagen M covered wagon; **Planwirtschaft** F planned economy

Plapperei [plapə'raɪ] F -, -en (*inf*) prattling (*esp Brit*)

Plappermaul NT (*inf*) (= *Mund*) big mouth (*inf*); (= *Kind*) chatterbox (*inf*); (= *Schwätzer*) windbag (*inf*)

plappern ['plapɐn] ❶ VI to chatter; (= *Geheimnis verraten*) to blab (*inf*) ❷ VT **was plapperst du denn da für Blödsinn?** don't talk nonsense

Plaque [plak] F -, -s (*Med*) plaque

plärren ['plɛrən] VTI (*inf*: = *weinen*) to howl; (*Radio*) to blare (out); (= *schreien*) to yell

Pläsierchen [plɛ'zi:ɐçən] NT -s, - **jedem Tierchen sein ~** (*hum*) each to his own

Plasma ['plasma] NT -s, **Plasmen** [-mən] plasma

Plastik¹ ['plastɪk] NT -s, NO PL (= *Kunststoff*) plastic

Plastik² F -, -en (a) (= *Bildhauerkunst*) sculpture
(b) (= *Skulptur*) sculpture (c) (*Med*) plastic surgery (d) (*fig*: = *Anschaulichkeit*) vividness

Plastik-: Plastikbeutel M plastic bag; **Plastikbombe** F plastic bomb; **Plastikfolie** F plastic film; **Plastikgeld** NT (*inf*) plastic money; **mit ~ bezahlen** to pay with plastic (*inf*); **Plastiksprengstoff** M plastic explosive; **Plastiktüte** F plastic bag

Plastilin [plasti'li:n] NT -s, -e Plasticine®

plastisch ['plastɪʃ] ❶ ADJ (a) (= *dreidimensional*) three-dimensional, 3-D; (*fig*: *anschaulich*) vivid; **~es Vorstellungsvermögen** ability to imagine things in three dimensions
(b) (*Art*) plastic; **die ~e Kunst** plastic art
(c) (*Med*) *Chirurgie* plastic
❷ ADV (a) (*räumlich*) three-dimensionally; **~ wirken** or **erscheinen** to appear three-dimensional; **etw ~ ausformen** to mould (*Brit*) or mold (*US*) sth into shape
(b) (*fig*: *anschaulich*) **etw ~ schildern** to give a graphic description of sth; **sich** (*dat*) **etw ~ vorstellen** to picture sth clearly; **das kann ich mir ~ vorstellen** I can just imagine it

Platane [pla'ta:nə] F -, -n plane tree

Plateau [pla'to:] NT -s, -s (a) plateau (b) (*von Schuh*) platform

Plateauschuh [pla'to:-] M platform shoe

Plateausohle [pla'to:-] F platform sole

Platin ['pla:ti:n, pla'ti:n] NT -s, NO PL (*abbr* Pt) platinum

Platine [pla'ti:nə] F -, -n (*Comput*) circuit board

platonisch [pla'to:nɪʃ] ❶ ADJ Platonic; (= *nicht sexuell*) platonic ❷ ADV platonically

platsch [platʃ] INTERJ splash

platschen ['platʃn] VI (*inf*) to splash; (= *regnen*) to pelt

plätschern ['plɛtʃɐn] VI (*Bach*) to babble; (*Brunnen*) to splash; (*Regen*) to patter; **eine ~de Unterhaltung** light conversation

platschnass ADJ (*inf*) soaking (wet)

platt [plat] ❶ ADJ (a) (= *flach*) flat; **einen Platten** (*inf*) or **einen ~en Reifen haben** to have a flat tyre (*Brit*) or tire (*US*); **das ~e Land** the flat country; (*nicht Stadt*) the country
(b) (*fig*: = *geistlos*) dull
(c) (*inf*: = *verblüfft*) **~ sein** to be flabbergasted (*inf*); **da bist du ~, nicht?** that surprised you, didn't it?
(d) (*sl*: = *high*) wasted (*sl*)
❷ ADV *pressen, walzen* flat; **etw ~ drücken** to press sth flat

Platt [plat] NT -(s), NO PL (*inf*) Low German, Plattdeutsch

Plättchen ['plɛtçən] NT -s, - little tile

plattdeutsch ADJ Low German

Platte ['platə] F -, -n (a) (= *Holzplatte*) piece of wood, board; (*zur Wandverkleidung*) panel; (= *Tischtennisplatte*) ping-pong table; (= *Glasplatte/Metallplatte/Plastikplatte*) piece of glass/metal/plastic; (= *Betonplatte, Steinplatte*) slab; (*zum Pflastern*) paving stone, flag(stone); (= *Kachel, Fliese*) tile; (= *Grabplatte*) gravestone; (= *Herdplatte*) hotplate; (= *Tischplatte*) (table) top; (*ausziehbare*) leaf; (*Geol*: = *tektonische ~*) (tectonic) plate; (*Phot*) plate; (*von Gebiss*) (dental) plate; (= *Gedenktafel*) plaque; (*Comput*) disk; **ein Ereignis auf die ~ bannen** to capture an event on film
(b) (= *Serviertellter*) serving dish; (= *Tortenplatte*) cake plate; (*mit Fuß*) cake stand
(c) (= *Schallplatte*) record; **die ~ kenne ich schon** (*fig inf*) I've heard all that before; **leg doch mal eine neue ~ auf!** (*fig inf*) change the record, can't you!; **die ~ hat einen Sprung** the record's stuck
(d) (*inf*) (= *Glatze*) bald head; (= *kahle Stelle*) bald spot
(e) (*sl*) **auf ~ sein** (= *obdachlos*) to be on the streets; **~ machen** (= *als Obdachloser schlafen*) to sleep rough on the streets

plätten ['plɛtn] VT (*dial*) to iron; *siehe auch* **geplättet**

Platten-: Plattenbau M, *pl* **-bauten** (*inf*: = *Haus*) *building made from prefabricated slabs*; **Plattenlabel** NT record label; **Plattenlaufwerk** NT (*Comput*) disk drive; **Plattenleger** [-le:gɐ] M -s, -, **Plattenlegerin** [-ərɪn] F -, -nen paver; **Plattensammlung** F record collection; **Plattensee** M der ~ Lake Balaton; **Plattenspieler** M record player; **Plattenteller** M turntable

Platt-: Plattfisch M flatfish; **Plattform** F platform; (*fig*: = *Grundlage*) basis; **Plattfuß** M flat foot; (*inf*: = *Reifenpanne*) flat (*inf*); **plattfüßig** ADJ, ADV flat-footed

Plattheit F -, -en (a) NO PL (= *Flachheit*) flatness; (= *Geistlosigkeit*) dullness (b) USU PL (= *Redensart etc*) platitude, cliché

plattmachen VT SEP (*sl*) (= *dem Erdboden gleichmachen*) to level; (= *Pleite gehen lassen*) *Firma* to bankrupt; (= *töten*) to do in (*inf*)

Platz [plats] M **-es**, **ⁱe** ['plɛtsə] (a) (= *freier Raum*) room; **~ für jdn/etw schaffen** to make room for sb/sth; **in dem Zelt finden** or **haben zwei Personen ~** there is room for two people in the tent; **~ greifen** to spread; **~ einnehmen** or **brauchen** to take up room; **~ raubend** space-consuming; **~ sparend** space-saving *attr*; *bauen, einbauen, unterbringen* (in order) to save space; **das ist ~ sparender** (that saves more space; **etw ~ sparend stapeln** to stack sth (away) with a minimum use of space; **jdm den (ganzen) ~ wegnehmen** to take up all the room; **jdm ~ machen** to make room for sb; (= *vorbeigehen lassen*) to make way for sb (*auch fig*); **~ machen** to get out of the way (*inf*); **mach mal ein bisschen ~** make a bit of room; **~ da!** (*inf*) gangway! (*inf*)
(b) (= *Sitzplatz*) seat; **~ nehmen** to take a seat; **bitte ~ nehmen zum Mittagessen** please take your seats for lunch; **behalten Sie doch bitte ~!** (*form*) please remain seated (*form*); **ist hier noch ein ~ frei?** is there a free seat here?; **dieser ~ ist belegt** or **besetzt** this seat's taken; **der Saal hat 2.000 Plätze** the hall seats 2,000; **mit jdm den ~ tauschen** or **wechseln** to change places with sb; **erster/zweiter ~** front/rear stalls; **~! (*zum Hund*) lie down!
(c) (= *Stelle, Standort, Rang*) place; **das Buch steht nicht an seinem ~** the book isn't in (its) place; **etw (wieder) an seinen ~ stellen** to put sth (back) in (its) place; **fehl or nicht am ~(e) sein** to be out of place; **am ~(e) sein** to be appropriate; **auf die Plätze, fertig, los!** (*beim Sport*) on your marks, get set, go!; **er wich nicht vom ~(e)** he wouldn't yield (an inch); **seinen ~ behaupten** to stand one's ground; **alles hat seinen festen ~** everything has its proper place; **die Literatur hat einen festen ~ in ihrem Leben** literature is very much a part of her life; **den ersten ~ einnehmen** (*fig*) to take first place; **auf ~ zwei** in second place; **jdn auf die Plätze verweisen** (*fig*) to beat sb
(d) (= *Arbeitsplatz, Studienplatz, Heimplatz etc*) place; (= *unbesetzter Arbeitsplatz*) vacancy
(e) (= *umbaute Fläche*) square; **auf dem ~** in the square
(f) (= *Sportplatz*) playing field; (*Ftbl, Hockey*) pitch; (= *Handballplatz, Tennisplatz*) court; (= *Golfplatz*) (golf) course; **einen Spieler vom ~ stellen** or **verweisen** to send a player off (*Brit*), to eject a player (*US*); **auf gegnerischem ~** away; **auf eigenem ~** at home; **jdn vom ~ fegen** (*inf*: = *vernichtend schlagen*) to wipe the floor with sb (*inf*)

(g) (= *Ort*) town, place; (= *Handelsplatz*) centre (*Brit*), center (*US*); **das erste Hotel** *or* **Haus am ~(e)** the best hotel in town **(h)** (= *Lagerplatz*) (store *or* storage) yard **(I)** (= *Bauplatz*) site

Platz-: Platzangst F (*inf*: = *Beklemmung*) claustrophobia; (*auf offenen Plätzen*) agoraphobia; **Platzanweiser** [-anvaizɐ] M **-s, -** usher; **Platzanweiserin** [-anvaizərɪn] F **-, -nen** usherette

Plätzchen ['plɛtsçən] NT **-s, -** **(a)** DIM *von* **Platz** spot **(b)** (*Gebäck*) biscuit (*Brit*), cookie (*US*)

platzen ['platsn] VI AUX SEIN **(a)** (= *aufreißen*) to burst; (*Naht, Hose, Augenbraue, Haut*) to split; (= *explodieren*: *Granate, Stinkbombe*) to explode; (= *einen Riss bekommen*) to crack; **mir ist unterwegs ein Reifen geplatzt** I had a blowout on the way (*inf*); **ihm ist eine Ader geplatzt** he burst a blood vessel; **wir sind vor Lachen fast geplatzt** we split our sides laughing; **ins Zimmer ~** (*inf*) to burst into the room; **jdm ins Haus ~** (*inf*) to descend on sb; (**vor Wut/Neid/Ungeduld**) ~ (*inf*) to be bursting (with rage/envy/impatience) **(b)** (*inf*: = *scheitern*) (*Plan, Geschäft, Termin, Vertrag*) to fall through; (*Freundschaft, Koalition*) to break up; (*Theorie*) to fall down; (*Wechsel*) to bounce (*inf*); **die Verlobung ist geplatzt** the engagement is (all) off; **etw ~ lassen** *Plan, Geschäft, Termin, Vertrag* to make sth fall through; *Freundschaft, Verlobung* to break sth off; *Koalition* to break sth up; *Vorstellung* to call sth off; *Theorie* to explode sth; *Wechsel* to make sth bounce (*inf*)

Platz-: Platzhalter M place marker; (*Comput*) free variable parameter; **Platzhirsch** M (*lit, fig*) dominant male

platzieren [pla'tsi:rən], *ptp* **platziert** **1** VT **(a)** (= *Platz anweisen*) to put; *Soldaten, Wächter* to put, to place; (*Tennis*) to seed; **der Kellner platzierte uns in die** *or* **der Nähe der Band** the waiter put us near the band **(b)** (= *zielen*) *Ball* to place; *Schlag, Faust* to land **(c)** (= *anlegen*) *Geld* to put, to place; *Aktien* to place **2** VR **(a)** (*inf*: = *sich setzen, stellen etc*) to plant oneself (*inf*) **(b)** (*Sport*) to be placed; (*Tennis*) to be seeded; **der Läufer konnte sich gut/nicht ~** the runner was well-placed/wasn't even placed

Platzierung F (*bei Rennen*) order; (*Tennis*) seeding; (= *Platz*) place; (*von Aktien, Geld*) placing; **welche ~ hatte er?** where did he come in?

Platz-: Platzkarte F (*Rail*) seat reservation (ticket); **Platzmangel** M, NO PL shortage of space; **wir leiden sehr unter ~** we're terribly short of space; **Platzpatrone** F blank (cartridge); **platzraubend** ADJ *siehe* **Platz**; **Platzregen** M cloudburst; **Platzreservierung** F seat reservation; **platzsparend** ADJ *siehe* **Platz**; **Platzverweis** M sending-off (*Brit*), ejection (*US*); **es gab drei ~e** three players were sent off (*Brit*) *or* ejected (*US*); **Platzwart** [-vart] M **-s, -e**, **Platzwartin** [-vartɪn] F **-, -nen** (*Sport*) groundsman; **Platzwunde** F cut

Plauderei [plaudə'rai] F **-, -en** chat; (*Press*) feature; (*TV, Rad*) talk show

Plauderer ['plaudərɐ] M **-s, -**, **Plauderin** [-ərɪn] F **-, -nen** conversationalist

plaudern ['plaudɐn] VI to chat, to talk (*über +acc, von* about); (= *verraten*) to talk

Plausch [plauʃ] M **-(e)s, -e** (*inf*) chat; **das war ein ~** (*Sw*: = *Freude, Amüsement*) that was a good laugh

plauschen ['plauʃn] VI (*inf*) to chat

plausibel [plau'zi:bl] ADJ *Erklärung, Grund* plausible **2** ADV plausibly; **jdm etw ~ machen** to explain sth to sb

Plausibilität [plauzibili'tɛːt] F **-**, NO PL plausibility

Plausibilitätskontrolle F (*von Daten, Statistik*) plausibility check

Play-: Play-back ['ple:bɛk] NT **-s, -s**, **Playback** NT **-s, -s** (= *Band*) (*bei Musikaufnahme*) backing track; (*TV*) recording; (= *Playbackverfahren*) (*bei Musikaufnahme*) double-tracking *no pl*; (*TV*) miming *no pl*; **Playback singen** to mime; **Playboy** ['ple:-] M playboy; **Playgirl** ['ple:-] NT playgirl

Plazenta [pla'tsɛnta] F **-, -s** *or* **Plazenten** [-'tsɛntn] placenta

Plazet ['pla:tsɛt] NT **-s, -s** (*geh*) approval; **sein ~ zu etw geben** to give sth one's approval

plazieren [pla'tsi:rən] VT *siehe* **platzieren**

Plebiszit [plebɪs'tsi:t] NT **-(e)s, -e** plebiscite

pleite ['plaitə] ADJ PRED, ADV (*inf*) *Mensch* broke (*inf*)

Pleite ['plaitə] F **-, -n** (*inf*) bankruptcy; (*fig*) flop (*inf*); **~ machen** to go bankrupt; **damit/mit ihm haben wir eine ~ erlebt** it/he was a disaster; **~ gehen** to go bust

plemplem [plɛm'plɛm] ADJ PRED (*inf*) nuts (*inf*)

Plena PL *von* **Plenum**

Plenar- [ple'na:ɐ-]: **Plenarsaal** M chamber; **Plenarsitzung** F, **Plenarversammlung** F plenary session

Plenum ['ple:nʊm] NT **-s, Plena** [-na] plenum

Pleuelstange ['plɔyəl-] F connecting rod

plissieren [plɪ'si:rən], *ptp* **plissiert** VT to pleat

PLO [pe:lɛl'lo:] F - PLO

Plombe ['plɔmbə] F **-, -n (a)** (= *Siegel*) lead seal **(b)** (= *Zahnplombe*) filling

plombieren [plɔm'bi:rən], *ptp* **plombiert** VT **(a)** (= *versiegeln*) to seal **(b)** *Zahn* to fill; **er hat mir zwei Zähne plombiert** he did two fillings

Plot [plɔt] M *or* NT **-s, -s** (*Liter*) plot

Plotter ['plɔtɐ] M **-s, -** (*Comput*) plotter

plötzlich ['plœtslɪç] **1** ADJ sudden **2** ADV suddenly; **aber etwas ~!** (*inf*), **aber ein bisschen ~!** (*inf*) (and) make it snappy! (*inf*)

Plötzlichkeit F **-**, NO PL suddenness

Pluderhose ['plu:də-] F harem pants *pl*

Plug-and-Play ['plagand'ple:] NT **-s**, NO PL (*Comput*) plug-and-play

plump [plʊmp] **1** ADJ *Figur, Hände, Form* ungainly *no adv*; *Ausdruck* clumsy; *Bemerkung, Benehmen* crass; *Mittel, Schmeichelei, Lüge, Betrug, Trick* obvious; *Film, Roman* crude; **~e Annäherungsversuche** obvious and crude advances **2** ADV *sich bewegen, tanzen* awkwardly; *sagen, sich ausdrücken* clumsily; **~ lügen** to tell a blatant lie; **der Film ist sehr ~ gemacht** the film is very crudely made

> *Vorsicht!* **plump** *wird nicht mit dem englischen Wort* **plump** *übersetzt.*

Plumpheit F **-, -en** (*von Figur, Form*) ungainliness; (*von Ausdruck*) clumsiness; (*von Bemerkung, Benehmen*) crassness; (*von Lüge, Trick*) obviousness

plumps [plʊmps] INTERJ bang; (*lauter*) crash

Plumps [plʊmps] M **-es, -e** (*inf*) (= *Fall*) fall; (*Geräusch*) bump; **mit einem ~ ins Wasser fallen** to fall into the water with a splash

plumpsen ['plʊmpsn] VI AUX SEIN (*inf*) (= *fallen*) to tumble; **ich ließ mich einfach aufs Bett ~** I just flopped (down) onto the bed

Plumpsklo(sett) NT (*inf*) earth closet

plumpvertraulich ADJ overly chummy (*inf*)

Plunder ['plʊndɐ] M **-s**, NO PL junk

plündern ['plʏndɐn] VTI to loot; (= *ausrauben*) to raid; *Obstbaum* to strip

Plünderung F **-, -en** looting

Plural ['plu:ra:l] M **-s, -e** plural; **im ~ stehen** to be (in the) plural; **den ~ zu etw bilden** to form the plural of sth

Pluralismus [plura'lɪsmʊs] M **-**, NO PL pluralism

pluralistisch [plura'lɪstɪʃ] **1** ADJ pluralistic (*form*) **2** ADV pluralistically (*form*)

plus [plʊs] **1** PREP +GEN plus **2** ADV plus; **bei ~ 5 Grad** *or* **5 Grad ~** at 5 degrees (above freezing); **~ minus 10** plus or minus 10; **das Ergebnis war ~ minus null** nothing was gained, nothing was lost; **mit ~ minus null abschließen** to break even

Plus [plʊs] NT **-, - (a)** (= *~zeichen*) plus (sign); **ein ~ machen** to put a plus (sign) **(b)** (*Phys inf*: = *~pol*) positive (pole) **(c)** (*esp Comm*) (= *Zuwachs*) increase; (= *Gewinn*) profit; (= *Überschuss*) surplus **(d)** (*fig*: = *Vorteil*) advantage; **das ist ein ~ für dich** that's a point in your favour (*Brit*) *or* favor (*US*); **das können Sie als ~ für sich buchen** that's one up for you (*inf*)

Plüsch [plyʃ, ply:ʃ] M **-(e)s, -e** plush; (*pej*) ostentation; **Stofftiere aus ~** soft toys made of fur fabric

Plüsch- IN CPDS plush; (*von ~tier*) furry; **Plüschbär** M furry teddy bear; **Plüschtier** NT ≈ soft toy

Plus-: Pluspol M (*Elec*) positive pole; **Pluspunkt** M (*Sport*) point; (*Sch*) extra mark; (*fig*) advantage; **einen ~ machen** to win a point; **deine Erfahrung ist ein ~ für dich** your experience counts in your favour (*Brit*) *or* favor (*US*); **~e**

sammeln (inf) to score Brownie points; **Plusquamperfekt** ['pluskvampɛrfɛkt] NT pluperfect
plustern ['pluːstɐn] VT Federn to fluff up
Pluszeichen NT plus sign
Plutonium [pluˈtoːniʊm] NT **-s**, NO PL (abbr **Pn**) plutonium
PLZ [peːlɛˈt͡sɛt] F - ABBR von **Postleitzahl**
Pneu [pnøː] M **-s**, **-s** (esp Sw) tyre (Brit), tire (US)
pneumatisch [pnɔyˈmaːtɪʃ] **1** ADJ pneumatic; **~e Kammer** pressure chamber **2** ADV pneumatically
Po [poː] M **-s**, **-s** (inf) bottom
Pöbel ['pøːbl] M **-s**, NO PL rabble
Pöbelei [pøːbeˈlai] F **-**, **-en** vulgarity, bad language no pl
pöbeln ['pøːbln] VI to swear
pochen ['pɔxn] VI to knock; (leise auch) to tap; (heftig) to thump; (Herz, Blut) to pound; **auf etw** (acc) **~** (fig) to insist on sth
Pocke ['pɔkə] F **-**, **-n** (a) pock (b) **Pocken** PL smallpox
Pocken-: **Pockennarbe** F pockmark; **pockennarbig** ADJ pockmarked; **Pocken(schutz)impfung** F smallpox vaccination
Pocket- ['pɔkət] IN CPDS pocket; **Pocketkamera** F pocket camera
Podest [poˈdɛst] NT or M **-(e)s**, **-e** (= Sockel) pedestal (auch fig); (= Podium) platform
Podium ['poːdiʊm] NT **-s**, **Podien** [-diən] (lit, fig) platform; (des Dirigenten) podium; (bei Diskussion) panel
Podiumsdiskussion F, **Podiumsgespräch** NT panel discussion
Poesie [poeˈziː] F **-**, **-n** [-ˈziːən] (lit, fig) poetry
Poesiealbum NT autograph book
Poetik [poˈeːtɪk] F **-**, **-en** poetics sing
poetisch [poˈeːtɪʃ] **1** ADJ poetic **2** ADV poetically
Pointe ['poɛ̃tə] F **-**, **-n** (eines Witzes) punch line; (einer Geschichte) point
pointiert [poɛ̃ˈtiːɐt] **1** ADJ pithy **2** ADV pithily; **~ antworten** to give a pithy answer
Pokal [poˈkaːl] M **-s**, **-e** (zum Trinken) goblet; (Sport) cup; **das Endspiel um den ~** the cup final
Pokal-: **Pokalsieger(in)** M(F) cup winners pl; **Pokalspiel** NT cup tie
Pökelfleisch NT salt meat
pökeln ['pøːkln] VT Fleisch, Fisch to salt
Poker ['poːkɐ] NT **-s**, NO PL poker
Pokerface ['poːkɐfeːs] NT **-**, **-s**, **Pokermiene** F poker face
pokern ['poːkɐn] VI to play poker; (fig) to gamble; **um etw ~** (fig) to haggle for sth; **hoch ~** (fig) to take a big risk
Pol [poːl] M **-s**, **-e** pole; **der ruhende ~** (fig) the calming influence
polar [poˈlaːɐ] ADJ polar; **~e Kälte** arctic coldness
Polar- [poˈlaːɐ] IN CPDS polar; **Polareis** NT polar ice; **Polarfuchs** M arctic fox
polarisieren [polariˈziːrən], ptp **polarisiert** **1** VT to polarize **2** VR to polarize
Polarisierung F **-**, **-en** polarization
Polar-: **Polarkreis** M polar circle; **nördlicher/südlicher ~** Arctic/Antarctic circle; **Polarlicht** NT polar lights pl; **Polarstern** M Pole Star
Polder ['pɔldɐ] M **-s**, - polder
Pole ['poːlə] M **-n**, **-n** Pole
Polemik [poˈleːmɪk] F **-**, **-en** polemics sing (gegen against); (= Streitschrift) polemic; **die ~ dieses Artikels** the polemic nature of this article
Polemiker [poˈleːmikɐ] M **-s**, -, **Polemikerin** [-ərɪn] F **-**, **-nen** controversialist, polemicist
polemisch [poˈleːmɪʃ] **1** ADJ polemic(al) **2** ADV polemically; **~ argumentieren** to be polemical
Polen ['poːlən] NT **-s** Poland; **noch ist ~ nicht verloren** (prov) all is not yet lost
Police [poˈliːsə] F **-**, **-n** (insurance) policy
polieren [poˈliːrən], ptp **poliert** VT to polish; **jdm die Fresse ~** (vulg) to smash sb's face in (inf)
Polier-: **Poliermittel** NT polish; **Polierscheibe** F polishing wheel

Poliklinik ['poːli-] F (= Krankenhaus) clinic (for outpatients only); (Abteilung) outpatients' department
Polin ['poːlɪn] F **-**, **-nen** Pole
Polio ['poːlio] F **-**, NO PL polio
Polit- [poˈlɪt-] IN CPDS (inf) political; **Politbarometer** NT (fig) political barometer; **Politbüro** NT Politburo
Politesse [poliˈtɛsə] F **-**, **-n** (woman) traffic warden
Politik [poliˈtiːk] F **-**, **-en** (a) NO PL politics sing; (= politischer Standpunkt) politics pl; **welche ~ vertritt er?** what are his politics?; **in die ~ gehen** to go into politics (b) (= bestimmte ~) policy; **eine ~ der starken Hand treiben** to take a tough line; **eine ~ verfolgen** or **betreiben** to pursue a policy
Politiker [poˈliːtikɐ] M **-s**, -, **Politikerin** [-ərɪn] F **-**, **-nen** politician; **führender ~** leading politician
Politik-: **Politikverdrossenheit** F disenchantment with politics; **die wachsende ~ der Bevölkerung** the people's growing disenchantment with politics; **Politikwissenschaft** F political science
politisch [poˈliːtɪʃ] **1** ADJ political; (= klug) politic; **er ist ein Politischer** he's a political prisoner **2** ADV politically; **sich ~ betätigen** to be involved in politics; **~ interessiert sein** to be interested in politics
politisieren [politiˈziːrən], ptp **politisiert** **1** VI to politicize **2** VT to politicize; jdn to make politically aware
Politologe [politoˈloːgə] M **-n**, **-n**, **Politologin** [-ˈloːgɪn] F **-**, **-nen** political scientist
Politologie [politoloˈgiː] F **-**, NO PL political science
Politur [poliˈtuːɐ] F **-**, **-en** polish
Polizei [poliˈt͡sai] F **-**, **-en** police pl; (Gebäude) police station; **auf die** or **zur ~ gehen** to go to the police; **er ist bei der ~** he's in the police (force)
Polizei- IN CPDS police; **Polizeiapparat** M police force; **Polizeiaufgebot** NT police presence; **Polizeibeamte(r)** M DECL AS ADJ, **Polizeibeamtin** F police official; (= Polizist) police officer; **Polizeifunk** M police radio; **Polizeigewahrsam** M police custody; **jdn in ~ nehmen** to take sb into police custody; **Polizeigriff** M arm lock; **jdn in den ~ nehmen** to put sb in an arm lock; **Polizeihaft** F detention; **Polizeihund** M police dog; **Polizeikette** F police cordon; **Polizeiknüppel** M truncheon
polizeilich [poliˈt͡sailɪç] **1** ADJ police attr; **~es Führungszeugnis** certificate issued by the police, stating that the holder has no criminal record **2** ADV ermittelt werden by the police; **~ überwacht werden** to be under police surveillance; **sie wird ~ gesucht** the police are looking for her; **sich ~ melden** to register with the police; **~ verboten** against the law; **„Parken ~ verboten"** "police notice - no parking"
Polizei-: **Polizeirevier** NT (a) (= Polizeiwache) police station (b) (Bezirk) (police) district, precinct (US); **Polizeischutz** M police protection; **Polizeispitzel** M (police) informer; **Polizeistaat** M police state; **Polizeistreife** F police patrol; **Polizeistunde** F closing time; **Polizeiwache** F police station; **Polizeiwesen** NT, NO PL police force; **polizeiwidrig** **1** ADJ illegal **2** ADV **sich ~ verhalten** to break the law
Polizist [poliˈt͡sɪst] **-en**, **-en**, M policeman
Polizistin [poliˈt͡sɪstɪn] F **-**, **-nen** policewoman
Polkappe F polar icecap
Pollen ['pɔlən] M **-s**, - pollen
Pollen-: **Pollenbericht** M pollen forecast; **Pollenfalle** F pollen trap; **Pollenflug** M pollen count; **Pollenwarnung** F pollen warning
polnisch ['pɔlnɪʃ] ADJ Polish
Polohemd NT sports shirt; (für Frau) casual blouse
Polster ['pɔlstɐ] NT or (AUS) M **-s**, - (a) cushion; (= Polsterung) upholstery no pl; (bei Kleidung) pad (b) (fig) (= Fettpolster) flab no pl (inf); (= Bauch) spare tyre (Brit) or tire (US); (= Reserve) reserve; (= Geldreserve) reserves pl
Polstergarnitur F three-piece suite
Polstermöbel PL upholstered furniture sing
polstern ['pɔlstɐn] VT to upholster; Kleidung, Tür to pad; **sie ist gut gepolstert** she's well-padded
Polsterung ['pɔlstəʊŋ] F **-**, **-en** (= Polster) upholstery; (= das Polstern) upholstering

Polterabend M party on the eve of a wedding, at which old crockery is smashed to bring good luck

POLTERABEND

Polterabend is the evening before a wedding, when crockery is smashed outside the door of the bride's parents or of the bride and groom. According to tradition, the broken pieces are supposed to bring luck to the happy couple. Often the *Polterabend* is extended into an informal party for friends and acquaintances and is sometimes held a week before the wedding to allow guests time to recover.

Poltergeist M poltergeist

poltern ['pɔltɐn] VI **(a)** (= *Krach machen*) to crash about; (= *polternd umfallen*) to go crash; **was hat da eben so gepoltert?** what was that crash?; **es fiel ~d zu Boden** it crashed to the floor; **es polterte fürchterlich, als er ... there** was a terrific crash when he ...; **an die Tür ~** to thump on the door
(b) AUX SEIN (= *sich laut bewegen*) to crash; **über das Pflaster ~** to clatter over the cobbles
(c) (*inf:* = *schimpfen*) to rant (and rave)
(d) (*inf:* = *Polterabend feiern*) to celebrate on the eve of a wedding

Poly-: Polyamid [polyla'mi:t] NT **-(e)s, -e** [-də] polyamide; **Polyester** [poly'lɛstɐ] M **-s, -** polyester; **polygam** [poly'ga:m] **1** ADJ polygamous **2** ADV **~ leben** to be polygamous; **Polygamie** [polyga'mi:] F **-,** NO PL polygamy

Polynesien [poly'ne:ziən] NT **-s** Polynesia

polynesisch [poly'ne:zɪʃ] ADJ Polynesian

Polyp [po'ly:p] M **-en, -en (a)** (Zool) polyp; (old: = *Krake*) octopus **(b)** (*Med*) **~en** adenoids

Polypol [poli'po:l] NT **-s, -e** polypoly

Polytechnikum [poly'tɛçnikum] NT polytechnic

pommerisch ['pɔmərɪʃ] ADJ, **pommersch** ['pɔmɛʃ] ADJ Pomeranian

Pommern ['pɔmɐn] NT **-s** Pomerania

Pommes ['pɔməs] PL (*inf*) chips *pl* (*Brit*), (French) fries *pl*

Pommesbude F (*inf*) fast food stand

Pommes frites [pɔm 'frit] PL chips *pl* (*Brit*), French fries *pl*

Pomp [pɔmp] M **-(e)s,** NO PL pomp

pompös [pɔm'pø:s] **1** ADJ grandiose **2** ADV grandiosely

Poncho ['pɔntʃo] M **-s, -s** poncho

Pontius ['pɔntsiʊs] M **von ~ zu Pilatus laufen** to rush from one place to another; **jdn von ~ zu Pilatus schicken** to pass sb from one place to another

Pony[1] ['pɔni] NT **-s, -s** pony

Pony[2] M **-s, -s** (*Frisur*) fringe (*Brit*), bangs *pl* (*US*)

Pool [pu:l] M **-s, -s** pool; **Mitarbeiter-~** pool of workers

Pool(billard) ['pu:l-] NT **-s,** NO PL pool

Pop [pɔp] M **-s,** NO PL (*Mus*) pop; (*Art*) pop art

Popcorn ['pɔpkɔːn] NT **-s,** NO PL popcorn

Popel ['po:pl] M **-s, -** - (*inf:* = *Nasenpopel*) bogey (*Brit inf*), booger (*US inf*)

popelig ['po:pəlɪç] (*inf*) **1** ADJ **(a)** (= *knauserig*) stingy (*inf*); **~e zwei Euro** a lousy two euros (*inf*) **(b)** (= *dürftig*) crummy (*inf*) **(c)** (= *spießig*) small-minded **2** ADV **(a)** (= *knauserig*) stingily **(b)** (= *dürftig*) **~ leben** to live on the cheap (*inf*); **ihr Haus war recht ~ eingerichtet** her house had really crummy furniture (*inf*)

Popelin [popə'li:n] M **-s, -e**, **Popeline** [popə'li:nə] F **-,** - poplin

popeln ['po:pln] VI (*inf*) **(in der Nase) ~** to pick one's nose

Popgruppe F pop group

Popo [po'po:] M **-s, -s** (*inf*) bottom

poppen ['pɔpn] VI (*sl:* = *koitieren*) to pump (*sl*)

poppig ['pɔpɪç] (*inf*) **1** ADJ (*Art, Mus*) pop *no adv*; *Kleidung* loud and trendy; *Farben* bright and cheerful **2** ADV **sich ~ kleiden** to wear loud, trendy clothes; **das Buch war total ~ aufgemacht** the book was brightly presented

Pop-: Popsänger(in) M(F) pop singer; **Popstar** M pop star; **Popszene** F pop scene

populär [popu'lɛ:ɐ] **1** ADJ popular (*bei* with) **2** ADV *schreiben, darstellen* in an accessible way

Popularität [populari'tɛ:t] F **-,** NO PL popularity

populärwissenschaftlich **1** ADJ *Buch* popular science; *Literatur* popular scientific **2** ADV **etw ~ darstellen** to present sth in a popular scientific way

Population [popula'tsio:n] F **-, -en** (*Biol, Sociol*) population

Populismus [popu'lɪsmʊs] M **-,** NO PL (*Pol*) populism

Populist [popu'lɪst] M **-en, -en, Populistin** [-'lɪstɪn] F **-, -nen** populist

populistisch [popu'lɪstɪʃ] **1** ADJ populist **2** ADV in a populist way

Pore ['po:rə] F **-, -n** pore

-porig ADJ SUF with ... pores; **feinporige Haut** skin with fine pores

Porno ['pɔrno] M **-s, -s** (*inf*) porn (*inf*)

Porno- IN CPDS (*inf*) porn (*inf*); **Pornofilm** M porn movie

Pornografie [pɔrnogra'fi:] F **-, -n** [-'fi:ən] pornography

pornografisch [pɔrno'gra:fɪʃ] ADJ pornographic

porös [po'rø:s] ADJ (= *durchlässig*) porous; (= *brüchig*) *Gummi, Leder* perished; **~ werden** to perish

Porree ['pɔre] M **-s, -s** leek

Port[1] [pɔrt] M **-(e)s, -e** (= *~wein*) port

Port[2] M **-s, -s** (*Comput*) port

Portal [pɔr'ta:l] NT **-s, -e** portal

Portemonnaie [pɔrtmɔ'ne:, pɔrtmo'ne:] NT **-s, -s** purse

Portier [pɔr'tie:] M **-s, -s = Pförtner[2]**

Portion [pɔr'tsio:n] F **-, -en (a)** (*beim Essen*) portion, helping; **eine halbe ~** a half portion; (*fig inf*) a half pint (*inf*); **eine zweite ~** a second helping; **eine ~ Kaffee** a pot of coffee **(b)** (*fig inf:* = *Anteil*) amount; **er besitzt eine gehörige ~ Mut** he's got a fair amount of courage

Portmonee [pɔrtmɔ'ne:, pɔrtmo'ne:] NT **-s, -s = Portemonnaie**

Porto ['pɔrto] NT **-s, -s** *or* **Porti** [-ti] postage *no pl* (*für* on, for); (*für Kisten etc*) carriage; **~ zahlt Empfänger** postage paid

Porto-: portofrei ADJ, ADV postage paid; **Portokasse** F ≈ petty cash (*for postal expenses*)

Porträt [pɔr'trɛ:, pɔr'trɛ:t] NT **-s, -s** (*lit, fig*) portrait

porträtieren [pɔrtrɛ'ti:rən], *ptp* **porträtiert** VT (*fig*) to portray; **jdn ~** to paint sb's portrait; (*mit Fotoapparat*) to do a portrait of sb

Portugal ['pɔrtugal] NT **-s** Portugal

Portugiese [pɔrtu'gi:zə] M **-n, -n, Portugiesin** [-'gi:zɪn] F **-, -nen** Portuguese

portugiesisch [pɔrtu'gi:zɪʃ] ADJ Portuguese

Portwein ['pɔrt-] M port

Porzellan [pɔrtse'la:n] NT **-s, -e** (*Material*) china; (= *Geschirr*) china; (**unnötig**) **~ zerbrechen** *or* **zerschlagen** (*fig*) to cause a lot of (unnecessary) bother

Porzellan- IN CPDS china; **Porzellangeschirr** NT china, crockery

Posaune [po'zaunə] F **-, -n** trombone; (*fig*) trumpet

Posaunenbläser(in) M(F) trombonist

Posaunist [pozau'nɪst] M **-en, -en, Posaunistin** [-'nɪstɪn] F **-, -nen** trombonist

Pose ['po:zə] F **-, -n** pose

posieren [po'zi:rən], *ptp* **posiert** VI to pose; **er posiert in der Rolle des Wohltäters** he's playing the benefactor

Position [pozi'tsio:n] F **-, -en** position; (*Comm:* = *Posten einer Liste*) item

positionieren [pozitsio'ni:rən], *ptp* **positioniert** VT to position

Positionierung F **-, -en** positioning

Positionslampe F, **Positionslicht** NT navigation light

positiv ['po:ziti:f, pozi'ti:f] **1** ADJ positive; **eine ~e Antwort** an affirmative (answer); **ich weiß nichts Positives** I don't know anything definite **2** ADV positively; **etw ~ wissen** to know sth for certain; **~ denken** to think positively; **etw ~ (auf)laden** (*Phys*) to put a positive charge on sth; **~ zu etw stehen** to be in favour (*Brit*) *or* favor (*US*) of sth

Positiv[1] ['po:ziti:f, pozi'ti:f] M **-s, -e** [-və] (*Gram*) positive

Positiv[2] NT **-s, -e** [-və] (*Phot*) positive

Positur [pozi'tu:r] F **-, -en** posture; (*stehend auch*) stance; **sich in ~ setzen/stellen** to take up a posture; **sie setzte sich vor den Fernsehkameras in ~** she posed for the TV cameras; **sich in ~ werfen** to strike a pose

Posse ['pɔsə] F **-, -n** farce

possessiv ['pɔsɛsiːf, pɔse'siːf] ADJ possessive

Possessiv ['pɔsɛsiːf, pɔse'siːf] NT **-s, -e**, **Possessivpronomen** ['pɔsɛsiːf-, pɔse'siːf-] NT possessive pronoun

possierlich [pɔ'siːɐlɪç] **1** ADJ comical **2** ADV comically

Post [pɔst] F **-, -en** post (*Brit*), mail; (= ~*amt*, ~*wesen*) post office; **etw mit der ~ schicken** to send sth by mail; **etw auf or in die ~ geben** to post (*Brit*) *or* mail sth; **mit gleicher ~** by the same post (*Brit*), in the same mail (*US*); **mit getrennter ~** under separate cover; **etw durch die ~ beziehen** to order sth by mail *Brit* **die ~ geht ab** (*fig inf*) things really happen

postalisch [pɔs'taːlɪʃ] **1** ADJ postal **2** ADV by mail *Brit*

Post-: **Postamt** NT post office; **Postanschrift** F postal address; **Postanweisung** F *remittance paid in at a Post Office and delivered by post*, ≈ money order *Brit*; **Postausgang** M outgoing mail; **Ablage für Postausgänge** out-tray; **Postausgangskorb** M out-tray; **Postbank** F Post Office Savings Bank; **Postbeamte(r)** M DECL AS ADJ, **Postbeamtin** F post office official; **Postbezirk** M postal district *or* zone (*US*); **Postboot** NT mail boat; **Postbote** M postman, mailman (*US*); **Postbotin** F postwoman, mailwoman (*US*); **Postbus** M mail bus; **Posteingang** M incoming mail; **Ablage für Posteingänge** in-tray; **Posteingangskorb** M in-tray

posten ['pɔstn] (*Sw*: = *einkaufen*) **1** VT to buy **2** VI to shop

Posten ['pɔstn] M **-s, -** (a) (= *Anstellung*) position (b) (*Mil*: = *Wachmann*) guard; (= *Stelle*) post; **~ stehen** to stand guard; **~ aufstellen** to post guards (c) (*fig*) **auf dem ~ sein** (= *aufpassen*) to be awake; (= *gesund sein*) to be fit; **nicht ganz auf dem ~ sein** to be (a bit) under the weather (d) (= *Streikposten*) picket (e) (*Comm*: = *Warenmenge*) quantity (f) (*Comm*: *im Etat*) item

Poster ['pɔstɐ] NT **-s, -(s)** poster

Postf. ABBR *von* **Postfach**

Post-: **Postfach** NT PO box; **Postfachnummer** F (PO *or* post office) box number; **Postflugzeug** NT mail plane; **postfrisch** ADJ *Briefmarke* mint; **Postgeheimnis** NT secrecy of the post (*Brit*) *or* mail; **Posthorn** NT post horn

posthum [pɔst'huːm, pɔs'tuːm] ADJ, ADV = **postum**

postieren [pɔs'tiːrən], *ptp* **postiert** **1** VT to post, to station **2** VR to position oneself

Post-: **Postkarte** F postcard; **Postkutsche** F stagecoach; **postlagernd** ADJ, ADV poste restante (*Brit*), general delivery (*US*); **Postleitzahl** F post(al) code, Zip code (*US*)

postmodern [pɔstmo'dɛrn] ADJ postmodern

Postmoderne [pɔstmo'dɛrnə] F postmodern era

Post-: **Postnachnahme** F cash (*Brit*) *or* collect (*US*) on delivery, COD; **Postpaket** NT parcel (*sent by post*); **Postsache** F matter *no pl* sent postage paid; **Postsack** M postbag (*Brit*), mailbag; **Postschalter** M post office counter

Postskript [pɔst'skrɪpt] NT **-(e)s, -e** postscript, PS

Post-: **Postsparbuch** NT Post Office savings book; **Poststelle** F sub-post office; **Poststempel** M postmark; **Datum des ~s** date as postmark; **Einsendungen bis zum 17. Juni (Datum des ~s)** entries to be postmarked no later than 17th June

postum [pɔs'tuːm] **1** ADJ posthumous **2** ADV posthumously

Post-: **Postvermerk** M postmark; **postwendend** ADV by return mail; (*fig*) straight away; **Postwertzeichen** NT (*form*) postage stamp (*form*); **Postwesen** NT, NO PL Post Office; **Postwurfsendung** F direct-mail advertising; **Postzustellung** F mail delivery; **Postzustellungsurkunde** F registered post (*Brit*) *or* certified mail (*US*) certificate

potemkinsch [po'tɛmkɪnʃ] ADJ sham; **~e Dörfer** façade

potent [po'tɛnt] ADJ (a) (*sexuell*) potent (b) (= *leistungsfähig, stark*) *Gegner, Waffe, Fantasie* powerful (c) (= *einflussreich*) high-powered; (= *zahlungskräftig*) financially powerful

Potential [potɛn'tsiaːl] NT **-s, -e** = **Potenzial**

potentiell [potɛn'tsiɛl] ADJ, ADV = **potenziell**

Potenz [po'tɛnts] F **-, -en** (a) (*Med*) potency; (*fig*) ability; (*wirtschaftlich, schöpferisch etc*) power (b) (*Math*) power; **zweite ~** square; **dritte ~** cube; **eine Zahl in die sechste ~ erheben** to raise a number to the sixth power *esp Brit* **die sechste ~ zu zwei** two to the sixth power *esp Brit* **die sechste ~ zu zwei** two to the sixth power; **in höchster ~** (*fig*) to the highest degree

Potenzial [potɛn'tsiaːl] NT **-s, -e** potential

potenziell **1** ADJ potential **2** ADV potentially

potenzieren [potɛn'tsiːrən], *ptp* **potenziert** VT (*Math*) to raise to the power of; (*fig*: = *steigern*) to multiply; **2 potenziert mit 4** 2 to the power of 4 (*esp Brit*)

Potpourri ['pɔtpuri] NT **-s, -s** (*Mus, fig*) potpourri (*aus* +*dat* of)

Pott [pɔt] M **-(e)s, ⸚e** ['pœtə] (*inf*) pot; (= *Schiff*) ship; **mit etw zu ~e kommen** to see sth through

Pott-: **potthässlich** (*inf*) **1** ADJ ugly as sin **2** ADV **sie war ~ angezogen** the way she was dressed made her look plug-ugly (*inf*); **wie kann man sein Haus nur so ~ anstreichen?** who would ever paint a house like that, it's ugly as sin (*inf*); **Pottwal** M sperm whale

Poularde [pu'lardə] F **-, -n** poulard(e)

Poulet [pu'leː] NT **-s, -s** (*Sw*) chicken

Power ['pauɐ] F **-**, NO PL (*inf*) power

Powerfrau ['pauɐ-] F (*inf*) high-powered career woman

powern ['pauɐn] VI (*inf*) to get things moving

PR [peː'ɛr] ABBR *von* **Public Relations** PR

Prä-, prä- [prɛ] PREF pre-; **Präambel** [prɛ'ambl] F **-, -n** preamble (+*gen* to)

Pracht [praxt] F **-**, NO PL splendour (*Brit*), splendor (*US*); (*fig*: = *Herrlichkeit*) splendo(u)r; **es ist eine wahre ~** it's (really) fantastic

Pracht-: **Prachtbau** M, *pl* **-bauten** magnificent building; **Prachtexemplar** NT prime specimen; (*von Buch*: = *Prachtausgabe*) de luxe copy; (*fig*: *Mensch*) fine specimen; **mein ~ von Sohn** (*iro*) my brilliant son (*iro*)

prächtig ['prɛçtɪç] **1** ADJ (= *prunkvoll*) splendid; (= *großartig*) marvellous (*esp Brit*), marvelous (*US*) **2** ADV (a) (= *prunkvoll*) magnificently (b) (= *großartig*) marvellously (*esp Brit*), marvelously (*US*); **sich ~ amüsieren** to have a marvellous (*esp Brit*) *or* marvelous (*US*) time

prädestinieren [predɛsti'niːrən], *ptp* **prädestiniert** VT to predestine (*für* for); **er ist für diese Aufgabe wie or geradezu prädestiniert** he seems to have been made for the job

Prädikat [predi'kaːt] NT **-(e)s, -e** (*Gram*) predicate; (= *Bewertung*) **Wein mit ~** special quality wine

prädikativ ['preːdikatiːf, predika'tiːf] **1** ADJ predicative **2** ADV predicatively

Prädikats-: **Prädikatsnomen** NT predicative noun/pronoun; **Prädikatswein** M top quality wine

prädisponieren [predɪspo'niːrən], *ptp* **prädisponiert** VT to predispose (*für* to)

Präfix [prɛ'fɪks, 'prɛːfɪks] NT **-es, -e** prefix

Prag [praːk] NT **-s** Prague; **der ~er Frühling** (*Pol*) the Prague Spring

Präge ['prɛːgə] F **-, -n**, **Prägeanstalt** F mint

prägen ['prɛːgn] VT (a) *Münzen* to mint; *Leder, Papier, Metall* to emboss; (= *erfinden*) *Begriffe, Wörter* to coin (b) (*fig*: = *formen*) *Charakter* to shape; (*Erlebnis, Kummer, Erfahrungen*) *jdn* to leave its/their mark on; **ein vom Leid geprägtes Gesicht** a face marked by suffering; **ein katholisch geprägtes Land** a predominantly Catholic country; **das moderne Drama ist durch Brecht geprägt worden** Brecht had a formative influence on modern drama (c) (= *kennzeichnen*) to characterize

PR-Agentur [peː'ɛr-] F PR agency

Pragmatiker [pra'gmaːtikɐ] M **-s, -**, **Pragmatikerin** [-ərɪn] F **-, -nen** pragmatist

pragmatisch [pra'gmaːtɪʃ] **1** ADJ pragmatic **2** ADV pragmatically; **~ eingestellt sein** to be pragmatic

prägnant [prɛ'gnant] **1** ADJ *Worte* succinct; *Beispiel, Unterschied* striking **2** ADV succinctly

Prägnanz [prɛ'gnants] F **-**, NO PL succinctness

Prägung ['prɛːgʊŋ] F **-, -en** (a) (= *das Prägen*) stamping; (*von Münzen*) minting; (*von Leder, Papier, Metall*) embossing; (*von Begriffen, Wörtern*) coining; (*fig*: *von Charakter*) shaping (b) (*auf Münzen*) strike; (*auf Leder, Metall, Papier*) embossing (c) (= *Eigenart*) character; **Kommunismus sowjetischer ~** soviet-style communism

prähistorisch ADJ prehistoric

prahlen ['praːlən] VI to boast (*mit* about)

Prahlerei [praːlə'rai] F **-, -en** (= *Großsprecherei*) boasting *no pl*; (= *das Zurschaustellen*) showing-off; **-en** boasts

prahlerisch ['praːlərɪʃ] **1** ADJ (= großsprecherisch) boastful, bragging attr; (= großtuerisch) flashy (inf) **2** ADV boastfully; ~ **reden** to brag; **sich ~ verhalten** to strut around (inf)

Präimplantationsdiagnostik F pre-implantation diagnosis

Praktik ['praktɪk] F -, -en (= Methode) procedure; (usu pl: = Kniff) practice; **undurchsichtige ~en** shady or dark practices

Praktika PL von **Praktikum**

praktikabel [prakti'kaːbl] ADJ practicable

Praktikant [prakti'kant] M -en, -en, **Praktikantin** [-'kantɪn] F -, -nen student doing a period of practical training

Praktikum ['praktikʊm] NT -s, **Praktika** [-ka] (period of) practical training

praktisch ['praktɪʃ] **1** ADJ practical; (= nützlich auch) handy; **sie hat einen ~en Verstand** she's practically minded; **~er Arzt** general practitioner; **~es Beispiel** concrete example **2** ADV (= in der Praxis) in practice; (= geschickt) practically; (= so gut wie) practically

praktizieren [prakti'tsiːrən], ptp **praktiziert** VI to practise (Brit), to practice (US); **sie praktiziert als Ärztin** she is a practising (Brit) or practicing (US) doctor

Praline [pra'liːnə] F -, -n (Aus) **Praliné** [prali'neː] NT -s, -s, **Pralinee** [prali'neː] NT -s, -s chocolate, chocolate candy (US)

prall [pral] **1** ADJ Sack, Beutel, Brieftasche bulging; Segel, Wange full; Tomaten firm; Euter swollen; Luftballon hard; Brüste, Hintern well-rounded; Arme, Schenkel big strong attr; Sonne blazing **2** ADV **etw ~ aufblasen** to blow sth up until it is ready to burst; **~ gefüllt** Tasche, Kasse etc full to bursting; Arbeitstag chock-full (inf); **die Sonne brannte ~ auf den Strand** the sun beat down onto the beach

Prall [pral] M -(e)s, -e collision (gegen with)

prallen ['pralən] VI AUX SEIN **gegen etw ~** to collide with sth; (Ball) to bounce against sth; **er prallte mit dem Kopf gegen die Windschutzscheibe** he hit his head against the windscreen; **die Sonne prallte auf** or **gegen die Fenster** the sun beat down on the windows

prallvoll ADJ full to bursting; Brieftasche bulging

Prämie ['prɛːmiə] F -, -n premium; (= Belohnung) bonus; (= Preis) prize

Prämien-: prämienbegünstigt [-bəgʏnstɪçt] ADJ carrying a premium; **prämiensparen** VI SEP INFIN, PTP ONLY to save on a system benefiting from government premiums in addition to interest

prämieren [prɛ'miːrən], ptp **prämiert** VT (= auszeichnen) to give an award; (= belohnen) to give a bonus; **der prämierte Film** the award-winning film

Prämisse [prɛ'mɪsə] F -, -n premise

pränatal [prena'taːl] ADJ ATTR Diagnostik prenatal; Vorsorge, Untersuchung antenatal, prenatal (esp US)

Pranger ['praŋɐ] M -s, - stocks pl; **jdn/etw an den ~ stellen** (fig) to pillory sb/sth; **am ~ stehen** (lit) to be in the stocks; (fig) to be being pilloried

Pranke ['praŋkə] F -, -n paw

PR-Anzeige [peː'ʔɛr-] F promotional advert

Präparat [prepa'raːt] NT -(e)s, -e preparation; (für Mikroskop) slide preparation

Präposition [prepozi'tsioːn] F -, -en preposition

präpositional [prepozitsio'naːl] ADJ prepositional

Prärie [prɛ'riː] F -, -n [-'riːən] prairie

Präriewolf M prairie wolf

Präsens ['prɛːzɛns] NT -, Präsenzien [prɛ'zɛntsiən] present (tense)

präsent [prɛ'zɛnt] ADJ (= anwesend) present; (= geistig rege) alert; **etw ~ haben** to have sth at hand; **sein Name ist mir nicht ~** his name escapes me

präsentabel [prɛzɛn'taːbl] **1** ADJ presentable **2** ADV presentably; **~ aussehen** to look presentable; **etw ~ herrichten** to make sth look presentable

Präsentation [prɛzɛnta'tsioːn] F -, -en presentation

präsentieren [prɛzɛn'tiːrən], ptp **präsentiert** VT to present; **jdm etw ~** to present sb with sth; **jdm die Rechnung (für etw) ~** (fig) to make sb pay the price (for sth); **präsentiert das Gewehr!** present arms!

Präsentierteller M (old) salver; **auf dem ~ sitzen** (fig) to be on show

Präsenzliste F (attendance) register

Präservativ [prezɛrva'tiːf] NT -s, -e [-və] condom

*Vorsicht! **Präservativ** wird nicht mit dem englischen Wort **preservative** übersetzt.*

Präsident [prɛzi'dɛnt] M -en, -en, **Präsidentin** [-'dɛntɪn] F -, -nen president; **Herr ~** Mister President; **Frau ~in** Madam President

Präsidentenwahl F presidential election

Präsidentschaft [prɛzi'dɛntʃaft] F -, -en presidency

Präsidentschaftskandidat(in) M(F) presidential candidate

Präsidium [prɛ'ziːdiʊm] NT -s, Präsidien [-diən] (= Vorsitz) presidency; (= Führungsgruppe) committee; (= Gebäude) headquarters (building); (= Polizeipräsidium) (police) headquarters pl

prasseln ['prasl̩] VI (a) AUX SEIN to clatter; (Regen, Hagel) to drum; (fig: Vorwürfe, Fragen) to rain down (b) (Feuer) to crackle

prassen ['prasn̩] VI (= schlemmen) to feast; (= in Luxus leben) to live the high life

Prasserei [prasə'rai] F -, -en (= Schlemmerei) feasting; (= Luxusleben) high life

Präteritum [prɛ'teːritʊm] NT -s, Präterita [-ta] preterite

präventiv [prevɛn'tiːf] **1** ADJ prevent(at)ive **2** ADV prevent(at)ively; wirken, operieren as a prevent(at)ive measure; **etw ~ bekämpfen** to use prevent(at)ive measures against sth; **die Polizei hat ~ eingegriffen** the police took prevent(at)ive measures

Präventiv-: Präventivbehandlung F (Med) prevent(at)ive treatment; **Präventivkrieg** M prevent(at)ive war; **Präventivmedizin** F prevent(at)ive medicine; **Präventivschlag** M (Mil) pre-emptive strike

Praxis ['praksɪs] F -, Praxen ['praksn̩] (a) NO PL practice; (= Erfahrung) experience; (= Brauch) practice; **in der ~** in practice; **die ~ sieht anders aus** the facts are different; **etw in die ~ umsetzen** to put sth into practice; **ein Mann der ~** a man with practical experience; **ein Beispiel aus der ~** an example from real life (b) (eines Arztes, Rechtsanwalts) practice; (= Behandlungsräume) surgery (Brit), doctor's office (US); (= Anwaltsbüro) office (c) (= Sprechstunde) consultation (hour), surgery (Brit)

praxis-: praxisfern, praxisfremd **1** ADJ Ausbildung lacking in practical relevance **2** ADV **jdn ~ ausbilden** to provide sb with training lacking in practical relevance; **praxisnah** **1** ADJ Ausbildung practically relevant **2** ADV **jdn ~ ausbilden** to provide sb with practically relevant training; **praxisorientiert** [-orienti:ɐt] **1** ADJ Ausbildung, Lösung, Software practically orientated **2** ADV **jdn ~ ausbilden** to provide sb with a practically orientated training; **dort wird ~er gearbeitet** their work is practically orientated

Präzedenzfall M precedent

präzis [prɛ'tsiːs], **präzise** [prɛ'tsiːzə] **1** ADJ precise **2** ADV precisely; formulieren, schneiden exactly; **sie arbeitet sehr ~** her work is very precise

präzisieren [prɛtsi'ziːrən], ptp **präzisiert** VT to state more precisely; (= zusammenfassen) to summarize

Präzision [prɛtsi'zioːn] F -, NO PL precision

predigen ['preːdɪgn̩] **1** VT (a) (Rel) to preach (b) (fig) **jdm etw ~** to lecture sb on sth **2** VI to give a sermon; (fig: = mahnen) to preach; **tauben Ohren ~** to preach to deaf ears

Predigt ['preːdɪçt] F -, -en (lit, fig) sermon

Preis [prais] M -es, -e (a) price (für of); (= Fahrgeld) fare (für for); (= Gebühr, Honorar) fee (für of); **(weit) unter(m) ~** cut-price; **etw unter ~ verkaufen/verschleudern** to sell/flog (Brit inf) sth off cheap; **zum halben ~** half-price; **um jeden ~** (fig) at all costs; **Qualität hat ihren ~** you have to pay for quality; **ich gehe um keinen ~ hier weg** (fig) I'm not leaving here at any price; **auch um den ~ seines eignen Glücks** even at the expense of his own happiness (b) (bei Wettbewerben) prize; (= Auszeichnung) award; **der Große ~ von Deutschland** the German Grand Prix (c) (= Belohnung) reward; **einen ~ auf jds Kopf aussetzen** to put a price on sb's head

Preis-: Preisabsprache F price-fixing no pl; **Preisänderung** F price change; **Preisangabe** F price quotation; **alle Kleider sind mit ~** all dresses are priced; **Preisaufgabe** F prize competition; **Preisaufschlag** M supplementary charge; **Preisausschreiben** NT competition; **Preisbindung** F price fixing; **~ der zweiten Hand** retail price maintenance; **Preiseinbruch** M price collapse

Preiselbeere ['praɪzl-] F cranberry

Preis-: **Preisdifferenzierung** F price discrimination; **Preiselastizität** F price elasticity; **Preisentwicklung** F price trend; **Preiserhöhung** F price increase; **Preisfrage** F **(a)** question of price **(b)** (beim Preisausschreiben) prize question (in a competition); (inf: = schwierige Frage) big question

preisgeben VT SEP IRREG (geh) **(a)** (= ausliefern) to expose; **jdm/einer Sache preisgegeben sein** to be exposed to sb/sth **(b)** (= aufgeben) to abandon **(c)** (= verraten) to betray

Preis-: **Preisgefälle** NT price gap; **Preisgefüge** NT price structure; **preisgekrönt** [-gəkrøːnt] ADJ award-winning; **~ werden** to be given an award; **Preisgericht** NT jury; **Preisgleitklausel** F escalator clause; **preisgünstig** ■ ADJ inexpensive ■ ADV kaufen inexpensively; **etw ~ bekommen** to get sth at a low price; **am ~sten kauft man im Supermarkt ein** you get the most for your money at the supermarket; **Preisklasse** F price range; **die gehobene/mittlere/untere ~** the upper/medium/lower price range; **Preiskrieg** M price war; **Preislage** F price range; **in jeder ~** at all prices; **im mittleren ~** in the medium-priced range; **Preis-Leistungs-Verhältnis** NT cost-effectiveness

preislich ['praɪslɪç] ■ ADJ price attr, in price; **~e Wettbewerbsfähigkeit** price competitiveness ■ ADV **niedriger/vorteilhaft** lower/favourably (Brit) or favorably (US) priced; **~ vergleichbar** similarly priced; **sie sind ~ unterschiedlich** they differ in price; **dieses Angebot ist ~ sehr günstig** this offer is a bargain

Preis-: **Preisliste** F price list; **Preisnachlass** M price reduction; **10% ~ bei Barzahlung** 10% off cash sales; **Preisobergrenze** F price ceiling; **Preisgleitklausel** F escalator clause; **Preisrätsel** NT prize competition; **Preisrichter(in)** M(F) judge (in a competition); **Preisschild** NT price tag; **Preisschlager** M (all-time) bargain; **Preissenkung** F price cut; **Preissturz** M sudden drop in prices; **Preisträger(in)** M(F) prizewinner; (= Kulturpreisträger) award-winner; **Preistreiber(in)** M(F) person who forces prices up; **Preistreiberei** [-traɪbə'raɪ] F -, -en forcing up of prices; (= Wucher) profiteering; **Preisuntergrenze** F price floor; **Preisverfall** M drop-off in prices; **Preisvergleich** M price comparison; **einen ~ machen** to shop around; **Preisverleihung** F presentation (of prizes); (von Auszeichnung) presentation (of awards); **preiswert** ■ ADJ good value pred; **ein (sehr) ~es Angebot** a (real) bargain; **ein ~es Kleid** a dress which is good value (for money) ■ ADV inexpensively; **hier kann man ~ einkaufen** you get good value (for money) here; **am ~esten kauft man im Supermarkt ein** you get the most for your money at the supermarket

prekär [pre'kɛːɐ] ADJ (= peinlich) awkward; (= schwierig) precarious

prellen ['prɛlən] ■ VT **(a)** Körperteil to bruise; (= anschlagen) to hit **(b)** (fig inf: = betrügen) to swindle; **jdm um etw ~** to swindle sb out of sth **(c)** (Sport) to bounce ■ VR to bruise oneself; **ich habe mich am** or **mir den Arm geprellt** I've bruised my arm

Prellung ['prɛlʊŋ] F -, -en bruise

Premier [prə'mieː, pre-] M -s, -s premier

Premiere [prə'mieːrə, pre-, -'mieːrə] F -, -n premiere

Premierminister(in) [prə'mieː-, pre-] M(F) prime minister

Presbyterianer [presbyte'riaːne] M -s, -, **Presbyterianerin** [-ərɪn] F -, -nen Presbyterian

presbyterianisch [presbyte'riaːnɪʃ] ADJ Presbyterian

preschen ['prɛʃn] VI AUX SEIN (inf) to tear

Presse ['prɛsə] F -, -n **(a)** (= mechanische ~, Druckmaschine) press; **in die ~ gehen** to go to press; **frisch** or **eben aus der ~** hot from the press **(b)** (= Zeitungen) press; **eine gute/schlechte ~ haben** to get a good/bad press; **von der ~ sein** to be (a member of the) press

Presse-: **Presseagentur** F press agency; **Presseausweis** M press card; **Pressebericht** M press report; **Presseerklärung** F statement to the press; (schriftlich) press release; **Pressefotograf(in)** M(F) press photographer; **Pressefreiheit** F freedom of the press; **Pressekonferenz** F press conference;

Pressemeldung F press report; **Pressemitteilung** F press release or announcement

pressen ['prɛsn] VT (= quetschen) to press; Obst, Saft to squeeze; (fig: = zwingen) to force (in +acc, zu into); **frisch gepresster Orangensaft** freshly squeezed orange juice; **eine CD ~** to press a CD; **etw auf CD-ROM ~** to put sth onto CD-ROM; **mit gepresster Stimme** in a strained voice

Presse-: **Pressenotiz** F paragraph in the press; **Pressereferent(in)** M(F) press officer; **Pressesprecher(in)** M(F) press officer

pressieren [prɛ'siːrən], ptp pressiert (S Ger, Aus, Sw) ■ VI to be in a hurry ■ VI IMPERS **es pressiert** it's urgent; **(bei) ihm pressiert es immer** he's always in a hurry

Pression [prɛ'sioːn] F -, -en pressure

Pressluft F compressed air

Pressluft-: **Pressluftbohrer** M pneumatic drill; **Presslufthammer** M pneumatic hammer

Prestige [prɛs'tiːʒə] NT -s, NO PL prestige

Prêt-à-porter- [prɛtapɔr'teː] IN CPDS ready-to-wear

Preuße ['prɔysə] M -n, -n, **Preußin** [-sɪn] F -, -nen Prussian; (fig) strict disciplinarian; **so schnell schießen die ~n nicht** (inf) things don't happen that fast

Preußen ['prɔysn] NT -s Prussia

preußisch ['prɔysɪʃ] ADJ Prussian

PR-Fachmann [peːˈɛr-] M, **PR-Fachfrau** F PR specialist

prickeln ['prɪkln] VI (= kribbeln) to tingle; (= kitzeln) to tickle; (= Bläschen bilden) to bubble; **die Limonade prickelt in der Nase** the lemonade's tickling my nose; **ein angenehmes Prickeln auf der Haut** a pleasant tingling of the skin

prickelnd ADJ (= kribbelnd) tingling; (= kitzelnd) tickling; (= Bläschen bildend) bubbling; (fig) (= würzig) piquant; (= erregend) Gefühl tingling; **der ~e Reiz der Neuheit** the thrill of novelty

Priel [priːl] M -(e)s, -e narrow channel (in North Sea mud flats), tideway

pries PRET von **preisen**

Priester ['priːstɐ] M -s, - priest

Priesterin ['priːstərɪn] F -, -nen (woman) priest; (Hist) priestess

Priester-: **Priesterschaft** ['priːstɐʃaft] F -, -en priesthood; **Priesterseminar** NT seminary; **Priesterweihe** F ordination (to the priesthood)

prima ['priːma] ■ ADJ INV **(a)** (inf) fantastic (inf), great no adv (inf) **(b)** (Comm) first-class ■ ADV (inf: = sehr gut) fantastically; **das hast du ~ gemacht** you did that fantastically (well)

Prima-: **Primaballerina** [primabalə'riːna] F prima ballerina; **Primadonna** [prima'dɔna] F -, **Primadonnen** [-'dɔnən] prima donna

primär [pri'mɛːɐ] ■ ADJ primary ■ ADV primarily

Primär-: **Primärenergie** F primary energy; **Primärkreislauf** F primary circuit

Primarlehrer(in) [pri'maːɐ-] M(F) (Sw) primary school teacher

Primärliteratur F primary literature pl

Primarschule [pri'maːɐ-] F (Sw) primary or junior school

Primat M -en, -en (Zool) primate

Primel ['priːml] F -, -n (= Waldprimel) (wild) primrose; (= farbige Gartenprimel) primula; **wie eine ~ eingehen** (fig) to wither away

primitiv [primi'tiːf] ■ ADJ primitive; Maschine auch crude ■ ADV primitively

Primitivität [primitivi'tɛːt] F -, -en primitiveness; (von Maschine auch) crudeness

Primzahl ['priːm-] F prime (number)

Printmedium ['prɪntmeːdiʊm] NT USU PL printed medium

Prinz [prɪnts] M -en, -en prince

Prinzessin [prɪn'tsɛsɪn] F -, -nen princess; **die ~ auf der Erbse** (Liter) the Princess and the Pea; **eine ~ auf der Erbse** (fig) a hothouse plant

Prinzgemahl M prince consort

Prinzip [prɪn'tsiːp] NT -s, -ien [-piən] or (rare) -e principle; **aus ~** on principle; **im ~** in principle; **das funktioniert nach einem einfachen ~** it works on a simple principle; **er ist ein Mann von** or **mit ~ien** he is a man of principle; **das ~ Hoffnung** the principle of hope

prinzipiell [prɪntsi'piɛl] **1** ADJ (= *im Prinzip*) in principle; (= *aus Prinzip*) on principle **2** ADV **(a)** (= *im Prinzip*) *möglich* theoretically; *dafür/dagegen sein* basically; ~ **bin ich einverstanden** I agree in principle **(b)** (= *aus Prinzip*) on principle; **das tue ich ~ nicht** I won't do that on principle

Prinzipien- [prɪn'tsi:piən-]: **Prinzipienfrage** F matter of principle; **Prinzipienreiter(in)** M(F) (*pej*) stickler for one's principles; **Prinzipienreiterei** F (*pej*) going-on about principles (*pej*)

Priorität [priori'tɛ:t] F **-, -en (a)** priority; ~ **vor etw** (*dat*) **haben** to have priority *or* precedence over sth; **erste** *or* **höchste ~ haben** to have top priority; **~en setzen** to establish one's priorities; **die richtigen/falschen ~en setzen** to get one's priorities right/wrong **(b) Prioritäten** PL (*Comm*) preference shares *pl*, preferred stock (*US*)

Prioritätenliste F list of priorities

Prioritätsaktie F (*St Ex*) preference share

Prise ['pri:zə] F **-, -n (a)** (= *kleine Menge*) pinch; **eine ~ Salz** a pinch of salt; **eine ~ Humor** a touch of humour (*Brit*) *or* humor (*US*) **(b)** (*Naut*) prize

Prisma ['prɪsma] NT **-s, Prismen** [-mən] prism

prismatisch [prɪs'ma:tɪʃ] ADJ prismatic

Prismen PL *von* **Prisma**

privat [pri'va:t] **1** ADJ private; **etw an Privat verkaufen/von Privat kaufen** (*Comm*) to sell sth to/to buy sth from private individuals; **aus ~er Hand** from private individuals **2** ADV privately; ~ **wohnt sie in einer Villa** she lives in a villa; ~ **ist der Chef sehr freundlich** the boss is very friendly out(side) of work; ~ **ist er ganz anders** he's quite different socially; **ich sagte es ihm ganz ~** I told him in private; ~ **versichert sein** to be privately insured; ~ **behandelt werden** to have private treatment; ~ **liegen** to be in a private ward

Privat- IN CPDS private; **Privatadresse** F private *or* home address; **Privatangelegenheit** F private matter; **das ist meine ~** that's my own business; **Privatbesitz** M private property; **viele Gemälde sind** *or* **befinden sich in ~** many paintings are privately owned; **Privatdetektiv(in)** M(F) private investigator; **Privatdiskontsatz** M prime (lending) rate

privatisieren [privati'zi:rən], *ptp* **privatisiert 1** VT to privatize **2** VI to live on a private income

Privatisierung F **-, -en** privatization

Privat-: **Privatklinik** F private clinic, nursing home; **Privatkredit** M personal *or* consumer credit; **Privatleben** NT private life; **Privatpatient(in)** M(F) private patient; **Privatplatzierung** F (*Fin*) private placing; **Privatsache** F private matter; **das ist meine ~** that's my own business; **das ist reine ~** that's a strictly private matter; **Privatschule** F private school; **Privatunterricht** M private tuition; **Privatvergnügen** NT (*inf*) private pleasure; **Privatversicherung** F private insurance; **Privatweg** M private way; **Privatwirtschaft** F private industry

Privileg [privi'le:k] NT **-(e)s, -gien** *or* **-e** [-giən, -gə] privilege

privilegieren [privile'gi:rən], *ptp* **privilegiert** VT to favour (*Brit*), to favor (*US*); **steuerlich privilegiert sein** to enjoy tax privileges

pro [pro:] PREP per; ~ **Tag/Stunde** a *or* per day/hour; ~ **Jahr** a *or* per year; ~ **Quadratmeter** a *or* per square metre (*Brit*) *or* meter (*US*); ~ **Person** per person; ~ **Kopf** per person; ~ **Stück** each

Pro [pro:] NT **(das)** ~ **und (das) Kontra** the pros and cons *pl*

Proband [pro'bant] M **-en, -en** [-dn], **Probandin** [-'bandɪn] F **-, -nen** guinea pig

Probe ['pro:bə] F **-, -n (a)** (= *Prüfung*) test; **eine ~ auf etw** (*acc*) **machen** to test sth; **die ~ (auf eine Rechnung) machen** to check a calculation; **ein Beamter auf ~** a probationary civil servant; **er ist auf ~ angestellt** he's employed for a probationary period; **jdn/etw auf ~ nehmen** to take sb/sth on trial; ~ **fahren** to go for a test drive; **ein Auto ~ fahren** to test-drive a car; **jdn/etw auf die ~ stellen** to put sb/sth to the test; **meine Geduld wurde auf eine harte ~ gestellt** my patience was sorely tried; **zur ~** to try out **(b)** (*Theat, Mus*) rehearsal **(c)** (= *Teststück, Beispiel*) sample; **er gab eine ~ seines Könnens** he showed what he could do

---

Vorsicht! **Probe** *wird nicht mit dem englischen Wort* **probe** *übersetzt.*

Probe-: **Probearbeit** F specimen piece; **Probebohrung** F test drill, probe; **Probeexemplar** NT specimen (copy); **probefahren** VT, VI *siehe* **Probe**; **Probefahrt** F test drive; (*mit Boot*) trial sail; (*mit Fahrrad*) test ride; **eine ~ machen** to go for a test drive *etc*; **probehalber** ADV for a test; **Probejahr** NT probationary year; **Probelehrer(in)** M(F) (*Aus*) probationary teacher

proben ['pro:bn] VTI to rehearse

Probe-: **Probenummer** F trial copy; **Probeseite** F specimen page; **Probestück** NT sample, specimen; **probeweise** ADV on a trial basis; **ich habe mir ~ einen anderen Kaffee gekauft** I've bought another kind of coffee to try (out); **Probezeit** F probationary *or* trial period

probieren [pro'bi:rən], *ptp* **probiert 1** VT to try; **lass (es) mich mal ~!** let me have a try! *Brit* **2** VI **(a)** (= *versuchen*) to try; **Kinder lernen durch Probieren** children learn by trial and error; **Probieren geht über Studieren** (*Prov*) the proof of the pudding is in the eating (*Prov*) **(b)** (= *kosten*) to have a taste; **probier mal** try some

Problem [pro'ble:m] NT **-s, -e** problem; **das wird zum ~** it's becoming (something of) a problem; **~e wälzen** to turn problems over in one's mind

Problematik [proble'ma:tɪk] F **-, -en (a)** (= *Schwierigkeit, Problem*) problem (+*gen* with); **die ~ der modernen Soziologie** the problems of modern sociology **(b)** (= *Fragwürdigkeit*) problematic nature

problematisch [proble'ma:tɪʃ] ADJ problematic; (= *fragwürdig*) questionable

Problem-: **Problembewusstsein** NT appreciation of the difficulties; **Problemkind** NT problem child; **problemlos 1** ADJ trouble-free, problem-free **2** ADV without any problems; ~ **ablaufen** to go smoothly; **Problemstellung** F problem

Product-Placement ['prɔdakt'ple:smənt] NT **-s, -s**, **Productplacement** NT **-s, -s** product placement

Produkt [pro'dʊkt] NT **-(e)s, -e** (*lit, fig*) product; **landwirtschaftliche ~e** agricultural produce *no pl*; **das ~ aus 2 mal 2** the product of 2 times 2; **ein ~ seiner Phantasie** a figment of his imagination

Produkt-: **Produktdifferenzierung** F product differentiation; **Produkterpressung** F extortion (*involving threats to poison goods*); **Produktgestaltung** F product design; **Produkthaftung** F product liability

Produktion [prodʊk'tsio:n] F **-, -en** production

Produktions- IN CPDS production; **Produktionsanlagen** PL production plant; **Produktionsfaktor** M factor of production; **Produktionsmenge** F output; **Produktionsmittel** PL means of production *pl*; **produktionsreif** ADJ ready to go into production; **Produktionsstätte** F production centre (*Brit*) *or* center (*US*)

produktiv [prodʊk'ti:f] ADJ productive

Produktivität [prodʊktivi'tɛ:t] F **-, -en** productivity

Produktivkräfte PL (*Sociol*) productive forces *pl*

Produktivvermögen NT productive assets *pl*

Produkt-: **Produktmanager(in)** M(F) product manager; **Produktpalette** F product spectrum; **Produktpiraterie** F product piracy

Produzent [produ'tsɛnt] M **-en, -en**, **Produzentin** [-'tsɛntɪn] F **-, -nen** producer

produzieren [produ'tsi:rən], *ptp* **produziert 1** VT **(a)** AUCH VI to produce; **~des Gewerbe** production industry **(b)** (*inf*: = *hervorbringen*) *Lärm* to make; *Entschuldigung* to come up with (*inf*); *Romane* to churn out (*inf*); **wer hat denn das produziert?** who's responsible for that? **2** VR (*pej*) to show off

Prof [prɔf] M **-s, -s** (*Univ inf*) prof (*inf*)

Prof. ABBR *von* **Professor**

Professionalität [profesionali'tɛ:t] F **-, NO PL** professionalism

professionell [profesio'nɛl] **1** ADJ professional; **eine Professionelle** (*inf*) a pro (*inf*) **2** ADV professionally

Professor [pro'fɛso:ɐ] M **-s, Professoren** [-'so:rən] **(a)** (= *Hochschulprofessor*) professor; **ordentlicher ~ für Philosophie** (full) professor of philosophy; **außerordentlicher ~** professor not holding a chair, ≈ associate professor (*US*); **Herr/Frau ~!** Professor!; **Herr ~ Vogel**

Professor Vogel **(b)** *(Aus, S Ger.* = *Gymnasiallehrer)* teacher; **Herr ~!** Sir!; **Frau ~!** Miss!

Professorenschaft [profe'so:rənʃaft] F **-, -en** professors *pl*

Professorin [profe'so:rɪn] F **-, -nen (a)** (= *Hochschulprofessorin)* professor **(b)** *(Aus, S Ger.* = *Gymnasiallehrerin)* teacher

Professur [profe'su:ɐ] F **-, -en** chair *(für* in, of)

Profi ['pro:fi] M **-s, -s** *(inf)* pro *(inf)*

Profil [pro'fi:l] NT **-s, -e (a)** *(von Gesicht)* profile; *(Archit)* elevation; *(fig:* = *Ansehen)* image; **im ~** in profile; **~ haben** *or* **besitzen** *(fig)* to have a (distinctive) image; **die Partei hat in den letzten Jahren mehr ~ bekommen** over the last few years the party has sharpened its image; **dadurch hat er an ~ gewonnen/verloren** that improved/damaged his image **(b)** *(von Reifen, Schuhsohle)* tread

profilieren [profi'li:rən], *ptp* **profiliert** VR (= *sich ein Image geben)* to create a distinctive image for oneself; (= *Besonderes leisten)* to distinguish oneself; **er will sich akademisch/ politisch** *etc* **~** he wants to make a name for himself academically/in politics *etc*

profiliert [profi'li:ɐt] ADJ *Schuhe, Reifen* with a tread; *(fig:* = *scharf umrissen)* clear-cut *no adv; (fig:* = *hervorstechend)* distinctive; *Persönlichkeit* prominent; **ein ~er Politiker/ Wissenschaftler** a politician/scientist who has made his mark

Profil-: Profilneurose F *(hum)* image neurosis; **Profilsohle** F treaded sole

Profit [pro'fi:t, pro'fɪt] M **-(e)s, -e** profit; **~ aus etw schlagen** *or* **ziehen** *(lit)* to make a profit from sth; *(fig)* to profit from sth; **~ machen** to make a profit; **~ bringend** *(adjektivisch)* profitable; *(adverbial)* profitably; **den/keinen ~ von etw haben** to profit/not to profit from sth; **ohne/mit ~ arbeiten** to work unprofitably/profitably

profitabel [profi'ta:bl] ADJ profitable

Profit-: Profitbringend ADJ *siehe* **Profit**; **Profitcenter** ['profitsentɐ] NT *(Comm)* profit centre *(Brit) or* center *(US)*

profitieren [profi'ti:rən], *ptp* **profitiert** VTI *(von* from, by) to profit; *(fig auch)* to gain; **viel/etwas ~** *(lit)* to make a large profit/to make something of a profit; *(fig)* to profit greatly/ somewhat; **dabei kann ich nur ~** I only stand to gain from it; **und was profitierst du dabei** *or* **davon?** what do you stand to gain from it?

Profit-: Profitmaximierung F maximization of profit(s); **Profitstreben** NT profit seeking

pro forma [pro 'fɔrma] ADV as a matter of form

Pro-forma-Rechnung [pro'fɔrma-] F pro forma invoice

Prognose [pro'gno:zə] F **-, -n** prognosis; (= *Wetterprognose)* forecast; **genetische ~** genetic prognosis

prognostizieren [prognɔsti'tsi:rən], *ptp* **prognostiziert** VT to predict, to prognosticate *(form)*

Programm [pro'gram] NT **-s, -e (a)** programme *(Brit)*, program *(US)*; (= *Tagesordnung)* agenda; *(TV:* = *Sender)* channel; (= *Sendefolge)* program(me)s *pl*; (= *gedrucktes Radio-~)* program(me) guide; (= *gedrucktes TV-~)* TV guide; (= *~heft)* program(me); (= *Verlagsprogramm)* list; (= *Kollektion, Sortiment)* range; **nach ~** as planned; **auf dem ~ stehen** to be on the program(me)/agenda; **für heute habe ich schon ein ~** I've already got something planned for today; **ein volles ~ haben** to have a full schedule; **unser ~ für den heutigen Abend** *(TV, Rad)* our program(me)s for this evening **(b)** *(Comput)* program

Programmanbieter M *(TV)* programme *(Brit) or* program *(US)* maker

Programm-: Programmfolge F order of programmes *(Brit) or* programs *(US); (Theat)* order of acts; **programmgemäß** ADJ, ADV according to plan *or* programme *(Brit) or* programme *(US)*; **Programmhandel** M *(Fin)* programme *(Brit) or* program *(US)* trading; **Programmheft** NT program(me) *or* program *(US)*; **Programmhinweis** M *(Rad, TV)* programme *(Brit) or* program *(US)* announcement; **wir bringen noch einige ~e für morgen** and now a look at some of tomorrow's programmes *(Brit) or* programs *(US)*

programmierbar ADJ programmable

programmieren [progra'mi:rən], *ptp* **programmiert** VT AUCH VI to programme *(Brit)*, to program *(US); (Comput)* to program; *(fig:* = *konditionieren)* to programme *(Brit)*, to program *(US)*, to

condition; **auf etw** *(acc)* **programmiert sein** *(fig)* to be conditioned to sth

Programmierer [progra'mi:rɐ] M **-s, -, Programmiererin** [-ərɪn] F **-, -nen** programmer *(Brit)*, programer *(US)*

Programmierfehler M programming *(Brit) or* programing *(US)* error

Programmiersprache F programming *(Brit) or* programing *(US)* language

Programmierung [progra'mi:rʊŋ] F **-, -en** programming *(Brit)*, programing *(US); (fig auch)* conditioning

Programm-: Programmkino NT arts *or* repertory *(US)* cinema; **Programmpunkt** M item on the agenda; *(TV)* programme *(Brit)*, program *(US); (bei Show)* act; **Programmübersicht** F rundown of the programmes *(Brit) or* programs *(US)*; **Programmvorschau** F preview *(für* of); *(Film)* trailer; **Programmzeitschrift** F TV guide

Progression [progre'sio:n] F **-, -en** progression

progressiv [progre'si:f] **1** ADJ progressive **2** ADV **(a)** (= *fortschrittlich)* progressively; **~ eingestellt sein** to be progressive **(b)** *(in Bezug auf Steuern)* **der Steuertarif ist ~ gestaltet** the tax rates are progressive

Progymnasium ['pro:-] NT secondary school *(for pupils up to 16)*

Projekt [pro'jɛkt] NT **-(e)s, -e** project

Projektfinanzierung F project financing

Projektion [projɛk'tsio:n] F **-, -en** projection

Projektleiter(in) M(F) project leader

Projektor [pro'jɛkto:ɐ] M **-s, Projektoren** [-'to:rən] projector

projizieren [proji'tsi:rən], *ptp* **projiziert** VT to project

Pro-Kopf- [pro:'kɔpf] IN CPDS per capita; **Pro-Kopf-Einkommen** NT per capita income

Prokura [pro'ku:ra] F **-, Prokuren** [-rən] *(form)* procuration *(form)*

Prokurist [proku'rɪst] M **-en, -en, Prokuristin** [-'rɪstɪn] F **-, -nen** holder of a general power of attorney

Prolet [pro'le:t] M **-en, -en, Proletin** [-'le:tɪn] F **-, -nen** *(pej)* prole *(esp Brit pej inf)*

Proletariat [proleta'ria:t] NT **-(e)s, NO PL** proletariat

Proletarier [prole'ta:riɐ] M **-s, -, Proletarierin** [-iərɪn] F **-, -nen** proletarian; **~ aller Länder, vereinigt euch!** workers of the world, unite!

proletarisch [prole'ta:rɪʃ] ADJ proletarian

proletenhaft *(pej)* **1** ADJ plebeian *(pej)* **2** ADV like a pleb *(inf)*

Proletin F *siehe* **Prolet**

Proll [prɔl] M **-s, -s, Prolo** ['pro:lo] M **-s, -s** *(pej inf:* = *Prolet)* prole *(esp Brit inf)*

Prolog [pro'lo:k] M **-(e)s, -e** [-gə] prologue *(Brit)*, prolog *(US)*

Prolongation [prolɔŋga'tsio:n] F **-, -en** *(St Ex)* carryover

prolongieren [prolɔŋ'gi:rən], *ptp* **prolongiert** VT to prolong

Promi ['pro:mi] M **-s, -s** *or* f **-, -s** *(inf)* VIP; (= *Politiker)* star politician

Promille [pro'mɪlə] NT **-(s), -** thousandth; *(inf:* = *Alkoholspiegel)* alcohol level; **er hat zu viel ~ (im Blut)** he has too much alcohol in his blood; **0,5 ~ (Alkohol im Blut)** a blood-alcohol level of 50 millilitres *(Brit)*, a blood-alcohol content of 0.5 *(US)*

Promille-: Promillegrenze F legal (alcohol) limit; **Promillemesser** M **-s, -** Breathalyzer®

prominent [promi'nɛnt] ADJ prominent

Prominenten- IN CPDS VIP; *(inf:* = *vornehm)* posh *(inf)*; **Prominentenherberge** F *(inf)* posh hotel *(inf)*; **Prominentensuite** F VIP suite

Prominente(r) [promi'nɛntə] MF DECL AS ADJ prominent figure, VIP

Prominenz [promi'nɛnts] F **-** VIPs *pl*, prominent figures *pl*

promisk [pro'mɪsk] ADJ promiscuous

Promiskuität [promɪskui'tɛ:t] F **-, NO PL** promiscuity

Promotion [promo'tsio:n] F **-, -en (a)** *(Univ)* doctorate; *(Aus:* = *Feier)* doctoral degree ceremony; **nach seiner ~** after he got his PhD **(b)** *(Sw Sch:* = *Versetzung)* moving up

promovieren [promo'vi:rən], *ptp* **promoviert** VI to do a doctorate *(über* +acc in); (= *Doktorwürde erhalten)* to receive a doctorate *etc*

prompt [prɔmpt] **1** ADJ prompt **2** ADV promptly; (= *natürlich)* naturally

Pronomen [proˈnoːmən] NT **-s, -** *or* **Pronomina** [-mina] pronoun

pronominal [pronomiˈnaːl] ADJ pronominal

Propaganda [propaˈganda] F -, NO PL propaganda

Propagandafeldzug M propaganda campaign; (= *Werbefeldzug*) publicity campaign

propagandistisch [propaganˈdɪstɪʃ] **1** ADJ propagandist(ic) **2** ADV as propaganda; **etw ~ ausnutzen** to use sth as propaganda

propagieren [propaˈɡiːrən], *ptp* **propagiert** VT to propagate

Propan [proˈpaːn] NT **-s,** NO PL propane

Propangas NT, NO PL propane gas

Propeller [proˈpɛlɐ] M **-s, -** (= *Luftschraube, Schiffsschraube*) propeller

Propeller-: Propellerflugzeug NT, **Propellermaschine** F propeller-driven plane; **Propellerturbine** F turboprop

Prophet [proˈfeːt] M **-en, -en** prophet

Prophetin [proˈfeːtɪn] F **-, -nen** prophetess

prophetisch [proˈfeːtɪʃ] **1** ADJ prophetic **2** ADV prophetically

prophezeien [profeˈtsaɪən], *ptp* **prophezeit** VT to prophesy; **jdm eine glänzende Zukunft ~** to predict a brilliant future for sb

Prophezeiung F **-, -en** prophecy

Prophylaktikum [profyˈlaktikʊm] NT **-s, Prophylaktika** [-ka] (*Med*) prophylactic

prophylaktisch [profyˈlaktɪʃ] **1** ADJ preventative **2** ADV as a preventative measure

Prophylaxe [profyˈlaksə] F **-, -n** prophylaxis

Proportion [propɔrˈtsioːn] F **-, -en** proportion

proportional [propɔrtsioˈnaːl] **1** ADJ proportional; **umgekehrt ~** (*Math*) in inverse proportion **2** ADV proportionally

Proportional-: Proportionaldruck M, NO PL proportional printing; **Proportionalschrift** F proportionally spaced font

proportioniert [propɔrtsioˈniːɐt] ADJ proportioned

proppe(n)voll ADJ (*inf*) jam-packed (*inf*)

Prosa [ˈproːza] F -, NO PL prose; (*fig*) prosaicness

prosaisch [proˈzaːɪʃ] **1** ADJ **(a)** (= *nüchtern*) prosaic **(b)** (*Liter*) prose *attr*, prosaic (*form*) **2** ADV (= *nüchtern*) prosaically

Proseminar [ˈproː-] NT *introductory seminar course for students in their first and second year*

prosit [ˈproːzɪt] INTERJ your health; **~ Neujahr!** Happy New Year!

Prosit [ˈproːzɪt] NT **-s, -s** toast; **ein ~ der Köchin!** here's to the cook!; **ein ~ auf die Treue** let's drink to loyalty; **auf jdn ein ~ ausbringen** to toast sb

Prospekt [proˈspɛkt] M **-(e)s, -e** (= *Reklameschrift*) brochure (+*gen* about); (= *Werbezettel*) leaflet; (= *Verzeichnis*) catalogue (*Brit*), catalog (*US*)

Vorsicht! **Prospekt** *wird nicht mit dem englischen Wort* **prospect** *übersetzt.*

Prospektmaterial NT brochures *pl*

prost [proːst] INTERJ cheers; (*hum: beim Niesen*) bless you; **na denn ~!** (= *Prosit*) cheers then!; (*iro inf*) that's just great (*inf*); **~ Neujahr!** (*inf*) Happy New Year!

Prostata [ˈprɔstata] F -, NO PL prostate gland; (*inf*: = *~leiden*) prostate

prosten [ˈproːstn] VI to say cheers

prostituieren [prostituˈiːrən], *ptp* **prostituiert** VR (*lit, fig*) to prostitute oneself

Prostituierte(r) [prostituˈiːɐtə] MF DECL AS ADJ prostitute

Prostitution [prostituˈtsioːn] F **-, -en** prostitution

protegieren [proteˈʒiːrən], *ptp* **protegiert** VT *Künstler, Persönlichkeit, Projekt* to sponsor; *Land, Regime* to support; **er wird vom Chef protegiert** he's the boss's protégé

Protein [proteˈiːn] NT **-s, -e** protein

Protektion [protɛkˈtsioːn] F **-, -en** (= *Schutz*) protection; (= *Begünstigung*) patronage

Protektionismus [protɛktsioˈnɪsmʊs] M -, NO PL **(a)** (*Econ*) protectionism **(b)** (= *Günstlingswirtschaft*) nepotism

protektionistisch [protɛktsioˈnɪstɪʃ] ADJ protectionist

Protest [proˈtɛst] M **-(e)s, -e (a)** protest; (**gegen etw**) **~ einlegen** to register a protest (about sth); **etw aus ~ tun** to do sth in protest *or* as a protest; **unter ~** protesting; (*gezwungen*) under protest **(b)** (*Fin*) protest; **~ mangels Annahme/Zahlung** protest

for non-acceptance/non-payment; **einen Wechsel zu ~ gehen lassen** to protest a bill

Protestant [protɛsˈtant] M **-en, -en, Protestantin** [-ˈtantɪn] F **-, -nen** Protestant

protestantisch [protɛsˈtantɪʃ] **1** ADJ Protestant **2** ADV **~ denken** to have Protestant beliefs; **Kinder ~ erziehen** to raise one's children as Protestants; **~ heiraten** to be married in the Protestant church; **~ beerdigt werden** to be buried as a Protestant; **~ beeinflusst** influenced by Protestantism

protestieren [protɛsˈtiːrən], *ptp* **protestiert** **1** VI to protest (*gegen* against, about) **2** VT (*Fin*) to protest

Protest-: Protestkundgebung F (protest) rally; **Protestmarsch** M protest march; **Protestwähler(in)** M(F) protest voter

Prothese [proˈteːzə] F **-, -n** artificial limb *or* (*Gelenk*) joint; (= *Gebiss*) set of dentures

Protokoll [protoˈkɔl] NT **-s, -e (a)** (= *Niederschrift*) record; (= *Bericht*) report; (*von Sitzung*) minutes *pl*; (*bei Polizei*) statement; (*bei Gericht*) transcript; (= *Vertragsanhang*) protocol; **das ~ aufnehmen** (*bei Polizei*) to take (down) a statement; **(das) ~ führen** (*bei Sitzung*) to take the minutes; (*bei Gericht*) to keep a record of the proceedings; (*beim Unterricht*) to write a report; **etw zu ~ geben** to have sth put on record; (*bei Polizei*) to say sth in one's statement; **etw zu ~ nehmen** to take sth down **(b)** NO PL (*diplomatisch*) protocol **(c)** (= *Strafzettel*) ticket **(d)** (*Comput*) protocol

Protokollant [protokɔˈlant] M **-en, -en, Protokollantin** [-ˈlantɪn] F **-, -nen** secretary; (*Jur*) clerk (of the court)

protokollarisch [protokɔˈlaːrɪʃ] **1** ADJ **(a)** (= *protokolliert*) on record; (*in Sitzung*) minuted **(b)** (= *zeremoniell*) **~e Vorschriften** rules of protocol **2** ADV **(a)** (= *per Protokoll*) **folgende Maßnahmen wurden ~ festgelegt** the following measures were agreed on **(b)** (= *zeremoniell*) according to protocol; **~ ist das so geregelt, dass ...** protocol requires that ...

protokollieren [protokɔˈliːrən], *ptp* **protokolliert** **1** VI (*bei Sitzung*) to take the minutes (down); (*bei Polizei*) to take a/the statement (down); (*in der Schule*) to write notes **2** VT to take down; *Sitzung* to minute; *Unfall, Verbrechen* to take (down) statements about; *Vorgang, Vernehmung, Gerichtsverhandlung* to keep a record of; *Bemerkung* to put in the minutes; *Stunde* to write up; (*Comput*) to keep a log of

Proton [ˈproːtɔn] NT **-s, Protonen** [proˈtoːnən] proton

Protoplasma [protoˈplasma] NT protoplasm

Prototyp [ˈproːtotyːp] M prototype

Protz [prɔts] M **-es** *or* **-en, -e(n)** (*inf*) swank (*inf*)

protzen [ˈprɔtsn] VI (*inf*) to show off; **mit etw ~** to show sth off

protzig [ˈprɔtsɪç] (*inf*) **1** ADJ showy (*inf*) **2** ADV extravagantly; **wohnen** ostentatiously; **~ auftreten** to show off

Proviant [proˈviant] M **-s,** (*rare*) **-e** provisions *pl*; (= *Reiseproviant*) food for the journey; **sich mit ~ versehen** to lay in provisions; (*für Reise*) to buy food for the journey

Provider [proˈvaɪdɐ] M **-s, -** provider

Provinz [proˈvɪnts] F **-, -en** province; (*im Gegensatz zur Stadt*) provinces *pl* (*auch pej*); **das ist finsterste** *or* **hinterste ~** (*pej*) it's so provincial

provinziell [provɪnˈtsiel] ADJ provincial (*auch pej*)

Provision [proviˈzioːn] F **-, -en** commission; (*bei Bank*) bank charges *pl*; **auf ~** on commission

Provisionsbasis F, NO PL commission basis

provisorisch [proviˈzoːrɪʃ] **1** ADJ provisional; **~e Regierung** caretaker government; **das ist alles noch sehr ~ in unserem Haus** things are still very makeshift in our house; **Straßen mit ~em Belag** roads with a temporary surface **2** ADV temporarily; **wir wollen es ~ so lassen** let's leave it like that for the time being; **ich habe den Stuhl ~ repariert** I've fixed the chair up for the time being

Provisorium [proviˈzoːriʊm] NT **-s, Provisorien** [-riən] stopgap

Provokation [provokaˈtsioːn] F **-, -en** provocation

provozieren [provoˈtsiːrən], *ptp* **provoziert** VTI to provoke

Prozedur [protseˈduːɐ] F **-, -en (a)** (= *Vorgang*) procedure **(b)** (*pej*) carry-on (*inf*); **die ganze ~, bis man endlich zur Universität zugelassen wird** all the rigmarole before you are finally admitted to university; **die ~ beim Zahnarzt** the ordeal at the dentist's **(c)** (*Comput*) procedure

Prozent [pro'tsɛnt] NT **-(e)s, -e** or (nach Zahlenangaben) **-** per cent no pl (Brit), percent no pl (US); **~e** percentage; **fünf ~** five per cent (Brit) or percent (US); **wie viel ~?** what percentage?; **zu zehn ~** at ten per cent (Brit) or percent (US); **zu hohen ~en** at a high percentage; **dieser Whisky hat 35 ~ (Alkoholgehalt)** this whisky contains 35 per cent (Brit) or percent (US) alcohol; **~e bekommen** (= Rabatt) to get a discount

-prozentig [prɔtsɛntɪç] ADJ SUF per cent; **hochprozentig** high percentage; **eine zehnprozentige Lohnerhöhung** a ten per cent (Brit) or percent (US) pay rise

Prozent-: Prozentpunkt M point; **Prozentrechnung** F percentage calculation; **Prozentsatz** M percentage; (= Zins) rate of interest

prozentual [prɔtsɛn'tuaːl] **1** ADJ percentage attr; **~er Anteil** percentage **2** ADV **etw ~ ausdrücken/rechnen** to express/calculate sth as a percentage; **sich an einem Geschäft ~ beteiligen** to have a percentage (share) in a business; **~ gut abschneiden** to get a good percentage

Prozentzeichen NT percent sign

Prozess [pro'tsɛs] M **-es, -e (a)** (= Strafprozess) trial (wegen for; um in the matter of); (= Rechtsfall) (court) case; **der ~ gegen XY** the trial of XY; **einen ~ gewinnen/verlieren** to win/lose a case; **gegen jdn einen ~ anstrengen** to institute legal proceedings against sb; **er führt zur Zeit gegen fünf Firmen einen ~** at the moment he's taking five companies to court; **es ist sehr teuer, einen ~ zu führen** taking legal action is very expensive; **jdm den ~ machen** (inf) to take sb to court; **mit jdm/etw kurzen ~ machen** (fig inf) to make short work of sb/sth (inf)
(b) (= Vorgang) process

Prozess-: prozessführend ADJ **~e Partei** litigant; **die ~e Strafkammer** the criminal court conducting the case; **Prozessführung** F conducting of a case

prozessieren [protsɛ'siːrən], ptp **prozessiert** VI to go to court; **er prozessiert mit fünf Firmen** he's got cases going on against five firms; **gegen jdn ~** to bring an action against sb

Prozession [protsɛ'sioːn] F **-, -en** procession

Prozesskosten PL legal costs pl; **er musste die ~ tragen** he had to pay costs

Prozessor [pro'tsɛsoːɐ] M **-s, Prozessoren** [-'soːrən] (Comput) processor

prüde ['pryːdə] ADJ prudish

Prüderie [prydə'riː] F **-, NO PL** prudishness

prüfen ['pryːfn] **1** VT **(a)** AUCH VI (Sch, Univ) jdn, Kenntnisse to examine, to test; **jdn in etw** (dat) **~** to examine sb in sth; **wer hat bei dir geprüft?** who examined you?; **morgen wird in Englisch geprüft** the English exams are tomorrow; **schriftlich geprüft werden** to have a written examination; **ein staatlich geprüfter Dolmetscher** a state-certified interpreter
(b) (= überprüfen) to check (auf +acc for); (durch Ausprobieren) to test; Lebensmittel, Wein to inspect; **Metall auf den Anteil an Fremdstoffen ~** to check the level of impurities in metal; **wir werden die Beschwerde/Sache ~** we'll look into the complaint/matter; **sie wollte ihn nur ~** she only wanted to test him; **drum prüfe, wer sich ewig bindet** (prov) marry in haste, repent at leisure (Prov)
(c) (= erwägen) to consider; **etw nochmals ~** to reconsider sth
(d) (= mustern) to scrutinize; **ein ~der Blick** a searching look
(e) (= heimsuchen) to try; **ein schwer geprüfter Vater** a sorely tried father
2 VI (Sch, Univ) to give exams; **er prüft sehr streng** he's a strict examiner
3 VR (geh) to search one's heart; **du musst dich selber ~, ob ...** you must decide for yourself whether ...

Prüfer ['pryːfɐ] M **-s, -, Prüferin** [-ərɪn] F **-, -nen** examiner; (= Wirtschaftsprüfer) inspector

Prüfling ['pryːflɪŋ] M **-s, -e** examinee

Prüfstand M test bed; (Space) test stand; **auf dem ~ stehen** to be being tested

Prüfung ['pryːfʊŋ] F **-, -en (a)** (Sch, Univ) exam; **eine ~ machen** or **ablegen** to take or do an exam
(b) (= Überprüfung) checking no indef art; (= Untersuchung) examination; (von Geschäftsbüchern) audit; (von Lebensmitteln, Wein) testing no indef art; **jdn/etw einer ~ unterziehen** to subject sb/sth to an examination; **bei nochmaliger ~ der Rechnung** on rechecking the account; **er führt ~en bei Firmen durch** (von Geschäftsbüchern) he audits

firms' books; **nach/bei ~ Ihrer Beschwerde/dieser Sache ...** after/on looking into your complaint/the matter
(c) (= Erwägung) consideration
(d) (= Heimsuchung) trial

Prüfungs-: Prüfungsanforderung F examination requirement; **Prüfungsangst** F exam nerves pl; **Prüfungsarbeit** F dissertation; **Prüfungsaufgabe** F exam(ination) question; **Prüfungsausschuss** M board of examiners; **Prüfungsfrage** F examination question; **Prüfungskandidat(in)** M(F) examinee; **Prüfungskommission** F board of examiners; **Prüfungsordnung** F exam(ination) regulations pl; **Prüfungstermin** M (Sch, Univ) date of examination; (Jur) meeting of creditors; **Prüfungsunterlagen** PL exam(ination) papers pl

Prüfverfahren NT test procedure

Prügel ['pryːgl] M **-s, - (a)** pl auch **-n** (= Stock) club **(b)** PL (inf: = Schläge) beating; **~ bekommen** or **beziehen** (lit, fig) to get a beating; **jetzt gibt** or **setzt es ~** you're/he's etc in for a (good) thrashing **(c)** (sl: = Penis) tool (sl)

Prügelei [pryːgə'lai] F **-, -en** (inf) fight

Prügelknabe M (fig) whipping boy

prügeln ['pryːgln] **1** VTI to beat; **unser Lehrer prügelt grundsätzlich nicht** our teacher doesn't use corporal punishment on principle **2** VR to fight; **sich mit jdm ~** to fight sb; **Eheleute, die sich ~** married people who come to blows; **sich um etw** (acc) **~** to fight over sth

Prügelstrafe F corporal punishment

Prunk [prʊŋk] M **-s, NO PL** (= Pracht) splendour (Brit), splendor (US); **Protz und ~** pomp and splendo(u)r; **Ludwig XIV liebte ~** Louis XIV had a passion for grandeur; **großen ~ entfalten** to put on a show of great splendo(u)r

Prunk- IN CPDS magnificent; **Prunkbau** M, pl **-bauten** magnificent building; **Prunksaal** M sumptuous room; **Prunkstück** NT showpiece; **prunkvoll** **1** ADJ splendid **2** ADV splendidly

prusten ['pruːstn] VI (inf) to snort; **vor Lachen ~** to snort with laughter

PS [peː'ʔɛs] NT **-, -** ABBR von **Pferdestärke** hp

P.S., PS [peː'ʔɛs] NT **-, -** ABBR von **Postskript(um)** PS

Psalm [psalm] M **-s, -en** psalm

pseudo- ['psɔydo] IN CPDS pseudo

Pseudokrupp [-krʊp] M **-, NO PL** (Med) pseudocroup

Pseudonym [psɔydo'nyːm] NT **-s, -e** pseudonym

psst [pst] INTERJ psst; (= Ruhe!) sh

Psyche ['psyːçə] F **-, -n** psyche; (Myth) Psyche

psychedelisch [psyça'deːlɪʃ] ADJ psychedelic

Psychiater [psy'çiaːtɐ] M **-s, -, Psychiaterin** [-ərɪn] F **-, -nen** psychiatrist

Psychiatrie [psyçia'triː] F **-, -n** [-'triːən] psychiatry

psychiatrisch [psy'çiaːtrɪʃ] **1** ADJ psychiatric **2** ADV psychiatrically; behandeln, untersuchen by a psychiatrist; **~ behandelt werden** to be under psychiatric treatment

psychisch ['psyːçɪʃ] **1** ADJ Belastung, Auswirkungen, Defekt emotional; Phänomen, Erscheinung psychic; Vorgänge psychological; **~e Erkrankung** mental illness; **~ unter großem Druck stehen** or **unter großem ~en Druck stehen** to be under a great deal of emotional or psychological pressure **2** ADV abnorm, auffällig psychologically; krank, gestört, labil mentally; **sich ~ auswirken** to have psychological effects; **~ belastet sein** to be under psychological pressure; **~ erschöpft** emotionally exhausted; **sich ~ schlecht fühlen** to feel bad; **eine ~ bedingte Krankheit** a psychosomatic illness; **jdn ~ beanspruchen** to make emotional demands on sb; **er ist ~ völlig am Ende** his nerves can't take any more

Psycho-, psycho- ['psyːço] IN CPDS psycho-; **Psychoanalyse** [psyço-] F psychoanalysis; **Psychoanalytiker(in)** [psyço-] M(F) psychoanalyst; **Psychodrama** ['psyːço-] NT psychodrama; **Psychogramm** [psyço-] NT, pl **-gramme** profile (auch fig); **Psychologe** [psyço'loːgə] M **-n, -n, Psychologin** [-'loːgɪn] F **-, -nen** psychologist; **Psychologie** [psyçolo'giː] F **-, NO PL** psychology; **psychologisch** [psyço'loːgɪʃ] **1** ADJ psychological; **~e Kriegsführung** psychological warfare **2** ADV psychologically; **~ erfahrene Kräfte** personnel with experience in psychology; **Psychoneurose** [psyço-] F psychoneurosis; **Psychopath** [psyço'paːt] M **-en, -en, Psychopathin** [-'paːtɪn] F **-, -nen** psychopath; **psychopathisch** [psyço'paːtɪʃ] **1** ADJ psychopathic **2** ADV like a psychopath; **~ reagieren** to react psychopathically; **Psychopharmakon** [psyço'farmakɔn] NT **-s, -pharmaka** [-ka] USU PL psychiatric drug

Psychose [psy'ço:zə] F **-, -n** psychosis

Psycho-: psychosomatisch [psyçozo'ma:tɪʃ] **1** ADJ psychosomatic **2** ADV psychosomatically; **Psychoterror** ['psyːço-] M psychological terror; **Psychotest** ['psyːço-] M psychological test; **Psychotherapeut(in)** [psyço-] M(F) psychotherapist; **psychotherapeutisch** [psyço-] **1** ADJ psychotherapeutic **2** ADV psychotherapeutically; **Psychotherapie** [psyço-] F psychotherapy

Psychotiker [psy'ço:tɪkɐ] M **-s, -**, **Psychotikerin** [-ərɪn] F **-, -nen** psychotic

psychotisch [psy'ço:tɪʃ] ADJ psychotic

pubertär [puber'tɛːɐ] **1** ADJ adolescent; **ein Junge im ~en Alter** a boy in puberty **2** ADV **~ bedingte Störungen** disorders caused by puberty

Pubertät [puber'tɛːt] F **-**, NO PL puberty; **er steckt mitten in der ~** he's going through his adolescence

Pubertäts-: Pubertätserscheinung F symptom of puberty; **Pubertätsstörungen** PL adolescent disturbances *pl*

pubertieren [puber'tiːrən], *ptp* **pubertiert** VI to reach puberty; **~d** pubescent

Public-Domain-Programm [pablɪkdɔ'meːn-] NT (*Comput*) public domain program

Publicity [pa'blɪsɪti] F **-**, NO PL publicity

Public Relations [pablɪk rɪ'leːʃəns] PL public relations *pl*

publik [pu'bliːk] ADJ PRED public; **~ werden** to become public knowledge; **etw ~ machen** to make sth public; **die Sache ist längst ~** that's long been common knowledge

Publikation [publika'tsioːn] F **-, -en** publication

Publikum ['puːblɪkʊm] NT **-s**, NO PL public; (= *Zuschauer, Zuhörer*) audience; (= *Leser*) readers *pl*; (*Sport*) crowd; **er muss ja immer ein ~ haben** (*fig*) he always has to have an audience; **das ~ in dem Restaurant ist sehr gemischt** you get a very mixed group of people using this restaurant; **sein ~ finden** to find a public

Publikums-: Publikumserfolg M success with the public; **Publikumsmagnet** M crowd puller; **Publikumsverkehr** M **~ im Rathaus ist von 8 bis 12 Uhr** the town hall is open to the public from 8 till 12 o'clock; **„heute kein ~"** "closed today for public business"; **wir haben heute viel ~** we've a lot of people coming in today; **publikumswirksam** **1** ADJ **~ sein** to have public appeal; **sehr ~e Tricks** tricks which appeal to the public **2** ADV **ein Stück ~ inszenieren** to produce a play with a view to public appeal

publizieren [publi'tsiːrən], *ptp* **publiziert** VTI (a) (= *veröffentlichen*) to publish (b) (= *publik machen*) to publicize

Puck [pʊk] M **-s, -s** puck

Pudding ['pʊdɪŋ] M **-s, -s** thick custard-based dessert often tasting of vanilla, chocolate etc; **kaltgerührter ~** instant whip

Puddingpulver NT custard powder

Pudel ['puːdl] M **-s, -** (= *Hund*) poodle; **das ist des ~s Kern** (*fig*) that's what it's really all about

Pudel-: Pudelmütze F bobble cap; **pudelnass** ADJ drenched; **pudelwohl** ADJ (*inf*) **sich ~ fühlen** to feel completely contented; **nach der Sauna fühle ich mich ~** after the sauna I feel like a million dollars (*inf*)

Puder ['puːdɐ] M or (INF) NT **-s, -** powder

Puderdose F powder tin; (*für Gesichtspuder*) (powder) compact

pudern ['puːdɐn] **1** VT to powder; **sich** (*dat*) **das Gesicht ~** to powder one's face **2** VR (= *Puder auftragen*) to powder oneself; (= *Puder benutzen*) to use powder; **sich stark ~** to use a lot of powder

Puderzucker M icing sugar

puertoricanisch [pʊertori'kaːnɪʃ] ADJ Puerto Rican

Puerto Rico [pu'erto 'riːko] NT **- -s** Puerto Rico

Puff[1] [pʊf] M **-(e)s, ⁻e** ['pʏfə] (a) (= *Stoß*) thump; (*in die Seite*) prod; (*vertraulich*) nudge (b) (*Geräusch*) phut (*inf*)

Puff[2] M **-(e)s, -e** (a) (= *Wäschepuff*) linen basket (b) (= *Bausch*) puff (c) (= *Sitzpuff*) pouffe (*Brit*), pouf (*US*)

Puff[3] M or NT **-s, -s** (*inf*) brothel

Puffärmel M puff(ed) sleeve

Puffer ['pʊfɐ] M **-s, -** (a) (*Rail, Comput*) buffer (b) (*Cook:* = *Kartoffelpuffer*) potato fritter

Puffer-: Pufferspeicher M (*Comput*) buffer memory; **Pufferzone** F buffer zone

puh [puː] INTERJ (*Abscheu*) ugh; (*Erleichterung*) phew

Pulk [pʊlk] M **-s, -s** or (*rare*) **-e** (a) (*Mil*) group (b) (= *Menge*) (*von Menschen*) throng; (*von Dingen*) pile; **im ~** in a throng

Pull-down-Menü [pʊl'daun-] NT pull-down menu

Pulle ['pʊlə] F **-, -n** (*inf*) bottle; **volle ~ fahren/arbeiten** (*inf*) to drive/work flat out (*esp Brit*); **das Radio volle ~ aufdrehen** (*inf*) to turn the radio on at full blast

Pulli ['pʊli] M **-s, -s** (*inf*), **Pullover** [pʊ'loːvɐ] M **-s, -** jumper (*Brit*), sweater

Pullunder [pʊ'lʊndɐ, pʊl'lʊndɐ] M **-s, -** tank top

Puls [pʊls] M **-es, -e** [-zə] (*lit, fig*) pulse; **sein ~ geht** or **schlägt regelmäßig** his pulse is regular; **jdm den ~ fühlen** (*lit*) to feel sb's pulse; (*fig*) to take sb's pulse; **am ~ der Zeit sein** to have one's finger on the pulse of the time(s)

Pulsader F artery; **sich** (*dat*) **die ~(n) aufschneiden** to slash one's wrists

pulsieren [pʊl'ziːrən], *ptp* **pulsiert** VI (*lit, fig*) to pulsate; **~der Gleichstrom** intermittent direct current

Pult [pʊlt] NT **-(e)s, -e** desk

Pulver ['pʊlfɐ, -və] NT **-s, -** powder; **er hat das ~ nicht erfunden** (*fig*) he'll never set the Thames on fire (*prov*); **sein ~ verschossen haben** (*fig*) to have shot one's bolt

Pulverfass NT powder keg; (*fig*) powder keg, volcano; **(wie) auf einem ~ sitzen** (*fig*) to be sitting on (top of) a volcano; **Russland gleicht einem ~** Russia is like a powder keg

pulverig ['pʊlfərɪç, -vərɪç] **1** ADJ powdery *no adv* **2** ADV **den Kaffee ~ mahlen** to grind the coffee to a powder

pulverisieren [pʊlveri'ziːrən], *ptp* **pulverisiert** VT to pulverize

Pulverkaffee M (*inf*) instant coffee

Pulverschnee M powder snow

Puma ['puːma] M **-s, -s** puma

pummelig ['pʊməlɪç], **pummlig** ['pʊmlɪç] ADJ (*inf*) chubby

Pump [pʊmp] M **-(e)s**, NO PL (*inf*) credit; **etw auf ~ kaufen** to buy sth on credit

Pumpe ['pʊmpə] F **-, -n** (a) pump (b) (*inf*: = *Herz*) ticker (*inf*)

pumpen ['pʊmpn] **1** VT (a) (*mit Pumpe*) to pump (b) (*inf*: = *entleihen*) to borrow; (= *verleihen*) to lend; (**sich** *dat*) **Geld bei jdm ~** to borrow money from sb **2** VI to pump

Pumpernickel ['pʊmpɐnɪkl] M **-s, -** pumpernickel

Pumphose F knickerbockers *pl*; (= *Unterhose*) bloomers *pl*

Pumps [pœmps] M **-, -** pump

Pump-: Pumpspeicherkraftwerk NT, **Pumpspeicherwerk** NT pumped storage works *sing or pl*; **Pumpstation** F pumping station

Punk [paŋk] M **-s**, NO PL punk

Punker ['paŋkɐ] M **-s, -**, **Punkerin** ['paŋkərɪn] F **-, -nen** punk

Punkt [pʊŋkt] M **-(e)s, -e** (a) (= *Tupfen*) spot
(b) (= *Satzzeichen*) full stop (*Brit*), period (*esp US*); (*Typ*) point; (*auf dem i, Mus*: = *Auslassungszeichen, von ~linie, Comput*) dot; **der ~ auf dem i sein** (*fig*) to be the final touch; **nun mach aber mal einen ~!** (*inf*) come off it! (*inf*); **ohne ~ und Komma reden** (*inf*) to talk nineteen to the dozen (*Brit inf*), to talk up a storm (*US inf*)
(c) (= *Stelle, Zeitpunkt, auch Math*) point; **~ 12 Uhr** at 12 o'clock on the dot; **wir sind auf** or **an dem ~ angelangt, wo ...** we have reached the stage where ...; **ein dunkler ~** (*fig*) a dark chapter; **bis zu einem gewissen ~** up to a certain point
(d) (= *Bewertungseinheit*) point; (*bei Prüfung*) mark; **nach ~en siegen/führen** to win/lead on points
(e) (*bei Diskussion, von Vertrag etc*) point; **in diesem ~** on this point; **etw für ~ widerlegen** to disprove sth point by point; **etw in allen ~en widerlegen** to refute sth in every respect; **etw auf den ~ bringen** to get to the heart of sth; **damit brachte er das Problem auf den ~** he put his finger on it

Pünktchen ['pʏŋktçən] NT **-s, -** little dot; **drei ~** three dots

punktieren [pʊŋk'tiːrən], *ptp* **punktiert** VT (a) (*Med*) to aspirate (b) (= *mit Punkten versehen*) to dot; (*Mus*) *Note* to dot; **punktierte Linie** dotted line

Punktion [pʊŋk'tsioːn] F **-, -en** (*Med*) aspiration

Punktlandung F precision landing

pünktlich [ˈpʏŋktlɪç] **1** ADJ **(a)** punctual **(b)** (= *genau*) exact **2** ADV on time; **er kam ~ um 3 Uhr** he came at 3 o'clock sharp; **der Zug kommt immer sehr ~** the train is always dead on time; **~ da sein** to be there on time

Pünktlichkeit F -, NO PL punctuality

Punkt-: Punktlinie F dotted line; **Punktniederlage** F defeat on points

punkto [ˈpʊŋkto] PREP +GEN **in ~** with regard to; **~ X** where X is concerned; **~ meiner Anfrage** concerning *or* re (*Comm*) my inquiry

Punkt-: Punktrichter(in) M(F) judge; **Punktsieg** M win on points

punktuell [pʊŋkˈtuɛl] **1** ADJ *Maßnahmen, Streik* selective; *Zusammenarbeit* on certain points; **einige ~e Ergänzungen anbringen** to expand a few points; **~e Verkehrskontrollen** spot checks on traffic **2** ADV *kritisieren* in a few points; **wir haben uns nur ~ mit diesem Thema befasst** we only dealt with certain points of this topic

Punsch [pʊnʃ] M -es, -e (hot) punch

pupen [ˈpuːpn] VI (*inf*) to let off (*Brit inf*), to pass gas (*US inf*)

Pupille [puˈpɪlə] F -, -n pupil

Pupillen-: Pupillenerweiterung F dilation of the pupil; **Pupillenverengung** F contraction of the pupil, miosis (*spec*)

Püppchen [ˈpʏpçən] NT -s, - **(a)** (= *kleine Puppe*) little doll **(b)** (= *hübsches Mädchen*) little sweetie; **ein süßes kleines ~** a sweet little thing

Puppe [ˈpʊpə] F -, -n **(a)** (= *Kinderspielzeug*) doll; (= *Marionette*) puppet; (= *Schaufensterpuppe*) (*Mil:* = *Übungspuppe*) dummy; (*inf:* = *Mädchen*) doll (*inf*); (*als Anrede*) baby (*inf*); **die ~n tanzen lassen** (*inf*) to live it up (*inf*); **bis in die ~n schlafen** (*inf*) to sleep to all hours **(b)** (*Zool*) pupa

Puppen- IN CPDS doll's; **Puppenhaus** NT doll's house (*Brit*), dollhouse (*US*); **Puppenspiel** NT puppet show; **Puppenspieler(in)** M(F) puppeteer; **Puppenstube** F doll's house (*Brit*), dollhouse (*US*); **Puppentheater** NT puppet theatre (*Brit*) *or* theater (*US*); **Puppenwagen** M doll's pram (*Brit*), toy baby carriage (*US*)

pupsen [ˈpuːpsn] VI (*inf*) to let off (*Brit inf*), to pass gas (*US inf*)

pur [puːɐ] **1** ADJ (= *rein*) pure; (= *unverdünnt*) neat; (= *bloß, völlig*) sheer; **~er Unsinn** absolute nonsense; **~er Wahnsinn** sheer madness; **~er Zufall** sheer coincidence; **Whisky ~** straight whisky **2** ADV *anwenden* pure; *trinken* straight

Püree [pyˈreː] NT -s, -s puree; (= *Kartoffelpüree*) mashed *or* creamed potatoes *pl*

pürieren [pyˈriːrən], *ptp* **püriert** VT to puree

puristisch [puˈrɪstɪʃ] ADJ puristic

Puritaner [puriˈtaːnɐ] M -s, -, **Puritanerin** [-ərɪn] F -, -nen Puritan

puritanisch [puriˈtaːnɪʃ] **1** ADJ (*Hist*) Puritan; (*pej*) puritanical **2** ADV (*pej*) puritanically; **bei uns geht es ~ zu** ours is a puritanical household; **sie verhält sich sehr ~** she is really puritanical

Purpur [ˈpʊrpʊr] M -s, NO PL crimson; (= *purpurner Umhang*) purple

purpurfarben [-farbn], **purpurfarbig** ADJ crimson

purpurrot ADJ crimson (red)

Purzelbaum [ˈpʊrtslbaum] M somersault; **einen ~ machen** *or* **schlagen** *or* **schießen** to turn a somersault

purzeln [ˈpʊrtsln] VI AUX SEIN to tumble; **über etw** (*acc*) **~** to trip over sth

puschen, pushen [ˈpʊʃn] VT (*inf*) to push

pusseln [ˈpʊsln] VI (*inf*) **(a)** (= *geschäftig sein*) to fuss; **sie pusselt den ganzen Tag im Haus** she fusses about the house all day **(b)** (= *herumbasteln*) to fiddle around (*an etw* (*dat*)) with sth)

Puste [ˈpuːstə] F -, NO PL (*inf*) puff (*inf*); **aus der** *or* **außer ~ kommen** *or* **geraten** to get out of breath; **außer ~ sein** to be out of puff (*inf*)

Pusteblume F (*inf*) dandelion clock

Pustekuchen INTERJ (*inf*) fiddlesticks (*dated inf*); **(ja) ~!** (*inf*) no chance! (*inf*)

Pustel [ˈpʊstl] F -, -n (= *Pickel*) spot; (*Med*) pustule

pusten [ˈpuːstn] (*inf*) **1** VI (= *blasen*) to puff; (= *keuchen*) to puff (and pant) **2** VT **(a)** (= *blasen*) to puff **(b)** (*inf*) **dem werd' ich was ~!** I'll tell him where he can get off! (*inf*)

Pute [ˈpuːtə] F -, -n turkey (hen); **dumme ~** (*inf*) silly goose (*inf*); **eingebildete ~** (*inf*) conceited little madam (*Brit inf*) *or* missy (*US inf*)

Putenschnitzel NT (*Cook*) turkey breast in breadcrumbs

Puter [ˈpuːtɐ] M -s, - turkey (cock)

Put-Option [ˈpʊt-] F (*St Ex*) put option

Putsch [pʊtʃ] M -(e)s, -e putsch

putschen [ˈpʊtʃn] VI to rebel; **in Südamerika wird permanent geputscht** they're always having coups in South America; **sich an die Macht ~** to take power by a military coup

Putschist [pʊˈtʃɪst] M -en, -en, **Putschistin** [-ˈtʃɪstɪn] F -, -nen rebel

Putschversuch M attempted coup (d'état)

Putz [pʊts] M -es, NO PL **(a)** (*Build*) plaster; (= *Rauputz*) roughcast; **eine Mauer mit ~ verkleiden** *or* **bewerfen** to plaster a wall; **unter ~** under the plaster **(b)** **auf den ~ hauen** (*inf*) (= *angeben*) to show off; (= *ausgelassen feiern*) to have a rave-up (*inf*)

Putzdienst M cleaning duty; (= *Dienstleistung*) cleaning service; **~ haben** to be on cleaning duty

putzen [ˈpʊtsn] **1** VT **(a)** (= *säubern*) to clean; (= *polieren*) to polish; (= *wischen*) to wipe; **Fenster ~** to clean the windows; **sich** (*dat*) **die Nase ~** to wipe one's nose; (= *sich schnäuzen*) to blow one's nose; **sich** (*dat*) **die Zähne ~** to clean (*Brit*) *or* brush one's teeth; **einem Baby den Hintern/die Nase ~** to wipe a baby's bottom/nose; **~ gehen** to work as a cleaner **(b)** *Mauer* to plaster **2** VR (= *sich säubern*) to wash oneself

Putzfrau F cleaner

putzig [ˈpʊtsɪç] (*inf*) **1** ADJ (= *komisch*) funny; (= *niedlich*) cute; (= *merkwürdig*) funny, strange **2** ADV (= *niedlich*) cutely; **das klingt ganz ~** that sounds so cute

Putz-: Putzkolonne F team of cleaners; **Putzlappen** M cloth; **Putzmann** M, *pl* **-männer** cleaning man; **Putzmittel** NT (*zum Scheuern*) cleanser; (*zum Polieren*) polish; (*pl*) cleaning things *pl*; **putzmunter** ADJ (*inf*) full of beans (*Brit inf*), lively; **Putztuch** NT, *pl* **-tücher** (= *Staubtuch*) duster; (= *Wischlappen*) cloth; **Putzzeug** NT cleaning things *pl*

puzzeln [pasəln] VI to do a jigsaw (puzzle)

Puzzle [ˈpazl, ˈpasl] NT -s, -s jigsaw (puzzle)

PVC [peːfauˈtseː] NT -(s) PVC

PX-Laden [peːˈʔɪks-] M (*US Mil*) PX store

Pygmäe [pyˈɡmɛːə] M -n, -n, **Pygmäin** [pyˈɡmɛːɪn] F -, -nen Pygmy

Pyjama [pyˈdʒaːma, pyˈʒaːma, piˈdʒaːma, piˈʒaːma] M -s, -s pair of pyjamas (*Brit*) *or* pajamas (*US*) *sing*

Pylon [pyˈloːn] M -en, -en, **Pylone** [pyˈloːnə] F -, -n (*Archit*) (*von Brücke, Eingangstor*) pylon; (= *Absperrmarkierung*) traffic cone

Pyramide [pyraˈmiːdə] F -, -n pyramid

pyramidenförmig **1** ADJ pyramid-shaped *no adv*, pyramidal (*form*) **2** ADV in the shape of a pyramid; **die Artisten hatten sich ~ aufgebaut** the acrobats had formed a pyramid

Pyrenäen [pyreˈnɛːən] PL **die ~** the Pyrenees *pl*

Pyrenäenhalbinsel F Iberian Peninsula

Pyro-: Pyrolyse [pyroˈlyːzə] F -, -n pyrolysis; **Pyromane** [pyroˈmaːnə] M -n, -n, **Pyromanin** [-ˈmaːnɪn] F -, -nen pyromaniac; **Pyrotechnik** [pyroˈtɛçnɪk] F pyrotechnics *sing*; **Pyrotechniker(in)** [pyroˈtɛçnɪkɐ, -ərɪn] M(F) pyrotechnist; **pyrotechnisch** [pyroˈtɛçnɪʃ] ADJ pyrotechnic

Python [ˈpyːtɔn] M -s, -s python

Qq

Q, q [kuː] NT **-**, **-** Q, q

qkm ABBR *von* **Quadratkilometer**

qm ABBR *von* **Quadratmeter**

quabbelig ['kvabəlɪç] ADJ *Frosch, Qualle* slimy; *Pudding* wobbly

Quacksalber ['kvakzalbɐ] M **-s**, **-**, **Quacksalberin** [-ərɪn] F **-**, **-nen** (*pej*) quack (doctor)

Quacksalberei [kvakzalbə'rai] F **-**, **-en** quackery

Quaddel ['kvadl] F **-**, **-n** hives *pl*, rash; (*durch Insekten*) bite; (*von Sonne*) heat spot

Quader ['kvaːdɐ] M **-s**, **-** *or* f **-**, **-n** (*Math*) cuboid; (*Archit: auch* **Quaderstein**) ashlar

Quadrat [kva'draːt] NT **-(e)s**, **-e** (a) NO PL (*Fläche*) square; **drei Meter im ~** three metres (*Brit*) *or* meters (*US*) square (b) NO PL (*Potenz*) square; **eine Zahl ins ~ erheben** to square a number; **vier zum ~** four squared (c) (= *quadratische Fläche*) square; **magisches ~** magic square

Quadrat- IN CPDS square;

quadratisch [kva'draːtɪʃ] ADJ *Form* square; (*Math*) *Gleichung* quadratic

Quadrat-: **Quadratkilometer** M square kilometre (*Brit*) *or* kilometer (*US*); **Quadratmeter** M *or* NT square metre (*Brit*) *or* meter (*US*)

Quadratur [kvadra'tuːɐ] F **-**, **-en** quadrature; **die ~ des Kreises** *or* **Zirkels** the squaring of the circle

Quadrat-: **Quadratwurzel** F square root; **Quadratzahl** F square number

Quai [keː, keː] M *or* NT **-s**, **-s** quay

quak [kva:k] INTERJ (*von Frosch*) croak; (*von Ente*) quack

quaken ['kva:kn] VI (*Frosch*) to croak; (*Ente*) to quack; (*inf: Mensch*) to screech (*inf*)

quäken ['kvɛːkn] VTI (*inf*) to screech

Quäker ['kvɛːkɐ] M **-s**, **-**, **Quäkerin** [-ərɪn] F **-**, **-nen** Quaker

Qual [kva:l] F **-**, **-en** agony; **tapfer ertrug er alle ~en** he bore all his suffering bravely; **jds ~(en) lindern** *or* **mildern** (*liter*) to lessen sb's suffering; **~en erleiden** *or* **leiden** to suffer agonies; **unter großen ~en sterben** to die in agony; **sein Leben war eine einzige ~** his life was a living death; **die letzten Monate waren für mich eine (einzige) ~** the last few months have been sheer agony for me; **es ist eine ~, das mit ansehen zu müssen** it is agonizing to watch; **er machte ihr den Aufenthalt/das Leben/die Tage zur ~** he made her stay/her life/her days a misery

quälen ['kvɛːlən] **1** VT to torment; (*mit Bitten etc*) to pester; **jdn zu Tode ~** to torture sb to death; *siehe auch* **gequält 2** VR (a) (*seelisch*) to torture oneself; (= *leiden*) to suffer **2** (= *sich abmühen*) to struggle; **er musste sich ~, damit er das schaffte** it was a struggle for him to do it; **er quälte sich aus dem Sessel** he heaved himself out of the chair

quälend 1 ADJ agonizing **2** ADV agonizingly

Quälerei [kvɛːlə'rai] F **-**, **-en** (a) (= *Grausamkeit*) torture *no pl*; (= *seelische, nervliche Belastung*) agony; **diese Tierversuche sind in meinen Augen ~** in my view these experiments on animals are cruel; **das ist doch eine ~ für das Tier** that is cruel to the animal; **die letzten Monate waren eine einzige ~** the last few months were sheer agony (b) (= *mühsame Arbeit*) struggle

Quälgeist M (*inf*) pest (*inf*)

Quali¹ ['kva:li] M (*Sch inf*) special secondary school leaving certificate

Quali² ['kva:li] F ABBR *von* **Qualifikation** (*Sport inf*) qualification; (= *Runde*) qualifying round

Qualifikation [kvalifika'tsioːn] F **-**, **-en** qualification; (= *Ausscheidungswettkampf*) qualifying round; **für diese Arbeit fehlt ihm die nötige ~** he lacks the necessary qualifications for this work; **zur ~ fehlten ihr nur wenige Sekunden** she only failed to qualify by a few seconds

qualifizieren [kvalifi'tsiːrən] *ptp* **qualifiziert 1** VT to qualify (*für, zu* for) **2** VR (*allgemein, Sport*) to qualify; **er hat sich zum Facharbeiter qualifiziert** he qualified as a specialist; **sich wissenschaftlich ~** to gain academic qualifications

qualifiziert [kvalifi'tsiːɐt] ADJ **(a)** *Arbeiter, Nachwuchs* qualified; *Arbeit* expert **(b)** (*Pol*) *Mehrheit* requisite

Qualität [kvali'tɛːt] F **-**, **-en** quality; **von der ~ her** as far as quality is concerned; **die Ware ist von ausgezeichneter ~** the product is top quality

qualitativ [kvalita'tiːf] **1** ADJ qualitative **2** ADV qualitatively; **hochwertige Produkte** high-quality products; **~ ausgezeichnet/minderwertig sein** to be of (an) excellent/(a) substandard quality

Qualitäts- IN CPDS quality; **Qualitätsarbeit** F quality work; **unsere Firma hat sich durch (ihre) ~ einen Namen gemacht** our firm made its name by the quality of its work; **Qualitätskontrolle** F quality check; **Qualitätsmanagement** NT quality management; **Qualitätsware** F quality goods *pl*; **Qualitätswein** M *wine of certified origin and quality*

Qualle ['kvalə] F **-**, **-n** jellyfish

Qualm [kvalm] M **-(e)s**, NO PL (thick *or* dense) smoke; (= *Tabaksqualm*) fug

qualmen ['kvalmən] VI **(a)** (*Feuer*) to give off smoke; **es qualmt aus dem Schornstein/hinten aus dem Auto** clouds of smoke are coming from the chimney/from the back of the car **(b)** (*inf: Mensch*) to smoke; **sie qualmt einem die ganze Bude voll** she fills the whole place with smoke

qualmig ['kvalmɪç] ADJ smoky

qualvoll 1 ADJ painful; *Schmerzen, Vorstellung, Gedanke* agonizing; *Anblick* harrowing **2** ADV **~ sterben** to die an agonizing death

Quanten ['kvantn] PL *von* **Quantum**

Quanten-: **Quantenmechanik** F quantum mechanics *sing*; **Quantenphysik** F quantum physics *sing*; **Quantensprung** M quantum leap; **Quantentheorie** F quantum theory

Quantität [kvanti'tɛːt] F **-**, **-en** quantity

quantitativ [kvantita'tiːf] **1** ADJ quantitative **2** ADV quantitatively

Quantum ['kvantʊm] NT **-s**, **Quanten** [-tn] (= *Menge, Anzahl*) quantum; (= *Anteil*) quota (*an* +*dat* of)

Quappe ['kvapə] F **-**, **-n** **(a)** (= *Kaulquappe*) tadpole **(b)** (= *Aalquappe*) burbot

Quarantäne [karan'tɛːnə] F **-**, **-n** quarantine; **unter ~ stellen** to put in quarantine; **unter ~ stehen** to be in quarantine; **über das Gebiet wurde sofort ~ verhängt** the area was immediately placed under quarantine

Quark [kvark] M **-s**, NO PL **(a)** (= *Käse*) quark **(b)** (*inf*) (= *Unsinn*) rubbish (*Brit*), nonsense; (= *unbedeutende Sache*) (little) trifle; **so ein ~!** stuff and nonsense!; **~ reden** to talk nonsense

Quart [kvart] F **-**, **-en** (*Mus: auch* **Quarte**) fourth

Quartal [kvar'ta:l] NT **-s**, **-e** quarter; **Kündigung zum ~** quarterly notice date; **es muss jedes ~ bezahlt werden** it has to be paid quarterly

Quartal(s)-: **Quartal(s)abschluss** M end of the quarter; **Quartal(s)ende** NT end of the quarter; **zum ~ kündigen** to give notice to the end of the quarter; **Quartal(s)säufer(in)** M(F) (*inf*) periodic heavy drinker; **sein Vater ist ein ~** every so often his father goes on a binge (*inf*); **quartal(s)weise 1** ADJ quarterly **2** ADV quarterly

Quarte ['kvartə] F **-**, **-n** = **Quart**

Quartett [kvar'tɛt] NT **-(e)s**, **-e** **(a)** (*Mus*) quartet **(b)** (*Cards*) (= *Spiel*) ≈ happy families; (= *Karten*) set of four cards

Quartier [kvar'tiːɐ] NT **-s**, **-e** **(a)** (= *Unterkunft*) accommodation (*Brit*), accommodations *pl* (*US*); **wir sollten uns ein ~ suchen** we should look for accommodation; **wir hatten unser ~ in einem alten Bauernhof** we stayed in an old farmhouse **(b)** (*Mil*) quarters *pl* **(c)** (= *Stadtviertel*) district

Quarz [kvarts] M **-es**, **-e** quartz

Quarz-: **Quarzglas** NT quartz glass; **quarzhaltig** ADJ which contains quartz; **Quarzuhr** F quartz clock; (= *Armbanduhr*) quartz watch

quasi ['kva:zi] **1** ADV virtually **2** PREF quasi; **~-wissenschaftlich** quasi-scientific

Quasselei [kvasə'lai] F **-**, **-en** (*inf*) gabbing (*inf*)

quasseln ['kvasln] VTI to blather (*inf*); **was quasselst du denn da für ein dummes Zeug?** what are you blathering about now? (*inf*)

Quaste ['kvastə] F -, -n (= *Troddel*) tassel; (*von Pinsel*) bristles *pl*; (= *Schwanzquaste*) tuft; (= *Puderquaste*) powder puff

Quatsch [kvatʃ] M -es, NO PL (*inf*) (a) (= *Unsinn*) nonsense; **das ist der größte ~, den ich je gehört habe** that is the biggest load of nonsense I have ever heard *Brit* **ach ~!** nonsense!; **ohne ~!** (= *ehrlich*) no kidding! (*inf*); **alles ~!, so ein ~!** what (a load of) nonsense *Brit* (b) (= *Dummheiten*) nonsense; **hört doch endlich mit dem ~ auf!** stop being so stupid!; **lass den ~** cut it out! (*inf*); **~ machen** to mess about around (*inf*); **etw aus ~ machen** to do sth for a laugh; **mach damit keinen ~** don't do anything stupid with it

quatschen ['kvatʃn] (*inf*) ▮ VTI (= *dummes Zeug reden*) to gab (away) (*inf*), to blather (*inf*); **sie quatscht mal wieder einen Blödsinn** she's talking a load of nonsense again ▮ VI (a) (= *plaudern*) to blather (*inf*); **ich hab mit ihm am Telefon gequatscht** I had a good chat with him on the phone (b) (= *etw ausplaudern*) to squeal

Quatschkopf M (*pej inf*) (= *Schwätzer*) windbag (*inf*); (= *Dummkopf*) fool

Quecksilber ['kvɛkzɪlbɐ] NT (*abbr* **Hg**) mercury

Quellcode M (*Comput*) source code

Quelle ['kvɛlə] F -, -n (a) spring; (*von Fluss*) spring, source; (= *Erdölquelle, Gasquelle*) well (b) (*fig*) (= *Ursprung, Informant*) source; (*für Waren*) source (of supply), supplier; **die ~ allen Übels** the root of all evil; **aus zuverlässiger/sicherer ~** from a reliable/trustworthy source; **an der ~ sitzen** (*fig*) to be well-placed; (*in Organisation*) to be able to get inside information

quellen ['kvɛlən] VI, *pret* **quoll** [kvɔl], *ptp* **gequollen** [gə'kvɔlən] AUX SEIN (a) (= *herausfließen*) to pour (*aus* out of); **die Augen quollen ihm aus dem Kopf** his eyes were popping out of his head (b) (*Holz, Reis, Erbsen*) to swell; **lassen Sie die Bohnen über Nacht ~** leave the beans to soak overnight

Quellen-: **Quellenangabe** F reference; **achten Sie bei der ~ darauf, dass ...** make sure when doing the references that ...; **Quellensteuer** F (*Econ*) tax at source

Quell-: **Quellsprache** F source language; **Quellwasser** NT spring water

Quengelei [kvɛŋə'lai] F -, -en (*inf*) whining

quengelig ['kvɛŋəlɪç], **quenglig** ['kvɛŋlɪç] ADJ whining; **die Kinder wurden ~** the children started to whine

quengeln ['kvɛŋln] VI (*inf*) to whine

quer [kveːɐ] ADV (= *schräg*) crossways, diagonally; (= *rechtwinklig*) at right angles; **~ gestreift** horizontally striped; **er legte sich ~ aufs Bett** he lay down across the bed; **die Straße/Linie verläuft ~** the road/the line runs at right angles; **~ durch etw gehen/laufen** *etc* to go through sth; **~ über etw** (*acc*) **gehen/laufen** to cross sth

Quer-: **querbeet** [kveːɐ'beːt, 'kveːɐbeːt] ADV (*inf*) (= *wahllos*) at random; (= *durcheinander*) all over the place (*inf*); (= *querfeldein*) across country; **Querdenker(in)** M(F) open-minded thinker

Quere ['kveːrə] F -, NO PL **der ~ nach** widthways; **jdm in die ~ kommen** (= *begegnen*) to cross sb's path; (*also fig*: = *in den Weg geraten*) to get in sb's way

Querele [kve're:lə] F -, -n USU PL (*geh*) dispute

queren ['kveːrən] VTI to cross

querfeldein [kveːɐfɛlt'lain] ADV across country

Querfeldeinrennen NT cross-country; (*Autorennen*) autocross; (*Motorradrennen*) motocross; (*Fahrradrennen*) cyclecross

Quer-: **Querflöte** F (transverse) flute; **Querformat** NT landscape format; **im ~** in landscape format; **quergestreift** ADJ ATTR *siehe* **quer**; **Querlatte** F crossbar; **quer legen** VR (*fig inf*) to be awkward; **Querpass** M cross; **Querschläger** M ricochet (shot)

Querschnitt M (*lit, fig*) cross section

Querschnitt(s)-: **querschnitt(s)gelähmt** ADJ paraplegic; **seit dem Autounfall ist er ~** since the car accident he has been paralyzed from the waist down; **Querschnitt(s)gelähmte(r)** [-gəlɛːmtə] MF DECL AS ADJ paraplegic; **Querschnitt(s)lähmung** F paraplegia

Quer-: **quer stellen** VR (*fig inf*) to be awkward; **Querstraße** F (= *Nebenstraße*) side street; (= *Abzweigung*) turning; **bei** *or* **an der zweiten ~ fahren Sie links ab** take the second road on your left; **Querstreifen** M horizontal stripe; **Quersumme** F (*Math*) sum of digits (of a number); **die ~ bilden** to add the digits in a number; **Quertreiber(in)** M(F) (*inf*) troublemaker

Querulant [kveru'lant] M -en, -en, **Querulantin** [-'lantɪn] F -, -nen grumbler

Quer-: **Querverbindung** F connection; (*von Eisenbahn*) connecting line; (*von Straße*) link road; **Querverweis** M cross-reference

quetschen ['kvɛtʃn] ▮ VT (= *drücken*) to squash; (*aus einer Tube*) to squeeze; (*Med*: USU PASS) to crush; **etw in etw** (*acc*) **~** to squeeze sth into sth; **jdn halbtot ~** to crush sb (nearly) to death; **jdm/sich den Finger ~** to squash sb's/one's finger ▮ VR (= *sich klemmen*) to be caught; (= *sich zwängen*) to squeeze (oneself)

Quetschung ['kvɛtʃʊŋ] F -, -en, **Quetschwunde** F (*Med*) bruise; **~en erleiden** to suffer bruising; **der Fahrer kam mit ~en davon** the driver escaped with bruises; **Quetschung innerer Organe** internal bruising

Queue [køː] NT *or* M -s, -s (*Billard*) cue

Quickie ['kvɪki] M -s, -s (*inf*: = *Sex*) quickie (*inf*)

quicklebendig ADJ (*inf*) lively

quieken ['kviːkən], **quieksen** ['kviːksn] VI to squeal

quietschen ['kviːtʃn] VI (*Tür, Schloss, Schuhe*) to squeak; (*Reifen, Straßenbahn, Mensch*) to squeal; (*Bremsen*) to screech; **das Kind quietschte vergnügt** *or* **vor Vergnügen** (*inf*) the child squealed with delight; **das** *or* **es war zum Quietschen!** (*inf*) it was a (real) scream! (*inf*)

quietschfidel ['kviːtʃfi'deːl], **quietschvergnügt** ADJ (*inf*) happy as a sandboy

quillt [kvɪlt] 3. PERS SING PRES *von* **quellen**

Quintessenz ['kvɪntɛsɛnts] F quintessence

Quintett [kvɪn'tɛt] NT -(e)s, -e quintet

quirlen ['kvɪrlən] VT to whisk

quitt [kvɪt] ADJ **~ sein (mit jdm)** to be quits (with sb); **jdn/etw ~ sein** (*dial*) to be rid of sb/sth

Quitte ['kvɪtə] F -, -n quince

quitte(n)gelb ADJ (sickly) yellow

quittieren [kvɪ'tiːrən], *ptp* **quittiert** ▮ VT (a) (= *bestätigen*) to give a receipt for; **lassen Sie sich** (*dat*) **die Rechnung ~** get a receipt for the bill (b) (= *beantworten*) to counter (*mit* with) (c) (= *verlassen*) **Dienst** to quit ▮ VI (= *bestätigen*) to sign

Quittung ['kvɪtʊŋ] F -, -en (a) receipt; **gegen ~** on production of a receipt; **eine ~ über 500 Euro** a receipt for 500 euros; **jdm eine ~ für etw ausstellen** to give sb a receipt for sth (b) (*fig*) **das ist die ~ dafür, dass ...** that's the price you have to pay for ...; **die ~ für etw bekommen** *or* **erhalten** to pay the penalty for sth

Quittungsblock M, *pl* **-blöcke** receipt book

Quiz [kvɪs] NT -, - quiz

Quizmaster ['kvɪsmaːstɐ] M -s, -, **Quizmasterin** [-ərɪn] F -, -nen quizmaster

quoll PRET *von* **quellen**

Quorum ['kvoːrʊm] NT -s, NO PL quorum

Quote ['kvoːtə] F -, -n (a) (*Statistik*) (= *Anteilsziffer*) proportion; (= *Rate*) rate; (*TV etc*) ratings *pl* (b) (*Econ*: = *Quantum*) quota

Quotenfrau F (*pej inf*) woman who has been given a post just to fulfil the quota system requirements

Quotenregelung F quota system

Quotient [kvo'tsiɛnt] M -en, -en quotient

Rr

R, r [ɛr] NT **-, -** R, r; **das R rollen** to roll one's r's
Rabatt [ra'bat] M **-(e)s, -e** discount (*auf* on)
Rabattaktion NT sale
Rabauke [ra'baukə] M **-n, -n** (*inf*) hooligan
Rabbi ['rabi] M **-(s), -s** *or* **Rabbinen** [ra'bi:nən] rabbi
Rabbiner [ra'bi:nɐ] M **-s, -, Rabbinerin** [-ərɪn] F **-, -en** rabbi
Rabe ['ra:bə] M **-n, -n** raven; **wie ein ~ stehlen** (*inf*) to thieve like a magpie
Raben-: Rabeneltern PL (*inf*) bad parents *pl*; **Rabenmutter** F, *pl* **-mütter** (*inf*) bad mother; **rabenschwarz** ADJ *Nacht* pitch-black; *Haare* jet-black; (*fig*) *Tag, Humor* black; **Rabenvater** M (*inf*) bad father
rabiat [ra'bia:t] **1** ADJ *Kerl* violent; *Autofahrer* wild; *Geschäftsleute* ruthless; *Umgangston* aggressive; *Methoden, Konkurrenz* ruthless; **~ werden** (*wütend*) to go wild; (*aggressiv*) to get violent **2** ADV (= *rücksichtslos*) roughly; *vorgehen* ruthlessly; (= *aggressiv*) violently
Rache ['raxə] F **-**, NO PL revenge; **die ~ des kleinen Mannes** (*inf*) sweet revenge; **auf ~ sinnen** to contemplate revenge; **~ schwören** to swear vengeance; **(an jdm) ~ nehmen** *or* **üben** to take revenge (*on or upon* sb); **etw aus ~ tun** to do sth in revenge; **~ ist süß** (*prov*) revenge is sweet (*prov*); **Montezumas ~** (*hum inf: = Durchfall*) Montezuma's revenge (*hum*)
Rachen ['raxn] M **-s, -** throat; (*von großen Tieren*) jaws *pl*; (*fig*) jaws *pl*, abyss; **jdm etw in den ~ werfen** *or* **schmeißen** (*inf*) to shove sth down sb's throat (*inf*)
rächen ['rɛçn] **1** VT *jdn, Untat* to avenge (*etw an jdm* sth on sb); **dieses Unrecht werde ich noch an ihm ~** I intend to avenge myself on him for this injustice **2** VR (*Mensch*) to get one's revenge (*an jdm für etw* on sb for sth); (*Schuld, Sünde, Untat*) to have dire consequences; **deine Faulheit/Unehrlichkeit wird sich ~** you'll pay for being so lazy/dishonest
Rachenblütler [-bly:tlɐ] M **-s, -** (*Bot*) figwort
Rachitis [ra'xi:tɪs] F **-, Rachitiden** [raxi'ti:dn] rickets
rachitisch [ra'xi:tɪʃ] ADJ *Kind* with rickets; *Symptom* of rickets
Rach-: Rachsucht F vindictiveness; **rachsüchtig** ADJ vindictive
Racker ['rakɐ] M **-s, -** (*inf: Kind*) rascal (*inf*)
Rackerei [rakə'rai] F **-, -en** (*inf*) grind (*inf*)
rackern ['rakɐn] VIR (*inf*) to slave (away) (*inf*)
Racket ['rɛkət, ra'kɛt] NT **-s, -s** (*Aus*) racket, racquet (*Brit*)
Raclette ['raklɛt] NT *or* F **-s, -s** raclette
Rad [ra:t] NT **-(e)s, ⁻er** ['rɛ:dɐ] **(a)** wheel; (= *Rolle*) caster; (= *Zahnrad*) gearwheel; (*Sport*) cartwheel; **ein ~ schlagen** (*Sport*) to do a cartwheel; **der Pfau schlägt ein ~** the peacock is fanning out its tail; **alle Räder greifen ineinander** (*fig*), **ein ~ greift ins andere** (*fig*) all the parts knit together; **nur ein ~** *or* **Rädchen im Getriebe sein** (*fig*) to be only a cog in the works; **das ~ der Geschichte** the wheels of history; **das ~ der Geschichte** *or* **Zeit lässt sich nicht zurückdrehen** you can't turn the clock back; **unter die Räder kommen** *or* **geraten** (*inf*) to get into bad ways; **das ~ neu** *or* **noch einmal erfinden** (*inf*) to reinvent the wheel; **das fünfte ~ am Wagen sein** (*inf*) to be in the way; **ein ~ abhaben** (*inf*) to have a screw loose (*inf*) **(b)** (= *Fahrrad*) bicycle, bike (*inf*); **~ fahren** to cycle; (*pej inf: = kriechen*) to suck up (*inf*); **kannst du ~ fahren?** can you ride a bike?; **mit dem ~ fahren/kommen** to go/come by bicycle
Radachse F axle(tree)
Radar [ra'da:ɐ, 'ra:da:ɐ] M *or* NT **-s, -e** radar
Radar- IN CPDS radar; **Radaranlage** F radar (equipment) *no indef art*; **Radarfalle** F speed trap; **Radarkontrolle** F radar speed check
Radau [ra'dau] M **-s**, NO PL (*inf*) racket (*inf*); **~ machen** *or* **schlagen** to kick up a row; (= *Unruhe stiften*) to cause trouble; (= *Lärm machen*) to make a racket
Radaufhängung F (*Aut*) (wheel) suspension
Rädchen ['rɛ:tçən] NT **-s, -** DIM *von* **Rad** small wheel; (*für Schnittmuster*) tracing wheel; (*Cook*) pastry wheel
Raddampfer M paddle steamer
radebrechen ['ra:dəbrɛçn] INSEP **1** VI to speak broken English/German *etc* **2** VT **Englisch/Deutsch ~** to speak broken

English/German; **er radebrechte auf Italienisch, er wolle ...** he said in broken Italian that he wanted ...
radeln ['ra:dln] VI AUX SEIN (*inf*) to cycle
Rädelsführer(in) ['rɛ:dls-] M(F) ringleader
-räderig [rɛdərɪç] ADJ SUF **-wheeled; zwei-/vierräderig** two-/four-wheeled
radfahren ['ra:tfa:rən] VI SEP IRREG AUX SEIN *siehe* **Rad**
Radfahren NT **-s**, NO PL **~ verboten** no cycling
Radfahrer(in) M(F) **(a)** cyclist **(b)** (*pej inf*) crawler (*Brit inf*), brown-noser (*esp US sl*)
Radfahrweg M cycleway; (*in der Stadt*) cycle lane
Radgabel F fork
Radhelm M cycle helmet
radial [ra'dia:l] **1** ADJ radial **2** ADV radially
Radiator [ra'dia:to:ɐ] M **-s, Radiatoren** [-'to:rən] radiator
Radicchio [ra'dɪkjo] M **-s, Radicchi** [-'diki] radicchio
radieren [ra'di:rən] *ptp* **radiert** **1** VT **(a)** (*mit Radiergummi*) to erase; (*mit Messer*) to erase **(b)** (*Art*) to etch **2** VI **(a)** (*mit Radiergummi*) to erase **(b)** (*Art*) to etch
Radiergummi M rubber (*Brit*), eraser (*esp US, form*)
Radierung [ra'di:rʊŋ] F **-, -en** (*Art*) etching
Radieschen [ra'di:sçən] NT **-s, -** radish; **sich** (*dat*) **die ~ von unten ansehen** *or* **besehen** (*hum*) to be pushing up the daisies (*hum*)
radikal [radi'ka:l] **1** ADJ radical; *Vertilgung, Entfernen* total; *Verneinung* categorical; *Ablehnung* flat **2** ADV **(a)** (*Pol*) *sich verhalten* radically; **~ denken, ~ eingestellt** *or* **gesinnt sein** to be politically radical **(b)** (= *völlig*) *ausrotten, beseitigen, mit jdm brechen* radically; *ablehnen* flatly; *verneinen* categorically **(c)** (= *tief greifend*) *ändern, verfahren* radically; **mit diesem Missbrauch muss ~ Schluss gemacht werden** a definitive stop must be put to this abuse; **etw ~ ablehnen** to refuse sth flatly; **~ vorgehen** to be drastic; **~ gegen etw vorgehen** to take radical steps against sth
Radikale(r) [radi'ka:lə] MF DECL AS ADJ radical
Radikalkur F (*inf*) drastic remedy
Radio ['ra:dio] NT *or* (SW, S GER AUCH) M **-s, -s** radio; **~ hören** to listen to the radio; **im ~, am ~** (*Sw*) on the radio; **aus dem ~ ertönte ein Beatles-Hit** a Beatles hit was playing on the radio
Radio- IN CPDS radio; **radioaktiv** [radioak'ti:f] **1** ADJ radioactive; **~er Niederschlag** radioactive fallout **2** ADV radioactively; **~ verseucht** contaminated with radioactivity; **Radioaktivität** [radioaktivi'tɛ:t] F radioactivity; **Radioapparat** M radio (set); **Radiodurchsage** F radio announcement; **Radioempfänger** M radio (set); (*von Funkamateur*) radio receiver; **Radiografie** [radiogra'fi:] F **-, -n** [-'fi:ən] radiography; **Radioisotop** NT radioisotope
Radiologe [radio'lo:gə] M **-n, -n, Radiologin** [-'lo:gɪn] F **-, -nen** (*Med*) radiologist
Radiologie [radiolo'gi:] F **-**, NO PL (*Med*) radiology
radiologisch [radio'lo:gɪʃ] **1** ADJ radiological **2** ADV radiologically; **~ behandelt werden** to undergo radiotherapy; **~ untersucht werden** to undergo a radiological examination
Radio-: Radiorekorder M radio recorder; **Radiosender** M (= *Rundfunkanstalt*) radio station; (= *Sendeeinrichtung*) radio transmitter; **Radiosendung** F radio programme (*Brit*) *or* program (*US*); **Radiotherapeut(in)** M(F) radiotherapist; **Radiotherapie** F radiotherapy; **Radioübertragung** F (radio) broadcast; **Radiowecker** M radio alarm (clock)
Radium ['ra:diʊm] NT **-**, NO PL (*abbr* **Ra**) radium
Radius ['ra:diʊs] M **-, Radien** [-diən] radius
Rad-: Radkappe F hubcap; **Radlager** NT wheel bearing
Radler ['ra:dlɐ] M **-s, -, Radlerin** [-ərɪn] F **-, -nen** (*inf*) cyclist
Radlerhose F cycling shorts *pl*
Radlermaß F (*S Ger inf*) shandy (*esp Brit*), radler (*US*)
Radon ['ra:dɔn, ra'do:n] NT **-s**, NO PL (*abbr* **Rn**) radon
Rad-: Radrennbahn F cycle (racing) track; **Radrennen** NT (*Sportart*) cycle racing; (*einzelnes Rennen*) cycle race;

Radrennfahrer(in) M(F) racing cyclist; **Radrennsport** M cycle racing

-rädrig [rɛːdrɪç] ADJ SUF = **-räderig**

Rad-: **Radsport** M cycling; **Radsportler(in)** M(F) cyclist; **Radstand** M (Aut, Rail) wheelbase; **Radtour** F bike ride; (länger) cycling tour; **Radwechsel** M wheel change; **Radweg** M cycleway

RAF [ɛrlaːˈlɛf] F -, NO PL ABBR von **Rote-Armee-Fraktion**

raffen [ˈrafn] VT **(a)** (= anhäufen) to pile; (hastig) to grab; **er will immer nur (Geld)** – he's always after money; **sein ganzes Leben hat er nur (Geld) gerafft** he spent his whole life making money; **etw an sich** (acc) – to grab sth **(b)** Stoff, Gardine to gather; langes Kleid, Rock to gather up **(c)** (zeitlich) to shorten **(d)** (sl: = verstehen) to get (inf)

Raffinade [rafiˈnaːdə] F -, -n (Zucker) refined sugar

Raffination [rafinaˈtsioːn] F -, -en refining

Raffinerie [rafinəˈriː] F -, -n [-ˈriːən] refinery

Raffinesse [rafiˈnɛsə] F -, -n **(a)** (= Feinheit) refinement **(b)** (= Schlauheit, Durchtriebenheit) cunning no pl; **mit aller** – with all one's cunning

raffinieren [rafiˈniːrən], ptp **raffiniert** VT to refine

raffiniert [rafiˈniːrt] **1** ADJ **(a)** Zucker, Öl refined **(b)** Methoden, Techniken, Mechanismen, Apparat sophisticated; (inf) Kleid, Frisur, Kleidung stylish **(c)** (= schlau) clever; (= durchtrieben) crafty **2** ADV **(a)** (= durchtrieben) cleverly; – **vorgehen** to be cunning; **da musst du dich –er anstellen** you have to be a little more clever; – **einfach** cunningly simple **(b)** (= ausgesucht) gewürzt exquisitely; **sie kleidet sich sehr** – she certainly knows how to dress

Raffiniertheit F -, NO PL **(a)** (von Kleidung, Frisur) stylishness **(b)** (= Schlauheit) cleverness; (= Durchtriebenheit) craftiness

Rage [ˈraːʒə] F -, NO PL (= Wut) rage; **jdn in** – **bringen** to infuriate sb; **sich in** – **reden** to talk oneself into a rage

ragen [ˈraːɡn] VI to rise, to loom; (= herausragen) to jut

Ragout [raˈɡuː] NT -s, -s ragout

Rah [raː] F -, -en, **Rahe** [ˈraːə] F -, -en (Naut) yard

Rahm [raːm] M -(e)s, NO PL (dial) cream

rahmen [ˈraːmən] VT to frame; Dias to mount

Rahmen [ˈraːmən] M -s, - **(a)** (= Rahme) frame **(b)** (fig) (= Bereich) (Liter: = ~handlung) framework; (= Atmosphäre) setting; (= Größe) scale; **den** – **zu** or **für etw bilden** to provide a backdrop for sth; **im** – **within the** framework (+gen of); **seine Verdienste wurden im** – **einer kleinen Feier gewürdigt** his services were honoured (Brit) or honored (US) in a small ceremony; **im** – **des Möglichen** within the bounds of possibility; **im** – **bleiben, sich im** – **halten** to keep within the limits; **aus dem** – **fallen** to be strikingly different; **musst du denn immer aus dem** – **fallen!** do you always have to show yourself up?; **in den** – **von etw passen, sich in den** – **von etw einfügen** to fit (in) with sth; **den** – **von etw sprengen, über den** – **von etw hinausgehen** to go beyond the scope of sth; **einer Feier einen würdigen** or **den richtigen** – **geben** to provide the appropriate setting for a celebration; **in größerem/kleinerem** – on a large/small scale; **die Feier fand nur in engem** or **in engstem** – **statt** the celebration was just a small-scale affair

Rahmen-: **Rahmenbedingung** F basic condition; **Rahmenkredit** M bank credit line, line of credit; **Rahmentarifvertrag** M ≈ general agreement on conditions of employment; **Rahmenvertrag** M (Ind) general agreement

rahmig [ˈraːmɪç] ADJ (dial) creamy

Rahsegel [ˈraː-] NT (Naut) square sail

räkeln [ˈrɛːkln] VR = **rekeln**

Rakete [raˈkeːtə] F -, -n rocket (auch Space); (Mil auch) missile

Raketen-: **Raketenabschussbasis** F (Mil) missile base; (Space) launch site Brit; **Raketenabwehr** F antimissile defence (Brit) or defense (US); **Raketensilo** M rocket silo; **Raketenstart** M (rocket) launch; (= Start mittels Raketen) rocket-assisted takeoff; **Raketenstützpunkt** M missile base; **Raketenwerfer** M rocket launcher

Rallye [ˈrali, ˈrɛli] F -, -s rally; **eine** – **fahren** to drive in a rally; – **fahren** to go rallying

Rallyefahrer(in) M(F) rally driver

RAM [ram] NT -s, -s (Comput) RAM

Rambazamba [ˈrambaˈtsamba] NT -s, NO PL (inf) – **machen** to kick up a fuss

Rambo [ˈrambo] M -s, -s Rambo

Ramme [ˈramə] F -, -n ram(mer); (für Pfähle) pile-driver

rammeln [ˈramln] **1** VT siehe **gerammelt 2** VI (Hunt) to mate; (sl) to do it (inf)

rammen [ˈramən] VT to ram

Rammler [ˈramlɐ] M -s, - (a) (= Kaninchen) buck (b) (sl: = Mann) stud (inf)

Rampe [ˈrampə] F -, -n (a) ramp (b) (Theat) forestage

Rampenlicht NT (Theat) footlights pl; (fig) limelight; **im** – **der Öffentlichkeit stehen** (fig) to be in the limelight

ramponieren [rampoˈniːrən], ptp **ramponiert** VT (inf) to ruin; Möbel to bash about (inf); **er sah ziemlich ramponiert aus** he looked the worse for wear (inf)

Ramsch [ramʃ] M -(e)s, NO PL (a) (inf) junk (b) (Skat) (einen) – **spielen** to play (a) ramsch

RAM-Speicher [ˈram-] M (Comput) RAM memory

ran [ran] INTERJ (inf) come on (inf); – **an den Feind!** let's go get 'em! (inf); – **an die Arbeit!** down to work; siehe auch **heran**

Rand¹ [rant] M -es, ⁼er [ˈrɛndə] (a) edge; (von Weg, Straße, Schwimmbecken etc) side, edge; (von Brunnen, Gefäß, Tasse) top, rim; (von Abgrund) brink; **voll bis zum** – full to the brim; **am ~e erwähnen, zur Sprache kommen** in passing; **interessieren** marginally; **beteiligt sein** marginally; **miterleben** from the sidelines; **am ~e des Waldes** at the edge of the forest; **am ~e der Stadt** on the outskirts of the town; **am ~e der Verzweiflung/des Wahnsinns** on the verge of despair/madness; **am ~e des Grabes** or **Todes stehen** to be at death's door; **am ~e des Untergangs** or **Ruins** on the brink of ruin; **am ~e eines Krieges** on the brink of war; **die Schweizer haben den Krieg nur am ~e miterlebt** the Swiss were only marginally involved in the war; **am ~e der Gesellschaft/der politischen Landschaft** on the fringes of society/the political scene; **an den** – **der Gesellschaft gedrängt werden** to be marginalized by society; **am äußersten rechten** – **des politischen Spektrums** on the extreme right of the political spectrum **(b)** (= Umrandung) border; (= Tellerrand) edge; (= Brillenrand) rim; (von Hut) brim; (= Seitenrand, Buchrand, Heftrand) margin; **mit schwarzem** – black-edged, with a black border; **etw an den** – **schreiben** to write sth in the margin **(c)** (= Schmutzrand) ring; (um Augen) circle; **rote Ränder um die Augen haben** to have red rims around one's eyes **(d)** (fig) **sie waren außer** – **und Band** they were going wild; (sl) **halt den ~!** (sl) shut your face! (sl); **zu ~e = zurande**

Rand² M -s, -(s) (= Währung) rand

Randale [ranˈdaːlə] F -, NO PL rioting; – **machen** to riot

randalieren [randaˈliːrən], ptp **randaliert** VI to rampage (about); **~de Jugendliche** (young) hooligans; **~de Studenten** rioting students; **die Gefangenen fingen an zu** – the prisoners started to go on the rampage

Randalierer [randaˈliːrɐ] M -s, -, **Randaliererin** [-ərɪn] F -,-nen hooligan

Rand-: **Randausgleich** M (Comput) justification; **Randbemerkung** F (schriftlich: auf Seite) note in the margin; (mündlich, fig) (passing) comment

Rande [ˈrandə] F -, -n (Sw) beetroot

Rand-: **Randeinstellung** F margin setting; **Randerscheinung** F marginal matter; (= Nebenwirkung) side effect; **Randfigur** F minor figure; **Randgruppe** F fringe group; **randlos 1** ADJ Brille rimless; Hut brimless **2** ADV (Comput) drucken, bedrucken without margins; **randständig** ADJ Personen, Position marginal(ized); Bevölkerungsgruppen minority; **Randstein** M kerb; **den** – **mitnehmen** (inf) to hit the kerb; **randvoll** ADJ Glas full to the brim; Behälter full to the top; (fig) Terminkalender, Programm packed; (inf: = betrunken) smashed (inf)

rang PRET von **ringen**

Rang [raŋ] M -(e)s, ⁼e [ˈrɛŋə] (a) (Mil) rank; (in Firma) position; (= gesellschaftliche Stellung) position; (in Wettbewerb) place; **im** – **höher/tiefer stehen** to have a higher/lower rank/position; **einen hohen** – **haben** to hold a high office; (Mil) to have a high rank; **ein Mann von** – **und Würden** a man of status; **ein Mann ohne** – **und Namen** a man without any standing; **alles, was** – **und Namen hat** everybody who is anybody; **jdm den** – **streitig machen** (fig) to challenge sb's position; **jdm den** –

ablaufen (*fig*) to outstrip sb
(b) (= *Qualität*) quality; **ein Künstler/Wissenschaftler von** ~ an artist/scientist of standing; **von hohem** ~ high-class; **eine Touristenattraktion ersten ~es** a first-class tourist attraction; **ein Skandal ersten ~es** a scandal of the highest order; **minderen ~es** second-rate
(c) (*Theat*) circle; **erster/zweiter** ~ dress/upper circle, first/second circle (*US*); **vor leeren/überfüllten Rängen spielen** to play to an empty/a packed house
(d) Ränge PL (*Sport*: = *Tribünenränge*) stands *pl*

rangeln [ˈraŋln] (*inf*) 🔢 VI to scrap; (*um Posten*) to wrangle (*um* for) 🔢 VR to sprawl about

Rangierbahnhof [raˈʒiːɐ-] M marshalling (*Brit*) *or* marshaling (*US*) yard

rangieren [raˈʒiːrən], *ptp* **rangiert** 🔢 VT (*Rail*) to shunt (*Brit*), to switch (*US*) 🔢 VI (*inf*: = *Rang einnehmen*) to rank; **er rangiert gleich hinter** *or* **unter dem Abteilungsleiter** he comes directly beneath the head of department; **Mathilde rangiert bei mir unter „ferner liefen"** (*inf*) as far as I'm concerned Mathilde is a "has-been" (*inf*); **an erster/letzter Stelle** ~ to come first/last

Rang-: Rangliste F **(a)** (*Mil*) active list **(b)** (*Sport, fig*) (results) table; **er steht auf der ~ der weltbesten Boxer** he ranks among the world's top boxers; **rangmäßig** 🔢 ADJ according to rank 🔢 ADV higher in rank; **jdm ~ übergeordnet/ untergeordnet sein** to be sb's superior/subordinate; **~ stehe ich unter ihm** I'm lower than him in rank

ranhalten [ˈranhaltn] VR SEP IRREG (*inf*) **(a)** (= *sich beeilen, sich umtun*) to get a move on (*inf*) **(b)** (= *schnell zugreifen*) to get stuck in (*inf*)

Ranke [ˈraŋkə] F **-, -n** tendril; (*von Brom-, Himbeeren*) branch; (*von Erdbeeren*) stalk; (*von Weinrebe*) shoot

ranken [ˈraŋkn] 🔢 VR **sich um etw** ~ to entwine itself around sth; (*fig: Geschichten etc*) to have grown up around sth 🔢 VI AUX HABEN *or* SEIN **an etw** (*dat*) ~ to entwine itself around sth

Ranking [ˈrɛŋkɪŋ] NT **-s, -s** (*inf*: = *Rangordnung*) ranking

ranklotzen [ˈranklɔtsn] VI SEP (*inf*) to get stuck in (*inf*)

rankommen [ˈrankɔmən] VI SEP IRREG AUX SEIN (*inf*) **an etw** (*acc*) ~ to get at sth; **an die Helga ist nicht ranzukommen** you won't get anywhere with Helga (*inf*); **an unseren Chef ist schwer ranzukommen** our boss isn't very easy to get through to; **niemanden an sich ~ lassen** to be standoffish (*inf*); **nichts an sich ~ lassen** not to be fazed by anything; *siehe auch* **herankommen**

ranlassen [ˈranlasn] VT SEP IRREG (*inf*) **jdn** ~ (*an eine Aufgabe etc*) to let sb have a try; **sie lässt jeden ran** (*inf*) she's an easy lay (*sl*); **sie lässt keinen mehr (an sich** *acc***) ran** (*inf*) she won't let anybody near her

ranmachen [ˈranmaxn] VR SEP (*inf*) = **heranmachen**

rann PRET *von* **rinnen**

rannte PRET *von* **rennen**

ranschmeißen [ˈranʃmaisn] VR SEP IRREG (*inf*) **sich an jdn** ~ to throw oneself at sb (*inf*)

Ranunkel [raˈnʊŋkl] F **-, -n** (*Bot*) ranunculus

Ranzen [ˈrantsn] M **-s, -** **(a)** (= *Schulranzen*) satchel **(b)** (*inf*: = *Bauch*) belly (*Brit inf*); **sich** (*dat*) **den ~ voll schlagen** to stuff oneself (*inf*)

ranzig [ˈrantsɪç] 🔢 ADJ rancid 🔢 ADV **~ schmecken/riechen** to taste/smell rancid

Rap [rɛp] M **-(s), -s** (*Mus*) rap

rapid [raˈpiːt], **rapide** [raˈpiːdə] 🔢 ADJ rapid 🔢 ADV rapidly

Rappe [ˈrapə] M **-n, -n** black horse

Rappel [ˈrapl] M **-s, -** (*inf*) **(a)** (= *Fimmel*) craze; (= *Klaps*) crazy mood; **seinen ~ kriegen** *or* **bekommen** to go completely crazy; **du hast wohl einen ~!** you must be crazy! **(b)** (= *Wutanfall*) **einen ~ haben** to be in a foul mood *or* temper; **einen ~ kriegen** *or* **bekommen** to throw a fit; **dabei kann man ja einen ~ kriegen** it's enough to drive you mad (*inf*)

rappen [ˈrɛpn] VI (*Mus*) to rap

Rappen [ˈrapn] M **-s, -** (*Sw*) centime

Rapper [ˈrɛpɐ] M **-s, -, Rapperin** [-ərɪn] F **-, -nen** (*Mus*) rapper; (= *Fan*) rap fan

Rapport [raˈpɔrt] M **-(e)s, -e** **(a)** report; **sich zum ~ melden** to report **(b)** (*Psych*) rapport

Raps [raps] M **-es, -e** (*Bot*) rape

Rapsöl NT rape(seed) oil

Rapunzel [raˈpʊntsl] F **-, -n (a)** (*Bot*) lamb's lettuce **(b)** (*Märchen*) Rapunzel

rar [raːɐ] ADJ rare; **sich ~ machen** (*inf*) to keep away; (= *sich zurückziehen*) to make oneself scarce

Rarität [rariˈtɛːt] F **-, -en** rarity

rasant [raˈzant] 🔢 ADJ **(a)** *Tempo, Spurt* terrific, lightning *attr* (*inf*); *Auto, Fahrer* fast; *Aufstieg, Karriere* meteoric; *Entwicklung, Wachstum, Fortschritt, Abnahme, Zerfall* rapid **(b)** (= *imponierend*) *Frau* vivacious; *Leistung* terrific 🔢 ADV **(a)** (= *sehr schnell*) fast; **sie fuhr ~ die Straße hinunter** she tore down the street **(b)** (= *stürmisch*) dramatically

rasch [raʃ] 🔢 ADJ **(a)** (= *schnell*) quick; *Tempo* great **(b)** (= *übereilt*) rash 🔢 ADV **(a)** (= *schnell*) quickly; **nicht so ~!** not so fast; **~ machen** to hurry (up); **es muss ~ gehen** it's got to be fast; **ich habe so ~ wie möglich gemacht** I was as quick as I could be; **ein bisschen ~, bitte!** make it quick **(b)** (= *vorschnell*) **mit etw ~ bei der Hand sein** to be rash about sth

rascheln [ˈraʃln] VI to rustle; **es raschelt (im Stroh/Laub)** there's something rustling (in the straw/leaves); **mit etw ~** to rustle sth

rasen [ˈraːzn] VI **(a)** (= *wüten, toben*) to rave; (*Sturm*) to rage; **er raste vor Wut** he was mad with rage; **er raste vor Eifersucht** he was half-crazed with jealousy; **die Zuschauer rasten vor Begeisterung** the spectators were wild with excitement **(b)** AUX SEIN (= *sich schnell bewegen*) to race; (*Puls, Herz*) to race; **der Rennwagen raste in die Menge/gegen einen Baum** the racing car crashed into the crowd/a tree; **ras doch nicht so!** (*inf*) don't go so fast!; **die Zeit rast** time flies **(c)** AUX SEIN (*inf*: = *herumhetzen*) to race around

Rasen [ˈraːzn] M **-s, -** lawn, grass *no indef art, no pl*; (*von Sportplatz*) turf; (= *Sportplatz*) field; (*Tennis*) court; **einen ~ anlegen** to lay (down) a lawn; **„bitte den ~ nicht betreten"** "please keep off the grass"

rasend 🔢 ADJ **(a)** (= *enorm*) terrific; *Beifall* rapturous; *Eifersucht* burning; **~e Kopfschmerzen** a splitting headache **(b)** (= *wütend*) furious; **er macht mich noch ~** he'll drive me crazy (*inf*); **es ist zum Rasendwerden** it's absolutely infuriating 🔢 ADV (*inf*) terrifically; *schnell* incredibly; *wehtun, sich beeilen, applaudieren* like mad (*inf*); *lieben, verliebt, eifersüchtig sein* madly (*inf*); **~ viel Geld** heaps of money (*inf*); **~ gern!** I'd simply love to!

Rasen-: Rasenmäher [-mɛːɐ] M **-s, -, Rasenmähmaschine** F lawn mower; **Rasenplatz** M (*Ftbl etc*) field; (*Tennis*) grass court

Raser [ˈraːzɐ] M **-s, -, Raserin** [-ərɪn] F **-, -nen** (*inf*) speed maniac (*esp Brit inf*), speed demon (*US inf*)

Raserei [razəˈrai] F **-, -en (a)** (= *Wut*) fury **(b)** (*inf*: = *schnelles Fahren, Gehen*) mad rush

Rasier- [raˈziːɐ] IN CPDS shaving; **Rasierapparat** M razor; (*elektrisch auch*) shaver; **Rasiercreme** F shaving cream

rasieren [raˈziːrən], *ptp* **rasiert** 🔢 VT **(a)** *Haare, Kopf, Bart* to shave; **sich ~ lassen** to get a shave; **sie rasiert sich** (*dat*) **die Beine** she shaves her legs **(b)** (*inf*: = *streifen*) to scrape 🔢 VR to (have a) shave; **sich nass ~** to have a wet shave; **sich trocken ~** to use an electric shaver

Rasier-: Rasierklinge F razor blade; **Rasiermesser** NT (open) razor; **Rasierpinsel** M shaving brush; **Rasierschaum** M shaving foam; **Rasierwasser** NT, *pl* **-wasser** *or* **-wässer** aftershave (lotion); (*vor der Rasur*) pre-shave (lotion); **Rasierzeug** NT, *pl* **-zeuge** shaving things *pl*

Räson [rɛˈzõː] F **-, NO PL er will keine ~ annehmen** he won't listen to reason; **jdn zur ~ bringen** to make sb listen to reason; **zur ~ kommen** to see reason

Raspel [ˈraspl] F **-, -n (a)** (= *Holzfeile*) rasp **(b)** (*Cook*) grater

raspeln [ˈraspln] VT to grate; *Holz* to rasp

Rasse [ˈrasə] F **-, -n** (= *Menschenrasse*) race; (= *Tierrasse*) breed; (*fig*) spirit, hot-bloodedness; **das Mädchen hat ~** she's a hot-blooded girl; **das Pferd/der Hund hat ~** that horse/dog has spirit

Rassehund M pedigree dog

Rassel [ˈrasl] F **-, -n** rattle

rasseln [ˈrasln] VI **(a)** (= *Geräusch erzeugen*) to rattle; **mit** *or* **an etw** (*dat*) ~ to rattle sth **(b)** AUX SEIN (*inf*) **durch eine Prüfung ~** to flunk an exam (*inf*)

Rassen- IN CPDS racial; **Rassendiskriminierung** F racial discrimination; **Rassenhass** M race hatred; **Rassenkampf** M racial struggle; **Rassenkonflikt** M racial conflict; **Rassenkrawall** M race riot; **Rassenproblem** NT race problem; **Rassenschranke** F racial barrier; (*Farbige betreffend*) colour (*Brit*) *or* color (*US*) bar; **Rassentrennung** F racial segregation; **Rassenunruhen** PL racial disturbances *pl*; **Rassenvorurteil** NT racial prejudice; **~e haben** to be racially biased

rassig ['rasıç] ADJ *Pferd, Auto* sleek; *Frau* sexy; *Erscheinung, Gesichtszüge* striking; *Zigeuner, Südländer* fiery

rassisch ['rasıʃ] **1** ADJ racial **2** ADV racially; **~ anders sein** not to belong to the same race; **jdn ~ verfolgen** to persecute sb because of his/her race

Rassismus [ra'sısmus] M **-**, NO PL racism

Rassist [ra'sıst] M **-en, -en, Rassistin** [-'sıstın] F **-, -nen** racist

rassistisch [ra'sıstıʃ] **1** ADJ racist **2** ADV **sich ~ äußern** to make racist remarks; **sich ~ verhalten** to act like a racist; **~ eingestellt sein** to be a racist; **~ angehauchte Texte** racist sounding texts

Rast [rast] F **-, -en** rest; (*auf Autofahrt*) stop (for a rest); **~ machen** to stop (for a rest)

Rastalocken ['rasta-] PL dreadlocks *pl*

Raste ['rastə] F **-, -n** notch

rasten ['rastn] VI to rest; (*Mil*) to make a halt

Raster ['rastɐ] NT **-s, -** (*Archit: auf Landkarte*) grid; (*Typ*) halftone *or* raster screen; (*Phot*: = *Gitter*) screen; (*TV*) raster; (*fig*) framework

Rasterfahndung F computer search

rastern ['rastɐn] VT (*Typ*) to print in halftone; (*TV*) to scan

Rasterpunkt M (*Typ*) (halftone) dot; (*TV*) picture element

Rasterung F **-, -en** (*TV*) scanning

Rast-: **Rasthaus** NT (travellers' (*Brit*) *or* travelers' (*US*)) inn; (*an Autobahn: auch* **Rasthof**) service area (*including motel*); **rastlos** **1** ADJ (= *unruhig*) restless; (= *unermüdlich*) tireless **2** ADV tirelessly; **Rastplatz** M resting place; (*an Autostraßen*) picnic area; **Raststätte** F (*Mot*) service area

Rasur [ra'zu:ɐ] F **-, -en** (= *Bartrasur*) shave; (= *das Rasieren*) shaving

Rat¹ [ra:t] M **-(e)s (a)** *pl* **Ratschläge** ['ra:tʃlɛːgə] (= *Empfehlung*) advice *no pl*; **jdm einen ~ geben** to give sb a piece of advice; **jdm den ~ geben, etw zu tun** to advise sb to do sth; **jdn um ~ fragen** *or* **bitten, sich** (*dat*) **bei jdm ~ holen** to ask sb's advice; **~ suchend** seeking advice; **sich ~ suchend an jdn wenden** to turn to sb for advice; **~ Suchende** people seeking advice; **einem ~ folgen, einem ~ befolgen** to take a piece of advice; **auf jds ~** (*acc*) **(hin)** on *or* following sb's advice; **jdm mit ~ und Tat beistehen** *or* **zur Seite stehen** to support sb in (both) word and deed; **da ist guter ~ teuer** it's hard to know what to do; **zu ~e zurate**
(b) NO PL (= *Abhilfe*) **~ (für etw) wissen** to know what to do (about sth); **sie wusste sich** (*dat*) **keinen ~ mehr** she was at her wits' end; **sich** (*dat*) **keinen ~ mit etw wissen** not to know what to do about sth; **kommt Zeit, kommt ~** (*Prov*) things work themselves out, given time
(c) *pl* **Räte** ['rɛːtə] (= *Körperschaft*) council; **der Große ~** (*Sw*) the cantonal parliament

Rat² M **-(e)s, ¨-e, Rätin** ['rɛːtın] F **-, -nen** senior official; (= *Titel*) Councillor (*Brit*), Councilor (*US*); *siehe* **wissenschaftlich**

rät [rɛːt] 3. PERS SING PRES *von* **raten**

Rate ['ra:tə] F **-, -n (a)** (= *Geldbetrag*) instalment (*Brit*), installment (*US*); **auf ~n kaufen** to buy on hire purchase (*Brit*) *or* on the installment plan (*US*); **auf ~n** (*fig*) bit by bit; **Tod auf ~n** slow death; **in ~n zahlen** to pay in instal(l)ments
(b) (= *Verhältnis*) rate

raten ['ra:tn], *pret* **riet** [ri:t], *ptp* **geraten** [gə'ra:tn] VTI
(a) (= *Ratschläge geben*) to advise; **jdm ~** to advise sb; **jdm gut/richtig/schlecht ~** to give sb good/correct/bad advice; **(jdm) zu etw ~** to recommend sth (to sb); **zu dieser langen Reise kann ich dir nicht ~** I must advise you against making this long journey; **das würde ich dir nicht ~** I wouldn't advise it; **das möchte ich dir nicht ~** or nicht geraten haben I wouldn't if I were you; **das möchte ich dir auch geraten haben!** you better had (*inf*); **was** *or* **wozu ~ Sie mir?** what do you advise?
(b) (= *erraten, herausfinden*) to guess; *Kreuzworträtsel etc* to solve; **hin und her ~** to make all sorts of guesses; **rate mal!**

(have a) guess; **dreimal darfst du ~** I'll give you three guesses (*auch iro*); **(gut) geraten!** good guess!; **falsch geraten!** wrong!

Raten-: **Ratenkauf** M (= *Kaufart*) HP (*Brit inf*), the installment plan (*US*); **Ratensparvertrag** M (*Fin*) premium-aided saving; **ratenweise** ADV in instalments (*Brit*) *or* installments (*US*); **Ratenzahlung** F (= *Zahlung einer Rate*) payment of an instalment (*Brit*) *or* installment (*US*); (= *Zahlung in Raten*) payment by instal(l)ments

Raterei [ra:tə'rai] F **-, -en (a)** (= *das Schätzen*) guessing; **lass mal die ~** must we have these guessing games? **(b)** (= *Rätselraten*) puzzle-solving

Ratespiel NT guessing game; (*TV*) quiz; (*Beruferaten etc*) panel game, quiz

Rat-: **Ratgeber** M (*Buch, TV-Sendung etc*) guide; **ein ~ für den Garten** a book of gardening tips; **Ratgeber(in)** M(F) adviser; **Rathaus** NT town hall; (*einer Großstadt*) city hall

ratifizieren [ratifi'tsi:rən], *ptp* **ratifiziert** VT to ratify

Ratifizierung F **-, -en** ratification

Rätin F *siehe* **Rat²**

Ration [ra'tsio:n] F **-, -en** ration

rational [ratsio'na:l] **1** ADJ rational **2** ADV rationally

rationalisieren [ratsionali'zi:rən], *ptp* **rationalisiert** VTI to rationalize

Rationalisierung F **-, -en** rationalization

Rationalisierungs-: **Rationalisierungsmaßnahme** F rationalization measure; **Rationalisierungsschutz** M job protection measures *pl*

rationalistisch [ratsiona'lıstıʃ] ADJ rationalist(ic)

Rationalität [ratsionali'tɛ:t] F **-**, NO PL rationality; (= *Leistungsfähigkeit*) efficiency

rationell [ratsio'nɛl] **1** ADJ *Methode, Energienutzung etc* efficient **2** ADV efficiently

rationieren [ratsio'ni:rən], *ptp* **rationiert** VT to ration

ratlos **1** ADJ helpless; **ich bin völlig ~(, was ich tun soll)** I just don't know what to do; **~e Eltern** parents who are at a loss to know what to do with their children; **sie machte ein ~es Gesicht** she looked helpless **2** ADV helplessly; **einer Sache** (*dat*) **~ gegenüberstehen** to be at a loss when faced with sth

Ratlosigkeit F **-**, NO PL helplessness; **in meiner ~ ...** not knowing what to do ...

Rätoromane [rɛtoro'ma:nə] M **-n, -n, Rätoromanin** [-'ma:nın] F **-, -nen** Rhaetian

rätoromanisch [rɛtoro'ma:nıʃ] ADJ Rhaetian; *Sprache* Rhaeto-Romanic

ratsam ['ra:tza:m] ADJ advisable

Ratschlag M piece of advice; **Ratschläge** advice; **drei Ratschläge** three pieces of advice; **deine klugen Ratschläge kannst du dir sparen** keep your advice for yourself; **jdm einen ~ geben** *or* **erteilen** to give sb a piece of advice

Rätsel ['rɛ:tsl] NT **-s, - (a)** riddle; (= *Kreuzworträtsel*) crossword (puzzle); (= *Silbenrätsel, Bilderrätsel etc*) puzzle; **in ~n sprechen** to talk in riddles
(b) (*fig*: = *Geheimnis*) riddle, mystery (*um* of); **die Polizei konnte das ~ lösen** the police have solved the mystery; **vor einem ~ stehen** to be baffled; **das plötzliche Verschwinden des Zeugen gab der Polizei ~ auf** the sudden disappearance of the witness baffled the police; **es ist mir ein ~, wie ...** it's a mystery to me how ...; **das ist des ~s Lösung!** that's the answer

Rätsel-: **rätselhaft** ADJ mysterious; **auf ~e Weise** mysteriously; **es ist mir ~** it's a mystery to me; **Rätselheft** NT puzzle book

rätseln ['rɛ:tsln] VI to puzzle (over sth)

Rätselraten NT **-s**, NO PL guessing game; (= *Rätseln*) guessing

Ratsversammlung F **(a)** (= *Sitzung*) council meeting
(b) (= *Rat*) council

Rattan ['ratan] NT **-s**, NO PL rattan

Ratte ['ratə] F **-, -n (a)** (= *Tier*) rat; **die ~n verlassen das sinkende Schiff** (*prov*) the rats are deserting the sinking ship **(b)** (*inf*: = *Mensch*) rat (*inf*)

Ratten-: **Rattenfänger(in)** M(F) rat-catcher; (*Hund*) ratter; (*fig*) rabble-rouser; **der ~ von Hameln** the Pied Piper of Hamelin; **Rattengift** NT rat poison; **Rattenschwanz** M **(a)** (*lit*) rat's tail **(b)** USU PL (*inf*: = *Zopf*) bunch **(c)** (*fig inf*: = *Serie, Folge*) string

rattern ['ratɐn] VI (*als Bewegungsverb: aux sein*) to rattle; (*Maschinengewehr*) to chatter

rau [rau] ADJ **(a)** rough; (= *hart*) *Mann* tough; *Ton, Worte, Behandlung* harsh; **~, aber herzlich** bluff; *Begrüßung, Ton* rough but jovial; **er ist ~, aber herzlich** he's a rough diamond; **in unserer Familie geht es ~, aber herzlich zu** we're a pretty hale and hearty lot in our family; **eine ~e Schale haben** (*fig*) to be a rough diamond; **~e Schale, weicher Kern** (*fig*) tough exterior, soft centre (*Brit*) *or* center (*US*) **(b)** *Hals, Kehle* sore; *Stimme* husky; (= *heiser*) hoarse **(c)** (= *nicht mild, streng*) *Wetter* inclement; *Wind, Luft* raw; *See* rough; *Klima, Winter* harsh, raw; **im ~en Norden** in the rugged north; **(die) ~e Wirklichkeit** harsh reality **(d)** (*inf*) **in ~en Mengen** galore (*inf*)

Raub [raup] M **-(e)s** [-bəs], NO PL **(a)** (= *das Rauben*) robbery; (= *Diebstahl*) theft; **schwerer ~** aggravated robbery **(b)** (= *Entführung*) abduction; **der ~ der Sabinerinnen** the rape of the Sabine women **(c)** (= *Beute*) booty, spoils *pl*

Raub-: Raubbau M, NO PL overexploitation (of natural resources); (*am Wald*) overfelling; (*an Äckern*) overcropping; (*an Weideland*) overgrazing; (*an Fischbeständen*) overfishing; **~ an etw** (*dat*) **treiben** to overexploit *etc* sth; **mit seiner Gesundheit ~ treiben** to ruin one's health; **Raubdruck** M, *pl* **-drucke** pirate(d) copy; (= *das Drucken*) pirating

rauben ['raubn] **1** VT (= *wegnehmen*) to steal; (= *entführen*) to abduct; **jdm etw ~** (*lit, fig*) to rob sb of sth; **das hat uns viel Zeit geraubt** it cost us a lot of time; **jdm einen Kuss ~** to steal a kiss from sb; **jdm den Schlaf/den Verstand ~** to rob sb of his/her sleep/reason; **jdm den Atem ~** to take sb's breath away; **du raubst mir noch den letzten Nerv!** you'll drive me crazy (*inf*) **2** VI to rob

Räuber ['raubɐ] M **-s, -**, **Räuberin** [-ərɪn] F **-, -nen** robber; (= *Wegelagerer*) highwayman; **Ali Baba und die vierzig ~** Ali Baba and the forty thieves; **der Fuchs ist ein ~** the fox is a beast of prey; **~ und Gendarm** cops and robbers

Räuberei [rɔybə'rai] F **-, -n** (*inf*) robbery

räuberisch ['rɔybərɪʃ] ADJ rapacious; **~er Diebstahl** (*Jur*) theft in which force or the threat of violence is used to remain in possession of the stolen goods; **~e Erpressung** (*Jur*) armed robbery; **in ~er Absicht** with intent to rob

räubern ['rɔybɐn] VI (*inf*) to thieve; **in der Speisekammer ~** to raid the larder

Raub-: Raubfisch M predatory fish; **Raubkatze** F (predatory) big cat; **Raubkopie** F pirate(d) copy; **Raubmord** M robbery with murder; **Raubmörder(in)** M(F) robber and murderer; **Raubpressung** F pirate(d) copy; **Raubritter** M robber baron; **Raubtier** NT predator, beast of prey; **Raubüberfall** M robbery; **einen ~ auf jdn begehen** *or* **verüben** to hold sb up; **„~ auf Taxifahrer"** "taxi driver attacked and robbed"; **Raubvogel** M bird of prey

Rauch [raux] M **-(e)s**, NO PL smoke; (*giftig auch*) fumes *pl*; **in ~ aufgehen** (*lit, fig*), **sich in ~ auflösen** (*fig*) to go up in smoke; **Würste in den ~ hängen** to hang sausages up to smoke

Rauch-: Rauchabzug M smoke outlet; **raucharm** ADJ smokeless; **Rauchbildung** F production of smoke; **mit großer ~ verbrennen** to burn giving off a lot of smoke; **Rauchbombe** F smoke bomb

rauchen ['rauxn] **1** VI (= *Rauch abgeben*) to smoke; **sie sah, dass es aus unserer Küche rauchte** she saw smoke coming from our kitchen; **mir raucht der Kopf** my head's spinning **2** VTI (*Mensch*) to smoke; **möchten Sie ~?** do you want to smoke?; (*Zigarette anbietend*) would you like a cigarette?; **eine ~ to** have a smoke; **hast du was zu ~?** have you got a smoke?; **„Rauchen verboten"** "no smoking"; **sich** (*dat*) **das Rauchen angewöhnen/abgewöhnen** to take up/give up smoking; **viel** *or* **stark ~** to be a heavy smoker

Rauchentwicklung F production of smoke; **mit starker/geringer ~** giving off high/low smoke levels

Raucher[1] ['rauxɐ] M **-s, -** (*Rail*: = **~abteil**) smoking compartment

Raucher[2] ['rauxɐ] M **-s, -**, **Raucherin** [-ərɪn] F **-, -nen** smoker; **sind Sie ~?** do you smoke?

Raucheraal ['rɔyçɐ-] M smoked eel

Raucher-: Raucherabteil NT smoking compartment; **Raucherbein** NT hardening of the arteries (in the leg) (*caused by smoking*)

Raucherin F smoker; *siehe auch* **Raucher**[2]

Räucher-: Räucherkammer ['rɔyçɐ-] F smokehouse; **Räucherkerze** ['rɔyçɐ-] F incense cone; **Räucherlachs** ['rɔyçɐ-] M smoked salmon

räuchern ['rɔyçɐn] VT to smoke

Räucher-: Räucherschinken M smoked ham; **Räucherstäbchen** NT joss stick

Raucherzone F smoking area

Rauch-: Rauchfahne F trail of smoke; **Rauchfang** M **(a)** (= *Rauchabzug*) chimney hood **(b)** (*Aus*) chimney; **Rauchfleisch** NT smoked meat; **rauchfrei** ADJ *Zone* smokeless; *Aufenthaltsraum* no-smoking; **Rauchgase** PL fumes *pl*; **Rauchgasentschwefelungsanlage** F flue gas desulphurization (*Brit*) *or* desulfurization (*US*) plant; **Rauchglas** NT smoked glass

rauchig ['rauxɪç] ADJ smoky

Rauch-: rauchlos ADJ smokeless; **Rauchmelder** M smoke alarm; **Rauchschwaden** PL drifts *pl* of smoke; **Rauchschwalbe** F swallow; **Rauchsignal** NT smoke signal; **Rauchverbot** NT smoking ban; **hier herrscht ~** smoking is not allowed here; **Rauchvergiftung** F fume poisoning; **eine ~ erleiden** to be overcome by fumes; **Rauchwaren**[1] PL tobacco (products *pl*); **Rauchwaren**[2] PL (= *Pelze*) furs *pl*; **Rauchwolke** F cloud of smoke; **Rauchzeichen** NT smoke signal

Räude ['rɔydə] F **-, -n** (*Vet*) mange

räudig ['rɔydɪç] ADJ mangy

rauf [rauf] ADV (*inf*) **~!** (get) up!; *siehe auch* **herauf**, **hinauf**

Raufasertapete F woodchip paper

raufen ['raufn] **1** VT **sich** (*dat*) **die Haare ~** to tear (at) one's hair **2** VIR to scrap; **sich um etw ~** to fight over sth

Rauferei [raufə'rai] F **-, -en** scrap

rauh [rau] ADJ *siehe* **rau**

Rauhaardackel M wire-haired dachshund

rauhaarig ADJ coarse-haired; *Hund auch* wire-haired; *Fell, Wolle* coarse

Rauheit ['rauhait] F **-**, NO PL roughness; (*von Hals, Kehle*) soreness; (*von Stimme*) huskiness; (= *Heiserkeit*) hoarseness; (*von Wind, Luft*) rawness; (*von Klima, Winter*) harshness; (*von Gegend*) bleakness; (= *Härte*) toughness

Rauke ['raukə] F (*Bot*) rocket

Raum [raum] M **-(e)s, Räume** ['rɔymə] **(a)** NO PL (= *Platz*) room, space; (= *Weite*) expanse; **~ sparend** space-saving *attr*; **bauen, einbauen, unterbringen** to save space; **das ist ~ sparender** that saves more space; **etw ~ sparend stapeln** to stack sth (away) with a minimum use of space; **auf engstem ~ leben** to live in a very confined space; **eine Frage in den ~ stellen** to pose a question; **eine Frage im ~ stehen lassen** to leave a question unresolved **(b)** (= *Spielraum*) scope **(c)** (= *Zimmer*) room **(d)** (= *Gebiet, Bereich*) area; (*größer*) region; (*fig*) sphere; **der mitteleuropäische ~** the Central European region; **~ gewinnen** (*Mil, fig*) to gain ground **(e)** NO PL (*Phys, Space*) space *no art*; **der offene** *or* **leere ~** the void

Raum-: Raumanzug M spacesuit; **Raumaufteilung** F floor plan; **Raumausstatter** [-lausʃtatɐ] M **-s, -**, **Raumausstatterin** [-ərɪn] F **-, -nen** interior decorator

Räumboot NT minesweeper

räumen ['rɔymən] **1** VT **(a)** (= *verlassen*) *Gebäude, Gebiet, Posten* to vacate; (*Mil: Truppen*) to withdraw from; **wir müssen das Haus bis Mittwoch ~** we have to be out of the house by Wednesday **(b)** (= *leeren*) *Gebäude, Straße, Warenlager* to clear (*von* of); **„wir ~"** "clearance sale" **(c)** (= *woanders hinbringen*) to shift; (= *entfernen*) *Schnee, Schutt* to clear (away); *Minen* to clear; (*auf See*) to sweep; **räum deine Sachen in den Schrank** put your things away in the cupboard **2** VI (= *aufräumen*) to clear up; (= *umräumen*) to rearrange things

Raum-: Raumersparnis F space-saving; **aus Gründen der ~ to** save space; **Raumfähre** F space shuttle; **Raumfahrer(in)** M(F) astronaut; (*russisch*) cosmonaut

Raumfahrt F space travel *no art or* flight *no art*; **die Ausgaben für die ~ erhöhen** to increase the space budget; **das Zeitalter der ~** the space age; **die bemannte ~** manned space travel

Raumfahrt- IN CPDS space; **Raumfahrtbehörde** F space authority; **Raumfahrtingenieur(in)** M(F) astronautical engineer; **Raumfahrtstation** F space station;

Raumfahrttechnik F space technology; **Raumfahrtzentrum** NT space centre (*Brit*) *or* center (*US*)

Raumfahrzeug NT spacecraft

Räumfahrzeug NT bulldozer; (*für Schnee*) snow-clearer

Raum-: Raumflug M space flight; **Raumforschung** F space research; **Raumgestaltung** F interior design; **Raumgleiter** M orbiter; **Rauminhalt** M volume; **Raumkapsel** F space capsule; **Raumlabor** NT space lab; **Raumlehre** F geometry

räumlich ['rɔymlıç] **1** ADJ **(a)** (= *den Raum betreffend*) spatial; **~e Verhältnisse** physical conditions; **~e Nähe** physical closeness; **~e Entfernung** physical distance
(b) (= *dreidimensional*) three-dimensional
2 ADV **(a)** (= *platzmäßig*) **~ beschränkt sein** to have very little room; **sich ~ beschränken** to make do with very little room; **rein ~ ist das unmöglich** (just) from the point of view of space it's impossible
(b) (= *dreidimensional*) **~ sehen** to see in three dimensions; **Menschen, die auf einem Auge blind sind, können nicht ~ sehen** people who are blind in one eye have no depth perception

Räumlichkeit F -, -en **(a)** NO PL three-dimensionality
(b) (= *Zimmer*) room; **~en** pl premises pl

Raum-: Raummangel M lack of space; **Raummaß** NT unit of volume; **Raummeter** M or NT cubic metre (*Brit*) *or* meter (*US*) (*of stacked wood*); **Raumpfleger(in)** M(F) cleaner

Räumpflug M snowplough (*Brit*), snowplow (*US*)

Raum-: Raumschiff NT spaceship; **Raumschifffahrt** F = Raumfahrt; **Raumsonde** F space probe; **raumsparend** ADJ *siehe* Raum; **Raumstation** F space station; **Raumtransporter** M space shuttle

Räumung ['rɔymʊŋ] F -, -en clearing; (*von Wohnung, Gebäude, Stelle, Posten*) vacation; (*wegen Gefahr etc*) evacuation; (*unter Zwang*) eviction; (*Mil: von besetztem Gebiet*) withdrawal (*gen* from); (*von Lager, Vorräten, Geschäft*) clearance; **„wegen ~ alle Preise radikal herabgesetzt!"** "all prices reduced to clear"

Raupe ['raupə] F -, -n **(a)** caterpillar **(b)** (= *Planierraupe*) caterpillar®; (= *Kette*) caterpillar® track

Raupen-: Raupenfahrzeug NT caterpillar® (vehicle); **Raupenkette** F caterpillar® track

Rauputz M roughcast

Raureif M hoarfrost; (= *gefrorener Nebel*) rime

raus [raus] ADV (*inf*) **~!** (get) out!; *siehe auch* heraus, hinaus

Rausch [rauʃ] M -(e)s, Räusche ['rɔyʃə] (= *Trunkenheit*) intoxication; (= *Drogenrausch*) high (*inf*); **sich** (*dat*) **einen ~ antrinken** to get drunk; **einen ~ haben** to be drunk; **etw im ~ tun/sagen** to do/say sth while under the influence of alcohol *or* drink); **seinen ~ ausschlafen** to sleep it off

rauschen ['rauʃn] VI **(a)** (*Wasser, Meer, Wasserfall*) to roar; (*sanft*) to murmur; (*Baum, Wald*) to rustle; (*Wind*) to murmur; (*Seide*) to swish; (*Regen*) to pour down; (*Radio, Lautsprecher etc*) to hiss; (*Muschel*) to sing; **weißes Rauschen** (*Rad*) white noise **(b)** AUX SEIN (= *sich schnell bewegen*) (*Bach*) to rush; (*Bumerang, Geschoss, Auto*) to whoosh (*inf*) **(c)** AUX SEIN (*inf*: *Mensch*) to sweep

rauschend ADJ *Fest* grand; *Beifall, Erfolg* resounding; **eine ~e Ballnacht** a glittering ball

rauschfrei ADJ (*Rad, Tech*) noiseless

Rauschgift NT drug, narcotic; (= *Drogen*) drugs pl; **~ nehmen** to take drugs

Rauschgift-: Rauschgiftdezernat NT narcotics *or* drug squad; **Rauschgifthandel** M drug trafficking; **Rauschgifthändler(in)** M(F) drug trafficker; **rauschgiftsüchtig** ADJ drug-addicted; **er ist ~** he's addicted to drugs; **Rauschgiftsüchtige(r)** MF DECL AS ADJ drug addict

rausekeln ['raus|e:kln] VT SEP (*inf*) to freeze out (*inf*)

rausfliegen ['rausfli:gn] VI SEP IRREG AUX SEIN (*inf*) to be chucked out (*inf*)

rauskriegen ['rauskri:gn] VT SEP (*inf*) = herausbekommen

rauspauken ['rauspaukn] VT SEP (*inf*) **jdn ~** to get sb out of trouble; **mein Anwalt hat mich rausgepaukt** my lawyer got me off

räuspern ['rɔyspɐn] VR to clear one's throat

rausreißen ['rausraisn] VT SEP IRREG (*inf*) **jdn ~** to save sb; **der Torwart/das hat noch alles rausgerissen** the goalkeeper/that saved the day; *siehe auch* herausreißen

rausschmeißen ['rausʃmaisn] VT SEP IRREG (*inf*) to chuck *or* kick out (*aus* of) (*all inf*); (= *wegwerfen*) to chuck out (*inf*); *Geld* to chuck away (*inf*)

Rausschmeißer ['rausʃmaisɐ] M -s, -, **Rausschmeißerin** [-ərın] F -, -nen (*inf*) bouncer

Rausschmiss ['rausʃmıs] M (*inf*) booting out (*inf*); **man drohte uns mit dem ~** they threatened us with the boot (*inf*)

Raute ['rautə] F -, -n **(a)** (*Bot*) rue **(b)** (*Math*) rhombus

rautenförmig ADJ rhomboid

Rave [re:v] M OR NT -(s), -s **(a)** (= *Party*) rave **(b)** NO PL (*Musikrichtung*) rave (music)

Rave-Party ['re:v-] F rave (party)

Raver ['re:vɐ] M -s, -, **Raverin** [-ərın] F -, -nen raver

Ravioli [ravi'o:li] PL ravioli sing

Rayon [re'jõ:] M -s, -s (*Aus*) department

Razzia ['ratsia] F -, **Razzien** [-tsiən] raid (*gegen* on) *inf* **eine ~ durchführen** to carry out a raid

Re [re:] NT -s, -s (*Cards*) redouble; **Re ansagen** to redouble

Reagens [re'a:gens, re'la:gens] NT -, **Reagenzien** [rea'gentsian], **Reagenz** [rea'gents] NT -es, -ien [-tsian] (*Chem*) reagent

Reagenzglas NT, **Reagenzröhrchen** NT (*Chem*) test tube

reagieren [rea'gi:rən], *ptp* **reagiert** VI to react (*auf* +acc to; *mit* with); (*Chem*) to react (*mit* with)

Reaktion [reak'tsio:n] F -, -en **(a)** reaction (*auf* +acc to); (*Chem*) reaction (*mit* with) **(b)** (*Pol pej*) reaction

reaktionär [reaktsio'nɛ:ɐ] (*Pol pej*) **1** ADJ reactionary **2** ADV **~ denken** to be a reactionary

Reaktions-: Reaktionsfähigkeit F ability to react; (*Chem, Physiol*) reactivity; **Alkohol vermindert die ~** alcohol slows down the reactions; **Reaktionsgeschwindigkeit** F speed of reaction; **reaktionsschnell** **1** ADJ with fast reactions; **~ sein** to have fast reactions **2** ADV **er bremste ~** he reacted quickly and braked; **Reaktionszeit** F reaction time

reaktivieren [reakti'vi:rən], *ptp* **reaktiviert** VT (*Sci*) to reactivate; (*Agr, Biol, fig*) to revive; *Kenntnisse, Können* to brush up; *Kontakte* to renew; *Markt* to revive; *Sportler, Beamte* to bring back

Reaktivierung F -, -en (*Sci*) reactivation; (*Agr, Biol*) (*fig*) revival; (*von Kenntnissen, Können*) brushing up

Reaktor [re'akto:ɐ] M -s, **Reaktoren** [-'to:rən] reactor

Reaktor-: Reaktorblock M, pl **-blöcke** reactor block; **Reaktorkern** M reactor core; **Reaktorsicherheit** F reactor safety; **Reaktorunglück** NT nuclear disaster

real [re'a:l] **1** ADJ real; (= *wirklichkeitsbezogen*) realistic **2** ADV *sinken, steigen* actually; **der ~ existierende Sozialismus** socialism as it exists in reality

Real-: Realbüro NT (*Aus*) estate agency (*Brit*), real estate agency (*US*); **Realeinkommen** NT real income; **Realgymnasium** NT ≈ grammar school (*Brit*), ≈ high school (*esp US*) (*stressing modern languages, maths and science*)

Realisation [realiza'tsio:n] F -, -en (= *Verwirklichung, auch Fin*) realization; (*TV, Rad, Theat*) production

realisierbar ADJ *Idee, Projekt* feasible (*Fin*) realizable

realisieren [reali'zi:rən], *ptp* **realisiert** VT **(a)** *Pläne, Ideen, Programm, Projekt* to carry out; (*TV, Rad, Theat*) to produce **(b)** (*Fin*) to realize; *Verkauf* to make **(c)** (= *erkennen*) to realize

Realismus [rea'lısmʊs] M -, NO PL realism

Realist [rea'lıst] M -en, -en, **Realistin** [-'lıstın] F -, -nen realist

realistisch [rea'lıstıʃ] **1** ADJ realistic **2** ADV realistically

Realität [reali'tɛ:t] F -, -en **(a)** reality; **die ~ anerkennen** to face facts; **die ~en** pl (= *Gegebenheiten*) the realities pl; **virtuelle ~** virtual reality **(b) Realitäten** PL (*Aus*: = *Immobilien*) real estate

Realitäts-: realitätsfern ADJ unrealistic; **Realitätsferne** F lack of contact with reality; **realitätsnah** ADJ realistic; **Realitätsnähe** F contact with reality; **Realitätssinn** M sense of realism; **er hat einen ausgeprägten ~** he has a firm hold on reality

Reality-Fernsehen [ri'ɛlıti-] NT, **Reality-TV** [ri'ɛlıtiti:vi:] NT reality TV (*esp US*)

Real-: Realkanzlei F (*Aus*) estate agency (*Brit*), estate agency (*US*); **Realkreditinstitut** NT mortgage bank

Realo [re'a:lo] M -s, -s (*Pol sl*) political realist (*of the Green Party*)

Real-: Realpolitik F political realism, Realpolitik; **realpolitisch** ADJ pragmatic; **Realschule** F ≈ secondary school, ≈ secondary modern school (*Brit*); **Realschüler(in)** M(F) ≈ secondary modern pupil (*Brit*), ≈ student in secondary school (*US*)

*A **Realschule** is a type of German secondary school. It normally covers a period of six school years (only four years in many **Länder** that have a separate **Orientierungsstufe**) and is designed to provide a general education that goes beyond that of a **Hauptschule**. Pupils work towards the **mittlere Reife**, after which they can for example try for a **Fachabitur** at a **Fachoberschule** or serve an apprenticeship. If pupils from a **Realschule** achieve good examination results, they may move up to the eleventh year of a **Gymnasium** and try for the **Abitur**.*

*In Austria the functions of **Realschulen** are performed by mathematische Realgymnasien and extended **Hauptschulen***
▶ ABITUR, GYMNASIUM, HAUPTSCHULE, MITTLERE REIFE, ORIENTIERUNGSSTUFE

Reassekuranz [reːlasekuˈrants] F reinsurance

Rebe [ˈreːbə] F **-, -n** (= *Ranke*) shoot; (= *Weinstock*) vine

Rebell [reˈbɛl] M **-en, -en, Rebellin** [-ˈbɛlɪn] F **-, -nen** rebel

rebellieren [rebɛˈliːrən], *ptp* **rebelliert** VI to rebel

Rebellion [rebɛˈliːoːn] F **-, -en** rebellion

rebellisch [reˈbɛlɪʃ] ADJ rebellious

Reb-: Rebhuhn [ˈreːp-, ˈrɛp-] NT (common) partridge; **Rebstock** [ˈreːp-] M vine

Rechaud [reˈʃoː] M or NT **-s, -s** hotplate; (*für Tee/Kaffee*) tea/coffee warmer; (*für Fondue*) spirit burner (*Brit*), ethanol burner (*US*)

rechen [ˈrɛçn] VT (*S Ger*) to rake

Rechen [ˈrɛçn] M **-s, -** (*S Ger*) (= *Harke*) rake; (= *Gitter an Bächen, Flüssen*) grill

Rechen-: Rechenart F type of calculation; **die vier ~en** the four arithmetical operations; **Rechenaufgabe** F sum (*esp Brit*), (arithmetical) problem; **Rechenfehler** M miscalculation; **Rechenmaschine** F adding machine

Rechenschaft [ˈrɛçnʃaft] F **-,** NO PL account; **jdm über etw** (*acc*) **~ geben** or **ablegen** to account to sb for sth; **jdm ~ schuldig sein** or **schulden** to have to account to sb; **dafür bist du mir ~ schuldig** you owe me an explanation for that; **jdn (für etw) zur ~ ziehen** to call sb to account (for or over sth); **(von jdm) ~ verlangen** or **fordern** to demand an explanation (from sb)

Rechenschaftsbericht M report

Rechen-: Rechenschieber M slide rule; **Rechenzentrum** NT computer centre (*Brit*) or center (*US*)

Recherche [reˈʃɛrʃə, rə-] F **-, -n** investigation; (*in Datenbank, Katalog*) search

recherchieren [reʃɛrˈʃiːrən, rə-], *ptp* **recherchiert** VTI to investigate

rechnen [ˈrɛçnən] **1** VT (a) (= *addieren etc*) to work out; **rund gerechnet** in round figures; **was für einen Unsinn hast du da gerechnet!** how did you get that absurd result?
(b) (= *einstufen*) to count; **jdn/etw zu etw ~, jdn/etw unter etw** (*acc*) **~** to count sb among sth; **alles in allem gerechnet** all in all; **den Ärger/die Unkosten mit dazu gerechnet** what with all the trouble/expense too
(c) (= *veranschlagen*) to estimate; **wir hatten nur drei Tage gerechnet** we were only reckoning on three days; **für vier Personen rechnet man ca. zwei Pfund Fleisch** for four people you should reckon on about two pounds of meat; **das ist zu hoch/niedrig gerechnet** that's too high/low (an estimate)
2 VI (a) (= *addieren etc*) to do a calculation/calculations; (*esp Sch*) to do sums (*esp Brit*) or adding; **falsch ~** to make a mistake (in one's calculations); **richtig ~** to calculate correctly; (**da hast du**) **falsch gerechnet!** you got that wrong; **gut/schlecht ~ können** to be good/bad at arithmetic; (*esp Sch*) to be good/bad at sums (*esp Brit*) or adding; **~ lernen** to learn arithmetic
(b) (= *sich verlassen*) **auf jdn/etw ~** to count on sb/sth
(c) **mit jdm/etw ~** to reckon with sb/sth; **es wird damit gerechnet, dass ...** it is reckoned that ...; **du musst damit ~, dass es regnet** you must reckon with it raining; **damit hatte ich nicht gerechnet** I wasn't expecting that; **er rechnet mit einem Sieg** he reckons he'll win; **mit allem/dem Schlimmsten ~** to be prepared for anything/the worst; **wir hatten nicht**

mehr mit ihm or **seinem Kommen gerechnet** we hadn't reckoned on him coming any more; **damit ~ müssen, dass ...** to have to expect that ...; **ich rechne morgen fest mit dir** I'll be expecting you tomorrow
(d) (*inf*: = *haushalten*) to be thrifty
3 VR to pay off; **etw rechnet sich/rechnet sich nicht** sth is economical/not economical

Rechnen [ˈrɛçnən] NT **-s,** NO PL arithmetic

Rechner [ˈrɛçnɐ] M **-s, -** (= *Elektronenrechner*) computer; (= *Taschenrechner*) calculator

rechner-: rechnergesteuert [-ɡəʃtɔyɐt] ADJ computer-controlled; **rechnergestützt** [-ɡəʃtʏtst] ADJ computer-aided

rechnerisch **1** ADJ arithmetical; (*Pol*) *Mehrheit* numerical; **ein ~es Beispiel** an example with some figures **2** ADV
(a) (= *kalkulatorisch*) **~ falsch sein** to be wrongly calculated; **~ richtig** correctly calculated; **rein ~** just on the basis of the figures (b) (= *durch Rechnen*) through calculation

Rechnung [ˈrɛçnʊŋ] F **-, -en** (a) (= *Berechnung*) calculation; (*als Aufgabe*) sum; **die ~ geht nicht auf** (*lit*) the sum doesn't work out; (*fig*) it won't work (out)
(b) (= *schriftliche Kostenforderung*) bill (*Brit*), check (*US*); (*esp von Firma*) invoice; (*für Kundenkonto*) statement of account; **das geht auf meine ~** this one's on me; **auf ~ kaufen/bestellen** to buy/order on account; **laut ~ vom 5. Juli** as per our invoice of July 5th; **auf** or **für eigene ~** on one's own account; **(jdm) etw in ~ stellen** to charge (sb) for sth; **einer Sache** (*dat*) **~ tragen, etw in ~ ziehen** to take sth into account; **auf seine ~ kommen** to get one's money's worth; **aber er hatte die ~ ohne den Wirt gemacht** (*inf*) but there was one thing he hadn't reckoned with

Rechnungs-: Rechnungsabschluss M making-up of (the) accounts; **den ~ machen** to do the books; **Rechnungsart** F = **Rechenart; Rechnungsbetrag** M *siehe* Rechnung (b) (total) amount of a bill (*Brit*) or check (*US*)/invoice/account; **Rechnungseinheit** F unit of account; **Rechnungsjahr** NT financial or fiscal year; **Rechnungsposten** M invoice item; **Rechnungspreis** M invoice price; **Rechnungsprüfung** F audit; **Rechnungswesen** NT (*Führung*) accountancy; (*Prüfung*) auditing

recht [rɛçt] **1** ADJ (a) (= *richtig*) right; **es soll mir ~ sein, mir solls ~ sein** (*inf*) it's OK (*inf*) by me; **ganz ~!** quite right; **alles, was ~ ist** (*empört*) there is a limit; **hier geht es nicht mit ~en Dingen zu** there's something not right here; **ich habe keine ~e Lust** I don't particularly feel like it; **nichts Rechtes** no good; **aus dem Jungen kann nichts Rechtes werden** that boy will come to no good; **aus ihm ist nichts Rechtes geworden** (*beruflich etc*) he never really made it; **er hat nichts Rechtes gelernt** he didn't learn any real trade; **nach dem Rechten sehen** to see that everything's OK (*inf*); **was dem einen ~ ist, ist dem andern billig** (*Prov*) what's sauce for the goose is sauce for the gander (*Brit Prov*), what's good for the goose is good for the gander (*US Prov*)
(b) **~ haben/bekommen/behalten/geben** *siehe* Recht (d)
2 ADV (a) (= *richtig*) properly; (= *wirklich*) really; **verstehen Sie mich ~** don't get me wrong (*inf*); **wenn ich Sie ~ verstehe** if I understand you rightly; **sehe/höre ich ~?** am I seeing/hearing things?; **ich werde daraus nicht ~ klug** I can't really know what to make of it; **das geschieht ihm ~** it serves him right; **nun** or **jetzt mache ich es erst ~/erst ~ nicht** now I'm definitely/definitely not going to do it; **du kommst gerade ~, um ...** you're just in time to ...; **das ist** or **kommt mir gerade ~** (*inf*) that suits me fine; **du kommst mir gerade ~** (*iro*) you're all I needed; **gehe ich ~ in der Annahme, dass ...?** am I right in assuming that ...?; **man kann ihm nichts ~ machen** you can't do anything right for him; **man kann es nicht allen ~ machen** you can't please all of the people all of the time; **~ daran tun, zu ...** to be right to ...
(b) (= *ziemlich, ganz*) quite; **~ viel** quite a lot
(c) (= *sehr*) very; **~ herzlichen Dank!** thank you very much indeed

Recht [rɛçt] NT **-(e)s, -e** (a) (= *Rechtsordnung, sittliche Norm*) law; (= *Gerechtigkeit*) justice; **~ sprechen** to administer justice; **nach geltendem ~** in law; **nach englischem ~** under or according to English law; **das Schwurgericht hat für ~ erkannt ...** the court has reached the following verdict ...; **von ~s wegen** legally; (*inf*: = *eigentlich*) by rights (*inf*)
(b) **Rechte** PL (*form*: = *Rechtswissenschaft*) jurisprudence; **Doktor der** or **beider ~e** Doctor of Laws

(c) (= *Anspruch, Berechtigung*) right (*auf +acc* to, *zu* to); **ich nehme mir das ~, das zu tun** I shall make so bold as to do that; **sein ~ bekommen** *or* **erhalten** *or* **kriegen** (*inf*) to get what is one's by right; **zu seinem ~ kommen** (*lit*) to gain one's rights; (*fig*) to come into one's own; **auch das Vergnügen muss zu seinem ~ kommen** there has to be a place for pleasure too; **gleiches ~ für alle!** equal rights for all!; **mit** *or* **zu ~ rightly; Sie stellen diese Frage ganz zu ~** you are quite right to ask this question; **im ~ sein** to be in the right; **das ist mein gutes ~** it's my right; **es ist unser gutes ~, zu erfahren ...** we have every right to know ...; **mit welchem ~?** by what right? **(d) ~ haben** to be right; **er hat ~ bekommen** he was right; **~ behalten** to be right; **er will immer ~ behalten** he always has to be right; **ich hatte ~, und ich habe ~ behalten** I was right and I'm still right; **jdm ~ geben** to agree with sb, to admit that sb is right

Rechte ['rɛçtə] F DECL AS ADJ **(a)** (*Hand*) right hand; (*Seite*) right(-hand) side; (*Boxen*) right; **zur ~n (des Königs) saß ...** to the right (of the king) sat ... **(b)** (*Pol*) **die ~ the Right**

Recht-: Rechteck NT rectangle; **rechteckig** ADJ rectangular

rechte(r, s) ['rɛçtə] ADJ ATTR **(a)** right; *Rand, Spur etc auch* right-hand; **auf der ~n Seite** on the right-hand side; **jds ~ Hand sein** to be sb's right-hand man **(b) ein ~r Winkel** a right angle **(c)** (= *konservativ*) right-wing, rightist; **der ~ Flügel** the right wing **(d)** (*beim Stricken*) plain; **eine ~ Masche stricken** to knit one

rechtfertigen ['rɛçtfɛrtɪgn] INSEP **1** VT to justify **2** VR to justify oneself

Rechtfertigung F justification; **etw zur ~ vorbringen** to say sth to justify oneself

Recht-: Rechthaberei [rɛçthaːbəˈraɪ] F -, NO PL (*pej*) know-all (*Brit inf*) *or* know-it-all (*US inf*) attitude; **rechthaberisch** ['rɛçthaːbərɪʃ] **1** ADJ know-all *attr* (*Brit inf*), know-it-all *attr* (*US inf*) **2** ADV **~ bestand er darauf** he insisted on it in his self-opinionated way

rechtlich ['rɛçtlɪç] **1** ADJ (= *gesetzlich*) legal **2** ADV (= *gesetzlich*) legally; **~ zulässig** permissible in law; **~ unmöglich** impossible for legal reasons; **jdn ~ belangen** to take legal action against sb

Recht-: rechtmäßig **1** ADJ (= *legitim*) legitimate; (= *dem Gesetz entsprechend*) legal; **etw für ~ erklären** to legitimize sth; to declare sth legal **2** ADV legally; **jdm etw ~ zuerkennen** to recognize sb's legal right to sth; **jdm ~ zustehen** to belong to sb legally; **~ gewählt** legally elected; **Rechtmäßigkeit** ['rɛçtmɛːsɪçkaɪt] F -, NO PL (= *Legitimität*) legitimacy; (= *Legalität*) legality

rechts [rɛçts] **1** ADV **(a)** on the right; **nach ~** (to the) right; **von ~** from the right; **~ von etw** (on *or* to the) right of sth; **~ von jdm** to sb's right; (*Pol*) to the right of sb; **sich ~ einordnen** to move into the right-hand lane; **~ vor links** right before left (*rule of the priority system for driving*); **sich ~ halten** to keep to (the) right; **~ stehend** right-hand, on the right; (*Pol*) right-wing **(b) ~ stricken** to knit (plain); **ein ganz ~ gestrickter Pullover** a pullover knitted in garter stitch; **zwei ~, zwei links** (*beim Stricken*) knit two, purl two **2** PREP +GEN **~ des Rheins** on the right of the Rhine

Rechts- IN CPDS (*Jur*) legal; **Rechtsabbieger** M -s, -, **Rechtsabbiegerin** [-ərɪn] F -, -nen motorist/cyclist/car *etc* turning right; **Rechtsabbiegerspur** F right-hand turn-off lane; **Rechtsangelegenheit** F legal matter; **Rechtsanspruch** M legal right; **Rechtsanwalt** M, **Rechtsanwältin** F lawyer, attorney (*US*); (*als Berater auch*) solicitor (*Brit*), attorney (*US*); (*vor Gericht auch*) barrister (*Brit*), attorney (*US*); **sein ~ behauptete vor Gericht, ...** his counsel maintained in court ...; **Rechtsaußen** [-ˈʔaʊsn] M -, - (*Ftbl*) outside-right; (*Pol inf*) extreme right-winger; **Rechtsbeistand** M legal advice; (*Mensch*) legal adviser; **Rechtsberater(in)** M(F) legal adviser; **Rechtsberatung** F **(a)** legal advice (*Brit*) (*auch* **Rechtsberatungsstelle**) ≈ citizens' advice bureau (*Brit*), ≈ ACLU (*US*); **Rechtsbrecher(in)** M(F) lawbreaker; **rechtsbündig** (*Typ*) **1** ADJ right-aligned **2** ADV aligned right

rechtschaffen ['rɛçtʃafn] **1** ADJ (= *ehrlich, redlich*) honest **(b)** (*inf*: = *stark, groß*) **~en Durst/Hunger haben** to be really thirsty/hungry **2** ADV **(a)** (= *redlich*) honestly **(b)** (*inf*: = *sehr*) really; **sich ~ bemühen** to try really hard

rechtschreiben ['rɛçtʃraɪbn] VI INFIN ONLY to spell

Rechtschreib-: Rechtschreibfehler M spelling mistake; **Rechtschreibhilfe** F (*Comput*) spelling aid; **Rechtschreibkontrolle** F, **Rechtschreibprüfung** F (*Comput*) spell check; (= *Programm*) spellchecker; **Rechtschreibreform** F spelling reform

Rechtschreibung F spelling

Rechts-: Rechtsempfinden NT sense of justice; **Rechtsextremist(in)** M(F) right-wing extremist; **Rechtsfall** M court case; (*in der Rechtsgeschichte auch*) legal case; **Rechtsform** F legal form; **Rechtsfrage** F legal question *or* issue; **rechtsfrei** ADJ **~er Raum** unlegislated area; **Rechtsgeschäft** NT legal transaction; **Rechtsgrund** M legal justification; **Rechtsgrundlage** F legal basis; **rechtsgültig** ADJ legally valid, legal; **Rechtshänder** [-hɛndə] M -s, -; **Rechtshänderin** [-ərɪn] F -, -nen right-handed person, right-hander (*esp Sport*); **~ sein** to be right-handed; **rechtshändig** ADJ, ADV right-handed; **Rechtshandlung** F legal act; **Rechtshilfe** F (mutual) assistance in law enforcement; **Rechtshilfeabkommen** NT law enforcement treaty; **Rechtskraft** F, NO PL (*von Gesetz, Urteil*) legal force, force of law; (= *Gültigkeit*: *von Vertrag etc*) legal validity; **~ erlangen** (*Gesetz*) to become law; (*Urteil*) to come into force; **rechtskräftig** **1** ADJ having the force of law; *Urteil* final; *Vertrag* legally valid; **~ sein/werden** (*Verordnung*) to have the force of law/to become law; (*Urteil*) to be/become final; (*Gesetz*) to be in/come into force **2** ADV **~ verurteilt sein** to be issued with a final sentence; **rechtskundig** ADJ familiar with the law; **Rechtskurve** F right-hand bend; **Rechtslage** F legal position; **rechtslastig** [-lastɪç] ADJ listing to the right; *Auto auch* down at the right; (*fig*) leaning to the right; **~ sein** to list to/be down at/lean to the right; **Rechtsmittel** NT means *sing* of legal redress; **~ einlegen** to lodge an appeal; **auf ~ verzichten** to relinquish one's right to appeal; **Rechtsmittelbelehrung** F statement of rights of redress; **Rechtsordnung** F **eine ~** a system of laws; **die ~** the law; **die staatliche ~** state laws *pl*; **Rechtspflege** F administration of justice

Rechtsprechung ['rɛçtʃprɛçʊŋ] F -, -en **(a)** (= *Rechtspflege*) administration of justice; (= *Gerichtsbarkeit*) jurisdiction **(b)** (= *richterliche Tätigkeit*) administering of justice **(c)** (= *bisherige Urteile*) precedents *pl*

Rechts-: rechtsradikal **1** ADJ radical right-wing; **die Rechtsradikalen** the right-wing radicals **2** ADV **~ eingestellt sein** to be a right-wing radical; **~ klingen** to sound radically right-wing; **Rechtsreferendar(in)** M(F) articled clerk (*Brit*), legal intern (*US*); **~ sein** to be under articles (*Brit*), to be a legal intern (*US*); **rechtsrheinisch** ADJ on the right of the Rhine; **Rechtsruck** M, **Rechtsrutsch** M (*Pol*) swing to the right; **Rechtssache** F legal matter; (= *Fall*) case; **Rechtsschutz** M legal protection; **Rechtsschutzversicherung** F legal costs insurance; **rechtsseitig** [-zaɪtɪç] ADJ, ADV on the right(-hand) side; **~ gelähmt** paralyzed on the right side; **~ blind** blind in the right eye; **Rechtsspruch** M verdict; **Rechtsstaat** M state under the rule of law; **rechtsstaatlich** ADJ of a state under the rule of law; **~e Ordnung** law and order; **seine ~e Gesinnung** his predisposition for law and order; **rechtsstehend** ADJ ATTR *siehe* **rechts**; **Rechtsstellung** F legal position; **Rechtssteuerung** F right-hand drive; **Rechtsstreit** M lawsuit; **Rechtstitel** M legal title

rechtsuchend ADJ ATTR seeking justice

Rechts-: Rechtsunsicherheit F legal uncertainty; **rechtsverbindlich** **1** ADJ legally binding; *Auskunft* legally valid **2** ADV **~ festgelegt** laid down so as to be legally binding; **Rechtsverdreher** [-fɛːdreːɐ] M -s, -, **Rechtsverdreherin** [-ərɪn] F -, -nen (*pej*) shyster (*inf*); (*hum inf*) legal eagle (*inf*); **Rechtsverkehr** M driving on the right *no def art*; **in Deutschland ist ~** in Germany they drive on the right; **im ~ muss man ...** when driving on the right one must ...; **Rechtsvertreter(in)** M(F) legal representative; **Rechtsweg** M legal action; **den ~ beschreiten** *or* **einschlagen** to take legal action; **auf dem ~** by taking legal action; **unter Ausschluss des ~es** without possibility of recourse to legal action; **der ~ ist ausgeschlossen** ≈ the judges' decision is final; **rechtswidrig** **1** ADJ illegal **2** ADV illegally; **Rechtswidrigkeit** F **(a)** NO PL illegality **(b)** (*Handlung*) illegal act; **Rechtswissenschaft** F jurisprudence

Recht-: rechtwinkelig, rechtwinklig ADJ right-angled; **rechtzeitig** **1** ADJ (= *früh genug*) timely; (= *pünktlich*)

punctual; **um ~e Anmeldung wird gebeten** you are requested to apply in good time **2** ADV (= *früh genug*) in (good) time; (= *pünktlich*) on time; **gerade noch ~ ankommen** to arrive just in time

Reck [rɛk] NT **-(e)s, -e** (*Sport*) horizontal bar

recken ['rɛkn̩] **1** VT (= *aus-, emporstrecken*) to stretch; **den Kopf** *or* **Hals ~** to crane one's neck; **die Arme in die Höhe ~** to raise one's arms in the air **2** VR to stretch (oneself); **sich ~ und strecken** to have a good stretch

Recorder [re'kɔrdɐ] M **-s, -** *siehe* **Rekorder**

recycelbar [riː'saɪkəlbaːɐ] ADJ recyclable

recyceln [riː'saɪkl̩n], *ptp* **recycelt** [riː'saɪkl̩t] VT to recycle

Recycling [riː'saɪklɪŋ] NT **-s**, NO PL recycling

Recycling- [riː'saɪklɪŋ-]: **Recyclinghof** M transfer facility for recyclable waste; **Recyclingpapier** NT recycled paper; **Recyclingwerk** NT recycling plant

Redakteur [redak'tøːɐ] M **-s, -e**, **Redakteurin** [-'tøːrɪn] F **-, -nen** editor

Redaktion [redak'tsioːn] F **-, -en (a)** (= *das Redigieren*) editing; **die ~ dieses Buches hatte ...** this book was edited by ...; **~: XY** editor: XY **(b)** (= *Personal*) editorial staff **(c)** (= *Büro*) editorial office(s)

redaktionell [redaktsio'nɛl] **1** ADJ editorial; **die ~e Leitung im Ressort Wirtschaft hat Herr Müller** Mr Müller is the editor responsible for business and finance **2** ADV *überarbeiten* editorially; **ein Projekt ~ betreuen** to be the editor of a project; **etw ~ bearbeiten** to edit sth

Redaktionsschluss M time of going to press; (= *Einsendeschluss*) copy deadline; **bei ~** at the time of going to press; **diese Nachricht ist vor/nach ~ eingegangen** this news item arrived before/after the paper went to press *or* bed (*inf*)

Redaktor [re'daktoːɐ] M **-s, Redaktoren** [-'toːrən], **Redaktorin** [-'toːrɪn] F **-, -nen** (*Sw*) editor

Redaktrice [redak'triːsə] F **-, -n** (*Aus*) editor

Rede ['reːdə] F **-, -n (a)** speech; (= *Ansprache*) address; **eine ~ halten** *or* **schwingen** (*inf*) to make a speech; **der langen ~ kurzer Sinn** (*prov*) the long and the short of it; **direkte** *or* **wörtliche/indirekte ~** (*Ling, Liter*) direct/indirect speech *or* discourse (*US*)

(b) (= *Äußerungen, Worte*) words *pl*, language *no pl*; **seine frechen ~n** his cheek (*Brit*) *or* impudence; **große ~n führen** *or* **schwingen** (*inf*) to talk big (*inf*); **das ist meine ~!** that's what I've always said; **das ist nicht der ~ wert** it's not worth mentioning; **(es ist) nicht der ~ wert!** don't mention it **(c)** (= *das Reden, Gespräch*) conversation; **es war von einer Gehaltserhöhung die ~** there was talk of a salary increase; **aber davon war doch nie die ~** but no-one was ever talking about that; **von einer Gehaltserhöhung kann keine** *or* **kann nicht die ~ sein** there can be no question of a salary increase; **davon kann keine** *or* **kann nicht die ~ sein** it's out of the question

(d) (= *Gerücht, Nachrede*) rumour (*Brit*), rumor (*US*); **kümmere dich doch nicht um die ~n der Leute!** don't worry (about) what people say

(e) (= *Rechenschaft*) **(jdm) ~ (und Antwort) stehen** to justify oneself (to sb); **(jdm) für etw ~ und Antwort stehen** to account (to sb) for sth; **jdn zur ~ stellen** to take sb to task

Rede-: **Redefreiheit** F freedom of speech; **redegewandt** ADJ eloquent

reden ['reːdn̩] **1** VI **(a)** (= *sprechen*) to talk, to speak; **Reden während des Unterrichts** talking in class; **mit sich selbst/jdm ~** to talk to oneself/sb; **wie red(e)st du denn mit deiner Mutter!** that's no way to talk *or* speak to your mother; **so lasse ich nicht mit mir ~!** I won't be spoken to like that!; **mit jdm über jdn/etw ~** to talk to sb about sb/sth; **(viel) von sich ~ machen** to become (very much) a talking point; **das Buch/ er macht viel von sich ~** everyone is talking about the book/ him; **du hast gut** *or* **leicht ~!** it's all very well for you (to talk); **ich habe mit Ihnen zu ~!** I would like a word with you; **ich rede gegen eine Wand** *or* **Mauer** it's like talking to a brick wall (*inf*); **darüber lässt** *or* **ließe sich ~** that's a possibility; (*über Preis, Bedingungen*) I think we could discuss that; **darüber lässt** *or* **ließe sich eher ~** that's more like it; **er lässt mit sich ~** he could be persuaded; (*in Bezug auf Preis*) he's open to offers; (= *gesprächsbereit*) he's open to discussion; **sie lässt nicht mit sich ~** she is adamant; **Reden ist Silber, Schweigen**

ist Gold (*Prov*) (speech is silver but) silence is golden (*Prov*); **das ist ja mein Reden (seit 33)** (*inf*) I've been saying that for (donkey's (*Brit inf*)) years; *siehe* **Wasserfall**

(b) (= *klatschen*) to talk (*über* +*acc* about); **schlecht von jdm ~** to speak ill of sb; **in so einem Dorf wird natürlich viel geredet** in a village like that naturally people talk a lot

(c) (= *eine Rede halten*) to speak; **er redet nicht gerne öffentlich** he doesn't like public speaking; **er kann gut ~** he is a good speaker; **frei ~** to speak without notes

2 VT **(a)** (= *sagen*) to talk; *Worte* to say; **sich** (*dat*) **etw von der Seele** *or* **vom Herzen ~** to get sth off one's chest

(b) (= *klatschen*) to say; **Schlechtes von jdm** *or* **über jdn ~** to say bad things about sb; **damit die Leute wieder was zu ~ haben** so that people have something to talk about again

3 VR **sich heiser ~** to talk oneself hoarse; **sich in Zorn** *or* **Wut ~** to talk oneself into a fury

Redensart F (= *Phrase*) cliché; (= *Redewendung*) expression; (= *Sprichwort*) saying; (= *leere Versprechung*) empty promise; **das ist nur so eine ~** it's just a way of speaking

Redenschreiber(in) M(F) speechwriter

Rede-: **Redeverbot** NT ban on speaking; **jdm ~ erteilen** to ban sb from speaking; **(allgemeines) ~!** (= *keine Gespräche erlaubt*) no talking!; **Redewendung** F idiom

redigieren [redi'giːrən], *ptp* **redigiert** VT to edit

Rediskont M rediscounting

redlich ['reːtlɪç] **1** ADJ honest **2** ADV **(a)** (= *ehrlich*) honestly; **er meint es ~** he is being honest; **sich** (*dat*) **etw ~ verdient haben** to have really earned sth; *Geld, Gut* to have acquired sth by honest means; **~ (mit jdm) teilen** to share (things) equally (with sb) **(b)** (= *ziemlich*) really

Redlichkeit F **-**, NO PL honesty

Redner ['reːdnɐ] M **-s, -**, **Rednerin** [-ərɪn] F **-, -nen** speaker; (= *Rhetoriker*) orator; **ich bin kein (großer) ~** I'm not much of a speaker

rednerisch ['reːdnərɪʃ] **1** ADJ rhetorical; **~e Begabung** talent for public speaking **2** ADV rhetorically

Rednerpult NT lectern

redselig ['reːtzeːlɪç] ADJ talkative

Reduktion [redʊk'tsioːn] F **-, -en** reduction

redundant [redʊn'dant] **1** ADJ redundant (*auch Comput*) **2** ADV *schreiben* redundantly; **er drückt sich ~ aus** a lot of what he says is redundant

Redundanz [redʊn'dants] F **-, -en** redundancy

reduzieren [redu'tsiːrən], *ptp* **reduziert** **1** VT to reduce (*auf* +*acc* to) **2** VR to decrease

Reede ['reːdə] F **-, -n** (*Naut*) roads *pl*; **auf der ~ liegen** to be (lying) in the roads

Reeder ['reːdɐ] M **-s, -**, **Reederin** [-ərɪn] F **-, -en** shipowner

Reederei [reːdə'raɪ] F **-, -en** shipping company

reell [re'ɛl] **1** ADJ **(a)** (= *ehrlich*) honest, on the level (*inf*); (*Comm*) *Geschäft, Firma* sound; *Preis* fair; *Bedienung* good; **das ist etwas Reelles!** it's pretty much on the level! (*inf*) **(b)** (= *wirklich, echt*) *Chance* real **(c)** (*Math*) *Zahlen* real **2** ADV (= *tatsächlich*) when it comes down to it; (= *nicht betrügerisch*) on the level (*inf*)

Reet [reːt] NT **-s**, NO PL (*N Ger*) reed

Reetdach NT thatched roof

Reexport M re-export

Referat [refe'raːt] NT **-(e)s, -e (a)** (*Univ*) seminar paper; (*Sch*) project; (= *Vortrag*) paper; **ein ~ vortragen** *or* **halten** to give a paper/to present a project **(b)** (*Admin*: = *Ressort*) department

Referendar [referen'daːɐ] M **-s, -e**, **Referendarin** [-'daːrɪn] F **-, -nen** trainee (in civil service); (= *Studienreferendar*) student teacher; (= *Gerichtsreferendar*) articled clerk (*Brit*), legal intern (*US*)

Referendare are candidates for a higher civil-service post who are undergoing practical training. These might, for example, be prospective *Gymnasium* teachers who have already taken the first *Staatsexamen* and are now doing two years of teaching experience. At the end of the *Referendar* period they take the second *Staatsexamen*, and only then is their teacher training complete ▶ GYMNASIUM, STAATSEXAMEN

Referendarzeit F traineeship; (= *Studienreferendarzeit*) teacher training; (= *Gerichtsreferendarzeit*) time under articles (*Brit*), legal internship (*US*)

Referendum [refe'rɛndʊm] NT **-s, Referenden** *or* **Referenda** [-dn, -da] referendum

Referent [refe'rɛnt] M **-en, -en, Referentin** [-'rɛntɪn] F **-, -nen** (= *Sachbearbeiter*) expert; (= *Redner, Berichterstatter*) speaker

Referenz [refe'rɛnts] F **-, -en** reference (*auch Comput*); **jdn als ~ angeben** to give sb as a referee

referieren [refe'ri:rən], *ptp* **referiert** VI to (give a) report (*über +acc* on)

Reflation [re:fla'tsio:n] F **-, -en** reflation

reflektieren [reflɛk'ti:rən], *ptp* **reflektiert** ■ VT **(a)** (*lit, fig*: *widerspiegeln*) to reflect **(b)** (*überdenken*) to reflect on ■ VI **(a)** (*Phys*) to reflect **(b)** (= *nachdenken*) to reflect (*über +acc* (up)on); **auf etw** (*acc*) **~** to be interested in sth

Reflex [re'flɛks] M **-es, -e (a)** (*Phys*) reflection **(b)** (*Physiol*) reflex **(c)** (*Soziol*) reflection

Reflexbewegung F reflex action

reflexiv [reflɛ'ksi:f] (*Gram*) ■ ADJ reflexive ■ ADV reflexively

Reflexivpronomen NT reflexive pronoun

Reflexzonenmassage F reflexology

Reform [re'fɔrm] F **-, -en** reform

Reformation [refɔrma'tsio:n] F **-, -en** Reformation

Reformator [refɔr'ma:to:ɐ] M **-s, Reformatoren** [-'to:rən], **Reformatorin** [-'to:rɪn] F **-, -nen** Reformer

reformatorisch [refɔrma'to:rɪʃ] ADJ (= *reformierend*) reforming; (= *aus der Zeit der Reformation*) Reformation *attr*

Reform-: reformbedürftig ADJ in need of reform; **Reformbestrebungen** PL striving for reform; **Reformhaus** NT health-food shop

---

REFORMHAUS

Reformhaus sells everything for a healthy diet and lifestyle, including Reformkost (natural foodstuffs without chemical additives), health products such as essential oils and natural bath salts, and medicinal herbs. The first Reformhäuser were established as early as 1890 out of a desire to encourage healthy living. Nowadays, however, they have to contend with competition from the Bioläden ▶ BIOLADEN

---

reformieren [refɔr'mi:rən], *ptp* **reformiert** VT to reform

reformiert [refɔr'mi:ɐt] ADJ (*Eccl*) Reformed

Reform-: Reformkurs M policy of reform; **einen ~ steuern** to follow a policy of reform; **Reformplan** M plan for reform; **Reformstau** M (*Pol*) reform bottleneck

Refrain [rə'frɛ̃:, re-] M **-s, -s** (*Mus*) chorus

Regal [re'ga:l] NT **-s, -e (a)** (= *Bord*) shelves *pl* **(b)** (*Mus*) (= *tragbare Orgel*) regal; (*Orgelteil*) vox humana

Regatta [re'gata] F **-, Regatten** [-tn] regatta

Reg. Bez. ABBR *von* Regierungsbezirk

rege ['re:gə] ■ ADJ **(a)** (= *betriebsam*) busy; *Handel* flourishing; *Briefwechsel* lively; **ein ~s Treiben** a hustle and bustle; *Tendenz ~* (*St Ex*) brisk activity **(b)** (= *lebhaft*) lively; *Fantasie* vivid; **ein ~r Geist** a lively soul; (= *Verstand*) an active mind; **körperlich und geistig ~ sein** to be active in mind and body; **noch sehr ~ sein** to be very active still; **~ Beteiligung** lively participation; (*zahlreich*) good turnout **(c)** (= *zahlreich*) numerous; (= *häufig*) frequent; **~r Besuch** high attendance ■ ADV (= *lebhaft*) **das Museum wurde nach der Eröffnung ~ besucht** when it opened the museum was very well visited; **sich ~ an etw** (*dat*) **beteiligen** to actively take part in sth

Regel ['re:gl] F **-, -n (a)** (= *Vorschrift, Norm*) rule; (= *Verordnung*) regulation; **nach allen ~n der Kunst** (*fig*) thoroughly; **sie überredete ihn nach allen ~n der Kunst, ...** she used every trick in the book to persuade him ... **(b)** (= *Gewohnheit*) habit; **sich** (*dat*) **etw zur ~ machen** to make a habit of sth; **in der** *or* **aller ~** as a rule; **zur ~ werden** to become a habit **(c)** (= *Monatsblutung*) period; **die ~ haben/bekommen** to have/get one's period

Regel-: Regelarbeitszeit F core working hours *pl*; **Regelfall** M rule; **im ~** as a rule; **regelmäßig** ■ ADJ regular ■ ADV **(a)** (*in gleichmäßiger Folge*) regularly; **das Herz schlägt ~** the heartbeat is normal; **sein Herz schlägt wieder ~er** his

heartbeat is more regular now; **etw ~ jeden Tag tun** to do sth every day; **~ spazieren gehen** to take regular walks **(b)** (= *andauernd*) always; **er kommt ~ zu spät** he's always late; **Regelmäßigkeit** ['re:glmɛ:sɪçkait] F **-,** NO PL regularity; **er kommt mit sturer ~ zu spät** he is persistently late; **in** *or* **mit schöner ~** as regular as clockwork

regeln ['re:gln] ■ VT **(a)** (= *regulieren*) *Prozess, Vorgang, Temperatur* to regulate; *Verkehr* to control; *siehe auch* **geregelt (b)** (= *erledigen*) to see to; *Problem etc* to sort out; (= *in Ordnung bringen*) *Unstimmigkeiten, Nachlass* to settle; *Finanzen* to put in order; *Finanzierung* to deal with; **das werde ich schon ~** I'll see to it; **wir haben die Sache so geregelt ...** we have arranged things like this ...; **dieses Gesetz regelt ...** this law deals with ...; **gesetzlich geregelt sein** to be laid down by law ■ VR to sort itself out

Regel-: regelrecht ■ ADJ real; *Betrug, Erpressung, Beleidigung etc* downright; **das Spiel artete in eine ~e Schlägerei aus** the match degenerated into a regular brawl ■ ADV really; *unverschämt, beleidigend* downright; (= *buchstäblich*) literally; **Regelstudienzeit** F *period of time within which a student should complete his studies*

Regelung ['re:gəlʊŋ] F **-, -en (a)** (= *Regulierung*) regulation **(b)** (= *Erledigung*) settling; (*von Unstimmigkeiten*) resolution; **ich habe die ~ meiner finanziellen Angelegenheiten meinem Bruder übertragen** I have entrusted my brother with the management of my financial affairs; **ich werde für die ~ dieser Angelegenheit sorgen** I shall see to this matter **(c)** (= *Abmachung*) arrangement; (= *Bestimmung*) ruling; **gesetzliche ~en** legal *or* statutory regulations

Regel-: regelwidrig ■ ADJ against the rules; (= *gegen Verordnungen verstoßend*) against the regulations; **~es Verhalten im Verkehr** breaking the traffic regulations ■ ADV **~ spielen** to infringe the rules; (= *foulen*) to commit a foul; **Regelwidrigkeit** F irregularity

regen ['re:gn] ■ VT (= *bewegen*) to move; **keinen Finger (mehr) ~** (*fig*) not to lift a finger (any more) ■ VR to stir; **unter den Zuhörern regte sich Widerspruch** there were mutterings of disapproval from the audience; **er kann sich nicht/kaum ~** he is not/hardly able to move

Regen ['re:gn] M **-s, -** rain; (*fig: von Schimpfwörtern, Blumen etc*) shower; **in** *or* **bei strömendem ~** in the pouring rain; **bei ~ entfällt das Konzert** if it rains the concert will be cancelled (*esp Brit*) *or* canceled (*US*); **ein warmer ~** (*fig*) a windfall; **jdn im ~ stehen lassen** (*fig*) to leave sb out in the cold; **vom ~ in die Traufe kommen** (*prov*) to jump out of the frying pan into the fire (*prov*)

Regenbogen M rainbow

Regenbogen-: Regenbogenforelle F rainbow trout; **Regenbogenpresse** F trashy (*inf*) magazines *pl*

Regeneration [regenera'tsio:n] F regeneration

regenerieren [regene'ri:rən], *ptp* **regeneriert** ■ VR (*Biol*) to regenerate; (*fig*) to revitalize oneself/itself; (*nach Anstrengung, Schock etc*) to recover ■ VT (*Biol*) to regenerate; (*fig auch*) to revitalize

Regen-: Regenfall M USU PL (fall of) rain; **ein ~** rain, a shower; **tropische Regenfälle** tropical rains; **heftige Regenfälle** heavy rain; **Regenguss** M downpour; **Regenkleidung** F rainwear; **Regenmantel** M raincoat, mac (*Brit inf*); **Regenrinne** F gutter; **Regenschauer** M shower (of rain); **Regenschirm** M umbrella

Regent [re'gɛnt] M **-en, -en, Regentin** [-'gɛntɪn] F **-, -nen** sovereign; (= *Stellvertreter*) regent

Regen-: Regentag M rainy day; **Regentonne** F rain barrel; **Regentropfen** M raindrop

Regentschaft [re'gɛntʃaft] F **-, -en** reign; (= *Stellvertretung*) regency

Regen-: Regenwald M (*Geog*) rain forest; **Regenwasser** NT, NO PL rainwater; **Regenwetter** NT rainy weather; **er macht ein Gesicht wie drei** *or* **sieben Tage ~** (*inf*) he's got a face as long as a month of Sundays (*inf*); **Regenwurm** M earthworm; **Regenzeit** F rainy season

Regie [re'ʒi:] F **-, NO PL (a)** (= *künstlerische Leitung*) direction; (*Theat, Rad, TV*) production; **die ~ bei etw haben** *or* **führen** to direct/produce sth; (*fig*) to be in charge of sth; **unter der ~ von** directed/produced by; **„~: A.G. Meier"** "Director/ Producer A.G. Meier" **(b)** (= *Leitung, Verwaltung*) management; **unter jds ~** (*dat*) under sb's control; **etw in eigener ~ tun** to do sth oneself

regieren [re'giːrən], *ptp* **regiert** ◼ VI (= *herrschen*) to rule; (*Monarch auch, fig*) to reign; **der Regierende Bürgermeister von Berlin** the Mayor of Berlin ◼ VT (= *beherrschen, lenken*) *Staat* to rule (over); (*Monarch auch*) to reign over; (*Gram*) to govern; **SPD-regierte Länder** states governed by the SPD

Regierung [re'giːrʊŋ] F **-, -en (a)** (= *Kabinett*) government; **die ~ Blair** the Blair government **(b)** (= *Herrschaft*) government; (= *Zeitabschnitt*) period of government; (*nicht demokratisch*) rule; (*von Monarch*) reign; (= *Führung*) leadership; **an die ~ kommen** to come to power; (*durch Wahl auch*) to come into office; **jdn an die ~ bringen** to put sb into power; **die ~ antreten** to take power

Regierungs-: Regierungsantritt M coming to power; (*nach Wahl auch*) taking of office; **bei ~** when the government took power/office; **Regierungsbezirk** M *primary administrative division of a Land*, ≈ region (*Brit*), ≈ county (*US*); **Regierungschef(in)** M(F) head of a/the government; **der belgische ~** the head of the Belgian government; **Regierungserklärung** F inaugural speech; (*in GB*) King's/Queen's Speech; **regierungsfeindlich** ◼ ADJ anti-government *no adv* ◼ ADV **sich ~ verhalten/äußern** to act/speak against the government; **Regierungsform** F form of government; **Regierungskreise** PL government circles *pl*; **Regierungskrise** F government(al) crisis; **regierungsnah** ADJ *Kreise* close to the government; *Zeitung* pro-government; **Regierungssitz** M seat of government; **Regierungssprecher(in)** M(F) government spokesperson; **Regierungsumbildung** F cabinet reshuffle; **Regierungswechsel** M change of government; **Regierungszeit** F rule; (*von Monarch auch*) reign; (*von gewählter Regierung, Präsident*) period or term of office

Regime [re'ʒiːm] NT **-s, -s** (*pej*) regime

Regime-: Regimegegner(in) M(F) opponent of the regime; **Regimekritiker(in)** M(F) critic of the regime

Regiment [regi'ment] NT **-(e)s, -e** or (*Einheit*) **-er (a)** (*old*: = *Herrschaft*) rule; **das ~ führen** (*inf*) to be the boss (*inf*); **ein strenges** or **straffes ~ führen** (*inf*) to be strict **(b)** (*Mil*) regiment

Region [re'gioːn] F **-, -en** region

regional [regio'naːl] ◼ ADJ regional ◼ ADV regionally; **~ verschieden** or **unterschiedlich sein** to vary from one region to another

Regionalismus [regionaˈlɪsmʊs] M **-, Regionalismen** [-mən] regionalism

Regisseur [reʒɪˈsøːɐ] M **-s, -e, Regisseurin** [-ˈsøːrɪn] F **-, -nen** director; (*Theat, Rad, TV*) producer

Register [reˈɡɪstɐ] NT **-s, - (a)** (= *amtliche Liste*) register **(b)** (= *Stichwortverzeichnis*) index **(c)** (*Mus*) register; (*von Orgel*) stop; **alle ~ ziehen** or **spielen lassen** (*fig*) to pull out all the stops

Registertonne F (*Naut*) register ton

Registrierballon M (*Met*) sounding balloon

registrieren [rɛɡɪsˈtriːrən], *ptp* **registriert** VT **(a)** (= *erfassen*) to register; (= *zusammenzählen*) to calculate; **amtlich registriert** officially registered; **sie ist registriert** (*als Prostituierte*) she is a registered prostitute **(b)** (= *feststellen*) to note; **sie hat überhaupt nicht registriert, dass ich nicht da war** the fact that I wasn't there didn't register with her at all

Registrierkasse F cash register

Registrierung F **-, -en** registration

reglementieren [reglemenˈtiːrən], *ptp* **reglementiert** VT to regulate; *jdn* to regiment; **staatlich reglementiert** state-regulated

Regler [ˈreːglɐ] M **-s, -** regulator; (*an Fernseher, Stereoanlage etc*) control; (*von Elektromotor, Fernsteuerung*) control(ler); (*von Benzinmotor*) governor

reglos [ˈreːkloːs] ADJ, ADV motionless

regnen [ˈreːɡnən] VTI IMPERS to rain; **es regnet Glückwünsche/Proteste** congratulations/protests are pouring in; **es regnete Vorwürfe** reproaches hailed down

regnerisch [ˈreːɡnərɪʃ] ADJ *Wetter, Tag* rainy

Regress [reˈgrɛs] M **-es, -e** (*Jur*) recourse; **~ anmelden** to seek recourse; **einen ~ auf jdn** or **an jdm nehmen, jdn in ~ nehmen** to have recourse against sb

Regress-: Regressanspruch M (*Jur*) claim for compensation; **Regresspflicht** F liability for compensation; **regresspflichtig** [-pflɪçtɪç] ADJ liable for compensation

regulär [reguˈlɛːɐ] ◼ ADJ (= *üblich*) normal; (= *vorschriftsmäßig*) proper; *Arbeitszeit* normal; **~e Truppen** regular troops; **die ~e Spielzeit** (*Sport*) normal time ◼ ADV (= *zum normalen Preis*) normally; **etw ~ kaufen/verkaufen** (= *zum normalen Preis*) to buy/sell sth at the normal price; (= *auf normale Weise*) to buy/sell sth in the normal way

regulieren [reguˈliːrən], *ptp* **reguliert** VT (= *einstellen*) to regulate; (= *nachstellen*) to adjust

Regulierung F **-, -en** regulation; (= *Nachstellung*) adjustment

Regulierungsbehörde F regulatory body

Regung [ˈreːɡʊŋ] F **-, -en** (= *Bewegung*) movement; (*des Gefühls, des Gewissens, von Mitleid*) stirring; **ohne jede ~** without a flicker (of emotion); **zu keiner ~ fähig sein** (*fig*) to be paralyzed; **eine menschliche ~ verspüren** (*hum*) to have to answer a call of nature (*hum*)

regungslos ADJ, ADV motionless

Reh [reː] NT **-s, -e** deer; (*im Gegensatz zu Hirsch etc*) roe deer; **scheu wie ein ~** (as) timid as a fawn

Reha- [ˈreːha] IN CPDS ABBR *von* **Rehabilitations-**

Rehabilitation [rehabilitaˈtsioːn] F rehabilitation; (*von Ruf, Ehre*) vindication

Rehabilitations-: Rehabilitationsklinik F rehabilitation clinic; **Rehabilitationszentrum** NT rehabilitation centre (*Brit*) or center (*US*)

rehabilitieren [rehabiliˈtiːrən], *ptp* **rehabilitiert** ◼ VT to rehabilitate ◼ VR to rehabilitate oneself

Reh-: Rehbock M roebuck; **Rehbraten** M roast venison; **Rehleder** NT deerskin; **Rehrücken** M (*Cook*) saddle of venison

Reibach [ˈraɪbax] M **-s**, NO PL (*inf*) killing (*inf*); **einen ~** or **den großen ~ machen** (*inf*) to make a killing (*inf*)

Reibe [ˈraɪbə] F **-, -n** (*Cook*) grater

Reibeisen NT rasp; (*Cook*) grater

Reibe-: Reibekuchen M (*Cook dial*) ≈ potato fritter; **Reibelaut** M (*Ling*) fricative

reiben [ˈraɪbn̩], *pret* **rieb** [riːp], *ptp* **gerieben** [gəˈriːbn̩] ◼ VT **(a)** (= *frottieren*) to rub; **etw blank ~** to rub sth till it shines; **sich** (*dat*) **die Augen (vor Müdigkeit) ~** to rub one's eyes (because one is tired) **(b)** (= *zerkleinern*) to grate ◼ VI **(a)** (= *frottieren*) to rub; **an etw** (*dat*) **~** to rub sth **(b)** (= *zerkleinern*) to grate ◼ VR to rub oneself (*an +dat* on, against); (= *sich verletzen*) to scrape oneself (*an +dat* on); **ich würde mich ständig an ihm ~** there would always be friction between him and me; **sich an etw** (*dat*) **wund ~** to rub oneself raw on sth

Reiberei [raɪbəˈraɪ] F **-, -en** USU PL (*inf*) friction *no pl*; (*kleinere*) **~en** (short) periods of friction; **ihre ständigen ~en** the constant friction between them

Reibung [ˈraɪbʊŋ] F **-, -en (a)** (= *das Reiben*) rubbing; (*Phys*) friction **(b)** (*fig*) friction *no pl*

Reibungs-: reibungslos ◼ ADJ frictionless; (*fig inf*) trouble-free ◼ ADV (= *problemlos*) smoothly; **~ verlaufen** to go off smoothly; **Reibungswiderstand** M (*Phys*) frictional resistance

reich [raɪç] ◼ ADJ **(a)** (= *vermögend, wohlhabend*) rich; *Erbschaft* substantial; *Partie, Heirat* good **(b)** (= *kostbar*) costly *no adv* **(c)** (= *ergiebig, üppig*) rich, copious; *Mahl* sumptuous; **~ an etw** (*dat*) **sein** to be rich in sth; **~ an Fischen/Wild/Steinen** full of fish/game/stones; **er ist ~ an Erfahrungen** he has had a wealth of experiences **(d)** (= *groß, vielfältig*) copious; *Auswahl, Erfahrungen, Kenntnisse* wide; *Blattwerk, Vegetation* luxuriant; **in ~em Maße vorhanden sein** to abound ◼ ADV **(a)** (= *wohlhabend*) **~ heiraten** (*inf*) to marry (into) money **(b)** (= *großzügig*) **jdn ~ belohnen** to reward sb well; **damit bin ich ~ belohnt** (*fig*) I am richly rewarded; **jdn ~ beschenken** to shower sb with presents; **eine mit Kindern ~ beschenkte Familie** a family blessed with many children **(c)** (*~haltig*) richly; **eine ~ ausgestattete Bibliothek** a well-stocked library; **~ illustriert** richly illustrated

Reich [raɪç] NT **-(e)s, -e (a)** (= *Herrschaft(sgebiet), Imperium*) empire; (= *Königreich*) realm; **das Deutsche ~** the German

Reich; (*bis 1918 auch*) the German Empire; **das Dritte ~** the Third Reich **(b)** (= *Bereich, Gebiet*) realm; **das ~ der Tiere/ Pflanzen** the animal/vegetable kingdom; **das ist mein ~** (*fig*) that is my domain; **da bin ich in meinem ~** that's where I'm in my element

reichen ['raɪçn] **1** VI **(a)** (= *sich erstrecken*) to reach (*bis zu etw* sth); **sein Swimmingpool reicht bis an mein Grundstück** his swimming pool comes right up to my land; **der Garten reicht bis ans Ufer** the garden stretches right down to the riverbank; **das Wasser reicht mir bis zum Hals** (*lit*) the water comes up to my neck; **so weit der Himmel reichte** in the whole sky; **das Spektrum reicht von der Volksmusik bis zum Jazz** the spectrum ranges from folk music to jazz; **so weit ~ meine Beziehungen nicht** my connections are not that extensive; **so weit ~ meine Fähigkeiten nicht** my skills are not that wide-ranging

(b) (= *langen*) to be enough; **der Saal reicht nicht für so viele Leute** the room isn't big enough for so many people; **der Zucker reicht nicht** there won't be enough sugar; **reicht mein Geld noch bis zum Monatsende?** will my money last until the end of the month?; **reicht das Licht zum Lesen?** is there enough light to read by?; **dazu ~ meine Fähigkeiten nicht** I'm not skilled enough for that; **das muss für vier Leute ~** that will have to do (*inf*) for four people; **mir reichts** (*inf*) (= *habe die Nase voll*) I've had enough (*inf*); (= *habe genug gehabt*) that's enough for me; **als das dann noch passierte, reichte es ihm** when that happened it was just too much for him; **jetzt reichts (mir aber)!** that's the last straw!; (= *Schluss!*) that's enough!; **es reichte ja schon, dass er faul war** it was bad enough that he was lazy

2 VT (= *entgegenhalten*) to hand; (= *anbieten*) to serve; **jdm die Hand ~** to hold out one's hand to sb; (*fig*) to extend the hand of friendship to sb; **sich die Hände ~** to join hands; (*zur Begrüßung*) to shake hands

Reiche(r) ['raɪçə] MF DECL AS ADJ rich man/woman; **die ~n** the rich

reichhaltig ADJ extensive; *Auswahl, Angebot auch* wide, large; *Essen* rich; *Informationen* comprehensive; *Programm* varied

reichlich ['raɪçlɪç] **1** ADJ **(a)** (= *sehr viel, groß*) ample, large; *Vorrat* plentiful; *Portion, Trinkgeld* generous; *Alkoholgenuss* substantial; *Geschenke* numerous

(b) (= *mehr als genügend*) *Zeit, Geld, Platz* plenty of; *Belohnung* ample

(c) (*inf*: = *mehr als*) good; **eine ~e Stunde** a good hour **2** ADV **(a)** (= *sehr viel*) *belohnen, sich eindecken* amply; *verdienen* richly; **jdn ~ beschenken** to give sb lots of presents; **~ Trinkgeld geben** to tip generously; **~ Zeit/Geld haben** to have plenty of *or* ample time/money; **~ vorhanden sein** to abound; **mehr als ~ belohnt** more than amply rewarded; **mehr als ~ bezahlt** paid more than enough; **der Mantel ist ~ ausgefallen** the coat is on the big side; **das war ~ gewogen/ abgemessen** that was very generously weighed out/ measured out

(b) (*inf*: = *mehr als*) **~ 1.000 Euro** a good 1,000 euros **(c)** (*inf*: = *ziemlich*) pretty

Reichs-: Reichsadler M (*Her, Hist*) imperial eagle; **Reichshauptstadt** F (*1933-45*) capital of the Reich; (*vor 1933*) imperial capital; **Reichskanzler** M (*bis 1918*) Imperial Chancellor; (*1918-34*) German Chancellor; **Reichsmark** F, *pl* **-mark** (*Hist*) reichsmark; **Reichsstadt** F (*Hist*) free city (of the Holy Roman Empire); **freie ~** free city; **Reichstag** M Parliament; (*in Deutschland 1871-1945*) Reichstag; (*in Deutschland vor 1871, in Japan*) Imperial Diet; **Reichstagsbrand** M burning of the Reichstag

Reichtum ['raɪçtuːm] M **-s**, **Reichtümer** [-tyːmɐ] **(a)** wealth *no pl*; (= *Besitz*) riches *pl*; **zu ~ kommen** to become rich; **die Reichtümer der Erde/des Meeres** the riches of the earth/sea; **damit kann man keine Reichtümer gewinnen** you won't get rich that way **(b)** (*fig*: = *Fülle, Reichhaltigkeit*) wealth (*an +dat* of); **der ~ an Fischen** the abundance of fish

Reichweite F range; (= *greifbare Nähe*) reach; (*fig*: = *Einflussbereich*) scope; **in ~** within range/reach (+*gen* of); **jd ist in ~** sb is around; **außer ~** out of range/reach (+*gen* of); (*fig*) out of reach

reif [raɪf] ADJ (= *voll entwickelt*) *Früchte, Getreide* ripe; *Mensch, Ei, Arbeit* mature; **in ~(er)em Alter, in den ~eren Jahren** in one's mature(r) years; **die ~ere Jugend** those of mellower years; **im ~eren Alter von ...** at the ripe old age of ...; **die Zeit ist ~/noch**

nicht ~ the time is ripe/not yet ripe; **eine ~e Leistung** (*inf*) a brilliant achievement; **für etw ~ sein** (*inf*) to be ready for sth; **~ sein** (*inf*) to be in for it (*inf*); (*sl: für Geschlechtsverkehr*) to be dying for it (*sl*)

Reif¹ [raɪf] M **-(e)s**, NO PL (= *Raureif*) hoarfrost; (= *gefrorener Nebel*) rime

Reif² M **-(e)s**, **-e** (*old*) (*liter*) (= *Stirnreif, Diadem*) circlet; (= *Armreif*) bangle; (= *Fingerring*) ring; (*im Rock*) hoop

Reife ['raɪfə] F -, NO PL (= *das Reifen*) ripening; (= *das Reifsein*) ripeness; (= *Geschlechtsreife, von Ei, fig*) maturity; **ihm fehlt die (sittliche) ~** he's too immature; **Zeugnis der ~** (*Sch form*) = **Reifezeugnis**

reifen VI AUX SEIN (*Obst*) to ripen; (*Mensch, Ei, Plan*) to mature; **zur Gewissheit ~** to turn into certainty; **langsam reifte in ihm der Entschluss, ...** he slowly reached the decision ...

Reifen ['raɪfn] M **-s**, **-** tyre (*Brit*), tire (*US*); (= *Spielreifen*) (*von Fass, von Rock*) hoop; (= *Armreifen*) bangle

Reifen-: Reifendruck M, *pl* **-drücke** tyre (*Brit*) *or* tire (*US*) pressure; **Reifenpanne** F puncture (*Brit*), flat (*inf*); (*geplatzt auch*) blowout (*inf*); **Reifenwechsel** M tyre (*Brit*) *or* tire (*US*) change

Reife-: Reifeprüfung F (*Sch*) *siehe* **Abitur**; **Reifezeugnis** NT (*Sch*) *Abitur certificate*, ≈ A Level certificate (*Brit*), ≈ high school diploma (*US*)

reiflich ['raɪflɪç] **1** ADJ thorough; **nach ~er Überlegung** after careful consideration **2** ADV *nachdenken* thoroughly; **sich** (*dat*) **etw ~ überlegen** to consider sth carefully

Reihe ['raɪə] F -, **-n (a)** (= *geregelte Anordnung*) row; **in ~n zu (je) drei antreten/marschieren** to line up/march in rows of three *or* in threes; **sich in einer ~ aufstellen** to line up; **sich in die ~ stellen** to join the row; **in einer ~ stehen** to stand in a row *or* line; **in Reih und Glied antreten** to line up in formation; **sie standen in Reih und Glied vor dem Lehrer** they stood lined up in front of their teacher; **aus der ~ tanzen** (*fig inf*) to be different; (= *gegen Konventionen verstoßen*) to step out of line; **die ~n lichten sich** (*fig*) the ranks are thinning; **in den eigenen ~n** within our/their *etc* own ranks; **in der vordersten ~ stehen** (*fig*) to be in the topmost rank

(b) (= *Reihenfolge*) **er ist an der ~** it's his turn; **die ~ ist an jdm** it's sb's turn; **er kommt an die ~** he's next; **der ~ nach, nach der ~** in order, in turn; **sie sollen der ~ nach hereinkommen** they are to come in one by one; **erzähl mal der ~ nach, wie alles war** tell us how it was in the order it all happened; **außer der ~** out of order; (*bei Spielen auch*) out of turn; (= *zusätzlich, nicht wie gewöhnlich*) out of the usual way of things; **wenn ich das Auto mal außer der ~ brauche** if I should happen to need the car at a time when I don't normally have it

(c) (= *Serie: Math, Mus*) series *sing*; (*Biol*: = *Ordnung*) order **(d)** (= *unbestimmte Anzahl*) number; **in die ~ der Mitgliedsstaaten eintreten** to join the ranks of the member states; **in der ~ der Stars** amongst the ranks of the stars; **eine ganze ~ (von)** a whole lot (of)

(e) (*inf*: = *Ordnung*) **aus der ~ kommen** (= *in Unordnung geraten*) to get out of order; (= *verwirrt werden*) to lose one's equilibrium; (*gesundheitlich*) to fall ill; **jdn aus der ~ bringen** to confuse sb; **wieder in die ~ kommen** to get one's equilibrium back; (*gesundheitlich*) to get back on form; **in die ~ bringen** to put in order; **nicht alle auf der ~ haben** (*sl*) to have a screw loose (*inf*); **etw auf die ~ kriegen** (*inf*) to handle sth

reihen ['raɪən] **1** VT **(a)** **Perlen auf eine Schnur ~** to string beads (on a thread) **(b)** (*Sew*) to tack **2** VR **etw reiht sich an etw** (*acc*) sth follows (after) sth; **eine Enttäuschung reihte sich an die andere** letdown followed letdown

Reihenfolge F order; (= *notwendige Aufeinanderfolge*) sequence; **der ~ nach** in sequence; **alphabetische/zeitliche ~** alphabetical/chronological order

Reihen-: Reihenhaus NT terraced house (*Brit*), town house (*esp US*); **Reihen(haus)siedlung** F estate of terraced houses (*Brit*) *or* town houses (*esp US*); **Reihenuntersuchung** F mass screening; **reihenweise** ADV (= *in Reihen*) in rows **(b)** (*fig*: = *in großer Anzahl*) by the dozen

Reiher ['raɪɐ] M **-s**, **-** heron

reihern ['raɪɐn] VI (*sl*) to puke (up) (*inf*)

-reihig [raɪç] ADJ SUF -rowed; **zweireihige Jacke** double-breasted jacket

reihum [rai'Um] ADV round; **es geht ~** everybody takes their turn; **etw ~ gehen lassen** to pass sth round

Reim [raim] M **-(e)s, -e** rhyme; **ein ~ auf „Hut"** a rhyme for "hat"; **~e bilden** *or* **machen** *or* **drechseln** (*hum*) *or* **schmieden** (*hum*) to make *or* write rhymes; **sich** (*dat*) **einen ~ auf etw** (*acc*) **machen** (*inf*) to make sense of sth; **ich mache mir so meinen ~ darauf** (*inf*) I can put two and two together (*inf*); **ich kann mir keinen ~ darauf machen** (*inf*) I can't make head (n)or tail of it

reimen ['raimən] █ VT to rhyme (*auf +acc, mit* with) █ VI to make up rhymes █ VR to rhyme (*auf +acc, mit* with); **das reimt sich nicht** (*fig*) it doesn't make sense

Reimport [reIm'pɔrt, 'reImpɔrt] M (*Fin, Comm*) reimportation

rein¹ [rain] ADV (*inf*) = **herein, hinein**

rein² █ ADJ (a) pure; (= *absolut, völlig*) sheer; *Wahrheit* plain; *Gewinn, Gewissen* clear; **das ist die ~ste Freude/der ~ste Hohn** *etc* it's sheer joy/mockery *etc*; **er ist der ~ste Künstler/Akrobat** he's a real artist/acrobat; **er ist die ~ste Bestie** he's an absolute brute; **mit ihren Kindern hat sie nicht immer die ~ste Freude** she sometimes finds her children a mixed blessing; **eine ~e Jungenklasse** an all boys' class
(b) (= *sauber*) clean; *Haut, Teint* clear; **etw ~ machen** to clean sth; **~en Tisch machen** (*fig*) to get things straight
(c) (= *klar, übersichtlich*) **etw ins Reine schreiben** to write out a fair copy of sth; **etw ins Reine bringen** to clear sth up; **mit sich selbst ins Reine kommen** to get things straight with oneself; **mit etw ins Reine kommen** to get straight about sth; **mit jdm/sich selbst im Reinen sein** to have got things straightened out with sb/oneself; **mit etw im Reinen sein** to have got sth straightened out; **mit seinem Gewissen im Reinen sein** to have a clear conscience; **er ist mit sich selbst nicht im Reinen** he is at odds with himself
█ ADV (a) (= *ausschließlich*) purely; **~ hypothetisch gesprochen** speaking purely hypothetically
(b) (= *pur*) **~ leinen** pure linen; **~ seiden** pure silk
(c) (= *sauber*) **~ klingen** to make a pure sound; **~ singen** to have a pure voice
(d) (*inf*: = *ganz, völlig*) absolutely; **~ gar nichts** absolutely nothing

Reineclaude [rɛːnə'kloːdə] F **-, -n** greengage

Reinemachefrau F cleaner

Reinerlös M, **Reinertrag** M net profit(s *pl*)

Reinfall M (*inf*) disaster (*inf*); **mit der Waschmaschine/dem Kollegen haben wir einen ~ erlebt** we had real problems with the washing machine/this colleague

reinfallen ['rainfalən] VI SEP IRREG AUX SEIN (*inf*) = **hereinfallen, hineinfallen**

Rein-: Reingewicht NT net(t) weight; **Reingewinn** M net(t) profit; **Reinhaltung** F keeping clean; (*von Wasser, Luft auch, von Sprache*) keeping pure; **reinhängen** VR SEP (*sl*: = *sich anstrengen*) to get stuck in (*inf*)

Reinheit F -, NO PL purity; (= *Sauberkeit*) cleanness; (*von Haut*) clearness; **Rohstoffe in hoher ~** high-purity raw materials

Reinheitsgebot NT purity law (*regulating the production of beer and various other food and drink items*)

reinigen ['rainIgn] █ VT (a) (= *sauber machen, putzen*) to clean; **etw chemisch ~** to dry-clean sth (b) (= *säubern*) to purify; *Metall* to refine; **ein ~des Gewitter** (*fig inf*) a row which clears the air █ VR (= *rein sein selbst*; (*Mensch*) to cleanse oneself

Reiniger ['rainIgɐ] M **-s, -** cleaner

Reinigung ['rainIgʊŋ] F **-, -en (a)** (= *das Saubermachen*) cleaning (b) (= *chemische ~*) (*Vorgang*) dry cleaning; (*Anstalt*) (dry) cleaner's (c) (= *das Säubern*) purification; (*von Metall*) refining

Reinigungs-: Reinigungsmilch F cleansing milk; **Reinigungsmittel** NT cleansing agent

Reinkarnation [reInkarna'tsioːn] F reincarnation

Reinkultur F (*Biol*) pure culture; **Kitsch/Faschismus** *etc* **in ~** (*inf*) pure unadulterated kitsch/fascism *etc*

reinlegen ['rainleːgn] VT SEP (*inf*) = **hereinlegen, hineinlegen**

reinlich ['rainlIç] █ ADJ (a) = *sauberkeitsliebend*) cleanly (b) (= *ordentlich*) tidy (c) (= *gründlich, klar*) clear █ ADV (a) (= *sauber*) cleanly (b) (= *genau*) *trennen, unterscheiden* clearly

Reinlichkeit F -, NO PL (a) (= *Sauberkeitsliebe*) cleanliness (b) (= *Ordentlichkeit*) tidiness

Rein-: Reinluftgebiet NT pollution-free zone; **reinrassig** ADJ pure-blooded; *Tier* thoroughbred; (*fig*) *Sportwagen etc* thoroughbred; **Reinrassigkeit** F -, NO PL racial purity; (*von Tier*) pure breeding; **Reinraum** M clean room; **reinstressen** VR SEP (*sl*) to get stressed out (*sl*); (= *hart arbeiten*) to work like hell (*inf*); **reintun** ['raintuːn] VT (*inf*) **sich** (*dat*) **etw ~** to imagine sth; **das muss man sich mal ~** just imagine that; *siehe auch* **hineintun**

reinvestieren *ptp* **reinvestiert** VTI to reinvest

rein-: rein waschen ['rainvaʃn] IRREG █ VT (*von* of) to clear; (*von Sünden*) to cleanse; *schmutziges Geld* to launder █ VR (*fig*) to clear oneself; (*von Sünden*) to cleanse oneself; **reinwürgen** ['rainvʏrgn] (*inf*) *Essen etc* to force down; **jdm einen** *or* **eins ~** to do the dirty on sb (*inf*); **reinziehen** ['raintsiːən] VT (*inf*) **sich** (*dat*) **etw ~** *Drogen* to take sth; *Musik* to listen to sth; *Film, Video* to watch sth; *siehe auch* **hineinziehen**

Reis M **-es, -e** [-zə] rice; **Huhn auf ~** chicken with rice

Reise ['raizə] F **-, -n** journey, trip; (= *Schiffsreise*) voyage; (*Space*) voyage; (= *Geschäftsreise*) trip; **seine ~n durch Europa** his travels through Europe; **seine ~ nach Spanien** his trip to Spain; **er plant eine ~ durch Afrika** he's planning to travel through Africa; **eine ~ machen** to go on a journey; **wir konnten die geplante ~ nicht machen** we couldn't go away as planned; **wann machst du die nächste ~?** when's the next trip?; **ich muss mal wieder eine ~ machen** I must go away again; **auf ~n sein** to be away (travelling (*Brit*) *or* traveling (*US*)); **er ist viel auf ~n** he does a lot of travelling (*Brit*) *or* traveling (*US*); **jeden Sommer gehen wir auf ~n** we go away every summer; **er geht viel auf ~n** he travels a lot; **etw auf die ~ schicken** *Brief etc* to send sth off; **wohin geht die ~?** where are you off to?; **glückliche** *or* **gute ~!** have a good journey!; **wenn einer eine ~ tut, so kann er was erzählen** (*prov*) strange things happen when you're abroad; **die ~ nach Jerusalem** (= *Spiel*) musical chairs *sing*

Reise-: Reiseandenken NT souvenir; **Reiseapotheke** F first-aid kit; **Reisebedarf** M travel requisites *pl*; **Reisebegleiter(in)** M(F) travelling (*Brit*) *or* traveling (*US*) companion; (= *Reiseleiter*) courier; (*für Kinder*) chaperon; **Reisebüro** NT travel agency; **Reisebürokauffrau** F, **Reisebürokaufmann** M travel agent; **Reisecar** M (*Sw*) bus; **reisefertig** ADJ ready (to go *or* leave); **~e Gäste warten bitte in der Hotelhalle** would guests who are ready to leave please wait in the hotel foyer; **Reiseflughöhe** F cruising altitude; **Reiseführer** M (*Buch*) guidebook; **Reiseführer(in)** M(F) tour guide; **Reisegepäckversicherung** F baggage insurance; **Reisegeschwindigkeit** F cruising speed; **Reisegesellschaft** F (tourist) party; (*im Bus auch*) coach party; (*inf*. = *Veranstalter*) tour operator; **eine japanische ~** a party of Japanese tourists

Reisekosten PL travelling (*Brit*) *or* traveling (*US*) expenses *pl*

Reisekosten-: Reisekostenabrechnung F claim for travelling (*Brit*) *or* traveling (*US*) expenses; **Reisekostenvergütung** F reimbursement of travelling (*Brit*) *or* traveling (*US*) expenses; **500 Euro ~** 500 euros (in respect of) travelling (*Brit*) *or* traveling (*US*) expenses

Reise-: Reisekrankheit F travel sickness; **Reiseland** NT holiday (*esp Brit*) *or* travel destination; **Reiseleiter(in)** M(F) tour guide; **Reiselust** F wanderlust; **mich packt die ~** I've got the travel bug (*inf*); **reiselustig** ADJ fond of travel *or* travelling (*Brit*) *or* traveling (*US*); **Reisemitbringsel** NT souvenir

reisen ['raizn] VI AUX SEIN to travel; **in den Urlaub ~** to go away on holiday (*esp Brit*) *or* vacation (*US*); **in etw** (*dat*) **~** (*Comm*) to travel in sth; **viel gereist sein** to have travelled (*Brit*) *or* traveled (*US*) a lot

Reisende(r) ['raizndə] MF DECL AS ADJ traveller (*Brit*), traveler (*US*); (= *Fahrgast*) passenger; (*Comm*) travelling (*Brit*) *or* traveling (*US*) salesman/-woman

Reise-: Reisenecessaire NT (*für Nagelpflege*) travelling (*Brit*) *or* traveling (*US*) manicure set; (= *Nähzeug*) travelling (*Brit*) *or* traveling (*US*) sewing kit; **Reisepass** M passport; **Reiseprospekt** M travel brochure; **Reiseproviant** M food for the journey; **Reiseruf** M personal message; **Reisescheck** M traveller's cheque (*Brit*), traveler's check (*US*); **Reisespesen** PL travelling (*Brit*) *or* traveling (*US*) expenses *pl*; **Reisetablette** F travel sickness pill; **Reisetasche** F holdall; **Reiseveranstalter(in)** M(F) tour operator; **Reiseversicherung** F travel insurance; **Reisewecker** M travelling (*Brit*) *or* traveling (*US*) alarm clock; **Reisewelle** F (surge of) holiday traffic; **die ~ setzt ein** the holiday season is under way; **Reisewetter** NT travelling (*Brit*) *or* traveling (*US*) weather; **Reisewetterbericht** M holiday (*Brit*) *or* travel weather forecast; **Reisezeit** F (= *günstige Zeit*) time for travelling (*Brit*) *or* traveling (*US*); (= *Saison*) holiday (*esp Brit*) *or* vacation (*US*) season; (= *Fahrzeit, Fahrtdauer*) travel time; **Reiseziel** NT destination

Reisfeld NT paddy field

Reisig ['raizɪç] NT **-s**, NO PL brushwood

Reis-: Reiskorn NT, *pl* **-körner** grain of rice; **Reismehl** NT ground rice; **Reispapier** NT (*Art, Cook*) rice paper

Reißaus [raisˈlaus] M ~ **nehmen** (*inf*) to clear off *or* out (*inf*)

Reißbrett ['rais-] NT drawing board

reißen ['raisn], *pret* **riss** [rɪs], *ptp* **gerissen** [gəˈrɪsn] **1** VT
(a) (= *zerreißen, abreißen*) to tear, to rip (*etw von etw* sth off sth); (= *mitreißen, zerren*) to pull, to drag; **jdn zu Boden ~** to pull *or* drag sb to the ground; **jdn/etw in die Tiefe ~** to pull *or* drag sb/sth down into the depths; **der Fluss hat die Brücke mit sich gerissen** the river swept the bridge away; **jdm etw aus den Händen/der Hand ~** to snatch sth out of sb's hands/hand; **jdn aus seinen Gedanken ~** to interrupt sb's thoughts; (= *aufmuntern*) to make sb snap out of it; **jdn aus dem Schlaf/seinen Träumen ~** to wake sb from his sleep/dreams; **jdn ins Verderben ~** to ruin sb; **jdn in den Tod ~** to claim sb's life; (*Flutwelle, Lawine*) to sweep sb to his/her death; **hin und her gerissen werden/sein** (*fig*) to be torn
(b) **etw an sich** (*acc*) ~ to seize sth; *Unterhaltung* to monopolize sth
(c) (*Sport*) (*Gewichtheben*) to snatch; (*Hochsprung, Pferderennen*) to knock down
(d) (= *töten*) to kill
(e) (*inf*: = *machen*) *Witze* to crack (*inf*); *Possen* to play
(f) *siehe* **gerissen**
2 VI (a) AUX SEIN (= *zerreißen*) to tear, to rip; (*Muskel, Bänder*) to tear; (*Seil*) to tear, to break, to snap; (= *Risse bekommen*) to crack; **mir ist die Kette/der Faden gerissen** my chain/thread has broken; **da riss mir die Geduld** *or* **der Geduldsfaden** my patience gave out; **es reißt mir in allen Gliedern** (*inf*) I'm aching all over; **wenn alle Stricke** *or* **Stränge ~** (*fig inf*) if all else fails
(b) (= *zerren*) (*an* +*dat* at) to pull, to tug; (*wütend*) to tear
(c) (*Sport*) (*Gewichtheben*) to snatch; (*Hochsprung*) to knock the bar off; (*Springreiten*) to knock the bar/top brick(s) *etc* off
3 VR (a) (= *sich verletzen*) to cut oneself (*an* +*dat* on)
(b) (*inf*) **sich um jdn/etw ~** to scramble to get sb/sth

reißend ADJ *Fluss* raging; *Tier* rapacious; *Schmerzen* searing; *Verkauf, Absatz* massive

reißerisch ['raisərɪʃ] **1** ADJ *Bericht, Titel* sensational **2** ADV sensationally

Reiß- ['rais-]: **reißfest** ADJ tear-proof; **Reißfestigkeit** F (tensile) strength; **Reißleine** F ripcord; **Reißnagel** M drawing pin (*Brit*), thumbtack (*US*); **Reißschiene** F T-square; **Reißverschluss** M zip (fastener) (*Brit*), zipper (*US*); **den ~ an etw** (*dat*) **zumachen** *or* **zuziehen** to zip sth up; **den ~ an etw** (*dat*) **aufmachen** *or* **aufziehen** to unzip sth; **Reißverschlussprinzip** NT principle of alternation; **Reißwolf** M shredder; **Reißzahn** M fang; **Reißzeug** NT, *pl* **-zeuge** drawing instruments *pl*; **Reißzwecke** F drawing pin (*Brit*), thumbtack (*US*)

reiten ['raitn], *pret* **ritt** [rɪt], *ptp* **geritten** [gəˈrɪtn] **1** VI AUX SEIN (*auf Tier*) to ride; **auf etw** (*dat*) ~ to ride (on) sth; **im Schritt/Trab/Galopp ~** to ride at a walk/trot/gallop; **geritten kommen** to ride up **2** VT to ride; **Schritt/Trab/Galopp ~** to ride at a walk/trot/gallop; **ein schnelles Tempo ~** to ride at a fast pace; **Prinzipien ~** (*inf*) to insist on one's principles

Reiter ['raitɐ] M **-s**, **-** (a) rider; (*Mil*) cavalryman (b) (*an Waage*) rider; (= *Karteireiter*) index tab

Reiterin ['raitərɪn] F **-**, **-nen** rider

Reiterstandbild NT equestrian statue

Reit- ['rait-]: **Reitgerte** F riding crop; **Reithose** F riding breeches *pl*; (*Hunt, Sport*) jodhpurs *pl*; **Reitkunst** F horsemanship; **Reitpeitsche** F riding whip; **Reitpferd** NT mount; **Reitsattel** M (riding) saddle; **Reitschule** F riding school; **Reitsitz** M riding position; (*rittlings*) straddling position; **im ~ sitzen** to sit astride (*auf etw* (*dat*) sth); **Reitsport** M (horse-)riding; **Reitstall** M riding stable; **Reitstiefel** M riding boot; **Reitweg** M bridle path; **Reitzeug** NT, *pl* **-zeuge** riding equipment *or* things *pl*

Reiz [raits] M **-es**, **-e** (a) (*Physiol*) stimulus; **einen ~ auf etw** (*acc*) **ausüben** to act as a stimulus on sth

(b) (= *Verlockung*) attraction, appeal; (*des Unbekannten, Fremdartigen, der Großstadt*) appeal; (= *Zauber*) charm; (**auf jdn**) **einen ~ ausüben** to have great attraction (for sb); **das erhöht den ~** it adds to the thrill; **diese Idee hat auch ihren ~** this idea also has its attractions; **seinen** *or* **den ~ verlieren** to lose all one's/its charm; **an ~ verlieren** to be losing one's/its charm; **seine ~e spielen lassen** to display one's charms; **weibliche ~e** feminine charms; **seine ~e zeigen** (*euph iro*) to reveal one's charms

Reiz-: reizbar ADJ (= *empfindlich*) touchy (*inf*); (*Med*) sensitive; (= *erregbar*) irritable; **Reizbarkeit** ['raitsbaːɐkait] F **-**, NO PL (= *Empfindlichkeit*) touchiness (*inf*); (*Med*) sensitivity; (= *Erregbarkeit*) irritability; **reizempfänglich** ADJ responsive; (*Physiol*) receptive to stimuli

reizen ['raitsn] **1** VT (a) (*Physiol*) to irritate; (= *stimulieren*) to stimulate
(b) (= *verlocken*) to appeal to; **es würde mich ja sehr ~, ...** I'd love to ...; **es reizt mich, nach Skye zu fahren** I've got an itch to go to Skye; **es hat mich ja immer sehr gereizt, ...** I've always had an itch to ...; **Ihr Angebot reizt mich sehr** I find your offer very tempting; **sie versteht es, Männer zu ~** she knows how to appeal to men; **was reizt Sie daran?** what do you like about it?
(c) (= *ärgern*) to annoy; *Tier* to tease; (= *herausfordern*) to provoke; **ein gereiztes Nashorn ...** a rhinoceros when provoked ...; **jdn bis aufs Blut ~** to push sb to breaking point; **die Kinder reizten sie bis zur Weißglut** the children really made her see red; *siehe auch* **gereizt**
2 VI (a) (*Med*) to irritate; (= *stimulieren*) to stimulate; **auf der Haut** *etc* ~ to irritate the skin *etc*; **zum Widerspruch ~** to invite contradiction
(b) (*Cards*) to bid; **hoch ~** (*lit, fig*) to make a high bid

reizend **1** ADJ charming; **das ist ja ~** (*iro*) (that's) charming **2** ADV *einrichten, schmücken* attractively; **~ aussehen** to look charming; **sie haben sich ~ um uns gekümmert** they took such good care of us

Reiz-: Reizgas NT irritant gas; **Reizhusten** M chesty (*Brit*) *or* deep (*US*) cough; (*nervös*) nervous cough; **Reizklima** NT bracing climate; (*fig*) charged atmosphere; **reizlos** ADJ dull, uninspiring; **das ist ja ~** that's no fun; **Reizthema** NT controversial issue; **Reizüberflutung** F overstimulation

Reizung ['raitsʊŋ] F **-**, **-en** (*Med*) stimulation; (*krankhaft*) irritation

Reiz-: reizvoll ADJ delightful; *Aufgabe, Beruf* attractive; **die Aussicht ist nicht gerade ~** the prospect is not particularly appealing; **es wäre ~, mal dahin zu fahren** it would be lovely to go there some time; **es wäre ~, das ganz anders zu machen** it would be interesting to do it quite differently; **Reizwäsche** F (*inf*) sexy underwear; **Reizwort** NT, *pl* **-wörter** emotive word

rekeln ['reːkln] VR (*inf*) (= *sich herumlümmeln*) to loll around; (= *sich strecken*) to stretch; **sich noch ein paar Minuten im Bett ~** to stretch out in bed for a few more minutes; **er rekelte sich im behaglichen Sessel vor dem Feuer** he snuggled down in the comfortable chair in front of the fire

Reklamation [reklamaˈtsioːn] F **-**, **-en** query; (= *Beschwerde*) complaint; **„spätere ~en können nicht anerkannt werden"** "please check your change/money immediately since mistakes cannot be rectified later"

Reklame [reˈklaːmə] F **-**, **-n** (a) (= *Werbewesen, Werbung*) advertising; **~ für jdn/etw machen** to advertise sb/sth; (*fig*) to do a bit of advertising for sb/sth (b) (= *Einzelwerbung*) advertisement; (*esp TV, Rad*) commercial

Reklame-: Reklamerummel M (*pej*) advertising frenzy (*inf*); **Reklameschild** NT, *pl* **-schilder** advertising sign; **Reklamespot** M (advertising) spot

reklamieren [reklaˈmiːrən], *ptp* **reklamiert** **1** VI (= *Einspruch erheben*) to complain; **bei jdm wegen etw ~** to complain to sb about sth; **die Rechnung kann nicht stimmen, da würde ich ~** the bill can't be right, I would query it **2** VT (a) (= *bemängeln*) to complain about (*etw bei jdm* sth to sb); (= *infrage stellen*) *Rechnung, Rechnungsposten* to query (*etw bei jdm* sth with sb) (b) (= *in Anspruch nehmen*) to claim; **jdn/etw für sich ~** to lay claim to sb/sth

rekommandieren [rekɔmanˈdiːrən], *ptp* **rekommandiert** VT (*Aus*) *Brief, Sendung* to register

Rekompens [rekɔm'pɛns] **-, -en** [-zn] F, (*Aus* **Rekompenz** *Admin*) [rekɔm'pɛnts] F **-, -en** compensation

rekonstruieren [rekɔnstru'i:rən], *ptp* **rekonstru<u>ie</u>rt** VT to reconstruct

Rekonstruktion [rekɔnstrʊk'tsio:n] F reconstruction

Rekord [re'kɔrt] M **-s, -e** [-də] record; **einen ~ aufstellen** to set a record

Rekord- IN CPDS record; **Rek<u>o</u>rdbrecher(in)** M(F) record breaker

Rekorder [re'kɔrdɐ] M **-s, -** (cassette) recorder

Rekord-: Rek<u>o</u>rdhalter(in) M(F), **Rek<u>o</u>rdinhaber(in)** M(F) record holder; **Rek<u>o</u>rdzeit** F record time

Rekrut [re'kru:t] M **-en, -en**, **Rekrutin** [-'kru:tɪn] F **-, -nen** (*Mil*) recruit

rekrutieren [rekru'ti:rən], *ptp* **rekrut<u>ie</u>rt** VT (*Mil, fig*) to recruit **2** VR (*fig*) **sich ~ aus** to be recruited from

Rekrutin F **-, -nen** (*Mil*) recruit

rektal [rɛk'ta:l] **1** ADJ (*Med*) rectal **2** ADV **~ einführen** to insert through the rectum; **die Temperatur ~ messen** to take the temperature rectally

Rektor ['rɛkto:ɐ] M **-s, Rektoren** [-'to:rən], **Rektorin** [-'to:rɪn, 'rɛktorɪn] F **-, -nen** (*Sch*) head teacher, principal (*esp US*); (*Univ*) vice chancellor (*Brit*), rector (*US*); (*von Fachhochschule*) principal

Rektorat [rɛkto'ra:t] NT **-(e)s, -e** (*Sch*) (= *Amt, Amtszeit*) headship, principalship (*esp US*); (= *Zimmer*) head teacher's study, principal's room (*esp US*); (*Univ*) vice chancellorship (*Brit*), rectorship (*US*); vice chancellor's (*Brit*) or rector's (*US*) office; (*in Fachhochschule*) principalship; principal's office

Relais [rə'lɛ:] NT **-, -** [rə'lɛ:(s), rə'lɛ:s] (*Elec*) relay

Relation [rela'tsio:n] F **-, -en** relation; **in einer/keiner ~ zu etw stehen** to bear some/no relation to sth; **etw in ~ (zu** or **mit etw) setzen** to compare sth (to or with sth)

relational [relatsio'na:l] (*Comput*) **1** ADJ relational **2** ADV relationally

relativ [rela'ti:f] **1** ADJ relative **2** ADV relatively

relativieren [relati'vi:rən], *ptp* **relativ<u>ie</u>rt** (*geh*) **1** VT *Begriff, Behauptung etc* to qualify **2** VI to think in relative terms **3** VR to become relative

Relativität [relativi'tɛ:t] F **-**, NO PL relativity

Relativitätstheorie F theory of relativity

Relativ-: Relat<u>i</u>vpronomen NT relative pronoun; **Relat<u>i</u>vsatz** M relative clause

relaxen [ri'lɛksn] VI (*inf*) to take it easy (*inf*)

relaxt [ri'lɛkst] (*inf*) **1** ADJ laid-back (*inf*) **2** ADV **~ auf etw** (*acc*) **reagieren** to be laid-back about sth (*inf*); **sie ist alles andere als ~ in die Prüfung gegangen** she was anything but relaxed when she went to take her exam

relevant [rele'vant] ADJ relevant

Relevanz [rele'vants] F **-**, NO PL relevance

Reli ['rɛli] F **-**, NO PL (*Sch inf*: = *Religion*) RE

Relief [reli'ef] NT **-s, -s** or **-e** relief

Religion [reli'gio:n] F **-, -en** (*lit, fig*) religion; (*Schulfach*) religious instruction or education

Religions-: Relig<u>i</u>onsfreiheit F freedom of worship; **Relig<u>i</u>onsführer(in)** M(F) religious leader; **relig<u>i</u>onslos** ADJ not religious; (= *bekenntnislos*) nondenominational; **Relig<u>i</u>onsstifter(in)** M(F) founder of a religion; **Relig<u>i</u>onsunterricht** M religious education or instruction; (*Sch*) RE or RI lesson

religiös [reli'giøːs] **1** ADJ religious **2** ADV **~ motiviert** religiously motivated or inspired; **sie werden ~ verfolgt** they are being persecuted because of their religion; **~ erzogen werden** to have a religious upbringing

Relikt [re'lɪkt] NT **-(e)s, -e** relic

Reling ['re:lɪŋ] F **-, -s** or **-e** (*Naut*) (deck) rail

Relocate-Funktion [ri:lo'ke:t-] F relocate function

Rem NT, **rem** [rɛm] NT **-, -** (= *Einheit*) rem

remis [rə'mi:] ADJ INV drawn; **~ spielen** to draw

Remis [rə'mi:] NT **- or -en** [rə'mi:(s)], **-en** [rə'mi:s, rə'mi:zn] (*Chess, Sport*) draw; **gegen jdn ein ~ erzielen** to hold sb to a draw

Remittende [remi'tɛndə] F **-, -n** (*Comm*) return

Remittent [remi'tɛnt] M **-en, -en**, **Remittentin** [-'tɛntɪn] F **-, -nen** (*Fin*) payee

remittieren [remi'ti:rən], *ptp* **remitt<u>ie</u>rt** VT (*Comm*) *Waren* to return; *Geld* to remit

Remmidemmi ['rɛmi'dɛmi] NT **-s**, NO PL (*inf*) (= *Krach*) rumpus (*inf*); (= *Trubel*) to-do (*inf*); **~ machen** to cause a rumpus (*inf*)

Remoulade [remu'la:də] F **-, -n**, **Remoul<u>a</u>densoße** F (*Cook*) remoulade

rempeln ['rɛmpln] (*inf*) **1** VT to barge (*jdn* into sb) (*inf*); (= *foulen*) to push **2** VI to barge (*inf*); (*Sport*: = *foulen*) to push

REM-Phase ['rɛm-] F REM sleep

Remuneration [remunera'tsio:n] F **-, -en** (*Aus*) (= *Gratifikation*) bonus; (= *Vergütung*) remuneration

Ren [ren, re:n] NT **-s, -e** or **-s** ['re:nə, rens] reindeer

Renaissance [rəne'sãːs] F **-, -en** (a) (*Hist*) renaissance (b) (*fig*: *von Kunstformen*) renaissance, revival; **eine ~ erleben** to experience a revival

Renaissance- [rəne'sãːs] IN CPDS renaissance

Rendezvous [rãde'vuː, 'rãːdevu] NT **- -** [-'vuː(s), -'vuːs] rendezvous (*liter, hum*), date (*inf*); (*Space*) rendezvous

Rendite [rɛn'diːtə] F **-, -n** (*Fin*) yield, return on capital

Reneklode [re:nə'klo:də] F **-, -n** greengage

renitent [reni'tɛnt] **1** ADJ defiant **2** ADV defiantly

Renitenz [reni'tɛnts] F **-, -en** defiance

Renn- IN CPDS race; **R<u>e</u>nnbahn** F (race)track; **R<u>e</u>nnboot** NT powerboat

rennen ['rɛnən], *pret* **rannte** ['rantə], *ptp* **gerannt** [gə'rant] **1** VI AUX SEIN (= *schnell laufen*) to run; (*Auto etc*) to race; **um die Wette ~** to have a race; **(mit offenen Augen) ins Verderben** or **Unglück ~** to rush into disaster (with one's eyes wide open); **sie rennt wegen jeder Kleinigkeit zum Chef** (*inf*) she goes running (off) to the boss at the slightest little thing; **an** or **gegen jdn/etw ~** to run or bump into sb/sth; **er rannte mit dem Kopf gegen ...** he bumped his head against ... **2** VT AUX HABEN or SEIN (*Sport*) to run; **einen neuen Rekord über 100 Meter ~** to set a new record for the 100 metres (*Brit*) or meters (*US*); **jdn zu Boden** or **über den Haufen ~** to knock sb over

Rennen ['rɛnən] NT **-s, -** running; (*Sport*) (*Vorgang*) racing; (*Veranstaltung*) race; (*fig*) race (*um* for); **totes ~** dead heat; **gut im ~ liegen** (*lit, fig*) to be well-placed; **das ~ machen** (*lit, fig*) to win (the race); **aus dem ~ ausscheiden** (*lit, fig*) to drop out

Renner ['rɛnɐ] M **-s, -** (*inf*: = *Verkaufsschlager*) winner

Rennerei [rɛnə'rai] F **-, -en** (*inf*) (*lit, fig*: = *das Herumrennen*) running around; (= *Hetze*) mad chase (*inf*); **nach meinem Umzug hatte ich tagelange ~en** after moving I was running around for days; **diese ~ zum Klo** this running to the toilet

Renn-: R<u>e</u>nnfahrer(in) M(F) (= *Rennradfahrer*) racing cyclist; (= *Motorradrennfahrer*) racing motorcyclist; (= *Autorennfahrer*) racing driver; **R<u>e</u>nnpferd** NT racehorse; **aus einem Ackergaul kann man kein ~ machen** (*prov*) you can't make a silk purse out of a sow's ear (*Prov*); **R<u>e</u>nnpiste** F (race)track; **R<u>e</u>nnrad** NT racing bicycle; **R<u>e</u>nnsport** M racing; **R<u>e</u>nnstall** M (*Tiere, Zucht*) stable; (*Rennsport, Radrennen*) team; **R<u>e</u>nnwagen** M racing car

Renommee [renɔ'me:] NT **-s, -s** reputation, name

renommiert [renɔ'mi:ɐt] ADJ famous (*wegen* for)

renovieren [reno'vi:rən], *ptp* **renov<u>ie</u>rt** VT to renovate; (= *tapezieren etc*) to redecorate

Renov<u>ie</u>rung F **-, -en** renovation

rentabel [rɛn'ta:bl] **1** ADJ profitable; **es ist nicht ~, das reparieren zu lassen** it is not worth(while) having it repaired; **das ist eine rentable Sache** or **Angelegenheit** it will pay (off) **2** ADV profitably; **~ wirtschaften** (= *gut einteilen*) to spend one's money sensibly; (= *mit Gewinn arbeiten*) to show a profit

Rentabilität [rɛntabili'tɛ:t] F **-, -en** profitability

Rente ['rɛntə] F **-, -n** (= *Altersrente, Invalidenrente*) pension; (*aus Versicherung*) (= *Lebensrente*) annuity; (*aus Vermögen*) income; **in** or **auf** (*inf*) **~ gehen** to start drawing one's pension; **in** or **auf** (*inf*) **~ sein** to be on a pension; **jdn in ~ schicken** (*inf*) to pension sb off (*inf*)

Vorsicht! **Rente** *wird nicht mit dem englischen Wort* **rent** *übersetzt.*

Renten-: R<u>e</u>ntenalter NT retirement age; **R<u>e</u>ntenanspruch** M pension entitlement; **R<u>e</u>ntenbemessungsgrundlage** F basis of calculation of a pension/the pensions; **rentenberechtigt** ADJ entitled to a pension; *Alter* pensionable; **Rentenbescheid** M notice of the amount of one's pension; **Rentenbezüger(in)** M(F) (*Sw*) pensioner; **Rentenempfänger(in)** M(F) pensioner; **Rentenfonds** M fixed-income fund; **Rentenmarkt** M market in fixed-interest securities; **Rentenoptionshandel** M bond option dealing; **Rentenpapier** NT fixed-interest security; **Rentenreform** F reform of pensions; **Rentenversicherung** F pension scheme (*Brit*), retirement plan (*US*); **Rentenversicherungsbeitrag** M pension scheme (*Brit*) or retirement plan (*US*) contribution

Rentier ['rɛntiːɐ, 'rɛːntiːɐ] NT (*Zool*) reindeer
rentieren [rɛn'tiːrən], *ptp* **rentiert** 🔢 VI to be worthwhile; (*Wertpapier*) to yield a return 🔢 VR to be worthwhile; (*Geschäft, Unternehmen etc auch, Maschine*) to pay; **das rentiert sich nicht** it's not worth it; **ein Auto rentiert sich für mich nicht** it's not worth my having a car
Rentner ['rɛntnɐ] M **-s, -**, **Rentnerin** [-ərɪn] F **-, -nen** pensioner
Reorganisation [reɔrganiza'tsioːn] F, **Reorganisierung** F **-, -en** reorganization
reorganisieren [reɔrgani'ziːrən], *ptp* **reorganisiert** VT to reorganize
Rep [rɛp] M **-s, -s(e)** USU PL (*inf*) ABBR *von* **Republikaner** Republican, *member of the right-wing German Republikaner party*
reparabel [repa'raːbl] ADJ repairable
Reparatur [repara'tuːɐ] F **-, -en** repair; **~en am Auto** car repairs; **~en am Haus vornehmen** *or* **ausführen** to do some repairs to the house; **in ~ sein** to be being repaired; **etw in ~ geben** to have sth repaired
Reparatur-: reparaturanfällig ADJ prone to break down; **reparaturbedürftig** ADJ in need of repair; **Reparaturkosten** PL repair costs *pl*; **Reparaturwerkstatt** F workshop; (= *Autowerkstatt*) garage, auto repair shop (*US*)
reparieren [repa'riːrən], *ptp* **repariert** VT to repair
repatriieren [repatri'iːrən], *ptp* **repatriiert** VT (a) (= *wieder einbürgern*) to renaturalize (b) (= *heimschicken*) to repatriate
Repertoire [reper'toaːɐ] NT **-s, -s** repertoire (*auch fig*)
Repetent [repe'tɛnt] M **-en, -en**, **Repetentin** [-'tɛntɪn] F **-, -nen** (*Aus form*) pupil who has to repeat a year
repetieren [repe'tiːrən], *ptp* **repetiert** VT to repeat
Repetition [repeti'tsioːn] F **-, -en** (= *Wiederholung*) repetition
Repetitor [repe'tiːtoːɐ] M **-s**, **Repetitoren** [-'toːrən], **Repetitorin** [-'toːrɪn] F **-, -nen** (*Univ*) coach, tutor
Report [re'pɔrt] M **-(e)s, -e** (a) report (b) (*Fin*) contango
Reportage [repɔr'taːʒə] F **-, -n** report
Reporter [re'pɔrtɐ] M **-s, -**, **Reporterin** [-ərɪn] F **-, -nen** reporter; **Sport-/Wirtschaftsreporter** sports/economics correspondent
repräsentabel [reprɛzɛn'taːbl] ADJ prestigious; *Frau* (highly) presentable
Repräsentant [reprɛzɛn'tant] M **-en, -en**, **Repräsentantin** [-'tantɪn] F **-, -nen** representative
Repräsentantenhaus NT (*US Pol*) House of Representatives
Repräsentation [reprɛzɛnta'tsioːn] F (a) (= *Vertretung, Vorhandensein*) representation; (*von Firma*) office (b) (= *Darstellung*) **der ~ dienen** to create a good image; **die Diplomatenfrau fand die Repräsentation der ~ sehr anstrengend** the diplomat's wife found her life of official functions very tiring; **die einzige Funktion des Monarchen ist heute die ~** the sole function of the monarch today is that of an official figurehead
repräsentativ [reprɛzɛnta'tiːf] 🔢 ADJ (a) (= *stellvertretend, typisch*) representative (*für* of) (b) *Haus, Auto, Ausstattung* prestigious; *Erscheinung* presentable; **die ~en Pflichten eines Botschafters** the social duties of an ambassador; **ein großes**

Konferenzzimmer für ~e Zwecke a large conference room to provide a suitable setting for functions 🔢 ADV **bauen** prestigiously; **sie sind sehr ~ eingerichtet** their decor is very impressive
repräsentieren [reprɛzɛn'tiːrən], *ptp* **repräsentiert** 🔢 VT to represent 🔢 VI to perform official duties
Repressalie [repre'saːliə] F **-, -n** reprisal
Repro ['reːpro] F **-s** (*Typ sl*) ABBR *von* **Reproduktion**
Reproduktion [reprodʊk'tsioːn] F reproduction
Reproduktions-: Reproduktionsmedizin F reproductive medicine; **Reproduktionstechnik** F reproduction technology
reproduzieren [reprodu'tsiːrən], *ptp* **reproduziert** VT to reproduce
repro-: reprofähig ADJ camera-ready; **Reprofilm** M repro film; **Reprografie** [reprogra'fiː] F **-, -n** [-'fiːən] (*Typ*) reprography
Reptil [rɛp'tiːl] NT **-s, -ien** [-liən] reptile
Reptilienfonds M slush fund
Republik [repu'bliːk] F **-, -en** republic
Republikaner [republi'kaːnɐ] M **-s, -**, **Republikanerin** [-ərɪn] F **-, -nen** republican; (*Pol*) Republican

republikanisch [republi'kaːnɪʃ] ADJ republican
Requisit [rekvi'ziːt] NT **-s, -en** equipment *no pl*; **ein unerlässliches ~** an indispensable piece of equipment; **~en** (*Theat*) props
resch [rɛʃ] ADJ (*Aus*) (= *knusprig*) *Brötchen etc* crispy; (*fig*: = *lebhaft*) *Frau* dynamic
Reservat [rezer'vaːt] NT **-(e)s, -e** (a) (= *Naturschutzgebiet*) reserve; (*fig*) preserve (b) (*für Indianer, Ureinwohner etc*) reservation
Reserve [re'zɛrvə] F **-, -n** (a) (= *Vorrat*) reserve(s *pl*) (*an +dat* of); (= *angespartes Geld*) savings *pl*; (= *Kapitalrücklagen*) reserve(s *pl*); (*Mil, Sport*) reserves *pl*; **offene ~n** (*Fin*) disclosed reserves; **(noch) etw/jdn in ~ haben** to have sth/sb (still) in reserve (b) (= *Zurückhaltung*) reserve; (= *Bedenken*) reservation; **jdn aus der ~ locken** to bring sb out of his/her shell
Reserve-: Reservebank F, *pl* **-bänke** (*Sport*) substitutes *or* reserves bench; **er saß nur auf der ~** he only sat on the bench; **Reservefonds** M reserve fund; **Reservekanister** M spare can; **Reserverad** NT spare (wheel); **Reservespieler(in)** M(F) (*Sport*) reserve; **Reservetank** M reserve tank
reservieren [rezer'viːrən], *ptp* **reserviert** VT to reserve
reserviert [rezer'viːɐt] ADJ *Platz, Mensch* reserved
Reservierung F **-, -en** reservation
Reservoir [rezer'voaːɐ] NT **-s, -e** reservoir
Reset-Taste [riː'set-] F (*Comput*) reset key
resident [rezi'dɛnt] ADJ (*Comput*) resident
Residenz [rezi'dɛnts] F **-, -en** (= *Wohnung*) residence
Residenzstadt F royal seat
Resignation [rezigna'tsioːn] F **-, NO PL** (*geh*) resignation; **(über etw** *acc*) **in ~ verfallen, sich der ~ überlassen** to become resigned (to sth)
resignieren [rezi'gniːrən], *ptp* **resigniert** VI to give up; **resigniert** resigned; **... sagte er ~d** *or* **resigniert ...** he said with resignation
resistent [rezɪs'tɛnt] ADJ resistant (*gegen* to)
Resistenz [rezɪs'tɛnts] F **-, -en** resistance (*gegen* to)
Reskription [reskrip'tsioːn] F **-, -en** treasury bond
resolut [rezo'luːt] 🔢 ADJ resolute 🔢 ADV resolutely
Resolution [rezolu'tsioːn] F **-, -en** (*Pol*) (= *Beschluss*) resolution; (= *Bittschrift*) petition
Resonanz [rezo'nants] F **-, -en** (a) (*Mus, Phys*) resonance (b) (*fig*) response (*auf +acc* to); **keine/wenig/große ~ finden** to get no/little/a good response

Resonanz-: Resonanzboden M sounding board; **Resonanzkasten** M soundbox

Resopal® [rezo'paːl] NT **-s**, NO PL Formica®

resozialisieren [rezotsiali'ziːrən], *ptp* **resozialisiert** VT to rehabilitate

Resozialisierung F rehabilitation

Respekt [re'spɛkt, res'pɛkt] M **-s**, NO PL (= *Achtung*) respect; (= *Angst*) fear; **jdm ~ einflößen** (*Achtung*) to command respect from sb; (*Angst*) to put the fear of God into sb; **~ einflößend** authoritative; **ein wenig ~ einflößender Mensch** a person who commands little respect; **bei allem ~ (vor jdm/ etw)** with all due respect (to sb/for sth); **vor jdm/etw ~ haben** (*Achtung*) to have respect for sb/sth; (*Angst*) to be afraid of sb/sth; **sich** (*dat*) **~ verschaffen** to make oneself respected; **allen ~!** well done!

respektabel [respɛk'taːbl, res-] ADJ respectable

respektieren [respɛk'tiːrən, res-], *ptp* **respektiert** VT to respect; *Wechsel* to honour (*Brit*), to honor (*US*)

respektive [respɛk'tiːvə, res-] ADV (*geh, Comm*) **(a)** (= *jeweils*) and ... respectively **(b)** (= *anders ausgedrückt*) or rather; (= *genauer gesagt*) (or) more precisely **(c)** (= *oder*) or

Respekt-: respektlos ▌▌ ADJ disrespectful ▌▌ ADV disrespectfully; **Respektlosigkeit** F **-, -en (a)** (*no pl: Verhalten*) lack of respect **(b)** (*Bemerkung*) disrespectful remark *or* comment

Respektsperson F person to be respected; (= *Beamter etc*) person in authority

Ressentiment [resɑ̃ti'mãː, rə-] NT **-s, -s** resentment *no pl* (*gegen* towards)

Ressort [re'soːɐ] NT **-s, -s** department; **in das ~ von jdm/etw fallen** to be sb's/sth's department

Ressource [re'sʊrsə] F **-, -n** (*auch Comput*) resource

Rest [rest] M **-(e)s, -e (a)** rest; **die ~e einer Kirche/Stadt/Kultur** the remains of a church/city/civilization; **der ~ der Welt** the rest of the world; **am Anfang hatte ich 25 Schüler, die 3 hier sind noch der ~ (davon)** at the beginning I had 25 pupils, these 3 are all that is left; **der letzte ~** the last bit; **der letzte ~ vom Schützenfest** (*hum*) the last little bit; **bis auf einen ~** except for a little bit; **der kümmerliche** *or* **klägliche** *or* **schäbige ~** (*von meinem Geld*) all that's left; (*vom Essen*) the sad remnants; **der ~ ist Schweigen** the rest is silence; **der ~ ist für Sie** (*beim Bezahlen*) keep the change; **jdm/einer Sache den ~ geben** (*inf*) to finish sb/sth off **(b) Reste** PL (= *Essensreste*) leftovers *pl* **(c)** (= *Stoffrest*) remnant **(d)** (*Math*) remainder; **2 ÷ 3** 2 remainder 3

Rest- IN CPDS remaining; **Restalkohol** M, NO PL residual alcohol; **Restauflage** F remainder(ed) stock

Restaurant [resto'rãː] NT **-s, -s** restaurant

Restaurator [restau'raːtoːɐ, res-] M **-s, Restauratoren** [-'toːrən], **Restauratorin** [-'toːrɪn] F **-, -nen** restorer

restaurieren [restau'riːrən, res-], *ptp* **restauriert** VT to restore

Restaurierung F **-, -en** restoration

Rest-: Restbestand M remaining stock; (*fig*) remnant; **wir haben noch einen kleinen ~ an Bikinis** we still have a few bikinis left; **Restbetrag** M balance; **Restlaufzeit** F (*Fin*) remaining term

restlich ['restlɪç] ADJ remaining, rest of the ...; **die ~e Welt** the rest of the world; **die ~en** the rest

Restlieferung F (*Comm*) rest of the/a delivery

restlos ▌▌ ADJ complete ▌▌ ADV completely; **ich war ~ begeistert** I was completely bowled over (*inf*)

Restposten M **(a)** (*Comm*) remaining stock; **ein ~ remaining** stock; **ein großer ~ Bücher/Zucker** a lot of books/sugar left in stock; **„~"** "reduced to clear" **(b)** (*Fin: in Bilanz*) residual item

restriktiv [restrɪk'tiːf, res-] (*geh*) ▌▌ ADJ restrictive ▌▌ ADV restrictively; **die Werbebeschränkungen wurden ~ gehandhabt** advertising restrictions were rigorously applied

Rest-: Restrisiko NT residual risk; **Restsumme** F balance, amount remaining; **Restwert** M residual; **Restzahlung** F payment of the balance

Resultat [rezʊl'taːt] NT **-(e)s, -e** result; (*von Prüfung auch*) results *pl*; **zu einem ~ kommen** to come to a conclusion

resultieren [rezʊl'tiːrən], *ptp* **resultiert** VI (*geh*) to result (*in +dat* in); (*Sw: sich ergeben*) to result; **aus etw ~** to result from sth; **aus dem Gesagten resultiert, dass ...** from what was said one must conclude that ...; **die daraus ~den ...** the resulting ...; **daraus resultiert ...** the result (of this) is ...

Resümee [rezy'meː] NT **-s, -s** (*Aus, Sw*) **Resumé** [rezy'meː] NT **-s, -s** (*geh*) résumé

resümieren [rezy'miːrən], *ptp* **resümiert** VTI (*geh*) to summarize

Retorte [re'tɔrtə] F **-, -n** (*Chem*) retort; **aus der ~** (*fig inf*) synthetic; **Baby aus der ~** test-tube baby

Retortenbaby NT test-tube baby

retour [re'tuːɐ] ADV (*Aus, dial*) back

Retourbillett [re'tuːrbɪl'jet] NT (*Sw*) return (ticket) (*esp Brit*), round-trip ticket (*US*)

Retoure [re'tuːrə] F **-, -n** USU PL return

Retour- [re'tuːɐ-]: **Retourgang** M, *pl* **-gänge** (*Aus*) reverse (gear); **Retourkarte** F (*Aus*) return (ticket) (*esp Brit*), round-trip ticket (*US*); **Retourkutsche** F (*inf*) (*Worte*) retort; (*Handlung*) retribution; **Retourspiel** NT (*Aus*) return (match) (*Brit*), rematch (*US*)

Retrovirus [retro'viːrʊs] NT *OR* M retrovirus

retten ['rɛtn] ▌▌ VT to save; (*aus Gefahr auch*) (= *befreien*) to rescue; (*Comput*) *Datei* to recover; **jdn/etw vor jdm/etw ~** to save sb/sth from sb/sth; **jdm das Leben ~** to save sb's life; **ein ~der Gedanke** a bright idea that saved the situation; **er hat wieder geheiratet? er ist nicht mehr zu ~** he got married again? he's past saving; **bist du noch zu ~?** (*inf*) are you out of your mind? (*inf*) ▌▌ VR to escape; **sich auf/unter etw** (*acc*)**/aus etw ~** to escape onto/under/from sth; **sich vor jdm/etw ~** to escape (from) sb/ sth; **sich durch die Flucht ~** to escape; **sich vor etw nicht mehr ~ können** *or* **zu ~ wissen** (*fig*) to be swamped with sth; **rette sich, wer kann!** (it's) every man for himself!

Retter ['rɛtɐ] M **-s, -**, **Retterin** [-ərɪn] F **-, -nen** (*aus Notlage*) rescuer; **der ~** (*Rel*) the Saviour (*Brit*) *or* Savior (*US*); **ach mein ~!** oh my hero!; **der ~ des Unternehmens** the saviour (*Brit*) *or* savior (*US*) of the business

Rettich ['rɛtɪç] M **-s, -e** radish

Rettung ['rɛtʊŋ] F **-, -en** (*aus Notlage*) rescue; (= *Erhaltung*) saving; (*von Waren*) recovery; (*Rel*) salvation; **die ~ und Erhaltung historischer Denkmäler** the saving and preservation of historical monuments; **Gesellschaft zur ~ Schiffbrüchiger** Lifeboat Service; **die ~ kam in letzter Minute** the situation was saved at the last minute; (*für Schiffbrüchige etc*) help came in the nick of time; **an seine (eigene) ~ denken** to worry about one's own safety; **für den Patienten/ unsere Wirtschaft gibt es keine ~ mehr** the patient/our economy is beyond saving; **das war meine ~** that saved me; **das war meine letzte ~** that was my last hope; (= *hat mich gerettet*) that was my salvation

Rettungs-: Rettungsaktion F rescue operation; **Rettungsanker** M sheet anchor; (*fig*) anchor; **Rettungsarzt** M, **Rettungsärztin** F emergency doctor; **Rettungsboot** NT lifeboat; **Rettungsdienst** M rescue service; **Rettungsflugwacht** F air rescue service; **Rettungsflugzeug** NT rescue aircraft; **Rettungshubschrauber** M rescue helicopter; **Rettungsinsel** F inflatable life raft; **Rettungsleine** F lifeline; **rettungslos** ▌▌ ADJ beyond saving; *Lage* irretrievable; *Verlust* irrecoverable ▌▌ ADV *verloren* irretrievably; **er ist ihr ~ verfallen** he is completely under her spell; **Rettungsmannschaft** F rescue party; **Rettungsring** M life belt; (*hum: = Bauch*) spare tyre (*Brit hum*), spare tire (*US hum*); **Rettungssanitäter(in)** M(F) paramedic; **Rettungsschuss** M *finaler* = fatal shot (*fired by the police*); **Rettungsschwimmen** NT lifesaving; **Rettungsschwimmer(in)** M(F) lifesaver; (*an Strand, Pool*) lifeguard; **Rettungstrupp** M rescue squad; **Rettungswagen** M ambulance; **Rettungswesen** NT rescue services *pl*

Retusche [re'tʊʃə] F **-, -n** (*Phot*) retouching

retuschieren [retu'ʃiːrən], *ptp* **retuschiert** VT (*Phot*) to retouch

Reue ['rɔyə] F **-**, NO PL remorse (*über +acc* at, about), repentance (*auch Rel*) (*über +acc* of); (= *Bedauern*) regret (*über +acc* at, about)

Reufracht F = **Fautfracht**

reumütig ['rɔymyːtɪç] ▌▌ ADJ (= *voller Reue*) remorseful, repentant; *Sünder* contrite, penitent; (= *betreten, zerknirscht*) rueful ▌▌ ADV *gestehen, bekennen* full of remorse; **du wirst bald ~ zu mir zurückkommen** you'll soon come back to me feeling sorry

Reuse [ˈrɔyzə] F **-, -n** fish trap

Revanche [reˈvãːʃ(ə)] F **-, -n (a)** (*Sport*) revenge (*für* for); (= ~*partie*) return match (*Brit*), rematch (*US*) **(b)** NO PL (= *Rache*) revenge

revanchieren [revãˈʃiːrən], *ptp* **revanchiert** VR **(a)** (= *sich rächen*) to get one's revenge (*bei jdm für etw* on sb for sth) **(b)** (= *sich erkenntlich zeigen*) to reciprocate; **ich werde mich bei Gelegenheit mal ~** I'll return the compliment some time; (*für Hilfe*) I'll do the same for you one day; **das Problem bei Geschenken ist, dass man meint, sich ~ zu müssen** the problem with getting presents is that one always feels one has to give something in return; **sich bei jdm für eine Einladung/seine Gastfreundschaft ~** to return sb's invitation/ hospitality

revanchistisch [revãˈʃɪstɪʃ] ADJ revanchist

Revers [reˈveːɐ, reˈveːr, rəˈ-] NT or (AUS) M **-, - [-ɐ(s), -ɐs]** (*an Kleidung*) lapel

reversibel [reverˈziːbl] ADJ reversible

revidieren [reviˈdiːrən], *ptp* **revidiert** VT to revise; (*Comm*) to audit, to check; **die Wachstumsprognosen wurden nach oben/ unten revidiert** the growth forecasts were revised upwards/ downwards

Revier [reˈviːɐ] NT **-s, -e (a)** (= *Polizeidienststelle*) (police) station; (= *Dienstbereich*) beat, district; (*von Prostituierter*) patch (*inf*) **(b)** (*Zool*: = *Gebiet*) territory; **die Küche ist mein ~** the kitchen is my territory **(c)** (*Hunt*: = *Jagdrevier*) hunting ground **(d)** (*Min*: = *Kohlenrevier*) coalfields *pl*; **das ~** (= *Ruhrgebiet*) the Ruhr; (= *Saarland*) the Saar

Revirement [reviˈrmãː, revirˈmãː] NT **-s, -s** (*Pol*) reshuffle

Revision [reviˈzioːn] F **-, -en (a)** (*von Meinung, Politik etc*) revision; **sich in ~ befinden** to be undergoing revision **(b)** (*Comm*: = *Prüfung*) audit **(c)** (*Typ*: = *letzte Überprüfung*) final (proof)read **(d)** (*Jur*: = *Urteilsanfechtung*) appeal (*an* +acc to); **in die ~ gehen, ~ einlegen** to lodge an appeal

revisionistisch [revizioˈnɪstɪʃ] ADJ (*Pol*) revisionist

Revisor [reˈviːzoːɐ] M **-s, Revisoren** [-ˈzoːrən], **Revisorin** [-ˈzoːrɪn] F **-, -nen** (*Comm*) auditor; (*Typ*) proofreader

Revolte [reˈvɔltə] F **-, -n** revolt

revoltieren [revɔlˈtiːrən], *ptp* **revoltiert** VI to revolt, to rebel (*gegen* against); (*fig: Magen*) to rebel

Revolution [revoluˈtsioːn] F **-, -en** (*lit, fig*) revolution; **die sanfte/ friedliche ~** the velvet/peaceful revolution

revolutionär [revolutsioˈnɛːɐ] **1** ADJ (*lit, fig*) revolutionary **2** ADV **etw als ~ betrachten** to view sth as revolutionary; **etw als ~ bezeichnen** to call sth revolutionary

Revolutionär [revolutsioˈnɛːɐ] M **-s, -e, Revolutionärin** [-ˈnɛːrɪn] F **-, -nen** revolutionary

revolutionieren [revolutsioˈniːrən], *ptp* **revolutioniert** VT to revolutionize

Revolutions- IN CPDS revolutionary; **Revolutionsführer(in)** M(F) revolutionary leader

Revoluzzer [revoˈlʊtsɐ] M **-s, -, Revoluzzerin** [-ərɪn] F **-, -nen** (*pej*) would-be revolutionary

Revolver [reˈvɔlvɐ] M **-s, -** revolver

Revolver-: Revolverheld(in) M(F) (*pej*) gunslinger; **Revolvermündung** F mouth (of a/the revolver); **plötzlich starrte er in eine ~** he suddenly found himself staring down the barrel of a revolver

revolvierend [revɔlˈviːrənt] ADJ (*Fin*) revolving

Revolvingkredit [reˈvɔlvɪŋ-] M revolving credit (facility)

Revue [rəˈvyː] F **-, -n** [-ˈvyːən] (*Theat*) revue; **etw ~ passieren lassen** (*fig*) to let sth parade before one

Revuetänzer(in) [rəˈvyː-] M(F) chorus boy/girl

Reykjavik [ˈraikjaviːk] NT **-s** Reykjavik

Rezensent [retsɛnˈzɛnt] M **-en, -en, Rezensentin** [-ˈzɛntɪn] F **-, -nen** reviewer

rezensieren [retsɛnˈziːrən], *ptp* **rezensiert** VT to review

Rezension [retsɛnˈzioːn] F **-, -en** review

Rezept [reˈtsɛpt] NT **-(e)s, -e (a)** (*Med*) prescription; (*fig*: = *Heilmittel*) cure (*für, gegen* for); **auf ~** on prescription **(b)** (*Cook, fig*: = *Anleitung*) recipe (*zu* for)

Vorsicht! **Rezept** *wird nicht mit dem englischen Wort* **receipt** *übersetzt.*

rezeptfrei **1** ADJ available without prescription **2** ADV without a prescription

Rezeption [retsɛpˈtsioːn] F **-, -en** (*von Hotel*: = *Empfang*) reception

Rezept-: Rezeptpflicht F prescription requirement; **der ~ unterliegen** *or* **unterstehen** to be available only on prescription; **dafür besteht jetzt keine ~ mehr** you don't need a prescription for it any more; **rezeptpflichtig** [-pflɪçtɪç] ADJ available only on prescription; **etw ~ machen** to put sth on prescription

Rezession [retsɛˈsioːn] F **-, -en** (*Econ*) recession

rezitieren [retsiˈtiːrən], *ptp* **rezitiert** VTI to recite

R-Gespräch [ˈɛr-] NT reverse charge call (*Brit*), collect call (*US*)

rh [ɛrˈhaː] ABBR *von* **Rhesusfaktor negativ**

Rh [ɛrˈhaː] ABBR *von* **Rhesusfaktor positiv**

Rhabarber¹ [raˈbarbɐ] M **-s**, NO PL rhubarb

Rhabarber² NT **-s**, NO PL (*inf*: = *Gemurmel*) rhubarb

Rhein [rain] M **-s** Rhine

Rhein-: rheinab(wärts) [rainˈlap(vɛrts)] ADV down the Rhine; **Rheinarmee** F British Army of the Rhine; **rheinauf(wärts)** [rainˈlauf(vɛrts)] ADV up the Rhine; **Rheinfall** M Rhine Falls *pl*, Falls *pl* of the Rhine

rheinisch [ˈrainɪʃ] ADJ ATTR Rhenish

Rhein-: Rheinländer [ˈrainlɛndɐ] M **-s, -, Rheinländerin** [-ərɪn] F **-, -nen** Rhinelander; **rheinländisch** [ˈrainlɛndɪʃ] ADJ Rhineland; **Rheinland-Pfalz** [ˈrainlantˈpfalts] NT Rhineland-Palatinate; **Rheinwein** M Rhine wine; (*weißer auch*) hock

Rhesus- [ˈreːzʊs-]: **Rhesusaffe** M rhesus monkey; **Rhesusfaktor** M (*Med*) rhesus *or* Rh factor; **Rhesus(faktor) positiv/negativ** rhesus positive/negative

Rhetorik [reˈtoːrɪk] F **-, -en** rhetoric

rhetorisch [reˈtoːrɪʃ] **1** ADJ rhetorical; **~e Frage** rhetorical question **2** ADV **(a)** (*als Redner*) rhetorically; **~ begabt sein** to have a gift for rhetoric **(b)** **rein ~** rhetorically; **verstehen Sie diese Frage bitte rein ~** of course, you understand this question is purely rhetorical

Rheuma [ˈrɔyma] NT **-s**, NO PL rheumatism

Rheumatiker [rɔyˈmaːtikɐ] M **-s, -, Rheumatikerin** [-ərɪn] F **-, -nen** rheumatic

rheumatisch [rɔyˈmaːtɪʃ] **1** ADJ rheumatic **2** ADV **~ bedingte Schmerzen** rheumatic pains

Rheumatismus [rɔymaˈtɪsmʊs] M **-, Rheumatismen** [-mən] rheumatism

Rhinozeros [riˈnoːtserɔs] NT **-(ses), -se** rhinoceros, rhino (*inf*); (*inf*: = *Dummkopf*) fool

Rhodesien [roˈdeːziən] NT **-s** (*Hist*) Rhodesia

rhodesisch [roˈdeːzɪʃ] ADJ (*Hist*) Rhodesian

Rhododendron [rodoˈdɛndrɔn] M or NT **-s, Rhododendren** [-drən] rhododendron

Rhodos [ˈroːdɔs, ˈrɔdɔs] NT **-'** Rhodes

Rhombus [ˈrɔmbʊs] M **-, Rhomben** [-bn] rhombus

Rhythmik [ˈrʏtmik] F **-, -en** rhythmics *sing*; (*inf*: = *Rhythmus*) rhythm

rhythmisch [ˈrʏtmɪʃ] **1** ADJ rhythmic(al); **~e Prosa** rhythmic prose; **~e (Sport)gymnastik** rhythmic gymnastics *sing* **2** ADV rhythmically; **sie bewegten sich ~ zum Schlagen der Trommeln** they moved to the rhythm of the drums

Rhythmus [ˈrʏtmʊs] M **-, Rhythmen** [-mən] (*Mus, Poet, fig*) rhythm

Ribisel [ˈriːbiːzl] F **-, -n, Ribisl** [ˈriːbiːzl] F **-, -n** (*Aus*: = *Johannisbeere*) (*rot*) redcurrant; (*schwarz*) blackcurrant

Ribonukleinsäure [ribonukleˈiːn-] F (*abbr* **RNS**) ribonucleic acid

richten [ˈrɪçtn] **1** VT **(a)** (= *lenken*) to direct (*auf* +acc towards); **den Kurs nach Norden/Osten** *etc* **~** to set *or* steer a northerly/ easterly *etc* course; **einen Verdacht gegen jdn ~** to suspect sb **(b)** (= *ausrichten*) **etw nach jdm/etw ~** to suit *or* fit sth to sb/ sth; *Lebensstil, Verhalten* to orientate sth to sth/sth **(c)** (= *adressieren*) to address (*an* +acc to); *Kritik, Vorwurf* to direct (*gegen* at, against); **das Wort an jdn ~** to address sb **(d)** (*esp S Ger*) (= *zurechtmachen*) to get ready; (= *in Ordnung bringen*) to fix; (= *reparieren*) to fix; *Haare* to do **(e)** (= *einstellen*) to set; (*S Ger*: = *gerade biegen*) to straighten (out); **einen Knochenbruch ~** to set a fracture **2** VR **(a)** (= *sich hinwenden*) to be directed (*auf* +acc towards,

gegen at)
(b) (= *sich wenden*) to consult (*an jdn* sb); (*Maßnahme, Vorwurf etc*) to be directed (*gegen* at)
(c) (= *sich anpassen*) to follow (*nach jdm/etw* sb/sth); **sich nach den Vorschriften ~** to go by the rules; **sich nach jds Wünschen ~** to comply with sb's wishes; **ich richte mich nach dir** I'll fit in with you; **wir ~ uns ganz nach unseren Kunden** we are guided entirely by our customers' wishes; **warum sollte die Frau sich immer nach dem Mann ~?** why should the woman always do what the man wants?; **sich nach den Sternen/der Wettervorhersage/dem, was er behauptet, ~** to go by the stars/the weather forecast/what he maintains; **und richte dich (gefälligst) danach!** (*inf*) (kindly) do as you're told
(d) (= *abhängen von*) to depend (*nach* on)
(e) (*esp S Ger*: = *sich zurechtmachen*) to get ready
⊠ VI (*liter.* = *urteilen*) to pass judgement (*über +acc* on); **milde/streng ~** to be mild/harsh in one's judgement
Richter ['rɪçtɐ] M **-s, -**, **Richterin** [-ərɪn] F **-, -nen** judge; **jdn/einen Fall vor den ~ bringen** or **zerren** to bring sb/a case before a judge; **der vorsitzende ~** the presiding judge; **sich zum ~ aufwerfen** or **machen** (*fig*) to set (oneself) up in judgement
richterlich ['rɪçtɐlɪç] ADJ ATTR judicial
Richter-Skala ['rɪçtɐ-] F (*Geol*) Richter scale
Richter-: **Richterspruch** M **(a)** (*Jur*) ≈ judgement **(b)** (*Sport*) judges' decision; (*Pferderennen*) stewards' decision; **Richterstuhl** M Bench; (= *Richteramt*) judicial office; **auf dem ~ sitzen** to be on the Bench
Richt-: **Richtfest** NT topping-out ceremony; **Richtfeuer** NT (*Naut*) leading lights *pl*; (*Aviat*) approach lights *pl*
Richtfunk M directional radio
Richtfunkverbindung F microwave link
Richtgeschwindigkeit F recommended speed
richtig ['rɪçtɪç] **⊠ ADJ (a)** right *no comp*; (= *zutreffend*) correct, right; **der ~e Mann am ~en Ort** the right man for the job; **ich halte es für ~/das Richtigste, ...** I think it would be right/best ...; **nicht ganz ~ (im Kopf) sein** (*inf*) to be not quite right (in the head) (*inf*); **bin ich hier ~ bei Müller?** (*inf*) is this right for the Müllers?
(b) (= *wirklich, echt*) real; **der ~e Vater** the real father; **die ~e Mutter** the real mother; **ein ~er Idiot** a real idiot
⊠ ADV (a) (= *korrekt*) right; *passen, funktionieren, liegen etc* properly, correctly, right; **ich habe ihn ~ eingeschätzt** I was right about him; **~ gehend** *Uhr, Waage* accurate; **die Uhr geht ~** the clock is right or correct; **habe ich ~ gehört?** (*iro*) do my ears deceive me?; (*Gerücht betreffend*) is it right what I've heard?; **du kommst gerade ~!** you're just in time; (*iro*) you're just what I need
(b) (*inf*: = *ganz und gar*) really, real (*esp US inf*)
(c) (= *wahrhaftig*) right, correct; **das ist doch Paul! – ach ja, ~** that's Paul – oh yes, so it is; **wir dachten, es würde gleich regnen, und ~, kaum ...** we thought it would soon start raining and, sure enough, scarcely ...
Richtige(r) ['rɪçtɪɡə] MF DECL AS ADJ right person, right man/woman *etc*; (*zum Heiraten etc*) Mr/Miss Right; **du bist mir der ~!** (*iro*) you're a fine one (*inf*); **sechs ~ im Lotto** six right in the lottery
Richtige(s) ['rɪçtɪɡə] NT DECL AS ADJ right thing; **das ist das ~** that's right; **das ist genau das ~** that's just right; **das ist auch nicht das ~** that's not right either; **ich habe nichts ~s gegessen** I haven't had a proper meal; **ich habe nichts ~s gelernt** I didn't really learn anything; **ich habe noch nicht das ~ gefunden** I haven't found anything suitable
richtiggehend **⊠** ADJ ATTR (*inf*: = *regelrecht*) real, proper; *siehe auch* **richtig ⊠** ADV (*inf*) **~ intelligent** really intelligent; **das ist ja ~ Betrug** that's downright deceit
Richtigkeit F **-**, NO PL correctness; **an der ~ von etw zweifeln, bei etw an der ~ zweifeln** (*inf*) to doubt whether sth is correct or right; **die ~ einer Abschrift bescheinigen** to certify a copy as being accurate; **damit hat es** or **das hat schon seine ~** that's (quite) right
richtig-: **richtig liegen** VI IRREG (*inf*) to fit in; (= *recht haben*) to be right; **bei jdm ~** to get on well with sb; **richtig stellen** VT to correct; **ich muss Ihre Behauptung ~** I must put you right there; **Richtigstellung** F correction
Richt-: **Richtlinie** F guideline; **Richtlinienkompetenz** F (*Pol*) authority in matters of general policy; **Richtmikrofon** NT

directional microphone; **Richtpreis** M (**unverbindlicher**) **~** recommended price
Richtung ['rɪçtʊŋ] F **-, -en (a)** direction; **in ~ Hamburg** towards (*Brit*) or toward (*US*) Hamburg; **in ~ Süden** in a southerly direction; (*auf Autobahn*) on the southbound carriageway (*Brit*) or lane; **in nördliche ~** northwards, in a northerly direction; **die Autobahn/der Zug ~ Hamburg** the Hamburg autobahn/train; **nach allen ~en, in alle ~en** in all directions; **eine ~ nehmen** or **einschlagen** to head or drive/walk *etc* in a direction; **eine neue ~ bekommen** to take a new turn; **einem Gespräch eine bestimmte ~ geben** to turn a conversation in a particular direction; **in die gleiche ~ gehen** or **zielen** (*fig*) to point in the same direction; **er will sich nach keiner ~ hin festlegen** he won't commit himself in any way at all; **ein Schritt in die richtige/falsche ~** a step in the right/wrong direction; **ein Schritt in ~ Frieden und Stabilität** a step toward(s) peace and stability; **irgend etwas in der** or **dieser ~** something along those lines
(b) (= *Tendenz*) trend; (= *die Vertreter einer ~*) movement; (= *Denkrichtung, Lehrmeinung*) school of thought; **Picasso begann eine völlig neue ~ in der Malerei** Picasso started a completely new direction in painting; **sie gehören den verschiedensten politischen ~en an** they have the most varied political sympathies; **die ganze ~ passt uns nicht!** that's not the sort of thing we want
Richtungs-: **Richtungskampf** M (*Pol*) factional dispute; **richtungslos** ADJ lacking a sense of direction; **Richtungsstreit** M (*Pol*) factional dispute; **Richtungswechsel** M (*lit, fig*) change of direction
richtung(s)weisend ADJ pointing the way; **~ sein** to point the way (ahead)
rieb PRET *von* **reiben**
riechen ['riːçn], *pret* **roch** [rɔx], *ptp* **gerochen** [ɡəˈrɔxn] **⊠ VT** to smell; **ich rieche das Gewürz gern** I like the smell of this spice; **Lunte** or **den Braten ~** (*inf*) to smell a rat (*inf*); **ich kann das nicht ~** (*inf*) I can't stand the smell of it; (*fig*: = *nicht leiden*) I can't stand it; **jdn nicht ~ können** (*inf*) not to be able to stand sb; **das konnte ich doch nicht ~!** (*inf*) how was I (supposed) to know?
⊠ VI (a) (= *Geruchssinn haben*) to have a sense of smell; **nicht mehr ~ können** to have lost one's sense of smell; **Hunde können gut ~** dogs have a good sense of smell
(b) (= *bestimmten Geruch haben*) to smell; **gut/schlecht ~** to smell good/bad; **nach etw ~** to smell of sth; **aus dem Mund ~** to have bad breath; **das riecht nach Betrug/Verrat** (*fig inf*) that smacks of deceit/treachery
(c) (= *schnüffeln*) to sniff; **an jdm/etw ~** to sniff (at) sb/sth; **riech mal** have a sniff
⊠ VI IMPERS to smell; **es riecht angebrannt** there's a smell of burning; **es riecht nach Gas** there's a smell of gas
Riecher ['riːçɐ] M **-s, -** (*inf*) **einen ~ (für etw) haben** to have a nose (for sth); **da habe ich doch den richtigen ~ gehabt!** I knew it all along!
Riechnerv M olfactory nerve
Ried [riːt] NT **-s, -e** [-də] **(a)** (= *Schilf*) reeds *pl* **(b)** (*S Ger*: = *Moor*) marsh
Riedgras NT sedge
rief PRET *von* **rufen**
Riege ['riːɡə] F **-, -n** team
Riegel ['riːɡl] M **-s, - (a)** (= *Verschluss*) bolt; **den ~ an etw** (*dat*) **vorlegen** to bolt sth; **den ~ an etw** (*dat*) **zurückschieben** to unbolt sth; **einer Sache** (*dat*) **einen ~ vorschieben** or (*Sw*) **schieben** (*fig*) to put a stop to sth; **ein ~ gegen aggressive Politik** a restraint against aggressive policies
(b) (= *Schokoladenriegel, Seifenstück*) bar
Riemen¹ ['riːmən] M **-s, -** (= *Treibriemen, Gürtel*) belt; (*an Schuhen, Kleidung, Koffer, Gepäck*) strap; (= *Schnürsenkel*) leather shoelace; (= *Peitschenriemen*) thong; **den ~ enger schnallen** (*fig*) to tighten one's belt; **sich am ~ reißen** (*fig inf*) to get a grip on oneself
Riemen² M **-s, -** (*Sport*) oar; **sich in die ~ legen** (*lit, fig*) to put one's back into it
Riese¹ ['riːzə] M **das macht nach Adam ~ £ 3,50** (*hum inf*) the way I learned it at school that makes £3.50
Riese² M **-n, -n** (*lit, fig*) giant; (*sl*: = *Geldschein*) big one (*inf*); **ein böser ~** an ogre
Rieselfelder PL sewage farm

rieseln ['ri:zln] VI AUX SEIN (*Wasser, Sand*) to trickle; (*Regen*) to drizzle; (*Schnee*) to flutter down; (*Staub*) to fall down; (*Musik*) to filter; **der Kalk rieselt von der Wand** lime is crumbling off the wall; **Schuppen ~ ihm vom Kopf** dandruff is flaking off his head

Riesen- PREF gigantic, colossal; (*Zool, Bot etc auch*) giant; **Riesenameise** F carpenter ant; **Riesenarbeit** F (= *Pensum*) gigantic *etc* job; (= *Anstrengung*) gigantic *etc* effort; **Riesenchance** F tremendous chance; **Riesenerfolg** M gigantic *etc* success; (*Theat, Film*) smash hit; **Riesengebirge** NT (*Geog*) Sudeten Mountains *pl*; **riesengroß, riesenhaft** ADJ = riesig; **Riesenhai** M basking shark; **Riesenhunger** M (*inf*) enormous appetite; **ich habe einen ~** (*inf*) I could eat a horse (*inf*); **Riesenrad** NT big wheel, Ferris wheel; **Riesenschildkröte** F giant tortoise; **Riesenschlange** F boa; **Riesenschritt** M giant step; **wir nähern uns mit ~en dem amerikanischen System** we are moving swiftly toward(s) the American system; **einer Sache** (*dat*) **einen ~ näher kommen** to take a giant step towards sth; **Riesenslalom** M giant slalom

riesig ['ri:zɪç] **1** ADJ (a) (= *sehr groß, gigantisch*) enormous, huge; *Spaß* tremendous (b) (*inf*: = *toll*) fantastic (*inf*) **2** ADV (*inf*: = *sehr, überaus*) incredibly

Riesin ['ri:zɪn] F -, -nen giantess

Riesling ['ri:slɪŋ] M -s, -e Riesling

riet PRET *von* **raten**

Riff¹ [rɪf] NT -(e)s, -e (= *Felsklippe*) reef

Riff² M -(e)s, -s (*Mus*) riff

Rigg [rɪg] NT -s, -s (*Naut*) rigging

rigoros [rigo'ro:s] **1** ADJ rigorous; **ich bleibe dabei, da bin ich ganz ~** I'm sticking to that, I'm adamant **2** ADV *ablehnen* rigorously; *kürzen* drastically; **~ durchgreifen** to take decisive action

Rigorosum [rigo'ro:zʊm] NT -s, **Rigorosa** *or* (*Aus*) **Rigorosen** [-za, -zn] (*Univ*) (doctoral *or* PhD) viva (*Brit*) *or* oral

Rikscha ['rɪkʃa] F -, -s rickshaw

Rille ['rɪlə] F -, -n groove; (*in Säule*) flute

rin- [rɪn] PREF (*dial*) = **herein-, hinein-**

Rind [rɪnt] NT -(e)s, -er [-dɐ] (a) (= *Tier*) cow; (= *Bulle*) bull; **~er** cattle *pl*; **10 ~er** 10 head of cattle (b) (*inf*: = *~fleisch*) beef; **vom ~** beef *attr*; **Hackfleisch vom ~** minced (*esp Brit*) *or* ground (*US*) beef

Rinde ['rɪndə] F -, -n (= *Baumrinde*) bark; (= *Brotrinde*) crust; (= *Käserinde*) rind; (*Anat*) cortex

Rinder-: Rinderbraten M (*roh*) joint of beef; (*gebraten*) roast beef *no indef art*; **Rinderbremse** F horsefly; **Rinderbrust** F brisket (of beef); **Rinderfilet** NT fillet of beef; **Rinderherde** F herd of cattle; **Rinderpest** F (*Vet*) rinderpest; **Rinderseuche** F epidemic cattle disease; (= *BSE*) mad cow disease; **Rinderwahn(sinn)** M mad cow disease; **Rinderzucht** F cattle farming

Rindfleisch NT beef

Rinds- IN CPDS (*Aus, S Ger*) = **Rinder-: Rindsleder** NT cowhide; **rindsledern** ADJ ATTR cowhide

Rindvieh NT (a) NO PL cattle; **10 Stück ~** 10 head of cattle (b) *pl* **Rindviecher** (*inf*: = *Idiot*) ass (*inf*)

Ring [rɪŋ] M -(e)s, -e ring; (= *Kettenring*) link; (= *Wurfring*) quoit; (= *Einweckring*) seal; (= *Rettungsring*) life belt; (*auf dem Wasser, von Menschen*) circle; (= *~straße*) ring road; (**dunkle**) **~e unter den Augen haben** to have (dark) rings under one's eyes; **~e** (*Turnen*) rings; **~ frei!** (*Sport*) seconds out *or* away!; (*fig*) clear the decks!; **der ~ (des Nibelungen)** the Ring (of the Nibelung)

Ring-: ringartig ADJ ring-like; **Ringbuch** NT ring binder; **Ringbucheinlage** F loose-leaf pad

Ringelblume F marigold

Ringelgans F Brent goose

ringeln ['rɪŋln] **1** VT (*Pflanze*) to (en)twine; *Schwanz etc* to curl; *siehe auch* **geringelt 2** VR to curl; (*Rauch*) to curl up(wards); **der Schwanz des Schweins ringelt sich** the pig has a curly tail; **die Schlange ringelte sich um den Baum** the snake coiled itself around the tree

Ringel-: Ringelnatter F grass snake; **Ringelschwanz** M, **Ringelschwänzchen** NT (*inf*) curly tail; **Ringelspiel** NT (*Aus*) merry-go-round

ringen ['rɪŋən] *pret* **rang** [raŋ], *ptp* **gerungen** [gə'rʊŋən] **1** VT **die Hände ~** to wring one's hands; **er rang ihr das Messer aus der**

Hand he wrenched the knife from her hand **2** VI (a) (*lit, fig*: = *kämpfen*) to wrestle (*mit* with); **mit sich/dem Tode ~** to wrestle with oneself/death; **mit den Tränen ~** to struggle to keep back one's tears (b) (= *streben*) **nach** *or* **um etw ~** to struggle for sth

Ringen ['rɪŋən] NT -s, NO PL (*Sport*) wrestling; (*fig*) struggle

Ringer ['rɪŋɐ] M -s, -, **Ringerin** [-ərɪn] F -, -nen wrestler

Ring-: Ringfahndung F dragnet; **Ringfinger** M ring finger; **Ringkampf** M fight; (*Sport*) wrestling match; **Ringkämpfer(in)** M(F) wrestler

Ringlein ['rɪŋlain] NT -s, - ring

Ring-: Ringordner M ring binder; **Ringrichter(in)** M(F) (*Sport*) referee

rings [rɪŋs] ADV (all) around; **die Stadt ist ~ von Bergen umgeben** the town is completely surrounded by mountains; **wir mussten uns alle ~ im Kreis aufstellen** we all had to form a circle

ringsherum ['rɪŋsɛ'rʊm] ADV all (the way) around

Ringstraße F ring road

rings-: ringsum ['rɪŋs'ʊm] ADV (all) around; **~ konnte ich nichts sehen** I could see nothing around me; **ringsumher** ['rɪŋsʊm'heːɐ] ADV around

Rinne ['rɪnə] F -, -n (= *Rille*) groove; (= *Furche, Abflussrinne, Fahrrinne*) channel; (= *Dachrinne*) (*inf*: = *Rinnstein*) gutter; (*Geog*) gap

rinnen ['rɪnən], *pret* **rann** [ran], *ptp* **geronnen** [gə'rɔnən] VI AUX SEIN (= *fließen*) to run; **das Blut rann ihm in Strömen aus der Wunde** blood streamed from his wound; **das Geld rinnt ihm durch die Finger** (*fig*) money slips through his fingers

Rinn-: Rinnsal ['rɪnzaːl] NT -(e)s, -e rivulet; **Rinnstein** M (= *Gosse*) gutter

Rippchen ['rɪpçən] NT -s, - (*Cook*) *slightly cured pork rib*

Rippe ['rɪpə] F -, -n (a) (*Anat, Cook, Bot*) rib; **bei ihm kann man die ~n zählen** (*inf*) you could play a tune on his ribs (*inf*); **er hat nichts auf den ~n** (*inf*) he's just skin and bone(s); **... damit du was auf die ~n kriegst** (*inf*) ... to put a bit of flesh on you; **ich kann es mir nicht aus den ~n schneiden** (*inf*), **ich kann es doch nicht durch die ~n schwitzen** (*inf*) I can't just produce it from nowhere (b) (*von Heizkörper, Kühlaggregat*) fin

Rippen-: Rippenbruch M broken *or* fractured rib; **Rippenfell** NT pleura; **Rippenfellentzündung** F pleurisy; **Rippenspeer** M *or* NT (*Cook*) spare rib; **Kass(e)ler ~** *slightly cured pork spare rib*; **Rippenstrickpulli** M ribbed sweater; **Rippenstück** NT (*Cook*) *joint of meat including ribs*

Rippli ['rɪpli] PL (*Sw*) ribs *pl*

Risiko ['ri:ziko] NT -s, -s *or* **Risiken** *or* (*Aus*) **Risken** ['ri:zikn, 'rɪskn] risk; **auf eigenes ~** at one's own risk; **ohne ~** without risk; **etw ohne ~ tun** to do sth without taking a risk; **es ist nicht ohne ~, das zu tun** doing that is not without risk; **die Sache ist ohne ~** there's no risk involved; **als gutes ~ gelten** to be a good (credit) risk

Risiko-: Risikobereitschaft F readiness to take risks; **sie hat eine hohe ~** she is prepared to take big risks; **Risikofaktor** M risk factor; **risikofreudig** ADJ prepared to take risks; **sie ist sehr ~** she likes to take risks; **Risikogeburt** F (*Med*) high-risk birth; **Risikogruppe** F (high-)risk group; **Risikokapital** NT (*Fin*) risk *or* venture capital; **Risikolebensversicherung** F (renewable) term life insurance; **Risikoschwangerschaft** F (*Med*) high-risk pregnancy; **Risikoträger(in)** M(F) (*von Krankheit*) high-risk carrier; (*Insur, Fin*) risk bearer; **~ von Lungenkrebs sein** to be in a high-risk category for lung cancer; **Risikoversicherung** F term insurance

riskant [rɪs'kant] ADJ risky

riskieren [rɪs'ki:rən], *ptp* **riskiert** VT (a) (= *aufs Spiel setzen*) to risk; **etwas/nichts ~** to take risks/no risks; **seine Stellung/sein Geld ~** to put one's job/money at risk; **sein Geld bei etw ~** to risk one's money on sth (b) (= *wagen*) to venture; **traust du dich, hier runterzuspringen? – ja, ich riskiers!** do you think you dare jump down? – yes, I'll risk it!; **in Gegenwart seiner Frau riskiert er kein Wort** when his wife is present he dare not say a word

riss PRET *von* **reißen**

Riss [rɪs] M -es, -e (*in Stoff, Papier etc*) tear, rip; (*in Erde, Gestein*) fissure; (= *Sprung: in Wand, Behälter etc*) crack; (= *Hautriss*) chap; (*fig*: = *Kluft*) rift, split; **die Freundschaft hat einen (tiefen) ~ bekommen** a (deep) rift has developed in their friendship; **durch das Volk geht ein tiefer ~** there is a deep split in the people

rissig ['rɪsɪç] ADJ *Boden, Wand, Leder* cracked; *Haut, Hände, Lippen* chapped

Risswunde F laceration

Riten PL *von* **Ritus**

ritt PRET *von* **reiten**

Ritt [rɪt] M **-(e)s, -e** ride

Rittberger ['rɪtbɛrɡɐ] M **-s, -** (*Eiskunstlauf*) Rittberger

Ritter ['rɪtɐ] M **-s, -** **(a)** (*im Mittelalter, im alten Rom*) knight; (= *Kavalier*) cavalier; (*fig, hum*: = *Kämpfer*) champion; **fahrender ~** knight errant; **jdn zum ~ schlagen** to knight sb; **ein ~ ohne Furcht und Tadel** (*lit*) a doughty knight; (*fig*) a knight in shining armour (*Brit*) *or* armor (*US*) **(b)** (*Adelstitel*) ≈ Sir; **X ~ von Y** ≈ Sir X of Y; (*Cook*) **arme ~** *pl* ≈ bread-and-butter pudding

Ritter-: Ritterburg F knight's castle; **Rittergut** NT ≈ manor; **ritterlich** ['rɪtɐlɪç] ADJ (*lit*) knightly; (*fig*) chivalrous; **Ritterorden** M order of knights; **der Deutsche ~** the Teutonic Order; **Ritterrüstung** F knight's armour (*Brit*) *or* armor (*US*); **Ritterschaft** ['rɪtɐʃaft] F **-, -en (a)** (= *die Ritter*) knights *pl* **(b)** (= *Ritterehre*) knighthood; **Ritterschlag** M (*Hist*) dubbing; (*fig*) ennoblement; **den ~ empfangen** to be knighted; **(jdm) den ~ erteilen** to confer a knighthood (on sb); **Rittersporn** M, *pl* **-sporne** (*Bot*) larkspur, delphinium; **Ritterstand** M knighthood; **Rittertum** ['rɪtɐtuːm] NT **-s,** NO PL knighthood

rittlings ['rɪtlɪŋs] ADV astride (*auf etw* (*dat*) sth)

Ritual [ri'tuaːl] NT **-s, -e** *or* **-ien** [-liən] (*lit, fig*) ritual

Ritualmord M ritual murder

rituell [ri'tuɛl] ADJ (*Rel, fig*) ritual

Ritus ['riːtʊs] M **-, Riten** [-tn] rite; (*fig*) ritual

Ritze ['rɪtsə] F **-, -n** (= *Riss, Poritze*) crack; (= *Fuge*) gap; **auf der ~ schlafen** (*hum inf*) to sleep in the middle

Ritzel ['rɪtsl] NT **-s, -** (*Tech*) pinion

ritzen ['rɪtsn] **1** VT to scratch **2** VR to scratch oneself

Rivale [ri'vaːlə] M **-n, -n, Rivalin** [ri'vaːlɪn] F **-, -nen** rival

rivalisieren [rivali'ziːrən], *ptp* **rivalisiert** VI **mit jdm (um etw) ~** to compete with sb (for sth); **34 ~de Parteien** 34 rival parties

Rivalität [rivali'tɛːt] F **-, -en** rivalry

Riviera [ri'vieːra] F - Riviera

Rizinus ['riːtsinʊs] M **-, -** *or* **-se (a)** (*Bot*) castor-oil plant **(b)** (*auch* **Rizinusöl**) castor oil

RNS [ɛrɛn'lɛs] F **-,** ABBR *von* **Ribonukleinsäure** RNA

Roastbeef ['roːstbiːf] NT **-s, -s** (*roh*) beef; (*gebraten*) roast beef

Robbe ['rɔbə] F **-, -n** seal

robben ['rɔbn] VI AUX SEIN (*Mil*) to crawl

Robben-: Robbenfang M sealing, seal hunting; **Robbenfänger(in)** M(F) sealer, seal hunter; **Robbenjagd** F sealing, seal hunting

Robe ['roːbə] F **-, -n (a)** (= *Abendkleid*) evening gown; **in großer ~** in evening dress **(b)** (= *Amtstracht*) robes *pl*

Robinie [ro'biːniə] F **-, -n** robinia

Robotbild ['rɔbɔt-] NT (*Sw*) Identikit® (picture)

Roboter ['rɔbɔtɐ] M **-s, -** robot

Robotertechnik F, **Robotik** [ro'boːtɪk] F **-,** NO PL robotics *sing or pl*

robust [ro'bʊst] ADJ robust; *Material* tough

Robustheit F **-,** NO PL robustness; (*von Material*) toughness

roch PRET *von* **riechen**

röcheln ['rœçln] VI to groan; (*Sterbender*) to give the death rattle; **~d atmen** to breathe with a rasping sound

Rochen ['rɔxn] M **-s, -** ray

Rock¹ [rɔk] M **-(e)s, ⸚e** ['rœkə] (= *Damenrock*) skirt; (= *Schottenrock*) kilt; (*Sw:* = *Kleid*) dress

Rock² M **-s,** NO PL (*Mus*) rock

rocken ['rɔkn] VI (*Mus*) to rock

Rocker ['rɔkɐ] M **-s, -, Rockerin** [-ərɪn] F **-, -nen** rocker

rockig ['rɔkɪç] **1** ADJ *Musik* which sounds like (hard) rock **2** ADV **~ klingender Blues** blues which sounds like (hard) rock

Rock-: Rockmusik F rock music; **Rocksaum** M hem of a/the skirt; **Rockstar** M rock star; **Rockzipfel** M **der Mutter am ~ hängen, an Mutters ~ hängen** (*inf*) to be tied to (one's)

mother's apron strings (*inf*); **an jds ~** (*dat*) **hängen** (*inf*) to cling to sb's coat-tails (*inf*)

Rodel ['roːdl] M **-s, -** *or* (*S Ger, Aus*) F **-, -n** toboggan

Rodelbahn F toboggan run

rodeln ['roːdln] VI AUX SEIN *or* HABEN to toboggan (*auch Sport*)

Rodel-: Rodelschlitten M toboggan; **Rodelsport** M tobogganing

roden ['roːdn] VT *Wald, Land* to clear; *Kartoffeln* to lift

Rodung ['roːdʊŋ] F **-, -en** clearing

Rogen ['roːɡn] M **-s, -** roe

Roggen ['rɔɡn] M **-s,** NO PL rye

roh [roː] **1** ADJ **(a)** (= *ungebraten, ungekocht*) raw; *Milch* unpasteurized **(b)** (= *unbearbeitet*) *Bretter, Stein etc* rough; *Diamant* uncut; *Eisen, Metall* crude; *Felle* untreated **(c)** (= *unkultiviert, brutal*) rough; **~e Gewalt** brute force; **wo ~e Kräfte sinnlos walten ...** (*prov*) brute force does it **2** ADV **(a)** (= *ungekocht*) raw **(b)** (= *grob*) *behauen, zusammen nageln* roughly **(c)** (= *brutal*) brutally

Roh-: Rohbau M, *pl* **-bauten** (*Bauabschnitt*) shell (of a/the building); **das Haus ist im ~ fertig (gestellt)** the house is structurally complete; **Rohdiamant** M rough *or* uncut diamond; **Roheisen** NT pig iron

Roheit ['roːhait] F **-, -en** *siehe* **Rohheit**

Roh-: Rohentwurf M rough draft; **Rohfaser** F raw fibre (*Brit*) *or* fiber (*US*); **Rohgewinn** M gross profit; **Rohheit** ['roːhait] F **-, -en (a)** NO PL (*Eigenschaft*) roughness; (= *Brutalität*) brutality **(b)** (*Tat*) brutality **(c)** (= *ungekochter Zustand*) rawness; **Rohkost** F raw fruit and vegetables *pl*; **Rohleder** NT untanned leather, rawhide (*US*); **Rohling** ['roːlɪŋ] M **-s, -e (a)** (= *Grobian*) brute **(b)** (*Tech*) blank; **Rohmaterial** NT raw material; **Rohöl** NT crude oil

Rohr [roːɐ] NT **-(e)s, -e (a)** (= *einzelnes Schilfrohr*) reed; (= *Röhricht, Schilf*) reeds *pl*; (= *Zuckerrohr*) cane; (*für Stühle etc*) cane, wicker *no pl* **(b)** (*Tech, Mech*) pipe; (= *Geschützrohr*) (gun) barrel; (= *Blasrohr*) blowpipe; **aus allen ~en feuern** (*lit*) to fire with all its guns; (*fig*) to use all one's fire power; **volles ~** (*inf*) flat out, at full speed **(c)** (*S Ger, Aus:* = *Backröhre*) oven

Röhrchen ['røːɐçən] NT **-s, -** tube; (*Chem*) test tube; (*inf: zur Alkoholkontrolle*) Breathalyzer®; **ins ~ blasen** (*inf*) to be breathalyzed

Röhre ['røːrə] F **-, -n (a)** (= *Ofenröhre*) warming oven; (= *Backröhre*) oven; (= *Drainageröhre*) drainage pipe; **in die ~ gucken** (*inf*) to be left out **(b)** (= *Neonröhre*) (neon) tube; (= *Elektronenröhre*) valve (*Brit*), tube (*US*); (= *Fernsehröhre*) tube **(c)** (= *Höhlung, Hohlkörper*) tube; (*in Knochen*) cavity; (*von Tunnel, U-Bahn*) tube

röhren ['røːrən] VI (*Hunt*) to bell; (*Motorrad, Mensch*) to roar

Röhren-: röhrenförmig ADJ tubular; *Hosenbein* drainpipe *attr*; **Röhrenhose** F (*inf*) drainpipe trousers *pl* (*esp Brit*), drainpipes *pl*; **Röhrenknochen** M long bone; **Röhrenpilz** M boletus

Rohr-: Rohrgeflecht NT wickerwork, basketwork; **Rohrkolben** M (*Bot*) reed mace, cat's tail; **Rohrleitung** F conduit; **Rohrleitungssystem** NT system of pipes

Röhrling ['røːrlɪŋ] M **-s, -e** (*Bot*) boletus

Rohr-: Rohrmöbel PL cane (*esp Brit*) *or* wicker furniture *sing*; **Rohrmuffe** F (*Tech*) socket; **Rohrpost** F pneumatic dispatch system; **Rohrstock** M cane; **Rohrstuhl** M basketwork *or* wickerwork chair; **Rohrzange** F pipe wrench; **Rohrzucker** M cane sugar

Roh-: Rohseide F wild silk; **rohseiden** ADJ wild silk

Rohstoff M raw material; (*St Ex*) commodity

Rohstoff-: Rohstoffabkommen NT commodity agreement; **Rohstoffbörse** F commodities market; **Rohstoffmangel** M shortage of raw materials; **Rohstoffmarkt** M commodities market; **Rohstoffpreis** M commodity price; **Rohstoffreserven** PL reserves *pl* of raw materials

Rohzustand M natural state *or* condition; **im ~** (*Denkmal etc*) in its initial stages; (*Übersetzung*) in its first draft

Rokoko ['rɔkoko, ro'kɔko, roko'koː] NT **-(s),** NO PL Rococo period; (= *Stil*) rococo

Rolladen M *siehe* **Rollladen**

Rollbahn F (*Aviat*) taxiway; (= *Start-, Landebahn*) runway

Röllchen ['rœlçən] NT **-s, -** little roll; (*von Garn*) reel

Rolle ['rɔlə] F -, -n **(a)** (= Zusammengerolltes) roll; (= Garnrolle, Zwirnrolle, Papierrolle) reel; (= Urkunde) scroll; **eine ~ Garn/ Zwirn** a reel of thread; **eine ~ Bindfaden** a ball of string; **eine ~ Toilettenpapier** a toilet roll; **eine ~ Film** a roll of film; (im Kino) a reel of film
(b) (= kleines Rad, Walze) roller; (an Möbeln, Kisten) caster, castor; (an Flaschenzug) pulley; (= Gardinenrolle) runner; **von der ~ sein** (fig inf) to have lost it (inf)
(c) (Sport, Aviat) roll; **eine ~ machen** to do a roll
(d) (Theat, Film, fig) role, part; (Sociol) role; **ein Stück mit verteilten ~n lesen** to read a play with the parts cast; (in Schule) to read a play with the parts given out; **eine Ehe mit streng verteilten ~n** a marriage with strict allocation of roles; **jds ~ bei** or **in etw** (fig) sb's role or part in sth; **er gefällt sich** (dat) **in der ~ des ...** (fig) he likes to see himself in the role of the ...; **sich in die ~ eines anderen versetzen** (fig) to put oneself in sb else's place; **bei** or **in etw** (dat) **eine ~ spielen** to play a part in sth; **etw spielt eine große ~ (bei jdm)** sth is very important (to sb); **es spielt keine ~, (ob) ...** it doesn't matter (whether) ...; **das spielt hier keine ~** that is irrelevant; **bei ihm spielt Geld keine ~** with him money is no object; **aus der ~ fallen** (fig) to do/say the wrong thing; **du bist aber gestern wirklich aus der ~ gefallen!** you really behaved badly yesterday!

rollen ['rɔlən] ▮ VI **(a)** AUX SEIN to roll; (Flugzeug) to taxi; **der Stein kommt ins Rollen** (fig) the ball has started rolling; **die Ermittlungen sind ins Rollen gekommen** the investigation has gathered momentum; **etw/den Stein ins Rollen bringen** (fig) to set or start sth/the ball rolling; **es werden einige Köpfe ~** heads will roll; **die Privatisierungswelle rollt** privatizations are in full flow
(b) mit den Augen ~ to roll one's eyes
▮ VT to roll; Teig to roll out; Teppich, Papier to roll up
Rollen-: **Rollenbesetzung** F (Theat, Film) casting; **Rollenlager** NT roller bearings pl; **Rollenprüfstand** M (Tech) rolling road dynamometer; **rollenspezifisch** ADJ role-specific; **Rollenspiel** NT role play; **Rollentausch** M exchange of roles; **Rollenverständnis** NT understanding of one's role; **Rollenverteilung** F (Sociol) role allocation
Roller ['rɔlɐ] M -s, - **(a)** (= Motorroller, für Kinder) scooter **(b)** (Aus: = Rollo) (roller) blind
Rollerblades® ['rɔlɐbleɪdz] PL Rollerblades® pl
Rollerfahren NT -s, NO PL riding a scooter
Roll-: **Rollfeld** NT runway; **Rollfuhrdienst** M road-rail haulage; **Rollgeld** NT freight charge; **Rollgut** NT (Rail) freight
rollig ['rɔlɪç] ADJ (inf) Katze on (Brit) or in heat; (sl) Mensch horny (inf)
Roll-: **Rollkommando** NT raiding party; **Rollkragen** M polo neck; **Rollkragenpullover** M polo-neck sweater; **Rollladen** M (an Fenster, Tür etc) (roller) shutters pl; (von Schreibtisch) roll top; (von Schrank) roll front; **Rollmops** M rollmops
Rollo ['rɔlo, rɔ'lo:] NT -s, -s (roller) blind
Roll-over-Kredit [rɔl'o:vɐ-] M rollover loan
Rollschuh M roller skate; **~ laufen** to roller-skate
Rollschuh-: **Rollschuhlaufen** NT -s, NO PL roller-skating; **Rollschuhläufer(in)** M(F) roller skater
Roll-: **Rollsplitt** M loose chippings pl; **Rollsteg** M moving pavement (Brit), mobile walkway (US)
Rollstuhl M wheelchair
Rollstuhl-: **Rollstuhlfahrer(in)** M(F) wheelchair user; **rollstuhlgerecht** ADJ, ADV suitable for wheelchairs
Rolltreppe F escalator
Rom [ro:m] NT -s Rome; **~ ist auch nicht an einem Tag erbaut worden** (prov) Rome wasn't built in a day (Prov); **viele** or **alle Wege führen nach ~** (Prov) all roads lead to Rome (Prov); **das sind Zustände wie im alten ~** (inf) (unmoralisch) it's disgraceful; (primitiv) it's medieval (inf)
ROM [rɔm] NT -s, -s (Comput) ROM
Roma ['ro:ma] PL (= Zigeuner) Romanies pl
Roman [ro'ma:n] M -s, -e novel
romanartig ADJ novelistic
Romanautor(in) M(F), **Romancier** [romã'sie:] M -s, -s novelist
Romandie [roman'di:] F - (esp Sw) **die ~** French-speaking Switzerland
Roman-: **Romanheld** M hero of a/the novel; **Romanheldin** F heroine of a/the novel

Romanik [ro'ma:nɪk] F -, NO PL (Archit, Art) Romanesque period; (Stil) Romanesque (style)
romanisch [ro'ma:nɪʃ] ADJ Volk, Sprache Romance; (Art, Archit) Romanesque
Romanist [roma'nɪst] M -en, -en, **Romanistin** [-'nɪstɪn] F -, -nen (Univ) student of or (Wissenschaftler) expert on Romance languages and literature
Romanistik [roma'nɪstɪk] F -, NO PL (Univ) Romance languages and literature
romanistisch [roma'nɪstɪʃ] ADJ Romance; **~es Institut** (Univ) Institute for Romance Languages and Literature
Romantik [ro'mantɪk] F -, NO PL **(a)** (Liter, Art, Mus) Romanticism; (Epoche) Romantic period **(b)** (fig) romance; (Gefühl, Einstellung) romanticism; **keinen Sinn für ~ haben** to have no sense of romance
Romantiker [ro'mantɪkɐ] M -s, -, **Romantikerin** [-ərɪn] F -, -nen (Liter, Art, Mus) Romantic; (fig) romantic
romantisch [ro'mantɪʃ] ▮ ADJ romantic; (Liter etc) Romantic ▮ ADV romantically; **~ liegen** to be in a romantic spot
romantsch [ro'mantʃ] ADJ = rätoromanisch
Romanze [ro'mantsə] F -, -n (Liter, Mus, fig) romance
Römer¹ ['rø:mɐ] M -s, - wineglass with clear glass bowl and green or brown coiled stem
Römer² ['rø:mɐ] M -s, -, **Römerin** [-ərɪn] F -, -nen Roman; **die alten ~** the (ancient) Romans
Römer-: **Römerreich** NT Roman Empire; **Römertopf®** M (Cook) clay casserole dish; **Römertum** ['rø:mɐtu:m] NT -s, NO PL Roman culture etc; **die Haupttugenden des ~s** the main virtues of Rome
römisch ['rø:mɪʃ] ADJ Roman; **~ 12** 12 in Roman numerals
römisch-katholisch ['rø:mɪʃka'to:lɪʃ] ADJ Roman Catholic
Rommé [rɔ'me:, 'rɔme] NT -s, -s, **Rommee** NT -s, -s rummy
röntgen ['rœntgn] VT to X-ray
Röntgen NT -s, NO PL X-raying; **er ist gerade beim ~** he's just being X-rayed
Röntgen-: **Röntgenapparat** M X-ray equipment no indef art, no pl; **Röntgenaufnahme** F X-ray (plate); **Röntgendiagnostik** F X-ray diagnosis; **Röntgenfilm** M X-ray film
röntgenisieren [rœntgeni'zi:rən], ptp **röntgenisiert** VT (Aus) to X-ray
Röntgenlaser M X-ray laser
Röntgenologe [rœntgeno'lo:gə] M -n, -n, **Röntgenologin** [-'lo:gɪn] F -, -nen radiologist
Röntgenologie [rœntgenolo'gi:] F -, NO PL radiology
Röntgen-: **Röntgenpass** M X-ray registration card; **Röntgenreihenuntersuchung** F X-ray screening; **Röntgenstrahlen** PL X-rays pl; **Röntgentherapie** F X-ray therapy; **Röntgenuntersuchung** F X-ray examination
RoRo-Verkehr ['ro:ro:-] M roll-on/roll-off service, RORO
rosa ['ro:za] ADJ INV pink; **ein ~** or **~nes** (inf) Kleid a pink dress; **die Welt durch eine ~(rote) Brille sehen** to see the world through rose-coloured (Brit) or rose-colored (US) glasses; **in ~(rotem) Licht** in a rosy light; **er malt die Zukunft ~rot** he paints a rosy picture of the future
Röschen ['rø:sçən] NT -s, - (little) rose; (von Broccoli, Blumenkohl) floret; (von Rosenkohl) sprout
Rose ['ro:zə] F -, -n **(a)** (Blume) rose; (Archit) rose window; **er ist nicht auf ~n gebettet** (fig) life isn't a bed of roses for him **(b)** (Med) erysipelas (spec)
rosé [ro'ze:] ADJ INV pink; **Schuhe in ~** pink shoes
Rosé [ro'ze:] M -s, -s rosé (wine)
Rosen-: **rosenfarben** [-farbn], **rosenfarbig** ADJ pink; **Rosengarten** M rose garden; **Rosengewächse** PL rosaceae pl (spec); **Rosenholz** NT rosewood; **Rosenkohl** M Brussel(s) sprouts pl; **Rosenkranz** M (Eccl) rosary; **Rosenkriege** PL (Hist) the Wars of the Roses pl; **Rosenmontag** M Monday preceding

Ash Wednesday; **Rosenmontagszug** M *Carnival parade which takes place on the Monday preceding Ash Wednesday*

ROSENMONTAG

Rosenmontag *is the last Monday of* ***Karneval***. *Traditional processions take place on this day: bands and carnival club members go through the streets wearing costumes and throwing toffees (***Kamellen***), sweets and flowers into the crowd, who are also dressed up for the occasion. There are also big carnival floats which pass comment on the year's events and carry huge papier-mâché figures which poke fun at local and national politicians* ▶ KARNEVAL

Rosen-: Rosenquarz M rose quartz; **Rosenstock** M rose (tree); **Rosenstrauch** M rosebush

Rosette [ro'zetə] F **-, -n** rosette

Roséwein M rosé wine

rosig ['ro:zɪç] ADJ (*lit, fig*) rosy; *Braten* pink; **etw in ~em Licht sehen** (*inf*) to see sth in a rosy light; **etw in ~en Farben schildern** (*inf*) to show sth in a rosy light

Rosine [ro'zi:nə] F **-, -n** raisin; **(große) ~n im Kopf haben** (*inf*) to have big ideas; **sich** (*dat*) **die (besten** *or* **größten) ~n (aus dem Kuchen) herauspicken** (*inf*) to take the pick of the bunch

Rosmarin ['ro:smari:n, ro:sma'ri:n] M **-s,** NO PL rosemary

Ross [rɔs] NT **-es, -e** *or* (*S Ger, Aus, Sw*) **Rösser** ['ræse] (*liter*) steed; (*S Ger, Aus, Sw*) horse; **~ und Reiter nennen** (*fig geh*) to name names; **auf dem hohen ~ sitzen** (*fig*) to be on one's high horse

Rössel ['ræsl] NT **-s, -** (*Chess*) knight

Rösselsprung M (*Chess*) knight's move

Ross-: Rosshaar NT horsehair; **Rosskastanie** F horse chestnut; **Rosskur** F (*hum*) kill-or-cure remedy; **eine ~ (durch)machen** to follow a drastic cure

Rössl ['ræsl] NT **-s, -** (*Chess*) knight

Rösslispiel ['ræsli-] NT (*Sw*) merry-go-round

Rost¹ [rɔst] M **-(e)s,** NO PL (*auch Bot*) rust; **~ ansetzen** to start to rust

Rost² M **-(e)s, -e** (= *Ofenrost*) grill; (= *Gitterrost*) grating, grille; (*dial* = *Bettrost*) frame; **auf dem ~ braten** (*Cook*) to barbecue

Rost-: Rostbraten M (*Cook*) ≈ roast; **Rostbratwurst** F barbecue sausage; **rostbraun** ADJ russet; *Haar* auburn

rosten ['rɔstn] VI AUX SEIN *or* HABEN to rust, to get rusty (*auch fig*)

rösten [(*S Ger*) 'rø:stn, (*N Ger*) 'ræstn] VT *Kaffee, Erdnüsse, Kastanien* to roast; *Brot* to toast

Rost-: rostfarben, rostfarbig ADJ = **rostbraun**; **Rostfleck** M patch of rust; **Rostfraß** M rust corrosion; **rostfrei** ADJ *Stahl* stainless

röstfrisch [(*S Ger*) 'rø:st-, (*N Ger*) 'ræst-] ADJ *Kaffee* freshly roasted

Rösti [(*S Ger*) 'rø:sti, (*N Ger*) 'ræsti] PL *fried grated potatoes*

rostig ['rɔstɪç] ADJ (*lit, fig*) rusty

Röstigraben M (*esp Sw hum*) *lack of understanding between the German-speaking and French-speaking Swiss*

Röstkartoffeln [(*S Ger*) 'rø:st-, (*N Ger*) 'ræst-] PL sauté potatoes *pl*

Rostschutz M antirust protection

Rostschutz-: Rostschutzfarbe F antirust paint; **Rostschutzmittel** NT rustproofer

Röstzwiebeln [(*S Ger*) 'rø:st-, (*N Ger*) 'ræst-] PL fried onions *pl*

rot [ro:t] **1** ADJ, *comp* **röter** ['rø:te], *superl* **röteste(r, s)** ['rø:təstə] red (*auch Pol*); **Rote Bete** *or* **Rüben** beetroot (*Brit*), beets *pl* (*US*); **~e Karte** (*Ftbl*) red card; **das Rote Kreuz** the Red Cross; **der Rote Halbmond** the Red Crescent; **der Rote Platz** Red Square; **das Rote Meer** the Red Sea; **die Roten** (*pej*) the reds; **~e Zahlen schreiben, in den ~en Zahlen stecken** to be in the red; **Gewalt zieht sich wie ein ~er Faden durch die Geschichte** violence runs like a thread through history; **~ werden** to blush, to go red; **bis über beide Ohren ~ werden** to blush scarlet, to turn crimson; **~ wie ein Krebs** red as a lobster; **~e Ohren bekommen** (*hum*), **einen ~en Kopf bekommen** *or* **kriegen** (*inf*) to blush, to go red; **~ sein** (*Pol inf*) to be a socialist

2 ADV, *comp* **röter**, *superl* **am rötesten (a)** (= *mit ~er Farbe*) *anmalen* red; *schreiben, unterstreichen, anstreichen* in red; **die Lippen ~ schminken** to use a red lipstick; **sich** (*dat*) **etw ~ (im Kalender) anstreichen** (*inf*) to mark sth a red-letter day; **den Tag werde ich mir ~ im Kalender anstreichen** that will be a red-letter day

(b) (= *in ~er Farbe*) *glühen, leuchten* a bright red; **~ anlaufen** to

turn red; **~ gerändert** red-rimmed; **~ glühend** *Metall* red-hot; **der ~ glühende Abendhimmel** the red glow of the evening sky; **~ verheulte Augen** eyes red from crying

(c) (*Pol inf*) **~ angehaucht sein** to have left-wing leanings

Rot [ro:t] NT **-s, -s** *or* **-** red; (= *Wangenrot*) rouge; **bei** *or* **auf ~** at red; **bei ~ anhalten!** stop (when the lights are) at red; **die Ampel stand auf ~** the lights were (at) red; **bei ~ über die Ampel fahren/gehen** to go through the lights/cross at a red light

Rotation [rota'tsio:n] F **-, -en** rotation

Rot-: Rotauge NT (*Zool*) roach; **rotbackig** [-bakɪç], **rotbäckig** [-bɛkɪç] ADJ rosy-cheeked; **Rotbarsch** M rosefish; **Rotbart** M red-beard; **Kaiser ~** Emperor Frederick Barbarossa; **rotblond** ADJ (*Männer*)*haar* sandy; *Mann* sandy-haired; *Frau, Tönung* strawberry blonde; **rotbraun** ADJ reddish brown

Röte ['rø:tə] F **-,** NO PL redness, red; (= *Erröten*) blush; **die ~ stieg ihr ins Gesicht** her face reddened

Rote-Armee-Fraktion [ro:təlar'me:-] F Red Army Faction

Rote Khmer [kme:ɐ] PL Khmer Rouge *pl*

Röteln ['rø:tln] PL German measles *sing*

röten ['rø:tn] **1** VT to make red; *Himmel* to turn red; **ein gerötetes Gesicht** a flushed face; **gerötete Augen** red eyes **2** VR to turn *or* become red

Rot-: rotgerändert [-gərɛndɐt] ADJ siehe **rot**; **rotgesichtig** [-gəzɪçtɪç] ADJ red-faced; **rotglühend** ADJ siehe **rot**; **rotgrün** ADJ red-green; **die ~e Koalition** the Red-Green coalition; **Rotgrünblindheit** F red-green colour (*Brit*) *or* color (*US*) blindness; **rothaarig** ADJ red-haired

rotieren [ro'ti:rən], *ptp* **rotiert** VI (*auch Pol*) to rotate; (*inf:* = *hektisch handeln*) to flap (*inf*); **anfangen zu ~** (*inf*) to get into a flap (*inf*); **am Rotieren sein** (*inf*) to be in a flap (*inf*)

Rot-: Rotkabis M (*Sw*) red cabbage; **Rotkäppchen** [-kɛpçən] NT **-s,** NO PL (*Liter*) Little Red Riding Hood; **Rotkehlchen** [-ke:lçən] NT **-s, -** robin; **Rotkohl** M red cabbage; **Rotkraut** NT (*S Ger, Aus*) red cabbage

rötlich ['rø:tlɪç] ADJ reddish

Rotlicht NT red light

Rotlicht-: Rotlichtmilieu NT demimonde; **Rotlichtviertel** NT red-light district

Rotor ['ro:to:ɐ] M **-s, Rotoren** [-'to:rən] rotor

Rot-: rotsehen ['ro:tze:ən] VI SEP IRREG (*inf*) to see red (*inf*); **Rotstift** M red pencil; **den ~ ansetzen** (*fig*) to cut back drastically; **dem ~ zum Opfer fallen** (*fig*) to be scrapped; **Rottanne** F Norway spruce

Rottweiler ['rɔtvaile] M **-s, -** Rottweiler

Rötung ['rø:tʊŋ] F **-, -en** reddening

Rot-: rotverheult ADJ siehe **rot**; **rotwangig** [-vaŋɪç] ADJ *Mensch* rosy-cheeked; *Apfel* rosy; **Rotwein** M red wine; **Rotwild** NT red deer

Rotz [rɔts] M **-es,** NO PL (*inf*) snot (*inf*); **~ und Wasser heulen** (*inf*) to blubber; **Baron** *or* **Graf ~** (*inf*) His Highness (*inf*)

Rotz-: Rotzbengel M, (*S Ger, Aus*) **Rotzbub** M (*inf*) snotty-nosed brat (*inf*); **rotzbesoffen** ADJ (*sl*) wasted (*sl*); **rotzfrech** (*inf*) **1** ADJ cocky (*inf*) **2** ADV **~ antworten** to give a cocky answer (*inf*); **~ auftreten** to act cocky (*inf*); **Rotznase** F **(a)** (*inf*) snotty nose (*inf*) **(b)** (*inf:* = *Kind*) snotty-nosed brat (*inf*); **rotznäsig** [-nɛːzɪç] ADJ (*inf*) **(a)** snotty-nosed (*inf*) **(b)** (= *frech*) snotty (*inf*)

Rotzunge F (*Zool*) witch flounder

Rouge [ru:ʒ] NT **-s, -s** blusher

Roulade [ru'la:də] F **-, -n** (*Cook*) ≈ beef olive

Rouleau [ru'lo:] NT **-s, -s** (roller) blind

Roulett [ru'lɛt] NT **-(e)s, -e** *or* **-s, Roulette** [ru'lɛtə] NT **-s, -s** roulette

Route ['ru:tə] F **-, -n** route (*auch Comput*)

Routine [ru'ti:nə] F **-, -n (a)** (= *Erfahrung*) experience; (= *Gewohnheit, Trott*) routine **(b)** (*Comput*) routine

Routine-: Routineangelegenheit F routine matter; **routinemäßig 1** ADJ routine **2** ADV **ich gehe ~ zum Zahnarzt** I make routine visits to the dentist's; **das wird ~ überprüft** it's checked as a matter of routine; **Routinesache** F routine matter

routiniert [ruti'ni:ɐt] **1** ADJ experienced **2** ADV expertly

Rowdy ['raudi] M **-s, -s** hooligan; (*zerstörerisch*) vandal; (*lärmend*) rowdy (type); (= *Verkehrsrowdy*) road hog (*inf*)

Royalismus [roaja'lɪsmʊs] M -, NO PL royalism
royalistisch [roaja'lɪstɪʃ] ADJ royalist
Rubbel- ['rʊbl-]: **Rubbelkarte** F, **Rubbellos** NT scratch card; **Rubbellotterie** F scratch card lottery
rubbeln ['rʊbln] VTI to rub; *Los* to scratch
Rübchen ['ry:pçən] NT -s, - DIM *von* **Rübe** small turnip; **Teltower** ~ *(Cook) glazed turnip with bacon*
Rübe ['ry:bə] F -, -n (a) turnip; **Gelbe** ~ *(S Ger, Sw: = Mohrrübe)* carrot; **Rote** ~ beetroot *(Brit),* beet *(US);* **Weiße** ~ white turnip **(b)** *(inf: = Kopf)* nut *(inf);* **nichts in der** ~ **haben** to have nothing up top *(inf);* ~ **ab!** off with his/her head!
Rubel ['ru:bl] M -s, - rouble; **der** ~ **rollt** *(inf)* the money's rolling in *(inf)*
Rüben-: **Rübensaft** M, **Rübenkraut** NT sugar beet syrup; **Rübenzucker** M beet sugar
rüber- ['ry:be-] IN CPDS *(inf) siehe auch* **herüber-, hinüber-**: **rüberbringen** VT SEP IRREG *(inf) Botschaft, Feeling* to get across; **rüberkommen** VI SEP **(a)** *siehe* **herüberkommen (b)** *(inf)* to come across; **sie kam gut rüber** she came across well; **mit etw** ~ **to come out with sth**
Rübezahl ['ry:bətsa:l] M -s *spirit of the Sudeten Mountains*
Rubin [ru'bi:n] M -s, -e ruby
Rubrik [ru'bri:k] F -, -en **(a)** *(= Kategorie)* category; **das läuft unter der** ~ **Spesen** that comes under expenses **(b)** *(= Zeitungsrubrik)* section
Ruck [rʊk] M -(e)s, -e jerk; *(von Fahrzeug)* jolt, jerk; *(Pol)* swing; **auf einen** *or* **mit einem** ~ in one go; **er stand mit einem** ~ **auf** he stood up suddenly; **sich** *(dat)* **einen** ~ **geben** *(inf)* to make an effort; **durch die Gesellschaft muss ein** ~ **gehen** society needs to be jolted out of its complacency
Rück-: **Rückansicht** F rear view; **Rückantwort** F reply, answer; **um** ~ **wird gebeten** please reply; **Telegramm mit** ~ reply-paid telegram
ruckartig 🔲 ADJ jerky; **das Auto machte einige ~e Bewegungen** the car jerked a few times 🔲 ADV jerkily; **er stand** ~ **auf** he shot to his feet; **sie drehte sich** ~ **um** she turned round jerkily
Rück-: **Rückbesinnung** F **eine** ~ **auf die Werte der Vergangenheit** a return to past values; **rückbezüglich** ADJ *(Gram)* reflexive; **Rückblende** F flashback; **Rückblick** M look back *(auf +acc* at); **im** ~ **auf etw** *(acc)* looking back on sth; **im** ~ **lässt sich sagen** ... in retrospect one can say ...; **rückblickend** 🔲 ADJ retrospective; **ein auf das vergangene Jahr ~er Bericht** a report that looks back at the last year 🔲 ADV in retrospect; **rückdatieren** ['rʊkdati:rən], *ptp* **rückdatiert** VT SEP INFIN, PTP ONLY to backdate
rücken ['rʊkn] 🔲 VI AUX SEIN to move; *(= Platz machen)* to move up *or (zur Seite auch)* over; *(= weiterrücken: Zeiger)* to move on *(auf +acc* to); **näher** ~ to move closer; *(Zeit)* to get closer; **mit etw** ~ to move sth; **sie rückten ungeduldig mit den Stühlen** they shuffled their chairs about impatiently; **an etw** *(dat)* ~ *an Uhrzeiger* to move sth; *an Krawatte* to pull sth (straight); *(= schieben)* to push at sth; *(= ziehen)* to pull at sth; **an jds Stelle** *(acc)* ~ to take sb's place; **nicht von der Stelle** ~ not to budge an inch *(inf);* **in weite Ferne** ~ *(lit, fig)* to recede into the distance; **in greifbare Nähe** ~ *(fig)* to come within reach; **jdm auf den Leib** *or* **Pelz** *or* **die Pelle** ~ *(inf)* *(= zu nahe kommen)* to crowd sb; *(= sich jdn vornöpfen)* to get on at sb; *(hum: = besuchen)* to move in on sb 🔲 VT to move
Rücken ['rʊkn] M -s, - back; *(= Nasenrücken)* ridge; *(= Fußrücken)* instep; *(= Hügelrücken, Bergrücken)* crest; *(= Buchrücken)* spine; **auf dem/den** ~ on one's back; **er hat doch die Firma des Vaters im** ~ but he's got his father's firm behind him; **ich habe nicht gern jemanden im** ~ I don't like having somebody sitting/standing right behind my back; **mit dem** ~ **zur Wand stehen** *(fig) (aus Feigheit)* to cover oneself; *(aus Unterlegenheit)* to have one's back to the wall; **der verlängerte** ~ *(hum inf)* one's posterior *(hum inf);* **an** ~ back to back; **ein schöner** ~ **kann auch entzücken** *(hum inf)* you've/she's *etc* got a lovely back; **hinter jds** ~ *(dat) (fig)* behind sb's back; **jdm/einer Sache den** ~ **kehren** *(lit, fig)* or **zuwenden** *(lit)* or **wenden** *(fig)* or **zudrehen** *(lit)* to turn one's back on sb/sth *(lit, fig);* **jdm in den** ~ **fallen** *(fig)* to stab sb in the back; *(Mil)* to attack sb from the rear; **den** ~ **frei haben** *(fig)* to be free of ties; **jdm den** ~ **decken** *(fig inf)* to back sb up *(inf);* **die Sparpolitik wird auf dem** ~ **der Sozialhilfeempfänger**

ausgetragen the cost-cutting policy is being carried out at the expense of people on benefit; **jdm den** ~ **stärken** *or* **steifen** *(fig inf)* to give sb encouragement
Rücken-: **Rückendeckung** F *(fig)* backing; **jdm** ~ **geben** to back sb; **Rückenflosse** F dorsal fin; **Rückenlage** F supine position; **er musste 3 Monate in** ~ **verbringen** he had to spend 3 months lying (flat) on his back; **er schläft in** ~ he sleeps on his back; **Rückenlehne** F back (rest); **Rückenmark** NT spinal cord; **Rückenmark(s)entzündung** F myelitis; **Rückenmuskel** M back muscle; **Rückenmuskulatur** F back muscles *pl;* **Rückenschmerzen** PL backache; **ich habe** ~ I've got backache; **rückenschwimmen** ['rʊknʃvɪmən] VI SEP INFIN ONLY to swim on one's back; **Rückenschwimmen** NT backstroke; **Rückenstärkung** F *(fig)* moral support
Rückentwicklung F *(allgemein)* fall-off *(+gen* in); *(Biol)* degeneration
Rücken-: **Rückenwind** M tailwind; **Rückenwirbel** M dorsal vertebra
Rück-: **rückerstatten** ['rʊkleeʃtatn], *ptp* **rückerstattet** VT SEP INFIN, PTP ONLY to refund; *Ausgaben* to reimburse; **Rückerstattung** F refund; *(von Ausgaben)* reimbursement; **Rückfahrkarte** F, **Rückfahrschein** M return ticket *(Brit),* round-trip ticket *(US);* **Rückfahrscheinwerfer** M *(Aut)* reversing light; **Rückfahrt** F return journey; **Rückfall** M *(Med) (fig)* relapse; *(Jur)* repetition of an/the offence *(Brit) or* offense *(US);* **rückfällig** ADJ *(Med)* *(fig)* relapsed; *(Jur)* recidivistic *(form);* **ein ~er Dieb** a thief who repeats his offence *(Brit) or* offense *(US);* ~ **werden** *(Med)* to have a relapse; *(fig)* to relapse; *(Jur)* to lapse back into crime; **Rückfalltäter(in)** M(F) recidivist *(form);* **Rückflug** M return flight; **Rückfrage** F question; **nach** ~ **bei der Zentrale** ... after querying this with the exchange ...; **bei jdm wegen etw** ~ **halten** to query sth with sb; **auf** ~ **wurde uns erklärt** ... when we queried this, we were told ...; **rückfragen** ['rʊkfra:gn] VI SEP INFIN, PTP ONLY to check; **ich muss beim Chef** ~ I'll have to check with the boss; **Rückführgebühr** F *(bei Leihwagen)* drop-off charge; **Rückgabe** F return; **Rückgaberecht** NT right of return; **Rückgang** M, *pl* -gänge fall, drop *(+gen* in); **einen** ~ *or* **Rückgänge zu verzeichnen haben** to report a drop *or* fall; **rückgängig** ADJ **(a)** *(= zurückgehend)* falling, dropping **(b)** ~ **machen** *(= widerrufen)* to undo; *Bestellung, Geschäft, Vertrag, Termin* to cancel; *Entscheidung* to go back on; *Verlobung, Hochzeit* to call off; *chemischen Prozess* to reverse; **Rückgängigmachung** ['rʊkgeniçmaxʊŋ] F -, -en *(form)* cancellation; *(Chem)* reversal; **Rückgebäude** NT rear building; **Rückgewinnung** F recovery; *(von Land, Gebiet)* reclamation; *(aus verbrauchten Stoffen)* recycling
Rückgrat ['rʊkgra:t] NT -(e)s, -e spine, backbone; **das** ~ **der Wirtschaft** the backbone of the economy
Rückgratverkrümmung F curvature of the spine
Rück-: **Rückgriff** M **durch einen** *or* **unter** ~ **auf jdn/etw** by reverting to sb/sth; **wenn ein** ~ **auf vorhandene Reserven nicht möglich ist** if it is not possible to fall back on available resources; **Rückhalt** M **(a)** *(= Unterstützung)* support; **an jdm einen** ~ **haben** to find a support in sb **(b)** *(= Einschränkung)* **ohne** ~ without reservation; **Rückhaltebecken** NT storage pond; **rückhaltlos** 🔲 ADJ complete 🔲 ADV completely; *ermitteln* thoroughly; **sich** ~ **zu etw bekennen** to proclaim one's total allegiance to sth; **Rückhand** F *(Sport)* backhand; ~ **spielen** to play backhand; **er kann erstklassig** ~ **spielen** he has a first-rate backhand; **den Ball (mit der)** ~ **schlagen** to hit the ball (on one's) backhand; **Rückhandschlag** M *(Sport)* backhand (stroke)
Rückkauf M repurchase
Rückkaufs-: **Rückkaufsrecht** NT right of repurchase; **Rückkaufswert** M repurchase value
Rückkehr ['rʊkke:e] F -, NO PL return; **bei seiner** ~ on his return; **jdn zur** ~ **(nach X/zu jdm) bewegen** to persuade sb to return (to X/to sb)
Rück-: **Rückkoppelung** F, **Rückkopplung** F feedback; **Rücklage** F *(Fin: = Reserve)* reserve, reserves *pl;* **rückläufig** ADJ declining; *Tendenz* downward; **eine ~e Entwicklung** a decline; **Rücklicht** NT tail-light, rear light; *(bei Fahrrad auch)* back light; **rücklings** ['rʊklɪŋs] ADV *(= rückwärts)* backwards; *(= von hinten)* from behind; *(= auf den Rücken)* on one's back; **Rückmeldung** F *(Univ)* re-registration; **Rücknahme** [-na:mə] F -, -n taking back; *(von Verordnung, Gesetz)* revocation; *(von Geldkürzungen)* reversal; *(= Senkung)* reduction; **die** ~ **des**

Gerätes ist unmöglich it is impossible for us to take this set back; **Rücknahmepreis** M repurchase price; **Rückporto** NT return postage; **Rückreise** F return journey; **Rückreiseverkehr** M homebound traffic; **Rückruf** M **(a)** (am Telefon) **Herr X hat angerufen und bittet um ~** Mr X called and asked you to call (him) back; **automatischer** = automatic callback **(b)** (Jur) rescission of permission to manufacture under licence (Brit) or license (US) **(c)** (von Botschafter, Auto, Waren) recall; **Rückrufaktion** F call-back campaign

Rucksack ['rʊkzak] M rucksack

Rucksacktourist(in) M(F) backpacker

Rück-: Rückschalttaste F backspace key; **Rückschau** F reflection (auf +acc on); (in Medien) review (auf +acc of); ~ **halten** to reminisce, to reflect; **auf etw** (acc) ~ **halten** to look back on sth; **Rückschein** M ≈ recorded delivery slip; **Rückschläger(in)** M(F) (Sport) receiver; **Rückschlagventil** NT check valve; **Rückschluss** M conclusion; **den ~ ziehen, dass ...** to draw the conclusion that ...; **Rückschlüsse auf etw** (acc) **zulassen** to allow conclusions to be drawn about sth; **Rückschlüsse ziehen** to draw one's own conclusions (aus from); **Rückschritt** M (fig) step backwards; **rückschrittlich** ['rʊkʃrɪtlɪç] ADJ reactionary; Entwicklung retrograde

Rückseite F back; (von Buchseite, Münze) reverse; (von Zeitung) back page; **siehe ~** see over(leaf)

rückseitig ['rʊkzaitɪç] **1** ADJ on the back; **die ~en Bemerkungen** the remarks overleaf **2** ADV (= auf der Rückseite) on the back; **das Papier soll auch ~ beschrieben werden** you should write on both sides of the paper; **der Garten liegt ~** the garden is at the back

Rücksendung F return

Rücksicht ['rʊkzɪçt] F **-, -en (a)** (= Schonung, Nachsicht) consideration; **aus** or **mit ~ auf jdn/etw** out of consideration for sb/sth; **ohne ~ auf jdn/etw** with no consideration for sb/sth; **ohne ~ auf Verluste** (inf) regardless; **auf jdn/etw ~ nehmen** to show consideration for sb/sth; **er kennt keine ~** he's ruthless **(b) Rücksichten** PL (= Gründe, Interessen) considerations pl

Rücksichts-: rücksichtslos **1** ADJ **(a)** inconsiderate; (im Verkehr) reckless **(b)** (= unbarmherzig) ruthless **2** ADV **(a)** (= ohne Nachsicht) inconsiderately; **er verfolgt ~ seine Interessen** he follows his own interests without consideration for others **(b)** (= schonungslos) ruthlessly; **Rücksichtslosigkeit** F **-, -en (a)** (= rücksichtslose Tat) inconsiderate act; **das ist doch eine ~!** how inconsiderate **(b)** NO PL (= das Rücksichtslossein) lack of consideration; (= Unbarmherzigkeit) ruthlessness; **rücksichtsvoll** **1** ADJ considerate, thoughtful; (gegenüber, gegen towards) **2** ADV considerately, thoughtfully; **behandeln Sie ihn etwas ~er** show him a little more consideration

Rück-: Rücksitz M (von Fahrrad, Motorrad) pillion; (von Auto) back seat; **Rückspiegel** M (Aut) rear-(view) mirror; (außen) outside mirror; **Rückspiel** NT (Sport) return match (Brit), rematch (US); **Rücksprache** F consultation; **nach ~ mit Herrn Müller ...** after consulting Mr Müller ...; **mit jdm halten** or **nehmen** to consult (with) sb; **rückspulen** ['rʊkʃpuːlən] VT SEP INFIN, PTP ONLY Tonband, Film to rewind

Rückstand ['rʊkʃtant] M **(a)** (= Überrest) remains pl; (bei Verbrennung: = Bodensatz) residue **(b)** (= Verzug) delay; (bei Aufträgen) backlog; (bei Entwicklung) slow progress; **im ~ sein** to be behind; **seinen ~ aufholen** to make up for one's delay; (bei Aufträgen) to catch up on a backlog; (bei Zahlungen) to catch up on one's payments; (in Leistungen) to catch up **(c)** (= Außenstände) arrears pl **(d)** (Sport) amount by which one is behind; **mit 0:2 (Toren) im ~ sein** to be 2-0 down; **ihr ~ auf den Tabellenführer beträgt 4 Punkte** they are 4 points behind the leader; **seinen ~ aufholen** to catch up

rückständig ['rʊkʃtɛndɪç] **1** ADJ **(a)** (= überfällig) Betrag overdue; Mensch in arrears **(b)** (= zurückgeblieben) backward **2** ADV **~ denken** to have antiquated ideas

Rückständigkeit F **-,** NO PL backwardness

rückstand(s)frei **1** ADJ residue-free **2** ADV **ein Diamant verbrennt ~** a diamond burns without leaving any residue; **dieses Öl verbrennt nahezu ~** this oil burns cleanly

Rück-: Rückstau M (von Wasser) backwater; (von Autos) tailback; (von Unerledigtem) backlog; **Rückstellung** F (Fin)

reserve; **Rückstoß** M repulsion; (bei Gewehr) recoil; (von Rakete) thrust; **Rückstrahler** M reflector; **Rücktaste** F (an Tastatur) backspace key

Rücktritt M **(a)** (= Amtsniederlegung) resignation; (von König) abdication **(b)** (Jur: von Vertrag) withdrawal (von from)

Rücktrittbremse F backpedal brake

Rücktritts-: Rücktrittsdrohung F threat to resign; (von König) threat to abdicate; **Rücktrittsklausel** F withdrawal clause; **Rücktrittsrecht** NT right of withdrawal; **Rücktrittsvorbehalt** M option of withdrawal

Rück-: rückübersetzen ['rʊkly:bezɛtsn], ptp **rückübersetzt** VT SEP INFIN, PTP ONLY to translate back into the original language; **Rückvergütung** F refund; **Rückversicherer** M reinsurer; (fig) hedger; **rückversichern** ['rʊkfɛɐzɪçɐn], ptp **rückversichert** SEP **1** VTI to reinsure **2** VR to check (up or back); **Rückversicherung** F reinsurance; **Rückwand** F (von Zimmer, Gebäude etc) back wall; (von Möbelstück etc) back; **rückwärtig** ['rʊkvɛrtɪç] ADJ back; (Mil) rear

rückwärts ['rʊkvɛrts] ADV **(a)** (= zurück, rücklings) backwards; **Rolle ~** backward roll; **Salto ~** back somersault; **~ einparken** to reverse into a parking space **(b)** (Aus: = hinten) behind

Rückwärts-: Rückwärtsfahren NT **-s,** NO PL reversing; **Rückwärtsgang** M, pl **-gänge** (Aut) reverse gear; **den ~ einlegen** to change (Brit) or shift (US) into reverse; **im ~ fahren** to reverse

Rückweg M way back; **den ~ antreten, sich auf den ~ begeben** to set off back; **sich auf den ~ machen** to head back

ruckweise ['rʊkvaizə] ADV jerkily

Rück-: rückwirkend ['rʊkvɪrknt] **1** ADJ (Jur) retrospective; Lohn-, Gehaltserhöhung backdated **2** ADV **es wird ~ vom 1. Mai bezahlt** it will be backdated to 1st May; **das Gesetz tritt ~ vom** or **zum 1. Januar in Kraft** the law is made retrospective to 1st January; **etw ist ~ fällig** sth is backdated; **Rückwirkung** F repercussion; **eine Zahlung mit ~ vom ...** a payment backdated to ...; **eine Gesetzesänderung mit ~ vom ...** an amendment made retrospective to ...; **rückzahlbar** ADJ repayable; **Rückzahlung** F repayment; **Rückzieher** ['rʊktsiːɐ] M **-s, -** (inf) backing down; **einen ~ machen** to back down

ruck, zuck ['rʊk'tsʊk] **1** INTERJ (beim Ziehen) heave; (beim Schieben) push **2** ADV in a flash; (Imperativ) jump to it; **das geht ~** it won't take a second

Rückzug M (Mil) retreat; (fig) withdrawal

Rucola ['ruːkola] F (esp Sw Bot) rocket

rüde ['ryːdə], (Aus) **rüd** [ryːt] **1** ADJ impolite; Antwort curt; Methoden crude; Angriff, Foul rough; **das war sehr ~ von dir** that was very rude of you **2** ADV rudely

Rüde ['ryːdə] M **-n, -n** (= Männchen) male; (= Hetzhund) hound

Rudel ['ruːdl] NT **-s, -** (von Hunden, Wölfen) pack; (von Wildschweinen, Hirschen) herd

Ruder ['ruːdɐ] NT **-s, -** (von ~boot, Galeere etc) oar; (Naut, Aviat: = Steuerruder) rudder; (fig: = Führung) helm; **das ~ fest in der Hand haben** (fig) to be in control of the situation; **am ~ sein** (lit, fig) to be at the helm; **ans ~ kommen** or **das ~ übernehmen** (lit, fig) to take over (at) the helm; **das ~ herumwerfen** or **herumreißen** (fig) to change tack; **aus dem ~ laufen** (fig) to get out of hand

Ruderboot NT rowing boat (Brit), rowboat (US)

Ruderer ['ruːdərə] M **-s, -** oarsman

Rudergerät NT rowing machine

Ruderin ['ruːdərɪn] F **-, -nen** oarswoman

rudern ['ruːdɐn] **1** VI AUX HABEN or SEIN to row **(b)** (Schwimmvögel) to paddle **2** VT to row

Ruder-: Ruderpinne F tiller; **Ruderregatta** F rowing regatta; **Rudersport** M rowing no def art

Rudiment [rudi'mɛnt] NT **-(e)s, -e** rudiment

rudimentär [rudimɛn'tɛːɐ] **1** ADJ rudimentary **2** ADV rudimentarily; **~ ausgebildet** rudimentary; **~ vorhanden sein** to be vestigial

Ruf [ruːf] M **-(e)s, -e (a)** (= Ausruf, Vogelruf) (fig: = Aufruf) call (nach for); (lauter) shout; (= gellender Schrei) cry; **der ~ des Muezzins** the call of the muezzin; **der ~ der Wildnis** the call of the wild; **der ~ zur Ordnung** (fig) the call to order **(b)** (= Ansehen, Leumund) reputation; **einen guten ~ haben** or **genießen, sich eines guten ~es erfreuen** (geh) to enjoy a good reputation; **einen schlechten ~ haben** to have a bad reputation; **dem ~ nach** by reputation; **eine Firma von ~ a**

firm with a good reputation; **seinem ~ (als etw) gerecht werden** to live up to one's reputation (as sth); **von üblem** or **zweifelhaftem ~** with a bad reputation; **jdn/etw in schlechten ~ bringen** to give sb/sth a bad name; **sie/das ist besser als ihr/sein ~** she/it is better than she/it is made out to be; **ist der ~ erst ruiniert, lebt man völlig ungeniert** (prov) you live freely if you haven't a reputation to lose

(c) (Univ: = Berufung) offer of a chair

(d) (= Fernruf) telephone number; **„~: 2785"** "Tel 2785"

rufen [ˈruːfn̩], pret **rief** [riːf], ptp **gerufen** [gəˈruːfn̩] **1** VI to call; (Mensch: = laut ~) to shout; (Gong, Glocke, Horn etc) to sound (zu for); **um Hilfe ~** to call for help; **die Pflicht ruft** duty calls; **die Arbeit ruft** my/your etc work is waiting; **nach jdm/etw ~** to call for sb/sth

2 VT (= laut sagen) **(a)** to call; (= ausrufen) to cry; (Mensch: = laut ~) to shout; **jdm etw in Erinnerung** or **ins Gedächtnis ~** to bring back (memories of) sth to sb; **sich** (dat) **etw in Erinnerung** or **ins Gedächtnis ~** to recall sth; **jdn zur Ordnung ~** to call sb to order; **jdn zur Sache ~** to bring sb back to the point; **jdn zu den Waffen ~** to call sb to arms; **bravo/da capo ~** to shout bravo/encore

(b) (= kommen lassen) to send for; Arzt, Polizei, Taxi to call; **jdn zu sich ~** to send for sb; **Sie haben mich ~ lassen?** you called, sir/madam?; **~ Sie ihn bitte!** please send him to me; **jdn zu Hilfe ~** to call on sb to help; **du kommst wie gerufen** you're just the man/woman I wanted; **das kommt mir wie gerufen** that's just what I needed; (= kommt mir gelegen) that suits me fine (inf)

Rüffel [ˈrʏfl̩] M **-s, -** (inf) telling-off (inf)

Ruf-: Rufmord M character assassination; **Rufmordkampagne** F smear campaign; **Rufname** M forename (by which one is generally known); **Rufnummer** F telephone number; **Rufnummernanzeige** F (Telec) caller ID display; **Rufnummernspeicher** M (von Telefon) memory; **Rufsäule** F (für Taxi) telephone; (Mot: = Notrufsäule) emergency telephone; **Rufumleitung** F (Telec) call diversion; **Rufweite** F **in ~** within earshot; **außer ~** out of earshot; **Rufzeichen** NT **(a)** (Telec) call sign; (von Telefon) ringing tone **(b)** (Aus) exclamation mark

Rugby [ˈrakbi] NT -, NO PL rugby

Rüge [ˈryːɡə] F **-, -n** (= Verweis) reprimand; (= Kritik) criticism no indef art; (= scharfe Kritik) censure no indef art; **jdm eine ~ erteilen** to reprimand/criticize/censure sb (für, wegen for)

Ruhe [ˈruːə] F **-,** NO PL **(a)** (= Schweigen, Stille) quiet; **~! quiet!**, silence!; **~, bitte!** quiet, please; **sich** (dat) **~ verschaffen** to get quiet; **es herrscht ~** all is silent; (fig: = Disziplin, Frieden) all is quiet; **~ halten** (lit, fig) to keep quiet; **die ~ der Natur** the stillness of nature; **himmlische ~** heavenly peace; **~ und Frieden** peace and quiet; **die ~ vor dem Sturm** (fig) the calm before the storm

(b) (= Ungestörtheit, Frieden) peace; (= ~stätte) resting place; **~ ausstrahlen** to radiate a sense of calm; **in ~ und Frieden leben** to live a quiet life; **~ und Ordnung** law and order; **nach tagelangen Krawallen ist wieder ~ eingekehrt** after days of rioting, calm has returned; **~ ist die erste Bürgerpflicht** (prov) the main thing is to keep calm; **die ~ wieder herstellen** to restore quiet; **ich brauche meine ~** I need a bit of peace; **lass mich in ~!** leave me in peace; **vor jdm ~ haben wollen** to want a rest from sb; (endgültig) to want to get rid of sb; **jdm keine ~ lassen** or **gönnen** (Mensch) not to give sb any peace; **keine ~ geben** to keep on and on; **das lässt ihm keine ~** he can't stop thinking about it; **zur ~ kommen** to get some peace; (= solide werden) to settle down; **jdn zur ~ kommen lassen** to give sb a chance to rest; **keine ~ finden (können)** to know no peace

(c) (= Erholung, Stillstand) rest; (= ~stand) retirement; **jdm keine ~ gönnen** not to give sb a minute's rest; **angenehme ~!** sleep well!; **sich zur ~ setzen** to retire

(d) (= Gelassenheit) calm(ness); (= Disziplin) order; **die ~ weghaben** (inf) to be unflappable (inf); **~ bewahren** to keep calm; **die ~ selbst sein** to be calmness itself; **jdn aus der ~ bringen** to throw sb (inf); **sich nicht aus der ~ bringen lassen**, **nicht aus der ~ zu bringen sein** not to (let oneself) get worked up; **in aller ~** calmly; **überlege es dir in (aller) ~** take your time and think about it; **sich** (dat) **etw in ~ ansehen** to look at sth in one's own time; **immer mit der ~** (inf) don't panic

Ruhe-: Ruhebedürfnis NT need for rest; **ruheliebend** ADJ fond of peace and quiet; **ruhelos** ADJ restless; **eine ~e Zeit** a time of unrest

ruhen [ˈruːən] VI **(a)** (= ausruhen) to rest; **nach dem Essen soll man ruhn oder tausend Schritte tun** (Prov) after a meal one should either rest or take some exercise; **nicht (eher) ~ or nicht ~ und rasten, bis ...** (fig) not to rest until ...

(b) (geh: = liegen) to rest (an or auf +dat on); (Fluch) to lie (auf +dat on); **unsere Hoffnung ruht auf ...** (dat) our hopes rest on ...

(c) (= stillstehen) to stop; (Maschinen) to stand idle; (Verkehr) to be at a standstill; (Arbeit) to stop; (Waffen) to be laid down; (= unterbrochen sein: Verfahren, Verhandlung, Vertrag) to be suspended

(d) (= tot und begraben sein) to be buried; **„hier ruht (in Gott) ..."** "here lies ..."; **„ruhe in Frieden!"** "Rest in Peace"; **„ruhe sanft!"** "rest eternal"

ruhend ADJ resting; Kapital dormant; Maschinen idle; Verkehr stationary; **~e Venus** Venus reclining

ruhen lassen VT, ptp **ruhen lassen** or (rare) **ruhen gelassen** IRREG Vergangenheit, Angelegenheit to let rest; Verhandlungen, Prozess to adjourn; Teig to allow to rest; Amt to leave temporarily vacant

Ruhe-: Ruhepause F break; (wenig Betrieb, Arbeit) quiet period; **eine ~ einlegen** to take a break; **Ruhestand** M retirement; **im ~ sein** or **leben** to be retired; **er ist Bankdirektor im ~** he is a retired bank director; **in den ~ treten** or **gehen** to retire; **jdn in den ~ versetzen** to retire sb; **Ruhestörer(in)** M(F) disturber of the peace; **Ruhestörung** F (Jur) disturbance of the peace; **Ruhetag** M day off; (von Geschäft etc) closing day; **einen ~ einlegen** to take a day off; **„Mittwoch ~"** "closed (on) Wednesdays"

ruhig [ˈruːɪç] **1** ADJ **(a)** (= still) quiet; Wetter, Meer calm; (= geruhsam) quiet; Farbe restful; (= ohne Störung) Überfahrt, Verlauf smooth; **seid ~!** be quiet!; **ihr sollt ~ sein!** (will you) be quiet!; **gegen 6 Uhr wird es ~er** it quietens (Brit) or quiets (US) down around 6 o'clock

(b) (= gelassen) calm; Gewissen easy; (= sicher) Hand, Blick steady; **nur ~ (Blut)!** keep calm; **bei ~er Überlegung** on (mature) consideration; **du wirst auch noch ~er!** you'll calm down one day; **du kannst/Sie können ganz ~ sein** I can assure you

2 ADV **(a)** (= still) sitzen, stehenbleiben, dastehen still

(b) (= untätig) **etw ~ mitansehen** to stand by and watch sth; **~ dabeistehen** just to stand by; **sich ~ verhalten** to keep calm

(c) (inf) **du kannst ~ hier bleiben** feel free to stay here; **ihr könnt ~ gehen, ich passe schon auf** you just go and I'll look after things; **man kann ~ behaupten/sagen/annehmen, dass ...** (= mit Recht) one may well assert/say/assume that ...; **die können ~ etwas mehr zahlen** (= leicht) they could easily pay a little more; **wir können ~ darüber sprechen** we can talk about it if you want; **du könntest ~ mal etwas für mich tun!** it's about time you did something for me!

(d) (= ohne Turbulenzen) laufen very quietly; **das Flugzeug liegt ~ in der Luft** the plane is flying smoothly; **ihr Leben verläuft sehr ~** she leads a very quiet life

(e) (= gelassen) **wenn du etwas ~er überlegen würdest** if you took more time to think things over; **lass uns ~ nachdenken** let's think things over calmly

(f) (= beruhigt) schlafen peacefully; **du kannst ~ ins Kino gehen** go ahead, go to the cinema; **jetzt kann ich in Urlaub fahren** now I can go on holiday (esp Brit) or vacation (US) with an easy mind

ruhig stellen VT (Med) (bei Knochenbruch etc) to immobilize; (mit Drogen) to sedate

Ruhm [ruːm] M **-(e)s,** NO PL glory; (= Berühmtheit) fame; (= Lob) praise; **zu ~ gelangen** to become famous; **sich in seinem ~ sonnen** to rest on one's laurels

rühmen [ˈryːmən] **1** VT (= preisen, empfehlen) to praise; **jdn ~d erwähnen** to give sb an honourable (Brit) or honorable (US) mention **2** VR **sich einer Sache** (gen) **~** (= prahlen) to boast about sth; (= stolz sein) to pride oneself on sth; **sich einer Sache** (gen) **~ können** to be able to boast of sth; **ohne mich zu ~** without wishing to boast

rühmlich [ˈryːmlɪç] ADJ praiseworthy; Ausnahme notable; **kein ~es Ende finden** or **nehmen** to meet a bad end; **sich ~ hervortun** to distinguish oneself

Ruhr¹ [ruːɐ] F - (Geog) Ruhr

Ruhr² F -, NO PL (Krankheit) dysentery

Rührei [ˈryːɐlai] NT scrambled egg; (als Gericht) scrambled eggs pl

rühren ['ry:rən] **1** VI **(a)** (= *umrühren*) to stir
(b) an etw (*acc or dat*) ~ (= *anfassen*) to touch sth; (*fig*:
= *erwähnen*) to touch on sth; **daran wollen wir nicht ~** let's not
go into it; (*in Bezug auf Vergangenes*) let sleeping dogs lie
(c) von etw ~ to stem from sth; **das rührt daher, dass ...** that
is because ...; **daher rührt sein Misstrauen!** so that is the
reason for his distrust!
2 VT **(a)** (= *umrühren*) to stir; (= *schlagen*) *Eier* to beat
(b) (= *bewegen*) to move; **er rührte keinen Finger or keine
Hand, um mir zu helfen** (*inf*) he didn't lift a finger to help me
(*inf*); **das kann mich nicht ~!** that leaves me cold; (= *stört mich
nicht*) that doesn't bother me; **jdn zu Tränen ~** to move sb to
tears; **sie war äußerst gerührt** she was extremely moved; **ihn
hat der Schlag gerührt** (*inf*) he was thunderstruck; **ich
glaubte, mich rührt der Schlag** (*inf*) you could have knocked
me down with a feather (*inf*)
3 VR (= *sich bewegen*) (*Blatt, Mensch*) to stir; (*Körperteil*) to
move; (= *sich von der Stelle bewegen*) to move; (= *aktiv sein*) to
buck up (*inf*); **kein Lüftchen rührte sich** the air was still; **er
rührt sich nicht mehr** (*inf*) he won't get up again; **nichts hat
sich gerührt** nothing happened; **sie hat sich schon zwei Jahre
nicht gerührt** (*inf*) she hasn't been in touch for two years
rührend **1** ADJ touching; **das ist ~ von Ihnen** that is sweet of
you **2** ADV **sie kümmert sich ~ um das Kind** it's touching how
she looks after the child
Ruhrgebiet NT, NO PL Ruhr (area)
ruhrig ['ry:rɪç] ADJ active
Ruhrpott M, NO PL (*inf*) Ruhr (Basin *or* Valley)
Rühr-: rührselig ADJ (*pej*) tear-jerking (*pej inf*); *Person* weepy;
Stimmung sentimental; **Rührseligkeit** F, NO PL sentimentality;
Rührstück NT (*Theat*) melodrama; **Rührteig** M sponge
mixture
Rührung ['ry:rʊŋ] F -, NO PL emotion
Ruin [ru'i:n] M -s, NO PL ruin; **vor dem ~ stehen** to be on the
brink of ruin; **jdn in den ~ treiben** to ruin sb
Ruine [ru'i:nə] F -, -n (*lit, fig*) ruin
ruinieren [rui'ni:rən], *ptp* **ruiniert** VT to ruin; **sich ~** to ruin
oneself
ruinös [rui'nø:s] ADJ ruinous
rülpsen ['rʏlpsn] VI to belch; **das Rülpsen** belching
Rülpser ['rʏlpsɐ] M -s, - (*inf*) belch
rum [rʊm] ADV (*inf*) = **herum**
Rum [rʊm, (*S Ger, Aus auch*) ru:m] M -s, -s rum
Rumäne [ru'mɛ:nə] M -n, -n, **Rumänin** [-'mɛ:nɪn] F -, -nen
Romanian
Rumänien [ru'mɛ:niən] NT -s Romania
rumänisch [ru'mɛ:nɪʃ] ADJ Romanian
Rumba ['rʊmba] F -, -s *or* (*inf*) m -s, -s rumba
Rumbakugel F, **Rumbarassel** F maraca
rumgiften VI SEP (*sl*) to bitch (*inf*)
rumgraben VI SEP IRREG (*sl*: = *Annäherungsversuche machen*) to
try it on (*inf*)
rumgurken VI SEP (*sl*: = *herumfahren*) to drive around
rumkriegen ['rʊmkri:gn] VT SEP (*inf*) **jdn ~** to talk sb round (*Brit*),
to bring sb around (*US*)
rummachen VI SEP (*inf*) to mess around (*mit jdm*
with sb, *an etw* (*dat*) with sth)
Rummel ['rʊml] M -s, NO PL **(a)** (*inf*) (= *Betrieb*) (hustle and)
bustle; (= *Getöse*) racket (*inf*); (= *Aufheben*) fuss (*inf*); **der
ganze ~** the whole business (*inf*); **großen ~ um jdn/etw
machen** *or* **veranstalten** to make a great fuss about sb/sth (*inf*)
(b) (= *~platz*) fair; **auf den ~ gehen** to go to the fair
Rummelplatz M (*inf*) fairground
rummotzen VI SEP (*inf*) to moan
Rummy ['rœmi] NT -s, -s (*Aus*) rummy
rumnüssen ['rʊmnʏsn] VI SEP (*sl*: = *Sex haben*) to shag (*sl*)
rumoren [ru'mo:rən], *ptp* **rumort** **1** VI to make a noise; (*Mensch*)
to rumble about; (*Magen, Vulkan*) to rumble; (*Gewissen*) to
play up; (*Gedanke*) to float about; **etw rumort in den Köpfen**
sth is going through people's minds **2** VI IMPERS **es rumort in
meinem Magen or Bauch** my stomach's rumbling; **es rumort
in der Mannschaft** (*fig*) there is growing unrest in the team
rumorgeln VI SEP (*sl*: = *Sex haben*) to screw (*sl*)
Rumpelkammer F (*inf*) junk room (*inf*)
Rumpelstilzchen ['rʊmpl̩ʃtɪltsçən] NT -s Rumpelstiltskin

Rumpf [rʊmpf] M -(e)s, ⸚e ['rʏmpfə] trunk; (*Sport*) body; (*von
geschlachtetem Tier*) carcass; (*von Statue*) torso; (*von Schiff*)
hull; (*von Flugzeug*) fuselage
rümpfen ['rʏmpfn] VT **die Nase ~** to turn up one's nose (*über
+acc* at)
Rumpsteak ['rʊmpste:k] NT rump steak
rums [rʊms] INTERJ bang
rumstänkern VI SEP (*inf*) to stir (*inf*)
Rum-: Rumtopf M rumpot (*soft fruit in rum*); **Rumverschnitt** M
blended rum
rumzicken ['rʊmtsɪkn] VI SEP (*sl*) to turn awkward
Run [ran] M -s, -s run (*auf +acc* on)
rund [rʊnt] **1** ADJ round; *Figur, Arme* plump; *Ton, Klang* full;
Wein mellow; **~e 50 Jahre/500 Euro** a good 50 years/500
euros; **ein ~es Dutzend Leute** a dozen or more people; **~er
Tisch** round table; **Konferenz am ~en Tisch** round-table talks
pl; **das ist eine ~e Sache** that's pretty good
2 ADV **(a)** (= *herum*) (a)round; **~ um** right (a)round; **~ um die
Uhr** right (a)round the clock
(b) (= *ungefähr*) (round) about; **~ gerechnet 200** call it 200
(c) (*Aut*) **der Motor läuft ~** the engine runs smoothly
Rund-: Rundblick M panorama; **Rundbogen** M (*Archit*) round
arch; **Rundbrief** M circular
Runde ['rʊndə] F -, -n **(a)** (= *Gesellschaft*) company; (*von
Teilnehmern*) circle; **sich zu einer gemütlichen ~ treffen** to
meet informally
(b) (= *Rundgang*) walk; (*von Wachmann*) rounds *pl*; (*von
Briefträger etc*) round; **die/seine ~ machen** to do the/one's
rounds; (*Gastgeber*) to circulate; (= *herumgegeben werden*) to
be passed (a)round; **das Gerücht machte die ~** the rumour
(*Brit*) or rumor (*US*) went around; **eine ~ durch die Lokale
machen** to go on a pub crawl (*Brit*), to go bar-hopping (*US*);
eine ~ machen to go for a walk; (*mit Fahrzeug*) to go for a ride;
eine ~ um etw machen to go for a walk (a)round sth; (*mit
Fahrzeug*) to ride (a)round sth
(c) (= *Gesprächsrunde, Sport*) round; (*bei Rennen*) lap; (*Cards*)
game; **über die ~n kommen** (*Sport, fig*) to pull through; **etw
über die ~n bringen** (*fig*) to manage sth; **eine ~ schlafen** (*inf*)
to have a nap
(d) (*von Getränken*) round; **(für jdn) eine ~ spendieren** *or*
ausgeben *or* **schmeißen** (*inf*) to buy (sb) a round *Brit*
runden ['rʊndn] **1** VT *Lippen* to round; *Zahl* (= *abrunden*) to
round down; (= *aufrunden*) to round up; **nach oben/unten ~**
(*Math*) to round up/down **2** VR (*lit*: = *rund werden*) to become
round; (*Lippen*) to grow round; (*fig*: = *konkrete Formen
annehmen*) to take shape
Rund-: runderneuern ['rʊntlɛ̯ɐnɔyɐn], *ptp* **runderneuert** VT SEP
INFIN, PTP ONLY (*lit, fig*) to remould (*Brit*), to remold (*US*);
runderneuerte Reifen remo(u)lds; **Rundfahrt** F tour; **eine ~
machen or an ~ teilnehmen** to go on a tour; **Rundflug** M
(= *Besichtigungsflug*) sightseeing flight; (= *Reiseroute*) round
trip; **Rundfrage** F survey (*an +acc, unter +dat* of)
Rundfunk M broadcasting; (= *Hörfunk*) radio; (= *Organisation*)
broadcasting company; **der ~ überträgt etw** sth is broadcast;
im/über ~ on the radio
Rundfunk- IN CPDS radio; **Rundfunkanstalt** F (*form*)
broadcasting corporation; **Rundfunkempfänger** M radio
receiver; **Rundfunkgebühr** F radio licence (*Brit*) or license (*US*)
fee; **Rundfunkgerät** NT radio; **Rundfunksatellit** M TV satellite;
Rundfunksender M **(a)** (= *Sendeanlage*) radio transmitter
(b) (= *Sendeanstalt*) radio station; **Rundfunksendung** F radio
programme (*Brit*) *or* program (*US*); **Rundfunksprecher(in)** M(F)
radio announcer; **Rundfunkstation** F radio station;
Rundfunkzeitschrift F radio programme (*Brit*) or program (*US*)
guide
Rundgang M, *pl* **-gänge (a)** (= *Spaziergang*) walk; (*zur
Besichtigung*) tour (*durch* of); (*von Wachmann*) rounds *pl*; (*von
Briefträger etc*) round; **einen ~ machen** to go for a walk; to go
on a tour; **seinen ~ machen** to do one's rounds/round
(b) (*Archit*) circular gallery
rundgehen ['rʊntge:ən] VI SEP IRREG (*inf*) **jetzt gehts rund** this is
where the fun starts (*inf*); **wenn er das erfährt, gehts rund** all
hell will break loose when he finds out (*inf*); **es geht rund,
wenn sie zu Besuch kommen** there's never a dull moment
when they come to visit; **es geht rund im Büro** there's a lot
(going) on at the office

Rund-: Rundheit F -, NO PL roundness; **rundheraus** ['rʊnthɛ'raus] ADV straight out; **~ gesagt** frankly; **Rundkopfschraube** F round-headed screw; **rundlich** ['rʊntlɪç] ADJ *Mensch, Gesicht* plump; *Form* roundish; **Rundreise** F tour (*durch* of); **Rundruf** M per **~** with a series of phone calls; **Rundschau** F (*Rad, TV*) magazine programme (*Brit*), news magazine (show) (*US*); **Rundschreiben** NT circular

rundum ['rʊnt'lʊm] ADV all around; (*fig*) completely

Rundumschlag M (*lit, fig*) sweeping blow

Rundung ['rʊndʊŋ] F -, -en curve

Rund-: Rundwanderweg M circular route; **Rundzange** F round-nosed pliers *pl*

Rune ['ruːnə] F -, -n rune

Runkel ['rʊŋkl] F -, -n (*Aus*), **Runkelrübe** F mangelwurzel

runter ['rʊntɐ] ADV (*inf*) = **herunter, hinunter**; **~!** down!

runter- PREF (*inf*) down; **runterhauen** ['rʊntɐhauən] VT SEP (*inf*) **(a)** (= *ohrfeigen*) **jdm eine** *or* **ein paar ~** to give sb a clip (a)round the ear **(b)** (= *schreiben*) **einen Text ~** to bang out a text (*inf*); **runterholen** ['rʊntɐhoːlən] VT SEP to get down; **jdm/sich einen ~** (*inf*) to jerk sb/(oneself) off (*sl*); *siehe auch* **herunterholen; runterkommen** ['rʊntɐkɔmən] VI SEP IRREG AUX SEIN **von etw ~** (*inf: von Drogen/Heroin etc*) to come off sth; *siehe auch* **herunterkommen**

runter sein VI SEP IRREG AUX SEIN (*inf: = erschöpft sein*) to be run down; **von etw ~** (*inf: von Drogen/Heroin etc*) to be off sth; **gesundheitlich ~** to be under the weather (*inf*); **mit den Nerven ~** to be at the end of one's tether (*Brit inf*) *or* rope (*US inf*)

Runzel ['rʊntsl] F -, -n wrinkle; (*auf Stirn auch*) line

runzelig ['rʊntsəlɪç] ADJ wrinkled

runzeln ['rʊntsln] 1 VT *Stirn* to wrinkle; *Brauen* to knit 2 VR to become wrinkled

runzlig ['rʊntslɪç] ADJ = **runzelig**

Rüpel ['ryːpl] M -s, - lout

rüpelhaft 1 ADJ loutish 2 ADV **sich ~ benehmen** to behave like a lout

rupfen ['rʊpfn] VT *Geflügel, Federn* to pluck; *Gras, Unkraut* to pull up; **sie sieht aus wie ein gerupftes Huhn** (= *schlecht frisiert*) she looks as if she's been dragged through a hedge backwards; (= *schlechter Haarschnitt*) she looks like a half-shorn sheep

ruppig ['rʊpɪç] 1 ADJ (= *grob*) rough; *Antwort* gruff; *Autofahren* reckless; **~es Benehmen** uncouth behaviour (*Brit*) *or* behavior (*US*) 2 ADV *behandeln, sagen* gruffly; *Auto fahren* recklessly; **~ spielen** to play rough; **~ antworten** to give a gruff answer; **sich ~ benehmen** to behave in an uncouth way

Rüsche ['ryːʃə] F -, -n ruche

Ruß [ruːs] M -es, NO PL soot; (*von Kerze*) smoke; (*von Petroleumlampe*) lampblack; (*von Dieselmotor*) exhaust particulate (*spec*)

Russe ['rʊsə] M -n, -n, **Russin** ['rʊsɪn] F -, -nen Russian

Rüssel ['rʏsl] M -s, - (*auch inf: = Nase*) snout; (*von Elefant*) trunk; (*von Insekt*) proboscis

rußen ['ruːsn] VI (*Öllampe, Kerze*) to smoke; (*Ofen*) to produce soot; **es rußt** there's a lot of soot; **eine stark ~de Lampe** a very smoky lamp

Ruß-: Rußfilter M (*esp Aut*) particulate filter (*spec*); **Rußfleck** M sooty mark; **Rußflocke** F soot particle; **rußgeschwärzt** [-ɡəʃvɛrtst] ADJ soot-blackened

rußig ['ruːsɪç] ADJ sooty

Russin F -, -nen Russian

russisch ['rʊsɪʃ] ADJ Russian; **~es Roulett** Russian roulette; **~e Eier** (*Cook*) egg(s) mayonnaise

Russland ['rʊslant] NT -s Russia

Russlanddeutsche(r) MF DECL AS ADJ *ethnic German living in Russia and the Republics*

rüsten ['rʏstn] 1 VI (*Mil*) to arm; (*fig*) to arm oneself; **zum Krieg/Kampf ~** to arm for war/battle; **gut/schlecht gerüstet sein** to be well/badly armed; (*fig*) to be well/badly prepared; **um die Wette ~** to be involved in an arms race 2 VR to prepare (*zu* for); (*lit, fig: = sich wappnen*) to arm oneself (*gegen* for); **sich zur Abreise ~** to get ready to leave

rüstig ['rʏstɪç] ADJ sprightly; **geistig/körperlich ~** mentally/physically active

Rüstigkeit F -, NO PL sprightliness

rustikal [rʊstiˈkaːl] 1 ADJ *Möbel* rustic; *Speisen* country-style 2 ADV *wohnen* rustically; **sich ~ einrichten** to furnish one's home in a rustic style

Rüstung ['rʏstʊŋ] F -, -en **(a)** (= *das Rüsten*) armament; (= *Waffen*) arms *pl*, weapons *pl* **(b)** (= *Ritterrüstung*) armour (*Brit*), armor (*US*)

Rüstungs- IN CPDS arms; **Rüstungsbegrenzung** F arms limitation; **Rüstungsgegner(in)** M(F) supporter of disarmament; **Rüstungsindustrie** F armaments industry; **Rüstungskontrolle** F arms control; **Rüstungswettlauf** M arms race; **Rüstzeit** F set-up time

Rute ['ruːtə] F -, -n **(a)** (= *Gerte*) switch; (= *esp Stock zum Züchtigen*) rod; (= *Birkenrute*) birch (rod) **(b)** (= *Wünschelrute*) divining rod; (= *Angelrute*) fishing rod **(c)** (*Aus:* = *Schneebesen*) whisk

Rütlischwur ['ryːtli-] M, NO PL (*Hist*) *oath taken on the Rütli Mountain by the founders of Switzerland*

Rutsch [rʊtʃ] M -es, -e slip, fall; (= *Erdrutsch*) landslide; (*von Steinen*) rock fall; (*fig*) (*Pol*) shift, swing; (*Fin*) slide, fall; (*inf:* = *Ausflug*) trip, outing; **guten ~!** (*inf*) have a good New Year!; **in einem ~** in one go

Rutschbahn F, **Rutsche** ['rʊtʃə] F -, -n (*Mech*) chute; (= *Kinderrutschbahn*) slide

rutschen ['rʊtʃn] VI AUX SEIN **(a)** (= *gleiten*) to slide; (= *ausrutschen, entgleiten*) to slip; (*Aut*) to skid; (*fig*) (*Preise, Kurse*) to slip; **auf dem Stuhl hin und her ~** to fidget (around) in one's chair; **ins Rutschen kommen** *or* **geraten** (*lit, fig*) to start to slip

(b) (*inf:* = *rücken*) to move up (*inf*); **zur Seite ~** to shove up *or* over (*inf*); **ein Stück(chen) ~** to shove up a bit (*inf*)

(c) (= *herunterrutschen*) to slip down; (*Essen, Tablette*) to go down

Rutsch-: rutschfest ADJ nonslip; **Rutschgefahr** F danger of skidding; **„~"** "slippery road"

rutschig ['rʊtʃɪç] ADJ slippery

rütteln ['rʏtln] 1 VT to shake; *Getreide etc* to sieve; **jdn am Arm/an der Schulter ~** to shake sb's arm/shoulder; *siehe auch* **gerüttelt** 2 VI to shake; (*Fahrzeug*) to jolt; (*Fenster, Tür: im Wind*) to rattle; **an etw** (*dat*) **~** *an Tür, Fenster etc* to rattle (at) sth; (*fig*) *an Grundsätzen, Ergebnis etc* to call sth into question; **daran ist nicht zu ~, daran gibt es nichts zu ~** (*inf*) there's no doubt about that

Ss

S, s [ɛs] NT -, - S, s

s. ABBR *von* **siehe** see

S ABBR *von* **Süden** S

S. ABBR *von* **Seite** p

SA [ɛs'|a:] F -, NO PL (*NS*) ABBR *von* **Sturmabteilung**

Saal [za:l] M -(e)s, **Säle** ['zɛ:lə] hall; (*für Sitzungen etc*) room

Saar [za:ɐ] F - Saar

Saar-: Saargebiet NT, **Saarland** NT -s Saarland; **Saarländer** ['za:ɐlɛndɐ] M -s, -, **Saarländerin** [-ərɪn] F -, -nen Saarlander; **saarländisch** ['za:ɐlɛndɪʃ] ADJ (of the) Saarland

Saat [za:t] F -, -en (a) (= *das Säen*) sowing (b) (= *Samen, ~gut*) seed(s *pl*) (*auch fig*)

Saat-: Saatgut NT, NO PL seed(s *pl*); **Saatkartoffel** F seed potato; **Saatzeit** F sowing time

Sabbat ['zabat] M -s, -e Sabbath

sabbern ['zabɐn] (*inf*) **1** VI to slobber; **vor sich hin ~** (*fig*) to mutter away to oneself **2** VT to blather; **dummes Zeug ~** to talk drivel (*inf*)

Säbel ['zɛ:bl] M -s, - sabre (*Brit*), saber (*US*); (= *Krummsäbel*) scimitar

säbeln ['zɛ:bln] (*inf*) **1** VT to saw away at **2** VI to saw away (*an* +*dat* at)

Säbelrasseln NT -s, NO PL sabre-rattling (*Brit*), saber-rattling (*US*)

Sabotage [zabo'ta:ʒə] F -, -n sabotage (*an* +*dat* of); **~ treiben** to perform acts of sabotage

Sabotageakt M act of sabotage

Saboteur [zabo'tø:ɐ] M -s, -e, **Saboteurin** [-'tø:rɪn] F -, -nen saboteur

sabotieren [zabo'ti:rən], *ptp* **sabotiert** VT to sabotage

Sa(c)charin [zaxa'ri:n] NT -s, NO PL saccharin

Sach-: Sachanlagevermögen NT (*Econ*) tangible fixed assets *pl*; **Sachbearbeiter(in)** M(F) specialist; (= *Beamter*) official in charge (*für* of); **der ~ für Anträge ist nicht da** the person who deals with applications isn't here; **Sachbereich** M (specialist) area; **Sachbeschädigung** F damage to property; **sachbezogen** **1** ADJ *Wissen, Fragen, Angaben, Politik* relevant **2** ADV with reference to the relevant issue/issues; **Sachbuch** NT nonfiction book

Sache ['zaxə] F -, -n (a) thing; (= *Gegenstand*) object, thing; (*Jur*: = *Eigentum*) article of property; **der Mensch wird zur ~** man is becomes an object; **~n gibts(, die gibts gar nicht)!** (*inf*) would you credit it! (*inf*)
(b) Sachen PL (*inf*: = *Zeug*) things *pl*; (*Jur*) property; **seine ~n packen** to pack ones bags
(c) (= *Angelegenheit*) matter; (= *Rechtsstreit, Fall*) case; (= *Vorfall*) business; (= *Anliegen*) cause; (= *Aufgabe*) job; **eine ~ der Polizei/der Behörden** a matter for the police/authorities; **es ist ~ der Polizei/der Behörden, das zu tun** it's up to the police/authorities to do that; **das ist eine ganz tolle/ unangenehme ~** it's really fantastic/unpleasant; **die ~ macht sich** (*inf*) things are coming along; **ich habe mir die ~ anders vorgestellt** I had imagined things differently; **das ist eine andere ~** that's a different matter; **das ist meine/seine ~** that's my/his affair; **in eigener ~** on one's own account; **in ~n** *or* **in der ~ A versus B** (*Jur*) in the case (of) A versus B; **das ist nicht jedermanns ~** it's not everyone's cup of tea (*inf*); **er versteht seine ~** he knows what he's doing; **er macht seine ~ gut** he's doing very well; (*beruflich*) he's doing a good job; **das ist so eine ~** (*inf*) it's a bit tricky; **das ist 'ne ~** (*inf*: = *prima*) great (*inf*); **der ~ zuliebe** for the love of it; **die ~ mit der Bank ist also geplatzt** so the bank job fell through; **er ist für illegale ~n nicht zu haben** you won't get him to do anything illegal; **solche ~n liegen mir nicht** I don't like things like that; **machst du bei der ~ mit?** are you with us?; **bei der ~ mache ich nicht mit** I'll have nothing to do with it; **was hat die Polizei zu der ~ gesagt?** what did the police say about all this business?; **das ist (eine) beschlossene ~** it's (all) settled; **die ~ hat geklappt/ist schief gegangen** everything worked/went wrong; **mach keine ~n!** (*inf*) don't be silly!; **was machst du bloß für ~n!** (*inf*) the things you do!; **um die ~ herumreden** to talk (all) round the subject; **zur ~!** let's get on with it; (*Parl,*
Jur etc) come to the point!; **zur ~ kommen** to come to the point; **das tut nichts zur ~** that doesn't matter; **sich** (*dat*) **seiner ~ sicher** *or* **gewiss sein** to be sure of one's ground; **bei der ~ sein** to be on the ball (*inf*); **sie war nicht bei der ~** her mind was elsewhere; **bei der ~ bleiben** to keep one's mind on the job; (*bei Diskussion*) to keep to the point; **die ~ ist die, dass ...** the thing is that ...; **jdm sagen, was ~ ist** (*inf*) to tell sb what's what
(d) (= *Tempo*) **mit 60/100 ~n** (*inf*) at 60/100

-sache F SUF IN CPDS a matter of ...; **das ist Ansichtssache/ Geschmackssache** that's a matter of opinion/taste

Sach-: Sachfrage F question regarding the matter itself; **Sach- und Personalfragen** questions relating to work and to personnel matters; **Sachgebiet** NT subject area; **sachgemäß, sachgerecht** **1** ADJ proper; **bei ~er Anwendung** if used properly **2** ADV properly; **sachkundig** **1** ADJ (well-)informed; *Beratung, Information* expert; *Erklärung* competent; **sich ~ machen** to inform oneself **2** ADV **~ antworten** to give an informed answer; **jdn ~ beraten** to give sb expert advice; **etw ~ erklären** to give a competent explanation of sth; **Sachlage** F situation

sachlich ['zaxlɪç] **1** ADJ (= *faktisch*) factual; *Grund, Einwand* practical; (= *sachbezogen*) *Frage, Wissen* relevant; (= *objektiv*) *Kritik, Bemerkung* objective; (= *nüchtern*) matter-of-fact; (= *schmucklos*) functional; **bleiben Sie mal ~** don't get carried away; (= *nicht persönlich werden*) don't get personal, stay objective **2** ADV (= *faktisch*) *unzutreffend* factually; (= *objektiv*) objectively; **die Auskunft war ~ falsch/richtig** the information was wrong/correct

sächlich ['zɛçlɪç] ADJ (*Gram*) neuter

Sachschaden M damage (to property); **bei dem Unfall hatte ich nur ~** only the car was damaged in the accident; **es entstand ~ in Höhe von ...** there was damage amounting to ...

Sachse ['zaksə] M -n, -n, **Sächsin** ['zɛksɪn] F -, -nen Saxon

sächseln ['zɛksln] VI (*inf*) (*mit Akzent*) to speak with a Saxon accent; (*in Mundart*) to speak in the Saxon dialect

Sachsen ['zaksn] NT -s Saxony

Sachsen-Anhalt ['zaksn'|anhalt] NT -s Saxony-Anhalt

sächsisch ['zɛksɪʃ] ADJ Saxon; **die Sächsische Schweiz** *area southeast of Dresden known for its health resorts and unusual rock formations*

sacht [zaxt], **sachte** ['zaxtə] **1** ADJ (= *leise*) soft; (= *sanft*) gentle; (= *vorsichtig*) careful; (= *allmählich*) gentle **2** ADV softly, gently; *ansteigen, abfallen* gently; (= *vorsichtig*) *anfragen* carefully

Sach-: Sachverhalt [-fɛɐhalt] M -(e)s, -e facts *pl* (of the case); **Sachverständige(r)** [-fɛɐʃtɛndɪgə] MF DECL AS ADJ expert; (*Jur*) expert witness

Sack [zak] M -(e)s, ̈e ['zɛkə] (a) sack; (*aus Papier, Plastik*) bag; **drei ~ Kartoffeln/Kohlen** three sacks of potatoes/coal; **in ~ und Asche** in sackcloth and ashes; **mit ~ und Pack** (*inf*) with bag and baggage; **gelber ~** yellow bag (*for the collection of recyclable packaging material*)
(b) (*Anat, Zool*) sac
(c) (*vulg*: = *Hoden*) balls *pl* (*sl*); **jdm auf den ~ gehen** (*sl*) to get on sb's tits (*sl*)
(d) (*inf*: = *Kerl, Bursche*) bastard (*sl*)

Sackbahnhof M terminus

sacken VI AUX SEIN (*lit, fig*) to sink; (*Flugzeug*) to lose height; (= *durchhängen*) to sag; **die Aktienkurse sackten in den Keller** share prices hit rock bottom

Sack-: Sackgasse F dead end, cul-de-sac (*esp Brit*); (*fig*) dead end; **in eine ~ geraten** (*fig*) to finish up a blind alley; (*Verhandlungen*) to reach an impasse; **in einer ~ stecken** (*fig*) to be (stuck) up a blind alley; (*mit Bemühungen etc*) to have come to a dead end; **Sackhüpfen** NT -s, NO PL sack race; **Sackkarre** F barrow; **Sackwichser** M (*sl*) wanker (*vulg*)

Sadismus [za'dɪsmʊs] M -, **Sadismen** [-mən] (a) NO PL sadism (b) (*Handlung*) sadistic act

Sadist [za'dɪst] M -en, -en, **Sadistin** [-dɪstɪn] F -, -nen sadist

sadistisch [za'dɪstɪʃ] **1** ADJ sadistic **2** ADV sadistically

Sadomaso [zado'ma:zo] M -, NO PL (*sl*) SM

Sadomasochismus [zadomazɔ'xɪsmʊs] M sadomasochism

säen ['zɛːən] VTI to sow; (fig) to sow (the seeds of); **dünn gesät** (fig) thin on the ground

Safari [za'faːri] F **-, -s** safari; **eine ~ machen** to go on safari

Safari-: Safarianzug M safari suit; **Safaripark** M safari park

Safe [zeːf] M or NT **-s, -s** safe

Safersex ['zeːfɐˈzeks] M **- -(es)**, NO PL, **Safer Sex** M **- -(e)s**, NO PL safe sex

Safran ['zafraːn, 'zafran] M **-s, -e** saffron

Saft [zaft] M **-(e)s, ̈e** ['zɛftə] juice; (= *Pflanzensaft*) sap; (= *Flüssigkeit*) liquid; (= *Hustensaft etc*) syrup; (*inf: = Strom, Benzin*) juice (*inf*); (*sl: = Sperma*) spunk (*vulg*); **voll im ~ stehen** to be full of sap; **von ~ und Kraft** (*fig*) dynamic; **ohne ~ und Kraft** (*fig*) wishy-washy (*inf*)

saftig ['zaftɪç] ADJ **(a)** (*= voll Saft*) *Obst, Fleisch* juicy; *Wiese, Grün* lush **(b)** (*inf: = kräftig*) *Witz* juicy (*inf*); *Rechnung, Strafe, Ohrfeige* hefty (*inf*); *Brief, Antwort, Ausdrucksweise* potent

Saft-: Saftladen M (*pej inf*) dump (*pej inf*); **Saftpresse** F fruit press; **Saftsack** M (*inf*) stupid bastard (*sl*)

Sage ['zaːgə] F **-, -n** legend; (*altnordische*) saga

Säge ['zɛːgə] F **-, -n (a)** (*Werkzeug*) saw **(b)** (*Aus: = ~werk*) sawmill

Säge-: Sägeblatt NT saw blade; **Sägebock** M sawhorse; **Sägefisch** M sawfish; **Sägemehl** NT sawdust; **Sägemesser** NT serrated knife

---

sagen ['zaːgn]

TRANSITIVES VERB

(a) (= *äußern*) to say; **wie kannst du so etwas sagen?** how can you say such things?; **wie gesagt** as I say; **das kann ich Ihnen nicht sagen** I couldn't say; **das sage ich nicht!** I'm not saying!; **so was sagt man doch nicht!** you can't say things like that!; (*bei Schimpfen, Fluchen*) (mind your) language!; **was soll man dazu sagen?** what can you say?; **was sagen Sie dazu?** what do you think about it?; **sich** (*dat*) **etw sagen** to say sth to oneself; **ich sags ja immer ...** I always say ...; **damit ist alles gesagt** that says it all; **sag bloß!** you don't say!; **was Sie nicht sagen!** you don't say!; **ich sage gar nichts mehr!** I'm not saying another word!; (*verblüfft*) good heavens!; **das kann man wohl sagen!** you can say that again!; **ich muss schon sagen** I must say; **wie man so sagt** as the saying goes; **das ist nicht gesagt** that's by no means certain; **leichter gesagt als getan** easier said than done; **gesagt, getan** no sooner said than done; **ich bin, sagen wir, in einer Stunde da** I'll be there in an hour, say; **da soll noch einer sagen, wir Deutschen hätten keinen Humor!** never let it be said that we Germans have no sense of humour (*Brit*) or humor (*US*)!

---

*Das englische Verb **to tell** kann von einem Personalpronomen gefolgt werden, **to say** jedoch nicht.*

---

jdm etw sagen to say sth to sb, to tell sb sth; **ich sags ihm** I'll tell him; **ich kann dir sagen ...** (*inf*) I can tell you ...; **das ist schnell gesagt** I can tell you in two words; **wem sagen Sie das!** you don't need to tell ME that!
(b) (= *bedeuten, meinen*) to mean; **das hat nichts zu sagen** that doesn't mean anything; **sagt dir der Name etwas?** does the name mean anything to you?; **ich will damit nicht sagen, dass ...** I don't mean to imply that ...; **willst du vielleicht sagen, dass ...** are you trying to say that ...?; **sein Gesicht sagte alles** it was written all over his face
(c) (= *befehlen*) to tell; **jdm sagen, er solle etw tun** to tell sb to do sth; **du hast hier (gar) nichts zu sagen** you're not the boss; **hat er im Betrieb etwas zu sagen?** does he have a say in the firm?; **das Sagen haben** to be the boss

◆sagen lassen ich habe mir sagen lassen, ... (= *ausrichten lassen*) I've been told ...; **was ich mir von ihm nicht alles sagen lassen muss!** the things I have to take from him!; **lass dir von mir sagen** or **gesagt sein, ...** let me tell you ...; **er lässt sich** (*dat*) **nichts sagen** he won't be told; **das lass ich mir von dem nicht sagen** I won't take that from him; **sie ließen es sich** (*dat*) **nicht zweimal sagen** they didn't need to be told twice
(d) (*andere Redewendungen*) **im Vertrauen gesagt** in confidence; **unter uns gesagt** between you and me; **genauer/deutlicher gesagt** to put it more precisely/clearly; **sag nicht**

---

so etwas or **so was!** (*inf*) don't talk like that!; **sag das nicht!** (*inf*) don't you be so sure!; **was ich noch sagen wollte, ...** another point I would like to make is that ...; **was ich noch sagen wollte, vergiss nicht ...** (*inf*) by the way, don't forget ...; **dann will ich nichts gesagt haben** in that case forget I said anything; **sage und schreibe 800 Euro** 800 euros, would you believe it

◆sag mal/sagen Sie mal du, Veronika, sag mal, wollen wir ... hey Veronika, listen, shall we ...; **sag mal, willst du nicht endlich Schluss machen?** come on, isn't it time to stop?; **nun sagen Sie/sag mal selber, ist das nicht unpraktisch?** you must admit that's impractical

sägen ['zɛːgn] **◼** VTI to saw **◼** VI (*inf: = schnarchen*) to snore

sagenhaft ◼ ADJ **(a)** (= *nach Art einer Sage*) legendary **(b)** (= *enorm*) *Summe* fabulous **(c)** (*inf: = hervorragend*) fantastic (*inf*) **◼** ADV (*inf: = unglaublich*) incredibly

Säge-: Sägespäne PL wood shavings *pl*; **Sägewerk** NT sawmill; **Sägezahn** M sawtooth

sah PRET *von* **sehen**

Sahara [za'haːra, 'zaːhara] F - Sahara (Desert)

Sahel-Zone F, **Sahelzone** F Sahel region

Sahne ['zaːnə] F **-, NO PL** cream; **(aller)erste ~ sein** (*inf*) to be top-notch (*inf*)

Sahne-: Sahnebonbon M or NT toffee; **Sahnehäubchen** NT (*lit*) cream topping; (*fig*) icing on the cake; **Sahnequark** [-kvark] M creamy quark; **Sahnetorte** F cream gateau

sahnig ['zaːnɪç] **◼** ADJ creamy **◼** ADV **etw ~ schlagen** to beat sth until creamy

Saison [sɛ'zõː, zɛ'zɔŋ, (*Aus*) zɛ'zoːn] F **-, -s** or (*Aus*) **-en** [-'zoːnən] season; **außerhalb der ~, in der stillen** or **toten ~** in the off season

Saison- [sɛ'zõː, zɛ'zɔŋ, (*Aus*) zɛ'zoːn] IN CPDS seasonal; **Saisonarbeit** F seasonal work; **Saisonarbeiter(in)** M(F) seasonal worker; **saisonbedingt** ADJ seasonal; **saisonbereinigt** [-bəraɪnɪçt] ADJ *Zahlen etc* seasonally adjusted; **Saisonschluss** M end of the season; **Saisonschwankung** F seasonal fluctuation; **Saisonzuschlag** M in-season supplement

Saite ['zaɪtə] F **-, -n** (*Mus, Sport*) string; **andere ~n aufziehen** (*inf*) to get tough

Saiten-: Saiteninstrument NT string(ed) instrument; **Saitenwurst** F *type of frankfurter*

Saitling ['zaɪtlɪŋ] M **-s, -e** sausage skin (*for frankfurters*)

Sakko ['zako] M or NT **-s, -s** sports jacket (*esp Brit*), sport coat (*US*); (*aus Samt etc*) jacket

Sakrament [zakra'mɛnt] NT **-(e)s, -e** sacrament

Sakrament(s)häuschen [-hɔɪsçən] NT tabernacle

Sakrileg [zakri'leːk] NT **-s, -e** [-gə] (*geh*) sacrilege

Sakristei [zakrɪs'taɪ] F **-, -en** sacristy

Salamander [zala'mandɐ] M **-s, -** salamander

Salami [za'laːmi] F **-, -s** salami

Salamitaktik (*inf*) policy of small steps

Salär [za'lɛːɐ] NT **-s, -e** (*old, Sw*) salary

Salat [za'laːt] M **-(e)s, -e (a)** (= *Pflanze, Kopfsalat*) lettuce **(b)** (= *Gericht*) salad; **da haben wir den ~!** (*inf*) now we're in a fine mess

Salat-: Salatbesteck NT salad servers *pl*; **Salatdressing** [-drɛsɪŋ] NT **-s, -s** salad dressing; **Salatgurke** F cucumber; **Salatkartoffel** F potato (*used for potato salad*); **Salatmajonäse** F salad cream; **Salatöl** NT salad oil; **Salatplatte** F salad; **Salatrauke** F rucola; **Salatschleuder** F salad drainer (*Brit*) or strainer (*US*); **Salatschüssel** F salad bowl; **Salatsoße** F salad dressing

Salbe ['zalbə] F **-, -n** ointment

Salbei ['zalbaɪ, zal'baɪ] M **-s** or f **-, NO PL** sage

salbungsvoll (*pej*) **◼** ADJ *Worte, Ton* unctuous (*pej*) **◼** ADV *sprechen, predigen* unctuously (*pej*)

Salchow ['zalço] M **-s, -s** (*Eiskunstlauf*) salchow

saldieren [zal'diːrən], *ptp* **saldiert** VT (*Comm*) to balance; (*Aus*) to confirm payment

Saldo ['zaldo] M **-s, -s** or **Saldi** or **Salden** [-di, -dn] (*Fin*) balance; **per saldo** (*lit, fig*) on balance; **per saldo bezahlen** or **remittieren** to pay off the balance in full

Saldoübertrag M, **Saldovortrag** M (*Fin*) balance brought forward *or* carried forward

Säle PL *von* **Saal**

Salmiak [zal'miak, 'zalmiak] M *or* NT **-s**, NO PL sal ammoniac

Salmiakgeist M, NO PL (liquid) ammonia

Salmonellen [zalmo'nɛlən] PL salmonellae *pl*

Salmonellenvergiftung F salmonella (poisoning)

Salmonellose [zalmonɛ'lo:zə] F **-**, **-n** salmonellosis

Salon [sa'lõ:, za'lɔŋ, (*Aus*) za'lo:n] M **-s**, **-s** (a) (= *Gesellschaftszimmer*) drawing room; (*Naut*) saloon (b) (= *Friseursalon, Modesalon, Kosmetiksalon etc*) salon (c) (= *Messe, Ausstellung*) show; (= *Messestand*) (exhibition) stand (d) (= *Kunstsalon*) exhibition room

salonfähig ADJ (*iro*) socially acceptable; *Leute, Aussehen* presentable; **ein nicht ~er Witz** an objectionable joke; **nicht ~e Ausdrucksweise** uncouth language

salopp [za'lɔp] **1** ADJ (a) (= *nachlässig*) sloppy, slovenly; *Manieren* slovenly; *Ausdruck, Sprache* slangy (b) (= *ungezwungen*) casual **2** ADV *sich kleiden, sich ausdrücken* casually; **~ gesagt, ...** to put it crudely ...

Salpeter [zal'pe:tɐ] M **-s**, NO PL saltpetre (*Brit*), saltpeter (*US*), nitre (*Brit*), niter (*US*)

Salpetersäure F nitric acid

Salsa ['zalza] M **-**, NO PL (*Mus*) salsa

Salsa-Musik F, **Salsamusik** F salsa (music)

Salto ['zalto] M **-s**, **-s** *or* **Salti** [-ti] somersault; **~ vorwärts/rückwärts** forward/backward somersault; **einen ~ mortale machen** (*im Zirkus*) to perform a death-defying leap; (*Aviat*) to loop the loop

Salut [za'lu:t] M **-(e)s**, **-e** (*Mil*) salute; **~ schießen** *or* **feuern** to fire a salute; **21 Schuss ~** 21-gun salute

salutieren [zalu'ti:rən], *ptp* **salutiert** VTI (*Mil*) to salute

Salve ['zalvə] F **-**, **-n** salvo, volley; (= *Ehrensalve*) salute; (*fig:* = *Lachsalve*) burst of laughter

Salz [zalts] NT **-es**, **-e** salt; **jodiertes ~** iodized salt; **das ist das ~ in der Suppe** (*fig*) that's what gives it that extra something

salzen ['zaltsn], *ptp* **gesalzen** [gə'zaltsn] VT to salt; *siehe auch* **gesalzen**

Salz-: **salzfrei** **1** ADJ salt-free **2** ADV **~ essen** not to eat salt; **~ kochen** to cook without salt; **Salzgebäck** NT savoury (*Brit*) *or* savory (*US*) biscuits *pl*; **salzhaltig** ADJ *Boden, Luft, Wasser* salty; **Salzhering** M salted herring

salzig ['zaltsɪç] ADJ *Speise, Wasser* salty

Salz-: **Salzkartoffeln** PL boiled potatoes *pl*; **Salzkorn** NT, *pl* **-körner** grain of salt; **Salzlake** F brine; **salzlos** **1** ADJ salt-free **2** ADV **~ essen** not to eat salt; **~ kochen** to cook without salt; **Salzlösung** F saline solution; **Salzsäule** F **zur ~ erstarren** (*Bibl*) to turn into a pillar of salt; (*fig*) to stand as though rooted to the spot; **Salzsäure** F hydrochloric acid; **Salzsee** M salt lake; **Salzstange** F pretzel stick; **Salzstock** M salt mine; **Salzstreuer** [-ʃtrɔyɐ] M **-s**, **-** salt shaker, saltcellar (*esp Brit*); **Salzwasser** NT, NO PL salt water

SA-Mann [ɛs'la:-] M, *pl* **SA-Leute** storm trooper

Samba ['zamba] M **-s**, **-s** *or* F **-**, **-s** samba

Sambesi [zam'be:zi] M **-(s)** Zambezi

Sambia ['zambia] NT **-s** Zambia

sambisch ['zambɪʃ] ADJ Zambian

Samen ['za:mən] M **-s**, **-** (a) (*Bot, fig*) seed (b) (= *Menschensamen, Tiersamen*) sperm

Samen-: **Samenanlage** F (*Bot*) ovule; **Samenbank** F, *pl* **-banken** sperm bank; **Samenerguss** M ejaculation; **Samenkorn** NT, *pl* **-körner** seed; **Samenspender** M sperm donor; **Samenstrang** M spermatic cord

sämig ['zɛ:mɪç] ADJ *Soße* thick

Sammel-: **Sammelalbum** NT (collector's) album; **Sammelanschluss** M (*Telec*) private (branch) exchange; (*von Privathäusern*) party line; **Sammelband** [-bant] M, *pl* **-bände** anthology; **Sammelbecken** NT collecting tank; (*Geol*) catchment area; (*fig*) melting pot (*von* for); **Sammelbestellung** F joint order; **Sammelbüchse** F collecting tin; **Sammeldepot** NT (*Fin*) collective securities deposit; **Sammelfahrschein** M, **Sammelkarte** F (*für mehrere Fahrten*) multi-journey ticket; (*für mehrere Personen*) group ticket; **Sammelmappe** F folder

sammeln ['zamln] **1** VT to collect; *Blumen, Pilze etc* to pick; *Truppen, Anhänger* to assemble; **neue Kräfte ~** to build up one's energy again; **Punkte ~** (*Sport, fig*) to score points **2** VR (a) (= *zusammenkommen*) to gather; (= *sich anhäufen: Wasser, Geld etc*) to accumulate (b) (= *sich konzentrieren*) to collect oneself; *siehe auch* **gesammelt** **3** VI to collect (*für* for)

Sammelplatz M (a) (= *Treffpunkt*) assembly point (b) (= *Lagerplatz*) collecting point; (= *Deponie*) dump

Sammelsurium [zaml'zu:riʊm] NT **-s**, **Sammelsurien** [-riən] conglomeration

Sammeltaxi NT share-a-ride taxi

Sammler ['zamlɐ] M **-s**, **-**, **Sammlerin** [-ərɪn] F **-**, **-nen** collector; (*von Beeren*) picker

Sammlung ['zamlʊŋ] F **-**, **-en** (a) collection (b) (*fig:* = *Konzentration*) composure; **ihm fehlt die innere ~** he lacks composure; **zur ~ (meiner Gedanken)** to collect my thoughts

Sammlungsbewegung F coalition movement

Samstag ['zamsta:k] M Saturday; *siehe auch* **Dienstag**

samstägig ['zamstɛ:gɪç] ADJ Saturday

samstags ['zamsta:ks] ADV on Saturdays

samt [zamt] **1** PREP +DAT along *or* together with; **sie kam ~ Katze** (*hum*) she came complete with cat **2** ADV **~ und sonders** the whole lot (of them/us/you), the whole bunch (*inf*); **die Teilnehmer wurden ~ und sonders verhaftet** all the participants were arrested, the whole lot of them

Samt [zamt] M **-(e)s**, **-e** velvet

Samt- IN CPDS velvet; **samtartig** ADJ velvety; **Samthandschuh** M velvet glove; **jdn mit ~en anfassen** (*inf*) to handle sb with kid gloves (*inf*)

samtig ['zamtɪç] ADJ velvety

sämtlich ['zɛmtlɪç] **1** ADJ (= *alle*) all; (= *vollständig*) complete; **Schillers ~e Werke** the complete works of Schiller; **~e Anwesenden** all those present **2** ADV all; **die Unterlagen waren ~ verschwunden** all the documents had disappeared

Samurai [zamʊ'rai] M **-(s)**, **-(s)** samurai

Samuraibond M (*Fin*) Samurai bond

Sanatorium [zana'to:riʊm] NT **-s**, **Sanatorien** [-riən] sanatorium (*Brit*), sanitarium (*US*)

Sand [zant] M **-(e)s**, **-e** [-də] sand; **das/die gibts wie ~ am Meer** (*inf*) there are heaps of them (*inf*); **auf ~ bauen** (*fig*) to build upon sandy ground; **jdm ~ in die Augen streuen** (*fig*) to throw dust (*Brit*) *or* dirt (*US*) in sb's eyes; **~ ins Getriebe streuen** to throw a spanner in the works (*Brit*), to throw a (monkey) wrench into the works (*US*); **im ~ verlaufen** (*inf*) to come to nothing; **den Kopf in den ~ stecken** to bury one's head in the sand; **etw in den ~ setzen** (*inf*) *Projekt, Prüfung* to blow sth (*inf*); *Geld* to squander sth

Sandale [zan'da:lə] F **-**, **-n** sandal

Sandalette [zanda'lɛtə] F **-**, **-n** high-heeled sandal

Sand-: **Sandbank** F, *pl* **-bänke** sandbank; **Sandgrube** F sandpit (*esp Brit*), sandbox (*US*); (*Golf*) bunker

sandig ['zandɪç] ADJ sandy

Sand-: **Sandkasten** M sandpit (*esp Brit*), sandbox (*US*); (*Mil*) sand table; **Sandkastenspiele** PL (*Mil*) sand-table exercises *pl*; (*fig*) tactical manoeuvrings (*Brit*) *or* maneuverings (*US*) *pl*; **Sandkorn** NT, *pl* **-körner** grain of sand; **Sandmann** M, NO PL, **Sandmännchen** NT, NO PL (*in Geschichten*) sandman; **Sandpapier** NT sandpaper; **Sandplatz** M (*Tennis*) clay court; **Sandstein** M sandstone; **Sandstrahl** M jet of sand; **sandstrahlen** *ptp* **gesandstrahlt** *or* (*spec*) **sandgestrahlt** VTI to sandblast; **Sandstrahlgebläse** NT sandblasting equipment *no indef art, no pl*; **Sandstrand** M sandy beach; **Sandsturm** M sandstorm

sandte PRET *von* **senden**[1]

Sandwüste F sandy waste; (*Geog*) (sandy) desert

sanft [zanft] **1** ADJ gentle; *Berührung, Stimme, Farbe, Licht, Wind, Regen auch, Haut* soft; *Schlaf, Tod* peaceful; **mit ~er Gewalt** gently but firmly; **mit ~er Hand** with a gentle hand; **~ wie ein Lamm** (as) gentle as a lamb; **~er Tourismus** green tourism **2** ADV softly; *abfallen, ansteigen, hinweisen* gently; *tadeln, ermahnen* mildly; **sich ~ anfühlen** to feel soft; **~ mit jdm umgehen** to be gentle with sb; **~ schlafen** to be sleeping peacefully; **er ist ~ entschlafen** he passed away peacefully

Sanftheit F **-**, NO PL gentleness; (*von Stimme, Farbe, Licht auch, von Haut*) softness

sang PRET *von* **singen**

Sang [zaŋ] M **-(e)s, ⸚e** ['zɛŋə] **mit ~ und Klang** (*lit*) with drums drumming and pipes piping; (*fig iro*) **durchfallen** catastrophically; **entlassen werden** with a lot of hullaballoo

Sänger ['zɛŋɐ] M **-s, -** , **Sängerin** [-ərɪn] F **-, -nen** singer; (= *esp Jazzsänger, Popsänger*) vocalist

Sangria [zaŋˈgriːa, ˈzaŋgria] F **-, -s** sangria

sang- und klanglos ADV (*inf*) without any ado; **sie ist ~ verschwunden** she just simply disappeared

sanieren [zaˈniːrən], *ptp* **saniert** ▮ VT **(a)** (= *gesunde Lebensverhältnisse schaffen*) **Gebäude** to renovate; **Stadtteil, Gelände** to redevelop; **Fluss** to clean up **(b)** (*Econ*) to put (back) on its feet, to rehabilitate; **Haushalt** to turn (a)round ▮ VR (*Unternehmen, Wirtschaft, Industrie*) to put itself (back) in good shape; **bei dem Geschäft hat er sich saniert** (*inf*) he made a killing on the deal (*inf*)

Sanierung F **-, -en (a)** (*von Gebäude*) renovation; (*von Stadtteil*) redevelopment; (*von Fluss*) cleaning-up **(b)** (*Econ*) rehabilitation; (*von Rentensystem etc*) modernization; **Maßnahmen zur ~ des Dollars** measures to put the dollar back on its feet again

Sanierungs-: Sanierungsgebiet NT redevelopment area; **Sanierungsmaßnahme** F (*für Gebiete etc*) redevelopment measure; (*Econ*) rehabilitation measure

sanitär [zaniˈtɛːɐ] ▮ ADJ NO PRED sanitary; **~e Anlagen** sanitation (facilities), sanitary facilities ▮ ADV **ein Haus ~ ausstatten** to install sanitation in a house

Sanitäter [zaniˈtɛːtɐ] M **-s, -** , **Sanitäterin** [-ərɪn] F **-, -nen** first-aid attendant; (*Mil*) (medical) orderly; (*in Krankenwagen*) ambulanceman/-woman

Sanitäts-: Sanitätsdienst M (*Mil*) medical duty; (= *Heeresabteilung*) medical corps; **Sanitätsflugzeug** NT air ambulance; **Sanitätswagen** M ambulance

sank PRET *von* **sinken**

Sanka [ˈzaŋka] M **-s, -s** (*Mil inf*) ambulance

Sankt [zaŋkt] ADJ INV saint; **~ Nikolaus** Santa (Claus), Father Christmas; (*Rel*) St *or* Saint Nicholas

Sankt Gallen [zaŋkt ˈgalən] NT **- -s** (= *Kanton, Stadt*) St Gall

Sanktion [zaŋkˈtsioːn] F **-, -en** sanction

sanktionieren [zaŋktsioˈniːrən], *ptp* **sanktioniert** VT to sanction

sann PRET *von* **sinnen**

Sansibar [ˈzanzibaːɐ, zanziˈbaːɐ] NT **-s** Zanzibar

Sanskrit [ˈzanskrɪt] NT **-s**, NO PL Sanskrit

Saphir [ˈzaːfɪr, ˈzaːfiːɐ, zaˈfiːɐ] M **-s, -e** sapphire

Sarde [ˈzardə] M **-n, -n** , **Sardin** [ˈzardɪn] F **-, -nen** Sardinian

Sardelle [zarˈdɛlə] F **-, -n** anchovy

Sardin F **-, -nen** Sardinian

Sardine [zarˈdiːnə] F **-, -n** sardine

Sardinenbüchse F sardine tin; **wie in einer ~** (*fig inf*) like sardines (*inf*)

Sardinien [zarˈdiːniən] NT **-s** Sardinia

Sardinier [zarˈdiːniɐ] M **-s, -** , **Sardinierin** [-ərɪn] F **-, -nen** Sardinian

sardinisch [zarˈdiːnɪʃ], **sardisch** [ˈzardɪʃ] ADJ Sardinian

Sarg [zark] M **-(e)s, ⸚e** [ˈzɛːrgə] coffin, casket (*US*)

Sarg-: Sargdeckel M coffin lid, casket lid (*US*); **Sargnagel** M coffin nail, casket nail (*US*); (*fig inf auch:* = *Zigarette*) cancer stick (*hum inf*)

Sari [ˈzaːri] M **-(s), -s** sari

Sarin [zaˈriːn] NT **-s**, NO PL (*Chem*) sarin

Sarkasmus [zarˈkasmʊs] M **-, Sarkasmen** [-mən] **(a)** NO PL sarcasm **(b)** (= *Bemerkung*) sarcastic comment *or* remark

sarkastisch [zarˈkastɪʃ] ▮ ADJ sarcastic ▮ ADV sarcastically

Sarkom [zarˈkoːm] NT **-s, -e** (*Med*) sarcoma

Sarkophag [zarkoˈfaːk] M **-(e)s, -e** [-gə] sarcophagus

Sarong [ˈzaːrɔŋ] M **-(s), -s** sarong

saß PRET *von* **sitzen**

Satan [ˈzaːtan] M **-s, -e** (*Bibl, fig*) Satan

satanisch [zaˈtaːnɪʃ] ▮ ADJ satanic ▮ ADV satanically

Satanismus [zataˈnɪsmʊs] M **-**, NO PL Satanism

Satellit [zatɛˈliːt] M **-en, -en** satellite

Satelliten- IN CPDS satellite; **Satellitenabwehrwaffe** F antisatellite weapon; **Satellitenantenne** F (*TV*) satellite dish;

Satellitenbild NT (*TV*) satellite picture; **Satellitenfernsehen** NT satellite television; **Satellitenfoto** NT satellite picture; **Satellitennavigation** F satellite navigation; **Satellitennavigationssystem** NT Global Positioning System; **Satellitenschüssel** F (*TV inf*) satellite dish; **Satellitenstadt** F satellite town; **Satellitenübertragung** F (*Rad, TV*) satellite transmission

Satin [zaˈtɛ̃ː] M **-s, -s** satin; (= *Baumwollsatin*) sateen

Satire [zaˈtiːrə] F **-, -n** satire (*auf +acc* on)

Satiriker [zaˈtiːrikɐ] M **-s, -** , **Satirikerin** [-ərɪn] F **-, -nen** satirist

satirisch [zaˈtiːrɪʃ] ▮ ADJ satirical ▮ ADV satirically

satt [zat] ▮ ADJ **(a)** (= *gesättigt*) **Mensch** full (up) (*inf*); **Magen, Gefühl** full; **~ sein** to have had enough (to eat), to be full (up) (*inf*); **~ werden** to have enough to eat; **das macht ~** it's filling; **sich (an etw** *dat*) **~ essen** to eat one's fill (of sth); **wie soll sie ihre Kinder ~ kriegen?** (*inf*) how is she supposed to feed her children?; **er ist kaum ~ zu kriegen** (*inf: lit, fig*) he's insatiable; **er konnte sich an ihr nicht ~ sehen** he could not see enough of her; **sie konnte sich an der Musik nicht ~ hören** she could not get enough of the music; **wie ein ~er Säugling** (*inf*) with a look of contentment

(b) **jdn/etw ~ haben** *or* **sein** to be fed up with sb/sth (*inf*); **jdn/ etw ~ bekommen** *or* **kriegen** (*inf*) to get fed up with sb/sth (*inf*)

(c) (= *blasiert, übersättigt*) well-fed

(d) (= *kräftig, voll*) **Farben, Klang** rich; (*inf*) **Applaus** resounding; (*inf*) **Mehrheit** comfortable; **~e 1000 Euro** (*inf*) a cool 1000 euros (*inf*)

(e) (*inf:* = *im Überfluss*) **... ~ ...** galore

▮ ADV (*inf*) **verdienen, da sein** more than enough; **es gab Champagner ~** there was more than enough champagne

Sattel [ˈzatl] M **-s, ⸚** [ˈzɛtl] saddle; **sich im ~ halten** (*lit, fig*) to stay in the saddle; **jdn in den ~ heben** (*lit*) to lift sb into the saddle; (*fig*) to help sb to power; **fest im ~ sitzen** (*fig*) to be firmly in the saddle

Sattel-: Satteldach NT saddle roof; **Satteldecke** F saddlecloth; **sattelfest** ADJ **~ sein** (*Reiter*) to have a good seat; **in etw** (*dat*) **~ sein** (*fig*) to have a firm grasp of sth; **Sattelgurt** M girth; **Sattelknopf** M pommel

satteln [ˈzatln] VT **Pferd** to saddle (up)

Sattel-: Sattelschlepper M articulated lorry (*Brit*), semitrailer (*US*); **Satteltasche** F saddlebag; (= *Gepäcktasche am Fahrrad, aus Stroh*) pannier; **Sattelzeug** NT, *pl* **-zeuge** saddlery; **Sattelzug** M = **Sattelschlepper**

Sattheit F **-**, NO PL **(a)** (*Gefühl*) full feeling **(b)** (*von Farben, Klang*) richness

sättigen [ˈzɛtɪgn] ▮ VT **(a)** **Hunger, Neugier** to satisfy; **jdn** to make replete; (= *ernähren*) to feed **(b)** (*Comm, Chem*) to saturate ▮ VI to be filling

sättigend ADJ **Essen** filling

Sättigungs-: Sättigungsgrad M degree of saturation; **Sättigungspunkt** M saturation point

Sattler [ˈzatlɐ] M **-s, -** , **Sattlerin** [-ərɪn] F **-, -nen** saddler; (= *Polsterer*) upholsterer

Sattlerei [zatləˈrai] F **-, -en** saddlery; (= *Polsterei*) upholstery; (= *Werkstatt*) saddler's; upholsterer's

sattsam [ˈzatzaːm] ADV amply; **bekannt** sufficiently

saturiert [zatuˈriːɐt] (*geh*) ▮ ADJ **Markt** saturated; **Klasse** prosperous ▮ ADV **~ leben** to prosper

Saturn [zaˈtʊrn] M **-s** (*Myth, Astron*) Saturn; **die Ringe des ~s** the rings of Saturn

Satz [zats] M **-es, ⸚e** [ˈzɛtsə] **(a)** sentence; (= *Teilsatz*) clause; (= *Lehrsatz*) proposition; (*Math*) theorem; **ich kann nur ein paar Sätze Italienisch** I only know a few phrases of Italian; **mitten im ~** in mid-sentence; **der ~ des Pythagoras** Pythagoras' theorem

(b) (*Typ*) (= *das Setzen*) setting; (= *das Gesetzte*) type *no pl*; **etw in ~ geben** to send sth for setting; **in ~ gehen** to go for setting; **das Buch ist im ~** the book is being set

(c) (*Mus:* = *Abschnitt*) movement

(d) (= *Bodensatz*) dregs *pl*; (= *Kaffeesatz*) grounds *pl*; (= *Teesatz*) leaves *pl*

(e) (= *Zusammengehöriges*) (*Sport*) set; (*Comput:* = *Datensatz*) record; (= *Tarifsatz*) charge; (= *Spesensatz*) allowance; (= *Zinssatz*) rate

(f) (= *Sprung*) leap; **einen ~ machen** *or* **tun** to leap; **mit einem ~** in one leap

Satz-: Satzaussage F (*Gram*) predicate; **Satzball** M (*Sport*) set point; (*Tischtennis*) game point; **Satzbau** M, NO PL sentence construction; **Satzergänzung** F (*Gram*) object; **Satzgefüge** NT (*Gram*) complex sentence; **Satzgegenstand** M (*Gram*) subject; **Satzlehre** F (*Gram*) syntax; **Satzmelodie** F (*Phon*) intonation; **Satzteil** M part of a/the sentence

Satzung ['zatsʊŋ] F -, -en constitution; (*von Verein*) rules pl

Satz-: Satzverlust M (*Tennis*) loss of a set; **Satzzeichen** NT punctuation mark

Sau [zaʊ] F -, **Säue** ['zɔʏə] *or* (*Hunt*) -en **(a)** sow; (*inf:* = *Schwein*) pig; (*Hunt*) wild boar; **die ~ rauslassen** (*fig inf*) to let it all hang out (*inf*); **wie eine gesengte ~** (*inf*), **wie die ~** (*inf*) like a maniac (*inf*)
(b) (*pej inf*) (= *Schmutzfink*) dirty swine (*inf*); **du ~!** you dirty swine! (*inf*); **miese ~** bastard (*sl*); **dumme ~** stupid cow (*inf*)
(c) (*fig inf*) **da war keine ~ zu sehen** there wasn't a bloody (*Brit*) *or* goddamn soul to be seen (*inf*); **das interessiert keine ~** nobody gives a damn about that (*inf*); **jdn zur ~ machen** to bawl sb out (*inf*); **unter aller ~** bloody (*Brit*) *or* goddamn awful (*inf*); **wie die ~** (= *wie verrückt*) like mad *or* crazy

sauber ['zaʊbɐ] **1** ADJ **(a)** (= *rein, reinlich*) clean; **~ sein** (*Hund etc*) to be house-trained; (*Kind*) to be (potty-)trained
(b) (= *ordentlich*) neat, tidy; (*Aus, Sw, S Ger:* = *hübsch*) Mädel pretty; (= *exakt*) accurate
(c) (= *anständig*) honest; **~ bleiben** to keep one's hands clean; **bleib ~!** (*inf*) keep your nose clean (*inf*)
(d) (*inf:* = *großartig*) fantastic; **~! ~!** that's the stuff! (*inf*); **du bist mir ja ein ~er Freund!** (*iro*) a fine friend YOU are! (*iro*)
2 ADV **(a)** (= *rein*) **etw ~ putzen** to clean sth; **~ singen/spielen** to sing/play on key
(b) (= *sorgfältig*) very thoroughly
(c) (= *genau*) *analysieren, darstellen* carefully; **etw ~ lösen** to find a neat solution for sth

sauber halten VT IRREG to keep clean

Sauberkeit F -, NO PL **(a)** (= *Hygiene, Ordentlichkeit*) cleanliness; (= *Reinheit*) (*von Wasser, Luft etc*) cleanness; (*von Tönen*) accuracy **(b)** (= *Anständigkeit*) honesty; (*im Sport*) fair play

säuberlich ['zɔʏbɐlɪç] **1** ADJ neat and tidy **2** ADV neatly; *auseinander halten, trennen* clearly; **fein ~** neatly and tidily

sauber machen VT to clean

Saubermann M, pl -männer (*fig inf*) decent and upstanding sort; (*in Politik etc*) squeaky-clean man (*inf*); **die Saubermänner** the squeaky-clean brigade (*inf*)

säubern ['zɔʏbɐn] VT **(a)** (= *reinigen*) to clean; **das Wasser (von Verschmutzung) ~** to cleanse the water (*fig euph*) *Partei, Buch* to purge (*von* of); *Saal* to clear (*von* of); (*Mil*) *Gegend* to clear (*von* of); **eine Region ethnisch ~** to ethnically cleanse a region

Säuberung F -, -en **(a)** (= *Reinigung*) cleaning; (*von Wasser*) cleansing **(b)** (*fig: von Partei, Buch*) purging; (*von Gegend*) clearing; (*Pol: Aktion*) purge; **ethnische ~** ethnic cleansing

Sau-: saublöd, saublöde (*inf*) **1** ADJ bloody (*Brit*) *or* damn stupid (*inf*) **2** ADV **~ anstellen** to behave like a bloody (*Brit*) *or* damn idiot (*inf*); **~ fragen** to ask a damn stupid question (*inf*); **Saubohne** F broad bean

Sauce ['zo:sə] F -, -n sauce; (= *Bratensauce*) gravy

Saudi ['zaʊdi, za'u:di] M -(s), -(s) *or* f -, -s Saudi

Saudi-: Saudiaraber(in) ['zaʊdi'arabɐ, zaʊdila'ra:bɐ] M(F) Saudi; **Saudi-Arabien** ['zaʊdila'ra:biən] NT Saudi Arabia; **saudi-arabisch** ADJ Saudi *attr*, Saudi Arabian

saudisch ADJ Saudi *attr*, Saudi Arabian

saudumm (*inf*) **1** ADJ damn stupid (*inf*) **2** ADV **sich ~ benehmen** to behave like a stupid idiot; **~ fragen** to ask a damn stupid question (*inf*)

sauer ['zaʊɐ] **1** ADJ **(a)** (= *nicht süß*) sour; *Wein* acid(ic); *Gurke, Hering* pickled; *Sahne* soured; **saure Drops** acid drops
(b) (= *verdorben*) off *pred* (*Brit*), bad; *Milch* sour, off *pred* (*Brit*); *Geruch* sickly; **~ werden** to go off (*Brit*) *or* sour
(c) (*Chem*) acid(ic); **saurer Regen** acid rain
(d) (*inf:* = *schlecht gelaunt*) (*auf* +acc with) mad (*inf*), cross; **eine ~e Miene machen** to look annoyed
2 ADV **(a)** (= *verdorben*) **es roch so ~** there was a sickly smell
(b) (*Chem*) **~ reagieren** to react acidically

(c) (= *mühselig*) **das habe ich mir ~ erworben** I got that the hard way; **~ erworbenes Geld** hard-earned money; **mein ~ erspartes Geld** money I had painstakingly saved
(d) (*inf:* = *übel gelaunt*) **~ reagieren** to get annoyed; **~ antworten** to give a cross answer

Sauer-: Sauerampfer [-ampfɐ] M -s, - sorrel; **Sauerbraten** M braised beef (marinaded in vinegar), sauerbraten (*US*)

Sauerei [zaʊə'raɪ] F -, -en (*inf*) **(a)** (= *Unflätigkeit*) **~en erzählen** to tell dirty stories; **eine einzige ~** a load of filth
(b) (= *Gemeinheit*) **das ist eine ~!, so eine ~!** it's a downright disgrace **(c)** (= *Dreck, Unordnung*) mess

Sauer-: Sauerkirsche F sour cherry; **Sauerkraut** NT sauerkraut

säuerlich ['zɔʏɐlɪç] **1** ADJ (*lit, fig*) sour **2** ADV (*Cook*) **~ schmecken** to taste a little sour

Sauermilch F sour milk

Sauerrahm M thick sour(ed) cream

Sauerstoff M, NO PL (*abbr* O) oxygen

Sauerstoff- IN CPDS oxygen; **Sauerstoffflasche** F oxygen cylinder *or* (*kleiner*) bottle; **Sauerstoffgerät** NT breathing apparatus; (*Med*) (*für künstliche Beatmung*) respirator; (*für erste Hilfe*) resuscitator; **Sauerstoffmangel** M lack of oxygen; (*akut*) oxygen deficiency; **Sauerstoffmaske** F oxygen mask

Sauerteig M sour dough

saufen ['zaʊfn] *pret* **soff** [zɔf], *ptp* **gesoffen** [gə'zɔfn] VTI **(a)** (*Tiere*) to drink **(b)** (*inf: Mensch*) to booze (*inf*); **das Saufen** boozing; **wie ein Loch ~** to drink like a fish

Säufer ['zɔʏfɐ] M -s, -, **Säuferin** [-ərɪn] F -, -nen (*inf*) boozer (*inf*)

Sauferei [zaʊfə'raɪ] F -, -en (*inf*) **(a)** (= *Trinkgelage*) booze-up (*inf*) **(b)** NO PL (= *Trunksucht*) boozing (*inf*)

säuft [zɔʏft] 3. PERS SING PRES *von* **saufen**

saugen ['zaʊgn], *pret* **sog** *or* **saugte** [zo:k, 'zaʊktə], *ptp* **gesogen** *or* **gesaugt** [gə'zo:gn, gə'zaʊkt] VTI to suck; (*Pflanze, Schwamm*) to absorb; (*inf: mit Staubsauger*) to vacuum; **an etw** (*dat*) **~** to suck sth; **an Pfeife** to draw on sth; **etw aus dem Internet ~** to download sth from the Internet

säugen ['zɔʏgn] VT to suckle

Sauger ['zaʊgɐ] M -s, - **(a)** (*auf Flasche*) teat (*Brit*), nipple (*US*) **(b)** (*von Krake*) sucker

Säuger ['zɔʏgɐ] M -s, -, **Säugetier** NT mammal

Saug-: saugfähig ADJ absorbent; **Saugfähigkeit** F absorbency; **Saugglocke** F **(a)** (*Med*) ventouse (*spec*) **(b)** (*zur Abflussreinigung*) plunger

Säugling ['zɔʏklɪŋ] M -s, -e baby, infant

Säuglings- IN CPDS baby, infant (*form*); **Säuglingsalter** NT babyhood; **das Kind ist noch im ~** the child is still a baby; **Säuglingspflege** F babycare; **Säuglingsschwester** F infant nurse; **Säuglingssterblichkeit** F infant mortality

Sau-: Sauhaufen M (*inf*) bunch of slobs; **saukalt** ADJ (*inf*) damn cold (*inf*); **Saukälte** F (*inf*) damn cold weather (*inf*); **Saukerl** M (*inf*) bastard (*sl*)

Säule ['zɔʏlə] F -, -n column; (*fig* = *Stütze*) pillar

Säulen-: Säulendiagramm NT bar chart, histogram; **Säulengang** M, pl -gänge colonnade; (*um einen Hof*) peristyle; **Säulenhalle** F columned hall

Saum [zaʊm] M -(e)s, **Säume** ['zɔʏmə] (= *Stoffumschlag*) hem; (= *Naht*) seam; (*fig:* = *Waldsaum etc*) edge

saumäßig ['zaʊmɛ:sɪç] (*inf*) **1** ADJ lousy (*inf*); (*zur Verstärkung*) hell of a (*inf*) **2** ADV lousily (*inf*); (*zur Verstärkung*) damn (*inf*); **das hat er ~ gemacht** he made a real mess of it

säumen ['zɔʏmən] VT (*Sew*) to hem; (*fig geh*) to line

säumig ['zɔʏmɪç] ADJ (*geh*) *Schuldner* defaulting; *Zahlung* overdue; *Schüler* dilatory; **~ sein/bleiben/werden** to be/ remain/get behind

Sauna ['zaʊna] F -, -s *or* **Saunen** [-nən] sauna

Saupack NT (*pej inf*) scum (*pej inf*)

Säure ['zɔʏrə] F -, -n (= *Magensäure*) (*auch Chem*) acid; (= *saurer Geschmack*) sourness; (*von Wein, Bonbons*) acidity; (*von Obst*) sharpness; **dieser Wein hat zu viel ~** this wine is too acidic

Sauregurkenzeit F bad time; (*in den Medien*) silly season (*Brit*), off season (*US*)

säurehaltig ADJ acidic

Saure(s) ['zaʊrə] NT DECL AS ADJ **gib ihm ~!** (*inf*) let him have it! (*inf*)

Saurier ['zaʊriɐ] M -s, - dinosaur

Saus [zaus] M **in ~ und Braus leben** to live like a king

Sause ['zauzə] F **-, -n** (inf) (= Party) bash (inf); (= Kneipentour) pub crawl (esp Brit inf), bar hop (US inf)

säuseln ['zɔyzln] **1** VI (Wind) to murmur; (Blätter) to rustle; (Mensch) to purr; **mit ~der Stimme** in a purring voice **2** VT to murmur

sausen ['zauzn] VI **(a)** (Ohren, Kopf) to buzz; (Wind) to whistle; (Sturm) to roar **(b)** AUX SEIN (Geschoss, Peitsche) to whistle **(c)** AUX SEIN (inf: Mensch) to tear (inf); (Fahrzeug) to roar; (Schlitten, Gegenstand) to hurtle; **durch eine Prüfung ~** to fail or flunk (inf) an exam

Sauser ['zauzɐ] M **-s, -** (S Ger) fermented apple/grape juice

Sau-: Saustall M (inf) (unordentlich) pigsty (esp Brit inf); (chaotisch) mess; **Sauwetter** NT (inf) damn awful weather (inf); **sauwohl** ADJ PRED (inf) really good; **mir ist ~, ich fühle mich ~** I feel really good; **Sauwut** F (inf) absolute rage (inf); **eine ~ (im Bauch) haben** to be raging mad; **eine ~ auf jdn/etw haben** to be raging mad at sb/sth

Savanne [za'vanə] F **-, -n** savanna(h)

Saxophon [zakso'foːn, 'zaksofoːn] NT **-(e)s, -e**, **Saxofon** NT **-(e)s, -e** saxophone, sax (inf)

Saxophonist [zaksofo'nɪst] M **-en, -en**, **Saxophonistin** [-'nɪstɪn] F **-, -nen** saxophonist

SB- [ɛs'beː] IN CPDS self-service

S-Bahn ['ɛs-] F ABBR von **Schnellbahn, Stadtbahn**

S-Bahnhof ['ɛs-] M suburban line station

S-Bahn-Netz ['ɛs-] NT suburban rail network

SBB [ɛsbeː'beː] F ABBR von **Schweizerische Bundesbahn**

s. Br. ABBR von **südlicher Breite**

scannen ['skɛnən] VT to scan

Scanner ['skɛnɐ] M **-s, -** (Med, Comput) scanner

Schabe ['ʃaːbə] F **-, -n** cockroach

schaben ['ʃaːbn] VT to scrape; Fleisch to chop finely; Leder, Fell to shave

Schaber ['ʃaːbɐ] M **-s, -** scraper

Schabernack ['ʃaːbɐnak] M **-(e)s, -e** practical joke; **jdm einen ~ spielen, mit jdm einen ~ treiben** to play a prank on sb; **ich bin zu jedem ~ bereit** I'm always ready for a laugh

schäbig ['ʃɛːbɪç] **1** ADJ **(a)** (= unansehnlich) Wohnung, Teppich, Aussehen shabby **(b)** (= niederträchtig) mean; (= geizig) stingy (inf); Bezahlung poor **2** ADV **(a)** (= unansehnlich) shabbily; **~ aussehen** to look shabby **(b)** (= gemein) **jdn ~ behandeln** to treat sb shabbily **(c)** (= dürftig) bezahlen poorly

Schablone [ʃa'bloːnə] F **-, -n (a)** stencil; (= Muster) template; (Comput) template **(b)** (fig pej) (bei Arbeit, Arbeitsweise) routine; (beim Reden) cliché; **in ~n denken** to think in a stereotyped way

Schach [ʃax] NT **-s**, NO PL chess; (= Stellung im Spiel) check; **~ (dem König)!** check; **~ (und) matt** checkmate; **im ~ stehen** or **sein** to be in check; **jdm ~ bieten** (lit) to put sb in check; (fig) to thwart sb; **jdn in ~ halten** (fig) to keep sb in check; (mit Pistole etc) to cover sb

Schach-: Schachbrett NT chessboard; **schachbrettartig** **1** ADJ chequered (Brit), checkered (US) **2** ADV **~ gemustert** chequered (Brit), checkered (US)

schachern ['ʃaxɐn] VI (pej) **um etw ~** to haggle over sth

Schach-: Schachfigur F chesspiece; (fig) pawn; **schachmatt** ADJ (lit) (check)mated; (fig: = erschöpft) exhausted; **~!** (check)mate; **jdn ~ setzen** (lit) to (check)mate sb; (fig) to snooker sb (inf); **Schachpartie** F game of chess; **Schachspiel** NT (= Spiel) game of chess; (= Spielart) chess no art; (= Brett und Figuren) chess set; **Schachspieler(in)** M(F) chess player

Schacht [ʃaxt] M **-(e)s, ¨e** (a) shaft; (= Brunnenschacht) well; (= Straßenschacht) manhole; (= Kanalisationsschacht) drain; (Comput: von Laufwerk) bay, slot; (= Druckerschacht) tray

Schachtel ['ʃaxtl] F **-, -n (a)** box; (= Zigarettenschachtel) packet; **eine ~ Streichhölzer/Pralinen** a box of matches/chocolates **(b)** (inf: = Frau) **alte ~** old bag (inf)

Schachtelbeteiligung F (Fin) intercorporate stockholdings pl

schächten ['ʃɛçtn] VT to slaughter according to religious rites

Schachzug M (fig) move

schade ['ʃaːdə] ADJ PRED **(das ist aber) ~!** what a pity or shame; **es ist ~ um jdn/etw** it's a pity or shame about sb/sth; **um ihn ist es nicht ~** he's no great loss; **für etw zu ~ sein** to be too

good for sth; **sich** (dat) **für etw zu ~ sein** to consider oneself too good for sth; **sich** (dat) **für nichts zu ~ sein** to consider nothing (to be) beneath one

Schädel ['ʃɛːdl] M **-s, -** skull; **ein kahler ~** a bald head; **jdm den ~ einschlagen** to beat sb's skull in; **mir brummt der ~** (inf) my head is going round and round; (vor Kopfschmerzen) my head is throbbing; **einen dicken ~ haben** (fig inf) to be stubborn

schaden ['ʃaːdn] **1** VI +DAT to damage; einem Menschen to harm, to hurt; jds Ruf to damage; **das/Rauchen schadet Ihrer Gesundheit/Ihnen** that/smoking is bad for your health/you; **das schadet nichts** it does no harm; (= macht nichts) that doesn't matter; **das kann nicht(s) ~** that won't do any harm; **das schadet dir gar nichts** it serves you right; **was schadet es, wenn ...?** what harm can it do if ...?; **mehr ~ als nützen** to do more harm than good

2 VR **sich** (dat) **selbst ~** to harm or hurt oneself

Schaden ['ʃaːdn] M **-s, ¨** ['ʃɛːdn] **(a)** (= Beschädigung, Zerstörung) damage no pl, no indef art (durch caused by, an +dat to); (= Personenschaden) injury; (= Verlust) loss; (= Unheil, Leid) harm; **einen ~ verursachen, ~/Schäden anrichten** to cause damage; **den ~ begrenzen** to limit the damage; **ich habe einen ~ am Auto** my car has been damaged; **es soll sein ~ nicht sein** it will not be to his disadvantage; **zu ~ kommen** to suffer; (physisch) to be hurt or injured; **nicht zu ~ kommen** not to come to any harm; **jdm ~ zufügen** to harm sb; **einer Sache** (dat) **~ zufügen** to damage sth; **geringe/einige Schäden aufweisen** to have suffered little/some damage; **aus** or **durch ~ wird man klug** (Prov) you learn by or from your mistakes; **wer den ~ hat, braucht für den Spott nicht zu sorgen** (Prov) don't mock the afflicted

(b) (= Defekt) fault; (= körperlicher Mangel) defect; **Schäden aufweisen** to be defective; (Organ) to be damaged

Schaden-: Schadenfreiheitsrabatt M no-claims bonus; **Schadenfreude** F gloating; **... sagte er mit einer gewissen ~ ...** he gloated; **schadenfroh** **1** ADJ gloating **2** ADV with malicious delight; sagen gloatingly

Schadensersatz M damages pl, compensation; **jdn auf ~ verklagen** to sue sb for damages etc; **~ leisten** to pay damages etc

Schadensersatz-: Schadensersatzanspruch M claim for damages etc; **schadensersatzpflichtig** [-pflɪçtɪç] ADJ liable for damages etc

Schadens-: Schadensfall M (Insur) case of damage; **im ~** in the event of damage; **Schadensregulierung** F settlement of damages

schadhaft ADJ NO ADV faulty, defective; (= beschädigt) damaged

schädigen ['ʃɛːdɪɡn] VT to damage; Gesundheit, Umwelt auch to harm; jdn to hurt, to harm

schädlich ['ʃɛːtlɪç] ADJ harmful; Wirkung, Einflüsse damaging; **~ für etw sein** to be damaging to sth; **~es Tier** pest

Schädlichkeit F **-**, NO PL harmfulness

Schädling ['ʃɛːtlɪŋ] M **-s, -e** pest

Schädlings-: Schädlingsbekämpfung F pest control no art; **Schädlingsbekämpfungsmittel** NT pesticide

schadlos ADJ **(a) sich an jdm/etw ~ halten** to take advantage of sb/sth **(b) etw ~ überstehen** to survive sth unharmed

Schador [ʃa'doːɐ] M **-s, -s** (= Schleier) chador

Schadstoff M harmful substance

Schadstoff-: schadstoffarm ADJ **~ sein** to contain a low level of harmful substances; **ein ~es Auto** a clean-air car; **Schadstoffbelastung** F (von Umwelt) pollution; **schadstofffrei** ADJ **~ sein** to contain no harmful substances

Schaf [ʃaːf] NT **-(e)s, -e** sheep; (inf: = Dummkopf) dope (inf); **das schwarze ~ sein** to be the black sheep (in +dat, gen of)

Schafbock M ram

Schäfchen ['ʃɛːfçən] NT **-s, -** lamb, little sheep; **~** pl (= Gemeinde, Anvertraute) flock sing; **sein ~ ins Trockene bringen** (prov) to look after number one (inf)

Schäfchenwolken PL cotton wool clouds pl

Schäfer ['ʃɛːfɐ] M **-s, -** shepherd

Schäferhund M Alsatian (dog) (Brit), German shepherd (dog)

Schäferin ['ʃɛːfərɪn] F **-, -nen** shepherdess

Schaffell NT sheepskin

schaffen¹ ['ʃafn], pret **schuf** [ʃuːf], ptp **geschaffen** [ɡə'ʃafn] VT **(a)** (= hervorbringen) to create; **dafür ist er wie geschaffen** he's just made for it **(b)** *pret auch* **schaffte** [ˈʃaftə] (= *herstellen*) to make; *Bedingungen, Möglichkeiten, Arbeitsplätze* to create; (= *verursachen*) *Ärger* to cause; **Probleme** ~ to create problems; **Ruhe** ~ to establish order; **Klarheit** ~ to provide clarification

schaffen² 🔢 VT **(a)** (= *bewältigen, zustande bringen*) *Aufgabe, Hürde, Portion etc* to manage; *Prüfung* to pass; ~ **wir das zeitlich?** are we going to make it?; **wir habens geschafft** we've managed it; (= *Arbeit erledigt*) there, that's done; (= *gut angekommen*) we've made it; **so, das hätten wir** *or* **das wäre geschafft!** there, that's done; **das hast du wieder mal geschafft** you've done it again; **er schafft es noch, dass ich ihn rauswerfe/er rausgeworfen wird** he'll end up with me throwing him out/(by) being thrown out

(b) (*inf*: = *überwältigen*) *jdn* to see off (*inf*); **das hat mich geschafft** it took it out of me; (*nervlich*) it got on top of me; **geschafft sein** to be exhausted

(c) (= *bringen*) **etw in etw** (*acc*) ~ to put sth in sth; **wie sollen wir das in den Keller/auf den Berg ~?** how will we manage to get that into the cellar/up the mountain?; **etw aus der Welt ~** to settle sth (for good); **sich** (*dat*) **jdn/etw vom Hals(e)** *or* **Leib(e)** ~ to get sb/sth off one's back

🔢 VI **(a)** (= *tun*) to do; **ich habe nichts mit ihm zu ~** I don't have anything to do with him; **sich** (*dat*) **an etw** (*dat*) **zu ~ machen** to fiddle around with sth

(b) (= *zusetzen*) **jdm (sehr** *or* **schwer) zu ~ machen** to cause sb (a lot of) trouble; (= *bekümmern*) to worry sb (a lot)

(c) (*S Ger*: = *arbeiten*) to work

Schaffen NT **-s**, NO PL **die Freude am** ~ the joy of creation; **sein musikalisches/künstlerisches** ~ his musical/artistic creations *pl*; **auf dem Höhepunkt seines ~s** at the peak of his creative powers

Schaffleisch NT mutton

Schaffner [ˈʃafnɐ] M **-s, -**, **Schaffnerin** [-ərɪn] F **-, -nen** (*im Bus*) conductor/conductress; (*Rail*) ticket collector; (*im Zug*) guard (*Brit*), conductor (*US*); (*im Schlafwagen*) attendant; (= *Fahrkartenkontrolleur*) ticket inspector

Schaffung [ˈʃafʊŋ] F **-, -en** creation

Schäflein [ˈʃeːflaɪn] NT **-s, -** = **Schäfchen**

Schafs-: **Schafskäse** M sheep's milk cheese; **Schafsmilch** F sheep's milk

Schafstall M sheepfold

Schaft [ʃaft] M **-(e)s, ⁼e** [ˈʃɛftə] **(a)** shaft (*auch Archit*); (*von Gewehr*) stock; (*von Stiefel*) leg; (*von Schraube, Schlüssel*) shank; (*Bot*) stalk **(b)** (*Sw, S Ger*) (= *Regal*) shelves *pl*; (= *Schrank*) cupboard

Schaftstiefel PL high boots *pl*; (*Mil*) jackboots *pl*

Schaf-: **Schafwolle** F sheep's wool; **Schafzucht** F sheep breeding *no art*

Schah [ʃaː] M **-s, -s** Shah

Schakal [ʃaˈkaːl] M **-s, -e** jackal

schäkern [ˈʃɛːkɐn] VI to flirt; (= *necken*) to play around

schal [ʃaːl] ADJ *Getränk* flat; *Wasser, Geschmack* stale; (*fig*: = *geistlos*) *Witz* weak; *Leben* empty; *Gerede* vapid

Schal [ʃaːl] M **-s, -s** *or* **-e** scarf; (= *Umschlagtuch*) shawl

Schale¹ [ˈʃaːlə] F **-, -n** bowl; (*flach, zum Servieren etc*) dish; (*von Waage*) pan; (= *Sektschale*) champagne glass

Schale² F **-, -n** (*von Obst, Gemüse*) skin; (*abgeschält*) peel *no pl*; (= *Rinde*) (*von Käse*) rind; (*von Nuss, Ei, Muschel, Krebs*) shell; (*von Getreide*) husk, hull; (*fig*: = *äußeres Auftreten*) appearance; **sich in** ~ **werfen** *or* **schmeißen** (*inf*) to get dressed up

schälen [ˈʃɛːlən] 🔢 VT to peel; *Tomate, Mandel* to skin; *Erbsen, Eier, Nüsse* to shell; *Getreide* to husk 🔢 VR to peel

Schall [ʃal] M **-s, -e** *or* **⁼e** [ˈʃɛlə] sound; **Name ist** ~ **und Rauch** (*Prov*) what's in a name?; **das ist alles** ~ **und Rauch** it's all hollow words

Schall-: **Schalldämmung** F sound absorption; (= *Abdichtung gegen Schall*) soundproofing; **schalldämpfend** ADJ *Wirkung* sound-muffling; *Material* soundproofing; **Schalldämpfer** M (*von Auto*) silencer (*Brit*), muffler (*US*); (*von Gewehr etc*) silencer; (*Mus*) mute

schallen [ˈʃalən] VI to sound; (*Stimme, Glocke, Beifall*) to ring (out); (= *widerhallen*) to resound

schallend 🔢 ADJ *Beifall, Ohrfeige* resounding; *Gelächter* ringing 🔢 ADV ~ **lachen** to roar with laughter; **jdn** ~ **ohrfeigen** to give sb a resounding slap

Schall-: **Schallgeschwindigkeit** F speed of sound; **Schallgrenze** F sound barrier; **Schallmauer** F sound barrier; **Schallplatte** F record; **Schallschutzfenster** NT soundproof window; **Schalltrichter** M horn; (*von Trompeten etc*) bell

Schalotte [ʃaˈlɔtə] F **-, -n** shallot

schalt PRET *von* **schelten**

Schalt-: **Schaltbild** NT circuit *or* wiring diagram; **Schaltbrett** NT switchboard, control panel

schalten [ˈʃaltn] 🔢 VT **(a)** *Gerät* to switch, to turn; (= *in Gang bringen*) to switch *or* turn on; *Leitung* to connect; **etw auf „2"** ~ to turn *or* switch sth to "2"; **etw auf die höchste Stufe** ~ to turn sth on full; **in Reihe/parallel** ~ (*Elec*) to connect in series/in parallel; **das Auto schaltet sich leicht** it's easy to change (*esp Brit*) *or* shift (*US*) gear in this car

(b) *Werbung, Anzeige* to place; *Hotline* to set up

🔢 VI **(a)** (*Gerät, Ampel*) to switch (*auf +acc* to); (*Aut*) to change (*esp Brit*) *or* shift (*US*) gear; **in den 2. Gang** ~ to change (*esp Brit*) *or* shift (*US*) into 2nd gear; **auf stur** ~ (*fig*) to dig one's heels in

(b) (*fig*: = *verfahren, handeln*) ~ **und walten** to bustle around; **frei** ~ **(und walten) können** to have a free hand (to do as one pleases); **jdn frei** ~ **und walten lassen** to give sb a free hand

(c) (*inf*) (= *begreifen*) to get it (*inf*); (= *reagieren*) to react

Schalter [ˈʃaltɐ] M **-s, - (a)** (*Elec etc*) switch **(b)** (*in Post, Bank, Amt*) counter; (*im Bahnhof*) ticket window

Schalter-: **Schalterdienst** M counter duty; **Schalterhalle** F (*in Post*) hall; (*in Bank*) (banking) hall; (*im Bahnhof*) ticket hall; **Schalterleiste** F (*Comput*) toolbar; **Schalterstunden** PL hours *pl* of business

Schalt-: **Schaltfläche** F (*Comput*) button; **Schaltgetriebe** NT manual transmission, stick shift (*US*); **Schalthebel** M switch lever; (*Aut*) gear lever (*Brit*), gear shift (*US*); **an den ~n der Macht sitzen** to hold the reins of power; **Schaltjahr** NT leap year; **alle ~e** (*inf*) once in a blue moon; **Schaltknüppel** M (*Aut*) gear lever (*Brit*), gear shift (*US*); (*Aviat*) joystick; **Schaltkreis** M (*Tech*) (switching) circuit; **Schaltplan** M circuit *or* wiring diagram; **Schalttag** M leap day

Schaltung [ˈʃaltʊŋ] F **-, -en** switching; (*Elec*) wiring; (*Aut*) gear change (*Brit*), gearshift (*US*)

Scham [ʃaːm] F **-,** NO PL shame; **ich hätte vor** ~ **(in den Boden) versinken können** I wanted the floor to swallow me up; **aus falscher** ~ from a false sense of shame; **ohne** ~ unashamedly

schämen [ˈʃɛːmən] VR to be ashamed; **du solltest dich** ~!, **du sollst dich was** ~ (*inf*) you ought to be ashamed of yourself!; **sich einer Sache** (*gen*) *or* **für etw** ~ to be ashamed of sth; **sich jds/einer Sache** *or* **wegen jdm/etw** (*inf*) ~ to be ashamed of sb/sth; **sich für jdn** ~ to be ashamed for sb; **schäme dich!** shame on you!

Scham-: **Schamfrist** F decent interval; **Schamgegend** F pubic region; **Schamhaar** NT pubic hair; **Schamlippen** PL labia *pl*; **schamlos** 🔢 ADJ shameless; *Frechheit, Lüge* brazen 🔢 ADV shamelessly; **sich** ~ **zeigen** to flaunt oneself shamelessly; **sich** ~ **kleiden** to dress indecently; **Schamlosigkeit** F **-, -en** shamelessness; **Schamröte** F flush of shame; **die** ~ **stieg ihr ins Gesicht** her face flushed with shame; **Schamteile** PL genitals *pl*

Schande [ˈʃandə] F **-,** NO PL disgrace; **er ist eine** ~ **für seine Familie** he is a disgrace to his family; **das ist eine (wahre)** ~! this is a(n absolute) disgrace!; ~! (*euph inf*) sugar! (*euph inf*); **jdm/einer Sache** ~ **machen** to be a disgrace to sb/sth; **zu meiner (großen)** ~ **muss ich gestehen, ...** to my great shame I have to admit that ...

schänden [ˈʃɛndn] VT to violate; *Sabbat, Sonntag etc* to desecrate; *Ansehen, Namen* to dishonour (*Brit*), to dishonor (*US*)

Schandfleck M blot (*in +dat* on); **er war der** ~ **der Familie** he was the disgrace of his family

schändlich [ˈʃɛntlɪç] 🔢 ADJ shameful 🔢 ADV shamefully; *behandeln* disgracefully; **er hat sie** ~ **verlassen** it was a disgrace the way he left her

Schandtat F scandalous deed; (*hum*) escapade; **zu jeder** ~ **bereit sein** (*inf*) to be always ready for mischief

Schändung [ˈʃɛndʊŋ] F **-, -en** violation; (*von Sabbat*) desecration; (*von Namen, Ansehen*) dishonouring (*Brit*), dishonoring (*US*)

Schankbetrieb M bar service; **nach 24 Uhr kein ~ mehr** the bar closes at 12 midnight

Schänke ['ʃɛŋkə] F **-, -n** inn

Schank-: **Schankkonzession** F licence (*of publican*) (*Brit*), excise license (*US*); **Schankstube** F (public) bar (*esp Brit*), saloon (*US dated*); **Schanktisch** M bar

Schanze ['ʃantsə] F **-, -n** (*Mil*) entrenchment; (*Sport*) (ski) jump; (*für Skateboarder*) ramp

Schar¹ [ʃaːɐ] F **-, -en** crowd; (*von Vögeln*) flock; (*von Insekten, Heuschrecken etc*) swarm; (= *Reiterschar, Soldatenschar etc*) band; (*von Pfadfindern*) company; (*von Engeln*) host; **die Fans verließen das Stadion in (hellen) ~en** the fans left the stadium in droves; **der Partei laufen die Mitglieder in ~en davon** members are leaving the party in droves; **die Menschen kamen in (hellen) ~en nach Lourdes** people flocked to Lourdes

Schar² F **-, -en** (= *Pflugschar*) (plough)share (*Brit*), (plow)share (*US*)

Scharade [ʃaˈraːdə] F **-, -n** charade

Schäre ['ʃɛːrə] F **-, -n** skerry

scharen ['ʃaːrən] 🔢 VT **Menschen/Anhänger um sich ~** to gather people/to rally supporters around one 🔢 VR **sich um jdn/etw ~** to gather around sb/sth

scharf [ʃarf] 🔢 ADJ, *comp* ⁼**er** ['ʃɛrfə], *superl* ⁼**ste(r, s)** ['ʃɛrfstə]
(a) (*lit, fig*) sharp; *Wind, Kälte* biting; *Luft, Frost, Beobachter* keen; *Brille, Linse* sharply focusing; **ein Messer ~ machen** to sharpen a knife; **mit ~em Blick** (*fig*) with penetrating insight
(b) (= *stark gewürzt*) hot; *Geruch, Geschmack* pungent; *Käse* strong; (= *ätzend*) *Waschmittel, Lösung* caustic; **~e Sachen** (*inf*) hard stuff (*inf*)
(c) (= *hart, streng*) *Mittel, Maßnahmen* severe; (*inf*) *Prüfung, Untersuchung, Lehrer, Polizist* tough; *Bewachung* close; *Hund* fierce; *Worte, Kritik* harsh; *Widerstand, Konkurrenz, Protest* strong; *Auseinandersetzung* bitter; **etw in schärfster Form verurteilen** to condemn sth in the strongest possible terms
(d) (= *heftig, schnell*) *Ritt, Trab* hard; **ein ~es Tempo fahren** (*inf*) to drive hell for leather (*inf*)
(e) (= *echt*) *Munition etc, Schuss* live; **etw ~ machen** to arm sth; **~e Schüsse abgeben** to fire live bullets
(f) (*inf*: = *geil*) randy (*Brit inf*), horny (*inf*); **jdn ~ machen** to turn sb on (*inf*); **auf jdn/etw ~ sein** to fancy sb/sth (*inf*); **der Kleine/Alte ist ~ wie Nachbars Lumpi** *or* **tausend Russen** *or* **sieben Sensen** (*dated*) he's a randy (*Brit*) *or* horny little/old man (*inf*); *siehe auch* **scharfmachen**
🔢 ADV, *comp* ⁼**er**, *superl* **am** ⁼**sten** (a) (= *intensiv*) **~ nach etw riechen** to smell strongly of sth; **~ würzen** to season highly; *Fleisch* **~ anbraten** to sear meat; **sie kocht sehr ~** her cooking is very spicy; **sie hat das Curry ~ zubereitet** she made the curry hot (*inf*)
(b) (= *heftig*) *attackieren, kritisieren* sharply; *ablehnen* adamantly; *protestieren* emphatically
(c) (= *präzise*) *analysieren* carefully; *hören, sehen* clearly; *bewachen, zuhören* closely; **~ beobachten** to be very observant; **etw ~ betrachten** to look at sth intensely; **~ aufpassen** to pay close attention; **jdn ~ ansehen** to give sb a scrutinizing look; (*missbilligend*) to look sharply at sb; **~ nachdenken** to have a good think
(d) (= *genau*) **etw ~ einstellen** *Bild, Diaprojektor etc* to bring sth into focus; *Sender* to tune sth in (properly); **~ eingestellt** in (sharp) focus; (properly) tuned in; **~ sehen/hören** to have sharp eyes/ears
(e) (= *abrupt*) *bremsen* hard
(f) (= *hart*) **~ vorgehen/durchgreifen** to take decisive action; **etw ~ bekämpfen** to take strong measures against sth
(g) (*Mil*) **~ schießen** (*lit*) (= *mit ~er Munition*) to shoot with live ammunition; (= *auf den Mann*) to aim to hit; (*fig*) to let fly

Scharfblick M (*fig*) keen insight

Schärfe ['ʃɛrfə] F **-, -n** (a) (*lit, fig*) sharpness; (*von Brille, Linse*) strength; (*von Wind, Frost, Gehör, Verstand*) keenness (b) (*von Essen*) spiciness; (*von Geruch, Geschmack*) pungency; (*von Lösung*) causticity (c) (= *Härte, Strenge*) severity; (*von Worten, Kritik*) harshness; (*von Widerstand, Konkurrenz*) toughness; (*von Protest*) strength; (*von Auseinandersetzung*) bitterness; **etw/jdn in** *or* **mit aller ~ kritisieren** to be sharply critical of sth/sb

schärfen ['ʃɛrfn] VT (*lit, fig*) to sharpen

Scharf-: **scharfmachen** VT SEP (*inf*) (= *aufstacheln*) to stir up; (= *aufreizen*) to turn on (*inf*); **Scharfmacher(in)** M(F) (*inf*) rabble-rouser; **Scharfrichter** M executioner; **Scharfschütze** M marksman; **Scharfschützin** F markswoman; **Scharfsinn** M astuteness; **scharfsinnig** 🔢 ADJ astute 🔢 ADV astutely

Scharia [ʃaˈriːa] F **-**, NO PL sharia

Scharlach ['ʃarlax] M **-s**, NO PL (a) (*Farbe*) scarlet (b) (= *~fieber*) scarlet fever

scharlachrot ADJ scarlet (red)

Scharlatan ['ʃarlatan] M **-s, -e** charlatan

Scharnier [ʃarˈniːɐ] NT **-s, -e**, **Scharniergelenk** NT hinge

Schärpe ['ʃɛrpə] F **-, -n** sash

scharren ['ʃarən] VTI to scrape; (*Pferd, Hund*) to paw; (*Huhn*) to scratch; (= *verscharren*) to bury (hurriedly); **mit den Füßen ~** to shuffle one's feet

Scharte ['ʃartə] F **-, -n** nick; (= *Schießscharte*) embrasure

Schaschlik ['ʃaʃlɪk] NT **-s, -s** (shish) kebab

schassen ['ʃasn] VT (*inf*) to chuck out (*inf*)

Schatten ['ʃatn] M **-s, -** (*lit, fig*) shadow; (= *schattige Stelle*) shade; (= *Geist*) shade; **40 Grad im ~** 40 degrees in the shade; **~ geben** *or* **spenden** to give *or* provide shade; **~ spendend** *Baum, Dach* shady; **große Ereignisse werfen ihre ~ voraus** great events are often foreshadowed; **in jds ~ stehen** (*fig*) to be in sb's shadow; **jdn/etw in den ~ stellen** (*fig*) to put sb/sth in the shade; **man kann nicht über seinen eigenen ~ springen** (*fig*) the leopard cannot change his spots (*prov*); **nur noch ein ~ (seiner selbst) sein** to be (only) a shadow of one's former self; **~ unter den Augen** shadows under the eyes

Schatten-: **Schattenboxen** NT shadow-boxing; **Schattendasein** NT shadowy existence; **schattenhaft** 🔢 ADJ shadowy 🔢 ADV *sehen, erkennen* vaguely; *sichtbar* barely; **Schattenkabinett** NT (*Pol*) shadow cabinet; **Schattenmorelle** [-mɔrɛlə] F **-, -n** morello cherry; **schattenreich** ADJ shady; **Schattenriss** M silhouette; **Schattenseite** F shady side; (*von Planeten*) dark side; (*fig*: = *Nachteil*) drawback; **die ~(n) des Lebens** the dark side of life; (*in Milieu, Slums etc*) the seamy side of life; **schattenspendend** ADJ ATTR *siehe* **Schatten**; **Schattenwirtschaft** F black economy

schattieren [ʃaˈtiːrən], *ptp* **schattiert** VT to shade

Schattierung F **-, -en** (*lit, fig*) shade; (= *das Schattieren*) shading; **aller politischen ~en** of every political shade; **in allen ~en** (*fig*) of every shade

schattig ['ʃatɪç] ADJ shady

Schatulle [ʃaˈtʊlə] F **-, -n** casket; (= *Geldschatulle*) coffer; (*pej inf*) bag (*pej inf*)

Schatz [ʃats] M **-es,** ⁼**e** ['ʃɛtsə] (a) (*lit, fig*) treasure; **Schätze** *pl* (= *Bodenschätze*) natural resources *pl*; (= *Reichtum*) riches *pl*; **du bist ein ~!** (*inf*) you're a (real) treasure *or* gem! (b) (= *Liebling*) sweetheart

Schatz-: **Schatzamt** NT Treasury; **Schatzanweisung** F treasury bond

schätzbar ADJ assessable; **gut/schlecht/schwer ~** easy/hard/difficult to estimate

Schätzchen ['ʃɛtsçən] NT **-s, -** darling

schätzen ['ʃɛtsn] 🔢 VT (a) (= *veranschlagen*) to estimate; *Wertgegenstand, Gemälde etc* to value, to appraise; (= *annehmen*) to reckon; **wie alt ~ Sie mich denn?** how old do you reckon I am then?; **was schätzt du, wie lange/wie viele/wie alt ...?** how long/how many/how old do you reckon ...?; **ich hätte sie älter geschätzt** I'd have thought her older (*esp Brit*)
(b) (= *würdigen*) to value; **jdn ~** to think highly of sb; **etw besonders ~** to hold sth in very high esteem; **etw zu ~ wissen** to appreciate sth; **das schätzt er (überhaupt) nicht** he doesn't appreciate that (at all); **sich glücklich ~** to consider oneself lucky
🔢 VI (= *veranschlagen, raten*) to guess; **schätz mal** have a guess

Schätzpreis M valuation price

Schätzung ['ʃɛtsʊŋ] F **-, -en** estimate; (= *das Schätzen*) estimation; (*von Wertgegenstand*) valuation

schätzungsweise ADV (= *so vermutet man*) it is estimated; (= *ungefähr*) approximately; (= *so schätze ich*) I reckon; **es werden ~ 3.000 Zuschauer kommen** an estimated 3,000 spectators will come; **wann wirst du ~ kommen?** when do you reckon you'll come?

Schätzwert M estimated value

Schau [ʃau] F **-, -en (a)** (= *Vorführung*) show; (= *Ausstellung*) display, exhibition; **etw zur ~ stellen** (= *ausstellen*) to put sth on show; (*fig*) to make a show of sth; (= *protzen mit*) to show off sth; **zur ~ gestellter Wohlstand** display of wealth; **etw zur ~ tragen** to display sth **(b)** (*inf*) **eine ~ abziehen** to put on a display; (= *Theater machen*) to make a big show (*inf*); **das war eine ~!** that was fantastic (*inf*); **das ist nur ~** it's only show; **er macht nur (eine) ~** he's (only) putting it on; **jdm die ~ stehlen** *or* **klauen** to steal the show from sb

Schaubild NT diagram; (= *Kurve*) graph

Schauder [ˈʃaudɐ] M **-s, -** shudder

schauderhaft 1 ADJ (*lit*) horrible, terrible; (*fig inf*) terrible, awful 2 ADV *verstümmeln* gruesomely; (*fig inf*) awfully; **er spricht ~ schlecht Italienisch** his Italian is terrible

schaudern [ˈʃaudɐn] VI to shudder; (*vor Ehrfurcht*) to tremble; **ihr schaudert vor ihm** he makes her shudder; **mit Schaudern** with a shudder

schauen [ˈʃauən] VI (*esp dial*) to look; **verärgert/traurig** *etc* **~** to look angry/sad *etc*; **auf etw** (*acc*) **~** to look at sth; **um sich ~** to look around (one); **jdm (fest) in die Augen ~** to look sb (straight) in the eye; **nach jdm/etw ~** (= *suchen*) to look for sb/sth; (= *sich kümmern um*) to look after sb/sth; **da schaust du aber!** there, see!; **schau, schau!** (*inf*), **da schau her!** (*S Ger inf*) well, well!; **schau, dass du ...** see *or* mind (that) you ...

Schauer [ˈʃauɐ] M **-s, - (a)** (= *Regenschauer*) shower **(b)** = **Schauder**

Schauergeschichte F horror story

schauerlich [ˈʃauɐlɪç] 1 ADJ (*lit*) horrible; *Schrei* bloodcurdling; (= *gruselig*) eerie **(b)** (*inf*: = *fürchterlich*) terrible, awful 2 ADV horribly; **sie spricht ~ schlecht Englisch** her English is terrible

schauern [ˈʃauɐn] 1 VI (= *schaudern*) to shudder 2 VT IMPERS **mich schauert** I shudder; **mich schauert bei dem bloßen Gedanken** the very thought (of it) makes me shudder

Schaufel [ˈʃaufl] F **-, -n** shovel; (*kleiner: für Mehl, Zucker*) scoop; (*von Bagger*) scoop; (*von ~rad*) paddle; (*von Wasserrad, Turbine*) vane; **zwei ~n (voll) Sand/Kies** two shovel(ful)s of sand/gravel

schaufeln [ˈʃaufln] VTI to shovel; *Grab, Grube* to dig

Schaufenster NT display window; (*von Geschäft auch*) shop window; (*fig*) shop window

Schaufenster-: Schaufensterauslage F window display; **Schaufensterbummel** M window-shopping expedition; **einen ~ machen** to go window-shopping; **Schaufensterdekorateur(in)** M(F) window-dresser; **Schaufensterpuppe** F display dummy

Schau-: Schaugeschäft NT show business; **Schaukampf** M exhibition fight; **Schaukasten** M showcase

Schaukel [ˈʃaukl] F **-, -n** swing

schaukeln [ˈʃaukln] 1 VI **(a)** (*mit Schaukel*) to swing; (*im Schaukelstuhl*) to rock; **auf** *or* **mit dem Stuhl ~** to rock back and forth in one's chair **(b)** (= *sich hin und her bewegen*) to sway (back and forth); (= *sich auf und ab bewegen*) to rock up and down; (*Fahrzeug*) to bounce (up and down); (*Schiff*) to pitch and toss 2 VT to rock; **wir werden das Kind** *or* **die Sache** *or* **das schon ~** (*inf*) we'll manage it

Schaukel-: Schaukelpferd NT rocking horse; **Schaukelstuhl** M rocking chair

Schau-: schaulustig ADJ curious; **Schaulustige** [-lʊstɪɡə] PL DECL AS ADJ (curious) onlookers *pl*

Schaum [ʃaum] M **-s, Schäume** [ˈʃɔymə] foam, froth; (= *Seifenschaum, Shampooschaum*) lather; (*von Waschmittel*) lather; (*zum Feuerlöschen*) foam; (*Cook*) (*auf Speisen, Getränken*) froth; (*auf Marmelade, Flüssen, Sümpfen*) scum; (*von Bier*) head, froth; **~ vor dem Mund haben** (*lit, fig*) to foam at the mouth

Schaumbad NT bubble *or* foam bath

schäumen [ˈʃɔymən] VI to foam, to froth; (*Seife, Shampoo, Waschmittel*) to lather (up); (*Limonade, Wein*) to bubble; (*inf*: = *wütend sein*) to foam at the mouth; **das Waschmittel schäumt stark/schwach** it's a high-lather/low-lather detergent; **vor Wut ~** to be foaming at the mouth

Schaum-: Schaumfestiger M mousse; **Schaumgummi** NT or M foam rubber

schaumig [ˈʃaumɪç] ADJ foamy, frothy; *Seife, Shampoo, Waschmittel* lathery; *Speise, Getränk, Bier* frothy; *Marmelade, Fluss, Sumpf* scummy; **ein Ei ~ schlagen** to beat an egg until frothy

Schaum-: Schaumkrone F whitecap; **Schaumlöscher** [-lœʃɐ] M **-s, -, Schaumlöschgerät** NT foam extinguisher; **Schaumschläger(in)** M(F) (*fig inf*) man/woman full of hot air (*inf*); **Schaumstoff** M foam material; **Schaumtönung** F colour (*Brit*) *or* color (*US*) mousse; **Schaumwein** M sparkling wine

Schau-: Schauplatz M scene; **vom ~ berichten** to give an on-the-spot report; **am ~ sein** to be at the scene; **auf dem ~ erscheinen** to appear on the scene; **Schauprozess** M show trial

schaurig [ˈʃaurɪç] 1 ADJ gruesome; *Schrei* bloodcurdling; (*inf*: = *sehr schlecht*) dreadful 2 ADV (*inf*) dreadfully; **er spricht ~ schlecht Japanisch** his Japanese is dreadful

Schauspiel NT (*Theat*) drama, play; (*fig*) spectacle; **Leipziger ~** (= *Theater*) Leipzig Playhouse

Schauspieler M actor; (*fig*) (play-)actor

Schauspielerin F (*lit*) actress; (*fig*) (play-)actress

schauspielerisch 1 ADJ acting *attr*; *Talent* for acting; **eine überzeugende ~e Leistung** a convincing piece of acting 2 ADV as regards acting

schauspielern [ˈʃauʃpiːlɐn] VI INSEP to act; (*fig*) to (play-)act

Schauspiel-: Schauspielhaus NT playhouse; **Schauspielschule** F drama school

Schau-: Schausteller [ˈʃauʃtɛlɐ] M **-s, -, Schaustellerin** [-ərɪn] F **-, -nen** showman; **Schautafel** F (*zur Information*) (notice) board (*Brit*), bulletin board (*US*); (= *Schaubild*) diagram

Scheck [ʃɛk] M **-s, -s** *or* (*rare*) **-e** cheque (*Brit*), check (*US*); **mit (einem)** *or* **per ~ bezahlen** to pay by cheque *etc*; **ein ~ auf** *or* **über 200 Euro** a cheque *etc* for 200 euros

Scheck-: Scheckbetrug M cheque (*Brit*) *or* check (*US*) fraud; **Scheckheft** NT chequebook (*Brit*), checkbook (*US*)

scheckig [ˈʃɛkɪç] ADJ spotted; *Pferd* dappled; (*inf*) (= *kunterbunt*) gaudy; (= *verfärbt*) patchy

Scheckkarte F cheque card (*Brit*), check card (*US*)

scheel [ʃeːl] 1 ADJ (= *missgünstig*) envious; (= *abschätzig*) disparaging; **ein ~er Blick** a dirty look 2 ADV **jdn ~ ansehen** to give sb a dirty look; (= *abschätzig*) to look askance at sb

Scheffel [ˈʃɛfl] M **-s, -** (= *Gefäß, Hohlmaß*) ≈ bushel (*containing anything from 30 to 300 litres*); **sein Licht unter den ~ stellen** (*inf*) to hide one's light under a bushel

scheffeln [ˈʃɛfln] VT *Geld* to rake in (*inf*); *Gold, Orden* to accumulate

Scheibe [ˈʃaibə] F **-, -n (a)** disc (*esp Brit*), disk; (= *Schießscheibe*) target; (*Eishockey*) puck; (= *Wählscheibe*) dial; (= *Kupplungsscheibe, Bremsscheibe*) disc (*esp Brit*), disk; (= *Töpferscheibe*) wheel; (*inf*: = *Schallplatte*) disc (*esp Brit inf*), disk **(b)** (= *abgeschnittene ~*) slice; (= *Längsscheibe: von Orange etc*) segment; **etw in ~n schneiden** to slice sth (up); **von ihm könntest du dir eine ~ abschneiden** (*fig inf*) you could take a leaf out of his book (*inf*) **(c)** (= *Glasscheibe*) (window)pane; (= *Fenster, auch von Auto*) window; (*inf*: = *Windschutzscheibe*) windscreen (*Brit*), windshield (*US*); (= *Spiegelscheibe*) glass

Scheiben-: Scheibenbremse F disc (*esp Brit*) *or* disk brake; **Scheibenwaschanlage** F windscreen (*Brit*) *or* windshield (*US*) washers *pl*; **Scheibenwischer** M windscreen (*Brit*) *or* windshield (*US*) wiper

Scheich [ʃaiç] M **-s, -e** sheik(h)

Scheichtum [ˈʃaiçtuːm] NT **-s, Scheichtümer** [-tyːmɐ] sheik(h)dom

Scheide [ˈʃaidə] F **-, -n** sheath; (*von Schwert*) sheath; (= *Vagina*) vagina

scheiden [ˈʃaidn], *pret* **schied** [ʃiːt], *ptp* **geschieden** [ɡəˈʃiːdn] 1 VT **(a)** (= *auflösen*) *Ehe* to dissolve; *Eheleute* to divorce; **sich ~ lassen** to get divorced; **er will sich von ihr ~ lassen** he wants to get a divorce (from her); *siehe auch* **geschieden (b)** (*geh*: = *trennen*) to separate; (*Chem*) to separate (out) 2 VR (*Wege*) to divide; (*Meinungen*) to diverge

Scheideweg M (*fig*) crossroads *sing*; **am ~ stehen** to be at a crossroads

Scheidung [ˈʃaidʊŋ] F **-, -en (a)** (= *das Scheiden*) separation **(b)** (= *Ehescheidung*) divorce; **die ~ dieser Ehe** the dissolution of this marriage; **in ~ leben** *or* **liegen** to be in the middle of divorce proceedings; **die ~ einreichen** to file a petition for divorce

Scheidungsgrund M grounds pl for divorce; (hum: Mensch) reason for his/her etc divorce

Schein[1] [ʃaɪn] M **-s**, NO PL **(a)** (= Licht) light; (matt) glow; (von Gold, Schwert etc) glint; **einen (hellen) ~ auf etw** (acc) **werfen** to shine (brightly) on sth
(b) (= Anschein) appearances pl; (= Vortäuschung) pretence; **~ und Sein/Wirklichkeit** appearance and reality; **das ist mehr ~ als Sein** it's all (on the) surface; **der ~ trügt** or **täuscht** appearances are deceptive; **den ~ wahren** to keep up appearances; **etw nur zum ~ tun** only to pretend to do sth

Schein[2] M **-s, -e** (= Geldschein) note, bill (US); (= Bescheinigung) certificate; (Univ) credit; (= Fahrschein) ticket; **~e machen** (Univ) to get credits

Schein-: Scheinasylant(in) M(F) bogus asylum-seeker; **scheinbar** ① ADJ apparent, seeming attr; (= vorgegeben) feigned ② ADV apparently, seemingly; **er hörte ~ interessiert zu** he listened with apparent or seeming/feigned interest; **Scheinehe** F sham marriage

scheinen [ʃaɪnən], pret **schien** [ʃiːn], ptp **geschienen** [ɡəˈʃiːnən] VI **(a)** (= leuchten) to shine **(b)** AUCH VI IMPERS (= den Anschein geben) to seem, to appear; **mir scheint, (dass) ...** it seems to me that ...; **er kommt scheints nicht mehr** (dial inf) it would seem that he won't come now; **du hast scheints vergessen, dass ...** (dial inf) you seem to have forgotten that ...

Schein-: Scheinfecht NT sham fight; **Scheingeschäft** NT fictitious or artificial transaction; **scheinheilig** ① ADJ hypocritical; (= Arglosigkeit vortäuschend) innocent ② ADV fragen, sagen, grinsen innocently; **~ tun** to be hypocritical; (= Arglosigkeit vortäuschen) to act innocent; **Scheinheilige(r)** MF DECL AS ADJ hypocrite; (Arglosigkeit vortäuschend) sham; **Scheinhinrichtung** F mock execution; **Scheinselbstständige(r)** MF DECL AS ADJ person who has adopted freelance status so that his employer avoids paying social security contributions; **Scheinselbstständigkeit** F freelance status (to avoid employer paying social security contributions)

Scheinwerfer M (zum Beleuchten) floodlight; (im Theater) spotlight; (= Suchscheinwerfer) searchlight; (Aut) (head)light

Scheiß [ʃaɪs] M **-**, NO PL (sl) shit (sl), crap (sl); **ein ~** a load of shit (sl) or crap (sl); **einen ~** (= nichts) fuck-all (vulg); **~ machen** (= herumalbern) to mess around (inf); (= Fehler machen) to screw up (sl); **mach keinen ~!** don't do anything so damn silly (inf); **red doch keinen ~!** don't talk crap! (esp Brit inf); **was soll der ~?** what the hell's the matter with you/him etc? (inf)

Scheiß- IN CPDS (inf) **(a)** (= verdammt) damn(ed) (inf)
(b) (= miserabel) crap (inf), shitty (sl); **so ein ~wetter!** what crap weather! (inf)

Scheißdreck M (vulg: = Kot) shit (sl), crap (sl); (sl) (= blödes Gerede, schlechtes Buch, schlechte Ware etc) load of shit (sl); (= unangenehme Sache, Arbeit) effing (sl) or bloody (Brit inf) thing; **~!** shit! (sl); **wegen jedem ~** about every effing (sl) or bloody (Brit inf) little thing; **das geht dich einen ~ an** it's none of your effing (sl) or bloody (Brit inf) business; **einen ~ werd ich tun!** like hell I will! (inf); **sich einen ~ um jdn/etw kümmern** not to give a shit about sb/sth (sl)

Scheiße [ʃaɪsə] F **-**, NO PL (vulg: = Kot) shit (sl), crap (sl); (inf: = unangenehme Lage) shit (sl); (inf: = Unsinn) shit (sl), crap (inf); **(echt) ~ sein** (inf) to be bloody awful (Brit) or goddamn awful (inf); (sl: = ärgerlich) to be a bloody (Brit) or damn nuisance (inf); **das ist doch alles ~** (inf) it's all shit (sl); (= Unsinn) it's all a load of shit (sl); **in der ~ sitzen** (inf) to be up shit creek (sl); **~ bauen** (inf) to screw up (sl); siehe auch **Scheiß**

scheißegal [ʃaɪsəˈɡaːl] ADJ (inf) **das ist mir doch ~!** I don't give a shit (sl) or a damn (inf)

scheißen [ʃaɪsn], pret **schiss** [ʃɪs], ptp **geschissen** [ɡəˈʃɪsn] VI (vulg) to shit (sl), to crap (sl); **auf jdn/etw** (acc) **~** (fig sl) not to give a shit about sb/sth (sl)

Scheißerei [ʃaɪsəˈraɪ] F **-, -en** (inf) **die ~** the runs (inf)

Scheiß-: scheißfreundlich [ˈʃaɪsˈfrɔyntlɪç] ADJ (inf) as nice as pie (iro inf); **Scheißhaus** NT (sl) shithouse (sl); **Scheißkerl** M (inf) bastard (sl); **Scheißwut** F (sl) **eine ~ (auf jdn/etw) haben** to be mad as hell (with sb/sth) (inf)

Scheit [ʃaɪt] M **-(e)s, -e** or (Aus, Sw) **-er** piece of wood

Scheitel [ʃaɪtl] M **-s, -** **(a)** (= Haarscheitel) parting (Brit), part (US); **vom ~ bis zur Sohle** (fig) through and through **(b)** (= höchster Punkt) vertex

scheiteln [ʃaɪtln] VT to part

Scheiterhaufen [ʃaɪtɐ-] M (funeral) pyre; (Hist: zur Hinrichtung) stake

scheitern [ʃaɪtɐn] VI AUX SEIN (an +dat because of) to fail; (Verhandlungen, Ehe) to break down; (Regierung) to founder (an +dat on); (Mannschaft) to be defeated (an +dat by); **die Partei scheiterte an der Fünf-Prozent-Hürde** the party fell at the five-percent hurdle

Scheitern [ʃaɪtɐn] NT **-s**, NO PL failure; (von Verhandlungen, Ehe) breakdown; (von Regierung) foundering; (von Mannschaft) defeat; **das war zum ~ verurteilt** or **verdammt** that was doomed to failure

Schelle [ʃɛlə] F **-, -n** **(a)** bell; (dial: = Klingel) (door)bell **(b)** (Tech) clamp **(c)** (= Handschelle) handcuff

Schellfisch [ʃɛl-] M haddock

Schelm [ʃɛlm] M **-(e)s, -e** (dated: = Spaßvogel) joker; **den ~ im Nacken haben** to be up to mischief

schelmisch [ʃɛlmɪʃ] ① ADJ Blick, Lächeln mischievous ② ADV mischievously

Schelte [ʃɛltə] F **-, -n** scolding; (= Kritik) attack

schelten [ʃɛltn], pret **schalt** [ʃalt], ptp **gescholten** [ɡəˈʃɔltn] ① VT to scold; **jdn einen Dummkopf ~** to call sb an idiot; **(als) faul gescholten werden** to be called lazy ② VI (= schimpfen) to curse; **über** or **auf jdn/etw ~** to curse sb/sth; **mit jdm ~** to scold sb

Schema [ʃeːma] NT **-s, Schemen** or **-ta** [-mən, -ta] scheme; (= Darstellung) diagram; (= Ordnung, Vorlage) plan; (= Muster) pattern; (Philos, Psych) schema; **nach ~ F** in the same (old) way; **etw nach einem ~ machen** to do sth according to a pattern

schematisch [ʃeːˈmaːtɪʃ] ① ADJ schematic; (= mechanisch) mechanical ② ADV **etw ~ darstellen** to show sth schematically; **~ vorgehen** to work methodically; **er arbeitet zu ~** he works too mechanically

Schemel [ʃeːml] M **-s, -** stool

schemenhaft ① ADJ shadowy; Erinnerungen hazy ② ADV **etw ~ sehen/erkennen** to see/make out the outlines of sth; **die Bäume hoben sich ~ gegen den Himmel ab** the trees were silhouetted against the sky

Schenke [ʃɛŋkə] F **-, -n** inn

Schenkel [ʃɛŋkl] M **-s, -** **(a)** (Anat) (= Oberschenkel) thigh; (= Unterschenkel) lower leg; **sich** (dat) **auf die ~ schlagen** to slap one's thighs **(b)** (von Zirkel) leg; (von Zange, Schere) shank; (Math: von Winkel) side

Schenkel-: Schenkelhals M neck of the femur; **Schenkelhalsbruch** M fracture of the neck of the femur

schenken [ʃɛŋkn] ① VT **(a)** (= Geschenk geben) **jdm etw ~** to give sb sth or give sth to sb (as a present or gift); **etw geschenkt bekommen** to get sth as a present or gift; **etw zum Geburtstag/zu Weihnachten geschenkt bekommen** to get sth for one's birthday/for Christmas; **ich möchte nichts geschenkt haben!** (lit) I don't want any presents!; (fig: = bevorzugt werden) I don't want any special treatment!; **das ist geschenkt!** (inf) (= ist ein Geschenk) it's a present; (= nicht der Rede wert) that's no great shakes (inf); (sl: = nichts wert) forget it! (inf); **das ist (fast** or **glatt) geschenkt!** (inf: = billig) that's a giveaway (inf); **das möchte ich nicht mal geschenkt haben!** I wouldn't want it if it was given to me; **jdm das Leben ~** (= begnadigen) to spare sb's life; **jdm die Freiheit ~** to set sb free; **jdm seine Liebe/seine Aufmerksamkeit ~** to give sb one's love/one's attention; **einem geschenkten Gaul sieht man nicht ins Maul** (Prov) don't look a gift horse in the mouth (Prov)
(b) (= erlassen) **jdm etw ~** to let sb off sth; **ihm ist nie etwas geschenkt worden** (fig) he never had it easy; **deine Komplimente kannst du dir ~!** you can keep your compliments (inf); **sich** (dat) **die Mühe ~** to save oneself the trouble
② VI to give presents

Schenkung [ʃɛŋkʊŋ] F **-, -en** (Jur) gift

Schenkungs-: Schenkungssteuer F gift tax; **Schenkungsurkunde** F deed of gift

Scherbe ['ʃɛrbə] F **-, -n** fragment; (= Glasscherbe/Porzellan-scherbe/Keramikscherbe) broken piece of glass/china/pottery; (Archeol) shard; **etw in ~n schlagen** to shatter sth; **in ~n gehen** to shatter; (fig) to go to pieces; **~n bringen Glück** (Prov) broken crockery brings you luck

Schere ['ʃeːrə] F **-, -n (a)** (Werkzeug) (klein) scissors pl; (groß) shears pl; (fig: = Kluft) divide; **eine ~** a pair of scissors/shears **(b)** (Zool) pincer; (von Hummer, Krebs etc) claw, pincer

scheren¹ ['ʃeːrən], pret **schor** [ʃoːɐ], ptp **geschoren** [gə'ʃoːrən] VT to clip; Schaf to shear; Haare to crop; Bart = rasieren) to shave; (= stutzen) to trim; (Tech) to shear

scheren² VTR (= kümmern) **sich nicht um jdn/etw ~** not to care about sb/sth; **was schert mich das?** what do I care (about that)?; **er scherte sich nicht im Geringsten darum** he couldn't have cared less about it **2** VR (inf) **scher dich (weg)!** beat it! (inf); **scher dich heim!** go home!

Scherenschnitt M silhouette

Schererei [ʃeːrə'raɪ] F **-, -en** USU PL (inf) trouble no pl

Scherflein ['ʃɛrflaɪn] NT **-s**, NO PL (Bibl) mite; **sein ~ (zu etw) beitragen** or **dazu geben** or **dazu beisteuern** (Geld) to pay one's bit (towards sth); (fig) to do one's bit (for sth) (inf)

Scherz [ʃɛrts] M **-es, -e** joke; (= Unfug) tomfoolery no pl; **aus** or **zum ~** as a joke; **im ~** in jest; **einen ~ machen** to make a joke; (= Streich) to play a joke; **mach keine ~e!** (inf) you're joking!; **mit so etwas macht man keine ~e** you don't joke about things like that; **seine ~e über jdn/etw machen** to make jokes about sb/sth; **sich** (dat) **(mit jdm) einen (schlechten) ~ erlauben** to play a (dirty) trick (on sb); **... und solche ~e** (inf) ... and what have you (inf); **(ganz) ohne ~!** (inf) no kidding! (inf); **~ beiseite!** joking aside

Scherz-: Scherzartikel M USU PL joke (article); **Scherzfrage** F riddle; **scherzhaft** ADJ jocular; Angelegenheit joking; (= spaßig) Einfall playful **2** ADV jokingly; **etw ~ meinen** to mean sth as a joke; **Scherzkeks** M (inf) joker (inf)

scheu [ʃɔy] **1** ADJ (= schüchtern) shy; (= zaghaft) Versuche, Worte cautious; **mach doch die Pferde** or **Gäule nicht ~** (fig inf) keep your hair (Brit) or head (US) on (inf) **2** ADV shyly

Scheu [ʃɔy] F **-**, NO PL fear (vor +dat of); (= Schüchternheit) shyness; (von Reh, Tier) timidity; (= Hemmung) inhibition; (= Ehrfurcht) awe; **seine ~ verlieren** to lose one's inhibitions; **ohne jede ~** without any inhibition; **sprechen** quite freely

scheuchen ['ʃɔyçn] VT to shoo (away); (= verscheuchen) to scare off; (= antreiben) Tiere to drive; Menschen to shoo (along)

scheuen ['ʃɔyən] **1** VT Kosten, Arbeit, Vergleich, Konflikt, Risiko to shy away from; Menschen, Licht to shun; **weder Mühe noch Kosten ~** to spare neither trouble nor expense; **keine Mühe(n) ~** to go to endless trouble; **wir brauchen den Vergleich mit ihnen nicht zu ~** we don't have to be afraid of the comparison with them **2** VR **sich vor etw** (dat) **~** (= Angst haben) to be afraid of sth; (= zurückschrecken) to shy away from sth; **und ich scheue mich nicht, das zu sagen** and I'm not afraid to say it **3** VI (Pferd etc) to shy (vor +dat at)

Scheuer ['ʃɔyɐ] F **-, -n** barn

scheuern ['ʃɔyɐn] **1** VTI **(a)** (= putzen) to scour; (mit Bürste) to scrub **(b)** (= reiben) to chafe; **der Rucksack scheuert mich am Rücken** the rucksack is chafing my back **2** VT (inf) **jdm eine ~** to smack sb (one) (inf) **3** VR **sich (an etw** dat) **~** to rub (against sth); **sich** (acc) **(wund) ~** to chafe oneself

Scheuklappe F blinker (Brit), blinder (US); **~n haben** or **tragen** (lit, fig) to wear blinkers (Brit) or blinders (US)

Scheune ['ʃɔynə] F **-, -n** barn

Scheusal ['ʃɔyzaːl] NT **-s, -e** or (inf) **Scheusäler** [-zɛːlɐ] monster

scheußlich ['ʃɔyslɪç] **1** ADJ dreadful; (= abstoßend hässlich) hideous **2** ADV **(a)** (= widerlich) kochen terribly; speisen badly; **~ riechen/schmecken** to smell/taste terrible **(b)** (= gemein) sich benehmen dreadfully **(c)** (inf: = furchtbar) dreadfully

Scheußlichkeit F **-, -en (a)** NO PL (= das Scheußlichsein) dreadfulness; (= Hässlichkeit) hideousness **(b)** (= Gräueltat etc) monstrosity

Schi [ʃiː] M **-s, -er** ['ʃiːɐ] or **-** = Ski

Schicht [ʃɪçt] F **-, -en (a)** (= Lage) layer; (= dünne ~) film; (Geol, Sci) layer; (= Farbschicht) coat; (der Gesellschaft) stratum; **breite ~en der Bevölkerung** large sections of the population; **aus allen ~en (der Bevölkerung)** from all walks of life **(b)** (= Arbeitsabschnitt, -gruppe etc) shift; **er hat jetzt ~** (inf), **er**

ist auf ~ (inf) he's on shift; **zur ~ gehen** to go on shift; **er muss ~ arbeiten** he has to work shifts

Schicht-: Schichtarbeit F shiftwork; **Schichtarbeiter(in)** M(F) shiftworker

schichten ['ʃɪçtn] **1** VT to layer; Holz, Steine, Bücher etc to stack **2** VR (Geol) to form layers; (Gestein) to stratify

schick [ʃɪk] **1** ADJ smart; Frauenmode, Kleidung chic; (inf: = prima) great **2** ADV smartly

Schick [ʃɪk] M **-s**, NO PL style

schicken ['ʃɪkn] **1** VTI to send; **(jdm) etw ~** to send sth (to sb), to send (sb) sth; **jdn einkaufen ~** to send sb to do the shopping; **(jdn) nach jdm/etw ~** to send (sb) for sb/sth; **jdn in den Ruhestand ~** to pension sb off **2** VR IMPERS (= sich ziemen) to be fitting; **das schickt sich nicht für ein Mädchen** it does not become a girl

Schickeria [ʃɪkə'riːa] F **-**, NO PL (iro) in-crowd (inf)

Schickimicki [ʃɪki'mɪki] M **-(s), -s** (inf) trendy (inf)

Schicksal ['ʃɪkzaːl] NT **-s, -e** fate; **~ spielen** to influence fate; **manche schweren ~e** many a difficult fate; **das sind (schwere) ~e** those are tragic cases; **er hat ein schweres ~ gehabt** or **durchgemacht** fate has been unkind to him; **(das ist) ~** (inf) that's life; **jdn seinem ~ überlassen** to abandon sb to his fate; **das ~ hat es gut mit uns gemeint** fortune has smiled on us

schicksalhaft ADJ fateful

Schicksalsschlag M great misfortune

Schiebe-: Schiebedach NT sunroof; **Schiebefenster** NT sliding window

schieben ['ʃiːbn], pret **schob** [ʃoːp], ptp **geschoben** [gə'ʃoːbn] **1** VT **(a)** (= bewegen) to push; (in den Ofen) to put; **etw von sich** (dat) **~** (fig) to put sth aside; Schuld, Verantwortung to reject sth; **etw vor sich her ~** (fig) to put sth off; **etw auf jdn/etw ~** to blame sb/sth for sth; **die Schuld auf jdn ~** to put the blame on sb; **die Verantwortung auf jdn ~** to place the responsibility at sb's door
(b) (inf: = handeln mit) to traffic in; Drogen to push (inf)
(c) (inf) **Dienst/Wache ~** to do duty/guard duty
2 VI **(a)** (= drücken, schubsen) to push
(b) (inf) **mit etw ~** to traffic in sth; **mit Drogen ~** to push drugs (inf)
3 VR (= sich bewegen) to move; **sich an die Spitze ~** to push one's way to the front

Schieber ['ʃiːbɐ] M **-s, -**, **Schieberin** [-ərɪn] F **-, -nen** (= Schwarzhändler) black marketeer; (= Waffenschieber) gunrunner; (= Drogenschieber) pusher (inf)

Schiebetür F sliding door

Schiebung ['ʃiːbʊŋ] F **-, -en** (= Begünstigung) string-pulling no pl; (Sport) rigging; **das war doch ~** that was a fix; **die Zuschauer riefen „~!"** the spectators shouted "fix!"

schied PRET von **scheiden**

Schieds-: Schiedsgericht NT court of arbitration; **Schiedsklausel** F arbitration clause; **Schiedsrichter(in)** M(F) arbitrator, arbiter; (Fußball, Eishockey, Boxen) referee; (Hockey, Tennis, Federball, Kricket, Mil) umpire; (= Preisrichter) judge; **schiedsrichtern** ['ʃiːtsrɪçtɐn] VI INSEP (inf) to arbitrate/referee/umpire/judge; **Schiedsspruch** M (arbitral) award; **Schiedsstelle** F arbitration service

schief [ʃiːf] **1** ADJ crooked, not straight pred; (= nach einer Seite geneigt) lopsided; Winkel oblique; Blick, Lächeln wry; Absätze worn(-down); (fig: = unzutreffend) inappropriate; Bild distorted; **~e Ebene** (Phys) inclined plane; **auf die ~e Bahn geraten** or **kommen** (fig) to leave the straight and narrow; **der Schiefe Turm von Pisa** the Leaning Tower of Pisa **2** ADV **(a)** (= schräg) halten, wachsen crooked; hinstellen at an angle; **er hatte den Hut ~ auf** he wore his hat at an angle; **~ laufen** to walk lopsidedly; **das Bild hängt ~** the picture is crooked or isn't straight; **jdn ~ ansehen** (fig) to look askance at sb
(b) (= unrichtig) übersetzen badly; **du siehst die Sache ganz ~!** (fig) you're looking at it all wrong!; **~ gewickelt** on the wrong track; **da bist du ~ gewickelt** you're in for a surprise there (inf)

Schiefe ['ʃiːfə] F **-**, NO PL crookedness; (= Neigung) lopsidedness; (von Ebene) inclination

Schiefer ['ʃiːfɐ] M **-s, -** (Gesteinsart) slate; (esp Aus: = Holzsplitter) splinter

Schiefer-: Schieferdach NT slate roof; **schiefergrau** ADJ slate-grey (Brit), slate-gray (US); **Schiefertafel** F slate

schief-: schief gehen VI IRREG AUX SEIN to go wrong; **es wird schon ~!** (hum) it'll be OK (inf); **schieflachen** VR SEP (inf) to kill oneself (laughing) (inf); **Schieflage** F (fig) difficulties pl; **schief liegen** VI IRREG (inf) to be wrong; **mit einer Meinung ~** to be on the wrong track

schielen ['ʃiːlən] VI to squint, to be cross-eyed; **auf** or **mit einem Auge ~** to have a squint in one eye; **auf etw** (acc) **~** (inf) to steal a glance at sth; **nach jdm/etw ~** (inf) to look at sb/sth out of the corner of one's eye; (begehrlich) to look sb/sth up and down; (heimlich) to sneak a look at sb/sth

schien PRET von **scheinen**

Schienbein ['ʃiːnbaɪn] NT shin; (= ~knochen) shinbone

Schiene ['ʃiːnə] F **-, -n (a)** rail; (Med) splint; **auf oberster ~ backen** (im Backofen) to bake at the top of the oven **(b) Schienen** PL (Rail) track sing, rails pl; **aus den ~n springen** to leave the rails; **Verkehr auf die ~(n) verlagern** to transfer traffic onto the rails **(c)** (fig) **auf der politischen ~** along political lines; **ein Problem auf der pragmatischen/politischen ~ lösen** to solve a problem pragmatically/by political means; **auf der emotionalen ~** on an emotional level

schienen ['ʃiːnən] VT to splint

Schienen-: Schienenfahrzeug NT track vehicle; **Schienennetz** NT (Rail) rail network

schier [ʃiːɐ] ADJ (= rein) pure; (fig) sheer

Schieß-: Schießbefehl M order to fire or shoot; **Schießbude** F shooting gallery; **Schießbudenfigur** F target figure; (fig inf) clown; **du siehst ja aus wie eine ~** you look like something out of a pantomime

schießen ['ʃiːsn] pret **schoss** [ʃɔs], ptp **geschossen** [gəˈʃɔsn] **🔟** VT to shoot; Kugel, Rakete to fire (auf jdn/etw at sb/sth); (Ftbl etc) to kick; Tor to score; (mit Stock, Schläger) to hit; **ein paar Bilder ~** (Phot inf) to shoot a few pictures; **eine Filmszene ~** (inf) to shoot a film scene

🔢 VI **(a)** (mit Waffe, Ball) to shoot; **auf jdn/etw ~** to shoot at sb/sth; **nach etw ~** to shoot at sth; **aufs Tor/ins Netz ~** to shoot at goal/into the net; **das ist zum Schießen** (inf) that's a scream (inf) **(b)** AUX SEIN (= in die Höhe ~) to shoot up; (Bot: = Samenstand entwickeln) to go to seed; **die Pflanzen/Kinder sind in die Höhe geschossen** the plants/children have shot up; **die Preise schossen in die Höhe** prices rocketed; **(wie Pilze) aus dem Boden ~** (lit, fig) to spring up **(c)** AUX SEIN (Flüssigkeit) to shoot; (= spritzen) to spurt; (inf: = sich schnell bewegen) to shoot; **die Tränen schossen ihr in die Augen** tears flooded her eyes; **er ist** or **kam um die Ecke geschossen** he shot (a)round the corner; **jdm durch den Kopf ~** (fig) to flash through sb's mind

Schießerei [ʃiːsəˈraɪ] F **-, -en** shoot-out; (= das Schießen) shooting

Schieß-: Schießplatz M (shooting or firing) range; **Schießpulver** NT gunpowder; **Schießscharte** F embrasure; **Schießscheibe** F target; **Schießstand** M shooting range; (= Schießbude) shooting gallery

Schiff [ʃɪf] NT **-(e)s, -e (a)** ship **(b)** (Archit) (= Mittelschiff) nave; (= Seitenschiff) aisle; (= Querschiff) transept

Schifffahrt F siehe **Schifffahrt**

Schiff-: schiffbar ADJ Gewässer navigable; **Schiffbau** M, NO PL shipbuilding; **Schiffbauer(in)** M(F), pl **-bauer(innen)** shipwright; **Schiffbruch** M shipwreck; **~ erleiden** (lit) to be shipwrecked; (fig) to fail; (Firma) to founder; **schiffbrüchig** ADJ shipwrecked; **~ werden** to be shipwrecked

Schiffchen ['ʃɪfçən] NT **-s, -** (a) (zum Spielen) little boat **(b)** (Mil, Fashion) forage cap **(c)** (Tex, Sew) shuttle

Schiffeversenken NT **-** (= Spiel) battleships sing

Schifffahrt F shipping; (= Schifffahrtskunde) navigation; **die ~ wurde eingestellt** all shipping movements were halted

Schifffahrts-: Schifffahrtsgesellschaft F shipping company; **Schifffahrtsstraße** F, **Schifffahrtsweg** M (= Kanal) waterway; (= Schifffahrtslinie) shipping route

Schiffschaukel F swingboat

Schiffs-: Schiffsjunge M ship's boy; **Schiffskarte** F chart; **Schiffsladung** F shipload; **Schiffsrumpf** M hull; **Schiffstaufe** F

christening of a/the ship; **Schiffsverkehr** M shipping; **Schiffswerft** F shipyard

Schiit [ʃiˈiːt] M **-en, -en, Schiitin** [-ˈiːtɪn] F **-, -nen** Shiite

schiitisch [ʃiˈiːtɪʃ] ADJ Shiite

Schikane [ʃiˈkaːnə] F **-, -n (a)** harassment no pl; (von Mitschülern) bullying no pl; **das hat er aus reiner ~ gemacht** he did it out of sheer pig-headedness **(b) mit allen ~n** (inf) with all the trimmings **(c)** (Sport) chicane

schikanieren [ʃikaˈniːrən], ptp **schikaniert** VT to harass; Mitschüler to bully

Schikoree ['ʃikore] F **-** or m **-s**, NO PL chicory

Schild¹ [ʃɪlt] M **-(e)s, -e** [-də] shield; (= Wappenschild) escutcheon; (von ~kröte) shell; **etwas im ~e führen** (fig) to be up to something; **nichts Gutes im ~e führen** (fig) to be up to no good

Schild² NT **-(e)s, -er** [-dɐ] (= Aushang, Warenschild, Verkehrsschild) sign; (= Wegweiser) signpost; (= Namensschild, Türschild) nameplate; (= Kennzeichen) number plate (Brit), license plate (US); (= Preisschild) ticket; (= Etikett: an Käfig, Gepäck etc) label; (= Plakette) badge; (= Plakat) placard; (von Plakatträger) board; (an Monument, Haus, Grab) plaque; (von Mütze) peak

Schilddrüse F thyroid gland; **an der ~ leiden** to have a thyroid complaint

schildern ['ʃɪldɐn] VT Ereignisse, Situation, Erlebnisse, Vorgänge to describe; (= skizzieren) to outline; Menschen, Landschaften to portray; **~ Sie den Verlauf des Unfalls** give an account of how the accident happened

Schilderung [ʃɪldərʊŋ] F **-, -en** (= Beschreibung) description; (= Bericht: auch von Zeuge) account

Schilderwald M (hum) forest of traffic signs

Schild-: Schildkröte F (= Landschildkröte) tortoise; (= Wasserschildkröte) turtle; **Schildlaus** F scale insect

Schilf [ʃɪlf] NT **-(e)s, -e** reed; (= mit ~ bewachsene Fläche) reeds pl

schillern ['ʃɪlɐn] VI to shimmer

schillernd ADJ Farben, Stoffe shimmering; (in Regenbogenfarben) iridescent; (fig) Charakter enigmatic; **~e Seide** shot silk

Schilling ['ʃɪlɪŋ] M **-s, -** or (bei Geldstücken) **-e** shilling; (Aus) schilling

schilt [ʃɪlt] 3. PERS SING PRES von **schelten**

Schimäre [ʃiˈmɛːrə] F **-, -n** chimera

Schimmel¹ ['ʃɪml] M **-s, -** (= Pferd) grey (Brit), gray (US)

Schimmel² M **-s**, NO PL (auf Nahrungsmitteln) mould (Brit), mold (US); (auf Leder, Papier etc) mildew

schimmelig ['ʃɪməlɪç] ADJ Nahrungsmittel mouldy (Brit), moldy (US); Leder, Papier etc mildewy; **~ riechen** to smell mo(u)ldy; **~ werden** (Nahrungsmittel) to go mo(u)ldy; (Leder, Papier etc) to become covered with mildew

schimmeln ['ʃɪmln] VI AUX SEIN or HABEN (Nahrungsmittel) to go mouldy (Brit) or moldy (US); (Leder, Papier etc) to go mildewy; **die Wand schimmelt** the wall has mo(u)ld on it

Schimmelpilz M mould (Brit), mold (US)

Schimmer ['ʃɪmɐ] M **-s**, NO PL glimmer; (von Licht auf Wasser, von Perlen, Seide) shimmer; (von Metall) gleam; (im Haar) sheen; **keinen (blassen)** or **nicht den geringsten ~ von etw haben** (inf) not to have the faintest idea about sth (inf)

schimmern ['ʃɪmɐn] VI to glimmer; (Licht auf Wasser auch, Perlen, Seide) to shimmer; (Metall) to gleam; **der Stoff/ihr Haar schimmert rötlich** the material/her hair has a tinge of red

schimmlig ['ʃɪmlɪç] ADJ = **schimmelig**

Schimpanse [ʃɪmˈpanzə] M **-n, -n, Schimpansin** [-ˈpanzɪn] F **-, -nen** chimpanzee, chimp (inf)

schimpfen ['ʃɪmpfn] **🔟** VI to get angry; (= sich beklagen) to moan; (= fluchen) to curse; (Vögel, Affen etc) to bitch (inf); **mit jdm ~** to tell sb off; **auf** or **über jdn/etw ~** to curse (about or at) sb/sth; **vor sich hin ~** to grumble **🔢** VT (= ausschimpfen) to tell off; **jdn einen Idioten ~** to call sb an idiot **🔼** VR **sich etw ~** (inf) to call oneself sth

Schimpfwort NT, pl **-wörter** swearword; **mit Schimpfwörtern um sich werfen** to curse and swear

Schindel ['ʃɪndl] F **-, -n** shingle

schinden ['ʃɪndn], pret **schindete** or (rare) **schund** ['ʃɪndətə, ʃʊnt], ptp **geschunden** [gəˈʃʊndn] **🔟** VT **(a)** (= quälen) Gefangene, Tiere to maltreat; (= ausbeuten) to overwork, to drive hard; **jdn zu**

Tode ~ to work sb to death
(b) (*inf*: = *herausschlagen*) *Zeilen* to pad (out); *Arbeitsstunden* to pile up; **Zeit ~** to play for time; **(bei jdm) Eindruck ~** to make a good impression (on sb)
② VR (= *hart arbeiten*) to struggle; (= *sich quälen*) to strain; **sich mit etw ~** to slave away at sth

Schindluder [ˈʃɪntluːdɐ] NT (*inf*) **mit jdm ~ treiben** to make sb suffer; **mit etw ~ treiben** to misuse sth; *mit Gesundheit, Kräften* to abuse sth

Schinken [ˈʃɪŋkn] M **-s, -** **(a)** ham **(b)** (*pej inf*) (= *großes Buch*) tome; (= *großes Bild*) great daub (*pej inf*)

Schinken-: **Schinkenspeck** M bacon; **Schinkenwurst** F ham sausage

Schippe [ˈʃɪpə] F **-, -n** (*esp N Ger*: = *Schaufel*) shovel; **jdn auf die ~ nehmen** (*fig inf*) to pull sb's leg (*inf*)

schippen [ˈʃɪpn] VT to shovel; **Schnee ~** to shovel the snow away

Schirm [ʃɪrm] M **-(e)s, -e** **(a)** (= *Regenschirm*) umbrella; (= *Sonnenschirm*) sunshade; (*von Pilz*) cap
(b) (= *Mützenschirm*) peak **(c)** (= *Röntgenschirm, Wandschirm, Ofenschirm*) screen; (= *Lampenschirm*) shade

Schirm-: **Schirmherr(in)** M(F) patron; (*Frau auch*) patroness; **Schirmherrschaft** F patronage; **unter der ~ von** under the patronage of; (*von Organisation*) under the auspices of; **die ~ übernehmen** to become patron; **Schirmmütze** F peaked cap; **Schirmständer** M umbrella stand

Schirokko [ʃiˈrɔko] M **-s, -s** sirocco

schiss PRET *von* **scheißen**

Schiss [ʃɪs] M **-es**, NO PL (*sl*) **(fürchterlichen) ~ haben** to be scared to death (*vor* +*dat* of) (*inf*); **~ kriegen** to get scared

schizophren [ʃitsoˈfreːn, sçi-] ADJ (*Med*) schizophrenic; (*pej*: = *widersinnig*) contradictory, topsy-turvy

Schizophrenie [ʃitsofreˈniː, sçi-] F **-**, NO PL (*Med*) schizophrenia; (*pej*: = *Widersinn*) contradictoriness; **das ist die reinste ~** that's a flat contradiction

Schlacht [ʃlaxt] F **-, -en** battle; **die ~ bei** *or* **um X** the battle of X; **jdm eine ~ liefern** to fight sb, to battle with sb

schlachten [ˈʃlaxtn] **①** VT to slaughter; (*hum*) *Sparschwein* to break into; **heilige Kühe ~** (*fig*) to slaughter sacred cows **②** VI to do one's slaughtering

Schlachtenbummler(in) M(F) (*Sport inf*) away supporter

Schlachter [ˈʃlaxtɐ] M **-s, -**, **Schlachterin** [-ərɪn] F **-, -nen** (*esp N Ger*) butcher

Schlächter [ˈʃlɛçtɐ] M **-s, -**, **Schlächterin** [-ərɪn] F **-, -nen** (*dial, fig*) butcher

Schlachterei [ʃlaxtəˈraɪ] F **-, -en** (*esp N Ger*) butcher's (shop)

Schlächterei [ʃlɛçtəˈraɪ] F **-, -en** **(a)** (*dial*) butcher's (shop) **(b)** (*fig*: = *Blutbad*) massacre

Schlacht-: **Schlachtfeld** NT battlefield; **auf dem ~ bleiben** (*lit*) to fall in battle; (*fig*) (*nach Schlägerei etc*) to be left lying; (*esp Pol*) to be finished; **Schlachtfest** NT *country feast to eat up meat from freshly slaughtered pigs*; **Schlachtgetümmel** NT thick of the battle; **Schlachthaus** NT, **Schlachthof** M slaughterhouse; **Schlachtplan** M battle plan; (*für Feldzug*) campaign plan; (*fig*) plan of action; **Schlachtvieh** NT, NO PL animals pl for slaughter

Schlacke [ˈʃlakə] F **-, -n** (= *Verbrennungsrückstand*) clinker no pl; (= *Aschenteile auch*) cinders pl; (*Metal, Geol*) slag no pl; (*Physiol*) waste products pl

schlackern [ˈʃlakɐn] VI (*inf*) to tremble; (*Kleidung*) to hang loosely; **mit den Knien ~** to tremble at the knees; **mit den Ohren ~** (*fig*) to be (left) speechless

Schlaf [ʃlaːf] M **-(e)s**, NO PL sleep; (= *Schläfrigkeit auch*) sleepiness; **einen leichten/festen/tiefen ~ haben** to be a light/sound/deep sleeper; **keinen ~ finden** to be unable to sleep; **um seinen ~ kommen** *or* **gebracht werden** to lose sleep; (= *überhaupt nicht schlafen*) not to get any sleep; **jdn um seinen ~ bringen** to keep sb awake; **im ~** (= *während des Schlafens*) while he sleeps/they slept *etc*; **halb im ~** half asleep; **im ~ reden** to talk in one's sleep; **es fällt mir nicht im ~(e) ein, das zu tun** I wouldn't dream of doing that; **das macht** *or* **tut** *or* **kann er (wie) im ~** (*fig inf*) he can do that in his sleep

Schlaf-: **Schlafanzug** M pyjamas pl (*Brit*), pajamas pl (*US*); **schlafbedürftig** ADJ **(besonders) ~ sein** to need a lot of sleep;

Kinder sind ~er als Erwachsene children need more sleep than adults

Schläfchen [ˈʃlɛːfçən] NT **-s, -** nap; **ein ~ machen** to have a nap

Schläfe [ˈʃlɛːfə] F **-, -n** temple

schlafen [ˈʃlaːfn] pret **schlief** [ʃliːf], ptp **geschlafen** [ɡəˈʃlaːfn] **①** VI to sleep; (*inf*: = *nicht aufpassen*) to be asleep; **tief** *or* **fest ~** (*zu diesem Zeitpunkt*) to be fast *or* sound asleep; (*immer*) to be a deep *or* sound sleeper; **~ gehen** to go to bed; **sich ~ legen** to lie down to sleep; **jdn ~ legen** to put sb to bed; **schläfst du schon?** are you asleep?; **schlaf gut** *or* (*geh*) **wohl** sleep well; **mittags** *or* **über Mittag ~** to have an afternoon nap; **~ wie ein Murmeltier** *or* **Bär** *or* **Sack** *or* **Stein** *or* **eine Ratte** (*all inf*) to sleep like a log; **bei jdm ~** to stay overnight with sb; **wir können ruhig ~** (*fig*) we can sleep easy; **er kann nachts nicht mehr ~** (*fig*) he can't sleep nights; **ich konnte die ganze Nacht nicht ~** I couldn't sleep at all last night; **das lässt ihn nicht ~** (*fig*) it gives him no peace; **darüber muss ich erst mal ~** (*fig*: = *überdenken*) I'll have to sleep on it; **mit jdm ~** (= *euph*) to sleep with sb; **miteinander ~** (*euph*) to sleep with each other; **sie schläft mit jedem** she sleeps around; **schlaf nicht!** wake up! **②** VR IMPERS **auf dieser Matratze schläft es sich schlecht** this mattress is terrible to sleep on

Schläfenlocke F sidelock

Schlafenszeit F bedtime

schlaff [ʃlaf] **①** ADJ limp; (= *locker*) *Seil, Segel* slack; *Moral, Disziplin* lax; *Haut, Muskeln* flabby; (= *erschöpft*) worn-out; (= *energielos*) listless **②** ADV limply; (*bei Seil, Segel*) loosely

Schlaf-: **Schlafgelegenheit** F place to sleep; **wir haben ~ für mehrere Leute** we have room for several people to sleep over; **Schlafkrankheit** F sleeping sickness; **Schlaflied** NT lullaby; **schlaflos** **①** ADJ (*lit, fig*) sleepless; **~ liegen** to lie awake; **jdm ~e Nächte bereiten** to give sb many a sleepless night **②** ADV sleeplessly; **Schlaflosigkeit** F **-**, NO PL sleeplessness, insomnia; **Schlafmittel** NT sleeping drug; (*fig iro*) soporific; **Schlafmütze** F **(a)** nightcap **(b)** (*inf*: *Person*) dozy devil (*inf*); (= *jd, der viel schläft*) sleepyhead (*inf*); **diese ~n im Parlament** that dozy lot in Parliament (*inf*); **Schlafraum** M dormitory, dorm (*inf*)

schläfrig [ˈʃlɛːfrɪç] ADJ sleepy

Schläfrigkeit F **-**, NO PL sleepiness

Schlaf-: **Schlafsaal** M dormitory; **Schlafsack** M sleeping bag; **Schlafstadt** F dormitory town; **Schlafstelle** F place to sleep; **Schlafstörung** F sleeplessness, insomnia

schläft [ʃlɛːft] 3. PERS SING *von* **schlafen**

Schlaf-: **Schlaftablette** F sleeping pill; **schlaftrunken** (*geh*) **①** ADJ drowsy **②** ADV drowsily

Schlafwagen M sleeping car

Schlafwagen-: **Schlafwagenkarte** F ticket for a/the sleeping car; **Schlafwagenplatz** M berth

Schlaf-: **schlafwandeln** VI INSEP AUX SEIN *or* HABEN to sleepwalk; **Schlafwandler** [-vandlɐ] M **-s, -**, **Schlafwandlerin** [-ərɪn] F **-, -nen** sleepwalker; **Schlafzimmer** NT bedroom

Schlag [ʃlaːk] M **-(e)s, ⸚e** [ˈʃlɛːɡə] **(a)** (*lit, fig*) blow (*gegen* against); (*mit der Handfläche*) smack, slap; (*leichter*) pat; (= *Handkantenschlag*) (*auch Judo etc*) chop (*inf*); (= *Ohrfeige*) cuff; (*mit Rohrstock etc*) stroke; (= *Peitschenschlag*) lash; (= *einmaliges Klopfen*) knock; (*dumpf*) thud; (= *Glockenschlag*) chime; (= *Standuhrschlag*) stroke; (= *Gehirnschlag, ~anfall, Kolbenschlag, Ruderschlag*) stroke; (= *Herzschlag, Pulsschlag, Trommelschlag, Wellenschlag*) beat; (= *Donnerschlag*) clap; (= *Stromschlag*) shock; (= *Militärschlag*) strike; **Schläge kriegen** to get a beating; **zum entscheidenden ~ ausholen** (*fig*) to strike the decisive blow; **~ auf ~** one after the other; **~ acht Uhr** (*inf*) at eight on the dot (*inf*); **jdm/einer Sache einen schweren ~ versetzen** (*fig*) to deal a severe blow to sb/sth; **ein ~ ins Gesicht** (*lit, fig*) a slap in the face; **ein ~ ins Wasser** (*inf*) a letdown (*inf*); **mit einem** *or* **auf einen ~** (*inf*) all at once; **mit einem ~ berühmt werden** to become famous overnight; **die haben keinen ~ getan** (*inf*) they haven't done a stroke (of work); **einen ~ weghaben** (*sl*: = *blöd sein*) to have a screw loose (*inf*); **ihn hat der ~ getroffen** (*Med*) he had a stroke; **ich dachte, mich rührt** *or* **trifft der ~** (*inf*) I was flabbergasted (*inf*); **ich glaube, mich trifft der ~** I don't believe it; **wie vom ~ gerührt** *or* **getroffen sein** to be flabbergasted (*inf*)
(b) (*inf*: = *Wesensart*) type (of person *etc*); **vom ~ der Südländer sein** to be a Southern type; **vom gleichen ~ sein** to be cast in the same mould (*Brit*) *or* mold (*US*); (*pej*) to be tarred

with the same brush; **vom alten ~** of the old school
(c) (Aus: = ~sahne) cream
(d) (= Hosenschlag) flare; **eine Hose mit ~** flares pl (inf)
Schlag-: Schlagabtausch M (Boxen) exchange of blows; (fig)
(verbal) exchange; **offener ~** public exchange (of views);
Schlagader F artery; **Schlaganfall** M stroke; **schlagartig** █ ADJ
sudden █ ADV suddenly; **Schlagbaum** M barrier;
Schlagbohrer M, **Schlagbohrmaschine** F hammer drill

schlagen [ˈʃlaːgn], pret **schlug** [ʃluːk], ptp **geschlagen** [gəˈʃlaːgn]
█ VTI (a) (= zuschlagen, prügeln) to hit; (= hauen) to beat; (mit
der flachen Hand) to slap, to smack; (mit der Faust) to punch;
(mit Hammer, Pickel etc) Loch to knock; **die Bombe schlug ein
Loch in die Straße** the bomb blew a hole in the road; **jdn
bewusstlos ~** to knock sb out; (mit vielen Schlägen) to beat sb
unconscious; **etw in Stücke** or **kurz und klein ~** to smash sth
up or to pieces; **nach jdm/etw ~** to lash out at sb/sth; **um sich
~** to lash out; **mit dem Hammer auf den Nagel ~** to hit the nail
with the hammer; **mit der Faust an die Tür/auf den Tisch ~** to
beat on the door/table with one's fist; **gegen die Tür ~** to
hammer on the door; **jdm** or (rare) **jdn auf die Schulter ~** to
slap sb on the back; (leichter) to pat sb on the back; **jdm etw
aus der Hand ~** to knock sth out of sb's hand; **jdm** or (rare)
jdn ins Gesicht ~ to hit/slap/punch sb in the face; **einer
Sache** (dat) **ins Gesicht ~** (fig) to be a slap in the face for sth;
na ja, ehe ich mich ~ lasse! (hum inf) I suppose you could
twist my arm (hum inf)
(b) (= läuten) to chime; Stunde to strike; **eine geschlagene
Stunde** a full hour
(c) (= heftig flattern) **mit den Flügeln ~** to beat its wings
█ VT (a) (= besiegen, übertreffen) Gegner, Konkurrenz, Rekord to
beat; **jdn in etw** (dat) **~** to beat sb at sth; **sich geschlagen
geben** to admit defeat
(b) (Cook) to beat; (mit Schneebesen) to whisk; Sahne to whip;
ein Ei in die Pfanne ~ to crack an egg into the pan; **ein Ei in
die Suppe ~** to beat an egg into the soup
(c) (= hinzufügen) to add (auf +acc, zu to); Gebiet to annexe
(d) **den Kragen nach oben ~** to turn up one's collar; **die
Hände vors Gesicht ~** to cover one's face with one's hands;
Profit aus etw ~ to make a profit from sth; (fig) to profit from
sth
█ VI (a) (Herz, Puls) to beat; (heftig) to pound; **sein Puls schlug
unregelmäßig** his pulse was irregular; **ihr Herz schlägt für den
FC Bayern** she's passionate about FC Bayern; **jds Herz höher
~ lassen** (fig) to make sb's heart beat faster
(b) AUX SEIN (= auftreffen) **mit dem Kopf auf/gegen etw** (acc) **~**
to hit one's head on/against sth
(c) (Regen) to beat; (Wellen) to pound; (Blitz) to strike (in etw
acc sth)
(d) AUX SEIN or HABEN (Flammen) to shoot out (aus of); (Rauch)
to pour out (aus of)
(e) AUX SEIN (inf: = ähneln) **er schlägt sehr nach seinem Vater**
he takes after his father a lot
█ VR (= sich prügeln) to fight; (= sich duellieren) to duel (auf
+dat with); **um etw ~** (lit, fig) to fight over sth; **er schlägt
sich nicht um die Arbeit** he's not crazy about work (inf); **sich
tapfer** or **gut ~** to make a good showing; **sich auf jds Seite**
(acc) **~** to side with sb; (= die Fronten wechseln) to go over to
sb

Schlager [ˈʃlaːgɐ] M **-s, -** (a) (Mus) pop song; (erfolgreich) hit
(song) (b) (inf) (= Erfolg) hit; (= Waren) bargain;
(= Verkaufsschlager, Buch) bestseller
Schläger¹ [ˈʃlɛːgɐ] M **-s, -** (= Tennisschläger, Federballschläger)
racquet (Brit), racket (US); (= Hockeyschläger, Eishockeyschläger)
stick; (= Golfschläger) club; (= Baseballschläger,
Tischtennisschläger) bat
Schläger² [ˈʃlɛːgɐ] M **-s, -**, **Schlägerin** [-ərɪn] F **-, -nen**
(= Raufbold) thug
Schlägerei [ʃlɛːgəˈraɪ] F **-, -en** brawl
Schlagermusik F pop music
Schlager-: Schlagersänger(in) M(F) pop singer; **Schlagertext**
M (pop music) lyrics pl; **Schlagertexter(in)** M(F) pop lyricist
Schlag-: schlagfertig █ ADJ Antwort quick and clever; **er ist
ein ~er Mensch** he is always ready with a quick(-witted) reply
█ ADV **~ reagieren** to give a quick-witted reply; **~ antworten**
to be quick with an answer; **... bemerkte sie ~ ...** she said
smartly; **Schlagfertigkeit** F, NO PL (von Mensch) quick-
wittedness; (von Antwort) cleverness; **Schlaghose** F flares pl
(inf); **Schlaginstrument** NT percussion instrument;

Schlagloch NT pothole; **Schlagmann** M, pl **-männer** (Rudern)
stroke; (Kricket) batsman; (Baseball) batter; **Schlagobers**
[ˈʃlaːkloːbɐs] NT **-, -** (Aus), **Schlagrahm** M (S Ger) (whipping)
cream; (geschlagen) whipped cream; **Schlagring** M
(a) knuckle-duster (b) (Mus) plectrum; **Schlagsahne** F
(whipping) cream; (geschlagen) whipped cream; **Schlagseite**
F (Naut) list; **~ haben** (Naut) to be listing; (fig) to be one-
sided; (hum inf: = betrunken sein) to be three sheets to the
wind (inf); **Schlagstock** M (form) baton
schlägt [ʃlɛːkt] 3. PERS SING PRES von schlagen
Schlag-: Schlagwort NT (a) pl **-wörter** (= Stichwort) headword
(b) pl **-worte** (= Parole) slogan; **Schlagzeile** F headline; **~n
machen** (inf) to hit the headlines; **in die ~n geraten** to make
the headlines; **für ~n sorgen** to make headlines; **etw/jdn aus
den ~n bringen** to get sth/sb out of the media spotlight; **aus
den ~n verschwinden** not to be big news anymore;
Schlagzeug NT, pl **-zeuge** drums pl; (in Orchester) percussion
no pl; **Schlagzeuger** [-tsɔygɐ] M **-s, -**, **Schlagzeugerin** [-ərɪn] F
-, -nen drummer; (in Orchester) percussionist
Schlamassel [ʃlaˈmasl] M or NT **-s, -** (inf) (= Durcheinander) mix-
up; (= missliche Lage) mess (inf); **da haben wir den** or **das ~**
now we're in a right mess (inf)
Schlamm [ʃlam] M **-(e)s, -e** or **¨e** [ˈʃlɛmə] mud
schlammig [ˈʃlamɪç] ADJ muddy
Schlammlawine F mudslide
Schlammschlacht F (inf) mud bath
Schlampe [ˈʃlampə] F **-, -n** (pej inf) slut (inf)
schlampen [ˈʃlampn] VI (inf) to be sloppy (in one's work); **bei
einer Arbeit ~** to do a piece of work sloppily; **die Behörden
haben wieder einmal geschlampt** (once again) the authorities
have done a sloppy job
Schlamperei [ʃlampəˈraɪ] F **-, -en** (inf) sloppiness; (= schlechte
Arbeit) sloppy work; (= Unordentlichkeit) untidiness; **das ist
eine ~!** that's a disgrace!
schlampig [ˈʃlampɪç], (Aus, S Ger) **schlampert** [ˈʃlampɐt] █ ADJ
sloppy; (= unordentlich) untidy █ ADV (= nachlässig)
carelessly; (= ungepflegt) slovenly; **die Arbeit ist ~ erledigt
worden** the work has been sloppily done
schlang PRET von schlingen¹, schlingen²
Schlange [ˈʃlaŋə] F **-, -n** (a) snake; (fig: = Frau) Jezebel; **eine
falsche ~** a snake in the grass (b) (= Menschenschlange,
Autoschlange) queue (Brit), line (US); **~ stehen** to queue (up)
(Brit), to stand in line (US) (c) (Tech) coil
schlängeln [ˈʃlɛŋln] VR (Weg, Menschenmenge) to wind (its
way); (Fluss auch) to meander; (Schlange) to wriggle; **sich um
etw ~** to wind around sth; **sich durch etw ~** to worm
one's way through sth; **eine geschlängelte Linie** a wavy line
Schlangen-: Schlangenbiss M snakebite; **Schlangengift** NT
snake venom; **Schlangenhaut** F snake's skin; (= Leder)
snakeskin; **Schlangenleder** NT snakeskin; **Schlangenlinie** F
wavy line; **(in) ~n fahren** to swerve about
Schlangestehen NT **-s**, NO PL queueing (Brit), standing in line
(US)
schlank [ʃlaŋk] ADJ (a) slim; **~ werden** to slim; **ihr Kleid macht
sie ~** her dress makes her look slim; **Joghurt macht ~** yoghurt
is slimming (b) (fig: = effektiv) lean; **~er Staat** (Pol) lean state
Schlankheit F, NO PL slimness
Schlankheitskur F diet; (Med) course of slimming treatment;
eine ~ machen/anfangen to be/go on a diet
schlapp [ʃlap] ADJ (inf) (= erschöpft, kraftlos) worn-out;
(= energielos) listless; (nach Krankheit etc) run-down; (= gering,
unbedeutend) measly (inf); **sich ~ lachen** to laugh oneself
silly; **~e 300 Euro** a measly 300 euros
Schlappe [ˈʃlapə] F **-, -n** (inf) setback; (esp Sport) defeat; **eine ~
einstecken (müssen)** or **erleiden** to suffer a setback/defeat;
jdm eine ~ beibringen or **erteilen** to defeat sb
Schlapp-: schlappmachen VI SEP (inf) to wilt;
(= zusammenbrechen, ohnmächtig werden) to collapse; **Leute,
die bei jeder Gelegenheit ~, können wir nicht gebrauchen** we
can't use people who can't take it; **Schlappschwanz** M (pej
inf) wimp (inf)
schlau [ʃlau] ADJ smart; (= gerissen) cunning; Sprüche clever;
er ist ein ~er Kopf he has a good head on his shoulders; **ein
~er Bursche** a crafty devil (inf); **ein ~es Buch** (inf) a clever
book; **sich über etw** (acc) **~ machen** (inf) to inform oneself
about sth; **ich werde nicht ~ aus ihm/dieser Sache** I can't

make him/it out **2** ADV cleverly; **sie tut immer so ~** she always thinks she's so clever

Schlauch [ʃlaux] M **-(e)s, Schläuche** [ˈʃlɔyçə] hose; (*Med*) tube; (= *Fahrradschlauch, Autoschlauch*) (inner) tube; (= *Weinschlauch etc*) skin; **auf dem ~ stehen** (*inf*) (= *nicht begreifen*) not to have a clue (*inf*); (= *nicht weiterkommen*) to be stuck (*inf*)

Schlauch-: schlauchartig ADJ tubular; *Zimmer* narrow; **Schlauchboot** NT rubber dinghy

schlauchen [ˈʃlauxn] **1** VT (*inf*) *jdn* (*Reise, Arbeit etc*) to wear out; (*Chef, Feldwebel etc*) to drive hard **2** VI (*inf*: = *Kraft kosten*) to take it out of you/one *etc* (*inf*); **das schlaucht echt!** it really takes it out of you (*inf*)

schlauchlos ADJ *Reifen* tubeless

schlauerweise [ˈʃlauɐˈvaizə] ADV cleverly; (= *gerissen*) cunningly

Schlaufe [ˈʃlaufə] F **-, -n** (*an Kleidungsstück, Schuh etc*) loop; (= *Aufhänger*) hanger; (= *Strecke*) loop

Schlauheit [ˈʃlauhait] F **-, -en (a)** NO PL cleverness; (*von Mensch, Idee auch*) shrewdness; (= *Gerissenheit*) cunning **(b)** (= *Bemerkung*) clever remark

Schlaumeier [-maiɐ] M **-s, -** smart aleck (*inf*)

Schlawiner [ʃlaˈviːnɐ] M **-s, -** (*hum inf*) villain

schlecht [ʃlɛçt] **1** ADJ **(a)** bad; *Gesundheit, Durchblutung* poor; **das Schlechte in der Welt/im Menschen** the evil in the world/ in man; **das ist ein ~er Scherz** that is a dirty trick; **er ist in Latein ~er als ich** he is worse at Latin than I am; **sich zum Schlechten wenden** to take a turn for the worse; **nur Schlechtes von jdm** *or* **über jdn sagen** not to have a good word to say for sb; **jdm ist (es)** ~ sb feels ill; **in ~er Verfassung sein** to be in a bad way; **~ aussehen** to look bad; **mit jdm/etw sieht es ~ aus** sb/sth looks in a bad way

(b) PRED (= *ungenießbar*) off *pred* (*Brit*), bad; **die Milch/das Fleisch ist** ~ the milk/meat has gone bad *or* is bad; **~ werden** to go off (*Brit*) *or* bad

2 ADV badly; *lernen, begreifen* with difficulty; **~ beraten sein** to be ill-advised; **sich ~ vertragen** (*Menschen*) to get along badly; (*Dinge, Farben etc*) not to go well together; **~ über jdn sprechen/von jdm denken** to speak/think ill of sb; **~ gelaunt** bad-tempered; **~ gelaunt sein** to be in a bad mood; **er kann ~ nein sagen** he finds it hard to say no; **da kann man ~ nein sagen** it's hard to say no to that; **heute geht es ~** today is not very convenient; **das lässt sich ~ machen, das geht ~** that's not really possible *or* on (*inf*); **er ist ~ zu verstehen** he is hard to understand; **sie kann sich ~ anpassen** she finds it difficult to adjust; **ich kann sie ~ sehen** I can't see her very well; **auf jdn/etw ~ zu sprechen sein** not to have a good word to say for sb/sth; **~ und recht** (*hum*), **mehr ~ als recht** (*hum*) after a fashion; **er hat nicht ~ gestaunt** (*inf*) he was very surprised

schlechterdings [ˈʃlɛçtɐdɪŋs] ADV (= *völlig*) absolutely; (= *nahezu*) virtually

schlecht-: schlecht gehen VI IMPERS IRREG AUX SEIN **es geht jdm schlecht** sb is in a bad way; (*finanziell*) sb is doing badly; **wenn er das erfährt, gehts dir schlecht** if he hears about that you'll be for it (*inf*); **schlechtgelaunt** ADJ ATTR *siehe* **schlecht**; **schlechthin** [ʃlɛçtˈhɪn] ADV (= *vollkommen*) quite; (= *als solches, in seiner Gesamtheit*) per se; **er gilt als** *or* **er ist der romantische Komponist ~** he is the epitome of the Romantic composer

Schlechtigkeit [ˈʃlɛçtɪçkait] F **-, -en (a)** NO PL badness; (*esp qualitativ*) inferiority **(b)** (= *schlechte Tat*) misdeed

Schlecht-: schlecht machen VT (= *herabsetzen*) to denigrate; **Schlechtwettergeld** NT bad-weather pay

schlecken [ˈʃlɛkn] (*Aus, S Ger*) VTI **= lecken²**

Schlehe [ˈʃleːə] F **-, -n** sloe

schleichen [ˈʃlaiçn] , *pret* **schlich** [ʃlɪç], *ptp* **geschlichen** [ɡəˈʃlɪçn] **1** VI AUX SEIN to creep; (*heimlich auch*) to sneak; (*Fahrzeug*) to crawl; (*fig: Zeit*) to crawl (by); **um das Haus ~** to prowl around the house

2 VR **(a)** (= *leise gehen*) to creep; (*fig: Misstrauen*) to enter; **sich in jds Vertrauen** (*acc*) **~** to worm one's way into sb's confidence

(b) (*S Ger, Aus*: = *weggehen*) to go away; **schleich dich!** get lost! (*inf*)

schleichend ADJ ATTR creeping; *Krankheit, Gift* insidious; *Fieber* lingering

Schleich-: Schleichpfad M, **Schleichweg** M secret path; (= *wenig befahrene Straßenverbindung*) short cut (*avoiding traffic*); **auf Schleichwegen** (*fig*) on the quiet

Schleie [ˈʃlaiə] F **-, -n** (*Zool*) tench

Schleier [ˈʃlaiɐ] M **-s, -** (*lit, fig*) veil; **einen ~ vor den Augen haben, wie durch einen ~ sehen** to have a mist in front of one's eyes; **den ~ (des Geheimnisses) lüften** to lift the veil of secrecy

Schleier-: Schleiereule F barn owl; **schleierhaft** ADJ (*inf*) baffling; **es ist mir völlig ~** it's a complete mystery to me; **Schleierkraut** NT (*Bot*) gypsophila; **Schleierschwanz** M goldfish

Schleife [ˈʃlaifə] F **-, -n (a)** loop; (= *Straßenschleife*) twisty bend **(b)** (*von Band*) bow; (= *Schuhschleife*) bow(knot); (= *Fliege*) bow tie; (= *Kranzschleife*) ribbon

schleifen¹ [ˈʃlaifn] **1** VT **(a)** (*lit, fig*) to drag; (*Mus*) *Töne, Noten* to slur; **jdn vor Gericht ~** (*fig*) to drag sb into court **(b)** (= *niederreißen*) to raze (to the ground) **2** VI **(a)** AUX SEIN or HABEN to trail, to drag **(b)** (= *reiben*) to rub; **die Kupplung ~ lassen** (*Aut*) to slip the clutch; **die Zügel ~ lassen** (*lit, fig*) to slacken the reins; **wir haben die Sache ~ lassen** (*fig*) we let things slide

schleifen² *pret* **schliff** [ʃlɪf], *ptp* **geschliffen** [ɡəˈʃlɪfn] VT *Messer, Schere* to sharpen; *Sense, Werkstück, Linse* to grind; *Parkett* to sand; *Edelstein, Glas, Spiegel* to cut; *siehe auch* **geschliffen**

Schleif-: Schleiflack M (coloured (*Brit*) *or* colored (*US*)) lacquer; **Schleiflackmöbel** PL lacquered furniture *sing*; **Schleifmaschine** F grinding machine; **Schleifpapier** NT abrasive paper; **Schleifrad** NT, **Schleifscheibe** F grinding wheel; **Schleifstein** M grinding stone, grindstone

Schleim [ʃlaim] M **-(e)s, -e (a)** slime; (*Med*) mucus; (*in Atemorganen*) phlegm; (*Bot*) mucilage **(b)** (*Cook*) gruel

schleimen [ˈʃlaimən] VI to leave a coating; (*fig inf*: = *schmeicheln*) to crawl (*inf*)

Schleimer [ˈʃlaimɐ] M **-s, -, Schleimerin** [-ərɪn] F **-, -nen** (*inf*) crawler (*inf*)

Schleimhaut F mucous membrane

schleimig [ˈʃlaimɪç] ADJ **(a)** slimy; (*Med*) mucous; (*Bot*) mucilaginous **(b)** (*pej*: = *unterwürfig*) slimy (*inf*)

schleimlösend ADJ expectorant

schlemmen [ˈʃlɛmən] **1** VI (= *üppig essen*) to feast; (= *üppig leben*) to live it up **2** VT to feast on

Schlemmer [ˈʃlɛmɐ] M **-s, -, Schlemmerin** [-ərɪn] F **-, -nen** bon vivant

schlendern [ˈʃlɛndɐn] VI AUX SEIN to stroll

Schlendrian [ˈʃlɛndriaːn] M **-(e)s**, NO PL (*inf*) casualness; (= *Trott*) rut

Schleppe [ˈʃlɛpə] F **-, -n** (*von Kleid*) train

schleppen [ˈʃlɛpn] **1** VT (= *tragen*) *Lasten, Gepäck* to lug; (= *zerren*) to drag; *Auto, Schiff* to tow; *Flüchtlinge* to smuggle **2** VI (*inf*: = *nachschleifen*) to drag **3** VR to drag oneself; (*Verhandlungen etc*) to drag on

schleppend **1** ADJ *Gang* shuffling; *Bedienung, Abfertigung, Nachfrage, Geschäft* sluggish; *Stimme* drawling; **nach ein paar Stunden wurde die Unterhaltung immer ~er** after a few hours the conversation began to drag **2** ADV **nur ~ vorankommen** to progress very slowly; **die Unterhaltung kam nur ~ in Gang** conversation was very slow to start

Schlepper¹ [ˈʃlɛpɐ] M **-s, - (a)** (*Aut*) tractor **(b)** (*Naut*) tug

Schlepper² [ˈʃlɛpɐ] M **-s, -, Schlepperin** [-ərɪn] F **-, -nen (a)** (*sl: für Lokal*) tout **(b)** (= *Fluchthelfer*) people smuggler

Schlepp-: Schleppkahn M (canal) barge; **Schlepplift** M ski tow; **Schleppnetz** NT trawl (net); **Schleppnetzfahndung** F dragnet; **Schlepptau** NT (*Naut*) tow rope; (*Aviat*) dragrope; **ein Schiff/jdn ins ~ nehmen** to take a ship/sb in tow

Schlesien [ˈʃleːziən] NT **-s** Silesia

Schlesier [ˈʃleːziɐ] M **-s, -, Schlesierin** [-iərɪn] F **-, -nen** Silesian

schlesisch [ˈʃleːzɪʃ] ADJ Silesian

Schleswig-Holstein [ˈʃleːsvɪçˈhɔlʃtain] NT **-s** Schleswig-Holstein

Schleuder [ˈʃlɔydɐ] F **-, -n (a)** (*Waffe*) sling; (= *Wurfmaschine*) catapult **(b)** (= *Zentrifuge*) centrifuge; (*für Honig*) extractor; (= *Wäscheschleuder*) spin-dryer

Schleudergefahr F (*Mot*) risk of skidding; **„Achtung ~"** "slippery road ahead"

schleudern ['ʃlɔydɐn] **1** VTI **(a)** (= *werfen*) to hurl; **durch die Luft geschleudert werden** to be flung through the air **(b)** (*Tech*) to centrifuge; *Honig* to extract; *Wäsche* to spin-dry; **kalt geschleuderter Honig** cold-pressed honey **2** VI AUX SEIN or HABEN (*Aut*) to skid; **ins Schleudern kommen** *or* **geraten** to go into a skid; (*fig inf*) to run into trouble

Schleuder-: Schleuderpreis M giveaway price; **Schleudersitz** M (*Aviat*) ejector seat; (*fig*) hot seat

schleunigst ['ʃlɔynɪçst] ADV straight away; **verschwinde, aber ~!** beat it, on the double!; **ein Bier, aber ~!** a beer, and make it snappy! (*inf*)

Schleuse ['ʃlɔyzə] F -, -n (*für Schiffe*) lock; (*zur Regulierung des Wasserlaufs, für Abwasser*) sluice; (= *Sicherheitsschleuse*) double door system; **die ~n öffnen** (*fig*) to open the floodgates

schleusen ['ʃlɔyzn] VT *Schiffe* to pass through a lock; *Wasser* to channel; (*langsam*) *Menschen* to filter; *Antrag* to channel; (*fig: heimlich*) *Flüchtlinge* to smuggle

schlich PRET *von* **schleichen**

Schlich [ʃlɪç] M -(e)s, -e USU PL ruse; **alle ~e kennen** to know all the tricks; **jdm auf** *or* **hinter die ~e kommen** to catch on to sb

schlicht [ʃlɪçt] **1** ADJ simple; **~ und einfach** plain and simple **2** ADV **(a)** (= *einfach*) simply **(b)** (= *glattweg*) *gelogen, erfunden* simply; *falsch* just; *vergessen* completely; **das ist ~ und einfach nicht wahr** that's just simply not true

schlichten ['ʃlɪçtn] **1** VT **(a)** *Streit* (= *vermitteln*) to mediate, to arbitrate (*esp Ind*); (= *beilegen*) to settle **(b)** (= *glätten*) to dress; *Holz* to smooth (off) **2** VI to mediate, to arbitrate (*esp Ind*); **zwischen zwei Ländern ~** to mediate between two countries; **er wollte ~d in den Streit eingreifen** he wanted to intervene in the quarrel (to settle it)

Schlichter ['ʃlɪçtɐ] M -s, -, **Schlichterin** [-ərɪn] F -, -nen mediator; (*Ind*) arbitrator

Schlichtheit F -, NO PL simplicity

Schlichtung ['ʃlɪçtʊŋ] F -, -en (= *Vermittlung*) mediation, arbitration (*esp Ind*); (= *Beilegung*) settlement

schlief PRET *von* **schlafen**

Schließe ['ʃliːsə] F -, -n fastening

schließen ['ʃliːsn], *pret* **schloss** [ʃlɔs], *ptp* **geschlossen** [gə'ʃlɔsn] **1** VT **(a)** (= *zumachen, beenden*) to close; (= *verriegeln*) to bolt; (= *Betrieb einstellen*) to close down; *Stromkreis* to close; **eine Lücke ~** (*lit*) to close a gap **(b)** (= *eingehen*) *Vertrag* to conclude; *Frieden* to make; *Bündnis* to enter into; *Freundschaft* to form; **wo wurde Ihre Ehe geschlossen?** where did your marriage take place?; **wer hat Ihre Ehe geschlossen?** who married you? **(c)** (= *befestigen*) **etw an etw** (*acc*) **~** to fasten sth to sth; **daran schloss er eine Bemerkung** he added a remark (to this) **2** VR (= *zugehen*) to close; **daran schließt sich eine Diskussion** this is followed by a discussion **3** VI **(a)** (= *zugehen, enden*) to close; (= *Betrieb einstellen*) to close down; (*Schlüssel*) to fit; **„geschlossen"** "closed" **(b)** (= *schlussfolgern*) to infer; **aus etw auf etw** (*acc*) **~** to infer sth from sth; **auf etw** (*acc*) **~ lassen** to indicate sth; **von sich auf andere ~** to judge others by one's own standards; *siehe auch* **geschlossen**

Schließfach NT locker; (= *Postschließfach*) post office box; (= *Bankschließfach*) safe-deposit box

schließlich ['ʃliːslɪç] ADV (= *endlich*) in the end, eventually; (= *immerhin*) after all; **er kam ~ doch** he came after all; **~ und endlich** at long last

Schließmuskel M (*Anat*) sphincter

Schließung ['ʃliːsʊŋ] F -, -en **(a)** (= *das Schließen*) closing; (= *Betriebseinstellung*) closure **(b)** (= *Beendigung*) (*einer Versammlung*) breaking-up; (*von Debatte etc*) conclusion; (= *Geschäftsschluss*) closing (time); (*Parl*) closure

schliff PRET *von* **schleifen²**

Schliff [ʃlɪf] M -(e)s, -e (*von Glas, von Edelstein*) (*Prozess*) cutting; (*Ergebnis*) cut; (*von Linse*) grinding; (*fig: = Umgangsformen*) polish; **jdm den letzten ~ geben** (*fig*) to perfect sb; **einer Sache den letzten ~ geben** (*fig*) to put the finishing touch(es) to sth

schlimm [ʃlɪm] **1** ADJ bad; *Krankheit, Wunde* nasty; *Nachricht* awful; (= *unartig*) naughty; **es gibt Schlimmere als ihn** there are worse than him; **~, ~!** terrible, terrible!; **~ genug, dass ...** it is/was bad enough that ...; **das finde ich nicht ~** I don't find that so bad; **eine ~e Geschichte** (*inf*) a nasty state of affairs; **eine ~e Zeit** bad times *pl*; **das ist halb so *or* nicht so ~!** that's not so bad!; **zu Anfang war es ~ für ihn** in the beginning he had a hard time of it; **ist es ~** *or* **etwas Schlimmes?** is it bad?; **wenn es nichts Schlimmeres ist!** if that's all it is!; **es gibt Schlimmeres** it could be worse; **im ~sten Fall** if (the) worst comes to (the) worst; **das Schlimmste** the worst **2** ADV *sich benehmen, zurichten* horribly; *zerstören* totally; **er ist ~ dran** (*inf*) he's in a bad way; **wenn es ganz ~ kommt** if things get really bad; **es hätte ~er kommen können** it could have been worse; **umso** *or* **desto ~er** all the worse; **sie haben ~ gehaust** they wreaked havoc; **mit der neuen Frisur siehst du ~ aus** you look awful with that new hairdo; **es steht ~ (um ihn)** things aren't looking too good (for him)

schlimmstenfalls ['ʃlɪmstnfals] ADV at (the) worst

Schlinge ['ʃlɪŋə] F -, -n loop; (*an Galgen*) noose; (*Med*: = *Armbinde*) sling; (= *Falle*) snare

Schlingel ['ʃlɪŋl] M -s, - rascal

schlingen¹ ['ʃlɪŋən], *pret* **schlang** [ʃlaŋ], *ptp* **geschlungen** [gə'ʃlʊŋən] (*geh*) **1** VT (= *binden*) *Knoten* to tie; (= *umbinden*) *Schal etc* to wrap (*um* +*acc* around) **2** VR **sich um etw ~** to coil (itself) around sth

schlingen² *pret* **schlang** [ʃlaŋ], *ptp* **geschlungen** [gə'ʃlʊŋən] VI to gobble

schlingern ['ʃlɪŋɐn] VI (*Schiff*) to roll; (*Auto etc*) to lurch from side to side; **ins Schlingern geraten** (*Auto etc*) to go into a skid; (*fig*) to run into trouble

Schlips [ʃlɪps] M -es, -e tie, necktie (*US*)

Schlitten ['ʃlɪtn] M -s, - **(a)** sledge, sled; (= *Pferdeschlitten*) sleigh; (= *Rodelschlitten*) toboggan; (= *Rennschlitten*) bobsleigh; **mit jdm ~ fahren** (*inf*) to bawl sb out (*inf*) **(b)** (*inf*: = *Auto*) big car

schlittern ['ʃlɪtɐn] VI **(a)** AUX SEIN or HABEN (*absichtlich*) to slide **(b)** AUX SEIN (= *ausrutschen*) to slip; (*Wagen*) to skid; (*fig*) to slide, to stumble; **in den Konkurs/Krieg ~** to slide into bankruptcy/war

Schlittschuh M (ice) skate; **~ laufen** *or* **fahren** (*inf*) to (ice-)skate

Schlittschuh-: Schlittschuhlaufen NT -s, NO PL (ice-)skating; **Schlittschuhläufer(in)** M(F) (ice-)skater; **Schlittschuhschritt** M skating step

Schlitz [ʃlɪts] M -es, -e slit; (= *Einwurfschlitz*) slot; (= *Hosenschlitz*) fly, flies *pl* (*Brit*)

Schlitz-: Schlitzauge NT slant eye; (*pej*: = *Chinese*) Chink (*pej*); **schlitzäugig** **1** ADJ slant-eyed **2** ADV **er grinste ~** he grinned a slant-eyed grin

schlitzen ['ʃlɪtsn] VT to slit

Schlitzohr NT (*fig*) sly fox

schloss PRET *von* **schließen**

Schloss [ʃlɔs] NT -es, ̈er ['ʃlœsə] **(a)** (= *Gebäude*) castle; (= *Palast*) palace; (= *großes Herrschaftshaus*) mansion; (*in Frankreich*) château; **Schlösser und Burgen** castles and stately homes **(b)** (= *Türschloss, Gewehrschloss etc*) lock; (= *Vorhängeschloss*) padlock; (*an Handtasche etc*) clasp; **hinter ~ und Riegel sitzen/bringen** to be/put behind bars

Schlosser ['ʃlɔsɐ] M -s, -, **Schlosserin** [-ərɪn] F -, -nen fitter, metalworker; (*für Schlösser*) locksmith

Schlosserei [ʃlɔsə'rai] F -, -en (= *Werkstatt*) metalworking shop

Schlot [ʃloːt] M -(e)s, -e *or* (*rare*) ̈e (= *Schornstein*) chimney (stack); (*Naut, Rail*) funnel; **rauchen** *or* **qualmen wie ein ~** (*inf*) to smoke like a chimney (*inf*)

schlottern ['ʃlɔtɐn] VI **(a)** (*vor* with) (= *zittern*) to shiver; (*vor Angst, Erschöpfung*) to tremble; **an allen Gliedern ~** to shake all over; **ihm schlotterten die Knie** his knees were knocking **(b)** (*Kleider*) to hang loose

Schlucht [ʃlʊxt] F -, -en gorge

schluchzen ['ʃlʊxtsn] VTI (*lit, fig*) to sob

Schluchzer ['ʃlʊxtsɐ] M -s, - sob

Schluck [ʃlʊk] M -(e)s, -e *or* (*rare*) ̈e ['ʃlʏkə] drink; (= *ein bisschen*) drop; (= *das Schlucken*) swallow; (*großer*) gulp; (*kleiner*) sip; **der erste ~ war mir ungewohnt** the first mouthful tasted strange; **er stürzte das Bier in einem ~ herunter** he downed the beer in one go; **einen ~ aus der Flasche/dem Glas nehmen** to take a drink from the bottle/the glass

Schluckauf ['ʃlʊkauf] M -s, NO PL hiccups *pl*; **einen/den ~ haben** to have (the) hiccups

schlucken [ˈʃlʊkn̩] **1** VT **(a)** (= *hinunterschlucken*) to swallow; (*hastig*) to gulp down; **Alkohol ~** (*sl*) to booze (*inf*); **Pillen ~** (*sl*) to pop pills (*inf*)
(b) (*Comm inf*: = *absorbieren*) to swallow up; *Benzin, Öl* to guzzle
(c) (*inf*: = *hinnehmen, glauben*) to swallow
2 VI to swallow; (*hastig*) to gulp; **da musste ich erst mal (trocken** *or* **dreimal) ~** (*inf*) I had to take a deep breath; **daran hatte er schwer zu ~** (*fig*) he found that difficult to swallow
Schlucker [ˈʃlʊkɐ] M **-s, -** (*inf*) **armer ~** poor devil
Schluck-: Schluckimpfung F oral vaccination; **Schluckspecht** M (*dated inf*) boozer (*inf*)
schluderig [ˈʃluːdərɪç] (*inf*) **1** ADJ *Arbeit* sloppy **2** ADV sloppily
schludern [ˈʃluːdɐn] (*inf*) **1** VT to skimp; **das ist geschludert!** this is a sloppy piece of work! **2** VI to do sloppy work
schludrig [ˈʃluːdrɪç] ADJ, ADV (*inf*) **= schluderig**
Schludrigkeit F **-, -en** (*inf*) sloppiness
schlug PRET *von* **schlagen**
schlummern [ˈʃlʊmɐn] VI (*geh*) to slumber (*liter*)
Schlummertaste F (*an Radiowecker*) snooze button
Schlund [ʃlʊnt] M **-(e)s, ⁼e** [ˈʃlʏndə] (*Anat*) pharynx; (*fig liter*) maw (*liter*)
Schlupf [ʃlʊpf] M **-(e)s**, NO PL slip
schlüpfen [ˈʃlʏpfn̩] VI AUX SEIN to slip; (*Küken*) to hatch (out)
Schlüpfer [ˈʃlʏpfɐ] M **-s, -** panties *pl*, knickers *pl* (*Brit*)
Schlupfloch NT hole, gap; (= *Versteck*) hideout; (*fig*) loophole; **ein ~ stopfen** (*fig*) to close a loophole
schlüpfrig [ˈʃlʏpfrɪç] ADJ **(a)** slippery **(b)** (*fig*) *Bemerkung* suggestive
schlurfen [ˈʃlʊrfn̩] VI AUX SEIN to shuffle
schlürfen [ˈʃlʏrfn̩] **1** VT to slurp; (*mit Genuss*) to savour (*Brit*), to savor (*US*) **2** VI to slurp
Schluss [ʃlʊs] M **-es, ⁼e** [ˈʃlʏsə] **(a)** NO PL (= *Ende*) end; **~! that'll do!; ~ damit!** stop it!; **... und damit ~!** ... and that's that!; **nun ist aber ~!, ~ jetzt!** that's enough now!; **dann ist ~** that'll be it; **~ folgt** to be concluded; **am/zum ~ des Jahres** at the end of the year; **zum ~ sangen wir ...** at the end we sang ...; **zum ~ hat sies dann doch erlaubt** finally *or* in the end she allowed it after all; **bis zum ~ bleiben** to stay to the end; **zum ~ kommen** to conclude; **zum ~ möchte ich noch darauf hinweisen, dass ...** in conclusion I would like to point out that ...; **~ machen** (*inf*) (= *aufhören*) to finish; (= *zumachen*) to close; (= *Selbstmord begehen*) to end it all; (= *Freundschaft beenden*) to break it off; **ich muss ~ machen** (*in Brief*) I'll have to finish off now; (*am Telefon*) I'll have to go now; **mit der Arbeit ~ machen** to stop work
(b) NO PL (= *das Schließen*) closing
(c) (= *Folgerung*) conclusion; **zu dem ~ kommen, dass ...** to come to the conclusion that ...; **aus etw die richtigen/ falschen Schlüsse ziehen** to draw the right/wrong conclusions from sth
(d) (*St Ex*) minimum amount allowed for dealing
Schluss-: Schlussabrechnung F final statement; **Schlussakkord** M final chord; **Schlussdividende** F final dividend
Schlüssel [ˈʃlʏsl̩] M **-s, -** (*lit, fig*) key (*zu* to); (*Tech*) spanner (*Brit*), wrench; (= *Verteilungsschlüssel*) ratio (of distribution); (*Mus*) clef
Schlüssel-: Schlüsselbein NT collarbone; **Schlüsselblume** F cowslip; **Schlüsselbund** M or NT, *pl* **-bunde** bunch of keys; **Schlüsseldienst** M key cutting service; **Schlüsselerlebnis** NT (*Psych*) crucial experience; **Schlüsselindustrie** F key industry; **Schlüsselkind** NT (*inf*) latchkey kid (*inf*); **Schlüsselloch** NT keyhole; **Schlüssellochchirurgie** F keyhole surgery; **Schlüsselposition** F key position
Schluss-: schlussfolgern VI INSEP to conclude; **Schlussfolgerung** F conclusion; **Schlussformel** F (*in Brief*) complimentary close; (*bei Vertrag*) final clause
schlüssig [ˈʃlʏsɪç] **1** ADJ *Beweis* conclusive; *Konzept* logical; **sich** (*dat*) (**über etw** *acc*) **~ sein** to have made up one's mind (about sth) **2** ADV *begründen* conclusively
Schluss-: Schlusskapitel NT concluding chapter; **Schlusskurs** M (*St Ex*) closing prices *pl*; **Schlusslicht** NT tail-light; (*inf: bei Rennen etc*) back marker; **~ der Tabelle/in der Klasse sein** to be bottom of the table/class; **Schlussnotierung** F (*St Ex*) closing quotation; **Schlusspfiff** M final whistle;

Schlussstrich M (*fig*) final stroke; **einen ~ unter etw** (*acc*) **ziehen** to consider sth finished; **Schlussverkauf** M (end-of-season) sale (*Brit*), season close-out sale (*US*)
Schmach [ʃmaːx] F **-**, NO PL (*geh*) disgrace
schmachten [ˈʃmaxtn̩] VI (*geh*) **(a)** (= *leiden*) to languish; **vor Durst ~** to be parched; **vor Hunger ~** to starve; **vor Liebeskummer ~** to pine with love **(b)** (= *sich sehnen*) **nach jdm/etw ~** to pine for sb/sth
schmachtend ADJ *Stimme, Blick* soulful; *Liebhaber* languishing
schmächtig [ˈʃmɛçtɪç] ADJ slight
schmackhaft ADJ (= *wohlschmeckend*) tasty; (= *appetitanregend*) appetizing; **jdm etw ~ machen** (*fig*) to make sth palatable to sb
Schmäh [ʃmɛː] M **-s, -(s)** (*Aus inf*) **(a)** (= *Trick*) con (*inf*); **jdn am ~ halten** to make a fool out of sb **(b)** (= *Scherzhaftigkeit*) jokiness
Schmähbrief M defamatory letter
schmähen [ˈʃmɛːən] VT (*geh*) to abuse
schmählich [ˈʃmɛːlɪç] (*geh*) **1** ADJ ignominious; (= *demütigend*) humiliating **2** ADV shamefully; *versagen* miserably; **~ im Stich gelassen werden** to be left in the lurch in a humiliating way
Schmähung [ˈʃmɛːʊŋ] F **-, -en** (*geh*) abuse; (**gegen jdn**) **~en ausstoßen** to hurl abuse (at sb)
schmal [ʃmaːl] ADJ, *comp* **-er** *or* **⁼er** [ˈʃmɛːlə], *superl* **-ste(r, s)** *or* **⁼ste(r, s)** [ˈʃmɛːlstə], *adv superl* **am -sten** *or* **⁼sten (a)** narrow; *Hüfte, Taille* slender, narrow; *Mensch, Band, Buch* slim; *Gelenke, Lippen* thin; **er ist sehr ~ geworden** he has got (*Brit*) *or* gotten (*US*) very thin
(b) (*fig*: = *karg*) meagre (*Brit*), meager (*US*); **~e Kost** slender fare

Vorsicht! **schmal** *wird nicht mit dem englischen Wort* **small** *übersetzt.*

schmälern [ˈʃmɛːlɐn] VT to diminish
Schmal-: Schmalfilm M cine film (*Brit*), movie film (*US*); **schmalschultrig** ADJ narrow-shouldered; **Schmalseite** F narrow side
Schmalspur F (*Rail*) narrow gauge
Schmalspur- IN CPDS (*Rail*) narrow-gauge; (*pej*) small-time
schmalspurig [-ʃpuːrɪç] **1** ADJ (*Rail*) *Strecke* narrow-gauge; (*fig*) *Fachmann* overspecialized **2** ADV *ausgebildet* narrowly; **der Lehrplan ist sehr ~ angelegt** the curriculum is very narrow
Schmalz¹ [ʃmalts] NT **-es, -e (a)** fat; (= *Schweineschmalz*) lard; (= *Bratenschmalz*) dripping (*Brit*), drippings *pl* (*US*)
(b) (= *Ohrenschmalz*) earwax
Schmalz² M **-es**, NO PL (*pej inf*) schmaltz (*inf*)
schmalzig [ˈʃmaltsɪç] (*pej inf*) **1** ADJ schmaltzy (*inf*) **2** ADV **er singt mir zu ~** his songs are too schmaltzy for me (*inf*); **seine Liebesbriefe sind ziemlich ~ geschrieben** his love letters are pretty schmaltzy (*inf*)
Schmand [ʃmant] M **-(e)s** [-dəs], NO PL sour(ed) cream
Schmankerl [ˈʃmaŋkɐl] NT **-s, -n** (*S Ger, Aus*) **(a)** (= *Speise*) delicacy **(b)** (*fig*) gem
schmarotzen [ʃmaˈrɔtsn̩], *ptp* **schmarotzt** VI to sponge, to scrounge (*bei* off); (*Biol*) to be parasitic (*bei* on)
Schmarotzer¹ [ʃmaˈrɔtsɐ] M **-s, -** (*Biol*) parasite
Schmarotzer² [ʃmaˈrɔtsɐ] M **-s, -**, **Schmarotzerin** [-ərɪn] F **-, -nen** (*fig*) sponger
Schmarren [ˈʃmarən] M **-s, -**, **Schmarrn** [ʃmarn] M **-s, - (a)** (*S Ger, Aus*: *Cook*) pancake cut up into small pieces **(b)** (*inf*: = *Quatsch*) rubbish (*Brit*); **das geht dich einen ~ an!** that's none of your business!
schmatzen [ˈʃmatsn̩] VI (*beim Essen*) to eat noisily, to smack (*US*); (*beim Trinken*) to slurp; **er aß ~d seine Suppe** he slurped his soup
schmecken [ˈʃmɛkn̩] **1** VI (= *Geschmack haben*) to taste (*nach* of); (= *gut ~*) to be good, to taste good; (= *probieren*) to taste; **ihm schmeckt es** (= *gut finden*) he likes it; (= *Appetit haben*) he likes his food; **ihm schmeckt es nicht** (= *keinen Appetit haben*) he's lost his appetite; **das schmeckt ihm nicht** (*lit, fig*) he doesn't like it; **diese Arbeit schmeckt ihm nicht** he has no taste for this work; **nach etw ~** (*fig*) to smack of sth; **das schmeckt nach nichts** it's tasteless; **das schmeckt nach mehr!** (*inf*) it tastes moreish (*Brit hum inf*), it tastes like I want some more; **schmeckt es (Ihnen)?** do you like it?; **das hat**

geschmeckt that was good; **das schmeckt nicht (gut)** it doesn't taste good; **es schmeckt mir ausgezeichnet** it tastes really excellent; **Hauptsache, es schmeckt** (*inf*) the main thing is it tastes nice; **es sich** (*dat*) **~ lassen** to tuck in; **sich** (*dat*) **etw ~ lassen** to tuck into sth **2** VT to taste

Schmeichelei [ʃmaiçə'lai] F **-, -en** flattery

schmeichelhaft ADJ flattering; **wenig ~** not very flattering

schmeicheln ['ʃmaiçln] VI **(a) jdm ~** to flatter sb; **... sagte sie ~d ...** she wheedled **(b)** (= *verschönen*) to flatter; **das Bild ist aber geschmeichelt!** the picture is very flattering

Schmeichler ['ʃmaiçlɐ] M **-s, -**, **Schmeichlerin** [-ərɪn] F **-, -nen** flatterer; (= *Kriecher*) sycophant

schmeichlerisch ['ʃmaiçlərɪʃ] ADJ flattering

schmeißen ['ʃmaisn], *pret* **schmiss** [ʃmɪs], *ptp* **geschmissen** [gə'ʃmɪsn] (*inf*) **1** VT **(a)** (= *werfen*) to sling (*inf*), to chuck (*inf*); **die Tür (ins Schloss) ~** to slam the door **(b)** (*inf*) **eine Runde** *or* **Lage ~** to stand a round; **eine Party ~** to throw a party; **den Laden ~** to run the (whole) show **(c)** (= *aufgeben*) to chuck in (*inf*) **2** VI (= *werfen*) to throw; **mit Steinen ~** to throw stones; **mit etw um sich ~** to throw sth about, to chuck sth around (*inf*); **mit Fremdwörtern um sich ~** to bandy foreign words about **3** VR **sich auf etw** (*acc*) **~** to throw oneself into sth; **sich jdm an den Hals ~** (*fig*) to throw oneself at sb

Schmeißfliege F bluebottle

Schmelze ['ʃmɛltsə] F **-, -n (a)** (*Metal, Geol*) melt **(b)** (= *Schmelzen*) melting; (*Metal: von Erz*) smelting **(c)** (= *Schmelzhütte*) smelting plant

schmelzen ['ʃmɛltsn], *pret* **schmolz** [ʃmɔlts], *ptp* **geschmolzen** [gə'ʃmɔltsn] **1** VI AUX SEIN (*lit, fig*) to melt; (*Reaktorkern*) to melt down **2** VT *Metall, Fett, Schnee* to melt; *Erz* to smelt

Schmelz-: Schmelzkäse M cheese spread; **Schmelzofen** M melting furnace; (*für Erze*) smelting furnace; **Schmelzpunkt** M melting point; **Schmelztiegel** M (*lit, fig*) melting pot; **Schmelzwasser** NT, *pl* **-wasser** melted snow and ice; (*Geog, Phys*) meltwater

Schmerz [ʃmɛrts] M **-es, -en** pain *pl rare*; (= *Kummer auch*) grief *no pl*; **ihre ~en** her pain; **dumpfer ~** ache; **~en haben** to be in pain; **~en in der Nierengegend haben** to have a pain in the kidneys; **~en in den Ohren haben** to have (an (*US*)) earache; **~en im Hals haben** to have a sore throat; **wo haben Sie ~en?** where does it hurt?; **wenn der Patient wieder ~en bekommt ...** if the patient starts feeling pain again ...; **jdm ~en bereiten** to cause sb pain; **mit ~en** (*fig*) regretfully; **jdn/etw mit ~en erwarten** to wait impatiently for sb/sth; **unter ~en** while in pain; (*fig*) regretfully

Schmerz-: schmerzbetäubend ADJ pain-killing; **schmerzempfindlich** ADJ *Mensch* sensitive to pain; *Wunde, Körperteil* sensitive, tender

schmerzen ['ʃmɛrtsn] (*geh*) VTI (*geh*) to hurt; **es schmerzt** (*lit, fig*) it hurts; **eine ~de Stelle** a painful spot

-schmerzen PL SUF IN CPDS **-ache**; **Bauch-/Kopfschmerzen haben** to have stomach ache/a headache; **Herzschmerzen haben** to have pains in the chest; **ich habe Halsschmerzen** I have a sore throat

Schmerzensgeld NT (*Jur*) damages *pl*

Schmerz-: schmerzfrei ADJ free of pain; *Operation* painless; **Schmerzgrenze** F (*lit, fig*) pain barrier; **schmerzhaft** ADJ (*lit, fig*) painful; **Schmerzkranke(r)** MF DECL AS ADJ *person suffering from chronic pains*; **schmerzlindernd** ADJ pain-relieving, analgesic (*Med*); **schmerzlos** ADJ (*lit, fig*) painless; **~er** less painful; **Schmerzmittel** NT painkiller; **schmerzstillend** ADJ pain-killing, analgesic (*Med*); **~es Mittel** painkiller; **Schmerztablette** F painkiller; **schmerzunempfindlich** ADJ insensitive to pain; **schmerzverzerrt** [-fɛɐtsɛrt] ADJ *Gesicht* distorted with pain; **mit ~em Gesicht** his/her face twisted with pain; **schmerzvoll** ADJ (*fig*) painful

Schmetterball M smash

Schmetterling ['ʃmɛtɐlɪŋ] M **-s, -e** (*Zool, inf: Schwimmart*) butterfly; **kannst du ~ schwimmen?** can you do the butterfly?

schmettern ['ʃmɛtɐn] **1** VT **(a)** (= *schleudern*) to smash; *Tür* to slam; (*Sport*) *Ball* to smash; **etw in Stücke ~** to smash sth to pieces **(b)** *Lied, Arie* to bellow out; (*Vogel*) to sing **2** VI **(a)** (*Sport*) to hit a smash (*esp Brit*) **(b)** (*Trompete etc*) to blare (out); (*Sänger*) to bellow

Schmied [ʃmiːt] M **-(e)s, -e** [-də], **Schmiedin** ['ʃmiːdɪn] F **-, -nen** (black)smith

Schmiede ['ʃmiːdə] F **-, -n** forge

Schmiede-: Schmiedeeisen NT wrought iron; **schmiedeeisern** ADJ wrought-iron

schmieden ['ʃmiːdn] VT (*lit, fig*) to forge (*zu* into); (= *ersinnen*) *Plan, Komplott* to hatch; (*hum*) *Verse* to concoct; **geschmiedet sein** (*Gartentür etc*) to be made of wrought iron

Schmiedin ['ʃmiːdɪn] F **-, -nen** (black)smith

schmiegen ['ʃmiːgn] **1** VR **sich an jdn ~** to cuddle up to sb; **sich an/in etw** (*acc*) **~** to nestle into sth; **sich um etw ~** to hang gracefully on sth; (*Haare*) to fall gracefully (a)round sth **2** VT **etw an/in etw** (*acc*) **~** to nestle sth into sth; **etw um etw ~** to wrap sth around sth

schmiegsam ['ʃmiːkzaːm] ADJ supple; *Stoff* soft; (*fig*: = *anpassungsfähig*) adaptable

Schmiere ['ʃmiːrə] F **-, -n (a)** (*inf*) grease; (= *Salbe*) ointment; (= *feuchter Schmutz*) mud; (= *Aufstrich*) spread **(b)** (*inf*) **~ stehen** to be the look-out

schmieren ['ʃmiːrən] **1** VT **(a)** (= *streichen*) to smear; *Butter, Aufstrich* to spread; *Brot* (*mit Butter*) to butter; *Salbe, Make-up* to rub in (*in +acc* -to); (= *einfetten, ölen*) to grease; (*Tech*) to lubricate; **sie schmierte sich ein Brot** she made herself a sandwich; **es geht** *or* **läuft wie geschmiert** it's going like clockwork; **jdm eine ~** (*inf*) to smack sb one (*inf*) **(b)** (*pej*: = *schreiben*) to scrawl; (= *malen*) to daub **(c)** (*inf*: = *bestechen*) **jdn ~** to grease sb's palm (*inf*) **2** VI **(a)** (*pej*: = *schreiben*) to scrawl; (= *malen*) to daub **(b)** (*Stift, Radiergummi, Scheibenwischer*) to smear

Schmiererei [ʃmiːrə'rai] F **-, -en** (*pej*) (= *Geschriebenes*) scrawl; (= *Parolen etc*) graffiti *pl*; (= *Malerei*) daubing

Schmier-: Schmierfett NT (lubricating) grease; **Schmierfink** M (*pej*) **(a)** (= *Autor, Journalist*) hack; (= *Skandaljournalist*) muckraker (*inf*) **(b)** (= *Schüler*) messy writer; **Schmiergeld** NT bribe; **Schmierheft** NT notebook

schmierig ['ʃmiːrɪç] ADJ greasy; (*fig*) (= *unanständig*) filthy; (= *schleimig*) smarmy (*Brit inf*)

Schmier-: Schmiermittel NT lubricant; **Schmieröl** NT lubricating oil; **Schmierpapier** NT jotting paper (*Brit*), scratch paper (*US*); **Schmierseife** F soft soap

schmilzt [ʃmɪltst] 3. PERS SING PRES *von* **schmelzen**

Schminke ['ʃmɪŋkə] F **-, -n** make-up

schminken ['ʃmɪŋkn] **1** VT to make up; **sich** (*dat*) **die Lippen/Augen ~** to put on lipstick/eye make-up **2** VR to put on make-up; **sich stark ~** to wear a lot of make-up

schmirgeln ['ʃmɪrgln] VTI to sand

Schmirgel-: Schmirgelpapier NT sandpaper; **Schmirgelscheibe** F sanding disc

schmiss PRET *von* **schmeißen**

Schmöker ['ʃmøːkɐ] M **-s, -** book (*usu of light literature*); (*dick*) tome

schmökern ['ʃmøːkɐn] (*inf*) **1** VI to bury oneself in a book/magazine *etc*; (= *in Büchern blättern*) to browse **2** VT to bury oneself in

schmollen ['ʃmɔlən] VI to pout; (= *gekränkt sein*) to sulk; **mit jdm ~** to be annoyed with sb

schmolz PRET *von* **schmelzen**

Schmorbraten M pot roast

schmoren ['ʃmoːrən] **1** VT to braise; **geschmorte Kalbshaxe** braised knuckle of veal **2** VI (*Cook*) to braise; (*inf*: = *schwitzen*) to roast; **jdn (im eigenen Saft** *or* **Fett) ~ lassen** to leave sb to stew (in his/her own juice); **in der Hölle ~** to roast in hell

Schmu [ʃmuː] M **-s**, NO PL (*inf*) cheating; **das ist ~!** that's cheating!; **~ machen** to cheat

Schmuck [ʃmʊk] M **-(e)s**, (*rare*) **-e (a)** (= *~stücke*) jewellery (*Brit*) *no pl*, jewelry (*US*) *no pl* **(b)** (= *Verzierung*) decoration; (*fig*) embellishment; **der ~ am Christbaum** the decorations on the Christmas tree

schmücken ['ʃmʏkn] **1** VT to decorate; *Rede* to embellish; **die mit Blumenkränzen geschmückten Tänzerinnen** the dancers adorned with garlands of flowers; **mit Juwelen geschmückt** bejewelled (*Brit*), bejeweled (*US*); **~des Beiwerk** embellishment **2** VR (*zum Fest etc*) (*Mensch*) to adorn oneself; (*Stadt*) to be decorated; **sich mit etw ~** (*lit, fig*) to adorn oneself with sth; **sich mit Blumenkränzen ~** to garland oneself with flowers

Schmuck-: **Schmuckgegenstand** M ornament; (= *Ring etc*) piece of jewellery (*Brit*) *or* jewelry (*US*); **schmucklos** ADJ plain; *Fassade* unadorned; *Einrichtung, Stil, Prosa* simple; **Schmucklosigkeit** F -, NO PL plainness; (*von Einrichtung, Stil, Prosa*) simplicity; **Schmuckstück** NT (= *Ring etc*) piece of jewellery; (= *Schmuckgegenstand*) ornament; (*fig*: = *Prachtstück*) gem; (*fig inf*: = *Frau*) better half (*hum inf*)

schmuddelig [ˈʃmʊdəlɪç] ADJ messy; (= *schmierig, unsauber*) filthy; (= *schlampig*) sloppy

Schmuggel [ˈʃmʊgl] M -s, NO PL smuggling; (= *einzelne ~operation*) smuggling operation; **~ treiben** to smuggle; **der ~ von Heroin** heroin smuggling

Schmuggelei [ʃmʊgəˈlai] F -, -en smuggling *no pl*

schmuggeln [ˈʃmʊgln] VTI (*lit, fig*) to smuggle; **mit etw ~** to smuggle sth

Schmuggeln NT -s, NO PL smuggling

Schmuggelware F smuggled goods *pl*

Schmuggler [ˈʃmʊglɐ] M -s, -, **Schmugglerin** [-ərɪn] F -, -nen smuggler; **~ von Rauschgift** drug smuggler; **~ von Waffen** arms smuggler

schmunzeln [ˈʃmʊntsln] VI to smile

Schmunzeln NT -s, NO PL smile

Schmusekurs M (*inf*) friendly overtures *pl*; **mit jdm auf ~ gehen** to cosy up to sb; **der ~ zwischen SPD und Unternehmern** the friendly noises between the SPD and the employers; **sich mit jdm auf ~ begeben** to try to ingratiate oneself with sb

schmusen [ˈʃmuːzn] VI (*inf*) (= *zärtlich sein*) to cuddle; **mit jdm ~** to cuddle sb

schmusig [ˈʃmuːzɪç] ADJ (*inf*) smoochy (*inf*)

Schmutz [ʃmʊts] M -es, NO PL (a) dirt; **die Handwerker haben viel ~ gemacht** the workmen have made a lot of mess; **sie leben in ~** they live in real squalor; **der Stoff nimmt leicht ~ an** the material dirties easily (b) (*fig*) filth; **~ und Schund** offensive material; **jdn/etw in den ~ ziehen** *or* **zerren** to drag sb/sth through the mud

schmutzen [ˈʃmʊtsn] VI to get dirty

Schmutz-: **Schmutzfink** M (*inf*) (= *unsauberer Mensch*) dirty slob (*inf*); (= *Kind*) mucky pup (*Brit inf*), messy thing (*esp US inf*); (*fig*) (= *Mann*) dirty old man; (= *Journalist*) muckraker (*inf*); **Schmutzfleck** M dirty mark; **Schmutzfracht** F dirty cargo

schmutzig [ˈʃmʊtsɪç] ADJ dirty; **sich ~ machen** to get oneself dirty

Schnabel [ˈʃnaːbl] M -s, ¨ [ˈʃnɛːbl] (a) (= *Vogelschnabel*) beak, bill (b) (*von Kanne*) spout; (*von Krug*) lip (c) (*inf*: = *Mund*) mouth; **halt den ~!** shut your mouth! (*inf*); **reden, wie einem der ~ gewachsen ist** to say exactly what comes into one's head; (*unaffektiert*) to talk naturally

Schnack [ʃnak] M -(e)s, -s (*N Ger*) (*inf*) (= *Unterhaltung*) chat; (= *Ausspruch*) silly phrase; **das ist ein dummer ~** that's a silly phrase

schnacken [ˈʃnakn] VI (*N Ger*) to chat

Schnake [ˈʃnaːkə] F -, -n (a) (*inf*: = *Stechmücke*) gnat, midge (*Brit*) (b) (= *Weberknecht*) daddy-longlegs

Schnalle [ˈʃnalə] F -, -n (a) (= *Schuhschnalle, Gürtelschnalle*) buckle (b) (*an Handtasche, Buch*) clasp (c) (*Aus, S Ger*: = *Türklinke*) handle (d) (*sl*: = *Frau, Mädchen*) bird (*esp Brit inf*), chick (*esp US inf*) (e) (*vulg*: = *Vagina*) fanny (*sl*)

schnallen [ˈʃnalən] VT (a) (= *befestigen*) to strap; *Gürtel* to fasten (b) (*inf*: = *begreifen*) **etw ~** to catch on to sth

Schnäppchen [ˈʃnɛpçən] NT -s, - bargain; **ein ~ machen** to get a bargain

schnappen [ˈʃnapn] VI (a) **nach jdm/etw ~** to snap at sb/sth; (= *greifen*) to snatch at sb/sth (b) AUX SEIN (= *sich bewegen*) to spring up; **die Tür schnappt ins Schloss** the door clicks shut VT (*inf*) (a) (= *ergreifen*) to grab; **sich** (*dat*) **jdn/etw ~** to grab sb/sth (*inf*) (b) (= *fangen*) to catch

Schnapp-: **Schnappschloss** NT (*an Tür*) spring lock; (*an Schmuck*) spring clasp; **Schnappschuss** M (= *Foto*) snap(shot)

Schnaps [ʃnaps] M -es, ¨e [ˈʃnɛpsə] (= *klarer ~*) schnapps; (*inf*) (= *Branntwein*) spirits *pl*; (= *Alkohol*) drink

Schnaps-: **Schnapsbrenner(in)** M(F) distiller; **Schnapsbrennerei** F (a) (*Gebäude*) distillery (b) NO PL (= *das*

Brennen) distilling of spirits *or* liquor; **Schnapsidee** F (*inf*) crazy idea; **Schnapszahl** F (*inf*) *multidigit number with all digits identical*

schnarchen [ˈʃnarçn] VI to snore

schnattern [ˈʃnatɐn] VI (*Gans*) to gabble; (*Ente*) to quack; (*Affen*) to chatter; (*inf*: = *schwatzen*) to natter (*inf*); **sie schnattert vor Kälte** her teeth are chattering with (the) cold

schnauben [ˈʃnaubn], *pret* **schnaubte** *or* (*old*) **schnob** [ʃnauptə, ʃnoːp], *ptp* **geschnaubt** *or* (*old*) **geschnoben** [gəˈʃnaupt, gəˈʃnoːbn] VI (a) (*Tier*) to snort (b) (= *fauchen*) to snort; **vor Wut/Entrüstung ~** to snort with rage/indignation VT (a) (= *schnäuzen*) **sich** (*dat*) **die Nase ~** to blow one's nose (b) (= *fauchen*) to snort

schnaufen [ˈʃnaufn] VI (a) (= *schwer atmen*) to wheeze; (= *keuchen*) to puff; (*fig*) (*Lokomotive*) to puff; (*inf*: *Auto*) to struggle (b) (*esp S Ger*: = *atmen*) to breathe

Schnauferl [ˈʃnaufɐl] NT -s, - *or* (*Aus*) -n (*hum*: = *Oldtimer*) veteran car

Schnauzbart M walrus moustache (*Brit*) *or* mustache (*US*)

Schnauze [ˈʃnautsə] F -, -n (a) (*von Tier*) snout; **eine feuchte ~ haben** to have a wet nose; **mit einer Maus in der ~** with a mouse in its mouth (b) (= *Ausguss*) (*an Kaffeekanne etc*) spout; (*an Krug etc*) lip (c) (*inf*) (= *Mund*) gob (*Brit inf*), trap (*inf*); (= *respektlose Art zu reden*) bluntness; (**halt die**) **~!** shut your trap! (*inf*); **auf die ~ fallen** (*lit*) to fall flat on one's face; (*fig auch*) to come a cropper (*Brit inf*); **jdm die ~ einschlagen** *or* **polieren** to smash sb's face in (*sl*); **die ~ (von jdm/etw) (gestrichen) voll haben** to be fed up (to the back teeth) (with sb/sth) (*inf*); **eine große ~ haben** to have a big mouth; **die ~ halten** to hold one's tongue; **etw frei nach ~ machen** to do sth any old (*Brit*) *or* ole (*US*) how (*inf*); **Berliner ~** endearing Berlin bluntness

schnauzen [ˈʃnautsn] VI (*inf*) to shout; (= *jdn anfahren*) to snap

schnäuzen [ˈʃnɔytsn] VR to blow one's nose VT **einem Kind/sich die Nase ~** to blow a child's/one's nose

Schnauzer [ˈʃnautsɐ] M -s, - (a) (= *Hundeart*) schnauzer (b) (*inf*: = *Schnauzbart*) walrus moustache (*Brit*) *or* mustache (*US*)

Schnecke [ˈʃnɛka] F -, -n (a) (*Zool*) (*fig*) snail; (= *Nacktschnecke*) slug; (*Cook*) escargot; **jdn zur ~ machen** (*inf*) to bawl sb out (*inf*) (b) (*Archit*: *an Säule*) volute (c) (*Tech*) (= *Schraube*) worm; (= *Förderschnecke*) screw conveyor (d) (*Cook*: *Gebäck*) ≈ Chelsea bun

Schnecken-: **Schneckengehäuse** NT, **Schneckenhaus** NT snail shell; **sich in sein Schneckenhaus zurückziehen** (*fig inf*) to retreat into one's shell; **Schneckenpost** F (*inf*) snail mail (*inf*); **Schneckentempo** NT (*inf*) **im ~** at a snail's pace

Schnee [ʃneː] M -s, NO PL (a) (*auch TV*) snow; **im Jahre ~** (*Aus*) ages ago; **das ist ~ von gestern** (*inf*) that's old hat (b) (= *Eischnee*) whisked egg white; **Eiweiß zu ~ schlagen** to whisk the egg white(s) till stiff (c) (*inf*: = *Heroin, Kokain*) snow (*sl*)

Schneeball M snowball; (*Bot*) guelder rose

Schneeball-: **Schneeballprinzip** NT snowball effect; **Schneeballschlacht** F snowball fight; **eine ~ machen** to have a snowball fight; **Schneeballsystem** NT accumulative process; (*Comm*) pyramid selling; **das vermehrt sich nach dem ~** it snowballs

Schnee-: **schneebedeckt** ADJ snow-covered; **Schneebesen** M (*Cook*) whisk; **schneeblind** ADJ snow-blind; **Schneebrett** NT windslab (*Brit*), snow/ice slab (*US*); **Schneebrettgefahr** F danger of windslab (*Brit*) *or* snow/ice slab (*US*) avalanches; **Schneebrille** F snow goggles *pl*; **Schneedecke** F blanket *or* (*Met*) covering of snow; **Schneeflocke** F snowflake; **Schneefräse** F snow blower; **schneefrei** ADJ *Gebiet, Bergpass* free of snow; **in der ~en Zeit** when there is no snow; **Schneegans** F snow goose; **Schneegestöber** NT (*leicht*) snow flurry; (*stark*) snowstorm; **Schneeglätte** F hard-packed snow *no pl*; **Schneeglöckchen** NT snowdrop; **Schneegrenze** F snow line; **Schneekanone** F snow cannon; **Schneekette** F (*Aut*) snow chain; **Schneemann** M, *pl* **-männer** snowman; **Schneematsch** M slush; **Schneemensch** M abominable snowman; **Schneemobil** [-mobiːl] NT -s, -e snowmobile; **Schneepflug** M (*Tech, Ski*) snowplough (*Brit*), snowplow (*US*); **Schneeregen** M sleet; **Schneeschaufel** F, **Schneeschippe** F snow shovel, snowpusher (*US*); **Schneeschmelze** F thaw; **Schneeschuh** M snowshoe; (*dated Ski*) ski; **Schneesturm** M snowstorm; (*stärker*) blizzard; **Schneetreiben** NT driving

snow; **Schneeverhältnisse** PL snow conditions *pl*;
Schneeverwehung F snowdrift; **Schneewächte** [-vɛçtə] F -, -n
snow cornice; **Schneewehe** F snowdrift; **schneeweiß** ADJ
snow-white; *Haare* snowy-white; *Hände* lily-white; *Gewissen*
clear; **Schneeweißchen** ['-vaisçən] NT -s, NO PL,
Schneewittchen ['-vɪtçən] NT -s, NO PL Snow White

Schneid [ʃnait] M -(e)s [-dəs] (*S Ger, Aus*) *f* -, NO PL (*inf*) guts *pl*
(*inf*); ~/keinen ~ haben to have/not to have guts (*inf*); den ~
verlieren to lose one's nerve; jdm den ~ abkaufen (*fig*) to
knock the stuffing out of sb (*inf*)

Schneidbrenner M (*Tech*) cutting torch

Schneide ['ʃnaidə] F -, -n (sharp *or* cutting) edge; (*von Messer,
Schwert*) blade

schneiden ['ʃnaidn], *pret* **schnitt** [ʃnɪt], *ptp* **geschnitten** [gə'ʃnɪtn]
1 VI to cut; (*Med*) to operate; (*bei Geburt*) to do an
episiotomy
2 VT (a) *Papier etc, Haare, Hecke* to cut; *Getreide* to mow;
(= *klein ~*) *Schnittlauch, Gemüse etc* to chop; (*Sport*) *Ball* to
slice; (= *schnitzen*) *Namen, Figuren* to carve; (*Math*) to
intersect with; (*Weg*) to cross; eine Kurve ~ to cut a corner;
jdn ~ (*beim Überholen*) to cut in on sb; (= *ignorieren*) to cut sb
dead (*Brit*) *or* off; sein schön/scharf geschnittenes Gesicht his
clean-cut/sharp features; Gesichter *or* Grimassen ~ to make
faces; weit/eng geschnitten sein (*Sew*) to be cut wide/narrow
(b) *Film, Tonband* to edit
(c) (*fig*: = *meiden*) to cut
3 VR (a) (*Mensch*) to cut oneself; sich in den Finger ~ to cut
one's finger
(b) (*inf*: = *sich täuschen*) da hat er sich aber geschnitten! he's
made a big mistake
(c) (*Linien, Straßen etc*) to intersect

schneidend ADJ biting; *Schmerz* sharp; *Stimme, Ton* piercing

Schneider¹ ['ʃnaidɐ] M -s, - (*Gerät*) cutter; (*inf: für Brot etc*)
slicer; aus dem ~ sein (*fig*) to be out of the woods

Schneider² ['ʃnaidɐ] M -s, -, **Schneiderin** ['ʃnaidərɪn] F -, -nen
tailor; (= *Damenschneider auch*) dressmaker

Schneiderei [ʃnaidə'rai] F -, -en (= *Werkstatt*) tailor's/
dressmaker's

schneidern ['ʃnaidɐn] **1** VI (*beruflich*) to be a tailor;
(*Damenschneider*) to be a dressmaker; (*als Hobby*) to do
dressmaking **2** VT to make; *Anzug, Kostüm* to tailor, to make;
(*fig*) *Plan, Programm* to draw up; jdm (wie) auf den Leib
geschneidert sein (*fig*) to be tailor-made for sb

Schneidersitz M im ~ sitzen to sit cross-legged

Schneidezahn M incisor

schneien ['ʃnaian] **1** VI IMPERS to snow **2** VT IMPERS es schneit
dicke Flocken big flakes (of snow) are falling; es schneite
Konfetti confetti rained down **3** VI AUX SEIN (*fig*) to rain
down; jdm ins Haus ~ (*Besuch*) to drop in on sb;
(*Rechnung, Brief*) to arrive in the post

Schneise ['ʃnaizə] F -, -n break; (= *Waldschneise*) lane;
(= *Feuerschneise*) firebreak; (= *Flugschneise*) path; eine ~
schlagen (*lit*) to cut a lane

schnell [ʃnɛl] **1** ADJ quick; *Auto, Zug, Verkehr, Fahrer, Strecke*
fast; *Abreise, Bote, Hilfe* speedy; er ist sehr ~ mit seinem Urteil/
seiner Kritik he's very quick to judge/to criticize; ~es Geld
(machen) (*inf*) (to make) a fast buck (*inf*)
2 ADV (= *mit hoher Geschwindigkeit*) quickly; *arbeiten, handeln,
durchführen, erwärmen* fast; ~er als der Schall fliegen to fly
faster than the speed of sound; wie ~ ist er die 100 Meter
gelaufen? how fast did he run the 100 metres (*Brit*) *or* meters
(*US*)?; geh ~er! hurry up!; nicht so ~! not so fast!; sein Puls
ging ~ his pulse was very fast; das geht ~ (*grundsätzlich*) it
doesn't take long; das mache ich gleich, das geht ~ I'll do
that now, it won't take long; das ging ~ that was quick; mach
~/-er! hurry up!; es ist mit dem Patienten ~ gegangen it was
all over quickly; an der Grenze ist es ~ gegangen things went
very quickly at the border; das ging alles viel zu ~ it all
happened much too quickly *or* fast; das werden wir ~ erledigt
haben we'll soon have that finished; das werden wir ~ sehen
(= *bald*) we'll soon see about that; das sagt sich so ~ that's
easy to say; sie wird ~ böse, sie ist ~ verärgert she loses her
temper quickly; das werde ich so ~ nicht vergessen/wieder
tun I won't forget that/do that again in a hurry; diese
dünnen Gläser gehen ~ kaputt these thin glasses break easily;
ich gehe noch ~ beim Bäcker vorbei I'll just stop by at the
baker's; kannst du das vorher noch ~ machen? (*inf*) can you

do that quickly first?; ich muss mir nur noch ~ die Haare
kämmen I must just give my hair a quick comb

Schnell-: **Schnellboot** NT speedboat; **Schnelldienst** M express
service

Schnelle ['ʃnɛlə] F -, -n (a) NO PL (= *Schnelligkeit*) speed; etw auf
die ~ machen to do sth quickly *or* in a rush; das lässt sich
nicht auf die ~ machen that will take time
(b) (= *Stromschnelle*) rapids *pl*

schnellebig ADJ *siehe* **schnelllebig**

Schnell-: **Schnellgaststätte** F fast-food restaurant, fast-food
store (*US*); **Schnellhefter** M spring folder

Schnelligkeit ['ʃnɛlɪçkait] F -, -en speed; (*von Puls*) rapidity;
(*von Bote, Hilfe*) speediness; (*von Antwort*) promptness

Schnell-: **Schnellimbiss** M (a) (*Essen*) (quick) snack
(b) (*Raum*) snack bar; **Schnellkochplatte** F high-speed ring;
Schnellkochtopf M (= *Dampfkochtopf*) pressure cooker;
(= *Wasserkochtopf*) ≈ electric kettle; **Schnellkurs** M crash
course; **schnelllebig** [-le:bɪç] ADJ *Zeit, Geschäft, Markt* fast-
moving; **Schnellrücklauf** M fast rewind

schnellstens ['ʃnɛlstns] ADV as quickly as possible

Schnell-: **Schnellstraße** F expressway; **Schnellsuchlauf** M
rapid search; **Schnellvorlauf** M fast forward; **Schnellzug** M
fast train

Schnepfe ['ʃnɛpfə] F -, -n snipe; (*pej inf*) silly cow (*inf*)

schneuzen ['ʃnɔytsn] VTR *siehe* **schnäuzen**

Schnickschnack ['ʃnɪkʃnak] M -s, NO PL (*inf*) (= *Unsinn*) twaddle
(*inf*) *no indef art*; (= *Kinkerlitzchen*) paraphernalia (*inf*) *no indef
art*

schniefen ['ʃni:fn] VI (*dial*) (*bei Schnupfen*) to sniff(le); (*beim
Weinen*) to sniffle

Schnippchen ['ʃnɪpçən] NT -s, - (*inf*) jdm ein ~ schlagen to play
a trick on sb; dem Tod ein ~ schlagen to cheat death

schnippeln ['ʃnɪpln] (*inf*) **1** VI to snip (*an +dat* at); (*mit Messer*)
to hack (*an +dat* at) **2** VT to snip; (*mit Messer*) to hack;
Gemüse to chop up

schnippen ['ʃnɪpn] **1** VI mit den Fingern ~ to snap one's
fingers **2** VT etw (von etw) ~ to flick sth (off *or* from sth)

schnippisch ['ʃnɪpɪʃ] **1** ADJ saucy **2** ADV saucily

Schnipsel ['ʃnɪpsl] M *or* NT -s, - (*inf*) scrap; (= *Papierschnipsel*)
scrap of paper

schnitt PRET *von* **schneiden**

Schnitt [ʃnɪt] M -(e)s, -e (a) cut; (*von Gesicht, Augen*) shape;
(*von Profil*) line; (= *Kerbe*) notch; (*Med*) incision; (*von Heu,
Getreide*) crop; (= *~muster*) pattern
(b) (*Film*) editing *no pl*; der Film ist jetzt beim ~ the film is
now being edited
(c) (*Math*) (= *~punkt*) (point of) intersection; (= *~fläche*)
section; (*inf*: = *Durchschnitt*) average; im ~ on average; unter/
über dem ~ below/above average
(d) (*inf*: = *Gewinn*) profit

Schnittblumen PL cut flowers *pl*; (*im Garten*) flowers *pl*
(suitable) for cutting

Schnitte ['ʃnɪtə] F -, -n (a) slice; (*belegt*) open sandwich;
(*zusammenklappt*) sandwich (b) (*sl*: = *Frau, Mädchen*) bird
(*esp Brit inf*), chick (*esp US inf*)

schnittig ['ʃnɪtɪç] **1** ADJ smart **2** ADV er ist ganz schön ~
gefahren he zipped along (*inf*)

Schnitt-: **Schnittlauch** M, NO PL chives *pl*; **Schnittmuster** NT
(*Sew*) (paper) pattern; **Schnittpunkt** M (*von Straßen*)
intersection; (*Math auch*) point of intersection; (*fig*)
interface; **Schnittstelle** F cut; (*Comput, fig*) interface;
Schnittwinkel M angle of intersection; **Schnittwunde** F cut;
(*tief*) gash

Schnitzarbeit F (wood)carving

Schnitzel¹ ['ʃnɪtsl] NT *or* M -s, - (= *Papierschnitzel*) bit of paper;
(= *Holzschnitzel*) shaving

Schnitzel² NT -s, - (*Cook*) veal/pork cutlet

Schnitzeljagd F paper chase

schnitzeln ['ʃnɪtsln] VT *Gemüse* to shred

schnitzen ['ʃnɪtsn] VTI to carve

Schnitzer¹ ['ʃnɪtsɐ] M -s, - (*inf*) (*in Benehmen*) blunder;
(= *Fauxpas*) gaffe; (= *Fehler*) howler (*Brit inf*), blooper (*US inf*)

Schnitzer² ['ʃnɪtsɐ] M -s, -, **Schnitzerin** ['ʃnɪtsərɪn] F -, -nen
woodcarver

Schnitzerei [ʃnɪtsə'rai] F -, -en (wood)carving

schnodderig [ˈʃnɔdərɪç], **schnoddrig** [ˈʃnɔdrɪç] ADJ (inf) Mensch, Bemerkung brash

schnöde [ˈʃnøːdə] **1** ADJ (= niederträchtig) despicable; Geiz, Verrat base; Behandlung, Ton, Antwort contemptuous; **~s Geld** filthy lucre **2** ADV behandeln despicably; **jdn ~ verlassen** to leave sb in a most despicable fashion

Schnorchel [ˈʃnɔrçl] M **-s, -** (von U-Boot, Taucher) snorkel

Schnörkel [ˈʃnœrkl] M **-s, -** flourish; (an Möbeln, Säulen) scroll; (fig: = Unterschrift) squiggle (hum), signature

schnörkelig [ˈʃnœrkəlɪç] ADJ ornate

schnorren [ˈʃnɔrən] VTI (inf) to scrounge (inf) (bei from)

Schnorrer [ˈʃnɔrɐ] M **-s, -**, **Schnorrerin** [-ərɪn] F **-, -nen** (inf) scrounger (inf)

Schnösel [ˈʃnøːzl] M **-s, -** (inf) snotty(-nosed) little upstart (inf)

schnöselig [ˈʃnøːzəlɪç] (inf) **1** ADJ Benehmen, Jugendlicher snotty (inf) **2** ADV sich benehmen snottily

schnüffeln [ˈʃnʏfln] **1** VI (a) to sniff; **an etw** (dat) **~** to sniff (at) sth (b) (fig inf: = spionieren) to snoop around (inf) **2** VT Drogen, Klebstoff to sniff

Schnüffler [ˈʃnʏflɐ] M **-s, -**, **Schnüfflerin** [-ərɪn] F **-, -nen** (inf) (fig) snooper (inf); (= Detektiv) private eye (inf)

Schnuller [ˈʃnʊlɐ] M **-s, -** (inf) dummy (Brit), pacifier (US); (auf Flasche) teat (Brit), nipple (US)

Schnulze [ˈʃnʊltsə] F **-, -n** (inf) schmaltzy film/book/song (inf); **das sind alles ~n** it's all schmaltz (inf)

schnulzig [ˈʃnʊltsɪç] **1** ADJ slushy (inf) **2** ADV schreiben soppily (inf); **er singt so ~** his songs are so schmaltzy (inf)

schnupfen [ˈʃnʊpfn] VTI Kokain to snort; **Tabak ~** to take snuff

Schnupfen [ˈʃnʊpfn] M **-s, -** cold; **(einen) ~ bekommen, sich** (dat) **einen ~ holen** (inf) to catch a cold; **(einen) ~ haben** to have a cold

Schnupftabak M snuff

schnuppe [ˈʃnʊpə] ADJ PRED (inf) **jdm ~ sein** to be all the same to sb; **das Wohl seiner Angestellten ist ihm völlig ~** he couldn't care less about the welfare of his employees (inf)

Schnupper- IN CPDS (inf) trial, taster; **Schnupperkurs** M (inf) taster course

schnuppern [ˈʃnʊpɐn] **1** VI to sniff; (Hund auch) to snuffle; **an etw** (dat) **~** to sniff (at) sth; **wir kamen nur zum Schnuppern** (fig inf) we only came to get a taste of it **2** VT to sniff; (fig) Atmosphäre etc to sample

Schnur [ʃnuːɐ] F **-, "e** [ˈʃnyːrə] (= Bindfaden) string; (= Kordel, an Vorhang) cord; (= Zeltschnur) guy (rope)

Schnürchen [ˈʃnyːrçən] NT **-s, -** es läuft or geht or klappt alles wie am **~** everything's going like clockwork

schnüren [ˈʃnyːrən] VT Paket, Strohbündel to tie up; Schuhe, Mieder to lace (up); Körper to lace in; (fig) Maßnahmenpaket etc to put together; **Schuhe zum Schnüren** lace-up shoes, lace-ups

schnurgerade **1** ADJ (dead) straight **2** ADV straight as an arrow; **~ auf jdn/etw zugehen** to go straight up to sb/sth

schnurlos **1** ADJ Telefon, Apparat cordless **2** ADV **~ telefonieren** to use a cordless phone

Schnurrbart M moustache (Brit), mustache (US)

schnurrbärtig ADJ with a moustache (Brit) or mustache (US)

schnurren [ˈʃnʊrən] VI (Katze) to purr; (Spinnrad etc) to hum

Schnür-: Schnürschuh M lace-up shoe; **Schnürsenkel** M shoelace; (für Stiefel) bootlace

schnurstracks [ˈʃnuːɐˈʃtraks] ADV straight; **~ auf jdn/etw zugehen** to go straight up to sb/sth

schnurz [ʃnʊrts], **schnurz(piep)egal** ADJ (inf) **das ist ihm ~** he couldn't give a damn (about it) (inf); **das ist ~!** it doesn't matter a damn! (inf)

Schnute [ˈʃnuːtə] F **-, -n** (inf) (= Mund) mouth; (= Schmollmund) pout; **eine ~ ziehen** or **machen** to pout

schob PRET von schieben

Schock M **-(e)s, -s** (= Schreck, elektrisch) shock; **unter ~ stehen** to be in (a state of) shock

Schock-: Schockeinwirkung F state of shock; **unter ~ stehen** to be in (a state of) shock

schocken [ˈʃɔkn] VT (inf) to shock

Schocker [ˈʃɔkɐ] M **-s, -** (inf: = Film/Roman) shock film/novel

schockieren [ʃɔˈkiːrən], ptp **schockiert** VTI to shock; (stärker) to scandalize; **sich leicht ~ lassen** to be easily shocked; **~d** shocking; **schockiert sein** to be shocked (über +acc at)

schofel [ˈʃoːfl], **schofelig** [ˈʃoːfəlɪç] (inf) **1** ADJ Behandlung, Ausrede rotten no adv (inf); Spende, Geschenk, Mahlzeit miserable **2** ADV miserably

Schöffe [ˈʃœfə] M **-n, -n**, **Schöffin** [ˈʃœfɪn] F **-, -nen** ≈ juror

Schöffengericht NT court (with jury); **einen Fall vor einem ~ verhandeln** ≈ to try a case by jury

Schöffin F **-, -nen** ≈ juror

schoflig [ˈʃoːflɪç] ADJ, ADV (inf) = schofel

Schokolade [ʃokoˈlaːdə] F **-, -n** chocolate

Schokoladen- IN CPDS chocolate; **Schokoladenguss** M chocolate icing; **Schokoladenriegel** M chocolate bar

Schokoriegel [ˈʃoko-] M chocolate bar

Scholle¹ [ˈʃɔlə] F **-, -n** (Fisch) plaice

Scholle² F **-, -n** (= Eisscholle) (ice) floe; (= Erdscholle) clod (of earth)

ADVERB

(a) (= bereits) already; **schon vor 100 Jahren kämpften Frauen um das Wahlrecht** 100 years ago women were already fighting for the vote

*Im Englischen wird **schon** oft nicht übersetzt.*

er ist schon hier! he's (already) here!; **danke, ich habe schon** (inf) no thank you, I have (already) got some; **es ist schon 11 Uhr** it's (already) 11 o'clock; **wie schon erwähnt** as has (already) been mentioned; **ich warte nun schon seit drei Wochen!** I've been waiting three whole weeks!; **ich bin schon drei Jahre alt** I'm THREE (years old); **der Milchmann kommt schon um 6 Uhr!** the milkman comes at 6 o'clock!; **das habe ich dir doch schon hundertmal gesagt** I've told you that a hundred times; **schon vor drei Wochen** three weeks ago; **schon am frühen Morgen** early in the morning; **ich werde schon bedient** I'm being served; **er wollte schon die Hoffnung aufgeben, als ...** he was about to give up hope when ...; **schon damals** even then; **schon damals, als ...** even when ...; **schon früher wusste man ...** even in years gone by they knew ...; **schon im 13. Jahrhundert** as early as the 13th century; **schon am nächsten Tag** the very next day; **das habe ich schon oft gehört** I've often heard that; **das ist schon längst erledigt** that was done a long time ago; **ich bin schon lange fertig** I've been ready for ages; **wie schon so oft** as ever; **schon immer** always

◆**schon einmal, schon mal** before; (= je: in Fragen) ever; **ich habe das schon mal gehört** I've heard that before; **warst du schon (ein)mal dort?** have you ever been there?; **ich habe dir schon (ein)mal gesagt, dass ...** I've already told you once that ...

◆**schon wieder schon wieder zurück** back already; **da ist sie schon wieder** (= zum x-ten Male) there she is again; (= schon zurück) she's back already; **was, schon wieder?** what - AGAIN?; **was denn nun schon wieder?** what is it NOW?

(b) (= bereits: in Fragen) ever; (= je) ever; **warst du schon dort?** have you been there (yet)?; (= je) have you (ever) been there?; **ist er schon hier?** is he here yet?; **musst du schon gehen?** must you go so soon?

*In Fragesätzen wird **schon** oft nicht übersetzt.*

kommt er schon heute? is he coming today?; **wie lange wartest du schon?** how long have you been waiting?
(c) (= allein, bloß) just; **der braucht kein Geld, der hat (ohnehin) schon genug** he doesn't need any money, he's got (quite) enough as it is; **allein schon der Gedanke, dass ...** just the thought that ...; **wenn ich das schon sehe/höre/lese!** if I even see/hear/read that!; **schon deswegen** if only because of that; **schon weil** if only because
(d) (= bestimmt) all right; **du wirst schon sehen** you'll see (all right); **das wirst du schon noch lernen** you'll learn that one day; **sie wird es schon machen** (don't worry,) she'll do it; (= schaffen) she'll manage (it) all right

(e) (= *tatsächlich, allerdings*) really; **das ist schon etwas, (wenn ...)** it's really something (if ...); **da gehört schon Mut/ Geschick** *etc* **dazu** that takes real courage/skill *etc*; **da müssten wir schon großes Glück haben** we'd be very lucky; **das ist schon möglich** that's quite possible; **das musst du schon machen!** you really ought to do that!

(f) (*ungeduldig*) **hör schon auf damit!** will you stop that!; **so antworte schon!** come on, answer!; **geh schon** go on; **nun sag schon!** come on, tell me/us *etc*!; **mach schon!** get a move on! (*inf*); **wenn doch schon ...!** if only ...!; **ich komme ja schon!** I'm just coming!

(g) (*einschränkend*) **schon** *or* **ja schon, aber ...** (*inf*) yes (well), but ...

(h) (*in rhetorischen Fragen*) **was macht das schon, wenn ...** what does it matter if ...; (= *was hilft das schon*) what(ever) use is it if ...; **wer fragt schon danach, ob ...** who wants to know if ...; **aber wer fragt schon danach** (*resignierend*) but no-one wants to know; **fünf Euro, was ist das schon?, was sind heute schon fünf Euro?** what's five euros these days?; **drei Seiten schreiben, was ist das schon?** write three pages? that's nothing!

(l) (*Füllwort*) (*inf*) **schon gut!** okay! (*inf*); **ich verstehe schon** I understand; **ich weiß schon** I know; **danke, es geht schon** thank you, I'll/we'll *etc* manage; **für Krimis gebe ich kein Geld aus und für Pornoheftchen schon gar nicht** I won't spend money on thrillers and certainly not on pornography

schön [ʃøːn] **1** ADJ **(a)** (= *hübsch anzusehen*) beautiful; *Mann* handsome; **das Schöne** beauty

(b) (= *nett, angenehm*) good; *Gelegenheit* great; (*inf:* = *gut*) nice; **die ~en Künste** the fine arts; **das ist ein ~er Tod** that's a good way to die; **eines ~en Tages** one fine day; **(wieder) in ~ster Ordnung** (*nach Krach etc*) back to normal (again); **das Schöne beim Skilaufen ist ...** the nice thing about skiing is ...; **~e Ferien!, ~en Urlaub!** have a good holiday (*esp Brit*) *or* vacation (*US*); **~es Wochenende** have a good weekend; **war es ~ im Urlaub?** did you have a nice holiday (*esp Brit*) *or* vacation (*US*)?; **war es ~ bei Tante Veronika?** did you have a good time at Aunt Veronika's?; **zu ~, um wahr zu sein** (*inf*) too good to be true; **~, ~, (also) ~, na** ~ fine, okay; **und gut, aber ...** that's all very well but ...

(c) (*iro*) *Unordnung* fine; *Überraschung, Wetter* lovely; *Unsinn, Frechheit* absolute; **da hast du etwas Schönes angerichtet** you've made a fine mess; **du bist mir ein ~er Freund/Vater/ Held** *etc* a fine friend/father/hero *etc* you are; **du machst** *or* **das sind mir ja ~e Sachen** *or* **Geschichten** this is a pretty state of things; **von dir hört man ~e Sachen** *or* **Geschichten** I've been hearing some nice things about you; **das wäre ja noch ~er** (*inf*) that's (just) too much!; **es wird immer ~er** (*inf*) things are going from bad to worse

(d) (= *beträchtlich, groß*) *Erfolg* great; *Strecke, Stück Arbeit, Alter* good; **eine ganz ~e Leistung** quite an achievement; **eine ganz ~e Arbeit** quite a lot of work; **eine ganz ~e Menge** quite a lot; **das hat eine ~e Stange Geld gekostet** (*inf*) that cost a pretty penny

2 ADV **(a)** (= *gut*) well; *sich waschen, verarbeiten lassen* easily; *scheinen* brightly; *schreiben* beautifully; (= *richtig, genau*) *ansehen, durchlesen etc* carefully; **sich ~ anziehen** to get dressed up; **es ~ haben** to be well off; (*im Urlaub etc*) to have a good time (of it); **~ weich/warm/stark** nice and soft/warm/ strong; *schlaf* ~ sleep well; **amüsiere dich** ~ have a nice time; **erhole dich** ~ have a good rest

(b) (*inf*) (= *brav, lieb*) nicely; (= *sehr, ziemlich*) really; **iss mal ~ deinen Teller leer** eat it all up nicely (now); **sei ~ still/ ordentlich** *etc* (*als Aufforderung*) be nice and quiet/tidy *etc*; **sei ~ brav** be a good boy/girl; **sich** (*dat*) ~ **wehtun** to hurt oneself a lot; **sich ~ täuschen** to make a big mistake; **sich ~ ärgern** to be very angry; **jdn ~ erschrecken** to give sb quite a *or* real fright; **ganz ~ teuer/kalt** pretty expensive/cold; **(ganz) ~ weit weg** quite a distance away; **ganz ~ lange** quite a while; **(ganz) ~ viel Geld kosten** to cost a pretty penny

schonen [ˈʃoːnən] **1** VT *Gesundheit, Herz, Körperteil, Buch, Kleider* to look after; *Ressourcen, eigene Kraft* to conserve; *Umwelt* to protect; *jds Nerven, Gefühle, Kraft* to spare; *Gegner, Kind* to be easy on; (= *nicht stark beanspruchen*) *Teppich, Schuhsohlen, Füße* to save; *Bremsen, Auto, Batterie* to go easy on; **ein Waschmittel, das die Hände/Wäsche schont** a detergent that is kind to your hands/washing; **er muss den Arm noch ~** he

still has to be careful with his arm; **um seine Nerven/die Nerven seiner Mutter zu ~** for the sake of his/his mother's nerves; **ein Beruf, der die Nerven nicht gerade schont** a job that isn't exactly easy on the nerves; **du brauchst mich nicht zu ~, sag ruhig die Wahrheit** you don't need to spare my feelings - just tell me the truth

2 VR to look after oneself; (*Patient auch*) to take things easy; **er schont sich für das nächste Rennen** he's saving himself for the next race

schönen [ˈʃøːnən] VT *Statistik, Zahlen* to dress up

schonend **1** ADJ gentle; (= *rücksichtsvoll*) considerate; *Waschmittel, Politur* mild; *Nutzung* (*von Ressourcen etc*) careful **2** ADV **jdm etw ~ beibringen** to break sth to sb gently; **jdn ~ behandeln** to be *or* go easy on sb; *Kranken* to treat sb gently; **etw ~ behandeln** to treat sth with care

Schön-: **schönfärben** SEP **1** VT (*fig*) to gloss over **2** VI to gloss things over; **Schönfärberei** F (*fig*) glossing things over

Schönheit F **-, -en** beauty

Schönheits-: **Schönheitschirurgie** F cosmetic surgery; **Schönheitsfarm** F beauty farm; **Schönheitsfehler** M blemish; (*von Gegenstand*) flaw; **Schönheitskönigin** F beauty queen; **Schönheitswettbewerb** M beauty contest

Schonkost F light diet; (= *Spezialdiät*) special diet

Schönling [ˈʃøːnlɪŋ] M **-s, -e** (*pej*) pretty boy (*inf*)

Schön-: **schönmachen** SEP **1** VT *Kind* to dress up; *Wohnung, Straßen* to decorate **2** VR to get dressed up; (= *sich schminken*) to make (oneself) up; **Schönschrift** F, NO PL **in ~** in one's best (hand)writing; **schöntun** VI SEP IRREG **jdm ~** (= *schmeicheln*) to flatter sb; (= *sich lieb Kind machen*) to suck up to sb (*inf*)

Schonung [ˈʃoːnʊŋ] F **-, -en (a)** (= *Waldbestand*) (protected) forest plantation area

(b) NO PL (= *das Schonen*) (*von Gefühlen, Kraft*) sparing; (*von Teppich, Schuhsohlen, Kleidern, Ressourcen*) saving; (*von Umwelt*) protection; **der Patient/Arm braucht noch ein paar Wochen ~** the patient/arm still needs looking after for a few weeks; **zur ~ meiner Gefühle/der Gefühle anderer** to spare my feelings/the feelings of others; **zur ~ des Magens sollten Sie nur Tee trinken** in order not to irritate your stomach you should only drink tea; **zur ~ Ihrer Augen/Waschmaschine** to look after your eyes/washing machine

(c) NO PL (= *Nachsicht, Milde*) mercy

schonungslos **1** ADJ ruthless; *Wahrheit* blunt; *Ehrlichkeit, Offenheit* brutal; *Kritik* savage **2** ADV ruthlessly; **jdm ~ die Wahrheit sagen** to tell sb the truth with no holds barred

Schonzeit F close season; (*fig*) honeymoon period

Schopf [ʃɔpf] M **-(e)s, ⸚e** [ˈʃœpfə] (shock of) hair; (*von Vogel*) tuft; **eine Gelegenheit beim ~ ergreifen** *or* **packen** to seize an opportunity with both hands

schöpfen [ˈʃœpfn] VT **(a)** AUCH VI (*aus* from) *Wasser* to scoop; *Suppe* to ladle; *Papier* to dip; **Wasser aus einem Boot ~** to bale out a boat

(b) *Kraft* to summon up; *Vertrauen, Hoffnung* to find; **Atem ~** to draw breath; *Verdacht* ~ to become suspicious; **Vertrauen/ Hoffnung/Mut** *etc* **aus etw ~** to draw confidence/hope/ courage *etc* from sth

(c) AUCH VI (= *schaffen*) *Kunstwerk* to create; *neuen Ausdruck, Wörter* to coin

Schöpfer [ˈʃœpfɐ] M **-s, -**, **Schöpferin** [-ərɪn] F **-, -nen** creator; (= *Gott*) Creator

schöpferisch [ˈʃœpfərɪʃ] **1** ADJ creative; **~e Pause** (*hum*) pause for inspiration **2** ADV creatively; **~ tätig sein** to do creative work; **sie ist ~ veranlagt** she is creative; (= *künstlerisch*) she is artistic

Schöpfkelle F, **Schöpflöffel** M ladle

Schöpfung [ˈʃœpfʊŋ] F **-, -en** creation; (= *Wort, Ausdruck*) coinage

Schöps [ʃœps] M **-es, -e** (*Aus*) = **Hammel**

schor PRET *von* **scheren¹**

Schorf [ʃɔrf] M **-(e)s, -e** crust; (= *Wundschorf*) scab

Schorle [ˈʃɔrlə] F **-, -n** *or* NT **-s, -s** spritzer

Schornstein [ˈʃɔrnʃtaɪn] M chimney; (*von Schiff, Lokomotive*) funnel, (smoke)stack

Schornsteinfeger [-feːgɐ] M **-s, -**, **Schornsteinfegerin** [-ərɪn] F **-, -nen** chimney sweep

schoss PRET *von* **schießen**

Schoß [ʃoːs] **-es, ⸚e** [ˈʃøːsə] M **(a)** lap; **die Hände in den ~ legen** (lit) to put one's hands in one's lap; (fig) to sit back (and take it easy); **das ist ihm nicht in den ~ gefallen** (fig) it wasn't handed (to) him on a plate **(b)** (liter) (= Mutterleib) womb; **im ~e der Familie/Kirche** in the bosom of one's family/of the church; **im ~ der Erde** in the bowels of the earth **(c)** (an Kleidungsstück) tail

Schoßhund M lapdog

Schössling [ˈʃœslɪŋ] M **-s, -e** (Bot) shoot

Schote [ˈʃoːtə] F **-, -n** (Bot) pod

Schott [ʃɔt] NT **-(e)s, -e(n)** (Naut) bulkhead; **die ~en dichtmachen** (inf) to close up shop

Schotte [ˈʃɔtə] M **-n, -n** Scot; **er ist ~** he's a Scot; **die ~n** the Scots

Schotten-: Schottenkaro NT, **Schottenmuster** NT tartan; **Rock mit** or **im ~** tartan skirt; **Schottenrock** M tartan skirt; (= Kilt) kilt

Schotter [ˈʃɔtɐ] M **-s, -** gravel; (im Straßenbau) (road) metal; (Rail) ballast

schottern [ˈʃɔtɐn] VT to gravel (over); (im Straßenbau) to metal; (Rail) to ballast

Schottin [ˈʃɔtɪn] F **-, -nen** Scot

schottisch [ˈʃɔtɪʃ] ADJ Scottish; Sprache Scots

Schottland [ˈʃɔtlant] NT **-s** Scotland

schraffieren [ʃraˈfiːrən] ptp **schraffiert** VT to hatch

Schraffierung F **-, -en**, **Schraffur** [ʃraˈfuːrə] F **-, -en** hatching

schräg [ʃrɛːk] **1** ADJ **(a)** (= schief, geneigt) sloping; Augen slanting; Kante bevelled (Brit), beveled (US); (= nicht gerade, nicht parallel) oblique
(b) (inf) (= verdächtig) fishy (inf); (= seltsam) Musik, Vorstellungen, Leute weird
2 ADV **(a)** (= geneigt) at an angle; halten on the slant; (= krumm) slanting; (= nicht gerade, nicht parallel) obliquely; überqueren, gestreift diagonally; (Sew) on the bias; **~ gegenüber/hinter** diagonally opposite/behind; **~ rechts/links** diagonally to the right/left; **~ rechts/links abbiegen** (Auto, Fähre) to bear right/left; **die Straße biegt ~ ab** the road forks off; **den Kopf ~ halten** to hold one's head at an angle; **~ parken** to park at an angle; **jdn ~ ansehen** or **angucken** (fig) to look at sb out of the corner of one's eye; (fig) to look askance at sb

Schräge [ˈʃrɛːgə] F **-, -n** (= schräge Fläche) slope; (= schräge Kante) bevel; (im Zimmer) sloping ceiling

Schräg-: Schrägkante F bevelled (Brit) or beveled (US) edge; **Schräglage** F angle; (von Flugzeug) bank(ing); (im Mutterleib) oblique position; **etw in ~ bringen/aufbewahren** to put/keep sth at an angle; **Schrägstrich** M oblique

schrak (old) PRET von **schrecken**

Schramme [ˈʃramə] F **-, -n** scratch

schrammen [ˈʃramən] **1** VT to scratch; **sich** (dat) **den Arm/sich ~** to scratch one's arm/oneself **2** VI **über den Boden ~** to scrape across the floor

Schrank [ʃraŋk] M **-(e)s, ⸚e** (Brit), closet (US); (= Küchenschrank) cupboard; (= Kleiderschrank) wardrobe (Brit), closet (US); (für Bücher) bookcase; (= Umkleideschrank, Mil: = Spind) locker

Schränkchen [ˈʃrɛŋkçən] NT **-s, -** DIM von **Schrank** small cupboard (Brit) or closet (US); (= Arzneischränkchen, im Badezimmer) cabinet; (neben dem Bett) bedside cupboard, night stand (US)

Schranke [ˈʃraŋkə] F **-, -n** barrier; (= Barrikade) barricade (fig) (= Grenze) limit; (= Hindernis) barrier; **keine ~n kennen** to know no bounds; (Mensch) not to know when to stop; **er kennt keine ~n mehr** there's no restraining him; **sich in ~n halten** to keep within reasonable limits; **meine Begeisterung hält sich in ~n** I'm not exactly overwhelmed by it; **etw in ~n halten** to keep sth within reasonable limits

Schranken [ˈʃraŋkn] M **-s, -** (Aus) (level-crossing (Brit) or grade-crossing (US)) barrier

Schranken-: schrankenlos ADJ (fig) unbounded, boundless; Vertrauen total; Verhalten, Forderungen, Ansprüche unrestrained; **Schrankenwärter(in)** M(F) attendant (at level crossing)

Schrank-: Schrankkoffer M clothes trunk; **Schrankwand** F wall unit

Schraubdeckel M screw(-on) lid

Schraube [ˈʃraubə] F **-, -n (a)** screw; (ohne Spitze) bolt; **bei ihr ist eine ~ locker** (inf) she's got a screw loose (inf) **(b)** (Naut, Aviat) propeller **(c)** (Sport) twist

schrauben [ˈʃraubn] VTI to screw; **etw fester ~** to screw sth tighter; **etw in die Höhe ~** (fig) Preise, Rekorde, Gewinn to push sth up; Ansprüche, Erwartungen to raise; **etw niedriger ~** (fig) to lower sth

Schrauben-: Schraubengewinde NT screw thread; **Schraubenkopf** M screw head; **Schraubenmutter** F, pl **-muttern** nut; **Schraubenschlüssel** M spanner (Brit), wrench (US); **Schraubenzieher** [-tsiːɐ] M **-s, -** screwdriver

Schraub-: Schraubstock M vice; **Schraubverschluss** M screw top

Schrebergarten [ˈʃreːbɐ-] M allotment (Brit), garden plot

Schreck [ʃrɛk] M **-s,** (rare) **-e** fright; (= ~figur) terror; **vor ~** in fright; zittern with fright; **zu meinem großen ~(en)** to my great horror; **einen ~(en) bekommen** to get a fright; **jdm einen ~(en) einjagen** to give sb a fright; **mir sitzt** or **steckt der ~ noch in den** or **allen Gliedern** or **Knochen** my knees are still like jelly (inf); **auf den ~ (hin)** to get over the fright; **mit dem ~(en) davonkommen** to get off with no more than a fright; **ach du ~!** (inf) blast! (inf); **(o) ~, lass nach!** (hum inf) for goodness sake! (inf)

schrecken [ˈʃrɛkn] pret **schreckte** [ˈʃrɛktə] ptp **geschreckt** [gəˈʃrɛkt] **1** VT (= ängstigen) to frighten; (stärker) to terrify; **jdn aus dem Schlaf/aus seinen Träumen ~** to startle sb out of his sleep/dreams **2** pret auch (old) **schrak** [ʃraːk], ptp auch (old) **geschrocken** [gəˈʃrɔkn] VI AUX SEIN **aus dem Schlaf ~** to be startled out of one's sleep; **aus den Gedanken ~** to be startled

Schrecken [ˈʃrɛkn] M **-s, -** **(a)** (= plötzliches Erschrecken) = Schreck **(b)** (= Furcht, Entsetzen) terror; **einer Sache** (dat) **den ~ nehmen** to make a thing less frightening; **er war der ~ der ganzen Lehrerschaft** he was the terror of all the teachers; **jdn in Angst und ~ versetzen** to frighten and terrify sb; **ein Land in Angst und ~ versetzen** to spread fear and terror throughout a country

Schreckens-: schreckensblass, schreckensbleich ADJ as white as a sheet; **Schreckensnachricht** F terrible news no pl

Schreck-: Schreckgespenst NT nightmare; **das ~ des Krieges/der Inflation** the bogey of war/inflation; **schreckhaft** ADJ easily startled; **Schreckhaftigkeit** [ˈʃrɛkhaftɪçkait] F **-, NO PL** nervousness

schrecklich [ˈʃrɛklɪç] **1** ADJ terrible **2** ADV **(a)** (= entsetzlich) horribly; **~ schimpfen** to swear dreadfully **(b)** (inf: = sehr) terribly; **~ gerne** I'd absolutely love to; **~ viel** an awful lot (of); **~ wenig** very little

Schreck-: Schreckschuss M (lit) warning shot; **einen ~ abgeben** (lit, fig) to fire a warning shot; **Schreckschusspistole** F blank gun; **Schrecksekunde** F moment of shock

Schredder [ˈʃrɛdɐ] M **-s, -** shredder

Schrei [ʃrai] M **-(e)s, -e** cry; (brüllender) yell; (gellender) scream; (kreischender) shriek; (von Eule etc) screech; (von Hahn) crow; **der ~ nach Freiheit/Rache** the call for freedom/revenge; **ein ~ der Entrüstung** an (indignant) outcry; **der letzte ~** (inf) the latest thing; **nach dem letzten ~ gekleidet** (inf) dressed in the latest style

Schreibblock M, pl **-blöcke** or **-blocks** (writing) pad

Schreibe [ˈʃraibə] F **-, -en** (inf) writing

schreiben [ˈʃraibn] pret **schrieb** [ʃriːp], ptp **geschrieben** [gəˈʃriːbn] **1** VT **(a)** to write; Klassenarbeit, Übersetzung, Examen to do; **schwarze/rote Zahlen ~** (Comm) to be in the black/red; **etw auf Diskette ~** to save sth to disk; **sich** (dat) **etw vor der Seele** or **dem Herzen ~** to get sth off one's chest; **wo steht das geschrieben?** where does it say that?; **es steht Ihnen im Gesicht** or **auf der Stirn geschrieben** it's written all over your face
(b) (orthografisch) to spell; **wie schreibt man das?** how do you spell that?
2 VI to write; (= berichten) to say; **jdm ~** to write to sb, to write sb (US); **ich schrieb ihm, dass ...** I wrote and told him that ...; **er schreibt orthografisch richtig** his spelling is correct; **an einem Roman** etc **~** to be working on or writing a novel etc; **über etw** (acc) **~** (= abhandeln) to write about sth; **mit Tinte ~** to write in ink; **hast du was zum Schreiben?** have you anything to write with?
3 VR IMPERS to write; **mit diesem Bleistift schreibt es sich gut/**

schlecht this pencil writes well/doesn't write properly; **auf diesem Papier schreibt es sich gut/schlecht** this paper is easy *or* good/difficult to write on

4 VR **(a)** (= *korrespondieren*) to write (to each other); **ich schreibe mich schon lange mit ihm** (*inf*) I've been writing to him for a long time

(b) (= *geschrieben werden*) to be spelt (*esp Brit*) *or* spelled; **wie schreibt er sich?** how does he spell his name?; **wie schreibt sich das?** how is that spelled?

Schreiben ['ʃraibn] NT **-s, -** (a) NO PL writing **(b)** (= *Mitteilung*) communication (*form*); (= *Brief*) letter

Schreiber[1] ['ʃraibɐ] M **-s, -** (*inf*: = *Schreibgerät*) writing implement; **einen/keinen ~ haben** to have something/nothing to write with

Schreiber[2] ['ʃraibɐ] M **-s, -**, **Schreiberin** [-ərɪn] F **-, -nen** writer; (*Hist*) scribe; (= *Angestellter, Gerichtsschreiber*) clerk/clerkess; (*Sw*: = *Schriftführer*) secretary; (*pej*: = *Schriftsteller*) scribbler

Schreib-: schreibfaul ADJ lazy (about letter writing); **ich bin ~** I'm no great letter writer, I'm a poor correspondent; **Schreibfehler** M (spelling) mistake; (*aus Flüchtigkeit*) slip of the pen; (= *Tippfehler*) (typing) mistake; **schreibgeschützt** ADJ (*Comput*) write-protected; **Schreibkraft** F typist; **Schreibkrampf** M writer's cramp; **Schreib-/Lesekopf** M (*Comput*) read-write head; **Schreibmaschine** F typewriter; **auf** *or* **mit der ~ schreiben** to type; **mit der ~ geschrieben** typewritten; **Schreibmaterial** NT stationery *no pl*; **Schreibschrift** F cursive (hand)writing; (*Typ*) script; **Schreibschutz** M (*Comput*) write protection; **schreibschützen** VT (*Comput*) to write-protect; **Schreibstelle** F (*Comput*) (cursor) position; **Schreibtisch** M desk; **Schreibtischtäter(in)** M(F) mastermind behind the scenes (of a/the crime)

Schreibung ['ʃraibʊŋ] F **-, -en** spelling; **falsche ~ eines Namens** misspelling of a name

Schreib-: Schreibwaren PL stationery *sing*; **Schreibwarenhändler(in)** M(F) stationer; **Schreibwarenhandlung** F stationer's (shop); **Schreibweise** F (= *Stil*) style; (= *Rechtschreibung*) spelling; **Schreibzeug** NT, *pl* **-zeuge** writing things *pl*

schreien ['ʃraiən], *pret* **schrie** [ʃriː], *ptp* **geschrie(e)n** [ɡə'ʃriː(ə)n] **1** VI to shout; (*gellend*) (*vor Angst, Schmerzen*) to scream; (*kreischend*) to shriek; (= *brüllen*) to yell; (= *heulen, weinen*: *Kind*) to howl; (*Esel*) to bray; (*Vogel, Wild*) to call; (*Eule, Käuzchen etc*) to screech; (*Hahn*) to crow; **vor Lachen ~** to roar with laughter; (*schrill*) to scream with laughter; **es war zum Schreien** (*inf*) it was a scream (*inf*); **nach jdm ~** to shout for sb; **nach etw ~** (*fig*) to cry out for sth **2** VR **sich heiser ~** to shout oneself hoarse; (*Baby*) to cry itself hoarse

Schreierei [ʃraiə'rai] F **-, -en** (*inf*) bawling *no pl* (*inf*)

Schrei-: Schreihals M (*inf*) (= *Baby*) bawler (*inf*); (= *Unruhestifter*) noisy troublemaker; **Schreikrampf** M screaming fit

Schreiner ['ʃrainɐ] M **-s, -**, **Schreinerin** [-ərɪn] F **-, -nen** (*esp S Ger*) carpenter

schreiten ['ʃraitn], *pret* **schritt** [ʃrɪt], *ptp* **geschritten** [ɡə'ʃrɪtn] VI AUX SEIN (*geh*) (= *schnell gehen*) to stride; (= *feierlich gehen*) to walk; (*vorwärts*) to proceed; (= *stolzieren*) to strut; **zu etw ~** (*fig*) to get down to sth; **es wird Zeit, dass wir zur Tat ~** it's time we got down to work; **zum Äußersten ~** to take extreme measures; **zur Abstimmung/Wahl ~** to proceed to a vote

schrie PRET *von* **schreien**

schrieb PRET *von* **schreiben**

Schrift [ʃrɪft] F **-, -en (a)** writing; (= *~system*) script; (*Typ*) type **(b)** (= *~stück*) document; (= *Bericht*) report; (= *Eingabe*) petition **(c)** (= *Broschüre*) leaflet; (= *Buch*) work; (= *kürzere Abhandlung*) paper; **die (Heilige) ~** the (Holy) Scriptures *pl*

Schrift-: Schriftart F (= *Handschrift*) script; (*Typ*) typeface; **Schriftbild** NT script; **Schriftdeutsch** NT (*nicht Umgangssprache*) written German; (*nicht Dialekt*) standard German; **Schriftform** F (*Jur*) **dieser Vertrag erfordert die ~** this contract must be drawn up in writing; **Schriftführer(in)** M(F) secretary; **Schriftgrad** M type size

schriftlich ['ʃrɪftlɪç] **1** ADJ written; **in ~er Form** in writing; **auf ~em Wege** in writing; **die ~e Prüfung, das Schriftliche** (*inf*) the written exam; **ich habe nichts Schriftliches darüber** I haven't got anything in writing

2 ADV in writing; **ich bin ~ eingeladen worden** I have had a

written invitation; **etw ~ festhalten/niederlegen/machen** (*inf*) to put sth down in writing; **das kann ich Ihnen ~ geben** (*fig inf*) I can tell you that for free (*inf*)

Schrift-: Schriftsatz M **(a)** (*Jur*) legal document **(b)** (*Typ*) form(e); **Schriftsetzer(in)** M(F) typesetter; **Schriftsprache** F (= *nicht Umgangssprache*) written language; (= *nicht Dialekt*) standard language; **die französische ~** written/(good) standard French

Schriftsteller [-ʃtɛlɐ] M **-s, -** author

Schriftstellerin [-ʃtɛlərɪn] F **-, -nen** author(ess)

schriftstellerisch [-ʃtɛlərɪʃ] **1** ADJ *Arbeit, Werk, Talent* literary **2** ADV **~ tätig sein** to write; **er ist ~ begabt** he has talent as a writer

Schrift-: Schriftstück NT paper; (*Jur*) document; **Schriftverkehr** M, **Schriftwechsel** M correspondence; **im ~ stehen** to be in correspondence

schrill [ʃrɪl] **1** ADJ *Ton, Stimme* shrill; (*fig*) (*Misston, Missklang*) jarring; *Fest, Musik, Persönlichkeit* brash; *Farbe, Accessoires, Outfit* garish **2** ADV shrilly; **gekleidet** loudly; **sie lachte ~ auf** she gave a shriek of laughter

schritt PRET *von* **schreiten**

Schritt [ʃrɪt] M **-(e)s, -e (a)** (*lit, fig*) step (*zu* towards); (*weit ausholend*) stride; (*hörbar*) footstep; (= *Gang*) walk; (= *Tempo*) pace; **mit schleppenden ~en** dragging one's feet; **einen ~ zur Seite gehen** to step aside; **einen ~ machen** *or* **tun** to take a step; **ich habe seit Wochen keinen/kaum einen ~ aus dem Haus getan** I haven't/have hardly set foot outside the house for weeks; **die ersten ~e machen** *or* **tun** to take one's first steps; (*fig*) to take the first step; **den ersten ~ tun** (*fig*) to make the first move; (= *etw beginnen*) to take the first step; **den ~ tun** (*fig*) to take the plunge; **~e gegen jdn/etw unternehmen** to take steps against sb/sth; **ich würde sogar noch einen ~ weiter gehen und behaupten ...** I would go even further and maintain ...; **auf ~ und Tritt** (*lit, fig*) wherever one goes; **~ für** *or* **um ~** step by step; **Politik der kleinen ~e** step-by-step policy; **ein ~ in Richtung Frieden** a step towards peace; **~ halten** (*lit, fig*) to keep up; **mit der Zeit ~ halten** to keep abreast of the times; **einen schnellen/unwahrscheinlichen ~ am Leib** (*inf*) *or* **an sich** (*dat*) **haben** to walk quickly/incredibly quickly

(b) (= *~geschwindigkeit*) walking pace; **(im) ~ fahren** to drive at walking speed; **„~ fahren"** "dead slow" (*Brit*), "slow"

(c) (= *Hosenschritt*) crotch; (= *~weite*) crotch measurement

Schrittempo NT *siehe* **Schritttempo**

Schritt-: Schrittmacher M (*Med*) pacemaker; **Schrittmacher(in)** M(F) (*Sport*) pacemaker (*esp Brit*), pacer; (*fig auch*) pacesetter; **die Universitäten waren ~ der Revolution** the universities were in the vanguard of the revolution; **Schritttempo** NT walking speed; **im ~ fahren** to crawl along; **schrittweise 1** ADV gradually **2** ADJ gradual

schroff [ʃrɔf] **1** ADJ = *rau, barsch* curt; (= *krass, abrupt*) *Übergang, Bruch* abrupt; (= *steil, jäh*) precipitous; **~e Gegensätze** stark contrasts **2** ADV **(a)** (= *barsch*) curtly **(b)** (= *steil*) steeply

schröpfen ['ʃrœpfn] VT (= *Blut absaugen*) to bleed; **jdn ~** (*fig*) to rip sb off (*inf*)

Schrot [ʃroːt] M *or* NT **-(e)s, -e (a)** grain (*coarsely ground*); (= *Weizenschrot*) ≈ wholemeal (*Brit*), ≈ whole-wheat (*US*); **vom alten ~ und Korn** (*fig*) of the old school **(b)** (*Hunt*) shot

schroten ['ʃroːtn] VT *Getreide* to grind coarsely

Schrot-: Schrotflinte F shotgun; **Schrotkugel** F pellet; **Schrotladung** F round of shot; **Schrotschuss** M round of shot

Schrott [ʃrɔt] M **-(e)s**, NO PL scrap metal; (*aus Eisen auch*) old iron; (*fig*) rubbish (*Brit*), garbage

Schrott-: Schrottauto NT car that is ready for the scrap heap; **Schrotthaufen** M (*lit*) scrap heap; (*fig*: = *Auto*) pile of scrap; **Schrottplatz** M scrap yard; **schrottreif** ADJ ready for the scrap heap; **Schrottwert** M scrap value

schrubben ['ʃrʊbn] VTI to scrub

Schrubber ['ʃrʊbɐ] M **-s, -** (long-handled) scrubbing (*Brit*) *or* scrub (*US*) brush

Schrulle ['ʃrʊlə] F **-, -n (a)** quirk **(b)** (*pej*: = *alte Frau*) old crone

schrullig ['ʃrʊlɪç] **1** ADJ odd **2** ADV **sich benehmen** oddly

schrumpelig ['ʃrʊmpəlɪç] ADJ (*inf*) wrinkled

schrumpeln ['ʃrʊmpln] VI AUX SEIN (*inf*) to go wrinkled

schrumpfen ['ʃrʊmpfn] VI AUX SEIN (*lit, fig*) to shrink; (*Leber, Niere*) to atrophy; (*Muskeln*) to waste, to atrophy; (*Metall, Gestein etc*) to contract; (*Exporte, Mitgliederschaft, Interesse*) to dwindle; (*Industriezweig*) to decline

Schrumpfung ['ʃrʊmpfʊŋ] F **-, -en** shrinking; (= *Raumverlust*) shrinkage; (*von Fundamenten, Metall*) contraction; (*Med*) atrophy(ing); (*von Kapital, Arbeitskräften, Exporten*) dwindling, diminution; (*von Industriezweig etc*) decline

schrumplig ['ʃrʊmplɪç] ADJ (*inf*) wrinkled

Schub [ʃuːp] M **-(e)s, -e** ['ʃyːbə] (a) (= *Stoß*) push, shove (b) (*Phys*) (= *Vortriebskraft*) thrust; (*fig*: = *Impuls, Anstoß*) impetus (c) (*Med*) phase (d) (= *Anzahl*) batch

Schub-: Schubfach NT drawer; **Schubkarre** F, **Schubkarren** M wheelbarrow

Schublade ['ʃuːplaːdə] F **-, -n** drawer; (*fig*) pigeonhole, compartment; **in der ~ liegen** (*fig*) to be in reserve

Schubs [ʃʊps] M **-es, -e** (*inf*) shove (*inf*), push; (*Aufmerksamkeit erregend*) nudge

schubsen ['ʃʊpsn] VTI (*inf*) to shove (*inf*), to push; (*Aufmerksamkeit erregend*) to nudge

schubweise ADV in batches; (*Med*) in phases

schüchtern ['ʃʏçtɐn] **1** ADJ shy; **einen ~en Versuch unternehmen** (*iro*) to make a half-hearted attempt **2** ADV shyly

Schüchternheit F **-, NO PL** shyness

schuf PRET *von* **schaffen**[1]

Schufa ['ʃuːfa] F **-, NO PL** ABBR *von* **Schutzgemeinschaft für allgemeine Kreditsicherung** ≈ credit investigation company (*Brit*), ≈ credit bureau (*US*)

Schuft [ʃʊft] M **-(e)s, -e** heel (*inf*)

schuften ['ʃʊftn] VI (*inf*) to slave away

Schufterei [ʃʊftəˈrai] F **-, -en** (*inf*) graft (*inf*)

Schuh [ʃuː] M **-(e)s, -e** shoe; **jdm etw in die ~e schieben** (*inf*) to put the blame for sth on sb; **wissen, wo jdn der ~ drückt** to know what is bothering sb; **umgekehrt wird ein ~ d(a)raus** (*fig*) exactly the opposite is the case

Schuh-: Schuhcreme F shoe polish; **Schuhgröße** F shoe size; **Schuhlöffel** M shoehorn; **Schuhmacher(in)** M(F) shoemaker; (= *Flickschuster*) cobbler; **Schuhnummer** F (*inf*) shoe size; **jds ~ sein** (*fig*) to be sb's cup of tea (*inf*); **ein paar or mindestens zwei ~n zu groß für jdn** (*fig*) out of sb's league; **Schuhsohle** F sole (of a/one's shoe); **Schuhwerk** NT, NO PL, **Schuhzeug** NT, NO PL footwear

Schul-: Schulabgänger [-lapgɛŋə] M **-s, -**, **Schulabgängerin** [-ərɪn] F **-, -nen** school-leaver (*Brit*), graduate (*US*); **Schulalter** NT school age; **im ~ of** school age; **ins ~ kommen** to reach school age; **Schulanfang** M beginning of (the (*esp US*)) term; (= *Schuleintritt*) first day at school; **morgen ist ~** school starts tomorrow; **Schulanfänger(in)** M(F) child just starting school; **Schularbeit** F (a) USU PL homework no pl (b) (*Aus*) test; **Schulaufgaben** PL homework sing; **Schulausflug** M school trip, field trip (*US*); **Schulbank** F, pl **-bänke** school desk; **die ~ drücken** (*inf*) to go to school; **Schulbeginn** M (= *Schuljahrsbeginn*) beginning of the school year; (*nach Ferien*) beginning of (the (*esp US*)) term; (**der**) **~ ist um neun** school starts at nine; **Schulbeispiel** NT (*fig*) classic example (*für* of); **Schulbesuch** M school attendance; **Schulbildung** F (school) education; **Schulbuch** NT schoolbook; **Schulbus** M school bus

schuld [ʃʊlt] ADJ PRED **~ sein** to be to blame (*an +dat* for); **er war ~ an dem Streit** the argument was his fault; **bin ich denn ~, wenn ...?** is it my fault if ...?; **du bist selbst ~** that's your own fault

Schuld [ʃʊlt] F **-, -en** [-dn] (a) NO PL (= *Verantwortlichkeit*) **~ haben** to be to blame (*an +dat* for); **er hatte ~ an dem Streit** the argument was his fault; **du hast selbst ~** that's your own fault; **die ~ auf sich** (*acc*) **nehmen** to take the blame; **jdm die ~ geben or zuschreiben** to blame sb; **die ~ auf jdn abwälzen or schieben** to put the blame on sb; **die ~ bei anderen suchen** to try to blame somebody else; **das ist meine/deine ~** that is my/your fault; **durch meine/deine ~** because of me/you; **jdm/ einer Sache ~ geben** to blame sb/sth

(b) (= *haftigkeit, gefühl*) guilt; (= *Unrecht*) wrong; (*Rel*: = *Sünde*) sin; (*im Vaterunser*) trespasses pl; **sich frei von ~ fühlen** to consider oneself completely blameless; **ich bin mir keiner ~ bewusst** I'm not aware of having done anything

wrong; **ich bin mir meiner ~ bewusst** I know that I have done wrong; **ihm konnte keine ~ nachgewiesen werden** it couldn't be proved that he had done anything wrong; **~ und Sühne** crime and punishment

(c) (= *Zahlungsverpflichtung*) debt; **ich stehe tief in seiner ~** (*lit*) I'm deeply in debt to him; (*fig*) I'm deeply indebted to him; **~en machen** to run up debts; **~en haben** to be in debt; **in ~en geraten** to get into debt

schuldbewusst **1** ADJ *Mensch* feeling guilty; *Gesicht, Miene* guilty **2** ADV guiltily; **jdn ~ ansehen** to give sb a guilty look; **~ erröten** to blush from guilt

Schuldbrief M IOU

schulden ['ʃʊldn] VT to owe; **das schulde ich ihm** I owe it to him; **jdm Dank ~** to owe sb a debt of gratitude

Schulden-: Schuldenberg M mountain of debts; **Schuldendienst** M (*Econ*) debt servicing; **schuldenfrei** ADJ free of debt(s); *Besitz* unmortgaged

Schuld-: schuldfähig ADJ (*Jur*) criminally responsible; **Schuldgefühl** NT sense no pl or feeling of guilt; **schuldhaft** (*Jur*) **1** ADJ culpable **2** ADV culpably

Schuldienst M (school)teaching no art; **in den ~ treten or gehen** to go into teaching; **im ~ (tätig) sein** to be a teacher

schuldig ['ʃʊldɪç] ADJ (a) (= *schuldhaft, straffällig, schuldbeladen*) guilty; (= *verantwortlich*) to blame pred (*an +dat* for); (*Rel*) sinful; **einer Sache** (*gen*) **~ sein** to be guilty of sth; **jdn ~ sprechen** to find sb guilty; **sich ~ bekennen** to admit one's guilt; (*Jur*) to plead guilty

(b) (= *verpflichtet*) **jdm etw** (*acc*) **~ sein** (*lit, fig*) to owe sb sth; **ich muss Ihnen zwei Euro ~** I'll have to owe you two euros; **was bin ich Ihnen ~?** how much do I owe you?; **jdm Dank ~ sein** to owe sb a debt of gratitude; **sie blieb mir die Antwort ~** she didn't answer me

Schuldige(r) ['ʃʊldɪgə] MF DECL AS ADJ guilty person; (*zivilrechtlich*) guilty party

schuldlos **1** ADJ (*an Verbrechen*) innocent (*an +dat* of); (*an Fehler, Unglück etc*) blameless; **er war vollständig ~ an dem Unglück** he was in no way to blame for the accident **2** ADV (*in etw geraten*) innocently; **~ in einen Unfall verwickelt sein** to be involved in an accident without being at fault

Schuldner ['ʃʊldnɐ] M **-s, -**, **Schuldnerin** [-ərɪn] F **-, -nen** debtor

Schuldnerstaat M debtor nation

Schuld-: Schuldschein M IOU; **Schuldspruch** M verdict of guilty; **schuldunfähig** ADJ (*Jur*) not criminally responsible; **Schuldverschreibung** F (*Fin*) debenture bond; **Schuldwechsel** M bills pl payable, notes pl payable (*US*); **Schuldzuweisung** F accusation

Schule ['ʃuːlə] F **-, -n** (= *Lehranstalt, Lehrmeinung, künstlerische Richtung*) school; **in die or zur ~ kommen** to start school; **in die or zur ~ gehen** to go to school; **auf or in der ~ at** school; **von der ~ abgehen** to leave school; **die ~ ist aus** school is over; **durch eine harte ~ gegangen sein** (*fig*) to have learned in a hard school; **~ machen** to become the accepted thing; **aus der ~ plaudern** to tell tales; **ein Kavalier der alten ~** a gentleman of the old school

schulen ['ʃuːlən] VT to train

Schulenglisch NT schoolboy/schoolgirl English; **zwei Jahre ~** two years' English at school; **mein ~** the English I learned at school

Schüler ['ʃyːlɐ] M **-s, -**, **Schülerin** [-ərɪn] F **-, -nen** schoolboy/ -girl; (*einer bestimmten Schule, eines Künstlers*) pupil; (*einer Oberschule*) student; (= *Jünger*) follower; **als ~ habe ich ...** when I was at school I ...; **alle ~ und ~innen dieser Stadt** all the schoolchildren of this town; **ein ehemaliger ~ (der Schule)** an old boy or pupil (of the school)

Schüler-: Schüleraustausch M school exchange; **Schülerausweis** M (school) student card

Schülerin F siehe **Schüler**

Schüler-: Schülerkarte F school season ticket; **Schülerlotse** M, **Schülerlotsin** F pupil acting as warden at a crossing, lollipop man/lady (*Brit inf*), crossing guard (*US*); **Schülermitverwaltung** F school council; **Schülerschaft** ['ʃyːlɐʃaft] F **-, -en** pupils pl; **Schülervertretung** F pupil or student representation; **Schülerzeitung** F school magazine or newspaper

Schul-: Schulfach NT school subject; **Schulferien** PL school holidays pl (*Brit*) or vacation (*US*); **Schulfest** NT school function; **schulfrei** ADJ **ein ~er Nachmittag** an afternoon when one doesn't have to go to school; **an ~en Samstagen** on Saturdays when there's no school; **nächsten Samstag ist ~** there's no school next Saturday; **die Kinder haben morgen ~** the children don't have to go to school tomorrow; **Schulfreund(in)** M(F) schoolfriend; **Schulgegenstand** M (*Aus*) school subject; **Schulgelände** NT school grounds *pl*; **Schulheft** NT exercise book; **Schulhof** M school playground, schoolyard

schulisch ['ʃuːlɪʃ] **1** ADJ *Leistungen, Probleme, Verbesserung* at school; (= *rein akademisch*) scholastic; *Bildung, Einrichtung* school *attr*; **seine ~en Leistungen/Probleme** his progress/problems at school; **~e Angelegenheiten** school matters **2** ADV scholastically

Schul-: Schuljahr NT school year; (= *Klasse*) year; **ihre ~e** her school days; **Schuljunge** M schoolboy; **Schulkamerad(in)** M(F) schoolfriend; **Schulkenntnisse** PL knowledge *sing* acquired at school; **Schulkind** NT schoolchild; **Schulklasse** F (school) class; **Schullandheim** NT *country house used by school classes for short visits*; **Schulleiter** M headmaster, principal; **Schulleiterin** F headmistress, principal; **Schulmädchen** NT schoolgirl; **Schulmappe** F schoolbag; **Schulmedizin** F orthodox medicine; **Schulmeinung** F received opinion; **schulmeisterlich** (*pej*) **1** ADJ schoolmasterish **2** ADV like a schoolmaster; **sich ~ aufspielen** to play the schoolmaster; **Schulpflicht** F compulsory school attendance *no art*; **allgemeine ~** compulsory school attendance for all children; **es besteht ~** school attendance is compulsory; **schulpflichtig** [-pflɪçtɪç] ADJ *Kind* required to attend school; **im ~en Alter** of school age; **Schulpsychologe** M, **Schulpsychologin** F educational psychologist; **Schulrat** M, **Schulrätin** F schools inspector (*Brit*), ≈ school board superintendent (*US*); **Schulschiff** NT training ship; **Schulschluss** M, NO PL end of school; (*vor den Ferien*) end of term; **~ ist um 13.10** school finishes at 13.10; **kurz nach ~** just after school finishes; **Schulsprecher** M head boy (*Brit*), school representative; **Schulsprecherin** F head girl (*Brit*), school representative; **Schulstress** M stress at school; **im ~ sein** to be under stress at school; **Schulstunde** F (school) period; **Schultasche** F schoolbag

Schulter ['ʃʊltɐ] F -, -n shoulder; **breite ~n haben** (*lit*) to be broad-shouldered; (*fig*) to have a broad back; **jdm auf die ~ klopfen** *or* **schlagen** to give sb a slap on the back; (*lobend*) to pat sb on the back; **sich** (*dat*) **selbst auf die ~ klopfen** (*fig*) to blow one's own trumpet; **~ an ~** (= *dicht gedrängt*) shoulder to shoulder; (= *gemeinsam, solidarisch*) side by side; **die** *or* **mit den ~n zucken** to shrug one's shoulders; **dem Künstler beim Arbeiten über die ~ sehen** to look over the artist's shoulder while he works; **die Verantwortung ruht auf seinen ~n** the responsibility rests on his shoulders; **etw auf die leichte ~ nehmen** to take sth lightly

Schulter-: Schulterblatt NT shoulder blade; **Schultergelenk** NT shoulder joint

schulterlang ADJ shoulder-length

schultern ['ʃʊltɐn] VT (*lit, fig*) to shoulder

Schulterschluss M, NO PL solidarity; (= *Solidarisierung*) closing of ranks

Schulung ['ʃuːlʊŋ] F -, -en (= *Ausbildung, Übung*) training; (*Pol*) political instruction

Schul-: Schuluniform F school uniform; **Schulunterricht** M school lessons *pl*; **Schulverweigerer** M, **Schulverweigerin** F school refuser; **Schulweg** M way to school; (*Entfernung*) distance to school; (*Route*) route to school; **ich habe einen ~ von 20 Minuten** it takes me 20 minutes to get to school; **Schulwesen** NT school system; **Schulzeit** F (= *Schuljahre*) school days *pl*; **nach 13-jähriger ~** after 13 years at school; **Schulzeitung** F school magazine *or* newspaper; **Schulzeugnis** NT school report

schummeln ['ʃʊmln] VI (*inf*) to cheat

schummerig ['ʃʊmərɪç], **schummrig** ['ʃʊmrɪç] ADJ *Beleuchtung* dim; *Raum* dimly-lit; **bei ~em Licht** in the half-light; **es war schon ~** it was already getting dark

Schund [ʃʊnt] M -(e)s [-dəs], NO PL (*pej*) trash, rubbish (*Brit*); **was für ~/einen ~ hast du denn da?** what's that trash/trashy book you're reading?

Schunkellied NT German drinking song

schunkeln ['ʃʊŋkln] VI to link arms and sway from side to side

Schuppe ['ʃʊpə] F -, -n **(a)** (*Bot*) (*Zool*) scale; (*von Ritterrüstung, Tierpanzer*) plate; **es fiel mir wie ~n von den Augen** the scales fell from my eyes **(b) Schuppen** PL (= *Kopfschuppen*) dandruff *sing*

schuppen ['ʃʊpn] **1** VT *Fische* to scale **2** VR to flake

Schuppen ['ʃʊpn] M -s, - **(a)** shed; (= *Flugzeugschuppen*) hangar **(b)** (*inf*) (= *übles Lokal*) dive (*inf*) **(c)** (*sl*: = *Disko etc*) club

Schuppen-: Schuppenbildung F, NO PL dandruff; **Schuppenflechte** F (*Med*) psoriasis (*spec*); **Schuppentier** NT scaly anteater

Schur [ʃuːr] F -, -en (= *das Scheren*) shearing; (= *geschorene Wolle*) clip

schüren ['ʃyːrən] VT **(a)** *Feuer, Glut* to rake **(b)** (*fig*) to stir up; *Zorn, Eifersucht, Leidenschaft, Hass* to fan the flames of

schürfen ['ʃʏrfn] **1** VI (*Min*) to prospect (*nach* for); **tief ~** (*fig*) to dig deep **2** VT *Bodenschätze* to mine **3** VR to graze oneself; **sich** (*dat*) **die Haut ~, sich ~** to graze oneself *or* one's skin; **sich am Knie ~** to graze one's knee

Schürfwunde F graze

Schürhaken M poker

Schurke ['ʃʊrkə] M -n, -n, **Schurkin** ['ʃʊrkɪn] F -, -nen (*dated*) villain

Schurwolle ['ʃuːr-] F virgin wool; **„reine ~"** "pure new wool"

Schurz [ʃʊrts] M -es, -e loincloth; (*von Schmied, Arbeiter etc, dial*) apron

Schürze ['ʃʏrtsə] F -, -n apron; (= *Kittelschürze*) overall

Schuss [ʃʊs] M -es, ⸗e ['ʃʏsə] **(a)** shot; (= ~ *Munition*) round; **sechs ~** *or* **Schüsse** six shots/rounds; **einen ~ auf jdn/etw abgeben** to fire a shot at sb/sth; **ein ~ ins Schwarze** (*lit, fig*) a bull's-eye; **weit (ab) vom ~ sein** (*fig inf*) to be miles from where the action is (*inf*); **der ~ ging nach hinten los** it backfired; **ein ~ in den Ofen** (*inf*) a complete waste of time **(b)** (*Ftbl*) kick; (*esp zum Tor*) shot; **zum ~ kommen** to get the ball; (*zum Tor*) to get a chance to shoot **(c)** (= *Spritzer*) (*von Wein, Essig etc*) dash; (*von Whisky*) shot; (*von Humor, Leichtsinn etc*) touch **(d)** (*inf*: *mit Rauschgift*) shot; (**sich** *dat*) **einen ~ setzen** to shoot up (*inf*); **sich** (*dat*) **den goldenen ~ setzen** to OD (*inf*) **(e)** (*inf*) **in ~ sein/kommen** to be in/get into (good) shape; (*Schüler, Klasse*) to be/get up to the mark (*esp Brit*) *or* up to snuff; **etw in ~ bringen/halten** to knock sth into shape/keep sth in good shape; **Schulklasse** to bring/keep sth up to the mark (*esp Brit*) *or* up to snuff

Schussbereich M (firing) range; **im ~** within range

Schussel ['ʃʊsl] M -s, - (*inf*) *or* f -, -n (*inf*) dolt (*inf*); (*zerstreut*) scatterbrain (*inf*); (*ungeschickt*) clumsy clot (*inf*)

Schüssel ['ʃysl] F -, -n bowl; (= *Servierschüssel auch*, = *Satellitenschüssel*) dish; (= *Waschschüssel*) basin

schusselig ['ʃʊsəlɪç] ADJ (= *zerstreut*) scatterbrained (*inf*); (= *ungeschickt*) clumsy

Schuss-: Schusslinie F firing line; **Schussverletzung** F bullet wound; **Schusswaffe** F firearm; **Schusswechsel** M exchange of shots; **Schussweite** F range (of fire); **in/außer ~** within/out of range; **Schusswunde** F bullet wound

Schuster ['ʃuːstɐ] M -s, -, **Schusterin** [-ərɪn] F -, -nen shoemaker; (= *Flickschuster*) cobbler

Schusterei [ʃuːstə'raɪ] F -, -en (*Werkstatt*) shoemaker's; (*von Flickschuster*) cobbler's

Schutt [ʃʊt] M -(e)s, NO PL (= *Trümmer, Bauschutt*) rubble; (*Geol*) debris; **„~ abladen verboten"** "no tipping" (*Brit*), "no dumping" (*US*); **eine Stadt in ~ und Asche legen** to reduce a town to rubble; **in ~ und Asche liegen** to be in ruins

Schuttabladeplatz M dump

Schüttel-: Schüttelfrost M (*Med*) shivering fit; **Schüttellähmung** F (*Med*) Parkinson's disease

schütteln ['ʃʏtln] **1** VT to shake; (= *rütteln*) to shake about; **den** *or* **mit dem Kopf ~** to shake one's head; **von Fieber geschüttelt werden** to be racked with fever **2** VR to shake oneself; (*vor Kälte*) to shiver (*vor* with); (*vor Ekel*) to shudder (*vor* with, in); **sich vor Lachen ~** to shake with laughter

schütten ['ʃʏtn] **1** VT to tip; *Flüssigkeiten* to pour; (= *verschütten*) to spill **2** VI IMPERS (*inf*) **es schüttet** it's pouring (with rain)

schütter ['ʃʏtɐ] ADJ *Haar, Schneedecke, Pflanzen* thin

Schutthaufen M pile of rubble; **etw in einen ~ verwandeln** to reduce sth to a pile of rubble

Schutz [ʃʊts] M **-es**, NO PL protection (*vor +dat, gegen* against, from); (*der Natur, Umwelt etc*) protection; (*esp Mil: = Deckung*) cover; **unter einem Baum ~ suchen** to shelter under a tree; **im ~(e) der Nacht** *or* **Dunkelheit/des Artilleriefeuers** under cover of night/artillery fire; **zum ~ der Augen** to protect the eyes; **jdn in ~ nehmen** (*fig*) to take sb's part

Schutz-: Schutzanzug M protective clothing *no indef art, no pl*; **schutzbedürftig** ADJ in need of protection; **Schutzbefohlene(r)** [-bəfoːlənə] MF DECL AS ADJ protégé; (= *esp Kind*) charge; **Schutzbehauptung** F lie to cover oneself; **Schutzblech** NT mudguard; **Schutzbrief** M **(a)** (letter of) safe-conduct **(b)** = **Auslandsschutzbrief; Schutzbrille** F protective goggles *pl*

Schütze [ˈʃʏtsə] M **-n, -n (a)** marksman; (= *Schießsportler*) rifleman; (*Hunt*) hunter; (= *Bogenschütze*) archer; (*Ftbl:* = *Torschütze*) scorer; **er ist der beste ~** he is the best shot **(b)** (*Mil*) (= *Dienstgrad*) private; (= *Maschinengewehrschütze*) gunner **(c)** (*Astrol, Astron*) Sagittarius *no art*; **sie ist ~** she's Sagittarius

schützen [ˈʃʏtsn̩] **1** VT to protect (*vor +dat, gegen* from, against); (*esp Mil: = Deckung geben*) to cover; **urheberrechtlich geschützt** protected by copyright; **gesetzlich geschützt** registered; **patentrechtlich geschützt** patented; **vor Hitze/ Sonnenlicht ~!** keep away from heat/sunlight; **vor Nässe ~!** keep dry; *siehe auch* **geschützt** **2** VR to protect oneself (*vor +dat, gegen* from, against); **er weiß sich zu ~** he knows how to look after himself

schützend 1 ADJ protective; **ein ~es Dach** (*gegen Wetter*) a shelter; **ein ~es Dach über sich** (*dat*) **haben** to be under cover; **der ~e Hafen** (*lit*) the protection of the harbour (*Brit*) *or* harbor (*US*); (*fig*) a/the safe haven; **seine ~e Hand über jdn halten** *or* **breiten** to take sb under one's wing **2** ADV protectively

Schutzengel M guardian angel

Schützen-: Schützengraben M trench; **Schützenhilfe** F (*fig*) support; **jdm ~ geben** to back sb up; **Schützenverein** M shooting club

Schutz-: Schutzfarbe F, **Schutzfärbung** F (*Biol*) protective colouring (*Brit*) *or* coloring (*US*); **Schutzgebiet** NT (*Pol*) protectorate; **Schutzgebühr** F (token) fee; **Schutzgeld** NT protection money; **Schutzgelderpressung** F extortion of protection money; **Schutzhaft** F (*Jur*) protective custody; (*Pol*) preventive detention; **Schutzheilige(r)** MF DECL AS ADJ patron saint; **Schutzhelm** M safety helmet; (*von Bauarbeiter auch*) hard hat (*inf*); **Schutzherr** M patron; **Schutzherrin** F patron, patroness; **Schutzherrschaft** F (*Pol*) protection; (= *Patronat*) patronage; **Schutzhülle** F protective cover; (= *Buchumschlag*) dust cover; **Schutzhütte** F shelter; **Schutzimpfung** F vaccination, inoculation

Schützin [ˈʃʏtsɪn] F **-, -nen** markswoman; (= *Schießsportlerin*) riflewoman; (*Hunt*) huntress; (= *Bogenschützin*) archer; (*Ftbl:* = *Torschützin*) scorer

Schutz-: Schutzkleidung F protective clothing; **Schutzkontakt** M (*Elec*) safety contact

Schützling [ˈʃʏtslɪŋ] M **-s, -e** protégé; (*esp Kind*) charge

schutzlos 1 ADJ (= *wehrlos*) defenceless (*Brit*), defenseless (*US*); (*gegen Kälte etc*) unprotected **2** ADV **jdm/einer Sache ~ ausgeliefert** *or* **preisgegeben sein** to be at the mercy of sb/sth

Schutz-: Schutzmacht F (*Pol*) protecting power; **Schutzmann** M, *pl* **-leute** policeman; **Schutzmaske** F (protective) mask; **Schutzmaßnahme** F precaution; (*vorbeugend*) preventive measure; **Schutzpatron** M, **Schutzpatronin** F patron saint; **Schutzpolizei** F (*form*) police force; **Schutzpolizist(in)** M(F) (*form*) police officer; **Schutzprogramm** M **(a)** conservation programme (*Brit*) *or* program (*US*) **(b)** (*Comput*) (= *Virenschutzprogramm*) antivirus program; (= *Daten-schutzprogramm*) privacy and security program; **Schutzraum** M shelter; **Schutzschicht** F protective layer; (= *Überzug*) protective coating; **Schutzstaffel** F (*Hist*) SS; **Schutztruppe** F protection force; (*Hist*) colonial army; **Schutzumschlag** M dust cover; **Schutzvorrichtung** F safety device; **Schutzwald** M barrier woodland; **Schutzwall** M protective wall (*gegen* to keep out); **Schutzweg** M (*Aus*) pedestrian crossing (*Brit*), crosswalk (*US*); **Schutzweste** F protective jacket; (= *schusssichere Weste*) bulletproof vest

Schwa [ʃvaː] NT **-s**, NO PL (*Ling*) schwa

Schwabe [ˈʃvaːbə] M **-n, -n**, **Schwäbin** [ˈʃveːbɪn] F **-, -nen** Swabian

Schwaben [ˈʃvaːbn̩] NT **-s** Swabia

schwäbisch [ˈʃveːbɪʃ] ADJ Swabian; **die Schwäbische Alb** the Swabian mountains *pl*; **das Schwäbische Meer** (*hum*) Lake Constance

schwach [ʃvax] **1** ADJ, *comp* **er** [ˈʃveçɐ], *superl* **ste(r, s)** [ˈʃveçstə] weak (*auch Gram*); *Gesundheit, Beteiligung, Gedächtnis, Gehör* poor; *Ton, Anzeichen, Hoffnung, Bewegung* faint; *Licht* dim; *Wind* light; (*Comm*) *Nachfrage, Geschäft* slack; **das ist ein ~es Bild** (*inf*) *or* **eine ~e Leistung** (*inf*) that's a poor show (*inf*); **jds ~e Seite/Stelle** sb's weak point/spot; **ein ~er Trost** cold comfort; **in einem ~en Augenblick, in einer ~en Stunde** in a weak moment; **jdn ~ machen** (*inf*) to soften sb up; **mach mich nicht ~!** (*inf*) don't say that! (*inf*); **in etw** (*dat*) **~ sein** to be weak in sth; **auf ~en Beinen** *or* **Füßen stehen** (*fig*) to be on shaky ground; (*Theorie*) to be shaky; **nur nicht ~ werden!** don't weaken!; **schwächer werden** to grow weaker; (*Augen*) to fail; (*Stimme*) to grow fainter; (*Licht*) to (grow) dim; (*Ton*) to fade; (*Nachfrage*) to fall off; **die Schwachen** the weak; **der Schwächere** the weaker (person); (*gegenüber Gegner*) the underdog **2** ADV, *comp* **er**, *superl* **am ~sten (a)** (= *leicht*) *schlagen* weakly; *vibrieren, radioaktiv* slightly; *spüren, riechen, hören* barely **(b)** (= *spärlich*) *besucht, bestückt* poorly; **~ besiedelt** *or* **bevölkert** sparsely populated **(c)** (= *geringfügig*) *sich beteiligen* very little; **~ aktiv** *Atommüll etc* low-level; **~ radioaktiv** with low-level radioactivity **(d)** (= *mild*) *salzen, süßen* slightly; *würzen* lightly; *pfeffern* mildly

Schwäche [ˈʃveçə] F **-, -n** weakness; (*von Stimme*) feebleness; (*von Licht*) dimness; (*von Wind*) lightness; (= *-anfall*) feeling of weakness; **sie brach vor ~ zusammen** she was so weak she collapsed; **jeder Mensch hat seine ~n** we all have our little weaknesses

schwächen [ˈʃveçn̩] **1** VT (*lit, fig*) to weaken **2** VR to weaken oneself

Schwach-: Schwachkopf M (*inf*) dimwit (*inf*); **schwachköpfig** (*inf*) **1** ADJ idiotic **2** ADV idiotically

schwächlich [ˈʃveçlɪç] ADJ weakly

Schwächling [ˈʃveçlɪŋ] M **-s, -e** (*lit, fig*) weakling

Schwach-: Schwachpunkt M weak point; **Schwachsinn** M (*Med*) mental deficiency; (*fig inf*) (= *unsinnige Tat*) idiocy *no indef art*; (= *Quatsch*) rubbish (*Brit inf*), garbage; **schwachsinnig 1** ADJ (*Med*) mentally deficient; (*fig inf*) idiotic **2** ADV (*fig inf*) idiotically; **Schwachsinnige(r)** [ˈʃvaxzɪnɪgə] MF DECL AS ADJ mental defective; (*fig inf*) moron (*inf*), imbecile (*inf*); **Schwachstelle** F weak point; **Schwachstrom** M (*Elec*) low-voltage current

Schwächung [ˈʃveçʊŋ] F **-, -en** weakening

Schwaden [ˈʃvaːdn̩] M **-s, -** USU PL (= *Dunst*) cloud

Schwafelei [ʃvafəˈlai] F **-, -en** (*pej inf*) drivel *no pl* (*inf*); (= *das Schwafeln*) drivelling (*Brit*) *or* driveling (*US*) on (*inf*)

schwafeln [ˈʃvaːfln̩] (*pej inf*) **1** VI to drivel (on) (*inf*); (*in einer Prüfung*) to waffle (*inf*) **2** VT *dummes Zeug* **~** to talk drivel (*inf*); **was schwafelst du da?** what are you drivelling (*Brit*) *or* driveling (*US*) on about? (*inf*)

Schwafler [ˈʃvaːflɐ] M **-s, -**, **Schwaflerin** [-ərɪn] F **-, -nen** (*pej inf*) windbag *inf*

Schwager [ˈʃvaːgɐ] M **-s, -** [ˈʃveːgɐ] brother-in-law

Schwägerin [ˈʃveːgərɪn] F **-, -nen** sister-in-law

Schwalbe [ˈʃvalbə] F **-, -n** swallow; **eine ~ machen** (*Ftbl sl*) to take a dive; **eine ~ macht noch keinen Sommer** (*Prov*) one swallow doesn't make a summer (*Prov*)

Schwall [ʃval] M **-(e)s, -e** flood

schwallen [ˈʃvalən] (*sl*) **1** VI to chatter on **2** VT to chatter about

schwamm PRET *von* **schwimmen**

Schwamm [ʃvam] M **-(e)s, -e** [ˈʃvemə] **(a)** sponge; **~ drüber!** (*inf*) (let's) forget it! **(b)** (*dial:* = *Pilz*) fungus; (*essbar*) mushroom; (*giftig*) toadstool **(c)** (= *Hausschwamm*) dry rot; **den ~ haben** to have dry rot

schwammig [ˈʃvamɪç] **1** ADJ **(a)** (*lit*) spongy **(b)** (*fig*) *Gesicht, Hände* puffy; (= *vage*) *Begriff, Gesetz, Regelung* woolly **2** ADV (= *vage*) vaguely

Schwan [ʃvaːn] M -(e)s, ¨e [ʃveːnə] swan

schwand PRET von **schwinden**

schwanen [ʃvaːnən] VI IMPERS **ihm schwante etwas** he sensed something might happen; **mir schwant nichts Gutes** I don't like it

Schwanen-: Schwanengesang M (fig) swan song; **Schwanenhals** M swan's neck; (fig) swanlike neck; (Tech) gooseneck; **schwanenweiß** ADJ (geh) lily-white

schwang PRET von **schwingen**

schwanger [ʃvaŋɐ] ADJ pregnant; **~ sein** or **gehen** to be pregnant; **mit etw ~ gehen** (fig) to be big with sth

Schwangere [ʃvaŋərə] F DECL AS ADJ pregnant woman

schwängern [ʃvɛŋɐn] VT to make pregnant; **mit etw geschwängert sein** (fig) to be impregnated with sth

Schwangerschaft [ʃvaŋɐʃaft] F -, -en pregnancy

Schwangerschafts-: Schwangerschaftsabbruch M termination of pregnancy; **Schwangerschaftsgymnastik** F antenatal (esp Brit) or prenatal exercises pl; **Schwangerschaftsstreifen** M stretchmark; **Schwangerschaftstest** M pregnancy test; **Schwangerschaftsunterbrechung** F termination of pregnancy

schwanken [ʃvaŋkn] VI **(a)** (= wanken, sich wiegen) to sway; (Schiff) (auf und ab) to pitch; (seitwärts) to roll; (Preise, Temperatur etc) to fluctuate; (Gebrauch, Schätzungen, Angaben) to vary; (Phys, Math) to fluctuate; **ins Schwanken kommen** or **geraten** (Baum, Gebäude etc) to start to sway; (Erde) to start to shake; (Preise, Kurs, Temperatur etc) to start to fluctuate; (Autorität, Überzeugung etc) to begin to waver **(b)** AUX SEIN (= gehen) to stagger **(c)** (= hin und her gerissen werden) to vacillate; (= wechseln) to alternate; **sie schwankte zwischen Stolz und Mitleid** she alternated between pride and pity **(d)** (= zögern) to hesitate; (= sich nicht schlüssig sein) to waver **~, ob** to hesitate as to whether

schwankend ADJ **(a)** (= wankend, sich wiegend) swaying; Schiff (auf und ab) pitching; (seitwärts) rolling; Preise, Temperatur, Stimmung etc fluctuating esp attr; Gebrauch varying; **auf ~en Füßen stehen** (fig) to be shaky **(b)** Mensch staggering; Gang rolling; Schritt unsteady **(c)** (= unschlüssig) uncertain; (= zögernd) hesitant; (= unbeständig) unsteady

Schwankung [ʃvaŋkʊŋ] F -, -en **(a)** (hin und her) swaying no pl; (auf und ab) shaking no pl, rocking no pl **(b)** (von Preisen, Temperatur etc) fluctuation (+gen in); **seelische ~en** mental ups and downs (inf)

Schwankungsbereich M range

Schwanz [ʃvants] M -es, ¨e [ʃvɛntsə] **(a)** (lit, fig) tail; (inf: von Zug) (tail) end; **das Pferd** or **den Gaul beim** or **am ~ aufzäumen** to do things back to front **(b)** (sl: = Penis) prick (sl)

schwänzen [ʃvɛntsn] (inf) **1** VT Stunde, Vorlesung to skip (inf); Schule to play truant (esp Brit) or hooky (esp US inf) from **2** VI to play truant (esp Brit inf) or hooky (esp US inf)

Schwanz-: Schwanzende NT tip of the tail; (fig) tail end; (von Flugzeug) tail; **Schwanzfeder** F tail feather; **Schwanzflosse** F tail fin

schwappen [ʃvapn] VI **(a)** (Flüssigkeit) to slosh around **(b)** AUX SEIN (= überschwappen) to splash; (fig) to spill; **die Modewelle schwappt nach Europa** the fashion spills over into Europe

Schwarm [ʃvarm] M -(e)s, ¨e [ʃvɛrmə] **(a)** swarm; (= Flugzeugformation) flight **(b)** (inf: = Angebeteter) idol; (= Vorliebe) passion; **der neue Englischlehrer ist ihr ~** she's got a crush on the new English teacher (inf)

schwärmen [ʃvɛrmən] VI **(a)** AUX SEIN to swarm **(b)** (= begeistert reden) to enthuse (von about); **für jdn/etw ~** to be crazy about sb/sth (inf); **ins Schwärmen kommen** or **geraten** to go into raptures

Schwärmer [ʃvɛrmɐ] M -s, -, **Schwärmerin** [-ərɪn] F -, -nen (= Begeisterter) enthusiast; (= Fantast) dreamer; (= sentimentaler ~) sentimentalist

Schwärmerei [ʃvɛrmə'rai] F -, -en (= Begeisterung) enthusiasm; (in Worten ausgedrückt) effusion no pl; (= Leidenschaft) passion; (= Verzückung) rapture

schwärmerisch [ʃvɛrmərɪʃ] **1** ADJ (= begeistert) enthusiastic; Worte, Übertreibung effusive; (= verliebt) infatuated **2** ADV enthusiastically; (verliebt) infatuated

Schwärmzeit F swarming time

Schwarte [ʃvartə] F -, -n **(a)** (= Speckschwarte) rind **(b)** (inf) (= Buch) tome (hum); (= Gemälde) daub(ing) (pej)

Schwartenmagen M (Cook) brawn

schwarz [ʃvarts] **1** ADJ, comp ¨er [ʃvɛrtsə], superl ¨este(r, s) [ʃvɛrtsəstə] **(a)** (lit, fig) black; (= stark sonnengebräunt) deeply tanned; **der Schwarze Erdteil** the Dark Continent; **der Schwarze Freitag** Black Friday; **~es Gold** (fig) black gold; **~er Humor** black humour (Brit) or humor (US); **~er Kaffee/Tee** black coffee/tea; (= Magie) the Black Art; **~e Liste** blacklist; **~es Loch** black hole; **~e Magie** black magic; **der ~e Mann** (= Schornsteinfeger) the (chimney) sweep; (= Kinderschreck) the bogeyman; **das Schwarze Meer** the Black Sea; **Schwarzer Peter** (Cards) children's card game, ≈ old maid; **jdm den ~en Peter zuschieben** or **zuspielen** (fig) (= die Verantwortung abschieben) to pass the buck to sb (inf); (= etw Unangenehmes abschieben) to give sb the worst of the deal; **das ~e Schaf (in der Familie)** the black sheep (of the family); **die Schwarze Witwe** the Black Widow (spider); **etw ~ auf weiß haben** to have sth in black and white; **etw in den schwärzesten Farben** or **~ in ~ schildern/darstellen** to describe/present sth in the blackest terms; **wie die Nacht/wie Ebenholz** jet-black; **in den ~en Zahlen sein, ~e Zahlen schreiben** (Comm) to be in the black; **sich ~ ärgern** to get extremely annoyed; **mir wurde ~ vor den Augen** I blacked out; **da kannst du warten, bis du ~ wirst** (inf) you can wait till the cows come home (inf) **(b)** (inf: = ungesetzlich) illicit; **der ~e Markt** the black market; **~e Geschäfte machen** to do shady deals; **~es Konto** secret account

2 ADV, comp ¨er, superl **am ¨esten (a)** (= mit schwarzer Farbe) anstreichen black; einrichten, sich kleiden in black; **~ gestreift** with black stripes

(b) (= illegal) erwerben illegally; **sich** (dat) **etw ~ besorgen** to get sth illicitly; (= auf dem Schwarzmarkt) to get sth on the black market; **etw ~ verdienen** to earn sth on the side (inf)

Schwarz [ʃvarts] NT -, NO PL INV black; **in ~ gehen** to wear black

Schwarz-: Schwarzafrika NT Black Africa; **Schwarzarbeit** F illicit work; (nach Feierabend) moonlighting (inf); **schwarzarbeiten** VI SEP to do illicit work; (nach Feierabend) to moonlight (inf); **Schwarzarbeiter(in)** M(F) person doing illicit work; (nach Feierabend) moonlighter (inf); **schwarzbraun** ADJ dark brown; **Schwarzbrenner(in)** M(F) moonshiner (inf); **Schwarzbrennerei** F moonshine still (inf); **Schwarzbrot** NT (braun) brown rye bread; (schwarz, wie Pumpernickel) black bread

Schwarze [ʃvartsə] F DECL AS ADJ black woman/girl; (= Schwarzhaarige) black-haired woman/girl

Schwärze [ʃvɛrtsə] F -, -n **(a)** (no pl: = Dunkelheit) blackness **(b)** (Farbe) black dye; (= Druckerschwärze) printer's ink

schwärzen [ʃvɛrtsn] VTR to blacken

Schwarze(r) [ʃvartsə] M DECL AS ADJ black; (= Schwarzhaariger) dark(-haired) man/boy; (pej sl: = Katholik) Catholic; (Aus: = schwarzer Mokka) black (mocha) coffee

Schwarze(s) [ʃvartsə] NT DECL AS ADJ black; (auf Zielscheibe) bull's-eye; **das kleine ~** (inf) one's/a little black dress; **ins ~ treffen** (lit, fig) to score a bull's-eye

Schwarz-: schwarzfahren VI SEP IRREG AUX SEIN (ohne zu zahlen) to travel without paying; (ohne Führerschein) to drive without a licence (Brit) or license (US); **Schwarzfahrer(in)** M(F) fare dodger (inf); (ohne Führerschein) driver without a licence (Brit) or license (US); **Schwarzgeld** NT illegal earnings pl; **schwarzhaarig** ADJ black-haired; **eine Schwarzhaarige** a black-haired woman/girl; **Schwarzhandel** M, NO PL black market; (= Tätigkeit) black marketeering; **im ~ on** the black market; **Schwarzhändler(in)** M(F) black marketeer; **schwarzhören** VI SEP (Rad) to use a radio without having a licence (Brit) or license (US)

Schwarzkonto NT secret account

schwärzlich [ʃvɛrtslɪç] ADJ blackish; Haut dusky

Schwarz-: schwarz malen 1 VI to be pessimistic **2** VT to be pessimistic about; **Schwarzmalerei** F pessimism; **Schwarzmarkt** M black market; **Schwarzmarktpreis** M black-market price; **Schwarzpulver** NT black (gun)powder; **schwarz sehen** IRREG **1** VI to be pessimistic about **2** VI to be pessimistic; **für jdn/etw ~** to be pessimistic about sb/sth; **schwarzsehen** VI SEP IRREG (TV) to watch TV without a licence (Brit) or license (US); **Schwarzseherei** [-zeːə'rai] F -, NO PL pessimism; **Schwarztee** M black tea; **Schwarzwald** M Black

Forest; **Schwarzwälder** [-vɛldə] ADJ ATTR Black Forest; ~ **Kirschtorte** Black Forest gateau (*Brit*) *or* cake (*US*); ~ **Kirschwasser** kirsch

schwarzwei̱ß, schwarz-wei̱ß 🔟 ADJ black-and-white *attr*, black and white **🔟** ADV black and white; ~ **gepunktet/ gestreift** with black and white polka dots/stripes

Schwarzwei̱ß-: Schwarzwei̱ßaufnahme F black-and-white (shot); **Schwarzwei̱ßfilm** M black-and-white film; **Schwarzwei̱ßfoto** NT black-and-white (photo)

Schwarz-: Schwarzwild NT wild boars *pl*; **Schwarzwurzel** F viper's grass; (*Cook*) salsify

Schwatz [ʃvats] M **-es, -e** (*inf*) chat; **auf einen ~ kommen** to come (round (*Brit*) *or* by) for a chat

Schwätzchen [ʃvɛtsçən] NT **-s, -** DIM *von* **Schwatz**

schwatzen [ʃvatsn] **🔟** VI to talk; (*pej*) (*unaufhörlich*) to chatter; (*über belanglose, oberflächliche Dinge, kindisch*) to prattle; (= *Unsinn reden*) to blather (*inf*); (= *klatschen*) to gossip; **über Politik ~** to prattle on about politics (*pej*) **🔟** VT to talk; **dummes Zeug ~** to talk a lot of rubbish (*esp Brit inf*)

schwätzen [ʃvɛtsn] VTI (*S Ger, Aus*) = **schwatzen**

Schwätzer [ʃvɛtsɐ] M **-s, -, Schwätzerin** [-ərɪn] F **-, -nen** (*pej*) chatterbox (*inf*); (= *Schwafler*) windbag (*inf*); (= *Klatschmaul*) gossip

Schwätzerei [ʃvɛtsə'rai] F **-, -en** (*pej*) (= *Gerede, im Unterricht*) chatter; (*über Belanglosigkeiten, kindisch*) prattle; (= *Unsinn*) drivel (*inf*); (= *Klatsch*) gossip

Schwebe [ʃveːbə] F **-, NO PL in der ~ sein/bleiben** (*fig*) to be/ remain in the balance; (*Jur, Comm*) to be/remain pending

Schwebe-: Schwebebahn F suspension railway; (= *Seilbahn*) cable railway; **Schwebebalken** M, **Schwebebaum** M (*Sport*) beam

schweben [ʃveːbn] VI **(a)** (= *frei im Raum stehen, hängen*) (*Nebel, Rauch*) to hang; (*Wolke*) to float; (= *sich unbeweglich in der Luft halten: Geier etc*) to hover; (= *nachklingen, zurückbleiben: Klänge, Parfüm*) to linger (on); **etw schwebt jdm vor Augen** (*fig*) sb has sth in mind; (*Bild*) sb sees sth in his mind's eye; **in großer Gefahr ~** to be in great danger; **der Verletzte schwebt in Lebensgefahr** the injured man is in a critical condition
(b) AUX SEIN (= *durch die Luft gleiten*) to float; (= *hochschweben*) to soar; (= *niederschweben*) to float down; (*an Seil etc*) to swing; (= *sich leichtfüßig bewegen*) to glide

schwebend ADJ (*Tech, Chem*) suspended; (*fig*) *Fragen etc* unresolved; *Musik, Rhythmus* floating; (*Jur, Comm*) *Verfahren, Geschäft* pending

Schwede [ʃveːdə] M **-n, -n, Schwedin** F [ʃveːdɪn] **-, -nen** Swede

Schweden [ʃveːdn] NT **-s** Sweden

schwedisch [ʃveːdɪʃ] ADJ Swedish; **hinter ~en Gardinen** (*inf*) behind bars; **hinter ~e Gardinen kommen** (*inf*) to be put behind bars

Schwefel [ʃveːfl] M **-s, NO PL** (*abbr* **S**) sulphur (*Brit*), sulfur (*US*)

Schwefel- IN CPDS sulphur (*Brit*), sulfur (*US*); **schwefelartig** ADJ sulphur(e)ous (*Brit*), sulfurous (*US*); **Schwefelblume** F, **Schwefelblüte** F flowers of sulphur (*Brit*) *or* sulfur (*US*); **Schwefeldioxid** NT sulphur (*Brit*) *or* sulfur (*US*) dioxide; **schwefelhaltig** ADJ containing sulphur (*Brit*) *or* sulfur (*US*)

schwefeln [ʃveːfln] VT to sulphurize (*Brit*), to sulfurize (*US*)

Schwefelsäure F sulphuric (*Brit*) *or* sulfuric (*US*) acid

schweflig [ʃveːflɪç] **🔟** ADJ sulphurous (*Brit*), sulfurous (*US*) **🔟** ADV **es roch ~** there was a smell of sulphur (*Brit*) *or* sulfur (*US*)

Schweif [ʃvaif] M **-(e)s, -e** (*auch Astron*) tail

schweifen [ʃvaifn] VI AUX SEIN (*lit gehfig*) to roam; **seine Gedanken in die Vergangenheit ~ lassen** to let one's thoughts roam over the past; **seinen Blick ~ lassen** to let one's eyes wander (*über etw (acc)* over sth)

Schweige-: Schweigegeld NT hush money; **Schweigeminute** F one minute('s) silence

schweigen [ʃvaign], *pret* **schwieg** [ʃviːk], *ptp* **geschwiegen** [gə'ʃviːgn] VI to be silent; (= *aufhören: Musik, Geräusch, Wind*) to stop; **kannst du ~?** can you keep a secret?; **seit gestern ~ die Waffen** yesterday the guns fell silent; **plötzlich schwieg er** suddenly he fell silent; **er kann ~ wie ein Grab** he knows how to keep quiet; **auf etw (acc)/zu etw ~** to make no reply to sth; **ganz zu ~ von ..., von ... ganz zu ~** to say nothing of ...

Schweigen NT **-s, NO PL** silence; **jdn zum ~ bringen** to silence sb (*auch euph*); **(es herrscht) ~ im Walde** (there is) dead silence

schweigend 🔟 ADJ silent **🔟** ADV in silence; ~ **über etw** (*acc*) **hinweggehen** to pass over sth in silence

Schweigepflicht F pledge of secrecy; (*von Anwalt*) requirement of confidentiality; **die ärztliche ~** medical confidentiality; **die priesterliche ~** a priest's duty to remain silent; **unter ~ stehen** to be bound to observe confidentiality; **jdn von der ~ entbinden** to release sb from his/her duty of confidentiality

schweigsam [ʃvaikzaːm] ADJ silent; (*als Charaktereigenschaft*) taciturn; (= *verschwiegen*) discreet

Schweigsamkeit F **-, NO PL** silence; (*als Charaktereigenschaft*) silent manner

Schwein [ʃvain] NT **-s, -e (a)** pig, hog (*US*); (*Fleisch*) pork; **sich wie die ~e benehmen** (*inf*) to behave like pigs (*inf*); **bluten wie ein ~** (*inf*) to bleed like a stuck pig **(b)** (*inf: Mensch*) pig (*inf*), swine; (= *Schweinehund*) bastard (*sl*); **ein armes/faules ~** a poor/lazy bastard (*sl*); **kein ~** nobody **(c)** NO PL (*inf: = Glück*) ~ **haben** to be lucky; ~ **gehabt!** that's a stroke of luck

Schweine-: Schweinebauch M (*Cook*) belly of pork; **Schweinebraten** M joint of pork; (*gekocht*) roast pork; **Schweinefleisch** NT pork; **Schweinefraß** M (*fig inf*) muck (*inf*); **Schweinegeld** NT (*inf*) **ein ~** a packet (*Brit inf*), a fistful (*US inf*); **Schweinehund** M (*inf*) bastard (*sl*); **den inneren ~ überwinden** (*inf*) to conquer one's weaker self; **Schweinemast** F pig-fattening; (*Futter*) pig food; **Schweinepest** F (*Vet*) swine fever

Schweinerei [ʃvainə'rai] F **-, -en** (*inf*) **(a)** NO PL mess; **es ist eine ~, wenn ...** it's disgusting if ...; **so eine ~!** how disgusting! **(b)** (= *Skandal*) scandal; (= *Gemeinheit*) dirty trick (*inf*); **ich finde es eine ~, wie er sie behandelt** I think it's disgusting the way he treats her; **(so eine) ~!** what a dirty trick! (*inf*) **(c)** (= *Zote*) smutty joke; (= *unzüchtige Handlung*) indecent act; ~**en machen** to do dirty things; **das Buch besteht nur aus ~en** the book is just a lot of dirt

Schweine-: Schweineschnitzel NT pork cutlet; **Schweinestall** M (*lit, fig*) pigsty, pigpen (*esp US*); **Schweinezucht** F pig-breeding; (*Hof*) pig farm

Schweinigel [ʃvainiːgl] M (*inf*) dirty pig (*inf*)

schweinisch [ʃvainɪʃ] (*inf*) **🔟** ADJ *Benehmen* piggish (*inf*); *Witz* dirty **🔟** ADV like a pig; **benimm dich nicht so ~!** stop behaving like a pig!

Schweinkram M (*inf*) dirt, filth

Schweins-: Schweinshaxe F (*S Ger Cook*) knuckle of pork; **Schweinsleder** NT pigskin; **schweinsledern** ADJ pigskin; **Schweinsohr** NT pig's ear; (*Gebäck*) (kidney-shaped) pastry

Schweiß [ʃvais] M **-es, NO PL** sweat; **der ~ brach ihm aus** he broke out in a sweat; **nass von ~** soaked with perspiration; **kalter ~** cold sweat; **das hat viel ~ gekostet** it was a sweat (*inf*)

Schweiß-: Schweißapparat M welding equipment *no indef art, no pl*; **Schweißausbruch** M sweating *no indef art, no pl*; **Schweißband** [-bant] NT, *pl* **-bänder** sweatband; **schweißbedeckt** ADJ covered in sweat; **Schweißbrenner** M (*Tech*) welding torch; **Schweißdrüse** F (*Anat*) sweat gland

schweißen [ʃvaisn] VTI (*Tech*) to weld

Schweißer [ʃvaisɐ] M **-s, -, Schweißerin** [-ərɪn] F **-, -nen** (*Tech*) welder

Schweiß-: Schweißfleck M sweat stain; **Schweißfuß** M sweaty foot; **schweißgebadet** [-gəbaːdət] ADJ bathed in sweat; **Schweißgeruch** M smell of sweat

schweißig [ʃvaisɪç] ADJ sweaty

Schweiß-: Schweißnaht F (*Tech*) weld; **schweißnass** ADJ sweaty; **Schweißperle** F bead of perspiration; **Schweißstelle** F weld; **Schweißtechnik** F welding (engineering); **schweißtreibend** ADJ *Tätigkeit* that makes one sweat; ~**es Mittel** sudorific (*spec*); **Schweißtropfen** M drop of sweat; **schweißüberströmt** [-ly:bɐʃtrøːmt] ADJ streaming with sweat

Schweiz [ʃvaits] F **- die ~** Switzerland

Schweizer [ʃvaitsɐ] ADJ ATTR Swiss; ~ **Käse** Swiss cheese

Schweizer [ʃvaitsɐ] M **-s, -, Schweizerin** [-ərɪn] F **-, -nen** Swiss

schweizerdeutsch ADJ Swiss-German

schweizerisch [ʃvaitsərɪʃ] ADJ Swiss

Schweizermesser NT Swiss army knife

Schwelbrand M smouldering (*Brit*) *or* smoldering (*US*) fire

schwelen [ʃveːlən] VI (*lit, fig*) to smoulder (*Brit*), to smolder (*US*)

schwelgen [ˈʃvɛlɡn̩] VI to indulge oneself (*in +dat* in); **wir schwelgten in Kaviar und Sekt** we feasted on caviar and champagne; **in Erinnerungen ~** to indulge in reminiscences; **im Überfluss ~** to live in the lap of luxury

Schwelle [ˈʃvɛlə] F -, -n (a) (= *Türschwelle*) (*fig*) (*Psych*) threshold; (= *Stein etc*) sill; (*auf Straße*) bump; **an der ~ (zu) einer neuen Zeit** on the threshold of a new era; **an der ~ des Grabes** *or* **Todes** at death's door (b) (*Rail*) sleeper (*Brit*), crosstie (*US*)

schwellen [ˈʃvɛlən] ■ VI, *pret* **schwoll** [ʃvɔl], *ptp* **geschwollen** [ɡəˈʃvɔlən] AUX SEIN to swell; (*lit: Körperteile auch*) to swell up; **der Wind schwoll zum Sturm** the wind grew into a storm; *siehe auch* **geschwollen** ■ VT (*geh*) Segel to swell (out)

Schwellen-: Schwellenangst F (*Psych*) fear of entering a place; (*fig*) fear of embarking on something new; **Schwellenland** NT fast-developing nation; **Schwellenmacht** F rising power

Schwellkörper M (*Anat*) erectile tissue

Schwellung [ˈʃvɛlʊŋ] F -, -en swelling

Schwemme [ˈʃvɛmə] F -, -n (a) (*für Tiere*) watering place (b) (= *Überfluss*) glut (*an +dat* of) (c) (= *Kneipe*) bar (d) (*Aus: im Warenhaus*) bargain basement

schwemmen [ˈʃvɛmən] VT (= *treiben*) Sand etc to wash; Vieh to water; (= *wässern*) Felle to soak; (*Aus:* = *spülen*) Wäsche to rinse; **etw an(s) Land ~** to wash sth ashore

Schwengel [ˈʃvɛŋl̩] M -s, - (= *Glockenschwengel*) clapper; (= *Pumpenschwengel*) handle

Schwenk [ʃvɛŋk] M -(e)s, -s (= *Drehung*) wheel; (*Film*) pan; (*fig*) about-turn; **einen ~ machen** (*Kolonne*) to wheel around

Schwenk-: Schwenkarm M swivel arm; **schwenkbar** ADJ swivelling (*Brit*), swiveling (*US*); Lampe *auch* swivel *attr*; Geschütz traversable; **Schwenkbereich** M jib range

schwenken [ˈʃvɛŋkn̩] ■ VT (a) (= *schwingen*) to wave; (= *herumfuchteln mit*) to brandish (b) Lampe etc to swivel; Kran to swing; Geschütz to traverse; Kamera to pan (c) (*Cook*) Kartoffeln, Nudeln to toss ■ VI AUX SEIN to swing; (*Kolonne von Soldaten, Autos etc*) to wheel; (*Geschütz*) to traverse; (*Kamera*) to pan; (*fig*) to swing over

Schwenkung [ˈʃvɛŋkʊŋ] F -, -en swing; (*Mil*) wheel; (*von Kran*) swing; (*von Geschütz*) traverse; (*von Kamera*) pan(ning)

schwer [ʃveːɐ] ■ ADJ (a) (*lit, fig*) heavy; (= *massiv*) Fahrzeug, Maschine powerful; **ein 10 kg ~er Sack** a sack weighing 10 kgs; **die Beine wurden mir ~** my legs grew heavy; **er ist fünf Millionen ~** (*inf*) he is worth five million
(b) (= *ernst*) serious, grave; Zeit, Leben, Schicksal hard; Leiden, Strafe, Buße severe; **~e Verluste** heavy losses; **Schweres erlebt** *or* **durchgemacht haben** to have been through (some) hard times; **das war ein ~er Schlag für ihn** it was a hard blow for him
(c) (= *hart, anstrengend*) Amt, Aufgabe, Tag hard; Geburt, Tod difficult
(d) (= *schwierig*) hard
(e) (*inf*) **~es Geld machen** to make a packet (*inf*)
■ ADV (a) (= *mit schwerer Last*) beladen, bepackt, bewaffnet heavily; **~ auf jdm/etw liegen/lasten** to lie/weigh heavily on sb/sth; **~ an etw** (*dat*) **zu tragen haben** (*sich abschleppen*) to be loaded down with sth; (*fig*) an Schuld etc to be heavily burdened with sth
(b) (= *hart*) arbeiten, schuften hard; bestrafen, tadeln, missbilligen severely; **~ geprüft sein** to be sorely tried; **~ verdientes Geld** hard-earned money; **es ~ haben** to have a hard time of it; **es mit jdm ~ haben** to have a hard time with sb
(c) (= *ernstlich*) seriously; behindert severely; beleidigen, kränken, treffen, gekränkt deeply; **~ beschädigt** severely disabled; **~ erkältet sein** to have a bad cold; **~ stürzen** to have a bad fall; **~ verunglücken** to have a serious accident
(d) (= *nicht einfach*) **~ zu sehen/sagen** hard to see/say; **es lässt sich ~ abschätzen/voraussagen** it's hard to estimate/to predict; **sich ~ entschließen können** to find it hard to decide; **er lernt ~** he's a slow learner; **~ hören** to be hard of hearing; **ein ~ erziehbares Kind** a maladjusted child; **~ verdaulich** Speisen indigestible; (*fig auch*) difficult; **etw ist ~ verdaulich** sth is hard to digest; **~ verständlich** difficult to understand; **~ verträglich sein** (Speise) to be indigestible; (Medikament) to have side effects; (Klima) to be unhealthy
(e) (*inf:* = *sehr*) really; **da musste ich ~ aufpassen** I really had to watch out; **~ betrunken** completely drunk; **sich ~**

blamieren to make a proper fool (*Brit*) *or* an ass (*esp US*) of oneself; **ich werde mich ~ hüten** there's no way (I will) (*inf*); **er ist ~ in Ordnung** he's OK (*inf*)

Schwer-: Schwerarbeit F heavy labour (*Brit*) *or* labor (*US*); **Schwerarbeiter(in)** M(F) labourer (*Brit*), laborer (*US*); **Schwerathletik** F *weightlifting sports, boxing, wrestling etc*; **Schwerbehinderte(r)** MF DECL AS ADJ severely disabled person; **Schwerbeschädigte(r)** MF DECL AS ADJ severely disabled person

Schwere [ˈʃveːrə] F -, NO PL (a) heaviness (b) (= *Ernsthaftigkeit, von Krankheit*) seriousness (c) (= *Schwierigkeit*) difficulty; **das hängt von der ~ der Aufgabe ab** it depends on how difficult the task is (d) (*Phys:* = *Schwerkraft*) gravitation

Schwere-: schwerelos ADJ weightless; **Schwerelosigkeit** F -, NO PL weightlessness

schwererziehbar ADJ ATTR *Kind siehe* schwer

schwer fallen VI IRREG AUX SEIN to be difficult (*jdm* for sb); **das dürfte dir doch nicht ~** you shouldn't find that too difficult

schwerfällig ■ ADJ (= *unbeholfen*) Gang, Bewegungen heavy (in one's movements); (= *langsam*) Verstand slow; Stil, Übersetzung ponderous; Verwaltung, Staatsapparat cumbersome; **~ sein** (Mensch) to move heavily ■ ADV heavily; sprechen ponderously; **sich bewegen** with difficulty; **du bewegst dich so ~** you seem to have so much trouble moving

Schwer-: Schwergewicht NT (a) (*Sport, fig*) heavyweight (b) (= *Nachdruck*) stress; **das ~ auf etw** (*acc*) **legen** to put the stress on sth; **schwerhörig** ADJ hard of hearing; **du bist wohl ~!** (*inf*) are you deaf? (*inf*); **Schwerhörigkeit** F hardness of hearing; **Schwerindustrie** F heavy industry; **Schwerkraft** F, NO PL gravity

schwerlich [ˈʃveːɐlɪç] ADV hardly

Schwer-: schwer machen VT (a) **jdm das Herz ~** to make sb's heart heavy; **jdm das Leben ~** to make life difficult for sb (b) **es jdm/sich ~** to make it *or* things difficult for sb/oneself; **Schwermetall** NT heavy metal

Schwermut [ˈʃveːɐmuːt] F -, NO PL melancholy

schwermütig [ˈʃveːɐmyːtɪç] ADJ melancholy

schwer nehmen VT SEP IRREG **etw ~** to take sth hard

Schwerpunkt M (*Phys*) centre (*Brit*) *or* center (*US*) of gravity; (*fig*) (= *Zentrum*) centre (*Brit*), center (*US*); (= *Hauptgewicht*) main emphasis *or* stress; **politische/thematische ~e** main political/thematic emphases; **~e setzen** to set priorities

schwerreich ADJ (*inf*) stinking rich (*inf*)

Schwert [ʃveːɐt] NT -(e)s, -er sword

Schwert-: Schwertfisch M swordfish; **Schwerthieb** M sword stroke; **Schwertlilie** F (*Bot*) iris

Schwer-: schwer tun VR IRREG (*inf*) **sich** (*dat*) **mit** *or* **bei etw ~** to make a big deal of sth (*inf*); **Schwertwal** M killer whale; **Schwerverbrecher(in)** M(F) criminal, felon (*esp Jur*); **schwerverdaulich** etc ADJ ATTR *siehe* schwer; **Schwerverkehr** M heavy goods traffic; **Schwerverkehrsabgabe** F heavy goods vehicle supplement; **Schwerverletzte(r)** MF DECL AS ADJ serious casualty; **Schwerverwundete(r)** MF DECL AS ADJ major casualty; **Schwerwasserreaktor** M heavy water reactor; **schwerwiegend** ADJ (*fig*) Fehler, Mängel, Folgen serious

Schwester [ˈʃvɛstɐ] F -, -n sister; (= *Krankenschwester*) nurse; (= *Ordensschwester*) nun

Schwesterchen [ˈʃvɛstɐçən] NT -s, - little sister

Schwesterfirma F, **Schwestergesellschaft** F sister company

schwesterlich [ˈʃvɛstɐlɪç] ■ ADJ sisterly ■ ADV like sisters; **ich bin ihr ~ verbunden** she's like a sister to me

Schwesterliebe F sisterly love

Schwestern-: Schwesternheim NT nurses' home; **Schwesternhelfer(in)** M(F) nursing auxiliary (*Brit*) *or* assistant (*US*)

Schwester-: Schwesterpartei F sister party; **Schwesterschiff** NT sister ship

schwieg PRET *von* schweigen

Schwieger- [ˈʃviːɡɐ-]: **Schwiegereltern** PL parents-in-law *pl*; **Schwiegersohn** M son-in-law; **Schwiegertochter** F daughter-in-law; **Schwiegervater** M father-in-law

Schwiele [ˈʃviːlə] F -, -n callus; (= *Vernarbung*) welt

schwielig [ˈʃviːlɪç] ADJ Hände callused

schwierig [ˈʃviːrɪç] **ⓐ** ADJ difficult; **er ist ein ~er Fall** he is a problem **ⓑ** ADV **= zu übersetzen** difficult to translate; **das Gespräch verlief ~** the discussion didn't go well

Schwierigkeit F -, -en difficulty; **in ~en geraten** or **kommen** to get into difficulties; **jdm ~en machen** to make trouble for sb; **es macht mir überhaupt keine ~en** it won't be at all difficult for me; **jdn in ~en** (acc) **bringen** to create difficulties for sb; **mach keine ~en!** (inf) don't be difficult; **ohne ~en** without any difficulty; **ohne große ~(en)** without any great difficulty; **~en haben, etw zu tun** to have difficulties doing sth

Schwierigkeitsgrad M degree of difficulty

schwillt [ʃvɪlt] 3. PERS SING PRES von **schwellen**

Schwimm-: **Schwimmbad** NT swimming pool; (= Hallenbad) swimming baths pl; **Schwimmbecken** NT (swimming) pool

schwimmen [ˈʃvɪmən], pret **schwamm** [ʃvam], ptp **geschwommen** [gəˈʃvɔmən] AUX SEIN **ⓐ** VI (a) AUCH AUX HABEN to swim (b) (inf: = überschwemmt sein) (Boden) to be swimming (inf); **in Fett** (dat) **~** to be swimming in fat; **in seinem Blut ~** to be soaked in blood; **in** or **im Geld ~** to be rolling in it (inf) (c) (fig: = unsicher sein) to be at sea **ⓑ** VT AUCH AUX HABEN (Sport) to swim

Schwimmen NT -s, NO PL swimming; **zum ~ gehen** to go swimming; **ins ~ geraten** or **kommen** (fig) to begin to flounder

Schwimmer[1] M -s, - (Tech, Angeln) float

Schwimmer[2] [ˈʃvɪmɐ] M -s, -, **Schwimmerin** [-ərɪn] F -, -nen swimmer

Schwimm-: **Schwimmflosse** F fin; (von Taucher auch, von Wal, Robbe) flipper; **Schwimmflügel** M water wing; **Schwimmhaut** F (Orn) web; **Schwimmkran** M floating crane; **Schwimmsport** M swimming no art; **Schwimmstil** M stroke; (= Technik) (swimming) style; **Schwimmvogel** M water bird; **Schwimmweste** F life jacket

Schwindel [ˈʃvɪndl̩] M -s, NO PL (a) (= Gleichgewichtsstörung) dizziness; (esp nach Drehen) giddiness; **~ erregend** Höhe dizzy; Tempo dizzying; (inf) Preise astronomical; **in ~ erregender Höhe** at a dizzy height (b) (= Lüge) lie; (= Betrug) swindle, fraud; (= Vertrauensmissbrauch) con (inf); **das ist alles ~, was er da sagt** what he says is all a pack of lies; **mit Subventionen wird viel ~ getrieben** a lot of cheating goes on with subsidies (c) (inf: = Kram) **der ganze ~** the whole (kit and) caboodle (inf); **ich will von dem ganzen ~ nichts mehr wissen!** I don't want to hear another thing about the whole damn business (inf)

Schwindelanfall M dizzy turn

Schwindelei [ʃvɪndəˈlai] F -, -en (inf) (= leichte Lüge) fib (inf); (= leichter Betrug) swindle; **seine ständige ~** his constant fibbing (inf)

Schwindel-: **schwindelerregend** ADJ siehe **Schwindel**; **schwindelfrei** ADJ **Wendy ist nicht ~** Wendy can't stand heights; **sie ist völlig ~** she has a good head for heights

schwindelig [ˈʃvɪndəlɪç] ADJ dizzy; (esp nach Drehen) giddy; **mir ist** or **ich bin ~** I feel dizzy/giddy; **mir wird leicht ~** I get dizzy/giddy easily

schwindeln [ˈʃvɪndl̩n] **ⓐ** VI (a) **mir** or **mich** (rare) **schwindelt** I feel dizzy; **in ~der Höhe** at a dizzy height (b) (inf: = lügen) to fib (inf) **ⓑ** VT (inf) **das ist alles geschwindelt** it's all lies **ⓒ** VR **sich durch die Kontrollen/in den Saal ~** to con one's way through the checkpoint/into the hall (inf)

schwinden [ˈʃvɪndn̩], pret **schwand** [ʃvant], ptp **geschwunden** [gəˈʃvʊndn̩] VI AUX SEIN (a) (= abnehmen) to dwindle; (Schönheit) to fade; (Ton) to fade (away); (Erinnerung, Angst, Chance, Zeit) to fade away; (Kräfte) to fail; **im Schwinden begriffen sein** to be dwindling; **sein Mut schwand** his courage failed him (b) (Tech: Holz, Metall, Ton) to shrink

Schwindler [ˈʃvɪndlɐ] M -s, -, **Schwindlerin** [-ərɪn] F -, -nen swindler; (= Hochstapler) con man; (= Lügner) liar, fraud

schwindlerisch [ˈʃvɪndlərɪʃ] ADJ fraudulent

schwindlig [ˈʃvɪndlɪç] ADJ = **schwindelig**

schwingen [ˈʃvɪŋən], pret **schwang** [ʃvaŋ], ptp **geschwungen** [gəˈʃvʊŋən] **ⓐ** VT Schläger to swing; (drohend) Schwert, Stock etc to brandish; Hut, Zauberstab, Fahne to wave; siehe auch **geschwungen**

ⓑ VR **sich auf etw** (acc) **~** to leap onto sth; **sich über etw** (acc)

~ to vault across sth; **sich in die Luft or **Höhe ~** (geh) to soar (up) into the air; **die Brücke schwingt sich elegant über das Tal** the bridge sweeps elegantly over the valley **ⓒ** VI to swing; (= vibrieren) (Brücke, Saite) to vibrate; (Wellen) to oscillate; (geh: = nachklingen) to linger; **in ihren Worten schwang leichte Kritik** her words had a tone of mild criticism

Schwing-: **Schwingflügel** M casement window; **Schwingtür** F swing door

Schwingung [ˈʃvɪŋʊŋ] F -, -en (Phys) vibration; (von Wellen) oscillation; (fig) vibration; **in ~ kommen** to begin to swing or (Saite) to vibrate or (Wellen) to oscillate; **etw in ~(en) versetzen** to set sth swinging; to start sth vibrating; to start sth oscillating

Schwips [ʃvɪps] M -es, -e (inf) **einen (kleinen) ~ haben** to be (slightly) tipsy

schwirren [ˈʃvɪrən] VI AUX SEIN to whizz (Brit), to whiz (US); (Bienen, Fliegen etc) to buzz; **unzählige Gerüchte ~ durch die Presse** the press is buzzing with countless rumours (Brit) or rumors (US); **die Gedanken/Zahlen schwirrten mir durch den Kopf** thoughts/figures were buzzing through my head; **mir schwirrt der Kopf** my head is buzzing

Schwitze [ˈʃvɪtsə] F -, -n (Cook) roux

schwitzen [ˈʃvɪtsn̩] **ⓐ** VI (lit, fig) to sweat; (Fenster) to steam up **ⓑ** VR **sich halb tot ~** (inf) to get drenched in sweat; **sich nass ~** to get drenched in sweat

Schwitzen NT -s, NO PL sweating; **ins ~ kommen** or **geraten** (lit) to break out in a sweat; (fig) to get into a sweat; **jdn ins ~ bringen** (lit, fig) to make sb sweat

Schwitz-: **Schwitzkasten** M (Ringen) headlock; **jdn in den ~ nehmen** to get sb in a headlock; **Schwitzwasser** NT, NO PL condensation

schwofen [ˈʃvoːfn̩] VI (inf) to dance; **~ gehen** to go to a dance

schwoll PRET von **schwellen**

schwören [ˈʃvøːrən], pret **schwor** [ʃvoːɐ], ptp **geschworen** [gəˈʃvoːrən] **ⓐ** VT to swear; Eid auch to take; **ich schwöre es(, so wahr mir Gott helfe)** I swear it (so help me God); **er schwor bei Gott/seiner Ehre, nichts davon gewusst zu haben** he swore by God/on his honour (Brit) or honor (US) that he knew nothing about it; **ich kann darauf ~, dass ...** I could swear to it that ...; **ich hätte ~ mögen** or **hätte geschworen, dass ...** I could have sworn that ...; **jdm/sich etw ~** to swear sth to sb/oneself; **ich spreche nie mehr mit ihm, das habe ich mir geschworen** I have sworn never to speak to him again; **aber das hast du mir geschworen!** but you swore ...!; **sie schworen sich** (dat) **ewige Liebe** they swore (each other) eternal love **ⓑ** VI to swear; **auf jdn/etw ~** (fig) to swear by sb/sth; **auf die Bibel/die Verfassung** etc **~** to swear on the Bible/the Constitution etc

Schwuchtel [ˈʃvʊxtl̩] F -, -n (pej inf) queen (sl); (sl: Schimpfwort) dick (sl)

schwul [ʃvuːl] ADJ (inf) gay, queer (pej inf)

schwül [ʃvyːl] ADJ (lit, fig) Wetter, Tag etc sultry, muggy; Träume, Fantasien sensuous

Schwüle [ˈʃvyːlə] F -, NO PL (lit, fig) sultriness; **in dieser ~** in this sultry weather

Schwule(r) [ˈʃvuːlə] MF DECL AS ADJ gay

Schwulität [ʃvuliˈtɛːt] F -, -en (inf) trouble no indef art, difficulty; **in ~en geraten** or **kommen** to get in a fix (inf); **jdn in ~en bringen** to get sb into trouble

Schwulst [ʃvʊlst] M -(e)s, NO PL (pej) bombast

schwülstig [ˈʃvʊlstɪç] (pej) **ⓐ** ADJ bombastic **ⓑ** ADV bombastically

Schwund [ʃvʊnt] M -(e)s [-dəs], NO PL (a) (= Abnahme, Rückgang) decrease (+gen in) (b) (von Material) shrinkage; (Tech: = Abfall) waste; **~ machen** (inf) to produce scrap (c) (Med) atrophy

Schwung [ʃvʊŋ] M -(e)s, -̈e [ˈʃvʏŋə] (a) swing; (= ausholende Handbewegung) flourish; (= Sprung) leap; **etw in ~ setzen** to set sth in motion

(b) NO PL (lit: = Antrieb) momentum; (fig: = Elan) verve; **~ holen** (lit, fig) to build up momentum; **in ~ kommen** (lit: Schlitten etc) to gain momentum; (fig auch) to get going; **an ~ gewinnen/verlieren** (fig) to gain/lose momentum; **jdn/etw in ~ bringen** (lit, fig) to get sb/sth going; **jdm/einer Sache ~ geben** or **verleihen** (lit) to give sb/sth momentum; (fig auch) to get sb/sth going; **in ~ sein** (lit: Schlitten etc) to be going at full speed; (*fig*) to be in full swing; **etw mit ~ tun** (*fig*) to do sth with zest; **voller/ohne ~** (*fig*) full of/lacking life **(c)** NO PL (*inf:* = *Menge*) (*Sachen*) stack; (*Leute*) bunch

Schwung-: Schwungfeder F (*Orn*) wing feather; **schwunghaft** 🔟 ADJ *Handel* flourishing 🔢 ADV **sich ~ entwickeln** to grow hand over fist

schwungvoll 🔟 ADJ **(a)** *Linie, Bewegung, Handschrift* sweeping **(b)** (= *mitreißend*) *Rede, Aufführung* lively 🔢 ADV (= *mit Schwung*) energetically; *werfen, schaukeln* powerfully; **etw ~er spielen** to play sth with more verve

Schwur [ʃvuːɐ] M **-(e)s, ⁼e** [ʃvyːrə] (= *Eid*) oath; (= *Gelübde*) vow

Schwurgericht NT *court with a jury*; **vor das ~ kommen** to be tried by jury

Schwyz [ʃviːts] NT - (= *Kanton*) Schwyz

Schwyzerdütsch [ˈʃviːtsədyːtʃ] NT **-(s)**, NO PL (*Sw*) Swiss German

Sciencefiction [ˈsaiənsˈfikʃn] F **-, -s** science fiction, sci-fi (*inf*)

Scientologe [saiəntoˈloːgə] M **-n, -n, Scientologin** [-ˈloːgɪn] F **-, -nen** Scientologist

scientologisch [saiəntoˈloːgɪʃ] ADJ Scientologist

Scientology [saiənˈtɔlədʒi] F -, NO PL Scientology

Scirocco [ʃiˈrɔko] M **-s, -s** sirocco

Scotchterrier [ˈskɔtʃteriə] M Scotch terrier

scrollen [ˈskrɔlən] VTI (*Comput*) to scroll

sechs [zɛks] NUM six; *siehe auch* **vier**

Sechs- [zɛks] IN CPDS *six; siehe auch* **vier-; Sechseck** NT hexagon; **sechseckig** ADJ hexagonal

Sechser [ˈzɛksɐ] M **-s, -** six; *siehe auch* **Vierer**

sechserlei [ˈzɛksɐlai] ADJ INV six kinds of; *siehe auch* **viererlei**

Sechserpack [-pak] M **-s, -s** six-pack

Sechs- [zɛks-]: **sechsfach** 🔟 ADJ sixfold 🔢 ADV sixfold, six times; *siehe auch* **vierfach; sechshundert** NUM six hundred; **sechsmal** ADV six times; **Sechstagerennen** NT six-day (bicycle) race; **sechstägig** ADJ six-day; **sechstausend** NUM six thousand

Sechstel [ˈzɛkstl] NT **-s, -** sixth; *siehe auch* **Viertel[1]**

sechstens [ˈzɛkstns] ADV sixth(ly)

sechste(r, s) [ˈzɛkstə] ADJ sixth; **einen ~n Sinn für etw haben, den ~n Sinn haben** to have a sixth sense (for sth); *siehe auch* **vierte(r, s)**

sechzehn [ˈzɛçtseːn] NUM sixteen; *siehe auch* **vierzehn**

sechzig [ˈzɛçtsɪç] NUM sixty; *siehe auch* **vierzig**

Secondhand- [sekəndˈhend] IN CPDS second-hand; **Secondhandladen** M second-hand shop

SED [esleːˈdeː] F - (*DDR*) ABBR *von* **Sozialistische Einheitspartei Deutschlands**

See[1] [zeː] F **-, -n** [ˈzeːən] sea; **raue** *or* **schwere ~** rough *or* heavy seas; **an der ~** by the sea; **an die ~ fahren** to go to the sea(side); **auf hoher ~** on the high seas; **auf ~** at sea; **in ~ gehen** *or* **stechen** to put to sea; **zur ~ fahren** to be a merchant seaman

See[2] M **-s, -n** lake; (*in Schottland*) loch; (= *Teich*) pond

See-: Seeaal M **(a)** (*Zool*) conger (eel) **(b)** (*Comm*) dogfish; **Seeadler** M sea eagle; **Seeanemone** F sea anemone; **Seebad** NT (= *Kurort*) seaside resort; **Seebär** M **(a)** (*hum inf*) seadog (*inf*) **(b)** (*Zool*) fur seal; **Seebeben** NT seaquake; **See-Elefant** M sea elephant; **seefahrend** ADJ ATTR *Volk* seafaring; **Seefahrer(in)** M(F) seafarer; **Sindbad der ~** Sinbad the Sailor; **Seefahrt** F **(a)** (= *Fahrt*) (sea) voyage; (= *Vergnügungsseefahrt*) cruise **(b)** (= *Schifffahrt*) seafaring *no art*; **Seefisch** M saltwater fish; **Seefischerei** F sea fishing; **Seefracht** F sea freight; **Seefrachtbrief** M (*Comm*) bill of lading; **Seegang** [-ɡaŋ] M, NO PL swell; **starker** *or* **hoher ~** heavy *or* rough seas; **seegestützt** [-ɡəʃtʏtst] ADJ (*Mil*) sea-based; **Seegras** NT (*Bot*) eelgrass; **Seehafen** M seaport; **Seehandel** M maritime trade; **Seehund** M seal; **Seeigel** M sea urchin; **Seekarte** F nautical chart; **Seekonnossement** NT ocean bill of lading; **seekrank** ADJ seasick; **Paul wird leicht ~** Paul is a bad sailor; **Seekrankheit** F seasickness; **Seekrieg** M naval war; **Seekuh** F (*Zool*) sea cow; **Seelachs** M (*Cook*) pollack

Seele [ˈzeːlə] F **-, -n** (*Rel*) (*fig*) soul; (= *Herzstück, Mittelpunkt*) life and soul; **in tiefster** *or* **innerster ~** (*geh*) in one's heart of hearts; **mit ganzer ~** with all one's soul; **von ganzer ~** with all one's heart (and soul); **aus tiefster** *or* **innerster ~** with all one's heart and with all one's soul; *danken* from the bottom of one's heart; **jdm aus der ~** *or* **aus tiefster ~ sprechen** to

express exactly what sb feels; **das liegt mir auf der ~** it weighs heavily on my mind; **sich** (*dat*) **etw von der ~ reden** to get sth off one's chest; **sich** (*dat*) **die ~ aus dem Leib reden/schreien** (*inf*) to talk/shout until one is blue in the face (*inf*); **das tut mir in der ~ weh** I am deeply distressed; **eine ~ von Mensch** *or* **von einem Menschen** an absolute dear

Seelen-: Seelenforscher(in) M(F) psychologist; **seelengut** ADJ kind-hearted; **Seelenheil** NT spiritual salvation; (*fig*) spiritual welfare; **Seelenlage** F inner state; **Seelenleben** NT inner life; **er versteht ihr ~ überhaupt nicht** he does not understand her emotions at all; **seelenlos** ADJ soulless; **Seelenruhe** F calmness; **in aller ~** calmly; (= *kaltblütig*) as cool as ice; **seelenruhig** 🔟 ADJ calm; (= *kaltblütig*) as cool as ice 🔢 ADV calmly; (= *kaltblütig*) callously; **seelenverwandt** ADJ congenial (*liter*); **sie waren ~** they were kindred spirits; **Seelenwanderung** F (*Rel*) transmigration of souls; **Seelenzustand** M psychological state

See-: Seeleute PL *von* **Seemann; Seelilie** F sea lily

seelisch [ˈzeːlɪʃ] 🔟 ADJ (*Rel*) spiritual; (= *geistig*) *Gesundheit, Gleichgewicht* mental; *Schaden* psychological; *Erschütterung, Belastung* emotional; *Grausamkeit* mental; **~e Abgründe** the blackest depths of the human soul 🔢 ADV psychologically; **~ bedingt sein** to have psychological causes; **~ krank** mentally ill

Seelöwe M sea lion

Seelsorge [ˈzeːlzɔrgə] F, NO PL spiritual welfare; **in der ~ arbeiten** to do spiritual welfare work with a church

Seelsorger [-zɔrgɐ] M **-s, -, Seelsorgerin** [-ərɪn] F **-, -nen** pastor

seelsorgerisch [-zɔrgərɪʃ] 🔟 ADJ *Tätigkeit, Betreuung* pastoral 🔢 ADV **~ tätig sein** to do pastoral work; **jdn ~ betreuen** to be a religious counsellor (*Brit*) *or* counselor (*US*) to sb

See-: Seeluft F sea air; **Seemacht** F naval *or* maritime power

Seemann M, *pl* **-leute** sailor

seemännisch [-mɛnɪʃ] ADJ nautical

Seemanns-: Seemannsbrauch M seafaring custom; **Seemannsgarn** NT, NO PL (*inf*) sailor's yarn; **~ spinnen** to spin a yarn; **Seemannslied** NT sea shanty; **Seemannstod** M sailor's death; **den ~ sterben** to die a sailor's death

Seemeile F sea mile

Seengebiet [ˈzeːən-] NT lakeland district

Seenot F, NO PL distress; **in ~ geraten** to get into distress

Seenplatte [ˈzeːən-] F *lowland plain full of lakes*

See-: Seeotter M sea otter; **Seepferd** NT, **Seepferdchen** [-pfeːɐtçən] NT **-s, -** sea horse; **Seeräuberei** F piracy; **Seereise** F (sea) voyage; (= *Kreuzfahrt*) cruise; **Seerose** F water lily; **Seesack** M seabag; **Seesalz** NT sea salt; **Seeschaden** M damage at sea; **Seeschifffahrt** F maritime shipping; **Seeschildkröte** F sea turtle; **Seeschlacht** F sea battle; **Seestern** M (*Zool*) starfish; **Seestreitkräfte** PL naval forces *pl*; **Seetang** M seaweed; **Seetaucher** M (*Orn*) grebe; **Seeteufel** M (*Zool*) monkfish; **Seetransport** M sea transport; **seetüchtig** ADJ seaworthy; **Seetüchtigkeit** F seaworthiness; **Seeungeheuer** NT sea monster; **seeuntüchtig** ADJ unseaworthy; **Seeverkehr** M maritime traffic; **Seeversicherung** F marine insurance; **Seevogel** M sea bird; **Seevolk** NT (*Nation*) seafaring nation; (*inf:* = *Seeleute*) seafaring people *pl*; **Seeweg** M sea route; **auf dem ~ reisen** to go by sea; **Seewesen** NT maritime affairs *pl, no art*; **Seewolf** M (*Zool*) wolffish; **Seezunge** F sole

Segel [ˈzeːgl] NT **-s, -** sail; **die ~ setzen** to set the sails; **mit vollen ~n** under full sail; (*fig*) with gusto; **die ~ streichen** (*Naut*) to strike sail; (*fig*) to give in

Segel-: Segelboot NT sailing boat (*Brit*), sailboat (*US*); **segelfliegen** VI INFIN ONLY to glide; **~ gehen** to go gliding; **Segelfliegen** NT **-s**, NO PL gliding; **Segelflieger(in)** M(F) glider pilot; **Segelflugplatz** M gliding field; **Segelflugzeug** NT glider; **Segeljacht** F (sailing) yacht, sailboat (*US*); **Segelklub** M sailing club

segeln [ˈzeːgln] 🔟 VTI AUX HABEN *or* SEIN (*lit, fig*) to sail; **eine Strecke ~** to sail a course; **eine Regatta ~** to sail in a regatta; **als junger Mensch hat** *or* **ist er viel gesegelt** in his younger days he did a lot of sailing; **~ gehen** to go for a sail 🔢 VI AUX SEIN (*inf*) **durch eine Prüfung ~** to fail an exam

Segeln NT **-s**, NO PL sailing

Segel-: Segelohren PL (*hum*) flappy ears *pl* (*inf*); **Segelpartie** F sailing trip; **Segelregatta** F sailing *or* yachting regatta;

Segelschiff NT sailing ship; **Segelschulschiff** NT training sailing ship; **Segelsport** M sailing *no art*; **Segeltuch** NT, *pl* **-tuche** canvas

Segen ['zeːgn̩] M **-s, -** (*lit, fig*) blessing; **es ist ein ~, dass ...** it is a blessing that ...; **jdm/einer Sache seinen ~ erteilen** *or* **geben** (*fig*) to give sb/sth one's blessing; **meinen ~ hat er, er hat meinen ~** he has my blessing; **~ bringend** beneficent; **ein wahrer ~** a real blessing

Segler ['zeːglɐ] M **-s, -**, **Seglerin** [-ərɪn] F **-, -nen** (= *Segelsportler*) yachtsman/-woman, sailor

Segment [zɛ'ɡmɛnt] NT **-(e)s, -e** segment

segnen ['zeːɡnən] VT (*Rel*) to bless; *siehe auch* **gesegnet**

Segnung F **-, -en** (*Rel*) blessing

sehbehindert ADJ partially sighted

---

sehen ['zeːən]

1 TRANSITIVES VERB	**3** INTRANSITIVES VERB
2 REFLEXIVES VERB	

pret **sah** [zaː], *ptp* **gesehen** [ɡə'zeːən]

1 TRANSITIVES VERB

(a) (= *mit den Augen wahrnehmen*) to see; (= *ansehen*) to look at, to see; **siehst du irgendwo mein Buch?** can you see my book anywhere?; **ich sehe was, was du nicht siehst** (= *Spiel*) I spy (with my little eye (*Brit*)); **gut zu sehen sein** to be clearly visible; **schlecht zu sehen sein** to be difficult to see; **sieht man das?** does it show?; **von ihm war nichts mehr zu sehen** he was no longer to be seen; **da gibt es nichts zu sehen** there is nothing to see; **darf ich das mal sehen?** can I have a look at that?; **jdn kommen/weggehen sehen** to see sb coming/leaving; **jdn/etw zu sehen bekommen** to get to see sb/sth; **sich/jdn als etw sehen** to see oneself/sb as sth; **etw in jdm sehen** to see sb as sth; **ich kann den Mantel/Mann nicht mehr sehen** (= *nicht mehr ertragen*) I can't stand the sight of that coat/the man any more; **das muss man gesehen haben** it has to be seen to be believed; (= *lässt sich nicht beschreiben*) you have to see it for yourself; **den möchte ich sehen, der ...** I'd like to meet the man who ...; **hat man so was schon gesehen!** (*inf*) did you ever see anything like it!

✦**sich sehen lassen** to put in an appearance; **er lässt sich kaum noch bei uns sehen** he hardly ever comes to see us now; **lassen Sie sich doch mal wieder sehen!** do come again!; **er kann sich in dieser Gegend nicht mehr sehen lassen** he can't show his face in the area any more; **kann ich mich in diesem Anzug sehen lassen?** do I look all right in this suit?; **mit diesem Mann kannst du dich doch nirgends sehen lassen!** you don't want to be seen with this man!; **mit diesem Ergebnis kann sich die Mannschaft sehen lassen** the team can be proud of this result

(b) (= *treffen*) to see; **sich** *or* **einander sehen** to see each other; **ich freue mich, Sie zu sehen!** nice to see you!; **also, wir sehen uns morgen** right, I'll see you tomorrow

(c) (= *feststellen*) to see; **das wird man noch sehen** we'll see; **das wollen wir (doch) erst mal sehen, ob ...** we'll see if ...; **das müssen wir erst mal sehen** that remains to be seen; **da sieht man es mal wieder!** that's typical!

(d) (= *beurteilen*) to see; (= *deuten, interpretieren*) to look at, to see; **wie siehst du das?** how do you see it?; **das sehe ich anders, so sehe ich das nicht** that's not how I see it; **du hast wohl keine Lust, oder wie sehe ich das?** (*inf*) you don't feel like it, do you?; **du siehst das/ich nicht richtig** you've got it/him wrong; **rein menschlich/wirtschaftlich gesehen** from a purely personal/economic point of view; **so gesehen** looked at in this way

2 REFLEXIVES VERB

✦**sich sehen sich betrogen/getäuscht sehen** to see oneself cheated/deceived; **sich enttäuscht sehen** to feel disappointed; **sich genötigt** *or* **veranlasst sehen, zu ...** to find it necessary to ...; **sich gezwungen sehen, zu ...** to find oneself obliged to ...

3 INTRANSITIVES VERB

(a) (*mit den Augen*) to see; **er sieht gut/schlecht** he can/cannot see very well; **er sieht nur mit einem** *or* **auf einem Auge**

he only has sight in one eye; **jdm tief in die Augen sehen** to look deep into sb's eyes; **siehe oben/unten** see above/below; **sieh(e) da!** (*liter*) behold! (*liter*); **siehst du (wohl)!, siehste!** (*inf*) you see!; **sieh doch!** look (here)!; **sehen Sie mal!** look!; **willst du mal sehen?** do you want to have a look?; **lass mal sehen** let me see, let me have a look

(b) (= *feststellen*) **na siehst du** (there you are,) you see?; **wie ich sehe ...** I see that ...; **wie ich sehe, hast du schon angefangen** I see you have already started; **Sie sind beschäftigt, wie ich sehe** I can see you're busy; **wir werden schon sehen** we'll see; **da kann man mal sehen, da kannste mal sehen** (*inf*) that just goes to show (*inf*); **wir wollen sehen** we'll have to see; **mal sehen, ob ...** (*inf*) let's see if ...; **mal sehen!** (*inf*) we'll see; **jeder muss sehen, wo er bleibt** (it's) every man for himself; **sieh, dass du ...** make sure you..., see (that) you ...

✦**auf etw (*acc*) sehen** (= *hinsehen*) to look at sth; (= *achten*) to consider sth important; **auf die Uhr sehen** to look at one's watch; **darauf sehen, dass ...** to make sure (that) ...; **er sieht auf Pünktlichkeit** he's a stickler for punctuality; **er sieht nur auf seinen eigenen Vorteil** he only cares about what's good for him

✦**sehen nach jdm sehen** (= *betreuen*) to look after sb; (= *besuchen*) to go to see sb; **nach etw sehen** to look after sth; **ich muss nur mal eben nach den Kartoffeln sehen** I've just got to have a look at the potatoes; **nach der Post sehen** to see if there are any letters

---

Sehen NT **-s**, NO PL seeing; (= *Sehkraft*) sight; **ich kenne ihn nur vom ~** I only know him by sight

sehenswert, sehenswürdig ADJ worth seeing

Sehenswürdigkeit [-vyrdɪçkaɪt] F **-, -en** sight; **dieses Gebäude ist wirklich eine ~!** that building is really (a sight) worth seeing!; **die ~en (einer Stadt) besichtigen** to go sightseeing (in a city)

seherisch ['zeːərɪʃ] ADJ ATTR *Fähigkeit* prophetic

Seh-: **Sehfehler** M visual defect; **Sehfeld** NT field of vision; **Sehkraft** F, NO PL (eye)sight

Sehne ['zeːnə] F **-, -n** **(a)** (*Anat*) tendon **(b)** (= *Bogensehne*) string **(c)** (*Math*) chord

sehnen ['zeːnən] VR **sich nach jdm/etw ~** to long for sb/sth; (*schmachtend*) to pine for sb/sth

Sehnen-: **Sehnenscheidenentzündung** F tendinitis; **Sehnenzerrung** F pulled tendon

Sehnerv M optic nerve

sehnlich ['zeːnlɪç] **1** ADJ *Wunsch* ardent; *Erwartung* eager; **sein ~ster Wunsch** his fondest wish **2** ADV *hoffen, wünschen* ardently

Sehnsucht ['zeːnzʊxt] F longing (*nach* for); (*schmachtend*) pining; **~ haben** to have a longing

sehnsüchtig **1** ADJ longing; *Verlangen, Wunsch etc* ardent; *Erwartung, Ungeduld* eager; *Brief* full of longing **2** ADV *hoffen, wünschen* ardently; **~ auf jdn warten** to yearn for sb; **~ auf etw (*acc*) warten** to long for sth

Sehorgan NT visual organ

sehr [zeːɐ] ADV, *comp* **mehr** [meːɐ], *superl* **am meisten** ['maɪstn̩] **(a)** (*mit adj, adv*) very; **er ist ~ dagegen** he is very much against it; **er hat ~ viel getrunken** he drank a lot; **~ zu meiner Überraschung** very much to my surprise; **es geht ihm ~ viel besser** he is very much better **(b)** (*mit vb*) very much, a lot; **so ~** so much; **wie ~** how much; **wie ~ er sich auch ...** however much he ...; **sich (*dat*) etw ~ überlegen** to consider sth very carefully; **sich ~ anstrengen** to try very hard; **~ weinen** to cry a lot; **es regnet ~** it's raining hard; **regnet es ~?** is it raining a lot?; **freust du dich? – ja, ~!** are you pleased? – yes, very; **freust du dich darauf? – ja, ~** are you looking forward to it? – yes, very much; **zu ~** too much

Seh-: **Sehschwäche** F poor eyesight; **Sehstörung** F visual defect; **wenn ~en auftreten** when the vision becomes disturbed; **Sehtest** M eye test; **Sehvermögen** NT powers *pl* of vision

sei [zaɪ] IMPER SING, 1. AND 3. PERS SING SUBJUNC *von* **sein**

seicht [zaɪçt] ADJ (*lit, fig*) shallow; *Unterhaltung, TV-Programm* trivial; **die ~e Stelle** the shallows *pl*

seid [zaɪt] 2. PERS PL PRES, IMPER PL *von* **sein**

Seide ['zaɪdə] F **-, -n** silk

Seidel ['zaidl] NT **-s, -** (*Gefäß*) stein

seiden ['zaidn] ADJ ATTR (= *aus Seide*) silk

Seiden- IN CPDS silk; **seidenartig** ADJ silky; **Seidenfaden** M, **Seidengarn** NT silk thread; **Seidengewebe** NT silk fabric; **Seidenglanz** M silky sheen; **Seidenmalerei** F silk painting; **Seidenpapier** NT tissue paper; **Seidenraupe** F silkworm; **Seidenraupenzucht** F silkworm breeding; **Seidenschwanz** M (*Orn*) waxwing; **Seidenspinner** M (*Zool*) silk(worm) moth; **Seidenspinner(in)** M(F) silk spinner; **Seidenspinnerei** F **(a)** silk spinning **(b)** (*Betrieb*) silk mill; **seidenweich** ADJ soft as silk

seidig ['zaidɪç] ADJ (= *wie Seide*) silky

Seife ['zaifə] F **-, -n** soap

Seifen-: Seifenblase F soap bubble; (*fig*) bubble; **~n machen** to blow (soap) bubbles; **Seifenflocken** PL soap flakes *pl*; **Seifenkistenrennen** NT soapbox derby; **Seifenlauge** F (soap)suds *pl*; **Seifenoper** F (*inf*) soap (opera); **Seifenpulver** NT soap powder; **Seifenschale** F soap dish; **Seifenschaum** M lather; **Seifenspender** M soap dispenser

seifig ['zaifɪç] ADJ soapy

seihen ['zaiən] VT (= *sieben*) to sieve; (*S Ger, Aus*: = *Flüssigkeit abgießen von*) to strain

Seiher ['zaiɐ] M **-s, -** (*esp S Ger, Aus*) strainer

Seil [zail] NT **-(e)s, -e** rope; (= *Kabel*) cable; (= *Hochseil*) tightrope, high wire

Seil-: Seilbahn F cable railway; **Seilschaft** ['zailʃaft] F **-, -en** (*Bergsteigen*) roped party; (*fig*: in *Politik, Industrie etc*) clique; **seilspringen** VI SEP AUX SEIN, USU INFIN or PTP to skip; **Seiltanz** M tightrope act; **Seiltänzer(in)** M(F) tightrope walker

sein¹ [zain], *pres* **ist** [ɪst], *pret* **war** [vaːɐ], *ptp* **gewesen** [gə've:zn] AUX SEIN **1** VI **(a)** to be; **sei (mir)/seien Sie (mir) nicht böse, aber ...** don't be angry (with me) but ...; **sei/seid so nett und ...** be so kind as to ...; **du bist wohl verrückt!** (*inf*) you must be crazy (*inf*); **das wäre gut** that would be a good thing; **es wäre schön gewesen** it would have been nice; **er ist Lehrer/ Inder/ein Verwandter/der Chef** he is a teacher/(an) Indian/a relative/the boss; **was sind Sie (beruflich)?** what do you do?; **drei und vier ist** or **sind sieben** three and four is seven; **x sei 4** let x be or equal 4; **wenn ich Sie/er wäre** if I were or was you/ him or he (*form*); **er war es nicht** it wasn't him; **niemand will es gewesen** – nobody admits that it was him/her or them (*inf*); **ich will mal nicht so ~ und ...** I don't want to be awkward and ...; **das kann schon ~** that may well be; **wer ist da?** who's there?; **ist da jemand?** is (there) anybody there?; **er ist aus Genf/aus guter Familie** he comes from Geneva/a good family; **morgen bin ich im Büro/in Rom** I'll be in the office/in Rome tomorrow; **waren Sie (schon) mal in Rom?** have you ever been to Rome?; **wir waren baden/essen** we went swimming/out for a meal; **wo warst du so lange?** where have you been all this time?; **was nicht ist, kann ja noch werden** things can change

(b) **was ist?** what's the matter?, what's up (*inf*); **ist was?** what is it?; (= *passt dir was nicht*) is something the matter?; **was ist mit dir/ihm?** what about you/him?; (= *was hast du/hat er?*) what's wrong or up (*inf*) with you/him?; **das kann nicht ~** that can't be (true); **wie wäre es mit ...?** how about ...?; **wenn du nicht gewesen wärest ...** if it hadn't been for you ...; **mir ist kalt** I'm cold; **mir ist, als wäre ich zehn Jahre jünger** I feel ten years younger; **mir ist, als hätte ich ihn früher schon einmal gesehen** I have a feeling I've seen him before

2 V AUX to have; **er ist/war jahrelang krank gewesen** he's/he'd been ill for years; **er ist verschwunden** he's disappeared; **er ist geschlagen worden** he has been beaten; *siehe auch* **gewesen**

sein² POSS PRON (*adjektivisch*) (*bei Männern*) his; (*bei Dingen, Abstrakta*) its; (*bei Mädchen*) her; (*bei Tieren*) its, his/her; (*bei Ländern, Städten*) its, her; (*auf „man" bezüglich*) one's, his (US), your; **wenn man ~ Leben betrachtet** when one looks at one's or his (US) life, when you look at your life; **jeder hat ~e Probleme** everybody has their problems; **er wiegt gut ~e zwei Zentner** (*inf*) he weighs a good two hundred pounds

Sein [zain] NT **-s,** NO PL being *no art*; (*Philos*) (= *Existenz, Dasein auch*) existence *no art*; **~ und Schein** appearance and reality; **~ oder Nichtsein** to be or not to be

seine(r, s) ['zainə] POSS PRON (*substantivisch*) his; **er hat das ~** or **Seine getan** (*geh*) he did his bit; **jedem das ~** or **Seine** each to his own (*Brit*), to each his own; **die ~n** or **Seinen** (*geh*) his family; (*auf „man" bezüglich*) one's or his (US) family; **das ~** or

Seine (*geh*: = *Besitz*) what is his; (*auf „man" bezüglich*) what is one's own or his (US)

seinerseits ['zainɐ'zaits] ADV (= *von ihm*) on his part; (= *er selbst*) for his part

seinesgleichen ['zainəs'glaiçn] PRON INV (*gleichgestellt*) his equals *pl*; (*auf „man" bezüglich*) one's or his (US) equals; (*gleichartig*) his kind *pl*; of one's own kind; (*pej*) the likes of him *pl*; **jdn wie ~ behandeln** to treat sb as an equal; **das hat nicht** or **das sucht ~** it is unparalleled

seinet-: seinetwegen ['zainət've:gn] ADV **(a)** (= *wegen ihm*) because of him; (= *ihm zuliebe*) for his sake; (= *um ihn*) about him; (= *für ihn*) on his behalf **(b)** (= *von ihm aus*) as far as he is concerned; **seinetwillen** ['zainət'vɪlən] ADV **um ~** for his sake

sein lassen *ptp* **sein lassen** VT IRREG **etw ~** (= *aufhören*) to stop sth/doing sth; (= *nicht tun*) to leave sth; **jdn/etw ~** to leave sb/ sth alone; **lass das sein!** stop that!; **du hättest es ~ sollen** you should have left well (enough (US)) alone; **sie kann es einfach nicht ~** she just can't stop herself

seins [zains] POSS PRON his

seismisch ['zaismɪʃ] ADJ seismic

Seismograf [zaismo'gra:f] M **-en, -en** seismograph

Seismologe [zaismo'lo:gə] M **-n, -n**, **Seismologin** [-'lo:gɪn] F **-, -nen** seismologist

seit [zait] **1** PREP +DAT (*in Bezug auf Zeitpunkt*) since; (*in Bezug auf Zeitdauer*) for, in (*esp US*); **~ wann?** since when?; **~ Jahren** for years; **ich bin ~ zwei Jahren hier** I have been here for two years; **schon ~ zwei Jahren nicht mehr** not for two years, not since two years ago; **wir warten schon ~ zwei Stunden** we've been waiting (for) two hours; **~ etwa einer Woche** since about a week ago, for about a week **2** CONJ since

seitdem [zait'de:m] **1** ADV since then; **~ ist die Strecke nicht mehr in Betrieb** the line has been closed down since then **2** CONJ since

Seite ['zaitə] F **-, -n (a)** (= *auch Abstammungslinie, Charakterzug*) side; **die hintere/vordere ~** the back/front; **~ an ~** side by side; **er ging** or **wich uns nicht von der ~** he never left our side; **jdn von der ~ ansehen** to give sb a sidelong glance; **auf die** or **zur ~ gehen** or **treten** to step aside; **die ~n wechseln** (*Sport*) to change ends or over; (*fig*) to change sides; **jdn auf seine ~ bringen** or **ziehen** (*fig*) to get sb on one's side; **auf einer ~ gelähmt sein** to be paralyzed down one side; **jedes Ding** or **alles hat zwei ~n** there are two sides to everything; **jdm zur ~ stehen** (*fig*) to stand by sb's side; **auf jds** (*dat*) **~ stehen** or **sein** (*fig*) to be on sb's side; **das Recht ist auf ihrer ~** she has right on her side; **etw auf die ~ legen** (*lit, fig*) to put sth aside; (= *umkippen*) to put sth on its side; **jdn zur ~ nehmen** to take sb aside; **auf der einen ~..., auf der anderen (~) ...** on the one hand ..., on the other (hand) ...; **jds starke ~** sb's strong point; **jds schwache ~** sb's weak spot; **sich von seiner besten ~ zeigen** to show oneself at one's best; **von dieser ~ kenne ich ihn gar nicht** I didn't know that side of him

(b) (= *Richtung*) **von allen ~n** (*lit, fig*) from all sides; **nach allen ~n auseinander gehen** to scatter in all directions; **sich nach allen ~n umsehen** to look around on all sides; **das habe ich von einer anderen ~ erfahren** (*fig*) I heard it from another source or from elsewhere; **er erfuhr es von dritter ~** (*fig*) he heard it from a third party; **bisher wurden von keiner ~ Einwände erhoben** so far no objections have been voiced from any quarter; **die Behauptung wurde von keiner ~ bestritten** nobody challenged the claim; **auf ~n** +*gen* = **aufseiten**; **von ~n** +*gen* = **vonseiten**

(c) (= *Buchseite, Zeitungsseite*) page; **die erste/letzte ~** the first/last page; (*von Zeitung*) the front/back page

Seiten- IN CPDS side; (*esp Tech, Sci etc*) lateral; **Seitenairbag** M (*Aut*) side-impact airbag; **Seitenaltar** M side altar; **Seitenangabe** F page reference; **Seitenansicht** F side view; (*Tech*) side elevation; **Seitenaufprallschutz** M (*Aut*) side impact protection system; **Seitenausgang** M side exit; **Seitenblick** M sidelong glance; **mit einem ~ auf** (+*acc*) (*fig*) with one eye on; **Seitenhieb** M (*Fechten*) side cut; (*fig*) sideswipe; **Seitenlage** F side position; **in ~ schlafen** to sleep on one's side; **stabile ~** recovery position; **seitenlang 1** ADJ several pages long **2** ADV *darstellen* over pages and pages; **etw ~ beschreiben** to devote pages to describing sth; **sich ~ über etw** (*acc*) **auslassen** to go on for pages about sth; **Seitenlinie** F **(a)** (*Rail*) branch line **(b)** (*Tennis*) sideline; (*Ftbl etc*) touchline (*Brit*), sideline; **Seitenruder** NT (*Aviat*) rudder

seitens ['zaitns] PREP +GEN (form) on the part of

Seiten-: Seitenscheitel M side parting (Brit), side part (US); **Seitenschiff** NT (Archit) (side) aisle; **Seitensprung** M (fig) bit on the side (inf) no pl; **die Versuchung, Seitensprünge zu machen** the temptation to have a bit on the side (inf); **Seitenstechen** NT, NO PL stitch; **~ haben/bekommen** to have/get a stitch; **Seitenstiche** PL = Seitenstechen; **Seitenstraße** F side street; **Seitenstreifen** M verge; (der Autobahn) hard shoulder (Brit), shoulder (US); „**~ nicht befahrbar**" "soft verges" (Brit), "soft shoulder" (US); **seitenverkehrt** ADJ, ADV the wrong way round; **Seitenvorschub** M (beim Drucker) form feed; **Seitenwagen** M sidecar; **Seitenwechsel** M (Sport) changeover; **Seitenwind** M crosswind; **Seitenzahl** F (a) page number (b) (= Gesamtzahl) number of pages

seither ['zait'he:ɐ] ADV since then

seitlich ['zaitlıç] ⊞ ADJ lateral (esp Sci, Tech), side attr; **die ~e Begrenzung der Straße wird durch einen weißen Streifen markiert** the side of the road is marked by a white line; **bei starkem ~en Wind** in a strong crosswind ⊠ ADV at the side; (= von der Seite) from the side; **~ von** at the side of; **~ stehen** to stand sideways on; **etw/sich ~ stellen** to put sth/stand sideways on

Sek., sek. ABBR von Sekunde sec

Sekret [ze'kre:t] NT -(e)s, -e (Physiol) secretion

Sekretär[1] [zekre'tɛ:ɐ] M -s, -e (= Schreibschrank) bureau (Brit), secretary desk (US)

Sekretär[2] [zekre'tɛ:ɐ] M -s,-e, **Sekretärin** [-'tɛ:rɪn] F -, -nen secretary

Sekretariat [zekreta'ria:t] NT -(e)s, -e office

Sekretion [zekre'tsio:n] F -, -en (Physiol) secretion

Sekt [zɛkt] M -(e)s, -e sparkling wine, champagne

Sekte ['zɛktə] F -, -n sect

Sektierer [zɛk'ti:rɐ] M -s, -, **Sektiererin** [-ərɪn] F -, -nen sectarian

sektiererisch [zɛk'ti:rərıʃ] ⊞ ADJ sectarian ⊠ ADV in a sectarian way; **~ denken** to think in a sectarian way

Sektion [zɛk'tsio:n] F -, -en section; (= Abteilung) department

Sektkelch M champagne flute

Sektor ['zɛkto:ɐ] M -s, **Sektoren** [-'to:rən] sector (auch Comput); (= Sachgebiet) field

Sektschale F champagne glass

sekundär [zekʊn'dɛ:ɐ] ⊞ ADJ secondary ⊠ ADV secondarily; **nur ~ von Bedeutung sein** to be of secondary importance

Sekundär- IN CPDS secondary; **Sekundärenergie** F secondary energy; **Sekundärkreislauf** M (in Atomkraftwerk) secondary circuit

Sekundarlehrer(in) [zekʊn'da:ɐ-] M(F) (Sw) secondary school teacher

Sekundär-: Sekundärliteratur F secondary literature; **Sekundärmarkt** M (Fin) secondary market

Sekundar- [zekʊn'da:ɐ-]: **Sekundarschule** F (Sw) secondary school; **Sekundarstufe** F secondary or high (esp US) school level

Sekunde [ze'kʊndə] F -, -n second; **auf die ~ genau** to the second

Sekunden-: sekundenlang ⊞ ADJ of a few seconds ⊠ ADV for a few seconds; **Sekundenzeiger** M second hand

selber ['zɛlbɐ] DEM PRON = selbst 1

Selbermachen NT -s, NO PL **Möbel zum ~** do-it-yourself furniture

selbst [zɛlpst] ⊞ DEM PRON (a) **ich ~** I myself; **er ~** he himself; **Sie ~** (sing) you yourself; (pl) you yourselves; **sie ~** she herself; **das Haus ~** the house itself; **wir ~** we ourselves; **sie ~** they themselves; **die Häuser ~** the houses themselves; **er ist gar nicht mehr er ~** he's not himself any more; **sie ist die Güte/Tugend ~** she's kindness/virtue itself; **~ ist der Mann/die Frau!** self-reliance is the name of the game (inf); **eine Sache um ihrer ~ willen tun** to do sth for its own sake

(b) (= ohne Hilfe) by oneself/himself/yourself etc; **von ~** by myself/yourself/himself/itself/ourselves etc; **das regelt sich alles von ~** it'll sort itself out (by itself); **er kam ganz von ~** he came of his own accord

⊠ ADV **(a)** (= eigen) **~ ernannt** self-appointed; (in Bezug auf Titel) self-styled; **~ gebacken** home-baked, home-made; **~ gebastelt** home-made; **~ gebaut** home-made; Haus self-

built; **~ gebraut** Bier home-brewed; **~ gemacht** home-made; **~ gestrickt** Pullover etc hand-knitted; (inf) Methode etc homespun; **~ verdientes Geld** money one has earned oneself; **sein ~ verdientes Motorrad** the motorbike he bought with the money he earned

(b) (= sogar) even; **~ der Minister/Gott** even the Minister/God (himself); **~ wenn** even if

Selbstachtung F self-respect

selbständig etc ['zɛlpʃtɛndıç] ADJ, ADV = selbstständig etc

Selbst-: Selbstanzeige F (a) (steuerlich) voluntary declaration **(b) ~ erstatten** to come forward oneself; **Selbstauslöser** M (Phot) delayed-action shutter release; **Selbstbedienung** F self-service; (fig: finanziell) helping oneself to funds; **Selbstbedienungsladen** M self-service shop (esp Brit) or store; **Selbstbefriedigung** F masturbation; **Selbstbehauptung** F self-assertion; **Selbstbeherrschung** F self-control; **die ~ wahren/verlieren** to keep/lose one's self-control; **selbstbestimmt** ADJ self-determined; **~ leben** to be independent; **Selbstbestimmungsrecht** NT right of self-determination; **Selbstbeteiligung** F (Insur) (percentage) excess; **Selbstbetrug** M self-deception; **selbstbewusst** ⊞ ADJ (= selbstsicher) self-assured; (= eingebildet) self-important ⊠ ADV self-confidently; **Selbstbewusstsein** NT self-confidence; (= Einbildung) self-importance; **Selbstbildnis** NT self-portrait; **Selbsteinschätzung** F self-assessment; **eine gesunde ~** a healthy self-awareness; **Selbsterfahrung** F self-awareness; **Selbsterfahrungsgruppe** F encounter group; **Selbsterhaltungstrieb** M survival instinct; **Selbsterkenntnis** F self-knowledge; **~ ist der erste Schritt zur Besserung** (prov) self-knowledge is the first step toward(s) self-improvement; **selbsternannt** ['-lɛnant] ADJ self-appointed; **selbstgebacken** ADJ siehe selbst; **selbstgebraut** [-gəbraut] ADJ siehe selbst; **Selbstgedrehte** [-gədre:tə] F DECL AS ADJ roll-up (inf); **~ rauchen** to roll one's own; **selbstgefällig** ⊞ ADJ self-satisfied ⊠ ADV smugly; **Selbstgefälligkeit** F smugness, complacency; **selbstgemacht** ADJ siehe selbst; **selbstgerecht** ⊞ ADJ self-righteous ⊠ ADV self-righteously; **Selbstgerechtigkeit** F self-righteousness; **Selbstgespräch** NT **~ e führen** or **halten** to talk to oneself; **selbstgestrickt** [-gəʃtrıkt] ADJ siehe selbst; **Selbstheilungskraft** F self-healing power; **selbstherrlich** (pej) ⊞ ADJ (= eigenwillig) high-handed; (= selbstgefällig, selbstgerecht) arrogant ⊠ ADV (= eigenwillig) high-handedly; (= selbstgefällig) arrogantly; **Selbstherrlichkeit** F (pej) (= Eigenwilligkeit) high-handedness; (= Selbstgerechtigkeit) arrogance; **Selbsthilfe** F self-help; **zur ~ greifen** to take matters into one's own hands; **Selbsthilfegruppe** F self-help group; **selbstklebend** ADJ self-adhesive

Selbstkosten PL (Econ) prime costs pl

Selbstkosten-: Selbstkostenbeteiligung F (Insur) excess; **Selbstkostenpreis** M cost price; **zum ~** at cost

Selbst-: Selbstkritik F self-criticism; **selbstkritisch** ⊞ ADJ self-critical ⊠ ADV self-critically; **Selbstlaut** M vowel; **Selbstlerner(in)** M(F) autodidact (form); **er ist ~** he is self-taught; **dies Buch ist geeignet für ~** this book is suitable for people teaching themselves; **selbstlos** ⊞ ADJ selfless ⊠ ADV selflessly; **Selbstlosigkeit** F -, NO PL selflessness; **Selbstmedikation** [-medikatsio:n] F -, NO PL self-medication; **Selbstmitleid** NT self-pity

Selbstmord M (lit, fig) suicide

Selbstmörder(in) M(F) suicide; **ich bin doch kein ~!** (inf) I have no desire to commit suicide

selbstmörderisch ADJ (lit, fig) suicidal; **in ~er Absicht** intending to commit suicide

Selbstmord-: selbstmordgefährdet ADJ suicidal; **Selbstmordversuch** M attempted suicide

Selbst-: Selbstporträt NT self-portrait; **selbstredend** ADV of course; **Selbstschutz** M self-protection; **selbstsicher** ⊞ ADJ self-assured ⊠ ADV self-confidently; **Selbstsicherheit** F self-assurance; **selbstständig** ['zɛlpstʃtɛndıç] ADJ ⊞ ADJ independent; (beruflich) self-employed; **~ sein** (beruflich) to be self-employed; **sich ~ machen** (beruflich) to set up on one's own; (hum) to go off on its own; (= verschwinden) to grow legs (hum) ⊠ ADV independently; **~ denken** to think for oneself; **das entscheidet er ~** he decides that on his own; **Selbstständige(r)** ['zɛlpstʃtɛndıgə] MF DECL AS ADJ self-employed person; **die ~n** the self-employed; **Selbstständigkeit** F -, NO PL independence; (beruflich) self-employment; **~ im Denken lernen** to learn to think for oneself; **Selbststudium** NT private study; **etw im ~ lernen** to learn sth by studying on one's own; **Selbstsucht** F, NO PL egoism; **selbstsüchtig** ADJ egoistic; **selbsttätig** ◼ ADJ **(a)** (= *automatisch*) automatic **(b)** (= *eigenständig*) independent ◻ ADV (= *automatisch*) automatically; **Selbsttest** M (*von Maschine*) self-test; **Selbstverbraucher** M **Verkauf nur an ~** goods not for resale; **selbstverdient** ADJ *siehe* **selbst**; **selbstvergessen** ◼ ADJ absent-minded; *Blick* faraway ◻ ADV **~ dasitzen** to sit there lost to the world; **Selbstverlag** M **im ~ erschienen** published oneself; **Selbstverpfleger** [-fɛɐˌpfleːɡə] M **-s, -, Selbst-verpflegerin** [-ərɪn] F **-, -nen** self-caterer; **Ferien für ~** self-catering holiday(s); **Selbstverpflegung** F self-catering; **Selbstverschulden** NT one's own fault; **wenn ~ vorliegt ...** if the claimant is himself at fault ...; **selbstverschuldet** [-fɛɐˌʃʊldət] ADJ *Unfälle, Notlagen* for which one is oneself responsible; **der Unfall war ~** the accident was his/her own fault; **wenn der Unfall/Verlust ~ ist** if the claimant is himself/herself responsible for the accident/loss; **Selbst-versorger(in)** M(F) **(a)** **~ sein** to be self-sufficient **(b)** (*im Urlaub etc*) sb who is self-catering (*Brit*); **Appartements für ~** self-catering apartments (*Brit*), condominiums (*US*); **selbstverständlich** ◼ ADJ *Freundlichkeit* natural; *Wahrheit* self-evident; **das ist doch ~!** that goes without saying; **vielen Dank für Ihre Hilfe – aber das ist doch ~** thanks for your help – it's no more than anybody would have done; **es war für uns ~, dass Sie ...** we took it for granted that you ...; **das ist keineswegs ~** it cannot be taken for granted ◻ ADV of course; **wie ~** as if it were the most natural thing in the world; **Selbstverständlichkeit** [-fɛɐˌʃtɛntlɪçkaɪt] F **-, -en** naturalness; (= *Unbefangenheit*) casualness *no indef art*; **das war doch eine ~, dass wir ...** it was only natural that we ...; **etw für eine ~ halten** to take sth as a matter of course; **Meinungsfreiheit ist für uns eine ~** we take freedom of speech for granted; **mit der größten ~** as if it were the most natural thing in the world; **Selbstversuch** M experiment on oneself; **Selbstverteidigung** F self-defence (*Brit*), self-defense (*US*); **Selbstvertrauen** NT self-confidence; **Selbstverwaltung** F self-administration; (*Verwaltungskörper*) self-governing body; **Selbst-verwirklichung** F self-realization; **Selbstwertgefühl** NT self-esteem; **Selbstzweck** M end in itself; **als ~** as an end in itself

selchen [ˈzɛlçn] VTI (*S Ger, Aus*) *Fleisch* to smoke

selektieren [zelɛkˈtiːrən], *ptp* **selektiert** VT to select

Selektion [zelɛkˈtsioːn] F **-, -en** selection

selektiv [zelɛkˈtiːf] ◼ ADJ selective ◻ ADV selectively

selig [ˈzeːlɪç] ◼ ADJ **(a)** (*Rel*) blessed **(b)** (= *überglücklich*) overjoyed; *Lächeln, Stunden* blissful ◻ ADV blissfully

Selige(r) [ˈzeːlɪɡə] MF DECL AS ADJ (*Eccl*) blessed (*inf*); **die ~n** the Blessed

Seligkeit F **-, -en (a)** NO PL (*Rel*) salvation; **ewige ~** eternal salvation **(b)** (= *Glück*) (supreme) happiness, bliss

Sellerie [ˈzɛləri] M **-s, -(s)** *or* f **-, -** celeriac; (= *Stangensellerie*) celery

selten [ˈzɛltn] ◼ ADJ rare; **du bist ja in letzter Zeit ein ~er Gast** you're a stranger here these days ◻ ADV (= *nicht oft*) rarely; (= *besonders*) exceptionally; **nur/höchst ~** very/extremely rarely; **~ so gelacht!** (*inf*) what a laugh! (*inf*)

Seltenheit F **-, -en** rarity; **das ist keine ~ bei ihr** it's nothing unusual with her

Seltenheitswert M rarity value

Selters [ˈzɛltəs] NT **-, -** (*inf*), **Selter(s)wasser** NT, *pl* **-wässer** soda (water)

seltsam [ˈzɛltzaːm] ◼ ADJ strange ◻ ADV strangely; **~ klingen/aussehen/schmecken/riechen** to sound/look/taste/smell strange

seltsamerweise [ˈzɛltzaːmɐˌvaɪzə] ADV strangely enough

Seltsamkeit F **-, -en (a)** NO PL (= *Sonderbarkeit*) strangeness **(b)** (= *seltsame Sache*) oddity

Semantik [zeˈmantɪk] F **-,** NO PL semantics *sing*

semantisch [zeˈmantɪʃ] ◼ ADJ semantic ◻ ADV semantically

Semester [zeˈmɛstɐ] NT **-s, -** (*Univ*) semester (*esp US*), term (*of a half-year's duration*); **im 7./8. ~ sein** to be in one's 4th year; **die älteren ~** the senior students; **sie ist auch schon ein älteres ~** she's no spring chicken (*inf*)

Semesterferien PL vacation *sing*

Semi-, semi- [ˈzemi] IN CPDS semi-; **Semifinale** [ˈzeːmi-] NT (*Sport*) semifinal(s); **Semikolon** [zemiˈkoːlɔn] NT **-s, -s** *or* **Semikola** [-la] semicolon

Seminar [zemiˈnaːɐ] NT **-s, -e** *or* (*Aus*) **-rien** [-ian] **(a)** (*Univ*) department; (= *~übung*) seminar **(b)** (= *Priesterseminar*) seminary **(c)** (= *Lehrerseminar, Studienseminar*) teacher training college

Semit [zeˈmiːt] M **-en, -en, Semitin** [-ˈmiːtɪn] F **-, -nen** Semite

semitisch [zeˈmiːtɪʃ] ADJ Semitic

Semmel [ˈzɛml] F **-, -n** (*dial*) roll

Semmel-: Semmelbrösel(n) [-brøːzl(n)] PL breadcrumbs *pl*; **Semmelknödel** M (*S Ger, Aus*) bread dumpling

sen. ABBR *von* **senior** sen.

Senat [zeˈnaːt] M **-(e)s, -e (a)** (*Pol, Univ*) senate **(b)** (*Jur*) Supreme Court

Senator [zeˈnaːtoːɐ] M **-s, Senatoren** [-ˈtoːrən], **Senatorin** [-ˈtoːrɪn] F **-, -nen** senator

Senats- IN CPDS of the senate; **Senatsausschuss** M senate committee; **Senatspräsident(in)** M(F) chairman/-woman of the senate

Sende-: Sendeanlage F transmitting installation; **Sendebereich** M transmission range; **Sendebericht** M (*von Fax*) journal; **Sendefolge** F **(a)** (= *Sendung in Fortsetzungen*) series *sing*; (= *einzelne Folge*) episode **(b)** (= *Programmfolge*) programmes *pl* (*Brit*), programs *pl* (*US*); **Sendegebiet** NT transmission area; **Sendeleiter(in)** M(F) producer

senden[1] [ˈzɛndn], *pret* **sandte** *or* **sendete** [ˈzantə, ˈzɛndətə], *ptp* **gesandt** *or* **gesendet** [ɡəˈzant, ɡəˈzɛndət] ◼ VT to send (*an +acc* to); **jdm etw ~** to send sb sth, to send sth to sb ◻ VI **nach jdm ~** to send for sb

senden[2] VTI (*Rad, TV*) to broadcast; *Signal etc* to transmit

Sendepause F interval; (*fig inf*) deathly silence; **auf meine Frage hin herrschte ~** my question was met by deathly silence

Sender [ˈzɛndɐ] M **-s, -** transmitter; (= *~kanal*) (*Rad*) station; (*TV*) channel (*esp Brit*), station (*esp US*); **der ~ Prag** Radio Prague; **über den ~ gehen** to go on the air

---

Vorsicht! **Sender** *wird nicht mit dem englischen Wort* **sender** *übersetzt.*

Sende-: Senderaum M studio; **Sendereihe** F (radio/television) series; **Sendeschluss** M (*Rad, TV*) close-down; **Sendezeit** F broadcasting time; **und damit geht unsere heutige ~ zu Ende** and that concludes our programmes (*Brit*) *or* programs (*US*) for today; **in der besten ~** in prime time

Sendung [ˈzɛndʊŋ] F **-, -en (a)** NO PL (= *das Senden*) sending **(b)** (= *Postsendung*) letter; (= *Päckchen*) packet; (= *Paket*) parcel; (*Comm*) consignment **(c)** (*TV*) programme (*Brit*), program (*US*); (*Rad*) broadcast; (= *das Senden*) broadcasting; (*von Signal etc*) transmission; **auf ~ gehen/sein** to go/be on the air

Senegal NT **-s** Senegal

Senegalese [zeneɡaˈleːzə] M **-n, -n, Senegalesin** [-ˈleːzɪn] F **-, -nen** Senegalese

senegalesisch [zeneɡaˈleːzɪʃ] ADJ Senegalese

Senf [zɛnf] M **-(e)s, -e** mustard; **seinen ~ dazugeben** (*inf*) to have one's say

Senf-: senffarben [-farbn], **senffarbig** ADJ mustard(-coloured) (*Brit*), mustard(-colored) (*US*); **Senfgas** NT (*Chem*) mustard gas; **Senfkorn** NT, *pl* **-körner** mustard seed; **Senfsoße** F, **Senftunke** F (*dial*) mustard sauce

sengen [ˈzɛŋən] ◼ VT to singe ◻ VI to scorch

senil [zeˈniːl] ADJ (*pej*) senile

Senilität [zeniliˈtɛːt] F **-,** NO PL senility

senior [ˈzeːnioːɐ] ADJ *Franz Schulz* **~** Franz Schulz senior

Senior [ˈzeːnioːɐ] M **-s, Senioren** [-ˈnioːrən], **Seniorin** [-ˈnioːrɪn] F **-, -nen (a)** (*auch* **Seniorchef(in)**) boss; **kann ich mal den ~ sprechen?** can I speak to Mr X senior? **(b)** (*Sport*) senior player; **die ~en** the seniors **(c)** **Senioren** PL senior citizens *pl*; (*hum*) old folk *pl*

Senioren-: Seniorenkarte F senior citizen's ticket; **Seniorenpass** M senior citizen's travel pass; **Senioren(wohn)heim** NT old people's home

Seniorin F *siehe* **Senior**

Senkblei NT plumb line; (= *Gewicht*) plummet

Senkel ['zɛŋkl] M **-s, -** (= *Schnürsenkel*) lace

senken ['zɛŋkn] **1** VT to lower; *Lanze, Fahne* to dip; *Kopf* to bow; (*Tech*) *Schraube, Loch, Schacht* to sink; **den Blick ~** to lower one's gaze **2** VR to sink; (*Grab, Haus, Boden, Straße auch*) to subside; (*Stimme*) to drop; **dann senkte sich ihr Blick** then she looked down

senkrecht ['zɛŋkrɛçt] **1** ADJ vertical; (*Math*) perpendicular; (*in Kreuzworträtsel*) down; **immer schön ~ bleiben!** (*inf*) keep your end up (*inf*) **2** ADV vertically, perpendicularly; *aufsteigen, in die Höhe steigen* straight up; **sie stehen ~ aufeinander** they are perpendicular to each other

Senkrechte ['zɛŋkrɛçtə] F DECL AS ADJ vertical; (*Math*) perpendicular

Senkrechtstarter M (*Aviat*) vertical takeoff aircraft

Senkrechtstarter(in) M(F) (*fig inf*) whiz(z) kid (*inf*)

Senkung ['zɛŋkʊŋ] F **-, -en (a)** lowering; (*von Arbeitslosigkeit*) fall (*von in*) (*inf*) **(b)** (= *Vertiefung*) hollow **(c)** (*Poet*) thesis **(d)** (*Med*) = **Blutsenkung**

Senner ['zɛnɐ] M **-s, -** (*S Ger, Aus*) Alpine dairyman

Sennerei [zɛnə'raɪ] F **-, -en** (*S Ger, Aus*) (*Gebäude*) Alpine dairy; (*Wirtschaftsform*) Alpine dairy farming

Sennerin ['zɛnərɪn] F **-, -nen** (*S Ger, Aus*) Alpine dairymaid

Sensation [zɛnza'tsioːn] F **-, -en** sensation

sensationell [zɛnzatsio'nɛl] **1** ADJ sensational **2** ADV sensationally; **er wurde ~ Dritter** he came a sensational third; **~ schnell** incredibly fast

Sensations-: **Sensationsblatt** NT sensational paper; **Sensationslust** F desire for sensation; **sensationslüstern** ADJ sensation-seeking; **Sensationsmeldung** F, **Sensationsnachricht** F sensational news *sing*; **eine ~** a sensational piece of news; **Sensationspresse** F sensational papers *pl*

Sense ['zɛnzə] F **-, -n (a)** scythe **(b)** (*inf*) **jetzt/dann ist ~!** that's the end!

sensibel [zɛn'ziːbl] **1** ADJ sensitive **2** ADV sensitively; **~ auf etw** (*acc*) **reagieren** to be sensitive to sth

> *Vorsicht!* **sensibel** *wird nicht mit dem englischen Wort* **sensible** *übersetzt.*

sensibilisieren [zɛnzibili'ziːrən], *ptp* **sensibilisiert** VT to sensitize

Sensibilisierung F **, -en** sensitization

Sensibilität [zɛnzibili'tɛːt] F **-, NO PL** sensitivity

Sensor ['zɛnzoːɐ̯] M **-s, Sensoren** [-'zoːrən] sensor

sensorisch [zɛn'zoːrɪʃ] **1** ADJ sensory **2** ADV *aktivieren, steuern* by a sensor; **~ gestört sein** to have a sensory disability

Sensortaste F touch-sensitive button

sentimental [zɛntimɛn'taːl] **1** ADJ sentimental **2** ADV sentimentally; **~ klingen** to sound sentimental

Sentimentalität [zɛntimɛntali'tɛːt] F **-, -en** sentimentality

separat [zepa'raːt] **1** ADJ separate; *Wohnung, Zimmer* self-contained **2** ADV separately

Sepia ['zeːpia] F **-, Sepien** [-pian] **(a)** (*Zool*) cuttlefish **(b)** NO PL (*Farbstoff*) sepia (ink)

September [zɛp'tɛmbɐ] M **-(s), -** September; *siehe auch* **März**

Septett [zɛp'tɛt] NT **-(e)s, -e** (*Mus*) septet(te)

Sequenz [ze'kvɛnts] F **-, -en** sequence

sequenziell [zekvɛn'tsiɛl] ADJ **1** ADJ sequential **2** ADV sequentially

Sera PL *von* **Serum**

Serbe ['zɛrbə] M **-n, -n, Serbin** ['zɛrbɪn] F **-, -nen** Serbian

Serbien ['zɛrbiən] NT **-s** Serbia

serbisch ['zɛrbɪʃ] ADJ Serbian

Serbokroatisch(e) [zɛrbokro'aːtɪʃ] NT Serbo-Croat; *siehe auch* **Deutsch(e)**

Seren PL *von* **Serum**

Serie ['zeːriə] F **-, -n** series *sing*; (*von Waren auch*) line; (*Billard*) break; **13 Siege in ~** 13 wins in a row; **in ~ gehen** to go into production; **in ~ hergestellt werden** to be mass-produced; **in ~ schalten** (*Elec*) to connect in series

seriell [ze'riɛl] **1** ADJ *Herstellung* series *attr*; (*Comput*) serial; **~e Musik** serial music **2** ADV serially; **~ hergestellt werden** to be mass-produced

Serien- ['zeːriən-]: **Serienbrief** M (*Comput*) mail-merge letter; **Serienfabrikation** F, **Serienfertigung** F series production; **Serienfax** NT series mail-merge fax; **serienmäßig** **1** ADJ *Autos* production *attr*; *Ausstattung* standard; *Herstellung* series *attr* **2** ADV *herstellen* in series; **das wird ~ eingebaut** it's a standard fitting; **Serienmörder(in)** M(F) serial killer; **Seriennummer** F serial number; **serienreif** ADJ (*esp Aut*) ready to go into production; **Serienreife** F readiness for production; **etw zur ~ entwickeln** to develop sth so that it is ready for production; **Serientäter(in)** M(F) serial offender; **serienweise** [-vaɪzə] ADV *produzieren* in series; (*inf*: = *in Mengen*) wholesale

serifenlos ADJ (*Typ*) sanserif

seriös [ze'riøːs] **1** ADJ serious; (= *anständig*) respectable; *Firma* reputable **2** ADV **~ auftreten** to appear respectable; **~ wirken** to give the impression of being respectable; **~ klingen** to sound serious

> *Vorsicht!* **seriös** *wird im Allgemeinen nicht mit dem englischen Wort* **serious** *übersetzt.*

Seriosität [zeriozi'tɛːt] F **-, NO PL** seriousness; (= *Anständigkeit*) respectability; (*von Firma*) integrity

Serpentine [zɛrpɛn'tiːnə] F **-, -n** winding road, zigzag; (= *Kurve*) double bend

Serum ['zeːrʊm] NT **-s, Seren** or **Sera** ['zeːrən, 'zeːra] serum

Server ['zœrvɐ] M **-s, -** (*Comput*) server

Service¹ ['zœrvɪːs] NT **-(s), -** [-'viːs(əs), -'viːs(ə)] (= *Essgeschirr*) dinner service; (= *Kaffee-/Teeservice*) coffee/tea service; (= *Gläserservice*) set

Service² ['sœːɐ̯vɪs, 'zœrvɪs] M or NT **-, -s** (*Comm*) service; (*Sport*) service, serve

Serviceprovider ['zœrvɪsprɔ'vaɪdɐ, 'sœːɐ̯vɪs-] M **-s, -** (*für Mobilfunk, Internet*) service provider

servieren [zɛr'viːrən], *ptp* **serviert** **1** VT to serve (*jdm etw* sb sth, *sth to sb*); (*inf:* = *anbieten*) to serve up (*inf*) (*jdm* for sb); (*Tennis*) to serve; **jdm etw auf dem Silbertablett ~** (*fig*) to hand sth to sb on a plate (*Brit*) **2** VI to serve; **nach 24 Uhr wird nicht mehr serviert** there is no waiter service after midnight; **es ist serviert!** lunch/dinner *etc* is served

Serviererin [zɛr'viːrərɪn] F **-, -nen** waitress

Servier- [zɛr'viːɐ̯-]: **Serviertochter** F (*Sw*) waitress; **Servierwagen** M trolley

Serviette [zɛr'viɛtə] F **-, -n** napkin

Servo- ['zɛrvo-] (*Tech*): **Servobremse** F power brake; **Servolenkung** F power steering

servus ['zɛrvʊs] INTERJ (*Aus, S Ger*) (*beim Treffen*) hello; (*beim Abschied*) cheerio (*Brit inf*), see ya (*esp US inf*)

Sesam ['zeːzam] M **-s, -s** sesame; **~, öffne dich!** open Sesame!

Sessel ['zɛsl] M **-s, -** easy chair; (= *Polstersessel*) armchair; (*Aus*: = *Stuhl*) chair; **am ~ kleben** (*fig*) to cling to one's position; **seinen ~ räumen** (*fig*) to clear one's desk

Sessellift M chairlift

sesshaft ADJ settled; (= *ansässig*) resident; **~ werden, sich ~ machen** to settle down

Set¹ [zɛt, sɛt] M or NT **-s, -s (a)** (*Tennis*: = *Satz*) set **(b)** (= *Deckchen*) place mat

Set² M **-(s), -s** (*TV, Film*) set

Setter [zɛtɐ] M **-s, -** setter

Setup ['sɛtap] NT **-s, -s** (*Comput*) setup

Setup- ['sɛtap-]: **Setup-Datei** F setup file; **Setupprogramm** NT (*Comput*) setup program

setzen ['zɛtsn] **1** VT **(a)** (= *hintun, hinbringen*) to put, to set; (= *sitzen lassen*) to sit, to place, to put; **etw auf die Rechnung/Speisekarte** *etc* **~** to put sth on the bill/menu *etc*; **jdn an Land ~** to put sb ashore; **etw auf die Tagesordnung ~** to put sth on the agenda; **etw in die Zeitung ~** to put sth in the paper; **sich** (*dat*) **etw in den Kopf** or **Schädel ~** (*inf*) to take sth into one's head; **dann setzt es was** or **Hiebe** or **Prügel** (*all inf*) there'll be trouble; **seine Hoffnung/sein Vertrauen in jdn/etw ~** to put one's hopes/trust in sb/sth; **seinen Ehrgeiz in etw** (*acc*) **~** to make sth one's goal

(b) (*Naut*) *Segel* to set; (*Typ*) to set; **ein Gedicht/einen Text in Musik ~** to set a poem/words to music

(c) *Preis, Summe* to put (*auf* +*acc* on); *Stein, Figur* to move; **Geld auf ein Pferd ~** to put money on a horse

(d) (= *errichten, aufstellen*) to build; (*fig*) *Norm etc* to set

(e) (= *schreiben*) *Komma, Punkt* to put; **seinen Namen unter etw** (*acc*) ~ to put one's signature to sth
(f) (= *bestimmen*) *Ziel, Grenze, Termin, Preis, Prioritäten etc* to set; **jdm/sich ein Ziel/eine Frist** ~ to set sb/oneself a goal/deadline
(g) jdm eine Spritze ~ to give sb an injection; **sich** (*dat*) **einen Schuss** ~ (*inf*) to shoot up (*inf*)
(h) (= *einstufen*) *Sportler* to place; (*Tennis*) to seed; **der an Nummer eins/zwei gesetzte Spieler** (*Tennis*) the top/second seed
(i) (*Hunt*: = *gebären*) to bear
(j) *siehe* **gesetzt**
2 VR **(a)** (= *Platz nehmen*) to sit down; (*Vogel*) to perch; **sich ins Auto** ~ to get into the car; **sich in die Sonne/ins Licht** ~ to sit in the sun/light; **sich jdm auf den Schoß** ~ to sit on sb's lap; **sich zu jdm** ~ to sit with sb; **wollen Sie sich nicht zu uns ~?** won't you join us?; **darf ich mich zu Ihnen ~?** may I join you?; **bitte** ~ **Sie sich** please take a seat; **setz dich doch** sit yourself down (*inf*)
(b) (*Kaffee, Tee, Lösung*) to settle
(c) (*Staub, Geruch, Läuse*) to get (*in* +*acc* into)
3 VI **(a)** (*bei Glücksspiel, Wetten*) to bet; **auf ein Pferd** ~ to bet on a horse; **auf jdn/etw** ~ (*lit, fig*) to put one's money on sb/sth
(b) AUX SEIN *or* HABEN (= *springen*) (*Pferd, Läufer*) to jump; (*Mil*) to cross

Setzer [ˈzɛtsɐ] M **-s**, **-**, **Setzerin** [-ərɪn] F **-**, **-nen** (*Typ*) typesetter
Setzerei [zɛtsəˈraɪ] F **-**, **-en** (= *Firma*) typesetter's
Setz-: Setzfehler M (*Typ*) printer's error; **Setzkasten** M case; **Setzling** [ˈzɛtslɪŋ] M **-s**, **-e** (*Hort*) seedling
Seuche [ˈzɔʏçə] F **-**, **-n** epidemic; (*fig pej*) scourge
Seuchen-: seuchenartig **1** ADJ epidemic **2** ADV **sich ~ ausbreiten** to spread like an epidemic; **Seuchenbekämpfung** F epidemic control; **Seuchengebiet** NT epidemic area; **Seuchengefahr** F danger of epidemic; **Seuchenherd** M centre (*Brit*) *or* center (*US*) of an/the epidemic
seufzen [ˈzɔʏftsn̩] VTI to sigh
Seufzer [ˈzɔʏftsɐ] M **-s**, **-** sigh
Sex [zɛks] M **-(es)**, NO PL sex
Sex-: sexaktiv ADJ sexually active; **Sex-Appeal** [-ləˈpiːl] M **-s**, NO PL sex appeal; **sexbesessen** ADJ sex-obsessed; **Sexbombe** F (*inf*) sex bomb (*inf*); **Sexfilm** M sex film
Sexismus [zɛˈksɪsmʊs] M **-**, **Sexismen** [-mən] sexism
Sexist [zɛˈksɪst] M **-en**, **-en**, **Sexistin** [-ˈksɪstɪn] F **-**, **-nen** sexist
sexistisch [zɛˈksɪstɪʃ] **1** ADJ sexist **2** ADV **~ eingestellt sein** to be sexist; **sich** ~ **verhalten** to act in a sexist way; **~ klingen** to sound sexist
Sex-: Sexmagazin NT sex magazine; **Sexobjekt** NT sex object; **Sexshop** [ˈzɛksʃɔp] M **-s**, **-s** sex shop
Sextett [zɛksˈtɛt] NT **-(e)s**, **-e** (*Mus*) sextet(te)
Sextourismus M sex tourism
Sexual-: Sexualatlas M illustrated sex handbook; **Sexualerziehung** F sex education
Sexualität [zɛksualiˈtɛːt] F **-**, NO PL sexuality
Sexual-: Sexualkunde F (*Sch*) sex education; **Sexualleben** NT sex life; **Sexualpartner(in)** M(F) sexual partner; **Sexualpraktik** F sexual practice *usu pl*; **Sexualtrieb** M sex(ual) drive
sexuell [zɛˈksuɛl] **1** ADJ sexual **2** ADV sexually
sexy [ˈzɛksi] ADJ INV (*inf*) sexy (*inf*)
Seychellen [zeˈʃɛlən] PL (*Geog*) Seychelles *pl*
sezieren [zeˈtsiːrən] *ptp* **seziert** VTI (*lit, fig*) to dissect
SFOR, Sfor [ˈɛsfɔːɐ] F ABBR *von* **Stabilization Force** SFOR
S-förmig [ˈɛs-] ADJ S-shaped
sfr ABBR *von* **Schweizer Franken** sfr
SGML [ɛsɡeːɛmˈɛl] ABBR *von* **Standardized Generalized Mark-up Language** SGML
Shakehands [ˈʃeːkhɛndz] NT **-**, **-** (*inf*) handshake; **~ machen** to shake hands
Shampoo [ˈʃampuː, ˈʃampoː] NT **-s**, **-s** shampoo
shampoonieren [ʃampoˈniːrən, ʃampuˈniːrən], *ptp* **shampooniert** VT to shampoo
Shareware [ˈʃeːɛvɛːɐ] F **-**, NO PL (*Comput*) shareware
Shareware-Programm [ˈʃeːɛvɛːɐ-] NT shareware program
Sherpa [ˈʃɛrpa] M **-s**, **-s** Sherpa
Sherry [ˈʃɛrɪ] M **-s**, **-s** sherry

Shetland- [ˈʃɛtlant-]: **Shetlandinseln** PL Shetland Islands *pl*; **Shetlandpony** NT Shetland pony; **Shetlandwolle** F Shetland wool
Shift-Taste [ˈʃɪft-] F, **Shifttaste** F (*Comput*) shift key
Shit [ʃɪt] NT **-s**, NO PL (*sl*: = *Haschisch*) dope (*inf*)
Shootingstar [ˈʃuːtɪŋstaːɐ] M shooting star
shoppen [ˈʃɔpn̩] VI (*inf*) to shop
Shopping [ˈʃɔpɪŋ] NT **-s**, NO PL shopping (*for luxury items*); **~ gehen** *or* **machen** (*inf*) to go shopping (*for luxury items*)
Shoppingcenter [ˈʃɔpɪŋsɛntɐ] NT **-s**, **-** shopping centre (*Brit*) *or* center (*US*)
Shorts [ʃoːɐts, ʃɔrts] PL (pair of) shorts *pl*
Show [ʃoː] F **-**, **-s** show; **eine ~ abziehen** (*inf*) to put on a show (*inf*)
Show-: Show-down [ˈʃoːdaun] M *or* NT **-(s)**, **-s**, **Showdown** M *or* NT **-(s)**, **-s** showdown; **Showgeschäft** [ˈʃoː-] NT show business; **Showmaster** [ˈʃoːmaːstɐ] M **-s**, **-**, **Showmasterin** [-ərɪn] F **-**, **-nen** compère, emcee (*US*)
Shredder [ˈʃrɛdɐ] M **-s**, **-**, **Shredderanlage** F shredder
Shuttle [ˈʃatl] M **-s**, **-s** (*Aut, Aviat, Space*) shuttle
Shuttle-Flug [ˈʃatl-] M (*Space*) shuttle flight
siamesisch [ziaˈmeːzɪʃ] ADJ **(a)** (*Hist*) Siamese **(b)** **~e Katze** Siamese cat; **~e Zwillinge** Siamese twins
Sibirien [ziˈbiːrɪən] NT **-s** Siberia
sibirisch [ziˈbiːrɪʃ] ADJ Siberian; **~e Kälte** Siberian *or* arctic conditions *pl*
sich [zɪç] REFL PRON **(a)** (*acc*) (+*infin, bei „man“*) oneself; (*3. pers sing*) himself; herself; itself; (*Höflichkeitsform sing*) yourself; (*Höflichkeitsform pl*) yourselves; (*3. pers pl*) themselves; **nur an ~** (*acc*) **denken** to think only of oneself
(b) (*dat*) (+*infin, bei „man“*) to oneself; (*3. pers sing*) to himself; to herself; to itself; (*Höflichkeitsform sing*) to yourself; (*Höflichkeitsform pl*) to yourselves; (*3. pers pl*) to themselves; ~ **die Haare waschen/färben** *etc* to wash/dye *etc* one's hair; **wann hat sie ~ das gekauft?** when did she buy that?; **wenn man keinen Pass bei** ~ (*dat*) **hat** if you haven't got a passport with you
(c) (= *einander*) each other; **sie schreiben ~ schon viele Jahre** they have been writing to each other for many years
(d) (*impers*) **hier sitzt/singt es ~ gut** it's good to sit/sing here; **diese Wolle strickt ~ gut** this wool knits well; **dieses Auto fährt ~ gut** this car drives well
Sichel [ˈzɪçl] F **-**, **-n** sickle; (= *Mondsichel*) crescent
sicher [ˈzɪçɐ] **1** ADJ **(a)** (= *gewiss*) certain; (**sich** *dat*) **einer Sache** (*gen*) ~ **sein** to be sure of sth; **so viel ist ~** this much is certain; **das ist uns** ~ that is for sure; **mit der guten Zeit ist uns der zweite Platz** ~ with such a good time we're sure of second place
(b) (= *geschützt, gefahrlos*) safe; (= *geborgen*) secure; *Investition* secure; **vor jdm/etw** ~ **sein** to be safe from sb/sth; ~ **ist** ~ you can't be too sure
(c) (= *zuverlässig*) reliable; (= *fest*) *Gefühl, Zusage* definite; *Hand, Einkommen, Job* steady; *Stellung* secure
(d) (= *selbstbewusst*) (self-)confident
2 ADV **(a)** *fahren, aufbewahren etc* safely; ~ **wirkend** reliable; ~ **leben** to live a secure life
(b) (= *selbstbewusst*) ~ **wirken/auftreten** to give an impression of (self-)confidence
(c) (= *natürlich*) of course; **~!** sure (*esp US*)
(d) (= *bestimmt*) **das wolltest du ~ nicht sagen** surely you didn't mean that; **du hast dich ~ verrechnet** you must have counted wrong; **das weiß ich ganz ~** I know that for certain; **das ist ganz ~ das Beste** it's quite certainly the best; **aber er kommt ~ noch** I'm sure he'll come; **das hat er ~ vergessen** I'm sure he's forgotten it; (= *garantiert*) he's sure to have forgotten it; **er kommt ~ auch mit** he's bound to want to come too
sichergehen VI SEP IRREG AUX SEIN to be sure
Sicherheit F **-**, **-en (a)** NO PL (= *Gewissheit*) certainty; **sich** (*dat*) ~ **darüber verschaffen, dass …** to assure oneself that …; **verschaffen Sie sich persönlich ~ darüber** you have to make certain for yourself; **mit an ~ grenzender Wahrscheinlichkeit** almost certainly; **das ist mit ~ richtig** that is definitely right; **das lässt sich nicht mit ~ sagen/beweisen** that cannot be said/proved with any degree of certainty
(b) NO PL (= *Schutz, das Sichersein*) safety; (*als Aufgabe von*)

Sicherheitsbeamten *etc*) security; **~ und Ordnung** law and order; **die öffentliche ~** public safety; **innere ~** internal security; **die ~ der Bevölkerung** the safety of the people; **jdn/ etw in ~ bringen** to get sb/sth to safety; **sich in ~ bringen** to get (oneself) to safety; **~ im Straßen-/Flugverkehr** road/air safety; **in ~ sein, sich in ~ befinden** to be safe; **sich in ~ wiegen** *or* **wähnen** to think oneself safe

(c) NO PL (= *Zuverlässigkeit*) (*von Mittel, Methode, Geschmack, Instinkt*) reliability; (*von Fahrer, Schwimmer*) competence; (*von Hand, Job, Einkommen*) steadiness; (*von Stellung*) security **(d)** (= *Treffsicherheit im Umgang mit Sprache*) sureness **(e)** NO PL (= *Selbstsicherheit*) (self-)confidence; **~ im Auftreten** self-confident manner **(f)** (*Comm, Fin*) security; (= *Pfand*) surety; **~ leisten** (*Comm, Fin*) to offer security; (*Jur*) to stand bail

Sicherheits-: Sicherheitsabstand M safe distance; **Sicherheitsbeamte(r)** M DECL AS ADJ, **Sicherheitsbeamtin** F security officer; **Sicherheitsbehälter** M (*von Atomreaktor*) containment dome; **Sicherheitsbehörde** F security service; **Sicherheitsbestimmungen** PL safety regulations *pl*; (*betrieblich, Pol etc*) security controls *pl*; **Sicherheitsbindung** F (*Ski*) safety binding; **Sicherheitsfaktor** M security factor; **Sicherheitsglas** NT safety glass; **Sicherheitsgurt** M (*in Flugzeug*) seat belt; (*in Auto auch*) safety belt; **sicherheitshalber** ADV to be on the safe side; **Sicherheitskopie** F (*Comput*) backup copy; **Sicherheitskräfte** PL security forces *pl*; **Sicherheitsmaßnahme** F safety precaution; (*betrieblich, Pol etc*) security measure; **Sicherheitsnadel** F safety pin; **Sicherheitsrat** M security council; **Sicherheitsrisiko** NT security risk; **Sicherheitsschloss** NT Yale® lock; **Sicherheittruppen** PL security troops *pl*; **Sicherheitsvorkehrung** F safety precaution; (*betrieblich, Pol etc*) security precaution

sicherlich ['zɪçɐlɪç] ADV **= sicher 2(c, d)**

sichern ['zɪçɐn] **1** VT **(a)** (*gegen, vor +dat* against) to safeguard; (= *absichern*) to protect; (= *sicher machen*) Tür, Wagen, Fahrrad, Unfallstelle to secure; Bergsteiger etc to belay; (*Mil*) to protect; (*Comput*) Daten to save; **eine Feuerwaffe ~** to put the safety catch of a firearm on; **den Frieden ~** to maintain the peace **(b)** **jdm/sich etw ~** to secure sth for sb/oneself **2** VR to protect oneself; (*Bergsteigen*) to belay oneself; **sich vor etw** (*dat*) *or* **gegen etw ~** to protect oneself against sth

sicherstellen VT SEP **(a)** (= *in Gewahrsam nehmen*) Waffen, Drogen to take possession of; Beweismittel to secure; **das Tatfahrzeug wurde sichergestellt** the vehicle used in the crime was found (and taken in) **(b)** (= *garantieren*) to guarantee

Sicherung ['zɪçɐrʊŋ] F **-, -en (a)** NO PL (= *das Sichern*) (*gegen, vor +dat* against) safeguarding; (= *Absicherung*) protection; (*von Tür, Wagen, Fahrrad*) securing **(b)** (= *Schutz*) safeguard **(c)** (*Elec*) fuse; (*von Waffe*) safety catch; **da ist (bei) ihm die ~ durchgebrannt** (*fig inf*) he blew a fuse (*inf*)

Sicherungs-: Sicherungskopie F (*Comput*) backup copy; **Sicherungsverwahrung** F (*Jur*) preventive detention

Sicht [zɪçt] F **-,** NO PL **(a)** (= *Sehweite*) visibility; **in ~ sein/ kommen** to be in/come into sight; **aus meiner/seiner** *etc* **~** (*fig*) as I see/he sees it; **aus heutiger ~** from today's perspective; **auf lange/kurze ~** (*fig*) in the long/short term; *planen* for the long/short term **(b)** (= *Ausblick*) view **(c)** (*Comm*) **auf** *or* **bei ~** at sight; **acht Tage nach ~** one week after sight

sichtbar **1** ADJ (*lit, fig*) visible; **~ werden** (*fig*) to become apparent **2** ADV altern visibly; *Fortschritte machen* obviously; *sich verändern* noticeably; *sich verbessern, sich verschlechtern* clearly; **sie hat ~ abgenommen/zugenommen** it's obvious that she's lost/gained weight

sichten ['zɪçtn] VT **(a)** (= *erblicken*) to sight **(b)** (= *durchsehen*) to look through

Sicht-: Sichtflug M contact flight; **Sichtgeld** NT (*Fin*) demand *or* sight deposit; **Sichtgerät** NT monitor; (*Comput*) VDU; **Sichtguthaben** NT **= Sichtgeld**

sichtlich ['zɪçtlɪç] **1** ADJ obvious **2** ADV obviously; *beeindruckt* visibly

Sicht-: Sichtverhältnisse PL visibility *sing*; **Sichtvermerk** M endorsement; (*im Pass*) visa stamp; **Sichtweite** F visibility *no art*; **außer ~** out of sight

Sickergrube F soakaway

sickern ['zɪkɐn] VI AUX SEIN to seep; (*in Tropfen*) to drip; (*fig*) to leak out

sie [zi:] PERS PRON 3. PERS **(a)** SING *gen* **ihrer** ['i:rɐ], *dat* **ihr** [i:ɐ], *acc* **sie** (*nom*) she; (*acc*) her; (*von Dingen*) it; **wenn ich ~ wäre ...** if I were her; **~ ist es** it's her; **wer hat das gemacht? – ~** who did that? – she did *or* her!; **~ war es nicht, ich wars** it wasn't her, it was me **(b)** PL *gen* **ihrer** ['i:rɐ], *dat* **ihnen** ['i:nən], *acc* **sie** (*nom*) they; (*acc*) them; **~ sind es** it's them; **~ sind es, die ...** it's them who ...

Sie [zi:] **1** PERS PRON 2. PERS SING *or* PL WITH 3. PERS VB *gen* **ihrer** ['i:rɐ], *dat* **Ihnen** ['i:nən], *acc* **Sie** you; **beeilen ~ sich!** hurry up!; **he, ~!** (*inf*) hey, you!; **~, wissen ~ was ...** (*inf*) do you know what ... **2** NT **-s,** NO PL polite *or* "Sie" form of address; **jdn per** *or* **mit ~ anreden** to use the polite form of address to sb

Sieb [zi:p] NT **-(e)s, -e** [-bə] sieve; (= *Teesieb*) strainer; (= *Gemüsesieb*) colander; **ein Gedächtnis wie ein ~ haben** to have a memory like a sieve

sieben¹ ['zi:bn] **1** VT to pass through a sieve; Korn, Gold to screen; (*Cook*) to sieve **2** VI (*fig inf*) **es wird stark gesiebt** they are very selective

sieben² NUM seven; *siehe auch* **vier**

Sieben ['zi:bn] F **-,** *or* **-en** seven; *siehe* **Vier**

sieben-, Sieben- IN CPDS *siehe auch* **Vier-**: **siebenarmig** ADJ *Leuchter* seven-armed; **Siebenbürgen** [zi:bn'bʏrgn] NT **-s** (*Geog*) Transylvania; **Siebeneck** NT heptagon; **siebenhundert** ['zi:bn'hʊndɐt] NUM seven hundred; **siebenjährig** ADJ seven-year-old; (= *sieben Jahre dauernd*) seven-year *attr*; **siebenmal** ['zi:bnma:l] ADV seven times; **Siebensachen** PL (*inf*) belongings *pl*, things *pl*; **seine ~ packen** to pack one's bits and pieces; **Siebenschläfer** [-ʃlɛːfɐ] M **-s, -** **(a)** (*Zool*) edible dormouse **(b)** 27th June (*day which is said to determine the weather for the next seven weeks*); **siebentausend** ['zi:bn'tauznt] NUM seven thousand

siebentens ['zi:bntəns], **siebtens** ['zi:ptns] ADV seventh(ly)

Siebtel ['zi:ptl] NT **-s, -** seventh

siebte(r, s) ['zi:ptə] ADJ seventh; *siehe auch* **vierte(r, s)**

siebzehn ['zi:ptse:n] NUM seventeen; **Siebzehn und Vier** (*Cards*) pontoon; *siehe auch* **vierzehn**

siebzig ['zi:ptsɪç] NUM seventy; *siehe auch* **vierzig**

sieden ['zi:dn] *pret* **siedete** *or* **sott** ['zi:dətə, zɔt], *ptp* **gesiedet** *or* **gesotten** [gə'zi:dət, gə'zɔtn] **1** VI to boil; **~d heiß** boiling hot **2** VT Seife, Leim to produce by boiling; *siehe auch* **gesotten**

Siede-: Siedepunkt M (*Phys, fig*) boiling point; **Siedewasserreaktor** M boiling-water reactor

Siedler ['zi:dlɐ] M **-s, -, Siedlerin** [-ərɪn] F **-, -nen** settler; (= *Bauer*) smallholder

Siedlung ['zi:dlʊŋ] F **-, -en (a)** (= *Ansiedlung*) settlement **(b)** (= *Wohnsiedlung*) housing estate *or* development (*US*)

Sieg [zi:k] M **-(e)s, -e** [-gə] victory (*über +acc* over); **den ~ davontragen** *or* **erringen** to be victorious; **einer Sache ~** (*dat*) **zum ~ verhelfen** to help sth to triumph

Siegel ['zi:gl] NT **-s, -** seal; **unter dem ~ der Verschwiegenheit** under the seal of secrecy

Siegel-: Siegellack M sealing wax; **Siegelring** M signet ring; **Siegelwachs** NT sealing wax

siegen ['zi:gn] VI (*Mil*) to be victorious; (*fig auch*) to triumph; (*in Wettkampf*) to win; **über jdn/etw ~** (*Mil*) to vanquish sb/ sth; (*fig*) to triumph over sb/sth; (*in Wettkampf*) to beat sb/ sth; **ich kam, sah und siegte** I came, I saw, I conquered

Sieger ['zi:gɐ] M **-s, -, Siegerin** [-ərɪn] F **-, -nen** victor; (*in Wettkampf*) winner; **zweiter ~** runner-up; **~ werden** to be the winner

Sieger-: Siegerehrung F (*Sport*) presentation ceremony; **Siegermacht** F USU PL (*Pol*) victorious power; **Siegerstraße** F road to victory

Sieges-: siegesbewusst ADJ confident of victory; **siegessicher** **1** ADJ certain of victory **2** ADV confidently; **Siegeszug** M triumphal march

siegreich **1** ADJ triumphant; (*in Wettkampf*) winning *attr*, successful **2** ADV triumphantly

sieh [zi:], **siehe** ['zi:ə] IMPER SING *von* **sehen**

sieht [zi:t] (*inf*) 3. PERS SING PRES *von* **sehen**

siezen ['zi:tsn] VT **jdn/sich ~** to address sb/each other as "Sie"; *siehe auch* **duzen**

Sightseeing ['saitsi:ɪŋ] NT -, NO PL sightseeing; ~ **machen** to do some sightseeing

Signal [zɪ'gna:l] NT **-s, -e** (*auch Rail*) signal; **~e setzen** (*fig*) to blaze a trail; **falsche ~e setzen** (*fig*) to point in the wrong direction

Signalanlage F signals *pl*

signalisieren [zɪgnali'zi:rən], *ptp* **signalisiert** VT (*lit, fig*) to signal

Signatur [zɪgna'tu:ɐ] F **-, -en (a)** (= *Unterschrift, Buchsignatur*) signature **(b)** (*auf Landkarten*) symbol **(c)** (= *Bibliothekssignatur*) shelf mark

signieren [zɪ'gni:rən], *ptp* **signiert** VT to sign

Silbe ['zɪlbə] F **-, -n** syllable; **~ für ~** (*fig*) word for word; **er hat es mit keiner ~ erwähnt/verraten** he didn't say/breathe a word about it

Silben-: Silbentrennprogramm NT (*Typ, Comput*) hyphenation program; **Silbentrennung** F syllabification; (*Typ, Comput*) hyphenation

Silber ['zɪlbɐ] NT **-s,** NO PL (*abbr* **Ag**) silver

Silber- IN CPDS silver; **Silberbesteck** NT silver(ware); **Silberfischchen** [-fɪʃçən] NT **-s,** - silverfish; **Silbergeld** NT silver; **silbergrau** ADJ silver(y)-grey (*Brit*), silver(y)-gray (*US*); **silberhaltig** ADJ silver-bearing; **Silberhochzeit** F silver wedding (anniversary); **Silberlöwe** M puma (*esp Brit*), mountain lion; **Silbermedaille** F silver medal

silbern ['zɪlbɐn] **1** ADJ silver; (*liter*) *Licht, Stimme, Haare* silvery (*liter*); **~e Hochzeit** silver wedding (anniversary) **2** ADV **~ schimmern** to have a silvery gleam

Silber-: Silberpappel F white poplar; **Silberstreif** [-ʃtraif] M **-en, -en, Silberstreifen** M (*fig*) **es zeichnete sich ein ~(en) am Horizont ab** you/they *etc* could see light at the end of the tunnel; **Silbertanne** F noble fir; **Silberwährung** F currency based on the silver standard; **silberweiß** ADJ silvery white

-silbig [zɪlbɪç] ADJ SUF **fünfsilbig/zehnsilbig sein** to have five/ten syllables; **ein sechssilbiges Wort** a word with six syllables

silbrig ['zɪlbrɪç] **1** ADJ silvery **2** ADV **~ schimmern/glänzen** to shimmer/gleam like silver; **~ weißes Haar** silvery white hair

Silhouette [zi'lu̯ɛtə] F **-, -n** silhouette

Silikon [zili'ko:n] NT **-s, -e** silicone

Silizium [zi'li:tsiom] NT **-s,** NO PL (*abbr* **Si**) silicon

Silo ['zi:lo] M **-s, -s** silo

Silvester [zɪl'vɛstɐ] M or NT **-s,** - New Year's Eve, Hogmanay (*esp Scot*)

SILVESTER

*December 31st is known as **Silvester** after the saint commemorated on that day. The old year is seen out with friends, often with a special **Silvester** meal. At midnight **Sekt** is drunk and fireworks let off to welcome the New Year. There is also the custom of **Bleigießen**, in which small amounts of lead are melted down and dropped into cold water. The resulting shapes are used as the basis for prophecies about the coming year. In some parts of Switzerland the old year is seen out with noisy processions in which the participants wear traditional masks.*

Simbabwe [zɪm'bapvə] NT **-s** Zimbabwe

simpel ['zɪmpl] **1** ADJ simple; *Mensch auch* simple-minded; (= *vereinfacht*) simplistic **2** ADV simply

Sims [sɪms] M or NT **-es, -e** [-zə] (= *Fenstersims*) (window)sill; (*außen auch*) (window) ledge; (= *Gesims*) ledge; (= *Kaminsims*) mantlepiece

simsen ['zɪmzn] VTI (*inf*) to text

Simulant [zimu'lant] M **-en, -en, Simulantin** F **-, -nen** malingerer

Simulation [zimula'tsio:n] F **-, -en** simulation

Simulator [zimu'la:to:ɐ] M **-s, Simulatoren** [-'to:rən] (*Sci*) simulator

simulieren [zimu'li:rən], *ptp* **simuliert** **1** VI (= *sich krank stellen*) to feign illness; **er simuliert nur** he's shamming; (*um sich zu drücken auch*) he's malingering **2** VT **(a)** (*Sci, Tech, Comput*) to simulate **(b)** (= *vorgeben*) *Krankheit, Empörung, Frohsinn* to feign

simultan [zimol'ta:n] **1** ADJ simultaneous **2** ADV simultaneously

Simultandolmetscher(in) M(F) simultaneous translator

sin. ABBR *von* Sinus

Sinai ['zi:nai] M **-(s), Sinaihalbinsel** F Sinai (Peninsula)

---

sind [zɪnt] 1. AND 3. PERS PL, WITH SIE SING AND PL PRES *von* **sein**

Sinfonie [zɪnfo'ni:] F **-, -n** [-'ni:ən] symphony

Sinfoniker [zɪn'fo:nikɐ] M **-s, -, Sinfonikerin** [-ərɪn] F **-, -nen** member of a symphony orchestra; **die Bamberger ~** the Bamberg Symphony Orchestra

sinfonisch [zɪn'fo:nɪʃ] ADJ symphonic

Singapur ['zɪŋgapu:ɐ] NT **-s** Singapore

singen ['zɪŋən], *pret* **sang** [zaŋ], *ptp* **gesungen** [gə'zʊŋən] **1** VI **(a)** to sing; (*Telegrafendrähte*) to hum; **ein ~der Tonfall** a lilt **(b)** (*inf*: = *gestehen*) to squeal (*inf*) **2** VT (*lit*) (*fig*) to sing; (*esp Eccl*) *Psalmen, Kanon* to chant **3** VR **sich heiser/in den Schlaf ~** to sing oneself hoarse/to sleep; **sich müde ~** to sing until one is tired

Singhalese [zɪŋga'le:zə] M **-n, -n, Singhalesin** [-'le:zɪn] F **-, -nen** Sin(g)halese

singhalesisch [zɪŋga'le:zɪʃ] ADJ Sin(g)halese

Single¹ ['sɪŋgl] F **-, -(s)** (= *Schallplatte*) single

Single² M **-s, -s** (= *Alleinlebender*) single; **Urlaub für ~s** singles' holiday (*Brit*), vacation for singles (*US*)

Singular ['zɪŋgula:ɐ] M **-s, -e** (*Gram*) singular; **im ~ stehen** to be (in the) singular

Singvogel M songbird

sinken ['zɪŋkn], *pret* **sank** [zaŋk], *ptp* **gesunken** [gə'zʊŋkn] VI AUX SEIN **(a)** (*Mensch, Gegenstand*) to sink; (*Ballon*) to descend; (*Nebel*) to come down; **ins Bett ~** to fall into bed; **sein Stern ist im or am Sinken** (*geh*) his star is waning; **die Arme/den Kopf ~ lassen** to let one's arms/head drop **(b)** (*Boden, Gebäude*) to subside; (*Fundament*) to settle **(c)** (= *niedriger werden: Wasserspiegel, Temperatur, Preise etc*) to fall **(d)** (= *schwinden*) to diminish; (*Hoffnung, Stimmung, moralisch*) to sink; **den Mut/die Hoffnung ~ lassen** to lose courage/hope; **tief gesunken sein** to have sunk low; **in jds Meinung/Achtung** (*dat*) **~** to go down in sb's estimation

Sinn [zɪn] M **-(e)s, -e (a)** (= *Wahrnehmungsfähigkeit*) sense **(b) Sinne** PL (= *Bewusstsein*) senses *pl*; **er war von ~en** he was out of his mind; **wie von ~en** like one demented; **bist du noch bei ~en?** have you taken leave of your senses? **(c)** (= *Gedanken, Denkweise*) mind; **sich** (*dat*) **jdn/etw aus dem ~ schlagen** to forget all about sb/sth; **es kommt or geht or will mir nicht aus dem ~** (*geh*) I can't get it out of my mind; **das will mir einfach nicht in den ~** I just can't understand it; **jdm durch den ~ gehen** to occur to sb; **etw im ~ haben** to have sth in mind; **mit etw nichts im ~ haben** to want nothing to do with sth **(d)** (= *Verständnis, Empfänglichkeit*) feeling; **dafür fehlt ihm der ~** he has no feeling for that sort of thing; **~ für Proportionen/Gerechtigkeit** *etc* **haben** to have a sense of proportion/justice *etc* **(e)** (= *Geist*) spirit; **im ~e des Gesetzes** according to the spirit of the law; **in jds** (*dat*) **handeln** to act as sb would have wished; **im ~e des Verstorbenen** in accordance with the wishes of the deceased; **das ist nicht in meinem/seinem ~e** that is not what I myself/he himself would have wished; **das wäre nicht im ~e unserer Kunden** it would not be in the interests of our customers **(f)** (= *Zweck*) point; **das ist nicht der ~ der Sache** that is not the point; **~ und Unsinn dieser Maßnahmen/des Geschichtsunterrichts** reasoning or lack of it behind these measures/behind history teaching; **der ~ des Lebens** the meaning of life; **ohne ~ und Verstand sein** to make no sense at all; **das hat keinen ~** there is no point in that; **was hat denn das für einen ~?** what's the point of that? **(g)** (= *Bedeutung*) meaning; **im übertragenen/weiteren ~** in the figurative/broader sense; **~ machen** to make sense; **das macht keinen/wenig ~** that makes no/little sense

sinnen ['zɪnən], *pret* **sann** [zan], *ptp* **gesonnen** [gə'zɔnən] (= *planen*) **auf etw** (*acc*) **~** to think of sth; **auf Abhilfe ~** to think up a remedy; *siehe auch* **gesonnen**

Sinnes-: Sinnesänderung F change of mind; **Sinneseindruck** M sensory impression; **Sinnesorgan** NT sense organ; **Sinnestäuschung** F hallucination; **Sinneswahrnehmung** F sensory perception *no pl*; **Sinneswandel** M change of mind

sinngemäß **1** ADJ (= *inhaltlich*) **eine ~e Zusammenfassung** a summary which gives the gist (of it) **2** ADV (= *dem Sinn nach*) **etw ~ wiedergeben** to give the gist of sth

sinnig ['zɪnɪç] ADJ apt; *Vorrichtung* practical; (*iro*: = *wenig sinnvoll*) clever

sinnigerweise ADV (*iro*) naturally (*iro*)

sinnlich ['zɪnlɪç] **1** ADJ **(a)** (*Philos*) *Empfindung, Eindrücke* sensory; **die ~e Welt** the material world **(b)** (= *vital, sinnenfroh*) sensuous; (= *erotisch*) sensual **2** ADV **(a)** (= *sexuell*) sexually **(b)** (= *mit den Sinnen*) ~ **wahrnehmbar** perceptible by the senses

Sinnlichkeit F -, NO PL (= *Vitalität, Sinnenfreude*) sensuousness; (= *Erotik*) sensuality

sinnlos **1** ADJ **(a)** (= *unsinnig*) *Redensarten, Geschwätz* meaningless; *Verhalten, Töten* senseless **(b)** (= *zwecklos*) futile; *Hoffnung* forlorn; **es ist/wäre ~, zu ...** it is/would be futile to ...; **das ist völlig ~** there's no sense in that **2** ADV **(a)** (= *ohne Sinn*) *zerstören, morden* senselessly **(b)** (= *äußerst*) ~ **betrunken** blind drunk; **sich ~ betrinken** to get blind drunk

Sinnlosigkeit F -, -en (= *Unsinnigkeit*) (*von Redensart, Geschwätz*) meaninglessness; (*von Verhalten, Töten*) senselessness; (= *Zwecklosigkeit*) futility

Sinn-: **sinnverwandt** ADJ synonymous; **~e Wörter** synonyms; **sinnvoll** **1** ADJ **(a)** *Satz* meaningful **(b)** (*fig*) (= *vernünftig*) sensible; (= *nützlich*) useful **2** ADV **sein Geld ~/~er anlegen** to invest one's money sensibly/more sensibly; **sein Geld ~ verwenden** to use one's money for something useful

Sinologie [zinolo'giː] F -, NO PL Sinology

Sintflut ['zɪntfluːt] F (*Bibl*) Flood; **nach mir/uns die ~** (*inf*) it doesn't matter what happens when I've/we've gone

sintflutartig ADJ **~e Regenfälle** torrential rain

Sinto ['zɪnto] M -, **Sinti** ['zɪnti] USU PL Sinto (gypsy); **Sinti und Roma** Sinti and Romanies

Sinus ['ziːnʊs] M -, **-se** *or* - [-nuːs] **(a)** (*Math*) sine **(b)** (*Anat*) sinus

Sioux ['ziːʊks] M -, - Sioux

Siphon ['ziːfõ, zi'fõ, zi'foːn] M -s, -s siphon

Sippe ['zɪpə] F -, -n (extended) family; (*inf*: = *Verwandtschaft*) clan (*inf*)

Sippschaft ['zɪpʃaft] F -, -en (*pej inf*) (= *Familie*) tribe (*inf*); (= *Bande, Gesindel auch*) bunch (*inf*)

Sirene [zi'reːnə] F -, -n (*Myth, Tech, fig*) siren

Sirup ['ziːrʊp] M -s, -e syrup

Sisal(hanf) ['ziːzal-] M -s sisal (hemp)

Sitte ['zɪtə] F -, -n **(a)** (= *Brauch*) custom; (= *Mode*) practice; **~ sein** to be the custom/the practice; **~n und Gebräuche** customs and traditions; **was sind denn das für ~n?** what's all this? **(b)** USU PL (= *gutes Benehmen*) manners *pl*; (= *Sittlichkeit*) morals *pl* **(c)** (*sl*: = *Sittenpolizei*) vice squad

Sitten-: **Sittendezernat** NT vice squad; **Sittenpolizei** F vice squad; **Sittenstrolch** M (*Press inf*) sex fiend; **sittenwidrig** ADJ (*form*) immoral

Sittich ['zɪtɪç] M -s, -e parakeet

sittlich ['zɪtlɪç] ADJ moral; **ihm fehlt die ~e Reife** he's morally immature

Sittlichkeit F -, NO PL morality

Sittlichkeits-: **Sittlichkeitsdelikt** NT sexual offence (*Brit*) *or* offense (*US*); **Sittlichkeitsverbrechen** NT sex crime; **Sittlichkeitsverbrecher(in)** M(F) sex offender

Situation [zitua'tsioːn] F -, -en situation

Situationskomik F comedy of the situation/situations; (= *Art der Komik*) situation comedy, sitcom (*inf*)

situiert [zitu'iːrt] ADJ **gut ~** (*attr*) well-off; **gut/schlecht ~ sein** to be well/poorly situated financially

Sitz [zɪts] M -es, -e **(a)** (= *~platz*) (*Parl*) seat; (= *Wohnsitz*) residence, domicile (*form*); (*von Firma, Verwaltung*) headquarters *pl* **(b)** NO PL (*Tech, von Kleidungsstück*) sit; (*von der Größe her*) fit; **einen guten ~ haben** to sit/fit well; **einen schlechten ~ haben** to sit/fit badly

Sitz-: **Sitzbank** F, *pl* **-bänke** bench; **Sitzblockade** F sit-in; **Sitzdemonstrant(in)** M(F) sit-down demonstrator

sitzen ['zɪtsn] *pret* **saß** [zaːs], *ptp* **gesessen** [gə'zɛsn] VI AUX HABEN *or* (*Aus, S Ger, Sw*) SEIN **(a)** (*Mensch, Tier*) to sit; (*Vogel*) to perch; **~ Sie bequem?** are you comfortable?; **hier sitzt man sehr bequem** it's very comfortable sitting here; **etw im Sitzen tun** to do sth sitting down; **beim Frühstück/Mittagessen ~** to be having breakfast/lunch; **an einer Aufgabe/über einer Arbeit ~** to sit over a task/a piece of work; **der Deckel sitzt fest** the lid is on tightly; **die Schraube sitzt fest** the screw is in tightly; **locker ~** to be loose; **deine Krawatte sitzt nicht richtig** your tie isn't straight; **sein Hut saß schief** his hat was (on) crooked; *siehe auch* **sitzen bleiben** **(b)** (= *seinen Sitz haben*) (*Regierung, Gericht etc*) to sit; (*Firma*) to have its headquarters **(c)** (= *Mitglied sein*) (*im Parlament*) to have a seat (*in +dat* in); (*im Vorstand, Aufsichtsrat etc*) to be *or* sit (*in +dat* on) **(d)** (*inf*: = *im Gefängnis ~*) to do time (*inf*), to be inside (*inf*); **er musste zwei Jahre ~** he had to do two years (*inf*) **(e)** (= *im Gedächtnis ~*) to have sunk in **(f)** (*inf*: = *treffen*) to hit home; **das saß!, das hat gesessen!** that hit home

sitzen bleiben VI IRREG AUX SEIN (*inf*) **(a)** (= *nicht aufstehen*) to remain seated; **bleiben Sie bitte sitzen!, bitte bleiben Sie sitzen!** please don't get up **(b)** (*Sch*) to have to repeat a year **(c)** **auf einer Ware ~** to be left with a product **(d)** (*Mädchen*) (*beim Tanz*) to be left sitting; (= *nicht heiraten*) to be left on the shelf (*inf*)

sitzend **1** ADJ ATTR *Lebensweise etc* sedentary **2** ADV sitting down; **ich verbringe die meiste Zeit ~** I sit most of the time

sitzen lassen *ptp* **sitzen lassen** *or* (*rare*) **sitzen gelassen** VT IRREG (*inf*) **(a)** (*Sch*: = *nicht versetzen*) to keep down (a year) **(b)** jdn ~ (= *im Stich lassen*) to leave sb in the lurch; (= *warten lassen*) to leave sb waiting; *Freund/in* (*durch Nichterscheinen*) to stand sb up; (*für immer*) to walk out on sb; **eine Beleidigung** *etc* **auf sich** (*dat*) **~** to take an insult *etc*

Sitz-: **Sitzgelegenheit** F seats *pl*; **eine ~ suchen** to look for somewhere to sit; **Sitzkissen** NT (floor) cushion; **Sitzordnung** F seating plan; **Sitzpinkler** M -s, - (*pej inf*) wimp (*inf*), wuss (*esp US inf*); **Sitzplatz** M seat

Sitzung ['zɪtsʊŋ] F -, -en **(a)** (= *Konferenz*) meeting; (*Jur*: = *Gerichtsverhandlung*) session; (= *Parlamentssitzung*) sitting **(b)** (= *Einzelsitzung*) (*bei Künstler*) sitting; (*bei Zahnarzt*) visit; (*inf*: = *Toilettenbesuch*) session; **spiritistische ~** séance

Sizilianer [zitsi'liːanɐ] M -s, -, **Sizilianerin** [-ərɪn] F -, -nen Sicilian

sizilianisch [zitsi'liːanɪʃ] ADJ Sicilian

Sizilien [zi'tsiːliən] NT -s Sicily

Skala ['skaːla] F -, **Skalen** ['skaːlən] *or* -s (= *Gradeinteilung*) (*auch Mus*) scale; (= *Reihe gleichartiger Dinge*) range

Skalpell [skal'pɛl] NT -s, -e scalpel

skalpieren [skal'piːrən], *ptp* **skalpiert** VT to scalp

Skandal [skan'daːl] M -s, -e scandal; (*inf*: = *Krach*) to-do (*inf*)

skandalös [skanda'løːs] **1** ADJ scandalous **2** ADV scandalously

Skandinavien [skandi'naːviən] NT -s Scandinavia

Skandinavier [skandi'naːviɐ] M -s, -, **Skandinavierin** [-iərɪn] F -, -nen Scandinavian

skandinavisch [skandi'naːvɪʃ] ADJ Scandinavian

Skat [skaːt] M -(e)s, -e (*Cards*) skat; **~ spielen** to play skat

Skat is a card game that is extremely popular in Germany. It is played amongst friends at regular *Skatrunden* or *Skatabende* and requires a pack of 32 German or French cards. There are also *Skat* competitions between clubs which have been organized into leagues, with the German championship being decided every year. Since 1927 *Skat* has had its own special panel in Altenburg for settling disputes.

Skateboard ['skeːtbɔːɐd] NT -s, -s skateboard

Skelett [ske'lɛt] NT -(e)s, -e (*lit, fig*) skeleton

Skepsis ['skɛpsɪs] F -, NO PL scepticism (*Brit*), skepticism (*US*); **mit** *or* **voller ~** sceptically (*Brit*), skeptically (*US*)

Skeptiker ['skɛptikɐ] M -s, -, **Skeptikerin** [-ərɪn] F -, -nen sceptic (*Brit*), skeptic (*US*)

skeptisch ['skɛptɪʃ] **1** ADJ sceptical (*Brit*), skeptical (*US*) **2** ADV sceptically (*Brit*), skeptically (*US*)

Sketch [skɛtʃ] M -(es), -e(s) (*Art, Theat*) sketch

Ski [ʃiː] M -s, - *or* **-er** ['ʃiːɐ] ski; **~ laufen** *or* **fahren** to ski

Ski- IN CPDS ski; **Skianzug** M ski suit; **Skiausrüstung** F skiing gear; **eine komplette ~** a complete set of skiing gear; **Skibob** M skibob; **Skibrille** F ski goggles *pl*

Skier PL *von* **Ski**

Ski-: **Skifahrer(in)** M(F) skier; **Skigebiet** NT ski(ing) area; **Skigymnastik** F skiing exercises *pl*; **Skihose** F (pair of) ski pants *pl*; **Skikurs** M skiing course; **Skilauf** M skiing;

Skiläufer(in) M(F) skier; **Skilehrer** M ski instructor; **Skilift** M ski lift

Skin [skɪn] M **-s, -s** (*inf*) skin (*inf*)

Skinhead ['skɪnhɛd] M **-s, -s** skinhead

Ski-: Skipass M ski pass; **Skipiste** F ski run; **Skischuh** M ski boot; **Skischule** F ski school; **Skisport** M skiing; **Skispringen** NT ski jumping; **Skistock** M ski stick; **Skiträger** M (*Aut*) ski rack; **Skizirkus** M ski circus

Skizze ['skɪtsə] F **-, -n** sketch; (*fig*: = *Grundriss*) outline

skizzenhaft ADJ *Zeichnung etc* roughly sketched; *Beschreibung etc* (given) in broad outline **2** ADV **etw ~ zeichnen** to sketch sth roughly; **etw ~ beschreiben** to describe sth in broad outline

skizzieren [skɪ'tsiːrən], *ptp* **skizziert** VT to sketch; (*fig*) *Plan etc* to outline

Sklave ['sklaːvə, 'sklaːfə] M **-n, -n**, **Sklavin** ['sklaːvɪn, 'sklaːfɪn] F **-, -nen** slave; **~ einer Sache** (*gen*) **sein** (*fig*) to be a slave to sth

Sklaven-: Sklavenarbeit F slavery; (= *Arbeit von Sklaven*) work of slaves; **Sklaventreiber(in)** M(F) (*lit, fig*) slave-driver

Sklaverei [sklaːvə'rai, sklaːfə'rai] F **-**, NO PL (*lit, fig*) slavery *no art*

Sklavin F slave; *siehe auch* **Sklave**

sklavisch ['sklaːvɪʃ, 'sklaːfɪʃ] **1** ADJ slavish **2** ADV slavishly

Sklerose [skle'roːzə] F **-, -n** sclerosis

Skonto ['skɔnto] NT *or* M **-s, -s** *or* **Skonti** [-ti] cash discount; **bei Barzahlung 3% ~** 3% discount for cash

Skorbut [skɔr'buːt] M **-(e)s**, NO PL scurvy

Skorpion [skɔr'pioːn] M **-s, -e** (*Zool*) scorpion; (*Astrol*) Scorpio

Skript [skrɪpt] NT **-(e)s, -s** (*Film*) (film) script

Skrupel ['skruːpl] M **-**, - USU PL scruple; **keine ~ haben** *or* **kennen** to have no scruples; **er hatte keine ~, das zu tun** he didn't scruple to do it; **ohne (jeden) ~** without (the slightest) scruple

Skrupel-: skrupellos **1** ADJ unscrupulous **2** ADV unscrupulously; **Skrupellosigkeit** F **-**, NO PL unscrupulousness

Skulptur [skʊlp'tuːɐ] F **-, -en** sculpture

Skunk [skʊŋk] M **-s, -s** *or* **-e** skunk

S-Kurve ['ɛs-] F S-bend

Slalom ['slaːlɔm] M **-s, -s** slalom; **(im) ~ fahren** (*fig inf*) to drive a crazy zigzag course (*inf*)

Slang [slɛn] M **-s**, NO PL slang

Slapstick ['slɛpstɪk] M **-s, -s** slapstick

Slawe ['slaːvə] M **-n, -n**, **Slawin** ['slaːvɪn] F **-, -nen** Slav

slawisch ['slaːvɪʃ] ADJ Slavonic, Slavic

Slawistik [sla'vɪstɪk] F **-**, NO PL Slavonic studies *sing*

Slip [slɪp] M **-s, -s** (pair of) briefs *pl*

Slipeinlage F panty liner

Slipper ['slɪpə] M **-s, -** slip-on shoe

Slogan ['sloːgn] M **-s, -s** slogan

Slot [slɔt] M **-s, -s** (*Comput, Aviat*) slot

Slowake [slo'vaːkə] M **-n, -n**, **Slowakin** [-'vaːkɪn] F **-, -nen** Slovak

Slowakei [slova'kai] F **- die ~** Slovakia

slowakisch [slo'vaːkɪʃ] ADJ Slovakian, Slovak

Slowene [slo'veːnə] M **-n, -n**, **Slowenin** [-'veːnɪn] F **-, -nen** Slovene

Slowenien [slo'veːniən] NT **-s** Slovenia

slowenisch [slo'veːnɪʃ] ADJ Slovenian, Slovene

Slum [slam] M **-s, -s** slum

SM [ɛs'lɛm] M **-(s)** ABBR *von* **Sadomasochismus** SM

Smalltalk ['smɔːltɔːk] M **-(s)**, NO PL, **Small Talk** M **- -(s)**, NO PL small talk

Smaragd [sma'rakt] M **-(e)s, -e** [-də] emerald

smart [sma:ɐt, smart] (*inf*) **1** ADJ smart **2** ADV *gekleidet* smartly; **~ klingen** to sound smart

Smart-Card F **-, -s**, **Smartcard** ['sma:ɐtka:ɐd] F **-, -s** (*inf*) smart card

Smiley ['smaili] NT **-s, -s** (*Comput*) smiley

Smog [smɔk] M **-(s), -s** smog

Smogalarm M smog alert

Smoking ['smoːkɪŋ] M **-s, -s** dinner jacket (*esp Brit*), tuxedo (*esp US*)

SMS [ɛslɛm'lɛs] F **-, -** ABBR *von* **Short Message Service** SMS

SMS-Nachricht [ɛslɛm'lɛs-] F text message

Snack [snɛk] M **-s, -s** snack (meal)

Snob [snɔp] M **-s, -s** snob

Snobismus [sno'bɪsmʊs] M **-**, **Snobismen** [-mən] **(a)** NO PL snobbishness **(b)** (= *Bemerkung*) snobbish remark *or* comment

snobistisch [sno'bɪstɪʃ] ADJ snobbish

Snow-: Snowboard ['snoːbɔːɐd] NT **-s, -s** snowboard; **Snowboarding** ['snoːbɔːɐdɪŋ] NT **-s**, NO PL snowboarding; **Snowboarder** ['snoːbɔːɐdə] M **-s, -**, **Snowboarderin** [-ərɪn] F **-, -nen** snowboarder

so [zoː] **1** ADV **(a)** (*mit adj, adv*) so; (*mit vb*: = *so sehr*) so much; **so groß** *etc* so big *etc*; **eine so große Frau** such a big woman; **so groß** *etc* **wie ...** as big *etc* as ...; **so gut es geht** as best *or* well as I/he *etc* can; **ich wusste nicht, dass es ihn so ärgern würde** I didn't know that it would annoy him so much; **ich freue mich so sehr, dass du kommst** I'm so pleased you're coming **(b)** (= *auf diese Weise, von dieser Art*) like this/that, this/that way; **mach es nicht so, sondern so** don't do it like this but like that; **mach es so, wie er es vorgeschlagen hat** do it the way he suggested; **ist es dort tatsächlich so?** is it really like that there?; **ist das tatsächlich so?** is that really so?; **so ist sie nun einmal** that's the way she is; **sei doch nicht so** don't be like that; **so ist es nicht gewesen** that's not how it was; **(ach) so ist das!** I see!; **so oder so** either way; **und so weiter (und so fort)** and so on (and so forth); **gut so!** fine!, good!; **das ist gut so** that's fine; **das ist auch gut so!** (and) a good thing too!; **mir ist (es) so, als ob ...** it seems to me as if ...; **so geht es, wenn ...** that's what happens if ...; **das habe ich nur so gesagt** I didn't really mean it; **so genannt** (= *angeblich*) so-called
(c) (= *etwa*) about, or so; **ich komme so um 8 Uhr** I'll come at 8 or thereabouts; **sie heißt doch Malitzki oder so** she's called Malitzki or something
(d) (*inf*: = *umsonst*) for nothing
(e) **so dann und wann** now and then; **so beeil dich doch!** do hurry up!; **so mancher** quite a few people *pl*; **so ein Gebäude/ Fehler** a building/mistake like that; **so ein guter Lehrer/ schlechtes Bild** *etc* such a good teacher/bad picture *etc*; **so ein Idiot!** what an idiot!; **hast du so etwas schon einmal gesehen?** have you ever seen anything like it?; **na so was!** well I never!; **so etwas Schönes** such a beautiful thing; **so einer wie ich/er** somebody like me/him
2 CONJ **(a) so dass** so that
(b) so wie es jetzt ist the way things are at the moment; **so klein er auch sein mag** however small he may be; **so wahr ich lebe** as true as I'm standing here
3 INTERJ so; (= *wirklich*) oh, really; (*abschließend*) well, right; **so, das wärs für heute** well *or* right, that's it for today; **so, jetzt habe ich die Nase voll** I've had enough; **so, so!** well, well

SO ABBR *von* **Südosten** SE

s. o. ABBR *von* **siehe oben**

sobald [zo'balt] CONJ as soon as

Socke ['zɔkə] F **-, -n** sock; **sich auf die ~n machen** (*inf*) to get going (*inf*); **von den ~n sein** (*inf*) to be flabbergasted (*inf*)

Sockel ['zɔkl] M **-s, -** base; (*von Denkmal, Statue*) plinth, pedestal; (*Elec*) socket; (*für Birne*) holder

Sockelbetrag M basic sum

Socken ['zɔkn] M **-s, -** (*S Ger, Aus*) sock

Sockenhalter M (sock) suspender (*Brit*), garter

Soda ['zoːda] F **-,** *no pl or* nt **-s**, NO PL soda

sodass [zo'das] CONJ so that

Sodawasser NT, *pl* **-wässer** soda water

Sodbrennen ['zoːtbrɛnən] NT **-s**, NO PL heartburn

Sodomie [zodo'miː] F **-**, NO PL buggery

Vorsicht! **Sodomie** *wird nicht mit dem englischen Wort* **sodomy** *übersetzt.*

---

soeben [zo'leːbn] ADV just (this moment); **~ hören wir** *or* **haben wir gehört ...** we have just (this moment) heard ...; **~ erschienen** just published

Sofa ['zoːfa] NT **-s, -s** sofa

sofern [zo'fɛrn] CONJ provided (that); **~ ... nicht** if ... not

soff PRET *von* **saufen**

sofort [zo'fɔrt] ADV immediately; **~ nach ...** immediately after ...; **(ich) komme ~!** (I'm) just coming!; (*Kellner etc*) I'll be right with you

Sofort-: Sofortbildkamera F Polaroid® camera; **Soforthilfe** F emergency aid

sofortig [zo'fɔrtɪç] ADJ immediate

Sofortmaßnahme F immediate measure

Softdrink ['zɔftdrɪŋk] M **-s, -s**, **Soft Drink** M **- -s, - -s** soft drink

Softeis ['zɔftlais] NT soft ice cream

Softie ['zɔfti] M **-s, -s** (*inf*) caring type

Software ['sɔftwɛːɐ] F **-, -s** (*Comput*) software

Softwarepaket ['sɔftwɛːɐ-] NT software package

sog PRET *von* **saugen**

Sog [zo:k] M **-(e)s, -e** [-ɡə] (= *saugende Kraft*) suction; (*bei Schiff*) wake; (*bei Flugzeug, Fahrzeug*) slipstream; (*von Strudel*) vortex; (*von Brandungswelle*) undertow; (*fig*) maelstrom

sogar [zo'ɡaːɐ] ADV even; **er kam ~** he even came; **schön, ~ sehr schön** beautiful, in fact very beautiful

sogenannt ['zo:ɡənant] ADJ ATTR *siehe* **so**

Sogwirkung F suction; (*fig*) knock-on effect

Sohle ['zo:lə] F **-, -n (a)** (= *Fußsohle etc*) sole; (= *Einlage*) insole **(b)** (= *Boden*) bottom; (= *Talsohle*) floor

sohlen ['zo:lən] VT to sole

Sohn [zo:n] M **-(e)s, ⁻e** ['zøːnə] (*lit, fig*) son

Soja ['zo:ja] F **-, Sojen** ['zo:jən] soya (*esp Brit*), soy

Soja-: Sojabohne F soya bean (*esp Brit*), soybean; **Sojabohnenkeime** PL bean sprouts *pl*; **Sojasoße** F soya (*esp Brit*) *or* soy sauce

Soko ['zo:ko] F **-, -s** ABBR *von* **Sonderkommission**

solang [zo'laŋ], **solange** [zo'laŋə] CONJ as *or* so long as

Solar- [zola:ɐ-] IN CPDS solar; **Solarenergie** F solar energy

Solarium [zo'la:riʊm] NT **-s, Solarien** [-riən] solarium

Solarzelle F solar cell

Solawechsel ['zo:la-] M promissory note

solch [zɔlç] ADJ INV, **solche(r, s)** ['zɔlçə] ADJ such; **ein ~er Mensch, ~ ein Mensch** such a person; **~es Wetter/Glück** such weather/luck; **wir haben ~en Durst/~e Angst** we're so thirsty/afraid; **der Mensch als ~er** man as such; **~es** that kind of thing; **~e** (*Leute*) such people; **Rechtsanwälte gibt es ~e und ~e** there are lawyers and lawyers

Sold [zɔlt] M **-(e)s** [-dəs], NO PL (*Mil*) pay

Soldat [zɔl'daːt] M **-en, -en**, **Soldatin** [-'daːtɪn] F **-, -nen** soldier; **~ werden** to join the army

soldatisch [zɔl'daːtɪʃ] **1** ADJ (= *militärisch*) military; (= *soldatengemäß*) soldierly **2** ADV *sich verhalten* like a soldier; **~ stramm stehen** to stand up straight like a soldier; **~ grüßen** to salute

Söldner ['zœldnɐ] M **-s, -**, **Söldnerin** [-ərɪn] F **-, -nen** mercenary

Sole ['zo:lə] F **-, -n** brine

Solei ['zo:lai] NT pickled egg

Soli¹ PL *von* **Solo**

Soli² ['zo:li] M **-s**, NO PL (*inf*) = **Solidaritätszuschlag**

solid [zo'liːt] ADJ, ADV = **solide**

solidarisch [zoli'daːrɪʃ] **1** ADJ showing solidarity; **sich mit jdm ~ erklären** to declare one's solidarity with sb; **eine ~e Haltung zeigen** to show (one's) solidarity; **sich mit jdm ~ fühlen** to feel solidarity with sb **2** ADV in/showing solidarity; **~ mit jdm handeln** to act in solidarity with sb

solidarisieren [zolidari'ziːrən], *ptp* **solidarisiert** VR **sich ~ mit** to show (one's) solidarity with

Solidarität [zolidari'tɛːt] F **-**, NO PL solidarity; **~ üben** to show solidarity

Solidaritätszuschlag M (*Fin*) solidarity surcharge on income tax (*for the reconstruction of eastern Germany*)

Solidar-: Solidarpakt [zoli'daːɐ-] M solidarity pact; **Solidarschuld** F (*Com*) joint and several liability

solide [zo'liːdə] **1** ADJ *Haus, Möbel etc* solid; *Arbeit, Wissen, Politik, Basis, Finanzen, Ausbildung* sound; *Mensch, Leben, Lokal* respectable; *Firma, Mehrheit* solid; *Preise* reasonable **2** ADV **(a)** (= *untadelig*) **~ leben** to lead a well-ordered life **(b)** (= *stabil*) **~ gebaut** solidly built; **~ konstruiert** well-constructed **(c)** (= *gründlich*) *arbeiten* thoroughly; **~ ausgebildet** well-trained

Solidität [zolidi'tɛːt] F **-**, NO PL (*von Haus, Möbeln etc, Firma*) solidness; (*von Arbeit, Wissen, Finanzen*) soundness

Solist [zo'lɪst] M **-en, -en**, **Solistin** [-'lɪstɪn] F **-, -nen** (*Mus*) soloist

Soll [zɔl] NT **-(s), -(s) (a)** (= *Schuld*) debit; (= *Schuldseite*) debit side; **~ und Haben** debit and credit **(b)** (*Comm:* = *Planaufgabe*) target

sollen ['zɔlən]

1 HILFSVERB	**3** TRANSITIVES VERB
2 INTRANSITIVES VERB	

1 HILFSVERB, *pret* **sollte** ['zɔltə], *ptp* **sollen**
(a) (*Befehl, Verpflichtung, Plan*) **was soll ich/er tun?** what should I/he do?; **soll ich Ihnen helfen?** can I help you?; **soll ich (gehen/singen)? – ja, du sollst (gehen/singen)** shall I (go/sing)? – yes, do; **du weißt, dass du das nicht tun sollst** you know that you're not supposed to do that; **er weiß nicht, was er tun soll** he doesn't know what to do; **sie sagte ihm, er solle draußen warten** she told him (that he was) to wait outside; **er wurde wütend, weil er draußen warten sollte** he was livid that he had to wait outside; **was ich (nicht) alles tun/wissen soll!** the things I'm meant *or* supposed to do/know!; **es soll nicht wieder vorkommen** it won't happen again; **er soll reinkommen** tell him to come in; **der soll nur kommen!** just let him come!; **niemand soll sagen, dass ...** let no-one say that ...; **ich soll Ihnen sagen, dass ...** I've been asked to tell you that ...; **ich soll dir schöne Grüße von Renate bestellen** Renate asked me to give you her best wishes; **du sollst nicht töten** (*Bibl*) thou shalt not kill
(b) (*konjunktivisch*) **was sollte ich/er deiner Meinung nach tun?** what do you think I/he should do *or* ought to do?; **das hättest du nicht tun sollen** you shouldn't have done that; **das hättest du sehen sollen!** you should have seen it!
(c) (*konditional*) **sollte das passieren, ...** if that should happen ...; **sollte das happen ...**; **sollte ich Unrecht haben, tut es mir Leid** I'm sorry if I am wrong
(d) (*Vermutung, Erwartung*) to be supposed *or* meant to; **sie soll krank/verheiratet sein** apparently she's ill/married; **er soll angeblich sehr reich sein** he's supposed to be very rich
(e) (= *können, mögen*) **mir soll es gleich sein** it's all the same to me; **so etwas soll es geben** these things happen; **man sollte glauben, dass ...** you would think that ...
(f) (*in Prophezeihung*) (*geh*) **er sollte sie nie wiedersehen** he was never to see her again; **es hat nicht sollen sein** it wasn't to be

2 INTRANSITIVES VERB, *pret* **sollte** ['zɔltə], *ptp* **gesollt** [ɡə'zɔlt]
(= *bewirken, bedeuten, in Fragen*) **was soll das?** what's all this?; (= *warum denn das*) **was soll das?** what for?; **was sollst!** (*inf*) what the hell! (*inf*); **was soll der Quatsch** *or* **Mist?** (*inf*) what's this stupid nonsense? (*inf*); **was soll ich dort?** what would I do there?

3 TRANSITIVES VERB, *pret* **sollte** ['zɔltə], *ptp* **gesollt** [ɡə'zɔlt] **das sollst/solltest du nicht** you shouldn't do that; **was man nicht alles soll!** (*inf*) the things you're expected to do!

Sollseite F (*Fin*) debit side

solo ['zo:lo] ADV (*Mus*) solo; (*fig inf*) on one's own

Solo ['zo:lo] NT **-s, Soli** ['zo:li] (*alle Bedeutungen*) solo

Solothurn ['zo:loturn] NT **-s** (= *Kanton, Stadt*) Solothurn

solvent [zɔl'vɛnt] ADJ (*Fin*) solvent

Somali [zo'ma:li] M **-(s), -(s)** *or* f **-, -s** Somali

Somalia [zo'ma:lia] NT **-s** Somalia

somalisch [zo'ma:lɪʃ] ADJ Somali

somit [zo'mɪt, 'zo:mɪt] ADV consequently, therefore

Sommer ['zɔmɐ] M -s, - summer; **im ~, des ~s** (geh) in (the) summer; **im nächsten** ~ next summer; **im ~ (des Jahres) 1951** in the summer of 1951; ~ **wie** or **und Winter** all year round

Sommer- IN CPDS summer; **Sommeranfang** M beginning of summer; **Sommerfahrplan** M summer timetable; **Sommerferien** PL summer holidays pl (Brit) or vacation (US); (Jur, Parl) summer recess; **Sommerflugplan** M summer flight schedule; **Sommerhalbjahr** NT summer semester, ≈ summer term (Brit); **Sommerkleidung** F summer clothing; (esp Comm) summerwear

sommerlich ['zɔmɐlɪç] **1** ADJ (= sommerartig, heiter) summery; (= Sommer-) summer attr **2** ADV **es ist ~ warm** it's as warm as it is in summer; ~ **heiße Temperaturen** hot summery temperatures; ~ **gekleidet sein** to be in summer clothes

Sommer-: **Sommerloch** NT (inf) silly season (Brit), off season (US); **Sommerolympiade** F Summer Olympics pl; **Sommerpause** F summer break; (Jur, Parl) summer recess; **Sommerreifen** M normal tyre (Brit) or tire (US); **Sommerschlussverkauf** M summer sale; **Sommersemester** NT (Univ) summer semester, ≈ summer term (Brit); **Sommerspiele** PL Summer Games pl; **die Olympischen** ~ the Summer Olympics, the Summer Olympic Games; **Sommersprosse** F freckle; **sommersprossig** [-ʃprɔsɪç] ADJ freckled; **Sommerzeit** F summer time no art; (geh: = Sommer) summertime

Sonate [zoˈnaːtə] F -, -n sonata

Sonde ['zɔndə] F -, -n (Space, Med: zur Untersuchung) probe; (Med: zur Ernährung) tube; (Met) sonde

Sonder- ['zɔndɐ-] IN CPDS special; **Sonderabdruck** M (Typ) offprint; **Sonderangebot** NT special offer; **im ~ sein** to be on special offer; **Sonderausführung** F special model; **Sonderausgabe** F (a) special edition (b) **Sonderausgaben** PL (Fin) additional or extra expenses pl

sonderbar 1 ADJ strange **2** ADV strangely; ~ **klingen** to sound strange

sonderbarerweise ['zɔndɐbaːrɐ'vaɪzə] ADV strangely enough

Sonder-: **Sonderbeauftragte(r)** MF DECL AS ADJ (Pol) special emissary; **Sonderdruck** M, pl **-drucke** offprint; **Sonderfall** M special case; (= Ausnahme) exception; **Sondergenehmigung** F special permission; (Schein) special permit; **sondergleichen** ['zɔndɐˈglaɪçn] ADJ INV **eine Geschmacklosigkeit** ~ the height of bad taste; **mit einer Arroganz** ~ with unparalleled arrogance

sonderlich ['zɔndɐlɪç] **1** ADJ ATTR particular, especial; **ohne ~e Begeisterung** without much enthusiasm **2** ADV particularly, especially

Sonder- ['zɔndɐ-]: **Sondermarke** F special issue (stamp); **Sondermüll** M hazardous waste

sondern ['zɔndɐn] CONJ but; ~? where/who/what etc then?; **wir fahren nicht nach Spanien,** ~ **nach Frankreich** we're not going to Spain, we're going to France; **nicht nur ...,** ~ **auch** not only ... but also

sonders ['zɔndɐs] ADV siehe **samt**

Sonder- ['zɔndɐ-]: **Sonderschicht** F special shift; (zusätzlich) extra shift; **Sonderschule** F special school

SONDERSCHULE

A **Sonderschule** is a school for disabled and special-needs children. By offering support and assistance and by focusing on the children's disabilities, the aim is to develop their abilities and help to compensate for their disability. Opportunities also exist for children to move to a conventional school at a later stage. There are different kinds of **Sonderschulen** catering for the physically and mentally disabled, and for blind, deaf and developmentally retarded children.

Sonder- ['zɔndɐ-]: **Sonderwünsche** PL special requests pl; **Sonderzeichen** NT (Comput) special character; **Sonderziehungsrechte** PL (Fin) special drawing rights pl; **Sonderzug** M special train

sondieren [zɔnˈdiːrən], ptp **sondiert 1** VT to sound out; **das Terrain** or **Gelände** ~ to spy out the land; **die Lage** ~ to find out how the land lies **2** VI to sound things out; ~, **ob ...** to try to sound out whether ...

Sondierungsgespräch NT exploratory talk

Sonett [zoˈnet] NT -(e)s, -e sonnet

Song [zɔŋ] M -s, -s song

Sonnabend ['zɔnlaːbnt] M Saturday; siehe auch Dienstag

sonnabends ['zɔnlaːbnts] ADV on Saturdays, on a Saturday; siehe auch dienstags

Sonne ['zɔnə] F -, -n sun; (= Sonnenlicht) sun(light); **unter der** ~ (fig geh) under the sun; **an** or **in die** ~ **gehen** to go out in the sun(shine); **er kommt viel/wenig an die** ~ he goes/doesn't go out in the sun a lot; **die** ~ **bringt es an den Tag** (prov) truth will out (esp Brit prov)

sonnen ['zɔnən] VR to sun oneself; **sich in etw** (dat) ~ (fig) to bask in sth

Sonnen-: **Sonnenanbeter(in)** M(F) (lit, fig) sun worshipper; **Sonnenaufgang** M sunrise; **Sonnenbad** NT sunbathing no pl; **ein** ~ **nehmen** to sunbathe; **sonnenbaden** VI SEP INFIN, PTP ONLY to sunbathe; **Sonnenbank** F, pl **-bänke** sun bed; **Sonnenblende** F (Aut) sun visor; (Phot) lens hood; **Sonnenblume** F sunflower; **Sonnenblumenöl** NT sunflower oil; **Sonnenbrand** M sunburn no art; **Sonnenbrille** F (pair of) sunglasses pl; **Sonnencreme** F suntan cream; **Sonnenenergie** F solar energy; **Sonnenfinsternis** F solar eclipse; **sonnengebräunt** ADJ suntanned; **Sonnengel** NT suntan gel; **Sonnengenerator** M (an Satellit) solar generator; **Sonnengott** M sun-god; **Sonnenhitze** F heat of the sun; **Sonnenhut** M sunhat; **sonnenklar** ADJ (inf) crystal-clear; **Sonnenkollektor** M solar panel; **Sonnenkraftwerk** NT solar power station; **Sonnenlicht** NT sunlight; **Sonnenmilch** F suntan lotion; **Sonnenöl** NT suntan oil; **Sonnenschein** M sunshine; **bei** ~ in the sunshine; **bei strahlendem** ~ in brilliant sunshine; **Sonnenschirm** M sunshade; **Sonnenschutzfaktor** M protection factor; **Sonnenschutzmittel** NT sunscreen; **Sonnensegel** NT (a) (= Schutzdach) awning (b) (bei Raumfahrzeug) solar sail; **Sonnenstich** M sunstroke no art; **Sonnenstrahl** M ray of sunshine; (esp Astron, Phys) sun ray; **Sonnenstudio** NT tanning salon (esp US) or studio; **Sonnensystem** NT solar system; **Sonnenuhr** F sundial; **Sonnenuntergang** M sunset; **Sonnenwende** F solstice

sonnig ['zɔnɪç] ADJ (lit, fig) sunny

Sonntag ['zɔntaːk] M Sunday; siehe auch **Dienstag**

sonntägig ['zɔntɛːgɪç] ADJ ATTR Sunday

sonntäglich ['zɔntɛːklɪç] **1** ADJ Sunday attr **2** ADV ~ **gekleidet** dressed in one's Sunday best; ~ **ruhig** as quiet as a Sunday

sonntags ['zɔntaːks] ADV on Sundays, on a Sunday; siehe auch **dienstags**

Sonntags- IN CPDS Sunday; **Sonntagsarbeit** F Sunday working; **Sonntagsbeilage** F Sunday supplement; **Sonntagsfahrer(in)** M(F) (pej) Sunday driver; **Sonntagsfahrverbot** NT Sunday driving ban; **Sonntagsfrage** F (inf) question about voting intentions; **Sonntagsruhe** F **die** ~ **stören/einhalten** to contravene the observance of/to observe Sunday as a day of rest; **Sonntagszeitung** F Sunday paper

Sonn- und Feiertage PL Sundays and public holidays pl

sonn- und feiertags ['zɔnlunt'faɪɐtaːks] ADV on Sundays and public holidays

sonst [zɔnst] **1** ADV (a) (= außerdem) (mit pron, adv) else; (mit n) other; ~ **keine Besucher/Zeitungen** etc no other visitors/ papers etc; ~ **noch Fragen?** any other questions?; **wer/wie** etc **(denn)** ~? who/how etc else?; ~ **niemand** or **keiner(noch)** jemand or wer (inf) nobody/somebody else; **das kannst du** ~ **jemandem** or **wem** (inf) **erzählen** tell that to the marines (Brit inf) or to the judge (US); **da kann** ~ **wer kommen, wir machen keine Ausnahme** (inf) it doesn't matter who it is, we're not making any exceptions; **er und** ~ **keiner** nobody else but he; ~ **wann** (inf) some other time; **er denkt, er ist** ~ **wer** (inf) he thinks he's somebody special; ~ **nichts/noch etwas** nothing/ something else; **ich werde weder das tun noch** ~ **was** (inf) I won't do that or anything else; ~ **noch etwas?** is that all?, anything else?; ~ **wie** (inf) (in) some other way; (= sehr) like mad (inf) or crazy (inf); ~ **wo** (inf) somewhere else; ~ **wo, nur nicht hier** anywhere (else) but here; ~ **wohin** (inf) somewhere else; **das kannst du dir** ~ **wohin stecken!** (inf) you can stuff that! (inf); ~ **gehts dir gut?** (inf) are you feeling okay? (inf) **(b)** (= andernfalls, im übrigen) otherwise; (= in anderer Hinsicht) in other ways; **wie gehts** ~? how are things otherwise?; **wenn ich Ihnen** ~ **noch behilflich sein kann** if I can help you in any other way

(c) (= gewöhnlich) usually; **genau wie es** ~ **ist** just as it usually is; **genau wie** ~ the same as usual; **anders als** ~ different from usual; **mehr/weniger als** ~ more/less than usual; **alles war wie**

~ everything was as it always used to be; **war das auch ~ der Fall?** was that always the case?; **wenn er ~ zu Besuch hier war** when he has visited us before **2** CONJ otherwise, or (else)

sonstig ['zɔnstɪç] ADJ ATTR other; *Fragen, Auskünfte etc* further; „**Sonstiges**" "other"

sonstjemand *etc* INDEF PRON (*inf*) *siehe* **sonst**

sooft [zo'lɔft] CONJ whenever

Sopran [zo'praːn] M **-s, -e** soprano

Sopranistin [zopra'nɪstɪn] F **-, -nen** soprano

Sorbe ['zɔrbə] M **-n, -n**, **Sorbin** ['zɔrbɪn] F **-, -nen** Sorb

Sorbinsäure [zɔr'biːn-] F sorbic acid

sorbisch ['zɔrbɪʃ] ADJ Sorbian

Sorge ['zɔrgə] F **-, -n** worry; (= *Ärger*) trouble; (= *Kummer*) worry; **keine ~!** (*inf*) don't (you) worry!; **~ haben, ob/dass ...** to be worried whether/that ...; **wir betrachten diese Entwicklung mit ~** we view this development with concern; **~n haben** to have problems; **ich habe solche ~** I'm so worried; **du hast ~n!** (*iro*), **deine ~n möchte ich haben!** (*inf*) you think you've got problems!; **~n haben die Leute!** the worries people have!; **ich habe andere ~n, als ...** I have other things to worry about than ...; **jdm ~n machen** *or* **bereiten** (= *Kummer bereiten*) to cause sb a lot of worry; (= *beunruhigen*) to worry sb; **es macht mir ~n, dass ...** it worries me that ...; **in ~ ~** (*dat*) **sein** to be worried; **sich** (*dat*) **~n machen** to worry; **lassen Sie das meine ~ ~ sein** let me worry about that; **das ist nicht meine ~** that's not my problem; **für etw ~ tragen** (*geh*) to attend *or* see to sth; **dafür ~ ~ tragen, dass ...** (*geh*) to see to it that ...

Sorge-: **sorgeberechtigt** ADJ **~ sein** to have custody; **Sorgeberechtigte(r)** [-bəreçtɪçtə] MF DECL AS ADJ person having custody

sorgen ['zɔrgn] **1** VR to worry; **sich ~ um** to be worried about **2** VI **~ für** (= *sich kümmern um*) to take care of; (= *vorsorgen für*) to provide for; (= *herbeischaffen*) *Proviant, Musik* to provide; (= *bewirken*) *Aufregung* to cause; **dafür ~, dass ...** to see to it that ...; **für Schlagzeilen ~** to make headlines; **für Wirbel ~** to cause a commotion; **für Ruhe/einen reibungslosen Ablauf ~** to make sure that things are quiet/go smoothly; **für Aufsehen ~** to cause a sensation; **dafür ist gesorgt** that's taken care of

Sorgen-: **Sorgenfalte** F worry line; **Sorgenkind** NT (*inf*) problem child; **Sorgentelefon** NT helpline

Sorgerecht NT (*Jur*) custody

Sorgfalt ['zɔrkfalt] F **-**, NO PL care; **ohne ~ arbeiten** to work carelessly; **viel ~ auf etw** (*acc*) **verwenden** to take a lot of care over sth

sorgfältig ['zɔrkfɛltɪç] **1** ADJ careful **2** ADV carefully

sorglos **1** ADJ (= *unbekümmert*) carefree; (= *leichtfertig, nachlässig*) careless **2** ADV in a carefree way; carelessly

Sorglosigkeit F **-**, NO PL (= *Unbekümmertheit*) carefreeness; (= *Leichtfertigkeit*) carelessness

sorgsam ['zɔrkzaːm] **1** ADJ careful **2** ADV carefully; **ein ~ gehütetes Geheimnis** a well-guarded secret

Sorte ['zɔrtə] F **-, -n** (a) sort, type; (*von Waren*) type; (= *Qualität, Klasse*) grade; (= *Marke*) brand; **beste** *or* **erste ~** top quality *or* grade (b) (*Fin*) USU PL foreign currency

Sortenfertigung F, **Sortenproduktion** F (*Ind*) batch production

sortieren [zɔr'tiːrən], *ptp* **sortiert** VT to sort

Sortier-: **Sortierfeld** NT (*Comput*) sort field; **Sortierschlüssel** M (*Comput*) sort key

Sortierung [zɔr'tiːrʊŋ] F **-, -en** sorting; (*Comput: von Daten*) sort

Sortiment [zɔrti'mɛnt] NT **-(e)s, -e** (a) assortment; (= *Sammlung*) collection; **etw ins ~ nehmen** to add sth to one's range; **etw aus dem ~ nehmen** to drop sth from one's range (b) (= *Buchhandel*) retail book trade

SOS [ɛslo:'ɛs] NT **-, -** SOS; **~ funken** to put out an SOS

sosehr [zo'zeːɐ] CONJ however much

SOS-Kinderdorf [ɛslo:'ɛs-] NT *children's home organized into family units*

soso [zo'zo:] **1** ADV (*inf*. = *einigermaßen*) so-so (*inf*) **2** INTERJ **~!** I see!; (*erstaunt*) well, well!; (*drohend*) well!

Soße ['zo:sə] F **-, -n** sauce; (= *Bratensoße*) gravy

sott PRET *von* **sieden**

Soufflé [zu'fle:] NT **-s, -s**, **Soufflee** NT **-s, -s** (*Cook*) soufflé

Souffleur [zu'fløːɐ] M **-s, -e** (*Theat*) prompter

Souffleuse [zu'fløːzə] F **-, -n** (*Theat*) prompter

soufflieren [zu'fliːrən], *ptp* **souffliert** VTI (*Theat*) to prompt; **jdm (den Text) ~** to prompt sb

Sound [saund] M **-s, -s** (*inf*) sound

Soundkarte ['saund-] F (*Comput*) sound card

soundso ['zo:ʊntzo:] ADV **~ lange** for such and such a time; **~ groß/breit** of such and such a size/width; **~ oft** n (number of) times; **~ viele** so and so many; **Paragraf ~** article such-and-such

soundsovielte(r, s) ['zo:ʊntzo'fiːltə] ADJ umpteenth; **am/bis zum Soundsovielten** (*Datum*) on/by such and such a date

Soundtrack ['saundtrɛk] M **-s, -s** (*inf*) soundtrack

Souvenir [zuvə'niːɐ] NT **-s, -s** souvenir

souverän [zuvə'rɛːn] **1** ADJ sovereign *no adv*; (*fig*) supremely good; (= *überlegen*) (most) superior *no adv*; *Sieg* commanding **2** ADV (a) **~ regieren** to be sovereign (b) (= *überlegen*) **handhaben** supremely well; **etw ~ meistern** to resolve sth masterfully; **~ siegen** to win a commanding victory; **sein Gebiet ~ beherrschen** to have a commanding knowledge of one's field; **die Lage ~ beherrschen** to be in full command of the situation

Souveränität [zuvərɛni'tɛːt] F **-**, NO PL sovereignty; (*fig*: = *Überlegenheit*) superiority

soviel [zo'fiːl] **1** ADV *siehe* **viel 2** CONJ as *or* so far as; **~ ich weiß, nicht!** not as *or* so far as I know; **~ ich auch ...** however much I ...

soweit [zo'vait] **1** ADV *siehe* **weit 2** CONJ as *or* so far as; (= *insofern*) in so far as

sowie [zo'viː] CONJ (a) (= *sobald*) as soon as (b) (= *und auch*) as well as

sowieso [zovi'zo:] ADV anyway, anyhow; **das ~!** that goes without saying

Sowjet [zɔ'vjet, 'zɔvjet] M (*Hist*) **-s, -s** Soviet

sowjetisch [zɔ'vjetɪʃ, zɔ'vjeːtɪʃ] ADJ (*Hist*) Soviet

Sowjet- (*Hist*): **Sowjetrepublik** F Soviet Republic; **Union der Sozialistischen ~en** Union of Soviet Socialist Republics; **Sowjetunion** F Soviet Union

sowohl [zo'vo:l] CONJ **~ ... als** *or* **wie (auch)** both ... and, ... as well as

sozial [zo'tsiaːl] **1** ADJ social; (= *~ bewusst*) socially conscious; (= *an das Gemeinwohl denkend*) public-spirited; **die ~en Berufe** the caring professions; **~e Dienste** social services; **~er Wohnungsbau** ≈ council (*Brit*) *or* public (*US*) housing; **~es Jahr** year spent by young person as voluntary assistant in hospitals, with social services etc; **~e Indikation** (*bei Abtreibung*) social factor; **~e Marktwirtschaft** social market economy; **ich habe heute meinen ~en Tag!** (*hum*) I'm feeling charitable today **2** ADV **~ eingestellt sein** to be public-spirited; **~ handeln** to act for the good of all; **~ denken** to be socially minded

Sozial-: **Sozialabbau** M, NO PL cuts *pl* in social services; **Sozialabgaben** PL social security (*Brit*) *or* social welfare (*US*) contributions *pl*; **Sozialamt** NT social security (*Brit*) *or* social welfare (*US*) office; **Sozialarbeit** F social work; **Sozialarbeiter(in)** M(F) social worker; **Sozialausgaben** PL public spending *sing*; **Sozialbeiträge** PL social security (*Brit*) *or* social welfare (*US*) contributions *pl*; **Sozialdemokrat(in)** M(F) social democrat; **Sozialdemokratie** F social democracy; **sozialdemokratisch** **1** ADJ social democratic **2** ADV **die ~ regierten Bundesländer** the states controlled by the Social Democrats; **~ wählen** to vote for the Social Democrats; **Sozialeinrichtungen** PL social facilities *pl*; **Sozialfall** M hardship case; **Sozialhilfe** F income support (*Brit*), welfare (aid) (*US*); **Sozialhilfeempfänger(in)** M(F) person receiving income support (*Brit*) *or* welfare (aid) (*US*)

Sozialismus [zotsia'lɪsmʊs] M **-**, **Sozialismen** [-mən] socialism

Sozialist [zotsia'lɪst] M **-en, -en**, **Sozialistin** [-'lɪstɪn] F **-, -nen** socialist

sozialistisch [zotsia'lɪstɪʃ] **1** ADJ socialist **2** ADV socialistically

Sozial-: **Sozialleistungen** PL employers' contribution (*sometimes including pension scheme payments*); **Sozialpartner** PL unions and management *pl*; **wenn einer der ~ ...** if either unions or management ...; **Sozialplan** M redundancy payments scheme; **Sozialprodukt** NT national product; **Sozialstaat** M welfare state; **Sozialversicherung** F national

insurance (*Brit*), social security (*US*);
Sozialversicherungsausweis M ≈ national insurance card (*Brit*), ≈ social security card (*US*); **Sozialwohnung** F state-subsidized apartment, ≈ council flat (*Brit*)

Soziologe [zotsio'lo:gə] M **-n, -n**, **Soziologin** [-'lo:gɪn] F **-, -nen** sociologist

Soziologie [zotsiolo'gi:] F **-**, NO PL sociology

soziologisch [zotsio'lo:gɪʃ] **1** ADJ sociological **2** ADV sociologically; **~ gesehen/betrachtet** from a sociological point of view

Soziussitz M pillion (seat)

sozusagen [zo:tsu'za:gn, 'zo:tsuza:gn] ADV so to speak

Spachtel ['ʃpaxtl] M **-s, -** *or* f **-, -n** (*Werkzeug*) spatula

Spachtelmasse F filler

Spagat [ʃpa'ga:t] M *or* NT **-(e)s, -e** (*lit*) splits *pl*; (*fig*) balancing act; **~ machen** to do the splits

Spagetti [ʃpa'gɛti, sp-] PL, **Spaghetti** PL spaghetti *sing*

Spag(h)ettiwestern M (*inf*) spaghetti western

spähen ['ʃpe:ən] VI to peer; **nach jdm/etw ~** to look out for sb/sth

Spalier [ʃpa'li:ɐ] NT **-s, -e (a)** trellis; **am ~ ziehen** to train on a trellis **(b)** (*von Menschen*) row; (*zur Ehrenbezeigung*) guard of honour (*Brit*), honor guard (*US*); **~ stehen/ein ~ bilden** to form a guard of honour (*Brit*) *or* honor guard (*US*)

Spalt [ʃpalt] M **-(e)s, -e (a)** (= *Öffnung*) gap; (= *Riss*) crack; (= *Felsspalt*) crevice; **die Tür stand einen ~ offen** the door was slightly ajar; **die Tür/Augen einen ~ öffnen** to open the door/one's eyes slightly **(b)** (*fig*: = *Kluft*) split

spaltbar ADJ (*Phys*) *Material* fissile

Spalte ['ʃpaltə] F **-, -n (a)** (*esp Geol*) fissure; (= *esp Felsspalte*) crevice; (= *Gletscherspalte*) crevasse; (*in Wand*) crack **(b)** (*Typ, Press*) column

spalten ['ʃpaltn], *ptp auch* **gespalten** [gə'ʃpaltn] **1** VT (*lit, fig*) to split; *Holz* to chop **2** VR to split; (*Meinungen*) to be split; *siehe auch* **gespalten**

Spaltung ['ʃpaltʊŋ] F **-, -en** (*lit, fig*) splitting; (*von Atomkernen auch*) fission; (*in Partei etc*) split; **die ~ der Persönlichkeit** the split in his/her personality

Spam [spɛm] M **-s, -s** (*Comput*) spam

spammen ['spɛmən] VI to spam

Spamming ['spɛmɪŋ] NT **-s** spamming

Span [ʃpa:n] M **-(e)s, ˶e** ['ʃpe:nə] shaving; (= *Metallspan*) filing

Spanferkel NT sucking pig

Spange ['ʃpaŋə] F **-, -n** clasp; (= *Haarspange*) hair slide (*Brit*), barrette (*US*); (= *Schuhspange*) strap; (= *Schnalle*) buckle; (= *Armspange*) bracelet

Spaniel ['ʃpa:niəl] M **-s, -s** spaniel

Spanien ['ʃpa:niən] NT **-s** Spain

Spanier ['ʃpa:niɐ] M **-s, -**, **Spanierin** [-iərɪn] F **-, -nen** Spaniard; **die ~** the Spanish, the Spaniards

spanisch ['ʃpa:nɪʃ] ADJ Spanish; **~e Wand** (folding) screen; **das kommt mir ~ vor** (*inf*) that seems odd to me

spann PRET *von* **spinnen**

Spann [ʃpan] M **-(e)s, -e** instep

Spann-: **Spannbeton** M prestressed concrete; **Spannbetttuch** NT fitted sheet

Spanne ['ʃpanə] F **-, -n** (*geh*: = *Zeitspanne*) while; (= *Verdienstspanne*) margin

spannen ['ʃpanən] **1** VT *Saite, Seil, Geigenbogen* to tighten; *Bogen* to draw; *Feder* to tension; *Muskeln* to tense, to flex; *Gewehr, Abzugshahn, Kameraverschluss* to cock; *Werkstück* to clamp; *Wäscheleine* to put up; *Netz, Plane, Bildleinwand* to stretch; *Zugtier* to hitch up (an +*acc*, vor +*acc* to); *siehe auch* **gespannt**
2 VR (*Haut*) to become taut; (*Muskeln*) to tense; **sich über etw** (*acc*) **~** *Regenbogen, Brücke* to span sth; (*Haut*) to stretch over sth
3 VI (*Kleidung*) to be (too) tight; (*Haut*) to be taut

spannend 1 ADJ exciting; (*stärker*) thrilling; (*inf*: = *interessant*) fascinating; **machs nicht so ~!** (*inf*) don't keep me/us in suspense **2** ADV full of suspense; **der Bericht liest sich ~** the report is thrilling to read

Spanner ['ʃpanɐ] M **-s, - (a)** (*für Tennisschläger*) press; (= *Hosenspanner*) hanger; (= *Schuhspanner*) shoetree; (= *Stiefelspanner*) boot tree **(b)** (*inf*: = *Voyeur*) Peeping Tom

Spannkraft F (*von Feder, Bremse*) tension; (*von Muskel*) tone; (*fig*) vigour (*Brit*), vigor (*US*)

Spannung ['ʃpanʊŋ] F **-, -en (a)** NO PL (*von Seil, Feder, Muskel etc*) tautness; (*Mech*: = *innerer Druck*) stress **(b)** (*Elec*) voltage; **unter ~ stehen** to be live **(c)** NO PL (*fig*) excitement; (= *Spannungsgeladenheit*) suspense; **mit großer/atemloser ~** with great/breathless excitement; **etw mit ~ erwarten** to await sth full of suspense; **seine mit ~ erwarteten Memoiren sind endlich erschienen** his eagerly awaited memoirs have appeared at last **(d)** NO PL (= *innerliche, nervliche Anspannung*) tension **(e)** USU PL (= *Feindseligkeit*) tension *no pl*

Spannungs-: **Spannungsgebiet** NT (*Pol*) flash point; **Spannungsmesser** M **-s, -** (*Elec*) voltmeter; **Spannungsprüfer** M voltage detector

Spannweite F (*Math*) range; (*Archit*) span; (*Aviat, von Vogelflügeln*) (wing)span

Spanplatte F chipboard

Spar-: **Sparbrief** M (*Fin*) savings certificate; **Sparbuch** NT savings book; **Sparbüchse** F, **Spardose** F piggy bank; **Spareinlage** F savings deposit

sparen ['ʃpa:rən] **1** VT to save; **keine Kosten/Mühe ~** to spare no expense/effort; **spar dir deine guten Ratschläge!** (*inf*) you can keep your advice!; **diese Bemerkung hätten Sie sich** (*dat*) **~ können!** you should have kept that remark to yourself! **2** VI to save; (= *sparsam sein*) to economize; **an etw** (*dat*) **~ to** be sparing with sth; (= *mit etw Haus halten*) to economize on sth; **bei etw ~** to save on sth; **er hat nicht mit Lob gespart** he was unstinting in his praise; **für** *or* **auf etw** (*acc*) **~** to save up for sth; **am falschen Ort ~** to make false economies

> *Vorsicht!* **sparen** *wird im Allgemeinen nicht mit dem englischen Wort* **to spare** *übersetzt.*

Sparer ['ʃpa:rɐ] M **-s, -**, **Sparerin** [-ərɪn] F **-, -nen** (*bei Bank etc*) saver

Sparflamme F low flame; (= *Zündflamme*) pilot light; **auf ~** (*fig inf*) just ticking over (*Brit inf*) *or* coming along (*US*)

Spargel ['ʃpargl] M **-s, -** *or* (*Sw*) f **-, -n** asparagus

Spar-: **Spargelder** PL savings *pl*; **Sparguthaben** NT savings account; **Sparkasse** F savings bank; **Sparkonto** NT savings account

spärlich ['ʃpe:ɐlɪç] **1** ADJ sparse; *Ausbeute, Reste, Einkünfte, Kenntnisse* sketchy; *Beleuchtung* poor; *Kleidung* scanty; *Mahl* meagre (*Brit*), meager (*US*); *Nachfrage* low **2** ADV *bevölkert, eingerichtet* sparsely; *beleuchtet, besucht* poorly; **~ bekleidet** scantily clad *or* dressed

Spar-: **Sparmaßnahme** F economy (*Brit*) *or* budgeting (*US*) measure; **Sparpaket** NT savings package; (*Pol*) package of austerity measures; **Sparprämie** F savings premium

Sparren ['ʃparən] M **-s, -** rafter

Sparring ['ʃparɪŋ, 'sp-] NT **-s**, NO PL (*Boxen*) sparring

sparsam ['ʃpa:rza:m] **1** ADJ *Mensch* thrifty; (= *haushälterisch, wirtschaftlich*) *Hausfrau, Motor, Verbrauch* economical; **~ im Verbrauch** economical; **von einer Möglichkeit nur ~en Gebrauch machen** to make little use of an opportunity **2** ADV *leben, essen* economically; *verwenden* sparingly; **~ wirtschaften** to keep expenses as low as possible; **mit etw ~ umgehen** *or* **sein** to be economical with sth

Sparsamkeit F **-**, NO PL thrift; (= *sparsames Haushalten*) economizing; **~ im Verbrauch** economy

Sparschwein NT piggy bank

Sparte ['ʃpartə] F **-, -n (a)** (*Comm*) (= *Branche*) line of business; (= *Teilgebiet*) area **(b)** (= *Rubrik*) section

Spartenkanal M (*TV*) specialist channel

Spaß [ʃpa:s] M **-es, ˶e** ['ʃpe:sə] (*no pl*: = *Vergnügen*) fun; (= *Scherz*) joke; (= *Streich*) prank; **lass die dummen Späße!** stop fooling around!; **~ beiseite** joking apart; **viel ~!** have fun! (*auch iro*); **wir haben viel ~ gehabt** we had a really good time; **an etw** (*dat*) **~ haben** to enjoy sth; **es macht mir ~/keinen ~ (, das zu tun)** I enjoy *or* like/don't enjoy *or* like (doing) it; **wenns dir ~ macht** if it turns you on (*inf*); **~/keinen ~ machen** to be fun/no fun; **ich hab doch nur ~ gemacht!** I was only joking!; **(nur**

so,) zum *or* aus **~** (just) for fun; **etw aus** *or* **im** *or* **zum ~ sagen** to say sth as a joke; **da hört der ~ auf, das ist kein ~ mehr** that's going beyond a joke; **sich** (*dat*) **einen ~ daraus machen, etw zu tun** to get enjoyment out of doing sth; **er versteht keinen ~** he has no sense of humor (*Brit*) *or* humor (*US*); (= *er lässt nicht mit sich spaßen*) he doesn't stand for any nonsense; **da verstehe ich keinen ~!** I won't stand for any nonsense; **das war ein teurer ~** (*inf*) that was an expensive business (*inf*)

Spaßbad NT leisure pool

spaßeshalber ADV for fun

spaßhaft, spaßig ['ʃpaːsɪç] ADJ funny

Spaß-: Spaßverderber [-fɛɐdɐbɐ] M **-s, -**, **Spaßverderberin** [-ərɪn] F **-, -nen** spoilsport; **Spaßvogel** M joker

Spasti ['ʃpasti] M **-s, -s** (*sl*) spastic (*sl*)

Spastiker ['ʃpastikɐ, 'sp-] M **-s, -**, **Spastikerin** [-ərɪn] F **-, -nen** spastic

spastisch ['ʃpastɪʃ, 'sp-] ❶ ADJ spastic ❷ ADV *sich bewegen* spastically; **~ gelähmt** suffering from spastic paralysis

spät [ʃpɛːt] ❶ ADJ late; *Reue, Ruhm, Glück* belated; **am ~en Nachmittag** in the late afternoon ❷ ADV late; **~ in der Nacht/am Tage** late at night/in the day; **es ist schon ~** it is late; **es wird schon ~** it is getting late; **heute Abend wird es ~** it'll be a late night tonight; (*nach Hause kommen*) I/he *etc* will be late this evening; **wie ~ ist es?** what's the time?; **zu ~** too late; **der Zug ist zu ~ angekommen** the train arrived late; **wir sind ~ dran** we're late; **besser ~ als nie** (*prov*) better late than never (*prov*); *siehe auch* **später**

Spaten ['ʃpaːtn] M **-s, -** spade

später ['ʃpɛːtɐ] COMP *von* **spät** ❶ ADJ later; (= *zukünftig*) future ❷ ADV later (on); **ein paar Minuten ~** a few minutes later; **~ als** later than; **an ~ denken** to think of the future; **bis ~!, also dann, auf ~!** see you later!

spätestens ['ʃpɛːtəstns] ADV at the latest

Spät-: Spätfolge F USU PL late effect; **Spätherbst** M late autumn, late fall (*US*); **Spätlese** F late vintage; **Spätschaden** M USU PL long-term damage; **Spätschicht** F late shift; **Spätsommer** M late summer

Spatz [ʃpats] M **-en, -en** sparrow; **besser ein ~ in der Hand als eine Taube auf dem Dach** (*Prov*) a bird in the hand is worth two in the bush (*Prov*)

Spatzenhirn NT (*pej*) birdbrain (*inf*)

Spätzle ['ʃpɛtslə] PL (*S Ger Cook*) spaetzle, *sort of pasta*

spazieren [ʃpa'tsiːrən], *ptp* **spaziert** VI AUX SEIN to stroll; (= *stolzieren*) to strut; **wir waren ~** we went for a stroll

spazieren: spazieren fahren IRREG VI AUX SEIN to go for a ride ❷ VT **jdn ~** to take sb for a drive; **das Baby (im Kinderwagen) ~** to take the baby for a walk (in the pram (*Brit*) *or* baby carriage (*US*)); **spazieren gehen** VI IRREG AUX SEIN to go for a walk

Spazier-: Spazierfahrt F ride; **eine ~ machen** to go for a ride; **Spaziergang** M, *pl* **-gänge** walk; (*fig*) child's play *no art*; (*Match*) walkover; **einen ~ machen** to go for a walk; **~ im All** space walk; **Spaziergänger** [-gɛŋɐ] M **-s, -**, **Spaziergängerin** [-ərɪn] F **-, -nen** stroller; **Spazierstock** M walking stick

SPD [espeː'deː] F - ABBR *von* **Sozialdemokratische Partei Deutschlands**

Specht [ʃpɛçt] M **-(e)s, -e** woodpecker

Speck [ʃpɛk] M **-(e)s, -e** (= *Schinkenspeck, durchwachsener ~*) bacon; (= *Walspeck*) blubber; (*inf: bei Mensch*) flab (*inf*); **mit ~ fängt man Mäuse** (*Prov*) you have to use a sprat to catch a mackerel (*prov*)

Speckgürtel M (*fig*) affluent areas outside city boundaries

speckig ['ʃpɛkɪç] ADJ *Kleidung, Haar* greasy

Speck-: Speckscheibe F (bacon) rasher; **Speckschwarte** F bacon rind; **Speckstein** M (*Miner*) soapstone

Spediteur [ʃpedi'tøːɐ] M **-s, -e**, **Spediteurin** [-'tøːrɪn] F **-, -nen** haulier (*Brit*), hauler (*US*); (= *Zwischenspediteur*) forwarding agent; (*von Schiffsfracht*) shipping agent; (= *Umzugsfirma*) furniture remover

Spedition [ʃpedi'tsioːn] F **-, -en** (a) (= *das Spedieren*) transporting; (*auf dem Wasserweg*) shipping (b) (= *Firma*) haulier (*Brit*), hauler (*US*); (= *Zwischenspedition*) forwarding agency; (= *Schiffskontor*) shipping agency; (= *Umzugsfirma*) furniture remover; (= *Versandabteilung*) forwarding department

Speer [ʃpeːɐ] M **-(e)s, -e** spear; (*Sport*) javelin

Speerwerfen NT **-s**, NO PL (*Sport*) **das ~** the javelin; **im ~** in the javelin

Speiche ['ʃpaiçə] F **-, -n** (a) spoke (b) (*Anat*) radius

Speichel ['ʃpaiçl] M **-s**, NO PL saliva

Speicher ['ʃpaiçɐ] M **-s, -** (= *Lagerhaus*) storehouse; (*im Haus*) loft, attic; (= *Wasserspeicher*) tank; (*Comput*) memory, store; **auf dem ~** in the loft *or* attic

Speicher-: Speicherchip M (*Comput*) memory chip; **Speicherdichte** F (*Comput*) storage density; **Speichereinheit** F (*Comput*) (= *Gerät*) storage device; (= *Einheit*) storage unit; **Speichererweiterung** F (*Comput*) memory expansion; **Speicherfunktion** F (*Comput*) memory function; **Speicherkapazität** F storage capacity; (*Comput*) memory capacity; **Speicherkraftwerk** NT storage power station

speichern ['ʃpaiçɐn] ❶ VT *Vorräte, Energie, Daten* to store; (= *abspeichern*) to save ❷ VR to accumulate

Speicher-: Speicherofen M storage heater; **Speicherplatte** F (*Comput*) storage disk; **Speicherplatz** M (*Comput*) storage space; **speicherresident** ADJ (*Comput*) memory-resident

Speicherung ['ʃpaiçərʊŋ] F **-, -en** storage

Speicherverwaltung F (*Comput*) memory management

speien ['ʃpaiən], *pret* **spie** [ʃpiː], *ptp* **gespie(e)n** [gə'ʃpiː(ə)n] ❶ VT to spit; *Lava, Feuer* to spew (forth); *Wasser* to spout; *Flammen, Dämpfe* to belch (out); (= *erbrechen*) to vomit ❷ VI (= *sich übergeben*) to vomit

Speise ['ʃpaizə] F **-, -n** (= *Gericht*) dish; (= *Süßspeise*) dessert; **~n und Getränke** meals and beverages; **kalte und warme ~n** hot and cold meals

Speise-: Speiseeis NT ice cream; **Speisekammer** F pantry; **Speisekarte** F menu

speisen ['ʃpaizn] ❶ VI (*geh*) to eat; **zu Abend/Mittag ~** to have dinner/lunch ❷ VT (a) (*geh: = essen*) to eat; **was wünschen Sie zu ~?** what do you wish to eat, sir/madam? (b) (*liter, Tech*) to feed ❸ VR **sich aus etw ~** (= *seinen Ursprung haben*) to have its source in sth; (= *finanziert werden*) to be financed by sth

Speise-: Speiseöl NT salad oil; (*zum Braten*) edible oil; **Speisequark** [-kvark] M quark; **Speiseröhre** F (*Anat*) gullet; **Speisesaal** M dining hall; (*in Hotel etc*) dining room; (*auf Schiffen*) dining saloon; **Speisewagen** M (*Rail*) dining *or* restaurant car

Spektakel [ʃpɛk'taːkl] M **-s, -** (*inf*) rumpus (*inf*); (= *Aufregung*) palaver (*inf*)

spektakulär [ʃpɛktaku'lɛːɐ, sp-] ❶ ADJ spectacular ❷ ADV spectacularly

Spektrum ['ʃpɛktrʊm, 'sp-] NT **-s, Spektren** *or* **Spektra** [-trən, -tra] spectrum

Spekulant [ʃpeku'lant] M **-en, -en**, **Spekulantin** [-'lantɪn] F **-, -nen** speculator

Spekulation [ʃpekula'tsioːn] F **-, -en** (a) (*Fin*) speculation (*mit* in); **~ mit Grundstücken** property speculation (b) (= *Vermutung*) speculation (*über* about); **das ist reine ~** that is pure speculation; **~en anstellen** to speculate

Spekulations-: Spekulationsgeschäft NT speculative transaction; **Spekulationsgewinn** M speculative profit; **Spekulationsobjekt** NT object of speculation

Spekulatius [ʃpeku'laːtsios] M **-, -** spiced biscuit (*Brit*) *or* cookie (*US*)

spekulativ [ʃpekula'tiːf, sp-] ADJ speculative

spekulieren [ʃpeku'liːrən], *ptp* **spekuliert** VI (a) (*Fin*) to speculate (*mit* in) (b) (= *Vermutungen anstellen*) to speculate; **auf etw** (*acc*) **~** (*inf*) to have hopes of sth

Spelunke [ʃpe'lʊŋkə] F **-, -n** (*pej inf*) dive (*inf*)

spendabel [ʃpɛn'daːbl] ADJ (*inf*) generous

Spende ['ʃpɛndə] F **-, -n** donation; (= *Beitrag*) contribution

spenden ['ʃpɛndn] ❶ VT *Lebensmittel, Blut, Geld, Hilfsgüter* to donate, to give; (= *beitragen*) *Geld* to contribute; *Abendmahl,*

Segen to administer; *Schatten* to offer; *Trost* to give **2** VI to donate; (= *Geld beitragen*) to contribute

---

Vorsicht! **spenden** *wird nicht mit dem englischen Wort to spend übersetzt.*

Spenden-: Spendenaffäre F donations scandal; **Spendenbescheinigung** F charitable donation certificate; **Spendenkonto** NT donations account; **Spendensammler(in)** M(F) fundraiser; **Spendenwaschanlage** F (*Pol*) donation-laundering scheme

Spender[1] [ˈʃpɛndɐ] M **-s, -** (= *Seifenspender etc*) dispenser

Spender[2] [ˈʃpɛndɐ] M **-s, -, Spenderin** [-ərɪn] F **-, -nen** donator; (= *Beitragsleistender*) contributor; (*Med*) donor

Spender- IN CPDS (*Med*) donor; **Spenderblut** NT donor blood; **Spenderherz** NT donor heart

spendieren [ʃpɛnˈdiːrən], *ptp* **spendiert** VT to buy (*jdm etw sb sth, sth for sb*); **spendierst du mir einen?** (*inf*) are you going to buy me a drink?

Sperling [ˈʃpɛrlɪŋ] M **-s, -e** sparrow

Sperma [ˈʃpɛrma, ˈsp-] NT **-s, Spermen** *or* **-ta** [-mən, -ta] sperm

Spermizid [ʃpɛrmiˈtsiːt, sp-] NT **-(e)s, -e** [-də] spermicide

sperrangelweit [ˈʃpɛrʔaŋlˈvait] ADV (*inf*) **~ offen** wide open

Sperre [ˈʃpɛrə] F **-, -n (a)** (= *Hindernis, Schlagbaum, Bahnsteigsperre etc*) barrier; (= *Polizeisperre*) roadblock; (*Mil*) obstacle; (*Tech*) locking device **(b)** (= *Verbot*) (*auch Sport*) ban; (= *Blockierung*) blockade; (*Comm*) embargo **(c)** (*Psych*) mental block; **eine psychologische/emotionale ~** a mental/emotional block

sperren [ˈʃpɛrən] **1** VT **(a)** (= *schließen*) to close; *Platz, Gegend* to close (off); (*Tech*) to lock **(b)** (*Comm*) *Konto, Gelder* to block; *Scheck, Kreditkarte* to stop; (*Comput*) *Daten, Zugriff* to lock; **jdm das Gehalt ~** to stop sb's salary; **jdm den Strom/das Telefon ~** to disconnect sb's electricity/telephone **(c)** (*Sport*: = *ausschließen*) to ban **(d)** (= *einschließen*) **jdn in etw** (*acc*) **~** to shut sb in sth **(e)** (*Typ*) to space out **2** VR **sich (gegen etw) ~** to ba(u)lk (at sth)

Sperr-: Sperrfrist F waiting period (*auch Jur*); (*Sport*) (period of) suspension; **Sperrgebiet** NT prohibited area *or* zone; **Sperrholz** NT plywood

sperrig [ˈʃpɛrɪç] ADJ bulky; (= *unhandlich*) unwieldy; (*fig*) *Sprache, Text, Musik* unwieldy; *Thema, Charakter* awkward; **sich ~ zeigen** to be awkward

Sperr-: Sperrklausel F exclusion clause; **Sperrkonto** NT blocked account; **Sperrminorität** F (*Fin*) blocking minority; **Sperrmüll** M bulky refuse; **Sperrstunde** F closing time

Sperrung [ˈʃpɛrʊŋ] F **-, -en** (= *Schließung*) closing; (*von Platz, Gegend*) closing off; (*Tech*) locking; (*von Konto*) blocking; (*von Scheck*) stopping; (*Sport*: = *Ausschluss*) banning; (= *Verbot*) banning; (*von Urlaub, Gehalt*) stopping; (*von Strom, Gas, Telefon*) disconnection

Spesen [ˈʃpeːzn] PL (*auch Fin*) expenses *pl*; **auf ~ reisen/essen** to travel/eat on expenses; **außer ~ nichts gewesen** nothing doing (*inf*)

Spezi[1] [ˈʃpeːtsi] M **-s, -s** (*S Ger inf*) pal (*inf*)

Spezi[2] NT **-s, -s** (*Getränk*) cola and orangeade

Spezial- [ʃpeˈtsiaːl-]: **Spezialausbildung** F specialized training; **Spezialeffekt** M special effect; **Spezialfall** M special case; **Spezialgebiet** NT special field

spezialisieren [ʃpetsialiˈziːrən], *ptp* **spezialisiert** VR **sich (auf etw** *acc***) ~** to specialize (in sth)

Spezialisierung F **-, -en** specialization

Spezialist [ʃpetsiaˈlɪst] M **-en, -en, Spezialistin** [-ˈlɪstɪn] F **-, -nen** specialist (*für in*)

Spezialität [ʃpetsialiˈtɛːt] F **-, -en (a)** speciality (*Brit*), specialty (*US*) **(b) Spezialitäten** PL (*Cook*) specialities *pl* (*Brit*), specialties *pl* (*US*)

speziell [ʃpeˈtsiɛl] **1** ADJ special **2** ADV (e)specially

Spezifikation [ʃpetsifikaˈtsioːn, sp-] F **-, -en** specification; (= *Aufgliederung*) classification

spezifisch [ʃpeˈtsiːfɪʃ, sp-] **1** ADJ specific **2** ADV specifically; (= *typisch*) typically

spezifizieren [ʃpetsifiˈtsiːrən, sp-], *ptp* **spezifiziert** VT to specify; (= *einzeln aufführen auch*) to itemize

---

Sphäre [ˈsfɛːrə] F **-, -n** (*lit, fig*) sphere

spicken [ˈʃpɪkn] **1** VT (*Cook*) *Braten* to baste; **mit Zitaten gespickt** peppered with quotations *esp Brit* **2** VI (*Sch inf*) to copy (*bei* off, *from*)

Spickzettel M crib (*Brit*), cheat sheet (*US*)

spie PRET *von* **speien**

Spiegel [ˈʃpiːɡl] M **-s, -** **(a)** mirror; **glatt wie ein ~** like glass; **im ~ der Öffentlichkeit** *or* **der öffentlichen Meinung** as reflected in public opinion; **jdm den ~ vorhalten** (*fig*) to hold up a mirror to sb **(b)** (= *Wasserspiegel, Alkoholspiegel*) level; (= *Wasseroberfläche*) surface

Spiegel-: Spiegelbild NT (*lit, fig*) reflection; (= *seitenverkehrtes Bild*) mirror image; **Spiegelei** [ˈʃpiːɡllai] NT fried egg; **spiegelfrei** ADJ *Brille, Bildschirm etc* nonreflecting; **spiegelglatt** ADJ *Fahrbahn, Meer etc* glassy

spiegeln [ˈʃpiːɡln] **1** VI (= *reflektieren*) to reflect (the light); (= *glitzern*) to shine **2** VT to reflect **3** VR to be reflected

Spiegel-: Spiegelreflexkamera F reflex camera; **Spiegelschrift** F mirror writing; **etw in ~ schreiben** to write sth backwards

Spiegelung [ˈʃpiːɡəlʊŋ] F **-, -en** reflection; (= *Luftspiegelung*) mirage

Spiel [ʃpiːl] NT **-(e)s, -e (a)** (= *Unterhaltungsspiel*) (*Sport*) game; (= *Wettkampfspiel, Fußballspiel*) match; (*Theat*: = *Stück*) play; **ein ~ spielen** (*lit, fig*) to play a game; **im ~ sein** (*lit*) to be in the game; (*fig*) to be involved; **stör die Kinder nicht beim ~** don't disturb the children while they're playing **(b)** (= *Bewegung, Zusammenspiel*) play; **das (freie) ~ der Kräfte** the (free) (inter)play of forces **(c)** (= *~zubehör*) (*Karten*) deck, pack; (*Satz*) set **(d)** (*Tech*) (free) play; (= *~raum*) clearance **(e)** (*fig*) **das ist ein ~ mit dem Feuer** that's playing with fire; **leichtes ~ (mit** *or* **bei jdm) haben** to have an easy job of it (with sb); **das ~ ist aus** the game's up; **die Hand** *or* **Finger im ~ haben** to have a hand in it; **jdn/etw aus dem ~ lassen** to leave sb/sth out of it; **jdn/etw ins ~ bringen** to bring sb/sth into it; **etw aufs ~ setzen** to put sth at stake; **auf dem ~(e) stehen** to be at stake; **sein ~ mit jdm treiben** to play games with sb

Spiel-: Spielautomat M gambling *or* gaming machine; (*zum Geldgewinnen*) fruit machine; **Spielball** M (*Volleyball*) match ball; (*Tennis*) game point; (*Billard*) cue ball; (*fig*) plaything; **Spielbank** F, *pl* **-banken** casino; **Spielchen** [ˈʃpiːlçən] NT **-s, -** (*inf*) little game; **Spielcomputer** M (*für Computerspiele*) games computer; (= *Lerncomputer*) educational computer; **Spieldose** F music box

spielen [ˈʃpiːlən] **1** VT to play; **Klavier/Flöte ~** to play the piano/the flute; **was wird heute im Theater gespielt?** what's on at the theatre (*Brit*) *or* theater (*US*) today?; **sie ~ einen Film von ...** they're showing a film by ...; **das Stück war sehr gut gespielt** the play was very well acted; **den Beleidigten ~** to act all offended; **sie spielt die große Dame** she's acting the grand lady; **was wird hier gespielt?** (*inf*) what's going on here?

2 VI to play; (*Theat*) (*Schauspieler*) to act; (*Stück, Film*) to be on; (*beim Glücksspiel*) to gamble; **bei ihm spielt das Radio den ganzen Tag** he has the radio on all day; **seine Beziehungen ~ lassen** to bring one's connections into play; **seine Muskeln ~ lassen** to ripple one's muscles; **wie das Leben so spielt** life's funny like that; **das Stück spielt im 18. Jahrhundert/in Italien** the play is set in the 18th century/in Italy; **mit dem Gedanken ~, etw zu tun** to toy with the idea of doing sth **3** VR **sich müde ~** to tire oneself out playing; **sich warm ~** to warm up; *siehe auch* **gespielt**

spielend 1 ADJ playing **2** ADV easily; **das ist ~ leicht** that's very easy

Spieler [ˈʃpiːlɐ] M **-s, -, Spielerin** [-ərɪn] F **-, -nen** player; (= *Glücksspieler*) gambler

Spielerei [ʃpiːləˈrai] F **-, NO PL** (= *das Spielen*) playing; (*beim Glücksspiel*) gambling; (= *das Herumspielen*) playing around; (= *Kinderspiel*) child's play *no art*

spielerisch [ˈʃpiːlərɪʃ] **1** ADJ **(a)** (= *verspielt*) *Geste, Katze etc* playful; **mit ~er Leichtigkeit** with the greatest of ease **(b)** (*Sport*) playing; (*Theat*) acting; **~es Können** playing/acting ability; **die ~e Leistung** the playing/acting **2** ADV **(a)** (= *verspielt*) playfully; (= *mit Leichtigkeit*) with the greatest of ease **(b)** (*Sport*) in playing terms; (*Theat*) in acting terms

Spiel-: Spielfeld NT field; (*Tennis, Squash, Basketball*) court; **Spielfigur** F piece; **Spielfilm** M feature film; **Spielgeld** NT **(a)** (= *Einsatz*) stake **(b)** (= *unechtes Geld*) play money; **Spielgestalter** [-gəʃtaltɐ] M **-s, -**, **Spielgestalterin** [-ərɪn] F **-, -nen** (*Sport*) key player; **Spielhalle** F amusement arcade (*Brit*), arcade; **Spielhölle** F gambling den; **Spielkamerad(in)** M(F) playmate; **Spielkarte** F playing card; **Spielkasino** NT (gambling) casino; **Spielklasse** F division; **Spielkonsole** F game(s) console; **Spielleiter(in)** M(F) **(a)** (= *Regisseur*) director **(b)** (*Sport*) organizer **(c)** (= *Conférencier*) master of ceremonies, emcee (*esp US inf*); **Spielmacher(in)** M(F) key player

Spielothek [ʃpiːloˈteːk] F **-, -en** amusement arcade (*Brit*), arcade

Spiel-: Spielplan M (*Theat, Film*) programme (*Brit*), program (*US*); **Spielplatz** M (*für Kinder*) playground; (*Sport*) playing field; **Spielraum** M room to move; (*fig*) scope; (*zeitlich*) time; (*bei Planung etc*) leeway; (*Tech*) (free) play; **Spielregel** F (*lit, fig*) rule of the game; **sich an die ~n halten, die ~n beachten** to stick to the rules of the game; **gegen die ~n verstoßen** to break the rules; **Spielsachen** PL toys *pl*; **Spielsaison** F (*Theat, Sport*) season; **Spielschuld** F gambling debt; **Spielstand** M score; **bei einem ~ von ...** with the score (standing) at ...; **Spielsucht** F compulsive gambling; **Spielsüchtige(r)** MF DECL AS ADJ compulsive gambler; **Spieltag** M (*Ftbl etc*) day; **Spieltisch** M games table; (*beim Glücksspiel*) gaming *or* gambling table; **Spieluhr** F music box; **Spielverderber** [-fɛɐdɛrbɐ] M **-s, -**, **Spielverderberin** [-ərɪn] F **-, -nen** spoilsport; **Spielverlauf** M play; **Spielwaren** PL toys *pl*; **Spielwarengeschäft** NT, **Spielwarenhandlung** F toy shop (*esp Brit*) *or* store (*esp US*); **Spielzeit** F **(a)** (= *Saison*) season **(b)** (= *Spieldauer*) playing time; **die normale ~** (*Sport*) normal time

Spielzeug NT, *pl* **-zeuge** toys *pl*; (*einzelnes*) toy; **er hat viel ~** he has a lot of toys

Spielzeug- IN CPDS toy; **Spielzeugeisenbahn** F (toy) train set

Spieß [ʃpiːs] M **-es, -e** (= *Stich- und Wurfwaffe*) spear; (= *Bratspieß*) spit; (*kleiner*) skewer; **wie am ~(e) schreien** (*inf*), **den ~ umkehren** *or* **umdrehen** (*fig*) to turn the tables

Spießbürger(in) M(F) (*pej*) (petit) bourgeois; **ihre Eltern sind richtige ~** her parents are typically middle-class

spießbürgerlich (*pej*) ▮ ADJ (petit) bourgeois ▮ ADV in a bourgeois way

spießen [ʃpiːsn] VT **etw auf etw** (*acc*) ~ (*auf Pfahl etc*) to impale sth on sth; (*auf Gabel etc*) to skewer sth on sth; (*auf größeren Bratspieß*) to spit sth on sth; (*auf Nadel*) to pin sth on sth

Spießer [ʃpiːsɐ] M **-s, -**, **Spießerin** [-ərɪn] F **-, -nen** (*pej*) = **Spießbürger(in)**

spießig [ʃpiːsɪç] ADJ, ADV (*pej*) = **spießbürgerlich**

Spießrute F switch; **~n laufen** (*fig*) to run the gauntlet

Spießrutenlauf M (*fig*) running the gauntlet

Spikes [ʃpaiks, sp-] PL (= *Sportschuhe, Stifte*) spikes *pl*

spinal [ʃpiˈnaːl, sp-] ADJ (*Med*) spinal; **~e Kinderlähmung** poliomyelitis

Spinat [ʃpiˈnaːt] M **-(e)s**, NO PL spinach

Spind [ʃpɪnt] M *or* NT **-(e)s, -e** [-də] (*Mil, Sport*) locker

Spindel [ʃpɪndl] F **-, -n** spindle

Spinne [ʃpɪnə] F **-, -n** spider; (= *Wäschespinne*) rotary clothesline

spinnen [ʃpɪnən], *pret* **spann** [ʃpan], *ptp* **gesponnen** [ɡəˈʃpɔnən] ▮ VT to spin ▮ VI **(a)** (*lit*) to spin **(b)** (*inf*) (= *leicht verrückt sein*) to be crazy; (= *Unsinn reden*) to talk garbage (*inf*); (= *Lügengeschichten erzählen*) to tell tall stories; **stimmt das oder spinnst du?** is that true, or are you having (*Brit*) *or* putting (*US*) me on? (*inf*); **sag mal, spinn ich, oder ...?** am I imagining things or ...?; **spinnst du?** you must be crazy!

Spinnennetz NT cobweb, spider's web

Spinner [ʃpɪnɐ] M **-s, -**, **Spinnerin** [-ərɪn] F **-, -nen (a)** (*Tex*) spinner **(b)** (*inf*) nutcase (*inf*)

Spinnerei [ʃpɪnəˈrai] F **-, -en (a)** (= *Spinnwerkstatt*) spinning mill **(b)** (*inf*) crazy behaviour (*Brit*) *or* behavior (*US*) *no pl*; (= *Unsinn*) garbage (*inf*)

Spinn-: Spinngewebe NT cobweb, spider's web; **Spinnrad** NT spinning wheel

Spion[1] [ʃpioːn] M **-s, -e** (*inf*) (= *Guckloch*) spyhole; (= *Fensterspiegel*) window mirror

Spion[2] [ʃpioːn] M **-s, -e**, **Spionin** [ʃpioːnɪn] F **-, -nen** spy

Spionage [ʃpioˈnaːʒə] F **-**, NO PL spying, espionage; **~ treiben** to spy

Spionage-: Spionageabwehr F counterintelligence *or* counterespionage (service); **Spionagesatellit** M spy satellite

spionieren [ʃpioˈniːrən], *ptp* **spioniert** VI to spy; (*fig inf*: = *nachforschen*) to snoop around (*inf*)

Spionin F **-, -nen** spy

Spirale [ʃpiˈraːlə] F **-, -n** spiral; (*Med*) coil

Spiritismus [ʃpiriˈtɪsmʊs, sp-] M **-**, NO PL spiritualism

spiritistisch [ʃpiriˈtɪstɪʃ, sp-] ADJ **~e Sitzung** seance

spirituell [ʃpiriˈtuɛl, sp-] ▮ ADJ spiritual ▮ ADV spiritually

Spirituosen [ʃpiriˈtuoːzn, sp-] PL spirits *pl*

Spiritus M **-**, NO PL [ʃpiːritʊs] (= *Alkohol*) spirit; **mit ~ kochen** to cook on a spirit stove; **etw in ~ legen** to put sth in alcohol

Spital [ʃpiˈtaːl] NT **-s, Spitäler** [-ˈtɛːlɐ] (*old, Aus, Sw*: = *Krankenhaus*) hospital

spitz [ʃpɪts] ▮ ADJ **(a)** (= *mit einer Spitze*) pointed; (= *nicht stumpf*) Bleistift, Nadel etc sharp; (*Math*) Winkel acute; **~e Klammern** angle brackets; **etw mit ~en Fingern anfassen** (*inf*) to pick sth up gingerly **(b)** (= *gehässig*) barbed; Zunge sharp ▮ ADV **(a)** feilen, zuhauen to a point **(b)** (= *~züngig*) bemerken, kontern, antworten sharply

Spitz [ʃpɪts] M **-es, -e** (*Hunderasse*) spitz

Spitz-: Spitzbart M goatee; **spitzbekommen** *ptp*
spitzbekommen VT SEP IRREG (*inf*) **etw ~** to catch on to sth (*inf*); **Spitzbogen** M pointed arch; **spitzbübisch** ▮ ADJ mischievous ▮ ADV mischievously

Spitze [ʃpɪtsə] F **-, -n (a)** top; (= *von Gegenstand, Kinn*) point; (= *Schuhspitze*) toe; (= *Fingerspitze, Nasenspitze*) tip; (= *Haarspitze*) end; **etw auf die ~ treiben** to carry sth to extremes **(b)** (*fig*) (= *Höchstwert*) peak; (*inf*: = *Höchstgeschwindigkeit*) top speed **(c)** (= *Führung*) head; (= *vorderes Ende*) front; (= *Tabellenspitze*) top; **an der ~ stehen** to be at the head; (*auf Tabelle*) to be (at the) top (of the table); **an der ~ liegen** (*Sport, fig*) to be in the lead **(d)** (*fig*: = *Stichelei*) dig (*esp Brit*), cut (*US*); **das ist eine ~ gegen Sie** that's a dig (*esp Brit*) *or* cut (*US*) at you **(e)** (*Gewebe*) lace **(f)** (*inf*: = *prima*) great (*inf*); **das war einsame** *or* **absolute ~!** that was really great! (*inf*)

Spitzel [ʃpɪtsl] M **-s, -** (= *Informant*) informer; (= *Spion*) spy; (= *Schnüffler*) snooper; (= *Polizeispitzel*) police informer

spitzen [ʃpɪtsn] VT (= *spitz machen*) Bleistift to sharpen; Lippen, Mund to purse; (*zum Küssen*) to pucker (up); Ohren (*lit, fig*) to prick up

Spitzen- IN CPDS top; (= *aus Spitze*) lace; **Spitzenbelastung** F peak (load); **die Zeit der ~** the peak period; **Spitzenerzeugnis** NT top(-quality) product; **Spitzengehalt** NT top salary; **Spitzengeschwindigkeit** F top speed; **Spitzenhöschen** [-høːsçən] NT lace panties *pl*; **Spitzenkandidat(in)** M(F) top candidate; **Spitzenklasse** F top class; **Sekt/ein Auto** *etc* **der ~** top-class champagne/a top-class car *etc*; **Spitzenleistung** F top performance; (*von Maschine, Auto*) peak performance; (*fig*: = *ausgezeichnete Leistung*) top-class performance; **Spitzenlohn** M top wage(s *pl*); **spitzenmäßig** (*inf*) ▮ ADJ fantastic (*inf*) ▮ ADV fantastically (*inf*); **Spitzenposition** F leading *or* top position; **Spitzenreiter** M (*Ware*) top seller; (*Film, Stück etc*) hit; (= *Schlager*) number one; **Spitzensportler(in)** M(F) top(-class) sportsman/-woman; **Spitzenstellung** F leading position; **Spitzensteuersatz** M top rate of income tax; **Spitzentechnologie** F state-of-the-art technology; **Spitzenverband** M leading organization; **Spitzenverdiener(in)** M(F) top earner; **Spitzenverkehrszeit** F peak period; **Spitzenwein** M top-quality wine

Spitzer [ʃpɪtsɐ] M **-s, -** (*inf*) (pencil) sharpener

Spitz-: spitzfindig ▮ ADJ over(ly)-subtle ▮ ADV in an over(ly)-subtle way; **Spitzhacke** F pickaxe (*Brit*), pickax (*US*); **spitzkriegen** VT SEP (*inf*) = **spitzbekommen**; **Spitzname** M nickname; **mit dem ~n nicknamed**; **Spitzwegerich** M ribwort; **spitzwinklig 🔢** ADJ (*Math*) *Dreieck* acute-angled **🔢** ADV *abzweigen, auslaufen* at a sharp angle

Spleen [ʃpliːn] M **-s, -s** (*inf*) (= *Angewohnheit*) strange habit; (= *Idee*) crazy idea (*inf*); (= *Fimmel*) obsession

spleenig [ˈʃpliːnɪç] ADJ (*inf*) crazy (*inf*)

Spliss [ʃplɪs] M **-es, -e (a)** (*dial:* = *Splitter*) splinter **(b)** NO PL (= *gespaltene Haarspitzen*) split ends *pl*

Splitt [ʃplɪt] M **-(e)s, -e** stone chippings *pl*; (= *Streumittel*) grit

Splitter [ˈʃplɪtɐ] M **-s, -** splinter

Splitter-: splitterfasernackt ADJ (*inf*) stark-naked; **splitterfrei** ADJ *Glas* shatterproof; **Splittergruppe** F (*Pol*) splinter group

splittern [ˈʃplɪtɐn] VI AUX SEIN or HABEN (*Holz, Glas, Knochen*) to splinter

splitternackt ADJ stark-naked

SPÖ [ɛsˈpeːˈøː] F - ABBR *von* Sozialdemokratische Partei Österreichs

Spoiler [ˈʃpɔylɐ, ˈspɔy-] M **-s, -** spoiler

sponsern [ˈʃpɔnsɐn, ˈspɔn-] VT to sponsor

Sponsion [ʃpɔnˈzioːn] F (*Aus Univ*) academic degree ceremony in which the title of Magister is awarded

Sponsor [ˈʃpɔnzɐ, ˈspɔn-] M **-s, Sponsoren** [-ˈzoːrən], **Sponsorin** [-ˈzoːrɪn] F **-, -nen** sponsor

spontan [ʃpɔnˈtaːn, sp-] **🔢** ADJ spontaneous **🔢** ADV spontaneously

Spontaneität [ʃpɔntaneiˈtɛːt, sp-] F -, NO PL spontaneity

sporadisch [ʃpoˈraːdɪʃ, sp-] **🔢** ADJ sporadic **🔢** ADV sporadically

Sport [ʃpɔrt] M **-(e)s, (*rare*) -e** sport; (= *Zeitvertreib*) hobby; **treiben Sie ~?** do you do any sport?; **er treibt viel ~** he does a lot of sport; **etw aus** *or* **zum ~ betreiben** to do sth as a hobby; **sich** (*dat*) **einen ~ aus etw machen** (*inf*) to get a kick out of sth (*inf*)

Sport-: Sportart F (kind of) sport; **Sportbericht** M sports report; **Sportfeld** NT sports ground; **Sportflugzeug** NT sporting aircraft; **Sportfreund(in)** M(F) sport(s) fan; **Sporthalle** F sports hall; **Sporthemd** NT sports shirt

sportiv [spɔrˈtiːf, ʃp-] ADJ *Mensch, Kleidung, Auto* sporty

Sport-: Sportjackett NT sports jacket; **Sportkleidung** F sportswear

Sportler [ˈʃpɔrtlɐ] M **-s, -** sportsman

Sportlerherz NT athlete's heart

Sportlerin [ˈʃpɔrtlərɪn] F **-, -nen** sportswoman

sportlich [ˈʃpɔrtlɪç] ADJ **(a)** sporting; *Mensch, Auto* sporty; (= *durchtrainiert*) athletic **(b)** *Kleidung* casual; (= ~-*schick*) smart but casual; (= *wie Sportkleidung aussehend*) sporty **🔢** ADV **(a) sich ~ betätigen, ~ aktiv sein** to do sport **(b)** (= *fair*) sportingly; **er hat sich ihr gegenüber nicht besonders ~ verhalten** he wasn't particularly sporting in the way he behaved toward(s) her **(c)** (= *leger*) casually; **~ gekleidet** casually dressed **(d)** (= *rasant*) *fahren* fast

Sport-: Sportmedizin F sports medicine; **Sportnachrichten** PL sports news *with sing vb*; **Sportplatz** M sports field; (*in der Schule*) playing field(s *pl*); **Sportschuh** M casual shoe

Sports-: Sportsfrau F sportswoman; **Sportsfreund(in)** M(F) (*inf*) pal (*inf*); **Sportskanone** F (*inf*) sporting ace (*inf*); **Sportsmann** M, *pl* **-männer** sportsman; (*inf: als Anrede*) pal (*inf*)

Sport-: Sportstudio NT fitness centre (*Brit*) *or* center (*US*); **Sportunfall** M sporting accident; **Sportveranstaltung** F sporting event; **Sportverein** M sports club; **Sportwagen** M sports car; (*für Kind*) pushchair (*Brit*), (baby) stroller (*US*); **Sportzeug** NT, NO PL (*inf*) sport(s) stuff (*inf*)

Spot [spɔt, ʃpɔt] M **-s, -s** commercial

Spot- [ˈspɔt-]: **Spotgeschäft** NT (*Fin*) spot transaction; **Spotlight** [ˈspɔtlait] NT **-s, -s** spotlight; **Spotmarkt** M (*Fin*) spot market

Spott [ʃpɔt] M **-(e)s**, NO PL mockery; **jdn dem ~ preisgeben** to hold sb up to ridicule; **seinen ~ mit jdm treiben** to make fun of sb

spottbillig (*inf*) **🔢** ADJ dirt-cheap (*inf*) **🔢** ADV **das habe ich ~ gekauft** I bought it dirt-cheap (*inf*)

Spöttelei [ʃpœtəˈlai] F **-, -en** (= *das Spotten*) mocking; (= *ironische Bemerkung*) mocking remark

spötteln [ˈʃpœtln] VI to mock (*über jdn/etw* sb/sth)

spotten [ˈʃpɔtn] VI (= *sich lustig machen*) to mock; **über jdn/etw ~** to mock sb/sth; **das spottet jeder Beschreibung** that simply defies description

Spötter [ˈʃpœtɐ] M **-s, -, Spötterin** [-ərɪn] F **-, -nen** mocker; (= *satirischer Mensch*) satirist

spöttisch [ˈʃpœtɪʃ] **🔢** ADJ mocking **🔢** ADV mockingly

Spottpreis M ridiculously low price; **für einen ~** for a song (*inf*)

sprach PRET *von* sprechen

Sprach-: Sprachbarriere F language barrier; **sprachbegabt** ADJ linguistically talented; **Sprachbegabung** F talent for languages; **Sprachcomputer** M computer with speech synthesizer; (= *Taschenübersetzer*) pocket electronic dictionary

Sprache [ˈʃpraːxə] F **-, -n** language; (= *das Sprechen*) speech; (= *Fähigkeit, zu sprechen*) power of speech; **in französischer** *etc* **~** in French *etc*; **die gleiche ~ sprechen** (*lit, fig*) to speak the same language; **mit der ~ herausrücken** to come out with it; **die ~ auf etw** (*acc*) **bringen** to bring the conversation (a)round to sth; **zur ~ kommen** to be brought up; **etw zur ~ bringen** to bring sth up; **die ~ verlieren** to lose the power of speech; **die ~ wiederfinden** to be able to speak again; **es raubt** *or* **verschlägt einem die ~** it takes your breath away; **mir blieb die ~ weg** I was speechless

Sprachenschule F language school

Sprach-: Spracherkennung F (*Comput*) speech recognition; **Spracherwerb** M language acquisition; **Sprachfehler** M speech impediment; **Sprachforscher(in)** M(F) linguist(ic researcher); (= *Philologe*) philologist; **Sprachforschung** F linguistic research; (= *Philologie*) philology; **Sprachführer** M phrase book; **Sprachgebrauch** M (linguistic) usage; **moderner deutscher ~** modern German usage; **Sprachgefühl** NT feeling for language; **Sprachgenie** NT linguistic genius; **sprachgesteuert** [-ɡəʃtɔyɐt] ADJ (*Comput*) voice-activated; **Sprachkenntnisse** PL knowledge *sing* of languages/the language/a language; **mit englischen ~n** with a knowledge of English; **haben Sie irgendwelche ~?** do you know any languages?; **~ erwünscht** (knowledge of) languages desirable; **Sprachkurs** M language course; **Sprachlabor** NT language laboratory; **Sprachlehre** F grammar

sprachlich [ˈʃpraːxlɪç] **🔢** ADJ linguistic; *Unterricht, Schwierigkeiten* language *attr*; *Fehler* grammatical **🔢** ADV linguistically; **~ hatten die Einwanderer keine Schwierigkeiten** the immigrants had no language difficulties; **~ falsch/richtig** grammatically incorrect/correct; **eine intelligente Analyse, auch ~ gut** an intelligent analysis, well written too

sprachlos ADJ speechless; **ich bin ~!** I'm speechless; **da ist man (einfach) ~** (*inf*) that's really something (*inf*)

Sprachlosigkeit F -, NO PL speechlessness

Sprach-: Sprachmelodie F intonation; **Sprachmittler(in)** M(F) translator and interpreter; **Sprachregelung** F **(a)** (= *Bestimmung*) linguistic ruling **(b)** (= *Version*) **offizielle ~** official version; **Sprachreise** F language(-learning)trip; **Sprachrohr** NT (*fig*) mouthpiece; **Sprachschule** F language school; **Sprachunterricht** M language teaching; **der französische ~** the teaching of French; **Sprachurlaub** M language-learning trip; **Sprachwissenschaft** F linguistics *sing*; (= *Philologie*) philology; **vergleichende ~en** comparative linguistics/philology; **Sprachwissenschaftler(in)** M(F) linguist; (= *Philologe*) philologist; **sprachwissenschaftlich** **🔢** ADJ linguistic **🔢** ADV linguistically

sprang PRET *von* springen

Spray [ʃpreː, spreː] M or NT **-s, -s** spray

Spraydose [ˈʃpreː-, ˈspreː-] F aerosol (can)

sprayen [ˈʃpreːən, ˈsp-] VTI to spray

Sprech-: Sprechanlage F intercom; **Sprechblase** F balloon

sprechen [ˈʃprɛçn], *pret* **sprach** [ʃpraːx], *ptp* **gesprochen** [ɡəˈʃprɔxn] **🔢** VI to speak (*über +acc, von* about, of); (= *reden, sich unterhalten*) to talk, to speak (*über +acc, von* about); **viel ~** to talk a lot; **frei ~** to extemporize; **er spricht wenig** he doesn't say very much; **~ Sie!** (*form*) speak away!; **sprich doch endlich!** (*geh*) say something; **im Traum** *or* **Schlaf ~** to talk in one's sleep; **es spricht ...** the speaker is ...; **schlecht** *or* **nicht gut auf jdn/etw zu ~ sein** not to have a good thing to say about sb/sth; **mit jdm ~** to speak *or* talk to sb; **mit sich selbst ~** to talk to oneself; **ich habe mit dir zu ~** I want to have a word with you; **wie sprichst du mit mir?** who do you think you're talking to?; **so spricht man nicht mit seinem Großvater** that's no way to talk or speak to your grandfather; **mit wem spreche ich?** to whom am I speaking, please?; **wir haben gerade von dir gesprochen** we were just talking about you; **es wird kaum noch von ihm gesprochen** he's hardly mentioned now; **auf jdn/etw zu ~ kommen** to get to talking about sb/sth; **für jdn/etw** to speak for sb/sth; **gegen jdn/etw ~** to speak against sb/sth; **es spricht für jdn/etw(, dass ...)** it says something for sb/sth (that ...); **das spricht für sich (selbst)** that speaks for itself; **es spricht vieles dafür/dagegen** there's a lot to be said for/against it; **es spricht vieles dafür, dass ...** there is every reason to believe that ...; **was spricht dafür/dagegen?** what is there to be said for/against it?; **aus seinen Worten sprach Verachtung/Hoffnung** his words expressed contempt/hope; **ganz allgemein gesprochen** generally speaking

2 VT **(a)** (= sagen) to say, to speak; eine Sprache, Mundart to speak; (= aufsagen) Gebet to say; **es wurde viel gesprochen** a lot of talking was done; **~ Sie Japanisch?** do you speak Japanese?; **hier spricht man Spanisch** Spanish spoken **(b)** Urteil to pronounce **(c)** (= mit jdm reden) to speak to; **kann ich bitte Herrn Kurz ~?** may I speak to Mr Kurz, please?; **er ist nicht zu ~** he can't see anybody; **ich bin für niemanden zu ~** I can't see anybody, I'm not available; **ich hätte gern Herrn Bremer gesprochen** could I speak to Mr Bremer?; **kann ich Sie einen Augenblick or kurz ~?** can I have a quick word?; **wir ~ uns noch!** you haven't heard the last of this!

sprechend ADJ Augen, Gebärde eloquent
Sprecher ['ʃprɛçɐ] M **-s, -**, **Sprecherin** [-ərɪn] F **-, -nen** speaker; (= Nachrichtensprecher) newscaster; (für Dokumentarfilme, Stücke etc) narrator; (= Ansager) announcer; (= Wortführer) spokesperson; **sich zum ~ von jdm/etw machen** to become the spokesperson for sb/sth
Sprech-: Sprechfunk M radiotelephone system; **Sprechfunkgerät** NT radiotelephone; (tragbar auch) walkie-talkie; **Sprechstunde** F consultation (hour); (von Arzt) surgery (Brit), consultation (US); **~n** consultation hours; (von Arzt) surgery (Brit) or consulting hours; **~ halten** to hold surgery (Brit), to be available for consultation; **Sprechstundenhilfe** F (doctor's) receptionist; **Sprechtaste** F "talk" button; **Sprechübung** F speech exercise; **Sprechweise** F way of speaking; **Sprechzeit** F **(a)** (= Sprechstunde) consulting time; (von Arzt) surgery (Brit) or consultation time **(b)** (Telec) call time; **Sprechzimmer** NT consulting room
spreizen ['ʃpraitsn̩] **1** VT to spread; (Sport) to straddle; siehe auch **gespreizt** **2** VR (= sich sträuben) to kick up (inf)
Spreizfuß M splayfoot
sprengen ['ʃprɛŋən] **1** VT **(a)** (mit Sprengstoff) to blow up; Fels to blast; **etw in die Luft ~** to blow sth up **(b)** Türschloss, Tor to force (open); Tresor to break open; Bande, Fesseln to burst; Eisdecke, Versammlung to break up; (Spiel)bank to break; **die Grenzen von etw ~** (fig) to go beyond the boundaries of sth **(c)** (= abspritzen) Beete, Rasen to water **2** VI (= Sprengarbeiten vornehmen) to blast
Spreng-: Sprengkapsel F detonator; **Sprengkopf** M warhead; **Sprengkörper** M explosive device; **Sprengkraft** F explosive force; **Sprengladung** F explosive charge; **Sprengsatz** M explosive device
Sprengstoff M explosive; (fig) dynamite
Sprengstoffanschlag M, **Sprengstoffattentat** NT bomb attack; (erfolgreich auch) bombing; **auf ihn wurde ein ~ verübt** he was the subject of a bomb attack
Sprengung ['ʃprɛŋʊŋ] F **-, -en (a)** blowing-up; (von Felsen) blasting **(b)** (von Tür, Schloss) forcing (open); (von Tresor) breaking open
sprenkeln ['ʃprɛŋkln̩] VT Farbe to sprinkle spots of; siehe auch **gesprenkelt**
Spreu [ʃprɔy] F **-**, NO PL chaff; **die ~ vom Weizen trennen** or **sondern** (fig) to separate the wheat from the chaff
spricht [ʃprɪçt] 3. PERS SING PRES von **sprechen**
Sprichwort NT, pl **-wörter** proverb
sprichwörtlich ADJ (lit, fig) proverbial
sprießen ['ʃpriːsn̩], pret **spross** or **sprießte** [ʃprɔs, 'ʃpriːstə], ptp **gesprossen** [gə'ʃprɔsn̩] VI AUX SEIN (aus der Erde) to come up; (Knospen, Blätter) to shoot

Springbrunnen M fountain
springen ['ʃprɪŋən], pret **sprang** [ʃpraŋ], ptp **gesprungen** [gə'ʃprʊŋən] **1** VI AUX SEIN **(a)** (lit, fig, Sport, bei Brettspielen) to jump; (esp mit Schwung) to leap; (beim Stabhochsprung) to vault; (Raubtier) to pounce; **jdm an den Hals or die Kehle or die Gurgel** (inf) **~** to fly at sb's throat; (fig) to fly at sb; **aus dem Gleis or aus den Schienen ~** to jump the rails **(b)** **etw ~ lassen** (inf) to fork out for sth (inf); Runde to stand sth; Geld to fork out sth (inf); **für jdn etw ~ lassen** (inf) to treat sb to sth **(c)** (Glas, Porzellan, Saite) to break; (= Risse bekommen) to crack; (= sich lösen: Knopf) to come off (von etw sth) **2** VT AUX HABEN **einen (neuen) Rekord ~** (Sport) to make a record jump
Springen NT **-s, -** (Sport) jumping; (= Stabhochspringen) vaulting; (Wassersport) diving
springend ADJ **der ~e Punkt** the crucial point
Springer[1] ['ʃprɪŋɐ] M **-s, -** (Chess) knight
Springer[2] ['ʃprɪŋɐ] M **-s, -**, **Springerin** [-ərɪn] F **-, -nen (a)** jumper; (= Stabhochspringer) vaulter; (Wassersport) diver **(b)** (Ind) stand-in
Springerstiefel PL Doc Martens® (boots) pl
Spring-: Springflut F spring tide; **Springreiten** NT **-s**, NO PL show jumping; **Springrollo** NT roller blind; **Springseil** NT skipping-rope (Brit), jump rope (US)
Sprinkler ['ʃprɪŋklɐ] M **-s, -** sprinkler
Sprinkleranlage F sprinkler system
Sprint [ʃprɪnt] M **-s, -s** sprint
sprinten ['ʃprɪntn̩] VTI AUX SEIN to sprint
Sprit [ʃprɪt] M **-(e)s, -e** (inf: = Benzin) gas (inf)
Spritz-: Spritzbesteck NT (für Drogen) needles pl; **Spritzdüse** F nozzle; (Tech) jet
Spritze ['ʃprɪtsə] F **-, -n** syringe; (= Feuerspritze, Gartenspritze) hose; (= Injektion) injection; **eine ~ bekommen** to have an injection
spritzen ['ʃprɪtsn̩] **1** VT **(a)** Flüssigkeit to spray; (Cook) Zuckerguss etc to pipe; (= verspritzen) Wasser, Schmutz etc to splash; (Fahrzeug) to spray **(b)** (= lackieren) Auto, Gegenstand to spray **(c)** (= injizieren) to inject; (= eine Injektion geben) to give injections/an injection; **wir müssen dem (Kranken) Morphium ~** we have to give the patient a morphine injection; **sich** (dat) **Heroin ~** to inject (oneself with) heroin **2** VI AUX HABEN or SEIN (Wasser, Schlamm, Blut) to spray; (heißes Fett) to spit; (aus einer Tube, Wasserpistole etc) to squirt
Spritzer ['ʃprɪtsɐ] M **-s, -** splash
Spritzfahrt F (inf) spin (inf); **eine ~ machen** to go for a spin (inf)
spritzig ['ʃprɪtsɪç] **1** ADJ Wein tangy; Auto, Aufführung, Dialog lively; (= witzig) witty **2** ADV aufführen, darstellen with sparkle; schreiben racily; (= witzig) wittily
spröd [ʃprøːt], **spröde** ['ʃprøːdə] ADJ Glas, Stein, Haar brittle; Haut rough; Stimme thin; (fig) Material obdurate, recalcitrant; (= abweisend) Mensch, Charakter aloof; Sprache, Worte offhand; Atmosphäre, Stimmung chilly; Charme austere
spross PRET von **sprießen**
Sprosse ['ʃprɔsə] F **-, -n** (lit, fig) rung; (= Fenstersprosse) (senkrecht) mullion; (waagerecht) transom; (= Geweihsprosse) branch
Sprossen-: Sprossenfenster NT lattice window; **Sprossenwand** F (Sport) wall bars pl
Sprössling ['ʃprœslɪŋ] M **-s, -e** shoot; (fig hum) offspring pl
Sprotte ['ʃprɔtə] F **-, -n** sprat
Spruch [ʃprʊx] M **-(e)s, ⸚e** ['ʃprʏçə] **(a)** saying; (= Sinnspruch) saying, aphorism; (= Wahlspruch) motto; **flotte Sprüche** wisecracks; **Sprüche klopfen** (inf) to talk posh (inf); (= angeben) to talk big (inf); (Verkäufer) spiel (inf); **mach keine Sprüche!** (inf) come off it! (inf); **das sind doch nur Sprüche!** that's just talk **(b)** (= Richterspruch) judgement; (= Freispruch/Schuldspruch) verdict; (= Strafurteil) sentence; (= Schiedsspruch) ruling
Spruchband [-bant] NT, pl **-bänder** banner
spruchreif ADJ (inf) **die Sache ist noch nicht ~** it's not definite yet so we'd better not talk about it; **die Sache wird erst ~, wenn ...** we can only start talking about it definitely when ...
Sprudel ['ʃpruːdl̩] M **-s, -** mineral water; (= süßer ~) fizzy drink

Sprudelbad NT whirlpool (bath)

sprudeln [ˈʃpruːdln] VI **(a)** (= *schäumen*) (*Wasser, Quelle*) to bubble; (*Sekt, Limonade*) to fizz; (*fig: vor Freude, guten Ideen etc*) to bubble **(b)** AUX SEIN (= *hervorsprudeln*) (*Wasser etc*) to bubble; (*fig*) (*Worte*) to pour out; (*Steuern, Einnahmen*) to pour in

sprudelnd ADJ (*lit*) *Getränke* fizzy; *Quelle* bubbling; (*fig*) *Temperament, Witz* bubbly; *Geldquelle, Gewinne* inexhaustible

Sprühdose F spray (can)

sprühen [ˈʃpryːən] **1** VI **(a)** AUX HABEN or SEIN to spray; (*Funken*) to fly **(b)** (*fig*) (*vor Witz, Ideen etc*) to bubble over (*vor +dat* with); (*Augen*) (*vor Freude etc*) to sparkle (*vor +dat* with); (*vor Zorn etc*) to flash (*vor +dat* with) **2** VT to spray

Sprühregen M fine rain

Sprung [ʃprʊŋ] M **-(e)s, ̈-e** [ˈʃprʏŋə] **(a)** jump; (*schwungvoll*) (*fig:* = *Gedankensprung*) leap; (= *Hüpfer*) skip; (*auf einem Bein*) hop; (= *Satz*) bound; (*von Raubtier*) pounce; (= *Stabhochsprung*) vault; (*Wassersport*) dive; **einen ~ machen** to jump; **zum ~ ansetzen** (*lit*) to get ready to jump *etc*; (*fig*) to get ready to pounce; **sie wagte den ~ (ins kalte Wasser) nicht** (*fig*) she didn't dare (to) take the plunge; **damit kann man keine großen Sprünge machen** (*inf*) you can't exactly live it up on that (*inf*); **jdm auf die Sprünge helfen** (*wohlwollend*) to give sb a (helping) hand; (*drohend*) to show sb what's what **(b)** (*inf: = kurze Strecke*) stone's throw (*inf*); **auf einen ~ bei jdm vorbeikommen/-gehen** to drop in to see sb (*inf*) **(c)** (= *Riss*) crack; **einen ~ haben** to be cracked; **einen ~ bekommen** to crack; **einen ~ in der Schüssel haben** (*fig inf*) to be off one's rocker (*inf*)

Sprung-: Sprungbein NT **(a)** (*Anat*) anklebone **(b)** (*Sport*) takeoff leg; **Sprungbrett** NT (*lit, fig*) springboard; **Sprungfeder** F spring; **Sprunggelenk** NT ankle joint; (*von Pferd*) hock; **sprunghaft 1** ADJ **(a)** *Mensch, Charakter* volatile; *Denken* disjointed **(b)** (= *rapide*) rapid **2** ADV *ansteigen, entwickeln* by leaps and bounds; **Sprungschanze** F (*Ski*) ski jump; **Sprungturm** M diving platform

Spucke [ˈʃpʊkə] F -, NO PL (*inf*) spit; **da bleibt einem die ~ weg!** (*inf*) it's flabbergasting (*inf*); **mit Geduld und ~** (*hum inf*) with blood, sweat and tears (*hum*)

spucken [ˈʃpʊkn] **1** VT to spit; (*inf: = erbrechen*) to throw up (*inf*); *Lava, Flammen* to spew (out) **2** VI to spit; (*inf: = sich übergeben*) to throw up (*inf*); **in die Hände ~** (*lit*) to spit on one's hands; (*fig*) to roll up one's sleeves

Spuk [ʃpuːk] M **-(e)s, -e** (= *Geistererscheinung*) **der ~ fing um Mitternacht an** the ghosts started to walk at midnight

spuken [ˈʃpuːkn] VI to haunt; **an einem Ort/in einem Schloss ~** to haunt a place/castle; **es spukt auf dem Friedhof/im alten Haus** *etc* the cemetery/old house *etc* is haunted; **hier spukt es** this place is haunted; **das spukt noch immer in den Köpfen** or **durch die Köpfe** that still has a hold on people's minds

Spülbecken NT sink

Spule [ˈʃpuːlə] F -, -n spool; (= *Nähmaschinenspule*) (*Ind*) bobbin; (*Elec*) coil

Spüle [ˈʃpyːlə] F -, -n sink

spulen [ˈʃpuːlən] VT to spool (*auch Comput*)

spülen [ˈʃpyːlən] **1** VT **(a)** (= *ausspülen, abspülen*) *Mund* to rinse; *Wunde* to wash; *Darm* to irrigate; *Vagina* to douche; (= *abwaschen*) *Geschirr* to wash up **(b)** (*Wellen etc*) to wash; (*fig*) *Menschen* to bring; **etw an Land ~** to wash sth ashore; **Geld in die Kassen ~** to bring money pouring into the coffers **2** VI (*Waschmaschine*) to rinse; (= *Geschirr ~*) to wash up; (*auf der Toilette*) to flush; **du spülst und ich trockne ab** you wash and I'll dry

Spül-: Spülkasten M cistern; **Spüllappen** M dishcloth; **Spülmaschine** F (automatic) dishwasher; **spülmaschinenfest** ADJ dishwasher-proof; **Spülmittel** NT washing-up liquid; **Spülschüssel** F washing-up bowl

Spülung [ˈʃpyːlʊŋ] F -, -en rinsing; (= *Wasserspülung*) flush; (= *Haarspülung*) conditioner; (*Med*) (= *Darmspülung*) irrigation; (= *Vaginalspülung*) douche

Spulwurm M roundworm

Spund [ʃpʊnt] M **-(e)s, ̈-e** [ˈʃpʏndə] stopper; (*Holztechnik*) tongue

spunden [ˈʃpʊndn] VT *Fass* to stop up

Spur [ʃpuːɐ] F -, -en **(a)** (= *Abdruck im Boden etc*) track; (= *hinterlassenes Zeichen*) trace; (= *Bremsspur*) skidmarks *pl*;

(= *Blutspur etc, Fährte*) trail; **von den Tätern fehlt jede ~** there is no clue as to the whereabouts of the persons responsible; **der Täter hat keine ~en hinterlassen** the culprit left no traces; **auf der richtigen/falschen ~ sein** (*lit, fig*) to be on the right/wrong track; **jdm/einer Sache auf der ~ sein/auf die ~ kommen** to be/get onto sb/sth; **~en hinterlassen** (*fig*) to leave one's/its mark; **nicht ohne ~(en) an jdm vorübergehen** to leave its mark on sb

(b) (*fig:* = *kleine Menge*) trace; (*von Vernunft, Talent etc*) scrap; **von Anstand/Takt keine ~** (*inf*) no decency/tact at all; **von Liebe keine ~** (*inf*) love doesn't/didn't come into it; **keine ~!** (*inf*) not at all; **keine ~ davon ist wahr** (*inf*) there's not a scrap of truth in it; **wir hatten nicht die ~ einer Chance** we didn't have a ghost of a chance (*inf*); **eine ~ zu laut/grell** a touch too loud/garish

(c) (= *Fahrbahn*) lane

(d) (*Comput*) track

spürbar 1 ADJ noticeable, perceptible **2** ADV noticeably, perceptibly

spuren [ˈʃpuːrən] VI (*Ski*) to make a track; (*Aut*) to track; (*inf*) to obey; (= *sich fügen*) to toe the line; **bei dem Lehrer wird gespurt** (*inf*) he makes you obey, that teacher

spüren [ˈʃpyːrən] **1** VT to feel; **sie ließ mich ihr Missfallen ~** she made no attempt to hide her displeasure; **etw in allen Gliedern ~** (*lit, fig*) to feel sth in every bone of one's body; **davon ist nichts zu ~** there is no sign of it; **etw zu ~ bekommen** (*lit*) to feel sth; (*fig*) to feel the (full) force of sth; *jds Spott, Anerkennung etc* to meet with sth; **es zu ~ bekommen, dass ...** to feel the effects of the fact that ... **2** VTI (*Hunt*) (*nach*) **etw ~** to track sth

Spuren-: Spurenelement NT trace element; **Spurensicherung** F securing of evidence; **die Leute von der ~** the forensic people

Spürhund M tracker dog; (*inf: Mensch*) sleuth

spurlos ADJ, ADV without trace; **das ist nicht ~ an ihm vorübergegangen** it left its mark on him

Spurrille F (*Mot*) rut

Spürsinn M, NO PL (*Hunt*) (*fig*) nose; (*fig:* = *Gefühl*) feel

Spurt [ʃpʊrt] M **-s, -s** or **-e** spurt; (= *Endspurt, fig*) final spurt; **zum ~ ansetzen** (*lit, fig*) to make a final spurt

Spur-: Spurwechsel M (*Mot*) lane change; **Spurweite** F (*Rail*) gauge; (*Aut*) track

Squash [skvɔʃ] NT -, NO PL squash

Squash- [skvɔʃ-]: **Squashhalle** F squash courts *pl*; **Squashschläger** M squash racket

Sri Lanka [sriˈlaŋka] NT -, -s Sri Lanka

Srilanker [sriˈlaŋkɐ] M **-s, -**, **Srilankerin** [-ərɪn] F -, **-nen** Sri Lankan

srilankisch [sriˈlaŋkɪʃ] ADJ Sri Lankan

SS¹ [ɛsˈlɛs] NT -, - (*Univ*) ABBR *von* **Sommersemester**

SS² [ɛsˈlɛs] F -, NO PL (*NS*) ABBR *von* **Schutzstaffel** SS

SSV [ɛslɛsˈfau] M **-s, -s** ABBR *von* **Sommerschlussverkauf**

s. t. [ɛsˈteː] ADV ABBR *von* **sine tempore**

St. 1 ABBR *von* **Stück 2** ABBR *von* **Sankt** St

Staat [ʃtaːt] M **-(e)s, -en (a)** state; (= *Land*) country; **die ~en** (*inf*) the States (*inf*); **ein ~ im ~e** a state within a state; **von ~s wegen** on a governmental level; **zum Wohl des ~es** for the good of the nation; **beim ~ arbeiten** or **sein** (*inf*) to be employed by the state **(b)** (= *Ameisenstaat, Bienenstaat*) colony **(c)** (*fig*) (= *Pracht*) pomp; (= *Kleidung, Schmuck*) finery; **(großen) ~ machen (mit etw)** to make a show (of sth); **damit ist kein ~ zu machen** that's nothing to write home about (*inf*)

Staaten-: Staatenbund M, *pl* **-bünde** confederation (of states); **staatenlos** ADJ stateless; **Staatenlose(r)** [ˈʃtaːtnloːzə] MF DECL AS ADJ stateless person

staatl. gepr. ABBR *von* **staatlich geprüft**

staatlich [ˈʃtaːtlɪç] **1** ADJ state *attr*; (= ~ *geführt*) state-run **2** ADV by the state; **~ subventioniert** state-subsidized; **~ anerkannt** state-approved; **~ geprüft** state-certified

staatlicherseits [ˈʃtaːtlɪçɐzaɪts] ADV on the part of the state

Staats-: Staatsaffäre F **(a)** (*lit*) affair of state **(b)** (*fig*) major operation; **Staatsaktion** F major operation; **Staatsangehörige(r)** MF DECL AS ADJ national; **Staatsangehörigkeit** [-laŋɡəhøːrɪçkaɪt] F -, **-en** nationality; **Staatsanleihe** F government bond; **Staatsanwalt** M,

Staatsanwältin F district attorney (US), public prosecutor (esp Brit); **Staatsausgaben** PL public expenditure sing; **Staatsbeamte(r)** M DECL AS ADJ, **Staatsbeamtin** F public servant; **Staatsbegräbnis** NT state funeral; **Staatsbesuch** M state visit; **Staatsbürger(in)** M(F) citizen; **staatsbürgerlich** ADJ ATTR Pflicht civic; Rechte civil; **Staatsbürgerschaft** F nationality; **doppelte ~** dual nationality; **Staatschef(in)** M(F) head of state; **Staatsdienst** M civil service; **staatseigen** ADJ state-owned; **Staatsempfang** M state reception; **Staatsexamen** NT university degree required for the teaching profession

STAATSEXAMEN

The **Staatsexamen**, or Staatsprüfung to give it its official name, is an examination set by state-run examination boards. It has to be taken by everyone trying to get into certain professions, such as those of lawyer, teacher, doctor, pharmacist or nurse. A course of study, if required, leads to the first **Staatsexamen**. This is followed by a two- to three-year period of practical training and the second **Staatsexamen** or, in the case of doctors and pharmacists, the **Approbation**.

Staats-: Staatsfeind(in) M(F) enemy of the state; **staatsfeindlich** 🔢 ADJ Person, Gruppe hostile to the state; Tätigkeit, Hetze against the state 🔢 ADV **sich ~ betätigen** to engage in activities hostile to the state; **Staatsform** F type of state; **Staatsgeheimnis** NT (lit, fig hum) state secret; **Staatsgelder** PL public funds pl; **Staatshoheit** F sovereignty; **Staatskosten** PL public expenses pl; **auf ~** at the public expense; **Staatsmann** M, pl -männer statesman; **staatsmännisch** [-menɪʃ] 🔢 ADJ statesmanlike 🔢 ADV in a statesmanlike manner; **Staatsoberhaupt** NT head of state; **Staatspräsident(in)** M(F) president; **Staatsrat¹** M council of state; (Sw) cantonal government; **Staatsrat²** M, **Staatsrätin** F councillor (Brit) or councilor (US) of state; (Sw) member of the cantonal government; **Staatsschuld** F (Fin) national debt; **Staatssekretär(in)** M(F) (= Beamter) ≈ permanent secretary (Brit), ≈ undersecretary (US); **Staatssicherheit** F state security; **Staatssicherheitsdienst** M (DDR) state security service; **Staatsstreich** M coup (d'état); **Staatsverbrechen** NT political crime; (fig) major crime; **Staatsverschuldung** F national debt; **Staatsvertrag** M international treaty

Stab [ʃtaːp] M -(e)s, ⁼e [ˈʃtɛːbə] (a) rod; (= Gitterstab) bar; (= Spazierstock, Wanderstab) stick; (= Hirtenstab) crook; (= Dirigentenstab, für Staffellauf etc) baton; (für ~hochsprung, = Zeltstab) pole; (= Zauberstab) wand; **den ~ über jdn brechen** (fig) to condemn sb (b) (= Mitarbeiterstab) (Mil) staff; (von Experten) panel; (Mil: = Hauptquartier) headquarters sing or pl

Stäbchen [ˈʃtɛːpçən] NT -s, - DIM von Stab (= Essstäbchen) chopstick

Stab-: Stabdiagramm NT bar chart, histogram; **Stabhochspringer(in)** M(F) pole-vaulter; **Stabhochsprung** M pole vault

stabil [ʃtaˈbiːl, st-] 🔢 ADJ Möbel, Schuhe, Kind sturdy; Währung, Beziehung, Charakter stable; Gesundheit sound; (euph: = korpulent) well-built 🔢 ADV gebaut sturdily

Stabilisation [ʃtabiliˈzaˈtsioːn, st-] F **-, -en** stabilization

Stabilisator [ʃtabiliˈzaːtoːɐ, st-] M **-s, Stabilisatoren** [-ˈtoːrən] stabilizer

stabilisieren [ʃtabiliˈziːrən, st-], ptp **stabilisiert** 🔢 VT to stabilize 🔢 VR to stabilize, to become stable

Stabilität [ʃtabiliˈtɛːt, st-] F **-, NO PL** stability

Stab-: Stablampe F (electric) torch (Brit), flashlight; **Stabreim** M alliteration

stach PRET von stechen

Stachel [ˈʃtaxl̩] M **-s, -n** (von Rosen, Ginster etc) thorn; (von Kakteen, ~häutern, Igel) spine; (von ~schwein) quill; (auf ~draht) barb; (= Giftstachel: von Bienen etc) sting

Stachelbeere F gooseberry

Stacheldraht M barbed wire

Stacheldraht-: Stacheldrahtverhau M barbed-wire entanglement; **Stacheldrahtzaun** M barbed-wire fence

stachelig [ˈʃtaxəlɪç] ADJ Rosen, Ginster etc thorny; Kaktus, Igel etc spiny; (= sich ~ anfühlend) prickly; Kinn, Bart bristly

Stachelschwein NT porcupine

Stadel [ˈʃtaːdl̩] M **-s, -** (S Ger, Aus, Sw) barn

Stadion [ˈʃtaːdiɔn] NT **-s, Stadien** [-diən] stadium

Stadium [ˈʃtaːdiʊm] NT **-s, Stadien** [-diən] stage; **er hat Krebs im vorgerückten/letzten ~** he has advanced/terminal cancer

Vorsicht! **Stadium** wird nicht mit dem englischen Wort **stadium** übersetzt.

Stadt [ʃtat] F **-, ⁼e** [ˈʃtɛːtə, ˈʃtɛtə] (a) town; (= Großstadt) city; **die ~ Paris** the city of Paris; **Mexiko-~** Mexico City; **~ und Land** town and country; **in die ~ gehen** to go into town (b) (= ~verwaltung) (town) council; (von Großstadt) (city) council; **bei der ~ angestellt sein** to be working for the council; **die ~ Ulm** Ulm City Council

städt. ABBR von städtisch

Stadt-: stadtauswärts ADV out of town; **für den Verkehr ~ gesperrt** closed to traffic going out of town; **Stadtautobahn** F urban motorway (Brit) or freeway (US); **Stadtbad** NT municipal swimming pool; **Stadtbahn** F suburban railway (Brit), city railroad (US); **stadtbekannt** ADJ well-known, known all over town; **Stadtbewohner(in)** M(F) town dweller (esp Brit) or resident; (von Großstadt) city dweller (esp Brit) or resident; **~ pl** townspeople pl; (von Großstadt) city people pl; **Stadtbezirk** M municipal district; **Stadtbücherei** F public library; **Stadtbummel** M stroll through town

Städtchen [ˈʃtɛːtçən, ˈʃtɛtçən] NT **-s, -** DIM von Stadt small town

Städte-: Städtebau M, NO PL urban development; **städtebaulich** 🔢 ADJ Entwicklung of urban building; Maßnahme for urban development; Veränderungen in urban development 🔢 ADV as regards urban development

stadteinwärts ADV into town; **für den Verkehr ~ gesperrt** closed to traffic going into town

Städte-: Städtepartnerschaft F town twinning (Brit), sister city agreement (US); **Städteplanung** F town planning

Städter [ˈʃtɛːtɐ, ˈʃtɛtɐ] M **-s, -**, **Städterin** [-ərɪn] F **-, -nen** town resident; (= Großstädter) city resident

Städtetag M convention or congress of municipal authorities

Stadtgespräch NT (a) (das) **~ sein** to be the talk of the town (b) (Telec) local call

städtisch [ˈʃtɛːtɪʃ, ˈʃtɛtɪʃ] ADJ municipal, town attr; (= einer Großstadt auch) city attr; (= nach Art einer Stadt) urban; **die ~e Bevölkerung** the town/city or urban population

Stadt-: Stadtkasse F siehe Stadt (a) town/city treasury; **Stadtkern** M siehe Stadt (a) town/city centre (Brit) or center (US); **Stadtkreis** M siehe Stadt (a) town/city borough; **Stadtmauer** F city wall; **Stadtmitte** F siehe Stadt (a) town/city centre (Brit) or center (US); **Stadtplan** M siehe Stadt (a) (street) map (of a/the town/city); (Archit) town/city plan; **Stadtplanung** F town planning; **Stadtrand** M siehe Stadt (a) outskirts pl (of a/the town/city); **am ~** on the outskirts (of the town/city); **Stadtrandsiedlung** F suburban housing scheme; **Stadtrat¹** M siehe Stadt (a) (town/city) council; **Stadtrat²** M, **Stadträtin** F siehe Stadt (a) (town/city) councillor (Brit) or councilor (US); **Stadtrundfahrt** F siehe Stadt (a) (sightseeing) tour of a/the town/city; **eine ~ machen** to go on a (sightseeing) tour of a/the town/city; **Stadtstaat** M city state; **Stadtstreicher** [-ʃtraɪçɐ] M **-s, -**, **Stadtstreicherin** [-ərɪn] F **-, -nen** siehe Stadt (a) (town/city) tramp; **Stadtstreicherei** [-ʃtraɪçəˈraɪ] F **-, NO PL** urban vagrancy; **Stadtteil** M district; **Stadtverwaltung** F siehe Stadt (a) (town/city) council; **Stadtwerke** PL siehe Stadt (a) town's/city's department of works; **Stadtzentrum** NT siehe Stadt (a) town/city centre (Brit) or center (US)

Staffel [ˈʃtafl̩] F **-, -n** (a) (= Formation) (Mil, Naut, Aviat) echelon; (Aviat: = Einheit) squadron; **~ fliegen** to fly in echelon formation (b) (Sport) relay (race); (= Mannschaft) relay team; (fig) relay; **~ laufen/schwimmen** to run/swim in a relay (race)

Staffelei [ʃtafəˈlaɪ] F **-, -en** easel

Staffellauf M relay (race)

staffeln [ˈʃtafl̩n] VT Gehälter, Tarife, Fahrpreise to grade; Anfangszeiten, Startplätze to stagger; **die Gehaltserhöhung wird zeitlich gestaffelt** the salary increase is being phased (over a period of time)

Staffelung [ˈʃtafəlʊŋ] F **-, -en**, **Stafflung** [ˈʃtaflʊŋ] F **-, -en** (von Gehältern, Tarifen, Preisen) grading; (von Zeiten, Startplätzen) staggering

Stagflation [ʃtakflaˈtsioːn, st-] F **-, -en** (Econ) stagflation

Stagnation [ʃtagnaˈtsioːn, st-] F **-, -en** stagnation; **es kam zu einer ~** there was a period of stagnation

stagnieren [ʃtaˈgniːrən, st-], *ptp* **stagniert** VI to stagnate

stahl PRET *von* **stehlen**

Stahl [ʃtaːl] M **-(e)s, -e** *or* **Stähle** [ˈʃtɛːlə] steel; **Nerven aus** *or* **wie ~** nerves of steel

Stahl- IN CPDS steel; **Stahlbeton** M reinforced concrete; **stahlblau** ADJ steel-blue

stählern [ˈʃtɛːlɛn] ADJ steel; (*fig*) *Muskeln, Wille* of iron, iron *attr*; *Nerven* of steel; *Blick* steely

Stahl-: Stahlhelm M (*Mil*) steel helmet; **Stahlhelm-Fraktion** F (*Pol*) hawks *pl*; **Stahlrohr** NT tubular steel; (*Stück*) steel tube; **Stahlrohrmöbel** PL tubular steel furniture *sing*; **Stahlträger** M steel girder; **Stahlwolle** F steel wool

Stakkato [ʃtaˈkaːto, st-] NT **-s, -s** *or* **Stakkati** [-ti] staccato

staksen [ˈʃtaːksn] VI AUX SEIN (*inf*) to stalk; (*unsicher*) to teeter; (*steif*) to hobble; **mit ~den Schritten gehen** to stalk/teeter/hobble

staksig [ˈʃtaːksɪç] **1** ADJ *Beine* spindly; (= *unbeholfen*) gawky **2** ADV **~ gehen** (= *steif*) to hobble; (= *unsicher*) to teeter; **jdm ~ entgegenkommen** to teeter toward(s) sb

Stalagmit [stalaˈgmiːt, ʃt-, -mɪt] M **-en** *or* **-s, -en** stalagmite

Stalaktit [stalakˈtiːt, ʃt-, -tɪt] M **-en** *or* **-s, -en** stalactite

Stalinismus [staliˈnɪsmʊs, ʃt-] M **-**, NO PL Stalinism

stalinistisch [staliˈnɪstɪʃ, ʃt-] **1** ADJ Stalinist **2** ADV *geführt* along Stalinist lines; in a Stalinist way; **~ klingend** Stalinist sounding; **~ gesinnt** Stalinist; **~ beeinflusst** influenced by (the teachings of) Stalin

Stall [ʃtal] M **-(e)s, -e** [ˈʃtɛlə] (*lit*) (*fig*) stable; (= *Kuhstall*) cowshed; (= *Hühnerstall*) henhouse; (= *Kaninchenstall*) hutch; (= *Schafstall*) (sheep)cote; (= *Schweinestall*) (pig)sty, (pig)pen (*US*); **ein (ganzer) ~ voll Kinder** (*inf*) a (whole) pack of children

Stallung [ˈʃtalʊŋ] F **-, -en, Stallungen** PL stables *pl*

Stamm [ʃtam] M **-(e)s, -e** [ˈʃtɛmə] (a) (= *Baumstamm*) trunk (b) (*Ling*) stem (c) (= *Volksstamm*) tribe; (= *Abstammung*) line; (= *Bakterienstamm*) strain (d) (= *Kern, fester Bestand*) regulars *pl*; (= *Kunden*) regular customers *pl*; (*von Mannschaft*) regular team members *pl*; (= *Arbeiter*) permanent workforce; (= *Angestellte*) permanent staff *pl*; **ein fester ~ von Kunden** regular customers

Stamm-: Stammaktie F (*St Ex*) ordinary share; **Stammbaum** M family tree; (*von Zuchttieren*) pedigree; **Stammbelegschaft** F permanent workforce; (= *Angestellte*) regular staff *pl*; **Stammbuch** NT (a) *book recording family events with some legal documents* (b) (*fig*) **jdm etw ins ~ schreiben** to make sb take note of sth; **Stammdaten** PL (*Comput*) master data

stammeln [ˈʃtamln] VTI to stammer

stammen [ˈʃtamən] VI to come (*von, aus* from); (*zeitlich*) to date (*von, aus* from); **die Bibliothek/Uhr stammt von seinem Großvater** the library/watch originally belonged to his grandfather

Stammes- IN CPDS tribal; **Stammesgenosse** M, **Stammesgenossin** F member of a/the tribe, tribesman/-woman; **Stammeszugehörigkeit** F tribal membership

Stamm-: Stammform F base form; **Stammgast** M regular; **Stammhalter** M son and heir

stämmig [ˈʃtɛmɪç] ADJ (= *gedrungen*) stocky; (= *kräftig*) sturdy

Stamm-: Stammkapital NT (*Fin*) ordinary share (*Brit*) *or* common stock (*US*) capital; **Stammkneipe** F (*inf*) local (*Brit inf*), local bar; **Stammkunde** M, **Stammkundin** F regular (customer); **Stammkundschaft** F regulars *pl*; **Stammland** NT place of origin; **Stammpersonal** NT permanent staff *pl*; **Stammplatz** M usual seat; **Stammsilbe** F radical; **Stammsitz** M (*von Firma*) headquarters *sing or pl*; (*von Geschlecht*) ancestral seat; (*im Theater etc*) regular seat; **Stammtisch** M (= *Tisch in Gasthaus*) table reserved for the regulars; (= *~runde*) group of regulars; **er hat mittwochs seinen ~** Wednesday is his night

for meeting his friends at the pub; **Stammtischpolitiker(in)** M(F) (*pej*) armchair politician

Stamm-: Stammwähler(in) M(F) (*Pol*) staunch supporter; **Stammzelle** F stem cell; **embryonale ~n** embryonic stem cells

stampfen **1** VI (a) (= *laut auftreten*) to stamp; (= *auf und nieder gehen: Maschine*) to pound; **mit dem Fuß ~** to stamp one's foot; **mit den Hufen ~** to paw (*Brit*) *or* stamp (*US*) the ground (with its hooves) (b) AUX SEIN (= *gehen*) (*mit schweren Schritten*) to tramp; (*wütend*) to stamp; (= *stapfen*) to trudge (c) AUX HABEN or SEIN (*Schiff*) to pitch, to toss **2** VT (a) (= *festtrampeln*) *Lehm, Sand* to stamp; *Trauben* to press; (*mit den Füßen*) to tread (b) (*mit Stampfer*) to mash; (*im Mörser*) to pound

stand PRET *von* **stehen**

Stand [ʃtant] M **-(e)s, -e** [ˈʃtɛndə] (a) NO PL (= *das Stehen*) standing position; (= *~fläche*) place to stand; (*für Gegenstand*) stand; **aus dem ~** from a standing position; **ein Sprung/Start aus dem ~** a standing jump/start; **bei jdm** *or* **gegen jdn/bei etw einen schweren ~ haben** (*fig*) to have a hard time with sb/in sth; **aus dem ~ (heraus)** (*fig inf*) off the cuff (b) (= *Marktstand etc*) stand; (= *Taxistand*) rank (c) NO PL (= *Lage*) state; (= *Niveau*) (*Fin*: = *Kurs*) level; (= *Zählerstand, Thermometerstand, Barometerstand etc*) reading; (= *Kassenstand, Kontostand*) balance; (*Sport*: = *Spielstand*) score; **beim jetzigen ~ der Dinge** the way things stand at the moment; **der neueste ~ der Forschung** the latest developments in research; **etw auf dem neuesten ~ bringen** to bring sth up to date; **auf dem neuesten ~ der Technik sein** (*Gerät*) to be state-of-the-art technology; **~ November 1997** as at November 1997; **außer ~e = außerstande; im ~e = imstande; in ~ = instand; zu ~e = zustande** (d) (= *soziale Stellung*) status; (= *Klasse*) class; (= *Beruf, Gewerbe*) profession

Standard [ˈʃtandart, ˈst-] M **-s, -s** standard

Standard- IN CPDS standard;

standardisieren [ʃtandardiˈziːrən, st-], *ptp* **standardisiert** VT to standardize

Standardisierung F **-, -en** standardization

Standardsituation F (*esp Ftbl*) set piece

Stand-: Standbein NT (*Sport*) pivot leg; (*Art*) standing leg; (*fig*) pillar; **Standbild** NT statue; (*TV*) freeze frame

Stand-by- [ˈstɛndbai] IN CPDS stand-by; **Stand-by-Betrieb** M (*Comput*) stand-by; **Stand-by-Modus** M (*Comput*) stand-by mode; **Stand-by-Ticket** NT (*Aviat*) stand-by ticket

Ständchen [ˈʃtɛntçən] NT **-s, -** serenade; **jdm ein ~ bringen** to serenade sb

Ständer [ˈʃtɛndɐ] M **-s, -** stand; (*inf*: = *Erektion*) hard-on (*sl*)

Ständerat¹ M (*Sw Parl*) upper chamber

Ständerat² M, **Ständerätin** F (*Sw Parl*) member of the upper chamber

Standes-: Standesamt NT registry office (*Brit*), *official building where civil marriages take place*; **auf dem ~** at the registry office (*Brit*); **standesamtlich** **1** ADJ **~e Trauung** civil wedding **2** ADV **sich ~ trauen lassen** to get married in a registry office (*Brit*), to have a civil wedding; **Standesbeamte(r)** M DECL AS ADJ, **Standesbeamtin** F registrar; **Standesunterschied** M class difference

Stand-: standfest ADJ *Tisch, Leiter* stable; (*fig*) steadfast; **Standfoto** NT still (photograph); **Standgeld** NT stallage; **Standgericht** NT (*Mil*) drumhead court martial; **vor ein ~ gestellt werden** *or* **kommen** to be summarily court-martialled (*Brit*) *or* court-martialed (*US*); **standhaft** ◨ ADJ steadfast ◨ ADV **etw ~ verteidigen** *or* **vertreten** to defend sth staunchly; **er weigerte sich ~, er lehnte ~ ab** he steadfastly refused; **Standhaftigkeit** [ˈʃtanthaftɪçkait] F -, NO PL steadfastness; **standhalten** [ˈʃtanthaltn] VI SEP IRREG (*Mensch*) to stand firm; (*Gebäude, Brücke etc*) to hold; **jdm ~** to stand up to sb; **einer Sache** (*dat*) **~** to withstand sth; **der Versuchung** (*dat*) **~** to resist temptation; **einer/der Prüfung ~** to stand up to close examination; **Standheizung** F (*Aut*) stationary heating

ständig [ˈʃtɛndɪç] ◨ ADJ (a) (= *dauernd*) permanent; *Praxis, Regel* established; *Korrespondent* (*von Zeitung*) resident (b) (= *unaufhörlich*) constant ◨ ADV (a) (= *andauernd*) constantly; **sie beklagt sich ~** she's always complaining; **sie ist ~ krank** she's always ill; **passiert das oft? – ~** does it happen often? – all the time (b) (= *permanent*) **wohnen** permanently; **sich ~ niederlassen** to settle (down)

Standleitung F (*Telec*) direct line
Standlicht NT sidelights *pl*; **mit ~ fahren** to drive on sidelights
Standort M, *pl* **-orte** location; (*von Schütze, Schiff etc*) position; (*Mil*) garrison; (*Bot*) habitat; (*von Pflanzungen, Industriebetrieb*) site; (*fig*) position
Standort-: Standortfaktor M USU PL (*Econ*) locational factor; **Standortwahl** F (*Comm*) choice of site or location
Stand-: Standpunkt M (= *Meinung*) point of view; **auf dem ~ stehen** *or* **den ~ vertreten** *or* **sich auf den ~ stellen, dass ...** to take the view that ...; **von meinem ~ aus** from my point of view; **das ist vielleicht ein ~!** (*iro*) what kind of attitude is that!; **Standspur** F (*Aut*) hard shoulder (*Brit*), shoulder (*US*); **Standuhr** F grandfather clock

Stange [ˈʃtaŋə] F **-, -n (a)** (= *langer, runder Stab*) pole; (= *Querstab*) bar; (= *Ballettstange*) barre; (= *Kleiderstange, Teppichstange*) rail; (= *Gardinenstange, Leiste für Treppenläufer*) rod; (= *Vogelstange*) perch; (= *Hühnerstange*) roost; (*fig*: = *dünner Mensch*) beanpole (*inf*) **(b)** (= *länglicher Gegenstand*) stick; **eine ~ Zigaretten** a carton of 200 cigarettes **(c)** (*Redewendungen*) **ein Anzug von der ~** a suit off the peg (*Brit*) *or* rack (*US*); **etw von der ~ kaufen** to buy off the peg (*Brit*) *or* rack (*US*); **jdn bei der ~ halten** (*inf*) to keep sb; **bei der ~ bleiben** (*inf*) to stick at it (*inf*); **jdm die ~ halten** (*inf*) to stand up for sb; **eine (schöne** *or* **ganze) ~ Geld** (*inf*) a tidy sum (*inf*)

Stängel [ˈʃtɛŋl] M **-s, -** stem
Stangen-: Stangenbohne F runner (*Brit*) *or* pole (*US*) bean; **Stangenbrot** NT French bread; (= *Laib*) French loaf; **Stangensellerie** M or F celery
stank PRET *von* **stinken**
Stanniol [ʃtaˈnioːl, st-] NT **-s, -e** silver foil
Stanniolpapier NT silver paper
Stanze [ˈʃtantsə] F **-, -n** (*für Prägestempel, Bleche*) die; (= *Lochstanze*) punch
stanzen [ˈʃtantsn] VT to press; (= *prägen*) to stamp; *Löcher* to punch
Stapel [ˈʃtaːpl] M **-s, - (a)** (= *geschichteter Haufen*, fig: = *Vorrat*) stack **(b)** (*Comm*) (= *~platz*) store **(c)** (*Naut*: = *Schiffsstapel*) stocks *pl*; **auf ~ legen** to lay down; **auf ~ liegen** to be on the stocks; **vom ~ laufen** to be launched; **vom ~ lassen** to launch; (*fig*) to come out with (*inf*)
Stapellauf M (*Naut*) launching
stapeln [ˈʃtaːpln] ◨ VT to stack; (= *lagern*) to store ◨ VR to pile up
Stapelung [ˈʃtaːpəlʊŋ] F **-, -en** stacking; (= *Lagerung*) storing
Stapel-: Stapelverarbeitung F (*Comput*) batch processing; **Stapelware** F staple commodity
Stapfe [ˈʃtapfə] F **-, -n, Stapfen** [ˈʃtapfn] M **-s, -** footprint
stapfen [ˈʃtapfn] VI AUX SEIN to trudge
Star[1] [ʃtaːɐ] M **-(e)s, -e** (*Orn*) starling
Star[2] [ʃtaːɐ] M **-(e)s, -e** (*Med*) **grauer ~** cataract; **grüner ~** glaucoma; **schwarzer ~** amaurosis (*spec*); **jdm den ~ stechen** (*fig*) to tell sb some home truths
Star[3] [ʃtaːɐ, staːɐ] M **-s, -s** (*Film etc*) star
Starallüren [ˈʃtaːɐ-, ˈstaːɐ-] PL (*inf*) airs and graces *pl*
starb PRET *von* **sterben**

Starbesetzung [ˈʃtaːɐ-, ˈstaːɐ-] F star cast
Starenkasten M **(a)** nesting box (for starlings) **(b)** (*Aut inf*: = *Überwachungsanlage*) police camera
Star- [ˈʃtaːɐ-, ˈstaːɐ-] (*Press*): **Stargage** F top fee; **Stargast** M star guest

stark [ʃtark] ◨ ADJ, *comp* ⁼**er** [ˈʃtɛrkə], *superl* ⁼**ste(r, s)** [ˈʃtɛrkstə] **(a)** (= *kräftig, konzentriert*) strong (*auch Gram*); **~ bleiben** to be strong; (*im Glauben*) to hold firm; **sich für etw ~ machen** (*inf*) to stand up for sth; **den ~en Mann spielen** *or* **markieren** *or* **mimen** (*all inf*) to play the big guy (*inf*); **das ist seine ~e Seite** that is his strong point; **das ist ~** *or* **ein ~es Stück!** (*inf*) that's a bit much!
(b) (= *dick*) thick; (*euph*: = *korpulent*) *Dame, Herr* large, well-built (*euph*); *Arme, Beine* large; **Kostüme für stärkere Damen** suits for the fuller figure
(c) (= *beträchtlich, heftig*) *Schmerzen, Kälte* intense; *Frost* severe; *Regen, Schneefall, Verkehr, Raucher, Trinker, Druck* heavy; *Sturm* violent; *Erkältung* bad; *Wind, Strömung, Eindruck* strong; *Appetit, Esser* hearty; *Beifall* loud; *Fieber, Nachfrage* high; *Trauer, Schmerz* deep; *Übertreibung, Widerhall, Bedenken* considerable; **~e Abneigung** strong dislike
(d) (= *leistungsfähig*) *Motor* powerful; *Sportler* able; *Mannschaft, Brille, Arznei* strong; **er ist in Englisch nicht sehr ~** he's quite weak in English
(e) (= *zahlreich*) *Auflage, Gefolge* large; *Nachfrage* great; **wir hoffen auf ~e Beteiligung** we are hoping that a large number of people will take part; **zehn Mann ~** ten strong; **300 Seiten ~** 300 pages long
(f) (*inf*: = *hervorragend*) *Leistung, Werk* great (*inf*)
◨ ADV, *comp* ⁼**er** [ˈʃtɛrkə], *superl* **am** ⁼**sten (a)** (*mit vb*) a lot; (*mit adj, ptp*) very; *applaudieren* loudly; *pressen, drücken, ziehen* hard; *regnen* heavily; *beeindruckt, vergrößert, verkleinert* greatly; *vertreten, dagegen sein* strongly; *abgenutzt, beschmutzt, beschädigt, entzündet etc* badly; *bluten* profusely; **es hat ~ gestürmt** there was a severe storm; **~ wirken** to have a strong effect; **~ wirkend** *Medikament, Alkohol* potent; **~ gesalzen** very salty; **~ gewürzt** highly spiced; **~ verschuldet** heavily in debt; **~ behaart sein** to be very hairy; **stärker befahrene Straßen** busier roads; **die Ausstellung wurde ~ besucht** the exhibition was well attended; **Frauen sind stärker vertreten** there are more women
(b) (*inf*: = *hervorragend*) really well

Vorsicht! **stark** *wird nicht mit dem englischen Wort* **stark** *übersetzt.*

Starkbier NT strong beer
Stärke[1] [ˈʃtɛrkə] F **-, -n (a)** strength (*auch fig*); (*von Stimme, Land, Regierung*) power
(b) (= *Dicke, Durchmesser*) thickness
(c) (= *Heftigkeit*) (*von Strömung, Wind, Einfluss*) strength; (*von Eindruck, Leid, Kälte, Schmerzen, Druck*) intensity; (*von Regen, Verkehr*) heaviness; (*von Sturm, Abneigung*) violence
(d) (= *Leistungsfähigkeit*) (*von Motor*) power; (*von Sportmannschaft, Arznei, Brille*) strength
(e) (= *Anzahl*) (*von Gefolge, Heer, Mannschaft, Klasse*) size; (*von Beteiligung, Nachfrage*) level
(f) (*fig*: = *starke Seite*) strength
Stärke[2] F **-, -n** (*Chem*) starch
Stärkemehl NT (*Cook*) ≈ cornflour (*Brit*), ≈ cornstarch (*US*)
stärken [ˈʃtɛrkn] ◨ VT **(a)** (= *kräftigen*) (lit, fig) to strengthen; *Selbstbewusstsein* to boost; *Gesundheit* to improve; **gestärkt** *Mensch* strengthened **(b)** (= *erfrischen*) to fortify **(c)** *Wäsche* to starch ◨ VI to be fortifying; **das stärkt** it fortifies you; **~des Mittel** tonic ◨ VR to fortify oneself
Starkstrom M (*Elec*) heavy current
Stärkung [ˈʃtɛrkʊŋ] F **-, -en (a)** strengthening (*auch fig*); (*des Selbstbewusstseins*) boosting; **das dient der ~ der Gesundheit** it is beneficial to the health **(b)** (= *Erfrischung*) refreshment; **eine ~ zu sich nehmen** to take some refreshment
Stärkungsmittel NT (*Med*) tonic
starr [ʃtar] ◨ ADJ **(a)** stiff; (= *unbeweglich*) rigid; **~ vor Frost** stiff with frost; **meine Finger sind vor Kälte ganz ~** my fingers are frozen stiff
(b) (= *unbewegt*) *Augen* glassy; *Blick* fixed
(c) (= *regungslos*) paralyzed; **~ vor Schrecken/Entsetzen** paralyzed with fear/horror
(d) (= *nicht flexibel*) inflexible

⊠ ADV (a) (= *unbeweglich*) ~ **miteinander verbunden** joined rigidly; ~ **abstehen** to stand up stiffly
(b) (= *bewegungslos*) *lächeln* stiffly; **jdn ~ ansehen** to stare at sb
(c) (= *rigide*) ~ **an etw** (*dat*) **festhalten** to cling to sth

Starre ['ʃtarə] F -, NO PL stiffness

starren ['ʃtarən] VI (a) (= *starr blicken*) to stare (*auf* +*acc* at); **ins Leere** ~ to stare into space; **vor sich** (*acc*) **hin** ~ to stare straight ahead (b) **von Gewehren** ~ to bristle with guns; **vor Dreck** ~ to be covered with dirt; (*Kleidung*) to be stiff with dirt; **Moskau starrt vor Kälte** Moscow is in the grip of the cold

Starrheit F -, NO PL (a) (*von Gegenstand*) rigidity
(b) (= *Sturheit*) inflexibility

Starr-: starrköpfig 🔳 ADJ stubborn 🔳 ADV stubbornly; **Starrsinn** M, NO PL stubbornness; **starrsinnig** 🔳 ADJ stubborn 🔳 ADV stubbornly

Start [ʃtart] M -s, -s (a) (*lit, fig*) start; **das Zeichen zum ~ geben** to give the starting signal; **einen guten/schlechten ~ haben** to get (off to) a good/bad start (b) (= *~platz, ~linie*) start(ing line); (*bei Pferderennen*) start(ing post); (*bei Autorennen*) (starting) grid (c) (*Aviat*) takeoff; (= *Raketenstart*) launch; (= *~platz*) runway; **der Maschine den ~ freigeben** to clear the plane for takeoff

Start-: Startautomatik F (*Aut*) automatic choke; **Startbahn** F (*Aviat*) runway; **Start- und Landebahn** runway; **Startblock** M, pl **-blöcke** (*Sport*) starting block

starten ['ʃtartn] 🔳 VI AUX SEIN to start; (*Aviat*) to take off; (= *zum Start antreten*) to take part; (*bei Pferde-/Autorennen*) to race; (*inf*: = *abreisen*) to set off; **in die letzte Runde** ~ to go into the last lap 🔳 VT to start; *Satelliten, Rakete* to launch; *Expedition* to get under way; **den Computer neu** ~ to restart the computer

Starter ['ʃtartɐ] M -s, - (*Aut*) starter

Start-: Starterlaubnis F (*Sport*) permission to take part; (*Aviat*) clearance for takeoff; **Starthilfe** F (*Aviat*) rocket-assisted takeoff; (*fig*) initial aid; **im Winter braucht mein Auto** ~ my car won't start on its own in winter; **jdm ~ geben** to help sb get off the ground; **Starthilfekabel** NT jump leads pl (*Brit*), jumper cables pl (*US*); **Startkapital** NT starting capital; **startklar** ADJ (*Aviat*) clear(ed) for takeoff; (*Sport, fig*) ready to start; **Startrampe** F (*Space*) launch(ing) pad; **Startschuss** M (*Sport*) starting signal; (*fig*) signal (*zu* for); **vor dem** ~ before the gun; **den** ~ **geben** to fire the (starting) pistol; (*fig*) to open the door; (= *Erlaubnis geben*) to give the go-ahead; **Startseite** F (*im Internet*) start page

Stasi ['ʃtaːzi] M -, NO PL (*DDR*) ABBR *von* **Staatssicherheitsdienst** Stasi

Statik ['ʃtaːtɪk, 'st-] F -, NO PL (a) (*Sci*) statics *sing* (b) (*Build*) structural engineering

Statiker ['ʃtaːtikɐ, 'st-] M -s, -, **Statikerin** [-ərɪn] F -, -nen (*Tech*) structural engineer

Station [ʃtaˈtsioːn] F -, -en (a) station; (= *Haltestelle*) stop; (*fig*: = *Abschnitt*) (*von Reise*) stage; (*von Leben*) phase; ~ **machen** to stop off (b) (= *Krankenstation*) ward

stationär [ʃtatsioˈnɛːɐ] 🔳 ADJ (*Astron, Comput, Sociol*) stationary; (*Med*) *Behandlung, Pflegeeinrichtungen* inpatient *attr*; **~er Patient** inpatient 🔳 ADV *entbinden* in hospital; **jdn ~ behandeln** to treat sb in hospital *or* as an inpatient; **jdn ~ einweisen** to hospitalize sb

stationieren [ʃtatsioˈniːrən], *ptp* **stationiert** VT *Truppen, Beobachter* to station; *Atomwaffen etc* to deploy

Stationierung F -, -en (*von Truppen*) stationing; (*von Atomwaffen etc*) deployment

Stations-: Stationsarzt M, **Stationsärztin** F ward doctor; **Stationsschwester** F senior nurse (*in a ward*)

statisch ['ʃtaːtɪʃ, 'st-] 🔳 ADJ (*lit, fig*) static; *Gesetze* of statics 🔳 ADV **das Gebäude ist** ~ **einwandfrei** the building is

structurally sound; **die Brücke ist** ~ **falsch berechnet** the design of this bridge is structurally unsound; **etw** ~ **berechnen** to do the structural design work for sth; **meine Haare haben sich** ~ **aufgeladen** my hair is full of static electricity

Statist [ʃtaˈtɪst] M **-en, -en**, **Statistin** [-ˈtɪstɪn] F -, -nen (*Film*) extra; (*Theat*) supernumerary; (*fig*) cipher; **er war nur ein kleiner** ~ (*fig*) he only played a minor role

Statistik [ʃtaˈtɪstɪk] F -, -en statistics *sing*; **eine** ~ a set of statistics; **die ~en** the statistics *pl*

Statistiker [ʃtaˈtɪstikɐ] M **-s, -**, **Statistikerin** [-ərɪn] F -, -nen statistician

Statistin F *siehe* Statist

statistisch [ʃtaˈtɪstɪʃ] 🔳 ADJ statistical; **~es Amt** statistics office 🔳 ADV statistically; ~ **gesehen** statistically

Stativ [ʃtaˈtiːf] NT **-s, -e** [-və] tripod

statt [ʃtat] 🔳 PREP +GEN or (*INF*) +DAT instead of; ~ **meiner/ seiner/ihrer** *etc* instead of me/him/her *etc*; **an Kindes ~ annehmen** (*Jur*) to adopt; *siehe auch* **stattdessen** 🔳 CONJ instead of; ~ **zu bleiben, wollte ich lieber ...** rather than stay I wanted to ...

stattdessen ADV instead

Stätte ['ʃtɛtə] F -, -n place

Statt-: stattfinden ['ʃtatfɪndn] VI SEP IRREG to take place; **stattgeben** ['ʃtatgeːbn] VI SEP IRREG +DAT (*form*) to grant; **statthaft** ['ʃtathaft] ADJ PRED permitted

stattlich ['ʃtatlɪç] ADJ (a) (= *hochgewachsen, ansehnlich*) *Tier, Gebäude, Anwesen, Park* magnificent; *Bursche* strapping; (= *eindrucksvoll*) *Erscheinung, Fünfziger* imposing; **ein ~er Mann** a fine figure of a man (b) (= *umfangreich*) *Sammlung* impressive; *Familie* large; (= *beträchtlich*) handsome

Statue ['ʃtaːtuə, 'st-] F -, -n statue

statuieren [ʃtatuˈiːrən, st-], *ptp* **statuiert** VT **ein Exempel an jdm** ~ to make an example of sb; **ein Exempel mit etw** ~ to use sth as a warning; **um ein Exempel zu** ~ as an example to others

Statur [ʃtaˈtuːɐ] F -, -en build

Status ['ʃtaːtʊs, 'st-] M -, - [-tuːs] status; ~ **quo** status quo; ~ **quo ante** status quo

Status-: Statussymbol NT status symbol; **Statuszeile** F (*Comput*) status line

Stau [ʃtau] M **-(e)s, -e** *or* **-s (a)** (= *Wasserstauung*) build-up; (= *Windstau*) barrier effect; (= *Verkehrsstauung*) traffic jam; **ein ~ von 3 km** a 3km tailback (*Brit*), a 3km backup (of traffic) (*US*) (b) = **Stauung**

Staub [ʃtaup] M **-(e)s, -e** *or* **Stäube** [-bə, 'ʃtɔybə] dust; (*Bot*) pollen; ~ **saugen** to vacuum, to hoover® (*Brit*); ~ **wischen** to dust; **vor jdm im** ~ **kriechen** (*lit, fig*) to grovel before sb; **sich aus dem ~(e) machen** (*inf*) to clear off (*inf*)

Staubecken NT reservoir

stäuben ['ʃtɔybn] VT *Mehl/Puder etc* **auf etw** (*acc*) ~ to dust sth with flour/powder *etc* (*esp Brit*)

Stauberater(in) M(F) traffic problem adviser

staubig ['ʃtaubɪç] ADJ dusty

Staub-: Staublappen M duster; **Staublunge** F (*Med*) dust on the lung; (*von Kohlenstaub*) black lung; **staubsaugen** ['ʃtaupzaʊgn], *ptp* **staubgesaugt** ['ʃtaupgəzaukt] VI INSEP to vacuum, to hoover® (*Brit*); **Staubsauger** M vacuum cleaner, Hoover® (*Brit*); **Staubschicht** F layer of dust; **Staubtuch** NT, pl **-tücher** duster; **Staubwolke** F cloud of dust

stauchen ['ʃtauxn] VT to compress (*auch Tech*)

Staudamm M dam

Staude ['ʃtaudə] F -, -n (*Hort*) herbaceous perennial (plant); (= *Busch*) shrub; (= *Bananenstaude, Tabakstaude, Rosenkohlstaude*) plant

stauen ['ʃtauən] 🔳 VT *Wasser, Fluss* to dam (up); *Blut* to stop the flow of 🔳 VR (= *sich anhäufen*) to pile up; (= *ins Stocken geraten*) to get jammed; (*Verkehr, Wasser*) (*fig*) to build up; (*Blut*) to accumulate; (*durch Abbinden*) to be cut off; **die Menschen stauten sich in den Gängen** people were jamming the corridors; **der Verkehr staute sich** *or* **die Autos stauten sich über eine Strecke von 2 km** there was a 2km tailback (*Brit*) *or* backup (of traffic) (*US*)

Stau-: Staugefahr F risk of congestion; „~" "delays likely"; **Staumauer** F dam wall

staunen [ˈʃtaunən] VI to be astonished (*über +acc* at); **~d** in astonishment; **ich staune(, ich staune)!** (*inf*) well, I never!; **man staunt, wie ...** it's amazing how ...; **da kann man nur noch ~** it's just amazing; **da staunst du, was?** (*inf*) you didn't expect that, did you!; **da hat er nicht schlecht gestaunt** (*inf*) he was flabbergasted (*inf*)

Staunen NT **-s**, NO PL astonishment (*über +acc* at); **jdn in ~ versetzen** to amaze sb

staunenswert **1** ADJ astonishing **2** ADV astonishingly

Stau-: **Stauraum** M storage space; **Stausee** M reservoir

Stauung [ˈʃtauʊŋ] F **-, -en (a)** (= *Stockung*) pile-up; (*in Lieferungen, Post etc*) hold-up; (*von Menschen*) jam; (*von Verkehr*) tailback (*Brit*), backup (*US*); **eine ~ des Verkehrs** a traffic jam **(b)** (*von Wasser*) build-up (of water); **zur ~ eines Flusses** to dam a river **(c)** (= *Blutstauung*) congestion *no pl*; **bei ~(en) (des Blutes) in den Venen** when the veins become congested

Std. ABBR *von* **Stunde** hr

stdl. ABBR *von* **stündlich**

Steak [steːk, ʃteːk] NT **-s, -s** steak

Stearin [ʃteaˈriːn, st-] NT **-s, -e** stearin

stechen [ˈʃtɛçn̩], *pret* **stach** [ʃtax], *ptp* **gestochen** [ɡəˈʃtɔxn̩] **1** VI **(a)** (*Dorn, Stachel etc*) to prick; (*Wespe, Biene*) to sting; (*Mücken, Moskitos*) to bite; (*mit Messer etc*) to (make a) stab (*nach* at); (*Sonne*) to beat down; (*mit Stechkarte*) (*bei Ankunft*) to clock in; (*bei Weggang*) to clock out; **der Geruch sticht in die Nase** the smell stings one's nose; **mit etw in etw** (*acc*) **~** to stick sth in(to) sth **(b)** (*Cards*) to trump **(c)** (*Farbe: = spielen*) **die Farbe sticht ins Rötliche** the colour (*Brit*) *or* color (*US*) has a tinge of red **2** VT **(a)** (*Dorn, Stachel etc*) to prick; (*Wespe, Biene*) to sting; (*Mücken, Moskitos*) to bite; (*mit Messer etc*) to stab; **Löcher** to pierce **(b)** (*Cards*) to trump **(c)** **Spargel, Torf, Rasen** to cut **(d)** (= *gravieren*) to engrave; *siehe auch* **gestochen** **3** VR to prick oneself (*an +dat* on, *mit* with); **sich** (*acc or dat*) **in den Finger ~** to prick one's finger

Stechen [ˈʃtɛçn̩] NT **-s, - (a)** (*Sport*) play-off; (*bei Springreiten*) jump-off **(b)** (= *Schmerz*) sharp pain

stechend ADJ piercing; *Sonne* scorching; *Schmerz* sharp; *Geruch* pungent

Stecher [ˈʃtɛçɐ] M **-s, -** (*sl*: = *Freund*) shagging partner (*sl*)

Stech-: **Stechkarte** F clocking-in card; **Stechmücke** F gnat, midge (*Brit*); **Stechpalme** F holly; **Stechuhr** F time clock

Steck-: **Steckbrief** M "wanted" poster; (*fig*) personal description; **steckbrieflich** ADV **jdn ~ verfolgen** to put up "wanted" posters for sb; **~ gesucht werden** to be wanted; **Steckdose** F (*Elec*) (wall) socket

stecken **1** VI **(a)** (= *festsitzen*) to be stuck; (= *an- or eingesteckt sein*) to be; (*Nadel, Splitter etc*) to be (sticking); (*Brosche, Abzeichen etc*) to be (pinned); **einen Ring am Finger ~ haben** to have a ring on one's finger; **der Stecker steckt in der Dose** the plug is in the socket; **der Schlüssel steckt** the key is in the lock **(b)** (= *verborgen sein*) to be (hiding); **wo steckt er?** where has he got to?; **wo hast du die ganze Zeit gesteckt?** where have you been (hiding) all this time?; **darin steckt viel Mühe** a lot of work has gone into that; **da steckt etwas dahinter** (*inf*) there's something behind it; **in ihm steckt etwas** he certainly has it in him; **zeigen, was in einem steckt** to show what one is made of **(c)** (= *strotzen vor*) **voll** *or* **voller Fehler/Nadeln/Witz** *etc* **~** to be full of mistakes/pins/wit *etc* **(d)** (= *verwickelt sein in*) **in Schwierigkeiten ~** to be in difficulties; **tief in Schulden ~** to be deep(ly) in debt; **in einer Krise ~** to be in the throes of a crisis **2** VT **(a)** (= *hineinstecken*) to put; **Brosche** to pin (*an +acc* onto); **das Hemd in die Hose ~** to tuck one's shirt in (one's trousers (*esp Brit*) *or* pants (*esp US*)); **jdn ins Bett ~** (*inf*) to put sb to bed (*inf*); **jdn ins Gefängnis ~** (*inf*) to stick sb in prison (*inf*) **(b)** (*Sew*) to pin **(c)** (*inf*: = *investieren*) **Geld, Mühe** to put (*in +acc* into); **Zeit** to devote (*in +acc* to) **(d)** (*sl*: = *aufgeben*) to jack in (*Brit inf*), to chuck (*inf*)

(e) **jdm etw ~** (*inf*) to tell sb sth; **es jdm ~** (*inf*) to give sb a piece of one's mind

Stecken [ˈʃtɛkn̩] M **-s, -** stick

Stecken-: **stecken bleiben** VI IRREG AUX SEIN to stick fast; (*Kugel*) to be lodged; (*in der Rede*) to falter; (*beim Gedichtaufsagen etc*) to get stuck; **etw bleibt jdm im Halse stecken** (*lit, fig*) sth sticks in sb's throat; **stecken lassen** *ptp* **stecken lassen** *or* (*rare*) **stecken gelassen** VT IRREG to leave; **den Schlüssel ~** to leave the key in the lock; **lass dein Geld stecken!** leave your money where it is!; **Steckenpferd** NT (*lit, fig*) hobbyhorse; **sein ~ reiten** (*fig*) to be on one's hobbyhorse

Stecker [ˈʃtɛkɐ] M **-s, -** (*Elec*) plug

Steck-: **Steckkarte** F (*Comput*) expansion card; **Steckkontakt** M (*Elec*) plug

Stecknadel F pin; **etw mit ~n befestigen** to pin sth (*an +dat* to); **man hätte eine ~ fallen hören können** (*fig*) you could have heard a pin drop; **eine ~ im Heuhaufen** *or* **Heuschober suchen** (*fig*) to look for a needle in a haystack

Stecknadelkissen NT pincushion

Steck-: **Steckplatz** M (*Comput*) (expansion) slot; **Steckrübe** F swede (*Brit*), rutabaga (*US*); **Steckschloss** NT bicycle lock; **Steckzwiebel** F bulb

Steg [ʃteːk] M **-(e)s, -e** [-ɡə] **(a)** (= *Brücke*) footbridge; (= *Landungssteg*) landing stage **(b)** (*Mus*: = *Brillensteg*) bridge **(c)** (= *Hosensteg*) stirrup

Steghose F stirrup pants *pl*

Stegreif [ˈʃteːkraif] M **aus dem ~ spielen** (*Theat*) to improvise; **eine Rede aus dem ~ halten** to make an impromptu speech; **etw aus dem ~ tun** to do sth just like that

Steh- IN CPDS stand-up

Stehaufmännchen [ˈʃteːlauf-] NT (*Spielzeug*) tumbler; (*fig*) somebody who always bounces back; **er ist ein richtiges ~** he always bounces back

---

stehen [ˈʃteːən]

1 INTRANSITIVES VERB	**3** REFLEXIVES VERB
2 TRANSITIVES VERB	**4** UNPERSÖNLICHES VERB

pret **stand** [ʃtant], *ptp* **gestanden** [ɡəˈʃtandn̩] AUX HABEN *or* (*S Ger, Aus, Sw*) SEIN

1 INTRANSITIVES VERB

(a) (= *in aufrechter Stellung sein*) to stand; (= *warten*) to wait; (*Penis*) to be erect; **fest/sicher stehen** to stand firm(ly)/securely; (*Mensch*) to have a firm/safe foothold; **unter der Dusche stehen** to be in the shower; **vor der Tür stand ein Fremder** there was a stranger (standing) at the door; **neben jdm zu stehen kommen** (*Mensch*) to end up beside sb; **ich kann nicht mehr stehen** I can't stay on my feet any longer; **mit jdm/etw stehen und fallen** to depend on sb/sth; **mit ihm steht und fällt die Firma** he's the kingpin of the organization; **sein Hemd steht vor Dreck** (*inf*) his shirt is stiff with dirt; **er hat einen stehen** (*inf*) he has a hard-on (*sl*)

(b) (= *sich befinden*) to be; **die Vase/Tasse steht auf dem Tisch** the vase/cup is on the table; **meine alte Schule steht noch** my old school is still standing; **ihm steht der Schweiß auf der Stirn** his forehead is covered in sweat; **unter Schock stehen** to be in a state of shock; **unter Drogen/Alkohol stehen** to be under the influence of drugs/alcohol; **vor einer Entscheidung stehen** to be faced with a decision; **die Frage steht vor der Entscheidung** the question is about to be decided; **ich tue, was in meinen Kräften/meiner Macht steht** I'll do everything I can/in my power; **das steht zu erwarten** (*geh*) that is to be expected

(c) (= *geschrieben, gedruckt sein*) to be; **was steht da/in dem Brief?** what does it/the letter say?; **es stand im „Kurier"** it was in the "Courier"; **das steht in der Bibel (geschrieben)** it says that in the Bible; **das steht im Gesetz** that is what the law says

(d) (= *angehalten haben*) to have stopped; **meine Uhr steht** my watch has stopped; **der ganze Verkehr steht** traffic is at a complete standstill; **wo stehen Sie?** (*inf*: = *geparkt*) where have you parked?

(e) (= *bewertet werden*) (*Währung, Kurs*) to be (*auf +dat* at); **wie steht das Pfund?** what's the exchange rate for the pound?;

das Pfund steht auf EUR 1,60 the pound stands at EUR 1.60; **am besten steht der Schweizer Franken** the Swiss franc is strongest

(f) (= *in bestimmter Position sein*) (*Rekord*) to stand (*auf +dat* at); (*Mannschaft etc*) to be (*auf +dat* in); **der Zeiger steht auf 4 Uhr** the clock says 4 (o'clock); **die Kompassnadel steht auf** *or* **nach Norden** the compass needle is pointing north; **wie steht das Spiel?** what is the score?; **es steht 2:1 für München** the score is *or* it is 2-1 to Munich

(g) (= *passen zu*) **jdm stehen** to suit sb; **ich finde, diese Farbe steht mir gar nicht** I don't think this colour (*Brit*) *or* color (*US*) suits me

(h) (*grammatikalisch*) (*bei Satzstellung*) to come; (*bei Zeit, Fall, Modus*) to be; (= *gefolgt werden von*) to take; **dieses Verb steht im Perfekt** this verb is in the perfect tense; **nach „in" steht der Akkusativ oder der Dativ** "in" takes the accusative or the dative; **mit dem Dativ/Akkusativ stehen** to take the dative/accusative

(I) (*Belohnung, Strafe*) **auf Betrug steht Gefängnis** *or* **eine Gefängnisstrafe** fraud is punishable by imprisonment; **auf sachdienliche Hinweise steht eine Belohnung** there is a reward for useful information

(j) *siehe* **gestanden**

(k) (*Redewendungen*) **das/die Sache steht** (*inf*) that/the whole business is settled; **es steht mir bis hier (oben)** (*inf*) I've had it up to here with it (*inf*); **für etw stehen** to stand for sth; **hinter jdm/etw stehen** to be behind sb/sth; **auf jdn/etw stehen** (*inf*) to be mad about sb/sth (*inf*)

✦**stehen zu zu jdm stehen** to stand by sb; **zu seinem Versprechen stehen** to stand by one's promise; **zu seinen Behauptungen/seiner Überzeugung stehen** to stand by what one says/by one's convictions; **zu dem, was man gesagt hat, stehen** to stick to what one has said; **wie stehen Sie dazu?** what are your views on that?

2 TRANSITIVES VERB **Posten stehen** to stand guard; **Wache stehen** to mount watch; **sich** (*dat*) **die Beine in den Bauch stehen** (*inf*) to stand until one is ready to drop

3 REFLEXIVES VERB
(a) (*in bestimmten Verhältnissen leben*) **sich gut/schlecht stehen** to be well/badly off
(b) (= *sich verstehen*) **sich mit jdm gut/schlecht stehen** to get on well/badly with sb

4 UNPERSÖNLICHES VERB **wie stehts?** how are *or* how's things?; **wie steht es damit?** how about it?; **wie stehts mit ...?** what's the state of play with ...?; **es steht schlecht/gut/besser um jdn** (*bei Aussichten*) things look bad/good/better for sb; (*gesundheitlich, finanziell*) sb is doing badly/well/better; **es steht schlecht/gut/besser um etw** things look bad/good/better for sth

Stehen NT -s, NO PL **(a)** standing; **das viele ~** all this standing; **etw im ~ tun** to do sth standing up **(b)** (= *Halt*) stop, standstill; **zum ~ bringen/kommen** to stop

stehen bleiben VI IRREG AUX SEIN **(a)** (= *anhalten*) to stop; **~!** (= *nicht weitergehen*) to stay; (*Zeit*) to stand still, stop!; (*Mil*) halt! **(b)** (= *zurück gelassen werden*) to be left (behind); **mein Regenschirm muss im Büro stehen geblieben sein** I must have left my umbrella in the office **(c)** (= *unverändert bleiben*) to be left (in); **soll das so ~?** should that stay as it is?

stehend ADJ ATTR *Fahrzeug* stationary; *Wasser, Gewässer* stagnant; **~e Redensart** stock phrase

stehen lassen ptp **stehen lassen** *or* (*rare*) **stehen gelassen** VT IRREG to leave; (*Cook*) to let stand; *Essen, Getränk* to leave (untouched); *Fehler* to leave (in); **alles stehen und liegen lassen** to drop everything; (*Flüchtlinge etc*) to leave everything behind; **jdn einfach ~** to leave sb standing (there); **sich** (*dat*) **einen Bart ~** to grow a beard

Steh-: **Stehimbiss** M stand-up snack bar; **Stehkneipe** F stand-up bar; **Stehlampe** F standard lamp

stehlen ['ʃteːlən], pret **stahl** [ʃtaːl], ptp **gestohlen** [gəˈʃtoːlən] **1** VTI to steal; **hier wird viel gestohlen** there's a lot of stealing around here; **jdm die Zeit ~** to waste sb's time **2** VR to steal; **sich aus der Verantwortung ~** to evade one's responsibility; *siehe auch* **gestohlen**

Steh-: **Stehparty** F buffet party; **Stehplatz** M **ich bekam nur noch einen ~** I had to stand; **ein ~ kostet zehn Euro** it costs ten euros to stand; **Stehplätze** standing room *sing*; **zwei Stehplätze, bitte** two standing, please; **Stehvermögen** NT staying power

Steiermark ['ʃtaiɐmark] F - Styria

steif [ʃtaif] **1** ADJ **(a)** stiff; *Penis* hard; **ein ~er Hals** a stiff neck; **sich ~ (wie ein Brett) machen** to go rigid; **ein Steifer** (*inf*: = *Erektion*) a hard-on (*sl*); (*sl*: = *Toter*) a stiff (*inf*) **(b)** (= *förmlich*) stiff; *Empfang, Konventionen, Begrüßung, Abend* formal **2** ADV **(a)** (= *hart*) **das Eiweiß ~ schlagen** to beat the egg white until stiff; **~ und fest auf etw** (*dat*) **beharren** to insist stubbornly on sth; **sie behauptete ~ und fest, dass ...** she insisted that ...; **etw ~ und fest glauben** to be convinced of sth **(b)** (= *förmlich*) stiffly; **~ lächeln** to smile stiffly; **jdn ~ behandeln** to be standoffish to sb

steifen ['ʃtaifn] VT to stiffen; *Wäsche* to starch

Steifheit F -, NO PL stiffness

Steigbügel M stirrup; **jdm den ~ halten** (*fig*) to help sb on

Steigbügelhalter(in) M(F) (*esp Pol pej*) **jds ~ sein** to help sb to come to power

Steige ['ʃtaigə] F -, -n (*dial*) **(a)** (= *Steig*) steep track **(b)** (= *Treppe*) (narrow) staircase **(c)** (= *Lattenkiste*) crate

Steigeisen NT climbing iron *usu pl*; (*Bergsteigen*) crampon; (*an Mauer*) rung (in the wall)

steigen ['ʃtaign], pret **stieg** [ʃtiːk], ptp **gestiegen** [gəˈʃtiːgn] AUX SEIN **1** VI **(a)** (= *klettern*) to climb; **auf einen Berg/Turm/Baum/ eine Leiter ~** to climb (up) a mountain/tower/tree/ladder; **aufs Fahrrad ~** to get on(to) the/one's bicycle; **aufs Pferd ~** to get on(to) the/one's horse; **ins Bett/in den Straßenbahn ~** to get into bed/on the tram; **vom Fahrrad/Pferd ~** to get off the/ one's bicycle/horse; **aus dem Wasser/der Badewanne/dem Bett ~** to get out of the water/the bath/bed; **aus dem Zug/Bus/ Flugzeug ~** to get off the train/bus/plane **(b)** (= *sich aufwärts bewegen*) to rise; (*Flugzeug, Straße*) to climb; (= *sich erhöhen*) (*Preis, Zahl, Gehalt, Fieber*) to go up; (= *zunehmen*) (*Chancen, Misstrauen, Ungeduld etc*) to increase; (= *sich auflösen*: *Nebel*) to lift; **Drachen ~ lassen** to fly kites; **das Blut stieg ihm in den Kopf/das Gesicht** the blood rushed to his head/face; **in jds Achtung** (*dat*) **~** to rise in sb's estimation **(c)** (*inf*: = *stattfinden*) to be; **steigt die Demo/Prüfung oder nicht?** is the demo/exam on or not? **2** VT *Treppen, Stufen* to climb (up)

steigern ['ʃtaigɐn] **1** VT **(a)** (= *erhöhen*) to increase (*auf +acc* to, *um* bei); (= *verschlimmern*) *Übel, Zorn* to aggravate; (= *verbessern*) *Leistung* to improve **(b)** (*Gram*) *Adjektiv* to compare **(c)** (= *ersteigern*) to buy at an auction **2** VI to bid (*um* for) **3** VR **(a)** (= *sich erhöhen*) to increase; **sein Ärger steigerte sich zu Zorn** his annoyance turned into rage; **seine Schmerzen steigerten sich ins Unerträgliche** his pain became unbearable **(b)** (= *sich verbessern*) to improve **(c)** (= *hineinsteigern*) **sich in etw** (*acc*) **~** to work oneself (up) into sth

Steigerung ['ʃtaigərʊŋ] F -, -en **(a)** (= *das Steigern*) increase (*+gen* in); (= *Verschlimmerung*) aggravation; (= *Verbesserung*) improvement **(b)** (*Gram*) comparative

Steigerungs-: **steigerungsfähig** ADJ improvable; **Steigerungsform** F (*Gram*) (= *Komparativ*) comparative form; (= *Superlativ*) superlative form; **Steigerungsstufe** F (*Gram*) degree of comparison

Steigung ['ʃtaigʊŋ] F -, -en (= *Hang*) slope; (*von Hang, Straße, Math*) gradient (*Brit*), grade (*esp US*)

steil [ʃtail] **1** ADJ **(a)** (*lit, fig*) *Abhang, Treppe, Anstieg, Rückgang* steep; **eine ~e Karriere** a rapid rise **(b)** (= *senkrecht*) upright **(c)** (*Sport*) **~e Vorlage, ~er Pass** through ball **2** ADV steeply

Steil-: **Steilhang** M steep slope; **Steilheck** NT hatchback; **Steilheit** F, NO PL steepness; **Steilküste** F steep coast; (= *Klippen*) cliffs *pl*; **Steilpass** M, **Steilvorlage** F (*Sport*) through ball; **Steilwand** F steep face

Stein [ʃtain] M -(e)s, -e stone; (= *Feuerstein*) flint; (*in Uhr*) jewel; (= *Spielstein*) piece; (= *Ziegelstein*) brick; **heißer ~** (*Cook*) hot stone; **es blieb kein ~ auf dem anderen** everything was smashed to pieces; (*bei Gebäuden, Mauern*) not a stone was left standing; **mir fällt ein ~ vom Herzen!** (*fig*) that's a load off my mind!; **bei jdm einen ~ im Brett haben** (*fig inf*) to be well in with sb (*inf*); **ein Herz aus ~** (*fig*) a heart of stone; **~ und Bein schwören** (*fig inf*) to swear to God (*inf*)

Stein-: **Steinadler** M golden eagle; **Steinbock** M **(a)** (*Zool*) ibex **(b)** (*Astrol*) Capricorn; **Steinbruch** M quarry; **Steinbutt** M (*Zool*) turbot; **Steineiche** F holm oak, holly oak

steinern ['ʃtainɐn] ADJ stone; (*fig*) stony

Stein-: **Steinfraß** M stone erosion; **Steinfrucht** F stone fruit; **Steinfußboden** M stone floor; **Steingarten** M rockery; **Steingut** NT, NO PL stoneware

steinhart ADJ (as) hard as a rock

steinig ['ʃtainɪç] ADJ stony; **ein ~er Weg** (*fig*) a path of trial and tribulation

steinigen ['ʃtainɪɡn] VT to stone

Stein-: **Steinkohle** F hard coal; **Steinkrug** M (= *Kanne*) stoneware jug; **Steinmetz** [-mɛts] M **-en, -en**, **Steinmetzin** [-mɛtsɪn] F **-, -nen** stonemason; **Steinobst** NT stone fruit; **Steinpilz** M boletus edulis (*spec*); **Steinplatte** F stone slab; (*zum Pflastern*) flagstone; **steinreich** ADJ (*inf*) stinking rich (*Brit inf*); **Steinsalz** NT rock salt; **Steinschlag** M rockfall; **„Achtung ~"** "danger falling stones"; **Steinwurf** M (*fig*) stone's throw; **Steinzeit** F (*lit, fig*) Stone Age; **steinzeitlich** ADJ Stone Age *attr*; **Steinzeug** NT, NO PL stoneware

Steirer ['ʃtaire] M **-s, -**, **Steirerin** [-ərɪn] F **-, -nen** Styrian

steirisch ['ʃtairɪʃ] ADJ Styrian

Steiß [ʃtais] M **-es, -e** (*Anat*) coccyx; (*hum inf*) tail (*inf*)

Steiß-: **Steißbein** NT (*Anat*) coccyx; **Steißlage** F (*Med*) breech presentation

Stelle ['ʃtɛlə] F **-, -n (a)** place; (= *Fleck: rostend, nass, faul etc*) patch; (*in Tabelle, Hierarchie*) position; (*in Text, Musikstück*) passage; (= *Bibelstelle*) verse; **an dieser ~** in this place; **an erster ~** in the first place; **eine gute ~ zum Parken/Picknicken** a good place to park/for a picnic; **diese ~ muss repariert werden** it needs to be repaired here; **eine entzündete ~ am Finger** an inflammation on one's finger; **eine empfindliche ~** (*lit*) a sensitive spot; (*fig*) a sensitive point; **eine schwache ~** a weak spot; (*fig auch*) a weak point; **auf der ~ treten** (*lit*) to mark time; (*fig*) not to make any progress; **auf der ~** (*fig* = *sofort*) on the spot; **kommen, gehen** straight away; **nicht von der ~ kommen** not to make any progress; **sich nicht von der ~ rühren** *or* **bewegen, nicht von der ~ weichen** to refuse to budge (*inf*); **zur ~ sein** to be on the spot; (= *bereit, etw zu tun*) to be at hand; **an dieser ~** here; **an anderer ~** in another place **(b)** (= *Zeitpunkt*) point; **an dieser ~** at this point; **an anderer ~** on another occasion; **an passender ~** at an appropriate moment **(c)** (*Math*) figure; (*hinter Komma*) place; **drei ~n hinter dem Komma** three decimal places **(d)** (= *Lage, Platz, Aufgabenbereich*) place; **an ~ von** in place of; **an jds ~** (*acc*)/**an die ~ einer Sache** (*gen*) **treten** to take sb's place/the place of sth; **das erledige ich an deiner ~** I'll do that for you; **ich gehe an deiner ~** I'll go in your place; **ich möchte jetzt nicht an seiner ~ sein** I wouldn't like to be in his position now; **an deiner ~ würde ich ...** if I were you I would ...; *siehe auch* **anstelle** **(e)** (= *Posten*) job; **eine freie** *or* **offene ~** a vacancy; **wir haben zur Zeit keine ~n zu vergeben** we haven't any vacancies at present **(f)** (= *Dienststelle*) office; (= *Behörde*) authority; **da bist du bei mir/uns an der richtigen ~!** (*inf*) you've come to the right place; **bei ihm/ihnen bist du an der richtigen ~!** (*inf*) you went to the right place; **sich an höherer ~ beschweren** to complain to somebody higher up

stellen ['ʃtɛlən] **1** VT **(a)** (= *hinstellen*) to put; (= *an bestimmten Platz legen*) to place; **auf sich** (*acc*) **selbst** *or* **allein gestellt sein** (*fig*) to have to fend for oneself **(b)** (= *in senkrechte Position bringen*) to stand; **du solltest es ~, nicht legen** you should stand it up, not lay it down **(c)** (= *anordnen, arrangieren*) to arrange; **das sollten Sie anders ~** you should put it in a different position; **gestellt** *Bild, Foto* posed; **die Szene war gestellt** they posed for the scene; **eine gestellte Pose** a pose **(d)** (= *erstellen*) **(jdm) eine Diagnose ~** to make a diagnosis (for sb); **jdm sein Horoskop ~** to draw up sb's horoscope

(e) (= *beschaffen, aufbieten*) to provide; **die CDU stellt zwei Minister** the CDU has two ministers **(f)** (= *einstellen*) to set (*auf +acc* at); **das Radio lauter/leiser ~** to turn the radio up/down; **die Heizung höher/kleiner ~** to turn the heating up/down **(g)** (*finanziell*) **gut/besser/schlecht gestellt sein** to be well/better/badly off **(h)** (= *erwischen*) to catch; (*fig inf*) to corner **(i)** *Aufgabe, Thema, Bedingung, Termin* to set (*jdm* sb); *Frage* to put (*jdm, an jdn* to sb); *Antrag, Forderung* to make; **jdn unter jds Aufsicht** (*acc*) **~** to place sb under sb's care; **jdn vor ein Problem/eine Aufgabe** *etc* **~** to confront sb with a problem/task *etc*; **jdn vor eine Entscheidung ~** to put sb in the position of having to make a decision

2 VR **(a)** (= *sich hinstellen*) to (go and) stand (*an +acc* at, by); (= *sich aufstellen, sich einordnen*) to position oneself; (= *sich aufrecht hinstellen*) to stand up; **sich auf (die) Zehenspitzen ~** to stand on tiptoe; **sich auf den Standpunkt ~, ...** to take the view ...; **sich gegen jdn/etw ~** (*fig*) to oppose sb/sth; **sich hinter jdn/etw ~** (*fig*) to support *or* back sb/sth **(b)** (*fig:* = *sich verhalten*) **sich positiv/anders zu etw ~** to have a positive/different attitude toward(s) sth; **wie stellst du dich zu ...?** what do you think of ...?; **sich gut mit jdm ~** to put oneself on good terms with sb **(c)** (*inf: finanziell*) **sich gut/schlecht ~** to be well/badly off **(d)** (= *sich einstellen: Gerät etc*) to set itself (*auf +acc* at); **die Heizung stellt sich von selbst kleiner** the heating turns itself down **(e)** (= *sich ausliefern*) to give oneself up (*jdm* to sb); **sich den Fragen der Journalisten ~** to be prepared to answer reporters' questions; **sich einer Herausforderung ~** to take up a challenge; **sich einem Herausforderer ~** to take on a challenger; **sich (jdm) zum Kampf ~** to be prepared to do battle (with sb) **(f)** (= *sich verstellen*) **sich krank/schlafend** *etc* **~** to pretend to be ill/asleep *etc* **(g)** (*fig:* = *entstehen*) to arise (*für* for); **es stellten sich uns** (*dat*) **allerlei Probleme** we were faced with all sorts of problems; **es stellt sich die Frage, ob ...** the question arises whether ...

Stellen-: **Stellenangebot** NT job offer; **„~e"** "situations vacant", "vacancies"; **Stellenanzeige** F, **Stellenausschreibung** F job advertisement; **Stellenbeschreibung** F job description; **Stellengesuch** NT advertisement seeking employment; **„~e"** "situations wanted" (*Brit*), "employment wanted"; **Stellenmarkt** M job market; (*in Zeitung*) appointments section; **Stellennachweis** M, **Stellenvermittlung** F employment bureau; **stellenweise** ADV in places; **Stellenwert** M (*Math*) place value; (*fig*) status; **einen hohen ~ haben** to play an important role

Stellfläche F area; **10.000 Quadratmeter ~** an area of 10,000 square metres (*Brit*) *or* meters (*US*); **der Drucker benötigt nur eine kleine ~** the printer does not take up much space

Stell-: **Stellplatz** M (*für Auto*) parking space; **Stellschraube** F (*Tech*) adjusting screw

Stellung ['ʃtɛlʊŋ] F **-, -en** (*lit, fig, Mil*) position; **die ~ halten** (*Mil*) to hold one's position; (*hum*) to hold the fort; **~ beziehen** (*Mil*) to move into position; (*fig*) to declare one's position; **zu etw ~ nehmen** *or* **beziehen** to comment on sth; **die rechtliche ~ des Mieters** the legal status of the tenant; **gesellschaftliche ~** social status; **bei jdm in ~ sein** to be in sb's employment

Stellungnahme [-naːmə] F **-, -n** statement (*zu* on); **eine ~ zu etw abgeben** to make a statement on sth

Stellungs-: **Stellungssuche** F search for employment; **auf ~ sein** to be looking for employment; **Stellungswechsel** M change of job

Stell-: **stellvertretend** **1** ADJ (*von Amts wegen*) deputy *attr*; (= *vorübergehend*) acting *attr* **2** ADV **~ für jdn** for sb; (*Rechtsanwalt*) on behalf of sb; **ich bin ~ für ihn da** I'm here in his place; **~ für jdn handeln** to deputize for sb; **~ für etw stehen** to stand in place of sth; **Stellvertretung** F (= *Stellvertreter*) representative; (*von Amts wegen*) deputy; (*von Arzt*) locum; **die ~ für jdn übernehmen** to represent sb; (*von Amts wegen*) to stand in for sb; **in ~** (*+gen*) for, on behalf of

Stelze ['ʃtɛltsə] F **-, -n (a)** stilt **(b)** (*Orn*) wagtail **(c)** (*Aus*: = *Schweinsstelze*) pig's trotter

Stemmbogen M (*Ski*) stem turn

Stemmeisen NT crowbar

stemmen [ˈʃtɛmən] **1** VT **(a)** (= *stützen*) to press; *Ellenbogen* to prop **(b)** (= *hochstemmen*) to lift (above one's head); *Gewichte* ~ to lift weights **2** VR **sich gegen etw** ~ to brace oneself against sth; (*fig*) to oppose sth

Stemmschwung M (*Ski*) stem turn

Stempel [ˈʃtɛmpl̩] M **-s, -** **(a)** (= *Gummistempel*) (rubber) stamp **(b)** (= *Abdruck*) stamp; (= *Poststempel*) postmark; (= *Viehstempel*) brand; (*auf Silber, Gold*) hallmark; **jdm/einer Sache** (*dat*) **einen/seinen** ~ **aufdrücken** *or* **aufprägen** (*fig*) to make a/one's mark on sb/sth; **jds** ~/**den** ~ **einer Sache** (*gen*) **tragen** to bear the stamp of sb/sth **(c)** (*Tech*) (= *Prägestempel*) die; (*stangenförmig*, = *Lochstempel*) punch **(d)** (*Bot*) pistil

Stempel-: **Stempelkarte** F punch card; **Stempelkissen** NT ink pad

stempeln [ˈʃtɛmpl̩n] **1** VT to stamp; *Brief* to postmark; *Briefmarke* to frank; *Gold, Silber* to hallmark; **jdn zum Lügner/Verbrecher** ~ (*fig*) to brand sb (as) a liar/criminal **2** VI (*inf*) **(a)** ~ **gehen** (= *arbeitslos sein*) to be on the dole (*Brit inf*), to be on welfare (*US*); (= *sich arbeitslos melden*) to go on the dole (*Brit inf*) *or* on welfare (*US*) **(b)** (= *Stempeluhr betätigen*) (*beim Hereinkommen*) to clock in; (*beim Hinausgehen*) to clock out

Stempeluhr F time clock

Stengel [ˈʃtɛŋl̩] M **-s, -** *siehe* **Stängel**

Steno [ˈʃteːno] F **-,** NO PL (*inf*) shorthand

Steno-: **Stenoblock** M, *pl* **-blöcke** *or* **-blocks** shorthand pad; **Stenografie** [ʃtenoɡraˈfiː] F **-,** NO PL shorthand; **stenografieren** [ʃtenoɡraˈfiːrən], *ptp* **stenografiert** **1** VT to take down in shorthand **2** VI to take shorthand; **können Sie** ~**?** can you take shorthand?; **Stenogramm** [ʃtenoˈɡram] NT, *pl* **-gramme** text in shorthand; (= *Diktat*) shorthand dictation; **ein** ~ **aufnehmen** to take shorthand; **Stenotypist** [ʃtenotyˈpɪst] M **-en, -en**, **Stenotypistin** [-ˈpɪstɪn] F **-, -nen** shorthand typist

Stepp [ʃtɛp, st-] M **-s, -s** tap dance; ~ **tanzen** to tap-dance

Steppanorak M quilted anorak (*esp Brit*)

Steppdecke F quilt

Steppe [ˈʃtɛpə] F **-, -n** steppe

Stepp-: **Steppfuß** M foot; **Steppjacke** F quilted jacket; **Steppstich** M (*Sew*) backstitch; (*mit Maschine*) lockstitch; **Stepptanz** M tap dance

Sterbe-: **Sterbefall** M death; **Sterbehilfe** F **(a)** death benefit **(b)** (= *Euthanasie*) euthanasia; **jdm** ~ **geben** *or* **gewähren** to administer euthanasia to sb (*form*)

sterben [ˈʃtɛrbn̩], *pret* **starb** [ʃtarp], *ptp* **gestorben** [ɡəˈʃtɔrbn̩] VTI AUS SEIN to die; **einen schnellen Tod** ~ to die quickly; **einen leichten Tod** ~ to have an easy death; **eines natürlichen/gewaltsamen Todes** ~ to die a natural/violent death; **an einer Krankheit/Verletzung** ~ to die of an illness/from an injury; **daran wirst du nicht** ~**!** (*hum*) it won't kill you!; **vor Angst/Durst/Hunger** ~ to die of fright/thirst/hunger (*auch fig*); **er stirbt vor Angst** (*fig*) he's frightened to death; **gestorben sein** to be dead; (*fig*: *Projekt*) to be over and done with; **er ist für mich gestorben** (*fig inf*) he doesn't exist as far as I'm concerned; **und wenn sie nicht gestorben sind, so leben sie noch heute** and they lived happily ever after

Sterben NT **-s,** NO PL death; **wenn es ans** ~ **geht** when it comes to dying; **im** ~ **liegen** to be dying; **zum Leben zu wenig, zum** ~ **zu viel** barely enough to keep body and soul together

sterblich [ˈʃtɛrplɪç] **1** ADJ mortal; **jds** ~**e Hülle** *or* **(Über)reste** sb's mortal remains *pl* **2** ADV (*inf*) terribly (*inf*), dreadfully (*inf*)

Sterbliche(r) [ˈʃtɛrplɪçə] MF DECL AS ADJ mortal

Sterblichkeit F **-,** NO PL mortality; (*Zahl*) mortality (rate)

stereo [ˈʃteːreo, ˈst-] ADV (*in*) stereo

Stereo- IN CPDS stereo; (= *stereoskopisch*) stereoscopic; **Stereoanlage** F stereo (*inf*); **Stereogerät** NT stereo unit; **Stereokamera** F stereoscopic camera; **stereophon** [ʃtereoˈfoːn, st-] **1** ADJ stereophonic **2** ADV stereophonically; **Stereoskop** [ʃtereoˈskoːp, st-] NT **-s, -e** stereoscope; **stereoskopisch** [ʃtereoˈskoːpɪʃ, st-] ADJ stereoscopic; (= *dreidimensional*) 3-D; **Stereoturm** M hi-fi stack; **stereotyp** [ʃtereoˈtyːp, st-] **1** ADJ (*fig*) stereotyped, stereotypical; *Lächeln* (= *gezwungen*) stiff; (= *unpersönlich*) impersonal **2** ADV in stereotyped fashion; ~ **darstellen** to represent as stereotypes; **Stereotyp** NT (*Psych*) stereotype

steril [ʃteˈriːl, st-] ADJ (*lit, fig*) sterile

Sterilisation [ʃteriliˈzatsioːn, st-] F **-, -en** sterilization

sterilisieren [ʃteriliˈziːrən, st-], *ptp* **sterilisiert** VT to sterilize

Sterilität [ʃteriliˈtɛːt, st-] F **-,** NO PL (*lit, fig*) sterility

Sterling [ˈʃtɛrlɪŋ, ˈst-] M **-s, -e** sterling; **30 Pfund** ~ 30 pounds sterling

Stern [ʃtɛrn] M **-(e)s, -e** star; **in den** ~**en** (**geschrieben**) **stehen** (*fig*) to be (written) in the stars; **das steht (noch) in den** ~**en** (*fig*) it's in the lap of the gods; **unter einem guten** *or* **glücklichen** *or* **günstigen** ~ **geboren sein** to be born under a lucky star; **unter einem guten** *or* **glücklichen** *or* **günstigen** ~ **stehen** to be blessed with good fortune; **unter einem unglücklichen** ~ **stehen** to be ill-fated; **mit ihr ging am Theaterhimmel ein neuer** ~ **auf** with her coming a new star was born in the theatrical world; ~**e sehen** (*inf*) to see stars (*inf*); **ein Hotel/Cognac mit drei** ~**en** a three-star hotel/brandy; **ein Vier-~-e-General** a four-star general

Sternbild NT (*Astron*) constellation; (*Astrol*) sign (of the zodiac)

Sternchen [ˈʃtɛrnçən] NT **-s, -** DIM *von* **Stern** **(a)** little star **(b)** (*Typ*) asterisk, star (*Brit*) **(c)** (*Film*) starlet

Sternen-: **Sternenbanner** NT Stars and Stripes *sing*; **sternenbedeckt** ADJ starry; **Sternenhimmel** M starry sky; **Veränderungen am** ~ changes in the star formation

Stern-: **Sternfahrt** F (*Pol*) rally (*where participants commence at different points*); **eine** ~ **nach Ulan Bator** a rally converging on Ulan Bator; **Sternfrucht** F star fruit; **sternhagelvoll** [ˈʃtɛrnˈhaːɡlˈfɔl] ADJ (*inf*) roaring drunk (*inf*); **sternhell** ADJ starlit, starry *attr*; **Sternjahr** NT sidereal year; **sternklar** ADJ *Himmel, Nacht* starry *attr*, starlit; **Sternkunde** F astronomy; **Sternmarsch** M (*Pol*) protest march with marchers converging on assembly point from different directions; **Sternschnuppe** [-ˌʃnʊpə] F **-, -n** shooting star; **Sternsinger** PL carol singers *pl*; **Sternstunde** F great moment; **das war meine** ~ that was a great moment in my life; **Sternsystem** NT galaxy; **Sternwarte** F observatory; **Sternzeichen** NT (*Astrol*) sign of the zodiac; **im** ~ **der Jungfrau** under the sign of Virgo

Steroid [ʃteroˈiːt, st-] NT **-(e)s, -e** [-də] steroid

stet [ʃteːt] ADJ ATTR constant; ~**er Tropfen höhlt den Stein** (*Prov*) constant dripping wears away the stone

Stethoskop [ʃtetoˈskoːp, st-] NT **-s, -e** stethoscope

stetig [ˈʃteːtɪç] **1** ADJ steady; (*Math*) *Funktion* continuous; ~**es Meckern** constant moaning **2** ADV *wachsen, sinken etc* steadily

stets [ʃteːts] ADV always

Steuer¹ [ˈʃtɔyɐ] NT **-s, -** (*Naut*) helm; (*Aut*) (steering) wheel; (*Aviat*) controls *pl*; **am** ~ **sein** (*fig*) to be at the helm; **am** ~ **sitzen** *or* **sein, hinter dem** ~ **sitzen** (*inf*) (*Aut*) to be at the wheel, to drive; (*Aviat*) to be at the controls; **das** ~ **übernehmen** (*lit, fig*) to take over; **das** ~ **fest in der Hand haben** (*fig*) to be firmly in control

Steuer² F **-, -n** (= *Abgabe*) tax; (*an Gemeinde*) council tax (*Brit*), local tax (*US*); (*von Firmen*) rates *pl* (*Brit*), corporate property tax (*US*); ~**n** tax; (= *Arten von* ~*n*) taxes; ~**n zahlen** to pay tax; **Gewinn vor/nach** ~**n** pre-/after-tax profit

Steuer-: **Steueraufkommen** NT tax revenue; **steuerbar** ADJ **(a)** (= *versteuerbar*) taxable **(b)** (= *lenkbar, bedienbar*) controllable; *Schiff, Auto* steerable; *Flugzeug* flyable; **leicht/schwer** ~ easy/difficult to control/steer/fly; **Steuerbeamte(r)** M DECL AS ADJ, **Steuerbeamtin** F tax officer; **steuerbegünstigt** [-bəɡʏnstɪçt] ADJ *Investitionen, Hypothek, Spende* tax-deductible; *Waren* taxed at a lower rate; ~**es Sparen** form of saving entitling the saver to tax relief; *Investitionen* **sind** ~ you get tax relief on investments; **Steuerberater(in)** M(F) tax consultant; **Steuerbescheid** M tax assessment; **Steuerbilanz** F tax balance sheet; **Steuerbord** [ˈʃtɔybɔrt] NT **-s,** NO PL (*Naut*) starboard; **steuerbord(s)** [ˈʃtɔybɔrt(s)] ADV (*Naut*) to starboard; **steuerehrlich** ADJ ~ **sein** to be honest in tax matters; **Steuerehrlichkeit** F honesty in tax matters; **Steuereinnahmen** PL revenue from taxation; **Steuererhöhung** F tax increase; **Steuererklärung** F tax return; **Steuerfahndung** F investigation of (suspected) tax evasion; (*Behörde*) commission for investigation of suspected tax evasion; **Steuerflucht** F tax evasion (*by leaving the country*); **Steuerflüchtling** M tax exile; **Steuerfrau** F (*Rudersport*) cox(swain); **steuerfrei** **1** ADJ tax-free **2** ADV tax-free; **er hat den Nebenverdienst** ~ **kassiert** he didn't pay taxes on his additional earnings; **Steuerfreibetrag** M tax-exempt income; **Steuergelder** PL taxes *pl*; **warum soll das aus ~n finanziert werden?** why should it be paid for with taxpayers' money?; **Steuergerät** NT tuner-amplifier; (*Comput*) control unit; **Steuerharmonisierung** F harmonization of taxes; **Steuerhinterziehung** F tax evasion; **Steuerjahr** NT tax year; **Steuerklasse** F tax bracket; **Steuerknüppel** M control column; (*Aviat auch*) joystick

steuerlich [ˈʃtɔyəlɪç] **◼1** ADJ tax *attr*; **~e Belastung** tax burden; **aus ~en Überlegungen** for tax reasons **◼2** ADV **es ist ~ günstiger ...** for tax purposes it is better ...; **das wirkt sich ~ ganz günstig aus** taxwise it works out very well; **das ist ~ vorteilhaft** that's a good way to save on taxes; **~ abzugsfähig** tax-deductible; **~ stark belastet werden** (*Mensch*) to pay high taxes; **~ entlastet werden** (*Mensch*) to get a tax reduction

Steuer-: Steuermann M, *pl* **-männer** *or* **-leute** helmsman; (*als Rang*) (first) mate; (*Rudersport*) cox(swain); **Zweier mit/ohne ~** coxed/coxless pairs; **Steuermarke** F revenue stamp; (*für Hunde*) dog licence disc (*Brit*), dog tag (*US*); **Steuermittel** PL tax revenue(s *pl*); **etw aus ~n finanzieren** to finance sth out of public funds; **Steuermoral** F honesty in tax matters

steuern [ˈʃtɔyən] **◼1** VT **(a)** *Schiff* to steer; *Flugzeug* to pilot; *Auto* to steer; (*fig*) *Wirtschaft, Politik* to run; (*Comput*) to control; **einen Kurs ~** (*lit, fig*) to steer a course; **eine Diskussion/die Wirtschaft in eine bestimmte Richtung ~** to steer a discussion/the economy in a certain direction
(b) (= *regulieren*) to control
◼2 VI **(a)** AUX SEIN to head; (*Aut*) to drive; (*Naut*) to make for, to steer; **wohin steuert die Wirtschaft?** where is the economy heading (for)?
(b) (= *am Steuer sein*) (*Naut*) to be at the helm; (*Aut*) to be at the wheel; (*Aviat*) to be at the controls

Steuer-: Steueroase F, **Steuerparadies** NT tax haven; **Steuerpflicht** F liability to tax; **der ~ unterliegen** to be liable to tax; **steuerpflichtig** [-pflɪçtɪç] ADJ taxable; **Steuerpflichtige(r)** [-pflɪçtɪgə] MF DECL AS ADJ taxpayer; **Steuerprogression** F progressive taxation; **Steuerprüfer(in)** M(F) tax inspector, tax auditor (*esp US*); **Steuerprüfung** F tax inspector's investigation (*Brit*), tax audit (*esp US*); **Steuerrad** NT (*Aviat*) control wheel; (*Aut*) (steering) wheel; **Steuerreform** F tax reform; **Steuersatz** M rate of taxation; **Steuerschuld** F tax(es *pl*) owing *no indef art*; **Steuersenkung** F tax cut; **Steuersparmodell** NT tax relief scheme; **Steuersünder(in)** M(F) tax evader

Steuerung [ˈʃtɔyərʊŋ] F **-, -en (a)** NO PL (= *das Steuern*) (*von Schiff*) steering; (*von Flugzeug*) piloting; (*fig*) (*von Politik, Wirtschaft*) running; (*Comput*) control; (= *Regulierung*) regulation; (= *Bekämpfung*) control **(b)** (= *Steuervorrichtung*) (*Aviat*) controls *pl*; (*Tech*) steering apparatus; (*elektronisch*) control; **automatische ~** (*Aviat*) automatic pilot; (*Tech*) automatic steering (device)

Steuer-: Steuerveranlagung F tax assessment; **Steuervergünstigung** F tax relief; **Steuerwerk** NT (*Comput*) control unit; **Steuerzahler(in)** M(F) taxpayer; **Steuerzeichen** NT (*Comput*) control character

Steward [ˈstjuːɐt, ˈʃt-] M **-s, -s** (*Naut, Aviat*) steward

Stewardess [ˈstjuːɐdɛs, stjuːɐˈdɛs, ʃt-] F **-, -en** stewardess

StGB [esteːgeːˈbeː] NT **-s** ABBR *von* **Strafgesetzbuch**

stich [ʃtɪç] IMPER SING *von* **stechen**

Stich [ʃtɪç] M **-(e)s, -e (a)** (= *Insektenstich*) sting; (= *Mückenstich*) bite; (= *Nadelstich*) prick; (= *Messerstich*) stab **(b)** (= *~wunde*) (*von Messer etc*) stab wound; (= *Einstichloch*) prick **(c)** (= *stechender Schmerz*) stabbing pain; (= *Seitenstich*) stitch **(d)** (*Sew*) stitch **(e)** (= *Kupferstich, Stahlstich*) engraving **(f)** (= *Schattierung*) tinge (*in +acc* of); (= *Tendenz*) hint (*in +acc* of); **ein ~ ins Rote** a tinge of red **(g)** (*Cards*) trick; **einen ~ machen** *or* **bekommen** to get a trick **(h)** **jdn im ~ lassen** to let sb down; (= *verlassen*) to abandon sb; **etw im ~ lassen** to abandon sth **(i)** (*Aus*) **~ halten** to hold water

Stichel [ˈʃtɪçl] M **-s, -** (*Art*) gouge

Stichelei [ʃtɪçəˈlai] F **-, -en** (*pej inf*: = *boshafte Bemerkung*) snide (*inf*) or sneering remark

sticheln [ˈʃtɪçln] VI **(a)** (= *nähen*) to sew; (= *sticken*) to embroider **(b)** (*pej inf*: = *boshafte Bemerkungen machen*) to

make snide remarks (*inf*); **gegen jdn ~** to make digs (*Brit*) or pokes (*US*) at sb

Stich-: stichfest ADJ *siehe* **hiebfest**; **Stichflamme** F tongue of flame; **stichhalten** [ˈʃtɪçhaltn] VI SEP IRREG (*Aus*) *siehe* **Stich**; **stichhaltig**, (*Aus*) **stichhältig ◼1** ADJ valid; *Beweis* conclusive; **sein Alibi ist nicht ~** his alibi doesn't hold water **◼2** ADV conclusively

Stichling [ˈʃtɪçlɪŋ] M **-s, -e** (*Zool*) stickleback

Stichprobe F spot check; (*Sociol*) (random) sample survey; **~n machen** to carry out spot checks; (*Sociol*) to carry out a (random) sample survey

Stichsäge F fret saw

sticht [ʃtɪçt] 3. PERS SING PRES *von* **stechen**

Stich-: Stichtag M qualifying date; **Stichwaffe** F stabbing weapon

Stichwort NT **(a)** *pl* **-wörter** (*in Nachschlagewerken*) headword **(b)** *pl* **-worte** (*Theat, fig*) cue **(c)** *pl* **-worte** USU PL notes *pl*; (*bei Nacherzählung etc*) key words *pl*

Stichwort-: Stichwortkatalog M classified catalogue (*Brit*) or catalog (*US*); **Stichwortverzeichnis** NT index

Stichwunde F stab wound

sticken [ˈʃtɪkn] VTI to embroider

Sticker [ˈʃtɪkɐ, ˈst-] M **-s, -** (*inf*: = *Aufkleber*) sticker

Stickerei [ʃtɪkəˈrai] F **-, -en (a)** NO PL (= *das Sticken*) embroidering **(b)** (*Gegenstand*) embroidery

Stickgarn NT embroidery thread

stickig [ˈʃtɪkɪç] ADJ *Luft, Zimmer* stuffy; *Klima* sticky; (*fig*) *Atmosphäre* oppressive

Sticknadel F embroidery needle

Stickoxid [ˈʃtɪkɔksiːt] NT nitric oxide

Stickstoff [ˈʃtɪkʃtɔf] M (*abbr* **N**) nitrogen

Stiefbruder [ˈʃtiːf-] M stepbrother

Stiefel [ˈʃtiːfl] M **-s, -** boot; **das sind zwei Paar ~** (*fig*) they are two completely different things

Stiefelette [ʃtiːfəˈlɛtə] F **-, -n** (= *Frauenstiefelette*) bootee; (= *Männerstiefelette*) half-boot

Stiefelknecht M bootjack

Stief- [ˈʃtiːf-]: **Stiefeltern** [ˈʃtiːf-] PL step-parents *pl*; **Stiefgeschwister** PL stepbrother(s *pl*) and sister(s *pl*); **Stiefkind** NT stepchild; (*fig*) poor cousin; **sie fühlt sich immer als ~ des Glücks** she always feels that fortune never smiles upon her; **Stiefmutter** F, *pl* **-mütter** stepmother; **Stiefmütterchen** NT (*Bot*) pansy; **stiefmütterlich** ADV (*fig*) **jdn/etw ~ behandeln** to pay little attention to sb/sth; **die Natur hat ihn ~ behandelt** Nature has not been kind to him; **Stiefschwester** F stepsister; **Stiefsohn** M stepson; **Stieftochter** F stepdaughter; **Stiefvater** M stepfather

stieg [ʃtiːk] PRET *von* **steigen**

Stiege [ˈʃtiːgə] F **-, -n (a)** (= *schmale Treppe*) (narrow) flight of stairs **(b)** (= *Lattenkiste*) crate

Stieglitz [ˈʃtiːglɪts] M **-es, -e** goldfinch

stiehlt [ʃtiːlt] 3. PERS SING PRES *von* **stehlen**

Stiel [ʃtiːl] M **-(e)s, -e** (= *Griff*) handle; (= *Pfeifenstiel, Glasstiel, Blütenstiel*) stem; (= *Stängel*) stalk; (= *Blattstiel*) leafstalk

Stielaugen PL (*fig inf*) **~ machen** *or* **kriegen** to gawp; **er machte ~** his eyes (nearly) popped out of his head

Stiel-: Stielglas NT stemmed glass; **Stielkamm** M tail comb; **Stielpfanne** F frying pan with a (long) handle

stier [ʃtiːɐ] **◼1** ADJ **(a)** *Blick* vacant **(b)** (*inf*: *Aus, Sw*) *Geschäft* slow; *Mensch* broke (*inf*) **◼2** ADV *starren* vacantly; **~ blicken** to have a blank stare

Stier [ʃtiːɐ] M **-(e)s, -e (a)** bull; (= *junger ~*) bullock; **wie ein ~ brüllen** to bawl one's head off (*inf*); **den ~ bei den Hörnern packen** *or* **fassen** (*prov*) to take the bull by the horns (*prov*) **(b)** (*Astrol*) Taurus *no art*; **ich bin (ein) ~** I'm (a) Taurus

stieren [ˈʃtiːrən] VI (*auf +acc* at) to stare; **sein Blick stierte ins Leere** he stared vacantly into space

Stier-: Stierkampf M bullfight; **Stierkampfarena** F bullring; **Stierkämpfer(in)** M(F) bullfighter

stieß [ʃtiːs] PRET *von* **stoßen**

Stift¹ [ʃtɪft] M **-(e)s, -e (a)** (= *Metallstift*) pin; (= *Holzstift*) peg; (= *Nagel*) tack **(b)** (= *Bleistift*) pencil; (= *Buntstift*) crayon; (= *Filzstift*) felt-tipped pen; (= *Kugelschreiber*) ballpoint (pen); (*Comput*) pen **(c)** (*inf*: = *Lehrling*) apprentice (boy)

Stift² NT -(e)s, -e (= *Domstift*) cathedral chapter; (= *Theologiestift*) seminary

stiften ['ʃtɪftn] VT (a) (= *gründen*) *Kirche, Universität* to found; (= *spenden, spendieren*) to donate; *Preis, Stipendium etc* to endow (b) *Verwirrung, Unfrieden, Unheil* to cause; *Frieden* to bring about; *Ehe* to arrange; **Gutes/Schaden** ~ to do good/damage

Stifter ['ʃtɪftɐ] M -s, -, **Stifterin** [-ərɪn] F -, -nen (= *Gründer*) founder; (= *Spender*) donator

Stiftung ['ʃtɪftʊŋ] F -, -en foundation; (= *Schenkung*) donation; (*von Universität, Stipendium etc*) endowment

Stiftzahn M post crown

Stigma ['ʃtɪgma, st-] NT -s, -ta [-ta] (*Biol, Rel, fig*) stigma

Stil [ʃtiːl, stiːl] M -(e)s, -e (= *Eigenart*) style; **in großem** *or* **im großen** ~ in a big way; **... alten ~s** old-style ...; **schlechter** ~ bad style; **das ist schlechter** ~ (*fig*) that is bad form

Stil-: **Stilblüte** F (*hum*) stylistic howler (*Brit inf*) *or* blooper (*US inf*); **Stilbruch** M stylistic incongruity; (*in Roman etc*) abrupt change in style; **das ist ein glatter** ~ (*inf*) that is really incongruous; **Stilebene** F (*Liter, Ling*) style level

stilisieren [ʃtili'ziːrən, st-], *ptp* **stilisiert** VT to stylize

Stilistik [ʃti'lɪstɪk, st-] F -, -en (*Liter*) stylistics *sing*; (= *Handbuch*) guide to good style

stilistisch [ʃti'lɪstɪʃ, st-] ◼ ADJ stylistic ◼ ADV **ich muss meine Vorlesung** ~ **überarbeiten** I must go over my lecture from the point of view of style; **etw** ~ **ändern/verbessern** to change/improve the style of sth; ~ **gesehen** *or* **betrachtet ist der Artikel brillant** the style of this article is brilliant

still [ʃtɪl] ◼ ADJ (a) (= *ruhig*) quiet; *Gebet, Vorwurf, Beobachter* silent; ~ **werden** to go quiet; **ein ~es Eckchen** a quiet corner; **um ihn/darum ist es ~ geworden** you don't hear anything about him/it any more; **Stille Nacht** Silent Night; **in ~em Gedenken** in silent tribute; **in ~em Schmerz/in ~er Trauer** in silent suffering/grief; **im Stillen** without saying anything; **ich dachte mir im Stillen** I thought to myself; **sei doch ~!** be quiet (b) (= *unbewegt*) *Luft* still; *See* calm; (= *ohne Kohlensäure*) *Mineralwasser* still; **die Stille Ozean** the Pacific (Ocean); **~e Wasser sind tief** (*Prov*) still waters run deep (*Prov*) (c) (= *heimlich*) secret; **im Stillen** in secret (d) (*Comm*) *Gesellschafter, Teilhaber* sleeping (*Brit*), silent (*US*); *Reserven, Rücklagen* secret ◼ ADV (a) (= *leise*) *weinen, arbeiten, nachdenken* quietly; *leiden* in silence; *auseinander gehen, weggehen* silently; ~ **lächeln** to give a quiet smile; **ganz ~ und leise** *erledigen* discreetly; **er hat sich ~ und leise aus dem Staub gemacht** he just disappeared (b) (= *unbewegt*) *daliegen, dasitzen, liegen bleiben* still; ~ **halten** to keep still; ~ **sitzen** to sit still

Stille ['ʃtɪlə] F -, NO PL (a) (= *Ruhe*) quiet(ness); (= *Schweigen*) silence; **in der** ~ **der Nacht** in the still of the night; **in aller** ~ quietly; **die Beerdigung fand in aller** ~ **statt** it was a quiet funeral (b) (= *Unbewegtheit*) calm(ness); (*der Luft*) stillness (c) (= *Heimlichkeit*) secrecy; **in aller** ~ secretly

Stilleben NT *siehe* **Stillleben**

stillegen VT *siehe* **stilllegen**

stillen ['ʃtɪlən] ◼ VT (a) (= *zum Stillstand bringen*) *Tränen* to stop; *Schmerzen* to ease; *Blutung* to staunch (b) (= *befriedigen*) to satisfy; *Durst* to quench (c) *Säugling* to breast-feed ◼ VI to breast-feed; **~de Mutter** nursing mother

Stillhalteabkommen NT (*Fin, fig*) moratorium

stillhalten VI SEP IRREG (a) *siehe* **still** (b) (*fig*) to keep quiet

Still-: **Stillleben** NT still life; **stilllegen** VT SEP to close down; **stillgelegtes Bergwerk** disused mine; **Stilllegung** [-leːgʊŋ] F -, -en closure

stillos ◼ ADJ lacking in style; (= *fehl am Platze*) incongruous ◼ ADV with no sense of style; **völlig ~ servierte sie Hummersuppe in Teetassen** showing absolutely no sense of style she served up lobster soup in tea cups

Stillosigkeit F -, -en lack of style *no pl*; **solche ~en ist man von ihr gewohnt** we're used to her having no sense of style

stillschweigen VI SEP IRREG to remain silent; **zu etw** ~ to remain silent in the face of sth; **schweig still!** be silent

Stillschweigen NT silence; **auf sein ~ kann man sich verlassen** one can rely on his keeping silent; **jdm** ~ **auferlegen**, **jdn zum** ~ **verpflichten** to swear sb to silence; **beide Seiten haben** ~ **vereinbart** both sides have agreed not to say anything

stillschweigend ◼ ADJ silent; *Einverständnis* tacit ◼ ADV tacitly; **über etw** (*acc*) ~ **hinweggehen** to pass over sth in silence; **etw** ~ **hinnehmen** to accept sth silently

stillsitzen VI SEP IRREG AUX SEIN *or* HABEN *siehe* **still**

Stillstand M standstill; (*vorübergehend*) interruption; (*in Entwicklung*) halt; **bei ~ der Maschine ...** when the machine is stopped ...; **ein ~ des Herzens** a cardiac arrest; **zum ~ kommen** to come to a standstill; (*Produktion auch, Maschine, Motor, Herz, Blutung*) to stop; (*Prozess, Entwicklung*) to come to a halt; **etw zum ~ bringen** *Verkehr* to bring sth to a standstill; *Produktion auch, Maschine, Motor* to stop sth; *Blutung* to stop sth; *Prozess, Entwicklung* to bring sth to a halt

stillstehen VI SEP IRREG AUX SEIN *or* HABEN (a) (*Verkehr, Produktion, Handel etc*) to be at a standstill; (*Fabrik, Maschine*) to be idle; (*Herz*) to have stopped; **die Zeit schien stillzustehen** time seemed to stand still (b) (= *stehen bleiben*) to stop; (*Maschine*) to stop working

stillvergnügt ◼ ADJ contented ◼ ADV happily

Stil-: **Stilmittel** NT stylistic device; **Stilmöbel** PL period furniture *sing*; **stilsicher** ◼ ADJ stylistically confident ◼ ADV ~ **schreiben** to write with a good consistent style; **sich ~ ausdrücken** to be a stylistically confident speaker; **stilvoll** ◼ ADJ stylish ◼ ADV stylishly; **Stilwörterbuch** NT dictionary of correct usage

Stimm-: **Stimmabgabe** F voting; **sie kommen zur ~** they come to vote; **Stimmband** [-bant] NT, *pl* **-bänder** USU PL vocal chord; **seine Stimmbänder strapazieren** to strain one's voice; (*fig*) to talk one's head off; **stimmberechtigt** ADJ entitled to vote; **Stimmbruch** M = **Stimmwechsel**

Stimme ['ʃtɪmə] F -, -n (a) (*lit*) (*fig*) voice; (*Mus: = Part*) part; (= *Orgelstimme*) register; **mit leiser/lauter ~** in a soft/loud voice; **die erste/zweite ~ singen** to sing the top part *or* the melody/the descant; **die ~n mehren sich, die ...** there is a growing number of people calling for ...; **der ~ des Gewissens folgen** to act according to one's conscience; **der ~ des Herzens folgen** to follow the dictates of one's heart (b) (= *Wahlstimme, Votum*) vote; **eine ~ haben** to have the vote; (= *Mitspracherecht*) to have a say; **keine ~ haben** not to be entitled to vote; (= *Mitspracherecht*) to have no say; **seine ~ abgeben** to cast one's vote; **jdm/einer Partei seine ~ geben** to vote for sb/a party; **die abgegebenen ~n** the votes cast

stimmen ['ʃtɪmən] ◼ VI (a) (= *richtig sein*) to be right; **stimmt es, dass ...?** is it true that ...?; **das stimmt** that's right; **das stimmt nicht** that's not right, that's wrong; **hier stimmt was nicht!** there's something wrong here; **mit ihr stimmt etwas nicht** there's something wrong with her; **das stimmt schon, aber ...** that's true, but ...; **stimmt so!** keep the change (b) (= *zusammenpassen*) to go (together) (c) (= *wählen, sich entscheiden*) to vote; **für/gegen jdn/etw ~** to vote for/against sb/sth ◼ VT *Instrument* to tune; **jdn froh/traurig ~** to make sb (feel) cheerful/sad; *siehe auch* **gestimmt**

Stimmen-: **Stimmenfang** M (*inf*) canvassing; **auf ~ sein/gehen** to be/go canvassing; **Stimmengewirr** NT babble of voices; **Stimmengleichheit** F tie

Stimm-: **Stimmenthaltung** F abstention; **Stimmgabel** F tuning fork; **stimmhaft** (*Ling*) ◼ ADJ voiced ◼ ADV ~ **ausgesprochen werden** to be voiced

stimmig ['ʃtɪmɪç] ADJ *Umfeld* ordered; *Argumente* coherent

Stimmigkeit F -, NO PL coherence

Stimm-: **Stimmlage** F (*Mus*) voice, register; **stimmlos** (*Ling*) ◼ ADJ voiceless ◼ ADV ~ **ausgesprochen werden** not to be voiced; **Stimmrecht** NT right to vote; **Stimmrechtsaktie** F voting share

Stimmung ['ʃtɪmʊŋ] F -, -en (a) (= *Gemütszustand*) mood; (= *Atmosphäre*) atmosphere; (*bei der Truppe, unter den Arbeitern*) morale; **in (guter) ~** in a good mood; **in gehobener ~** in high spirits; **in schlechter ~** in a bad mood; **wir hatten eine tolle ~** we were in a tremendous mood; **in ~ kommen** to liven up; **für ~ sorgen** to make sure there is a good atmosphere; **in ~ sein** to be in a good mood; **~!** have a good time! (b) (= *Meinung*) opinion; **~ gegen/für jdn/etw machen** to stir up (public) opinion against/in favour (*Brit*) *or* favor (*US*) of sb/sth (c) (*St Ex*) mood

Stimmungs-: **Stimmungsmache** F, NO PL (*pej*) cheap propaganda; **Stimmungsumschwung** M change of atmosphere; (*Pol*) swing (in public opinion); (*St Ex*) change in trend; **Stimmungswandel** M change of atmosphere; (*Pol*) change in (public) opinion

Stimm-: **Stimmverzerrer** [-fɛɐtsɛʀə] M **-s, -** voice distorter; **Stimmwechsel** M **nach dem ~** after one's voice has broken; **er ist im ~** his voice is breaking; **Stimmzettel** M ballot paper

Stimulation [ʃtimula'tsɪoːn, st-] F **-, -en** (*Med, fig*) stimulation

stimulieren [ʃtimu'liːrən, st-], *ptp* **stimuliert** VT (*Med, fig*) to stimulate

Stink-: **Stinkbombe** F stink bomb; **Stinkdrüse** F (*Zool*) scent gland

Stinkefinger M (*inf*) finger (*inf*) (*held up as rude gesture*), bird (*US inf*); **jdm den ~ zeigen** to give sb the finger (*inf*) *or* the bird (*US inf*)

stinken [ˈʃtɪŋkn̩], *pret* **stank** [ʃtaŋk], *ptp* **gestunken** [gəˈʃtʊŋkn̩] VI **(a)** (*nach of*) to stink; **wie der Teufel** *or* **die Pest ~** (*inf*) to stink to high heaven (*inf*)
(b) (*fig inf*) **er stinkt nach Geld** he's stinking rich (*inf*); **er stinkt vor Faulheit** he's bone idle (*Brit*) *or* extremely lazy; **das stinkt zum Himmel** it's an absolute scandal; **an der Sache stinkt etwas** there's something fishy about it (*inf*); **die Sache stinkt mir** (*inf*), **mir stinkts (gewaltig)!** (*inf*) I'm fed up to the back teeth (with it) (*Brit inf*) *or* to the back of my throat (with it) (*US inf*)

stinkfaul ADJ (*inf*) bone idle (*Brit*)

stinkig [ˈʃtɪŋkɪç] ADJ (*inf*) stinking (*inf*); (= *verärgert*) pissed off (*sl*)

Stink-: **stinklangweilig** ADJ (*inf*) deadly boring; **Stinkmorchel** F (*Bot*) stinkhorn; **stinknormal** ADJ (*inf*) boringly normal; **stinkreich** ADJ (*inf*) stinking rich (*Brit inf*), rolling in it (*inf*); **stinksauer** ADJ (*sl*) pissed off (*inf*); **Stinktier** NT skunk; **Stinkwut** F (*inf*) raging temper; **eine ~ (auf jdn) haben** to be livid (with sb)

Stint [ʃtɪnt] M **-(e)s, -e** (*Zool*) smelt

Stipendiat [ʃtipɛn'diaːt] M **-en, -en**, **Stipendiatin** [-'diaːtɪn] F **-, -nen** *siehe* **Stipendium** person receiving a scholarship/grant

Stipendium [ʃti'pɛndiʊm] NT **-s, Stipendien** [-diən] (*als Auszeichnung etc erhalten*) scholarship; (*zur allgemeinen Unterstützung des Studiums*) grant

stirbt [ʃtɪrpt] 3. PERS SING PRES *von* **sterben**

Stirn [ʃtɪrn] F **-, -en** forehead; **die ~ runzeln** to wrinkle one's brow; **es steht ihm auf der ~ geschrieben** it is written all over his face; **die ~ haben** *or* **besitzen, zu ...** to have the effrontery to ...; **jdm/einer Sache die ~ bieten** (*geh*) to defy sb/sth

Stirn-: **Stirnband** [-bant] NT, *pl* **-bänder** headband; **Stirnglatze** F receding hairline; **Stirnhöhle** F frontal sinus; **Stirnhöhlenkatarr(h)** M, **Stirnhöhlenvereiterung** F sinusitis; **Stirnlocke** F quiff (*Brit*), cowlick; **Stirnrunzeln** NT **-s**, NO PL frown

stöbern [ˈʃtøːbɐn] VI to rummage (*in* +*dat* in, *durch* through)

Stocherkahn M punt

stochern [ˈʃtɔxɐn] VI to poke (*in* +*dat* at); (*im Essen*) to pick (*in* +*dat* at); **sich** (*dat*) **in den Zähnen ~** to pick one's teeth

Stock [ʃtɔk] M **-(e)s, ⸚e** [ˈʃtœkə] **(a)** stick; (= *Rohrstock*) cane; (= *Taktstock*) baton; (= *Zeigestock*) pointer; (= *Billardstock*) cue; **am ~ gehen** to walk with (the aid of) a stick; (*fig inf*) to be in a bad way; (*nach viel Arbeit*) to be dead beat (*Brit inf*) *or* dead (*US inf*)
(b) (*Pflanze*) (= *Rebstock*) vine; (= *Rosenstock*) rose bush; (*Bäumchen*) rose tree; (= *Blumenstock*) pot plant
(c) *pl* **-** (= ~*werk*) floor; **im ersten ~** on the first floor (*Brit*), on the second floor (*US*)
(d) (*Sw*: = *Kartoffelbrei*) mashed potato(es *pl*)

Stock-: **stockbesoffen** ADJ (*inf*) dead drunk (*inf*); **Stockbett** NT bunk bed; **stockdunkel** ADJ (*inf*) pitch-dark; **im Stockdunkeln** in the pitch dark

Stöckelschuh M stiletto

stocken [ˈʃtɔkn̩] VI **(a)** (*Herz, Puls*) to skip a beat; (*Gedanken, Worte*) to falter; (= *nicht vorangehen*) (*Arbeit, Entwicklung*) to make no progress; (*Unterhaltung, Gespräch*) to flag; (*Verhandlungen*) to grind to a halt; (*Konjunktur, Geschäfte, Handel*) to stagnate; (*Verkehr*) to be held up; **ihm stockte der Atem** he caught his breath

(b) (= *innehalten*) (*in der Rede*) to falter; (*im Satz*) to break off; **ihre Stimme stockte** she *or* her voice faltered

stockend ⓐ ADJ faltering; *Verkehr* stop-go ⓑ ADV *sprechen* haltingly; **der Verkehr kam nur ~ voran** traffic was stop and go

Stock-: **Stockente** F mallard; **Stockfisch** M dried cod; (*pej*: *Mensch*) stick-in-the-mud (*pej inf*); **stockfleckig** ADJ mouldy (*Brit*), moldy (*US*), mildewed

Stockholm [ˈʃtɔkhɔlm] NT **-s** Stockholm

-stöckig [ʃtœkɪç] ADJ SUF -storey *attr* (*Brit*), -storeyed (*Brit*), -story *attr* (*US*), -storied (*US*); **ein zweistöckiges Haus** a two-stor(e)y house

Stock-: **stockkatholisch** ADJ (*inf*) Catholic through and through; **stockkonservativ** ADJ (*inf*) archconservative; **stocknüchtern** ADJ (*inf*) stone-cold sober (*inf*); **stocksauer** ADJ (*inf*) pissed off (*inf*); **Stockschirm** M stick umbrella; **stocktaub** ADJ (*inf*) as deaf as a post

Stockung [ˈʃtɔkʊŋ] F **-, -en (a)** (= *vorübergehender Stillstand*) interruption (+*gen, in* +*dat* in); (= *Verkehrsstockung*) congestion **(b)** (*von Verhandlungen*) breakdown (+*gen* of, in); (*von Geschäften, Handel*) slackening off (+*gen* in) **(c)** (= *Pause, Unterbrechung*) (*im Gespräch*) lull; (*in der Rede*) pause

Stockwerk NT floor; **im 5. ~** on the 5th (*Brit*) *or* 6th (*US*) floor

Stoff [ʃtɔf] M **-(e)s, -e (a)** material; (*als Materialart*) cloth **(b)** (*no pl*: = *Materie*) matter
(c) (= *Substanz, Chem*) substance; **tierische ~e** animal substance; **pflanzliche ~e** vegetable matter
(d) (= *Gegenstand, Thema*) subject (matter); (= *Unterhaltungsstoff, Diskussionsstoff*) topic; (= *Material*) material; **~ für ein** *or* **zu einem Buch sammeln** to collect material for a book; **~ zum Lesen** reading matter; **~ zum Nachdenken** food for thought
(e) (*inf*: = *Rauschgift*) dope (*inf*)

Stoffel [ˈʃtɔfl̩] M **-s, -** (*pej inf*) lout (*inf*)

stoffelig [ˈʃtɔfəlɪç] (*pej inf*) ⓐ ADJ uncouth ⓑ ADV *sich benehmen* uncouthly

stofflich [ˈʃtɔflɪç] ⓐ ADJ **(a)** (*Philos, Chem*) material **(b)** (= *den Inhalt betreffend*) as regards subject matter ⓑ ADV **(a)** (*Chem*) **etw ~ (wieder) verwerten** to (re)use the materials in sth **(b)** (*von der Materie her*) **ein ~ hochinteressanter Bericht** a report with a very interesting subject matter

stofflig ADJ, ADV (*pej inf*) = **stoffelig**

Stoff-: **Stoffpuppe** F rag doll; **Stoffrest** M remnant; **Stofftier** NT soft toy

Stoffwechsel M metabolism

Stoffwechsel-: **Stoffwechselkrankheit** F metabolic disease; **Stoffwechselstörung** F metabolic disturbance

stöhnen [ˈʃtøːnən] VI to groan; **~d** with a groan

stoisch [ˈʃtoːɪʃ, st-] ⓐ ADJ (*Philos*) Stoic; (*fig*) stoic(al) ⓑ ADV (*fig*) stoically

Stollen [ˈʃtɔlən] M **-s, - (a)** (*Min, Mil*) gallery **(b)** (*Cook*) stollen **(c)** (= *Zapfen*) (*an Hufeisen*) calk(in); (= *Schuhstollen*) stud

stolpern [ˈʃtɔlpɐn] VI AUX SEIN to stumble (*über* +*acc* over); (*fig*: = *zu Fall kommen*) to come unstuck (*esp Brit inf*); **jdn zum Stolpern bringen** (*lit*) to trip sb up; (*fig*) to be sb's downfall; **über einen Hinweis ~** (*fig*) to stumble upon a clue; **über einen Bekannten ~** (*fig*) to bump into an acquaintance

stolz [ʃtɔlts] ⓐ ADJ **(a)** proud (*auf* +*acc* of); **darauf kannst du ~ sein** that's something to be proud of **(b)** (= *imposant*) *Bauwerk, Schiff* majestic; (*iro*: = *stattlich*) *Preis, Summe* princely ⓑ ADV proudly

Stolz [ʃtɔlts] M **-es**, NO PL pride; **sein Garten/Sohn** *etc* **ist sein ganzer ~** his garden/son *etc* is his pride and joy; **voller ~ auf etw** (*acc*) **sein** to be very proud of sth; **seinen ~ in etw** (*acc*) **setzen** to take a pride in sth

stolzieren [ʃtɔl'tsiːrən], *ptp* **stolziert** VI AUX SEIN to strut; (*hochmütig, beleidigt*) to stalk

stop [ʃtɔp, st-] INTERJ stop

Stop-and-go-Verkehr [stɔpənd'goː-] M stop-and-go traffic

stopfen [ˈʃtɔpfn̩] ⓐ VT **(a)** (= *ausstopfen, füllen*) to stuff; *Pfeife, Loch, Wurst* to fill; **jdm den Mund** (*inf*) *or* **das Maul** (*inf*) **~ to** silence sb; **sich** (*dat*) **Watte in die Ohren ~** to plug one's ears with cotton wool (*Brit*) *or* cotton (*US*)
(b) (= *ausbessern, flicken*) *Loch, Strümpfe etc* to mend; (*fig*) *Haushaltslöcher etc* to plug
ⓑ VI **(a)** (*Speisen*) (= *verstopfen*) to cause constipation;

(= *sättigen*) to be filling **(b)** (= *flicken*) to darn

stopp [ʃtɔp] INTERJ stop

Stopp [ʃtɔp] M **-s, -s** stop; (= *Lohnstopp*) freeze

Stoppball M (*Tennis etc*) dropshot

Stoppel [ʃtɔpl] F **-, -n** stubble

Stoppel-: **Stoppelbart** M stubbly beard; **Stoppelfeld** NT stubble field

stoppelig [ʃtɔpəlɪç] ADJ stubbly

stoppen [ʃtɔpn] **1** VT **(a)** (= *anhalten, aufhalten*) to stop **(b)** (= *Zeit abnehmen*) to time **2** VI **(a)** (= *anhalten*) to stop **(b) ihr beide lauft und ich stoppe** you two run and I'll time you

Stopplicht NT stoplight; (*Aut*) brake light

stopplig [ʃtɔplɪç] ADJ stubbly

Stopp-: **Stoppschild** NT, *pl* **-schilder** stop sign; **Stoppstraße** F road with stop signs, stop street (*US*); **Stoppuhr** F stopwatch

Stöpsel [ʃtœpsl] M **-s, -** plug; (= *Pfropfen*) stopper; (= *Korken*) cork; (*inf:* = *Knirps*) little fellow

Stopselzieher [-tsiːɐ] M **-s, -** (*Aus*) corkscrew

Stör [ʃtøːɐ] M **-(e)s, -e** (*Zool*) sturgeon

Stör-: **Störaktion** F disruptive action *no pl*; **störanfällig** ADJ Technik, Bauteil, Kraftwerk susceptible to faults; Gerät, Verkehrsmittel liable to break down; Zündung, Lenkung etc unreliable; (*fig*) Verhältnis shaky; **Störanfälligkeit** F (*von Technik, Bauteil, Kraftwerk*) susceptibility to faults; (*von Gerät, Verkehrsmittel*) liability to break down; (*von Zündung, Lenkung etc*) unreliability; (*fig: von Verhältnis*) shakiness

Storch [ʃtɔrç] M **-(e)s, -e** [ʃtœrçə] stork; **wie der ~ im Salat gehen** (*inf*) to pick one's way carefully

Störchin F **-, -nen** female stork

Storchschnabel M **(a)** (*Bot*) cranesbill **(b)** (*Tech*) pantograph

stören [ʃtøːrən] **1** VT **(a)** (= *beeinträchtigen*) to disturb; Verhältnis, Harmonie, Gesamteindruck etc to spoil; Rundfunkempfang to interfere with; (*absichtlich*) to jam; **jds Pläne ~** to interfere with sb's plans; *siehe auch* **gestört (b)** Prozess, Vorlesung, Feier to disrupt **(c)** (= *unangenehm berühren*) to disturb; **was mich an ihm/ daran stört** what I don't like about him/it; **entschuldigen Sie, wenn ich Sie störe** I'm sorry if I'm disturbing you; **stört es Sie, wenn ich rauche?** do you mind if I smoke?; **würden Sie bitte aufhören zu rauchen, es stört mich** would you mind not smoking, I find it annoying; **das stört mich nicht** that doesn't bother me; **sie lässt sich durch nichts ~** she doesn't let anything bother her **2** VR **sich an etw** (*dat*) **~** to be bothered about sth; **ich störe mich an seiner Unpünktlichkeit** I take exception to his unpunctuality **3** VI **(a)** (= *lästig sein, im Weg sein*) to get in the way; (= *unterbrechen*) to interrupt; (= *Belästigung darstellen:* Musik, Lärm etc) to be disturbing; **bitte nicht ~!** please do not disturb!; **ich möchte nicht ~** I don't want to be a nuisance; (*in Privatsphäre*) I don't want to intrude; **störe ich?** am I disturbing you?; **stört das sehr, wenn ich jetzt fernsehe?** would it disturb you if I watch television?; **etw als ~d empfinden** to find sth bothersome; **ein ~der Lärm** a disturbing noise; **ein ~der Umstand** a nuisance; **eine ~de Begleiterscheinung** a troublesome side effect **(b)** (= *unangenehm auffallen*) to spoil the effect

Störenfried [-friːt] M **-(e)s, -e** [-də], **Störer** [ʃtøːrɐ] M **-s, -**, **Störerin** [-ərɪn] F **-, -nen** troublemaker

Stör-: **Störfall** M (*in Kernkraftwerk etc*) malfunction, accident; **Störmanöver** NT disruptive action

Storni PL *von* **Storno**

stornieren [ʃtɔrˈniːrən, st-], *ptp* **storniert** VTI (*Comm*) Auftrag, Reise, Flug to cancel; Buchungsfehler to reverse

Storno [ʃtɔrno, ˈst-] M *or* NT **-s, Storni** [-ni] (*Comm*) (*von Buchungsfehler*) reversal; (*von Auftrag*) cancellation

störrisch [ʃtœrɪʃ] **1** ADJ obstinate; Kind, Haare unmanageable; Pferd refractory **2** ADV **sich ~ verhalten** *or* **anstellen** to act stubborn

Störsender M (*Rad*) jamming transmitter

Störung [ʃtøːrʊŋ] F **-, -en (a)** disturbance **(b)** (*von Ablauf, Verhandlungen etc*) disruption **(c)** (= *Verkehrsstörung*) holdup; **es kam immer wieder zu ~en des Verkehrs** the traffic was continually held up **(d)** (*Tech*) fault; **eine ~** a fault; **in der**

Leitung muss eine **~** sein there must be a fault on the line **(e)** (*Rad*) interference; (*absichtlich*) jamming; **atmosphärische ~en** atmospherics *pl* **(f)** (*Med*) disorder

Störungs-: **Störungsanzeige** F fault indicator; **störungsfrei** ADJ trouble-free; (*Rad*) free from interference; **der Verkehr ist** *or* **läuft wieder ~** the traffic is moving freely again; **Störungsstelle** F (*Telec*) faults service

Stoß [ʃtoːs] M **-es, -e** [ʃtøːsə] **(a)** push; (*leicht*) poke; (*mit Faust*) punch; (*mit Fuß*) kick; (*mit Ellbogen*) nudge; (*mit Kopf, Hörnern*) butt; (= *Dolchstoß etc*) stab; (*Fechten*) thrust; (= *Schwimmstoß*) stroke; (= *Atemstoß*) gasp; **sich** (*dat*) *or* **seinem Herzen einen ~ geben** to pluck up courage **(b)** (= *Anprall*) impact; (= *Erdstoß*) tremor **(c)** (*Med*) intensive course of drugs **(d)** (= *Stapel*) pile, stack

Stoßdämpfer M (*Aut*) shock absorber

stoßen [ʃtoːsn], *pret* **stieß** [ʃtiːs], *ptp* **gestoßen** [gəˈʃtoːsn] **1** VT **(a)** (= *einen Stoß versetzen*) to push; (*leicht*) to poke; (*mit Faust*) to punch; (*mit Fuß*) to kick; (*mit Ellbogen*) to nudge; (*mit Kopf, Hörnern*) to butt; (= *stechen*) Dolch to thrust; **sich** (*dat*) **den Kopf** *etc* **or sich** (*acc*) **an den Kopf** *etc* **~** to hit one's head *etc*; **jdm** *or* **jdn in die Seite ~** to nudge sb; **jdn von sich ~** to push sb away; (*fig*) to cast sb aside **(b)** (*werfen*) to push; (*Sport*) Kugel to put; **jdn von der Treppe/aus dem Zug ~** to push sb down the stairs/out of *or* off the train **(c)** (= *zerkleinern*) Zimt, Pfeffer, Zucker to pound **2** VR to bump *or* bang oneself; **sich an etw** (*dat*) **~** (*lit*) to bump etc oneself on sth; (*fig*) to take exception to sth **3** VI **(a)** AUX SEIN (= *treffen, prallen*) to run into (*auch fig*); (= *herabsinken:* Vogel) to swoop down (*auf +acc* on); **an etw** (*acc*) **~** to bump into sth; (= *grenzen*) to border on sth; **gegen etw ~** to run into sth; **zu jdm ~** to meet up with sb; **auf jdn ~** to bump into sb; **auf etw** (*acc*) **~** (*Straße*) to lead into *or* onto sth; (*Schiff*) to hit sth; (*fig:* = *entdecken*) to come upon sth; **auf Erdöl ~** to strike oil; **auf Grundwasser ~** to discover underground water; **auf Widerstand ~** to meet with resistance; **an seine Grenzen ~** to reach one's limits **(b)** (*mit den Hörnern*) to butt (*nach* at) **(c)** (*Tech*) to butt (*an +acc* against) **(d)** (*Gewichtheben*) to jerk

Stoß-: **stoßfest** ADJ shockproof; **Stoßkarrette** F (*Sw:* = *Schubkarre*) wheelbarrow; **Stoßseufzer** M deep sigh; **Stoßstange** F (*Aut*) bumper

stößt [ʃtøːst] 3. PERS SING PRES *von* **stoßen**

Stoß-: **Stoßzahn** M tusk; **Stoßzeit** F (*im Verkehr*) rush hour; (*in Geschäft etc*) peak period

Stotterer [ʃtɔtərə] M **-s, -**, **Stotterin** [-ərɪn] F **-, -nen** stutterer

stottern [ʃtɔtɐn] VTI to stutter; (*Motor*) to splutter; **ins Stottern kommen** to start stuttering

Stövchen [ʃtøːfçən] NT **-s, -** (*teapot etc*) warmer

StPO [eˈstepeˈʔoː] F - ABBR *von* **Strafprozessordnung**

Str. ABBR *von* **Straße** St

stracks [ʃtraks] ADV straight

Straf-: **Strafanstalt** F prison; **Strafanzeige** F **~ gegen jdn erstatten** to bring a charge against sb; **Strafarbeit** F (*Sch*) punishment; (*schriftlich*) lines *pl*; **Strafbank** F, *pl* **-bänke** (*Sport*) penalty bench

strafbar ADJ Vergehen punishable; **~e Handlung** punishable offence (*Brit*) *or* offense (*US*); **das ist ~!** that's an offence (*Brit*) *or* offense (*US*); **sich ~ machen** to commit an offence (*Brit*) *or* offense (*US*)

Strafe [ʃtraːfə] F **-, -n** punishment; (*Jur, Sport*) penalty; (= *Geldstrafe*) fine; (= *Gefängnisstrafe*) sentence; **... bei ~ verboten ...** forbidden; **es ist bei ~ verboten, ...** it is a punishable offence (*Brit*) *or* offense (*US*) ...; **etw unter ~ stellen** to make sth a punishable offence (*Brit*) *or* offense (*US*); **unter ~ stehen** to be a punishable offence (*Brit*) *or* offense (*US*); **seine ~ abbüßen** *or* **absitzen** *or* **abbrummen** (*inf*) to serve one's sentence, to do one's time (*inf*); **eine ~ von drei Jahren Gefängnis** a three-year prison sentence; **100 Dollar ~ zahlen** to pay a 100 dollar fine; **zur ~ as** a punishment; **seine verdiente ~ bekommen** to get one's just deserts; **dieses Kind/Wetter ist eine ~** this child/weather is a pain (in the neck) (*inf*)

strafen [ʃtraːfn] **1** VT (= *bestrafen*) to punish; **jdn (für etw/mit etw) ~** to punish sb (for sth/with sth); **mit etw gestraft sein** to be cursed with sth; **mit seinen Kindern ist er wirklich**

gestraft his children are a real trial to him; **mit dieser Arbeit ist er wirklich gestraft** his work is a chore **2** VI to punish; **orientalische Richter ~ hart** oriental judges give severe sentences; **das Strafen** punishment

strafend 1 ADJ ATTR punitive; *Blick, Worte* reproachful **2** ADV **jdn ~ ansehen** to give sb a reproachful look

Straf-: Strafentlassene(r) [-lɛntlasənə] MF DECL AS ADJ ex-prisoner; **Strafentlassung** F discharge, release (from prison); **Straferlass** M remission (of sentence)

straff [ʃtraf] **1** ADJ *Seil* taut; *Haut* smooth; *Busen* firm; *Haltung, Gestalt* erect; (= ~ *sitzend*) *Hose etc* tight; (*fig*: = *streng*) *Disziplin, Organisation, Politik* strict; *Zeitplan* tight **2** ADV (= *stramm*) tightly; (= *streng*) *organisieren, reglementieren* strictly; **~ sitzen** to fit tightly; **etw ~ spannen** *or* **ziehen** to tighten sth; *Decke, Laken etc* to pull sth tight; **die Leine muss ~ gespannt sein** the line has to be tight

straffällig ADJ **~ werden** to commit a criminal offence (*Brit*) *or* offense (*US*); **wenn Sie wieder ~ werden ...** if you commit a further offence (*Brit*) *or* offense (*US*) ...

Straffällige(r) [ˈʃtraˌfɛɛlɪɡə] MF DECL AS ADJ offender

straffen [ˈʃtrafn] **1** VT to tighten; (= *raffen*) *Handlung, Darstellung* to tighten up; **sich** (*dat*) **die Gesichtshaut ~ lassen** to have a face-lift; **sich** (*dat*) **den Busen ~ lassen** to have one's breasts lifted; **die Zügel ~** (*fig*) to tighten the reins **2** VR to tighten; (*Haut*) to become smooth; (*Busen*) to become firm; (= *sich aufrichten*) to stiffen

Straf-: straffrei ADJ, ADV not subject to prosecution; **~ bleiben** *or* **ausgehen** to go unpunished; **Straffreiheit** F immunity from prosecution; **Strafgebühr** F surcharge; **Strafgeld** NT fine; **Strafgesetz** NT criminal law; **Strafgesetzbuch** NT Penal Code; **Strafgesetzgebung** F penal legislation; **Strafkammer** F division for criminal matters (of a court)

sträflich [ˈʃtrɛːflɪç] **1** ADJ (*lit, fig*) criminal **2** ADV *vernachlässigen etc* criminally

Sträfling [ˈʃtrɛːflɪŋ] M **-s, -e** prisoner

Straf-: Strafmandat NT ticket; **Strafmaß** NT sentence; **strafmildernd** ADJ extenuating; **Strafmündigkeit** F age of criminal responsibility; **Strafporto** NT excess postage; **Strafpredigt** F reprimand; **jdm eine ~ halten** to give sb a lecture; **Strafprozess** M criminal proceedings *pl*; **Strafprozessordnung** F code of criminal procedure; **Strafpunkt** M (*Sport*) penalty point; **Strafraum** M (*Sport*) penalty area *or* (*Ftbl auch*) box; **Strafrecht** NT criminal law; **strafrechtlich 1** ADJ criminal; **das ist aber kein ~es Problem** but that is not a problem of criminal law **2** ADV **jdn/etw ~ verfolgen** *or* **belangen** to prosecute sb/sth; **Strafregister** NT police records *pl*; (*hum inf*) record; **er hat ein langes ~** he has a long (criminal) record; (*hum inf*) he's got a bad record; **Strafsache** F criminal matter; **Strafschuss** M (*Sport*) penalty (shot); **Strafstoß** M (*Ftbl etc*) penalty (kick); (*Hockey etc*) penalty (shot); **Straftat** F criminal offence (*Brit*) *or* offense (*US*); **Straftäter(in)** M(F) offender; **Strafverfahren** NT criminal proceedings *pl*; **strafversetzen** *ptp* **strafversetzt** VT INSEP *Beamte* to transfer for disciplinary reasons; **Strafversetzung** F (disciplinary) transfer; **Strafverteidiger(in)** M(F) defence (*Brit*) *or* defense (*US*) counsel *or* lawyer; **Strafvollzug** M penal system; **offener ~** non-confinement; **Strafvollzugsanstalt** F (*form*) penal institution; **Strafzettel** M (*Jur*) ticket

Strahl [ʃtraːl] M **-(e)s, -en (a)** (*lit, fig*) ray; (= *Sonnenstrahl*) shaft of light; (= *Radiostrahl, Laserstrahl etc*) beam; **im ~ einer Taschenlampe** by the light of a torch **(b)** (= *Wasserstrahl, Luftstrahl*) jet

Strahlemann M, *pl* **-männer** (*inf*) golden boy (*inf*)

strahlen [ˈʃtraːlən] VI **(a)** (*Sonne, Licht etc*) to shine; (*Sender*) to beam; (= *glühen*) to glow (*vor +dat* with); (*Heizofen etc*) to radiate; (*radioaktiv*) to give off radioactivity **(b)** (= *leuchten*) to gleam; (*fig*) (*Gesicht*) to beam; (*Augen*) to shine; **das ganze Haus strahlte vor Sauberkeit** the whole house was sparkling clean; **was strahlst du so?** what are you so happy about?; **er strahlte vor Freude** he was beaming with happiness; **er strahlte (übers ganze Gesicht)** he was beaming all over his face; *siehe* **strahlend**

Strahlen-: Strahlenbehandlung F (*Med*) ray treatment; **Strahlenbelastung** F radiation

strahlend 1 ADJ radiant; *Wetter, Tag* glorious; *Farben* brilliant; (= *radioaktiv*) radioactive; **~es Lachen** beaming smile; **mit ~en Augen** with shining eyes; **mit ~em Gesicht**

with a beaming face **2** ADV **jdn ~ ansehen** (= *lächelnd*) to beam at sb; (= *glücklich*) to look at sb, beaming with happiness; **der Tag war ~ schön, es war ein ~ schöner Tag** it was a glorious day

Strahlen-: Strahlendosis F dose of radiation; **strahlenförmig 1** ADJ radial **2** ADV **sich ~ ausbreiten** to radiate out; **~ von etw wegführen** to radiate from sth; **strahlengeschädigt** [-ɡəʃɛːdɪçt] ADJ suffering from radiation damage; *Organ* damaged by radiation; **die Strahlengeschädigten** the radiation victims; **strahlenkrank** ADJ radiation sick; **Strahlenkrankheit** F radiation sickness; **Strahlenschäden** PL radiation injuries *pl*; **Strahlenschutz** M radiation protection; **Strahlentod** M death through radiation; **strahlenverseucht** [-fɛɛʐɔʏçt] ADJ contaminated (with radiation)

Strahler [ˈʃtraːlə] M **-s, -** (= *Lampe*) spotlight

Strahl-: Strahlmaterial NT radioactive material; **Strahltriebwerk** NT jet engine

Strahlung [ˈʃtraːlʊŋ] F **-, -en** radiation

strahlungsarm ADJ *Monitor* low-radiation

Strähnchen [ˈʃtrɛːnçən] NT **-s, -** streak

Strähne [ˈʃtrɛːnə] F **-, -n** (*Aus*) **Strähn** [ʃtrɛːn] M **-(e)s, -e** (= *Haarsträhne*) strand; (*Längenmaß,* = *Wollsträhne, Garnsträhne*) skein; **ich habe schon eine weiße ~** I already have a white streak

strähnig [ˈʃtrɛːnɪç] **1** ADJ *Haar* straggly **2** ADV **das Haar fiel ihr ~ auf die Schultern** her hair straggled down over her shoulders

stramm [ʃtram] **1** ADJ (= *straff*) tight; *Haltung, Soldat* erect; (= *kräftig, drall*) *Mädchen, Junge* strapping; *Junge, Beine* sturdy; *Brust* firm; (= *tüchtig*) *Marsch, Arbeit* strenuous; *Tag, Programm* packed; *Leistung* solid; *Tempo* brisk; (= *überzeugt*) staunch; **~e Haltung annehmen** to stand to attention **2** ADV *binden* tightly; **~ sitzen** to be tight; **~ arbeiten** (*inf*) to work hard; **~ marschieren** (*inf*) to march hard; **~ konservativ** (*inf*) staunchly conservative; **die Politiker sind weiter ~ auf Atomkurs** (*inf*) the politicians are continuing to support nuclear power unreservedly

stramm-: strammstehen VI SEP IRREG (*Mil inf*) to stand to attention; **stramm ziehen** VT SEP IRREG *Seil, Hose* to pull tight; *Socken* to pull up; **jdm den Hosenboden ~** (*inf*) to give sb a good hiding (*inf*)

Strampelhöschen [-høːsçən] NT rompers *pl*

strampeln [ˈʃtrampln] VI **(a)** (*mit Beinen*) to flail about; (*Baby*) to thrash about; **das Baby strampelte mit Armen und Beinen** the baby was kicking its feet and waving its arms about **(b)** AUX SEIN (*inf*: = *Rad fahren*) to pedal **(c)** (*inf*: = *sich abrackern*) to (sweat and) slave

Strampelsack M (*für Säuglinge*) carry-nest (*Brit*), pup sack (*US*)

Strand [ʃtrant] M **-(e)s, ⸚e** [ˈʃtrɛndə] (= *Meeresstrand*) beach; (= *Seeufer*) shore; **am ~** (= *am Meer*) on the beach; (= *am Seeufer*) on the shore; **auf ~ geraten** *or* **laufen** to run aground; **auf ~ setzen** to beach

stranden [ˈʃtrandn] VI AUX SEIN to be stranded; (*fig*) to fail

Strand-: Strandgut NT, NO PL (*lit, fig*) flotsam and jetsam; **Strandhafer** M marram (grass); **Strandkorb** M wicker beach chair with a hood; **Strandläufer** M (*Orn*) sandpiper; **Strandpromenade** F promenade

Strang [ʃtraŋ] M **-(e)s, ⸚e** [ˈʃtrɛŋə] (= *Nervenstrang, Muskelstrang*) cord; (= *DNA-~*) strand; (= *Wollstrang, Garnstrang*) hank; **der Tod durch den ~** death by hanging; **an einem** *or* **am gleichen** *or* **an demselben ~ ziehen** (*fig*) to pull together; **über die Stränge schlagen** *or* **hauen** (*inf*) to run wild (*inf*)

Strapaze [ʃtraˈpaːtsə] F **-, -n** strain

strapazfähig ADJ (*Aus*) = **strapazierfähig**

strapazieren [ʃtrapaˈtsiːrən], *ptp* **strapaziert 1** VT to be a strain on; *Schuhe, Kleidung* to be hard on; (*fig inf*) *Redensart, Begriff* to flog (to death) (*inf*); *Nerven* to strain; *Geduld* to try; **er sah strapaziert aus** he looked worn out **2** VR to tax oneself

strapazierfähig ADJ *Schuhe, Kleidung, Material* hard-wearing; (*fig inf*) *Nerven* strong

strapaziös [ʃtrapaˈtsiøːs] ADJ (*lit, fig*) exhausting

Straps [ʃtraps] M **-es, -e** suspender belt (*Brit*), garter belt (*US*)

Straßburg [ˈʃtraːsbʊrk] NT **-s** Strasbourg, Strassburg

Sträßchen [ˈʃtrɛːsçən] NT **-s, -** DIM *von* **Straße**

Straße [ˈʃtraːsə] F **-, -n (a)** road; (*in Stadt, Dorf*) street; (= *kleine Landstraße*) lane; **an der ~** by the roadside; **auf die ~ gehen** (*lit*) to go out on the street; (*als Demonstrant*) to take to the streets; (als Prostituierte) to go on the streets; **auf die ~ gesetzt werden** (inf) to be turned out (onto the streets); (als Arbeiter) to be sacked (Brit inf); **über die ~ gehen** to cross the road/street); **er wohnt drei ~n weiter** he lives three blocks further on; **Verkauf über die ~** takeaway (Brit) or takeout (US) sales; (von Getränken) off-licence sales pl (Brit), package store sales pl (US); **etw über die ~ verkaufen** to sell sth to take away (Brit) or to take out (US); **das Geld liegt auf der ~** money is there for the asking; **das Geld liegt nicht auf der ~** money doesn't grow on trees; **der Mann auf der ~** (fig) the man in the street **(b)** (= Meerenge) strait(s pl); **die ~ von Dover/Gibraltar/Messina** etc the Straits of Dover/Gibraltar/Messina etc **(c)** (Tech) (= Fertigungsstraße) (production) line; (= Walzstraße) train

Straßen-: Straßenarbeiten PL roadworks pl; **Straßenarbeiter(in)** M(F) roadworker

Straßenbahn F (= Wagen) tram (esp Brit), streetcar (US); (= Netz) tramway(s) (esp Brit), streetcar system (US); **mit der ~** by tram (esp Brit) or streetcar (US)

Straßenbahn-: Straßenbahnhaltestelle F tram (esp Brit) or streetcar (US) stop; **Straßenbahnlinie** F tramline (esp Brit), streetcar line (US); **mit der ~ 11 fahren** to take the number 11 tram (esp Brit) or streetcar (US); **Straßenbahnschaffner(in)** M(F) tram (esp Brit) or streetcar (US) conductor/conductress; **Straßenbahnwagen** M tram (esp Brit), streetcar (US)

Straßen-: Straßenbau M, NO PL road construction; **Straßenbauarbeiten** PL roadworks pl; **Straßenbelag** M road surface; **Straßenbeleuchtung** F street lighting; **Straßenbenutzungsgebühr** F (road) toll; **Straßenfeger** [-fe:gɐ] M **-s, -**, **Straßenfegerin** [-ərɪn] F **-, -nen** road sweeper; **Straßenfest** NT street party; **Straßenführung** F route; **Straßenglätte** F slippery road surface; **Straßengraben** M ditch; **Straßenjunge** M (pej) street urchin; **Straßenkarte** F road map; **Straßenkehrer** [-ke:rɐ] M **-s, -**, **Straßenkehrerin** [-ərɪn] F **-, -nen** road sweeper; **Straßenkreuzer** M (inf) limo (inf); **Straßenkreuzung** F crossroads sing or pl, intersection (US); **Straßenlage** F (Aut) road holding; **Straßenlaterne** F streetlamp; **Straßenmädchen** NT prostitute; **Straßenmusikant(in)** M(F) street musician; **Straßenname** M street name; **Straßennetz** NT road network; **Straßenrand** M roadside; **Straßenreinigung** F street cleaning; **Straßensänger** M street singer; **Straßenschäden** PL damage sing to the road surface; „**Achtung ~**" "uneven road surface"; **Straßenschild** NT, pl **-schilder** street sign; **Straßenschlacht** F street battle; **Straßensperre** F roadblock; **Straßenstrich** M (inf) walking the streets; (Gegend) red-light district; **auf den ~ gehen** to walk the streets; **Straßentransport** M road transport or haulage; **im ~ road;** **Straßenverhältnisse** PL road conditions pl; **Straßenverkauf** M street trading; (= Außerhausverkauf) takeaway (Brit) or takeout (US) sales pl; (von alkoholischen Getränken) off-licence sales pl (Brit), package store sales pl (US); (= Verkaufsstelle) takeaway (Brit), takeout (US); (für alkoholische Getränke) off-licence (Brit), package store (US); **Zeitungen werden im ~ angeboten** newspapers are sold on the streets; **Straßenverkäufer(in)** M(F) street vendor; **Straßenverkehr** M traffic; **Straßenverkehrsordnung** F ≈ Highway Code (Brit), traffic rules and regulations pl; **Straßenwacht** F road patrol; **Straßenwalze** F steamroller; **Straßenzustand** M road conditions pl; **Straßenzustandsbericht** M road report

Stratege [ʃtra'te:gə, st-] M **-n, -n**, **Strategin** [-'te:gɪn] F **-, -nen** strategist

Strategie [ʃtrate'gi:, st-] F **-, -n** [-'gi:ən] strategy

strategisch [ʃtra'te:gɪʃ, st-] **1** ADJ strategic **2** ADV strategically

Stratosphäre [ʃtrato'sfɛ:rə, st-] F, NO PL stratosphere

sträuben ['ʃtrɔybn] **1** VR **(a)** (Haare, Fell) to stand on end; (Gefieder) to become ruffled; **da ~ sich einem die Haare** it's enough to make your hair stand on end **(b)** (fig) to resist (gegen etw sth); **es sträubt sich alles in mir, das zu tun** I am most reluctant to do it **2** VT Gefieder to ruffle

Strauch [ʃtraux] M **-(e)s, Sträucher** ['ʃtrɔyçɐ] bush

Strauch-: Strauchtomate F vine-ripened tomato; **Strauchwerk** NT, NO PL (= Gebüsch) bushes pl; (= Gestrüpp) undergrowth

Strauß¹ {ʃtraus} M **-es, -e** ostrich; **wie der Vogel ~** like an ostrich

Strauß² M **-es, Sträuße** ['ʃtrɔysə] (= Blumenstrauß) bunch (of flowers); (= kleiner ~, Biedermeierstrauß) posy

Sträußchen ['ʃtrɔysçən] NT **-s, -** DIM von **Strauß²**

Streamer ['stri:mɐ] M **-s, -** (Comput) streamer

Strebe ['ʃtre:bə] F **-, -n** brace; (= Deckenstrebe) joist; (von Flugzeug) strut

streben ['ʃtre:bn] VI (geh) **(a)** (= den Drang haben, sich bemühen) to strive (nach, an +acc, zu for); (Sch pej) to swot (inf); **danach ~, etw zu tun** to strive to do sth; **die Pflanze strebt nach dem Licht** the plant seeks the light; **in die Ferne ~** to be drawn to distant parts **(b)** AUX SEIN (= sich bewegen) **nach** or **zu etw ~** to make one's way to sth **(c)** AUX SEIN **in die Höhe** or **zum Himmel ~** to rise aloft

Streben ['ʃtre:bn] NT **-s**, NO PL (= Drängen, Sinnen) striving (nach for); (nach Ruhm, Geld) aspiration (nach to); (= Bemühen) efforts pl

Strebepfeiler M buttress

Streber ['ʃtre:bɐ] M **-s, -**, **Streberin** [-ərɪn] F **-, -nen** (pej inf) pushy person; (Sch) swot (Brit inf), grind (US inf)

Streberei [ʃtre:bə'rai] F **-**, NO PL (pej inf) pushiness (inf); (Sch) cramming (inf)

strebsam ['ʃtre:pza:m] ADJ assiduous

Strecke ['ʃtrɛkə] F **-, -n (a)** (= Entfernung zwischen zwei Punkten) (Sport) distance; (Math) line (between two points); **eine ~ zurücklegen** to cover a distance; **eine ziemliche** or **gute ~ entfernt sein** (lit, fig) to be a long way away **(b)** (= Abschnitt) (von Straße, Fluss) stretch; (von Bahnlinie) section **(c)** (= Weg, Route, Flugstrecke) route; (= Straße) road; (= Bahnlinie) (Sport: = Bahn) track; (fig: = Passage) passage; **für die ~ London-Glasgow brauchen wir 5 Stunden** the journey from London to Glasgow will take us 5 hours; **auf** or **an der ~ Paris-Brüssel** on the way from Paris to Brussels; **die ~ Wien-München führt durch ...** the road/track etc between Vienna and Munich goes through ...; **auf freier** or **offener ~** (esp Rail) on the open line; **auf weite ~n (hin)** (lit, fig) for long stretches; **auf der ~ bleiben** (bei Rennen) to drop out of the running; (in Konkurrenzkampf) to fall by the wayside **(d)** (Hunt: = Jagdbeute) kill; **zur ~ bringen** to kill; (fig) Verbrecher to hunt down

strecken ['ʃtrɛkn] **1** VT **(a)** Arme, Beine, Oberkörper to stretch; Hals to crane; (Sch: um sich zu melden) Finger, Hand to raise; **die Zunge aus dem Mund ~** to stick out one's tongue; **den Kopf aus dem Fenster/durch die Tür ~** to stick one's head out of the window/through the door **(b)** (inf: = absichtlich verlängern) Vorräte, Geld to eke out; Arbeit to drag out (inf); Essen, Suppe to make go further; (= verdünnen) to thin down, to dilute **2** VR **(a)** (= sich recken) to stretch **(b)** (= sich hinziehen) to drag on

Strecken-: Streckenabschnitt M (Rail) track section; **Streckenarbeiter(in)** M(F) (Rail) platelayer; **Streckenführung** F (Rail) route; **Streckengeschäft** NT drop shipping; **Streckennetz** NT rail network; **Streckenstilllegung** F (Rail) line closure; **streckenweise** ADV in parts

Streckverband M (Med) bandage used in traction

Streetball ['stri:tbɔ:l] M **-s**, NO PL streetball

Streetworker ['stri:twœ:ɐkɐ, -wœrkɐ] M **-s, -**, **Streetworkerin** [-ərɪn] F **-, -nen** outreach worker

Streich [ʃtraiç] M **-(e)s, -e** (= Schabernack) prank, trick; **jdm einen ~ spielen** (lit) to play a trick on sb; (fig: Gedächtnis etc) to play tricks on sb

Streicheleinheiten PL (= Zärtlichkeit) tender loving care sing; (= Lob, Anerkennung) words pl of praise

streicheln ['ʃtraiçln] VTI to stroke; (= liebkosen) to caress

streichen ['ʃtraiçn], pret **strich** [ʃtrɪç], ptp **gestrichen** [gə'ʃtrɪçn] **1** VT **(a)** (mit der Hand) to stroke; **etw glatt ~** to smooth sth (out); **sich** (dat) **die Haare aus dem Gesicht ~** to push one's hair back from one's face **(b)** (= auftragen) Butter, Marmelade etc to spread; Salbe, Farbe etc to apply; **sich** (dat) **ein Brot (mit Butter) ~** to butter oneself a slice of bread; **sich ~ lassen** (Butter etc) to spread easily **(c)** (= anstreichen: mit Farbe) to paint; **frisch gestrichen!** wet (Brit) or fresh (US) paint **(d)** (= tilgen) Zeile, Satz to delete; Auftrag, Plan, Zug, freier Tag etc to cancel; Schulden to write off; Zuschuss, Gelder, Arbeitsplätze etc to cut; **etw aus dem Protokoll ~** to delete sth from the minutes; **jdn/etw von** or **aus der Liste ~** to take sb/sth off the list

(e) (*Naut*) *Segel, Flagge, Ruder* to strike
(f) *siehe* **gestrichen**
⧓ VI **(a)** (= *über etw hinfahren*) to stroke; **mit der Hand über etw** *acc* ~ to stroke sth (with one's hand); **sie strich ihm über das Haar** she stroked his hair
(b) AUX SEIN (= *streifen*) to brush past (*an* +*dat* sth); (*Wind*) to waft; **um/durch etw** ~ (= *herumstreichen*) to prowl around/through sth; **die Katze strich mir um die Beine** the cat rubbed against my legs
(c) (= *malen*) to paint

Streicher ['ʃtraiçɐ] PL (*Mus*) strings *pl*

Streich-: Streichholz NT match; **Streichholzschachtel** F matchbox; **Streichinstrument** NT string(ed) instrument; **die ~e** the strings; **Streichkäse** M cheese spread; **Streichorchester** NT string orchestra; **Streichquintett** NT string quintet

Streichung ['ʃtraiçʊŋ] F **-, -en** (= *Tilgung*) (*von Zeile, Satz*) deletion; (= *Kürzung*) cut; (*von Auftrag, Plan, Zug, freiem Tag etc*) cancellation; (*von Schulden*) writing off; (*von Zuschüssen, Arbeitsplätzen etc*) cutting; **die drastischen ~en bei den Subventionen** the drastic cuts in subsidies

Streichwurst F ≈ meat paste

Streife ['ʃtraifə] F **-, -n** (= *Patrouille*) patrol; **auf ~ gehen/sein** to go/be on patrol; **ein Polizist auf ~** a policeman on his beat

streifen ['ʃtraifn] **⧓** VT **(a)** (= *flüchtig berühren*) to touch, to brush (against); (*Kugel*) to graze; (*Billardkugel*) to kiss; (*Auto*) to scrape; **jdn mit einem Blick ~** to glance fleetingly at sb; **ein flüchtiger Blick streifte mich** he/she glanced fleetingly at me
(b) (*fig*: = *flüchtig erwähnen*) to touch (up)on
(c) (= *abstreifen, überziehen*) **die Butter vom Messer ~** to scrape the butter off the knife; **die Schuhe von den Füßen ~** to slip one's shoes off; **den Ring vom Finger ~** to slip the ring off one's finger; **sich** (*dat*) **die Handschuhe über die Finger ~** to pull on one's gloves; **er streifte sich** (*dat*) **den Pullover über den Kopf** (= *an-/ausziehen*) he slipped the pullover over his head
⧓ VI (*geh*) **(a)** AUX SEIN (= *wandern*) to roam
(b) AUX SEIN (= *flüchtig berühren: Blick etc*) **sie ließ ihren Blick über die Menge ~** she scanned the crowd; **sein Blick streifte über seine Besitztümer** he gazed at his possessions

Streifen ['ʃtraifn] M **-s, -** **(a)** (= *Stück, Band, Landstreifen*) strip; (= *Speckstreifen*) rasher; **ein ~ Land/Speck** a strip of land/bacon **(b)** (= *Strich*) stripe; (= *Farbstreifen*) streak
(c) (= *Lochstreifen, Klebestreifen etc*) tape **(d)** (*Film*) film

Streifen-: Streifendienst M patrol duty; **Streifenpolizei** F patrol police (*Brit*) *or* officers (*US*); **Streifenpolizist(in)** M(F) policeman/-woman on patrol; **Streifenwagen** M patrol car

streifig ['ʃtraifɪç] ADJ streaky

Streif-: Streifschuss M graze; **Streifzug** M raid; (= *Bummel*) expedition

Streik [ʃtraik] M **-(e)s, -s** *or* (*rare*) **-e** strike; **zum ~ aufrufen** to call a strike; **jdn zum ~ aufrufen** to call sb out on strike; **in (den) ~ treten** to go on strike

Streik-: Streikaufruf M strike call; **Streikbrecher** [-brɛçɐ] M **-s, -**, **Streikbrecherin** [-ərɪn] F **-, -nen** strikebreaker, scab (*pej*)

streiken ['ʃtraikn] VI to strike; (*hum inf*) (= *nicht funktionieren*) to pack up (*inf*); (*Magen*) to protest; (*Gedächtnis*) to fail; **die Waschmaschine/das Auto streikt schon wieder** (*inf*) the washing machine/car has packed up again (*inf*); **da streike ich** (*inf*) I refuse!

Streikende(r) ['ʃtraiknda] MF DECL AS ADJ striker

Streik-: Streikgeld NT strike pay; **Streikkasse** F strike fund; **Streikposten** M picket; **~ aufstellen** to put up pickets; **~ stehen** to picket

Streit [ʃtrait] M **-(e)s, -e** argument (*um, über* +*acc* about, over); (*leichter*) quarrel, squabble; (= *Auseinandersetzung*) dispute; **~ haben** to be arguing; **wegen etw mit jdm (einen) ~ haben** to argue with sb about sth; **wegen einer Sache ~ bekommen** to get into an argument over sth

streiten ['ʃtraitn], *pret* **stritt** [ʃtrɪt], *ptp* **gestritten** [gə'ʃtrɪtn] **⧓** VI (= *eine Auseinandersetzung haben*) to argue (*um, über* +*acc* about, over); (*leichter*) to quarrel; (*Jur*: = *prozessieren*) to take legal action; **die Streitenden** the arguers, the people fighting; **es wird immer noch gestritten, ob ...** the argument about whether ... is still going on; **darüber kann man** *or* **lässt sich ~** that's a debatable point; **die ~den Parteien** (*Jur*) the litigants

⧓ VR to argue; (*leichter*) to quarrel; **habt ihr euch schon wieder gestritten?** have you been fighting again?; **wir wollen uns deswegen nicht ~!** don't let's fall out over that!

Streiterei [ʃtraitə'rai] F **-, -en** (*inf*) arguing *no pl*; **eine ~** an argument

Streit-: Streitfrage F dispute; **Streitgespräch** NT debate; **Streithahn** M (*inf*) squabbler; **Streithammel** M, (*S Ger, Aus*) **Streithansel** [-hanzl] M **-s, -** (*inf*) quarrelsome person

streitig ['ʃtraitɪç] ADJ **jdm das Recht auf etw** (*acc*) **~ machen** to dispute sb's right to sth; **jdm das Geschäft/den ersten Platz ~ machen** to vie with sb for business/for first place

Streitigkeiten PL quarrels *pl*

Streit-: Streitkräfte PL forces *pl*; **Streitkultur** F culture of debate; **eine ~ entwickeln** to debate things in a civilized manner; **Streitmacht** F armed forces *pl*; **Streitpunkt** M contentious issue; **streitsüchtig** ADJ quarrelsome; **Streitwert** M (*Jur*) amount in dispute

streng [ʃtrɛŋ] **⧓** ADJ **(a)** strict; *Maßnahmen* stringent; *Bestrafung, Richter* severe; *Anforderungen* rigorous; *Ausdruck, Blick, Gesicht* stern; *Stillschweigen, Diskretion* absolute; *Kritik, Urteil* harsh; *Lebensführung, Schönheit, Form* austere; *Examen* stiff; **~ aber gerecht** severe but just
(b) (= *durchdringend*) *Geruch, Geschmack* pungent; *Frost, Kälte, Winter* severe
(c) (= *~gläubig*) *Katholik, Moslem etc* strict
⧓ ADV **(a)** (= *unnachgiebig*) *befolgen, einhalten* strictly; *tadeln, bestrafen* severely; *vertraulich, wissenschaftlich* strictly; **~ genommen** strictly speaking; (= *eigentlich*) actually; **~ gegen jdn/etw vorgehen** to deal severely with sb/sth; **~ durchgreifen** to take rigorous action; **~ geheim** top secret; **~(stens) verboten!** strictly prohibited
(b) (*intensiv*) **~ riechen/schmecken** to have a pungent smell/taste; **der Käse schmeckt mir zu ~** this cheese tastes too strong for me
(c) (*Sw*) **es ~ haben** to be under a lot of pressure

Strenge ['ʃtrɛŋə] F **-, NO PL (a)** strictness; (*von Regel, Kontrolle, Maßnahmen*) stringency; (*von Bestrafung, Richter*) severity; (*von Ausdruck, Blick*) sternness; (*von Kritik, Urteil*) harshness; **mit ~ regieren** to rule strictly **(b)** (= *Schärfe*) (*von Geruch, Geschmack*) pungency; (*von Frost, Kälte, Winter*) severity

streng-: strenggenommen ADV *siehe* **streng**; **strenggläubig** ADJ strict; **streng nehmen** VT SEP IRREG to take seriously; **es mit etw ~** to be strict about sth; **wenn man es streng nimmt** strictly speaking

Stress [ʃtrɛs, st-] M **-es, -e** (*alle Bedeutungen*) stress; **(voll) im ~ sein** *or* **stehen** to be under (a lot of) stress; **ich bin heute im ~** I'm feeling hassled today (*inf*)

Stressbewältigung F stress management

stressen ['ʃtrɛsn] VT to put under stress; **gestresst sein** to be under stress

stress-: stressfrei ADJ stress-free; **stressgeplagt** [-gəplaːkt] ADJ under stress; **~e Manager** highly stressed executives

stressig ['ʃtrɛsɪç] ADJ (*inf*) stressful

Stretching ['strɛtʃɪŋ] NT **-s, NO PL** (*Gymnastik*) stretching exercises *pl*

Stretch- ['strɛtʃ-]: **Stretchhose** F stretch trousers *pl*; **Stretchlimousine** F stretch limousine; **Stretchstoff** M stretch fabric

Streu [ʃtrɔy] F **-, NO PL** straw; (*aus Sägespänen*) sawdust

streuen ['ʃtrɔyən] **⧓** VT to scatter; *Dünger, Stroh, Sand, Kies* to spread; *Gewürze, Zucker etc* to sprinkle; *Straße, Gehweg etc* (*mit Sand*) to grit; (*mit Salz*) to salt; (*fig*) *Gerüchte etc* to spread; *Aktien* to make widely available; **die Regierung ließ ~, dass ...** the government gave reason to believe that ... **⧓** VI
(a) (= *Streumittel anwenden*) to grit; to put down salt
(b) (*Salzstreuer etc*) to sprinkle

Streuer ['ʃtrɔyɐ] M **-s, -** (= *Salzstreuer*) shaker; (= *Pfefferstreuer*) pot

Streufahrzeug NT gritter

streunen ['ʃtrɔynən] VI **(a)** (= *nicht sesshaft sein*) to roam about; (*Hund, Katze*) to stray **(b)** AUX SEIN **durch etw/in etw** (*dat*) **~** to roam through/around sth

Streu-: Streusalz NT salt (*for icy roads*); **Streusand** M sand; (*für Straße*) grit

Streusel ['ʃtrɔyzl] NT **-s, -** (*Cook*) crumble (*Brit*) *or* crumb (*US*) (mixture)

Streuselkuchen M *thin sponge cake with crumble topping*

Streuung ['ʃtrɔyʊŋ] F -, -en (*Statistik*) mean variation; (*Phys*) scattering

strich PRET *von* **streichen**

Strich [ʃtrɪç] M -(e)s, -e (a) line; (= *Querstrich*) dash; (= *Schrägstrich*) oblique; (= *Federstrich, Pinselstrich*) stroke; (*von Land*) stretch; **jdm einen ~ durch die Rechnung/einen Plan machen** to thwart sb's plans/plan; **einen ~ (unter etw** *acc*) **machen** *or* **ziehen** (*fig*) to forget sth; **unterm ~** at the final count; **sie ist nur noch ein ~ (in der Landschaft** *hum*) (*inf*) she's as thin as a rake (*Brit*) *or* rail (*US*) now (*inf*); **keinen ~ tun** (*inf*) not to do a stroke (of work) (b) (*von Teppich, Samt*) pile; (*von Gewebe*) nap; (*von Fell, Haar*) direction of growth; **gegen den ~ bürsten** (*lit*) to brush the wrong way; **es geht (mir) gegen den ~** (*inf*) it goes against the grain; **nach ~ und Faden** (*inf*) thoroughly (c) (*Mus*: = *Bogenstrich*) stroke (d) (*inf*: = *Prostitution*) prostitution *no art*; (= *Bordellgegend*) red-light district; **auf den ~ gehen** to be on the game (*Brit inf*), to be a prostitute

Strichcode M = **Strichkode**

stricheln ['ʃtrɪçln] VT to sketch in; (= *schraffieren*) to hatch; **eine gestrichelte Linie** a broken line

Stricher ['ʃtrɪçɐ] M -s, - (*pej inf*) rent boy (*Brit*), boy prostitute

Stricherin ['ʃtrɪçərɪn] F -, -nen (*pej inf*) hooker (*esp US inf*)

Strich-: **Strichjunge** M (*inf*) rent boy (*Brit*), boy prostitute; **Strichkode** M bar code (*Brit*), universal product code (*US*); **Strichmädchen** NT (*inf*) hooker (*esp US inf*); **Strichpunkt** M semicolon; **strichweise** ADV (*auch Met*) here and there; **~ Regen** rain in places

Strick [ʃtrɪk] M -(e)s, -e rope; (*dünner, als Gürtel*) cord; **jdm aus etw einen ~ drehen** to use sth against sb; **am gleichen** *or* **an einem ~ ziehen** (*fig*) to pull together

Strickarbeit F knitting *no pl*; **eine ~** a piece of knitting

stricken ['ʃtrɪkn] VTI to knit; (*fig*) to construct; **an etw** (*dat*) **~** (*lit, fig*) to work on sth

Strickerei [ʃtrɪkə'raɪ] F -, -en (a) knitting *no indef art, no pl* (b) (*Betrieb*) knitwear factory

Strick-: **Strickjacke** F cardigan; **Strickkleid** NT knitted dress; **Strickleiter** F rope ladder; **Strickmaschine** F knitting machine; **Strickmuster** NT (*lit*) knitting pattern; (*fig*) pattern; **Stricknadel** F knitting needle; **Strickwaren** PL knitwear *sing*; **Strickzeug** NT, NO PL knitting

Striegel ['ʃtriːgl] M -s, - currycomb

striegeln ['ʃtriːgln] VT *Tier* to curry(comb); *siehe auch* **gestriegelt**

Strieme ['ʃtriːmə] F -, -n, **Striemen** ['ʃtriːmən] M -s, - weal

striemig ['ʃtriːmɪç] ADJ *Haut* marked with weals

strikt [ʃtrɪkt, st-] **1** ADJ strict; *Ablehnung* categorical **2** ADV strictly; *ablehnen* categorically; **~ gegen etw sein** to be totally opposed to sth

Strip [ʃtrɪp, st-] M -s, -s (*inf*) strip(tease)

Strippe ['ʃtrɪpə] F -, -n (*inf*) (a) (= *Bindfaden*) string; **die ~n ziehen** (*fig*) to pull the strings (b) (= *Telefonleitung*) phone; **an der ~ hängen** to be on the phone; **sich an die ~ hängen** to get on the phone; **jdn an der ~ haben** to have sb on the line

strippen ['ʃtrɪpn, 'st-] VI to strip

Strippenzieher ['ʃtrɪpəntsiːɐ] M -s, -, **Strippenzieherin** [-ərɪn] F (*inf*) **er war der ~** he was the one pulling the strings

Stripper ['ʃtrɪpɐ, 'st-] M -s, -, **Stripperin** [-ərɪn] F -, -nen (*inf*) stripper

Striptease ['ʃtrɪptiːs, 'st-] M or NT -, NO PL striptease

Stripteasetänzer(in) ['ʃtrɪptiːs-, st-] M(F) stripper

stritt PRET *von* **streiten**

strittig ['ʃtrɪtɪç] ADJ contentious; **noch ~** still in dispute

Strizzi ['ʃtrɪtsi] M -s, -s (*Aus inf*) pimp

Stroboskop [ʃtrobo'skoːp, st-] NT -s, -e stroboscope

Stroboskoplampe F strobe light

Stroh [ʃtroː] NT -(e)s, NO PL straw; (= *Dachstroh*) thatch

Stroh-: **Strohballen** M bale of straw; **strohblond** ADJ *Mensch* flaxen-haired; *Haare* flaxen; **Strohblume** F strawflower; **Strohdach** NT thatched roof; **strohdumm** ADJ thick (*inf*); **Strohfeuer** NT **ein ~ sein** (*fig*) to be a passing fancy; **Strohfrau** F (*fig*) front woman; **strohgedeckt** ADJ thatched; **Strohhalm**

M straw; **sich an einen ~ klammern, nach einem ~ greifen** to clutch at straws; **Strohhut** M straw hat

strohig ['ʃtroːɪç] ADJ *Gemüse* tough; *Orangen etc* dry; *Haar* dull and lifeless

Stroh-: **Strohmann** M, *pl* **-männer** (*fig*) front man; **Strohwitwe** F grass widow; **Strohwitwer** M grass widower

Strom [ʃtroːm] M -(e)s, ⸚e ['ʃtrøːmə] (a) (large) river; (= *Strömung*) current; (*von Schweiß, Blut*) river; (*von Besuchern, Flüchen etc*) stream; **ein reißender ~** a raging torrent; **Ströme und Flüsse Europas** rivers of Europe; **es regnet in Strömen** it's pouring (with rain); **der Wein floss in Strömen** the wine flowed like water; **mit dem/gegen den ~ schwimmen** (*lit*) to swim with/against the current; (*fig*) to swim *or* go with/against the tide (b) (*Elec*) (**elektrischer**) **~** current; (= *Elektrizität*) electricity; **~ führen** to be live; **unter ~ stehen** (*lit*) to be live; (*fig*) to be high (*inf*); **mit ~ heizen** to have electric heating

Strom-: **stromabwärts** [ʃtroːm'apvɛrts] ADV downstream; **Stromanschluss** M **~ haben** to be connected to the electricity mains; **stromauf(wärts)** [ʃtroːm'aʊf(vɛrts)] ADV upstream; **Stromausfall** M power failure

strömen ['ʃtrøːmən] VI AUX SEIN to stream; (*Blut auch, Gas*) to flow; (*Menschen*) to pour (*in* into, *aus* out of); **bei ~dem Regen** in (the) pouring rain

Strom-: **Stromkabel** NT electric cable; **Stromkreis** M (electrical) circuit; **Stromleitung** F electric cables *pl*; **stromlinienförmig** ADJ (*lit, fig*) streamlined; **Strommesser** M -s, - (*Elec*) ammeter; **Stromnetz** NT electricity supply system; **Stromschnelle** F rapids *pl*; **Stromsperre** F power cut

Strömung ['ʃtrøːmʊŋ] F -, -en current; (*fig auch*) trend

Strom-: **Stromverbrauch** M electricity consumption; **Stromversorgung** F electricity supply; **Stromzähler** M electricity meter

Strontium ['ʃtrɔntsiʊm, 'st-] NT -s, NO PL (*abbr* **Sr**) strontium

Strophe ['ʃtroːfə] F -, -n verse

strotzen ['ʃtrɔtsn] VI to be full (*von, vor +dat* of), to abound (*von, vor +dat* with); (*von Kraft, Gesundheit, Lebensfreude*) to be bursting (*von* with); (*vor Ungeziefer*) to be crawling (*vor +dat* with); (*von Waffen*) to be bristling (*von* with); **von Schmutz ~** to be covered with dirt

strubbelig ['ʃtrʊbəlɪç], **strubblig** ['ʃtrʊblɪç] ADJ (*inf*) *Haar, Fell* tousled

Strudel ['ʃtruːdl] M -s, - (a) (*lit, fig*) whirlpool; (*von Ereignissen, Vergnügen*) whirl (b) (*Cook*) strudel

strudeln ['ʃtruːdln] VI to whirl

Struktur [ʃtrʊk'tuːɐ, st-] F -, -en structure; (*von Stoff etc*) texture; (= *Webart*) weave

Strukturanalyse F structural analysis

strukturell [ʃtrʊktu'rɛl, st-] **1** ADJ structural **2** ADV **~ bedingt** structurally; **~ gesehen** looking at the infrastructure; **sich ~ auswirken** to have an effect on the infrastructure; **ein ~ schwaches Gebiet** a region with a weak infrastructure

strukturieren [ʃtrʊktu'riːrən, st-], *ptp* **strukturiert** VT to structure

Strukturierung F -, -en structuring

Struktur-: **Strukturkrise** F structural crisis; **strukturschwach** ADJ lacking in infrastructure; **die ~en Gebiete Bayerns** the parts of Bavaria with less well-developed infrastructure; **Strukturschwäche** F lack of infrastructure; **Strukturwandel** M structural change (+*gen* in)

strullern ['ʃtrʊlɐn] VI (*sl*: = *pinkeln*) to take a leak (*inf*)

Strumpf [ʃtrʊmpf] M -(e)s, ⸚e ['ʃtrʏmpfə] (a) sock; (= *Damenstrumpf*) stocking; **ein Paar Strümpfe** a pair of socks/stockings; **auf Strümpfen** in one's stockinged feet (b) (= *Glühstrumpf*) mantle

Strumpf-: **Strumpfband** [-bant] NT, *pl* **-bänder** garter; **Strumpfhalter** M suspender (*Brit*), garter (*US*); **Strumpfhaltergürtel** M suspender belt (*Brit*), garter belt (*US*); **Strumpfhose** F tights *pl* (*esp Brit*), pantihose; **eine ~** a pair of tights (*esp Brit*) *or* pantihose tights; **Strumpfmaske** F stocking mask; **Strumpfwaren** PL hosiery *sing*

Strunk [ʃtrʊŋk] M -(e)s, ⸚e ['ʃtrʏŋkə] stalk

struppig ['ʃtrʊpɪç] ADJ unkempt; *Tier* shaggy

Struwwelpeter ['ʃtrʊvl-] M tousle-head; **der ~** (*Liter*) shock-headed Peter

Stübchen ['ʃtyːpçən] NT -s, - DIM *von* **Stube** little room

Stube [ˈʃtuːbə] F -, -n (dated) (dial) room; (dial: = Wohnzimmer) lounge; (in Kaserne) barrack room (Brit), quarters; **die gute ~** the parlour (dated Brit) or parlor (dated US); **in der ~ hocken** (inf) to sit around indoors

Stuben-: Stubenfliege F (common) housefly; **Stubengelehrte(r)** MF DECL AS ADJ (pej) armchair scholar; **Stubenhocker** [-hɔkɐ] M -s, -, **Stubenhockerin** [-ərɪn] F -, -nen (pej inf) stay-at-home; **er ist ein richtiger ~** he sits at home all the time; **stubenrein** ADJ Katze, Hund house-trained; (hum) Witz clean

Stüberl [ˈʃtyːbɐl] NT -s, - (Aus) small room

Stuck [ʃtʊk] M -(e)s, NO PL stucco; (zur Zimmerverzierung) moulding (Brit), molding (US)

Stück [ʃtʏk] NT -(e)s, -e or (nach Zahlenangaben) - (a) piece; (von Vieh, Wild) head; (von Zucker) lump; (= Seifenstück) bar; (= abgegrenztes Land) plot; **ich nehme fünf ~** I'll take five; **12 ~ (Eier)** a dozen (eggs); **drei Euro das ~, pro ~ drei Euro** three euros each; **im** or **am ~** in one piece; Käse, Wurst auch unsliced; **aus einem ~** in one piece; **~ für ~** (= ein Exemplar nach dem andern) one by one; **ein ~ Garten** a patch of garden; **das ist unser bestes ~** (hum) that is our pride and joy **(b)** (= Teil, Abschnitt) piece; (von Buch, Rede, Reise etc) part; (von Straße etc) stretch; **~ für ~** (= einen Teil um den andern) bit by bit; **in ~e gehen/zerspringen** to be broken/smashed to pieces; **etw in ~e schlagen** to smash sth to pieces; **ein ~ Heimat** a piece of home; **ich komme ein ~ (des Weges) mit** I'll come part of the way with you **(c) ein gutes ~ weiterkommen** to make considerable progress; **ein schweres ~ Arbeit** a tough job; **das ist (doch) ein starkes ~!** (inf) that's a bit much (inf); **große ~e auf jdn halten** to think highly of sb; **große ~e auf etw** (acc) **halten** to be very proud of sth; **aus freien ~en** of one's own free will **(d)** (= Bühnenstück) play; (= Musikstück) piece **(e)** (inf: Mensch) so-and-so (inf); **mein bestes ~** (hum inf) my pride and joy; **ein ~ Dreck** (inf) (Frau) a bitch (sl); (Mann) a bastard (sl)

Stückarbeit F piecework

Stuckateur [ʃtʊkaˈtøːɐ] M -s, -e, **Stuckateurin** [-ˈtøːrɪn] F -, -nen plasterer (who works with stucco)

Stuckatur [ʃtʊkaˈtuːɐ] F -, -en stucco (work), ornamental plasterwork

Stückchen [ˈʃtʏkçən] NT -s, - DIM von **Stück (a, b)**

Stuckdecke F stucco(ed) ceiling

stückeln [ˈʃtʏkln] **1** VT to patch **2** VI to patch it together

Stückelung F -, -en (= Aufteilung) splitting up; (von Geld, Aktien) denomination; **in kleiner ~** (Geldbetrag) in small denominations

Stück-: Stückgut NT (Rail) parcel service; **etw als ~ schicken** to send sth as a parcel (Brit) or package; **Stücklohn** M piece(work) rate; **Stücknotierung** F quotation per unit; **Stückpreis** M unit price; **Stückwerk** NT, NO PL unfinished work; **~ sein/bleiben** to be/remain unfinished; **Stückzahl** F number of pieces; **Stückzins** M (Fin) accrued interest

stud. ABBR von studiosus; **~ med./phil.** etc student of medicine/ humanities etc

Student [ʃtuˈdɛnt] M -en, -en student; (Aus: = Schüler) schoolboy; (einer bestimmten Schule) pupil

Studenten-: Studentenausweis M student (ID) card; **Studentenbude** F (inf) student housing; **Studentenfutter** NT nuts and raisins pl; **Studentenheim** NT hall of residence (Brit), dormitory (US); **Studentenleben** NT student life; **Studentenschaft** [ʃtuˈdɛntnʃaft] F -, -en students pl; **Studentenwerk** NT student administration; **Studentenwohnheim** NT hall of residence (Brit), dormitory (US)

Studentin [ʃtuˈdɛntɪn] F -, -nen student; (Aus: = Schülerin) schoolgirl; (einer bestimmten Schule) pupil

studentisch [ʃtuˈdɛntɪʃ] ADJ ATTR student attr; **~e Hilfskraft** student assistant

Studie [ˈʃtuːdiə] F -, -n study (über +acc of); (= Entwurf auch) sketch; (= Abhandlung) essay (über +acc on)

Studien-: Studienabbrecher(in) M(F) dropout; **Studienabschluss** M completion of a course of study; **Volkswirtschaftler mit ~** graduate economist; **die Universität ohne ~ verlassen** to leave university without graduating; **Studienanfänger(in)** M(F) first year (student), freshman (US),

fresher (Brit); **Studienberatung** F course guidance service; **Studienfach** NT subject; **Studienfahrt** F study trip; (Sch) educational trip; **Studiengang** M, pl -gänge course of studies; **Studiengebühren** PL tuition fees pl; **Studienjahr** NT academic year; **Studienjahre** PL university/college years pl; **Studienplatz** M university/college place; **ein ~ in Medizin** a place (at university/college) to study medicine; **Studienrat** M, **Studienrätin** F teacher at a secondary school; **Studienreferendar(in)** M(F) student teacher; **Studienreise** F study trip; (Sch) educational trip; **Studienseminar** NT teacher training course; **sie ist im ~ in Essen** she is doing her teacher training in Essen; **Studienzeit** F **(a)** student days pl **(b)** (= Dauer) duration of a/one's course of studies; **Studienzeitbegrenzung** F limitation on the length of courses of study

studieren [ʃtuˈdiːrən] ptp **studiert 1** VI to study; (= Student sein) to be a student; **ich studiere an der Universität Bonn** I am (a student) at Bonn University; **nicht jeder kann ~** not everyone can go to university/college; **wo haben Sie studiert?** what university/college did you go to?; **bei jdm ~** to study under sb; **jdn ~ lassen** to send sb to university/ college **2** VT to study; (an Uni auch) to read; (= genau betrachten) to scrutinize

Studierende(r) [ʃtuˈdiːrəndə] MF DECL AS ADJ student

Studio [ˈʃtuːdio] NT -s, -s studio

Studium [ˈʃtuːdiʊm] NT -s, **Studien** [-diən] study; (= Hochschulstudium) studies pl; **das ~ hat fünf Jahre gedauert** the course (of study) lasted five years; **das ~ ist kostenlos/ teuer** studying (at university) is free/expensive; **während seines ~s** while he is/was etc a student; **er ist noch im ~** he is still a student; **er war gerade beim ~ des Börsenberichts, als ...** he was just studying the stock exchange report when ...; **seine Studien zu etw machen** to study sth

Studium generale [ˈʃtuːdiʊm genəˈraːlə, ˈst-] NT - -, NO PL general course of studies; **ein ~ machen** to do a general degree

Stufe [ˈʃtuːfə] F -, -n (a) step; (Mus: = Tonstufe) degree; (an Rock, Kleid etc) tier; (zum Kürzen) tuck; (im Haar) layer; (von Rakete) stage; **mehrere ~n auf einmal nehmen** to run up the stairs two or three at a time **(b)** (fig) (= Phase) stage; (= Niveau) level; (= Rang) grade; (Gram: = Steigerungsstufe) degree; **eine ~ höher als ... a** step up from ...; **die höchste ~** the height; **die tiefste ~** the depths pl; **mit jdm auf gleicher ~ stehen** to be on a level with sb; **jdn/sich mit jdm/etw auf die gleiche** or **eine ~ stellen** to put sb/oneself on a par with sb/sth

stufen [ˈʃtuːfn] VT Schüler, Preise, Gehälter to grade; Haare to layer; Land etc to terrace; siehe auch **gestuft**

Stufen-: Stufenbarren M asymmetric bar; **stufenförmig 1** ADJ (lit) stepped; Landschaft terraced; (fig) gradual **2** ADV (lit) in steps; angelegt in terraces; (fig) in stages; **Stufenführerschein** M (graded) motorcycle licence (Brit) or license (US); **Stufenheck** NT ein Auto mit ~ a saloon car; **Stufenleiter** F (fig) ladder (+gen to); **stufenlos** ADJ Schaltung, Regelung infinitely variable; (fig: = gleitend) smooth; **stufenweise 1** ADV step by step **2** ADJ ATTR gradual

stufig [ˈʃtuːfɪç] **1** ADJ stepped; Land etc terraced; Haar layered **2** ADV **das Haar ~ schneiden** to layer sb's hair

-stufig ADJ SUF -stage attr

Stuhl [ʃtuːl] M -(e)s, ⸚e [ˈʃtyːlə] **(a)** chair; **ist dieser ~ noch frei?** is this chair taken?; **sich zwischen zwei Stühle setzen** (fig), **zwischen zwei Stühlen sitzen** (fig) to fall between two stools; **ich wäre fast vom ~ gefallen** (inf) I nearly fell off my chair (inf) **(b)** (= Königsstuhl) throne; **der Apostolische** or **Heilige** or **Päpstliche ~** the Apostolic or Holy or Papal See **(c)** (= Lehramt) chair (+gen of, für of, in) **(d)** (= ~gang) bowel movement; (= Kot) stool; **~/keinen ~ haben** to have had/not to have had a bowel movement

Stuhl-: Stuhlgang [-gaŋ] M, NO PL bowel movement; **regelmäßig ~ haben** to have regular bowels; **Stuhllehne** F back of a chair

Stukkateur [ʃtʊkaˈtøːɐ] M -s, -e **Stukkateurin** [-ˈtøːrɪn] F -, -en siehe **Stuckateur**

Stukkatur [ʃtʊkaˈtuːɐ] F -, -en siehe **Stuckatur**

Stulle [ˈʃtʊlə] F -, -n (N Ger) slice of bread and butter; (= Doppelstulle) sandwich

stülpen [ˈʃtʏlpn] VT **den Kragen nach oben ~** to turn up one's collar; **etw auf/über etw** (acc) **~** to put sth on/over sth; **etw**

nach innen/außen ~ to turn sth to the inside/outside; **sich** (*dat*) **den Hut auf den Kopf ~** to put on one's hat

stumm [ʃtʊm] **1** ADJ **(a)** (*lit, fig*) dumb **(b)** (= *schweigend*) mute; *Anklage, Blick, Gebet* silent; **~ bleiben** to stay silent **(c)** (*Gram*) mute **(d)** *Rolle* nonspeaking; *Film, Szene* silent **2** ADV (= *schweigend*) silently; **sie sah mich ~ an** she looked at me without saying a word

Stummel [ˈʃtʊml] M **-s, -** **(a)** (= *Zigarettenstummel, Zigarrenstummel*) stub; (= *Kerzenstummel*) stub; (*von Gliedmaßen, Zahn*) stump **(b)** (= *~schwanz*) dock

Stumme(r) [ˈʃtʊmə] MF DECL AS ADJ dumb *or* mute person; **die ~n** the dumb

Stummfilm M silent film

Stümper [ˈʃtʏmpɐ] M **-s, -**, **Stümperin** [-ərɪn] F **-, -nen** (*pej*) **(a)** amateur **(b)** (= *Pfuscher*) bungler

Stümperei [ʃtʏmpəˈraɪ] F **-, -en** (*pej*) **(a)** amateur work **(b)** (= *Pfuscherei*) bungling; (= *stümperhafte Arbeit*) botched job (*inf*)

stümperhaft (*pej*) **1** ADJ (= *nicht fachmännisch*) amateurish; (= *schlecht auch*) botched (*inf*) **2** ADV *ausführen, malen* crudely; *arbeiten* poorly; *übersetzen* clumsily; **~ vorgehen** to be clumsy

stumpf [ʃtʊmpf] **1** ADJ **(a)** *Messer* blunt **(b)** (*fig*) *Haar, Farbe, Mensch* dull; *Blick, Sinne* dulled; **einer Sache gegenüber ~ sein** to remain impassive about sth **(c)** (*Math*) *Winkel* obtuse; *Kegel etc* truncated **2** ADV *ansehen* dully; **~ vor sich hin brüten** to sit brooding impassively

Stumpf [ʃtʊmpf] M **-(e)s, ⸚e** [ˈʃtʏmpfə] stump; (= *Bleistiftstumpf*) stub; **etw mit ~ und Stiel ausrotten** to eradicate sth root and branch

Stumpfheit F **-, NO PL** bluntness; (*fig*) dullness

Stumpf-: Stumpfsinn M, NO PL mindlessness; (= *Langweiligkeit*) monotony; **das ist doch ~** that's a tedious business; **stumpfsinnig** ADJ mindless; (= *langweilig*) monotonous; **stumpfwinkelig, stumpfwinklig** ADJ (*Math*) *Winkel, Dreieck* obtuse

Stündchen [ˈʃtʏntçən] NT **-s, -** DIM *von* **Stunde**; **ein paar ~** an hour or so

Stunde [ˈʃtʊndə] F **-, -n** **(a)** hour; **eine viertel ~** a quarter of an hour; **eine halbe ~** half an hour; **drei ~n lang** for three hours; **jede ~** every hour; **~um ~, ~um um ~n** hour after hour; **von ~ zu ~** hourly; **sein Befinden wird von ~ zu ~ schlechter** his condition is becoming worse every hour; **130 Kilometer in der ~** 130 kilometers (*Brit*) *or* kilometers (*US*) per *or* an hour **(b)** (= *Augenblick, Zeitpunkt*) time; **zu dieser ~** at this/that time; **zu jeder ~** at any time; **zu später ~** at a late hour; **zur ~** at present; **bis zur ~** as yet; **die ~ X** (*Mil*) the impending onslaught; **sich auf die ~ X vorbereiten** (*fig*) to prepare for the inevitable; **eine schwache ~** a moment of weakness; **eine schwere ~** a time of difficulty; **seine ~ hat geschlagen** (*fig*) his hour has come; **die ~ der Entscheidung/Wahrheit** the moment of decision/truth **(c)** (= *Unterricht*) lesson; **in der zweiten ~ haben wir Latein** in the second period we have Latin; **~n geben/nehmen** to give/ have *or* take lessons

stunden [ˈʃtʊndn] VT **jdm etw ~** to give sb time to pay sth; **jdm etw zwei Wochen/bis Mittwoch ~** to give sb two weeks/until Wednesday to pay sth

Stunden-: Stundengeschwindigkeit F speed per hour; **eine ~ von 90 km** a speed of 90 km per hour; **Stundenkilometer** PL kilometres *pl* (*Brit*) *or* kilometers *pl* (*US*) per *or* an hour; **stundenlang** **1** ADJ lasting several hours; **eine ~e Verspätung** a delay of several hours; **nach ~em Warten** after hours of waiting **2** ADV for hours; **Stundenlohn** M hourly wage; **~ bekommen** to be paid by the hour; **Stundenplan** M (*Sch*) timetable; **Stundentakt** M hourly frequency; **im ~** at hourly intervals; **stundenweise** ADV (= *pro Stunde*) by the hour; (= *stündlich*) every hour; **Kellner ~ gesucht** part-time waiters required; **der Patient darf ~ aufstehen** the patient may get up for an hour at a time; **Stundenzeiger** M hour hand

stündlich [ˈʃtʏntlɪç] **1** ADJ hourly **2** ADV every hour

Stundung [ˈʃtʊndʊŋ] F **-, -en** deferment of payment

Stunk [ʃtʊŋk] M **-s, NO PL** (*inf*) stink (*inf*); **~ machen** to kick up a stink (*inf*)

Stunt [stant] M **-s, -s** stunt

Stuntman [ˈstantmən] M **-s, Stuntmen** [-mən] stunt man

Stuntwoman [ˈstantwʊmən] F **-, Stuntwomen** [-vɪmɪn] stunt woman

Stups [ʃtʊps] M **-es, -e** nudge

stupsen [ˈʃtʊpsn] VT to nudge

Stupsnase F snub nose

stur [ʃtuːɐ] **1** ADJ pig-headed; *Nein, Arbeiten* dogged; **sich ~ stellen** (*inf*), **auf ~ stellen** *or* **schalten** (*inf*) to dig one's heels in; **ein ~er Bock** (*inf*) a pig-headed fellow **2** ADV *beharren, bestehen* stubbornly; **~ weitermachen/weiterreden/ weitergehen** to carry on regardless; **er fuhr ~ geradeaus** he just carried straight on

Sturheit F **-, NO PL** pig-headedness, stubbornness

Sturm [ʃtʊrm] M **-(e)s, ⸚e** [ˈʃtʏrmə] **(a)** (*lit, fig*) storm; **in ~ und Regen** in wind and rain; (*fig*) there's a storm brewing; **die Ruhe** *or* **Stille vor dem ~** the calm before the storm; **ein ~ im Wasserglas** (*fig*) a storm in a teacup (*Brit*), a tempest in a teapot (*US*); **~ läuten** to keep one's finger on the doorbell; (= *Alarm schlagen*) to ring the alarm bell; **ein ~ der Begeisterung/Entrüstung** a wave of enthusiasm/indignation; **~ und Drang** (*Liter*) Sturm und Drang; (*fig*) emotion **(b)** (= *Angriff*) attack (*auf* on); (*Sport*: = *Stürmerreihe*) forward line; **etw im ~ nehmen** (*Mil, fig*) to take sth by storm; **gegen etw ~ laufen** (*fig*) to be up in arms against sth; **ein ~ auf die Banken/Aktien** a run on the banks/shares

stürmen [ˈʃtʏrmən] **1** VI **(a)** (*Meer*) to rage; (*Wind auch*) to blow; (*Mil*) to attack (*gegen etw* sth) **(b)** (*Sport*) (= *als Stürmer spielen*) to play forward; (= *angreifen*) to attack **(c)** AUX SEIN (= *rennen*) to storm **2** VI IMPERS **es stürmt** to be blowing a gale **3** VT (*Mil, fig*) to storm; *Bank etc* to make a run on

Stürmer [ˈʃtʏrmɐ] M **-s, -**, **Stürmerin** [-ərɪn] F **-, -nen** (*Sport*) forward; (*Ftbl auch*) striker

Sturm-: Sturmflut F storm tide; **sturmfrei** ADJ (*lit*) storm-free; (*Mil*) unassailable; **ich habe eine ~e Bude** (*inf*) where I live I can do as I please

stürmisch [ˈʃtʏrmɪʃ] **1** ADJ **(a)** *Meer, Überfahrt* rough; *Wetter, Tag* blustery; (*mit Regen*) stormy **(b)** (*fig*) tempestuous; (= *aufregend*) *Zeit, Jugend* stormy; *Entwicklung, Wachstum* rapid; *Liebhaber* passionate; *Jubel, Beifall* tumultuous; **nicht so ~ take it easy 2** ADV enthusiastically; **jdn ~ bejubeln/feiern** to give sb a tumultuous reception

Sturm-: Sturmschaden M storm damage *no pl*; **Sturmtief** NT (*Met*) deep depression; **Sturmwarnung** F gale warning

Sturz [ʃtʊrts] M **-es, ⸚e** [ˈʃtʏrtsə] **(a)** (*lit*, *fig*) fall; **~ tun** to have a fall **(b)** (*in Temperatur, Preis*) drop; (*von Börsenkurs*) slump **(c)** (*von Regierung, Minister*) fall; (*durch Coup, von König*) overthrow **(d)** (*Archit*) lintel **(e)** (= *Radsturz*) camber

stürzen [ˈʃtʏrtsn] **1** VI AUX SEIN **(a)** (= *fallen, abgesetzt werden*) to fall; **ins Wasser ~** to plunge into the water; **zu Boden ~** to crash to the ground; **zu Tode** *or* **in den Tod ~** to fall to one's death; **er ist schwer** *or* **heftig/unglücklich gestürzt** he had a heavy/bad fall **(b)** (= *rennen*) to rush; **sie kam ins Zimmer gestürzt** she burst into the room **2** VT **(a)** (= *werfen*) to fling; **jdn ins Unglück** *or* **Verderben ~** to bring disaster to sb; **jdn/etw in eine Krise ~** to plunge sb/sth into a crisis **(b)** (= *kippen*) to turn upside down; *Pudding* to turn out; **„nicht ~!"** "this side up"; **etw über etw** (*acc*) **~** to put sth over sth **(c)** (= *absetzen*) *Regierung, Minister* to bring down; (*durch Coup*) to overthrow; *König* to depose **3** VR **sich zu Tode ~** to fall to one's death; (*absichtlich*) to jump to one's death; **sich auf jdn/etw ~** to pounce on sb/sth; *auf Essen* to fall on sth; *auf Zeitung etc* to grab sth; *auf den Feind* to attack sb/sth; **sich ins Wasser ~** to fling oneself into the water; **sich in die Arbeit ~** to throw oneself into one's work; **sich in Schulden ~** to plunge into debt; **sich ins Unglück/Verderben ~** to plunge headlong into disaster/ruin; **sich ins Vergnügen ~** to fling oneself into a round of pleasure; **sich in Unkosten ~** to go to great expense

Sturz-: Sturzflug M (nose) dive; **Sturzhelm** M crash helmet

Stuss [ʃtʊs] M **-es, NO PL** (*inf*) nonsense; **was für ein ~** what a load of nonsense (*inf*); **~ lallen** (*sl*) to talk crap (*inf*)

Stute [ˈʃtuːtə] F **-, -n** mare

Stutz [ʃtʊts] M **-es, Stütze** *or* (*nach Zahlenangabe*) **-** [ˈʃtʏtsə] (*Sw inf*: = *Franken*) (Swiss) franc

Stützbalken M beam; (*in Decke*) joist; (*quer*) crossbeam

Stütze [ˈʃtʏtsə] F -, -n (a) support; (= *Pfeiler*) pillar; (*für Wäscheleine etc*) prop; (= *Buchstütze*) rest; (= *Fußstütze*) footrest (b) (*fig*) (= *Hilfe*) help (*für* to); (= *wichtiger Mensch*) mainstay; **die ~n der Gesellschaft** the pillars of society (c) (*inf*: = *Arbeitslosengeld*) dole (*Brit inf*), welfare (*US*); **~ bekommen** to be on the dole (*Brit inf*), to be on welfare (*US*)

stutzen¹ [ˈʃtʊtsn] VI to stop short; (= *zögern*) to hesitate

stutzen² VT to trim; *Flügel, Ohren, Hecke* to clip; *Schwanz* to dock

Stutzen [ˈʃtʊtsn] M -s, - (a) (= *Rohrstück*) connecting piece; (= *Endstück*) nozzle (b) (= *Strumpf*) woollen (*Brit*) *or* woolen (*US*) gaiter

stützen [ˈʃtʏtsn] 🔳 VT to support; *Gebäude, Mauer* to shore up; **einen Verdacht auf etw** (*acc*) **~** to found a suspicion on sth; **die Ellbogen auf den Tisch ~** to prop one's elbows on the table; **den Kopf in die Hände ~** to hold one's head in one's hands 🔳 VR **sich auf jdn/etw ~** (*lit*) to lean on sb/sth; (*fig*) to count on sb/sth; (*Beweise, Verteidigung, Theorie etc*) to be based on sb/sth; **können Sie sich auf Fakten ~?** can you produce facts to bear out what you're saying?

stutzig [ˈʃtʊtsɪç] ADJ PRED **~ werden** (= *argwöhnisch*) to become suspicious; (= *verwundert*) to begin to wonder; **jdn ~ machen** to make sb suspicious; **das hat mich ~ gemacht** that made me wonder; (= *argwöhnisch*) that made me suspicious

Stütz-: Stützkurs M (*Sch*) extra classes *pl*; **Stützpreis** M (*Econ*) support price; **Stützpunkt** M (*Mil*) (*fig*) base; (= *Ausbildungsstätte*) centre

Stützung [ˈʃtʏtsʊŋ] F -, -en support

StVO [ɛsteˈfauˈloː] ABBR *von* Straßenverkehrsordnung

stylen [ˈstailən] 🔳 VT *Wagen, Wohnung* to design; *Frisur* to style; *jdn* to do up 🔳 VR to do oneself up

Styling [ˈstailɪŋ] NT -s, NO PL styling

Styropor® [ˈʃtyroˈpoːɐ, st-] NT -s polystyrene

s. u. ABBR *von* siehe unten

Suaheli [zuaˈheːli] NT -(s), NO PL (*Ling*) Swahili

Sub-, sub- IN CPDS sub-; **subaltern** [zʊplalˈtɛrn] ADJ (*pej*) *Stellung, Beamter* subordinate; *Gesinnung* subservient; **Subdominante** [zʊpdomiˈnantə, ˈzʊp-] F (*Mus*) subdominant

Subjekt [zʊpˈjɛkt, ˈzʊp-] NT -(e)s, -e (a) subject (b) (*pej*: = *Mensch*) customer (*inf*)

subjektiv [zʊpjɛkˈtiːf, ˈzʊp-] 🔳 ADJ subjective 🔳 ADV subjectively

Subjektivität [zʊpjɛktiviˈtɛːt] F -, NO PL subjectivity

Sub-: Subkontinent M subcontinent; **Subkultur** F subculture; **subkutan** [zʊpkuˈtaːn] (*Med*) 🔳 ADJ subcutaneous 🔳 ADV *spritzen* subcutaneously; **Submission** F -, -en (*von Projekt*) tendering

Subsidiarität [zʊpzidiariˈtɛːt] F -, -en (*Pol*) subsidiarity

Subsidiaritätsprinzip NT (*Pol*) subsidiarity principle

Subsistenzwirtschaft [zʊpzɪsˈtɛnts-] F subsistence farming

subskribieren [zʊpskriˈbiːrən], *ptp* **subskribiert** VTI (*auf*) **etw** (*acc*) **~** to subscribe to sth

Subskription [zʊpskrɪpˈtsioːn] F -, -en subscription (+*gen, auf* +*acc* to)

Substantiv [ˈzʊpstantiːf] NT -s, -e *or* (*rare*) -a [-və, -va] noun

substantivieren [zʊpstantiˈviːrən], *ptp* **substantiviert** VT to nominalize

substantivisch [ˈzʊpstantiːvɪʃ] 🔳 ADJ nominal 🔳 ADV *verwenden* nominally

Substanz [zʊpˈstants] F -, -en (a) substance; (= *Wesen*) essence; **etw in seiner ~ treffen** to affect the substance of sth (b) (*Fin*) capital assets *pl*; **von der ~ zehren** *or* **leben** to live on one's capital

Substanzwert M net asset value, NAV

substituieren [zʊpstituˈiːrən], *ptp* **substituiert** VT (*geh*) **A durch B ~** to substitute B for A

Substitution [zʊpstituˈtsioːn] F -, -en (*geh*) **die ~ von A durch B** the substitution of B for A

Substrat [zʊpˈstraːt] NT -(e)s, -e substratum

subtil [zʊpˈtiːl] (*geh*) 🔳 ADJ subtle 🔳 ADV subtly; **es wird ~ unterschieden zwischen ...** there is a subtle difference between ...

Subtrahend [zʊptraˈhɛnt] M -en, -en [-dn] (*Math*) subtrahend

subtrahieren [zʊptraˈhiːrən], *ptp* **subtrahiert** VTI to subtract

Subtraktion [zʊptrakˈtsioːn] F -, -en subtraction

Subtraktionszeichen NT subtraction sign

Subtropen PL subtropics *pl*

subtropisch ADJ subtropical

Subunternehmer(in) M(F) subcontractor

Subvention [zʊpvɛnˈtsioːn] F -, -en subsidy

subventionieren [zʊpvɛntsioˈniːrən], *ptp* **subventioniert** VT to subsidize

subversiv [zʊpvɛrˈziːf] 🔳 ADJ subversive 🔳 ADV **sich ~ betätigen** to engage in subversive activities

Such-: Suchaktion F search operation; **Suchanfrage** F (*Comput*) search enquiry; **Suchanzeige** F missing person/dog *etc* report; **eine ~ aufgeben** to report sb/sth missing; **Suchbegriff** M (*Comput*) search item; **Suchdauer** F (*Comput*) search time

Suche [ˈzuːxə] F -, NO PL search (*nach* for); **auf die ~ nach jdm/etw gehen, sich auf die ~ nach jdm/etw machen** to go in search of sb/sth; **auf der ~ sein** to be looking for sth

suchen [ˈzuːxn] 🔳 VT (a) (*um zu finden*) to look for; (*stärker, intensiv*) to search for (*auch Comput*); **Abenteuer ~** to go out in search of adventure; **Verkäufer(in) gesucht** sales person wanted; **gesucht!** wanted (*wegen* for); **er wurde mit *or* per Haftbefehl gesucht** there was a warrant out for his arrest; **Streit/Ärger (mit jdm) ~** to be looking for trouble/a quarrel (with sb); **Schutz vor etw** (*dat*) **~** to seek shelter from sth; **Zuflucht ~ bei jdm** to seek refuge with sb; **etw zu tun ~** (*geh*) to seek to do sth; **was suchst du hier?** what are you doing here?; **du hast hier nichts zu ~** you have no business being here; **seinesgleichen ~** to be unparalleled; *siehe auch* **gesucht** (b) (= *wünschen, streben nach*) to seek; (= *versuchen*) to strive; **sein Recht/seinen Vorteil ~** to be out for one's rights/one's own advantage; **ein Gespräch ~** to try to have a talk 🔳 VI to search; **nach etw ~** to look for sth; (*stärker*) to search for sth; **nach Worten ~** to search for words; (= *sprachlos sein*) to be at a loss for words; **Suchen und Ersetzen** (*Comput*) search and replace; **such!** (*zu Hund*) seek!, find!

Sucher [ˈzuːxɐ] M -s, - (*Phot*) viewfinder

Such-: Suchergebnis NT (*Comput*) search result; **Suchfunktion** F (*Comput*) search function; **Suchlauf** M (*bei Hi-Fi-Geräten*) search; **Suchmannschaft** F search party; **Suchmaschine** F (*Comput*) search engine; **Suchmodus** M (*Comput*) search mode; **Suchprogramm** NT (*Comput*) search program; **Suchscheinwerfer** M searchlight

Sucht [zʊxt] F -, ⸚e [ˈzʏçtə] addiction (*nach* to); (*fig*) obsession (*nach* with); **~ erzeugend** addictive; **das kann zur ~ werden** you'll get addicted to that; **an einer ~ leiden** to be an addict

-sucht F, NO PL SUF IN CPDS **Drogensucht** addiction to drugs; **Trinksucht** addiction to drink

Sucht-: Suchtbeauftragte(r) MF DECL AS ADJ anti-drugs coordinator; **Suchtberater(in)** M(F) addiction counsellor (*Brit*) *or* counselor (*US*); **Suchtdroge** F addictive drug; **suchterzeugend** ADJ *siehe* **Sucht**; **Suchtgefahr** F danger of addiction

süchtig [ˈzʏçtɪç] ADJ addicted (*nach* to); **von** *or* **nach etw ~ werden/sein** to get/be addicted to sth; **~ machen** (*Droge*) to be addictive

Süchtige(r) [ˈzʏçtɪgə] MF DECL AS ADJ addict

Sucht-: Suchtklinik F detox(ification) centre (*Brit*) *or* center (*US*); **Suchtkranke(r)** MF DECL AS ADJ addict; **Suchtkrankheit** F addictive illness

Süd- IN CPDS (*in Ländernamen, politisch*) South; (*geografisch auch*) the South of ..., Southern; **Südafrika** NT South Africa; **Südamerika** NT South America

Sudan [zuˈdaːn, ˈzuːdan] M -s **der ~** the Sudan

Sudaner [zuˈdaːnɐ] M -s, -, **Sudanerin** [-ərɪn] F -, -nen, **Sudanese** [zudaˈneːzə] M -n, -n, **Sudanesin** [-ˈneːzɪn] F -, -nen Sudanese

sudanesisch [zudaˈneːzɪʃ], **sudanisch** [zuˈdaːnɪʃ] ADJ Sudanese

Süd-: süddeutsch ADJ South German; *Dialekt, Spezialität, Mentalität auch* Southern German; **die Süddeutschen** the South Germans; **Süddeutschland** NT South(ern) Germany

sudeln [ˈzuːdln] VTI (= *schreiben*) to scrawl; (= *zeichnen*) to daub

Süden [ˈzyːdn] M -s, NO PL south; (*von Land*) South; **aus dem ~, vom ~ her** from the south; **gegen** *or* **gen** (*liter*) *or* **nach ~** south(wards), to the south; **nach ~ hin** to the south; **im ~ der Stadt/des Landes** in the south of the town/country; **im tiefen**

~ in the deep south; **weiter** or **tiefer im** ~ further south; **im** ~ **Frankreichs** in southern France

Südengland NT the South of England

Sudeten [zu'de:tn] PL (*Geog*) **die** ~ the Sudeten(land)

Sudetenland NT **das** ~ the Sudetenland

Süd-: Südeuropa NT Southern Europe; **Südfrankreich** NT the South of France; **Südfrüchte** PL citrus and tropical fruit(s *pl*); **Südhalbkugel** F southern hemisphere; **auf der** ~ in the southern hemisphere; **Süditalien** NT Southern Italy; **Südkorea** NT South Korea; **Südküste** F south(ern) coast; **die** ~ **Englands** the south coast of England; **Südlage** F southern aspect; **Südländer** [ʾzy:tlɛndɐ] M **-s, -, Südländerin** [-ərɪn] F **-, -nen** southerner; (= *Italiener, Spanier etc*) Mediterranean type; **südländisch** [-lɛndɪʃ] **1** ADJ southern; (= *italienisch, spanisch etc*) Mediterranean; *Temperament* Latin **2** ADV ~ **aussehen** to look Mediterranean

südlich [ʾzy:tlɪç] **1** ADJ **(a)** southern; *Kurs, Wind, Richtung* southerly; **der** ~**e Polarkreis** the Antarctic Circle; **der** ~**e Wendekreis** the Tropic of Capricorn; **52 Grad** ~**er Breite** 52 degrees south; ~**es Eismeer** Antarctic Ocean **(b)** (= *mediterran*) Mediterranean; *Temperament* Latin **2** ADV (to the) south; ~ **von Wien (gelegen)** (to the) south of Vienna; **es liegt** ~**er** or **weiter** ~ it is further (to the) south **3** PREP +GEN (to the) south of

Südlicht NT, NO PL southern lights *pl*; (*fig hum: Mensch*) Southerner

Südost- IN CPDS southeast; (*bei Namen*) Southeast

Südosten [zy:tʾɔstn] M southeast; (*von Land*) South East; **aus** or **von** ~ from the southeast; **nach** ~ to the southeast

südöstlich [zy:tʾœstlɪç] **1** ADJ *Gegend* southeastern; *Wind* southeast(erly) **2** ADV (to the) southeast (*von* of) **3** PREP +GEN (to the) southeast of

Süd-: Südpol M South Pole; **Südpolargebiet** NT Antarctic (region), area of the South Pole; **Südpolarmeer** NT Antarctic Ocean; **Südpolexpedition** F South Pole expedition; **Südsee** [ʾzy:tze:] F South Pacific; **Südseeinsulaner(in)** M(F) South Sea Islander; **Südseite** F south(ern) side; (*von Berg*) south(ern) face; **Südstaat** M southern state; **die** ~**en** (*US*) the Southern States; **Südstaatler** [ʾzy:tʃta:tlɐ] M **-s, -, Südstaatlerin** [-ərɪn] F **-, -nen** (*US*) Southerner; (*US Hist*) Confederate; **Südtirol** NT South(ern) Tyrol; **Südtiroler(in)** M(F) South Tyrolean; **Südvietnam** NT (*Hist*) South Vietnam; **Südwand** F (*von Berg*) south face

südwärts [ʾzy:tvɛrts] ADV south(wards); **der Wind dreht** ~ the wind is moving round to the south

Südwest- IN CPDS south-west; (*bei Namen*) South-west;

Südwesten [zy:tʾvɛstn] M southwest; (*von Land*) South West; **aus** or **von** ~ from the southwest; **nach** ~ to the southwest

Südwester [zy:tʾvɛstɐ] M **-s, -** (*Hut*) sou'wester

südwestlich [zy:tʾvɛstlɪç] **1** ADJ *Gegend* southwestern; *Wind* southwest(erly) **2** ADV (to the) southwest (*von* of) **3** PREP +GEN (to the) southwest of

Südwind M south wind

Sueskanal [ʾzu:ɛs-] M Suez Canal

Suff [zʊf] M **-(e)s,** NO PL (*inf*) **dem** ~ **verfallen** to hit the bottle (*inf*); **dem** ~ **ergeben** or **verfallen sein** to be on the bottle (*inf*); **im** ~ while under the influence (*inf*)

süffig [ʾzyfɪç] ADJ *Wein, Bier* drinkable; *Melodie, Ballade* lovely

süffisant [zyfiʾzant] **1** ADJ smug **2** ADV smugly

Suffix [zoʾfɪks, ʾzʊfɪks] NT **-es, -e** suffix

suggerieren [zʊgeʾri:rən] *ptp* **suggeriert** VT to suggest; **jdm etw** ~ to influence sb by suggesting sth; **jdm** ~**, dass ...** to get sb to believe that ...

suggestiv [zʊgesʾti:f] **1** ADJ suggestive **2** ADV suggestively

Suggestivfrage F leading question

suhlen [ʾzu:lən] VR (*lit, fig*) to wallow

Sühne [ʾzy:nə] F **-, -n** (*Rel, geh*) atonement; (*von Schuld*) expiation; **als** ~ **für etw** to atone for sth

sühnen [ʾzy:nən] **1** VT *Unrecht, Verbrechen* to atone for **2** VI to atone

Suizid [zuiʾtsi:t] M or NT **-(e)s, -e** [-də] (*form*) suicide

Suizid-: Suizidgefahr F risk of suicide; **suizidgefährdet** ADJ suicidal; **Suizidversuch** M suicide attempt

sukzessiv [zʊktseʾsi:f], **sukzessive** [zʊktseʾsi:və] **1** ADJ gradual **2** ADV gradually

Sulfat [zʊlʾfa:t] NT **-(e)s, -e** sulphate (*Brit*), sulfate (*US*)

Sulfid [zʊlʾfi:t] NT **-(e)s, -e** [-də] sulphide (*Brit*), sulfide (*US*)

Sulfit [zʊlʾfi:t] NT **-s, -e** sulphite (*Brit*), sulfite (*US*)

Sulfonamid [zʊlfonaʾmi:t] NT **-(e)s, -e** [-də] sulphonamide (*Brit*), sulfonamide (*US*)

Sultanine [zʊltaʾni:nə] F **-, -n** (= *Rosine*) sultana

Sülze [ʾzyltsə] F **-, -n** brawn

sülzen [ʾzyltsn] VI (*sl*) to go on and on (*inf*)

Sumatra [zuʾma:tra, ʾzu:matra] NT **-s** Sumatra

sumerisch [zuʾme:rɪʃ] ADJ (*Hist*) Sumerian

summ [zʊm] INTERJ buzz; ~ **machen** to buzz

summa cum laude [ʾzʊma kʊm ʾlaʊdə] ADV (*Univ*) summa cum laude (*US*), with distinction

summarisch [zʊʾma:rɪʃ] **1** ADJ (*auch Jur*) summary; *Zusammenfassung* summarizing **2** ADV **etw** ~ **zusammenfassen** to summarize sth; ~ **lässt sich sagen, dass ...** to summarize, we can say that ...

Sümmchen [ʾzʏmçən] NT **-s, -** DIM *von* **Summe**; **ein nettes** ~ (*hum*) a tidy sum (*inf*)

Summe [ʾzʊmə] F **-, -n** sum; (= *Gesamtsumme auch*) total; (*fig*) sum total

summen [ʾzʊmən] **1** VT *Melodie etc* to hum **2** VI to buzz; (*Mensch, Motor, Gerät*) to hum **3** VI IMPERS **es summt** there is a buzzing/humming noise

summieren [zʊʾmi:rən], *ptp* **summiert** **1** VT to sum up **2** VR to mount up; **das summiert sich** it (all) adds up

Sumoringen NT sumo wrestling

Sumoringer M sumo wrestler

Sumpf [zʊmpf] M **-(e)s, -e** [ʾzʏmpfə] marsh; (= *Morast*) mud; (*in tropischen Ländern*) swamp; (*fig*) morass; **im** ~ **der Großstadt** in the squalor and corruption of the big city

Sumpfdotterblume F marsh marigold

sumpfig [ʾzʊmpfɪç] ADJ marshy

Sumpf-: Sumpfland NT marshland; (*in tropischen Ländern*) swampland; **Sumpfpflanze** F marsh plant

Sünde [ʾzyndə] F **-, -n** sin; **ökologische** ~**n** ecological sins or crimes

Sünden-: Sündenbock M (*inf*) scapegoat; **jdn zum** ~ **machen** to make sb one's scapegoat; **Sündenfall** M (*Rel*) Fall (of Man); (*fig*) sin; **Sündenregister** NT (*fig*) list of sins; **jds** ~ the list of sb's sins

Sünder [ʾzyndɐ] M **-s, -, Sünderin** [-ərɪn] F **-, -nen** sinner

sündhaft **1** ADJ (*lit*) sinful; (*fig inf*) *Preise* wicked; **ein** ~**es Geld** (*inf*) a ridiculous amount of money **2** ADV (*inf*) ~ **teuer** wickedly expensive

sündigen [ʾzyndɪgn] VI to sin (*an* +*dat* against); (*hum*) to indulge; **gegen die Natur** ~ to commit a crime against nature

sündteuer ADJ (*Aus*) wickedly expensive

Sunnit [zʊʾni:t] M **-en, -en, Sunnitin** [zʊʾni:tɪn] F **-, -nen** Sunnite

super [ʾzu:pɐ] **1** ADJ INV super (*inf*), great (*inf*) **2** ADV (*mit adj*) really; (*mit vb*) really well

Super [ʾzu:pɐ] NT **-s,** NO PL (= *Benzin*) ≈ four-star (petrol) (*Brit*), ≈ premium (*US*)

Super- [zu:pɐ-] IN CPDS super-; (= *sehr*) ultra-; **Super-8-Film** [zu:pɐʾlaxt-] M Super 8 film; **Superbenzin** NT = **Super**; **Superfrau** F superwoman; **Super-GAU** M ultimate MCA; (*fig*) total meltdown

Superlativ [ʾzu:pɐlati:f] M **-s, -e** [-və] (*Gram, fig*) superlative

superlativisch [ʾzu:pɐlati:vɪʃ] ADJ (*Gram*) superlative; (*fig*) grand; **ins Superlativische geraten** to assume massive proportions

Super-: superleicht ADJ (*inf*) *Zigaretten* extra mild; (= *kinderleicht*) very easy; (= *wenig wiegend*) ultralight; **Supermacht** F superpower; **Supermann** M, *pl* **-männer** superman; **Supermarkt** M supermarket; **supermodern** [-modɛrn] ADJ ultramodern **2** ADV ultramodernly; **superschnell** (*inf*) **1** ADJ ultrafast **2** ADV incredibly fast (*inf*); **Superstar** M (*inf*) superstar

Süppchen [ʾzypçən] NT **-s, -** DIM *von* **Suppe**; **sein eigenes** ~ **kochen** (*fig*) to do one's own thing (*inf*)

Suppe [ʾzʊpə] F **-, -n** soup; (*sämig mit Einlage*) broth; (= *klare Brühe*) bouillon; (*fig inf*: = *Nebel*) dense fog; **klare** ~ consommé; **jdm ein schöne** ~ **einbrocken** (*fig inf*) to get sb into a pickle (*inf*); **du musst die** ~ **auslöffeln, die du dir**

eingebrockt hast (inf) you've made your bed, now you must lie on it (prov)

Suppen- IN CPDS soup; **Suppengrün** NT herbs and vegetables pl for making soup; **Suppenhuhn** NT boiling fowl; **Suppenkaspar** [-kaspar] M **-s, -e**, **Suppenkasper** M (inf) poor eater; (= Suppenfreund) soup fan (inf); **Suppenkelle** F soup ladle; **Suppenküche** F soup kitchen; **Suppenlöffel** M soup spoon; **Suppennudel** F vermicelli pl; **Suppenteller** M soup plate; **Suppenwürfel** M stock cube

Support [zu'pɔrt] M **-s** (technical) support

Supra- ['zu:pra-]: **supraleitend** ADJ (Phys) superconductive; **Supraleiter** M (Phys) superconductor

Sure ['zu:rə] F **-, -n** (im Koran) sura(h)

Surfbrett ['zœ:ef-, 'zœrf-, s-] NT surfboard

surfen ['zœ:efn, 'zœrfn, s-] VI to surf; **im Internet ~** to surf the Internet

Surfer ['zœ:efe, 'zœrfe, s-] M **-s, -**, **Surferin** [-ərɪn] F **-, -nen** surfer

Surfing ['zœ:efɪŋ, 'zœr-, s-] NT **-s**, NO PL (Sport) surfing

Surinam [zuri'nam] NT **-s** Dutch Guiana

surren ['zʊrən] VI **(a)** (Projektor, Computer) to hum; (Ventilator, Kamera) to whir(r) **(b)** AUX SEIN (= sich bewegen: Insekt) to buzz

suspekt [zʊs'pɛkt] ADJ suspicious; **jdm ~ sein** to seem suspicious to sb

suspendieren [zʊspɛn'di:rən], ptp **suspendiert** VT to suspend (von from)

Suspensorium [zʊspɛn'zo:riom] NT **-s, Suspensorien** [-riən] (Med) suspensory

süß [zy:s] **1** ADJ (lit, fig) sweet; **etw ~ machen** to sweeten sth; Tee, Kaffee (mit Zucker) to sugar sth; **sie ist eine Süße** (inf) (= isst gerne ~) she has a sweet tooth; (= ist nett) she's a sweetie(-pie) (inf); **das ~e Leben** the good life; **(mein) Süßer**, **(meine) Süße** (inf) my sweetheart **2** ADV sich bedanken, sagen sweetly; **gern ~ essen** to have a sweet tooth; **den Kaffee ~ trinken** to put sugar in one's coffee; **etw sehr ~ zubereiten** to make sth very sweet; **~ aussehen** to look sweet

Süße ['zy:sə] F **-**, NO PL (lit, fig) sweetness

süßen ['zy:sn] **1** VT to sweeten; (mit Zucker) Tee, Kaffee to sugar **2** VI mit Honig etc ~ to use honey etc as a sweetener

Süßigkeit ['zy:sɪçkait] F **-, -en (a)** NO PL (lit, fig) sweetness **(b)** ~en PL sweets pl (Brit), candy (US)

Süßkartoffel F sweet potato

süßlich ['zy:slɪç] ADJ **(a)** Geruch, Geschmack (= leicht süß) slightly sweet; (= unangenehm süß) sickly (sweet) **(b)** (fig) Töne, Miene, Worte sweet; Lächeln, Schlager sugary; Farben, Modegeschmack overly pretty; (= kitschig) mawkish, tacky

Süß-: **Süßmost** M unfermented fruit juice; **Süßrahmbutter** F creamery butter; **süßsauer** **1** ADJ sweet-and-sour; Gurken etc pickled; (fig: = gezwungen freundlich) Lächeln forced; Miene artificially friendly; **Ente ~** sweet-and-sour duck **2** ADV würzen, einlegen in a sweet-and-sour sauce; **~ schmecken** to taste sweet-and-sour; **~ lächeln** to give a bittersweet smile; **Süßspeise** F sweet dish; **Süßstoff** M sweetener; **Süßwasser** NT, pl **-wasser** freshwater; **Süßwasserfisch** M freshwater fish

SVP [es'fau'pe:] F **-** ABBR von Schweizerische Volkspartei

Swapgeschäft ['svɔp-] NT (Fin) swap (transaction)

Swasiland ['sva:zilant] NT **-s** Swaziland

Sweatshirt ['svɛtʃœrt, -ʃœːt] NT **-s, -s** sweatshirt

Swift ABBR von Society for Worldwide Interbank Financial Telecommunications SWIFT

Swimmingpool ['svɪmɪŋpuːl] M **-s, -s** swimming pool

Sylt [zylt] NT **-s** Sylt

Sylvester [zyl'veste] NT **-s, -** = Silvester

Symbiose [zym'bio:zə] F **-, -n** symbiosis

symbiotisch [zym'bio:tɪʃ] **1** ADJ symbiotic **2** ADV **~ zusammenleben** to have a symbiotic relationship; (Menschen) to live together symbiotically

Symbol [zym'bo:l] NT **-s, -e** symbol

Symbolfigur F symbolic figure

Symbolik [zym'bo:lɪk] F **-**, NO PL symbolism

symbolisch [zym'bo:lɪʃ] **1** ADJ symbolic(al) (für of) **2** ADV symbolically

symbolisieren [zymboli'zi:rən], ptp **symbolisiert** VT to symbolize

Symbol-: **Symbolleiste** F (Comput) toolbar; **symbolträchtig** ADJ heavily symbolic

Symmetrie [zyme'tri:] F **-, -n** [-'tri:ən] symmetry

Symmetrie-: **Symmetrieachse** F axis of symmetry; **Symmetrieebene** F plane of symmetry

symmetrisch [zy'me:trɪʃ] **1** ADJ symmetric(al) **2** ADV symmetrically

Sympathie [zympa'ti:] F **-, -n** [-'ti:ən] (= Zuneigung) liking; (= Mitgefühl, Solidaritätsgefühl) sympathy; **für jdn/etw ~ haben** to have a liking for/a certain amount of sympathy with sb/sth; **diese Maßnahmen haben meine volle ~** I sympathize completely with these measures; **~n gewinnen** to win favour (Brit) or favor (US)

Sympathisant [zympati'zant] M **-en, -en**, **Sympathisantin** [-'zantɪn] F **-, -nen** sympathizer

sympathisch [zym'pa:tɪʃ] ADJ **(a)** nice; **er/es ist mir ~** I like him/it; **das ist mir gar nicht ~** I don't like it at all **(b)** (Anat, Physiol) sympathetic

---

Vorsicht! **sympathisch** *wird im Allgemeinen nicht mit dem englischen Wort* **sympathetic** *übersetzt.*

---

sympathisieren [zympati'zi:rən], ptp **sympathisiert** VI to sympathize (mit with)

Symphoniker [zym'fo:nike] M **-s, -**, **Symphonikerin** [-ərɪn] F **-, -nen** = Sinfoniker

symphonisch [zym'fo:nɪʃ] ADJ = sinfonisch

Symptom [zymp'to:m] NT **-s, -e** symptom

symptomatisch [zympto'ma:tɪʃ] ADJ symptomatic (für of)

Synagoge [zyna'go:gə] F **-, -n** synagogue

synchron [zyn'kro:n] **1** ADJ synchronous; (Ling) synchronic **2** ADV synchronologically

Synchrongetriebe NT (Aut) synchromesh gearbox

Synchronisation [zynkroniza'tsio:n] F **-, -en** (Film, TV) synchronization; (= Übersetzung) dubbing

synchronisieren [zynkroni'zi:rən], ptp **synchronisiert** VT to synchronize; (= übersetzen) Film to dub

Syndrom [zyn'dro:m] NT **-s, -e** syndrome

Synergie [zyner'gi:, zynler'gi:] F **-**, NO PL synergy

Synode [zy'no:də] F **-, -n** (Eccl) synod

synonym [zyno'ny:m], **synonymisch** [zyno'ny:mɪʃ] ADJ synonymous

Synonym [zyno'ny:m] NT **-s, -e** synonym

syntaktisch [zyn'taktɪʃ] **1** ADJ syntactic(al) **2** ADV **das ist ~ korrekt/falsch** the syntax (of this) is correct/wrong; **~ schwierige Übersetzungen** translations with difficult syntax

Syntax ['zyntaks] F **-, -en** syntax

Synthese [zyn'te:zə] F **-, -n** synthesis

Synthesizer ['zyntəsaize] M **-s, -** synthesizer

synthetisch [zyn'te:tɪʃ] **1** ADJ synthetic; Stoff, Faser auch manmade **2** ADV **etw ~ herstellen** to make sth synthetically

Syphilis ['zy:fɪlɪs] F **-**, NO PL syphilis

Syrer ['zy:re] M **-s, -**, **Syrerin** [-ərɪn] F **-, -nen** Syrian

Syrien ['zy:riən] NT **-s** Syria

Syrier ['zy:riе] M **-s, -**, **Syrierin** [-iərɪn] F **-, -nen** Syrian

syrisch ['zy:rɪʃ] ADJ Syrian

System [zys'te:m] NT **-s, -e** system (auch Comput); (= Ordnung, Ordnungsprinzip auch) method; **etw mit ~ machen** to do sth systematically; **etw mit einem ~ machen** to do sth according to a system; **hinter dieser Sache steckt ~** there's method behind it; **Apparate verschiedener ~e** machinery of different designs

System-: **Systemabsturz** M (Comput) system crash; **Systemanalyse** F systems analysis; **Systemanalytiker(in)** M(F) systems analyst

Systematik [zyste'ma:tɪk] F **-**, NO PL **(a)** (= systematisches Ordnen) system **(b)** (= Lehre, Klassifikation) systematology

systematisch [zyste'ma:tɪʃ] **1** ADJ systematic **2** ADV systematically

System-: **systembedingt** ADJ determined by the system; **Systembetreuer(in)** M(F) (Comput) systems administrator; **Systemdiskette** F systems disk; **Systemfehler** M (Comput)

system error; **Systeminformationen** PL (*Comput*) system information *sing*; **Systemkritiker(in)** M(F) critic of the system; **systemkritisch** ▮ ADJ critical of the system ▮ ADV **sich ~ äußern** to make remarks critical of the system; **~ eingestellt sein** to be critical of the system; **systemlos** ▮ ADJ unsystematic ▮ ADV unsystematically; **Systemmanager** M (*Comput: = Programm*) system manager program; **Systemsoftware** F systems software; **Systemspezialist(in)** M(F) (*Comput*) systems specialist; **Systemsteuerung** F (*Comput*) control panel; **Systemtechniker(in)** M(F) (*Comput*) systems engineer; **Systemveränderer** [-fɛɐlɛndərə] M **-s, -,** **Systemveränderin** [-ərɪn] F **-, -nen** (*Pol pej*) **die Partei besteht aus lauter ~n** the whole party is just a bunch of people out to change the system; **Systemzwang** M obligation to conform to the system

Szenario [stse'naːrio] NT **-s, -s** scenario

Szene ['stseːnə] F **-, -n** (*Theat*) (*fig*) scene; (*Theat: = Bühnenausstattung*) set; (*sl: = Drogenszene etc*) scene (*inf*); (*sl: = Milieu*) subculture; **hinter der ~** backstage; (*fig*) behind the scenes; **etw in ~ setzen** (*lit, fig*) to stage sth; **sich in ~ setzen** (*fig*) to play to the gallery; **die rechte/linke ~** (*inf*) the right-/left-wing scene; **jdm eine ~ machen** to make a scene in front of sb

-szene F SUF IN CPDS (*inf*) scene (*inf*); **die Drogenszene** the drugs (*Brit*) *or* drug scene

Szene- IN CPDS (*inf*) in-; **ein ~kenner** somebody who knows the in places (*inf*)

Szenerie [stsenə'riː] F **-, -n** [-'riːən] (*Theat, fig*) scenery

Szintigraf [stsɪnti'graːf] M **-en, -en** scintigraph

Szintigrafie [stsɪntigra'fiː] F **-, -n** [-'fiːən] scintigraphy

Szintigramm [stsɪnti'gram] NT, *pl* **-gramme** scintigram

Tt

T, t [te:] NT **-, -** T, t

t ABBR *von* **Tonne**

Tab [tɛb] M **-s, -s** tab

Tabak ['ta:bak, 'tabak, (*Aus*) ta'bak] M **-s, -e** tobacco; (= *Schnupftabak*) snuff

Tabak- ['ta:bak] IN CPDS tobacco; **Tabakdose** F tobacco tin; (*für Schnupftabak*) snuffbox; **Tabakgenuss** M (tobacco) smoking; **Tabakladen** M tobacconist's; **Tabakmischung** F blend (of tobaccos); **Tabaksteuer** F duty on tobacco; **Tabaktrafik** [ta'bak-] F (*Aus*) tobacconist's; **Tabaktrafikant(in)** [ta'bak-] M(F) (*Aus*) tobacconist

tabellarisch [tabɛ'la:rɪʃ] **◫** ADJ tabular; **bitte fügen Sie einen ~en Lebenslauf bei** please write out your curriculum vitae (*Brit*) *or* résumé (*US*) in tabular form **◫** ADV in tabular form

Tabelle [ta'bɛlə] F **-, -n** table; (= *Diagramm*) chart; (*Sport*) (league) table

Tabellen-: Tabellenform F in ~ in tabular form, in tables/a table; (*Diagramm*) as a chart; **tabellenförmig** **◫** ADJ tabular; (= *als Diagramm*) as a chart **◫** ADV in a table; as a chart; **Tabellenführer(in)** M(F) (*Sport*) league leaders *pl*; **~ sein** to be at the top of the (league) table; **Tabellenkalkulation** F (*Comput*) spreadsheet; **Tabellenkalkulationsprogramm** NT (*Comput*) spreadsheet (program); **Tabellenplatz** M (*Sport*) position in the league; **auf den letzten ~ fallen** to drop to the bottom of the table; **Tabellenstand** M (*Sport*) league situation

Tablett [ta'blɛt] NT **-(e)s, -s** *or* **-e** tray; **jdm etw auf einem silbernen ~ servieren** (*fig*: = *einfach machen*) to hand sb sth on a silver platter

Tablette [ta'blɛtə] F **-, -n** tablet

Tabletten-: Tablettenmissbrauch M pill abuse; **Tablettensucht** F addiction to pills; **tablettensüchtig** ADJ addicted to pills

tabu [ta'bu:, 'ta:bu] ADJ PRED taboo

Tabu [ta'bu:, 'ta:bu] NT **-s, -s** taboo

tabuisieren [tabui'zi:rən], *ptp* **tabuisiert** VT to make taboo

Tabulator [tabu'la:to:r] M **-s, Tabulatoren** [-'to:rən] tabulator

Tacheles ['taxələs] NO ART (*inf*) **(mit jdm) ~ reden** to have a talk (with sb)

tachinieren [taxi'ni:rən], *ptp* **tachiniert** VI (*Aus inf*) to laze about (*inf*)

Tacho ['taxo] M **-s, -s** (*inf*) speedo (*Brit inf*)

Tachometer [taxo'me:tɐ] M *or* NT **-s, -** speedometer

Tacker ['takɐ] M **-s, -** (*inf*) stapler

Tadel ['ta:dl] M **-s, -** (= *Verweis*) reprimand; (= *Vorwurf*) reproach; (= *Kritik*) criticism; (*geh*: = *Makel*) blemish; (*Sch*: = *Eintragung*) black mark

tadellos **◫** ADJ perfect; *Deutsch etc auch* faultless; *Leben* blameless; (*inf*) splendid **◫** ADV perfectly; *sprechen auch* faultlessly; *gekleidet* immaculately

tadeln ['ta:dln] VT *jdn* to rebuke; *jds Benehmen* to criticize

tadelnd ADJ ATTR reproachful

Tadschikistan [tad'ʒi:kɪsta:n] M **-s** Tajikistan

Tafel ['ta:fl] F **-, -n (a)** (= *Platte*) slab; (= *Holztafel*) panel; (= ~ *Schokolade etc*) bar; (= *Gedenktafel*) plaque; (= *Wandtafel*) (black)board; (= *Schiefertafel*) slate; (*Elec*: = *Schalttafel*) control panel; (= *Anzeigetafel*) board; (= *Verkehrstafel*) sign **(b)** (*form*: = *festlicher Speisetisch*) table; (= *Festmahl*) meal; (*mittags*) luncheon (*form*); (*abends*) dinner; **die ~ aufheben** to officially end the meal

Tafel-: Tafelapfel M eating apple; **Tafelberg** M (*Geog*) table mountain; **Tafelgeschäft** NT (*Fin*) counter transactions *pl*; **Tafelgeschirr** NT tableware; **Tafelland** NT plateau

täfeln ['tɛ:fln] VT *Wand* to wainscot; *Decke, Raum* to panel

Tafel-: Tafelobst NT (dessert) fruit; **Tafelöl** NT cooking oil; (= *Salatöl*) salad oil; **Tafelsalz** NT table salt; **Tafelsilber** NT silver; **Tafelspitz** M (*Cook*) soured boiled rump

Täfelung ['tɛ:fəlʊŋ] F **-, -en** (*von Wand*) wainscoting; (*von Decke*) (wooden) panelling (*Brit*) *or* paneling (*US*)

Tafel-: Tafelwasser NT, *pl* **-wässer** mineral water; **Tafelwein** M table wine

Taft [taft] M **-(e)s, -e** taffeta

Tag [ta:k] M **-(e)s, -e** [-gə] **(a)** day; **am ~(e) des/der ...** (on) the day of ...; **am ~** during the day; **alle ~e** (*inf*), **jeden ~** every day; **auf den ~ (genau)** to the day; **auf ein paar ~e** for a few days; **auf seine alten ~e** at his age; **bei ~ und Nacht** night and day; **in den letzten ~en** in the last few days; **bis die ~e!** (*inf*) so long (*inf*); **diese** (*inf*) *or* **dieser ~e** (= *bald*) in the next few days; **den ganzen ~ (lang)** (*lit, fig*) all day long; **eines ~es** one day; **eines schönen** *or* **guten ~es** one fine day; **sich** (*dat*) **einen schönen/faulen ~ machen** to have a nice/lazy day; **~ für** *or* **um ~** day by day; **in unseren ~en, in den heutigen ~en** these days, nowadays; **von ~ zu ~** from day to day; **~ der Arbeit** Labour Day (*Brit*), Labor Day (*US*); **welcher ~ ist heute?** what day is it today?; **guten ~!** hello (*inf*); (*esp bei Vorstellung*) how-do-you-do; **~!** (*inf*) hi (*inf*); **zweimal am ~(e)** *or* **pro ~** twice a day; **von einem ~ auf den anderen** overnight; **der ~ X** D-Day (*fig*); **er erzählt** *or* **redet viel, wenn der ~ lang ist** (*inf*) he'll tell you anything if you let him; **seinen guten/schlechten ~ haben** to have a good/bad *or* off day; **das war heute wieder ein ~!** (*inf*) what a day!; **das Ereignis/Thema des ~es** the event/talking point of the day; **Sie hören jetzt die Nachrichten des ~es** and now the news; **in den ~ hinein leben** to live from day to day; **~ und Nacht** night and day; **das ist ein Unterschied wie ~ und Nacht** they are as different as chalk and cheese (*Brit*) *or* night and day (*US*)

(b) (= *Tageslicht*) **bei ~(e) ankommen** while it's light; *arbeiten, reisen* during the day; **es wird schon ~** it's getting light already; **es ist ~** it's light; **an den ~ kommen** (*fig*) to come to light; **etw an den ~ bringen** to bring sth to light; **er legte großes Interesse an den ~** he showed great interest; **zu ~e** = **zutage**

(c) (*inf*: = *Menstruation*) **meine/ihre ~e** my/her period

(d) (*Min*) **über ~e arbeiten** to work above ground; **unter ~e arbeiten** to work underground; **etw unter ~e abbauen** to mine sth; **etw über ~e abbauen** to quarry (*esp Brit*) *or* excavate sth

-tag M SUF IN CPDS (= *Konferenz*) conference; **Weltfrauentag** International Women's Conference

tagaus [ta:k'laus] ADV *siehe* **tagein**

Tage-: Tagebau M, *pl* **-baue** (*Min*) opencast mining; **Tagebuch** NT diary; **(über etw** *acc*) **~ führen** to keep a diary (of sth); **Tagegeld** NT daily allowance

tagein [ta:k'lain] ADV **~, tagaus** day in, day out

tagelang **◫** ADJ lasting for days; **~e Regenfälle** several days' rain **◫** ADV for days

tagen ['ta:gn] VI (*Parlament, Rat, Gericht*) to sit; (*Minister, Leiter*) to meet

Tagereise F day's journey

Tages-: Tagesablauf M day; **Tagesanbruch** M daybreak; **Tagesausflug** M day trip *or* excursion; **Tagesbedarf** M daily requirement; **Tagescreme** F day cream; **Tagesdecke** F bedspread; **Tagesgeschehen** NT events *pl* of the day; **Tagesgespräch** NT talk of the town; **Tageskarte** F **(a)** (= *Speisekarte*) menu of the day; specialties *pl* of the day (*US*) **(b)** (= *Fahr-, Eintrittskarte*) day ticket; **Tageskasse** F **(a)** (*Theat*) box office **(b)** (*Econ*) day's takings *pl*; **Tageskurs** M (*St Ex*) (*von Effekten*) current price; (*von Devisen*) current rate; **Tageslicht** NT, NO PL daylight; **ans ~ kommen** (*fig*) to come to light; **Tageslichtprojektor** M overhead projector; **Tageslohn** M day's wages; **Tagesmenü** NT menu of the day (*Brit*), specialties *pl* of the day (*US*); **Tagesmutter** F, *pl* **-mütter** child minder (*Brit*), nanny; **Tagesordnung** F agenda; **zur ~!** keep to the agenda!; **etw auf die ~ setzen** to put sth on the agenda; **auf der ~ stehen** to be on the agenda; **zur ~ übergehen** to proceed to the agenda; (= *an die Arbeit gehen*) to get down to business; (= *wie üblich weitermachen*) to carry on as usual; **an der ~ sein** (*fig*) to be the order of the day; **Tagesordnungspunkt** M item on the agenda; **Tagespresse** F daily (news)papers *pl*; **Tagesration** F daily rations *pl*; **Tagesreise** F **(a)** (= *Entfernung*) day's journey **(b)** (= *Ausflug*) day trip; **Tagessatz** M daily rate; **Tagesschau** F (*TV*) news *sing*;

Tageswert M current cost; **Tageszeit** F time (of day); **zu jeder Tages- und Nachtzeit** at all hours of the day and night; **Tageszeitung** F daily (paper)

tageweise ['taːɡəvaizə] ADV for a few days at a time

taghell ◼ ADJ (as) bright as day; **es war schon ~** it was already broad daylight ◼ ADV **etw ~ erleuchten** to light sth up very brightly

-tägig [tɛːɡɪç] ADJ SUF -day; **eine dreitägige Konferenz** a three-day conference

tägl. ABBR *von* **täglich**

täglich ['tɛːɡlɪç] ◼ ADJ daily; (*attr.* = *gewöhnlich*) everyday; **~e Gelder** (*Comm*) call money; **~e Zinsen** (*Comm*) daily interest; **sein ~(es) Brot verdienen** to earn a living; **das ist unser ~(es) Brot** (*fig*: *Ärger etc*) it is our stock in trade; **unser ~ Brot gib uns heute** (*Bibl*) give us this day our daily bread ◼ ADV every day; **einmal ~** once a day

tags [taːks] ADV (a) **~ zuvor** the day before; **~ darauf** or **danach** the next day (b) (= *bei Tag*) in the daytime

Tagschicht F day shift; **~ haben** to be on (the) day shift

tagsüber ['taːksyːbə] ADV during the day

Tag-: tagtäglich ◼ ADJ daily ◼ ADV every (single) day; **Tagtraum** M daydream; **Tagträumer(in)** M(F) daydreamer; **Tagundnachtgleiche** ['taːklʊntˈnaxtɡlaiçə] F DECL AS ADJ equinox

Tagung ['taːɡʊŋ] F **-, -en** conference; (*von Ausschuss*) sitting

Tahiti [taˈhiːti] NT **-s** Tahiti

tahitisch [taˈhiːtɪʃ] ADJ Tahitian

Tai Chi ['tai ˈtʃiː] NT **-, NO PL** t'ai chi

Taifun [taiˈfuːn] M **-s, -e** typhoon

Taille ['taljə] F **-, -n** waist; (*bei Kleidungsstücken auch*) waistline; **auf seine ~ achten** to watch one's waistline

Taillenweite ['taljən-] F waist measurement

tailliert [taˈljiːɐt] ADJ waisted, fitted

Taiwan ['taivan, taiˈvaː(ː)n] NT **-s** Taiwan

Taiwanese [taivaˈneːzə] M **-n, -n**, **Taiwanesin** [-ˈneːzɪn] F **-, -nen** Taiwanese

taiwanesisch [taivaˈneːzɪʃ] ADJ Taiwan(ese)

Takelage [takəˈlaːʒə] F **-, -n** (*Naut*) rigging

Takt [takt] M **-(e)s, -e (a)** (= *Einheit*) (*Mus*) bar; (*Phon, Poet*) foot; **mit jdm ein paar ~e reden** (*inf:* = *die Meinung sagen*) to give sb a good talking-to (*inf*)
(b) (= *Rhythmus*) time; **den ~ schlagen** to beat time; **den ~ verlieren** to lose the beat; **im ~ singen/tanzen** to sing/dance in time (with the music); **den ~ angeben** (*lit*) to give the beat; (*fig*) to call the tune; **das Publikum klatschte den ~ dazu** the audience clapped in time to the music
(c) (*Aut*) stroke
(d) (*Ind*) phase
(e) NO PL (= *Taktgefühl*) tact; **mit dem ihm eigenen ~** with his great tact(fulness); **er hat keinen ~ im Leibe** (*inf*) he hasn't an ounce of tact in him
(f) (= *Taktverkehr*) regular service; **im ~ fahren** to go at regular intervals; **alle Linien verkehren im Einstundentakt** there is an hourly service on all routes
(g) (*Comput*) (clock) pulse

takten ['taktn] VT (*Comput*) to clock; **ein mit 60 MHz getakteter Prozessor** a processor with a clock speed of 60 MHz

Takt-: Taktfrequenz F (*Comput*) clock speed; **Taktgefühl** NT sense of tact

taktieren [takˈtiːrən], *ptp* **taktiert** VI (= *Taktiken anwenden*) to manoeuvre (*Brit*), to maneuver (*US*); **so kann man nicht ~** you can't use these tactics

Taktik ['taktɪk] F **-, -en** tactics *pl*; **eine ~** tactics *pl*, a tactical approach; **man muss mit ~ vorgehen** you have to use tactics

Taktiker ['taktikɐ] M **-s, -**, **Taktikerin** [-ərɪn] F **-, -nen** tactician

taktisch ['taktɪʃ] ◼ ADJ tactical ◼ ADV tactically; **~ vorgehen** to use tactics; **~ klug** good tactics

Takt-: taktlos ◼ ADJ tactless ◼ ADV tactlessly; **Taktlosigkeit** F **-, -en** tactlessness; **es war eine ~ sondergleichen** it was a particularly tactless thing to do/say; **Taktstock** M baton; **taktvoll** ◼ ADJ tactful ◼ ADV tactfully

Tal [taːl] NT **-(e)s, ⁻er** ['tɛːlə] valley

tal-: talab(wärts) [taˈlʔap(vɛrts)] ADV (a) down into the valley (b) (= *flussabwärts*) downriver; **talauf(wärts)** ADV (a) up the valley (b) (= *flussaufwärts*) upriver

Talent [taˈlɛnt] NT **-(e)s, -e (a)** (= *Begabung*) talent (*zu* for); **ein großes ~ haben** to be very talented **(b)** (= *begabter Mensch*) talented person; **junge ~e** young talent; **er ist ein großes ~** he is very talented

talentiert [talɛnˈtiːɐt] ADJ talented

Talent-: talentlos ADJ untalented; **Talentscout** [-skaut] M **-(s), -s** talent scout; **Talentsuche** F search for talent; **wir sind auf ~** we are looking for new talent

Taler ['taːlɐ] M **-s, -** (*Hist*) T(h)aler

Talfahrt F (*bergabwärts*) descent; (*flussabwärts*) downriver trip; (*fig*) decline

Talg [talk] M **-(e)s, -e** [-ɡə] tallow; (*Cook*) suet; (= *Hautabsonderung*) sebum

Talgdrüse F (*Physiol*) sebaceous gland

Taliban [taliˈbaːn] F **-, -** Taliban

Talisman ['talɪsman] M **-s, -e** talisman; (= *Maskottchen*) mascot

talken ['tɔːkn] VI (*inf*) to talk

Talkessel M basin

Talkmaster ['tɔːkmaːstɐ] M **-s, -**, **Talkmasterin** [-ərɪn] F **-, -nen** talk show host

Talkshow ['tɔːkʃoː] F (*TV*) talk show

Talkum ['talkʊm] NT **-s, NO PL (a)** (= *Talk*) talc(um) **(b)** (= *Puder*) talc

Talmud ['talmuːt] M **-(e)s, -e** [-də] Talmud

Talon [taˈlõː] M **-s, -s** (*St Ex*) renewal coupon

Tal-: Talsohle F bottom of a/the valley; (*fig*) rock bottom; **in der ~** (*fig*) at rock bottom; **Talsperre** F dam; **Talstation** F base camp; (*von Skilift etc*) station at the bottom of a ski lift *etc*

Tamburin [tambuˈriːn, ˈtam-] NT **-s, -e** tambourine

Tamile [taˈmiːlə] M **-n, -n**, **Tamilin** [-ˈmiːlɪn] F **-, -nen** Tamil

tamilisch [taˈmiːlɪʃ] ADJ Tamil

Tampon ['tampɔn, tamˈpoːn] M **-s, -s** tampon

tamponieren [tampoˈniːrən], *ptp* **tamponiert** VT to plug

Tamtam [tamˈtam, ˈtam-] NT **-s, -s** (*Mus*) tom-tom; (*inf*) (= *Wirbel*) fuss; (= *Lärm*) row; **der Faschingszug zog mit großem ~ durch die Straßen** the Fasching procession paraded loudly through the streets

Tandem ['tandɛm] NT **-s, -s** tandem

Tandler ['tandlɐ] M **-s, -**, **Tandlerin** [-ərɪn] F **-, -nen** (*Aus*) **(a)** (= *Trödler*) second-hand dealer **(b)** (= *langsamer Mensch*) slowcoach (*Brit inf*), slowpoke (*US inf*)

Tang [taŋ] M **-(e)s, -e** seaweed

Tanganjika [taŋanˈjiːka] NT **-s** Tanganyika

Tangens ['taŋɡɛns] M **-, -** (*Math*) tan(gent)

Tangente [taŋˈɡɛntə] F **-, -n** (*Math*) tangent; (= *Straße*) ring road (*Brit*), expressway

tangential [taŋɡɛnˈtsiaːl] ADJ tangential

tangieren [taŋˈɡiːrən], *ptp* **tangiert** VT **(a)** (*Math*) to be tangent to **(b)** (= *berühren*) *Problem* to touch on; *Stadt, Gebiet* to skirt; **das tangiert das Problem nur** that is merely tangential to the problem **(c)** (= *betreffen*) to affect; (*inf:* = *kümmern*) to bother

Tango ['taŋɡo] M **-s, -s** tango

Tank [taŋk] M **-(e)s, -s** or **-e** (= *Behälter, Panzer*) tank

Tank-: Tankanzeige F fuel gauge; **Tankdeckel** M filler cap (*Brit*), gas cap (*US*)

tanken ['taŋkn] ◼ VI (*Autofahrer*) to get petrol (*Brit*) or gas (*US*); (*Rennfahrer, Flugzeug*) to refuel; **wo kann man hier ~?** where can I get petrol (*Brit*) or gas (*US*) (a)round here?; **hier kann man billig ~** you can get cheap petrol (*Brit*) or gas (*US*) here; **ich muss noch ~** I have to get some petrol (*Brit*) or gas (*US*); **ich tanke nur für 15 Euro** I'll just put 15 euros' worth in ◼ VT *Super, Diesel* to get; **ich tanke bleifrei** I use unleaded; **ich habe 30 Liter getankt** I put 30 litres (*Brit*) or liters (*US*) in (the tank); **er hat einiges ~** or **ganz schön getankt** (*inf*) he's had a few

Tanker ['taŋkɐ] M **-s, -** (*Naut*) tanker

Tank-: Tankfahrzeug NT (*Aut*) tanker; **Tankfüllmenge** F tank capacity; **Tanklaster** M, **Tanklastzug** M tanker; **Tankmöglichkeit** F **letzte ~ vor ...** last petrol (*Brit*) or gas (*US*) station before ...; **Tanksäule** F petrol pump (*Brit*), gas(oline) pump (*US*); **Tankschiff** NT tanker; **Tankstelle** F filling (*Brit*) or gas(oline) (*US*) station; **Tankstutzen** M filler pipe; **Tankuhr** F fuel gauge; **Tankverschluss** M petrol (*Brit*) or gas (*US*) cap; **Tankwagen** M tanker; (*Rail*) tank wagon; **Tankwart(in)** M(F) petrol pump (*Brit*) *or* gas station (*US*) attendant; **Tankzug** M tanker

Tanne ['tanə] F **-, -n** fir; (*Holz*) pine

Tannen-: Tannenbaum M **(a)** fir tree **(b)** (= *Weihnachtsbaum*) Christmas tree; **Tannennadel** F fir needle; **Tannenzapfen** M fir cone

Tannin [ta'niːn] NT **-s**, NO PL tannin

Tansania [tanza'niːa, tan'zaːnia] NT **-s** Tanzania

tansanisch [tan'zaːnɪʃ] ADJ Tanzanian

Tantchen ['tantçən] NT **-s, -** (*inf*) **(a)** (*Verwandte*) auntie, aunty **(b)** (= *alte Dame*) old dear (*Brit inf*) *or* lady

Tante ['tantə] F **-, -n (a)** (*Verwandte*) aunt **(b)** (*pej inf*: = *Frau*) woman (*inf*), old lady **(c)** (*baby-talk*) (= *Frau*) lady; (= *Kindergartenschwester etc*) teacher; (= *Krippenschwester*) nurse; ~ **Schneider/Monika** aunty Schneider/Monika

Tante-Emma-Laden [tantə'lɛma-] M (*inf*) corner shop

Tantieme [tãˈtieːmə, -ˈtiːmə] F **-, -n** percentage (of the profits); (*für höhere Angestellte*) director's fee; (*für Künstler*) royalty

Tanz [tants] M **-es, ⸚e** ['tɛntsə] dance; **jdn zum ~ auffordern** to ask sb to dance; **ein ~ auf dem Vulkan** (*fig*) living on the edge

Tanz-: Tanzabend M dance; **Tanzbar** F bar with dancing; **Tanzbein** NT (**mit jdm**) **das ~ schwingen** (*hum*) to trip the light fantastic (with sb) (*hum*)

tänzeln ['tɛntsln] VI AUX HABEN *or* (*bei Richtungsangabe*) SEIN to mince (*Brit*), to sashay (*esp US*); (*Boxer*) to skip; (*Pferd*) to step delicately

tanzen ['tantsn] **1** VI AUX HABEN *or* (*bei Richtungsangabe*) SEIN to dance; ~ **gehen, zum Tanzen gehen** to go dancing **2** VT *Walzer, Tango etc* to dance; **er hat mit mir einen Walzer getanzt** he danced a waltz with me

Tänzer ['tɛntsɐ] M **-s, -, Tänzerin** [-ərɪn] F **-, -nen** dancer; (= *Tanzpartner*) (dancing) partner

tänzerisch ['tɛntsərɪʃ] **1** ADJ *Grazie, Beschwingtheit etc* dance-like; **eine große ~e Leistung** a tremendous piece of dancing; **~e Darbietungen** dance acts; **sein ~es Können** his dancing ability **2** ADV ~ **veranlagt sein** to have a talent for dancing; ~ **ausgebildet** trained as a dancer; **die Darsteller waren ~ hervorragend** the dancing was excellent; **die Kür war ~ miserabel** the dance technique in the free section was terrible

Tanz-: Tanzfläche F dance floor; **Tanzkapelle** F dance band; **Tanzkurs** M dancing course; **Tanzlokal** NT café with dancing; **Tanzmusik** F dance music; **Tanzorchester** NT dance orchestra; **Tanzpartner(in)** M(F) dancing partner; **Tanzschritt** M (dance) step; **Tanzschule** F dancing school; **Tanzsport** M competitive dancing; **Tanzstunde** F dancing lesson; **sie haben sich in der ~ kennengelernt** they met at dancing lessons; **Tanzturnier** NT dancing *or* dance contest; **Tanzveranstaltung** F, **Tanzvergnügen** NT dance

Taoismus [tao'ɪsmʊs, tau-] M **-**, NO PL Taoism

Tapet [ta'peːt] NT (*inf*) **etw aufs ~ bringen** to bring sth up; **aufs ~ kommen** to be brought up

Tapete [ta'peːtə] F **-, -n** wallpaper; **ohne ~n** without wallpaper; **die ~n wechseln** (*fig inf*) to have a change of scenery

Tapeten-: Tapetentür F concealed door; **Tapetenwechsel** M (*inf*) change of scenery

tapezieren [tape'tsiːrən], *ptp* **tapeziert** VT to (wall)paper; (*inf*: *mit Bildern*) to plaster (*inf*); **neu ~** to repaper

Tapezierer [tape'tsiːrɐ] M **-s, -, Tapeziererin** [-ərɪn] F **-, -nen (a)** paperhanger, decorator (*Brit*) **(b)** (= *Polsterer*) upholsterer

Tapeziertisch M trestle table

tapfer ['tapfɐ] **1** ADJ brave; (= *wacker*) steadfast **2** ADV bravely; **wir marschierten immer ~ weiter, ohne zu merken …** we marched on blithely, not realizing …; **sich ~ schlagen** (*inf*) to put on a brave show

Tapferkeit F **-**, NO PL bravery

Tapioka [ta'pioːka] F **-**, NO PL tapioca

Tapir ['taːpiːɐ] M **-s, -e** (*Zool*) tapir

tapsen ['tapsn] VI AUX SEIN (*inf*) (*Kind*) to toddle; (*Bär*) to lumber; (*Kleintier*) to waddle

tapsig ['tapsɪç] (*inf*) **1** ADJ awkward **2** ADV awkwardly

Tara ['taːra] F **-, Taren** [-rən] (*Comm*) tare

Tarantel [ta'rantl] F **-, -n** tarantula; **wie von der ~ gestochen** as if stung by a bee

tarieren [ta'riːrən], *ptp* **tariert** VT to tare

Tarif [ta'riːf] M **-(e)s, -e** rate; (= *Fahrpreis*) fare; **die ~e für Telefonanschlüsse** telephone line rental; **neue ~e für Löhne/ Gehälter** new wage rates/salary scales; **die Gewerkschaft hat die ~e für Löhne und Gehälter gekündigt** the union has put in a new wage claim; **nach/über/unter ~ bezahlen** to pay according to/above/below the (union) rate(s)

Tarif-: Tarifabschluss M wage settlement; **Tarifautonomie** F (right to) free collective bargaining; **Tarifgehalt** NT union rates *pl*; **Tarifgruppe** F grade

tariflich [ta'riːflɪç] **1** ADJ *Arbeitszeit, Regelung* agreed **2** ADV **die Gehälter sind ~ festgelegt** there are fixed rates for salaries; **etw ~ festschreiben** to include sth in the labour (*Brit*) *or* labor (*US*) contract; **~ vereinbart sein** to be in the labour (*Brit*) *or* labor (*US*) contract

Tarif-: Tariflohn M standard wage; **tariflos** ADJ **~er Zustand** period when new rates are being negotiated; **Tarifpartei** F party to a wage agreement; **die ~en** unions and management; **Tarifpartner(in)** M(F) party to the wage *or* (*für Gehälter*) salary agreement; **die ~** union and management; (= *Sozialpartner*) both sides of industry; **Tarifrunde** F pay round; **Tarifverhandlungen** PL negotiations *pl* on pay; **Tarifvertrag** M pay agreement; **Tarifzone** F fare zone

tarnen ['tarnən] **1** VT to camouflage; (*fig*) *Absichten, Identität etc* to disguise; **Saunas sind oft getarnte Bordelle** saunas are often a cover for brothels; **als Polizist getarnt** disguised as a policeman **2** VR (*Tier*) to camouflage itself; (*Mensch*) to disguise oneself

Tarn-: Tarnfarbe F camouflage colour (*Brit*) *or* color (*US*); (*Anstrich*) camouflage paint; **Tarnkappe** F magic hat; **Tarnkappenbomber** M Stealth bomber

Tarnung ['tarnʊŋ] F **-, -en** camouflage; (*von Agent etc*) disguise; **die Arztpraxis ist nur eine ~** the doctor's practice is just a cover

Tartar[1] [tar'taːɐ] NT **-(s)**, NO PL, **Tartarbeefsteak** NT steak tartare

Tartar[2] [tar'taːɐ] M **-en, -en, Tartarin** [-'taːrɪn] F **-, -nen** Tartar

Täschchen ['tɛʃçən] NT **-s, -** DIM *von* **Tasche**

Tasche ['taʃə] F **-, -n (a)** (= *Handtasche*) bag (*Brit*), purse (*US*); (= *Reisetasche etc*) bag; (= *Aktentasche*) case **(b)** (*bei Kleidungsstücken*, = *Billardtasche*) pocket; **in die eigene ~ arbeiten** *or* **wirtschaften** to line one's own pockets; **etw in der ~ haben** (*inf*) to have sth in the bag (*inf*); **jdm das Geld aus der ~ locken** *or* **ziehen** *or* **lotsen** to get sb to part with his money; **etw aus der eigenen ~ bezahlen** to pay for sth out of one's own pocket; **sich** (*dat*) **etwas in die ~ lügen** (*inf*) to kid oneself (*inf*); **jdm auf der ~ liegen** (*inf*) to live off sb; **jdn in die ~ stecken** (*inf*) to put sb in the shade (*inf*)

Taschelzieher ['taʃltsiːɐ] M **-s, -, Taschelzieherin** [-ərɪn] F **-, -nen** (*Aus inf*: = *Taschendieb*) pickpocket

Taschen-: Taschenausgabe F pocket edition; **Taschenbuch** NT paperback (book); **Taschenbuchausgabe** F paperback (edition); **Taschendieb(in)** M(F) pickpocket; **Taschendiebstahl** M pickpocketing; **Taschenfeitel** M (*Aus inf*) penknife, pocketknife; **Taschenformat** NT pocket size; **Taschengeld** NT pocket money; **Taschenlampe** F torch, flashlight; **Taschenmesser** NT pocketknife; **Taschenrechner** M pocket calculator; **Taschentuch** NT, *pl* **-tücher** hanky (*inf*)

Tasmanien [tas'maːniən] NT **-s** Tasmania

tasmanisch [tas'maːnɪʃ] ADJ Tasmanian

Tässchen ['tɛsçən] NT **-s, -** DIM *von* **Tasse** (little) cup; **ein ~ Tee** a quick cup of tea

Tasse ['tasə] F **-, -n** cup; (*mit Untertasse*) cup and saucer; (= *Henkeltasse*) mug; (= *Suppentasse*) bowl; **eine ~ Kaffee** a cup of coffee; **er hat nicht alle ~n im Schrank** (*inf*) he's a sandwich short of a picnic (*Brit inf*), he's one card shy of a full deck (*US inf*)

Tastatur [tasta'tuːɐ] F **-, -en** keyboard

Taste ['tastə] F **-, -n** key; (= *Knopf an Gerät auch*) button; „~ **drücken**" "push button"

Vorsicht! **Taste** *wird nicht mit dem englischen Wort* **taste** *übersetzt.*

tasten ['tastn] **1** VI to feel; **nach etw ~** (*lit, fig*) to feel for sth; **vorsichtig ~d** feeling one's way carefully; **~de Schritte** (*lit, fig*) tentative steps **2** VR to feel one's way **3** VT (= *drücken*) to press; *Nummer auch* to punch out; *Text* to key; (*Typ:* = *setzen*) to key(board)

Tasten-: **Tastenfeld** NT (*Comput*) keypad; **Tasteninstrument** NT (*Mus*) keyboard instrument; **Tastentelefon** NT push-button telephone

Tast-: **Tastorgan** NT organ of touch; **Tastsinn** M sense of touch

tat PRET *von* **tun**

Tat [taːt] F -, -en (= *das Handeln*) action; (= *Einzeltat auch*) act; (= *Heldentat, Untat*) deed; (= *Leistung*) feat; (= *Verbrechen*) crime; **ein Mann der ~** a man of action; **eine ~ der Verzweiflung/Nächstenliebe** an act of desperation/charity; **als er sah, was er mit dieser ~ angerichtet hatte** when he saw what he had done by this; **eine geschichtliche/verbrecherische ~** an historic/a criminal act; **eine gute/böse ~** a good/wicked deed; **etw in die ~ umsetzen** to put sth into action; **zur ~ schreiten** to proceed to action; (*hum*) to get on with it; **in der ~** indeed; (*wider Erwarten, erstaunlicherweise etc*) actually

Tatar¹ [taˈtaːɐ] NT -(s), NO PL, **Tatarbeefsteak** NT steak tartare

Tatar² [taˈtaːɐ] M -en, -en, **Tatarin** [-ˈtaːrɪn] F -, -nen Tartar

Tat-: **Tatbestand** M (*Jur*) facts *pl* (of the case); (= *Sachlage*) facts *pl* (of the matter); **den ~ des Betrugs erfüllen** (*Jur*) to constitute fraud; **Tateinheit** F (*Jur*) **in ~ mit** concomitantly with

Taten-: **Tatendrang** M thirst for action; **tatenlos** 1 ADJ idle 2 ADV **~ herumstehen** to stand idly by; **wir mussten ~ zusehen** we could only stand and watch; **Tatenlosigkeit** F -, NO PL inaction

Täter [ˈtɛːtɐ] M -s, -, **Täterin** [-ərɪn] F -, -nen culprit; (*Jur*) perpetrator (*form*); **als ~ verdächtigt werden** to be a suspect; **als ~ in Frage kommen** to be a possible suspect; **nach dem ~ wird noch gefahndet** the police are still searching for the person responsible; **wer war der ~?** who did it?; **unbekannte ~** person or persons unknown; **jugendliche ~** young offenders

Täterprofil NT suspect profile

Täterschaft [ˈtɛːtɐʃaft] F -, -en guilt; **die Frage (nach) der ~** (*form*) the question of who was responsible; **die ~ leugnen/zugeben** to deny/admit one's guilt; (*vor Gericht*) to plead not guilty/guilty

tätig [ˈtɛːtɪç] ADJ (a) ATTR active; **in einer Sache ~ werden** (*form*) to take action in a matter (b) (= *arbeitend*) **~ sein** to work; **als was sind Sie ~?** what do you do?; **er ist im Bankwesen ~** he's in banking

tätigen [ˈtɛːtɪgn̩] VT (*Comm*) to conclude; (*geh*) *Einkäufe* to carry out; (*geh*) *Anruf* to make

Tätigkeit [ˈtɛːtɪçkait] F -, -en activity; (= *Beschäftigung*) occupation; (= *Arbeit*) work; (= *Beruf*) job; **während meiner ~ als Lehrer** while I was working as a teacher; **zur Zeit übt er eine andere ~ aus** at present he has a different occupation; **auf eine langjährige ~ (als ...) zurückblicken** to look back on many years of active life (as ...)

Tätigkeits-: **Tätigkeitsbereich** M field of activity; **Tätigkeitsbeschreibung** F job description; **Tätigkeitsmerkmale** PL job characteristics *pl*

Tat-: **Tatkraft** F, NO PL energy, drive; **tatkräftig** 1 ADJ energetic; *Hilfe* active 2 ADV actively; **etw/jdn ~ unterstützen** to actively support sth/sb

tätlich [ˈtɛːtlɪç] 1 ADJ violent; **~e Beleidigung** (*Jur*) assault (and battery); **~ werden** to become violent; **gegen jdn ~ werden** to assault sb 2 ADV **jdn ~ angreifen** to attack sb physically

Tätlichkeit F violent act; **~en** violence *sing*; **es kam zu ~en** there was violence

Tat-: **Tatmotiv** NT motive (for the crime); **Tatort** M, *pl* -orte scene of the crime

tätowieren [tɛtoˈviːrən], *ptp* **tätowiert** VT to tattoo; **sich ~ lassen** to have oneself tattooed

Tätowierung F -, -en (a) NO PL (= *das Tätowieren*) tattooing (b) (= *Darstellung*) tattoo

Tatsache F fact; **~ ist aber, dass ...** but the fact of the matter is that ...; **~?** (*inf*) really?; **das ist ~** (*inf*) that's a fact; **nackte ~n** (*inf*) the hard facts; (*hum*) girlie pictures; **jdn vor vollendeten ~n stellen** to present sb with a fait accompli; **(unter) Vorspiegelung falscher ~n** (under) false pretences (*Brit*) or pretenses (*US*)

tatsächlich [ˈtaːtzɛçlɪç, taːtˈzɛçlɪç] 1 ADJ ATTR real 2 ADV (a) (= *in Wirklichkeit, objektiv*) actually, in fact; **~ war es aber ganz anders** in (actual) fact it was quite different (b) (= *sage und schreibe*) really; **~?** really?; **~!** oh yes, so it/he *etc* is/was *etc*; **da kommt er!** – **~!** here he comes! – so he does!

tätscheln [ˈtɛtʃln̩] VT to pat

tatschen [ˈtatʃn̩] VI (*pej inf*) **auf etw** (*acc*) **~** to paw sth

Tatterich [ˈtatərɪç] M -(e)s, NO PL (*inf*) **den ~ haben/bekommen** to have/get the shakes (*inf*)

tatütata [tatyːtaˈtaː] INTERJ **~! die Feuerwehr ist da!** da-da-da-da! here comes the fire engine!; **das Tatütata des Polizeiautos** the (wailing) siren of the police car

Tat-: **Tatverdacht** M suspicion (*of having committed a crime*); **unter ~ stehen** to be under suspicion; **tatverdächtig** ADJ suspected; **Tatverdächtige(r)** MF DECL AS ADJ suspect; **Tatwaffe** F weapon (used in the crime); (= *bei Mord*) murder weapon

Tatze [ˈtatsə] F -, -n (*lit, fig*) paw

Tau¹ [tau] M -(e)s, NO PL dew

Tau² NT -(e)s, -e (= *Seil*) rope; (*Naut auch*) hawser

taub [taup] ADJ deaf; *Glieder* numb; *Gestein* dead; *Metall* dull; *Ähre* unfruitful; *Nuss* empty; **sich ~ stellen** to pretend not to hear; **gegen** or **für etw ~ sein** (*fig*) to be deaf to sth

Taube [ˈtaubə] F -, -n (a) (*Zool*) pigeon; (= *Turteltaube*) dove (b) (*fig*) dove; **~n und Falken** (*Pol inf*) hawks and doves

Tauben-: **taubengrau** ADJ dove grey (*Brit*) or gray (*US*); **Taubenpost** F mit der ~ by pigeon post (*esp Brit*); **Taubenschießen** NT -s, NO PL (*Sport*) pigeon shooting; **Taubenschlag** M (*fig*) **hier geht es zu wie im ~** it's mobbed here (*inf*)

Taube(r) [ˈtaubə] MF DECL AS ADJ deaf person or man/woman *etc*; **die ~n** the deaf

Tauber [ˈtaubɐ] M -s, -, **Täuber** [ˈtɔybɐ] M -s, -, **Täuberich** [ˈtɔybərɪç] M -s, -e cock pigeon

Taubheit F -, NO PL (a) deafness (b) (*von Körperteil*) numbness

Taub-: **Taubnessel** F dead-nettle; **taubstumm** ADJ deaf-mute; **Taubstummensprache** F sign language; **Taubstumme(r)** [-ʃtumə] MF DECL AS ADJ deaf-mute

Tauchboot NT submersible

tauchen [ˈtauxn̩] 1 VI AUX HABEN or SEIN to dive (*nach* for); (= *kurz ~*) to duck under; (= *unter Wasser sein*) to stay under water; *U-Boot* to dive (b) AUX SEIN (*fig*) to disappear (*in* +*acc* into) 2 VT (= *kurz ~*) to dip; *Menschen, Kopf* to duck; (= *eintauchen, auch bei Taufe*) to immerse; **in Licht getaucht** (*geh*) bathed in light

Tauchen NT -s, NO PL diving

Taucher [ˈtauxɐ] M -s, -, **Taucherin** [-ərɪn] F -, -nen diver

Taucher-: **Taucheranzug** M diving (*Brit*) or dive (*US*) suit; **Taucherausrüstung** F diving (*Brit*) or dive (*US*) equipment or gear; **Taucherbrille** F diving (*Brit*) or dive (*US*) goggles *pl*; **Taucherflosse** F (diving (*Brit*) or dive (*US*)) flipper; **Taucherglocke** F diving (*Brit*) or dive (*US*) bell

Taucherin F -, -nen diver

Tauch-: **Tauchmaske** F diving (*Brit*) or dive (*US*) mask; **Tauchsieder** [-ziːdɐ] M -s, - immersion coil (*for boiling water*); **Tauchsport** M (skin) diving; **Tauchstation** F **auf ~ gehen** (*U-Boot*) to dive; (*fig: = sich verstecken*) to make oneself scarce; **auf ~ sein** (*U-Boot*) to be submerged

tauen [ˈtauən] VTI (*vi: aux haben or sein*) (*Eis, Schnee*) to melt, to thaw; **es taut** it is thawing

Taufbecken NT font

Taufe [ˈtaufə] F -, -n baptism; (*christliche auch, esp von Kindern*) christening; (= *Schiffstaufe*) launching (ceremony); **etw aus der ~ heben** (*hum*) *Verein, Firma* to start sth up; *Zeitung, Projekt* to launch sth

taufen [ˈtaufn̩] VT to baptize; (*bei Äquatortaufe*) to duck; (= *nennen*) *Kind, Schiff, Hund etc* to christen; **sich ~ lassen** to be baptized; **jdn auf den Namen Rufus ~** to christen sb Rufus

Täufling [ˈtɔyflɪŋ] M -s, -e child/person to be baptized

Tauf-: **Taufpate** M godfather; **Taufpatin** F godmother

taufrisch ADJ (*geh*) dewy; (*fig*) fresh; (= *fit für sein Alter*) sprightly

taugen [ˈtaugn̩] VI (a) (= *geeignet sein*) to be suitable (*zu, für* for); **wozu soll denn das ~?** what is that supposed to be for?; **er taugt zu gar nichts** he is useless; **er taugt nicht zum Arzt** he wouldn't make a good doctor

(b) (= *wert sein*) **etwas ~** to be good *or* all right; **nichts** *or* **nicht viel ~** to be not much good *or* no good; **taugt der Neue etwas?** is the new bloke any good?; **der Bursche taugt nicht viel/gar nichts** that bloke is a (real) bad lot (*inf*)

tauglich ['tauklıç] ADJ *Kandidat, Bewerber, Material* suitable (*zu* for); (*Mil*) fit (*zu* for); **jdn für ~ erklären** (*Mil*) to declare sb fit for service

Tauglichkeit F -, NO PL suitability; (*Mil*) fitness (for service)

taumeln ['taumln] VI AUX SEIN to stagger; (*zur Seite*) to sway

Tausch [tauʃ] M -(e)s, -e exchange; (= *~handel*) barter; **im ~ gegen** *or* **für etw** in exchange for sth; **jdm etw zum ~ für etw anbieten** to offer to exchange sth for sth; **einen guten/ schlechten ~ machen** to get a good/bad deal

tauschen ['tauʃn] ■ VT to exchange; *Güter* to barter; (= *austauschen*) *Briefmarken, Münzen etc* to swap; *Geld* to change (*in +acc* into); (*inf:* = *umtauschen*) *Gekauftes* to change; **einen Blick mit jdm ~** (*geh*) to exchange glances with sb; **die Rollen ~** to swap roles; **wollen wir die Plätze ~?** shall we swap places? ☑ VI to swap; (*in Handel*) to barter; **wollen wir ~?** shall we swap (places *etc*)?; **ich möchte nicht mit ihm ~** I wouldn't like to change places with him

täuschen ['tɔyʃn] ■ VT to deceive; **man kann ihn nicht ~** you can't fool him; **er wurde in seinen Erwartungen/Hoffnungen getäuscht** his expectations/hopes were disappointed; **wenn mich mein Gedächtnis nicht täuscht** if my memory serves me right; **wenn mich nicht alles täuscht** unless I'm completely wrong; **sie lässt sich leicht/nicht ~** she is easily/not easily fooled (*durch* by) ☑ VR to be wrong (*in +dat, über +acc* about); **dann hast du dich getäuscht!** then you are mistaken; **so kann man sich ~!** it shows how wrong you can be ☒ VI **(a)** (= *irreführen*) (*Aussehen etc*) to be deceptive; (*Sport*) to feint; **das täuscht** that is deceptive; **der Eindruck täuscht** things are not what they seem **(b)** (*Sch form:* = *betrügen*) to cheat

täuschend ■ ADJ *Ähnlichkeit* remarkable ☑ ADV **sich** (*dat*) **~ ähnlich sehen/sein** to look/be remarkably alike; **jdm ~ ähnlich sehen** to look remarkably like sb; **eine ~ echte Fälschung/ Nachahmung** a remarkably convincing fake/imitation

Tausch-: Tauschgeschäft NT exchange; (= *Handel*) barter (deal); **mit etw ein ~ machen** to exchange/barter sth; **Tauschhandel** M barter; **~ treiben** to barter; **Tauschobjekt** NT barter *no pl*

Täuschung ['tɔyʃʊŋ] F -, -en **(a)** (= *das Täuschen*) deception **(b)** (= *Irrtum*) mistake; (= *Irreführung*) deceit; (= *falsche Wahrnehmung*) illusion; (= *Selbsttäuschung*) delusion; **er gab sich einer ~** (*dat*) **hin** he was deluding himself

Tauschwirtschaft F, NO PL (*Econ*) barter economy

tausend ['tauznt] NUM a thousand; **~ Dank/Grüße/Küsse** a thousand thanks/greetings/kisses

Tausend¹ ['tauznt] F -, -en [-dn] (*Zahl*) thousand

Tausend² NT -s, -e [-da] thousand; **vom ~** in a thousand

Tausender ['tauzndɐ] M -s, - **(a)** (= *Zahl*) **ein ~** a figure in the thousands; **die ~** the thousands **(b)** (= *Geldschein*) thousand (euro/dollar *etc* note or bill)

tausenderlei ['tauzndɐ'lai] ADJ INV a thousand kinds of

Tausend-: Tausendfüßer [-fy:sɐ] M -s, - (*form*), **Tausendfüßler** [-fy:slɐ] M -s, - centipede; **die ~** the myriapods (*spec*); **Tausendjahrfeier** F millenary; **tausendjährig** ADJ ATTR thousand-year-old; (= *tausend Jahre lang*) thousand-year(-long); **Hitlers „~es Reich"** Hitler's "thousand-year empire"; **tausendmal** ADV a thousand times; **ich bitte ~ um Entschuldigung** a thousand pardons

Tausendstel ['tauzntstl] NT -s, - thousandth

tausendste(r, s) ['tauzntsta] ADJ thousandth

Tausend-: tausendundeine(r, s) ['tauznt'lunt'lainə] ADJ a thousand and one; **Märchen aus Tausendundeiner Nacht** the Arabian Nights; **tausend(und)eins** ['tauznt(lunt)'lains] NUM one thousand and one

Tau-: Tautropfen M dewdrop; **Tauwerk** NT, NO PL (*Naut*) rigging; **Tauwetter** NT thaw; (*fig auch*) relaxation; **wir haben** *or* **es ist ~** it is thawing; **bei ~** during a thaw; **Tauziehen** NT -s, NO PL (*lit, fig*) tug-of-war

Taxameter [taksa'me:tɐ] M -s, - taximeter

Taxe ['taksə] F -, -n **(a)** (= *Schätzung*) valuation **(b)** (= *Gebühr*) charge; (= *Kurtaxe etc*) tax; (= *Gebührenordnung*) scale of charges **(c)** (*dial*) = **Taxi**

Taxi ['taksi] NT -s, -s taxi; **~ fahren** to drive a taxi; (*als Fahrgast*) to go by taxi

Taxichauffeur(in) M(F) taxi driver

taxieren [ta'ksi:rən], *ptp* **taxiert** VT **(a)** *Preis, Wert* to estimate (*auf +acc* at); *Haus, Gemälde etc* to value (*auf +acc* at); **etw zu hoch ~** to overestimate/overvalue sth; **etw zu niedrig ~** to underestimate/undervalue sth **(b)** (*geh:* = *einschätzen*) *Situation* to assess

Taxi-: Taxifahrer(in) M(F) taxi *or* cab driver, cabby (*inf*); **Taxifahrt** F taxi ride; **Taxistand** M taxi rank (*Brit*) *or* stand

Tax- ['taks-]: **Taxkurs** M rate of taxation; **Taxpreis** M estimated price (*according to valuation*); **Taxwert** M estimated value

Tb(c) [te:(')be:('tse:)] F -, -s ABBR *von* **Tuberkulose** TB

Tb(c)-krank [te:(')be:('tse:)-] ADJ **~ sein** to have TB; **die ~en Patienten** TB patients *or* cases

Teakholz ['ti:k-] NT teak; **ein Tisch aus ~** a teak table

Team [ti:m] NT -s, -s team

Team- ['ti:m-]: **Teamarbeit** F teamwork; **etw in ~ machen** to do sth through teamwork; **teamfähig** ADJ able to work in a team; **sie ist nicht ~** she's not a team player; **Teamfähigkeit** F ability to work in a team; **Teamwork** ['ti:mwɔːɛk, -wœrk] NT -s, NO PL = **Teamarbeit**

Technik ['tɛçnɪk] F -, -en **(a)** (*no pl:* = *Technologie*) technology; (*esp als Studienfach*) engineering; **der Mensch und die ~** man and technology; **verfluchte ~!** stupid technology! **(b)** (= *Arbeitsweise, Verfahren*) technique; **die ~ des Dramas/ der Musik** dramatic/musical techniques **(c)** (*no pl:* = *Funktionsweise und Aufbau*) (*von Auto, Motor etc*) mechanics *pl*

technikbegeistert ADJ technology-mad (*Brit inf*), techno-crazy (*US inf*)

Techniker ['tɛçnikɐ] M -s, -, **Technikerin** [-ərɪn] F -, -nen engineer; (= *Beleuchtungstechniker, Labortechniker*) technician; (*fig:* = *Fußballspieler, Künstler*) technician

Technik-: technikfeindlich ADJ technophobic; **Technikfolgenabschätzung** F technology assessment; **technikfreundlich** ADJ receptive to new technology

technisch ['tɛçnɪʃ] ■ ADJ technical; (= *technologisch*) technological; *Studienfach* technical; (= *mechanisch*) mechanical; **~e Hochschule/Universität** technological university; **~er Zeichner** engineering draughtsman (*Brit*) *or* draftsman (*US*); **~er Leiter** technical director; **~e Einzelheiten** (*fig*) technicalities; **~e Daten** specifications ☑ ADV technically; **er ist ~ begabt** he is technically minded; **~ versiert sein** to have technical skills; **das ist ~ unmöglich** it is technically impossible; (*inf:* = *das geht nicht*) it is absolutely impossible

technisieren [tɛçni'zi:rən], *ptp* **technisiert** VT to mechanize

Techno ['tɛçno] M -, NO PL (*Mus*) techno

Technokrat [tɛçno'kra:t] M -en, -en, **Technokratin** [-'kra:tɪn] F -, -nen technocrat

technokratisch [tɛçno'kra:tɪʃ] ■ ADJ technocratic ☑ ADV technocratically

Technologie-: Technologiepark M technology park; **Technologietransfer** M technology transfer; **Technologiezentrum** NT technology park

technologisch [tɛçno'lo:gɪʃ] ■ ADJ technological ☑ ADV technologically; **eine ~ führende Nation** a leading technological nation

Techno-: Techno-Musik F, **Technomusik** F techno music; **Techno-Party** F, **Technoparty** F techno party

Techtelmechtel [tɛçtl'mɛçtl] NT -s, - (*inf*) affair

TED [tɛt] M -(s) ABBR *von* **Teledialog** computer used to work out results of telephone polls

Teddy ['tɛdi] M -s, -s **(a)** (*auch* **Teddybär**) teddy (bear) **(b)** (*auch* **Teddystoff**) fur fabric

Tee [te:] M -s, -s tea; **einen im ~ haben** (*inf*) to be tipsy (*inf*)

Tee-: Teebeutel M tea bag; **Teeblatt** NT tea leaf; **Tee-Ei** NT, **Teeei** NT (tea) infuser (*esp Brit*), tea ball (*esp US*); **Teefilter** M tea filter; **Teegebäck** NT, NO PL sweet biscuits *pl* (*Brit*), cookies *pl* (*esp US*); **Teeglas** NT tea glass; **Teekanne** F teapot; **Teekessel** M **(a)** kettle **(b)** (= *Gesellschaftsspiel*) guessing game based on

puns; **Teeküche** F kitchenette; **Teelicht** NT night-light;
Teelöffel M teaspoon; (*Menge*) teaspoonful; **teelöffelweise**
ADV by the teaspoonful

Teen [tiːn] M **-s, -s** (*Press sl*) teenager

Teenager ['tiːneːdʒɐ] M **-s, -** teenager

Teeny ['tiːni] M **-s, -s** (*inf*) teenybopper (*inf*)

Teer [teːɐ] M **-(e)s, -e** tar

Teerdachpappe F (bituminous) roofing felt

teeren ['teːrən] VT to tar

Teer-: Teergehalt M tar content; **teerhaltig** ADJ **eine wenig/
stark ~e Zigarette** a low/high tar cigarette; **~ sein** to contain
tar

Teerose F tea rose

Teer-: Teerpappe F (bituminous) roofing felt; **Teerstraße** F
tarred road

Tee-: Teeservice [-zɛrviːs] NT tea set; **Teesieb** NT tea strainer;
Teestrumpf M tea filter; **Teestube** F tearoom; **Teetasse** F
teacup; **Teewagen** M tea trolley

Teflon® ['teflɔ:n, tɛf'lo:n] NT **-s** Teflon®

Teheran ['teːhəraːn, tehaˈraːn] NT **-s** Teh(e)ran

Teich [taiç] M **-(e)s, -e** pond

Teig [taik] M **-(e)s, -e** [-gə] dough; (= *Mürbteig, Blätterteig etc*)
pastry; (= *Pfannkuchenteig*) batter

teigig ['taigiç] ADJ doughy; (= *voller Teig*) **Hände** covered in
dough/pastry

Teigwaren PL (= *Nudeln*) pasta *sing*

Teil¹ [tail] M **-(e)s, -e (a)** part; (*von Zeitung*) section; **der Bau/
das Projekt ist zum ~ fertig** the building/project is partly
finished; **wir hörten zum ~ interessante Reden** some of the
speeches we heard were interesting; **200 Menschen wurden
zum ~ schwer verletzt** 200 people were injured, some of
them badly; **zum ~ ..., zum ~ ...** partly ..., partly ...; **zum
großen/größten ~** for the most part; **er hat die Bücher
darüber zum großen/größten ~ gelesen** he has read many/
most of the books about that; **ein großer ~ stimmte dagegen**
a large number (of people) voted against it; **der dritte/vierte/
fünfte** *etc* **~** (= *ein Drittel/Viertel/Fünftel etc*) a third/quarter/
fifth *etc* (*von* of); **in zwei ~e zerbrechen** to break in two
(b) (*Jur*: = *Partei, Seite*) party
(c) AUCH NT (= *Anteil*) share; **ein gut ~ Arbeit** (*dated*) quite a
bit of work; **zu gleichen ~en erben** to get an equal share of
an inheritance; **zu gleichen ~en beitragen** to make an equal
contribution; **er hat sein(en) ~** dazu beigetragen he did his
bit; **er hat sein(en) ~ bekommen** *or* **weg** (*inf*) he has (already)
had his due; **sich** (*dat*) **sein(en) ~ denken** (*inf*) to draw one's
own conclusions
(d) AUCH NT **ich für mein(en) ~** for my part, I ...

Teil² NT **-(e)s, -e** part; (= *Bestandteil*) component; (= *Ersatzteil*)
(spare) part; (*sl*: = *Ding*) thing; **etw in seine ~e zerlegen** Tier,
Leiche to cut sth up; Motor, Möbel etc to take sth apart; *siehe
auch* **Teil¹** (c) (d)

Teil-: teilbar ADJ divisible (*durch* by); **Teilbereich** M part; (*in
Abteilung*) section; **Teilbetrag** M part (of an amount); (*auf
Rechnung*) item; (= *Rate*) instalment; (= *Zwischensumme*)
subtotal

Teilchen ['tailçən] NT **-s, -** particle; (*dial*: = *Gebäckstück*) cake

Teilchen-: Teilchenbeschleuniger M (*Phys*) particle
accelerator; **Teilchenphysik** F particle physics *sing*

teilen ['tailən] **1** VT **(a)** (= *zerlegen, trennen*) to divide (up);
(*Math*) to divide (*durch* by); **27 geteilt durch 9** 27 divided by
9; **(politisch) geteilter Meinung sein** to have different
(political) opinions; **darüber sind die Meinungen geteilt**
opinions differ on that; **darüber kann man geteilter Meinung
sein** one can disagree about that
(b) (= *aufteilen*) to share (out) (*unter* +*dat* amongst); **etw mit
jdm ~** to share sth with sb; **sich** (*dat*) **etw ~** to share sth; **teilt
euch das!** share that between you
(c) (= *an etw teilhaben*) to share; **geteilte Freude ist doppelte
Freude** (*prov*) a joy shared is a joy doubled (*prov*); **geteilter
Schmerz ist halber Schmerz** (*prov*) a trouble shared is a
trouble halved (*prov*); **sie teilten unser Schicksal** *or* **Los** they
shared the same fate as us; **sie teilten das Zimmer mit ihm**
they shared the room with him
2 VR **(a)** (*in Gruppen*) to split up
(b) (*Straße, Fluss*) to fork; (*Vorhang*) to part
(c) (*fig*: = *auseinander gehen*) **in diesem Punkt ~ sich die**

Meinungen opinion is divided on this
3 VI to share; **er teilt nicht gern** he doesn't like sharing

Teiler ['tailɐ] M **-s, -** (*Math*) factor

Teil-: Teilerfolg M partial success; **Teilgebiet** NT **(a)** (= *Bereich*)
branch **(b)** (*räumlich*) area; **teilhaben** VI SEP IRREG (*geh*) (*an
+dat* in) (= *mitwirken*) to participate; **Teilhaber** ['tailhaːbɐ] M
-s, -, Teilhaberin [-ərɪn] F **-, -nen** (*Comm*) partner;
Teilhaberschaft ['tailhaːbɐʃaft] F **-, -en** (*Comm*) partnership

-teilig [tailiç] ADJ SUF (*von Kleidung, Geschirr etc*) -piece; **ein
zweiteiliges Kostüm** a two-piece suit; **ein dreiteiliges
Fernsehspiel** a three-part TV drama

Teilkasko-: teilkaskoversichert [-fɛɐzɪçɐt] ADJ **~ sein** to be
insured third party, fire and theft; **Teilkaskoversicherung** F
third party, fire and theft

Teillieferung F part delivery

Teilnahme [-naːmə] F **-, -n (a)** (= *Anwesenheit*) attendance (*an
+dat* at); (= *Beteiligung an Wettbewerb etc*) participation (*an
+dat* in); **seine ~ absagen** to withdraw; **~ am Straßenverkehr**
(*form*) road use **(b)** (= *Interesse*) interest (*an +dat* in);
(= *Mitgefühl*) sympathy; **jdm seine herzliche** *or* **aufrichtige ~
aussprechen** to offer sb one's heartfelt condolences

Teilnahms-: teilnahmslos **1** ADJ (= *gleichgültig*) indifferent;
(= *stumm leidend*) listless **2** ADV indifferently; (= *stumm
leidend*) listlessly; **Teilnahmslosigkeit** F **-,** NO PL indifference;
teilnahmsvoll **1** ADJ compassionate **2** ADV compassionately

teilnehmen VI SEP IRREG **(a) an etw** (*dat*) **~** to take part in sth;
(= *anwesend sein*) to attend sth; **an einem Ausflug ~** to go on
an outing; **am Krieg ~** to fight in the war; **am Unterricht ~** to
attend classes; **lebhaft am Unterricht ~** to take an active part
in the lessons; **an einem Kurs ~** to do a course **(b)** (= *Anteil
nehmen*) to share (*an +dat* in)

Teilnehmer ['tailneːmɐ] M **-s, -, Teilnehmerin** [-ərɪn] F **-, -nen
(a)** (= *Beteiligter bei Kongress etc*) participant; (= *Kriegsteilnehmer*) combatant; (*bei Wettbewerb, Preisausschreiben etc*)
competitor, contestant; (= *Kursteilnehmer*) student; (*bei
Ausflug etc*) member of a party; **alle ~ an dem Ausflug** all those
going on the outing **(b)** (*Telec*) subscriber; **der ~ meldet sich
nicht** there is no reply

Teilnehmerzahl F attendance

teils [tails] ADV partly; **~ ... ~ ...** partly ... partly ...; (*inf*:
= *sowohl ... als auch*) both ... and ...; **die Demonstranten
waren ~ Arbeiter, ~ Studenten** some of the demonstrators
were workers and the others were students; **~ heiter, ~
wolkig** cloudy with sunny periods

Teilung ['tailʊŋ] F **-, -en** division

teilweise ['tailvaizə] **1** ADV partly; (= *manchmal*) sometimes;
nicht alle Schüler sind so faul, ~ sind sie sehr interessiert not
all the pupils are so lazy, some of them are very interested;
der Film war ~ gut the film was good in parts; **~ bewölkt**
cloudy in parts **2** ADJ ATTR partial

Teilwert M (*im Steuerrecht*) going concern value

Teilzahlung F hire-purchase (*Brit*), installment plan (*US*);
(= *Rate*) instalment (*Brit*), installment (*US*); **auf ~** on hire-
purchase (*Brit*) *or* (an) installment plan (*US*)

Teilzahlungsgeschäft NT = **Abzahlungsgeschäft**

Teilzeit-: Teilzeitarbeit F part-time work; (= *Stelle*) part-time
job; **Teilzeitarbeitsplatz** M part-time job; **teilzeitbeschäftigt**
ADJ employed part time; **Teilzeitbeschäftigte(r)** MF DECL AS
ADJ part-time employee; **Teilzeitbeschäftigung** F part-time
work; (= *Stelle*) part-time job; **Teilzeitkraft** F part-time
worker

Teint [tɛ̃ː] M **-s, -s** complexion

Tel. ABBR *von* **Telefon**

Tele- ['teːleː]-: **Telearbeit** F telecommuting; **Telearbeiter(in)**
M(F) telecommuter; **Telearbeitsplatz** M job for
telecommuters; **Telebanking** [-bɛŋkɪŋ] NT **-s,** NO PL
telebanking; **Telefax** NT (= *Kopie, Gerät*) fax; **Telefaxgerät** NT
fax machine; **Telefaxteilnehmer(in)** M(F) fax subscriber

Telefon [teleˈfoːn, ˈteːlefoːn] NT **-s, -e** (tele)phone; **am ~ (verlangt
werden)** (to be wanted) on the phone; **~ haben** to be on the
phone; **ans ~ gehen** to answer the phone

Telefon- IN CPDS (tele)phone; *siehe auch* **Fernsprech-**;
Telefonansage F telephone information service;
Telefonapparat M telephone

Telefonat [telefoˈnaːt] NT **-(e)s, -e** (tele)phone call

Telefon-: Telefonauskunft F directory inquiries *pl* (*Brit*) *or* assistance (*US*); **Telefonbanking** [-bɛŋkɪŋ] NT **-s**, NO PL telephone banking; **Telefonbuch** NT (tele)phone book; **Telefongebühr** F call charge; (= *Grundgebühr*) telephone rental; **Telefongespräch** NT (tele)phone call; (= *Unterhaltung*) telephone conversation; **Telefonhäuschen** [-hɔysçən] NT (*inf*) phone booth

telefonieren [telefoˈniːrən], *ptp* **telefoniert** VI to make a (tele)phone call; **wir haben stundenlang telefoniert** we talked on the phone for hours; **mit jdm ~** to speak to sb on the phone; **miteinander ~** to speak (to each other) on the phone; **bei jdm ~** to use sb's phone; **es wird entschieden zu viel telefoniert** the phones are definitely used too much; **ins Ausland ~** to make an international call; **nach Amerika/Hamburg ~** to call America/Hamburg; **er telefoniert den ganzen Tag** he is on the phone all day long

telefonisch [teleˈfoːnɪʃ] **1** ADJ telephonic; **~e Auskunft/Beratung** telephone information/advice service; **eine ~e Mitteilung** a (tele)phone message
2 ADV *Auskunft geben* over the phone; *beraten, erpressen, bedrohen* on the phone; **jdm etw ~ mitteilen** to tell sb sth over the phone; **~ anfragen** to call to ask; **er hat sich ~ entschuldigt** he phoned to apologize; **jdn ~ belästigen** to make crank phone calls to sb; **ich bin ~ erreichbar** *or* **zu erreichen** I can be contacted by phone; **bitte melden Sie sich ~ unter ...** please phone on ...

Telefonist [telefoˈnɪst] M **-en, -en**, **Telefonistin** [-ˈnɪstɪn] F **-, -nen** telephonist

Telefonitis [telefoˈniːtɪs] F **-**, NO PL (*hum inf*) **die ~ haben** to be a telephone addict (*inf*)

Telefon-: Telefonkarte F phonecard; **Telefonkonferenz** F telephone conference; **Telefonleitung** F telephone line; **Telefonmarketing** NT telemarketing; **Telefonnetz** NT telephone network; **Telefonnummer** F (tele)phone number; **Telefonrechnung** F (tele)phone bill; **Telefonseelsorge** F ≈ Samaritans *pl* (*Brit*), ≈ advice hotline (*US*); **Telefonsex** M telephone sex; **Telefonterror** M nuisance phone calls *pl*; **Telefonüberwachung** F telephone tapping, wiretapping; **Telefonverbindung** F telephone line; (*zwischen Orten*) telephone link; **Telefonverstärker** M telephone amplifier; **Telefonverzeichnis** NT telephone directory; **Telefonwerbung** F telephone advertising; (*im Wahlkampf*) telephone canvassing; **Telefonzelle** F (tele)phone box (*Brit*) *or* booth; **Telefonzentrale** F (telephone) switchboard

telegen [teleˈgeːn] ADJ telegenic

telegrafieren [telegraˈfiːrən], *ptp* **telegrafiert** VTI to send a telegram, to cable

telegrafisch [teleˈgraːfɪʃ] **1** ADJ telegraphic **2** ADV **jdm ~ Geld überweisen** to wire sb money

Telegramm [teleˈgram] NT, *pl* **-gramme** telegram

Telekolleg [ˈteːlə-] NT ≈ Open University (*esp Brit*), ≈ Distance Education (*US*)

Telekom [ˈteːlekɔm] F **-**, NO PL **die ~** German telecommunications service

Tele- [ˈteːlə-]: **Telekommunikation** F telecommunications *pl or* (*als Fachgebiet*) *sing*; **Telekopie** F fax; **Telekopierer** M fax machine; **Teleobjektiv** NT (*Phot*) telephoto lens

Telepathie [telepaˈtiː] F **-**, NO PL telepathy

telepathisch [teleˈpaːtɪʃ] **1** ADJ telepathic **2** ADV telepathically

Telephon *etc* NT = **Telefon** *etc*

Teleprompter [ˈteːleprɔmptɐ] M **-s, -** Autocue® (*Brit*), Teleprompter® (*US*)

Teleshopping [ˈteːlə-] NT teleshopping

Teleskop [teleˈskoːp] NT **-s, -e** telescope

teleskopisch [teleˈskoːpɪʃ] ADJ telescopic

Telex [ˈteːlɛks] NT **-, -e** telex

Teller [ˈtɛlɐ] M **-s, -** (a) plate; **ein ~ Suppe** a plate of soup (b) (*sl*: = *Plattenteller*) turntable (c) (*Ski*) basket

Teller-: Tellergericht NT (*Cook*) one-course meal; **Tellermine** F (*Mil*) flat antitank mine; **Tellerwäscher(in)** M(F) dishwasher; **Tellerwäscherkarriere** F (*inf*) rags-to-riches career

Tempel [ˈtɛmpl] M **-s, -** temple (*auch fig*)

Tempera [ˈtɛmpera] F **-, -s** tempera (colour (*Brit*) *or* color (*US*))

Temperament [tempera'ment] NT **-(e)s, -e (a)** (= *Wesensart*) temperament; **ein hitziges ~ haben** to be hot-tempered **(b)** NO PL (= *Lebhaftigkeit*) vitality; **viel/kein ~ haben** to be very/not to be vivacious; **sein ~ ist mit ihm durchgegangen** he lost his temper

Temperament-: temperamentlos **1** ADJ lifeless **2** ADV listlessly; **Temperamentlosigkeit** F **-**, NO PL lifelessness; **temperamentvoll** **1** ADJ vivacious; *Auto, Fahrer* nippy (*Brit inf*), speedy (*US inf*) **2** ADV exuberantly; **ein Lied ~ vortragen** to give a spirited rendering of a song

Temperatur [tempera'tuːɐ] F **-, -en** temperature; **erhöhte ~ haben** to have a temperature; **die ~en sind angestiegen/gesunken** the temperature has risen/fallen; **bei diesen/solchen ~en** in these/such temperatures; **bei ~en von bis zu 42 Grad Celsius** in temperatures of up to 42°C

Temperatur-: Temperaturanstieg M rise in temperature; **Temperaturregler** M thermostat; **Temperaturrückgang** M fall in temperature; **Temperaturschwankung** F variation in temperature; **Temperatursturz** M sudden drop in temperature

Tempo [ˈtɛmpo] NT **-s, -s (a)** (= *Geschwindigkeit*) speed; **~!** (*inf*) hurry up!; **bei jdm ~ (dahinter** *or* **hinter etw** *acc*) **machen** (*inf*) to make sb get a move on (with sth) (*inf*); **~ 100** speed limit (of) 100 km/h; **im ~ zulegen** to speed up; **im ~ nachlassen** to slow down; **aufs ~ drücken** (*inf*) to step on the gas (*inf*) **(b)** (*Mus*) *pl* **Tempi** [ˈtɛmpi] tempo; **das ~ halten** to keep time; **das ~ angeben** to set the tempo; (*fig*) to set the pace **(c) Tempo**® (*inf*: = *Taschentuch*) Kleenex®

Tempo-30-Zone [tempoˈdraisɪç-] F ≈ 20 mph zone

Tempolimit NT speed limit

Tempora PL *von* **Tempus**

temporal [tempoˈraːl] ADJ (*Gram*) temporal

Temporalsatz M temporal clause

temporär [tempoˈrɛːɐ] (*geh*) **1** ADJ temporary **2** ADV temporarily

Tempo-: Temposünder(in) M(F) person caught for speeding; **Tempotaschentuch**® NT tissue, Kleenex®

Tempus [ˈtɛmpʊs] NT **-, Tempora** [ˈtɛmpora] (*Gram*) tense

Tendenz [tɛnˈdɛnts] F **-, -en** trend (*auch St Ex*); (= *Neigung*) tendency; (= *Absicht*) intention; (*no pl*: = *Parteilichkeit*) bias; **die ~ haben, zu ...** to have a tendency to ...; **er hat nationalistische ~en** he has nationalist leanings; **vier Millionen Menschen sind arbeitslos, ~ steigend** the number of people out of work is four million and rising

tendenziell [tɛndɛnˈtsiel] **1** ADJ **eine ~e Veränderung** a change in direction **2** ADV **~ ist Ruritanien ein faschistischer Staat** Ruritania is a country which shows fascist tendencies; **die Ziele der beiden Parteien unterscheiden sich ~ kaum voneinander** the aims of the two parties are broadly similar (in direction)

tendenziös [tɛndɛnˈtsiøːs] **1** ADJ tendentious **2** ADV tendentiously; **etw ist ~ gefärbt** sth has a tendentious cast to it

Tenderverfahren NT (*Fin*) tendering

tendieren [tɛnˈdiːrən], *ptp* **tendiert** VI **(a) dazu ~, etw zu tun** (= *neigen*) to tend to do sth; (= *beabsichtigen*) to be moving toward(s) doing sth; **zum Kommunismus/Katholizismus ~** to have communist/Catholic leanings; **zu Erkältungen/Wutausbrüchen ~** to tend to get colds/fits of anger **(b)** (*Fin, St Ex*) to tend; **freundlich/fester/schwächer ~** to show a favourable (*Brit*) *or* favorable (*US*)/stronger/weaker tendency

Teneriffa [teneˈrɪfa] NT **-s** Tenerife

Tennis [ˈtɛnɪs] NT **-**, NO PL tennis

Tennis- IN CPDS tennis; **Tennishalle** F indoor tennis centre (*Brit*) *or* center (*US*); **Tennisplatz** M tennis court; **Tennisschläger** M tennis racket; **Tennisspieler(in)** M(F) tennis player; **Tenniszirkus** M tennis circus

Tenor[1] [ˈteːnoːɐ] M **-s**, NO PL tenor

Tenor[2] [teˈnoːɐ] M **-s, -e** [-ˈnoːrə] (*Mus*) tenor

Tensid [tɛnˈziːt] NT **-(e)s, -e** [-də] (*Chem*) surfactant

Tentakel [tɛnˈtaːkl] M *or* NT **-s, -** tentacle

Teppich [ˈtɛpɪç] M **-s, -e** carpet (*auch fig*); (= *Ölteppich*) (oil) slick; **etw unter den ~ kehren** *or* **fegen** (*lit, fig*) to sweep sth under the carpet; **bleib auf dem ~!** (*inf*) be reasonable!; **den roten ~ ausrollen** to bring out the red carpet

Teppich-: Teppichboden M carpet(ing); **das Zimmer ist mit ~ ausgelegt** the room has a fitted carpet; **Teppichfliese** F carpet tile; **Teppichklopfer** M carpet-beater

Termin [tɛrˈmiːn] M **-s, -e** date; (*für Fertigstellung*) deadline; (*Comm:* = *Liefertag*) delivery date; (*bei Arzt, Besprechung etc*) appointment; (*Sport*) fixture; (*Jur:* = *Verhandlung*) hearing; **der letzte ~** the deadline; (*bei Bewerbung etc*) the closing date; **sich** (*dat*) **einen ~ geben lassen** to make an appointment; **sich** (*dat*) **einen ~ in der Autowerkstatt geben lassen** to book one's car/van *etc* into the garage; **schon einen anderen ~ haben** to have a prior engagement

Terminal [ˈtøːɛminəl, ˈtœr-] NT or M **-s, -s** terminal

Termin-: **Terminbörse** F futures market; **Termineinlage** F (*Fin*) time deposit; **Termingeld** NT fixed-term deposit; **termingemäß, termingerecht** ADJ, ADV on schedule; **Termingeschäft** NT deal on the futures market; **~e** futures; **Terminhandel** M (*St Ex*) forward *or* futures trading

Termini PL *von* **Terminus**

Termin-: **Terminkalender** M (appointments) diary; **Terminkurs** M forward price

terminlich [tɛrˈmiːnlɪç] **1** ADJ **aus ~en Gründen absagen** to cancel because of problems with one's schedule; **~e Verpflichtungen** commitments; **ich habe schon zu viele ~e Verpflichtungen** I have too many prior commitments **2** ADV **etw ~ einrichten** to fit sth in (to one's schedule); **~ in Anspruch genommen sein** to have a full schedule; **das ist ~ zu schaffen** the scheduling is no problem

Terminmarkt M (*St Ex*) futures market

Terminologie [tɛrminoloˈgiː] F **-, -n** [-ˈgiːən] terminology

terminologisch [tɛrminoˈloːgɪʃ] **1** ADJ terminological **2** ADV terminologically; **~ arbeiten** to work in terminology; **sich ~ abstimmen** to agree on the terminology one is using

Terminplaner M appointments calendar

Terminus [ˈtɛrminʊs] M **-, Termini** [-ni] term; **~ technicus** technical term

Termite [tɛrˈmiːtə] F **-, -n** termite

Terpentin [tɛrpɛnˈtiːn] NT or (AUS) M **-s, -e** turpentine; (*inf:* = *~öl*) turps (*inf*)

Terpentinöl NT turps *sing* (*inf*)

Terrain [tɛˈrɛ̃ː] NT **-s, -s** terrain; (*fig*) territory; **das ~ sondieren** (*Mil*) to reconnoitre (*Brit*) *or* reconnoiter (*US*) the terrain; (*fig*) to see how the land lies; **sich auf unsicheres ~ begeben** to get onto shaky ground; **verlorenes ~ (wieder) gutmachen** (*lit, fig*) to regain lost ground

Terrarium [tɛˈraːriʊm] NT **-s, Terrarien** [-riən] terrarium

Terrasse [tɛˈrasə] F **-, -n (a)** (*Geog*) terrace **(b)** (= *Veranda*) patio; (= *Dachterrasse*) roof garden

terrassenartig, terrassenförmig **1** ADJ terraced **2** ADV in terraces

terrestrisch [tɛˈrɛstrɪʃ] ADJ terrestrial

Terrier [ˈtɛriɐ] M **-s, -** terrier

Terror [ˈtɛrɔːɐ] M **-s,** NO PL terror; (= *Terrorismus*) terrorism; (= *~herrschaft*) reign of terror; (= *brutale Einschüchterung*) intimidation; (= *Belästigung*) menace; **die Stadt steht unter dem ~ der Mafia** the town is being terrorized by the Mafia; **~ machen** (*inf*) to raise hell (*inf*)

Terror-: **Terrorakt** M act of terrorism; **Terrorangriff** M terrorist raid; **Terroranschlag** M terrorist attack

terrorisieren [tɛroriˈziːrən], *ptp* **terrorisiert** VT to terrorize

Terrorismus [tɛroˈrɪsmʊs] M **-,** NO PL terrorism

Terrorismus-: **Terrorismusbekämpfung** F counterterrorism; **Terrorismusexperte** M, **Terrorismusexpertin** F expert on terrorism

Terrorist [tɛroˈrɪst] M **-en, -en, Terroristin** [-ˈrɪstɪn] F **-, -nen** terrorist

terroristisch [tɛroˈrɪstɪʃ] ADJ terrorist *attr*

tertiär [tɛrˈtsiɛːɐ] ADJ tertiary

Terz [tɛrts] F **-, -en** (*Mus*) third; (*Fechten*) tierce

Tesafilm® [ˈteːza-] M Sellotape® (*Brit*), Scotch tape® (*esp US*)

Tessin [tɛˈsiːn] NT **-s das** ~ Ticino

Test [tɛst] M **-(e)s, -s** *or* **-e** test

Testament [tɛstaˈmɛnt] NT **-(e)s, -e (a)** (*Jur*) will; (*fig*) legacy; **das ~ eröffnen** to read the will; **sein ~ machen** to make one's will **(b)** (*Bibl*) Testament; **Altes/Neues ~** Old/New Testament

testamentarisch [tɛstamɛnˈtaːrɪʃ] **1** ADJ testamentary; **eine ~e Verfügung** an instruction in the will **2** ADV in one's will; **etw ~ festlegen** *or* **verfügen** to write sth in one's will; **~ festgelegt** (written) in the will

Testaments-: **Testamentseröffnung** F reading of the will; **Testamentsvollstrecker(in)** M(F) executor; (*Frau auch*) executrix

Testbild NT (*TV*) test card

testen [ˈtɛstn] VT to test (*auf +acc* for); **jdn auf seine Intelligenz ~** to test sb's intelligence

Tester [ˈtɛstɐ] M **-s, -, Testerin** [-ərɪn] F **-, -nen** tester

Testosteron [tɛstosteˈroːn] NT **-s** testosterone

Test-: **Testperson** F subject (of a test); **Testpilot(in)** M(F) test pilot; **Testprogramm** NT (*Comput*) test program; **Testreihe** F, **Testserie** F series of tests; **Teststopp** M test ban; **Teststoppabkommen** NT test ban treaty

Tetanus [ˈteːtanʊs, ˈtɛtanʊs] M **-,** NO PL tetanus

Tetraeder [tetraˈleːdɐ] NT **-s, -** (*Math*) tetrahedron

teuer [ˈtɔyɐ] **1** ADJ expensive; (*fig*) dear; **etw für teures Geld kaufen** to pay good money for sth; **teurer werden** to go up (in price) **2** ADV **anbieten, speisen** expensively; **etw ~ kaufen/verkaufen** to buy/sell sth for a high price; **etw zu ~ kaufen** to pay too much for sth; **in Tokio lebt man ~** life is expensive in Tokyo; **das wird ihn ~ zu stehen kommen** (*fig*) that will cost him dear; **~ erkauft** dearly bought; **etw ~ bezahlen** (*fig*) to pay a high price for sth

Teuerung [ˈtɔyərʊŋ] F **-, -en** rise in prices

Teuerungs-: **Teuerungsrate** F rate of price increases; **Teuerungszulage** F cost of living bonus; **Teuerungszuschlag** M surcharge

Teufel [ˈtɔyfl] M **-s, - (a)** (*lit, fig*) devil; **den ~ durch Beelzebub austreiben** to replace one evil with another; **der ~ der Eifersucht** *etc* a jealous *etc* devil **(b)** (*inf*) **~ (noch mal** *or* **aber auch)!** damn it (all)! (*inf*); **~ auch** (*bewundernd*) well I'll be damned (*inf*), I'll be a sun-of-a-gun (*US inf*); **scher dich** *or* **geh zum ~, hol dich der ~!** go to hell! (*inf*); **der ~ soll ihn/es holen!, hol ihn/es der ~** to hell with him/it (*inf*); **jdn zum ~ wünschen** to wish sb in hell; **jdn zum ~ jagen** *or* **schicken** to send sb packing (*inf*); **zum ~!** damn! (*inf*); **wer zum ~?** who the devil? (*inf*); **zum ~ mit dem Ding!** to hell with the thing! (*inf*); **zum ~ sein** (= *kaputt sein*) to have had it (*inf*); (= *verloren sein*) to have gone to the devil (*inf*); **den ~ an die Wand malen** (= *schwarz malen*) to think the worst; (= *Unheil heraufbeschwören*) to tempt fate; **wenn man vom ~ spricht(, dann ist er nicht weit)** (*prov*) talk (*Brit*) *or* speak of the devil (and he's sure to appear) (*inf*); **dann kommst** *or* **gerätst du in ~s Küche** then you'll be in a hell of a mess (*inf*); **wie der ~** like hell (*inf*); **er ist hinter dem Geld her wie der ~** hinter der armen Seele he's money mad (*Brit inf*), he loves money like the devil loves souls (*US*); **auf ~ komm raus** like crazy (*inf*); **ich mache das auf ~ komm raus** I'll do that come hell or high water; **da ist der ~ los** all hell's been let loose (*inf*); **den ~ werde ich (tun)!** I'll be damned if I will! (*inf*); **der ~ steckt im Detail** the devil is in the detail

Teufelei [tɔyfəˈlai] F **-, -en** (*inf*) devilish trick; (= *Streich*) piece of devilry

Teufels-: **Teufelsaustreibung** F exorcism; **Teufelsbeschwörung** F exorcism; (*Anrufen*) invocation of the devil; **Teufelskreis** M vicious circle; **Teufelskult** M devil worship

teuflisch [ˈtɔyflɪʃ] **1** ADJ fiendish **2** ADV fiendishly

TEURO

Teuro is the German nickname for the euro, a combination of **teuer** meaning expensive, and **Euro**. The word was coined in an atmosphere of growing public concern over profiteering following the changeover from the mark to the euro in 2002, with the retail, catering and service industries being accused of cleverly exploiting a lack of consumer knowledge about the euro to increase prices.

Teutone [tɔyˈtoːnə] M **-n, -n, Teutonin** [-ˈtoːnɪn] F **-, -nen** Teuton

teutonisch [tɔyˈtoːnɪʃ] ADJ Teutonic

Text [tɛkst] M **-(e)s, -e** text; (*eines Gesetzes*) wording; (*von Lied*) words *pl*; (*von Schlager*) lyrics *pl*; (*von Film, Hörspiel, Rede etc*) script; (*Mus:* = *Operntext*) libretto; (*unter Bild*) caption; (*auf Plakat*) words *pl*; **weiter im ~** (*inf*) (let's) get on with it

Text-: **Textaufgabe** F problem; **Textbaustein** M (*Comput*) template; **Textbuch** NT script; (*für Lieder*) songbook; **Texteingabe** F (*Comput*) text input

texten ['tɛkstn] 🔢 VTI to write; (mit Handy) to text 🔢 VI siehe **Texter** to write songs/copy

Texter ['tɛkstɐ] M **-s, -**, **Texterin** [-ərɪn] F **-, -nen** (für Schlager) songwriter; (für Werbesprüche) copywriter

Texterfasser [-lɛɐfasɐ] M **-s, -**, **Texterfasserin** [-ərɪn] F **-, -nen** keyboarder

Textil- [tɛks'tiːl] IN CPDS textile; **Textilarbeiter(in)** M(F) textile worker; **Textilbranche** F textile trade; **Textilfabrik** F textile factory

Textilien [tɛks'tiːliən] PL linen, clothing, fabrics etc; (Ind) textiles pl

Textil-: **Textilindustrie** F textile industry; **Textilwaren** PL textiles pl

Text-: **Textkritik** F textual criticism; **Textmarke** F (Comput) marker; **Textmodus** M (Comput) text mode; **Textnachricht** F (Telec) text message; **Textspeicher** M (Comput) memory; **Textstelle** F passage; **Textsystem** NT (Comput) word processor, word processing system

Textverarbeitung F word processing

Textverarbeitungs-: **Textverarbeitungsprogramm** NT word processor, word processing program; **Textverarbeitungssystem** NT word processor

TH [teːˈhaː] F **-, -s** ABBR von **Technische Hochschule**

Thai¹ [tai] M **-(s), -(s)** Thai

Thai² [tai] F **-, -** Thai

Thai³ [tai] NT **-, NO PL** (Ling) Thai

Thailand ['tailant] NT **-s** Thailand

Thailänder ['tailɛndɐ] M **-s, -**, **Thailänderin** [-ərɪn] F **-, -nen** Thai

thailändisch ['tailɛndɪʃ] ADJ Thai

Thalassotherapie [talaso-] F (Med) thalassotherapy

Theater [teˈaːtɐ] NT **-s, -** (a) theatre (Brit), theater (US); (= Schauspielbühne) theatre (Brit) or theater (US) company; (= Zuschauer) audience; **beim** or **am ~ arbeiten** to work in the theatre (Brit) or theater (US); **er ist** or **arbeitet beim Ulmer ~** he's with the Ulm theatre (Brit) or theater (US) company; **das ~ fängt um 8 Uhr an** the performance begins at 8 o'clock; **zum ~ gehen** to go on the stage; **ins ~ gehen** to go to the theatre (Brit) or theater (US); **das französische ~** French theatre (Brit) or theater (US); **~ spielen** (lit) to act; (= Stück aufführen) to put on a play; (fig) to put on an act; **jdm ein ~ vormachen** or **vorspielen** (fig) to put on an act for sb's benefit; **das ist doch alles nur ~** (fig) it's all just play-acting
(b) (fig) to-do (inf), fuss; **das war vielleicht ein ~, bis ich ...** what a palaver I had to ... (inf); **das ist (vielleicht) immer ein ~, wenn er kommt** there's always a big fuss when he comes; **(ein) ~ machen** to make a (big) fuss (mit jdm of sb)

Theater- IN CPDS theatre (Brit), theater (US); **Theateraufführung** F stage production; (= Vorstellung, Darbietung) performance; **Theaterbesuch** M visit to the theatre; **Theaterbesucher(in)** M(F) theatregoer (Brit), theatergoer (US); **Theaterkarte** F theatre ticket; **Theaterkasse** F theatre box office; **Theaterstück** NT (stage) play

theatralisch [teaˈtraːlɪʃ] 🔢 ADJ theatrical 🔢 ADV theatrically

Theke ['teːkə] F **-, -n** (= Schanktisch) bar; (= Ladentisch) counter

T-Helfer-Zelle ['teː-] F T helper cell

Thema ['teːma] NT **-s, Themen** or **-ta** [-mən, -ta] (= Gegenstand) subject; (= Leitgedanke, auch Mus) theme; **beim ~ bleiben** to stick to the subject; **das ~ wechseln** to change the subject; **ein/kein ~ sein** to be/not to be an issue; **Geld ist für sie kein ~ money** is no object for her; **aus etw ein ~ machen** to make an issue of sth; **zum ~ werden** to become an issue; **wir wollen das ~ begraben** (inf) let's not talk about it any more; **das ~ ist (für mich) erledigt** (inf) as far as I'm concerned the matter's closed

Thematik [teˈmaːtɪk] F **-, -en** topic

thematisch [teˈmaːtɪʃ] 🔢 ADJ thematic; (= vom Thema her) as regards subject matter; **~es Verzeichnis** subject index 🔢 ADV **~ interessant sein** to be an interesting subject; **~ geordnet** arranged according to subject

Themen PL von **Thema**

Themen-: **Themenbereich** M, **Themenkreis** M topic; **in den ~ „Tiere" gehören** to come under the heading of "animals"; **Themenpark** M theme park; **Themenstellung** F subject

Themse ['tɛmzə] F **- die ~** the Thames

Theologe [teoˈloːgə] M **-n, -n**, **Theologin** [-ˈloːgɪn] F **-, -nen** theologian

Theologie [teoloˈgiː] F **-, NO PL** theology; **Doktor der ~** Doctor of Divinity (Brit), Doctor of Theology (US)

theologisch [teoˈloːgɪʃ] 🔢 ADJ theological 🔢 ADV theologically; **sich ~ gut auskennen** to know quite a bit about theology; **~ interessiert sein** to be interested in theology; **eine ~ interessante Frage** a question which is interesting from a theological point of view

Theoretiker [teoˈreːtikɐ] M **-s, -**, **Theoretikerin** [-ərɪn] F **-, -nen** theoretician

theoretisch [teoˈreːtɪʃ] 🔢 ADJ theoretical 🔢 ADV theoretically; **~ gesehen** theoretically

theoretisieren [teoretiˈziːrən], ptp **theoretisiert** VI to theorize

Theorie [teoˈriː] F **-, -n** [-ˈriːən] theory

Therapeut [teraˈpɔyt] M **-en, -en**, **Therapeutin** [-ˈpɔytɪn] F **-, -nen** therapist

Therapeutik [teraˈpɔytɪk] F **-, NO PL** therapeutics sing

therapeutisch [teraˈpɔytɪʃ] 🔢 ADJ therapeutic(al) 🔢 ADV therapeutically; **~ umstrittene Methoden** controversial therapeutic methods

Therapie [teraˈpiː] F **-, -n** [-ˈpiːən] therapy (auch fig), treatment; (= Behandlungsmethode) (method of) treatment (gegen for)

Therapieplatz M place in therapy

therapieren [teraˈpiːrən], ptp **therapiert** VT to give therapy to

Thermal- [tɛrˈmaːl]: **Thermalbad** NT thermal bath; (Gebäude) thermal baths pl; (= Badeort) spa; **jdm Thermalbäder verschreiben** to prescribe hydrotherapy for sb; **Thermalquelle** F thermal spring

thermisch ['tɛrmɪʃ] ADJ ATTR (Phys) thermal

Thermo- ['tɛrmo] IN CPDS thermo-; **Thermodrucker** M thermal printer; **Thermodynamik** F thermodynamics sing; **thermodynamisch** ADJ thermodynamic; **Thermokanne** F Thermos® jug

Thermometer NT **-s, -** thermometer

Thermometerstand M temperature; **bei ~ 60°** when the temperature reaches 60°

thermonuklear ADJ thermonuclear

Thermopapier NT thermal paper

Thermosflasche F vacuum flask

Thermostat [tɛrmoˈstaːt] M **-(e)s, -e** thermostat

thesaurieren [tezauˈriːrən] VT (Econ, St Ex) to accumulate; **~der Fonds** accumulated fund

Thesaurierung F **-, -en** (Econ, St Ex) accumulation

These ['teːzə] F **-, -n** hypothesis; (inf: = Theorie) theory; **Luthers 95 ~n** Luther's 95 propositions

Thora ['toːra] F **-, NO PL** (Rel) Torah

Thriller ['θrɪlɐ] M **-s, -** thriller

Thrombose [trɔmˈboːzə] F **-, -n** thrombosis

Thron [troːn] M **-(e)s, -e** throne; (hum inf: = Nachttopf) pot

thronen ['troːnən] VI (lit) to sit enthroned; (fig) to sit in state

Thron-: **Thronfolge** F line of succession; **die ~ antreten** to succeed to the throne; **Thronfolger** [-fɔlgɐ] M **-s, -**, **Thronfolgerin** [-ərɪn] F **-, -nen** heir to the throne

Thuja ['tuːja] F **-, Thujen** [-jən] thuja

Thunfisch ['tuːn-] M tuna (fish)

Thurgau ['tuːɐgau] M **-s der ~** the Thurgau

Thüringen ['tyːrɪŋən] NT **-s** Thuringia

Thüringer ['tyːrɪŋɐ] ADJ Thuringian

THW [teːhaˈveː] ABBR von **Technisches Hilfswerk**

THW

*THW - short for **Technisches Hilfswerk** - was founded in 1950, under the organizational control of the Ministry of the Interior. It provides technical assistance in response to cases of civil defence, major accidents and natural disasters both in Germany and abroad. It also supports humanitarian relief work outside the country. It has about 80,000 voluntary helpers.*

Thymian ['tyːmian] M **-s, -e** thyme

Tibet [ˈtiːbɛt, tiˈbɛt] NT **-s** Tibet

tibetanisch [tibeˈtaːnɪʃ], **tibetisch** [tiˈbeːtɪʃ] ADJ Tibetan

tick [tɪk] INTERJ tick; **~ tack!** ticktock!

Tick [tɪk] M **-(e)s, -s (a)** (*Med*) tic; **nervöser ~** nervous tic **(b)** (*inf: = Schrulle*) quirk (*inf*); **Uhren sind sein ~** he has a thing about clocks (*inf*); **einen ~ haben** (*inf*) to be crazy; **er hat einen ~ mit seiner Ordnung** he has this thing about tidiness (*inf*); **einen ~ besser/schneller** *etc* **sein** (*inf*) to be a shade better/faster *etc*

-tick M SUF IN CPDS (*inf*) **ein Autotick** a thing about cars (*inf*)

ticken ['tɪkn] **1** VI to tick (away); (*fig inf*) to have a different mentality; **du tickst ja nicht richtig** (*inf*) you're off your rocker! (*inf*) **2** VT (*Press sl: = zusammenschlagen*) to bash (*inf*)

Ticket ['tɪkət] NT **-s, -s** (plane) ticket

Tie-Break M **-s, -s**, **Tiebreak** ['taibreːk] M **-s, -s** (*Tennis*) tie-break (*esp Brit*), tie-breaker

tief [tiːf] **1** ADJ deep; *Verbeugung, Ausschnitt, Lage, Ton, Temperatur* low; *Schmerz* intense; *Not* dire; *Verlassenheit, Einsamkeit, Elend* utter; **~er Teller** soup plate; **ein ~er Eingriff in jds Rechte** (*acc*) a gross infringement of sb's rights; **die ~eren Ursachen** the underlying causes; **aus ~stem Herzen** from the bottom of one's heart; **bis in den ~sten Winter** (till) well into winter; **bis in die ~ste Nacht** (till) late into the night; **im ~en Wald** deep in the forest; **im ~en Winter** in the depths of winter; **in der ~en Nacht** at dead of night; **im ~sten Afrika** in darkest Africa; **im ~sten Innern** in one's heart of hearts; **der ~ere Sinn** the deeper meaning

2 ADV **(a)** (= *weit nach unten, innen, hinten*) a long way; *bohren, graben, eindringen, tauchen* deep; *sich bücken* low; *untersuchen* in depth; **3 m ~ fallen** to fall 3 metres (*Brit*) or meters (*US*); **~ gehend** (*lit, fig*) deep; *Schmerz* acute; *Kränkung* extreme; **~ sinken** (*fig*) to sink low; **~ fallen** (*fig*) to go downhill; **~ liegend** *Augen* deep-set; (*nach Krankheit*) sunken; **bis ~ in etw** (*acc*) **hinein** (*örtlich*) a long way down/deep into sth; **(ganz) ~ unter uns** far below us; **~ verschneit** deep with snow; **~ in Gedanken (versunken)** deep in thought; **~ in Schulden stecken** to be deep in debt; **jdm ~ in die Augen sehen** to look deep into sb's eyes; **~ in die Tasche** or **den Beutel greifen müssen** (*inf*) to have to reach deep in one's pocket; **das geht bei ihm nicht sehr ~** (*inf*) it doesn't go very deep with him

(b) (= *sehr stark*) deeply; *erschrecken* terribly; **~ greifend** *Reform, Veränderung* far-reaching; *sich verändern* significantly; *reformieren* thoroughly; **die Gesellschaft hat sich ~ greifend gewandelt** society has done a basic turnaround

(c) (= *~gründig*) *nachdenken* deeply; **~ blickend** (*fig*) perceptive; **~ schürfend** profound

(d) (= *niedrig*) low; **ein Stockwerk ~er** on the floor below; **~ liegend** *Gegend, Häuser* low-lying; **im Winter steht die Sonne ~er** the sun is lower (in the sky) in winter

(e) (= *mit ~er Stimme*) *sprechen* in a deep voice; **so ~ kann ich nicht singen** I can't sing that low; **~er singen** to sing lower; **etw zu ~ singen** to sing sth flat; **~er stimmen** to tune down

Tief [tiːf] NT **-(e)s, -e** (*Met*) depression; (*im Kern, fig*) low; **ein moralisches ~** (*fig*) a low

Tief-: Tiefbau M, NO PL civil engineering (*excluding the construction of buildings*); *siehe* **Hoch- und Tiefbau**; **tiefblau** ADJ ATTR deep blue; **tiefblickend** ADJ ATTR *siehe* **tief**

Tiefe ['tiːfə] F **-, -n (a)** depth; **unten in der ~** far below; **das U-Boot ging auf ~** the submarine dived; **in 450 Metern ~** at a depth of 450 metres (*Brit*) or meters (*US*) **(b)** (= *Intensität*) deepness; (*von Schmerz*) intensity; (*von Not*) direness; (*von Elend*) depths *pl* **(c)** (= *Tiefgründigkeit*) profundity **(d)** (= *niedriger Stand*) lowness **(e)** (*von Farbton, Stimme*) deepness; (*von Ton*) lowness

Tiefebene F lowland plain; **die Oberrheinische ~** the Upper Rhine Valley

Tiefen-: Tiefenpsychologie F depth psychology; **Tiefenrausch** M (*Med*) rapture(s *pl*) of the deep; **Tiefenschärfe** F (*Phot*) depth of field

Tief-: Tiefflieger M low-flying aircraft; **geistiger ~** (*pej inf*) numskull (*inf*); **Tiefflug** M low-altitude flight; **er überquerte den Kanal im ~** he crossed low over the Channel; **Tiefgang** [-gaŋ] M, NO PL (*Naut*) draught (*Brit*), draft (*US*); (*fig inf*) depth; **Tiefgarage** F underground car park (*Brit*), underground parking garage (*esp US*); **tiefgefrieren** VT IRREG to (deep-)freeze; **tiefgehend** ADJ *siehe* **tief**; **tiefgekühlt 1** ADJ (= *gefroren*) frozen; (= *sehr kalt*) chilled **2** ADV **Spinat ~ kaufen** to buy frozen spinach; **~ halten Erdbeeren ein Jahr** frozen

strawberries can be stored for a year; **~ servieren** to serve frozen; **tiefgreifend** ADJ *siehe* **tief**; **tiefgründig** [-grʏndɪç] ADJ profound; (= *durchdacht*) well-grounded

Tiefkühl-: Tiefkühlfach NT freezer compartment; **Tiefkühlkost** F frozen food; **Tiefkühltruhe** F (chest) freezer

Tief-: Tiefland NT lowlands *pl*; **tiefliegend** ADJ ATTR *siehe* **tief**; **Tiefpunkt** M low; **Tiefschlag** M (*Boxen, fig*) hit below the belt; **jdm einen ~ verpassen** (*lit, fig*) to hit sb below the belt; **das war ein ~** (*lit, fig*) that was below the belt; **tiefschürfend** ADJ *siehe* **tief**; **Tiefsee** F deep sea; **Tiefstand** M low; **Tiefstapelei** [-ʃtaːpəˈlai] F **-, -en** understatement; (*auf eigene Leistung bezogen*) modesty; **tiefstapeln** VI SEP to understate the case; to be modest; **Tiefstart** M crouch start

Tiefstpreis M lowest price; **„~e"** "rock bottom prices"

tieftraurig ADJ very sad

Tiegel ['tiːgl] M **-s, -** (*zum Kochen*) (sauce)pan; (*in der Chemie*) crucible

Tier [tiːɐ] NT **-(e)s, -e (a)** animal; (*inf: = Ungeziefer*) bug (*inf*) **(b)** (*inf: = Mensch*) (*grausam*) brute; (*grob*) animal; (*gefräßig*) pig (*inf*); **großes** or **hohes ~** (*inf*) big shot (*inf*); **das ~ im Menschen** the beast in man; **da wird der Mensch zum ~** it brings out man's bestiality

Tier- IN CPDS (*Med*) veterinary; (*für Haustiere*) pet; **Tierarzt** M, **Tierärztin** F vet; **Tierasyl** NT (animal) pound

Tierchen ['tiːɐçən] NT **-s, -** DIM *von* **Tier** little animal; **ein niedliches ~** a sweet little creature

Tier-: Tierfreund(in) M(F) animal lover; (*von Haustier auch*) pet lover; **Tierfutter** NT animal food; (*für Haustiere*) pet food; **Tiergarten** M zoo; **Tierhandlung** F pet shop; **Tierheim** NT animal home

tierisch ['tiːrɪʃ] **1** ADJ animal *attr*; (*fig*) *Rohheit, Grausamkeit* bestial; (= *unzivilisiert, fig inf:* = *unerträglich*) deadly (*inf*); **~er Ernst** (*inf*) deadly seriousness **2** ADV (*inf: = ungeheuer*) horribly (*inf*); *wehtun, nerven* like hell (*inf*); *ernst* deadly; *gut* incredibly; **ich habe mich ~ geärgert** I got really furious; **~ wenig verdienen** to earn practically nothing

Tier-: Tierkreis M zodiac; **Tierkreiszeichen** NT sign of the zodiac; **im ~ des Skorpions geboren sein** to be born under Scorpio; **Tierkunde** F zoology; **Tiermedizin** F veterinary medicine; **Tierpark** M zoo; **Tierpfleger(in)** M(F) zoo keeper; **Tierquälerei** F cruelty to animals; (*fig inf*) cruelty to dumb animals; **Tierschutz** M protection of animals; **Tierschutzverein** M society for the prevention of cruelty to animals; **Tierversuch** M animal experiment; **Tierzucht** F stockbreeding

Tiger ['tiːgɐ] M **-s, -** tiger; *siehe auch* **Tigerin**

Tigerin ['tiːgərɪn] F **-, -nen** tigress

tigern ['tiːgɐn] **1** VT *siehe* **getigert** **2** VI AUX SEIN (*inf*) to mooch (about (*Brit*))

Tilde ['tɪldə] F **-, -n** tilde

tilgen ['tɪlgn] VT (*geh*) **(a)** *Schulden* to pay off **(b)** (= *beseitigen*) *Sünde, Unrecht, Spuren* to wipe out; *Erinnerung, Druckfehler* to erase; *Strafe* to remove

Tilgung ['tɪlgʊŋ] F **-, -en (a)** (*von Schulden*) repayment **(b)** (*fig*) (*von Sünde, Unrecht, Spuren*) wiping out; (*von Erinnerung, Druckfehler*) erasure; (*von Strafe*) removal

Tilgungs-: Tilgungsfonds M sinking fund; **tilgungsfrei** ADJ redemption-free; **Tilgungsrate** F redemption instalment (*Brit*) or installment (*US*)

Tilsiter ['tɪlzɪtɐ] M **-s, -** Tilsit cheese

timen ['taimən] VT to time

Timing ['taimɪŋ] NT **-**, NO PL timing

Tinktur [tɪŋkˈtuːɐ] F **-, -en** tincture

Tinnitus ['tɪnitʊs] M **-, -** (*Med*) tinnitus

Tinte ['tɪntə] F **-, -n** ink; **in der ~ sitzen** (*inf*) to be in the soup (*inf*)

Tinten-: Tintenfass NT inkpot; (*eingelassen*) inkwell; **Tintenfisch** M cuttlefish; (= *Kalmar*) squid; (*achtarmig*) octopus; **Tintenkartusche** F ink cartridge; **Tintenkiller** M (*inf*) correction pen; **Tintenklecks** M ink blot; **Tintenpatrone** F (*von Füller, Drucker*) ink cartridge; **Tintenstrahldrucker** M ink-jet (printer)

Tipp [tɪp] M **-s, -s** (= *Empfehlung*) (*Sport, St Ex*) tip; (= *Andeutung*) hint; (*an Polizei*) tip-off; **unser ~ für diesen Sommer ...** this summer we recommend ...; **unser Garten-~ für August** our gardening tip for August

tippen ['tɪpn] **1** VT **(a)** (inf: = schreiben) to type
(b) (= klopfen) **jdn auf die Schulter** ~ to tap sb on the shoulder **2** VI **(a)** (= klopfen) **an/auf/gegen etw** (acc) ~ to tap sth; **an** or **auf etw** (acc) ~ (= zeigen) to touch sth; **jdm auf die Schulter** ~ to tap sb on the shoulder
(b) (inf: auf der Schreibmaschine, am Computer) to type
(c) (= wetten) to fill in one's coupon; (esp im Toto) to do the pools; **im Lotto** ~ to play the lottery
(d) (inf: = raten) to guess; **auf jdn/etw** ~ to put one's money on sb/sth (inf); **ich tippe darauf, dass ...** I bet (that) ...

Tipp-Ex® ['tɪpɛks] NT -, NO PL Tipp-Ex®, whiteout (US); **etw mit** ~ **entfernen** to Tipp-Ex® sth out (Brit), to white sth out (US)

Tipp-: **Tippfehler** M (inf) typing mistake; **Tippgemeinschaft** F (im Lotto) lottery syndicate; (im Fußballtoto) pools syndicate

tipptopp ['tɪp'tɔp] (inf) **1** ADJ immaculate; (= prima) first-class **2** ADV immaculately; (= prima) really well; ~ **sauber** spotless

Tippzettel M (im Toto) football or pools coupon; (im Lotto) lottery coupon

Tirana [ti'ra:na] NT -s Tirana

Tirol [ti'ro:l] NT -s Tyrol

Tiroler [ti'ro:lɐ] M -s, -, **Tirolerin** [-ərɪn] F -, -nen Tyrolese, Tyrolean

Tirolerhut M Tyrolean hat

Tisch [tɪʃ] M -(e)s, -e table; (= Schreibtisch) desk; (= Werktisch) bench; (= Mahlzeit) meal; **bei** ~ at (the) table; **die Gäste zu** ~ **bitten** to ask the guests to take their places; **bitte zu** ~! lunch/dinner is served!; **vor/nach** ~ before/after the meal; **bei** ~ at the table; **zu** ~ **sein** to be having one's lunch/dinner; **zu** ~ **gehen** to go to lunch/dinner; **er zahlte bar auf den** ~ he paid cash down; **etw auf den** ~ **bringen** (inf) to serve sth (up); **die Beine** or **Füße unter jds** ~ (acc) **strecken** (inf) to eat at sb's table; **getrennt von** ~ **und Bett leben** to be separated; **unter den** ~ **fallen** (inf) to go by the board; **vom** ~ **sein** (fig) to be cleared out of the way; **vom** ~ **müssen** (fig) to have to be cleared out of the way; **etw vom** ~ **wischen** (fig) to dismiss sth; **zwei Parteien an einen** ~ **bringen** (fig) to get two parties (a)round the conference table; **jdn über den** ~ **ziehen** (fig inf) to take sb to the cleaners (inf)

Tisch- IN CPDS table; **Tischdecke** F tablecloth; **Tischfußball** NT table football; **Tischgrill** M table grill

Tischler ['tɪʃlɐ] M -s, -, **Tischlerin** [-ərɪn] F -, -nen joiner (esp Brit), carpenter; (= Möbeltischler) cabinet-maker

Tischlerei [tɪʃlə'rai] F -, -en **(a)** (Werkstatt) carpenter's workshop; (= Möbeltischlerei) cabinet-maker's workshop
(b) NO PL (inf) (= Handwerk) carpentry; (von Möbeltischler) cabinet-making

tischlern ['tɪʃlɐn] (inf) **1** VI to do woodwork **2** VT Tisch, Regal etc to make

Tisch-: **Tischordnung** F seating plan; **Tischplatte** F tabletop; **Tischrechner** M desk calculator

Tischtennis NT table tennis

Tischtennis- IN CPDS table-tennis; **Tischtennisplatte** F table-tennis table; **Tischtennisschläger** M table-tennis bat

Tischtuch NT, pl -tücher tablecloth

Titan NT -s, NO PL (abbr Ti) titanium

Titel ['ti:tl, 'tɪtl] M -s, - **(a)** title **(b)** (= ~blatt) title page

Titel-: **Titelanwärter(in)** M(F) (main) contender for the title; **Titelbild** NT cover (picture); **Titelmelodie** F (von Film) theme tune

Titel-: **Titelseite** F cover, front page; **Titelverteidiger(in)** M(F) title holder

Titte ['tɪtə] F -, -n (sl) tit (sl)

tja [tja, tja:] INTERJ well

T-Lymphozyt ['te:-] M (Med, Biol) T-lymphocyte

Toast [to:st] M -(e)s, -e **(a)** (= Brot) toast; **ein** ~ a slice of toast **(b)** (= Trinkspruch) toast; **einen** ~ **auf jdn ausbringen** to propose a toast to sb

Toastbrot ['to:st-] NT sliced white bread for toasting

toasten ['to:stn] **1** VI to drink a toast (auf +acc to) **2** VT Brot to toast

Toaster ['to:stɐ] M -s, - toaster

Toastständer ['to:st-] M toast rack

toben ['to:bn] VI **(a)** (= wüten) to rage; (Mensch) to throw a fit; (vor Wut, Begeisterung etc) to go wild (vor with)
(b) (= ausgelassen spielen) to rollick (about)

Tobsucht ['to:pzʊxt] F (bei Tieren) madness; (bei Menschen) maniacal rage

tobsüchtig ADJ mad; Mensch auch raving mad

Tobsuchtsanfall M (inf) fit of rage; **einen** ~ **bekommen** to blow one's top (inf)

Tochter ['tɔxtɐ] F -, ⸚ ['tœçtɐ] daughter; (= ~firma) subsidiary; (Sw: = Bedienstete) girl

Töchterchen ['tœçtɐçən] NT -s, - baby daughter

Tochter-: **Tochterfirma** F subsidiary (firm); **Tochtergeschwulst** F secondary growth or tumour; **Tochtergesellschaft** F subsidiary (company)

töchterlich ['tœçtɐlɪç] ADJ ATTR daughterly; Pflicht, Gehorsam, Liebe filial

Tod [to:t] M -(e)s, -e [-də] death; **der schwarze** ~ (= die Pest) the Black Death; ~ **durch Erschießen/Ersticken/Erhängen** death by firing squad/suffocation/hanging; **eines natürlichen/ gewaltsamen ~es sterben** to die of natural causes/a violent death; **sich** (dat) **den** ~ **holen** to catch one's death (of cold); **den** ~ **finden, zu** ~**e kommen** to die; **jdn/etw auf den** ~ **nicht leiden** or **ausstehen können** (inf) to be unable to stand sb/sth; **sich zu** ~**(e) langweilen** to be bored to death; **zu** ~**e betrübt sein** to be in the depths of despair

tod-: **todelend** ADJ (inf) as miserable as sin (inf); **todernst** (inf) **1** ADJ deadly serious; **es ist mir** ~ (damit) I'm deadly serious (about it) **2** ADV **jdn** ~ **ansehen** to give sb a deadly serious look; **und das alles sagte er** ~ and the way he said it all was deadly serious

Todes-: **Todesangst** F mortal agony; **eine** ~ **haben** (inf), **Todesängste ausstehen** (inf) to be scared to death (inf); **Todesanzeige** F (als Brief) letter announcing sb's death; (= Annonce) obituary (notice); „~n" "Deaths"; **Todesfall** M death; **Todesgefahr** F mortal danger; **Todeskampf** M death throes pl; **Todesopfer** NT death, casualty; **Todesschwadron** F death squad; **Todesstrafe** F death penalty; **Todesursache** F cause of death; **Todesurteil** NT death sentence; **Todeszelle** F death cell; (inf) cell on Death Row (US)

Tod-: **Todfeind(in)** M(F) deadly enemy; **todgeweiht** [-gəvait] ADJ Mensch, Patient doomed; **todkrank** ADJ (= sterbenskrank) critically ill; (= unheilbar krank) terminally ill

tödlich ['tø:tlɪç] **1** ADJ fatal; Gefahr, Beleidigung mortal; Gift, Waffe, Dosis lethal; (inf) Langeweile, Ernst, Sicherheit deadly **2** ADV **(a)** (mit Todesfolge) ~ **verunglücken** to be killed in an accident; ~ **abstürzen** to die in a fall **(b)** (inf: = äußerst) horribly (inf); **langweilen** to death

Tod-: **todmüde** ADJ (inf) dead tired (inf); **todschick** (inf) **1** ADJ dead smart (inf) **2** ADV **gekleidet** ravishingly; eingerichtet exquisitely; **er hat sich** ~ **zurechtgemacht** he was dressed to kill (inf); **todsicher** (inf) **1** ADJ dead certain (inf); Methode, Tipp sure-fire (inf); **eine ~e Angelegenheit** or **Sache** a dead cert (Brit inf), a cinch (esp US inf) **2** ADV for sure; **Todsünde** F mortal sin; **todunglücklich** ADJ (inf) desperately unhappy

Toeloop ['to:lu:p] M -s, -s (Eiskunstlauf) toe loop

Tofu ['to:fu] NT -, NO PL tofu

Togo ['to:go] NT -s Togo

Toilette [toa'lɛtə] F -, -n **(a)** (= Abort) toilet, lavatory (esp Brit), bathroom (esp US); **öffentliche** ~ public conveniences pl (Brit), rest stop (US); **auf die** ~ **gehen** to go to the toilet; **auf der** ~ **sein** to be in the toilet **(b)** (geh: = Kleidung) outfit; **in großer** ~ in full dress

Toiletten- IN CPDS toilet; **Toilettenartikel** M USU PL toiletry; **Toilettenfrau** F toilet attendant; **Toilettenmann** M, pl -männer toilet attendant; **Toilettenpapier** NT toilet paper

toi, toi, toi ['tɔy 'tɔy 'tɔy] INTERJ (inf) (vor Prüfung etc) good luck; (unberufen) touch wood (Brit), knock on wood (US)

Tokio ['to:kio] NT -s Tokyo

Tokioter [to'kio:tɐ] ADJ ATTR Tokyo

tolerant [tole'rant] ADJ tolerant (gegen of)

Toleranz [tole'rants] F -, -en tolerance (gegen of)

tolerieren [tole'ri:rən] ptp **toleriert** VT to tolerate

toll [tɔl] **1** ADJ **(a)** (= wild, ausgelassen) wild; **die (drei) ~en Tage** (the last three days) of Fasching
(b) (inf: = verrückt) crazy
(c) (inf: = schlimm) terrible
(d) (inf: = großartig) fantastic (inf) **2** ADV **(a)** (inf: = großartig) fantastically; **schmecken** fantastic
(b) (= wild, ausgelassen) **es ging** ~ **her** or **zu** things were pretty

wild (*inf*)
(c) (*inf*: = *verrückt*) **(wie) ~ regnen** to rain like mad (*inf*); **(wie) ~ fahren** *etc* to drive *etc* like a madman
(d) (*inf*: = *schlimm*) **es kommt noch ~er!** there's more or worse to come; **es zu ~ treiben** to go too far

Toll-: Tollkirsche F deadly nightshade; **tollkühn 🔢** ADJ *Person, Plan, Fahrt* daredevil *attr*, daring **🔢** ADV daringly; *fahren* like a real daredevil; **Tollpatsch** ['tɔlpatʃ] M **-s, -e** (*inf*) clumsy creature; **tollpatschig** ['tɔlpatʃɪç] **🔢** ADJ clumsy **🔢** ADV clumsily; **Tollwut** F rabies *sing*; **Tollwutgefahr** F danger of rabies; **tollwütig** ADJ rabid

Tolpatsch ['tɔlpatʃ] M **-es, -e** *siehe* **Tollpatsch**

Tölpel ['tœlpl] M **-s, -** (*inf*) fool

Tomahawk ['tɔmahaːk, -hoːk] M **-s, -s** tomahawk

Tomate [to'maːtə] F **-, -n** tomato; **du treulose ~!** (*inf*) you're a fine friend!

Tomaten- IN CPDS tomato; **Tomatenmark** NT, **Tomatenpüree** NT tomato puree

Tombola ['tɔmbola] F **-, -s** or **Tombolen** [-lən] tombola (*Brit*), raffle (*US*)

Tomograf [tomo'graːf] M **-en, -en** (*Med*) tomograph

Tomografie [tomogra'fiː] F **-, -n** [-'fiːən] tomography

Tomogramm [tomo'gram] NT, *pl* **-gramme** (*Med*) tomogram

Ton¹ [toːn] M **-(e)s, -e** (= *Erdart*) clay

Ton² M **-(e)s, ⸚e** ['tøːnə] **(a)** sound (*auch Rad, Film*); (*von Zeitzeichen, im Telefon*) pip; (= *Klangfarbe*) tone; (*Mus*) tone; (= *Note*) note; **halber ~** semitone; **ganzer ~** tone; **den ~ angeben** (*lit*) to give the note; (*fig*) (*Mensch*) to set the tone; **keinen ~ herausbringen** or **hervorbringen** not to be able to say a word; **keinen ~ sagen** or **von sich geben** not to make a sound; **aus dem Regierungslager kamen kritische Töne** criticism came from the government camp; **dicke** or **große Töne spucken** or **reden** (*inf*) to talk big; **jdn in (den) höchsten Tönen loben** (*inf*) to praise sb to the skies
(b) (= *Betonung*) stress; (= ~*fall*) intonation
(c) (= *Redeweise, Umgangston*) tone; **ich verbitte mir diesen ~** I will not be spoken to like that; **der ~ macht die Musik** (*prov*) it's not what you say but the way that or how you say it; **der gute ~** good form
(d) (= *Farbton*) tone; (= *Nuance*) shade

Ton-: Tonabnehmer M pick-up; **Tonarm** M pick-up arm; **Tonart** F (*Mus*) key; (*fig*: = *Tonfall*) tone; **eine andere ~ anschlagen** to change one's tune

Tonband [-bant] NT, *pl* **-bänder** tape (*mit of*); (*inf*: = *Gerät*) tape recorder

Tonband-: Tonbandaufnahme F tape recording; **Tonbandgerät** NT tape recorder

tönen¹ ['tøːnən] VI (*lit, fig*: = *klingen*) to sound; (= *großspurig reden*) to boast; **nach etw ~** (*fig*) to contain (over)tones of sth

tönen² VT to tint; **sich** (*dat*) **die Haare ~** to tint one's hair; **etw leicht rot** *etc* **~** to tinge sth (with) red *etc*; *siehe auch* **getönt**

Toner ['toːnɐ] M **-s, -** toner

Tonerkassette F toner cartridge

tönern ['tøːnɐn] ADJ ATTR clay; **auf ~en Füßen stehen** (*fig*) to be shaky

Ton-: Tonfall M tone of voice; (= *Intonation*) intonation; **Tonfilm** M sound film; **tonhaltig** ADJ clayey; **Tonhöhe** F pitch

Tonika ['toːnika] F **-, Toniken** [-kn] (*Mus*) tonic

Ton-: Toningenieur(in) M(F) sound engineer; **Tonlage** F pitch (level); (= *Tonumfang*) register; **eine ~ höher** one note higher; **Tonleiter** F scale; **tonlos 🔢** ADJ toneless; *Stimme auch* flat **🔢** ADV in a flat voice

Tonnage [tɔ'naːʒə] F **-, -n** (*Naut*) tonnage

Tonne ['tɔnə] F **-, -n (a)** (= *Behälter*) barrel; (*aus Metall*) drum; (= *Mülltonne*) bin (*Brit*), trash can (*US*); (*inf*: *Mensch*) fatty (*inf*); **gelbe ~** yellow bin (*Brit*) or trash can (*US*) (*for recyclable material*); **grüne ~** green bin (*Brit*) or trash can (*US*) (*for paper*); **braune ~** brown bin (*Brit*) or trash can (*US*) (*for biodegradable waste*)
(b) (= *Gewicht*) metric ton(ne)
(c) (= *Registertonne*) (register) ton

tonnenweise ADV by the ton; **~ Fische fangen** (*fig*) to catch tons (and tons) of fish

Ton-: Tonspur F soundtrack; **Tonstörung** F sound interference; **Tonstudio** NT recording studio; **Tontaube** F clay pigeon;

Tontaubenschießen NT **-s**, NO PL clay pigeon shooting; **Tontechniker(in)** M(F) sound technician

Tönung ['tøːnʊŋ] F **-, -en** (= *Haartönung*) hair colour (*Brit*) or color (*US*); (= *das Tönen*) tinting; (= *Farbton*) shade, tone

Top [tɔp] NT **-s, -s** (*Fashion*) top

Top-, top- ['tɔp] IN CPDS top; **Topagent(in)** M(F) top agent; **topaktuell** ADJ up-to-the-minute

Topas [to'paːs] M **-es, -e** [-zə] topaz

Topf [tɔpf] M **-(e)s, ⸚e** ['tœpfə] pot; (= *Kochtopf auch*) (sauce)pan; (= *Nachttopf*) potty (*inf*); (= *Toilette*) loo (*Brit inf*), john (*US inf*); **alles in einen ~ werfen** (*fig*) to lump everything together

Topfen ['tɔpfn] M **-s, -** (*Aus, S Ger*) quark

Töpfer ['tœpfɐ] M **-s, -**, **Töpferin** [-ərɪn] F **-, -nen** potter

Töpferei [tœpfɐ'rai] F **-, -en** pottery

töpfern ['tœpfɐn] **🔢** VI to do pottery **🔢** VT to make (in clay); **wir sahen zu, wie er auf der Scheibe eine Vase töpferte** we watched him throwing a vase

Töpfer-: Töpferofen M kiln; **Töpferscheibe** F potter's wheel

topfit ADJ PRED in top form; (*gesundheitlich*) as fit as a fiddle

Topf-: Topflappen M oven cloth; (*kleiner*) pan holder; **Topfpflanze** F potted plant

Topografie [topogra'fiː] F **-, -n** [-'fiːən] topography

topografisch [topo'graːfɪʃ] **🔢** ADJ topographic(al) **🔢** ADV *vermessen* topographically; **das Land ist ~ und klimatisch ungeeignet** the topography and the climate of this country are ill suited

topp [tɔp] INTERJ it's a deal

Tor NT **-(e)s, -e (a)** (*lit, fig*) gate; (= *Durchfahrt*) (*fig: zum Glück etc*) gateway; (= ~*bogen*) archway; (*von Garage, Scheune*) door
(b) (*Sport*) goal; (*bei Skilaufen*) gate; **im ~ stehen** to be in goal

Tor-: Torbogen M arch; **Toreinfahrt** F entrance gate

Toresschluss M = **Torschluss**

Torf [tɔrf] M **-(e)s**, NO PL peat

torfig ['tɔrfɪç] ADJ peaty

Torf-: Torfmoor NT peat bog or (*trocken*) moor; **Torfmull** M (loose) garden peat

Torfrau F goalkeeper

Torhüter(in) M(F) goalkeeper

töricht ['tøːrɪçt] (*geh*) **🔢** ADJ foolish; *Wunsch, Hoffnung* idle **🔢** ADV foolishly

Torjäger(in) M(F) (goal)scorer

torkeln ['tɔrkln] VI AUX SEIN to stagger, to reel

Tor-: Torlatte F crossbar; **Tormann** M, *pl* **-männer** goalkeeper

Törn [tœrn] M **-s, -s** (*Naut*) cruise

Tornado [tɔr'naːdo] M **-s, -s** tornado

torpedieren [tɔrpe'diːrən], *ptp* **torpediert** VT (*Naut, fig*) to torpedo

Torpedo [tɔr'peːdo] M **-s, -s** torpedo

Tor-: Torpfosten M gatepost; (*Sport*) goalpost; **Torschluss** M, NO PL (*fig*) **kurz vor ~** at the last minute; **nach ~** too late; **Torschlusspanik** F (*inf*) last minute panic; (*von Unverheirateten*) fear of being left on the shelf; **Torschütze** M, **Torschützin** F (goal)scorer

Torte ['tɔrtə] F **-, -n** gâteau; (= *Obsttorte*) flan

Torten-: Tortenboden M flan case or (*ohne Seiten*) base; **Tortendiagramm** NT pie chart; **Tortenguss** M glaze; **Tortenheber** [-heːbɐ] M **-s, -** cake slice

Tortur [tɔr'tuːɐ] F **-, -en** torture; (*fig auch*) ordeal

Tor-: Torverhältnis NT score; **Torwächter(in)** M(F), **Torwart** [-vart] M **-(e)s, -e**, **Torwartin** [-vartɪn] F **-, -nen** goalkeeper

tosen ['toːzn] VI (*Wasserfall, Wellen, Verkehr*) to thunder; (*Wind, Sturm*) to rage; **~der Beifall** thunderous applause

tot [toːt] ADJ (*lit, fig*) dead; (*inf*: = *erschöpft*) beat (*inf*); *Augen* blind; *Haus, Stadt* deserted; *Landschaft etc* bleak; *Wissen* useless; *Farbe* drab; (*Rail*) *Gleis* disused; **~ geboren** stillborn; **ein ~ geborenes Kind sein** (*fig*) to be doomed (to failure); **~ umfallen, ~ zu Boden fallen** to drop dead; **~ zusammenbrechen** to collapse and die; **er war auf der Stelle ~** he died instantly; **den ~en Mann machen** (*inf*) to float on one's back; **ein ~er Mann sein** (*fig inf*) to be a goner (*inf*); **~er Winkel** blind spot; (*Mil*) dead angle; **das Tote Meer** the Dead Sea; **~er Punkt** (= *Stillstand*) standstill, halt; (*in Verhandlungen*) deadlock; (= *körperliche Ermüdung*) low point; **ich habe im Moment meinen ~en Punkt** I'm at a low ebb just now; **den**

~en Punkt überwinden to break the deadlock; (*körperlich*) to get one's second wind

total [to'ta:l] **1** ADJ total; *Staat* totalitarian **2** ADV totally

Totalisator [totali'za:tɔːɐ] M **-s, Totalisatoren** [-'tɔːrən] totalizator

totalitär [totali'tɛːɐ] **1** ADJ totalitarian **2** ADV in a totalitarian way

Total-: Totaloperation F extirpation; (*von Gebärmutter*) hysterectomy; (*mit Eierstöcken*) hysterosaphorectomy; **Totalschaden** M write-off; **~ machen** (*inf*) to write a car *etc* off

tot-: totarbeiten VR SEP (*inf*) to work oneself to death; **totärgern** VR SEP (*inf*) to be/become livid

Totempfahl M totem pole

töten ['tøːtn] VTI (*lit, fig*) to kill; *Zahnnerv* to deaden

Toten-: Totenbett NT deathbed; **totenblass** ADJ deathly pale; **Totengräber(in)** M(F) gravedigger; **Totenkopf** M skull; (*als Zeichen*) death's-head; (*auf Piratenfahne, Arzneiflasche etc*) skull and crossbones; **Totenstarre** F rigor mortis; **Totenstille** F deathly silence

Tote(r) ['toːtə] MF DECL AS ADJ dead person; (*bei Unfall etc*) fatality, casualty; (*Mil*) casualty; **die ~n** the dead; **es gab 3 ~** 3 people died *or* were killed

Tot-: totfahren VT SEP IRREG (*inf*) to knock down and kill; **totgeboren** ADJ ATTR *siehe* tot; **Totgeburt** F stillbirth; (= *Kind*) stillborn child; **totkriegen** VT SEP (*inf*) **nicht totzukriegen sein** to go on for ever; **totlachen** VR SEP (*inf*) to kill oneself (laughing; (*Brit inf*); **es ist zum Totlachen** it is hilarious

Toto ['toːto] M *or* (INF, AUS, SW) NT **-s, -s** (football) pools *pl* (*Brit*); **(im) ~ spielen** to do the pools (*Brit*)

Toto- IN CPDS pools (*Brit*); **Totoschein** M, **Totozettel** M pools coupon (*Brit*)

Tot-: totschießen VT SEP IRREG (*inf*) to shoot dead; **Totschlag** M (*Jur*) manslaughter; *siehe* **Mord**; **totschlagen** VT SEP IRREG (*lit, fig*) to kill; **du kannst mich ~, ich weiß es nicht** (*inf*) for the life of me I don't know; **Totschläger** M cudgel; **totschweigen** VT SEP IRREG to hush up (*inf*); **tot stellen** VR to pretend to be dead

Tötung ['tøːtʊŋ] F **-, -en** killing; **fahrlässige ~** manslaughter (through culpable negligence (*esp Brit*))

Touch [tatʃ] M **-s, -s** (= *Atmosphäre*) air; (= *Flair*) touch; (= *Tendenz*) leanings *pl*

Touch-Screen ['tatʃskriːn] M **-s, -s**, **Touchscreen** M **-s, -s** (*Comput*) touch screen

Toupet [tu'peː] NT **-s, -s** toupée

toupieren [tu'piːrən], *ptp* **toupiert** VT to backcomb

Tour [tuːɐ] F **-, -en (a)** (= *Fahrt*) trip; (= *Ausflug, Tournee*) tour; (= *Spritztour*) (*mit Auto*) drive; (*mit Rad*) ride; (= *Wanderung*) walk; (= *Bergtour*) climb **(b)** (= *Umdrehung*) revolution; **auf ~en kommen** (*Auto*) to reach top speed; (*fig inf*) to get into top gear; (= *sich aufregen*) to get worked up (*inf*); **jdn/etw auf ~en bringen** (*fig*) to get sb/ sth going; **in einer ~** (*inf*) incessantly **(c)** (*inf*: = *Art und Weise*) ploy; **mit der ~ brauchst du mir gar nicht zu kommen** don't try that one on me; **auf die krumme** *or* **schiefe** *or* **schräge ~** by dishonest means; **etw auf die weiche** *or* **sanfte ~ versuchen** to try using soft soap (*Brit*) *or* sweet talk to get sth (*inf*); **jdm die ~ vermasseln** (*inf*) to put paid to sb's plans

Touren- ['tuːrən-]: **Tourenrad** NT tourer; **Tourenski** M crosscountry ski; **Tourenwagen** M (*im Motorsport*) touring car; **Tourenzähler** M rev counter

Tourismus [tu'rɪsmʊs] M **-**, NO PL tourism

Tourismusindustrie F tourist industry

Tourist [tu'rɪst] M **-en, -en, Touristin** [-'rɪstɪn] F **-, -nen** tourist

Touristenklasse F tourist class

Touristik [tu'rɪstɪk] F **-**, NO PL tourism

Touristikunternehmen NT tour company

Touristin F **-, -nen** tourist

Tournee [tʊr'neː] F **-, -s** *or* **-n** [-'neːən] tour; **auf ~ gehen** to go on tour; **auf ~ sein** to be on tour

Tower ['taʊɐ] M **-s, -** (*Aviat*) control tower

Toxikologe [tɔksiko'loːgə] M **-n, -n, Toxikologin** [-'loːgɪn] F **-, -nen** toxicologist

toxikologisch [tɔksiko'loːgɪʃ] **1** ADJ toxicological **2** ADV toxicologically; **etw ~ untersuchen** to do a toxicological analysis of sth; **~ unbedenklich** nontoxic

toxisch ['tɔksɪʃ] **1** ADJ toxic **2** ADV toxically; **~ wirken** to be toxic

Toxoplasmose [tɔksoplas'moːzə] F **-, -n** toxoplasmosis

Trab [traːp] M **-(e)s** [-bəs], NO PL trot; **im ~** at a trot; **(im) ~ reiten** to trot; **auf ~ sein** (*inf*) to be on the go (*inf*); **jdn in ~ halten** (*inf*) to keep sb on the go (*inf*)

traben ['traːbn] VI **(a)** AUX HABEN *or* SEIN to trot; **mit dem Pferd ~** to trot one's horse **(b)** AUX SEIN (*inf*: = *laufen*) to trot

Trab-: Trabrennbahn F trotting course; **Trabrennen** NT trotting; (*Veranstaltung*) trotting race

Tracht [traxt] F **-, -en (a)** (= *Kleidung*) dress; (= *Volkstracht etc*) costume; (= *Schwesterntracht*) uniform **(b)** **jdm eine ~ Prügel verabfolgen** *or* **verabreichen** (*inf*) to give sb a beating

trachten ['traxtn] VI (*geh*) to strive (*nach* for, after); **jdm nach dem Leben ~** to be after sb's blood

trächtig ['trɛçtɪç] ADJ *Tier* pregnant

Trächtigkeit F (*von Tier*) pregnancy

Trackball ['trɛkbɔːl] M **-s, -s** (*Comput*) trackball

Tradition [tradi'tsioːn] F **-, -en** tradition; **(bei jdm) ~ haben** to be a tradition (for sb)

traditionell [traditsio'nɛl] **1** ADJ USU ATTR traditional **2** ADV traditionally

Traditions-: traditionsbewusst ADJ tradition-conscious; **Traditionsbewusstsein** NT consciousness of tradition; **traditionsgemäß** ADV traditionally; **Traditionspapier** NT document of title

traf PRET *von* **treffen**

Trafik [tra'fɪk] F **-, -en** (*Aus*) tobacconist's (shop)

Trafikant [trafi'kant] M **-en, -en, Trafikantin** [-'kantɪn] F **-, -nen** (*Aus*) tobacconist

Trafo ['traːfo] M **-(s), -s** (*inf*) transformer

Trag-: Tragbahre F stretcher; **tragbar** ADJ **(a)** *Apparat, Gerät* portable; *Kleid* wearable **(b)** (= *annehmbar*) acceptable (*für* to); (= *erträglich*) bearable

Trage ['traːgə] F **-, -n** (= *Bahre*) litter; (= *Tragkorb*) pannier

träge ['trɛːgə] **1** ADJ **(a)** sluggish; *Mensch, Handbewegung etc* lethargic; (= *faul*) lazy; **geistig ~** mentally lazy **(b)** (*Phys*) *Masse* inert **2** ADV *sich bewegen* sluggishly; *sich rekeln* lethargically

tragen ['traːgn], *pret* **trug** [truːk], *ptp* **getragen** [gə'traːgn] **1** VT **(a)** (= *befördern, dabeihaben*) to carry; (= *an einen Ort bringen*) to take; **den Brief zur Post ~** to take the letter to the post office; **den Arm in der Schlinge ~** to have one's arm in a sling **(b)** (= *am Körper ~*) to wear; *Bart, Gebiss* to have; *Waffen* to carry; **getragene Kleider** second-hand clothes; (= *abgelegt*) castoffs (*Brit*), throwouts (*US*) **(c)** (= *stützen, halten*) to support; *siehe* **tragend** **(d)** (= *aushalten, Tragfähigkeit haben*) to take (the weight of) **(e)** (= *hervorbringen*) *Zinsen, Ernte* to yield; (*lit, fig*) *Früchte* to bear; **der Baum trägt viele Früchte** the tree produces a good crop of fruit; (*in dieser Saison*) the tree is full of fruit **(f)** (= *trächtig sein*) to be carrying **(g)** (= *ertragen*) *Schicksal, Leid etc* to bear **(h)** (= *übernehmen*) *Verluste* to defray; *Kosten* to bear, to carry; *Risiko, Folgen* to take; **die Verantwortung für etw ~** to be responsible for sth; **die Schuld für etw ~** to be to blame for sth **(i)** (= *unterhalten*) *Verein, Organisation* to support, to back **(j)** (= *haben*) *Titel, Namen, Aufschrift etc* to bear; *Vermerk* to contain; *Etikett* to have **2** VI **(a)** (*Baum, Acker etc*) to produce a crop **(b)** (= *trächtig sein*) to be pregnant **(c)** (= *reichen: Geschütz, Stimme*) to carry **(d)** (*Eis*) to take weight; **das Eis trägt noch nicht** the ice won't take anyone's weight yet **(e)** **schwer an etw** (*dat*) **~** to have a job carrying sth; (*fig*) to find sth hard to bear; **schwer zu ~ haben** to have a lot to carry; (*fig*) to have a heavy cross to bear **(f)** **zum Tragen kommen** to come to fruition; (= *nützlich werden*) to come in useful; **etw zum Tragen bringen** to bring sth to bear (*in* +*dat* on) **3** VR **(a)** **sich gut** *or* **leicht/schwer** *or* **schlecht ~** to be easy/ difficult to carry; **schwere Lasten ~ sich besser auf dem Rücken** it is better to carry heavy loads on one's back **(b)** (*Kleid, Stoff*) to wear **(c)** (= *ohne Zuschüsse auskommen*) to be self-supporting

tragend ADJ **(a)** (= *stützend*) *Säule, Bauteil, Chassisteil* load-bearing; (*fig:* = *bestimmend*) *Bedeutung, Idee, Motiv* fundamental **(b)** (*Theat*) *Rolle* major

Träger¹ ['trɛːgɐ] M **-s, -** **(a)** (*an Kleidung*) strap; (= *Hosenträger*) braces *pl* (*Brit*), suspenders *pl* (*US*) **(b)** (*Build*) (*Holzträger, Betonträger*) (supporting) beam; (= *Stahlträger, Eisenträger*) girder **(c)** (*Tech:* = *Stütze von Brücken etc*) support **(d)** (= *Flugzeugträger*) carrier **(e)** (= *Kostenträger*) funding provider

Träger² ['trɛːgɐ] M **-s, -**, **Trägerin** [-ərɪn] F **-, -nen** **(a)** (*von Lasten, Namen, Titel*) bearer; (*von Kleidung*) wearer; (*eines Preises*) winner; (*von Krankheit, Gen*) carrier **(b)** (*fig*) (*der Kultur, Staatsgewalt etc*) representative; (*einer Bewegung, Entwicklung*) supporter; (*einer Veranstaltung*) sponsor; (*Mittel*) vehicle; ~ **einer Einrichtung sein** to be in charge of an institution

Trägerrakete F carrier rocket

Tragetasche F carrier bag

Trag-: tragfähig ADJ able to take a weight; (*fig*) *Kompromiss, Konzept, Lösung* workable; **Tragfläche** F wing; (*von Boot*) hydrofoil; **Tragflächenboot** NT hydrofoil; **Tragflügel** M wing; (*von Boot*) hydrofoil; **Tragflügelboot** NT hydrofoil

Trägheit F **-, -en** sluggishness; (*von Mensch*) lethargy; (= *Faulheit*) laziness; (*Phys*) inertia

Tragik ['traːgɪk] F **-, NO PL** tragedy

Tragikomik [tragi'koːmɪk, 'traːgi-] F tragicomedy

tragikomisch [tragi'koːmɪʃ, 'traːgi-] ADJ tragicomical

Tragikomödie [tragiko'møːdiə, 'traːgi-] F tragicomedy

tragisch ['traːgɪʃ] **1** ADJ tragic; **das ist nicht so ~** (*inf*) it's not the end of the world **2** ADV tragically; **etw ~ nehmen** (*inf*) to take sth to heart

Tragödie [tra'gøːdiə] F **-, -n** (*Liter, fig*) tragedy

trägt [trɛːkt] 3. PERS SING PRES *von* **tragen**

Trag-: Tragweite F (*von Geschütz etc*) range; (*fig*) consequences *pl*; (*von Gesetz*) scope; **von großer ~ sein** to have far-reaching consequences; **Tragwerk** NT (*Aviat*) wing assembly

Trailer ['trɛːlɐ] M **-s, -** (= *Filmwerbung*) trailer

Trainer¹ ['trɛːnɐ, 'trɛːnɐ] M **-s, -** (*Sw:* = *Trainingsanzug*) tracksuit

Trainer² ['trɛːnɐ, 'trɛːnɐ] M **-s, -**, **Trainerin** [-ərɪn] F **-, -nen** trainer; (*von Schwimmer, Tennisspieler*) coach; (*bei Fußball*) manager

trainieren [trɛ'niːrən, trɛ-], *ptp* **trainiert** **1** VT to train; *Mannschaft, Sportler auch* to coach; *Sprung, Übung, Sportart* to practise (*Brit*), to practice (*US*); *Muskel, Kreislauf* to exercise; **Fußball/Tennis** ~ to do some football/tennis practice; **ein (gut) trainierter Sportler** an athlete who is in training; **jdn auf** *or* **für etw** (*acc*) ~ to train sb for sth **2** VI (*Sportler*) to train; (*Rennfahrer*) to practise (*Brit*), to practice (*US*); (= *Übungen machen*) to exercise; (= *üben*) to practise (*Brit*), to practice (*US*); **auf** *or* **für etw** (*acc*) ~ to train/practise (*Brit*) *or* practice (*US*) for sth

Training ['trɛːnɪŋ, 'trɛː-] NT **-s, -s** training *no pl*; (= *Fitnesstraining*) workout; (*fig:* = *Übung*) practice; **er geht jeden Abend zum** ~ he goes for a workout every evening; **ein 2-stündiges** ~ a 2-hour training session; (= *Fitnesstraining*) a 2-hour workout; **im** ~ **stehen** to be in training; **durch regelmäßiges** ~ **lernen die Schüler ...** by regular practice the pupils learn ...

Trainings-: Trainingsanzug M tracksuit; **Trainingshose** F tracksuit trousers *pl* (*esp Brit*) *or* pants *pl* (*esp US*); **Trainingsjacke** F tracksuit top; **Trainingslager** NT training camp; **Trainingsschuh** M training shoe

Trakt [trakt] M **-(e)s, -e** (= *Gebäudeteil*) section; (= *Flügel*) wing; (*von Autobahn*) stretch

traktandieren [traktan'diːrən], *ptp* **traktandiert** VT (*Sw:* = *auf die Tagesordnung setzen*) to put on the agenda; **traktandiert sein** to be on the agenda

traktieren [trak'tiːrən], *ptp* **traktiert** VT (*inf*) (= *schlecht behandeln*) to maltreat; (= *quälen*) *kleine Schwester, Tier etc* to torment; **jdn mit Vorwürfen** ~ to keep on at sb (*inf*); **er hat ihn mit Fäusten/Füßen/Schlägen traktiert** he punched/kicked/hit him

Traktor ['traktoːɐ] M **-s, Traktoren** [-'toːrən] tractor

trällern ['trɛlɐn] VTI to warble; (*Vogel auch*) to trill; **vor sich hin** ~ to warble away to oneself

Tram [tram] F **-, -s** (*dial, Sw*), **Trambahn** F (*S Ger*) = **Straßenbahn**

Trampel ['trampl] M *or* NT **-s, -** *or* f **-, -n** clumsy clot (*inf*); ~ **vom Land** (country) bumpkin

trampeln ['trampln] **1** VI **(a)** (= *mit den Füßen stampfen*) to stamp; **die Zuschauer haben getrampelt** the audience stamped their feet **(b)** AUX SEIN (= *schwerfällig gehen*) to stamp along **2** VT **(a)** (= *mit Füßen bearbeiten*) *Weg* to trample; **jdn zu Tode** ~ to trample sb to death **(b)** (= *abschütteln*) to stamp (*von* from)

Trampel-: Trampelpfad M track; **Trampeltier** NT **(a)** (*Zool*) (Bactrian) camel **(b)** (*inf*) clumsy oaf (*inf*)

trampen ['trɛmpn, 'tram-] VI AUX SEIN to hitchhike

Tramper ['trɛmpɐ] M **-s, -**, **Tramperin** [-ərɪn] F **-, -nen** hitchhiker

Trampolin [trampo'liːn, 'tram-] NT **-s, -e** trampoline

Tramway ['tramvai] F **-, -s** (*Aus*) = **Straßenbahn**

Tran [traːn] M **-(e)s, -e** **(a)** (*von Fischen*) train oil **(b)** (*inf*) **im ~ dop(e)y** (*inf*); (= *leicht betrunken*) tipsy; **ich lief wie im ~ durch die Gegend** I was running around in a dream; **das habe ich im ~ ganz vergessen** it completely slipped my mind

Trance ['trãːsə)] F **-, -n** trance

Tranche ['trãːʃ(ə)] F **-, -n** **(a)** (*St Ex*) tranche of a bond issue; (= *Anleihe*) quota share **(b)** (= *Abschnitt*) tranche

Tranchierbesteck [trã'ʃiːɐ-] NT carving set

tranchieren [trã'ʃiːrən], *ptp* **tranchiert** VT to carve

Träne ['trɛːnə] F **-, -n** tear; (= *einzelne ~*) tear(drop); **unter ~n gestand er seine Schuld/Liebe** in tears he confessed his guilt/love; **ihm kamen die ~n** tears welled (up) in his eyes; **mir kommen die ~n** (*iro*) my heart bleeds for him/her *etc*; ~**n lachen** to laugh till one cries; **die Sache/der Mann ist keine ~ wert** the matter/man isn't worth crying over; **bittere ~n weinen** to shed bitter tears; **jdm/sich die ~n trocknen** *or* **abwischen** to wipe away sb's/one's tears

tränen ['trɛːnən] VI to water

Tränen-: Tränendrüse F lachrymal gland; **der Film drückt sehr auf die ~n** the film is a real tear-jerker (*inf*); **Tränengas** NT tear gas; **Tränensack** M lachrymal sac

Tranfunsel F, **Tranfunzel** F (*inf*) slowcoach (*Brit inf*), slowpoke (*US inf*)

tranig ['traːnɪç] **1** ADJ like train oil; (*inf*) sluggish **2** ADV **schmecken** oily; (*inf*) **sich bewegen** sluggishly; *fahren, arbeiten* slowly

trank PRET *von* **trinken**

Trans- IN CPDS trans-

Transaktion [translak'tsioːn] F transaction

transatlantisch [translat'lantɪʃ] ADJ transatlantic

Transchier- (*Aus*) = **Tranchier-**

Transfer [trans'feːɐ] M **-s, -s** transfer; (*Psych*) transference

Transformation [transfɔrma'tsioːn] F transformation

Transformator [transfɔr'maːtoːɐ] M **-s, Transformatoren** [-'toːrən] transformer

Transformatorenhäuschen NT transformer

Transfusion [transfu'zioːn] F transfusion

transgen [trans'geːn] ADJ transgenic

Transistor [tran'zɪstoːɐ] M **-s, Transistoren** [-'toːrən] transistor

Transistorradio NT transistor (radio)

Transit ['tranziːt, tran'zɪt, 'tranzɪt] M **-s, -e** transit

Transit-: Transitabkommen NT transit agreement; **Transithalle** F (*Aviat*) transit area

transitiv ['tranziːtiːf, tranzi'tiːf] (*Gram*) **1** ADJ transitive **2** ADV **gebrauchen** transitively

Transit-: Transitraum M (*Aviat*) transit lounge; **Transitverkehr** M transit traffic; (= *Transithandel*) transit trade; **Passagiere im ~ transit passengers** *pl*

transkribieren [transkri'biːrən], *ptp* **transkribiert** VT to transcribe; (*Mus*) to arrange

Transmission [transmɪ'sioːn] F (*Mech*) transmission

transparent [transpa'rɛnt] ADJ transparent

Transparent [transpa'rɛnt] NT **-(e)s, -e** (= *Reklameschild etc*) neon sign; (= *Durchscheinbild*) transparency; (= *Spruchband*) banner

Transparenz [transpa'rɛnts] F **-, NO PL** transparency; **sie fordern mehr ~ bei allen Vorgängen in der Politik** they demand more openness in political matters

Transplantat [transplan'taːt] NT **-(e)s, -e** (*Haut*) graft; (*Organ*) transplant

Transplantation [transplanta'tsio:n] F **-, -en (a)** (*Med*) transplant; (*von Haut*) graft; (*Vorgang*) transplantation; (*von Haut*) grafting **(b)** (*Bot*) grafting

transplantieren [transplan'ti:rən], *ptp* **transplantiert** VTI **(a)** (*Med*) *Organ, Gen* to transplant; *Haut* to graft **(b)** (*Bot*) to graft

Transport [trans'pɔrt] M **-(e)s, -e** transport; **ein ~ auf dem Landweg** road transport; **ein ~ des Kranken ist ausgeschlossen** moving the patient is out of the question; **beim** *or* **auf dem ~ beschädigte/verloren gegangene Waren** goods damaged/lost in transit

transportabel [transpɔr'ta:bl] ADJ *Fernseher, Computer etc* portable

Transport-: Transportband [-bant] NT, *pl* **-bänder** conveyor belt; **Transportbehälter** M container

Transporter [trans'pɔrtɐ] M **-s, -** (*Schiff*) cargo ship; (*Flugzeug*) transport plane; (*Auto*) van; (= *Autotransporter*) transporter

Transport-: transportfähig ADJ *Patient* moveable; **Transportflugzeug** NT transport plane

transportieren [transpɔr'ti:rən], *ptp* **transportiert** VT to transport; *Patienten* to move; *Film* to wind on

Transport-: Transportkosten PL carriage *sing*; **Transportmittel** NT means *sing* of transport; **Transportunternehmen** NT haulier (*Brit*), hauler (*US*); **Transportwesen** NT transport

Transrapid® [ˌtransra'pi:t] M (*Rail*) maglev (train)

Transsexuelle(r) [transzɛ'ksuɐlə] MF DECL AS ADJ transsexual

Transvestit [transvɛs'ti:t] M **-en, -en** transvestite

Trapez [tra'pe:ts] NT **-es, -e (a)** (*Math*) trapezium **(b)** (*von Artisten*) trapeze

Trapez-: Trapezakt M trapeze act; **trapezförmig** ADJ trapeziform; **Trapezkünstler(in)** M(F) trapeze artist

trappeln ['trapln] VI AUX SEIN to clatter; (*Pony*) to clip-clop

Trara [tra'ra:] NT **-s, -s** (*von Horn*) tantara; (*fig inf*) hullabaloo (*inf*) (*um* about)

Trassant [tra'sant] M **-en, -en, Trassantin** [-'santin] F **-, -nen** (*Fin*) drawer

Trassat [tra'sa:t] M **-en, -en, Trassatin** [-'sa:tɪn] M **-, -nen** (*Fin*) drawee

Trasse ['trasə] F **-, -n** (*Surv*) marked-out route

Trassenführung F route

trat PRET *von* **treten**

Tratsch [tra:tʃ] M **-(e)s**, NO PL (*inf*) gossip

tratschen ['tra:tʃn] VI (*inf*) to gossip

Tratscherei [tra:tʃə'rai] F **-, -en** (*inf*) gossip(ing) *no pl*

Tratte ['tratə] F **-, -n** (*Fin*) draft

Traualtar M altar

Traube ['traubə] F **-, -n** (*einzelne Beere*) grape; (*ganze Frucht*) bunch of grapes; (= *Blütenstand*) raceme (*spec*); (*fig*) (*von Bienen*) cluster; (= *Menschentraube*) bunch; **~n** (*Fruchtart*) grapes

Trauben-: Traubenlese F grape harvest; **Traubensaft** M grape juice; **Traubenzucker** M dextrose

trauen ['trauən] **1** VI +DAT to trust; **einer Sache** (*dat*) **nicht ~ to** be wary of sth; **ich traute meinen Augen/Ohren nicht** I couldn't believe my eyes/ears; **ich traue dem Frieden nicht** (I think) there must be something afoot **2** VR to dare; **sich** (*acc or* (*rare*) *dat*) **~, etw zu tun** to dare (to) do sth; **ich trau mich nicht** I daren't; **sich auf die Straße/nach Hause/zum Chef ~** to dare to go out/home/to one's boss **3** VT to marry; **sich standesamtlich/kirchlich ~ lassen** to get married in a registry office (*Brit*) *or* in a civil ceremony/in church

Trauer ['trauɐ] F **-**, NO PL mourning; (= *Schmerz, Leid*) sorrow, grief; **~ haben/tragen** to be in mourning

Trauer-: Traueranzeige F obituary; **Trauerfall** M bereavement; **Trauermarsch** M funeral march

trauern ['trauɐn] VI to mourn (*um jdn* (for) sb, *um etw* sth); (= *Trauerkleidung tragen*) to be in mourning; **die ~den Hinterbliebenen** his/her bereaved family

Trauer-: Trauerspiel NT tragedy; (*fig inf*) fiasco; **es ist ein ~ mit ihm** he's really pathetic; **es ist ein ~ mit dem Projekt** the project is in bad shape; **Trauerweide** F weeping willow

Traufe ['traufə] F **-, -n** eaves *pl*

träufeln ['trɔyfln] VT to dribble

Traum [traum] M **-(e)s, Träume** ['trɔymə] (*lit, fig*) dream; **es war immer sein ~, ein großes Haus zu besitzen** he had always dreamed of owning a large house; **aus der ~!, der ~ ist aus!** it's all over; **aus der ~ vom neuen Auto** that's put paid to your/my *etc* dreams of a new car; **der ~ meiner schlaflosen Nächte** (*hum inf*) the man/woman of my dreams

Trauma ['trauma] NT **-s, Traumen** *or* **-ta** [-mən, -ta] (*Med, Psych*) trauma; (*fig auch*) nightmare

traumatisch [trau'ma:tɪʃ] ADJ traumatic

traumatisieren [traumati'zi:rən], *ptp* **traumatisiert** VT to traumatize

Traumen PL *von* **Trauma**

träumen ['trɔymən] **1** VI to dream; **von jdm/etw ~** to dream about sb/sth; (= *sich ausmalen*) to dream of sb/sth; **vor sich hin ~, mit offenen Augen ~** to daydream; **das hätte ich mir nicht ~ lassen** I'd never have thought it possible **2** VT to dream; *Traum* to have; **etwas Schönes/Schreckliches ~ to** have a pleasant/an unpleasant dream

träumerisch ['trɔymərɪʃ] ADJ dreamy; (= *schwärmerisch*) wistful

Traum-: Traumfabrik F (*pej*) dream factory; **traumhaft 1** ADJ (= *fantastisch*) fantastic; (= *wie im Traum*) dreamlike **2** ADV (= *fantastisch*) fantastically; **~ aussehen** to look fantastic; **~ schönes Wetter** fantastic weather; **~ leere Strände** fantastic deserted beaches

Trauminet ['trauminɛt] M **-s, -e** (*Aus inf*) coward

Traum-: Traumpaar NT perfect couple; **Traumtänzer(in)** M(F) dreamer; **traumwandlerisch** [-vandlərɪʃ] **1** ADJ somnambulistic; **mit ~er Sicherheit** with instinctive certainty **2** ADV **~ sicher** instinctively certain

traurig ['trauriç] **1** ADJ sad; *Leistung, Erfolg, Rekord* pathetic; *Wetter* miserable; *Berühmtheit* notorious; **die ~e Bilanz** the tragic toll; **das ist doch ~, was er da geleistet hat** what he's done is pathetic

2 ADV sadly; (= *tief betrübt*) sorrowfully; **mit meinen Finanzen/ der Wirtschaft sieht es sehr ~ aus** my finances are/the economy is in a very sorry state; **~, ~ dear, dear; wie sieht es damit aus? – ~(, ~)** what are the prospects for that? – pretty bad; **um meine Zukunft sieht es ~ aus** my future doesn't look too bright

Traurigkeit F **-, -en** sadness; **allgemeine ~** a general feeling of sadness

Trauung ['trauʊŋ] F **-, -en** wedding

Trauzeuge M, **Trauzeugin** F witness (*at marriage ceremony*)

Travestie [travɛs'ti:] F **-, -n** [-'ti:ən] travesty

Treber ['tre:bɐ] PL (= *Biertreber*) spent hops *pl* (*Brit*), hop pulp (*US*); (= *Weintreber*) marc *sing*; (= *Fruchttreber*) pomace *sing*

Treck [trɛk] M **-s, -s** trek; (= *Leute*) train; (= *Wagen etc*) wagon train

Trecking ['trɛkɪŋ] NT **-s**, NO PL *siehe* **Trekking**

Treff M **-s, -s** (*inf*) (= *Treffen*) meeting; (= *~punkt*) haunt, meeting place

treffen ['trɛfn], *pret* **traf** [tra:f], *ptp* **getroffen** [gə'trɔfn] **1** VT **(a)** (*durch Schlag, Schuss etc*) to hit (*an/in +dat* on, *in +acc* in); (*Unglück*) to strike; **auf dem Foto bist du gut getroffen** (*inf*) that's a good photo of you **(b)** (*fig*: = *kränken*) to hurt **(c)** (= *betreffen*) **es trifft immer die Falschen** it's always the wrong people who are affected; **ihn trifft keine Schuld** he's not to blame **(d)** (= *finden*) to hit upon; (*lit, fig*) *Ton* to hit **(e)** (= *jdm begegnen, mit jdm zusammenkommen*) to meet; (= *antreffen*) to find **(f) es gut/schlecht ~** to be fortunate/unlucky (*mit* with); **es mit dem Wetter/der Unterkunft gut/schlecht ~** to have good/ bad weather/accommodation; **ich hätte es schlechter ~ können** it could have been worse **(g)** *Vorbereitungen, Anstalten etc* to make; *Vereinbarung* to reach; *Entscheidung, Vorsorge, Maßnahmen* to take **2** VI **(a)** (*Schlag, Schuss etc*) to hit; **der Schuss/er hat getroffen** the shot/he hit it/him *etc*; **tödlich getroffen** (*von Schuss, Pfeil etc*) fatally wounded; **nicht ~ to** miss; **gut/schlecht ~ to** aim well/badly; **getroffen!** a hit **(b)** AUX SEIN (= *stoßen*) **auf jdn/etw ~ to** meet sb/sth **(c)** (= *verletzen*) to hurt; **sich getroffen fühlen** to feel hurt; (= *auf sich beziehen*) to take it personally **3** VR (= *zusammentreffen*) to meet

4 VR IMPERS **es trifft sich, dass ...** it (just) happens that ...; **das trifft gut/schlecht, dass ...** it is convenient/inconvenient that ...

Treffen ['trefn] NT **-s, -** meeting; (*Sport, Mil*) encounter

treffend 1 ADJ *Beispiel, Bemerkung* apt; *Ähnlichkeit* striking **2** ADV aptly; **~ bemerken** to remark aptly; **etw ~ darstellen** to describe sth perfectly

Treffer ['trefe] M **-s, -** hit; (= *Tor*) goal; (*fig*) (= *Erfolg*) hit; (= *Gewinnlos*) winner; **das Geschenk/das Auto war ein ~ the** present/car was just right; **einen ~ erzielen** or **landen** (*inf*) to score a hit; (*Ftbl*) to score a goal

Treff-: Treffpunkt M meeting place; **einen ~ ausmachen** to arrange where or somewhere to meet; **treffsicher** ADJ *Stürmer etc* accurate; (*fig*) *Bemerkung* apt; *Urteil* sound

Treibeis NT drift ice

treiben ['traibn], *pret* **trieb** [tri:p], *ptp* **getrieben** [gə'tri:bn] **1** VT **(a)** (*lit, fig*) to drive; (*fig*: = *drängen*) to rush; (= *antreiben*) to push; **jdn zum** or **in den Wahnsinn/zur** or **in die Verzweiflung/ zum** or **in den Selbstmord ~** to drive sb mad/to despair/to (commit) suicide; **jdn zur Eile/Arbeit ~** to make sb hurry (up)/work; **jdn zum Äußersten ~** to push sb too far; **die Preise (in die Höhe) ~** to push prices up; **die ~de Kraft bei etw sein** to be the driving force behind sth **(b)** (= *Reaktion erzeugen*) to bring; **jdm den Schweiß/das Blut ins Gesicht ~** to make sb sweat/blush **(c)** (= *einschlagen*) *Nagel, Pfahl etc* to drive **(d)** (= *ausüben, betreiben*) *Handel, Geschäfte, Sport* to do; *Studien, Politik* to pursue; *Gewerbe* to carry on; *Schabernack, Unfug, Unsinn* to be up to; *Spaß* to have; *Aufwand* to create; *Unzucht* to commit; **was treibst du?** what are you up to?; **Missbrauch mit etw ~** to abuse sth; **Handel mit etw/jdm ~** to trade in sth/with sb; **Wucher ~** to profiteer; **wenn du es weiter so treibst ...** if you carry on like that ...; **es toll ~** to have a wild time; **es zu toll ~** to overdo it; **es schlimm ~** to behave badly; **es zu bunt** or **weit ~** to go too far; **er treibt es noch so weit, dass er hinausgeworfen wird** if he goes on like that, he'll get thrown out; **es mit jdm ~** (*inf*) to have sex with sb **(e)** (= *hervorbringen*) *Blüten, Knospen etc* to sprout; (*im Treibhaus*) to force **2** VI **(a)** AUX SEIN (= *sich fortbewegen*) to drift; **sich ~ lassen** (*lit, fig*) to drift; **die Dinge ~ lassen** to let things go **(b)** (= *wachsen*) to sprout **(c)** (*Bier, Kaffee, Medizin etc*) to have a diuretic effect

Treiben ['traibn] NT **-s, -** (a) (= *Getriebe*) hustle and bustle; (*von Schneeflocken*) swirling; **ich beobachte dein ~ schon lange** I've been watching what you've been (getting) up to for a long time **(b)** = **Treibjagd**

Treiber[1] ['traibe] M **-s, -** (*Comput*) driver

Treiber[2] ['traibe] M **-s, -**, **Treiberin** [-ərɪn] F **-, -nen** (= *Viehtreiber*) drover; (*Hunt*) beater

Treibgas NT (*bei Sprühdosen*) propellant

Treibhaus NT hothouse

Treibhaus-: Treibhauseffekt M (*Met*) greenhouse effect; **Treibhausgas** NT greenhouse gas

Treib-: Treibjagd F battue (*spec*); **Treibmittel** NT (*in Sprühdosen*) propellant; (*Cook*) raising agent; **Treibnetz** NT drift net; **Treibsand** M quicksand; **Treibstoff** M fuel

Trekking ['trekɪŋ] NT **-s**, NO PL trekking

Trekkingrad NT hybrid bike

Trema ['tre:ma] NT **-s, -s** or **-ta** [-ta] dieresis

Trend [trent] M **-s, -s** trend; **voll im ~ liegen** to follow the trend

Trend-: Trendscout ['trentskaut] M **-(s), -s** trend spotter; **Trendwende** F new trend

trennbar ADJ separable

trennen ['trenən] **1** VT **(a)** to separate (*von* from); (*Tod*) to take away (*von* from); *Kopf, Glied etc* to sever; (= *abmachen*) to detach (*von* from); *Partner, Freunde* to split up; *Begriffe* to differentiate (between); (*nach Rasse, Geschlecht*) to segregate; **etw in zwei Hälften ~** to divide sth into two halves; **voneinander getrennt werden** to be separated; **uns trennt zu vieles** we have too little in common; **jetzt kann uns nichts mehr ~** now nothing can ever come between us; *siehe auch* **getrennt** **(b)** (= *in Bestandteile zerlegen, Ling*) *Wort* to divide **2** VR **(a)** (= *auseinander gehen*) to separate; (= *Abschied nehmen*) to part; **sich von jdm/der Firma ~** to leave sb/the

firm; **die Firma trennte sich von ihrem Geschäftsführer** the firm parted company with its managing director; **die zwei Mannschaften trennten sich 2:0** the final score was 2-0; **sich von etw ~** to part with sth; **er konnte sich davon nicht ~** he couldn't bear to part with it; (*von Plan*) he couldn't give it up; (*von Anblick*) he couldn't take his eyes off it **(b)** (= *sich teilen*) (*Wege, Flüsse*) to divide; **hier ~ sich unsere Wege** (*fig*) now we must go our separate ways **3** VI (*zwischen Begriffen*) to draw a distinction

Trenn-: trennscharf ADJ **~ sein** to have good selectivity; **Trennschärfe** F selectivity

Trennung ['trenʊŋ] F **-, -en** (a) (= *Abschied*) parting **(b)** (= *Getrenntwerden, Getrenntsein*) separation; (*in Teile*) (*von Wort*) division; (*von Begriffen*) distinction; (*von Sender*) selectivity; (= *Rassentrennung, Geschlechtertrennung*) segregation; **die Partner entschlossen sich zu einer ~** the partners decided to split up; **in ~ leben** to be separated

Trennwand F partition (wall)

Trennzeichen NT hyphen

Treppe ['trepə] F **-, -n** (a) (= *Aufgang*) (flight of) stairs *pl*; (*im Freien*) (flight of) steps *pl*; **eine ~** a staircase **(b)** (*inf*: = *Stufe*) step; **~n steigen** to climb stairs

Treppen-: Treppenabsatz M half landing; **Treppengeländer** NT banister; **Treppenhaus** NT stairwell; **im ~** on the stairs

Tresen ['tre:zn] M **-s, -** (= *Theke*) bar; (= *Ladentisch*) counter

Tresor [tre'zo:ɐ] M **-s, -e** (= *Raum*) strongroom; (= *Schrank*) safe

Trester ['treste] PL (= *Biertrester*) spent hops *pl* (*Brit*), hop pulp (*US*); (= *Weintrester*) marc *sing*; (= *Fruchttrester*) pomace *sing*

Tret-: Tretauto NT pedal car; **Tretboot** NT pedal boat, pedalo (*Brit*); **Treteimer** M pedal bin

treten ['tre:tn], *pret* **trat** [tra:t], *ptp* **getreten** [gə'tre:tn] **1** VI **(a)** (= *ausschlagen, mit Fuß anstoßen*) to kick (*gegen etw* sth, *nach* out at) **(b)** AUX SEIN (*mit Raumangabe*) to step; **in den Vordergrund/ Hintergrund ~** to step forward/back; (*fig*) to come to the forefront/to recede into the background; **an jds Stelle** (*acc*) **~** to take sb's place **(c)** AUX SEIN or HABEN (*in Loch, Pfütze, auf Gegenstand etc*) to step; **jdm auf die Füße ~** (*fig*) to tread (*esp Brit*) or step on sb's toes; **jdm auf den Schlips** (*inf*) or **Schwanz** (*sl*) **~** to tread on sb's toes; **sich auf den Schlips** (*inf*) or **Schwanz** (*sl*) **getreten fühlen** to feel offended **(d)** AUX SEIN or HABEN (= *betätigen*) **in die Pedale ~** to pedal hard; **aufs Gas(pedal) ~** (= *Pedal betätigen*) to press the accelerator; (= *schnell fahren*) to put one's foot down (*inf*); **auf die Bremse ~** to brake **(e)** AUX SEIN (= *beginnen*) to start, to begin; (= *eintreten*) to enter; **Wasser trat aus allen Ritzen und Fugen** water was coming out of every nook and cranny; **der Schweiß trat ihm auf die Stirn** sweat appeared on his forehead; **Tränen traten ihr in die Augen** tears came to her eyes; **der Fluss trat über die Ufer** the river overflowed its banks; **in den Ruhestand ~** to retire; **in den Streik** or **Ausstand ~** to go on strike; **in den Staatsdienst/Stand der Ehe** or **Ehestand ~** to enter the civil service/into the state of matrimony; **mit jdm in Verbindung ~** to get in touch with sb **2** VT **(a)** (= *einen Fußtritt geben, stoßen*) to kick; (*Sport*) *Ecke, Freistoß* to take; **jdn mit dem Fuß ~** to kick sb; **sich** (*dat*) **in den Hintern ~** (*fig inf*) to kick oneself **(b)** (= *trampeln*) *Pfad, Weg, Bahn* to tread; **sich** (*dat*) **einen Splitter in den Fuß ~** to get a splinter in one's foot **(c)** (*fig*) (= *schlecht behandeln*) to shove around (*inf*); **jdn ~** (*inf*: = *antreiben*) to get at sb

Tret-: Tretmine F (*Mil*) (antipersonnel) mine; **Tretroller** M scooter

treu [trɔy] **1** ADJ *Freund, Sohn, Kunde etc* loyal; *Seele auch, Hund, Gatte etc* faithful; (= *~herzig*) trusting; *Miene* innocent; **jdm sein/bleiben** to be/remain faithful to sb; **sich** (*dat*) **selbst ~ bleiben** to be true to oneself; **seinen Grundsätzen ~ bleiben** to stick to one's principles; **der Erfolg ist ihr ~ geblieben** success kept coming her way; **das Glück ist ihr ~ geblieben** her luck held (out) **2** ADV faithfully; *dienen auch* loyally; *sorgen* devotedly; (= *~herzig*) trustingly; *ansehen* innocently; **jdm ~ ergeben sein** to be loyally devoted to sb; **~ sorgend** devoted; **~ und brav** (*Erwachsener*) dutifully; (*Kind*) like a good boy/girl

treudoof (*inf*) **1** ADJ stupidly naive **2** ADV stupidly and naively

Treue ['trɔyə] F -, NO PL (*von Freund, Sohn, Kunde etc*) loyalty; (*von Hund*) faithfulness; (= *eheliche* ~) fidelity; **jdm die ~ halten** to keep faith with sb; *Ehegatten etc* to remain faithful to sb; **auf Treu und Glauben** in good faith

treuergeben ADJ *siehe* **treu**

Treuhand F, NO PL (a) trust (b) = **Treuhandanstalt**

TREUHANDANSTALT

The **Treuhandanstalt**, also more informally known as the **Treuhand**, was an organization which, from 1990 to 1994, took over the state-owned firms of the former East Germany after re-unification and sought to bring them into the private sector. Many of the firms were actually closed down by the **Treuhandanstalt**, since the machinery was out of date and the company structure could not cope with the changed circumstances. The **Treuhandanstalt** was wound up in 1994 in accordance with the Unification Treaty, but since then various successor organizations have carried on its work.

Treuhänder [-hɛndɐ] M -s, -, **Treuhänderin** [-ərɪn] F -, -nen trustee

Treuhänderschaft F -, -en trusteeship

Treuhand-: Treuhandgesellschaft F trust company; **Treuhandschaft** F -, -en trusteeship

Treu-: treuherzig **1** ADJ innocent, trusting **2** ADV innocently, trustingly; **treulos** **1** ADJ disloyal; **du ~es Stück** (*inf*) you wretch **2** ADV disloyally; **~ an jdm handeln** to fail sb; **Treulosigkeit** F -, NO PL disloyalty; **treusorgend** ADJ ATTR *siehe* **treu**

Triangel ['tri:aŋl] M or (AUS) NT -s, - triangle

Triathlon ['tri:atlɔn] M -, -e (*Sport*) triathlon

Tribüne [tri'by:nə] F -, -n (= *Rednertribüne*) platform; (= *Zuschauertribüne*) stand; (= *Haupttribüne*) grandstand

Trichine [tri'çi:nə] F -, -n trichina

Trichter ['trɪçtɐ] M -s, - funnel; (= *Schüttgutbehälter*) hopper; (= *Bombentrichter*) crater; (*von Grammofon*) horn; (*von Trompete, Megafon etc*) bell; (*von Hörgerät*) trumpet; (*von Lautsprecher*) cone

trichterförmig ADJ funnel-shaped

Trick [trɪk] M -s, -s or (rare) -e trick; (*betrügerisch auch, raffiniert*) ploy; (= *Tipp, Rat*) tip; **ein fauler/gemeiner ~** a dirty trick; **keine faulen ~s!** no funny business! (*inf*); **das ist der ganze ~** that's all there is to it; **den ~ raushaben, wie man etw macht** (*inf*) to have got the knack of doing sth; **jdm einen ~ verraten** to give sb a tip

Trick-: Trickbetrüger(in) M(F), **Trickdieb(in)** M(F) confidence trickster; **Trickfilm** M trick film; (= *Zeichentrickfilm*) cartoon (film); **trickreich** (*inf*) ADJ tricky; (= *raffiniert*) clever **2** ADV *erschwindeln, abgaunern* through various tricks

tricksen ['trɪksn] (*inf*) **1** VI to fiddle (*inf*); (*Sport*) to feint **2** VT to fiddle (*inf*)

trieb PRET *von* **treiben**

Trieb [tri:p] M -(e)s, -e [-bə] (a) (= *Naturtrieb*) (*auch Psych*) drive; (= *Drang*) urge; (= *Verlangen*) desire; (= *Neigung, Hang*) inclination; (= *Selbsterhaltungstrieb, Fortpflanzungstrieb*) instinct (b) (*Bot*) shoot (c) (*Tech*) drive

Trieb-: triebartig ADJ ATTR *Verhalten* instinctive; (*von Sexualverbrecher etc*) compulsive; **Triebfeder** F (*fig*) motivating force (+*gen* behind); **Triebkraft** F (*Mech*) motive power; (*Bot*) germinating power; (*fig*) driving force; **Triebrad** NT driving wheel (*Brit*), gear wheel; **Triebtäter(in)** M(F), **Triebverbrecher(in)** M(F) sexual offender; **Triebwagen** M (*Rail*) railcar; **Triebwerk** NT power plant; (*in Uhr*) mechanism

Trief-: Triefauge NT (*Med*) bleary eye; **~n** (*pej*) watery eyes; (*von Mensch*) sheeplike eyes; **triefäugig** **1** ADJ watery-eyed **2** ADV **er schaute mich ~ an** (*pej*) he looked at me with dumb devotion

triefen ['tri:fn], *pret* **triefte** or (*geh*) **troff** ['tri:ftə, trɔf], *ptp* **getrieft** or (*rare*) **getroffen** [gə'tri:ft, gə'trɔfn] VI to be dripping wet; (*Nase*) to run; (*Auge*) to water; **~ vor** to be dripping with; (*fig pej*) to gush with; **~d vor Nässe, ~d nass** dripping wet; **~d** soaking (wet)

Triefnase F (*inf*) runny nose (*inf*)

trifft [trɪft] 3. PERS SING PRES *von* **treffen**

triftig ['trɪftɪç] **1** ADJ convincing **2** ADV convincingly

Trigonometrie [trigonome'tri:] F -, NO PL trigonometry

trigonometrisch [trigono'me:trɪʃ] ADJ trigonometric(al)

Trikot[1] [tri'ko:, 'triko] M or NT -s, NO PL (= ~*stoff*) cotton jersey

Trikot[2] NT -s, -s (= *Hemd*) shirt; **das gelbe ~** (*bei Tour de France*) the yellow jersey

Trikotwerbung [tri'ko:-] F shirt advertising

Triller ['trɪlɐ] M -s, - trill

trillern ['trɪlɐn] VTI to warble

Trillerpfeife F (pea) whistle

Trillion [trɪ'lio:n] F -, -en trillion (*Brit*), quintillion (*US*)

Trimaran [trima'ra:n] M or NT -s, -e (*Naut*) trimaran

Trimester [tri'mɛstɐ] NT -s, - term

Trimm-dich-Pfad M keep-fit trail

trimmen ['trɪmən] **1** VT *Hund, Schiff, Flugzeug* to trim; (*inf*) *Mensch, Tier* to teach, to train; *Funkgerät* to tune; **den Motor/das Auto auf Höchstleistung ~** (*inf*) to soup up the engine/car (*inf*); **etw auf alt ~** to make sth look old; **auf alt getrimmt** done up to look old **2** VR to do keep-fit (exercises); **trimm dich durch Sport** keep fit with sport

Trink-: trinkbar ADJ drinkable; **Trinkei** NT new-laid egg

trinken ['trɪŋkn], *pret* **trank** [traŋk], *ptp* **getrunken** [gə'trʊŋkn] **1** VT to drink; **alles/eine Flasche leer ~** to finish off all the drink/a bottle; **ich habe nichts zu ~ im Haus** I haven't any drink in the house; **er trinkt gern einen** (*inf*) he likes his drink; **(schnell) einen ~ gehen** (*inf*) to go for a (quick) drink **2** VI to drink; **jdm zu ~ geben** to give sb something to drink; **lass mich mal ~** let me have a drink; **auf jds Wohl/jdn/etw ~** to drink sb's health/to sb/to sth; **er trinkt** (= *ist Alkoholiker*) he's a drinker

3 VR **sich voll** or **satt ~** to drink one's fill

Trinker ['trɪŋkɐ] M -s, -, **Trinkerin** [-ərɪn] F -, -nen drinker; (= *Alkoholiker*) alcoholic

Trink-: trinkfest ADJ **so ~ bin ich nicht** I can't hold my drink (*Brit*) or liquor (*esp US*) very well; **seine ~en Freunde** his hard-drinking friends; **Trinkgeld** NT tip; **jdm ~ geben** to tip sb; **Trinkhalm** M drinking straw; **Trinkschokolade** F drinking chocolate; **Trinkwasser** NT, *pl* **-wässer** drinking water; **„kein ~"** "not for drinking"; **Trinkwasserversorgung** F provision of drinking water

Trio [tri:o] NT -s, -s trio

Trip [trɪp] M -s, -s (*inf*) trip

trippeln ['trɪpln] VI AUX HABEN or (*bei Richtungsangabe*) SEIN to trip (*esp Brit*), to skip; (*Kind, alte Dame*) to toddle; (*geziert*) to mince (*Brit*), to sashay (*esp US*); (*Boxer*) to dance around; (*Pferd*) to prance

Tripper ['trɪpɐ] M -s, - gonorrhoea *no art* (*Brit*), gonorrhea *no art* (*US*); **sich** (*dat*) **den ~ holen** (*inf*) to get a dose (of the clap) (*inf*)

trist [trɪst] ADJ dismal; *Farbe* dull

Tritium ['tri:tsiʊm] NT -s, NO PL (*abbr* **T**) tritium

tritt [trɪt] 3. PERS SING PRES *von* **treten**

Tritt [trɪt] M -(e)s, -e (a) (= *Schritt, Gang, Stufe*) step; **einen falschen ~ machen** to take a wrong step; **ich hörte ~e** I heard footsteps; **im ~ marschieren, ~ halten** to march in step (b) (= *Fußtritt*) kick; **jdm einen ~ geben** or **versetzen** to give sb a kick; (*fig*) (= *entlassen etc*) to kick sb out (*inf*); (*inf:* = *anstacheln*) to give sb a kick in the pants (*inf*); **einen ~ in den Hintern kriegen** (*inf*) to get a kick in the pants (*inf*); (*fig*) to get kicked out (*inf*)

(c) (= *Fußspur*) footprint; (*von Tier*) track

Tritt-: Trittbrett NT step; (*an Auto*) running board; (*an Nähmaschine*) treadle; **Trittbrettfahrer(in)** M(F) (*inf*) fare dodger; (*fig*) copycat (*inf*); **Trittleiter** F stepladder

Triumph [tri'ʊmf] M -(e)s, -e triumph; **im ~** in triumph; **~e feiern** to be very successful

Triumphbogen M triumphal arch

triumphieren [triʊm'fi:rən], *ptp* **triumphiert** VI (= *frohlocken*) to rejoice

triumphierend **1** ADJ triumphant **2** ADV triumphantly

trivial [tri'via:l] **1** ADJ trivial **2** ADV trivially; **sich ~ unterhalten** to have a trivial conversation

Trivialität [triviali'tɛ:t] F -, -en triviality; (= *triviale Bemerkung*) banality

Trivialliteratur F (*pej*) light fiction

trocken ['trɔkn] **1** ADJ dry; *Gedeck* without wine *etc*; **~er Dunst** (*Met*) haze; **~ werden** to dry; (*Brot*) to go or get dry; **auf dem**

Trockenen sitzen (*inf*) to be in a tight spot (*inf*) **2** ADV *aufbewahren, lagern* in a dry place; **sich ~ rasieren** to use an electric razor; **die Haare ~ schneiden** to cut one's/sb's hair dry; **die Gäste ~ sitzen lassen** to leave one's guests without a drink

Trocken-: Trockenblume F dried flower; **Trockendock** NT dry dock; **Trockenfutter** NT dried food; **Trockengebiet** NT arid region; **Trockengestell** NT drying rack; **Trockenhaube** F (salon) hairdryer; **Trockenheit** F -, -en (*lit, fig*) dryness; (= *Trockenperiode*) drought; **trockenlegen** VT SEP **(a)** *Sumpf, Gewässer* to drain **(b)** *Baby* to change; (*inf*) *Trinker* to dry out; **Trockenmilch** F dried milk; **Trockenrasierer** [-razi:rɐ] M **-s, -** (*inf*: = *Rasierapparat*) electric razor; **Trockenrasur** F dry shave; (= *das Rasieren*) shaving with an electric razor *no art*; **trockenreiben** VT SEP IRREG to rub dry; **Trockenzeit** F (= *Jahreszeit*) dry season

trocknen ['trɔknən] **1** VT to dry **2** VI AUX SEIN to dry

Trödel ['trø:dl] M **-s,** NO PL (*inf*) junk

Trödelei [trø:də'lai] F **-, -en** (*inf*) dawdling

trödeln ['trø:dln] VI to dawdle

Trödler ['trø:dlɐ] M **-s, -, Trödlerin** [-ərɪn] F **-, -nen (a)** (= *Händler*) junk dealer **(b)** (*inf*: = *langsamer Mensch*) slowcoach (*Brit inf*), slowpoke (*US inf*)

troff PRET *von* **triefen**

trog PRET *von* **trügen**

Trog [tro:k] M **-(e)s, ⁼e** ['trø:gə] trough; (= *Waschtrog*) tub

trojanisch [tro'ja:nɪʃ] ADJ Trojan; **Trojanisches Pferd** Trojan Horse

trollen ['trɔlən] VR (*inf*) to push off (*inf*)

Trommel ['trɔml] F **-, -n (a)** (*Mus*) drum **(b)** (*Tech*) (*in Maschine*) drum; (*in Revolver*) revolving breech

Trommel-: Trommelbremse F drum brake; **Trommelfell** NT eardrum; **da platzt einem ja das ~** (*fig*) the noise is earsplitting

trommeln ['trɔmln] **1** VI to drum; (*Regen*) to bear (down); **gegen die Tür ~** to bang on the door; **gegen die Brust ~** to beat one's chest; **mit den Fingern ~** to drum one's fingers; **der Regen trommelt gegen die Fensterscheiben** the rain is beating against the window panes **2** VT *Marsch, Lied* to play on the drum/drums, to drum; *Rhythmus* to beat out

Trommler ['trɔmlɐ] M **-s, -, Trommlerin** [-ərɪn] F **-, -nen** drummer

Trompete [trɔm'pe:tə] F **-, -n** trumpet

trompeten [trɔm'pe:tn] *ptp* **trompetet 1** VI to trumpet; (= *sich schnäuzen*) to blow one's nose loudly **2** VT *Marsch* to play on the trumpet

Trompeter [trɔm'pe:tɐ] M **-s, -, Trompeterin** [-ərɪn] F **-, -nen** trumpeter

Tropen ['tro:pn] PL tropics *pl*

Tropen- IN CPDS tropical; **Tropenanzug** M tropical suit; **Tropenhelm** M pith helmet; **Tropenkoller** M tropical madness; **Tropenkrankheit** F tropical disease

Tropf [trɔpf] M **-(e)s, ⁼e** ['trœpfə] (*inf*) **(a)** (= *Schelm*) rogue, rascal; **armer ~** poor devil **(b)** NO PL (= *Infusion*) drip (*inf*); **am ~ hängen** to be on a drip; (*fig inf: finanziell*) to be on a drip-feed

Tröpfchen- ** ['trœpfçən-]: **Tröpfcheninfektion F airborne infection; **tröpfchenweise** ADV in dribs and drabs

tröpfeln ['trœpfln] **1** VI **(a)** (*Leitung, Halm*) to drip; (*Nase*) to run **(b)** AUX SEIN (*Flüssigkeit*) to drip **2** VI IMPERS **es tröpfelt** it is spitting **3** VT to drip

tropfen ['trɔpfn] **1** VI to drip; (*Nase*) to run; **es tropft durch die Decke** there is water dripping through the ceiling; **es tropft aus der Leitung** the pipe is dripping **2** VT to drop, to drip

Tropfen ['trɔpfn] M **-s, - (a)** drop; (= *einzelner ~: an Kanne, Nase etc*) drip; (*inf*: = *kleine Menge*) drop; **ein guter** *or* **edler ~** (*inf*) a good wine; **bis auf den letzten ~** to the last drop; **ein ~ auf den heißen Stein** (*fig inf*) a drop in the ocean **(b)** Tropfen PL (= *Medizin*) drops *pl*

tropfenweise ADV drop by drop

Tropf-: Tropfinfusion F intravenous drip; **tropfnass** ['trɔpfnas] ADJ dripping wet; **Tropfstein** M dripstone; (*an der Decke*) stalactite; (*am Boden*) stalagmite; **Tropfsteinhöhle** F dripstone cave

Trophäe [tro'fɛ:ə] F **-, -n** trophy

tropisch ['tro:pɪʃ] **1** ADJ tropical **2** ADV tropically; **~ wuchernde** *or* **wachsende Vegetation** tropical growth

Trost [tro:st] M **-(e)s,** NO PL consolation; **jdm ~ zusprechen/ bringen** to console sb; **das Kind war ihr einziger ~** the child was her only comfort; **~ im Alkohol/in der Religion suchen** to seek solace in alcohol/religion; **zum ~ kann ich Ihnen sagen, dass ...** it may comfort you to know that ...; **das ist ein schwacher** *or* **schlechter ~** that's pretty cold comfort; **das ist ein schöner ~** (*iro*) some comfort that is!; **du bist wohl nicht ganz** *or* **recht bei ~!** (*inf*) you must be out of your mind!

trösten ['trø:stn] VT to comfort; **jdn/sich mit etw ~** to console sb/oneself with sth; **sich über etw** (*acc*) **~** to get over sth; **~ Sie sich!** never mind

tröstlich ['trø:stlɪç] ADJ comforting; **das ist ja sehr ~** (*iro*) that's some comfort

trostlos ADJ hopeless; *Jugend, Verhältnisse* miserable; (= *verzweifelt*) inconsolable; (= *öde, trist*) dreary; **~ langweilig** desperately boring

Trost-: Trostpflaster NT consolation; **als ~** by way of consolation; **Trostpreis** M consolation prize

Trott [trɔt] M **-(e)s,** NO PL (slow) trot; (*fig*) routine; **im ~** at a (slow) trot; **aus dem alten ~ herauskommen** to get out of one's rut

Trottel ['trɔtl] M **-s, -** (*inf*) idiot

trottelig ['trɔtəlɪç] (*inf*) **1** ADJ stupid **2** ADV stupidly

trotten ['trɔtn] VI AUX SEIN to trot along; (*Pferd*) to trot slowly

trotz [trɔts] PREP +GEN or (*INF*) +DAT in spite of, despite; **~ allem** *or* **alledem** in spite of everything

Trotz [trɔts] M **-es,** NO PL defiance; (= *trotziges Verhalten*) contrariness; **jdm/einer Sache zum ~** in defiance of sb/sth

Trotzalter NT defiant age; **sich im ~ befinden, im ~ sein** to be going through a defiant phase; **ins ~ kommen** to get to a defiant age

trotzdem ['trɔtsde:m, 'trɔts'de:m] **1** ADV nevertheless; **(und) ich mache das ~!** I'll do it all the same **2** CONJ (*strictly incorrect*) even though

trotzen ['trɔtsn] VI **(a)** +DAT to defy; *der Kälte, dem Klima etc* to withstand; **Wind und Wetter ~** to defy the elements **(b)** (= *trotzig sein*) to be awkward

trotzig ['trɔtsɪç] **1** ADJ defiant; *Kind etc* difficult; (= *widerspenstig*) contrary **2** ADV defiantly

Trotz-: Trotzkopf M (*inf*) (*Einstellung*) defiant streak; (*widerspenstig*) contrary streak; (*Mensch*) contrary so-and-so (*inf*); **trotzköpfig** ADJ *Kind* contrary; **Trotzreaktion** F act of defiance; **das war eine reine ~** he/she just reacted like that out of defiance

Troubleshooter ['trablʃu:tɐ] M **-s, -** troubleshooter

trüb [try:p], **trübe** ['try:bə] ADJ **(a)** (= *unklar*) *Flüssigkeit* cloudy; (= *glanzlos, matt*) *Glas, Augen, Himmel, Tag* dull; *Sonne, Mond, Licht* dim; **in ~en Wassern fischen, im Trüben fischen** (*inf*) to fish in troubled waters **(b)** (*fig*: = *bedrückend, unerfreulich*) cheerless; *Zeiten, Zukunft* bleak; *Stimmung, Gedanken, Aussichten, Vorahnung, Miene* gloomy; *Erfahrung* grim; **es sieht ~ aus** things are looking pretty bleak; **~e Tasse** (*inf*) drip (*inf*); (= *Spielverderber*) wet blanket (*inf*)

Trubel ['tru:bl] M **-s,** NO PL hurly-burly

trüben ['try:bn] **1** VT **(a)** *Flüssigkeit* to make cloudy; *Glas, Metall, Augen, Blick* to dull; *Himmel* to overcast; *Wasseroberfläche* to ruffle; **getrübt** *Flüssigkeit, Himmel* cloudy; *Spiegel, Metall* dull; *Verstand* dulled; *Stimmung, Laune* dampened **(b)** (*fig*) *Glück, Freude, Verhältnis, Bild* to spoil; *Beziehungen* to strain; *Laune* to dampen; *Bewusstsein, Verstand* to dull; *Erinnerung, Urteilsvermögen* to dim **2** VR (*Flüssigkeit*) to go cloudy; (*Spiegel, Metall*) to become dull; (*geh*) (*Verstand*) to become dulled; (*Augen*) to dim; (*Himmel*) to cloud over; (*fig*) (*Stimmung, Laune*) to be dampened; (*Beziehungen, Verhältnis*) to become strained; (*Glück, Freude*) to be marred; *siehe auch* **getrübt**

Trüb-: Trübsal ['try:pza:l] F **-,** NO PL (= *Stimmung*) sorrow; **~ blasen** (*inf*) to mope; **trübselig** ADJ gloomy; *Gegend* bleak; *Behausung* depressing; **Trübsinn** M, NO PL gloom; **trübsinnig** ADJ gloomy

Trübung ['try:bʊŋ] F **-, -en (a)** (*von Flüssigkeit*) clouding; (*von Glas, Metall*) dulling; (*von Himmel*) overcasting **(b)** (*fig*) (*von*

Glück, Freude, Verhältnis) spoiling; (*von Beziehungen*) straining; (*von Laune*) dampening

trudeln ['truːdln] VI AUX SEIN or HABEN (*Aviat*) to spin; (*fig*) to slide; **ins Trudeln kommen** or **geraten** to go into a spin; (*fig*) to go into a tailspin

True-Type-Schrift ['truːtaip-] F True Type font

trug PRET *von* **tragen**

trügen ['tryːgn], *pret* **trog** [troːk], *ptp* **getrogen** [gə'troːgn] **1** VT to deceive; **wenn mich nicht alles trügt** unless I am very much mistaken **2** VI to be deceptive

Truhe ['truːə] F **-, -n** chest

Trümmer ['trʏmɐ] PL rubble *sing*; (= *Ruinen*) (*fig: von Glück etc*) ruins *pl*; (*von Schiff, Flugzeug etc*) wreckage *sing*; (= *Überreste*) remnants *pl*; **in ~n liegen** to be in ruins; **in ~ gehen** to be ruined (*auch fig*); (*Schiff, Flugzeug*) to be wrecked

Trumpf [trʊmpf] M **-(e)s, ⁓e** ['trʏmpfə] (*Cards*) (= *~karte*) trump (card); (= *Farbe*) trumps *pl*; (*fig*) trump card; **noch einen ~ in der Hand haben** (*fig*) to have an ace up one's sleeve

Trumpfass NT ace of trumps

Trunken-: **Trunkenbold** ['trʊŋknbɔlt] M **-(e)s, -e** [-də] (*pej*) drunkard; **Trunkenheit** F **-,** NO PL intoxication; **~ am Steuer** drunk driving

Trunk-: **Trunksucht** F alcoholism; **trunksüchtig** ADJ alcoholic; **~ werden** to become an alcoholic

Trupp [trʊp] M **-s, -s** bunch; (= *Einheit*) group; (*Mil*) squad; (*esp beritten*) troop

Truppe ['trʊpə] F **-, -n** (a) NO PL (*Mil*) army; (= *Panzertruppe etc*) corps *sing*; **von der (ganz) schnellen ~ sein** (*inf*) to be a fast mover (*inf*); **nicht von der schnellen ~ sein** (*inf*) to be slow (b) **Truppen** PL troops (c) (= *Künstlertruppe*) troupe

Truppen-: **Truppenabzug** M withdrawal of troops; **Truppengattung** F corps *sing*; **Truppenübung** F field exercise; **Truppenübungsplatz** M military training area

Trust [trast] M **-(e)s, -s** or **-e** trust

Trut- ['truːt-]: **Truthahn** M turkey (cock); **Truthenne** F turkey (hen)

Tschad [tʃat, tʃaːt] M **- der ~** Chad

tschadisch ['tʃadɪʃ, 'tʃaːdɪʃ] ADJ Chad *attr*

Tschador [tʃa'doːɐ] M **-s, -s** chador

tschau [tʃau] INTERJ (*inf*) so long (*inf*)

Tscheche ['tʃɛçə] M **-n, -n**, **Tschechin** ['tʃɛçɪn] F **-, -nen** Czech

Tschechien ['tʃɛçiən] NT **-s** the Czech Republic

tschechisch ['tʃɛçɪʃ] ADJ Czech; **die Tschechische Republik** the Czech Republic

Tschechoslowakei [tʃɛçoslova'kai] F (*Hist*) **die ~** Czechoslovakia

tschechoslowakisch [tʃɛçoslo'vaːkɪʃ] ADJ (*Hist*) Czechoslovak(ian)

tschüs, tschüss [tʃʏs] INTERJ (*inf*) bye (*inf*), so long (*inf*)

Tsetsefliege ['tseːtse-, 'tsɛtse-] F tsetse fly

T-Shirt [tiːʃœrt, -ʃøːɐt] NT **-s, -s** T-shirt

T-Träger ['teː-] M T-bar

TU [teː'luː] F **-** ABBR *von* **technische Universität**

Tube ['tuːbə] F **-, -n** tube

Tuberkel [tu'bɛrkl] M **-s, -** or (*Aus auch*) f **-, -n** tubercle

tuberkulös [tubɛrku'løːs] ADJ tubercular

Tuberkulose [tubɛrku'loːzə] F **-, -n** tuberculosis

Tuberkulose-: **tuberkulosekrank** ADJ tubercular; **Tuberkulosekranke(r)** MF DECL AS ADJ TB sufferer

Tuch [tuːx] NT **-(e)s, ⁓er** ['tyːçɐ] (= *Stück Stoff, Tischtuch*) cloth; (= *Halstuch, Kopftuch*) scarf; (= *Schultertuch*) shawl; (= *Handtuch, Geschirrtuch*) towel; (*zum Abdecken von Möbeln*) dustsheet (*Brit*), dust cover; **das rote ~ (des Stierkämpfers)** the bullfighter's cape; **das wirkt wie ein rotes ~ auf ihn** it makes him see red

tüchtig ['tʏçtɪç] **1** ADJ (a) (= *fähig*) capable (*in +dat* at); (= *fleißig*) efficient; *Arbeiter* good (b) (*inf:* = *groß*) *Portion, Appetit, Esser* big; *Stoß, Schlag* hard; **eine ~e Tracht Prügel** a good hiding (*inf*); **eine ~e Portion Arroganz** *etc* a fair amount of arrogance *etc* **2** ADV (a) (= *fleißig, fest*) hard; *essen* heartily; **hilf ~ mit** lend us a hand (b) (*inf:* = *sehr*) good and proper (*inf*); **~ regnen** to pelt (*inf*);

jdm ~ die Meinung sagen to give sb a piece of one's mind; **~ ausschimpfen** to scold thoroughly; **~ zulangen** to tuck in (*inf*)

Tüchtigkeit F **-,** NO PL (= *Fähigkeit*) competence; (*von Arbeiter etc*) efficiency

Tücke ['tʏkə] F **-, -n** (a) (*no pl:* = *Bosheit*) malice; (= *böswillige Handlung*) malicious action (b) (= *Gefahr*) danger; (*von Krankheit*) perniciousness; **voller ~n stecken** to be difficult; (= *gefährlich*) to be dangerous or (*Berg, Fluss auch*) treacherous; **das ist die ~ des Objekts** these things have a will of their own!; **seine ~n haben** (*Maschine etc*) to be temperamental; (= *schwierig sein*) to be difficult; (= *gefährlich sein*) to be dangerous

tuckern ['tʊkɐn] VI AUX HABEN or (*bei Richtungsangabe*) SEIN to put-put

tückisch ['tʏkɪʃ] ADJ *Mensch, Blick, Lächeln* malicious; *Zufall* unhappy; *Berge, Strom etc* treacherous; *Krankheit* pernicious

tu(e) [tuː(ə)] IMPER SING *von* **tun**

Tuerei [tuːə'rai] F **-, -en** (*inf*) antics *pl*

Tüftelei [tʏftə'lai] F **-, -en** (*inf*) finicky job; **das ist eine ~** that's finicky

tüftelig ['tʏftəlɪç] ADJ (*inf*) finicky

tüfteln ['tʏftln] VI (*inf*) to puzzle; (= *basteln*) to fiddle about (*inf*); **an etw** (*dat*) **~** to fiddle about with sth; (*geistig*) to puzzle over sth

Tüftler ['tʏftlɐ] M **-s, -**, **Tüftlerin** [-ərɪn] F **-, -nen** (*inf*) *person who likes doing finicky things*; (= *Erfinder*) inventor

Tugend ['tuːgnt] F **-, -en** [-dən] virtue

Tugend-: **tugendhaft** **1** ADJ virtuous **2** ADV virtuously; **Tugendhaftigkeit** ['tuːgnthaftɪçkait] F **-,** NO PL virtuousness

Tüll [tʏl] M **-s, -e** tulle; (*für Gardinen*) net

Tülle ['tʏlə] F **-, -n** spout; (= *Spritzdüse*) pipe

Tüllgardine F net curtain

Tulpe ['tʊlpə] F **-, -n** (a) (*Bot*) tulip (b) (= *Glas*) tulip glass

Tulpenzwiebel F tulip bulb

Tumbler ['tamblɐ] M **-s, -** (*Sw:* = *Wäschetrockner*) tumble dryer

tummeln ['tʊmln] VR (a) (*Hunde, Kinder etc*) to romp (about) (b) (= *sich beeilen*) to hurry (up)

Tummelplatz ['tʊml-] M play area; (*fig*) hotbed

Tümmler ['tʏmlɐ] M **-s, -** (bottlenose) dolphin

Tumor ['tuːmoːɐ, tu'moːɐ] M **-s, Tumoren** [tu'moːrən] tumour (*Brit*), tumor (*US*)

Tümpel ['tʏmpl] M **-s, -** pond

Tumult [tu'mʊlt] M **-(e)s, -e** commotion; (= *Aufruhr auch*) disturbance; (*der Gefühle*) tumult

---

tun [tuːn]	
1 TRANSITIVES VERB	**3** INTRANSITIVES VERB
2 REFLEXIVES VERB	

pret **tat** [taːt], *ptp* **getan** [gə'taːn]

1 TRANSITIVES VERB

In Verbindungen mit Substantiv siehe auch Eintrag für das jeweilige Substantiv.

(a) (= *machen*) to do; **er tut nichts als faulenzen** he does nothing but laze around; **so etwas tut man nicht!** that is just not done!; **was tut man in dieser Situation?** what should one do in this situation?; **... aber er tut es einfach nicht** ... but he just won't (do it); **was tun?** what can be done?; **was kann ich für Sie tun?** what can I do for you?; **etw aus Liebe/Bosheit** *etc* **tun** to do sth out of love/malice *etc*; **etwas/nichts gegen etw tun** to do something/nothing about sth; **du kannst tun und lassen, was du willst** you can do what you like; **tu, was du nicht lassen kannst** well, if you have to; **damit ist es noch nicht getan** and that's not all; **was tust DU denn hier?** (*inf*) what are YOU doing here?; **seine Arbeit/Pflicht tun** to do one's job/duty; **einen Schrei tun** to cry (out); *siehe auch* **getan**

✦jdm etwas tun to do something to sb; (*stärker*) to hurt sb; **der Hund tut dir schon nichts** the dog won't hurt you; **was du nicht willst, dass man dir tu, das füg auch keinem andern zu** (*Prov*) do as you would be done by (*prov*)

◆es tun (inf) **es mit jdm tun** (euph inf) to do it with sb (inf); **die Uhr/das Auto tut es** or **tuts nicht mehr** the watch/car has had it (inf); **das tuts für heute** that'll do for today; **unser Auto muss es noch ein Weilchen tun** we'll have to make do with our car a bit longer

◆mit jdm/etw zu tun haben das hat etwas/nichts mit ihm/damit zu tun that's something/nothing to do with him/it; **mit ihm/damit habe ich nichts zu tun/will ich nichts zu tun haben** I have/want nothing to do with him/it; **er hat es mit der Leber/dem Herzen** etc **zu tun** (inf) he has liver/heart etc trouble

◆es mit jdm zu tun bekommen or **kriegen** (inf) to get into trouble with sb

(b) (= ausmachen) **was tuts?** what does it matter?; **das tut nichts** it doesn't matter; **das tut dir/mir nichts** it won't do you/him any harm; **das tut nichts zur Sache** that's beside the point

(c) (= an einen bestimmten Ort legen etc) (inf) to put; **jdn in eine andere Schule tun** to put sb in a different school

2 REFLEXIVES VERB

◆sich tun

(a) (= geschehen) **es tut sich etwas/nichts** there is something/nothing happening; **hier hat sich einiges getan** there have been some changes here; **hat sich in dieser Hinsicht schon etwas getan?** has anything been done about this?

(b) (mit Adjektiv)

◆sich schwer or **nicht leicht tun** sich (acc or dat) **mit etw schwer tun** to have problems with sth; **sich** (acc or dat) **mit etw nicht leicht tun** to have problems with sth

3 INTRANSITIVES VERB

(a) (= vorgeben) **so tun, als ob ...** to pretend that ...; **tu doch nicht so** stop pretending; **tust du nur so dumm?** are you just acting stupid?; **sie tut nur so** she's only pretending

(b) (andere Wendungen)

◆zu tun haben (= beschäftigt sein) to have things to do; **auf dem Finanzamt zu tun haben** to have business at the tax office; **mit jdm zu tun haben** to have dealings with sb

◆daran tun Sie täten gut daran, früh zu kommen you would do well to come early

Tun [tuːn] NT **-s**, NO PL conduct; **sein ganzes ~, sein ~ und Lassen, sein ~ und Treiben** everything he does

Tünche ['tʏnçə] F **-, -n** whitewash; (getönt) distemper; (fig) veneer

tünchen ['tʏnçn] VT to whitewash; (mit getönter Farbe) to distemper

tunen ['tjuːnən] VT to tune

Tuner ['tjuːnɐ] M **-s, -** tuner

Tunesien [tu'neːziən] NT **-s** Tunisia

Tunesier [tu'neːziɐ] M **-s, -**, **Tunesierin** [-iərɪn] F **-, -nen** Tunisian

tunesisch [tu'neːzɪʃ] ADJ Tunisian

Tunfisch [tuːn-] M tuna (fish)

Tuning ['tjuːnɪŋ] NT **-s**, NO PL tuning

Tunke ['tʊŋkə] F **-, -n** sauce; (= Bratentunke) gravy

tunken ['tʊŋkn] VT to dip; jdn to duck

tunlichst ['tuːnlɪçst] ADV **(a)** (= möglichst) if possible; **~ bald** as soon as possible; **ich werde es ~ vermeiden, ihm meine Meinung zu sagen** I'll do my best to avoid telling him what I think **(b)** (= gefälligst) **das wirst du ~ bleiben lassen** you'll do nothing of the kind

Tunnel ['tʊnl] M **-s, -** or **-s** tunnel

Tunte ['tʊntə] F **-, -n** (pej inf) fairy (pej inf)

Tüpfelchen ['tʏpflçən] NT **-s, -** dot

tupfen ['tʊpfn] VT to dab; **getupft** spotted

Tupfen ['tʊpfn] M **-s, -** spot; (klein) dot

Tupfer ['tʊpfɐ] M **-s, -** swab

Tür [tyːɐ] F **-, -en** door; (= Gartentür) gate; **in der ~** in the doorway; **~ an ~ mit jdm wohnen** to live next door to sb; **Weihnachten steht vor der ~** Christmas is just (a)round the corner; **jdn vor die ~ setzen** (inf) to throw sb out; **offene ~en einrennen** to preach to the converted; **mit der ~ ins Haus fallen** (inf) to blurt it out; **zwischen ~ und Angel** in passing; **einer Sache** (dat) **~ und Tor öffnen** (fig) to open the way to sth

Türangel F (door) hinge

Turban ['tʊrbaːn] M **-s, -e** turban

Turbine [tʊr'biːnə] F **-, -n** turbine

Turbo- ['tʊrbo-]: **Turbodiesel** M (Aut) turbo-diesel engine; **Turbolader** [-laːdɐ] M **-s, -** (Aut) turbocharger; **Turbomotor** M turbo-engine; **Turbo-Prop-Flugzeug** NT turboprop aircraft

turbulent [tʊrbu'lent] **1** ADJ turbulent **2** ADV turbulently; **auf der Versammlung ging es ~ zu** the meeting was turbulent

Turbulenz [tʊrbu'lents] F **-, -en (a)** NO PL turbulence **(b)** (= turbulentes Ereignis) excitement no pl **(c)** (= Wirbel, Luftstrom) turbulence no pl

Türdrücker M (= Knauf) doorknob; (inf: = Öffner) buzzer (for opening the door)

-türig [tyːrɪç] ADJ SUF **eintürig/zweitürig** etc with one door/two doors etc; **ein viertüriges Auto** a four-door car

Türke ['tʏrkə] M **-n, -n** Turk; siehe auch **Türkin**

Türkei [tʏr'kai] F **- die ~** Turkey

türken ['tʏrkn] VT (inf) etw to fiddle (inf); **die Statistik ~** to massage the figures; **Belege ~** to falsify documents

Türken ['tʏrkn] M **-s**, NO PL (Aus inf) maize

Türkin ['tʏrkɪn] F **-, -nen** Turk, Turkish woman/girl

türkis [tʏr'kiːs] ADJ turquoise

Türkis [tʏr'kiːs] M **-es, -e** [-zə] (= Edelstein) turquoise

türkisch ['tʏrkɪʃ] ADJ Turkish; **~er Honig** nougat

Türklinke F door handle

Turm [tʊrm] M **-(e)s, ¨e** ['tʏrmə] **(a)** tower; (= spitzer Kirchturm) spire; (im Schwimmbad) diving (Brit) or dive (US) tower **(b)** (Chess) rook

Türmchen ['tʏrmçən] NT **-s, -** DIM von **Turm** turret

türmen ['tʏrmən] **1** VT to pile (up) **2** VR to pile up; (Wolken) to build up; (Wellen) to tower up **3** VI AUX SEIN (inf: = davonlaufen) to run off

Turm-: **Turmfalke** M kestrel; **turmhoch** **1** ADJ towering **2** ADV **~ über jdm stehen, jdm ~ überlegen sein** to stand head and shoulders above sb

Turnanzug M leotard

turnen ['tʊrnən] VI **(a)** (an Geräten) to do gymnastics; (Sch) to do gym; **am Reck/an den Ringen/auf der Matte** etc **~** to work on the horizontal bar/rings/mat etc; **sie kann gut ~** she is good at gym **(b)** AUX SEIN (= herumklettern) to climb about; (Kind) to romp

Turnen NT **-s**, NO PL gymnastics sing; (inf: = Leibeserziehung) gym, PE (inf)

Turner ['tʊrnɐ] M **-s, -**, **Turnerin** [-ərɪn] F **-, -nen** gymnast

Turn-: **Turnfest** NT gymnastics display; (von Schule) sports day; **Turngerät** NT (= Reifen, Ball etc) (piece of) gymnastic equipment; (= Reck, Barren etc) (piece of) gymnastic apparatus; **Turnhalle** F gym(nasium); (Gebäude auch) sports hall; **Turnhemd** NT gym shirt; **Turnhose** F gym shorts pl

Turnier [tʊr'niːɐ] NT **-s, -e** (= Ritterturnier, sportliche Veranstaltung) tournament; (= Tanzturnier) competition; (= Reitturnier) show

Turn-: **Turnschuh** M gym shoe, sneaker (US); **Turnstunde** F gym lesson; (im Verein) gymnastics lesson; **Turnübung** F gymnastic exercise; **Turnunterricht** M gymnastics instruction; (= Turnstunde) gym; **Turnverein** M gymnastics club; **Turnzeug** NT, NO PL gym things pl or kit (Brit)

Tür-: **Türöffner** M **elektrischer ~** buzzer (for opening the door); **Türrahmen** M doorframe; **Türschild** NT, pl **-schilder** doorplate; **Türschloss** NT door lock; **Türsteher** [-ʃteːɐ] M **-s, -**, **Türsteherin** [-ərɪn] F **-, -nen** bouncer

turteln ['tʊrtln] VI to bill and coo

Türvorleger M doormat

Tusche ['tʊʃə] F **-, -n** (= Ausziehtusche) Indian ink; (= Tuschfarbe) watercolour (Brit), watercolor (US); (= Wimperntusche) mascara

tuscheln ['tʊʃln] VTI to whisper; **hinter seinem Rücken über jdn ~** to talk behind sb's back

Tuschkasten M paintbox

Tussi ['tʊsi] F **-, -s** (inf), **Tuss** [tʊs] F **-, -en** (sl) female (inf)

tut [tuːt] INTERJ toot

Tüte ['tyːtə] F **-, -n** (aus Papier, Plastik) bag; (= Eistüte) cone; (von Suppenpulver etc) packet; **in die ~ blasen** (inf) to be breathalyzed; **das kommt nicht in die ~!** (*inf*) no way! (*inf*)

tuten ['tu:tn] VI to toot; (*Schiff*) to sound its hooter *or* (*mit Nebelhorn*) foghorn; **von Tuten und Blasen keine Ahnung haben** (*inf*) not to have a clue (*inf*)

Tutor ['tu:to:ɐ] M **-s, Tutoren** [-'to:rən], **Tutorin** [-'to:rɪn] F **-, -nen** tutor

TÜV [tʏf] M **-s, -s** ABBR *von* **Technischer Überwachungs-Verein** ≈ MOT (*Brit*), ≈ inspection (*US inf*)

TÜV

The **TÜV** *- short for* **Technischer Überwachungs-Verein** *- is an organization that tests the safety of technical installations, machinery and motor vehicles. All vehicles over three years old must undergo a* **TÜV** *test every two years in order to prove they are safe and roadworthy. Should the vehicle fail the test, it must be deregistered and taken off the road. The* **TÜV** *also carries out safety tests on a wide range of other products. If they pass the test, products are permitted to carry the* **GS** *(Geprüfte Sicherheit) seal. The independence of the* **TÜV** *means that this seal is regarded as a guarantee of good quality and reliability.*

TÜV-Plakette F ≈ MOT certificate (*Brit*), ≈ inspection certificate (*US*)

TV [te:'fau] **(a)** ABBR *von* **Television (b)** ABBR *von* **Turnverein**

TV- [te:'fau] IN CPDS TV; **TV-Moderator** M, **TV-Moderatorin** F TV presenter; **TV-Programm** NT TV programmes (*Brit*) *or* programs (*US*) *pl*; **TV-Sendung** F TV broadcast

Twen [tvɛn] M **-(s), -s** *person in his/her twenties*

Typ [ty:p] M **-s, -en (a)** (= *Modell*) model **(b)** (= *Menschenart*) type **(c)** (*inf*: = *Mensch*) person, character; (*sl*: = *Mann, Freund*) guy (*inf*); **dein ~ wird verlangt** (*inf*) you're wanted; **dein ~ ist nicht gefragt** (*inf*) you're not wanted (a)round here

Typenrad NT daisy wheel

Typenraddrucker M daisy wheel (printer)

Typhus ['ty:fʊs] M **-,** NO PL typhoid (fever)

typisch ['ty:pɪʃ] **1** ADJ typical (*für* of) **2** ADV ~ **deutsch/Mann/Frau** typically German/male/female; **ein ~ deutsches Gericht** a typical German dish; ~ **Claire** that's so typical of Claire

Typografie [typogra'fi:] F **-, -n** [-'fi:ən] typography

typografisch [typo'gra:fɪʃ] **1** ADJ typographic(al) **2** ADV typographically

Typoskript [typo'skrɪpt] NT **-(e)s, -e** (*Typ*) typescript

Tyrann [ty'ran] M **-en, -en, Tyrannin** [-'ranɪn] F **-, -nen** (*lit, fig*) tyrant

tyrannisch [ty'ranɪʃ] **1** ADJ tyrannical **2** ADV tyranically

tyrannisieren [tyrani'zi:rən], *ptp* **tyrannisiert** VT to tyrannize

T-Zelle ['te:-] F (*Med, Biol*) T-cell

Uu

U, u [uː] NT -, - U, u

u. ABBR *von* **und**

u. a. ABBR *von* **und andere(s), unter anderem/anderen**

U. A. w. g. [uːlaːvɛˈgeː] ABBR *von* **Um Antwort wird gebeten** RSVP

UB [uːˈbeː] F -, -s ABBR *von* **Universitätsbibliothek**

U-Bahn [ˈuː-] F underground, subway (US)

U-Bahnhof [ˈuː-] M underground *or* subway (US) station; (*in* London) tube station

übel [ˈyːbl̩] **1** ADJ **(a)** (= *schlimm, unangenehm*) bad; **das ist gar nicht so** ~ that's not so bad at all

(b) (= *moralisch, charakterlich schlecht*) wicked; *Eindruck, Ruf* bad; *Tat* evil; **ein übler Bursche** *or* **Kunde** (*inf*) a bad lot (*inf*); **das ist eine üble Sache!** it's a bad business; **ein übler Streich** a nasty trick; **auf üble** *or* **in der ~sten Weise, in übler** *or* **~ster Weise** in a most unpleasant way

(c) (= *physisch schlecht, eklig*) *Geschmack, Geruch, Gefühl* nasty; **mir wird** ~ I feel ill; **es kann einem ~ werden** it's enough to make you feel ill

(d) (= *verkommen, ~ beleumdet*) evil

2 ADV **(a)** (= *schlimm, unangenehm, schlecht*) badly; **das ist ihm ~ bekommen** it did him no good at all; **dran sein** to be in a bad way; ~ **beraten** (*geh*) ill-advised; ~ **gelaunt** ill-humoured (*Brit*), ill-humored (*US*); ~ **riechend** foul-smelling; **jd ist ~ gelaunt** sb is in a bad mood; **etw riecht** ~ sth smells bad; **es steht ~ mit ihm** he's in bad shape; **das schmeckt gar nicht so** ~ it doesn't taste so bad

(b) (= *moralisch, charakterlich schlecht*) badly; **über jdn ~ reden** to say bad things about sb; ~ **beleumdet** disreputable

(c) (= *physisch schlecht*) ill, poorly; **das Essen ist ihm ~ bekommen** the food disagreed with him

Übel [ˈyːbl̩] NT -s, - **(a)** (*geh*: = *Krankheit, Leiden*) illness

(b) (= *Missstand, Schaden*) evil; **ein notwendiges/das kleinere** *or* **geringere** ~ a necessary/the lesser evil; **das alte** ~ the old trouble; **der Grund allen ~s ist, dass ...** the cause of all the trouble is that ...; **das ~ bei der Sache** the trouble; **von ~ sein** to be a bad thing; **zu allem ~ ...** to make matters worse ...; **ein ~ kommt selten allein** (*Prov*) misfortunes seldom come alone

Übelkeit F -, -en (*lit, fig*) nausea; **eine plötzliche** ~ a sudden feeling of nausea; ~ **erregen** to cause nausea

Übel-: übel nehmen VT IRREG to take badly; **jdm etw** ~ to hold sth against sb; **bitte nehmen Sie es (mir) nicht übel, aber ...** please don't take offence *or* offense (US), but ...; **ich habe ihm gar nicht einmal übel genommen, dass er gelogen hat, aber ...** I didn't even mind him lying but ...; **Übelsein** NT nausea; **übel wollen** VI (*geh*) **jdm** ~ to be ill-disposed toward(s) sb

üben [ˈyːbn̩] **1** VT **(a)** (= *praktisch erlernen*) *Aussprache, Musik, Sport* to practise (*Brit*), to practice (US); (*Mil*) to drill; *Geige/Klavier* to practise (*Brit*) *or* practice (US) the violin/piano **(b)** (= *schulen, trainieren*) *Gedächtnis, Muskeln etc* to exercise; *siehe auch* **geübt (c)** *Kritik an etw* (*dat*) ~ to criticize sth; **Geduld** ~ to be patient **2** VI (= *praktisch lernen*) to practise (*Brit*), to practice (US)

über [ˈyːbɐ] **1** PREP **(a)** +ACC (*räumlich*) over; (= *quer* ~) across; (= *weiter als*) beyond; **es wurde ~ alle Sender ausgestrahlt** it was broadcast over all transmitters; **er lachte ~ das ganze Gesicht** he was beaming all over his face

(b) +DAT (*räumlich*) (*Lage, Standort*) over, above; (= *jenseits*) over; **zwei Grad ~ null** two degrees (above zero); **er trug den Mantel ~ dem Arm** he was carrying his coat over his arm; ~ **jdm stehen** *or* **sein** (*fig*) to be over sb; **er steht ~ der Situation** (*fig*) he is above it all

(c) +DAT (*zeitlich*: = *bei, während*) over; **etw ~ einem Glas Wein besprechen** to discuss sth over a glass of wine; ~ **all der Aufregung/unserer Unterhaltung habe ich ganz vergessen, dass ...** in all the excitement/what with all this chatting I quite forgot that ...; ~ **Mittag geht er meist nach Hause** he usually goes home at lunch

(d) +ACC *Cäsars Sieg ~ die Gallier* Caesar's victory over the Gauls; **es kam plötzlich ~ ihn** it suddenly came over him; **sie liebt ihn ~ alles** she loves him more than anything

(e) +ACC (= *vermittels, auf dem Wege* ~) via; **die Nummer erfährt man ~ die Auskunft** you'll get the number from information;

wir sind ~ die Autobahn gekommen we came by the autobahn

(f) +ACC (*zeitlich*) (= *innerhalb eines Zeitraums, länger als*) over; ~ **Weihnachten** over Christmas; **bis ~ Ostern** until after Easter; **den ganzen Sommer** ~ all summer long; ~ **Wochen (ausgedehnt)** for weeks on end; **die ganze Zeit** ~ all the time; **das ganze Jahr** ~ all through the year; ~ **kurz oder lang** sooner or later; **es ist ~ vierzehn Tage her, dass ...** it's over fourteen days since ...

(g) +ACC (*bei Zahlenangaben*) (= *in Höhe von*) for; (= *mehr als*) over; **Kinder ~ 14 Jahre** children over 14 years; **Städte ~ 50.000 Einwohner** towns of over 50,000 inhabitants

(h) +ACC (= *wegen*) over; (= *betreffend*) about; **was wissen Sie ~ ihn?** what do you know about him?; ~ **welches Thema schreiben Sie Ihr neues Buch?** what's your new book about?; ~ **jdn/etw lachen** to laugh about *or* at sb/sth; **sich ~ etw freuen/ärgern** to be pleased/angry about sth

(i) +ACC (*steigernd*) upon; **Fehler ~ Fehler** mistake upon mistake

2 ADV ~ **und** ~ all over; **ich stecke ~ und ~ in Schulden** I am up to my ears in debt; **jdm in etw** (*dat*) ~ **sein** (*inf*) to be better than sb at sth

überaktiv ADJ hyperactive, overactive

überall [yːbɐˈlal] ADV everywhere; ~ **herumliegen** to be lying all over the place; ~ **wo** wherever; ~ **Bescheid wissen** (*wissensmäßig*) to have a wide-ranging knowledge; (*in Stadt etc*) to know one's way around; **es ist ~ dasselbe** it's the same wherever you go; **so ist es** ~ it's the same everywhere; ~ **und nirgends zu Hause sein** to be at home everywhere and nowhere

überall-: überallher [yːbɐlalˈheːɐ, yːbɐˈlalheːɐ] ADV from all over; **überallhin** [yːbɐlalˈhɪn, yːbɐˈlalhɪn] ADV everywhere

Über-: überaltert [yːbɐˈlaltɐt] ADJ **(a)** (*Sociol*) having too high a percentage of old people **(b)** = **veraltet**; **Überalterung** F (*Sociol*) increase in the percentage of old people; **Überangebot** NT surplus (*an* +*dat* of); **überängstlich** ADJ overanxious; **überanstrengen** [yːbɐˈlanʃtrɛŋən], *ptp* **überanstrengt** INSEP **1** VT to overstrain, to overexert; *Kräfte* to overtax; *Augen* to strain **2** VR to overstrain oneself; **überanstrenge dich nicht!** (*iro*) don't strain yourself! (*iro*); **Überanstrengung** F overexertion; **eine ~ der Nerven/Augen** a strain on the nerves/eyes; **überarbeiten** [yːbɐˈlarbaitn̩], *ptp* **überarbeitet** INSEP **1** VT to rework; **in einer überarbeiteten Fassung** in a revised edition **2** VR to overwork; **Überarbeitung** F -, -en **(a)** (*Vorgang*) reworking; (*Ergebnis*) revision **(b)** NO PL (= *Überanstrengung*) overwork; **überaus** [ˈyːbɐlaus, yːbɐˈlaus] ADV extremely; **überbacken** [yːbɐˈbakn̩], *ptp* **überbacken** VT INSEP IRREG (*im Backofen*) to put in the oven; (*im Grill*) to put under the grill; **mit Käse ~** au gratin; **~e Käseschnitten** cheese on toast

Überbein NT (*an Gelenk*) ganglion

Über-: überbekommen *ptp* **überbekommen** VT SEP IRREG (*inf*) **jdn/etw ~** to get sick of sb/sth (*inf*); **überbelegen** *ptp* **überbelegt** VT INSEP USU PTP to overcrowd; *Kursus, Fach etc* to oversubscribe; **Überbelegung** F overcrowding; (*von Kursus, Fach etc*) oversubscription; **überbelichten** *ptp* **überbelichtet** VT INSEP (*Phot*) to overexpose; **Überbeschäftigung** F overemployment; **überbesetzt** ADJ *Behörde, Abteilung* overstaffed; **überbetrieblich** **1** ADJ industry-wide **2** ADV industry-wide; **überbewerten** *ptp* **überbewertet** VT INSEP (*lit*) to overvalue; (*fig auch*) to overrate; *Schulleistung etc* to mark too high; **wollen wir doch eine so vereinzelte Äußerung nicht ~** let's not attach too much importance to such an isolated remark; **Überbezahlung** F overpayment

überbietbar ADJ (*fig*) **kaum noch ~** sb to take some beating; **ein an Vulgarität nicht mehr ~er Pornofilm** a porn film of unsurpassable vulgarity

überbieten [yːbɐˈbiːtn̩], *ptp* **überboten** [yːbɐˈboːtn̩] INSEP IRREG **1** VT (*bei Auktion*) to outbid (*um* by); (*fig*) to outdo; *Leistung, Rekord* to beat; **das ist kaum noch zu ~** (*fig*) it's outrageous; **diese Geschichte ist an Peinlichkeit kaum noch zu ~** the incident could scarcely have been more embarrassing **2** VR sich in etw (*dat*) (**gegenseitig**) ~ to vie with one another in sth; **sich** (**selber**) ~ to surpass oneself

überblättern [y:bɐ'blɛtɐn], *ptp* **überblättert** VT INSEP *Buch* to flick through; *Stelle* to skip over

Überbleibsel [y:bɐblaipsl] NT **-s, -** remnant; (= *Speiserest*) leftover *usu pl*; (= *Brauch, Angewohnheit etc*) survival, hangover; (= *Spur*) trace

Überblick M (*über* +*acc* of) (**a**) (= *freie Sicht*) view (**b**) (= *Einblick*) perspective, overview; **er hat keinen ~, ihm fehlt der ~, es fehlt ihm an ~** he has no overall picture; **den ~ verlieren** to lose track (of things) (**c**) (= *Abriss*) survey; (= *Übersicht, Zusammenhang*) synopsis; **sich** (*dat*) **einen ~ verschaffen** to get a general idea; **Weltgeschichte im ~** compendium of world history

überblicken [y:bɐ'blɪkn], *ptp* **überblickt** VT INSEP (**a**) (*lit*) *Platz, Stadt, Gebiet* to overlook (**b**) (*fig*) to see; **die Entwicklung lässt sich leicht ~** the development can be seen at a glance; **bis ich die Lage besser überblicke** until I have a better view of the situation

überbringen [y:bɐ'brɪŋən], *ptp* **überbracht** [y:bɐ'braxt] VT INSEP IRREG **jdm etw** ~ to bring sb sth; *Brief etc auch* to deliver sth to sb

Überbringer [y:bɐ'brɪŋɐ] M **-s, -**, **Überbringerin** [-ərɪn] F **-, -nen** bringer; (*von Scheck etc*) bearer

überbrücken [y:bɐ'brʏkn], *ptp* **überbrückt** VT INSEP (*fig*) *Kluft, Zeitraum* to bridge; *Krisenzeiten* to get through; *Gegensätze* to reconcile; **die Gegensätze zwischen … ~** to bridge the gap between …

Überbrückung F **-, -en** (*fig*) bridging; (*von Krisenzeiten*) getting through; (*von Gegensätzen*) reconciliation; **100 Euro zur ~** 100 euros to tide me/him *etc* over

Überbrückungskredit [-kredi:t] M bridging loan

Über-: überbuchen [y:bɐ'bu:xn], *ptp* **überbucht** VT INSEP to overbook; **Überbuchung** F overbooking; **Überdach** NT roof; **überdachen** [y:bɐ'daxn], *ptp* **überdacht** VT INSEP to cover over; **überdachte Fahrradständer/Bushaltestelle** covered bicycle stands/bus shelter; **überdauern** [y:bɐ'dauɐn], *ptp* **überdauert** VT INSEP to survive; **überdenken** [y:bɐ'dɛŋkn], *ptp* **überdacht** VT INSEP IRREG to think over; **etw noch einmal ~** to reconsider sth; **überdeutlich** ADJ all too obvious ADV **es ist mir ~ klar geworden** it has become perfectly clear to me; **jdm etw ~ zu verstehen geben** to make sth perfectly clear to sb

überdies [y:bɐ'di:s] ADV (*geh*) (**a**) (= *außerdem*) moreover (**b**) (= *ohnehin*) anyway

Über-: überdosieren *ptp* **überdosiert** VT INSEP **dieses Mittel wird oft überdosiert** an excessive dose of this medicine is often given; **nicht ~** do not exceed the dose; **Überdosis** F overdose; (= *zu große Zumessung*) excessive amount; **sich** (*dat*) **eine ~ Heroin spritzen** to overdose on heroin

überdreht [y:bɐ'dre:t] ADJ (*inf*) overexcited; (*ständig*) highly charged; (= *verrückt*) weird; **ein ~er Typ** a weirdo (*inf*)

Überdruck M, *pl* **-drücke** (*Tech*) excess pressure *no pl*

Überdruck-: Überdruckkabine F (*Aviat*) pressurized cabin; **Überdruckventil** NT pressure relief valve

Überdruss [y:bɐdrʊs] M **-es**, NO PL (= *Übersättigung*) surfeit (*an* +*dat* of); (= *Widerwille*) aversion (*an* +*dat* to); **bis zum ~** ad nauseam; **er aß Kaviar bis zum ~** he ate caviar until he was sick of it; **~ am Leben** weariness of life

überdrüssig [y:bɐdrʏsɪç] ADJ **jds/einer Sache ~ sein** to be weary of sb/sth; **jds/einer Sache ~ werden** to (grow) weary of sb/sth

Über-: überdüngen [y:bɐ'dʏŋən], *ptp* **überdüngt** VT SEP to over-fertilize; **Überdüngung** F over-fertilization; **überdurchschnittlich** ADJ above-average ADV exceptionally; **er arbeitet ~ gut** his work is above average; **sie verdient ~ gut** she earns more than the average; **übereck** [y:bɐ'ɛk] ADV at right angles (to each other); **Übereifer** M overzealousness; (*pej*: = *Wichtigtuerei*) officiousness; **übereifrig** ADJ overzealous; (*pej*: = *wichtigtuerisch*) officious; **übereilen** [y:bɐ'lailən], *ptp* **übereilt** VT INSEP to rush; **~ Sie nichts!** don't rush things!; **übereilt** [y:bɐ'lailt] ADJ overhasty ADV overhastily

übereinander [y:bɐlai'nandɐ] ADV (**a**) (*räumlich*) on top of each other, one on top of the other; **hängen** one above the other (**b**) *reden etc* about each other

übereinander: übereinander legen VT to put one on top of the other; **übereinander liegen** VI IRREG to lie one on top of

the other; **übereinander schlagen** VT IRREG **die Beine ~** to cross one's legs; **die Arme ~** to fold one's arms

übereinkommen [y:bɐ'lain-] VI SEP IRREG AUX SEIN to agree; **wir sind darin übereingekommen, dass …** we have agreed that …

Übereinkommen [y:bɐ'lainkɔmən] NT, **Übereinkunft** [y:bɐ'lainkʊnft] F **-, ⸚e** [-kʏnftə] agreement; **ein ~ *or* eine Übereinkunft treffen** to enter into an agreement; **ein ~ *or* eine Übereinkunft erzielen** to come to an agreement

übereinstimmen [y:bɐ'lain-] VI SEP to agree; (*Meinungen*) to tally; (*Angaben, Messwerte, Rechnungen etc*) to tally, to agree; **mit jdm in etw** (*dat*) ~ to agree with sb on sth

übereinstimmend ADJ corresponding; *Meinungen, Vermutungen etc* concurring; **nach ~en Angaben/Meldungen** according to all accounts/reports; **nach ~en Zeugenaussagen** according to mutually corroborative testimonies ADV **alle erklärten ~, dass …** everybody agreed that …; **wir sind ~ der Meinung, dass …** we unanimously agree that …; **sie bestritten ~, dass …** they are in agreement in denying that …; **~ mit** in agreement with

Übereinstimmung F (**a**) (= *Einklang, Gleichheit*) correspondence; **bei den Zeugenaussagen gab es nur in zwei Punkten ~** the testimonies only agreed *or* tallied in two particulars; **zwei Dinge in ~ bringen** to bring two things into line; **es besteht *or* herrscht keine ~ zwischen X und Y** X and Y do not agree (**b**) (*von Meinung*) agreement; **darin besteht bei allen Beteiligten ~** all parties involved are agreed on that; **in ~ mit jdm** in agreement with sb; **in ~ mit etw** in accordance with sth (**c**) (*Gram*) agreement

Über-: überempfindlich ADJ (*gegen* to) oversensitive, hypersensitive (*auch Med*) ADV **~ auf etw** (*acc*) **reagieren** to be oversensitive to sth; **Überempfindlichkeit** F (*gegen* to) oversensitivity, hypersensitivity (*auch Med*); **übererfüllen** *ptp* **übererfüllt** VT INSEP *Norm, Soll, Plan* to exceed (*um* by); **Überernährung** F (*no pl*: = *das Überernähren*) overfeeding; (*Krankheit*) overeating; **überessen** [y:bɐ'lɛsn], *pret* **überaß** [y:bɐ'la:s], *ptp* **übergessen** [y:bɐ'gɛsn] VR INSEP to overeat; **ich habe mich an Käse übergessen** I've eaten too much cheese

überfahren [y:bɐ'fa:rən], *ptp* **überfahren** VT INSEP IRREG (**a**) *jdn, Tier* to run over (**b**) (= *hinwegfahren über*) to go over; *Fluss etc* to cross (over) (**c**) (= *übersehen und weiterfahren*) *Ampel etc* to go through; (*inf*: = *übertölpeln*) **jdn ~** to railroad sb into it

Überfahrt F crossing

Überfall M (**a**) (= *Angriff*) attack (*auf* +*acc* on); (*esp auf offener Straße*) mugging (*auf* +*acc* of); (*auf Bank etc*) raid (*auf* +*acc* on); (*auf Land*) invasion (*auf* +*acc* of); **dies ist ein ~, keine Bewegung!** this is a hold-up *or* stick-up (*esp US inf*), freeze! (**b**) (*hum*: = *unerwartetes Erscheinen*) invasion; **er hat einen ~ auf uns vor** he's planning to descend on us

überfallen [y:bɐ'falən], *ptp* **überfallen** VT INSEP IRREG (**a**) (= *angreifen*) to attack; (*esp auf offener Straße*) to mug; *Bank etc* to raid, to hold up; *Land, Stadt* to invade (**b**) (*fig inf*) (= *überraschend besuchen*) to descend (up)on; (= *bestürmen*) to pounce upon; **jdn mit Fragen/Wünschen ~** to bombard sb with questions/requests

Über-: überfällig ADJ overdue *usu pred*; **seit einer Woche ~ sein** to be a week overdue; **Überfischung** F **-, -en** overfishing; **überfliegen** [y:bɐ'fli:gn], *ptp* **überflogen** [y:bɐ'flo:gn] VT INSEP IRREG (*lit*) to fly over; (= *flüchtig ansehen*) *Buch etc* to glance through; **Überflieger(in)** M(F) (*fig*) high-flyer; **überflügeln** [y:bɐ'fly:gln], *ptp* **überflügelt** VT INSEP to outdistance; (*in Leistung, bei Wahl*) to outdo

Überfluss M, NO PL (**a**) (= *super*)abundance (*an* +*dat* of); (= *Luxus*) affluence; **Arbeit/Geld im ~** an abundance of work/money; **im ~ leben** to live in luxury; **im ~ vorhanden sein** to be in plentiful supply; **~ an etw** (*dat*) **haben, etw im ~ haben** to have an abundance of sth (**b**) **zu allem *or* zum ~** (= *unnötigerweise*) superfluously; (= *obendrein*) into the bargain

Überflussgesellschaft F affluent society

überflüssig ADJ superfluous; (= *frei, entbehrlich*) spare; (= *unnötig*) unnecessary; (= *zwecklos*) useless; **~ zu sagen, dass …** it goes without saying that …

Über-: Überflutung [y:bɐ'flu:tʊŋ] F **-, -en** (**a**) (*lit*) flood; (= *das Überfluten*) flooding *no pl* (**b**) (*fig*) flooding *no pl*, inundation; **überfordern** [y:bɐ'fɔrdɐn], *ptp* **überfordert** VT INSEP to overtax;

jdn auch to ask too much of; **damit ist er überfordert** that's asking too much of him; **als Abteilungsleiter wäre er doch etwas überfordert** being head of department would be too much for him; **Überforderung** F excessive demand(s *pl*) (*für* on); (*no pl*: = *das Überfordern*) overtaxing; **überfrachten** [y:bɐˈfraxtn̩], *ptp* **überfrachtet** VT INSEP (*fig*) to overload; **ein mit Emotionen überfrachteter Begriff** a concept fraught with emotions; **überfragt** [y:bɐˈfra:kt] ADJ PRED stumped (for an answer); **da bin ich ~** there you've got me; **Überfremdung** F -, -en foreign infiltration; (*Econ*) swamping; **überfrieren** [y:bɐˈfri:rən], *ptp* **überfroren** [y:bɐˈfro:rən] VI INSEP IRREG to freeze over; **Glatteisgefahr durch ~de Nässe** slippery roads due to black ice; **überführen** [y:bɐˈfy:rən], *ptp* **überführt** VT INSEP **(a)** to transfer; *Leichnam* to transport; *Wagen* to drive **(b)** *Täter* to convict (*+gen* of); **ein überführter Verbrecher** a convicted criminal; **Überführung** F **(a)** transportation **(b)** NO PL (*Jur*) conviction **(c)** (= *Brücke über Straße etc*) bridge (*auch Rail*); (= *Fußgängerüberführung*) footbridge; **überfüllt** [y:bɐˈfʏlt] ADJ overcrowded; *Kurs* oversubscribed; (*Comm*) *Lager* overstocked; **Überfunktion** F hyperactivity

Übergabe F handing over *no pl*; (*von Neubau*) opening; (*Mil*) surrender

Übergang M, *pl* -gänge **(a)** (= *das Überqueren*) crossing **(b)** (= *Fußgängerübergang*) crossing; (= *Brücke*) footbridge; (= *Bahnübergang*) level crossing (*Brit*), grade crossing (*US*) **(c)** (= *Grenzübergangsstelle*) checkpoint **(d)** (*fig*: = *Wechsel, Überleitung*) transition

Übergangs-: **übergangslos** ADJ, ADV without a transition; **Übergangslösung** F interim solution; **Übergangsphase** F transitional phase; **Übergangszeit** F **(a)** transitional period **(b)** (*zwischen Jahreszeiten*) in-between season

Übergardine F curtain, drape (*US*)

übergeben [y:bɐˈge:bn̩], *ptp* **übergeben** INSEP IRREG **1** VT (= *überreichen*) to hand over; *Dokument, Zettel, Einschreiben* to hand (*jdm* sb); **ein Gebäude der Öffentlichkeit/eine Straße dem Verkehr ~** to open a building to the public/a road to traffic; **eine Angelegenheit einem Rechtsanwalt ~** to place a matter in the hands of a lawyer **2** VR (= *sich erbrechen*) to vomit; **ich muss mich ~** I'm going to be sick

übergehen[1] [ˈy:bɐge:ən] VI SEP IRREG AUX SEIN **(a)** **in etw** (*acc*) ~ (*in einen anderen Zustand*) to turn into sth; (*Farben*) to merge into sth; **in jds Besitz** (*acc*) ~ to become sb's property; **in andere Hände ~** to pass into other hands **(b)** **auf jdn ~** (= *übernommen werden*) to pass to sb **(c)** **zu etw ~** to go over to sth; **wir sind dazu übergegangen, Computer zu benutzen** we went over to (using) computers

übergehen[2] [y:bɐˈge:ən], *ptp* **übergangen** [y:bɐˈɡaŋən] VT INSEP IRREG to pass over

Über-: **übergenau** ADJ overprecise; **übergeordnet** ADJ **(a)** *Behörde, Dienststelle, Recht* higher; **die uns ~e Behörde** the next authority above us **(b)** (*Gram*) *Satz* superordinate; (*Ling, Philos*) *Begriff* generic **(c)** (*fig*) **von ~er Bedeutung sein** to be of overriding importance; **Übergepäck** NT (*Aviat*) excess baggage; **übergeschnappt** ADJ (*inf*) crazy; *siehe auch* **überschnappen**; **Übergewicht** NT overweight; (*fig*) predominance; **~ haben** (*Paket etc*) to be overweight; **an ~ leiden**, **~ haben** (*Mensch*) to be overweight; **5 Gramm ~** 5 grammes excess weight; **das ~ haben** (*fig*) to predominate; **übergewichtig** ADJ overweight; **übergießen** [y:bɐˈɡi:sn̩], *ptp* **übergossen** [y:bɐˈɡɔsn̩] VT INSEP IRREG to pour over; *jdn* to douse; *Braten* to baste; **jdn/sich mit etw ~** to pour sth over sb/oneself; **überglücklich** ADJ overjoyed; **übergreifen** VI SEP IRREG **(a)** (*beim Klavierspiel*) to cross one's hands (over) **(b)** (*auf Rechte etc*) to infringe (*auf +acc* on); (*Feuer, Streik, Krankheit etc*) to spread (*auf +acc* to); **ineinander ~** to overlap; **Übergriff** M (= *Einmischung*) infringement (*auf +acc* of), interference *no pl* (*auf +acc* with or in); (*Mil*) attack (*auf +acc* upon); (= *Ausschreitung*) excess; **übergroß** ADJ oversize(d); *Mehrheit* overwhelming; **Übergröße** F (*bei Kleidung etc*) outsize; **überhaben** VT SEP IRREG (*inf*) **(a)** (= *satt haben*) to be sick (and tired) of (*inf*) **(b)** (= *übrig haben*) to have left (over); **für etw nichts ~** not to like sth

überhand nehmen [y:bɐˈhantne:mən] VI IRREG to get out of hand; (*Meinungen, Ideen etc*) to gain the upper hand

Über-: **Überhang** M **(a)** (= *Felsüberhang*) overhang **(b)** (= *Überschuss*) surplus (*an +dat* of); **überhängen** VT SEP **sich** (*dat*) **ein Gewehr ~** to sling a rifle over one's shoulder; **sich** (*dat*) **einen Mantel ~** to put a coat round one's

---

shoulders; **Überhangmandat** NT (*Pol*) seat gained as a result of votes for a specific candidate over and above the seats to which a party is entitled by the number of votes cast for the party; **überhäufen** [y:bɐˈhɔyfn̩], *ptp* **überhäuft** VT INSEP *jdn* to overwhelm; *Schreibtisch etc* to pile high; **jdn mit Geschenken/Glückwünschen/Titeln ~** to heap presents/congratulations/titles (up)on sb; **ich bin völlig mit Arbeit überhäuft** I'm completely snowed under (with work); **jdn mit Vorwürfen ~** to heap reproaches (up)on sb('s head)

überhaupt [y:bɐˈhaupt] ADV **(a)** (= *sowieso, im Allgemeinen*) in general; (= *überdies, außerdem*) anyway; **und ~, warum nicht?** and after all, why not?; **nicht nur Rotwein, sondern Wein ~ mag ich nicht** it's not only red wine I don't like, I don't like wine at all
(b) (*in Fragen, Verneinungen*) at all; **~ nicht** not at all; **ich denke ~ nicht daran mitzukommen** I've (absolutely) no intention whatsoever of coming along; **~ nie** never (ever); **~ kein Grund** no reason whatsoever; **hast du denn ~ keinen Anstand?** have you no decency at all?
(c) (= *erst, eigentlich*) **dann merkt man ~ erst, wie schön ...** then you really notice for the first time how beautiful ...; **waren Sie ~ schon in dem neuen Film?** have you actually been to the latest film?; **da fällt mir ~ ein, ...** now I remember ...; **wenn ~** if at all; **wie ist das ~ möglich?** how is that possible?; **gibt es das ~?** is there really such a thing?; **was wollen Sie ~ von mir?** (*herausfordernd*) what do you want from me?; **wer sind Sie ~?** who do you think you are?; **wissen Sie ~, wer ich bin?** do you realize who I am?

Über-: **überheblich** [y:bɐˈhe:plɪç] ADJ arrogant; **Überheblichkeit** F -, NO PL arrogance; **überheizen** [y:bɐˈhaitsn̩], *ptp* **überheizt** VT INSEP to overheat; **überhitzen** [y:bɐˈhɪtsn̩], *ptp* **überhitzt** VT INSEP to overheat; **überhitzt** [y:bɐˈhɪtst] ADJ (*fig*) *Konjunktur, Markt, Fantasie* overheated; *Gemüter, Diskussion* very heated *pred*; **Überhitzungsschutz** M cutout switch (*to prevent overheating*); **überhöht** [y:bɐˈhø:t] ADJ *Kurve* banked; *Forderungen, Preise, Geschwindigkeit* excessive

überholen [y:bɐˈho:lən], *ptp* **überholt** INSEP **1** VT **(a)** *Fahrzeug* to overtake (*esp Brit*), to pass; (*fig*: = *übertreffen*) to overtake **(b)** (*Tech*) *Maschine, Motor etc* to overhaul **2** VI to overtake

Überholmanöver NT (*Aut*) overtaking manoeuvre (*Brit*), passing maneuver (*US*)

Überholspur F (*Aut*) overtaking (*esp Brit*) *or* fast lane

überholt [y:bɐˈho:lt] ADJ out-dated

Überhol- [y:bɐˈho:l-]: **Überholverbot** NT restriction on overtaking (*esp Brit*); (*als Schild etc*) no overtaking (*esp Brit*); **auf dieser Strecke besteht ~** no overtaking (*esp Brit*) *or* passing on this stretch; **Überholvorgang** M (*form*) overtaking (*esp Brit*); **vor Beginn des ~es** before starting to overtake (*esp Brit*)

Über-: **Überich** NT (*Psych*) superego; **überirdisch** **1** ADJ **(a)** *Wesen, Schönheit* heavenly **(b)** (= *oberirdisch*) above ground **2** ADV **(a)** **~ schön** heavenly **(b)** (= *oberirdisch*) above ground; **überkandidelt** ADJ (*inf*) eccentric; **Überkapazität** F overcapacity; **überkochen** VI SEP AUX SEIN (*lit, fig*) to boil over

überkommen [y:bɐˈkɔmən], *ptp* **überkommen** VT INSEP IRREG (= *überfallen, ergreifen*) to come over; *Furcht etc* **überkam ihn** he was overcome with fear *etc*

Über-: **überkompensieren** *ptp* **überkompensiert** VT INSEP to overcompensate for; **überkreuzen** [y:bɐˈkrɔytsn̩], *ptp* **überkreuzt** **1** VT (= *überqueren*) to cross **2** VR (= *sich überschneiden*: *Linien etc*) to intersect; **überkriegen** VT SEP (*inf*: = *überdrüssig werden*) to get sick (and tired) (*inf*) of; **eins ~** to get hit; **überladen**[1] [y:bɐˈla:dn̩], *ptp* **überladen** VT INSEP IRREG to overload; **überladen**[2] [y:bɐˈla:dn̩] ADJ *Wagen* overloaded; (*fig*) *Stil* over-ornate; *Bild* cluttered; **Überladung** F overload; **überlang** ADJ *Oper, Stück etc* overlength; *Arme, Mantel, Netze, Schnüre etc* too long; **Überlänge** F excessive length; **~ haben** to be overlength; **überlappen** [y:bɐˈlapn̩], *ptp* **überlappt** VIR INSEP to overlap

überlassen [y:bɐˈlasn̩], *ptp* **überlassen** VT INSEP IRREG **(a)** (= *haben lassen*) **jdm etw ~** to let sb have sth **(b)** (= *anheim stellen*) **es jdm ~, etw zu tun** to leave it (up) to sb to do sth; **das bleibt (ganz) Ihnen ~** that's (entirely) up to you; **jdm die Initiative/Wahl ~** to leave the initiative/choice (up) to sb
(c) (= *in Obhut geben*) **jdm etw ~** to leave sth with sb; **sich** (*dat*) **selbst ~ sein** to be left to one's own devices; **jdn sich** (*dat*) **selbst ~** to leave sb to his/her own devices
(d) (= *preisgeben*) **sich seinem Schmerz/seinen Gedanken/**

Gefühlen ~ to abandon oneself to one's pain/thoughts/feelings; **jdn seinem Schicksal** ~ to leave sb to his fate

Überlassung [yːbɐˈlasʊn] F **-, -en** (*von Recht, Anspruch*) surrender

überlasten [yːbɐˈlastn], *ptp* **überlastet** VT INSEP to put too great a strain on; *jdn* to overtax; (*Elec*) *Telefonnetz, (durch Gewicht) Brücke* to overload; **überlastet sein** to be under too great a strain; (= *überfordert sein*) to be overtaxed; (*Elec etc*) to be overloaded

Überlastung F **-, -en** (*von Mensch*) overtaxing; (= *Überlastetsein*) strain; (*Elec, durch Gewicht*) overloading; **bei ~ der Leber** when there is too much strain on the liver

überlaufen¹ [ˈyːbɐlaufn] VI SEP IRREG AUX SEIN **(a)** (*Wasser, Gefäß*) to overflow; (= *überkochen*) to boil over; **zum Überlaufen voll** full to overflowing **(b)** (*Mil, fig:* = *überwechseln*) to desert; **zum Feind** ~ to go over to the enemy

überlaufen² [yːbɐˈlaufn] ADJ overcrowded; (*mit Touristen*) overrun

Überläufer(in) M(F) turncoat

überleben [yːbɐˈleːbn], *ptp* **überlebt** INSEP **1** VT to survive; **das überlebe ich nicht!** (*inf*) it'll be the death of me (*inf*); **ums Überleben kämpfen** to fight for survival **2** VI to survive **3** VR **das hat sich überlebt** that's had its day; **diese Mode überlebt sich ganz schnell** this fashion will soon be a thing of the past

Überlebende(r) [yːbɐˈleːbndə] MF DECL AS ADJ survivor

Überlebenschance F chance of survival

überlebensgroß ADJ *Denkmal etc* larger-than-life

Überlebenstraining NT survival training

überlegen¹ [yːbɐˈleːgn], *ptp* **überlegt** INSEP **1** VI (= *nachdenken*) to think; **überleg doch mal!** think!; **hin und her** ~ to deliberate; **ich habe hin und her überlegt** I've thought about it a lot; **ohne zu** ~ without thinking; (= *ohne zu zögern*) without thinking twice **2** VT (= *überdenken, durchdenken*) to think about, to consider; **das werde ich mir** ~ I'll think about it; **ich habe es mir anders überlegt** I've changed my mind (about it); **ich habe es mir noch mal überlegt** I've had second thoughts (about it); **wollen Sie es sich** (*dat*) **nicht noch einmal ~?** won't you think it over again?; **das hätten Sie sich** (*dat*) **vorher ~ müssen** you should have thought about that before *or* sooner; **es wäre zu** ~ it should be considered; **wenn man es sich recht überlegt** if you really think about it

überlegen² [yːbɐˈleːgn] **1** ADJ superior; **jdm** ~ **sein** to be superior to sb; **ein ~er Sieg** that was a convincing victory **2** ADV in a superior manner; **Bayern München hat ~ gesiegt** Bayern Munich won convincingly

Überlegenheit F **-**, NO PL superiority

überlegt [yːbɐˈleːkt] **1** ADJ (well-)considered **2** ADV in a considered way

Überlegung [yːbɐˈleːgʊn] F **-, -en (a)** (= *Nachdenken*) consideration, thought; **bei näherer** ~ on closer examination; (= *nüchterner* ~ on reflection; **das wäre wohl einer ~ wert** that would be worth thinking about; **ohne ~** without thinking **(b)** (= *Bemerkung*) observation; **~en anstellen** to make observations (*zu* about *or* on)

überleiten SEP **1** VT (*Thema, Abschnitt etc*) to link up (*in +acc* to, with) **2** VI **zu etw** ~ to lead up to sth

Überleitung F connection; (*zur nächsten Frage, Mus*) transition

überlesen [yːbɐˈleːzn], *ptp* **überlesen** VT INSEP IRREG (= *übersehen*) to miss

überliefern [yːbɐˈliːfɐn], *ptp* **überliefert** VT INSEP *Brauch, Tradition, Lied* to hand down; **das Manuskript ist nur als Fragment überliefert** the manuscript has only come down to us in fragmentary form; **etw der Nachwelt** ~ to preserve sth for posterity

Überlieferung F **(a)** tradition; **schriftliche ~en** (written) records **(b)** (= *Brauch*) tradition

überlisten [yːbɐˈlɪstn], *ptp* **überlistet** VT INSEP to outwit

überm [ˈyːbɐm] CONTR *von* über dem

Übermacht F, NO PL superior strength; (*fig: von Gefühlen, Ideologie etc*) predominance; **in der** ~ **sein** to have the greater strength

übermächtig ADJ *Gewalt, Stärke* superior; *Feind, Opposition* powerful; *Wunsch, Bedürfnis* overpowering; (*fig*) *Institution* all-powerful

Übermaß NT, NO PL excessive amount (*an +acc* of); **im** ~ to *or* in excess

übermäßig **1** ADJ excessive; *Schmerz, Sehnsucht* violent; *Freude* intense; **das war nicht** ~ that was not too brilliant **2** ADV excessively; **er hat sich nicht** ~ **bemüht** he didn't exactly overexert himself

übermenschlich ADJ superhuman; **Übermenschliches leisten** to perform superhuman feats

übermitteln [yːbɐˈmɪtln], *ptp* **übermittelt** VT INSEP to convey (*jdm* to sb); *Daten, Meldung* to transmit

Übermittlung [yːbɐˈmɪtlʊn] F **-, -en** conveyance; (*telefonisch etc, von Meldung*) transmission

übermorgen ADV the day after tomorrow; ~ **Abend/früh** the day after tomorrow in the evening/morning

Übermüdung F **-**, NO PL overtiredness

Übermut M high spirits *pl*; **vor lauter** ~ **wussten die Kinder nicht, was sie tun sollten** the children were so full of high spirits that they didn't know what to do with themselves; ~ **tut selten gut** (*Prov*) pride goes before a fall (*Prov*); (*zu Kindern*) it'll all end in tears

übermütig [ˈyːbɐmyːtɪç] **1** ADJ **(a)** (= *ausgelassen*) boisterous **(b)** (= *zu mutig*) cocky (*inf*) **2** ADV (= *ausgelassen*) boisterously

übernächste(r, s) ADJ ATTR next ... but one; **das** ~ **Haus** the next house but one; **die** ~ **Woche** the week after next; **am ~n Tag war er ...** two days later he was ...; **er kommt ~n Freitag** he's coming a week on Friday

übernachten [yːbɐˈnaxtn], *ptp* **übernachtet** VI INSEP to sleep; (*in Hotel, Privathaus etc auch*) to stay; (*eine Nacht*) to spend the night; **bei jdm** ~ to stay with sb; **wie viele Leute können bei dir ~?** how many people can you put up?

übernächtigt [yːbɐˈnɛçtɪçt], (*esp Aus*) **übernächtig** [ˈyːbɐnɛçtɪç] ADJ bleary-eyed

Übernachtung [yːbɐˈnaxtʊn] F **-, -en** overnight stay; ~ **und Frühstück** bed and breakfast

Übernachtungsmöglichkeit F overnight accommodation *no pl*; **sich nach einer** ~ **umsehen** to look for somewhere to spend the night

Übernahme [ˈyːbɐnaːmə] F **-, -n (a)** takeover (*auch Comm, Fin*); (= *das Übernehmen*) taking over; (*von Ausdruck, Ansicht*) adoption; (*von Zitat, Wort*) borrowing; **seit der** ~ **des Geschäfts durch den Sohn** since the son took over the business; **freundliche/feindliche** ~ (*Comm*) friendly/hostile takeover **(b)** (*von Amt*) assumption; **durch** ~ **dieser Aufgabe** by taking on this task; **er hat sich zur** ~ **der Kosten/Hypothek verpflichtet** he has agreed to pay the costs/mortgage; **bei** ~ **einer neuen Klasse** (*Sch*) when taking charge of a new class

Übernahmeangebot NT, **Übernahmeofferte** F takeover bid

übernatürlich ADJ supernatural

übernehmen [yːbɐˈneːmən], *ptp* **übernommen** [yːbɐˈnɔmən] INSEP IRREG **1** VT **(a)** (= *annehmen*) to take; *Aufgabe, Arbeit, Verantwortung, Funktion* to take on; *Kosten, Hypothek* to agree to pay; (= *kaufen*) to buy; **die Führung** ~ (*von Organisation etc*) to take charge (*gen* of); (*Sport*) to take over the lead; **seit er das Amt übernommen hat** since he assumed office; **er übernimmt Ostern eine neue Klasse** (*Sch*) he's taking charge of a new class at Easter; **lassen Sie mal, das übernehme ich!** let me take care of that; **es ~, etw zu tun** to undertake to do sth **(b)** (*stellvertretend, ablösend*) to take over (*von* from); *Ausdruck, Ansicht* to adopt; *Zitat, Wort* to borrow **(c)** *Geschäft, Praxis etc* to take over **2** VR to take on too much; (= *sich überanstrengen*) to overdo it; (*beim Essen*) to overeat; ~ **Sie sich nur nicht!** (*iro*) don't strain yourself! (*iro*)

übernervös ADJ highly strung

überparteilich **1** ADJ nonparty *attr*; (= *unvoreingenommen*) nonpartisan; (*Parl*) *Problem* all-party *attr*; *Amt, Präsident etc* above party politics **2** ADV *handeln, denken* in a nonpartisan way; **ein ~ zusammengesetztes Komitee** a nonpartisan committee

Überproduktion F overproduction

überprüfbar ADJ checkable

Überprüfbarkeit [yˈbɐˌpryːfbaːɐkait] F -, NO PL means *sing* of checking; **aufgrund der mangelnder ~** because there is no means of checking

überprüfen [yːbɐˈpryːfn], *ptp* **überprüft** VT INSEP (*auf +acc* for) to check; *Gepäck auch, Maschine, Waren, (Fin) Bücher* to inspect, to examine; *Entscheidung, Lage, Frage* to review; *Ergebnisse, Teilnehmer etc* to scrutinize; *(Pol) jdn* to screen

Überprüfung F **(a)** NO PL (= *das Überprüfen*) checking; (*von Maschinen, Waren, Fin: von Büchern*) inspection, examination; (*von Entscheidung*) review; (*Pol*) screening; **nach ~ der Lage** after reviewing the situation **(b)** (= *Kontrolle*) inspection

überqueren [yːbɐˈkveːrən], *ptp* **überquert** VT INSEP to cross

überragend ◫ ADJ (*fig*) outstanding; *Bedeutung auch* paramount ◪ ADV outstandingly well

überraschen [yːbɐˈraʃn], *ptp* **überrascht** VT INSEP to surprise; **jdn bei etw ~** to catch sb doing sth; **von einem Gewitter überrascht werden** to be caught in a storm; **lassen wir uns ~!** let's wait and see!; *siehe auch* **überrascht**

überraschend ◫ ADJ surprising; *Besuch surprise attr; Tod, Weggang* unexpected; **eine ~e Wendung nehmen** to take an unexpected turn ◪ ADV unexpectedly; **das kam (für uns) völlig ~** that came as a complete surprise *or* (*Sterbefall etc*) shock (to us)

überraschenderweise [yːbɐˈraʃndɐˈvaizə] ADV surprisingly

überrascht [yːbɐˈraʃt] ◫ ADJ surprised (*über +dat* at); **da bin ich aber ~!** that's quite a surprise ◪ ADV with surprise; **jdn ~ ansehen** to look at sb in surprise; *siehe auch* **überraschen**

Überraschung [yːbɐˈraʃʊŋ] F -, -en surprise; **zu meiner (größten) ~** to my (great) surprise; **für eine ~ sorgen** to have a surprise in store; **sie ist immer für eine ~ gut** she never ceases to amaze

überreagieren *ptp* **überreagiert** VI INSEP to overreact

Überreaktion F overreaction

überreden [yːbɐˈreːdn], *ptp* **überredet** VT INSEP to persuade; **jdn ~, etw zu tun** to persuade sb to do sth; **jdn zu etw ~** to talk sb into sth

Überredungskunst F persuasiveness; **all ihre Überredungskünste** all her powers of persuasion

überregional ◫ ADJ (= *national*) national ◪ ADV nationally

überreichen [yːbɐˈraiçn], *ptp* **überreicht** VT INSEP **(jdm) etw ~** to hand sth over (to sb); (*feierlich*) to present sth (to sb)

überreichlich ◫ ADJ ample, abundant; (= *zu reichlich*) overabundant; **in ~em Maße** in abundance ◪ ADV *Gebrauch machen* excessively; **~ essen/trinken** to eat/drink more than enough; **eine ~ bemessene Dosierung** an extremely high dose

Überreichung F -, -en presentation

überrepräsentiert ADJ overrepresented

Überrest M remains *pl*

Überrollbügel M (*Aut*) rollbar

überrumpeln [yːbɐˈrʊmpln], *ptp* **überrumpelt** VT INSEP (*inf*) to take by surprise; (= *überwältigen*) to overpower; **jdn mit einer Frage ~** to throw sb with a question

Überrumpelungstaktik F surprise tactics *pl*

überrunden [yːbɐˈrʊndn], *ptp* **überrundet** VT INSEP (*Sport*) to lap; (*fig*) to outstrip

übers [yːbɐs] CONTR *von* **über das**

übersättigen [yːbɐˈzɛtɪɡn], *ptp* **übersättigt** VT INSEP to satiate; *Markt* to oversaturate; (*Chem*) to supersaturate; **übersättigt sein** (*Menschen*) to be sated with luxuries

Übersättigung F satiety; (*des Marktes*) oversaturation; (*Chem*) supersaturation

Übersäuerung F -, -en excessive acidity; (*von Gewässer, Boden*) over-acidification

Überschall- IN CPDS supersonic; **Überschallflugzeug** NT supersonic aircraft, SST (*esp US*); **Überschallgeschwindigkeit** F supersonic speed; **mit ~ fliegen** to fly supersonic; **Überschallknall** M sonic boom

überschaubar ADJ *Plan, Gesetzgebung etc* easily understandable; *Grenzen, Größenordnung, Kundenkreis* manageable; *Zeitraum* reasonable; **damit die Abteilung ~ bleibt** so that one can keep a general overview of the department; **die Folgen sind noch nicht ~** the consequences cannot yet be clearly seen

Überschaubarkeit [yːbɐˈʃaubaːɐkait] F -, NO PL comprehensibility; **zum Zwecke der besseren ~** to give (you) a better idea

überschäumen VI SEP AUX SEIN to froth over; (*fig*) to bubble (over) (*vor +dat* with); (*vor Wut*) to seethe; **~de Begeisterung** *etc* bubbling enthusiasm *etc*

überschlafen [yːbɐˈʃlaːfn], *ptp* **überschlafen** VT INSEP IRREG *Problem etc* to sleep on

Überschlag M **(a)** (= *Berechnung*) (rough) estimate **(b)** (= *Drehung*) somersault (*auch Sport*)

überschlagen¹ [yːbɐˈʃlaːgn], *ptp* **überschlagen** INSEP IRREG ◫ VT **(a)** (= *auslassen*) to skip **(b)** (= *berechnen*) *Kosten etc* to estimate (roughly) ◪ VR (*Mensch*) to somersault; (*Auto*) to turn over; (*fig: Ereignisse*) to come thick and fast; **sich vor Hilfsbereitschaft** (*dat*)/**mit Vorschlägen ~** to fall over oneself to be helpful/to make suggestions

überschlagen² [yːbɐˈʃlaːgn] SEP IRREG ◫ VT *Beine* to cross; *Arme* to fold; *Decke* to turn back ◪ VI AUX SEIN **(a)** (*Wellen*) to break **(b)** (*Stimmung etc*) **in etw** (*acc*) **~** to turn into sth

überschlagen³ [yːbɐˈʃlaːgn] ADJ *Flüssigkeit* lukewarm; *Zimmer* slightly warm

überschnappen VI SEP AUX SEIN (*Stimme*) to crack; (*inf: Mensch*) to crack up (*inf*); *siehe auch* **übergeschnappt**

überschneiden [yːbɐˈʃnaidn], *ptp* **überschnitten** [yːbɐˈʃnɪtn] VR INSEP IRREG (*Linien*) to intersect; (*Flächen*) (*fig: Themen, Interessen, Ereignisse etc*) to overlap; (*völlig*) to coincide; (*unerwünscht*) to clash

Überschneidung F -, -en (*von Linien*) intersection; (*von Flächen*) (*fig*) overlap *no pl*; (*unerwünscht*) clash

Überschreibemodus M (*Comput*) typeover mode

überschreiben [yːbɐˈʃraibn], *ptp* **überschrieben** [yːbɐˈʃriːbn] VT INSEP IRREG **(a)** (= *betiteln*) to head **(b)** (= *übertragen*) **etw jdm** *or* **auf jdn ~** to sign sth over to sb **(c)** (*Comput*) *Daten, Diskette* to overwrite; *Text* to type over

überschreiten [yːbɐˈʃraitn], *ptp* **überschritten** [yːbɐˈʃrɪtn] VT INSEP IRREG to cross; (*fig*) to exceed; *Höhepunkt, Alter* to pass; **die Grenze des Erlaubten/des Anstands ~** to go beyond what is permissible/decent

Überschrift F heading; (= *Schlagzeile*) headline

überschuldet [yːbɐˈʃʊldət] ADJ *Person, Unternehmen* heavily in debt; *Grundstück* heavily mortgaged

Überschuldung [yːbɐˈʃʊldʊŋ] F -, -en excessive debts *pl*; (*von Grundstück*) heavy mortgaging

Überschuss M surplus (*an +dat* of)

Überschussbeteiligung F surplus sharing

überschüssig [-ʃʏsɪç] ADJ surplus

überschütten [yːbɐˈʃʏtn], *ptp* **überschüttet** VT INSEP **(a)** (= *bedecken*) **jdn/etw mit etw ~** to cover sb/sth with sth; *mit Flüssigkeit* to pour sth onto sb/sth **(b)** (= *überhäufen*) **jdn mit etw ~** to heap sth on sb

überschwänglich [yːbɐˈʃvɛŋlɪç] ◫ ADJ effusive ◪ ADV effusively

überschwappen VI SEP AUX SEIN to splash over; (= *sich ausbreiten*) to spill over

überschwemmen [yːbɐˈʃvɛman], *ptp* **überschwemmt** VT INSEP (*lit, fig*) to flood; *Verbraucher, Leser etc* to swamp

Überschwemmung F -, -en (*lit*) flood; (= *das Überschwemmen*) flooding *no pl*; (*fig*) inundation; (*von Verbrauchern, Lesern*) swamping; **es kam zu ~en** there was a lot of flooding

Überschwemmungs-: **Überschwemmungsgebiet** NT (= *überschwemmtes Gebiet*) flood area; (*Geog*) flood plain; **Überschwemmungsgefahr** F danger of flooding; **Überschwemmungskatastrophe** F flood disaster

überschwenglich [yːbɐˈʃvɛŋlɪç] ADJ, ADV *siehe* **überschwänglich**

Übersee NO ART **in/nach ~** overseas; **aus/von ~** from overseas; **Briefe nach ~** overseas letters

übersehbar ADJ **(a)** (*lit*) *Gegend etc* visible; **das Tal ist von hier schlecht ~** you don't get a good view of the valley from here **(b)** (*fig*) (= *erkennbar*) *Folgen, Zusammenhänge etc* clear; (= *abschätzbar*) *Kosten, Dauer etc* assessable; **dieses Fachgebiet ist nicht mehr ~** it is no longer possible to have an overall view of this subject; **die Folgen sind klar/schlecht ~** the consequences are quite/not very clear; **der Schaden ist noch gar nicht ~** the damage cannot be assessed yet

(c) solche Druckfehler sind leicht ~ misprints like that are easily overlooked

übersehen [yːbɐˈzeːən], *ptp* **übersehen** VT INSEP IRREG **(a)** (*lit*) *Gegend etc* to have a view of **(b)** (= *erkennen, Bescheid wissen über*) *Folgen, Zusammenhänge, Sachlage* to see clearly; *Fachgebiet* to have an overall view of; (= *abschätzen*) *Schaden, Kosten, Dauer* to assess **(c)** (= *ignorieren, nicht erkennen*) to overlook; (= *nicht bemerken*) to miss; **~, dass ...** to overlook the fact that ...; *etw* **stillschweigend/geflissentlich ~** to quietly/conveniently ignore sth

über sein VI IRREG AUX SEIN (*inf*) **jdm ist etw über** sb is fed up with sth (*inf*)

übersenden [yːbɐˈzɛndn̩], *ptp* **übersandt** *or* **übersendet** [yːbɐˈzant, yːbɐˈzɛndət] VT INSEP IRREG to send; **hiermit ~ wir Ihnen ...** please find enclosed ...

übersetzen¹ [yːbɐˈzɛtsn̩], *ptp* **übersetzt** VT INSEP **(a)** AUCH VI (*in andere Sprachen*) to translate; **aus dem** *or* **vom Englischen ins Deutsche ~** to translate from English into German; *etw* **falsch ~** to mistranslate sth; **sich leicht/schwer ~ lassen** to be easy/hard to translate; **sich gut/schlecht ~ lassen** to translate well/badly **(b)** (*Tech*) (= *umwandeln*) to translate; (= *übertragen*) to transmit

übersetzen² [ˈyːbɐzɛtsn̩] SEP **1** VT (*mit Fähre*) to ferry across **2** VI AUX SEIN to cross (over)

Übersetzer(in) M(F) translator

Übersetzung [yːbɐˈzɛtsʊŋ] F **-, -en (a)** translation **(b)** (*Tech*) (= *Umwandlung*) conversion; (= *Übertragung*) transmission; (= *Übersetzungsverhältnis*) gear ratio

Übersicht F **-, -en (a)** NO PL (= *Überblick*) overall view; **die ~ verlieren** to lose track of things **(b)** (= *Abriss, Resümee*) survey; (= *Tabelle*) table

übersichtlich **1** ADJ *Gelände etc* open; (= *erfassbar*) *Darstellung etc* clear; **eine Bibliothek muss ~ sein** a library should be clearly laid out **2** ADV clearly; **~ angelegt** *or* **geplant** clearly laid out; **~ gegliederte Einträge** well-structured entries

Übersichtlichkeit F **-,** NO PL (*von Gelände etc*) openness; (= *Verständlichkeit: von Darstellung etc*) clarity

Übersichtskarte F general map

überspannt [yːbɐˈʃpant] ADJ *Ideen, Forderungen* extravagant; (= *exaltiert*) eccentric; (= *hysterisch*) hysterical; *Nerven* overexcited

überspielen [yːbɐˈʃpiːlən], *ptp* **überspielt** VT INSEP **(a)** (= *verbergen*) to cover (up) **(b)** (= *übertragen*) *Aufnahme etc* to transfer; **eine CD (auf Kassette) ~** to tape a CD

überspitzt [yːbɐˈʃpɪtst] **1** ADJ *Formulierungen* (= *zu spitzfindig*) over(ly) subtle, fiddly (*Brit inf*); (= *übertrieben*) exaggerated; *Argument* overstated **2** ADV (= *übertrieben*) in an exaggerated fashion; **~ argumentieren** to overstate one's argument(s) *or* case

überspringen¹ [yːbɐˈʃprɪŋən], *ptp* **übersprungen** [yːbɐˈʃprʊŋən] VT INSEP IRREG **(a)** *Hindernis, Höhe* to clear; **die Fünfprozenthürde ~** to clear the five-percent hurdle **(b)** (= *weiter springen als*) to jump more than **(c)** (= *auslassen*) *Klasse, Kapitel, Lektion* to skip

überspringen² [ˈyːbɐʃprɪŋən] VI SEP IRREG AUX SEIN (*lit, fig: = sich übertragen*) to jump (*auf +acc* to); (*Begeisterung etc*) to spread quickly (*auf +acc* to)

überstaatlich ADJ supranational

überstehen¹ [yːbɐˈʃteːən], *ptp* **überstanden** VT INSEP IRREG (= *durchstehen*) to get through; (= *überleben*) to survive; (= *überwinden*) to overcome; *Unwetter* to weather; *Krankheit* to get over; **etw lebend ~** to survive sth; **das Schlimmste ist jetzt überstanden** the worst is over now; **das wäre überstanden!** thank heavens that's over

überstehen² [ˈyːbɐʃteːən] VI SEP IRREG AUX HABEN or SEIN (= *hervorstehen*) to jut *or* stick out

übersteigen [yːbɐˈʃtaign̩], *ptp* **überstiegen** VT INSEP IRREG **(a)** (= *klettern über*) to climb over **(b)** (= *hinausgehen über*) to exceed

übersteigert [yːbɐˈʃtaigɐt] ADJ excessive; **an einem ~en Selbstbewusstsein leiden** to have an inflated view of oneself

überstimmen [yːbɐˈʃtɪmən], *ptp* **überstimmt** VT INSEP to outvote; *Antrag* to vote down

überstrapazieren *ptp* **überstrapaziert** INSEP **1** VT to wear out; *Ausrede etc* to wear thin; **überstrapaziert** worn out; thin; **jds Geduld ~** to really try sb's patience **2** VR to wear oneself out

Überstunde F hour of overtime; **~n** overtime *sing*; **~n/zwei ~n machen** to do overtime/two hours overtime

Überstundenzuschlag M overtime allowance; **der ~ beträgt 50%** overtime is paid at time and a half

überstürzen [yːbɐˈʃtʏrtsn̩], *ptp* **überstürzt** INSEP **1** VT to rush into; **man soll nichts ~, nur nichts ~!** look before you leap (*Prov*) **2** VR (*Ereignisse etc*) to happen in a rush; (*Nachrichten*) to come fast and furious; (*Worte*) to come tumbling out

überstürzt [yːbɐˈʃtʏrtst] **1** ADJ overhasty **2** ADV rashly

übertariflich ADJ, ADV above the agreed rate

überteuert [yːbɐˈtɔyɐt] ADJ overexpensive; *Preise, Mieten* inflated

übertölpeln [yːbɐˈtœlpln̩], *ptp* **übertölpelt** VT INSEP to take in, to dupe

übertönen [yːbɐˈtøːnən], *ptp* **übertönt** VT INSEP to drown

Übertrag [ˈyːbɐtraːk] M **-(e)s, ⸚e** [-trɛːgə] amount carried forward (*esp Brit*) *or* over (*esp US*)

übertragbar ADJ transferable (*auch Jur, Comput*); *Methode, Maßstab* applicable (*auf +acc* to); *Ausdruck* applicable (*in +acc* into); *Krankheit* communicable (*form*) (*auf +acc* to), infectious; (*durch Berührung*) contagious

Übertragbarkeit [yːbɐˈtraːkbaːɐkait] F **-,** NO PL transferability (*auch Jur, Comput*); (*von Krankheit*) infectiousness; (*durch Berührung*) contagiousness

übertragen¹ [yːbɐˈtraːgn̩], *ptp* **übertragen** INSEP IRREG **1** VT **(a)** (= *an eine andere Stelle bringen, an jdn übergeben*) to transfer (*auch Jur, Psych, Comput*); *Krankheit* to pass on (*auf +acc* to); (*Tech*) *Bewegung, Kraft* to transmit **(b)** (= *kopieren*) to copy (out); (= *transkribieren*) to transcribe **(c)** (*TV, Rad*) to transmit; **etw im Fernsehen ~** to televise sth; **via** *or* **durch Satelliten ~ werden** to be broadcast by satellite **(d)** (= *übersetzen*) *Text* to render (*in +acc* into); **... aus dem Englischen ~ von ...** ... translated from the English by ... **(e)** *Methode, Maßstab* to apply (*auf +acc* to) **(f)** (= *verleihen*) *Auszeichnung, Würde* to confer (*jdm* on sb); *Vollmacht, Verantwortung, Amt* to give (*jdm* sb) **(g)** (= *auftragen*) *Aufgabe, Mission* to assign (*jdm* to sb) **2** VR (*Eigenschaft, Krankheit etc*) to be passed on (*auf +acc* to); (*Tech*) to be transmitted (*auf +acc* to); (*Heiterkeit etc*) to spread (*auf +acc* to); **seine Fröhlichkeit hat sich auf uns ~** we were infected by his happiness

übertragen² [yːbɐˈtraːgn̩] **1** ADJ **(a)** *Bedeutung etc* figurative **(b)** (*Aus*) worn; (= *gebraucht*) second-hand **2** ADV (= *figurativ*) figuratively

Übertragung F **-, -en (a)** (= *Transport*) transfer (*auch Comput*); (*von Krankheit*) passing on (*b*) (*schriftlich*) transference; (= *das Kopieren*) copying (out); (= *Transkription*) transcription **(c)** (*TV, Rad*) transmission **(d)** (= *Übersetzung*) rendering **(e)** (= *Anwendung*) application **(f)** **„~ auf andere Tonträger verboten**" "recording forbidden in any form"

Übertragungs-: **Übertragungsanzeige** F (*Comput*) transfer dialogue box; **Übertragungsbilanz** F transfer balance sheet; **Übertragungsfehler** M (*Comput*) transmission error; **Übertragungsgeschwindigkeit** F (*Comput*) transfer rate; **Übertragungsprotokoll** NT (*Comput*) transfer protocol; **Übertragungsrate** F (*Comput*) transmission rate; **Übertragungswagen** M outside broadcast unit

übertreffen [yːbɐˈtrɛfn̩], *ptp* **übertroffen** [yːbɐˈtrɔfn̩] INSEP IRREG **1** VT to surpass (*an +dat* in); *Rekord* to break; **jdn an Intelligenz/Schönheit** *etc* **~** to be more intelligent/beautiful *etc* than sb; **er ist nicht zu ~** he is unsurpassable **2** VR **sich selbst ~** to excel oneself

übertreiben [yːbɐˈtraibn̩], *ptp* **übertrieben** [yːbɐˈtriːbn̩] VT INSEP IRREG **(a)** AUCH VI (= *aufbauschen*) to exaggerate; **ohne zu ~** without exaggerating **(b)** (= *zu weit treiben*) to overdo; **es mit der Sauberkeit ~** to take cleanliness too far; *siehe auch* **übertrieben**

Übertreibung F **-, -en** exaggeration; **man kann ohne ~ sagen ...** it's no exaggeration to say ...

übertreten [yːbɐˈtreːtn̩], *ptp* **übertreten** VT INSEP IRREG *Grenze etc* to cross; (*fig*) *Gesetz, Verbot* to break

Übertretung [y:bɐˈtreːtʊŋ] F **-, -en** (von Gesetz etc) violation; (Jur. = strafbare Handlung) misdemeanour (Brit), misdemeanor (US)

übertrieben [y:bɐˈtriːbn] **1** ADJ exaggerated; (= zu stark, übermäßig) Vorsicht, Training excessive **2** ADV (= übermäßig) excessively; siehe auch **übertreiben**

Übertritt M (über Grenze) crossing (über +acc of); (zu anderem Glauben) conversion; (von Abtrünnigen, esp zu anderer Partei) defection; (von einer Schule) move (in +acc to); **die Zahl der ~e zur demokratischen Partei** the number of people going over to the democratic party

überübermorgen ADV (inf) in three days

übervölkern [y:bɐˈfœlkɐn], ptp **übervölkert** VT INSEP to overpopulate

Übervölkerung F **-, -en** overpopulation

übervoll ADJ too full; Glas full to the brim

übervorsichtig ADJ overcautious

übervorteilen [y:bɐˈfɔrtailən], ptp **übervorteilt** VT INSEP to cheat, to do down (inf)

überwachen [y:bɐˈvaxn], ptp **überwacht** VT INSEP (= kontrollieren) to supervise; (= beobachten) to observe; Verdächtigen to keep under surveillance; (auf Monitor, mit Radar, fig) to monitor

Überwachung F **-, -en** supervision; (= Beobachtung) observation; (von Verdächtigen) surveillance; (auf Monitor, mit Radar, fig) monitoring

Überwachungskamera F surveillance camera

Überwachungsstaat F Big Brother state

überwältigen [y:bɐˈvɛltɪɡn], ptp **überwältigt** VT INSEP (a) (lit) to overpower; (zahlenmäßig) to overwhelm; (= bezwingen) to overcome (b) (fig) (Schlaf, Mitleid, Angst etc) to overcome; (Musik, Schönheit etc) to overwhelm

überwältigend ADJ overwhelming; Schönheit stunning; Erfolg phenomenal; **nicht gerade ~** nothing to write home about (inf)

überwechseln VI SEP AUX SEIN to move (in +acc to); (zu Partei etc) to go over (zu to); (Wild) to cross over

Überweg M **-** für Fußgänger pedestrian crossing

überweisen [y:bɐˈvaizn], ptp **überwiesen** [y:bɐˈviːzn] VT INSEP IRREG Geld to transfer (an +acc, auf +acc to); Patienten to refer (an +acc to); **mein Gehalt wird direkt auf mein Bankkonto überwiesen** my salary is paid directly into my bank account

Überweisung F (= Geldüberweisung) (credit) transfer; (von Patient) referral

überwerfen¹ [y:bɐˈvɛrfn], ptp **überworfen** [y:bɐˈvɔrfn] VR INSEP IRREG (= zerstreiten) **sich (mit jdm) ~** to fall out (with sb)

überwerfen² [ˈyːbɐvɛrfn] VT SEP IRREG to put over; Kleidungsstück to put on; (sehr rasch) to throw on

überwiegen [y:bɐˈviːɡn], ptp **überwogen** [y:bɐˈvoːɡn] INSEP IRREG **1** VT to outweigh **2** VI (= das Übergewicht haben) to be predominant; (= das Übergewicht gewinnen) to prevail

überwiegend **1** ADJ predominant; Mehrheit vast; **der ~e Teil** (+gen) the majority (of); **zum ~en Teil** for the most part **2** ADV predominantly

überwinden [y:bɐˈvɪndn], ptp **überwunden** [y:bɐˈvʊndn] INSEP IRREG **1** VT to overcome; **überwunden** Standpunkt, Haltung etc of the past; Angst conquered; Krise, Rezession that has been overcome; **ein bis heute noch nicht überwundenes Vorurteil** a prejudice which is still prevalent today **2** VR to overcome one's inclinations; **sich ~, etw zu tun** to force oneself to do sth; **ich konnte mich nicht dazu ~** I couldn't bring myself to do it

Überwindung F, NO PL overcoming; (= Selbstüberwindung) will power; **das hat mich viel ~ gekostet** that took me a lot of will power; **selbst bei der größten ~ könnte ich das nicht tun** I simply couldn't bring myself to do it

Überzahl F, NO PL **in der ~ sein** to be in the majority; (Feind) to be superior in number; **die Frauen waren in der ~** the women outnumbered the men

überzählig ADJ (= überschüssig) surplus; (= überflüssig) superfluous; (= übrig) spare

überzeichnen [y:bɐˈtsaiçnən], ptp **überzeichnet** VT INSEP (a) (Fin) Aktie, Anleihe to oversubscribe (b) (fig: = übertrieben darstellen) to exaggerate

Überzeichnung F **-, -en** (St Ex) oversubscription

überzeugen [y:bɐˈtsɔygn], ptp **überzeugt** INSEP **1** VT to convince; (Jur) to satisfy; **er ließ sich nicht ~** he would not be convinced; **ich bin davon überzeugt, dass …** I am convinced that …; **Sie dürfen überzeugt sein, dass …** you may rest assured that …; **er ist sehr von sich überzeugt** he is very sure of himself **2** VI to be convincing **3** VR **sich (selbst) ~** to convince oneself (von of), to satisfy oneself (von as to); (mit eigenen Augen) to see for oneself; **~ Sie sich selbst!** see for yourself!

überzeugend **1** ADJ convincing **2** ADV convincingly; **~ klingen** to sound convincing

Überzeugung F (a) (= das Überzeugen) convincing (b) (= das Überzeugtsein) conviction; (= Prinzipien) convictions pl, beliefs pl; **meiner ~ nach …, nach meiner ~ …** I am convinced (that) …; **aus ~** out of principle; **ich bin der festen ~, dass …** I am firmly convinced that …; **zu der ~ gelangen** or **kommen, dass …, die ~ gewinnen, dass …** to become convinced that …

Überzeugungs-: Überzeugungskraft F persuasiveness; **Überzeugungstäter(in)** M(F) **~ sein** to commit an offence (Brit) or offense (US) for political/religious etc reasons

überziehen¹ [y:bɐˈtsiːən], ptp **überzogen** [y:bɐˈtsoːgn] INSEP IRREG **1** VT (a) (= bedecken) to cover; (mit Schicht, Belag) to coat; (mit Metall) to plate; (mit Zuckerguss) to ice (Brit), to frost (US) (b) Konto to overdraw; **er hat sein Konto (um 200 Euro) überzogen** he is (200 euros) overdrawn (c) Redezeit etc to overrun (d) (= übertreiben) to overdo; siehe auch **überzogen** **2** VI (a) (Fin) to overdraw one's account (b) (Redner, Moderator) to overrun

überziehen² [ˈyːbɐtsiːən] VT SEP IRREG (a) (= anziehen) (sich dat) **etw ~** to put sth on (b) (inf: = schlagen) **jdm eins ~** to belt sb (inf)

Überziehungskredit [y:bɐˈtsiːʊŋskrediːt] M overdraft provision

überzogen [y:bɐˈtsoːgn] ADJ (= übertrieben) excessive; **sein Benehmen wirkte ~** his behaviour (Brit) or behavior (US) seemed exaggerated; siehe auch **überziehen¹**

Überzug M cover

üblich [ˈyːplɪç] ADJ usual; (= herkömmlich) customary; (= typisch, normal) normal; **wie ~** as usual; **das ist bei ihm so ~** that's usual for him; **allgemein ~ sein** to be common practice; **die allgemein ~en Bedingungen/Methoden** the usual conditions/methods

üblicherweise [ˈyːplɪçɐˈvaizə] ADV normally

Übliche(s) [ˈyːplɪçə] NT DECL AS ADJ **das ~** the usual

U-Boot [ˈuː-] NT submarine, sub (inf); (esp Hist: der deutschen Marine) U-boat

übrig [ˈyːbrɪç] ADJ (a) ATTR (= verbleibend) rest of, remaining; (= andere) other; **meine/die ~en Sachen** the rest of my/the things; **alle ~en Bücher** all the remaining or all the rest of the books (b) PRED left (over); (= zu entbehren) spare; **etw ~ haben** to have sth left (over)/to spare (c) (= mögen) **für jdn/etw wenig ~ haben** not to have much time for sb/sth; **für jdn/etw nichts ~ haben** to have no time for sb/sth; **für jdn/etw etwas ~ haben** to have a liking for sb/sth; **für jdn/etw viel ~ haben** to be very fond of sb/sth (d) (substantivisch) **das Übrige** the rest, the remainder; **alles Übrige** all the rest, everything else; **die/alle Übrigen** the/all the rest or others; **im Übrigen** incidentally, by the way

übrig bleiben VI IRREG AUX SEIN to be left (over); **wie viel ist übrig geblieben?** how much is left?; **da wird ihm gar nichts anderes ~** he won't have any choice; **was blieb mir anderes übrig als …?** what choice did I have but …?

übrigens [ˈyːbrɪɡns] ADV incidentally, by the way

übrig lassen VT IRREG to leave (jdm for sb); **(einiges)/viel zu wünschen ~** to leave something/a lot to be desired

Übung [ˈyːbʊŋ] F **-, -en** (a) NO PL (= das Üben, Geübtsein) practice; **das macht die ~, das ist alles nur ~** it's a question of practice; **aus der ~ kommen** to get out of practice; **aus der or außer ~ sein** to be out of practice; **in ~ bleiben** to keep in practice; **zur ~** as practice; **~ macht den Meister** (Prov) practice makes perfect (Prov) (b) (Veranstaltung) practice; (Mil, Sport, Sch) exercise

UdSSR [uːdeːʔɛsʔɛsˈʔɛr] F **-** (Hist) ABBR von **Union der Sozialistischen Sowjetrepubliken** USSR

UEFA-Cup [uːˈleːfaːkap] M (*Ftbl*) UEFA cup

Ufer [ˈuːfɐ] NT **-s, -** (= *Flussufer*) bank; (= *Seeufer*) shore; (= *Küstenlinie*) shoreline; **direkt am ~ gelegen** right on the water's edge; **etw ans ~ spülen** to wash sth ashore; **der Fluss trat über die ~** the river burst its banks; **zu neuen ~n aufbrechen** (*fig*) to try something completely new

Ufer-: Uferböschung F embankment; **uferlos** ADJ (= *endlos*) endless; (= *grenzenlos*) boundless; **ins Uferlose gehen** (*Debatte etc*) to go on forever; (*Kosten*) to go up and up; **sonst geraten wir ins Uferlose** otherwise things will get out of hand

uff [ʊf] INTERJ (*inf*) phew

UFO, Ufo [ˈuːfo] NT **-(s), -s** UFO, Ufo

Ufologe [ufoˈloːgə] M **-n, -n, Ufologin** [-ˈloːgɪn] F **-, -nen** ufologist

Uganda [uˈganda] NT **-s** Uganda

ugandisch [uˈgandɪʃ] ADJ Ugandan

U-Haft [ˈuː-] F (*inf*) custody

Uhr [uːɐ] F **-, -en (a)** clock; (= *Armbanduhr, Taschenuhr*) watch; (= *Anzeigeinstrument*) gauge, dial; (= *Wasseruhr, Gasuhr*) meter; **nach meiner ~** by my watch; **rund um die ~** round the clock; **die innere ~** the body clock; **ein Rennen gegen die ~** a race against the clock
(b) (*bei Zeitangaben*) **um drei (~)** at three (o'clock); **ein ~ dreißig, 1.30 ~** half past one, 1.30 (*ausgesprochen "one-thirty"*); **zwei ~ morgens** *or* **nachts/nachmittags** two o'clock in the morning/afternoon; **wie viel ~ ist es?** what time is it?, what's the time?; **um wie viel ~?** (at) what time?

Uhr(arm)band [-bant] NT, *pl* **-bänder** watch strap; (*aus Metall*) watch bracelet

Uhrenvergleich M *siehe* **Uhr (a)** comparison of clock/watch times; **einen ~ machen** to synchronize watches

Uhr-: Uhrmacher(in) M(F) *siehe* **Uhr (a)** clockmaker; watchmaker; **Uhrzeiger** M *siehe* **Uhr (a)** (clock/watch) hand; **Uhrzeigersinn** M **im ~** clockwise; **entgegen dem ~** anticlockwise (*Brit*), counterclockwise (*US*); **Uhrzeit** F time (of day); **haben Sie die genaue ~?** do you have the correct time?

Uhu [ˈuːhu] M **-s, -s** eagle owl

Ukraine [ukraˈiːnə, uˈkrainə] F **- die ~** the Ukraine

ukrainisch [ukraˈiːnɪʃ, uˈkrainɪʃ] ADJ Ukrainian

UKW [uːkaːˈveː] ABBR *von* **Ultrakurzwelle** ≈ FM

Ulme [ˈʊlmə] F **-, -n** elm

Ulmenkrankheit F, **Ulmensterben** NT Dutch elm disease

Ultimaten PL *von* **Ultimatum**

ultimativ [ʊltimaˈtiːf] **1** ADJ **(a)** *Forderung etc* given as an ultimatum **(b)** (*inf*: = *beste*) *Film, Buch* ultimate (*inf*) **2** ADV **wir fordern ~ eine Lohnerhöhung von 9%** we demand a pay rise of 9% and this is an ultimatum; **jdn ~ zu etw auffordern** to give sb an ultimatum to do sth

Ultimatum [ʊltiˈmaːtʊm] NT **-s, -s** *or* **Ultimaten** [-tn] ultimatum; **jdm ein ~ stellen** to give sb an ultimatum

Ultimo [ˈʊltimo] M **-s, -s** (*Comm*) last (day) of the month; **per ~** by the end of the month

Ultra [ˈʊltra] M **-s, -s** (*pej*) extremist

Ultra-, ultra- [ˈʊltra] IN CPDS ultra

Ultrakurzwelle [ˈʊltraˈkʊrts-] F (*Phys*) ultrashort wave; (*Rad*) ≈ very high frequency

Ultrakurzwellen-: Ultrakurzwellenempfänger M VHF receiver; **Ultrakurzwellensender** M VHF station; (= *Apparat*) VHF transmitter

Ultra-: Ultramarin [ʊltramaˈriːn] NT **-s**, NO PL ultramarine; **ultramarin(blau)** [ʊltramaˈriːn-] ADJ ultramarine; **ultramodern** [-modɛrn] **1** ADJ ultramodern **2** ADV ultramodernly

Ultraschall M (*Phys*) ultrasound

Ultraschall- IN CPDS ultrasound; **Ultraschallaufnahme** F scan (*Brit*), ultrasound (picture); **Ultraschallgerät** NT ultrasound scanner; **Ultraschalluntersuchung** F scan (*Brit*), ultrasound

ultraviolett ADJ ultraviolet

um [ʊm] **1** PREP +ACC **(a)** **um ... (herum)** around
(b) (= *nach allen Seiten*) **um sich schauen** to look around one; **um sich schlagen** to hit out in all directions
(c) (*zur Zeitangabe*) at; **bitte kommen Sie (genau) um acht** please come at eight (sharp); **um ... (herum)** around about; (*bei Uhrzeiten auch*) at about; **um Weihnachten/Ostern** *etc* around Christmas/Easter *etc*
(d) (= *betreffend, über*) about; **es geht um das Prinzip** it's a question of principles; **es geht um alles** it's all or nothing; **es steht schlecht um seine Gesundheit** his health isn't very good
(e) (= *für, Ergebnis, Ziel bezeichnend*) for; **der Kampf um die Stadt/den Titel** the battle for the town/the title; **um Geld spielen** to play for money; **um etw rufen/bitten** *etc* to cry/ask *etc* for sth
(f) (= *wegen*) **die Sorge um die Zukunft** concern about the future; **(es ist) schade um das schöne Buch** (it's a) pity *or* shame about that nice book; **sich um etw sorgen** to worry about sth
(g) (*bei Differenzangaben*) by; **um 10% teurer** 10% more expensive; **er ist um zwei Jahre jünger als sie** he is two years younger than she is; **um vieles besser** far better; **um einiges besser** quite a bit better; **um nichts besser/teurer** *etc* no better/dearer *etc*; **etw um 4 cm verkürzen** to shorten sth by 4 cm
(h) (*bei Verlust*) **jdn um etw bringen** to deprive sb of sth; **um etw kommen** to be deprived of sth
(i) (= *nach*) after, upon; **Stunde um Stunde** hour after hour; **einer um den anderen, eine um die andere** one after the other **2** PREP +GEN **um ... willen** for the sake of; **um Gottes willen!** for goodness' *or* (*stärker*) God's sake!
3 CONJ **um ... zu** (*final*) (in order) to; **intelligent genug/zu intelligent, um ... zu** intelligent enough/too intelligent to ...; **er studierte jahrelang Jura, um dann Taxifahrer zu werden** he studied law for several years only to become a taxi driver **4** ADV (= *ungefähr*) **um (die) 30 Schüler** *etc* about *or* (a)round about 30 pupils *etc*

umadressieren *ptp* **umadressiert** VT SEP to readdress; (*und nachschicken*) to redirect

umändern VT SEP to alter

umarmen [ʊmˈarmən], *ptp* **umarmt** VT INSEP to embrace (*auch euph*), to hug

Umarmung F **-, -en** embrace (*auch euph*), hug

Umbau M, *pl* **-bauten (a)** (*von Gebäude*) rebuilding, renovation; (*zu etwas anderem*) conversion (*zu* into); (= *Umänderung*) alterations *pl*; (*von Maschine*) modification; (*von Organisation*) reorganization; **das Gebäude befindet sich im ~** the building is being renovated **(b)** (= *Gebäude*) renovated/converted building

umbauen [ˈʊmbaʊən] SEP **1** VT *Gebäude* to rebuild, to renovate; (*zu etwas anderem*) to convert (*zu* into); (= *umändern*) to alter; *Maschine etc* to modify; (*fig*) *Organisation, Firma* to restructure **2** VI to rebuild

umbenennen *ptp* **umbenannt** VT SEP IRREG to rename (*in etw* sth)

Umbenennung F renaming

umbesetzen *ptp* **umbesetzt** VT SEP (*Theat*) to recast; *Mannschaft* to reorganize; *Posten, Stelle* to find someone else for

Umbesetzung F (*Theat*) recasting; (*von Mannschaft*) reorganization; (*von Posten, Stelle*) reassignment; **eine ~ vornehmen** (*Theat*) to alter the cast; **~en vornehmen** (*Theat*) to recast roles; **~en im Kabinett vornehmen** to reshuffle (*Brit*) *or* shake up (*US*) the cabinet

umbilden VT SEP (*fig*) to reorganize; (*Pol*) *Kabinett* to reshuffle (*Brit*), to shake up (*US*)

Umbildung F reorganization; (*Pol*) reshuffle (*Brit*), shake up (*US*)

umbinden [ˈʊmbɪndn] VT SEP IRREG to put on; **sich** (*dat*) **einen Schal ~** to put a scarf on

umblättern VTI SEP to turn over

umbringen SEP IRREG **1** VT to kill (*auch fig*); **das ist nicht umzubringen** (*fig inf*) it's indestructible; **das bringt mich noch um!** (*inf*) it'll be the death of me! (*inf*) **2** VR to kill oneself; **er bringt sich fast um vor Höflichkeit** (*inf*) he falls over himself to be polite

Umbruch M **(a)** radical change **(b)** (*Typ*) make-up

umbuchen SEP **1** VT **(a)** *Reise, Flug, Termin* to alter one's booking for **(b)** (*Fin*) *Betrag* to transfer **2** VI **(a)** (= *Reisetermin ändern*) to alter one's booking (*auf +acc* for) **(b)** (*Fin*) to transfer (*auf +acc* to)

Umbuchung F **(a)** (*von Reise, Termin*) rebooking **(b)** (*Fin*) transfer

umdenken VI SEP IRREG to change one's ideas; **darin müssen wir ~** we'll have to rethink that

umdirigieren *ptp* **umdirigiert** VT SEP to redirect

umdisponieren *ptp* **umdisponiert** VI SEP to change one's plans

umdrehen SEP **1** VT (= *auf andere Seite drehen*) to turn over; (*auf den Kopf*) to turn up (the other way); (*mit der Vorderseite nach hinten*) to turn (a)round; (*von innen nach außen*) to turn inside out; (*von außen nach innen*) to turn back the right way; (*um die Achse*) to turn (a)round; *Schlüssel* to turn; **einem Vogel/jdm den Hals ~** to wring a bird's/sb's neck; **jdm den Arm ~** to twist sb's arm **2** VR to turn (a)round (*nach* to look at); (*im Bett etc*) to turn over; **dabei drehte sich ihm der Magen um** (*inf*) it turned his stomach **3** VI to turn (a)round

Umdrehung F turn; (*Phys*) revolution, rotation; (*Mot*) revolution, rev

Umdrehungszahl F (number of) revolutions *pl* (per minute/second)

umeinander ADV about each other *or* one another; (*räumlich*) (a)round each other

umfahren¹ ['ʊmfaːrən] VT SEP IRREG (= *überfahren*) to run over

umfahren² [ʊm'faːrən], *ptp* **umfahren** VT INSEP IRREG (= *fahren um*) to go (a)round; (*mit dem Auto*) to drive (a)round; (*auf Umgehungsstraße*) to bypass; (= *ausweichen*) to make a detour (a)round; *Kap* to round; *die Welt* to circumnavigate

Umfahrungsstraße F (*Aus*) bypass, beltway (*US*)

umfallen VI SEP IRREG AUX SEIN to fall over; (*Baum, Gegenstand*) to fall (down); (*inf:* = *ohnmächtig werden*) to pass out; (*fig inf:* = *nachgeben*) to give in; **vor Müdigkeit fast ~, zum Umfallen müde sein** to be ready to drop; **wir arbeiteten bis zum Umfallen** we worked until we were ready to drop; **vor Schreck fast ~** (*inf*) to almost die with fright; **~ wie die Fliegen** (*inf*) to drop like flies

Umfang M **(a)** (*von Kreis etc*) circumference; (= *Bauchumfang*) girth **(b)** (= *Fläche*) area; (= *Rauminhalt*) capacity; (= *Größe*) size; (*von Gepäck etc*) amount; **das Buch hat einen ~ von 800 Seiten** the book has 800 pages **(c)** (*fig*) (= *Ausmaß*) extent; (= *Reichweite, Stimmumfang*) range; (*von Untersuchung, Arbeit etc*) scope; (*von Verkehr, Verkauf etc*) volume; **in großem ~** on a large scale; **in vollem ~** fully, entirely; **das hat einen solchen ~ angenommen, dass ...** it has assumed such proportions that ...; **etw in vollem ~ übersehen können** to be able to see the full extent of sth

umfänglich ['ʊmfɛŋlɪç], **umfangreich** ADJ extensive; (= *geräumig*) spacious; *Buch* thick

umfassen [ʊm'fasn], *ptp* **umfasst** VT INSEP **(a)** (= *herumgreifen um*) to grasp; (= *umarmen*) to embrace **(b)** (*fig*) (= *einschließen*) *Zeitperiode* to cover; (= *enthalten*) to contain

umfassend **1** ADJ extensive; (= *vieles enthaltend*) comprehensive; *Vorbereitung* thorough; *Geständnis* full, complete **2** ADV comprehensively; **~ gestehen** to give a full confession

Umfeld NT surroundings *pl*; (*fig*) sphere; **zum ~ von etw gehören** to be associated with sth; **Personen aus dem ~ dieser terroristischen Vereinigung** people associated with this terrorist organization

umfliegen [ʊm'fliːɡn], *ptp* **umflogen** [ʊm'floːɡn] VT INSEP IRREG (= *fliegen um*) to fly (a)round

umformen VT SEP **(a)** (= *andere Form geben*) to reshape (*in +acc* into) **(b)** (*Elec*) to convert **(c)** (*Ling*) to transform

Umformung F reshaping; (*Elec*) conversion; (*Ling*) transformation

Umfrage F **(a)** (*Sociol*) survey; (*esp Pol*) (opinion) poll; **eine ~ halten** *or* **machen** *or* **veranstalten** to carry out a survey/a(n opinion) poll **(b)** **~ halten** to ask around

Umfrageergebnis NT *siehe* **Umfrage (a)** survey/poll result(s *pl*)

umfüllen VT SEP to transfer into another bottle/container *etc*

umfunktionieren *ptp* **umfunktioniert** VT SEP to change the function of; **etw in etw** (*acc*) *or* **zu etw ~** to turn sth into sth; **die Kinder haben das Wohnzimmer umfunktioniert** (*hum*) the children have done a conversion job on the living room (*hum*)

Umgang [-gaŋ] M, NO PL **(a)** (= *gesellschaftlicher Verkehr*) dealings *pl*; (= *Bekanntenkreis*) acquaintances *pl*; **schlechten ~**

haben to keep bad company; **~ mit jdm haben** *or* **pflegen** to associate with sb; **keinen/so gut wie keinen ~ mit jdm haben** to have nothing/little to do with sb; **sie hat nur ~ mit den besten gesellschaftlichen Kreisen** she only mixes in the best social circles; **er ist kein ~ für dich** he's not fit company for you **(b)** **im ~ mit Tieren/Jugendlichen/Vorgesetzten muss man ...** in dealing with animals/young people/one's superiors one must ...; **durch ständigen ~ mit Autos/Büchern/Kindern** through having a lot to do with cars/books/children; **an den ~ mit Tieren/Kindern gewöhnt sein** to be used to animals/children; **an den ~ mit Büchern/Nachschlagewerken gewöhnt sein** to be used to having books around (one)/to using reference books; **der ~ mit Tieren/Kindern muss gelernt sein** you have to learn how to handle animals/children

umgänglich ['ʊmgɛŋlɪç] ADJ affable

Umgänglichkeit F -, NO PL (= *entgegenkommende Art*) affability

Umgangs-: Umgangsformen PL manners *pl*; **Umgangsrecht** NT, NO PL (right of) access (*mit* to); **Umgangssprache** F colloquial language; **umgangssprachlich** ADJ colloquial; **Umgangston** M, *pl* **-töne** tone; **hier herrscht ein rüder/höflicher ~** people talk brusquely/politely here

umgeben [ʊm'geːbn], *ptp* **umgeben** INSEP IRREG **1** VT to surround (*auch fig*) **2** VR **sich mit jdm/etw ~** to surround oneself with sb/sth

Umgebung F -, -en (= *Umwelt*) surroundings *pl*; (= *Nachbarschaft*) neighbourhood (*Brit*), neighborhood (*US*); (= *gesellschaftlicher Hintergrund*) background; (= *Freunde, Kollegen etc*) people *pl* about one; **Hamburg und ~** Hamburg and the surrounding area; **in der näheren ~ Münchens** on the outskirts of Munich; **in der weiteren ~ Münchens** in the area around Munich; **zu jds (näherer) ~ gehören** (*Menschen*) to be one of the people closest to sb

umgehen¹ ['ʊmgeːən] VI SEP IRREG AUX SEIN **(a)** (*Gerücht etc*) to go (a)round; (*Grippe*) to be going round; (*Gespenst*) to walk; **in diesem Schloss geht ein Gespenst um** this castle is haunted (by a ghost); **es geht die Furcht um, dass ...** it is feared that ... **(b)** **mit jdm/etw ~ können** to know how to handle sb/sth; **mit jdm grob/behutsam ~** to treat sb roughly/gently; **sorgsam/verschwenderisch mit etw ~** to be careful/lavish with sth; **mit dem Gedanken ~, etw zu tun** to be thinking about doing sth

umgehen² [ʊm'geːən], *ptp* **umgangen** [ʊm'gaŋən] VT INSEP IRREG (*fig*) to avoid; *Gesetz* to get (a)round; **die Antwort auf etw** (*acc*) **~** to avoid answering sth

umgehend **1** ADJ immediate **2** ADV immediately

Umgehung [ʊm'geːʊŋ] F -, -en (= *Vermeidung*) avoidance; (*durch Straßenführung*) bypassing; (*von Gesetz*) circumvention; (*von Frage*) evasion; **unter ~ der Vorschriften** by getting (a)round the regulations

Umgehungsstraße F bypass, beltway (*US*)

umgekehrt ['ʊmgəkeːɐt] **1** ADJ reversed; *Reihenfolge* reverse; (*Math*) *Vorzeichen* opposite; (= *gegenteilig*) opposite, contrary; (= *andersherum*) the other way (a)round; **in die ~e Richtung fahren** to go in the opposite direction; **gerade** *or* **genau ~!** quite the contrary!; **die Sache war genau ~ und nicht so, wie er sie erzählte** the affair was exactly the reverse of what he said; **im ~en Verhältnis zu etw stehen** *or* **sein** to be in inverse proportion to sth; *siehe auch* **umkehren** **2** ADV (= *andersherum*) the other way (a)round; (*am Satzanfang:* = *dagegen*) conversely; *proportional* inversely; **... und/oder ~** ... and/or vice versa; **~ als** *or* **wie** (*inf*) the other way (a)round to what ...; **es kam ~** (*inf*) the opposite happened

umgestalten *ptp* **umgestaltet** VT SEP to alter; (= *reorganisieren*) to reorganize; (= *umbilden*) to remodel; (= *umordnen*) to rearrange; **etw in etw** (*acc*) *or* **zu etw ~** to redesign sth as sth; *Werk, Buch* to rewrite sth as sth

Umgestaltung F alteration; (= *Reorganisation*) reorganization; (= *Umbildung*) remodelling (*Brit*), remodeling (*US*); (= *Umordnung*) rearrangement

umgewöhnen *ptp* **umgewöhnt** VR SEP to readapt

umgraben VT SEP IRREG to dig over; *Erde* to turn (over)

umgruppieren *ptp* **umgruppiert** VT SEP *Möbel etc* to rearrange; *Mitarbeiter* to redeploy; (= *auf andere Gruppen verteilen*) to regroup

umgucken VR SEP = **umsehen**

umhaben VT SEP IRREG (*inf*) to have on

Umhang M cape; (*länger*) cloak; (= *Umhängetuch*) shawl

umhängen VT SEP **(a)** *Rucksack etc* to put on; *Jacke, Schal etc* to drape (a)round; *Gewehr* to sling on; **sich** (*dat*) **etw ~** to put sth on; to drape sth (a)round one *etc*; **jdm etw ~** to put sth on sb; to drape sth (a)round sb **(b)** *Bild* to rehang

Umhängetasche F shoulder bag

umhauen VT SEP IRREG **(a)** *Baum* to chop down **(b)** (*inf*: = *umwerfen*) to knock over **(c)** (*inf*) (= *erstaunen*) to bowl over (*inf*); (*Gestank etc*) to knock out

umher [ʊmˈheːɐ] ADV around, about (*Brit*); **weit ~** all around

umher- PREF *siehe auch* **herum-** around, about (*Brit*); **umherfahren** SEP IRREG ◼ VT (*mit Auto*) to drive around *etc*; (*in Kinderwagen*) to walk around *etc* ◼ VI AUX SEIN to travel around *etc*; (*mit Auto*) to drive around *etc*; (*mit Kinderwagen*) to walk around *etc*; **umherlaufen** VI SEP IRREG AUX SEIN to walk around *etc*; (= *rennen*) to run around *etc*; **im Garten ~** to walk/run around *etc* the garden; **umherstreifen** VI SEP AUX SEIN to roam around *etc* (*in etw* (*dat*) sth); **umherwandern** VI SEP AUX SEIN to wander around *etc* (*in etw* (*dat*) sth); **umherziehen** VI SEP IRREG AUX SEIN to move around *etc* (*in etw* (*dat*) sth)

umhinkönnen [ʊmˈhɪn-] VI SEP IRREG **ich/er** *etc* **kann nicht umhin, das zu tun** I/he *etc* can't avoid doing it; (*einem Zwang folgend*) I/he *etc* can't help doing it

umhören VR SEP to ask around; **sich unter seinen Kollegen ~** to ask (around) one's colleagues

umjubeln [ʊmˈjuːbln], *ptp* **umjubelt** VT INSEP to cheer; **ein umjubelter Popstar** a wildly acclaimed pop idol

umkämpfen [ʊmˈkɛmpfn], *ptp* **umkämpft** VT INSEP *Stadt, Gebiet* to fight over; *Entscheidung* to dispute; *Wahlkreis, Sieg* to contest; **ein hart umkämpfter Markt** a hotly contested market

Umkehr [ˈʊmkeːɐ] F -, NO PL **(a)** (*lit*) turning back; **jdn zur ~ zwingen** to force sb to turn back **(b)** (*fig geh*) (= *Änderung*) change; (*zur Religion etc*) changing one's ways; **zur ~ bereit sein** to be ready to change one's ways

umkehrbar ADJ reversible

umkehren SEP ◼ VI AUX SEIN to turn back; (= *auf demselben Weg zurückgehen*) to retrace one's steps; (*fig*) to change one's ways ◼ VT *Kleidungsstück, Tasche* to turn inside out; *Reihenfolge, Trend* to reverse; *Verhältnisse* (= *umstoßen*) to overturn; (= *auf den Kopf stellen*) to turn upside down; (*Gram, Math, Mus*) to invert; *siehe auch* **umgekehrt** ◼ VR (*Verhältnisse*) to become reversed; **dabei kehrt sich mir der Magen um** it turns my stomach

Umkehrschluss M inversion of an argument; **im ~ bedeutet das ...** to turn the argument on its head, it means ...

umkippen SEP ◼ VT (= *umwerfen*) to tip over; *Auto, Boot* to overturn; *Leuchter, Vase* to knock over; *volles Gefäß* to upset ◼ VI AUX SEIN **(a)** (= *zur Seite fallen*) to tip over; (*Auto, Boot*) to overturn; (*volles Gefäß, Bier*) to be spilled **(b)** (*inf*: = *ohnmächtig werden*) to pass out **(c)** (*inf*: = *aufgeben*) to back down **(d)** (= *sich umwandeln*) to tip over (*in* +acc into); **plötzlich kippte seine Fröhlichkeit in Depression um** suddenly his cheerfulness turned to depression **(e)** (*Fluss, See*) to become polluted

umklappbar ADJ *Rücksitz, Lehne* fold-down *attr*

umklappen VT SEP to fold down

Umkleidekabine F changing cubicle

Umkleideraum M changing room; (*esp mit Schließfächern*) locker room; (*Theat*) dressing room

umknicken ◼ VT *Ast, Mast* to snap; *Baum* to break; *Gras, Strohhalm* to bend over; *Papier* to fold (over) ◼ VI AUX SEIN (*Ast*) to snap; (*Gras, Strohhalm*) to get bent over; **mit dem Fuß ~** to twist one's ankle

umkommen VI SEP IRREG AUX SEIN **(a)** (= *sterben*) to be killed; **vor Langeweile ~** (*inf*) to be bored to death (*inf*); **da kommt man ja um!** (*inf*) (*vor Hitze*) the heat is killing (*inf*); (*wegen Gestank*) it's enough to knock you out (*inf*) **(b)** (*inf*: = *verderben: Lebensmittel*) to go off (*Brit*) *or* bad

Umkreis M (= *Umgebung*) surroundings *pl*; (= *Gebiet*) area; (= *Nähe*) vicinity; (*Math*) circumcircle; **im näheren ~** in the vicinity; **im ~ von 20 Kilometern** within a radius of 20 kilometres (*Brit*) *or* kilometers (*US*)

umkreisen [ʊmˈkraizn], *ptp* **umkreist** VT INSEP to circle (around); (*Astron, Space*) to orbit

Umkreisung F -, **-en** (*Space, Astron*) orbiting; **drei ~en der Erde** three orbits of the Earth

umkrempeln VT SEP **(a)** *Ärmel, Hosenbein* to turn up; (*mehrmals*) to roll up **(b)** (= *umwenden*) to turn inside out; (*inf*) *Zimmer* to turn upside down (*inf*); *Betrieb, System* to shake up (*inf*); **jdn ~** (*fig inf*) to change sb

umladen VT SEP IRREG to transfer; (*Naut*) to transship

Umlage F **eine ~ machen** to split the cost; **sie beschlossen eine ~ der Kosten** they decided to split the costs

umlagern [ʊmˈlaːgɐn], *ptp* **umlagert** VT INSEP (= *einkreisen*) to surround; (= *sich drängen um, auch Mil*) to besiege

Umland NT, NO PL surrounding countryside

Umlauf M **(a)** (*von Erde etc*) revolution; (*Sport*) (*auf Parcours etc*) round; (= *das Kursieren*) circulation (*auch fig*); **im ~ sein** to be in circulation; **in ~ bringen** *or* **setzen** to circulate **(b)** (= *Rundschreiben*) circular

Umlauf-: **Umlaufbahn** F orbit; **die ~ um den Mond/die Erde** lunar/earth orbit; **auf der ~ um die Erde sein** to be orbiting the earth; **Umlaufvermögen** NT (*Fin*) current assets *pl*

Umlaut M **(a)** NO PL umlaut **(b)** (*Laut*) vowel with umlaut

umlegen SEP ◼ VT **(a)** (= *umhängen, umbinden*) to put round; **jdm/sich eine Stola ~** to put a stole (a)round sb's/one's shoulders **(b)** (= *umklappen*) to tilt (over); *Kragen* to turn down; *Manschetten* to turn up; *Hebel* to turn **(c)** (= *verlegen*) *Kranke* to move; *Leitung* to re-lay **(d)** *Termin* to change (*auf* +acc to) **(e)** (= *verteilen*) **die 200 Euro wurden auf uns fünf umgelegt** the five of us each had to pay a contribution toward(s) the 200 euros **(f)** (*inf*: = *ermorden*) to bump off (*inf*) ◼ VR (*Boot*) to capsize; (*Getreide*) to be flattened

umleiten VT SEP to divert

Umleitung F diversion; (*Strecke auch*) detour

umlernen VI SEP to retrain; (*fig*) to change one's ideas

umliegend ADJ surrounding

Umluft F (*Tech*) circulating air

Umluftherd M fan-assisted oven

ummelden VTR SEP **jdn/sich ~** to notify (the police of) a change in sb's/one's address

Ummeldung F notification of (one's) change of address

ummodeln VT SEP (*inf*) to change

Umnachtung [ʊmˈnaxtʊŋ] F -, **-en geistige ~** mental derangement

umnieten VT SEP (*sl*: = *töten*) to blow away (*inf*)

umnummerieren umnummeriert *ptp* VT SEP to renumber

umordnen VT SEP to rearrange

Umorganisation F reorganization

umorganisieren *ptp* **umorganisiert** VT SEP to reorganize

umpflanzen [ˈʊmpflantsn] VT SEP (= *woanders pflanzen*) to transplant; *Topfpflanze* to repot

umpflügen VT SEP to plough (*Brit*) *or* plow (*US*) up

umquartieren *ptp* **umquartiert** VT SEP to move; *Truppen* (*in andere Kaserne etc*) to requarter; (*in anderes Privathaus*) to rebillet

umrahmen [ʊmˈraːmən], *ptp* **umrahmt** VT INSEP to frame; **die Ansprache war von musikalischen Darbietungen umrahmt** the speech was accompanied by musical offerings (before and after)

umranden [ʊmˈrandn], *ptp* **umrandet** VT INSEP to edge; **tragen Sie die Adresse in das stark umrandete Feld ein** write the address in the area marked in bold outline

umräumen SEP ◼ VT (= *anders anordnen*) to rearrange; (= *an anderen Platz bringen*) to shift ◼ VI to rearrange the furniture

umrechnen VT SEP to convert (*in* +acc into)

Umrechnung F conversion

Umrechnungs-: **Umrechnungskurs** M exchange rate; **Umrechnungstabelle** F conversion table

umreißen [ʊmˈraisn], *ptp* **umrissen** [ʊmˈrɪsn] VT INSEP IRREG (= *skizzieren*) to outline; **scharf umrissen** well defined

umrennen VT SEP IRREG to (run into and) knock down

umringen [ʊmˈrɪŋən], *ptp* **umringt** VT INSEP to surround; (*drängend*) to throng around

Umriss M outline; (= *Kontur*) contour(s *pl*); **etw in ~en zeichnen/erzählen** to outline sth; „**Geschichte in ~en**" "History - A Brief Outline"

umrühren VT SEP to stir

umrüsten VT SEP **(a)** (*Tech*) to adapt; **etw auf etw** (*acc*) ~ to convert sth to sth **(b)** (*Mil*) to re-equip

ums [ʊms] CONTR *von* um das

umsatteln VI SEP (*inf*) (*beruflich*) to change jobs; (*Univ*) to change courses; **von etw auf etw** (*acc*) ~ to switch from sth to sth

Umsatz M (*Comm*) turnover; **5000 Euro ~ machen** (*inf*) to do 5000 euros' worth of business

Umsatz-: **Umsatzanstieg** M increase in turnover; **Umsatzbeteiligung** F commission; **Umsatzeinbruch** M (*Econ*) drop in turnover; **Umsatzplus** NT (*Comm*) increase in turnover; **Umsatzrückgang** M drop in turnover; **Umsatzsteuer** F sales tax

umschalten VI SEP to flick the/a switch; (*auf anderen Sender*) to turn over (*auf +acc* to); (*im Denken*) (= *sich gewöhnen*) to change (*auf +acc* to); (*Ampel*) to change; „**wir schalten jetzt um nach Hamburg**" "and now we're going over to Hamburg"

Umschau F, NO PL (*fig*) review; (*TV, Rad*) magazine programme (*Brit*), news magazine (show) (*US*); ~ **halten** to look around (*nach* for)

umschauen VR SEP (*esp dial*) = umsehen

umschichten SEP 🔳 VT to restack; *Gelder* to reallocate 🔳 VR (*Sociol*) to restructure itself

umschiffen [ʊmˈʃɪfn], *ptp* **umschifft** VT INSEP to sail (a)round

Umschlag M **(a)** (= *Hülle*) cover; (= *Briefumschlag*) envelope; (*als Verpackung*) wrapping; (= *Buchumschlag*) jacket **(b)** (*Med*) compress; (= *Packung*) poultice; **jdm heiße/kalte Umschläge machen** to put hot poultices/cold compresses on sb **(c)** (= *Veränderung*) (sudden) change (+*gen* in, *in +acc* into) **(d)** (= *Ärmelumschlag*) cuff; (= *Hosenumschlag*) turn-up (*Brit*), cuff (*US*) **(e)** (= *umgeschlagene Gütermenge*) volume of traffic; **einen hohen ~ an Baumwolle** *etc* **haben** to handle a lot of cotton *etc*

umschlagen SEP IRREG 🔳 VT **(a)** *Seite etc* to turn over; *Ärmel, Hosenbein, Saum* to turn up; *Teppich, Decke* to fold back; *Kragen* to turn down **(b)** (= *umladen*) *Güter* to transship; **etw vom Schiff auf die Bahn** ~ to unload sth from the ship onto the train **(c)** (= *absetzen*) *Güter* to handle 🔳 VI AUX SEIN (= *sich ändern*) to change (suddenly); (*Wind*) to veer; **in etw** (*acc*) ~ to change into sth; **ins Gegenteil** ~ to become the opposite

Umschlag-: **Umschlaghafen** M port of transshipment; **Umschlagklappe** F jacket flap (*of book*); **Umschlagplatz** M trade centre (*Brit*) or center (*US*)

umschlungen [ʊmˈʃlʊŋən] ADJ **eng ~** with their *etc* arms tightly (a)round each other

umschmeicheln [ʊmˈʃmaɪçln], *ptp* **umschmeichelt** VT INSEP to flatter; (*fig*) to caress

umschmeißen VT SEP IRREG **(a)** (= *umwerfen*) to knock over **(b)** (= *erstaunen*) to bowl over (*inf*); (*Gestank etc*) to knock out **(c)** **das schmeißt meine Pläne um** that messes my plans up (*inf*)

umschnallen VT SEP to buckle on

umschreiben[1] [ˈʊmʃraɪbn] VT SEP IRREG **(a)** *Text etc* to rewrite; (*in andere Schrift*) to transcribe (*auch Phon*); (= *bearbeiten*) *Theaterstück etc* to adapt (*für* for) (= *umbuchen*) to change (*auf +acc* for) **(c)** *Hypothek etc* to transfer; **etw auf jdn ~/~ lassen** to transfer sth/have sth transferred to sb

umschreiben[2] [ʊmˈʃraɪbn], *ptp* **umschrieben** [ʊmˈʃriːbn] VT INSEP IRREG **(a)** (= *mit anderen Worten ausdrücken*) to paraphrase; (= *darlegen*) to describe; (= *abgrenzen*) to circumscribe **(b)** (*Ling*) *Verneinung* to construct

Umschreibung [ʊmˈʃraɪbʊŋ] F **(a)** (= *das Umschriebene*) paraphrase; (= *Darlegung*) description; (= *Abgrenzung*) circumscription **(b)** NO PL (*Gram: von Verneinung*) construction

Umschrift F (*Ling*: = *Transkription*) transcription

umschulden VT SEP (*Comm*) *Kredit* to convert, to fund; **ein Unternehmen ~** to change the terms of a firm's debt(s)

Umschuldung [ˈʊmʃʊldʊŋ] F -, -en funding *no pl*

umschulen VT SEP **(a)** (*beruflich*) to retrain; (*Pol euph*) to re-educate **(b)** (*auf andere Schule*) to transfer (to another school)

Umschulung F retraining; (*Pol euph*) re-education; (*auf andere Schule*) transfer

umschwärmen [ʊmˈʃvɛrmən], *ptp* **umschwärmt** VT INSEP to swarm (a)round; (= *verehren*) to idolize; **von Verehrern umschwärmt werden** (*fig*) to be surrounded by admirers; **eine umschwärmte Schönheit** a much-courted beauty

Umschweife [ˈʊmʃvaɪfə] PL **ohne ~** straight out; **mach keine ~!** don't beat about (*Brit*) or around the bush

umschwenken VI SEP **(a)** AUX SEIN or HABEN (*Anhänger, Kran*) to swing out; (*fig*) to do an about-turn (*Brit*) or about-face (*US*); **der Kran schwenkte nach rechts um** the crane swung to the right **(b)** (*Wind*) to veer

Umschwung M **(a)** (*Gymnastik*) circle **(b)** (*fig*) (= *Veränderung*) drastic change; (*ins Gegenteil*) about-turn (*Brit*), about-face (*US*)

umsegeln [ʊmˈzeːgln], *ptp* **umsegelt** VT INSEP to sail (a)round

Umsegelung [ʊmˈzeːgəlʊŋ] F -, -en, **Umseglung** [ʊmˈzeːglʊŋ] F -, -en sailing (a)round

umsehen VR SEP IRREG to look around (*nach* for); (*rückwärts*) to look back; **sich in der Stadt** ~ to have a look (a)round the town; **sich in der Welt** ~ to see something of the world; **ich möchte mich nur mal** ~ (*in Geschäft*) I'm just looking; **ohne mich wird er sich noch** ~ (*inf*) he's not going to find it easy without me

um sein VI IRREG AUX SEIN (*Frist, Zeit*) to be up

umseitig [ˈʊmzaɪtɪç] ADJ, ADV overleaf

umsetzen SEP 🔳 VT **(a)** *Pflanzen* to transplant; *Topfpflanze* to repot; *Schüler etc* to move (to another seat) **(b)** *Waren, Geld* to turn over **(c)** **etw in etw** (*acc*) ~ to convert sth into sth; (*Mus:* = *transponieren*) to transpose sth into sth; (*in Verse etc*) to translate sth into sth; **sein Geld in Alkohol** ~ to spend all one's money on alcohol; **etw in die Tat** ~ to translate sth into action 🔳 VR (*Schüler etc*) to change places

Umsicht F, NO PL circumspection, prudence

umsichtig [ˈʊmzɪçtɪç] 🔳 ADJ circumspect, prudent 🔳 ADV circumspectly, prudently

umsiedeln VTI SEP (*vi: aux sein*) to resettle; **von einem Ort an einen anderen** ~ to move from one place and settle in another

Umsiedler(in) M(F) resettler

Umsiedlung [ˈʊmziːdlʊŋ] F resettlement

umso [ˈʊmzoː] CONJ (= *desto*) ~ **besser/schlimmer!** so much the better/worse!; **je mehr ... ~ weniger/eher kann man ...** the more ... the less/sooner one can ...; ~ **mehr, als ...** all the more considering or as; **unser Aufenthalt ist sehr kurz, ~ besser muss er geplant werden** as our stay is so short, we have to plan it all the better

umsonst [ʊmˈzɔnst] ADV **(a)** (= *unentgeltlich*) free (of charge (*esp Comm*)); ~ **sein** to be free (of charge) **(b)** (= *vergebens*) in vain; (= *erfolglos*) without success **(c)** (= *ohne Grund*) for nothing

umsorgen [ʊmˈzɔrgn], *ptp* **umsorgt** VT INSEP to look after

umspannen [ˈʊmʃpanən] VT SEP (*Elec*) to transform

Umspannstation F, **Umspannwerk** NT (*Elec*) transformer (station)

umspringen [ˈʊmʃprɪŋən] VI SEP IRREG AUX SEIN **(a)** (*Wind*) to veer (*nach* to) **(b)** **mit jdm grob** *etc* ~ (*inf*) to treat sb roughly *etc*; **so kannst du nicht mit ihr** ~! (*inf*) you can't treat her like that!

Umstand M **(a)** circumstance; (= *Tatsache*) fact; **ein unvorhergesehener ~** unforeseen circumstances *pl*; **den Umständen entsprechend** much as one would expect (under the circumstances); **es geht ihm den Umständen entsprechend (gut)** he is as well as can be expected (under the circumstances); **nähere/die näheren Umstände** further details; **in anderen Umständen sein** to be expecting; **unter diesen/keinen/anderen Umständen** under these/no/any other circumstances; **unter Umständen** possibly **(b) Umstände** PL (= *Mühe, Schwierigkeiten*) bother *sing*;

(= *Förmlichkeit*) fuss *sing*; **ohne (große) Umstände** without (much) fuss; **das macht gar keine Umstände** it's no bother at all; **jdm Umstände machen** *or* **bereiten** to cause sb bother; **machen Sie bloß keine Umstände!** please don't go to any bother

umständehalber [ˈʊmʃtɛndəhalbɐ] ADV owing to circumstances; **„~ zu verkaufen"** "forced to sell"

umständlich [ˈʊmʃtɛntlɪç] ■ ADJ *Arbeitsweise, Methode* (awkward and) involved; (= *langsam und ungeschickt*) ponderous; *Vorbereitung* elaborate; *Begriff, Erklärung, Übersetzung, Titel, Anleitung* long-winded; *Abfertigung* laborious; *Arbeit, Reise* awkward; **sei doch nicht so ~!** don't make everything twice as hard as it really is!; **das ist vielleicht ~** what a lot of bother; **das ist mir zu ~** that's too much bother
■ ADV *erklären, fragen, formulieren* in a roundabout way; *arbeiten, vorgehen* awkwardly; **etw ~ machen** to make doing sth seem twice as hard; **etw ~ erzählen/beschreiben** *etc* to tell/describe *etc* sth in a roundabout way

Umständlichkeit F -, -en (*von Arbeitsweise, Methode*) involvedness; (*von Erklärung etc*) long-windedness; **ihre ~** the way she makes everything seem twice as hard

Umstands-: Umstandsbestimmung F adverbial phrase; **Umstandskleid** NT maternity dress; **Umstandskleidung** F maternity wear; **Umstandskrämer(in)** M(F) (*inf*) fusspot (*Brit inf*), fussbudget (*US*); **Umstandswort** NT, *pl* **-wörter** adverb

umstehend ■ ADJ ATTR **(a)** (= *in der Nähe stehend*) standing nearby; **die Umstehenden** the bystanders **(b)** (= *umseitig*) overleaf; **im Umstehenden** overleaf ■ ADV overleaf

Umsteige-: Umsteigebahnhof M interchange (station); **Umsteigemöglichkeit** F **dort haben Sie ~** you can change there (*nach* for)

umsteigen VI SEP IRREG AUX SEIN **(a)** (*in anderes Verkehrsmittel*) to change (*nach* for); (*in Bus, Zug etc*) to change (buses/trains *etc*); **in ein anderes Auto ~, von einem Auto ins andere ~** to change cars **(b)** (*fig inf*) to switch (over) (*auf* +*acc* to)

umstellen[1] [ˈʊmʃtɛlən] SEP ■ VT **(a)** *Möbel, Wörter* to change (a)round; (*Gram*) *Subjekt und Prädikat* to transpose **(b)** (= *anders einstellen*) *Hebel, Telefon, Fernsehgerät, Betrieb* to switch over; *Radio* to switch to another station; *Uhr* to change; *Währung* to change over; **etw auf Computer ~** to computerize sth
■ VI **auf etw** (*acc*) **~** (*Betrieb*) to switch over to sth; *auf Erdgas etc* to convert to sth
■ VR to move *or* shift around; (*fig*) to get used to a different lifestyle; **sich auf etw** (*acc*) **~** to adjust to sth

umstellen[2] [ʊmˈʃtɛlən], *ptp* **umstellt** VT INSEP (= *einkreisen*) to surround

Umstellung [ˈʊm-] F **(a)** (*von Möbel, Wörtern*) changing (a)round; (*Gram*) transposition **(b)** (*von Hebel, Telefon, Fernsehgerät, Betrieb*) switch-over; (*von Radio*) switching to another station; (*von Uhr*) changing; (*von Währung*) changeover; **~ auf Erdgas** conversion to natural gas; **~ auf Computer** computerization **(c)** (*fig*: = *das Sichumstellen*) adjustment (*auf* +*acc* to); **das wird eine große ~ für ihn sein** it will be a big change for him

umstimmen VT SEP **(a)** *Instrument* to retune **(b)** **jdn ~** to change sb's mind; **er war nicht umzustimmen, er ließ sich nicht ~** he was not to be persuaded

umstoßen VT SEP IRREG *Gegenstand* to knock over; (*fig*) (*Mensch*) *Plan, Testament, Bestimmung etc* to change; (*Umstände etc*) *Plan, Berechnung* to upset

umstritten [ʊmˈʃtrɪtn] ADJ (= *fraglich*) controversial; (= *wird noch debattiert*) disputed

umstrukturieren *ptp* **umstrukturiert** VT SEP to restructure

Umsturz M coup (d'état)

umstürzen SEP ■ VT to overturn; *Puddingform etc* to turn upside down; (*fig*) *Regierung, Staat, Verfassung* to overthrow; *Demokratie* to destroy ■ VI AUX SEIN to fall; (*Möbelstück, Wagen etc*) to overturn

umtaufen VT SEP to rebaptize; (= *umbenennen*) to rechristen

Umtausch M exchange; **diese Waren sind vom ~ ausgeschlossen** these goods cannot be exchanged; **beim ~ bitte den Kassenzettel vorlegen** please produce the receipt when exchanging goods

umtauschen VT SEP to (ex)change; *Geld, Aktien* to change (*in* +*acc* into)

umtopfen VT SEP *Blumen etc* to repot

Umtriebe PL machinations *pl*; **umstürzlerische ~** subversive activities

umtriebig [ˈʊmtriːbɪç] ADJ (= *betriebsam*) go-getting

UMTS [uːɛmteːˈʔɛs] NT - ABBR *von* **Universal Mobile Telecommunications System** UMTS

umtun VR SEP IRREG (*inf*) to look around (*nach* for)

U-Musik [ˈuː-] F ABBR *von* **Unterhaltungsmusik**

Umverpackung F external packaging

umverteilen *ptp* **umverteilt** VT SEP *or* INSEP to redistribute

Umverteilung F redistribution

Umwälzpumpe F circulating pump

umwandeln [ˈʊmvandln] SEP ■ VT to change (*in* +*acc* into); (*Comm, Fin, Sci*) to convert (*in* +*acc* to); (*Jur*) *Strafe* to commute (*in* +*acc* to); (*fig*) to transform (*in* +*acc* into); **er ist wie umgewandelt** he's a changed man ■ VR to be converted (*in* +*acc* into)

Umwandlung [ˈʊm-] F change; (*Comm, Fin, Sci*) conversion; (*von Strafe*) commutation; (*fig*) transformation

umwechseln VT SEP *Geld* to change (*in* +*acc* to, into)

Umwechslung [ˈʊmvɛkslʊŋ] F -, -en exchange (*in* +*acc* for)

Umweg [ˈʊmveːk] M detour; (*fig*) roundabout way; **einen ~ machen/fahren** to go a long way round (*Brit*) *or* around (*esp US*); (*absichtlich auch*) to make a detour; **wenn das für Sie kein ~ ist** if it doesn't take you out of your way; **auf dem ~ über jdn** indirectly via sb; **etw auf ~en erfahren** (*fig*) to find sth out indirectly

Umwegfinanzierung F indirect financing

Umwelt F, NO PL environment

Umwelt- IN CPDS environmental; **Umweltallergie** F environmental allergy; **Umweltauflage** F (*Admin*) environmental requirement; **Umweltauto** NT environmentally friendly car; **umweltbedingt** ADJ caused by the environment; *Faktoren, Einflüsse* determined by the environment; **Umweltbehörde** F environmental authority; **umweltbelastend** ADJ causing environmental pollution; **Umweltbelastung** F damage to the environment; **umweltbewusst** ■ ADJ *Person* environmentally aware; *Verhalten, Produkt* environmentally friendly ■ ADV in an environmentally friendly way; **Umweltbewusstsein** NT environmental awareness; **Umweltengel** M **der blaue ~** *symbol attached to a product guaranteeing environmental friendliness*; **umweltfreundlich** ADJ environmentally friendly; **Umweltfreundlichkeit** F environmental friendliness; **umweltgefährdend** ADJ harmful to the environment; **Umweltgefährdung** F endangering of the environment; **umweltgerecht** ■ ADJ compatible with the environment ■ ADV in an environmentally sound way; **Umweltgift** NT environmental pollutant; **Umweltkarte** F *cheap ticket to encourage use of public transport*; **Umweltkatastrophe** F ecological disaster; **Umweltkrankheiten** PL environmental illnesses *pl*; **Umweltkriminalität** F environmental crimes *pl*; **Umweltmedizin** F environmental medicine; **Umweltmobil** [-mobiːl] NT **-s, -e** environmental information bus; **Umweltnorm** F environmental standard; **Umweltpapier** NT recycled paper; **Umweltpolitik** F environmental policy; **umweltpolitisch** ■ ADJ relating to environmental policy; **~er Sprecher** environment spokesman ■ ADV in terms of environmental policy; **~ umstrittene Gesetzesvorlagen** (draft) bills which are controversial in terms of environmental policy; **Umweltqualität** F quality of the environment; **Umweltrecht** NT environmental law; **Umweltschaden** M damage to the environment; **umweltschädlich** ■ ADJ harmful to the environment ■ ADV in a way which is harmful to the environment; **umweltschonend** ■ ADJ environmentally friendly ■ ADV in an environmentally friendly way

Umweltschutz M conservation

Umweltschutz-: Umweltschutzauflage F environmental restriction; **Umweltschutzbeauftragte(r)** MF DECL AS ADJ environmental protection officer

Umweltschützer(in) M(F) conservationist, environmentalist
Umweltschutz-: **Umweltschutzorganisation** F
environmentalist group; **Umweltschutztechnik** F
conservation technology
Umwelt-: **Umweltsteuer** F ecology tax; **Umweltsünder(in)** M(F)
(*inf*) polluter; **Umwelttechnik** F environmental technology;
Umweltverschmutzung F pollution (of the environment);
Umweltverseuchung F contamination of the environment;
umweltverträglich 𝟙 ADJ *Produkte, Stoffe* not harmful to the
environment 𝟚 ADV in a way which is not harmful to the
environment; **Umweltverträglichkeit** F environmental
friendliness; **Umweltverträglichkeitsprüfung** F test for
environmental friendliness; **Umweltzerstörung** F
destruction of the environment
umwenden SEP IRREG 𝟙 VT to turn over 𝟚 VR to turn
((a)round) (*nach* to)
umwerben [ʊmˈvɛrbn], *ptp* **umworben** [ʊmˈvɔrbn] VT INSEP IRREG
to court
umwerfen VT SEP IRREG (a) *Gegenstand* to knock over;
Möbelstück etc to overturn (b) (*fig*: = *ändern*) to upset;
Strategie, Vorstellungen to throw over (c) *jdn (körperlich)* to
knock down; (*Ringen*) to throw down; (*fig inf*) to stun; **ein
Whisky wirft dich nicht gleich um** one whisky won't knock
you out (d) **sich** (*dat*) **etw ~** to throw sth (a)round one's
shoulders
umwerfend 𝟙 ADJ fantastic; **von ~er Komik** hilarious 𝟚 ADV
fantastically
umwittert [ʊmˈvɪtɐt] ADJ (*geh*) surrounded (*von* by); **von
Geheimnissen ~** shrouded in mystery
umwohnend ADJ neighbouring (*Brit*), neighboring (*US*); **die
Umwohnenden** the local residents
umwölken [ʊmˈvœlkn], *ptp* **umwölkt** VR INSEP (*geh*) to cloud
over; (*Berggipfel*) to become shrouded in cloud (*Brit*) *or* clouds
(*US*); (*fig*: *Stirn*) to cloud
umzäunen [ʊmˈtsɔʏnən], *ptp* **umzäunt** VT INSEP to fence
(a)round
Umzäunung F **-, -en** (= *das Umzäunen*) fencing (a)round;
(= *Zaun*) fence
umziehen [ˈʊmtsiːən] SEP IRREG 𝟙 VI AUX SEIN (= *Wohnung
wechseln*) to move (house (*Brit*)); (*Firma etc*) to move; **nach
Köln ~** to move to Cologne 𝟚 VT **die Kinder ~** to get the
children changed 𝟛 VR to change, to get changed
umzingeln [ʊmˈtsɪŋln], *ptp* **umzingelt** VT INSEP to surround, to
encircle
Umzug [ˈʊmtsuːk] M (a) (= *Wohnungsumzug*) move, removal
(*esp Brit*); **wann soll euer ~ sein?** when are you moving?
(b) (= *Festzug*) procession; (= *Demonstrationszug*) parade
Umzugs-: **Umzugskarton** M packing case; **Umzugskosten** PL
removal (*esp Brit*) *or* moving (*US*) costs *pl*
UN [uːˈɛn] PL UN *sing*, United Nations *sing*
unabänderlich [ʊnlapˈlɛndɐlɪç] 𝟙 ADJ (a) (= *unwiderruflich*)
unalterable; *Entschluss, Urteil* irrevocable; **etw als ~
hinnehmen** to accept sth as an unalterable fact (b) (= *ewig*)
Gesetze, Schicksal, Wahrheit immutable 𝟚 ADV **~ feststehen** to
be absolutely certain; **etw ist ~ passiert** sth is irreversible
unabdingbar [ʊnlapˈdɪŋbaːɐ, ˈʊn-] ADJ indispensable;
Notwendigkeit absolute
unabhängig ADJ independent (*von* of); *Journalist* freelance;
das ist ~ davon, ob/wann *etc* that does not depend on
whether/when *etc*; **~ davon, was Sie meinen** irrespective of
what you think; **sich ~ machen** to go one's own way; **sich von
jdm/etw ~ machen** to become independent of sb/sth
Unabhängigkeit F, NO PL independence; **ein Land in die ~
entlassen** to grant a country independence
Unabhängigkeits-: **Unabhängigkeitsbewegung** F
independence movement; **Unabhängigkeitserklärung** F
declaration of independence
unabkömmlich ADJ (*geh*) busy; (= *unverzichtbar*) *Person,
Gegenstand* indispensable
unablässig [ʊnlapˈlɛsɪç, ˈʊn-] 𝟙 ADJ continual 𝟚 ADV
continually; **~ für den Frieden kämpfen** to fight unceasingly
for peace
unabsehbar 𝟙 ADJ (*fig*) *Folgen etc* unforeseeable; *Schaden*
immeasurable; **der Schaden/die Zahl der Toten ist noch ~** the
amount of damage/the number of dead is not yet known;
auf ~e Zeit for an indefinite period 𝟚 ADV *sich verzögern* to

an unforeseeable extent; **~ lang sein** to seem to be
interminable
un-: **unabsichtlich** 𝟙 ADJ unintentional 𝟚 ADV
unintentionally; **unabwendbar** ADJ inevitable; **unachtsam**
𝟙 ADJ (= *unaufmerksam*) inattentive; (= *nicht sorgsam*)
careless; (= *unbedacht*) thoughtless 𝟚 ADV carelessly;
wegwerfen thoughtlessly; **benimm dich nicht so ~** don't be so
careless; **~ über die Straße laufen** to cross the road without
paying attention; **Unachtsamkeit** F (= *Unaufmerksamkeit*)
inattentiveness; (= *Sorglosigkeit*) carelessness;
(= *Unbedachtheit*) thoughtlessness; **unähnlich** ADJ dissimilar;
einander ~ dissimilar; **unanfechtbar** ADJ incontestable;
Argument etc unassailable; *Beweis* irrefutable; **unangebracht**
ADJ uncalled-for; (*für Kinder, Altersstufe etc*) unsuitable;
(= *unzweckmäßig*) *Maßnahmen* inappropriate;
unangefochten [ˈʊnlaŋɡəfɔxtn] 𝟙 ADJ unchallenged; *Urteil,
Entscheidung, Testament, Wahlkandidat* uncontested 𝟚 ADV
unchallenged; **unangemeldet** [ˈʊnlaŋɡəmɛldət] 𝟙 ADJ
unannounced *no adv*; *Besucher* unexpected; *Patient etc*
without an appointment 𝟚 ADV unannounced; *besuchen*
without letting sb know; (*in Bezug auf Patient*) without an
appointment
unangemessen 𝟙 ADJ (= *zu hoch*) unreasonable;
(= *unzulänglich*) inadequate; **einer Sache** (*dat*) **~ sein** to be
inappropriate to sth 𝟚 ADV *hoch, niedrig, teuer* unreasonably;
gekleidet, sich verhalten inappropriately; **sich ~ äußern** to
make inappropriate remarks
unangenehm 𝟙 ADJ unpleasant; *Frage* awkward; *Zwischenfall,
Begegnung* embarrassing; **das ist mir immer so ~** I don't like
that at all; **es ist mir ~, dass ich Sie gestört habe** I feel bad
about having disturbed you; **er kann ~ werden** he can get
quite nasty 𝟚 ADV unpleasantly; **jdn ~ berühren** to embarrass
sb; **~ schmecken/riechen** to taste/smell unpleasant
un-: **unangepasst** ADJ nonconformist; **unannehmbar** ADJ
unacceptable
Unannehmlichkeit F USU PL trouble *no pl*; **~en haben/
bekommen** *or* **kriegen** to be in/to get into trouble; **mit etw
~en haben** to have a lot of trouble with sth; **mit den
Behörden ~en haben** to get into trouble with the authorities
unansehnlich ADJ unsightly; *Frau etc* plain; *Tapete, Möbel*
shabby; *Nahrungsmittel* unappetizing
unanständig 𝟙 ADJ (a) (= *unkultiviert, unerzogen*) bad-
mannered; (= *frech, unverschämt*) rude; **so was
Unanständiges!** how rude! (b) (= *obszön, anstößig*) dirty;
Wörter rude; (= *vulgär*) *Kleidung* indecent; **~e Reden führen** to
talk smut 𝟚 ADV (a) (= *rüpelhaft*) in a rude way (b) (= *obszön*)
in a dirty way
Unanständigkeit F (a) (= *Unkultiviertheit, Unerzogenheit*) bad
manners *pl*; (= *Unverschämtheit*) rudeness *no pl*
(b) (= *Obszönität*) obscenity; **~en erzählen** to tell dirty jokes/
stories
Un-: **unantastbar** [ʊnlanˈtastbaːɐ, ˈʊn-] ADJ sacrosanct; *Rechte*
inviolable; **Unantastbarkeit** F **-**, NO PL sanctity; (*von Rechten,
Staat, Grenze, Wohnung*) inviolability; **unappetitlich** ADJ (*lit,
fig*) unappetizing
Unart F bad habit; (= *Ungezogenheit*) rude habit
unartig ADJ naughty
Unartigkeit F (a) NO PL (= *Unartigsein*) naughtiness
(b) (= *Handlungsweise*) naughty behaviour (*Brit*) *or* behavior
(*US*) *no pl*
Un-: **unästhetisch** ADJ unappetizing; **unaufdringlich** 𝟙 ADJ
unobtrusive; *Parfüm auch, Geste* discreet; *Mensch*
unassuming 𝟚 ADV discreetly
unauffällig 𝟙 ADJ inconspicuous; (= *unscheinbar, schlicht*)
unobtrusive; **die Narbe/sein Hinken ist ziemlich ~** the scar/
his limp isn't very noticeable; **er ist ein ziemlich ~er junger
Mann** he's not the kind of young man you notice
particularly 𝟚 ADV unobtrusively
Unauffälligkeit F **-**, NO PL inconspicuousness; (= *Schlichtheit*)
unobtrusiveness
unauffindbar ADJ nowhere to be found; *Verbrecher, vermisste
Person* untraceable
unaufgefordert [ˈʊnlaʊfɡəfɔrdɐt] 𝟙 ADJ unsolicited (*esp Comm*)
𝟚 ADV without being asked; **jdm ~ Prospekte zuschicken** to
send sb unsolicited brochures; **~ zugesandte Manuskripte**
unsolicited manuscripts

Un-: unaufgeklärt ADJ **(a)** unexplained; *Verbrechen* unsolved **(b)** *Mensch* ignorant; *(sexuell)* ignorant of the facts of life; **unaufgeregt** ① ADJ calm; *Erzählstil* sober ② ADV calmly; **unaufhaltsam** [ʊnlaufˈhaltzaːm, ˈʊn-] ① ADJ **(a)** (= *unaufhaltbar*) unstoppable **(b)** (= *unerbittlich*) inexorable ② ADV **(a)** (= *unaufhaltbar*) unstoppably **(b)** (= *unerbittlich*) inexorably; **unaufhörlich** [ʊnlaufˈhøːɛlɪç, ˈʊn-] ① ADJ incessant ② ADV incessantly; **unaufmerksam** ADJ inattentive; **da war ich einen Augenblick ~** I didn't pay attention for a moment; **Unaufmerksamkeit** F inattentiveness; **unaufrichtig** ADJ insincere; **unausbleiblich** [ʊnlausˈblaiplɪç, ˈʊn-] ADJ inevitable; **unausgefüllt** [ˈʊnlausgəfʏlt] ADJ **(a)** *Formular etc* blank **(b)** *Leben, Mensch* unfulfilled

unausgeglichen ADJ unbalanced; *Mensch* (= *launisch*) changeable; **ein Mensch mit ~em Wesen** a person of uneven temper

Unausgeglichenheit F imbalance; *(von Mensch)* changeable moods *pl;* **die ~ seines Wesens** the unevenness of his temper

Un-: unausgegoren ADJ immature; **unausgesprochen** ADJ unspoken; **unausgewogen** ADJ unbalanced; **Unausgewogenheit** F imbalance

unaussprechlich [ʊnlausˈʃpreçlɪç, ˈʊn-] ① ADJ **(a)** *Wort, Laut* unpronounceable **(b)** *Schönheit, Leid etc* inexpressible ② ADV *(enorm) schön* indescribably; *grausam, leiden* unspeakably

Un-: unausstehlich [ʊnlausˈʃteːlɪç, ˈʊn-] ADJ intolerable; **unausweichlich** [ʊnlausˈvaiçlɪç, ˈʊn-] ① ADJ unavoidable ② ADV unavoidably

unbändig [ˈʊnbɛndɪç] ① ADJ **(a)** *Kind* boisterous **(b)** *Freude, Lust, Hass, Zorn* unrestrained *no adv; Ehrgeiz, Fleiß* boundless; *Hunger* enormous ② ADV **(a)** *herumtoben* boisterously; **führt euch nicht so ~ auf** don't be so wild **(b)** (= *enorm*) enormously

Un-: unbar *(Comm)* ① ADJ **~e Zahlungsweise** non-cash payment ② ADV **etw ~ bezahlen** not to pay sth in cash; **unbarmherzig** ① ADJ merciless ② ADV mercilessly; **unbeabsichtigt** [ˈʊnbəlapzɪçtɪçt] ① ADJ unintentional ② ADV unintentionally

unbeachtet [ˈʊnbəlaxtət] ① ADJ unnoticed; *Warnung, Vorschläge* unheeded; **~ bleiben** to go unnoticed/unheeded; **jdn/etw ~ lassen** not to take any notice of sb/sth; **wir sollten die weniger wichtigen Punkte zunächst ~ lassen** let's leave the less important points aside for the time being; **das dürfen wir nicht ~ lassen** we mustn't overlook that ② ADV unnoticed; *daliegen* completely ignored

Un-: unbeantwortet [ˈʊnbəlantvɔrtət] ADJ, ADV unanswered; **unbebaut** [ˈʊnbəbaut] ADJ *Land* undeveloped; *Grundstück* vacant; *Feld* uncultivated; **unbedacht** ① ADJ (= *hastig*) rash; (= *unüberlegt*) thoughtless ② ADV rashly; **unbedarft** [ˈʊnbədarft] ADJ *(inf)* simple-minded; *Mensch (auf bestimmtem Gebiet)* clueless *(inf);* (= *dumm*) dumb *(inf);* **Unbedarftheit** F *(inf)* simple-mindedness; (= *Dummheit*) dumbness *(inf)*

unbedenklich ① ADJ (= *ungefährlich*) quite safe; (= *sorglos*) thoughtless ② ADV (= *ungefährlich*) quite safely; (= *ohne zu zögern*) without thinking (twice *(inf)*)

Unbedenklichkeit F (= *Ungefährlichkeit*) harmlessness

Unbedenklichkeitsbescheinigung F *(Jur)* document certifying that one has no taxes, loans etc outstanding

unbedeutend ① ADJ (= *unwichtig*) insignificant; (= *geringfügig*) *Rückgang, Änderung etc* minor ② ADV (= *geringfügig*) slightly

unbedingt ① ADJ ATTR absolute; *Reflex* unconditioned ② ADV (= *auf jeden Fall*) really; *nötig, erforderlich* absolutely; **ich muss ~ mal wieder ins Kino gehen** I really must go to the cinema again; **ich musste sie ~ sprechen** I really had to speak to her; *(äußerst wichtig)* it was imperative that I spoke to her; **müsst ihr denn ~ in meinem Arbeitszimmer spielen?** do you HAVE to play in my study?; **er wollte ~ mit Renate verreisen** he was (hell)bent on going away with Renate; **~!** of course!; **nicht ~** not necessarily

Un-: unbeeindruckt [ˈʊnbəˈlaindrʊkt, ˈʊn-] ADJ, ADV unimpressed *(von* by); **unbefahrbar** ADJ *Straße, Weg* impassable; *Gewässer* unnavigable; **unbefahren** ADJ *Straße, Fluss* unused; **unbefangen** ① ADJ **(a)** (= *unvoreingenommen*) impartial **(b)** (= *natürlich*) natural; (= *ungehemmt*) uninhibited ② ADV **(a)** (= *unvoreingenommen*) impartially **(b)** (= *ungehemmt*) naturally, without inhibition; **Unbefangenheit** F **(a)** (= *unparteiische Haltung*) impartiality **(b)** (= *Natürlichkeit*)

naturalness; (= *Ungehemmtheit*) uninhibitedness;

unbefriedigend ① ADJ unsatisfactory ② ADV unsatisfactorily; **unbefriedigt** ADJ unsatisfied; (= *unzufrieden*) dissatisfied;

unbefristet ① ADJ *Arbeitsverhältnis, Vertrag* for an indefinite period; *Aufenthaltserlaubnis, Visum* permanent ② ADV for an indefinite period; **etw ~ verlängern** to extend sth indefinitely; **unbefugt** ① ADJ unauthorized; **Eintritt für Unbefugte verboten, kein Zutritt für Unbefugte** no admittance to unauthorized persons ② ADV without authorization; **unbegabt** ADJ untalented; **für etw ~ sein** to have no talent for sth; **er ist handwerklich völlig ~** he's no handyman

unbegreiflich ADJ (= *unverständlich*) incomprehensible; *Leichtsinn, Irrtum, Dummheit* inconceivable; **es wird mir immer ~ bleiben, wie/dass ...** I shall never understand how/why ...; **es ist uns allen ~, wie das passieren konnte** none of us can understand how it happened

unbegrenzt ① ADJ unlimited; *Land, Meer etc* boundless; *Zeitspanne, Frist* indefinite; **zeitlich ~** indefinite; **auf ~e Zeit** indefinitely; **in ~er Höhe** of an unlimited amount; **es ist nach oben ~** there's no upper limit (on it) ② ADV indefinitely; **„~ haltbar"** "will keep indefinitely"

unbegründet ADJ unfounded; *Maßnahme* unwarranted; **eine Klage als ~ abweisen** to dismiss a case

unbehaart ADJ hairless; *(auf dem Kopf)* bald

Unbehagen NT uneasy feeling; (= *Unzufriedenheit*) discontent *(an +dat* with); *(körperlich)* discomfort

unbehaglich ADJ uncomfortable; *Gefühl auch* uneasy ② ADV **sich in jds Gesellschaft** *(dat)* **~ fühlen** to feel uncomfortable *or* ill at ease in sb's company

Un-: unbehelligt [ʊnbəˈhɛlɪçt, ˈʊn-] ① ADJ (= *unbelästigt*) unmolested; (= *unkontrolliert*) unchecked; **jdn ~ lassen** to leave sb alone; *(Polizei etc)* not to stop sb ② ADV (= *unkontrolliert*) unchecked; (= *ungestört*) in peace; **unbeherrscht** ① ADJ *Reaktion, Handlung, Bewegung* uncontrolled; *Mensch* lacking self-control; (= *gierig*) greedy ② ADV *essen* greedily; **sich ~ verhalten** to lose control; **~ reagieren** to react in an uncontrolled way; **Unbeherrschtheit** F **-, -en (a)** NO PL *(von Mensch)* lack of self-control; (= *Gier*) greediness **(b)** (= *unbeherrschte Handlung*) **diese ~ hat ihn seinen Job gekostet** losing his self-control just once cost him his job

unbeholfen [ˈʊnbəhɔlfn] ① ADJ clumsy; (= *hilflos*) helpless ② ADV clumsily

Unbeholfenheit F **-,** NO PL clumsiness; (= *Hilflosigkeit*) helplessness

unbeirrt [ʊnbəˈlɪrt, ˈʊn-] ① ADJ unwavering ② ADV *glauben, festhalten* unwaveringly; *weiterreden, weitermachen* undeterred

unbekannt ADJ unknown; *Flugzeug, Flugobjekt etc* unidentified; **das war mir ~** I didn't know that; **es wird Ihnen nicht ~ sein, dass ...** you will no doubt be aware that ...; **~e Größe** *(Math, fig)* unknown quantity; **nach ~ verzogen** moved – address unknown; **~e Täter** person or persons unknown; **Strafanzeige gegen ~** charge against person or persons unknown

Unbekannte F DECL AS ADJ *(Math)* unknown

Unbekannte(r) MF DECL AS ADJ stranger; **der große ~** *(hum)* the mystery man/person *etc*

unbekannterweise [ˈʊnbəkantəˈvaizə] ADV **grüße sie/ihn ~ von mir** give her/him my regards although I don't know her/him

unbekleidet ① ADJ bare; **sie war ~** she had nothing on ② ADV without any clothes on

unbekümmert [ʊnbəˈkʏmɛt, ˈʊn-] ① ADJ **(a)** (= *unbesorgt*) unconcerned; **sei ganz ~** don't worry **(b)** (= *sorgenfrei*) carefree ② ADV **(a)** (= *unbesorgt*) without worrying **(b)** (= *sorglos*) without a care in the world; *lachen* happily

Unbekümmertheit F **-,** NO PL **(a)** (= *Unbesorgtheit*) lack of concern **(b)** (= *Sorgenfreiheit*) carefreeness

unbelastet [ˈʊnbəlastət] ① ADJ **(a)** (= *ohne Last*) unladen; **das linke Bein ~ lassen** to keep one's weight off one's left leg **(b)** (= *ohne Schulden*) unencumbered **(c)** *(Pol:* = *ohne Schuld)* guiltless **(d)** (= *ohne Sorgen*) free from worries; **von Hemmungen** *etc* **~** free from inhibitions *etc* **(e)** (= *schadstofffrei*) unpolluted ② ADV (= *ohne Sorgen*) without any worries; (= *unvoreingenommen*) impartially

un-: unbelehrbar ADJ fixed in one's views; *Rassist etc* dyed-in-the-wool *attr*; **er ist ~** you can't tell him anything; **wenn du so ~ bist** if you won't be told; **unbeleuchtet** ['ʊnbəlɔʏçtət] ADJ *Straße, Weg* unlit; *Fahrzeug* without lights; **unbeliebt** ADJ unpopular (*bei* with); **sich ~ machen** to make oneself unpopular; **unbemannt** ['ʊnbəmant] ADJ unmanned; *Fahrzeug* driverless; (*inf*: = *ohne Mann*) without a husband; **unbemerkt** ['ʊnbəmɛrkt] ADJ, ADV unnoticed; **~ bleiben** to go unnoticed; **unbenommen** [ʊnbə'nɔmən, 'ʊn-] ADJ PRED (*form*) **es bleibt** *or* **ist Ihnen ~, zu ...** you are (quite) at liberty to ...; **unbenutzbar** [ʊnbə'nʊtsbaːɐ, 'ʊn-] ADJ unusable; **unbenutzt** ['ʊnbənʊtst] ADJ, ADV unused; **unbeobachtet** ['ʊnbəlo:baxtət] ADJ unnoticed; **in einem ~en Moment** when nobody was looking; **wenn er sich ~ fühlt ...** when he thinks nobody is looking ...

unbequem ADJ (= *ungemütlich*) uncomfortable; (= *lästig*) *Mensch, Frage, Situation* awkward; *Aufgabe* unpleasant; (= *mühevoll*) difficult; **diese Schuhe sind mir zu ~** these shoes are too uncomfortable; **der Regierung/den Behörden** *etc* **~ sein** to be an embarrassment to the government/authorities *etc*

Unbequemlichkeit F (a) NO PL (= *Ungemütlichkeit*) lack of comfort; (*von Situation*) awkwardness (b) USU PL inconvenience

unberechenbar ADJ unpredictable

unberechtigt 🔢 ADJ *Sorge, Zweifel etc* unfounded; *Kritik, Forderung* unjustified; (= *unbefugt*) unauthorized 🔢 ADV (= *unbefugt*) without authorization; **in Anspruch nehmen, kassieren** without entitlement

unberücksichtigt [ʊnbə'rʏkzɪçtɪçt, 'ʊn-] ADJ unconsidered; **etw ~ lassen** not to consider sth

unberufen ADV **~ (toi, toi, toi)!** touch wood! (*Brit*), knock on wood! (*US*); **sich ~ einmischen** to interfere without good reason

unberührt ['ʊnbəryːɐt] 🔢 ADJ (a) untouched; (*fig*) *Wald etc* virgin; *Natur* unspoiled; **~ sein** (*Mädchen*) to be a virgin (b) (= *mitleidlos*) unmoved; **das kann ihn nicht ~ lassen** he can't help but be moved by that (c) (= *unbetroffen*) unaffected 🔢 ADV (= *unangetastet*) **~ in die Ehe gehen** to be a virgin when one marries; **das Essen ~ stehen lassen** to leave one's food untouched

Unberührtheit F -, NO PL (*von Mädchen*) virginity; **wo finden Sie sonst noch diese ~ der Natur?** where else will you find nature so completely unspoiled?

un-: unbeschädigt ['ʊnbəʃeːdɪçt] ADJ, ADV undamaged; *Siegel* unbroken; **~ bleiben** not to be damaged/broken; (*seelisch etc*) to emerge unscathed; **unbescheiden** ADJ *Mensch, Plan* presumptuous; **darf ich mir die ~e Frage erlauben, ...?** I hope you don't think me impertinent but might I ask ...?; **unbescholten** ['ʊnbəʃɔltn] ADJ (*geh*) respectable; *Ruf* spotless; (*Jur*) with no previous convictions; **unbeschrankt** ADJ unguarded

unbeschränkt ADJ unrestricted; *Macht* absolute; *Geldmittel, Haftung, Zeit, Geduld* unlimited; **wie viel darf ich mitnehmen? – ~ ~** how much can I take? – there's no limit; **jdm ~e Vollmacht geben** to give sb carte blanche

unbeschreiblich [ʊnbə'ʃraɪplɪç, 'ʊn-] 🔢 ADJ indescribable; *Frechheit* enormous 🔢 ADV *schön, gut etc* indescribably

Un-: unbeschwert ['ʊnbəʃveːɐt] 🔢 ADJ (a) (= *sorgenfrei*) carefree; *Melodien* light; *Unterhaltung, Lektüre* light-hearted (b) (= *ohne Gewicht*) unweighted 🔢 ADV (= *sorgenfrei*) carefree;

unbesehen [ʊnbə'zeːən, 'ʊn-] ADV indiscriminately; (= *ohne es anzusehen*) without looking at it/them; **das glaube ich dir ~** I believe it if you say so; **das glaube ich dir nicht ~** I'll believe that when I see it; **unbesetzt** ADJ vacant; *Bus, Zug* empty; *Schalter* closed; **unbesiegbar** ADJ invincible; **unbesiegt** ['ʊnbəziːkt] ADJ undefeated; **unbesonnen** ADJ rash 🔢 ADV rashly; **Unbesonnenheit** F rashness

unbesorgt 🔢 ADJ unconcerned; **Sie können ganz ~ sein** you can set your mind at rest 🔢 ADV without worrying; **das können Sie ~ tun** you don't need to worry about doing that

Un-: unbeständig ADJ *Wetter* changeable; *Mensch* unsteady; (*in Leistungen*) erratic; *Liebhaber* inconstant; *Liebe, Gefühl* transitory; **Unbeständigkeit** F (*von Wetter*) changeability; (*von Mensch*) unsteadiness; (*in Leistungen*) erratic behaviour (*Brit*) *or* behavior (*US*); (*von Liebhaber*) inconstancy; **unbestechlich** ADJ (a) *Mensch* incorruptible (b) *Urteil, Blick* unerring; **Unbestechlichkeit** F (*von Mensch*) incorruptibility;

unbestellt ADJ **~e Ware** unsolicited goods *pl*; **~e Warensendung** unordered consigment of goods;

unbestimmt ADJ (a) (= *ungewiss*) uncertain; (= *unentschieden*) undecided (b) (= *unklar, undeutlich*) *Gefühl, Erinnerung etc* vague; **etw ~ lassen** to leave sth open; **auf ~e Zeit** for an indefinite period (c) (*Gram*) indefinite; **unbestreitbar** 🔢 ADJ *Tatsache* indisputable; *Verdienste, Fähigkeiten* unquestionable 🔢 ADV *richtig* indisputably; *fähig* unquestionably;

unbestritten ['ʊnbəʃtrɪtn, ʊnbə'ʃtrɪtn] 🔢 ADJ indisputable; **es ist ja ~, dass ...** nobody disputes that ... 🔢 ADV indisputably;

unbeteiligt ADJ (a) (= *uninteressiert*) indifferent; (*bei Diskussion*) uninterested (b) (= *nicht teilnehmend*) uninvolved *no adv* (*an* +*dat, bei* in); (*Jur, Comm*) disinterested; **es kamen auch Unbeteiligte zu Schaden** innocent bystanders were also injured; **unbetont** ADV unstressed; **unbewacht** ['ʊnbəvaxt] ADJ, ADV (*lit, fig*) unguarded; *Parkplatz* unattended by; **unbewaffnet** ADJ unarmed; **unbewältigt** ['ʊnbəvɛltçt, ʊnbə'vɛltçt] ADJ unconquered; **Deutschlands ~e Vergangenheit** the past with which Germany has not yet come to terms

unbeweglich 🔢 ADJ (a) (= *nicht zu bewegen*) immovable; (= *steif*) stiff; (*geistig*) rigid; **ohne Auto ist man ziemlich ~** you're not very mobile without a car; **~e Güter** (*Jur*) immovable property (b) (= *bewegungslos*) motionless 🔢 ADV *dastehen* motionless

un-: unbewohnbar ADJ uninhabitable; **unbewohnt** ADJ *Gegend, Insel, Planet* uninhabited; *Wohnung, Haus* unoccupied; **unbewusst** 🔢 ADJ unconscious; *Reflex* involuntary 🔢 ADV unconsciously; **unbezahlbar** ADJ (a) (*lit*: = *zu teuer*) prohibitively expensive; *Miete* prohibitively high; *Luxusartikel* absolutely unaffordable (b) (*fig*) (= *praktisch, nützlich*) invaluable; (= *komisch*) priceless; **unbezahlt** ADJ unpaid; **sein noch ~es Auto** the car he hasn't finished paying for yet; **unblutig** 🔢 ADJ *Sieg, Umsturz etc* bloodless; (*Med*) non-operative 🔢 ADV without bloodshed;

unbrauchbar ADJ (= *nutzlos*) useless; (= *nicht zu verwenden*) unusable; **unbürokratisch** 🔢 ADJ unbureaucratic 🔢 ADV without a lot of red tape; **unchristlich** 🔢 ADJ unchristian; **eine ~e Zeit** (*inf*) an ungodly hour 🔢 ADV in an unchristian way; **uncool** ADJ (*inf*) uncool (*inf*)

und [ʊnt] CONJ (a) and; **~? well?; ~ dann?** (and) what then *or* then what?; (= *danach*) and then?; **~ anderes** and other things; **er kann es nicht, ~ ich auch nicht** he can't do it, (and) nor *or* neither can I; **ich ~ ihm Geld leihen?** (*inf*) me, lend him money?; **du ~ tanzen können?** (*inf*) you dance?; **immer zwei ~ zwei** two at a time; **Gruppen zu fünf ~ fünf** groups of five; **er aß ~ aß** he ate and ate; **Unfälle, Staus, ~ ~ ~** accidents, traffic jams etc etc etc (b) (*konzessiv*) even if; **..., ~ wenn ich selbst bezahlen muss ...** even if I have to pay myself; **..., ~ wenn du auch noch so bettelst ...** no matter how much you beg; **~ selbst** even; **~ selbst dann** even then

Undank M ingratitude; **~ ernten** to get little thanks

undankbar 🔢 ADJ (a) *Mensch* ungrateful (b) (= *unerfreulich*) *Aufgabe, Arbeit etc* thankless 🔢 ADV **sich jdm gegenüber ~ zeigen** *or* **erweisen** to be ungrateful to sb

Undankbarkeit F (a) (*von Mensch*) ingratitude (b) (*von Aufgabe, Arbeit etc*) thanklessness

un-: undatiert ['ʊndatiːɐt] ADJ undated; **undefinierbar** ADJ *Begriff, Aroma, Art* indefinable; **das Essen war ~** nobody could say what the food was; **undemokratisch** 🔢 ADJ undemocratic 🔢 ADV undemocratically

undenkbar ADJ inconceivable

undeutlich 🔢 ADJ indistinct; *Schrift* illegible; *Ausdrucksweise, Erklärung* unclear 🔢 ADV **~ sprechen** to speak indistinctly; **ich konnte es nur ~ verstehen** I couldn't understand it very clearly; **bemüh dich mal, nicht so ~ zu schreiben** try to write more clearly; **Sie drücken sich sehr ~ aus** you don't express yourself very clearly; **sie/es war nur ~ zu erkennen** you couldn't see her/it at all clearly

undeutsch ADJ un-German

undicht ADJ (= *luftdurchlässig*) not airtight; (= *wasserdurchlässig*) not watertight; *Dach* leaky, leaking; **das Rohr ist ~** the pipe leaks; **das Fenster ist ~** the window lets in a draught (*Brit*) *or* draft (*US*); **es/er/sie muss eine ~e Stelle haben** (*Rohr etc*) it must have a leak in it; (*Reifen etc*) it must have a hole in it; (*Flasche etc*) the seal must be broken; **in der Regierung muss eine ~e Stelle sein** the government must have a leak somewhere

undifferenziert 1 ADJ simplistic; (= *nicht analytisch*) indiscriminate **2** ADV simplistically; *behandeln* in an over-generalized way; *Begriffe verwenden* indiscriminately

Unding NT, NO PL absurdity; **es ist ein ~, zu ...** it is preposterous *or* absurd to ...

Un-: undiplomatisch 1 ADJ undiplomatic **2** ADV undiplomatically; **undiszipliniert 1** ADJ undisciplined **2** ADV in an undisciplined way; **undurchlässig** ADJ impervious (*gegen* to); *Grenze* closed; **undurchschaubar** ADJ unfathomable; *Exot, Volk etc* inscrutable; **er ist ein ~er Typ** (*inf*) you never know what game he's playing (*inf*); **undurchsichtig** ADJ **(a)** *Fenster, Papier, Stoff* opaque **(b)** (*fig pej*) *Mensch, Methoden* devious; *Motive* obscure; *Vorgänge, Geschäfte* dark; **es ist eine ganze ~e Angelegenheit** you can't tell what's going on in that business

Und-Zeichen NT ampersand

uneben ADJ uneven; *Gelände* rough

Unebenheit F -, -en unevenness; (*von Gelände*) roughness; **kleine ~en** uneven patches

Un-: unecht 1 ADJ false; (= *vorgetäuscht*) fake; *Schmuck, Edelstein, Blumen etc* artificial; *Bruch* improper **2** ADV **~ klingen** to sound false; **~ wirken** to seem false; **unehelich 1** ADJ illegitimate **2** ADV **~ geboren sein** to be illegitimate; **unehrlich 1** ADJ dishonest **2** ADV dishonestly; **~ spielen** to cheat; **Unehrlichkeit** F dishonesty; **uneidlich** ADJ **~e Falschaussage** (*Jur*) false statement made while not under oath; **uneigennützig 1** ADJ unselfish **2** ADV unselfishly; **Uneigennützigkeit** F unselfishness

uneinbringlich ADJ **~e Forderungen** bad debts *pl*

uneingeschränkt 1 ADJ absolute, total; *Freiheit, Rechte* unlimited; *Annahme, Zustimmung* unqualified; *Vertrauen* absolute; *Lob* unreserved; *Handel* unrestricted; *Vollmachten* plenary **2** ADV absolutely, totally; *zustimmen, akzeptieren* without qualification; *loben, vertrauen* unreservedly; *Handel treiben* without restriction

Un-: uneingeweiht ADJ uninitiated; **für Uneingeweihte** for the uninitiated; **uneinheitlich 1** ADJ nonuniform; *Öffnungszeiten, Arbeitszeiten, Systeme, Reaktion* varied; (= *nicht für alle gleich*) *Arbeitszeiten, Schulferien* different; *Qualität* inconsistent; *Börse* irregular; *Preise* unsteady; **~ sein** to vary **2** ADV *gekleidet, beurteilen* differently; *sich entwickeln* in different ways; (*St Ex*) irregularly; **die New Yorker Börse hat am Donnerstag ~ tendiert** on Thursday shares on the New York Stock Exchange were mixed; **~ verlaufen** to vary; **uneinig** ADJ **(a)** (= *verschiedener Meinung*) in disagreement; **über etw** (*acc*) **~ sein** to disagree about sth; **ich bin mit mir selbst noch ~** I haven't made up my mind yet **(b)** (= *zerstritten*) divided; **uneins** ADJ PRED disagreed; (= *zerstritten*) divided; **(mit jdm) ~ sein/werden** to disagree with sb; **ich bin mit mir selbst ~** I cannot make up my mind; **unempfänglich** ADJ (*für* to) unsusceptible; (*für Eindrücke auch, für Atmosphäre*) insensitive; **unempfindlich** ADJ (*gegen* to) insensitive; (*durch Übung, Erfahrung*) inured; (*gegen Krankheiten, Bazillen etc*) immune; *Pflanze* hardy; *Baustoff* which weathers well; *Textilien, Teppich* hard-wearing and stain-resistant; **gegen Kälte ~e Pflanzen** plants which aren't sensitive to the cold; **Unempfindlichkeit** F, NO PL (*gegen* to) insensitivity; (*gegen Krankheiten, Bazillen etc*) immunity; (*von Pflanzen*) hardiness; (*von Textilien*) practicality; **dieser Baustoff ist wegen seiner ~ gegen Witterungseinflüsse besonders gut geeignet** this building material is particularly suitable because it weathers so well; **unendlich 1** ADJ infinite; (*zeitlich*) endless; **das Unendliche** infinity; **(bis) ins Unendliche** (*lit, Math*) to infinity; **auf ~ einstellen** (*Phot*) to focus on infinity; **~e Mal** endless times **2** ADV endlessly; infinitely; (*fig:* = *sehr*) terribly; **~ lange diskutieren** to argue endlessly; **~ viele Dinge/Leute** *etc* no end of things/people *etc*

Unendlichkeit F infinity; (*zeitlich*) endlessness; (*von Universum*) boundlessness; **~ von Raum und Zeit** infinity of time and space

Un-: unentbehrlich ADJ indispensable; **unentdeckt** ADJ undiscovered; **unentgeltlich 1** ADJ free of charge **2** ADV free of charge; *arbeiten* for nothing; **etw ~ tun** to do sth free of charge

unentschieden 1 ADJ (= *nicht entschieden*) undecided; (= *entschlusslos*) indecisive; (*Sport*) drawn; **ein ~es Rennen** a

dead heat **2** ADV **das Spiel steht immer noch 2:2 ~** the score is still level (*Brit*) *or* even (*US*) at 2 all; **~ enden** *or* **ausgehen** to end in a draw *or* tie; **~ spielen, sich ~ trennen** to draw, to tie

Unentschieden ['ʊnɛntʃiːdn] NT -s, - (*Sport*) draw

unentschlossen 1 ADJ (= *nicht entschieden*) undecided; *Mensch* indecisive; **ich bin noch ~** I haven't decided yet **2** ADV *sich verhalten* indecisively; **~ stand er vor dem Haus** he stood hesitating in front of the house

unentschuldigt ['ʊnɛntʃʊldɪçt] **1** ADJ unexcused; **~es Fernbleiben** *or* **Fehlen von der Arbeit** absenteeism; **~es Fernbleiben** *or* **Fehlen von der Schule** truancy **2** ADV without an excuse

unentwegt [ʊnɛntˈveːkt, 'ʊn-] **1** ADJ (*mit Ausdauer*) constant; *Kämpfer* untiring; **einige Unentwegte** a few stalwarts **2** ADV constantly; without tiring; **~ weitermachen** to continue unceasingly

unerbittlich [ʊnlɛɐˈbɪtlɪç] **1** ADJ *Kampf* relentless; *Härte* unyielding; *Mensch* pitiless **2** ADV (= *hartnäckig*) stubbornly; (= *gnadenlos*) ruthlessly; **~ auf jdn einschlagen** to beat sb pitilessly

Unerbittlichkeit F -, NO PL relentlessness

Un-: unerfahren ADJ inexperienced; **Unerfahrenheit** F inexperience; **unerfindlich** [ʊnlɛɐˈfɪntlɪç, 'ʊn-] ADJ incomprehensible; *Grund* obscure; **aus ~en Gründen** for some obscure reason; **unerfreulich** ADJ unpleasant; **Unerfreuliches** (= *schlechte Nachrichten*) bad news *sing*; (= *Übles*) bad things *pl* **2** ADV unpleasantly; **unerfüllbar** [ʊnlɛɐˈfʏlbaːɐ, 'ʊn-] ADJ unrealizable; **unerfüllt** ['ʊnlɛɐfʏlt] ADJ unfulfilled; **unergiebig** ADJ *Quelle, Thema* unproductive; *Boden, Ernte, Nachschlagewerk* poor; *Kaffee, Trauben* uneconomical; **unergründlich** [ʊnlɛɐˈɡrʏntlɪç, 'ʊn-] ADJ unfathomable; **unerheblich 1** ADJ insignificant; **nicht ~** not inconsiderable **2** ADV insignificantly; **nicht ~ verbessert** significantly improved

unerhört¹ ['ʊnlɛɐˈhøːɐt] **1** ADJ ATTR (= *ungeheuer, gewaltig*) enormous; (= *empörend*) outrageous; *Frechheit* incredible; **das ist ja ~!** that's quite outrageous **2** ADV incredibly; **~ viel** a tremendous amount (of); **~ viel arbeiten** to work tremendously hard; **~ aufpassen** to watch very carefully

unerhört² ['ʊnlɛɐˈhøːɐt] ADJ *Bitte, Gebet* unanswered; *Liebe* unrequited; *Liebhaber* rejected

un-: unerkannt ['ʊnlɛɐkant] **1** ADJ unrecognized; **~ bleiben** not to be recognized **2** ADV without being recognized; **unerklärbar, unerklärlich** ADJ inexplicable; **das ist mir ~ or** unerklärlich** I can't understand it; **unerlässlich** [ʊnlɛɐˈlɛslɪç, 'ʊn-] ADJ essential

unerlaubt ['ʊnlɛɐlaupt] **1** ADJ forbidden; *Betreten, Parken* unauthorized; (= *ungesetzlich*) illegal **2** ADV *betreten, verlassen* without permission; **etw ~ tun** to do sth without permission

unerlaubterweise ['ʊnlɛɐlauptɐˈvaɪzə] ADV without permission

unerledigt 1 ADJ unfinished; *Post* unanswered; *Rechnung* outstanding; *Auftrag* unfulfilled; **"~" "pending" **2** ADV *liegen bleiben* without being dealt with; **etw ~ lassen** not to deal with sth

un-: unermesslich [ʊnlɛɐˈmɛslɪç, 'ʊn-] **1** ADJ *Reichtum, Schaden, Leid* immense; *Weite, Himmel, Ozean* vast **2** ADV *reich, groß* immensely; **unermüdlich** [ʊnlɛɐˈmyːtlɪç, 'ʊn-] **1** ADJ tireless; *Versuche* unceasing **2** ADV tirelessly; **unernst** ADJ frivolous; **unerquicklich** ADJ (= *unerfreulich*) unedifying; **unerreichbar** ADJ *Ziel, Leistung, Qualität* unattainable; *Ort, Ferne* inaccessible; (*telefonisch*) unobtainable; **seine Beförderung war in ~e Ferne gerückt** promotion was now right out of his reach

unersättlich [ʊnlɛɐˈzɛtlɪç, 'ʊn-] ADJ insatiable

Unersättlichkeit [ʊnlɛɐˈzɛtlɪçkaɪt, 'ʊn-] F -, NO PL insatiability

un-: unerschöpflich [ʊnlɛɐˈʃœpflɪç, 'ʊn-] ADJ inexhaustible; **unerschrocken 1** ADJ courageous **2** ADV courageously; **unerschütterlich** [ʊnlɛɐˈʃʏtɐlɪç, 'ʊn-] **1** ADJ unshakeable; *Ruhe* imperturbable **2** ADV steadfastly; **sie glaubt ~ an ...** (*acc*) she has an unshakeable belief in ...; **unerschwinglich** ADJ prohibitive; **für jdn ~ sein** to be beyond sb's means; **unersetzbar** [ʊnlɛɐˈzɛtsbaːɐ, 'ʊn-], **unersetzlich** [ʊnlɛɐˈzɛtslɪç, 'ʊn-] ADJ irreplaceable; **unersprießlich** ADJ (= *unerfreulich*) unedifying; **unerträglich 1** ADJ unbearable **2** ADV *heiß, laut* unbearably; **er hat sich gestern ~ benommen** his behaviour (*Brit*) *or* behavior (*US*) was unbearable yesterday; **unerwähnt**

['ʊnlɛɛvɛ:nt] ADJ unmentioned; **~ bleiben** not to be mentioned; **unerwartet** ['ʊnlɛɛvartət, ʊnlɛɛ'vartət] **1** ADJ unexpected **2** ADV unexpectedly; **unerwünscht** ADJ *Kind* unwanted; *Besuch, Effekt* unwelcome; *Eigenschaften* undesirable; **du bist hier ~** you're not welcome here; **~e Personen** undesirables; **unerzogen** ['ʊnlɛɛtso:gn] ADJ ill-mannered

UNESCO [u'nɛsko] F **- die ~** UNESCO

unfachgemäß, unfachmännisch **1** ADJ unprofessional **2** ADV unprofessionally

unfähig ADJ **(a)** ATTR incompetent **(b) ~ sein, etw zu tun** to be incapable of doing sth; *(vorübergehend)* to be unable to do sth; **einer Sache** *(gen)* **or zu etw ~ sein** to be incapable of sth

Unfähigkeit F **(a)** (= *Untüchtigkeit*) incompetence **(b)** (= *Nichtkönnen*) inability

unfair **1** ADJ unfair *(gegenüber* to) **2** ADV unfairly

Unfall ['ʊnfal] M accident

Unfall-: Unfallarzt M, **Unfallärztin** F specialist for accident injuries; **Unfallbeteiligte(r)** MF DECL AS ADJ person/man/woman *etc* involved in an/the accident; **Unfallfahrer(in)** M(F) driver at fault in an/the accident; **Unfallflucht** F failure to stop after an accident; *(esp bei Verletzung von Personen)* hit-and-run driving; **~ begehen** to commit a hit-and-run offence *(Brit)* or offense *(US)*; **Unfallfolge** F result of an/the accident; **unfallfrei** **1** ADJ accident-free **2** ADV without an accident; **Unfallopfer** NT casualty; **Unfallort** M, *pl* **-orte** scene of an/the accident; **Unfallschaden** M damages *pl*; **Unfallstation** F accident *or* emergency ward *(Brit)*, emergency room *(US)*; **Unfallstelle** F scene of an/the accident; **Unfalltod** M accidental death; **bei ~** in the event of death by misadventure; **Unfallursache** F cause of an/the accident; **Unfallverhütung** F accident prevention; **Unfallwagen** M car involved in an/the accident; **der Wagen ist so billig, weil es ein ~ ist** the car is so cheap because it has been involved in an accident; **Unfallzeuge** M, **Unfallzeugin** F witness to an/the accident

unfassbar, unfasslich ADJ incomprehensible; **es ist mir** *or* **für mich ~, wie ...** I (simply) cannot understand how ...

Un-: unfehlbar **1** ADJ infallible; *Instinkt* unerring **2** ADV without fail; **Unfehlbarkeit** [ʊn'fe:lbaːɐkait, 'ʊn-] F **-**, NO PL infallibility; **unfein** **1** ADJ unrefined *no adv*; **das ist ~** that's bad manners; **das ist mehr als ~** that's most ungentlemanly/unladylike **2** ADV *sich ausdrücken* in an unrefined way; *sich benehmen* in an ill-mannered way; **unflätig** ['ʊnflɛ:tɪç] **1** ADJ offensive **2** ADV **sich ~ ausdrücken** to use obscene language; **unfolgsam** ADJ disobedient; **unformatiert** ['ʊnfɔrmatiːɐt] ADJ *(Comput)* unformatted

unförmig ADJ (= *formlos*) shapeless; *Möbel, Auto* inelegant; (= *groß*) cumbersome; *Füße, Gesicht* unshapely

Unförmigkeit F **-**, NO PL (= *Formlosigkeit*) shapelessness; *(von Möbeln, Auto)* inelegance; (= *Größe*) awkward size; *(von Füßen, Gesicht)* unshapeliness

unfrankiert ['ʊnfraŋkiːɐt] ADJ, ADV unfranked

Unfreiheit F lack of freedom; *(Hist)* bondage, serfdom

unfreiwillig **1** ADJ **(a)** (= *gezwungen*) compulsory; **ich war ~er Zeuge** I was an unwilling witness **(b)** (= *unbeabsichtigt) Witz, Fehler* unintentional **2** ADV involuntarily; **ich musste ~ zuhören** I was forced to listen

unfreundlich **1** ADJ unfriendly *(zu, gegen* to); *Wetter* inclement; *Landschaft, Zimmer, Farbe* cheerless; **ein ~er Akt** *(Pol)* a hostile act **2** ADV in an unfriendly way; **jdn ~ behandeln** to be unfriendly to sb; **jdn ~ begrüßen/ansehen** to give sb an unfriendly welcome/look; **~ reagieren** to react in an unfriendly way

Unfreundlichkeit F **(a)** unfriendliness; *(von Wetter)* inclemency **(b)** (= *Bemerkung*) unpleasant remark

Unfriede(n) M strife; **in Unfrieden (mit jdm) leben** to live in conflict (with sb)

unfruchtbar ADJ infertile; *(fig) Debatte etc* sterile; *Schaffenszeit* unproductive; **~ machen** to sterilize; **die ~en Tage** *(Med)* the days of infertility

Unfruchtbarkeit F infertility; *(fig: von Debatte etc)* sterility

Unfug ['ʊnfuːk] M **-s**, NO PL nonsense; **~ treiben** *or* **anstellen** *or* **machen** to get up to mischief; **lass den ~!** stop that nonsense!; **grober ~** *(Jur)* public nuisance

Ungar ['ʊŋar] M **-n, -n, Ungarin** ['ʊŋarɪn] F **-, -nen** Hungarian

ungarisch ['ʊŋarɪʃ] ADJ Hungarian

Ungarn ['ʊŋarn] NT **-s** Hungary

un-: ungastlich **1** ADJ inhospitable **2** ADV inhospitably; **ungeachtet** ['ʊngalaxtət, ʊnga'laxtət] PREP +GEN in spite of, despite; **~ dessen, dass es regnet** in spite of it raining; **~ aller Ermahnungen, aller Ermahnungen ~** despite all warnings; **ungeahnt** ['ʊngalaːnt, ʊnga'laːnt] ADJ undreamt-of; **ungebeten** **1** ADJ uninvited **2** ADV **er kam ~** he came uninvited; **ungebildet** ADJ uncultured; (= *ohne Bildung*) uneducated; **Ungebildete** uneducated people; **ungebleicht** ['ʊngablaiçt] ADJ unbleached; **ungeboren** ADJ unborn; **ungebräuchlich** ADJ uncommon; **ungebrochen** **1** ADJ *(fig) Rekord, Wille* unbroken; *Widerstand* unyielding; *Popularität* undiminished **(b)** *(Phys) Licht* unrefracted **2** ADV *weiterkämpfen, weitermachen* undiminished; **ungebührlich** **1** ADJ improper **2** ADV **(a)** (= *ungehörig*) improperly **(b)** (= *über Gebühr*) excessively; **sich ~ aufregen** to get unduly excited

ungebunden ADJ (= *unabhängig) Leben* (fancy-)free; (= *unverheiratet*) unattached; *(Pol)* independent; *(Comm) Kredit* untied; **frei und ~** footloose and fancy-free; **parteipolitisch ~** (politically) independent

ungedeckt ADJ **(a)** (= *schutzlos) Schachfigur etc* unguarded; *(Sport) Tor* undefended; *Spieler* unmarked; *Scheck, Kredit* uncovered **(b)** *Tisch* unlaid *(Brit)*, not set *pred*

Ungeduld F impatience; **vor ~** with impatience; **voller ~** impatiently

ungeduldig **1** ADJ impatient **2** ADV impatiently

ungeeignet ADJ unsuitable

ungefähr ['ʊngəfɛːɐ, ʊngə'fɛːɐ] **1** ADJ ATTR approximate, rough **2** ADV roughly; **von ~** from nowhere; (= *zufällig*) by chance; **das kommt nicht von ~** it's no accident; **diese Bemerkung kommt doch nicht von ~** he *etc* didn't make this remark just by chance; **wo ~?** whereabouts?; **wie ~?** approximately how?; **so ~!** more or less!; **können Sie mir (so) ~ sagen, wie ...?** can you tell me roughly how ...?; **~ (so) wie** a bit like; **dann weiß ich ~ Bescheid** then I've got a rough idea; **so ~ habe ich mir das gedacht** I thought it would be something like this; **so ~, als wären wir kleine Kinder** a bit as if we were little children; **das hat sich ~ so abgespielt** it happened something like this

Un-: ungefährlich ADJ safe; *Tier, Krankheit, Arzneimittel etc* harmless; **nicht ganz ~** not altogether safe/harmless; *Expedition* not altogether without its dangers; **Ungefährlichkeit** F safeness; *(von Tier, Krankheit, Arzneimittel etc)* harmlessness; **ungefragt** ADV unasked

ungehalten **1** ADJ indignant *(über +acc* about) **2** ADV indignantly

Ungehaltenheit ['ʊngəhaltnhait] F **-**, NO PL indignation

un-: ungehärtet ['ʊngəhɛrtət] ADJ *Stahl* untempered; **ungeheizt** ['ʊngəhaitst] ADJ unheated; **ungehemmt** **1** ADJ unrestrained **2** ADV without inhibition; **sich ~ benehmen** to behave in an uninhibited way

ungeheuer ['ʊngəhɔye, ʊngə'hɔye] **1** ADJ **(a)** *siehe* **ungeheuerlich (b)** (= *riesig*) enormous; *(in Bezug auf Länge, Weite)* vast; **sich ins Ungeheuere steigern** to take on enormous dimensions **(c)** (= *genial, kühn*) tremendous **(d)** (= *frevelhaft, vermessen*) dreadful **2** ADV (= *sehr*) enormously; *(negativ)* terribly, awfully; **~ viele Menschen** an enormous number of people

Ungeheuer ['ʊngəhɔye] NT **-s, -** monster

ungeheuerlich [ʊngə'hɔyɐlɪç, 'ʊn-] ADJ monstrous; *Verleumdung, Leichtsinn* outrageous; *Verdacht, Dummheit* dreadful

Ungeheuerlichkeit F **-, -en (a)** *(von Tat)* atrociousness; *(von Verleumdung)* outrageousness; **so eine ~!** how outrageous! **(b) Ungeheuerlichkeiten** PL (= *Verbrechen etc*) atrocities; (= *Behauptungen etc*) outrageous claims

Un-: ungehindert ['ʊngəhɪndɐt] **1** ADJ unhindered **2** ADV without hindrance; **ungehobelt** ['ʊngəhoːblt, ʊngə'hoːblt] ADJ *Brett etc* unplaned; *Mensch, Benehmen* boorish; **ungehörig** **1** ADJ impertinent **2** ADV impertinently; **Ungehörigkeit** F **-, -en** impertinence; **ungehorsam** ADJ disobedient; **Ungehorsam** M disobedience; *(Mil)* insubordination; **ziviler ~** civil disobedience; **ungeklärt** **1** ADJ *Abwasser etc* untreated **(b)** *Frage, Verbrechen* unsolved; *Ursache* unknown; **unter ~en Umständen** in mysterious circumstances; **die Finanzierung des Projekts ist ~** the financing of the project has not been settled **2** ADV

Abwässer ~ einleiten to discharge effluents in an untreated state; **ungekürzt** [ˈʊngəkʏrtst] **1** ADJ not shortened; *Buch* unabridged; *Film* uncut; *Ausgaben* not cut back **2** ADV *veröffentlichen* unabridged; *(Film)* uncut; **der Artikel wurde ~ abgedruckt** the article was printed in full; **ungeladen** ADJ *Gäste etc* uninvited; **ungeläufig** ADJ unfamiliar

ungelegen 1 ADJ inconvenient **2** ADV **komme ich (Ihnen) ~?** is this an inconvenient time for you?; **etw kommt jdm ~** sth is inconvenient for sb; **das kam (mir) gar nicht so ~** that was really rather convenient

Ungelegenheiten PL inconvenience *sing*; **jdm ~ bereiten** *or* **machen** to inconvenience sb

un-: ungelernt ADJ ATTR unskilled; **ungelesen** ADJ unread; **ungelogen** ADV honestly

ungemein 1 ADJ tremendous **2** ADV extraordinarily; **das freut mich ~** I'm really really pleased

ungemustert ADJ plain

ungemütlich 1 ADJ uncomfortable; *Wohnung, Zimmer* not very cosy; *Mensch* awkward; *Land, Wetter, Wochenende* unpleasant; **mir wird es hier ~** I'm getting a bit uncomfortable; **er kann ~ werden** he can get nasty; **ich kann auch ~ werden** I can be very unpleasant if I choose; **hier kann es gleich sehr ~ werden** things could get very nasty here in a moment **2** ADV uncomfortably; **seine Wohnung wirkt sehr ~** his apartment has a very uncomfortable feel about it

ungenannt ADJ **(a)** *Mensch* anonymous; **~ bleiben** to remain anonymous **(b)** *Zahl, Summe* unspecified; **Beträge in ~er Höhe** unspecified amounts

ungenau 1 ADJ (= *nicht fehlerfrei*) inaccurate; (= *nicht wahrheitsgetreu*) inexact; (= *vage*) vague; (= *ungefähr*) rough **2** ADV *formulieren* imprecisely; *arbeiten, messen* inaccurately; *rechnen* roughly

Ungenauigkeit F inaccuracy; (= *Vagheit*) vagueness

ungeniert [ˈʊnʒeniːɐt] **1** ADJ (= *frei, ungehemmt*) unembarrassed; (= *bedenkenlos, taktlos*) uninhibited **2** ADV openly; (= *bedenkenlos, taktlos*) without any inhibition; **greifen Sie bitte ~ zu** please feel free to help yourself/yourselves

ungenießbar ADJ (= *nicht zu essen*) inedible; (= *nicht zu trinken*) undrinkable; (= *unschmackhaft*) unpalatable; (*inf*) *Mensch* unbearable

ungenügend 1 ADJ inadequate, insufficient; (*Sch*) unsatisfactory; **ein Ungenügend** an "unsatisfactory" **2** ADV inadequately, insufficiently

Un-: ungenutzt [ˈʊngənʊtst], **ungenützt** [ˈʊngənʏtst] **1** ADJ unused; *Energien* unexploited; **eine Chance ~ lassen** to miss an opportunity **2** ADV *Energien* unused; **eine Chance ~ vorübergehen lassen** to miss an opportunity; **ungepflegt 1** ADJ *Mensch* unkempt; *Park, Rasen, Hände etc* neglected **2** ADV (= *unordentlich*) untidy; **der Garten sieht ~ aus** the garden looks neglected; **ungeprüft** [ˈʊngəpryːft] **1** ADJ untested; *Vorwürfe* unchecked **2** ADV without testing; without checking; **etw ~ übernehmen** to accept sth without testing it; *Bilanz* to accept sth without checking it; (*unkritisch*) to accept sth at face value; **ungeputzt** [ˈʊngəpʊtst] ADJ uncleaned; *Zähne* unbrushed; *Schuhe* unpolished; **ungerade** ADJ odd; **ungerechnet** [ˈʊngərɛçnət] PREP +GEN not including; **ungerecht 1** ADJ unjust, unfair **2** ADV unjustly, unfairly; **ungerechtfertigt 1** ADJ unjustified **2** ADV unjustly; **Ungerechtigkeit** F injustice; **ungeregelt** ADJ **(a)** *Zeiten* irregular; *Leben* disordered **(b)** (*Tech*) *Katalysator* open-loop; **Ungereimtheit** F -, -en inconsistency

ungern ADV reluctantly; **(höchst) ~!** if I/we really have to!; **das tue ich gar nicht ~** I don't mind doing that at all

un-: ungerührt [ˈʊngəryːɐt] ADJ, ADV unmoved; **ungesagt** [ˈʊngəzaːkt] ADJ unsaid; **etw ~ machen** to pretend sth has never been said; **ungesalzen** ADJ unsalted; **ungesättigt** ADJ *Hunger etc* unsatisfied; (*Chem*) *Fettsäuren etc* unsaturated; **ungeschehen** ADJ **etw ~ machen** to undo sth

Ungeschick NT -s, NO PL, **Ungeschicklichkeit** F clumsiness

ungeschickt 1 ADJ clumsy; (= *unbedacht*) careless **2** ADV clumsily

un-: ungeschlechtlich 1 ADJ asexual **2** ADV *sich vermehren* asexually; **ungeschmälert** [ˈʊngəʃmɛːlɐt] ADJ undiminished; **ungeschminkt** [ˈʊngəʃmɪŋkt] **1** ADJ without make-up; (*fig*) *Wahrheit* unvarnished **2** ADV (= *ohne Schminke*) without

make-up; (= *unverblümt*) bluntly; **du solltest ihr ~ die Wahrheit sagen** you should tell her the whole truth; **ungeschoren 1** ADJ unshorn; (*fig*) spared; **jdn ~ lassen** (*inf*) to spare sb; (= *ungestraft*) to let sb off (scot-free) **2** ADV **~ davonkommen** (*inf*) to escape unscathed; (*Verbrecher*) to get off (scot-free); **ungeschrieben** ADJ ATTR unwritten;

ungeschützt 1 ADJ unprotected (*auch Jur*); *Anlagen* undefended; (*Sport*) *Tor* undefended **2** ADV without protection; **~ (mit jdm) Geschlechtsverkehr haben** to have unprotected sex (with sb); **ungesellig** ADJ unsociable; *Tier* non-gregarious; **ungesetzlich** ADJ unlawful, illegal; **ungestempelt** [ˈʊngəʃtɛmplt] ADJ unstamped; *Briefmarke* unfranked; (*für Sammler*) mint; **ungestört 1** ADJ undisturbed; (*Rad, TV etc*) without interference; **hier sind wir ~** we won't be disturbed here **2** ADV *arbeiten, spielen, sprechen* without being interrupted; **ungestraft** [ˈʊngəʃtraːft] ADV with impunity

ungestüm [ˈʊngəʃtyːm] **1** ADJ impetuous **2** ADV impetuously

Ungestüm [ˈʊngəʃtyːm] NT -(e)s, NO PL impetuousness

un-: ungesühnt [ˈʊngəzyːnt] ADJ unatoned; **ungesund 1** ADJ unhealthy; (= *schädlich*) harmful **2** ADV unhealthily; **sie lebt sehr ~** she has a very unhealthy lifestyle; **ungesüßt** [ˈʊngəzyːst] ADJ unsweetened; **ungetan** ADJ undone; **etw ~ machen** to undo sth; **ungeteilt** [ˈʊngətaɪlt] ADJ undivided; *Beifall* universal; **ungetrübt** ADJ clear; *Glück, Freude* perfect

Ungetüm [ˈʊngətyːm] NT -(e)s, -e monster

ungewiss ADJ uncertain; (= *vage*) vague; **ein Sprung/eine Reise ins Ungewisse** (*fig*) a leap/a journey into the unknown; **jdn (über etw** *acc***) im Ungewissen lassen** to leave sb in the dark (about sth); **im Ungewissen bleiben/sein** to stay/be in the dark

Ungewissheit F uncertainty

ungewöhnlich 1 ADJ unusual **2** ADV unusually

ungewohnt ADJ (= *fremdartig*) unfamiliar; (= *unüblich*) unusual; **das ist mir ~** I am unaccustomed to it

ungewollt 1 ADJ unintentional **2** ADV unintentionally; **er musste ~ lachen** he couldn't help laughing

Ungeziefer [ˈʊngətsiːfɐ] NT -s, NO PL pests *pl*

ungezogen 1 ADJ ill-mannered **2** ADV badly; (*in Bezug auf Kinder*) naughtily

Ungezogenheit F -, -en **(a)** NO PL unmannerliness **(b)** (= *ungezogene Handlung*) bad manners *no indef art*; **so eine ~ von dir!** what manners!

ungezwungen 1 ADJ casual; *Benehmen* natural **2** ADV casually; **sich benehmen** naturally

ungläubig 1 ADJ unbelieving; (*Rel*) infidel; (= *zweifelnd*) doubting; **~er Thomas** (*Bibl, fig*) doubting Thomas **2** ADV doubtingly

Ungläubige(r) MF DECL AS ADJ unbeliever

unglaublich 1 ADJ unbelievable; **das grenzt ans Unglaubliche** that's almost incredible **2** ADV unbelievably

unglaubwürdig 1 ADJ implausible; *Dokument* dubious; *Mensch* unreliable **2** ADV *sich benehmen, sich verhalten* unreliably; **sich ~ machen** to lose credibility; **diese Regierung wirkt völlig ~** this government lacks credibility

ungleich 1 ADJ (= *nicht gleichartig*) *Charaktere* dissimilar, unlike *pred*; *Größe, Farbe* different; (= *nicht gleichwertig, nicht vergleichbar*) *Mittel, Waffen, Kampf* unequal; *Partner* very different; (*Math*) not equal; **sie sind ein ~es Paar** they are very different; **das Zeichen für ~** the not-equals (*Brit*) *or* inequality (*US*) sign **2** ADV **(a)** (= *unterschiedlich*) unequally **(b)** (*vor Komparativ*) much

Ungleich-: Ungleichbehandlung F, NO PL discrimination; **Ungleichgewicht** NT (*fig*) imbalance

Ungleichheit F (= *Ungleichartigkeit*) (*von Charakteren*) dissimilarity; (*von Größe, Farbe*) difference; (*von Mitteln, Waffen, Kampf*) inequality

Ungleichheitszeichen NT (*Math*) not-equals sign (*Brit*), inequality sign (*US*)

ungleichmäßig 1 ADJ uneven; *Atem, Gesichtszüge, Puls* irregular **2** ADV unevenly; **~ lang** of uneven length

Unglück NT -(e)s, -e (= *Unfall, Vorfall*) accident; (= *Schicksalsschlag*) disaster; (= *Unheil*) misfortune; (= *Pech: im Aberglauben, bei Glücksspiel*) bad luck; (= *Unglücklichsein*) unhappiness; **in sein ~ rennen** to head for disaster; **das ist auch kein ~** that is not a disaster; **er hat im Leben viel ~**

gehabt he has experienced a great deal of misfortune in life; **es ist ein ~, dass ...** it is bad luck that ...; **das bringt ~** that brings bad luck; **zum ~, zu allem ~** to make matters worse; **ein ~ kommt selten allein** (*prov*) it never rains but it pours (*Brit prov*), when it rains, it pours (*US prov*); **~ im Spiel, Glück in der Liebe** (*prov*) unlucky at cards, lucky in love

unglücklich ▨ ADJ **(a)** (= *traurig*) unhappy; *Liebe* unrequited **(b)** (= *bedauerlich*) unfortunate; **eine ~e Figur abgeben** to cut a sorry figure ▨ ADV **(a)** (*traurig*) unhappily; **~ verliebt sein** to be crossed in love **(b)** (*ungünstig*) unfortunately; **~ enden** *or* **ausgehen** to turn out badly **(c)** *stürzen, fallen* awkwardly

unglücklicherweise [ˈʊnɡlʏklɪçəˈvaɪzə] ADV unfortunately

Unglücks-: **Unglücksfall** M accident; **Unglücksrabe** M (*inf*) unlucky thing (*inf*); **Unglückstag** M fateful day

Ungnade F disgrace; **bei jdm in ~ fallen** to fall out of favour (*Brit*) *or* favor (*US*) with sb

ungnädig ▨ ADJ ungracious; (*hum*) unkind ▨ ADV ungraciously; (*hum*) unkindly; **etw ~ aufnehmen** to take sth with bad grace

ungrammatisch ▨ ADJ ungrammatical ▨ ADV ungrammatically

ungültig ADJ (= *nicht gültig*) invalid; (= *nicht mehr gültig*) no longer valid; (= *nichtig*) void; *Stimmzettel* spoiled; (*Sport*) *Tor* disallowed; **„~"** (*in Pass*) "cancelled"; **~ werden** (*Pass*) to expire; **~er Sprung** no-jump; **etw für ~ erklären** to declare sth null and void

Ungültigkeit F (*von Pass, Visum*) invalidity; (*von Ehe*) nullity; **die ~ einer Wahl** an election's being null and void

ungünstig ADJ unfavourable (*Brit*), unfavorable (*US*); *Auswirkungen, Entwicklung* undesirable; *Termin* inconvenient; *Augenblick, Wetter* bad; *Licht* unflattering; **im ~sten Fall** if (the) worst comes to (the) worst

ungut ADJ bad; **nichts für ~!** no offence (*Brit*) *or* offense (*US*)!

un-: **unhaltbar** ADJ *Zustand* intolerable; *Vorwurf, Behauptung etc* untenable; *Torschuss* unstoppable; **unhandlich** ADJ unwieldy

Unheil NT disaster; **~ stiften** *or* **anrichten** to do damage; **~ bringend** fateful

unheilbar ▨ ADJ incurable ▨ ADV incurably, terminally; **~ krank sein** to be terminally ill

unheimlich [ˈʊnhaɪmlɪç, ʊnˈhaɪmlɪç] ▨ ADJ **(a)** (= *Angst erregend*) frightening; **~e Begegnung** (= *übernatürlich etc*) close encounter; **das/er ist mir ~** it/he gives me the creeps (*inf*); **mir ist ~ (zumute** *or* **zu Mute)** it is uncanny **(b)** (*inf*) tremendous (*inf*) ▨ ADV (*inf*: = *sehr*) incredibly (*inf*); **~ viel Geld/viele Menschen** a tremendous amount of money/number of people (*inf*)

Un-: **unhöflich** ▨ ADJ impolite ▨ ADV impolitely; **Unhöflichkeit** F impoliteness; **deine ~en** your impoliteness; **es war eine ~ von dir** that was not polite of you; **unhygienisch** ADJ unhygienic

uni [yˈniː] ADJ PRED self-coloured (*Brit*), self-colored (*US*), plain

Uni [ˈʊni] F **-, -s** (*inf*) uni (*inf*), U (*US inf*)

UNICEF [ˈuːnitsɛf] F **- (die) ~** UNICEF

unidiomatisch ▨ ADJ unidiomatic ▨ ADV unidiomatically

Uniform [uniˈfɔrm, ˈʊnifɔrm, ˈuːnifɔrm] F **-, -en** uniform

uniformiert [unifɔrˈmiːɐt] ADJ uniformed

Uniformierte(r) [unifɔrˈmiːɐtə] MF DECL AS ADJ person/man/woman in uniform

Unikum [ˈuːnikʊm] NT **-s, -s** *or* **Unika** [-ka] **(a)** (= *Einmaliges*) unique thing *etc*; **ein ~** a curiosity; (= *Seltenheit*) a rarity **(b)** (*inf*) real character

unilateral [unilateˈraːl] ▨ ADJ unilateral ▨ ADV unilaterally

un-: **unintelligent** ▨ ADJ unintelligent; **uninteressant** ADJ uninteresting; **sein Angebot ist für uns ~** his offer is of no interest to us; **das ist doch völlig ~** that's of absolutely no interest

Union [uˈnioːn] F **-, -en** union; **die ~** (*Pol*) the CDU and CSU

Unionsparteien PL (*Ger Pol*) CDU and CSU parties *pl*

unisono [uniˈzoːno] ADV (*Mus, fig*) in unison

Univ. ABBR *von* **Universität**

universal [univɛrˈzaːl] ▨ ADJ universal ▨ ADV universally

Universal- [univɛrˈzaːl-] IN CPDS universal; (*Mech*) universal; *Bildung etc* general; **Universalbank** F, *pl* **-banken** universal bank; **Universalgenie** NT universal genius

universell [univɛrˈzɛl] ▨ ADJ universal ▨ ADV universally

Universität [univɛrziˈtɛːt] F **-, -en** university; **die ~ Freiburg, die Freiburger ~** the University of Freiburg, Freiburg University; **auf die ~ gehen, die ~ besuchen** to go to university

Universitäts- IN CPDS university; *siehe auch* **Hochschul-**; **Universitätsbibliothek** F university library; **Universitätsdozent(in)** M(F) senior lecturer (*Brit*), associate professor (*US*); **Universitätsgelände** NT university campus; **Universitätsklinik** F university clinic; **Universitätsstadt** F university town; **Universitätsstudium** NT (*Ausbildung*) university training; **dazu ist ein ~ erforderlich** you need a degree for that

Universum [uniˈvɛrzʊm] NT **-s,** NO PL universe

unkameradschaftlich ▨ ADJ uncomradely; *Schüler, Verhalten* unfriendly ▨ ADV in an uncomradely way

Unke [ˈʊŋkə] F **-, -n** toad; (*inf*: = *Schwarzseher*) Jeremiah

unken [ˈʊŋkn] VI (*inf*) to foretell gloom

Unkenntlichkeit F **-,** NO PL **bis zur ~** beyond recognition

Unkenntnis F, NO PL ignorance; **in ~ über etw** (*acc*) **sein** to be ignorant about sth; **aus ~** out of ignorance; **~ schützt nicht vor Strafe** (*prov*) ignorance is no excuse

unklar ▨ ADJ (= *unverständlich*) unclear; (= *ungeklärt*) unclarified; (= *undeutlich*) blurred; *Wetter* hazy; **es ist mir völlig ~, wie das geschehen konnte** I (just) can't understand how that could happen; **ich bin mir darüber noch im Unklaren** I'm not quite clear about that yet; **über etw** (*acc*) **völlig im Unklaren sein** to be completely in the dark about sth; **jdn über etw** (*acc*) **im Unklaren lassen** to leave sb in the dark about sth ▨ ADV *sich ausdrücken, formulieren* unclearly; **nur ~ zu erkennen sein** not to be easily discernible

Unklarheit F **(a)** lack of clarity; (*über Tatsachen*) uncertainty; **darüber herrscht noch ~** this is still uncertain *or* unclear **(b)** (= *unklarer Punkt*) unclear point

Un-: **unklug** ▨ ADJ unwise ▨ ADV unwisely; **unkollegial** ▨ ADJ uncooperative ▨ ADV uncooperatively; **sich ~ verhalten** to behave uncooperatively (*towards one's colleagues*); **unkompliziert** ▨ ADJ uncomplicated ▨ ADV in an uncomplicated way; **unkontrollierbar** ADJ uncontrollable; **~ werden** (*Missbrauch etc*) to get out of hand; **unkontrolliert** [ˈʊnkɔntrɔliːɐt] ADJ, ADV unchecked; **unkonventionell** ▨ ADJ unconventional ▨ ADV unconventionally; **unkonzentriert** ▨ ADJ lacking in concentration; **er ist so ~** he can't concentrate ▨ ADV without concentrating; **~ arbeiten** to lack concentration in one's work

Unkosten PL costs *pl*; (= *Ausgaben*) expenses *pl*; **das ist mit großen ~ verbunden** that involves a great deal of expense; **sich in ~ stürzen** (*inf*) to go to a lot of expense

Unkostenbeitrag M *siehe* **Unkosten** contribution toward(s) costs/expenses

Unkraut NT weed; **Unkräuter** weeds; **~ vergeht nicht** (*Prov*) it would take more than that to finish me/him *etc* off! (*hum*)

Unkraut-: **Unkrautbekämpfung** F weed control; **Unkrautbekämpfungsmittel** NT weed killer; **Unkrautvernichtung** F, **Unkrautvertilgung** F weed killing

Un-: **unkritisch** ▨ ADJ uncritical ▨ ADV uncritically; **unkultiviert** ▨ ADJ uncultivated ▨ ADV in an uncultivated manner; **unkündbar** ADJ *Beamter, Mitarbeiter* permanent; *Vertrag* binding; *Anleihe* irredeemable; **in ~er Stellung** in a permanent position; **Unkündbarkeit** F (*von Mitarbeiter*) permanent status

unkundig ADJ ignorant (+*gen* of); **einer Sprache ~ sein** to have no knowledge of a language; **des Lesens/Schreibens ~ sein** to be illiterate

un-: **unlauter** ADJ dishonest; *Wettbewerb* unfair; **unleidlich** ADJ disagreeable; **unleserlich** ADJ *Handschrift etc* illegible; **unlieb** ADJ **es ist mir nicht ~, dass ...** I am quite glad that ...

unliebsam [ˈʊnliːpzaːm] ▨ ADJ unpleasant; *Konkurrent* irksome; **das ist mir noch in ~er Erinnerung** that's still an unpleasant memory ▨ ADV *auffallen* unpleasantly; **er ist dem Lehrer ~ aufgefallen** his behaviour (*Brit*) *or* behavior (*US*) made a bad impression on the teacher

Un-: **unlogisch** ▨ ADJ illogical ▨ ADV illogically; **unlösbar** ADJ (*fig*) (= *untrennbar*) indissoluble; (= *nicht lösbar*) *Problem etc* insoluble; *Widerspruch* irreconcilable; **unlöslich** ADJ (*Chem*) insoluble

Unlust F, NO PL **(a)** (= *Widerwille*) reluctance **(b)** (= *Lustlosigkeit, Langeweile*) listlessness; (*St Ex*) slackness

Unmasse F (*inf*) load (*inf*); **eine ~ Leute/Bücher** *or* **an Büchern, ~n von Leuten/Büchern** loads *or* masses of people/books (*inf*)

unmaßgeblich 1 ADJ (= *nicht entscheidend*) *Urteil* not authoritative; (= *unwichtig*) *Äußerung, Mensch* inconsequential; **nach meiner ~en Meinung** (*hum*) in my humble opinion (*hum*) 2 ADV insignificantly; **nicht ~** to a significant degree

unmäßig 1 ADJ excessive 2 ADV *essen, trinken* to excess; *rauchen* excessively

Unmenge F vast number; (*bei unzählbaren Mengenbegriffen*) vast amount; **~n von Leuten, eine ~ Leute** a vast number of people; **~n essen** to eat an enormous amount

Unmensch M monster; **ich bin ja kein ~** I'm not an ogre

unmenschlich 1 ADJ **(a)** *Verhalten, Behandlung* inhuman **(b)** (*inf*: = *unerträglich*) terrible 2 ADV **(a)** *behandeln, foltern* in an inhuman way **(b)** *heiß, kalt, schwül* unbearably

Unmenschlichkeit F inhumanity; **~en** inhumanity

un-: unmerklich 1 ADJ imperceptible 2 ADV imperceptibly; **unmissverständlich** 1 ADJ unequivocal 2 ADV unequivocally; **jdm etw ~ zu verstehen geben** to tell sb sth in no uncertain terms; **unmittelbar** 1 ADJ *Nähe, Nachbarschaft etc* immediate; (= *direkt*) direct; (*Jur*) *Besitz, Besitzer* direct, actual; **aus ~er Nähe schießen** to fire at close range 2 ADV immediately; (= *ohne Umweg*) directly; **~ vor** (+*dat*) (*zeitlich*) immediately before; (*räumlich*) right in front of; **das berührt mich ~** it affects me directly; **unmöbliert** [ˈʊnmøbliːɐt] 1 ADJ *Zimmer* unfurnished 2 ADV *mieten, vermieten* unfurnished; **~ wohnen** to live in unfurnished accommodation; **unmodern** [-ˈmɔdɐn] 1 ADJ old-fashioned; **~ werden** to go out of fashion 2 ADV *eingerichtet, gekleidet* in an old-fashioned way

unmöglich 1 ADJ impossible; **Unmögliches, das Unmögliche** the impossible; **jdm etw ~ machen** to make it impossible for sb to do sth; **das Unmögliche möglich machen** to do the impossible; **jdn/sich ~ machen** to make sb/oneself look ridiculous 2 ADV (= *keinesfalls*) not possibly; (*pej inf*: = *unpassend*) impossibly; **sich anziehen** ridiculously; **ich kann es ~ tun** I cannot possibly do it; **~ aussehen** (*inf*) to look ridiculous

Unmöglichkeit F impossibility; **das ist ein Ding der ~!** that's quite impossible!

Un-: unmoralisch ADJ immoral; **unmündig** ADJ under-age; (*fig*: = *geistig unselbstständig*) sheep-like; **Unmündige(r)** [ˈʊnmʏndɪɡə] MF DECL AS ADJ minor; **Unmündigkeit** F minority; (*fig*: = *geistige Unselbstständigkeit*) mental immaturity; **unmusikalisch** ADJ unmusical; **unnachgiebig** 1 ADJ inflexible 2 ADV inflexibly; **sich ~ verhalten** to be obstinate; **unnachsichtig** 1 ADJ severe; (*stärker*) merciless; *Strenge* unrelenting 2 ADV *hinrichten, verfolgen* mercilessly; *bestrafen* severely; **unnahbar** ADJ *Mensch* unapproachable; **unnatürlich** 1 ADJ unnatural; *Tod* violent 2 ADV unnaturally; **unnormal** ADJ abnormal; **unnötig** 1 ADJ unnecessary 2 ADV unnecessarily; **unnötigerweise** [ˈʊnnøːtɪɡɐˈvaɪzə] ADV unnecessarily

unnütz [ˈʊnnʏts] 1 ADJ useless; *Geschwätz* idle; (= *umsonst*) pointless 2 ADV pointlessly; **sich Sorgen machen** unnecessarily

UNO [ˈuːno] F -, NO PL **die ~** the UN *sing*

unökonomisch ADJ uneconomic; *Fahrweise, Konsumverhalten* uneconomical

unordentlich 1 ADJ untidy; *Lebenswandel* disorderly 2 ADV untidily

Unordnung F disorder *no indef art*; (*in Zimmer etc auch*) untidiness *no indef art*; (= *Durcheinander*) mess; **etw in ~ bringen** to mess sth up; **in etw bringen** *in Leben, System* to bring disorder to sth

Un-: unorganisch ADJ inorganic; **unorthodox** 1 ADJ unorthodox 2 ADV in an unorthodox way; **unpädagogisch** ADJ educationally unsound; *Lehrer etc* bad (as a teacher); **unparteiisch** 1 ADJ impartial 2 ADV impartially; **Unparteiische(r)** [ˈʊnpartaɪʃə] MF DECL AS ADJ impartial *or* neutral person; **der ~** (*Sport*) the referee; **unpassend** ADJ inappropriate; *Augenblick* inconvenient; **unpassierbar** ADJ impassable; **unpersönlich** ADJ impersonal (*auch Ling*); *Mensch* aloof; **unpolitisch** ADJ unpolitical; **unpraktisch** ADJ *Mensch* unpractical; *Maschine, Lösung* impractical; **unproblematisch**

1 ADJ (= *ohne Probleme*) unproblematic; (= *einfach, leicht*) uncomplicated; **das wird nicht ganz ~ sein** it won't be without its problems 2 ADV without any problems; **unproduktiv** ADJ unproductive; *Kapital auch* idle

unpünktlich 1 ADJ *Mensch* unpunctual; *Zug* not on time; **er ist immer ~** he's never on time 2 ADV late; **die Züge fahren immer ~** the trains never run on time

Unpünktlichkeit F unpunctuality

un-: unqualifiziert 1 ADJ *Arbeitskraft* unqualified; *Arbeiten, Jobs* unskilled; *Äußerung* incompetent 2 ADV *sich äußern, sich auslassen* incompetently; **unrasiert** [ˈʊnraziːɐt] ADJ unshaven; **unrationell** 1 ADJ inefficient 2 ADV inefficiently; **unrealistisch** 1 ADJ unrealistic 2 ADV unrealistically

unrecht 1 ADJ wrong; **das ist mir gar nicht so ~** I don't really mind 2 ADV **~ handeln** to do wrong

Unrecht NT, NO PL wrong, injustice; **zu ~ verdächtigt** unjustly; **diese Vorurteile bestehen ganz zu ~** these prejudices are quite unfounded; **nicht zu ~** not without good reason; **im ~ sein** to be wrong; **ihm ist im Leben viel ~ geschehen** he has suffered many injustices in life; **~ bekommen** to be shown to be wrong; **~ haben** to be wrong; **jdm ~ geben** to contradict sb; **~ tun** to do wrong; **jdm ein ~ tun** to do sb an injustice; **Sie haben nicht ganz ~** you're not entirely wrong

unrechtmäßig 1 ADJ unlawful; *Thronfolger* wrongful 2 ADV *besitzen* unlawfully; **sich etw ~ aneignen** to misappropriate sth

Unrechtsbewusstsein NT awareness of wrongdoing

unregelmäßig 1 ADJ irregular 2 ADV irregularly; **~ essen/schlafen** not to eat/sleep regularly

Unregelmäßigkeit F irregularity

Un-: unreif 1 ADJ *Obst* unripe; *Mensch, Plan, Gedanke, Verhalten, Werk* immature 2 ADV *ernten, verarbeiten* before becoming ripe; **Unreife** F (*von Mensch, Werk*) immaturity; **unrentabel** 1 ADJ unprofitable 2 ADV unprofitably; **unrichtig** 1 ADJ incorrect; *Vorwurf* false; (*Admin*) *Angaben etc* false 2 ADV incorrectly; **Unrichtigkeit** F incorrectness; (*Admin*: *von Angaben etc*) falseness; (= *Fehler*) error; **unromantisch** ADJ unromantic

Unruhe F -, -n **(a)** NO PL restlessness; (= *Nervosität*) agitation; (= *Besorgnis*) agitation; **in ~ sein** to be restless; (= *besorgt*) to be agitated **(b)** NO PL (= *Lärm*) noise; (= *Geschäftigkeit*) (hustle and) bustle **(c)** NO PL (= *Unfrieden*) unrest *no pl*; **~ stiften** to create unrest; (*in Familie, Schule*) to make trouble **(d)** (*politische*) **~n** (political) disturbances

Unruhestifter(in) M(F) troublemaker

unruhig 1 ADJ restless; (= *laut, belebt*) noisy; *Schlaf, Zeit, Meer* troubled; **ein ~er Geist** (*inf*) a restless creature 2 ADV *schlafen* fitfully; (*ungleichmäßig*) unevenly; **ihr Herz schlägt zu ~** her heart is beating too irregularly

unrühmlich 1 ADJ inglorious; **ein ~es Ende nehmen** to have an inglorious end 2 ADV ingloriously

uns [ʊns] 1 PERS PRON ACC, DAT *von* **wir** us; (*dat auch*) to us; **bei ~** (= *zu Hause, im Betrieb etc*) at our place; (= *in unserer Beziehung*) between us; (= *in unserem Land*) in our country; **bei ~ zu Hause** at our house; **bei ~ im Garten** in our garden; **einer von ~** one of us; **ein Freund von ~** a friend of ours; **das gehört ~** that is ours; **viele Grüße von ~ beiden/allen** best wishes from both/all of us 2 REFL PRON ACC, DAT ourselves; (= *einander*) each other; **wir freuten ~** we were glad; **wir wollen ~ ein neues Auto kaufen** we want to buy (ourselves) a new car; **~ selbst** ourselves; **wann sehen wir ~ wieder?** when will we see each other again?; **mitten unter ~** in our midst; **hier sind wir unter ~** we are alone here; **das bleibt unter ~** it won't go any further

unsachgemäß 1 ADJ improper 2 ADV improperly

unsanft 1 ADJ rough; *Druck* ungentle; (= *unhöflich*) rude 2 ADV rudely; *durchrütteln* roughly; **~ aus dem Schlaf gerissen werden** to be rudely awakened

unsauber 1 ADJ **(a)** (= *ungewaschen, schmutzig*) dirty **(b)** (= *unordentlich*) *Handschrift, Arbeit* untidy; (= *nicht exakt*) *Schuss, Schlag, Schnitt* inaccurate; *Ton, Klang* impure **(c)** (= *unmoralisch*) shady 2 ADV (= *unordentlich*) untidily

unschädlich ADJ harmless; **eine Bombe ~ machen** to make a bomb safe; (= *entschärfen*) to defuse a bomb; **jdn ~ machen** (*inf*) to take care of sb (*inf*)

unscharf ADJ **(a)** blurred; *Justierung* unsharp; *(Rad)* indistinct; *Erinnerung, Vorstellung* hazy **(b)** *Munition* blank; *Bomben etc* unprimed ② ADV indistinctly; **der Sender/das Radio ist ~ eingestellt** the station/the radio is not tuned clearly

Unschärfe F fuzziness; *(von Erinnerung, Vorstellung)* haziness; **begriffliche ~** lack of conceptual clarity

unschätzbar ADJ *Wert, Verlust* incalculable; *Hilfe, Vorteil* invaluable; **von ~em Wert** invaluable; *Schmuck etc* priceless

unscheinbar ADJ inconspicuous; *(= unattraktiv) Aussehen, Mensch* unprepossessing

unschlagbar ADJ unbeatable

unschlüssig ① ADJ *(= unentschlossen)* undecided; *(= zögernd)* irresolute; **sich** *(dat)* **~ über etw** *acc)* **sein** to be undecided (about sth); to be hesitant (about sth) ② ADV *(= unentschlossen)* undecided; *(= zögernd)* hesitantly; **er blieb ~ stehen** he stopped, uncertain what to do

unschön ADJ *(= hässlich)* unsightly; *(stärker)* ugly; *Gesicht* plain; *Bilder* unattractive; *(= unangenehm)* unpleasant; *Streit, Auseinandersetzung, Szenen* ugly

Unschuld F, NO PL **(a)** *(= Schuldlosigkeit)* innocence **(b)** *(= Jungfräulichkeit)* virginity **(c)** *(= Naivität, Unverdorbenheit)* innocence; **die ~ vom Lande** *(inf)* a real innocent; **in aller ~** in all innocence

unschuldig ① ADJ **(a)** innocent; **an etw** *(dat)* **~ sein** not to be guilty of sth; **er war völlig ~ an dem Unfall** he was in no way responsible for the accident; **sind Sie schuldig oder ~? – ~** how do you plead, guilty or not guilty? – not guilty **(b)** *(= jungfräulich)* virginal; **er/sie ist noch ~** he/she is still a virgin ② ADV **(a)** *(Jur)* when innocent; **jdn ~ verurteilen** to convict sb when he is innocent; **er sitzt ~ im Gefängnis** he is being held, an innocent man, in prison **(b)** *(= arglos) fragen, sagen* innocently

Unschuldige(r) MF DECL AS ADJ innocent person/man/ woman/child *etc*; **die ~n** the innocent

unselbstständig, unselbständig ① ADJ lacking in independence; **eine ~e Tätigkeit ausüben** to work as an employee; **Einkünfte aus ~er Arbeit** income from (salaried) employment; **sei doch nicht immer so ~!** show a bit of independence once in a while! ② ADV *(= mit fremder Hilfe)* not independently

Unselbstständigkeit F, **Unselbständigkeit** F lack of independence

unser ['ʊnzɐ] ① POSS PRON *(adjektivisch)* our; **~e** *or* **unsre Bücher** our books ② PERS PRON GEN *von* **wir** *(old, Bibl, geh)* of us; **~ beider gemeinsame Zukunft** our common future; **~ aller heimlicher Wunsch** the secret wish of all of us

unsereiner ['ʊnzɐlainɐ], **unsereins** ['ʊnzɐlains] INDEF PRON *(inf)* the likes of us *(inf)*

unsere(r, s) ['ʊnzərə] POSS PRON *(substantivisch)* ours; **der/die/ das ~** *or* **Unsere** *(geh)* ours; **wir tun das ~** *or* **Unsere** *(geh)* we are doing our bit; **die ~n** *or* **Unseren** *(geh)* our family; **das ~** *or* **Unsere** *(geh: = Besitz)* what is ours

unsererseits ['ʊnzərəˈzaits] ADV *(= auf unserer Seite)* for our part; *(= von unserer Seite)* on our part; **den Vorschlag haben wir ~ gemacht** we made the suggestion ourselves

unseresgleichen ['ʊnzərəsˈɡlaiçn] INDEF PRON people like us; **Menschen ~** people like us

unseriös ADJ *Mensch* slippery; *Auftreten, Aussehen, Kleidung, Bemerkung* frivolous; *Methoden, Firma, Bank* shady; *Zeitung, Wissenschaftler, Angebot* not serious; *Verlag* lowbrow; *Gutachten, Angaben* untrustworthy

unserseits ['ʊnzɐzaits] ADV = **unsererseits**

unsertwegen ['ʊnzɐtˈveːɡn] ADV *(= wegen uns)* because of us; *(= uns zuliebe auch)* for our sake; *(= um uns)* about us; *(= für uns)* on our behalf

unsertwillen ['ʊnzɐtˈvɪlən] ADV **um ~** for our sake

Unservater ['ʊnzɐfaːtɐ] NT **-s, -** *(Sw)* Lord's Prayer

unsicher ① ADJ **(a)** *(= gefährlich)* dangerous; **die Gegend ~ machen** *(fig inf)* to hang out *(inf)*; **sich ~ fühlen** to feel unsafe **(b)** *(= nicht selbstbewusst, verunsichert)* insecure, unsure (of oneself); **jdn ~ machen** to make sb feel unsure of himself/ herself **(c)** *(= ungewiss, ungeübt)* unsure; *(= unstabil)* uncertain, unstable; *Hand* unsteadily; *Kenntnisse* shaky

② ADV **(a)** *(= schwankend)* unsteadily **(b)** *(= nicht selbstsicher)* uncertainly; **sie blickte ~ im Kreise umher** she looked around timidly

Unsicherheit F *(= Gefahr)* danger; *(= mangelndes Selbstbewusstsein)* insecurity; *(= Ungewissheit)* uncertainty; *(= Instabilität)* instability

unsichtbar ADJ *(lit, fig)* invisible

Unsinn M, NO PL nonsense *no indef art*; **~ machen** *or* **treiben** to do silly things; **lass den ~!** stop fooling about!; **wirklich? mach keinen ~!** really? - stop messing around! *(inf)*

unsinnig ① ADJ *(= sinnlos)* foolish; *(= ungerechtfertigt)* unreasonable; *(stärker)* absurd ② ADV foolishly; *(= ungerechtfertigterweise)* unreasonably; *(stärker)* absurdly; **~ viel** *(inf)* an incredible amount *(inf)*; **~ hohe Preise** *(inf)* ridiculously high prices *(inf)*

Un-: Unsitte F *(= schlechte Gewohnheit)* bad habit; **unsolid, unsolide** ① ADJ *Mensch* free-living; *(= unredlich) Firma, Angebot, Geschäftsmann* unreliable; *Politik* without a solid basis; **~(e) leben** to have an unhealthy lifestyle; **ein ~es Leben führen** to be free-living ② ADV *(etwas ausschweifend)* dissolutely; **unsolidarisch** ① ADJ lacking in solidarity; **sich ~ verhalten** to show a lack of solidarity; **unsozial** ① ADJ *Verhalten, Mensch* antisocial; *Maßnahmen, Politik* unsocial ② ADV antisocially; **unspezifisch** ADJ nonspecific; **unsportlich** ADJ **(a)** *(= ungelenkig)* unsporty **(b)** *(= unfair)* unsporting

unsre ['ʊnzrə] PRON *siehe* **unser**

unsrerseits ['ʊnzrɐˈzaits] ADV = **unsererseits**

unsresgleichen ['ʊnzrəsˈɡlaiçn] INDEF PRON = **unseresgleichen**

unsretwegen ['ʊnzrɐtˈveːɡn] ADV = **unsertwegen**

unsretwillen ['ʊnzrɐtˈvɪlən] ADV = **unsertwillen**

unsterblich ① ADJ immortal; *Liebe* undying; **jdn ~ machen** to immortalize sb ② ADV *(inf)* utterly; **sich ~ blamieren** to make a complete idiot of oneself; **~ verliebt sein** to be madly in love *(inf)*

Un-: unstimmig ADJ *Aussagen etc* at variance, differing *attr*; **in einem Punkt sind wir noch ~** we still disagree on one point; **Unstimmigkeit** F *(= Ungenauigkeit, Fehler)* discrepancy; *(= Streit)* difference; **Unsumme** F vast sum

unsympathisch ADJ unpleasant; **er ist ~** he's unpleasant; **das/ er ist mir ~** I don't like that/him

unsystematisch ① ADJ unsystematic ② ADV unsystematically

Untat F atrocity; **~en begehen** *(im Krieg etc)* to commit atrocities

untätig ① ADJ *(= müßig)* idle; *(= nicht handelnd)* passive; *Vulkan* dormant ② ADV idly; **sie sah ~ zu, wie er verblutete** she stood idly by as he bled to death

Untätigkeit F *(= Müßiggang)* idleness; *(= Passivität)* passivity

Un-: untauglich ADJ *(zu, für* for) unsuitable; *(für Wehrdienst)* unfit; **unteilbar** ADJ indivisible

unten ['ʊntn] ADV *(= im unteren Teil, am unteren Ende)* *(in Rangfolge)* at the bottom; *(= tiefer, drunten)* (down) below; *(= an der Unterseite)* underneath; *(in Gebäude)* downstairs; *(inf: geografisch)* down south; *(= tiefer gelegen)* down there/ here; **von ~** from below; **die Frau von ~ war gekommen** the woman from downstairs had come; **nach ~** down; **die Säule wird nach ~ hin breiter** the column broadens out toward(s) the base; **bis ~** to the bottom; **~ am Berg** at the bottom of the hill; **~ am Fluss** down by the river(side); **~ im Glas** at the bottom of the glass; **~ auf dem Bild** at the bottom of the picture; **dort** *or* **da/hier ~** down there/here; **weiter ~** further down; **~ bleiben** to stay down; **~ erwähnt, ~ genannt** mentioned below; **rechts/links ~** down on the right/left; **siehe ~** see below; **er ist bei mir ~ durch** *(inf)* I'm through with him *(inf)*; **ich weiß schon nicht mehr, was** *or* **wo oben und ~ ist** *(inf)* I don't know whether I'm coming or going *(inf)*; **~ stehend** following; *(lit)* standing below; **~ Stehendes** the following; **das ~ Stehende** what follows; **~ wohnen** to live downstairs

Unten-: untendrunter ['ʊntn'drʊntɐ] ADV *(inf)* underneath; **untenerwähnt** [-lɛːvveːnt], **untengenannt** ADJ ATTR *siehe* **unten**; **untenherum** ['ʊntnhə'rʊm] ADV *(inf)* down below *(inf)*; **untenstehend** ADJ *siehe* **unten**

unter ['ʊntɐ] PREP **(a)** +DAT *(= ~halb von)* under; *(= drunter)* underneath, below; *(= zwischen, innerhalb)* among(st); **~ 18**

Jahren/50 Euro under 18 years (of age)/50 euros; **~ dem Durchschnitt** below average; **Temperaturen ~ 25 Grad** temperatures below 25 degrees; **~ sich** (*dat*) **sein** to be by themselves; **~ etw leiden** to suffer from sth; **~ anderem** among other things **(b)** +ACC under; **bis ~ das Dach voll mit ...** full to bursting with ...; **~ Verbrecher geraten** to fall in with criminals

Unter-: **Unterabteilung** F subdivision; **Unterarm** M forearm; **Unterausschuss** M subcommittee; **Unterbegriff** M member of a conceptual class; **unterbelegt** ADJ *Hotel, Schule etc* not full; *Fortbildungskurs* undersubscribed; **das Hotel ist ziemlich ~** the hotel is not very full; **unterbelichtet** ['ʊntɐbəlɪçtət] ADJ (*Phot*) underexposed; **geistig ~ sein** (*hum*) to be a bit dim (*inf*); **Unterbeschäftigung** F underemployment; **unterbesetzt** ADJ understaffed; **Unterbeteiligung** F (*Fin*) sub-participation; **unterbewusst** ▨ ADJ subconscious; **das Unterbewusste** the subconscious ▨ ADV subconsciously; **Unterbewusstsein** NT subconscious; **im ~** subconsciously; **unterbezahlt** ADJ underpaid; **unterbieten** *ptp* **unterboten** VT INSEP IRREG *Konkurrenten, Preis* to undercut; (*fig*) to surpass; **sich gegenseitig ~** to undercut each other; **eine kaum noch zu ~de Leistung** an unsurpassable achievement (*iro*); **unterbinden** [ʊntɐˈbɪndn̩], *ptp* **unterbunden** [ʊntɐˈbʊndn̩] VT INSEP IRREG to stop; (*Med*) *Blutung* to ligature; **unterbleiben** [ʊntɐˈblaɪbn̩], *ptp* **unterblieben** [ʊntɐˈbliːbn̩] VI INSEP IRREG AUX SEIN **(a)** (= *aufhören*) to cease; **das hat zu ~** that will have to stop **(b)** (= *nicht geschehen*) not to happen **(c)** (= *versäumt werden*) to be omitted; **Unterbodenschutz** M (*Mot*) protective undercoating; **unterbrechen** [ʊntɐˈbrɛçn̩], *ptp* **unterbrochen** [ʊntɐˈbrɔxn̩] INSEP IRREG ▨ VT to interrupt; *Stille, Reise, Eintönigkeit, Langeweile* to break; (*langfristig*) to break off; *Telefonverbindung* to disconnect; *Spiel* to suspend; *Schwangerschaft* to terminate; **entschuldigen Sie bitte, wenn ich Sie unterbreche** forgive me for interrupting; **wir sind unterbrochen worden** (*am Telefon*) we've been cut off ▨ VR to break off; **Unterbrechung** F interruption; (*von Stille, Reise, Langeweile*) break (+*gen* in); (*von Telefonverbindung*) disconnection; (*von Spiel*) stoppage; **bei ~ der Reise** when breaking the journey; **ohne ~** without a break; **nach einer kurzen ~** (*Rad, TV*) after a short break; **mit ~en** with a few breaks in between; **Unterbrechungsbefehl** M (*Comput*) break command; **unterbringen** VT SEP IRREG **(a)** (= *verstauen, Platz geben*) to put; (*in Heim, Krankenhaus etc*) to put; *Arbeitslose etc* to fix up (*bei* with); *Zitat* (*in Text etc*) to get in (*in etw* (*acc*) sth); **ich kann in meinem Auto noch einen ~** I can get one more in my car; **etw bei jdm ~** to leave sth with sb; **ich kenne ihn, aber ich kann ihn nirgends ~** (*inf*) I know him, but I just can't place him **(b)** (= *Unterkunft geben*) *Menschen* to accommodate; *Ausstellung, Sammlung* to house; **gut/schlecht untergebracht sein** to have good/bad accommodation; (= *versorgt werden*) to be well/badly looked after; **Unterbringung** F **-**, **-en** accommodation (*Brit*), accommodations *pl* (*US*); **Unterbruch** M (*Sw*) = **Unterbrechung**; **unterderhand** [ʊntɐdeːɐˈhant] ADV *siehe* **Hand**; **unterdes(sen)** [ʊntɐˈdɛs(n̩)] ADV meanwhile; **Unterdruck** M, *pl* **-drücke** (*Phys*) below atmospheric pressure; (*Med*) low blood pressure; **unterdrücken** [ʊntɐˈdrʏkn̩], *ptp* **unterdrückt** VT INSEP **(a)** (= *beherrschen*) *Volk, Sklaven* to oppress; *Freiheit, Meinung* to suppress; *Revolution* to put down; **die Unterdrückten** the oppressed **(b)** (= *zurückhalten*) *Neugier, Gähnen, Lachen, Gefühle* to suppress; *Tränen, Antwort, Bemerkung* to hold back; **Unterdrückung** F **-**, **-en (a)** (*von Volk, Sklaven*) oppression; (*von Freiheit, Revolution*) suppression **(b)** (*von Neugier, Gähnen, Lachen, Gefühlen*) suppression; (*von Tränen, Antwort, Bemerkung*) holding back; **unterdurchschnittlich** ▨ ADJ below average ▨ ADV below the average; **untereinander** [ʊntɐlaɪˈnandɐ] ADV **(a)** (= *gegenseitig*) each other; (= *miteinander*) among ourselves/themselves *etc*; **Familien, die ~ heiraten** families that intermarry **(b)** (*räumlich*) one below the other

untere(r, s) ['ʊntərə] ADJ, *superl* **unterste(r, s)** ['ʊntɐstə] lower

Unter-: **unterernährt** [-ˈɛɐnɛːɐt] ADJ undernourished; **Unterernährung** F malnutrition; **Unterfranken** NT (*Geog*) Lower Franconia; **Unterführung** F underpass; **Unterfunktion** F insufficient function *no indef art*; **(eine) ~ der Schilddrüse** thyroid insufficiency

Untergang M, *pl* **-gänge (a)** (*von Schiff*) sinking **(b)** (*von Gestirn*) setting **(c)** (= *das Zugrundegehen*) (*allmählich*)

decline; (*völlig*) destruction; (*der Welt*) end; (*von Individuum*) downfall; **dem ~ geweiht sein** to be doomed; **du bist noch mal mein ~!** you'll be the death of me! (*inf*)

Untergangsstimmung F feeling of doom

untergeben [ʊntɐˈgeːbn̩] ADJ subordinate

Untergebene(r) [ʊntɐˈgeːbənə] MF DECL AS ADJ subordinate

untergegangen ADJ *Schiff* sunken; *Gestirn* set; *Volk etc* extinct; *Zivilisation, Kultur, Epoche* lost

untergehen VI SEP IRREG AUX SEIN **(a)** (= *versinken*) to sink; (*fig: im Lärm etc*) to be submerged *or* drowned **(b)** (*Gestirn*) to set **(c)** (= *zugrunde gehen*) (*Kultur*) (*allmählich*) to decline; (*völlig*) to be destroyed; (*Welt*) to come to an end; (*Individuum*) to perish; **dort muss man sich durchsetzen, sonst geht man unter** you've got to assert yourself there or you'll go under

Unter-: **untergeordnet** ADJ *Dienststelle, Stellung* subordinate; *Bedeutung* secondary; *siehe auch* **unterordnen**; **Untergeschoss** NT basement; **untergewichtig** ADJ underweight; **untergliedern** [ʊntɐˈgliːdɐn], *ptp* **untergliedert** VT INSEP to subdivide; **untergraben** [ʊntɐˈgraːbn̩], *ptp* **untergraben** VT INSEP IRREG (= *zerstören*) to undermine

Untergrund M, NO PL **(a)** (*Geol*) subsoil **(b)** (= *Farbschicht*) undercoat; (= *Hintergrund*) background **(c)** (*Liter, Pol etc*) underground; **in den ~ gehen** to go underground

Untergrund- IN CPDS (*Liter, Pol*) underground

Untergrundbahn F underground (*Brit*), subway (*US*)

Unter-: **Untergruppe** F subgroup; **unterhaken** SEP ▨ VT **jdn ~** to link arms with sb ▨ VR **sich bei jdm ~** to link arms with sb; **untergehakt gehen** to walk arm in arm; **unterhalb** ['ʊntɐhalp] ▨ PREP +GEN below ▨ ADV below; **~ von** below

Unterhalt M, NO PL **(a)** (= *Lebensunterhalt*) maintenance (*esp Brit Jur*), alimony; **für jds ~ aufkommen** to pay for sb's keep; **für seine Kinder ~ zahlen** to pay maintenance (*Brit*) *or* child support for one's children; **für seine Ex-Ehefrau ~ zahlen** to pay alimony to one's ex-wife; **seinen ~ verdienen** to earn one's living **(b)** (= *Instandhaltung*) upkeep

unterhalten [ʊntɐˈhaltn̩], *ptp* **unterhalten** INSEP IRREG ▨ VT **(a)** (= *versorgen, ernähren*) to support; *Angestellten* to maintain **(b)** (= *halten, betreiben*) *Geschäft, Gaststätte* to run; *Konto* to have; *Kfz* to run **(c)** (= *instand halten*) *Gebäude, Fahrzeug etc* to maintain **(d)** *Kontakte, Beziehungen* to maintain **(e)** *Gäste, Publikum* to entertain ▨ VR **(a)** (= *sprechen*) to talk (*mit* to, with); **man kann sich mit ihm gut/schlecht/glänzend ~** he's easy/not easy/really easy to talk to; **man kann sich mit ihm nicht ~** he's impossible to talk to; **sich mit jdm (über etw** *acc*) **~** to (have a) talk *or* chat with sb (about sth) **(b)** (= *sich vergnügen*) to have a good time; **sich mit etw ~** to amuse oneself with sth

Unterhalter [ʊntɐˈhaltɐ] M **-s**, **-**, **Unterhalterin** [-ərɪn] F **-**, **-nen** entertainer; (= *unterhaltsamer Mensch*) conversationalist

unterhaltsam [ʊntɐˈhaltzaːm] ADJ entertaining

Unterhalts-: **unterhaltsberechtigt** ADJ entitled to maintenance (*Brit*) *or* alimony; **Unterhaltsgeld** NT maintenance (*Brit*), alimony; **Unterhaltsklage** F action for maintenance (*Brit*), lawsuit for alimony (*esp US*); **Unterhaltskosten** PL (*von Gebäude, Anlage*) maintenance (*Brit*) *or* alimony costs *pl*; (*von Kfz*) running costs *pl*; **unterhaltspflichtig** [-pflɪçtɪç] ADJ under obligation to pay maintenance (*Brit*) *or* alimony; **Unterhaltspflichtige(r)** [-pflɪçtɪgə] MF DECL AS ADJ person legally responsible for paying maintenance (*Brit*) *or* alimony; **Unterhaltszahlung** F maintenance payment

Unterhaltung [ʊntɐˈhaltʊŋ] F **(a)** (= *Gespräch*) talk, conversation; **eine ~ (mit jdm) führen** to have a talk (with sb) **(b)** (= *Amüsement*) entertainment; **wir wünschen gute** *or* **angenehme ~** we hope you enjoy the programme (*Brit*) *or* program (*US*) **(c)** NO PL (= *Instandhaltung*) upkeep; (*von Kfz, Maschinen*) maintenance

Unterhaltungs-: **Unterhaltungselektronik** F (= *Industrie*) consumer electronics *sing*; (= *Geräte*) audio systems *pl*; **Unterhaltungsmusik** F light music

Unter-: **Unterhändler(in)** M(F) negotiator; **Unterhaus** NT Lower House, House of Commons (*Brit*); **Mitglied des ~es** member of parliament; **Unterhemd** NT vest (*Brit*), undershirt (*US*); **Unterhose** F (= *Herrenunterhose*) (pair of) underpants *pl*, briefs *pl*; (= *Damenunterhose*) (pair of) pants *pl* (*Brit*) *or* panties *pl* (*esp US*); **lange ~n** long johns *pl*; **unterirdisch** ADJ, ADV underground; **unterjubeln** VT SEP (*inf*) **(a)** (= *andrehen*) **jdm etw ~** to palm sth off on sb (*inf*) **(b)** (= *anlasten*) **jdm etw ~** to pin sth on sb (*inf*); **Unterkiefer** M lower jaw; **Unterklasse** F **(a)** subclass **(b)** (*Sociol*) lower class

unterkommen VI SEP IRREG AUX SEIN **(a)** (= *Unterkunft finden*) to find accommodation; (*inf*: = *Stelle finden*) to find a job (*als* as, *bei* with, at); **bei jdm ~** to stay at sb's (place) **(b)** (*inf*) **so etwas ist mir noch nie untergekommen!** I've never come across anything like it!

Unter-: Unterkörper M lower part of the body; **unterkriegen** VT SEP (*inf*) to bring down; (= *deprimieren*) to get down; **sich nicht ~ lassen** not to let things get one down; **lass dich von ihnen nicht ~** don't let them get you down; **unterkühlt** [ʊntɐˈkyːlt] ADJ *Flüssigkeit, Metall, Gas* supercooled; *Körper* affected by hypothermia; (*fig*) *Atmosphäre* chilly; *Mensch* cool; *Musik, Spielweise* subdued; **Unterkühlung** F, NO PL (*von Flüssigkeit, Metall, Gas*) supercooling; (*im Freien*) exposure; (*Med*) hypothermia

Unterkunft [ˈʊntɐkʊnft] F -, **Unterkünfte** [-kynftə] accommodation *no pl* (*Brit*), accommodations *pl* (*US*), lodging; **~ und Verpflegung** board and lodging

Unterlage F **(a)** (*für Teppich*) underlay; (*im Bett*) draw sheet; **du brauchst eine ~** you need to put something underneath; (*zum Schreiben*) you need something to rest on; (*zum Schlafen*) you need something to lie on **(b)** USU PL (= *Belege, Urkunden, Papiere*) document

unterlassen [ʊntɐˈlasn], *ptp* **unterlassen** VT INSEP IRREG (= *nicht tun*) to refrain from; (= *nicht durchführen*) not to carry out; (= *auslassen*) to omit; *Bemerkung, Zwischenrufe* to refrain from making; *etwas Dummes etc* to refrain from doing; *Trinken* to abstain from; **keine Anstrengung** *or* **nichts ~** to spare no effort; **~ Sie das!** don't do that!; **er hat es ~, mich zu benachrichtigen** he failed to notify me; **warum wurde das ~?** why was it not done?; **~e Hilfeleistung** (*Jur*) failure to give assistance

Unterlauf M lower reaches *pl* (of a river)

unterlaufen¹ [ʊntɐˈlaufn], *ptp* **unterlaufen** INSEP IRREG **1** VI +DAT AUX SEIN *Fehler, Irrtum, Versehen* to occur; **mir ist ein Fehler ~** I made a mistake **2** VT *Bestimmungen, Maßnahmen* to get (a)round; *Steuergesetze* to avoid; (= *umgehen*) to circumvent

unterlaufen² [ʊntɐˈlaufn] ADJ suffused with blood; **ein mit Blut ~es Auge** a bloodshot eye

Unterleder NT sole leather

unterlegen [ʊntɐˈleːɡn] ADJ inferior; (= *besiegt*) defeated; **jdm ~ sein** to be inferior to sb; **zahlenmäßig ~ sein** to be outnumbered; *siehe auch* **unterliegen**

Unterlegene(r) [ʊntɐˈleːɡənə] MF DECL AS ADJ underdog; **der ~ sein** to be in the weaker position

Unterlegscheibe F (*Tech*) washer

Unterleib M abdomen

Unterleibs- IN CPDS abdominal; (*in Bezug auf weibliche Geschlechtsorgane*) gynaecological (*Brit*), gynecological (*US*); **Unterleibskrebs** M cancer of the abdomen; (*bei Frau*) cancer of the womb; **Unterleibsschmerzen** PL abdominal pains *pl*

unterliegen [ʊntɐˈliːɡn], *ptp* **unterlegen** [ʊntɐˈleːɡn] VI INSEP IRREG AUX SEIN **(a)** (= *besiegt werden*) to be defeated (+*dat* by); (*fig*) *einer Versuchung etc* to succumb (+*dat* to) **(b)** +DAT (= *unterworfen sein*) to be subject to; *einer Gebühr, Steuer* to be liable to; **es unterliegt keinem Zweifel, dass ...** it is not open to any doubt that ...

Unterlippe F bottom lip

unterm [ˈʊntɐm] CONTR *von* **unter dem**

untermauern [ʊntɐˈmauɐn], *ptp* **untermauert** VT INSEP (*Build*) to underpin; (*fig auch*) *Behauptung, Theorie* to back up

untermengen VT SEP to mix in

Untermenü NT (*Comput*) submenu

Untermiete F subtenancy; **bei jdm zur** *or* **in ~ wohnen** to be sb's tenant

Untermieter(in) M(F) lodger (*esp Brit*), subtenant

unterminieren [ʊntɐmiˈniːrən], *ptp* **unterminiert** VT INSEP (*lit, fig*) to undermine

unternehmen [ʊntɐˈneːmən], *ptp* **unternommen** [ʊntɐˈnɔmən] VT INSEP IRREG to do; (= *durchführen auch*) to undertake; *Versuch, Vorstoß, Reise* to make; **einen Ausflug ~** to go on an outing;

Schritte ~ to take steps; **etwas/nichts gegen jdn/etw ~** to do something/nothing about sb/sth; **zu viel ~** to take on too much

Unternehmen [ʊntɐˈneːmən] NT -s, - (a) (= *Firma*) business, concern, enterprise **(b)** (= *Aktion, Vorhaben*) undertaking, enterprise, venture; (*Mil*) operation

Unternehmens-: Unternehmensberater(in) M(F) management consultant; **Unternehmensform** F type of enterprise; **Unternehmenszusammenschluss** M merger

Unternehmer(in) M(F) employer; (*alten Stils*) entrepreneur; (= *Industrieller*) industrialist; **die ~** the employers

unternehmerisch [ʊntɐˈneːmərɪʃ] **1** ADJ entrepreneurial **2** ADV *denken, handeln* in an entrepreneurial way

Unternehmerkredit M commercial *or* corporate loan

Unternehmung [ʊntɐˈneːmʊŋ] F -, -en **(a)** = **Unternehmen (b)** (= *Transaktion*) undertaking

Unternehmungs-: Unternehmungsgeist M, NO PL enterprise; **unternehmungslustig** ADJ (= *tatendurstig*) enterprising; (= *abenteuerlustig auch*) adventurous

Unteroffizier(in) M(F) **(a)** (= *Rang*) noncommissioned officer; **~ vom Dienst** duty NCO **(b)** (= *Dienstgrad*) (*bei der Armee*) sergeant; (*bei der Luftwaffe*) corporal (*Brit*), airman first class (*US*)

Unter-: unterordnen SEP **1** VT to subordinate (+*dat* to); *siehe auch* **untergeordnet 2** VR to subordinate oneself (+*dat* to); **unterordnend** ADJ (*Gram*) *Konjunktion* subordinating; **Unterordnung** F **(a)** NO PL subordination **(b)** (*Biol*) suborder; **unterprivilegiert** [-priviːleːgiːɐt] ADJ underprivileged; **Unterprogramm** NT (*Comput*) subroutine; **Unterredung** F -, -en discussion; (*Pol auch*) talks *pl*; **unterrepräsentiert** [-reprezɛntiːɐt] ADJ underrepresented

Unterricht [ˈʊntɐrɪçt] M -(e)s, NO PL classes *pl*; **theoretischer/praktischer ~** theoretical/practical classes; **~ in Fremdsprachen** foreign language teaching; (*jdm*) **~ geben** *or* **erteilen** to teach (sb) (*in etw* (*dat*) sth); (*bei jdm*) **~ nehmen** *or* **haben** to take *or* have lessons (with sb); **am ~ teilnehmen** to attend classes; **zu spät zum ~ kommen** to be late for class; **im ~ aufpassen** to pay attention in class; **der ~ beginnt um 8 Uhr** classes start at 8 o'clock

unterrichten [ʊntɐˈrɪçtn], *ptp* **unterrichtet** INSEP **1** VT **(a)** (= *Unterricht geben*) *Schüler, Klasse, Fach* to teach; **jdn in etw** (*dat*) **~** to teach sb sth **(b)** (= *informieren*) to inform (*von, über* +*acc* about) **2** VI to teach **3** VR **sich über etw** (*acc*) **~** to inform oneself about sth; **sich von jdm über etw** (*acc*) **~ lassen** to be informed by sb about sth

unterrichtet [ʊntɐˈrɪçtət] ADJ informed; **gut ~e Kreise** well-informed circles; **wie aus gut ~en Kreisen verlautet, ...** according to well-informed sources ...

Unterrichts-: Unterrichtsbetrieb M, NO PL classes *pl*; (= *Unterrichtsroutine*) teaching *no art*; **Unterrichtseinheit** F teaching unit; **Unterrichtsfach** NT subject; **Geschichte ist ~** history is on the curriculum; **unterrichtsfrei** ADJ *Stunde, Tag* free; **der Montag ist ~** there are no classes on Monday; **Unterrichtsstoff** M subject matter; **Unterrichtsstunde** F lesson, period; **während der ~n** during lessons; **Unterrichtsveranstaltung** F lesson; (*Univ*) lecture

Unterrichtung F, NO PL (= *Belehrung*) instruction; (= *Informierung*) information

Unterrock M underskirt

unters [ˈʊntɐs] CONTR *von* **unter das**

untersagen [ʊntɐˈzaːgn], *ptp* **untersagt** VT INSEP to forbid; **(das) Rauchen (ist hier) strengstens untersagt** smoking (is) strictly prohibited (here); **jdm etw gerichtlich ~** to enjoin sb to do sth

Untersatz M mat; (*für Gläser, Flaschen etc*) coaster (*esp Brit*); (*für Blumentöpfe etc*) saucer; **etw als ~ verwenden** to use sth to put underneath

unterschätzen [ʊntɐˈʃɛtsn], *ptp* **unterschätzt** VT INSEP to underestimate

unterscheidbar ADJ distinguishable

unterscheiden [ʊntɐˈʃaidn], *ptp* **unterschieden** [ʊntɐˈʃiːdn] INSEP IRREG **1** VT to distinguish; **A nicht von B ~ können** to be unable to tell the difference between A and B; **zwei Personen (voneinander) ~** to tell two people apart; **das ~de Merkmal** the distinguishing feature; **nach verschiedenen Merkmalen ~** to classify according to various characteristics

2 VI to differentiate
3 VR **sich von etw/jdm ~** to differ from sth/sb; **worin unterscheidet sich eine Amsel von einer Drossel?** what is the difference between a blackbird and a thrush?

Unterscheidung F differentiation; (= *Unterschied*) difference; **eine ~ treffen** to make a distinction

Unterschenkel M lower leg

unterschieben [ˈʊntɐʃiːbn] VT SEP IRREG **(a)** (*lit:* = *schieben unter*) to push underneath; **etw unter etw** (*acc*) ~ to push sth under(neath) sth **(b)** (*fig*) **jdm etw ~** (= *anlasten*) to palm sth off on sb; **er wehrte sich dagegen, dass man ihm das Kind ~ wollte** he defended himself against the charge that the child was his

Unterschied [ˈʊntɐʃiːt] M **-(e)s, -e** [-də] difference (*auch Math*); (= *Unterscheidung auch*) distinction; **einen ~ (zwischen zwei Dingen) machen** to make a distinction (between two things); **das macht keinen ~** that makes no difference; **es ist ein (großer) ~, ob ...** it makes a (big) difference whether ...; **ein feiner ~** a slight difference, a fine distinction; **im ~ zu (jdm/etw)** in contrast to (sb/sth); **mit dem ~, dass ...** with the difference that ...; **alle ohne ~ halfen mit** everyone without exception lent a hand; **der kleine ~** (*hum*) the difference between the sexes

unterschiedlich [ˈʊntɐʃiːtlɪç] **1** ADJ different; (= *veränderlich*) variable; (= *gemischt*) varied; **das ist sehr ~** it varies a lot **2** ADV differently; **~ gut/lang** of varying quality/length; **sie haben ~ reagiert** their reactions varied

unterschiedslos 1 ADJ (= *undifferenziert*) indiscriminate; (= *gleichberechtigt*) equal **2** ADV (= *undifferenziert*) indiscriminately; (= *gleichberechtigt*) equally

unterschlagen *ptp* **unterschlagen** VT INSEP IRREG *Geld* to embezzle; *Brief, Beweise, Tatsachen* to withhold; (*inf*) *Neuigkeit, Nachricht, Wort etc* to keep quiet about; **das hast du mir die ganze Zeit ~** and you've kept quiet about it all this time

Unterschlagung [ʊntɐˈʃlaːgʊŋ] F **-, -en** (*von Geld*) embezzlement; (*von Briefen, Beweisen etc*) withholding

Unterschlupf [ˈʊntɐʃlʊpf] M **-(e)s, Unterschlüpfe** [-ʃlʏpfə] (= *Obdach, Schutz*) shelter; (= *Versteck*) hiding place

unterschlupfen [ˈʊntɐʃlʊpfn] VI SEP AUX SEIN (= *Obdach oder Schutz finden*) to take shelter; (= *Versteck finden*) to hide out (*inf*) (**bei jdm** at sb's)

unterschreiben [ʊntɐˈʃraɪbn], *ptp* **unterschrieben** [ʊntɐˈʃriːbn] INSEP IRREG **1** VT to sign; **das kann or würde ich ~!** (*fig*) I'll subscribe to that! **2** VI to sign; **mit vollem Namen ~** to sign one's full name

Unterschrift F **(a)** signature; **eigenhändige ~** personal signature; **seine ~ unter etw** (*acc*) **setzen** to sign sth **(b)** (= *Bildunterschrift*) caption

Unterschriften-: Unterschriftenmappe F signature folder; **Unterschriftensammlung** F collection of signatures

Unterschrifts-: unterschriftsberechtigt ADJ authorized to sign; **Unterschriftsberechtigte(r)** [-bəʀɛçtɪçta] MF DECL AS ADJ authorized signatory; **Unterschriftsprobe** F specimen signature; **unterschriftsreif** ADJ *Vertrag* ready to be signed

Unter-: unterschwellig [-ʃvɛlɪç] **1** ADJ subliminal **2** ADV subliminally; **Unterseeboot** NT submarine; **Unterseite** F underside; (*von Blatt*) undersurface; **an der ~** on the underside/undersurface; **Untersetzer** M = **Untersatz**; **untersetzt** [ʊntɐˈzɛtst] ADJ stocky

unterstehen¹ [ʊntɐˈʃteːən], *ptp* **unterstanden** [ʊntɐˈʃtandn] INSEP IRREG **1** VI +DAT (= *unterstellt sein*) to be under (the control of); *jdm* to be subordinate to; **einer Behörde, dem Ministerium** to come under (the jurisdiction of); **dem Gesetz** to be subject to; (*in Firma*) to report to; **jds Aufsicht** (*dat*) ~ to be under sb's supervision; **dem Verkaufsdirektor ~ sechs Abteilungsleiter** the sales director is in charge of six departmental heads **2** VR (= *wagen*) to dare; **untersteh dich (ja nicht)!** (don't) you dare!; **was ~ Sie sich!** how dare you!

unterstehen² [ˈʊntɐʃteːən] VI SEP IRREG (*bei Regen etc*) to take shelter

unterstellen¹ [ˈʊntɐʃtɛlən], *ptp* **unterstellt** INSEP VT **(a)** (= *unterordnen*) to (make) subordinate (+*dat* to); *jdm* **unterstellt sein** to be under sb; (*in Firma*) to report to sb; **ihm sind vier Mitarbeiter unterstellt** he is in charge of four employees; **jdm etw ~** to put sb in charge of sth; (*Mil*) to put sth under the command of sb

(b) (= *annehmen*) to assume, to suppose; **einmal unterstellt, es sei so gewesen** supposing (that) it was so **(c)** (= *unterschieben*) **jdm etw ~** to insinuate that sb has done/said sth; **jdm Nachlässigkeit ~** to insinuate that sb has been negligent; **ihm wurde unterstellt, gesagt zu haben, ...** he was purported to have said ...

unterstellen² [ˈʊntɐʃtɛlən] SEP **1** VT (= *abstellen, unterbringen*) to keep; *Möbel* to store **2** VR to take shelter

Unterstellung [-ˈʃtɛlʊŋ] F **(a)** (= *falsche Behauptung*) misrepresentation; (= *Andeutung*) insinuation; (= *Annahme*) assumption **(b)** NO PL (= *Unterordnung*) subordination (*unter* +*acc* to)

unterste(r, s) [ˈʊntɐstə] ADJ SUPERL *von* **untere(r, s)** lowest; (= *tiefste auch*) bottom; (*rangmäßig*) lowest; (= *letzte*) last; **das Unterste zuoberst kehren** to turn everything upside down

unterstreichen [ʊntɐˈʃtraɪçn], *ptp* **unterstrichen** [ʊntɐˈʃtrɪçn] VT INSEP IRREG (*lit, fig*) to underline

Unterstreichung F underlining

Unterstufe F (*Sch*) lower school, lower grade (*US*)

unterstützen [ʊntɐˈʃtʏtsn], *ptp* **unterstützt** VT INSEP to support

Unterstützung F **(a)** NO PL support (*zu, für* for); **zur ~ seiner Behauptung** in support of his statement **(b)** (= *Zuschuss*) assistance; (*inf:* = *Arbeitslosenunterstützung*) (unemployment) benefit; **staatliche ~** state aid

Unterstützungsempfänger(in) M(F) person receiving benefit (*Brit*) or on welfare (*US*)

Untersuch [ʊntɐˈzuːx] M **-s, -e** (*Sw*) = **Untersuchung**

untersuchen [ʊntɐˈzuːxn], *ptp* **untersucht** VT INSEP **(a)** (= *inspizieren, prüfen*) to examine (*auf* +*acc* for); (= *erforschen*) to look into; (*genau*) *Dokumente etc* to scrutinize; (*statistisch, soziologisch etc*) to sound (out), to survey; (*chemisch, technisch etc*) to test (*auf* +*acc* for); **sich ärztlich ~ lassen** to have a medical (examination) **(b)** (= *nachprüfen*) to check

Untersuchung [ʊntɐˈzuːxʊŋ] F **-, -en (a)** (= *das Untersuchen*) examination (*auf* +*acc* for); (= *Erforschung*) investigation (+*gen, über* +*acc* into); (= *genaue Prüfung*) scrutiny; (*chemisch, technisch*) test (*auf* +*acc* for); (*ärztlich*) examination **(b)** (= *Nachprüfung*) check

Untersuchungs-: Untersuchungsausschuss M investigating committee; (*nach Unfall etc*) committee of inquiry; **Untersuchungsergebnis** NT (*Jur*) findings *pl*; (*Med*) result of an/the examination; (*Sci*) test result; **Untersuchungsgefängnis** NT prison (*for people awaiting trial*); **Untersuchungshaft** F (*period of*) *imprisonment while awaiting trial*; **in ~ sein** or **sitzen** (*inf*) to be in prison awaiting trial; **jdn in ~ nehmen** to commit sb for trial; **Untersuchungskommission** F investigating committee; (*nach schwerem Unfall etc*) board of inquiry; **Untersuchungsrichter(in)** M(F) examining magistrate

Untertage- [ʊntɐˈtaːgə] IN CPDS underground; **Untertagearbeiter(in)** M(F) (*coal*)face worker (*Brit*), belowground worker (*US*); **Untertagebau** M, NO PL underground mining

Unter-: untertariflich ADJ, ADV *Bezahlung* below an/the agreed rate; **~ bezahlt werden** to be paid less than the agreed rate; **Untertasse** F saucer; **fliegende ~** flying saucer

untertauchen SEP **1** VI AUX SEIN to dive (under); (*U-Boot auch*) to submerge; (*fig*) to disappear **2** VT to immerse; *jdn* to duck

Unterteil NT or M bottom part

unterteilen [ʊntɐˈtailən], *ptp* **unterteilt** VT INSEP to subdivide (*in* +*acc* into)

Unterteilung F subdivision (*in* +*acc* into)

Unter-: Unterteller M saucer; **Untertitel** M subtitle; (*für Bild*) caption; **Unterton** M, *pl* **-töne** (*Mus, fig*) undertone; **untertourig** [-tuːrɪç] **1** ADJ with low revs **2** ADV **~ fahren** to drive with low revs; **untertreiben** [ʊntɐˈtraibn], *ptp* **untertrieben** [ʊntɐˈtriːbn] INSEP IRREG **1** VT to understate **2** VI to play things down; **Untertreibung** F **-, -en (a)** understatement **(b)** (= *das Untertreiben*) playing things down *no art*; **untervermieten** *ptp* **untervermietet** VTI INSEP to sublet; **Unterversorgung** F inadequate provision; **Unterverzeichnis** NT (*Comput*) subdirectory

Unterwalden [ˈʊntɐvaldn] NT **-s** Unterwalden

unterwandern [ʊntɐˈvandɐn], *ptp* **unterwandert** VT INSEP to infiltrate

Unterwäsche F, NO PL underwear *no pl*
Unterwasser-: Unterwasserkamera F underwater camera; **Unterwasserlabor** NT underwater laboratory; **Unterwassermassage** F (*Med*) underwater massage
unterwegs [ʊntɐˈveːks] ADV on the *or* one's/its way (*nach, zu* to); (= *auf Reisen*) away; **eine Karte von ~ schicken** to send a card while one is away; **bei denen ist wieder ein Kind ~** they've got another child on the way; **bei ihr ist etwas (Kleines) ~** she's expecting
Unterwelt F (*lit, fig*) underworld
unterwerfen [ʊntɐˈvɛrfn], *ptp* **unterworfen** [ʊntɐˈvɔrfn] INSEP IRREG **1** VT **(a)** *Volk, Land* to conquer **(b)** (= *unterziehen*) to subject (*+dat* to); **einer Sache** (*dat*) **unterworfen sein** to be subject to sth **2** VR (*lit, fig*) **sich jdm/einer Sache ~** to submit to sb/sth
unterwürfig [ʊntɐˈvʏrfɪç, ˈʊntɐ-] ADJ (*pej*) obsequious
unterzeichnen [ʊntɐˈtsaiçnən], *ptp* **unterzeichnet** VT INSEP (*form*) to sign
Unterzeichner(in) M(F) signatory
Unterzeichnerstaat M signatory state
Unterzeichnete(r) [ʊntɐˈtsaiçnətə] MF DECL AS ADJ (*form*) **der/die ~** the undersigned
unterziehen¹ [ʊntɐˈtsiːən], *ptp* **unterzogen** [ʊntɐˈtsoːgn] INSEP IRREG **1** VR (= *unterwerfen*) **sich einer Sache** (*dat*) **~ (müssen)** to (have to) undergo sth; **sich einer Prüfung** (*dat*) **~** to take an examination **2** VT to subject (*+dat* to); **jdn einer Operation ~** to perform an operation on sb
unterziehen² [ˈʊntɐtsiːən] VT SEP IRREG **(a)** *Unterwäsche, Kleidung* to put on underneath; **sich** (*dat*) **etw ~** to put sth on underneath **(b)** (*Cook*) *Eischnee, Sahne* to fold in
Unterzuckerung [-ˈtsʊkərʊŋ] F **-, -en** (*Med*) hypoglycaemia (*Brit*), hypoglycemia (*US*)
Un-: Untiefe F (= *seichte Stelle*) shallow; **Untier** NT monster; **untragbar** ADJ *Zustände, Belastung* intolerable; *Risiko* unacceptable; **er ist politisch ~ geworden** he has become a political liability; **untrainiert** [ˈʊntrɛniːɐt, -trɛ-] ADJ untrained; **untrennbar 1** ADJ inseparable **2** ADV **~ zusammengesetzte Verben** inseparable verbs; **mit etw ~ verbunden sein** (*fig*) to be inextricably linked with sth
untreu ADJ *Liebhaber etc* unfaithful; (*einem Prinzip etc*) disloyal (*+dat* to); **sich** (*dat*) **selbst ~ werden** to be untrue to oneself; **jdm ~ werden** to be unfaithful to sb
Untreue F **(a)** (*von Liebhaber etc*) unfaithfulness **(b)** (*Jur*) embezzlement
untröstlich ADJ inconsolable (*über +acc* about)
untrüglich [ʊnˈtryːklɪç, ˈʊn-] ADJ *Gedächtnis, Instinkt, Gespür* infallible; *Zeichen* unmistakable
Untugend F (= *Laster*) vice; (= *schlechte Angewohnheit*) bad habit; (= *Schwäche*) weakness
un-: unübel ADJ **(gar) nicht (so) ~** not bad (at all); **unüberbietbar** ADJ *Preis, Rekord etc* unbeatable; *Leistung* unsurpassable; *Frechheit, Virtuosität, Eifer* unparalleled; **unüberbrückbar** ADJ (*fig*) *Gegensätze etc* irreconcilable; *Kluft* unbridgeable; **unüberlegt 1** ADJ rash **2** ADV rashly; **~ entscheiden** to make a rash decision; **unübersehbar** ADJ **(a)** *Schaden, Schwierigkeiten, Folgen* incalculable; *Menge, Häusermeer etc* vast **(b)** *Fehler etc* obvious; **unübersichtlich** ADJ **(a)** *Gelände* broken; *Kurve, Stelle* blind **(b)** (= *durcheinander*) *System, Plan* confused; **unübertrefflich 1** ADJ unsurpassable; *Rekord* unbeatable **2** ADV superbly; **unübertroffen** [ʊnlyːbɐˈtrɔfn, ˈʊn-] ADJ unsurpassed; **unüblich 1** ADJ not usual **2** ADV unusually; **unumgänglich** [ʊnlʊmˈgɛŋlɪç, ˈʊn-] ADJ essential; (= *unvermeidlich*) inevitable; *Notwendigkeit* absolute; **~ notwendig werden** to become absolutely essential/quite inevitable; **unumschränkt** [ʊnlʊmˈʃrɛŋkt, ˈʊn-] **1** ADJ unlimited; *Freiheit, Gewalt, Macht auch, Herrscher* absolute **2** ADV **~ herrschen** to have absolute rule; **unumstößlich** [ʊnlʊmˈʃtøːslɪç, ˈʊn-] **1** ADJ *Tatsache, Wahrheit* irrefutable; *Entschluss* irrevocable **2** ADV **~ feststehen** to be absolutely definite; **unumstritten 1** ADJ indisputable **2** ADV indisputably; **unumwunden** [ʊnlʊmˈvʊndn, ʊnlʊmˈvʊndn] ADV frankly
unveränderlich [ʊnfɛɐˈlɛndəlɪç, ˈʊn-] ADJ (= *gleichbleibend*) unchanging; (= *unwandelbar*) unchangeable; **eine ~e Größe** (*Math*), **eine Unveränderliche** (*Math*) an invariable
Unveränderlichkeit F unchanging nature

unverändert [ˈʊnfɛɐlɛndɐt, ʊnfɛɐˈlɛndɐt] **1** ADJ unchanged; **unsere Weine sind immer von ~er Güte** our wines are consistently good **2** ADV always; **du siehst ~ jung aus** you look just as young as ever; **das Wetter wird bis auf weiteres ~ heiter bleiben** the weather will remain fine for the time being
un-: unverantwortlich [ʊnfɛɐˈlantvɔrtlɪç, ˈʊn-] **1** ADJ irresponsible **2** ADV irresponsibly; **er hat sich ~ intensiv der Sonne ausgesetzt** he spent so much time in the sun, it was irresponsible; **du trinkst ~ viel** you're acting irresponsibly by drinking so much; **sie ist ~ schnell gefahren** she drove dangerously fast; **unveräußerlich** [ʊnfɛɐˈlɔysəlɪç, ˈʊn-] ADJ **(a)** *Rechte* inalienable **(b)** *Besitz* unsaleable; **unverbesserlich** [ʊnfɛɐˈbɛsəlɪç, ˈʊn-] ADJ incorrigible
unverbindlich [ˈʊnfɛɐbɪntlɪç, ʊnfɛɐˈbɪntlɪç] **1** ADJ **(a)** (= *nicht bindend*) *Angebot, Preisangabe, Richtlinie* not binding; *Besichtigung* free **(b)** (= *vage, allgemein*) noncommittal **2** ADV (= *nicht bindend*) noncommittally; **sich** (*dat*) **etw ~ schicken lassen** to have sth sent without obligation; **etw ~ ausrechnen** to give a nonbinding estimate for sth
unverdächtig [ˈʊnfɛɐdɛçtɪç, ʊnfɛɐˈdɛçtɪç] **1** ADJ unsuspicious; (= *nicht unter Verdacht stehend*) above suspicion; **das ist doch völlig ~** there's nothing suspicious about that **2** ADV **sich möglichst ~ benehmen** to arouse as little suspicion as possible; **benimm dich möglichst ~!** act as normally as possible
Un-: unverdaulich [ˈʊnfɛɐdaulɪç, ʊnfɛɐˈdaulɪç] ADJ (*lit, fig*) indigestible; **unverdorben** ADJ (*lit, fig*) unspoilt; **Unverdorbenheit** F (*fig*) purity; **unverdrossen** [ˈʊnfɛɐdrɔsn, ʊnfɛɐˈdrɔsn] **1** ADJ (= *nicht entmutigt*) undeterred; (= *unermüdlich*) indefatigable; (= *unverzagt*) undaunted **2** ADV (= *unverzagt*) undauntedly; *weitermachen* untiringly; **unverdünnt** [ˈʊnfɛɐdʏnt] **1** ADJ undiluted **2** ADV *anwenden, auftragen* undiluted; **Spirituosen ~ trinken** to drink spirits neat (*esp Brit*), to drink alcohol straight (*esp US*); **unvereinbar** [ʊnfɛɐˈlainbaːɐ, ˈʊn-] ADJ incompatible; **miteinander ~ sein** to be incompatible; **Unvereinbarkeit** F incompatibility; **unverfänglich** [ˈʊnfɛɐfɛŋlɪç, ʊnfɛɐˈfɛŋlɪç] ADJ harmless; **das ist ~** it doesn't commit you to anything
unvergessen ADJ unforgotten; **Roland wird (uns allen) ~ bleiben** we'll (all) remember Roland
unvergesslich [ʊnfɛɐˈgɛslɪç, ˈʊn-] ADJ unforgettable; **das wird mir ~ bleiben, das bleibt mir ~** I'll always remember that
Un-: unvergleichlich [ʊnfɛɐˈglaiçlɪç, ˈʊn-] **1** ADJ unique, incomparable **2** ADV incomparably; **unverhältnismäßig** [ˈʊnfɛɐhɛltnɪsmɛːsɪç, ʊnfɛɐˈhɛltnɪsmɛːsɪç] **1** ADV disproportionately; (= *übermäßig*) excessively **2** ADJ disproportionate; (= *übermäßig*) excessive; **Unverhältnismäßigkeit** F disproportion; (= *Übermäßigkeit*) excessiveness; **ihm wurde ~ der Strafe vorgeworfen** he was accused of imposing an excessive punishment; **unverhofft** [ˈʊnfɛɐhɔft, ʊnfɛɐˈhɔft] **1** ADJ unexpected **2** ADV unexpectedly; **das kam völlig ~** it was quite unexpected; **~ Besuch bekommen** to get an unexpected visit; **~ kommt oft** (*Prov*) what you least expect often happens; **unverkäuflich** [ʊnfɛɐˈkɔyflɪç, ʊnfɛɐˈkɔyflɪç] ADJ unsaleable; **~es Muster** free sample; „**~**" "not for sale"; **unverkennbar** [ʊnfɛɐˈkɛnbaːɐ, ˈʊn-] ADJ unmistak(e)able; **unverletzlich** [ʊnfɛɐˈlɛtslɪç, ˈʊn-] ADJ **(a)** (*fig*) *Rechte, Grenze* inviolable **(b)** (*lit*) invulnerable; **unverletzt** [ˈʊnfɛɐlɛtst] ADJ uninjured, unhurt; *Körperteil* undamaged; **unvermeidlich** [ʊnfɛɐˈmaitlɪç, ˈʊn-] ADJ inevitable; (= *nicht zu umgehen*) unavoidable; **unvermindert** [ˈʊnfɛɐmɪndɐt] ADJ, ADV undiminished
unvermittelt [ˈʊnfɛɐmɪtlt] **1** ADJ (= *plötzlich*) sudden **2** ADV suddenly
Unvernunft F (= *Torheit*) stupidity; (= *mangelnder Verstand*) irrationality; (= *Uneinsichtigkeit*) unreasonableness
unvernünftig ADJ (= *töricht*) stupid; (*aus mangelnder Vernunft*) irrational; (= *uneinsichtig*) unreasonable; **das war sehr ~ von ihr** it was very stupid of her
unverrichtet [ˈʊnfɛɐrɪçtət] ADJ **~er Dinge** *or* **Sache** without having achieved anything
unverschämt 1 ADJ outrageous; *Mensch, Frage, Benehmen etc* impudent; (*inf*) *Preis* outrageous; **~es Glück** unbelievable luck **2** ADV **(a)** (= *dreist*) *grinsen* impudently; *lügen* blatantly; **grins nicht so ~!** take that impudent grin off your face!; **lüg**

nicht so ~! don't tell such barefaced lies! **(b)** (*inf*: = *unerhört*) *teuer, hoch* outrageously

Unverschämtheit F **-, -en (a)** NO PL outrageousness; (*von Mensch, Frage, Benehmen etc*) impudence; **die ~ besitzen, etw zu tun** to have the impudence to do sth **(b)** (*Bemerkung*) impertinence; (*Tat*) outrageous thing; **das ist eine ~!** it's outrageous!

unverschuldet [ˈʊnfɛɐˌʃʊldət, ʊnfɛɐˈʃʊldət] **1** ADJ **(a) ein ~er Unfall** an accident which was not his/her *etc* fault **(b)** (= *ohne Schulden*) free from debt **2** ADV **~ in eine Notlage geraten** to get into difficulties through no fault of one's own

unversehens [ˈʊnfɛɐzeːəns, ʊnfɛɐˈzeːəns] ADV all of a sudden; (= *überraschend*) unexpectedly

Un-: unversehrt [ˈʊnfɛɐzeːɐt] ADJ *Mensch* (*lit, fig*) unscathed; (= *unbeschädigt*) intact *pred*; **Unversehrtheit** F **-,** NO PL (= *ohne Beschädigung*) intactness; **körperliche ~** freedom from bodily harm; **sie haben die ~ der Geiseln bestätigt** they have confirmed that the hostages are uninjured; **unversöhnlich** [ˈʊnfɛɐzøːnlɪç, ʊnfɛɐˈzøːnlɪç] ADJ *Standpunkte etc* irreconcilable; **unversorgt** [ˈʊnfɛɐzɔrkt] ADJ *Familie, Kinder* unprovided-for; *Patient, Verletzter* uncared-for

Unverstand M lack of judgement; (= *Torheit*) foolishness; **etw im ~ tun** to do sth to excess

unverstanden [ˈʊnfɛɐʃtandn] ADJ not understood; (= *missverstanden*) misunderstood; **er fühlt sich ~** he feels that nobody understands him

unverständlich ADJ (= *nicht zu hören*) inaudible; (= *unbegreifbar*) incomprehensible

Unverständnis NT, NO PL lack of understanding; (= *Nichterfassen, für Kunst etc*) lack of appreciation

un-: unversucht [ˈʊnfɛɐzuːxt, ʊnfɛɐˈzuːxt] ADJ **nichts ~ lassen** to try everything; **unverträglich** [ˈʊnfɛɐtrɛklɪç, ʊnfɛɐˈtrɛklɪç] ADJ **(a)** (= *streitsüchtig*) cantankerous **(b)** (= *unverdaulich*) indigestible; (*Med*) intolerable; (*mit anderer Substanz etc*) incompatible; **unverwechselbar** [ˈʊnfɛɐvɛkslbaːɐ, ʊn-] ADJ unmistak(e)able; **unverwundbar** ADJ (*lit, fig*) invulnerable

unverwüstlich [ˈʊnfɛɐvyːstlɪç, ʊn-] ADJ indestructible; *Gesundheit* robust; *Humor, Mensch* irrepressible

unverzeihlich [ˈʊnfɛɐˈtsailɪç, ʊn-] ADJ unforgivable

unverzichtbar [ˈʊnfɛɐˈtsɪçtbaːɐ, ʊn-] ADJ ATTR *Recht* inalienable; *Anspruch* undeniable; *Bedingung, Bestandteil* indispensable

unverzinslich [ˈʊnfɛɐˈtsɪnslɪç, ʊn-] ADJ interest-free

unverzüglich [ˈʊnfɛɐˈtsyːklɪç, ʊn-] **1** ADJ immediate **2** ADV immediately

unvollendet [ˈʊnfɔlɛndət, ʊnfɔlˈɛndət, ʊnfɔlˈlɛndət] ADJ unfinished; **Die „Unvollendete" von Schubert** Schubert's Unfinished (Symphony)

unvollkommen [ˈʊnfɔlkɔmən, ʊnfɔlˈkɔmən] **1** ADJ (= *unvollständig*) incomplete; (= *fehlerhaft, mangelhaft*) imperfect **2** ADV partially; *wiedergeben* incompletely; **er konnte seine Gefühle nur ~ beschreiben** he could only describe his feelings to a certain degree

unvollständig [ˈʊnfɔlʃtɛndɪç, ʊnfɔlˈʃtɛndɪç] **1** ADJ incomplete; (*Gram*) *Hilfsverb* defective **2** ADV partially; **er hat das Formular ~ ausgefüllt** he didn't fill the form out properly

Unvollständigkeit F incompleteness

Un-: unvorbereitet [ˈʊnfoːɐbəraitət] **1** ADJ unprepared (*auf +acc* for); **eine ~e Rede halten** to make an impromptu speech **2** ADV *reden, unterrichten* unprepared; **der Tod des Vaters traf sie ~** her father's death came unexpectedly; **unvoreingenommen** **1** ADJ impartial **2** ADV impartially; **Unvoreingenommenheit** F impartiality; **unvorhergesehen** [ˈʊnfoːɐheːɐgəzeːən] **1** ADJ unforeseen; *Besuch* unexpected; **wir bekamen ~en Besuch** we had unexpected visitors **2** ADV unexpectedly; **unvorschriftsmäßig** **1** ADJ not in keeping with the regulations **2** ADV improperly; **unvorsichtig** **1** ADJ careless; (= *voreilig*) rash **2** ADV carelessly; (= *unbedacht*) rashly; **unvorsichtigerweise** [ˈʊnfoːɐzɪçtɪgəˈvaizə] ADV carelessly; (= *voreilig*) rashly; **unvorstellbar** [ˈʊnfoːɐʃtɛlbaːɐ, ʊn-] **1** ADJ inconceivable **2** ADV *heiß, kalt* incredibly; *brutal, grausam* inconceivably; **unvorteilhaft** **1** ADJ unfavourable (*Brit*), unfavorable (*US*); *Kleid, Frisur etc* unbecoming **2** ADV *gekleidet, geschminkt* unbecomingly; **~ aussehen** not to look one's best; **unwahr** ADJ untrue; **Unwahrheit** F **(a)** NO PL (*von Äußerung*) untruthfulness **(b)** (= *unwahre Äußerung*) untruth; **die ~ sagen** not to tell the truth

unwahrscheinlich **1** ADJ (= *nicht zu erwarten, kaum denkbar*) unlikely; (= *unglaubhaft*) implausible; (*inf*: = *groß*) incredible (*inf*) **2** ADV (*inf*) incredibly (*inf*); **wir haben uns ~ beeilt** we hurried as much as we possibly could

Unwahrscheinlichkeit F unlikeliness

unwegsam ADJ *Gelände etc* rough

unweigerlich [ʊnˈvaigɐlɪç, ˈʊn-] **1** ADJ ATTR *Folge* inevitable **2** ADV inevitably; (= *fraglos*) undoubtedly; (= *grundsätzlich*) invariably

unweit PREP +GEN ADV not far from

Unwesen NT, NO PL (= *übler Zustand*) terrible state of affairs; **sein ~ treiben** to be up to mischief; (*Landstreicher etc*) to make trouble; (*Gespenst*) to walk abroad; (*Vampir etc*) to strike terror into people's hearts

unwesentlich **1** ADJ (= *nicht zur Sache gehörig*) irrelevant; (= *unwichtig*) unimportant **2** ADV *erhöhen, verringern* insignificantly; *sich unterscheiden, verändern* only slightly; *mehr, weniger, jünger, besser* just slightly; **zu einer Sache nicht/nur ~ beitragen** to make a not insignificant/only an insignificant contribution to sth

Un-: Unwetter NT (thunder)storm; **unwichtig** ADJ unimportant; (= *belanglos*) irrelevant; (= *verzichtbar*) nonessential; **Unwichtigkeit** F unimportance; (= *Belanglosigkeit*) irrelevance; **unwiderstehlich** [ʊnviˈdɐˈʃteːlɪç, ʊn-] ADJ irresistible

Unwille(n) M, NO PL displeasure (*über +acc* at); (= *Ungeduld*) irritation; **seinem Unwillen Luft machen** to give vent to one's indignation

unwillkürlich [ˈʊnvɪlkyːɐlɪç, ʊnvɪlˈkyːɐlɪç] **1** ADJ spontaneous; (= *instinktiv*) instinctive; (*Physiol, Med*) involuntary **2** ADV *zusammenzucken* instinctively; **ich musste ~ lachen/grinsen** I couldn't help laughing/smiling

Un-: unwirklich ADJ unreal; **unwirksam** ADJ (= *wirkungslos, auch Med*) ineffective; *Vertrag, Rechtsgeschäft* inoperative; (= *nichtig*) null, void; (*Chem*) inactive; **Unwirksamkeit** F (= *Wirkungslosigkeit*) ineffectiveness; (*Jur*) (the fact of) not being operative; **unwirsch** [ˈʊnvɪrʃ] **1** ADJ *Mensch, Benehmen, Bemerkung* surly, gruff; *Bewegung* brusque **2** ADV gruffly, brusquely; **unwirtlich** [ˈʊnvɪrtlɪç] ADJ inhospitable; **Unwirtlichkeit** F **-,** NO PL (*von Ort*) inhospitable feel; (*von Klima*) inhospitable nature; **unwirtschaftlich** **1** ADJ uneconomic **2** ADV uneconomically; **Unwirtschaftlichkeit** F **die ~ dieser Methode** because this method is/was uneconomic; **Unwissen** NT ignorance; **unwissend** ADJ ignorant; (= *ahnungslos*) unsuspecting; (= *unerfahren*) inexperienced; **Unwissenheit** F **-,** NO PL ignorance; (= *Unerfahrenheit*) inexperience; **~ schützt nicht vor Strafe** (*prov*) ignorance is no excuse *or* (*Jur*) is no defence (*Brit*) *or* defense (*US*) in law; **unwissentlich** ADV unwittingly

unwohl ADJ (= *unpässlich*) unwell; (= *unbehaglich*) uneasy; **mir ist ~, ich fühle mich ~** I don't feel well; **in ihrer Gegenwart fühle ich mich ~** I feel uneasy in her presence

Unwohlsein NT indisposition; (= *unangenehmes Gefühl*) unease; **von einem (plötzlichen) ~ befallen werden** to be taken ill suddenly

unwürdig ADJ unworthy (+*gen* of); *Verhalten* undignified; (= *schmachvoll*) degrading

Unzahl F **eine ~ von** a host of

unzählig [ʊnˈtsɛːlɪç, ˈʊn-] **1** ADJ innumerable; **~e Mal(e)** countless times **2** ADV **~ viele** huge numbers; **~ viele Bücher/Mädchen** innumerable books/girls

Unze [ˈʊntsə] F **-, -n** ounce

un-: unzeitgemäß ADJ (= *altmodisch*) old-fashioned; (= *nicht in die Zeit passend*) anachronistic; **unzerbrechlich** [ʊntsɛɐˈbrɛçlɪç, ʊn-] ADJ unbreakable; **unzerkaut** [ˈʊntsɛɐkaut] ADJ unchewed **2** ADV without chewing; *hinunterschlucken* whole; **unzertrennlich** [ʊntsɛɐˈtrɛnlɪç, ʊn-] ADJ inseparable; **unzivilisiert** [ˈʊntsiviliziːɐt] ADJ (*lit, fig*) uncivilized **2** ADV *sich benehmen* in an uncivilized manner

Unzucht F, NO PL (*esp Jur*) sexual offence (*Brit*) *or* offense (*US*); **~ treiben** to fornicate; **~ mit Abhängigen/Kindern/Tieren** (*Jur*) illicit sexual relations with dependants/children/animals; **gewerbsmäßige ~** prostitution; **~ mit jdm treiben** to fornicate with sb; (*Jur*) to commit a sexual offence (*Brit*) *or* offense (*US*) with sb

unzüchtig ■ ADJ (*esp Jur*) indecent; *Reden, Schriften* obscene; **~e** Handlungen obscene acts; (*Jur*) illicit sexual acts ■ ADV **~ leben** to live licentiously

Un-: unzufrieden ADJ dissatisfied; (= *missmutig*) unhappy; **manche Leute sind immer ~** some people are never happy; **Unzufriedenheit** F, NO PL dissatisfaction, discontent; (= *Missmut*) unhappiness; **unzulänglich** ■ ADJ (= *nicht ausreichend*) insufficient; (= *mangelhaft*) inadequate ■ ADV inadequately; **~ unterstützt werden** to get inadequate support; **Unzulänglichkeit** F (a) NO PL insufficiency; (= *Mangelhaftigkeit*) inadequacy (b) **-en** shortcomings *pl*; **unzulässig** ADJ (*auch Jur*) inadmissible; *Gebrauch* improper; *Beeinflussung* undue; *Belastung, Geschwindigkeit* excessive; **für ~ erklären** (*Jur*) to rule out; **unzumutbar** ADJ *Bedingungen, Zustände* unreasonable; **unzurechnungsfähig** ADJ of unsound mind; **jdn für ~ erklären lassen** (*Jur*) to have sb certified (insane); **geistig ~** of unsound mind; **Unzurechnungsfähigkeit** F unsoundness of mind; **~ geltend machen** to enter a plea of insanity; **unzusammenhängend** ADJ incoherent; **unzutreffend** ADJ inappropriate, inapplicable; (= *unwahr*) incorrect; **Unzutreffendes bitte streichen** delete as applicable; **unzuverlässig** ADJ unreliable; **unzweideutig** ■ ADJ unambiguous; (*fig*: = *unanständig*) explicit ■ ADV explicitly; **jdm ~ zu verstehen geben, dass ...** to make it quite clear to sb that ...

Update [ˈapdeːt] NT **-s, -s** (*Comput*) update (*auf +acc* or *zu* to)
updaten [ˈapdeːtn], *ptp* **upgedatet** VTI SEP (*Comput*) to update

üppig [ˈʏpɪç] ■ ADJ *Wachstum* luxuriant; *Haar* thick; *Mahl, Ausstattung* sumptuous; *Rente, Gehalt* lavish; *Figur, Frau, Formen* voluptuous; *Busen* ample; *Leben* luxurious; *Fantasie* rich ■ ADV **die ~ ausfallenden Dividenden** the generous dividends; **ihre Bezüge sind sehr ~ bemessen** her earnings are very generously figured; **~ wucherndes Gestrüpp** lush verdant undergrowth; **350 ~ illustrierte Seiten** 350 lavishly illustrated pages; **~ leben** to live in style

Üppigkeit F -, NO PL (*von Wachstum*) luxuriance; (*von Haar*) thickness; (*von Mahl, Ausstattung*) sumptuousness; (*von Figur, Frau, Formen*) voluptuousness

up to date [ˈap tuː ˈdeːt] ADJ PRED (*inf*) up to date; *Kleidung* modern

Ur [uːɐ] M **-(e)s, -e** (*Zool*) aurochs

Ur- IN CPDS (= *erste*) first; (= *ursprünglich*) original; **Urabstimmung** F ballot

Ural [uˈraːl] M **-s** (*Geog*) (a) (*Fluss*) Ural (b) (*Gebirge*) **der ~** the Urals *pl*

uralt ADJ ancient; **seit -en Zeiten** from time immemorial; **aus -en Zeiten** from long (long) ago

Uran [uˈraːn] NT **-s,** NO PL (*abbr* **U**) uranium

uraufführen [ˈuːɐʔaʊffyːrən], *ptp* **uraufgeführt** [ˈuːɐʔaʊfɡəfyːɐt] VT to give the first performance (of), to play for the first time; *Film* to premiere *usu pass*

Uraufführung F premiere

urbanisieren [ʊrbaniˈziːrən], *ptp* **urbanisiert** VTR (*Sociol*) to urbanize

Urbanisierung F -, -en (*Sociol*) urbanization

urbar [ˈʊrbaːɐ] ADJ **einen Wald ~ machen** to clear a forest; **die Wüste ~ machen** to reclaim the desert; **Land ~ machen** to cultivate land

Ur-: Urbayer(in) M(F) (*inf*) typical Bavarian; **Urbeginn** M very beginning; **seit ~, von ~ an** from the beginning(s) of time; **Urbevölkerung** F natives *pl*; (*in Australien*) Aborigines *pl*; **Urbewohner(in)** M(F) native; (*in Australien*) Aborigine

urchig [ˈʊrçɪç] ADJ (*Sw*) = **urwüchsig**

Ur-: ureigen [ˈuːɐʔaɪɡn] ADJ very own; **es liegt in seinem -sten Interesse** it's in his own best interests; **ein dem Menschen ~er Hang** an inherent human quality; **Ureinwohner(in)** M(F) native; (*in Australien*) Aborigine; **Urenkel** M great-grandchild, great-grandson; **Urenkelin** F great-granddaughter; **urgemütlich** ADJ (*inf*) really cosy (*Brit*) or cozy (*US*); *Mensch* really easy-going; **Urgeschichte** F prehistory; **Urgestein** NT prehistoric rock; **politisches ~** (*fig*) a dyed-in-the-wool politician; **Urgewalt** F elemental force

Urgroß-: Urgroßeltern PL great-grandparents *pl*; **Urgroßmutter** F great-grandmother; **Urgroßvater** M great-grandfather

Urheber [ˈuːɐheːbɐ] M **-s, -**, **Urheberin** [-ərɪn] F **-, -nen** originator; (*Jur*: = *Verfasser*) author; **der geistige ~** the spiritual father

Urheber-: Urheberrecht NT copyright (*an +dat* on); **urheberrechtlich** ADJ, ADV on copyright *attr*; **~ geschützt** copyright(ed); **Urheberschaft** [ˈuːɐheːbɐʃaft] F **-, -en** authorship; **Urheberschutz** M copyright

Uri [ˈuːri] NT **-s** Uri

urig [ˈuːrɪç] ADJ (*inf*) *Mensch* earthy; *Lokal etc* ethnic

Urin [uˈriːn] M **-s, -e** urine; **etw im ~ haben** (*dated inf*) to have a gut feeling about sth (*inf*)

urinieren [uriˈniːrən], *ptp* **uriniert** VI to urinate

Ur-: Urknall M (*Astron*) big bang; **urkomisch** ADJ (*inf*) screamingly funny (*inf*)

Urkunde [ˈuːɐkʊndə] F **-, -n** document; (= *Kaufurkunde*) deed; (= *Gründungsurkunde etc*) charter; (= *Siegerurkunde, Diplomurkunde, Bescheinigung etc*) certificate; **eine ~ (über etw acc) ausstellen** or **ausfertigen** (*Jur*) to draw up a document about sth

Urkundenfälschung F falsification of a/the document/documents

Urlaub [ˈuːɐlaʊp] M **-(e)s, -e** [-bə] (= *Ferien*) holiday(s *pl*) (*esp Brit*), vacation (*US*); (*esp Mil*) leave (of absence), furlough (*US*); **~ haben** to have a holiday (*esp Brit*) or vacation (*US*); (*esp Mil*) to have leave; **in** or **im** or **auf** (*inf*) **~ sein** to be on holiday (*esp Brit*) or vacation (*US*)/on leave; **er macht zur Zeit ~** he's on holiday (*esp Brit*) or he's vacationing (*US*) at the moment; **in ~ fahren** to go on holiday (*esp Brit*) or vacation (*US*)/on leave; **(sich dat) einen Tag ~ nehmen** to take a day off

urlauben [ˈuːɐlaʊbn] VI (*inf*) to holiday (*esp Brit*), to vacation (*US*)

Urlauber [ˈuːɐlaʊbɐ] M **-s, -**, **Urlauberin** [-ərɪn] F **-, -nen** holiday-maker (*Brit*), vacationist (*US*)

Urlaubs-: Urlaubsanspruch M holiday (*esp Brit*) or vacation (*US*) entitlement; **Urlaubsgebiet** NT holiday (*esp Brit*) or vacation (*US*) area; **urlaubsreif** ADJ ready for a holiday (*esp Brit*) or vacation (*US*); **Urlaubssperre** F (*Mil*) ban on leave; **Urlaubsstimmung** F holiday mood; **Urlaubstag** M (one day of) holiday (*esp Brit*) or vacation (*US*); **die ersten drei -e hat es geregnet** it rained on the first three days of the/my/his *etc* holiday (*esp Brit*) or vacation (*US*); **ich habe noch drei -e gut** I've still got three days' holiday (*esp Brit*) or vacation (*US*) to come; **Urlaubsvertretung** F temporary replacement; **ich mache ~ für Frau Schumm** I'm filling in while Mrs Schumm is on holiday (*esp Brit*) or is vacationing (*US*); **Urlaubszeit** F holiday (*esp Brit*) or vacation (*US*) period or season

Ur-: Urlaut M elemental cry; **Urmensch** M primeval man; (*inf*) caveman (*inf*)

Urne [ˈʊrnə] F **-, -n** urn; (= *Losurne*) box; (= *Wahlurne*) ballot box; **zur ~ gehen** to go to the polls; **die Wähler wurden an die ~n gerufen** the voters were asked to go to the polls

Urnen-: Urnenfeld NT (*Archeol*) urnfield; **Urnenfriedhof** M cinerarium; **Urnengang** M, *pl* **-gänge** (*Pol*) going to the polls *no art*; **Urnengrab** NT urn grave

Urologe [uroˈloːɡə] M **-n, -n**, **Urologin** [-ˈloːgɪn] F **-, -nen** urologist

Urologie [uroloˈgiː] F -, NO PL urology

urologisch [uroˈloːgɪʃ] ADJ urological

Ur-: Uroma F (*inf*) great-granny (*inf*); **Uropa** M (*inf*) great-grandpa (*inf*); **urplötzlich** (*inf*) ■ ADJ ATTR very sudden ■ ADV all of a sudden; **Urproduktion** F primary production

Ursache [ˈuːɐzaxə] F cause (*auch Philos*); (= *Grund*) reason; (= *Beweggrund*) motive; (= *Anlass*) occasion; **~ und Wirkung** cause and effect; **kleine ~, große Wirkung** (*prov*) big oaks from little acorns grow (*prov*); **keine ~!** (*auf Dank*) don't mention it!; (*auf Entschuldigung*) that's all right; **ohne (jede) ~** for no reason (at all); **aus ungeklärter ~** for reasons unknown; **alle/keine ~ zu etw haben** to have every/no reason for sth; **alle/keine ~ haben, etw zu tun** to have every/no reason to do sth

ursächlich [ˈuːɐzɛçlɪç] ADJ (*esp Philos*) causal; **~ für etw sein** to be the cause of sth; **in -em Zusammenhang stehen** to be causally related

Ur-: Urschlamm M primeval mud; **Urschleim** M protoplasm; **Urschrei** M (*Psych*) primal scream

urspr. ABBR *von* **ursprünglich**

Ursprache F **(a)** proto-language **(b)** (*bei Übersetzungen*) original (language)

Ursprung ['uːɐʃprʊŋ] M origin; (= *Anfang auch*) beginning; (= *Abstammung*) extraction; **er ist keltischen ~s** he is of Celtic extraction; **dieses Wort ist keltischen ~s** this word is of Celtic origin; **seinen ~ in etw** (*dat*) **haben, einer Sache** (*dat*) **seinen ~ verdanken** to originate in sth

ursprünglich ['uːɐʃprʏŋlɪç, uːɐʃp-] ⬛ ADJ **(a)** ATTR original; (= *anfänglich*) initial **(b)** (= *urwüchsig*) natural; *Natur* unspoilt ⬛ ADV originally; (= *anfänglich*) initially

Ursprünglichkeit F -, NO PL naturalness

Ursprungs-: Ursprungsland NT (*Comm*) country of origin; **Ursprungszeugnis** NT certificate of origin

Urteil ['ʊrtail] NT **-s, -e (a)** judgement (*auch Philos*); (= *Entscheidung*) decision; (= *Meinung*) opinion; **nach meinem ~ in** my judgement/opinion; **ich kann darüber kein ~ abgeben** I am no judge of this; **sich** (*dat*) **ein ~ über jdn/etw erlauben, ein ~ über jdn/etw fällen** to pass judgement on sb/sth; **sich** (*dat*) **kein ~ über etw** (*acc*) **erlauben können** to be in no position to judge sth; **(sich) mit seinem ~ zurückhalten** to reserve judgement; **zu dem ~ kommen, dass ...** to come to the conclusion that ...; **sich** (*dat*) **ein ~ über jdn/etw bilden** to form an opinion about sb/sth

(b) (*Jur*) (= *Gerichtsurteil*) verdict; (= *Richterspruch*) judgement; (= *Strafmaß*) sentence; (= *Schiedsspruch*) award; (= *Scheidungsspruch*) decree; **das ~ über jdn sprechen** (*Jur*) to pass judgement on sb

urteilen ['ʊrtailən] VI to judge (*nach* by); **über etw** (*acc*) ~ to judge sth; (= *seine Meinung äußern*) to give one's opinion on sth; **hart über jdn** ~ to judge sb harshly; **abfällig über jdn** ~ to be disparaging about sb; **nach seinem Aussehen zu** ~ judging by his appearance; **vorschnell** ~ to make a hasty judgement

Urteils-: Urteilsbegründung F (*Jur*) opinion; **Urteilsfindung** [-fɪndʊŋ] F **-, -en** (*Jur*) reaching a verdict *no art*; **Urteilskraft** F, NO PL power of judgement; (= *Umsichtigkeit*) discernment; **Urteilsspruch** M (*Jur*) judgement; (*von Geschworenen*) verdict; (*von Strafgericht*) sentence; (*von Schiedsgericht*) award; **Urteilsverkündung** F (*Jur*) pronouncement of judgement;

Urteilsvermögen NT faculty of judgement; (= *Umsichtigkeit*) discernment

Ur-: Urtext M original (text); **Urtier** NT, **Urtierchen** NT protozoan; (*in der Morphologie*) primordial animal; **urtümlich** ['uːrtyːmlɪç] ADJ = **urwüchsig; Urtyp** M, **Urtypus** M prototype

Uruguay ['uːrʊgvai, 'ʊr-, urʊ'guai] NT **-s** Uruguay

Urur- ['uːrʊr-] IN CPDS great-great-;

Ur-: Urvater M forefather; **Urvogel** M archaeopteryx; **Urvolk** NT first people; **Urwald** M primeval forest; (*in den Tropen*) jungle; **urwüchsig** ['uːrvyːksɪç] ADJ (= *unverbildet, naturhaft*) natural; *Natur* unspoilt; (= *urweltlich*) *Flora, Fauna* primeval; (= *ursprünglich*) original; (= *bodenständig*) rooted in the soil; (= *derb, kräftig*) sturdy; *Mensch* rugged; *Humor, Sprache* earthy; **Urzeit** F primeval times *pl*; **seit ~en** since primeval times; (*inf*) for aeons (*Brit inf*) *or* eons (*US inf*); **vor ~en** in primeval times; (*inf*) ages ago; **urzeitlich** ADJ primeval; **Urzelle** F (*Biol*) primordial cell; **Urzustand** M original state

USA [uːlɛsˈlaː] PL **die ~** the USA *sing*; **in die ~ fahren** to travel to the USA

Usambaraveilchen [uzamˈbaːra-] NT African violet

Usbekistan [ʊsˈbeːkɪstaːn] NT **-s** Uzbekistan

User ['juːze] M **-s, -, Userin** ['juːzərɪn] F **-, -nen** (*Comput*) user

usw. ABBR *von* **und so weiter** etc

Utensil [utenˈziːl] NT **-s, -ien** [-liən] utensil

Uterus ['uːterʊs] M **-, Uteri** [-ri] uterus

Utopia [uˈtoːpia] NT **-s, -s** Utopia

Utopie [utoˈpiː] F **-, -n** [-ˈpiːən] utopia; (= *Wunschtraum*) utopian dream

utopisch [uˈtoːpɪʃ] ADJ utopian; (= *von Utopia*) Utopian

utopistisch [utoˈpɪstɪʃ] ADJ (*pej*) utopian

u. U. ABBR *von* **unter Umständen**

UV [uːˈfau] ABBR *von* **ultraviolett**

UV- [uːˈfau] IN CPDS ultraviolet

u. v. a. (m.) ABBR *von* **und vieles andere (mehr)**

UV-Strahlen [uːˈfau-] PL ultraviolet rays *pl*

Ü-Wagen [yː-] M (*Rad, TV*) outside broadcast vehicle

Vv

V, v [fau] NT **-,** - V, v

V ABBR *von* **Volt, Volumen**

Vaduz [fa'dʊts, va'duːts] NT **-'** Vaduz

vag [vaːk] ADJ = **vage**

Vagabund [vaga'bʊnt] M **-en, -en** [-dn], **Vagabundin** [-'bʊndɪn] F **-, -nen** vagabond

vage ['vaːgə] **1** ADJ vague **2** ADV vaguely; *etw* ~ *andeuten* to give a vague indication of sth; **drück dich nicht so ~ aus!** don't be so vague!

Vagheit ['vaːkhait] F **-, -en** vagueness

Vagina [va'giːna] F **-, Vaginen** [-nən] vagina

vaginal [vagi'naːl] **1** ADJ vaginal **2** ADV vaginally; *ertasten* through the vaginal canal; ~ *untersucht werden* to have a vaginal examination

Vakuum ['vaːkuɔm] NT **-s, Vakuen** or **Vakua** [-kuən, -kua] (*lit, fig*) vacuum; *unter/im* ~ in a vacuum

Vakuum-, vakuum- IN CPDS vacuum; **Vakuumpumpe** F vacuum pump; **vakuumverpackt** [-fɛɛpakt] ADJ vacuum-packed; **vakuumversiegelt** [-fɛɛziːglt] ADJ vacuum-sealed

Valentinstag ['vaːlɛntiːns-] M (St) Valentine's Day

Valenz [va'lɛnts] F **-, -en** valency

Valoren [va'loːrən] PL (*Sw Fin*) securities *pl*

Valuta [va'luːta] F **-, Valuten** [-tn] **(a)** (= *Währung*) foreign currency **(b)** (*im Zahlungsverkehr*) value; (= *Datum*) value date

Valutakonto NT foreign currency account

Vamp [vɛmp] M **-s, -s** vamp

Vampir [vam'piːɐ] M **-s, -e** vampire

Van-Allen-Gürtel [vɛn'ɛlɪn-] M Van Allen belt

Vandale [van'daːlə] M **-n, -n**, **Vandalin** [-'daːlɪn] F **-, -nen** vandal; (*Hist*) Vandal

Vandalismus [vanda'lɪsmʊs] M **-**, NO PL vandalism

Vanille [va'nɪljə, va'nɪlə] F **-**, NO PL vanilla

Vanille-: Vanilleeis NT vanilla ice cream; **Vanillegeschmack** M vanilla flavour (*Brit*) or flavor (*US*); *mit* ~ vanilla-flavoured (*Brit*), vanilla-flavored (*US*); **Vanillesauce** F custard; **Vanillestange** F vanilla pod; **Vanillezucker** M vanilla sugar, **Vanillinzucker** [vanɪ'liːn-] M vanilla sugar

variabel [va'riaːbl] **1** ADJ variable **2** ADV ~ **verzinsliche Anleihen** loans at a variable interest rate

Variabilität [variabili'tɛːt] F **-**, NO PL variability

Variable [va'riaːblə] F DECL AS ADJ variable

Variante [va'riantə] F **-, -n** variant (*zu* on)

Variation [varia'tsioːn] F **-, -en** (*alle Bedeutungen*) variation; **~en zu einem Thema** variations on a theme

Varietee [varie'teː] NT **-s, -s, Varieté** NT **-s, -s (a)** variety (entertainment), vaudeville (*esp US*) **(b)** (= *Theater*) music hall (*Brit*), vaudeville theater (*US*)

variieren [vari'iːrən], *ptp* **variiert** VTI to vary

Vase ['vaːzə] F **-, -n** vase

Vasektomie [vazɛkto'miː] F **-, -n** [-'miːən] (*spec*) vasectomy

Vaselin [vaze'liːn] NT **-s**, NO PL, **Vaseline** [vaze'liːnə] F **-**, NO PL Vaseline®

Vater ['faːtɐ] M **-s, ⁼** ['fɛːtɐ] (*lit, fig*) father; (*Gott, bei Namen*) Father; (*von Zuchttieren*) sire; ~ **von zwei Kindern sein** to be the father of two children; ~ **unser** (*Rel*) Our Father; **wie der ~, so der Sohn** (*prov*) like father, like son (*prov*); **er ist ganz der ~** he's very like his father; ~ **Staat** (*hum*) the State

Väterchen ['fɛːtɐçən] NT **-s, -** DIM *von* **Vater** (= *Vater*) dad(dy) (*inf*); (= *alter Mann*) grandad (*inf*)

Vaterland NT native country; (*esp Deutschland*) Fatherland; **dem ~ dienen** to serve one's country

vaterländisch [-lɛndɪʃ] ADJ (= *national*) national; (= *patriotisch*) patriotic

Vaterlands-: Vaterlandsliebe F patriotism; **Vaterlandsverräter(in)** M(F) traitor to one's country

väterlich ['fɛːtɐlɪç] **1** ADJ (= *vom Vater*) paternal; (= *wie ein Vater auch*) fatherly **2** ADV like a father; **er klopfte ihm ~ auf die Schulter** he gave him a fatherly pat on the shoulder

väterlicherseits ADV on one's father's side; **meine Großeltern** ~ my paternal grandparents

Vater-: Vaterliebe F paternal love; ~ **ist unersetzbar** a father's love is irreplaceable; **Vatermord** M patricide; **Vatermörder** M (*hum*: *Kragen*) stand-up collar

Vaterschaft ['faːtɐʃaft] F **-, -en** fatherhood *no art*; (*esp Jur*) paternity; **gerichtliche Feststellung der ~** (*Jur*) affiliation

Vaterschafts-: Vaterschaftsklage F paternity suit; **Vaterschaftsnachweis** M proof of paternity

Vätersitte F tradition of one's forefathers

Vater-: Vatertag M Father's Day; **Vaterunser** ['faːtɐ'ʊnzɐ, faːtɐ'ʊnzɐ] NT **-s, -** Lord's Prayer

Vati ['faːti] M **-s, -s** (*inf*) dad(dy) (*inf*)

Vatikan [vati'kaːn] M **-s** Vatican

Vatikanstadt F, NO PL Vatican City

V-Ausschnitt ['fau-] M V-neck; **ein Pullover mit ~** a V-neck pullover

v. Chr. ABBR *von* **vor Christus** BC

VE ABBR *von* **Verrechnungseinheit**

Veganer [ve'gaːnɐ] M **-s, -**, **Veganerin** [-ərɪn] F **-, -nen** vegan

Vegetabile(r) [vegeta'biːlə] MF DECL AS ADJ vegetarian

Vegetarier [vege'taːriɐ] M **-s, -**, **Vegetarierin** [-iərɪn] F **-, -nen** vegetarian

vegetarisch [vege'taːrɪʃ] **1** ADJ vegetarian **2** ADV ~ **leben** to be a vegetarian; **sich ~ ernähren** to live on a vegetarian diet; ~ **kochen** to cook vegetarian meals

Vegetarismus [vegeta'rɪsmʊs] M **-**, NO PL vegetarianism

Vegetation [vegeta'tsioːn] F **-, -en** vegetation

vegetativ [vegeta'tiːf] **1** ADJ (= *pflanzlich*) vegetative; *Nervensystem* autonomic **2** ADV (*Bot*) vegetatively; ~ **bedingt** (*Med*) caused by the autonomic nervous system

vegetieren [vege'tiːrən], *ptp* **vegetiert** VI to vegetate; (= *kärglich leben*) to eke out a bare existence

Veilchen ['failçən] NT **-s, -** violet; (*inf*: = *blaues Auge*) black eye

veilchenblau ADJ violet

Vektor ['vɛktoːɐ] M **-s, Vektoren** [-'toːrən] vector

Velo ['veːlo] NT **-s, -s** (*Sw*) bike (*inf*); (*motorisiert*) moped

Velour [və'luːɐ, ve'luːɐ] NT **-s, -s** or **-e**, **Velours** [və'luːɐ, ve'luːɐ] NT **-, -** (*auch* **Veloursleder**) suede

Velours M **-, -** (*Tex*) velour(s)

Vene ['veːnə] F **-, -n** vein

Venedig [ve'neːdɪç] NT **-s** Venice

Venenentzündung F phlebitis

venezianisch [vene'tsiaːnɪʃ] ADJ Venetian

Venezolaner [venetso'laːnɐ] M **-s, -**, **Venezolanerin** [-ərɪn] F **-, -nen** Venezuelan

venezolanisch [venetso'laːnɪʃ] ADJ Venezuelan

Venezuela [vene'tsueːla] NT **-s** Venezuela

Ventil [vɛn'tiːl] NT **-s, -e** (*Tech, Mus*) valve; (*fig*) outlet

Ventilation [vɛntila'tsioːn] F **-, -en** ventilation; (*Anlage*) ventilation system

Ventilator [vɛnti'laːtoːɐ] M **-s, Ventilatoren** [-'toːrən] ventilator

verabreden [fɛɐ'apreːdn], *ptp* **verabredet** **1** VT to arrange; **es war eine verabredete Sache** it was arranged beforehand; **ein vorher verabredetes Zeichen** a prearranged signal; **zum verabredeten Zeitpunkt** at the agreed time; **am verabredeten Ort** at the agreed place; **wir haben verabredet, dass wir uns um 5 Uhr treffen** we have arranged to meet at 5 o'clock; **schon verabredet sein** to have something else on (*inf*); **mit jdm verabredet sein** to have arranged to meet sb; (*esp mit Freund/Freundin*) to have an appointment with sb; (*esp mit Freund/Freundin*) to have a date with sb
2 VR **sich mit jdm ~** to arrange to meet sb; (*geschäftlich, formell*) to arrange an appointment with sb; (*esp mit Freund/Freundin*) to make a date with sb; **sich miteinander ~** to arrange to meet; (*geschäftlich, formell*) to arrange an appointment; (*esp mit Freund/Freundin*) to make a date

Verabredung F **-, -en** (= *Vereinbarung*) arrangement; (= *Treffen*) engagement (*form*); (*geschäftlich, formell*) appointment; (*esp mit Freund/Freundin*) date; **ich habe eine ~** I'm meeting somebody

verabreichen [fɛɐ'apraiçn], *ptp* **verabreicht** VT *Tracht Prügel etc* to give; *Arznei, Droge auch* to administer (*form*) (*jdm* to sb); (= *verordnen*) to prescribe (*jdm* for sb)

verabscheuen [fɛɐ'apʃɔyən], *ptp* **verabscheut** VT to detest

verabscheuenswert ADJ detestable

verabschieden [fɛɐ'apʃiːdn], *ptp* **verabschiedet** **1** VT to say goodbye to; (= *Abschiedsfeier veranstalten für*) to hold a farewell ceremony for; (= *entlassen*) *Beamte, Truppen* to discharge; (*Pol*) *Haushaltsplan* to adopt; *Gesetz, Erklärung* to pass **2** VR **sich (von jdm) ~** to say goodbye (to sb); **sich von etw ~** (*fig*) to turn one's back on sth; **sich aus etw ~** (*fig*) to withdraw from sth

Verabschiedung F **-, -en** (*von Beamten etc*) discharge; (*Pol*) (*von Gesetz*) passing; (*von Haushaltsplan*) adoption

verachten *ptp* **verachtet** VT to despise; **nicht zu ~** (*inf*) not to be sneezed at (*inf*); **einen guten Whisky hat er nie verachtet** (*inf*) he never said no to a good drop of whisky

verachtenswert ADJ despicable

verächtlich [fɛɐ'lɛçtlɪç] **1** ADJ contemptuous; (= *verachtenswert*) despicable; **jdn/etw ~ machen** to run sb down/belittle sth **2** ADV contemptuously

Verachtung F, NO PL contempt (*von* for); **jdn mit ~ strafen** to treat sb with contempt

verallgemeinern [fɛɐʔalgə'mainɐn], *ptp* **verallgemeinert** VTI to generalize

Verallgemeinerung F **-, -en** generalization

veralten [fɛɐ'altn], *ptp* **veraltet** VI AUX SEIN to become obsolete; (*Ansichten, Methoden*) to become antiquated; (*Mode*) to go out of date

veraltet [fɛɐ'altət] ADJ obsolete; *Ansichten* antiquated; *Mode* out-of-date

Veranda [ve'randa] F **-, Veranden** [-dn] veranda

veränderbar ADJ changeable

veränderlich [fɛɐ'lɛndəlɪç] ADJ variable; *Wetter, Mensch* changeable

Veränderlichkeit F **-, -en** variability

verändern *ptp* **verändert** **1** VT to change **2** VR to change; (= *Stellung wechseln*) to change one's job; (= *Wohnung wechseln*) to move; **sich zu seinem Vorteil/Nachteil ~** (*im Aussehen*) to look better/worse; (*charakterlich*) to change for the better/worse; **verändert aussehen** to look different

Veränderung F change; **eine berufliche ~** a change of job

verängstigen *ptp* **verängstigt** VT (= *erschrecken*) to frighten; (= *einschüchtern*) to intimidate

veranlagen [fɛɐ'lanlaːgn], *ptp* **veranlagt** VT to assess (*mit* at)

veranlagt [fɛɐ'lanlaːkt] ADJ **melancholisch/tuberkulös ~ sein** to have a melancholy/tubercular disposition; **technisch/ mathematisch/praktisch ~ sein** to be technically/ mathematically/practically minded; **künstlerisch/ musikalisch ~ sein** to have an artistic/a musical bent; **zu or für etw ~ sein** to be cut out for sth; **er ist so ~, dass ...** it's his nature to ...

Veranlagung F **-, -en (a)** (*körperlich*) (*esp Med*) predisposition; (*charakterlich*) nature; (= *Hang*) tendency; (= *allgemeine Fähigkeiten*) natural abilities *pl*; (= *künstlerisches, praktisches etc Talent*) bent; **eine ~ zum Dickwerden haben** to have a tendency to put on weight **(b)** (*von Steuern*) assessment

veranlassen [fɛɐ'lanlasn], *ptp* **veranlasst** VT (a) **etw ~** (= *in die Wege leiten*) to arrange for sth; (= *befehlen*) to order sth; **ich werde das Nötige ~** I will see (to it) that the necessary steps are taken; **wir werden alles Weitere ~** we will take care of everything else

(b) AUCH VI (= *bewirken*) to give rise (*zu* to); **jdn zu etw ~** (*Ereignis etc*) to lead sb to sth; (*Mensch*) to cause sb to do sth; **das veranlasst zu der Annahme, dass ...** that leads one to assume that ...; **sich (dazu) veranlasst fühlen, etw zu tun** to feel compelled to do sth

Veranlassung F **-, -en** cause; **auf ~ von** *or* **+gen** at the instigation of; **keine ~ zu etw haben** to have no cause for sth; **~ zu etw geben** to give cause for sth

veranschaulichen [fɛɐ'lanʃaulɪçn], *ptp* **veranschaulicht** VT to illustrate (*+dat* to, *an +dat, mit* with)

Veranschaulichung F **-, -en** illustration

veranschlagen *ptp* **veranschlagt** VT to estimate (*auf +acc* at); **etw zu hoch ~** to overestimate sth; **etw zu niedrig ~** to underestimate sth

veranstalten [fɛɐ'lanʃtaltn], *ptp* **veranstaltet** VT to organize; *Wahlen* to hold; *Umfrage* to do; (*kommerziell*) *Wettkämpfe, Konzerte etc* to promote; *Party etc* to hold; (*inf*) *Szene* to make

Veranstalter [fɛɐ'lanʃtaltɐ] M **-s, -, Veranstalterin** [-ərɪn] F **-, -nen** organizer; (*Comm: von Wettkämpfen, Konzerten etc*) promoter

Veranstaltung [fɛɐ'lanʃtaltʊŋ] F **-, -en (a)** event (*von* organized by); (*feierlich, öffentlich*) function **(b)** NO PL (= *das Veranstalten*) organization

Veranstaltungs-: Veranstaltungskalender M calendar of events; **Veranstaltungsprogramm** NT programme (*Brit*) *or* program (*US*) of events

verantworten *ptp* **verantwortet** **1** VT to accept (the) responsibility for; *die Folgen auch, sein Tun* to answer for (*vor +dat* to); **wie könnte ich es denn ~, ...?** it would be most irresponsible of me ...; **ein weiterer Streik/eine solche Operation wäre nicht zu ~** another strike/such an operation would be irresponsible; **eine nicht zu ~de Fahrlässigkeit/ Schlamperei** inexcusable negligence/sloppiness **2** VR **sich für** *or* **wegen etw ~** to justify sth (*vor +dat* to); **für Missetaten etc** to answer for sth (*vor +dat* before)

verantwortlich [fɛɐ'lantvɔrtlɪç] ADJ responsible (*für* for); (= *haftbar*) liable; **jdm (gegenüber) ~ sein** to be responsible *or* answerable to sb; **jdn für etw ~ machen** to hold sb responsible for sth; **der ~e Leiter des Projekts** the person in charge of the project

Verantwortliche(r) [fɛɐ'lantvɔrtlɪçə] MF DECL AS ADJ person responsible; **die ~n** *pl* those responsible

Verantwortung [fɛɐ'lantvɔrtʊŋ] F **-, -en** responsibility (*für* for); **auf eigene ~** on one's own responsibility; **auf deine ~!** on your own head be it! (*Brit*), it's your ass! (*US inf*); **die ~ (für etw) tragen** to take responsibility (for sth); **jdn zur ~ ziehen** to call sb to account

Verantwortungs-: verantwortungsbewusst **1** ADJ responsible **2** ADV responsibly; **Verantwortungsbewusstsein** NT sense of responsibility; **verantwortungslos** **1** ADJ irresponsible **2** ADV irresponsibly; **verantwortungsvoll** **1** ADJ responsible **2** ADV responsibly

verarbeiten *ptp* **verarbeitet** VT to use (*zu etw* to make sth); (*Tech, Biol etc*) to process; *Gold etc* to work; (= *verbrauchen*) to consume; (= *verdauen*) to digest; (*fig*) to use (*zu* for); *Stoff* to treat; *Daten* to process; *Erlebnis etc* to assimilate; (= *bewältigen*) to overcome; **~de Industrie** processing industries *pl*; **etw geistig ~** to assimilate sth; **gut/schlecht verarbeitet** *Rock etc* well/badly finished

Verarbeitung [fɛɐ'larbaitʊŋ] F **-, -en (a)** use, using; (*Tech, Biol, Comput*) processing; (*von Ton, Gold*) working; (= *Verdauen*) digestion; (*fig*) (*von Stoff*) treating; (*von Erlebnis etc*) assimilation; (= *Bewältigung*) overcoming **(b)** (= *Aussehen*) finish; (= *Qualität*) workmanship *no indef art*

verärgern *ptp* **verärgert** VT **jdn ~** to annoy sb; (*stärker*) to anger sb

verärgert [fɛɐ'lɛrgɐt] **1** ADJ annoyed; (*stärker*) angry; **~ über jdn/etw** annoyed/angry with *or* at sb/about sth **2** ADV *reagieren* angrily

Verärgerung [fɛɐ'lɛrgərʊŋ] F **-, -en** annoyance; (*stärker*) anger

verarschen [fɛɐ'larʃn, -'laːɐʃn], *ptp* **verarscht** VT (*inf*) to take the piss out of (*Brit sl*), to make fun of; (= *für dumm verkaufen*) to mess around (*inf*)

verarzten [fɛɐ'laːɐtstn, -'laːrtstn], *ptp* **verarztet** VT (*inf*) to fix up (*inf*); (*mit Verband*) to patch up (*inf*)

verausgaben [fɛɐ'lausgaːbn], *ptp* **verausgabt** VR to overexert oneself; (*finanziell*) to overspend

veräußerlich ADJ (*form:* = *verkäuflich*) saleable

veräußern *ptp* **veräußert** VT (*form:* = *verkaufen*) to dispose of; *Rechte, Land* to alienate (*form*)

Verb [vɛrp] NT **-s, -en** [-bn] verb

verbal [vɛr'baːl] **1** ADJ verbal (*auch Gram*) **2** ADV verbally

Verband [fɛɐ'bant] M **-(e)s, ~e** [-'bɛndə] **(a)** (*Med*) dressing; (*mit Binden*) bandage **(b)** (= *Bund*) association

Verband(s)-: Verband(s)kasten M first-aid box; **Verband(s)material** NT dressing material; **Verband(s)päckchen** NT gauze bandage; **Verband(s)stoff** M dressing; **Verband(s)watte** F surgical cotton wool (*Brit*), absorbent cotton (*US*); **Verband(s)zeug** NT, *pl* **-zeuge** dressing material

verbannen *ptp* **verbannt** VT to banish (*auch fig*), to exile (*aus* from, *auf* to)

Verbannte(r) [fɛɐ̯ˈbantə] MF DECL AS ADJ exile

Verbannung [fɛɐ̯ˈbanʊŋ] F **-, -en** banishment *no art*; (= *das Verbannen*) banishment

verbarrikadieren *ptp* **verbarrikadiert** **1** VT to barricade **2** VR to barricade oneself in (*in etw* (*dat*) sth)

verbauen *ptp* **verbaut** VT (= *versperren*) to obstruct; **sich** (*dat*) **die Zukunft ~** to spoil one's prospects for the future; **jdm die Möglichkeit ~, etw zu tun** to ruin sb's chances of doing sth

verbeamten [fɛɐ̯ˈlamtn], *ptp* **verbeamtet** VT to give the status of civil servant to

verbeißen *ptp* **verbissen** IRREG **1** VT (*fig inf*) **sich** (*dat*) **etw ~** *Zorn etc* to stifle sth; *Bemerkung* to bite back sth; *Schmerz* to hide sth; **sich** (*dat*) **das Lachen ~** to keep a straight face **2** VR **sich in etw** (*acc*) **~** (*Hund*) to sink its teeth into sth; (*fig*) to become fixed on sth; *siehe auch* **verbissen**

verbergen *ptp* **verborgen** [fɛɐ̯ˈbɔrgn] IRREG **1** VT (+*dat*, *vor* +*dat* from) (*lit*, *fig*) to hide; **sein Gesicht in den Händen ~** to bury one's face in one's hands; **jdm etw ~** (= *verheimlichen*) to keep sth from sb **2** VR to hide (oneself); *siehe auch* **verborgen²**

verbessern *ptp* **verbessert** **1** VT (**a**) (= *besser machen*) to improve; *Leistung, Bestzeit, Rekord* to improve (up)on; *die Welt* to reform; **eine neue, verbesserte Auflage** a new revised edition (**b**) (= *korrigieren*) to correct **2** VR (**a**) to improve; (*beruflich, finanziell*) to better oneself (**b**) (= *sich korrigieren*) to correct oneself

Verbesserung F **-, -en** (**a**) improvement (*von* in); (*von Leistung, Bestzeit*) improvement (*von* on); (*von Buch*) revision; (= *berufliche, finanzielle ~*) betterment (**b**) (= *Berichtigung*) correction

verbeugen *ptp* **verbeugt** VR to bow (*vor* +*dat* to)

Verbeugung F bow; **eine ~ vor jdm machen** to (make a) bow to sb

verbeulen *ptp* **verbeult** VT to dent

verbiegen *ptp* **verbogen** IRREG **1** VT to bend (out of shape); (*fig*) *Idee, Wahrheit* to distort; *Mensch* to corrupt; **verbogen** bent; *Rückgrat* curved; (*fig*) twisted **2** VR to bend; (*Holz*) to warp; (*Metall*) to buckle

verbieten *ptp* **verboten** [fɛɐ̯ˈboːtn] VT IRREG to forbid; *Zeitung, Partei, Organisation etc* to ban; **jdm ~, etw zu tun** to forbid sb to do sth; **mein Taktgefühl/die Höflichkeit verbietet mir eine derartige Bemerkung** tact/politeness prevents me from making such a remark

verbilligen *ptp* **verbilligt** **1** VT to reduce the cost of; *Kosten, Preis* to reduce; **verbilligte Waren** reduced goods; **verbilligte Karten** tickets at reduced prices; **verbilligte Darlehen** reduced-rate loans; **etw verbilligt abgeben** to sell sth at a reduced price **2** VR to become cheaper

verbinden *ptp* **verbunden** [fɛɐ̯ˈbʊndn] IRREG **1** VT (**a**) (*Med*) to dress; (*mit Binden*) to bandage; **jdm die Augen ~** to blindfold sb; **mit verbundenen Augen** blindfold(ed)
(**b**) (= *verknüpfen, in Kontakt bringen*) (*lit, fig*) to connect; *Punkte* to join (up); (*emotional*) *Menschen* to join together
(**c**) (*Telec*) **jdn (mit jdm) ~** to put sb through (to sb); **ich verbinde!** I'll put you through; **(Sie sind hier leider) falsch verbunden!** (I'm sorry, you've got the) wrong number!; **mit wem bin ich verbunden?** who am I speaking to?
(**d**) (= *gleichzeitig haben or tun, anschließen*) to combine
(**e**) (= *assoziieren*) to associate
(**f**) (= *mit sich bringen*) **mit etw verbunden sein** to involve sth **2** VR (**a**) (= *zusammenkommen*) to combine (*auch Chem*) (*mit* with, *zu* to form), to join (together); (= *sich zusammentun*) to join forces
(**b**) (= *assoziiert werden*) to be associated; (= *hervorgerufen werden*) to be evoked (*mit* by)
3 VI (*emotional*) to form a bond

verbindlich [fɛɐ̯ˈbɪntlɪç] **1** ADJ (**a**) obliging; **~sten Dank!** (*form*) thank you kindly!
(**b**) (= *verpflichtend*) obligatory; *Regelung, Zusage* binding; (= *verlässlich*) *Auskunft* reliable
2 ADV (**a**) (= *bindend*) **etw ~ vereinbart haben** to have a binding agreement (regarding sth); **etw ~ reservieren** to make a confirmed reservation for sth; **etw ~ erklären** to

officially state sth; **~ zusagen** to accept definitely
(**b**) (= *freundlich*) **~ lächeln** to give a friendly smile; **etwas ~er auftreten** to act a little more friendly

Verbindlichkeit F **-, -en** (**a**) (= *Entgegenkommen*) obliging ways *pl*; (= *höfliche Redensart*) civility *usu pl* (**b**) NO PL (= *verpflichtender Charakter*) obligatory nature; (*von Regelung, Zusage*) binding nature; (= *Verlässlichkeit: von Auskunft*) reliability (**c**) **Verbindlichkeiten** PL (*Comm, Jur*) obligations *pl*; (*finanziell auch*) liabilities *pl*; **~en gegen jdn haben** to have (financial) commitments to sb

Verbindung F (**a**) connection; (= *Kontakt*) contact (*zu, mit* with); **in ~ mit** (= *zusammen mit*) in conjunction with; (= *im Zusammenhang mit*) in connection with; **jdn/etw mit etw in ~ bringen** to connect sb/sth with sth; (= *assoziieren*) to associate sb/sth with sth; **er/sein Name wurde mit dem Mord/ der Affäre in ~ gebracht** he/his name was mentioned in connection with the murder/the affair; **seine ~en spielen lassen** to use one's connections; **~ mit jdm aufnehmen** to contact sb; **mit jdm in ~ bleiben** to stay in touch with sb; **sich (mit jdm) in ~ setzen, (mit jdm) in ~ treten** to get in touch (with sb); **mit jdm in ~ stehen, mit jdm ~ haben** to be in touch or contact with sb; **mit etw in ~ stehen** to be connected with sth; **die ~ von Berlin nach Warschau** the connections *pl* from Berlin to Warsaw
(**b**) (*Telec: = Anschluss*) line; **telefonische ~** telephonic communication; **~ durch Funk** radio communication; **eine ~ (zu einem Ort) bekommen** to get through (to a place); **unsere ~ wurde unterbrochen** we were cut off; **eine ~ zwischen zwei Rechnern aufbauen** or **herstellen** (*Comput*) to connect two computers
(**c**) (= *Kombination*) combination
(**d**) (= *Vereinigung, Bündnis*) association; (*ehelich*) union; (*Univ*) society; (*für Männer auch*) ≈ fraternity (*US*); (*für Frauen auch*) ≈ sorority (*US*); **eine schlagende/nicht schlagende ~** (*Univ*) a duelling (*Brit*) or dueling (*US*)/nonduelling (*Brit*) or nondueling (*US*) fraternity
(**e**) (*Chem*) (= *Prozess*) combination; (= *Ergebnis*) compound (*aus* formed out of); **eine ~ mit etw eingehen** to form a compound with sth

Verbindungs- IN CPDS (*esp Tech, Archit*) connecting; **Verbindungsfrau** F, **Verbindungsmann** M, *pl* **-leute** or **-männer** intermediary; (= *Agent*) contact; **Verbindungsstraße** F connecting road

verbissen [fɛɐ̯ˈbɪsn] **1** ADJ *Arbeiter* determined; *Kampf* dogged; *Gesicht, Miene* determined; *Hartnäckigkeit* grim **2** ADV determinedly; *kämpfen* doggedly; **du solltest das nicht so ~ sehen** you shouldn't take things so seriously; *siehe auch* **verbeißen**

Verbissenheit F **-**, NO PL (*von Arbeiter, Kampf*) doggedness; (*von Gesicht, Miene*) determination

verbittern [fɛɐ̯ˈbɪtɐn], *ptp* **verbittert** **1** VT to embitter; **jdm das Leben ~** to make sb's life a misery **2** VI AUX SEIN to become embittered

verbittert [fɛɐ̯ˈbɪtɐt] **1** ADJ embittered **2** ADV bitterly; **sich ~ verhalten** to act embittered

verblassen [fɛɐ̯ˈblasn], *ptp* **verblasst** VI AUX SEIN (*lit, fig*) to fade; **alles andere verblasst daneben** (*fig*) everything else pales into insignificance beside it

Verbleib [fɛɐ̯ˈblaip] M **-(e)s** [-bəs], NO PL (*form*) whereabouts *pl*

verbleiben *ptp* **verblieben** [fɛɐ̯ˈbliːbn] VI IRREG AUX SEIN to remain; **etw verbleibt jdm** sb has sth left; **... verbleibe ich Ihr ...** (*form*) ... I remain, Yours sincerely (*Brit*) or Sincerely (yours) (*US*) ...; **wir sind so verblieben, dass wir ...** we agreed to ...

verbleichen [fɛɐ̯ˈblaiçn], *pret* **verblich** [fɛɐ̯ˈblɪç], *ptp* **verblichen** [fɛɐ̯ˈblɪçn] VI AUX SEIN (*lit, fig*) to fade

verbleit [fɛɐ̯ˈblait] ADJ *Benzin* leaded

verblenden *ptp* **verblendet** VT (**a**) (*fig*) to blind; **verblendet sein** to be blind (**b**) (*Archit*) to face

Verblendung F (**a**) (*fig*) blindness (**b**) (*Archit*) facing

verblich PRET *von* **verbleichen**

verblichen PTP *von* **verbleichen**

verblöden [fɛɐ̯ˈbløːdn], *ptp* **verblödet** VI AUX SEIN (*inf*) to become a zombi(e) (*inf*)

Verblödung F **-**, NO PL (*inf*) stupefaction; **diese Arbeit führt noch zu meiner völligen ~** this job will turn me into a zombi(e) (*inf*); **die dauernde Reklame führt noch zu unserer**

völligen ~ the long-term effect of advertising is to make us totally uncritical

verblüffen [fɛɐ̯'blʏfn], *ptp* **verblüfft** VT (= *erstaunen*) to stun; (= *verwirren*) to baffle; **sich durch** *or* **von etw** ~ **lassen** to be taken in by sth

verblüfft [fɛɐ̯'blʏft] **⓵** ADJ amazed; **~e Miene** astounded expression **⓶** ADV *aufsehen, schauen* perplexed; *sich umdrehen* in surprise; ~ **reagieren** to be amazed

Verblüffung F -, NO PL (= *Erstaunen*) amazement; (= *Verwirrung*) bafflement

verbluten *ptp* **verblutet** VI AUX SEIN to bleed to death

verbocken *ptp* **verbockt** VT (*inf*) (= *verpfuschen*) to botch (*inf*); (= *anstellen*) to get up to (*inf*)

verbohren *ptp* **verbohrt** VR (*inf*) **sich in etw** (*acc*) ~ to become obsessed with sth; (= *unbedingt wollen*) to become (dead) set on sth (*inf*)

verbohrt [fɛɐ̯'boːɐ̯t] ADJ *Haltung* stubborn; *Politiker auch, Meinung* inflexible

Verbohrtheit F -, NO PL inflexibility

verborgen[1] [fɛɐ̯'bɔrgn], *ptp* **verborgt** VT to lend out (*an* +*acc* to)

verborgen[2] ADJ hidden; **etw** ~ **halten** to hide sth; **sich** ~ **halten** to hide; **im Verborgenen leben** to live hidden away; **so manches große Talent blüht im Verborgenen** great talents flourish in obscurity; *siehe auch* **verbergen**

Verbot [fɛɐ̯'boːt] NT -(e)s, -e ban (+*gen* on); **er ging trotz meines ~s** he went even though I had forbidden him to do so; **trotz des ärztlichen ~es** against doctor's orders

verboten [fɛɐ̯'boːtn] ADJ forbidden; (*amtlich*) prohibited; (= *gesetzeswidrig*) *Handel* illegal; *Zeitung, Partei, Buch etc* banned; **jdm ist etw** ~ sb is forbidden to do sth; **Rauchen/ Parken** ~ no smoking/parking; **er sah** ~ **aus** (*inf*) he was a real sight (*inf*); *siehe auch* **verbieten**

verbotenerweise [fɛɐ̯'boːtnɐ'vaizə] ADV against orders; (= *gesetzeswidrig*) illegally; **er hat ~ geraucht** he smoked even though it was forbidden

Verbotsschild NT, *pl* **-schilder**, **Verbotstafel** F (*allgemein*) notice (prohibiting something); (*im Verkehr*) prohibition sign

Verbrauch [fɛɐ̯'braux] M -(e)s, NO PL consumption (*von, an* +*dat* of); (*von Geld*) expenditure; (*von Kräften*) drain (*von, an* +*dat* on); **im Winter ist der ~ an Kalorien/Energie höher** we use up more calories/energy in winter; **sparsam im ~** economical; **zum baldigen ~ bestimmt** to be used immediately

verbrauchen *ptp* **verbraucht** **⓵** VT (a) (= *aufbrauchen*) to use; *Energie, Strom etc* to consume; *Vorräte* to use up; **der Wagen verbraucht 10 Liter Benzin auf 100 km** the car does 10 kms to the litre (*Brit*) *or* liter (*US*), ≈ the car does 24 miles to the gallon (b) (= *abnützen*) *Kräfte* to exhaust; *Kleidung etc* to wear out; **verbrauchte Luft** stale air **⓶** VR to wear oneself out

Verbraucher [fɛɐ̯'brauxɐ] M -s, -, **Verbraucherin** [-ərɪn] F -, -nen consumer

Verbraucher- IN CPDS consumer; **Verbraucherberatung** F consumer advice centre (*Brit*) *or* center (*US*); **Verbrauchermarkt** M large supermarket; **Verbraucherschutz** M consumer protection; **Verbraucherverband** M consumer council; **Verbraucherzentrale** F consumer advice centre (*Brit*) *or* center (*US*)

Verbrauchsgüter PL consumer goods *pl*

verbrechen [fɛɐ̯'brɛçn], *ptp* **verbrochen** [fɛɐ̯'brɔχn] VT IRREG (a) *Straftat, Greueltat* to commit; **etwas** ~ to commit a crime (b) (*inf*: = *anstellen*) **etwas** ~ to be up to something (*inf*); **was habe ich denn jetzt schon wieder verbrochen?** what on earth have I done now? (c) (*hum inf*) *Gedicht, Kunstwerk, Übersetzung etc* to be the perpetrator of (*hum*)

Verbrechen [fɛɐ̯'brɛçn] NT -s, - (*lit, fig*) crime (*gegen, an* +*dat* against)

Verbrechensbekämpfung F combating crime *no art*

Verbrecher [fɛɐ̯'brɛçɐ] M -s, -, **Verbrecherin** [-ərɪn] F -, -nen criminal

verbrecherisch [fɛɐ̯'brɛçərɪʃ] **⓵** ADJ criminal; **in ~er Absicht** with criminal intent **⓶** ADV *verraten, im Stich lassen* vilely

Verbrecher-: **Verbrecherjagd** F chase after a/the criminal/ criminals; **Verbrecherkartei** F criminal records *pl*; **Verbrechertum** [fɛɐ̯'brɛçətuːm] NT -s, NO PL criminality

verbreiten [fɛɐ̯'braitn], *ptp* **verbreitet** **⓵** VT to spread; *Zeitung* to distribute; (= *ausstrahlen*) *Wärme* to radiate; *Licht* to shed; *Ruhe* to radiate; **eine (weit) verbreitete Ansicht** a widely held opinion **⓶** VR (a) (= *sich ausbreiten*) to spread (b) **sich über ein Thema** ~ to expound on a subject

verbreitern *ptp* **verbreitert** **⓵** VT to widen **⓶** VR to get wider

Verbreiterung F -, -en widening

Verbreitung [fɛɐ̯'braitʊŋ] F -, NO PL spreading; (*von Zeitung*) distribution

verbrennen *ptp* **verbrannt** [fɛɐ̯'brant] IRREG **⓵** VT (a) (*mit Feuer*) to burn; (= *einäschern*) *Tote* to cremate; **verbrannt** burned; **verbrannte Erde** (*fig*) scorched earth (b) (= *versengen*) to scorch; *Finger, Haut etc* to burn; *Haar* to singe; (= *verbrühen*) to scald; **sich** (*dat*) **die Zunge/den Mund** ~ (*lit*) to burn one's tongue/mouth; **sich** (*dat*) **den Mund** *or* **Schnabel** (*inf*) ~ (*fig*) to open one's big mouth **⓶** VR to burn oneself; (= *sich verbrühen*) to scald oneself **⓷** VI AUX SEIN to burn; (= *niederbrennen: Haus etc*) to burn down; (*durch Sonne, Hitze*) to be scorched; **das Fleisch ~ lassen** to burn the meat; **alles verbrannte, alles war verbrannt** everything was destroyed in the fire

Verbrennung [fɛɐ̯'brɛnʊŋ] F -, -en (a) NO PL (= *das Verbrennen*) burning; (*von Treibstoff*) combustion; (*von Leiche*) cremation (b) (= *Brandwunde*) burn; (= *Verbrühung*) scald; **starke/leichte ~en davontragen** to be badly/not seriously burned

Verbrennungs-: **Verbrennungsanlage** F incineration plant; **Verbrennungsmotor** M internal combustion engine; **Verbrennungsofen** M furnace; (*für Müll*) incinerator

verbringen *ptp* **verbracht** [fɛɐ̯'braxt] VT IRREG *Zeit etc* to spend

verbrüdern [fɛɐ̯'bryːdɐn], *ptp* **verbrüdert** VR to swear eternal friendship (*mit* to); (*politisch*) to ally oneself (*mit* to, with)

Verbrüderung F -, -en avowal of friendship; (*politisch*) alliance

verbrühen *ptp* **verbrüht** **⓵** VT to scald **⓶** VR to scald oneself

Verbrühung [fɛɐ̯'bryːʊŋ] F -, -en (*no pl*: = *das Verbrühen*) scalding; (= *Wunde*) scald

verbuchen *ptp* **verbucht** VT to enter (up) (in a/the book); **einen Betrag auf ein Konto** ~ to credit a sum to an account; **einen Erfolg (für sich)** ~ to notch up a success (*inf*); **etw für sich** *or* **auf sein Konto** ~ **können** (*fig*) to be able to credit oneself with sth

verbuddeln *ptp* **verbuddelt** VT (*inf*) to bury

Verbund M -(e)s, NO PL (*Econ*) combine; **im ~ arbeiten** to cooperate

verbünden [fɛɐ̯'bʏndn], *ptp* **verbündet** VR to ally oneself (*mit* to); (*Staaten*) to form an alliance; **alle haben sich gegen mich verbündet** everyone is against me; **verbündet sein** to be allies

Verbundenheit F -, NO PL (*von Völkern*) solidarity; (*von Menschen*) (*mit Menschen, Natur*) closeness (*mit* to); (*mit Land, Tradition*) attachment (*mit* to); **in tiefer ~, ...** very affectionately yours, ...

Verbündete(r) [fɛɐ̯'bʏndətə] MF DECL AS ADJ ally

Verbund-: **Verbundfahrausweis** M travel pass (*valid for all forms of public transport*); **Verbundglas** NT laminated glass; **Verbundstoff** M composite (*material*)

verbürgen *ptp* **verbürgt** **⓵** VR **sich für jdn/etw** ~ to vouch for sb/sth; **ich will mich nicht dafür ~, dass das stimmt** I cannot guarantee that this is correct **⓶** VT (a) (= *gewährleisten*) *Freiheit, Recht, Unterstützung* to guarantee; **ein verbürgtes Recht** an established right (b) (*Fin*: = *bürgen für*) *Kredit, Mietausfälle* to guarantee (c) (= *dokumentieren*) **eine verbürgte Nachricht** a confirmed report; **historisch verbürgt sein** to be historically documented; **dokumentarisch verbürgt sein** to be backed up by documentary evidence

verbüßen *ptp* **verbüßt** VT to serve

Verbüßung [fɛɐ̯'byːsʊŋ] F -, NO PL serving; **zur ~ einer Haftstrafe von zwei Jahren verurteilt werden** to be sentenced to serve two years in prison

verchromen [fɛɐ̯'kroːmən], *ptp* **verchromt** VT to chromium-plate

Verchromung F -, -en chromium-plating

Verdacht [fɛɐ̯'daxt] M -(e)s, -e *or* **~e** [-'dɛçtə] suspicion; (*hum*: = *Vermutung*) hunch; **jdn in** *or* **im ~ haben** to suspect sb; **im ~ stehen, etw getan zu haben** to be suspected of having done sth; **den ~ auf jdn lenken** to throw suspicion on sb; (*gegen jdn*) ~ **schöpfen** to become suspicious (of sb); ~ **erregen** to arouse suspicion; **es besteht ~ auf Krebs** (*acc*) cancer is suspected; **bei ~ auf Krebs** in the case of suspected cancer; **etw auf ~ tun** (*inf*) to do sth on spec (*inf*)

verdächtig [fɛɐˈdɛçtɪç] **1** ADJ suspicious; (= *~ aussehend*) suspicious-looking; **sich ~ machen** to arouse suspicion; **die drei ~en Personen** the three suspects; **einer Sache** (*gen*) **~ sein** to be suspected of sth **2** ADV suspiciously; *schnell* unbelievably; **~ aussehen** to look suspicious

verdächtigen [fɛɐˈdɛçtɪɡn], *ptp* **verdächtigt** VT to suspect (+*gen* of); **ich will niemanden ~, aber ...** I don't want to cast suspicion on anyone, but ...; **er wird verdächtigt, gestohlen zu haben, er wird des Diebstahls verdächtigt** he is suspected of theft

Verdächtige(r) [fɛɐˈdɛçtɪɡɐ] MF DECL AS ADJ suspect

verdammen [fɛɐˈdaman], *ptp* **verdammt** VT (*esp Rel*: = *verfluchen*) to damn; (= *verurteilen*) to condemn

verdammt [fɛɐˈdamt] (*inf*) **1** ADJ damned (*inf*); **~er Mist!** screw it! (*sl US sl*); **~e Scheiße!** (*sl*) shit! (*sl*) **2** ADV damn (*inf*); **das tut ~ weh** that hurts like hell (*inf*); **~ viel Geld** a hell of a lot of money (*inf*); **mir gehts ~ gut** I'm on top of the world (*inf*); **mir gehts ~ schlecht** I'm in a bad way **3** INTERJ **verdammt!** damn (it) (*inf*); **~ noch mal!** damn it all (*inf*); **du wirst dich ~ noch mal entschuldigen!** apologize, damn you! (*inf*)

verdampfen *ptp* **verdampft** VTI (*vi: aux sein*) to vaporize; (*Cook*) to boil away

verdanken *ptp* **verdankt** VT **jdm etw ~** to owe sth to sb; **es ist jdm/einer Sache zu ~(, dass ...)** it is thanks to sb/sth (that ...); **das verdanke ich dir** (*iro*) I've got you to thank for that

Verdankung [fɛɐˈdaŋkʊŋ] F **-,** NO PL (*Sw*) **unter ~ seiner Verdienste** grateful thanks for his contribution

verdarb PRET *von* **verderben**

verdattert [fɛɐˈdatɐt] ADJ, ADV (*inf*: = *verwirrt*) flabbergasted (*inf*)

verdauen [fɛɐˈdauan], *ptp* **verdaut** VT (*lit, fig*) to digest

verdaulich [fɛɐˈdauliç] ADJ (*lit, fig*) digestible; **leicht ~** easily digestible; **schwer ~** hard to digest

Verdauung [fɛɐˈdauʊŋ] F **-, -en** digestion

Verdauungs-: Verdauungsbeschwerden PL digestive trouble *sing*; **Verdauungsspaziergang** M constitutional; **Verdauungsstörung** F USU PL indigestion *no pl*

Verdeck [fɛɐˈdɛk] NT **-(e)s, -e** (a) (= *Dach*) (*von Kutsche, Kinderwagen*) hood (*Brit*), canopy; (*von Auto*) soft top; (*hart*) roof (b) (*von Passagierdampfer*) sun deck; (*von Doppeldeckerbus*) open top deck

verdecken *ptp* **verdeckt** VT to hide; (= *zudecken*) to cover (up); *Sicht* to block; (*fig*) to conceal; **eine Wolke verdeckte die Sonne** a cloud hid the sun

verdeckt [fɛɐˈdɛkt] **1** ADJ concealed; *Widerspruch* hidden; *Ermittler, Einsatz* undercover **2** ADV **~ agieren** to operate undercover; **~ ermitteln** to investigate undercover

verdenken *ptp* **verdacht** VT IRREG **jdm etw ~** to hold sth against sb; **ich kann es ihm nicht ~(, dass er es getan hat)** I can't blame him (for doing it)

verderben [fɛɐˈdɛrbn], *pret* **verdarb** [fɛɐˈdarp], *ptp* **verdorben** [fɛɐˈdɔrbn] **1** VT to spoil; (*stärker*) to ruin; *Luft* to pollute; *jdn* (*moralisch*) to corrupt; (= *verwöhnen*) to spoil; **jdm etw ~** *Abend, Urlaub* to spoil sth for sb; *Chancen, Leben, Witz* to ruin sth for sb; **jdm** (*dat*) **den Magen ~** to give oneself an upset stomach; **sich** (*dat*) **die Augen/Stimme/Lungen ~** to ruin one's eyes *or* eyesight/voice/lungs; **die Preise ~** (= *verbilligen*) to force prices down; (= *verteuern*) to force prices up; **jdm das Geschäft ~** to damage sb's business; **jds Laune ~, jdm die Laune ~** to put sb in a bad mood; **es (sich** *dat*) **mit jdm ~** to fall out with sb

2 VI AUX SEIN (*Material*) to become spoiled/ruined; (*Nahrungsmittel*) to go off (*Brit*) *or* bad; (*Ernte*) to be ruined; (*Mensch*) to become depraved; **da** *or* **daran ist nichts mehr zu ~** it *or* things couldn't get any worse; **an dem Kuchen/Hemd ist nichts mehr zu ~** the cake/shirt is absolutely ruined anyway; *siehe auch* **verdorben**

Verderben [fɛɐˈdɛrbn] NT **-s,** NO PL (= *Untergang, Unglück*) undoing; **in sein ~ rennen** to be heading for disaster; **jdn ins ~ stürzen** to bring ruin (up)on sb

verderblich [fɛɐˈdɛrplɪç] ADJ pernicious; *Einfluss auch* corrupting; *Lebensmittel* perishable

verdeutlichen [fɛɐˈdɔʏtlɪçn], *ptp* **verdeutlicht** VT to show clearly; (= *deutlicher machen*) to clarify; (= *erklären*) to

explain; **sich** (*dat*) **etw ~** to think sth out for oneself; **etw besser/näher ~** to clarify sth further

ver.di [ˈvɛrdi] F **-** ABBR *von* **Vereinigte Dienstleistungsgewerkschaft** service sector union

verdichten *ptp* **verdichtet** **1** VT (*Phys*) to compress; (*fig*: = *komprimieren*) to condense **2** VR to thicken; (*Schneetreiben*) to worsen; (*Gas*) to become compressed; (*fig*: = *häufen*) to increase; (*Verdacht, Eindruck*) to deepen; **die Handlung verdichtet sich** the plot thickens; **der Verdacht verdichtet sich, dass ...** the suspicion that ... is growing; **es ~ sich die Hinweise, dass ...** there is growing evidence that ...

verdienen *ptp* **verdient** **1** VT (a) (= *einnehmen*) to earn; (= *Gewinn machen*) to make; **sein Brot** *or* **seinen Unterhalt ~** to earn one's living; **er hat an dem Auto 500 Euro verdient** he made 500 euros on the car; **dabei ist nicht viel zu ~** there's not much money in that; **sich** (*dat*) **etw ~** to earn the money for sth; **sich** (*dat*) **das Studium ~** to pay for one's own studies (b) (*fig*) *Lob, Strafe* to deserve; **sich** (*dat*) **etw (redlich) verdient haben** to deserve sth; **er verdient es nicht anders/besser** he doesn't deserve anything else/any better; **eine Reform, die diesen Namen verdient** a reform which lives up to its name; *siehe auch* **verdient**

2 VI to earn; (= *Gewinn machen*) to make (a profit) (*an* +*dat* on); **in dieser Familie ~ drei Personen** there are three wage earners in this family; **er verdient gut/besser** he earns a lot/more; **er verdient schlecht** he doesn't earn much; **am Krieg ~** to profit from war

Verdiener [fɛɐˈdiːnɐ] M **-s,** -, **Verdienerin** [-ərɪn] F **-, -nen** wage earner; **der einzige ~** the sole breadwinner

Verdienst[1] [fɛɐˈdiːnst] M **-(e)s, -e** (= *Einkommen*) income; (= *Profit*) profit; **einen besseren ~ haben** to earn more

Verdienst[2] NT **-(e)s, -e (a)** (= *Anspruch auf Anerkennung*) merit; (= *Dank*) credit; **es ist sein ~/das ~ der Wissenschaftler(, dass ...)** it is thanks to him/the scientists (that ...); **nach ~** on merit; **sich** (*dat*) **etw als** *or* **zum ~ anrechnen** to take the credit for sth

(b) USU PL (= *Leistung*) contribution; (*national*) service; **ihre ~e um die Wissenschaft** *or* **als Wissenschaftlerin** her services to science; **seine ~e um das Vaterland/die Stadt** his services to his country/town; **er hat sich** (*dat*) **große ~e um das Vaterland erworben** he has rendered his country great service

Verdienst-: Verdienstausfall M loss of earnings; **Verdienstkreuz** NT highest decoration awarded for military or other service; **Verdienstmöglichkeit** F opportunity for earning money; **Verdienstorden** M order of merit; **verdienstvoll** ADJ commendable

verdient [fɛɐˈdiːnt] **1** ADJ (a) *Lohn, Strafe* rightful; *Ruhe, Lob* well-deserved (b) *Wissenschaftler, Künstler, Politiker, Sportler* of outstanding merit; **sich um etw ~ machen** to render outstanding services to sth **2** ADV *gewinnen, siegen* deservedly; *siehe auch* **verdienen**

verdientermaßen [fɛɐˈdiːntɐˈmaːsn], **verdienterweise** [fɛɐˈdiːntɐˈvaizə] ADV deservedly

Verdingung F **-, -en** (*Comm*) tendering

verdirbt [fɛɐˈdɪrpt] 3. PERS SING PRES *von* **verderben**

verdolmetschen *ptp* **verdolmetscht** VT to interpret

verdonnern *ptp* **verdonnert** VT (*inf*: *zu Haft etc*) to sentence (*zu* to); **jdn zu etw ~, jdn dazu ~, etw zu tun** to order sb to do sth as a punishment; **jdn zu einer Geldstrafe von ... ~** to fine sb ...

verdoppeln *ptp* **verdoppelt** **1** VT to double; (*fig*) *Anstrengung etc* to redouble **2** VR to double

Verdoppelung [fɛɐˈdɔpəlʊŋ] F **-, -en**, **Verdopplung** [fɛɐˈdɔplʊŋ] F **-, -en** doubling; (*von Anstrengung*) redoubling

verdorben [fɛɐˈdɔrbn] **1** PTP *von* **verderben** **2** ADJ **(a)** *Lebensmittel* bad; *Wasser, Luft* polluted; *Magen* upset **(b)** *Stimmung, Urlaub, Freude* spoiled **(c)** (*moralisch*) corrupt; (*sittlich*) depraved; (= *verzogen*) *Kind* spoiled

Verdorbenheit F **-,** NO PL depravity

verdorren *ptp* **verdorrt** VI AUX SEIN to wither

verdrängen *ptp* **verdrängt** VT *jdn* to drive out; (= *ersetzen*) to replace; (*Phys*) *Wasser, Luft* to displace; (*Met*) to drive; (*fig*) *Sorgen, Angst* to dispel; (*Psych*) to repress; **jdn aus dem Amt/von der Macht ~** to oust sb (from office/power); **das habe ich**

völlig verdrängt (*hum*: = *vergessen*) it completely slipped my mind (*inf*)

Verdrängung [fɛɐ̯'drɛŋʊŋ] F **-, -en** driving out; (= *Ersetzung*) replacing; (*Phys*) displacement; (*Met*) driving; (*von Sorgen*) dispelling; (*Psych*) repression

verdrecken [fɛɐ̯'drɛkn] *ptp* **verdreckt** VTI (*vi: aux sein*) (*inf*) to get dirty; **verdreckt** filthy (dirty)

verdrehen *ptp* **verdreht** VT to twist; (= *anders einstellen*) *Radio, Regler, Lampe* to adjust; (= *verknacksen*) to sprain; *Hals* to crick; *Augen* to roll; *jds Worte, Tatsachen* to distort

verdreht [fɛɐ̯'dreːt] ADJ (*inf*) crazy (*inf*); *Bericht* confused

verdreifachen [fɛɐ̯'draifaxn], *ptp* **verdreifacht** VTR to triple

verdreschen *ptp* **verdroschen** [fɛɐ̯'drɔʃn] VT IRREG (*inf*) to beat up; (*als Strafe*) to thrash

verdrießlich [fɛɐ̯'driːslɪç] ADJ morose; *Arbeit, Angelegenheit* irksome

verdrossen [fɛɐ̯'drɔsn] 🗗 ADJ (= *schlecht gelaunt*) morose; (= *unlustig*) *Mensch, Gesicht* unwilling 🗗 ADV (= *schlecht gelaunt*) morosely; (= *unlustig*) unwillingly

Verdrossenheit F **-, NO PL** (= *schlechte Laune*) moroseness; (= *Lustlosigkeit*) unwillingness; (*über Politik etc*) dissatisfaction (*über +acc* with); **mit ~ arbeiten** to work unwillingly

verdrücken *ptp* **verdrückt** 🗗 VT (*inf*) *Essen* to polish off (*inf*); **der kann was ~** he's got some appetite (*inf*) 🗗 VR (*inf*) to beat it (*inf*); **sich heimlich ~** to slip away (unnoticed)

Verdruss [fɛɐ̯'drɔs] M **-es, -e** frustration; **~ mit jdm haben** to get frustrated with sb; **zu jds ~** to sb's annoyance; **jdm ~ bereiten** to cause annoyance to sb

verduften *ptp* **verduftet** VI AUX SEIN (a) (= *seinen Duft verlieren*) to lose its smell; (*Parfüm*) to lose its scent; (*Tee, Kaffee*) to lose its aroma (b) (*inf: = verschwinden*) to beat it (*inf*)

verdummen [fɛɐ̯'dʊmən], *ptp* **verdummt** 🗗 VT *jdn ~* (= *für dumm verkaufen*) to make sb out to be stupid; (= *dumm machen*) to dull sb's mind 🗗 VI AUX SEIN to stultify

Verdummung F **-, -en (a)** (= *Verblödung*) dulling (of the mind) **(b)** (= *das Dummwerden*) stultification

verdunkeln *ptp* **verdunkelt** 🗗 VT to darken; (*im Krieg*) to black out; (*fig*) *Zusammenhänge, Motive etc* to obscure; *jds Glück* to cloud; **die Sonne ~** (*Mond*) to eclipse the sun; (*Wolken*) to obscure the sun 🗗 VR to darken

Verdunkelung [fɛɐ̯'dʊŋkəlʊŋ] F **-, -en (a)** (= *das Dunkelmachen*) darkening; (*von Bühne auch*) (*im Krieg*) blacking out; (*fig*) obscuring; (*von Glück*) clouding; **die ~ nicht einhalten** not to keep to the blackout **(b)** (*Jur*) suppression of evidence

Verdunkelungsgefahr F, NO PL (*Jur*) danger of suppression of evidence

Verdunklung [fɛɐ̯'dʊŋklʊŋ] F **-, -en** = **Verdunkelung**

verdünnen [fɛɐ̯'dʏnən], *ptp* **verdünnt** 🗗 VT to thin (down); (*mit Wasser*) to water down; *Lösung* to dilute; *Gas* to rarefy; **den Teig mit Wasser ~** to add water to the dough 🗗 VR (*Lösung*) to become diluted; (*Luft*) to become rarefied; (*Vegetation*) to become thinner; (= *schmaler werden*) to become thinner; (*Rohr*) to become narrower

Verdünner [fɛɐ̯'dʏnɐ] M **-s, -** thinner

Verdünnung F **-, -en (a)** thinning; (*von Lösung*) dilution; (*mit Wasser*) watering down; (*von Luft*) rarefaction (*form*); (= *Verengung*) narrowing **(b)** (= *Flüssigkeit zum Verdünnen*) thinner

verdunsten *ptp* **verdunstet** VI AUX SEIN to evaporate

Verdunster [fɛɐ̯'dʊnstɐ] M **-s, -** humidifier

Verdunstung [fɛɐ̯'dʊnstʊŋ] F **-, -en** evaporation

Verdunstungsröhrchen NT aromatherapy tube (*hung over radiator in order to allow contents to slowly evaporate*)

verdursten *ptp* **verdurstet** VI AUX SEIN to die of thirst

verdüstern [fɛɐ̯'dyːstɐn], *ptp* **verdüstert** VTR to darken

verdutzt [fɛɐ̯'dʊtst] ADJ, ADV (*inf*) taken aback; (= *verwirrt*) baffled

Verdutztheit F **-, NO PL** (*inf*) bafflement

veredeln [fɛɐ̯'leːdln], *ptp* **veredelt** VT *Metalle, Erdöl* to refine; *Fasern* to finish; (*Bot*) to graft; *Boden, Geschmack* to improve

Veredelung [fɛɐ̯'leːdəlʊŋ] F **-, -en, Veredlung** [fɛɐ̯'leːdlʊŋ] F **-, -en** (*von Metallen, Erdöl*) refining; (*von Fasern*) finishing; (*Bot*) grafting; (*von Boden, Geschmack*) improving

verehelicht [fɛɐ̯'leːəlɪçt] ADJ (*form*) married; **Eva Schmidt, ~e Meier** Eva Meier née Schmidt

Verehelichung [fɛɐ̯'leːəlɪçʊŋ] F **-, -en** (*form*) marriage

verehren *ptp* **verehrt** VT **(a)** (= *hoch achten*) to admire; *Gott, Maria, Heiligen* to honour; (= *ehrerbietig lieben*) to worship; *siehe auch* **verehrt (b)** (= *schenken*) **jdm etw ~** to give sb sth

Verehrer [fɛɐ̯'leːrɐ] M **-s, -, Verehrerin** [-ərɪn] F **-, -nen** admirer

verehrt [fɛɐ̯'leːɐt] ADJ (*in Anrede*) **(sehr) ~e Anwesende/Gäste/~es Publikum** Ladies and Gentlemen; **(sehr) ~e gnädige Frau** (*in Brief*) (dear) Madam; *siehe auch* **verehren**

vereidigen [fɛɐ̯'laidɪgn], *ptp* **vereidigt**, **vereiden** [fɛɐ̯'laidn], *ptp* **vereidet** (*dated*) VT to swear in; **jdn auf etw** (*acc*) ~ to make sb swear on sth; **vereidigter Übersetzer** *etc* sworn translator *etc*

Vereidigung F **-, -en** swearing in

Verein [fɛɐ̯'lain] M **-(e)s, -e** organization; (= *Sportverein*) club; (*inf*) crowd; **ein wohltätiger ~** a charity; **eingetragener ~** registered society *or* (*wohltätig*) charity

vereinbar ADJ compatible; *Aussagen* consistent; **nicht (miteinander) ~** incompatible; *Aussagen* inconsistent; **eine mit meinem Gewissen nicht ~e Tat** a deed which I cannot reconcile with my conscience

vereinbaren [fɛɐ̯'lainbaːrən], *ptp* **vereinbart** VT **(a)** (= *miteinander absprechen*) to agree; *Zeit, Treffen, Tag* to arrange; **(es) ~, dass ...** to agree/arrange that ... **(b) etw mit etw ~** to reconcile sth with sth; **Arbeit und Familie miteinander ~** to reconcile the demands of work and family; **sich mit etw ~ lassen** to be compatible with sth; **mit etw zu ~ sein** to be compatible with sth; (*Aussagen*) to be consistent with sth; (*Ziele, Ideale*) to be reconcilable with sth

Vereinbarung F **-, -en** (= *das Vereinbaren*) agreeing; (*von Zeit, Treffen, Tag*) arranging; (= *Abmachung*) agreement; **laut ~** as agreed; **nach ~** by arrangement

vereinbarungsgemäß ADV as agreed

vereinen [fɛɐ̯'lainən], *ptp* **vereint** 🗗 VT to unite; (= *miteinander vereinbaren*) *Ideen, Prinzipien* to reconcile; **eine Familie wieder ~** to reunite a family; **sich nicht mit etw ~ lassen** to be irreconcilable with sth; *siehe auch* **vereint** 🗗 VR to join together

vereinfachen [fɛɐ̯'lainfaxn], *ptp* **vereinfacht** VT to simplify; (*Math*) to reduce

vereinheitlichen [fɛɐ̯'lainhaitlɪçn], *ptp* **vereinheitlicht** VT to standardize

Vereinheitlichung F **-, -en** standardization

vereinigen *ptp* **vereinigt** 🗗 VT to unite; *Kräfte auch* to combine; *Eigenschaften* to bring together; (*Comm*) *Firmen* to merge (*zu* into); *Kapital* to pool; **etw mit etw ~** (= *vereinbaren*) to reconcile sth with sth; **Schönheit mit Intelligenz (in sich** *dat*) ~ to combine beauty with intelligence; **die beiden Standpunkte lassen sich nicht ~** the two points of view are incompatible; **alle Stimmen auf sich** (*acc*) ~ to collect all the votes 🗗 VR to unite; (*Firmen*) to merge; (= *zusammenkommen*) to combine; (*Töne*) to blend; (*Flüsse*) to meet; (*Zellen etc*) to fuse; (= *sich versammeln*) to assemble; **sich zu einem harmonischen Ganzen ~** to merge into a harmonious whole

vereinigt ADJ united; **Vereinigtes Königreich** United Kingdom; **Vereinigte Staaten** United States; **Vereinigte Arabische Emirate** United Arab Emirates

Vereinigung F **(a)** (= *das Vereinigen*) uniting; (*von Eigenschaften*) bringing together; (*von Firmen*) merging; (*von Kapital*) pooling; (*Math, geh: = körperliche, eheliche ~*) union; **die deutsche ~** (*Pol*) the unification of Germany **(b)** (= *Organisation*) organization

vereinsamen [fɛɐ̯'lainzaːmən], *ptp* **vereinsamt** VI AUX SEIN to become lonely *or* isolated; **vereinsamt sterben** to die lonely

Vereinsamung F **-, NO PL** loneliness

Vereins-: Vereinshaus NT clubhouse; **Vereinsmitglied** NT club member

vereint [fɛɐ̯'laint] 🗗 ADJ united; **Vereinte Nationen** United Nations *sing* 🗗 ADV together, in unison; **~ rufen** to shout in unison; **~ handeln** to act together; *siehe auch* **vereinen**

vereinzelt [fɛɐ̯'laintsl̩t] 🗗 ADJ occasional; (*Met auch*) isolated; *Schauer auch* scattered; **die Faulheit ~er Schüler** the laziness of the occasional pupil 🗗 ADV occasionally; **... ~ bewölkt ...** with cloudy patches

vereisen *ptp* **vereist** 🗗 VT (*Med*) to freeze 🗗 VI AUX SEIN to freeze; (*Straße*) to freeze over; (*Fensterscheibe*) to ice over

vereist [fɛɐˈlaist] ADJ *Straßen, Fenster* icy; *Bäche* frozen; *Türschloss, Tragfläche, Piste* iced-up; *Land* covered in ice

vereiteln [fɛɐˈlaitln], *ptp* **vereitelt** VT to foil

vereitern *ptp* **vereitert** VI AUX SEIN to go septic; **vereitert sein** to be septic; **vereiterter Zahn** abscess; **vereiterte Mandeln haben** to have tonsillitis

verenden *ptp* **verendet** VI AUX SEIN to perish

verengen [fɛɐˈlɛŋən], *ptp* **verengt** 🔢 VR to narrow; *(Gefäße, Pupille)* to contract; *(Kleid, Taille)* to go in; *(fig: Horizont)* to narrow 🔢 VT to make narrower; *Blutgefäß, Pupille etc* to make contract; *Kleid* to take in; *Horizont* to narrow

Verengung F -, **-en (a)** narrowing; *(von Pupille, Gefäß)* contraction **(b)** (= *verengte Stelle*) narrow part *(in +dat* of); *(in Adern)* stricture *(in +dat* of)

vererben *ptp* **vererbt** 🔢 VT **(a)** *Besitz* to leave, to bequeath *(+dat, an +acc* to); *(hum)* to hand on *(jdm* to sb) **(b)** *Anlagen, Eigenschaften* to pass on *(+dat, auf +acc* to); *Krankheit* to transmit 🔢 VR to be passed on/transmitted *(auf +acc* to)

vererblich [fɛɐˈlɛrplɪç] ADJ *Anlagen, Krankheit* hereditary

Vererbung [fɛɐˈlɛrbʊŋ] F -, NO PL **(a)** (= *das Vererben*) *(von Besitz)* bequeathing; *(von Anlagen)* passing on; *(von Krankheit)* transmission **(b)** *(Lehre)* heredity; **das ist ~** *(inf)* it's hereditary

Vererbungslehre F genetics *sing*

verewigen [fɛɐˈleːvɪgn], *ptp* **verewigt** 🔢 VT to immortalize; *Zustand, Verhältnisse* to perpetuate; **seine schmutzigen Finger auf der Buchseite ~** to leave one's dirty fingermarks on the page for posterity 🔢 VR *(lit, fig)* to immortalize oneself

Verf. ABBR *von* **Verfasser**

Verfahren [fɛɐˈfaːrən] NT -s, - (= *Vorgehen*) actions *pl*; (= *Verfahrensweise*) procedure; *(Tech)* process; (= *Methode*) method; *(Jur)* proceedings *pl*; **ein ~ gegen jdn anhängig machen** *or* **einleiten** to take *or* initiate legal proceedings against sb

verfahren[1] [fɛɐˈfaːrən], *ptp* **verfahren** VI IRREG AUX SEIN (= *vorgehen*) to act; **mit jdm/etw streng/schlecht ~** to deal strictly/badly with sb/sth

verfahren[2] *ptp* **verfahren** IRREG 🔢 VT (= *verbrauchen*) *Geld, Zeit* to spend in travelling *(Brit)* or traveling *(US)*; *Benzin* to use up 🔢 VR (= *sich verirren*) to lose one's way

verfahren[3] [fɛɐˈfaːrən] ADJ *Angelegenheit, Situation* muddled; **eine ~e Sache** a muddle

Verfahrens-: Verfahrenstechnik F process engineering; **Verfahrensweise** F procedure

Verfall M, NO PL **(a)** (= *Zerfall*) decay; *(von Gebäude)* dilapidation; *(gesundheitlich, geistig)* decline **(b)** *(von Kultur, der Sitten, sittlich)* decline; *(des Römischen Reichs)* fall **(c)** (= *das Ungültigwerden*) lapsing; *(von Scheck, Karte)* expiry

verfallen[1] *ptp* **verfallen** VI IRREG AUX SEIN **(a)** (= *zerfallen*) to decay; *(Bauwerk)* to fall into disrepair; *(Zellen)* to die; *(körperlich und geistig)* to deteriorate; *(Sitten, Kultur, Reich)* to decline; **der Patient verfällt zusehends** the patient has gone into a rapid decline **(b)** (= *ungültig werden*) *(Briefmarken, Geldscheine, Gutschein)* to become invalid; *(Scheck, Fahrkarte)* to expire; *(Strafe, Recht, Termin, Anspruch, Patent)* to lapse **(c)** (= *abhängig werden*) **jdm/einer Sache ~/~ sein** to become/ be a slave to sb/sth; *dem Alkohol etc* to become/be addicted to sth; *dem Wahnsinn* to fall/have fallen victim to; *jds Zauber etc* to become/be enslaved by sth; **jdm völlig ~ sein** to be completely under sb's spell; **einem Irrtum ~** to make a mistake **(d)** *auf etw (acc)* **~** to think of sth; *(aus Verzweiflung)* to resort to sth; **auf abstruse Gedanken ~** to start having abstruse thoughts; **wer ist denn bloß auf diesen Gedanken ~?** whoever thought this up? **(e)** *in etw (acc)* **~** to sink into sth; **in einen tiefen Schlaf ~** to fall into a deep sleep; **in einen Fehler ~** to make a mistake; **in Panik ~** to get into a panic

verfallen[2] [fɛɐˈfalən] ADJ *Gebäude* dilapidated; *Mensch (körperlich)* emaciated; *(geistig)* senile; (= *abgelaufen*) *Karten, Briefmarken* invalid; *Strafe* lapsed; *Scheck* expired

Verfalls-: Verfallsdatum NT expiry date; *(der Haltbarkeit)* best-before date; **Verfallserscheinung** F symptom of decline *(+gen* in)

verfälschen *ptp* **verfälscht** VT to distort; *Wahrheit, Aussage auch, Daten* to falsify; *Lebensmittel, Wein, Geschmack* to adulterate

verfänglich [fɛɐˈfɛŋlɪç] ADJ *Situation* awkward; *Aussage, Beweismaterial, Blicke, Andeutungen* incriminating; (= *gefährlich*) dangerous; *Angewohnheit* insidious; *Frage* tricky

verfärben *ptp* **verfärbt** 🔢 VT to discolour *(Brit)*, to discolor *(US)*; **etw rot ~** to turn sth red 🔢 VR to change colour *(Brit)* or color *(US)*; *(Blätter auch)* to turn; *(Metall, Wäsche, Stoff)* to discolour *(Brit)*, to discolor *(US)*; **sich grün/rot ~** to turn green/red

Verfärbung F change in colour *(Brit)* or color *(US)*; *(von Blättern auch)* turning; *(von Metall, Wäsche, Stoff)* discolouring *(Brit)*, discoloring *(US)*

verfassen *ptp* **verfasst** VT to write; *Gesetz, Urkunde* to draw up

Verfasser [fɛɐˈfasɐ] M -s, -, **Verfasserin** [-ərɪn] F -, **-nen** writer; *(von Buch, Artikel etc auch)* author

Verfassung F **(a)** *(Pol)* constitution; **gegen die ~ handeln** to act unconstitutionally **(b)** (= *Zustand*) state; *(seelisch)* state of mind; **sie ist in guter/schlechter ~** she is in good/bad shape; **sie ist nicht in der ~ zu arbeiten** she is in no shape to work; **die Firma/Wirtschaft ist in guter ~** the company/ economy is in good shape

Verfassungs-: Verfassungsänderung F constitutional amendment; **Verfassungsbeschwerde** F *complaint about infringement of the constitution*; **verfassungsfeindlich** ADJ anticonstitutional; **verfassungsmäßig** ADJ constitutional; **etw ~ garantieren** to guarantee sth in the constitution; **eine ~e Ordnung** a constitutional law; **Verfassungsschutz** M *(Aufgabe)* defence *(Brit)* or defense *(US)* of the constitution; *(Organ, Amt)* office responsible for defending the constitution; **verfassungswidrig** ADJ unconstitutional

verfaulen *ptp* **verfault** VI AUX SEIN to decay; *(Körper, organische Stoffe)* to decompose

verfault [fɛɐˈfault] ADJ decayed; *Fleisch, Obst etc* rotten; *Zähne* bad

verfechten *ptp* **verfochten** [fɛɐˈfɔxtn] VT IRREG to defend; *Lehre* to advocate; *Meinung* to maintain

Verfechter [fɛɐˈfɛçtɐ] M -s, -, **Verfechterin** [-ərɪn] F -, **-nen** advocate

verfehlen *ptp* **verfehlt** VT **(a)** (= *verpassen, nicht treffen*) to miss; **den Zweck ~** not to achieve its purpose; **das Thema ~** to be completely off the subject **(b)** (= *versäumen*) **nicht ~, etw zu tun** not to fail to do sth

verfehlt [fɛɐˈfeːlt] ADJ (= *unangebracht*) inappropriate; (= *misslungen*) unsuccessful; **es ist ~, das zu tun** you are mistaken in doing that

Verfehlung [fɛɐˈfeːlʊŋ] F -, **-en (a)** *(des Ziels)* missing; **bei ~ des Themas bekommt der Schüler ...** if the essay is off the subject the pupil will get ... **(b)** (= *Vergehen*) misdemeanour *(Brit)*, misdemeanor *(US)*; (= *Sünde*) transgression

verfeinern [fɛɐˈfainɐn], *ptp* **verfeinert** VTR to improve

verfeinert [fɛɐˈfainɐt] ADJ sophisticated

Verfeinerung F -, **-en** improvement; **die zunehmende ~ technischer Geräte** the increasing sophistication of technical equipment

verfestigen *ptp* **verfestigt** 🔢 VT to harden; *Flüssigkeit* to solidify; (= *verstärken*) to strengthen 🔢 VR to harden; *(Flüssigkeit)* to solidify; *(fig)* *(Hass, Feindschaft)* to harden; *(Kenntnisse)* to be reinforced; *(Ideen, Gewohnheiten)* to become fixed; *(Demokratie, Strukturen)* to be strengthened

Verfettung [fɛɐˈfɛtʊŋ] F -, **-en** *(Med)* *(von Körper)* obesity; *(von Organ, Muskeln)* fatty degeneration

verfilmen *ptp* **verfilmt** VT *Buch, Geschichte* to make a film of

Verfilmung [fɛɐˈfɪlmʊŋ] F -, **-en** (= *das Verfilmen*) filming; (= *Film*) film (version)

verfilzen *ptp* **verfilzt** VI AUX SEIN *(Wolle, Pullover, Teppich)* to become felted; *(Haare)* to become matted; *(fig: Pol etc)* to become corrupt

verfilzt [fɛɐˈfɪltst] ADJ felted; *Haare* matted

verfinstern [fɛɐˈfɪnstɐn], *ptp* **verfinstert** 🔢 VT to darken; *Sonne, Mond* to eclipse 🔢 VR *(lit, fig)* to darken

Verfinsterung F -, **-en** darkening; *(von Sonne etc)* eclipse

verflachen [fɛɐˈflaxn], *ptp* **verflacht** VI AUX SEIN to flatten out; *(fig: Diskussion, Gespräch, Mensch)* to become superficial

verflechten *ptp* **verflochten** [fɛɐ̯ˈflɔxtn̩] IRREG VT to interweave; *Bänder* to interlace; (*auch fig*) *Methoden* to combine; *Firmen* to interlink; **eng mit etw verflochten sein** (*fig*) to be closely connected with sth; **jdn in etw** (*acc*) ~ **in Gespräch, Unternehmen** to involve sb in sth

Verflechtung [fɛɐ̯ˈflɛçtʊŋ] F **-, -en** (= *das Verflochtensein*) interconnection (+*gen* between); (*Pol, Econ*) integration

verfliegen *ptp* **verflogen** [fɛɐ̯ˈfloːɡn̩] IRREG **1** VI AUX SEIN (*Stimmung, Zorn etc*) to blow over (*inf*), to pass; (*Heimweh, Kummer, Hoffnung etc*) to vanish; (*Alkohol*) to evaporate; (*Duft*) to fade (away); (*Zeit*) to fly **2** VR to stray; (*Pilot, Flugzeug*) to lose one's/its bearings

verflixt [fɛɐ̯ˈflɪkst] (*inf*) **1** ADJ blessed (*inf*), darned (*inf*), (= *kompliziert*) tricky; **du ~er Kerl!** you devil; **das ~e siebte Jahr** ≈ the seven-year itch **2** ADV darned (*inf*) **3** INTERJ **verflixt!** blow! (*Brit inf*), darn! (*US inf*)

verflossen [fɛɐ̯ˈflɔsn̩] ADJ **(a)** *Jahre, Tage* bygone; (= *letzte*) last **(b)** (*inf*: = *ehemalig*) one-time *attr* (*inf*); **ihr Verflossener** her ex (*inf*)

verfluchen *ptp* **verflucht** VT to curse; **sei verflucht** curses on you

verflucht [fɛɐ̯ˈfluːxt] ADJ (*inf*) damn (*inf*); **~ (noch mal)!** damn (it) (*inf*)

verflüchtigen [fɛɐ̯ˈflʏçtɪɡn̩], *ptp* **verflüchtigt** VR (*Alkohol, Kohlensäure etc*) to evaporate; (*Duft*) to disappear; (*Gase*) to volatilize; (*fig*) (*Bedenken, Ärger*) to be dispelled; (*hum*) (*Mensch, Gegenstand, Hoffnungen etc*) to vanish; (*Geld*) to go up in smoke (*inf*)

verflüssigen [fɛɐ̯ˈflʏsɪɡn̩], *ptp* **verflüssigt** VTR to liquefy

Verflüssigung F **-, -en** liquefaction

verfolgen *ptp* **verfolgt** VT *Ziel, Idee, Interessen, Karriere, Straftat* to pursue; (= *jds Spuren folgen*) *jdn* to trail; *Tier* to track; (*mit Hunden etc*) to hunt; *Unterricht, Entwicklung, Geschichte, Spur* to follow; *Vorschlag, Gedanken* to follow up; (*politisch, religiös*) to persecute; (*Gedanke, Erinnerung etc*) *jdn* to haunt; **vom Unglück/Schicksal** *etc* **verfolgt werden** *or* **sein** to be dogged by ill fortune/by fate *etc*; **jdn politisch** ~ to persecute sb for political reasons; **jdn gerichtlich** ~ to prosecute sb; **welche Absicht verfolgt er?** what is his intention?

Verfolger [fɛɐ̯ˈfɔlɡɐ] M **-s, -**, **Verfolgerin** [-ərɪn] F **-, -nen** **(a)** pursuer **(b)** (*politisch, wegen Gesinnung*) persecutor

Verfolgte(r) [fɛɐ̯ˈfɔlktə] MF DECL AS ADJ quarry; (*politisch, wegen Gesinnung*) victim of persecution

Verfolgung [fɛɐ̯ˈfɔlɡʊŋ] F **-, -en** (*von Ziel, Idee, Karriere, Verbrecher, Fahrzeug*) pursuit; (= *Spurensuche*) trailing; (*von Tier*) tracking; (= *politische* ~) persecution *no pl*; **die ~ aufnehmen** to take up the chase; **~ eines Ziels** pursuance of an aim

Verfolgungswahn M persecution mania

verfrachten [fɛɐ̯ˈfraxtn̩], *ptp* **verfrachtet** VT (*Comm*) to transport; (*Naut*) to ship; (*inf*) *jdn* to bundle off (*inf*); **etw in den Keller/eine Kiste** ~ (*inf*) to dump sth in the cellar/a crate

verfranzen [fɛɐ̯ˈfrantsn̩], *ptp* **verfranzt** VR (*inf*) to lose one's way; (*Aviat sl*) to lose one's bearings

verfremden [fɛɐ̯ˈfrɛmdn̩], *ptp* **verfremdet** VT *Thema, Stoff* to make unfamiliar; *Werkstoffe* to use in an unusual way

Verfremdung F **-, -en** defamiliarization; (*Theat, Liter*) alienation; **die ~ vertrauter Formen** using familiar forms in an unfamiliar way

Verfremdungseffekt M distancing effect; (*Theat, Liter*) alienation effect

verfressen [fɛɐ̯ˈfrɛsn̩] ADJ (*inf*) greedy

verfroren [fɛɐ̯ˈfroːrən] ADJ (*inf*) sensitive to cold; (= *durchgefroren*) frozen; **~ sein** (= *kälteempfindlich*) to feel the cold

verfrüht [fɛɐ̯ˈfryːt] ADJ (= *zu früh*) premature; (= *früh*) early; **solche Aufgaben sind für dieses Alter ~** exercises like this are too advanced for this age group

verfügbar ADJ available

Verfügbarkeit F availability

verfügen *ptp* **verfügt** **1** VI **über etw** (*acc*) ~ to have sth at one's disposal; (= *besitzen*) to have sth; **du kannst über mein Auto ~, wenn ich nicht da bin** you can use my car while I'm away; **du kannst doch nicht über meine Zeit ~** you can't tell me how to spend my time; **über etw** (*acc*) **frei ~ können** to be

able to do as one wants with sth; **~ Sie über mich** I am at your disposal **2** VT to order; (*gesetzlich*) to decree

Verfügung F **(a)** NO PL (= *das Verfügen*) possession; **jdm etw zur ~ stellen** to put sth at sb's disposal; (= *leihen*) to lend sb sth; **jdm zur ~ stehen, zu jds ~ stehen** to be at sb's disposal; (**jdm**) **zur ~ stehen** (= *verfügbar sein*) to be available (to sb); **sich zur ~ halten** to be available (to sb); **halte dich ab 7 Uhr zur ~** be ready from 7 o'clock; **etw zur ~ haben** to have sth at one's disposal
(b) (*behördlich*) order; (*von Gesetzgeber*) decree; (*testamentarisch*) provision; (= *Anweisung*) instruction

Verfügungsrahmen M (*Fin*) credit limit

verführen *ptp* **verführt** VT to tempt; (*esp sexuell*) to seduce; *die Jugend, das Volk etc* to lead astray; **jdn zu etw ~, jdn ~, etw zu tun** to encourage sb to do sth; **ich lasse mich gern ~** you can twist my arm (*inf*); **diese offenen Kisten ~ ja direkt zum Diebstahl** these open boxes are an invitation to steal

Verführer M seducer

Verführerin F seductress

verführerisch [fɛɐ̯ˈfyːrərɪʃ] **1** ADJ seductive; (= *verlockend*) tempting **2** ADV seductively; *duften, riechen, aussehen* seductive

Verführung F seduction; (*von Jugend, Volk*) tempting; (= *Verlockung*) enticement

Verführungskunst F seductive manner; (*von Werbung*) persuasiveness; **ein Meister der ~** a master of seduction/persuasion; **Verführungskünste** seductive/persuasive charms

verfünffachen [fɛɐ̯ˈfʏnffaxn̩], *ptp* **verfünffacht** **1** VT *Zahl* to multiply by five **2** VR to increase five times

verfüttern *ptp* **verfüttert** VT to use as animal/bird food; (= *aufbrauchen*) to feed (*an* +*acc* to); **etw an die Schweine/Vögel ~** to feed sth to the pigs/birds

Vergabe F **-,** (*rare*) **-n** (*von Arbeiten*) allocation; (*von Stipendium, Auftrag etc*) award

Vergabestelle F (*für Studienplätze*) central universities admissions council

vergammeln *ptp* **vergammelt** (*inf*) **1** VI AUX SEIN **(a)** (= *verderben*) to get spoiled; (*Speisen*) to go bad; **vergammeltes Obst** mouldy (*Brit*) *or* moldy (*US*) fruit **(b)** (= *verlottern*) to go to the dogs (*inf*); *Gebäude* to become run down; **vergammelt aussehen** to look scruffy; **eine vergammelte Kneipe** a seedy bar **2** VT to waste; **ich möchte mal wieder einen Tag ~** I'd like to have a day doing nothing

vergangen [fɛɐ̯ˈɡaŋən] ADJ **(a)** (= *letzte*) last **(b)** *Jahre* past; *Zeiten, Bräuche* bygone; *Größe* past; **das Vergangene** the past; **das ist alles ~ und vergessen** that is all in the past now; *siehe auch* **vergehen**

Vergangenheit F **-, -en** past; (*Gram*) past (tense); **die erste** *or* **einfache/zweite** *or* **vollendete/dritte ~** (*Gram*) the simple past/perfect/pluperfect (tense); **eine Frau mit ~** a woman with a past; **der ~ angehören** to be a thing of the past

Vergangenheitsbewältigung F process of coming to terms with the past

vergänglich [fɛɐ̯ˈɡɛŋlɪç] ADJ transitory

Vergänglichkeit F **-,** NO PL transitoriness

vergasen [fɛɐ̯ˈɡaːzn̩], *ptp* **vergast** VT (*Tech: in Motor*) to carburet; *Kohle* to gasify; (= *durch Gas töten*) to gas

Vergaser [fɛɐ̯ˈɡaːzɐ] M **-s, -** (*Aut*) carburettor (*Brit*), carburetor (*US*)

vergaß PRET *von* **vergessen**

Vergasung F **-, -en** (*Tech*) carburation; (*von Kohle*) gasification; (= *Tötung*) gassing; **etw bis zur ~ diskutieren** (*inf*) to discuss sth ad nauseam

vergeben *ptp* **vergeben** IRREG **1** VT **(a)** (= *weggeben*) *Auftrag, Stipendium, Preis* to award (*an* +*acc* to); *Plätze, Studienplätze, Stellen* to allocate; *Kredit* to give out; *Karten* to give away; *Arbeit* to assign; (*fig*) *Chance, Möglichkeit* to throw away; **zu ~ sein** to be available; **er/sie ist schon ~** (*inf*) he/she is already spoken for (*inf*); **der nächste Tanz ist schon ~** I've already promised the next dance
(b) (= *verzeihen*) to forgive; **jdm etw ~** to forgive sb (for) sth **(c)** **sich** (*dat*) **etwas/nichts ~** to lose/not to lose face; **was vergibst du dir, wenn du ein bisschen netter bist?** what have you got to lose by being a bit friendlier? **2** VR (*Cards*) to misdeal

vergebens [fɛɐ̯ˈɡeːbns] ADJ PRED, ADV in vain

vergeblich [fɛɐˈgeːplɪç] **1** ADJ futile; **alle Bitten/Versuche waren ~** all requests/attempts were in vain **2** ADV in vain

Vergeblichkeit F -, NO PL futility

Vergebung [fɛɐˈgeːbʊŋ] F -, -en forgiveness

vergehen ptp **vergangen** [fɛɐˈgaŋən] IRREG **1** VI AUX SEIN
(a) (= vorbeigehen) to pass; (Liebe, Leidenschaft) to die; (Schönheit, Glück) to fade; (Duft) to wear off; **wie doch die Zeit vergeht** how time flies; **mir ist die Lust/Laune dazu vergangen** I don't feel like it any more; **mir ist der Appetit vergangen** I have lost my appetite; **es werden noch Monate ~, ehe ...** it will be months before ...; **damit die Zeit vergeht** in order to pass the time; siehe auch **vergangen**
(b) vor etw (dat) ~ to be dying of sth; **vor Angst ~** to be scared to death; **vor Kälte ~** to be frozen; **vor Sehnsucht ~** to pine away
2 VR **sich an jdm ~** to do sb wrong; (unsittlich) to assault sb indecently

Vergehen [fɛɐˈgeːən] NT -s, - (= Verstoß) offence (Brit), offense (US); **~ im Amt** professional misconduct no pl; **das ist doch kein ~, oder?** that's not a crime, is it?

vergelten ptp **vergolten** [fɛɐˈgɔltn] VT IRREG to repay; **jdm etw ~** to repay sb for sth

Vergeltung F (= Rache) retaliation; **~ üben** to take revenge (an jdm on sb)

Vergeltungs-: Vergeltungsmaßnahme F reprisal, retaliatory measure; **Vergeltungsschlag** M act of reprisal

vergessen [fɛɐˈgɛsn], pret **vergaß** [fɛɐˈgaːs], ptp **vergessen** **1** VT to forget; (= liegen lassen) to leave (behind); **dass ich es nicht vergesse, ehe ich es vergesse** before I forget; **das werde ich dir nie ~** I will never forget that; **das kannst du (voll) ~!** (inf) forget it! **2** VI to forget; **auf jdn/etw ~** (Aus) to forget sb/sth **3** VR (Mensch) to forget oneself; **Zahlen ~ sich leicht** numbers are easy to forget

Vergessenheit F -, NO PL oblivion; **in ~ geraten, der ~ anheimfallen** (geh) to vanish into oblivion

vergesslich [fɛɐˈgɛslɪç] ADJ forgetful

Vergesslichkeit F -, NO PL forgetfulness

vergeuden [fɛɐˈgɔydn], ptp **vergeudet** VT to waste

Vergeudung F -, -en wasting; **diese ~!** what a waste!

vergewaltigen [fɛɐgəˈvaltɪgn], ptp **vergewaltigt** VT to rape; (fig) Sprache etc to murder

Vergewaltiger [fɛɐgəˈvaltɪgɐ] M -s, - rapist

Vergewaltigung F -, -en rape; (fig) (von Sprache) murder(ing)

vergewissern [fɛɐgəˈvɪsɐn], ptp **vergewissert** VR to make sure; **sich einer Sache** (gen) **or über etw** (acc) **~** to make sure of sth

vergießen ptp **vergossen** [fɛɐˈgɔsn] VT IRREG Kaffee, Wasser to spill; Blut auch, Tränen to shed; **ich habe bei der Arbeit viel Schweiß vergossen** I sweated blood over that job

vergiften ptp **vergiftet** **1** VT (lit, fig) to poison **2** VR to poison oneself (mit, durch, an +dat with)

Vergiftung F -, -en poisoning no pl; (der Luft) pollution; **an einer ~ sterben** to die of poisoning

vergiss [fɛɐˈgɪs] IMPER SING von **vergessen**

Vergissmeinnicht [fɛɐˈgɪsmaɪnnɪçt] NT -(e)s, -(e) forget-me-not

verglasen [fɛɐˈglaːzn], ptp **verglast** VT to glaze

Vergleich [fɛɐˈglaɪç] M -(e)s, -e **(a)** comparison; (Liter) simile; **im ~ zu** or **mit** in comparison with, compared with or to; **in keinem ~ zu etw stehen** to be out of all proportion to sth; (Leistungen) not to compare with sth; **dem ~ mit jdm/etw standhalten, den ~ mit jdm/etw aushalten** to stand comparison with sb/sth; **der ~ hinkt** the comparison is misleading
(b) (Jur) settlement; **einen gütlichen ~ schließen** to reach an amicable settlement; **einen außergerichtlichen ~ schließen** to settle out of court

vergleichbar ADJ comparable

vergleichen ptp **verglichen** [fɛɐˈglɪçn] IRREG **1** VT to compare; **etw mit etw ~** (prüfend) to compare sth with sth; (= einen Vergleich herstellen zwischen) to compare sth to sth; **verglichen mit** compared with; **vergleiche oben** compare above; **sie sind nicht (miteinander) zu ~** they cannot be compared (to one another)
2 VR **(a) sich mit jdm ~** to compare oneself with sb
(b) (Jur) to reach a settlement (mit with)

vergleichend ADJ comparative

Vergleichs-: Vergleichsform F (Gram) comparative form; **Vergleichsweg** M (Jur) **auf dem ~** by reaching a settlement; **vergleichsweise** ADV comparatively

verglühen ptp **verglüht** VI AUX SEIN (Feuer, Feuerwerk) to die away; (Draht) to burn out; (Raumkapsel, Meteor etc) to burn up

vergnügen [fɛɐˈgnyːgn], ptp **vergnügt** **1** VT to amuse **2** VR to enjoy oneself; **sich mit jdm/etw ~** to amuse oneself with sb/ sth; **sich mit Lesen/Tennis ~** to amuse oneself by reading/ playing tennis; **sich an etw** (dat) **~** to be amused by sth; siehe auch **vergnügt**

Vergnügen [fɛɐˈgnyːgn] NT -s, - (= Freude, Genuss) pleasure; (= Spaß) fun no indef art; (= Erheiterung) amusement; **das macht** or **bereitet mir ~** I enjoy it; **sich** (dat) **ein ~ aus etw machen** to get pleasure from (doing) sth; **für ihn ist es ein ~, nachts durch die menschenleeren Straßen zu wandern** he enjoys wandering around the empty streets at night; **ich laufe jeden Tag eine halbe Stunde nur zum ~** I run for half an hour each day just for pleasure; **das war ein teures ~** (inf) that was an expensive bit of fun; **mit ~** with pleasure; **mit größtem** or **dem größten ~** with the greatest of pleasure; **(na dann) viel ~!** (auch iro) enjoy yourself/yourselves!; **wir wünschen Ihnen bei der Show viel ~** we hope you enjoy the show; **mit wem habe ich das ~?** (form) with whom do I have the pleasure of speaking? (form); **es ist mir ein ~** it is a pleasure for me

vergnügt [fɛɐˈgnyːkt] **1** ADJ Abend, Stunden enjoyable; Mensch, Gesichter, Lachen, Stimmung cheerful; **über etw** (acc) **~ sein** to be pleased about sth **2** ADV happily; **~ aussehen** to look cheerful; **~ lachen** to laugh happily; siehe auch **vergnügen**

Vergnügung F -, -en pleasure; (= Veranstaltung) entertainment

Vergnügungs-: Vergnügungsfahrt F pleasure trip; **Vergnügungsindustrie** F entertainment industry; **Vergnügungspark** M amusement park; **vergnügungssüchtig** ADJ pleasure-loving

vergolden [fɛɐˈgɔldn], ptp **vergoldet** VT (= mit Gold bemalen) Nüsse etc to paint gold; (mit Blattgold) Statue, Buchkante to gild; (= mit Gold überziehen) Schmuck to gold-plate; (fig: = verschönern) Zeit, Alter, Erinnerung to enhance; **sich** (dat) **etw ~ lassen** (fig) to accept a financial inducement to do sth

vergoldet [fɛɐˈgɔldət] ADJ Nüsse gold-painted; Buchseiten gilt; Schmuck gold-plated; Kuppeln, Spitzen gilded; Natur, Stadt, Erinnerung etc golden

vergöttern [fɛɐˈgœtɐn], ptp **vergöttert** VT to idolize

vergraben ptp **vergraben** IRREG **1** VT to bury **2** VR (Maulwurf etc) to bury oneself; (fig: = zurückgezogen leben) to hide oneself (away); **sich hinter seinen Büchern ~** to bury oneself in one's books

vergrätzen [fɛɐˈgrɛtsn], ptp **vergrätzt** VT (inf) to vex

vergraulen ptp **vergrault** VT (inf) to put off; (= vertreiben) to scare off

vergreifen ptp **vergriffen** [fɛɐˈgrɪfn] VR IRREG
(a) (= danebengreifen) to make a mistake; (Sport: bei Gerät) to miss one's grip; **sich im Ton ~** (fig) to adopt the wrong tone; **sich im Ausdruck ~** (fig) to use the wrong expression; siehe auch **vergriffen**
(b) sich an etw (dat) **~** an fremdem Eigentum to misappropriate sth; (euph: = stehlen) to help oneself to sth (euph); **sich an jdm ~** (= angreifen) to lay hands on sb; (= missbrauchen) to assault sb (sexually)

vergreisen [fɛɐˈgraɪzn], ptp **vergreist** VI AUX SEIN (Bevölkerung) to age; (Mensch) to become senile; **Deutschland vergreist immer mehr** the German population is getting older and older; **vergreist** aged; senile

Vergreisung F -, NO PL (von Bevölkerung) ageing; (von Organismen) senescence; (von Mensch) senility

vergriffen [fɛɐˈgrɪfn] ADJ unavailable; Buch out of print; siehe auch **vergreifen**

vergrößern [fɛɐˈgrøːsɐn], ptp **vergrößert** **1** VT (räumlich) Raum, Gebäude, Fläche, Gebiet to extend; Abstand auch, Vorsprung, Produktion to increase; (größenmäßig) Maßstab, Wissen, Foto, Bekanntenkreis to enlarge; Firma, Absatzmarkt to expand; (Lupe, Brille) to magnify
2 VR to increase; (räumlich) to be extended; (Bekanntenkreis) to be enlarged; (Firma, Absatzmarkt) to expand; (Pupille, Gefäße) to dilate; (Organ) to become enlarged; **wir wollen uns**

~ (*inf*) we want to move to a bigger place
8 VI (*Lupe, Brille*) to magnify

Vergrößerung F -, -en (a) (*räumlich*) extension; (*von Abstand*) (*umfangmäßig, zahlenmäßig*) increase; (*von Maßstab, Wissen, Fotografie, Bekanntenkreis*) enlargement; (*von Firma, Absatzmarkt*) expansion; (*mit Lupe, Brille*) magnification; **in 1.000-facher ~** magnified 1,000 times (b) (*von Pupille, Gefäß*) dilation; (*von Organ*) enlargement (c) (= *vergrößertes Bild*) enlargement

vergünstigt [fɛɐˈɡʏnstɪçt] **8** ADJ *Lage* improved; *Preis* reduced **2** ADV **etw ~ kaufen** to buy sth at a reduced price

Vergünstigung F -, -en (= *Vorteil*) privilege; (= *Preisermäßigung*) reduction; **besondere ~en für Rentner** special rates for pensioners

vergüten [fɛɐˈɡyːtn], *ptp* **vergütet** VT **jdm etw ~** *Unkosten* to reimburse sb for sth; *Preis* to refund sb sth; *Schaden* to compensate sb for sth; *Arbeit, Leistung* to pay sb for sth

Vergütung F -, -en (*von Unkosten*) reimbursement; (*von Preis*) refunding; (*für Verlust, Schaden*) compensation; (*für Arbeit, Leistung*) payment

verh. ABBR *von* **verheiratet**

verhaften *ptp* **verhaftet** VT to arrest; **Sie sind verhaftet!** you are under arrest!

Verhaftete(r) [fɛɐˈhaftətə] MF DECL AS ADJ **der ~ wurde abgeführt** the arrested man was taken away; **die zehn ~n** the ten people under arrest

Verhaftung F arrest

verhageln *ptp* **verhagelt** VI AUX SEIN to be damaged by hail

Verhalten [fɛɐˈhaltn] NT -s, NO PL (= *Benehmen*) behaviour (*Brit*), behavior (*US*); (= *Vorgehen*) conduct; (*Chem*) reaction; **falsches Parken ist rechtswidriges ~** unauthorized parking is an offence (*Brit*) *or* offense (*US*); **faires ~** fair conduct

verhalten¹ *ptp* **verhalten** IRREG **8** VR (a) (= *sich benehmen*: *Mensch, Maschine, Preise etc*) to behave; (= *handeln*) to act; **wie ~ Sie sich dazu?** what is your attitude to that?; **sich ruhig ~** to keep quiet; (= *sich nicht bewegen*) to keep still; **sich rechtswidrig ~** to commit an offence (*Brit*) *or* offense (*US*) (b) (*Sachen, Marktlage*) to be; (*Chem*) to react; **wie verhält sich die Sache?** how do things stand?; **2 verhält sich zu 4 wie 1 zu 2** 2 is to 4 as 1 is to 2 **2** VR IMPERS **wie verhält es sich damit?** (= *wie ist die Lage?*) how do things stand?; (= *wie wird das gehandhabt?*) how do you go about it?; **anders/ähnlich verhält es sich mit** *or* **bei ...** the situation is different/the same with regard to ...; **mit den anderen verhält es sich genauso** (= *die anderen denken auch so*) the others feel exactly the same; **wenn sich das so verhält, ...** if that is the case ...

verhalten² [fɛɐˈhaltn] **8** ADJ restrained; *Stimme* muted; *Atem* bated; *Wut* suppressed; *Interesse, Optimismus* guarded; *Tempo, Schritte, Rhythmus* measured **2** ADV *sprechen* in a restrained manner; *kritisieren, sich äußern, lachen, weinen* with restraint; *laufen* at a measured pace

Verhaltens-: **verhaltensauffällig** ADJ (*Psych*) displaying behavioural (*Brit*) *or* behavioral (*US*) problems; **Verhaltensforscher(in)** M(F) behavioural (*Brit*) *or* behavioral (*US*) scientist; **Verhaltensforschung** F behavioural (*Brit*) *or* behavioral (*US*) research; **verhaltensgestört** ADJ disturbed; **Verhaltensstörung** F behavioural (*Brit*) *or* behavioral (*US*) disturbance; **Verhaltensweise** F behaviour (*Brit*), behavior (*US*)

Verhältnis [fɛɐˈhɛltnɪs] NT -ses, -se (a) (= *Proportion*) proportion; (*Math*: = *Mischungsverhältnis*) ratio; **im ~ zu** in relation to; **im ~ zu früher** (= *verglichen mit*) in comparison with earlier times; **im ~ 2 zu 4** in the ratio of 2 to 4; **in keinem ~ zu etw stehen** to be out of all proportion to sth (b) (= *Beziehung*) relationship (*mit jdm/etw* with sb/to sth); (*zwischen Ländern, innerhalb einer Gruppe*) relations *pl* (*zu* with); (= *Einstellung*) attitude (*zu* to); **ein freundschaftliches ~ zu jdm haben, mit jdm in freundschaftlichem ~ stehen** to be on friendly terms with sb; **sie hat ein gestörtes ~ zur Wirklichkeit** her grasp on reality is distorted (c) (= *Liebesverhältnis*) affair (d) **Verhältnisse** PL (= *Umstände, Bedingungen*) conditions *pl*; (*finanzielle*) circumstances *pl*; **unter** *or* **bei normalen ~sen** under normal circumstances; **so wie die ~se liegen ...** as things stand ...; **die akustischen ~se** the acoustics *pl*; **über seine ~se leben** to live beyond one's means; **ich bin für klare**

~se I want to know how we stand; **für klare ~se sorgen, klare ~se schaffen** to get things straight

Verhältnis-: **verhältnismäßig** **8** ADJ (a) (= *proportional*) proportional; (*esp Jur*: = *angemessen*) commensurate (b) (= *relativ*) comparative; (*inf*: = *ziemlich*) reasonable **2** ADV (a) (= *proportional*) proportionally (b) (= *relativ, inf*: = *ziemlich*) relatively; **Verhältniswahl** F proportional representation *no art*; **eine ~ abhalten** to hold a proportional election; **Verhältniswahlrecht** NT (system of) proportional representation

verhandeln *ptp* **verhandelt** **8** VT (a) (= *aushandeln*) to negotiate (b) (*Jur*) *Fall* to hear **2** VI (a) (= *Verhandlungen führen*) to negotiate (*über* +*acc* about); (*inf*: = *diskutieren*) to argue; **da gibts doch nichts zu ~** (*inf*) there's nothing to argue about; **über den Preis lässt sich ~** (*inf*) we can discuss the price (b) (*Jur*) to hear a/the case; **gegen jdn ~** to hear sb's case; **in einem Fall ~** to hear a case

Verhandlung F (a) negotiations *pl*; (= *das Verhandeln*) negotiation; **mit jdm in ~(en) stehen** to be negotiating with sb; **(mit jdm) in ~(en) treten** to enter into negotiations (with sb); **~en führen** to negotiate; **ich lasse mich auf keine ~(en) ein** (*inf*) I don't propose to enter into any long debates (b) (*Jur*) hearing; (= *Strafverhandlung*) trial

Verhandlungs-: **Verhandlungsbasis** F basis for negotiation(s); **~ EUR 2.500** (price) EUR 2,500 or near(est) offer; **verhandlungsfähig** ADJ (*Jur*) able to stand trial; **Verhandlungsführer(in)** M(F) chief negotiator; **Verhandlungstisch** M negotiating table; **verhandlungsunfähig** ADJ (*Jur*) unable to stand trial

verhängen *ptp* **verhängt** VT (a) *Embargo, Strafe, Hausarrest etc* to impose (*über* +*acc* on); *Ausnahmezustand, Notstand* to declare (*über* +*acc* in); (*Sport*) *Elfmeter etc* to award (b) (= *zuhängen*) to cover (*mit* with); *Kruzifix, Statue* to veil

Verhängnis [fɛɐˈhɛŋnɪs] NT -ses, -se (= *schlimmes Schicksal*) undoing; (= *Katastrophe*) disaster; **jdm zum ~ werden, jds ~ werden** to be sb's undoing

verhängnisvoll ADJ disastrous; *Irrtum, Fehler auch, Zögern, Entschlusslosigkeit* fatal; *Tag* fateful

verharmlosen [fɛɐˈharmloːzn], *ptp* **verharmlost** VT to play down

verharren *ptp* **verharrt** VI AUX HABEN *or* SEIN to pause; (*in einer bestimmten Stellung*) to remain; **auf einem Standpunkt/in** *or* **bei einem Entschluss ~** to adhere to a viewpoint/to a decision

verhärten *ptp* **verhärtet** VTR to harden

verhasst [fɛɐˈhast] ADJ hated; *Arbeit auch, Pflicht* hateful; **sich ~ machen** to make oneself hated (*bei* by); **das ist ihm ~** he hates that

verhätscheln *ptp* **verhätschelt** VT to pamper

Verhau [fɛɐˈhau] M -(e)s, -e (*zur Absperrung*) barrier; (= *Käfig*) coop; (= *Bretterbude etc*) shack; (*inf*: = *Unordnung*) mess

verhauen *pret* **verhaute**, *ptp* **verhauen** (*inf*) **8** VT (a) (= *verprügeln*) to beat up; (*zur Strafe*) to beat (b) *Klassenarbeit, Prüfung etc* to make a mess of (*inf*) **2** VR (a) (= *sich verprügeln*) to have a fight (b) (= *Fehler machen*) to make a mistake; (= *sich irren*) to slip up (*inf*)

verheddern [fɛɐˈheːdɐn], *ptp* **verheddert** VR (*inf*) to get tangled up; (*beim Sprechen*) to get in a muddle

verheeren [fɛɐˈheːrən], *ptp* **verheert** VT to devastate

verheerend **8** ADJ (a) *Sturm, Folgen, Niederlage, Katastrophe* devastating; *Anblick* ghastly (b) (*inf*: = *schrecklich*) ghastly (*inf*) **2** ADV (*inf*: = *schrecklich*) frightfully (*inf*)

Verheerung F -, -en devastation *no pl*

verhehlen [fɛɐˈheːlən], *ptp* **verhehlt** VT to conceal; **jdm etw ~** to conceal sth from sb; **ich möchte Ihnen nicht ~, dass ...** I have no wish to conceal the fact that ...

verheilen *ptp* **verheilt** VI AUX SEIN to heal

verheimlichen [fɛɐˈhaimlɪçn], *ptp* **verheimlicht** VT to keep secret (*jdm* from sb); **es lässt sich nicht ~, dass ...** it is impossible to conceal the fact that ...; **ich habe nichts zu ~** I have nothing to hide

verheiraten *ptp* **verheiratet** **8** VT to marry (*mit, an* +*acc* to) **2** VR to get married; **sich mit jdm ~** to marry sb, to get married to sb

verheiratet [fɛɐ̯'haɪratət] ADJ married; **glücklich ~ sein** to be happily married; **mit jdm/etw ~ sein** (hum inf) to be married to sb/sth

verheizen ptp **verheizt** VT to burn, to use as fuel; (fig inf) Sportler to burn out; Minister, Untergebene to crucify; **Soldaten im Kriege ~** (inf) to send soldiers to the slaughter

verhelfen ptp **verholfen** [fɛɐ̯'hɔlfn̩] VI IRREG **jdm zu etw ~** to help sb to get sth; **jdm zu seinem Glück ~** to help to make sb happy; **jdm zum Sieg ~** to help sb to victory

verherrlichen [fɛɐ̯'hɛrlɪçn̩], ptp **verherrlicht** VT Gewalt, Krieg, Taten, Regime, jdn to glorify; Gott to praise; Tugenden to extol; (in Gedichten) to celebrate

verheult [fɛɐ̯'hɔʏlt] ADJ Augen, Gesicht puffy, swollen from crying; **du siehst so ~ aus** you really look as if you have been crying

verhexen ptp **verhext** VT to bewitch; (inf) Maschine etc to put a jinx on (inf); **jdn in etw** (acc) **~** to turn sb into sth (by magic); **der verhexte Prinz** the enchanted prince; **das verhexte Schloss** the bewitched castle; **heute ist alles wie verhext** (inf) there's a jinx on everything today (inf); **das ist doch wie verhext** (inf) it's maddening (inf)

verhindern ptp **verhindert** VT to prevent; Versuch, Plan to foil; **ich konnte es nicht ~, dass er die Wahrheit erfuhr** I couldn't prevent him from finding out the truth; **das lässt sich nicht ~** it can't be helped; **er war an diesem Abend** (dienstlich or geschäftlich) **verhindert** he was unable to come that evening (for reasons of work); **ein verhinderter Politiker** (inf) a would-be politician

Verhinderung F prevention; (von Versuch, Plan) foiling, stopping; **im Falle seiner ~** if he is unable to come

verhökern ptp **verhökert** VT (inf) to get rid of (inf)

Verhör [fɛɐ̯'høːɐ̯] NT -(e)s, -e questioning; (bei Gericht) examination

verhören ptp **verhört** **1** VT to question, to interrogate; (bei Gericht) to examine; (inf) to quiz (inf) **2** VR to mishear

verhüllen ptp **verhüllt** **1** VT to veil; Haupt, Körperteil, Gebäude to cover; (fig) to mask **2** VR (Frau) to veil oneself; (Berge etc) to become veiled

verhundertfachen [fɛɐ̯'hʊndɐtfaxn̩], ptp **verhundertfacht** VTR to increase a hundredfold

verhungern ptp **verhungert** VI AUX SEIN to starve, to die of starvation; (inf: = Hunger haben) to be starving (inf); **er sah völlig verhungert aus** he looked half-starved (inf); (inf) he looked absolutely famished (inf); **ich bin am Verhungern** (inf) I'm starving (inf)

verhunzen [fɛɐ̯'hʊntsn̩], ptp **verhunzt** VT (inf) to ruin

verhüten ptp **verhütet** **1** VT to prevent; **das verhüte Gott!** God forbid!; **möge Gott ~, dass ...** God forbid that ...; **~de Maßnahmen** preventive measures; (zur Empfängnisverhütung) precautions **2** VI (= Empfängnisverhütung betreiben) to take precautions

Verhüterli [fɛɐ̯'hyːtəli] NT -(s), - (Sw: = Verhütungsmittel) contraceptive; (hum inf: = Kondom) rubber (esp US inf)

Verhütung [fɛɐ̯'hyːtʊŋ] F -, -en prevention; (= Empfängnisverhütung) contraception

Verhütungsmittel NT contraceptive

verinnerlichen [fɛɐ̯'ɪnɐlɪçn̩], ptp **verinnerlicht** VT to internalize; jdn to spiritualize

verirren ptp **verirrt** VR to get lost; (fig) to go astray; (Tier, Kugel) to stray; **hierhin ~ sich die Touristen nur selten** (fig) tourists don't venture out here very often

Verirrung F losing one's way no art; (fig) aberration

verjagen ptp **verjagt** VT (lit, fig) to chase away

verjähren ptp **verjährt** VI AUX SEIN to come under the statute of limitations; (Anspruch) to be in lapse; **verjährtes Verbrechen** statute-barred crime; **Totschlag verjährt nach 20 Jahren** the statute of limitations for manslaughter is 20 years; **Mord verjährt nie** there is no statute of limitations for murder; **das ist schon längst verjährt** (inf) that's all over and done with

Verjährung [fɛɐ̯'jɛːrʊŋ] F -, -en limitation; (von Anspruch) lapse

Verjährungsfrist F limitation period

verjazzen [fɛɐ̯'dʒɛsn̩, -'jatsn̩], ptp **verjazzt** VT to jazz up

verjüngen [fɛɐ̯'jʏŋən], ptp **verjüngt** **1** VT to rejuvenate; (= jünger aussehen lassen) to make look younger; Baumbestand to regenerate; **eine Mannschaft/das Personal ~** to build up a younger team/staff; **die neue Stelle hat ihn um Jahre verjüngt** the new job gave him a new lease of life; **er kam (um Jahre) verjüngt von der Gesundheitsfarm zurück** he came back from the health farm looking (years) younger **2** VR **(a)** (= jünger werden) to become younger; (Haut, Erscheinung) to become rejuvenated; (= jünger aussehen) to look younger

(b) (= dünner werden) to taper; (Tunnel, Rohr) to narrow

verkabeln ptp **verkabelt** VT (Telec) to link up to the cable network

Verkabelung [fɛɐ̯'kaːbəlʊŋ] F -, -en (Telec) linking up to the cable network

verkalken ptp **verkalkt** VI AUX SEIN (Arterien) to harden; (Gewebe) to calcify; (Kessel, Wasserleitung etc) to fur up; (inf: Mensch) to become senile

verkalkt [fɛɐ̯'kalkt] ADJ (inf) senile

verkalkulieren ptp **verkalkuliert** VR to miscalculate

Verkalkung [fɛɐ̯'kalkʊŋ] F -, -en (von Arterien) hardening; (von Gewebe) calcification; (von Kessel, Wasserleitung etc) furring; (inf) senility

verkannt [fɛɐ̯'kant] ADJ unrecognized; siehe auch **verkennen**

verkappt [fɛɐ̯'kapt] ADJ ATTR hidden; Lungenentzündung undiagnosed

verkarsten [fɛɐ̯'karstn̩], ptp **verkarstet** VI AUX SEIN to develop to karst (spec)

Verkarstung F -, -en karst development (spec)

verkatert [fɛɐ̯'kaːtɐt] ADJ (inf) hung over usu pred (inf); **einen ~en Eindruck machen** to look hung over (inf)

Verkauf M **(a)** sale; (= das Verkaufen) selling; **zum ~ stehen** to be up for sale; **beim ~ des Hauses** when selling the house **(b)** (= Abteilung) sales sing, no art

verkaufen ptp **verkauft** **1** VTI (lit, fig) to sell (für, um for); „**zu ~**" "for sale"; **jdm etw ~, etw an jdn ~** to sell sb sth, to sell sth to sb; **er würde sogar seine Großmutter ~** he'd even sell his own grandmother **2** VR **(a)** (Ware) to sell; (Mensch) to sell oneself **(b)** (= einen schlechten Kauf machen) to make a bad buy; **damit habe ich mich verkauft** that was a bad buy **(c)** (fig: = sich anpreisen) to sell oneself

Verkäufer(in) M(F) seller; (in Geschäft) sales assistant; (im Außendienst) salesman/saleswoman/salesperson; (Jur: von Grundbesitz etc) vendor

Verkäufermarkt M seller's market

verkäuflich ADJ sal(e)able; (= zu verkaufen) for sale; **leicht** or **gut/schwer ~** easy/hard to sell

Verkaufs- IN CPDS sales; **Verkaufsabteilung** F sales department; **Verkaufsautomat** M vending machine; **Verkaufsfläche** F sales area; **Verkaufsförderung** F sales promotion; (= Abteilung) sales promotion department; **verkaufsoffen** ADJ open for business; **~er Samstag** Saturday on which the shops are open all day; **Verkaufspreis** M retail price; **Verkaufsschlager** M big seller; **Verkaufswert** M market value or price

Verkehr [fɛɐ̯'keːɐ̯] M -(e)s, NO PL **(a)** traffic; (= Beförderung, Verkehrsmittel) transport, transportation (US); **für den ~ freigeben, dem ~ übergeben** Straße etc to open to traffic; Transportmittel to bring into service

(b) (= Verbindung) contact; (= Umgang) company; (= Geschlechtsverkehr) intercourse; **in brieflichem ~ stehen** to correspond

(c) (= Geschäftsverkehr, Handelsverkehr) trade; (= Umsätze, Zahlungsverkehr) business; (= Postverkehr) service; (= Umlauf) circulation; **etw in (den) ~ bringen** to put sth into circulation; **etw aus dem ~ ziehen** Banknoten to take sth out of circulation; schadhafte Produkte, Fahrzeuge to withdraw sth; altes Schiff to take sth out of commission; Blutkonserven, medizinische Präparate to remove sth

verkehren ptp **verkehrt** **1** VI **(a)** AUX HABEN or SEIN (= fahren) to run; (Flugzeug) to fly; **der Bus/das Flugzeug verkehrt regelmäßig zwischen A und B** the bus runs regularly/the plane goes regularly between A and B

(b) (= Gast sein, Kontakt pflegen) **bei jdm ~** to frequent sb's house; **mit jdm ~** to associate with sb; **in einem Lokal ~** to frequent a pub; **in Künstlerkreisen ~** to move in artistic circles; **mit jdm brieflich** or **schriftlich ~** (form) to correspond with sb

⊠ VT to turn (*in +acc* into); **etw ins Gegenteil ~** to reverse sth; *siehe auch* **verkehrt**

⊠ VR to turn (*in +acc* into); **sich ins Gegenteil ~** to become reversed

Verkehrs- IN CPDS traffic; **Verkehrsampel** F traffic lights *pl*; **Verkehrsanbindung** F transport links *pl*; **die Stadt hat eine gute ~** the town has good transport links; **verkehrsarm** ADJ *Zeit, Straße* quiet; **ein ~es Gebiet** an area with little traffic; **Verkehrsaufkommen** NT volume of traffic; **Verkehrsbehinderung** F (*Jur*) obstruction (of traffic); **verkehrsberuhigt** [-bəru:ɪçt] ADJ traffic-calmed; **Verkehrsberuhigung** F traffic calming; **Verkehrsbetriebe** PL transport services *pl*; **Verkehrsbüro** NT tourist information office; **Verkehrschaos** NT chaos on the roads; **Verkehrsdelikt** NT traffic offence (*Brit*) *or* offense (*US*); **Verkehrsdurchsage** F traffic announcement; **Verkehrserziehung** F road safety training; **Verkehrsführung** F traffic management system; **Verkehrsfunk** M radio traffic service; **Verkehrsgefährdung** F (*Jur.* = *verkehrswidriges Fahren*) dangerous driving; **eine ~ darstellen** to be a hazard to other traffic; **verkehrsgünstig** **⊠** ADJ *Lage* convenient; *Ort, Viertel* conveniently situated **⊠** ADV *liegen* conveniently; *wohnen* in a convenient location; **Verkehrshinweis** M traffic announcement; **Verkehrshypothek** F ordinary *or* regular mortgage; **Verkehrsinfarkt** M total gridlock; **Verkehrskollaps** M total gridlock; **Verkehrslärm** M traffic noise; **Verkehrsleitsystem** NT traffic guidance system; **Verkehrsmittel** NT means *sing* of transport; **öffentliche/private ~** public/private transport; **Verkehrsnetz** NT traffic network; **Verkehrsopfer** NT road casualty; **Verkehrsordnung** F ≈ Highway Code (*Brit*), traffic rules and regulations *pl*; **Verkehrspolizei** F traffic police *pl*; **Verkehrspolizist(in)** M(F) traffic policeman/-woman; **Verkehrsregel** F traffic regulation; **Verkehrsregelung** F traffic control; **Verkehrsschild** NT, *pl* **-schilder** road sign; **verkehrsschwach** ADJ *Zeit* off-peak; *Gebiet* with little traffic; **die Nachmittagsstunden sind sehr ~** there is very little traffic in the afternoons; **verkehrssicher** ADJ *Fahrzeug* roadworthy; *Straße, Brücke* safe (for traffic); **Verkehrssprache** F lingua franca; **Verkehrsstau** M, **Verkehrsstauung** F traffic jam; **Verkehrsstockung** F traffic jam; **Verkehrssünder(in)** M(F) (*inf*) traffic offender (*Brit*) *or* violator (*US*); **Verkehrssünderkartei** F (*inf*) central index of road traffic offenders; **Verkehrsteilnehmer(in)** M(F) road user; **Verkehrstote(r)** MF DECL AS ADJ road casualty; **die Zahl der ~n** the number of deaths on the road; **verkehrstüchtig** ADJ *Fahrzeug* roadworthy; *Mensch* fit to drive; **Verkehrsunfall** M road accident; (*hum inf*) accident; **Verkehrsunterricht** M traffic instruction; **verkehrsuntüchtig** ADJ *Fahrzeug* unroadworthy; *Mensch* unfit to drive; **Verkehrsverbindung** F link; (= *Anschluss*) connection; **Verkehrsverbund** M integrated transport system; **Verkehrsverein** M *local organization concerned with upkeep of tourist attractions, facilities etc*; **Verkehrsverhältnisse** PL traffic situation *sing*; (= *Straßenzustand*) road conditions *pl*; **Verkehrsverstoß** M motoring offence (*Brit*), traffic violation (*US*); **Verkehrswacht** F traffic patrol; **Verkehrsweg** M highway; **Verkehrswert** M (*Fin*) current market value; **verkehrswidrig** **⊠** ADJ contrary to road traffic regulations **⊠** ADV **sich ~ verhalten** to break the road traffic regulations; **Verkehrszählung** F traffic census; **Verkehrszeichen** NT road sign; **Verkehrszentralregister** NT *central index of traffic offenders*

verkehrt [fɛɐˈkeːɐt] **⊠** ADJ wrong; *Vorstellung auch, Welt* topsy-turvy; **das ist gar nicht (so) ~** (*inf*) that can't be bad (*inf*); **der ist gar nicht (so) ~** (*inf*) he's not such a bad sort; **das Verkehrte** the wrong thing; **das Verkehrteste, was du tun könntest** the worst thing you could do; **der/die Verkehrte** the wrong person

⊠ ADV wrongly; **etw ~ (herum) anhaben** (= *linke Seite nach außen*) to have sth on inside out; (= *vorne nach hinten*) to have sth on back to front; **etw ~ halten** to hold sth wrongly; (= *falsch herum*) to hold sth the wrong way (a)round; (= *oben nach unten*) to hold sth upside down; *siehe auch* **verkehren**

verkennen *ptp* **verkannt** [fɛɐˈkant] VT IRREG to misjudge; **ein Dichter, der zeit seines Lebens verkannt wurde** a poet who remained unrecognized in his lifetime; **es ist nicht zu ~, dass ...** it is undeniable that ...; **seine schlechte Laune/seine Absicht war nicht zu ~** his bad temper/his intention was obvious; *siehe auch* **verkannt**

Verkennung F misjudgement; (*von Genie, Künstler*) failure to appreciate (*jds* sb); **in ~ der wahren Sachlage ...** misjudging the real situation ...

verkitten *ptp* **verkittet** VT to cement; *Fenster* to put putty (a)round

verklagen *ptp* **verklagt** VT to sue (*wegen* for); **jdn auf etw** (*acc*) **~** to take sb to court for sth

verklappen *ptp* **verklappt** VT *Abfallstoffe* to dump

Verklappung [fɛɐˈklapʊŋ] F **-, -en** dumping

verklärt [fɛɐˈklɛːɐt] ADJ transfigured

verkleben *ptp* **verklebt** **⊠** VT (= *zusammenkleben*) to stick together; (= *zukleben*) to cover (*mit* with); *Tapeten* to stick; *Plakate* to stick up; *Haare, Verband* to make sticky; (= *verbrauchen*) to use up **⊠** VI AUX SEIN (*Wunde, Eileiter*) to close; (*Augen*) to get gummed up; (*Mehl, Briefmarken, Bonbons*) to stick together; (*Haare*) to become matted; **mit etw ~** to stick to sth

verklebt [fɛɐˈkleːpt] ADJ *Verband, Wunde* sticky; *Augen* gummed up; *Haare* matted; *Eileiter* blocked

verkleiden *ptp* **verkleidet** **⊠** VT **(a)** *jdn* to disguise; (= *kostümieren*) to dress up; **alle waren verkleidet** everyone was in fancy dress **(b)** (= *verschalen*) *Wand, Schacht, Tunnel* to line; (= *vertäfeln*) to panel; (= *bedecken, verdecken*) to cover; (= *ausschlagen, auslegen*) *Kiste etc* to line **⊠** VR to disguise oneself; (= *sich kostümieren*) to dress (oneself) up; **muss man sich ~?** do you have to wear fancy dress?

Verkleidung F **(a)** (= *das Verkleiden von Menschen*) disguising; (= *Kostümierung*) dressing up; (= *Kleidung*) disguise; (= *Kostüm*) fancy dress **(b)** (= *das Verkleiden*) (*Material*) lining; (*mit Holz*) panelling (*Brit*), paneling (*US*); (= *das Bedecken*) covering

verkleinern [fɛɐˈklainɐn], *ptp* **verkleinert** **⊠** VT to reduce; *Raum, Gebiet, Firma, Linse, Brille* to make smaller; *Maßstab* to scale down; *Abstand* to decrease; *Not, Probleme, Schuld* to minimize; *jds Leistungen, Verdienste* to belittle **⊠** VR to be reduced; (*Raum, Gebiet, Firma*) to become smaller; (*Abstand*) to decrease; (*Not, Probleme, Schuld*) to become less; **wir haben uns verkleinert** (*wohnungsmäßig*) we have moved into a smaller apartment **⊠** VI (*Linse etc*) to make everything seem smaller

Verkleinerung F **-, -en (a)** (= *das Verkleinern*) reduction; (*von Gebiet, Firma*) (*durch Linse, Brille*) making smaller; (*von Maßstab*) scaling down; (*von Abstand*) decreasing; (*von Not, Problemen, Schuld*) minimizing; (*von Leistungen, Verdiensten*) belittling; (*Gram*) formation of the diminutive **(b)** (= *Bild*) reduced size reproduction; (= *Foto*) reduction; (= *Wort*) diminutive (form); (*Mus*) diminution

Verkleinerungsform F diminutive form

verklemmt [fɛɐˈklɛmt] ADJ (*inf*) *Mensch* inhibited

Verklemmtheit F **-, -en** (*inf*), **Verklemmung** F **-, -en** inhibitions *pl*; **Sex ohne ~** uninhibited sex

verklingen *ptp* **verklungen** [fɛɐˈklʊŋən] VI IRREG AUX SEIN to fade away; (*fig*) to fade

verklumpen *ptp* **verklumpt** VI AUX SEIN to get lumpy

verknacksen [fɛɐˈknaksn], *ptp* **verknackst** VT (**sich** *dat*) **den Knöchel** *or* **Fuß ~** to twist one's ankle

verknallen *ptp* **verknallt** (*inf*) VR **sich (in jdn) ~** to fall for sb (*inf*); **ich war damals unheimlich (in ihn) verknallt** I was head over heels in love (with him) then

verknappen *ptp* **verknappt** **⊠** VT to cut back; *Rationen* to cut down (on) **⊠** VR to run short

verkneifen *ptp* **verkniffen** [fɛɐˈknifn] VT IRREG (*inf*) **sich** (*dat*) **etw ~** to stop oneself (from) saying/doing *etc* sth; *Lächeln* to keep back sth; *Bemerkung* to bite back sth; **ich konnte mir das Lachen nicht ~** I couldn't help laughing; **das kann ich mir ~** I can manage without that (*iro*)

verkniffen [fɛɐˈknifn] **⊠** ADJ *Gesicht, Miene* (= *angestrengt*) strained; (= *verbittert*) pinched; *Ansichten* narrow-minded **⊠** ADV **etw ~ sehen** to take a narrow view of sth

verknoten *ptp* **verknotet** **⊠** VT to tie, to knot; (*inf*) *Paket* to tie up **⊠** VR to become knotted

verknüpfen *ptp* **verknüpft** VT **(a)** (= *verknoten*) to knot (together); (*Comput*) to integrate **(b)** (*fig*) to combine; (= *in Zusammenhang bringen*) to link; *Gedanken, Geschehnisse* to associate; **etw mit Bedingungen ~** to attach conditions to sth; **mit diesem Ort sind für mich schöne Erinnerungen verknüpft**

this place has happy memories for me; **ein Hauskauf ist immer mit großen Ausgaben verknüpft** buying a house always involves a lot of expense

Verknüpfung [fɛɐ̯ˈknʏpfʊŋ] F **-, -en** (*von Bändern, Schnur*) knotting (together); (*Comput*) integration; (*fig*) combining; (= *Assoziieren*) linking; (*von Gedanken, Geschehnissen*) association

verknusen [fɛɐ̯ˈknuːzn̩], *ptp* **verknust** VT (*inf*) **ich kann ihn/das nicht ~** I can't stick him/that (*inf*)

verkochen *ptp* **verkocht** **1** VI AUX SEIN (*Flüssigkeit*) to boil away; (*Kartoffeln, Gemüse*) to overcook **2** VT *Gemüse* to overcook

verkohlen *ptp* **verkohlt** **1** VI AUX SEIN to become charred; (*Braten*) to burn to a crisp **2** VT (**a**) *Holz* to char; (*Tech*) to carbonize (**b**) (*inf*) **jdn ~** to pull sb's leg (*inf*)

Verkohlung [fɛɐ̯ˈkoːlʊŋ] F **-, -en** carbonization

verkommen[1] [fɛɐ̯ˈkɔmən], *ptp* **verkommen** VI IRREG AUX SEIN (**a**) (*Mensch*) to go to pieces; (*moralisch*) to become dissolute; (*Kind*) to run wild; **zu etw ~** to degenerate into sth (**b**) (*Gebäude, Auto*) to fall to pieces; (*Stadt, Land*) to become run-down; (*Gelände, Anlage etc*) to run wild (**c**) (= *nicht genutzt werden: Lebensmittel, Begabung, Fähigkeiten etc*) to go to waste; (= *verderben: Lebensmittel*) to go bad (**d**) (*Sw.* = *übereinkommen*) to agree (**e**) (*Aus inf.* = *verschwinden*) to clear off (*inf*)

verkommen[2] ADJ *Mensch* depraved; *Auto, Gebäude* dilapidated; *Garten* wild

Verkommenheit F **-,** NO PL (*von Mensch*) depravity; (*von Auto, Gebäude*) dilapidation; (*von Garten*) wildness

verkoppeln *ptp* **verkoppelt** VT to connect; (*Space*) to link (up)

Verkoppelung F, **Verkopplung** F connection, coupling; (*Space*) linkup

verkorksen [fɛɐ̯ˈkɔrksn̩], *ptp* **verkorkst** VT (*inf*) to screw up (*inf*); **sich** (*dat*) **den Magen ~** to upset one's stomach

verkorkst [fɛɐ̯ˈkɔrkst] ADJ (*inf*) messed-up (*inf*); *Magen* upset; *Mensch* screwed up (*inf*); **eine völlig ~e Sache** a real mess

verkörpern [fɛɐ̯ˈkœrpɐn], *ptp* **verkörpert** VT to embody; (*Theat*) to play (the part of)

verköstigen [fɛɐ̯ˈkœstɪɡn̩], *ptp* **verköstigt** VT to feed

verkrachen *ptp* **verkracht** VR (*inf*) **sich (mit jdm) ~** to fall out (with sb)

verkracht [fɛɐ̯ˈkraxt] ADJ (*inf*) *Leben* ruined; *Typ, Mensch* dead beat (*inf*); (= *zerstritten*) *Nachbarn, Freunde* who have fallen out with each other

verkraften [fɛɐ̯ˈkraftn̩], *ptp* **verkraftet** VT to cope with; (*finanziell*) to afford; (*inf:* = *essen, trinken können*) to manage

verkrampfen *ptp* **verkrampft** VR to become cramped; (*Hände*) to clench up; (*Mensch*) to go tense; **verkrampft** (*fig*) tense

verkriechen *ptp* **verkrochen** [fɛɐ̯ˈkrɔxn̩] VR IRREG to creep away; (*fig*) to hide (oneself away); **sich unter den** or **dem Tisch ~** to crawl under the table; **am liebsten hätte ich mich vor Scham verkrochen** I wanted the ground to open up and swallow me

verkrümeln *ptp* **verkrümelt** VR (*inf*) to disappear

verkrümmen *ptp* **verkrümmt** **1** VT to bend **2** VR to bend; (*Rückgrat*) to become curved; (*Holz*) to warp

verkrümmt [fɛɐ̯ˈkrʏmt] ADJ bent; *Wirbelsäule* curved; *Finger, Knochen, Bäume* crooked; *Holz* warped

Verkrümmung F bend (+*gen* in), distortion (*esp Tech*); (*von Holz*) warp; (*von Fingern, Knochen, Bäumen*) crookedness *no pl*; **~ der Wirbelsäule** curvature of the spine

verkrüppeln [fɛɐ̯ˈkrʏpl̩n], *ptp* **verkrüppelt** **1** VT to cripple **2** VI AUX SEIN to become crippled; (*Zehen, Füße*) to become deformed; (*Baum etc*) to grow stunted

verkrusten [fɛɐ̯ˈkrʊstn̩], *ptp* **verkrustet** VIR (*vi: aux sein*) to become encrusted

verkrustet [fɛɐ̯ˈkrʊstət] ADJ *Wunde* scabby; *Strukturen, Ansichten* decrepit

verkühlen *ptp* **verkühlt** (*inf*) **1** VR to get a chill **2** VT **sich** (*dat*) **die Nieren ~** to get a kidney infection (*resulting from a chill*)

Verkühlung F (*inf*) chill; **~ der Blase** bladder infection (*resulting from a chill*)

verkümmern *ptp* **verkümmert** VI AUX SEIN (*Glied, Organ*) to atrophy; (= *eingehen: Pflanze*) to die; (*Talent*) to go to waste; (*Schönheitssinn, Interesse etc*) to wither away; (*Mensch*) to

waste away; **emotionell/geistig ~** to become emotionally/intellectually stunted

verkünden *ptp* **verkündet** VT to announce; *Urteil* to pronounce; *Evangelium* to preach; *nichts Gutes, Unwetter etc* to forebode; *neue Zeit* to herald

verkünsteln [fɛɐ̯ˈkʏnstl̩n], *ptp* **verkünstelt** VR (*inf*) to overdo it; **sich an etw** (*dat*) **~** to overdo sth

verkupfern [fɛɐ̯ˈkʊpfɐn], *ptp* **verkupfert** VT to copper(-plate); **verkupfert** copper-plated

verkuppeln *ptp* **verkuppelt** VT (*pej*) to pair off; **jdn an jdn ~** (*Zuhälter*) to procure sb for sb

Verkuppelung F, NO PL, **Verkupplung** F, NO PL pairing off; (*durch Zuhälter*) procuring

verkürzen *ptp* **verkürzt** **1** VT to shorten; *Abstand, Vorsprung* to narrow; *Aufenthalt* to cut short; *Haltbarkeit* to reduce; *Schmerzen, Leiden* to end; **sich** (*dat*) **die Zeit ~** to pass the time; **jdm die Zeit ~** to help sb pass the time; **verkürzte Arbeitszeit** shorter working hours; **verkürzter Nebensatz** (*Gram*) elliptical subordinate clause **2** VR to be shortened; (*Abstand*) to be narrowed; (*Haltbarkeit*) to be reduced; (*Leiden*) to be ended; (*Urlaub, Aufenthalt*) to be cut short

Verkürzung F shortening; (*von Abstand, Vorsprung*) narrowing; (*von Aufenthalt*) cutting short; (*von Haltbarkeit*) reduction; (*von Schmerzen, Leiden*) ending

Verl. ABBR *von* **Verlag, Verleger**

verladen *ptp* **verladen** VT IRREG (**a**) *Güter, Menschen* to load; (*Mil*) (*in Eisenbahn*) to entrain; (*auf Schiff*) to embark; (*in Flugzeug*) to enplane; **die Güter vom Eisenbahnwaggon aufs Schiff ~** to offload the goods from the train onto the ship (**b**) (*fig inf*) to con (*inf*)

Verlader [fɛɐ̯ˈlaːdɐ] M **-s, -** shipper

Verlag [fɛɐ̯ˈlaːk] M **-(e)s, -e** [-ɡə] (**a**) (= *Buchverlag*) publishing house; (= *Zeitungsverlag*) newspaper publisher's *sing*; **~ HarperCollins** HarperCollins Publishers *sing*; **einen ~ finden** to find a publisher; **in** or **bei welchem ~ ist das erschienen?** who published it?; **der ~ zahlt nicht viel** the publishers do not pay much (**b**) (= *Zwischenhandelsgeschäft*) (firm of) distributors *pl*

verlagern *ptp* **verlagert** **1** VT (*lit, fig*) to shift; (*lit: an anderen Ort*) to move **2** VR (*lit*) (*fig*) to shift; (*Met: Tief, Hoch etc*) to move; (*fig: Problem, Frage*) to change in emphasis (*auf +acc* to)

Verlags-: Verlagskauffrau F, **Verlagskaufmann** M publishing manager; **Verlagsleiter(in)** M(F) publishing director; **Verlagsprogramm** NT list; **Verlagsredakteur(in)** M(F) (publishing) editor; **Verlagswesen** NT, NO PL publishing *no art*

verlangen *ptp* **verlangt** **1** VT (**a**) (= *fordern*) to demand; (= *wollen*) to want; *Preis* to ask; *Qualifikationen, Erfahrung* to require (**b**) (= *erwarten*) to ask (*von* of); **es wird von jdm verlangt, dass ...** it is required of sb that ...; **das ist nicht zu viel verlangt** it's not asking too much; **das ist ein bisschen viel verlangt** that's asking rather a lot (**c**) (= *erfordern*) to require (**d**) (= *fragen nach*) to ask for; **Sie werden am Telefon verlangt** you are wanted on the phone; **ich verlange den Geschäftsführer (zu sprechen)** I demand to see the manager **2** VI **~ nach** to ask for; (= *sich sehnen nach*) to long for; (*stärker*) to crave

Verlangen [fɛɐ̯ˈlaŋən] NT **-s, -** (*nach* for) desire; (= *Sehnsucht*) yearning; (= *Begierde*) craving; **kein ~ nach etw haben** to have no desire for sth; **auf ~** on demand; **auf ~ des Gerichts** by order of the court; **auf ~ der Eltern** at the request of the parents

verlängern [fɛɐ̯ˈlɛŋɐn], *ptp* **verlängert** **1** VT (**a**) (= *länger machen*) to extend; *Leben, Schmerzen, Leiden etc* to prolong; *Hosenbein, Ärmel etc* to lengthen; *Pass, Abonnement etc* to renew; **die Suppe/Soße ~** (*fig inf*) to make the soup/gravy go further; **ein verlängertes Wochenende** a long weekend; **verlängerte Werkbank** (*fig inf*) extended production line (**b**) (*Sport*) *Ball, Pass* to touch (*zu jdm* to sb) **2** VR to be extended; (*zeitlich auch, Leiden etc*) to be prolonged **3** VI (*Sport*) to play on

Verlängerung F **-, -en (a)** (= *das Verlängern*) extension; (*von Pass, Abonnement etc*) renewal **(b)** (*Gegenstand*) extension **(c)** (*Sport*) (*von Spielzeit*) extra time (*Brit*), over time (*US*); (= *nachgespielte Zeit*) injury time (*Brit*), over time (*US*); (*von Pass*) play-on (*zu* to); **das Spiel geht in die ~** they're going to play extra time *etc*; **eine ~ von fünf Minuten** five minutes' extra time *etc*

Verlängerungskabel NT, **Verlängerungsschnur** F (*Elec*) extension lead

verlangsamen [fɛɐˈlaŋzaːmən], *ptp* **verlangsamt** ⓵ VT to slow down; **er musste das Tempo/seine Schritte ~** he had to slow down ⓶ VR to slow down

Verlass [fɛɐˈlas] M **-es**, NO PL **auf jdn/etw ist kein ~**, **es ist kein ~ auf jdn/etw** there is no relying on sb/sth

verlassen[1] *ptp* **verlassen** IRREG ⓵ VT to leave; (*fig: Mut, Kraft, Hoffnung*) *jdn* to desert; (= *im Stich lassen*) to desert; (*Comput*) *Datei, Programm* to exit; **... und da verließen sie mich/ihn** *etc* (*iroinf*) ... that's as far as I/he *etc* got ⓶ VR **sich auf jdn/etw ~** to rely on sb/sth; **darauf können Sie sich ~** you can be sure of that; **worauf du dich ~ kannst!** you bet!

verlassen[2] [fɛɐˈlasn] ADJ deserted; (= *öd*) desolate; (= *einsam*) lonely; *Auto* abandoned

Verlassenschaft [fɛɐˈlasnʃaft] F **-, -en** (*Aus, Sw*) estate; (*literarisch*) legacy

verlässlich ADJ reliable

Verlässlichkeit [fɛɐˈlɛslɪçkait] F **-**, NO PL reliability

Verlauf M course; (= *Ausgang*) end; **im ~ der Jahre/Monate** over the (course of the) years/months; **einen guten/schlechten ~ nehmen** to go well/badly; **im weiteren ~ der Sache zeichnete sich folgende Tendenz ab** as things developed the following tendency became apparent

verlaufen *ptp* **verlaufen** IRREG ⓵ VI AUX SEIN **(a)** (= *ablaufen*) (*Tag, Prüfung, Entwicklung*) to go; (*Feier, Demonstration*) to go off; (*Kindheit*) to pass; (*Untersuchung*) to proceed; **beschreiben Sie, wie diese Krankheit normalerweise verläuft** describe the course this illness usually takes; **die Verhandlungen verliefen in angespannter Atmosphäre** the negotiations took place in a tense atmosphere
(b) (= *sich erstrecken*) to run
(c) (= *auseinander fließen*) to run; **die Spur verlief im Sand/Wald** the track disappeared in the sand/forest; **~e Farben** runny colours (*Brit*) *or* colors (*US*)
⓶ VR **(a)** (= *sich verirren*) to get lost
(b) (= *verschwinden*) (*Menschenmenge*) to disperse; (*Wasser*) to drain away

Verlaufsform F (*Gram*) progressive form

verlaust [fɛɐˈlaust] ADJ lice-ridden

verlautbaren [fɛɐˈlautbaːrən], *ptp* **verlautbart** (*form*) VTI to announce; **etw ~ lassen** to let sth be announced

Verlautbarung F **-, -en** announcement; (*inoffiziell*) report

verlauten *ptp* **verlautet** ⓵ VI **etwas/nichts ~ lassen** to give an/ no indication; **er hat ~ lassen, dass ...** he indicated that ...; **er hat keinen Ton** *or* **kein Wort ~ lassen** he hasn't said a word ⓶ VI IMPERS AUX SEIN *or* HABEN **es verlautet, dass ...** it is reported that ...; **wie aus Bonn verlautet** according to reports from Bonn

verleben *ptp* **verlebt** VT to spend; **eine schöne Zeit ~** to have a nice time

verlebt [fɛɐˈleːpt] ADJ worn-out

verlegen[1] *ptp* **verlegt** ⓵ VT **(a)** (*an anderen Ort*) to move **(b)** (= *verschieben*) to postpone (*auf +acc* until); (= *vorverlegen*) to bring forward (*auf +acc* to) **(c)** (= *an falschen Platz legen*) to mislay **(d)** (= *anbringen*) *Kabel, Fliesen etc* to lay **(e)** (= *drucken lassen*) to publish ⓶ VR **sich auf etw** (*acc*) **~** to resort to sth; **er hat sich neuerdings auf Golf verlegt** he has taken to golf recently; **sich aufs Unterrichten ~** to take up teaching

verlegen[2] [fɛɐˈleːgn] ⓵ ADJ **(a)** embarrassed *no adv* **(b)** **um Worte/eine Antwort ~ sein** to be lost for words/an answer; **um Geld ~ sein** to be financially embarrassed ⓶ ADV in embarrassment; **das habe ich vergessen, sagte sie ~** I forgot about that, she said, embarrassed

Verlegenheit F **-, -en (a)** NO PL (= *Betretenheit, Befangenheit*) embarrassment; **jdn in ~ bringen** to embarrass sb; **in ~ kommen** *or* **geraten** to get embarrassed **(b)** (= *unangenehme*

Lage) embarrassing situation; **wenn er in finanzieller ~ ist** when he's in financial difficulties; **ich bin (finanziell) zur Zeit leider etwas in ~** I'm afraid I'm rather short (of funds) at the moment

Verlegenheitslösung F stopgap

Verleger [fɛɐˈleːgɐ] M **-s**, **-**, **Verlegerin** [-ərɪn] F **-, -nen** publisher; (= *Händler*) distributor

Verlegung [fɛɐˈleːgʊŋ] F **-, -en (a)** (*räumlich*) transfer; (*von Schauplatz*) shifting **(b)** (*zeitlich*) postponement (*auf +acc* until); (= *Vorverlegung*) bringing forward (*auf +acc* to) **(c)** (*von Kabeln etc*) laying

Verleih [fɛɐˈlai] M **-(e)s, -e (a)** (= *Unternehmen*) rental company; (= *Autoverleih*) car hire (*Brit*) *or* rental; (= *Filmverleih*) distributor(s *pl*) **(b)** (= *das Verleihen*) renting (out), hiring (out) (*Brit*); (= *Filmverleih*) distribution; **der ~ von Büchern** the lending of books

verleihen *ptp* **verliehen** [fɛɐˈliːən] VT IRREG **(a)** (= *ausleihen*) to lend (*an jdn* to sb); (*gegen Gebühr*) to rent (out), to hire (out) (*Brit*) **(b)** (= *zuerkennen*) to award (*jdm* (to) sb); *Titel, Ehrenbürgerwürde* to confer (*jdm* on sb) **(c)** (= *geben, verschaffen*) to give; **einer Sache** (*dat*) **Gewicht ~** to lend weight to sth

Verleihung F **-, -en (a)** (= *das Ausleihen*) lending; (*gegen Gebühr*) renting, rental **(b)** (*von Preis etc*) award(ing); (*von Titel, Ehrenbürgerwürde*) conferment; **die ~ des Preises findet am 26. September statt** the prize will be awarded on 26 September

verleiten *ptp* **verleitet** VT **(a)** (= *verlocken*) to tempt; (= *verführen*) to lead astray; **jdn zum Stehlen/Lügen ~** to lead sb to steal/lie; **jdn dazu ~, die Schule zu schwänzen** to encourage sb to play truant **(b)** (= *veranlassen*) **jdn zu etw ~** to lead sb to sth

verlernen *ptp* **verlernt** VT to forget; **das Tanzen ~** to forget how to dance

verlesen *ptp* **verlesen** IRREG ⓵ VT **(a)** (= *vorlesen*) to read (out); *Namen* to read out **(b)** *Gemüse, Linsen, Früchte etc* to sort; *Feldsalat* to clean ⓶ VR (*beim Vorlesen*) to make a slip; **ich habe mich wohl ~** I must have misread it

verletzbar ADJ (*lit, fig*) vulnerable

verletzen [fɛɐˈlɛtsn], *ptp* **verletzt** ⓵ VT **(a)** to injure; (*in Kampf etc, mit Kugel, Messer*) to wound; (*fig*) *jdn, jds Stolz, Gefühle* to hurt; *jds Schönheitssinn, zarte Ohren* to offend **(b)** *Gesetz* to break; *Pflicht, Rechte, Intimsphäre* to violate ⓶ VR to injure oneself

verletzend ADJ *Bemerkung* hurtful

Verletzte(r) [fɛɐˈlɛtstə] MF DECL AS ADJ injured person; (= *Unfallverletzter auch*) casualty; (*bei Kampf*) wounded man; **die ~n** the injured/wounded; **es gab drei ~** three people were injured

Verletzung F **-, -en (a)** (= *Wunde*) injury **(b)** (= *das Verletzen*) injuring; (*in Kampf, mit Waffe*) wounding; (*fig*) hurting; (*von Ehrgefühl, Schönheitssinn*) offending; **zur ~ des Knies führen** to cause a knee injury

verleugnen *ptp* **verleugnet** VT to deny; **es lässt sich nicht ~, dass ...** there is no denying that ...; **er lässt sich immer (vor ihr) ~** he always pretends not to be there (when she calls)

verleumden [fɛɐˈlɔymdn], *ptp* **verleumdet** VT to slander; (*schriftlich*) to libel

verleumderisch [fɛɐˈlɔymdərɪʃ] ADJ slanderous; (*in Schriftform*) libellous (*esp Brit*), libelous (*US*)

Verleumdung F **-, -en** slandering; (*schriftlich*) libelling (*esp Brit*), libeling (*US*); (= *Bemerkung*) slander; (= *Bericht*) libel

Verleumdungskampagne F smear campaign

verlieben *ptp* **verliebt** VR to fall in love (*in +acc* with)

verliebt [fɛɐˈliːpt] ⓵ ADJ *Benehmen, Blicke, Worte* amorous; **(in jdn/etw) ~ sein** to be in love (with sb/sth); **die Verliebten** the lovers ⓶ ADV *ansehen* lovingly

verlieren [fɛɐˈliːrən], *pret* **verlor** [fɛɐˈloːɐ], *ptp* **verloren** [fɛɐˈloːrən] ⓵ VT to lose; **kein Wort über jdn/etw ~** not to say a word about sb/sth; **das/er hat hier nichts verloren** (*inf*) that/he has no business to be here
⓶ VI to lose; **sie hat an Schönheit/Charme verloren** she has lost some of her beauty/charm; **sie/die Altstadt** *etc* **hat sehr verloren** she/the old town *etc* is not what she/it *etc* used to be; **durch etw ~** to lose (something) by sth
⓷ VR **(a)** (*Menschen*) to lose each other

(b) (= *verschwinden*) to disappear; (= *verhallen*) to fade away; *siehe auch* **verloren**

Verlierer [fɛɐˈliːrə] M **-s, -, Verliererin** [-ərɪn] F **-, -nen** loser

Verliererstraße F **auf der ~ sein** (*inf*) to be on the downward slope

Verlies [fɛɐˈliːs] NT **-es, -e** [-zə] dungeon

verlinken VT to hyperlink

verloben *ptp* **verlobt** VR (*mit* to) to get engaged

Verlobte(r) [fɛɐˈloːptə] MF DECL AS ADJ **mein ~r** my fiancé; **meine ~** my fiancée; **die ~n** the engaged couple

Verlobung [fɛɐˈloːbʊŋ] F **-, -en** engagement

verlocken *ptp* **verlockt** VTI to entice

Verlockung F enticement; (= *Reiz*) allure

verlogen [fɛɐˈloːɡn] ADJ *Mensch* lying; *Komplimente, Versprechungen* false; *Moral, Freundlichkeit, Gesellschaft* hypocritical

Verlogenheit F **-, -en** (*von Mensch*) mendacity (*form*); (*von Versprechungen*) falseness; (*von Moral, Gesellschaft*) hypocrisy

verlor PRET *von* **verlieren**

verloren [fɛɐˈloːrən] **1** PTP *von* **verlieren 2** ADJ lost; *Mühe* vain; (*Cook*) *Eier* poached; **der ~e Sohn** (*Bibl*) the prodigal son; **jdn/etw ~ geben** to give sb/sth up for lost; **auf ~em Posten kämpfen** *or* **stehen** to be fighting a losing battle; *siehe auch* **verlieren**

verloren gehen VI IRREG AUX SEIN to get lost; (*Zeit, Geld*) to be wasted; **an ihm ist ein Sänger verloren gegangen** he would have made a (good) singer

verlosen *ptp* **verlost** VT to raffle (off); **wir ~ das letzte Stück Kuchen** we'll draw lots *or* straws for the last piece of cake

Verlosung F (= *das Verlosen*) raffling; (= *Lotterie*) raffle; (= *Ziehung*) draw

Verlust [fɛɐˈlʊst] M **-(e)s, -e (a)** loss; **~ bringend** lossmaking; **~ bringend arbeiten** to work at a loss; **mit ~ verkaufen** to sell at a loss **(b) Verluste** PL losses *pl*; **schwere ~e haben/machen** to sustain/make heavy losses

Verlust-: verlustbringend ADJ *siehe* **Verlust**; **Verlustgeschäft** NT (= *Firma*) lossmaking business (*Brit*), business operating in the red; **ich habe es schließlich verkauft, aber das war ein ~** I sold it eventually, but I made a loss; **verlustreich** ADJ **(a)** (*Comm*) *Firma* heavily loss-making; **ein ~es Jahr** a year of heavy losses; **ein ~es Geschäft** a deal on which heavy losses were made **(b)** (*Mil*) *Schlacht* involving heavy losses; **Verlustzuweisung** F (*Econ*) allocation of losses

vermachen *ptp* **vermacht** VT **jdm etw ~** (*lit, fig*) to bequeath sth to sb

Vermächtnis [fɛɐˈmɛçtnɪs] NT **-ses, -se** bequest; (*fig*) legacy

vermählen [fɛɐˈmɛːlən] *ptp* **vermählt** (*form*) **1** VT to marry; **frisch vermählt sein** to be newly married **2** VR **sich (mit jdm) ~** to marry (sb); **„wir haben uns vermählt ..."** "the marriage is announced of ..."

vermarkten [fɛɐˈmarktn] *ptp* **vermarktet** VT to market; (*fig*) to commercialize

Vermarktung F **-, -en** marketing; (*fig*) commercialization

vermasseln [fɛɐˈmasln] *ptp* **vermasselt** VT (*inf*) to mess up (*inf*); *Prüfung, Klassenarbeit* to make a mess of

vermehren *ptp* **vermehrt 1** VT to increase; (= *fortpflanzen*) to breed; *Bakterien* to multiply; **vermehrt** increased; **diese Fälle treten vermehrt auf** these cases are occurring with increasing frequency **2** VR to increase; (= *sich fortpflanzen*) to reproduce; (*Bakterien, Zellen*) to multiply; (*Pflanzen*) to propagate

Vermehrung F increase; (= *Fortpflanzung*) reproduction; (*von Bakterien*) multiplying; (*von Pflanzen*) propagation

vermeidbar ADJ avoidable

vermeiden *ptp* **vermieden** [fɛɐˈmiːdn] VT IRREG to avoid; **es lässt sich nicht ~** it is inevitable *or* unavoidable; **es lässt sich nicht ~, dass ...** it is inevitable *or* unavoidable that ...

vermeintlich [fɛɐˈmaɪntlɪç] **1** ADJ ATTR supposed; *Täter, Vater eines Kindes* putative **2** ADV supposedly

vermengen *ptp* **vermengt** VT to mix; (*fig inf*: = *durcheinander bringen*) *Begriffe etc* to mix up

Vermerk [fɛɐˈmɛrk] M **-(e)s, -e** remark; (*in Pass*) observation; (= *Stempel*) stamp

vermerken *ptp* **vermerkt** VT (= *aufschreiben*) to note (down); (*in Pass, Karte*) *Namen, Datum etc* to record; **alle Verkehrssünder**

werden in Flensburg vermerkt a record of (the names of) all traffic offenders is kept in Flensburg

vermessen¹ *ptp* **vermessen** IRREG **1** VT to measure; *Land, Gelände* to survey **2** VR (= *falsch messen*) to measure wrongly

vermessen² [fɛɐˈmɛsn] ADJ (= *anmaßend*) presumptuous; *Diener* impudent; (= *kühn*) *Unterfangen* bold

Vermessenheit F **-, -en** (= *Anmaßung*) presumption; (= *Kühnheit*) boldness; **es wäre eine ~, das zu tun** that would be a presumptuous thing to do

Vermessung F measurement; (*von Land, Gelände*) survey

vermiesen [fɛɐˈmiːzn] *ptp* **vermiest** VT (*inf*) **jdm etw ~** to spoil sth for sb

vermieten *ptp* **vermietet 1** VT to rent (out), to lease (*Jur*); **Zimmer zu ~** room for rent **2** VI to rent (out) a room/rooms; **„zu ~"** "to let" (*esp Brit*), "for rent"

Vermieter M lessor; (*von Wohnung etc*) landlord

Vermieterin F lessor; (*von Wohnung etc*) landlady

Vermietung [fɛɐˈmiːtʊŋ] F **-, -en** renting (out); (*von Auto, Boot*) rental, hiring (out) (*Brit*)

vermindern *ptp* **vermindert 1** VT to reduce; *Gefahr, Anfälligkeit, Einfluss etc auch, Ärger, Zorn* to lessen; (*Mus*) to diminish; **verminderte Zurechnungsfähigkeit** (*Jur*) diminished responsibility **2** VR to decrease; (*Gefahr, Anfälligkeit, Einfluss auch, Ärger, Zorn*) to lessen; (*Reaktionsfähigkeit*) to diminish; (*Schmerzen*) to ease off

Verminderung F reduction (+*gen* of); (*von Gefahr, Anfälligkeit, Einfluss auch, von Ärger, Zorn*) lessening; (*von Reaktionsfähigkeit*) diminishing; (*von Schmerzen*) easing

vermischen *ptp* **vermischt 1** VT to mix; *Tabaksorten, Teesorten etc* to blend; **„Vermischtes"** "miscellaneous" **2** VR to mix; (*Elemente, Klänge, Farben*) to blend

vermissen *ptp* **vermisst** VT to miss; **vermisst werden** to be missing; **vermisst sein, als vermisst gemeldet sein** to be reported missing; **ich vermisse die Blumen auf den Tischen** I see you don't have the flowers on the tables; **etw an jdm/etw ~** to find sb/sth lacking in sth; **wir haben dich bei der Party vermisst** we didn't see you at the party; **entschuldige, dass ich zu spät komme – wir hatten dich noch gar nicht vermisst** sorry I'm late – we hadn't even noticed you weren't here; **etw ~ lassen** to be lacking in sth

Vermisstenanzeige F missing persons report; **eine ~ aufgeben** to report someone (as) missing

Vermisste(r) [fɛɐˈmɪstə] MF DECL AS ADJ missing person

vermitteln [fɛɐˈmɪtln] *ptp* **vermittelt 1** VT to arrange (*jdm* for sb); *Stelle, Partner, Privatschüler, Kontakte* to find (*jdm* for sb); *Aushilfskräfte, Lehrer etc* to find jobs for; (*Telec*) *Gespräch* to put through; *Hypotheken, Kredite, Geschäfte* to arrange (*jdm* for sb); *Gefühl, Bild, Idee, Einblick* to convey, to give (*jdm* to sb); *Verständnis* to give (*jdm* (to) sb); *Wissen* to impart (*jdm* to sb); **jdm etw ~** to get sth for sb; **eine Stelle, die Hotelunterkunft vermittelt** an office which finds hotel accommodation; **wir ~ Geschäftsräume** we are agents for business premises **2** VI to mediate; **~d eingreifen** to intervene; **~de Worte** conciliatory words

Vermittler(in) M(F) **(a)** mediator **(b)** (*Comm*) agent; (*Fin*: = *Heiratsvermittler*) broker

Vermittlergebühr F commission; (*Fin auch*) brokerage

Vermittlung [fɛɐˈmɪtlʊŋ] F **-, -en** (= *das Vermitteln*) arranging; (*von Stelle, Briefpartner, Privatschüler*) finding; (*von Arbeitskräften*) finding of jobs (+*gen* for); (*Telec: von Gespräch*) connection; (*von Hypothek, Kredit, Geschäft, Wertpapier*) negotiation; (*in Streitigkeiten*) mediation; (*von Gefühl, Bild, Idee, Einblick*) conveying; (*von Verständnis*) giving; (*von Wissen*) imparting; **sie haben sich durch die ~ einer Agentur kennen gelernt** they met through an agency; **ich habe das Zimmer/die Stelle durch ~ eines Freundes bekommen** I got the room/job through a friend; **durch seine freundliche ~** with his kind help; **eine ~ zwischen den beiden ist mir leider nicht gelungen** unfortunately I was unable to reconcile them **(a)** (= *Stelle, Agentur*) agency; (= *Wohnungsvermittlung*) estate agent's (*Brit*), realtor (*US*), real estate agent's (*esp US*) **(b)** (*Telec*) (= *Amt*) exchange; (*in Firma etc*) switchboard; (= *Mensch*) operator; **~, bitte geben Sie mir Göhren 487** give me Göhren 487 please, operator

Vermittlungs-: **Vermittlungsgebühr** F commission; **Vermittlungsversuch** M attempt at mediation

vermöbeln [fɛɐ'møːbln], *ptp* **vermöbelt** VT (*inf*) to beat up; (*als Strafe*) to thrash

vermodern [fɛɐ'moːdɐn], *ptp* **vermodert** VI AUX SEIN to moulder (*Brit*), to molder (*US*)

Vermögen [fɛɐ'møːgn] NT **-s, -** (**a**) (= *Reichtum, viel Geld*) fortune; **eine Frau, die ~ hat** a woman who has money (**b**) (= *Besitz*) property; **mein ganzes ~ besteht aus ...** my entire assets consist of ...

vermögend ADJ (= *reich*) wealthy

Vermögens-: **Vermögensberater(in)** M(F) investment analyst; **vermögensbildend** ADJ wealth-creating; **Vermögensbildung** F creation of wealth; (*durch Prämiensparen*) wealth formation by long-term saving with tax concessions; **Vermögenssteuer** F wealth tax; **Vermögensverhältnisse** PL financial circumstances *pl*; **Vermögensverwaltung** F asset management; **vermögenswirksam** ADJ profitable; **~e Leistungen** employer's contributions to tax-deductible savings scheme ☑ ADV **Geld ~ investieren** to invest money profitably

vermummen [fɛɐ'momən], *ptp* **vermummt** VR (**a**) (= *sich warm anziehen*) to wrap (oneself) up (warm); **vermummte Gestalten in einer Winterlandschaft** muffled-up figures in a winter landscape (**b**) (= *sich verkleiden*) to disguise oneself; **eine vermummte Gestalt betrat den Raum** a cloaked figure entered the room; **tief vermummt** heavily disguised; **vermummte Demonstranten** masked demonstrators

Vermummung F **-, -en** disguise; (*von Demonstranten*) covering of the face

Vermummungsverbot NT **das ~ bei Demonstrationen** the law requiring demonstrators to leave their faces uncovered

vermuten [fɛɐ'muːtn], *ptp* **vermutet** VT to suspect; **ich vermute es nur** that's only an assumption; **wir haben ihn dort nicht vermutet** we did not expect him to be there; **ich hatte dich nicht so früh vermutet** I didn't suspect you would be so early; **es ist zu ~, dass ...** we may assume that ...; **die Entwicklung lässt ~, dass ...** developments lead one to assume that...

vermutlich [fɛɐ'muːtlɪç] ☑ ADJ ATTR presumable; *Täter* suspected ☑ ADV presumably

Vermutung F **-, -en** (= *Annahme*) assumption; (= *Mutmaßung*) conjecture; (= *Verdacht*) hunch; **die ~ liegt nahe, dass ...** there are grounds for the assumption that ...; **das sind alles nur ~en** that is pure conjecture; **wir sind nur auf ~en angewiesen** we have to rely on assumptions *or* guesswork; **meine ~en waren doch richtig** my hunch was right

vernachlässigen [fɛɐ'naːxlɛsɪgn], *ptp* **vernachlässigt** ☑ VT to neglect; **das können wir ~** (= *nicht berücksichtigen*) we can ignore that ☑ VR to neglect oneself *or* one's appearance

vernarben [fɛɐ'narbn], *ptp* **vernarbt** VI AUX SEIN to heal (up)

vernarren *ptp* **vernarrt** VR (*inf*) **sich in jdn/etw ~** to fall for sb/sth; **in jdn/etw vernarrt sein** to be crazy about sb/sth (*inf*)

vernaschen *ptp* **vernascht** VT (*inf*) *Mädchen, Mann* to make it with (*inf*)

vernehmbar ☑ ADJ (**a**) (= *hörbar*) audible (**b**) (= *vernehmungsfähig*) able to be questioned ☑ ADV (= *hörbar*) audibly

vernehmen *ptp* **vernommen** [fɛɐ'nɔmən] VT IRREG (**a**) (= *hören*) to hear (**b**) (= *erfahren*) to hear; **das Presseamt hat ~ lassen, dass ...** the press agency has given to understand that ...; **er hat über seine Pläne nichts ~ lassen** he has let nothing be known about his plans (**c**) (*Jur*) *Zeugen, Angeklagte* to examine; (*Polizei*) to question; **zu diesem Fall wurden fünfzig Zeugen vernommen** fifty witnesses were heard in connection with this case

vernehmlich [fɛɐ'neːmlɪç] ☑ ADJ clear ☑ ADV audibly; **es tönte laut und ~ ...** it sounded loud and clear ...

Vernehmung [fɛɐ'neːmʊŋ] F **-, -en** (*Jur: von Zeugen, Angeklagten*) examination; (*durch Polizei*) questioning

verneigen *ptp* **verneigt** VR to bow; **sich vor jdm/etw ~** (*lit*) to bow to sb/sth; (*fig*) to bow down before sb/sth

Verneigung F bow (*vor +dat* before); **eine ~ machen** to bow

verneinen [fɛɐ'nainən], *ptp* **verneint** VTI *Frage* to answer in the negative; (= *leugnen*) *Tatsache, Existenz Gottes etc* to deny; *These, Argument* to dispute; (*Gram, Logik*) to negate; **die verneinte Form** the negative (form)

verneinend ☑ ADJ (*auch Gram*) negative ☑ ADV *antworten* in the negative; **er schüttelte ~ den Kopf** he shook his head

Verneinung F **-, -en** (= *Leugnung*) denial; (*von These etc*) disputing; (*Gram, Philos*) negation; (= *verneinte Form*) negative; **die ~ meiner Frage** the negative answer to my question

vernetzen *ptp* **vernetzt** VT (*esp Mot*) to link up; (*Comput*) to network

Vernetzung [fɛɐ'nɛtsʊŋ] F **-, -en** (*esp Mot*) linking-up; (*Comput*) networking

vernichten [fɛɐ'nɪçtn], *ptp* **vernichtet** VT (*lit, fig*) to destroy

vernichtend ☑ ADJ *Kritik, Urteil* devastating; *Blick auch* withering; *Niederlage* crushing ☑ ADV **~ über jdn urteilen** to make a devastating appraisal of sb; **jdn ~ schlagen** (*Mil, Sport*) to annihilate sb

Vernichtung F **-, -en** destruction

Vernichtungs-: **Vernichtungslager** NT extermination camp; **Vernichtungsschlag** M devastating blow; **zum ~ ausholen** (*Mil, fig*) to prepare to deliver the final blow

vernickeln [fɛɐ'nɪkln], *ptp* **vernickelt** VT to nickel-plate

verniedlichen [fɛɐ'niːtlɪçn], *ptp* **verniedlicht** VT to trivialize

vernieten *ptp* **vernietet** VT to rivet

Vernissage [vɛrnɪ'saːʒə] F **-, -n** opening (*at art gallery*)

Vernunft [fɛɐ'nʊnft] F **-**, NO PL reason (*auch Philos*), good sense; **zur ~ kommen** to come to one's senses; **~ annehmen** to see reason; **nimm doch ~ an!** why don't you see sense?; **gegen alle (Regeln der) ~** against all (the laws of) reason; **~ beweisen** to show (good) sense; **etw mit/ohne ~ tun** to do sth sensibly/foolishly; **etw mit ~ essen/trinken** to eat/drink sth appreciatively; **jdn zur ~ bringen** to make sb see sense

vernünftig [fɛɐ'nʏnftɪç] ☑ ADJ sensible; (= *logisch denkend*) rational; (*inf*) (= *ordentlich, anständig*) decent; (= *annehmbar*) reasonable; **ich kann keinen ~en Gedanken fassen** I can't think properly ☑ ADV sensibly; (= *logisch*) rationally; (*inf*) (= *anständig, ordentlich*) decently; (= *annehmbar*) reasonably; (= *tüchtig*) properly (*inf*); **~ reden** (*inf*) to speak properly

vernünftigerweise [fɛɐ'nʏnftɪgɐ'vaizə] ADV **etw ~ tun** to have the (good) sense to do sth; **du solltest dich ~ ins Bett legen** you should be sensible and go to bed

Vernünftigkeit F **-**, NO PL good sense

veröden [fɛɐ'løːdn], *ptp* **verödet** ☑ VT (*Med*) *Krampfadern* to sclerose ☑ VI AUX SEIN to become desolate; (*fig: = geistig ~*) to become stultified

veröffentlichen [fɛɐ'œfntlɪçn], *ptp* **veröffentlicht** VTI to publish

Veröffentlichung F **-, -en** publication

verordnen *ptp* **verordnet** VT to prescribe (*jdm etw* sth for sb)

Verordnung F (**a**) (*Med*) prescription; **nach ~ des Arztes einzunehmen** to be taken as directed by the doctor (**b**) (*form: = Verfügung*) decree

verpachten *ptp* **verpachtet** VT to lease (*an +acc* to)

Verpächter(in) M(F) lessor

verpacken *ptp* **verpackt** VT to pack; (*verbrauchergerecht*) to package; (= *einwickeln*) to wrap

Verpackung F (**a**) (= *Material*) packaging *no pl* (**b**) NO PL (= *das Verpacken*) packing; (*verbrauchergerecht*) packaging; (= *das Einwickeln*) wrapping

Verpackungs-: **Verpackungsindustrie** F packaging industry; **Verpackungskosten** PL packing *or* packaging costs *pl*; **Verpackungsmaterial** NT, **Verpackungsmittel** PL packaging (material); **Verpackungsmüll** M packaging waste

verpassen *ptp* **verpasst** VT (**a**) (= *versäumen*) to miss (**b**) (*inf*: = *zuteilen*) **jdm etw ~** to give sb sth; (= *aufzwingen*) to make sb have sth; **jdm eins** *or* **eine** *or* **eine Ohrfeige ~** to smack sb one (*inf*); **jdm eine Tracht Prügel ~** to give sb a good hiding (*inf*); **jdm einen Denkzettel ~** to give sb something to think about (*inf*)

verpatzen *ptp* **verpatzt** VT (*inf*) to spoil; **sich** (*dat*) **etw ~** to spoil sth/make a mess of sth

verpennen *ptp* **verpennt** (*inf*) ☑ VT (= *verschlafen*) *Termin, Zeit* to miss by oversleeping; (= *schlafend verbringen*) *Tag, Morgen etc* to sleep through; (= *verpassen*) *Einsatz* to miss; *Leben* to waste away; (*fig: = nicht bemerken*) to sleep through ☑ VIR to oversleep

verpesten [fɛɐ'pɛstn], *ptp* **verpestet** VT to pollute; **die Luft im Büro ~** (*inf*) to stink out (*Brit*) *or* up (*US*) the office (*inf*)

verpetzen *ptp* **verpetzt** VT (*inf*) to tell on (*inf*) (*bei* to)

verpfänden *ptp* **verpfändet** VT to pawn; (*Jur*) to mortgage

verpfeifen *ptp* **verpfiffen** [fɛɐ̯'pfaɪfn̩] VT IRREG (*inf*) to grass on (*bei* to) (*inf*)

verpflanzen *ptp* **verpflanzt** VT (*Bot, Med, fig*) to transplant; *Haut* to graft

Verpflanzung F (*Med*) transplant; (*von Haut*) grafting

verpflegen *ptp* **verpflegt** ■ VT to feed ■ VR **sich (selbst)** ~ to feed oneself; (= *selbst kochen*) to cater for oneself

Verpflegung [fɛɐ̯'pfleːɡʊŋ] F -, -en (a) (= *das Verpflegen*) catering; (*Mil*) rationing; **die ~ von 4 Leuten** feeding 4 people (b) (= *Essen*) food; (*Mil*) provisions *pl*; **mit voller ~** including food; (= *mit Vollpension*) with full board

verpflichten [fɛɐ̯'pflɪçtn̩], *ptp* **verpflichtet** ■ VT (a) (= *moralische Pflicht auferlegen*) to oblige; **sich verpflichtet fühlen, etw zu tun, sich zu etw verpflichtet fühlen** to feel obliged to do sth; **der Tradition verpflichtet** bound by tradition; **jdm verpflichtet sein** to be under an obligation to sb (b) (= *binden*) to commit; (*vertraglich, durch Eid, durch Handschlag etc*) to bind; (*durch Gesetz*) to oblige; **jdn auf die Verfassung ~** to make sb swear to uphold the constitution; **auf die Verfassung verpflichtet werden** to be sworn to uphold the constitution; **~d** binding (c) (= *einstellen*) to engage; *Sportler* to sign on; (*Mil*) to enlist ■ VI (= *moralische Pflicht darstellen*) to carry an obligation (*zu etw* to do sth); (= *bindend sein*) to be binding; **das verpflichtet zu nichts** there is no obligation involved ■ VR (*moralisch*) to make a commitment; (*eidlich, vertraglich*) to commit oneself; (*Mil*) to enlist; **sich zu etw ~** to undertake to do sth; (*vertraglich, eidlich*) to commit oneself to doing sth

Verpflichtung F -, -en (a) obligation (*zu etw* to do sth); (*finanziell*) commitment (*zu etw* to do sth); (= *Aufgabe*) duty; **dienstliche ~en** official duties (b) (= *Einstellung*) engaging; (*von Sportlern*) signing on; (*Mil*) enlistment (c) (= *das Sich-Verpflichten*) (*für, auf +acc* for) signing on; (*Mil*) signing up

verpfuschen *ptp* **verpfuscht** VT (*inf*) *Arbeit etc* to bungle; *Leben, Erziehung, Urlaub etc* to screw up (*sl*), to ruin; *Mensch* to ruin; *Kind* to spoil; **jdm/sich den Abend** *etc* ~ to ruin sb's/one's evening *etc*

verpissen *ptp* **verpisst** VR (*sl*) to clear out (*inf*)

verplanen *ptp* **verplant** ■ VT *Zeit* to book up; *Geld* to budget; **jdn ~** (*inf*) to fill up all sb's spare time (for him/her) ■ VR to plan badly; (= *falsch berechnen*) to miscalculate

verplappern *ptp* **verplappert** VR (*inf*) to open one's mouth too wide (*inf*)

verplempern *ptp* **verplempert** VT (*inf*) to waste

verplomben [fɛɐ̯'plɔmbn̩], *ptp* **verplombt** VT to seal

verpönt [fɛɐ̯'pøːnt] ADJ frowned (up)on (*bei* by)

verprassen *ptp* **verprasst** VT to blow (*inf*) (*für* on); **etw sinnlos ~** to fritter sth away

verprellen *ptp* **verprellt** VT to put off

verprügeln *ptp* **verprügelt** VT to beat up

verpulvern [fɛɐ̯'pʊlvɐn, -fɐn], *ptp* **verpulvert** VT (*inf*) to fritter away

verpuppen [fɛɐ̯'pʊpn̩], *ptp* **verpuppt** VR (*inf*) to pupate

Verputz M plaster; (= *Rauputz*) roughcast; **über/unter ~** on top of/under plaster

verputzen *ptp* **verputzt** VT (a) *Gebäude, Wand* to plaster; (*mit Rauputz*) to roughcast (b) (*inf*: = *aufessen*) to polish off (*inf*); **ich kann ihn/das nicht ~** (*inf*) I can't stomach him/it

verqualmen *ptp* **verqualmt** VT *Zimmer, Luft* to fill with smoke; **ein verqualmtes Zimmer** a room full of smoke

verquirlen *ptp* **verquirlt** VT to whisk

verrammeln *ptp* **verrammelt** VT to barricade

verramschen [fɛɐ̯'ramʃn̩], *ptp* **verramscht** VT (*Comm*) to sell off cheap; (*inf auch*) to flog (*Brit inf*)

Verrat M, NO PL betrayal (*an +dat* of); (*Jur*) treason (*an +dat* against); **~ an jdm üben** to betray sb

verraten *ptp* **verraten** IRREG ■ VT *Geheimnis, Absicht, jdn, Vaterland* to betray; (= *bekannt geben, ausplaudern*) to tell; (*fig*: = *erkennen lassen*) to reveal; **nichts ~!** don't say a word!; **er hat es ~** he let it out; **~ und verkauft** (*inf*) well and truly sunk (*inf*) ■ VR to give oneself away

Verräter [fɛɐ̯'rɛːtɐ] M -s, -, **Verräterin** [-ərɪn] F -, -nen traitor (+*gen* to)

verräterisch [fɛɐ̯'rɛːtərɪʃ] ■ ADJ treacherous; (*Jur*) treasonable; (= *verdächtig*) *Hinweis, Blick, Lächeln etc* telltale *attr* ■ ADV (= *etwas erkennen lassend*) revealingly; **ihre Augen zwinkerten ~** her eyes twinkled conspiratorially

verrauchen *ptp* **verraucht** VI AUX SEIN (*fig: Zorn, Enttäuschung*) to subside

verräuchern *ptp* **verräuchert** VT to fill with smoke

verraucht [fɛɐ̯'rauxt] ADJ smoky

verrechnen *ptp* **verrechnet** ■ VT (= *begleichen*) to settle; *Scheck* to clear; (= *gutschreiben*) to credit to an account; (= *belasten*) to debit to an account; *Gutschein* to redeem; **etw mit etw ~** (= *zusammen abrechnen*) to settle sth (together) with sth; (= *gegeneinander aufrechnen*) to balance sth with sth ■ VR to miscalculate; (= *Rechenfehler machen*) to make a mistake/mistakes; (*inf*: = *sich täuschen*) to be mistaken; **sich um zwei Euro ~** to be out by two euros

Verrechnung F settlement; (*von Scheck*) clearing; (= *Gutschrift*) crediting to an account; (= *Belastung*) debiting to an account; **„nur zur ~"** "A/C payee only"

Verrechnungs-: Verrechnungseinheit F clearing unit; **Verrechnungsscheck** M crossed cheque (*Brit*), voucher check (*US*); **Verrechnungsstelle** F clearing house

verrecken *ptp* **verreckt** VI AUX SEIN (*vulg*) to croak (*inf*); (*sl*: = *kaputtgehen*) to give up the ghost (*inf*); **er ist elend(ig)** or **elendiglich verreckt** he died like a dog (*inf*); **soll er doch ~!** let him damn well die! (*inf*); **zu tausenden** or **Tausenden ~** to perish in their thousands; **etw ums Verrecken nicht tun** (*sl*) damn well refuse to do sth (*inf*)

verregnet [fɛɐ̯'reːɡnət] ADJ rainy

verreiben *ptp* **verrieben** [fɛɐ̯'riːbn̩] VT IRREG to rub (*auf +dat* into); *Salbe* to massage (*auf +dat* into)

verreisen *ptp* **verreist** VI AUX SEIN to go away (on a trip *or* journey); **er ist verreist** he's away; **er ist geschäftlich verreist** he's away on business; **wohin ~ Sie in diesem Jahr?** where are you going (on holiday (*esp Brit*) *or* vacation (*US*)) this year?; **mit dem Auto/der Bahn ~** to go on a car/train journey; (*in Urlaub*) to go on holiday (*esp Brit*) *or* vacation (*US*) by car/train

verreißen *ptp* **verrissen** [fɛɐ̯'rɪsn̩] VT IRREG (a) (= *kritisieren*) to tear to pieces (b) (*dial*) = **zerreißen**

verrenken [fɛɐ̯'rɛŋkn̩], *ptp* **verrenkt** ■ VT to dislocate; *Hals* to crick ■ VR to contort oneself

Verrenkung F -, -en (a) contortion; **~en machen** to contort oneself (b) (*Med*: = *das Verrenken*) dislocation

Verrentung [fɛɐ̯'rɛntʊŋ] F -, -en retirement

verrichten *ptp* **verrichtet** VT *Arbeit* to perform; *Andacht* to perform; *Gebet* to say

verriegeln [fɛɐ̯'riːɡln̩], *ptp* **verriegelt** VT to bolt

verringern [fɛɐ̯'rɪŋɐn], *ptp* **verringert** ■ VT to reduce ■ VR to decrease

Verringerung F -, -en (= *das Verringern*) reduction; (= *Abnahme*) decrease; (*von Qualität, Leistung*) deterioration; (*von Abstand, Vorsprung*) lessening

verrinnen *ptp* **verronnen** [fɛɐ̯'rɔnən] VI IRREG AUX SEIN (*Wasser*) to trickle away (*in +dat* into); (*Zeit*) to elapse

Verriss M slating review

verrohen [fɛɐ̯'roːən], *ptp* **verroht** ■ VT to brutalize ■ VI AUX SEIN to become brutalized; (*Sitten*) to coarsen

Verrohung F -, -en brutalization

verrosten *ptp* **verrostet** VI AUX SEIN to rust; (*fig*: = *steif werden*) to get rusty; **verrostet** rusty

verrotten [fɛɐ̯'rɔtn̩], *ptp* **verrottet** VI AUX SEIN to rot; (= *sich organisch zersetzen*) to decompose

verrücken *ptp* **verrückt** VT to move

verrückt [fɛɐ̯'rʏkt] ADJ (a) (= *geisteskrank*) mad (b) (*inf*) crazy; **~ auf** (+*acc*) *or* **nach** crazy about (*inf*); **wie ~** like crazy (*inf*); **so etwas Verrücktes!** what a crazy idea!; **jdn ~ machen** to drive sb crazy *or* wild (*inf*); **~ werden** to go crazy; **ich werd ~!** (*inf*) (well,) I'll be blowed damned! (*inf*); **du bist wohl ~!** you must be crazy!; **~ spielen** to play up

Verrückte(r) [fɛɐ̯'rʏktə] MF DECL AS ADJ (*inf*) lunatic

Verrücktheit F -, -en (*inf*) madness, craziness; (*Handlung*) crazy thing

Verrücktwerden NT **zum ~** enough to drive one mad *or* crazy

Verruf M, NO PL **in ~ kommen** or **geraten** to fall into disrepute; **jdn/etw in ~ bringen** to bring sb/sth into disrepute

verrufen [fɛɐˈruːfn̩] ADJ disreputable

verrühren ptp **verrührt** VT to mix

verrutschen ptp **verrutscht** VI AUX SEIN to slip

Vers [fɛrs] M **-es, -e** [-zə] verse (auch Bibl); (= Zeile) line; **ich kann mir keinen ~ darauf machen** (fig) there's no rhyme or reason to it

versacken ptp **versackt** VI AUX SEIN (fig inf) (= lange zechen) to get involved in a booze-up (inf); (= nicht wegkommen) to stay on

versagen ptp **versagt** 🟦 VT **jdm/sich etw ~** to deny sb/oneself sth; (= verweigern) to refuse sb/oneself sth; **etw bleibt** or **ist jdm versagt** sb is denied sth 🟦 VI to fail; (Maschine) to break down; (Gewehr) to fail to function; **die Beine/Nerven** etc **versagten ihm** his legs/nerves etc gave way; **da versagt diese Methode** this method doesn't work there

Versagen [fɛɐˈzaːgn̩] NT **-s**, NO PL failure; (von Maschine) breakdown; **menschliches ~** human error

Versager [fɛɐˈzaːgɐ] M **-s, -**, **Versagerin** [-ərɪn] F **-, -nen** failure

versalzen ptp **versalzen** VT IRREG to put too much salt in/on; (inf = verderben) to spoil; **~ sein** to be too salty; **~es Essen** oversalty food

versammeln ptp **versammelt** 🟦 VT to assemble (auch Mil); **Leute um sich ~** to gather people around one; **vor versammelter Mannschaft** (inf) in front of the assembled company 🟦 VR to assemble; (Parlament) to sit; (Ausschuss, Mitglieder) to meet; (Tagung) to convene

Versammlung F (= Veranstaltung) meeting; (= versammelte Menschen) assembly; **verfassunggebende ~** legislative assembly

Versammlungsfreiheit F freedom of assembly

Versand [fɛɐˈzant] M **-(e)s** [-dəs], NO PL **(a)** (= das Versenden) dispatch (esp Brit), shipment; (= das Vertreiben) distribution; **der ~ per Land/Schiene** shipment by land/rail **(b)** (Abteilung) shipping department

Versand-: Versandabteilung F shipping department; **Versandgeschäft** NT **(a)** (= Firma) mail-order firm **(b)** (= Handel) mail-order business; **Versandhandel** M mail-order business; **Versandhaus** NT mail-order firm; **Versandkosten** PL transport(ation) costs pl; **Versandschein** M consignment note

versauen ptp **versaut** VT (inf) **(a)** (= verschmutzen) to make a mess of; Umwelt to mess up **(b)** (= verderben, ruinieren) to ruin; Kinder, Moral, Mensch to screw up (inf); (= schlecht machen) Arbeit to make a mess of; **der Chirurg hat ihn versaut** the surgeon made a mess of him

versauern [fɛɐˈzauɐn], ptp **versauert** (inf) 🟦 VI AUX SEIN to stagnate; **eine versauerte alte Jungfer** an embittered old spinster 🟦 VT **jdm etw ~** to mess sth up for sb (inf)

versaufen ptp **versoffen** [fɛɐˈzɔfn̩] IRREG (inf) VT Geld to spend on booze (inf); **seinen Verstand ~** to drink oneself silly; siehe auch **versoffen**

versäumen ptp **versäumt** VT to miss; Zeit to lose; Pflicht to neglect; (Sw: = aufhalten) jdn to delay; **(es) ~, etw zu tun** to fail to do sth; **das Versäumte** what one has missed; **die versäumte Zeit aufholen** to make up for lost time

Versäumnis [fɛɐˈzɔymnɪs] NT **-ses, -se** (= Fehler, Nachlässigkeit) failing; (= Unterlassung) omission; (= versäumte Zeit) (Sch) absence (+gen from); (Jur) default (+gen in); **bei ~ rechtzeitiger Bezahlung** in the event that payment is not made punctually

versaut ADJ (sl: = schweinisch) filthy

verschachtelt [fɛɐˈʃaxtlt] ADJ Satz complex; (Comput) Menü, Befehle nested; **ineinander ~** interlocking

verschaffen ptp **verschafft** VT **(a)** jdm etw ~ Geld, Kapital, Alibi to provide sb with sth; Erleichterung, Genugtuung, Vergnügen to give sb sth; Ansehen, Respekt to earn sb sth **(b)** sich (dat) etw ~ to obtain sth; Kenntnisse to acquire sth; Ansehen, Vorteil to gain sth; Ruhe, Respekt to get sth; **sich mit Gewalt Zutritt ~** to force an entry; **ich muss mir darüber Gewissheit ~** I must be certain about it; **ich muss mir darüber Klarheit ~** I must clarify the matter

verschandeln [fɛɐˈʃandl̩n], ptp **verschandelt** VT to ruin

Verschandelung [fɛɐˈʃandəlʊŋ] F **-, -en**, **Verschandlung** [fɛɐˈʃandlʊŋ] F **-, -en** ruining

verschanzen ptp **verschanzt** VR (Mil) (fig) to entrench oneself (hinter +dat behind); (= sich verbarrikadieren) to barricade oneself in (in etw (dat) sth); (= Deckung suchen) to take cover (hinter +dat behind)

verschärfen ptp **verschärft** 🟦 VT (= erhöhen) Tempo, Aufmerksamkeit to increase; Gegensätze to intensify; (= verschlimmern) Lage to aggravate; Spannungen to heighten; (= strenger machen) to tighten 🟦 VR (Tempo, Aufmerksamkeit) to increase; (Wettbewerb, Gegensätze) to intensify; (Lage) to become aggravated; (Spannungen) to heighten; (Kontrollen, Gesetze, Maßnahmen, Prüfungen) to become tighter

verschärft [fɛɐˈʃɛrft] 🟦 ADJ **(a)** (= erhöht) Tempo, Aufmerksamkeit, Wettbewerb increased; Gegensätze intensified; (= verschlimmert) Lage aggravated; Spannungen heightened; (= strenger) Kontrollen, Strafe, Maßnahmen tightened; Arrest close **(b)** (inf: = gut) brilliant (inf) 🟦 ADV (= intensiver) more intensively; (= strenger) more severely; prüfen more closely; **~ aufpassen** to keep a closer watch; **~ kontrollieren** to keep a tighter control; **~ vorgehen** to take more stringent measures

verscharren ptp **verscharrt** VT to bury

verschätzen ptp **verschätzt** VR to misjudge, to miscalculate (in etw (dat) sth); **sich um zwei Monate ~** to be out by two months

verschauen ptp **verschaut** VR (Aus) **(a)** (= nicht richtig sehen) to make a mistake **(b)** (= sich verlieben) **sich in jdn ~** to fall for sb

verscheißern [fɛɐˈʃaisɐn], ptp **verscheißert** VT (inf) **jdn ~** to make fun of sb

verschenken ptp **verschenkt** VT (lit, fig) to give away

verscherzen ptp **verscherzt** VT **sich** (dat) **etw ~** to lose sth; **sich** (dat) **seine Chancen ~** to throw away one's chances; **sich** (dat) **jds Gunst** or **Wohlwollen ~** to lose sb's favour (Brit) or favor (US); **es sich** (dat) **mit jdm ~** to spoil things (for oneself) with sb

verscheuchen ptp **verscheucht** VT to scare away; Fliegen to chase away; (fig) Sorgen, Gedanken etc to drive away

verscheuern ptp **verscheuert** VT (inf) to sell off

verschicken ptp **verschickt** VT **(a)** (= versenden) to send off **(b)** (zur Kur etc) to send away **(c)** (= deportieren) to deport

verschieben ptp **verschoben** IRREG 🟦 VT **(a)** (= verrücken) to move (auch Comput), to shift; Truppen to displace; (Rail) to shunt **(b)** (= aufschieben) to change; (auf später) to postpone (um for) **(c)** (inf) Waren, Devisen to traffic in 🟦 VR **(a)** (= verrutschen) to move out of place; (fig: Perspektive, Schwerpunkt) to shift **(b)** (zeitlich) to be postponed

Verschiebung F **(a)** (= das Verschieben) moving; (von Truppen) displacement; (fig: von Perspektiven) alteration **(b)** (von Termin) postponement **(c)** (inf: von Waren, Devisen) trafficking **(d)** (Geol) displacement **(e)** (Ling: von Lauten) shift

verschieden [fɛɐˈʃiːdn̩] 🟦 ADJ **(a)** (= unterschiedlich) different; (= unähnlich) dissimilar; **die ~sten Sorten** many different kinds; **das ist ganz ~** (= wird ~ gehandhabt) that varies **(b)** (= mehrere, einige) several **(c)** (substantivisch) **Verschiedene** various or several people; **Verschiedenes** different things; (in Zeitungen, Listen) miscellaneous 🟦 ADV differently; **die Häuser sind ~ lang/breit/hoch** the houses vary in length/breadth/height

verschiedenartig ADJ different; (= mannigfaltig) diverse; **die ~sten Dinge** all sorts of things

verschiedenerlei [fɛɐˈʃiːdənɐˈlai] ADJ INV **(a)** ATTR many different **(b)** (substantivisch) many different things

Verschiedenheit F **-, -en** difference (+gen of, in); (= Unähnlichkeit) dissimilarity; (= Vielfalt) variety

verschiedentlich [fɛɐˈʃiːdntlɪç] ADV (= mehrmals) several times; (= vereinzelt) occasionally

verschießen ptp **verschossen** [fɛɐˈʃɔsn̩] IRREG 🟦 VT **(a)** Munition to use up; Pfeile to shoot off; (inf) Fotos, Film to take, to use up **(b)** (Sport) to miss 🟦 VR **sich in jdn ~** to fall for sb (inf); **in jdn verschossen sein** to be crazy about sb (inf) 🟦 VI AUX SEIN (Stoff, Farbe) to fade

verschimmeln ptp **verschimmelt** VI AUX SEIN (Nahrungsmittel) to go mouldy (Brit) or moldy (US); (Wand, Leder, Papier etc) to become mildewed; **verschimmelt** (*lit*) mouldy (*Brit*), moldy (*US*); mildewed, mildewy

verschlafen¹ *ptp* **verschlafen** IRREG 🔳 VIR to oversleep 🔳 VT *Termin* to miss by oversleeping; (= *schlafend verbringen*) *Tag, Morgen* to sleep through; (= *verpassen*) *Einsatz* to miss

verschlafen² ADJ sleepy; (= *trottelig*) *Mensch* dozy (*inf*); **~ sein** (= *Vielschläfer sein*) to like one's sleep

Verschlag M (= *abgetrennter Raum*) partitioned area; (= *Schuppen*) shed; (*grob gezimmert*) shack; (*esp für Kaninchen*) hutch; (*ans Haus angebaut*) lean-to; (= *elende Behausung*) hovel; (= *Verpackung*) crate

verschlagen *ptp* **verschlagen** VT IRREG **(a)** *etw mit Brettern ~* to board sth up **(b)** (= *nehmen*) *Atem* to take away; **das hat mir die Sprache ~** it left me speechless **(c)** (= *geraten lassen*) to bring; **auf eine einsame Insel ~ werden** to be cast up on a lonely island; **an einen Ort ~ werden** to end up somewhere

verschlampen *ptp* **verschlampt** (*inf*) 🔳 VT (= *verlieren*) to go and lose (*inf*) 🔳 VI AUX SEIN (*Mensch*) to go to seed (*inf*)

verschlechtern [fɛɐ̯'ʃlɛçtɐn], *ptp* **verschlechtert** 🔳 VT to make worse; *Qualität* to impair; *Aussicht* to decrease 🔳 VR to get worse; **sich finanziell ~** to be worse off financially; **sich beruflich ~** to take a worse job

Verschlechterung F -, -en worsening; (*von Leistung*) decline; **eine finanzielle ~** a financial setback; **eine berufliche ~** a retrograde step professionally

verschleiern [fɛɐ̯'ʃlaiɐn], *ptp* **verschleiert** 🔳 VT to veil; *Blick* to blur 🔳 VR (*Frau*) to veil oneself; (*Himmel*) to become hazy; (*Blick*) to become blurred; (= *träumerisch werden*) to become hazy

Verschleierung F -, -en veiling; (*fig auch*) disguising

verschleimen *ptp* **verschleimt** 🔳 VT to congest with phlegm; **verschleimt sein** (*Patient*) to be congested with phlegm 🔳 VI AUX SEIN to become congested with phlegm

Verschleimung [fɛɐ̯'ʃlaimʊŋ] F -, -en mucous congestion

Verschleiß [fɛɐ̯'ʃlais] M -es, -e **(a)** (*lit, fig*) wear and tear; (= *Verbrauch*) consumption; (= *Verluste*) loss; **eingeplanter ~** built-in obsolescence; **sein ~ an Frauen** (*hum*) the rate he goes through women **(b)** (*Aus*: = *Kleinverkauf*) retail trade

verschleißen [fɛɐ̯'ʃlaisn], *pret* **verschliss** [fɛɐ̯'ʃlɪs], *ptp* **verschlissen** [fɛɐ̯'ʃlɪsn] 🔳 VT **(a)** (= *kaputtmachen*) to wear out; (= *verbrauchen*) to use up; **der Verein hat dieses Jahr schon drei Trainer verschlissen** the club has already gone through three managers this year **(b)** (*Aus*) to retail 🔳 VI AUX SEIN to wear out; *siehe auch* **verschlissen** 🔳 VR to wear out; (*Menschen*) to wear oneself out

verschleppen *ptp* **verschleppt** VT **(a)** (= *entführen*) *jdn* to abduct; *Gefangene, Kriegsopfer etc* to displace; *Kunstschätze etc* to carry off; (*inf*) *etw* to go off with **(b)** (= *hinauszögern*) *Prozess, Verhandlung, Ermittlungen* to draw out; (*Pol*) to delay; *Krankheit* to protract

Verschleppte(r) [fɛɐ̯'ʃlɛptə] MF DECL AS ADJ displaced person; **die ~n** the displaced *pl*

Verschleppung [fɛɐ̯'ʃlɛpʊŋ] F -, -en **(a)** (*von Menschen*) abduction; (*von Kunstschätzen*) carrying off **(b)** (= *Verzögerung*) (*von Krankheit*) protraction; (*von Gesetzesänderung*) delay

Verschleppungstaktik F delaying tactics *pl*

verschleudern *ptp* **verschleudert** VT (*Comm*) to dump; (= *vergeuden*) *Vermögen, Geld, Energie, Ressourcen* to squander

verschließbar ADJ *Dosen, Gläser etc* sealable; *Tür, Schublade, Zimmer etc* lockable

verschließen *ptp* **verschlossen** [fɛɐ̯'ʃlɔsn] IRREG 🔳 VT **(a)** (= *abschließen*) to lock (up); (*fig*) to close; (= *versperren*) to bar; (*mit Riegel*) to bolt; **jdm etw ~** (*fig*) to deny sb sth; *siehe auch* **verschlossen** **(b)** (= *zumachen*) to close; (*dauerhaft*) *Einmachglas, Karton, Brief* to seal; (*mit Pfropfen*) *Flasche* to cork; **die Augen/Ohren/sein Herz (vor etw** *dat***) ~** to shut one's eyes/ears/heart (to sth) 🔳 VR (*Reize, Sprache, Möglichkeit*) to be closed (+*dat* to); (*Mensch*: = *reserviert sein*) to shut oneself off (+*dat* from); **sich einer Sache** (*dat*) *or* **gegen etw ~** to close one's mind to sth; **ich kann mich der Tatsache nicht ~, dass ...** I can't close my eyes to the fact that ...

verschlimmbessern [fɛɐ̯'ʃlɪmbɛsɐn], *ptp* **verschlimmbessert** VT INSEP (*hum*) to make worse

verschlimmern [fɛɐ̯'ʃlɪmɐn], *ptp* **verschlimmert** 🔳 VT to make worse 🔳 VR to get worse

Verschlimmerung F -, -en worsening

verschlingen *ptp* **verschlungen** [fɛɐ̯'ʃlʊŋən] IRREG 🔳 VT **(a)** (= *verflechten*) to intertwine; **er stand mit verschlungenen Armen da** he stood there with his arms folded; **ein verschlungener Pfad** a winding path **(b)** (= *fressen, gierig essen*) to devour; (*fig*) (*Welle, Dunkelheit*) to engulf; (= *verbrauchen*) *Geld, Strom etc* to eat up; (*inf*) *Buch, jds Worte* to devour; **jdn mit Blicken** *or* **den Augen ~** to devour sb with one's eyes 🔳 VR to become intertwined; (*zu einem Knoten etc*) to become entangled; (*Därme*) to become twisted

verschliss PRET *von* **verschleißen**

verschlissen [fɛɐ̯'ʃlɪsn] 🔳 PTP *von* **verschleißen** 🔳 ADJ worn (out); (*fig*) *Arbeiter, Politiker etc* burned-out (*inf*)

verschlossen [fɛɐ̯'ʃlɔsn] ADJ closed; (*mit Schlüssel*) *Tür, Fach etc* locked; (*mit Riegel*) bolted; *Dose* closed; *Briefumschlag* sealed; (*fig*: = *unzugänglich*) reserved; **gut ~ aufbewahren** keep tightly closed; **hinter ~en Türen** behind closed doors; **wir standen vor ~er Tür** we were left standing on the doorstep; *siehe auch* **verschließen**

Verschlossenheit F -, NO PL (*von Mensch*) reserve

verschlucken *ptp* **verschluckt** 🔳 VT to swallow; (*fig auch*) *Wörter, Silben, Buchstaben* to slur; *Geld* to consume; *Schall* to deaden 🔳 VR to swallow the wrong way; (*fig*) to splutter

Verschluss M **(a)** (= *Schloss*) lock; (*luft-, wasserdicht, für Zoll*) seal; (= *Deckel, Klappe*) top; (= *Pfropfen, Stöpsel*) stopper; (*an Kleidung*) fastener; (*an Schmuck*) catch; (*an Tasche, Buch, Schuh*) clasp; **etw unter ~ halten** to keep sth under lock and key **(b)** (*Phot*) shutter **(c)** (*Med, Phon*) occlusion

verschlüsseln [fɛɐ̯'ʃlʏsln], *ptp* **verschlüsselt** VT to (put into) code

Verschlüsselung [fɛɐ̯'ʃlʏsəlʊŋ] F -, -en coding

verschmachten *ptp* **verschmachtet** VI AUX SEIN to languish (*vor* +*dat* for); **vor Durst/Hitze ~** (*inf*) to be dying of thirst/heat (*inf*)

verschmähen *ptp* **verschmäht** VT to spurn; **verschmähte Liebe** unrequited love; **einen Whisky verschmähe ich nie** I never say no to a whisky

verschmelzen *ptp* **verschmolzen** [fɛɐ̯'ʃmɔltsn] IRREG VI AUX SEIN to melt together; (*Metalle*) to fuse; (*Farben*) to blend; (*Betriebe etc*) to merge; (*fig*) to blend (*zu* into); **zu einer Einheit ~** to blend into one

Verschmelzung [fɛɐ̯'ʃmɛltsʊŋ] F -, -en **(a)** (= *Verbindung*) fusion; (*von Reizen, Eindrücken, Farben*) blending **(b)** (*fig*: *von Völkern, Begriffen etc*) fusion **(c)** (*Comm*) merger

verschmerzen *ptp* **verschmerzt** VT to get over

verschmieren *ptp* **verschmiert** 🔳 VT **(a)** (= *verstreichen*) to spread (*in* +*dat* over) **(b)** (= *verputzen*) *Löcher* to fill in **(c)** *Fenster, Gesicht* to smear; *Geschriebenes, Schminke* to smudge 🔳 VI to smudge

verschmiert [fɛɐ̯'ʃmiːɐ̯t] ADJ *Hände, Gesicht* smeary; *Schminke* smudged

verschmitzt [fɛɐ̯'ʃmɪtst] 🔳 ADJ mischievous 🔳 ADV mischievously

verschmutzen *ptp* **verschmutzt** 🔳 VT to dirty; *Luft, Wasser, Umwelt* to pollute; *Fahrbahn* to make muddy; *Straße, Bürgersteig* (*Hund*) to foul 🔳 VI AUX SEIN to get dirty; (*Luft, Wasser, Umwelt*) to become polluted

verschmutzt [fɛɐ̯'ʃmʊtst] ADJ dirty, soiled; *Luft etc* polluted; **stark ~** very dirty, badly soiled; **„~e Fahrbahn"** "mud on road"

Verschmutzung [fɛɐ̯'ʃmʊtsʊŋ] F -, -en NO PL (= *das Verschmutzen*) dirtying; (*von Luft, Wasser, Umwelt*) pollution; (*von Fahrbahn*) muddying **(b)** (= *das Verschmutztsein*) dirtiness *no pl*; (*von Luft etc*) pollution; **starke ~en auf der Straße** a great deal of mud on the road

verschnaufen *ptp* **verschnauft** VIR (*inf*) to take a breather (*inf*)

verschneit [fɛɐ̯'ʃnait] ADJ snow-covered; **tief ~** thick with snow

verschnupft [fɛɐ̯'ʃnʊpft] ADJ (*inf*) **(a)** (= *erkältet*) *Mensch* with a cold; *Nase* bunged up (*inf*) **(b)** (*usu pred*: = *beleidigt*) peeved (*inf*)

verschollen [fɛɐ̯'ʃɔlən] ADJ *Schiff, Flugzeug, Gemälde, Mensch etc* missing; *Literaturwerk* forgotten; **ein lange ~er Freund** a long-lost friend; **er ist ~** (*im Krieg*) he is missing, presumed dead

verschonen *ptp* **verschont** VT to spare (*jdn von etw* sb sth); **verschone mich damit!** spare me that!; **von etw verschont bleiben** to escape sth

verschönern [fɛɐ̯'ʃøːnɐn], *ptp* **verschönert** VT to improve (the appearance of); *Wohnung, Haus, Zimmer* to brighten (up)

Verschönerung [fɛɐ̯'ʃøːnərʊŋ] F **-, -en** improvement; (*von Wohnung, Zimmer*) brightening up

Verschonung F sparing; (*von Steuern*) exemption

verschränken [fɛɐ̯'ʃrɛŋkn̩], *ptp* **verschränkt** VT to cross over; *Arme* to fold; *Beine* to cross; *Hände* to clasp

verschrecken *ptp* **verschreckt** VT to frighten off

verschreckt [fɛɐ̯'ʃrɛkt] ADJ frightened

verschreiben *ptp* **verschrieben** [fɛɐ̯'ʃriːbn̩] IRREG **1** VT **(a)** (= *verordnen*) to prescribe **(b)** *Papier* to use up **2** VR **(a)** (= *falsch schreiben*) to make a slip (of the pen) **(b) sich einer Sache** (*dat*) **~** to devote oneself to sth

verschreibungspflichtig [-pflɪçtɪç] ADJ only available on prescription

verschrieen [fɛɐ̯'ʃriːən], **verschrien** [fɛɐ̯'ʃriːn] ADJ notorious; **als etw ~** notorious for being sth

verschrotten [fɛɐ̯'ʃrɔtn̩], *ptp* **verschrottet** VT to scrap

verschrumpeln *ptp* **verschrumpelt** VI AUX SEIN to shrivel

verschüchtern [fɛɐ̯'ʃʏçtɐn], *ptp* **verschüchtert** VT to intimidate

verschulden *ptp* **verschuldet** **1** VT (= *schuldhaft verursachen*) to be to blame for; *Unfall, Unglück* to cause **2** VI AUX SEIN (= *in Schulden geraten*) to get into debt; **immer mehr ~** to get deeper and deeper into debt; **verschuldet sein** to be in debt **3** VR to get into debt

Verschulden [fɛɐ̯'ʃʊldn̩] NT **-s**, NO PL fault; **durch eigenes ~** through one's own fault; **ohne sein/mein ~** through no fault of his (own)/of my own *or* of mine

Verschuldung [fɛɐ̯'ʃʊldʊŋ] F **-, -en (a)** (= *Schulden*) indebtedness **(b)** (= *schuldhafte Verursachung*) blame (+*gen* for); **bei eigener ~ eines Schadens** if one is (oneself) to blame for damage caused

verschütten *ptp* **verschüttet** VT **(a)** *Flüssigkeit* to spill **(b)** (= *begraben*) **verschüttet werden** (*Mensch*) to be buried (alive); (*fig*) to be submerged **(c)** (= *blockieren*) *Weg* to block

verschüttet [fɛɐ̯'ʃʏtət] ADJ buried (alive); (*fig*) submerged

Verschüttete(r) [fɛɐ̯'ʃʏtətə] MF DECL AS ADJ person buried in the disaster/accident

verschütt gehen VI IRREG AUX SEIN (*inf*) to get lost

verschweigen *ptp* **verschwiegen** [fɛɐ̯'ʃviːgn̩] VT IRREG to withhold (*jdm etw* sth from sb); **ich habe nichts zu ~** I've nothing to hide; *siehe auch* **verschwiegen**

verschwenden [fɛɐ̯'ʃvɛndn̩], *ptp* **verschwendet** VT to waste (*auf* +*acc, an* +*acc, für* on); (= *leichtsinnig vertun*) *Geld* to squander

Verschwender [fɛɐ̯'ʃvɛndɐ] M **-s, -**, **Verschwenderin** [-ərɪn] F **-, -nen** spendthrift

verschwenderisch [fɛɐ̯'ʃvɛndərɪʃ] **1** ADJ wasteful; *Leben* extravagant; (= *üppig*) lavish; *Fülle* lavish **2** ADV wastefully; (= *üppig*) lavishly; **mit etw ~ umgehen** to be lavish with sth

Verschwendung F **-, -en** wastefulness; **~ von Geld/Zeit** waste of money/time

verschwiegen [fɛɐ̯'ʃviːgn̩] ADJ *Mensch* discreet; *Ort* secluded; *siehe auch* **verschweigen**

Verschwiegenheit F **-**, NO PL (*von Mensch*) discretion; (*von Ort*) seclusion; **zur ~ verpflichtet** bound to secrecy

verschwinden *ptp* **verschwunden** [fɛɐ̯'ʃvʊndn̩] VI IRREG AUX SEIN to disappear, to vanish; **verschwinde!** clear out! (*inf*); **etw ~ lassen** (*Zauberer*) to make sth disappear *or* vanish; (= *verstecken*) to dispose of sth; (= *stehlen*) to steal sth; **von der Landkarte ~** to disappear *or* vanish (*dat*) **~ lassen** to slip sth into sth; **(mal) ~ müssen** (*euph inf*) to have to go to the bathroom; *siehe auch* **verschwunden**

Verschwinden [fɛɐ̯'ʃvɪndn̩] NT **-s**, NO PL disappearance

verschwindend **1** ADJ *Anzahl, Menge* insignificant; *Minderheit* tiny **2** ADV **~ wenig** very, very few; **~ klein** *or* **gering** minute

verschwitzen *ptp* **verschwitzt** VT **(a)** *Kleidung* to make sweaty **(b)** (*fig inf*) to forget

verschwitzt [fɛɐ̯'ʃvɪtst] ADJ *Kleidungsstück* sweat-stained; (= *feucht*) sweaty

verschwommen [fɛɐ̯'ʃvɔmən] **1** ADJ *Foto, Umrisse* fuzzy; *Berge* hazy; *Erinnerung, Vorstellung, Argumente, Begriffe* vague **2** ADV

wahrnehmen, sehen blurred; *sich erinnern, sich vorstellen, sprechen, reden* vaguely; **ich sehe alles ~** everything looks hazy to me

Verschwommenheit F **-**, NO PL (*von Foto, Umrissen*) fuzziness; (*von Anblick*) haziness; (*von Erinnerung, Vorstellung, Argumenten, Begriffen*) vagueness

verschwören *ptp* **verschworen** [fɛɐ̯'ʃvoːrən] VR IRREG **(a)** (= *ein Komplott schmieden*) to plot (*mit* with, *gegen* against); **sich zu etw ~** to plot sth; **alles hat sich gegen mich verschworen** (*fig*) there's a conspiracy against me **(b)** (= *sich verschreiben*) **sich einer Sache** (*dat*) **~** to give oneself over to sth

Verschwörer [fɛɐ̯'ʃvøːrɐ] M **-s, -**, **Verschwörerin** [-ərɪn] F **-, -nen** conspirator

Verschwörung [fɛɐ̯'ʃvøːrʊŋ] F **-, -en** conspiracy, plot

verschwunden [fɛɐ̯'ʃvʊndn̩] ADJ missing; **das ~e Mädchen/Auto** the missing girl/car; *siehe auch* **verschwinden**

versechsfachen [fɛɐ̯'zɛksfaxn̩], *ptp* **versechsfacht** **1** VT to multiply by six **2** VR to increase sixfold

versehen *ptp* **versehen** IRREG **1** VT **(a)** (= *ausüben*) *Amt, Stelle etc* to occupy; *Dienst* to perform; (= *sich kümmern um*) to take care of; (*Bus, Schiff etc*) *Route* to provide the/a service on; *Dienst* to provide; **den Dienst eines Kollegen ~** to take a colleague's place **(b)** (= *ausstatten*) **jdn mit etw ~** to provide sb with sth; (= *ausrüsten auch*) to equip sb with sth; **etw mit etw ~** to put sth on/in sth; (= *montieren*) to fit sth with sth; **ein Buch mit einem Umschlag ~** to provide a book with a dust jacket; **mit etw ~ sein** to have sth; **mit Etiketten/Wegweisern ~ sein** to be labelled (*Brit*) *or* labeled (*US*)/signposted **(c)** (*Eccl*) **jdn (mit den Sterbesakramenten) ~** to administer the last rites to sb **(d)** (= *geben*) to give; **jdn mit einer Vollmacht ~** to invest sb with full powers; **etw mit seiner Unterschrift ~** to sign sth; **etw mit einem Stempel ~** to stamp sth; **etw mit Akzept ~** (*Fin*) to accept sth **2** VR **(a)** (= *sich irren*) to be mistaken **(b) sich mit etw ~** (= *sich versorgen*) to provide oneself with sth; (= *sich ausstatten*) to equip oneself with sth **(c) ehe man sichs versieht** before you could turn (a)round

Versehen [fɛɐ̯'zeːən] NT **-s, -** (= *Irrtum*) mistake; (= *Unachtsamkeit*) oversight; **aus ~** by mistake

versehentlich [fɛɐ̯'zeːəntlɪç] **1** ADJ ATTR inadvertent; (= *irrtümlich*) erroneous **2** ADV inadvertently, by mistake

Versehrte(r) [fɛɐ̯'zeːɐtə] MF DECL AS ADJ disabled person/man/woman *etc*

versenden *ptp* **versendet** (*rare*) *or* **versandt** [fɛɐ̯'zant] VT IRREG *or* REG to send

Versender(in) M(F) consignor, shipper

Versendung F sending; (*von Heiratsanzeige*) sending out; **die ~ der Kataloge** sending (out) the catalogues (*Brit*) *or* catalogs (*US*)

Versendungs-: Versendungsland NT country of consignment; **Versendungsort** M place of consignment

versengen *ptp* **versengt** VT (*Sonne*) (*mit Bügeleisen*) to scorch; (*Feuer*) to singe

versenkbar ADJ that can be lowered; *Scheinwerfer* retractable; *Nähmaschine, Tischplatte* foldaway *attr*

versenken *ptp* **versenkt** **1** VT **(a)** *Schatz, Behälter, Bohrinsel* to sink; *Leiche, Sarg* to lower; *Schiff* to sink; *das eigene Schiff* to scuttle; **den Kopf in ein Buch ~** to bury one's head in a book **(b)** *Schraube* to countersink; *Tischplatte* to fold away; (*Theat*) to lower; **eine Nähmaschine, die man ~ kann** a foldaway sewing machine **2** VR **sich in etw** (*acc*) **~** to become immersed in sth; *in Gedanken auch, in Anblick* to lose oneself in sth

Versenkung F **(a)** (= *das Versenken*) sinking; (*von Leiche, Sarg*) lowering; (*von eigenem Schiff*) scuttling **(b)** (*Theat*) trap(door) **(c)** (= *das Sichversenken*) immersion; **jdn aus seiner ~ reißen** to tear sb from (his immersion in) his book/work *etc* **(d)** (*inf*) **in der ~ verschwinden** to vanish; **aus der ~ auftauchen** to reappear

versessen [fɛɐ̯'zɛsn̩] ADJ (*fig*) **auf etw** (*acc*) **~ sein** to be very keen on sth

Versessenheit F **-, -en** keenness (*auf* +*acc* on)

versetzen *ptp* **versetzt** **1** VT **(a)** (= *an andere Stelle setzen*) to move; *Pflanzen* to transplant; (= *nicht geradlinig anordnen*) to

stagger
(b) (*beruflich*) to move; **jdn in einen höheren Rang ~** to promote sb
(c) (*Sch: in höhere Klasse*) to move up
(d) (*inf*: = *verkaufen*) to sell; (= *verpfänden*) to pawn
(e) (*inf*: = *nicht erscheinen*) **jdn ~** to stand sb up (*inf*)
(f) **etw in Bewegung ~** to set sth in motion; **etw in Schwingung ~** to set sth swinging; **jdn in Wut ~** to send sb into a rage; **jdn in fröhliche Stimmung ~** to put sb in a cheerful mood; **jdn in Sorge/Unruhe ~** to worry/disturb sb; **jdn in Angst (und Schrecken) ~** to frighten sb; **jdn in die Lage ~, etw zu tun** to put sb in a position to do sth
(g) (= *geben*) *Stoß, Schlag, Tritt etc* to give; **jdm eins ~** (*inf*) to belt sb (*inf*)
2 VR sich in jdn/jds Lage/Gefühle ~ to put oneself in sb's place *or* position; **sich in eine frühere Zeit/seine Jugend** *etc* ~ to take oneself back to an earlier period/one's youth *etc*

Versetzung [fɛɐˈzɛtsʊŋ] F **-, -en (a)** (*beruflich*) transfer; **seine ~ in einen höheren Rang** his promotion (to a higher rank) **(b)** (*Sch*) moving up; **bei nicht erfolgter ~** when the pupil isn't moved up **(c)** (= *nicht geradlinige Anordnung*) staggering

verseuchen [fɛɐˈzɔyçn̩], *ptp* **verseucht** VT (*mit Bakterien*) to infect; (*mit Gas, Giftstoffen, fig*) to contaminate; (*Comput*) to infect with a virus

Verseuchung F **-, -en** (*mit Bakterien, Viren*) infection; (*mit Gas, Giftstoffen, fig*) contamination *no pl*

Vers-: Versform F (*Poet*) verse form; **Versfuß** M (*Poet*) (metrical) foot

Versicherer [fɛɐˈzɪçɐɐ] M **-s, -** insurer; (*bei Schiffen*) underwriter

versichern *ptp* **versichert** VT **(a)** (= *bestätigen*) to assure; (= *beteuern*) to protest; **jdm ~, dass ...** to assure sb that ...; **jdm etw ~** to assure sb of sth; **seine Unschuld ~** to protest sth to sb **(b)** (*Insur: gegen Betrag*) to insure; **gegen etw versichert sein** to be insured against sth
2 VR **(a)** (= *Versicherung abschließen*) to insure oneself (*mit* for); (*Lebensversicherung*) to take out a life insurance policy; **sich gegen Unfall ~** to take out accident insurance **(b)** (= *sich vergewissern*) to make sure *or* certain

Versichertenkarte F health insurance card

Versicherte(r) [fɛɐˈzɪçɐtə] MF DECL AS ADJ insured (party)

Versicherung F **(a)** (= *Bestätigung*) assurance; (= *Beteuerung*) protestation **(b)** (= *Feuerversicherung etc*) insurance **(c)** (= *Gesellschaft*) insurance company

Versicherungs-: Versicherungsbeginn M policy inception; **Versicherungsbeitrag** M **(a)** (*bei staatlicher Versicherung etc*) insurance contribution **(b)** (*bei Haftpflichtversicherung etc*) insurance premium; **Versicherungsbetrug** M insurance fraud; **Versicherungsdauer** F period of insurance; **Versicherungsfall** M (= *Verlust*) event of loss; (= *Schaden*) event of damage; **Versicherungskarte** F insurance card; **die grüne ~** (*Mot*) the green card (*Brit*), *insurance document for driving abroad*; **Versicherungsmakler(in)** M(F) insurance broker; **Versicherungsmathematik** F actuarial theory; **Versicherungsnehmer(in)** M(F) (*form*) policy holder; **Versicherungspflicht** F compulsory insurance; **jeder Autofahrer unterliegt der ~** insurance is compulsory for every driver; **versicherungspflichtig** [-pflɪçtɪç] ADJ subject to compulsory insurance; **Versicherungspolice** F insurance policy; **Versicherungsschein** M insurance policy; **vorläufiger ~** cover note (*Brit*), binder (*US*); **Versicherungsschutz** M insurance cover; **Versicherungssumme** F sum insured; **Versicherungsverein** M insurance company; **~ auf Gegenseitigkeit** mutual insurance company; **Versicherungsvertrag** M insurance contract; **Versicherungswesen** NT, NO PL insurance (business); **Versicherungszertifikat** NT insurance certificate

versickern *ptp* **versickert** VI AUX SEIN to seep away; (*fig*) (*Gespräch, Unterstützung*) to dry up; (*Interesse, Teilnahme*) to peter out; (*Geld*) to trickle away

versiebenfachen [fɛɐˈziːbn̩faxn̩], *ptp* **versiebenfacht** **1** VT to multiply by seven **2** VR to increase sevenfold

versiegeln *ptp* **versiegelt** VT to seal

versiegen *ptp* **versiegt** VI AUX SEIN (*Fluss, Quelle, Gespräch*) to dry up; (*Interesse*) to peter out; (*gute Laune, Humor, Kräfte*) to fail; **nie ~de Hoffnung** never-failing *or* undying hope

versiert [vɛrˈziːɐt] ADJ experienced; **in etw** (*dat*) **~ sein** to be experienced *or* (*in Bezug auf Wissen*) (well) versed in sth

versifft [fɛɐˈzɪft] ADJ (*sl*) yucky (*inf*)

versilbern [fɛɐˈzɪlbɐn], *ptp* **versilbert** VT (= *silbern bemalen*) to paint silver; (= *mit Silber überziehen*) to silver(-plate); (*fig inf*: = *verkaufen*) to sell

versinken *ptp* **versunken** [fɛɐˈzʊŋkn̩] VI IRREG AUX SEIN (= *untergehen*) to sink; **ich hätte im Boden** *or* **in der Erde/vor Scham ~ mögen** I wished the ground would (open and) swallow me up; **in etw** (*acc*) **~** (*fig*) *in Trauer, Melancholie, Chaos* to sink into sth; *in Anblick, Gedanken, Musik* to lose oneself in sth; *siehe auch* **versunken**

Version [vɛrˈzioːn] F **-, -en** version

versklaven [fɛɐˈsklaːvn̩, -aːfn̩], *ptp* **versklavt** VT (*lit, fig*) to enslave

verslumen [fɛɐˈslamən] VI *Stadtzentrum, Stadtteil* to become a slum

Verslumung [fɛɐˈslaːmʊŋ] F **die ~ ganzer Stadtteile** the deterioration of whole parts of a/the city into slums

Versmaß NT metre (*Brit*), meter (*US*)

versoffen [fɛɐˈzɔfn̩] ADJ (*inf*) boozy (*inf*); **ein ~es Genie** a drunken genius; *siehe auch* **versaufen**

versohlen *ptp* **versohlt** VT (*inf*) to belt (*inf*)

versöhnen [fɛɐˈzøːnən], *ptp* **versöhnt** **1** VT to reconcile; (= *besänftigen*) *jdn, Götter* to appease; **~de Worte** conciliatory words; (*besänftigend*) placatory words; **das versöhnt einen dann wieder** it almost makes up for it **2** VR to be(come) reconciled; (*Streitende*) to make it up; **sich mit etw ~** to reconcile oneself to sth

versöhnlich [fɛɐˈzøːnlɪç] ADJ conciliatory; *Schluss* (*von Film, Roman*) upbeat; (= *nicht nachtragend*) forgiving

Versöhnung F **-, -en** reconciliation; (= *Beschwichtigung*) appeasement

versonnen [fɛɐˈzɔnən] **1** ADJ *Gesichtsausdruck* pensive; (= *träumerisch*) *Blick* dreamy **2** ADV *blicken* pensively; (= *träumerisch*) dreamily

versorgen *ptp* **versorgt** **1** VT **(a)** (= *sich kümmern um, bedienen*) to look after; **jdn medizinisch ~** to give sb medical treatment **(b)** (= *beliefern*) to supply; **jdn mit etw ~** (= *versehen*) to supply sb with sth; **das Gehirn mit Sauerstoff ~** to supply oxygen to the brain **(c)** (= *unterhalten*) *Familie* to provide for; **versorgt sein** to be provided for **2** VR **sich mit etw ~** to provide oneself with sth; **sich selbst ~** to look after oneself

Versorgung [fɛɐˈzɔrgʊŋ] F **-, -en (a)** (= *Pflege*) care; **die ~ des Haushalts** looking after the house; **medizinische ~** medical care **(b)** (= *Belieferung*) supply; **die ~ mit Strom/Gas/Wasser** the supply of electricity/gas/water; **die ~ der Truppen (mit Munition)** supplying the troops (with ammunition); **Probleme mit der ~ haben** to have supply problems **(c)** (= *Unterhalt*) **die ~ im Alter/einer sechsköpfigen Familie** providing for one's old age/a family of six; **der Staat übernimmt die ~ von Witwen und Waisen** the state undertakes to provide for widows and orphans

Versorgungs-: Versorgungsengpass M supply bottleneck; **Versorgungsgüter** PL supplies *pl*; **Versorgungsschwierigkeiten** PL supply problems *pl*; **Versorgungsstaat** M all-providing state; **Versorgungsweg** M supply channel

verspannt [fɛɐˈʃpant] ADJ *Muskeln* tense

verspäten [fɛɐˈʃpɛːtn̩], *ptp* **verspätet** VR **(a)** (= *zu spät kommen*) to be late **(b)** (= *nicht rechtzeitig wegkommen*) to be late leaving; (= *aufgehalten werden*) to be delayed

verspätet [fɛɐˈʃpɛːtət] **1** ADJ *Zug, Flugzeug* delayed; *Ankunft, Eintreten, Frühling, Entwicklung* late; *Glückwunsch, Bewerbung* belated **2** ADV late; *sich bewerben, gratulieren* belatedly

Verspätung F **-, -en** (*von Verkehrsmitteln*) delay; (*von Mensch*) late arrival; (*von Glückwunsch etc*) belatedness; **(10 Minuten) ~ haben** to be (10 minutes) late; **eine zweistündige ~** a two-hour delay; **die ~ aufholen** to catch up lost time; **mit ~ abfahren/ankommen** to leave/arrive late; **ohne ~ ankommen** to arrive on time; **mit zwanzig Minuten ~** twenty minutes late behind schedule

verspekulieren *ptp* **verspekuliert** **1** VT to lose through speculation **2** VR to ruin oneself by speculation; (*fig*) to miscalculate

versperren *ptp* **versperrt** VT **(a)** *Weg, Durchgang* to block **(b)** (*dial:* = *verschließen*) to lock up

verspielen *ptp* **verspielt** ◼ VT (*lit, fig*) *Geld, Chancen, Zukunft* to gamble away; *Vorteile* to bargain away; *Vertrauen, Glaubwürdigkeit* to lose ◼ VI (*fig*) **jetzt hast du verspielt** you've had it now (*inf*); **er hatte bei ihr verspielt** he had had it as far as she was concerned (*inf*)

verspielt [fɛɐˈʃpiːlt] ADJ *Kind, Katze etc* playful; *Frisur, Muster, Kleid* pretty; *Verzierung* dainty

verspotten *ptp* **verspottet** VT to mock; (*höhnisch*) to jeer at

Verspottung [fɛɐˈʃpɔtʊŋ] F -, -en **(a)** NO PL (= *das Verspotten*) mocking *no indef art*; (*höhnisch*) jeering *no indef art* **(b)** (= *spöttische Rede*) mockery *no indef art, no pl*; (= *höhnische Rede*) jeer

versprechen *ptp* **versprochen** [fɛɐˈʃprɔxn] IRREG ◼ VT to promise (*jdm etw* sb sth); **aber er hat es doch versprochen!** but he promised!; **das verspricht interessant zu werden** it promises to be interesting; **nichts Gutes ~** to be ominous; **sich** (*dat*) **viel/wenig von jdm/etw ~** to have high hopes/no great hopes of sb/sth; **was versprichst du dir davon?** what do you expect to achieve (by that)? ◼ VR (= *falsch sagen, aussprechen*) to pronounce a word/ words wrong(ly); (= *etwas Nichtgemeintes sagen*) to make a slip (of the tongue)

Versprechen [fɛɐˈʃprɛçn̩] NT -s, - promise

Versprecher M (*inf*) slip (of the tongue); **ein freudscher ~** a Freudian slip

Versprechung [fɛɐˈʃprɛçʊŋ] F -, -en promise

versprühen *ptp* **versprüht** VT to spray; *Charme* to exude; (= *verbrauchen*) to use; **Witz/Geist ~** to scintillate

verspüren *ptp* **verspürt** VT to feel

verstaatlichen [fɛɐˈʃtaːtlɪçn̩], *ptp* **verstaatlicht** VT to nationalize; *Schulen* to put under state control

Verstaatlichung F -, -en nationalization; (*von Schulen*) putting under state control

Verstand [fɛɐˈʃtant] M -(e)s [-dəs], NO PL (= *Fähigkeit zu denken*) reason; (= *Intellekt*) mind; (= *Vernunft*) (common) sense; (= *Urteilskraft*) (powers *pl* of) judgement; **das müsste dir dein ~ sagen** your common sense should tell you that; **den ~ verlieren** to lose one's mind; **hast du denn den ~ verloren?**, **bist du denn noch bei ~?** are you out of your mind? (*inf*); **jdn um den ~ bringen** to drive sb out of his/her mind (*inf*); **nicht recht** *or* **ganz bei ~ sein** not to be in one's right mind; **mit seinem ~ am Ende sein** to be at one's wits' end; **das geht über meinen ~** it's beyond me; **etw ohne ~ tun** to do sth mindlessly; **etw ohne ~ essen/trinken** to eat/drink sth without paying attention; **etw mit ~ genießen/essen/trinken** to savour (*Brit*) *or* savor (*US*) sth

verständig [fɛɐˈʃtɛndɪç] ADJ (= *vernünftig*) sensible; (= *einsichtig*) understanding

verständigen [fɛɐˈʃtɛndɪɡn̩], *ptp* **verständigt** ◼ VT to notify (*von* of, about) ◼ VR to communicate (with each other); (= *sich einigen*) to come to an understanding; **sich mit jdm ~** to communicate with sb

Verständigung F -, (*rare*) -en **(a)** (= *Benachrichtigung*) notification **(b)** (= *das Sichverständigen*) communication *no indef art*; **die ~ am Telefon war schlecht** the (telephone) line was bad **(c)** (= *Einigung*) understanding

verständlich [fɛɐˈʃtɛntlɪç] ◼ ADJ (= *begreiflich*) *Reaktion etc* understandable; (= *intellektuell erfassbar*) comprehensible; (= *hörbar*) audible; (= *klar*) *Erklärung, Ausdruck* intelligible; **allgemein ~** readily comprehensible; **eine schwer ~e Unterscheidung** a distinction that is difficult to understand; **jdm etw ~ machen** to make sb understand sth; **sich ~ machen** to make oneself understood; (= *sich klar ausdrücken*) to make oneself clear; (*gegen Lärm*) to make oneself heard ◼ ADV clearly

verständlicherweise [fɛɐˈʃtɛntlɪçɐˈvaɪzə] ADV understandably (enough)

Verständnis [fɛɐˈʃtɛntnɪs] NT -ses, NO PL **(a)** (= *das Begreifen*) (*für* of) understanding, comprehension; (= *Einfühlungsvermögen, Einsicht*) understanding (*für* för); (= *Mitgefühl*) sympathy (*für* for); **für etw kein ~ aufbringen** to show understanding/sympathy for sth; **für etw kein ~ haben** to have no understanding/ sympathy for sth; **für so was habe ich kein ~** I have no time for that kind of thing; **dafür hast du mein vollstes ~** you have

my fullest sympathy; **wir bitten um Ihr ~** we apologize for any inconvenience **(b)** (= *Kunstverständnis etc*) appreciation (*für* of)

Verständnis-: **verständnislos** ◼ ADJ uncomprehending; (= *ohne Mitgefühl*) unsympathetic (*für* towards); (*für Kunst*) unappreciative (*für* of) ◼ ADV uncomprehendingly; (= *ohne Mitgefühl*) unsympathetically; (*gegenüber Kunst*) unappreciatively; **verständnisvoll** ◼ ADJ understanding; *Blick* knowing *no pred* ◼ ADV understandingly; **sie gibt sich gern ~** she likes to seem sympathetic

verstärken *ptp* **verstärkt** ◼ VT to reinforce; *Spannung, Zweifel, Zusammenarbeit* to intensify; (*Chem*) to concentrate; *Signal, Strom, Spannung, Stimme, Musik, Musikinstrument* to amplify ◼ VR (*fig*) to intensify; (= *sich vermehren*) to increase

Verstärker [fɛɐˈʃtɛrkɐ] M -s, - (*Rad, Elec*) amplifier; (*Telec*) repeater; (*von Signalen etc*) booster

Verstärkung F reinforcement; (*von Spannung, Zweifel*) intensification; (*Chem*) concentration; (*Elec, Mus*) amplification

verstauben *ptp* **verstaubt** VI AUX SEIN to get dusty; (*Möbel, Bücher auch, fig*) to gather dust; **verstaubt** covered in dust; (*fig*) *Ideen, Ansichten* fuddy-duddy (*inf*)

verstauchen *ptp* **verstaucht** VT to sprain; **sich** (*dat*) **die Hand/ den Fuß** *etc* **~** to sprain one's hand/foot *etc*

Verstauchung [fɛɐˈʃtauxʊŋ] F -, -en sprain; (= *das Verstauchen*) spraining

verstauen *ptp* **verstaut** VT (*in* +*dat* in(to)) *Gepäck* to load; (*Naut*) to stow; (*hum*) *Menschen* to pile; **etw im Kofferraum ~** to load sth into the boot (*Brit*) *or* trunk (*US*)

Versteck [fɛɐˈʃtɛk] NT -(e)s, -e hiding place; (*von Verbrechern*) hide-out; **~ spielen** to play hide-and-seek (*Brit*) *or* hide-and-go-seek (*US*)

verstecken *ptp* **versteckt** ◼ VT to hide (*vor* from) ◼ VR to hide; **sich vor jdm ~** to hide from sb; **sich vor** *or* **neben jdm ~ können/müssen** (*fig*) to be no match for sb; **sich** (*vor* *or* **neben jdm*) **nicht zu ~ brauchen** (*fig*) not to need to fear comparison (with sb); **sich hinter etw** (*dat*) **~** (*fig*) *hinter Pseudonym* to write under sth; *hinter falschem Namen, Maske* to hide behind sth; **Verstecken spielen** to play hide-and-seek (*Brit*) *or* hide-and-go-seek (*US*)

Versteckspiel NT (*lit, fig*) hide-and-seek (*Brit*), hide-and-go-seek (*US*)

versteckt [fɛɐˈʃtɛkt] ADJ hidden; *Eingang, Tür, Winkel* concealed; *Lächeln, Blick* furtive; *Bemerkung, Andeutung* veiled

verstehen *ptp* **verstanden** [fɛɐˈʃtandn̩] IRREG ◼ VTI to understand; **jdn/etw falsch** *or* **nicht recht ~** to misunderstand sb/sth; **versteh mich recht** don't get me wrong; **wenn ich recht verstehe ...** if I understand correctly ...; **jdm zu ~ geben, dass ...** to give sb to understand that ...; **ein ~der Blick** a knowing look; (**ist das**) **verstanden?** (is that) understood? ◼ VT **(a)** (= *können, beherrschen*) to know; **es ~, etw zu tun** to know how to do sth; **es mit Kindern ~** to be good with children; **es mit seinen Kollegen ~** to know how to get on (*Brit*) *or* along with one's colleagues; **etwas/nichts von etw ~** to know something/nothing about sth **(b)** (= *auslegen*) to understand, to see; **etw unter etw** (*dat*) **~** to understand sth by sth; **wie soll ich das ~?** how am I supposed to take that?; **das ist bildlich** *or* **nicht wörtlich zu ~** that isn't to be taken literally ◼ VR **(a)** (= *kommunizieren können*) to understand each other **(b)** (= *miteinander auskommen*) to get on (*Brit*) *or* along (with each other *or* together); **sich mit jdm ~** to get on (*Brit*) *or* along with sb **(c)** (= *klar sein*) to go without saying; **versteht sich!** (*inf*) of course! **(d)** **sich als etw ~** (*Mensch*) to think of oneself as sth; **sich auf etw** (*acc*) **~** to be (an) expert at sth; **die Preise ~ sich einschließlich Lieferung** prices are inclusive of delivery

versteigern *ptp* **versteigert** VT to auction (off); **etw ~ lassen** to put sth up for auction

Versteigerung F (sale by) auction

versteinern [fɛɐˈʃtainɐn], *ptp* **versteinert** ◼ VI AUX SEIN (*Geol*) (*Pflanzen, Tiere*) to fossilize; (*Holz*) to petrify; (*fig: Miene*) to harden; **versteinerte Pflanzen/Tiere** fossilized plants/animals ◼ VR (*fig*) (*Miene, Gesicht*) to harden; (*Lächeln*) to become fixed

Versteinerung F -, -en (*Vorgang*) fossilization; (*von Holz*) petrification; (= *versteinertes Tier etc*) fossil

verstellbar ADJ adjustable; **in der Höhe** ~ adjustable for height

verstellen *ptp* **verstellt** ▊ VT **(a)** (= *anders einstellen, regulieren*) to adjust; *Signal, Zahlen* to change; *Möbel, Gegenstände* to move (out of position); (= *in Unordnung bringen*) to put in the wrong place; (= *falsch einstellen*) to adjust wrongly; *Radio* to alter the tuning of; *Uhr* to set wrong **(b)** *Stimme* to disguise **(c)** (= *versperren*) to block ▊ VR to move (out of position); (*fig*) to play a part; (= *Gefühle verbergen*) to hide one's (true) feelings; **er kann sich gut ~** he's good at playing a part

versteppen [fɛɐˈʃtɛpn̩], *ptp* **versteppt** VTI to turn into desert

Versteppung F -, -en desertification

versteuern *ptp* **versteuert** VT to pay tax on; **versteuerte Waren** taxed goods; **das versteuerte Einkommen** taxed income; **das zu ~de Einkommen** taxable income

verstimmen *ptp* **verstimmt** VT (*lit*) to put out of tune; (*fig*) to put out

verstimmt [fɛɐˈʃtɪmt] ADJ *Klavier etc* out of tune; (*fig*) (= *verdorben*) *Magen* upset; (= *verärgert*) put out

Verstimmung F disgruntlement; (*zwischen Parteien*) ill will

verstohlen [fɛɐˈʃtoːlən] ▊ ADJ furtive ▊ ADV furtively

verstopfen *ptp* **verstopft** VT to stop up; *Straße* to block; *Blutgefäß* to block

verstopft [fɛɐˈʃtɔpft] ADJ blocked; *Nase* stuffed up, blocked (up); *Mensch* constipated

Verstopfung [fɛɐˈʃtɔpfʊŋ] F -, -en blockage; (= *Verkehrsstauung*) jam; (*Med*) constipation

verstorben [fɛɐˈʃtɔrbn̩] ADJ deceased; **mein ~er Mann** my late husband; **eine 1995 ~e Frau** a woman who died in 1995

Verstorbene(r) [fɛɐˈʃtɔrbənə] MF DECL AS ADJ deceased

verstören *ptp* **verstört** VT to disturb

verstört [fɛɐˈʃtøːɐt] ▊ ADJ disturbed; (*vor Angst*) distraught ▊ ADV in a disturbed way; (*vor Angst*) in a distraught way

Verstoß M violation (*gegen* of)

verstoßen *ptp* **verstoßen** IRREG ▊ VT *jdn* to disown; **jdn aus einem Verein/einer Gruppe** ~ to expel sb from a club/group ▊ VI **gegen etw** ~ to offend against sth

verstrahlen *ptp* **verstrahlt** VT **(a)** *Licht, Wärme* to give off **(b)** (*radioaktiv*) to expose to radiation; *Gebäude, Gebiet* to make (highly) radioactive

verstrahlt [fɛɐˈʃtraːlt] ADJ contaminated (by radiation); **lebensgefährlich ~ sein** to have had a potentially lethal dose of radiation

Verstrahlung F radiation

verstreichen *ptp* **verstrichen** [fɛɐˈʃtrɪçn̩] IRREG ▊ VT *Salbe, Farbe* to apply (*auf +dat* to); *Butter etc* to spread (*auf +dat* on); (= *verbrauchen*) to use ▊ VI AUX SEIN *Zeit* to elapse; (*Frist, Ultimatum*) to expire

verstreuen *ptp* **verstreut** VT to scatter; (*versehentlich*) to spill

verströmen *ptp* **verströmt** VT (*lit, fig*) to exude

verstümmeln [fɛɐˈʃtʏmln̩], *ptp* **verstümmelt** VT to mutilate; *Nachricht, Bericht* to garble

Verstümmelung F -, -en mutilation; (*von Nachricht, Bericht*) garbling *no pl*

verstummen [fɛɐˈʃtʊmən], *ptp* **verstummt** VI AUX SEIN (*Mensch*) to go or fall silent; (*Geräusch, Gespräch, Musik, Beifall*) to stop; (*Wind, Glocken, Instrumente, Kritik*) to become silent; (= *langsam verklingen*) to die away; (*fig: = sich langsam legen*) to subside; **jdn/etw ~ lassen** *or* **zum Verstummen bringen** to silence sb/sth

Versuch [fɛɐˈzuːx] M -(e)s, -e attempt (*zu tun* at doing, to do); (*wissenschaftlich*) experiment; (= *Test*) trial, test; (*Rugby*) try; **einen ~ machen** to make an attempt; to carry out an experiment/a trial; **mit jdm/etw einen ~ machen** to give sb/sth a try *or* trial; (*Forscher*) to do a trial/an experiment with sb/sth; **das käme auf einen ~ an** we'll have to (have a) try; **wir sollten es auf einen ~ ankommen lassen** we should give it a try

versuchen *ptp* **versucht** ▊ VT **(a)** AUCH VI (= *probieren, kosten*) to try; **es mit etw ~** to try sth; **versuchs doch!** (give it a) try; **es mit jdm ~** to give sb a try; **versuchter Mord/Diebstahl**

attempted murder/theft **(b)** (= *in Versuchung führen*) to tempt ▊ VR **sich an** *or* **in etw** (*dat*) ~ to try one's hand at sth

Versuchs-: **Versuchsabteilung** F experimental department; **Versuchsanlage** F experimental plant; **Versuchsballon** M sounding balloon; **einen ~ steigen lassen, es mit einem ~ probieren** (*fig*) to fly a kite; **Versuchskaninchen** NT (*lit*) laboratory rabbit; (*fig*) guinea pig; **Versuchsobjekt** NT test object; (*fig: Mensch*) guinea pig; **Versuchsperson** F test *or* experimental subject; **Versuchsstadium** NT experimental stage; **versuchsweise** ADV on a trial basis; *einstellen, engagieren* on trial

Versuchung [fɛɐˈzuːxʊŋ] F -, -en temptation (*auch Rel*); **jdn in ~ führen** to lead sb into temptation; **in ~ geraten** *or* **kommen** to be tempted

versumpfen *ptp* **versumpft** VI AUX SEIN **(a)** (*Gebiet*) to become marshy *or* boggy **(b)** (*fig inf*) (= *verwahrlosen*) to go to pot (*inf*); (= *lange zechen*) to get involved in a booze-up (*inf*)

versunken [fɛɐˈzʊŋkn̩] ADJ sunken; *Kultur* submerged; (*fig*) engrossed; **in Gedanken ~** immersed in thought; **völlig in diesen Anblick ~** completely lost in this sight; *siehe auch* **versinken**

versüßen *ptp* **versüßt** VT (*fig*) to sweeten; **jdm etw ~** to sweeten sth for sb

vertagen *ptp* **vertagt** ▊ VTI to adjourn; (= *verschieben*) to postpone (*auf +acc* until, till) ▊ VR to be adjourned

Vertagung F adjournment; (= *Verschiebung auf später*) postponement; (*Parl*) prorogation (*form*)

vertauschbar ADJ exchangeable (*gegen* for); (*miteinander*) interchangeable

vertauschen *ptp* **vertauscht** VT **(a)** (= *austauschen*) to exchange (*gegen, mit* for); (*miteinander*) to interchange; *Auto, Plätze* to change (*gegen, mit* for); (*Elec*) *Pole* to transpose; **vertauschte Rollen** reversed roles **(b)** (= *verwechseln*) to mix up

verteidigen [fɛɐˈtaidɪɡn̩], *ptp* **verteidigt** ▊ VT to defend ▊ VR to defend oneself (*auch Sport*); **sich selbst ~** (*vor Gericht*) to conduct one's own defence (*Brit*) *or* defense (*US*)

Verteidiger [fɛɐˈtaidɪɡɐ] M -s, -, **Verteidigerin** [-ərɪn] F -, -nen defender (*auch Sport*); (= *Fürsprecher auch*) advocate; (= *Anwalt*) defence (*Brit*) *or* defense (*US*) lawyer; **der ~ des Angeklagten** the counsel for the defence (*Brit*) *or* defense (*US*)

Verteidigung F -, -en (*alle Bedeutungen*) defence (*Brit*), defense (*US*); **zur ~ von** *or* **gen** in defence (*Brit*) *or* defense (*US*) of; **zu ihrer/seiner eigenen ~** in her/one's own defence (*Brit*) *or* defense (*US*)

Verteidigungs- IN CPDS defence (*Brit*), defense (*US*); **Verteidigungsfall** M **wenn der ~ eintritt** if defence should be necessary; **Verteidigungsminister(in)** M(F) Minister of Defence (*Brit*), Secretary of Defense (*US*); **Verteidigungsministerium** NT Ministry of Defence (*Brit*), Department of Defense (*US*); **verteidigungsunfähig** ADJ defenceless (*Brit*), defenseless (*US*)

verteilen *ptp* **verteilt** ▊ VT (= *austeilen, anordnen*) to distribute; *Süßigkeiten etc* to share out; *Essen* to dish out; (*Theat*) *Rollen* to allocate; *Investitionen, soziale Lasten, Farbe* to spread; (*Mil*) to deploy; (= *verstreuen*) to spread out; (= *streuen*) to sprinkle; **verteilte Datenbank** (*Comput*) distributed database ▊ VR (*Zuschauer, Polizisten etc*) to spread (themselves) out; (*Bevölkerung, Farbe, Wasser*) to spread (itself) out; (*Med: Bakterien, Metastasen*) to spread; (*Reichtum etc*) to be distributed; (*zeitlich*) to be spread (*über +acc* over); **übers ganze Land verteilt** spread throughout the country

Verteiler [fɛɐˈtailɐ] M -s, - **(a)** (*Tech*) distributor **(b)** (= *~schlüssel*) distribution list

Verteiler-: **Verteilerdeckel** M distributor cap; **Verteilerkopf** M (*Aut*) distributor head; **Verteilernetz** NT (*Elec*) distribution system; (*Comm*) distribution network; **Verteilerschlüssel** M distribution list

Verteilung F distribution; (= *Zuteilung*) allocation; (*Mil*) deployment; (*Theat*) casting

Verteilungskampf M **einen ~ um etw führen** to battle for a share of sth

vertelefonieren *ptp* **vertelefoniert** VT (*inf*) *Geld, Zeit* to spend on the phone

verteuern [fɛɐˈtɔyən], *ptp* **verteuert** **1** VT to make more expensive **2** VR to become more expensive

Verteuerung F increase in price

vertiefen [fɛɐˈtiːfn], *ptp* **vertieft** **1** VT to deepen; *Zusammenarbeit* to intensify; *Kontakte* to strengthen; (*Sch*) *Unterrichtsstoff* to reinforce; (*Mus*) to flatten **2** VR (*lit, fig*) to deepen; (*fig: Lehrstoff*) to be reinforced; **sich in etw** (*acc*) **~** (*fig*) to become engrossed in sth; **in etw** (*acc*) **vertieft sein** (*fig*) to be engrossed in sth

Vertiefung F **-, -en (a)** (= *das Vertiefen*) deepening; (*von Unterrichtsstoff*) reinforcement; (*Mus*) flattening **(b)** (*in Oberfläche*) depression **(c)** (= *Vertieftsein*) engrossment

vertikal [vɛrtiˈkaːl] **1** ADJ vertical **2** ADV vertically

Vertikale [vɛrtiˈkaːlə] F **-, -n** vertical line; **in der -n** vertically

vertilgen *ptp* **vertilgt** VT **(a)** *Unkraut etc* to destroy **(b)** (*inf:* = *aufessen*) to demolish (*inf*)

Vertilgung F (*von Unkraut*) destruction; (*von Ungeziefer*) extermination

Vertilgungsmittel NT weedkiller; (= *Insektenvertilgungsmittel*) pesticide

vertippen *ptp* **vertippt** (*inf*) VR **(a)** (*beim Schreiben*) to make a typing error **(b)** (*beim Lotto, Toto etc*) to slip up (*inf*)

vertonen *ptp* **vertont** VT to set to music; *Film etc* to add a soundtrack to

Vertonung [fɛɐˈtoːnʊŋ] F **-, -en** (= *das Vertonen*) setting (to music); (*von Film*) adding a soundtrack (+*gen* to); (= *vertonte Fassung*) musical version

Vertrag [fɛɐˈtraːk] M **-(e)s, ⸚e** [-ˈtrɛːɡə] contract; (= *Abkommen*) agreement; (*Pol:* = *Friedensvertrag*) treaty; **laut ~** under the terms of the contract; **jdn unter ~ nehmen** to contract sb; (**bei jdm**) **unter ~ stehen** to be under contract (to sb)

vertragen *ptp* **vertragen** IRREG **1** VT to take; (= *aushalten*) to stand; (*viel*) to tolerate; **Eier vertrage ich nicht** *or* **kann ich nicht ~** eggs don't agree with me; **Kontaktlinsen/synthetische Stoffe vertrage ich nicht** *or* **kann ich nicht ~** I can't wear contact lenses/synthetics; **Patienten, die kein Penizillin ~** patients who are allergic to penicillin; **so etwas kann ich nicht ~** I can't stand that kind of thing; **er verträgt keinen Spaß** he can't take a joke; **viel ~ können** (*inf: Alkohol*) to be able to hold one's drink (*Brit*) *or* liquor (*US*); **er verträgt nichts** (*inf: Alkohol*) he can't take his drink (*Brit*) *or* liquor (*US*); **jd/etw könnte etw ~** (*inf*) sb/sth could do with sth **2** VR **sich (mit jdm) ~** to get on (*Brit*) *or* along (with sb); **sich wieder ~** to be friends again; **sich mit etw ~** (*Nahrungsmittel, Farbe*) to go with sth; (*Aussage, Verhalten*) to be consistent with sth; **diese Farben ~ sich nicht** these colours (*Brit*) *or* colors (*US*) don't go together; **diese Aussagen ~ sich nicht** these statements are inconsistent

vertraglich [fɛɐˈtraːklɪç] **1** ADJ contractual **2** ADV by contract; *festgelegt* in the/a contract; **ein ~ zugesichertes Recht** a contractual right

verträglich [fɛɐˈtrɛːklɪç] ADJ (= *friedlich, umgänglich*) good-natured; *Speise* digestible; (= *bekömmlich*) wholesome; (*Med*) well tolerated (*für* by); **gut ~** easily digestible; (*Med*) well tolerated; **ökologisch/sozial ~** ecologically/socially acceptable

Vertrags-: Vertragsbruch M *siehe* **Vertrag** breach of contract; breaking of an/the agreement; breaking of a/the treaty; **vertragsbrüchig** ADJ *siehe* **Vertrag** who is in breach of contract; who has broken an/the agreement; who has broken a/the treaty; **~ werden** to be in breach of contract; to break an/the agreement; to break a/the treaty; **Vertragsentwurf** M *siehe* **Vertrag** draft contract/agreement/treaty; **vertragsgemäß** *siehe* **Vertrag** ADJ, ADV as stipulated in the contract/agreement/treaty; **Vertragshändler(in)** M(F) appointed retailer; **Vertragspartner(in)** M(F) *siehe* **Vertrag** party to a/the contract/agreement/treaty; **vertragsschließend** ADJ contracting; **Vertragsspieler(in)** M(F) player under contract

vertrauen *ptp* **vertraut** VI **jdm/einer Sache ~** to trust sb/sth; **auf jdn/etw ~** to trust in sb/sth; **auf sein Glück ~** to trust to luck; *siehe auch* **vertraut**

Vertrauen [fɛɐˈtrauən] NT **-s**, NO PL trust, confidence (*zu, in* +*acc, auf* +*acc* in); **voll ~** full of confidence; **im ~** (*gesagt*) strictly in confidence; **im ~ auf etw** (*acc*) trusting in sth; **im ~ darauf, dass ...** confident that ...; **ein ~ erweckender Mensch/ Arzt** *etc* a person/doctor *etc* who inspires confidence; **einen**

~ erweckenden Eindruck machen, ~ erweckend aussehen to inspire confidence; **jdn ins ~ ziehen** to take sb into one's confidence; **jdm das ~ aussprechen/entziehen** (*Parl*) to pass a vote of confidence/no confidence in sb

Vertrauens-: vertrauensbildend ADJ confidence-building; **Vertrauensfrage** F question *or* matter of trust; **die ~ stellen** (*Parl*) to ask for a vote of confidence; **Vertrauensfrau** F *siehe* **Vertrauensmann**; **Vertrauenslehrer(in)** M(F) liaison teacher (*between pupils and staff*); **Vertrauensmann** M, *pl* **-leute** *or* **-männer** intermediary agent; (*in Gewerkschaft*) (union) negotiator *or* representative; **Vertrauenssache** F (= *vertrauliche Angelegenheit*) confidential matter; (= *Frage des Vertrauens*) question *or* matter of trust; **vertrauensvoll** **1** ADJ trusting **2** ADV trustingly; **wende dich ~ an mich** you know you can always turn to me (for help); **Vertrauensvotum** NT (*Parl*) vote of confidence; **vertrauenswürdig** ADJ trustworthy

vertraulich [fɛɐˈtraulɪç] **1** ADJ **(a)** (= *geheim*) confidential **(b)** (= *freundschaftlich*) friendly; (= *plumpvertraulich*) familiar; **~ werden** to take liberties **2** ADV **(a)** confidentially, in confidence **(b)** in a friendly/familiar way

Vertraulichkeit F **-, -en** confidentiality; (= *vertrauliche Mitteilung*) confidence; (= *Aufdringlichkeit*) familiarity

verträumt [fɛɐˈtrɔymt] ADJ dreamy

vertraut [fɛɐˈtraut] ADJ intimate; (= *bekannt*) *Gesicht, Umgebung* familiar; **sich mit etw ~ machen** to familiarize oneself with sth; **sich mit dem Gedanken ~ machen, dass ...** to get used to the idea that ...; **mit etw ~ sein** to be familiar with sth; **mit jdm ~ werden** to become friendly with sb; **mit jdm sehr ~ werden** to get on intimate terms with sb; *siehe auch* **vertrauen**

Vertraute(r) [fɛɐˈtrautə] MF DECL AS ADJ close friend

Vertrautheit F **-, (rare) -en** intimacy; (*von Freund*) closeness; (*von Gesicht, Umgebung*) familiarity

vertreiben *ptp* **vertrieben** [fɛɐˈtriːbn] VT IRREG *Tiere, Wolken, Einbrecher, Geister* to drive away; (*aus Haus etc*) to turn out (*aus* of); (*aus Land, Gebiet*) to expel (*aus* from); (*aus Amt, von Stellung*) to oust; *Feind* to repulse; (*fig*) *Sorgen, Schmerzen* to banish; (*Comm*) *Waren, Produkte* to sell; **ich wollte Sie nicht ~, bleiben Sie doch noch ein wenig** I didn't mean to chase you away – do stay a bit longer; **ich wollte Sie nicht von Ihrem Stuhl/Platz ~** I didn't mean to take your chair/seat; **jdm die Zeit mit etw ~** to help sb pass the time with sth; **sich** (*dat*) **die Zeit mit etw ~** to pass (away) the time with sth; *siehe auch* **vertrieben**

Vertreibung [fɛɐˈtraibʊŋ] F **-, -en** (*aus* from) expulsion; (*aus Amt etc*) ousting; (*von Feind*) repelling

vertretbar ADJ justifiable; *Theorie, Argument* tenable

vertreten *ptp* **vertreten** VT IRREG **(a)** (= *jds Stelle, Dienst übernehmen*) to replace, to stand in for; (*fig:* = *Funktion einer Sache übernehmen*) to take the place of **(b)** *jds Interessen, Firma, Land, Wahlkreis* to represent; *Sache* to attend to; (*Rechtsanwalt*) *Fall* to plead; **~ sein** to be represented **(c)** (= *verfechten, angehören*) *Standpunkt, Doktrin, Theorie* to support; *Meinung, Ansicht* to hold; *Kunstrichtung* to represent; (= *rechtfertigen*) to justify (*vor* to) **(d) sich** (*dat*) **den Fuß ~** to twist one's ankle; **sich** (*dat*) **die Beine** *or* **Füße ~** (*inf*) to stretch one's legs

Vertreter [fɛɐˈtreːtɐ] M **-s, -**, **Vertreterin** [-ərɪn] F **-, -nen (a)** (*von Land, Firma etc*) representative; (*Comm*) (*Firma*) agent **(b)** (= *Ersatz*) replacement; (*im Amt*) deputy; (*von Arzt*) locum **(c)** (= *Verfechter*) (*von Doktrin*) supporter; (*von Meinung*) holder; (*von Kunstrichtung*) representative

Vertretung [fɛɐˈtreːtʊŋ] F **-, -en (a)** (*von Menschen*) replacement; **die ~ (für jdn) übernehmen** to replace sb; **die ~ (für jdn) haben** to deputize (for sb); **X spielt in ~** X is appearing in his/her place; **in ~** (*in Briefen*) on behalf of **(b)** (*von Interessen, Firma, Land, Wahlkreis*) representation; **X übernimmt die ~ des Klienten/Falles** X is representing the client/pleading the case; **die ~ meiner Interessen** representing my interests **(c)** (= *das Verfechten*) supporting; (*von Meinung*) holding; (*von Kunstrichtung*) representation **(d)** (*Comm:* = *Firma*) agency **(e)** (= *Botschaft*) **diplomatische ~** embassy **(f)** = **Vertreter (a, b)**

Vertrieb [fɛɐˈtriːp] M **-(e)s, -e** [-bə] **(a)** NO PL sales *pl*; **der ~ eines Produktes** the sale of a product; **den ~ für eine Firma haben**

to have the (selling) agency for a firm **(b)** (= *Abteilung einer Firma*) sales department

vertrieben [fɛɐ̯'triːbn] ADJ (*aus Land*) expelled; **die nach dem Krieg ~en Deutschen** the Germans who were driven out of their homeland after the war; *siehe auch* **vertreiben**

Vertriebene(r) [fɛɐ̯'triːbənə] MF DECL AS ADJ exile

Vertriebs-: **Vertriebsabteilung** F sales department; **Vertriebskosten** PL marketing costs *pl*; **Vertriebsleiter(in)** M(F) sales manager; **Vertriebssystem** NT distribution system; **Vertriebsweg** M channel of distribution

vertrösten *ptp* **vertröstet** VT to put off; **jdn auf ein andermal/ auf später ~** to put sb off

vertun *ptp* **vertan** [fɛɐ̯'taːn] IRREG ■ VT to waste ■ VR (*inf*) to slip up (*inf*)

vertuschen *ptp* **vertuscht** VT to hush up; **etw vor jdm ~** to keep sth from sb

verübeln [fɛɐ̯'yːbln], *ptp* **verübelt** VT **jdm etw ~** to take sth amiss; **ich hoffe, Sie werden mir die Frage nicht ~** I hope you won't mind my asking (this); **das kann ich dir nicht ~** I can't blame you for that

verüben *ptp* **verübt** VT to commit

verulken *ptp* **verulkt** VT (*inf*) to make fun of

verunfallen [fɛɐ̯'ʊnfalən], *ptp* **verunfallt** VI AUX SEIN (*Sw*) to have an accident

verunglücken [fɛɐ̯'ʊnɡlʏkn], *ptp* **verunglückt** VI AUX SEIN (*Mensch*) to have an accident; (*Fahrzeug, Flugzeug*) to crash; (*fig inf*: = *misslingen*) to go wrong; **mit dem Flugzeug/Auto ~** to be in a plane/car crash

verunglückt [fɛɐ̯'ʊnɡlʏkt] ADJ (*fig*) Versuch, Aufführung etc unsuccessful

Verunglückte(r) [fɛɐ̯'ʊnɡlʏktə] MF DECL AS ADJ casualty; **10 Tote, 20 ~** 10 dead, 20 injured

verunreinigen [fɛɐ̯'ʊnraɪnɪɡn], *ptp* **verunreinigt** VT Fluss, Luft, Wasser to pollute; (= *beschmutzen*) to dirty; (*euph: Hund etc*) to foul

Verunreinigung F (*von Fluss, Luft, Wasser*) pollution; (= *Beschmutzung*) dirtying; (*euph: durch Hund*) fouling; **~en in der Luft/im Wasser** pollutants in the atmosphere/in the water

verunsichern [fɛɐ̯'ʊnzɪçɐn], *ptp* **verunsichert** VT to make unsure (*in +dat* of); **jetzt hast du mich völlig verunsichert** I just don't know at all any more; **sie versuchten, ihn zu ~** they tried to throw him; **verunsichert sein** to be uncertain; **verunsicherte Kunden/Patienten** confused customers/patients

veruntreuen [fɛɐ̯'ʊntrɔʏən], *ptp* **veruntreut** VT to embezzle

Veruntreuung F **-, -en** embezzlement

verursachen [fɛɐ̯'uːɐ̯zaxn], *ptp* **verursacht** VT to cause

Verursacher [fɛɐ̯'uːɐ̯zaxɐ] M **-s, -**, **Verursacherin** [-ərɪn] F **-, -nen** cause; **der ~ kommt für den Schaden auf** the party responsible is liable for the damage

Verursacherprinzip NT originator principle; (*bei Umweltschäden auch*) polluter pays principle

Verursachung F **-,** NO PL causing

verurteilen *ptp* **verurteilt** VT to condemn; (*Jur*: = *für schuldig befinden*) to convict (*für* of); (*zu Strafe*) to sentence; **jdn zu einer Geldstrafe von 1.000 Euro ~** to fine sb 1,000 euros; **jdn zum Tode ~** to condemn *or* sentence (*Jur*) sb to death; **jdn zu einer Gefängnisstrafe ~** to give sb a prison sentence

Verurteilte(r) [fɛɐ̯'ʊrtaɪltə] MF DECL AS ADJ convicted man/ woman, convict (*Jur*); **der zum Tode ~** the condemned man

Verurteilung F condemnation; (= *das Schuldigsprechen*) conviction; (*zu einer Strafe*) sentencing; **seine ~ zu 5 Jahren** his being sentenced to 5 years; **seine ~ zum Tode** his being condemned/sentenced to death

vervielfachen [fɛɐ̯'fiːlfaxn], *ptp* **vervielfacht** VTR to multiply

vervielfältigen [fɛɐ̯'fiːlfɛltɪɡn], *ptp* **vervielfältigt** VT to duplicate; (= *fotokopieren*) to photocopy

Vervielfältigung F **-, -en (a)** (= *das Vervielfältigen*) duplication; (= *Fotokopieren*) photocopying **(b)** (= *Abzug*) copy; (= *Fotokopie*) photocopy

vervierfachen *ptp* **vervierfacht** VTR to quadruple

vervollständigen [fɛɐ̯'fɔlʃtɛndɪɡn], *ptp* **vervollständigt** ■ VT to complete; Kenntnisse, gutes Essen auch to round off; Erlebnis to make complete ■ VR to be completed

Vervollständigung F **-, -en** completion

verwackeln *ptp* **verwackelt** VT to blur

verwählen *ptp* **verwählt** VR to misdial

verwahren *ptp* **verwahrt** ■ VT (= *aufbewahren*) to keep (safe); **jdm etw zu ~ geben** to give sth to sb for safekeeping ■ VR **sich gegen etw ~** to protest against sth

Verwahrer [fɛɐ̯'vaːrɐ] M **-s, -**, **Verwahrerin** [-ərɪn] F **-, -nen** (*von Wertpapieren*) depository; (= *Aufbewahrer*) custodian; (= *Nutznießer*) bailee

verwahrlosen [fɛɐ̯'vaːɐ̯loːzn], *ptp* **verwahrlost** VI AUX SEIN to go to seed; (*Park*) to become neglected; (*Mensch*) to neglect oneself; (= *verwildern*) to run wild; (= *auf die schiefe Bahn geraten*) to get into bad habits

verwahrlost [fɛɐ̯'vaːɐ̯loːst] ADJ neglected; Mensch, Äußeres auch unkempt; *sittlich* ~ decadent

Verwahrlosung F **-,** NO PL neglect; (= *Verwilderung*) wildness; (*moralisch*) waywardness

Verwahrung F, NO PL (*von Geld etc*) keeping; (*von Täter*) detention; **jdm etw in ~ geben, etw bei jdm in ~ geben** to give sth to sb for safekeeping; **etw in ~ nehmen** to take sth into safekeeping; (*Behörde*) to take possession of sth; **jdn in ~ nehmen** to take sb into custody

verwalten *ptp* **verwaltet** VT to manage; Treuhandsgut to hold in trust; Amt to hold; (*Pol*) Provinz etc to govern; **sich selbst ~** (*Pol*) to be self-governing

Verwalter [fɛɐ̯'valtɐ] M **-s, -**, **Verwalterin** [-ərɪn] F **-, -nen** administrator; (= *Treuhänder*) trustee

Verwaltung [fɛɐ̯'valtʊŋ] F **-, -en (a)** (= *das Verwalten*) management; (*von Treuhandgut*) holding in trust; (*von Amt*) holding; (*von Provinz*) government **(b)** (= *Behörde, Abteilung*) administration; (= *Hausverwaltung*) management; **städtische ~** municipal authorities *pl*

Verwaltungs-: **Verwaltungsakt** M administrative act; **Verwaltungsbehörde** F administration; **Verwaltungsbezirk** M administrative district; **Verwaltungsgebühr** F administrative charge

verwandelbar ADJ (*Math, Econ*) convertible

verwandeln *ptp* **verwandelt** ■ VT (= *umformen*) to change, to transform; (*Math, Econ, Chem*) to convert; (*Jur*) Strafe to commute; **jdn/etw in etw** (*acc*) **~** to turn sb/sth into sth; **die Vorlage ~** (*Ftbl*) to score from the pass; **einen Strafstoß ~** to score (from) a penalty; **Müller verwandelte den Pass zum 2:0** Müller put the pass away to make it 2-0; **den Matchball ~** (*Tennis*) to convert the match point; **ein Gebäude in einen Trümmerhaufen ~** to reduce a building to a pile of rubble; **er ist wie verwandelt** he's a changed man
■ VI (*Sport sl*) **zum 1:0 ~** to make it 1-0
■ VR to change; (*Zool*) to metamorphose; **sich in etw** (*acc*) or **zu etw ~** to change *or* turn into sth

Verwandlung F (= *das Verwandeln*) change, transformation; (*Math, Econ, Chem*) conversion; (*von Strafe*) commuting; (*Zool*) metamorphosis

verwandt [fɛɐ̯'vant] ■ PTP *von* **verwenden** ■ ADJ (*lit, fig*) related (*mit* to); Denker, Geister kindred *attr*; **~e Seelen** (*fig*) kindred spirits

verwandte PRET *von* **verwenden**

Verwandte(r) [fɛɐ̯'vantə] MF DECL AS ADJ relation, relative

Verwandtschaft [fɛɐ̯'vantʃaft] F **-, -en** relationship; (= *die Verwandten*) relations *pl*, relatives *pl*; (*fig*) affinity

verwandtschaftlich [fɛɐ̯'vantʃaftlɪç] ADJ family *attr*

verwanzt [fɛɐ̯'vantst] ADJ Betten, Kleider bug-infested; (*inf*: = *mit Abhörgeräten*) bugged

verwarnen *ptp* **verwarnt** VT to caution

Verwarnung F caution

Verwarnungsgeld NT exemplary fine

verwässern *ptp* **verwässert** VT to water down

verwechseln *ptp* **verwechselt** VT Gegenstände to mix up; Begriffe, Menschen auch to confuse; **jdn (mit jdm) ~** to confuse sb with sb; (= *für jdn halten auch*) to mistake sb for sb; **zum Verwechseln ähnlich sein** to be the spitting image of each other; **ich habe meinen Schirm verwechselt** I took somebody else's umbrella by mistake; **sie verwechselt mir und mich** (*lit*) she confuses "mir" and "mich"; (*fig*) she doesn't know her grammar

Verwechslung [fɛɐ̯'vɛkslʊŋ] F **-, -en** confusion; (= *Irrtum*) mistake; **die Polizei ist sicher, dass eine ~ (des Täters) völlig ausgeschlossen ist** the police are certain that there can be absolutely no mistake (about the culprit); **es kam deshalb zu einer ~, weil ...** there was a mix-up or confusion because ...; **da muss es sich um eine ~ handeln** there must be some mistake

Verwehung [fɛɐ̯'veːʊŋ] F -, -en (= Schneeverwehung) (snow)drift; (= Sandverwehung) (sand)drift

verweichlichen [fɛɐ̯'vaiçlɪçn̩], ptp **verweichlicht** ⬛ VT **jdn ~** to make sb soft; **ein verweichlichter Mensch** a weakling; **ein verweichlichtes Muttersöhnchen** a mollycoddled mummy's boy (Brit), a pampered momma's boy (US) ⬛ VI AUX SEIN to get soft

Verweichlichung F -, NO PL softness; **Zentralheizung führt zur ~** central heating makes you soft

Verweigerer [fɛɐ̯'vaigərə] M -s, -, **Verweigerin** [-ərɪn] F -, -nen refusenik (inf); (= Kriegsdienstverweigerer) conscientious objector

verweigern ptp **verweigert** VT to refuse; Befehl to refuse to obey; Kriegsdienst to refuse to do; **jdm etw ~** to refuse or deny sb sth; **die Zustimmung zu etw ~** to refuse to give approval to sth; **es war ihr verweigert, ihren Sohn wiederzusehen** she was denied seeing her son; **die Annahme eines Briefes ~** to refuse (to take delivery of) a letter; **er verweigerte die Unterschrift** he refused to sign

Verweigerung F refusal; **~ der Aussage** (Jur) refusal to make a statement; (von Zeuge) refusal to testify; **~ des Gehorsams** disobedience

verweint [fɛɐ̯'vaint] ADJ Augen tear-swollen; Gesicht tear-stained; Mensch with (a) tear-stained face; **~ aussehen** to look as though one has (just) been crying

Verweis [fɛɐ̯'vais] M -es, -e [-zə] **(a)** (= Rüge) reprimand, admonishment; **jdm einen ~ erteilen** or **aussprechen** to reprimand or admonish sb **(b)** (= Hinweis) reference (auf +acc to)

verweisen ptp **verwiesen** [fɛɐ̯'viːzn̩] IRREG ⬛ VT **(a)** (= hinweisen) **jdn auf etw** (acc)/**an jdn ~** to refer sb to sth/sb **(b)** (von der Schule) to expel; **jdn des Landes** or **aus dem Lande ~** to expel sb (from the country); **jdn vom Platz** or **des Spielfeldes ~** to send sb off; **jdn auf den zweiten Platz ~** (Sport) to relegate sb to second place **(c)** (Jur) to refer (an +acc to) ⬛ VI **auf etw** (acc) **~** to refer to sth

verwelken ptp **verwelkt** VI AUX SEIN (Blumen) to wilt; (fig) to fade; **ein verwelktes Gesicht** a worn face; **eine verwelkte Schönheit** a faded beauty

verwenden [fɛɐ̯'vɛndn̩], pret **verwendete** or **verwandte** [fɛɐ̯'vɛndətə, fɛɐ̯'vantə], ptp **verwendet** or **verwandt** [fɛɐ̯'vɛndət, fɛɐ̯'vant] ⬛ VT to use; **Mühe/Fleiß auf etw** (acc) **~** to put effort/hard work into sth; **Zeit auf etw** (acc) **~** to spend time on sth ⬛ VR **sich (bei jdm) für jdn ~** to intercede (with sb) on sb's behalf

Verwendung F use; (von Zeit, Geld) expenditure (auf +acc on); **keine ~ für etw haben** to have no use for sth; **~ finden** to come in useful; **für jdn/etw ~ finden** to find a use for sb/sth

verwerfen ptp **verworfen** [fɛɐ̯'vɔrfn̩] IRREG ⬛ VT **(a)** (= ablehnen) to reject; eigene Meinung, Ansicht, Gedanken to discard; (Jur) Klage, Antrag, Revision to dismiss; Urteil to quash; (= kritisieren) to condemn **(b)** Ball to lose ⬛ VR (Holz) to warp; (Geol) to fault

verwerflich [fɛɐ̯'vɛrflɪç] ADJ reprehensible

Verwerfung [fɛɐ̯'vɛrfʊŋ] F -, -en **(a)** (= Ablehnung) rejection; (Jur) dismissal; (von Urteil) quashing **(b)** (Geol) fault; (von Holz) warping

verwertbar ADJ usable

Verwertbarkeit [fɛɐ̯'veːɐ̯tbaːɐ̯kait] F -, NO PL usability

verwerten ptp **verwertet** VT (= verwenden) to make use of; Reste to use; Kenntnisse, Erfahrungen to utilize, to put to good use; (kommerziell) to exploit; (Körper) Nahrung to process; **dieser Stoff wird sich gut für ein Kleid ~ lassen** this material will make a nice dress

Verwertung F utilization; (von Resten) using; (kommerziell) exploitation

verwesen [fɛɐ̯'veːzn̩], ptp **verwest** VI AUX SEIN to decay; (Fleisch) to rot

Verwesung F -, NO PL decay; **in ~ übergehen** to start to decay

verwetten ptp **verwettet** VT to gamble away

verwickeln ptp **verwickelt** ⬛ VT Fäden etc to tangle (up); **jdn in etw** (acc) **~** to involve sb in sth; **in etw verwickelt sein** to be involved/mixed up/embroiled in sth ⬛ VR (Fäden etc) to become tangled; **sich in etw** (acc) **~** (lit) to become entangled in sth; (fig) in Widersprüche to get oneself tangled up in sth; **in Skandal** to get mixed up in sth

verwickelt [fɛɐ̯'vɪklt] ADJ (fig inf) (= schwierig) complicated; (= verwirrt) Mensch confused

Verwickelung [fɛɐ̯'vɪkəlʊŋ] F -, -en, **Verwicklung** [fɛɐ̯'vɪklʊŋ] F -, -en involvement (in +acc in); (= Komplikation) complication; (= Verwirrung) confusion

verwildern ptp **verwildert** VI AUX SEIN (Garten) to become overgrown; (Pflanzen) to grow wild; (Haustier) to become wild; (hum inf: Mensch) to run wild

verwildert [fɛɐ̯'vɪldɐt] ADJ wild; Garten overgrown; Aussehen unkempt

Verwilderung [fɛɐ̯'vɪldərʊŋ] F -, -en (von Garten) overgrowing; **Zustand der ~** state of neglect; **mangelnde Sorge führte zur ~ des Tieres/der Kinder** as a result of negligence the animal became wild/the children ran wild

verwinkelt [fɛɐ̯'vɪŋklt] ADJ Straße, Gasse winding; Gebäude, Raum full of nooks and crannies

verwirklichen [fɛɐ̯'vɪrklɪçn̩], ptp **verwirklicht** ⬛ VT to realize ⬛ VR to be realized; (Mensch) to fulfil (Brit) or fulfill (US) oneself

Verwirklichung F -, -en realization; (von Hoffnung, Selbstverwirklichung) fulfilment (Brit), fulfillment (US)

verwirren [fɛɐ̯'vɪrən], ptp **verwirrt** ⬛ VT **(a)** Haar to ruffle (up); Fäden etc to tangle (up) **(b)** (= durcheinander bringen) to confuse; (= konfus machen) to bewilder; Sinne, Verstand to confuse ⬛ VR (Fäden etc) to become tangled (up); (Haare) to become tousled; (fig) to become confused

Verwirrung F confusion; **jdn in ~ bringen** to confuse sb; (= verlegen machen) to fluster sb

verwittern ptp **verwittert** VI AUX SEIN to weather

verwitwet [fɛɐ̯'vɪtvət] ADJ widowed; **Frau Meier, ~e Schulz** Mrs Meier, the widow of Mr Schulz

verwöhnen [fɛɐ̯'vøːnən], ptp **verwöhnt** ⬛ VT to spoil; (Schicksal) to smile upon ⬛ VR to spoil oneself

verwohnt [fɛɐ̯'voːnt] ADJ Wohnung run-down; Möbel battered

verwöhnt [fɛɐ̯'vøːnt] ADJ spoiled; Kunde, Geschmack discriminating; **vom Schicksal/von den Göttern ~** smiled upon by fate/the gods

verworren [fɛɐ̯'vɔrən] ADJ confused; (= verwickelt) intricate

Verworrenheit F -, NO PL confusion; (= Verwickeltheit) intricacy

verwundbar ADJ (lit, fig) vulnerable

verwunden [fɛɐ̯'vʊndn̩], ptp **verwundet** VT to wound; (lit auch) to injure

verwunderlich ADJ surprising; (stärker) astonishing, amazing; (= sonderbar) strange, odd; **es ist nicht ~, dass ...** it is not surprising that ...

verwundern ptp **verwundert** ⬛ VT to astonish, to amaze ⬛ VR (über +acc at) to be amazed; **sich über etw** (acc) **sehr ~ müssen** to be most amazed at sth

verwundert ⬛ ADJ astonished, amazed ⬛ ADV in astonishment, in amazement

Verwunderung [fɛɐ̯'vʊndərʊŋ] F -, NO PL astonishment, amazement; **zu meiner größten ~** to my great astonishment or amazement

Verwundete(r) [fɛɐ̯'vʊndətə] MF DECL AS ADJ casualty; **die ~n** (Mil) the wounded

Verwundung F -, -en wound

verwunschen [fɛɐ̯'vʊnʃn̩] ADJ enchanted

verwünschen ptp **verwünscht** VT **(a)** (= verfluchen) to curse; **verwünscht** confounded **(b)** (in Märchen) (= verzaubern) to enchant; (= verhexen) to bewitch

Verwünschung [fɛɐ̯'vʏnʃʊŋ] F -, -en **(a)** (= Fluch) curse **(b)** NO PL (= Verzauberung) enchantment; (= Verhexung) bewitchment

verwüsten [fɛɐ̯'vyːstn̩], ptp **verwüstet** VT to devastate; (fig) Gesicht to ravage

Verwüstung F -, -en devastation no pl; (von Gesicht) ravages pl; **die ~en durch den Sturm** the devastation caused by the storm; **~en anrichten** to inflict devastation

verzagt [fɛɐ̯'tsaːkt] ⬛ ADJ despondent ⬛ ADV despondently

Verzagtheit F -, NO PL despondency

verzählen *ptp* **verzählt** ▮ VR to miscount ▮ VTI (*dial inf*) = **erzählen**

verzärteln [fɛɐˈtsɛːtln], *ptp* **verzärtelt** VT (*pej*) to mollycoddle (*esp Brit*), to pamper

verzaubern *ptp* **verzaubert** VT (*lit*) to put a spell on; **jdn in etw** (*acc*) ~ (*fig*) to turn sb into sth; **eine verzauberte Prinzessin** an enchanted princess

Verzauberung [fɛɐˈtsaubərʊŋ] F -, -en (*lit, fig*) enchantment; (= *Verhexung*) bewitchment; **die ~ des Prinzen in einen Frosch** turning the prince into a frog

verzehnfachen [fɛɐˈtseːnfaxn], *ptp* **verzehnfacht** VTR to increase tenfold

Verzehr [fɛɐˈtseːɐ] M -(e)s, NO PL consumption

verzehren *ptp* **verzehrt** VT (*form: lit, fig*) to consume

verzeichnen *ptp* **verzeichnet** VT (= *notieren, aufweisen*) to record; (*esp in Liste*) to enter; **gewaltige Änderungen sind zu ~** enormous changes are to be noted; **Todesfälle waren nicht zu ~** there were no fatalities; **einen Erfolg zu ~ haben** to have scored a success; **das kann die Regierung als (einen) Erfolg ~** the government can mark this up as a success

Verzeichnis [fɛɐˈtsaiçnɪs] NT -ses, -se index; (= *Tabelle*) table; (= *Namensverzeichnis: esp amtlich*) register; (= *Aufstellung*) list; (*Comput*) directory

verzeigen *ptp* **verzeigt** VT (*Sw*) **jdn ~** to report sb to the police

Verzeigung [fɛɐˈtsaigʊŋ] F -, -en (*Sw*) reporting

verzeihen *ptp* **verziehen** [fɛɐˈtsiːən] VTI IRREG (= *vergeben*) to forgive; (*Gott, Gebieter*) to pardon; (= *entschuldigen*) to excuse; **jdm (etw) ~** to forgive sb (for sth); **ich kann es mir nicht ~, dass ich sie geschlagen habe** I'll never forgive myself for hitting her; **das ist nicht zu ~** that's unforgivable; **es sei dir noch einmal verziehen** you're forgiven!; **~ Sie!** excuse me!; **~ Sie die Störung, ~ Sie, dass ich stören muss** excuse me for disturbing you

verzeihlich [fɛɐˈtsailıç] ADJ forgivable; (= *zu entschuldigen*) excusable

Verzeihung [fɛɐˈtsaiʊŋ] F -, NO PL forgiveness; (= *Entschuldigung*) pardon; **~! excuse me!; (als Entschuldigung auch) sorry!; (jdn) um ~ bitten** (= *sich entschuldigen*) to apologize (to sb); **ich bitte vielmals um ~** I do apologize (*für* for)

verzerren *ptp* **verzerrt** VT (*lit, fig*) to distort; **Gesicht etc** to contort; **etw verzerrt darstellen** (*fig*) to present a distorted picture of sth; **verzerrte Gitarren** distorted guitars

Verzicht [fɛɐˈtsıçt] M -(e)s, -e renunciation (*auf +acc* of); (*auf Anspruch*) abandonment (*auf +acc* of); (= *Opfer*) sacrifice; (*auf Recht, Eigentum, Amt*) relinquishment (*auf +acc* of); (*auf Thron*) abdication (*auf +acc* of); **der ~ auf Zigaretten fällt ihm schwer** he finds it hard to give up cigarettes; **~, der mir nicht schwer fällt** that's something I can easily do (*Brit*) or go without; **~ ist ein Fremdwort für sie** doing (*Brit*) or going without is foreign to her

verzichten [fɛɐˈtsıçtn], *ptp* **verzichtet** VI to do (*Brit*) or go without; (= *Opfer bringen*) to make sacrifices; **sie verzichtete zugunsten ihrer Schwester auf das Auto** she let her sister have the car; **der Kandidat hat zugunsten eines Jüngeren verzichtet** the candidate stepped down in favour (*Brit*) or favor (*US*) of a younger man; **dankend ~** (*iro*) to decline politely; **danke, ich verzichte** (*iro*) not for me, thanks; **auf jdn/ etw ~** (= *ohne auskommen müssen*) to do (*Brit*) or go without sb/sth; (= *aufgeben*) to give up sb/sth; **auf Erbschaft, Eigentum** to renounce sth; **auf Anspruch** to waive sth; **auf Recht** to relinquish sth; (*von etw absehen*) **auf Kommentar, Anzeige etc** to abstain from sth; **auf Kandidatur, Wiederwahl, Amt** to refuse sth; **auf jdn/etw ~ können** to be able to do (*Brit*) or go without sb/sth; **auf den Thron ~** to abdicate; **auf Einzelheiten ~ können** to be able to dispense with details

verziehen *ptp* **verzogen** [fɛɐˈtsoːgn] IRREG ▮ VT (a) **Mund, Züge etc** to twist (*zu* into); **das Gesicht ~** to pull (*Brit*) or make a face; **den Mund ~** to turn up one's mouth; **keine Miene ~** not to bat an eyelash (*Brit*) or eye (*US*)

(b) **Kinder** to bring up badly; (= *verwöhnen*) to spoil; **Tiere** to train badly; *siehe auch* **verzogen**

▮ VR (a) (*Stoff*) to go out of shape; (*Chassis*) to be bent out of shape; (*Holz*) to warp

(b) (*Mund, Gesicht etc*) to contort

(c) (= *verschwinden*) to disappear (*auch inf*); (*Gewitter*) to pass;

(*Nebel, Wolken*) to disperse; (*inf: = schlafen gehen*) to go to bed ▮ VI AUX SEIN to move (*nach* to); **„verzogen"** (= *unbekannt*) "no longer at this address"

verzieren *ptp* **verziert** VT to decorate; (= *verschönern*) to embellish; (*Mus*) to ornament

Verzierung [fɛɐˈtsiːrʊŋ] F -, -en decoration; (= *Verschönerung*) embellishment; (*Mus: = verzierende Noten*) ornament

verzinsen *ptp* **verzinst** ▮ VT to pay interest on; **jdm sein Kapital (mit or zu 5%) ~** to pay sb (5%) interest on his/her capital; **das Geld wird mit 3% verzinst** 3% interest is paid on the money ▮ VR **sich (mit 6%) ~** to yield or bear (6%) interest

verzinslich [fɛɐˈtsınslıç] ▮ ADJ interest-bearing *attr*; **~ sein** to yield or bear interest; **zu 3%/einem hohen Satz ~** yielding or bearing 3% interest/a high rate of interest; **nicht ~** free of interest ▮ ADV **Kapital ~ anlegen** to put capital out at interest

Verzinsung [fɛɐˈtsınzʊŋ] F -, -en (= *das Verzinsen*) payment of interest (*+gen, von* on); (= *Zinsertrag*) interest (yield or return) (*+gen, von* on); (= *Zinssatz*) interest rate

verzocken *ptp* **verzockt** VT (*inf*) to gamble away

verzogen [fɛɐˈtsoːgn] ADJ **Kind** badly brought up; (= *verwöhnt*) spoiled; **Tier** badly trained; *siehe auch* **verziehen**

verzögern *ptp* **verzögert** ▮ VT to delay; (= *verlangsamen*) to slow down ▮ VR to be delayed

Verzögerung [fɛɐˈtsøːgərʊŋ] F -, -en (a) delay, hold-up (b) NO PL (= *das Verzögern*) delaying; (= *Verlangsamung*) slowing down; (*Phys*) deceleration

Verzögerungstaktik F delaying tactics *pl*

verzollen *ptp* **verzollt** VT to pay duty on; **diese Waren müssen verzollt werden** you must pay duty on these articles; **haben Sie etwas zu ~?** have you anything to declare?; **verzollt** duty-paid

verzückt [fɛɐˈtsʏkt] ▮ ADJ enraptured, ecstatic ▮ ADV **ansehen** adoringly; **~ lauschte er der Musik** he listened enraptured to the music

Verzückung [fɛɐˈtsʏkʊŋ] F -, -en rapture, ecstasy; **in ~ geraten** to go into raptures or ecstasies (*wegen* over)

Verzug M, NO PL (a) delay; (= *Rückstand von Zahlung*) arrears *pl*; **im ~** in arrears *pl* (*esp Brit*), behind; **mit etw in ~ geraten** to fall behind with sth; *mit Zahlungen* to fall into arrears (*esp Brit*) or behind with sth (b) **es ist Gefahr im ~** there's danger ahead

Verzugszinsen PL interest *sing* payable (on arrears (*esp Brit*))

verzweifeln *ptp* **verzweifelt** VI AUX SEIN to despair (*an +dat* of); **am Leben ~** to despair of life; **nur nicht ~!** don't despair!; **es ist zum Verzweifeln!** it drives you to despair!

verzweifelt [fɛɐˈtsvaiflt] ▮ ADJ **Blick, Stimme etc** despairing *attr*, full of despair; **Mensch auch, Lage, Versuch, Kampf etc** desperate; **ich bin (völlig) ~** I'm in (the depths of) despair; (= *ratlos*) I'm at my wits' end ▮ ADV desperately; **..., sagte er ~ ...** he said despairingly; **schau nicht so ~** don't look so desperate

Verzweiflung [fɛɐˈtsvaiflʊŋ] F -, -en (*Gemütszustand*) despair; (= *Ratlosigkeit*) desperation; **etw in seiner ~ tun, etw aus ~ tun** to do sth in desperation; **jdn zur or in die ~ treiben** to drive sb to despair

verzweigt [fɛɐˈtsvaikt] ADJ **Baum, Familie, Firma, Straßennetz** branched; (*Anat, fig*) ramified

verzwickt [fɛɐˈtsvɪkt] ADJ (*inf*) tricky

Vesper NT -s, - (*dial*) (*auch* **Vesperpause, Vesperzeit**) break; (*auch* **Vesperbrot**) sandwiches *pl*

Veterinärmedizin F veterinary medicine

Veto [ˈveːto] NT -s, -s veto

Vetorecht NT right of veto

Vetter [ˈfɛtɐ] M -s, -n cousin; (*in Märchen*) Brother, Brer

Vetternwirtschaft F (*inf*) nepotism

V-Form [ˈfau-] F V-shape; **in ~** in a V-shape

v-förmig [ˈfau-], **V-förmig** ▮ ADJ V-shaped ▮ ADV in the shape of a V; **~ aussehen** to be V-shaped; **der Pullover ist ~ ausgeschnitten** this sweater has a V-neck

V-Frau [ˈfau-] F ABBR *von* **Verbindungsfrau**

VGA-Karte [fauge:ˈʔa:-] F (*Comput*) VGA card

vgl. ABBR *von* **vergleiche** cf

VHS[1] [fauha:ˈʔɛs] F -, NO PL ABBR *von* **Volkshochschule**

VHS[2] [fauha:ˈʔɛs] NT -, NO PL ABBR *von* **Video-Home-System** VHS

via ['viːa] ADV via

Viadukt [via'dʊkt] M -(e)s, -e viaduct

Viagra® [vi'aːgra] NT -s Viagra®

Vibration [vibra'tsioːn] F -, -en vibration

vibrieren [vi'briːrən], *ptp* **vibriert** VI to vibrate; (*Stimme*) to quiver; (*Ton*) to vary

Video ['viːdeo] NT -s, -s video; **etw auf ~ aufnehmen** to video sth

Video- IN CPDS video; **Videoaufnahme** F video recording; **Videoclip** M video clip; **Videogerät** NT video (recorder); **Videokamera** F video camera; **Videokassette** F video cassette; **Videokonferenz** F video conference; **Videoprint** [-prɪnt] NT -s, -s video print; **Videorekorder** M video recorder; **Videospiel** NT video game; **Videotechnik** F video technology; **Videotext** M Teletext®; **Videothek** [video'teːk] F -, -en video (tape) library

Vieh [fiː] NT -(e)s, NO PL (a) (= *Nutztiere*) livestock; (= *esp Rinder*) cattle *pl*; **10 Stück** ~ 10 head of livestock/cattle (b) (*inf.* = *Tier*) animal (c) (*pej inf: Mensch*) swine

Vieh-: **Viehbestand** M livestock; **Viehfutter** NT (animal) fodder *or* feed

viehisch ['fiːɪʃ] **1** ADJ brutish; *Schmerzen* beastly; (= *unzivilisiert*) *Benehmen* swinish **2** ADV (a) *jucken, brennen* unbearably; **~ wehtun** to be unbearably painful (b) *sich benehmen* like an animal/animals; **~ essen** to eat like a pig; **~ hausen** to live like animals/an animal

Vieh-: **Viehweide** F pasture; **Viehzucht** F (live)stock breeding; (= *Rinderzucht auch*) cattle breeding

viel [fiːl] INDEF PRON, ADJ, *comp* **mehr** [meːɐ], *superl* **meiste(r, s)** *or adv* **am meisten** ['maistə] (a) SING (*adjektivisch*) a lot of, a great deal of; (*substantivisch*) a lot, a great deal; (*esp fragend, verneint*) much; **~es** a lot of things; **in ~em, in ~er Hinsicht** *or* **Beziehung** in many respects; **mit ~em** with a lot of things; **um ~es besser** *etc* a lot *or* much *or* a great deal better *etc*; **so ~** so much; **halb/doppelt so ~** half/twice as much; **so ~ als** *or* **wie ...** as much as ...; **noch einmal so ~** the same again; (= *doppelt so ~*) twice as much; **das ist so ~ wie eine Zusage** that is tantamount to a promise; **so ~ für heute!** that's all for today; **so ~, was ihn betrifft** so much for him; **so ~ (Arbeit** *etc*) so much *or* such a lot (of work *etc*); **noch (ein)mal so ~ (Zeit** *etc*) as much (time *etc*) again; **zweimal so ~ (Arbeit** *etc*) twice as much (work *etc*); **gleich ~ (Gewinn** *etc*) the same amount (of profit *etc*); **wie ~** how much; (*bei Mehrzahl*) how many; (**um**) **wie ~ größer** how much bigger; **zu ~** too much; (*inf:* = *zu viele*) too many; **~ zu ~** much *or* far too much; **wenns dir zu ~ wird, sag Bescheid** say if it gets too much for you; **ihm ist alles zu ~** (*inf*) it's all too much for him; **da krieg ich zu ~** (*inf*) I blow my top (*inf*); **einer/zwei** *etc* **zu ~** one/two *etc* too many; **was zu ~ ist, ist zu ~** that's just too much; **ein bisschen ~ (Regen** *etc*) a bit too much (rain *etc*); **furchtbar ~ (Regen** *etc*) an awful lot (of rain *etc*); **~ Erfolg!** good luck!; **~ Spaß!** have fun!; **~ Neues/Schönes** *etc* a lot of *or* many new/beautiful *etc* things; **das ~e Geld** all that money; **das ~e Geld/Lesen** *etc* all this money/reading *etc*; **~ zu tun haben** to have a lot to do; **das will ~/nicht ~ heißen** *or* **sagen** that's saying a lot *or* a great deal/not saying much

(b) **~e** *pl* (*adjektivisch*) many, a lot of; (*substantivisch*) many, a lot; **da wir so ~e sind** since there are so many *or* such a lot of us; **davon gibt es nicht ~e** there aren't many *or* a lot about; **furchtbar ~e (Kinder/Bewerbungen** *etc*) an awful lot (of children/applications *etc*); **gleich ~e (Angestellte/Anteile** *etc*) the same number (of employees/shares *etc*); **so/zu ~e (Menschen/Fehler** *etc*) so/too many (people/mistakes *etc*); **er hat ~(e) Sorgen/Probleme** *etc* he has a lot of worries/problems *etc*; **~e hundert** *or* **Hundert Menschen** many hundreds of people; **die/seine ~en Fehler** *etc* the/his many mistakes *etc*; **die ~en Leute/Bücher!** all these people/books!; **~e glauben, ...** many (people) *or* a lot of people believe ...; **und ~e andere** and many others

(c) (*adverbial: mit vb*) a lot, a great deal; (*esp fragend, verneint*) much; **er arbeitet ~** he works a lot; **er arbeitet nicht ~** he doesn't work much; **er arbeitet zu ~** he works too much; **die Straße wird (sehr/nicht) ~ befahren** this street is (very/not very) busy; **dieses Thema wird ~ diskutiert** this subject is much debated; **sich ~ einbilden** to think a lot of oneself

(d) (*adverbial: mit adj, adv*) much, a lot; **~ größer** *etc* much *or* a lot bigger *etc*; **~ beschäftigt** very busy; **~ diskutiert** much discussed; **~ gekauft** frequently bought; **~ geliebt** much-loved *or* very; **~ genannt** much-cited; **~ geprüft** (*hum*) sorely tried; **~**

gereist much-travelled (*Brit*), much-traveled (*US*); **~ sagend** meaningful; (*adverbial*) meaningfully; **jdn ~ sagend ansehen** to give sb a meaningful look; **~ sagend lächeln** to give a meaningful smile; **~ verheißend** promising; *anfangen* promisingly; **sich ~ verheißend anhören** to sound promising; **~ versprechend** promising; *anfangen* promisingly; **~ versprechend klingen** to sound promising; **~ zu ...** much too ...; **~ zu ~** much *or* far too much; **~ zu ~e** far too many; **ich würde ~ lieber auf eine Party gehen** I'd much rather go to a party

Viel-: **vielbeschäftigt** *etc* ADJ ATTR *siehe* **viel**; **vieldeutig** [-dɔytɪç] ADJ ambiguous; **Vieldeutigkeit** F -, NO PL ambiguity; **Vieleck** NT polygon; **vieleckig** ADJ polygonal (*Math*), many-sided; **Vielehe** F polygamy

vielerlei ['fiːlɐ'lai] ADJ INV (a) various, all sorts of (b) (*substantivisch*) all kinds *or* sorts of things

vielfach ['fiːlfax] **1** ADJ multiple *attr*, manifold; **ein ~er Millionär** a multimillionaire; **auf ~e Weise** in many ways; **auf ~en Wunsch** at the request of many people **2** ADV many times; (= *in vielen Fällen*) in many cases; (= *auf vielfache Weise*) in many ways; (*inf:* = *häufig*) frequently; **~ bewährt** tried and tested many times

Vielfache(s) ['fiːlfaxə] NT DECL AS ADJ (*Math*) multiple; **das kleinste gemeinsame ~** (*Math*) the least *or* lowest common multiple; **um ein ~s** many times over; **um ein ~s besser** *etc* many times better *etc*; **der Gewinn hat sich um ein ~s vermehrt** *or* **ist um ein ~s gestiegen** the profit has been multiplied several times; **er verdient ein ~s von dem, was ich verdiene** his salary is many times higher than mine

Vielfahrer(in) M(F) (*mit öffentlichen Verkehrsmitteln*) frequent traveller (*Brit*) *or* traveler (*US*) (*on public transport*); (*mit Auto*) frequent car user

Vielfalt ['fiːlfalt] F -, NO PL (great) variety

vielfältig ['fiːlfɛltɪç] ADJ varied, diverse

Viel-: **vielfarbig**, (*Aus*) **vielfärbig** ADJ multicoloured (*Brit*), multicolored (*US*); (*Tech*) polychromatic; **Vielflieger(in)** M(F) frequent flier; **Vielfraß** M (a) (*fig*) glutton (b) (*Zool*) wolverine; **vielgekauft** *etc* [-gəkauft] ADJ ATTR *siehe* **viel**; **vielköpfig** ADJ many-headed; (*inf*) *Familie, Schar* large

vielleicht [fi'laiçt] ADV (a) perhaps; (*esp in Bitten*) by any chance; **könnten Sie mir ~ sagen, wie spät es ist?** could you possibly tell me the time?; **~ sagst du mir mal, warum** you'd better tell me why; **~ hältst du mal den Mund!** keep your mouth shut; **hat er sich ~ verirrt/wehgetan?** maybe he has got lost/has hurt himself; **hast du ihm das ~ erzählt?** did you perhaps tell him that?; (*entsetzt:* = *denn etwa*) you didn't tell him that, did you?; **~, dass ...** it could be that ...

(b) (= *wirklich, tatsächlich, inf: verstärkend*) really; **soll ich ~ 24 Stunden arbeiten?!** am I supposed to work 24 hours then?; **willst du mir ~ erzählen, dass ...?!** do you really mean to tell me that ...?; **du bist ~ ein Idiot!** you really are an idiot!; **ich war ~ nervös!** was I nervous!; **das ist ~ ein Haus!** that's some house! (*inf*)

(c) (= *ungefähr*) perhaps, about

vielmal ['fiːlmaːl] ADV (*Sw*) = **vielmals**

vielmals ['fiːlmaːls] ADV **danke ~!** thank you very much!, many thanks!; **ich bitte ~ um Entschuldigung!** I do apologize!; **er lässt ~ grüßen** he sends his best regards

vielmehr [fiːl'meːɐ, 'fiːl-] ADV rather; (= *sondern, nur*) just; **nicht dumm, ~ faul** not stupid just lazy

Viel-: **vielsagend** [-zaːgnt] ADJ *siehe* **viel**; **vielseitig** [-zaitɪç] **1** ADJ (*lit*) many-sided; *Mensch, Gerät, Verwendung* versatile; *Interessen* varied; *Ausbildung* broad; **dieser Beruf ist sehr ~** there are many different sides to this job; **auf ~en Wunsch** by popular request **2** ADV **~ interessiert/anwendbar** *etc* to have varied interests/many uses *etc*; **~ ausgebildet sein** to have a broad education; **~ anwendbar/einsetzbar sein** to be versatile; **Kompost ist ~ verwendbar** compost can be used for many purposes; **Vielseitigkeit** F -, NO PL (*von Mensch, Gerät, Verwendung*) versatility; (*von Interessen*) multiplicity; (*von Ausbildung*) broadness; **vielsprachig** ADJ multilingual; **vielverheißend** *etc* [-fɛhaisnt] ADJ *siehe* **viel**; **Vielvölkerstaat** [fiːl'fœlkɐ-] M multiracial state; **Vielzahl** F multitude; **eine ~ von Abbildungen** a wealth of illustrations

Vielzweck- IN CPDS multipurpose; **Vielzweckreiniger** M multipurpose cleaner

vier [viːɐ] NUM **(a)** four; **die ersten/nächsten/letzten ~** the first/next/last four; **sie ist ~ (Jahre)** she's four (years old); **mit ~ (Jahren)** at the age of four; **~ Millionen** four million; **es ist ~ (Uhr)** it's four (o'clock); **um/gegen ~ (Uhr)** or **-e** (inf) at/around four (o'clock); **~ Uhr ~** four minutes past four; **~/fünf Minuten vor/nach ~** four minutes/five (minutes) to/past four; **halb ~** half past three; **~ Minuten vor halb ~** twenty-six minutes past three; **~ Minuten nach halb ~** twenty-six minutes to four; **~ zu drei** (geschrieben 4:3) four-three; **wir waren ~** or **zu ~t** or **zu ~en** there were four of us; **wir fahren zu ~t** or **mit ~en in Urlaub** there are four of us going on holiday (esp Brit) or vacation (US) together; **sie kamen zu ~t** or **zu ~en** four of them came; **stellt euch ~ und ~** or **zu je ~** or **zu ~t** or **zu ~en auf** line up in fours

(b) **jdn unter ~ Augen sprechen** to speak to sb in private; **ein Gespräch unter ~ Augen** a private conversation; **~ Augen sehen mehr als zwei** (prov) two heads are better than one (prov); **alle ~e von sich strecken** (inf) (= ausgestreckt liegen) to stretch out; (= tot sein) to have given up the ghost; **auf allen ~en** (inf) on all fours

Vier [viːɐ] F **-, -en** four; (Buslinie etc) (number) four

Vier-: **Vierachser** [-laksɐ] M **-s, -** (Aut) four-axle vehicle; **vierarmig** ADJ with four arms; Leuchter with four branches; **Vier-Augen-Gespräch** NT, **Vieraugengespräch** NT private discussion; **vierbändig** ADJ four-volume attr, in four volumes; **Vierbeiner** [-bainɐ] M **-s, -** (hum) four-legged friend (hum); **vierbeinig** ADJ four-legged; **vierblätterig, vierblättrig** ADJ four-leaved; **vierdimensional** ADJ four-dimensional; **Viereck** NT four-sided figure, quadrilateral (Math); (= Rechteck) rectangle; **viereckig** ADJ square; (esp Math) quadrilateral; (= rechteckig) rectangular; **viereinhalb** [ˈfiːɐˈain'halp] NUM four and a half

Vierer [ˈfiːrɐ] M **-s, -** (Rudern, Sch) four; (Golf) foursome; (inf: = Linie) (number) four; (Aus, S Ger: Ziffer) four; **einen ~ im Lotto haben** to have four numbers in the lottery

Vierer-: **Viererbob** M four-man bob (Brit) or bobsled (US); **viererlei** [ˈfiːrɐ'lai] ADJ INV **(a)** ATTR Brot, Käse, Wein four kinds or sorts of; Möglichkeiten, Fälle, Größen four different **(b)** (substantivisch) four different things; (= vier Sorten) four different kinds; **Viererpasch** M (all) fours no indef art; **Viererreihe** F row of four

vierfach [ˈfiːɐfax] **1** ADJ fourfold, quadruple (esp Math); **die ~e Größe/Menge/Anzahl** four times the size/amount/number; **in ~er Ausfertigung** in quadruplicate; **in ~er Vergrößerung** enlarged four times **2** ADV four times, fourfold; **das Papier ~ legen** or **nehmen** to fold the paper in four; **den Faden ~ nehmen** to take four threads together; **er hat den Band ~** he has four copies of the book

Vierfache(s) [ˈfiːɐfaxə] NT DECL AS ADJ four times the amount, quadruple (Math); **das ~ von 3 ist 12** four times 3 is 12; **um das ~ zunehmen** to quadruple; **das ~ von jdm verdienen** to earn four times as much as sb

Vier-: **Vierfachsteckdose** F (Elec) 4-socket plug; **Vierfarbendruck** M, pl **-drucke** (Verfahren) four-colour (Brit) or four-color (US) printing; (Erzeugnis) four-colo(u)r print; **vierfarbig** **1** ADJ four-colour attr (Brit), four-color attr (US) **2** ADV in four colo(u)rs; **Vierfelderwirtschaft** F four-course rotation; **Vierflach** [-flax] NT **-(e)s, -e** (Math) tetrahedron; **vierflächig** ADJ Körper, Gebilde tetrahedral; **Vierfüßer** [-fyːsɐ] M **-s, -** (Zool) quadruped; **vierfüßig** ADJ four-legged; (Poet) tetrameter attr; **Vierfüßler** [-fyːslɐ] M **-s, -** (Zool) quadruped; **Vierganggetriebe** NT four-speed gearbox; **viergeschossig, viergeschoßig** ADJ (Aus, S Ger) **viergeschoßig** ADJ, ADV four-storey attr (Brit), four-story attr (US); **~ bauen** to build houses with four storeys (Brit) or stories (US); **Viergespann** NT (= vier Tiere, Wagen mit vier Tieren) four-in-hand; (Hist: = Quadriga) quadriga; (= vier Menschen) foursome; **viergliedrig** [-ɡliːdrɪç] ADJ (Math) quadrinomial; **vierhändig** **1** ADJ (Mus) four-handed **2** ADV **~ spielen** to play something for four hands

vierhundert [ˈfiːɐˈhʊndɐt] NUM four hundred

Vierhundertjahrfeier F quatercentenary (Brit), quadricentennial (US)

vierhundertste(r, s) [ˈfiːɐˈhʊndɐtstə] ADJ four hundredth

vierhunderttausend NUM four hundred thousand

Vier-: **Vierjahresplan** M (Econ) four-year plan; **vierjährig, 4-jährig** ADJ (= 4 Jahre alt) four-year-old attr; (= 4 Jahre dauernd) four-year attr; **ein ~es Kind** a four-year-old child;

Vierjährige(r) [-jɛːrɪɡə] MF DECL AS ADJ four-year-old; **Vierkampf** M (Sport) four-part competition; **Vierkant** [-kant] M or NT **-(e)s, -e** (Tech) square; (Math) tetrahedron; **Vierkanteisen** NT square steel bar; **Vierkantholz** NT squared timber; **vierkantig** ADJ square(-headed); **Vierkantschlüssel** M square box spanner (Brit) or wrench (US); **vierköpfig** ADJ Ungeheuer four-headed; **eine ~e Familie** a family of four

Vierling [ˈfiːrlɪŋ] M **-s, -e** quadruplet, quad (inf)

viermal [ˈfiːɐmaːl] ADV four times; **~ so viele** four times as many

viermalig [ˈfiːɐmaːlɪç] ADJ done four times; Weltmeister, Olympiasieger etc four-times attr; **~es Klingeln** four rings; **~e Vorstellungen** four performances; **nach ~em Versuch** after the fourth attempt; **nach ~er Aufforderung** after the fourth time of asking

Viermaster [-mastɐ] M **-s, -** (Naut) four-master

viermonatig ADJ ATTR Säugling four-month-old; Abstände four-monthly; Lieferungsfrist, Aufenthalt, Waffenstillstand four-month

viermonatlich **1** ADJ ATTR Erscheinen four-monthly **2** ADV erscheinen, sich wiederholen every four months

Vier-: **viermotorig** ADJ four-engined; **Vierpfünder** M four-pounder; **vierphasig** ADJ (Elec) four-phase; **Vierradantrieb** M four-wheel drive; **vierräderig, vierrädrig** ADJ four-wheeled; **das Auto ist ~** that car is a four-wheeler; **viersaitig** ADJ four-stringed; **~ sein** to have four strings; **vierseitig** [-zaitɪç] ADJ four-sided; Abkommen, Verhandlungen etc quadripartite; Brief, Broschüre four-page attr; **Viersilber** [-zɪlbɐ] M **-s, -** (Poet) tetrasyllable; **viersilbig** ADJ four-syllable attr, tetrasyllabic; **Viersitzer** M four-seater; **viersitzig** [-zɪtsɪç] ADJ four-seater attr; **~ sein** to have four seats; **vierspaltig** [-ʃpaltɪç] **1** ADJ four-column attr; **~ sein** to have four columns **2** ADV in four columns; **Vierspänner** [-ʃpɛnɐ] M **-s, -** four-in-hand; **vierspännig** **1** ADJ Wagen four-horse attr **2** ADV **~ fahren** to drive a team of four horses; **viersprachig** ADJ Mensch, Wörterbuch quadrilingual; Speisekarte in four languages; **das Buch wird ~ angeboten** the book is available in four languages; **vierspurig** [-ʃpuːrɪç] **1** ADJ four-lane attr; **~ sein** to have four lanes **2** ADV **eine Straße ~ bauen/planen** to build/plan a four-lane road; **etw ~ ausbauen** to expand sth to four lanes; **vierstellig** ADJ four-figure attr; (Math) Funktion, Dezimalbruch four-place attr; **~ sein** to have four figures/places; **Rechnungen in ~er Höhe** four-figure bills; **Viersternehotel** NT 4-star hotel; **vierstimmig** **1** ADJ four-part attr, for four voices **2** ADV **~ singen** to sing a song for four voices; **vierstöckig** **1** ADJ Haus four-storeyed (Brit), four-storied (US) **2** ADV **~ bauen** to build houses with four storeys (Brit) or stories (US); **vierstrahlig** ADJ Flugzeug four-engined; **Vierstufenrakete** F four-stage rocket; **vierstufig** ADJ four-stage attr; **~ sein** to have four stages; **vierstündig** ADJ ATTR Reise, Vortrag four-hour; **vierstündlich** **1** ADJ ATTR four-hourly **2** ADV every four hours

viert [fiːɐt] ADJ **zu ~** siehe auch **vier**

Vier-: **Viertagewoche** F four-day week; **viertägig** ADJ ATTR (= 4 Tage dauernd) four-day; (= 4 Tage alt) four-day-old; **viertäglich** ADJ, ADV every four days; **Viertakter** [-taktɐ] M **-s, -** (inf), **Viertaktmotor** M four-stroke (engine); **viertausend** [ˈfiːɐˈtauznt] NUM four thousand; **Viertausender** [ˈfiːɐˈtauzndɐ] M **-s, -** (Berg) four-thousand-metre (Brit) or four-thousand-meter (US) mountain

vierte ADJ siehe **vierte(r, s)**

vier-: **vierteilen** [ˈfiːɐˌtailən] VT **(a)** INSEP (Hist) to quarter **(b)** SEP = vierteilen; **vierteilig** ADJ (= mit vier einzelnen Teilen) four-piece attr; Roman, Fernsehserie four-part attr, in four parts; **~ sein** to have four pieces/parts; **ich habe dieses Service nur ~** I only have four settings of this dinner service

viertel [fɪrtl] ADJ INV quarter; **ein ~ Liter/Pfund** a quarter (of a) litre (Brit) or liter (US)/pound; **drei ~ Liter** three quarters of a litre (Brit) or liter (US); **drei ~ voll** three-quarters full; siehe auch **Viertel[1]**

Viertel[1] [fɪrtl] NT (SW AUCH M) **-s, - (a)** (Bruchteil) quarter; (inf) (= ~pfund) ≈ quarter; (= ~liter) quarter litre (Brit) or liter (US); **drei ~ der Bevölkerung** three quarters of the population; **der Mond ist im ersten/letzten ~** the moon is in the first/last quarter; **ein ~ Wein** a quarter litre (Brit) or liter (US) of wine; **ein ~ Butter** a quarter of butter

(b) (Uhrzeit) **(ein) ~ nach/vor sechs** (a) quarter past/to six; **(ein) ~ sechs** (a) quarter past five; **drei viertel sechs** (dial) (a) quarter to six; **um viertel/drei viertel sechs** (*dial*) at (a) quarter past five/(a) quarter to six; **fünf Minuten vor ~/drei ~** ten past/ twenty to; **es ist ~** it's (a) quarter past; **die Uhr schlug ~** the clock struck (a) quarter past

Viertel² ['fɪrtl] NT **-s, -** (= *Stadtbezirk*) quarter, district

Viertel- ['fɪrtl-]: **Vierteldrehung** F quarter turn; **Viertelfinale** NT quarterfinals *pl*

Vierteljahr NT three months *pl*, quarter (*Comm, Fin*)

Vierteljahres- IN CPDS quarterly; **Vierteljahresschrift** F quarterly

Viertel-: **Vierteljahrhundert** NT quarter of a century; **vierteljährig** ADJ ATTR *Kind etc* three-month-old; *Aufenthalt, Frist* three months'; **vierteljährlich** ❶ ADJ quarterly; *Kündigungsfrist* three months' *attr* ❷ ADV quarterly; **~ kündigen** to give three months' notice; **Viertelkreis** M quadrant; **Viertelliter** M or NT quarter of a litre (*Brit*) *or* liter (*US*)

vierteln ['fɪrtln] VT (= *in vier Teile teilen*) to divide into four; *Kuchen, Apfel etc auch* to divide into quarters; (= *durch vier teilen*) to divide by four

Viertel- ['fɪrtl-]: **Viertelnote** F crotchet (*Brit*), quarter note (*US*); **Viertelpause** F crotchet rest (*Brit*), quarter-note rest (*US*); **Viertelpfund** NT ≈ quarter (of a pound); **Viertelstunde** F quarter of an hour; **viertelstündig** ADJ ATTR *Abstand* quarter-hour; *Vortrag* lasting quarter of an hour; **viertelstündlich** ❶ ADJ ATTR *Abstand* quarter-hour ❷ ADV every quarter of an hour; **Viertelton** M, *pl* **-töne** quarter tone

viertens ['fiːɐtns] ADV fourth(ly), in the fourth place

Vierte(r) ['fiːɐtə] MF DECL AS ADJ fourth; **~r werden** to be *or* come fourth; **am ~n** (des Monats) on the fourth (of the month); **Karl IV.** *or* **der ~** Charles IV *or* the Fourth; **er war ~r im Rennen** he was *or* came fourth in the race; **als ~r durchs Ziel gehen** to be fourth at the finish; **du bist der ~, der mich das fragt** you're the fourth person to ask me that; **jeder ~ muss ...** every fourth person/boy *etc* has to ...

vierte(r, s) ['fiːɐtə] ADJ fourth; **der ~ Oktober** the fourth of October; **den 4. Oktober** October 4th, October the fourth; **am ~n Oktober** on the fourth of October; **der ~ Stock** the fourth (*Brit*) *or* fifth (*US*) floor; **im ~n Kapitel/Akt** in chapter/ act four; *siehe auch* **Vierte(r)**

viertletzte(r, s) ['fiːɐtˈlɛtstə] ADJ fourth (from) last

Vier-: **Viertonner** [-tɔnɐ] M **-s, -** ≈ four-ton truck; **Viertürer** [-tyːrɐ] M **-s, -** (*Aut*) four-door model; **viertürig** ADJ four-door *attr*; **~ sein** to have four doors; **Vieruhrzug** M, **4-Uhr-Zug** M four o'clock (train); **vierundeinhalb** NUM four and a half; **Vierundsechzigstelnote** F hemidemisemiquaver (*Brit*), sixty-fourth note (*US*); **Vierundsechzigstelpause** F hemidemisemiquaver rest (*Brit*), sixty-fourth note rest (*US*); **vierundzwanzig** NUM twenty-four; **Viervierteltakt** [-ˈfɪrtl-] M four-four *or* common time

Vierwaldstätter See [fiːɐˈvaltʃtɛtɐ] M Lake Lucerne

vier-: **vierwertig** ADJ (*Chem*) tetravalent; (*Ling*) four-place; **vierwöchentlich** ADJ ADV every four weeks; **vierwöchig** [-vœçɪç] ADJ four-week *attr*, four weeks long

vierzehn ['fɪrtseːn] NUM fourteen; **~ Uhr** 2 pm; (*auf Fahrplan, Mil*) fourteen hundred hours; **~ Tage** two weeks, a fortnight *sing* (*Brit*)

Vierzehn- ['fɪrtseːn-]: **Vierzehnender** M (*Hunt*) fourteen-pointer; **vierzehntägig** ADJ two-week *attr*, lasting a fortnight (*Brit*) *or* two weeks; **nach ~er Dauer** after a fortnight (*Brit*) *or* two weeks; **vierzehntäglich** ADJ, ADV fortnightly (*Brit*), every two weeks

vierzehnte(r, s) ['fɪrtseːntə] ADJ fourteenth; *siehe* **vierte(r, s)**

Vier-: **Vierzeiler** [-tsaɪlɐ] M **-s, -** four-line poem; (= *Strophe*) four-line stanza; **vierzeilig** ADJ four-line *attr*; **~ sein** to have four lines

vierzig ['fɪrtsɪç] NUM forty; **(mit) ~ (km/h) fahren** to drive at forty (km/h); **etwa ~ (Jahre alt)** about forty (years old); (*Mensch auch*) fortyish (*inf*); **mit ~ (Jahren)** at forty (years of age); **Mitte ~** in one's mid-forties; **über ~** over forty; **der Mensch über ~** people *pl* over forty; **im Jahre ~** in forty; (= *~ nach/vor Christi Geburt*) in (the year) forty (AD)/BC

Vierzig ['fɪrtsɪç] F **-, -en** forty

vierziger, 40er ['fɪrtsɪgɐ] ADJ ATTR INV **die ~ Jahre** the forties; **ein ~ Jahrgang** (*Mensch*) a person born in nineteen forty; (*Wein*) a vintage forty

Vierziger¹ ['fɪrtsɪgɐ] M **-s, -** (a) (*Wein*) wine of vintage forty (b) (*Aus, S Ger: Geburtstag*) fortieth (birthday) (c) **die ~** *pl* (= *~jahre*) one's forties; **er ist in den ~n** he is in his forties; **er ist Mitte der ~** he is in his mid-forties; **in die ~ kommen** to be getting on for forty

Vierziger² ['fɪrtsɪgɐ] M **-s, -**, **Vierzigerin** [-ərɪn] F **-, -nen** forty-year-old; **die ~** *pl* people in their forties

Vierzigerjahre PL **die ~** one's forties

Vierzig-: **vierzigfach** ['fɪrtsɪçfax] ❶ ADJ forty-fold ❷ ADV forty times; *siehe* **vierfach**; **vierzigjährig** ['fɪrtsɪç-] ADJ ATTR (= *40 Jahre alt*) forty-year-old; (= *40 Jahre dauernd*) forty-year; **das ~e Jubiläum** the 40th anniversary; **ein Vierzigjähriger** a forty-year-old; **vierzigmal** ['fɪrtsɪçmaːl] ADV forty times

vierzigstel ['fɪrtsɪçstl] ADJ INV fortieth; **eine ~ Sekunde** a *or* one fortieth of a second

Vierzigstel ['fɪrtsɪçstl] NT **-s, -** fortieth

vierzigste(r, s) ['fɪrtsɪçstə] ADJ fortieth

Vierzigstundenwoche F forty-hour week

Vier-: **Vierzimmerwohnung** F four-room flat (*Brit*) *or* apartment; **Vierzylindermotor** M four-cylinder engine; **vierzylindrig** ADJ four-cylinder *attr*

Vietnam [viɛtˈnam] NT **-s** Vietnam

Vietnamese [viɛtnaˈmeːzə] M **-n, -n**, **Vietnamesin** [-ˈmeːzɪn] F **-, -nen** Vietnamese

vietnamesisch [viɛtnaˈmeːzɪʃ] ADJ Vietnamese

Vignette [vɪnˈjɛtə] F **-, -n** vignette; (*Aut*) permit (*for motorway driving*)

Villa ['vɪla] F **-, Villen** [-lən] villa

Viola ['viːola] F **-, Violen** ['vioːlən] (*Mus*) viola

violett [vioˈlɛt] ADJ purple, violet; (*im Spektrum, Regenbogen*) violet

Violine [vioˈliːnə] F **-, -n** violin

VIP [vɪp] M **-, -s** (*inf*), **V. I. P.** [viːlaɪˈpiː] M **-, -s** (*inf*) ABBR *von* **Very Important Person** VIP

Viren PL *von* **Virus**

Virensuchprogramm NT (*Comput*) virus checker (*Brit*) *or* scanner

Virologe [viroˈloːgə] M **-n, -n**, **Virologin** [-ˈloːgɪn] F **-, -nen** virologist

Virologie [viroloˈgiː] F **-, NO PL** virology

virologisch [viroˈloːgɪʃ] ADJ virological

virtuell [vɪrtuˈɛl] ❶ ADJ *Realität etc* virtual ❷ ADV in virtual reality

virtuos [vɪrˈtuoːs] ❶ ADJ virtuoso *attr* ❷ ADV *beherrschen* like a virtuoso; **~ spielen** to give a virtuoso performance

Virus ['viːrʊs] NT or M **-, Viren** [-rən] (*auch Comput*) virus

Virus-: **Virusinfektion** F viral *or* virus infection; **Virusprogramm** NT (*Comput*) virus (program)

Visa PL *von* **Visum**

Visage [viˈzaːʒə] F **-, -n** (*inf*) face

Visen PL *von* **Visum**

Visier [viˈziːɐ] NT **-s, -e (a)** (*am Helm*) visor **(b)** (*an Gewehren*) sight; **jdn/etw im ~ haben** (*fig*) to have sb/sth in one's sights; **in jds ~** *acc* **geraten** (*fig*) to become a target for sb

Vision [viˈzioːn] F **-, -en** vision

Visite [viˈziːtə] F **-, -n** (*Med*) (*im Krankenhaus*) round; (*zu Hause*) house call; **~ machen** to do one's round/to do house calls

Visitenkarte [viˈziːtn-] F (*lit, fig*) visiting *or* calling (*US*) card

Viskose [vɪsˈkoːzə] F **-, NO PL** viscose

visuell [viˈzuɛl] ADJ visual

Visum ['viːzʊm] NT **-s, Visa** *or* **Visen** [-za, -zn] visa

vital [viˈtaːl] ADJ vigorous; (= *lebenswichtig*) vital

Vitalität [vitaliˈtɛːt] F **-, NO PL** vitality

Vitamin [vitaˈmiːn] NT **-s, -e** vitamin; **~ B** (*lit*) vitamin B; (*fig inf*) contacts *pl*

Vitamin-: **vitaminarm** ❶ ADJ poor in vitamins; **eine ~e Zeit** a time when there are/were few vitamins available ❷ ADV **~ leben/essen** to live on/have a vitamin-deficient diet; **vitaminhaltig**, (*Aus*) **vitaminhältig** ADJ containing vitamins; **~ sein** to contain vitamins; **Vitaminmangel** M vitamin deficiency

Vitrine [viˈtriːnə] F **-, -n** (= *Schrank*) glass cabinet; (= *Schaukasten*) display case

Vize ['fiːtsə] M **-s, -** (*inf*) number two (*inf*); (= *~meister*) runner-up

Vize- IN CPDS vice-; **Vizemeister(in)** M(F) runner-up

V-Mann ['faʊ-] M, *pl* **-Männer** *or* **-Leute** ABBR *von* **Verbindungsmann**

Vogel ['foːgl] M **-s, ¨** ['føːgl] (*lit*, *fig*) bird; **ein seltsamer ~** (*inf*) a strange bird (*inf*); **ein lustiger ~** (*inf*) a lively character (*inf*); **~ friss oder stirb** (*prov*) do or die! (*prov*); **den ~ abschießen** (*inf*) to surpass everyone (*iro*); **einen ~ haben** (*inf*) to be crazy (*inf*); **jdm den ~ zeigen** (*inf*) to tap one's forehead (*to indicate to sb that he/she's not quite right in the head*)

Vogel-: Vogelbauer NT, *pl* **-bauer** birdcage; **Vogelbeere** F (*auch* **Vogelbeerbaum**) rowan (tree); (= *Frucht*) rowan(berry); **Vogelfutter** NT bird food; (= *Samen*) birdseed; **Vogelhäuschen** [-hɔʏsçən] NT (= *Futterhäuschen*) birdhouse; **Vogelkäfig** M birdcage; **Vogelkunde** F ornithology

vögeln ['føːgln] VTI (= to screw (*sl*)

Vogel-: Vogelscheuche [-ʃɔʏçə] F **-, -n** (*lit*, *fig inf*) scarecrow; **Vogel-Strauß-Politik** F head-in-the-sand policy; **~ treiben** to bury one's head in the sand

Vogerlsalat ['foːgɐl-] M (*Aus*) corn salad

Vogesen [vo'geːzn] PL Vosges *pl*

Voice-Mail ['vɔɪsmeːl] F **-,** NO PL, **Voicemail** F **-,** NO PL (*Telec*) voice mail

Voice-Rekorder ['vɔɪsrekɔrdɐ] M **-s, -**, **Voicerekorder** M **-s, -** (*Aviat*) (cockpit) voice recorder

Vokabel [vo'kaːbl] F **-, -n** *or* (*Aus*) nt **-s, -** word; **~n** *pl* vocabulary *sing*, vocab *sing* (*Sch inf*)

Vokabular [vokabu'laːɐ] NT **-s, -e** vocabulary

Vokal [vo'kaːl] M **-s, -e** vowel

vokalisch [vo'kaːlɪʃ] ADJ (*Ling*) vocalic

Volk [fɔlk] NT **-(e)s, ¨er** ['fœlkɐ] (a) NO PL people *pl*; (= *Nation*) nation; (*inf: = Gruppe*) crowd *pl*; (*pej: = Pack*) rabble *pl*; **viel ~** lots of people *pl*; **etw unters ~ bringen** *Nachricht* to spread sth; *Geld* to spend sth (b) (= *ethnische Gemeinschaft*) people *sing*; **die Völker Afrikas** the peoples of Africa (c) (*Zool*) colony

Völker- ['fœlkɐ-]: **Völkerbund** M, NO PL (*Hist*) League of Nations; **Völkerfreundschaft** F friendship among nations; **Völkerkunde** F ethnology; **völkerkundlich** [-kʊntlɪç] ADJ ethnological; **Völkermord** M genocide; **Völkerrecht** NT international law; **völkerrechtlich** ADJ under international law; *Frage, Thema, Hinsicht, Standpunkt* of international law; *Anspruch, Haftung* international; **~e Anerkennung eines Staates** recognition of a state ADV *regeln, entscheiden* by international law; *klären* according to international law; *bindend sein* under international law; **Völkerverständigung** F international understanding; **Völkerwanderung** F (*Hist*) migration of the peoples; (*hum*) mass exodus

Volks- IN CPDS popular; (= *auf ein Land bezogen*) national; (*Pol*) people's; **Volksabstimmung** F plebiscite; **Volksbegehren** NT petition for a referendum; **Volksbelustigung** F public entertainment; **Volksbrauch** M national custom; **Volksdemokratie** F people's democracy; **volkseigen** ADJ (*DDR*) nationally-owned; (*in Namen*) People's Own; **Volksentscheid** M referendum; **Volksfest** NT public festival; (= *Jahrmarkt*) funfair; **Volksglaube(n)** M popular belief; **Volkshochschule** F adult education centre (*Brit*) *or* center (*US*); **einen Kurs an der ~ machen** to do an adult education class

Volks-: Volkskrankheit F widespread disease; **Volkslauf** M (*Sport*) open cross-country race; **Volkslied** NT folk song; **Volksmusik** F folk music; **Volksrepublik** F people's republic; **Volksseuche** F epidemic; **Volksstamm** M tribe; **Volkstanz** M folk dance; **Volkstrauertag** M national day of mourning, ≈ Remembrance Day (*Brit*), ≈ Veterans' Day (*US*)

volkstümlich ['fɔlkstyːmlɪç] 1 ADJ folk *attr*, folksy; (= *traditionell, überliefert*) traditional; (= *beliebt*) popular; **ein ~er König** a king with the common touch 2 ADV **etw ~ darstellen** to popularize sth; **sich ~ ausdrücken** to express oneself in plain language

Volks-: Volksverhetzung F **-, -en** incitement (of the people); **Volksversammlung** F people's assembly; (= *Kundgebung*) public gathering; **Volksvertreter(in)** M(F) representative of the people; **Volksvertretung** F representative body (of the people); **Volkswirt(in)** M(F) economist; **Volkswirtschaft** F national economy; (*Fach*) economics *sing*, political economy; **Volks- und Betriebswirtschaft** economics and business studies; **volkswirtschaftlich** ADJ *Schaden, Nutzen* economic; **Volkswirtschaftslehre** F economics *sing*, political economy; **Volkszählung** F (national) census; **Volkszugehörigkeit** F ethnic origin

voll [fɔl] 1 ADJ (a) full; *Satz, Service, Erfolg* complete; *Woche, Jahr, Wahrheit* whole; *Wangen* chubby; *Haar* thick; **~er ... full of ...;** **~ (von** *or* **mit) etw** full of sth; (= *bedeckt mit*) covered with sth; **aus dem Vollen schöpfen** to draw on unlimited resources; **~e drei Jahre/Tage** three whole years/days; **in ~er Größe** (*Bild*) life-size; (*bei plötzlicher Erscheinung etc*) large as life; **sich zu ~er Größe aufrichten** to draw oneself up to one's full height; **jdn nicht für ~ nehmen** not to take sb seriously; **mit dem ~en Namen unterschreiben** to sign one's full name (b) **~ sein** (*inf*) (= *satt*) to be full, to be full up (*Brit*); (= *betrunken*) to be tight (*Brit inf*) 2 ADV fully; (= *vollkommen auch*) completely; (*sl:* = *total*) dead (*Brit inf*), real (*US inf*); **~ und ganz** completely, wholly; **eine Rechnung ~ bezahlen** to pay a bill in full; **~ hinter jdm/ etw stehen** to be fully behind sb/sth; **den Mund ~ nehmen** (*fig*) to exaggerate; **etw ~ ausnützen** to take full advantage of sth; **~ zuschlagen** (*inf*) to hit out; **~ durcharbeiten** (*inf*) to work solidly (throughout); **~ (Stoff) gegen etw fahren** (*inf*) to run full tilt into sth; **nicht ~ da sein** (*inf*) not to be quite with it (*inf*); **~ dabei sein** (*inf*) to be totally involved

Voll-: vollautomatisch 1 ADJ fully automatic 2 ADV (completely) automatically; **Vollbad** NT (proper) bath; **Vollbart** M (full) beard; **Vollbeschäftigung** F full employment; **Vollbesitz** M **im ~ +gen** in full possession of; **Vollbild** NT (*Med: von Krankheit*) full-blown form; **Vollbild-Aids** NT full-blown Aids

Vollblut NT, NO PL thoroughbred

Vollblut- IN CPDS (*lit: Tier*) thoroughbred; (*fig*) full-blooded

Voll-: Vollbremsung F emergency stop; **eine ~ machen** to do an emergency stop; **vollbringen** [fɔl'brɪŋən], *ptp* **vollbracht** [fɔl'braxt] VT INSEP IRREG (= *ausführen*) to achieve; *Wunder* to work; **eine große Leistung ~** to achieve a lot; **vollbusig** [-buːzɪç] ADJ full-bosomed; **Volldampf** M (*Naut*) full steam; **mit ~ at full steam;** (*inf*) flat out (*esp Brit*)

voll dröhnen VTR = zudröhnen

vollenden [fɔl'lɛndn], *ptp* **vollendet** INSEP 1 VT (= *abschließen*) to complete; (= *vervollkommnen*) to make complete 2 VR (= *zum Abschluss kommen*) to come to an end; (= *vollkommen werden*) to be completed

vollendet [fɔl'lɛndət] 1 ADJ (= *vollkommen*) completed; *Tugend, Schönheit* perfect; *Mensch* accomplished; (*Jur*) *Straftat* completed; **nach ~em 18. Lebensjahr** upon completion of one's 18th year; **bis zum ~en 6. Lebensjahr** until one turns 6 2 ADV perfectly; **~ Klavier spielen** to be an accomplished pianist

vollends ['fɔlɛnts] ADV (a) (= *völlig*) completely (b) (= *besonders*) especially, particularly

Vollendung F completion; (= *Vervollkommnung, Vollkommenheit*) perfection

voller ['fɔlɐ] ADJ *siehe* voll

voll essen VR IRREG (*inf*) to gorge oneself

Volleyball M volleyball

Voll-: voll fressen VR IRREG (*pej inf*) to stuff oneself (*inf*); **Vollgas** NT, NO PL full throttle; **~ geben** to open it right up; **mit ~ fahren** to drive at full throttle; **mit ~** (*fig inf*) full tilt; **voll gießen** VT IRREG (= *auffüllen*) to fill (up); **Vollidiot(in)** M(F) (*inf*) complete idiot

völlig ['fœlɪç] 1 ADJ complete; **das ist mein ~er Ernst** I'm completely *or* absolutely serious 2 ADV completely; **es genügt ~** that's quite enough; **er hat ~ Recht** he's absolutely right

Voll-: volljährig ADJ of age; **~ werden/sein** to come/be of age; **sie hat drei ~e Kinder** she has three children who are of age; **Volljährige(r)** [-jɛːrɪɡə] MF DECL AS ADJ major; **Volljährigkeit** [-jɛːrɪçkait] F -, NO PL majority *no art*; **bei (Erreichen der) ~** on attaining one's majority; **Vollkasko** NT -, NO PL fully comprehensive insurance; **vollkaskoversichert** [-fɛɐzɪçɐt] ADJ comprehensively insured; **~ sein** to have fully comprehensive insurance; **Vollkaskoversicherung** F -, NO PL fully comprehensive insurance

vollkommen [fɔlˈkɔmən, ˈfɔl-] **1** ADJ perfect; (= *völlig*) complete, absolute; (*Math*) *Zahl* perfect; **sein Glück war ~** his happiness was complete **2** ADV completely

Voll-: Vollkornbrot NT coarse wholemeal (*Brit*) *or* wholegrain bread; **Vollkostenrechnung** F (*Comm, Fin*) absorption costing; **voll kotzen** VT (*sl*) to puke (up) over (*inf*); **voll labern** VT (*inf*) to chatter (on) to; **voll laden** VT IRREG to load up; **voll geladen** fully-laden; **Volllastbetrieb** M, NO PL (*Tech*) **im ~** at full load; **voll laufen** VI IRREG AUX SEIN to fill up; **etw ~ lassen** to fill sth (up); **sich ~ lassen** (*inf*) to get tanked up (*inf*); **voll machen** VT (a) *Gefäß* to fill (up); *Zahl, Dutzend* to make up; *Sammlung, Set* to complete (b) (*inf*) *Hosen* to make a mess in; *Windeln* to fill (*Brit*), to dirty (*US*); **sich** (*dat*) **die Hosen ~** (*fig inf*) to wet oneself (*inf*)

Vollmacht F -, -en (legal) power *or* authority *no pl, no indef art*; (*Urkunde*) power of attorney; **jdm eine ~ erteilen** to grant sb power of attorney

Voll-: Vollmilch F full-cream milk; **Vollmilchschokolade** F full-cream milk chocolate; **Vollmond** M full moon; **heute ist ~** there's a full moon today; **vollmundig** **1** ADJ *Wein* full-bodied; *Unterstützung, Versprechen* wholehearted; *Ankündigung, Erklärung* grandiose **2** ADV (= *großsprecherisch*) grandiosely; **etw ~ bestreiten** to dispute sth vehemently; **Vollnarkose** F general anaesthetic (*Brit*) *or* anesthetic (*US*); **Vollpension** F full board; **voll pfropfen** VT (*inf*) to cram full; **voll pissen** VT (*vulg*) to piss on (*sl*); *Hose* to piss in (*sl*); **voll saugen** VR REG *or* IRREG (*inf*) to become saturated; **voll schlagen** VT IRREG (*inf*) **sich** (*dat*) **den Bauch ~** to stuff oneself (with food) (*inf*); **voll schreiben** VT IRREG *Heft, Seite* to fill (with writing); *Tafel* to cover (with writing)

vollständig **1** ADJ complete; *Adresse* full *attr*; **nicht ~** incomplete; **etw ~ machen** to complete sth **2** ADV completely

Vollständigkeit [-ʃtɛndɪçkait] F -, NO PL completeness; **der ~ halber** to complete the picture

voll stopfen VT to cram full

vollstrecken [fɔlˈʃtrɛkn], *ptp* **vollstreckt** VT INSEP to execute; *Urteil, Haftbefehl* to carry out; *Pfändung* to enforce; **~de Gewalt** executive (power)

Vollstreckung F -, -en execution; (*von Todesurteil*) carrying out; (*von Pfändung*) enforcement

Vollstreckungsbescheid M writ of execution

Voll-: Vollstudium NT complete course of study; **voll tanken** VTI to fill up; **bitte ~** fill her up, please

Volltext M (*Comput*) full text

Volltext- (Comput**): Volltextdatenbank** F full text database; **Volltextsuche** F full text search

Voll-: Volltreffer M (*lit, fig*) bull's eye; **volltrunken** ADJ completely drunk; **in ~em Zustand Auto fahren** to drive in a drunken state; **Vollversammlung** F general assembly; (*von Stadtrat etc*) full meeting; **Vollversion** F (*Comput*) complete version; **Vollwaschmittel** NT detergent; **vollwertig** ADJ *Mitglied, Partner* full *attr*; *Stellung* equal; *Ersatz, Kost* (fully) adequate; **jdn als ~ behandeln/betrachten** to treat/regard sb as an equal; **Vollwertkost** F wholefoods *pl*; **vollzählig** [-tsɛːlɪç] **1** ADJ USU PRED *Satz, Anzahl, Mannschaft* complete; (= *ausnahmslos anwesend*) all present *pred*; **um ~es Erscheinen wird gebeten** everyone is requested to attend **2** ADV **sie sind ~ erschienen** everyone came; **~ versammelt sein** to be assembled in full force; **Vollzähligkeit** F -, NO PL full number; (= *ausnahmslose Anwesenheit*) full attendance

Vollzeit- IN CPDS full-time

vollziehen [fɔlˈtsiːən], *ptp* **vollzogen** [fɔlˈtsoːɡn] INSEP IRREG **1** VT to carry out; *Opferung, Trauung* to perform; *Bruch* to make **2** VR to take place; (*Trauung*) to be performed; (*jds Schicksal*) to be fulfilled

Vollzug [fɔlˈtsuːk] M, NO PL (= *Strafvollzug*) penal system; **offener ~** daytime release for prisoners pending parole

Vollzugs-: Vollzugsanstalt F (*form*) penal institution; **Vollzugsbeamte(r)** M DECL AS ADJ, **Vollzugsbeamtin** F (*form*) warder

Volontariat [volɔntaˈriaːt] NT **-(e)s, -e** (*Zeit*) practical training (b) (*Stelle*) position as a trainee

volontieren [volɔnˈtiːrən], *ptp* **volontiert** VI to be training (*bei* with)

Volt [vɔlt] NT **-(e)s, -** volt

Volt-: Voltmeter NT voltmeter; **Voltzahl** F voltage

Volumen [voˈluːmən] NT **-s, -** *or* **Volumina** [-na] (*lit, fig*: = *Inhalt*) volume

vom [fɔm] CONTR *von* **von dem**; **~ 10. September an** from the 10th September (*Brit*), from September 10th; **das kommt ~ Rauchen** that comes from smoking; **~ Kochen hat er keine Ahnung** he has no idea about cooking

von [fɔn] PREP +DAT (a) from; **nördlich ~** to the North of; **~ ... an** from ...; **~ Jugend an** from early on; **vom 10. Lebensjahr an** since he/she was ten years old; **~ heute ab** *or* an from today; **~ ... aus** from ...; **~ dort aus** from there; **etw ~ sich aus wissen** to know sth by oneself; **etw ~ sich aus tun** to do sth of one's own accord; **~ ... bis** from ... to; **~ morgens bis abends** from morning till night; **Ihr Brief ~ vor zwei Wochen** your letter of two weeks ago; **~ ... zu** from ... to; **wo/wann/was** where/when/what ... from, from where/when/what (*form*); **etw ~ etw nehmen/abreißen** to take/tear sth off sth; **alles ~ sich werfen** to throw everything aside

(b) (*Ursache, Urheberschaft ausdrücken*) by; **das Gedicht ist ~ Schiller** the poem is by Schiller; **ein Kleid ~ Dior** a Dior dress; **das Kind ist ~ ihm** the child is his; **~ etw müde** tired from sth; **~ etw begeistert** enthusiastic about sth

(c) (*partitiv, bestehend aus*) of; **jeweils zwei ~ zehn** two out of every ten; **ein Riese ~ einem Mann** (*inf*) a giant of a man; **dieser Dummkopf ~ Gärtner!** (*inf*) that idiot of a gardener!; **~ 50 m Länge** 50 m in length; **im Alter ~ 50 Jahren** at the age of 50; **Kinder ~ 10 Jahren** ten-year-old children; **~ Dauer sein** to be lasting; **das ist sehr freundlich ~ Ihnen** that's very kind of you

(d) (*in Titel*) of; (*bei deutschem Adelstitel*) von; **Otto ~ Bismarck** Otto von Bismarck; **ein „~" (und zu) „ sein** to have a handle to one's name; **da kannst du dich aber „~" schreiben** (*fig*) you can be really proud yourself (there)

(e) (*inf*) **~ dem halte ich gar nichts** I don't think much of him; **da weiß ich nichts ~** I don't know anything about it; **~ wegen** no way! (*inf*); **~ wegen der Karte/dem Buch** (*incorrect*) about the map/the book

voneinander [fɔnlaiˈnandɐ] ADV of each other, of one another; **etwas/nichts ~ haben** to see something/nothing of each other *or* one another; (= *Zusammensein genießen*) to be able/not to be able to enjoy each other's company; **sich ~ trennen** to part *or* separate (from each other *or* one another)

vonseiten [fɔnˈzaitn] PREP +GEN on the part of

vor [foːɐ] **1** PREP +ACC or DAT (a) +DAT (*räumlich, in Gegenwart von*) in front of; (= *außerhalb von*) outside; (= *~ Hintergrund*) against; (*bei Reihenfolge*) before; **der See/die Stadt lag ~ uns** the lake/town lay before us; **~ der Kirche rechts abbiegen** turn right before the church; **sich ~ jdm/etw verneigen** (*lit, fig*) to bow before *or* to sb/sth; **~ allen Dingen, ~ allem** above all; **~ dem Fernseher sitzen** *or* **hocken** (*inf*) to sit in front of the TV

(b) +DAT (*zeitlich*) before; (*Ursache angebend*) with; **zwanzig (Minuten) ~ drei** twenty (minutes) to three; **heute ~ acht Tagen** a week ago today; **das ist ~ liegt noch ~ uns** this is still to come; **ich war ~ ihm an der Reihe** I was in front of him; **~ einigen Tagen/langer Zeit/fünf Jahren** a few days/a long time/five years ago; **~ Hunger sterben** to die of hunger; **~ Kälte zittern** to tremble with cold; **~ lauter Arbeit** because of work

(c) +ACC **~ sich hin summen/lachen/sprechen** *etc* to hum/laugh/talk *etc* to oneself; **~ sich hin schreiben/arbeiten** to write/work away

(d) **~ jdm/etw sicher sein** to be safe from sb/sth; **Achtung ~ jdm/etw haben** to have respect for sb/sth; **wie ist das ~ sich gegangen?** how did it happen?

2 ADV **~ und zurück** backwards and forwards; **alle kleinen Kinder ~!** all small children to the front!

vorab [foːɐˈlap] ADV to begin *or* start with; **lassen Sie mich ~ erwähnen ...** first let me mention ...

Vor-: Vorabend M evening before; **das war am ~** that was the evening before; **am ~ der Revolution** (fig) on the eve of revolution; **Vorahnung** F presentiment, premonition; **Voralpen** PL foothills pl of the Alps

voran [fo'ran] ADV **(a)** (= vorn, an der Spitze) first; **ihm/ihr ~** in front of him/her **(b)** (= vorwärts) forwards; **immer langsam ~!** easy does it!

voran-: vorangehen VI SEP IRREG AUX SEIN **(a)** (= an der Spitze gehen) to go first or in front; (= anführen) to lead the way; **jdm ~** to go ahead of sb **(b)** (= zeitlich vor jdm gehen) to go on ahead **(c)** (zeitlich) **einer Sache** (dat) **~** to precede sth; **das Vorangegangene** what has gone before **(d)** AUCH VI IMPERS (= Fortschritte machen) to come along; **vorangestellt** [-gəʃtɛlt] ADJ (Gram) preceding attr; **~ sein** to precede; **vorankommen** VI SEP IRREG AUX SEIN to make progress; **im Leben/beruflich ~** to get on in life/in one's job; **nur langsam ~** to make slow progress

Vor-: Voranmeldung F appointment; (von Telefongespräch) booking; **Voranschlag** M estimate; **Vorarbeit** F groundwork; **gute ~ leisten** to do good groundwork; **vorarbeiten** SEP **1** VI (inf) to (do) work in advance **2** VT to work in advance **3** VR to work one's way forward; **Vorarbeiter** M foreman; **Vorarbeiterin** F forewoman

Vorarlberg ['fo:ɐlarlbɛrk, fo:ɐ'larl-] NT **-s** Vorarlberg

voraus [fo'raus] ADV **(a)** (= voran) in front (+dat of); (Naut, fig) ahead (+dat of) **(b)** (= vorher) **im Voraus** in advance

Voraus-: vorausbezahlt ADJ prepaid; **vorausfahren** VI SEP IRREG AUX SEIN to go in front (+dat of); (Fahrer) to drive in front (+dat of); (= früher fahren) to go on ahead; (Fahrer) to drive on ahead; **vorausgehen** VI SEP IRREG AUX SEIN = vorangehen; **vorausgesetzt** ADJ **~, (dass)** ... provided (that) ...; **voraushaben** VT SEP IRREG **jdm etw ~** to have the advantage of sth over sb; **jdm viel ~** to have a great advantage over sb; **vorausplanen** VTI SEP to plan ahead; **Voraussage** F prediction; (= Wettervoraussage) forecast; **voraussagen** VT SEP to predict (jdm for sb); **Wahlergebnisse auch, Wetter** to forecast; **jdm die Zukunft ~** to foretell sb's future; **voraussehen** VT SEP IRREG to foresee; **ich habe es ja vorausgesehen, dass** ... I knew that ...; **das war vorauszusehen!** that was (only) to be expected!

voraussetzen VT SEP to presuppose; **Interesse, Zustimmung, jds Liebe, Verständnis** to take for granted; (= erfordern) to require; **wenn wir einmal ~, dass** ... let us assume that ...; **etw als selbstverständlich ~** to take sth for granted; **etw als bekannt ~** to assume that everyone knows sth

Voraussetzung [-zɛtsʊŋ] F **-, -en** prerequisite, precondition; (= Qualifikation) qualification; (= Erfordernis) requirement; (= Annahme) assumption; **unter der ~, dass** ... on condition that ...

voraussichtlich **1** ADJ expected **2** ADV probably; **er wird ~ gewinnen** he is expected to win; **~ wird es keine Schwierigkeiten geben** we don't anticipate any difficulties

vorbauen VI SEP (= Vorkehrungen treffen) to take precautions; **einer Sache** (dat) **~** to provide against sth

Vorbehalt [-bahalt] M **-(e)s, -e** reservation; **unter dem ~, dass** ... with the reservation that ...

vorbehalten ptp **vorbehalten** VT SEP IRREG **sich** (dat) **etw ~** to reserve sth (for oneself); **Recht** to reserve sth; **jdm etw ~** to leave sth (up) to sb; **alle Rechte ~** all rights reserved; **Änderungen (sind) ~** subject to alterations; **Irrtümer ~** errors excepted

vorbehaltlos [-bahaltlo:s] **1** ADJ unconditional **2** ADV without reservations; **lieben** unconditionally

vorbei [fo:ɐ'bai] ADV **(a)** (räumlich) past, by; **~ an** (+dat) past; **~!** (= nicht getroffen) missed!
(b) (zeitlich) **~ sein** to be past; (= vergangen auch, beendet) to be over; (Schmerzen) to be gone; **es ist schon 8 Uhr ~** it's already past or after 8 o'clock; **damit ist es nun ~** that's all over now; **~ die schöne Zeit!** gone are the days!; **aus und ~** over and done with; **~ ist ~** what's past is past; (= reden wir nicht mehr davon) let bygones be bygones

vorbei-: vorbeibringen VT SEP IRREG (inf) to drop by or in; **vorbeidürfen** VI SEP IRREG (inf) to be allowed past; **dürfte ich bitte vorbei?** could I get past or by, please?; **vorbeifahren** SEP IRREG **1** VI AUX SEIN (an jdm/etw sb/sth) to go/drive/sail past; **im Vorbeifahren** in passing; **bei jdm ~** (inf) to drop in on sb **2** VT **jdn an etw** (dat) **~** to drive sb past sth; **ich kann dich ja schnell dort/bei ihnen ~** (inf) I can run you over there/to their

place; **vorbeigehen** VI SEP IRREG AUX SEIN **(a)** (lit, fig) (an jdm/etw sb/sth) to go past or by; **an etw** (dat) **~** (fig: = nicht beachten) to overlook sth; **bei jdm ~** (inf) to drop in on sb; **eine Gelegenheit ~ lassen** to let an opportunity pass by; **das Leben geht an ihm vorbei** life is passing him by; **im Vorbeigehen** (lit, fig) in passing **(b)** (= vergehen) to pass **(c)** (= danebengehen) to miss (an etw (dat) sth);
vorbeikommen VI SEP IRREG AUX SEIN **(a)** (an jdm/etw sb/sth) to pass, to go past; (an einem Hindernis) to get past; **an einer Sache/Aufgabe nicht ~** to be unable to avoid a thing/task; **wir kommen nicht an der Tatsache vorbei, dass** ... there's no escaping the fact that ... **(b)** **bei jdm ~** (inf) to drop in on sb; **vorbeilassen** VT SEP IRREG to let past (an jdm/etw sb/sth); **vorbeischauen** VI SEP (esp dial inf) = vorbeikommen **(b)**

vorbelastet [-bəlastət] ADJ handicapped; **von den Eltern/vom Milieu her ~ sein** to be at a disadvantage because of one's parents/background; **da bin ich ~** (= voreingenommen) I'm biased

vorbereiten ptp **vorbereitet** SEP **1** VT to prepare **2** VR (Mensch) to prepare (oneself) (auf +acc for); (Ereignisse) to be in the offing (inf)

Vorbereitung ['fo:ɛbəraitʊŋ] F **-, -en** preparation; **~en (für** or **zu etw) treffen** to make preparations (for sth)

Vorbereitungs- IN CPDS preparatory; **Vorbereitungszeit** F preparation time

Vor-: vorbestellen ptp **vorbestellt** VT SEP to order in advance; **Vorbestellung** F advance order; (von Platz, Tisch, Zimmer) (advance) booking; **bei ~** when ordering/booking in advance; **vorbestraft** [-bəʃtra:ft] ADJ previously convicted; **wegen Körperverletzung ~ sein** to have a previous conviction for bodily harm

vorbeugen SEP **1** VI to prevent (einer Sache dat sth); **~ ist besser als heilen** (prov) prevention is better than cure (prov) **2** VT **Kopf, Oberkörper** to bend forward **3** VR to bend forward

vorbeugend **1** ADJ preventive **2** ADV as a preventive measure

Vorbeugung F prevention (gegen, von of); **zur ~** (Med) as a prophylactic

Vorbild NT model; (= Beispiel) example; **nach dem ~** +gen based on the model of; **nach amerikanischem ~** following the American example; **sich** (dat) **jdn zum ~ nehmen** to model oneself on sb; (= sich ein Beispiel nehmen an) to take sb as an example

vorbildlich **1** ADJ exemplary **2** ADV exemplarily; **sich ~ benehmen** to be on one's best behaviour (Brit) or behavior (US); **sich ~ verhalten** to act in an exemplary fashion

Vorbildlichkeit F exemplary nature

Vor-: Vorbörse F before-hours market; **Vorbote** M, **Vorbotin** F (fig) harbinger, herald

vorbringen VT SEP IRREG **(a)** (inf: = nach vorn bringen) to take up or forward
(b) (= äußern) to say; **Plan** to propose; **Meinung, Wunsch, Anliegen, Forderung** to state; **Klage, Beschwerde** to lodge; **Entschuldigung, Kritik, Einwand** to make; **Bedenken** to express; **Argument, Beweis** to produce; **Grund** to put forward; **können Sie dagegen etwas ~?** have you anything to say against it?; **was hast du zu deiner Entschuldigung vorzubringen?** what have you to say in your defence (Brit) or defense (US)?

Vor-: Vordach NT canopy; **vordatieren** ptp **vordatiert** VT SEP to postdate; **Ereignis** to predate

Vordenker(in) M(F) mentor

Vorder-: Vorderachse F front axle; **Vorderasien** NT Near East; **Vorderbein** NT foreleg

Vordere(r) ['fɔrdərə] MF DECL AS ADJ person/man/woman etc in front

vordere(r, s) ['fɔrdərə] ADJ front; **die ~ Seite des Hauses** the front of the house; **der Vordere Orient** the Near East; siehe **vorderste(r, s)**

Vorder-: Vordergrund M foreground; **im ~ stehen** (fig) to be to the fore; **sich in den ~ schieben** or **drängen** (fig) to push oneself to the fore(front); **etw in den ~ rücken** or **stellen** (fig) to give priority to sth; **in den ~ rücken/treten** (fig) to come to the fore; **sich in den ~ spielen** (fig) to push oneself forward; **vordergründig** [-gryndɪç] **1** ADJ (fig) (= oberflächlich) superficial **2** ADV **behandeln** superficially; **~ geht es darum, dass sie mehr Geld wollen** it appears at first that they want more money; **Vordermann** M, *pl* **-männer** person in front; (*Auto*) car in front; **sein** ~ the person/car in front of him; **jdn auf ~ bringen** (*fig inf*) to get sb to shape up; (*gesundheitlich*) to get sb fighting fit (*inf*); **etw auf ~ bringen** (*fig inf*) Haushalt, *Auto etc* to get sth shipshape; Kenntnisse, Wissen to brush sth up; Finanzen to get sth straightened out; (= *auf neuesten Stand bringen*) Listen, Garderobe to bring sth up-to-date; **Vorderrad** NT front wheel; **Vorderradantrieb** M front-wheel drive; **Vorderseite** F front; (*von Münze*) head; **Vordersitz** M front seat

vorderste(r, s) ['fɔrdəstə] ADJ SUPERL *von* **vordere(r, s)** front(most); **der/die Vorderste in der Schlange** the first man/woman in the queue (*Brit*) *or* line (*US*)

Vorder-: Vorderteil M *or* NT front; **Vordertür** F front door
Vordiplom NT first diploma

vordrängen VR SEP to push to the front; **sich in einer Schlange** ~ (*Brit*), to push to the front of a line (*US*)

vordringen VI SEP IRREG AUX SEIN to advance; **bis zu jdm/etw ~** to get as far as sb/sth

vordringlich 1 ADJ urgent 2 ADV **Dinge, die ich ~ erledigen muss** things that I must take care of first; **~ zu besprechende Punkte** points that are most urgent

Vordruck M, *pl* **-drucke** form

voreilig 1 ADJ rash; **~e Schlüsse ziehen** to jump to conclusions 2 ADV rashly; **~ urteilen** to be rash in one's judgement

voreinander [fɔrɛlaiˈnandə] ADV (*räumlich*) in front of one another; (= *einander gegenüber*) face to face; **wir haben keine Geheimnisse** ~ we have no secrets from each other

voreingenommen ADJ prejudiced, biased

Voreingenommenheit F (a) NO PL prejudice, bias (b) USU PL (= *Vorurteil*) prejudice *no pl*

voreingestellt ADJ (*esp Comput*) preset
Voreinstellung F (*esp Comput*) presetting

vorenthalten *ptp* **vorenthalten** VT SEP IRREG **jdm etw ~** to withhold sth from sb

vorerst ['foːrʔeːɐst, foːrˈʔeːɐst] ADV for the time being

Vorfahr ['foːrfaːɐ] M **-en, -en** ancestor

vorfahren SEP IRREG 1 VI AUX SEIN (a) (= *nach vorn fahren*) to drive move forward (b) (= *ankommen*) to drive up; **den Wagen ~ lassen** to have the car brought (up) (c) (= *früher fahren*) to go on ahead; **wir fahren schon mal vor** we'll go on ahead (d) (= *an der Spitze fahren*) to drive in front 2 VT (a) (= *weiter nach vorn fahren*) to move up (b) (= *vor den Eingang fahren*) to drive up

Vorfahrt F, NO PL right of way; **~ haben** to have (the) right of way; **die ~ beachten/nicht beachten** to observe/ignore the right of way; **„~ (be)achten** *or* **gewähren"** "give way" (*Brit*), "yield" (*US*); **jdm die ~ nehmen** to ignore sb's right of way

Vorfahrts-: Vorfahrtsschild NT, *pl* **-schilder** give way (*Brit*) *or* yield (*US*) sign; **Vorfahrtsstraße** F major road

Vorfall M (a) incident (b) (*Med*) prolapse

vorfallen VI SEP IRREG AUX SEIN (a) (= *sich ereignen*) to happen (b) (*inf*: = *nach vorn fallen*) to fall forward

Vor-: vorfeiern VTI SEP to celebrate early; **Vorfeld** NT (*Aviat*) apron; (*fig*) run-up (+*gen* to); **im ~ der Wahlen** in the run-up to the elections; **im ~ der Verhandlungen** in the preliminary stages of the negotiations; **etw im ~ klären** to clear sth up beforehand; **Vorfilm** M supporting film, short; **Vorfreude** F anticipation

vorfühlen VI SEP (*fig*) to put out (a few) feelers; **bei jdm ~** to sound or feel (*US*) sb out

vorführen VT SEP (a) Angeklagten etc to bring forward; **den Gefangenen dem Haftrichter ~** to bring the prisoner up before the magistrate (b) (= *zeigen*) to present; Kunststücke to perform (*dat* to); Film to show; Mode to model; Übung, Modell, Gerät to demonstrate (*dat* to)

Vorführung F presentation; (*von Angeklagten, Zeugen etc*) production *no pl*; (*von Filmen*) showing; (*von Mode*) modelling (*esp Brit*), modeling (*US*); (*von Geräten, Modellen, Übungen*) demonstration; (*von Theaterstück, Kunststücken*) performance

Vorgang M, *pl* **-gänge** (a) (= *Ereignis*) event; (= *Ablauf, Hergang*) series of events; **jdm den genauen ~ eines Unfalls schildern** to tell sb exactly what happened in an accident (b) (*Biol, Chem, Tech, Comput*) process

Vorgänger [-gɛŋɐ] M **-s, -, Vorgängerin** [-ərɪn] F **-, -nen** predecessor

vorgeben VT SEP IRREG (a) (= *vortäuschen*) to pretend; (= *fälschlich beteuern*) to profess; **sie gab Zeitmangel vor, um …** she pretended to be pressed for time in order to … (b) (*Sport*) to give (a start of) (c) (*inf*: = *nach vorn geben*) to pass forward

vorgefasst ADJ Meinung preconceived

vorgehen VI SEP IRREG AUX SEIN (a) (= *handeln*) to act; **gerichtlich/energisch gegen jdn ~** to take legal action/assertive action against sb; **die Polizei ging gegen die Demonstranten vor** the police took action against the demonstrators (b) (= *geschehen, vor sich gehen*) to go on (c) (*Uhr*) (= *spätere Zeit anzeigen*) to be fast; (= *zu schnell gehen*) to gain (d) (= *nach vorn gehen*) to go forward; (= *als Erster gehen*) to go first; (= *früher gehen*) to go on ahead (e) (= *den Vorrang haben*) to come first

Vorgehen NT action

Vor-: Vorgeschichte F (a) (*eines Falles*) past history (b) (= *Urgeschichte*) prehistoric times *pl*; **aus der ~** from prehistoric times; **vorgeschichtlich** ADJ prehistoric; **Vorgeschmack** M (*fig*) foretaste

Vorgesetzte(r) ['foːrɡəzɛtstə] MF DECL AS ADJ superior

vorgestern ADV the day before yesterday; **von ~** (*fig*) antiquated; Methoden, Ansichten auch, Kleidung old-fashioned; **~ Abend/Morgen** the evening/morning before last; **~ Mittag** midday the day before yesterday

vorgestrig ADJ ATTR of the day before yesterday

vorgreifen VI SEP IRREG to anticipate; (= *verfrüht handeln*) to act prematurely; **jdm ~** to forestall sb; **einer Sache** (*dat*) **~** to anticipate sth

vorhaben VT SEP IRREG to intend; (= *geplant haben*) to have planned; **was haben Sie heute vor?** what are your plans for today?; **hast du heute Abend schon etwas vor?** have you already got something planned this evening?; **wenn du nichts Besseres vorhast …** if you've nothing better to do …; **etw mit jdm/etw ~** to intend doing sth with sb/sth; (= *etw geplant haben*) to have sth planned for sb/sth; **die ehrgeizigen Eltern haben viel mit dem Kind vor** the ambitious parents have great plans for the child; **was hast du jetzt wieder vor?** what are you up to now?

vorhalten SEP IRREG 1 VT (a) = **vorwerfen** (a) (b) (*als Beispiel*) **jdm jdn/etw ~** to hold sb/sth up to sb (c) (= *vor den Körper halten*) to hold up; (*beim Niesen etc*) Hand, Taschentuch to put in front of one's mouth 2 VI (= *anhalten*) to last

Vorhaltung F USU PL reproach; **jdm/sich (wegen etw) ~en machen** to reproach sb/oneself (with *or* for sth)

Vorhand F (*Sport*) forehand

vorhanden [foːrˈhandn] ADJ (= *verfügbar*) available; (= *existierend*) in existence; **eine Dusche ist hier leider nicht ~** I'm afraid there isn't a shower here; **davon ist genügend/nichts mehr ~** there's plenty/no more of that

Vorhang M curtain

Vorhängeschloss ['foːrhɛŋə-] NT padlock

Vorhaut F foreskin

vorher [foːɐˈheːɐ, ˈfoːɐ-] ADV before; **konntest du das nicht ~ sagen?** couldn't you have said that earlier?

Vorher-: vorherbestimmen *ptp* **vorherbestimmt** VT SEP to determine in advance; Schicksal, Zukunft to predetermine; (*Gott*) to preordain; **es war ihm vorherbestimmt …** he was predestined …; **vorhergehend** ADJ Tag, Ereignisse preceding

vorherig [foːɐˈheːrɪç, ˈfoːɐ-] ADJ ATTR previous; (= *ehemalig*) former; (= *vorhergehend*) Anmeldung, Genehmigung, Vereinbarung prior

vorherrschen VI SEP to predominate

vorherrschend ADJ predominant; (= *weitverbreitet*) prevalent

Vorher-: Vorhersage F forecast; **vorhersagen** VT SEP = **voraussagen**; **vorhersehen** VT SEP IRREG to foresee

vorhin [foːɐˈhɪn, ˈfoːɐ-] ADV just now

Vorhinein ['foːɐhɪnain] ADV **im ~** in advance

vorig [ˈfoːrɪç] ADJ ATTR (= *früher*) Besitzer, Wohnsitz previous; (= *vergangen*) Jahr, Woche etc last

Vor-: **Vorjahr** NT previous year; **vorjammern** VTI SEP jdm (etwas) ~ to moan to sb (von about); **Vorkalkulation** F cost estimation; **Vorkämpfer(in)** M(F) (für of) pioneer; **Vorkasse** F advance payment; **per ~ zahlen** to pay in advance; „**Zahlung nur gegen ~**" "advance payment only"; **Vorkaufsrecht** NT option of purchase

Vorkehrung ['fo:ɐke:rʊŋ] F **-, -en** precaution; **~en treffen** to take precautions

Vorkenntnis F previous knowledge no pl; (= Erfahrung) previous experience no pl; **sprachliche ~se** previous knowledge of languages/the language

vorkommen VI SEP IRREG AUX SEIN (a) AUCH VI IMPERS (= sich ereignen) to happen; **so etwas ist mir noch nie vorgekommen** such a thing has never happened to me before; **dass mir das nicht noch einmal vorkommt!** don't let it happen again!; **das kann schon mal ~** it can happen; (= das ist nicht ungewöhnlich) that happens; **so was soll ~!** that's life! (b) (= vorhanden sein, auftreten) to occur; (Pflanzen, Tiere) to be found; **in dem Aufsatz dürfen keine Fehler ~** there mustn't be any mistakes in the essay (c) (= erscheinen) to seem; **das kommt mir bekannt/merkwürdig vor** that seems familiar/strange to me; **sich** (dat) **überflüssig/dumm ~** to feel superfluous/silly; **sich** (dat) **klug ~** to think one is clever; **das kommt dir nur so vor** it just seems that way to you; **wie kommst du mir denn vor?** (inf) who do you think you are? (d) (= nach vorn kommen) to come forward

Vorkommnis ['fo:ɐkɔmnɪs] NT **-ses, -se** incident

Vorkriegs- IN CPDS prewar; **Vorkriegszeit** F prewar period

Vorladung F summons

Vorlage F (a) NO PL (= das Vorlegen) presentation; (von Beweismaterial) submission; **gegen ~ einer Sache** (gen) (up)on production or presentation of sth; **zahlbar bei ~** payable on demand (b) (= Muster) (zum Stricken, Nähen) pattern; (Liter) model; **etw von einer ~ abzeichnen/nach einer ~ machen** to copy sth (c) (= Entwurf) draft; (Parl: = Gesetzesvorlage) bill (d) (Comm: = geliehene Summe) advance; **mit 500 Euro in ~ treten** to pay 500 euros in advance

vorlassen VT SEP IRREG (a) (inf) jdn ~ (= nach vorn gehen lassen) to let sb go in front; (= vorbeigehen lassen) to let sb pass; **ein Auto ~** (= einbiegen lassen) to let a car in; (= überholen lassen) to let a car pass (b) (= Empfang gewähren) to allow in

vorläufig **1** ADJ temporary; Urteil preliminary; Verfügung des Gerichts interim **2** ADV (= einstweilig) temporarily; (= fürs erste) for the time being

vorlaut ADJ cheeky (Brit), impertinent

Vorlegebesteck NT serving cutlery; (= Tranchierbesteck) carvers pl

vorlegen SEP VT (a) (= präsentieren) to present; Pass, Schulzeugnis to show; Beweismaterial to submit; Bewerbungsunterlagen to produce; Schularbeit to hand in; (Pol) Entwurf to introduce; **ein schnelles Tempo ~** to go at a fast pace; **ein schnelleres Tempo ~** to speed up (b) Riegel to put across; Schloss, Kette to put on; (inf: = davorlegen) to put in front (c) (= vorstrecken) Geld to advance

Vorleger ['fo:ɐle:gɐ] M **-s, -** mat

vorlehnen VR SEP to lean forward

Vorleistung F (Econ) (= Vorausbezahlung) advance (payment); (= finanzielle Aufwendung) outlay no pl (an +dat on); (= vorausgehende Arbeit) preliminary work

vorlesen VTI SEP IRREG to read aloud; **jdm (etw) ~** to read (sth) to sb

Vorlesung F (Univ) lecture; (= Vorlesungsreihe) course (of lectures); **über etw** (acc) **~en halten** to give (a course of) lectures on sth; **~en hören** to go to lectures

vorletzte(r, s) ['fo:ɐlɛtstə] ADJ next to last, penultimate; **im ~n Jahr** the year before last

Vorliebe F preference; **etw mit ~ tun** to particularly like doing sth

vorlieb nehmen ['fo:ɐli:p-] VI IRREG **mit jdm/etw ~** to make do with sb/sth

vorliegen SEP IRREG **1** VI (= zur Verfügung stehen: Beweise, Katalog, Erkenntnisse) to be available; (Urteil) to be known; (= eingereicht, vorgelegt sein: Unterlagen, wissenschaftliche Arbeit) to be in; (Pol) (Gesetzesvorlage) to be before the house;

(Haushalt) to be published; (= vorhanden sein) (Irrtum, Schuld etc) to be; (Symptome) to be present; (Gründe, Voraussetzungen) to exist; **jdm ~** (Unterlagen, Akten etc) to be with sb; **die Ergebnisse liegen der Kommission vor** the commission has the results; **das Beweismaterial liegt dem Gericht vor** the evidence is before the court; **etw liegt gegen jdn vor** sth is against sb; (gegen Angeklagten) sb is charged with sth **2** VI IMPERS to be; **es liegen fünf Bewerbungen vor** there are five applications; **es muss ein Irrtum ~** there must be some mistake

vorm. ABBR von vormittags

vormachen VT SEP (a) (jdm) etw ~ (= zeigen) to show (sb) how to do sth; (fig: = als Beispiel dienen) to show sb sth (b) jdm etwas ~ (fig: = täuschen) to fool sb; **ich lasse mir so leicht nichts ~** you/he etc can't fool me so easily; **er lässt sich** (dat) **von niemandem etwas ~** he's nobody's fool; **sich** (dat) **(selbst) etwas ~** to fool oneself

Vormacht(stellung) F supremacy (gegenüber over); **eine Vormachtstellung haben** to have supremacy

Vormarsch M (Mil) advance; **im ~ sein** to be on the advance; (fig) to be gaining ground

vormerken VT SEP to note down; Plätze to reserve; **ich werde Sie für Mittwoch ~** I'll put you down for Wednesday; **sich für einen Kursus ~ lassen** to put one's name down for a course

Vormittag M morning; **am ~** in the morning; **heute/gestern/morgen ~** this/yesterday/tomorrow morning

vormittags ADV in the morning; (= jeden Morgen) in the morning(s)

Vormund M **-(e)s, -e** or **Vormünder** guardian

vorn [fɔrn] ADV (a) in front; **von ~** from the front; **nach ~** (= ganz nach ~) to the front; (= weiter nach ~) forwards; **~ im Buch/in der Schlange** at the front of the book/queue (Brit) or line (US); **sich ~ anstellen** to join the front of the queue (Brit) or line (US); **im Bild** in the front of the picture; **nach ~ laufen** to run to the front; **das Auto da ~** the car in front there; **sie waren ziemlich weit ~** they were quite far ahead (b) (= am Anfang) **von ~** from the beginning; **wie schon ~ erklärt** as explained above; **von ~ anfangen** to begin at the beginning; (= von neuem) to start again from scratch; (neues Leben) to start afresh; **etw ~ anfügen** to add sth at the beginning (c) (= am vorderen Ende) at the front; (Naut) fore; **von ~** from the front; **jdn von ~ sehen** to see sb's face; **~ im Auto/Bus** in the front of the car/bus; **der Blinker ~** the front indicator (esp Brit) or blinker (US); **nach ~** to the front; fallen, ziehen forwards; **ein nach ~ gelegenes Zimmer** a room facing the front (d) **ich kann doch nicht ~ und hinten gleichzeitig sein** I can't be everywhere at once; **sich von ~(e) bis or und hinten bedienen lassen** to be waited on hand and foot; **er betrügt sie von ~ bis hinten** he deceives her right, left and centre (Brit) or center (US)

Vorname M first name

vorne ['fɔrnə] ADV = **vorn**

vornehm ['fo:ɐne:m] **1** ADJ (a) (kultiviert, von hohem Rang) distinguished; Manieren, Art, Benehmen genteel; **die ~e Gesellschaft** high society; **ihr seid mir eine ~e Gesellschaft** (iro) you're a fine lot! (inf); **so was sagt/tut man nicht in ~en Kreisen** one doesn't say/do that in polite society (b) (= elegant, luxuriös) Wohngegend, Haus posh (inf); Geschäft exclusive; Kleid, Äußeres elegant; Auto smart; Geschmack refined **2** ADV wohnen grandly; schweigen, sich zurückhalten grandly; **~ tun** (pej inf) to act posh (inf); **~ geht die Welt zugrunde** (iro) aren't we going up in the world! (iro)

vornehmen VT SEP IRREG (a) (= ausführen) to carry out; Umfrage, Änderungen to do; Messungen to take; Einsparungen to make; (sich dat) **etw ~** (= in Angriff nehmen) to get to work on sth; (= planen, vorhaben) to intend to do sth; (= Vorsatz fassen) to have resolved to do sth; **ich habe mir vorgenommen, das nächste Woche zu tun** I intend to do that next week; **ich habe mir zu viel vorgenommen** I've taken on too much; **sich** (dat) **jdn ~** (inf) to have a word with sb (b) (= früher drannehmen) to attend to first

Vornehmheit F **-**, NO PL (a) (= hoher Rang: von Familie etc) high rank; (= Kultiviertheit) (von Mensch) distinguished ways pl; (von Art, Benehmen) refinement (b) (= Eleganz) (von

Wohngegend, Haus) poshness (*inf*); (*von Kleid, Äußerem*) elegance

vornherein ['fɔrnhɛrain, fɔrnhe'rain] ADV **von** ~ from the start

vorn-: vornüber [fɔrn'lyːbɐ] ADV forwards; **vornüberfallen** VI SEP to fall (over) forwards; **vornweg** ['fɔrnvɛk, fɔrn'vɛk] ADV = **vorneweg**

Vorort ['foːʔɔrt] M, *pl* -**orte** (= *Vorstadt*) suburb

Vor-Ort- [foːʔ'ɔrt] IN CPDS on-site

Vorort- ['foːʔɔrt-]: **Vorortverkehr** M suburban traffic; (*von öffentlichen Verkehrsmitteln*) suburban service; **Vorortzug** M suburban train; (*im Berufsverkehr*) commuter train

Vor-: Vorplatz M forecourt; **Vorprogramm** NT supporting bill, warm-up act (*US*); **im** ~ on the supporting bill (*Brit*), as the warm-up act (*US*); **vorprogrammieren** *ptp* **vorprogrammiert** VT SEP to preprogram; **vorprogrammiert** [-prɔgramiːet] ADJ *Erfolg, Antwort* automatic; *Verhaltensweise* preprogrammed; *Weg* predetermined; **die nächste Krise ist** ~ the seeds of the next crisis have been sown

Vorrang M, NO PL **(a)** ~ **haben** to have priority; **den** ~ **vor etw** (*dat*) **haben** to take precedence over sth; **jdm/einer Sache den** ~ **geben** *or* **einräumen** to give sb/a matter priority; **mit** ~ (= *vorrangig*) as a matter of priority **(b)** (*Aus:* = *Vorfahrt*) right of way

vorrangig ['foːʔraŋɪç] **1** ADJ priority *attr*; ~ **sein** to have (top) priority **2** ADV as a matter of priority; **eine Angelegenheit** ~ **erledigen/behandeln** to give a matter priority treatment

Vorrat ['foːʔraːt] M -**(e)s**, **Vorräte** [-rɛːtə] (*an* +*dat* of) stock; (*esp Comm*) stocks *pl*; (= *Geldvorrat*) reserves *pl*; (*an Atomwaffen*) stockpile; **Vorräte anlegen** *or* **ansammeln** to build up reserves; **solange der** ~ **reicht** (*Comm*) while stocks last; **etw auf** ~ **haben** to have sth in reserve; (*Comm*) to have sth in stock

vorrätig ['foːʔrɛːtɪç] ADJ in stock; (= *verfügbar*) available; **etw nicht mehr** ~ **haben** to be out of sth

Vorratsvermögen NT inventories *pl*

vorrechnen VT SEP **jdm etw** ~ to calculate sth for sb; **er rechnet mir dauernd vor, wie viel alles kostet** he's always pointing out to me how much everything costs; **jdm seine Fehler** ~ (*fig*) to enumerate sb's mistakes

Vorrecht NT prerogative; (= *Vergünstigung*) privilege

Vorrichtung F device

vorrücken SEP **1** VT to move forward; *Schachfigur* to advance **2** VI AUX SEIN to move forward; (*Mil*) to advance; (*Sport, im Beruf etc*) to move up; (*Uhrzeiger*) to move on; **mit dem Stuhl** ~ to move one's chair forward; **in vorgerücktem Alter** in later life; **zu vorgerückter Stunde** at a late hour

Vorruhestand M early retirement

Vorruheständler(in) M(F) person taking early retirement

Vorruhestandsregelung F early retirement scheme

vorsagen SEP **1** VT **jdm etw** ~ *Gedicht* to recite sth to sb; *Antwort, Lösung* to tell sb sth **2** VI (*Sch*) **jdm** ~ to tell sb the answer

Vorsaison F low season

Vorsatz M **(a)** (firm) intention; **mit** ~ (*Jur*) with intent; **den** ~ **haben, etw zu tun** to (firmly) intend to do sth **(b)** (*von Buch*) endpaper

vorsätzlich [-zɛtslɪç] **1** ADJ deliberate; (*Jur*) *Mord, Brandstiftung etc* wilful **2** ADV deliberately; **jdn** ~ **töten** to kill sb intentionally

Vorschau F preview; (*für Film*) trailer; (= *Wettervorschau*) forecast

Vorschein M **zum** ~ **bringen** (*lit:* = *zeigen*) to produce; *Fleck* to show up; (*fig:* = *deutlich machen*) to bring to light; **zum** ~ **kommen** (*lit:* = *sichtbar werden*) to appear; (*fig:* = *entdeckt werden*) to come to light

vorschieben SEP IRREG VT **(a)** (= *davorschieben*) to push in front; *Riegel* to put across; (= *nach vorn schieben*) to push forward **(b)** (*fig:* = *vorschützen*) to put forward as an excuse; **vorgeschobene Gründe** pretexts *pl*, excuses *pl* **(c)** **jdn** ~ to put sb forward as a front man

vorschießen SEP IRREG **1** VT **jdm Geld** ~ to advance sb money **2** VI AUX SEIN to shoot forward

Vorschlag M **(a)** (= *Rat*) advice; (= *Angebot*) proposition; (*Pol: von Kandidaten*) proposal; **auf** ~ **von** *or* +*gen* at *or* on the suggestion of; **das ist ein** ~! that's an idea! **(b)** (*Sw:* = *Gewinn*) profit

vorschlagen VT SEP IRREG (= *als Vorschlag unterbreiten*) to suggest; **jdn für ein Amt** ~ to propose sb for a position; **jdm** ~, **dass er etw tut** to suggest that sb do(es) sth

vorschreiben VT SEP IRREG (= *befehlen*) to stipulate; (*Med*) *Dosis* to prescribe; **jdm** ~, **wie/was** ... to dictate to sb how/what ...; **ich lasse mir nichts** ~ I won't be dictated to; **vorgeschriebene Lektüre** (*Sch, Univ*) prescribed texts; **gesetzlich vorgeschrieben** stipulated by law

Vorschrift F (= *gesetzliche etc Bestimmung*) regulation; (= *Anweisung*) instruction; **nach** ~ **des Arztes** according to doctor's orders; **jdm** ~**en machen** to give sb orders; **ich lasse mir (von dir) keine** ~**en machen lassen** I won't take orders (from you); **sich an die** ~**en halten** to observe the regulations; **Arbeit nach** ~ work to rule; **das ist** ~ that's the regulation

vorschrifts-: vorschriftsgemäß, vorschriftsmäßig **1** ADJ regulation *attr*; *Signal, Parken, Verhalten* correct, proper *attr*; (*Med*) *Dosis* prescribed **2** ADV (= *laut Anordnung*) according to (the) regulations; (*Med*) as directed; ~ **gekleidet sein** to be in regulation dress; **vorschriftswidrig** ADJ, ADV contrary to (the) regulations; (*Med*) *Dosis* contrary to the prescription

Vorschub M **jdm** ~ **leisten** to encourage sb; **einer Sache** (*dat*) ~ **leisten** to encourage sth

Vorschuss M advance

Vorschuss-: Vorschusslorbeeren PL premature praise *sing*; **Vorschusszinsen** PL (*Fin*) penalty interest on early settlement

vorschützen VT SEP to plead as an excuse; *Unwissenheit* to plead; **er schützte vor, dass** ... he pretended that ...

vorschwärmen VTI SEP **jdm von jdm/etw** ~ to go into raptures over sb/sth

vorschweben VI SEP **jdm schwebt etw vor** sb has sth in mind

vorsehen SEP IRREG **1** VT (= *planen*) to plan; (= *einplanen*) *Kosten, Anschaffungen* to allow for; *Zeit* to allow; (*im Gesetz, Vertrag*) to provide for; **etw für etw** ~ (= *bestimmen*) to intend sth for sth; *Geld* to earmark sth for sth; **jdn für etw** ~ (= *beabsichtigen*) to have sb in mind for sth; (= *bestimmen*) to designate sb for sth **2** VR (= *sich in Acht nehmen*) to watch out; **sich vor jdm/etw** ~ to beware of sb/sth **3** VI (= *sichtbar sein*) to appear; **hinter/unter etw** (*dat*) ~ to peep out from behind/under sth

Vorsehung ['foːʔezeːʊŋ] F -, NO PL **die (göttliche)** ~ (divine) Providence

vorsetzen SEP **1** VT **(a)** (*nach vorn*) to move forward; *Fuß* to put forward; *Schüler* to move (up) to the front **(b) jdm etw** ~ (= *geben*) to give sb sth; (= *anbieten*) to offer sb sth **2** VR to sit in (the) front; **sich in die erste Reihe** ~ to move to the front row

Vorsicht ['foːzɪçt] F -, NO PL care; (*bei Gefahr*) caution; (= *Überlegtheit*) circumspection; (= *Behutsamkeit*) guardedness; ~ **walten lassen** *or* **üben** to be careful; (*bei Gefahr*) to exercise caution; (= *überlegt handeln*) to be circumspect; (= *behutsam vorgehen*) to be wary; **zur** ~ **raten/ mahnen** to advise caution; ~! watch out!; „~ **bei Einfahrt des Zuges**" "stand back when the train approaches the platform"; „~ **Gift**" "Poison"; „~ **feuergefährlich**" "danger - inflammable"; „~ **zerbrechlich/Glas**" "fragile/glass - with care"; „~ **Stufe**" "mind the step"; **mit** ~ carefully; (*bei Gefahr*) cautiously; (= *überlegt*) prudently; (= *behutsam*) guardedly; **etw zur** ~ **tun** to do sth to be on the safe side; **was er sagt/ dieser Artikel ist mit** ~ **zu genießen** (*hum inf*) you have to take what he says/this article with a pinch of salt (*inf*); ~ **ist besser als Nachsicht** (*Prov*) better safe than sorry; ~ **ist die Mutter der Porzellankiste** (*inf*) better safe than sorry

vorsichtig ['foːzɪçtɪç] **1** ADJ careful; (= *besonnen*) cautious; (= *überlegt*) prudent; (= *misstrauisch*) wary; *Äußerung* guarded; *Schätzung* cautious **2** ADV **(a)** (*umsichtig*) carefully **(b)** (*zurückhaltend*) **sich** ~ **äußern** to be very careful what one says; **ich schätze die Kosten** ~ **auf 20.000 Euro** to give you a conservative estimate of the costs I would say 20,000 euros

Vorsichts-: vorsichtshalber ADV as a precaution; **Vorsichtsmaßnahme** F precaution

Vor-: Vorsilbe F prefix; **vorsintflutlich** [-zɪntfluːtlɪç] ADJ (*inf*) antiquated

Vorsitz M chairmanship; (= *Amt eines Präsidenten*) presidency; **unter dem** ~ **von** under the chairmanship of; **(bei etw) den** ~ **haben** *or* **innehaben** *or* **führen** to be chairman (of sth); **bei**

einer Sitzung den ~ haben or führen to chair a meeting; den ~ übernehmen to take the chair

Vorsitzende(r) [ˈfoːɛzɪtsnda] MF DECL AS ADJ chairperson; (*Mann auch*) chairman; (*Frau auch*) chairman, chairwoman; (*von Firma, Verein*) president; (*von Partei, Gewerkschaft etc*) leader; **der ~ Mao** Chairman Mao

Vorsorge F, NO PL (= *Vorsichtsmaßnahme*) precaution; (= *vorherplanende Fürsorge*) provision(s *pl*) *no def art*; **zur** ~ as a precaution; **~ tragen** to make provision; **~ treffen** to take precautions; (*fürs Alter*) to make provision

vorsorgen VI SEP to make provision (*dass* so that); **für etw** ~ to provide for sth

Vorsorgeuntersuchung F (*Med*) medical checkup

vorsorglich [-zɔrklɪç] **1** ADJ precautionary; *Mensch* cautious **2** ADV as a precaution

Vorspeise F hors d'œuvre, starter (*Brit*)

Vorspiegelung F pretence (*Brit*), pretense (*US*); **unter ~ von etw** under the pretence (*Brit*) or pretense (*US*) of sth; **das ist nur (eine) ~ falscher Tatsachen** (*hum*) it's all sham

Vorspiel NT (= *Einleitung*) prelude; (= *Ouvertüre*) overture; (*Theat*) prologue (*Brit*), prolog (*US*); (*Sport*) preliminary match; (*bei Geschlechtsverkehr*) foreplay

vorspielen SEP **1** VT **jdm etw** ~ (*Mus*) to play sth to sb; (*Theat*) to act sth to sb; (*fig*) to act out a sham of sth in front of sb; **jdm eine Komödie** ~ (*fig*) to act out a farce in front of sb; **jdm ~, dass ...** to pretend to sb that ...; **spiel mir doch nichts vor** don't try and pretend to me **2** VI (*vor Zuhörern*) to play; (*Mus, Theat*) (*zur Prüfung*) to do one's practical (exam); (= *Vorgabe*) start; **jdm 2 Meter/10 Minuten ~ geben** to give sb a 2-metre (*Brit*) or 2-meter (*US*)/a 10-minute start; **einen ~ vor jdm haben** to be ahead of sb

Vorstand M **(a)** (= *leitendes Gremium*) board; (*von Verein*) committee; (*von Partei*) executive **(b)** (= *Leiter*) chairman **(c)** (*Aus*) = **Vorsteher**

Vorstands-: **Vorstandsmitglied** NT member of the board; (*von Verein*) committee member; (*von Partei*) member of the executive; **Vorstandsvorsitzende(r)** MF DECL AS ADJ chairperson of the board of directors

vorstehen VI SEP IRREG AUX HABEN or SEIN **(a)** (= *hervorragen*) to jut out; (*Zähne*) to protrude; (*Backenknochen, Kinn, Nase*) to be prominent **(b) einer Sache** ~ *dem Haushalt* to preside over sth; *einer Firma, einer Partei, einem Gremium* to be the chairperson of sth; *der Regierung* to be the head of sth; *einer Schule* to be the head(master/mistress) or principal (*US*) of sth; *einem Geschäft* to manage sth; *einer Abteilung, einer Behörde* to be in charge of sth

Vorsteherdrüse F prostate (gland)

vorstellbar ADJ conceivable; **das ist nicht ~** that is inconceivable

vorstellen SEP **1** VT **(a)** (*nach vorn*) to move forward; *Bein* to put out; *Uhr* to put forward (*um* by) **(b)** (= *darstellen*) to represent; (= *bedeuten*) to mean; **was soll das ~?** (*inf*) what is that supposed to be?; **etwas ~** (*fig*) (= *gut aussehen*) to look good; (= *Ansehen haben*) to count for something **(c)** (= *bekannt machen, vorführen*) to present (*jdm* to sb); **jdm etw ~** to show sb sth; **jdn jdm ~** to introduce sb to sb **(d) sich** (*dat*) **etw ~** to imagine; **stell dir mal vor** just imagine; **das kann ich mir gut ~** I can imagine that (well); **das muss man sich** (*dat*) **mal** (**bildlich** or **plastisch**) **~** just imagine it!; **sich** (*dat*) **etw unter etw** (*dat*) **~** *Begriff, Wort* to understand sth by sth; **darunter kann ich mir nichts ~** it doesn't mean anything to me; **das Kleid ist genau, was ich mir vorgestellt hatte** the dress is just what I had in mind; **was haben Sie sich** (**als Gehalt**) **vorgestellt?** what (salary) did you have in mind?; **ich kann sie mir gut als Lehrerin ~** I can just imagine her as a teacher; **stell dir das nicht so einfach vor** don't think it's so easy **2** VR **(a)** (= *sich nach vorn stellen*) to move forward; (*in Schlange*) to stand at the front **(b)** (= *sich bekannt machen*) to introduce oneself (*jdm* to sb); (*bei Bewerbung*) to come/go for an interview

vorstellig ADJ **bei jdm ~ werden** to go to sb; (*wegen Beschwerde*) to complain to sb

Vorstellung F **(a)** (= *Gedanke*) idea; (*bildlich*) picture; (= *Einbildung*) illusion; (= *Vorstellungskraft*) imagination; **in meiner ~ sah das größer aus** I imagined it bigger; **du hast falsche ~en** you are wrong (in your ideas); **es übertrifft alle ~en** it's incredible; **das entspricht ganz meiner ~** that is just how I imagined it; **sich** (*dat*) **eine ~ von etw machen** to form an idea or (*Bild*) picture of sth; **du machst dir keine ~, wie schwierig das ist** you have no idea how difficult that is **(b)** (*Theat etc*) performance **(c)** (= *das Bekanntmachen*) (*zwischen Leuten*) introduction; (*bei Bewerbung, Antrittsbesuch*) interview (*bei* with)

Vorstellungs-: **Vorstellungsgespräch** NT (*job*) interview; **Vorstellungskraft** F imagination; **Vorstellungsvermögen** NT powers *pl* of imagination

Vorsteuer F (= *Mehrwertsteuer*) input tax

Vorsteuerabzug M input tax deduction

Vorstopper [ˈfoːɛʃtɔpɐ] M -s, -, **Vorstopperin** [-ərɪn] F -, -NEN (*Ftbl*) centre half (*Brit*), center half (*US*)

Vorstoß M (= *Vordringen*) venture; (*Mil*) advance; (*fig*: = *Versuch*) attempt

Vorstrafe F previous conviction

Vorstrafenregister NT criminal record; (= *Kartei*) police records *pl*

vorstrecken VT SEP to stretch forward; *Arme, Hand* to stretch out; *Bauch* to stick out; *Krallen* to put out; *Geld* to advance (*jdm* sb)

Vorstufe F preliminary stage; (*von Entwicklung*) early stage

Vortag M day before, eve; **am ~ der Konferenz** (on) the day before the conference

vortäuschen VT SEP *Krankheit, Armut* to feign; *Schlag, Straftat, Orgasmus* to fake; **sie hat mir eine glückliche Ehe vorgetäuscht** she pretended to me that her marriage was happy

Vortäuschung F pretence (*Brit*), pretense (*US*); **die ~ einer Krankheit** feigning an illness; **~ von Tatsachen** (*Jur*) misrepresentation of the facts; **unter ~ falscher Tatsachen** under false pretences (*Brit*) or pretenses (*US*)

Vorteil [ˈfoːɛtail] M **-s, -e** advantage (*auch Tennis*); **die Vor- und Nachteile** the pros and cons; **auf den eigenen ~ bedacht sein** to have an eye to one's own interests; **jdm gegenüber im ~ sein** to have an advantage over sb; **sich zu seinem ~ ändern** to change for the better; **von ~ sein** to be advantageous; **das kann für dich nur von ~ sein** it can only be to your advantage; **ich habe dabei an deinen ~ gedacht** I was thinking of your interests; **im ~ sein** to have the advantage (*jdm gegenüber* over sb); **"~ Agassi"** (*Tennis*) "advantage Agassi"

vorteilhaft **1** ADJ advantageous; *Kleid, Frisur* flattering; *Geschäft* lucrative; **ein ~er Kauf** a good buy **2** ADV **~ aussehen** to look one's best; **der helle Teppich wirkt ~** the light carpet looks good; **sie war nicht sehr ~ geschminkt** her make-up wasn't very flattering; **du solltest dich ~er kleiden** you should wear more flattering clothes

Vortrag [ˈfoːɛtraːk] M **-(e)s, Vorträge** [-trɛːɡə] **(a)** (= *Vorlesung*) lecture; (= *Bericht, Beschreibung*) talk; **einen ~ halten** to give a lecture/talk; **halt keine Vorträge** (*inf*) don't give a whole lecture **(b)** (= *Art des Vortragens*) performance **(c)** (*Fin*) balance carried forward

vortragen VT SEP IRREG **(a)** (*lit*) to carry forward **(b)** (= *berichten*) to report; *Fall, Angelegenheit, Forderungen* to present; *Meinung, Bedenken, Wunsch* to express **(c)** (= *vorsprechen*) *Gedicht* to recite; *Rede* to give; (*Mus*) to perform; *Lied* to sing **(d)** (*Fin*) to carry forward

vortrefflich [foːɛˈtrɛflɪç] **1** ADJ excellent **2** ADV excellently; **~ schmecken** to taste excellent

vortreten VI SEP IRREG AUX SEIN **(a)** (*lit*) to step forward **(b)** (= *hervorragen*) to project; (*Augen*) to protrude; **~de Backenknochen** prominent cheekbones

Vortritt M, NO PL precedence; (*Sw*: = *Vorfahrt*) right of way; **in etw** (*dat*) **den ~ haben** (*fig*) to have precedence in sth (*vor +dat* over); **jdm den ~ lassen** (*lit*) to let sb go first; (*fig auch*) to let sb go ahead

vorüber [foˈryːbɐ] ADV **~ sein** (*räumlich*) (*Jugend*) to be past; (*zeitlich auch*) (*Gewitter, Winter, Kummer*) to be over; (*Schmerz*) to have gone

vorüber- PREF *siehe auch* **vorbei-**: **vorübergehen** VI SEP IRREG AUX SEIN **(a)** (*räumlich*) (*an etw* (*dat*) sth) to go past; **im Vorübergehen** in passing; **an jdm/etw ~** (*fig*: = *ignorieren*) to ignore sb/sth **(b)** (*zeitlich*) to pass; (*Gewitter*) to blow over; **eine Gelegenheit ~ lassen** to let an opportunity slip **(c) an jdm ~** (= *sich nicht bemerkbar machen*) to pass sb by; **an jdm nicht ~** (*Erlebnis etc*) to leave its/their mark on sb; **vorübergehend 1** ADJ (= *flüchtig*) passing *attr*; *Krankheit* short; (= *zeitweilig*) temporary **2** ADV temporarily; **sich ~ im Ausland aufhalten** to stay abroad for a short time

Vorurteil NT prejudice (*gegenüber* against); **das ist ein ~** it's prejudice; **~e haben** to be prejudiced

vorurteilsfrei, vorurteilslos 1 ADJ unprejudiced **2** ADV without prejudice

Vor-: **Vorväter** PL forefathers *pl*, ancestors *pl*; **Vorvergangenheit** F (*Gram*) pluperfect; **Vorverkauf** M (*Theat, Sport*) advance booking; **sich** (*dat*) **Karten im ~ besorgen** to buy tickets in advance; **Vorverkaufskasse** F, **Vorverkaufsstelle** F advance booking office

vorverlegen *ptp* **vorverlegt** VT SEP *Termin* to bring forward

Vor-: **Vorverurteilung** F prejudgement; **vorvorgestern** ADV (*inf*) three days ago; **vorvorletzte(r, s)** ADJ last but two

vorwagen VR SEP to venture forward

Vorwahl F **(a)** preliminary election; (*US*) primary **(b)** (*Telec*) dialling (*Brit*) *or* area (*US*) code

vorwählen VT SEP (*Telec*) to dial first

Vorwahlnummer F, **Vorwählnummer** F dialling (*Brit*) *or* area (*US*) code

Vorwand [ˈfoːɐvant] M **-(e)s, Vorwände** [-vɛndə] pretext; **unter dem ~, dass ...** under the pretext that ...

Vorwarnung F (prior *or* advance) warning; (*Mil: vor Angriff*) early warning

vorwärts [ˈfoːɐvɛrts] ADV forwards, forward; **~!** (*inf*) let's go (*inf*); (*Mil*) forward march!; **weiter ~** further ahead; **~ und rückwärts** backwards and forwards; **wir kamen nur langsam ~** we made slow progress; **Rolle/Salto ~** forward roll/somersault

Vorwärts-: **Vorwärtsgang** M, *pl* **-gänge** forward gear; **vorwärts gehen** IRREG AUX SEIN (*fig*) **1** VI to progress, to come on **2** VI IMPERS **es geht wieder vorwärts** things are looking up; **mit etw geht es vorwärts** sth is progressing; **vorwärts kommen** VI IRREG AUX SEIN (*fig*) to make progress (*in, mit* with); (*beruflich, gesellschaftlich*) to get on; **im Leben/Beruf ~** to get on in life/one's job

Vorwäsche F, **Vorwaschgang** M prewash

vorweg [foˈrɛvɛk] ADV (= *voraus, an der Spitze*) at the front; (= *vorher*) before(hand); (= *als Erstes, von vornherein*) at the outset

vorwegnehmen VT SEP IRREG to anticipate; **um das Wichtigste vorwegzunehmen** to come to the most important point first

Vorweihnachtszeit F pre-Christmas period

vorweisen VT SEP IRREG to produce; **etw ~ können** (*fig*) to have sth

vorwerfen VT SEP IRREG **(a)** (*fig*) **jdm etw/Unpünktlichkeit ~** (= *anklagen*) to reproach sb for sth/for being unpunctual; (= *beschuldigen*) to accuse sb of sth/of being unpunctual; **jdm ~, dass er etw getan hat** to reproach sb for having done sth; **jdm ~, dass er etw nicht getan hat** to accuse sb of not having done sth; **das wirft er mir heute noch vor** he still holds it against me; **ich habe mir nichts vorzuwerfen** my conscience is clear; **muss ich mir das ~ lassen?** do I have to listen to these accusations?
(b) (*lit*) **Tieren/Gefangenen etw ~** to throw sth down for the animals/prisoners

vorwiegend [ˈfoːɐviːgnt] **1** ADJ ATTR predominant **2** ADV predominantly

Vorwort NT **(a)** *pl* **-worte** foreword; (*esp von Autor*) preface **(b)** *pl* **-wörter** (*Aus*: = *Präposition*) preposition

Vorwurf M reproach; (= *Beschuldigung*) accusation; **jdm/sich große Vorwürfe machen, dass ...** to reproach sb/oneself for ...; **jdm etw zum ~ machen** to reproach sb with sth; **jdm (wegen etw) Vorwürfe machen** to reproach sb (for sth)

vorwurfsvoll 1 ADJ reproachful **2** ADV reproachfully

Vorzeichen NT (= *Omen*) omen; (*Med*) early symptom; (*Math*) sign; (*Mus*) (*Kreuz/b*) sharp/flat (sign); (*vor einzelner Note*) accidental; (*von Tonart*) key signature; **unter umgekehrtem/dem gleichen ~** (*fig*) under different/the same circumstances

vorzeigbar ADJ presentable

Vorzeige- IN CPDS (= *vorbildlich*) model; (= *führend*) leading; **Vorzeigefrau** F (= *Vorbild*) female role model; (= *Alibifrau*) token woman

vorzeigen VT SEP to show; *Zeugnisse* to produce; **jdm die Hände ~** to show sb one's hands

Vorzeigeobjekt NT, **Vorzeigestück** NT showpiece

Vorzeit F prehistoric times *pl*; **in der ~** in prehistoric times; (= *vor langem*) in the dim and distant past

vorzeitig 1 ADJ early; *Geburt, Altern etc* premature **2** ADV early; prematurely

Vorzeitigkeit F -, NO PL (*Gram*) anteriority

Vorzelt NT awning

vorziehen VT SEP IRREG **(a)** (= *hervorziehen*) to pull out; (= *nach vorne ziehen*) *Stuhl etc* to pull up; (= *zuziehen*) *Vorhänge* to draw; **etw hinter/unter etw** (*dat*) **~** to pull sth out from behind/under sth
(b) (*fig*) (= *lieber mögen*) to prefer; (= *bevorzugen*) *jdn* to favour (*Brit*), to favor (*US*); **etw einer anderen Sache ~** to prefer sth to sth else; **es ~, etw zu tun** to prefer to do sth; (*allgemein gesehen*) to prefer doing sth
(c) *Wahlen, Termin* to bring forward; **vorgezogener Ruhestand** early retirement

Vorzug¹ M **(a)** preference; (= *Vorteil*) advantage; (= *gute Eigenschaft*) merit; **einer Sache** (*dat*) **den ~ geben** (*form*) to give sth preference; (= *Vorrang geben*) to give sth precedence; **den ~ haben, dass ...** to have the advantage that ... **(b)** (*Aus Sch*) distinction

Vorzug² M (*Rail*) train in front; (= *früher fahrend*) train before; (= *Entlastungszug*) relief train

vorzüglich [foːɐˈtsyːklɪç, (*esp Aus*) ˈfoːɐ-] **1** ADJ excellent **2** ADV excellently; (= *vornehmlich*) especially; **der Wein schmeckt ~** the wine tastes excellent

Vorzüglichkeit F -, NO PL excellence

Vorzugs-: **Vorzugsaktie** F (*St Ex*) preference share; **Vorzugspreis** M special discount price; **vorzugsweise** ADV preferably; (= *hauptsächlich*) mainly; **etw ~ trinken** to prefer to drink sth

Vostrokonto [ˈvɔstro-] NT vostro account

V-Pullover [ˈfau-] M V-neck pullover

VR [fauˈʔɛr] **(a)** ABBR *von* **Volksrepublik** VR **(b)** ABBR *von* **virtuelle Realität**

vulgär [vʊlˈgɛːɐ] **1** ADJ vulgar **2** ADV vulgarly; **~ aussehen** to look vulgar; **drück dich nicht so ~ aus** don't be so vulgar

Vulgarität [vʊlgariˈtɛːt] F -, **-en** vulgarity

Vulkan [vʊlˈkaːn] M **-(e)s, -e** volcano; **auf einem ~ leben** (*fig*) to be living on the edge of a volcano

Vulkanausbruch M volcanic eruption

vulkanisch [vʊlˈkaːnɪʃ] ADJ volcanic

vulkanisieren [vʊlkaniˈziːrən], *ptp* **vulkanisiert** VT to vulcanize

Vulkanologe [vʊlkanoˈloːgə] M **-n, -n, Vulkanologin** [-ˈloːgɪn] F **-, -nen** volcanologist

Vulkanologie [vʊlkanoloˈgiː] F -, NO PL volcanology

WaG ABBR *von* **Versicherungsverein auf Gegenseitigkeit**

Ww

W, w [ve:] NT -, - W, w

W ABBR *von* **Westen**

WAA [ve:laː'laː] F ABBR *von* **Wiederaufbereitungsanlage**

Waadt [vaː(ː)t] F - Vaud

Waage ['vaːɡə] F **-, -n (a)** (*Gerät*) scales *pl*; (= *Federwaage, Apothekerwaage*) balance; (*für Lastwagen, Autos*) weigh station; **eine ~** a pair of scales; **sich** (*dat*) **die ~ halten** (*fig*) to balance one another; **einer Sache** (*dat*) **die ~ halten** to balance sth (out) **(b)** (*Astron, Astrol*) Libra; **er ist (eine) ~** he's (a) Libra

Waage-: waagerecht 1 ADJ horizontal; (*im Kreuzworträtsel*) across 2 ADV levelly

Waag-: waagerecht ADJ, ADV = **waagerecht**; **Waagrechte** F DECL AS ADJ = **Waagerechte; Waagschale** F scale; **(schwer) in die ~ fallen** (*fig*) to carry weight; **jedes Wort auf die ~ legen** to weigh every word (carefully); **seinen Einfluss/seine Autorität/ sein ganzes Gewicht in die ~ werfen** (*fig*) to bring one's influence/one's authority/one's full weight to bear

wabbelig ['vabəlɪç] ADJ *Pudding, Gelee* wobbly; *Mensch* flabby

wabbeln ['vabln] VI to wobble

Wabe ['vaːbə] F **-, -n** honeycomb

wach [vax] ADJ awake *pred*; (*fig*: = *aufgeweckt*) alert; *Nacht* sleepless; **in ~em Zustand** in the waking state; **sich ~ halten** to stay awake; **~ werden** to wake up; **~ liegen** to lie awake

Wache ['vaxə] F **-, -n (a)** (= *Wachdienst*) guard (duty); **auf ~** on guard (duty); **(bei jdm) ~ halten** to keep guard (over sb); (= *Krankenwache, Totenwache*) to watch over sb; **~ stehen** *or* **schieben** (*inf*) to be on guard (duty); (*Dieb, Schüler etc*) to keep a lookout **(b)** (*Mil*: = *Wachtposten*) guard **(c)** (= *Polizeiwache*) (police) station

wachen ['vaxn] VI **(a)** (= *wach sein*) to be awake; (= *nicht schlafen können*) to lie awake **(b)** (= *Wache halten*) to keep watch; **bei jdm ~** to sit up with sb; **über etw** (*acc*) **~** to (keep) watch over sth; **über Verkehr** to supervise sth; **der Polizist wachte darüber, dass niemand ...** the policeman watched that no-one ...

Wach-: wach halten IRREG 1 VT (*fig*) *Erinnerung* to keep alive; *Interesse auch* to keep up 2 VR to keep oneself awake; **Wachhund** M (*lit, fig*) watchdog; (*lit auch*) guard dog; **Wachleute** PL *von* **Wachmann; Wachlokal** NT guardroom; **Wachmacher** M (*Med inf*) stimulant; **Wachmann** M, *pl* **-leute** watchman; (*Aus*) policeman; **Wachmannschaft** F men on guard; (*Naut*) watch

Wacholder [va'xɔldɐ] M **-s, - (a)** (*Bot*) juniper (tree) **(b)** = **Wacholderschnaps**

Wacholder-: Wacholderbeere F juniper berry; **Wacholderbranntwein** M (*form*), **Wacholderschnaps** M alcohol made from juniper berries, ≈ gin; **Wacholderstrauch** M juniper (tree)

Wachposten M sentry; (= *Schüler, Dieb etc*) lookout

Wachs [vaks] NT **-es, -e** wax; **~ in jds Händen sein** (*fig*) to be putty in sb's hands

wachsam ['vaxzaːm] 1 ADJ vigilant; (= *vorsichtig*) on one's guard; **ein ~es Auge auf jdn/etw haben** to keep a watchful eye on sb/sth 2 ADV vigilantly

Wachsamkeit F -, NO PL vigilance; (= *Vorsichtigkeit*) guardedness

wachseln ['vaksln] VT (*Aus*) to wax

wachsen¹ ['vaksn], *pret* **wuchs** [vuːks], *ptp* **gewachsen** VI AUX SEIN to grow; **in die Länge ~** to get *or* grow longer; **in die Höhe ~** to grow taller; (*Kind*) to shoot up (*inf*); **sich** (*dat*) **einen Bart ~ lassen** to grow a beard; **sich** (*dat*) **die Haare ~ lassen** to grow one's hair; **ich lese dieses Buch mit ~der Begeisterung** I'm really getting into this book; *siehe auch* **gewachsen**

wachsen² VT to wax

wächsern ['vɛksɐn] ADJ (*lit, fig*) waxen

Wachs-: Wachsfarbe F (= *Farbstift*) wax crayon; **Wachsfigur** F wax figure; **Wachsfigurenkabinett** NT waxworks *pl*; **Wachsmalstift** M, **Wachsmalkreide** F wax crayon; **Wachsstock** M wax taper

wächst [vɛkst] 3. PERS SING PRES *von* **wachsen**

Wachstube ['vaxʃtuːbə] F guardroom; (*von Polizei*) duty room

Wachstuch [vaks-] NT, *pl* **-tücher** oilcloth

Wachstum [vakstuːm] NT **-s**, NO PL growth; **im ~ zurückgeblieben** stunted

Wachstums-: Wachstumsbranche F growth industry; **wachstumsfördernd** ADJ (*Econ, Biol*) growth-promoting; **wachstumshemmend** ADJ (*Econ, Biol*) growth-inhibiting; **Wachstumshormon** NT growth hormone; **Wachstumspolitik** F growth policy; **Wachstumsrate** F (*Biol, Econ*) growth rate; **Wachstumsstörung** F disturbance of growth; **Wachstumswert** M growth share *or* stock

wachsweich ADJ (as) soft as butter; *Ausrede* lame; *Erklärung, Formulierung* vague; **~ werden** (*Mensch*) to melt; (*Knie*) to turn to jelly

Wachtel ['vaxtl] F **-, -n** quail

Wächter ['vɛçtɐ] M **-s, -, Wächterin** [-ərɪn] F **-, -nen** guardian; (= *Nachtwächter*) watchman; (= *Turmwächter*) watch; (= *Museumswächter, Parkplatzwächter*) attendant

Wachtraum M daydream

Wach(t)turm M watchtower

Wach-: Wach- und Schließgesellschaft F security corps; **Wachzustand** M **im ~** in the waking state

wackelig ['vakəlɪç] 1 ADJ wobbly; (*fig*) *Firma, Unternehmen, Kompromiss* shaky; *Mehrheit* flimsy; **auf ~en Füßen stehen** (*fig*) to have no sound basis 2 ADV **~ stehen** (*lit*) to be unsteady; (*fig: Unternehmen, Schüler*) to be shaky

Wackelkontakt M loose connection

wackeln ['vakln] VI (= *sich bewegen*) to wobble; (= *zittern*) to shake; (*Zahn, Schraube*) to be loose; (*fig*) (*Thron*) to totter; (*Position*) to be shaky; **du hast gewackelt** (*beim Fotografieren*) you moved; **mit den Ohren ~** to wiggle one's ears; **mit den Hüften/dem Hintern ~** to wiggle one's hips/bottom; **mit dem Kopf/Schwanz ~** to wag one's head/its tail

Wackelpeter [-peːtɐ] M **-s, -** (*inf*) jelly (*Brit*), Jell-O® (*US*)

wacker ['vakɐ] 1 ADJ (= *tapfer*) brave 2 ADV (= *tapfer*) bravely; **sich ~ halten** (*inf*) to hold one's ground; **sich ~ schlagen** (*inf*) to put up a brave fight

Wackerstein M boulder

wacklig ['vaklɪç] ADJ, ADV = **wackelig**

Wade ['vaːdə] F **-, -n** calf

Waden-: Wadenbein NT fibula; **Wadenkrampf** M cramp in the/one's calf

Waffe ['vafə] F **-, -n** (*lit, fig*) weapon; (= *Schusswaffe*) gun; **~n** (*Mil*) arms; **die ~n strecken** (*lit, fig*) to surrender; **jdn mit seinen eigenen ~n schlagen** (*fig*) to beat sb at his own game

Waffel ['vafl] F **-, -n** waffle; (= *Keks, Eiswaffel*) wafer; (= *Eistüte*) cornet; **einen an der ~ haben** (*sl*: = *verrückt sein*) to be off one's nut (*inf*)

Waffeleisen NT waffle iron

Waffen- IN CPDS **Waffenbesitz** M possession of firearms; **waffenfähig** ADJ *Uran, Plutonium* weapons-grade; **Waffengattung** F (*Mil*) arm of the service; **Waffengewalt** F force of arms; **mit ~** by force of arms; **Waffenhandel** M arms trade; (*illegal auch*) gunrunning; **Waffenhändler(in)** M(F) arms dealer; (*illegal auch*) gunrunner; **Waffenhilfe** F military assistance; **Waffenlager** NT (*von Armee*) ordnance depot; (*von Terroristen*) cache; **Waffenruhe** F ceasefire; **Waffenschein** M firearms licence (*Brit*) *or* license (*US*); **Waffenschmied** M (*Hist*) armourer (*Brit*), armorer (*US*); **Waffenschmuggel** M gunrunning; **Waffen-SS** [-lesles] F (*NS*) Waffen-SS; **Waffenstillstand** M armistice

waffnen ['vafnən] VR = **wappnen**

wagen ['vaːgn] 1 VT to venture; (= *riskieren*) *hohen Einsatz, sein Leben* to risk; (= *sich getrauen*) to dare; **es ~, etw zu tun** to venture to do sth; to risk doing sth; to dare (to) do sth; **wage nicht, mir zu widersprechen!** don't you dare (to) contradict me!; **ich wags** I'll risk it; **davon hätte ich nicht zu träumen gewagt** I would never even have dreamed it; **wer wagt, gewinnt** (*Prov*), **wer nicht wagt, der nicht gewinnt** (*Prov*) nothing ventured, nothing gained (*Prov*) 2 VR to dare; **sich ~, etw zu tun** to dare (to) do sth; **sich an**

etw (*acc*) ~ to venture to do sth; **ich wage mich nicht daran** I dare not do it; **bei dem schönen Wetter kann ich mich aus dem Haus/ins Wasser ~** in this lovely weather I can venture out of doors/into the water; *siehe auch* **gewagt**

Wagen [ˈvaːgn] M **-s, -** *or (S Ger, Aus)* ≃ [ˈvɛːgn] **(a)** (= *Personenwagen*) car; (= *Lieferwagen*) van; (= *Planwagen, Zirkuswagen, Zigeunerwagen*) wagon; (*von Pferden gezogen*) cart; (= *Kutsche*) coach; (= *Puppenwagen, Kinderwagen*) pram (*Brit*), baby carriage (*US*); (= *Handwagen*) (hand)cart; (= *Kofferkuli, Einkaufswagen*) trolley; **sich nicht vor jds ~ spannen lassen** (*fig*) not to allow oneself to be used by sb **(b)** (*Astron*) **der Große ~** the Big Dipper; **der Kleine ~** the Little Dipper

Wagen-: Wagenburg F barricade (of wagons); **Wagendeichsel** F shaft; **Wagenführer(in)** M(F) driver; **Wagenheber** M jack; **Wagenladung** F (*von Lastwagen*) truckload; (*von Eisenbahn*) wagonload; **Wagenpark** M fleet of cars; (= *Lieferwagen*) fleet of vans; **Wagenrennen** NT (*Hist*) chariot racing; (*einzelner Wettkampf*) chariot race; **Wagentyp** M type of car; **Wagenwäsche** F car wash; (= *das Waschen*) car washing

Waggon [vaˈgõː, vaˈgɔŋ] M **-s, -s** (goods) wagon; (= *Ladung*) wagonload/carload

waggonweise [vaˈgõː-, vaˈgɔŋ-] ADV by the wagonload *or* carload (*US*)

waghalsig ADJ daredevil *attr*

Wagnis [ˈvaːknɪs] NT **-ses, -se** hazardous business; (= *Risiko*) risk

Wagniskapital NT (*Fin*) venture *or* risk capital

Wagon [vaˈgoːn] M **-s, -s** *siehe* **Waggon**

Wahl [vaːl] F **-, -en (a)** (= *Auswahl*) choice; **die ~ fiel auf ihn/dieses Buch** he/this book was chosen; **aus freier ~** of one's own free choice; **wir hatten keine (andere) ~(, als)** we had no alternative (but); **jdm die ~ lassen** to leave (it up to) sb to choose; **jdm etw zur ~ stellen** to give sb the choice of sth; **drei Kandidaten stehen zur ~** there is a choice of three candidates; **seine/eine ~ treffen** to make one's/a choice *or* selection; **du hast die ~** take your pick; **sie hat die ~, ob sie ...** the choice is hers whether she ...; **wer die ~ hat, hat die Qual** (*Prov*) he is/you are *etc* spoiled for choice **(b)** (*Pol etc*) election; (= *Abstimmung*) vote; (*geheim*) ballot; **geheime ~** secret ballot; **freie ~en** free elections; **~ durch Handerheben** vote by (a) show of hands; **(die) ~en** (the) elections; **seine ~ in den Vorstand/zum Präsidenten** his election to the board/as president; **die ~ gewinnen** to win the election; **zur ~ gehen** to go to the polls; **sich zur ~ stellen** to stand (as a candidate) **(c)** (= *Qualität*) quality; **erste ~** top quality; *Gemüse, Eier* class one; **zweite/dritte ~** second/third quality; *Gemüse, Eier* class two/three; **Waren erster ~** top-quality goods; **Fleisch erster ~** prime meat; **Waren zweiter ~** seconds *pl*; **Gemüse zweiter ~** class-two vegetables; **der Teller war zweite ~** the plate was a second

Wahlautomatik F (*Telec*) automatic dialling (*Brit*) *or* dialing (*US*)

wählbar ADJ **(a)** eligible (for office) **(b)** (= *auswählbar*) **frei ~** of one's choice

Wahl-: Wahlbenachrichtigung F, **Wahlbenachrichtigungskarte** F polling card; **wahlberechtigt** ADJ entitled to vote; **Wahlberechtigte(r)** [-bəreçtɪçtɐ] MF DECL AS ADJ person entitled to vote; **Wahlbeteiligung** F poll; **eine hohe ~** a heavy poll; **Wahlbezirk** M ward; **Wahlbrief** M letter containing completed postal vote

wählen [ˈvɛːlən] **1** VT **(a)** (*von* from, out of) to choose; (= *auswählen*) to select; *siehe auch* **gewählt** **(b)** (*Telec*) Nummer to dial **(c)** (= *durch Wahl ermitteln*) Regierung, Sprecher etc to elect; (= *sich entscheiden für*) Partei, Kandidaten to vote for; **jdn ins Parlament ~** to elect sb to Parliament; **jdn in den Vorstand ~** to elect sb onto the board; **jdn zum Präsidenten ~** to elect sb president **2** VI **(a)** (= *auswählen*) to choose **(b)** (*Telec*) to dial **(c)** (= *Wahlen abhalten*) to hold elections; (= *Stimme abgeben*) to vote; **wann wird gewählt?** when are the elections?; **man darf ab 18 ~** you can vote at 18; **durch Handerheben ~** to vote by (a) show of hands; **~ gehen** to go to the polls

Wähler [ˈvɛːlɐ] M **-s, -**, **Wählerin** [-ərɪn] F **-, -nen** (*Pol*) voter; **der** *or* **die ~** the electorate *sing or pl*

Wahlergebnis NT election result

wählerisch [ˈvɛːlərɪʃ] ADJ particular; *Geschmack, Kunde* discriminating; **sei nicht so ~!** don't be so choosy

Wählerschaft [ˈvɛːlɐʃaft] F **-, -en** electorate *sing or pl*; (*eines Wahlkreises*) constituents *pl*

Wähler-: Wählerschicht F section of the electorate; **Wählerstimme** F vote; **wählerwirksam** ADJ *Politik, Parole* vote-winning

Wahl-: Wahlfach NT (*Sch*) option, elective (*US*); **Wahlfrau** F delegate; **wahlfrei** ADJ (*Sch*) optional; **~er Zugriff** (*Comput*) random access; **Wahlfreiheit** F (*Pol*) electoral freedom; (*Sch*) freedom of choice; **Wahlgang** M, *pl* **-gänge** ballot; **Wahlgeschenk** NT pre-election promise; **Wahlheimat** F adopted country; **Wahlhelfer(in)** M(F) (*im Wahlkampf*) electoral assistant; (*bei der Wahl*) polling officer; **Wahlkabine** F polling booth; **Wahlkampf** M election(eering) campaign; **einen ~ führen** to conduct an election campaign; **Wahlkreis** M constituency; **Wahlleiter(in)** M(F) returning officer (*Brit*), chief election official (*US*); **Wahllokal** NT polling station; **wahllos** **1** ADJ indiscriminate **2** ADV at random; (= *nicht wählerisch*) indiscriminately; **Wahlmann** M, *pl* **-männer** delegate; **Wahlmöglichkeit** F choice; **Wahlniederlage** F election defeat; **Wahlperiode** F lifetime of a/the parliament; **Wahlpflichtfach** NT (*Sch*) (compulsory) optional subject; **ich muss zwei Wahlpflichtfächer belegen** I have to take two optional subjects; **Wahlplakat** NT election poster; **Wahlrecht** NT (right to) vote; **allgemeines ~** universal suffrage; **das kommunale ~ haben** to have the right to vote in local elections; **das aktive ~** the right to vote; **das passive ~** eligibility (for political office); **mit 21/18 bekommt man das passive ~** at 21/18 one becomes eligible for political office; **Wahlrede** F election speech; **Wahlreform** F electoral reform

Wählscheibe F (*Telec*) dial

Wahl-: Wahlschein M polling card; **Wahlsieg** M election victory; **Wahlsonntag** M polling Sunday; **Wahlspruch** M **(a)** (= *Motto*) motto **(b)** (= *Wahlslogan*) election slogan; **Wahlsystem** NT electoral system; **Wahltag** M election day; **Wahlurne** F ballot box; **Wahlversammlung** F election meeting; **Wahlversprechungen** PL election promises *pl*; **Wahlvolk** M, NO PL **das ~** the electorate; **wahlweise** ADV alternatively; **~ Kartoffeln oder Reis** (a) choice of potatoes or rice; **Sie können ~ Wasserski fahren oder reiten** you have a choice between water-skiing and riding; **die Modelle sind ~ mit Sechs- oder Zwölfzylindermotor ausgestattet** the models have the option of a six- or a twelve-cylinder engine; **Wahlwiederholung** F (*Telec*) **(automatische) ~** (automatic) redial

Wahlzelle F polling booth

Wahn [vaːn] M **- (e)s**, NO PL **(a)** illusion, delusion; **in dem ~ leben, dass ...** to labour (*Brit*) *or* labor (*US*) under the delusion that ... **(b)** (= *Manie*) mania

wähnen [ˈvɛːnən] (*geh*) **1** VT to imagine (wrongly) **2** VR **sich sicher ~** to imagine oneself (to be) safe

Wahnidee F delusion; (= *verrückte Idee*) crazy notion

Wahnsinn M, NO PL madness; **jdn in den ~ treiben** to drive sb mad; **das ist doch (heller) ~, so ein ~!** that's sheer madness!; **einfach ~!** (*inf*: = *prima*) way out (*inf*), wicked! (*Brit sl*)

wahnsinnig **1** ADJ mad; (= *toll, super*) brilliant (*inf*); (*attr*: = *sehr groß, viel*) terrible; **eine ~e Arbeit** a crazy amount of work; **wie ~** (*inf*) like mad; **das macht mich ~** (*inf*) it's driving me crazy (*inf*); **~ werden** to go crazy (*inf*); **ich werde ~!** it's mind-blowing! (*inf*) **2** ADV (*inf*) incredibly (*inf*); **~ verliebt** madly in love; **~ viele/viel** an incredible number/amount (*inf*)

Wahnsinnige(r) [-zɪnɪgə] MF DECL AS ADJ madman/-woman

Wahnsinnigwerden NT **zum ~** enough to drive you round (*Brit*) *or* around (*US*) the bend (*inf*)

Wahnsinns- IN CPDS (*inf*) (= *verrückt*) crazy; (= *prima*) fantastic (*inf*); **Wahnsinnsarbeit** F **eine ~** a crazy amount of work (*inf*)

Wahnvorstellung F delusion

wahr [vaːɐ] ADJ true; (*attr*: = *wirklich*) real; **im ~sten Sinne des Wortes** in the true sense of the word; **daran ist kein ~es Wort, davon ist kein Wort ~** there's not a word of truth in it; **da hast du ein ~es Wort gesprochen** there is, there's a lot of truth in that; **etw ~ machen** *Pläne* to make sth a reality; *Versprechung, Drohung* to carry sth out; **~ werden** to come true; **so ~ mir Gott helfe!** so help me God!; **so ~ ich lebe/hier**

stehe as sure as I'm alive/standing here; **das darf** or **kann doch nicht ~ sein!** (inf) it can't be true!; **das ist schon gar nicht mehr ~** (inf) (verstärkend) it's not true! (inf); (= schon lange her) that was ages ago; **das ist nicht der ~e Jakob** or **Otto** (inf), **das ist nicht das Wahre** (inf) it's no great shakes (inf)

wahren ['vaːrən] VT **(a)** (= wahrnehmen) Interessen, Rechte to look after **(b)** (= erhalten) Autorität, Ruf, Würde to preserve; Geheimnis to keep; Chancen to keep alive; gute Manieren to observe; **die Form ~** to adhere to correct form; **den Anstand ~** to observe the proprieties

während ['vɛːrənt] **1** PREP +GEN or DAT during; **~ eines Zeitraums** over a period of time; **~ der ganzen Nacht** all night long **2** CONJ while

währenddem [vɛːrənt'deːm] (inf), **währenddessen** [vɛːrənt'dɛsn] ADV meanwhile

Wahr-: wahrhaben VT SEP IRREG **etw nicht ~ wollen** not to want to admit sth; **wahrhaft 1** ADJ (= ehrlich) truthful; (= echt) Freund true; (attr: = wirklich) real **2** ADV really; **wahrhaftig** [vaːɐ'haftɪç, 'vaːɐ-] **1** ADJ (geh) (= aufrichtig) truthful; Gemüt honest; Worte etc true **2** ADV really; (= tatsächlich) actually

Wahrheit F -, -en truth; **in ~** in reality; **die ~ sagen** to tell the truth; **er nimmt es mit der ~ nicht so genau** (inf) you have to take what he says with a pinch (esp Brit) or grain (US) of salt

Wahrheits-: Wahrheitsfindung [-fɪndʊŋ] F -, NO PL establishment of the truth; **wahrheitsgetreu 1** ADJ Bericht truthful; Darstellung faithful **2** ADV truthfully; **Wahrheitsliebe** F love of truth; **wahrheitsliebend** ADJ truth-loving; (= ehrlich) truthful

wahrlich ['vaːɐlɪç] ADV really, indeed; (= garantiert) certainly

Wahr-: wahrnehmbar ADJ perceptible; **nicht ~** imperceptible; **mit bloßem Auge ~/nicht ~** visible/invisible to the naked eye; **wahrnehmen** VT SEP IRREG **(a)** (= mit den Sinnen erfassen) to perceive; (= bemerken) Vorgänge, Veränderungen etc to be aware of; Geräusch to hear; Licht to see; Geruch to detect; (= heraushören) Unterton, Stimmung to detect; **nichts mehr/ alles um sich herum ~** to be no longer aware of anything/to be aware of everything around one **(b)** Frist, Termin to observe; Gelegenheit to take; Interessen, Angelegenheiten to look after; Verantwortung to exercise; **Wahrnehmung** [-neːmʊŋ] F -, -en **(a)** (mit den Sinnen) perception; (von Vorgängen etc) awareness; (von Geruch, Stimmung) detection **(b)** (von Interessen, Angelegenheiten) looking after; **wahrsagen** SEP or INSEP **1** VI to tell fortunes; **aus dem Kaffeesatz/aus den Teeblättern/aus den Karten ~** to read coffee grounds/tea leaves/cards; **jdm ~** to tell sb's fortune; **sich** (dat) **~ lassen** to have one's fortune told **2** VT **(jdm) die Zukunft ~** to tell sb's fortune; **er hat mir wahrgesagt** or **gewahrsagt, dass ...** he predicted (to me) that ...; **Wahrsager** [-zaːgɐ] M -s, -, **Wahrsagerin** [-ərɪn] F -, -nen fortune-teller; **Wahrsagerei** [-zaːgə'raɪ] F -, -en **(a)** NO PL fortune-telling **(b)** prediction; **Wahrsagung** [-zaːgʊŋ] F -, -en prediction

währschaft ['vɛːɐʃaft] ADJ (Sw) (= gediegen) Ware, Arbeit reliable; (= reichhaltig) Essen wholesome

wahrscheinlich [vaːɐ'ʃaɪnlɪç, 'vaːɐ-] **1** ADJ probable, likely; (= glaubhaft) plausible; **es liegt im Bereich des Wahrscheinlichen** it is quite within the bounds of probability **2** ADV probably

Wahrscheinlichkeit F -, -en probability; (= Glaubhaftigkeit) plausibility; **mit großer ~, aller ~ nach, in aller ~** in all probability

Wahrscheinlichkeitsrechnung F theory of probabilities

Wahrung ['vaːrʊŋ] F -, NO PL **(a)** (= Wahrnehmung) safeguarding **(b)** (= Erhaltung) preservation; (von Geheimnis) keeping; **~ der guten Manieren** observance of good manners

Währung ['vɛːrʊŋ] F -, -en currency

Währungs- IN CPDS currency, monetary; **Währungsblock** M, pl -blöcke monetary bloc; **Währungseinheit** F monetary unit; **Währungsfonds** M Monetary Fund; **Währungskonto** NT foreign currency account; **Währungspolitik** F monetary policy; **Währungsraum** M currency area; **Währungsreserve** F currency reserve; **Währungssystem** NT monetary system; **Währungsunion** F monetary union; **europäische ~** European monetary union

Wahrzeichen NT (von Stadt, Verein) emblem; (= Gebäude, Turm etc) symbol

Waid- [vaɪt] IN CPDS = **Weid-**

Waise F -, -n orphan

Waisen-: Waisenhaus NT orphanage; **Waisenkind** NT orphan; **Waisenrente** F orphan's allowance

Wal [vaːl] M -(e)s, -e whale

Wald [valt] M -(e)s, =er ['vɛldɐ] wood(s pl); (großer) forest; **ich glaub, ich steh im ~** (inf) I must be seeing/hearing things! (inf); **er sieht den ~ vor lauter Bäumen nicht** he can't see the wood (Brit) or forest (US) for the trees (Prov); **der Thüringer ~** the Thuringian Forest

Wald-: Waldameise F red ant; **Waldbestand** M forest land; **Waldblume** F woodland flower; **Waldboden** M forest soil; **Waldbrand** M forest fire

Wäldchen ['vɛltçən] NT -s, - DIM von **Wald** little wood

Waldhorn NT (Mus) French horn

waldig ['valdɪç] ADJ wooded

Wald-: Waldland NT woodland(s pl); **Waldlauf** M cross-country running; (einzelner Lauf) cross-country run; **Waldmeister** M (Bot) woodruff

Waldorf- ['valdɔrf-]: **Waldorfsalat** M (Cook) Waldorf salad; **Waldorfschule** F ≈ Rudolf Steiner School

Wald-: waldreich ADJ densely wooded; **Waldsterben** NT dying of the forests (due to pollution)

Wald-und-Wiesen- IN CPDS (inf) common-or-garden (Brit inf), garden-variety (US inf)

Wales [weːls, weːlz] NT -' Wales

Wal-: Walfang M whaling; **Walfangboot** NT whaler; **Walfänger(in)** M(F) whaler; **Walfisch** M (inf) whale; **Walfischspeck** M blubber; **Walfischtran** M sperm oil

Waliser [va'liːzɐ] M -s, - Welshman

Waliserin [va'liːzərɪn] F -, -nen Welshwoman

walisisch [va'liːzɪʃ] ADJ Welsh

Walkie-Talkie ['wɔːki'tɔːki] NT -(s), -s walkie-talkie

Walking ['wɔːkɪŋ] NT -s, NO PL speed walking

Walkman® ['wɔːkmən] M -s, -s or **Walkmen** (Rad) Walkman®

Walküre [val'kyːrə, 'valkyːrə] F -, -n (Myth, fig) Valkyrie

Wall [val] M -(e)s, =e ['vɛlə] embankment; (Mil) rampart; (fig) bulwark

Wallfahrer(in) M(F) pilgrim

Wallfahrt F pilgrimage

Wallgraben M moat

Wallis ['valɪs] NT -' Valais

Walliser ['valɪzɐ] M -s, -, **Walliserin** [-ərɪn] F -, -nen inhabitant of the Valais

Walliser Alpen PL **die ~** the Valais Alps pl

walliserisch [valɪzərɪʃ] ADJ Valaisan

Wallone [va'loːnə] M -n, -n, **Wallonin** [-'loːnɪn] F -, -nen Walloon

Wallung ['valʊŋ] F -, -en **(a)** (geh) **in ~ geraten** (See, Meer) to begin to surge; (Mensch) (vor Leidenschaft) to be in a turmoil; (vor Wut) to fly into a rage; **jds Blut** or **jdn in ~ bringen** to make sb's blood surge through his/her veins **(b)** (Med) (hot) flush (Brit) or flash (US) usu pl

Walnuss [val-] F walnut

Walnussbaum M walnut (tree)

Walross ['val-] NT walrus

walten [valtn] VI (geh) to prevail (in +dat over); (= wirken: Mensch, Naturkräfte) to be at work; **Vernunft ~ lassen** to let reason prevail; **Vorsicht/Milde ~ lassen** to exercise caution/leniency; **Gnade ~ lassen** to show mercy; **jdn ~ lassen** to let sb have a free rein; **das walte Gott!** amen (to that)!

Walzblech NT sheet metal

Walze ['valtsə] F -, -n roller; (= Drehorgelwalze) barrel; (von Spieluhr) cylinder

walzen [valtsn] VT to roll

wälzen ['vɛltsn] **1** VT **(a)** (= rollen) to roll; (Cook) (in Ei, Mehl) to coat (in +dat with); (in Butter, Petersilie) to toss **(b)** (inf) Akten, Bücher to pore over; Probleme, Gedanken, Pläne to turn over in one's mind; **die Schuld/Verantwortung auf jdn ~** to shift the blame/responsibility onto sb **2** VR to roll; (vor Schmerzen) to writhe (vor +dat with); (schlaflos im Bett) to toss and turn

walzenförmig ADJ cylindrical

Walzer ['valtsə] M -s, - waltz; **Wiener ~** Viennese waltz; **~ tanzen** to (dance the/a) waltz

Wälzer ['vɛltsə] M -s, - (inf) heavy tome (hum)

Walz-: Walzstraße F rolling train; **Walzwerk** NT rolling mill

wand PRET *von* **winden¹**

Wand [vant] F -, ⁼e ['vɛndə] wall (*auch Anat*); (= *nicht gemauerte Trennwand*) partition (wall); (*von Gefäß, Behälter, Schiff*) side; (= *Felswand*) (rock) face; (*fig*) barrier; **spanische ~** (folding) screen; **~ an ~** wall to wall; **in seinen vier Wänden** (*fig*) within one's own four walls; **weiß wie die ~** as white as a sheet; **wenn die Wände reden könnten** if walls could speak; **mit dem Kopf gegen die ~ rennen** (*fig*) to bang one's head against a brick wall; **jdn an die ~ spielen** (*fig*) to outdo sb; (*Theat*) to steal the show from sb; **er lachte/tobte** *etc***, dass die Wände wackelten** (*inf*) or **zitterten** (*inf*) he raised the roof (with his laughter/ranting and raving *etc*) (*inf*); **die ~** or **Wände hochgehen** (*inf*) to go up the wall (*inf*)

> *Vorsicht!* **Wand** *wird nicht mit dem englischen Wort* **wand** *übersetzt.*

Wandale [van'daːlə] M -n, -n, **Wandalin** [-'daːlɪn] F -, -nen (*Hist*) Vandal

Wandalismus [vanda'lɪsmʊs] M -, NO PL vandalism

Wand-: Wandbehang M wall hanging; **Wandbord** NT, **Wandbrett** NT (wall) shelf

Wandel ['vandl] M -s, NO PL change; **im ~ der Zeiten** throughout the ages; **im ~ der Jahrhunderte** down the centuries

wandeln¹ ['vandln] VTR (= *ändern*) to change

wandeln² VI AUX SEIN (*geh*: = *gehen*) to walk; **ein ~des Wörterbuch** (*hum*) a walking dictionary

Wandel-: Wandelobligation F convertible bond; **Wandelschuldverschreibung** F convertible bond

Wander-: Wanderarbeiter(in) M(F) migrant worker; **Wanderausstellung** F touring exhibition; **Wanderdüne** F shifting (sand) dune

Wanderer ['vandərɐ] M -s, -, **Wanderin** [-ərɪn] F -, -nen hiker

Wander-: Wanderfalke M peregrine (falcon); **Wanderheuschrecke** F migratory locust

Wanderin F *siehe* **Wanderer**

Wander-: Wanderjahre PL years *pl* of travel; **Wanderkarte** F map of walks; **Wanderleber** F floating liver; **Wanderlust** F wanderlust

wandern ['vandɐn] VI AUX SEIN (a) (= *gehen*) to wander; (*Wanderbühne, Zigeuner*) to travel
(b) (= *sich bewegen*) to move; (*Wolken, Gletscher*) to drift; (*Düne*) to shift; (*Blick, Gedanken*) to wander; (= *weitergegeben werden*) to be passed (on)
(c) (*Vögel, Tiere, Völker*) to migrate
(d) (*zur Freizeitgestaltung*) to hike; (*esp in Verein*) to ramble (*esp Brit*), to hike
(e) (*inf: ins Bett, in den Papierkorb, ins Feuer*) to go; **hinter Schloss und Riegel ~** to be put behind bars; **ins Krankenhaus/ins Leihhaus ~** to end up in hospital/at the pawnbroker's

Wander-: Wanderniere F floating kidney; **Wanderpokal** M challenge cup

Wanderschaft ['vandɐʃaft] F -, NO PL travels *pl*; **auf ~ gehen** to go off on one's travels; (*Tier*) to set off on the move

Wander-: Wanderschuhe PL walking shoes *pl*; **Wandertag** M day in German schools on which pupils go hiking; **Wandertrieb** M (*von Tier*) migratory instinct; (*fig*) wanderlust

Wanderung ['vandərʊŋ] F -, -en (a) (= *Ausflug*) walk; **eine ~ machen** to go on a walk *or* hike (b) (*von Vögeln, Tieren, Völkern*) migration; (*Sociol*: = *Wohnortwechsel*) population shift

Wander-: Wanderverein M hiking club; **Wandervogel** M (= *begeisterter Wanderer*) hiker; **Wanderweg** M walk, (foot)path; **Wanderzirkus** M travelling (*esp Brit*) or traveling (*US*) circus

Wandgemälde NT mural

-wandig [vandɪç] ADJ SUF -walled; **dünnwandig** *Gebäude* thin-walled

Wand-: Wandkalender M wall calendar; **Wandkarte** F wall map; **Wandlampe** F wall lamp; **Wandleuchter** M wall bracket

Wandlung ['vandlʊŋ] F -, -en (a) (= *Wechsel, Wandel*) change; (= *völlige Umwandlung*) transformation (b) (*Eccl*) transubstantiation; (= *Teil der Messe*) consecration

wandlungsfähig ADJ adaptable; *Schauspieler etc* versatile

Wandrer ['vandrɐ] M -s, -, **Wandrerin** [-ərɪn] F -, -nen *siehe* **Wanderer**

Wand-: Wandschirm M screen; **Wandschrank** M wall cupboard; **Wandtafel** F (black)board

wandte PRET *von* **wenden**

Wand-: Wandteppich M tapestry; **Wanduhr** F wall clock; **Wandzeitung** F wall newssheet

Wange ['vaŋə] F -, -n (*geh*) cheek; **~ an ~** cheek to cheek

Wankelmotor ['vaŋkl-] M Wankel engine

wanken ['vaŋkn] VI (a) (= *schwanken*) (*Mensch, Gebäude*) to sway; (*Boden*) to rock; (*fig: Thron, Regierung*) to totter; (= *unsicher sein/werden*) to waver; **ins Wanken geraten** (*lit*) to begin to sway/rock; (*fig*) to begin to totter/waver; **etw ins Wanken bringen** (*lit*) to cause sth to sway/rock; (*fig*) *Thron, Regierung* to cause sth to totter; *Glauben, Mut* to shake sth; *Weltbild* to shake sth; **jds Entschluss ins Wanken bringen** to make sb waver in his decision
(b) AUX SEIN (= *gehen*) to stagger; (*alter Mensch*) to totter

wann [van] INTERROG ADV when; ~ (**auch**) **immer** whenever; **bis ~ ist das fertig?** when will that be ready (by)?; **bis ~ gilt der Ausweis?** until when is the pass valid?; **seit ~ bist/hast du ...?** (*zeitlich*) how long have you been/had ...?; (*bezweifelnd, entrüstet etc*) since when are you/do you have ...?; **von ~ an bist du in Deutschland?** from when will you be in Germany?; **von ~ bis ~?** when?, during what times?

Wanne ['vanə] F -, -n bath; (= *Badewanne auch*) (bath)tub; (= *Ölwanne*) reservoir; (*im Auto*) sump (*Brit*), oil pan (*US*)

Wanze ['vantsə] F -, -n bug

WAP [vap] NT (*Comput*) ABBR *von* **Wireless Application Protocol** WAP

WAP-Handy ['vap-] NT WAP phone

Wappen ['vapn] NT -s, - coat of arms; (*auf Münze*) heads *no art*

Wappen-: Wappenkunde F heraldry; **Wappentier** NT heraldic animal

wappnen ['vapnən] VR (*fig*) **sich (gegen etw) ~** to prepare (oneself) (for sth); **gewappnet sein** to be prepared

WAP-Technologie ['vap-] F WAP technology

war PRET *von* **sein¹**

warb PRET *von* **werben**

Ware ['vaːrə] F -, -n (a) product; (*einzelne ~*) article; (*als Sammelbegriff*) goods *pl* (b) **Waren** PL goods *pl*

wäre ['vɛːrə] PRET SUBJUNC *von* **sein¹**

Waren-: Warenangebot NT range of goods for sale; **Warenanlagefonds** M commodity fund; **Warenannahme** F receipt of goods; (= *Abteilung*) receiving office; **die ~ verweigern** to refuse to take delivery; **Warenaufzug** M goods hoist; **Warenausgangsbuch** NT (*für Außenstände*) sales ledger; (*für gelieferten Ware*) sales day book; **Warenbegleitpapiere** PL shipping documents *pl*; **Warenbestand** M stocks *pl* of goods; **Warenbörse** F commodity exchange; **Warenhaus** NT (*department*) store; **Warenkorb** M (*Econ*) basket of goods; **Warenlager** NT warehouse; (= *Bestand*) stocks *pl*; **Warenmuster** NT, **Warenprobe** F trade sample; **Warenterminbörse** F (*St Ex*) commodity futures exchange; **Warentermingeschäft** NT (*St Ex*) commodity futures *pl*; **Warentest** M test of goods; **Warenverkehrsbescheinigung** F movement certificate; **Warenwechsel** M commercial *or* trade bill; **Warenwert** M goods *or* commodity value; **Warenzeichen** NT trademark

warf PRET *von* **werfen**

warm [varm] **1** ADJ, *comp* ⁼er ['vɛrmə], *superl* ⁼ste(r, s) ['vɛrmstə] (*lit, fig*) warm; *Wetter auch, Getränk, Speise* (*auch Wasserhahn*) hot; **mir ist ~** I'm warm; **das hält ~** it keeps you warm; **das macht ~** it warms you up; **das Essen ~ stellen** to keep the food hot; **~e Miete** rent including heating; **wie ~e Semmeln weggehen** (*inf*) to go like hot cakes; **~ werden** (*fig inf*) to thaw out (*inf*); **mit jdm ~ werden** (*inf*) to get close to sb; **mit etw ~ werden** to get used to sth

2 ADV, *comp* ⁼er, *superl* **am** ⁼**sten** *sitzen* in a warm place; *schlafen* in a warm room; **am Kamin sitzen wir wärmer** we'll be warmer by the fireplace; **~ duschen** to take a warm shower; **die Milch ~ trinken** to drink warm milk; **sich ~ anziehen** to dress up warmly; (*fig inf: bei Schwierigkeiten*) to prepare oneself for a rough ride; **jdn/etw wärmstens empfehlen** to recommend sb/sth warmly

Warm-: Warmblut NT, pl **-blüter** crossbreed; **Warmblüter** [-bly:tɐ] M **-s, -** (Zool) warm-blooded animal; **warmblütig** ADJ warm-blooded; **Warmduscher** [-duːʃɐ] M **-s, -** (sl: = Weichling) wimp (inf)

Wärme [ˈvɛrmə] F **-, (rare) -n** (lit, fig) warmth; (von Wetter etc) (Phys) heat; (Wetterlage) warm weather; **10 Grad ~** 10 degrees above zero; **ist das eine ~!** isn't it warm!

Wärme-: wärmebeständig ADJ heat-resistant; **Wärmedämmung** F (heat) insulation; **Wärmeenergie** F thermal energy; **Wärmekraftwerk** NT thermal power station; **Wärmelehre** F theory of heat

wärmen [ˈvɛrmən] 🚺 VT to warm; Essen, Kaffee etc to warm up; **das wärmt einem das Herz** it's heartwarming 🚹 VI to be warm 🚼 VR to warm oneself (up), to warm up; **sich gegenseitig ~** to keep each other warm

Wärme-: Wärmepumpe F heat pump; **Wärmeregler** M thermostat; **Wärmeschutz** M heat shield; **Wärmespeicher** M storer of heat; (Gerät) heat storer; **Wärmetauscher** [-tauʃɐ] M **-s, -** heat exchanger; **Wärmetechnik** F heat technology

Wärmflasche F hot-water bottle

Warm-: Warmfront F (Met) warm front; **warm halten** VT IRREG **sich** (dat) **jdn ~** (fig inf) to keep in with sb (inf); **Warmhalteplatte** F hot plate; **warmherzig** ADJ warm-hearted; **Warmherzigkeit** [ˈvarmhɛrtsɪçkait] F **-, NO PL** warm-heartedness; **warm laufen** VI IRREG AUX SEIN to warm up; **Warmluft** F warm air; **Warmmiete** F rent including heating; **Warmstart** M (Aut, Comput) warm start

Warmwasser-: Warmwasserbereiter [varmˈvasəbəraitɐ] M **-s, -** water heater; **Warmwasserheizung** F hot-water central heating; **Warmwasserleitung** F hot-water pipe; **Warmwasserspeicher** M hot-water tank

Warn-: Warnanlage F warning system; **Warnblinkanlage** F flashing warning lights pl; (an Auto) hazard (warning) lights pl; **Warnblinkleuchte** F flashing warning light; **Warnblinklicht** NT flashing warning light; (an Auto) hazard warning light; **Warndreieck** NT warning triangle

warnen [ˈvarnən] VTI to warn (vor +dat of); **jdn (davor) ~, etw zu tun** to warn sb against doing sth; **vor Taschendieben wird gewarnt!** beware of pickpockets!

Warn-: Warnhinweis M (= Aufdruck) warning; **Warnkreuz** NT warning cross (before level crossing (Brit) or grade crossing (US)); **Warnmeldung** F warning (announcement); **Warnruf** M warning cry; **Warnschild** NT, pl **-schilder** warning sign; **Warnschuss** M warning shot; **Warnstreik** M token strike

Warnung [ˈvarnʊŋ] F **-, en** warning; **~ vor etw** (dat) warning about sth; **vor Gefahr** warning of sth

Warnvorrichtung F warning system

Warschau [ˈvarʃau] NT **-s** Warsaw

Warte-: Wartefrist F waiting period; (für Lieferung) delivery time; **Wartehalle** F waiting room; (im Flughafen) departure lounge; **Warteliste** F waiting list

warten¹ [ˈvartn] VI to wait (auf +acc for); **warte mal!** hold on; (überlegend) let me see; **na warte!** (inf) just you wait!; **bitte ~** (Telec) hold the line please; (Zeichen) please wait; **da kannst du ~, bis du schwarz wirst** (inf), **da(rauf) kannst du lange ~** (iro) you can wait till the cows come home; **auf Antwort/Einlass ~** to wait for an answer/to be let in; **mit dem Essen auf jdn ~** to wait for sb (to come) before eating; **auf sie/darauf habe ich gerade noch gewartet!** (iro) she/that was all I needed!; **lange auf sich ~ lassen** (Sache) to be a long time (in) coming; (Mensch) to take one's time; **nicht lange auf sich ~ lassen** (Sache) to be not long in coming; (Mensch) to not take long; **das lange Warten hatte ihn müde gemacht** the long wait had made him tired

warten² VT Auto, Maschine to service

Wärter [ˈvɛrtɐ] M **-s, -**, **Wärterin** [-ərɪn] F **-, -nen** attendant; (= Leuchtturmwärter, Tierwärter) keeper; (= Krankenwärter) orderly; (= Gefängniswärter) warder (Brit), guard

Warte-: Warteraum M waiting room; **Wartesaal** M waiting room; **Warteschleife** F (Aviat) holding pattern; **~n ziehen** or **drehen** to circle; **Wartezimmer** NT waiting room

-wärts [verts] ADV SUF -wards; **südwärts** southwards

Wartung [ˈvartʊŋ] F **-, -en** (von Auto) servicing; (von Maschine auch) maintenance

wartungsfrei ADJ maintenance-free

warum [vaˈrʊm] INTERROG ADV why; **~ nicht?** why not?; **~ nicht gleich so!** that's better; **nach dem Warum fragen** to ask why

Warze [ˈvartsə] F **-, -n** wart; (= Brustwarze) nipple

Warzenschwein NT warthog

was [vas] 🚻 INTERROG PRON **(a)** what; (= wie viel) how much; **~ ist** or **gibts?** what is it?, what's up?; **~ ist, kommst du mit?** well, are you coming?; **~ hast du denn?, ~ ist denn los?** what's the matter (with you)?; **~ willst** or **hast du denn?** what are you talking about?; **~ denn?** (ungehalten) what (is it)?; (um Vorschlag bittend) but what?; **das ist gut, ~?** (inf) that's good, isn't it?; **~ haben wir gelacht!** (inf) how we laughed! **(b)** (inf: = warum) why, what ... for; **~ lachst du denn so?** what are you laughing for? **(c)** **~ für ...** what sort or kind of ...; **~ für ein schönes Haus!** what a lovely house!; **~ für ein Wahnsinn!** what madness! 🚹 REL PRON (auf ganzen Satz bezogen) which; **das, ~ ...** that which ..., what ...; **~ auch (immer)** whatever; **das ist etwas, ~ ich nicht verstehe** that is something (which) I don't understand; **alles, ~ ...** everything (that) ...; **das Beste/Schönste/wenige/Einzige, ~ ich ...** the best/prettiest/little/only thing (that) I ...; **lauf, ~ du kannst!** (inf) run as fast as you can!; **~ du immer hast!** you do go on! 🚼 INDEF PRON (inf) ABBR von **etwas** something; (fragend, bedingend auch, verneint) anything; (unbestimmter Teil einer Menge) some, any; **(na,) so ~!** well I never!; **so ~ von Blödheit** such stupidity; **er ist so ~ von doof** he's so incredibly stupid; **kann ich dir ~ helfen?** (inf) can I give you a hand?; **ist (mit dir) ~?** is something the matter (with you)?; siehe auch etwas

Wasch-: Waschanlage F (für Autos) car wash; (= Scheibenwaschanlage) wipers pl; (fig inf: für Geld) laundering facility; **waschbar** ADJ washable; **Waschbär** M raccoon; **Waschbecken** NT washbasin

Wäsche [ˈvɛʃə] F **-, NO PL (a)** washing; (= Schmutzwäsche, bei Wäscherei) laundry; **in der ~ sein** to be in the wash **(b)** (= Stoffzeug) (= Bettwäsche, Tischwäsche, Küchenwäsche) linen; (= Unterwäsche) underwear; **dumm aus der ~ gucken** (inf) to look stupid

waschecht ADJ Farbe fast; Stoff auch colourfast (Brit), colorfast (US); (fig) genuine

Wäsche-: Wäscheklammer F clothes peg (Brit), clothes pin (US); **Wäschekorb** M dirty clothes basket; **Wäscheleine** F (clothes)line

waschen [ˈvaʃn] pret **wusch** [vuːʃ], ptp **gewaschen** [gəˈvaʃn] 🚻 VT to wash; Gold etc to pan; (fig inf) Geld, Spenden to launder; (Wäsche) **~** to do the washing; **etw** (acc) **warm/kalt ~** to wash sth in hot/cold water; **sich** (dat) **die Hände/Haare** etc **~** to wash one's hands/hair etc; **Waschen und Legen** (beim Friseur) shampoo and set 🚹 VR (Mensch/Tier) to wash (oneself/itself); (Stoff) to wash; **das hat sich gewaschen** (inf) that really had an effect; **eine Geldbuße, die sich gewaschen hat** (inf) a really heavy fine; **eine Ohrfeige, die sich gewaschen hat** (inf) a hard slap in the face; **eine Klassenarbeit, die sich gewaschen hat** (inf) a real stinker of a test (inf)

Wäscherei [vɛʃəˈrai] F **-, -en** laundry

Wäsche-: Wäscheschleuder F spin-drier; **Wäscheständer** M clotheshorse; **Wäschetrockner** M **-s, -** (= Ständer) clotheshorse; (= Trockenautomat) drier

Wasch-: Waschgang M, pl **-gänge** stage of the washing programme (Brit) or program (US); **Waschgelegenheit** F washing facilities pl; **Waschküche** F washroom, laundry; (inf: = Nebel) dense fog; **Waschlappen** M flannel; (für Gesicht auch) face cloth (Brit), washcloth (US); (inf: = Feigling) sissy (inf); **Waschmaschine** F washing machine; **Waschmittel** NT detergent; **Waschpulver** NT washing powder; **Waschsalon** M laundry; (zum Selbstwaschen) laundrette (Brit), Laundromat® (US); **Waschseide** F washable silk; **Waschstraße** F (zur Autowäsche) car wash

wäscht [vɛʃt] 3. PERS SING PRES von waschen

Wasch-: Waschtag M washday; **~ haben** to have one's washday; **Waschtisch** M washstand; **Waschzettel** M (Typ) blurb; **Waschzeug** NT, NO PL toilet things pl

Wasser [ˈvasɐ] NT **-s, -** or ˝ [ˈvɛsɐ] **(a)** NO PL water; **~ abstoßend, ~ abweisend** water-repellent; **das ist ~ auf seine Mühle** (fig) this is all grist for his mill; **bis dahin fließt noch viel ~ den Bach** or **den Rhein** or **die Donau** etc **hinunter** a lot of water will have flowed under the bridge by then; **dort wird auch nur mit**

~ **gekocht** (*fig*) they're no different from anybody else (there); **ihr kann er nicht das ~ reichen** (*fig*) he's not a patch on her (*Brit*); **~ lassen** (*Med*) to pass water; **etw unter ~ setzen** to flood sth; **unter ~ stehen** to be flooded; **zu ~ on** the water *or* (*Meer*) sea; (= *auf dem ~weg*) by water/sea; **ein Boot zu ~ lassen** to launch a boat; **ins ~ fallen**, **zu ~ werden** (*fig*) to fall through; **nahe ans** *or* **am ~ gebaut haben** (*inf*) to be inclined to tears; **sich über ~ halten** (*fig*) to keep one's head above water; **er ist mit allen ~n gewaschen** he knows all the tricks
(b) *pl* **Wässer** (= *Flüssigkeit, Abwaschwasser etc*) water; (*medizinisch*) lotion; (= *Mineralwasser*) mineral water; (= *Speichel*) saliva; (= *Schweiß*) sweat; (*Med: in Beinen etc*) fluid; (= *Abwasser*) sewage *no pl*; **dabei läuft mir das ~ im Mund(e) zusammen** it makes my mouth water
Wasser-: wasserabstoßend, **wasserabweisend** ADJ *siehe* **Wasser**; **Wasseranschluss** M mains water supply; (*auf Zeltplatz*) water point; **wasserarm** ADJ *Gegend, Zeitraum* arid; **Wasserbad** NT water bath; (*Cook*) bain-marie; **im ~** (*Cook*) in a bain-marie; **Wasserball** M **(a)** NO PL (*Spiel*) water polo **(b)** (*Ball*) beach ball; (*fürs ~spiel*) water polo ball; **Wasserbett** NT water bed; **Wasserbob** M jet ski; **~ fahren** to ride on a jet ski
Wässerchen ['vesəçən] NT **-s, -** little stream; (= *Parfüm*) scent; (*kosmetisch*) lotion; **er sieht aus, als ob er kein ~ trüben könnte** he looks as if butter wouldn't melt in his mouth
Wasser-: Wasserdampf M steam; **wasserdicht** ADJ (*lit, fig*) watertight; *Uhr, Stoff etc* waterproof; **Wassereimer** M bucket; **Wasserenthärter** M water softener; **Wasserfahrzeug** NT watercraft; **Wasserfall** M waterfall; **wie ein ~ reden** (*inf*) to talk nineteen to the dozen (*Brit inf*), to talk a blue streak (*US inf*); **Wasserfarbe** F watercolour (*Brit*), watercolor (*US*); **Wasserflugzeug** NT seaplane; **wassergekühlt** ADJ water-cooled; **Wassergraben** M (*Sport*) water jump; (*um Burg*) moat; **Wasserhahn** M water tap (*esp Brit*), faucet (*US*); (= *Haupthahn*) stopcock; **Wasserhaushalt** M (*Biol etc*) water balance
wässerig ['vesərɪç] ADJ (*lit, fig*) watery; *Augen* pale-coloured (*Brit*), pale-colored (*US*); (*Chem*) aqueous; **jdm den Mund ~ machen** (*inf*) to make sb's mouth water
Wasser-: Wasserjungfrau F (*Myth*) naiad; **Wasserkessel** M kettle; (*Tech*) boiler; **Wasserkopf** M water on the brain *no indef art*; **bürokratischer ~** (*fig*) top-heavy bureaucracy; **Wasserkraft** F water power; **Wasserkraftwerk** NT hydroelectric power station; **Wasserkühlung** F (*Aut*) water-cooling; **mit ~** water-cooled; **~ haben** to be water-cooled; **Wasserlassen** NT **-s**, NO PL (*Med*) passing water, urination; **Wasserleiche** F drowned body; **Wasserleitung** F (= *Rohr*) water pipe; (= *Anlagen*) plumbing *no pl*; (*inf*: = *Hahn*) tap, faucet (*US*); **wasserlöslich** ADJ water-soluble; **Wassermangel** M water shortage; **Wassermann** M, *pl* **-männer (a)** (*Myth*) water sprite **(b)** (*Astrol*) Aquarius *no art*; **~ sein** to be (an) Aquarius; **Wassermelone** F watermelon
wassern ['vasən] VI (*Aviat*) to land on water *or* (*im Meer auch*) in the sea; (*Space*) to splash down
wässern ['vesən] 🟦 VT *Heringe, Erbsen etc* to soak; (*Phot*) to rinse; (= *bewässern*) *Pflanzen, Felder, Rasen* to water 🟦 VI to water; **mir ~ die Augen** my eyes are watering
Wasser-: Wassernixe F (*Myth*) water nymph; **Wasserpfeife** F hookah (*Brit*), (water) bong (*US*); **Wasserpflanze** F aquatic plant; **Wasserpistole** F water pistol; **Wasserpocken** PL (*Med*) chickenpox *sing*; **Wasserreservoir** NT reservoir; **Wasserrohr** NT water pipe; **Wasserschaden** M water damage; **Wasserscheide** F watershed; **wasserscheu** ADJ scared of water; **Wasserscheu** F fear of water; (*Psych*) water phobia; **Wasserschi** M, NT = **Wasserski**; **Wasserschildkröte** F turtle; **Wasserschutzpolizei** F (*auf Flüssen, Wasserwegen*) river police; (*im Hafen*) harbour (*Brit*) *or* harbor (*US*) police; (*auf der See*) coastguard service; **Wasserski** 🟦 M water-ski 🟦 NT water-skiing; **Wasserspeier** [-ʃpaiɐ] M **-s, -** gargoyle; **Wasserspiegel** M (= *Oberfläche*) surface of the water; (= *Wasserstand*) water level; **Wassersport** M der ~ water sports *pl*; **Wassersportler(in)** M(F) water sportsman/-woman; **Wasserspülung** F flush; **Klosett mit ~** flush toilet; **Wasserstand** M water level; **niedriger/hoher ~** low/high water
Wasserstoff M hydrogen
Wasserstoff-: Wasserstoffbombe F hydrogen bomb; **Wasserstoffsuperoxid** NT hydrogen peroxide
Wasser-: Wasserstrahl M jet of water; **Wasserstraße** F waterway; **Wassersucht** F dropsy; **Wassertank** M water tank;

(*für WC*) cistern; **Wassertier** NT aquatic animal; **Wasserturm** M water tower; **Wasseruhr** F (= *Wasserzähler*) water meter
Wasserung ['vasərʊŋ] F **-, -en** water landing; (*im Meer*) sea landing; (*Space*) splashdown
Wässerung ['vesərʊŋ] F **-, -en** (*von Fisch, Gemüse etc*) soaking; (*Phot*) rinsing; (= *Bewässerung*) watering
Wasser-: Wasserversorgung F water supply; **Wasserverunreinigung** F water pollution; **Wasservogel** M waterfowl; **Wasserwaage** F spirit level (*Brit*), water level gauge (*US*); **Wasserweg** M waterway; **auf dem ~** by water *or* (*Meer*) sea; **Wasserwelle** F water wave; **Wasserwerfer** M water cannon; **Wasserwerk** NT waterworks *sing or pl*; **Wasserzähler** M water meter; **Wasserzeichen** NT watermark
wässrig ['vesrɪç] ADJ = **wässerig**
waten ['va:tn] VI AUX SEIN to wade
watscheln ['va:tʃln, 'vat-] VI AUX SEIN to waddle
Watschen ['va:tʃn, 'vat-] F **-, -** (*Aus, S Ger: inf*) = **Ohrfeige**
Watstiefel ['va:t-] M wader
Watt¹ [vat] NT **-s, -** (*Elec*) watt
Watt² NT **-(e)s, -en** (*Geog*) mud flats *pl*
Watte ['vatə] F **-, -n** cotton wool (*Brit*), cotton (*US*); (*zur Polsterung*) padding
Wattebausch M cotton-wool (*Brit*) *or* cotton (*US*) ball
Wattenmeer NT mud flats *pl*
Watte-: Wattepad [-pɛt] M **-s, -s** cotton wool pad; **Wattestäbchen** NT cotton bud
wattieren [va'ti:rən], *ptp* **wattiert** VT to pad; (= *füttern*) to line with padding; (*und absteppen*) *Stoff, Steppdecke* to quilt; **wattierte Umschläge** padded envelopes; **wattierte Jacken** quilted jackets
Wattierung F **-, -en** padding
Watt-: Wattmeter NT wattmeter; **Wattsekunde** F watt-second; **Wattstunde** F watt-hour; **Wattzahl** F wattage
Watvogel ['va:t-] M wading bird
wau wau ['vau 'vau] INTERJ bow-wow
WC [ve:'tse:] NT **-s, -s** WC
Web [wɛb] NT **-(s)**, NO PL Web; **im ~** on the Web
Web- [wɛb-]: **Webadresse** F website address; **Webcam** ['wɛbkɛm] F **-, -s** webcam; **Webdesigner(in)** M(F) web designer
weben ['ve:bn], *pret* **webte** *or* (*liter, fig*) **wob** ['ve:ptə, vo:p], *ptp* **gewebt** *or* (*liter, fig*) **gewoben** [gə've:pt, gə'vo:bn] VTI (*lit, fig*) to weave; *Spinnnetz, Lügennetz* to spin
Weber ['ve:bɐ] M **-s, -**, **Weberin** [-ərɪn] F **-, -nen** weaver
Weberei [ve:bə'rai] F **-, -en (a)** NO PL (= *das Weben*) weaving **(b)** (= *Betrieb*) weaving mill
Webkamera ['wɛb-] F web camera
Weberknecht M (*Zool*) crane fly
Webkante F selvage
Webseite ['wɛb-] F Web page
Webserver ['wɛb-] M Internet server
Webstuhl M loom
Websurfer ['wɛb-]**(in)** M(F) web surfer
Wechsel ['vɛksl] M **-s, - (a)** (= *Änderung*) change; (*abwechselnd*) alternation; (= *Geldwechsel*) exchange; (*der Jahreszeiten, Agr*: = *Fruchtwechsel*) rotation; **im ~** (= *abwechselnd*) in turn **(b)** (*Sport*) (= *Staffelwechsel*) (baton) change; (*Ftbl etc*) substitution **(c)** (*Fin*) bill of (exchange); (*inf*: = *Geldzuwendung*) allowance
Wechsel-: Wechselbeziehung F correlation; **in ~ miteinander** *or* **zueinander stehen** to be correlated; **Wechselgeld** NT change; **wechselhaft** 🟦 ADJ changeable 🟦 ADV **~ verlaufen** to be changeable; **Wechselhaftigkeit** F changeability; **Wechseljahre** PL menopause *sing*; **in die ~ kommen** to start the menopause; **in den ~n sein** to be suffering from the menopause; **Wechselkurs** M rate of exchange
wechseln ['vɛksln] 🟦 VT to change (*in +acc* into); (= *austauschen*) to exchange; (*Ftbl etc*) to substitute (*gegen* for); **den Tisch/die Schule/das Hemd ~** to change tables/schools/one's shirt; **die Farbe ~** to change colour (*Brit*) *or* color (*US*); **den Platz mit jdm ~** to exchange one's seat with sb; **Briefe ~** to correspond (*mit* with); **den Wohnung ~** to move; **können Sie (mir) zehn Euro ~?** can you change ten euros (for me)?; **Wäsche zum Wechseln** a change of underwear

2 VI to change; (*Sport*) to change (over); (= *einander ablösen*) to alternate; **ich kann Ihnen leider nicht ~** I'm sorry, I don't have any change

wechselnd [ˈvɛkslnt] **1** ADJ changing; (= *einander ablösend, abwechselnd*) alternating; *Launen, Stimmungen* changeable; *Winde, Bewölkung* variable; **mit ~em Erfolg** with varying (degrees of) success **2** ADV alternately; **~ bewölkt** cloudy with sunny intervals

Wechsel-: **Wechselregress** M, **Wechselrückgriff** M (*Fin*) recourse; **Wechselschalter** M **(a)** (*Elec*) changeover switch **(b)** (*in Bank*) counter for foreign currency exchange; **wechselseitig** [-zaitɪç] **1** ADJ reciprocal; (= *gegenseitig auch*) mutual **2** ADV reciprocally; **sich beschimpfen, sich hassen** one another; **Wechselstrom** M alternating current; **Wechselstube** F bureau de change (*Brit*), exchange; **Wechselwähler(in)** M(F) floating voter; **Wechselwirkung** F interaction; **in ~ stehen** to interact

Weckdienst M wake-up call service

wecken [ˈvɛkn] VT to wake (up); (*fig*) to arouse; *Bedarf* to create; *Erinnerungen* to bring back; **sich ~ lassen** to have sb wake one up; (*telefonisch*) to get an alarm call

Wecken[1] [ˈvɛkn] NT **-s**, NO PL waking-up time; (*Mil*) reveille; **Ausgang bis zum ~** overnight leave (until reveille)

Wecken[2] M **-s, -** (*dial*) (bread) roll

Wecker [ˈvɛkɐ] M **-s, -** alarm clock; **jdm auf den ~ fallen** *or* **gehen** (*inf*) to get on sb's nerves

Weck-: [ˈvɛk-]: **Weckglas**® NT preserving *or* Kilner® (*Brit*) jar; **Weckring**® M rubber ring (*for preserving jars*); **Weckruf** M (*Telec*) alarm call; (*Mil*) reveille

Wedel [ˈveːdl] M **-s, -** fly whisk; (= *Fächer*) fan; (= *Staubwedel aus Federn*) feather duster; (= *Zweig*) twig

wedeln [ˈveːdln] **1** VI **(a)** (**mit dem Schwanz**) **~** (*Hund*) to wag its tail; **mit etw ~** (= *winken*) to wave sth **(b)** (*Ski*) to wedel; **das Wedeln** wedel(l)ing **2** VT to waft

weder [ˈveːdɐ] CONJ **~ ... noch ...** neither ... nor ...; **~ das eine noch das andere** (*als Antwort*) neither

weg [vɛk] ADV (= *fort*) **~ sein** (= *fortgegangen, abgefahren, verschwunden*) to have gone; (= *nicht hier, entfernt*) to be away; (*inf*) (= *geistesabwesend*) to be not quite with it (*inf*); (= *begeistert*) to be bowled over (*von* by); **von zu Hause ~ sein** to be away from home; (*erwachsene Kinder*) to have left home; **über etw** (*acc*) **~ sein** (*inf*) to have got over sth; **über den Tisch ~** across the table; **über meinen Kopf ~** over my head; **weit ~ von hier** far (away) from here; **~ mit euch!** away with you!; **nichts wie** *or* **nur ~ von hier!** let's scram (*inf*); **~ da!** (get) out of the way!; **~ damit!** (*mit Schere etc*) put it away!; **immer ~ damit** throw it all out!; **~ mit den alten Traditionen!** away with these old traditions!; **Hände ~!** hands off!

Weg [veːk] M **-(e)s, -e** [-ɡə] **(a)** (= *Pfad*) (*fig*) path; (= *Straße*) road; **am ~e** by the wayside; **jdm in den ~ treten, jdm den ~ versperren** *or* **verstellen** to block sb's way; **jdm/einer Sache im ~ stehen** (*fig*) to stand in the way of sb/sth; **sich selbst im ~ stehen** (*fig*) to be one's own worst enemy; **jdm Hindernisse** *or* **Steine in den ~ legen** to put obstructions in sb's way; **den ~ des geringsten Widerstandes gehen** to follow the line of least resistance; **der ~ zur Hölle ist mit guten Vorsätzen gepflastert** (*Prov*) the road to Hell is paved with good intentions (*prov*)

(b) (*lit, fig*: = *Route*) way; (= *Entfernung*) distance; (= *Reise*) journey; (*zu Fuß*) walk; (= *Bildungsweg*) road; (= *Methode*) method; **ich muss diesen ~ jeden Tag zweimal gehen/fahren** I have to walk/drive this stretch twice a day; **auf dem ~ nach London/zur Arbeit** on the way to London/work; **sich auf den ~ machen** to set off; **6 km ~** 6 kms away; **mein erster ~ war zur Bank** the first thing I did was go to the bank; **den falschen/richtigen ~ einschlagen** to follow the wrong/right path *or* (*fig*) avenue; **jdn etw mit auf den ~ geben** (*lit*) to give sb sth to take with him/her *etc*; **jdm einen guten Rat mit auf den ~ geben** to give sb good advice to follow in life; **jdm/einer Sache aus dem ~ gehen** (*lit*) to get out of sb's way/the way of sth; (*fig*) to avoid sb/sth; **jdm über den ~ laufen** (*fig*) to run into sb; **seinen ~ (im Leben/Beruf) machen** (*fig*) to make one's way in life/one's career; **etw in die ~e leiten** to arrange sth; **jdm/sich den ~ verbauen** to ruin sb's chances (*für* of); **auf dem besten ~ sein, etw zu tun** to be well on the way to doing sth; **auf welchem ~ kommt man am schnellsten zu Geld?** what's the fastest way of making money?; **auf welchem ~**

---

sind Sie zu erreichen? how can I get in touch with you?; **auf diesem ~e** this way; **auf diplomatischem ~e** through diplomatic channels; **auf gesetzlichem** *or* **legalem ~e** legally; **zu ~e = zuwege**

(c) (*inf*: = *Besorgung*) errand

weg-: [ˈvɛk-]: **wegbekommen** ptp **wegbekommen** VT SEP IRREG **(a)** (= *entfernen, loswerden*) to get rid of (*von* from); *Klebstoff, Fleck etc* to remove (*von* from); (*von bestimmtem Ort*) *jdn, Hund* to get away (*von* from) **(b)** (*inf*: = *erhalten*) to get; *Grippe* to catch; **wegblasen** VT SEP IRREG to blow away; **wie weggeblasen sein** (*fig*) to have vanished; **wegbleiben** VI SEP IRREG AUX SEIN to stay away; (= *nicht mehr kommen*) to stop coming; (*Satz, Wort etc*) to be left out; **mir bleibt die Spucke** *or* **Luft weg!** (*inf*) I'm absolutely speechless; **wegbringen** VT SEP IRREG to take away; (*zur Reparatur*) to take in; **wegdürfen** VI SEP IRREG to be allowed to go; (*inf*: = *ausgehen dürfen*) to be allowed to go out

wegen [ˈveːɡn] PREP +GEN *or* (*INF*) +DAT because of; **jdn ~ einer Sache bestrafen/verurteilen/entlassen** *etc* to punish/sentence/dismiss *etc* sb for sth; **von ~!** (*inf*) you've got to be kidding!; **er ist krank – von ~ krank!** (*inf*) he's ill – since when? (*iro*)

Wegerich [ˈveːɡərɪç] M **-s, -e** (*Bot*) plantain

wegessen [ˈvɛk-] VT SEP IRREG **jdm den Kuchen** *etc* **~** to eat sb's cake *etc*; **er hat (mir) alles weggegessen** he's eaten all my food

wegfahren [ˈvɛk-] **1** VI SEP IRREG AUX SEIN (= *abfahren*) to leave; (*Auto, Bus, Fahrer*) to drive off; (*im Boot*) to sail away; (*zum Einkaufen, als Ausflug*) to go out; (= *verreisen*) to go away **2** VT *Menschen, Gegenstände* to take away; *Fahrzeug* to drive away; (= *umstellen*) to move

Wegfahrsperre [ˈvɛk-] F (*Aut*) (**elektronische**) **~** (electronic) immobilizer

wegfallen [ˈvɛk-] VI SEP IRREG AUX SEIN to be discontinued; (*Arbeitsplätze*) to be lost; (*Kontrollen*) to be removed; (*Bestimmung, Regelung*) to cease to apply; (= *ausgelassen werden*) to be omitted; **~ lassen** to discontinue; (= *auslassen*) to omit; **wir haben den Nachtisch ~ lassen** we did without dessert

weg-: [ˈvɛk-]: **wegfliegen** VI SEP IRREG AUX SEIN to fly away; (*Hut*) to fly off; (*mit Flugzeug*) to fly out; **wann bist du denn in Frankfurt weggeflogen?** when did you fly out of Frankfurt?; **wegfressen** VT SEP (*inf*) siehe **wegessen**

Weggabelung [ˈvɛk-] F fork (in the road)

Weggang [ˈvɛkɡaŋ] M, NO PL departure

weg-: [ˈvɛk-]: **weggeben** VT SEP IRREG (= *verschenken*) to give away; (*in Pflege geben*) to have looked after; **eine kaputte Uhr ~** to take in a broken watch; **seine Wäsche (zum Waschen) ~** to have one's washing done; **weggehen** VI SEP IRREG AUX SEIN to go; (= *verreisen, umziehen etc*) to go away; (= *ausgehen*) to go out; (*inf*) (*Fleck*) to come off; (*Ware*) to sell; **über etw** (*acc*) **~** (*inf*) to ignore sth; **aus Heidelberg/aus dem Büro/von der Firma/von zu Hause ~** to leave Heidelberg/the office/the firm/home; **weghaben** VT SEP IRREG (*inf*) (= *erledigt haben*) to have got done; (= *entfernt haben*) *Fleck etc* to have got rid of (*inf*); **jdn/etw ~ wollen** (*inf*) to want to get rid of sb/sth; **du hast deine Strafe/deinen Denkzettel weg** you have had your punishment; **weghelfen** VI SEP IRREG **jdm über etw** (*acc*) **~** (*fig*) to help sb (to) get over sth; **weghören** VI SEP not to listen; **wegjagen** VT SEP to chase away; (*aus Land*) to drive out; **wegknacken** VT SEP (*sl*: = *einschlafen*) to crash (out) (*inf*)

wegkommen [ˈvɛk-] VI SEP IRREG AUX SEIN **(a)** (*inf*) (= *entfernt werden*) to go; (= *abhanden kommen*) to disappear; (= *weggehen können*) to get away; (*aus dem Haus*) to get out; **was ich nicht brauche, kommt weg** what I don't want can go; **mach, dass du wegkommst!** hop it! (*inf*); **gut/schlecht (bei etw) ~** to come off well/badly (with sth); **über etw** (*acc*) **~/nicht ~** to get over/be unable to get over sth; **ich komme nicht darüber weg, dass ...** (*inf*) I can't get over the fact that ... **(b)** (*dial*: = *herkommen*) to come from

weg-: [ˈvɛk-]: **weglassen** VT SEP IRREG (= *auslassen*) to leave out; (= *nicht benutzen*) not to use; (*inf*: = *gehen lassen*) to let go; **ich lasse heute den Zucker im Kaffee weg** I won't take any sugar in my coffee today; **weglaufen** VI SEP IRREG AUX SEIN to run away (*vor* +*dat* from); **das läuft (dir) nicht weg!** (*fig hum*) that can wait; **weglegen** VT SEP (*in Schublade etc*) to put away; (*zur Seite, zum späteren Verbrauch*) to put aside; **wegmachen** VT SEP (*inf*) to get rid of; **sie ließ sich** (*dat*) **das Kind ~** (*sl*) she got rid of the baby (*inf*)

wegmüssen ['vɛk-] VI SEP IRREG to have to go; (= *entfernt werden*) to have to be removed; **ich muss eine Zeit lang von/aus New York weg** I must get away from/get out of New York for a while; **du musst da weg, du behinderst ja den ganzen Verkehr** you'll have to move (from there), you're blocking all the traffic; **die paar Reste müssen weg** we/you *etc* can't leave those little bits

Wegnahme ['vɛkna:mə] F -, NO PL taking; (= *Entziehung*) taking away; (*von Sicht*) blocking

wegnehmen ['vɛk-] VT SEP IRREG to take (*auch Chess*); (= *fortnehmen, entfernen, entziehen*) to take away; (= *verdecken*) *Licht, Sonne* to block out; *Aussicht, Sicht* to block; (= *beanspruchen*) *Zeit, Platz* to take up; **Gas ~** (*Aut*) to ease off the accelerator *or* gas (*US*); **fünf Tage vom Urlaub ~** to take five days off the holiday (*esp Brit*) *or* vacation (*US*); **jdm seine Kinder ~** to take sb's children away (from him/her); **jdm seine Frau ~** to steal sb's wife

Wegrand ['ve:k-] M wayside

weg- ['vɛk-]: **wegrationalisieren** *ptp* **wegrationalisiert** VT SEP *Arbeitsplätze* to rationalize away; **wegräumen** VT SEP to clear away; (*in Schrank*) to put away; **wegrennen** VI SEP IRREG AUX SEIN (*inf*) to run away; **wegrücken** VTI SEP (*vi: aux sein*) to move away; **wegschaffen** VT SEP (= *beseitigen, loswerden*) to get rid of; (= *wegräumen*) to clear away; (= *wegtragen, wegfahren*) to remove; (= *erledigen*) *Arbeit* to get done; **wegschauen** VI SEP (*esp dial*) = **wegsehen**

Wegscheide ['ve:k-] F parting of the ways (*liter*)

weg- ['vɛk-]: **wegschicken** VT SEP *Brief etc* to send off; *jdn* to send away; (*um etwas zu holen etc*) to send off; **wegschließen** VT SEP IRREG to lock away; **wegschmeißen** VT SEP IRREG (*inf*) to chuck away (*inf*); **wegschnappen** VT SEP (*inf*) **jdm etw ~** to snatch sth (away) from sb; **die andere Kundin hat mir das Kleid weggeschnappt** the other customer snapped up the dress before I could; **jdm die Freundin/den Job ~** to pinch (*Brit*) *or* snatch (*US*) sb's girlfriend/job (*inf*); **wegschütten** VT SEP to tip away; **wegschwemmen** VT SEP to wash away; **wegsehen** VI SEP IRREG to look away; **über etw** (*acc*) **~** (*lit*) to look over sth; (*fig inf*) to overlook sth; **wegsetzen** VR SEP to move away; **sich über etw** (*acc*) **~** (*inf*) to ignore sth; **wegstecken** VT SEP (*lit*) to put away; (*inf*) *Niederlage, Kritik* to take; *Enttäuschung, Verlust* to get over; **wegstehlen** VR SEP IRREG to steal away; **wegstellen** VT SEP to put away; (= *abstellen*) to put down; **wegsterben** VI SEP IRREG AUX SEIN (*inf*) to die off; **jdm ~** to die on sb (*inf*); **wegstoßen** VT SEP IRREG to push away; (*mit Fuß*) to kick away; **wegtragen** VT SEP IRREG to carry away; **wegtun** VT SEP IRREG to put away; (= *wegwerfen*) to throw away; (= *verstecken*) to hide away; **tu die Hände weg!** take your hands off!

Weg- ['ve:k-]: **Wegwarte** F (*Bot*) chicory; **wegweisend** ADJ pioneering *attr*, revolutionary; **Wegweiser** ['ve:kvaizɐ] M -s, - sign; (*an einem Pfosten*) signpost; (*fig: Buch etc*) guide

Wegwerf- ['vɛkvɛrf] IN CPDS disposable

weg- ['vɛk-]: **wegwerfen** VT SEP IRREG to throw away; **weggeworfenes Geld** money down the drain; **wegwerfend** ADJ dismissive

Wegwerf-: **Wegwerfgesellschaft** F throwaway society; **Wegwerfverpackung** F disposable packaging

weg- ['vɛk-]: **wegwischen** VT SEP to wipe off; (*fig*) to dismiss; **wegwollen** VI SEP IRREG (= *verreisen*) to want to go away; (= *weggehen von Haus, Party etc*) to want to leave; (= *hinausgehen*) to want to go out; **wegziehen** SEP IRREG VT to pull away (*jdm from sb*); *Vorhang* to draw back VI AUX SEIN to move away; (*Vögel*) to migrate

weh [ve:] ADJ (a) (= *wund*) sore (b) **~ tun** *siehe* **wehtun** INTERJ **o ~!** oh dear!; **~ mir, wenn ...** woe betide me if ...

wehe ['ve:ə] INTERJ **~ (dir), wenn du das tust** you'll be sorry if you do that; **darf ich das anfassen? - ~ (dir)!** can I touch? - you dare! (*inf*); **~ dem, der ...!** woe betide anyone who ...!

Wehe ['ve:ə] F -, -n (a) (= *Schneewehe etc*) drift (b) **Wehen** PL (*lit:* = *Geburtswehen*) (labour (*Brit*) *or* labor (*US*)) pains *pl*; (*fig*) birth pangs *pl*; **in den ~n liegen** to be in labour (*Brit*) *or* labor (*US*); **die ~n setzten ein** the contractions started, she went into labour (*Brit*) *or* labor (*US*)

wehen ['ve:ən] VI (a) (*Wind*) to blow; (*Fahne*) to wave; (*Haare*) to blow about; **es weht ein warmer Wind** there's a warm wind (blowing); **kein Lüftchen wehte** there wasn't even a breeze (b) AUX SEIN (*Geruch, Klang*) to drift; (*Duft*) to waft

Wehenschreiber M tocograph (*spec*)

Weh-: **wehleidig** ADJ over-sensitive to pain; (= *jammernd*) whining *attr*; (= *voller Selbstmitleid*) sorry for oneself; **er ist ja so ~** he whines at the least little thing; he's always feeling sorry for himself; **Wehleidigkeit** F self-pity; **wehmütig** ['ve:my:tɪç] ADJ melancholy; (= *sehnsuchtsvoll*) wistful; (= *nostalgisch*) nostalgic ADV (= *traurig*) sadly; (= *sehnsuchtsvoll*) wistfully; (= *nostalgisch*) nostalgically; **du wirst dich noch ~ nach mir zurücksehnen** you'll miss me terribly

Wehr[1] [ve:ɐ] F -, -en **sich zur ~ setzen** to defend oneself

Wehr[2] NT -(e)s, -e weir

Wehr- IN CPDS defence (*Brit*), defense (*US*); **Wehrbeauftragte(r)** MF DECL AS ADJ commissioner for the armed forces; **Wehrdienst** M military service; **seinen ~ (ab)leisten** to do one's military service; **jdn zum ~ einberufen** to call sb up (*Brit*), to draft sb (*US*); **Wehrdienstverweigerer** M, **Wehrdienstverweigerin** F conscientious objector

wehren ['ve:rən] VR to defend oneself; (= *sich aktiv widersetzen*) to (put up a) fight; **sich gegen einen Plan** *etc* **~** to fight (against) a plan *etc*; **dagegen weiß ich mich zu ~** I know how to deal with that VI +DAT (*geh*) to fight; (= *Einhalt gebieten*) to check; **wehret den Anfängen!** these things must be nipped in the bud

Wehr-: **Wehrersatzdienst** M alternative national service; **Wehrexperte** M, **Wehrexpertin** F defence (*Brit*) *or* defense (*US*) expert; **wehrlos** ADJ defenceless (*Brit*), defenseless (*US*); (*fig: gegenüber Gemeinheiten etc*) helpless ADV defencelessly (*Brit*), defenselessly (*US*), helplessly; **jdm ~ ausgeliefert sein** to be at sb's mercy; **Wehrlosigkeit** F -, NO PL defencelessness (*Brit*), defenselessness (*US*); (*fig: gegenüber Gemeinheiten etc*) helplessness; **Wehrmacht** F armed forces *pl*; (*Hist*) Wehrmacht; **Wehrpflicht** F (*allgemeine*) **~** (*universal*) conscription; **Wehrsportgruppe** F paramilitary group

wehtun VT SEP IRREG (*lit, fig*) to hurt; **mir tut der Rücken weh** my back hurts; **mir tut mein verbrannter Finger weh** my finger is sore where I burned it; **sich/jdm ~** (*lit, fig*) to hurt oneself/sb; **was tut dir denn nun schon wieder weh?** what's the matter now?; **wo tut es denn weh?** (*fig inf*) what's up? (*inf*)

Wehwehchen [ve:'ve:çən, 've:-] NT -s, - (*inf*) (minor) complaint; **seine tausend ~** all his little aches and pains

Weib [vaip] NT -(e)s, -er [-bɐ] woman; **sie ist ein tolles ~** (*inf*) she's quite a woman

Weibchen ['vaipçən] NT -s, - (*Zool*) female; (*hum:* = *Ehefrau*) little woman (*hum*); (*pej:* = *nicht emanzipierte Frau*) dumb female

Weiber-: **Weiberfastnacht** F *day during the carnival period when women assume control*; **Weiberheld** M (*pej*) lady-killer; **Weiberkram** M (*pej*) women's stuff (*inf*)

weibisch ['vaibɪʃ] ADJ effeminate

Weiblein ['vaiplain] NT -s, - little woman; **ein altes ~** a little old woman

weiblich ['vaiplɪç] ADJ (*Zool, Bot,* = *von Frauen*) female; (*Gram, Poet:* = *fraulich, wie Frauen*) feminine

Weiblichkeit F -, NO PL femininity; (= *Frauen*) women *pl*; **die holde ~** (*hum*) the fair sex

Weib(s)stück NT (*pej*) bitch (*inf*)

weich [vaiç] ADJ soft (*auch fig, Ling, Phot*); *Ei* soft-boiled; *Fleisch, Gemüse* tender; *Energietechnik* non-nuclear; (= *mitleidig*) soft-hearted; **~e Drogen** soft drugs; **~ werden** (*lit, fig*) to soften; **die Knie wurden mir ~** my knees turned to jelly; **~ machen** to soften; **eine ~e Birne** *or* **einen ~en Keks haben** (*inf*) to be soft in the head (*inf*); **~e Währung** soft currency ADV softly; **~ geklopft** *Fleisch* hammered tender; **~ gekocht** *Ei* soft-boiled; *Fleisch, Gemüse* boiled until tender; *Nudeln* cooked until soft; **die Kupplung ~ kommen lassen** to let out the clutch smoothly; **~ landen** to land softly; (= *auf ~em Untergrund*) to have a soft landing

Weiche F -, -n (*Rail*) points *pl* (*Brit*), switch (*US*); **die ~n stellen** (*lit*) to switch the points (*Brit*), to change the switch (*US*); (*fig*) to set the course

Weichei NT (*pej sl:* = *Weichling, Feigling*) wimp (*inf*)

weichen[1] VTI (*vi: aux haben or sein*) to soak

weichen[2] ['vaiçn], *pret* **wich** [vɪç], *ptp* **gewichen** [gə'vɪçn] VI AUX SEIN (a) (= *weggehen, verlassen*) to move; (= *zurückweichen*) to retreat (+*dat, vor* +*dat* from); (= *Platz machen, fig:* = *nachgeben*) to give way (+*dat* to); **nicht von jdm** *or* **jds Seite**

~ not to leave sb's side; **sie wich nicht von der Stelle** she refused to budge (an inch); **die Begeisterung ist der Ernüchterung gewichen** enthusiasm has given way to disillusionment
(b) (*Gefühl, Druck, Schmerz*) (= *nachlassen*) to ease; (= *verschwinden*) to go

Weichheit F **-**, NO PL softness (*auch fig, Ling, Phot*); (*von Fleisch, Gemüse*) tenderness

Weich-: weichherzig ADJ soft-hearted; **Weichherzigkeit** ['vaiçhertsıçkait] F **-**, NO PL soft-heartedness; **Weichholz** NT softwood; **Weichkäse** M soft cheese

weichlich ['vaiçlıç] ◼ ADJ (*lit*) soft; (*fig*) weak; (= *weibisch*) effeminate; (= *verhätschelt*) soft ◼ ADV **ein Kind zu ~ erziehen** to pamper a child

Weichling ['vaiçlıŋ] M **-s**, **-e** (*pej*) weakling

Weich-: weich machen VT (*fig*) to soften up; **Weichmacher** M (*Chem*) softener

Weichsel ['vaiksl] F **-** Vistula

Weichselkirsche ['vaiksl-] F St Lucie cherry

Weich-: weichspülen VT SEP to condition; *Wäsche* to use (fabric) conditioner on; **Weichspüler** M conditioner; **Weichteile** PL soft parts *pl*; (*inf*: = *Geschlechtsteile*) private parts *pl*; **Weichtier** NT mollusc

Weide¹ ['vaidə] F **-**, **-n** (*Bot*) willow

Weide² F **-**, **-n** (*Agr*) pasture; (= *Wiese*) meadow; **auf der ~ sein** to be grazing

Weideland NT (*Agr*) pasture(land)

weiden ['vaidn] ◼ VI to graze ◼ VT to (put out to) graze; **seine Blicke** *or* **Augen an etw** (*dat*) **~** to feast one's eyes on sth ◼ VR **sich an etw** (*dat*) **~** (*fig*) to revel in sth; (*sadistisch auch*) to gloat over sth

Weiden-: Weidenkätzchen NT pussy willow; **Weidenkorb** M wicker basket

weidlich ['vaitlıç] ADV (*mit adj*) pretty; **sich über etw** (*acc*) **~ amüsieren** to be highly amused at sth; **etw ~ ausnutzen** to make full use of sth; **er hat sich ~ bemüht** he tried pretty hard

weidmännisch [-menıʃ] ◼ ADJ huntsman's *attr*; **das ist nicht ~** that's not done in hunting ◼ ADV in a huntsman's manner; *ausgebildet* as a huntsman

weigern ['vaigən] VR to refuse

Weigerung ['vaigərʊŋ] F **-**, **-en** refusal

Weihbischof M suffragan bishop

Weihe F **-**, **-n** (*Eccl*) consecration; (= *Priesterweihe*) ordination; **die niederen/höheren ~n** minor/major orders; **höhere ~n** (*fig*) greater glory

weihen ['vaiən] VT **(a)** (*Eccl*) to consecrate; *Priester* to ordain; **jdn zum Bischof ~** to consecrate sb (as a) bishop; **jdn zum Priester ~** to ordain sb (as a) priest **(b)** (= *widmen*) **etw jdm/ einer Sache ~** to dedicate sth to sb/sth; **dem Tod(e)/ Untergang geweiht** doomed (to die/fall)

Weiher ['vaiə] M **-s**, **-** pond

Weihnacht ['vainaxt] F **-**, NO PL **= Weihnachten**

weihnachten ['vainaxtn] VI IMPERS (*poetiro*) **es weihnachtet sehr** Christmas is very much in evidence

Weihnachten ['vainaxtn] NT **-**, **-** Christmas; (*geschrieben auch*) Xmas (*inf*); **fröhliche** *or* **gesegnete** *or* **schöne** *or* **frohe(s)** *or* **ein fröhliches ~!** happy (*esp Brit*) *or* merry Christmas!; **(zu** *or* **an) ~** at Christmas; **(zu** *or* **an) ~ nach Hause fahren** to go home for Christmas; **etw zu ~ bekommen** to get sth for Christmas; **etw zu ~ schenken** to give sth as a Christmas present; **weiße ~** (a) white Christmas; **grüne ~** (a) Christmas without snow; **das ist ein Gefühl wie ~** (*iro inf*) it's an odd feeling

weihnachtlich ['vainaxtlıç] ◼ ADJ Christmassy (*inf*), festive ◼ ADV *geschmückt* festively; **~ gestimmt sein** to be feeling Christmassy (*inf*)

Weihnachts- IN CPDS Christmas; **Weihnachtsabend** M Christmas Eve; **Weihnachtsbaum** M Christmas tree; **Weihnachtsfeier** F Christmas celebration(s *pl*); **Weihnachtsfeiertag** M (*erster*) Christmas Day; (*zweiter*) Boxing Day; **Weihnachtsfest** NT Christmas; **Weihnachtsgans** F Christmas goose; **jdn ausnehmen wie eine ~** (*inf*) to fleece sb (*inf*); **Weihnachtsgeld** NT Christmas money; (= *Weihnachtsgratifikation*) Christmas bonus; (*für Briefträger etc*) Christmas box; **Weihnachtsgeschenk** NT Christmas present; **Weihnachtsgratifikation** F Christmas bonus; **Weihnachtsinsel** F Christmas Island; **Weihnachtskaktus** M

(*Bot*) Christmas cactus; **Weihnachtskarte** F Christmas card; **Weihnachtslied** NT (Christmas) carol; **Weihnachtsmann** M, *pl* **-männer** Father Christmas (*Brit*), Santa Claus; **Weihnachtsmärchen** NT (Christmas) pantomime; **Weihnachtsmarkt** M Christmas fair

Weihnachts-: Weihnachtsstern M **(a)** (*Bot*) poinsettia **(b)** (*Rel*) star of Bethlehem; **Weihnachtstag** M **= Weihnachtsfeiertag**; **Weihnachtsteller** M *plate of biscuits, chocolates etc*; **Weihnachtstisch** M table for Christmas presents; **Weihnachtszeit** F Christmas (time)

Weih-: Weihrauch M incense; **Weihwasser** NT, NO PL holy water

weil [vail] CONJ because

Weilchen ['vailçən] NT **-s**, **-** **ein ~** a (little) while

Weile ['vailə] F **-**, NO PL while; **wir können eine ~ Karten spielen** we could play cards for a while; **vor einer (ganzen) ~, eine (ganze) ~ her** quite a while ago

Weiler ['vailə] M **-s**, **-** hamlet

Weimarer Republik [vaima:re] F Weimar Republic

Wein [vain] M **-(e)s**, **-e** wine; (*no pl*: **= ~stöcke**) vines *pl*; (*no pl*: **= ~trauben**) grapes *pl*; **offener ~** draught (*Brit*) *or* draft (*US*) wine; **wilder ~** Virginia creeper; **jdm reinen** *or* **klaren ~ einschenken** to tell sb the truth

Wein- IN CPDS (*auf Getränk bezogen*) wine; (*auf Pflanze bezogen*) vine; **Weinbau** M, NO PL wine growing; **Weinbauer** M, *pl* **-bauern**, **Weinbäuerin** F wine grower; **Weinbeere** F grape; (= *Rosine*) raisin; **Weinberg** M vineyard; **Weinbergschnecke** F snail; (*auf Speisekarte*) escargot; **Weinbrand** M brandy

weinen ['vainən] VTI to cry; **etw nass ~** to make sth wet with one's tears; **sich** (*dat*) **die Augen rot ~**, **sich** (*dat*) **die Augen aus dem Kopf ~** to cry one's eyes out; **es ist zum Weinen!**, **man könnte ~!** it's enough to make you weep! (*esp Brit*); **es ist zum Weinen mit dieser Frau** that woman is enough to make you want to cry; **leise ~d** crying softly; (*inf*: = *kleinlaut*) rather subdued; (*inf*: = *resigniert*) resignedly

Weinerei [vainə'rai] F **-**, NO PL (*inf*) crying

weinerlich ['vainɐlıç] ◼ ADJ whining ◼ ADV whinily; **~ reden/ sagen** to whine

Wein-: Weinernte F grape harvest; **Weinessig** M wine vinegar; **Weingegend** F wine-growing area; **Weingummi** NT *or* M wine gum; **Weingut** NT wine-growing estate; **Weinhandlung** F wine shop (*esp Brit*) *or* store; **Weinhauer(in)** M(F) (*esp Aus*) wine grower; **Weinjahr** NT **ein gutes/schlechtes ~** a good/bad year for wine; **Weinkarte** F wine list; **Weinkeller** M wine cellar; (= *Lokal*) wine bar; **Weinkenner(in)** M(F) connoisseur of wine

Weinkrampf M crying fit; (*Med*) uncontrollable fit of crying

Wein-: Weinkraut NT sauerkraut; **Weinlaub** NT vine leaves *pl*; **Weinlaune** F **in einer ~ beschlossen sie ...** after a few glasses of wine they decided ...; **Weinlese** F grape harvest; **Weinlokal** NT wine bar; **Weinprobe** F wine tasting; **Weinrebe** F (grape)vine; **weinrot** ADJ claret; **Weinsorte** F sort of wine; **Weinstein** M tartar; **Weinstock** M vine; **Weinstube** F wine tavern; **Weintraube** F grape; **Weinzierl** [-tsiːɐl] M **-s, -(n)** (Aus) wine grower

weise [ˈvaizə] ADJ wise

Weise [ˈvaizə] F **-, -n** (= Verfahren etc) way; **auf diese ~** in this way; **auf geheimnisvolle** etc **~** in a mysterious etc way, mysteriously etc; **in gewisser/keiner** or **keinster** (inf) **~** in a/no way

-weise [vaizə] ADV SUF (an Substantiv) as a ...; (bei Maßangabe) by the ...; (an Adjektiv) -ly; **ausnahmsweise** as an exception; **meterweise** by the metre (Brit) or meter (US); **bedauerlicherweise** regrettably; **er hat mir netterweise ...** it was kind of him to ...

weisen [ˈvaizn], pret **wies** [viːs], ptp **gewiesen** [gəˈviːzn] (geh) ◨ VT **jdm etw ~** (lit, fig) to show sb sth; **jdn vom Feld** or **Platz ~** (Sport) to order sb off (the field); **jdn von der Schule ~** to expel sb (from school); **etw (weit) von sich ~** (fig) to reject sth (emphatically) ◨ VI to point (nach towards, auf +acc at)

Weise(r) [ˈvaizə] MF DECL AS ADJ wise man/woman; **die drei ~n aus dem Morgenland** the three Wise Men from the East; **die Fünf ~n** (Ger Pol) panel of five experts advising government on economic policy

DIE FÜNF WEISEN

Die Fünf Weisen is the popular name of the Sachverständigenrat zur Begutachtung der gesamtwirtschaftlichen Entwicklung. This is an independent body, set up in 1964 and consisting of five recognized economists appointed by the Bundespräsident for a period of five years. Each year they present a report on the economy and the likely course of its development. ▶ BUNDESPRÄSIDENT

Weisheit [ˈvaishait] F **-, -en (a)** NO PL wisdom; **das war der ~ letzter Schluss** that was all they/we etc came up with; **das ist auch nicht der ~ letzter Schluss** that's not exactly the ideal solution; **er glaubt, er hat die ~ gepachtet** or **mit Löffeln gegessen** or **gefressen** he thinks he knows it all **(b)** (= weiser Spruch) wise saying, pearl of wisdom (usu iro); **eine alte ~** a wise old saying

Weisheitszahn M wisdom tooth

weismachen [ˈvais-] VT SEP **jdm etw ~** to make sb believe sth; **wie konnten sie ihm ~, dass ...?** how could they fool him into believing that ...?; **das kannst du mir nicht ~!** you can't expect me to believe that

weiß[1] [vais] ◨ ADJ white; **ein ~es (Blatt) Papier** a blank sheet of paper; **ein ~er Fleck (auf der Landkarte)** a blank area (on the map); **das Weiße Haus** the White House; **~ wie Kreide** or **die Wand** white as chalk or a sheet; **das Weiße des Eis** or **vom Ei** egg white; **das Weiße von drei Eiern** the white(s) of three eggs ◨ ADV (mit ~er Farbe) anstreichen, lackieren white; tapezieren auch, einrichten, sich kleiden, umranden in white; **~ glühend** white-hot

weiß[2] [vais] 3. PERS SING PRES von **wissen**

Weis-: weissagen [ˈvais-] VT INSEP to prophesy; **Weissagung** [ˈvaizaːɡʊŋ] F **-, -en** prophecy

Weiß-: Weißbier NT light, fizzy beer made using top-fermentation yeast; **weißblau** ADJ (inf: = bayrisch) Bavarian; (farblich) in the Bavarian colours (Brit) or colors (US); **Weißblech** NT tinplate; **weißblond** ADJ ash blond(e); **Weißbrot** NT white bread; (= Laib) loaf of white bread

weißen [ˈvaisn] VT to whiten; (= weiß tünchen) to whitewash

Weiße(r) [ˈvaizə] MF DECL AS ADJ white, white man/woman; **die ~n** white people

Weiß-: weißglühend ADJ siehe **weiß**; **Weißglut** F white heat; **jdn zur ~ bringen, jdn bis zur ~ reizen** to make sb livid (with rage); **Weißgold** NT white gold; **weißhaarig** ADJ white-haired

Weißheit [ˈvaishait] F **-,** NO PL whiteness

Weiß-: Weißherbst M ≈ rosé; **Weißkabis** M (Sw) white cabbage; **Weißkäse** M (dial) quark; **Weißkohl** M, (S Ger, Aus) **Weißkraut** NT white cabbage

weißlich [ˈvaislɪç] ADJ whitish

Weiß-: Weißmacher M (in Waschmittel) brightening agent; (in Papier) whitener; **Weißrusse** M, **Weißrussin** F White Russian;

weißrussisch ADJ White Russian; **Weißrussland** NT White Russia; **Weißwein** M white wine; **Weißwurst** F veal sausage; **Weißzeug** NT, NO PL linen

Weisung [ˈvaizʊŋ] F **-, -en** directive; (Jur) ruling; **auf ~** on instructions

Weisungs-: Weisungsbefugnis F authority to issue directives; **weisungsberechtigt** ADJ (Jur) authorized to issue directives; **Weisungsrecht** NT authority to issue directives

---

weit [vait]

◨ ADJEKTIV	◨ ADVERB

◨ ADJEKTIV

Siehe auch Einträge **weitere, weitgehend, weitreichend, weitverbreitet**.

(a) (= breit) wide; Pupille dilated; Meer open; Begriff broad; Unterschied, Herz big; **weite Kreise** or **Teile der Bevölkerung** large sections of the population

(b) (= lang) Weg, Reise, Wurf etc long; **in weiten Abständen** widely spaced; (zeitlich) at long intervals; **man hat hier einen weiten Blick** or **eine weite Sicht** you can see a long way from here; **in weiter Ferne** a long way away

◆**so weit sein** (= bereit) to be ready; **es ist/war bald so weit** the time has/had nearly come; **wie lange dauert es noch, bis der Film anfängt? – es ist gleich so weit** how long will it be till the film starts? – not long, it'll start any minute now

◨ ADVERB

(a) (Entfernung) far; **weiter** further; **am weitesten** (the) furthest; **Bremen ist 10 km weit** Bremen is 10 kms away; **es ist noch weit bis Bremen** it's still a long way to Bremen; **3,60 m weit springen** to jump 3m 60; **wie weit bist du gesprungen?** how far did you jump?; **(sehr) weit springen/fahren** to jump/drive a (very) long way; **weit gereist** widely travelled (Brit) or traveled (US); **weit hergeholt** far-fetched; **weit und breit** for miles around; **weit ab** or **weg (von)** far away (from); **weit am Anfang/Ende/Rand** right at the beginning/end/edge; **ziemlich weit am Ende** fairly near the end; **von weitem** from a long way away; **von weit her** from a long way away; **weit schauend** or **blickend** far-sighted

◆**weit entfernt** a long way away; **weiter entfernt** further away; **ich bin weit davon entfernt, das zu tun** I have no intention of doing that; **weit entfernt** or **gefehlt!** far from it! **(b)** (= breit) offen, öffnen wide; verzweigt, herumkommen widely; **10 cm weit** 10cm wide; **weit verbreitet** widespread; **weit ausholend** Geste etc expansive; (fig) Erzählung etc long-drawn-out

(c) (in Entwicklung) **weit fortgeschritten** far advanced; **wie weit bist du?** how far have you got?; **so weit, so gut** so far so good; **sie sind nicht weit gekommen** they didn't get far; **jdn so weit bringen, dass ...** to bring sb to the point where ...

◆**es weit bringen** er wird es weit bringen he will go far; **er hat es weit gebracht** he has achieved a lot; **es so weit bringen, dass ...** to bring it about that ...; **sie hat es so weit gebracht, dass man sie entließ** she drove them to dismiss her

(d) (zeitlich) **es ist noch weit (hin) bis Ostern** Easter is still a long way off; **(bis) weit in die Nacht** (till) far into the night; **weit nach Mitternacht** well after midnight; **weit zurückliegen** to be a long way back

(e) (= erheblich) far; **das hat unsere Erwartungen weit übertroffen** it far exceeded our expectations; **weit über 60** well over 60

(f) (andere Wendungen)

◆**zu weit zu weit gehen** to go too far; **das geht zu weit!** that's going too far!; **das würde zu weit führen** that would be taking things too far

◆**so weit** (= im Großen und Ganzen) by and large; (= bis jetzt) up to now; (= bis zu diesem Punkt) thus far; **so weit ganz gut** (inf) not too bad; **so weit wie** or **als möglich** as far as possible; **ich bin so weit fertig** I'm more or less ready

◆**bei weitem** bei weitem besser etc als far better etc than; **bei weitem der Beste** by far the best; **bei weitem nicht so gut** etc **(wie...)** not nearly as good etc (as ...)

Weit-: **weitab** ['vait'lap] ADV ~ **von** far (away) from; **weitaus** ['vait'laus] ADV (*vor comp*) far; (*vor superl*) (by) far; **weitausholend** ADJ *siehe* **weit**; **Weitblick** M, NO PL (*fig*) vision
Weite[1] ['vaitə] F **-, -n** (= *Entfernung, Ferne*) distance; (= *Länge*) length; (= *Größe*) expanse; (= *Durchmesser, Breite*) width; **in der ~ passt das Hemd** the shirt fits as regards width; **etw in die ~ ziehen** to pull sth out; *Pullover* to stretch sth out
Weite[2] NT **-n**, NO PL distance; **das ~ suchen** to take to one's heels
weiten ['vaitn] **1** VT to widen **2** VR to broaden (*auch fig*); (*Pupille, Gefäße*) to dilate
weiter ['vaitɐ] **1** COMP *von* **weit**
2 ADJ (*fig*) further; (= *zusätzlich auch*) additional; (= *andere*) other; **~e Auskünfte** further information
3 ADV (= *noch hinzu*) further; (= *außerdem*) furthermore; (= *sonst*) otherwise; (= *nachher*) afterwards; **nichts ~, ~ nichts** (= *darüber hinaus nichts*) nothing further or more; **~ nichts?** is that all?; **nichts ~ als ..., ~ nichts als ...** nothing more than ..., nothing but ...; **ich brauche ~ nichts** I don't need anything else; **ich brauche nichts ~ als ...** all I need is ...; **wenn es ~ nichts ist, ...** well, if that's all (it is), ...; **außer uns war ~ niemand** *or* **niemand ~ da** there was nobody else there besides us; **nicht ~, ~ nicht** (= *eigentlich*) not really; **das hat ~ nichts** *or* **nichts ~ zu sagen** that doesn't really matter; **etw ~ tun** to continue to do sth, to continue doing sth; **immer ~** on and on; (*Anweisung*) keep on (going); **er hat sich immer ~ verbessert** he kept on improving; **und ~?** and then?; **und so ~ and so on; und so ~ und so fort** and so on and so forth; *siehe* **Weitere(s)**

Weiter-: **weiterarbeiten** VI SEP *siehe* **weiter-** to carry on *etc* working; **an einer Sache** (*dat*) **~** to do some more work on sth; **weiter bestehen** VI IRREG to continue to exist; **weiterbilden** SEP **1** VT **jdn ~** to educate sb further **2** VR to continue one's education; **Weiterbildung** F continuation of one's education; (*an Hochschule*) further education; **weiterbringen** VT SEP IRREG to take further; **das bringt uns auch nicht weiter** that doesn't get us any further; **weiterempfehlen** ptp **weiterempfohlen** VT SEP IRREG to recommend (to one's friends *etc*); **weiterentwickeln** ptp **weiterentwickelt** SEP **1** VT to develop; *Idee* to develop (further) **2** VR to develop (*zu* into); **Weiterentwicklung** F development; **weitererzählen** ptp **weitererzählt** VT SEP *siehe* **weiter-** to carry on *etc* telling; *Geheimnis etc* to repeat, to pass on; **das hat er der ganzen Klasse weitererzählt** he told the whole class

Weitere(s) ['vaitərə] NT DECL AS ADJ further details *pl*; **ich habe nichts ~s zu sagen** I have nothing further to say; **das ~** the rest; **alles ~** everything else; **bis auf weiteres** for the time being; (*amtlich, auf Schildern etc*) until further notice; **im ~n** subsequently

Weiter-: **weiterfahren** VI SEP IRREG AUX SEIN (= *Fahrt fortsetzen*) to go on; (= *durchfahren*) to drive on; (= *weiterreisen*) to travel on; **Weiterfahrt** F continuation of the/one's journey; **vor der ~ sahen wir ...** before continuing our journey we saw ...; **Weiterflug** M continuation of the/one's flight; **auf dem ~** after we'd taken off again; **Passagiere zum ~ nach ...** passengers continuing their flight to ...; **weiterführen** SEP **1** VT to continue **2** VI to continue; **das führt nicht weiter** (*fig*) that doesn't get us anywhere; **weiterführend** ADJ *Schule* secondary; *Bildungsgang, Qualifikation* higher; *Entwicklung, Lektüre* further; **weitergeben** VT SEP IRREG to pass on; to transmit; **weitergehen** VI SEP IRREG AUX SEIN to go on; **bitte ~!** (*Polizist etc*) move along (there), please!; **so kann es nicht ~** (*fig*) things can't go on like this; **wie soll es nun ~?** (*fig*) what's going to happen now?; **weiterhin** ['vaitɐ'hɪn] ADV **etw ~ tun** to carry on *etc* doing sth; **weiterkommen** VI SEP IRREG AUX SEIN to get further; (*fig auch*) to make progress; **nicht ~** (*fig*) to be stuck; **wir kommen einfach nicht weiter** we're just not getting anywhere; **weiterleiten** VT SEP to pass on (*an +acc* to); (= *weiterbefördern, -senden*) to forward; **weitermachen** VTI SEP to carry on (*etw* with sth); **~!** carry on!; **Weiterreise** F continuation of the/one's journey; **ich wünsche Ihnen eine gute ~** I hope the rest of the journey goes well; **auf der ~ nach ...** when I *etc* was travelling (*Brit*) *or* traveling (*US*) on to ...

weiters ['vaitɐs] ADV (*Aus*) = **ferner**
Weiter-: **weitersagen** VT SEP to repeat; **~!** pass it on!; **nicht ~!** don't tell anyone!; **weiterverarbeiten** ptp **weiterverarbeitet**

VT SEP to process; **Weiterverarbeitung** F reprocessing; **Weiterverkauf** M resale; **nicht zum ~ bestimmt** not for resale; **weitervermieten** ptp **weitervermietet** VT SEP to sublet; **weiterwissen** VI SEP IRREG **nicht (mehr) ~** not to know how to go on; (*bei Rätsel, Prüfung*) to be stuck; (= *verzweifelt sein*) to be at one's wits' end; **weiterzahlen** VTI SEP to continue paying
weitestgehend ['vaitəst-] ADV to the greatest possible extent
weit-: **weitgehend**[1] *comp* **weitgehender**, *superl* **weitgehendste(r,s)**, **weit gehend** *comp* **weiter gehend**, *superl* **am weitesten gehend** ADJ *Vollmachten etc* far-reaching; *Übereinstimmung etc* a large degree of; **er hatte viel ~ere** *or* **weiter gehende Befürchtungen** his fears went a lot further than that; **weitgehend**[2] *comp* **weitgehender**, *superl* **weitgehendst** ADV to a great extent; *siehe auch* **weitestgehend**; **weitgereist** [-gəraist] ADJ ATTR *siehe* **weit**; **weither** ['vait'heːɐ, 'vait'heːɐ] ADV (*auch* **von weit her**) from a long way away; **weithergeholt** ['vait'heːɐgəhoːlt] ADJ ATTR *siehe* **weit**; **weithin** ['vait'hɪn] ADV for a long way; (*fig*) *bekannt, beliebt* widely; *unbekannt* largely

Weit-: **weitläufig 1** ADJ (a) *Park, Gebäude* spacious; (= *verzweigt*) rambling; *Dorf* sprawling *attr* (b) *Verwandte* distant **2** ADV **sie sind ~ verwandt** they are distant relatives; **ich bin mit ihm ~ verwandt** I am distantly related to him; **weiträumig** [-rɔymɪç] **1** ADJ wide-ranging **2** ADV **ein Gelände ~ absperren** to cordon off a wide area around a site; **die Unfallstelle ~ umfahren** to keep well away from the scene of the accident; **der Verkehr wird ~ umgeleitet** traffic is being diverted well away from the obstruction; **weitreichend** *comp* **weitreichender**, *superl* **weitreichendste(r, s)**, **weit reichend** *comp* **weiter reichend**, *superl* **am weitesten reichend** ADJ (*fig*) far-reaching; (*Mil*) long-range *attr*; **weiter reichend** *comp* reaching; **weitschweifig** [-ʃvaifɪç] **1** ADJ long-winded **2** ADV long-windedly; **Weitsicht** F (*fig*) far-sightedness; **weitsichtig** [-zɪçtɪç] ADJ (*Med*) long-sighted (*Brit*), far-sighted (*esp US*); (*fig*) far-sighted; **Weitsichtigkeit** F, NO PL (*Med*) long-sightedness (*Brit*), far-sightedness (*esp US*); **Weitspringen** NT (*Sport*) long jump; **Weitspringer(in)** M(F) (*Sport*) long jumper; **Weitsprung** M (*Sport*) long jump; **weitverbreitet** [-feːbraitət], *comp* **weitverbreiteter**, *superl* **weitverbreiteteste(r, s)**, **weit verbreitet** *comp* **weiter verbreitet**, *superl* **am weitesten verbreitet** ADJ widespread; *Zeitung* with a wide circulation; **Weitwinkelobjektiv** NT wide-angle lens

Weizen ['vaitsn] M **-s**, NO PL wheat
Weizen-: **Weizenbier** NT *light, very fizzy beer made by using wheat, malt and top-fermentation yeast*; **Weizenmehl** NT wheat flour
welch [vɛlç] INTERROG PRON INV (a) (*geh: in Ausrufen*) what; **~ friedliches Bild!** what a peaceful scene! (b) (*in indirekten Fragesätzen*) (= **ein**) what
welche(r, s) ['vɛlçə] **1** INTERROG PRON (a) (*adjektivisch*) what; (*bei Wahl aus einer begrenzten Menge*) which; **~s Kleid soll ich anziehen, das rote oder das grüne?** which dress shall I wear, the red one or the green one?
(b) (*substantivisch*) which (one); **~s sind die Symptome dieser Krankheit?** what are the symptoms of this illness?
(c) (*in Ausrufen*) **~ Schande!** what a disgrace!; **~ Freude!** what joy!
2 INDEF PRON some; (*in Fragen, konditional auch, verneint*) any; **ich habe keine Tinte/Äpfel, haben Sie ~?** I don't have any ink/apples, do you have any?
welches ['vɛlçəs] PRON *siehe* **welche(r, s)**
welk [vɛlk] ADJ *Blume, Pflanze* wilted; *Blatt* dead; (*fig*) *Schönheit* fading; *Haut, Gesicht* tired-looking; (= *schlaff*) flaccid; *Hände* withered
welken ['vɛlkn] VI AUX SEIN (*lit, fig*) to wilt; (*Haut, Gesicht*) to grow tired-looking
Welkheit F **-**, NO PL wilted state; (*von Haut, Gesicht*) tired look
Wellblech ['vɛl-] NT corrugated iron
Welle ['vɛlə] F **-, -n** (a) wave (*auch fig, Phys, im Haar etc*); (*Rad: = Frequenz*) wavelength; (**hohe**) **~n schlagen** (*fig*) to create (quite) a stir (b) (*fig: = Mode*) craze; **die Neue ~** (*Film*) the nouvelle vague; (*Mus*) the New Wave (c) (*Tech*) shaft
wellen ['vɛlən] **1** VT *Haar* to wave; *Blech* to corrugate **2** VR (= *gewellt sein*) to be wavy; (= *Wellen bekommen*) to become wavy; **gewelltes Haar** wavy hair
Wellen-: **wellenartig 1** ADJ wave-like; *Linie etc* wavy **2** ADV like a wave; **Wellenbad** NT *swimming pool with wave machine*;

Wellenbereich M (*Phys, Telec*) frequency range; (*Rad*) waveband; **wellenförmig** 1 ADJ wave-like; *Linie* wavy 2 ADV in the form of waves; **Wellengang** [-gaŋ] M, NO PL waves *pl*, swell; **starker ~** heavy swell; **leichter ~** light swell; **Wellenlänge** F (*Phys, Telec*) wavelength; **auf der gleichen ~ sein** *or* **liegen, die gleiche ~ haben** (*inf*) to be on the same wavelength (*inf*); **Wellenlinie** F wavy line; **Wellenschliff** M (*am Messer*) serrated edge; **Wellensittich** M budgie (*inf*)

wellig [ˈvɛlɪç] ADJ *Haar etc* wavy; *Oberfläche, Fahrbahn* uneven; *Hügelland* undulating

Wellness [ˈwɛlnɛs] F -, NO PL wellness

Wellpappe [ˈvɛl-] F corrugated cardboard

Welpe [ˈvɛlpə] M **-n, -n** pup; (*von Wolf, Fuchs*) cub

Wels [vɛls] M **-es, -e** [-zə] catfish

welsch [vɛlʃ] ADJ **(a)** (= ~*sprachig*) Romance-speaking **(b)** (*Aus pej:* = *italienisch*) wop (*pej sl*) **(c)** (*Sw*) (Swiss-)French; **die ~e Schweiz** French Switzerland

Welsch-: **Welschland** NT **-s** (*Sw*) French Switzerland; **Welschschweizer(in)** M(F) (*Sw*) French Swiss; **welschschweizerisch** ADJ (*Sw*) Swiss-French

Welt [vɛlt] F **-, -en** (*lit, fig*) world; **die Alte/Neue/freie/Dritte ~** the Old/New/Free/Third World; **alle ~, Gott und die ~** everybody; **eine ~ brach für ihn zusammen** his whole world collapsed around him; **das ist doch nicht die ~** it isn't as important as all that; **davon** *or* **deswegen geht die ~ nicht unter** (*inf*) it isn't the end of the world; **das kostet doch nicht die ~** it won't cost a fortune; **uns/sie trennen ~en** (*fig*), **zwischen uns/ihnen liegen ~en** (*fig*) we/they are worlds apart; **auf der ~** in the world; **aus aller ~** from all over the world; **aus der ~ schaffen** to eliminate; **in aller ~** all over the world; **in alle ~ zerstreut** scattered all over the world; **warum/wer in aller ~ ...?** why/who on earth ...?; **um nichts in der ~, nicht um alles in der ~, um keinen Preis der ~** not for all the tea in China (*inf*); **ein Kind in die ~ setzen** to bring a child into the world; **ein Gerücht in die ~ setzen** to spread a rumour (*Brit*) *or* rumor (*US*); **ein Mann/eine Frau von ~** a man/woman of the world; **die beste Frau** *etc* **(von) der ~** the best woman *etc* in the world; **vor aller ~** in front of everybody; **auf die** *or* **zur ~ kommen** to come into the world

Welt- IN CPDS world; **Weltall** NT universe; **Weltanschauung** F philosophy of life; (*Philos, Pol*) world view; **Weltausstellung** F world exhibition; **Weltbank** F, NO PL World Bank; **weltbekannt** ADJ world-famous; **weltberühmt** ADJ world-famous; **Weltbeste(r)** [-bɛstə] MF DECL AS ADJ world's best; **weltbeste(r, s)** ADJ ATTR world's best; **Weltbestleistung** F world's best performance; **weltbewegend** ADJ world-shattering

Weltenbummler(in) M(F) globetrotter

Weltergewicht NT (*Boxen*) welterweight

Welt-: **welterschütternd** ADJ world-shattering; **weltfremd** ADJ unworldly; **Weltgerichtshof** M International Court; **Weltgeschichte** F world history; **in der ~ herumfahren** (*inf*) to travel around all over the place; **Weltgesundheitsorganisation** F World Health Organization; **weltgewandt** ADJ sophisticated; **Welthandel** M world trade; **Weltherrschaft** F world domination; **Weltklasse** F **ein Hochspringer der ~** a world-class high jumper; **~ sein** to be world class; (*inf*) to be fantastic (*inf*); **Weltkrieg** M world war; **der erste** *or* **Erste/zweite** *or* **Zweite ~** the First/Second World War; **Weltkulturerbe** NT world cultural heritage; (= *einzelnes Kulturgut*) World Heritage Site; **weltläufig** ADJ cosmopolitan; **weltlich** [ˈvɛltlɪç] ADJ worldly; (= *nicht kirchlich, geistlich*) secular; *Macht* temporal; **Weltliteratur** F world literature; **Weltmacht** F world power; **Weltmeer** NT ocean; **die sieben ~e** the seven seas; **Weltmeister(in)** M(F) world champion; **Weltmeisterschaft** F world championship; (*Ftbl*) World Cup; **weltoffen** ADJ cosmopolitan; **Weltöffentlichkeit** F general public; **was meint die ~ dazu?** what is world opinion on this?; **etw der ~ zugänglich machen** to make sth accessible to the world at large; **Weltpolitik** F world politics *pl*; **weltpolitisch** 1 ADJ **eine/die ~e Entwicklung** a development in/the development of world politics; **die ~e Rolle Deutschlands** Germany's role in world politics; **von ~er Bedeutung** of importance in world politics 2 ADV *gesehen* from the standpoint of world politics; **eine ~ wichtige Situation** an important international political situation; **~ nicht von Interesse** *or* **nicht bedeutsam** unimportant in the

realm of world politics; **Weltrang** M **von ~** world-famous; **~ genießen** to have world status; **Weltrangliste** F world rankings *pl*

Weltraum M (outer) space

Weltraum- IN CPDS space; *siehe auch* **Raum-**; **Weltraumbahnhof** M (*inf*) space mission launch centre; **Weltraumbehörde** F space agency; **Weltraumforschung** F space research; **weltraumgestützt** [-gəʃtʏtst] ADJ space-based; **Weltraumlabor** NT space laboratory; **Weltraumstation** F space station; **Weltraumteleskop** NT space telescope

Welt-: **Weltreich** NT world empire; **Weltreise** F world tour; **eine ~ machen** to go (a)round the world; **Weltrekord** M world record; **Weltschmerz** M world-weariness; **Weltsicherheitsrat** M (*Pol*) (United Nations) Security Council; **Weltstadt** F cosmopolitan city; **Weltuntergang** M (*lit, fig*) end of the world; **Weltuntergangsstimmung** F apocalyptic mood; **weltweit** ADJ, ADV worldwide; **Weltwirtschaftsgipfel** M World Economic Summit; **Weltwirtschaftskrise** F world economic crisis; **Weltwunder** NT **die sieben ~** the Seven Wonders of the World

wem [veːm] DAT *von* **wer** 1 INTERROG PRON who ... to, to whom; **mit/von** *etc* **~ ...** who ... with/from *etc*, with/from *etc* whom; **~ von euch soll ich den Schlüssel geben?** which (one) of you should I give the key to? 2 REL PRON (= *derjenige, dem*) the person (who ...) to, the person to whom ...; (= *jeder, dem*) anyone to whom ..., anyone ... to; **~ ... auch (immer)** whoever ... to 3 INDEF PRON (*inf:* = *jemandem*) to somebody; (*in Fragen auch*) (to) anybody

Wemfall M dative (case)

wen [veːn] ACC *von* **wer** 1 INTERROG PRON who, whom; **an ~ hast du geschrieben?** who did you write to?, to whom did you write?; **~ von den Schülern kennst du?** which (one) of these pupils do you know? 2 REL PRON (= *derjenige, den*) the person (who); (= *jeder, den*) anybody (who); **~ ... auch immer** whoever ... 3 INDEF PRON (*inf:* = *jemanden*) somebody; (*in Fragen auch*) anybody

Wende [ˈvɛndə] F **-, -n** turn; (= *Veränderung*) change; (= ~*punkt*) turning point; (*Turnen: am Pferd*) face or front vault; (*Pol*) (political) watershed; **die ~ vom 19. zum 20. Jahrhundert** the transition from the 19th to the 20th century

Wende-: **Wendefläche** F (*Mot*) turning area; **Wendehals** M (*Orn*) wryneck; (*fig inf*) turncoat (*pej*); **er ist einer der Wendehälse** he's one of those who have done a (complete) U-turn; **Wendekreis** M **(a)** tropic; **der nördliche ~** (*Geog*), **der ~ des Krebses** (*Astrol*) the Tropic of Cancer; **der südliche ~** (*Geog*), **der ~ des Steinbocks** (*Astrol*) the Tropic of Capricorn **(b)** (*Aut*) turning circle

Wendeltreppe F spiral staircase

wenden [ˈvɛndn] *pret* **wendete** *or* (*liter*) **wandte** [ˈvɛndətə, ˈvantə], *ptp* **gewendet** *or* (*liter*) **gewandt** [gəˈvɛndət, gəˈvant] 1 VT (= *umdrehen*) to turn (auch *Sew*); (*Cook*) *Eierpfannkuchen* to toss; *Schnitzel etc* to turn (over); **bitte ~!** please turn over; **wie man es auch wendet ..., man kann die Sache** *or* **es drehen und ~, wie man will ...** (*fig*) whichever way you (care to) look at it ...
2 VR **(a)** (= *sich umdrehen*) to turn (around); (*Wetter, Glück*) to change; **sich ins Gegenteil ~** to become the opposite; **seine Liebe wendete sich in Gegenteil** his love turned to hate; **das Gespräch wendete sich** the conversation took another turn; **sich zu jdm/etw ~** to turn toward(s) sb/sth; **sich zum Guten** *or* **Besseren/Schlimmeren ~** to take a turn for the better/worse **(b)** **sich an jdn ~** (*um Auskunft*) to consult sb; (*um Hilfe*) to turn to sb; (*Buch, Fernsehserie etc*) to be directed at sb; **sich gegen jdn/etw ~** to oppose sb/sth
3 VI to turn (*auch Sport*); (= *umkehren*) to turn (a)round; „**~ verboten**" "no U-turns"

Wende-: **Wendeplatz** M turning area; **Wendepunkt** M turning point; (*Math*) point of inflection

wendig ['vɛndɪç] ADJ agile; *Auto* manoeuvrable (*Brit*), maneuverable (*US*); (*fig*) *Politiker etc* agile

Wendigkeit F -, NO PL agility; (*von Auto etc*) manoeuvrability (*Brit*), maneuverability (*US*); (*fig: von Politiker etc*) agility

Wendung ['vɛndʊŋ] F -, -en (a) turn (*auch Mil*); (= *Veränderung*) change; **eine interessante/unerwartete ~ nehmen** (*fig*) to take an interesting/unexpected turn; **eine ~ zum Besseren** *or* **Guten/Schlechten nehmen** to change for the better/worse; **das gab seinem Leben eine neue ~** that changed the direction of his life (b) (= *Redewendung*) expression

Wenfall M accusative (case)

wenig ['ve:nɪç] *siehe auch* **weniger, wenigste(r, s)** ■ ADJ, INDEF PRON (a) SING little; **ich habe ~** I have only a little; **hast du Zeit? – ~!** have you got time? – not much; **das ist ~** that isn't much; **so ~ wie** *or* **als möglich** as little as possible; **sie ist mir so ~ sympathisch wie dir** I don't like her any more than you do; **du sagst so ~** you're not saying much; **mein ~es Geld** what little money I have; **das ~e Geld muss ausreichen** we'll have to make do with this small amount of money; **es fehlte (nur) ~, und er wäre überfahren worden** he was very nearly run over; **sie hat zu ~ Geld** *etc* she doesn't have enough money *etc*; **ein Exemplar zu ~ haben** to have one copy too few; **ich habe ihm £ 20 zu ~ geboten** I offered him £20 too little

(b) ~e *pl* (= *ein paar*) a few; (*einschränkend:* = *nicht viele*) few; **in ~en Tagen** in (just) a few days; **nicht ~e (waren da)** quite a few people (were there); **einige ~e Leute** a few people (c) (*auch adv*) **ein ~** a little; **ein ~ Salz/besser** a little salt/better

■ ADV little; **sie kommt (nur) ~ raus** she doesn't get out very often; **das überraschte ihn nicht ~** he was more than a little surprised; **besser** little better; **~ bekannt** little-known *attr*, little known *pred*; **~ mehr** little more; **~ erfreulich** not very pleasant; **zu ~** not enough; **einer/zwei** *etc* **zu ~** one/two *etc* too few

weniger ['ve:nɪɡɐ] COMP *von* **wenig** ■ ADJ, INDEF PRON less; (+*pl*) fewer; **~ werden** to get less and less; **mein Geld wird immer ~** my money is dwindling away; **~ Geld** less money; **~ Unfälle** fewer accidents

■ ADV less; **die Vorlesung war ~ lehrreich als belustigend** the lecture was not so much instructive as amusing; **das finde ich ~ schön!** that's not so nice!; **je mehr ... desto** *or* **umso ~ ...** the more ... the less ...; **ich glaube ihm umso ~, weil ...** I believe him all the less because ...

■ CONJ, PREP +ACC *or* GEN less; **sieben ~ drei ist vier** seven less three is four

wenigstens ['ve:nɪçstns] ADV at least

wenigste(r, s) ['ve:nɪçstɐ] SUPERL *von* **wenig** ADJ, INDEF PRON, ADV **am ~n** least; (*pl*) fewest; **er hat von uns allen das ~** *or* **am ~n Geld** he has the least money of any of us; **sie hat von uns allen die ~n** *or* **am ~n Sorgen** she has the fewest worries of any of us; **das konnte er am ~n vertragen** he could tolerate that least of all; **die ~n (Leute) glauben das** very few (people) believe that; **das ist (doch) das ~, was du tun könntest** that's the (very) least you could do; **das ist noch das ~!** (*inf*) that's the least of it!; **das am ~n!** that least of all!

wenn [vɛn] CONJ (a) (*konditional, konzessiv bei Wünschen*) if; **~ er nicht gewesen wäre, hätte ich meine Stelle verloren** if it had not been for him, I'd have lost my job; **selbst** *or* **und ~ even if**; **~ das Wörtchen ~ nicht wär(, wär mein Vater Millionär)** (*Prov*) if ifs and ans were pots and pans (there'd be no need for tinkers) (*Prov*); **~ ... auch ...** even though *or* if ...; **~ er auch noch so dumm sein mag, ...** however stupid he may be, ...; **~ auch!** (*inf*) even so!; **es ist nicht gut, ~ man mit vollem Magen schwimmt** it's not good to swim on a full stomach; **~ man bedenkt, dass ...** when you consider that ...; **~ wir erst das neue Haus haben** once we get the new house; **~ ich doch** *or* **nur** *or* **bloß ...** if only I ...; **~ er nur da wäre!** if only he were here!; **es ist, als** *or* **wie** (*inf*) **~ ...** it's as if ...; **außer ~** except if; *siehe* **wennschon**

(b) (*zeitlich*) when; **jedes Mal** *or* **immer ~** whenever; **außer ~** except when

Wenn [vɛn] NT -s, - (**die** *pl or* **das**) **~ und Aber** (the) ifs and buts; **ohne ~ und Aber** without any ifs and buts

wennschon ['vɛnʃoːn] ADV (*inf*) (**na** *or* **und**) **~!** so what? (*inf*); **~, dennschon!** in for a penny, in for a pound! (*esp Brit prov*)

wer [veːɐ] ■ INTERROG PRON who; **~ von ...** which (one) of ...; **~ ist da?** (*an Tür*) who's there?

■ REL PRON (= *derjenige, der*) the person who; (= *jeder, der*) anyone who; (*esp in Sprichwörtern*) he who; **~ ... auch (immer)** whoever ...

■ INDEF PRON (*inf:* = *jemand*) somebody; (*in Fragen auch*) anybody; **ist da ~?** is anybody there?; **~ sein** to be somebody (*inf*)

> *Vorsicht!* **wer** *wird nicht mit dem englischen Wort* **where** *übersetzt.*

Werbe- ['vɛrbə] IN CPDS advertising; **Werbeabteilung** F publicity department; **Werbeagentur** F advertising agency; **Werbebanner** NT banner; **Werbeblock** M, *pl* **-blocks** *or* **-blöcke** (*TV*) commercial break; **Werbebrief** M mailshot, mailing; **Werbebudget** NT advertising budget; **Werbefachfrau** F advertising woman; **Werbefachmann** M advertising man; **Werbefernsehen** NT commercial television; (*Sendung*) TV advertisements *pl*; **Werbegag** M publicity stunt; **Werbegeschenk** NT gift (*from company*); (*zu Gekauftem*) free gift; **Werbegrafiker(in)** M(F) commercial artist; **Werbekampagne** F publicity campaign; (*für Verbrauchsgüter*) advertising campaign; **Werbekosten** PL advertising *or* promotional costs *pl*; **Werbeleiter(in)** M(F) advertising manager

werben ['vɛrbn], *pret* **warb** [varp], *ptp* **geworben** [ɡə'vɔrbn] ■ VT Mitglieder, Mitarbeiter to recruit; *Kunden, Abonnenten, Stimmen* to attract ■ VI to advertise; **für etw ~** to advertise sth; **Plakate, die für den linken Kandidaten ~** placards supporting the left-wing candidate; **um etw ~** to solicit sth; **um Unterstützung/Verständnis ~** to try to enlist support/understanding; **um ein Mädchen ~** to court a girl

Werber ['vɛrbɐ] M **-s, -** (*um Kunden, Wähler*) canvasser; (*um Mädchen*) suitor; (*für Mitglieder etc, Mil Hist*) recruiter

werberisch ['vɛrbərɪʃ] ■ ADJ advertising *attr*, promotional ■ ADV publicity-wise

Werbe-: **Werbeslogan** M publicity slogan; (*für Verbrauchsgüter*) advertising slogan; **Werbespot** M commercial; **Werbetext** M advertising copy *no pl*; **zwei ~e** two pieces of advertising copy; **~e verfassen** to write (advertising) copy; **Werbetexter(in)** M(F) (advertising) copywriter; **Werbeträger** M advertising medium; **Werbetrommel** F **die ~ (für etw) rühren** (*inf*) to push sth (*inf*); **werbewirksam** ADJ effective (for advertising purposes); **der Skandal erwies sich als äußerst ~** the scandal proved to be excellent publicity; **Werbewirksamkeit** F publicity value

werblich ['vɛrplɪç] ■ ADJ advertising *attr*, promotional ■ ADV in advertising terms; **~ gesehen** from an advertising point of view

Werbung ['vɛrbʊŋ] F -, -en (*esp Comm*) advertising; (= *Werbeabteilung*) publicity department; (*Pol:* = *Propaganda*) pre-election publicity; (*von Kunden, Stimmen*) winning; (*von Mitgliedern, Soldaten etc*) recruitment; (*um Mädchen*) courting (*um* of); **~ für etw machen** to advertise sth

Werbungskosten PL (*von Mensch*) professional outlay *sing*; (*von Firma*) business expenses *pl*

Werdegang M, *pl* **-gänge** development; (*beruflich*) career

werden ['veːɐdn]	
■ HILFSVERB	■ INTRANSITIVES VERB

pret **wurde** ['vʊrdə], *ptp* **geworden** [ɡə'vɔrdn] AUX SEIN

■ HILFSVERB
(a) (*zur Bildung des Futurs*)

> *Die Kurzform* **'ll** *(für* **will**) *ist im gesprochenen Englisch sehr gebräuchlich, ebenfalls* **won't** *(=* **will not**). *Die unveränderliche Vollform* **will** *wird in der Schriftsprache sowie zur Betonung verwendet.*

ich werde es tun I'll do it; **ich werde das nicht tun** I won't do that; **er wird es tun, das verspreche ich euch** he will do it, I promise you

going to *drückt Sicherheit aus. Es wird ebenfalls für Voraussagen verwendet.*

es wird gleich regnen it's going to rain; **wer wird denn gleich weinen!** you're not going to cry now, are you?; **wer wird denn gleich!** (*inf*) come on, now!

♦**es wird ... werden es wird schon werden** (*inf*) it's going to be okay (*inf*); **es wird schon wieder (gut) werden** it'll turn out all right; **es wird sicher ein Junge werden** it's bound to be a boy **(b)** (*zur Bildung des Konjunktivs*)

Die Kurzformen **'d** (*für* **would**) *und* **wouldn't** (*für* **would not**) *sind sehr gebräuchlich; zur Betonung wird jedoch die Vollform* **would** *verwendet.*

das würde ich gerne tun I'd like to do that; **das würde ich nicht gerne tun** I wouldn't like to do that; **er würde kommen, wenn es nicht regnete** he would come if it wasn't raining; **er hat gesagt, er werde** *or* **würde kommen** he said he'd come; **würden Sie mir bitte das Buch geben?** would you give me the book, please?
(c) (*zur Bildung des Passivs*) *ptp* **worden** ['vɔrdn] **geschlagen werden** to be beaten; **was ist mit ihm? – er ist erschossen worden** what happened to him? – he has been shot dead; **er ist gestern erschossen worden** he was shot dead yesterday; **das Haus wird (gerade) renoviert** the house is being redecorated; **mir wurde gesagt, dass ...** I was told that ...; **es wurde gesungen** there was singing
(d) (*bei Vermutung*) **sie wird wohl in der Küche sein** she'll probably be in the kitchen; **er wird sicher gerade auf dem Heimweg sein** he will definitely be on his way home; **das wird etwa 20 Euro kosten** it will cost roughly 20 euros

2 INTRANSITIVES VERB
(a) (*mit Adjektiv*) to get; **mir wird kalt/warm** I'm getting cold/warm; **verrückt/blind werden** to go crazy/blind; **rot/sauer/blass/kalt werden** to go red/sour/pale/cold; **mir wird schlecht/besser** I feel bad/better; **anders werden** to change; **die Fotos sind gut geworden** the photos have come out well
(b) (*mit Substantiv, Pronomen*) to become; (= *sich verwandeln in*) to turn into; **Lehrer werden** to become a teacher; **was willst du einmal werden?** what do you want to be when you grow up?; **ich will Lehrer werden** I want to be a teacher; **Erster werden** to come first; **er ist etwas geworden** he's got somewhere in life; **das ist nichts geworden** it came to nothing; **das Eis wird Wasser** the ice is turning into water; **das wird bestimmt ein guter Eintopf** the stew is going to be good
(c) (*bei Altersangaben*) **er wird am 8. Mai 36 (Jahre alt)** he will be 36 on the 8th of May; **er ist gerade 40 geworden** he has just turned 40
(d) (*in festen Wendungen*)
♦**es wird ... es wird bald ein Jahr, dass ...** it's almost a year since ...; **es wird jetzt 13 Uhr** in a moment it will be 1 o'clock; **es wurde 10 Uhr, und ...** 10 o'clock came, and ...; **es wird Zeit, dass er kommt** it's time (that) he came; **es wird kalt/dunkel/spät** it's getting cold/dark/late; **es wird Nacht** it's getting dark; **es wird Tag** it's getting light; **es wird Winter** winter is coming
♦**werden + aus was ist aus ihm geworden?** what has become of him?; **aus ihm ist ein großer Komponist geworden** he has become a great composer; **aus ihm ist etwas geworden** he has got (*Brit*) *or* gotten (*US*) somewhere in life; **aus ihm wird noch einmal was!** he'll make something of himself yet!; **aus dir wird nie etwas!** you'll never be anything!; **daraus wird nichts** nothing will come of that; (= *das kommt nicht infrage*) that's out of the question
♦**werden + zu zu etw werden** to turn into sth
♦**werden + wie er wird mal wie sein Vater** he's going to be like his father
(e) (*andere Wendungen*) **was nicht ist, kann (ja) noch werden** (*prov inf*) my/your *etc* day will come; **was soll nun werden?** so what's going to happen now?

werdend ADJ nascent; **~e Mutter** expectant mother; **~er Vater** father-to-be

Werfall M nominative (case)
werfen ['vɛrfn], *pret* **warf** [varf], *ptp* **geworfen** [gə'vɔrfn] **1** VT
(a) to throw (*nach* at); *Tor, Korb* to score; **Bomben ~** (*von Flugzeug*) to drop bombs; **eine Münze ~** to toss a coin; **„nicht ~"** "handle with care"; **etw auf jdn/etw ~** to throw sth at sb/sth; **etw auf den Boden ~** to throw sth to the ground; **billige Waren auf den Markt ~** to dump cheap goods on the market; **jdn aus der Firma/dem Haus** *etc* **~** to throw sb out (of the firm/house *etc*); **Geld in den Automaten ~** to put money in the machine
(b) (= *Junge kriegen*) to have
2 VI **(a)** (= *schleudern*) to throw; **mit etw (auf jdn/etw) ~** to throw sth (at sb/sth); **mit Geld (nur so) um sich ~** (*inf*) to throw one's money around; **mit Komplimenten (nur so) um sich ~** to be lavish with one's compliments; **mit Fremdwörtern (nur so) um sich ~** to bandy foreign words about (*Brit*), to toss foreign words around (*esp US*)
(b) (*Tier*) to have its young; (*esp Katze, Hund etc*) to have a litter; (*bei einzelnen Jungen*) to have a pup *etc*
3 VR to throw oneself (*auf +acc* (up)on, at); (*Holz*) to warp; (*Metall, Asphalt etc*) to buckle
Werfer ['vɛrfe] M -s, -, **Werferin** [-ərɪn] F -, **-nen** thrower; (*Cricket*) bowler; (*Baseball*) pitcher
Werft [vɛrft] F -, **-en** shipyard; (*für Flugzeuge*) hangar
Werk [vɛrk] NT **-(e)s, -e (a)** (= *Arbeit, Tätigkeit, Buch etc*) work; (*geh:* = *Tat*) deed; (= *Gesamtwerk*) works *pl*; **das ~ eines Augenblicks** the work of a moment; **das ist sein ~** this is his doing; **das ~ jahrelanger Arbeit/seines Fleißes** the product of many years of work/of his industry; **gute ~e tun** to do good works; **ein gutes ~ (an jdm) tun** to do a good deed (for sb); **ans ~ gehen, sich ans ~ machen** to set to work; **am ~ sein** to be at work
(b) (= *Betrieb, Fabrik*) works *sing or pl* (*Brit*), factory; **ab ~** (*Comm*) ex works (*Brit*), ex factory
(c) (= *Triebwerk*) mechanism
Werk- IN CPDS factory; *siehe auch* **Werk(s)-**; **Werkbank** F, *pl* **-bänke** workbench
Werkel [vɛrkl] NT **-s, -(n)** (*Aus*) hurdy-gurdy
werken ['vɛrkn] **1** VI to work; (*handwerklich*) to do handicrafts; **Werken** (*Sch*) handicrafts **2** VT to make
Werk(s)-: **Werk(s)angehörige(r)** MF DECL AS ADJ factory employee; **Werk(s)arzt** M, **Werk(s)ärztin** F company doctor
Werkschutz M factory security service
Werks-: **werkseigen** ADJ company *attr*; **~ sein** to be company-owned; **Werksgelände** NT factory premises *pl*; **Werksleitung** F factory management; **Werksschließung** F plant closure
Werkstatt F, *pl* **-stätten** [-ʃtɛtn], **Werkstätte** F workshop (*auch fig*); (*für Autoreparaturen*) garage; (*von Künstler*) studio; **geschützte** *or* **beschützende ~** (*für Behinderte*) sheltered workshop
Werk-: **Werkstoff** M material; **Werkstück** NT (*Tech*) workpiece; **Werkstudent(in)** M(F) working student; **~ sein** to work one's way through college
Werktag M working day
werktags ['vɛrktaːks] ADV on weekdays
werktätig ADJ working
Werkvertrag M contract for work and services; **im ~ übergebene/übernommene Arbeit** contract work
Werkzeug NT, *pl* **-zeuge** (*lit, fig, Comput*) tool
Werkzeug-: **Werkzeugkasten** M toolbox; **Werkzeugleiste** F (*Comput*) toolbar
Wermut ['veːrmuːt] M **-(e)s**, NO PL **(a)** (*Bot*) wormwood
(b) (= *~wein*) vermouth
Wermutstropfen M (*fig geh*) drop of bitterness
wert [veːrt] ADJ **(a)** (*oldform: Anrede*) dear; **Ihr ~es Schreiben** (*form*) your esteemed letter (*form*); **wie war doch gleich Ihr ~er Name?** (*form*) what was the name, sir/madam?
(b) **etw ~ sein** to be worth sth; **nichts ~ sein** to be worthless; (= *untauglich*) to be no good; **sie war ihm offenbar nicht viel ~** she obviously didn't mean all that much to him; **Glasgow ist eine Reise ~** Glasgow is worth a visit; **einer Sache** (*gen*) **~ sein** (*geh*) to be worthy of sth; **es ist der Mühe ~** it's worth the trouble; **es ist nicht der Rede ~** it's not worth mentioning
(c) (= *nützlich*) useful; **das ist schon viel ~** (= *erfreulich*) that's very encouraging

Wert [veːɐt] M **-(e)s, -e (a)** value; (*esp menschlicher*) worth; (*von Banknoten, Briefmarken*) denomination; (= ~*sache*) valuable object; **einen ~ von fünf Euro haben** to be worth five euros; **im ~(e) von** to the value of; **an ~ verlieren/zunehmen, im ~ sinken/steigen** to decrease/increase in value, to depreciate/appreciate (*esp Econ*); **eine Sache unter/über (ihrem wirklichen) ~ verkaufen** to sell sth for less/more than its true value; **sie hat innere ~e** she has certain inner qualities; **~ auf etw** (*acc*) **legen** (*fig*) to set great store by sth (*esp Brit*); **das hat keinen ~** (*inf*) there's no point
(b) USU PL (*von Test, Analyse*) result

Wert-: **Wertangabe** F declaration of value; **Wertarbeit** F craftsmanship

werten [veːɐtn] VTI (= *einstufen*) to rate (*als* as); *Klassenarbeit etc* to grade; (= *beurteilen*) to judge (*als* to be); (*Sport*) (= *als gültig ~*) to allow; (= *Punkte geben*) to give a score; **ein Tor nicht ~** (*Ftbl etc*) to disallow a goal; **ohne (es) ~ zu wollen ...** without wanting to make any judgement (on it) ...

Werte-: **Wertesystem** NT system of values; **Wertewandel** M change in values

wertfrei 1 ADJ neutral 2 ADV in a neutral way

Wertgegenstand M object of value; **Wertgegenstände** *pl* valuables *pl*

Wertigkeit [veːɐtɪçkait] F **-, -en (a)** (*Chem, Ling*) valency **(b)** (= *Wert*) importance

Wert-: **wertlos** ADJ worthless; **Wertlosigkeit** F **-**, NO PL worthlessness; **Wertminderung** F reduction in value; **wertneutral** 1 ADJ value-free 2 ADV avoiding (making) value judgements; **Wertpapier** NT security; **~e** *pl* stocks and shares *pl*; **Wertsache** F object of value; **Wertschöpfung** F (*Econ*) net product; **Wertschriftenanalyse** F security rating; **Wertsicherungsklausel** F index *or* escalator clause; **Wertsteigerung** F increase in value; **Wertstellung** F (*Fin*) value; **Wertstoff** M reusable material; **Wertstofftonne** F bin for reusable materials

Wertung [veːɐtʊŋ] F **-, -en (a)** (= *Bewertung*) evaluation; (*von Jury etc*) judging; (= *Punkte*) score **(b)** (= *das Werten*) rating; (*von Klassenarbeit*) grading; (= *das Beurteilen*) judging; (*Sport*: = *Punktvergabe*) scoring

Wert-: **Werturteil** NT value judgement; **wertvoll** ADJ valuable; (*moralisch*) *Mensch* worthy; **Wertzoll** M ad valorem duty

werweißen [veːɐvaisn] VI INSEP (*Sw*) to guess

Werwolf [veːɐvɔlf] M werewolf

wes [ves] PRON (*old*) 1 GEN *von* **wer** whose 2 GEN *von* **was** of which

Wesen [veːzn] NT **-s, - (a)** NO PL nature; (= *Wesentliches*) essence; **es liegt im ~ einer Sache ...** it's in the nature of a thing ... **(b)** (= *Geschöpf*) being; (= *tierisches ~*) creature; (= *Mensch*) person; **das höchste ~** the Supreme Being; **ein menschliches ~** a human being; **ein weibliches ~** a female; **ein männliches ~** a male

wesentlich [veːzntlɪç] 1 ADJ (= *den Kern der Sache betreffend, sehr wichtig*) essential; (= *grundlegend*) fundamental; (= *erheblich*) substantial; (= *wichtig*) important; **das Wesentliche** the essential part; (*von dem, was gesagt wurde*) the gist; **im Wesentlichen** basically; (= *im Großen und Ganzen*) in the main
2 ADV (= *grundlegend*) fundamentally; (= *erheblich*) considerably; **es ist mir ~ lieber, wenn wir ...** I would much rather we ...; **sie hat sich nicht ~ verändert** she hasn't changed much

Wesfall M genitive case

weshalb [ves'halp, 'ves-] 1 INTERROG ADV why 2 REL ADV which is why; **der Grund, ~ ...** the reason why ...; **das ist es ja, ~ ...** that is why ...

Wespe [vespə] F **-, -n** wasp

Wespennest NT wasp's nest; **in ein ~ stechen** (*fig*) to stir up a hornets' nest

wessen [vesn] PRON 1 GEN *von* **wer (a)** INTERROG whose **(b)** REL, INDEF **~ Handschrift das auch (immer) sein mag, ...** no matter whose handwriting it may be, ... 2 GEN *von* **was** (*liter*) **(c)** INTERROG **~ hat man dich angeklagt?** of what have you been accused? **(d)** REL, INDEF **~ man dich auch (immer) anklagt, ...** whatever they accuse you of ...

Wessi [vesi] M **-s, -s** (*inf*) Westerner, West German

West- IN CPDS (*in Ländernamen*) (*politisch*) West; (*geografisch auch*) the West of ..., Western; **westdeutsch** ADJ (*Geog*) Western German; (*Pol Hist*) West German

Weste [vestə] F **-, -n** waistcoat (*Brit*), vest (*US*); **eine reine** *or* **saubere** *or* **weiße ~ haben** (*fig*) to have a clean slate

Westen [vestn] M **-s**, NO PL west; (*von Land*) West; **der ~** (*Pol*) the West; **aus dem ~, von ~ (her)** from the west; **gegen** *or* **gen** (*liter*) *or* **nach ~** west(wards); **nach ~ (hin)** to the west; **im ~ der Stadt/des Landes** in the west of the town/country; **weiter im ~** further west; **im ~ Frankreichs** in the west of France

Westentasche F waistcoat (*Brit*) *or* vest (*US*) pocket; **etw wie seine ~ kennen** (*inf*) to know sth like the back of one's hand (*inf*)

Western [vestɐn] M **-(s), -** western

West-: **Westeuropa** NT Western Europe; **westeuropäisch** ADJ West(ern) European; **~e Zeit** Greenwich Mean Time; **die Westeuropäische Union** the Western European Union

Westfale [vest'faːlə] M **-n, -n**, **Westfälin** [-'fɛːlɪn] F **-, -nen** Westphalian

Westfalen [vest'faːlən] NT **-s** Westphalia

Westfälin F **-, -nen** Westphalian (woman)

westfälisch [vest'fɛːlɪʃ] ADJ Westphalian

Westfriesische Inseln PL West Frisians *pl*

West-: **Westgermanen** PL (*Hist*) West Germanic peoples *pl*; **westgermanisch** ADJ (*Hist, Ling*) West Germanic; **Westgoten** PL (*Hist*) Visigoths *pl*; **Westintegration** F (*Pol*) integration with the West; **Westjordanland** [vest'jɔrdan-] NT **das ~** the West Bank; **Westküste** F west coast

westlich [vestlɪç] 1 ADJ western; *Kurs, Wind, Richtung* westerly; (*Pol*) Western; **der ~ste Ort** the westernmost place 2 ADV (to the) west; **~ von ...** to the west of ...; **es liegt ~er** *or* **weiter ~** it is further (to the) west 3 PREP +GEN (to the) west of

West-: **Westmächte** PL (*Pol*) **die ~** the western powers *pl*; **westöstlich** ADJ west-to-east; **in ~er Richtung** from west to east; **Westrom** NT (*Hist*) Western Roman Empire; **westwärts** [vestverts] ADV westward(s); **Westwind** M west wind

weswegen [ves've:gn, 'ves-] INTERROG ADV why

wett [vet] ADJ PRED **~ sein** to be quits

Wettbewerb M competition

Wettbewerbs-: **wettbewerbsfähig** ADJ competitive; **wettbewerbswidrig** 1 ADJ anticompetitive 2 ADV **~ handeln** (*unlauter*) to violate fair trade practices; (*ungesetzlich*) to violate competition law (*Brit*) *or* antitrust law (*US*)

Wettbüro NT betting office

Wette [vetə] F **-, -n** bet (*auch Sport*); wager; **darauf gehe ich jede ~ ein** I'll bet you anything you like; **was gilt die ~?** what are you betting?; **die ~ gilt!** done!; **um die ~ laufen/schwimmen** to run/swim a race (with each other); **mit jdm um die ~ laufen** *or* **rennen** to race sb

wetteifern VI INSEP **mit jdm um etw ~** to compete with sb for sth

wetten [vetn] VTI to bet (*auch Sport*), to wager; (**wollen wir**) **~?** (do you) want to bet?; **auf etw** (*acc*) **~** to bet on sth; **mit jdm ~** to bet with sb; (**mit jdm**) (**darauf**) **~, dass ...** to bet (sb) that ...; **ich wette 100 gegen 1(, dass ...)** I'll bet (you) 100 to 1 (that ...)

Wetter¹ [vetɐ] NT **-s, - (a)** weather *no indef art*; **bei jedem ~** in all weathers; **bei so einem ~** in such weather; **was haben wir heute für ~?** what's the weather like today?; **übers** *or* **vom ~ sprechen** to talk about the weather; (**bei jdm**) **gut ~ machen** (*inf*) to make up to sb **(b)** (= *Unwetter*) storm **(c)** USU PL (*Min*) air; **schlagende ~** *pl* firedamp *sing*

Wetter² [vetɐ] M **-s, -**, **Wetterin** [-ərɪn] F **-, -nen** better

Wetter-: **Wetteraussichten** PL weather outlook *sing*; **Wetterbericht** M weather report; **wetterbeständig** ADJ weatherproof; **wetterempfindlich** ADJ sensitive to (changes in) the weather; **wetterfest** ADJ weatherproof; **Wetterfrosch** M **(a)** *type of barometer using a frog* **(b)** *(hum inf)* weatherman *(inf)*; **wetterfühlig** [-fyːlɪç] ADJ sensitive to (changes in) the weather; **wettergeschützt** ADJ sheltered

Wetterin F -, -nen better

Wetter-: Wetterkarte F weather map; **Wetterkunde** F meteorology; **Wetterlage** F weather situation; **Wetterleuchten** NT -s, NO PL sheet lightning; *(fig)* storm clouds *pl*

wettern ['vɛtɐn] **1** VI IMPERS **es wettert** it's thundering and lightening **2** VI to curse and swear; **gegen** *or* **auf etw** *(acc)* ~ to rail against sth

Wetter-: Wetterprognose F *(Aus)* weather forecast; **Wetterstation** F weather station; **Wettersturz** M sudden fall in temperature and atmospheric pressure; **Wetterumbruch** M *(esp Sw)*, **Wetterumschwung** M sudden change in the weather; **Wettervoraussage** F, **Wettervorhersage** F weather forecast; **Wetterwarte** F weather station; **wetterwendisch** ADJ *(fig)* changeable

Wett-: Wettfahrt F race; **Wettkampf** M competition; **Wettkämpfer(in)** M(F) competitor; **Wettlauf** M race; **ein ~ mit der Zeit** *or* **gegen die Zeit** a race against time

wettmachen VT SEP to make up for; *Verlust etc* to make good; *Rückstand, Vorsprung* to make up

Wett-: Wettrennen NT *(lit, fig)* race; **ein ~ machen** to run a race; **Wettrüsten** NT -s, NO PL arms race; **Wettschein** M betting slip; **Wettschwimmen** NT swimming competition; **Wettzettel** M betting slip

wetzen ['vɛtsn] VT to whet

Wetz-: Wetzstahl M steel; **Wetzstein** M whetstone

WEU [veːeːˈʔuː] F - ABBR *von* **Westeuropäische Union** WEU

WEZ [veːleːˈtseːt] ABBR *von* **Westeuropäische Zeit** GMT

WG [veːˈgeː] F -, -s ABBR *von* **Wohngemeinschaft**

WG- [veːˈgeː-]: **WG-Bewohner(in)** M(F) apartment *or* house sharer; **WG-Zimmer** NT room in a shared flat *etc*

Whirlpool ['wœːrlpuːl, 'wøːɛl-] M -s, -s Jacuzzi®

Whisky ['wɪskɪ] M -s, -s whisky, whiskey (US); *(irischer)* whiskey; *(amerikanischer Maiswhisky)* bourbon (whiskey); *(amerikanischer Roggenwhisky)* rye (whiskey)

wich PRET *von* **weichen²**

Wichsbirne ['vɪks-] F *(sl)* wanker *(Brit sl)*, jerk-off *(US sl)*

wichsen ['vɪksn] VI *(sl: = onanieren)* to jerk off *(sl)*

Wichser ['vɪksɐ] M -s, - *(sl)* wanker *(Brit sl)*, jerk-off *(US sl)*

Wicht [vɪçt] M -(e)s, -e *(= Kobold)* goblin; *(= kleiner Mensch)* titch *(inf)*; *(= Kind)* (little) creature; *(fig: = verachtenswerter Mensch)* scoundrel

wichtig ['vɪçtɪç] **1** ADJ important; **sich ~ machen** *or* **tun** to be full of one's own importance; **er will sich nur ~ machen** he just wants to get attention; **sich mit etw ~ machen** *or* **tun** to go on and on about sth; **alles Wichtige** everything of importance; **Wichtigeres zu tun haben** to have more important things to do; **nichts Wichtigeres zu tun haben** to have nothing better to do; **das Wichtigste** *(= die wichtigste Sache)* the most important thing; *(= die wichtigsten Einzelheiten)* the most important details **2** ADV **sich selbst/etw (zu) ~ nehmen** to take oneself/sth (too) seriously; **~ tun** *(inf: sich aufspielen)* to be full of one's own importance; **sich** *(dat)* **~ vorkommen** to be full of oneself

Wichtigkeit F -, -en importance

Wichtigtuer [-tuːɐ] M -s, -, **Wichtigtuerin** [-ərɪn] F -, -nen **Wichtigmacher(in)** *(Aus)* M(F) *(pej)* pompous idiot

Wicke ['vɪkə] F -, -n *(Bot)* vetch; *(= Gartenwicke)* sweet pea

Wickel ['vɪkl] M -s, - **(a)** *(Med)* compress **(b)** *(= Rolle)* reel; *(= Lockenwickel)* curler

wickeln ['vɪkln] **1** VT **(a)** *(= schlingen)* to wind *(um* round); *Verband etc* to bind; **sich** *(dat)* **eine Decke um die Beine ~** to wrap a blanket around one's legs; **wenn du das denkst, bist du schief gewickelt!** *(fig inf)* if you think that, you're very much mistaken **(b)** *(= einwickeln)* to wrap *(in +acc* in); **einen Säugling ~** to change a baby's nappy *(Brit)* or diaper *(US)* **2** VR to wrap oneself *(in +acc* in); **sich um etw ~** to wrap itself around sth; *(Schlange, Pflanze)* to wind itself around sth

Wickel-: Wickelraum M *(in Kaufhaus etc)* mothers' (and babies') room *(Brit)*, (baby) changing room; **Wickelrock** M wraparound skirt; **Wickeltisch** M baby's changing table

Widder ['vɪdɐ] M -s, - *(Zool)* ram; *(Astrol)* Aries; **er/sie ist (ein) ~** *(Astrol)* he's/she's (an) Aries; **der ~** *(Astron, Astrol)* Aries, the Ram

wider ['viːdɐ] PREP +ACC *(geh)* against; *(= entgegen auch)* contrary to; **~ Erwarten** contrary to expectations

Wider-: widerborstig ADJ contrary; **Widerborstigkeit** ['viːdɐbɔrstɪçkaɪt] F -, NO PL contrariness; **widerhallen** VI SEP *or (rare)* INSEP to echo *(von* with); **Widerhandlung** F *(Sw)* contravention

widerlegen [viːdɐˈleːgn], *ptp* **widerlegt** VT INSEP *Behauptung etc* to refute; **jdn ~** to prove wrong

Widerlegung F -, -en refutation, disproving

widerlich ['viːdɐlɪç] **1** ADJ disgusting; *Mensch* repulsive; *Kopfschmerzen* nasty **2** ADV **sich benehmen** disgustingly; **~ riechen/schmecken** to smell/taste disgusting

Wider-: widernatürlich ADJ unnatural; **widerrechtlich** **1** ADJ illegal **2** ADV illegally; **etw ~ betreten** *Gelände* to trespass (up)on sth; *Gebäude* to enter sth illegally; **sich** *(dat)* **etw ~ aneignen** to misappropriate sth; **Widerrede** F **(a)** *(= Widerspruch)* contradiction; **keine ~!** don't argue!; **er duldet keine ~** he will not have any arguments about it; **ohne ~** without protest **(b)** *(= Antwort)* reply; **Rede und ~** dialogue *(Brit)*, dialog *(US)*

Widerruf M revocation *(auch Jur)*; *(von Aussage, Geständnis, Behauptung)* retraction *(auch Jur)*, withdrawal; *(von Befehl)* cancellation

widerrufen [viːdɐˈruːfn], *ptp* **widerrufen** INSEP IRREG **1** VT *Erlaubnis, Anordnung etc* to revoke *(auch Jur)*, to withdraw; *Aussage, Geständnis, Behauptung* to retract *(auch Jur)*, to withdraw; *Befehl* to cancel **2** VI *(bei Verleumdung etc)* to withdraw

Wider-: Widersacher ['viːdɐzaxɐ] M -s, -, **Widersacherin** [-ərɪn] F -, -nen adversary; **widersetzen** [viːdɐˈzɛtsn], *ptp* **widersetzt** VR INSEP **sich jdm/einer Sache ~** to oppose sb/sth; *einem Polizisten, der Festnahme* to resist sb/sth; *einem Befehl, einer Aufforderung* to refuse to comply with sth; **widersinnig** ADJ absurd; **widerspenstig** ADJ stubborn; *Kind, Haar* unruly; *Material, Plastik* difficult to work with; **„Der Widerspenstigen Zähmung"** "The Taming of the Shrew"; **widerspiegeln** SEP **1** VT *(lit, fig)* to reflect **2** VR *(lit, fig)* to be reflected

widersprechen [viːdɐˈʃprɛçn], *ptp* **widersprochen** [viːdɐˈʃprɔxn] INSEP IRREG **1** VI **jdm/einer Sache ~** to contradict sb/sth; **das widerspricht meinen Grundsätzen** that goes against my principles **2** VR *(einander)* to contradict each other; **sich (selbst) ~** to contradict oneself

widersprechend ADJ **(sich** *or* **einander) ~** contradictory

Widerspruch M **(a)** *(= Gegensätzlichkeit, Widerrede)* contradiction; *(= Unvereinbarkeit)* inconsistency; **ein ~ in sich selbst** a contradiction in terms; **in** *or* **im ~ zu** contrary to; **in** *or* **im ~ zu** *or* **mit etw stehen** to be contrary to sth **(b)** *(= Protest)* protest; *(= Ablehnung)* opposition; *(Jur)* appeal; **kein ~!** don't argue!; **er duldet keinen ~** he won't have any argument *(Brit)*, he won't stand for any back talk *(US)*; **es erhob sich ~** there was opposition *(gegen* to); **~ erheben** to protest; **~ einlegen** *(Jur)* to appeal; **~ erfahren, auf ~ stoßen** to meet with opposition *(bei* from)

widersprüchlich [-ʃprʏçlɪç] **1** ADJ contradictory; *Erzählung, Theorie auch, Verhalten* inconsistent **2** ADV contradictorily; **sich verhalten auch** inconsistently

Widersprüchlichkeit F -, -en contradictoriness; *(von Erzählung, Theorie auch, von Verhalten)* inconsistency

Widerspruchs-: Widerspruchsgeist M, NO PL spirit of opposition; **widerspruchslos** **1** ADJ *(= unangefochten)* unopposed; *(= ohne Einwände)* without contradiction; *(= folgsam)* unprotesting; *(= nicht widersprüchlich)* Theorie, Mensch, Verhalten consistent **2** ADV *(= unangefochten)* without opposition; *(= ohne Einwände)* without contradiction; *(= folgsam)* without protest

Widerstand M resistance *(auch Pol, Elec etc)*; *(im 2. Weltkrieg)* Resistance; *(= Ablehnung)* opposition; *(Elec: Bauelement)* resistor; **zum ~ aufrufen** to call upon people to resist; **es erhebt sich ~** there is resistance; **jdm/einer Sache** *or* **gegen jdn/etw ~ leisten** to resist sb/sth; **~ gegen die Staatsgewalt** obstructing an officer in the line of duty

Widerstands-: Widerstandsbewegung F resistance movement; (*im 2. Weltkrieg*) Resistance movement; **widerstandsfähig** ADJ robust; *Pflanze* hardy; (*Med, Tech etc*) resistant (*gegen* to); **Widerstandsfähigkeit** F robustness; (*von Pflanze*) hardiness; (*Med, Tech etc*) resistance (*gegen* to); **Widerstandskämpfer(in)** M(F) member of the resistance; (*im 2. Weltkrieg*) member of the Resistance; **widerstandslos** ADJ, ADV without resistance; (*Phys*) non-resistant

widerstehen [viːdɐˈʃteːən], *ptp* **widerstanden** [viːdɐˈʃtandn] VI INSEP IRREG +DAT **(a)** (= *nicht nachgeben*) to resist; (= *standhalten*) to withstand; **einer Versuchung/einem Erdbeben ~ können** to be able to resist a temptation/ withstand an earthquake **(b)** (= *anekeln*) **etw widersteht jdm** sb loathes sth

widerstreben [viːdɐˈʃtreːbn], *ptp* **widerstrebt** VI INSEP +DAT **jds sittlichem Empfinden/jds Interessen** *etc* **~** to go against sb's moral sense/sb's interests *etc*; **es widerstrebt mir, so etwas zu tun** (= *lehne ich ab*) it goes against the grain (*Brit*) *or* my grain (*US*) to do anything like that; (= *möchte ich nicht*) I am reluctant to do anything like that

widerstrebend 🔳 ADJ (= *gegensätzlich*) *Interessen* conflicting; (= *widerwillig, zögernd*) reluctant; **mit ~en Gefühlen** with (some) reluctance 🔳 ADV (*widerwillig*) unwillingly

widerwärtig [-vɛrtɪç] 🔳 ADJ (= *ekelhaft*) objectionable; disgusting 🔳 ADV **~ schmecken/stinken** to taste/smell disgusting

Widerwille M (= *Abscheu, Ekel*) disgust (*gegen* for); (= *Abneigung*) distaste (*gegen* for); (= *Widerstreben*) reluctance

widerwillig 🔳 ADJ reluctant 🔳 ADV reluctantly

Widerworte PL answering back *sing*; **~ geben** *or* **machen** to answer back; **er tat es ohne ~** he did it without protest

widmen [ˈvɪtmən] 🔳 VT **jdm etw ~** to dedicate sth to sb 🔳 VR +DAT to devote oneself to; (= *sich kümmern um*) **den Gästen etc** to attend to; **einem Problem, einer Aufgabe** to apply oneself to; **nun kann ich mich dir/dieser Aufgabe ganz ~** I can now give you/this task my undivided attention

Widmung [ˈvɪtmʊŋ] F **-, -en** (*in Buch etc*) dedication (*an +acc* to)

widrig [ˈviːdrɪç] ADJ adverse

Widrigkeit F **-, -en** adversity; **allen ~en zum Trotz** in the face of great adversity

wie [viː] 🔳 INTERROG ADV **(a)** how; **~ anders ...?** how else ...?; **~ das?** how come?; **aber frag (mich) nicht ~!** but don't ask me how!; **~ wärs (mit uns beiden etc)** (*inf*) how about it? (*inf*); **~ wärs mit einem Whisky?** (*inf*) how about a whisky? **(b)** (= *welcher Art*) **~ wars auf der Party/in Italien?** what was the party/Italy like?; **~ ist er (denn)?** what's he like?; **~ ist es eigentlich, wenn ...?** what happens if ...?; **~ war das (noch mal genau) mit dem Unfall?** what (exactly) happened in the accident?; **und ~ ist es mit deinem Job?** and what about your job?; **Sie wissen ja, ~ das so ist** well, you know how it is **(c)** (= *was*) **~ heißt er/das?** what's he/it called?; **~?** what?; **bitte?, ~ war das?** (*inf*), **meinen** *or* **belieben?** (*inf*) sorry?; **~ bitte?!** (*entrüstet*) I beg your pardon! **(d)** (*in Ausrufen*) how; **und ~!, aber ~!** and how! (*inf*); **~ groß er ist!** how big he is!; **~ haben wir gelacht, als ...** how we laughed when ... **(e)** (= *nicht wahr?*) eh; **das macht dir Spaß, ~?** you like that, don't you?; **das macht dir keinen Spaß, ~?** you don't like that, do you?

🔳 ADV **(a)** (*relativ*) **die Art, ~ sie geht** the way (in which) she walks; **es war ein Sonnenuntergang, ~ er noch nie einen gesehen hatte** it was a sunset the like of which he had never seen before **(b)** (*in Verbindung mit auch*) **~ stark du auch sein magst** however strong you may be; **~ sehr ... auch** however much; **~ sie auch alle heißen** whatever they're called

🔳 CONJ **(a)** (*vergleichend*) (*auf adj, adv bezüglich*) as; (*auf n bezüglich*) like; **so ... ~** as ... as; **so lang ~ breit** as long as it *etc* is wide; **weiß ~ Schnee** (as) white as snow; **eine Nase ~ eine Kartoffel** a nose like a potato; **er ist Lehrer, ~ sein Vater es war** he is a teacher like his father was (*inf*); **T ~ Theodor** "t" as in "Tommy"; (*bei Rundfunk etc*) t for Tommy; **~ gewöhnlich/immer** as usual/always *or* ever; **ich fühlte mich ~ im Traum** I felt as if I were dreaming; **~ du weißt/man sagt** as you know/ they say; **~ noch nie** as never before **(b)** (*incorrect: = als*) **größer ~** bigger than; **nichts ~ Ärger** *etc* nothing but trouble *etc*

(c) (= *und*) as well as; **Alte ~ Junge** old and young alike **(d)** (*inf*) **~ wenn** as if **(e)** **er sah, ~ es geschah** he saw it happen; **sie spürte, ~ es kalt wurde** she felt it getting cold; **~ ich mich umdrehte, sah ich ...** as I turned around, I saw ...

Wiedehopf [ˈviːdəhɔpf] M **-(e)s, -e** hoopoe

wieder [ˈviːdɐ] ADV again; **~ nüchtern/glücklich** *etc* sober/happy *etc* again; **immer ~, ~ und ~** again and again; **~ mal, (ein)mal ~** (once) again; **komm doch ~ mal vorbei** come and see me/us again; **~ ist ein Jahr vorbei** another year has passed; **wie, schon ~?** what, again?; **~ da** back (again); **das ist auch ~ wahr** that's true; **da sieht man mal ~, ...** it just shows ...; **das fällt mir schon ~ ein** I'll remember it again; **das Boot tauchte ~ auf** the boat resurfaced; **~ geboren** (*lit, fig*) reborn; **~ geboren werden** to be reborn; **~ verwendbar** reusable; **~ verwertbar** recyclable

Wieder-, wieder- PREF re; (*bei Verben*) = *erneut, noch einmal*) again; (= *zurück*) back; **wieder aufarbeiten** *etc* VT *siehe* **wieder aufbereiten; wieder aufbauen** VTI to reconstruct; **wieder aufbereiten** VT to recycle; *Atommüll, Abwasser* to reprocess; **Wiederaufbereitung** F recycling; (*von Atommüll*) reprocessing; **Wiederaufbereitungsanlage** F recycling plant; (*für Atommüll*) reprocessing plant; **wieder aufleben** VI AUX SEIN to revive; **Wiederaufnahme** [ˈviːdɐʔaufnaːmə] F **(a)** (*von Tätigkeit, Gespräch etc*) resumption; (*von Gedanken, Idee*) readoption; (*von Thema*) reversion (+*gen* to); **die ~ des Verfahrens** (*Jur*) the reopening of proceedings **(b)** (*von verstoßenem Menschen*) taking back; (*im Verein etc*) readmittance; (*von Patienten*) readmission; **wieder aufnehmen** VT SEP IRREG **(a)** (= *wieder beginnen*) to resume; *Gedanken, Idee, Hobby* to take up again; *Thema* to revert to; (*Jur*) *Verfahren* to reopen **(b)** *verstoßenen Menschen* to take back; *Vereinsmitglied, Patienten* to readmit; **Wiederbeginn** M recommencement; (*von Schule*) reopening; **wiederbekommen** *ptp* **wiederbekommen** VT SEP IRREG to get back; **wieder beleben** VT (*lit, fig*) to revive; **Wiederbelebung** F (*lit, fig*) revival; **Wiederbelebungsversuch** M attempt at resuscitation; (*fig*) attempt at revival

wiederbeschaffen *ptp* **wiederbeschafft** VT SEP to replace; (= *zurückbekommen*) to recover

Wiederbeschaffung F replacement; (= *Zurückbekommen*) recovery

Wiederbeschaffungs- (*Comm*): **Wiederbeschaffungskosten** PL replacement cost *sing*; **Wiederbeschaffungspreis** M replacement cost; **Wiederbeschaffungswert** M replacement value

Wieder-: wiederbringen VT SEP IRREG to bring back; **wieder einführen** VT to reintroduce; (*Comm*) *Waren* to reimport; **Wiedereingliederung** F reintegration; **die ~ eines Straftäters in die Gesellschaft** the rehabilitation of a criminal offender; **wieder einstellen** VT SEP to re-employ; (*nach ungerechtfertigter Entlassung*) to reinstate; **Wiedereintritt** M reentry (*auch Space*) (*in +acc* into); **wieder entdecken** VT (*lit, fig*) to rediscover; **Wiederentdeckung** F rediscovery; **wieder erkennen** VT IRREG to recognize; **das/er war nicht wieder zu erkennen** it/he was unrecognizable; **wieder eröffnen** VTI to reopen; **Wiedereröffnung** F reopening; **wiedererstatten** *ptp* **wiedererstattet** VT SEP *Unkosten etc* to refund (*jdm etw* sb for sth); **Wiedererstattung** F refund(ing); **wieder finden** IRREG 🔳 VT to find again; (*fig*) *Selbstachtung, Mut etc* to regain; **die Sprache ~** (*fig*) to find one's tongue again (*Brit*), to regain one's speech (*US*) 🔳 VR **sich irgendwo ~** to find oneself somewhere; **sich** *or* **einander ~** to find each other again

Wiedergabe F **(a)** (*von Rede, Ereignis, Vorgang*) account; (= *Beschreibung*) description; (= *Wiederholung: von Äußerung etc*) repetition **(b)** (= *Darbietung: von Stück etc*) rendition **(c)** (= *Übersetzung*) translation **(d)** (= *Reproduktion*) (*von Gemälde, Farben, akustisch*) reproduction; **bei der ~** in reproduction **(e)** (= *Rückgabe*) return; (*von Rechten, Freiheit etc*) restitution

wiedergeben VT SEP IRREG **(a)** *Gegenstand, Geld, Rechte, Mut etc* to give back; **jdm die Freiheit ~** to restore sb's freedom **(b)** (= *erzählen*) to give an account of; (= *beschreiben*) to describe; (= *wiederholen*) to repeat **(c)** (= *übersetzen*) to translate **(d)** (= *reproduzieren*) *Gemälde, Farbe, Ton* to reproduce **(e)** (= *vermitteln*) *Bedeutung, Gefühl, Erlebnis* to convey

Wieder-: wiedergeboren ADJ *siehe* **wieder; wiedergewinnen** *ptp* **wiedergewonnen** VT SEP IRREG (*lit, fig*) to regain; *jdn* to win back; *Land, Rohstoffe etc* to reclaim; *Geld, Selbstvertrauen* to recover; **wieder gutmachen** VT *Schaden* to compensate for; *Fehler* to rectify; *Beleidigung* to put right; (= *sühnen*) to atone for; (*Pol*) to make reparations for; (*Jur*) to redress; **das ist nie wieder gutzumachen** that can never be put right; **Wiedergutmachung** F **-, -en** compensation; (= *Sühne*) atonement; (*Pol*) reparations *pl*; (*Jur*) redress; **als ~ für den Schaden** to compensate for the damage; **als ~ für den Fehler** to rectify the fault; **wiederhaben** VT SEP IRREG (*inf*) to get back; **etw ~ wollen** to want sth back; **wieder herstellen** VT *Gebäude, Ordnung, Frieden, Demokratie* to restore; *Vertrauen, Glaubwürdigkeit auch, Beziehungen* to re-establish; **wiederherstellen** ptp **wiederhergestellt** VT SEP *Gesundheit* to restore; *Patienten* to restore to health; **von einer Krankheit wiederhergestellt sein** to have recovered from an illness; **Wiederherstellung** F (*von Gebäude, Ordnung, Frieden, Gesundheit*) restoration; (*von Beziehungen*) re-establishment

wiederholen[1] [viːdɐˈhoːlən], ptp **wiederholt** INSEP **1** VTI to repeat; (*zusammenfassend*) to recapitulate; *Lernstoff* to revise, to review (*US*); *Prüfung, Filmszene, Elfmeter* to retake; *Spiel* to replay; **wiederholt, was ich euch vorsage** repeat after me; **(eine Klasse** or **ein Jahr) ~** (*Sch*) to repeat a year **2** VR (*Mensch*) to repeat oneself; (*Thema, Ereignis*) to recur; (*Dezimalstelle*) to recur; **es wiederholt sich doch alles im Leben** life has a habit of repeating itself

wiederholen[2] [ˈviːdɐhoːlən] VT SEP (= *zurückholen*) to get back

wiederholt [viːdɐˈhoːlt] **1** ADJ repeated; **zu ~en Malen** repeatedly; **zum ~en Male** once again **2** ADV repeatedly

Wiederholung [viːdɐˈhoːlʊŋ] F **-, -en** repetition; (*von Prüfung, Filmszene, Elfmeter*) retaking; (*von Aufführung*) repeat performance; (*von Sendung*) repeat; (*von Spiel*) replay; (*von Lernstoff*) revision; (*zusammenfassend*) recapitulation

Wiederholungs-: Wiederholungsspiel NT (*Sport*) replay; **Wiederholungstäter(in)** M(F) (*Jur*) (*bei erster Wiederholung*) second offender; (*bei ständiger Wiederholung*) persistent offender

Wieder-: Wiederhören NT **(auf) ~!** (*am Telefon*) goodbye!; (*im Hörfunk*) goodbye for now!; **Wiederinstandsetzung** [viːdɐlɪnˈʃtantzɛtsʊŋ] F (*form*) repair (+*gen* to); **wiederkäuen** SEP **1** VT to ruminate; (*fig inf*) to go over again and again **2** VI to ruminate; (*fig inf*) to harp on; **Wiederkäuer** [-kɔyɐ] M **-s, -** ruminant

wiederkehren VI SEP AUX SEIN (= *zurückkehren*) to return; (= *sich wiederholen, wieder vorkommen*) to recur

wiederkehrend ADJ recurring; **regelmäßig/oft ~** recurrent; **immer ~** ever-recurring

Wieder-: wieder kennen VT IRREG (*inf*) to recognize; **wiederkommen** VI SEP IRREG AUX SEIN (*lit, fig*) to come back; **komm doch mal wieder!** you must come again!; **wiederkriegen** VT SEP (*inf*) to get back; **wiedersehen** VT SEP IRREG to see again; (= *wieder zusammentreffen mit auch*) to meet again; **wann sehen wir uns wieder?** when will we see each other again?; **Wiedersehen** [ˈviːdezeːən] NT **-s, -** (*nach kürzerer Zeit*) (another) meeting; (*nach längerer Zeit*) reunion; **ich freue mich auf das ~ mit meinen Freunden/mit der Heimat** I'm looking forward to seeing my friends/to being back home again; **irgendwo, irgendwann gibt es ein ~** we'll meet again, don't know where, don't know when; **(auf) ~!** goodbye!; **(auf** or **Auf) ~ sagen** to say goodbye; **~ macht Freude!** (*hum*) I wouldn't mind having it back again!

wiederum [ˈviːdɐʊm] ADV **(a)** (= *andrerseits*) on the other hand; (= *allerdings*) though; **das ist ~ richtig, daran habe ich nicht gedacht** that's quite correct, I didn't think of that **(b)** (*geh*: = *nochmals*) again

Wieder-: wieder vereinigen 1 VT *Menschen, Fraktionen* to reunite; *Kirche auch, Land* to reunify **2** VR to reunite; **Wiedervereinigung** F reunification; **Wiederverkaufswert** M resale value; **wiederverwendbar** ADJ siehe **wieder**; **wieder verwenden** VT to reuse; **wiederverwertbar** ADJ siehe **wieder**; **Wiederverwertbarkeit** F recyclability; **wieder verwerten** VT to recycle; **Wiederverwertung** F recycling

Wiege [ˈviːɡə] F **-, -n** (*lit, fig, Tech*) cradle; **es ist mir/ihm auch nicht an der ~ gesungen worden, dass ...** no-one could have foreseen that ...

Wiegemesser NT chopper, cleaver

wiegen[1] [ˈviːɡn] **1** VT **(a)** (= *hin und her bewegen*) to rock; *Hüften* to sway; **einen ~den Gang haben** to sway one's hips

when one walks **(b)** (= *zerkleinern*) to chop up **2** VR (*Boot etc*) to rock (gently); (*Mensch, Äste etc*) to sway; **sich in trügerischen Hoffnungen ~** to nurture false hopes

wiegen[2] pret **wog** [voːk], ptp **gewogen** [ɡəˈvoːɡn] VTI (= *abwiegen*) to weigh; **ein knapp gewogenes Kilo** something short of a kilo; **wie viel wiegst du?** how heavy are you?; **schwer ~** (*fig*) to carry a lot of weight; (*Irrtum etc*) to be serious; siehe auch **gewogen**

Wiegenlied NT lullaby

wiehern [ˈviːɐn] VI to neigh; (*leiser*) to whinny

Wien [viːn] NT **-s** Vienna

Wiener [ˈviːnɐ] ADJ ATTR Viennese; **~ Würstchen** frankfurter; **~ Schnitzel** Wiener schnitzel

wienerisch [ˈviːnərɪʃ] ADJ Viennese

wienerln [ˈviːnɐln], **wienern** [ˈviːnɐn] VI (*inf*) to speak Viennese

wienern VT (*usu pej*) to polish

wies PRET *von* **weisen**

Wiese [ˈviːzə] F **-, -n** meadow; (*inf*: = *Rasen*) grass; **auf der grünen ~** (*fig*) in the open countryside

Wiesel [ˈviːzl] NT **-s, -** weasel; **schnell** or **flink wie ein ~** quick as a flash

Wiesenblume F meadow flower

wieso [viˈzoː] INTERROG ADV why; (= *aus welchem Grund auch*) how come (*inf*); **~ nicht** why not; **~ sagst du das?** why do you say that?; **~ weißt du das?** how do you know that?

wieviel [viˈfiːl, ˈvi-] INTERROG ADV siehe **viel**

wievielerlei [viˈfiːleˈlai, ˈvi-] INTERROG ADJ INV how many sorts of

wievielmal [viˈfiːlmaːl, ˈvi-] INTERROG ADV how many times

Wievielte(r) [viˈfiːltə, ˈvi-] M DECL AS ADJ (*bei Datum*) **den ~n haben wir heute?, der ~ ist heute?** what's the date today?; **am ~n (des Monats)?** what date?; **der ~ ist Donnerstag?** what's the date on Thursday?

wievielte(r, s) [viˈfiːltə, ˈvi-] INTERROG ADJ **das ~ Kind ist das jetzt?** how many children is that now?; **das ~ Kind bist du? – das zweite** which child are you? – the second; **der ~ Band fehlt?** which volume is missing?; **den ~n Platz hat er im Wettkampf belegt?** where did he come in the competition?; **als Wievielter ging er durchs Ziel?** what place did he come?; **das ~ Mal** or **zum ~n Mal bist du schon in England?** how often have you been to England?; **am ~n September hast du Geburtstag?** what date in September is your birthday?; **das ~ Jahr bist du jetzt in Schottland?** how many years have you lived in Scotland now?; **ich habe morgen Geburtstag! – der ~ ist es denn?** it's my birthday tomorrow! – how old will you be?

wieweit [viˈvait] CONJ to what extent

Wikinger [ˈviːkɪŋɐ, ˈvɪkɪŋɐ] M **-s, -**, **Wikingerin** [-ərɪn] F **-, -nen** Viking

Wikingerschiff NT longboat

wild [vɪlt] **1** ADJ wild; *Stamm* savage; (= *laut, ausgelassen*) boisterous; (= *heftig*) *Kampf, Blick* fierce; (= *ungesetzlich*) *Parken, Zelten etc* illegal; *Streik* wildcat *attr*, unofficial; **der Wilde Westen** the Wild West; **seid nicht so ~!** calm down a bit!; **jdn ~ machen** to make sb furious, to drive sb crazy; (*esp vor Vergnügen etc*) to drive sb wild; **~ werden** to go wild (*auch inf*); **~ auf jdn/etw sein** (*inf*) to be mad about sb/sth (*inf*); **das ist nicht so** or **halb so ~** (*inf*) never mind **2** ADV **(a)** (= *unordentlich*) **~ durcheinander liegen** or **herumliegen** to be strewn all over the place; **dann ging alles ~ durcheinander** there was chaos then **(b)** (= *hemmungslos*) like crazy; **brüllen, auf jdn einschlagen, um sich schlagen** wildly; **wie ~ rennen/arbeiten** *etc* to run/work *etc* like mad; **~ entschlossen** (*inf*) really determined **(c)** (= *in der freien Natur*) **~ leben** to live in the wild; **~ wachsen** to grow wild; **~ wachsend** wild(-growing)

Wild [vɪlt] NT **-(e)s** [-dəs], NO PL (= *Tiere, Fleisch*) game; (= *Rotwild*) deer; (= *Fleisch von Rotwild*) venison

Wild-: Wildbach M torrent; **Wildbahn** F **auf** or **in freier ~** in the wild; **Wildbestand** M game population; **Wilddieb(in)** M(F) poacher; **Wilddiebstahl** M poaching

Wilde(r) [ˈvɪldə] MF DECL AS ADJ savage; (*fig*) madman; **die ~n** the savages

Wilderei [vɪldəˈrai] F **-, -en** poaching

Wilderer [ˈvɪldərɐ] M **-s, -**, **Wilderin** [-ərɪn] F **-, -nen** poacher

wildern [ˈvɪldən] VI (*Mensch*) to poach; (*Hund etc*) to kill game; ~der Hund dog which kills game

Wild-: Wildesel M wild ass; **Wildfleisch** NT game; (*von Rotwild*) venison; **wildfremd** [ˈvɪltˈfrɛmt] ADJ (*inf*) completely strange; ~e Leute/Menschen complete strangers; ein Wildfremder, ein ~er Mensch a complete stranger; **Wildgans** F wild goose

Wildheit F -, -en wildness; (*von Stamm etc*) savagery; (*von Kampf, Blick*) fierceness; (= *Leidenschaft*) wild passion

Wild-: Wildhüter(in) M(F) gamekeeper; **Wildkatze** F wildcat; **Wildleder** NT suede; **wildledern** ADJ suede

Wildnis [ˈvɪltnɪs] F -, -se (*lit, fig*) wilderness; in der ~ leben/geboren werden to live/be born in the wild

Wild-: Wildpark M game park; (*für Rotwild*) deer park; **wildromantisch** [ˈvɪltroˈmantɪʃ] ADJ (*iro*) terribly romantic; **Wildsau** F wild sow; (*fig sl*) pig (*inf*); **Wildschaden** M damage caused by game; **Wildschwein** NT wild boar; **Wildwasser** NT, *pl* -wasser white water; **Wildwasserfahren** NT white-water canoeing *or* rafting; **Wildwest** NO ART the Wild West; **Wildwestfilm** M western; **Wildwestmethoden** PL (*pej inf*) Mafia methods

Wilhelm [ˈvɪlhɛlm] M -s William; seinen (Friedrich) ~ unter etw (*dat*) setzen (*inf*) to put one's signature to sth

will 1. AND 3. PERS PRES *von* **wollen**[2]

Wille [ˈvɪlə] M -ns, NO PL will; (= *Absicht, Entschluss*) intention; nach jds ~n as sb wanted/wants; (*von Architekt etc*) as sb intended/intends; der ~ zur Zusammenarbeit the will to cooperate; wenn es nach ihrem ~n ginge if she had her way; das geschah gegen *or* wider meinen ~n (= *gegen meinen Wunsch*) that was done against my will; (= *unabsichtlich*) I didn't intend that to happen; er musste wider ~n *or* gegen seinen ~n lachen he couldn't help laughing; seinen ~n durchsetzen to get one's (own) way; jdm seinen ~n lassen to let sb have his own way; beim besten ~n nicht not with the best will in the world; ich hätte das beim besten ~n nicht machen können I couldn't have done that for the life of me; jdm zu ~n sein to comply with sb's wishes; (*Mädchen: = sich hingeben*) to yield to sb; wo ein ~ ist, ist auch ein Weg (*Prov*) where there's a will there's a way (*Prov*)

willen [ˈvɪlən] PREP *siehe* **um** 2

willenlos 1 ADJ weak-willed; **völlig ~ sein** to have no will of one's own 2 ADV jdm ~ ergeben sein to be totally submissive to sb

willens [ˈvɪləns] ADJ (*geh*) ~ sein to be willing

Willens-: Willenskraft F willpower; **willensschwach** ADJ weak-willed; **Willensschwäche** F weak will; **willensstark** ADJ strong-willed; **Willensstärke** F willpower

willentlich [ˈvɪləntlɪç] 1 ADJ wilful 2 ADV deliberately

willig [ˈvɪlɪç] 1 ADJ willing 2 ADV willingly

willkommen [vɪlˈkɔmən] ADJ welcome; du bist (mir) immer ~ you are always welcome; jdn ~ heißen to welcome sb; seid (herzlich) ~! welcome, welcome!; herzlich ~ welcome (*in +dat* to); es ist mir ganz ~, dass ... I quite welcome the fact that ...; die Gelegenheit, das zu sagen/zu tun, ist mir ~ I welcome the opportunity of saying/doing this

Willkommens-: Willkommensgruß M greeting; **Willkommenstrunk** M welcoming drink

Willkür [ˈvɪlkyːɐ̯] F -, NO PL capriciousness; (*politisch*) despotism; (*bei Entscheidungen, Handlungen*) arbitrariness; sie sind seiner ~ schutzlos preisgegeben *or* ausgeliefert they are completely at his mercy; das ist reinste ~ that is purely arbitrary; ein Akt der ~ an act of caprice/a despotic act/an arbitrary act

willkürlich [ˈvɪlkyːɐ̯lɪç] 1 ADJ (a) arbitrary; Herrscher autocratic (b) Muskulatur, Kontraktion voluntary 2 ADV anordnen, handeln, vorgehen arbitrarily; sie kann ~ Tränen produzieren she can produce tears at will

Willy [ˈvɪli] M -s, -s (*sl: = Penis*) willy (*Brit inf*), weenie (*US inf*)

wimmeln [ˈvɪmln] VI (a) AUCH VI IMPERS (= *in Mengen vorhanden sein*) der See wimmelt von Fischen, in dem See wimmelt es von Fischen the lake is teeming with fish; hier wimmelt es von Fliegen/Pilzen/Menschen this place is swarming with flies/overrun with mushrooms/teeming with people; der Käse wimmelt von Maden the cheese is crawling with maggots; dieses Buch wimmelt von Fehlern this book is riddled with mistakes (b) AUX SEIN (= *sich bewegen*) to teem; (*Mücken, Ameisen*) to swarm

wimmern [ˈvɪmɐn] VI to whimper

Wimpel [ˈvɪmpl] M -s, - pennant

Wimper [ˈvɪmpɐ] F -, -n (a) (eye)lash; ohne mit der ~ zu zucken (*fig*) without batting an eyelid (*Brit*) *or* eyelash (*US*) (b) (*Bot, Zool*) cilium

Wimperntusche F mascara

Wimpertierchen NT ciliate

Wind [vɪnt] M -(e)s, -e [-də] wind; bei *or* in ~ und Wetter in all weathers; ~ und Wetter ausgesetzt sein to be exposed to the elements; wissen/merken, woher der ~ weht *or* bläst (*fig*) to know/notice the way the wind is blowing; daher weht der ~! (*fig*) so that's the way the wind is blowing; ein neuer ~ weht durch das Land (*fig*) the wind of change is blowing in the country; frischen *or* neuen ~ in etw (*acc*) bringen (*fig*) to breathe new life into sth; mach doch nicht so einen ~ (*inf*) don't make such a to-do (*inf*); viel ~ um etw machen (*inf*) to make a lot of fuss about sth; vor dem ~ segeln (*lit*) to sail with the wind (behind one); gegen den ~ segeln (*lit*) to sail into the wind; (*fig*) to swim against the stream, to run against the wind (*US*); den Mantel *or* die Fahne nach dem ~ hängen *or* drehen to trim one's sails to the wind; jdm den ~ aus den Segeln nehmen (*fig*) to take the wind out of sb's sails; etw in den ~ schlagen Warnungen, Rat to turn a deaf ear to sth; Vorsicht, Vernunft to throw sth to the winds; in alle (vier) ~e to the four winds; in alle (vier) ~e zerstreut sein (*fig*) to be scattered to the four corners of the earth; von etw ~ bekommen *or* kriegen/haben (*fig inf*) to get/have wind of sth

Wind-: Windbeutel M (a) cream puff (b) (*inf: Mensch*) rake; **Windbluse** F windcheater; **Windbö(e)** F gust of wind

Winde[1] [ˈvɪndə] F -, -n (*Tech*) winch

Winde[2] F -, -n (*Bot*) bindweed

Windel [ˈvɪndl] F -, -n nappy (*Brit*), diaper (*US*)

Windel-: Windeleinlage F, **Windelfolie** F nappy (*Brit*) *or* diaper (*US*) liner; **Windelhöschen** [-høːsçən] NT plastic pants *pl*

windelweich [ˈvɪndlˈvaɪç] 1 ADV jdn ~ schlagen *or* hauen (*inf*) to beat sb black and blue 2 ADJ (= *nachgiebig*) softly-softly

winden[1] [ˈvɪndn] *pret* **wand** [vant], *ptp* **gewunden** [gəˈvʊndn] 1 VT to wind; Kranz to bind; (= *hochwinden*) Eimer, Last to winch; jdm etw aus der Hand ~ to wrest sth out of sb's hand 2 VR (*Pflanze, Schlange, Bach*) to wind; (*Mensch*) (*durch Menge, Gestrüpp etc*) to wind (one's) way; (*vor Schmerzen*) to writhe (*vor* with, in); (*vor Scham, Verlegenheit*) to squirm (*vor* with, in); (*fig: = ausweichen*) to try to wriggle out; sich ~ wie ein (getretener) Wurm to squirm; *siehe auch* **gewunden**

winden[2] VI IMPERS es windet the wind is blowing

Windenergie F wind energy

Windenergieanlage F wind energy plant

Windeseile F etw in *or* mit ~ tun to do sth in no time (at all); sich in *or* mit ~ verbreiten to spread like wildfire

Wind-: Windfarm F wind farm; **Windgenerator** M wind generator; **windgeschützt** 1 ADJ sheltered (from the wind) 2 ADV in a sheltered place; **Windhose** F vortex

Windhund M (a) (*Hund*) greyhound; (= *Afghanischer ~*) Afghan (hound) (b) (*fig pej*) rake

windig [ˈvɪndɪç] ADJ windy; (*fig*) Bursche, Sache dubious

Wind-: Windjacke F windcheater (*Brit*), windproof jacket; **Windkraft** F wind power; **Windkraftanlage** F, **Windkraftwerk** NT wind power station; **Windlicht** NT lantern; **Windmühle** F windmill; gegen ~n (an)kämpfen (*fig*) to tilt at windmills; **Wind(mühlen)park** M wind farm; **Windpocken** PL chickenpox *sing*; **Windrad** NT (*Tech*) wind turbine; **Windrichtung** F wind direction; **Windrose** F (*Naut*) compass card; (*Met*) wind rose; **Windschatten** M lee; (*von Fahrzeugen*) slipstream; **Windscheibe** F (*Sw, Aut*) windscreen (*Brit*), windshield (*US*); **windschief** ADJ crooked; **windschlüpfig, windschnittig** ADJ streamlined; **Windschutzscheibe** F windscreen (*Brit*), windshield (*US*); **Windstärke** F strength of the wind; (*Met*) wind force; **windstill** ADJ still; Platz, Ecke etc sheltered; wenn es völlig ~ ist when there is no wind at all; **Windstille** F calm; **Windstoß** M gust of wind; **Windsurfbrett** NT windsurfer; **windsurfen** VI INSEP to windsurf; ~ gehen to go windsurfing; **Windsurfen** NT -s, NO PL windsurfing; **Windsurfer(in)** M(F) windsurfer; **Windturbine** F wind turbine

Windung [ˈvɪndʊŋ] F -, -en (*von Weg, Fluss etc*) meander; (*von Schlange*) coil; (*Anat: von Darm*) convolution; (*Tech: von Schraube*) thread; (= *eine Umdrehung*) revolution; (*Elec: von Spule*) coil

Wink [vɪŋk] M **-(e)s, -e** (= *Zeichen*) sign; (*mit der Hand*) wave (*mit of*); (*mit dem Kopf*) nod (*mit of*); (= *Hinweis, Tip*) hint

Winkel [ˈvɪŋkl] M **-s, -** (a) (*Math*) angle (b) (*Tech*) square (c) (*fig*) (= *Stelle, Ecke*) corner; (= *Plätzchen: esp von Land, Wald etc*) spot

Winkel-: Winkeladvokat(in) M(F) (*pej*) incompetent lawyer; **Winkeleisen** NT angle iron; **winkelförmig** ◼ ADJ angled ◼ ADV ~ **gebogen** bent at an angle; **Winkelfunktion** F (*Math*) trigonometrical function; **Winkelhalbierende** [-halbiːrəndə] F DECL AS ADJ bisector of an/the angle

winkelig [ˈvɪŋkəlɪç] ADJ = **winklig**

Winkel-: Winkelmesser M **-s, -** protractor; **Winkelschleifer** [-ʃlaifə] M **-s, -** angle grinder

winken [ˈvɪŋkn], *ptp* **gewinkt** *or* (*dial*) **gewunken** [gəˈvʊŋkt, gəˈvʊŋkn] ◼ VI to wave (*jdm* to sb); **jdm ~, etw zu tun** to signal sb to do sth; **einem Taxi ~** to hail a taxi; **dem Kellner ~** to signal to the waiter; **jdm winkt etw** (*fig:* = *steht in Aussicht*) sb can expect sth; **bei der Verlosung ~ wertvolle Preise** valuable prizes are being offered in the draw; **dem Sieger winkt eine Reise nach Italien** the winner will receive (the attractive prize of) a trip to Italy
◼ VT to wave; (*esp Sport:* = *anzeigen*) to signal; *Kellner* to call; **jdn zu sich ~** to beckon sb over to one

winklig [ˈvɪŋklɪç] ADJ *Haus, Altstadt* full of nooks and crannies; *Gasse* twisty

winseln [ˈvɪnzln] VTI to whimper; (*pej: um Gnade etc*) to grovel

Winter [ˈvɪntɐ] M **-s, -** winter; **es ist/wird ~** winter is here/is coming; **im/über den ~** in (the)/over the winter; **der nächste ~ kommt bestimmt** (*inf*) you never know how long the good times are going to last; **der nukleare ~** nuclear winter

Winter- IN CPDS winter; **Winteranfang** M beginning of winter; **vor/seit ~** before/since the beginning of winter; **Winterdienst** M (*Mot*) winter road treatment; **Winterfahrplan** M winter timetable; **Winterflugplan** M winter flight schedule; **Wintergarten** M winter garden; **Winterhalbjahr** NT winter; **im ~** from September to March; **im ~ 1998/99** in the winter of 1998/99; **Winterlandschaft** F winter landscape

winterlich [ˈvɪntɐlɪç] ◼ ADJ wintry, winter *attr* ◼ ADV **es ist ~ kalt** it's as cold as it is in winter; **~ kalte Temperaturen** cold winter temperatures; **~ gekleidet** dressed for winter

Winter-: Winterolympiade F Winter Olympics *pl*; **Winterreifen** M winter tyre (*Brit*) *or* tire (*US*)

winters [ˈvɪntɐs] ADV in winter

Winter-: Wintersachen PL winter clothes *pl*; **Winterschlaf** M (*Zool*) hibernation; **(den) ~ halten** to hibernate; **Winterschlussverkauf** M winter (clearance) sale; **Wintersemester** NT winter semester; **Winterspiele** PL **(Olympische) ~** Winter Olympics *pl*; **Wintersport** M winter sports *pl*; (= *~art*) winter sport; **in den ~ fahren** to go on a winter sports holiday (*esp Brit*) *or* vacation (*US*); **Winterzeit** F winter time; (*Jahreszeit*) wintertime

Winzer [ˈvɪntsɐ] M **-s, -**, **Winzerin** [-ərɪn] F **-, -nen** wine grower; (= *Weinleser*) grape picker

winzig [ˈvɪntsɪç] ADJ tiny; **ein ~es bisschen** a tiny little bit; **~ klein** minute, tiny little *attr*

Winzigkeit F **-, -en** (a) NO PL tiny size (b) (= *winzige Menge*) tiny drop/bit/quantity *etc*; (= *Geschenk*) little thing

Winzling [ˈvɪntslɪŋ] M **-s, -e** (*inf*) mite

Wipfel [ˈvɪpfl] M **-s, -** treetop

Wippe [ˈvɪpə] F **-, -n** (*zum Schaukeln*) seesaw; (= *Babywippe*) bouncy chair

wippen [ˈvɪpn] VI (*auf und ab*) to bob up and down; (*hin und her*) to teeter; (*Schwanz*) to wag; (= *mit Wippe schaukeln*) to seesaw; **mit dem Fuß ~** to jiggle one's foot

wir [viːɐ] PERS PRON, *gen* **unser** [ˈʊnzɐ], *dat* **uns** [ʊns], *acc* **uns** [ʊns] we; **~ alle** all of us; **~ beide** both of us; **~ drei** the three of us; **~ Kommunisten** we Communists; **~, die ~ ...** we who ...; **immer sollen ~s gewesen sein** everyone always blames us; **wer war das? – ~ nicht** who was that? – it wasn't us; **wer kommt noch mit? – ~/~ nicht** who's coming along? – we are/not us; **wer ist da? – ~** (**sinds**) who's there? – (it's) us; **trinken ~ erst mal einen** let's have a drink first

wirb [vɪrp] IMPER SING *von* **werben**

Wirbel [ˈvɪrbl] M **-s, -** (a) (*lit, fig*) whirl; (*in Fluss etc*) whirlpool; (= *Aufsehen*) to-do; (**viel/großen**) **~ machen/verursachen** to make/cause (a lot of/a big) commotion (b) (= *Haarwirbel*)

crown; (*nicht am Hinterkopf*) cowlick (c) (= *Trommelwirbel*) (drum) roll (d) (*Anat*) vertebra

wirbellos ADJ (*Zool*) invertebrate; **die Wirbellosen** the invertebrates

wirbeln [ˈvɪrbln] VI (a) AUX SEIN (*Mensch, Wasser etc*) to whirl; (*Laub, Rauch*) to swirl (b) **mir wirbelt der Kopf** (*inf*) my head is spinning (c) (*Trommeln etc*) to roll

Wirbel-: Wirbelsäule F (*Anat*) spinal column; **Wirbelsturm** M whirlwind; **Wirbeltier** NT vertebrate; **Wirbelwind** M whirlwind

wirbt [vɪrpt] 3. PERS SING PRES *von* **werben**

wird [vɪrt] 3. PERS SING PRES *von* **werden**

wirf [vɪrf] IMPER SING *von* **werfen**

wirft [vɪrft] 3. PERS SING PRES *von* **werfen**

Wirgefühl NT community feeling

wirken [ˈvɪrkn] ◼ VI (a) (= *tätig sein*) (*Mensch*) to work; (*Einflüsse, Kräfte etc*) to be at work; (= *Wirkung haben*) to have an effect; (= *erfolgreich sein*) to work; **als Gegengift ~** to work as an antidote; **als Katalysator ~** to act as a catalyst; **schalldämpfend/abführend ~** to have a soundproofing/laxative effect; **eine stark ~de Droge** a strong drug; **auf etw** (*acc*) **~** (*esp Chem*) to act on sth; **etw auf sich** (*acc*) **~ lassen** to take sth in
(b) (= *erscheinen*) to seem; **das wirkt auf viele als Provokation** many people see that as a provocation
(c) (= *zur Geltung kommen*) to be effective; **neben diesen Gardinen wirkt das Muster nicht (richtig)** the pattern loses its effect next to those curtains; **ich finde, das Bild wirkt** I think the picture has something
◼ VT (*geh:* = *tun*) *Gutes* to do; *Wunder* to work

wirklich [ˈvɪrklɪç] ◼ ADJ real; *Freund auch* true; **im ~en Leben** in real life ◼ ADV really; **ich wüsste gern, wie es ~ war** I would like to know what really happened; **nicht ~** not really; **ich war das ~ nicht** it really was not me; **~?** (*als Antwort*) really?; **nein, ~?** (*als Antwort*) what, really?; **~ und wahrhaftig** really and truly

Wirklichkeit F **-, -en** reality; **~ werden** to come true; **in ~** in reality; **in ~ heißt er anders** his real name is different

Wirklichkeits-: wirklichkeitsfremd ADJ unrealistic; **wirklichkeitsgetreu, wirklichkeitsnah** ◼ ADJ realistic ◼ ADV realistically; **etw wirklichkeitsnah erzählen** to give a realistic account of sth

wirksam [ˈvɪrkzaːm] ◼ ADJ effective; **~ bleiben** to remain in effect; **mit (dem)** *or* **am 1. Januar ~ werden** (*form: Gesetz*) to take effect on January 1st ◼ ADV effectively; *verbessern* significantly

Wirksamkeit F **-**, NO PL effectiveness

Wirkstoff M (*esp Physiol*) active substance

Wirkung [ˈvɪrkʊŋ] F **-, -en** effect (*bei* on); (*von Tabletten etc*) effects *pl*; **ohne ~ bleiben** to have no effect; **seine ~ verfehlen** not to have the desired effect; **zur ~ kommen** (*Medikament*) to take effect; (*fig:* = *zur Geltung kommen*) to show to advantage; (*durch Kontrast*) to be set off; **mit ~ vom 1. Januar** (*form*) with effect from January 1st

Wirkungs-: wirkungslos ADJ ineffective; **Wirkungslosigkeit** F **-**, NO PL ineffectiveness; **wirkungsvoll** ◼ ADJ effective ◼ ADV effectively

Wirkwaren PL knitwear *sing*

wirr [vɪr] ◼ ADJ confused; *Blick* crazed; (= *unordentlich*) *Haare, Fäden* tangled; *Gedanken, Vorstellungen, Träume* weird; (= *unrealistisch, verstiegen*) wild; **er ist wirr im Kopf** he has crazy ideas; **~es Zeug reden** to talk gibberish ◼ ADV **alles lag ~ durcheinander** everything was in a mess; **das Haar hängt ihm ~ ins Gesicht** his hair is hanging in tangles in his face; **sich ~ ausdrücken** to express oneself in a confused way

Wirren [ˈvɪrən] PL confusion *sing*

Wirrwarr [ˈvɪrvar] M **-s**, NO PL confusion; (*von Verkehr*) chaos *no indef art*; (*von Fäden, Haaren etc*) tangle

Wirsing [ˈvɪrzɪŋ] M **-s**, NO PL, **Wirsingkohl** M savoy cabbage

Wirt [vɪrt] M **-(e)s, -e** *Gastwirt, Untervermieter*) landlord; (*Biol, rare:* = *Gastgeber*) host

wirten [ˈvɪrtn] VI (*Sw*) to be a/the landlord

Wirtin [ˈvɪrtɪn] F **-, -nen** landlady; (*Gastgeberin*) hostess; (= *Frau des Wirts*) landlord's wife

Wirtschaft [ˈvɪrtʃaft] F **-, -en** (a) (= *Volkswirtschaft*) economy; (= *Handel, Geschäftsleben*) industry and commerce;

(= *Finanzwelt*) business world; **freie** ~ free market economy; **er ist in der** ~ **tätig** he works in industry; he's a businessman **(b)** (= *Gastwirtschaft*) ≈ pub (*Brit*), ≈ bar (*US*) **(c)** (*inf:* = *Zustände*) state of affairs; **du hast vielleicht eine** ~ **in deinem Haus/auf deinem Schreibtisch** a fine mess your house/desk is in; **eine schöne** *or* **saubere** ~ (*iro*) a fine state of affairs

wirtschaften ['vɪrtʃaftn] **1** VI **(a)** (= *sparsam sein*) **(sparsam)** ~ to economize; **gut** ~ **können** to be economical **(b)** (= *den Haushalt führen*) to keep house **(c)** (*inf:* = *sich betätigen*) to busy oneself; (*gemütlich*) to potter about (*Brit*), to putter around (*US*); (= *herumfummeln*) to rummage about **2** VT **jdn/ etw zugrunde** ~ to ruin sb/sth financially

wirtschaftlich ['vɪrtʃaftlɪç] **1** ADJ **(a)** (= *die Wirtschaft betreffend*) economic **(b)** (= *sparsam*) economical; *Hausfrau* thrifty **2** ADV **(a)** (= *finanziell*) financially; **jdm geht es** ~ **gut/ schlecht** sb is in a good/bad financial position **(b)** (= *ökonomisch*) economically; **nicht** ~ **handeln** to be uneconomical

Wirtschaftlichkeit F -, NO PL **(a)** (= *Rentabilität*) profitability **(b)** (= *ökonomischer Betrieb*) economy

Wirtschaftlichkeitsberechnung F evaluation of economic efficiency

Wirtschafts- IN CPDS economic; **Wirtschaftsaufschwung** M economic upswing; **Wirtschaftsauskunftei** F credit investigation agency (*Brit*), credit bureau (*US*); **Wirtschaftsberater(in)** M(F) business consultant; **Wirtschaftsflüchtling** M economic refugee; **Wirtschaftsführer(in)** M(F) leading industrialist; **Wirtschaftsführung** F management; **Wirtschaftsgeld** NT housekeeping (money) (*Brit*), household allowance (*US*); **Wirtschaftsgemeinschaft** F economic community; **Wirtschaftsgipfel** M economic summit; **Wirtschaftsgüter** PL economic goods *pl*; **Wirtschaftsgymnasium** NT *grammar school or high school which places emphasis on economics, law, management studies etc*; **Wirtschaftindikatoren** PL economic indicators *pl*; **Wirtschaftsjahr** NT financial year, fiscal year; **Wirtschaftskreislauf** M business cycle; **Wirtschaftskriminalität** F white collar crime; **Wirtschaftskrise** F economic crisis; **Wirtschaftslage** F economic situation; **Wirtschaftsleben** NT business life; **Persönlichkeiten des ~s** business personalities; **Wirtschaftsminister(in)** M(F) minister of trade and industry (*Brit*), secretary of commerce (*US*); **Wirtschaftsministerium** NT ministry of trade and industry (*Brit*), department of commerce (*US*); **Wirtschaftsordnung** F economic order; **Wirtschaftsplan** M economic plan; **Wirtschaftspolitik** F economic policy; **wirtschaftspolitisch** **1** ADJ *Maßnahmen etc* economic policy *attr*, **~er Sprecher** spokesman on economic policy **2** ADV *geboten, sinnvoll* for the economy; *unerlässlich* to the economy; ~ **verfehlt** bad for the economy; ~ **ist es unmöglich ...** in terms of economic policy it is impossible ...; **Wirtschaftsprüfer(in)** M(F) accountant; (*zum Überprüfen der Bücher*) auditor; **Wirtschaftsraum** M (*Econ*) economic area; **Europäischer** ~ European Economic Area; **Wirtschaftsrecht** NT commercial *or* business law; **Wirtschaftssanktion** F USU PL economic sanction (*gegen* against); **Wirtschaftsspionage** F industrial espionage; **Wirtschaftsstandort** M business location; **der** ~ **Deutschland** Germany as a business location; **Wirtschaftsunion** F economic union; **Wirtschaftswachstum** NT economic growth; **Wirtschaftswissenschaft** F economics *sing*; **Wirtschaftswissenschaftler(in)** M(F) economist; **Wirtschaftswunder** NT economic miracle; **Wirtschaftszweig** M branch of industry

Wirts-: **Wirtshaus** NT ≈ pub (*Brit*), ≈ bar (*US*), ≈ saloon (*dated US*); (*esp auf dem Land*) inn; **Wirtsleute** PL landlord and landlady; **Wirtspflanze** F host (plant); **Wirtsprogramm** NT (*Comput*) host program; **Wirtsstube** F lounge; **Wirtstier** NT host (animal)

Wisch [vɪʃ] M **-(e)s, -e** (*pej inf*) piece of paper; (*mit Gedrucktem,* = *Dokument*) piece of bumph (*Brit inf*), piece of stuff for reading (*inf*); (= *Zettel mit Notiz*) note

wischen ['vɪʃn] **1** VTI to wipe; (= *mit Lappen reinigen*) to wipe clean; (*Sw:* = *fegen*) to sweep; **sie wischte ihm/sich den Schweiß mit einem Handtuch von der Stirn** she wiped the sweat from his/her brow with a towel; **Bedenken/Einwände (einfach) vom Tisch** ~ (*fig*) to sweep aside thoughts/ objections **2** VT (*inf*) **jdm eine** ~ to clout sb one (*Brit inf*), to

clobber sb (*inf*); **einen gewischt bekommen** (*Elec*) to get a shock

Wischer ['vɪʃe] M **-s, -** (*Aut*) (windscreen (*Brit*) or windshield (*US*)) wiper

Wischerblatt NT (*Aut*) wiper blade

Wischiwaschi [vɪʃi'vaʃi] NT **-s,** NO PL (*pej inf*) drivel (*inf*)

Wisent ['viːzɛnt] M **-s, -e** bison

Wismut ['vɪsmuːt] NT or (AUS) M **-(e)s,** NO PL (*abbr* **Bi**) bismuth

wispern ['vɪspɐn] VTI to whisper

Wissbegier(de) F thirst for knowledge

wissbegierig ADJ *Kind* eager to learn

wissen ['vɪsn], *pret* **wusste** ['vʊstə], *ptp* **gewusst** [gə'vʊst] **1** VTI **(a)** (= *informiert sein*) to know (*über +acc,* von about); **ich weiß (es) (schon)** I know; **ich weiß (es) nicht** I don't know; **weißt du schon das Neuste?** have you heard the latest?; **was ich alles ~ soll!, als ob ich das wüsste!** how should I know?; **von ihr weiß ich das Alter** I know her age; **von jdm/etw nichts ~ wollen** not to be interested in sb/sth; **er weiß es nicht anders/ besser** he doesn't know any different/better; **jdn/etw zu schätzen** ~ to appreciate sb/sth; **das musst du (selbst)** ~ it's your decision; **das hättest du ja ~ müssen!** you ought to have realized that; **man kann nie** ~ you never know; **das** ~ **die Götter** (*inf*), **das weiß der Henker** (*inf*) God only knows; **weiß Gott** (*inf*) God knows (*inf*); **sich für weiß Gott was halten** (*inf*) to think one is somebody really special; **sie hält sich für wer weiß wie klug** (*inf*) she thinks she's pretty clever; **er ist wieder wer weiß wo** (*inf*) goodness knows where he's got to (*Brit*) *or* gone to (*US*) again (*inf*); **(ja) wenn ich das wüsste!** goodness knows!; **wenn ich nur wüsste ...** if only I knew ...; **nicht, dass ich wüsste** not as far as I know; **gewusst wie/wo!** *etc* sheer brilliance!; **weißt du was?** (do) you know what?; **dass du es (nur) (gleich) weißt** just so you know; **was ich/er nicht weiß, macht mich/ihn nicht heiß** (*Prov*) what I don't/he doesn't know won't hurt me/him
(b) (= *sich erinnern*) to remember; (= *sich vor Augen führen*) to realize; **weißt du noch, wie schön es damals war?** do you remember how great things were then?; **du musst** ~, **dass ...** you must realize that ...
2 VT **(a)** (= *kennen*) to know; **ich weiß keinen größeren Genuss, als ...** I know (of) no greater delight than ...
(b) (= *erfahren*) **jdn etw ~ lassen** to let sb know sth
3 VI **um etw** (*acc*) ~ (*geh*), **von etw** ~ to know of *or* about sth; **ich/er weiß von nichts** I don't/he doesn't know anything about it

Wissen ['vɪsn] NT **-s,** NO PL knowledge; **meines ~s** to my knowledge; **etw gegen** *or* **wider** (*geh*) **(sein) besseres** ~ **tun** to do sth against one's better judgement; **nach bestem** ~ **und Gewissen** to the best of one's knowledge and belief; ~ **ist Macht** knowledge is power

wissend **1** ADJ *Blick etc* knowing **2** ADV knowingly

Wissenschaft ['vɪsnʃaft] F **-, -en** science

Wissenschaftler ['vɪsnʃaftle] M **-s, -**, **Wissenschaftlerin** [-ərɪn] F **-, -nen** scientist; (= *Geisteswissenschaftler*) academic

wissenschaftlich ['vɪsnʃaftlɪç] **1** ADJ scientific; (= *geisteswissenschaftlich*) academic **2** ADV *arbeiten, etw untersuchen* scientifically

Wissenschaftlichkeit F -, NO PL scientific nature; (*in Bezug auf Geisteswissenschaften*) academic nature; **der Arbeit mangelt es an** ~ this thesis lacks a scientific approach

Wissens-: **Wissensdrang** M, **Wissensdurst** M (*geh*) thirst for knowledge; **Wissensgebiet** NT field (of knowledge); **Wissenslücke** F gap in one's knowledge; **Wissensstand** M state of knowledge; **nach dem gegenwärtigen** ~ according to current knowledge; **Wissensstoff** M material; **das ist** ~ **der 3. Klasse** that's material learned in the 3rd form (*Brit*) *or* 7th grade (*US*); **ein enormer** ~ an enormous amount of material; **wissenswert** ADJ worth knowing; **das Buch enthält viel Wissenswertes** the book contains much valuable information

wissentlich ['vɪsntlɪç] **1** ADJ deliberate **2** ADV deliberately

Witterung F **-, -en (a)** (= *Wetter*) weather; **bei günstiger** *or* **guter** ~ if the weather is good **(b)** (*Hunt*) (= *Geruch*) scent (*von* of); (= *Geruchssinn*) sense of smell

Witterungs-: **Witterungseinflüsse** PL effects *pl* of the weather; **Witterungslage** F weather; **Witterungsverhältnisse** PL weather conditions *pl*

Witwe ['vɪtvə] F **-, -n** widow; **~ werden** to be widowed

Witwer ['vɪtvɐ] M **-s, -** widower

Witz [vɪts] M **-es, -e (a)** (= *Geist*) wit **(b)** (*Äußerung*) joke (*über +acc* about); **einen ~ machen** *or* **reißen** (*inf*) to make a joke; **mach keine ~e!** don't be funny; **ich mach keine ~e** I'm not being funny; **das soll doch wohl ein ~ sein, das ist doch wohl ein ~** that must be a joke, he/you *etc* must be joking **(c) der ~ an der Sache ist, dass ...** the great thing about it is that ...; **das ist der ganze ~** that's the thing

Witzbold ['vɪtsbɔlt] M **-(e)s, -e** [-də] joker; (= *unterhaltsamer Mensch*) comic; **du bist vielleicht ein ~!** (*iro*) you're a great one! (*iro*)

witzig ['vɪtsɪç] ADJ funny

Witzigkeit F **-**, NO PL humour (*Brit*), humor (*US*)

witzlos ADJ (*inf*: = *unsinnig*) pointless

WM [veːˈɛm] F **-, -s** ABBR *von* **Weltmeisterschaft**

wo [voː] **1** INTERROG, REL ADV **(a)** where; (= *irgendwo*) somewhere; **überall, wo** wherever; **wo immer ...** wherever ...; **der Tag/eine Zeit wo ...** (*inf*) the day/a time when ...; **ach** *or* **i wo!** (*inf*) nonsense!
(b) (*inf*: = *der/die/das*) that; **der Mann/die Frau/das Auto, wo ...** the man/woman/car that ...
2 CONJ **wo möglich** where possible; **wo er doch wusste, dass ich nicht kommen konnte** when he knew I couldn't come; **wo du doch in die Stadt gehst, könntest du ...?** (*inf*) seeing that you're going into town, could you ...?; **und das jetzt, wo ich doch dazu keine Lust habe** (*inf*) and that now when I'm just not in the mood

> *Vorsicht!* **wo** *wird nicht mit dem englischen Wort* **who** *übersetzt.*

wo-: **woanders** [voˈandɐs] ADV somewhere else; **woandersher** [voˈandɐsheːɐ] ADV from somewhere else; **woandershin** [voˈandɐshɪn] ADV somewhere else

wob PRET *von* **weben**

wobei [voˈbai] ADV **(a)** INTERROG **~ ist das passiert?** how did that happen?; **~ hast du ihn erwischt?** what did you catch him doing?
(b) REL in which; **ich erzähle mal, was passiert ist, ~ ich allerdings das Unwichtige auslasse** I will tell you what happened but I will leave out all the unimportant details; **~ man sehr aufpassen muss, dass man nicht betrogen wird** and you have to be very careful that you don't get cheated; **~ mir gerade einfällt** which reminds me; **das Auto prallte gegen einen Baum, ~ der Fahrer schwer verletzt wurde** the car hit a tree severely injuring the driver

Woche ['vɔxə] F **-, -n** week; **zweimal in der ~** twice a week; **in dieser ~** this week

Wochenarbeitszeit F working week

Wochenend- IN CPDS weekend; **Wochenendbeilage** F weekend supplement

Wochenende NT weekend; **schönes ~!** have a nice weekend; **langes** *or* **verlängertes ~** long weekend

Wochen-: **Wochenkarte** F weekly season ticket; **wochenlang** ADJ, ADV for weeks; **nach ~em Warten** after weeks of waiting; **Wochenlohn** M weekly wage

Wochentag M weekday (*including Saturday*); **was ist heute für ein ~?** what day (of the week) is it today?

wochentags ['vɔxntaːks] ADV on weekdays

wöchentlich ['vœçntlɪç] **1** ADJ weekly **2** ADV weekly; (= *einmal pro Woche*) once a week; **zwei Vormittage ~ kommen** to come two mornings a week; **sich ~ abwechseln** to take turns every week

Wodka ['vɔtka] M **-s, -s** vodka

wodurch [voˈdʊrç] ADV **(a)** INTERROG how **(b)** REL which

wofür [voˈfyːɐ] ADV **(a)** INTERROG for what, what ... for; (= *warum*) why **(b)** REL for which, which ... for

wog PRET *von* **wiegen²**

Woge ['voːgə] F **-, -n** wave; **wenn sich die ~n geglättet haben** (*fig*) when things have calmed down

wogegen [voˈgeːgn] ADV **(a)** INTERROG against what, what ... against; **~ ist dieses Mittel?** what's this medicine for? **(b)** REL against which, which ... against

woher [voˈheːɐ] ADV **(a)** INTERROG where ... from; **~ weißt du das?** how do you (come to) know that?; **~ kommt es eigentlich, dass ...** how come ... (*inf*) **(b)** REL where ... from

wohin [voˈhɪn] ADV **(a)** INTERROG where; **~, bitte?**, **~ solls gehen?** where are you off to so fast; **~ damit?** where shall I/we put it?; **ich muss mal ~** (*euph inf*) I've got to go somewhere (*euph inf*) **(b)** REL where; **~ man auch schaut** wherever you look

wohinein [vohɪˈnain] ADV = **worein**

wohingegen [vohɪnˈgeːgn] CONJ whereas

wohinter [voˈhɪntɐ] ADV **(a)** INTERROG what *or* where ... behind **(b)** REL behind which; **~ man sich auch versteckt** whatever you hide behind

wohl [voːl] **1** ADV **(a)** comp **-er**, superl **am -sten** (= *angenehm zumute*) happy; (= *gesund*) well; **sich ~/~er fühlen** to feel happy/happier; (= *wie zu Hause*) to feel at home/more at home; (*gesundheitlich*) to feel well/better; **bei dem Gedanken ist mir nicht ~** I'm not very happy at the thought; **~ oder übel** whether one likes it or not; **~ dem, der ...** happy the man who ...; **~ ihm, dass ...** it's a good thing for him that ...; **es sich** (*dat*) **~ gehen** *or* **sein** *or* **ergehen lassen** to enjoy oneself **(b)** (= *gut*) comp **besser**, superl **bestens** *or* **am besten** well; **~ bedacht** well considered; **~ bekannt** well-known; **sie ist mir ~ bekannt** I know her well; **~ durchdacht** well thought out; **~ überlegt** well thought out; **etw ~ überlegt machen** to do sth after careful consideration; **~ versorgt** well-provided-for **(c)** (= *wahrscheinlich*) probably; (*iro*: = *bestimmt*) surely; **das ist ~ nicht gut möglich** I should think it's unlikely; **es ist ~ anzunehmen, dass ...** it is to be expected that ...; **du bist ~ verrückt** you must be crazy!; **das ist doch ~ nicht dein Ernst!** you can't be serious!
(d) (= *vielleicht*) perhaps; (= *etwa*) about; **ob ~ noch jemand kommt?** I wonder if anybody else is coming?; **das mag ~ sein** that may well be; **willst du das ~ lassen!** I wish you'd stop (doing) that
(e) (= *durchaus*) well; **ich denke, ich verstehe dich sehr ~!** I think I understand you very well; **doch, das glaube ich ~** I certainly do believe it; **~!** (= *doch*) yes!; (*S Ger, Sw*: = *selbstverständlich*) of course!
2 CONJ (= *zwar*) **er hat es ~ versprochen, aber ...** he may have promised, but ...; **~, aber ...** that may well be, but ...

Wohl [voːl] NT **-(e)s**, NO PL welfare; **das öffentliche ~ und das ~ des Individuums** the public good and the welfare of the individual; **der Menschheit zum ~e** for the benefit of mankind; **zu eurem ~** for your benefit *or* good; **zum ~!** cheers!; **auf dein ~!** your health!; **auf jds ~ trinken** to drink sb's health

Wohl-: **wohlauf** [voːlˈlauf, voˈlauf] ADJ PRED well, in good health; **wohlbedacht** *etc* ADJ *siehe* **wohl**; **Wohlbefinden** NT feeling of wellbeing; **wohlbehalten** ADJ ankommen safe and sound; **wohldurchdacht** ADJ *siehe* **wohl**; **Wohlergehen** [-ˈɛɐɡeːən] NT **-s**, NO PL welfare; **wohlerzogen** [-ˈɛɐtsoːɡn] **1** ADJ, comp **besser erzogen**, superl **besterzogen** (*geh*) well-bred; *Kind* well-mannered; **~ sein** to be well-bred **2** ADV **sich ~ benehmen** to be well-mannered

Wohlfahrt F **-**, NO PL (= *Fürsorge*) welfare

Wohlfahrts-: **Wohlfahrtseinrichtung** F social service; **Wohlfahrtsmarke** F charity stamp; **Wohlfahrtsorganisation** F charitable organization; **Wohlfahrtsstaat** M welfare state

Wohl-: **wohlgeformt** [-ɡəˈfɔrmt] ADJ, comp **wohlgeformter**, superl **bestgeformt** well-shaped; *Körperteil* shapely; *Satz* well-formed; **Wohlgefühl** NT feeling of wellbeing; **wohlgemerkt** [-ɡəˈmɛrkt] ADV mind (you); **das waren ~ englische Pfund** that was English pounds, mind you; **wohlgenährt** [-ɡəˈnɛːɐt] ADJ, comp **wohlgenährter**, superl **wohlgenährteste(r, s)** well-fed; **wohlgesinnt** ADJ, comp **wohlgesinnter**, superl **wohlgesinnteste(r, s)** (*geh*) well-disposed (+*dat* towards); *Worte* well-meaning; **wohlhabend** ADJ, comp **wohlhabender**, superl **wohlhabendste(r, s)** well-to-do, prosperous

wohlig ['voːlɪç] **1** ADJ pleasant; (= *gemütlich*) cosy; *Ruhe* blissful **2** ADV warm comfortably; **~ rekelte er sich in der Sonne** he stretched luxuriously in the sun

Wohl-: **wohlmeinend** ADJ, *comp* **wohlmeinender**, *superl* **wohlmeinendste(r, s)** well-meaning; **wohlproportioniert** ADJ, *comp* **besser proportioniert** *or* **wohlproportionierter**, *superl* **bestproportioniert** well-proportioned; **Wohlsein** NT **zum ~!**, **auf Ihr ~!** your health!

Wohlstand M, NO PL affluence

Wohlstands-: **Wohlstandsbürger(in)** M(F) (*pej*) member of the affluent society; **Wohlstandsmüll** M refuse of the affluent society

Wohltat F **(a)** (= *Genuss*) relief **(b)** (= *Dienst, Gefallen*) favour (*Brit*), favor (*US*); (= *gute Tat*) good deed

Wohltäter M benefactor

Wohltäterin F benefactress

wohltätig ADJ charitable

Wohltätigkeit F charity

Wohltätigkeits-: **Wohltätigkeitsbasar** M charity bazaar; **Wohltätigkeitsverein** M charity; **Wohltätigkeitszweck** M charitable cause

Wohl-: **wohltuend** ADJ, *comp* **wohltuender**, *superl* **wohltuendste(r, s)** (most) agreeable; **wohl tun** VI IRREG (= *angenehm sein*) to do good (*jdm* sb); **das tut wohl** that's good; **wohlüberlegt** ADJ *siehe* **wohl**; **wohlverdient** ADJ well-deserved; **Wohlverhalten** NT (*usu iro*) good conduct; **wohlverstanden** [-vɛɐ̯ʃtandn̩] ADV mind you; **wohlweislich** [ˈvoːlvaislɪç, ˈvoːlˈvaislɪç] ADV very wisely; **ich habe das ~ nicht gemacht** I was careful not to do that; **Wohlwollen** NT **-s**, NO PL goodwill; **selbst bei dem größten** *or* **mit größtem ~** with the best will in the world; **jdn mit ~ betrachten** to regard sb benevolently; **wohlwollend** ADJ, *comp* **wohlwollender**, *superl* **wohlwollendste(r, s)** benevolent; **jdm gegenüber ~ sein** to be kindly disposed toward(s) sb ADV favourably (*Brit*), favorably (*US*); **jdm ~ geneigt** *or* **gesonnen sein** to be kindly disposed toward(s) sb; **einer Sache** (*dat*) **~ gegenüberstehen** to approve of sth

Wohn-: **Wohnbau** M, *pl* **-bauten** residential building; **Wohnblock** M, *pl* **-blocks** block of flats (*Brit*), apartment house (*US*); **Wohncontainer** M Portakabin® (*Brit*), trailer (*US*)

wohnen [ˈvoːnən] VI (= *Behausung haben*) to live; (*vorübergehend*) to stay; **wo ~ Sie?** where do you live/are you staying?; **wir ~ sehr schön** we have a very nice apartment/house *etc*; **wir ~ da sehr schön** it's very nice where we live

Wohn-: **Wohnfläche** F living space; **50 Quadratmeter ~** living room(, dining room) and bedroom(s) totalling 50 square metres (*Brit*) *or* totaling 50 square meters (*US*); **Wohngebäude** NT residential building; **Wohngebiet** NT residential area; **Wohngegend** F residential area; **Wohngeld** NT housing benefit (*Brit*), housing subsidy (*US*); **Wohngemeinschaft** F (*Menschen*) people sharing a flat (*Brit*) *or* apartment/house; **unsere ~** the people I share a flat *etc* with; **in einer ~ leben** to share a flat *etc*; **wohnhaft** ADJ (*form*) resident; **Wohnhaus** NT residential building; **Wohnheim** NT (*esp für Arbeiter*) hostel; (*für Studenten*) hall (of residence), dormitory (*US*); (*für alte Menschen*) home; **Wohnklo** NT (*hum inf*) **~ (mit Kochnische)** tiny flat (*Brit*) *or* apartment; **Wohnküche** F kitchen-cum-living-room; **Wohnlage** F residential area; **unsere ~ ist schön/ungünstig** our house/apartment is nicely/awkwardly situated; **wohnlich** [ˈvoːnlɪç] ADJ homely; **es sich** (*dat*) **~ machen** to make oneself comfortable; **Wohnmobil** [-mobiːl] NT **-s, -e** camper, RV (*US*); **Wohnort** M, *pl* **-orte** place of residence; **Wohnsilo** M (*pej*) concrete block; **Wohnsitz** M domicile; **ohne festen ~** of no fixed abode; **Wohnstube** F living room

Wohnung [ˈvoːnʊŋ] F **-, -en** flat (*Brit*), apartment; (= *Unterkunft*) lodging; **1.000 neue ~en** 1,000 new homes

Wohnungs-: **Wohnungsbau** M, NO PL house building *no def art*; **Wohnungsbedarf** M housing requirements *pl*; **Wohnungsinhaber(in)** M(F) householder; (= *Eigentümer auch*) owner-occupier; **wohnungslos** ADJ homeless; **Wohnungslose(r)** MF DECL AS ADJ homeless person; **für ~** for the homeless; **Wohnungslosigkeit** F homelessness; **Wohnungsmakler(in)** M(F) estate agent (*esp Brit*), real estate agent (*US*); **Wohnungsmangel** M housing shortage; **Wohnungsmarkt** M housing market; **Wohnungsnachweis** M accommodation registry; **Wohnungsnot** F serious housing shortage; **Wohnungssuche** F flat-hunting (*Brit*), apartment-hunting (*esp US*); **auf ~ sein** to be flat-hunting (*Brit*) *or* apartment-hunting (*esp US*); **Wohnungstür** F door (to the flat

(*Brit*) *or* apartment); **Wohnungswechsel** M change of address; **Wohnungswesen** NT housing

Wohn-: **Wohnviertel** NT residential area; **Wohnwagen** M caravan (*Brit*), trailer (*US*); **Wohnzimmer** NT living room; **Wohnzwecke** PL residential purposes *pl*

Wok [vɔk] M **-s, -s** (*Cook*) wok

wölben [ˈvœlbn̩] ■ VT to curve; *Blech etc* to bend ■ VR to curve; (*Asphalt*) to bend; (*Tapete*) to bulge out; (*Decke, Brücke*) to arch; *siehe auch* **gewölbt**

Wölbung F **-, -en** curvature; (*kuppelförmig*) dome; (*bogenförmig*) arch; (*von Körperteil*) curve; (*von Straße*) camber; (*von Tapete*) bulge

Wolf [vɔlf] M **-(e)s, ̈e** [ˈvœlfə] **(a)** wolf; **ein ~ im Schafspelz** a wolf in sheep's clothing **(b)** (*Tech*) shredder; (= *Fleischwolf*) mincer (*Brit*), grinder (*US*); **Fleisch durch den ~ drehen** to mince meat (*Brit*), to grind meat (*US*) **(c)** (*Med*) intertrigo *no art* (*spec*)

Wölfin [ˈvœlfɪn] F **-, -nen** she-wolf

Wolfram [ˈvɔlfram] NT **-s**, NO PL (*abbr* **W**) wolfram

Wolfs-: **Wolfsmilch** F (*Bot*) spurge; **Wolfsrachen** M (*Med*) cleft palate

Wolke [ˈvɔlkə] F **-, -n** (*lit, fig*) cloud; **aus allen ~n fallen** (*fig*) to be flabbergasted (*inf*)

Wolken-: **Wolkenbank** F, *pl* **-bänke** cloud bank; **Wolkenbildung** F cloud formation; **es kann zu ~ kommen** it may become cloudy; **Wolkenbruch** M cloudburst; **Wolkenkratzer** M skyscraper; **Wolkenkuckucksheim** NT cloud-cuckoo-land; **wolkenlos** ADJ cloudless; **wolkenverhangen** [-fɛɐ̯haŋən] ADJ overcast

wolkig [ˈvɔlkɪç] ADJ cloudy; (*fig*) obscure

Wolldecke F (woollen (*Brit*) *or* woolen (*US*)) blanket

Wolle [ˈvɔlə] F **-, -n** wool; **in der ~ gefärbt** (*fig*) dyed-in-the-wool; **mit jdm in die ~ kommen** *or* **geraten** (*fig inf*), **sich mit jdm in die ~ kriegen** (*fig inf*) to start squabbling with sb; **sich mit jdm in der ~ haben** (*fig inf*) to be at loggerheads with sb

wollen¹ [ˈvɔlən] ADJ ATTR woollen (*Brit*), woolen (*US*)

---

wollen² [ˈvɔlən]

■ HILFSVERB	■ INTRANSITIVES VERB
■ TRANSITIVES VERB	

pret **wollte** [ˈvɔltə], *ptp* **gewollt** [ɡəˈvɔlt]

wollen *wird normalerweise mit* **to want** *übersetzt.*

■ HILFSVERB, *ptp* **wollen**

(a) (= *Willen haben*) **sie will nach Hause gehen** she wants to go home; **sie will nicht nach Hause gehen** she doesn't want to go home; (= *weigert sich*) **sie will nicht** she won't go home; **etw haben wollen** to want (to have) sth; **ich will lieber ins Kino gehen** I'd prefer to go to the cinema; **er wollte unbedingt nach Frankreich ziehen** he was desperate to move to France; **das wollen wir doch erst mal sehen!** we'll see about that!; **was will man da schon machen/sagen?** what can you do/say?

(b) (= *beabsichtigen*) **etw gerade tun wollen** to be going to do sth; **ich wollte schon gehen/gerade aufhören, als ...** I was just going to leave/just about to stop when ...; **es will nicht besser/wärmer werden** it just won't get better/won't warm up

(c) (= *müssen*) **das will alles genauestens überlegt sein** *or* **werden** it all has to be most carefully considered

(d) (= *zugeben, behaupten*) **keiner wollte etwas gehört/gesehen haben** nobody would admit to hearing/seeing anything; **keiner will es gewesen sein** nobody will admit to it; **und so jemand will Lehrer sein!** and he calls himself a teacher

(e) (*Aufforderung*) **wollen wir uns nicht setzen?** why don't we sit down?; **wenn Sie bitte Platz nehmen wollen** if you would please take a seat; **na, wollen wir gehen?** well, shall we go?; **darauf wollen wir mal anstoßen!** let's drink to that; **wir wollen beten!** let us pray

(f) (*andere Wendungen*) **komme, was da wolle** come what may; **sei er, wer er wolle** whoever he may be

✦es will ... (*unpersönlich*) **es will mir nicht einleuchten, warum** I really can't see why; **es will mir scheinen, dass ...** it seems to me that ...

2 TRANSITIVES VERB
(a) (= *wünschen*) to want; **was wollen sie?** what do they want?; **was wollten sie denn von dir?** what did they want then?; **ohne es zu wollen** without wanting to; **das wollte ich nicht** (= *war unbeabsichtigt*) I didn't mean to (do that); **was willst du (noch) mehr!** what more do you want!; **ich weiß nicht, was du willst, das ist doch ausgezeichnet** I don't know what you're on about, it's excellent; **er hat gar nichts zu wollen** he has no say at all
(b) (= *bezwecken*) **was willst du mit dem Messer?** what are you doing with that knife?; **was willst du mit der Frage?** why are you asking that?; *siehe auch* **gewollt**
(c) (= *brauchen*) to need; **diese Pflanzen wollen viel Sonne** these plants need a lot of sun

3 INTRANSITIVES VERB
(a) (= *Willen haben*) **man muss nur wollen** you just have to want to; **da ist nichts zu wollen** there is nothing we/you can do (about it)
(b) (= *bereit sein*) **wenn er will** if he wants to; **er will nicht so recht** he seems rather unwilling; **so Gott will** God willing
(c) (= *mögen*) to want to; **wollen, dass jd etw tut** to want sb to do sth; **ich wollte, ich wäre ...** I wish I were ...; **ob du willst oder nicht** whether you like it or not

> *Nach* **wenn, wer** *und* **wie** *wird* **wollen** *mit* **to like** *übersetzt.*

wenn du willst if you like; **wenn man so will** as it were; **wer nicht will, der hat schon** if you don't/he doesn't like it, you/he can lump it (*inf*)
(d) (= *gehen wollen*) to want to go; **ich will nach Hause/hier raus/weg** I want to go home/to get out of here/to get away; **zu wem wollen Sie?** whom do you want to see?

Woll-: Wolljacke F cardigan; **Wollknäuel** NT ball of wool; **Wollmilchsau** F **Eier legende ~** all-providing genetically engineered animal; **Wollsachen** PL woollens *pl* (*Brit*), woolens *pl* (*US*); **Wollstoff** M woollen (*Brit*) or woolen (*US*) material

wollüstig [ˈvɔlʏstɪç] (*geh*) **1** ADJ (= *sinnlich*) sensual; (= *lüstern*) lascivious; (= *verzückt, ekstatisch*) ecstatic **2** ADV *streicheln, sich winden* sensually; *stöhnen* ecstatically; *etw ansehen* lustily

Woll-: Wollwaren PL woollens *pl* (*Brit*), woolens *pl* (*US*); **Wollwäsche** F washing woollens (*Brit*) or woolens (*US*) *no art*; (= *Wollartikel*) woollens *pl* (*Brit*), woolens *pl* (*US*); **Wollwaschmittel** NT detergent for woollens (*Brit*) or woolens (*US*)

womit [voˈmɪt] ADV **(a)** INTERROG with what, what ... with; **~ kann ich dienen?** what can I do for you? **(b)** REL with which; (*auf ganzen Satz bezüglich*) by which; **das ist es, ~ ich nicht einverstanden bin** that's what I don't agree with; **~ ich nicht sagen will, dass ...** by which I don't mean (to say) that ...

womöglich [voˈmøːklɪç] ADV possibly; *siehe auch* **wo**

wonach [voˈnaːx] ADV **(a)** INTERROG after what, what ... after; **~ sehnst du dich?** what do you long for?; **~ riecht das?** what does it smell of? **(b)** REL **das Land, ~ du dich sehnst** the land (which) you are longing for; **das war es, ~ ich mich erkundigen wollte** that was what I wanted to ask about

Wonne [ˈvɔnə] F **-, -n** (*geh*) (= *Glückseligkeit*) bliss *no pl*; (= *Vergnügen*) joy; **mit ~** with great delight; **(aber) mit ~!** with great pleasure!; **das ist ihre ganze ~** that's all her joy; **es ist eine wahre ~** it's a sheer delight

wonnig [ˈvɔnɪç] ADJ delightful; *Gefühl, Ruhe* blissful

woran [voˈran] ADV **(a)** INTERROG **~ soll ich den Kleiderbügel hängen?** what shall I hang the coat hanger on?; **~ denkst du?** what are you thinking about?; **man weiß bei ihm nie, ~ man ist** you never know where you are with him; **~ liegt das?** what's the reason for it?; **~ ist er gestorben?** what did he die of?
(b) REL (*auf vorausgehenden Satz bezogen*) by which; **das, ~ ich mich gerne erinnere** what I like to recall; **die Wand, ~ sie immer die Plakate kleben** the wall on which they are always sticking posters; **..., ~ ich schon gedacht hatte** ... which I'd

already thought of; **~ er auch immer gestorben ist ...** whatever he died of ...

worauf [voˈrauf] ADV **(a)** INTERROG (*räumlich*) on what, what ... on; **~ wartest du?** what are you waiting for? **(b)** REL (*zeitlich*) whereupon; **~ du dich verlassen kannst** of that you can be sure; **das ist etwas, ~ ich mich freue** that's something I'm looking forward to; **das, ~ er sich vorbereitet hatte** what he was prepared for

woraufhin [vorauf'hɪn] REL ADV whereupon

woraus [voˈraus] ADV **(a)** INTERROG out of what, what ... out of; **~ ist der Pullover?** what is the pullover made (out) of?; **~ schließt du das?** from what do you deduce that? **(b)** REL out of which, which ... out of; **das Buch, ~ ich gestern vorgelesen habe** the book I was reading from yesterday; **~ man das Öl auch gewinnt ...** whatever oil is obtained from ...

worden PTP *von* **werden** 1(c)

worin [voˈrɪn] ADV **(a)** INTERROG in what, what ... in; **~ war das eingewickelt?** what was it wrapped in?; **~ liegt der Unterschied/Vorteil?** what is the difference/advantage? **(b)** REL in which, which ... in; **das ist etwas, ~ wir nicht übereinstimmen** that's something we don't agree on; **~ du es auch einwickelst ...** whatever you wrap it in ...

Workshop [ˈwɔːɛkʃɔp, ˈwœrk-] M **-s, -s** workshop
Workstation [ˈwɔːɛksteːʃn, ˈwœrk-] F **-, -s** (*Comput*) work station
World Wide Web [wøːɛld ˈwaid ˈwɛb] NT **-, NO PL** (*Comput*) World Wide Web

Wort [vɔrt] NT **-(e)s, -e** or **=er** [ˈvœrtə] **(a)** *pl usu* **=er** (= *Vokabel*) word; **~ für ~** word for word
(b) *pl* **-e** (= *Äußerung*) word; **genug der ~e!** enough talk!; **das ist ein ~!** wonderful!; **in ~ und Schrift** in speech and writing; **er beherrscht die Sprache in ~ und Schrift** he has a command of the written and spoken language; **~en Taten folgen lassen** to suit the action to the word(s); **mit einem ~** in a word; **mit anderen/wenigen ~en** in other/a few words; **kein ~ mehr** not another word; **kein ~ von etw sagen** or **erwähnen** or **fallen lassen** not to say one word about sth; **keine ~e für etw finden** to find no words for sth; **ich verstehe kein ~!** I don't understand a word (of it); (= *kann nichts hören*) I can't hear a word (that's being said); **mit dir habe ich noch ein ~ zu reden!** I want a word with you!; **ein ernstes ~ mit jdm reden** to have a serious talk with sb; **hättest du doch ein ~ gesagt** if only you had said something; **davon hat man mir kein ~ gesagt** they didn't tell me anything about it; **man kann sein eigenes ~ nicht (mehr) verstehen** or **hören** you can't hear yourself speak; **ein ~ gab das andere** one thing led to another; **jdm das ~** or **die ~e im Mund (her)umdrehen** to twist sb's words; **du sprichst ein großes** or **wahres ~ gelassen aus** how true, too true; **jdm aufs ~ glauben** to believe sb implicitly; **das glaub ich dir aufs ~** I can well believe it; **ohne ein ~ (zu sagen)** without (saying) a word; **dein ~ in Gottes Ohr** let us hope so
(c) NO PL (= *Rede, Recht zu sprechen*) **das ~ nehmen** to speak; **das große ~ haben** or **führen** (*inf*) to shoot one's mouth off (*inf*); **einer Sache** (*dat*) **das ~ reden** to put the case for sth; **das ~ an jdn richten** to address (oneself to) sb; **jdm ins ~ fallen** to interrupt sb; **zu ~ kommen** to get a chance to speak; **ums ~ bitten, sich zu ~ melden** to ask to speak; **er hat das ~** it's his turn to speak; **jdm das ~ erteilen** or **geben** to allow sb to speak
(d) *pl* **-e** (= *Ausspruch*) saying; (= *Zitat*) quotation; (*Rel*) Word; **ein ~, das er immer im Munde führt** one of his favourite (*Brit*) or favorite (*US*) sayings; **ein ~ Goethes/aus der Bibel** a quotation from Goethe/the Bible; **das ~ zum Sonntag** short religious broadcast on Saturday night
(e) *pl* **-e** (= *Text, Sprache*) words *pl*; **in ~en** in words; **das geschriebene/gedruckte/gesprochene ~** the written/printed/spoken word
(f) *pl* **-e** (= *Befehl, Entschluss*) **das ~ des Vaters ist ausschlaggebend** the father's word is law; **jdm aufs ~ gehorchen** or **folgen** to obey sb's every word; **dabei habe ich auch (noch) ein ~ mitzureden** or **mitzusprechen** I (still) have something to say about that too; **das letzte ~ ist noch nicht gesprochen** the final decision hasn't been taken yet; **das letzte ~ haben** to have the last word
(g) NO PL (= *Versprechen*) word; **auf mein ~** I give (you) my word; **jdn beim ~ nehmen** to take sb at his word; **ich gebe mein ~ darauf** I give you my word on it; **sein ~ halten** to keep one's word

Wort-: Wortart F (*Gram*) part of speech; **wortbrüchig** ADJ false; **~ werden** to break one's word

Wörtchen ['vœrtçən] NT **-s, -** DIM *von* **Wort** little word; **da habe ich wohl ein ~ mitzureden** (*inf*) I think I have some say in that; **mit ihm habe ich noch ein ~ zu reden** (*inf*) I want a word with him

Wörter-: Wörterbuch NT dictionary; **Wörterverzeichnis** NT vocabulary; (*von Spezialbegriffen*) glossary

Wort-: Wortfolge F (*Gram*) word order; **Wortführer** M spokesman; **Wortführerin** F spokeswoman; **wortgetreu** ADJ, ADV verbatim; **wortgewandt** ADJ eloquent; **wortkarg** ADJ taciturn; **Wortlaut** M wording; **im ~** verbatim; **folgenden ~ haben** to read as follows

Wörtlein ['vœrtlain] NT **-s, - =** Wörtchen

wörtlich ['vœrtlɪç] ① ADJ literal; *Rede* direct ② ADV *wiedergeben, zitieren, abschreiben* verbatim; *übersetzen* literally; **das darf man nicht so ~ nehmen** you mustn't take it literally; **darf ich das ~ nehmen?** do you really mean that?; **das hat er ~ gesagt** those were his very words

Wort-: wortlos ① ADJ silent ② ADV without saying a word; **Wortmeldung** F request to speak; **wenn es keine weiteren ~en gibt** if nobody else wishes to speak; **Wortschatz** M vocabulary; **Wortschöpfung** F neologism; **Wortschwall** M torrent of words; **Wortspiel** NT pun; **Wortstellung** F (*Gram*) word order; **Wortwahl** F choice of words; **Wortwechsel** M exchange (of words); **wortweise** ADJ, ADV word for word; **wortwörtlich** ① ADJ word-for-word ② ADV word for word

worüber [vo'ry:bə] ADV **(a)** INTERROG about what, what ... about; (*örtlich*) over what, what ... over **(b)** REL about which, which ... about; (*örtlich*) over which, which ... over; (*auf vorausgehenden Satz bezogen*) which; **das Thema, ~ ich gerade einen Artikel gelesen habe** the subject I have just read an article about; **~ sie sich auch unterhalten, sie ...** whatever they talk about they ...

worum [vo'rʊm] ADV *siehe auch* **um (a)** INTERROG about what, what ... about; **~ handelt es sich?** what's it about? **(b)** REL about which, which ... about; **der Ast, ~ ich die Schnur gebunden hatte** the branch I tied the rope (a)round; **~ die Diskussion auch geht, ...** whatever the discussion is about ...

worunter [vo'rʊntɐ] ADV **(a)** INTERROG under what **(b)** REL under which

wovon [vo'fɔn] ADV **(a)** INTERROG from what, what ... from **(b)** REL from which, which ... from; (*auf vorausgehenden Satz bezogen*) about which, which ... about; **das ist ein Gebiet, ~ er viel versteht** that is a subject he knows a lot about; **~ du dich auch ernährst, ...** whatever you eat ...

wovor [vo'fo:ɐ] ADV **(a)** INTERROG (*örtlich*) before what, what ... before; **~ fürchtest du dich?** what are you afraid of? **(b)** REL before which, which ... before; **~ du dich auch fürchtest, ...** whatever you're afraid of ...

wozu [vo'tsu:] ADV **(a)** INTERROG to what, what ... to; (= *warum*) why; **~ hast du dich entschlossen?** what have you decided on?; **~ soll das gut sein?** what's the point of that?; **~ denn das?** what for?; **~ denn?** why should I/you? *etc* **(b)** REL to which, which ... to; **das Verfahren, ~ ich raten würde** the procedure I would advise; **sie haben geheiratet, ~ ich nichts weiter sagen möchte** they have got married, and I shall say no more about that; **~ du dich auch entschließt, ...** whatever you decide (on) ...

Wrack [vrak] NT **-s, -s** (*litfig*) wreck

wringen ['vrɪŋən], *pret* **wrang** [vraŋ], *ptp* **gewrungen** [gə'vrʊŋən] VTI to wring

WS ['ve:'ʔɛs] NT (*Univ*) ABBR *von* **Wintersemester**

Wucher ['vu:xɐ] M **-s**, NO PL profiteering; (*bei Geldverleih*) usury; **das ist doch ~!** that's daylight (*Brit*) *or* highway (*US*) robbery!

Wucherer ['vu:xərɐ] M **-s, -**, **Wucherin** [-ərɪn] F **-, -nen** profiteer; (= *Geldverleiher*) usurer

wucherisch ['vu:xərɪʃ] ADJ profiteering; *Geldverleih, Zinsen* usurious; *Bedingungen, Preis, Miete etc* exorbitant

wuchern ['vu:xɐn] VI **(a)** AUX SEIN *or* HABEN (*Pflanzen*) to grow rampant; (*Geschwür*) to grow rapidly; (*wildes Fleisch*) to proliferate; (*Bart, Haare*) to grow profusely **(b)** (*Kaufmann etc*) to profiteer; (*Geldverleiher*) to practise (*Brit*) *or* practice (*US*) usury; **mit seinen Talenten ~** (*fig*) to make the most of one's talents

Wucherpreis M exorbitant price

Wucherung F **-, -en** (*Med*) growth; (= *wildes Fleisch*) proud flesh

Wucherzins M exorbitant interest

wuchs PRET *von* **wachsen**[1]

Wuchs [vu:ks] M **-es**, NO PL (= *Wachstum*) growth; (= *Gestalt, Form*) stature; (*von Mensch*) build

Wuchsaktie F growth stock

Wucht [vʊxt] F **-**, NO PL **(a)** (*lit, fig*) force; **mit voller ~** with full force **(b)** (*inf*) **er/das ist die** *or* **eine ~!** he's/that's smashing! (*Brit inf*), he's/that's a hit (*US inf*)

wuchten ['vʊxtn] ① VT *Koffer, Karton, Paket* to heave, to drag; *Gewicht* to heave; **er wuchtete den Ball ins Tor** he belted the ball into the goal ② VR **er wuchtete sich aus dem Auto** he heaved himself out of the car; **Ikarus wuchtete sich in die Lüfte** Ikarus launched himself into the air

wühlen ['vy:lən] ① VI **(a)** (*nach* for) to dig; (*Maulwurf etc*) to burrow; (*Schwein, Vogel*) to root; **im Schmutz** *or* **Dreck ~** (*fig*) to wallow in the mire *or* mud **(b)** (= *suchen*) to rummage (*nach etw* for sth) **(c)** (= *Untergrundarbeit leisten*) to stir things up ② VR **sich durch die Menge/das Gestrüpp/die Akten ~** to burrow one's way through the crowd/the undergrowth/the files

Wühl-: Wühlmaus F vole; (*fig pej*) subversive; **Wühltisch** M (*inf*) bargain counter

Wulst [vʊlst] M **-es, ⁺e** ['vʏlstə] *or* F **-, ⁺e** bulge; (*an Reifen*) bead; (*an Flasche, Glas*) lip; **ein ~ von Fett** a roll of fat; **die dicken Wülste seiner Lippen** his thick lips

wulstig ['vʊlstɪç] ADJ bulging; *Rand, Lippen* thick

wund [vʊnt] ① ADJ sore; **ein ~er Punkt, eine ~e Stelle** a sore point ② ADV **etw ~ kratzen/scheuern/reiben** to scratch/chafe/rub sth until it's raw; **das Pferd/ich war vom Reiten ~ gescheuert** the horse/I was saddle-sore; **sich** (*dat*) **die Füße/Fersen ~ laufen** (*lit*) to walk until one's feet/heels are raw; (*fig*) to walk one's legs off; **sich** (*dat*) **die Finger ~ schreiben** (*fig*) to write one's fingers to the bone; **ein ~ gelegener Patient** a patient with bedsores; **eine ~ gelegene Stelle** a bedsore; **~ gelegen sein** to have bedsores; *siehe auch* **wund liegen**

Wundbrand M gangrene

Wunde ['vʊndə] F **-, -n** (*lit, fig*) wound; **alte ~n/eine alte ~ wieder aufreißen** (*fig*) to open up old sores; **Salz in eine/jds ~ streuen** (*fig*) to turn the knife in the wound; **Balsam** *or* **Öl in eine/jds ~ gießen** *or* **träufeln** (*fig geh*) to comfort sb

Wunder ['vʊndɐ] NT **-s, -** (= *übernatürliches Ereignis, Leistung*) miracle; (= *wunderbare Erscheinung*) wonder; (= *erstaunlicher Mensch*) marvel; **~ tun** *or* **wirken** (*Rel*) to work miracles; **das grenzt an ein ~** it's almost a miracle; **durch ein ~** by a miracle; **wie durch ein ~** as if by a miracle; **ein architektonisches ~** an architectural miracle; **meine Eltern denken ~ was passiert ist/~ was über mein Privatleben** my parents think goodness knows what has happened/goodness knows what about my private life; **er glaubt, ~ wer zu sein/~ was geleistet zu haben** he thinks he's marvellous (*Brit*) *or* marvelous (*US*)/done something marvel(l)ous; **er bildet sich ~ was ein** he thinks he's too wonderful for words; **~ tun** *or* **wirken** to do wonders; **diese Medizin wirkt ~** this medicine works wonders; **es ist ein/kein ~, dass ...** it's a wonder/no wonder that ...; **kein ~** no wonder

wunderbar ① ADJ **(a)** (= *schön*) wonderful **(b)** (= *übernatürlich, wie durch ein Wunder*) miraculous ② ADV (= *herrlich*) wonderfully

wunderbarerweise ['vʊndɐba:rɐ'vaizə] ADV miraculously

Wunder-: Wunderheiler(in) M(F) wonder doctor; (*pej*) faith healer; **wunderhübsch** ADJ wonderfully pretty; **Wunderkerze** F sparkler; **Wunderkind** NT child prodigy; **Wunderknabe** M (*usu iro*) wonder boy *or* child; **wunderlich** ['vʊndɐlɪç] ADJ (= *merkwürdig*) strange; **Wundermittel** NT miracle cure; (*von Fee etc*) magic potion

wundern ['vʊndɐn] ① VT IMPERS to surprise; **es wundert mich** *or* **mich wundert, dass er noch nicht hier ist** I'm surprised that he is not here yet; **das wundert mich nicht** I'm not surprised; **das würde mich nicht ~** I shouldn't be surprised; **mich wundert gar nichts mehr** nothing surprises me any more ② VR to be surprised (*über +acc* at); **du wirst dich ~!** you'll be amazed!; **du wirst dich noch einmal ~!** you're in for a shock!; **da wirst du dich aber ~!** you're in for a surprise; **ich muss mich doch sehr ~!** well, I am surprised (at you/him *etc*); **ich**

wundere mich über gar nichts mehr nothing surprises me any more

Wunder-: **wunderschön** ADJ beautiful; **einen ~en guten Morgen/Tag** *etc* a very good morning/day *etc* to you; **Wundertüte** F surprise packet; **wundervoll** 🔢 ADJ wonderful 🔢 ADV wonderfully; **Wunderwaffe** F wonder weapon; **Wunderwerk** NT miracle

Wund-: **Wundheit** F -, NO PL soreness; **wund liegen** VR IRREG to get bedsores; **Wundpflaster** NT adhesive plaster; **Wundsalbe** F ointment; **Wundsein** NT soreness; **Wundstarrkrampf** M tetanus

Wunsch [vʊnʃ] M -(e)s, ⸚e [ˈvynʃə] wish; (= *sehnliches Verlangen*) desire; (= *Bitte*) request; **ein Pferd war schon immer mein ~** I've always wanted a horse; **nach ~** just as he/she *etc* wants/wanted; (= *wie geplant*) according to plan; (= *nach Bedarf*) as required; **auf** *or* **nach ~ der Eltern** as his/her *etc* parents wish/wished; **alles geht nach ~** everything is going smoothly; **hier ist der ~ der Vater des Gedankens** (*prov*) the wish is father to the thought (*prov*); **ich habe einen ~ an dich** I've a request to make of you; **was haben Sie für einen ~?** what can I do for you?; **haben Sie (sonst) noch einen ~?** (*beim Einkauf etc*) is there anything else you would like?; **sonst noch Wünsche?** (*iro*) any other requests?; **auf ~ by** request; **auf jds (besonderen/ausdrücklichen) ~ hin** at sb's (special/express) request; **auf allgemeinen/vielfachen ~ hin** by popular request; **beste Wünsche zum Fest** the compliments of the season

wünschbar ADJ (*Sw*) = **wünschenswert**

Wunschdenken NT wishful thinking

Wünschelrute [ˈvynʃl-] F divining rod

Wünschelrutengänger [-gɛŋə] M -s, -, **Wünschelrutengängerin** [-ərɪn] F -, -nen diviner

wünschen [ˈvynʃn] 🔢 VT **(a)** **sich** (*dat*) **etw ~** to want sth; (= *den Wunsch äußern*) to ask for sth; (*im Stillen: bei Sternschnuppe etc*) to wish for sth; **ich wünsche mir, dass du ...** I would like you to ...; **das habe ich mir von meinen Eltern zu Weihnachten gewünscht** I asked my parents to give me that for Christmas; **ich wünsche mir einen Mantel von dir** I'd like a coat from you; **er wünscht sich** (*dat*)**, dass das Projekt erfolgreich sein wird** he wants the project to be successful; **er wünscht sich** (*dat*) **diesen Mann als Lehrer/Vater/als** *or* **zum Freund** he wishes that this man was his teacher/father/friend; **was wünschst du dir?** what do you want?; (*im Märchen*) what is your wish?; **du darfst dir was (zum Essen) ~** you can say what you'd like (to eat); **du darfst dir etwas ~** (= *Wunsch frei haben*) you can make a wish; **sie haben alles, was man sich** (*dat*) **nur ~ kann** they have everything you could possibly wish for; **man hätte es sich** (*dat*) **nicht besser ~ können** you couldn't have wished for anything better; **jdm etw ~** to wish sb sth; **wir ~ dir gute Besserung/eine gute Reise** we hope you get well soon/have a pleasant journey; **jdm den Tod/die Pest an den Hals ~** (*fig inf*) to wish sb would die/drop dead (*inf*); **das würde ich meinem schlimmsten Feind nicht ~** I wouldn't wish that on my worst enemy

(b) (= *ersehnen, hoffen*) to wish; **jdn fort/weit weg ~** to wish sb would go away/were far away; **es bleibt/wäre zu ~, dass ... it** is to be hoped that ...; **ich wünschte, ich hätte dich nie gesehen** I wish I'd never seen you

(c) (= *begehren, verlangen*) to want; **was ~ Sie?** (*Diener*) yes, Sir/Madam?; (*in Geschäft*) can I help you?; (*in Restaurant*) what would you like?

🔢 VI (= *begehren*) to wish; **Sie ~?** what can I do for you?; (*in Restaurant*) what would you like?; **ganz wie Sie ~** (just) as you wish; **zu ~/viel zu ~ übrig lassen** to leave something/a great deal to be desired

wünschenswert ADJ desirable

Wunsch-: **wunschgemäß** 🔢 ADJ desired; (= *erbeten*) requested; (= *geplant*) planned 🔢 ADV as desired; (= *wie erbeten*) as requested; (= *wie geplant*) as planned; **Wunschkind** NT planned child; **Wunschkonzert** NT (*Rad*) musical request programme (*Brit*) *or* program (*US*); **wunschlos** 🔢 ADJ **Mensch** content(ed); *Glück* perfect 🔢 ADV - **glücklich** perfectly happy; **Wunschpartner(in)** M(F) ideal partner; **Wunschsatz** M (*Gram*) optative clause; **Wunschtraum** M dream; (= *Illusion*) illusion; **das ist doch bloß ein ~** that's just a pipe dream; **Wunschzettel** M wish list; **das steht schon lange auf meinem ~** (*fig*) I've wanted that for a long time

wurde PRET *von* **werden**

Würde [ˈvyrdə] F -, -n **(a)** NO PL dignity; **unter aller ~ sein** to be beneath contempt; **unter jds ~ sein** to be beneath sb **(b)** (= *Auszeichnung*) honour (*Brit*), honor (*US*); (= *Titel*) title; (= *Amt*) rank

Würdenträger(in) M(F) dignitary

würdig [ˈvyrdɪç] 🔢 ADJ **(a)** (= *würdevoll*) dignified **(b)** (= *wert*) worthy; **jds/einer Sache ~/nicht ~ sein** to be worthy/unworthy of sb/sth 🔢 ADV **sich verhalten** with dignity; **beerdigen** respectfully; **jdn behandeln** with respect; **begrüßen, empfangen** with great respect; **vertreten** worthily

würdigen [ˈvyrdɪɡn] VT (= *anerkennen*) to appreciate; (= *lobend erwähnen*) to acknowledge; (= *respektieren*) to respect; (= *ehren*) to pay tribute to; **etw gebührend** *or* **nach Gebühr/richtig ~** to appreciate sth properly/fully; **etw zu ~ wissen** to appreciate sth

Wurf [vʊrf] M -(e)s, ⸚e [ˈvyrfə] **(a)** throw; (*beim Kegeln etc*) bowl; (*beim Baseball*) pitch; **drei ~** *or* **Würfe zwei Euro** three goes for two euros **(b)** NO PL (= *das Werfen*) throwing; **beim ~** when throwing; **zum ~ ansetzen/ausholen** to get ready to throw **(c)** (*fig*: = *Erfolg*) success; **mit dem Film ist ihm ein großer ~ gelungen** this film is a great success for him **(d)** (*Zool*) litter; (= *das Gebären*) birth

Wurfanker M grappling hook

Würfel [ˈvyrfl] M -s, - **(a)** (*auch Math*) cube; **etw in ~ schneiden** to dice sth **(b)** (= *Spielwürfel*) die; (*form*); **die ~ sind gefallen** (*fig*) the die is cast; **~ spielen** to play at dice

Würfel-: **Würfelbecher** M shaker; **würfelförmig** ADJ cube-shaped

würfelig [ˈvyrfəlɪç] 🔢 ADJ cubic 🔢 ADV **etw ~ schneiden** to cut sth into cubes

würfeln [ˈvyrfln] 🔢 VI to throw; (= *Würfel spielen*) to play at dice; **hast du schon gewürfelt?** have you had your throw?; **um etw ~** to throw dice for sth 🔢 VT **(a)** *Zahl* to throw **(b)** (= *in Würfel schneiden*) to dice

Würfel-: **Würfelspiel** NT (= *Partie*) game of dice; (= *Spielart*) dice; **beim ~** at dice; **Würfelzucker** M cube sugar

Wurfgeschoss NT projectile

würflig [ˈvyrflɪç] ADJ, ADV = **würfelig**

Wurf-: **Wurfpfeil** M dart; **Wurfring** M quoit; **Wurfsendung** F circular; **Reklame durch ~en** direct advertising; **Wurfspeer** M, **Wurfspieß** M javelin; **Wurfstern** M *spiked metal disc thrown as a weapon*

würgen [ˈvyrɡn] 🔢 VT **jdn** to strangle 🔢 VI **(a)** (= *mühsam schlucken*) to choke; (*Schlange*) to gulp; **an etw** (*dat*) **~** (*lit*) to choke on sth **(b)** (*beim Erbrechen*) to retch; **ein Würgen im Hals spüren** to feel one is going to be sick 🔢 VT IMPERS **es würgte sie (im Hals** *etc***)** she felt she was going to be sick

Wurm [vʊrm] M -(e)s, ⸚er [ˈvyrmə] **(a)** worm; (= *Made*) maggot; **da ist** *or* **steckt** *or* **sitzt der ~ drin** (*fig inf*) there's something wrong somewhere; (= *verdächtig*) there's something fishy about it (*inf*) **(b)** AUCH NT (*inf*: = *Kind*) (little) mite

wurmen [ˈvʊrmən] VT IMPERS (*inf*) to rankle with

Wurmfortsatz M (*Anat*) vermiform appendix

wurmig [ˈvʊrmɪç] ADJ worm-eaten; (= *madig*) *Obst* maggoty

Wurm-: **Wurmkur** F worming treatment; **die Katze braucht eine ~** the cat needs to be wormed; **eine ~ machen** to have worm treatment; **Wurmmittel** NT vermicide; **wurmstichig** [-ʃtɪçɪç] ADJ *Holz* full of wormholes; (= *madig auch*) *Obst* maggoty

Wurscht *etc* [vʊrʃt] (*inf*) = **Wurst** *etc*

Wurst [vʊrst] F -, ⸚e [ˈvyrstə] sausage; (= *Salami*) salami; **jetzt geht es um die ~** (*fig inf*) the moment of truth has come (*inf*); **das ist mir (vollkommen) ~** (*inf*) it's all the same to me

---

WURST

*German-speaking countries are famous for their wide variety of **Wurst**. It is eaten cold in slices, for example Zervelatwurst, or warm, for example Wiener Würstchen, Frankfurter Würstchen or Bratwurst. Less well known abroad are the various kinds of Streichwurst (eg Teewurst and Leberwurst): they are made from sausage that has been smoked and then chopped up so finely that it can be spread on bread.*

Wurstaufschnitt M *siehe* **Wurst** assortment of sliced sausage/salami

Würstchen [ˈvyrstçən] NT -s, - **(a)** DIM *von* **Wurst** small sausage; **heiße** *or* **warme ~** hot sausages; **Frankfurter/Wiener ~**

frankfurters/wienies **(b)** (*pej*: *Mensch*) squirt (*inf*); **ein armes ~** (*fig*) a poor soul

Würstchenbude F, **Würstchenstand** M ≈ hot-dog stand

wursteln [ˈvʊrstln] VI (*inf*) to muddle along; **sich durchs Leben ~** to muddle (one's way) through life

Wurstfinger PL (*pej inf*) pudgy fingers *pl*

wurstig [ˈvʊrstɪç] ADJ (*inf*) couldn't-care-less *attr* (*inf*); **sei doch nicht so ~!** don't be such a wet blanket! (*inf*)

Wurst-: **Wurstsalat** M sausage salad; **Wurstvergiftung** F sausage poisoning; **Wurstwaren** PL sausages *pl*; **Wurstzipfel** M sausage end

Württemberg [ˈvʏrtəmbɛrk] NT **-s** Württemberg

württembergisch [ˈvʏrtəmbɛrgɪʃ] ADJ Württembergian

Würze [ˈvʏrtsə] F **-, -n** (= *Gewürz*) seasoning, spice; (= *Aroma*) aroma; (*fig*: = *Reiz*) spice; (*von Bier*) wort

Wurzel [ˈvʊrtsl] F **-, -n (a)** (*lit, fig*) root; **das Übel an der ~ packen** to tackle the root of the problem; **~n schlagen** (*lit*) to root; (*fig*) (= *sich einleben*) to put down roots; (= *an einem Ort hängen bleiben*) to grow roots **(b)** (*Math*) root; **~n ziehen** to find the roots; **die ~ aus einer Zahl ziehen** to find the root of a number; **(die) ~ aus 4 ist 2** the square root of 4 is 2; **die vierte ~ aus 16 ist 2** the fourth root of 16 is 2

Wurzel-: **Wurzelbehandlung** F (*von Zahn*) root treatment; **Wurzelbürste** F (coarse) scrubbing brush; **Wurzelverzeichnis** NT (*Comput*) root directory; **Wurzelzeichen** NT (*Math*) radical sign; **Wurzelziehen** NT **-s**, NO PL (*Math*) root extraction

würzen [ˈvʏrtsn] VT to season; (*fig*) to add spice to; **eine Geschichte mit etw ~** to season a story with sth

würzig [ˈvʏrtsɪç] **1** ADJ *Speise* tasty; (= *scharf*) spicy; *Zigaretten, Tabak, Geruch etc* aromatic; *Luft* fragrant; **~ schmecken** to be spicy; (*Käse*) to have a sharp taste; **~ riechen** to smell spicy

wusch PRET *von* **waschen**

wuschelig [ˈvʊʃəlɪç] ADJ (*inf*) *Tier* shaggy; *Haare* fuzzy (*inf*)

Wuschelkopf M **(a)** (= *Haare*) mop of curly hair **(b)** (= *Mensch*) fuzzy head (*inf*)

wusste PRET *von* **wissen**

Wust [vuːst] M **-(e)s**, NO PL (*inf*) (= *Durcheinander*) jumble; (= *Menge*) pile; (= *unordentlicher Haufen*) heap; (= *Kram, Gerümpel*) junk (*inf*)

wüst [vyːst] **1** ADJ **(a)** (= *öde*) desolate; **die Erde war ~ und leer** (*Bibl*) the earth was without form, and void (*Bibl*) **(b)** (= *unordentlich*) chaotic; (= *ausschweifend*) wild **(c)** (= *rüde*) *Beschimpfung, Beleidigung etc* vile; (= *arg*) terrible **2** ADV **~ aussehen** to look a real mess; **~ feiern** to have a wild party; **jdn ~ beschimpfen** to use vile language to sb; **~ fluchen** to swear vilely

Wüste [ˈvyːstə] F **-, -n** (*Geog*) desert; (= *Ödland*) waste; (*fig*) waste(land); **die ~ Gobi** the Gobi Desert; **jdn in die ~ schicken** (*fig*) to send sb packing (*inf*)

Wüsten-: **Wüstenfuchs** M desert fox; **Wüstenklima** NT desert climate; **Wüstensand** M desert sand

Wut [vuːt] F **-**, NO PL **(a)** (= *Zorn, Raserei*) rage; (*fig*: *der Elemente*) fury; **vor ~ heulen** to yell with rage; **(auf jdn/etw) eine ~ haben** to be furious (with sb/sth); **eine ~ im Bauch haben** (*inf*) to be hopping mad (*inf*); **eine ~ haben/kriegen** *or* **bekommen** to be in/get into a rage; **jdn in ~ bringen** *or* **versetzen** to infuriate sb **(b)** (= *Verbissenheit*) frenzy; **mit einer wahren ~** as if possessed

Wut-: **Wutanfall** M fit of rage; (*esp von Kind*) tantrum; **Wutausbruch** M outburst of rage; (*esp von Kind*) tantrum

wüten [ˈvyːtn] VI (*lit, fig*) (= *toben*) to rage; (= *zerstörerisch hausen*) to cause havoc; (*verbal*) to storm (*gegen* at); (*Menge*) to riot

wütend [ˈvyːtnt] **1** ADJ furious; *Menge, Proteste* angry; *Kampf, Elemente* raging; **auf jdn/etw** (*acc*) **~ sein** to be mad at sb/sth; **über jdn/etw** (*acc*) **~ sein** to be furious about sb/sth **2** ADV in (a) rage, angrily; **~ raste der Stier auf ihn zu** the enraged bull raced toward(s) him

Wut-: **wutentbrannt** [-ʔɛntbrant] **1** ADJ furious **2** ADV in a rage; **Wutgeschrei** NT cries *pl* of rage

wutschen [ˈvʊtʃn] VI AUX SEIN (*inf*) to whoosh (*inf*); (= *schnell verschwinden*) to whiz (*inf*)

Wut-: **wutschnaubend** ADJ, ADV snorting with rage; **Wutschrei** M yell of rage; **wutverzerrt** [-fɛɐtsɛrt] ADJ distorted with rage

WWW [veːveːˈveː] NT **-**, NO PL (*Comput*) ABBR *von* **World Wide Web** WWW

Wz ABBR *von* **Warenzeichen**

Xx

X, x [ɪks] NT **-, -** X, x; **Herr X** Mr X; **jdm ein X für ein U vormachen** to put one over on sb (*inf*); **er lässt sich kein X für ein U vormachen** he's not easily fooled

x-Achse ['ɪks-] F x-axis

Xanthippe [ksan'tɪpə] F **-, -n** (*fig inf*) shrew

X-Beine ['ɪks-] PL knock-knees *pl*; **~ haben** to be knock-kneed

x-beinig ['ɪks-], **X-beinig** ADJ knock-kneed

x-beliebig [ɪks-] 🚹 ADJ any old (*inf*); **wir können uns an einem ~en Ort treffen** we can meet anywhere you like 🚺 ADV as you like

X-Chromosom ['ɪks-] NT X-chromosome

x-fach ['ɪks-] 🚹 ADJ **die ~e Menge** (*Math*) n times the amount; **trotz ~er Ermahnungen** (*inf*) in spite of umpteen warnings (*inf*) 🚺 ADV so many times

x-förmig ['ɪks-], **X-förmig** 🚹 ADJ X-shaped 🚺 ADV *angeordnet* in an X; **die Fäden X-förmig verkreuzen** to cross the threads to form an X

x-mal ['ɪksmaːl] ADV (*inf*) umpteen times (*inf*)

x-malig ['ɪksmaːlɪç] ADJ (*inf*) umpteen (*inf*); **wenn ein ~er Weltmeister ...** when somebody who has been world champion umpteen times ...

x-te(r, s) ['ɪkstə] ADJ (*Math*) nth; (*inf*) nth (*inf*), umpteenth (*inf*); **zum ~n Mal(e)** for the umpteenth time (*inf*)

Xylofon [ksylo'foːn] NT **-s, -e**, **Xylophon** NT **-s, -e** xylophone

Yy

Y, y [ˈʏpsilɔn] NT -, - Y, y
y-Achse [ˈʏpsilɔn-] F y-axis
Yacht [jaxt] F -, -en yacht
Yard [jaːɐt] NT -s, -s yard
Y-Chromosom [ˈʏpsilɔn-] NT Y-chromosome
Yen [jɛn] M -(s), -(s) yen
Yeti [ˈjeːti] M -s, -s yeti

Yoga [ˈjoːga] M or NT -(s) yoga
Yogi [ˈjoːgi] M -s, -s yogi ·
Ypsilon [ˈʏpsilɔn] NT -(s), -s y; (= *griechischer Buchstabe*) upsilon
Ytong® [ˈyːtɔŋ] M -s, -s breeze block (*Brit*), cinder block (*US*)
Yucca [ˈjʊka] F -, -s yucca
Yuppie [ˈjʊpiː, ˈjapiː] M -s, -s yuppie

Zz

Z, z [tset] NT **-,** - Z, z

zack [tsak] INTERJ (*inf*) pow; **~, ~!** chop-chop! (*inf*); **sei nicht so langsam, mach mal ein bisschen ~, ~** don't be so slow, get a move on (*inf*)

Zack [tsak] M **-s,** NO PL (*inf*) **auf ~ bringen** to knock into shape (*inf*); **auf ~ sein** to be on the ball (*inf*)

Zacke ['tsakə] F **-, -n** point; (*von Gabel*) prong; (*von Kamm*) tooth; (= *Bergzacke*) jagged peak; (= *Auszackung*) indentation; (*von Fieberkurve etc*) peak

zacken ['tsakn] VT to serrate; *Kleid, Saum, Papier* to pink; *siehe auch* **gezackt**

Zacken ['tsakn] M **-s,** - = **Zacke**

zackig ['tsakɪç] **1** ADJ **(a)** (= *gezackt*) jagged; *Stern* pointed **(b)** (*inf*) *Soldat, Bursche* smart; *Tempo, Musik* brisk; *Team, Manager etc* dynamic **2** ADV (*inf:* = *schnell*) *laufen* briskly; *fahren, bedienen* quickly; **bring mir meine Hausschuhe, aber ein bisschen ~!** fetch me my slippers, and make it snappy! (*inf*)

zaghaft 1 ADJ timid **2** ADV timidly

Zaghaftigkeit ['tsa:khaftɪçkait] F **-,** NO PL timidity

zäh [tsɛ:] **1** ADJ *Fleisch, Mensch, Verhandlungen* tough; (= *dickflüssig*) glutinous; (= *schleppend*) *Verkehr etc* slow-moving; (= *ausdauernd*) dogged **2** ADV *verhandeln* tenaciously; *sich widersetzen* doggedly; *fließen* slowly

zähflüssig ADJ thick; *Verkehr, Verhandlung* slow-moving

Zähigkeit ['tsɛ:ɪçkait] F **-,** NO PL toughness; (= *Ausdauer*) doggedness

Zahl [tsa:l] F **-, -en** (Math, Gram) number; (= *Verkaufszahl, Ziffer, Maßangabe, bei Geldmengen etc auch*) figure; **~en nennen** to give figures; **eine fünfstellige ~** a five-figure number; **~ oder Wappen** heads or tails; **in großer ~** in large numbers; **in voller ~** in full number; **der Aufsichtsrat war in voller ~ versammelt** there was a full turnout for the meeting of the board

zahlbar ADJ payable (*an* +*acc* to); **~ bei Lieferung** *or* **nach Erhalt** to be paid for on delivery *or* receipt

zählebig [-le:bɪç] ADJ hardy; (*fig*) *Gerücht, Vorurteil* persistent

zahlen ['tsa:lən] **1** VI to pay; **Herr Ober, (bitte) ~!** waiter, the bill (*esp Brit*) *or* check (*US*) please; **wenn er nicht bald zahlt, dann ...** if he doesn't pay up soon, then ... **2** VT (= *bezahlen*) to pay; **was habe ich (Ihnen) zu ~?** what do I owe you?; **ich zahle dir den Flug** I'll pay for your flight; **lass mal, ich zahls** no no, I'll pay *or* it's on me

zählen ['tsɛ:lən] **1** VI **(a)** to count; **bis hundert ~** to count (up) to a hundred; **auf jdn/etw ~** to count on sb/sth; **schon eine Stunde pro Woche zählt als Teilzeitjob** working just one hour per week counts as a part-time job **(b)** (= *gehören*) **zu einer Gruppe/Menge ~** to be one of a group/set; **er zählt zu den besten Schriftstellern unserer Zeit** he ranks as one of the best authors of our time; **zu welcher Sprachengruppe zählt Gälisch?** to which language group does Gaelic belong? **(c)** (= *wichtig sein*) to matter; **es zählt nicht, ob/dass ...** it doesn't matter if *or* whether/that ... **2** VT **(a)** to count; **bei diesem Spiel zählt der König 5 Punkte** in this game the king counts as 5 points; **seine Tage sind gezählt** his days are numbered; **die Stadt zählt 2 Millionen Einwohner** the town has two million inhabitants; **Stanford zählt 12.000 Studenten** Stanford has 12,000 students; **jdn/sich zu einer Gruppe ~** to regard sb/oneself as part of a group **(b)** (*geh*) **sie zählt 27 Jahre** she is 27 years old

Zahlen-: **Zahlenangabe** F figure; **ich kann keine genauen ~n machen** I can't give any precise figures; **Zahlenbeispiel** NT numerical example; **Zahlengedächtnis** NT memory for numbers; **zahlenmäßig 1** ADJ numerical **2** ADV **(a)** (= *der Anzahl nach*) **~ überlegen sein** to be greater in number; **schwach/unbedeutend** small in number; **~ stark** large in number; **Frauen sind ~ stärker vertreten** there's a greater number of women **(b)** (= *in Zahlen*) in figures; **Zahlenmaterial** NT figures *pl*; **Zahlenschloss** NT combination lock; **Zahlenverhältnis** NT (numerical) ratio

Zahler ['tsa:lɐ] M **-s,** -, **Zahlerin** [-ərɪn] F **-, -nen** payer

Zähler ['tsɛ:lɐ] M **-s,** - **(a)** (Math) numerator **(b)** (= *Messgerät*) meter

Zählerstand M meter reading

Zahl-: **Zahlkarte** F giro transfer form; **zahllos** ADJ countless; **zahlreich 1** ADJ numerous; **wir hatten mit einer ~eren Beteiligung gerechnet** we had expected more participants **2** ADV numerously; **die Veranstaltung war ~ besucht** the event was (very) well attended; **Zahlschein** M payment slip; **Zahltag** M payday

Zahlung ['tsa:lʊŋ] F **-, -en** payment; **in ~ nehmen** to take in part exchange; **in ~ geben** to trade in

Zählung ['tsɛ:lʊŋ] F **-, -en** count; (= *Volkszählung*) census

Zahlungs-: **Zahlungsanweisung** F giro transfer order (*Brit*), money transfer order (*US*); **Zahlungsaufforderung** F request for payment; **Zahlungsaufschub** M extension (of credit); **Zahlungsbedingungen** PL terms *pl* (of payment); **erleichterte ~** easy terms; **Zahlungsempfänger(in)** M(F) payee; **zahlungsfähig** ADJ able to pay; *Firma* solvent; **Zahlungsfähigkeit** F ability to pay; (*von Firma*) solvency; **Zahlungsfrist** F time allowed for payment; **zahlungskräftig** ADJ wealthy; **Zahlungsmittel** NT means *sing* of payment; (= *Münzen, Banknoten*) currency; **gesetzliches ~** legal tender; **Zahlungsschwierigkeiten** PL financial difficulties *pl*; **Zahlungssystem** NT method of payment; **zahlungsunfähig** ADJ unable to pay; *Firma* insolvent; **Zahlungsunfähigkeit** F inability *pl* to pay; (*von Firma*) insolvency; **Zahlungsverkehr** M payments *pl*; **Zahlungsweise** F method of payment; **Zahlungsziel** NT (*Comm*) period allowed for payment

Zählwerk NT counter

Zahlwort NT, *pl* **-wörter** numeral

zahm [tsa:m] ADJ (*lit, fig*) tame

zähmen ['tsɛ:mən] VT to tame; (*fig*) *Leidenschaft, Bedürfnisse* to control

Zähmung F **-,** (*rare*) **-en** taming

Zahn [tsa:n] M **-(e)s,** ⁺e ['tsɛ:nə] **(a)** (Anat) (= *Zacke*) tooth; (*von Briefmarke*) perforation; (= *Radzahn*) cog; **künstliche** *or* **falsche Zähne** false teeth *pl*; **Zähne bekommen** *or* **kriegen** (*inf*) to cut one's teeth; **die ersten Zähne** one's milk teeth; **die zweiten Zähne** one's second set of teeth; **die dritten Zähne** (*hum*) false teeth; **der ~ der Zeit** the ravages *pl* of time; **ich muss mir einen ~ ziehen lassen** I've got to have a tooth out; **den ~ kannst du dir ruhig ziehen lassen!** (*fig inf*) you can put that idea right out of your head!; **jdm auf den ~ fühlen** to sound sb out; **etw mit Zähnen und Klauen verteidigen** to defend sth tooth and nail **(b)** (*inf:* = *Geschwindigkeit*) **einen ~ draufhaben** to be going like the clappers (*inf*); **mit einem unheimlichen ~** at an incredible lick (*inf*)

Zahn-: **Zahnarzt** M, **Zahnärztin** F dentist; **Zahnarzthelfer(in)** M(F) dental nurse; **zahnärztlich 1** ADJ dental; **sich in ~e Behandlung begeben** (*form*) to have dental treatment **2** ADV by a dentist; **sich ~ behandeln lassen** to go to the dentist; **Zahnbehandlung** F dental treatment; **Zahnbelag** M film on the teeth; **Zahnbürste** F toothbrush; **Zahncreme** F toothpaste

Zähne-: **Zähneknirschen** NT **-s,** NO PL grinding one's teeth; (*fig*) gnashing of teeth; **zähneknirschend** ADJ ATTR, ADV grinding one's teeth; (*fig*) gnashing one's teeth; **er fand sich ~ damit ab** he agreed with (a) bad grace

zahnen ['tsa:nən] VI to teethe; **das Zahnen** teething

Zahn-: **Zahnersatz** M dentures *pl*; **Zahnfäule** F tooth decay; **Zahnfleisch** NT gum(s *pl*); **Zahnfleischbluten** NT **-s,** NO PL bleeding of the gums; **Zahnfüllung** F filling; **Zahnhals** M neck of a tooth; **Zahnklammer** F brace; **Zahnkranz** M (*Tech*) gear rim; **Zahnkrone** F crown; **zahnlos** ADJ (*lit, fig*) toothless; **Zahnlücke** F gap between one's teeth; **Zahnmedizin** F dentistry; **Zahnpasta** F, **Zahnpaste** F toothpaste; **Zahnpflege** F dental hygiene; **Zahnputzglas** NT toothbrush glass; **Zahnrad** NT cogwheel; **Zahnradbahn** F rack railway (*Brit*), rack railroad (*US*); **Zahnschmelz** M (tooth) enamel; **Zahnschmerzen** PL toothache *no pl*; **Zahnseide** F dental floss; **Zahnspange** F brace; **Zahnstein** M tartar; **Zahnstocher** [-ʃtɔxɐ]

M **-s, -** toothpick; **Zahntechniker(in)** M(F) dental technician; **Zahnweh** NT toothache

Zaire [zaˈiːr(ə)] NT (*Hist*) **-s** Zaire

zairisch [zaˈiːrɪʃ] ADJ (*Hist*) Zairean

Zampano [ˈtsampano] M **-s, -s** (*inf*) **der große ~** the big cheese (*inf*)

Zander [ˈtsandɐ] M **-s, -** (*Zool*) pikeperch

Zange [ˈtsaŋə] F **-, -n** (= *Flachzange, Rundzange*) (pair of) pliers *pl*; (= *Beißzange*) (pair of) pincers *pl*; (= *Greifzange, Kohlenzange, Zuckerzange*) (pair of) tongs *pl*; (*von Tier*) pincers *pl*; (*Med*) forceps *pl*; (*fig*) we've got him now; **ihn/das möchte ich nicht mit der ~ anfassen** (*inf*) I wouldn't touch him/it with a bargepole (*Brit inf*) *or* a ten-foot pole (*US inf*)

Zangengeburt F forceps delivery

Zankapfel M (*fig*) bone of contention

zanken [ˈtsaŋkn] VIR to quarrel; **wir haben uns gezankt** we've had a row; **(sich) um etw ~** to quarrel over sth

Zankerei [tsaŋkəˈrai] F **-, -en** quarrelling (*Brit*), quarreling (*US*)

zänkisch [ˈtsɛŋkɪʃ] ADJ (= *streitsüchtig*) quarrelsome; (= *tadelsüchtig*) *Frau* shrewish

Zäpfchen [ˈtsɛpfçən] NT **-s, -** DIM *von* Zapfen small plug *etc*; (= *Gaumenzäpfchen*) uvula; (= *Suppositorium*) suppository; **~-r, ~-R** (*Ling*) uvular "r"

zapfen [ˈtsapfn] VT to tap; **dort wird das Pils frisch gezapft** they have draught (*Brit*) *or* draft (*US*) Pilsener there

Zapfen [ˈtsapfn] M **-s, -** (= *Spund*) bung, spigot; (= *Pfropfen*) stopper; (= *Tannenzapfen etc*) cone; (= *Eiszapfen*) icicle; (*Mech: von Welle, Lager etc*) journal; (= *Holzverbindung*) tenon

Zapfenstreich M (*Mil*) tattoo, last post (*Brit*), taps *sing* (*US*); **der Große ~** the Ceremonial Tattoo; **um 12 Uhr ist ~** (*fig inf*) lights out is at 12 o'clock

Zapf-: Zapfhahn M tap; **Zapfpistole** F (petrol (*Brit*) *or* gas (*US*) pump) nozzle; **Zapfsäule** F petrol pump (*Brit*), gas pump (*US*)

Zaponlack [ˈtsaˈpoːnlak] M cellulose lacquer

zappelig [ˈtsapəlɪç] ADJ wriggly; (= *unruhig*) fidgety

zappeln [ˈtsapln] VI to wriggle; (*Hampelmann*) to jiggle; (= *unruhig sein*) to fidget; **jdn ~ lassen** (*fig inf*) to keep sb in suspense

Zappelphilipp [-fɪlɪp] M **-s, -e** *or* **-s** fidget(er)

zappen [ˈtsɛpn] VI (*TV inf*) to zap (*inf*); **in den Konkurrenzkanal ~** to zap over to the other channel (*inf*); **Zappen macht Spaß** zapping is fun (*inf*)

zappenduster [ˈtsapn̩ˈduːstɐ] ADJ (*inf*) pitch-black; **wie sieht es denn mit euren Plänen aus? – ~** how are your plans working out? – grim; **dann ist es ~** you'll/we'll *etc* be in trouble

zapplig [ˈtsaplɪç] ADJ = **zappelig**

Zar [tsaːɐ] M **-en, -en** tsar

Zarin [ˈtsaːrɪn] F **-, -nen** tsarina

zart [tsaːɐt] **1** ADJ (= *weich, leise, sanft*) soft; *Braten, Gemüse* tender; (= *fein, anfällig, feinfühlig*) delicate; **nichts für ~e Ohren** not for sensitive ears; **im ~en Alter von ...** at the tender age of ...; **das ~e Geschlecht** the gentle sex **2** ADV *umgehen, berühren, andeuten* gently; **~ schmecken** to have a delicate taste; **~ besaitet** highly sensitive; **~ besaitet sein** to be very sensitive; **~ fühlend** sensitive

Zart-: zartbitter ADJ *Schokolade* plain; **zartblau** ADJ pale blue; **Zartgefühl** NT sensitivity; **zartgliedrig** [-gliːdrɪç] ADJ dainty; **zartgrün** ADJ pale green

Zartheit F **-, -en** (*von Haut, Stimme*) softness; (*von Gemüse, Braten*) tenderness; (*von Farben, Teint*) delicateness; (*von Gemüt*) sensitivity; (*von Wind, Berührung*) gentleness

zärtlich [ˈtsɛːɐtlɪç] **1** ADJ tender, affectionate **2** ADV tenderly

Zärtlichkeit F **-, -en (a)** NO PL affection **(b)** (= *Liebkosung*) caress; **~en** (= *Worte*) tender words; **jdm ~en ins Ohr flüstern** to whisper sweet nothings in sb's ear

Zäsium [ˈtsɛːziʊm] NT **-s,** NO PL caesium (*Brit*), cesium (*US*)

Zast, ZAST [tsast] F ABBR *von* **Zinsabschlagsteuer**

Zauber [ˈtsaubɐ] M **-s, -** (= *Magie*) magic; (= *~bann*) (magic) spell; (*fig:* = *Reiz*) magic; **fauler ~** (*inf*) humbug *no indef art*; **der ganze ~** (*inf*) the whole lot (*inf*)

Zauberei [tsaubəˈrai] F **-, -en (a)** NO PL (= *das Zaubern*) magic **(b)** (= *Zauberkunststück*) conjuring trick

Zauberer [ˈtsaubərɐ] M **-s, -** magician; (*in Märchen etc auch*) sorcerer; (= *Zauberkünstler auch*) conjurer; *siehe auch* **Zauberin**

zauberhaft 1 ADJ enchanting **2** ADV fantastically

Zauberin [ˈtsaubərɪn] F **-, -nen** (female) magician; (*in Märchen etc auch*) sorceress; (= *Zauberkünstlerin auch*) (female) conjurer

Zauber-: Zauberkünstler(in) M(F) conjurer; **Zauberkunststück** NT conjuring trick

zaubern [ˈtsaubɐn] **1** VI to do magic; (= *Kunststücke vorführen*) to do conjuring tricks **2** VT **(a) etw aus etw ~** to conjure sth out of sth **(b)** (*fig*) *Lösung, Essen* to conjure up

Zauber-: Zauberspruch M (magic) spell; **Zauberstab** M (magic) wand; **Zaubertrank** M magic potion; **Zaubertrick** M conjuring trick; **Zauberwort** NT, *pl* **-worte** magic word

zaudern [ˈtsaudɐn] VI to hesitate

Zaum [tsaum] M **-(e)s, Zäume** [ˈtsɔymə] bridle; **jdn/etw im ~(e) halten** (*fig*) to keep a tight rein on sb/sth; **sich im ~(e) halten** (*fig*) to control oneself; **seine Ungeduld/seinen Zorn im ~e halten** (*fig*) to control one's impatience/anger

zäumen [ˈtsɔymən] VT to bridle

Zaumzeug NT, *pl* **-zeuge** bridle

Zaun [tsaun] M **-(e)s, Zäune** [ˈtsɔynə] fence

Zaun-: Zaungast M *sb who manages to get a free view of an event*; **Zaunkönig** M (*Orn*) wren; **Zaunpfahl** M (fencing) post; **jdm einen Wink mit dem ~ geben** to give sb a broad hint

z. B. [tsɛtˈbeː] ABBR *von* **zum Beispiel** eg

ZDF [tsɛtdeːˈlɛf] NT **-s** ABBR *von* **Zweites Deutsches Fernsehen**

Zebra [ˈtseːbra] NT **-s, -s** zebra

Zebrastreifen M pedestrian crossing

Zeche [ˈtsɛçə] F **-, -n (a)** (= *Rechnung*) bill (*esp Brit*), check (*US*); **die (ganze) ~ (be)zahlen** (*lit, fig*) to foot the bill *etc* **(b)** (= *Bergwerk*) (coal) mine

zechen [ˈtsɛçn] VI to booze (*inf*); (= *Zechgelage abhalten*) to carouse

Zech-: Zechgelage NT carousal (*old, hum*); **Zechprellerei** F *leaving without paying the bill at a restaurant etc*

Zecke [ˈtsɛkə] F **-, -n** (*Aus*) **Zeck** M **-(e)s, -en** tick

Zeder [ˈtseːdɐ] F **-, -n** cedar

Zeh [tseː] M **-s, -en**, **Zehe** [ˈtseːə] F **-, -n** toe; (= *Knoblauchzehe*) clove; **großer/kleiner ~**, **große/kleine ~e** big/little toe; **auf (den) ~en gehen/schleichen** to tiptoe; **jdm auf die ~en treten** (*fig inf*) to tread on sb's toes

Zehen-: Zehennagel M toenail; **Zehenspitze** F tip of the toe

zehn [tseːn] NUM ten; *siehe auch* **vier**

Zehn [tseːn] F **-, -en** ten; *siehe auch* **Vier**

Zehncentstück NT ten-cent piece

Zehner [ˈtseːnɐ] M **-s, - (a)** (*Math*) ten; *siehe auch* **Vierer (b)** (*inf*) (= *Münze*) ten; (= *Geldschein*) tenner (*inf*)

Zehner-: Zehnerkarte F (*für Bus etc*) 10-journey ticket; (*für Schwimmbad etc*) 10-visit ticket; **Zehnerpackung** F packet of ten; **Zehnerstelle** F ten's (place)

Zehn-: Zehneuroschein M ten-euro note (*Brit*) *or* bill (*US*); **Zehnfingersystem** NT touch-typing method; **Zehnkampf** M (*Sport*) decathlon; **Zehnkämpfer** M decathlete; **zehnmal** [ˈtseːnmaːl] ADV ten times; *siehe auch* **viermal**; **zehntausend** [ˈtseːnˈtauznt] NUM ten thousand; **~e** *or* **Zehntausende von Menschen** tens of thousands of people

zehntel [ˈtseːntl] ADJ tenth

Zehntel [ˈtseːntl] NT **-s, -** tenth

zehntens [ˈtseːntns] ADV tenth(ly)

zehnte(r, s) [ˈtseːntə] ADJ tenth; *siehe auch* **vierte(r, s)**

zehren ['tseːrən] VI **(a) von etw ~** (*lit*) to live off sth; (*fig*) to feed on sth **(b) an jdm/etw ~** to wear sb/sth out; **an Nerven** to ruin sth; (*Kummer*) to gnaw at sth; **an Gesundheit** to undermine sth

Zeichen ['tsaiçn] NT **-s, -** sign; (*Sci, algebraisch, auf Landkarte*) symbol; (= *Schriftzeichen*) (*Comput*) character; (= *Anzeichen*: = *Hinweis, Signal*) signal; (= *Erkennungszeichen*) identification; (= *Lesezeichen*) bookmark; (= *Vermerk*) mark; (*auf Briefköpfen*) reference; (= *Satzzeichen*) punctuation mark; **es ist ein ~ unserer Zeit, dass ...** it is a sign of the times that ...; **ein ~ setzen** to set an example; **es geschehen noch ~ und Wunder!** (*hum*) wonders will never cease! (*hum*); **als** *or* **zum ~** as a sign; **jdm ein ~ geben** *or* **machen** to give sb a signal *or* sign; **das ~ zum Aufbruch geben** to give the signal to leave; **unser/Ihr ~** (*form*) our/your reference; **seines ~s** (*oldhum*) by trade; **er ist im ~** *or* **unter dem ~ des Widders geboren** he was born under the sign of Aries; **unter dem ~ von etw stehen** (*fig*: *Konferenz etc*) to take place against a background of sth; **die ~ stehen auf Sturm** (*fig*) there's a storm brewing

Zeichen-: **Zeichenblock** M, *pl* **-blöcke** *or* **-blocks** sketch pad; **Zeichenbrett** NT drawing board; **Zeichendreieck** NT set square; **Zeichenerklärung** F (*auf Fahrplänen etc*) key (to the symbols); (*auf Landkarte*) legend; **Zeichenkette** F (*Comput*) character string; **Zeichensatz** M (*Comput*) character set; **Zeichensetzung** [-zetsʊŋ] F **-, -en** punctuation; **Zeichentrickfilm** M (animated) cartoon

zeichnen ['tsaiçnən] **1** VI to draw; (*form*: = *unterzeichnen*) to sign; **an dem Entwurf ist er lange gezeichnet** he has spent a long time drawing the blueprint; **gezeichnet XY** signed, XY **2** VT **(a)** (= *abzeichnen*) to draw; (= *entwerfen*) *Plan, Grundriss* to draw up; (*fig*: = *porträtieren*) to portray **(b)** (= *kennzeichnen*) to mark; **das Gefieder des Vogels ist hübsch gezeichnet** the bird's plumage has attractive markings; *siehe auch* **gezeichnet** **(c)** (*Fin*) *Betrag* to subscribe; *Aktien* to subscribe (for); *Anleihe* to subscribe to; **gezeichnet** *Kapital* subscribed

Zeichner ['tsaiçnɐ] M **-s, -, Zeichnerin** [-ərɪn] F **-, -nen (a)** artist; **muss ein Maler auch immer ein guter ~ sein?** must a painter always be a good draughtsman (*Brit*) *or* draftsman (*US*) too? **(b)** (*Fin*) subscriber (*von* to)

zeichnerisch ['tsaiçnərɪʃ] **1** ADJ *Darstellung, Gestaltung, Werk* graphic; **sein ~es Können** his drawing ability **2** ADV **~ begabt sein** to have a talent for drawing; **etw ~ festhalten** to draw sth; (*Polizei*) to make a diagram of sth; **etw ~ darstellen** to represent sth in a drawing

Zeichnung ['tsaiçnʊŋ] F **-, -en (a)** (= *Darstellung*) drawing; (= *Entwurf*) draft; (*fig*: = *Schilderung*) portrayal **(b)** (= *Muster*) patterning; (*von Gefieder, Fell*) markings *pl* **(c)** (*Fin*) subscription; **eine Anleihe zur ~ auflegen** to invite subscriptions for a loan

Zeichnungs-: **zeichnungsberechtigt** ADJ authorized to sign; **Zeichnungsvollmacht** F authority to sign

Zeigefinger M index finger

zeigen ['tsaign] **1** VI to point; **nach rechts ~** to point to the right; **auf jdn/etw ~** to point at sb/sth **2** VT to show; **jdm etw ~** to show sb sth; **dem werd ichs (aber) ~!** (*inf*) I'll show him! **3** VR to appear; (*Gefühle*) to show; **sich mit jdm ~** to let oneself be seen with sb; **er zeigt sich nicht gern in der Öffentlichkeit** he doesn't like being seen in public; **sich ~ als ...** to show oneself to be ...; **es zeigt sich, dass ...** it turns out that ...; **es zeigt sich (doch) wieder einmal, dass ...** it just goes to show ...; **es wird sich ~, wer Recht hat** we shall see who's right

Zeiger ['tsaigɐ] M **-s, -** indicator; (= *Uhrzeiger*) hand; **der große/ kleine ~** the big/little hand

Zeigestock M pointer

Zeile ['tsailə] F **-, -n** line; **zwischen den ~n lesen** to read between the lines; **vielen Dank für deine ~n** many thanks for your letter; **jdm ein paar ~n schreiben** to write sb a few lines

Zeilen-: **Zeilenabstand** M line spacing; **Zeilenlänge** F length (of a/the line); **Zeilenschaltung** F line spacing; **Zeilenumbruch** F (automatischer) – (*Comput*) wordwrap; **Zeilenvorschub** M (*Comput*) line feed; **zeilenweise** ADV in lines; (= *nach Zeilen*) by the line; **etw ~ vorlesen** to read sth out line by line

-zeilig [tsailıç] ADJ SUF with ... lines; **es ist vierzeilig** it has four lines

Zeisig ['tsaizıç] M **-s, -e** [-gə] (*Orn*) siskin

zeit [tsait] PREP +GEN **~ meines/seines Lebens** in my/his lifetime

Zeit [tsait] F **-, -en (a)** time; (= *Epoche*) age; **die gute alte ~** the good old days; **es erinnerte ihn an eine ~** it reminded him of the old days; **das waren noch ~en!** those were the days; **die ~en sind schlecht** times are bad; **die ~en haben sich geändert** times have changed; **die ~ Goethes** the age of Goethe; **für alle ~en** for ever; **etw für alle ~en entscheiden** to decide sth once and for all; **in seiner/ihrer besten ~** at his/her peak; **mit der ~ gehen** to move with the times; **vor jds** (*dat*) **~** before sb's time; **die ~ ist knapp bemessen** time is short; **eine lange ~ her sein** *or* **zurückliegen, dass ...** to be a long time (ago *or* back) since ...; **eine Stunde ~ haben** to have an hour (to spare); **Fräulein Glück, haben Sie vielleicht einen Augenblick ~?** Miss Glück, do you have a moment?; **~ raubend** time-consuming; **~ sparend** time-saving; (*adverbial*) expeditiously; **möglichst ~ sparend vorgehen** to save as much time as possible; **sich** (*dat*) **für jdn/etw ~ nehmen** to devote time to sb/sth; **dafür muss ich mir mehr ~ nehmen** I need more time for that; **du hast dir aber reichlich ~ gelassen** you certainly took your time; **keine ~ verlieren** to lose no time; **damit hat es noch ~** there's plenty of time; **das hat ~ bis morgen** that can wait until tomorrow; **lass dir ~** take your time; **... aller ~en ...** of all time; **in letzter ~** recently; **die ganze ~ über** the whole time; **eine ~ lang** a while; **eine ~ lang ist das ganz schön** for a while it's quite nice; **mit der ~** gradually; **nach ~ bezahlt werden** to be paid by the hour; **die ~ heilt alle Wunden** (*Prov*) time is a great healer (*prov*); **es wird langsam ~, dass ...** it's about time that ...; **hast du (die) genaue ~?** do you have the exact time?; **in der ~ von 10 bis 12** between 10 and 12 (o'clock); **Vertrag auf ~** fixed-term contract; **Beamter auf ~** ≈ nonpermanent civil servant; **Soldat auf ~** soldier serving for a set time; **seit dieser ~** since then; **zur** *or* **zu ~en Königin Viktorias** in Queen Victoria's time; **zu der ~, als ...** (at the time) when ...; **alles zu seiner ~** (*prov*) all in good time; **von ~ zu ~** from time to time; *siehe* **zurzeit** **(b)** (*Ling*) tense; **in welcher ~ steht das Verb?** what tense is the verb in?

Zeit-: **Zeitabschnitt** M period (of time); **Zeitangabe** F (= *Datum*) date; (= *Uhrzeit*) time (of day); **die ~ kommt vor der Ortsangabe** (*Gram*) time is given before place; **Zeitansage** F (*Rad*) time check; (*Telec*) speaking clock; **Zeitarbeit** F temporary work; **Zeitarbeiter(in)** M(F) temporary worker; **Zeitaufwand** M time (*needed to complete a task*); **mit möglichst wenig ~** taking as little time as possible; **mit großem ~ verbunden sein** to be extremely time-consuming; **Zeitbombe** F (*lit, fig*) time bomb; **Zeitdruck** M, NO PL pressure of time; **unter ~** under pressure; **Zeiteinheit** F time unit

Zeitenfolge F (*Gram*) sequence of tenses

Zeit-: **Zeitersparnis** F saving of time; **Zeitfahren** NT **-s**, NO PL (*Sport*) time trial; **Zeitform** F (*Gram*) tense; **Zeitfrage** F question of time; **Zeitgeist** M, NO PL Zeitgeist; **Zeitgeld** NT time *or* term deposit; **zeitgemäß** **1** ADJ up-to-date; **~ sein** to be in keeping with the times **2** ADV in keeping with the times; **Zeitgenosse** M, **Zeitgenossin** F contemporary; **zeitgenössisch** [-gənœsɪʃ] ADJ contemporary; **Zeitgeschmack** M prevailing taste; **Zeitgewinn** M gain in time; **sich um einen ~ bemühen** to try to gain time; **zeitgleich** **1** ADJ *Erscheinungen* contemporaneous; *Läufer* with the same time; (*Film*) synchronized **2** ADV at the same time (*mit* as); **~ den ersten Platz belegen** to tie for first place

zeitig ['tsaitıç] ADJ, ADV early

Zeit-: **Zeitkonto** NT record of hours worked; **Zeitlang** ['tsaitlaŋ] F *siehe* **Zeit**; **zeitlebens** [tsait'leːbns] ADV all one's life

zeitlich ['tsaitlıç] **1** ADJ temporal; *Verzögerungen* time-related; (= *chronologisch*) *Reihenfolge* chronological; **aus ~en Gründen** for reasons of time; **in kurzem/großem ~em Abstand** at short/ long intervals (of time); **einen hohen ~en Aufwand erfordern** to require a great deal of time **2** ADV timewise (*inf*); (= *chronologisch*) chronologically; **das passt ihr ~ nicht** the time isn't convenient for her; **~ befristet sein** to have a time limit; **~ zusammenfallen** to coincide; **die Uhren/Pläne ~ aufeinander abstimmen** to synchronize one's watches/plans

Zeit-: **zeitlos** ADJ timeless; **Zeitlupe** F slow motion *no art*; **etw in (der) ~ zeigen** to show sth in slow motion; **Wiederholung**

in (der) ~ slow-motion replay; **Zeitlupentempo** NT slow speed; **im** ~ (*lit*) in slow motion; (*fig*) at a snail's pace; **Zeitmangel** M lack of time; **aus** ~ for lack of time; **Zeitmaschine** F time machine; **Zeitmessung** F timekeeping (*auch Sport*), measurement of time; **zeitnah** 🔳 ADJ contemporary; *Bücher, Unterricht* relevant to present times 🔳 ADV in a contemporary way; **Zeitnot** F shortage of time; **in** ~ **sein** to be pressed for time; **Zeitplan** M schedule; **Zeitpunkt** M (= *Termin*) time; (= *Augenblick auch*) moment; **zu diesem** ~ at that time; **den** ~ **für etw festlegen** to set a time for sth; **Zeitraffer** [-rafɐ] M **-s**, NO PL time-lapse photography; **einen Film im** ~ **zeigen** to show a time-lapse film; **zeitraubend** ADJ *siehe* Zeit; **Zeitraum** M period of time; **in einem** ~ **von ...** over a period of ...; **Zeitrechnung** F calendar; **nach christlicher/jüdischer** ~ according to the Christian/Jewish calendar; **vor unserer** ~ before Christ; **nach unserer** ~ anno Domini; **Zeitschaltuhr** F timer; **Zeitschrift** F (= *Illustrierte*) magazine; (*wissenschaftlich*) periodical; **Zeitspanne** F period of time; **zeitsparend** ADJ *siehe* Zeit; **Zeittafel** F chronological table; **Zeitumstellung** F (= *Zeitänderung*) changing the clocks

Zeitung ['tsaitʊŋ] F **-, -en** (news)paper

Zeitungs- IN CPDS newspaper; **Zeitungsabonnement** NT subscription to a newspaper; **Zeitungsanzeige** F newspaper advertisement; (= *Familienanzeige*) announcement in the (news)paper; **Zeitungsausschnitt** M newspaper cutting; **Zeitungshändler(in)** M(F) newsagent, newsdealer (*US*); **Zeitungsjargon** M journalese; **Zeitungsleser(in)** M(F) newspaper reader; **Zeitungspapier** NT newsprint; (*als Altpapier*) newspaper; **Zeitungsredakteur(in)** M(F) newspaper editor; **Zeitungswesen** NT, NO PL press; **das** ~ **in Deutschland** the German press; **im** ~ **tätig sein** to be in the newspaper business; (*Journalist*) to be in journalism

Zeit-: **Zeitunterschied** M time difference; **Zeitverschiebung** F **(a)** (= *Zeitunterschied*) time difference **(b)** (*von Termin etc*) rescheduling; **Zeitverschwendung** F waste of time; **das wäre** ~ that would be a waste of time; **Zeitvertrag** M temporary contract; **Zeitvertreib** [-feetraip] M **-(e)s, -e** [-bə] way of passing the time; (= *Hobby*) pastime; **zum** ~ to pass the time; **zeitweilig** [-vailiç] 🔳 ADJ temporary 🔳 ADV for a while; (= *kurzzeitig*) temporarily; **zeitweise** ADV at times; **und** ~ **Regen** with rain at times; **Zeitwert** M (*Fin*) current value; (= *Marktwert*) market value; **Zeitwort** NT, *pl* **-wörter** verb; **Zeitzeichen** NT time signal; **Zeitzeuge** M, **Zeitzeugin** F contemporary witness; **Zeitzone** F time zone; **Zeitzünder** M time fuse

Zelle ['tsɛlə] F **-, -n** cell (*auch Sci, Pol*); (= *Kabine*) cabin; (= *Telefonzelle*) (phone) booth

Zell-: **Zellgewebe** NT cell tissue; **Zellgift** NT cytotoxin; **Zellkern** M nucleus (of a/the cell)

Zellophan [tselo'faːn] NT **-s**, NO PL cellophane

Zell-: **Zellstoff** M cellulose; **Zellstoffwindel** F disposable nappy (*Brit*) or diaper (*US*); **Zellteilung** F cell division

Zelluloid [tselu'byt, tselulo'iːt] NT **-s**, NO PL celluloid

Zellulose [tselu'loːzə] F **-, -n** cellulose

Zelt [tsɛlt] NT **-(e)s, -e** tent; (= *Bierzelt, Festzelt etc auch*) marquee; (= *Indianerzelt*) te(e)pee; (= *Zirkuszelt*) big top

Zeltbahn F strip of canvas

zelten ['tsɛltn] VI to camp; **Zelten verboten** no camping

Zelter ['tsɛltɐ] M **-s, -**, **Zelterin** [-ərɪn] F **-, -nen** camper

Zelt-: **Zelthering** M tent peg; **Zeltlager** NT camp; **wann fahrt ihr ins** ~? when are you going to camp?; **Zeltmast** M tent pole; **Zeltpflock** M tent peg; **Zeltplane** F tarpaulin; **Zeltplatz** M camp site

Zement [tse'mɛnt] M **-(e)s, -e** cement

zementieren [tsemen'tiːrən], *ptp* **zementiert** VT to cement; (= *verputzen*) to cement over; *Stahl* to carburize (*spec*); (*fig*) to reinforce; *Freundschaft* to cement

Zement(misch)maschine F cement mixer

Zenit [tse'niːt] M **-(e)s**, NO PL (*lit, fig*) zenith

zensieren [tsen'ziːrən], *ptp* **zensiert** VT **(a)** AUCH VI (= *benoten*) to mark; **einen Aufsatz mit einer Drei** ~ to give an essay a three **(b)** *Bücher etc* to censor

Zensur [tsen'zuːɐ] F **-, -en (a)** NO PL (= *Kontrolle*) censorship *no indef art*; (= *Prüfstelle*) censors *pl*; (*esp bei Film*) board of censors; **durch die** ~ **gehen** to be censored **(b)** (= *Note*) mark

(c) **Zensuren** PL (= *Zeugnis*) report *sing*; **wenn es auf die ~en zugeht** when report time approaches

zensurieren [tsenzu'riːrən], *ptp* **zensuriert** VT (*Aus, Sw*) to censor

Zenti-: **Zentigrad** [tsenti'graːt, 'tsenti-] M hundredth of a degree; **Zentigramm** [tsenti'gram, 'tsenti-] NT centigram(me); **Zentiliter** [tsenti'liːtɐ, -'lɪtɐ, 'tsenti-] M or NT centilitre (*Brit*), centileter (*US*); **Zentimeter** [tsenti'meːtɐ, 'tsenti-] M or NT centimetre (*Brit*), centimeter (*US*); **Zentimetermaß** [tsenti'meːtɐ-] NT (metric) tape measure

Zentner ['tsentnɐ] M **-s, -** (metric) hundredweight, 50 kg; (*Aus, Sw*) 100 kg

zentral [tsen'traːl] (*lit, fig*) 🔳 ADJ central 🔳 ADV centrally

Zentral- IN CPDS central; **Zentralabitur** NT centrally standardized final exam; **Zentralbank** F, *pl* **-banken** central bank

Zentrale [tsen'traːlə] F **-, -n** (*von Firma etc*) head office; (*für Taxis, Mil*) headquarters *sing or pl*; (*für Busse etc*) depot; (= *Schaltzentrale*) central control (office); (= *Telefonzentrale*) exchange; (*von Firma etc, Mil*) switchboard

Zentral-: **Zentraleinheit** F (*Comput*) central processing unit; **Zentralheizung** F central heating

Zentralisation [tsentraliza'tsioːn] F **-, -en** centralization

zentralisieren [tsentrali'ziːrən], *ptp* **zentralisiert** VT to centralize

Zentralismus [tsentra'lɪsmʊs] M **-**, NO PL centralism

zentralistisch [tsentra'lɪstɪʃ] 🔳 ADJ centralist 🔳 ADV from a centralist perspective

Zentral-: **Zentralnervensystem** NT central nervous system; **Zentralrechner** M (*Comput*) mainframe; **Zentralstelle** F ~ **für Arbeitsvermittlung** Central Employment Office (*Brit*), Employment and Training Administration (*US*); ~ **für die Vergabe von Studienplätzen** ≈ Universities and Colleges Admissions Service (*Brit*), ≈ Scholastic Aptitude Test Center (*US*); **Zentralverriegelung** [-feeri:gəlʊŋ] F **-, -en** (*Aut*) central (door) locking; **Zentralverwaltungswirtschaft** F command or controlled economy

Zentren PL *von* Zentrum

zentrieren [tsen'triːrən], *ptp* **zentriert** VT (*auch Comput*) to centre (*Brit*), to center (*US*)

Zentrifugalkraft F centrifugal force

Zentrifuge [tsentri'fuːgə] F **-, -n** centrifuge

Zentripetalkraft F centripetal force

Zentrum ['tsentrʊm] NT **-s, Zentren** [-trən] (*lit, fig*) centre (*Brit*), center (*US*); (= *Innenstadt*) (town) centre (*Brit*) or center (*US*); (*von Großstadt*) (city) centre (*Brit*) or center (*US*)

Zeppelin ['tsepəliːn] M **-s, -e** zeppelin

Zepter ['tsɛptɐ] NT **-s, -** sceptre (*Brit*), scepter (*US*)

zerbeißen *ptp* **zerbissen** [tsɛɐ'bɪsn] VT IRREG to chew; *Knochen, Bonbon, Keks etc* to crunch; (= *beschädigen*) *Pantoffel etc* to chew to pieces; (= *auseinander beißen*) *Kette, Leine* to chew through

zerbeulen *ptp* **zerbeult** VT to dent; **zerbeult** battered

zerbomben *ptp* **zerbombt** VT to flatten with bombs; **zerbombt** *Stadt, Gebäude* bombed out; **zerbombt werden** to be flattened by bombs

zerbrechen *ptp* **zerbrochen** [tsɛɐ'brɔxn] IRREG 🔳 VT (*lit*) to break into pieces; *Glas, Porzellan etc* to smash 🔳 VI AUX SEIN to break into pieces; (*Glas, Porzellan etc*) to smash; (*fig*) to be destroyed (*an +dat* by); (*Ehe*) to fall apart; **er ist am Leben zerbrochen** he has been broken by life

zerbrechlich [tsɛɐ'brɛçlɪç] ADJ fragile; *alter Mensch* frail; „**Vorsicht ~!**" "fragile, handle with care"

Zerbrechlichkeit F **-**, NO PL fragility; (*von altem Menschen*) frailness

zerbröckeln *ptp* **zerbröckelt** VTI (*vi: aux sein*) to crumble

zerdrücken *ptp* **zerdrückt** VT to squash; *Gemüse* to mash; (= *zerknittern*) to crush, to crease; (*inf*) *Träne* to squeeze out

Zeremonie [tseremo'niː, tsere'moːniə] F **-, -n** [-'niːən, -niən] ceremony

zeremoniell [tseremo'niɛl] 🔳 ADJ ceremonial 🔳 ADV ceremonially

Zerfall M, NO PL disintegration; (*von Gebäude auch, von Atom*) decay; (*von Leiche, Holz etc*) decomposition; (*von Land, Kultur*) decline; (*von Gesundheit*) decline

zerfallen¹ *ptp* **zerfallen** VI IRREG AUX SEIN **(a)** (= *sich auflösen*) to disintegrate; (*Gebäude*) to fall into ruin; (*Atomkern*) to decay; (= *auseinander fallen*) to fall apart; (*Leiche, Holz etc*) to decompose; (*Reich, Kultur, Moral, Gesundheit*) to decline **(b)** (= *sich gliedern*) to fall (*in +acc* into)

zerfallen² ADJ *Haus* tumbledown; *Gemäuer* crumbling

Zerfalls-: **Zerfallserscheinung** F sign of decay; **Zerfallsprodukt** NT daughter product

zerfetzen *ptp* **zerfetzt** VT to tear to pieces; *Brief etc* to rip up

zerfetzt [tsɛɐˈfɛtst] ADJ *Hose* tattered; *Körper, Arm* lacerated

zerfleischen [tsɛɐˈflaɪʃn], *ptp* **zerfleischt** ■ VT to tear to pieces; **einander ~** (*fig*) to tear each other apart ② VR (*fig*) **er zerfleischt sich in (Selbst)vorwürfen** he torments himself with self-reproaches; **sich gegenseitig ~** to tear each other apart

zerfließen *ptp* **zerflossen** [tsɛɐˈflɔsn] VI IRREG AUX SEIN (*Tinte, Make-up etc*) to run; (*Eis etc, fig: Reichtum etc*) to melt away; **in Tränen ~** to dissolve into tears; **vor Mitleid ~** to be overcome with pity

zerfranst [tsɛɐˈfranst] ADJ frayed

zergehen *ptp* **zergangen** [tsɛɐˈɡaŋən] VI IRREG AUX SEIN to dissolve; (= *schmelzen*) to melt; **auf der Zunge ~** (*Gebäck etc*) to melt in the mouth; (*Fleisch*) to fall apart; **vor Mitleid ~** to be overcome with pity

zerhacken *ptp* **zerhackt** VT to chop up

zerkauen *ptp* **zerkaut** VT to chew; (*Hund*) *Leine* to chew up

zerkleinern [tsɛɐˈklaɪnɐn], *ptp* **zerkleinert** VT to cut up; (= *zerhacken*) to chop (up); (= *zerbrechen*) to break up; (= *zermahlen*) to crush

zerklüftet [tsɛɐˈklʏftət] ADJ *Tal etc* rugged; *Ufer* indented; **tief ~es Gestein** deeply fissured rock

zerknautschen *ptp* **zerknautscht** VT (*inf*) to crease

zerknirscht [tsɛɐˈknɪrʃt] ADJ remorseful; *Gesicht* remorse-filled

Zerknirschtheit F -, NO PL, **Zerknirschung** [tsɛɐˈknɪrʃʊŋ] F -, NO PL remorse

zerknittern *ptp* **zerknittert** VT to crease

zerknüllen *ptp* **zerknüllt** VT to crumple up

zerkochen *ptp* **zerkocht** VTI (*vi: aux sein*) to cook to a pulp

zerkratzen *ptp* **zerkratzt** VT to scratch

zerlassen *ptp* **zerlassen** VT IRREG to melt

zerlaufen *ptp* **zerlaufen** VI IRREG AUX SEIN to melt

zerlegbar ADJ able to be taken apart; (*Gram*) analysable (*Brit*), analyzable (*US*); (*Math*) reducible; **die Möbel waren leicht ~** the furniture could easily be taken apart

zerlegen *ptp* **zerlegt** VT (= *auseinander nehmen*) to take apart; *Theorie, Argumente* to break down; (*Gram*) to analyse (*Brit*), to analyze (*US*); (= *zerschneiden*) to cut up; *Geflügel, Wild* to carve up; (*Biol*) to dissect; (*Chem*) to break down; **etw in seine Einzelteile ~** to take sth to pieces; to break sth down into its (individual) constituents; **eine Zahl in ihre Faktoren ~** to factorize a number

Zerlegung [tsɛɐˈleːɡʊŋ] F -, -en taking apart; (*Gram*) analysis; (*Math*) reduction; (*Biol*) dissection

zerlesen [tsɛɐˈleːzn] ADJ *Buch* well-thumbed

zerlumpt [tsɛɐˈlʊmpt] ADJ ragged

zermahlen *ptp* **zermahlen** VT to grind; (*in Mörser*) to crush

zermalmen [tsɛɐˈmalmən], *ptp* **zermalmt** VT (*lit, fig*) to crush; (*mit den Zähnen*) to crunch

zermartern *ptp* **zermartert** VT **sich** (*dat*) **den Kopf** *or* **das Hirn ~** to rack one's brains

zermürben [tsɛɐˈmʏrbn], *ptp* **zermürbt** VT (*fig*) **jdn ~** to wear sb down; **~d** wearing

Zerobond [ˈzeːroːbɔnt] M -s, -s (*St Ex*) zero-coupon bond

zerpflücken *ptp* **zerpflückt** VT (*lit, fig*) to pick to pieces

zerquetschen *ptp* **zerquetscht** VT to squash; (*mit Gabel*) *Kartoffeln etc* to mash; (*inf*) *Träne* to squeeze out

Zerquetschte [tsɛɐˈkvɛtʃtə] PL DECL AS ADJ (*inf*) **zehn Euro und ein paar ~** ten euros something (or other); **hundert** *or* **Hundert und ein paar ~** a hundred odd

Zerrbild NT distorted picture

zerreden *ptp* **zerredet** VT to beat to death (*inf*)

zerreiben *ptp* **zerrieben** [tsɛɐˈriːbn] VT IRREG to crumble; (*in Mörser etc*) to grind; (*fig*) to crush

zerreißen *ptp* **zerrissen** [tsɛɐˈrɪsn] IRREG ■ VT **(a)** to tear; (*in Stücke*) to tear to pieces; *Faden, Seil, Bindungen* to break; *Brief etc* to tear up; *Land* to tear apart; *siehe auch* **zerrissen** **(b)** (= *kritisieren*) *Autor, Stück, Film* to tear apart ② VI AUX SEIN (*Stoff*) to tear; (*Band, Seil etc*) to break

Zerreißprobe F (*lit*) pull test; (*fig*) real test; **eine ~ für ihre Ehe** *etc* a crucial test of their marriage *etc*; **eine ~ für meine Geduld** a real test of my patience

zerren [ˈtsɛrən] ■ VT to drag; *Sehne* to pull; **sich** (*dat*) **einen Muskel ~** to pull a muscle; **etw an die Öffentlichkeit ~** to drag sth into the public eye ② VI **an etw** (*dat*) **~** to tug at sth; **an den Nerven ~** to be nerve-racking

zerrinnen *ptp* **zerronnen** [tsɛɐˈrɔnən] VI IRREG AUX SEIN to melt (away); (*fig*) (*Träume, Pläne*) to fade away; (*Geld, Vermögen*) to disappear; **jdm unter den Händen** *or* **zwischen den Fingern ~** (*Geld*) to run through sb's hands like water; **die Zeit zerrinnt mir unter den Händen** the time just goes without me knowing where

zerrissen [tsɛɐˈrɪsn] ADJ (*fig*) *Volk, Partei* strife-torn; *Mensch* (inwardly) torn; *siehe auch* **zerreißen**

Zerrissenheit F -, NO PL (*fig*) (*von Volk, Partei*) disunity *no pl*; (*von Mensch*) (inner) conflict

Zerrung [ˈtsɛrʊŋ] F -, -en (= *das Zerren: von Sehne, Muskel*) pulling; (= *von Sehne*) a pulled ligament; (*von Muskel*) a pulled muscle

zerrütten [tsɛɐˈrʏtn], *ptp* **zerrüttet** VT to destroy; *Nerven* to shatter; **eine zerrüttete Ehe/Familie** a broken marriage/home; **ein zerrüttetes Verhältnis zu jdm haben** to have a disturbed relationship with sb; **sich in einem zerrütteten Zustand befinden** to be in terrible shape

Zerrüttung F -, -en destruction; (*von Ehe*) breakdown; (*von Nerven*) shattering; (*Zustand*) shattered state

Zerrüttungsprinzip NT principle of irretrievable breakdown

zersägen *ptp* **zersägt** VT to saw up

zerschlagen¹ *ptp* **zerschlagen** IRREG ■ VT **(a)** (*Mensch*) to smash (to pieces); *Stein, Porzellan, Glas etc* to shatter; (*Hagel*) *Ernte, Wein* to crush; (= *auseinander schlagen*) to break up **(b)** (*fig*) *Angriff, Widerstand, Opposition* to crush; *Hoffnungen, Pläne* to shatter; *Verbrecherring etc, Vereinigung* to break; *Großunternehmen* to break up; *Staat* to smash ② VR (= *nicht zustande kommen*) to fall through; (*Hoffnung, Aussichten*) to be shattered

zerschlagen² ADJ PRED washed out (*inf*); (*nach Anstrengung, langer Reise etc*) worn out

zerschmettern *ptp* **zerschmettert** ■ VT (*lit, fig*) to shatter; *Feind* to crush ② VI AUX SEIN to shatter

zerschneiden *ptp* **zerschnitten** [tsɛɐˈʃnɪtn] VT IRREG to cut; (*in zwei Teile*) to cut in two; (*in Stücke*) to cut up; (= *verschneiden*) *Stoff* to cut wrongly; (*fig*) *Stille* to pierce

zerschrammen *ptp* **zerschrammt** VT *Haut, Möbel* to scratch to pieces; *Lack* to scratch

zersetzen *ptp* **zersetzt** ■ VT to decompose; (*Säure*) to corrode; (*fig*) to undermine ② VR to decompose; (*durch Säure*) to corrode; (*fig*) to become undermined *or* subverted

Zersetzung [tsɛɐˈzɛtsʊŋ] F -, -en (*Chem*) decomposition; (*durch Säure*) corrosion; (*fig*) (= *Untergrabung*) undermining; (*von Gesellschaft*) decline (*von* in)

zersiedeln *ptp* **zersiedelt** VT to spoil (by development)

Zersiedelung [tsɛɐˈziːdəlʊŋ] F -, -en, **Zersiedlung** F overdevelopment

zersplittern *ptp* **zersplittert** ■ VT to shatter; *Holz* to splinter; (*fig*) *Kräfte, Zeit* to squander; *Gruppe, Partei* to fragment ② VI AUX SEIN to shatter; (*Holz, Knochen*) to splinter; (*fig*) to split up

zerspringen *ptp* **zersprungen** [tsɛɐˈʃprʊŋən] VI IRREG AUX SEIN to shatter; (*Saite*) to break; (= *einen Sprung bekommen*) to crack; **in tausend Stücke ~** to shatter in(to) a thousand pieces

zerstampfen *ptp* **zerstampft** VT (= *zertreten*) to stamp on; (= *zerkleinern*) to crush; (*im Mörser*) to grind; *Kartoffeln etc* to mash

zerstäuben *ptp* **zerstäubt** VT to spray

Zerstäuber [tsɛɐˈʃtɔybɐ] M -s, - spray; (= *Parfümzerstäuber auch*) atomizer

zerstechen *ptp* **zerstochen** [tsɛɐˈʃtɔxn] VT IRREG **(a)** (*Mücken*) to bite (all over); (*Bienen etc*) to sting (all over) **(b)** *Material, Haut, Reifen* to puncture; *Finger* to prick

zerstörbar ADJ destructible; **nicht ~** indestructible

zerstören ptp **zerstört 1** VT (lit, fig) to destroy; (Rowdys) to vandalize; Gesundheit to wreck **2** VI to destroy

zerstörerisch [tsɛɐ̯ˈʃtøːrərɪʃ] **1** ADJ destructive **2** ADV destructively; ~ **wirken** to wreak destruction

Zerstörung F (durch Rowdys) vandalizing

Zerstörungs-: Zerstörungsdrang M destructive urge; **Zerstörungslust** F delight in destruction; **Zerstörungstrieb** M destructive urge; **Zerstörungswut** F destructive mania

zerstoßen ptp **zerstoßen** VT IRREG **(a)** (= zerkleinern) to crush; (im Mörser) to grind **(b)** (= durch Stoßen beschädigen) to damage; Leder, Schuh to scuff

zerstreiten ptp **zerstritten** [tsɛɐ̯ˈʃtrɪtn] VR IRREG to quarrel; siehe auch **zerstritten**

zerstreuen ptp **zerstreut 1** VT **(a)** (= verstreuen) to scatter (in +dat over); Volksmenge etc to disperse; (fig) to dispel **(b)** (= ablenken) jdn ~ to take sb's mind off things **2** VR **(a)** (= sich verteilen) to scatter; (Menge) to disperse; (fig) to be dispelled **(b)** (= sich ablenken) to take one's mind off things; (= sich amüsieren) to amuse oneself

zerstreut [tsɛɐ̯ˈʃtrɔyt] ADJ (fig) Mensch absent-minded

Zerstreutheit F -, NO PL absent-mindedness

Zerstreuung F **(a)** NO PL (= das Zerstreuen) scattering; (von Menge) dispersal; (fig) dispelling **(b)** (= Ablenkung) diversion; **zur ~** as a diversion **(c)** (= Zerstreutheit) absent-mindedness

zerstritten [tsɛɐ̯ˈʃtrɪtn] ADJ ~ **sein** (Paar, Geschäftspartner) to have fallen out; (Partei) to be disunited; siehe auch **zerstreiten**

Zerstrittenheit F (von Paar, Geschäftspartnern) bad blood (+gen between); (von Partei) disunity

zerstückeln ptp **zerstückelt** VT (lit) to cut up; Leiche to dismember; Land to divide up

Zertifikat [tsɛrtifiˈkaːt] NT **-(e)s, -e** certificate

zertifizieren [tsɛrtifiˈtsiːrən] VT, ptp **zertifiziert** to certify

zertrampeln ptp **zertrampelt** VT to trample on

zertreten ptp **zertreten** VT IRREG to crush (underfoot); Rasen to ruin

zertrümmern [tsɛɐ̯ˈtrʏmɐn], ptp **zertrümmert** VT to smash; Gebäude auch to wreck; Einrichtung to smash up; Hoffnungen, Ordnung to destroy

Zervelatwurst [tsɛrvəˈlaːt-] F cervelat

Zerwürfnis [tsɛɐ̯ˈvʏrfnɪs] NT **-ses, -se** row

zerzausen ptp **zerzaust** VT to ruffle; Haar to tousle

zerzaust [tsɛɐ̯ˈtsaust] ADJ windswept; Haare auch dishevelled

Zessionar [tsesioˈnaːr] M **-s, -e**, **Zessionarin** [-ˈnaːrɪn] F **-, -nen** assignee

Zettel [ˈtsetl] M **-s, -** piece of paper; (= Notizzettel) note; (= Karteizettel) card; (= Anhängezettel) label; (mit Angabe über Inhalt, Anschrift etc) ticket; (= Bekanntmachung) notice; (= Handzettel) leaflet, handbill (esp US), flyer; (= Formular) form; (= Stimmzettel) ballot paper; (= Bestellzettel) coupon; (= Kassenzettel, Beleg) receipt; „**~ ankleben verboten**" "no posters allowed"

Zettel-: Zettelkasten M file-card box; **Zettelwirtschaft** F, NO PL (pej) **eine ~ haben** to have bits of paper everywhere

Zeug [tsɔyk] NT **-(e)s** [-gəs], NO PL **(a)** (inf) stuff no indef art, no pl; (= Ausrüstung) gear (inf); (= Kleidung) things pl (inf); (= Getier) things pl; **altes ~** junk, trash; **... und solches ~ ...** and such things **(b)** (inf: = Unsinn) nonsense; **ein/dieses ~** a/this load of nonsense; **dummes** or **ungereimtes ~ reden** to talk a lot of nonsense **(c)** (= Fähigkeit, Können) **das ~ zu etw haben** to have (got) what it takes to be sth (inf); **er hat nicht das ~ dazu** he hasn't got what it takes (inf) **(d)** (in Wendungen) **was das ~ hält** (inf) for all one is worth; **laufen, fahren** like mad; **sich für jdn ins ~ legen** (inf) to stand up for sb; **sich ins ~ legen** to go flat out (esp Brit) or all out (US)

Zeuge [ˈtsɔygə] M **-n, -n**, **Zeugin** [ˈtsɔygɪn] F **-, -nen** (Jur, fig) witness (+gen to); ~ **eines Unfalls/Gesprächs sein** to be a witness to an accident/a conversation; **sich als ~ zur Verfügung stellen** to come forward as a witness; **vor** or **unter ~n** in front of witnesses; **die ~n Jehovas** Jehovah's Witnesses

zeugen¹ [ˈtsɔygn] VT Kind to father

zeugen² VI **(a)** (vor +dat to) (= aussagen) to testify; (esp vor Gericht) to give evidence; **für/gegen jdn ~** to testify/give evidence for/against sb **(b) von etw ~** to show sth

Zeugen-: Zeugenaussage F testimony; **Zeugenbank** F, pl **-bänke** witness box (Brit), witness stand (US); **Zeugenschutz** M witness protection; **jdn unter ~** (dat) **stellen** to place sb under witness protection; **Zeugenschutzprogramm** NT witness protection programme (Brit) or program (US); **Zeugenstand** M witness box (Brit), witness stand (US); **in den ~ treten** to take the (witness) stand (US)

Zeugin F **-, -nen** witness; siehe auch **Zeuge**

Zeugnis [ˈtsɔyknɪs] NT **-ses, -se (a)** (= Zeugenaussage, Beweis) evidence; **für/gegen jdn ~ ablegen** to testify for/against sb; **für jds Ehrlichkeit** etc ~ **ablegen** to bear witness to sb's honesty etc **(b)** (= Schulzeugnis) report; (= Note) mark, grade (esp US) **(c)** (= Bescheinigung) certificate; (von Arbeitgeber) reference; **gute ~se haben** to have good qualifications; (von Arbeitgeber) to have good references

Zeugnis-: Zeugnisheft NT (Sch) report card; **Zeugniskonferenz** F (Sch) staff meeting to decide on marks etc; **Zeugnispapiere** PL certificates pl; (von Arbeitgeber) testimonials pl; **Zeugnisverweigerungsrecht** NT right of a witness to refuse to give evidence

Zeugs [tsɔyks] NT -, NO PL (pej inf) = **Zeug (a, b)**

Zeugung [ˈtsɔygʊŋ] F **-, -en** fathering

Zeugungs-: zeugungsfähig ADJ fertile; **Zeugungsfähigkeit** F, **Zeugungskraft** (geh) F fertility; **zeugungsunfähig** ADJ sterile; **Zeugungsunfähigkeit** F sterility

ZEVIS [ˈtseːvɪs] NT ABBR von **Zentrales Verkehrsinformationssystem**

z. H(d). ABBR von **zu Händen** attn

Zicke [ˈtsɪkə] F **-, -n (a)** nanny goat **(b)** (pej inf: = Frau) silly cow (inf)

Zicken [ˈtsɪkn] PL (inf) nonsense no pl; **mach bloß keine ~!** no nonsense now!; **~ machen** to make trouble

zickig [ˈtsɪkɪç] ADJ (inf: = prüde) awkward

Zickzack [ˈtsɪktsak] M **-(e)s, -e** zigzag; **zickzack** or **im ~ laufen** to zigzag; **~ nähen** to zigzag

Zickzack-: zickzackförmig 1 ADJ zigzag **2** ADV ~ **verlaufen** to zigzag; **Zickzackkurs** M zigzag course; (von Hase etc) zigzag path; **im ~ fahren/laufen** to zigzag

Ziege [ˈtsiːgə] F **-, -n (a)** goat; (weiblich) (nanny) goat **(b)** (pej inf: = Frau) cow (inf)

Ziegel [ˈtsiːgl] M **-s, -** (= Backstein) brick; (= Dachziegel) tile; **ein Dach mit ~n decken** to tile a roof

Ziegelei [tsiːgəˈlai] F **-, -en** brickworks sing or pl; (für Dachziegel) tilemaking works sing or pl

Ziegel-: ziegelrot ADJ brick-red; **Ziegelstein** M brick

Ziegen-: Ziegenbart M (an Hut) shaving brush (hum); (hum: = Bart) goatee (beard); **Ziegenbock** M billy goat; **Ziegenkäse** M goat's milk cheese; **Ziegenleder** NT kid (leather); **Ziegenmilch** F goat's milk; **Ziegenpeter** [-peːtɐ] M **-s, -** mumps sing

---

ziehen [ˈtsiːən]	
1 TRANSITIVES VERB	**3** UNPERSÖNLICHES VERB
2 INTRANSITIVES VERB	**4** REFLEXIVES VERB

pret **zog** [tsoːk], ptp **gezogen** [gəˈtsoːgn]

In Verbindungen mit Substantiv siehe auch Eintrag für das jeweilige Substantiv.

1 TRANSITIVES VERB
(a) (allgemein) to pull; Handbremse to put on; Hut to raise; **etw durch etw ziehen** to pull sth through sth; **jdn nach unten ziehen** to pull or (fig) drag sb down; **den Ring vom Finger ziehen** to pull one's ring off (one's finger); **die Vorhänge vors Fenster ziehen** to draw the curtains; **die Schultern in die Höhe ziehen** to raise one's shoulders; **das Flugzeug nach oben/unten ziehen** to put the plane into a climb/descent; **die Stirn kraus** or **in Falten ziehen** to knit one's brow **(b)** (= hinziehen) (fig) **was zieht dich denn nach Hause?** what

is drawing you home?; **es zog ihn in die weite Welt** he felt drawn toward(s) the big wide world; **etw ins Komische ziehen** to ridicule sth; **musst du immer alles ins Lächerliche ziehen?** must you always make fun of everything?; **unangenehme Folgen nach sich ziehen** to have unpleasant consequences; **die Aufmerksamkeit** *or* **die Blicke auf sich** (*acc*) **ziehen** to attract attention

(c) (= *herausziehen*) to pull out (*aus* of); *Zahn, Fäden* to take out; *Wasserproben* to take; (*Math*) *Wurzel* to work out; *Los, Spielkarte, Schlussfolgerungen* to draw; *Vergleich* to make; **Zigaretten (aus dem Automaten) ziehen** to get cigarettes from the machine; **ziehen und ablegen** (*Comput*) to drag and drop

(d) (= *zeichnen*) *Kreis, Linie* to draw

(e) (= *verlegen, anlegen*) *Kabel, Leitung etc* to lay; *Graben, Furchen* to dig; *Mauer* to build; *Zaun* to put up; *Grenze* to draw; **Perlen auf eine Schnur ziehen** to thread pearls

(f) (= *herstellen*) *Draht, Kerzen, Kopien* to make; **Kopien von etw ziehen** to copy sth

(g) (= *züchten*) *Blumen* to grow; *Tiere* to breed; **sie haben die Kinder gut gezogen** (*inf*) they brought the children up well

2 INTRANSITIVES VERB

(a) (= *zerren*) to pull; **an etw** (*dat*) **ziehen** to pull (on *or* at) sth; **ein ziehender Schmerz** an ache

(b) (= *umziehen*) AUX SEIN to move; **nach Bayern ziehen** to move to Bavaria; **zu jdm ziehen** to move in with sb

(c) (= *sich bewegen*) AUX SEIN to move; (*Soldaten, Volksmassen*) to march; (= *durchstreifen*) to wander; (*Wolken, Rauch*) to drift; (*Vögel*) to fly; (*während des Vogelzugs*) to migrate; **durch die Welt ziehen** to roam the world; **durch die Stadt ziehen** to wander about the town; **in den Krieg/die Schlacht ziehen** to go to war/battle; **mit dem Turm ziehen** (*Chess*) to move the rook

(d) (= *Zug haben*) (*Feuer, Ofen, Pfeife*) to draw; **an der Pfeife/ Zigarette ziehen** to take a drag on one's pipe/cigarette

(e) (= *Eindruck machen*) (*inf*) **so was zieht beim Publikum/bei mir nicht** the public/I don't like that sort of thing; **der Film zieht immer noch** the film is still popular; **so was zieht immer** that sort of thing always goes down well

(f) (= *sieden*) (*Tee*) to draw

3 UNPERSÖNLICHES VERB

✦**es zieht** there's a draught (*Brit*) *or* draft (*US*); **wenn es dir zieht** if you're in a draught (*Brit*) *or* draft (*US*); **mir ziehts im Nacken** there is a draught (*Brit*) *or* draft (*US*) round my neck; **mir ziehts im Rücken** (= *tut der Rücken weh*) my back hurts

4 REFLEXIVES VERB

✦**sich ziehen**

(a) (= *sich erstrecken*) to extend; **dieses Treffen zieht sich!** this meeting is dragging on!; **sich zickzackförmig durchs Land ziehen** to zigzag through the countryside; **dieses Thema zieht sich durch das ganze Buch** this theme runs throughout the whole book

(b) (= *sich dehnen*) to stretch; (*Holz*) to warp

Ziehharmonika F concertina; (*mit Tastatur*) accordion

Ziehung ['tsiːʊŋ] F -, -en draw

Ziel [tsiːl] NT -(e)s, -e **(a)** (= *Reiseziel*) destination; (= *Absicht, Zweck*) goal; (*von Wünschen, Spott*) object; **mit dem ~ ...** with the aim ...; **etw zum ~ haben** to have sth as one's goal; **jdm/ sich ein ~ stecken** *or* **setzen** to set sb/oneself a goal; **er hatte sich sein ~ zu hoch gesteckt** he had set his sights too high; **am ~ sein** to be at one's destination; (*fig*) to have reached *or* achieved one's goal

(b) (*Sport*) finish; (*bei Pferderennen*) finish(ing post), winning post; (*bei Rennen*) finish(ing line); **durchs ~ gehen** to pass the finishing post/to cross the finishing line

(c) (*Mil, Schießsport, fig*) target; **über das ~ hinausschießen** (*fig*) to overshoot the mark

(d) (*Comm*: = *Frist*) credit period; **mit drei Monaten ~** with a three-month credit period

zielen ['tsiːlən] VI (*Mensch*) to aim (*auf +acc, nach* at); (*Waffe, Schuss, fig: Bemerkung, Kritik, Tat*) to be aimed (*auf +acc* at); **das zielt auf uns** that's aimed at us; *siehe auch* **gezielt**

Ziel-: **Zielfernrohr** NT telescopic sight; **Zielgerade** F home straight; **Zielgruppe** F target group; **Zielhafen** M port of

destination; **Ziellinie** F (*Sport*) finishing line; **ziellos 1** ADJ aimless **2** ADV aimlessly; **Ziellosigkeit** F -, NO PL lack of purpose; **Zielort** M, *pl* **-orte** destination; **Zielscheibe** F target; (*von Spott auch*) object; **Zielsetzung** [-zetsʊŋ] F -, -en target; **zielsicher 1** ADJ unerring; *Handeln, Planen* purposeful **2** ADV unerringly; **~ auf jdn/etw zugehen** to go straight up to sb/sth; **Zielsprache** F target language; **zielstrebig** ['tsiːlʃtreːbɪç] **1** ADJ *Mensch, Handlungsweise* determined **2** ADV full of determination; **Zielstrebigkeit** F -, NO PL determination

ziemen ['tsiːmən] VR IMPERS (*geh*) **es ziemt sich nicht** it is not proper

ziemlich ['tsiːmlɪç] **1** ADJ ATTR (= *beträchtlich*) *Anzahl, Strecke* considerable; *Vermögen* sizable; *Genugtuung* reasonable; **das ist eine ~e Frechheit** that's a real cheek (*Brit*), that's really fresh (*US*); **eine ~e Zeit/Anstrengung/Arbeit** quite a time/an effort/a lot of work; **mit ~er Sicherheit** fairly certainly; *sagen, behaupten* with reasonable certainty

2 ADV **(a)** (= *beträchtlich*) quite; *sicher, genau* reasonably; **wir haben uns ~ beeilt** we've hurried quite a bit; **~ lange** quite a long time; **~ viel** quite a lot

(b) (*inf*: = *beinahe*) almost; **so ~** more or less; **so ~ alles** just about everything; **so ~ dasselbe** pretty well; **sie ist so ~ in meinem Alter** she is about the same age as me

Zierde ['tsiːɐdə] F -, -n ornament; (= *Schmuckstück*) adornment; (*fig*: = *Tugend*) virtue; **zur ~** for decoration; **das alte Haus ist eine ~ der Stadt** the old house is one of the beauties of the town; **die ~ der Familie** (*fig*) a credit to the family

zieren ['tsiːrən] **1** VT to adorn; *Speisen* to garnish; *Kuchen* to decorate; (*fig*: = *auszeichnen*) to grace

2 VR (*sich bitten lassen*) to make a fuss; (*Mädchen*) to act coyly; (= *sich gekünstelt benehmen*) to be affected; **du brauchst dich nicht zu ~, es ist genügend da** there's no need to be polite, there's plenty there; **er zierte sich nicht lange und sagte Ja** he didn't need much pressing before he agreed; **ohne sich zu ~** without having to be pressed; **zier dich nicht!** don't be shy; *siehe auch* **geziert**

Zier-: **Zierfarn** M decorative fern; **Zierfisch** M ornamental fish; **Ziergarten** M ornamental garden; **Ziergewächs** NT ornamental plant; **Zierleiste** F border; (*an Auto*) trim; (*an Möbelstück*) edging; (*an Wand*) moulding (*Brit*), molding (*US*)

zierlich ['tsiːɐlɪç] ADJ dainty; *Frau auch* petite; *Porzellanfigur, Möbel* delicate

Zierlichkeit F -, NO PL daintiness; (*von Porzellanfigur, Möbel etc*) delicateness

Ziffer ['tsɪfɐ] F -, -n **(a)** (= *Zahlzeichen*) digit; (= *Zahl*) figure; **römische/arabische ~n** roman/arabic numerals; **eine Zahl mit drei ~n** a three-figure number; **etw in ~n schreiben** to write sth in figures **(b)** (*eines Paragrafen*) clause

Zifferblatt NT (*an einer Uhr*) dial; (*von Armbanduhr*) (watch) face

zig [tsɪç] ADJ (*inf*) umpteen (*inf*)

zig- ['tsɪç] PREF (*inf*) umpteen (*inf*); **~tausend** umpteen thousand (*inf*)

Zigarette [tsigaˈrɛtə] F -, -n cigarette

Zigaretten- IN CPDS cigarette; **Zigarettenanzünder** M (*in Auto*) cigar lighter; **Zigarettenautomat** M cigarette machine; **Zigarettenlänge** F **auf** *or* **für eine ~ hinausgehen** to go out for a cigarette; **Zigarettenpapier** NT cigarette paper; **Zigarettenpause** F cigarette break; **Zigarettenspitze** F cigarette holder

Zigarillo [tsigaˈrɪlo, -ˈrɪljo] M *or* NT -s, -s cigarillo

Zigarre [tsiˈgarə] F -, -n **(a)** cigar **(b)** (*inf*: = *Verweis*) dressing-down; **jdm eine ~ verpassen** to give sb a dressing-down

Zigeuner [tsiˈgɔynɐ] M -s, -, **Zigeunerin** [-ərɪn] F -, -nen gypsy; (*Rasse auch*) Romany; (*pej inf*) vagabond; (= *Streuner*) gypsy

Zigeunerleben NT gypsy life; (*fig*) rootless life

zigeunern [tsiˈgɔynɐn], *ptp* **zigeunert** VI AUX HABEN *or* (*bei Richtungsangabe*) SEIN (*inf*) to rove

Zigeuner-: **Zigeunerschnitzel** NT (*Cook*) *cutlet served in a spicy sauce with green and red peppers*; **Zigeunerwagen** M gypsy caravan

zigmal ['tsɪçmaːl] ADV (*inf*) umpteen times (*inf*)

Zimbabwe [zɪmˈbabvə] NT -s Zimbabwe

Zimbabwer [zɪmˈbabvɐ] M -s, -, **Zimbabwerin** [-ərɪn] F -, -nen Zimbabwean

zimbabwisch [zɪmˈbabvɪʃ] ADJ Zimbabwean

Zimmer ['tsɪmɐ] NT -s, - room; **„~ frei"** "vacancies"

Zimmer-: Zimmerantenne F indoor aerial (*Brit*) *or* antenna (*US*); **Zimmerbrand** M fire in a/the room; **Zimmerdecke** F ceiling

Zimmerei [tsɪmə'raɪ] F **-, -en (a)** (= *Handwerk*) carpentry **(b)** (= *Werkstatt*) carpenter's shop

Zimmer-: Zimmereinrichtung F furniture; **Zimmerhandwerk** NT carpentry; **Zimmerherr** M (gentleman) lodger; **Zimmerkellner** M room waiter; **Zimmerkellnerin** F room waitress; **Zimmerlautstärke** F low volume; **Zimmerlehre** F apprenticeship in carpentry; **Zimmermädchen** NT chambermaid

Zimmermann M, *pl* **-leute** carpenter; **jdm zeigen, wo der ~ das Loch gelassen hat** (*inf*) to show sb the door

zimmern ['tsɪmɛn] **1** VT to make from wood; (*fig*) *Alibi, Lösung* to construct; *Ausrede* to make up **2** VI to do carpentry; **an etw** (*dat*) **~** (*lit*) to make sth from wood; (*fig*) to work on sth

Zimmer-: Zimmernachweis M accommodation service; **Zimmerpflanze** F house plant; **Zimmerservice** [-zøːɐ̯vɪs, -zœrvɪs] M room service; **Zimmersuche** F room hunting; **auf ~ sein** to be looking for rooms/a room; **Zimmervermittlung** F accommodation service

zimperlich ['tsɪmpɛlɪç] **1** ADJ (= *überempfindlich*) nervous (*gegen* about); (*beim Anblick von Blut etc*) squeamish; (= *prüde*) prissy; (= *wehleidig*) soft; **sei doch nicht so ~** don't be so silly; **da ist er gar nicht (so) ~** he doesn't have any qualms about that; **da darf man nicht so ~ sein** you can't afford to be soft **2** ADV oversensitively; **du behandelst ihn viel zu ~** you're much too soft with him

Zimt [tsɪmt] M **-(e)s, -e** (= *Gewürz*) cinnamon

Zimt-: zimtfarben [-farbn], **zimtfarbig** ADJ cinnamon-coloured (*Brit*), cinnamon-colored (*US*); **Zimtstange** F stick of cinnamon; **Zimtstern** M (*Cook*) *cinnamon-flavoured star-shaped biscuit*; **Zimtzicke** F (*inf*) stupid cow (*inf*)

Zink [tsɪŋk] NT **-(e)s**, NO PL (*abbr* **Zn**) zinc

Zinke ['tsɪŋkə] F **-, -n** (*von Gabel*) prong; (*von Kamm, Rechen*) tooth; (= *Holzzapfen*) tenon

zinken[1] ['tsɪŋkn] VT **(a)** *Karten* to mark **(b)** *Holz etc* to tenon

zinken[2] ADJ zinc *attr*, made of zinc

Zinn [tsɪn] NT **-(e)s**, NO PL **(a)** (*abbr* **Sn**) tin **(b)** (= *Legierung*, *~produkte*) pewter

Zinnbecher M pewter tankard

zinnen ['tsɪnən], **zinnern** ['tsɪnɛn] ADJ pewter

Zinn-: Zinnfigur F pewter figure; **Zinngeschirr** NT pewter ware; **Zinngießer(in)** M(F) pewterer

zinnoberrot ADJ vermilion

Zinn-: Zinnpest F tin disease; **Zinnsoldat** M tin soldier

Zins[1] [tsɪns] M **-es, -e** [-zə] (*Hist*: = *Abgabe*) tax; (*S Ger, Aus, Sw*: = *Pachtzins, Mietzins*) rent; (= *Wasserzins*) water rates *pl*

Zins[2] M **-es, -en** USU PL (= *Geldzins*) interest *no pl*; **~en bringen** to earn interest; **~en tragen** (*lit*) to earn interest; (*fig*) to pay dividends; **Darlehen zu 10% ~en** loan at 10% interest; **jdm etw mit ~en or mit ~ und ~eszins heimzahlen** *or* **zurückgeben** (*fig*) to pay sb back for sth with interest

Zins-: Zinsabschlagsteuer F tax on interest payments; **Zinsbindung** F pegging of interest rates; **Zinseinkünfte** PL interest income *no pl*

Zinseszins M compound interest

Zins-: zinsfrei **1** ADJ **(a)** (= *frei von Abgaben*) tax-free; (*S Ger, Aus, Sw*: = *pachtfrei, mietfrei*) rent-free; *Wasser* rate-free **(b)** *Darlehen* interest-free **2** ADV *Geld leihen* interest-free; **Zinsfuß** M interest rate; **zinslos** ADJ, ADV interest-free; **Zinsniveau** NT level of interest rates; **Zinsrechnung** F calculation of interest; **Zinssatz** M interest rate; (*bei Darlehen*) lending rate; **Zinssenkung** F reduction in the interest rate; **Zinsspanne** F *margin between interest rates paid by borrowers and to investors*; **Zinssteuer** F tax on interest; **Zinswucher** M usury

Zionismus [tsio'nɪsmʊs] M **-**, NO PL Zionism

zionistisch [tsio'nɪstɪʃ] ADJ Zionist

Zipfel ['tsɪpfl] M **-s, -** (*von Tuch, Decke, Stoff*) corner; (*von Mütze*) point; (*von Hemd, Jacke*) tail; (*am Saum*) dip (*an +dat* in); (*von Wurst*) end; (*von Land*) tip

Zipfelmütze F pointed cap

zipfeln ['tsɪpfln] VI (*Rock*) to be uneven

Zipp [tsɪp] M (*Aus*) zip

zippen ['tsɪpn] VTI (*Comput*: = *komprimieren*) to zip

Zippverschluss M (*Aus*) zip fastener

Zirbeldrüse ['tsɪrbl-] F pineal body

Zirbelkiefer F Swiss *or* stone pine

zirka ['tsɪrka] ADV about

Zirkel ['tsɪrkl] M **-s, - (a)** (= *Gerät*) pair of compasses; (= *Stechzirkel*) pair of dividers **(b)** (*lit, fig*: = *Kreis*) circle

Zirkelschluss M circular argument

Zirkulation ['tsɪrkula'tsioːn] F **-, -en** circulation

zirkulieren [tsɪrku'liːrən], *ptp* **zirkuliert** VI to circulate

Zirkumflex ['tsɪrkʊmflɛks, tsɪrkʊm'flɛks] M **-es, -e** (*Ling*) circumflex

Zirkus ['tsɪrkʊs] M **-, -se** circus; (= *Getue, Theater*) fuss; **in den ~ gehen** to go to the circus

Zirkus-: IN CPDS circus; **Zirkusartist(in)** M(F) circus performer; **Zirkuswagen** M circus caravan (*Brit*) *or* trailer (*US*); **Zirkuszelt** NT big top

Zirrhose [tsɪ'roːzə] F **-, -n** cirrhosis

Zirruswolke F cirrus (cloud)

zischeln ['tsɪʃln] VI to whisper

zischen ['tsɪʃn] **1** VI **(a)** (= *zischendes Geräusch machen*) to hiss; (*Limonade*) to fizz; (*Fett, Wasser*) to sizzle **(b)** AUX SEIN (*inf*: = *abzischen*) to whizz **2** VT **(a)** (= *zischend sagen*) to hiss **(b)** (*inf*: = *trinken*) **einen ~** to have a quick one (*inf*)

ziselieren [tsizə'liːrən], *ptp* **ziseliert** VTI to chase

Zisterne [tsɪs'tɛrnə] F **-, -n** well

Zitat [tsi'taːt] NT **-(e)s, -e** quotation; **ein falsches ~** a misquotation; **~ ... Ende des ~s** quote ... unquote

Zither ['tsɪtɐ] F **-, -n** zither

zitieren [tsi'tiːrən], *ptp* **zitiert** VT **(a)** *jdn, Ausspruch, Textstelle* to quote; *Beispiel* to cite **(b)** (= *vorladen, rufen*) to summon (*vor +acc* before, *an +acc, zu* to)

Zitronat [tsitro'naːt] NT **-(e)s, -e** candied lemon peel

Zitrone [tsi'troːnə] F **-, -n** lemon; (= *Getränk*) lemon drink; (= *Baum*) lemon tree; **jdn wie eine ~ auspressen** *or* **ausquetschen** to squeeze sb dry

Zitronen-: zitronengelb ADJ lemon yellow; **Zitronenlimonade** F lemonade; **Zitronenmelisse** F (lemon) balm; **Zitronenpresse** F lemon squeezer; **Zitronensaft** M lemon juice; **Zitronensäure** F citric acid; **Zitronenschale** F lemon peel

Zitrusfrucht F citrus fruit

zitterig ['tsɪtərɪç] ADJ shaky

zittern ['tsɪtɐn] VI to tremble (*vor +dat* with) (= *erschüttert werden*) to shake; (*inf*: = *Angst haben*) to tremble with fear; **an allen Gliedern ~** am ganzen Körper ~ to tremble all over; **mir ~ die Knie** my knees are shaking; **vor jdm ~** to be terrified of sb

Zittern NT **-s**, NO PL **(a)** (= *Beben*) shaking; (*vor Kälte*) shivering; (*von Stimme*) quavering; **ein ~ ging durch seinen Körper** a shiver ran through his body **(b)** (= *Erschütterung*) shaking; **ein ~ a tremor

Zitter-: Zitterpappel F aspen (tree); **Zitterpartie** F (*fig*) nail-biter (*inf*)

zittrig ['tsɪtrɪç] ADJ shaky

Zitze ['tsɪtsə] F **-, -n** teat

Zivi ['tsiːvi] M **-(s), -s** (*inf*) ABBR *von* **Zivildienst-leistende(r)**

zivil [tsi'viːl] ADJ **(a)** (= *nicht militärisch*) civilian; *Schaden* nonmilitary; **im ~en Leben** in civilian life; **~er Ersatzdienst** community service (*as alternative to military service*) **(b)** (*inf*: = *angemessen, anständig*) civil; *Bedingungen, Forderungen, Preise* reasonable

Zivil [tsi'viːl] NT **-s**, NO PL (*nicht Uniform*) civilian clothes *pl*; **Polizist in ~** plain-clothes policeman

Zivil-: Zivilbevölkerung F civilian population; **Zivilcourage** F courage (*to stand up for one's beliefs*); **der Mann hat ~** that man has the courage to stand up for his beliefs; **Zivildienst** M community service (*as alternative to military service*);

Zivildienstleistende(r) [-laistndə] MF DECL AS ADJ person doing community service (*instead of military service*); **Zivilfahnder(in)** M(F) plain-clothes policeman/-woman; **Zivilgesetzbuch** NT (*Sw*) code of civil law;

ZIVILDIENST

Zivildienst is community service carried out as an alternative to compulsory military service or Wehrdienst. The person seeking exemption from military service must first present his case at a special hearing. Zivildienst lasts three months longer than military service (two months longer in Austria). It is mainly carried out in the social services sector, where the Zivis – as those doing the community work are colloquially known – tend to be made very welcome, since they are an inexpensive and motivated workforce.

In Switzerland there is no way of avoiding compulsory military service.

▶ WEHRDIENST

Zivilisation [tsiviliza'tsio:n] F -, -en civilization (*especially its technological aspects*)
Zivilisationskrankheit F illness caused by today's lifestyle
zivilisieren [tsivili'zi:rən], *ptp* **zivilisiert** VT to civilize
zivilisiert [tsivili'zi:et] **1** ADJ civilized **2** ADV **sich ~ benehmen** to behave in a civilized manner
Zivilist [tsivi'list] M -en, -en, **Zivilistin** [-'listɪn] F -, -nen civilian
Zivil-: Zivilkammer F civil division; **Zivilperson** F civilian; **Zivilprozess** M civil action; **Zivilprozessordnung** F (*Jur*) code of civil procedure; **Zivilrecht** NT civil law; **zivilrechtlich** **1** ADJ civil law *attr*, of civil law; *Prozess, Auseinandersetzung, Anspruch* civil *attr* **2** ADV **etw ~ klären** to settle sth in a civil court; **jdn ~ verfolgen/belangen** to bring a civil action against sb
Zivilschutz M civil defence (*Brit*) *or* defense (*US*)
Zivil-: Zivilstandsamt NT (*Sw*) registry office; **Ziviltrauung** F civil marriage; **Zivilverfahren** NT civil proceedings *pl*
Zmittag ['tsmɪtaːk] M -, - (*Sw*) lunch
Zmorge ['tsmɔrgə] M -, - (*Sw*) breakfast
Znacht [tsnaxt] M -s, - (*Sw*) supper
Znüni ['tsny:ni] M -, - (*Sw*) morning break
zockeln ['tsɔkln] VI AUX SEIN (*inf*) = **zuckeln**
zocken ['tsɔkn] VI (*inf*) to gamble
Zocker ['tsɔkɐ] M -s, -, **Zockerin** [-ərɪn] F -, -nen (*inf*) gambler
Zoff [tsɔf] M -s, NO PL (*inf:* = *Ärger*) trouble; **dann gibts ~** then there'll be trouble
zog PRET *von* **ziehen**
zögerlich ['tsøːgɐlɪç] **1** ADJ hesitant **2** ADV hesitantly
zögern ['tsøːgɐn] VI to hesitate; **er zögerte lange mit der Antwort** he hesitated (for) a long time before replying; **sie zögerte nicht lange mit ihrer Zustimmung** she lost little time in agreeing
Zögern NT -s, NO PL hesitation
zögernd **1** ADJ hesitant **2** ADV hesitantly
Zölibat [tsøli'baːt] NT *or* M -(e)s, NO PL celibacy; (= *Gelübde*) vow of celibacy
Zoll¹ [tsɔl] M -(e)s, - (= *Längenmaß*) inch
Zoll² M -(e)s, ⁻e ['tsœlə] (a) (= *Warenzoll*) customs duty; (= *Brückenzoll, Straßenzoll*) toll; **einen ~ unterliegen** to carry duty; **darauf liegt (ein) ~, darauf wird ~ erhoben** there is duty to pay on that (b) (= *Stelle*) **der ~** customs *pl*; **durch den ~ gehen/kommen** to go/get through customs
Zoll-: Zollabfertigung F (a) (= *Vorgang*) customs clearance (b) (= *Dienststelle*) customs checkpoint; **Zollabgaben** PL customs duty; **Zollamt** NT customs house; **zollamtlich** **1** ADJ customs *attr* **2** ADV **~ geöffnet** opened by customs; **~ abgefertigt werden** to be cleared by customs; **Zollanmeldung** F customs declaration; **Zollbeamte(r)** M DECL AS ADJ, **Zollbeamtin** F customs officer; **Zollbegleitpapiere** PL customs documents *pl*; **Zollbestimmung** F USU PL customs regulation
zollen ['tsɔlən] VT **jdm Anerkennung/Achtung/Bewunderung ~** to acknowledge/respect/admire sb; **jdm Beifall ~** to applaud sb; **jdm Dank ~** to extend one's thanks to sb
Zoll-: Zollerklärung F customs declaration; **Zollfahnder(in)** M(F) customs investigator; **Zollfahndung** F customs investigation department; **zollfrei** **1** ADJ duty-free **2** ADV duty-free; **etw ~ einführen** to import sth free of duty;

Zollgebühr F (customs) duty; **Zollgrenzbezirk** M customs and border district; **Zollgut** NT dutiable goods *pl*; **Zollgutlager** NT bonded *or* customs warehouse; **Zollinhaltserklärung** F customs declaration; **Zollkontrolle** F customs check; **Zolllager** NT bonded warehouse
Zöllner ['tsœlnɐ] M -s, -, **Zöllnerin** [-ərɪn] F -, -nen (old, Bibl) tax collector; (inf: = *Zollbeamter*) customs officer
Zoll-: Zollpapiere PL customs documents *pl*; **zollpflichtig** [-pflɪçtɪç] ADJ dutiable; **Zollrückvergütung** F (*bei Wiederausfuhr*) customs drawback; **Zollschranke** F customs barrier; **Zollstock** M ruler; **Zolltarif** M customs tariff; **Zollunion** F customs union; **Zollwert** M declared value
Zombie ['tsɔmbi] M -(s), -s (lit, fig) zombie
Zone ['tsoːnə] F -, -n zone; (*von Fahrkarte*) fare stage
Zoo [tsoː] M -s, -s zoo
Zoologe [tsoo'loːgə] M -n, -n, **Zoologin** F -, -nen zoologist
Zoologie [tsoolo'giː] F -, NO PL zoology
zoologisch [tsoo'loːgɪʃ] **1** ADJ zoological **2** ADV zoologically
Zoom [zuːm] NT -s, -s zoom shot; (= *Objektiv*) zoom lens
zoomen [zuːmən] **1** VT to zoom in on **2** VI to zoom (in)
Zoomobjektiv ['zuːm-] NT zoom lens
Zopf [tsɔpf] M -(e)s, ⁻e ['tsœpfə] (a) (= *Haartracht*) pigtail, plait; **Zöpfe tragen** to wear one's hair in pigtails; **ein alter ~(, der abgeschnitten werden müsste)** (fig) an antiquated custom (that should be done away with) (b) (= *Gebäck*) plaited loaf
Zorn [tsɔrn] M -(e)s, NO PL anger; **der ~ Gottes** the wrath of God; **jdn in ~ bringen** to enrage sb; **in ~ geraten** *or* **ausbrechen** to fly into a rage; **der ~ packte ihn** he became angry; **im ~ in** a rage; **einen ~ auf jdn haben** to be furious with sb
Zornausbruch M fit of anger
zornig ['tsɔrnɪç] **1** ADJ angry; **(leicht) ~ werden** to lose one's temper (easily); **auf jdn ~ sein** to be angry with sb; **ein ~er junger Mann** (fig) an angry young man **2** ADV angrily
Zote ['tsoːtə] F -, -n dirty joke
zotig ['tsoːtɪç] ADJ dirty
Zottel ['tsɔtl] F -, -n (inf) rat's tail (inf); (an *Mütze*) pompom
zottelig ['tsɔtəlɪç] ADJ (inf) *Haar, Fell* shaggy
zotteln ['tsɔtln] VI AUX SEIN (inf) to amble
zottig ['tsɔtɪç] ADJ *Fell, Tier* shaggy
z. T. ABBR *von* **zum Teil**
Ztr. ABBR *von* **Zentner**

ZU [tsuː]

1 PRÄPOSITION	**3** ADJEKTIV
2 ADVERB	**4** BINDEWORT

---

1 PRÄPOSITION (+DAT)

(a) (örtlich: Richtung, Ziel) to; **zum Bahnhof** to the station; **zum Bäcker/Arzt gehen** to go to the baker's/doctor's; **bis zu** as far as; **(bis) zum Bahnhof sind es 5 km** it's 5 kms to the station; **zum Meer hin** toward(s) the sea; **zur Decke sehen** to look up at the ceiling; **zu jdm/etw hinaufsehen** to look up at sb/sth; **zu jdm herübersehen/hinübersehen** to look across at sb; **sie wandte sich zu ihm hin** she turned to him; **sie sah zu ihm hin** she looked toward(s) him; **die Tür zum Keller** the door to the cellar; **sich zu jdm setzen** to sit down next to sb; **setz dich doch zu uns** come and sit with us; **zur Tür hinaus/herein** out of/in the door; **das Zimmer liegt zur Straße hin** the room looks out onto the street; **der Dom zu Köln** Cologne cathedral; **zu Hause** at home; **zu beiden Seiten (des Hauses)** on both sides (of the house); **zu Lande und zu Wasser** on land and sea

(b) (zeitlich) at; **zu früher/später Stunde** at an early/late hour; **zu Mittag** (= am Mittag) at midday; (= bis Mittag) by midday; **(bis) zum 15. April/Donnerstag/Abend** until 15th April/Thursday/(this) evening; (= nicht später als) by 15th April/Thursday/(this) evening; **die Zahlung ist zum 15. April fällig** the payment is due on 15th April; **zum 31. Mai kündigen** to give in (Brit) *or* turn in (US) one's notice for 31st May

(c) (Zusammengehörigkeit, Zusatz) **Wein zum Essen trinken** to drink wine with one's meal; **der Deckel zu diesem Topf** the lid for this pan; **nehmen Sie Milch zum Kaffee?** do you take milk in your coffee?; **zur Gitarre singen** to sing to (Brit) *or* with

(US) a/the guitar; **Vorwort/Anmerkungen zu etw** preface/notes to sth; **zu dem kommt noch, dass ich ...** on top of that I ...; **etw zu etw tragen** (*Kleidung*) to wear sth with sth; **etw zu etw legen** to put sth with sth
(d) (*Zweck, Bestimmung*) for; **Wasser zum Waschen** water for washing; **Papier zum Schreiben** paper to write on; **ein Bett zum Schlafen** a bed to sleep in; **der Knopf zum Abstellen** the off button; **Stoff zu einem Kleid** material for a dress; **das Zeichen zum Aufbruch** the signal to leave; **zur Einführung ...** by way of (an) introduction ...; **zu seiner Entschuldigung muss man sagen ...** in his defence (*Brit*) or defense (*US*) one must say ...; **zu seiner Entschuldigung sagte er ...** by way of apology he said ...; **zur Erklärung** by way of explanation; **zu nichts taugen, zu nichts zu gebrauchen sein** to be no use to anyone (*inf*)
(e) (*Anlass*) **etw zum Geburtstag/zu Weihnachten bekommen** to get sth for one's birthday/for Christmas; **ein Geschenk zum Hochzeitstag** a wedding anniversary present; **zu Ihrem 60. Geburtstag** on your 60th birthday; **jdm zu etw gratulieren** to congratulate sb on sth; **jdn zum Essen einladen** to invite sb for a meal; **Ausstellung zum Jahrestag der Revolution** exhibition to mark the anniversary of the revolution; **was sagen Sie zu diesen Preisen?** what do you think of these prices?; **zum Thema Gleichberechtigung** on the subject of equal rights; **jdn zur Frage ...** to question sb about sth
(f) (*Folge, Umstand*) **zu seinem Besten** for his own good; **zum Glück** luckily; **zu meiner Schande/Freude** *etc* to my shame/joy *etc*; **es ist zum Lachen** it's really funny; **es ist zum Weinen** it's enough to make you cry
(g) (*Mittel, Art und Weise*) **zu Fuß/Pferd** on foot/horseback; **zu Schiff** by ship; **zu Deutsch** in German; **etw zu einem hohen Preis verkaufen** to sell sth at a high price
(h) (*Veränderung*) into; **zu etw werden** to turn into sth; **Leder zu Handtaschen verarbeiten** to make handbags out of leather; **jdn/etw zu etw machen** to make sb/sth (into) sth; **wieder zu Staub werden** to return to dust; **etw zu Pulver zermahlen** to grind sth into powder; **jdn zum Major befördern** to promote sb to (the rank of) major
(I) (= *als*) as; **jdn zum König wählen** to choose sb as king; **jdn zu etw ernennen** to nominate sb sth; **er machte mich zu seinem Stellvertreter** he made me his deputy
(J) (*Verhältnis, Beziehung*) **Liebe zu jdm** love for sb; **aus Freundschaft zu jdm** because of one's friendship with sb; **Vertrauen zu jdm/etw** trust in sb/sth; **meine Beziehung zu ihm** my relationship with him
(k) (*in Vergleichen*) **im Vergleich zu** in comparison with; **im Verhältnis drei zu zwei** (*Math*) in the ratio (of) three to two; **Wasser und Saft im Verhältnis drei zu eins mischen** take three parts water to one of juice; **das Spiel steht 3 zu 2** or (*geschrieben*) **3:2** the score is 3-2 or (*gesprochen*) three-two
(I) (*bei Zahlenangaben*) **zu zwei Prozent** at two per cent (*Brit*) or percent (*US*); **wir verkaufen die Gläser jetzt das Stück zu 99 Cent** we're selling the glasses now at or for 99 cents each; **fünf (Stück) zu 80 Pfennig** five for 80 pfennigs; **zwei Dritteln (gefüllt)** two-thirds (full); **zum halben Preis** at half price; **zum ersten Mal(e)** for the first time; **zum Ersten ..., zum Zweiten ...** (*Aufzählung*) first ..., second ...; **zum Ersten, zum Zweiten, zum Dritten** (*bei Auktion*) for the first time, for the second time, for the third time
(m) (*mit Fragepronomen*) **zu wem wollen Sie?** who do you want?; **zu wem gehen Sie?** who are you going to see?; **zu was** (*inf*) (*Zweck*) for what; (= *warum*) why
(n) (*bei Namen*) **der Graf zu Ehrenstein** the Count of Ehrenstein; **Gasthof zum goldenen Löwen** the Golden Lion (Inn)
(o) (*getrenntes "dazu"*) (*inf*) **da komme ich nicht zu** I can't get (a)round to it; *siehe auch* **dazu**
(p) (*andere Wendungen*) **zum Beispiel** for example; **zu jds Gedächtnis** in memory of sb; **zur Strafe** as a punishment; **zur Belohnung** as a reward; **zur Probe/Ansicht** on trial/approval

2 ADVERB
(a) (= *allzu*) too; **zu sehr** too much; **zu verliebt** too much in love; **das war einfach zu dumm!** (*inf*) it was so stupid!; **ich wäre zu gern mitgekommen** I'd have loved to come
(b) (= *geschlossen*) shut; **auf/zu** (*an Hähnen etc*) on/off; **Tür zu!** (*inf*) shut the door; **die Geschäfte haben jetzt zu** the shops are shut now
(c) (= *los, weiter*) (*inf*) **dann mal zu!** right, off we go!; **du**

wolltest mir was vorsingen, dann mal zu you wanted to sing me something? OK, go ahead; **immer** or **nur zu!** just keep on!; **mach zu!** get a move on!; **lauft schon zu, ich komme nach** you go on, I'll catch you up
(d) (*örtlich*) toward(s); **nach hinten zu** toward(s) the back; **auf den Wald zu** toward(s) the forest; **dem Ausgang zu** toward(s) the exit

3 ADJEKTIV (= *geschlossen, inf*) *Tür, Geschäft, Kiste etc* shut; *Kleid, Verschluss* done up; *siehe auch* **zu sein**

4 BINDEWORT
(a) (*mit Infinitiv*) to; **etw zu essen** sth to eat; **er hat zu gehorchen** he has to do as he's told; **jdm befehlen** or **den Auftrag erteilen, etw zu tun** to order sb to do sth; **das Material ist noch/nicht mehr zu gebrauchen** the material is still/is no longer usable; **diese Rechnung ist bis Montag zu bezahlen** this bill has to be paid by Monday; **zu stehen kommen** to come to a stop; **ich habe noch zu arbeiten** I still have some work to do; **ohne es zu wissen** without knowing it; **um besser sehen zu können** in order to see better; **ich komme, um mich zu verabschieden** I've come to say goodbye
(b) (*mit Partizip*) **noch zu bezahlende Rechnungen** outstanding bills; **nicht zu unterschätzende Probleme** problems (that are) not to be underestimated; **der zu prüfende Kandidat, der zu Prüfende** the candidate to be examined

zualler- [tsu'lalɐ-]: **zuallererst** [tsu'lalɐ'le:ɐst] ADV first of all; **zuallerletzt** [tsu'lalɐ'lɛtst] ADV last of all
zubauen VT SEP *Lücke* to fill in; *Platz, Gelände* to build up; *Blick* to block with buildings/a building
Zubehör ['tsu:bəhø:ɐ] NT or M **-(e)s,** (*rare*) **-e** equipment *no pl*; (= *Zusatzgeräte, Autozubehör, Kleidung*) accessories *pl*; (= ~*teil*) attachments *pl*; **Küche mit allem ~** fully equipped kitchen
zubeißen VI SEP IRREG to bite; (*beim Zahnarzt*) to bite (one's teeth) together
zubekommen *ptp* **zubekommen** VT SEP IRREG (*inf*) *Kleidung* to get done up; *Koffer auch, Tür, Fenster* to get shut
Zuber ['tsu:bɐ] M **-s, -** (*wash*)tub
zubereiten *ptp* **zubereitet** VT SEP to prepare
Zubereitung F **-, -en** preparation; **eine neue ~ für Blumenkohl** a new way of preparing cauliflower
Zubettgehen [tsu'bɛtge:ən] NT **vor dem ~** before (going to) bed; **beim ~** on going to bed
zubilligen VT SEP **jdm etw ~** to grant sb sth; **jdm mildernde Umstände ~** to recognize that there are/were mitigating circumstances for sb
zubinden VT SEP IRREG to tie up; *Schuhe auch* to lace up; **jdm die Augen ~** to blindfold sb
zubleiben VI SEP IRREG AUX SEIN (*inf*) to stay shut
zublinzeln VI SEP **jdm ~** to wink at sb
zubringen VT SEP IRREG **(a)** (= *verbringen*) to spend **(b)** (*inf*: = *zumachen können*) *Kiste, Koffer, Tür, Fenster* to get shut; *Knöpfe, Reißverschluss, Kleidung* to get done up
Zubringer ['tsu:brɪŋɐ] M **-s, -** **(a)** (*Tech*) conveyor **(b)** (= *Straße*) feeder road **(c)** (*auch* **Zubringerbus**) shuttle (bus); (*zum Flughafen*) airport bus
Zubringer-: **Zubringerdienst** M shuttle service; **Zubringerflug** M feeder flight; **Zubringerstraße** F feeder road
Zubrot NT, NO PL extra income; **ein kleines ~ verdienen** to make a bit on the side (*inf*)
Zucchini [tsʊ'ki:ni] F **-, -** courgette (*Brit*), zucchini (*US*)
Zucht [tsʊxt] F **-, -en** **(a)** (= *Disziplin*) discipline; **~ und Ordnung** discipline **(b)** NO PL (= *Aufzucht, das Züchten*) (*von Tieren*) breeding; (*von Pflanzen*) growing; (*von Bakterien, Perlen*) culture; (*von Bienen*) keeping; **die ~ von Pferden** horse breeding; **die ~ von Bienen** beekeeping **(c)** (= ~*generation*) (*von Tieren*) breed; (*von Pflanzen*) stock; (*von Bakterien, Perlen*) culture
züchten ['tsʏçtn] VT (*lit, fig*) to breed; *Bienen* to keep; *Pflanzen* to grow; *Perlen, Bakterien* to cultivate
Züchter ['tsʏçtɐ] M **-s, -**, **Züchterin** [-ərɪn] F **-, -nen** (*von Tieren*) breeder; (*von Pflanzen*) grower; (*von Bienen*) keeper; (*von Perlen, Bakterien*) culturist

Zuchthaus NT (= *Gebäude*) prison (*for serious offenders*), penitentiary (*US*); **zu 7 Jahren ~ verurteilt werden** to be sentenced to 7 years in prison; **dafür bekommt man ~, darauf steht ~** you'll go to prison for that

Züchtigung F **-, -en** beating; (*von Schüler*) ≈ caning; **körperliche ~** corporal punishment

Zucht-: Zuchtperle F cultured pearl; **Zuchttier** NT breeding animal

Züchtung ['tsʏçtʊŋ] F **-, -en** (a) (*von Tieren*) breeding; (*von Bienen*) keeping; (*von Pflanzen*) growing; (*von Kristallen*) synthesis (b) (= *Zuchtart*) (*Pflanzen*) strain; (*Tiere*) breed

Zucht-: Zuchtvieh NT breeding cattle; **Zuchtwahl** F selective breeding; **natürliche ~** natural selection

zuckeln ['tsʊkln] VI AUX SEIN (*inf*) to jog; **er zuckelte müde hinter den anderen drein** he trotted wearily along behind the others

zucken ['tsʊkn] **1** VI (a) (*nervös, krampfhaft*) to twitch; (*vor Schreck*) to start; (*vor Schmerzen*) to flinch; (*Fisch, verwundetes Tier*) to thrash about; **er zuckte ständig mit dem Mund** his mouth kept twitching; **mit den Schultern** *or* **Achseln ~** to shrug (one's shoulders) (b) (= *aufleuchten*) (*Blitz*) to flash; (*Flammen*) to flare up **2** VT **die Achseln** *or* **Schultern ~** to shrug (one's shoulders)

zücken ['tsʏkn] VT *Messer, Pistole* to pull out; *Schwert* to draw; (*inf: Notizbuch, Bleistift, Brieftasche*) to pull out

Zucker ['tsʊkɐ] M **-s**, NO PL (a) sugar; **ein Stück ~** a lump of sugar; **du bist doch nicht aus** *or* **von ~!** (*inf*) don't be such a softie! (*inf*) (b) (*Med*) (= *~gehalt*) sugar; (= *Krankheit*) diabetes *sing*; **~ haben** (*inf*) to be a diabetic

Zucker-: Zuckerdose F sugar bowl; **Zuckererbse** F mangetout (pea) (*Brit*), sweet pea (*US*); **zuckerfrei** ADJ sugar-free; **Zuckergehalt** M sugar content; **Zuckerguss** M icing, frosting (*esp US*); **mit ~ überziehen** to ice; **ein Kuchen mit ~** an iced cake; **Zuckerhut** M sugarloaf

zuckerig ['tsʊkərɪç] ADJ sugary

Zucker-: zuckerkrank ADJ diabetic; **Zuckerkranke(r)** MF DECL AS ADJ diabetic; **Zuckerkrankheit** F diabetes *sing*

Zuckerlecken NT **das ist kein ~** (*inf*) it's no picnic (*inf*)

Zuckermelone F muskmelon

zuckern ['tsʊkɐn] VT to put sugar in; **zu stark gezuckert sein** to have too much sugar in it

Zucker-: Zuckerrohr NT sugar cane; **Zuckerrübe** F sugar beet; **Zuckerschlecken** NT **das ist kein ~** (*inf*) it's no picnic (*inf*); **Zuckerspiegel** M (*Med*) (blood) sugar level; **zuckersüß** ADJ (*lit, fig*) as sweet as sugar; **Zuckerwatte** F candy floss; **Zuckerzange** F sugar tongs *pl*

zuckrig ['tsʊkrɪç] ADJ = **zuckerig**

Zuckung ['tsʊkʊŋ] F **-, -en** twitch; (*stärker: krampfhaft*) convulsion; (*von sterbendem Tier*) convulsive movement; **die letzten ~en** (*lit, fig*) the death throes

zudecken VT SEP to cover; (*im Bett*) to tuck up *or* in

zudem [tsu'de:m] ADV (*geh*) moreover

zudrehen SEP **1** VT *Wasserhahn etc* to turn off; (= *zuwenden*) to turn (+*dat* to) **2** VR to turn (+*dat* to)

zudringlich ADJ *Art* pushy (*inf*); *Nachbarn* intrusive; **~ werden** (*zu jdm*) to make advances (*zu* to)

Zudringlichkeit F **seine ~ (gegenüber jdm)** his way of forcing himself upon sb

zudröhnen (*sl*) **1** VT **jdn voll dröhnen** (*mit Drogen*) to dope sb up (*inf*); (*mit Alkohol*) to get sb tanked up (*inf*); **er war total zugedröhnt** (*mit Drogen*) he was doped up to the eyeballs (*inf*); (*mit Alkohol*) he was completely tanked up (*inf*) **2** VR (*mit Drogen*) to dope oneself up (*inf*); (*mit Alkohol*) to get tanked up (*inf*); (*inf: mit Musik*) to blast one's head off (*inf*)

zueinander [tsulaiˈnandɐ] ADV (= *gegenseitig*) to each other; *Vertrauen haben* in each other; (= *zusammen*) together; **~ passen** to go together; (*Menschen*) to suit each other; **Braun und Grün passen gut ~** brown and green go well together

zuerkennen ptp **zuerkannt** VT SEP IRREG to award (*jdm* to sb); *Sieg auch, Recht* to grant (*jdm etw* sb sth); (*vor Gericht*) *Entschädigung, Rente etc* to award (*jdm etw* sb sth)

zuerst [tsulˈeːrst] ADV (a) (= *als Erster*) first; **ich kam ~ an** I was (the) first to arrive; **~ an die Reihe kommen** to be first; **~ bin ich Geschäftsmann, dann Privatmann** I am first and foremost a businessman, and only then a private individual; **das muss ich morgen früh ~ machen** I must do that first thing to-morrow (morning) (b) (= *zum ersten Mal*) first, for the first time (c) (= *anfangs*) at first; **~ muss man ...** first (of all) you have to ...

zufahren VI SEP IRREG AUX SEIN (a) **auf jdn ~** (*mit Kfz*) to drive toward(s) sb; (*mit Fahrrad*) to ride toward(s) sb; (*direkt*) to drive/ride up to sb; **auf etw** (*acc*) **~** to drive/ride toward(s) sth; **er kam genau auf mich zugefahren** he drove/rode straight at me (b) (= *weiterfahren, losfahren*) **fahren Sie doch zu!** go on then!

Zufahrt F approach (road); (= *Einfahrt*) entrance; (*zu einem Haus*) drive(way); **„keine ~ zum Krankenhaus"** "no access to hospital"

Zufahrtsstraße F access road; (*zur Autobahn*) approach road

Zufall M chance, accident; (= *Zusammentreffen*) coincidence; **das ist ~** it's pure chance; **durch ~** (quite) by chance; **ich habe durch ~ gesehen, wie er das Geld in die Tasche gesteckt hat** I happened to see him putting the money in his pocket; **per ~** (*inf*) by a (pure) fluke (*inf*); **per ~ trafen wir uns im Bus** we happened to meet on the bus; **es ist kein ~, dass ...** it's no accident that ...; **es war ein glücklicher ~, dass ...** it was lucky that ...; **welch ein ~!** what a coincidence!; **wie es der ~ so will** as chance would have it; **etw dem ~ überlassen** to leave sth to chance

zufallen VI SEP IRREG AUX SEIN (a) (= *sich schließen*) (*Fenster etc*) to close; **die Tür fiel laut zu** the door slammed shut; **ihm fielen beinahe die Augen zu** he could hardly keep his eyes open (b) **jdm ~** (*Erbe*) to pass to sb; (*Preis, Geldsumme etc*) to go to sb; (*Aufgabe, Rolle*) to fall to sb

zufällig **1** ADJ chance *attr*; *Ergebnis auch* accidental; **das war rein ~** it was pure chance; **es ist nicht ~, dass er ...** it's no accident that he ...; **das kann doch nicht ~ gewesen sein** that can't have happened by chance; **„Ähnlichkeiten mit lebenden Personen sind rein ~"** ≈ "any similarities with persons living or dead are purely coincidental" **2** ADV by chance; (*esp bei Zusammentreffen von Ereignissen*) coincidentally; **er ging ~ vorüber** he happened to be passing; **wenn Sie das ~ wissen sollten** if you (should) happen to know; **~ auf ein Zitat stoßen** to happen to find a quotation; **kannst du mir ~ 20 Euro leihen?** can you lend me 20 euros by any chance?

zufälligerweise ['tsuːfɛlɪgɐˈvaizə] ADV = **zufällig 2**

Zufalls- IN CPDS chance; **Zufallsgenerator** M random generator; (*für Zahlen*) random-number generator; **Zufallstreffer** M fluke; **einen ~ machen** to make a lucky choice

zufassen VI SEP (a) (= *zugreifen*) to take hold of it/them; (*Hund*) to make a grab; (*fig: = schnell handeln*) to seize an/the opportunity (b) (= *helfen*) to lend a hand

zufliegen VI SEP IRREG AUX SEIN (a) **auf etw** (*acc*) **~** to fly toward(s) *or* (*direkt*) into sth; **auf etw** (*acc*) **zugeflogen kommen** to come flying toward(s) sth (b) +DAT to fly to; **der Vogel ist uns zugeflogen** the bird flew into our house; **„grüner Wellensittich zugeflogen"** "green budgerigar found"; **ihm fliegt alles nur so zu** (*fig*) everything comes so easily to him (c) (*inf: Fenster, Tür*) to bang shut

Zuflucht F refuge (*auch fig*), shelter (*vor +dat* from); **~ suchen** (*lit, fig*) to seek refuge; **zu etw ~ nehmen** (*fig*) to resort to sth; **zu Lügen ~ nehmen** to take refuge in lying; **du bist meine letzte ~** (*fig*) you are my last hope

Zufluss M, NO PL (*lit, fig: = Zufließen*) influx, inflow; (*Mech: = Zufuhr*) supply; **~ kalter Meeresluft** a stream of cold air from the sea

zufolge [tsuˈfɔlgə] PREP +DAT *or* GEN (*form*) (= *gemäß*) according to; (= *auf Grund*) as a consequence of; **dem Bericht ~, ~ des Berichtes** according to the report

zufrieden [tsuˈfriːdn] **1** ADJ contented, content *pred*; **ein ~es Gesicht machen** to look pleased; **mit jdm/etw ~ sein** to be satisfied with sb/sth; **wie gehts? – man ist ~** (*inf*) how are things? – can't complain; **er ist nie ~** he's never satisfied; **er ist mit nichts ~** there's no pleasing him (*inf*) **2** ADV contentedly; **~ lächeln** to smile contentedly

Zufrieden-: zufrieden geben VR IRREG **sich mit etw ~** to be content with sth; **Zufriedenheit** F **-**, NO PL contentedness; (= *Befriedigtsein*) satisfaction; **zur allgemeinen ~** to everyone's satisfaction; **zufrieden lassen** VT IRREG to leave alone; **zufrieden stellen** VT to satisfy; **schwer zufrieden zu stellen**

sein to be hard to please; **eine wenig ~de Antwort** a less than satisfactory answer

zufrieren VI SEP IRREG AUX SEIN to freeze (over)

zufügen VT SEP **(a)** *Kummer, Leid, Schmerz* to cause; *Verlust, Niederlage* to inflict; **jdm/einer Sache Schaden ~** to harm sb/ sth; **jdm etw ~** to cause sb sth/inflict sth on sb; **jdm eine Verletzung (mit einem Messer** *etc*) **~** to injure sb (with a knife *etc*) **(b)** (= *hinzufügen*) to add; (= *beilegen*) to enclose

Zufuhr ['tsu:fu:ɐ] F **-, -en** (= *Versorgung*) supply (*in* +*acc*, *nach* to); (*Met: von Luftstrom*) influx

zuführen SEP ▣ VT +DAT **(a)** (= *versorgen mit, beliefern*) to supply; (*Comput*) *Papier* to feed (+*dat* to); **jdm etw ~** to supply sb with sth
(b) (= *bringen, zur Verfügung stellen*) to bring; **die Abfälle der Wiederverwertung** (*dat*) **~** to supply refuse for recycling; **einem Geschäft Kunden ~** to bring customers to a business; **dem Magen Nahrung ~** to supply food to the stomach; **jdn dem Richter ~** to bring sb before the court
▣ VI SEP **auf etw** (*acc*) **~** (*lit, fig*) to lead to sth

Zug¹ [tsu:k] M **-(e)s, ⸚e** ['tsy:gə] **(a)** NO PL (= *Ziehen*) (*an* +*dat* on, at) pull; (= *~kraft, Spannung*) tension
(b) (= *Luftzug*) draught (*Brit*), draft (*US*); (= *Atemzug*) breath; (*an Zigarette, Pfeife*) puff; (= *Schluck*) gulp; **das Glas in einem ~ leeren** to empty the glass with one gulp; **in vollen Zügen genießen** to enjoy sth to the full; **in den letzten Zügen liegen** (*inf*) to be on one's last legs (*inf*); **er hat einen guten ~** (*inf*) he can really put it away (*inf*); **er hat ~ abbekommen** *or* **gekriegt** (*inf*) he got a stiff neck *etc* from sitting in a draught (*Brit*) *or* draft (*US*)
(c) (*beim Schwimmen*) stroke; (*beim Rudern*) pull (*mit* at); (*bei Brettspiel*) move; **~ um ~** (*fig*) step by step; **nicht zum ~ kommen** (*inf*) not to get a look-in (*inf*); **du bist am ~** (*bei Brettspiel, fig*) it's your move; **etw in großen Zügen darstellen/ umreißen** to outline sth; **das war kein schöner ~ von dir** that wasn't nice of you
(d) (= *~vorrichtung*) (= *Klingelzug*) bell pull; (*bei Feuerwaffen*) groove; (= *Orgelzug*) stop

Zug² M **-(e)s, ⸚e** (= *Eisenbahnzug*) train; (= *Lastzug*) truck and trailer; **mit dem ~ fahren** to go by train; **jdn zum ~ bringen** to take sb to the station; **auf den fahrenden ~ aufspringen** (*fig*) to jump on the bandwagon (*inf*)

Zug³ M **-(e)s, ⸚e** (= *Gesichtszug*) feature; (= *Charakterzug auch*) characteristic; (*sadistisch, brutal etc*) streak; (= *Anflug*) touch; **das ist ein schöner ~ von ihm** that's one of the nice things about him; **das ist kein schöner ~ von ihm** that's not one of his nicer characteristics

Zug⁴ NT **-s** (*Kanton*) Zug

Zugabe F extra; (*Comm*. = *Werbegeschenk etc*) free gift; (*Mus, Theat*) encore; **~! ~!** encore! encore!

Zugabteil NT train compartment

Zugang M, *pl* **-gänge (a)** (= *Eingang, Einfahrt*) entrance; (= *Zutritt*) admittance; (*fig*) access; **~ zu einem Tresor/ Informationen** *etc* **haben** to have access to a safe/information *etc*; **„kein ~"** "no entry" **(b)** (*von Patienten*) admission; (*von Schülern*) intake; (*von Waren*) receipt; (*von Abonnement*) new subscription; **in dieser Schule haben wir die meisten Zugänge im Frühling** our largest intake at this school is in spring

zugange [tsuˈɡaŋə] ADJ PRED (*esp N Ger*) **~ sein** (= *beschäftigt*) to be busy; (= *aufgestanden*) to be up and about; (*euph: in Nebenzimmer etc*) to be carrying on (*inf*)

zugänglich ['tsu:ɡɛŋlɪç] ADJ (+*dat, für* to) accessible; *öffentliche Einrichtungen* open; *Mensch, Vorgesetzter* approachable; **eine private Sammlung der Allgemeinheit ~ machen** to open a private collection to the public; **der Allgemeinheit/ Öffentlichkeit ~** open to the public; **für etw leicht/nicht ~ sein** to respond/not to respond to sth

Zug-: Zugbegleiter M (*Rail*. = *Zugfahrplan*) train timetable; **Zugbegleiter(in)** M(F) (*Rail*) guard (*Brit*), conductor (*US*); **Zugbrücke** F drawbridge

zugeben VT SEP IRREG **(a)** (= *zusätzlich geben*) **jdm etw ~** to give sb sth extra **(b)** (*Cook*) to add **(c)** (= *zugestehen, einräumen*) to admit; **jdm gegenüber etw ~** to confess sth to sb; **zugegeben** admittedly; **gib's zu!** admit it!

zugegebenermaßen ['tsu:ɡəge:bnɐˈmaːsn] ADV admittedly

zugehen SEP IRREG AUX SEIN ▣ VI **(a)** (*Tür, Deckel*) to shut; **der Koffer geht nicht zu** the case won't shut
(b) auf jdn/etw ~ to approach sb/sth; **direkt auf jdn/etw ~ to**

go straight up to sb/sth; **geradewegs auf etw** (*acc*) **~** (*fig*) to get straight down to sth; **aufeinander ~** to approach one another; (*fig auch*) to compromise; **es geht nun auf den Winter zu** winter is drawing in; **er geht schon auf die siebzig zu** he's getting on for seventy; **dem Ende ~** to near its end; (*Vorräte*) to be running out
(c) +DAT (*Nachricht, Brief etc*) to reach; **die Nachricht, die ich Ihnen gestern habe ~ lassen** the message I sent you yesterday
(d) (*inf*: = *weiter-, losgehen*) to get a move on (*inf*)
▨ VI IMPERS **(a)** dort geht es ... zu things are ... there; **es ging sehr lustig/fröhlich** *etc* **zu** (*inf*) we/they *etc* had a great time (*inf*); **du kannst dir nicht vorstellen, wie es dort zugeht** you can't imagine what goes on there (*inf*)
(b) (= *geschehen*) to happen; **hier geht es nicht mit rechten Dingen zu** there's something odd going on here

Zugehörigkeit F **-, -en (a)** (*zu Land, Glauben*) affiliation; (= *Mitgliedschaft*) membership (*zu* of)
(b) (= *Zugehörigkeitsgefühl*) sense of belonging

zugeknöpft ['tsu:ɡəknœpft] ADJ (*fig inf*) *Mensch* reserved; *siehe auch* **zuknöpfen**

Zügel ['tsy:ɡl] M **-s, -** rein (*auch fig*); **die ~ fest in der Hand haben/behalten** (*fig*) to have/keep things firmly in hand; **die ~ locker lassen** (*lit*) to slacken one's hold on the reins; (*fig*) to give free rein (*bei* to)

zügeln ['tsy:ɡln] ▣ VT *Pferd* to rein in; (*fig*) to curb ▨ VR to restrain oneself ▧ VI AUX SEIN (*Sw*: = *umziehen*) to move (house)

Zugeständnis NT concession (+*dat, an* +*acc* to); **er war zu keinem ~ bereit** he would make no concession(s)

zugestehen *ptp* **zugestanden** VT SEP IRREG (= *einräumen*) *Recht, Erlass etc* to concede; (= *zugeben*) to admit; **jdm etw ~** (= *einräumen*) to grant sb sth

zugetan ['tsu:ɡəta:n] ADJ **jdm/einer Sache ~ sein** to be fond of sb/sth

Zugewinn M (*Jur*) *increase in value of a married couple's property during the years of joint ownership through marriage*

Zugezogene(r) ['tsu:ɡətso:ɡənə] MF DECL AS ADJ newcomer

Zug-: Zugfolge F (*Rail*) succession of trains; **Zugführer(in)** M(F) **(a)** (*Rail*) chief guard (*Brit*) *or* conductor (*US*) **(b)** (*Aus Mil*) platoon leader

zugießen VT SEP IRREG **(a)** (= *hinzugießen*) to add; **darf ich Ihnen noch (etwas Kaffee) ~?** may I pour you a little more (coffee)?; **er goss sich** (*dat*) **ständig wieder zu** he kept topping up his glass/cup **(b)** (*mit Beton etc*) to fill (in)

zugig ['tsu:ɡɪç] ADJ draughty (*Brit*), drafty (*US*)

zügig ['tsy:ɡɪç] ▣ ADJ *Handschrift* smooth; *Studium* quickly completed ▨ ADV quickly

zugleich [tsu'ɡlaiç] ADV (= *zur gleichen Zeit*) at the same time; (= *ebenso auch*) both; **er ist ~ Gitarrist und Komponist** he is both a guitarist and a composer

Züglete ['tsy:ɡlətə] F **-, -n** (*Sw*: = *Umzug*) move

Zug-: Zugluft F draught (*Brit*), draft (*US*); **zu viel ~ bekommen** to be in too much of a draught (*Brit*) *or* draft (*US*); **Zugmaschine** F towing vehicle; (*von Sattelschlepper*) tractor; **Zugpersonal** NT (*Rail*) train personnel; **Zugpferd** NT carthorse; (*fig*) crowd puller

zugreifen VI SEP IRREG **(a)** (= *schnell nehmen*) to grab it/them; (*fig*) to get in quickly (*inf*); (*bei Tisch*) to help oneself; **greifen Sie bitte zu!** please help yourself! **(b)** (= *schwer arbeiten*) to get down to it **(c)** (*Comput*) **auf etw** (*acc*) **~** to access sth

Zugrestaurant NT dining car

Zugriff M **(a) durch raschen ~** by stepping in quickly; **sich dem ~ der Polizei/Gerichte entziehen** to evade justice **(b)** (*Fin, Comput*) access (*auf* to)

Zugriffs-: Zugriffsberechtigung F, **Zugriffserlaubnis** F access permission; **Zugriffszeit** F access time

zugrunde [tsu'ɡrʊndə] ADV **(a) ~ gehen** to perish; **jdn/etw ~ richten** to destroy sb/sth; (*finanziell*) to ruin sb/sth **(b) einer Sache** (*dat*) **~ liegen** to underlie sth; **~ liegend** underlying; **etw einer Sache** (*dat*) **~ legen** to base sth on sth

Zugs- IN CPDS (*Aus*) = **Zug-**

Zug-: Zugsalbe F (*Med*) poultice; **Zugtier** NT draught animal (*Brit*), draft animal (*US*)

zugucken VI SEP = **zusehen (a)**

Zugunglück NT train accident

zugunsten [tsu'ɡʊnstn] PREP +GEN or *(bei Nachstellung)* +DAT in favour *(Brit)* or favor *(US)* of; ~ **von** in favour *(Brit)* or favor *(US)* of

zugute [tsu'ɡuːtə] ADV **jdm etw ~ halten** to grant sb sth; *(= Verständnis haben)* to make allowances for sth; **einer Sache/jdm ~ kommen** to be of benefit to sth/sb; *(Geld, Erlös)* to benefit sth/sb; **das ist seiner Gesundheit ~ gekommen** his health benefited from it; **jdm etw ~ kommen lassen** to let sb have sth

Zug-: **Zugverbindung** F train connection; **Zugvogel** M migratory bird; **Zugwagen** M towing vehicle; **Zugzwang** M *(Chess)* zugzwang; *(fig)* tight spot; **jdn in ~ bringen** to put sb in zugzwang/on the spot; **in ~ geraten** to get into zugzwang/ be put on the spot; **unter ~ stehen** to be in zugzwang/in a tight spot; **die Gegenseite steht jetzt unter ~** the other side is now forced to move

zuhaben VI SEP IRREG *(inf: Geschäft, Museum, Behörde etc)* to be closed

zuhaken VT SEP to hook up

zuhalten SEP IRREG **1** VT to hold shut; **sich** *(dat)* **die Nase ~** to hold one's nose; **sich** *(dat)* **die Augen/Ohren/den Mund ~** to put one's hands over one's eyes/ears/mouth **2** VI **auf etw** *(acc)* **~** to head straight for sth

Zuhälter ['tsuːhɛltɐ] M **-s,** - pimp

zuhanden [tsu'handn] ADV *(form: Sw, Aus)* **(a)** *(auch old)* to hand; **es ist mir ~ gekommen** it came to hand **(b)** for the attention of; **~ (von) Herrn Braun** for the attention of Mr Braun

zuhauen SEP IRREG **1** VT Baumstamm to hew; Stein to trim **2** VI **(a)** *(mit Axt)* to strike; *(mit Fäusten, Schwert)* to strike out; **hau zu!** let him *etc* have it! **(b)** *(inf: Tür, Fenster)* to slam (shut)

zuhause [tsu'hauzə] *(Aus, Sw)*, **zu Hause** ADV *siehe* **Haus**

Zuhause [tsu'hauzə] NT **-s,** NO PL home

zuheilen VI SEP AUX SEIN to heal up

Zuhilfenahme [tsu'hɪlfənɑːmə] F **unter ~ von** or +gen with the aid of

zuhinterst [tsu'hɪntɐst] ADV at the very back

zuhören VI SEP to listen (+dat to); **hör mal zu!** *(drohend)* now (just) listen (to me)!; **gut ~ können** to be a good listener; **hör mir mal genau zu!** now listen carefully to me

Zuhörer(in) M(F) listener; **die ~** *(= das Publikum)* the audience *sing*; *(Rad auch)* the listeners

zujubeln VI SEP **jdm ~** to cheer sb

zukehren VT SEP *(= zuwenden)* to turn; **jdm den Rücken ~** *(lit, fig)* to turn one's back on sb

zuklappen VTI SEP *(vi: aux sein)* to snap shut; *(Tür, Fenster)* to click shut

zukleben VT SEP Loch etc to stick over; Briefumschlag to seal; Brief to seal (up); *(mit Klebstoff, Klebeband)* to stick up

zukleistern VT SEP *(inf: lit, fig)* to patch up

zuknallen VTI SEP *(vi: aux sein)* *(inf)* to slam

zukneifen VT SEP IRREG to pinch hard; Augen to screw up; Mund to shut tight(ly)

zuknöpfen VT SEP to button (up); **sich** *(dat)* **die Jacke/das Hemd ~** to button (up) one's jacket/shirt; *siehe auch* **zugeknöpft**

zukommen VI SEP IRREG AUX SEIN **(a)** **auf jdn/etw ~** to come toward(s) or *(direkt)* up to sb/sth; **das Gewitter kam genau auf uns zu** the storm was heading straight for us; **die Aufgabe, die nun auf uns zukommt** the task which is now in store for us; **die Dinge auf sich** *(acc)* **~ lassen** to take things as they come; **alles auf sich** *(acc)* **~ lassen** to let everything take its course

(b) **jdm etw ~ lassen** Brief etc to send sb sth; *(= schenken)* Hilfe to give sb sth

zukriegen VT SEP *(inf)* = **zubekommen**

Zukunft ['tsuːkʊnft] F **-,** NO PL **(a)** **die ~** the future; **in ~** in future; **in ferner/naher/nächster ~** in the remote/near/ immediate future; **ein Beruf mit/ohne ~** a career with/ without prospects; **das hat keine ~** there's no future in it; **das gilt für alle ~** that applies without exception from now on; **viel Glück für Ihre ~!** best wishes for the future! **(b)** *(Gram)* future (tense)

zukünftig **1** ADJ future; **der ~e Präsident/Bischof** the president/bishop elect **2** ADV in future

Zukunfts-: **Zukunftsangst** F *(vor der Zukunft)* fear of the future; *(um die Zukunft)* fear for the future; **Zukunfts- aussichten** PL future prospects *pl*; **Zukunftsforscher(in)** M(F) futurologist; **Zukunftsforschung** F futurology; **Zukunftsmusik** F *(fig inf)* pie in the sky *(inf)*; **Zukunftspläne** PL plans *pl* for the future; **Zukunftsroman** M *(naturwissen- schaftlich)* science fiction novel; *(gesellschaftspolitisch)* utopian novel; **Zukunftstechnik** F, **Zukunftstechnologie** F new technology; **zukunftsträchtig** ADJ with a promising future

Zukurzgekommene(r) [tsu'kʊrtsɡəkɔmənə] MF DECL AS ADJ loser

zulabern VT SEP *(inf)* **jdn ~** to rattle on at sb *(inf)*; **sie hat mich total zugelabert** she went on and on at me

zulächeln VI SEP **jdm ~** to smile at sb

zulachen VI SEP **jdm ~** to give sb a friendly laugh

zuladen VTI SEP IRREG to load more on/in

Zuladung F *(bei Kfz)* useful load; *(Naut)* deadweight

Zulage F **(a)** *(= Geldzulage)* extra pay *no indef art*; *(= Sonderzulage)* bonus (payment); *(= Gefahrenzulage)* danger money *no indef art* **(b)** *(= Gehaltserhöhung)* rise *(Brit)*, raise *(US)*; *(regelmäßig)* increment

zulangen VI SEP **(a)** *(inf: Dieb, Fiskus, beim Essen)* to help oneself; **kräftig ~** *(beim Essen)* to tuck in *(inf)* **(b)** *(inf: = zuschlagen)* to strike out

zulassen VT SEP IRREG **(a)** *(= Zugang gewähren)* to admit; **eine Partei zur Wahl ~** to permit a party to enter the/an election **(b)** *(amtlich)* to authorize; Arzt, Heilpraktiker to register; Arzneimittel to approve; Kraftfahrzeug to license; Rechtsanwalt to call (to the bar); Prüfling to admit; **amtlich zugelassen sein** to be authorized; **staatlich zugelassen sein** to be state- registered; **er ist an allen** or **für alle Gerichte zugelassen** he is authorized to practise *(Brit)* or practice *(US)* in any court; **eine nicht zugelassene Partei** an illegal party; **für Personenbeförderung nicht zugelassen** not licensed to carry passengers; **zugelassene Aktien** listed securities **(c)** *(= dulden, gestatten)* to allow; **das lässt nur den Schluss zu, dass ...** that leaves only one conclusion that ...; **sein Schweigen lässt keine andere Erklärung zu(, als dass ...)** there is no other explanation for his silence (but that ...) **(d)** *(= geschlossen lassen)* to keep shut

zulässig ['tsuːlɛsɪç] ADJ permissible; Beweis, Klage, Vorgehen admissible; Fangquote allowable; **~es Gesamtgewicht** *(Mot)* maximum laden weight; **~e Höchstgeschwindigkeit** (upper) speed limit; **~e Höchstbelastung** weight limit; **es ist nicht ~, hier zu parken** parking is prohibited here

Zulässigkeit F **-,** NO PL admissibility

Zulassung ['tsuːlasʊŋ] F **-, -en (a)** NO PL *(= Gewährung von Zugang)* admittance; *(amtlich)* authorization; *(als Rechtsanwalt)* licensing; *(als praktizierender Arzt)* registration; **Antrag auf ~ zu einer Prüfung** application to enter an examination; **seine ~ als Rechtsanwalt bekommen** to be called to the bar; **~ (von Aktien) zur Börse** listing on the Stock Exchange

(b) *(Dokument)* papers *pl*; *(esp von Kfz)* vehicle registration document; *(= Lizenz)* licence *(Brit)*, license *(US)*

Zulassungs-: **Zulassungsbeschränkung** F *(esp Univ)* restriction on admissions; **Zulassungsstelle** F registration office; **Zulassungsstopp** M *(esp Univ)* block on admissions

zulasten [tsu'lastn] ADV *siehe* **Last**

Zulauf M, NO PL **großen ~ haben** to be very popular

zulaufen VI SEP IRREG AUX SEIN **(a)** **auf jdn/etw ~**, **auf jdn/etw zugelaufen kommen** to run toward(s) sb/sth, to come running toward(s) sb/sth; *(direkt)* to run up to sb/sth, to come running up to sb/sth **(b)** *(Wasser etc)* to add; **lass noch etwas kaltes Wasser ~** add some more cold water **(c)** *(Hund etc)* **jdm ~** to stray into sb's house; **eine zugelaufene Katze** a stray (cat)

zulegen SEP **1** VT **(a)** *(= dazulegen)* to put on; Geld to add; *(bei Verlustgeschäft)* to lose; **der Chef hat mir 100 Euro im Monat zugelegt** the boss has given me an extra 100 euros a month; **die fehlenden 20 Euro legte meine Mutter zu** my mother made up the remaining 20 euros; **etwas Tempo** *(inf)* or **einen Zahn** *(inf)* **~** to get a move on *(inf)* **(b)** *(inf: an Gewicht)* to put on; **die SPD konnte 5% ~** the SPD managed to gain 5% **(c)** *(= anschaffen)* **sich** *(dat)* **etw ~** *(inf)* to get oneself sth **2** VI *(inf)* *(an Gewicht)* to put on weight;

(*Wirtschaftswachstum, Umsatz*) to increase; **die SPD hat in den Umfragen zugelegt** the SPD has gained support in the opinion polls

zuleide [tsu'laɪdə] ADV **jdm etwas ~ tun** to do sb harm; **was hat er dir ~ getan?** what (harm) has he done to you?

zuletzt [tsu'lɛtst] ADV **(a)** (= *schließlich, endlich, zum Schluss*) in the end; **~ kam sie doch** she came in the end; **wir blieben bis ~** we stayed to the very end; **ganz ~** right at the last moment **(b)** (= *an letzter Stelle, zum letzten Mal*) last; **ich kam ~** I came last; **wann haben Sie ihn ~ gesehen?** when did you last see him?; **ganz ~** last of all; **nicht ~ dank/wegen** not least thanks to/because of

zuliebe [tsu'liːbə] ADV **etw jdm ~ tun** to do sth for sb's sake *or* for sb; **das geschah nur ihr ~** it was done just for her

Zulieferer ['tsuːliːfərɐ] M **-s, -**, **Zulieferin** [-ərɪn] F **-, -nen** (*Econ*) supplier

Zulieferindustrie F (*Econ*) supply industry

Zulu ['tsuːlu] M **-(s), -(s)**, *or* f **-, -s** Zulu

zum [tsʊm] CONTR *von* **zu dem**; **geht es hier ~ Bahnhof?** is this the way to the station?; **„Gasthof Zum Löwen"** "The Lion Inn"; **~ Schwimmen gehen** to go swimming; **~ Essen gehen** to go and eat; **es ist ~ Verrücktwerden/Weinen** it's enough to drive you crazy (*inf*)/make you cry; **dieses Gerät ist ~ Messen des Blutdrucks** this apparatus is for measuring (the) blood pressure; **~ Spießbürger/Verräter werden** to become bourgeois/a traitor

zumachen SEP **1** VT (= *schließen*) to shut; *Flasche* to close; *Brief* to seal; (*inf:* = *auflösen*) *Laden etc* to close down; **die Augen ~** (*lit, fig*) to close one's eyes (*fig: bei etw* to sth) **2** VI (*inf*) **(a)** (= *den Laden ~*) to close (down) **(b)** (*inf:* = *sich beeilen*) to get a move on (*inf*)

zumal [tsu'maːl] **1** CONJ **~ (da)** particularly as *or* since **2** ADV (= *besonders*) particularly

zumauern VT SEP to brick up

zumeist [tsu'maɪst] ADV mostly

zumindest [tsu'mɪndəst] ADV at least

zumüllen ['tsuːmʏlən] VT SEP **(a)** (*inf*) to cover over with rubbish (*Brit*) *or* garbage; (*mit Werbesendungen, Junkmail, Spam*) to bombard (*inf*) **(b)** (*sl*) = zulabern

zumutbar ADJ reasonable; **jdm** *or* **für jdn ~ sein** to be reasonable for sb; **es ist ihm (durchaus) ~, dass er das tut** he can reasonably be expected to do that; **nicht ~ sein** to be unreasonable

Zumutbarkeit ['tsuːmuːtbaːɐkaɪt] F **-, NO PL** reasonableness

zumute [tsu'muːtə] ADV **wie ist Ihnen ~?** how do you feel?; **mir ist traurig/seltsam** *etc* ~ I feel sad/strange *etc*; **mir ist gar nicht lächerlich ~** I'm not in a laughing mood; **mir war dabei gar nicht wohl ~** I felt uneasy about it

zumuten VT SEP **jdm etw ~** to expect sth of sb; **das können Sie niemandem ~** you can't expect that of anyone; **Sie muten mir doch wohl nicht zu, das zu glauben!** you surely don't expect me to believe that; **sich** (*dat*) **zu viel ~** to take on too much; **seinem Körper zu viel ~** to overtax oneself

Zumutung ['tsuːmuːtʊŋ] F **-, -en** unreasonable demand; (= *Unverschämtheit*) nerve (*inf*); **das ist eine ~!** that's a bit much!

zunächst [tsu'nɛːçst] ADV **(a)** (= *zuerst*) first (of all); **~ einmal** first of all **(b)** (= *vorläufig*) for the time being

zunageln VT SEP *Fenster etc* to nail up; (*mit Brettern, Pappe etc*) to board up; *Sarg, Kiste etc* to nail down

zunähen VT SEP to sew up

Zunahme ['tsuːnaːmə] F **-, -n** (+*gen, an* +*dat* in) increase; (= *Anstieg auch*) rise

Zuname M surname

zündeln ['tsʏndln] VI to play (about) with fire; **mit Streichhölzern ~** to play (about) with matches

zünden ['tsʏndn] **1** VI to catch fire; (*Pulver*) to ignite; (*Streichholz*) to light; (*Motor*) to go off; (*Sprengkörper*) to go off; (*fig*) to kindle enthusiasm **2** VT to ignite; *Rakete* to fire; *Sprengkörper* to set off; *Feuerwerkskörper* to let off

zündend ADJ (*fig*) stirring; *Vorschlag* exciting

Zünder ['tsʏndɐ] M **-s, -** (*für Sprengstoff, Bombe, Torpedo etc*) fuse; (*für Mine*) detonator

Zünd-: Zündflamme F pilot light; **Zündholz** NT match(stick); **ein ~ anreißen** to strike a match; **Zündkabel** NT (*Aut*) plug

lead; **Zündkapsel** F detonator; **Zündkerze** F (*Aut*) spark(ing) plug; **Zündschlüssel** M (*Aut*) ignition key; **Zündschnur** F fuse; **Zündstoff** M inflammable matter; (= *Sprengstoff*) explosives *pl*; (*fig*) explosive stuff

Zündung ['tsʏndʊŋ] F **-, -en** ignition; (= *Zündvorrichtung bei Sprengkörpern*) detonator; **die ~ ist nicht richtig eingestellt** (*Aut*) the timing is out; **die ~ einstellen** (*Aut*) to adjust the timing

zunehmen VI SEP IRREG **1** VI (*an Zahl etc, beim Stricken*) to increase; (*Tage*) to draw out; (*an Weisheit, Erfahrung etc*) to gain (*an* +*dat* in); (*Mensch: an Gewicht*) to put on weight; (*Mond*) to wax **2** VT (*Mensch: an Gewicht*) to gain

zunehmend 1 ADJ increasing; *Mond* crescent; **bei** *or* **mit ~em Alter** with advancing age; **wir haben ~en Mond** there is a crescent moon; **in ~em Maße** to an increasing degree **2** ADV increasingly; **~ an Einfluss gewinnen** to gain increasing influence

Zuneigung F affection; **eine starke ~ zu jdm empfinden** to feel strong affection for sb; **~ zu jdm fassen** to grow fond of sb

Zunft [tsʊnft] F **-, ~e** ['tsʏnftə] (*Hist*) guild; (*hum inf*) brotherhood

zünftig ['tsʏnftɪç] ADJ **(a)** (*Hist*) belonging to a guild **(b)** (= *fachmännisch*) *Arbeit etc* expert; *Kleidung* professional(-looking); (*inf*) (= *ordentlich, regelrecht*) proper; (= *gut, prima*) great; **eine ~e Ohrfeige** a hefty slap across the face

Zunge ['tsʊŋə] F **-, -n** tongue; (*Mus: von Fagott, Akkordeon*) reed; (*von Waage*) pointer; (*Zool:* = *Seezunge*) sole; **mit der ~ anstoßen** to lisp; **die ~ herausstrecken** (*beim Arzt*) to stick out one's tongue; **mit schwerer ~ sprechen** to speak in a slurred voice; **eine böse** *or* **giftige/scharfe** *or* **spitze/lose ~ haben** to have an evil/a sharp/a loose tongue; **lose ~n behaupten, ...** rumour (*Brit*) *or* rumor (*US*) has it ...; **böse ~n behaupten, ...** malicious gossip has it ...; **das Wort liegt** *or* **schwebt mir auf der ~, ich habe das Wort auf der ~** the word is on the tip of my tongue; **mir hängt die ~ zum Hals heraus** (*inf*) my tongue is hanging out; **in fremden ~n reden** to speak in tongues

züngeln ['tsʏŋln] VI (*Schlange*) to dart its tongue in and out; (*Flamme, Feuer*) to lick

Zungen-: Zungenbrecher M tongue twister; **Zungenkuss** M French kiss; **Zungen-R** [-ɛr] NT, **Zungen-r** NT (*Ling*) rolled "r"; **Zungenspitze** F tip of the tongue

Zünglein ['tsʏŋlaɪn] NT **-s, -** DIM *von* **Zunge** tongue; (*rare: der Waage*) pointer; **das ~ an der Waage sein** (*fig*) to tip the scales; (*Pol*) to hold the balance of power

zunichte [tsu'nɪçtə] ADV **~ machen** to ruin; **~ werden** to be ruined

zunutze [tsu'nʊtsə] ADV **sich** (*dat*) **etw ~ machen** (= *verwenden*) to make use of sth; (= *ausnutzen*) to capitalize on sth

zuoberst [tsu'loːbɐst] ADV on *or* at the (very) top

zuordnen VT SEP +DAT to assign to; **ein Tier einer Gattung ~** to assign an animal to a genus; **jdn/etw jdm ~** to assign sb/sth to sb; **diesen Dichter ordnet man der Romantik zu** this poet is classified as a Romantic(ist)

Zuordnung F assignment (*zu einer Periode*), classification; (= *Beziehung zueinander*) relation

zupacken VI SEP (*inf*) **(a)** (= *zugreifen*) to make a grab for it *etc* **(b)** (*bei der Arbeit*) to get down to it **(c)** (= *helfen*) **mit ~** to give me/them *etc* a hand

zupackend 1 ADJ *Film, Theaterstück, Steuersystem* hard-hitting; (= *forsch*) straightforward; (= *aggressiv*) vigorous **2** ADV purposefully

Zupfinstrument NT (*Mus*) plucked string instrument

zuprosten VI SEP **jdm ~** to drink sb's health

zur [tsuːɐ, tsʊr] CONTR *von* **zu der**; **~ Schule gehen** to go to school; **~ See fahren** to go to sea; **„Gasthof Zur Post"** "The Post Inn"; **~ Zeit** at the moment; **~ Weihnachtszeit** at Christmas time; **~ Orientierung** for orientation; **~ Abschreckung** as a deterrent

zurande [tsu'randə] ADV **mit etw/jdm ~ kommen** (to be able) to cope with sth/sb

zurate [tsu'raːtə] ADV **jdn/etw ~ ziehen** to consult sb/sth

zuraten VI SEP IRREG **jdm ~, etw zu tun** to advise sb to do sth; **ich will weder ~ noch abraten** I won't advise you one way or the other; **auf sein Zuraten (hin)** on his advice

Zürcher ['tsʏrçɐ] M **-s, -**, **Zürcherin** [-ərɪn] F **-, -nen** native of Zurich

Zurechnungs-: zurechnungsfähig ADJ of sound mind; **Zurechnungsfähigkeit** F soundness of mind; **verminderte ~** diminished responsibility; **ich muss doch schon manchmal an seiner ~ zweifeln!** (*inf*) I sometimes wonder if he's quite right in the head (*inf*)

zurecht- [tsu'rɛçt-]: **zurechtbiegen** VT SEP IRREG to bend into shape; (*fig*) to twist; **zurechtfinden** VR SEP IRREG to find one's way (*in +dat* around); **sich in der Welt nicht mehr ~** not to be able to cope with the world any longer; **ich finde mich in dieser Tabelle nicht zurecht** I can't make head nor tail of this table; **sich mit etw ~** to get the hang of sth (*inf*); (*durch Gewöhnung*) to get used to sth; **zurechtkommen** VI SEP IRREG AUX SEIN **(a)** (*fig*) to get on; (= *schaffen, bewältigen*) to cope; (= *genug haben*) to have enough; **kommen Sie ohne das zurecht?** (*inf*) can you manage without it?; **er kam nie zurecht im Leben** he was never able to cope with life **(b)** (*finanziell*) to manage; **mit 100 Euro am Tag kann man gut ~** you can manage easily on 100 euros a day; **zurechtlegen** VT SEP IRREG to lay out ready; **sich** (*dat*) **etw ~** to lay sth out ready; (*fig*) to work sth out; **sich** (*dat*) **alle Argumente ~** to marshal all one's arguments; **zurechtmachen** SEP (*inf*) ◼ VT **(a)** *Zimmer, Essen etc* to prepare; *Bett* to make up **(b)** (= *anziehen*) to dress; (= *schminken*) to make up ◼ VR to get dressed; (= *sich schminken*) to put on one's make-up; **auf etw** (*acc*) **zurechtgemacht sein** (*inf*) to be done up as sth (*inf*); **zurechtweisen** VT SEP IRREG to rebuke; *Schüler etc* to reprimand; **Zurechtweisung** F rebuke; (*von Schüler*) reprimand

zureden VI SEP **jdm ~** (= *ermutigen*) to encourage sb; (= *überreden*) to persuade sb; **wenn du ihm gut zuredest, hilft er dir** if you talk to him nicely, he'll help you; **sie hat ihrem Vater so lange zugeredet, bis er ihr das Auto kaufte** she kept on at her father till he bought her the car; **auf mein Zureden (hin)** with my encouragement; (*Überreden*) with my persuasion; **gutes** or **freundliches Zureden** friendly persuasion

zureiten SEP IRREG ◼ VT *Pferd* to break in ◼ VI AUX SEIN (= *weiterreiten*) to ride on; (*schneller*) to ride faster; **auf jdn/etw ~**, **auf jdn/etw zugeritten kommen** to ride toward(s) or (*direkt*) up to sb/sth

Zürich ['tsyːrɪç] NT **-s** Zurich

Zürichsee M Lake Zurich

zurichten VT SEP (= *beschädigen, verunstalten*) to make a mess of; (= *verletzen*) to injure; **jdn übel ~** to beat sb up

zuriegeln ['tsuːriːgl̩n] VT SEP to bolt (shut)

Zurschaustellung [tsoːr'ʃaʊ-] F display, exhibition

zurück [tsu'rʏk] ADV back; (*mit Zahlungen*) behind; (= *~geblieben*) (*von Kind*) backward; **in Französisch (sehr) ~ sein** (*fig*) to be (really) behind in French; **fünf Punkte ~** (*Sport*) five points behind; **~ nach** *etc* back to *etc*; **~!** get back!; **~ an Absender** return to sender; **einmal München und ~** a return (*esp Brit*) or a round-trip ticket (*US*) to Munich; **seit wann ist Trevor ~?** when did Trevor get back?; **ich bin in zehn Minuten wieder ~** I will be back (again) in 10 minutes; **hinter jdm ~ sein** (*fig*) to lie behind sb; **es gibt kein Zurück (mehr)** there's no going back

Zurück-: zurückbehalten *ptp* **zurückbehalten** VT SEP IRREG to keep (back); **er hat Schäden/einen Schock ~** he suffered lasting damage/lasting shock; **zurückbekommen** *ptp* **zurückbekommen** VT SEP IRREG **(a)** (= *zurückerhalten*) to get back (*Brit*), to get back at **(b)** (*inf*: = *heimgezahlt bekommen*) **das wirst du (von mir) ~!** I'll get my own back on you for that! (*Brit*), I'll get back at you for that!; **zurückbeugen** SEP ◼ VT to bend back ◼ VR to lean back; **zurückbilden** VR SEP (*Geschwür*) to recede; (*Muskel*) to atrophy; (*Biol*) to regress; (*esp Sw*: = *abnehmen*) to decrease

zurückbleiben VI SEP IRREG AUX SEIN **(a)** (*an einem Ort*) to stay behind; (= *weiter hinten gehen*) to stay (back) behind **(b)** (= *übrig bleiben*: *Rest, Rückstand*) to be left; (*als Folge von Krankheit etc*: *Schaden, Behinderung*) to remain; **er blieb als Waise/Witwer zurück** he was left an orphan/a widower **(c)** (= *nicht Schritt halten*) (*auch fig*: *mit Arbeitsleistung etc*) to fall behind; (*in Entwicklung*) to be retarded; (*Sport*) to be behind; **die Einnahmen blieben hinter den Erwartungen zurück** the takings didn't come up to expectations; *siehe auch* **zurückgeblieben**

zurück-: zurückblenden VI SEP (*lit, fig*) to flash back (*auf +acc* to); **zurückblicken** VI SEP to look back (*auf +acc* at); (*fig*) to look back (*auf +acc* on); **zurückbringen** VT SEP IRREG (= *wieder herbringen*) to bring back (*lit, fig*); (= *wieder wegbringen*) to take back; **zurückdatieren** *ptp* **zurückdatiert** VT SEP to backdate; **zurückdenken** VI SEP IRREG to think back (*an +acc* to); **so weit ich ~ kann** as far as I can remember; **zurückdrehen** VT SEP to turn back; *Uhr* to put (*Brit*) or turn (*US*) back; **die Uhr** or **Zeit ~** to put (*Brit*) or turn (*US*) back the clock; **das Rad (der Geschichte) ~** to turn back the hands of time; **zurückdürfen** VI SEP IRREG (*inf*) to be allowed back; **zurückerstatten** VT SEP *ptp* **zurückerstattet** VT SEP to refund; *Ausgaben* to reimburse; **zurückerwarten** *ptp* **zurückerwartet** VT SEP **jdn ~** to expect sb back; **zurückfahren** SEP IRREG ◼ VI AUX SEIN **(a)** (*an einen Ort*) to go back; (*esp als Fahrer*) to drive back **(b)** (= *zurückweichen*) to start back ◼ VT **(a)** (*mit Fahrzeug*) to drive back **(b)** (= *drosseln*) *Produktion, Investitionen* to cut back; **zurückfallen** VI SEP IRREG AUX SEIN to fall back; (*Sport*) to drop back; (*fig*) (*Umsätze etc*) to fall; (*an Besitzer*) to revert (*an +acc* to); (*in Leistungen*) to fall behind; (*Schande, Vorwurf etc*) to reflect (*auf +acc* on); **in alte Gewohnheiten ~** to fall back into old habits; **er fällt immer wieder in seine alten Gewohnheiten zurück** he always lapses back into his old ways; **zurückfinden** VI SEP IRREG to find the way back; **zurückfliegen** VTI SEP IRREG (*vi: aux sein*) to fly back; **zurückfordern** VT SEP **etw ~** to ask for sth back; (*stärker*) to demand sth back; **zurückführbar** ADJ traceable (*auf +acc* to); **auf eine Formel ~** reducible to a formula

zurückführen SEP ◼ VT **(a)** (= *zurückbringen*) to lead back **(b)** (= *ableiten auf*) to put down to; **etw auf seine Ursache ~** to put sth down to its cause; **etw auf eine Formel/Regel ~** to reduce sth to a formula/rule; **das ist darauf zurückzuführen, dass ...** that can be put down to the fact that ... ◼ VI to lead back; **es führt kein Weg zurück** there's no way back; (*fig*) there's no going back

zurückgeben VT SEP IRREG to give back; *Wechselgeld* to give back; *Ball, Kompliment, Beleidigung* to return; (= *erwidern*) to retort; **das Geld kannst du dir von der Firma ~ lassen** you can ask the firm to give you the money back; **dieser Erfolg gab ihm seine Zuversicht wieder zurück** this success gave him back his confidence

zurückgeblieben ADJ geistig/körperlich **~** mentally/physically retarded; *siehe auch* **zurückbleiben**

zurückgehen VI SEP IRREG AUX SEIN **(a)** (= *zurückkehren*) to go back (*nach, in +acc, auf +acc* to); (= *seinen Ursprung haben*) to go back to (*auf +acc* to); **er ging zwei Schritte zurück** he stepped back two paces; **Waren/Essen** *etc* **~ lassen** to send back goods/food *etc*; **der Brief ging ungeöffnet zurück** the letter was returned unopened **(b)** (= *zurückweichen*) to retreat; (*fig*: = *abnehmen*) to go down; (*Geschäft, Umsatz, Produktion*) to fall off; (*Seuche, Schmerz, Sturm*) to die down

zurück-: zurückgezogen ◼ ADJ *Mensch* withdrawn, retiring; *Lebensweise* secluded ◼ ADV in seclusion; **er lebt sehr ~** he lives a very secluded life; *siehe auch* **zurückziehen**; **zurückgreifen** VI SEP IRREG (*fig*) to fall back (*auf +acc* upon); **zurückhaben** VT SEP IRREG (*inf*) to have (got (*Brit*) or gotten (*US*)) back; **ich will mein Geld ~** I want my money back

zurückhalten SEP IRREG ◼ VT to hold back; (= *nicht durchlassen, aufhalten*) *jdn* to hold up; (= *nicht freigeben*) *Manuskript, Film, Informationen* to withhold; (= *eindämmen*) *Gefühle, Ärger etc* to restrain; **jdn von etw** (*dat*) **~** to keep sb from sth ◼ VR (= *sich beherrschen*) to control oneself; (= *reserviert sein*) to be retiring; (= *im Hintergrund bleiben*) to keep in the background; (*bei Verhandlung, Demonstration etc*) to keep a low profile; (*bei Investitionen*) to be restrained; **sich mit seiner Kritik ~** to be restrained in one's criticism; **ich musste mich schwer ~** I had to take a firm grip on myself; **Sie müssen sich beim Essen sehr ~** you must cut down a lot on what you eat ◼ VI **mit etw ~** (= *verheimlichen*) to hold sth back

zurückhaltend ◼ ADJ **(a)** (= *beherrscht, kühl*) restrained; (= *reserviert*) reserved; (= *vorsichtig*) cautious; *Börse* dull **(b)** (= *nicht großzügig*) sparing; **mit Tadel** or **Kritik nicht ~ sein** to be unsparing in one's criticism ◼ ADV with restraint; **das Publikum reagierte ~** the audience's response was restrained

zurück-: zurückkaufen VT SEP to buy back; **zurückkehren** VI SEP AUX SEIN to return (*von, aus* from); to return (*nach, zu* to);

zurückkommen VI SEP IRREG AUX SEIN (*lit*, *fig*) to come back; (= *Bezug nehmen*) to refer (*auf* +*acc* to); **ich werde später auf deinen Vorschlag/dieses Angebot ~** I'll come back to your suggestion/this offer later; **zurückkönnen** VI SEP IRREG (*inf*) to be able to go back; **ich kann nicht mehr zurück** (*fig*) there's no going back!; **zurückkriegen** VT SEP (*inf*) = **zurückbekommen**; **zurücklassen** VT SEP IRREG **(a)** (= *hinterlassen*) to leave; (= *liegen lassen*) to leave behind **(b)** (*inf*: = *zurückkehren lassen*) to allow back

zurücklegen SEP **1** VT **(a)** (*an seinen Platz*) to put back **(b)** *Kopf* to lay back **(c)** (= *aufbewahren, reservieren*) to put aside; (= *sparen*) to put away; **jdm etw ~** to keep sth for sb **(d)** *Strecke* to cover **2** VR to lie back

zurück-: zurücklehnen VTR SEP to lean back; **zurückliegen** VI SEP IRREG (*örtlich*) to be behind; **der Unfall liegt etwa eine Woche zurück** the accident was about a week ago; **das liegt schon so weit zurück, dass ...** that is so long ago now that ...; **es liegt zwanzig Jahre zurück, dass ...** it is twenty years since ...; **zurückmüssen** VI SEP IRREG (*inf*) to have to go back

zurücknehmen VT SEP IRREG to take back; *Verordnung etc* to revoke; *Entscheidung* to reverse; *Angebot* to withdraw; *Auftrag, Bestellung* to cancel; **sein Wort/Versprechen ~** to break one's word/promise; **ich nehme alles zurück (und behaupte das Gegenteil)** I take it all back

zurück-: zurückreichen SEP **1** VT *Gegenstand* to hand back **2** VI (*Erinnerung, Tradition etc*) to go back (*in* +*acc* to); **zurückreisen** VI SEP AUX SEIN to travel back; **zurückrufen** SEP IRREG **1** VT to call back; (*am Telefon auch*) to ring back (*Brit*); *Botschafter, fehlerhafte Produkte* to recall; **jdn ins Leben ~** to bring sb back to life; **jdm etw in die Erinnerung** *or* **ins Gedächtnis ~** to conjure sth up for sb; **sich** (*dat*) **etw in die Erinnerung** *or* **ins Gedächtnis ~** to call sth to mind **2** VI to call back; (*am Telefon auch*) to ring back (*Brit*); **zurückscheuen** VI SEP AUX SEIN to shy away (*vor* +*dat* from); **vor nichts ~** to stop at nothing; **zurückschicken** VT SEP to send back

zurückschlagen SEP IRREG **1** VT *Ball* to return; *Feind, Angriff, Truppen etc* to beat back **2** VI (*lit*, *fig*) to hit back; (*Mil*) (*fig*) to retaliate; (*Flamme*) to flare back; (*Pendel*) to swing back; **auf jdn/etw ~** to have repercussions for sb/sth

zurück-: zurückschrauben VT SEP to screw back; (*fig inf*) *Erwartungen* to lower; *Subventionen* to cut back; **seine Ansprüche ~** to lower one's sights; **zurückschrecken** VI SEP IRREG AUX SEIN or HABEN to start back; (*fig*) to shy away (*vor* +*dat* from); **vor nichts ~** to stop at nothing; **zurücksehen** VI SEP IRREG to look back; **auf etw** (*acc*) **~** (*fig*) to look back on sth; **zurücksehnen** VR SEP IRREG to long to return (*nach* to); **sich nach der guten alten Zeit ~** to long for the good old days; **zurücksenden** VT SEP IRREG to send back

zurücksetzen SEP **1** VT **(a)** (*nach hinten*) to move back; *Auto* to reverse **(b)** (*an früheren Platz*) to put back **(c)** (*dial*) *Preis, Waren* to reduce; **zurückgesetzt** reduced **(d)** (*fig*: = *benachteiligen*) to neglect **2** VR to sit back **3** VI (*mit Fahrzeug*) to reverse

zurück-: zurückspringen VI SEP IRREG AUX SEIN to leap *or* jump back; **zurückstecken** SEP **1** VT to put back **2** VI **(a)** (= *weniger Ansprüche stellen*) to lower one's expectations; (= *weniger ausgeben*) to cut back **(b)** (= *nachgeben, einlenken*) to backtrack; **zurückstehen** VI SEP IRREG (= *hintangesetzt werden*) to take second place; **hinter etw** (*dat*) **~** to take second place to sth; **sie muss immer hinter ihm ~** she always comes off worse than he does; **zurückstellen** VT SEP **(a)** (*an seinen Platz*) *Uhr* to put back; (*nach hinten*) to move back **(b)** (*fig*: = *verschieben*) to defer; *Investitionen, Pläne* to postpone; *Bedenken, Forderungen etc* to put aside; *Sport, Privatleben, Hobbys etc* to spend less time on; **persönliche Interessen hinter etw** (*dat*) **~** to put one's personal interests after sth; **persönliche Interessen ~** to put one's own interests last; **zurückstrahlen** SEP **1** VT to reflect **2** VI to be reflected; **zurückströmen** VI SEP AUX SEIN to flow back; (*geh*: *Menschen*) to stream back; **zurückstufen** VT SEP to downgrade

zurücktreten SEP IRREG **1** VI AUX SEIN **(a)** (= *zurückgehen*) to step back; **bitte ~!** stand back, please!; **einen Schritt ~** to take a step back **(b)** (*Regierung, von Amt*) to resign **(c)** (*von Vertrag etc*) to withdraw (*von* from); **von einem Anspruch/einem Recht ~** to renounce a claim/a right **(d)** (*fig*: = *geringer werden*) to decline; (= *an Wichtigkeit verlieren*) to fade (in importance); (= *im Hintergrund bleiben*)

to come second (*hinter jdm/etw* to sb/sth) **2** VTI (*mit Fuß*) to kick back

zurück-: zurücktun VT SEP IRREG (*inf*) to put back; **zurückverfolgen** ptp **zurückverfolgt** VT SEP (*fig*) to trace back; **zurückverlangen** ptp **zurückverlangt** SEP VT to demand back; **zurückversetzen** ptp **zurückversetzt** SEP **1** VT **(a)** (*in seinen alten Zustand*) to restore (*in* +*acc* to); (*in eine andere Zeit*) to take back (*in* +*acc* to) **(b)** *Beamte etc* to transfer back; *Schüler* to move down (*in* +*acc* into) **2** VR to think oneself back (*in* +*acc* to); **zurückweichen** VI SEP IRREG AUX SEIN (*vor* +*dat* from) (*erschrocken*) to shrink back; (*ehrfürchtig*) to stand back; (*nachgeben*) to retreat; (*vor Verantwortung, Hindernis*) to shy away; (*Mil*) to withdraw; (*Hochwasser*) to subside; **zurückweisen** VT SEP IRREG to reject; *Angebot auch, Geschenk* to refuse; *Gäste, Bittsteller* to turn away; *Berichte, Vorwurf, Klage, Berufung* to dismiss; *Angriff* to repel; (*an der Grenze*) to turn back; **zurückwollen** VI SEP (*inf*) to want to go back; **zurückwünschen** VT SEP **sich** (*dat*) **jdn/etw ~** to wish sb/sth back; **zurückzahlen** VT SEP to repay; *Schulden auch* to pay off; *Spesen etc* to refund; **das werde ich ihm noch ~!** (*fig*) I'll pay him back for that!

zurückziehen SEP IRREG **1** VT to pull back; *Antrag, Bemerkung, Klage etc* to withdraw **2** VR to retire; (= *sich zur Ruhe begeben*) to retire; (*Mil*) to withdraw; (*vom Geschäft, von der Politik etc*) to retire (*von, aus* from); *siehe auch* **zurückgezogen** **3** VI AUX SEIN to move back; (*Truppen*) to march back; (*Vögel*) to fly back

Zurückziehung F withdrawal

zurückzucken VI SEP AUX SEIN to recoil; (*Hand, Fuß*) to jerk back

Zuruf M shout; (*aufmunternd*) cheer; **durch ~ abstimmen** *or* **wählen** to vote by acclamation

zurufen VTI SEP IRREG **jdm etw ~** to shout sth to sb

Zurverfügungstellung [tsuɐfeːˈfyːɡʊŋ-] F **-, -en** making available *no pl*

zurzeit [tsʊɐˈtsait] ADV at present

Zusage F **(a)** (= *Zustimmung*) consent **(b)** (= *Verpflichtung*) commitment **(c)** (= *Annahme*) acceptance; (= *Bestätigung*) confirmation **(d)** (= *Versprechen*) promise

zusagen SEP **1** VT (= *versprechen*) to promise; (= *bestätigen*) to confirm; **er hat sein Kommen fest zugesagt** he has promised firmly that he will come; **jdm etw auf den Kopf ~** (*inf*) to tell sb sth outright; **ich kann ihm auf den Kopf ~, wenn er mich belügt** I can tell straight away when he's lying **2** VI **(a)** (= *annehmen*) (*jdm*) **~** to accept; **eine ~de Antwort** a favourable (*Brit*) *or* favorable (*US*) reply **(b)** (= *gefallen*) **jdm ~** to appeal to sb

zusammen [tsuˈzamən] ADV together; **alle/alles ~** all together; **wir hatten ~ 100 Euro zum Ausgeben** between us we had 100 euros to spend; **~ mit** together with; **er zahlt mehr als wir alle ~** he pays more than the rest of us put together

Zusammen-: Zusammenarbeit F co-operation; (*mit dem Feind*) collaboration; **in ~ mit** in co-operation with; **zusammenarbeiten** VI SEP to co-operate; (*mit dem Feind*) to collaborate

Zusammenbau M, NO PL assembly; **zusammenbauen** VT SEP to assemble; **etw wieder ~** to reassemble sth; **zusammenbeißen** VT SEP IRREG **die Zähne ~** (*lit*) to clench one's teeth; (*fig*) to grit one's teeth; **zusammenbekommen** ptp **zusammenbekommen** VT SEP IRREG to get together; *Geld, Spenden* to collect; *Wortlaut* to remember; **zusammenbinden** VT SEP IRREG to tie together; **zusammenbleiben** VI SEP IRREG AUX SEIN to stay together; **zusammenbrauen** **1** VT SEP (*inf*) to concoct **2** VR (*Gewitter, Unheil etc*) to be brewing

zusammenbrechen VI SEP IRREG AUX SEIN to break down; (*Gebäude*) to cave in; (*Wirtschaft, Markt, Imperium*) to collapse; (*Widerstand*) to crumble; (= *zum Stillstand kommen*) (*Verkehr etc*) to come to a standstill

zusammenbringen VT SEP IRREG **(a)** (= *sammeln*) to bring together; *Geld* to raise **(b)** (*inf*: = *zustande bringen*) to manage; *Gedanken* to collect; *Worte, Sätze* to put together; (= *ins Gedächtnis zurückrufen*) to remember; (= *zusammenkriegen, -bauen*) to get together **(c)** (= *in Kontakt bringen*) *Stoffe* to bring into contact with each other; (= *bekannt machen*) *Menschen* to bring together; **wieder ~** (= *versöhnen*) to reconcile

Zusammenbruch M breakdown; (*fig*) collapse

zusammenfahren VI SEP IRREG AUX SEIN **(a)** (= *zusammenstoßen*) to collide **(b)** (= *erschrecken*) to start; (*vor Schmerz*) to flinch

zusammenfallen VI SEP IRREG AUX SEIN **(a)** (= *einstürzen*) to collapse; **in sich** (*acc*) ~ (*lit, fig*) to collapse; (*Hoffnungen*) to be shattered **(b)** (*durch Krankheit etc*) to waste away **(c)** (*Ereignisse*) to coincide

zusammenfalten VT SEP to fold up

zusammenfassen SEP ◘ VT **(a)** (= *verbinden*) to combine (*zu* in); (= *vereinigen*) to unite; (*Math*) to sum **(b)** *Bericht etc* to summarize; **etw in einem Satz** ~ to sum sth up in one sentence ◙ VI (= *das Fazit ziehen*) to summarize; **ein ~der Bericht** a summary; **~d kann man sagen, ...** to sum up, one can say ...; **wenn ich kurz ~ darf** just to sum up

Zusammen-: Zusammenfassung F **(a)** (= *verbinden*) combination, (= *Vereinigung*) union; (*Math*) summing **(b)** (= *Überblick*) summary; (*von Abhandlung*) abstract; **zusammenfließen** VI SEP IRREG AUX SEIN to flow together; (*Farben*) to run together; **Zusammenfluss** M confluence; **zusammenfügen** SEP ◘ VT to join together; (*Tech*) to fit together; **etw zu etw** ~ to join/fit sth together to make sth ◙ VR to fit together; **zusammengehören** *ptp* **zusammengehört** VI SEP (*Menschen, Städte, Firmen etc*) to belong together; (*Gegenstände, Themen*) to go together; (*als Paar*) to form a pair; **zusammengehörig** ADJ *Kleidungsstücke etc* matching; (= *verwandt*) related; **Zusammengehörigkeit** F -, NO PL common bond; **Zusammengehörigkeitsgefühl** NT (*in Gemeinschaft*) communal spirit; (*esp Pol*) feeling of solidarity; (*in Mannschaft*) team spirit; (*in Familie*) sense of a common bond

zusammengesetzt ADJ **aus etw ~ sein** to consist of sth; **~es Wort/Verb** compound (word)/verb; *siehe auch* **zusammensetzen**

Zusammen-: zusammengewürfelt [-gəvʏrflt] ADJ motley; *Mannschaft* scratch *attr*; **zusammenhaben** VT SEP IRREG (*inf*) **etw** ~ to have got (*Brit*) *or* gotten (*US*) sth together; **Zusammenhalt** M, NO PL (*fig: in einer Gruppe*) cohesion; (*esp Pol*) solidarity; (*fig: einer Mannschaft*) team spirit

zusammenhalten SEP IRREG ◘ VT **(a)** (= *verbinden*) to hold together; (*inf*) *Geld etc* to hold on to **(b)** (= *nebeneinander halten*) to hold side by side ◙ VI to hold together; (*fig: Freunde, Gruppe etc*) to stick together

Zusammenhang M (= *Beziehung*) connection (*von, zwischen* +*dat* between); (= *Wechselbeziehung*) correlation (*von, zwischen* +*dat* between); (*von Geschichte*) coherence; (*im Text*) context; **jdn/etw mit jdm/etw in** ~ **bringen** to connect sb/sth with sb/sth; **im** *or* **in** ~ **mit etw stehen** to be connected with sth; **etw aus dem** ~ **reißen** to take sth out of its context; **nicht im** ~ **mit etw stehen** to have no connection with sth; **in diesem** ~ in this context

zusammenhängen SEP ◘ VT *Kleider in Schrank etc* to hang (up) together ◙ VI IRREG to be joined (together); (*fig*) to be connected; **~d** *Rede, Erzählung* coherent; **das hängt damit zusammen, dass ...** that is connected with the fact that ...

zusammenhang(s)los ◘ ADJ incoherent ◙ ADV incoherently

Zusammen-: zusammenhauen VT SEP IRREG (*inf*) **(a)** (= *zerstören*) to smash to pieces; **jdn** ~ to beat sb up (*inf*) **(b)** (*fig: = pfuschen*) to knock together; *Geschriebenes* to scribble (down); **zusammenkehren** VT SEP to sweep together; **zusammenklappbar** ADJ folding

zusammenklappen SEP ◘ VT *Messer, Stuhl, Tisch etc* to fold up; *Schirm* to shut ◙ VI AUX SEIN **(a)** (*Stuhl etc*) to collapse **(b)** (*fig inf*) to flake out (*inf*); (*nach vorne*) to double up

Zusammen-: zusammenkleben VTI SEP (*vi: aux sein*) to stick together; **zusammenkneifen** SEP IRREG *Lippen, Pobacken etc* to press together; *Augen* to screw up; **zusammengekniffen** *Augen* screwed-up; *Mund* pinched; **zusammenknüllen** VT SEP to crumple up

zusammenkommen VI SEP IRREG AUX SEIN to meet (together); (*Umstände*) to combine; (*fig: = sich einigen*) to agree; (*fig* = *sich ansammeln: Schulden etc*) to mount up; (*Geld bei einer Sammlung*) to be collected; **er kommt viel mit Menschen zusammen** he meets a lot of people; **heute kommt wieder mal alles zusammen** (*inf*) it's all happening at once today

Zusammen-: zusammenkrachen VI SEP AUX SEIN (*inf*) **(a)** (= *einstürzen*) to crash down; (*fig: Börse, Wirtschaft*) to crash **(b)** (= *zusammenstoßen: Fahrzeuge*) to crash (into each other); **zusammenkratzen** VT SEP to scrape together; (*fig inf*) *Geld etc* to scrape together; **zusammenkriegen** VT SEP (*inf*) =

zusammenbekommen; **Zusammenkunft** [tsu'zamənkʊnft] F -, **-künfte** [-kʏnftə] meeting; (*zwanglos*) get-together; **zusammenläppern** VR SEP (*inf*) to add up

zusammenlaufen VI SEP IRREG AUX SEIN **(a)** (= *an eine Stelle laufen*) to gather; (*Flüssigkeit*) to collect **(b)** (*Farben*) to run together; (*Math*) to intersect; (*Straßen*) to converge; (*fig: Fäden etc*) to meet

zusammenleben SEP ◘ VI to live together ◙ VR to learn to live with each other

Zusammenleben NT living together *no art*; (*von Ländern etc*) coexistence; **eheliches** ~ married life; **außereheliches** ~ cohabitation

zusammenlegen SEP ◘ VT **(a)** (= *falten*) to fold (up) **(b)** (= *vereinigen*) to combine; *Aktien* to consolidate; *Grundstücke* to join; *Veranstaltungen* to hold together; *Häftlinge, Patienten* to put together; (= *zentralisieren*) to centralize; **sie legten ihr Geld zusammen** they clubbed (*Brit*) *or* pitched in (*US*) together ◙ VI (= *Geld gemeinsam aufbringen*) to club (*Brit*) *or* pitch in (*US*) together

zusammennehmen SEP IRREG ◘ VT to gather up; *Mut* to summon up; *Gedanken* to collect; **seine ganze Kraft** ~ to gather all one's strength; **alles zusammengenommen** all together ◙ VR (= *sich zusammenreißen*) to pull oneself together; (= *sich beherrschen*) to control oneself

zusammen-: zusammenpacken SEP ◘ VT to pack up together; **pack (deine Sachen) zusammen!** get packed! ◙ VI (= *einpacken*) to pack; **zusammenpassen** VI SEP (*Menschen*) to suit each other; (*Farben, Stile*) to go together; **gut** ~ to go well together; **überhaupt nicht** ~ not to go together at all; **das passt nicht mit den Tatsachen zusammen** it doesn't fit the facts; **zusammenpferchen** VT SEP to herd together; (*fig*) to pack together; **zusammenprallen** VI SEP AUX SEIN to collide; (*fig*) to clash; **zusammenraufen** VR SEP to achieve a viable working relationship; **zusammenrechnen** VT SEP to add up; **alles zusammengerechnet** all together; (*fig*) all in all; **zusammenreimen** SEP ◘ VT (*inf*) **sich** (*dat*) **etw** ~ to figure sth out (for oneself); **sich** (*dat*) **den Rest** ~ to put two and two together ◙ VR to make sense; **wie soll sich das ~?** it doesn't make sense; **zusammenreißen** VR SEP IRREG to pull oneself together; **zusammenrollen** SEP ◘ VT to roll up ◙ VR to curl up; (*Igel*) to roll (itself) up (into a ball); (*Schlange*) to coil up; **zusammenrücken** SEP ◘ VT *Möbel etc* to move closer together ◙ VI AUX SEIN to move closer together; **zusammenscheißen** VT SEP IRREG (*inf*) **jdn** ~ to give sb a bollocking (*Brit inf*), to kick sb's ass (*US sl*)

zusammenschlagen SEP IRREG ◘ VT **(a)** (= *aneinander schlagen*) to knock *or* bang together; *Becken* to clash; *Hacken* to click; *Hände* to clap **(b)** (= *verprügeln*) to beat up; (= *zerschlagen*) *Einrichtung* to smash up ◙ VI AUX SEIN **über jdm/etw** ~ (*Wellen etc*) to close over sb/sth; (*stärker*) to engulf sb/sth; (*fig: Unheil etc*) to descend upon sb/sth

Zusammen-: zusammenschließen VR SEP IRREG to join together; (*Comm*) to merge; **sich gegen jdn** ~ to band together against sb; **Zusammenschluss** M joining together; (*Comm*) merger; (*von politischen Gruppen*) amalgamation; **zusammenschreiben** VT SEP IRREG **(a)** *Wörter* (*orthographisch*) to write together; (*im Schriftbild*) to join up **(b)** (*pej: = verfassen*) to scribble down; **was der für einen Mist zusammenschreibt** what a load of garbage he writes; **zusammenschrumpfen** VI SEP AUX SEIN to shrivel up; (*fig*) to dwindle (*auf* +*acc* to); **zusammenschweißen** VT SEP (*lit*) to weld together; **zusammen sein** VI SEP IRREG AUX SEIN **mit jdm** ~ to be with sb; (*inf: = befreundet*) to be going out with sb; (*euph: = mit jdm schlafen*) to sleep with sb

Zusammensein NT being together *no art*; (*von Gruppe*) get-together

zusammensetzen SEP ◘ VT **(a)** *Schüler, Gäste etc* to put together **(b)** *Gerät, Gewehr etc* to assemble (*zu* to make) ◙ VR **(a)** (= *sich zueinander setzen*) to sit together; (*um etwas zu besprechen, zu trinken etc*) to get together; **sich gemütlich** ~ to have a cosy get-together; **sich auf ein Glas Wein** ~ to get together over a glass of wine **(b)** **sich** ~ **aus** to consist of; *siehe auch* **zusammengesetzt**

Zusammen-: Zusammensetzung [-zɛtsʊŋ] F -, **-en** putting together; (= *Struktur*) composition; (= *Mischung*) mixture (*aus* of); (*Gram*) compound; **das Team in dieser** ~ the team in this line-up; **zusammenstauchen** VT SEP (*inf*) to give a dressing-down (*inf*), to chew out (*US inf*); **zusammenstecken**

SEP ◼1 VT *Einzelteile* to fit together; (*mit Nadeln etc*) to pin together; **sie steckten die Köpfe zusammen** (*inf*) they put their heads together; (*um zu flüstern*) they whispered to each other ◼2 VI (*inf*) to be together; **immer ~** to be inseparable

zusammenstellen VT SEP to put together; (*nach einem Muster, System*) to arrange; (= *sammeln*) *Daten* to compile; *Liste, Fahrplan* to draw up; *Gruppe* to assemble; (*Sport*) *Mannschaft* to pick; **etw nach Gruppen** *etc* **~** to arrange sth in groups *etc*

Zusammenstellung F (a) NO PL putting together; (*nach Muster, System*) arranging; (*von Bericht, Programm, Daten*) compiling; (*von Liste, Fahrplan*) drawing up; (*von Mannschaft*) picking (b) (= *Kombination*) (*nach Muster, System*) arrangement; (*von Daten, Programm*) compilation; (= *Liste*) list; (= *Zusammensetzung*) composition; (= *Übersicht*) survey; (= *Gruppierung*) assembly; (*von Farben*) combination

Zusammenstoß M collision; (*Mil, fig*: = *Streit*) clash

zusammenstoßen SEP IRREG ◼1 VI AUX SEIN (= *zusammenprallen*) to collide; (*Mil*) (*fig*: = *sich streiten*) to clash; (= *sich treffen*) to meet; (= *gemeinsame Grenze haben*) to adjoin; **mit jdm ~** to collide with sb; (*fig*) to clash with sb; **sie stießen mit den Köpfen zusammen** they banged their heads together ◼2 VT to knock together

Zusammen-: zusammenstreichen VT SEP IRREG to cut (down) (*auf* +acc to); **zusammenstückeln** VT SEP to patch together; **zusammensuchen** VT SEP to collect (together); **sich** (*dat*) **etw ~** to find sth; **zusammentragen** VT SEP IRREG (*lit, fig*) to collect; **zusammentreffen** VI SEP IRREG AUX SEIN (*Menschen*) to meet; (*Ereignisse*) to coincide; **mit jdm ~** to meet sb; **Zusammentreffen** NT meeting; (*esp zufällig*) encounter; (*zeitlich*) coincidence; **zusammentrommeln** VT SEP (*inf*) to round up (*inf*); **zusammentun** SEP IRREG ◼1 VT (*inf*) to put together; (= *vermischen*) to mix ◼2 VR to get together; **zusammenwachsen** VI SEP IRREG AUX SEIN to grow together; (= *zuheilen*: *Wunde*) to heal (up); (*Knochen*) to knit; (*fig*) to grow close; **zusammenzählen** VT SEP to add up; **alles zusammengezählt macht es 50 Euro** that makes 50 euros altogether

zusammenziehen SEP IRREG ◼1 VT (a) *Muskel* to draw together; (= *verengen*) to narrow; *Knoten, Schlinge* to tighten; *Augenbrauen, Stirn* to knit; **~de Mittel** (*Med*) astringents (b) (*fig*) *Truppen, Polizei* to assemble ◼2 VR (*esp Biol*) (*Sci*) to contract; (= *enger werden*) to narrow; (*Gewitter, Unheil*) to be brewing ◼3 VI AUX SEIN to move in together; **mit jdm ~** to move in with sb

zusammenzucken VI SEP AUX SEIN to start

Zusatz M addition; (= *Bemerkung*) additional remark; (*zu Gesetz, Vertrag etc*) rider; (= *Beimischung*) addition

Zusatz- IN CPDS additional; **Zusatzgerät** NT attachment; (*Comput*) add-on; **Zusatzkosten** PL additional costs *pl*

zusätzlich ['tsuːzɛtslɪç] ◼1 ADJ additional ◼2 ADV in addition

Zusatz-: Zusatzmittel NT additive; **Zusatzstoff** M additive; **Zusatzzahl** F (*Lotto*) additional number, bonus number (*Brit*)

zusaufen VR SEP IRREG (*sl*: = *sich betrinken*) to get plastered (*inf*)

zuschalten SEP ◼1 VT to switch on (in addition); *Rundfunk-, Fernsehanstalt* to link up with ◼2 VR to come on; (*Rundfunk-, Fernsehanstalt*) to link into the network

zuschanzen VT SEP (*inf*) **jdm etw ~** to make sure sb gets sth

zuschauen VI SEP (*esp dial*) = **zusehen**

Zuschauer ['tsuːʃauɐ] M **-s, -**, **Zuschauerin** [-ərɪn] F **-, -nen** spectator (*auch Sport*); (*TV*) viewer; (*Theat*) member of the audience; (= *Beistehender*) onlooker; **die ~** *pl* the spectators *pl*; (*esp Ftbl auch*) the crowd *sing*; (*TV*) the viewers; (*Theat*) the audience *sing*

zuschicken VT SEP **jdm etw ~** to send sth to sb; **sich** (*dat*) **etw ~ lassen** to send for sth

zuschieben VT SEP IRREG **jdm etw ~** to push sth over to sb; (*heimlich*) to slip sb sth; (*fig*: = *zuschanzen*) to make sure sb gets sth; **jdm die Verantwortung/Schuld ~** to put the responsibility/blame on sb

Zuschlag M (a) (= *Erhöhung*) extra charge, surcharge (*esp Comm, Econ*); (*auf Briefmarke, Fahrpreis*) supplement (b) (*bei Versteigerung*) acceptance of a bid; (= *Auftragserteilung*) acceptance of a/the tender; **jdm den ~ erteilen** (*form*) *or* **geben** to knock down the lot to sb; (*nach Ausschreibung*) to award the contract to sb; **er erhielt den ~** the lot went to him; (*nach Ausschreibung*) he was awarded the contract

zuschlagen SEP IRREG ◼1 VT (a) *Tür, Fenster* to slam (shut), to bang shut; **die Tür hinter sich** (*dat*) **~** to slam the door behind one
(b) (*Sport*: = *zuspielen*) **jdm den Ball ~** to hit the ball to sb; (*Ftbl inf*) to kick the ball to sb
(c) (*bei Versteigerung*) **jdm etw ~** to knock sth down to sb; **einer Firma einen Vertrag ~** to award a contract to a firm ◼2 VI (a) (= *kräftig schlagen*) to strike (*auch fig*); (= *losschlagen*) to hit out; **schlag zu!** hit me/him/it *etc*!
(b) AUX SEIN (*Tür*) to slam (shut)
(c) (*fig inf*: = *zugreifen*) (*bei Angebot*) to go for it; (*beim Essen*) to get stuck in (*inf*); (*Polizei*) to pounce; **die EU-Bürokratie hat wieder zugeschlagen** EU bureaucracy has struck again (*inf*)

Zuschlag(s)-: Zuschlag(s)karte F (*Rail*) supplementary ticket (*for trains on which a supplement is payable*); **zuschlag(s)pflichtig** ADJ *Zug, Service* subject to a supplement

zuschließen SEP IRREG ◼1 VT to lock; *Laden* to lock up ◼2 VI to lock up

zuschnappen VI SEP (a) (= *zubeißen*) **der Hund schnappte zu** the dog snapped at me/him *etc* (b) (*fig*: *Polizei*) to pounce (c) AUX SEIN (*Schloss*) to snap shut; (*Falle*) (*lit*) to snap shut; (*fig*) to close

zuschneiden VT SEP IRREG to cut to size; (*Sew*) to cut out; **auf etw** (*acc*) **zugeschnitten sein** (*fig*) to be geared to sth; **auf jdn/etw genau zugeschnitten sein** (*lit, fig*) to be tailor-made for sb/sth

Zuschnitt M (a) NO PL (= *Zuschneiden*) cutting (b) (= *Form*) cut; (*fig*) calibre (*Brit*), caliber (*US*)

zuschreiben VT SEP IRREG (*fig*) to attribute (+*dat* to); **das hast du dir selbst zuzuschreiben** you've only got yourself to blame; **das ist nur seiner Dummheit zuzuschreiben** that can only be put down to his stupidity

Zuschrift F letter; (*auf Anzeige*) reply

zuschulden [tsuːˈʃʊldn] ADV **sich** (*dat*) **etwas ~ kommen lassen** to do something wrong

Zuschuss M subsidy; (*nicht amtlich*) contribution; (*esp regelmäßig von Eltern*) allowance; **mit einem kleinen ~ von meinen Eltern kann ich ...** if my parents give me something toward(s) it I can ...

Zuschuss-: Zuschussbetrieb M lossmaking (*Brit*) *or* losing (*US*) concern; **Zuschussgeschäft** NT lossmaking (*Brit*) *or* losing (*US*) deal; (*inf*: = *Zuschussunternehmen*) lossmaking (*Brit*) *or* losing (*US*) business

zuschütten SEP ◼1 VT to fill in; (= *hinzuschütten*) to add; (*fig*: = *verdecken*) to submerge ◼2 VR (*inf*) (*mit Alkohol*) to have a skinful (*Brit inf*), to be two sheets to the wind (*US*)

zuschwallen [ˈtsuːʃvalən] VT SEP (*sl*) to chatter (on) to

zusehen VI SEP IRREG (a) (= *beobachten, mit ansehen*) to watch; (= *unbeteiligter Zuschauer sein*) to look on; (= *etw dulden*) to sit back by (and watch); **jdm/einer Sache ~** to watch sb/sth; **bei etw ~** to watch sth; (= *etw dulden*) to sit back and watch sth; **jdm bei der Arbeit ~** to watch sb working; **er sah zu, wie ich das machte** he watched me doing it; **durch bloßes Zusehen** just by watching
(b) (= *dafür sorgen*) **~, dass ...** to see to it that ..., to make sure (that) ...; **sieh mal zu!** (*inf*) see what you can do

zusehends [ˈtsuːzeːənts] ADV visibly; (= *rasch*) rapidly

Zuseher(in) M(F) (*Aus TV*) viewer

zu sein VI IRREG AUX SEIN to be shut; (*inf*: = *betrunken, high sein*) to be stoned (*inf*)

zusenden VT SEP IRREG to send

zusetzen VI SEP **jdm ~** (= *unter Druck setzen*) to lean on sb (*inf*); *dem Gegner, Feind* to press sb hard; (= *drängen*) to pester sb; (= *schwer treffen*) to hit sb hard; (*Kälte, Krankheit etc*) to take a lot out of sb

zusichern VT SEP **jdm etw ~** to assure sb of sth

Zusicherung F assurance

zuspielen VT SEP *Ball* to pass (+*dat* to); **jdm etw ~** (*fig*) to pass sth on to sb; (*der Presse*) to leak sth to sb

zuspitzen VR SEP to be pointed; (*fig*: *Lage, Konflikt*) to intensify; **die Lage spitzt sich immer mehr zu** the situation is worsening

zusprechen SEP IRREG ◼1 VT (*Jur*) to award; *Preis, Gewinn etc* to award; *Kind* to award custody of; **das Kind wurde dem Vater zugesprochen** the father was granted custody (of the child);

jdm Mut/Trost ~ (fig) to encourage/comfort sb **2** VI **jdm (gut/besänftigend) ~** to talk or speak (nicely/gently) to sb

Zuspruch M, NO PL (= Anklang) **(großen) ~ finden** or **haben, sich großen ~s erfreuen** to be (very) popular; (Stück, Film) to meet with general acclaim; (Anwalt, Arzt) to be (very) much in demand

Zustand M state; (von Haus, Ware, Auto) (Med) condition; (= Lage) state of affairs; **in gutem/schlechtem ~** in good/poor condition; (Haus) in good/bad repair; **in angetrunkenem ~** under the influence of alcohol; **eine Frau in ihrem ~ ...** a woman in her condition ...; **Zustände bekommen** or **kriegen** (inf) to have a fit (inf); **das ist doch kein ~** that's not right; **das sind ja schöne** or **nette Zustände!** (iro) that's a fine state of affairs! (iro); **das sind ja Zustände!** (inf) it's terrible

zustande [tsuˈʃtandə] ADV **(a) ~ bringen** to manage; Arbeit to get done; Ereignis, Frieden etc to bring about; **es ~ bringen, dass jd etw tut** to (manage to) get sb to do sth **(b) ~ kommen** (= erreicht werden) to be achieved; (= geschehen) to come about; (= stattfinden) to take place; (Gewagtes, Schwieriges) to come off

Zustandekommen NT **die Chancen für das ~ eines Plans/einer Koalition** the chances of a plan materializing/of a coalition coming about; **die Ostdeutschen hatten einen wesentlichen Anteil am ~ der Wiedervereinigung** the East Germans played a significant part in bringing about reunification

zuständig [ˈtsuːʃtɛndɪç] ADJ (= verantwortlich) responsible; (= entsprechend) Amt etc appropriate; (= Kompetenz habend) competent (form, Jur); **dafür ist er ~** that's his responsibility; **der dafür ~e Beamte** the official responsible for such matters; **~ sein** (Jur) to have jurisdiction

Zuständigkeit F -, -en **(a)** (= Kompetenz) competence; (Jur) jurisdiction; (= Verantwortlichkeit) responsibility **(b)** = **Zuständigkeitsbereich**

Zuständigkeitsbereich M area of responsibility; (Jur) jurisdiction; **das fällt/fällt nicht in unseren ~** that is/isn't our responsibility; (Jur) that is within/outside our jurisdiction (Jur)

zustecken VT SEP **jdm etw ~** to slip sb sth

zustehen VI SEP IRREG **etw steht jdm zu** sb is entitled to sth; **darüber steht mir kein Urteil zu** it's not up to me to judge that; **es steht ihr nicht zu, das zu tun** it's not for her to do that

zustellen VT SEP **(a)** Brief, Paket etc to deliver; (Jur) to serve (jdm etw sb with sth) **(b)** Tür etc to block

Zusteller [ˈtsuːʃtɛlɐ] M -s, -, **Zustellerin** [-ərɪn] F -, -nen deliverer; (Jur) server; (= Briefträger) postman/-woman (Brit), mailman/-woman (US)

Zustellgebühr F delivery charge

Zustellung F delivery; (Jur) service (of a writ)

zustimmen VI SEP **(einer Sache** dat) **~** to agree (to sth); (= einwilligen) to consent (to sth); **jdm (in einem Punkt) ~** to agree with sb (on a point); **dem kann man nur ~** I/we etc quite agree with you/him etc; **er nickte ~** he nodded in agreement; **eine ~de Antwort** an affirmative answer

Zustimmung F (= Einverständnis) agreement; (= Einwilligung) consent; (= Beifall) approval; **allgemeine ~ finden** to meet with general approval; **das fand meine ~** I agreed with it completely; **mit/ohne ~** (+gen) with/without the agreement of

zustoßen SEP IRREG **1** VT Tür etc to push shut **2** VI **(a)** (mit Messer, Schwert etc) to plunge a/the knife/sword etc in; (Stier, Schlange) to strike; **stoß zu!** go on, stab him/her etc!; **der Mörder hatte (mit dem Messer) dreimal zugestoßen** the murderer had stabbed him/her etc three times **(b)** (= passieren) AUX SEIN **jdm ~** to happen to sb; **wenn mir einmal etwas zustößt ...** (euph) if anything should happen to me ...

zustürzen VI SEP AUX SEIN **auf jdn/etw ~** or **zugestürzt kommen** to rush up to sb/sth

zutage [tsuˈtaːgə] ADV **etw ~ fördern** to unearth sth (auch hum); (aus Wasser) to bring sth up; **etw ~ bringen** (fig) to bring sth to light; **(offen) ~ liegen** to be clear; **~ kommen** or **treten** (lit, fig) to come to light

Zutaten [ˈtsuːtaːtn] PL (Cook) ingredients pl

zuteilen VT SEP (jdm to sb) to allocate; Arbeitskraft, Leibwächter to assign; **etw zugeteilt bekommen** to be allocated sth; Lebensmittel to be apportioned sth

zutexten VT SEP (sl) (= viel schreiben) to write at length to; (= viel reden) to chatter (on) to

zutiefst [tsuˈtiːfst] ADV deeply; **er war ~ betrübt** he was greatly saddened

zutrauen VT SEP **jdm etw ~** Aufgabe, Tat, Sieg to think sb (is) capable of (doing) sth; **sich** (dat) **~, etw zu tun** to think one is capable of doing sth; **sich** (dat) **zu viel ~** to overrate one's own abilities; (= sich übernehmen) to take on too much; **sich** (dat) **nichts ~** to have no confidence in oneself; **den Mut/die Intelligenz (dazu) traue ich ihr nicht zu** I don't credit her with the courage/intelligence to do it; **das hätte ich ihm nie zugetraut!** I would never have thought him capable of it!; **jdm viel/wenig ~** to think/not to think a lot of sb; **ich traue ihnen viel** or **einiges/alles zu** (Negatives) I wouldn't put much/anything past them; **das ist ihm zuzutrauen!** (iro) I can well believe it (of him)!; (esp als Antwort auf Frage) I wouldn't put it past him!

zutraulich ADJ Kind trusting; Tier friendly

zutreffen VI SEP IRREG (= gelten) to apply (auf +acc, für to); (= richtig sein) to be accurate; (= wahr sein) to be true; **es trifft nicht immer zu, dass ...** it doesn't always follow that ...; **seine Beschreibung traf überhaupt nicht zu** his description was completely inaccurate; **das trifft zu** that is so

zutreffend **1** ADJ (= richtig) accurate; (= auf etw ~) applicable; **Zutreffendes bitte unterstreichen** underline where applicable **2** ADV accurately

Zutritt M, NO PL (= Einlass) entry; (= Zugang) access; **kein ~, ~ verboten** no entry

Zutun NT, NO PL assistance; **es geschah ohne mein ~** I did not have a hand in the matter

zuunterst [tsuˈʔʊntɛst] ADV right at the bottom

zuverlässig [ˈtsuːfɛɐlɛsɪç] **1** ADJ reliable; **aus ~er Quelle** from a reliable source **2** ADV funktionieren reliably; **etw ~ wissen** to know sth for sure; **seinen Pflichten ~ nachkommen** to reliably fulfil one's duties

Zuverlässigkeit F -, NO PL reliability

Zuversicht F, NO PL confidence; **in der festen ~, dass ...** confident that ...

zuversichtlich ADJ confident; **er zeigte sich ~, dass ...** he was confident that ...

Zuversichtlichkeit F -, NO PL confidence

zuviel [tsuˈfiːl] ADJ, ADV siehe viel

Zuviel [tsuˈfiːl] NT **ein ~ an etw** (dat) an excess of sth

zuvor [tsuˈvoːɐ] ADV before; (= zuerst) beforehand; **im Jahr ~** the year before; **am Tage ~** the day before

zuvorkommen VI SEP IRREG AUX SEIN +DAT to anticipate; (= verhindern) einer Gefahr, unangenehmen Fragen etc to forestall; **jdm ~** to beat sb to it; **jemand ist uns zuvorgekommen** somebody beat us to it

zuvorkommend **1** ADJ obliging (zu towards) **2** ADV obligingly

Zuwachs [ˈtsuːvaks] M **-es, Zuwächse** [-vɛksə] **(a)** NO PL (= Wachstum) growth (an +dat of) **(b)** (= Höhe, Menge des Wachstums) increase (an +dat in); **~ bekommen** (inf: ein Baby) to have an addition to the family

zuwachsen VI SEP IRREG AUX SEIN (Öffnung, Loch) to grow over; (Garten etc) (hum: Gesicht) to become overgrown; (Aussicht) to become blocked (by trees etc); (Wunde) to heal

zuwege [tsuˈveːgə] ADV **etw ~ bringen** to manage sth; (= erreichen) to achieve sth; **mit etw ~ kommen** to (be able to) cope with sth; **mit jdm ~ kommen** to get on with sb all right; **es ~ bringen, dass jd etw tut** to (manage to) get sb to do sth; **gut/schlecht ~ sein** (inf) to be in good/poor health

zuweisen VT SEP IRREG to assign (jdm etw sth to sb)

zuwenden SEP IRREG **1** VT **(a)** (lit, fig) to turn (+dat to, towards); (fig: = völlig widmen) to devote (+dat to); **jdm das Gesicht ~** to turn to face sb; **jdm seine ganze Liebe ~** to bestow all one's affections on sb **(b)** jdm Geld etc **~** to give sb money etc **2** VR **sich jdm/einer Sache ~** to turn to (face) sb/sth; (fig) to turn to sb/sth; (= sich widmen, liebevoll) to devote oneself to sb/sth

Zuwendung F **(a)** (fig: = das Sichzuwenden) turning (zu to); (= Liebe) care **(b)** (= Geldsumme) sum (of money); (= Beitrag) financial contribution; (= Schenkung) donation

zuwenig [tsu've:nɪç] ADJ, ADV siehe **wenig**

Zuwenig [tsu've:nɪç] NT **-s**, NO PL **ein ~ an etw** a lack of sth

zuwerfen VT SEP IRREG **(a)** (= schließen) Tür to slam (shut) **(b)** (= hinwerfen) jdm etw ~ to throw sth to sb; jdm einen Blick ~ to cast a glance at sb; jdm einen bösen or giftigen Blick ~ to give sb the evil eye; jdm Blicke ~ to make eyes at sb; jdm eine Kusshand ~ to blow sb a kiss

zuwider [tsu'vi:dɐ] ADV er/das ist mir ~ I find him/that unpleasant; (stärker) I detest or loathe him/that; (= Ekel erregend) I find him/that revolting

zuwinken VI SEP jdm ~ to wave to sb; (= Zeichen geben) to signal to sb

zuzahlen SEP **1** VT zehn Euro ~ to pay another ten euros **2** VI to pay extra

zuziehen SEP IRREG **1** VT **(a)** Vorhang to draw; Tür to pull shut; Knoten, Schlinge to pull tight; Arzt etc to call in; **einen weiteren Fachmann ~** to get a second opinion **(b)** sich (dat) jds Zorn/Hass etc ~ to incur sb's anger/hatred etc; **sich** (dat) **eine Krankheit ~** (form) to contract an illness; **sich** (dat) **eine Verletzung ~** (form) to sustain an injury **2** VR (Schlinge etc) to tighten; **es hat sich zugezogen** (Wetter) it has clouded over

Zuzug M (= Zustrom) influx; (von Familie etc) arrival (nach in), move (nach to)

zuzüglich [ˈtsuːtsyːklɪç] PREP +GEN plus

zuzwinkern VI SEP jdm ~ to wink at sb

Zvieri [ˈtsfiːri] M or NT **-s**, NO PL (Sw) afternoon snack

ZVS [tsetfauˈlɛs] F - ABBR von Zentralstelle für die Vergabe von Studienplätzen ≈ UCAS (Brit), ≈ SAT center (US)

zwang PRET von **zwingen**

Zwang [tsvaŋ] M **-(e)s, ¨e** [ˈtsvɛŋə] (= Notwendigkeit) compulsion; (= Gewalt) force; (= Verpflichtung) obligation; (= hemmender ~) constraint; **das ist ~** that is compulsory; **gesellschaftliche Zwänge** social constraints; **sich** (dat) **~ antun** to force oneself to be something one isn't; (= sich zurückhalten) to restrain oneself (etw nicht zu tun from doing sth); **tu dir keinen ~ an** don't feel you have to be polite; (iro) don't force yourself; **seinen Gefühlen ~ antun** to force oneself to ignore one's true feelings; **sie tut ihren Gefühlen keinen ~ an** she doesn't hide her feelings

zwängen [ˈtsvɛŋən] VT to cram; mehrere Sachen (in Koffer etc) to cram; **sich in/durch etw** (acc) **~** to squeeze into/through sth

Zwang-: **zwanghaft** (Psych) **1** ADJ compulsive **2** ADV compulsively; **zwanglos 1** ADJ (= ohne Förmlichkeit) informal; (= locker, unbekümmert) casual; (= frei) free **2** ADV informally; **da geht es recht ~ zu** things are very informal there; **Zwanglosigkeit** F -, NO PL informality; (= Lockerheit) casualness

Zwangs-: **Zwangsabgabe** F (Econ) compulsory levy; **Zwangsarbeit** F hard labour (Brit) or labor (US); (von Kriegsgefangenen) forced labo(u)r; **Zwangsarbeiter(in)** M(F) forced labourer (Brit) or laborer (US); **zwangsernähren** ptp zwangsernährt VT INSEP to force-feed; **Zwangsernährung** F force-feeding; **Zwangsjacke** F (lit, fig) straitjacket; **Zwangslage** F predicament; **zwangsläufig 1** ADJ inevitable **2** ADV inevitably; **das musste ja ~ so kommen** that had to happen; **Zwangsläufigkeit** [-lɔyfɪçkait] F -, **-en** inevitability; **Zwangspause** F (beruflich) **eine ~ machen** or **einlegen müssen** to have to stop work temporarily; **Zwangssparen** NT forced saving; **Zwangsvergleich** M (bei Konkurs) compulsory composition or settlement; **zwangsverpflichtet** [-fɛɐpflɪçtət] ADJ drafted (zu into); **Zwangsversteigerung** F compulsory auction; **Zwangsvorstellung** F (Psych) obsession; **zwangsweise 1** ADV compulsorily **2** ADJ compulsory

zwanzig [ˈtsvantsɪç] NUM twenty; siehe auch **vierzig**

Zwanzig [ˈtsvantsɪç] F -, **-en** [-gn] twenty; siehe auch **Vier**

Zwanziger [ˈtsvantsɪgɐ] M **-s, -** (inf: = Geldschein) twenty-euro etc note (Brit) or bill (US)

Zwanzigeuroschein M twenty-euro note (Brit) or bill (US)

zwanzigste(r, s) [ˈtsvantsɪçstə] ADJ twentieth

zwar [tsvaːɐ] ADV **(a)** (= wohl) er war ~ Zeuge des Unfalls, aber ... it's true he witnessed the accident but ...; **sie ist ~ sehr schön/krank, aber ...** it's true she's very beautiful/ill but ...;

ich weiß ~, dass es schädlich ist, aber ... I do know it's harmful but ... **(b)** (erklärend, betont) **und ~** in fact, actually; **er hat mir das anders erklärt, und ~ so ...** he explained it differently to me(, like this) ...; **und ~ einschließlich ...** inclusive of ...; **die Schulen, und ~ vor allem die Grundschulen** the schools, (and more) especially the primary schools; **das hat er gemacht, und ~ so gründlich, dass ...** he did it and (he did it) so thoroughly that ...; **ich werde ihm schreiben, und ~ noch heute** I'll write to him and I'll do it today

Zweck [tsvɛk] M **-(e)s, -e (a)** (= Ziel, Verwendung) purpose; **einem ~ dienen** to serve a purpose; **einem guten ~ dienen** to be for a good cause; **Spenden für wohltätige ~e** donations to charity; **seinen ~ erfüllen** to serve its/one's purpose **(b)** (= Sinn) point; **was soll das für einen ~ haben?** what's the point of that?; **das hat keinen ~** it's pointless; **das ist ja der ~ der Übung** that's what it's all about (inf) **(c)** (= Absicht) aim; **zum ~ der Völkerverständigung** (in order) to promote understanding between nations; **zu welchem ~?** for what purpose?; **zu diesem ~** to this end; **einen ~ verfolgen** to have a specific aim

Zweck-: **Zweckbau** M, pl **-bauten** functional building; **zweckdienlich** ADJ (= zweckentsprechend) appropriate; (= nützlich) useful; **~e Hinweise** (any) relevant information; **es wäre ~, das zu tun** it would be expedient to do that

Zwecke [ˈtsvɛkə] F **-, -n** tack; (= Schuhzwecke) nail; (= Reißzwecke) drawing pin (Brit), thumbtack (US)

Zweck-: **zweckgebunden** ADJ Geldmittel, Steuern etc for a specific purpose; **Zweckgemeinschaft** F partnership of convenience; **zwecklos** ADJ pointless; Versuch, Anstrengungen futile; **Zwecklosigkeit** F -, NO PL pointlessness; (von Versuch, Anstrengungen) futility; **zweckmäßig** ADJ (= nützlich) useful; (= ratsam) advisable; (= zweckentsprechend) Kleidung etc suitable; **Zweckmäßigkeit** [ˈtsvɛkmɛːsɪçkait] F -, NO PL (= Nützlichkeit) usefulness; (von Kleidung etc) suitability; **Zweckoptimismus** M calculated optimism; **Zweckpessimismus** M calculated pessimism

zwecks [tsvɛks] PREP +GEN (form) for the purpose of; **~ Wiederverwendung** for re-use

zwei [tsvai] NUM two; **wir ~ (beiden** (inf)) the two of us; **dazu gehören ~** (inf) it takes two; **~ Gesichter haben** (fig) to be two-faced; siehe auch **vier**

Zwei [tsvai] F **-, -en** two; siehe auch **Vier**

Zwei- IN CPDS siehe auch **Vier-**: **Zweibeiner** [-bainɐ] M **-s, -**, **Zweibeinerin** [-ərɪn] F **-, -nen** (hum inf) human being; **die ~** human beings; **zweibeinig** ADJ two-legged; **Zweibettzimmer** NT twin room; **zweideutig** [-dɔytɪç] **1** ADJ ambiguous; (= schlüpfrig) suggestive; **~e Reden führen** to use a lot of doubles entendres (esp Brit) **2** ADV ambiguously; **Zweideutigkeit** F **-, -en (a)** NO PL ambiguity; (= Schlüpfrigkeit) suggestiveness **(b)** (= Bemerkung) ambiguous remark; (= Witz) risqué joke; **zweidimensional 1** ADJ two-dimensional **2** ADV two-dimensionally; **Zweidrittelmehrheit** F (Parl) two-thirds majority; **zweieiig** [-laiç] ADJ Zwillinge nonidentical

Zweier-: **Zweierbeziehung** F relationship; **zweierlei** [ˈtsvaiɐˈlai] ADJ INV **(a)** Brot, Käse, Wein two kinds of; Möglichkeiten, Größen, Fälle two different; **auf ~ Art** in two different ways; **~ Handschuhe/Strümpfe** etc odd gloves/socks etc; **~ Meinung sein** to be of (two) different opinions **(b)** (substantivisch) two different things; (= zwei Sorten) two different kinds

zweifach [ˈtsvaifax] **1** ADJ double; (= zweimal) twice; **in ~er Ausfertigung** in duplicate **2** ADV **diesen Satz Briefmarken besitze ich ~** I have two sets of these stamps; **eine Urkunde ~ ausfertigen** to make up a document in duplicate; **~ gesichert** doubly secure; **ein Tuch ~ legen** to lay a cloth double

Zwei-: **Zweifamilienhaus** NT two-family house; **zweifarbig 1** ADJ two-colour (Brit), two-color (US) **2** ADV etw **~ anstreichen** to paint sth in two (different) colours (Brit) or colors (US); **es ist ~ gemustert** it has a two-colour (Brit) or two-color (US) pattern

Zweifel [ˈtsvaifl] M **-s, -** doubt; **außer ~** beyond doubt; **im ~** in doubt; **ohne ~** without doubt; **außer ~ stehen** to be beyond doubt; **über allen ~ erhaben** beyond all (shadow of a) doubt; **es besteht kein ~, dass ...** there is no doubt that ...; **~ an etw** (dat) **haben** to have one's doubts about sth; **etw in ~ ziehen**

to call sth into question; **ich bin mir im ~, ob ich das tun soll** I'm in two minds (*Brit*) *or* double-minded (*US*) *or* whether I should do that

zweifelhaft ADJ doubtful

zweifellos ADV undoubtedly

zweifeln ['tsvaifln] VI to doubt; **an etw/jdm ~** to doubt sth/sb; **daran ist nicht zu ~** there's no doubt about it; **ich zweifle noch, wie ich mich entscheiden soll** I am still in two minds (*esp Brit*) *or* double-minded (*US*) about it

Zweifels-: Zweifelsfall M borderline case; **im ~** when in doubt; (*inf*: = *gegebenenfalls*) if need be; **zweifelsfrei** 🚺 ADJ unequivocal 🚻 ADV beyond (all) doubt; **zweifelsohne** [tsvaifls'lo:nə] ADV undoubtedly

Zweig [tsvaik] M **-(e)s, -e** [-gə] (a) (= *Ast*) branch; (*dünner, kleiner*) twig (b) (*fig*) (*von Wissenschaft, Familie etc*) (*Rail*) branch; (= *Abteilung*) department

Zweiggeschäft NT branch

zweigleisig 🚺 ADJ double-tracked, double-track *attr* 🚻 ADV **~ fahren** (*lit*) to be double-tracked; (*fig inf*) to have two strings to one's bow; **~ argumentieren** to argue along two different lines

Zweig-: Zweigniederlassung F subsidiary; **Zweigstelle** F branch (office)

zweihändig 🚺 ADJ with two hands, two-handed; (*Mus*) for two hands 🚻 ADV (*Mus*) *spielen* two-handed; **die Rückhand ~ schlagen** (*Sport*) to use two hands for one's backhand

zweihundert ['tsvai'hʊndɐt] NUM two hundred

zweijährig ADJ (a) ATTR *Kind etc* two-year-old *attr*, two years old; *Dauer* two-year *attr*, of two years; **mit ~er Verspätung** two years late (b) (*Bot*) *Pflanze* biennial

Zwei-: Zweikammersystem [tsvai'kamɐ-] NT (*Pol*) two-chamber system; **Zweikampf** M single combat; (= *Duell*) duel; **jdn zum ~ (heraus)fordern** to challenge sb to a duel

zweimal ['tsvaima:l] ADV twice; **~ jährlich** *or* **im Jahr/täglich** *or* **am Tag** twice yearly *or* a year/twice daily *or* a day; **sich** (*dat*) **etw ~ überlegen** to think twice about sth; **das lasse ich mir nicht ~ sagen** I don't have to be told twice; **das mache ich bestimmt nicht ~** I certainly won't do that/it again

zweimalig ['tsvaima:lɪç] ADJ ATTR twice repeated; *Weltmeister etc* two-times *attr*; **nach ~er Aufforderung** after being told twice

Zwei-: Zweimaster [-mastɐ] M **-s, -** two-master; **zweimonatig** ADJ ATTR (a) *Dauer* two-month *attr*, of two months (b) *Säugling etc* two-month-old *attr*, two months old; **zweimonatlich** ADJ, ADV bimonthly (*esp Comm, Admin*); **zweimotorig** ADJ twin-engined; **Zweiparteiensystem** [tsvaipar'taian-] NT two-party system; **zweipolig** [-po:lɪç] ADJ (*Elec*) bipolar; **zweiräderig, zweirädrig** ADJ two-wheeled; **Zweireiher** [-raiɐ] M **-s, -** double-breasted suit *etc*; **zweireihig** 🚺 ADJ double-row *attr*, in two rows; *Anzug* double-breasted 🚻 ADV in two rows; **Zweisamkeit** ['tsvaiza:mkait] F **-, -en** (*literhum*) togetherness; **zweischneidig** ADJ double-edged (*auch fig*); **das ist ein ~es Schwert** (*fig*) it cuts both ways; **zweiseitig** [-zaitɪç] 🚺 ADJ *Brief, Erklärung etc* two-page *attr*; *Vertrag etc* bilateral 🚻 ADV on two sides; **zweisilbig** ADJ disyllabic; **Zweisitzer** M (*Aut, Aviat*) two-seater; **zweispaltig** [-ʃpaltɪç] 🚺 ADJ double-columned 🚻 ADV **der Artikel ist ~ (abgedruckt)** the article is printed in two columns; **zweisprachig** 🚺 ADJ bilingual; *Dokument* in two languages 🚻 ADV in two languages; **~ aufwachsen** to grow up bilingual; **Zweisprachigkeit** F **-, NO PL** bilingualism; **zweispurig** [-ʃpu:rɪç] ADJ double-tracked, double-track *attr*; *Autobahn* two-laned, two-lane *attr*; **zweistellig** 🚺 ADJ *Zahl* two-digit *attr*, with two digits; **~er Dezimalbruch** number with two decimal places; **~e Millionenbeträge** sums over ten million 🚻 ADV *steigen, zunehmen* by more than ten per cent (*Brit*) *or* percent (*US*); **~ gewinnen** to win by more than ten; **der Umsatz ist ~ gewachsen** the increase in turnover has reached double figures; **zweistöckig** 🚺 ADJ two-storey *attr* (*Brit*), two-story *attr* (*US*), two-storeyed (*Brit*), two-storied (*US*); **ein ~es Bett** bunk beds *pl*; *siehe auch* **doppelstöckig** 🚻 ADV **~ bauen** to build buildings with two storeys (*Brit*) *or* stories (*US*); **zweistrahlig** ADJ *Flugzeug* twin-jet *attr*; **zweistündig** ADJ two-hour *attr*, of two hours; **zweistündlich** ADJ, ADV every two hours

zweit [tsvait] ADV **zu ~** (= *in Paaren*) in twos; **wir gingen zu ~ spazieren** the two of us went for a walk; **ich gehe lieber zu ~**

auf Partys I prefer going to parties with somebody; **das Leben zu ~** living with someone; *siehe auch* **vier**

Zwei-: zweitägig ADJ two-day *attr*, of two days; **Zweitakter** [-taktɐ] M **-s, -** (*inf*) two-stroke (*inf*); **Zweitaktmotor** M two-stroke engine

zweitälteste(r, s) ['tsvait'ɛltəstə] ADJ second oldest; **unser Zweitältester** our second (child *or* son)

zweitausend ['tsvai'tauznt] NUM two thousand; **das Jahr ~** the year two thousand

Zweit-: Zweitausfertigung F (*form*) duplicate; **Zweitauto** NT second car; **Zweitbesetzung** F (*Theat*) understudy; **zweitbeste(r, s)** ['tsvait'bɛstə] ADJ second best

Zwei-: zweiteilen VT SEP, INFIN, PTP ONLY to divide (into two); **zweiteilig** ADJ *Roman* two-part *attr*, in two parts; *Plan* two-stage; *Kleidungsstück* two-piece; **Zweiteilung** F division; (*Math: von Winkel*) bisection

zweitens ['tsvaitns] ADV secondly

Zweite(r) [tsvaitə] MF DECL AS ADJ second; (*Sport etc*) runner-up; **wie kein ~r** like nobody else

zweite(r, s) ['tsvaitə] ADJ second; **~ Klasse** (*Rail etc*) second class; **~r Klasse fahren** to travel second (class); **jeden ~n Tag** every other day; **jeder Zweite** (*litinf*: = *sehr viele*) every other; **zum Zweiten** secondly; **ein ~r Caruso** another Caruso; **in ~r Linie** secondly; *siehe auch* **vierte(r, s)**

Zweit-: zweitgrößte(r, s) ['tsvait'grø:stə] ADJ second largest; *Zimmer auch, Mensch* second biggest; **zweithöchste(r, s)** ['tsvait'hø:çstə] ADJ second highest; (*fig: im Rang*) second most senior; **zweitklassig** ADJ (*fig*) second-class; **zweitletzte(r, s)** ['tsvait'lɛtstə] ADJ last but one *attr, pred*; **zweitrangig** [-ranɪç] ADJ = **zweitklassig**; **Zweitschlüssel** M duplicate key; **Zweitschrift** F copy; **Zweitstimme** F second vote; *siehe auch* **Erststimme**

Zweitürer [-ty:rɐ] M (*Aut*) **-s, -** two-door

zweitürig ADJ (*Aut*) two-door

Zweiunddreißigstel ['tsvaiʊnt'draisçstl] NT, **Zweiunddreißigstelnote** F (*Mus*) demisemiquaver (*Brit*), thirty-second note (*US*)

Zwei-: zweiwöchig [-vœçɪç] ADJ two-week *attr*, of two weeks; **zweizeilig** 🚺 ADJ two-line *attr*; (*Typ*) *Abstand* double-spaced 🚻 ADV **~ schreiben** to double-space; **Zweizimmerwohnung** ['tsvai'tsɪmɐ-] F two-room(ed) apartment; **Zweizylinder** M two-cylinder; **Zweizylindermotor** M two-cylinder engine; **zweizylindrig** ADJ two-cylinder *attr*

Zwerchfell ['tsvɛrçfɛl] NT (*Anat*) diaphragm

Zwerg [tsvɛrk] M **-(e)s, -e** [-gə], **Zwergin** ['tsvɛrgɪn] F **-, -nen** dwarf; (= *Gartenzwerg*) gnome; (*fig*: = *Knirps*) midget; (*pej*: = *unbedeutender Mensch*) squirt (*inf*)

Zwerg-: Zwergpudel M toy poodle; **Zwergstaat** M miniature state; **Zwergstamm** M, **Zwergvolk** NT pygmy tribe; **Zwergwuchs** M dwarfism; **zwergwüchsig** [-vy:ksɪç] ADJ ATTR *Mensch* dwarfish; *Baum* dwarf *attr*

Zwetschge ['tsvɛtʃgə] F **-, -n**, **Zwetschke** ['tsvɛtʃkə] (*Aus*) F **-, -n** plum

Zwickmühle ['tsvɪk-] F (*beim Mühlespiel*) double mill; **in der ~ sitzen** (*fig*) to be in a catch-22 situation (*inf*)

Zwieback ['tsvi:bak] M **-(e)s, -e** *or* **~e** [-beka] rusk

Zwiebel ['tsvi:bl] F **-, -n** onion; (= *Blumenzwiebel*) bulb

Zwiebel-: zwiebelförmig ADJ onion-shaped; **Zwiebelkuchen** M onion tart; **Zwiebelkuppel** F (*Archit*) imperial roof; **Zwiebelring** M onion ring; **Zwiebelschale** F onion skin; **Zwiebelsuppe** F onion soup; **Zwiebelturm** M onion dome

Zwie-: Zwielicht NT, NO PL twilight; (*abends auch*) dusk; (*morgens*) half-light; **ins ~ geraten sein** (*fig*) to appear in an unfavourable (*Brit*) *or* unfavorable (*US*) light; **zwielichtig** ['tsvi:lɪçtɪç] ADJ (*fig*) shady; **zwiespältig** ['tsvi:ʃpɛltɪç] ADJ *Gefühle* mixed; **mein Eindruck war ~** my impressions were very mixed; **ein ~er Mensch** a man/woman of contradictions; **Zwiespältigkeit** F (*von Gefühlen*) conflicting nature; (*in jds Verhalten*) contradiction; **Zwietracht** F, NO PL discord

Zwilling ['tsvɪlɪŋ] M **-s, -e** twin; **die ~e** (*Astrol, Astron*) Gemini; **~ sein** (*Astrol*) to be (a) Gemini

Zwillings-: Zwillingsbruder M twin brother; **Zwillingsgeburt** F twin birth; **Zwillingspaar** NT twins *pl*; **Zwillingsschwester** F twin sister

Zwinge ['tsvɪŋə] F **-, -n** (*Tech*) (screw) clamp

zwingen ['tsvɪŋən] *pret* **zwang** [tsvaŋ], *ptp* **gezwungen** [gə'tsvʊŋən] 🚺 VT (= *nötigen*) to force; **jdn ~, etw zu tun** to force

sb to do sth; **jdn zu etw ~** to force sb to do sth; **ich lasse mich nicht (dazu) ~** I won't be forced (to do it *or* into it); **jdn zum Handeln ~** to force sb into action; **jdn zum Gehorsam ~** to force sb to obey; **jdn zur Prostitution ~** to force sb into prostitution; **die Regierung wurde zum Rücktritt gezwungen** the government was forced to step down; **man kann niemanden zu seinem Glück ~** you can't force people; *siehe auch* **gezwungen**
⊞ VR to force oneself

zwingend ⊞ ADJ *Notwendigkeit* urgent; (= *logisch notwendig*) necessary; *Schluss, Beweis, Argumente* conclusive; *Argument* cogent; *Gründe* compelling; **dass B aus A resultiert, ist nicht ~** it isn't necessarily the case that B results from A **⊞** ADV **etwas ~ darlegen** to present sth conclusively; **etw ist ~ vorgeschrieben** sth is mandatory; **daraus folgert ~** the logical conclusion is

Zwinger ['tsvɪŋɐ] M **-s, -** (= *Käfig*) cage; (= *Bärenzwinger*) bear pit; (= *Hundezwinger*) kennels *pl*; (*von Burg*) (outer) ward

zwinkern ['tsvɪŋkɐn] VI to blink; (*um jdm etw zu bedeuten*) to wink; (*lustig*) to twinkle; **mit den Augen ~** to blink (one's eyes); to wink; to twinkle

Zwirn [tsvɪrn] M **-s, -e** (strong) thread

zwischen ['tsvɪʃn] PREP +DAT or (*mit Bewegungsverben*) +ACC between; (*von mehrere auch*) among; **mitten ~** right in the middle of; **die Kirche stand ~ Bäumen** the church stood among(st) trees

Zwischen-: **Zwischenablage** F (*Comput*) clipboard; **Zwischenaufenthalt** M stopover; **Zwischenbemerkung** F interjection; (= *Unterbrechung*) interruption; **wenn Sie mir eine kurze ~ erlauben** if I may just interrupt; **Zwischenbericht** M interim report; **Zwischenbescheid** M provisional notification *no indef art*; **Zwischenbilanz** F (*Comm*) interim balance; (*fig*) provisional appraisal; **Zwischending** NT cross (between the two); **was er schreibt, ist ein ~ zwischen Lyrik und Prosa** his writing is a cross between poetry and prose; **Zwischendividende** F interim dividend; **zwischendrin** ['tsvɪʃn'drɪn] ADV (*dial*) **(a)** = **zwischendurch (b)** = **dazwischen**; **zwischendurch** ['tsvɪʃn'dʊrç] ADV **(a)** (*zeitlich*) in between times; (= *inzwischen*) (in the) meantime; (= *nebenbei*) on the side; **das mache ich so ~** I'll do that on the side; **Schokolade für ~** chocolate for between meals **(b)** (*örtlich*) in between; **Zwischenergebnis** NT interim result; (*Sport*) latest score; **Zwischenfall** M incident; **ohne ~** without incident; **es kam zu schweren Zwischenfällen** there were clashes; **Zwischenfrage** F question; **Zwischenhandel** M intermediate trade; **Zwischenhändler(in)** M(F) middleman; **Zwischenkonto** NT suspense account; **Zwischenlager** NT temporary store; **zwischenlagern** VT INSEP INF AND PTP ONLY to store (temporarily); **Zwischenlagerung** F temporary storage; **zwischenlanden** VI SEP AUX SEIN (*Aviat*) to stop over; **Zwischenlandung** F (*Aviat*) stopover; **ohne ~** without a stopover; **zwischenmenschlich** ADJ ATTR interpersonal; **~e Beziehungen** interpersonal relations; **Zwischenprüfung** F intermediate examination; **Zwischenraum** M gap; (= *Wort-, Zeilenabstand*) space; (*zeitlich*) interval; **ein ~ von 5 m, 5 m ~** a gap/space of 5m; **Zwischenruf** M interruption; **~e heckling; einen Redner durch ~e stören** to heckle a speaker; **Zwischensaison** F low season; **Zwischenspeicher** M (*Comput*) cache (memory); **zwischenspeichern** VT SEP (*Comput*) to store in a/the cache (memory); **zwischenstaatlich** ADJ ATTR

international; (*zwischen Bundesstaaten*) interstate; **Zwischenstadium** NT intermediate stage; **Zwischenstation** F (intermediate) stop; **in London machten wir ~** we stopped off in London; **Zwischenstecker** M (*Elec*) adapter (plug); **Zwischenstufe** F (*fig*) intermediate stage; **Zwischensumme** F subtotal; **Zwischenwand** F dividing wall; (= *Stellwand*) partition; **Zwischenwirt** M (*Biol*) intermediate host; **Zwischenzeit** F **(a)** (= *Zeitraum*) interval; **in der ~** (in the) meantime **(b)** (*Sport*) intermediate time; **Zwischenzeugnis** NT (*Sch*) end of term report

Zwist [tsvɪst] M **-es,** (*rare*) **-e** (*geh*) discord; (= *Fehde, Streit*) dispute; **den alten ~ begraben** to bury the hatchet

Zwistigkeit ['tsvɪstɪçkait] F **-, -en** USU PL dispute

zwitschern ['tsvɪtʃɐn] VTI to twitter; (*Lerche*) to warble; **einen ~** (*inf*) to have a drink

Zwitter ['tsvɪtɐ] M **-s, -** hermaphrodite; (*fig*) cross (*aus* between)

zwölf [tsvœlf] NUM twelve; **~ Uhr mittags/nachts** (12 o'clock) midday/midnight; **fünf Minuten vor ~** (*fig*) at the eleventh hour; *siehe auch* **vier**

Zwölf-: **zwölffach** ['tsvœlffax] ADJ, ADV twelve-fold; *siehe auch* **vierfach**; **Zwölffingerdarm** [tsvœlf'fɪŋɐ-] M duodenum; **ein Geschwür am ~** a duodenal ulcer

Zwölftel ['tsvœlftl] NT **-s, -** twelfth; *siehe auch* **Viertel**[1]

zwölftens ['tsvœlftns] ADV twelfth(ly)

zwölfte(r, s) ['tsvœlftə] ADJ twelfth; *siehe auch* **vierte(r, s)**

Zwölfton-: **Zwölftonlehre** F twelve-tone system; **Zwölftonmusik** F twelve-tone music

Zyankali [tsyaːnˈkaːli] NT **-s,** NO PL (*Chem*) potassium cyanide

zyklisch ['tsyːklɪʃ] **⊞** ADJ cyclic(al) **⊞** ADV cyclically

Zyklon [tsyˈkloːn] M **-s, -e** cyclone

Zyklus ['tsyːklʊs] M **-, Zyklen** [-lən] cycle (*auch Physiol*)

Zykluszeit ['tsyːklʊs-] F (*Comput*) cycle time

Zylinder [tsiˈlɪndɐ, tsy-] M **-s, - (a)** (*Math, Tech*) cylinder **(b)** (= *Hut*) top hat

Zylinder-: **Zylinderblock** M, *pl* **-blöcke** (*Aut*) engine block; **zylinderförmig** ADJ = **zylindrisch**; **Zylinderkopf** M (*Aut*) cylinder head; **Zylinderkopfdichtung** F cylinder head gasket

-zylindrig [tsilɪndrɪç, tsy-] ADJ SUF -cylinder; **zweizylindrig** two-cylinder *attr*

zylindrisch [tsiˈlɪndrɪʃ, tsy-] **⊞** ADJ cylindrical **⊞** ADV cylindrically

Zyniker ['tsyːnikɐ] M **-s, -**, **Zynikerin** [-ərɪn] F **-, -nen** cynic

zynisch ['tsyːnɪʃ] **⊞** ADJ cynical **⊞** ADV cynically

Zynismus [tsyˈnɪsmʊs] M **-, Zynismen** [-mən] cynicism

Zypern ['tsyːpɐn] NT **-s** Cyprus

Zypresse [tsyˈprɛsə] F **-, -n** (*Bot*) cypress

Zyprier ['tsyːpriɐ] M **-s, -**, **Zyprierin** [-iərɪn] F **-, -nen** (*rare*), **Zypriot** [tsypriˈoːt] M **-en, -en**, **Zypriotin** [-ˈoːtɪn] F **-, -nen** Cypriot

zypriotisch [tsypriˈoːtɪʃ], **zyprisch** ['tsyːprɪʃ] ADJ Cypriot

Zyste ['tsʏstə] F **-, -n** cyst

Zytoplasma [tsytoˈplasma] NT (*Biol*) cytoplasm

Zytostatikum [tsytoˈstaːtikʊm] NT **-s, Zytostatika** [-ka] cytostatic drug

zz(t) ABBR *von* **zurzeit**

GERMAN IN ACTION
ENGLISCH AKTIV

contributors
Christine Bahr
Elspeth Jane Anderson

editor
Joyce Littlejohn

EINLEITUNG

In diesem Teil finden Sie alles, was Sie für gründliche Kenntnisse des Englischen benötigen.

Die Satzbausteine bieten Ihnen hunderte von Beispielsätzen, die Ihnen bei der fließenden und idiomatischen Verständigung auf Englisch behilflich sein werden.

Die Korrespondenzseiten zeigen authentische Beispiele für Privat– und Geschäftsbriefe und umfassen eine Vielzahl von Kommunikationssituationen – von der Hochzeitseinladung bis zur Bewerbung, von der Hotelzimmerbuchung bis hin zum Beschwerdebrief. Bitte beachten Sie, dass die englischen und deutschen Briefe keine direkten Übersetzungen sind. Vielmehr wurden Entsprechungen von typischen Wörtern und Wendungen, die Sie zum Verständnis und zum Verfassen von Briefen und Ankündigungen benötigen werden, grafisch durch Rasterung hervorgehoben. In einem separaten Abschnitt finden Sie alle Ausdrücke, die Ihnen bei verschiedenen Telefongesprächen von Nutzen sein werden. Das Senden und Empfangen von E-Mails wird ebenfalls behandelt.

Das Collins Handwörterbuch Englisch ist somit mehr als nur ein Wörterbuch – es ist ein unersetzliches Nachschlagewerk für jeden, der sich intensiv mit der englischen Sprache beschäftigt. Wir hoffen, dass Ihnen dieses Buch viel Freude bereiten wird.

INTRODUCTION

In this supplement you will find all you need to build a solid foundation for your knowledge of German.

The Sentence Builder section gives you hundreds of example phrases to show you how to communicate in fluent, natural German.

The section on correspondence provides practical models of personal and business letters. These cover everything from accepting a wedding invitation to applying for a job, from making a hotel booking to writing a letter of complaint. You should note that the German and English letters are not direct translations of each other. What we have done is highlight typical words and phrases you would need to write or understand letters and announcements. The shaded areas on the English letters correspond to the shaded areas in German and vice versa. Separate sections cover all the expressions you might need to make different types of phone calls and send and receive emails. The Collins German Concise Dictionary is more than just a dictionary – it is an essential reference work for any serious student of German. We hope you will enjoy using it.

INHALT

CONTENTS

1 VORLIEBEN UND ABNEIGUNGEN/ LIKES, DISLIKES AND PREFERENCES

1.1 Vorlieben erfragen

Do you like chips?
Do you like cooking?
Would you like to go to Crete?
What do you like best about him?
Do you prefer living in the town or in the country?
Which do you prefer: pop or classical music?
Which of the two proposed options **do you prefer?**

Asking what someone likes

Mögen Sie Pommes frites?
Kochen Sie **gerne?**
Würden Sie gerne nach Kreta fahren?
Was gefällt Ihnen an ihm **am besten?**
Wohnen Sie **lieber** in der Stadt oder auf dem Lande?
Was mögen Sie lieber: Pop oder klassische Musik?
Welcher der beiden Vorschläge **ist Ihnen lieber?**

1.2 Vorlieben ausdrücken

I like cakes
I like things to be tidy
I liked the film
I love going to discos
I don't mind being alone
I enjoyed the trip **very much**
I really appreciate it when people keep their promises
There's nothing I like better than an evening out with my friends
You can't beat candlelight at night

Saying what you like

Ich esse **gern** Kuchen
Ich habe es gern, wenn alles ordentlich ist
Der Film **hat mir gut gefallen**
Ich gehe **sehr gerne** in die Disko
Es macht mir nichts aus, allein zu sein
Der Ausflug **hat mir sehr gefallen**
Ich schätze es sehr, wenn Leute ihre Versprechen halten
Nichts mag ich lieber, als abends mit meinen Freunden auszugehen
Es **geht doch nichts über** Kerzenlicht bei Nacht

1.3 Abneigungen ausdrücken

I don't like fish
I'm not very keen on gardening
I'm not very keen on action films
I loathe spiders
I hate beetroot
I can't stand being lied to

I don't like his attitude **at all**
What I hate most is waiting for buses in the rain

I'm not particularly keen on the idea

Saying what you dislike

Ich mag keinen Fisch
Ich arbeite **nicht gern** im Garten
Ich mag keine Actionfilme
Ich hasse Spinnen
Ich kann Rote Bete **absolut nicht ausstehen**
Ich kann es nicht leiden, wenn man mich anlügt
Seine Einstellung **gefällt mir überhaupt nicht**
Am meisten hasse ich es, im Regen auf den Bus warten zu müssen
Ich kann nicht sagen, dass mir diese Idee **besonders gefällt**

1.4 Ausdrücken, was man bevorzugt

My favourite band is Oasis
What I like best about her **is** her charm
I would rather live in Bern
I'd rather not talk about it just now
I'd prefer you to leave now
I prefer red wine **to** white wine
I like the blue dress **better than** the red one
2 pm **would suit me better**

Saying what you prefer

Meine Lieblingsgruppe ist Oasis
Was mir an ihr **am besten gefällt** ist ihr Charme
Ich würde lieber in Bern wohnen
Ich würde jetzt **lieber nicht** darüber sprechen
Es wäre mir lieber, wenn Sie jetzt gingen
Ich mag Rotwein **lieber als** Weißwein
Das blaue Kleid **gefällt mir besser als** das rote
14 Uhr **würde mir besser passen**

1.5 Gleichgültigkeit ausdrücken

That **doesn't interest me in the slightest**
I have no particular **preference**
It **doesn't matter in the least**
I don't mind
It's all the same to me
I'm not bothered

Expressing indifference

Das **interessiert mich nicht im Geringsten**
Ich habe keine bestimmte **Vorliebe**
Das macht überhaupt nichts
Ich habe nichts dagegen
Das ist mir vollkommen egal
Mir ist alles recht

2 MEINUNGEN/OPINIONS

2.1 Meinungen erfragen · Asking for opinions

What do you think about it?
Was halten Sie davon?

What do you think about divorce?
Wie denken Sie über Ehescheidung?

What do you think of that sort of behaviour?
Was halten Sie von solch einem Benehmen?

What is your opinion on the chances of Germany winning the World Cup?
Wie sehen Sie Deutschlands Chancen, die Weltmeisterschaft zu gewinnen?

Could you give me your opinion on proportional representation?
Wie ist Ihre Meinung zum Verhältniswahlsystem?

I would be interested to know your personal opinion on the subject
Es würde mich interessieren, was Ihre persönliche Meinung zu diesem Thema ist

I should like to know your views on this subject
Ich würde gerne Ihre Meinung zu diesem Thema hören

I'd like to know what you think of his essay
Ich würde gerne wissen, was Sie von seinem Aufsatz **halten**

In your opinion, should young people be given greater freedom?
Sollten junge Leute **Ihrer Meinung nach** mehr Freiheiten haben?

2.2 Seine Meinung sagen · Expressing opinions

You are right
Sie haben Recht

He is wrong
Er hat Unrecht

He was wrong to resign
Es war falsch von ihm zurückzutreten

I'm sure he's lying
Ich bin (mir) sicher, dass er lügt

I'm convinced that there's another solution
Ich bin davon überzeugt, dass es noch eine andere Lösung gibt

I think it ought to be possible
Ich denke, das sollte möglich sein

I think it's a bit premature
Ich glaube, das ist ein bisschen voreilig

I think it's quite natural
Ich meine, das ist doch nur natürlich

In my opinion, he hasn't changed
Meiner Meinung nach hat er sich nicht verändert

I am of the opinion that whale hunting should be banned
Ich bin der Meinung, dass die Waljagd verboten werden sollte

In my view, he has made a mistake
Aus meiner Sicht hat er einen Fehler gemacht

In my view, activities like these should be illegal
Ich bin der Meinung, dass solche Aktivitäten verboten werden sollten

Personally, I believe that women make good engineers
Persönlich glaube ich, dass Frauen gute Ingenieure sind

I have the impression that her parents don't understand her
Ich habe den Eindruck, dass ihre Eltern sie nicht verstehen

2.3 Keine Meinung zum Ausdruck bringen · Avoiding expressing one's opinion

I have no definite opinion on the subject
Ich habe keine feste Meinung zu diesem Thema

I've never thought about it
Darüber habe ich noch nie nachgedacht

It (all) depends what you mean by that
Das hängt davon ab, was Sie darunter verstehen

I don't have any strong feelings about this novel
Ich habe eigentlich keine besondere Meinung über diesen Roman

I can't express an opinion on this subject
Ich kann mich zu diesem Thema **nicht äußern**

I'd prefer not to comment on this matter
Ich möchte mich lieber nicht zu dieser Angelegenheit **äußern**

3 ZUSTIMMUNG UND ÜBEREINSTIMMUNG/ APPROVAL AND AGREEMENT

I think it's an excellent idea	Ich denke, das ist eine hervorragende Idee
What a good idea!	Was für eine gute Idee!
You were right to travel with just a rucksack	Du hattest Recht, einfach nur mit dem Rucksack loszufahren
I was very impressed by his essay on racism	Sein Aufsatz über Rassismus hat mich sehr beeindruckt
I think you're right to be suspicious of him	Ich glaube, Sie haben Recht, wenn Sie ihm gegenüber misstrauisch sind
It's a very good thing	Das ist eine sehr gute Sache
You are not wrong to criticize the government	Sie haben durchaus Recht, die Regierung zu kritisieren
I share that view	Ich teile diese Ansicht
I share your fears about the disappearing forests	Ich teile Ihre Befürchtungen hinsichtlich der Zerstörung der Wälder
We are in favour of the job creation schemes	Wir befürworten die Arbeitsbeschaffungsmaßnahmen
We are in favour of a united Europe	Wir sind für ein vereintes Europa
Many people rightly believe that good qualifications are important	Viele Leute glauben berechtigterweise, dass gute Qualifikationen wichtig sind
I agree with you	Ich stimme Ihnen zu
I entirely agree with you	Ich bin ganz Ihrer Meinung
It is true that seven children escaped the bombing unharmed	Es stimmt, dass sieben Kinder bei dem Bombenanschlag unverletzt geblieben sind

4 ABLEHNUNG UND WIDERSPRUCH/ DISAPPROVAL AND DISAGREEMENT

4.1 Widerspruch — Disagreement

You are wrong!	Sie haben Unrecht!
I disagree	Ich bin anderer Meinung
I don't agree with you	Ich stimme Ihnen nicht zu
I don't agree with nuclear experiments	Ich lehne nukleare Experimente ab
I totally disagree with what he is saying	Ich bin mit dem, was er sagt, überhaupt nicht einverstanden
It is not true to say that traffic problems would be solved by raising petrol prices	Es wäre falsch zu behaupten, die Verkehrsprobleme ließen sich durch höhere Benzinpreise lösen
I don't share the Eurosceptics' point of view	Ich teile den Standpunkt der Euroskeptiker nicht

4.2 Ablehnung — Disapproval

I dislike the idea intensely	Diese Idee gefällt mir überhaupt nicht
I can't stand lies	Ich kann Lügen nicht ausstehen
We are against fanaticism and intolerance	Wir sind gegen Fanatismus und Intoleranz
I am opposed to compulsory screening of nurses for Aids	Ich bin dagegen, dass sich Krankenschwestern einem Aidstest unterziehen müssen
I think he was wrong to borrow money from his aunt	Ich denke, es war falsch von ihm, sich Geld von seiner Tante zu leihen
You shouldn't have spoken to him like that	Du hättest nicht so mit ihm reden sollen
I am disappointed by his attitude to his studies	Seine Einstellung zu seinem Studium enttäuscht mich
I am disappointed in you	Du enttäuschst mich
I am deeply disappointed	Ich bin zutiefst enttäuscht
It's a pity that he has such bad manners	Es ist schade, dass er so schlechte Manieren hat
It is regrettable that no solution has been found	Es ist bedauernswert, dass keine Lösung gefunden wurde

5 ENTSCHULDIGUNGEN/APOLOGIES

5.1 Sich entschuldigen

Sorry
Oh, sorry! I must have got the wrong number

I'm very sorry that I can't come on Friday

I'm sorry I woke you
I'm sorry for everything
I do apologize
We would ask our readers **to accept our apologies**

How to say sorry

Verzeihung
Oh, Entschuldigung! Ich muss mich verwählt **haben**
Es tut mir schrecklich Leid, dass ich am Freitag nicht kommen kann
Es tut mir Leid, wenn ich Sie geweckt habe
Das tut mir alles schrecklich Leid
Ich bitte um Entschuldigung
Wir möchten unsere Leser **um Entschuldigung bitten**

5.2 Verantwortung eingestehen

It's my fault; I should have come earlier

I shouldn't have hit her
It was a mistake not to check the tyres before setting off
I take full responsibility for what I did

I admit that it was my fault
If only I'd studied law instead of languages

Admitting responsibility

Das ist meine Schuld, ich hätte eher kommen **sollen**
Ich hätte sie **nicht** schlagen **dürfen**
Es war ein Fehler, den Reifendruck vor der Abfahrt nicht zu überprüfen
Ich übernehme die volle Verantwortung für das, was ich getan habe
Ich gebe zu, dass es mein Fehler war
Wenn ich doch bloß Jura statt Sprachen studiert **hätte**

5.3 Verantwortung ablehnen

It isn't my fault
It isn't my fault if we're late

I didn't do it on purpose
I had no option. I had to tell them what really happened.
I thought I was doing the right thing in refusing the donation

Disclaiming responsibility

Das ist nicht meine Schuld
Ich kann nichts dafür, wenn wir zu spät kommen
Ich habe das nicht mit Absicht getan
Ich hatte keine Wahl. Ich musste ihnen sagen, was wirklich passiert ist
Ich dachte, es wäre richtig, die Spende abzulehnen

5.4 Bedauern ausdrücken

I'm sorry but I can't come on Friday after all

There is no other option open to me
I understand your disappointment **but we cannot** allow you to sit the exam this year

Regrettably, we are unable to provide you with the information you requested
We regret that it will not be possible to guarantee uninterrupted power supplies in the next few months
The president **deeply regrets that** he is unable to attend the reception

Apologizing for being unable to do something

Es tut mir Leid, aber ich kann nun am Freitag doch nicht kommen
Ich habe keine andere Wahl
Ich verstehe Ihre Enttäuschung, **aber wir können** Ihnen wirklich **nicht** gestatten, die Prüfung dieses Jahr abzulegen
Leider können wir Ihnen die gewünschten Informationen **nicht** geben
Zu unserem Bedauern ist es uns nicht möglich, die Stromversorgung in den kommenden Monaten störungsfrei zu gewährleisten
Der Präsident **bedauert zutiefst** nicht an dem Empfang teilnehmen zu können

6 ERKLÄRUNGEN/EXPLANATIONS

6.1 Ursachen

I arrived late **because of** the heavy traffic

The club can afford to build a new clubhouse **thanks to** the generosity of the members

I can't buy any clothes **because** I haven't got any money

Since you insist, I'll go to the concert with you

I stayed in Switzerland for five years, **as** I enjoyed living there

Given his interest in architecture, I'm not surprised he wants visit Barcelona

Given that the government is short of money, we can't expect to build any new hospitals this year

It was a burst tyre **that caused** the crash

He resigned **for** health **reasons**

The youth club is closing down **due to** lack of funds

The train has been delayed **owing to** track repairs

Discontent amongst teachers **is linked to** lack of money for materials

The problem is that people are afraid of computers

The slowdown in exports **is the result of** the fall in European demand

Hatred **results from** a lack of understanding

Causes

Ich habe mich **wegen** des dichten Verkehrs verspätet

Dank der Großzügigkeit der Mitglieder kann es sich der Klub leisten, ein neues Klubhaus zu bauen

Ich kann keine Kleidung kaufen, **weil** ich kein Geld habe

Wenn du darauf bestehst, werde ich mit dir ins Konzert gehen

Ich blieb fünf Jahre in der Schweiz, **da** es mir dort gefallen hat

In Anbetracht seines Interesses für Architektur überrascht es mich nicht, dass er Barcelona besuchen möchte

In Anbetracht der Tatsache, dass die Regierung kein Geld hat, können wir nicht erwarten, in diesem Jahr neue Krankenhäuser bauen zu können

Ein geplatzer Reifen **hat** den Unfall **verursacht**

Er trat **aus** gesundheitlichen **Gründen** zurück

Der Jugendklub wird **wegen** fehlender finanzieller Mittel geschlossen

Der Zug hat sich **aufgrund von** Gleisbauarbeiten verspätet

Die Unzufriedenheit unter Lehrern **wird mit** dem Fehlen finanzieller Mittel für Lehrmaterialien **in Verbindung gebracht**

Das Problem liegt darin, dass die Leute Angst vor Computern haben

Der Rückgang des Exportgeschäfts **ist das Ergebnis** der sinkenden Nachfrage auf dem europäischen Markt

Hass **hat seine Ursache in** fehlendem Verständnis

6.2 Konsequenzen

I have to leave tonight, **so** I won't be able to come with you on Saturday

There has been another avalanche, **with the result that** the death toll has risen to 118

Distribution has been improved **so that** readers will get their newspapers earlier

This new cider is fermented for a very short time and is **consequently** very low in alcohol

Lack of consultation **has resulted in** a lot of wasted time

The lyrics of this song are beautiful. **That's why** they are easy to remember

Consequences

Ich muß heute Abend abreisen, **daher** kann ich Sie am Sonnabend nicht begleiten

Eine weitere Lawine **ließ** die Zahl der Todesopfer auf 118 steigen

Der Vertrieb ist verbessert worden, **so dass** die Leser ihre Zeitungen jetzt früher bekommen

Dieser neue Cider gärt nur kurze Zeit. **Folglich** ist der Alkoholgehalt sehr gering

Fehlende Absprache **hat dazu geführt, dass** viel Zeit verschwendet wurde

Der Text zu diesem Lied ist sehr schön. **Deshalb** kann man ihn sich so leicht merken

7 VERGLEICHE/COMPARISONS

7.1 Vergleichbare Dinge / Comparing similar things

As he is not very tall, **people compare him to** Napoleon
Da er nicht sehr groß ist, **vergleichen ihn die Leute mit** Napoleon

Television **can be compared** to a drug
Fernsehen **kann mit** einer Droge **verglichen werden**

The house looked **as if** it was falling down
Das Haus sah aus, **als ob** es einstürzen würde

The outline of Italy **is often compared to** a boot
Der Umriss von Italien **wird oft mit** einem Stiefel **verglichen**

The sound **was comparable to** the noise of a motorbike without a silencer
Der Lärm **war vergleichbar** dem Geräusch, das ein Motorrad ohne Schalldämpfer macht

My colleague **is like** a brother
Mein Kollege **ist wie** ein Bruder

He **reminds me of** my father's brother
Er **erinnert mich an** den Bruder meines Vaters

She **makes you think of** an old-fashioned schoolmistress
Sie **erinnert an** eine altmodische Schullehrerin

His facial expression **is reminiscent of** a Roman emperor in a bad Hollywood movie
Sein Gesichtsausdruck **erinnert in gewisser Weise an** einen römischen Kaiser in einem schlechten Hollywood-Film

Television **is the** modern day **equivalent of** the Roman circus
Das Fernsehen **ist das** moderne **Äquivalent zum** römischen Zirkus

The snowboard **is the equivalent** on snow of the skateboard
Ein Snowboard **ist wie** ein Skateboard auf Schnee

100 Pounds Sterling **is equivalent** to 160 euros
100 britische Pfund **entsprechen** 160 Euro

This amount **corresponds** to six months' rent
Diese Summe **entspricht** sechs Monatsmieten

A force field **is the same thing as** interatomic forces
Ein Kraftfeld **ist dasselbe wie** zwischenatomare Kräfte

It comes down to the same thing in terms of calories
Das läuft auf dasselbe hinaus, was die Kalorien **angeht**

7.2 Nicht vergleichbare Dinge / Comparing dissimilar things

Africa is still underpopulated **as compared to** Asia
Im Vergleich zu Asien ist Afrika immer noch unterbevölkert

His output seems small **by comparison with** Schiller's
Verglichen mit Schiller hat er wenig geschrieben

This catastrophe **cannot compare with** Chernobyl
Diese Katastrophe **lässt sich nicht mit** Tschernobyl **vergleichen**

My old armchair was **nowhere near as** comfortable **as** my new one
Mein alter Sessel war **in keiner Hinsicht so** bequem **wie** mein neuer

There is no comparison between the quality of the news in the local press and that in London
Die Qualität der Berichterstattung in der lokalen und der Londoner Presse **lässt sich nicht (miteinander) vergleichen**

Educational investment increased slightly **compared to** the previous year
Im Vergleich zum Vorjahr sind die Investitionen in das Bildungswesen leicht gestiegen

Saturated and unsaturated fats **differ in** their chemical composition
Gesättigte und ungesättigte Fette **unterscheiden sich in** ihrer chemischen Zusammensetzung

Present-day eating habits **bear little resemblance to** those of a 100 years ago
Die heutigen Essgewohnheiten **ähneln kaum mehr** denen vor 100 Jahren

There are worse things than losing a European Cup final
Es gibt Schlimmeres, als im Europacup-Finale zu verlieren

Gruyère is **better than** Edam for making fondues
Gruyère **eignet sich besser** für Fondues **als** Edamer

The centre of London is **less** crowded **than** the centre of Prague
Das Stadtzentrum von London ist **nicht so** überfüllt **wie** das Zentrum von Prag

Women's life expectancy is 81 years, **whereas** men's is 72
Die Lebenserwartung von Frauen beträgt 81 Jahre, **während** die der Männer 72 ist

While the consumption of meat is declining, vegetarianism is becoming increasingly popular
Während der Verbrauch von Fleisch sinkt, befindet sich die vegetarische Lebensweise auf dem Vormarsch

8 BITTEN UND ANGEBOTE/REQUESTS AND OFFERS

8.1 Bitten

I'd like three fruit tarts

I'd like another beer

I'd like to know the current exchange rate

Can you help me move this table?

Could you give us a hand?

Could you tell me the time, please?

Could you go and pick my dress up from the dry-cleaner's?

Be an angel and pop to the fruit shop for me

So we'll expect you next Sunday?

If you wouldn't mind waiting for a moment

Would you be so kind as to keep my seat for me?

Would you be so kind as to show me the way out?

Can I ask you for a few minutes of your time?

Would you mind opening the window?

Would you mind if I opened the window?

Do you mind if I smoke?

I would be grateful if you could publish my letter in full

We hope our listeners will forgive the delay

I should be obliged if in this personal matter you would observe the strictest discretion

Requests

Ich möchte drei Obsttorten

Ich möchte noch ein Bier

Ich wüsste gern den aktuellen Wechselkurs

Kannst du mir helfen, diesen Tisch zu tragen?

Könnten Sie uns bitte helfen?

Können Sie mir bitte sagen, wie spät es ist?

Könntest du bitte mein Kleid von der Reinigung holen?

Sei so lieb und gehe für mich zum Obstladen

Wir rechnen also nächsten Sonntag mit Ihnen?

Würden Sie bitte einen Moment warten, wenn es Ihnen nichts ausmacht

Würden Sie bitte so freundlich sein und meinen Platz für mich freihalten?

Könnten Sie mir bitte den Ausgang zeigen?

Hätten Sie vielleicht ein paar Minuten Zeit?

Würde es Ihnen etwas ausmachen, das Fenster zu öffnen?

Haben Sie etwas dagegen, wenn ich das Fenster öffne?

Stört es Sie, wenn ich rauche?

Ich wäre Ihnen dankbar, wenn Sie meinen Brief ungekürzt veröffentlichen würden

Wir hoffen, unsere Zuhörer werden die Verspätung entschuldigen

Ich wäre Ihnen sehr zu Dank verpflichtet, wenn Sie in dieser persönlichen Angelegenheit äußerste Diskretion wahren könnten

8.2 Angebote

I can come and pick you up if you want

I could go with you

Do you fancy some ice cream for dessert?

Do you fancy a beer?

How about a game of chess?

How about eating somewhere other than at the hotel?

How would you like to visit the White House?

We would be delighted if you came to visit us next summer

Do you want me to go and collect your car?

Would you like to go out with me to the cinema?

How about the 3rd of March at 10.30am?

Offers

Ich kann dich abholen, wenn du willst

Ich könnte Sie begleiten

Möchtest du etwas Eis zum Nachtisch?

Hast du Lust auf ein Bier?

Wie wäre es mit einer Partie Schach?

Was hältst du davon, woanders als im Hotel zu essen?

Was halten Sie davon, das Weiße Haus zu besuchen?

Wir wären sehr erfreut, wenn Sie uns nächsten Sommer besuchen würden

Soll ich dein Auto abholen?

Möchten Sie mit mir ins Kino gehen?

Wie wäre es am 3. März um 10.30 Uhr?

9 RATSCHLÄGE UND VORSCHLÄGE/ ADVICE AND SUGGESTIONS

9.1 Ratschläge erbitten / Asking for advice

What would you do, if you were me?	Was würden Sie an meiner Stelle tun?
What's your opinion on the matter?	Wie ist Ihre Meinung zu dieser Sache?
Which would you advise, the bracelet or the ring?	**Würden Sie mir zu** dem Armband **oder** dem Ring **raten?**
What would you advise?	Wozu würden Sie mir raten?
What would you advise me to do?	Was würden Sie mir raten zu tun?
We'd like to plant some fruit trees, **what would you recommend?**	Wir würden gerne ein paar Obstbäume pflanzen, **was würden Sie empfehlen?**
What action would you propose?	Welche Vorgehensweise würden Sie vorschlagen?
What, in your opinion, should be done to ensure an equitable outcome of the talks?	Was sollte Ihrer Meinung nach getan werden, **um** ein faires Verhandlungsergebnis zu erreichen?
How would you deal with this problem?	**Wie würden Sie** dieses Problem **lösen?**

9.2 Rat geben / Giving advice

If I may give you a piece of advice, keep your valuables in a safe place	**Wenn ich Ihnen einen Rat geben dürfte**, bewahren Sie Ihre Wertsachen an einem sicheren Ort auf
A word of advice: read the instructions	**Ein Hinweis:** Lesen Sie die Gebrauchsanweisung
A useful tip: feed your houseplants every two weeks	**Ein nützlicher Tip:** gießen Sie Ihre Zimmerpflanzen alle zwei Wochen mit Düngemittel
If I were you, **I'd** be a bit wary	**An Ihrer Stelle wäre ich** etwas vorsichtig
If I were you and I'd won the lottery, **I'd** buy a red BMW	**Wenn ich du wäre** und im Lotto gewonnen hätte, **würde ich** einen roten BMW kaufen
Why don't you telephone him?	**Warum** rufst du ihn **nicht (einfach)** an?
You've got a good sense of rhythm. **You ought to** learn to play percussion	Sie haben ein gutes Rhythmusgefühl. **Sie sollten** Schlagzeug lernen
You should see a specialist	**Sie sollten** einen Spezialisten aufsuchen
You would do better to speak to the professor yourself	**Sie sollten besser** selbst mit dem Professor sprechen
You could (perhaps) try being a little more understanding	**Du könntest (vielleicht)** versuchen, ein bisschen mehr Verständnis zu zeigen
Perhaps you should speak to your plumber about it	**Du solltest vielleicht mal** mit dem Klempner sprechen
It might be better to give her perfume rather than chocolates	**Es wäre vielleicht besser**, ihr Parfüm statt Pralinen zu schenken
It would be better to wait for the results	**Es wäre besser**, die Ergebnisse abzuwarten
You would be well-advised to keep the terms of the contract secret for the time being	**Sie wären gut beraten**, die Konditionen des Vertrages vorerst geheim zu halten
You would be ill-advised to give in now	**Sie wären schlecht beraten**, jetzt klein beizugeben

9.3 Warnende Hinweise / Warnings

Whatever you do, don't drink too much wine	**Was auch immer Sie tun**, trinken Sie **nicht** zu viel Wein
Beware of people offering to look after your house	**Nehmen Sie sich vor** Leuten **in Acht**, die Ihnen anbieten, auf Ihr Haus aufzupassen
You risk being fined **if** you park there	**Sie riskieren** ein Strafmandat, **wenn** Sie dort parken
I warn you, I'll get my own back	**Ich warne dich**, ich werde mich rächen
I'd better warn you that he takes offence very easily	**Ich sollte Sie besser warnen, dass** er sehr schnell beleidigt ist
Don't forget to keep a copy of your income tax return	**Vergessen Sie nicht**, eine Kopie Ihres Lohnsteuerjahresausgleichs zu behalten

10 ABSICHTEN UND VORHABEN/ INTENTIONS AND DESIRES

10.1 Nach Absichten fragen

Asking what someone intends to do

What do you intend to do?
Was beabsichtigen Sie zu tun?

What do you plan to do?
Was haben Sie vor?

What are you going to do when you get back? Do you have anything planned?
Was wollen Sie tun, wenn Sie zurückkommen? Haben Sie schon etwas geplant?

What are you going to do? Are you going to wait six months?
Was willst du tun? Willst du etwa sechs Monate warten?

What will you do if you fail your exams?
Was machst du, wenn du durch die Prüfung fällst?

Are you planning to go to Cyprus this year?
Haben Sie vor, dieses Jahr nach Zypern zu fahren?

Are you planning on staying long?
Wollen Sie lange bleiben?

What are you planning to do with your collection?
Was wollen Sie mit Ihrer Sammlung machen?

What do you propose to do?
Was schlagen Sie vor?

Do you intend to go to university?
Haben Sie die Absicht, zur Universität zu gehen?

Are you thinking of making another film?
Haben Sie vor, einen weiteren Film zu drehen?

10.2 Absichten ausdrücken

Saying what someone else intends to do

We are aiming to sell more than one hundred thousand CDs
Wir haben uns vorgenommen, mehr als einhunderttausend CDs zu verkaufen

I was planning to fly to Ajaccio on the 8th of July
Ich hatte vor, am 8. Juli nach Ajaccio zu fliegen

The bank intends to shut down more than 100 branches
Die Bank beabsichtigt, mehr als 100 Filialen zu schließen

I am thinking of giving up politics
Ich trage mich mit dem Gedanken, die Politik aufzugeben

She is thinking of giving up her career to have children
Sie spielt mit dem Gedanken, ihre Karriere aufzugeben, um Kinder zu haben

She plans to go and spend a year in India
Sie beabsichtigt, ein Jahr in Indien zu verbringen

I have decided to get a divorce
Ich habe beschlossen, die Scheidung einzureichen

I have made up my mind to stop smoking
Ich habe mich entschlossen, mit dem Rauchen aufzuhören

That's settled, I'm giving up acting
Es steht fest, ich gebe die Schauspielerei auf

We have every intention of retaining the title
Wir haben uns fest vorgenommen, den Titel erfolgreich zu verteidigen

10.3 Wünsche

Wishes

I want to go into acting
Ich möchte Schauspieler werden

I feel like a game of chess
Ich hätte jetzt Lust auf eine Partie Schach

I would like to go hang-gliding
Ich möchte gern drachenfliegen

I would like my photos to be published
Ich würde meine Fotos gerne veröffentlichen lassen

I would have liked to have been born earlier
Ich wäre gern früher geboren worden

What I'd really love would be a huge ice-cream
Ich würde jetzt wahnsinnig gerne eine Riesenportion Eis verschlingen

I hope to see you again soon
Ich hoffe, Sie bald einmal wieder zu treffen

I dream of owning a big house
Ich träume davon, ein großes Haus zu besitzen

We are hoping that children will watch this programme with their parents
Wir hoffen, dass die Kinder dieses Programm gemeinsam mit ihren Eltern ansehen

It is desirable that elite international athletes could be better supported
Es wäre wünschenswert, internationale Spitzensportler besser zu unterstützen

We wish to preserve our independence
Wir wollen uns unsere Unabhängigkeit bewahren

Peter wanted at all costs to fulfil his boyhood dream of learning to fly
Peter wollte sich unbedingt seinen Kindheitstraum erfüllen und fliegen lernen

11 VERPFLICHTUNG/OBLIGATION

I must find a job	**Ich muss** Arbeit finden
If you want to spend much time in the Ukraine, **you must** learn Ukrainian	Wenn Sie längere Zeit in der Ukraine bleiben wollen, **müssen Sie** Ukrainisch lernen
School **is compulsory**	Der Schulbesuch **ist Pflicht**
The minister **insisted on** his bodyguard sleeping in the same room as him	Der Minister **bestand darauf, dass** sein Leibwächter mit ihm in einem Raum schläft
The hijackers **demanded that** the plane should fly on to New York	Die Entführer **verlangten, dass** das Flugzeug nach New York weiterfliegen soll
A bad asthma attack meant that **I had to** stop off in Bern to see a doctor	Wegen eines schweren Asthmaanfalls **musste ich** in Bern Zwischenstation machen und den Arzt aufsuchen
My mother made me eat spinach when I was little	Als ich klein war, **hat meine Mutter mich gezwungen**, Spinat zu essen
You are obliged to report all road accidents to the police	**Sie sind dazu verpflichtet**, alle Verkehrsunfälle der Polizei zu melden
Whenever you go out **you're forced to** weave your way between the cars parked on the pavements	Wann immer man aus dem Haus geht, **man muss** sich immer einen Weg zwischen den auf dem Bürgersteig geparkten Autos bahnen
He was forced to ask his parents for money	**Er war gezwungen**, seine Eltern um Geld zu bitten
It is essential to know your career options before choosing a course of study	**Es ist unbedingt notwendig**, sich über die Berufschancen im Klaren zu sein, bevor man einen Studiengang wählt
You have no choice but to say no	**Es bleibt dir nichts anderes übrig, als** Nein zu sagen
In poor countries lots of children **have to** work; **they have no other option**	In armen Ländern **müssen** viele Kinder arbeiten, **sie haben keine andere Wahl**
You need to have a valid passport if you want to leave the country	Wenn Sie das Land verlassen wollen, **müssen Sie** im Besitz eines gültigen Passes sein
If no one claims the dogs, **we will be obliged to** destroy them	Wenn sich die Besitzer der Hunde nicht melden, **werden wir** die Tiere einschläfern **müssen**

12 ERLAUBNIS/PERMISSION

12.1 Um Erlaubnis bitten

Can I use the telephone, **please**?
Can I ask you something?
Can I pop round later for a chat?

Do you mind if I have a look in your beach bag, madam?
Do you mind if I come for lunch instead of dinner?

Do you mind if I smoke?
Do you have any objection to being named in my article?
With your permission I would like to make some changes to the floor plan

12.2 Erlaubnis erteilen

History students **are allowed to** visit the archives
You have my permission to be absent next week

You are authorized to take any measures necessary for the safety of the passengers

They allowed the old, the women and the children to leave the hijacked plane
Do as you please
I have nothing against it
I have no objection to your quoting me in your article

12.3 Erlaubnis verweigern

I forbid you to leave this room
It's forbidden
It's not allowed
No entry!
Smoking **is (strictly) forbidden** in the toilet
Child labour **is positively prohibited** by the UN convention for the rights of the child
It's a certificate 12 film
You are not allowed to smoke in the lecture hall
Don't leave the house
That's out of the question
Our superiors **are not authorized to** read our e-mail
You mustn't go anywhere near the new research lab

Asking for permission

Könnte ich bitte das Telefon benutzen?
Darf ich Sie etwas fragen?
Kann ich nachher auf einen kurzen Plausch vorbeikommen?
Dürfte ich bitte in ihre Strandtasche schauen?
Macht es Ihnen etwas aus, wenn ich zum Mittagessen komme statt zum Abendessen?
Stört es Sie, wenn ich rauche?
Haben Sie etwas dagegen, wenn ich Ihren Namen in meinem Artikel verwende?
Mit Ihrer Erlaubnis würde ich gerne einige Änderungen am Gebäudegrundriss vornehmen

Giving permission

Geschichtsstudenten **dürfen** das Archiv besuchen
Sie haben meine Erlaubnis, nächste Woche zu fehlen
Sie sind bevollmächtigt, alle notwendigen Maßnahmen zum Schutz der Passagiere zu ergreifen
Sie gestatteten den Alten, Frauen und Kindern, das entführte Flugzeug zu verlassen
Machen Sie, was Sie wollen
Ich habe nichts dagegen
Ich habe keinerlei Einwände dagegen, dass Sie mich in Ihrem Artikel zitieren

Refusing permission

Ich verbiete dir, das Zimmer zu verlassen
Das ist verboten
Das ist nicht gestattet
Zutritt verboten!
Auf der Toilette **ist** das Rauchen **(streng) verboten**
Die UN-Konvention über die Rechte der Kinder **verbietet** Kinderarbeit **eindeutig**
Dieser Film ist ab 12 Jahren
Sie dürfen im Hörsaal **nicht** rauchen
Geh nicht aus dem Haus
Das kommt gar nicht in Frage
Unsere Vorgesetzten **sind nicht berechtigt,** unsere E-Mail zu lesen
Sie dürfen sich **auf gar keinen Fall** in der Nähe des neuen Forschungslabors aufhalten

13 GEWISSHEIT, WAHRSCHEINLICHKEIT UND MÖGLICHKEIT/CERTAINTY, PROBABILITY AND POSSIBILITY

13.1 Gewissheit / Certainty

The economic situation will **undoubtedly** deteriorate further — **Zweifellos** wird sich die wirtschaftliche Lage noch verschlechtern

It is obvious that this actor doesn't work well with children — **Es ist offensichtlich, dass** dieser Schauspieler nicht gut mit Kindern arbeiten kann

It is undeniably true that the climate has changed considerably — **Es läßt sich nicht leugnen, dass** sich das Klima erheblich verändert hat

There is no doubt that low-fat cakes will be a real success — Kalorienarme Kuchen werden **ohne Zweifel** ein Renner werden

No-one can deny the unemployment rate is very high in this area — **Es lässt sich nicht bestreiten, dass** die Arbeitslosenzahlen in dieser Region sehr hoch sind

I am sure that you will like my brother — Du wirst meinen Bruder **bestimmt** mögen

I am certain that I will win — **Ich bin sicher, dass** ich gewinnen werde

I am sure that we are on the right track — **Ich bin ganz sicher, dass** wir auf dem richtigen Weg sind

I am certain that I will enjoy working here — **Gewiss** wird mir die Arbeit hier gefallen

I am convinced that there are other solutions — **Ich bin davon überzeugt, dass** es noch andere Lösungen gibt

I can assure you that we will have the problem solved by tomorrow morning — **Ich versichere Ihnen, dass** wir das Problem bis morgen früh gelöst haben

13.2 Wahrscheinlichkeit / Probability

The economic crisis will **probably** affect young people's employment opportunities — Die Wirtschaftskrise wird sich **wahrscheinlich** auf die Arbeitschancen junger Leute auswirken

The Swiss **probably** eat more chocolate than any other nation — Die Schweizer essen **wahrscheinlich** mehr Schokolade als jedes andere Volk

The rate of inflation will **very probably** exceed 5% — Die Inflationsrate wird **höchstwahrscheinlich** 5 % überschreiten

They were **no doubt** right — Sie hatten **zweifelsohne** recht

He must have forgotten to open the windows — **Er muß vergessen haben**, das Fenster zu öffnen

The construction work **should** start in April — Die Bauarbeiten **sollen** im April beginnen

It is quite possible that they are trying to test our reaction — **Es ist durchaus möglich, dass** sie nur mal sehen wollen, wie wir reagieren

It looks as if it's going to rain — **Es sieht nach** Regen **aus**

I wouldn't be at all surprised if he was late again — **Es würde mich überhaupt nicht wundern, wenn** er wieder zu spät kommt

13.3 Möglichkeit / Possibility

It is possible — **Das ist möglich**

That **might** be more expensive — Das **könnte** teurer sein

There is a possibility that our competitors have beaten us to it — **Es besteht die Möglichkeit, dass** uns die Konkurrenz zuvorgekommen ist

It should be possible to establish who committed this act — **Es sollte doch möglich sein** festzustellen, wer diese Tat verübt hat

He **may** have contracted an incurable disease — **Möglicherweise** hat er sich eine unheilbare Krankheit zugezogen

Perhaps I am mistaken — **Vielleicht** habe ich Unrecht

In a few months everything **may** have changed — In ein paar Monaten **kann** sich schon alles verändert haben

This virus **may** be extremely infectious — Das Virus **könnte** hochinfektiös sein

It may be that peace will not be concluded straightaway — **Es könnte sein**, dass es nicht sofort zum Friedensschluss kommen wird

It may well be that America was really discovered by the Chinese — **Es ist gut möglich, dass** Amerika in Wirklichkeit von den Chinesen entdeckt wurde

14 ZWEIFEL, UNWAHRSCHEINLICHKEIT UND UNMÖGLICHKEIT/DOUBT, IMPROBABILITY AND IMPOSSIBILITY

14.1 Zweifel

I'm not sure I'm right

I'm not convinced that this method will work

I wonder if we've made much progress in this field

I'm wondering if I should offer to help
He began to have doubts about his doctor's competence

I (very much) doubt he'll adapt to living in Africa

I'm not sure that it's a good idea

There is no guarantee that a vaccine can be developed
We still don't know exactly how we're going to decorate the living room
No one can say for sure how any child will develop

14.2 Unwahrscheinlichkeit

I'd be surprised if they had your size

We're not likely to get bored
They are not likely to get the Nobel Prize for Economics

He **probably won't** change his mind

There's not much chance of the interest rate exceeding 1.5%
It is unlikely that thousands of tourists would visit a bicycle factory
It would be surprising if everything went according to plan
It is (highly) improbable that Scotland will become independent within the next ten years

14.3 Unmöglichkeit

It's impossible
It is not possible for me to donate more than £50
This information **cannot possibly** be wrong

There is no chance of their coming to our assistance
I couldn't possibly invite Frank and not his wife

Such a solution **is completely out of the question**

Doubt

Ich bin nicht sicher, ob ich Recht habe

Ich bin nicht überzeugt, dass diese Methode funktioniert

Ich frage mich, ob wir auf diesem Gebiet große Fortschritte gemacht haben

Vielleicht sollte ich meine Hilfe anbieten?
Er begann, an der Kompetenz seines Arztes **zu zweifeln**

Ich bezweifle (sehr), dass er sich an das Leben in Afrika gewöhnen wird

Ich bin mir nicht sicher, ob das eine gute Idee ist

Es gibt keine Garantie dafür, dass ein Impfstoff entwickelt werden kann

Wir wissen noch nicht genau, wie wir das Wohnzimmer tapezieren wollen

Niemand kann mit Sicherheit sagen, wie sich ein Kind entwickeln wird

Improbability

Es würde mich überraschen, wenn sie Ihre Größe hätten

Wir werden uns wahrscheinlich nicht langweilen

Es ist höchst unwahrscheinlich, dass sie den Nobelpreis für Wirtschaftswissenschaften erhalten werden

Er wird seine Meinung **wahrscheinlich nicht** ändern

Der Zinssatz wird 1,5 % **wahrscheinlich nicht** überschreiten

Es ist unwahrscheinlich, dass tausende Touristen eine Fahrradfabrik besichtigen wollten

Es wäre eine Überraschung, wenn alles nach Plan laufen würde

Es ist (höchst) unwahrscheinlich, dass Schottland im Laufe der nächsten zehn Jahre seine Unabhängigkeit erlangen wird

Impossibility

Das ist unmöglich

Es ist mir nicht möglich, mehr als £ 50 zu spenden

Diese Information **kann unter keinen Umständen** falsch sein

Sie werden uns **ganz bestimmt nicht** zu Hilfe kommen

Ich kann unmöglich Frank einladen und seine Frau nicht

Eine solche Lösung **kommt überhaupt nicht in Frage**

15 TELEFONIEREN/THE TELEPHONE

15.1 Nach einer Nummer fragen

Getting a number

Could you get me Newhaven 465786, please?
(four-six-five-seven-eight-six)

Können Sie mich bitte mit Köln 465786 verbinden?
(vier-sechs-fünf-sieben-acht-sechs)

Could you give me directory enquiries *oder* directory assistance *(US)*, please?

Können Sie mich bitte mit der Auskunft verbinden?

Can you give me the number of Europost, of 54 Broad Street, Newham?

Ich hätte gern eine Nummer in Köln, Firma Europost, Breite Straße 54

It's not in the book

Ich kann die Nummer nicht finden

They're ex-directory *(Brit)* oder They're unlisted *(US)*

Das ist eine Geheimnummer

What is the code for Exeter?

Wie lautet die Vorwahl von Leipzig?

Can I dial direct to Peru?

Kann ich nach Peru durchwählen?

How do I make an outside call? *oder* What do I dial for an outside line?

Wie bekomme ich den Amtston?

What do I dial to get the speaking clock?

Wie lautet die Nummer der Zeitansage?

You'll have to look up the number in the directory

Sie müssen die Nummer im Telefonbuch nachschlagen

You should get the number from International Directory Enquiries

Sie können die Nummer bei der internationalen Auskunft erfragen

You omit the '0' when dialling England from Germany

Wenn Sie von Deutschland nach England anrufen, lassen Sie die Null weg

15.2 Verschiedene Arten von Anrufen

Different types of call

It's a local call

Es ist ein Ortsgespräch

It's a long-distance call from Worthing

Es ist ein Ferngespräch aus Hamburg

I want to make an international call

Ich möchte ins Ausland anrufen

I want to make a reverse charge call to a London number *(Brit) oder* I want to call a London number collect *(US)*

Ich möchte ein R-Gespräch nach London anmelden

I'd like to make a credit card call to Berlin

Ich möchte auf Kreditkarte nach Berlin anrufen

I'd like an alarm call for 7.30 tomorrow morning

Ich hätte gern einen Weckruf für morgen früh 7.30 Uhr

15.3 Vermittlung

The operator speaks

Number, please

Welche Nummer möchten Sie?

What number do you want? *oder* What number are you calling?

Welche Nummer wünschen Sie?

Where are you calling from?

Woher rufen Sie an?

Would you repeat the number, please?

Können Sie die Nummer bitte wiederholen?

You can dial the number direct

Sie können durchwählen

Replace the receiver and dial again

Legen Sie auf und wählen Sie noch einmal

There's a Mr Campbell calling you from Canberra and wishes you to pay for the call. Will you accept it?

Ich habe Herrn Campbell mit einem R-Gespräch aus Canberra für Sie. Nehmen Sie das Gespräch an?

Go ahead, caller

Ich verbinde

There's no listing under that name

Ich habe keine Eintragung unter diesem Namen

There's no reply from 45 77 57 84

Der Teilnehmer 45 77 57 84 antwortet nicht

I'll try to reconnect you

Ich versuche es noch einmal

Hold the line, caller

Bitte bleiben Sie am Apparat

All lines to Bristol are engaged – please try later

Alle Leitungen nach Bonn sind besetzt, bitte rufen Sie später noch einmal an

I'm trying it for you now

Ich versuche, Sie jetzt zu verbinden

It's ringing *oder* Ringing for you now

Wir haben ein Rufzeichen

The line is engaged *(Brit) oder* busy *(US)*

Die Leitung ist besetzt

15 TELEFONIEREN/THE TELEPHONE

15.4 Der Teilnehmer antwortet

When your number answers

Could I have extension 516?	Können Sie mich bitte mit Apparat 516 verbinden?
Is that Mr Lambert's phone?	Bin ich mit dem Apparat von Herrn Lambert verbunden?
Could I speak to Mr Swinton, please?	Kann ich bitte mit Herrn Schmiedel sprechen?
Could you put me through to Dr Henderson, please?	Können Sie mich bitte zu Herrn Dr. Graupner durchstellen?
Who's speaking?	Wer ist am Apparat?
I'll try again later	Ich versuche es später noch einmal
I'll call back in half an hour	Ich rufe in einer halben Stunde zurück
Could I leave my number for her to call me back?	Könnte ich bitte meine Nummer hinterlassen, damit sie mich zurückrufen kann?
I'm ringing from a callbox *(Brit)* oder I'm calling from a pay station *(US)*	Ich rufe aus einer Telefonzelle an
I'm phoning from England	Ich rufe aus England an
Would you ask him to ring me back?	Könnten Sie ihn bitten, mich zurückzurufen?

15.5 Die Zentrale antwortet

The switchboard operator speaks

Queen's Hotel, can I help you?	Hotel Maritim, guten Tag
Who is calling, please?	Wer ist am Apparat, bitte?
Who shall I say is calling?	Wen darf ich melden?
Do you know his extension number?	Wissen Sie, welchen Apparat er hat?
I am connecting you now *oder* I'm putting you through now	Ich verbinde Sie
I have a call from Tokyo for Mrs Thomas	Ein Gespräch aus Tokio für Frau Böhme
I've got Miss Trotter on the line for you	Frau Fehrmann für Sie
Mr Craig is talking on the other line	Herr Goy spricht gerade auf der anderen Leitung
Sorry to keep you waiting	Bitte bleiben Sie am Apparat
There's no reply	Es meldet sich niemand
You're through to our Sales Department	Sie sind mit unserer Verkaufsabteilung verbunden

15.6 Sich am Telefon melden

Answering the telephone

Hello, this is Anne speaking	Hallo, Anne hier
(Is that Anne?) Speaking	*(Kann ich mit Anne sprechen?)* Am Apparat
Would you like to leave a message?	Möchten Sie eine Nachricht hinterlassen?
Can I take a message for him?	Kann ich ihm etwas ausrichten?
Don't hang up yet	Bitte bleiben Sie am Apparat
Put the phone down and I'll call you back	Legen Sie bitte auf, ich rufe Sie zurück
This is a recorded message	Hier spricht der automatische Anrufbeantworter
Please speak after the tone	Bitte sprechen Sie nach dem Tonzeichen

15.7 Bei Schwierigkeiten

In case of difficulty

I can't get through	Ich komme nicht durch
The number is not ringing	Ich bekomme kein Rufzeichen
I'm getting 'number unobtainable' *oder* I'm getting the 'number unobtainable' signal	Ich bekomme immer nur „Kein Anschluss unter dieser Nummer"
Their phone is out of order	Das Telefon ist gestört
We were cut off	Wir sind unterbrochen worden
I must have dialled the wrong number	Ich muß mich verwählt haben
We've got a crossed line	Da ist noch jemand in der Leitung
I've called them several times with no reply	Ich habe mehrmals angerufen, aber es hat sich niemand gemeldet
You gave me a wrong number	Sie haben mir die falsche Nummer gegeben
I got the wrong extension	Ich bin mit dem falschen Apparat verbunden worden
This is a very bad line	Die Verbindung ist sehr schlecht

E-MAIL

Sending messages

Neue Nachricht								✉
Datei	**Bearbeiten**	**Ansicht**	**Extras**	**Verfassen**		**Hilfe**	**Senden**	

An: Marion.Beermann@bogner.com	**Nachricht erstellen**
Cc:	**Antworten**
Bcc:	**Allen antworten**
Betreff: Besprechung	**Weiterleiten**
	Anlage

Liebe Frau Beermann,

am Montag, den 19.05.03 findet von 11 Uhr bis 12 Uhr 30 eine

Besprechung zum JUMA-Projekt statt. Es wäre mir lieb, wenn Sie

daran teilnehmen könnten. Wenn Ihnen der Termin nicht passt, geben

Sie mir bitte Bescheid!

Rolf Hauser

Neue Nachricht	New
Datei	File
Bearbeiten	Edit
Ansicht	View
Extras	Tools
Verfassen	Compose
Hilfe	Help
Senden	Send
Nachricht erstellen	New Message
Antworten	Reply (to Sender)

E-MAIL

Receiving messages

Besprechung

| Datei | Bearbeiten | Ansicht | Extras | Verfassen | Hilfe |

Von: Marion Beermann (Marion.Beermann@bogner.com)

Datum: Montag, 12. Mai 2003 10:28

An: Rolf.Hauser@locatechnik.com

Betreff: Besprechung

> In German, when telling someone your e-mail address you say:
> **"Marion Punkt Beermann at Bogner Punkt Com".**

Lieber Herr Hauser,

leider bin ich die ganze nächste Woche geschäftlich in den USA.

Aber wir können uns gerne diese Woche einmal treffen, um die neuesten

Entwicklungen des Projektes zu besprechen. Wie wäre es mit Freitag

dieser Woche?

Marion Beermann

Allen antworten	Reply to All
Weiterleiten	Forward
An	To
Cc	Cc
Bcc	Bcc (Blind carbon copy)
Betreff	Subject
Anlage	Attachment
Von	From
Datum	Date

E-MAIL

E-Mails senden

```
┌─────────────────────── New Message ───────────────────────┐
│  File    Edit    View    Tools   Compose   Help   Send  ✉  │
├────────────────────────────────┬──────────────────────────┤
│ To: andrew@pmdesigns.co.uk     │ New                      │
│ Cc:                            │ Reply to Sender          │
│ Bcc:                           │ Reply to All             │
│ Subject: Meeting               │ Forward                  │
│                                │ Attachment               │
│                                                            │
│ Re our conversation this morning, would next Monday morning│
│ 10am be convenient for a meeting about the project's       │
│ progress? If this doesn't suit, I'm also free Wednesday    │
│ morning.                                                   │
│                                                            │
│ Mark                                                       │
│                                                            │
└────────────────────────────────────────────────────────────┘
```

New Message	=	Neue Nachricht
File	=	Datei
Edit	=	Bearbeiten
View	=	Ansicht
Tools	=	Extras
Compose	=	Verfassen
Help	=	Hilfe
Send	=	Senden
New	=	Nachricht erstellen
Reply to Sender	=	Antworten

E-MAIL

E-Mails bekommen

New Message						
File	**Edit**	**View**	**Tools**	**Compose**	**Help**	

From: Andrew Collins (andrew@pmdesigns.co.uk)

Sent: 19 May 2003 08.30

To: mark.gordon@typo.co.uk

Subject: Meeting

> Wenn Sie jemandem Ihre E-Mail-Adresse auf Englisch mitteilen wollen, sagen Sie: **„andrew at pmdesigns dot co dot uk"**

Mark,

Unfortunately I'm away on business all next week. Would it be possible to arrange a working lunch, Thursday or Friday of this week?

Sorry about this!

Andrew

Reply to All	=	Allen antworten
Forward	=	Weiterleiten
Attachment	=	Anlage
To	=	An
Cc (carbon copy)	=	Cc
Bcc (blind carbon copy)	=	Bcc
Subject	=	Betreff
From	=	Von
Sent	=	Datum

IRREGULAR GERMAN VERBS

Infinitive	Present Indicative 2nd pers sing ♦ 3rd pers sing	Imperfect Indicative	Past Participle
backen	bäckst, backst ♦ bäckt, backt	backte	gebacken
befehlen	befiehlst ♦ befiehlt	befahl	befohlen
beginnen	beginnst ♦ beginnt	begann	begonnen
beißen	beißt ♦ beißt	biss	gebissen
bergen	birgst ♦ birgt	barg	geborgen
bersten	birst ♦ birst	barst	geborsten
bewegen²	bewegst ♦ bewegt	bewog	bewogen
biegen	biegst ♦ biegt	bog	gebogen
bieten	bietest ♦ bietet	bot	geboten
binden	bindest ♦ bindet	band	gebunden
bitten	bittest ♦ bittet	bat	gebeten
blasen	bläst ♦ bläst	blies	geblasen
bleiben	bleibst ♦ bleibt	blieb	geblieben
braten	brätst ♦ brät	briet	gebraten
brechen	brichst ♦ bricht	brach	gebrochen
brennen	brennst ♦ brennt	brannte	gebrannt
bringen	bringst ♦ bringt	brachte	gebracht
denken	denkst ♦ denkt	dachte	gedacht
dreschen	drischst ♦ drischt	drosch	gedroschen
dringen	dringst ♦ dringt	drang	gedrungen
dürfen	1st darf ♦ 2nd darfst ♦ 3rd darf	durfte	gedurft ♦ (after infin) dürfen
empfangen	empfängst ♦ empfängt	empfing	empfangen
empfehlen	empfiehlst ♦ empfiehlt	empfahl	empfohlen
empfinden	empfindest ♦ empfindet	empfand	empfunden
erschrecken	erschrickst ♦ erschrickt	erschrak	erschrocken
essen	ist ♦ isst	aß	gegessen
fahren	fährst ♦ fährt	fuhr	gefahren
fallen	fällst ♦ fällt	fiel	gefallen
fangen	fängst ♦ fängt	fing	gefangen
fechten	fichtst ♦ ficht	focht	gefochten
finden	findest ♦ findet	fand	gefunden
flechten	flichtst ♦ flicht	flocht	geflochten
fliegen	fliegst ♦ fliegt	flog	geflogen
fliehen	fliehst ♦ flieht	floh	geflohen
fließen	fließt ♦ fließt	floss	geflossen
fressen	frisst ♦ frisst	fraß	gefressen
frieren	frierst ♦ friert	fror	gefroren
gebären	gebierst ♦ gebiert	gebar	geboren
geben	gibst ♦ gibt	gab	gegeben
gedeihen	gedeihst ♦ gedeiht	gedieh	gediehen
gehen	gehst ♦ geht	ging	gegangen
gelingen	gelingt	gelang	gelungen
gelten	giltst ♦ gilt	galt	gegolten
genesen	genest ♦ genest	genas	genesen
genießen	genießt ♦ genießt	genoss	genossen
geschehen	geschieht	geschah	geschehen
gewinnen	gewinnst ♦ gewinnt	gewann	gewonnen
gießen	gießt ♦ gießt	goss	gegossen
gleichen	gleichst ♦ gleicht	glich	geglichen
gleiten	gleitest ♦ gleitet	glitt	geglitten
glimmen	glimmst ♦ glimmt	glomm	geglommen
graben	gräbst ♦ gräbt	grub	gegraben
greifen	greifst ♦ greift	griff	gegriffen
haben	hast ♦ hat	hatte	gehabt
halten	hältst ♦ hält	hielt	gehalten
hängen	hängst ♦ hängt	hing	gehangen
hauen	haust ♦ haut	haute	gehauen
heben	hebst ♦ hebt	hob	gehoben
heißen	heißt ♦ heißt	hieß	geheißen
helfen	hilfst ♦ hilft	half	geholfen
kennen	kennst ♦ kennt	kannte	gekannt
klingen	klingst ♦ klingt	klang	geklungen
kneifen	kneifst ♦ kneift	kniff	gekniffen

Infinitive	Present Indicative	Imperfect	Past
	2nd pers sing ♦ 3rd pers sing	Indicative	Participle
kommen	kommst ♦ kommt	kam	gekommen
können	1st kann ♦ 2nd kannst ♦ 3rd kann	konnte	gekonnt ♦ (after infin) können
kriechen	kriechst ♦ kriecht	kroch	gekrochen
laden	lädst ♦ lädt	lud	geladen
lassen	lässt ♦ lässt	ließ	gelassen ♦ (after infin) lassen
laufen	läufst ♦ läuft	lief	gelaufen
leiden	leidest ♦ leidet	litt	gelitten
leihen	leihst ♦ leiht	lieh	geliehen
lesen	liest ♦ liest	las	gelesen
liegen	liegst ♦ liegt	lag	gelegen
lügen	lügst ♦ lügt	log	gelogen
mahlen	mahlst ♦ mahlt	mahlte	gemahlen
meiden	meidest ♦ meidet	mied	gemieden
melken	melkst ♦ melkt	melkte	gemolken
messen	misst ♦ misst	maß	gemessen
misslingen	misslingt	misslang	misslungen
mögen	1st mag ♦ 2nd magst ♦ 3rd mag	mochte	gemocht ♦ (after infin) mögen
müssen	1st muss ♦ 2nd musst ♦ 3rd muss	musste	müssen
nehmen	nimmst ♦ nimmt	nahm	genommen
nennen	nennst ♦ nennt	nannte	genannt
pfeifen	pfeifst ♦ pfeift	pfiff	gepfiffen
preisen	preist ♦ preist	pries	gepriesen
quellen	quillst ♦ quillt	quoll	gequollen
raten	rätst ♦ rät	riet	geraten
reiben	reibst ♦ reibt	rieb	gerieben
reißen	reißt ♦ reißt	riss	gerissen
reiten	reitest ♦ reitet	ritt	geritten
rennen	rennst ♦ rennt	rannte	gerannt
riechen	riechst ♦ riecht	roch	gerochen
ringen	ringst ♦ ringt	rang	gerungen
rinnen	rinnst ♦ rinnt	rann	geronnen
rufen	rufst ♦ ruft	rief	gerufen
salzen	salzt ♦ salzt	salzte	gesalzen
saufen	säufst ♦ säuft	soff	gesoffen
saugen	saugst ♦ saugt	sog	gesogen ♦ gesaugt
schaffen[1]	schaffst ♦ schafft	schuf	geschaffen
scheiden	scheidest ♦ scheidet	schied	geschieden
scheinen	scheinst ♦ scheint	schien	geschienen
scheißen	scheißt ♦ scheißt	schiss	geschissen
schelten	schiltst ♦ schilt	schalt	gescholten
scheren	scherst ♦ schert	schor	geschoren
schieben	schiebst ♦ schiebt	schob	geschoben
schießen	schießt ♦ schießt	schoss	geschossen
schinden	schindest ♦ schindet	schindete	geschunden
schlafen	schläfst ♦ schläft	schlief	geschlafen
schlagen	schlägst ♦ schlägt	schlug	geschlagen
schleichen	schleichst ♦ schleicht	schlich	geschlichen
schleifen	schleifst ♦ schleift	schliff	geschliffen
schließen	schließt ♦ schließt	schloss	geschlossen
schlingen	schlingst ♦ schlingt	schlang	geschlungen
schmeißen	schmeißt ♦ schmeißt	schmiss	geschmissen
schmelzen	schmilzt ♦ schmilzt	schmolz	geschmolzen
schneiden	schneid(e)st ♦ schneidet	schnitt	geschnitten
schreiben	schreibst ♦ schreibt	schrieb	geschrieben
schreien	schreist ♦ schreit	schrie	geschrie(e)n
schreiten	schreitest ♦ schreitet	schritt	geschritten
schweigen	schweigst ♦ schweigt	schwieg	geschwiegen
schwellen	schwillst ♦ schwillt	schwoll	geschwollen
schwimmen	schwimmst ♦ schwimmt	schwamm	geschwommen
schwinden	schwindest ♦ schwindet	schwand	geschwunden
schwingen	schwingst ♦ schwingt	schwang	geschwungen
schwören	schwörst ♦ schwört	schwor	geschworen

Infinitive	Present Indicative		Imperfect Indicative	Past Participle
	2nd pers sing ♦ *3rd pers sing*			
sehen	siehst ♦ sieht		sah	gesehen ♦ *(after infin)* sehen
sein	*1st* bin ♦ *2nd* bist ♦ *3rd* ist *1st pl* sind ♦ *2nd pl* seid ♦ *3rd pl* sind		war	gewesen
senden *(send)*	sendest ♦ sendet		sandte	gesandt
singen	singst ♦ singt		sang	gesungen
sinken	sinkst ♦ sinkt		sank	gesunken
sinnen	sinnst ♦ sinnt		sann	gesonnen
sitzen	sitzt ♦ sitzt		saß	gesessen
sollen	*1st* soll ♦ *2nd* sollst ♦ *3rd* soll		sollte	gesollt ♦ *(after infin)* sollen
spalten	spaltest ♦ spaltet		spaltete	gespalten ♦ gespaltet
speien	speist ♦ speit		spie	gespie(e)n
spinnen	spinnst ♦ spinnt		spann	gesponnen
sprechen	sprichst ♦ spricht		sprach	gesprochen
sprießen	sprießt ♦ sprießt		spross ♦ sprießte	gesprossen
springen	springst ♦ springt		sprang	gesprungen
stechen	stichst ♦ sticht		stach	gestochen
stecken *(vi)*	steckst ♦ steckt		steckte ♦ stak	gesteckt
stehen	stehst ♦ steht		stand	gestanden
stehlen	stiehlst ♦ stiehlt		stahl	gestohlen
steigen	steigst ♦ steigt		stieg	gestiegen
sterben	stirbst ♦ stirbt		starb	gestorben
stieben	stiebst ♦ stiebt		stob ♦ stiebte	gestoben ♦ gestiebt
stinken	stinkst ♦ stinkt		stank	gestunken
stoßen	stößt ♦ stößt		stieß	gestoßen
streichen	streichst ♦ streicht		strich	gestrichen
streiten	streitest ♦ streitet		stritt	gestritten
tragen	trägst ♦ trägt		trug	getragen
treffen	triffst ♦ trifft		traf	getroffen
treiben	treibst ♦ treibt		trieb	getrieben
treten	trittst ♦ tritt		trat	getreten
trinken	trinkst ♦ trinkt		trank	getrunken
trügen	trügst ♦ trügt		trog	getrogen
tun	*1st* tue ♦ *2nd* tust ♦ *3rd* tut		tat	getan
verderben	verdirbst ♦ verdirbt		verdarb	verdorben
verdrießen	verdrießt ♦ verdrießt		verdross	verdrossen
vergessen	vergisst ♦ vergisst		vergaß	vergessen
verlieren	verlierst ♦ verliert		verlor	verloren
verschleißen	verschleißt ♦ verschleißt		verschliss	verschlissen
verzeihen	verzeihst ♦ verzeiht		verzieh	verziehen
wachsen	wächst ♦ wächst		wuchs	gewachsen
wägen	wägst ♦ wägt		wog	gewogen
waschen	wäschst ♦ wäscht		wusch	gewaschen
weben	webst ♦ webt		webte, wob *(liter, fig)*	gewebt, gewoben *(liter, fig)*
weichen	weichst ♦ weicht		wich	gewichen
weisen	weist ♦ weist		wies	gewiesen
wenden	wendest ♦ wendet		wendete	gewendet ♦ gewandt
werben	wirbst ♦ wirbt		warb	geworben
werden	wirst ♦ wird		wurde	geworden ♦ *(after ptp)* worden
werfen	wirfst ♦ wirft		warf	geworfen
wiegen	wiegst ♦ wiegt		wog	gewogen
winden	windest ♦ windet		wand	gewunden
winken	winkst ♦ winkt		winkte	gewinkt ♦ gewunken
wissen	*1st* weiß ♦ *2nd* weißt ♦ *3rd* weiß		wusste	gewusst
wollen	*1st* will ♦ *2nd* willst ♦ *3rd* will		wollte	gewollt ♦ *(after infin)* wollen
wringen	wringst ♦ wringt		wrang	gewrungen
ziehen	ziehst ♦ zieht		zog	gezogen
zwingen	zwingst ♦ zwingt		zwang	gezwungen

UNREGELMÄSSIGE ENGLISCHE VERBEN

Präsens	Imperfekt	Partizip Perfekt	Präsens	Imperfekt	Partizip Perfekt
arise	arose	arisen	forget	forgot	forgotten
awake	awoke	awoken	forgive	forgave	forgiven
be (am, is, are; being)	was, were	been	forsake	forsook	forsaken
			freeze	froze	frozen
bear	bore	born(e)	get	got	got, (US) gotten
beat	beat	beaten	give	gave	given
become	became	become	go (goes)	went	gone
befall	befell	befallen	grind	ground	ground
begin	began	begun	grow	grew	grown
behold	beheld	beheld	hang	hung	hung
bend	bent	bent	hang (execute)	hanged	hanged
beset	beset	beset	have	had	had
bet	bet, betted	bet, betted	hear	heard	heard
bid (at auction, cards)	bid	bid	hide	hid	hidden
			hit	hit	hit
bid (say)	bade	bidden	hold	held	held
bind	bound	bound	hurt	hurt	hurt
bite	bit	bitten	keep	kept	kept
bleed	bled	bled	kneel	knelt, kneeled	knelt, kneeled
blow	blew	blown	know	knew	known
break	broke	broken	lay	laid	laid
breed	bred	bred	lead	led	led
bring	brought	brought	lean	leant, leaned	leant, leaned
build	built	built	leap	leapt, leaped	leapt, leaped
burn	burnt, burned	burnt, burned	learn	learnt, learned	learnt, learned
burst	burst	burst			
buy	bought	bought	leave	left	left
can	could	(been able)	lend	lent	lent
cast	cast	cast	let	let	let
catch	caught	caught	lie (lying)	lay	lain
choose	chose	chosen	light	lit, lighted	lit, lighted
cling	clung	clung	lose	lost	lost
come	came	come	make	made	made
cost	cost	cost	may	might	—
cost (work out price of)	costed	costed	mean	meant	meant
			meet	met	met
creep	crept	crept	mistake	mistook	mistaken
cut	cut	cut	mow	mowed	mown, mowed
deal	dealt	dealt	must	(had to)	(had to)
dig	dug	dug	pay	paid	paid
do (3rd person: he/she/it does)	did	done	put	put	put
			quit	quit, quitted	quit, quitted
			read	read	read
draw	drew	drawn	rid	rid	rid
dream	dreamed, dreamt	dreamed, dreamt	ride	rode	ridden
			ring	rang	rung
drink	drank	drunk	rise	rose	risen
drive	drove	driven	run	ran	run
dwell	dwelt	dwelt	saw	sawed	sawed, sawn
eat	ate	eaten	say	said	said
fall	fell	fallen	see	saw	seen
feed	fed	fed	seek	sought	sought
feel	felt	felt	sell	sold	sold
fight	fought	fought	send	sent	sent
find	found	found	set	set	set
flee	fled	fled	sew	sewed	sewn
fling	flung	flung	shake	shook	shaken
fly	flew	flown	shear	sheared	shorn, sheared
forbid	forbad(e)	forbidden	shed	shed	shed
forecast	forecast	forecast	shine	shone	shone

Präsens	Imperfekt	Partizip Perfekt	Präsens	Imperfekt	Partizip Perfekt
shoot	shot	shot	**stink**	stank	stunk
show	showed	shown	**stride**	strode	stridden
shrink	shrank	shrunk	**strike**	struck	struck
shut	shut	shut	**strive**	strove	striven
sing	sang	sung	**swear**	swore	sworn
sink	sank	sunk	**sweep**	swept	swept
sit	sat	sat	**swell**	swelled	swollen, swelled
slay	slew	slain	**swim**	swam	swum
sleep	slept	slept	**swing**	swung	swung
slide	slid	slid	**take**	took	taken
sling	slung	slung	**teach**	taught	taught
slit	slit	slit	**tear**	tore	torn
smell	smelt, smelled	smelt, smelled	**tell**	told	told
sow	sowed	sown, sowed	**think**	thought	thought
speak	spoke	spoken	**throw**	threw	thrown
speed	sped, speeded	sped, speeded	**thrust**	thrust	thrust
spell	spelt, spelled	spelt, spelled	**tread**	trod	trodden
spend	spent	spent	**wake**	woke, waked	woken, waked
spill	spilt, spilled	spilt, spilled	**wear**	wore	worn
spin	spun	spun	**weave**	wove	woven
spit	spat	spat	**weave** *(wind)*	weaved	weaved
spoil	spoiled, spoilt	spoiled, spoilt	**wed**	wedded, wed	wedded, wed
spread	spread	spread	**weep**	wept	wept
spring	sprang	sprung	**win**	won	won
stand	stood	stood	**wind**	wound	wound
steal	stole	stolen	**wring**	wrung	wrung
stick	stuck	stuck	**write**	wrote	written
sting	stung	stung			

CORRESPONDENCE/KORRESPONDENZ

Schweinfurter Stadtanzeiger
Samstag, 28. April 2001

Familienanzeigen

Traueranzeigen

Henriette hat ein Brüderchen bekommen.

Christian

23. April 2001 ✻ 8.30 Uhr ✻ 53 cm ✻ 3110 g

Mit ihr freuen sich die glücklichen Eltern

Gabi und Matthias Schulz

Ein herzliches Dankeschön an das gesamte Team der Entbindungsstation des Krankenhauses Oberndorf

Wir freuen uns über die Geburt unserer Tochter

Anna

▲ 24. April 2001
▲ 18.30 Uhr
▲ 49 cm
▲ 3280 g

Karsten und Maria Behrendt, geb. Lehmann

Geiersbergstr. 12,
97422 Schweinfurt

Wir heiraten
am Sonnabend, den 19. Mai 2001, um 14.30 Uhr
in der Evangelischen Stadtkirche Bad Kissingen

Jens Fiedler

Iris Fiedler, geb. Neumann

Tagesanschrift: Restaurant "Zum Stadtpfeifer", Bad Kissingen

Wir haben geheiratet.
Gerd Neubauer & Irene Neubauer, geb. Nolte
26. April 2001

Wir freuen uns, die Hochzeit unserer Kinder

Andrea Schmidt

Kai Seemann

bekanntgeben zu können.

Standesamt: Grimma, Freitag 25. Mai 2001, 11.00 Uhr
Kirchliche Trauung: Pfarrkirche St. Marien, Grimma,
Freitag 25. Mai 2001, 15.00 Uhr
Tagesanschrift: Gaststätte Seeblick, Dresdner Str. 103, Großsteinberg

Rita und Bernd Schmidt
Bergstr. 22
04668 Grimma

Isolde und Tristan Seemann
Zur Wasserleitung 65
97422 Schweinfurt

Plötzlich und unerwartet verstarb nach kurzer Krankheit meine liebe Frau, unsere liebe Mutter, Oma, Schwester und Schwägerin

Erika Walter

geb. Braun

* 29.2.1928   † 23.4.2001

In Liebe und Dankbarkeit nehmen Abschied
Rudolf Walter
Dieter Walter und Familie
sowie alle Angehörigen

Die Beerdigung findet am Sonnabend, den 5. Mai 2001, um 15.00 Uhr auf dem Neuen Stadtfriedhof in Eutritzsch statt.

Von Beileidsbekundungen am Grabe bitten wir Abstand zu nehmen.

Anstelle von Kränzen oder Blumen bitten wir im Sinne der Verstorbenen um eine Spende für das Deutsche Kinderhilfswerk (Konto Nummer 1004524, BLZ 860 700 00, Landeszentralbank Frankfurt).

Uns erreichte die traurige Nachricht, daß unser ehemaliger Mitarbeiter

✝ **Ewald Volkmann**
am 19. April 2001 im Alter von 83 Jahren verstorben ist.

In seiner langjährigen Tätigkeit hat er sich die Wertschätzung aller Mitarbeiter erworben.

Wir werden ihm ein ehrendes Angedenken bewahren.

Im Namen aller Mitarbeiter

Vorstand   Betriebsrat
Mitteldeutsche Braunkohle Bergbau AG

Danksagung

Für die vielen Beweise herzlicher Anteilnahme durch Wort, Schrift, Kranz, Blumen und Geldspenden sowie das ehrende Geleit zur letzten Ruhestätte unserer lieben Entschlafenen

✝ **Hilde Hagebock**
sagen wir allen Verwandten, Bekannten und Freunden unseren herzlichen Dank.

Unser besonderer Dank gilt Herrn Pfarrer Rein für seine trostreichen Abschiedsworte.

Aschaffenburg, im April 2001

ANNOUNCEMENTS/ANZEIGEN

Weekend News, Friday, November 9, 2001

Family Announcements

BIRTHS

RATTRAY

Tom and Karen (Melville) are delighted to announce the birth of their baby son (Aiden Thomas) a baby brother for Claire, born on 28th October, 2001 at Monkwell Maternity. Thanks to all staff.

JOHNSTONE

Iain and Alison (nee Lee) are pleased to announce the safe arrival of their daughter, (Cheryl) on 29th October, 2001 at Dumfries Maternity Hospital.

MARRIAGES

GREY – WALKER

Heather and Angus Grey are delighted to announce the marriage of their only daughter Helena to Johnny, youngest son of William and Sarah Walker, Barnsley, Yorkshire.

ROBERTS – FERRIER

Both families are pleased to announce the marriage of Josie, younger daughter of Janet and Ian Roberts, to Hugh Dean, younger son of Faith and Hugh Ferrier.

GREENHOLME – WILSON

At Portland Free Church on 30th October, 2001. Steven, younger son of Christine and the late John Greenholme (14, Elder Rd, Newtown) to Hannah, older daughter of Helen and Bob Wilson (189, Ralston Drive, Shieldhill). Congratulations from both families.

DEATHS

ADAM - Suddenly, after a short illness, on 2nd November, 2001, GRAHAM HOPE, aged 55 years, husband of Rita, father of John, Susan and Elsie. Grandfather of Graham and Scott. Funeral service at Holmsfield Crematorium on Wednesday 3rd November at 12.15 pm. No flowers please.

CHRISTIE - Peacefully at Harestone Nursing Home, on 29th October, 2001, CATHERINE, (Cathy McNee), aged 87 years, beloved mother and grandmother. Funeral service at St. Cuthbert's Church Tidewell at 12 noon on 4th November. Donations to Alzheimer's Society.

DAVIDSON - Quietly at Stonecross Hospital on Sunday 4th November, 2001, SANDY (Alexander), aged 83 years, beloved husband of the late Sarah Murray. The family would like to thank relatives, friends and neighbours for their support.

DOUGLAS - Suddenly, at Grangetown Infirmary on 29th October, 2001, Jim, aged 31 years, beloved son of Betty and Joe. Family only.

WEDDING INVITATIONS/ EINLADUNGEN ZUR HOCHZEIT

Wir freuen uns, Sie zur Hochzeit unserer Kinder

Cornelia Bunde und Jens Klein

recht herzlich einzuladen.

Standesamt: Kronsburg, Sonnabend 26. Mai 2001, 11.00 Uhr
Kirchliche Trauung: Sankt-Sebaldus-Kirche, 26. Mai 2001, 13.00 Uhr
Tagesanschrift: Hotel Stadthafen, Martensdamm 12, 24103 Kiel

Erika und Franz Bunde
Tulpenweg 34
24145 Kiel

Regina und Herbert Klein
Beethovenstraße 54
99880 Waltershausen

u. A. w. g.

Wir heiraten am Freitag,
den 25. Mai 2001, um 15.00 Uhr
in der St. Andreaskirche
in Neunkirchen

und würden uns freuen, Sie an diesem
Tag als unsere Gäste begrüßen zu können.

Tagesanschrift: Restaurant Bergwiese,
Schulstr. 109, 66540 Neunkirchen

Jana Wolf
Am Maikesselkopf 5
66539 Neunkirchen

Christian Schwarz
Zwickauer Str. 45
40627 Düsseldorf

Mr and Mrs James Cleland
request the pleasure of the company of

Miss Claire Stewart and partner

at the marriage of their daughter, Helen
to Mr Philip Bishop
at St Andrew's Parish Church, Thornton
on Saturday, 9th June 2001 at 2pm
and afterwards at Heatherfield Hotel, Thornton

RSVP   29 Milton Street
Thornton EH65 4EA

Martha Graupner
Hauptstraße 198
99094 Erfurt

Erfurt, 15. Mai 2001

Liebe Regina und Herbert

ich habe mich sehr über die freundliche Einladung zur Hochzeit Eurer Kinder Conny und Jens am 23. Mai in Kiel gefreut und bedanke mich recht herzlich dafür.

Natürlich werde ich gerne kommen, um diesen Festtag zusammen mit Euch und dem Brautpaar zu feiern.

Viele herzliche Grüße

Eure Martha

---

66 Buckingham Terrace,
London N10 3AG

12th August 2001

Dear Alastair and Margaret,

Thank you very much for the invitation to your Golden Wedding Anniversary party. Frank and I will be delighted to join you and we're very much looking forward to seeing you then.

With best wishes,

Alison

Uta Schwarz
Engelsweg 70
37339 Worbis

Worbis, 25. Juni 2001

Liebe Ina,

nochmals vielen Dank für die gelungene Garten-Party am vergangenen Sonntag. Es war sehr schön, so viele alte Freunde bei so gutem Essen wiederzutreffen und zu sehen, was über die Jahre aus allen geworden ist.

Ich lege einige Fotos bei. Wenn Du Zeit und Lust hast, kannst Du gerne mal bei mir vorbeischauen und die restlichen Bilder und das Video ansehen.

Viele liebe Grüße

Uta

---

346 London Road,
Birmingham
B21 6TY

Dear Jackie and Phil,

Thank you once again for the wonderful New Year party. James and I both really enjoyed seeing so many old friends again and catching up on what everyone has been up to over the past few years. I only hope that you were not left with too much mess to clean up the next day.

We are sorry you missed the Christening, but David took his camcorder along so you will be able to watch the recording. If you have time and the inclination, you're welcome to pop round to watch the video.

Many thanks again for such an enjoyable evening.

Love to all,

Carla

THANK YOU NOTES FOR GIFTS/
DANKSAGUNGEN FÜR GESCHENKE

Conny und Jens Klein
Dorfstr. 17
98663 Einöd

Einöd, 25. Juni 2001

Liebe Tante Martha,

unser großer Tag liegt nun schon wieder einen Monat zurück. Wir haben uns sehr gefreut, daß Du an diesem besonderen Tag unser Gast sein konntest.

Wir möchten Dir noch einmal recht herzlich danken für Dein Geschenk. Du mußt uns bald einmal in unserer neuen Wohnung besuchen, damit wir das schöne Fondue-Set auch gebührend einweihen können.

Herzliche Grüße

Conny & Jens

Dr and Mrs Lynn Preston
The Rushes
Bidewell Park Estate
Newton Milnes
Darlington DD7 2SY

Dear Uncle Andrew and Aunt Jayne,

Thank you so very much for your beautiful wedding gift. I have always admired your own Irish linen tablecloth so you can imagine how delighted I was to have one of my own. It will be the finishing touch to our dinner parties.

We will be sure to have you round as soon as you are on your feet again. Hope you enjoyed your piece of wedding cake!

All our love to you both,

Lynn.

Lübz, 24. Juni 2001

Liebe Oma und Opa,

vielen Dank für Euer Geburtstagsgeschenk. So eine Armbanduhr habe ich mir schon lange gewünscht. Meinen Geburtstag habe ich am Sonnabend mit meinen Freunden ganz groß gefeiert.

Ansonsten gibt es nicht viel Neues. Bald habe ich Prüfungen, dafür muß ich noch eine ganze Menge tun. Aber die Aussicht auf die großen Ferien macht es etwas leichter. Dann werde ich mit Mutti und Vati an die Ostsee fahren.

Viele Grüße auch von Mutti, Vati und Beate

Michael

---

18 Slateford Avenue
Leeds LS24 3PR
25th May 2001

Dear Gran and Grandpa,

Thank you both very much for the CDs which you sent me for my birthday. They are two of my favourite groups and I've wanted these CDs for a long time.

There's not really much news here. I seem to be spending most of my time studying for my exams which start in 2 weeks. I'm hoping to pass most of them but I'm not looking forward to the Maths exam as that's my worst subject.

Mum says that you're off to Crete on holiday next week, so I hope that you have a great time and come back with a good tan.

Tony sends his love too,

Lots of love from

Gary

SPECIAL OCCASIONS/
BESONDERE ANLÄSSE

Liebe Thekla und Andreas,

fröhliche Weihnachten und ein glückliches neues Jahr
wünscht Euch Eure

Christine

Dear John and Thomas,

Just a short note to wish you a
very happy new year.
We'll see you at the graduation.

Claire

Liebe Dorothee und Jürgen,

mit großer Freude haben wir von der Geburt Eurer Zwillinge
Wiebke und Henriette gehört. Wir hoffen, daß es Euch allen
gut geht.

Wir werden nächsten Monat kurz in Magdeburg sein.
Hoffentlich ergibt sich dann eine Gelegenheit, mal bei Euch
vorbeizuschauen. Wir werden Euch vorher noch anrufen.

Herzliche Grüße

Ines und Holger

Bromley 25.11.01

Dear Jackie and Andrew

Congratulations! We were delighted to hear about the birth of
your son, Peter. Alice must be thrilled to have a baby brother.

Send lots of photos soon!

Love,

Grace & Bob.

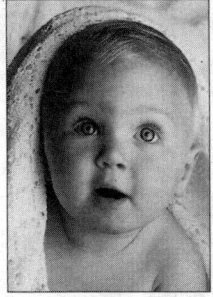

Hallo, da bin ich!
Maria Hermann

Ich wurde am 19. Mai 2001
um 18.30 Uhr im Anna-Hospital
in Hannover geboren.

Es freuen sich meine Eltern
Emma und Stefan Hermann

Leibnizufer 12
30169 Hannover

HOTEL BOOKINGS AND CONFIRMATION/
BUCHUNG UND BESTÄTIGUNG VON HOTELZIMMERN

Architekturbüro Hentschel
Burgstraße 12
51103 Köln

Hotel Ambassador
Zeil 34
60313 Frankfurt/Main

Köln, 7. Juni 2001

Sehr geehrte Damen und Herren,

zwei Mitarbeiter unseres Architekturbüros werden vom 15. bis 20. Juni dienstlich in Frankfurt sein. Wir möchten für diesen Zeitraum ein Doppelzimmer in Ihrem Hotel reservieren.

Bitte teilen Sie mir mit, ob Sie für den genannten Zeitraum noch freie Zimmer haben und wieviel die Übernachtung pro Person kostet.

Mit freundlichen Grüßen

Sekretärin

---

109 Bellview Road
Cumbernauld
CA7 4TX

14th June, 2001

Mrs Elaine Crawford
Manager
Poppywell Cottage
Devon DV3 8SP

Dear Mrs Crawford,

My sister stayed with you last year and has highly recommended your guest house.

We would like to reserve a double room for one week from 18th-24th August of this year. I would be obliged if you would let me know how much this would be for two adults and two children, and whether you have a room free on those dates.

I hope to hear from you soon,

Yours sincerely

Andrew Naismith

LETTERS OF COMPLAINT/
BESCHWERDEN

Nikolaus von Samson-Hohensterna
Flehbachmühlenweg 18
51109 Köln

Hotel Ambassador
Zeil 34
60313 Frankfurt/Main

Köln, 22. Juni 2001

Sehr geehrte Damen und Herren,

ich war vom 15. bis 20. Juni zusammen mit drei Kollegen Gast in Ihrem Hotel und muß Ihnen mitteilen, daß uns der Aufenthalt in Ihrem Haus in vielerlei Hinsicht nicht gefallen hat.

Die Empfangschefin an der Rezeption bediente uns erst nach 15 Minuten Wartezeit, denn sie mußte scheinbar erst ein persönliches Telefonat beenden. Danach stellten wir fest, daß uns noch keine Zimmer zugeteilt worden waren, obwohl unsere Firma bereits sieben Tage zuvor eine Reservierung gemacht hatte. Dies konnte erst nach weiteren 30 Minuten erledigt werden. Zu unserem Ärger mußten wir feststellen, daß die Zimmer noch nicht saubergemacht worden waren.

Was Ihr Personal betrifft, so mußten wir leider erkennen, daß die meisten Ihrer Angestellten den Gästen nicht gerade mit der für ein 4-Sterne-Hotel angemessenen Aufmerksamkeit und Höflichkeit entgegentreten, ja daß sie im Gegenteil sogar patzig auf kleine Bitten reagieren.

Ich kann Ihnen mitteilen, daß unsere Firma in Zukunft nicht mehr in Ihrem Hotel buchen wird.

Mit freundlichen Grüßen

N. von Samson-Hohensterna

Nikolaus von
Samson-Hohensterna
Architekt

Mr T. Greengage
85, Rush Lane
Triptown
Lancs LC4 2DT

WOODPECKER RESTAURANT
145 Main Street
Fallingwood FT1 6LB

20th February 2001

Dear Sir/Madam,

I was to dine in your restaurant last Thursday (15th) by way of celebrating my wedding anniversary with my wife and young son and am writing to let you know of our great dissatisfaction.

I had reserved a corner table for two with a view on the lake. However, when we arrived we had to wait for more than 20 minutes for a table and even then, not in the area which I had chosen. There was no high-chair for my son as was promised and your staff made no effort whatsoever to accommodate our needs. In fact, they were downright discourteous. Naturally we went elsewhere, and not only have you lost any future custom from me, but I will be sure to advise my friends and colleagues against your establishment.

Yours faithfully,

T. Greengage

LEBENSLAUF

PERSÖNLICHE DATEN:
Fehrmann, Dorothee
Genthiner Str. 22
10786 Berlin
Tel.: 030/855 452   Fax: 030/855 453
geb. am 17.11.1968 in Berlin
ledig

SCHULAUSBILDUNG:
1975 - 1979   Grundschule Charlottenburg II
1979 - 1988   Schiller-Gymnasium Berlin-Spandau

HOCHSCHULAUSBILDUNG:
10/1988 - 4/1993   Johannes-Gutenberg-Universität Mainz
Studium in der Fachrichtung Diplomübersetzer
für Englisch und Spanisch

AUSLANDSAUFENTHALTE:
10/1990 - 2/1991   University of Westminster, London
3/1991 - 7/1991   Universität Salamanca, Spanien

BERUFSPRAXIS:
5/1993 - 5/1995   Fremdsprachenkorrespondentin
Dr. Seeberger & Partner GmbH,
Management Consulting, München

seit 6/95   Übersetzerin
Hega Fremdsprachen-Service GmbH,
Berlin

BESONDERE KENNTNISSE:
EDV-Kenntnisse (Textverarbeitung,
Präsentationsprogramme)
gute polnische Sprachkenntnisse

Berlin,
3. Mai 2001

Dorothee Fehrmann
Genthiner Str. 22
10785 Berlin
Tel: 030/855 452
Fax: 030/852 453

Europäisches Patentamt
Personalabteilung
Hänflingweg 23
80973 München

Berlin, 3 Mai 2001

Sehr geehrte Frau Dembinski,

Ich bewerbe mich auf Ihr Stellenangebot in der heutigen Ausgabe der Süddeutschen Zeitung, weil ich sicher bin, Ihren Anforderungen an eine technische Übersetzerin zu entsprechen.

Ich arbeite seit drei Jahren als Übersetzerin in der Hega Fremdsprachen-Service GmbH in Berlin. Meine Aufgaben umfassen Übersetzungen sowohl allgemeinen als auch technischen Inhalts. Ich dolmetsche auch Geschäftstreffen unserer Kunden sowie auf Gerichtsverhandlungen am Landgericht Spandau.

Ich bin vom Landgericht als beeidigte Übersetzerin und Dolmetscherin für Englisch und Spanisch bestellt.

Ich interessiere mich besonders für diese Stelle, weil ich mich sehr gerne auf technische Übersetzungen spezialisieren möchte. Über die Möglichkeit, mein Können in einer Probeübersetzung unter Beweis zu stellen, würde ich mich sehr freuen.

Mit freundlichen Grüßen

Dorothee Fehrmann

Anlagen
Lebenslauf mit Foto
Zeugniskopien

JOB APPLICATIONS/
BEWERBUNGEN

```
                                              11 North Street
                                              Barnton
                                              BN7 2BT

                                              18th August 2001

The Personnel Director
Messrs. J. M. Kenyon Ltd.,
Firebrick House,
Clifton,
MC45 6RB

Dear Miss Paxman,

With reference to your advertisement in today's Guardian,
I wish to apply for the post of Personnel Manager.

I enclose my curriculum vitae. Please do not hesitate to
contact me if you require any further details.

            Yours sincerely,

            Rosalind Williamson
enc.
```

CURRICULUM VITAE

Name: Rosalind Anna WILLIAMSON

Address: 11 North Street, Barnton, BN7 2BT, England

Telephone: Barnton (01294) 476230

Date of Birth: 6.5.1968

Marital Status: Single

Nationality: British

Qualifications: A-levels (1986):
Italian (A), French (B), English (D)
O-levels (1984): 9 subjects

B.A. 2nd class Honours degree in Italian with French,
University of Newby, England (June 1990)

Present Post: Assistant Personnel Officer, Metal Company plc. Barnton
(since February 1992)

Previous Employment:

	Nov. 1990 - Jan. 1991:	Personnel trainee Metal Company plc.
	Oct. 1986 - June 1990:	Student, University of Newby

Skills, Interests and Experience: fluent Italian & French; good working knowledge of German; some Russian; car owner and driver (clean licence); riding & sailing.

The following have agreed to provide references:

Ms Alice Bluegown, Personnel Manager, Metal Company plc, Barnton, NB4 3KL
Dr I.O. Sono, Department of Italian, University of Newby, Newby, SR13 2RR

INVITATION TO INTERVIEW/
EINLADUNG ZUM VORSTELLUNGSGESPRÄCH

Infocomp International AG

Postfach 70, 10183 Berlin
Telefon: 030/433 4274   Telefax: 030/433 4271
E-Mail: infocomp@infocomp.intern.com

Frau Christiane Neugebauer
Koblenzer Str. 76
28325 Bremen

Berlin, 1. Juli 2001

Sehr geehrte Frau Neugebauer,

vielen Dank für Ihre Bewerbung um die von uns ausgeschriebene Stelle als Personalreferentin.

Wir laden Sie hiermit zu einem Vorstellungsgespräch ein und schlagen dafür Montag, 16. Juli 2001, 14.00 Uhr vor. Das Gespräch wird Herr Seidel führen. Unsere Geschäftsräume befinden sich in der Ungarnstraße 77 in 13591 Berlin.

Sollte Ihnen der vorgeschlagene Zeitpunkt nicht passen, melden Sie sich bitte bei Frau Nelkenbrecher (030/433 4265) zur Vereinbarung eines neuen Termins.

Die Fahrtkosten für eine Bahnfahrt 2. Klasse von und nach Berlin werden wir Ihnen unter Vorlage der Fahrkarte erstatten.

Mit freundlichen Grüßen

T. Dembinski

T. Dembinski
Leiterin Personalabteilung

Scottish Life Insurance Ltd

44 Clyde Street Glasgow G2 3GH
(0141) 345 1900

Ref: EA/LK

Ms Eleanor Aitken
210 Belmont Park
Glasgow G11 9TJ
E-mail: lynnekerr@scotlife.co.uk

18 February 2001

Dear Ms Aitken

Following your recent application for the position of Sales Adminstrator, I would like to invite you to attend an interview at the above office on Monday 26 February at 11am.

The interview will be conducted by Alan Murray and the District Sales Manager and should last approximately one hour.

If this date does not suit; please notify Mrs Simpson on extension 3200 to arrange an alternative date.

We look forward to meeting you,

Yours sincerely

Lynn Kerr

Lynn Kerr (Mrs)
Personnel Manager

OFFERING A JOB/
EINE STELLE ANBIETEN

Buschverlag
Gartenstr. 34 a
32105 Bad Salzuflen
Telefon: 0248/885 723
Telefax: 0248/531 766

Bad Salzuflen, 29. Juni 2001

Sehr geehrter Herr Franke,

bezugnehmend auf Ihr Vorstellungsgespräch am 18. Juni 2001 bieten wir Ihnen hiermit die Stelle als Cartoon-Zeichner an. Die Einzelheiten des Angebots entnehmen Sie bitte dem beigelegten Vertrag.

Sollten Sie sich für unser Angebot entscheiden, werden Sie zunächst für eine sechsmonatige Probezeit angestellt. Nach Ablauf dieser Frist können Sie in ein unbefristetes Arbeitsverhältnis übernommen werden.

Ich würde mich freuen, Sie demnächst als Mitarbeiter in unserem Verlag begrüßen zu können.

Mit freundlichen Grüßen

Astrid Meisenstein

Astrid Meisenstein
Leiterin Abt. Cartoon

---

date 27 February 2001

your ref

our ref

EXPRESS Art

Headquarters
42 West Port
EDINBURGH
EH3 1HS

Mr T Cairns
14, Greenknowe Lane
Bishopton, Glasgow G60 4BQ
Telephone 0141 226 7318

Dear Mr Cairns

Following your interview on February 3rd with Mr Davidson I am pleased to offer you the post of administrative assistant to the customer relations manager within our company.

Your employment will begin on a six month's fixed term contract, subject to review in six months. Mrs Boyle will meet you in her office at 8.45 on Monday 15th March for your induction.

If you require any further information please do not hesitate to call.

Yours sincerely,

Helen Bird

Helen Bird
Management Resources
Tel: 0131 226 7318 Personal line: 5408 7318

ACCEPTING A JOB/
EIN STELLENANGEBOT ANNEHMEN

Gerd Franke
Benrather Str. 68
42697 Solingen

Liebe Frau Meisenstein,

vielen Dank für Ihr Schreiben vom 29. Juni 2001.

Ich nehme das Angebot, in Ihrem Verlag als Cartoonist zu arbeiten, gerne an und freue mich, am 1. August meine Arbeit bei Ihnen beginnen zu können.

Ich werde mich telefonisch bei Ihnen melden, um Einzelheiten der Arbeitsaufnahme mit Ihnen zu besprechen.

Mit freundlichem Gruß

Gerd Franke

Gerd Franke

Mrs P Burns
Personnel Manager
Stocks and Chairs
Newholme 7YZ 2DD

15, Orchard Street
Greenmarket
Newholme 7YZ 3PB

22nd February 2001

Dear Mrs Burns,

Thank you for your letter of 20th February. I am pleased to accept your offer of the post of stock control officer, on a full-time permanent contract.

I understand that I will begin work at 9.15 am on Tuesday 5th March and will contact you when I arrive.

I look forward to working with you.

Yours sincerely,

E. Marriott.

NUMERALS ZAHLEN

CARDINAL NUMBERS / KARDINAL-ZAHLEN

nought, zero	0	null
one	1	eins*; (m, nt) ein, (f) eine
two	2	zwei
three	3	drei
four	4	vier
five	5	fünf
six	6	sechs
seven	7	sieben
eight	8	acht
nine	9	neun
ten	10	zehn
eleven	11	elf
twelve	12	zwölf
thirteen	13	dreizehn
fourteen	14	vierzehn
fifteen	15	fünfzehn
sixteen	16	sechzehn
seventeen	17	siebzehn
eighteen	18	achtzehn
nineteen	19	neunzehn
twenty	20	zwanzig
twenty-one	21	einundzwanzig
twenty-two	22	zweiundzwanzig
twenty-three	23	dreiundzwanzig
thirty	30	dreißig
thirty-one	31	einunddreißig
thirty-two	32	zweiunddreißig
forty	40	vierzig
fifty	50	fünfzig
sixty	60	sechzig
seventy	70	siebzig
eighty	80	achtzig
ninety	90	neunzig
ninety-nine	99	neunundneunzig
a (or one) hundred	100	(ein)hundert
a hundred and one	101	(ein)hundert(und)eins; -eine(r, s)
a hundred and two	102	(ein)hundert(und)zwei
a hundred and ten	110	(ein)hundert(und)zehn
a hundred and eighty-two	182	(ein)hundert(und)zweiundachtzig
two hundred	200	zweihundert
two hundred and one	201	zweihundert(und)eins; -eine(r, s)
two hundred and two	202	zweihundert(und)zwei
three hundred	300	dreihundert
four hundred	400	vierhundert
five hundred	500	fünfhundert
six hundred	600	sechshundert
seven hundred	700	siebenhundert
eight hundred	800	achthundert
nine hundred	900	neunhundert
a (or one) thousand	1000	(ein)tausend
a thousand and one	1001	(ein)tausend(und)eins, -eine(r, s)
a thousand and two	1002	(ein)tausend(und)zwei
two thousand	2000	zweitausend
ten thousand	10,000	zehntausend
a (or one) hundred thousand	100,000	(ein)hunderttausend
a (or one) million	1,000,000	eine Million
two million	2,000,000	zwei Millionen

Notes on the use of cardinal numbers

(a) *eins is used in counting or in listing; when 'one' directly replaces a noun, use the declined form.

(b) one, and the other numbers ending in one, agree in German with the noun (stated or implied): *ein Mann, eine Frau, (ein)hundert(und)ein Haus.*

(c) To divide thousands and above clearly, a point may be used in German where English places a comma: English 1,000 / German 1.000; English 2,304,700 / German 2.304.700.

Anstelle des im Deutschen zuweilen verwendeten Punktes zur Unterteilung von Zahlen über 1000 verwendet man in Englischen ein Komma: 1,000 statt 1.000 oder 1000, 2,304,700 statt 2.304.700.

ORDINAL NUMBERS / ORDINAL-ZAHLEN

first	1	erste(r, s)
second	2	zweite(r, s)
third	3	dritte(r, s)
fourth	4	vierte(r, s)
fifth	5	fünfte(r, s)
sixth	6	sechste(r, s)
seventh	7	siebte(r, s)
eighth	8	achte(r, s)
ninth	9	neunte(r, s)
tenth	10	zehnte(r, s)
eleventh	11	elfte(r, s)
twelfth	12	zwölfte(r, s)
thirteenth	13	dreizehnte(r, s)
fourteenth	14	vierzehnte(r, s)
fifteenth	15	fünfzehnte(r, s)
sixteenth	16	sechzehnte(r, s)
seventeenth	17	siebzehnte(r, s)
eighteenth	18	achtzehnte(r, s)
nineteenth	19	neunzehnte(r, s)
twentieth	20	zwanzigste(r, s)
twenty-first	21	einundzwanzigste(r, s)
twenty-second	22	zweiundzwanzigste(r, s)

NUMERALS   ZAHLEN

thirtieth	30	dreißigste(r, s)
thirty-first	31	einunddreißigste(r, s)
fortieth	40	vierzigste(r, s)
fiftieth	50	fünfzigste(r, s)
sixtieth	60	sechzigste(r, s)
seventieth	70	siebzigste(r, s)
eightieth	80	achtzigste(r, s)
ninetieth	90	neunzigste(r, s)
hundredth	100	(ein)hundertste(r, s)
hundred and first	101	(ein)hundert(und)erste(r, s)
hundred and tenth	110	(ein)hundert(und)zehnte(r, s)
two hundredth	200	zweihundertste(r, s)
three hundredth	300	dreihundertste(r, s)
four hundredth	400	vierhundertste(r, s)
five hundredth	500	fünfhundertste(r, s)
six hundredth	600	sechshundertste(r, s)
seven hundredth	700	siebenhundertste(r, s)
eight hundredth	800	achthundertste(r, s)
nine hundredth	900	neunhundertste(r, s)
thousandth	1000	(ein)tausendste(r, s)
two thousandth	2000	zweitausendste(r, s)
millionth	1,000,000	(ein)millionste(r, s)
two millionth	2,000,000	zweimillionste(r, s)

Notes on the use of ordinal numbers

(a) All ordinal numbers agree in German with the noun (stated or implied): *ihr erster Mann, die fünfte Frau, ein zweites Haus.*

(b) Abbreviations: English 1st, 2nd, 3rd 4th etc = German 1., 2., 3., 4. and so on.

(c) See also notes on dates below.

Siehe ebenfalls die Anmerkungen bezüglich Datum.

FRACTIONS   BRÜCHE

one half, a half	$\frac{1}{2}$	ein halb
one and a half helpings	$1\frac{1}{2}$	eineinhalb *oder* anderthalb Portionen
two and a half kilos	$2\frac{1}{2}$	zweieinhalb Kilo
one third, a third	$\frac{1}{3}$	ein Drittel

two thirds	$\frac{2}{3}$	zwei Drittel
one quarter, a quarter	$\frac{1}{4}$	ein Viertel
three quarters	$\frac{3}{4}$	drei Viertel
one sixth, a sixth	$\frac{1}{6}$	ein Sechstel
five and five sixths	$5\frac{5}{6}$	fünf fünf Sechstel
one twelfth, a twelfth	$\frac{1}{12}$	ein Zwölftel
seven twelfths	$\frac{7}{12}$	sieben Zwölftel
one hundredth, a hundredth	$\frac{1}{100}$	ein Hundertstel
one thousandth, a thousandth	$\frac{1}{1000}$	ein Tausendstel

DECIMALS   DEZIMALZAHLEN

In German, a comma is written where English uses a point: English 3.56 (three point five six) = German 3,56 (drei Komma fünf sechs); English .07 (point nought seven) = German 0,07 (null Komma null sieben). Note that a German number cannot start with *Komma* — *null* must preceed it.

Im Englischen wird anstelle des im Deutschen gebräuchlichen Kommas ein Punkt verwendet: 3.56 (three point five six). Bei Zahlen unter 1 kann die Null vor dem Punkt entfallen: 0.07 (nought point nought seven) oder .07 (point nought seven).

UNITS   EINHEITEN

3,684 is a four digit number
It contains 4 units, 8 tens, 6 hundreds and 3 thousands
The decimal .234 contains 2 tenths, 3 hundredths and 4 thousandths

3684 ist eine vierstellige Zahl. Sie enthält 4 Einer, 8 Zehner, 6 Hunderter und 3 Tausender. Die Dezimalzahl 0,234 enthält 2 Zehntel, 3 Hundertstel und 4 Tausendstel.

PERCENTAGES   PROZENTZAHLEN

$2\frac{1}{2}$%, two and a half per cent
18% of the people here are over 65
Production has risen by 8%
(See also the main text of the dictionary)

zweieinhalb Prozent

18% der Leute hier sind über 65 die Produktion ist um 8% gestiegen (Siehe ebenfalls die entsprechenden Einträge des Wörterbuchs)

NUMERALS

ZAHLEN

SIGNS   ZEICHEN

English

+   addition sign, plus sign (*eg* +7 = plus seven)
−   subtraction sign, minus sign (*eg* −3 = minus three)
×   multiplication sign
÷   division sign
√   square root sign
∞   infinity
≡   sign of identity, is equal to
=   equals sign
≈   is approximately equal to
≠   sign of inequality, is not equal to
>   is greater than
<   is less than

Deutsch

+   Additions-Zeichen, Plus-Zeichen (*z. B.* +7 = *plus sieben*)
−   Subtraktions-Zeichen, Minus-Zeichen (*z. B.* −3 = *minus drei*)
×   Multiplikations-Zeichen
:   Divisions-Zeichen
√   Quadratwurzel-Zeichen
∞   Unendlichkeits-Symbol
≡   Identitäts-Zeichen
=   Gleichheitszeichen, ist gleich
≈   ist ungefähr gleich
≠   Ungleichheitszeichen, ist nicht gleich
>   ist größer als
<   ist kleiner als

CALCULATIONS   RECHNEN

8+6 = 14 eight and (*or* plus) six are (*or* make) four-teen — *acht und* (oder *plus*) *sechs ist* (oder *macht* oder *gleich*) *vierzehn*

15−3 = 12 fifteen take away (*or* minus) three equals twelve, three from fifteen leaves twelve — *fünfzehn weniger drei ist* (oder *macht*) *zwölf, fünfzehn minus drei gleich zwölf*

3×3 = 9 three threes are nine, three times three is nine — *drei mal drei ist* (oder *macht* oder *gleich*) *neun*

32÷8 = 4 thirty-two divided by (*or* over) eight is (*or* equals) four — *zweiunddreißig geteilt durch acht ist* (oder *macht* oder *gleich*) *vier*

3² = 9 three squared is nine — *drei hoch zwei ist neun, drei zum Quadrat gleich neun*

2⁵ = 32 two to the fifth (*or* to the power of five) is (*or* equals) thirty two — *zwei hoch fünf ist* (oder *gleich*) *zweiunddreißig*

√16 = 4 the square root of sixteen is 4 — *die* (*Quadrat*)*wurzel aus sechzehn ist vier*

WEIGHTS AND MEASURES   MASSE UND GEWICHTE

METRIC SYSTEM — METRISCHES SYSTEM

deca-	10 times	10-mal	Deka-
hecto-	100 times	100-mal	Hekto-
kilo-	1000 times	1000-mal	Kilo-
deci-	one tenth	ein Zehntel	Dezi-
centi-	one hundredth	ein Hundertstel	Zenti-
milli-	one thousandth	ein Tausendstel	Milli-

Linear measures — Längenmaße

1 millimetre (Millimeter)	= 0.03937 inch
1 centimetre (Zentimeter)	= 0.3937 inch
1 metre (Meter)	= 39.37 inches
	= 1.094 yards
1 kilometre (Kilometer)	= 0.6214 mile ($\frac{5}{8}$ mile)

Square measures — Flächenmaße

1 square centimetre (Quadratzentimeter)	= 0.155 square inch
1 square metre (Quadratmeter)	= 10.764 square feet
	= 1.196 square yards
1 square kilometre (Quadratkilometer)	= 0.3861 square mile
	= 247.1 acres
1 are (Ar) = 100 square metres	= 119.6 square yards
1 hectare (Hektar) = 100 ares	= 2.471 acres

Cubic measures — Raummaße

1 cubic centimetre (Kubikzentimeter)	= 0.061 cubic inch
1 cubic metre (Kubikmeter)	= 35.315 cubic feet
	= 1.308 cubic yards

Measures of capacity — Hohlmaße

1 litre (Liter) = 1000 cubic centimetres	= 1.76 pints
	= 0.22 gallon

Weights — Gewichte

1 gram (Gramm)	= 15.4 grains
1 kilogram (Kilogramm)	= 2.2046 pounds
1 metric ton (Tonne) = 1000 kilograms	= 0.9842 ton

BRITISH SYSTEM — BRITISCHES SYSTEM

Linear measures — Längenmaße

1 inch (Zoll)	= 2,54 Zentimeter
1 foot (Fuß) = 12 inches	= 30,48 Zentimeter
1 yard (Yard) = 3 feet	= 91,44 Zentimeter
1 furlong = 220 yards	= 201,17 Meter
1 mile (Meile) = 1760 yards	= 1,609 Kilometer

Surveyor's measures — Feldmaße

1 link = 7.92 inches	= 20,12 Zentimeter
1 rod (or pole, perch) = 25 links	= 5,029 Meter
1 chain = 22 yards = 4 rods	= 20,12 Meter

Square measures — Flächenmaße

1 square inch (Quadratzoll)	= 6,45 cm^2
1 square foot (Quadratfuß) = 144 square inches	= 929,03 cm^2
1 square yard (Quadratyard) = 9 square feet	= 0.836 m^2
1 square rod = 30.25 square yards	= 25,29 m^2
1 acre = 4840 square yards	= 40.47 Ar
1 square mile (Quadratmeile) = 640 acres	= 2,59 km^2

Cubic measures — Raummaße

1 cubic inch (Kubikzoll)	= 16,387 cm^3
1 cubic foot (Kubikfuß) = 1728 cubic inches	= 0,028 m^3
1 cubic yard (Kubikyard) = 27 cubic feet	= 0,765 m^3
1 register ton (Registertonne) = 100 cubic feet	= 2,832 m^3

Measures of capacity — Hohlmaße

(a) Liquid — Flüssigkeitsmaße

1 gill	= 0,142 Liter
1 pint (Pint) = 4 gills	= 0,57 Liter
1 quart = 2 pints	= 1,136 Liter
1 gallon (Gallone) = 4 quarts	= 4,546 Liter

(b) Dry — Trockenmaße

1 peck = 2 gallons	= 9,087 Liter
1 bushel = 4 pecks	= 36,36 Liter
1 quarter = 8 bushels	= 290,94 Liter

Weights — Avoirdupois system — Handelsgewichte

1 grain (Gran)	= 0,0648 Gramm
1 drachm *or* dram = 27.34 grains	= 1,77 Gramm
1 ounce (Unze) = 16 drachms	= 28,35 Gramm
1 pound (britisches Pfund) = 16 ounces	= 453,6 Gramm
	= 0,453 Kilogramm
1 stone = 14 pounds	= 6,348 Kilogramm
1 quarter = 28 pounds	= 12,7 Kilogramm
1 hundredweight = 112 pounds	= 50,8 Kilogramm
1 ton (Tonne) = 2240 pounds = 20 hundredweight	= 1.016 Kilogramm

US MEASURES — AMERIKANISCHE MASSE

In the US, the same system as that which applies in Great Britain is used for the most part; the main differences are mentioned below:

In den Vereinigten Staaten gilt großenteils dasselbe System wie in Großbritannien; die Hauptunterschiede sind im Folgenden aufgeführt:

Measures of Capacity — Hohlmaße

(a) Liquid — Flüssigkeitsmaße

1 US liquid gill	= 0,118 Liter
1 US liquid pint = 4 gills	= 0,473 Liter
1 US liquid quart = 2 pints	= 0,946 Liter
1 US gallon = 4 quarts	= 3,785 Liter

(b) Dry — Trockenmaße

1 US dry pint	= 0,550 Liter
1 US dry quart = 2 dry pints	= 1,1 Liter
1 US peck = 8 dry quarts	= 8,81 Liter
1 US bushel = 4 pecks	= 35,24 Liter

Weights — Gewichte

1 hundredweight (*or* short hundredweight) = 100 pounds	= 45,36 Kilogramm
1 ton (*or* short ton) = 2000 pounds = 20 short hundredweights	= 907,18 Kilogramm

TEMPERATURE CONVERSION — TEMPERATURUMRECHNUNG

Fahrenheit — Celsius

Subtract 32 and multiply by 5/9
32 abziehen und mit 5/9 multiplizieren

Celsius — Fahrenheit

Multiply by 9/5 and add 32
Mit 9/5 multiplizieren und 32 addieren

°F		°C	°C		°F
0		-17.8	–10		14
32		0	0		32
50		10	10		50
70		21.1	20		68
90		32.2	30		86
98.4	≈	37	37	≈	98.4
212		100	100		212

TIME

2 hours 33 minutes and 14 seconds

half an hour
a quarter of an hour
three quarters of an hour
what's the time?
what time do you make it?
have you the right time?
I make it 2.20
my watch says 3.37
it's 1 o'clock
it's 2 o'clock
it's 5 past 4
it's 10 past 6
it's half past 8
it's (a) quarter past 9
it's (a) quarter to 2
at 10 a.m.
at 4 p.m.
at 11 p.m.
at exactly 3 o'clock, at 3 sharp, at 3 on the dot
the train leaves at 19.32
(at) what time does it start?
it is just after 3
it is nearly 9
about 8 o'clock
at (*or* by) 6 o'clock at the latest
have it ready for 5 o'clock
it is full each night from 7 to 9
"closed from 1.30 to 4.30"

until 8 o'clock
it would be about 11
it would have been about 10
at midnight
before midday, before noon

ZEIT

zwei Stunden, dreiunddreißig Minuten und vierzehn Sekunden

eine halbe Stunde
eine Viertelstunde, eine viertel Stunde
eine Dreiviertelstunde
wie spät ist es?
wie spät haben Sie es?
haben Sie die richtige Zeit?
nach meiner Uhr ist es 2 Uhr 20
auf meiner Uhr ist es 3 Uhr 37
es ist ein Uhr
es ist zwei Uhr
es ist fünf (Minuten) nach vier
es ist zehn (Minuten) nach sechs
es ist halb neun*
es ist Viertel nach neun
es ist Viertel vor zwei
um 10 Uhr (morgens)
um 4 Uhr nachmittags, um 16 Uhr
um 11 Uhr abends, um 23 Uhr
um Punkt drei Uhr

der Zug fährt um 19 Uhr 32 ab
um wie viel Uhr fängt es an?
es ist gerade drei (Uhr) vorbei
es ist fast neun (Uhr)
etwa acht Uhr, ungefähr acht Uhr
spätestens um sechs Uhr
es muss bis fünf Uhr fertig sein
es ist jeden Abend von 7 bis 9 Uhr voll
„geschlossen von ein Uhr dreißig bis vier Uhr dreißig"

bis acht Uhr
es wäre etwa 11 (Uhr)
es wäre etwa um zehn (Uhr) gewesen
um Mitternacht
vormittags, am Vormittag

*In German, the half hour is expressed by referring forward to the next full hour as opposed to backwards to the last full hour as in English.

DATES

DAS DATUM

N.B. The days of the week and the months are written with capitals as in English.

the 1st of July, July 1st
the 2nd of May, May 2nd
on June 21st, on the 21st (of) June
on Monday
he comes on Mondays
"closed on Fridays"
he lends it to me from Monday to Friday
from the 14th to the 18th
what's the date?, what date is it today?

der 1. Juli
der 2. Mai
am 21. Juni
am Montag
er kommt montags
„freitags geschlossen"
er leiht es mir von Montag bis Freitag

vom 14. bis (zum) 18.
welches Datum haben wir (heute)?

DATES

today's the 12th
one Thursday in October
about the 4th of July

Heading of letters:
19th May 2001
1978 nineteen (hundred and)
seventy-eight
2003 two thousand (and) three

4 B.C., B.C. 4
70 A.D., A.D. 70
in the 13th century
in (or during) the 1930s

in 1940 something

(See also the main text of the dictionary)

DAS DATUM

heute ist der 12.
an einem Donnerstag im Oktober
etwa am 4. Juli

Im Briefkopf:
19. Mai 2001
neunzehnhundert(und)achtundsiebzig

zweitausend(und)drei

4 v. Chr.
70 n. Chr.
im 13. Jahrhundert
in den 30er Jahren, während der 30er
Jahre
irgendwann in den vierziger Jahren or
Vierzi- gerjahren
(Siehe ebenfalls die entsprechenden Ein-
träge des Wörterbuchs)

Aa

A, a [eɪ] N A nt, a nt; (*Sch: as a mark*) Eins f, sehr gut; (*Mus*) A nt, a nt; **A sharp** (*Mus*) Ais nt, ais nt; **A flat** (*Mus*) As nt, as nt
A ABBR *of* **answer** Antw.

a [eɪ, ə] INDEF ART, *before vowel* **an (a)** ein(e); **so large a school** so eine große *or* eine so große Schule; **a young man** ein junger Mann
(b) (*in negative constructions*) **not a** kein(e); **he didn't want a present** er wollte kein Geschenk
(c) (*with profession, nationality etc*) **he's a doctor/Frenchman** er ist Arzt/Franzose; **he's a famous doctor/Frenchman** er ist ein berühmter Arzt/Franzose; **as a young girl** als junges Mädchen
(d) (= *the same*) **to be of an age/a size** gleich alt/groß sein
(e) (= *per*) pro; **50p a kilo** 50 Pence das *or* pro Kilo; **twice a month** zweimal im *or* pro Monat; **50 km an hour** 50 Stundenkilometer, 50 Kilometer pro Stunde

a- PREF (*privative*) **amoral** amoralisch; **atypical** atypisch

AA (a) ABBR *of* **Automobile Association** Britischer Automobilclub **(b)** ABBR *of* **Alcoholics Anonymous**

A & E ABBR *of* **accident and emergency**

AB ABBR (*US Univ*) = **BA**

aback [ə'bæk] ADV **to be taken ~** erstaunt sein

abandon [ə'bændən] **1** VT **(a)** (= *leave, forsake*) verlassen; *woman* sitzen lassen; *baby* aussetzen; *car* (einfach) stehen lassen; **to ~ ship** das Schiff verlassen **(b)** (= *give up*) *project, hope, attempt* aufgeben; **to ~ play** das Spiel abbrechen
(c) (*fig*) **to ~ oneself to sth** sich einer Sache (*dat*) hingeben **2** N, NO PL Hingabe f; **with ~** mit ganzer Seele, mit Leib und Seele

abandonment [ə'bændənmənt] N **(a)** (= *forsaking, desertion*) Verlassen nt **(b)** (= *giving-up*) Aufgabe f

abase [ə'beɪs] VT **to ~ oneself** sich (selbst) erniedrigen

abashed [ə'bæʃt] ADJ beschämt; **to feel ~** sich schämen

abate [ə'beɪt] VI nachlassen; (*flood*) zurückgehen

abatement [ə'beɪtmənt] N **the noise ~ society** die Gesellschaft zur Bekämpfung von Lärm

abattoir ['æbətwɑː[r]] N Schlachthof m

abbey ['æbɪ] N Abtei f

abbot ['æbət] N Abt m

abbr., abbrev. (a) ABBR *of* **abbreviation** Abk. **(b)** ABBR *of* **abbreviated** abgek.

abbreviate [ə'briːvɪeɪt] VT abkürzen (*to* mit); **~d dialling** (*Brit*) *or* **dialing** (*US*) (*Telec*) Kurzwahl f

abbreviation [ə,briːvɪ'eɪʃən] N Abkürzung f

ABC¹ N (*lit, fig*) Abc nt; **it's as easy as ~** das ist doch kinderleicht

ABC² ABBR *of* **American Broadcasting Company** *amerikanische Rundfunkgesellschaft*

ABD (*US Univ*) ABBR *of* **all but dissertation; she was still ~ after four years** nach vier Jahren als Doktorandin hatte sie ihre Dissertation immer noch nicht geschrieben

abdicate ['æbdɪkeɪt] **1** VT verzichten auf (+*acc*) **2** VI (*monarch*) abdanken; (*pope*) zurücktreten

abdication [æbdɪ'keɪʃən] N (*of monarch*) Abdankung f; (*of pope*) Verzicht m

abdomen ['æbdəmən] N Abdomen nt (*form*); (*of man, mammals also*) Unterleib m; (*of insects also*) Hinterleib m

abdominal [æb'dɒmɪnl] ADJ abdominal (*form*); **~ pain** Unterleibsschmerzen pl

abduct [æb'dʌkt] VT entführen

abduction [æb'dʌkʃən] N Entführung f

abductor [æb'dʌktə[r]] N Entführer(in) m(f)

aberration [æbə'reɪʃən] N Anomalie f; (*in statistics, from course*) Abweichung f; (= *mistake*) Irrtum m; (*moral*) Verirrung f; **in a moment of (mental) ~** (*inf*) in einem Augenblick geistiger Verwirrung

abet [ə'bet] **1** VT *crime, criminal* begünstigen; (*fig*) unterstützen **2** VI *see* **aid**

abeyance [ə'beɪəns] N, NO PL **to be in ~** (*law, rule, issue*) ruhen; (*custom, office*) nicht mehr ausgeübt werden

---

abhor [əb'hɔː[r]] VT verabscheuen

abhorrence [əb'hɒrəns] N Abscheu f (*of* vor +*dat*)

abhorrent [əb'hɒrənt] ADJ abscheulich; **the very idea is ~ to me** schon der Gedanke daran ist mir zuwider

abide [ə'baɪd] VT (*usu neg, interrog*) (= *tolerate*) ausstehen; (= *endure*) aushalten; **I cannot ~ living here** ich kann es nicht aushalten, hier zu leben
➤ **abide by** VI +PREP OBJ *rule, decision, results* sich halten an (+*acc*); **I abide by what I said** ich bleibe bei dem, was ich gesagt habe

abiding [ə'baɪdɪŋ] ADJ (*liter.* = *lasting*) unvergänglich

ability [ə'bɪlɪtɪ] N Fähigkeit f; **~ to pay/hear** Zahlungs-/Hörfähigkeit f; **to the best of my ~** nach (besten) Kräften; (*with mental activities*) so gut ich es kann

abject ['æbdʒekt] ADJ **(a)** (= *wretched*) *state, liar* elend, erbärmlich; *poverty* bitter; *failure* kläglich **(b)** (= *servile*) *submission, apology* demütig; *person, gesture* unterwürfig

abjectly ['æbdʒektlɪ] ADV *fail* kläglich

ablative ['æblətɪv] **1** N Ablativ m; **~ absolute** Ablativus absolutus **2** ADJ Ablativ-; *noun* im Ablativ

ablaze [ə'bleɪz] ADV, ADJ PRED **(a)** (*lit*) in Flammen; **to be ~ in Flammen stehen; **to set sth ~** etw in Brand stecken **(b)** (*fig:* = *animated*) **her eyes were ~** ihre Augen glühten; **to be ~ with light** hell erleuchtet sein; **to be ~ with colour** (*Brit*) *or* **color** (*US*) in leuchtenden Farben erstrahlen

able ['eɪbl] ADJ **(a)** (= *skilled, talented*) *person* fähig, kompetent; *piece of work, speech* gekonnt **(b)** **to be ~ to do sth** etw tun können; **if you're not ~ to understand that** wenn Sie nicht fähig sind, das zu verstehen; **I'm afraid I am not ~ to give you that information** ich bin leider nicht in der Lage, Ihnen diese Informationen zu geben

able-bodied [,eɪbl'bɒdɪd] ADJ (gesund und) kräftig; (*Mil*) tauglich

able(-bodied) seaman N Vollmatrose m

ablution [ə'bluːʃən] N **to perform one's ~s** (*esp hum*) seine Waschungen vornehmen; (= *go to lavatory*) seine Notdurft verrichten

ably ['eɪblɪ] ADV gekonnt, fähig

ABM ABBR *of* **anti-ballistic missile**

abnormal [æb'nɔːməl] ADJ anormal; (= *deviant, Med*) abnorm; **~ psychology** Psychologie f des Abnormen

abnormality [,æbnɔː'mælɪtɪ] N Anormale(s) nt; (= *deviancy, Med*) Abnormität f

abnormally [æb'nɔːməlɪ] ADV abnormal

aboard [ə'bɔːd] **1** ADV (*on plane, ship*) an Bord; (*on train*) im Zug; (*on bus*) im Bus; **all ~!** alle an Bord!; (*on train, bus*) alles einsteigen!; **to go ~** an Bord gehen **2** PREP **the ship/plane** an Bord des Schiffes/Flugzeugs; **~ the train/bus** im Zug/Bus

abode [ə'bəʊd] N (*Jur: also* **place of ~**) Wohnsitz m; **of no fixed ~** ohne festen Wohnsitz

abolish [ə'bɒlɪʃ] VT abschaffen

abolition [æbə'lɪʃən] N Abschaffung f

abominable [ə'bɒmɪnəbl] ADJ grässlich; **~ snowman** Schneemensch m

abominably [ə'bɒmɪnəblɪ] ADV grässlich; **~ rude** furchtbar unhöflich

abomination [ə,bɒmɪ'neɪʃən] N (= *loathsome act*) Abscheulichkeit f; (= *loathsome thing*) Scheußlichkeit f

aboriginal [,æbə'rɪdʒənl] **1** ADJ der (australischen) Ureinwohner; *tribe also* australisch **2** N = **aborigine**

aborigine [,æbə'rɪdʒɪnɪ] N Ureinwohner(in) m(f) (Australiens)

abort [ə'bɔːt] **1** VI (*fig:* = *go wrong*) scheitern; (*Comput*) abbrechen **2** VT (*Med*) *foetus* abtreiben; (*Space, Comput*) abbrechen; **an ~ed coup/attempt** ein abgebrochener Coup/Versuch

abortion [ə'bɔːʃən] N Abtreibung f; (*fig: of project etc*) Fehlschlag m; **to get** *or* **have an ~** eine Abtreibung vornehmen lassen

abortive [ə'bɔːtɪv] ADJ *attempt, plan* gescheitert

abound [əˈbaʊnd] VI (= *exist in great numbers*) im Überfluss vorhanden sein; (*persons*) sehr zahlreich sein; (= *have in great numbers*) reich sein (*in* an +*dat*)

about [əˈbaʊt] **1** ADV **(a)** (*esp Brit*) herum, umher; (= *present*) in der Nähe; **to run/walk ~** umherrennen/-gehen; **I looked (all) ~** ich sah ringsumher; **to leave things (lying) ~** Sachen herumliegen lassen; **to be (up and) ~ again** wieder auf den Beinen sein; **there's a thief ~** ein Dieb geht um; **there's plenty of money ~** es ist Geld in Mengen vorhanden; **there was nobody ~ who could help** es war niemand in der Nähe, der hätte helfen können

(b) to be ~ to im Begriff sein zu; (*esp US inf*: = *intending*) vorhaben, zu ...; **I was ~ to go out** ich wollte gerade ausgehen; **it's ~ to rain** es regnet gleich; **he's ~ to start school** er kommt demnächst in die Schule

(c) (= *approximately*) ungefähr; **he's ~ 40** er ist ungefähr 40; **he is ~ the same, doctor** sein Zustand hat sich kaum geändert, Herr Doktor; **that's ~ it** das ist so ziemlich alles; **that's ~ right** das stimmt (so) ungefähr; **I've had ~ enough (of this nonsense)** jetzt reicht es mir aber allmählich (mit diesem Unsinn) (*inf*)

2 PREP **(a)** (*esp Brit*) in (+*dat*) (... herum); **scattered ~ the room** im ganzen Zimmer verstreut; **there's something ~ him/ ~ the way he speaks** er/seine Art zu reden hat so etwas an sich; **while you're ~ it** wenn du gerade *or* schon dabei bist; **and be quick ~ it!** und beeil dich damit!

(b) (= *concerning*) über (+*acc*); **tell me all ~ it** erzähl doch mal; **he knows ~ it** er weiß davon; **what's it all ~?** worum geht es (eigentlich)?; **he's promised to do something ~ it** er hat versprochen, (in der Sache) etwas zu unternehmen; **how** *or* **what ~ me?** und ich, was ist mit mir? (*inf*); **how** *or* **what ~ it/ going to the cinema?** wie wärs damit/mit (dem) Kino?

about-face [ə,baʊtˈfeɪs], **about-turn** [ə,baʊtˈtɜːn] **1** N (*Mil*, *fig*) Kehrtwendung *f*; **to do an ~** kehrtmachen; (*fig*) sich um hundertachtzig Grad drehen **2** INTERJ **about face** *or* **turn!** (und) kehrt!

above [əˈbʌv] **1** ADV oben; (= *in a higher position*) darüber; **from ~** von oben; **look ~** schau nach oben; **the apartment ~** die Wohnung oben *or* (*above that one*) darüber

2 PREP über (+*dat*); (*with motion*) über (+*acc*); (= *upstream of*) oberhalb (+*gen*); **~ all** vor allem; **I couldn't hear ~ the din** ich konnte bei dem Lärm nichts hören; **he valued money ~ his family** er schätzte Geld mehr als seine Familie; **he's ~ that sort of thing** er ist über so etwas erhaben; **it's ~ my head** *or* **me** das ist mir zu hoch; **to get ~ oneself** (*inf*) größenwahnsinnig werden (*inf*)

3 ADJ ATTR **the ~ persons** die oben genannten Personen; **the ~ paragraph** der vorangehende Abschnitt

4 N **the ~** (= *statement etc*) Obiges *nt* (*form*); (= *person*) der/ die oben Genannte; (*several*) die oben Gennanten *pl*

above: **above-average** ADJ überdurchschnittlich; **above- board** ADJ PRED, **aboveboard** ADJ ATTR korrekt; **open and ~** offen und ehrlich; **above-mentioned** ADJ oben erwähnt; **above-named** ADJ oben genannt

abracadabra [,æbrəkəˈdæbrə] N Abrakadabra *nt*

abrasion [əˈbreɪʒən] N (*Med*) (Haut)abschürfung *f*

abrasive [əˈbreɪsɪv] **1** ADJ **(a)** *cleanser* scharf; *surface* rauh; **~ paper** Schmirgel- *or* Schleifpapier *nt* **(b)** (*fig*) *personality*, *person* aggressiv; *criticism*, *remarks* harsch **2** N (= *cleanser*) Scheuermittel *nt*; (= *substance*) Schleifmittel *nt*

abrasively [əˈbreɪsɪvlɪ] ADV *say* scharf; *criticize* harsch

abreast [əˈbrest] ADV Seite an Seite; **to march four ~** zu viert nebeneinander marschieren; **~ of sb/sth** neben jdm/etw; **to keep ~ of the times/news** *etc* mit seiner Zeit/den Nachrichten *etc* auf dem Laufenden bleiben

abridge [əˈbrɪdʒ] VT *book* kürzen

abridgement [əˈbrɪdʒmənt] N (*act*) Kürzen *nt*; (= *abridged work*) gekürzte Ausgabe

abroad [əˈbrɔːd] ADV **(a)** im Ausland; **to go/be sent ~** ins Ausland gehen/geschickt werden; **from ~** aus dem Ausland **(b) there is a rumour** (*Brit*) *or* **rumor** (*US*) **~ that ...** ein Gerücht geht um, dass ...

abrupt [əˈbrʌpt] ADJ **(a)** abrupt; *descent*, *drop* unvermittelt, jäh; *bend* plötzlich; **to come to an ~ end** ein abruptes Ende nehmen; **to bring sth to an ~ halt** (*lit*) etw abrupt zum Stehen bringen; (*fig*) etw plötzlich stoppen **(b)** (= *brusque*, *curt*) brüsk, schroff

abruptly [əˈbrʌptlɪ] ADV abrupt; *descend*, *drop* unvermittelt, jäh; *bend* plötzlich; *reply*, *ask* schroff, brüsk; (= *steeply*) *rise* steil

abs [æbz] PL (*inf*) Bauchmuskeln *pl*

ABS ABBR *of* **anti-lock braking system**; **~ brakes** ABS-Bremsen *pl*

abscess [ˈæbsɪs] N Abszess *m*

abscond [əbˈskɒnd] VI sich (heimlich) davonmachen

abseil [ˈæbseɪl] VI (*Brit Mountaineering*: *also* **~ down**) sich abseilen

absence [ˈæbsəns] N **(a)** Abwesenheit *f*; (*esp from school, work etc*) Fehlen *nt*; **in the ~ of the chairman** in Abwesenheit des Vorsitzenden; **~ makes the heart grow fonder** (*Prov*) die Liebe wächst mit der Entfernung (*Prov*) **(b)** (= *lack*) Fehlen *nt*; **~ of enthusiasm** Mangel *m* an Enthusiasmus; **in the ~ of further evidence/qualified staff** in Ermangelung weiterer Beweise/ von Fachkräften

absent [ˈæbsənt] **1** ADJ **(a)** (= *not present*) *person* abwesend; **to be ~ from school/work** in der Schule/am Arbeitsplatz fehlen; **~!** (*Sch*) fehlt!; **to be** *or* **go ~ without leave** (*Mil*) sich unerlaubt von der Truppe entfernen; **~ parent** nicht betreuender Elternteil; **to ~ friends!** auf unsere abwesenden Freunde! **(b)** (= *~-minded*) *expression*, *look* (geistes)abwesend **(c)** (= *lacking*) **to be ~** fehlen **2** [æbˈsent] VR **to ~ oneself (from)** (= *not go*, *not appear*) fernbleiben (+*dat*, von); (= *leave temporarily*) sich zurückziehen (von)

absentee [,æbsənˈtiː] N Abwesende(r) *mf*; **there were a lot of ~s** es fehlten viele

absentee ballot N (*esp US*) ≈ Briefwahl *f*

absenteeism [,æbsənˈtiːɪzəm] N häufige Abwesenheit; (*pej*) Krankfeiern *nt*; (*Sch*) Schwänzen *nt*; **the rate of ~ among workers** die Abwesenheitsquote bei Arbeitern

absentee voter N (*esp US*) ≈ Briefwähler(in) *m(f)*

absently [ˈæbsəntlɪ] ADV (geistes)abwesend

absent-minded [,æbsəntˈmaɪndɪd] ADJ (= *lost in thought*) geistesabwesend; (= *habitually forgetful*) zerstreut

absent-mindedly [,æbsəntˈmaɪndɪdlɪ] ADV *behave* zerstreut; *look* (geistes)abwesend

absent-mindedness [,æbsəntˈmaɪndɪdnɪs] N (*momentary*) Geistesabwesenheit *f*; (*habitual*) Zerstreutheit *f*

absolute [ˈæbsəluːt] ADJ absolut; *command* uneingeschränkt; *lie*, *idiot* ausgemacht; **the ~** das Absolute; **the divorce was made ~** die Scheidung wurde ausgesprochen

absolutely [,æbsəˈluːtlɪ] ADV absolut; *true* völlig; *amazing*, *fantastic* wirklich; *deny*, *refuse* strikt; *forbidden* streng; *necessary* unbedingt; *prove* eindeutig; **~!** durchaus; (= *I agree*) genau!; **do you agree? – ~** sind Sie einverstanden? – vollkommen; **you're ~ right** Sie haben völlig Recht

absolute: **absolute majority** N absolute Mehrheit; **absolute zero** N absoluter Nullpunkt

absolution [,æbsəˈluːʃən] N (*Eccl*) Absolution *f*

absolve [əbˈzɒlv] VT *person* (*from responsibility*) entlassen (*from* aus); (*from sins*) lossprechen (*from* von); (*from blame*) freisprechen (*from* von)

absorb [əbˈsɔːb] VT absorbieren; *shock* dämpfen; *costs etc* tragen; **to be ~ed in a book** *etc* in ein Buch *etc* vertieft sein; **she was completely ~ed in her family/job** sie ging völlig in ihrer Familie/Arbeit auf

absorbent [əbˈsɔːbənt] ADJ absorbierend

absorbent cotton N (*US*) Watte *f*

absorbing [əbˈsɔːbɪŋ] ADJ fesselnd

absorption [əbˈsɔːpʃən] N Absorption *f*; (*of shock*) Dämpfung *f*; **her total ~ in her studies** ihr vollkommenes Aufgehen in ihrem Studium; **~ costing** (*Fin*) Vollkostenkalkulation *f*

abstain [əbˈsteɪn] VI **(a)** (*from sex*, *smoking*) sich enthalten (*from* +*gen*); **to ~ from alcohol/drinking** sich des Alkohols/Trinkens enthalten (*geh*) **(b)** (*in voting*) sich der Stimme enthalten

abstemious [əbˈstiːmɪəs] ADJ *person*, *life* enthaltsam; *meal*, *diet* bescheiden

abstention [əbˈstenʃən] N (*in voting*) (Stimm)enthaltung *f*; **were you one of the ~s?** waren Sie einer von denen, die sich der Stimme enthalten haben?

abstinence [ˈæbstɪnəns] N Abstinenz *f* (*from* von), Enthaltung *f* (*from* von); (= *self-restraint*) Enthaltsamkeit *f*

abstract¹ ['æbstrækt] **1** ADJ abstrakt; **~ noun** Abstraktum *nt* **2** N (kurze) Zusammenfassung; **in the ~** abstrakt

abstract² [æb'strækt] VT abstrahieren; *information* entnehmen (*from* aus)

abstracted [æb'stræktɪd] ADJ abwesend

abstractedly [æb'stræktɪdlɪ] ADV abwesend; *gaze* wie abwesend

abstraction [æb'strækʃən] N Abstraktion *f*; (= *abstract term also*) Abstraktum *nt*

abstruse [æb'struːs] ADJ abstrus

absurd [əb'sɜːd] ADJ absurd; **don't be ~!** sei nicht albern; **what an ~ waste of time!** so eine blödsinnige Zeitverschwendung!

absurdity [əb'sɜːdɪtɪ] N Absurde(s) *nt, no pl* (*of* an +*dat*); (*thing etc*) Absurdität *f*

absurdly [əb'sɜːdlɪ] ADV *behave, react* absurd; *fast, rich, expensive etc* unsinnig

abundance [ə'bʌndəns] N (großer) Reichtum (*of* an +*dat*); (*of proof*) Fülle *f* (*of* von, +*gen*); **in ~** in Hülle und Fülle; **a country with an ~ of oil/raw materials** ein Land mit reichen Ölvorkommen/großem Reichtum an Rohstoffen; **with his ~ of energy** mit seiner ungeheuren Energie

abundant [ə'bʌndənt] ADJ reich; *growth, hair* üppig; *time, proof* reichlich; *energy, self-confidence etc* ungeheuer; **apples are in ~ supply** es gibt Äpfel in Hülle und Fülle

abundantly [ə'bʌndəntlɪ] ADV reichlich; *grow* üppig; **to make it ~ clear that ...** mehr als deutlich zu verstehen geben, dass ...

abuse [ə'bjuːs] **1** N **(a)** NO PL (= *insults*) Beschimpfungen *pl*; **a term of ~** ein Schimpfwort *nt*; **to shout ~ at sb** jdm Beschimpfungen an den Kopf werfen **(b)** (= *misuse*) Missbrauch *m*; (= *unjust practice*) Missstand *m*; **~ of authority** Amtsmissbrauch *m*; **the system is open to ~** das System lässt sich leicht missbrauchen **2** [ə'bjuːz] VT **(a)** (= *revile*) beschimpfen **(b)** (= *misuse*) missbrauchen

abuser [ə'bjuːzəʳ] N (*of person*) Missbraucher(in) *m(f)*

abusive [ə'bjuːsɪv] ADJ beleidigend; (*Psych*) *person, relationship* abusiv; **~ language** Beschimpfungen *pl*, Beleidigungen *pl*; **to be/become ~ (towards sb)** (jdm gegenüber) beleidigend sein/werden

abusively [ə'bjuːsɪvlɪ] ADV *refer to* beleidigend; **to shout ~ at sb** jdm Beleidigungen zurufen

abut [ə'bʌt] VI stoßen (*on(to)* an +*acc*); (*land*) grenzen (*on(to)* an +*acc*)

abutter [ə'bʌtəʳ] N (*US*) Anlieger(in) *m(f)*

abysmal [ə'bɪzməl] ADJ (*fig*) entsetzlich; *performance, work, taste etc* miserabel

abysmally [ə'bɪzməlɪ] ADV entsetzlich; *perform, work etc* miserabel

abyss [ə'bɪs] N (*lit, fig*) Abgrund *m*

AC ABBR *of* **alternating current**

A/C ABBR *of* **account** Kto.

acacia [ə'keɪʃə] N (*also* **~ tree**) Akazie *f*

academic [ækə'demɪk] **1** ADJ akademisch; *publisher, approach, interest* wissenschaftlich; *interests* geistig; *person, appearance* intellektuell; **~ advisor** (*US*) Studienberater(in) *m(f)*; **~ dean** (*US*) Dekan(in) *m(f)*; **~ officers** (*US*) akademisches Personal **2** N Akademiker(in) *m(f)*; (*Univ*) Universitätslehrkraft *f*

academically [ækə'demɪkəlɪ] ADV **(a)** wissenschaftlich; **to be ~ inclined** geistige Interessen haben; **~ gifted** intellektuell begabt **(b) she is not doing well ~** (*Sch*) sie ist in der Schule nicht gut; (*Univ*) sie ist mit ihrem Studium nicht sehr erfolgreich

academy [ə'kædəmɪ] N Akademie *f*; **naval/military ~** Marine-/ Militärakademie *f*

ACAS, Acas ['eɪkæs] ABBR *of* **Advisory Conciliation and Arbitration Service** Schlichtungsstelle für Arbeitskonflikte

acc. (*Fin*) ABBR *of* **account** Kto.

accede [æk'siːd] VI **(a) to ~ to the throne** den Thron besteigen **(b)** (= *agree*) zustimmen (*to* +*dat*); (= *yield*) einwilligen (*to* in +*acc*)

accelerate [æk'seləreɪt] **1** VT beschleunigen **2** VI beschleunigen; (*speed, change*) sich beschleunigen; (*growth, inflation etc*) zunehmen; **he ~d away** er gab Gas und fuhr davon; **~d depreciation** (*Fin*) Sonderabschreibung *f*

acceleration [æk‚selə'reɪʃən] N Beschleunigung *f*; **to have good/ poor ~** gut/schlecht beschleunigen

accelerator [æk'seləreɪtəʳ] N **(a)** (*also* **~ pedal**) Gaspedal *nt*; **to step on the ~** aufs Gas treten **(b)** (*Phys*) Beschleuniger *m*

accent ['æksənt] **1** N Akzent *m*; **to speak without/with an ~** akzentfrei/mit Akzent sprechen; **to put the ~ on sth** (*fig*) den Akzent auf etw (*acc*) legen **2** [æk'sent] VT betonen

accentuate [æk'sentjʊeɪt] VT betonen; (*in speaking, Mus*) akzentuieren

accept [ək'sept] **1** VT **(a)** akzeptieren; *apology, offer, gift, invitation* annehmen; *responsibility* übernehmen; *award* entgegennehmen; (= *believe*) *story* glauben; **to ~ sb into society** jdn in die Gesellschaft aufnehmen

(b) (= *recognize*) *need* einsehen; *person, duty* akzeptieren, anerkennen; **it is generally** *or* **widely ~ed that ...** es ist allgemein anerkannt, dass ...; **we must ~ the fact that ...** wir müssen uns damit abfinden, dass ...; **I ~ that it might take a little longer** ich sehe ein, dass es etwas länger dauern könnte; **to ~ that sth is one's responsibility/duty** etw als seine Verantwortung/Pflicht akzeptieren

(c) (= *allow, put up with*) *behaviour, fate, conditions* hinnehmen

(d) (*Comm*) *cheque, order* annehmen **2** VI annehmen

acceptability [ək‚septə'bɪlɪtɪ] N Annehmbarkeit *f*; (*of behaviour*) Zulässigkeit *f*

acceptable [ək'septəbl] ADJ annehmbar (*to* für), akzeptabel (*to* für); *behaviour* zulässig; (= *suitable*) *gift* passend; **any job would be ~ to him** ihm wäre jede Stelle recht

acceptably [ək'septəblɪ] ADV **(a)** (= *properly*) *behave, treat* anständig, korrekt **(b)** (= *sufficiently*) **~ safe** ausreichend sicher; **noise levels were ~ low** der Lärmpegel war erträglich

acceptance [ək'septəns] N **(a)** Annahme *f*; (*of report, findings*) Akzeptierung *f*; (*of responsibility*) Übernahme *f*; (= *believing: of story*) Glauben *nt*; (= *receiving: of award*) Entgegennahme *f*; **to find** *or* **win** *or* **gain ~** anerkannt werden **(b)** (= *recognition: of need, fact*) Anerkennung *f* **(c)** (= *toleration: of behaviour, fate, conditions*) Hinnahme *f* **(d)** (*Comm: of cheque, orders*) Annahme *f*

acceptance house N (*Fin*) Wechselbank *f*

accepted [ək'septɪd] ADJ *truth, fact* (allgemein) anerkannt; **it's the ~ thing** es ist üblich

access ['ækses] **1** N **(a)** Zugang *m* (*to* zu); (*esp to room, private grounds etc*) Zutritt *m* (*to* zu); **to give sb ~** jdm Zugang gewähren (*to* zu); **to refuse sb ~** jdm den Zugang verwehren (*to* zu); **to have ~ to sb/sth** Zugang zu jdm/etw haben; **to gain ~ to sb/sth** sich (*dat*) Zugang zu jdm/etw verschaffen; **"~ only"** „nur für Anlieger"; **right of ~ to one's children** Besuchsrecht für seine Kinder **(b)** (*Comput*) Zugriff *m* **2** VT (*Comput*) *file, data* zugreifen auf (+*acc*)

access: access code N Zugangskode *m*; **access course** N Brückenkurs *m*

accessibility [æk‚sesɪ'bɪlɪtɪ] N (*of place, information*) Zugänglichkeit *f*

accessible [æk'sesəbl] ADJ zugänglich (*to* +*dat*)

accession [æk'seʃən] N **(a)** (*also* **~ to the throne**) Thronbesteigung *f* **(b)** (= *addition: to library*) (Neu)anschaffung *f*

accessory [æk'sesərɪ] N **(a)** Extra *nt*; (*in fashion*) Accessoire *nt* **(b) accessories** PL Zubehör *nt*; **toilet accessories** Toilettenartikel *pl* **(c)** (*Jur*) Helfershelfer(in) *m(f)*; (*actively involved*) Mitschuldige(r) *mf* (*to* an +*dat*)

access: access road N Zufahrt(sstraße) *f*; **access time** N Zugriffszeit *f*

accident ['æksɪdənt] N (*Mot, in home, at work*) Unfall *m*; (*Rail, Aviat*) Unglück *nt*; (= *disaster*) Unglück *nt*; (= *mishap*) Missgeschick *nt*; (= *chance occurrence*) Zufall *m*; (*inf:* = *unplanned child*) (Verkehrs)unfall *m* (*inf*); **~ and emergency department/unit** Notaufnahme *f*; **she has had an ~** sie hat einen Unfall gehabt *or* (*caused it*) gebaut (*inf*); (*in kitchen etc*) ihr ist ein Missgeschick passiert; **by ~** (= *by chance*) zufällig; (= *unintentionally*) aus Versehen; **~s will happen** (*prov*) so was kann vorkommen; **it was an ~** es war ein Versehen

accidental [æksɪ'dentl] **1** ADJ **(a)** (= *unplanned*) *meeting, benefit* zufällig; (= *unintentional*) *blow, shooting* versehentlich **(b)** (= *resulting from accident*) *injury, death* durch Unfall; **~ damage** (*Insur*) Unfallschaden *m* **2** N (*Mus*) (= *sign*) Versetzungszeichen *nt*; (= *note*) erhöhter/erniedrigter Ton

accidentally [æksɪ'dentəlɪ] ADV (= *by chance*) zufällig; (= *unintentionally*) versehentlich

accident: **accident insurance** N Unfallversicherung *f*; **accident prevention** N Unfallverhütung *f*; **accident-prone** ADJ vom Pech verfolgt

acclaim [ə'kleɪm] **1** VT (= *applaud*) feiern (*as* als); (*critics*) anerkennen **2** N Beifall *m*; (*of critics*) Anerkennung *f*

acclimate ['æklaɪmeɪt] VT (*US*) = **acclimatize**

acclimatization [ə,klaɪmətaɪ'zeɪʃən], (*US*) **acclimation** [,æklaɪ'meɪʃən] N Akklimatisierung *f* (*to* an +*acc*); (*to new surroundings etc*) Gewöhnung *f* (*to* an +*acc*)

acclimatize [ə'klaɪmətaɪz], (*US*) **acclimate** [ə'klaɪmeɪt] **1** VT **to become ~d** sich akklimatisieren; (*person*) sich eingewöhnen **2** VI (*also vr*: **~ oneself**) sich akklimatisieren (*to* an +*acc*, *to a country etc* in einem Land *etc*)

accolade ['ækəʊleɪd] N (= *award*) Auszeichnung *f*; (= *praise*) Lob *nt, no pl*

accommodate [ə'kɒmədeɪt] VT **(a)** (= *provide lodging for*) unterbringen **(b)** (= *hold, have room for*) Platz haben für; (= *contain*) machine part *etc* enthalten **(c)** (= *be able to cope with*: *theory, plan*) Rechnung tragen (+*dat*) **(d)** (*form*: = *oblige*) dienen (+*dat*); *wishes* entgegenkommen (+*dat*); **I think we might be able to ~ you** ich glaube, wir können Ihnen entgegenkommen

accommodating [ə'kɒmədeɪtɪŋ] ADJ entgegenkommend

accommodation [ə,kɒmə'deɪʃən] N **(a)** (= *lodging*: *US also* **~s**) Unterkunft *f*; (= *room*) Zimmer *nt*; (= *flat*) Wohnung *f*; **hotel ~ is scarce** Hotelzimmer sind knapp; **~ wanted** Zimmer/Wohnung gesucht **(b)** (= *space*: *US also* **~s**) Platz *m*; **seating ~** Sitzplätze *pl*; **sleeping ~ for six** Schlafgelegenheit *f* für sechs Personen

accommodation: **accommodation bureau** N Wohnungsvermittlung *f*; (*Univ*) Zimmervermittlung *f*; **accommodation train** N (*US*) Personenzug *m*

accompaniment [ə'kʌmpənɪmənt] N Begleitung *f* (*also Mus*); **with piano ~** mit Klavierbegleitung; **to the ~ of** begleitet von

accompanist [ə'kʌmpənɪst] N Begleiter(in) *m(f)*

accompany [ə'kʌmpənɪ] VT begleiten (*also Mus*); **~ing letter** Begleitschreiben *nt*

accomplice [ə'kʌmplɪs] N Komplize *m*, Komplizin *f*; **to be an ~ to a crime** Komplize bei einem Verbrechen sein

accomplish [ə'kʌmplɪʃ] VT schaffen; **that didn't ~ anything** damit war nichts erreicht

accomplished [ə'kʌmplɪʃt] ADJ (= *skilled*) *player, carpenter* fähig; *performance* vollendet; *liar* versiert

accomplishment [ə'kʌmplɪʃmənt] N **(a)** NO PL (= *completion*) Bewältigung *f* **(b)** (= *skill*) Fertigkeit *f*; (= *achievement*) Leistung *f*

accord [ə'kɔːd] **1** N (= *agreement*) Übereinstimmung *f*; (*Pol*) Abkommen *nt*; **of one's/its own ~** von selbst; **with one ~** geschlossen; **sing, say etc** wie aus einem Mund(e); **to be in ~ with sth** mit etw in Einklang stehen **2** VT (*sb sth* jdm etw) gewähren; *honorary title* verleihen; *welcome* bieten **3** VI **to ~ with sth** einer Sache (*dat*) entsprechen

accordance [ə'kɔːdəns] N **in ~ with** entsprechend (+*dat*)

accordingly [ə'kɔːdɪŋlɪ] ADV (dem)entsprechend

according to [ə'kɔːdɪŋ'tuː] PREP (= *as stated or shown by*) zufolge (+*dat*), nach; (= *in agreement with, in proportion to*) entsprechend (+*dat*); **~ the map** der Karte nach; **~ Peter** laut Peter, Peter zufolge; **we did it ~ the rules** wir haben uns an die Regeln gehalten

accordion [ə'kɔːdɪən] N Akkordeon *nt*

accordion file N (*US*) Ordnungsmappe *f*

accordionist [ə'kɔːdɪənɪst] N Akkordeonspieler(in) *m(f)*

accost [ə'kɒst] VT ansprechen, anpöbeln (*pej*)

account [ə'kaʊnt] N **(a)** Darstellung *f*; (= *report*) Bericht *m*; **to keep an ~ of one's expenses** über seine Ausgaben Buch führen; **by** or **from all ~s** nach allem, was man hört; **to give an ~ of sth** über etw (*acc*) Bericht erstatten; **to give an ~ of oneself** Rede und Antwort stehen; **to give a good ~ of oneself** sich gut schlagen; **to be called** or **held to ~ for sth** über etw (*acc*) Rechenschaft ablegen müssen **(b)** (= *consideration*) **to take ~ of sb/sth, to take sb/sth into ~** jdn/etw in Betracht ziehen; **to take no ~ of sb/sth** jdn/etw außer Betracht lassen; **on no ~, not on any ~** auf (gar) keinen Fall; **on this/that ~** deshalb; **on ~ of the weather** wegen *or*

aufgrund des Wetters; **on my/their ~** meinet-/ihretwegen **(c)** (= *benefit*) **to turn sth to (good) ~** (guten) Gebrauch von etw machen **(d)** (= *importance*) **of no ~** ohne Bedeutung **(e)** (*Fin, Comm*) (*at bank, shop*) Konto *nt* (*with* bei); (= *client*) Kunde *m*, Kundin *f*; (= *bill*) Rechnung *f*; **to win sb's ~** jdn als Kunden gewinnen; **to buy sth on ~** etw auf (Kunden)kredit kaufen; **please charge it to my ~** stellen Sie es mir bitte in Rechnung; **£50 on ~** £ 50 als Anzahlung; **~(s) department** (*for customer ~s*) Kreditbüro *nt*; **to settle** or **square ~s** or **one's ~ with sb** (*fig*) mit jdm abrechnen; **~ payee only** (*Brit*) nur zur Verrechnung; **~s payable/receivable** (*on balance sheet*) Verbindlichkeiten *pl*/Forderungen *pl* aus Lieferungen und Leistungen **(f)** **accounts** PL (*of company, club*) (Geschäfts)bücher *pl*; (*of household*) Einnahmen und Ausgaben *pl*; **to keep the ~s** die Bücher führen

➤ **account for** VI +PREP OBJ **(a)** (= *explain*) erklären; (= *give account of*) *actions, expenditure* Rechenschaft ablegen über (+*acc*); **all the children were/all the money was accounted for** der Verbleib aller Kinder/des (ganzen) Geldes war bekannt; **there's no accounting for taste** über Geschmack lässt sich (nicht) streiten **(b)** (= *be the source of*) der Grund sein für; **this area accounts for most of the country's mineral wealth** aus dieser Gegend stammen die meisten Bodenschätze des Landes **(c)** (= *be the cause of defeat, destruction etc of*) zur Strecke bringen

accountability [ə,kaʊntə'bɪlɪtɪ] N Verantwortlichkeit *f* (*to sb* jdm gegenüber)

accountable [ə'kaʊntəbl] ADJ verantwortlich (*to sb* jdm); **to hold sb ~ (for sth)** jdn (für etw) verantwortlich machen

accountancy [ə'kaʊntənsɪ] N Buchführung *f*; (= *tax ~*) Steuerberatung *f*

accountant [ə'kaʊntənt] N Buchhalter(in) *m(f)*; (= *external financial adviser*) Wirtschaftsprüfer(in) *m(f)*; (= *auditor*) Rechnungsprüfer(in) *m(f)*; (= *tax ~*) Steuerberater(in) *m(f)*

account: **account book** N Geschäftsbuch *nt*; **account day** N (*Brit St Ex*) Zahlungstag *m*, Erfüllungstag *m*; **account executive** N Kundenbetreuer(in) *m(f)*; **account holder** N (*Fin*) Kontoinhaber(in) *m(f)*

accounting [ə'kaʊntɪŋ] N Buchhaltung *f*; **~ method** Buchhaltungsverfahren *nt*; **~ period** Abrechnungszeitraum *m*

accounting department N (*US*: *of company*) Buchhaltung *f*

account number N Kontonummer *f*

accounts department N (*Brit*: *of company*) Buchhaltung *f*

accoutrements [ə'kuːtrəmənts], (*US also*) **accouterments** [ə'kuːtərmənts] PL Ausrüstung *f*

accredit [ə'kredɪt] VT **(a)** *representative* akkreditieren (*form*), beglaubigen **(b)** (= *approve officially*) zulassen; *educational institution* anerkennen; **~ed agent** bevollmächtigter Vertreter

accrual [ə'kruːəl] N **(a)** (*Fin*: *of interest*) Auflaufen *nt* **(b)** **accruals** PL (*Fin*: = *liabilities*) Verbindlichkeiten *pl*

accrue [ə'kruː] VI (= *accumulate*) sich ansammeln; (*Fin*: *interest*) auflaufen; (= *be added to*) hinzukommen (*to* zu)

accumulate [ə'kjuːmjʊleɪt] **1** VT ansammeln; *evidence* sammeln; (*Fin*) *interest* akkumulieren lassen **2** VI sich ansammeln; (*evidence*) sich häufen

accumulation [ə,kjuːmjʊ'leɪʃən] N Ansammlung *f*; (*of evidence*) Häufung *f*

accumulative [ə'kjuːmjʊlətɪv] ADJ gesamt

accuracy ['ækjʊrəsɪ] N Genauigkeit *f*; (*of missile*) Zielgenauigkeit *f*

accurate ['ækjʊrɪt] ADJ genau, akkurat; *missile* zielgenau; **the clock is ~** die Uhr geht genau; **the test is 90% ~** der Test ist 90%ig sicher

accurately ['ækjʊrɪtlɪ] ADV genau

accusation [ækjʊ'zeɪʃən] N Beschuldigung *f*; (*Jur*) Anklage *f*; (= *reproach*) Vorwurf *m*

accusative [ə'kjuːzətɪv] **1** N Akkusativ *m*; **in the ~** im Akkusativ **2** ADJ Akkusativ-; **~ case** Akkusativ *m*

accusatory [ə'kjuːzətərɪ] ADJ anklagend

accuse [ə'kjuːz] VT **(a)** (*Jur*) anklagen (*of* wegen, +*gen*); **he is** or **stands ~d of murder** er ist des Mordes angeklagt **(b)** *person* beschuldigen; **to ~ sb of doing** or **having done sth** jdn beschuldigen, etw getan zu haben; **are you accusing me of lying?** willst du (damit) vielleicht sagen, dass ich lüge?

accused [ə'kjuːzd] N **the ~** der/die Angeklagte; (several) die Angeklagten pl

accusing [ə'kjuːzɪŋ] ADJ anklagend; **he had an ~ look on his face** sein Blick klagte an

accusingly [ə'kjuːzɪŋlɪ] ADV say, look anklagend

accustom [ə'kʌstəm] VT **to ~ sb/oneself to sth** jdn/sich an etw (acc) gewöhnen; **to be ~ed to sth** an etw (acc) gewöhnt sein; **to be ~ed to doing sth** gewöhnt sein, etw zu tun; **to become** or **get ~ed to sth** sich an etw (acc) gewöhnen; **to become** or **get ~ed to doing sth** sich daran gewöhnen, etw zu tun

accustomed [ə'kʌstəmd] ADJ ATTR (= usual) gewohnt

AC/DC ABBR of **alternating current/direct current** Allstrom

ace [eɪs] **1** N (lit, fig) Ass nt; **the ~ of clubs** das Kreuz-Ass; **to have an ~ up one's sleeve** noch einen Trumpf in der Hand haben; **to hold all the ~s** (fig) alle Trümpfe in der Hand halten; **to be an ~ at sth** ein Ass in etw (dat) sein; **to serve an ~** (Tennis) ein Ass servieren **2** ADJ ATTR (= excellent) Star-; **he's an ~ striker** (Ftbl) er ist ein Stürmer-Ass

acerbic [ə'sɜːbɪk] ADJ person gerissen; wit scharf; remark, style bissig

acetate ['æsɪteɪt] N Azetat nt

acetic acid [ə,siːtɪk'æsɪd] N Essigsäure f

acetylene [ə'setɪliːn] N Azetylen nt

ache [eɪk] **1** N (dumpfer) Schmerz m; **I have an ~ in my side** ich habe Schmerzen in der Seite **2** VI **(a)** (= hurt) wehtun, schmerzen; **my head ~s** mir tut der Kopf weh; **it makes my head/arms ~** davon tut mir der Kopf/tun mir die Arme weh; **I'm aching all over** mir tut alles weh; **it makes my heart ~ to see him** (fig) es tut mir in der Seele weh, wenn ich ihn sehe **(b)** (fig: = yearn) **to ~ to do sth** sich danach sehnen, etw zu tun

achieve [ə'tʃiːv] **1** VT erreichen, schaffen; success erzielen; victory erringen; title erlangen; **she ~d a great deal** (= did a lot of work) sie hat eine Menge geleistet; (= was quite successful) sie hat viel erreicht; **he will never ~ anything** er wird es nie zu etwas bringen **2** VI (Psych, Sociol) leisten

achievement [ə'tʃiːvmənt] N (= thing achieved) (of individual) Leistung f; (of society, technology) Errungenschaft f

achiever [ə'tʃiːvəʳ] N Leistungstyp m (inf); **to be an ~** leistungsorientiert sein; **high ~** (Sch) leistungsstarkes Kind

Achilles [ə'kɪliːz] N Achill(es) m; **~ heel** (fig) Achillesferse f

aching ['eɪkɪŋ] ADJ ATTR schmerzend; (fig) heart wund, weh (liter)

achy ['eɪkɪ] ADJ (inf) schmerzend; **I feel ~ all over** mir tut alles weh

acid ['æsɪd] **1** ADJ **(a)** (= sour, also Chem) sauer **(b)** (fig) ätzend, beißend **2** N **(a)** (Chem) Säure f **(b)** (inf: = LSD) Acid nt (sl)

acidic [ə'sɪdɪk] ADJ sauer

acidity [ə'sɪdɪtɪ] N Säure f; (of stomach) Magensäure f

acid rain N saurer Regen

acid test N Feuerprobe f

acknowledge [ək'nɒlɪdʒ] VT anerkennen; (= admit) truth, fault, defeat etc eingestehen, zugeben; (= note receipt of) letter etc den Empfang bestätigen von; (= respond to) cheers etc erwidern; **to ~ sb's presence** jds Anwesenheit zur Kenntnis nehmen

acknowledged [ək'nɒlɪdʒd] ADJ ATTR anerkannt

acknowledgement [ək'nɒlɪdʒmənt] N Anerkennung f; (= recognition: of truth, fault, defeat etc) Eingeständnis nt; (of letter) Empfangsbestätigung f; **he waved in ~** er winkte zurück; **in ~ of** in Anerkennung (+gen); **I received no ~** ich erhielt keine Antwort; **~s are due to …** (in book) mein/unser Dank gilt …

acknowledgement slip N (Comm) Empfangsbestätigung f

acne ['æknɪ] N Akne f

acorn ['eɪkɔːn] N Eichel f

acoustic [ə'kuːstɪk] ADJ akustisch; (= soundproof) tiles, panel schalldämpfend

acoustically [ə'kuːstɪkəlɪ] ADV akustisch

acoustic coupler N (Comput) Akustikkoppler m

acoustic guitar N Akustikgitarre f

acoustics [ə'kuːstɪks] N **(a)** SING (subject) Akustik f **(b)** PL (of room etc) Akustik f

ACP States ABBR of **African, Caribbean and Pacific States** AKP-Staaten pl

acquaint [ə'kweɪnt] VT **(a)** (= make familiar) bekannt machen; **to be ~ed/thoroughly ~ed with sth** mit etw bekannt/vertraut sein; **to become ~ed with sth** etw kennen lernen; facts, truth etw erfahren; **to ~ oneself** or **to make oneself ~ed with sth** sich mit etw vertraut machen **(b)** (with person) **to be ~ed with sb** mit jdm bekannt sein; **we're not ~ed** wir kennen uns nicht; **to become** or **get ~ed** sich (näher) kennen lernen

acquaintance [ə'kweɪntəns] N **(a)** (= person) Bekannte(r) mf; **we're just ~s** wir kennen uns bloß flüchtig; **a wide circle of ~s** ein großer Bekanntenkreis **(b)** (with person) Bekanntschaft f; (with subject etc) Kenntnis f (with +gen); **to make sb's ~** jds Bekanntschaft machen; **a woman of our ~** eine uns bekannte Dame

acquiesce [ækwɪ'es] VI einwilligen (in in +acc); (submissively) sich fügen (in +dat)

acquiescence [ækwɪ'esns] N Einwilligung f (in in +acc); (submissive) Fügung f (in in +acc)

acquire [ə'kwaɪəʳ] VT erwerben; (Fin) company also aufkaufen; (by dubious means) sich (dat) aneignen; habit annehmen; **where did you ~ that?** woher hast du das?; **to ~ a taste/liking for sth** Geschmack/Gefallen an etw (dat) finden; **caviar is an ~d taste** Kaviar ist (nur) für Kenner

acquirer [ə'kwaɪərəʳ] N (Fin) Erwerber(in) m(f)

acquisition [ækwɪ'zɪʃən] N **(a)** (= act) Erwerb m; (by dubious means) Aneignung f **(b)** (= thing acquired) Anschaffung f; **he's a useful ~ to the department** er ist ein Gewinn für die Abteilung

acquisitive [ə'kwɪzɪtɪv] ADJ auf Erwerb aus, habgierig (pej)

acquit [ə'kwɪt] **1** VT freisprechen; **to be ~ted of a crime/on a charge** von einem Verbrechen/einer Anklage freigesprochen werden **2** VR (= conduct oneself) sich verhalten; (= perform) seine Sache machen; **he ~ted himself well** er hat seine Sache gut gemacht; (= stood up well) er hat sich gut aus der Affäre gezogen

acquittal [ə'kwɪtl] N Freispruch m (on von)

acre ['eɪkəʳ] N ≈ Morgen m

acrid ['ækrɪd] ADJ taste bitter; (of wine) sauer; smell säuerlich; comment, smoke beißend

acrimonious [ækrɪ'məʊnɪəs] ADJ discussion, argument erbittert; divorce verbittert ausgefochten

acrimoniously [ækrɪ'məʊnɪəslɪ] ADV verbittert

acrimony ['ækrɪmənɪ] N (of discussion, argument) erbitterte Schärfe f

acrobat ['ækrəbæt] N Akrobat(in) m(f)

acrobatic [ækrəʊ'bætɪk] ADJ akrobatisch

acrobatics [ækrəʊ'bætɪks] PL Akrobatik f

acronym ['ækrənɪm] N Akronym nt

acropolis [ə'krɒpəlɪs] N Akropolis f

across [ə'krɒs] **1** ADV **(a)** (direction) (= to the other side) hinüber; (= from the other side) herüber; (= crosswise) (quer)durch; **shall I go ~ first?** soll ich zuerst hinüber(gehen/-schwimmen etc)?; **to throw sth ~** hinüberwerfen; **to help sb ~** jdm herüberhelfen; **~ from your house** gegenüber von eurem Haus, eurem Haus gegenüber **(b)** (measurement) breit; (of round object) im Durchmesser **(c)** (in crosswords) waagerecht **2** PREP **(a)** (direction) über (+acc); (= diagonally ~) quer durch (+acc); **to run ~ the road** über die Straße laufen; **to wade ~ a river** durch einen Fluss waten; **a tree fell ~ the path** ein Baum fiel quer über den Weg; **~ country** querfeldein; (over long distance) quer durch das Land; **to draw a line ~ the page** einen Strich durch die Seite machen **(b)** (position) über (+dat); **a tree lay ~ the path** ein Baum lag quer über dem Weg; **he was sprawled ~ the bed** er lag quer auf dem Bett; **with his arms (folded) ~ his chest** die Arme vor der Brust verschränkt; **from ~ the sea** von der anderen Seite des Meeres; **he lives ~ the street from us** er wohnt uns gegenüber; **you could hear him (from) ~ the hall** man konnte ihn von der anderen Seite der Halle hören

across-the-board [ə'krɒsðə'bɔːd] ADJ ATTR allgemein; see also **board**

acrylic [ə'krılık] **1** N Acryl *nt* **2** ADJ Acryl-; *dress* aus Acryl; ~ **paint** Acrylfarbe *f*

act [ækt] **1** N **(a)** (= *deed, thing done*) Tat *f*; (*official, ceremonial*) Akt *m*; **an ~ of mercy** ein Gnadenakt *m*; **an ~ of God** eine höhere Gewalt *no pl*; **an ~ of war** kriegerische Handlung; **an ~ of madness** ein Akt *m* des Wahnsinns
(b) (= *process of doing*) **to be in the ~ of doing sth** (gerade) dabei sein, etw zu tun; **to catch sb in the ~ of doing sth** jdn dabei ertappen, wie er etw tut
(c) (*Parl*) Gesetz *nt*
(d) (*Theat*) (*of play, opera*) Akt *m*; (= *turn*) Nummer *f*; **a one-~ play** ein Einakter *m*; **to get in on the ~** (*fig inf*) mit von der Partie sein; **he's really got his ~ together** (*inf*) (= *is organized, efficient with sth*) er hat die Sache wirklich im Griff; (*in lifestyle etc*) er hat im Leben erreicht, was er wollte; **she'll be a hard** *or* **tough ~ to follow** man wird es ihr nur schwer gleichmachen
(e) (*fig*: = *pretence*) Theater *nt*; **to put on an ~** Theater spielen **2** VT spielen; **to ~ the innocent** die gekränkte Unschuld spielen
3 VI **(a)** (*Theat*) (= *perform*) spielen; (= *to be an actor*) schauspielern, Theater spielen; (*fig*) Theater spielen; **he's only ~ing** er tut (doch) nur so; **to ~ innocent** *etc* sich unschuldig *etc* stellen
(b) (= *function*) (*brakes etc*) funktionieren; (*drug*) wirken; **to ~ as ...** wirken als ...; (= *have function*) fungieren als ...; (*person*) das Amt des/der ... übernehmen, fungieren als ...; **to ~ for** *or* **on behalf of sb** jdn vertreten
(c) (= *behave*) sich verhalten; **she ~ed as if** *or* **as though she was surprised** sie tat so, als ob sie überrascht wäre
(d) (= *take action*) handeln; **the police couldn't ~** die Polizei konnte nichts unternehmen

► **act on** VI +PREP OBJ **(a)** (= *affect*) wirken auf (+*acc*) **(b)** (= *take action on*) *warning, report, evidence* handeln auf (+*acc*) ... hin; *suggestion, advice* folgen (+*dat*); *orders* handeln aufgrund *or* auf Grund von; **acting on an impulse** einer plötzlichen Eingebung folgend

► **act out** VT SEP *fantasies, problems* durchspielen

► **act up** VI (*inf*) jdm Ärger machen; (*person*) Theater machen (*inf*); (*to attract attention*) sich aufspielen; (*machine*) verrückt spielen (*inf*); **my back is acting up** mein Rücken macht mir Ärger

► **act upon** VI +PREP OBJ = **act on**

acting ['æktıŋ] **1** ADJ **(a)** stellvertretend *attr* **(b)** ATTR (*Theat*) schauspielerisch **2** N (*Theat*) (= *performance*) Darstellung *f*; (= *activity*) Spielen *nt*; (= *profession*) Schauspielerei *f*; **what was his ~ like?** wie hat er gespielt?; **he's done some ~** er hat schon Theater gespielt

action ['ækʃən] N **(a)** NO PL (= *activity*) Handeln *nt*; (*of play, novel etc*) Handlung *f*; **a man of ~** ein Mann der Tat; **to take ~** etwas unternehmen; **have you taken any ~ on his letter?** haben Sie auf seinen Brief hin irgendetwas unternommen?; **course of ~** Vorgehen *nt*; **to take no further ~** keine weiteren Maßnahmen; (*label on file etc*) abgeschlossen; **the ~ of the play takes place ...** das Stück spielt ...; **~!** (*Film*) Achtung, Aufnahme!
(b) (= *deed*) Tat *f*
(c) (= *motion, operation*) **in/out of ~** in/nicht in Aktion; *machine* in/außer Betrieb; (= *operational*) einsatzfähig/nicht einsatzfähig; **to go into ~** in Aktion treten; **to put a plan into ~** einen Plan in die Tat umsetzen; **to put out of ~** außer Gefecht setzen; **he's been out of ~ since he broke his leg** er war nicht mehr einsatzfähig, seit er sich das Bein gebrochen hat
(d) (= *exciting events*) Action *f* (*sl*); **there's no ~ in this film** in dem Film passiert nichts; **a novel full of ~** ein handlungsreicher Roman; **that's where the ~ is** (*inf*) da ist was los (*inf*)
(e) (*Mil*) (= *fighting*) Aktionen *pl*; (= *battle*) Kampf *m*, Gefecht *nt*; **enemy ~** feindliche Handlungen *pl*; **killed in ~** gefallen; **he saw ~ in the desert** er war in der Wüste im Einsatz; **the first time they went into ~** bei ihrem ersten Einsatz
(f) (= *way of operating*) (*of machine*) Arbeitsweise *f*; (*of piano etc*) Mechanik *f*; (*of watch, gun*) Mechanismus *m*; (= *way of moving*) (*of athlete etc*) Bewegung *f*; (*of horse*) Aktion *f*
(g) (*esp Chem, Phys*: = *effect*) Wirkung *f* (*on* auf +*acc*)
(h) (*Jur*) Klage *f*; **to bring an ~ (against sb)** eine Klage (gegen jdn) anstrengen

(i) (*Fin inf*) **a piece** *or* **slice of the ~** ein Stück *nt* aus dem Kuchen (*sl*)

action: action film N Actionfilm *m*; **action group** N Aktionsgruppe *f*; **action movie** N (*esp US*) Actionfilm *m*; **action-packed** ADJ aktionsgeladen; **action point** N zu erledigende Aufgabe; **action replay** N Wiederholung *f*; **action shot** N (*Phot*) Actionfoto *nt*; (*Cine*) Actionszene *f*; **action stations** PL Stellung *f*; **~!** Stellung!; (*fig*) an die Plätze!

activate ['æktıveıt] VT *mechanism* (*person*) betätigen; (*heat*) auslösen; (*switch, lever*) in Gang setzen; *alarm* auslösen; *bomb* zünden; (*Chem, Phys*) aktivieren; (*US Mil*) mobilisieren

active ['æktıv] **1** ADJ aktiv (*also Gram, Comput*); *mind, social life* rege; *volcano* aktiv, tätig; *dislike* offen, unverhohlen; *file* im Gebrauch; **to be ~** (*terrorists, rebels*) operieren; (*lawyer, campaigner*) aktiv sein; **to be politically/sexually ~** politisch/ sexuell aktiv sein; **on ~ service** (*Mil*) im Einsatz; **to be on ~ duty** (*esp US Mil*) aktiven Wehrdienst leisten; **he played an ~ part in it** er war aktiv daran beteiligt; **~ assets** (*Comm*) Aktiva *pl*; **~ partner** (*Comm*) persönlich haftender Gesellschafter; **~ ingredient** (*Chem*) aktiver Bestandteil
2 N (*Gram*) Aktiv *nt*; **in the ~** im Aktiv

actively ['æktıvlı] ADV aktiv; *dislike* offen

activist ['æktıvıst] N Aktivist(in) *m(f)*

activity [æk'tıvıtı] N **(a)** NO PL Aktivität *f*; (*in market, town, office*) Geschäftigkeit *f*, geschäftiges Treiben; (*mental*) Betätigung *f*; **a new sphere of ~** ein neues Betätigungsfeld
(b) (= *pastime*) Betätigung *f*; **classroom activities** schulische Tätigkeiten *pl*; **the church organizes many activities** die Kirche organisiert viele Veranstaltungen; **business/social activities** geschäftliche/gesellschaftliche Unternehmungen *pl*; **criminal activities** kriminelle Aktivitäten *pl*; **a programme of activities** ein Veranstaltungsprogramm *nt*

activity holiday N (*Brit*) Aktivurlaub *m*

actor ['æktə'] N (*lit, fig*) Schauspieler(in) *m(f)*

actress ['æktrıs] N (*lit, fig*) Schauspielerin *f*

actual ['æktjʊəl] ADJ eigentlich; *result* tatsächlich; *case, example* konkret; **in ~ fact** eigentlich; **what were his ~ words?** was genau hat er gesagt?; **this is the ~ house** das ist hier das Haus; **~ size** Originalgröße *f*

> *Be careful!* **actual** *is not translated by the German word* ***aktuell***.

actual bodily harm N (*Jur*) einfache Körperverletzung

actuality [,æktjʊ'ælıtı] N (= *reality*) Wirklichkeit *f*

actually ['æktjʊəlı] ADV **(a)** (*used as a filler*) *usually not translated*; **~ I haven't started yet** ich habe noch (gar) nicht damit angefangen; **~ what we could do is to ...** (wissen Sie,) wir könnten doch ...
(b) (= *to tell the truth, in actual fact*) eigentlich; (= *by the way*) übrigens; **as you said before, and ~ you were quite right** wie Sie schon sagten, und eigentlich hatten Sie völlig Recht; **~ you were quite right, it was a bad idea** Sie hatten übrigens völlig Recht, es war eine schlechte Idee; **I'm going soon, tomorrow ~** ich gehe bald, nämlich morgen
(c) (= *truly, in reality: showing surprise*) tatsächlich; **if you ~ own an apartment** wenn Sie tatsächlich eine Wohnung besitzen; **oh, you're ~ in/ready!** oh, du bist sogar da/fertig!; **I haven't ~ started yet** ich habe noch nicht angefangen; **as for ~ doing it** wenn es dann daran geht, es auch zu tun; **it's the first time that I've ~ seen him** das ist das erste Mal, dass ich ihn mal gesehen habe
(d) **it's ~ taking place this very moment** das findet genau in diesem Augenblick statt

actuary ['æktjʊərı] N (*Insur*) Aktuar(in) *m(f)*

acumen ['ækjʊmen] N Scharfsinn *m*; **business ~** Geschäftssinn *m*; **political ~** politische Klugheit

acupuncture ['ækjʊ,pʌŋktʃə'] N Akupunktur *f*

acute [ə'kjuːt] **1** ADJ **(a)** (= *intense, serious*) *pain, shortage* akut **(b)** (= *extreme*) *situation, problem, anxiety* akut; *embarrassment* riesig **(c)** (= *keen*) *eyesight* scharf; *hearing, sense of smell* fein **(d)** (*Math*) *angle* spitz **(e)** (*Ling*) **~ accent** Akut *m*; **e ~** e Akut **2** N (*Ling*) Akut *m*

acutely [ə'kjuːtlı] ADV (= *intensely*) akut; *feel* intensiv; *embarrassed, sensitive* äußerst; *ill* akut; **to be ~ aware of sth** sich (*dat*) einer Sache (*gen*) genau bewusst sein

acuteness [əˈkjuːtnɪs] N (= *keenness*) (*of eyesight*) Schärfe *f*; (*of hearing, sense of smell*) Feinheit *f*

AD ABBR *of* **Anno Domini** n. Chr., A.D.

ad [æd] N ABBR *of* **advertisement** Anzeige *f*, Inserat *nt*

adage [ˈædɪdʒ] N Sprichwort *nt*

adagio [əˈdɑːdʒɪəʊ] **1** ADV adagio **2** N Adagio *nt*

Adam [ˈædəm] N Adam *m*; **~'s apple** Adamsapfel *m*; **I don't know him from ~** (*inf*) ich habe keine Ahnung, wer er ist (*inf*)

adamant [ˈædəmənt] ADJ *hart*; *refusal* hartnäckig; **to be ~ unnachgiebig sein**; **he was ~ about going** er bestand hartnäckig darauf zu gehen

adamantly [ˈædəməntlɪ] ADV (= *rigidly*) hartnäckig; **to be ~ opposed to sth** etw scharf ablehnen

adapt [əˈdæpt] **1** VT anpassen (*to +dat*); *machine* umstellen (*to, for* auf *+acc*); *vehicle, building* umbauen (*to, for* für); *text, book* bearbeiten (*for* für); **~ed to your requirements** nach Ihren Wünschen abgeändert; **~ed from the Spanish** aus dem Spanischen übertragen und bearbeitet **2** VI sich anpassen (*to +dat*)

adaptability [əˌdæptəˈbɪlɪtɪ] N (*of plant, animal, person*) Anpassungsfähigkeit *f*; (*of vehicle*) Vielseitigkeit *f*; (*of schedule*) Flexibilität *f*

adaptable [əˈdæptəbl] ADJ *plant, animal, person* anpassungsfähig; *vehicle* vielseitig; *schedule* flexibel

adaptation [ˌædæpˈteɪʃən] N (*of book, play etc*) Bearbeitung *f*

adapter [əˈdæptəʳ] N (a) (*of book etc*) Bearbeiter(in) *m(f)* (b) (*for connecting pipes etc*) Verbindungsstück *nt*; (*to convert machine etc*) Adapter *m* (c) (*Elec*) Adapter *m*; (*for several plugs*) Mehrfachstecker *m*; (*on appliance*) Zwischenstecker *m*

adapter card N (*Comput*) Adapterkarte *f*

adaptor [əˈdæptəʳ] N = **adapter**

ADD ABBR *of* **attention deficit disorder** ADS

add [æd] **1** VT (a) (*Math*) addieren; (= ~ *on*) dazuzählen (*to* zu); (= ~ *up*) addieren; **to ~ 8 to 5** 8 zu 5 hinzuzählen (b) *ingredients, money, name etc* hinzufügen (*to* zu); (= *say in addition*) hinzufügen, dazusagen; (= *build on*) anbauen; **~ed to which ...** hinzu kommt, dass ...; **it ~s nothing to our knowledge** unser Wissen wird dadurch nicht erweitert; **transport ~s 10% to the cost** es kommen 10% Transportkosten hinzu; **they ~ 10% for service** sie rechnen 10% für Bedienung dazu; **to ~ value to sth** den Wert einer Sache (*gen*) erhöhen **2** VI (a) (*Math*) addieren; **she just can't ~** sie kann einfach nicht rechnen (b) **to ~ to sth** zu etw beitragen; **to ~ to one's income** sein Einkommen aufbessern; **it will ~ to the time the job takes** es wird die Arbeitszeit verlängern

➤ **add on** VT SEP *number, amount* dazurechnen; *two weeks* mehr rechnen; *room* anbauen; *storey* aufstocken; (= *append*) *comments etc* anfügen

➤ **add up 1** VT SEP zusammenzählen **2** VI (a) (*figures etc*) stimmen; (*fig*: = *make sense*) sich reimen; **it all adds up** (*lit*) es summiert sich; (*fig*) es passt alles zusammen (b) **to add up to** (*figures*) ergeben; (*expenses*) sich belaufen auf (*+acc*); **that all adds up to a rather unusual state of affairs** alles in allem ergibt das eine recht ungewöhnliche Situation

added [ˈædɪd] ADJ ATTR zusätzlich; **~ value** Mehrwert *m*

addendum [əˈdendəm] N, *pl* **addenda** [əˈdendə] Nachtrag *m*

adder [ˈædəʳ] N Viper *f*, Natter *f*

addict [ˈædɪkt] N (*lit, fig*) Süchtige(r) *mf*, Suchtkranke(r) *mf*; **he's a television/heroin/real ~** er ist fernseh-/heroinsüchtig/ richtig süchtig

addicted [əˈdɪktɪd] ADJ süchtig; **to be/become ~ to heroin/ drugs/drink** heroin-/rauschgift-/trunksüchtig sein/werden; **he is ~ to sport/films** Sport ist/Filme sind bei ihm zur Sucht geworden

addiction [əˈdɪkʃən] N Sucht *f* (*to* nach); **~ to drugs/alcohol** Rauschgift-/Trunksucht *f*; **~ to sport** übermäßige Sportbegeisterung

addictive [əˈdɪktɪv] ADJ **to be ~** (*lit*) süchtig machen; (*fig*) zu einer Sucht werden können; **these drugs/watching TV can become ~** diese Drogen können/Fernsehen kann zur Sucht werden; **~ drug** Suchtdroge *f*

addition [əˈdɪʃən] N (a) (*Math*) Addition *f* (b) (= *adding, thing added*) Zusatz *m* (*to* zu); (*to list*) Ergänzung *f* (*to* zu); (*to building*) Anbau *m* (*to* an *+acc*); (*to bill*)

Zuschlag *m* (*to* zu); **the ~ of one more country to the EU** die Erweiterung der EU um ein weiteres Land (c) **in ~** außerdem; **in ~ (to this) he said ...** und außerdem sagte er ...; **in ~ to her other hobbies** zusätzlich zu ihren anderen Hobbys

additional [əˈdɪʃənl] ADJ zusätzlich; **~ charge** Aufpreis *m*

additionally [əˈdɪʃənlɪ] ADV außerdem; *say* ergänzend

additive [ˈædɪtɪv] N Zusatz *m*

addle [ˈædl] VT *brain* benebeln

add-on [ˈædɒn] N (*Comput*) Zusatz *m*

address [əˈdres] **1** N (a) (*of person, on letter etc*) Adresse *f*, Anschrift *f*; **home ~** Privatadresse *f*; (*when travelling*) Heimatanschrift *f*; **what's your ~?** wo wohnen Sie?; **I've come to the wrong ~** ich bin hier falsch *or* an der falschen Adresse; **at this ~** unter dieser Adresse; **"not known at this ~"** „Empfänger unbekannt" (b) (= *speech*) Ansprache *f* (c) **form of ~** (Form *f* der) Anrede *f* (d) (*Comput*) Adresse *f* **2** VT *letter, parcel* adressieren (*to* an *+acc*) (b) (= *direct*) *complaints, remarks* richten (*to* an *+acc*) (c) (= *speak to*) *meeting* sprechen zu; *jury* sich wenden an (*+acc*); *person* anreden; **don't ~ me as "Colonel"** nennen Sie mich nicht „Colonel" (d) *problem etc* angehen **3** VR **to ~ oneself to sb** (= *speak to*) jdn ansprechen

address: **address book** N Adressbuch *nt*; **address bus** N (*Comput*) Adressbus *m*

addressee [ˌædreˈsiː] N Empfänger(in) *m(f)*

address label N Adressenaufkleber *m*

Aden [ˈeɪdn] N Aden *nt*; **Gulf of ~** Golf *m* von Aden

adenoidal [ˌædɪˈnɔɪdl] ADJ *voice, adolescent* näselnd

adenoids [ˈædɪnɔɪdz] PL Rachenmandeln *pl*

adept [əˈdept] ADJ geschickt (*in, at* in *+dat*)

adequacy [ˈædɪkwəsɪ] N Adäquatheit *f*, Angemessenheit *f*

adequate [ˈædɪkwɪt] ADJ adäquat; (= *sufficient also*) *supply, heating system* ausreichend; *time* genügend *inv*; *excuse* angemessen; **to be ~** (= *sufficient*) (aus)reichen, genug sein; (= *good enough*) zulänglich *or* adäquat sein; **this is just not ~** das ist einfach unzureichend; **more than ~** mehr als genug; *heating* mehr als ausreichend

adequately [ˈædɪkwɪtlɪ] ADV (a) (= *sufficiently*) ausreichend; *insured* angemessen (b) (= *satisfactorily*) angemessen

adhere [ədˈhɪəʳ] VI (*to* an *+dat*) (= *stick*) haften; (*more firmly*) kleben

➤ **adhere to** VI +PREP OBJ (= *support, be faithful*) bleiben bei; *plan, principle* festhalten an (*+dat*); *rule* sich halten an (*+acc*)

adherence [ədˈhɪərəns] N Festhalten *nt* (*to* an *+dat*); (*to rule*) Befolgung *f* (*to +gen*)

adherent [ədˈhɪərənt] N Anhänger(in) *m(f)*

adhesion [ədˈhiːʒən] N (*of particles etc*) Adhäsion *f*, Haftfähigkeit *f*; (*more firmly: of glue*) Klebefestigkeit *f*

adhesive [ədˈhiːzɪv] **1** N Klebstoff *m* **2** ADJ haftend; (*more firmly*) klebend; **to be highly/not very ~** sehr/nicht gut haften/kleben; **~ label** Haftetikett *nt*

adhesive tape N Klebstreifen *m*

ad hoc [ædˈhɒk] ADJ, ADV ad hoc *inv*; **~ committee** Sonderausschuss *m*

ad infinitum [ˌædɪnfɪˈnaɪtəm] ADV ad infinitum (*geh*), für immer

adjacent [əˈdʒeɪsənt] ADJ angrenzend; **to be ~ to sth** an etw (*acc*) angrenzen; **the ~ room** das Nebenzimmer

adjectival ADJ, **adjectivally** ADV [ˌædʒekˈtaɪvəl, -ɪ] adjektivisch

adjective [ˈædʒɪktɪv] N Adjektiv *nt*

adjoin [əˈdʒɔɪn] **1** VT grenzen an (*+acc*) **2** VI aneinander grenzen

adjoining [əˈdʒɔɪnɪŋ] ADJ benachbart; (*esp Archit etc*) anstoßend; *field* angrenzend; (*of two things*) nebeneinander liegend; **the ~ room** das Nebenzimmer; **in the ~ office** im Büro nebenan

adjourn [əˈdʒɜːn] **1** VT (a) (*to another day*) vertagen (*until* auf *+acc*); **he ~ed the meeting for three hours** er unterbrach die Konferenz für drei Stunden (b) (*US*: = *end*) beenden **2** VI (a) (*to another day*) sich vertagen (*until* auf *+acc*); **to ~ for lunch/one hour** zur Mittagspause/für eine Stunde unterbrechen **(b)** (= *go to another place*) **to ~ to the living room** sich ins Wohnzimmer begeben

adjournment [əˈdʒɜːnmənt] N (*to another day*) Vertagung *f* (*until* auf +*acc*); (*within a day*) Unterbrechung *f*

adjudicate [əˈdʒuːdɪkeɪt] **1** VT **(a)** (= *judge*) *claim* entscheiden; *competition* Preisrichter(in) sein bei **(b)** (*Jur*: = *declare*) **to ~ sb bankrupt** jdn für bankrott erklären **2** VI entscheiden, urteilen (*on, in* bei); (*in dispute*) Schiedsrichter(in) sein (*on* bei, *in* +*dat*); (*in competition etc*) als Preisrichter(in) fungieren

adjudication [ədʒuːdɪˈkeɪʃən] N Entscheidung *f*; (= *result also*) Urteil *nt*; **~ of bankruptcy** Bankrotterklärung *f*

adjudicator [əˈdʒuːdɪkeɪtəʳ] N (*in competition etc*) Preisrichter(in) *m(f)*; (*in dispute*) Schiedsrichter(in) *m(f)*

adjust [əˈdʒʌst] **1** VT **(a)** (= *set*) *machine, brakes, height, speed etc* einstellen; *knob, lever* (richtig) stellen; (= *alter*) *height, speed* verstellen; *length of clothes* ändern; (= *correct, readjust*) nachstellen; *height, speed* regulieren; *figures* korrigieren; *plan, production, exchange rates, terms* ändern; *salaries* angleichen (*to* an +*acc*); *hat, tie* zurechtrücken; **you have to ~ this knob to regulate the ventilation** die Ventilation lässt sich an diesem Knopf regulieren; **do not ~ your set** ändern Sie nichts an der Einstellung Ihres Geräts
(b) to ~ oneself to sth *to new country, circumstances etc* sich einer Sache (*dat*) anpassen; *to new requirements, demands etc* sich auf etw (*acc*) einstellen
(c) (*Insur*) *claim* regulieren
2 VI (*to new country, circumstances etc*) sich anpassen (*to* +*dat*); (*to new requirements, demands etc*) sich einstellen (*to* auf +*acc*)

adjustable [əˈdʒʌstəbl] ADJ verstellbar; *shape* variabel; *speed, temperature* regulierbar; **~ rate mortgage** (*Fin*) variabel verzinsliches Hypothekendarlehen

adjuster [əˈdʒʌstəʳ] N (*Insur*) (Schadens)sachverständige(r) *mf*

adjustment [əˈdʒʌstmənt] N **(a)** (= *setting*) Einstellung *f*; (*of knob, lever*) (richtige) Stellung *f*; (= *alteration*) (*of height, speed*) Verstellung *f*; (*of length of clothes*) Änderung *f*; (= *correction, readjustment*) Nachstellung *f*; (*of height, speed*) Regulierung *f*; (*of plan, production, exchange rate, terms*) Änderung *f*; **to make ~s** Änderungen vornehmen; **to make ~s to one's plans** seine Pläne ändern; **brakes require regular ~** Bremsen müssen regelmäßig nachgestellt werden
(b) (*socially etc*) Anpassung *f*
(c) (*Insur*) Regulierung *f*

adjutant [ˈædʒətənt] N (*Mil*) Adjutant(in) *m(f)*

ad lib [ædˈlɪb] ADV aus dem Stegreif

ad-lib **1** N Improvisation *f* **2** VTI improvisieren

adman [ˈædmæn] N, *pl* **-men** [-men] (*inf*) Werbefachmann *m*; **admen** Werbeleute *pl*

admin [ˈædmɪn] ABBR *of* **administration**; **it involves a lot of ~** damit ist viel Verwaltung verbunden; **~ building** Verwaltungsgebäude *nt*

administer [ədˈmɪnɪstəʳ] VT **(a)** *institution, funds* verwalten; *business, affairs* führen; (= *run*) *company, department* die Verwaltungsangelegenheiten regeln von **(b)** (= *dispense*) *relief, alms* gewähren; *law* ausführen; *punishment* verhängen (*to* über +*acc*); **to ~ justice** Recht sprechen **(c)** (= *cause to take*) (*to sb* jdm) *medicine, drugs* verabreichen; *last rites* geben

administrate [ædˈmɪnɪstreɪt] VT = **administer**

administration [ədˌmɪnɪsˈtreɪʃən] N **(a)** NO PL Verwaltung *f*; (*of an election, a project etc*) Organisation *f*; **to spend a lot of time on ~** viel Zeit auf Verwaltungsangelegenheiten verwenden **(b)** (= *government*) Regierung *f*; **the Schmidt ~** die Regierung Schmidt **(c)** NO PL **the ~ of justice** die Rechtsprechung

administrative: **administrative** [ədˈmɪnɪstrətɪv] ADJ administrativ; **administrative body** N Verwaltungsbehörde *f*; **administrative costs** PL Verwaltungskosten *pl*; **administrative court** N (*US Jur*) Verwaltungsgericht *nt*; **administrative law** N Verwaltungsrecht *nt*

administrator [ədˈmɪnɪstreɪtəʳ] N Verwalter(in) *m(f)*; (*Jur*) Verwaltungsbeamte(r) *m*/-beamtin *f*

admirable ADJ, **admirably** ADV [ˈædmərəbl, -ɪ] (= *praiseworthy, laudable*) bewundernswert; (= *excellent*) ausgezeichnet

admiral [ˈædmərəl] N Admiral(in) *m(f)*

Admiralty [ˈædmərəltɪ] N (*Brit*) Admiralität *f*; (= *department, building*) britisches Marineministerium

admiration [ˌædməˈreɪʃən] N Bewunderung *f*; **to win the ~ of all/ of the world** (*person, object*) von allen/von aller Welt bewundert werden

admire [ədˈmaɪəʳ] VT bewundern

admirer [ədˈmaɪərəʳ] N Verehrer(in) *m(f)*

admiring ADJ, **admiringly** ADV [ədˈmaɪərɪŋ, -lɪ] bewundernd

admissible [ədˈmɪsɪbl] ADJ zulässig

admission [ədˈmɪʃən] N **(a)** (= *entry*) Zutritt *m*; (*to university*) Zulassung *f*; (*to hospital*) Einlieferung *f* (*to* in +*acc*); (= *price*) Eintritt *m*; **no ~ to minors** Zutritt für Minderjährige verboten; **to gain ~ to a building** Zutritt zu einem Gebäude erhalten; **~ fee** Eintrittspreis *m*
(b) (*Jur*: *of evidence etc*) Zulassung *f*
(c) (= *confession*) Eingeständnis *nt*; **on** *or* **by his own ~** nach eigenem Eingeständnis; **that would be an ~ of failure** das hieße, sein Versagen eingestehen

admit [ədˈmɪt] VT **(a)** (= *let in*) hereinlassen; (= *permit to join*) zulassen (*to* zu), aufnehmen (*to* in +*acc*); **children not ~ted** kein Zutritt für Kinder; **to be ~ted to hospital** ins Krankenhaus eingeliefert werden; **this ticket ~s two** die Karte ist für zwei (Personen) **(b)** (= *acknowledge*) zugeben; **do you ~ (to) stealing his hat?** geben Sie zu, seinen Hut gestohlen zu haben?
➤ **admit to** VI +PREP OBJ eingestehen; **I have to admit to a certain feeling of admiration** ich muss gestehen, dass mir das Bewunderung abnötigt

admittance [ədˈmɪtəns] N (*to building*) Zutritt *m* (*to* zu); (*to club*) Aufnahme *f* (*to* in +*acc*); **I gained ~ to the hall** mir wurde der Zutritt zum Saal gestattet; **I was denied ~** mir wurde der Zutritt verwehrt; **no ~ except on business** Zutritt für Unbefugte verboten

admittedly [ədˈmɪtɪdlɪ] ADV zugegebenermaßen; **~ this is true** zugegeben, das stimmt

admonish [ədˈmɒnɪʃ] VT ermahnen (*for* wegen)

admonishment [ədˈmɒnɪʃmənt], **admonition** [ˌædməʊˈnɪʃən] N (*form*) **(a)** (= *rebuke*) Tadel *m* **(b)** (= *warning*) Ermahnung *f*

ad nauseam [ædˈnɔːzɪæm] ADV bis zum Überdruss; **and so on ~** und so weiter, und so weiter

ado [əˈduː] N **much ~ about nothing** viel Lärm um nichts; **without more** *or* **further ~** ohne weiteres

adolescence [ˌædəʊˈlesns] N Jugend *f*; (= *puberty*) Pubertät *f*, Adoleszenz *f* (*form*)

adolescent [ˌædəʊˈlesnt] **1** N Jugendliche(r) *mf* **2** ADJ Jugend-; (= *in puberty*) pubertär; (= *immature*) unreif; **~ phase** Pubertätsphase *f*

adopt [əˈdɒpt] VT **(a)** *child* adoptieren; *child in a different country, family, city* die Patenschaft übernehmen für; **your cat has ~ed me** (*inf*) deine Katze hat sich mir angeschlossen **(b)** *idea, attitude, method* übernehmen; *mannerisms* annehmen **(c)** (*Pol*) *motion* annehmen; *candidate* nehmen

adopted [əˈdɒptɪd] ADJ Adoptiv-, adoptiert; **~ child** Adoptivkind *nt*; **her ~ country/home town** ihre Wahlheimat

adoption [əˈdɒpʃən] N **(a)** (*of child*) Adoption *f*; (*of city, child in other country*) Übernahme *f* der Patenschaft; **parents by ~** Adoptiveltern *pl* **(b)** (*of method, idea*) Übernahme *f*; (*of mannerisms*) Annahme *f*; **his country of ~** die Heimat seiner Wahl **(c)** (*of motion, candidate*) Annahme *f*

adoption agency N Adoptionsagentur *f*

adoptive [əˈdɒptɪv] ADJ Adoptiv-; **~ parents** Adoptiveltern *pl*; **~ home/country** Wahlheimat *f*

adorable [əˈdɔːrəbl] ADJ bezaubernd; **she is ~** sie ist ein Schatz

adoration [ˌædəˈreɪʃən] N **(a)** (*of God*) Anbetung *f* **(b)** (*of family, wife*) grenzenlose Liebe (*of* für)

adore [əˈdɔːʳ] VT **(a)** *God* anbeten **(b)** (= *love very much*) *family, wife* über alles lieben **(c)** (*inf*: = *like very much*) *French, whisky etc* (über alles) lieben

adoring ADJ, **adoringly** ADV [əˈdɔːrɪŋ, -lɪ] bewundernd

adorn [əˈdɔːn] VT schmücken

adornment [əˈdɔːnmənt] N Schmuck *m* no pl; (*act*) Schmücken *nt*; (*on dress, cake*) Verzierung *f*

adrenalin(e) [əˈdrenəlɪn] N **(a)** (*Med*) Adrenalin *nt* **(b)** (*phrases*) **it's impossible to relax now the ~'s going** es ist unmöglich abzuschalten, wenn man so aufgeregt ist; **working under pressure gets the ~ going** Arbeiten unter Druck weckt ungeahnte Kräfte

Adriatic (Sea) [ˌeɪdrɪˈætɪk(ˈsiː)] N Adria f, Adriatisches Meer

adrift [əˈdrɪft] ADV, ADJ PRED (a) (*Naut*) treibend; **to be ~** treiben (b) (*fig*) **to come ~** (*wire, hair etc*) sich lösen; (*plans, scheme*) fehlschlagen; (*theory*) zusammenbrechen

adroit [əˈdrɔɪt] ADJ geschickt; *mind* scharf; **to be ~ at sth/doing sth** geschickt in etw (*dat*) sein/darin sein, etw zu tun

adroitly [əˈdrɔɪtlɪ] ADV geschickt

adulation [ˌædjʊˈleɪʃən] N Verherrlichung f

adulatory [ˌædjʊˈleɪtərɪ, (US) ˈædʒələtɔːrɪ] ADJ (= *laudatory*) *comment* bewundernd; (*stronger*) vergötternd

adult [ˈædʌlt, (US) əˈdʌlt] ◼ N Erwachsene(r) mf; **~s only** nur für Erwachsene ◼ ADJ (a) *person* erwachsen; *animal* ausgewachsen; **he spent his ~ life in New York** er hat sein Leben als Erwachsener in New York verbracht (b) (= *for adults*) *film, classes* für Erwachsene; **~ education** Erwachsenenbildung f (c) (= *mature*) *decision* reif; **we were very ~ about it** wir waren sehr ruhig und vernünftig

adulterate [əˈdʌltəreɪt] VT *wine etc* panschen; *food* abwandeln

adulteration [əˌdʌltəˈreɪʃən] N (*of wine*) Pan(t)schen nt; (*of food*) Abwandlung f

adulterer [əˈdʌltərəʳ] N Ehebrecher m

adulteress [əˈdʌltərɪs] N Ehebrecherin f

adulterous [əˈdʌltərəs] ADJ ehebrecherisch

adultery [əˈdʌltərɪ] N Ehebruch m; **to commit ~** Ehebruch begehen

adulthood [ˈædʌlthʊd, (US) əˈdʌlthʊd] N Erwachsenenalter nt; **to reach ~** erwachsen werden

advance [ədˈvɑːns] ◼ N (a) (= *progress*) Fortschritt m (b) (= *movement forward*) (*of old age*) Voranschreiten nt; (*of science*) Weiterentwicklung f; (*of sea, ideas*) Vordringen nt; **with the ~ of old age** mit fortschreitendem Alter (c) (*Mil*) Vormarsch m (d) (= *money*) Vorschuss m (*on auf +acc*) (e) **advances** PL (*amorous, fig*) Annäherungsversuche pl (f) **in ~** im Voraus; **to send sb on in ~** jdn vorausschicken; **£100 in ~** £ 100 als Vorschuss; **to arrive in ~ of the others** vor den anderen ankommen; **to be (well) in ~ of sb** jdm (weit) voraus sein ◼ VT (a) (= *move forward*) *date, time* vorverlegen (b) (*Mil*) *troops* vorrücken lassen (c) (= *further*) *work, project* weiterbringen; *cause, interests, career* fördern; *knowledge* vergrößern; (= *accelerate*) *growth* vorantreiben; (= *promote*) *employee etc* befördern (d) (= *put forward*) *reason, opinion, plan* vorbringen (e) (= *pay beforehand*) (*sb* jdm) (als) Vorschuss geben; (= *lend*) als Kredit geben ◼ VI (a) (*Mil*) vorrücken (b) (= *move forward*) vorankommen; **to ~ toward(s) sb/sth** auf jdn/etw zugehen (c) (*fig*: = *progress*) Fortschritte pl machen

advance: **advance booking** N Reservierung f; (*Theat*) Vorverkauf m; **advance booking office** N (*Theat*) Vorverkaufsstelle f; **advance copy** N Vorausexemplar nt

advanced [ədˈvɑːnst] ADJ (a) *student, level, age, technology* fortgeschritten; *studies, mathematics etc* höher; *ideas* fortschrittlich; *version, model* weiterentwickelt; *position* vorgeschoben; *society, economy* hoch entwickelt; **he is very ~ for his age** er ist für sein Alter sehr weit (b) (= *developed*) *plan, programme* ausgefeilt; **in the ~ stages of the disease** im fortgeschrittenen Stadium der Krankheit (c) (*form*: = *mature*) **~ in years** in fortgeschrittenem Alter

advance man N (*US Pol*) Wahlhelfer m

advancement [ədˈvɑːnsmənt] N (a) (= *furtherance*) Förderung f (b) (= *promotion in rank*) Aufstieg m

advance: **advance notice** N frühzeitiger Bescheid; (*of sth bad*) Vorwarnung f; **to be given ~** frühzeitig Bescheid/eine Vorwarnung erhalten; **advance party** N (*Mil, fig*) Vorhut f; **advance payment** N Vorauszahlung f; **advance publicity** N Vorabwerbung f; **advance warning** N = **advance notice**

advantage [ədˈvɑːntɪdʒ] N Vorteil m; **to have an ~ (over sb)** (jdm gegenüber) im Vorteil sein; **that gives you an ~ over me** damit sind Sie mir gegenüber im Vorteil; **to have the ~ of sb** jdm überlegen sein; **she had the ~ of greater experience** sie war durch ihre größere Erfahrung im Vorteil; **to have the ~ of numbers** zahlenmäßig überlegen sein; **to take ~ of sb** (= *exploit*) jdn ausnutzen; (*euph: sexually*) jdn missbrauchen;

to take ~ of sth etw ausnutzen; **he turned it to his own ~** er machte es sich (*dat*) zunutze; **it is to my ~ to ...** es ist für mich von Vorteil ...; **to use sth to one's ~** etw für sich nutzen

advantageous [ˌædvənˈteɪdʒəs] ADJ vorteilhaft; **to be ~ to sb** für jdn von Vorteil sein

advent [ˈædvənt] N (a) (*of age, era*) Beginn m; (*of jet plane etc*) Aufkommen nt (b) (*Eccl*) **Advent** Advent m

Advent calendar N Adventskalender m

adventure [ədˈventʃəʳ] ◼ N (a) Abenteuer nt (b) NO PL **love/ spirit of ~** Abenteuerlust f; **to look for ~** (das) Abenteuer suchen ◼ ATTR Abenteuer-

adventure playground N Abenteuerspielplatz m

adventurer [ədˈventʃərəʳ] N Abenteurer(in) m(f)

adventurous [ədˈventʃərəs] ADJ (a) *person* abenteuerlustig; *journey* abenteuerlich (b) (= *bold*) gewagt

adventurously [ədˈventʃərəslɪ] ADV (= *boldly*) gewagt

adverb [ˈædvɜːb] N Adverb nt

adverbial ADJ, **adverbially** ADV [ədˈvɜːbɪəl, -ɪ] adverbial

adversary [ˈædvəsərɪ] N Widersacher(in) m(f); (*in contest*) Gegner(in) m(f)

adverse [ˈædvɜːs] ADJ ungünstig; *reaction* negativ

adversely [ˈædvɜːslɪ] ADV negativ

adversity [ədˈvɜːsɪtɪ] N, NO PL Not f; **in ~** im Unglück

advert [ˈædvɜːt] N (*inf*) ABBR of **advertisement** Anzeige f; (*on TV, radio*) Werbespot m

advertise [ˈædvətaɪz] ◼ VT (a) (= *publicize*) werben für; **I've seen that soap ~d on television** ich habe die Werbung für diese Seife im Fernsehen gesehen (b) (*in paper etc*) *flat, table etc* inserieren; *job* ausschreiben; **to ~ sth in a shop window/on local radio** etw durch eine Schaufensteranzeige/im Regionalsender anbieten (c) (= *make conspicuous*) *fact* publik machen ◼ VI (a) (*Comm*) Werbung machen, werben (b) (*in paper*) inserieren; **to ~ for sb/sth** jdn/etw (per Anzeige) suchen; **to ~ for sth on local radio/in a shop window** etw per Regionalsender/durch Anzeige im Schaufenster suchen

advertisement [ədˈvɜːtɪsmənt, (US) ˌædvəˈtaɪzmənt] N (a) (*Comm*) Werbung f; (*esp in paper*) Anzeige f; **he is not a good ~ for his school** er ist nicht gerade ein Aushängeschild für seine Schule (b) (= *announcement*) Anzeige f; **to put** *or* **place an ~ in the paper** eine Anzeige in die Zeitung setzen

advertiser [ˈædvətaɪzəʳ] N (*in paper*) Inserent(in) m(f); **TV ~s** Firmen, die im Fernsehen werben

advertising [ˈædvətaɪzɪŋ] N Werbung f; **he works in ~** er ist in der Werbung (tätig)

advertising IN CPDS Werbe-; **advertising agency** N Werbeagentur f; **advertising campaign** N Werbekampagne f; **advertising copy** N Werbetext m; **advertising manager** N Werbeleiter(in) m(f); **advertising rates** PL Anzeigenpreise pl; (*for TV, radio*) Preise pl für Werbespots; **advertising space** N Platz m für Anzeigen

advice [ədˈvaɪs] N (a) NO PL Rat m no pl; **a piece of ~** ein Rat(schlag) m; **let me give you a piece of ~** *or* **some ~** ich will Ihnen einen guten Rat geben; **to take sb's ~** jds Rat (be)folgen; **take my ~** höre auf mich; **to seek (sb's) ~** (jdn) um Rat fragen; (*from doctor, lawyer etc*) Rat (bei jdm) einholen; **to take medical/legal ~** einen Arzt/Rechtsanwalt zu Rate ziehen (b) (*Comm*: = *notification*) Mitteilung f

advice: **advice column** N Kummerkasten m; **advice columnist** N (*US*) Briefkastenonkel m (*inf*), Briefkastentante f (*inf*); **advice line** N Hotline f; **advice note** N Benachrichtigung f

advisability [ədˌvaɪzəˈbɪlɪtɪ] N Ratsamkeit f; **he questioned the ~ of going on strike** er bezweifelte, ob es ratsam wäre zu streiken

advisable [ədˈvaɪzəbl] ADJ ratsam

advise [ədˈvaɪz] ◼ VT (a) (= *give advice to*) *person* raten (+*dat*); (*professionally*) beraten; **I would ~ you to do it/not to do it** ich würde dir zuraten/abraten; **to ~ sb against doing sth** jdm abraten, etw zu tun; **what would you ~ me to do?** wozu würden Sie mir raten? (b) (*Comm*: = *inform*) verständigen; **to ~ sb of sth** jdn von etw in Kenntnis setzen ◼ VI (a) (= *give advice*) raten; **I shall do as you ~** ich werde tun, was Sie mir raten (b) (*US*) **to ~ with sb** sich mit jdm beraten

advisedly [ədˈvaɪzɪdlɪ] ADV richtig; **and I use the word ~** ich verwende bewusst dieses Wort

advisement [ədˈvaɪzmənt] N (US) **to keep sth under ~** etw im Auge behalten; **to take sth under ~** (= consider more carefully) sich (dat) etw genauer überlegen; (= consult experts) Experten zu etw zu Rate ziehen

adviser [ədˈvaɪzəʳ] N Ratgeber(in) m(f); (professional) Berater(in) m(f); **legal ~** Rechtsberater(in) m(f)

advisory [ədˈvaɪzərɪ] **1** ADJ beratend; **to act in a purely ~ capacity** rein beratende Funktion haben **2** N (esp US) Warnhinweis m

advocacy [ˈædvəkəsɪ] N Eintreten nt (of für); (of plan) Befürwortung f

advocate [ˈædvəkɪt] **1** N (a) (= upholder: of cause etc) Befürworter(in) m(f) (b) (esp Scot: Jur) (Rechts)anwalt m/-anwältin f **2** [ˈædvəkeɪt] VT eintreten für; plan etc befürworten; **what course of action would you ~?** welche Maßnahmen würden Sie empfehlen?

Aegean [iːˈdʒiːən] ADJ ägäisch; islands in der Ägäis; **the ~ (Sea)** die Ägäis, das Ägäische Meer

aegis [ˈiːdʒɪs] N **under the ~ of** unter der Schirmherrschaft von

aeon [ˈiːən] N Ewigkeit f

aerate [ˈɛəreɪt] VT liquid mit Kohlensäure anreichern; blood Sauerstoff zuführen (+dat); soil auflockern

aerial [ˈɛərɪəl] **1** N (esp Brit: = antenna) Antenne f **2** ADJ Luft-; **~ combat** Luftkampf m; **~ map** Luftbildkarte f; **~ photograph** Luftbild nt; **~ reconnaissance** Luftaufklärung f; **~ view** Luftansicht f; **~ warfare** Luftkrieg m

aerial: aerial camera N Luftbildkamera f; **aerial input** N (TV) Antennenanschluss m

aerialist [ˈɛərɪəlɪst] N (US) (on trapeze) Trapezkünstler(in) m(f); (on high wire) Seiltänzer(in) m(f)

aerial: aerial mast N Antennenmast m; **aerial railway** N Schwebebahn f; **aerial tram** N (US) Schwebebahn f

aerobatic [ˌɛərəʊˈbætɪk] ADJ Kunstflug-; **~ manoeuvre** (Brit) or **maneuver** (US) Kunstflugmanöver nt

aerobatics [ˌɛərəʊˈbætɪks] PL Kunstfliegen nt

aerobics [ɛəˈrəʊbɪks] N SING Aerobic nt

aerodrome [ˈɛərədrəʊm] N (Brit) Flugplatz m

aerodynamic ADJ, **aerodynamically** ADV [ˌɛərəʊdaɪˈnæmɪk, -lɪ] aerodynamisch

aerodynamics [ˌɛərəʊdaɪˈnæmɪks] N Aerodynamik f

aerofoil [ˈɛərəʊfɔɪl] N Tragflügel m; (on racing cars) Spoiler m

aeronautic(al) [ˌɛərəˈnɔːtɪk(əl)] ADJ aeronautisch

aeronautical engineering N Flugzeugbau m

aeronautics [ˌɛərəˈnɔːtɪks] N SING Luftfahrt f

aeroplane [ˈɛərəpleɪn] N (Brit) Flugzeug nt

aerosol [ˈɛərəsɒl] N (= can) Spraydose f; (= mixture) Aerosol nt; **~ paint** Sprayfarbe f; **~ spray** Aerosolspray nt

aerospace [ˈɛərəʊspeɪs] IN CPDS Raumfahrt-; **aerospace industry** N Raumfahrtindustrie f

Aertex® [ˈɛəteks] N Aertex® nt, Baumwolltrikotstoff mit Lochmuster

Aesop [ˈiːsɒp] N **~'s fables** die äsopischen Fabeln

aesthete, (US) **esthete** [ˈiːsθiːt] N Ästhet(in) m(f)

aesthetic(al), (US) **esthetic(al)** [iːsˈθetɪk(əl)] ADJ ästhetisch

aesthetically, (US) **esthetically** [iːsˈθetɪkəlɪ] ADV in ästhetischer Hinsicht; **~ pleasing** ästhetisch schön

aesthetics, (US) **esthetics** [iːsˈθetɪks] N SING Ästhetik f

afar [əˈfɑːʳ] ADV (liter) **from ~** aus der Ferne

affable [ˈæfəbl] ADJ, **affably** ADV [ˈæfəbl, -lɪ] umgänglich

affair [əˈfɛəʳ] N (a) (= event, concern, matter) Sache f, Angelegenheit f; **the Watergate/Profumo ~** die Watergate-/Profumo-Affäre; **this is a sorry state of ~s!** das sind ja schöne Zustände!; **your private ~s don't concern me** deine Privatangelegenheiten sind mir egal; **financial ~s have never interested me** Finanzfragen haben mich nie interessiert; **I never interfere with his business ~s** ich mische mich nie in seine geschäftlichen Angelegenheiten ein; **~s of state** Staatsangelegenheiten pl; **that's my/his ~!** das ist meine/seine Sache!

(b) (= love ~) Verhältnis nt; **to have an ~ with sb** ein Verhältnis mit jdm haben

(c) (inf: = object, thing) Ding nt; **what's this funny aerial ~?** was soll dieses komische Antennendings? (inf)

affect¹ [əˈfekt] VT (a) (= have effect on) sich auswirken auf (+acc); (detrimentally) nerves, material angreifen; health, person schaden (+dat) (b) (= concern) betreffen (c) (emotionally: = move) berühren (d) (diseases: = attack) befallen

affect² VT indifference vortäuschen

affectation [ˌæfekˈteɪʃən] N (= artificiality) Affektiertheit f no pl; **an ~** eine affektierte Angewohnheit

affected ADJ, **affectedly** ADV [əˈfektɪd, -lɪ] affektiert

affecting [əˈfektɪŋ] ADJ rührend

affection [əˈfekʃən] N (= fondness) Zuneigung f no pl (for, towards zu); **I have or feel a great ~ for her** ich mag sie sehr gerne; **you could show a little more ~ toward(s) me** du könntest mir gegenüber etwas mehr Gefühl zeigen; **he has a special place in her ~s** er nimmt einen besonderen Platz in ihrem Herzen ein

affectionate [əˈfekʃənɪt] ADJ liebevoll, zärtlich

affectionately [əˈfekʃənɪtlɪ] ADV liebevoll, zärtlich; **yours ~, Wendy** (letter-ending) in Liebe, deine Wendy

affidavit [ˌæfɪˈdeɪvɪt] N (Jur) eidesstattliche Erklärung; **to swear an ~ (that)** eine eidesstattliche Erklärung abgeben(, dass)

affiliate [əˈfɪlɪeɪt] **1** VT angliedern (to +dat); **the two banks are ~d** die zwei Banken sind aneinander angeschlossen; **~d company** Schwesterfirma f **2** VI sich angliedern (with an +acc) **3** N [əˈfɪlɪət] Schwestergesellschaft f; (= union) angegliederte Gewerkschaft

affiliation [əˌfɪlɪˈeɪʃən] N (a) Angliederung f (to, with an +acc); (state) Verbund m; **what are his political ~s?** was ist seine politische Zugehörigkeit? (b) (Brit Jur) **~ order** Verurteilung f zur Leistung des Regelunterhalts

affinity [əˈfɪnɪtɪ] N (a) (= liking) Neigung f (for, to zu); (for person) Verbundenheit f (for, to mit) (b) (= resemblance, connection) Verwandtschaft f

affirm [əˈfɜːm] VT (= assert) versichern; (very forcefully) beteuern; **he ~ed his innocence** er beteuerte seine Unschuld

affirmation [ˌæfəˈmeɪʃən] N (= assertion) Versicherung f; (very forceful) Beteuerung f

affirmative [əˈfɜːmətɪv] **1** N (Gram) Bejahung f; (sentence) bejahender Satz; **to answer in the ~** mit Ja antworten **2** ADJ bejahend; **the answer is ~** die Antwort ist bejahend or ja **3** INTERJ richtig

---

AFFIRMATIVE ACTION

Affirmative action ist der in den USA übliche Ausdruck für die bevorzugte Behandlung ethnischer Minderheiten und Frauen bei der Besetzung von Arbeits- und Ausbildungsplätzen. Diese Politik wurde in den sechziger Jahren unter Präsident Kennedy begonnen, als erstmals Quoten festgesetzt wurden, um den unterrepräsentierten Bevölkerungsgruppen mehr Arbeits- und Studienplätze zu garantieren. Mit dem Equal Employment Opportunities Act von 1972 wurde eine Kommission geschaffen, die für die Durchsetzung der Garantien sorgen sollte. Allerdings führte *affirmative action* später zu Klagen über Diskriminierung bei Angehörigen der Mehrheiten (z.B. Weißen oder Männern), was als *reverse discrimination* - „Diskriminierung unter umgekehrtem Vorzeichen" - bekannt geworden ist. Daraufhin wurden die strengen Quotenreglementierungen etwas gelockert.

---

affirmatively [əˈfɜːmətɪvlɪ] ADV bejahend

affix¹ [əˈfɪks] VT anbringen (to auf +dat); seal setzen (to auf +acc); signature setzen (to unter +acc)

affix² [ˈæfɪks] N (Gram) Affix nt

afflict [əˈflɪkt] VT plagen, zusetzen (+dat); (troubles, inflation, injuries) heimsuchen; **to be ~ed by a disease** an einer Krankheit leiden; **to be ~ed by doubts** von Zweifeln gequält werden

affliction [əˈflɪkʃən] N (= cause of suffering) (blindness etc) Gebrechen nt; (illness) Beschwerde f; (worry) Sorge f; **the ~s of old age** Altersbeschwerden pl

affluence [ˈæflʊəns] N Wohlstand m

affluent [ˈæflʊənt] ADJ reich, wohlhabend

afford [əˈfɔːd] VT (a) sich (dat) leisten; **I can't ~ to buy both of them/to make a mistake** ich kann es mir nicht leisten, beide zu kaufen/einen Fehler zu machen; **I can't ~ the time** ich habe einfach nicht die Zeit (b) (liter: = provide) (sb sth) jdm etw) gewähren; pleasure bereiten

afforestation [æˌfɒrɪsˈteɪʃən] N Aufforstung f

affray [əˈfreɪ] N (esp Jur) Schlägerei f

affront [əˈfrʌnt] **1** VT beleidigen **2** N Affront m (to gegen); **such poverty is an ~ to our national pride** solche Armut verletzt unseren Nationalstolz

Afghan [ˈæfgæn] **1** N (a) Afghane m, Afghanin f (b) (= language) Afghanisch nt (c) (also ~ **hound**) Afghane m **2** ADJ afghanisch

Afghanistan [æfˈgænɪstæn] N Afghanistan nt

aficionado [əˌfɪsjəˈnɑːdəʊ] N, pl **-s** Liebhaber(in) m(f)

afield [əˈfiːld] ADV **countries further ~** weiter entfernte Länder; **to venture further ~** (lit, fig) sich etwas weiter (vor)wagen

afire [əˈfaɪə] ADJ PRED, ADV in Brand; **to set sth ~** etw in Brand stecken; **~ with enthusiasm** hellauf begeistert

aflame [əˈfleɪm] ADJ PRED, ADV in Flammen; **to set sth ~** etw in Brand stecken

AFL-CIO ABBR of **American Federation of Labor and Congress of Industrial Organizations** amerikanischer Gewerkschafts-Dachverband

afloat [əˈfləʊt] ADJ PRED, ADV (a) (Naut) **to be ~** schwimmen; **to stay ~** sich über Wasser halten; (thing) schwimmen; **at last we were ~ again** endlich waren wir wieder flott (b) (fig) **to get/keep a business ~** ein Geschäft auf die Beine stellen/über Wasser halten

afoot [əˈfʊt] ADV im Gange; **there is something ~** da ist etwas im Gange

aforementioned [əˌfɔːˈmenʃənd], **aforesaid** [əˈfɔːsed] ADJ ATTR (form) oben genannt

afraid [əˈfreɪd] ADJ PRED (a) (= frightened) **to be ~ (of sb/sth)** (vor jdm/etw) Angst haben; **don't be ~!** keine Angst!; **it's quite safe, there's nothing to be ~ of** es ist ganz sicher, Sie brauchen keine Angst zu haben; **I am ~ of hurting him** or **that I might hurt him** ich fürchte, ich könnte ihm wehtun; **to make sb ~** jdm Angst machen; **I am ~ to leave her alone** ich habe Angst davor, sie allein zu lassen; **I was ~ of waking the children** ich wollte die Kinder nicht wecken; **he's not ~ of hard work** er hat keine Angst vor schwerer Arbeit; **he's not ~ to say what he thinks** er scheut sich nicht zu sagen, was er denkt; **that's what I was ~ of, I was ~ that would happen** das habe ich befürchtet; **to be ~ for sb/sth** (= worried) Angst um jdn/etw haben

(b) (expressing polite regret) **I'm ~ I can't do it** leider kann ich es nicht machen; **there's nothing I can do, I'm ~** ich kann da leider gar nichts machen; **are you going? – I'm ~ not/I'm ~ so** gehst du? – leider nicht/ja, leider

afresh [əˈfreʃ] ADV noch einmal von neuem

Africa [ˈæfrɪkə] N Afrika nt

African [ˈæfrɪkən] **1** N Afrikaner(in) m(f) **2** ADJ afrikanisch

African-American [ˌæfrɪkənəˈmerɪkən] **1** ADJ afroamerikanisch **2** N Afroamerikaner(in) m(f)

African violet N Usambaraveilchen nt

Afrikaans [ˌæfrɪˈkɑːns] N Afrikaans nt

Afrikaner [ˌæfrɪˈkɑːnə] N Afrika(a)nder(in) m(f)

Afro [ˈæfrəʊ] **1** PREF afro- **2** N (= hairstyle) Afrolook m

Afro-: **Afro-American 1** ADJ afroamerikanisch **2** N Afroamerikaner(in) m(f); **Afro-Asian** ADJ afroasiatisch; **Afro-Caribbean 1** ADJ afrokaribisch **2** N Afrokaribe m, Afrokaribin f

aft [ɑːft] (Naut) **1** ADV sit achtern; go nach achtern **2** ADJ Achter-, achter; **~ deck** Achterdeck nt

after [ˈɑːftə] **1** PREP nach (+dat); **~ dinner** nach dem Essen; **~ that** danach; **the day ~ tomorrow** übermorgen; **I'll be back the week ~ next** ich bin übernächste Woche wieder da; **ten ~ eight** (US) zehn nach acht; **I would put Keats ~ Shelley** für mich rangiert Keats unter Shelley; **~ you!** nach Ihnen; **I was ~ him** (in queue etc) ich war nach ihm dran; **he shut the door ~ him** er machte die Tür hinter ihm zu; **turn right about a mile ~ the village** biegen Sie etwa eine Meile nach dem Dorf rechts ab; **to shout ~ sb** hinter jdm herrufen; **~ what has happened** nach allem, was geschehen ist; **to do sth ~ all** etw schließlich doch tun; **~ all I've done for you!** und das nach allem, was ich für dich getan habe!; **~ all, he is your brother** er ist immerhin dein Bruder; **you tell me lie ~ lie** du erzählst mir eine Lüge nach der anderen; **it's just one thing ~ another** or **the other** es kommt eins zum anderen; **one ~ the other** eine(r, s) nach der/dem anderen; **day ~ day** Tag für Tag;

before us lay mile ~ mile of barren desert vor uns erstreckte sich meilenweit trostlose Wüste; **~ El Greco** in der Art von El Greco; **she takes ~ her mother** sie schlägt ihrer Mutter nach; **to be ~ sb/sth** hinter jdm/etw her sein; **she asked** or **inquired ~ you** sie hat sich nach dir erkundigt; **what are you ~?** was willst du?; **he's just ~ a free meal** er ist nur auf ein kostenloses Essen aus

2 ADV (time, order) danach; (place, pursuit) hinterher; **the year/week ~** das Jahr/die Woche darauf; **soon ~** kurz danach **3** CONJ nachdem; **~ he had closed the door he began to speak** nachdem er die Tür geschlossen hatte, begann er zu sprechen; **what will you do ~ he's gone?** was machst du, wenn er weg ist?; **~ finishing it I will ...** wenn ich das fertig habe, werde ich ... **4** N **afters** PL (Brit inf) Nachtisch m; **what's for ~s?** was gibts zum Nachtisch?

after: **afterbirth** N Nachgeburt f; **aftercare** N (of convalescent) Nachbehandlung f, Nachsorge f; (of ex-prisoner) Resozialisierungshilfe f; **after-dinner** ADJ coffee, conversation nach dem Essen; **~ walk/nap** Verdauungsspaziergang m/-schlaf m; **~ speech** Tischrede f; **aftereffect** N Nachwirkung f; **afterglow** N (fig) angenehme Erinnerung; **after-hours** ADJ nach Geschäftsschluss; **~ trading** (St Ex) nachbörsliches Geschäft, Nachbörse f; **afterlife** N Leben nt nach dem Tode; **aftermath** N Nachwirkungen pl; **in the ~ of sth** nach etw

afternoon [ˌɑːftəˈnuːn] **1** N Nachmittag m; **in the ~, ~s** (esp US) nachmittags; **at three o'clock in the ~** (um) drei Uhr nachmittags; **on Sunday ~** (am) Sonntag Nachmittag; **on Sunday ~s** am Sonntagnachmittag; **on the ~ of December 2nd** am Nachmittag des 2. Dezember; **this/tomorrow/yesterday ~** heute/morgen/gestern Nachmittag; **good ~!** Guten Tag!; **~! Tag!** (inf) **2** ADJ ATTR Nachmittags-; **~ performance** Nachmittagsvorstellung f

afternoon tea N (Brit) (Nachmittags)tee m

after: **after-sales service** N Kundendienst m; **aftershave (lotion)** N Aftershave nt; **aftershock** N (of earthquake) Nachbeben nt; **after-sun** ADJ **~ lotion/cream** After-Sun-Lotion f/-Creme f; **after-tax** ADJ profits etc nach Steuern, nach Steuerabzug; **afterthought** N nachträgliche Idee; **he added as an ~** fügte er hinzu; **the window was added as an ~** das Fenster kam erst später dazu

afterward [ˈɑːftəwəd] ADV (US) = **afterwards**

afterwards [ˈɑːftəwədz] ADV nachher; (= after that, after some event etc) danach; **this was added ~** das kam nachträglich dazu

Aga® [ˈɑːgə] N (Brit) eiserner, nach alter Vorlage gebauter Küchenherd

again [əˈgen] ADV (a) wieder; **~ and ~, time and ~** immer wieder; **to do sth ~** etw noch (ein)mal tun; **never** or **not ever ~** nie wieder; **if that happens ~** wenn das noch einmal passiert; **all over ~** noch (ein)mal von vorn; **what's his name ~?** wie heißt er noch gleich?; **to begin ~** von neuem anfangen; **not ~!** (nicht) schon wieder!; **it's me ~** (arriving) da bin ich wieder; (phoning) ich bins noch (ein)mal; **and these are different ~** und diese sind wieder anders; **here we are ~!** da wären wir wieder!; (finding another example etc) oh, schon wieder!

(b) (in quantity) **as much ~** noch (ein)mal so viel; **he's as old ~ as Mary** er ist doppelt so alt wie Mary

(c) (= on the other hand) wiederum; (= besides, moreover) außerdem; **but then** or **there ~, it may not be true** vielleicht ist es auch gar nicht wahr

against [əˈgenst] **1** PREP (a) gegen (+acc); **he's ~ her going** er ist dagegen, dass sie geht; **to have something/nothing ~ sb/sth** etwas/nichts gegen jdn/etw haben; **~ their wishes** entgegen ihrem Wunsch; **to hit one's head ~ the mantelpiece** mit dem Kopf gegen das Kaminsims stoßen; **push all the chairs right back ~ the wall** stellen Sie alle Stühle direkt an die Wand; **~ the light** gegen das Licht; **to draw money ~ security** gegen Sicherheit Geld abheben

(b) (= in preparation for) sb's arrival, one's old age für (+acc); misfortune, bad weather etc im Hinblick auf (+acc)

(c) (= compared with) (as) ~ gegenüber (+dat); **she had three prizes (as) ~ his six** sie hatte drei Preise, er hingegen sechs; **the advantages of flying (as) ~ going by boat** die Vorteile von Flugreisen gegenüber Schiffsreisen; **~ the euro** gegenüber dem Euro

2 ADJ PRED (= not in favour) dagegen

agate [ˈægət] N Achat m

age [eɪdʒ] **1** N **(a)** (= *attack*) Alter nt; **what is her ~?, what ~ is she?** wie alt ist sie?; **he is ten years of ~** er ist zehn Jahre alt; **at the ~ of 15, at ~ 15** mit 15 Jahren; **at your ~** in deinem Alter; **when I was your ~** als ich in deinem Alter war; **but he's twice your ~** aber er ist ja doppelt so alt wie du; **she doesn't look her ~** man sieht ihr ihr Alter nicht an; **be** *or* **act your ~!** sei nicht kindisch!; **bowed with ~** vom Alter gebeugt **(b)** (*Jur*) **to be of ~** volljährig sein; **to come of ~** volljährig werden; (*fig*) den Kinderschuhen entwachsen; **under ~** minderjährig; **~ of consent** (*for marriage*) Ehemündigkeitsalter nt; **intercourse with girls under the ~ of consent** Unzucht f mit Minderjährigen **(c)** (= *period, epoch*) Zeit(alter nt) f; **the ~ of technology** das technologische Zeitalter; **the Stone ~** die Steinzeit; **the Edwardian ~** die Zeit *or* Ära Edwards VII; **down the ~s** durch alle Zeiten **(d)** (*inf*: = *long time*) **~s, an ~** eine Ewigkeit (*inf*); **I haven't seen him for ~s** *or* **for an ~** ich habe ihn eine Ewigkeit nicht gesehen (*inf*); **to take ~s** eine Ewigkeit dauern (*inf*); (*person*) ewig brauchen (*inf*) **2** VI alt werden, altern; (*wine, cheese*) reifen; **you have ~d** du bist alt geworden **3** VT **(a)** (*worry etc*) altern lassen **(b)** *wine, cheese* reifen lassen

age bracket N Altersklasse f, Altersstufe f

aged [eɪdʒd] **1** ADJ **(a)** im Alter von; **a boy ~ ten** ein zehnjähriger Junge **(b)** [ˈeɪdʒɪd] *person* bejahrt, betagt **2** [ˈeɪdʒɪd] PL **the ~** die Alten pl

age: age difference, age gap N Altersunterschied m; **age group** N Altersgruppe f; **the forty to fifty ~** die (Alters)gruppe der Vierzig- bis Fünfzigjährigen

ag(e)ing [ˈeɪdʒɪŋ] **1** ADJ *person* alternd attr; *animal, population* älter werdend attr; **the ~ process** das Altern **2** N Altern nt

ageism [ˈeɪdʒɪzəm] N Altersdiskriminierung f

ageist [ˈeɪdʒɪst] ADJ altersdiskriminierend

age: ageless ADJ zeitlos; **she seems to be one of those ~ people** sie scheint zu den Menschen zu gehören, die nie alt werden; **age limit** N Altersgrenze f

agency [ˈeɪdʒənsɪ] N **(a)** (*Comm*) Agentur f; (= *subsidiary of a company*) Geschäftsstelle f; **translation/tourist ~** Übersetzungs-/Reisebüro nt **(b)** (= *instrumentality*) **through the ~ of friends** durch die Vermittlung von Freunden; **by the ~ of water** mithilfe von Wasser

agenda [əˈdʒendə] N Tagesordnung f; **a full ~** (*lit*) eine umfangreiche Tagesordnung; (*fig*) ein volles Programm; **to set the ~** (*lit*) die Tagesordnung festlegen; (*fig*) den Ton angeben; **they have their own ~** sie haben ihre eigenen Vorstellungen; **on the ~** auf dem Programm

agent [ˈeɪdʒənt] N **(a)** (*Comm*) (= *person*) Vertreter(in) m(f); (= *organization*) Vertretung f; **who is the ~ for this car in Scotland?** wer hat die schottische Vertretung für dieses Auto? **(b)** (= *literary ~, secret ~*) Agent(in) m(f); (*Pol*) Wahlkampfleiter(in) m(f); **business ~** Agent(in) m(f) **(c)** (= *person having power to act*) **you're a free ~, do what you want** du bist dein eigener Herr, tu was du willst **(d)** (= *means by which sth is achieved*) Mittel nt **(e)** (*Chem*) **cleansing ~** Reinigungsmittel nt

agent provocateur [ˌæʒɒŋprɒvɒkaˈtɜː] N, pl **-s -s** Agent provocateur m

age: age-old ADJ uralt; **age range** N Altersgruppe f; **age-related** ADJ altersbedingt; **~ allowance** (*Fin*) Altersfreibetrag m

aggrandizement [əˈɡrændɪzmənt] N (= *of power*) Vergrößerung f; (*of person, one's family*) Beförderung f

aggravate [ˈæɡrəveɪt] VT **(a)** (= *make worse*) verschlimmern **(b)** (= *annoy*) aufregen; (*deliberately*) reizen; **don't get ~d** regen Sie sich nicht auf

aggravating [ˈæɡrəveɪtɪŋ] ADJ ärgerlich; *child* lästig

aggravation [ˌæɡrəˈveɪʃən] N **(a)** (= *worsening*) Verschlimmerung f **(b)** (= *annoyance*) Ärger m; **she was a constant ~ to him** sie reizte ihn ständig

aggregate [ˈæɡrɪɡɪt] **1** N Gesamtmenge f; **on ~** (*Sport*) in der Gesamtwertung **2** ADJ gesamt, Gesamt-; **~ value** Gesamtwert m **3** [ˈæɡrɪɡeɪt] VT (= *amount to*) sich belaufen auf (+acc)

aggression [əˈɡreʃən] N **(a)** (= *attack*) Angriff m; **an act of ~** ein Angriff m **(b)** NO PL Aggression f; (= *aggressiveness*) Aggressivität f

aggressive [əˈɡresɪv] ADJ **(a)** (= *belligerent*) aggressiv **(b)** (= *forceful*) *salesman etc* aufdringlich (*pej*); *sales technique* aggressiv

aggressively [əˈɡresɪvlɪ] ADV (= *belligerently*) aggressiv; (= *forcefully*) energisch; *sell* aggressiv

aggressiveness [əˈɡresɪvnɪs] N Aggressivität f; (*of salesman etc*) Aufdringlichkeit f (*pej*)

aggressor [əˈɡresəʳ] N Aggressor(in) m(f)

aggrieved [əˈɡriːvd] ADJ betrübt (*at, by* über +acc); (= *offended*) verletzt (*at, by* durch); *voice, look* verletzt, gekränkt; **the ~ (party)** (*Jur*) die beschwerte Partei

aggro [ˈæɡrəʊ] N (*Brit inf*) **(a)** (= *aggression, bother*) Aggressionen pl; **don't give me any ~** mach keinen Ärger (*inf*); **she didn't want all the ~ of moving** sie wollte das ganze Theater mit dem Umziehen vermeiden **(b)** (= *fight*) Schlägerei f

aghast [əˈɡɑːst] ADJ PRED entgeistert (*at* über +acc)

agile [ˈædʒaɪl] ADJ *person, thinker* wendig; *body also, movements* gelenkig; *animal* flink, behände; **he has an ~ mind** er ist geistig sehr wendig

agility [əˈdʒɪlɪtɪ] N (*of person*) Wendigkeit f; (*of animal*) Flinkheit f, Behändigkeit f

aging ADJ, N = **ag(e)ing**

agitate [ˈædʒɪteɪt] **1** VT **(a)** (*lit*) *liquid* aufrühren; *surface of water* aufwühlen **(b)** (*fig*: = *excite, upset*) aufregen **2** VI agitieren; **to ~ for sth** sich für etw stark machen

agitated ADJ, **agitatedly** [ˈædʒɪteɪtɪd, -lɪ] aufgeregt, erregt

agitation [ˌædʒɪˈteɪʃən] N **(a)** (*fig*) (= *anxiety, worry*) Erregung f; (*on stock market*) Bewegung f **(b)** (*Pol*: = *incitement*) Agitation f

agitator [ˈædʒɪteɪtəʳ] N (= *person*) Agitator(in) m(f)

aglow [əˈɡləʊ] ADJ PRED **to be ~** glühen

AGM ABBR *of* **annual general meeting** JHV f

agnostic [æɡˈnɒstɪk] **1** ADJ agnostisch **2** N Agnostiker(in) m(f)

agnosticism [æɡˈnɒstɪsɪzəm] N Agnostizismus m

ago [əˈɡəʊ] ADV vor; **years/a week ~** vor Jahren/einer Woche; **a little while ~** vor kurzem; **that was years/a week ~** das ist schon Jahre/eine Woche her; **how long ~ is it since you last saw him?** wie lange haben Sie ihn schon nicht mehr gesehen?; **that was a long time** *or* **long ~** das ist schon lange her; **as long ~ as 1950** schon 1950

agog [əˈɡɒɡ] ADJ PRED gespannt; **the whole village was ~ (with curiosity)** das ganze Dorf platzte fast vor Neugierde

agonize [ˈæɡənaɪz] VI sich (*dat*) den Kopf zermartern (*over* über +acc)

agonized [ˈæɡənaɪzd] ADJ gequält

agonizing [ˈæɡənaɪzɪŋ] ADJ qualvoll

agonizingly [ˈæɡənaɪzɪŋlɪ] ADV qualvoll; **~ slow** aufreizend langsam

agony [ˈæɡənɪ] N **(a)** Qual f; **that's ~** das ist eine Qual; **to be in ~** Qualen leiden; **put him out of his ~** (*lit*) mach seiner Qual ein Ende; (*fig*) nun spann ihn doch nicht länger auf die Folter **(b)** (= *death ~*) Todeskampf m; (*of Christ*) Todesangst f

agony (*Brit Press inf*): **agony aunt** N Briefkastentante f (*inf*); **agony column** N Kummerkasten m

agoraphobia [ˌæɡərəˈfəʊbɪə] N (*Med*) Platzangst f

agoraphobic [ˌæɡərəˈfəʊbɪk] (*Med*) **1** ADJ agoraphobisch (*spec*) **2** N an Platzangst Leidende(r) mf

agrarian [əˈɡreərɪən] ADJ Agrar-

agree [əˈɡriː], pret, pt **agreed** **1** VT **(a)** *price, date etc* vereinbaren, abmachen **(b)** (= *consent*) **to ~ to do sth** sich bereit erklären, etw zu tun **(c)** (= *admit*) zugeben **(d)** (= *come to or be in agreement about*) zustimmen (+dat); **we all ~ that ...** wir sind alle der Meinung, dass ...; **it was ~d that ...** man einigte sich darauf, dass ...; **we ~d to do it** wir haben beschlossen, die zu tun; **we ~ to differ** wir sind uns einig, dass wir uns uneinig sind **2** VI **(a)** (= *hold same opinion*) (*two or more people*) einer Meinung sein; (*one person*) der gleichen Meinung sein; (= *come to an agreement*) sich einigen (*about* über +acc); **to ~ with sb** jdm zustimmen; **I ~!** der Meinung bin ich auch!; **I**

couldn't ~ more/less ich bin völlig/überhaupt nicht dieser Meinung; **it's too late now, don't** or **wouldn't you ~?** meinen Sie nicht auch, dass es jetzt zu spät ist?; **to ~ with sth** (= approve of) mit etw einverstanden sein; **to ~ with a theory/ the figures** etc (accept) eine Theorie/die Zahlen etc akzeptieren **(b)** (statements, figures etc. = tally) übereinstimmen **(c)** (food, climate etc) **whisky doesn't ~ with me** ich vertrage Whisky nicht **(d)** (Gram) übereinstimmen

➤ **agree on** VI +PREP OBJ solution sich einigen auf (+acc)

➤ **agree to** VI +PREP OBJ zustimmen (+dat); marriage also einwilligen in (+acc); terms also akzeptieren

agreeable [əˈɡriːəbl] ADJ **(a)** (= pleasant) angenehm; decor, behaviour nett **(b)** PRED (= willing to agree) einverstanden; **are you ~ to that?, is that ~ to you?** sind Sie damit einverstanden?

agreeably [əˈɡriːəbli] ADV angenehm; decorated, behave nett

agreed [əˈɡriːd] ADJ **(a)** PRED (= in agreement) einig; **to be ~ on sth** sich über etw einig sein; **to be ~ on doing sth** sich darüber einig sein, etw zu tun; **are we all ~?** sind wir uns da einig?; (on course of action) sind alle einverstanden? **(b)** (= arranged) vereinbart; **it's all ~** es ist alles abgesprochen; **~?** einverstanden?; **~!** (regarding price etc) abgemacht; (= I agree) stimmt

agreement [əˈɡriːmənt] N **(a)** (= understanding, arrangement) Übereinkunft f; (= treaty, contract) Abkommen nt; **to enter into an ~** einen Vertrag (ab)schließen; **to reach (an) ~** zu einer Einigung kommen; **General Agreement on Tariffs and Trade** Allgemeines Zoll- und Handelsabkommen **(b)** (= sharing of opinion) Einigkeit f; **by mutual ~** in gegenseitigem Einvernehmen; **to be in ~ with sb** mit jdm einer Meinung sein; **to be in ~ with sth** mit etw übereinstimmen; **to be in ~ about sth** über etw (acc) einig sein **(c)** (= consent) Einwilligung f (to zu) **(d)** (between figures, accounts etc) Übereinstimmung f **(e)** (Gram) Übereinstimmung f

agribusiness [ˈæɡrɪbɪznɪs] N Agroindustrie f

agricultural [æɡrɪˈkʌltʃərəl] ADJ landwirtschaftlich; land, reform Agrar-

agricultural college N Landwirtschaftsschule f

agricultural engineer N Agrartechniker(in) m(f)

agriculturally [æɡrɪˈkʌltʃərəli] ADV landwirtschaftlich

agricultural show N Landwirtschaftsausstellung f

agriculture [ˈæɡrɪkʌltʃəʳ] N Landwirtschaft f; **Minister of Agriculture** (Brit) Landwirtschaftsminister(in) m(f)

agronomist [əˈɡrɒnəmɪst] N Agronom(in) m(f)

aground [əˈɡraʊnd] ADV **to go** or **run ~** auf Grund laufen

ah [ɑː] INTERJ ah; (pain) au, autsch; (pity) o, ach

ahead [əˈhed] ADV **(a) the mountains lay ~** vor uns/ihnen etc lagen die Berge; **the German runner was/drew ~** der deutsche Läufer lag vorn/zog nach vorne; **he is ~ by about two minutes** er hat etwa zwei Minuten Vorsprung; **to stare straight ~** geradeaus starren; **keep straight ~** immer geradeaus; **full speed ~** (Naut, fig) volle Kraft voraus; **we sent him on ~** wir schickten ihn voraus; **in the months ~** in den bevorstehenden Monaten; **we've a busy time ~** vor uns liegt eine Menge Arbeit; **to plan ~** vorausplanen **(b) ~ of sb/sth** vor jdm/etw; **walk ~ of me** geh voran; **we arrived ten minutes ~ of time** wir kamen zehn Minuten vorher an; **to be/get ~ of schedule** schneller als geplant vorankommen; **to be ~ of one's time** (fig) seiner Zeit voraus sein

ahold [əˈhəʊld] N (esp US) **to get ~ of sb** jdn erreichen; **to get ~ of sth** (= procure) sich (dat) etw besorgen; **don't let him get ~ of this story** lass ihn diese Geschichte bloß nicht in die Finger kriegen (inf); **to get ~ of oneself** sich zusammenreißen

ahoy [əˈhɔɪ] INTERJ **ship ~!** Schiff ahoi!

AI ABBR of **artificial intelligence** KI f

aid [eɪd] **1** N **(a)** NO PL (= help) Hilfe f; **(foreign) ~** Entwicklungshilfe f; **with the ~ of a screwdriver** mithilfe eines Schraubenziehers; **to come** or **go to sb's ~** jdm zu Hilfe kommen; **a sale in ~ of the blind** ein Verkauf zugunsten der Blinden; **what's all this in ~ of?** (inf) wozu soll das gut sein?

(b) (= useful person, thing) Hilfe f (to für); (= piece of equipment, audio-visual ~ etc) Hilfsmittel nt; (= teaching ~) Lehrmittel nt **(c)** (esp US) = **aide**

2 VT unterstützen, helfen (+dat); **to ~ sb's recovery** jds Heilung fördern; **to ~ and abet sb** (Jur) jdm Beihilfe leisten; (after crime) jdn begünstigen; see **aiding and abetting**

aide [eɪd] N Helfer(in) m(f); (= adviser) (persönlicher) Berater

aide-de-camp [ˈeɪddəˈkɒŋ] N, pl **aides-de-camp (a)** (Mil) Adjutant(in) m(f) **(b)** = **aide**

aide-memoire [ˈeɪdmemˈwɑːʳ] N Gedächtnisstütze f; (= official memorandum) Aide-memoire nt

aiding and abetting [ˈeɪdɪŋəndəˈbetɪŋ] N (Jur) Beihilfe f; (after crime) Begünstigung f

AIDS, Aids [eɪdz] ABBR of **acquired immune deficiency syndrome** Aids nt

AIDS: **AIDS-related** ADJ illness, death aidsbedingt; **AIDS victim** N Aids-Kranke(r) mf

ailing [ˈeɪlɪŋ] ADJ (lit) kränklich; (fig) economy etc krankend

ailment [ˈeɪlmənt] N Leiden nt; **minor ~s** leichte Beschwerden pl

aim [eɪm] **1** N **(a)** Zielen nt; **to take ~** zielen (at auf +acc); **his ~ was bad/good** er zielte schlecht/gut **(b)** (= purpose) Ziel nt; **with the ~ of doing sth** mit dem Ziel, etw zu tun; **what is your ~ in life?** was ist Ihr Lebensziel?; **to achieve one's ~** sein Ziel erreichen

2 VT **(a)** (= direct) guided missile, camera richten (at auf +acc); stone, pistol etc zielen mit (at auf +acc); **he ~ed a punch at my stomach** sein Schlag zielte auf meinen Bauch **(b)** (fig) remark, insult richten (at gegen); **this book is ~ed at the general public** (Brit US) dieses Buch wendet sich an die Öffentlichkeit; **to be ~ed at sth** (cuts, new law etc) auf etw (acc) abgezielt sein

3 VI **(a)** (with gun, punch etc) zielen (at, for auf +acc) **(b)** (= try, strive for) **isn't that ~ing a bit high?** wollen Sie nicht etwas hoch hinaus?; **to ~ at** or **for sth** auf etw (acc) abzielen; **with this TV programme** (Brit) or **program** (US) **we're ~ing at a much wider audience** mit diesem Fernsehprogramm wollen wir einen größeren Teilnehmerkreis ansprechen; **we ~ to please** bei uns ist der Kunde König; **he ~s at only spending £50 per week** er hat sich zum Ziel gesetzt, mit £ 50 pro Woche auszukommen **(c)** (inf: = intend) **to ~ to do sth** vorhaben, etw zu tun

aimless ADJ, **aimlessly** ADV [ˈeɪmlɪs, -lɪ] ziellos; talk, act planlos

aimlessness [ˈeɪmlɪsnɪs] N Ziellosigkeit f; (of talk, action) Planlosigkeit f

ain't [eɪnt] (incorrect) = **am not, is not, are not, has not, have not**

air [ɛəʳ] **1** N **(a)** Luft f; **a change of ~** eine Luftveränderung; **to go out for a breath of (fresh) ~** frische Luft schnappen (gehen); **to go by ~** (person) fliegen, mit dem Flugzeug reisen; (goods) per Flugzeug transportiert werden **(b)** (fig phrases) **there's something in the ~** es liegt etwas in der Luft; **it's still all up in the ~** (inf) es ist noch alles offen; **to give sb the ~** (US inf) jdn abblitzen lassen (inf); **to clear the ~** die Atmosphäre reinigen; **to be walking** or **floating on ~** wie auf Wolken gehen; **to pull** or **pluck sth out of the ~** (fig) etw auf gut Glück nennen; see **thin**

(c) (Rad, TV) **to be on the ~** (programme) gesendet werden; (station) senden; **to go off the ~** (broadcaster) die Sendung beenden; (station) das Programm beenden **(d)** (= demeanour, manner) Auftreten nt; (= facial expression) Miene f; **with an ~ of bewilderment** mit bestürzter Miene; **there was** or **she had an ~ of mystery about her** sie hatte etwas Geheimnisvolles an sich **(e) airs** PL Getue nt, Gehabe nt; **to put on ~s, to give oneself ~s** sich zieren; **~s and graces** Allüren pl

2 VT **(a)** clothes, bed, room lüften **(b)** anger, grievance Luft machen (+dat); opinion darlegen **(c)** (esp US Rad, TV) story, series senden

3 VI (clothes etc) (after washing) nachtrocknen; (after storage) lüften

air IN CPDS Luft-; **air ambulance** N (= aeroplane) Rettungsflugzeug nt; (= helicopter) Rettungshubschrauber m; **air bag** N Airbag m; **air base** N Luftwaffenstützpunkt m; **air bed** N (Brit) Luftmatratze f; **airborne** ADJ **(a)** (= flying) **to be ~** sich in der Luft befinden **(b)** (Mil) **~ troops** Luftlandetruppen pl; **air brake** N (on truck) Druckluftbremse f; **airbrush** (Art) **1** N Spritzpistole f, Airbrush f **2** VT mit der

Spritzpistole bearbeiten; **Airbus®** N Airbus *m*; **air cargo** N Luftfracht *f*; **air-con** N = **air conditioning**; **air-conditioned** ADJ klimatisiert; **air conditioning** N (= *process*) Klimatisierung *f*; (= *system*) Klimaanlage *f*; **air consignment note** N Luftfrachtbrief *m*; **air-cooled** ADJ *engine* luftgekühlt; **aircraft** N, *pl* aircraft Flugzeug *nt*; **aircraft carrier** N Flugzeugträger *m*; **aircrew** N Flugpersonal *nt*; **air display** N Flugschau *f*; **airdrome** N (*US*) Flugplatz *m*

airer ['ɛərəʳ] N Trockenständer *m*

air: **airfield** N Flugplatz *m*; **airfoil** N (*US*) Tragflügel *m*; (*on racing cars*) Spoiler *m*; **air force** N Luftwaffe *f*; **Air Force One** N Air Force One *f*, *Dienstflugzeug des US-Präsidenten*; **air freight** N Luftfracht *f*; **air-freight** VT per Luftfracht senden; **air gun** N Luftgewehr *nt*; **air hole** N Luftloch *nt*; **air hostess** N Stewardess *f*

airily ['ɛərɪlɪ] ADV (= *casually*) *say etc* leichthin

airing ['ɛərɪŋ] N (*of linen, room etc*) lüften *nt*; **to give sth a good ~** etw gut durchlüften lassen; **to give an idea an ~** (*fig inf*) eine Idee darlegen

airing cupboard N (*Brit*) Trockenschrank *m*

air: **airless** ADJ (= *stuffy*) *room* stickig; **air letter** N Luftpostbrief *m*, Aerogramm *nt*; **airlift** 1 N Luftbrücke *f* 2 VT **to ~ sth in** etw über eine Luftbrücke hineinbringen; **airline** N Fluggesellschaft *f*; **airliner** N Verkehrsflugzeug *nt*; **airlock** N (*in pipe*) Luftsack *m*

airmail ['ɛəmeɪl] 1 N Luftpost *f*; **to send sth (by) ~** etw per Luftpost schicken 2 VT per Luftpost schicken

airmail: **airmail letter** N Luftpostbrief *m*; **airmail stamp,** **airmail sticker** N Luftpostaufkleber *m*

air: **airman** N (= *flier*) Flieger *m*; (*US*: *in air force*) Gefreite(r) *m*; **air mattress** N Luftmatratze *f*; **Air Miles** PL Flugmeilen *pl*; **airplane** N (*US*) Flugzeug *nt*; **air pocket** N Luftloch *nt*

airport ['ɛəpɔːt] N Flughafen *m*

airport: **airport bus** N Flughafenbus *m*; **airport tax** N Flughafengebühr *f*

air: **air pressure** N Luftdruck *m*; **air pump** N Luftpumpe *f*; **air rage** N aggressives Verhalten von Flugpassagieren, Flugkoller *m* (*inf*)

air raid N Luftangriff *m*

air-raid: **air-raid shelter** N Luftschutzkeller *m*; **air-raid warden** N Luftschutzwart *m*; **air-raid warning** N Fliegeralarm *m*

air: **air rescue service** N Luftrettungsdienst *m*; **air rifle** N Luftgewehr *nt*; **air route** N Flugroute *f*; **air-sea rescue** N Rettung *f* durch Seenotflugzeuge; **air-sea rescue service** N Seenotrettungsdienst *m*; **airship** N Luftschiff *nt*; **airshow** N Luftfahrtausstellung *f*; **airsick** ADJ luftkrank; **airspace** N Luftraum *m*; **airspeed** N Fluggeschwindigkeit *f*; **airstream** N (*of vehicle*) Luftsog *m*; (*Met*) Luftstrom *m*; **airstrip** N Start- und Lande-Bahn *f*; **air terminal** N Terminal *m* or *nt*; **airtight** ADJ (*lit*) luftdicht; (*fig*) *argument, case* hieb- und stichfest; **airtime** N (*Rad, TV*) Sendezeit *f*; **air-to-air** ADJ (*Mil*) Luft-Luft-; **air-to-ground** ADJ (*Mil*) Luft-Boden-; **air-to-sea** ADJ (*Mil*) Luft-See-; **air-traffic control** N Flugleitung *f*; **air-traffic controller** N Fluglotse *m*, Fluglotsin *f*; **air vent** N Ventilator *m*; (= *shaft*) Belüftungsschacht *m*; **airwaves** PL Radiowellen *pl*; **airway** N (a) (= *route*) Flugroute *f* (b) (*Med*) Atemwege *pl*; **airworthy** ADJ flugtüchtig

airy ['ɛərɪ] ADJ (+ER) (a) *room* luftig (b) (= *casual*) lässig, nonchalant

airy-fairy ['ɛərɪ'fɛərɪ] ADJ (*Brit inf*) versponnen; *excuse* windig

aisle [aɪl] N Gang *m*; (*in church*) Seitenschiff *nt*; (*central ~*) Mittelgang *m*; **~ seat** Sitz *m* am Gang; **to walk down the ~ with sb** jdn zum Altar führen; **he had them rolling in the ~s** (*inf*) er brachte sie so weit, dass sie sich vor Lachen kugelten (*inf*)

aitch [eɪtʃ] N H *nt*, H *nt*; **to drop one's ~es** den Buchstaben „h" nicht aussprechen; (= *be lower class*) ≈ „mir" und „mich" verwechseln

ajar [ə'dʒɑːʳ] ADJ, ADV angelehnt

aka ABBR *of* **also known as** alias

akin [ə'kɪn] ADJ PRED ähnlich (*to* +*dat*)

à la ['ɑːlɑː] PREP à la

alabaster ['æləbɑːstəʳ] 1 N Alabaster *m* 2 ADJ (*lit*) alabastern

à la carte [ɑːlɑː'kɑːt] ADJ, ADV à la carte

alacrity [ə'lækrɪtɪ] N (= *willingness*) Bereitwilligkeit *f*; (= *eagerness*) Eifer *m*; **to accept with ~** ohne zu zögern annehmen

Aladdin [ə'lædɪn] N Aladin *m*; **~'s cave** (*fig*: = *hoard*) Schatzhöhle *f*

à la mode [ɑːlɑː'məʊd] ADJ (*US*) mit Eis

alarm [ə'lɑːm] 1 N (a) NO PL (= *fear*) Sorge *f*; **to be in a state of ~** (= *worried*) besorgt sein; (= *frightened*) erschreckt sein; **to cause sb ~** jdn beunruhigen
(b) (= *warning*) Alarm *m*; **to raise** *or* **give** *or* **sound the ~** Alarm geben *or* (*fig*) schlagen
(c) (= *device*) Alarmanlage *f*; **~ (clock)** Wecker *m*; **car ~** Autoalarmanlage *f*
2 VT (= *worry*) beunruhigen; (= *frighten*) erschrecken; **don't be ~ed** erschrecken Sie nicht

alarm IN CPDS Alarm-; **alarm bell** N Alarmglocke *f*; **to set ~s ringing** (*fig*) die Alarmglocken klingeln lassen; **alarm call** N (*Telec*) Weckruf *m*; **alarm clock** N Wecker *m*

alarming [ə'lɑːmɪŋ] ADJ (= *worrying*) beunruhigend; (= *frightening*) erschreckend; *news* alarmierend

alarmingly [ə'lɑːmɪŋlɪ] ADV erschreckend

alarmist [ə'lɑːmɪst] 1 N Panikmacher(in) *m(f)* 2 ADJ *speech* Unheil prophezeiend *attr*; *politician* Panik machend *attr*

alas [ə'læs] INTERJ (*old*) leider

Alaska [ə'læskə] N Alaska *nt*

Alaskan [ə'læskən] 1 N Einwohner(in) *m(f)* von Alaska 2 ADJ Alaska-; *customs, winter* in Alaska; *fish, produce* aus Alaska

Albania [æl'beɪnɪə] N Albanien *nt*

Albanian [æl'beɪnɪən] 1 ADJ albanisch 2 N (a) Albaner(in) *m(f)* (b) (= *language*) Albanisch *nt*

albatross ['ælbətrɒs] N Albatros *m*; **to be an ~ around sb's neck** ein Mühlstein *m* um jds Hals sein

albeit [ɔːl'biːɪt] CONJ (*esp liter*) obgleich

albino [æl'biːnəʊ] 1 N Albino *m* 2 ADJ Albino-; **~ rabbit** Albinokaninchen *nt*

album ['ælbəm] N Album *nt*

alchemist ['ælkɪmɪst] N Alchemist(in) *m(f)*

alchemy ['ælkɪmɪ] N Alchemie *f*

alcohol ['ælkəhɒl] N Alkohol *m*; **~ by volume** Alkoholgehalt *m*

alcohol-free ['ælkəhɒl'friː] ADJ alkoholfrei

alcoholic [ælkə'hɒlɪk] 1 ADJ *drink* alkoholisch; *person* alkoholsüchtig 2 N (*person*) Alkoholiker(in) *m(f)*; **to be an ~** Alkoholiker(in) sein; **Alcoholics Anonymous** Anonyme Alkoholiker *pl*

alcoholism ['ælkəhɒlɪzəm] N Alkoholismus *m*

alcopop ['ælkəpɒp] N *alkoholisches kohlensäurehaltiges Getränk*

alcove ['ælkəʊv] N Nische *f*

alder ['ɔːldəʳ] N Erle *f*

ale [eɪl] N (*old*) Ale *nt*

aleck ['ælɪk] N *see* **smart aleck**

alert [ə'lɜːt] 1 ADJ aufmerksam; (*as character trait*) aufgeweckt; *mind* scharf; *dog* wachsam; **to be ~ to sth** vor etw (*dat*) auf der Hut sein 2 VT warnen (*to* vor +*dat*); *troops* in Gefechtsbereitschaft versetzen; *fire brigade etc* alarmieren 3 N Alarm *m*; **to be on (the) ~** einsatzbereit sein; (= *be on lookout*) auf der Hut sein (*for* vor +*dat*)

alertness [ə'lɜːtnɪs] N Aufmerksamkeit *f*; (*as character trait*) Aufgewecktheit *f*; (*of mind*) Schärfe *f*

A level ['eɪˌlevl] N (*Brit*) Abschluss *m* der Sekundarstufe 2; **to take one's ~s** ≈ das Abitur machen; **3 ~s** ≈ das Abitur in 3 Fächern

A LEVELS

A levels sind dem Abitur vergleichbare Hochschulqualifikationen. Zur Beendigung der höheren Schulbildung wählen Schülerinnen und Schüler in England, Wales und Nordirland zwei oder drei Fächer. Die Kurse schließen häufig an GCSE-Kurse der gleichen Fachbereiche an und dauern normalerweise zwei Jahre, die Abschlussprüfungen werden im Alter von 18 Jahren abgelegt. Zu den Universitäten werden Studenten im Allgemeinen nur dann zugelassen, wenn sie von den Universitäten festgelegte Notendurchschnitte in den ***A levels*** vorweisen können.

Das entsprechende schottische Pendant ist der **Higher Grade**, *der auch oft einfach nur* **Higher** *genannt wird. Schüler belegen dafür bis zu fünf Fächer und nehmen nach einem Jahr an der Abschlussprüfung teil.*
▶ GCSE

alfresco [ælˈfreskəʊ] ADJ PRED, ADV im Freien

algae [ˈælgiː] PL Algen pl

algebra [ˈældʒɪbrə] N Algebra f

Algeria [ælˈdʒɪərɪə] N Algerien nt

Algerian [ælˈdʒɪərɪən] **1** N Algerier(in) m(f) **2** ADJ algerisch

algorithm [ˈælgərɪðəm] N Algorithmus m

alias [ˈeɪlɪæs] **1** ADV alias **2** N Deckname m

alibi [ˈælɪbaɪ] N Alibi nt

alien [ˈeɪlɪən] **1** N (esp Pol) Ausländer(in) m(f); (Sci-Fi) außerirdisches Wesen **2** ADJ **(a)** (= foreign) ausländisch; (Sci-Fi) außerirdisch **(b)** (= different) fremd; **to be ~ to sb/sth** jdm/einer Sache fremd sein **(c)** (Comput) fremd

alienate [ˈeɪlɪəneɪt] VT people befremden; affections zerstören, sich (dat) verscherzen; public opinion gegen sich aufbringen; **to ~ oneself from sb/sth** sich jdm/einer Sache entfremden

alienation [ˌeɪlɪəˈneɪʃən] N Entfremdung f (from von)

alight¹ [əˈlaɪt] (form) VI **(a)** (person) aussteigen (from aus); (from horse) absitzen (from von) **(b)** (bird) sich niederlassen (on auf +dat); **his eyes ~ed on the ring** sein Blick fiel auf den Ring

alight² ADJ PRED **to be ~** brennen; **to keep the fire ~** das Feuer in Gang halten; **to set sth ~** etw in Brand setzen

align [əˈlaɪn] VT ausrichten; (Fin, Pol) currencies, policies aufeinander ausrichten; **to ~ sth with sth** etw auf etw (acc) ausrichten; **they have ~ed themselves against him/it** sie haben sich gegen ihn/dagegen zusammengeschlossen

alignment [əˈlaɪnmənt] N Ausrichtung f; **to be out of ~** nicht richtig ausgerichtet sein (with nach); **to be out of ~ with one another** (fig) nicht übereinstimmen, sich nicht aneinander orientieren; **his unexpected ~ with the Socialists** seine unerwartete Parteinahme für die Sozialisten

alike [əˈlaɪk] ADJ PRED, ADV gleich; **they're/they look very ~** sie sind/sehen sich (dat) sehr ähnlich; **they always think ~** sie sind immer einer Meinung; **winter and summer ~** Sommer wie Winter

alimentary [ˌælɪˈmentərɪ] ADJ (Anat) Verdauungs-; **~ canal** Verdauungskanal m

alimony [ˈælɪmənɪ] N Unterhaltszahlung f; **to pay ~** Unterhalt zahlen

A list N Hautevolee f

alive [əˈlaɪv] ADJ PRED **(a)** (= living, lively) lebendig; **dead or ~** tot oder lebendig; **to be ~** leben; **the greatest musician ~** der größte lebende Musiker; **to stay** or **keep ~** am Leben bleiben; **to keep sb/sth ~** (lit, fig) jdn/etw am Leben erhalten; **to be ~ and kicking** (hum inf) gesund und munter sein; **he's been found ~ and well** er ist gesund und munter aufgefunden worden; **to come ~** (= liven up) lebendig werden; (= prick up ears etc) wach werden; **to bring sth ~** story, character etw lebendig werden lassen **(b)** (= aware) **to be ~ to sth** sich (dat) einer Sache (gen) bewusst sein **(c)** **~ with** (= full of) erfüllt von; **to be ~ with tourists/insects** etc von Touristen/Insekten etc wimmeln

alkali [ˈælkəlaɪ] N, pl **-(e)s** Base f, Lauge f; (metal, Agr) Alkali nt

alkaline [ˈælkəlaɪn] ADJ alkalisch; **~ solution** Lauge f

---

all [ɔːl]

1 ADJECTIVE	**4** NOUN
2 PRONOUN	**5** SET STRUCTURES
3 ADVERB	

---

1 ADJECTIVE (with nouns) (plural) alle; (singular) ganze(r, s), alle(r, s)

---

*When **alle** is used to translate **all the** it is not followed by the German article.*

---

she brought all the children sie brachte alle Kinder mit; **all kinds** or **sorts of people** alle möglichen Leute; **all the tobacco** der ganze Tabak; **all you boys can come with me** ihr Jungen könnt alle mit mir kommen; **all the time** die ganze Zeit; **all day (long)** den ganzen Tag (lang); **all Spain** ganz Spanien; **to dislike all sport** jeglichen Sport ablehnen; **in all respects** in jeder Hinsicht

◆**all + possessive all my strength** meine ganze Kraft; **all my books/friends** alle meine Bücher/Freunde; **all my life** mein ganzes Leben (lang)

◆*pronoun + **all** **they all came** sie sind alle gekommen

---

*Note that **it all** is usually translated by **alles** alone.*

---

he took/spent it all er hat alles genommen/ausgegeben; **he's seen/done it all** für ihn gibt es nichts Neues mehr

◆**all this/that I don't understand all that** ich verstehe das alles nicht; **what's all this/that?** was ist denn das?; (annoyed) was soll denn das!; **what's all this I hear about you leaving?** was höre ich da! Sie wollen gehen?

◆**all possible/due with all possible speed** so schnell wie möglich; **with all due care** mit angemessener Sorgfalt; **they will take all possible precautions** sie werden alle möglichen Sicherheitsvorkehrungen treffen

2 PRONOUN

(a) (= everything) alles; **I'm just curious, that's all** ich bin nur neugierig, das ist alles; **that's all that matters** darauf allein kommt es an; **that is all (that) I can tell you** mehr kann ich Ihnen nicht sagen; **it was all I could do not to laugh** ich musste an mich halten, um nicht zu lachen

◆**all of all of Paris/of the house** ganz Paris/das ganze Haus; **all of it** alles; **all of 5 kms/£5** ganze 5 km/£ 5

◆**all or nothing** alles oder nichts

(b) (= everybody) alle pl; **all of them** (sie) alle; **the score was two all** es stand zwei zu zwei

3 ADVERB (= quite, entirely) ganz; **all dirty/excited** etc ganz schmutzig/aufgeregt etc; **that's all very fine** or **well** das ist alles ganz schön und gut

◆**all + adverb/preposition it was red all over** es war ganz rot; **all down the front of her dress** überall vorn auf ihrem Kleid; **all along the road** die ganze Straße entlang; **there were chairs all around the room** rundum im Zimmer standen Stühle; **he ordered whiskies/drinks all round** er hat für alle Whisky/Getränke bestellt; **I'll tell you all about it** ich erzähl dir alles

4 NOUN

◆**one's all** alles; **he staked his all on this race/deal** er setzte alles auf dieses Rennen/Unternehmen; **the horses were giving their all** die Pferde gaben ihr Letztes

5 SET STRUCTURES

◆**all along** (= from the start) von Anfang an

◆**all but** fast; **he all but died** er wäre fast gestorben; **the party won all but six of the seats** die Partei hat alle bis auf sechs Sitze gewonnen

◆**all for** (= in favour of) **I'm all for it!** ich bin ganz dafür

◆**all in** (inf: = exhausted) **to be** or **feel all in** total erledigt sein (inf)

◆**all in all** alles in allem

◆**all one** (= indifferent) **it's all one to me** das ist mir (ganz) egal

◆**all the +** comparative **all the hotter/happier** etc noch heißer/glücklicher etc; **all the funnier because ...** umso lustiger, weil ...

◆**all the same** trotz allem; **all the same, it's a pity** trotzdem ist es schade; **it's all the same to me** das ist mir (ganz) egal

◆**all there/not all there** (inf: person) **he's all there/not all there** er ist voll da/nicht ganz da (inf)

◆**all too +** adjective/adverb viel zu, allzu

◆**... and all** he ate the orange, peel and all er hat die ganze Orange gegessen, samt der Schale; **the whole family came, children and all** die Familie kam mit Kind und Kegel

◆**at all** (= whatsoever) überhaupt; **nothing at all** gar nichts; (= in the least) **I'm not at all sure** ich bin mir gar und gar nicht sicher; **I'm not at all angry** etc, **I'm not angry** etc **at all** ich bin überhaupt nicht wütend etc; **it's not bad at all** das ist gar nicht schlecht; **if at all possible** wenn irgend möglich

◆**for all** (= despite) trotz; **for all that** trotzdem

◆**for all I know** for all I know she could be ill was weiß ich, vielleicht ist sie krank

◆**in all** insgesamt; **ten people in all** insgesamt zehn Personen

◆**all that** (US inf) einfach super (inf)

✦**not all that** it's not all that bad, it's not as bad as all that so schlimm ist es nun auch wieder nicht

✦*of all ...!* of all the stupid things to do! so was Dummes!; **why me of all people?** warum ausgerechnet ich?

✦*superlative* + **of all** happiest/earliest *etc* of all am glücklichsten/frühsten *etc*; **I like him best of all** von allen mag ich ihn am liebsten; **most of all** am meisten; **the best car of all** das allerbeste Auto

✦**you all** (*US inf*) ihr (alle); (*to two people*) ihr (beide)

Allah ['ælə] N Allah *m*

all: **all-American** ADJ *team, player* uramerikanisch; **an ~ boy** ein durch und durch amerikanischer Junge; **all-around** ADJ (*US*) = **all-round**

allay [ə'leɪ] VT verringern; *doubt, fears, suspicion* zerstreuen

all: **all clear** N Entwarnung *f*; **to give/sound the ~** Entwarnung geben; **all-consuming** ADJ *passion* überwältigend; **all-day** ADJ ganztägig; **it was an ~ meeting** die Sitzung dauerte den ganzen Tag

allegation [ælɪ'geɪʃən] N Behauptung *f*

allege [ə'ledʒ] VT behaupten; **he is ~d to have said that ...** er soll angeblich gesagt haben, dass ...

alleged [ə'ledʒd] ADJ, **allegedly** [ə'ledʒɪdlɪ] ADV angeblich

allegiance [ə'liːdʒəns] N Treue *f* (*to* +*dat*); **oath of ~** Treueeid *m*

allegoric(al) [ælɪ'gɒrɪk(əl)] ADJ, **allegorically** [ælɪ'gɒrɪkəlɪ] ADV allegorisch

allegory ['ælɪgərɪ] N Allegorie *f*

allegro [ə'legrəʊ] **1** ADJ, ADV allegro **2** N Allegro *nt*

alleluia [ælɪ'luːjə] **1** INTERJ (h)alleluja **2** N (H)alleluja *nt*

all-embracing [ˌɔːlɪm'breɪsɪŋ] ADJ (all)umfassend

allergic [ə'lɜːdʒɪk] ADJ (*lit, fig*) allergisch (*to* gegen)

allergy ['ælədʒɪ] N Allergie *f* (*to* gegen)

alleviate [ə'liːvɪeɪt] VT lindern

alleviation [əˌliːvɪ'eɪʃən] N Linderung *f*

alley ['ælɪ] N **(a)** (enge) Gasse; (*in garden*) Laubengang *m* **(b)** (= *bowling ~*) Bahn *f*

Be careful! **alley** *is not translated by the German word* **Allee**.

alleyway ['ælɪweɪ] N Durchgang *m*

all: **all-fired** ADJ (*US inf*) furchtbar (*inf*); **All Fools' Day** N *der erste April*; **All Hallows' (Day)** N (*Brit*) = **All Saints' Day**

alliance [ə'laɪəns] N Verbindung *f*; (*of institutions also, of states*) Bündnis *nt*; (*in historical contexts*) Allianz *f*

allied ['ælaɪd] ADJ verbunden; (*for attack, defence etc*) verbündet; **the Allied forces** die Alliierten

alligator ['ælɪgeɪtə'] N Alligator *m*

all: **all-important** ADJ außerordentlich wichtig; **the ~ question** die Frage, auf die es ankommt; **all-in** ADJ ATTR, **all in** ADJ PRED (= *inclusive*) Inklusiv-; **~ price** Inklusivpreis *m*; *see also* **all**; **all-inclusive** ADJ Pauschal-; **all-in-one** ADJ *sleepsuit, wetsuit* einteilig; **all-in wrestling** N (*Sport*) Freistilringen *nt*

alliteration [əˌlɪtə'reɪʃən] N Alliteration *f*

all-night [ˌɔːl'naɪt] ADJ ATTR *café* (die ganze Nacht) durchgehend geöffnet; *vigil* die ganze Nacht andauernd *attr*; **we had an ~ party** wir haben die ganze Nacht durchgemacht; **there is an ~ bus service** die Busse verkehren die ganze Nacht über

allocate ['æləʊkeɪt] VT (= *allot*) zuteilen (*to sb* jdm); (= *apportion*) verteilen (*to* auf +*acc*); *tasks* vergeben (*to* an +*acc*); **to ~ money to or for a project** Geld für ein Projekt bestimmen

allocation [æləʊ'keɪʃən] N (= *allotting*) Zuteilung *f*; (= *apportioning*) Verteilung *f*; (= *sum allocated*) Zuwendung *f*

allot [ə'lɒt] VT zuteilen (*to sb/sth* jdm/etw); *time* vorsehen (*to* für); *money* bestimmen (*to* für)

allotment [ə'lɒtmənt] N (*Brit* = *plot of ground*) Schrebergarten *m*

all: **all out** ADV mit aller Kraft; **to go ~ to do sth** alles daransetzen, etw zu tun; **all-out** ADJ *strike, war* total; *attack* massiv; *effort, attempt* äußerste(r, s); **all-over** ADJ ganzflächig

allow [ə'laʊ] **1** VT **(a)** (= *permit*) *sth* erlauben; *behaviour etc* gestatten, zulassen; **to ~ sb sth** jdm etw erlauben; **to ~ sb to do sth** jdm erlauben, etw zu tun; **to be ~ed to do sth** etw tun dürfen; **smoking is not ~ed** Rauchen ist nicht gestattet; **"no**

dogs ~ed" „Hunde müssen draußen bleiben"; **to ~ oneself sth** sich (*dat*) etw erlauben; (= *treat oneself*) sich (*dat*) etw gönnen; **to ~ oneself to be waited on/persuaded** *etc* sich bedienen/überreden *etc* lassen; **~ me!** gestatten Sie (*form*); **to ~ sth to happen** zulassen, dass etw geschieht; **to be ~ed in/out** hinein-/hinausdürfen

(b) (= *recognize, accept*) *claim, appeal, goal* anerkennen

(c) (= *allocate, grant*) *discount, money* geben; *space* lassen; *time* einplanen; (*in tax, Jur*) zugestehen; **~ (yourself) an hour to cross the city** rechnen Sie mit einer Stunde, um durch die Stadt zu kommen; **~ 5 cms extra** geben Sie 5 cm zu

(d) (= *concede*) annehmen; **~ing** *or* **if we ~ that ...** angenommen, (dass) ...

2 VI **if time ~s** falls es zeitlich möglich ist

▸ **allow for** VI +PREP OBJ berücksichtigen; **allowing for the fact that ...** unter Berücksichtigung der Tatsache, dass ...; **after allowing for** nach Berücksichtigung (+*gen*)

allowable [ə'laʊəbl] ADJ zulässig; (*Fin: in tax*) absetzbar; **~ expenses** (*Fin*) abzugsfähige Kosten

allowance [ə'laʊəns] N **(a)** finanzielle Unterstützung; (*paid by state*) Beihilfe *f*; (*parent to child*) Unterhaltsgeld *nt*; (*as compensation*) (*for unsociable hours etc*) Zulage *f*; (*on business trip*) Spesen *pl*; (= *spending money*) Taschengeld *nt*; *clothing* **~** Kleidungsgeld *nt*; **he gave her an ~ of £500 a month** er stellte ihr monatlich £ 500 zur Verfügung

(b) (*Fin:* = *tax* ~) Freibetrag *m*

(c) (*Fin, Comm:* = *discount*) (Preis)nachlass *m* (*on* für); (= *quantity allowed: for shrinkage etc*) Zugabe *f*

(d) **to make ~(s) for sth** etw berücksichtigen; **to make ~s for sb** bei jdm Zugeständnisse machen

alloy ['ælɔɪ] N Legierung *f*

all: **all-party** ADJ (*Pol*) Allparteien-; **all-powerful** ADJ allmächtig; **all-purpose** ADJ Allzweck-

all right [ˌɔːl'raɪt] **1** ADJ PRED **(a)** (= *undamaged*) heil, okay (*inf*); **it's ~** (= *not too bad*) es geht; (= *working properly*) es ist in Ordnung; **that's** *or* **it's ~** (*after thanks, apology*) schon gut; **to taste/look ~** ganz gut schmecken/aussehen; **is it ~ for me to leave early/come out now?** kann ich früher gehen/jetzt rauskommen?; **it's ~ by me** ich habe nichts dagegen; **it's ~ for you (to talk)** du hast gut reden; **he's ~** (*inf:* = *is a good guy*) der ist in Ordnung (*inf*); **are you ~?** (= *healthy*) geht es Ihnen gut?; (= *unharmed*) ist Ihnen etwas passiert?; **are you feeling ~?** fehlt Ihnen was?

2 ADV **(a)** (= *satisfactorily*) ganz gut; (= *safely*) gut; **did I do it ~?** habe ich es recht gemacht?; **did you get home ~?** bist du gut nach Hause gekommen?; **did you get/find it ~?** haben Sie es denn bekommen/gefunden?

(b) (= *certainly*) schon; **he'll come ~** er wird schon kommen; **that's the boy ~** das ist der Junge; **oh yes, we heard you ~** o ja, und ob wir dich gehört haben

3 INTERJ gut, okay (*inf*); (*in agreement*) in Ordnung; **may I leave early? – ~** kann ich früher gehen? – ja; **~ that's enough!** komm, jetzt reichts (aber)!; **~, ~! I'm coming** schon gut, ich komme ja!

all: **all-round** ADJ (*esp Brit*) Allround-; *student* vielseitig begabt; *improvement* in jeder Hinsicht; **a good ~ performance** eine rundum gute Leistung; **all-rounder** N (*Brit*) Allroundmann *m*/-frau *f*; (*Sport*) Allroundsportler(in) *m(f)*; **All Saints' Day** N Allerheiligen *nt*; **all-seater** ADJ (*Brit Sport*) *stadium* ohne Stehplätze; **All Souls' Day** N Allerseelen *nt*; **allspice** N Piment *m or nt*; **all-star** ADJ Star-; **~ cast** Starbesetzung *f*; **all-terrain bike** N Mountainbike *nt*; **all-terrain vehicle** N Geländefahrzeug *nt*; **all-time** **1** ADJ aller Zeiten; **the ~ record** der Rekord aller Zeiten; **an ~ high/low** der höchste/niedrigste Stand aller Zeiten **2** ADV **~ best/worst** beste(r, s)/ schlechteste(r, s) aller Zeiten

allude [ə'luːd] VI +PREP OBJ **to ~ to** anspielen auf (+*acc*)

allure [ə'ljʊə'] N Reiz *m*

alluring ADJ, **alluringly** ADV [ə'ljʊərɪŋ, -lɪ] verführerisch

allusion [ə'luːʒən] N Anspielung *f* (*to* auf +*acc*)

all-weather [ˌɔːl'weðə'] ADJ Allwetter-; **~ pitch** Allwetterplatz *m*

ally ['ælaɪ] **1** N Verbündete(r) *mf*; (*Hist*) Alliierte(r) *m* **2** [ə'laɪ] VT verbinden (*with, to* mit); (*for attack, defence etc*) verbünden (*with, to* mit); **to ~ oneself with** *or* **to sb** sich mit jdm verbinden

alma mater ['ælmə'meɪtə'] N Alma Mater *f*

almanac ['ɔːlmənæk] N Almanach *m*

almighty [ɔːlˈmaɪtɪ] **1** ADJ **(a)** *god, person* allmächtig; **Almighty God** (*Eccl*), **God Almighty** (*Eccl*) der Allmächtige; (*address in prayer*) allmächtiger Gott; **God** *or* **Christ Almighty!** (*inf*) Allmächtiger! (*inf*) **(b)** (*inf*) *fool, row* mordsmäßig (*inf*); **there was an ~ bang and ...** es gab einen Mordsknall und ... (*inf*) **2** N **the Almighty** der Allmächtige

almond [ˈɑːmənd] N Mandel *f*

almost [ˈɔːlməʊst] ADV fast; **he ~ fell** er wäre fast gefallen; **she'll ~ certainly come** sie kommt ziemlich sicher

alms [ɑːmz] PL Almosen *pl*

almshouse [ˈɑːmzhaʊs] N Armenhaus *nt*

aloe vera [ˌæləʊˈvɪərə] N Aloe Vera *f*

aloft [əˈlɒft] ADV (= *into the air*) empor; (= *in the air*) hoch droben

alone [əˈləʊn] **1** ADJ PRED allein(e); **we're not ~ in thinking that** wir stehen mit dieser Meinung nicht allein **2** ADV allein(e); **the hotel ~ cost £300** das Hotel allein kostete (schon) £ 300; **Simon ~ knew the truth** nur Simon kannte die Wahrheit; **to stand ~** (*fig*) einzig dastehen; **to go it ~** (*inf*: = *be independent*) auf eigenen Beinen stehen

along [əˈlɒŋ] **1** PREP (*direction*) entlang (+*acc*), lang (+*acc*) (*inf*); (*position*) entlang (+*dat*); **he walked ~ the river** er ging den Fluss entlang; **somewhere ~ the way** irgendwo unterwegs *or* auf dem Weg; (*fig*) irgendwann einmal **2** ADV **(a)** (= *onwards*) weiter-; **to move ~** weitergehen; **run ~** nun lauf!; **he'll be ~ soon** er muss gleich da sein; **are you coming? – yes, I'll be ~ in a minute** kommst du? – ja, (ich komme) gleich **(b)** (= *together*) **~ with** zusammen mit; **to come/sing ~ with sb** mit jdm mitkommen/mitsingen; **take an umbrella ~** nimm einen Schirm mit

alongside [əˈlɒŋˈsaɪd] **1** PREP neben (+*dat*); **he parked ~ the kerb** (*Brit*) *or* **curb** (*US*) er parkte am Bordstein; **he works ~ me** (= *with me*) er ist ein Kollege von mir; (= *next to me*) er arbeitet neben mir **2** ADV daneben; **a police car drew up ~** ein Polizeiauto fuhr neben mich/ihn *etc* heran; **they brought their dinghy ~** sie brachten ihr Dingi heran

aloof [əˈluːf] **1** ADV (*lit, fig*) abseits; **to remain ~** sich abseits halten; **to keep** *or* **stand ~ (from sth)** sich (von etw) distanzieren **2** ADJ unnahbar

aloud [əˈlaʊd] ADV laut

alpaca [ælˈpækə] **1** N Alpaka *nt* **2** ATTR Alpaka-

alpha [ˈælfə] N **(a)** (= *letter*) Alpha *nt* **(b)** (*Brit Sch, Univ*) Eins *f*

alphabet [ˈælfəbet] N Alphabet *nt*; **does he know the** *or* **his ~?** kann er schon das Abc?

alphabetic(al) [ˌælfəˈbetɪk(əl)] ADJ alphabetisch; **in alphabetical order** in alphabetischer Reihenfolge

alphabetically [ˌælfəˈbetɪkəlɪ] ADV alphabetisch

alpine [ˈælpaɪn] ADJ **(a) Alpine** alpin; *dialects* der Alpen **(b)** (*general*) alpin; (*Geol*) alpinisch; **~ flower** Alpenblume *f*; **~ hut** Berghütte *f*; **~ scenery** Berglandschaft *f*

Alps [ælps] PL Alpen *pl*

already [ɔːlˈredɪ] ADV schon; **I've ~ seen it, I've seen it ~** ich habe es schon gesehen

alright [ɔːlˈraɪt] ADJ, ADV = **all right**

Alsace [ˈælsæs] N das Elsass

Alsace-Lorraine [ˈælsæsləˈreɪn] N Elsass-Lothringen *nt*

alsatian [ælˈseɪʃən] N (*Brit*: *also ~* **dog**) (Deutscher) Schäferhund

also [ˈɔːlsəʊ] ADV auch; (= *moreover*) außerdem; **her cousin ~ came** *or* **came ~** ihre Kusine kam auch; **not only ... but ~** nicht nur ... sondern auch; **~, I must explain that ...** außerdem muss ich erklären, dass ...

> *Be careful!* **also** *is not translated by the German word* **also***.*

also-ran [ˈɔːlsəʊˈræn] N **to be among the ~s, to be an ~** (*Sport, fig*) unter „ferner liefen" kommen

altar [ˈɒltəʳ] N Altar *m*; **to lead sb to the ~** jdn zum Altar führen; **she was left standing at the ~** sie wurde in letzter Minute sitzen gelassen (*inf*)

altar boy N Ministrant *m*

alter [ˈɒltəʳ] **1** VT **(a)** (= *change*) ändern; **to ~ sth completely** etw vollkommen verändern; **it does not ~ the fact that ...** das ändert nichts an der Tatsache, dass ... **(b)** (*US*: = *castrate, spay*) kastrieren **2** VI sich ändern

alteration [ˌɒltəˈreɪʃən] N (= *change*) Änderung *f*; (*of appearance*) Veränderung *f*; **to make ~s in sth** Änderungen an etw (*dat*) vornehmen; **(this timetable is) subject to ~** Änderungen (im Fahrplan sind) vorbehalten; **closed for ~s** wegen Umbau geschlossen

altercation [ˌɒltəˈkeɪʃən] N Auseinandersetzung *f*

alter ego [ˈæltərˈiːgəʊ] N Alter ego *nt*

alternate [ɒlˈtɜːnɪt] **1** ADJ **(a) they do their shopping on ~ days** (= *every other day*) sie machen ihre Einkäufe jeden zweiten Tag; (= *taking turns*) sie wechseln sich täglich mit dem Einkaufen ab; **they put down ~ layers of brick and mortar** sie schichteten (immer) abwechselnd Ziegel und Mörtel aufeinander **(b)** (= *alternative*) alternativ; **~ route** Ausweichstrecke *f* **2** [ˈɒltənɪt] N (*US*) Vertreter(in) *m(f)*; (*Sport*) Ersatzspieler(in) *m(f)* **3** [ˈɒltəneɪt] VT abwechseln lassen; *crops* im Wechsel anbauen; **to ~ one thing with another** zwischen einer Sache und einer anderen (ab)wechseln **4** [ˈɒltəneɪt] VI (sich) abwechseln; (*Elec*) alternieren

alternately [ɒlˈtɜːnɪtlɪ] ADV **(a)** (= *in turn*) wechselweise **(b)** = **alternatively**

alternating [ˈɒltɜːneɪtɪŋ] ADJ wechselnd; **a pattern with ~ stripes of red and white** ein Muster mit abwechselnd roten und weißen Streifen; **~ current** Wechselstrom *m*

alternation [ˌɒltɜːˈneɪʃən] N Wechsel *m*

alternative [ɒlˈtɜːnətɪv] **1** ADJ Alternativ-; **~ route** Ausweichstrecke *f* **2** N Alternative *f*; **I had no ~ (but ...)** ich hatte keine andere Wahl (als ...)

alternatively [ɒlˈtɜːnətɪvlɪ] ADV als Alternative; **or ~, he could come with us** oder aber, er kommt mit uns mit; **a prison sentence of three months or ~ a fine of £5000** eine Gefängnisstrafe von drei Monaten oder wahlweise eine Geldstrafe von £ 5000

alternative medicine N Alternativmedizin *f*

alternator [ˈɒltɜːneɪtəʳ] N (*Elec*) Wechselstromgenerator *m*; (*Aut*) Lichtmaschine *f*

although [ɔːlˈðəʊ] CONJ obwohl; **the house, ~ small ...** obwohl das Haus klein ist ...

altimeter [ˈæltɪmiːtəʳ] N Höhenmesser *m*

altitude [ˈæltɪtjuːd] N Höhe *f*; **what is our ~?** in welcher Höhe befinden wir uns?; **we are flying at an ~ of ...** wir fliegen in einer Höhe von ...

alt key [ˈɒltkiː] N (*Comput*) Alt-Taste *f*

alto [ˈæltəʊ] **1** N (= *voice, person*) Alt *m* **2** ADJ Alt- **3** ADV **to sing ~** Alt singen

altogether [ˌɔːltəˈgeðəʳ] **1** ADV **(a)** (= *including everything*) insgesamt; **taken ~,** *or* **~ it was very pleasant** alles in allem war es sehr nett **(b)** (= *wholly*) vollkommen; **he wasn't ~ pleased/surprised** er war nicht übermäßig zufrieden/überrascht; **it was ~ a waste of time** es war vollkommene Zeitverschwendung; **that is another matter ~** das ist etwas ganz anderes **2** N **in the ~** (*hum inf*) hüllenlos, im Adams-/Evaskostüm

alto sax(ophone) N Altsaxophon *nt*

altruism [ˈæltrʊɪzəm] N Altruismus *m*

altruistic ADJ, **altruistically** ADV [ˌæltrʊˈɪstɪk, -əlɪ] altruistisch

aluminium [ˌæljʊˈmɪnɪəm], (*US*) **aluminum** [əˈluːmɪnəm] N Aluminium *nt*; **~ foil** Alufolie *f*

alumna [əˈlʌmnə] N, *pl* **-e** [əˈlʌmniː] (*US*) ehemalige Schülerin/Studentin

alumnus [əˈlʌmnəs] N, *pl* **alumni** [əˈlʌmnaɪ] (*US*) ehemaliger Schüler/Student

always [ˈɔːlweɪz] ADV immer; **we could ~ go by train/sell the house** wir könnten doch auch den Zug nehmen/könnten ja auch das Haus verkaufen; **there's ~ the possibility that ...** es besteht immer noch die Möglichkeit, dass ...

Alzheimer's (disease) [ˈæltsˌhaɪməz(dɪˌziːz)] N Alzheimer-krankheit *f*

AM (a) (*Rad*) ABBR *of* **amplitude modulation** AM **(b)** (*Brit Pol*) ABBR *of* **Assembly Member** Mitglied *nt* der walisischen Versammlung

am [æm] 1ST PERS SING PRESENT *of* **be**

am, a.m. ABBR *of* **ante meridiem**; **2 am** 2 Uhr morgens; **12 am** 0 Uhr, Mitternacht

AM (*Brit Pol*) ABBR *of* **Assembly Member** Mitglied *nt* der walisischen Versammlung

amalgam [ə'mælgəm] N Amalgam *nt*; (*fig*) Mischung *f*

amalgamate [ə'mælgəmeɪt] **1** VT *companies, unions* fusionieren; *departments* zusammenlegen **2** VI (*companies etc*) fusionieren

amalgamation [ə,mælgə'meɪʃən] N (*of companies etc*) Fusion *f*

amass [ə'mæs] VT anhäufen

amateur ['æmətəʳ] **1** N **(a)** Amateur(in) *m(f)* **(b)** (*pej*) Dilettant(in) *m(f)* **2** ADJ **(a)** ATTR Amateur-; **~ painter** Hobbymaler(in) *m(f)* **(b)** (*pej*) = **amateurish**

amateur dramatics [,æmətədrə'mætɪks] PL Laiendrama *nt*

amateurish ADJ, **amateurishly** ADV ['æmətərɪʃ, -lɪ] (*pej*) dilettantisch

amaze [ə'meɪz] VT erstaunen; **I was ~d to learn that …** ich war erstaunt zu hören, dass …; **to be ~d at sth** über etw (*acc*) erstaunt sein; **you don't know that, you ~ me!** Sie wissen das nicht, das wundert mich aber; **it ~s me that he doesn't fall** ich finde es erstaunlich, dass er nicht fällt

amazement [ə'meɪzmənt] N Erstaunen *nt*; **much to my ~** zu meinem großen Erstaunen

amazing [ə'meɪzɪŋ] ADJ erstaunlich

amazingly [ə'meɪzɪŋlɪ] ADV erstaunlich; **~ (enough), he got it right first time** erstaunlicherweise hat er es gleich beim ersten Mal richtig gemacht

Amazon ['æməzən] N Amazonas *m*; (*Myth, fig*) Amazone *f*

ambassador [æm'bæsədəʳ] N Botschafter(in) *m(f)*; (*fig*) Vertreter(in) *m(f)*

ambassador extraordinary, (*esp US*) **ambassador-at-large** [æm'bæsədərət,lɑːdʒ] N Sonderbotschafter(in) *m(f)*

ambassadorial [æm,bæsə'dɔːrɪəl] ADJ Botschafter-; *rank, dignity* eines Botschafters

amber ['æmbəʳ] **1** N Bernstein *m*; (*colour*) Bernsteingelb *nt*; (*Brit: in traffic lights*) Gelb *nt* **2** ADJ aus Bernstein; (= *~-coloured*) bernsteinfarben; (*Brit*) *traffic light* gelb

ambidextrous [æmbɪ'dekstrəs] ADJ beidhändig

ambience ['æmbɪəns] N Atmosphäre *f*

ambiguity [æmbɪ'gjuːtɪ] N Zweideutigkeit *f*; (*with many possible meanings*) Mehrdeutigkeit *f*

ambiguous ADJ, **ambiguously** ADV [æm'bɪgjʊəs, -lɪ] zweideutig; (= *with many possible meanings*) mehrdeutig

ambition [æm'bɪʃən] N **(a)** (= *desire*) Ambition *f*; **she has ~s in that direction/for her son** sie hat Ambitionen in dieser Richtung/ehrgeizige Pläne für ihren Sohn; **my ~ is to become prime minister** es ist mein Ehrgeiz, Premierminister zu werden **(b)** (= *ambitious nature*) Ehrgeiz *m*

ambitious [æm'bɪʃəs] ADJ ehrgeizig; *idea, undertaking* kühn

ambitiously [æm'bɪʃəslɪ] ADV ehrgeizig; **rather ~, we set out to prove the following** wir hatten uns das ehrgeizige Ziel gesteckt, das Folgende zu beweisen

ambivalence [æm'bɪvələns] N Ambivalenz *f*

ambivalent [æm'bɪvələnt] ADJ ambivalent

amble ['æmbl] **1** VI (*person*) schlendern **2** N Schlendern *nt*; **he went for an ~ along the riverside** er machte einen gemütlichen Spaziergang am Fluss entlang

ambulance ['æmbjʊləns] N Krankenwagen *m*

ambulance: **ambulance driver** N Krankenwagenfahrer(in) *m(f)*; **ambulanceman** N Sanitäter *m*; **ambulance service** N Rettungsdienst *m*; (*system*) Rettungswesen *nt*

ambush ['æmbʊʃ] **1** N (= *attack*) Überfall *m* (aus dem Hinterhalt); **to lie in ~ for sb** (*Mil, fig*) jdm im Hinterhalt auflauern **2** VT (aus dem Hinterhalt) überfallen

ameba N (*US*) = **amoeba**

amen [ɑː'men] INTERJ amen; **~ to that!** (*fig inf*) ja, wahrlich *or* fürwahr! (*hum*)

amenable [ə'miːnəbl] ADJ (= *responsive*) zugänglich (*to* +*dat*)

amend [ə'mend] VT **(a)** *law, text* ändern; (*by addition*) ergänzen; **I'd better ~ that to "most people"** ich werde das lieber in „die meisten Leute" (ab)ändern **(b)** (= *improve*) *habits, behaviour* bessern

amendment [ə'mendmənt] N (*to law, in text*) Änderung *f* (*to* +*gen*); (= *addition*) Zusatz *m* (*to* zu); **the First/Second etc Amendment** (*US Pol*) Zusatz *m* 1/2 *etc*

amends [ə'mendz] PL **to make ~ for sth** etw wiedergutmachen; **to make ~ to sb for sth** jdn für etw entschädigen

amenity [ə'miːnɪtɪ] N (= *aid to pleasant living*) (**public**) **~** öffentliche Einrichtung; **close to all amenities** in günstiger Einkaufs- und Verkehrslage

Amerasian [æme'reɪʒn] N *Mensch amerikanisch-asiatischer Herkunft*

America [ə'merɪkə] N Amerika *nt*; **the ~s** Amerika *nt*, der amerikanische Kontinent

American [ə'merɪkən] **1** ADJ amerikanisch; **~ English** amerikanisches Englisch **2** N **(a)** Amerikaner(in) *m(f)* **(b)** (= *Ling*) Amerikanisch *nt*

AMERICAN DREAM

*Der **American Dream** ist ein Begriff, in dem all die positiven Werte und Grundsätze zusammengefasst werden, die viele Amerikaner empfinden, wenn sie ihr Leben als Nation beschreiben sollen, und die in der Unabhängigkeitserklärung von 1776 festgeschrieben wurden. Besonders betont werden dabei Individualismus, Fleiß, Aufstiegs- und Verbesserungsmöglichkeiten für alle und die umfassende Gültigkeit von Freiheit und Gerechtigkeit. Viele Einwanderer betrachteten den **American Dream** als eine Möglichkeit, ihr Glück zu versuchen und etwas aus ihrem Leben zu machen. Der Begriff wird auch ironisch verwendet, um auf den Gegensatz zwischen diesen Idealen und den materialistischen Einstellungen hinzuweisen, die nach Meinung vieler in der gegenwärtigen amerikanischen Gesellschaft vorherrschen.*

American Indian N Indianer(in) *m(f)*

Americanism [ə'merɪkənɪzəm] N (*Ling*) Amerikanismus *m*

Americanization [ə,merɪkənaɪ'zeɪʃən] N Amerikanisierung *f*

Americanize [ə'merɪkənaɪz] VT amerikanisieren

American plan N Vollpension *f*

Amerindian [æmə'rɪndɪən] **1** N Indianer(in) *m(f)* **2** ADJ indianisch

amethyst ['æmɪθɪst] N Amethyst *m*

AmEx® ['æmeks] (*US*) **1** N ABBR *of* **American Express** American Express *no art* **2** ADJ **~ card** American Express-Karte *f*

Amex ['æmeks] N (*US*) ABBR *of* **American Stock Exchange** Amex *f*

amiable ADJ, **amiably** ADV ['eɪmɪəbl, -lɪ] liebenswürdig

amicable ['æmɪkəbl] ADJ *person* freundlich; *relations* freundschaftlich; *discussion* friedlich; (*Jur*) *settlement* gütlich; **to be on ~ terms** freundschaftlich miteinander verkehren

amicably ['æmɪkəblɪ] ADV freundlich; *discuss* friedlich; (*Jur*) *settle* gütlich

amid(st) [ə'mɪd(st)] PREP inmitten (+*gen*)

amino acid [ə'miːnəʊˈæsɪd] N Aminosäure *f*

amiss [ə'mɪs] **1** ADJ PRED **there's something ~** da stimmt irgendetwas nicht **2** ADV **to take sth ~** (*Brit*) (jdm) etw übel nehmen; **a drink would not come** *or* **go ~** etwas zu trinken wäre gar nicht verkehrt

ammo ['æməʊ] N (*inf*) Munition *f*

ammonia [ə'məʊnɪə] N Ammoniak *nt*

ammunition [æmjʊ'nɪʃən] N (*lit, fig*) Munition *f*

ammunition: **ammunition belt** N Patronengurt *m*; **ammunition dump** N Munitionslager *nt*

amnesia [æm'niːzɪə] N Amnesie *f*

amnesty ['æmnɪstɪ] N Amnestie *f*; **during** *or* **under the ~** unter der Amnestie

amniocentesis [æmnɪəʊsen'tiːsɪs] N (*Med*) Fruchtwasseruntersuchung *f*

amoeba, (*US*) **ameba** [ə'miːbə] N Amöbe *f*

amok [ə'mɒk] ADV = **amuck**

among(st) [ə'mʌŋ(st)] PREP unter (+*acc or dat*); **~ other things** unter anderem; **she had sung with Madonna ~ others** sie hatte unter anderem mit Madonna gesungen; **to stand ~ the crowd** (mitten) in der Menge stehen; **they shared it out ~ themselves** sie teilten es untereinander auf; **talk ~ yourselves** unterhaltet euch; **he's ~ our best players** er gehört zu unseren besten Spielern; **to count sb ~ one's friends** jdn zu seinen Freunden zählen; **this habit is widespread ~ the French** diese Sitte ist bei den Franzosen weit verbreitet

amoral [eɪ'mɒrəl] ADJ amoralisch

amorous ['æmərəs] ADJ amourös; *look* verliebt

amorphous [ə'mɔːfəs] ADJ amorph, formlos; *style, ideas, novel* strukturlos

amortization [əˌmɔːtarˈzeɪʃən] N Amortisation f

amortize [əˈmɔːtaɪz] VT *debt* amortisieren, tilgen; *costs* amortisieren

amount [əˈmaʊnt] **1** N **(a)** *(of money)* Betrag m; **total ~** Gesamtsumme f; **debts to** *(Brit)* or in *(US)* **the ~ of £2000** Schulden in Höhe von £ 2000; **I was shocked at the ~ of the bill** ich war über die Höhe der Rechnung erschrocken; **in 12 equal ~s** in 12 gleichen Beträgen; **a large/a small ~ of money** eine große/geringe Summe (Geldes); **large ~s of money** Unsummen pl; **~ insured** *(Insur)* Versicherungssumme f **(b)** (= *quantity*) Menge f; *(of luck, skill etc)* Maß nt *(of* an +*dat)*; **an enormous ~ of work/time** sehr viel Arbeit/Zeit; **any ~ of time/food** beliebig viel Zeit/Essen; **no ~ of talking would persuade him** kein Reden würde ihn überzeugen
2 VI **(a)** (= *total*) sich belaufen *(to* auf +*acc)*
(b) (= *be equivalent*) gleichkommen *(to dat)*; **it ~s to the same thing** das kommt (doch) aufs Gleiche hinaus; **he will never ~ to much** aus ihm wird nie etwas werden

amp(ère) [ˈæmp(eəʳ)] N Ampere nt

ampersand [ˈæmpəsænd] N Et-Zeichen f, Und-Zeichen nt

amphetamine [æmˈfetəmiːn] N Amphetamin nt

amphibian [æmˈfɪbɪən] N Amphibie f

amphibious [æmˈfɪbɪəs] ADJ amphibisch; **~ vehicle/aircraft** Amphibienfahrzeug nt/-flugzeug nt

amphitheatre, *(US)* **amphitheater** [ˈæmfɪˌθɪətəʳ] N Amphitheater nt

ample [ˈæmpl] ADJ (+ER) **(a)** (= *plentiful*) reichlich; **that will be ~** das ist reichlich; **more than ~** überreichlich **(b)** (= *large*) *figure, proportions* üppig

amplification [ˌæmplɪfɪˈkeɪʃən] N Erläuterungen pl; *(Rad)* Verstärkung f

amplifier [ˈæmplɪfaɪəʳ] N *(Rad)* Verstärker m

amplify [ˈæmplɪfaɪ] **1** VT **(a)** *(Rad)* verstärken **(b)** (= *expand*) *statement, idea* näher erläutern **2** VI **to ~ on sth** etw näher erläutern

amply [ˈæmplɪ] ADV reichlich; *proportioned figure* üppig; *proportioned rooms* großzügig

amputate [ˈæmpjʊteɪt] VTI amputieren

amputation [ˌæmpjʊˈteɪʃən] N Amputation f

amputee [ˌæmpjʊˈtiː] N Amputierte(r) mf

amuck [əˈmʌk] ADV **to run ~** *(lit, fig)* Amok laufen

amuse [əˈmjuːz] **1** VT amüsieren; (= *entertain*) unterhalten; **let the children do it if it ~s them** lass die Kinder doch, wenn es ihnen Spaß macht **2** VR **the children can ~ themselves for a while** die Kinder können sich eine Zeit lang selbst beschäftigen; **to ~ oneself (by) doing sth** etw zu seinem Vergnügen tun; **how do you ~ yourself now you're retired?** wie vertreiben Sie sich *(dat)* die Zeit, wo Sie jetzt im Ruhestand sind?

amused [əˈmjuːzd] ADJ amüsiert; **she seemed ~ at my suggestion** sie schien über meinen Vorschlag amüsiert (zu sein); **I was ~ to see/hear that ...** es hat mich amüsiert zu sehen/hören, dass ...; **to keep sb/oneself ~** jdm/sich *(dat)* die Zeit vertreiben; **give him his toys, that'll keep him ~** gib ihm sein Spielzeug, dann ist er friedlich

amusement [əˈmjuːzmənt] N **(a)** (= *enjoyment, fun*) Vergnügen nt; (= *state of being entertained*) Belustigung f; **I see no cause for ~** ich sehe keinen Grund zur Heiterkeit; **to do sth for one's own ~** etw zu seinem Vergnügen tun; **to my great ~/to everyone's ~** zu meiner großen/zur allgemeinen Belustigung **(b)** **amusements** PL *(at fair)* Attraktionen pl; *(at the seaside)* Spielautomaten und Spiegelkabinett etc

amusement: amusement arcade N *(Brit)* Spielhalle f; **amusement park** N Vergnügungspark m

amusing [əˈmjuːzɪŋ] ADJ amüsant; **how ~** das ist aber lustig!; **I don't find that very ~** das finde ich gar nicht lustig

amusingly [əˈmjuːzɪŋlɪ] ADV amüsant

an [æn, ən, n] INDEF ART *see* **a**

anabolic steroid [ˌænəˈbɒlɪkˈstɪərɔɪd] N Anabolikum nt

anachronism [əˈnækrənɪzəm] N Anachronismus m

anachronistic [əˌnækrəˈnɪstɪk] ADJ anachronistisch; (= *not fitting modern times*) nicht zeitgemäß

anaemia, *(US)* **anemia** [əˈniːmɪə] N Anämie f, Blutarmut f

anaemic, *(US)* **anemic** [əˈniːmɪk] ADJ *(lit, fig)* anämisch

anaesthetic, *(US)* **anesthetic** [ˌænɪsˈθetɪk] **1** N Narkose f; (= *substance*) Narkosemittel nt; **general ~** Vollnarkose f; **local ~** örtliche Betäubung; **the nurse gave him a local ~** die Schwester gab ihm eine Spritze zur örtlichen Betäubung **2** ADJ *effect* betäubend; **~ drug** Betäubungsmittel nt

anaesthetist, *(US)* **anesthetist** [æˈniːsθɪtɪst] N Anästhesist(in) m(f)

anaesthetize, *(US)* **anesthetize** [æˈniːsθɪtaɪz] VT betäuben

anagram [ˈænəgræm] N Anagramm nt

anal [ˈeɪnəl] ADJ anal, Anal-; **~ intercourse** Analverkehr m

analgesic [ˌænælˈdʒiːsɪk] **1** N Schmerzmittel nt **2** ADJ schmerzstillend

analog [ˈænəlɒg] ADJ *(Tech)* analog

analog computer N Analogrechner m

analogous [əˈnæləgəs] ADJ analog *(to, with* zu)

analogue [ˈænəlɒg] ADJ *(Tech)* analog

analogy [əˈnælədʒɪ] N Analogie f; **to draw an ~** eine Analogie herstellen

anal-retentive [ˌeɪnəlrɪˈtentɪv] ADJ analfixiert

analyse, *(esp US)* **analyze** [ˈænəlaɪz] VT (= *examine*) analysieren *(also Psych)*; *(Gram) sentence* (zer)gliedern; **to ~ the situation** *(fig)* die Situation analysieren or *(to others)* erläutern

analysis [əˈnæləsɪs] N, pl **analyses** [əˈnæləsiːz] (= *examination*) Analyse f *(also Psych)*; *(Gram: of sentence also)* (Zer)gliederung f; **what's your ~ of the situation?** wie beurteilen Sie die Situation?; **in the last** or **final ~** letzten Endes; **on (closer) ~** bei genauerer Untersuchung

analyst [ˈænəlɪst] N Analytiker(in) m(f) *(also Psych)*; *(Chem)* Chemiker(in) m(f); *(St Ex)* Analyst(in) m(f); **food ~** Lebensmittelchemiker(in) m(f)

analytical ADJ, **analytically** ADV [ˌænəˈlɪtɪkəl, -ɪ] analytisch

analyze [ˈænəlaɪz] VT *(US)* = **analyse**

anaphylactic [ˌænəfɪˈlæktɪk] ADJ *(Med)* anaphylaktisch; **~ shock** anaphylaktischer Schock

anarchic(al) [æˈnɑːkɪk(əl)] ADJ anarchisch

anarchism [ˈænəkɪzəm] N Anarchismus m

anarchist [ˈænəkɪst] N Anarchist(in) m(f)

anarchy [ˈænəkɪ] N Anarchie f

anathema [əˈnæθɪmə] N *(fig: no art)* ein Gräuel m; **voting Labour was ~ to them** der Gedanke, Labour zu wählen, war ihnen ein Gräuel

anatomical ADJ, **anatomically** ADV [ˌænəˈtɒmɪkəl, -ɪ] anatomisch

anatomy [əˈnætəmɪ] N Anatomie f; *(fig)* Struktur f und Aufbau m; **on a certain part of her ~** *(euph)* an einer gewissen Stelle *(euph)*

ANC ABBR *of* **African National Congress** ANC m, südafrikanische nationalistische Bewegung

ancestor [ˈænsɪstəʳ] N Vorfahr m

ancestral [ænˈsestrəl] ADJ seiner/ihrer Vorfahren; **~ home** Stammsitz m

ancestry [ˈænsɪstrɪ] N (= *descent*) Abstammung f; (= *ancestors*) Ahnenreihe f; **to trace one's ~** seine Abstammung zurückverfolgen; **of royal ~** königlicher Abstammung

anchor [ˈæŋkəʳ] **1** N **(a)** *(Naut)* Anker m; *(fig)* Zuflucht f; **to cast** or **drop ~** vor Anker gehen; **to weigh** or **up ~** den Anker lichten; **to be** or **lie** or **ride at ~** vor Anker liegen **(b)** *(esp US TV: = presenter)* Anchorman m, Anchorwoman f **2** VT *(Naut, fig)* verankern; **to be ~ed in sth** *(fig)* in etw *(dat)* (fest) verankert sein **3** VI *(Naut)* vor Anker gehen

anchorage [ˈæŋkərɪdʒ] N *(Naut)* Ankerplatz m

anchorman [ˈæŋkəmæn] N, pl **-men** [-mən] *(esp US TV)* Anchorman m; *(Sport)* (*in relay race*) Letzte(r) m

anchorwoman [ˈæŋkəwʊmən] N, pl **-women** [-wɪmɪn] *(esp US TV)* Anchorwoman f; *(Sport: in relay race)* Letzte f

anchovy [ˈæntʃəvɪ] N Sardelle f, Anchovis f

ancient [ˈeɪnʃənt] **1** ADJ **(a)** alt; **in ~ times** im Altertum; **~ Rome** das alte Rom; **the ~ Romans** die alten Römer; **~ monument** *(Brit)* historisches Denkmal **(b)** *(inf) person, clothes etc* uralt **2** N **the ~s** die Völker or Menschen des Altertums

ancient history N *(lit)* Alte Geschichte; **that's ~** *(fig)* das ist schon längst Geschichte

ancillary [ænˈsɪlərɪ] ADJ (= *subordinate*) Neben-; (= *auxiliary*) Hilfs-; **~ course** *(Univ)* Begleitkurs m; **~ industry**

Zulieferindustrie f; ~ **staff/workers** Hilfskräfte pl; ~ **subject** (Univ) Nebenfach nt; ~ **troops** Hilfstruppen pl

and [ænd, ənd, nd, ən] CONJ **(a)** und; **nice ~ early/warm** schön früh/warm; **when I'm good ~ ready** wenn ich so weit bin; **try ~ come** versuch zu kommen; **wait ~ see!** abwarten!; **don't go ~ spoil it!** nun verdirb nicht alles!; **one more ~ I'm finished** noch eins, dann bin ich fertig; ~ **so on ~ so forth** und so weiter und so fort
(b) (in repetition, continuation) und; **better ~ better** immer besser; **for days ~ days** tagelang; **for miles ~ miles** meilenweit; **I rang ~ rang** ich klingelte und klingelte
(c) (with numbers) **three hundred ~ ten** dreihundert(und)zehn; **one ~ a half** anderthalb, eineinhalb

Andes ['ændiːz] PL Anden pl

Andorra [æn'dɔːrə] N Andorra nt

androgynous [æn'drɒdʒɪnəs] ADJ androgyn

android ['ændrɔɪd] N Androide m

anecdotal [ˌænɪk'dəʊtəl] ADJ anekdotisch

anecdote ['ænɪkdəʊt] N Anekdote f

anemia [ə'niːmɪə] N (US) = **anaemia**

anemic [ə'niːmɪk] ADJ (US) = **anaemic**

anemone [ə'nemənɪ] N (Bot) Anemone f

anesthesia etc (US) = **anaesthesia** etc

anew [ə'njuː] ADV **(a)** (= again) aufs neue; **let's start ~** fangen wir wieder von neuem an **(b)** (= in a new way) auf eine neue Art und Weise

angel ['eɪndʒəl] N (lit, fig) Engel m

> Be careful! **angel** is not translated by the German word **Angel**.

angel fish N Großer Segelflosser

angelic [æn'dʒelɪk] ADJ (= of an angel) Engels-; hosts himmlisch; (= like an angel) engelhaft

angelica [æn'dʒelɪkə] N (Cook) kandierte Angelika

anger ['æŋgə'] **1** N Ärger m; **a fit of ~** ein Wutanfall m; **public ~** öffentliche Entrüstung; **to speak/act in ~** im Zorn sprechen/handeln; **to be filled with ~** wütend sein **2** VT (stressing action) ärgern; (stressing result) verärgern; **what ~s me is ...** was mich ärgert, ist ...

angina [æn'dʒaɪnə] N Angina f

angina pectoris N Angina pectoris f

angle¹ ['æŋgl] **1** N **(a)** Winkel m; **at an ~ of 40°** in einem Winkel von 40°; **at an ~** schräg; **he was wearing his hat at an ~** er hatte seinen Hut schief aufgesetzt; **~ of elevation** (Math) Höhenwinkel m
(b) (= projecting corner) Ecke f; (= angular recess) Winkel m
(c) (of problem etc: = aspect) Seite f
(d) (= point of view) Standpunkt m; **an inside ~ on the story** die Geschichte vom Standpunkt eines direkt Beteiligten **2** VT lamp etc ausrichten; (Sport) shot im Winkel schießen/schlagen; (fig) information, report färben

angle² VI (esp Brit Fishing) angeln
➤ **angle for** VI +PREP OBJ (fig) compliments fischen nach; **to angle for sth** auf etw (acc) aus sein

angle bracket N **(a)** (for shelves) Winkelkonsole f **(b)** (Typ) spitze Klammer

Anglepoise (lamp)® ['æŋglpɔɪz('læmp)] N Gelenkleuchte f

angler ['æŋglə'] N Angler(in) m(f)

Anglican ['æŋglɪkən] **1** N Anglikaner(in) m(f) **2** ADJ anglikanisch

Anglicanism ['æŋglɪkənɪzəm] N Anglikanismus m

anglicism ['æŋglɪsɪzəm] N Anglizismus m

anglicize ['æŋglɪsaɪz] VT anglisieren

angling ['æŋglɪŋ] N (esp Brit) Angeln nt

Anglo- ['æŋgləʊ] PREF Anglo-; (between two countries) Englisch-; **Anglo-Asian** N Anglo-Asiat(in) m(f) **2** ADJ angloasiatisch; **Anglo-Catholic** **1** N Anglokatholik(in) m(f) **2** ADJ anglokatholisch; **Anglo-German** ADJ englisch-deutsch; **Anglo-Indian** **1** N (of British origin) in Indien lebender Engländer m/lebende Engländerin f; (= Eurasian) Angloinder(in) m(f) **2** ADJ angloindisch; **Anglo-Irish** **1** PL the ~ die Angloiren pl **2** ADJ angloirisch

Anglophile ['æŋgləʊfaɪl] **1** N Anglophile(r) mf **2** ADJ anglophil

Anglo-Saxon ['æŋgləʊ'sæksən] **1** N **(a)** (Hist: = person) Angelsachse m, Angelsächsin f **(b)** (= Ling) Angelsächsisch nt **2** ADJ angelsächsisch

Angola [æŋ'gəʊlə] N Angola nt

Angolan [æŋ'gəʊlən] **1** N Angolaner(in) m(f) **2** ADJ angolanisch

angora [æŋ'gɔːrə] **1** ADJ Angora-; **~ wool** Angorawolle f **2** N Angorawolle f; (Tex) Angoragewebe nt

angrily ['æŋgrɪlɪ] ADV wütend

angry ['æŋgrɪ] ADJ (+ER) **(a)** zornig; letter, look, animal wütend; **to be ~** wütend sein; **to be ~ with** or **at sb** über jdn verärgert sein; **to be ~ at** or **about sth** sich über etw (acc) ärgern; **to get ~ (with** or **at sb/about sth)** (mit jdm/über etw acc) böse werden; **you're not ~ (with me), are you?** du bist (mir) doch nicht böse(, oder)?; **to be ~ with oneself** sich über sich (acc) selbst ärgern; **to make sb ~** (stressing action) jdn ärgern; (stressing result) jdn verärgern
(b) (fig) sea aufgewühlt; sky, clouds finster

angst [æŋst] N (Existenz)angst f

anguish ['æŋgwɪʃ] N Qual f; **to be in ~** Qualen leiden; **he wrung his hands in ~** er rang die Hände in Verzweiflung; **the news caused her great ~** die Nachricht bereitete ihr großen Schmerz; **the decision caused her great ~** die Entscheidung bereitete ihr große Qual(en)

anguished ['æŋgwɪʃt] ADJ qualvoll

angular ['æŋgjʊlə'] ADJ shape eckig; features, prose kantig

animal ['ænɪməl] **1** N Tier nt; (= brutal person) Bestie f; **man is a social ~** der Mensch ist ein soziales Wesen; **there's no such ~** (fig) so was gibt es nicht! (inf); **the ~ in him** das Tier(ische) in ihm
2 ADJ ATTR Tier-; products, cruelty, lust tierisch; **~ behaviour** (Brit) or **behavior** (US) (lit) das Verhalten der Tiere; (fig: = brutal) tierisches Verhalten; **~ experiments/testing** Tierversuche pl; **~ magnetism** rein körperliche Anziehungskraft

animal: Animal Liberation Front N (Brit) militante Tierschützerorganisation; **animal lover** N Tierfreund(in) m(f); **animal rights** PL der Tierschutz, Tierrechte pl; **~ activist/campaigner** Tierschützer(in) m(f); **animal sanctuary** N Tierschutzgebiet nt; **animal welfare** N Tierschutz m

animate ['ænɪmɪt] **1** ADJ belebt; creation, creatures lebend **2** ['ænɪmeɪt] VT (fig) (= enliven) beleben; (Film) animieren

animated ['ænɪmeɪtɪd] ADJ (= lively) lebhaft; **~ cartoon/film** Zeichentrickfilm m

animatedly ['ænɪmeɪtɪdlɪ] ADV rege; talk lebhaft

animation [ænɪ'meɪʃən] N Lebhaftigkeit f; (Film) Animation f

animator ['ænɪmeɪtə'] N Animator(in) m(f)

animosity [ænɪ'mɒsɪtɪ] N Feindseligkeit f (towards gegenüber)

aniseed ['ænɪsiːd] N (= flavouring) Anis m

aniseed ball N Anisbonbon m or nt

ankle ['æŋkl] N Knöchel m

ankle: anklebone N Sprungbein nt; **ankle bracelet** N Fußkettchen nt; **ankle-deep** **1** ADJ knöcheltief **2** ADV he was **~ in water** er stand bis an die Knöchel im Wasser; **ankle sock** N Söckchen nt; **ankle strap** N Schuhriemchen nt

anklet ['æŋklɪt] N **(a)** Fußspange f **(b)** (US: = sock) Söckchen nt

annals ['ænəlz] PL Annalen pl; (of society etc) Bericht m

annex [ə'neks] **1** VT annektieren **2** ['æneks] N **(a)** (to document etc) Anhang m **(b)** (= building) Nebengebäude nt; (= extension) Anbau m

annexation [ˌænek'seɪʃən] N Annexion f

annexe ['æneks] N (Brit) = **annex 2(b)**

annihilate [ə'naɪɪleɪt] VT vernichten; (fig) hope zerschlagen; (inf) person, opponent fertig machen (inf)

annihilation [əˌnaɪɪ'leɪʃən] N Vernichtung f; **our team's ~** die vollständige Niederlage unserer Mannschaft

anniversary [ænɪ'vɜːsərɪ] N Jahrestag m; (= wedding ~) Hochzeitstag m; **~ gift** Geschenk nt zum Jahrestag/Hochzeitstag; **the ~ of his death** sein Todestag m

annotate ['ænəʊteɪt] VT mit Anmerkungen versehen; **~d text** kommentierter Text

annotation [ænəʊ'teɪʃən] N (no pl: = commentary, act) Kommentar m; (= comment) Anmerkung f

announce [ə'naʊns] VT (lit, fig: person) bekannt geben; arrival, departure, radio programme ansagen; (over intercom) durchsagen; (*formally*) *birth, marriage etc* anzeigen; **to ~ sb** jdn melden; **the arrival of flight BA 742 has just been ~d** soeben ist die Ankunft des Fluges BA 742 gemeldet worden

announcement [ə'naʊnsmənt] N (= *public declaration*) Bekanntmachung *f*; (*of impending event, speaker*) Ankündigung *f*; (*over intercom etc*) Durchsage *f*; (*giving information*) (*on radio etc*) Ansage *f*; (*written: of birth, marriage etc*) Anzeige *f*

announcer [ə'naʊnsəʳ] N (*Rad, TV*) Ansager(in) *m(f)*

annoy [ə'nɔɪ] VT (= *make angry, irritate*) ärgern; (= *upset: noise, questions etc*) aufregen; (= *pester*) belästigen; **to be ~ed that ...** ärgerlich *or* verärgert sein, weil ...; **to be ~ed with sb/about sth** sich über jdn/etw ärgern; **to get ~ed** sich ärgern, sich aufregen

annoyance [ə'nɔɪəns] N (a) NO PL (= *irritation*) Ärger *m*; **to his ~** zu seinem Ärger (b) (= *nuisance*) Ärgernis *nt*

annoying [ə'nɔɪɪŋ] ADJ ärgerlich; *habit* lästig; **the ~ thing (about it) is that ...** das Ärgerliche (daran) ist, dass ...

annoyingly [ə'nɔɪɪŋlɪ] ADV aufreizend; **~, the bus didn't turn up** ärgerlicherweise kam der Bus nicht

annual ['ænjʊəl] **1** N (a) (*Bot*) einjährige Pflanze (b) (= *book*) Jahresalbum *nt* **2** ADJ (= *happening once a year*) jährlich; (= *of or for the year*) Jahres-; **~ accounts** Jahresbilanz *f*; **~ percentage rate** (*Fin*) effektiver Jahreszins, Jahreszinssatz *m*

annual general meeting N Jahreshauptversammlung *f*

annually ['ænjʊəlɪ] ADV (= *once a year*) jährlich

annual report N Geschäftsbericht *m*

annuity [ə'nju:ɪtɪ] N (Leib)rente *f*; **to buy an ~** eine Rentenversicherung abschließen

annul [ə'nʌl] VT annullieren; *contract, marriage* auflösen

annulment [ə'nʌlmənt] N Annullierung *f*; (*of contract, marriage*) Auflösung *f*

Annunciation [ə,nʌnsɪ'eɪʃən] N (*Bibl*) Mariä Verkündigung *f*

anodyne ['ænəʊdaɪn] ADJ (*fig*) beruhigend

anoint [ə'nɔɪnt] VT salben; **to ~ sb king** jdn zum König salben; **to ~ sb as sth** (*fig*) jdn als etw auserwählen

anomaly [ə'nɒməlɪ] N Anomalie *f*; (*in law etc*) Besonderheit *f*

anon¹ [ə'nɒn] ADV **see you ~** (*hum*) bis demnächst

anon² ADJ ABBR *of* **anonymous; Anon** (*at end of text*) Anonymus *f*

anonymity [ænə'nɪmɪtɪ] N Anonymität *f*

anonymous ADJ, **anonymously** ADV [ə'nɒnɪməs, -lɪ] (*lit, fig*) anonym

anorak ['ænəræk] N (*Brit*) Anorak *m*; (*pej inf*: = *nerd*) Dumpfbacke *f* (*sl*)

anorexia (nervosa) [ænə'reksɪə(nɜː'vəʊsə)] N Magersucht *f*, Anorexie *f*

anorexic [ænə'reksɪk] ADJ magersüchtig

another [ə'nʌðəʳ] **1** ADJ (a) (= *additional*) noch eine(r, s); **~ one** noch eine(r, s); **take ~ ten** nehmen Sie noch (weitere) zehn; **I don't want ~ drink!** ich möchte nichts mehr trinken; **without ~ word** ohne ein weiteres Wort
(b) (= *similar, fig*: = *second*) ein zweiter, eine zweite, ein zweites; **there is not ~ man like him** so einen Mann gibt es nur einmal
(c) (= *different*) ein anderer, eine andere, ein anderes; **that's quite ~ matter** das ist etwas ganz anderes; **~ time** ein andermal
2 PRON ein anderer, eine andere, ein anderes; **have ~!** nehmen Sie (doch) noch einen!; **they help one ~** sie helfen einander; **at one time or ~** irgendwann; **what with one thing and ~** bei all dem Trubel

Ansaphone® ['ɑːnsəfəʊn] N Anrufbeantworter *m*

ANSI ABBR *of* **American National Standards Institute** *amerikanischer Normenausschuss*

answer ['ɑːnsəʳ] **1** N (a) (= *response*) Antwort *f* (*to* auf +*acc*) **to get an/no ~** Antwort/keine Antwort bekommen; **there was no ~** (*to telephone, doorbell*) es hat sich niemand gemeldet; **Germany's ~ to Concorde** Deutschlands Antwort auf die Concorde; **in ~ to your letter/my question** in Beantwortung Ihres Briefes (*form*)/auf meine Frage hin
(b) (= *solution*) Lösung *f* (*to* +*gen*); **there's no easy ~** es gibt dafür keine Patentlösung; **there's only one ~ for depression ...** es gibt nur ein Mittel gegen Depression ...
2 VT (a) antworten auf (+*acc*); *person* antworten (+*dat*); *exam questions, objections, criticism* beantworten; **to ~ the**

telephone das Telefon abnehmen; **to ~ the bell** *or* **door** die Tür öffnen; **shall I ~ it?** (*phone*) soll ich rangehen?; (*door*) soll ich hingehen?; **to ~ the call of nature** (*hum*) dem Ruf der Natur folgen; **the fire brigade ~ed the alarm call** die Feuerwehr rückte auf den Alarm hin aus; **~ me!** antworte (mir)!
(b) (= *fulfil*) *hope, expectation* erfüllen; *need* befriedigen; **people who ~ that description** Leute, auf die diese Beschreibung zutrifft; **this ~ed our prayers** das war (wie) ein Geschenk des Himmels
3 VI antworten; **if the phone rings, don't ~** wenn das Telefon läutet, geh nicht ran

➤ **answer back 1** VI widersprechen; **don't answer back!** keine Widerrede!; **it's not fair to criticize him because he can't answer back** es ist unfair, ihn zu kritisieren, weil er sich nicht verteidigen kann **2** VT SEP **to answer sb back** jdm widersprechen

➤ **answer for** VI +PREP OBJ (= *be responsible for*) verantwortlich sein für; **he has a lot to answer for** er hat eine Menge auf dem Gewissen

➤ **answer to** VI +PREP OBJ (a) (= *be accountable to*) **to answer to sb for sth** jdm für etw Rechenschaft schuldig sein (b) **to answer to a description** einer Beschreibung entsprechen (c) **to answer to the name of ...** auf den Namen ... hören

answerable ['ɑːnsərəbl] ADJ (= *responsible*) verantwortlich; **to be ~ to sb (for sth)** jdm gegenüber (für etw) verantwortlich sein

answering machine ['ɑːnsərɪŋmə'ʃiːn] N Anrufbeantworter *m*

answer paper N (*in exam*) Antwortbogen *m*

answerphone ['ɑːnsəfəʊn] N (*Brit*) Anrufbeantworter *m*

ant [ænt] N Ameise *f*

antacid [ænt'æsɪd] N säurebindendes Mittel

antagonism [æn'tægənɪzəm] N (*between people, theories etc*) Antagonismus *m*; (*towards sb, idea, change etc*) Feindseligkeit *f* (*to(wards)* gegenüber)

antagonist [æn'tægənɪst] N Gegner(in) *m(f)*, Antagonist(in) *m(f)*; (*esp Pol*) Gegenspieler(in) *m(f)*

antagonistic [æn,tægə'nɪstɪk] ADJ feindselig; **to be ~** *or* **toward(s) sb/sth** jdm/gegen etw feindselig gesinnt sein

antagonize [æn'tægənaɪz] VT *person* gegen sich aufbringen

Antarctic [ænt'ɑːktɪk] **1** ADJ antarktisch **2** N **the ~** die Antarktis

Antarctica [ænt'ɑːktɪkə] N die Antarktis

Antarctic Circle N südlicher Polarkreis

Antarctic Ocean N Südpolarmeer *nt*

ante ['æntɪ] N **to raise** *or* **up the ~** (*fig inf*) den Einsatz erhöhen

anteater ['ænt,iːtəʳ] N Ameisenbär *m*

antecedents [æntɪ'siːdənts] PL (= *ancestry*) Abstammung *f*; (*of event*) Vorgeschichte *f*

antediluvian [æntɪdɪ'luːvɪən] ADJ vorsintflutlich

antelope ['æntɪləʊp] N Antilope *f*

antenatal ['æntɪ'neɪtl] ADJ vor der Geburt; **~ care/exercises** Schwangerschaftsfürsorge *f*/-übungen *pl*; **~ clinic** Sprechstunde *f* für Schwangere

antenna [æn'tenə] N (a) *pl* **-e** [æn'teniː] (*Zool*) Fühler *m* (b) *pl* **-e** *or* **-s** (*Rad, TV*) Antenne *f*

anteroom ['æntɪruːm] N Vorzimmer *nt*

anthem ['ænθəm] N Hymne *f*

ant hill N Ameisenhaufen *m*

anthology [æn'θɒlədʒɪ] N Anthologie *f*

anthrax ['ænθræks] N Anthrax *m* (*spec*), Milzbrand *m*

anthropological [ænθrəpə'lɒdʒɪkəl] ADJ anthropologisch

anthropologist [ænθrə'pɒlədʒɪst] N Anthropologe *m*, Anthropologin *f*

anthropology [ænθrə'pɒlədʒɪ] N Anthropologie *f*

anti ['æntɪ] (*inf*) **1** ADJ PRED in Opposition (*inf*); **are you in favour** (*Brit*) *or* **favor** (*US*)**? – no, I'm ~** bist du dafür? – nein, ich bin dagegen **2** PREP gegen (+*acc*); **~ everything** grundsätzlich gegen alles

anti IN CPDS Anti-, anti-; **anti-abortionist** N Abtreibungsgegner(in) *m(f)*; **anti-aircraft** ADJ Flugabwehr-; **~ defence** (*Brit*) *or* **defense** (*US*) Luftverteidigung *f*; **~ gun** Flak *f*; **~ missile** Flugabwehrrakete *f*; **antiballistic missile** [æntɪbə'lɪstɪk-] N Antiraketenrakete *f*; **antibiotic** [æntɪbaɪ'ɒtɪk] N Antibiotikum *nt*; **antibody** N Antikörper *m*

antic [ˈæntɪk] N see **antics**

anticipate [ænˈtɪsɪpeɪt] VT (= expect) erwarten; (= see in advance) vorhersehen; (= do before sb else) zuvorkommen (+dat); **as ~d** wie erwartet; **don't ~ what I'm going to say** nimm nicht vorweg, was ich noch sagen wollte; **~d sales** voraussichtliche Verkaufszahlen pl

anticipation [ænˌtɪsɪˈpeɪʃən] N (a) (= expectation) Erwartung f; **thanking you in ~** herzlichen Dank im Voraus; **to wait in ~** gespannt warten (b) (= seeing in advance) Vorausberechnung f; **the driver showed good ~** der Fahrer zeigte gute Voraussicht

anticipatory [ænˈtɪsɪˌpeɪtərɪ] ADJ vorwegnehmend

anti: anticlimax N Enttäuschung f; **anticlockwise** ADV (esp Brit) gegen den Uhrzeigersinn

antics [ˈæntɪks] PL Eskapaden pl; (= tricks) Streiche pl; (= irritating behaviour) Mätzchen pl (inf); **he's up to his old ~ again** er macht wieder seine Mätzchen (inf)

anti: anticyclone N Hoch(druckgebiet) nt; **anti-dandruff** ADJ gegen Schuppen; **antidepressant** N Antidepressivum nt; **antidote** [ˈæntɪdəʊt] N (Med, fig) Gegenmittel nt (against, to, for gegen); **antifreeze** N Frostschutz(mittel nt) m; **antiglare** ADJ (US) blendfrei; **anti-globalization** ADJ Antiglobalisierungs-; **~ protester** Globalisierungsgegner(in) m(f); **antihistamine** N Antihistamin(ikum) nt; **antilock** ADJ **~ brakes** Blockierschutzbremsen pl; **antinuclear** ADJ (= against nuclear energy) Anti-Atom(kraft)-; (= against nuclear weapons) Anti-Atomwaffen-; **the ~ lobby/protesters** die Atomkraft-/Atomwaffengegner pl

antipathy [ænˈtɪpəθɪ] N Antipathie f (towards gegen)

anti: antipersonnel ADJ **~ mine** Antipersonenmine f; **antiperspirant** N Antitranspirant nt

antipodean [ænˌtɪpəˈdiːən] ADJ (Brit) australisch und neuseeländisch

Antipodes [ænˈtɪpədiːz] PL (Brit) Australien und Neuseeland

antiquarian [ˌæntɪˈkweərɪən] ■ ADJ books antiquarisch; studies der Antike; **~ bookshop** Antiquariat nt ② N = **antiquary**

antiquary [ˈæntɪkwərɪ] N (= collector) Antiquitätensammler(in) m(f); (= seller) Antiquitätenhändler(in) m(f)

antiquated [ˈæntɪkweɪtɪd] ADJ antiquiert

antique [ænˈtiːk] ■ ADJ antik; **~ pine** Kiefer f antik ② N Antiquität f

antique: antique dealer N Antiquitätenhändler(in) m(f); **antique shop** N Antiquitätengeschäft nt

antiquity [ænˈtɪkwɪtɪ] N (a) (= ancient times) das Altertum; (= Roman, Greek ~) die Antike; **in ~** im Altertum/in der Antike (b) (= great age) großes Alter (c) **antiquities** PL (= old things) Altertümer pl

anti: antiriot ADJ **~ police** Bereitschaftspolizei f; **anti-roll bar** N (Brit Aut) Stabilisator m; **antirust** ADJ Rostschutz-; **anti-Semitic** ADJ antisemitisch; **anti-Semitism** N Antisemitismus m; **antiseptic** ■ N Antiseptikum nt ② ADJ (lit, fig) antiseptisch; **anti-smoking** ADJ campaign Antiraucher-; **antisocial** ADJ person, behaviour etc unsozial; **I work ~ hours** ich arbeite zu Zeiten, wo andere freihaben; **antiterrorist** ADJ squad, measures zur Terrorismusbekämpfung; **antitheft device** N Diebstahlsicherung f

antithesis [ænˈtɪθɪsɪs] N, pl **antitheses** [ænˈtɪθɪsiːz] (= direct opposite) genaues Gegenteil (to, of +gen); (of idea, in rhetoric) Antithese f (to, of zu) (form); (= contrast) Gegensatz m

anti: antitrust ADJ (US) **~ legislation** Kartellgesetzgebung f; **antivivisectionist** N Gegner(in) m(f) der Vivisektion; **anti-wrinkle** ADJ Antifalten-; **~ cream** Antifaltencreme f

antler [ˈæntlə'] N (set or pair of) **~s** Geweih nt

antonym [ˈæntənɪm] N Antonym nt

anus [ˈeɪnəs] N After m

anvil [ˈænvɪl] N Amboss m (also Anat)

anxiety [æŋˈzaɪətɪ] N (a) Sorge f; **to cause sb ~** jdm Sorgen machen (b) (= keen desire) Verlangen nt; **in his ~ to get away** weil er unbedingt wegkommen wollte

anxious [ˈæŋkʃəs] ADJ (a) (= worried) besorgt; person, thoughts ängstlich; **to be ~ about sb/sth** um jdn/etw besorgt sein; **to be ~ about doing sth** Angst haben, etw zu tun
(b) (= worrying) moment, wait bang; **it's been an ~ time for us all** wir alle haben uns (in dieser Zeit) große Sorgen gemacht
(c) (= strongly desirous) **to be ~ to do sth** bestrebt sein, etw zu

tun; **I am ~ that he should do it** or **for him to do it** mir liegt viel daran, dass er es tut

anxiously [ˈæŋkʃəslɪ] ADV (a) besorgt (b) (= keenly) gespannt

any [ˈenɪ] ■ ADJ (a) (in interrog, conditional, neg sentences) not translated; (emph: = ~ at all) (with sing n) irgendein(e); (with pl n) irgendwelche; (with uncountable n) etwas; **not ~** kein/keine; **not ANY ... at all** überhaupt kein/keine ...; **if I had ~ plan/ideas/money** wenn ich einen Plan/Ideen/Geld hätte; **if I had ANY plan/ideas/money (at all)** wenn ich irgendeinen Plan/irgendwelche Ideen/(auch nur) etwas Geld hätte; **if it's ~ help (at all)** wenn das (irgendwie) hilft; **it won't do ~ good** es wird nichts nützen; **without ~ difficulty (at all)** ohne jede Schwierigkeit
(b) (= no matter which) jede(r, s) (beliebige ...); (with pl or uncountable n) alle; **~ one will do** es ist jede(r, s) recht; **~ one you like** was du willst; **~ one of us would have done the same** jeder von uns hätte dasselbe getan; **you can come at ~ time** du kannst jederzeit kommen; **thank you – ~ time** danke! – bitte!; **~ old ...** (inf) jede(r, s) x-beliebige ... (inf)
② PRON (a) (in interrog, conditional, neg sentences) welche; **I want to meet psychologists/a psychologist, do you know ~?** ich würde gerne Psychologen/einen Psychologen kennen lernen, kennen Sie welche/einen?; **I need some butter/stamps, do you have ~?** ich brauche Butter/Briefmarken, haben Sie welche?; **have you seen ~ of my ties?** haben Sie eine von meinen Krawatten gesehen?; **don't you have ~ (at all)?** haben Sie (denn) überhaupt keine/keinen/keines?; **he wasn't having ~ (of it/that)** (inf) er wollte nichts davon hören; **few, if ~, will come** wenn überhaupt, werden nur wenige kommen; **if ~ of you can sing** wenn (irgend)jemand von euch singen kann
(b) (= no matter which) alle; **~ who do come ...** alle, die kommen ...
③ ADV (a) colder, bigger etc noch; **not ~ colder/bigger** etc nicht kälter/größer etc; **we can't go ~ further** wir können nicht mehr weiter gehen; **are you feeling ~ better?** geht es dir etwas besser?; **do you want ~ more soup?** willst du noch etwas Suppe?; **don't you want ~ more tea?** willst du keinen Tee mehr?; **~ more offers?** noch weitere Angebote?; **I don't want ~ more (at all)** ich möchte (überhaupt) nichts mehr
(b) (esp US inf: = at all) überhaupt; **it didn't help them ~** es hat ihnen überhaupt nichts genützt

anybody [ˈenɪbɒdɪ] ■ PRON (a) (irgend)jemand; **not ... ~** niemand, keine(r); **is ~ there?** ist (irgend)jemand da?; **(does) ~ want my book?** will jemand mein Buch?; **I can't see ~** ich kann niemand(en) sehen
(b) (= no matter who) jede(r); **it's ~'s game** das Spiel kann von jedem gewonnen werden; **is there ~ else I can talk to?** gibt es sonst jemand(en), mit dem ich sprechen kann?; **I don't want to see ~ else** ich möchte niemand anderen sehen
② N (= person of importance) jemand; **he's not just ~** er ist nicht einfach irgendjemand; **everybody who is ~ was there** alles, was Rang und Namen hat, war dort

anyhow [ˈenɪhaʊ] ADV (a) (= at any rate) = **anyway**
(b) (= carelessly) irgendwie; (= at random) aufs Geratewohl; **the papers were scattered ~ on his desk** die Papiere lagen bunt durcheinander auf seinem Schreibtisch

anymore [ˈenɪˈmɔː'] ADV (+vb) nicht mehr; **I couldn't trust him ~** ich konnte ihm nicht mehr trauen; see **any**

anyone [ˈenɪwʌn] PRON, N = **anybody**

anyplace [ˈenɪpleɪs] ADV (US inf) = **anywhere**

anything [ˈenɪθɪŋ] ■ PRON (a) (irgend)etwas; **not ~ nichts; is it/isn't it worth ~?** ist es etwas/gar nichts wert?; **did/didn't he say ~ else?** hat er (sonst) noch etwas/sonst (gar) nichts gesagt?; **did/didn't they give you ~ at all?** haben sie euch überhaupt etwas/überhaupt nichts gegeben?; **are you doing ~ tonight?** hast du heute Abend schon etwas vor?; **he's as smart as ~** (inf) er ist clever wie noch was (inf)
(b) (= no matter what) alles; **~ you like** (alles,) was du willst; **not just ~** nicht bloß irgendetwas; **I wouldn't do it for ~** ich würde es um keinen Preis tun; **~ else is impossible** alles andere ist unmöglich; **this is ~ but pleasant** das ist alles andere als angenehm; **~ but that!** alles, nur das nicht!; **~ but!** von wegen!
② ADV (inf) **it isn't ~ like him** das sieht ihm überhaupt nicht ähnlich; **it didn't cost ~ like £100** es kostete bei weitem keine £ 100

anyway ['enɪweɪ] ADV jedenfalls; (= *regardless*) trotzdem; **~, that's what I think** das ist jedenfalls meine Meinung; **I told him not to, but he did it** ~ ich habe es ihm verboten, aber er hat es trotzdem gemacht; **who cares, ~?** überhaupt, wen kümmert es denn schon?

anyways ['enɪweɪz] ADV (*US dial*) = **anyway**

anywhere ['enɪweə'] ADV **(a)** *be, stay* irgendwo; *go* irgendwohin; **not** ~ nirgends/nirgendwohin; **he'll never get** ~ er wird es zu nichts bringen; **I wasn't getting** ~ ich kam (einfach) nicht weiter; **I haven't found** ~ **to live yet** ich habe noch nichts gefunden, wo ich wohnen kann; **the cottage was miles from** ~ das Häuschen lag jwd (*inf*); **there could be** ~ **between 50 and 100 people** es könnten (schätzungsweise) 50 bis 100 Leute sein

(b) (= *no matter where*) *be, stay* überall; *go* überallhin; **they could be** ~ sie könnten überall sein; ~ **you like** wo/wohin du willst

aorta [eɪˈɔːtə] N Aorta *f*

apace [əˈpeɪs] ADV geschwind (*geh*)

apart [əˈpɑːt] ADV **(a)** auseinander; **to stand/sit with one's legs** ~ mit gespreizten Beinen dastehen/dasitzen; **I can't tell them** ~ ich kann sie nicht auseinander halten; **to live** ~ getrennt leben; **to come** *or* **fall** ~ entzweigehen; **her marriage is falling** ~ ihre Ehe geht in die Brüche; **to take sth** ~ etw auseinander nehmen

(b) (= *to one side*) beiseite; (= *on one side*) abseits (*from* +*gen*); **he stood** ~ **from the group** er stand abseits von der Gruppe

(c) (= *excepted*) abgesehen von; **these problems** ~ abgesehen von diesen Problemen; ~ **from that, the gearbox is also faulty** außerdem ist (auch) das Getriebe schadhaft

apartheid [əˈpɑːteɪt] N Apartheid *f*

apartment [əˈpɑːtmənt] N **(a) apartments** PL (*Brit*: = *suite of rooms*) Appartement *nt* **(b)** (*esp US*: = *flat*) Wohnung *f*; ~ **house** *or* **block** *or* **building** Wohnblock *m*

apathetic [æpəˈθetɪk] ADJ apathisch; **they are completely** ~ **about their future** sie sind vollkommen apathisch, was ihre Zukunft angeht

apathy ['æpəθɪ] N Apathie *f*

APB (*US*) ABBR *of* **all points bulletin**; **to put out an** ~ **on sb** nach jdm eine Fahndung einleiten

ape [eɪp] **1** N (*lit, fig*) Affe *m* **2** VT nachmachen

apéritif [əˌperɪˈtiːf] N Aperitif *m*

aperture ['æpətjʊə'] N Öffnung *f*; (*Phot*) Blende *f*

apex ['eɪpeks] N, *pl* **-es** *or* **apices** Spitze *f*; (*fig*) Höhepunkt *m*

aphorism ['æfərɪzəm] N Aphorismus *m*

aphrodisiac [æfrəʊˈdɪzɪæk] N Aphrodisiakum *nt*

apiary ['eɪpɪərɪ] N Bienenhaus *nt*

apices ['eɪpɪsiːz] PL *of* **apex**

apiece [əˈpiːs] ADV pro Stück; (= *per person*) pro Person; **I gave them two** ~ ich gab ihnen je zwei; **they had two cakes** ~ sie hatten jeder zwei Kuchen

aplomb [əˈplɒm] N Gelassenheit *f*; **with** ~ gelassen

Apocalypse [əˈpɒkəlɪps] N Apokalypse *f*

apocalyptic [əˌpɒkəˈlɪptɪk] ADJ apokalyptisch

apocryphal [əˈpɒkrɪfəl] ADJ apokryph; **this story, which is almost certainly** ~ ... diese Geschichte, die höchstwahrscheinlich jeder Wahrheit entbehrt ...

apogee ['æpəʊdʒiː] N (*fig*: = *apex*) Höhepunkt *m*

apolitical [eɪpəˈlɪtɪkəl] ADJ apolitisch

apologetic [əˌpɒləˈdʒetɪk] ADJ (= *making an apology*) entschuldigend *attr*; (= *sorry, regretful*) bedauernd *attr*; **she wrote me an** ~ **letter** sie schrieb mir und entschuldigte sich vielmals; **he was most** ~ **(about it)** er entschuldigte sich vielmals (dafür)

apologetically [əˌpɒləˈdʒetɪkəlɪ] ADV entschuldigend

apologist [əˈpɒlədʒɪst] N Apologet(in) *m(f)*

apologize [əˈpɒlədʒaɪz] VI sich entschuldigen (*to* bei); **to** ~ **for sb/sth** sich für jdn/etw entschuldigen

apology [əˈpɒlədʒɪ] N **(a)** (= *expression of regret*) Entschuldigung *f*; **to make** *or* **offer sb an** ~ jdn um Verzeihung bitten; **Mr Jones sends his apologies** Herr Jones lässt sich entschuldigen; **I owe you an** ~ ich muss dich um Verzeihung bitten; **I make no** ~ *or* **apologies for the fact that** ... ich entschuldige mich nicht dafür, dass ... **(b)** (= *poor* *substitute*) trauriges Exemplar (*for* +*gen*); **an** ~ **for a breakfast** ein armseliges Frühstück

apoplectic [æpəˈplektɪk] ADJ (*inf*) cholerisch; ~ **fit** (*Med*) Schlaganfall *m*

apoplexy ['æpəpleksɪ] N Schlaganfall *m*

apostle [əˈpɒsl] N (*lit, fig*) Apostel *m*

apostrophe [əˈpɒstrəfɪ] N (*Gram*) Apostroph *m*

apotheosis [əˌpɒθɪˈəʊsɪs] N Apotheose *f* (*liter*) (*into* zu)

appal, (*US also*) **appall** [əˈpɔːl] VT entsetzen; **to be ~led (at** *or* **by sth)** (über etw *acc*) entsetzt sein

appalling ADJ, **appallingly** ADV [əˈpɔːlɪŋ, -lɪ] entsetzlich

apparatus [æpəˈreɪtəs] N (*lit, fig*) Apparat *m*; (*in gym*) Geräte *pl*; **a piece of** ~ ein Gerät *nt*

apparel [əˈpærəl] N, NO PL (*liter, US Comm*) Kleidung *f*

apparent [əˈpærənt] ADJ **(a)** (= *clear, obvious*) offensichtlich; **to be** ~ **to sb** jdm klar sein; **to become** ~ sich (deutlich) zeigen; **for no** ~ **reason** aus keinem ersichtlichen Grund

(b) (= *seeming*) scheinbar

apparently [əˈpærəntlɪ] ADV anscheinend

apparition [æpəˈrɪʃən] N Erscheinung *f*

appeal [əˈpiːl] **1** N **(a)** (= *request*) (*for help, money etc*) Appell *m* (*for* um); (*for mercy*) Gesuch *nt* (*for* um); ~ **for funds** Spendenappell *m*; **to make an** ~ **to sb** an jdn appellieren; (*charity etc*) einen Appell an jdn richten; **to make an** ~ **to sb for sth** jdn um etw bitten; (*charity etc*) jdn zu etw aufrufen **(b)** (*against decision*) Einspruch *m*; (*Jur*) (*against sentence*) Berufung *f*; (*actual trial*) Revision *f*; **he lost his** ~ er verlor in der Berufung; **to lodge an** ~ Einspruch erheben; (*Jur*) Berufung einlegen (*with* bei); **right of** ~ Einspruchsrecht *nt*; (*Jur*) Berufungsrecht *nt*; **Court of Appeal** Berufungsgericht *nt* **(c)** (= *power of attraction*) Reiz *m* (*to* für); **his music has (a) wide** ~ seine Musik spricht weite Kreise an

2 VI **(a)** (= *make request*) (dringend) bitten; **to** ~ **to sb for sth** jdn um etw bitten; **to** ~ **to the public to do sth** die Öffentlichkeit (dazu) aufrufen, etw zu tun

(b) (*against decision: to authority etc*) Einspruch erheben (*to* bei); (*Jur*) Berufung einlegen (*to* bei)

(c) (= *apply: for support, decision*) appellieren (*to an* +*acc*); (*Sport*) Beschwerde einlegen

(d) (= *be attractive*) reizen (*to sb* jdn); (*candidate, idea*) zusagen (*to sb* jdm); (*book, magazine*) ansprechen (*to sb* jdn)

3 VT **to** ~ **a case/verdict** (*Jur*) mit einem Fall/gegen ein Urteil in die Berufung gehen; **to** ~ **a decision** Einspruch gegen eine Entscheidung einlegen

appeal fund N Hilfsfonds *m*, Spendenfonds *m*

appealing [əˈpiːlɪŋ] ADJ **(a)** (= *attractive*) attraktiv; *house* reizvoll **(b)** (= *supplicating*) *look, voice* flehend

appeal judge N Richter(in) *m(f)* am Berufungsgericht

appear [əˈpɪə'] VI **(a)** (= *emerge*) erscheinen; **to** ~ **from behind sth** hinter etw (*dat*) auftauchen; **to** ~ **in public** sich in der Öffentlichkeit zeigen; **to** ~ **in court** vor Gericht erscheinen; **to** ~ **as a witness** als Zeuge/Zeugin auftreten

(b) (= *seem*) scheinen; **he ~ed (to be) drunk** er schien betrunken zu sein; **it ~s that** ... es hat den Anschein, dass ...; **it ~s not** anscheinend nicht; **there ~s** *or* **there would** ~ **to be a mistake** da scheint ein Irrtum vorzuliegen; **it ~s to me that** ... mir scheint, dass ...

appearance [əˈpɪərəns] N **(a)** (= *emergence*) Erscheinen *nt*; (*unexpected*) Auftauchen *nt no pl*; (*Theat*) Auftritt *m*; **many court ~s** viele Auftritte vor Gericht; **to put in** *or* **make an** ~ sich sehen lassen; **cast in order of** ~ Darsteller in der Reihenfolge ihres Auftretens

(b) (= *look, aspect*) Aussehen *nt*; (*esp of person*) Äußere(s) *nt*; ~**s** (= *outward signs*) der äußere (An)schein; **for ~s' sake, for the sake of ~s** um den Schein zu wahren; **to keep up ~s** den (äußeren) Schein wahren; **to give the ~ of being** ... sich (*dat*) den Anschein geben, ... zu sein; **by** *or* **from** *or* **to all ~s** allem Anschein nach

appease [əˈpiːz] VT (= *calm*) beschwichtigen

appeasement [əˈpiːzmənt] N Beschwichtigung *f*

append [əˈpend] VT *notes etc* anhängen (*to an* +*acc*) (*also Comput*); *signature* setzen (*to unter* +*acc*)

appendage [əˈpendɪdʒ] N (= *limb*) Gliedmaße *f*; (*fig*) Anhängsel *nt*

appendices [əˈpendɪsiːz] PL *of* **appendix**

appendicitis [əˌpendɪˈsaɪtɪs] N Blinddarmentzündung *f*

appendix [ə'pendɪks] N, *pl* **appendices** *or* **-es (a)** (*Anat*)
Blinddarm *m*; **to have one's ~ out** sich (*dat*) den Blinddarm
herausnehmen lassen **(b)** (*to book etc*) Anhang *m*
appertain [æpə'teɪn] VI (*form*) (= *belong*) gehören (*to* zu);
(= *relate*) betreffen (*to sb/sth* jdn/etw)
appetite ['æpɪtaɪt] N (*for food etc*) Appetit *m*; (*fig*: = *desire*)
Verlangen *nt*; **to have an/no ~ for sth** Appetit/keinen Appetit
auf etw (*acc*) haben; (*fig*) Verlangen/kein Verlangen nach
etw haben; **I hope you've got an ~** ich hoffe, ihr habt
Appetit!; **to take away** *or* **spoil one's ~** sich (*dat*) den Appetit
verderben
appetizer ['æpɪtaɪzə'] N (= *food*) Appetitanreger *m*; (= *hors
d'oeuvre*) Vorspeise *f*; (= *drink*) appetitanregendes Getränk
appetizing ['æpɪtaɪzɪŋ] ADJ appetitlich (*also fig*); *smell* lecker
applaud [ə'plɔːd] **1** VT (*lit, fig*) applaudieren; (*fig*) *efforts,
courage* loben; *decision* begrüßen **2** VI applaudieren
applause [ə'plɔːz] N, NO PL Applaus *m*
apple ['æpl] N Apfel *m*; **to be the ~ of sb's eye** jds Liebling sein
apple IN CPDS Apfel-; **applecart** N (*fig*) **to upset the ~** alles über
den Haufen werfen (*inf*); **apple-green** ADJ apfelgrün;
applejack N (*US*) Apfelschnaps *m*; **apple pie** N ≈ gedeckter
Apfelkuchen; **apple sauce** N **(a)** (*Cook*) Apfelmus *nt*
(b) (*dated US inf*: = *nonsense*) Schmus *m* (*inf*)
applet [æplɪt] N (*Comput*) Applet *nt*
appliance [ə'plaɪəns] N **(a)** Vorrichtung *f*; (= *household ~*)
Gerät *nt* **(b) the ~ of science** die Anwendung wissenschaftlicher Methoden
applicable [ə'plɪkəbl] ADJ anwendbar (*to* auf +*acc*); (*on forms*)
zutreffend (*to* für); **that isn't ~ to you** das trifft auf Sie nicht
zu, das gilt nicht für Sie
applicant ['æplɪkənt] N (*for job*) Bewerber(in) *m(f)* (*for* um, für);
(*for grant, loan etc*) Antragsteller(in) *m(f)* (*for* für, auf +*acc*)
application [æplɪ'keɪʃən] N **(a)** (*for job etc*) Bewerbung *f* (*for*
um, für); (*for grant, loan etc*) Antrag *m* (*for* auf +*acc*); **available
on ~** auf Anforderung erhältlich **(b)** (= *act of applying*) (*of
paint, ointment*) Auftragen *nt*; (*of dressing, plaster*) Anlegen *nt*;
(*of pressure, theory, rules, knowledge*) Anwendung *f*; **"for
external ~ only"** (*Med*) „nur zur äußerlichen Anwendung"
(c) (= *diligence, effort*) Fleiß *m*
application: application form N Antragsformular *nt*, Antrag
m; (*for job*) Bewerbungsbogen *m*; **application program** N
(*Comput*) Anwendungsprogramm *nt*; **application software** N
(*Comput*) Anwendersoftware *f*
applicator ['æplɪkeɪtə'] N Aufträger *m*; (*for tampons, pessaries*)
Applikator *m*
applied [ə'plaɪd] ADJ ATTR *maths etc* angewandt
appliqué [æ'pliːkeɪ] (*Sew*) **1** N Applikationen *pl* **2** ADJ ATTR **~
work** Stickerei *f*
apply [ə'plaɪ] **1** VT *paint, ointment* auftragen (*to* auf +*acc*);
dressing, plaster anlegen; *pressure, theory, rules, knowledge*
anwenden (*to* auf +*acc*); *brakes* betätigen; *sanctions*
verhängen (*to* über +*acc*); **to ~ oneself (to sth)** sich (bei etw)
anstrengen; **that term can be applied to many things** dieser
Begriff trifft auf viele Dinge zu
2 VI **(a)** (= *make an application*) sich bewerben (*for* um, für);
to ~ to sb for sth sich an jdn wegen etw wenden; (*for job,
grant*) sich bei jdm für etw bewerben; **~ next door/within**
Anfragen nebenan/im Laden; **she has applied to college/
university** sie hat sich um einen Studienplatz beworben
(b) (= *be applicable*) gelten (*to* für); (*description*) zutreffen (*to*
auf +*acc*, für)
appoint [ə'pɔɪnt] VT (*to a job*) einstellen; (*to a post*) ernennen;
to ~ sb to an office jdn in ein Amt berufen; **to ~ sb sth** jdn
zu etw ernennen; **to ~ sb to do sth** jdn dazu bestimmen, etw
zu tun
appointed [ə'pɔɪntɪd] ADJ *hour, place* festgesetzt; *task*
zugewiesen; *representative* ernannt
-appointed [-ə'pɔɪntɪd] ADJ SUF **well-/poorly-appointed** gut/
dürftig ausgestattet
appointee [əpɔɪn'tiː] N Ernannte(r) *mf*
appointment [ə'pɔɪntmənt] N **(a)** (= *pre-arranged meeting*)
Verabredung *f*; (= *business etc, with doctor, lawyer etc*) Termin
m (*with* bei); **to make** *or* **fix an ~ with sb** mit jdm eine
Verabredung treffen/einen Termin vereinbaren; **I made an ~
to see the doctor** ich habe mir beim Arzt einen Termin
geben lassen; **do you have an ~?** sind Sie angemeldet?; **to**

keep an ~ einen Termin einhalten; **by ~** auf Verabredung;
(*on business, to see doctor, lawyer etc*) nach Vereinbarung
(b) (= *act of appointing*) (*to a job*) Einstellung *f*; (*to a post*)
Ernennung *f*; (*to an office*) Berufung *f* (*to* zu); **his ~ to the
position of treasurer** seine Bestellung zum Schatzmeister;
"by ~ (to Her Majesty)" (*on goods*) „königlicher Hoflieferant"
(c) (= *post*) Stelle *f*
appointment(s) book N Terminkalender *m*
apportion [ə'pɔːʃən] VT aufteilen; *duties* zuteilen; **to ~ sth to sb**
jdm etw zuteilen; **the blame must be ~ed equally** die Schuld
muss allen zu gleichen Teilen angelastet werden
apportionment [ə'pɔːʃənmənt] N (*of costs*) Verteilung *f*
apposition [æpə'zɪʃən] N Apposition *f*; **A is in ~ to B, A and B
are in ~** A ist eine Apposition zu B
appraisal [ə'preɪzl] N (*of value, damage*) Abschätzung *f*; (*of
character, ability*) Beurteilung *f*
appraise [ə'preɪz] VT (= *estimate*) *value, damage* schätzen;
(= *weigh up*) *character, ability* einschätzen; *situation*
abschätzen; *poem etc* beurteilen; *performance* bewerten
appreciable ADJ, **appreciably** ADV [ə'priːʃəbl, -ɪ] beträchtlich
appreciate [ə'priːʃɪeɪt] **1** VT **(a)** (= *be aware of*) *dangers,
problems, value etc* sehen (+*gen*);
(= *understand*) *sb's wishes etc* Verständnis haben für; **I ~ that
you cannot come** ich verstehe, dass ihr nicht kommen
könnt
(b) (= *value, be grateful for*) zu schätzen wissen; **thank you, I ~
it** vielen Dank, sehr nett von Ihnen; **I would ~ it if you could
do this by tomorrow** könnten Sie das bitte bis morgen
erledigen?
(c) (= *enjoy*) *art, music* schätzen
2 VI (*Fin*) **to ~ (in value)** im Wert steigen
appreciation [ə.priːʃɪ'eɪʃən] N **(a)** (= *awareness: of problems,
dangers, value*) Erkennen *nt*
(b) (= *esteem, respect*) Anerkennung *f*; (*of person*)
Wertschätzung *f*; **in ~ of sth** zum Dank für etw; **to show one's
~** seine Dankbarkeit (be)zeigen
(c) (= *enjoyment, understanding, comprehension*) Verständnis
nt; (*of art*) Sinn *m* (*of* für); **to write an ~ of sb/sth** einen
Bericht über jdn/etw schreiben
(d) (= *increase*) (*Wert*)steigerung *f* (*in* bei)
appreciative [ə'priːʃɪətɪv] ADJ anerkennend; *audience* dankbar;
(= *grateful*) dankbar; **to be ~ of sth** etw zu schätzen wissen;
(*of music, art etc*) Sinn für etw haben
apprehend [æprɪ'hend] VT (= *arrest*) festnehmen
apprehension [æprɪ'henʃən] N **(a)** (= *fear*) Besorgnis *f*; **a
feeling of ~** eine dunkle Ahnung **(b)** (= *arrest*) Festnahme *f*
apprehensive [æprɪ'hensɪv] ADJ ängstlich; **to be ~ of sth** etw
befürchten; **to be ~ that ...** fürchten, dass ...; **he was ~ about
the future** er schaute mit ängstlicher Sorge in die Zukunft
apprehensively [æprɪ'hensɪvlɪ] ADV ängstlich
apprentice [ə'prentɪs] **1** N Lehrling *m*; **to be an ~** Lehrling
sein, in der Lehre sein; **~ electrician** Elektrikerlehrling *m*
2 VT **to be ~d to sb** bei jdm in die Lehre gehen *or* in der
Lehre sein
apprenticeship [ə'prentɪʃɪp] N Lehre *f*; **to serve one's ~** seine
Lehre absolvieren
apprise [ə'praɪz] VT (*form*) in Kenntnis setzen (*geh*)
approach [ə'prəʊtʃ] **1** VI (*physically*) sich nähern; (*date, summer
etc*) nahen
2 VT **(a)** (= *come near*) sich nähern (+*dat*); (*Aviat*) anfliegen;
(*in quality, stature*) herankommen an (+*acc*); (*fig*)
heranreichen an (+*acc*); **to ~ thirty** auf die dreißig zugehen;
the train is now ~ing platform 3 der Zug hat Einfahrt auf Gleis
3; **something ~ing a festive atmosphere** eine annähernd
festliche Stimmung
(b) (= *make an ~ to*) *person, organization* herantreten an
(+*acc*) (*about* wegen)
(c) (= *tackle*) *problem, task* angehen
3 N **(a)** (= *drawing near*) (*Heran*)nahen *nt*; (*of troops*)
Heranrücken *nt*; (*Aviat*) Anflug *m* (*to an* +*acc*)
(b) (*to person, organization*) Herantreten *nt*
(c) (= *way of tackling, attitude*) Ansatz *m* (*to* zu); **a positive ~
to mathematics/teaching** eine positive Einstellung zu
Mathematik/zum Unterrichten; **his ~ to the problem** seine
Art, an das Problem heranzugehen; **try a different ~** versuchs
doch mal anders

(d) (= *access*) Zugang *m*; (= *road*) Zufahrt(sstraße) *f*
(e) (= *approximation*) Annäherung *f* (*to* an +*acc*)

approachable [əˈprəʊtʃəbl] ADJ **(a)** *person* umgänglich, leicht zugänglich **(b)** *place* zugänglich **(c)** *text, idea* verständlich

approach: approach path N (*Aviat*) Einflugschneise *f*; **approach road** N (*to city etc*) Zufahrtsstraße *f*; (*to motorway*) (Autobahn)zubringer *m*; (= *slip road*) Auffahrt *f*

approbation [ˌæprəˈbeɪʃən] N Zustimmung *f*; (*from critics*) Beifall *m*

appropriate¹ [əˈprəʊprɪɪt] ADJ **(a)** (= *suitable, fitting*) geeignet (*for, to* für); (*to a situation, occasion*) angemessen (*to* +*dat*); *name, remark* treffend; **to be ~ for doing sth** geeignet sein, etw zu tun **(b)** (= *relevant*) entsprechend; *body, authority* zuständig; **put a tick where ~** Zutreffendes bitte ankreuzen; **delete as ~** Nichtzutreffendes streichen; **it may be ~ (for you) to discuss this with your lawyer** sie sollten das vielleicht mit Ihrem Anwalt besprechen

appropriate² [əˈprəʊprɪeɪt] VT (= *assume possession or control of*) beschlagnahmen; (= *take for oneself*) sich (*dat*) aneignen; *sb's ideas* sich (*dat*) zu Eigen machen

appropriately [əˈprəʊprɪɪtlɪ] ADV treffend; *dressed* passend (*for, to* für); *designed, equipped* entsprechend (*for, to* +*dat*)

appropriateness [əˈprəʊprɪɪtnɪs] N (= *suitability, fittingness*) Eignung *f*; (*of dress, remark, name, for a particular occasion*) Angemessenheit *f*

appropriation [əˌprəʊprɪˈeɪʃən] N (*of land, property*) Beschlagnahmung *f*; (*of sb's ideas*) Aneignung *f*; **~ account** (*Comm*) Gewinnverteilungsrechnung *f*

approval [əˈpruːvl] N **(a)** Anerkennung *f*, (= *consent*) Zustimmung *f* (*of* zu); **to win sb's ~ (for sth)** jds Zustimmung (für etw) gewinnen; **to give one's ~ for sth** seine Zustimmung zu etw geben; **to meet with/have sb's ~** jds Zustimmung finden/haben; **to show one's ~ of sth** zeigen, dass man einer Sache (*dat*) zustimmt **(b)** (*Comm*) **on ~** zur Probe; (*to look at*) zur Ansicht

approve [əˈpruːv] ▓ VT (= *consent to*) *decision* billigen; *minutes, motion* annehmen; *project, deal, plan* genehmigen; (= *recommend*) *hotel etc* empfehlen ▓ VI **to ~ of sb/sth** von jdm/etw etwas halten; **I don't ~ of him/it** ich halte nichts von ihm/davon; **I don't ~ of children smoking** ich billige nicht, dass Kinder rauchen

approving [əˈpruːvɪŋ] ADJ (= *satisfied, pleased*) anerkennend; (= *consenting*) zustimmend

approvingly [əˈpruːvɪŋlɪ] ADV anerkennend

approx. ABBR *of* **approximately** ca.

approximate [əˈprɒksɪmɪt] ▓ ADJ ungefähr; **these figures are only ~** dies sind nur ungefähre Werte; **three hours is the ~ time needed** man braucht ungefähr drei Stunden ▓ [əˈprɒksəmeɪt] VI **to ~ to sth** einer Sache (*dat*) in etwa entsprechen ▓ [əˈprɒksəmeɪt] VT **to ~ sth** einer Sache (*dat*) in etwa entsprechen

approximately [əˈprɒksɪmətlɪ] ADV ungefähr, etwa; *correct* in etwa

approximation [əˌprɒksɪˈmeɪʃən] N Annäherung *f* (*of, to* an +*acc*); (= *figure, sum etc*) (An)näherungswert *m*; **his story was an ~ of the truth** seine Geschichte entsprach in etwa der Wahrheit

APR ABBR *of* **annual percentage rate** Jahreszinssatz *m*

après-ski [ˌæprɛˈskiː] ▓ N Après-Ski *nt* ▓ ADJ ATTR Après-Ski-

apricot [ˈeɪprɪkɒt] ▓ N Aprikose *f* ▓ ADJ (*also* **~-coloured**) aprikosenfarben ▓ ATTR Aprikosen-

April [ˈeɪprəl] N April *m*; **~ shower** Aprilschauer *m*; *see also* **September**

April fool N Aprilnarr *m*; **~!** ≈ April, April!; **to play an ~ on sb** jdn in den April schicken

April Fools' Day N der erste April

a priori [ˌeɪpraɪˈɔːraɪ] ▓ ADV a priori *f* ▓ ADJ apriorisch

apron [ˈeɪprən] N Schürze *f*; (*Aviat*) Vorfeld *nt*; (*Theat*) Vorbühne *f*

apron strings PL **to be tied to sb's ~** jdm am Schürzenzipfel hängen (*inf*)

apropos [ˈæprəpəʊ] PREP (*also* **~ of**) apropos (+*nom*)

APT ABBR *of* **advanced passenger train** Hochgeschwindigkeitszug *m*

apt [æpt] ADJ (+ER) **(a)** (= *suitable, fitting*) passend **(b)** (= *liable, likely*) **to be ~ to do sth** dazu neigen, etw zu tun; **we are ~ to forget that ...** wir vergessen leicht, dass ...

Apt. ABBR *of* **apartment** Z, Zi

aptitude [ˈæptɪtjuːd] N Begabung *f*

aptitude test N Eignungsprüfung *f*

aptly [ˈæptlɪ] ADV passend

aqualung [ˈækwəlʌŋ] N Tauchgerät *nt*

aquamarine [ˌækwəməˈriːn] ▓ N Aquamarin *m*; (= *colour*) Aquamarin *nt* ▓ ADJ aquamarin

aquaplane [ˈækwəpleɪn] VI (*car etc*) (auf nasser Straße) ins Rutschen geraten; **in order to prevent the car from aquaplaning** um ein Aquaplaning zu verhindern

aquarium [əˈkwɛərɪəm] N Aquarium *nt*

Aquarius [əˈkwɛərɪəs] N Wassermann *m*

aquatic [əˈkwætɪk] ADJ Wasser-; **~ sports** Wassersport *m*

aqueduct [ˈækwɪdʌkt] N Aquädukt *m or nt*

aquiline [ˈækwɪlaɪn] ADJ *profile* mit Adlernase; **~ nose** Adlernase *f*

Arab [ˈærəb] ▓ N Araber *m* (*also horse*), Araberin *f*; **the ~s** die Araber ▓ ADJ ATTR arabisch; **~ horse** Araber *m*

arabesque [ˌærəˈbɛsk] N Arabeske *f*

Arabia [əˈreɪbɪə] N Arabien *nt*

Arabian [əˈreɪbɪən] ADJ arabisch

Arabic [ˈærəbɪk] ▓ N Arabisch *nt* ▓ ADJ arabisch; **~ numerals** arabische Ziffern *or* Zahlen

arable [ˈærəbl] ADJ Acker-; **~ farming** Ackerbau *m*; **~ land** bebaubares Land; (*in use*) Ackerland *nt*

arbiter [ˈɑːbɪtə] N **(a)** **they were the ~s of good taste** sie waren die Päpste des guten Geschmacks **(b)** = **arbitrator**

arbitral [ˈɑːbɪtrəl] ADJ Schiedsgerichts-; **~ tribunal** Schiedsgericht *nt*

arbitrarily [ˈɑːbɪtrərəlɪ] ADV willkürlich

arbitrary [ˈɑːbɪtrərɪ] ADJ willkürlich

arbitrate [ˈɑːbɪtreɪt] ▓ VT *dispute* schlichten ▓ VI (*in dispute*) vermitteln

arbitration [ˌɑːbɪˈtreɪʃən] N Schlichtung *f*; **to go to ~** vor eine Schlichtungskommission gehen; (*dispute*) vor eine Schlichtungskommission gebracht werden; **~ clause** Schiedsgerichtsklausel *f*

arbitrator [ˈɑːbɪtreɪtə] N Vermittler(in) *m(f)*; (*esp Ind*) Schlichter(in) *m(f)*

arbour, (*US*) **arbor** [ˈɑːbə] N Laube *f*

arc [ɑːk] N Bogen *m*

arcade [ɑːˈkeɪd] N (*Archit*) Arkade *f*; (= *shopping ~*) Passage *f*

arcane [ɑːˈkeɪn] ADJ obskur

arch¹ [ɑːtʃ] ▓ N **(a)** Bogen *m* **(b)** (*Anat: of foot*) Wölbung *f* ▓ VI sich wölben; (*arrow etc*) einen Bogen machen ▓ VT *back* krümmen; *eyebrows* hochziehen; **the cat ~ed its back** die Katze machte einen Buckel

arch² ADJ ATTR Erz-; **~ enemy** Erzfeind(in) *m(f)*

archaeological, (*US*) **archeological** [ˌɑːkɪəˈlɒdʒɪkəl] ADJ archäologisch

archaeologist, (*US*) **archeologist** [ˌɑːkɪˈɒlədʒɪst] N Archäologe *m*, Archäologin *f*

archaeology, (*US*) **archeology** [ˌɑːkɪˈɒlədʒɪ] N Archäologie *f*

archaic [ɑːˈkeɪɪk] ADJ veraltet; (*inf*: = *ancient*) vorsintflutlich

archaism [ˈɑːkeɪɪzəm] N veralteter Ausdruck

arch: archangel [ˈɑːkeɪndʒəl] N Erzengel *m*; **archbishop** N Erzbischof *m*; **archdeacon** N Erzdiakon *m*

arched [ɑːtʃt] ADJ gewölbt; **~ window** (Rund)bogenfenster *nt*

archeological *etc* (*US*) = **archaeological** *etc*

archer [ˈɑːtʃə] N Bogenschütze *m*/-schützin *f*

archery [ˈɑːtʃərɪ] N Bogenschießen *nt*

archetypal [ˈɑːkɪtaɪpəl] ADJ archetypisch (*geh*); (= *typical*) typisch; **he is the ~ millionaire** er ist ein Millionär, wie er im Buche steht

archetype [ˈɑːkɪtaɪp] N Archetyp(us) *m* (*form*); (= *original, epitome also*) Urtyp *m*

archipelago [ˌɑːkɪˈpɛlɪgəʊ] N, *pl* **~(e)s** Archipel *m*

architect [ˈɑːkɪtɛkt] N (*lit, fig*) Architekt(in) *m(f)*; **he was the ~ of his own downfall** er hat seinen Ruin selbst verursacht

architectural ADJ, **architecturally** ADV [ˌɑːkɪˈtektʃərəl, -ɪ] architektonisch

architecture [ˈɑːkɪtektʃəʳ] N Architektur f (also Comput)

archive [ˈɑːkaɪv] **1** N Archiv nt (also Comput); ~ **material** Archivmaterial nt **2** VT archivieren

archives [ˈɑːkaɪvz] PL Archiv nt

archivist [ˈɑːkɪvɪst] N Archivar(in) m(f)

arch-rival [ˌɑːtʃˈraɪvəl] N Erzrivale m, Erzrivalin f

archway [ˈɑːtʃweɪ] N Torbogen m

arc lamp, arc light N Bogenlampe f

arctic [ˈɑːktɪk] **1** ADJ (lit, fig) arktisch **2** N (a) **the Arctic** die Arktis (b) (US: = shoe) gefütterter, wasserundurchlässiger Überschuh

arctic: Arctic Circle N nördlicher Polarkreis; **Arctic Ocean** N Nordpolarmeer nt

ardent [ˈɑːdənt] ADJ leidenschaftlich; request inständig

ardently [ˈɑːdəntlɪ] ADV leidenschaftlich; desire, admire glühend

ardour, (US) **ardor** [ˈɑːdəʳ] N (of person) Leidenschaft f; (of poems, letters) Leidenschaftlichkeit f

arduous [ˈɑːdjʊəs] ADJ beschwerlich; course, work anstrengend; task mühselig

are [ɑːʳ] 2ND PERS SING, 1ST, 2ND, 3RD PERS PL PRESENT of **be**

area [ˈɛərɪə] N (a) (measure) Fläche f; **20 sq metres** (Brit) or **meters** (US) **in** ~ eine Fläche von 20 Quadratmetern (b) (= region, district) Gebiet nt; (= neighbourhood, vicinity) Gegend f; (separated off, piece of ground etc) Gelände nt; (on plan, diagram etc) Bereich m; **in the** ~ in der Nähe; **do you live in the** ~? wohnen Sie hier (in der Gegend)?; **in the London** ~ im Londoner Raum; **protected/prohibited** ~ Schutz-/ Sperrgebiet nt; **dining/sleeping** ~ Ess-/Schlafbereich m; **no smoking/recreation** ~ Nichtraucher-/Erholungszone f; **the goal** ~ (Ftbl) der Torraum; **the (penalty)** ~ (esp Brit Ftbl) der Strafraum; **a mountainous** ~ eine bergige Gegend; **a wooded** ~ ein Waldstück nt; (larger) ein Waldgebiet nt; **the infected** ~**s of the lungs** die befallenen Teile or (smaller) Stellen der Lunge (c) (fig) Bereich m; **his** ~ **of responsibility** sein Verantwortungsbereich m; ~ **of interest/study** Interessen-/ Studiengebiet nt

area: area code N (Telec) Vorwahl(nummer) f; **area manager** N Gebietsleiter m; **area office** N Bezirksbüro nt; **areaway** N (US) (a) Vorplatz m (b) (= passage) Durchgang m, Passage f

arena [əˈriːnə] N (lit, fig) Arena f; **to enter the** ~ (fig) auf den Plan treten

aren't [ɑːnt] = **are not, am not**; see **be**

Argentina [ˌɑːdʒənˈtiːnə] N Argentinien nt

Argentine [ˈɑːdʒəntaɪn] N **the** ~ Argentinien nt

Argentinian [ˌɑːdʒənˈtɪnɪən] **1** N (= person) Argentinier(in) m(f) **2** ADJ argentinisch

argon [ˈɑːgɒn] N Argon nt

arguable [ˈɑːgjʊəbl] ADJ (a) (= capable of being maintained) vertretbar; **it is** ~ **that** ... es lässt sich der Standpunkt vertreten, dass ... (b) (= open to discussion) **it is** ~ **whether** ... es ist (noch) die Frage, ob ...

arguably [ˈɑːgjʊəblɪ] ADV wohl; **this is** ~ **his best book** dies dürfte sein bestes Buch sein

argue [ˈɑːgjuː] **1** VI (a) (= dispute) streiten; (= quarrel) sich streiten; (about trivial things) sich zanken; **there's no arguing with him** mit ihm kann man nicht reden; **don't** ~ **with your mother!** du sollst deiner Mutter nicht widersprechen!; **there is no point in arguing** da erübrigt sich jede (weitere) Diskussion (b) (= present reasons) **to** ~ **for** or **in favour** (Brit) or **favor** (US) **of/against sth** für/gegen etw sprechen; (in book) sich für/ gegen etw aussprechen; **this** ~**s in his favour** (Brit) or **favor** (US) das spricht zu seinen Gunsten **2** VT (a) (= debate) case, matter diskutieren; (Jur) vertreten; **a well** ~**d case** ein gut begründeter Fall (b) (= maintain) behaupten; **he** ~**s that** ... er vertritt den Standpunkt, dass ... (c) (= persuade) **to** ~ **sb out of/into sth** jdm etw aus-/einreden

➤ **argue out** VT SEP problem, issue ausdiskutieren; **to argue sth out with sb** etw mit jdm durchsprechen

argument [ˈɑːgjʊmənt] N (a) (= discussion) Diskussion f; **for the sake of** ~ rein theoretisch; **this is open to** ~ darüber lässt sich streiten (b) (= quarrel) Auseinandersetzung f; **to have an** ~ sich streiten; (over sth trivial) sich zanken; **without** ~ widerspruchslos (c) (= reason) Beweis(grund) m, Argument nt; (= line of reasoning) Argumentation f; **one of the best** ~**s I have heard in favour** (Brit) or **favor** (US) **of private education** eines der besten Argumente zugunsten der Privatschule, die ich gehört habe (d) (= theme: of book etc) Aussage f; (= claim) These f (e) (= statement of proof) Beweis m; **Professor Ayer's** ~ **is that** ... Professor Ayers These lautet, dass ...

argumentative [ˌɑːgjʊˈmentətɪv] ADJ person streitsüchtig

argy-bargy [ˈɑːdʒɪˈbɑːdʒɪ] N (Brit inf) Hin und Her nt (inf)

aria [ˈɑːrɪə] N Arie f

arid [ˈærɪd] ADJ (lit) soil dürr; (fig) subject trocken

Aries [ˈɛəriːz] N (Astrol) Widder m; **she is (an)** ~ sie ist Widder

arise [əˈraɪz], pret **arose** [əˈrəʊz], ptp **arisen** [əˈrɪzn] VI (a) (= occur) sich ergeben; (question, problem) aufkommen; **should the need** ~ falls sich die Notwendigkeit ergibt (b) (= result) **to** ~ **out of** or **from sth** sich aus etw ergeben (c) (old, liter: = get up) ~ **Sir Humphrey** erhebt Euch, Sir Humphrey!

aristocracy [ˌærɪˈstɒkrəsɪ] N Aristokratie f

aristocrat [ˈærɪstəkræt] N Aristokrat(in) m(f)

aristocratic [ˌærɪstəˈkrætɪk] ADJ aristokratisch

arithmetic [əˈrɪθmətɪk] N Rechnen nt; (= calculation) Rechnung f; **could you check my** ~? kannst du mal gucken, ob ich richtig gerechnet habe?; **your** ~ **is wrong** du hast dich verrechnet

arithmetical [ˌærɪθˈmetɪkəl] ADJ rechnerisch

ark [ɑːk] N **Noah's** ~ die Arche Noah

ARM ABBR of adjustable rate mortgage

arm¹ [ɑːm] N (a) (Anat) Arm m; **in one's** ~**s** im Arm; **under one's** ~ unterm Arm; **to give sb one's** ~ (Brit) jdm den Arm geben; **to take sb in one's** ~**s** jdn in die Arme nehmen; **to hold sb in one's** ~**s** jdn umarmen; **to put** or **throw one's** ~**s around sb** die Arme um jdn schlingen (geh); ~ **in** ~ Arm in Arm; **to keep sb at** ~**'s length** (fig) jdn auf Distanz halten; **to receive** or **welcome sb with open** ~**s** jdn mit offenen Armen empfangen; **to receive** or **welcome sth with open** ~**s** etw mit Kusshand nehmen (inf); **within** ~**'s reach** in Reichweite; **the long** ~ **of the law** der lange Arm des Gesetzes; **a list as long as your** ~ eine ellenlange Liste; **it cost him an** ~ **and a leg** (inf) es kostete ihn ein Vermögen; **to put the** ~ **on sb** (dated US inf) jdn unter Druck setzen (b) (= sleeve) Ärmel m, Arm m (c) (of river) (Fluss)arm m; (of sea) Meeresarm m; (of armchair) (Arm)lehne f; (of record player) Tonarm m

arm² **1** VT bewaffnen; **to** ~ **sth with sth** etw mit etw ausrüsten; **to** ~ **oneself with sth** (lit, fig) sich mit etw bewaffnen; (fig: non-aggressively) sich mit etw wappnen **2** VI aufrüsten

armada [ɑːˈmɑːdə] N Armada f

armadillo [ˌɑːməˈdɪləʊ] N Gürteltier nt

Armageddon [ˌɑːməˈgedn] N (Bibl, fig) Armageddon nt

armaments [ˈɑːməmənts] PL Ausrüstung f

armband [ˈɑːmbænd] N Armbinde f

armchair [ˈɑːmtʃɛəʳ] **1** N Sessel m, Lehnstuhl m **2** ADJ **he is an** ~ **traveller** (Brit) or **traveler** (US) er reist nur mit dem Finger auf der Landkarte (inf)

armed [ɑːmd] ADJ bewaffnet

-armed [-ɑːmd] ADJ SUF -armig; **one-armed** einarmig

armed: armed forces PL Streitkräfte pl; **armed robbery** N bewaffneter Raubüberfall

Armenia [ɑːˈmiːnɪə] N Armenien nt

Armenian [ɑːˈmiːnɪən] **1** ADJ armenisch **2** N (a) (= person) Armenier(in) m(f) (b) (Ling) Armenisch nt

arm: armful N Arm m voll no pl; **armhole** N Armloch nt

armistice [ˈɑːmɪstɪs] N Waffenstillstand m

Armistice Day N 11.11., Tag des Waffenstillstands (1918)

armour, (US) **armor** [ˈɑːməʳ] N (a) Rüstung f; (of animal) Panzer m; **suit of** ~ Rüstung f (b) (no pl: = steel plates) Panzerplatte(n) f(pl)

armoured, (US) **armored** ['ɑːməd] ADJ Panzer-; *vehicle* gepanzert; **~ car** Panzerwagen *m*; **~ personnel carrier** Schützenpanzer(wagen) *m*

armour, (US) **armor**: **armour-plated** ADJ gepanzert; **armour plating** N Panzerung *f*

armoury, (US) **armory** ['ɑːmərɪ] N **(a)** Arsenal *nt*, Waffenlager *nt* **(b)** (US: = factory) Munitionsfabrik *f*

arm: **armpit** N Achselhöhle *f*; **armrest** N Armlehne *f*

arms [ɑːmz] PL **(a)** (= weapons) Waffen *pl*; **to take up ~ (against sb/sth)** (gegen jdn/etw) zu den Waffen greifen; (fig) (gegen jdn/etw) zum Angriff übergehen; **to be up in ~ (about sth)** (fig inf) (über etw *acc*) empört sein **(b)** (Her) Wappen *nt*

arms dealer N Waffenhändler(in) *m(f)*

arms race N Wettrüsten *nt*

army ['ɑːmɪ] **1** N **(a)** Armee *f*, Heer *nt*; **~ of occupation** Besatzungsarmee *f*; **to be in the ~** beim Militär sein; **to join the ~** zum Militär gehen **(b)** (fig) Heer *nt* **2** ATTR Militär-; *discipline* militärisch; **~ doctor** Stabsarzt *m*/-ärztin *f*; **~ life** Soldatenleben *nt*; **~ officer** Offizier(in) *m(f)* in der Armee

army: **army-issue** ADJ Armee-; **~ rifle** Armeegewehr *nt*; **army-surplus** ADJ Armee-, Army-; **~ store** Armee- *or* Armyladen *m*

A-road ['eɪrəʊd] N (Brit) ≈ Bundesstraße *f*

aroma [ə'rəʊmə] N Aroma *nt*

aromatherapy [ə,rəʊmə'θerəpɪ] N Aromatherapie *f*

aromatic [ærəʊ'mætɪk] ADJ aromatisch

arose [ə'rəʊz] PRET *of* **arise**

around [ə'raʊnd] **1** ADV herum, rum, (inf); **I looked all ~** ich sah mich nach allen Seiten um; **they came from all ~** sie kamen von überall her; **he turned ~** er drehte sich um; **for miles ~** meilenweit im Umkreis; **to stroll/travel ~** herumschlendern/-reisen; **is he ~?** ist er da?; **see you ~!** (inf) bis bald! **2** PREP **(a)** (= right round) (movement, position) um; (in a circle) um … herum

(b) (= in, through) **to wander ~ the city** durch die Stadt spazieren; **to travel ~ Scotland** durch Schottland reisen; **the church must be ~ here somewhere** die Kirche muss hier irgendwo sein

(c) (= approximately) (with date) um; (with time of day) gegen; (with weight, price) etwa; *see also* **round**

arouse [ə'raʊz] VT erregen

arr ABBR *of* **arrival**, **arrives** Ank.

arrange [ə'reɪndʒ] VT **(a)** (= order) ordnen; *furniture, objects* aufstellen; *items in a collection, books in library etc* anordnen; *flowers* arrangieren; *room* einrichten; (fig) *thoughts* ordnen **(b)** (= see to, decide on) vereinbaren; *details* regeln; *party* arrangieren; **to ~ a mortgage for sb** jdm eine Hypothek beschaffen; **I'll ~ for you to meet him** ich arrangiere für Sie ein Treffen mit ihm; **can you ~ an interview with the President for me?** können Sie mir ein Interview mit dem Präsidenten besorgen?; **an ~d marriage** eine arrangierte Ehe; **if you could ~ to be there at five** wenn du es so einrichten kannst, dass du um fünf Uhr da bist; **that's easily ~d** das lässt sich leicht einrichten *or* arrangieren; **a meeting has been ~d for next month** nächsten Monat ist ein Treffen angesetzt **(c)** (Mus) arrangieren

arrangement [ə'reɪndʒmənt] N **(a)** (of room) Anordnung *f*; (of room) Einrichtung *f*; (inf: = contrivance) Gerät *nt* (inf); **a floral** *or* **flower ~** ein Blumenarrangement *nt*

(b) (= agreement) Vereinbarung *f*; (to meet) Verabredung *f*; **by ~** nach Vereinbarung; **by ~ with** mit freundlicher Genehmigung (+gen); **a special ~** eine Sonderregelung; **to have/come to an ~ with sb** eine Regelung mit jdm getroffen haben/treffen

(c) (usu pl) (= plans) Pläne *pl*; (= preparations) Vorbereitungen *pl*; **to make ~s for sb/sth** für jdn/etw Vorbereitungen treffen; **to make ~s for sth to be done** veranlassen, dass etw getan wird; **to make one's own ~s** selber zusehen(, wie …); **seating ~s** Sitzordnung *f*

(d) (Mus) Bearbeitung *f*; (light music) Arrangement *nt*

array [ə'reɪ] **1** VT (= line up) aufstellen **2** N **(a)** (Mil: = arrangement) Aufstellung *f* **(b)** (= collection) Ansammlung *f*; (of objects) stattliche Reihe **(c)** (Comput) (Daten)feld *nt*, Array *nt*

arrears [ə'rɪəz] PL Rückstände *pl*; **to get** *or* **fall into ~** in Rückstand kommen; **to have ~ of £5000** mit £ 5000 im Rückstand sein; **to be paid in ~** rückwirkend bezahlt werden

arrest [ə'rest] **1** VT **(a)** (= apprehend) festnehmen; (with warrant) verhaften; (fig) *attention* erregen **(b)** (= check) hemmen **2** N (of suspect) Festnahme *f*; (with warrant) Verhaftung *f*; **to be under ~** festgenommen/verhaftet sein

arresting [ə'restɪŋ] ADJ **(a)** (= striking) atemberaubend; *features* markant **(b)** **the ~ officer** der festnehmende Beamte

arrest warrant N Haftbefehl *m*

arrival [ə'raɪvəl] N **(a)** Ankunft *f no pl*; (of goods, news) Eintreffen *nt no pl*; **on ~** bei Ankunft; **he was dead on ~** bei seiner Einlieferung ins Krankenhaus wurde der Tod festgestellt; **~ time, time of ~** Ankunftszeit *f*; **~s** (Rail, Aviat) Ankunft *f* **(b)** (= person) Ankömmling *m*; **new ~** Neuankömmling *m*; (in hotel) neu angekommener Gast; (in office) neuer Mitarbeiter, neue Mitarbeiterin

arrivals lounge [ə'raɪvəlz,laʊndʒ] N Ankunftshalle *f*

arrive [ə'raɪv] VI (= come, be born) ankommen; **to ~ home** nach Hause kommen; (esp after journey etc) zu Hause ankommen; **to ~ at a town/the airport** in einer Stadt/am Flughafen ankommen; **the train will ~ at platform 10** der Zug läuft auf Gleis 10 ein; **to ~ at a decision/result** zu einer Entscheidung/einem Ergebnis kommen

arrogance ['ærəgəns] N Arroganz *f*

arrogant ADJ, **arrogantly** ADV ['ærəgənt, -lɪ] arrogant

arrow ['ærəʊ] N (= weapon, sign) Pfeil *m*

arrow key N (Comput) Pfeiltaste *f*

arse [ɑːs] (Brit sl) **1** N Arsch *m* (sl); **get your ~ in gear!** setz mal deinen Arsch in Bewegung! (sl); **tell him to get his ~ into my office** sag ihm, er soll mal in meinem Büro antanzen (inf) **2** VT **I can't be ~d** ich hab keinen Bock (sl)

➤ **arse about** *or* **around** VI (Brit inf) rumblödeln (inf)

arsehole ['ɑːshəʊl] N (Brit vulg) Arschloch *nt* (vulg)

arsenal ['ɑːsɪnl] N (Mil) Arsenal *nt*; (fig) Waffenlager *nt*

arsenic ['ɑːsnɪk] N Arsen *nt*; **~ poisoning** Arsenvergiftung *f*

arson ['ɑːsn] N Brandstiftung *f*

arsonist ['ɑːsənɪst] N Brandstifter(in) *m(f)*

art [ɑːt] **1** N **(a)** Kunst *f*; **the ~s** die schönen Künste; **there's an ~ to it** das ist eine Kunst; **~s and crafts** Kunsthandwerk *nt* **(b)** **~s** (Univ) Geisteswissenschaften *pl*; **~s minister** Kulturminister(in) *m(f)* **2** ADJ ATTR Kunst-

art: **art college** N Kunsthochschule *f*; **art director** N (Ind) Artdirector *m*

artefact (Brit), **artifact** ['ɑːtɪfækt] N Artefakt *nt*

arterial [ɑː'tɪərɪəl] ADJ **~ road** (Aut) Fernverkehrsstraße *f*

artery ['ɑːtərɪ] N **(a)** (Anat) Arterie *f* **(b)** (also **traffic ~**) Verkehrsader *f*

artful ['ɑːtfʊl] ADJ raffiniert, schlau

art: **art gallery** N Kunstgalerie *f*; **art-house** ADJ ATTR **~ film** Experimentalfilm *m*; **~ cinema** ≈ Programmkino *nt*

arthritic [ɑː'θrɪtɪk] ADJ arthritisch; **she is ~** sie hat Arthritis

arthritis [ɑː'θraɪtɪs] N Arthritis *f*

artichoke ['ɑːtɪtʃəʊk] N Artischocke *f*

article ['ɑːtɪkl] **1** N **(a)** (= item) Gegenstand *m*; (in list) Posten *m*; (Comm) Artikel *m*; **~ of value** Wertgegenstand *m*; **~ of furniture** Möbelstück *nt*; **~s of clothing** Kleidungsstücke *pl*; **toilet ~** Toilettenartikel *pl* **(b)** (in newspaper, constitution, also Gram) Artikel *m*; (= encyclopedia entry) Eintrag *m*; (of treaty, contract) Paragraph *m*; **~ of faith** Glaubensartikel *m*; (fig) Kredo *nt*; **~s of association** Gesellschaftsvertrag *m*; (of company) Satzung *f*; **~s of incorporation** (US) Gründungsurkunde *f*; **~s of partnership** (US) Gesellschaftsvertrag *m* einer Handelsgesellschaft **(c)** (of articled clerk) **to take one's ~s** seine Referendarprüfung machen **2** VT **to be ~d to sb** bei jdm eine Lehre machen, bei jdm in die Lehre gehen; **~d clerk** (Brit Jur) ≈ Rechtsreferendar(in) *m(f)*

articulate [ɑː'tɪkjʊlɪt] **1** ADJ *sentence, book* klar; **to be ~** (of person) sich gut *or* klar ausdrücken können **2** [ɑː'tɪkjʊleɪt] VT **(a)** (= pronounce) artikulieren **(b)** (= state) *reasons etc* darlegen **3** [ɑː'tɪkjʊleɪt] VI artikulieren

articulated lorry (Brit), **articulated truck** [ɑː'tɪkjʊleɪtɪd-] N Sattelschlepper *m*

articulately [ɑː'tɪkjʊlɪtlɪ] ADV *pronounce* artikuliert; *write, express oneself* klar, flüssig

artifact N = **artefact**

artificial [ɑːtɪˈfɪʃəl] ADJ (*lit, fig*) künstlich; (*pej:* = *not sincere*) *smile, manner* gekünstelt; **~ hair/silk** Kunsthaar *nt*/-seide *f*; **~ limb** Prothese *f*; **you're so ~** du bist nicht echt

artificial: artificial insemination N künstliche Befruchtung; **artificial intelligence** N künstliche Intelligenz

artificiality [ˌɑːtɪfɪʃɪˈælɪtɪ] N (= *insincerity*) Gekünsteltheit *f*

artificially [ɑːtɪˈfɪʃəlɪ] ADV künstlich; (= *insincerely*) gekünstelt

artificial respiration N künstliche Beatmung *f*

artillery [ɑːˈtɪlərɪ] N Artillerie *f*

artisan [ˈɑːtɪzæn] N Handwerker(in) *m(f)*

artist [ˈɑːtɪst] N Künstler(in) *m(f)*; **~'s impression** Zeichnung *f*

Be careful! **artist** *is not translated by the German word* **Artist**.

---

artiste [ɑːˈtiːst] N Künstler(in) *m(f)*; (= *circus* ~) Artist(in) *m(f)*

artistic [ɑːˈtɪstɪk] ADJ künstlerisch; (= *tasteful*) *arrangements* kunstvoll; (= *appreciative of art*) *person* kunstverständig; **she's very ~** sie ist künstlerisch veranlagt *or* begabt/sehr kunstverständig

artistically [ɑːˈtɪstɪkəlɪ] ADV künstlerisch; (= *tastefully*) kunstvoll

artistic director N künstlerischer Direktor, künstlerische Direktorin

artistry [ˈɑːtɪstrɪ] N (*lit, fig*) Kunst *f*

artless ADJ, **artlessly** ADV [ˈɑːtlɪs, -lɪ] unschuldig

art lover N Kunstliebhaber(in) *m(f)*

Art Nouveau [ˈɑːnuːˈvəʊ] N Jugendstil *m*

Art-Nouveau [ˈɑːnuːˈvəʊ] ADJ ATTR Jugendstil-; **~ building** Jugendstilbau *m*

art school N Kunsthochschule *f*

Arts [ɑːts]: **Arts Council** N Kulturausschuss *m* (*der britischen Regierung*); **arts degree** N Abschlussexamen *nt* der philosophischen Fakultät; **Arts Faculty, Faculty of Arts** N philosophische Fakultät

artwork [ˈɑːtwɜːk] N (a) (*in book*) Bildmaterial *nt* (b) (*for advert etc:* = *material ready for printing*) Druckvorlage *f* (c) (= *painting etc*) Kunstwerk *nt*

arty [ˈɑːtɪ] ADJ (+ER) (*inf*) Künstler-; *tie, clothes* verrückt (*inf*); *person* auf Künstler machend (*pej*); *film, novel* geschmäcklerisch

arty-farty [ˈɑːtɪˈfɑːtɪ] ADJ (*hum inf*) = **arty**

Aryan [ˈɛərɪən] **1** N Arier(in) *m(f)* **2** ADJ arisch

as [æz, əz] **1** CONJ (a) (= *when, while*) als; (*two parallel actions*) während, als
(b) (= *since*) da
(c) (= *although*) **rich as he is I won't marry him** obwohl er reich ist, werde ich ihn nicht heiraten; **much as I admire her, ...** sosehr ich sie auch bewundere, ...; **be that as it may** wie dem auch sei *or* sein mag; **try as he might** sosehr er sich auch bemüht/bemühte
(d) (*manner*) wie; **do as you like** machen Sie, was Sie wollen; **leave it as it is** lass das so; **the first door as you go in** die erste Tür, wenn Sie hereinkommen; **knowing him as I do** so wie ich ihn kenne; **it is bad enough as it is** es ist schon schlimm genug; **as it were** sozusagen
(e) (*phrases*) **as if** *or* **though** als ob; **it isn't as if he didn't see me** schließlich hat er mich ja gesehen; **as for him** (und) was ihn angeht; **as from now** ab jetzt; **so as to** (= *in order to*) um zu +*infin*; (= *in such a way*) so, dass; **be so good as to ...** (*form*) hätten Sie die Freundlichkeit *or* Güte, ... zu ... (*form*); **he's not so silly as to do that** er ist so nicht so dumm, das zu tun **2** ADV (a) **as ... as** so ... wie; (*comparisons*) ebenso; **twice as old** doppelt so alt; **just as nice** genauso nett; **late as usual!** wie immer zu spät!; **as recently as yesterday** erst gestern; **she is very clever, as is her brother** sie ist sehr intelligent, genau(so) wie ihr Bruder; **as many/much as I could** so viele/so viel ich (nur) konnte; **there were as many as 100 people there** es waren bestimmt 100 Leute da; **this one is just as good** diese(r, s) ist genauso gut **3** REL PRON (*with same, such*) der/die/das; (*pl*) die; **the same man as was here yesterday** derselbe Mann, der gestern hier war **4** PREP (a) (= *in the capacity of*) als; **to treat sb as a child** jdn wie ein Kind behandeln
(b) (= *such as*) wie (zum Beispiel)

asap [ˈeɪsæp] ABBR *of* **as soon as possible** baldmöglichst

asbestos [æzˈbestəs] N Asbest *m*

ascend [əˈsend] **1** VI (= *rise*) aufsteigen; (= *slope upwards*) ansteigen (*to* auf +*acc*); **in ~ing order** in aufsteigender Reihenfolge **2** VT *stairs* hinaufsteigen; *mountain* erklimmen (*geh*)

ascendancy, ascendency [əˈsendənsɪ] N Vormachtstellung *f*; **to gain/have (the) ~ over sb** die Vorherrschaft über jdn gewinnen/haben

ascendant, ascendent [əˈsendənt] N **to be in the ~** (*Astrol*) im Aszendenten stehen; (*fig*) im Aufstieg begriffen sein

Ascension [əˈsenʃən] N **the ~** (*Christi*) Himmelfahrt *f*

Ascension Day N Himmelfahrt(stag *m*) *m*

ascent [əˈsent] N Aufstieg *m*; **the ~ of Ben Nevis** der Aufstieg auf den Ben Nevis

ascertain [æsəˈteɪn] VT ermitteln

ascetic [əˈsetɪk] **1** ADJ asketisch **2** N Asket *m*

asceticism [əˈsetɪsɪzəm] N Askese *f*

ASCII [ˈæskɪ] ABBR *of* **American Standard Code for Information Interchange**; **~ file** ASCII-Datei *f*

ascorbic acid [əˈskɔːbɪkˈæsɪd] N Askorbinsäure *f*

ascribe [əˈskraɪb] VT zuschreiben (*sth to sb* jdm etw); *importance, weight* beimessen (*to sth* einer Sache *dat*)

ASEAN [ˈæsɪˌæn] ABBR *of* **Association of Southeast Asian Nations** ASEAN *f*, Vereinigung *f* südostasiatischer Staaten

asexual [eɪˈseksjʊəl] ADJ *reproduction* ungeschlechtlich

ash[1] [æʃ] N (*also* ~ **tree**) Esche *f*

ash[2] N Asche *f*; **~es** Asche *f*; **to reduce sth to ~es** (= *burn down*) etw völlig niederbrennen; **to rise from the ~es** (*fig*) aus den Trümmern wieder auferstehen

ashamed [əˈʃeɪmd] ADJ beschämt; **to be** *or* **feel ~ (of sb/sth)** sich schämen (für jdn/etw); **it's nothing to be ~ of** deswegen braucht man sich nicht zu schämen; **he is ~ to do it** er schämt sich, das zu tun; **... I'm ~ to say** ..., muss ich leider zugeben; **you ought to be ~ (of yourself)** du solltest dich (was) schämen!

A shares [ˈeɪʃeəz] PL stimmrechtslose Aktien *pl*

ashen-faced [æʃnˈfeɪst] ADJ kreidebleich

ashore [əˈʃɔː] ADV an Land; **to run ~** stranden; **to put ~** an Land gehen

ash: ashtray N Aschenbecher *m*; **Ash Wednesday** N Aschermittwoch *m*

Asia [ˈeɪʃə] N Asien *nt*

Asia Minor N Kleinasien *nt*

Asian [ˈeɪʃn], **Asiatic** [ˌeɪʃɪˈætɪk] **1** ADJ (a) asiatisch (b) (*Brit:* = *from Indian subcontinent*) indopakistanisch **2** N (a) Asiat(in) *m(f)* (b) (*Brit:* = *person from the Indian subcontinent*) Indopakistaner(in) *m(f)*

Asian-American [ˌeɪʃnəˈmerɪkən] **1** ADJ asiatisch-amerikanisch **2** N Amerikaner(in) *m(f)* asiatischer Herkunft

Asian flu N asiatische Grippe

aside [əˈsaɪd] **1** ADV (a) (*with verbal element*) zur Seite, beiseite; **to set sth ~ for sb** etw für jdn beiseite legen; **to turn ~** (*lit, fig*) sich abwenden (b) (*esp US*) **~ from** außer; **~ from being chairman of this committee he is ...** außer Vorsitzender dieses Ausschusses ist er auch ...; **this criticism, ~ from being wrong, is ...** diese Kritik ist nicht nur falsch, sondern ... **2** N (*Theat*) **to say sth in an ~** etw beiseite sprechen

A-side [ˈeɪsaɪd] N (*of record*) A-Seite *f*

ask [ɑːsk] **1** VT (a) (= *inquire*) fragen; *question* stellen; **to ~ sb the way/his opinion** jdn nach dem Weg/seiner Meinung fragen; **don't ~ me!** (*inf*) frag mich nicht, was weiß ich! (*inf*) (b) (= *invite*) einladen; (*in dancing*) auffordern (c) (= *request*) bitten (*sb for sth* jdn um etw); (= *require, demand*) verlangen (*sth of sb* etw von jdm); **to ~ sb to do sth** jdn darum bitten, etw zu tun; **all I ~ is ...** ich will ja nur ...; **he ~ed to be excused** er bat, ihn zu entschuldigen; **that's ~ing too much** das ist zu viel verlangt (d) (*Comm*) *price* verlangen **2** VI (a) (= *inquire*) fragen; **to ~ about sb/sth** sich nach jdm/etw erkundigen
(b) (= *request*) bitten (*for sth* um etw); **you just have to ~** du brauchst nur zu fragen; **I'm not ~ing for sympathy** ich will kein Mitleid; **there's no harm in ~ing** Fragen kostet nichts!;

that's ~ing for trouble das kann ja nicht gut gehen; **to ~ for Mr X** Herrn X verlangen

➤ **ask after** VI +PREP OBJ sich erkundigen nach; **tell her I was asking after her** grüß sie schön von mir

➤ **ask around** VI herumfragen

➤ **ask back** VT SEP **(a)** (= *invite*) zu sich einladen **(b) they never asked me back again** sie haben mich nie wieder eingeladen

➤ **ask in** VT SEP (*to house*) hereinbitten

➤ **ask out** VT SEP einladen

➤ **ask over** VT SEP zu sich einladen

➤ **ask round** VT SEP (*esp Brit*) = **ask over**

askance [əˈskɑːns] ADV **to look ~ at sb** jdn entsetzt ansehen; **to look ~ at a suggestion** *etc* über einen Vorschlag *etc* die Nase rümpfen

askew [əˈskjuː] ADJ, ADV schief

asking price [ˈɑːskɪŋˌpraɪs] N Verkaufspreis *m*; (*for car, house etc also*) Verhandlungsbasis *f*

asleep [əˈsliːp] ADJ PRED **(a)** (= *sleeping*) schlafend; **to be (fast or sound) ~** (fest) schlafen; **to fall ~** einschlafen (*also euph*) **(b)** (*inf*: = *numb*) eingeschlafen

asocial [erˈsəʊʃəl] ADJ ungesellig

asparagus [əˈspærəgəs] N, NO PL Spargel *m*

asparagus tips PL Spargelspitzen *pl*

aspect [ˈæspekt] N **(a)** (*liter.*: = *appearance*) Erscheinung *f*; (*of thing*) Aussehen *nt* **(b)** (*of question, subject etc*) Aspekt *m*; **what about the security ~?** was ist mit der Sicherheit? **(c)** (*of building*) **to have a southerly ~** Südlage haben **(d)** (*Gram*) Aspekt *m*

aspersion [əsˈpɜːʃən] N **to cast ~s on sb/sth** abfällige Bemerkungen über jdn/etw machen

asphalt [ˈæsfælt] **1** N Asphalt *m* **2** VT asphaltieren **3** ADJ ATTR asphaltiert; **~ jungle** Asphaltdschungel *m*

asphyxiate [æsˈfɪksɪeɪt] VTI ersticken; **to be ~d** ersticken

asphyxiation [æsˌfɪksɪˈeɪʃən] N Erstickung *f*

aspic [ˈæspɪk] N (*Cook*) Aspik *m or nt*

aspirate [ˈæspəreɪt] VT aspirieren

aspiration [ˌæspəˈreɪʃən] N Aspiration *f*

aspire [əˈspaɪə'] VI **to ~ to sth** nach etw streben, etw erstreben; **to ~ to do sth** danach streben, etw zu tun

aspirin [ˈæsprɪn] N Kopfschmerztablette *f*, Aspirin® *nt*

aspiring [əˈspaɪərɪŋ] ADJ aufstrebend

ass¹ [æs] N (*lit, fig inf*) Esel *m*; **to make an ~ of oneself** sich lächerlich machen

ass² N (*US sl*) Arsch *m* (*vulg*); **to kick ~** (= *get tough*) mit der Faust auf den Tisch hauen (*inf*); **to work one's ~ off** sich zu Tode schuften (*inf*); **kiss my ~!** (*esp US sl*) du kannst mich mal am Arsch lecken! (*vulg*)

assail [əˈseɪl] VT (*lit, fig*) angreifen; (*fig: with questions etc*) überschütten; **to be ~ed by doubts** von Zweifeln geplagt werden

assailant [əˈseɪlənt] N Angreifer(in) *m(f)*

assassin [əˈsæsɪn] N Attentäter(in) *m(f)*

assassinate [əˈsæsɪneɪt] VT ein Attentat verüben auf (*+acc*); **JFK was ~d in Dallas** JFK wurde in Dallas ermordet

assassination [əˌsæsɪˈneɪʃən] N (geglücktes) Attentat (*of* auf *+acc*); **~ attempt** Attentat *nt*

assault [əˈsɔːlt] **1** N **(a)** (*Mil*) Sturm(angriff) *m* (*on* auf *+acc*); (*fig*) Angriff *m* (*on* gegen) **(b)** (*Jur*) Körperverletzung *f*; **sexual ~** Notzucht *f* **2** VT **(a)** (*Jur.*: = *attack*) tätlich werden gegen; (*sexually*) herfallen über (*+acc*); (= *rape*) sich vergehen an (*+dat*) **(b)** (*Mil*) angreifen

assault: **assault course** N Übungsgelände *nt*; **assault rifle** N Maschinengewehr *nt*; **assault troops** PL Sturmtruppen *pl*

assay [əˈseɪ] VT mineral, value prüfen

assemblage [əˈsemblɪdʒ] N (= *collection*) (*of things*) Sammlung *f*; (*of facts*) Anhäufung *f*

assemble [əˈsembl] **1** VT zusammensetzen; *facts* zusammentragen; *team* zusammenstellen **2** VI sich versammeln

assembler [əˈsemblə'] N (*Comput*) Assembler *m*

assembly [əˈsemblɪ] N **(a)** (= *gathering of people, Parl*) Versammlung *f*; **the Welsh/Northern Ireland Assembly** die walisische/nordirische Versammlung **(b)** (*Sch*)

Morgenandacht *f*, tägliche Versammlung **(c)** (= *putting together*) Zusammenbau *m*; (*esp of machine, cars*) Montage *f*

assembly: **assembly hall** N (*Sch*) Aula *f*; **assembly language** N (*Comput*) Assemblersprache *f*; **assembly line** N Montageband *nt*; **assemblyman** [əˈsemblɪmən] N (*US*) Abgeordnete(r) *m*; **Assembly Member** N Mitglied *nt* des walisischen Parlaments; **assembly point** N Sammelplatz *m*; **assemblywoman** [əˈsemblɪwʊmən] N (*US*) Abgeordnete *f*; **assembly worker** N Montagearbeiter(in) *m(f)*

assent [əˈsent] **1** N Zustimmung *f* **2** VI zustimmen; **to ~ to sth** einer Sache (*dat*) zustimmen; **~ed stock** (*St Ex*) abgestempelte Aktie

assert [əˈsɜːt] VT **(a)** (= *declare*) behaupten; **one's innocence** beteuern **(b)** (= *insist on*) **to ~ one's authority** seine Autorität geltend machen; **to ~ one's rights** sein Recht behaupten; **to ~ oneself** sich durchsetzen (*over* gegenüber)

assertion [əˈsɜːʃən] N (= *statement*) Behauptung *f*; **to make an ~** eine Behauptung aufstellen

assertive ADJ, **assertively** ADV [əˈsɜːtɪv, -lɪ] bestimmt

assertiveness [əˈsɜːtɪvnɪs] N Bestimmtheit *f*; **~ training course** Persönlichkeitstrainingskurs *m*

assess [əˈses] VT **(a)** *abilities, needs, situation* einschätzen; *proposal* abwägen; *damage* abschätzen **(b)** *property* schätzen; *person* (*for tax purposes*) veranlagen (*at* mit) **(c)** *fine, tax* festsetzen (*at* auf *+acc*); *damages* schätzen (*at* auf *+acc*)

assessment [əˈsesmənt] N **(a)** (= *evaluation*) Einschätzung *f*; (*of damage*) Schätzung *f*; **what's your ~ of the situation?** wie sehen *or* beurteilen Sie die Lage? **(b)** (*Fin*) (*of property*) Schätzung *f*; (*of person: for tax purposes*) Veranlagung *f* **(c)** (*Jur*) (*of fine, tax*) Festsetzung *f*; (*of damages*) Schätzung *f* **(d)** (*Sch, Univ: of student*) Einstufung *f*; (*Med: of patient*) Beurteilung *f*

assessor [əˈsesə'] N (*Insur*) (Schadens)gutachter(in) *m(f)*; (*Univ*) Prüfer(in) *m(f)*

asset [ˈæset] N **(a)** (*usu pl*) Vermögenswert *m*; (*on balance sheet*) Aktivposten *m*; **~ account** Bestandskonto *nt*, Aktivkonto *nt*; **~ turnover** Kapitalumschlag *m*; **~ value** Vermögenswert *m*; **~s** Vermögen *nt*; (*on balance sheet*) Aktiva *pl*; **personal ~s** persönlicher Besitz **(b)** (*fig*) **it would be an ~ ...** es wäre von Vorteil ...; **he is one of our great ~s** er ist einer unserer besten Leute

asset-stripping [ˈæsetstrɪpɪŋ] N Asset-Stripping *nt*, Aufkauf von finanziell gefährdeten Firmen und anschließender Verkauf ihrer Vermögenswerte

asshole [ˈæshəʊl] N (*US sl*) Arschloch *nt* (*vulg*)

assiduous ADJ, **assiduously** ADV [əˈsɪdjʊəs, -lɪ] gewissenhaft

assign [əˈsaɪn] VT **(a)** (= *allot*) zuweisen (*to sb* jdm); (*to a purpose*) *room* bestimmen (*to* für); (= *attribute*) *cause, novel* zuschreiben (*to +dat*) **(b)** (= *appoint*) berufen; (*to a case, task etc*) beauftragen (*to* mit); **she was ~ed to this school** sie wurde an diese Schule berufen **(c)** (*Jur*) übereignen (*to sb* jdm)

assignation [ˌæsɪgˈneɪʃən] N Rendezvous *nt*

assignment [əˈsaɪnmənt] N **(a)** (= *task*) Aufgabe *f*; (= *mission*) Auftrag *m*; **to be on (an) ~** einen Auftrag haben **(b)** (= *appointment*) Berufung *f*; (*to case, task etc*) Beauftragung *f* (*to* mit) **(c)** (= *allocation*) Zuweisung *f*; (*of room*) Bestimmung *f* (*to* für) **(d)** (*Jur*) Übereignung *f*

assimilate [əˈsɪmɪleɪt] VT aufnehmen

assimilation [əˌsɪmɪˈleɪʃən] N Aufnahme *f*

assist [əˈsɪst] **1** VT helfen (*+dat*); (= *act as an assistant to*) assistieren (*+dat*); *growth, progress* fördern; **to ~ sb with sth** jdm bei etw behilflich sein; **to ~ sb in doing** *or* **to do sth** jdm helfen, etw zu tun **2** VI (= *help*) helfen; **to ~ with sth** bei etw helfen; **to ~ in doing sth** helfen, etw zu tun

assistance [əˈsɪstəns] N Hilfe *f*; **to give ~ to sb** (= *come to aid of*) jdm Hilfe leisten; **to come to sb's ~** jdm zu Hilfe kommen; **can I be of any ~?** kann ich irgendwie helfen *or* behilflich sein?

assistant [əˈsɪstənt] **1** N Assistent(in) *m(f)*; (= *shop ~*) Verkäufer(in) *m(f)* **2** ADJ ATTR *manager etc* stellvertretend

assistant: **assistant priest** N Hilfspriester *m*; **assistant professor** N (*US*) Assistenz-Professor(in) *m(f)*; **assistant referee** N (*Ftbl*) Schiedsrichterassistent(in) *m(f)*

assistantship [əˈsɪstəntʃɪp] N (*Brit: at school*) Stelle *f* als Fremdsprachenassistent(in); (*US: at college*) Assistentenstelle *f*

associate [əˈsəʊʃɪɪt] **1** N **(a)** (= *colleague*) Kollege *m*, Kollegin *f*; (*Comm: = partner*) Teilhaber(in) *m(f)*; (= *accomplice*) Komplize *m*, Komplizin *f* **(b)** (*of a society*) außerordentliches Mitglied **2** [əˈsəʊʃɪeɪt] VT assoziieren (*also Psych*); **to ~ oneself with sb/sth** sich jdm/einer Sache anschließen, sich mit jdm/ einer Sache assoziieren; **~(d) company** Partnerfirma *f* **3** [əˈsəʊʃɪeɪt] VI **to ~ with** verkehren mit

associate: **associate director** N *Direktor einer Firma, der jedoch nicht offiziell als solcher ernannt wurde*; **associate member** N außerordentliches Mitglied; **associate partner** N (Geschäfts)partner(in) *m(f)*; **associate professor** N (*US*) außerordentlicher Professor, außerordentliche Professorin

association [əˌsəʊsɪˈeɪʃən] N NO PL (= *associating: with people*) Umgang *m*; (= *cooperation*) Zusammenarbeit *f*; **he has benefited from his ~ with us** er hat von seiner Beziehung zu uns profitiert; **published in ~ with ...** in Zusammenarbeit mit ... veröffentlicht **(b)** (= *organization*) Verband *m* **(c)** (= *connection in the mind*) Assoziation *f* (*with* an +*acc*) (*also Psych*); **~ of ideas** Gedankenassoziation *f*

association football N (*Brit*) Fußball *m*, Soccer *nt*

assorted [əˈsɔːtɪd] ADJ (= *mixed*) gemischt

assortment [əˈsɔːtmənt] N Mischung *f*; (*of goods*) Auswahl *f* (*of* an +*dat*), Sortiment *nt* (*of* von)

asst ABBR *of* **assistant**

assuage [əˈsweɪdʒ] VT *hunger, desire* stillen; *anger, fears etc* beschwichtigen; *guilt* vermindern

assume [əˈsjuːm] VT **(a)** annehmen; (= *presuppose*) voraussetzen; **let us ~ that you are right** nehmen wir an, Sie hätten Recht; **assuming (that) ...** angenommen(, dass) ...; **to ~ office** sein Amt antreten; **to ~ a look of innocence** eine unschuldige Miene aufsetzen **(b)** *power, control* übernehmen

assumed [əˈsjuːmd] ADJ **~ name** angenommener Name; (*for secrecy etc also*) Deckname *m*

assumption [əˈsʌmpʃən] N **(a)** Annahme *f*; (= *presupposition*) Voraussetzung *f*; **to go on the ~ that ...** von der Voraussetzung ausgehen, dass ... **(b)** (*of power, role etc*) Übernahme *f* **(c)** (*Eccl*) **the Assumption** Mariä Himmelfahrt *f*

assurance [əˈʃʊərəns] N **(a)** Versicherung *f*; (= *promise*) Zusicherung *f*; **he gave me his ~ that it would be done** er versicherte mir, dass es getan werden würde **(b)** (= *self-confidence*) Sicherheit *f* **(c)** (*Brit: = life ~*) Versicherung *f*

assure [əˈʃʊəʳ] VT **(a)** **to ~ sb of sth** (*of love, willingness etc*) jdn einer Sache (*gen*) versichern; (*of service, support*) jdm etw zusichern; **to ~ sb that ...** jdm versichern/zusichern, dass ...; **... I ~ you** ... versichere ich Ihnen **(b)** (= *make certain of*) *success, future* sichern; **he is ~d of a warm welcome wherever he goes** er kann sich überall eines herzlichen Empfanges sicher sein **(c)** (*Brit: = insure*) *life* versichern; **she ~d her life for £100,000** sie schloss eine Lebensversicherung über £ 100.000 ab

assured [əˈʃʊəd] **1** N (*Brit*) Versicherte(r) *mf* **2** ADJ sicher; **to rest ~ that ...** sicher sein, dass ...

assuredly [əˈʃʊərɪdlɪ] ADV mit Sicherheit

aster [ˈæstəʳ] N Aster *f*

asterisk [ˈæstərɪsk] N Sternchen *nt*

asteroid [ˈæstərɔɪd] N Asteroid *m*

asthma [ˈæsmə] N Asthma *nt*

asthmatic [æsˈmætɪk] **1** N Asthmatiker(in) *m(f)* **2** ADJ asthmatisch

astonish [əˈstɒnɪʃ] VT erstaunen; **to be ~ed** erstaunt sein

astonishing ADJ, **astonishingly** ADV [əˈstɒnɪʃɪŋ, -lɪ] erstaunlich; **~ly (enough)** erstaunlicherweise

astonishment [əˈstɒnɪʃmənt] N Erstaunen *nt* (*at* über +*acc*); **she looked at me in (complete) ~** sie sah mich (ganz) erstaunt an

astound [əˈstaʊnd] VT sehr erstaunen; **to be ~ed (at** or **by)** höchst erstaunt sein (über +*acc*)

astounding ADJ, **astoundingly** ADV [əˈstaʊndɪŋ, -lɪ] erstaunlich; **~ly (enough)** erstaunlicherweise

astral [ˈæstrəl] ADJ Stern-

astray [əˈstreɪ] ADJ **to go ~** (*person*) (*lit*) vom Weg abkommen; (*fig: morally*) vom rechten Weg abkommen; (*letter, object*) verloren gehen; **to lead sb ~** (*fig*) jdn vom rechten Weg abbringen; (= *mislead*) jdn irreführen

astride [əˈstraɪd] PREP rittlings auf (+*dat*)

astringent [əsˈtrɪndʒənt] ADJ *remark, humour* beißend

astrologer [əsˈtrɒlədʒəʳ] N Astrologe *m*, Astrologin *f*

astrological [ˌæstrəˈlɒdʒɪkəl] ADJ astrologisch; **~ sign** Tierkreiszeichen *nt*

astrology [əsˈtrɒlədʒɪ] N Astrologie *f*

astronaut [ˈæstrənɔːt] N Astronaut(in) *m(f)*

astronomer [əsˈtrɒnəməʳ] N Astronom(in) *m(f)*

astronomical ADJ, **astronomically** ADV [ˌæstrəˈnɒmɪkəl, -lɪ] (*lit, fig*) astronomisch

astronomy [əsˈtrɒnəmɪ] N Astronomie *f*

astrophysics [ˌæstrəʊˈfɪzɪks] N SING Astrophysik *f*

astute [əˈstjuːt] ADJ schlau; *child* aufgeweckt; *mind* scharf

astutely [əˈstjuːtlɪ] ADV scharfsinnig

astuteness [əsˈtjuːtnɪs] N Schlauheit *f*

asylum [əˈsaɪləm] N **(a)** Asyl *nt*; **to ask for (political) ~** um (politisches) Asyl bitten **(b)** (= *lunatic ~*) (Irren)anstalt *f*

asylum-seeker N [əˈsaɪləmˌsiːkəʳ] Asylbewerber(in) *m(f)*

asymmetric(al) [ˌeɪsɪˈmetrɪk(əl)] ADJ asymmetrisch

asymmetry [æˈsɪmɪtrɪ] N Asymmetrie *f*

at [æt] PREP **(a)** (*position*) an (+*dat*), bei (+*dat*); (*with place*) in (+*dat*); **at a table** an einem Tisch; **at the corner/top** an der Ecke/Spitze; **at home** zu Hause; **at the university** (*US*), **at university** an *or* auf der Universität; **at school** in der Schule; **at the hotel** im Hotel; **at my brother's** bei meinem Bruder; **at a party** auf *or* bei einer Party; **to arrive at the station** am Bahnhof ankommen; **this is where it's at** (*esp US inf*) da gehts ab (*sl*)
(b) (*direction*) **to shoot/point** *etc* **at sb/sth** auf jdn/etw schießen/zeigen *etc*; **to look/swear** *etc* **at sb/sth** jdn/etw ansehen/beschimpfen *etc*
(c) (*time, frequency, order*) **at ten o'clock** um zehn Uhr; **at night** bei Nacht; **at Christmas/Easter** *etc* zu Weihnachten/ Ostern *etc*; **at your age/16 (years of age)** in deinem Alter/mit 16 (Jahren); **three at a time** drei auf einmal; **at the start/end of sth** am Anfang/am Ende einer Sache (*gen*)
(d) (*activity*) **at play** beim Spiel; **at work** bei der Arbeit; **good/ an expert at sth** gut/ein Experte in etw (*dat*); **while we are at it** (*inf*) wenn wir schon mal dabei sind
(e) (*state, condition*) **to be at an advantage** im Vorteil sein; **at a loss/profit** mit Verlust/Gewinn; **I'd leave it at that** ich würde es dabei belassen
(f) (= *as a result of, upon*) auf (+*acc*) ... (hin); **at his request** auf seine Bitte (hin); **at that/this he left the room** daraufhin verließ er das Zimmer
(g) (*cause: = with*) *angry, delighted etc* über (+*acc*)
(h) (*rate, value, degree*) **at full speed/50 km/h** mit voller Geschwindigkeit/50 km/h; **at 50p a pound** für *or* zu 50 Pence pro Pfund; **at 5% interest** zu 5% Zinsen; **at a high price** zu einem hohen Preis; **when the temperature is at 90°** wenn die Temperatur auf 90° ist

ate [eɪt, et] PRET *of* **eat**

atheism [ˈeɪθɪɪzəm] N Atheismus *m*

atheist [ˈeɪθɪɪst] N Atheist(in) *m(f)*

atheistic [ˌeɪθɪˈɪstɪk] ADJ atheistisch

Athens [ˈæθɪnz] N Athen *nt*

athlete [ˈæθliːt] N Athlet(in) *m(f)*; (= *specialist in track and field events*) Leichtathlet(in) *m(f)*

athlete's foot [ˌæθliːtsˈfʊt] N Fußpilz *m*

athletic [æθˈletɪk] ADJ sportlich; (*referring to athletics*) *build* athletisch

athletics [æθˈletɪks] N SING or PL Leichtathletik *f*; **~ meeting** Leichtathletikwettkampf *m*

Atlantic [ətˈlæntɪk] **1** N (*also* **~ Ocean**) Atlantik *m* **2** ADJ ATTR atlantisch; **~ crossing** Atlantiküberquerung *f*

atlas [ˈætləs] N Atlas *m*

Atlas Mountains PL Atlas(gebirge *nt*) *m*

ATM ABBR *of* **automated telling machine**

atmosphere [ˈætməsfɪəʳ] N (*lit, fig*) Atmosphäre *f*

atmospheric [ˌætməsˈferɪk] ADJ atmosphärisch; (= *full of atmosphere*) *description* stimmungsvoll

atmospheric pressure N Luftdruck *m*

atom ['ætəm] N **(a)** Atom *nt* **(b)** (*fig*) **not an ~ of truth** kein Körnchen Wahrheit

atom bomb N Atombombe *f*

atomic [ə'tomɪk] ADJ atomar

atomic IN CPDS Atom-; **atomic bomb** N Atombombe *f*; **atomic energy** N Kernenergie *f*; **Atomic Energy Authority** N (*Brit*), **Atomic Energy Commission** N (*US*) Atomkommission *f*; **atomic number** N Ordnungszahl *f*; **atomic power** N Atomkraft *f*; (= *propulsion*) Atomantrieb *m*; **atomic-powered** ADJ atomgetrieben; **atomic structure** N Atombau *m*; **atomic weight** N Atomgewicht *nt*

atomizer ['ætəmaɪzə'] N Zerstäuber *m*

atone [ə'təʊn] VI **to ~ for sth** (für) etw büßen

atonement [ə'təʊnmənt] N Sühne *f*; **in ~ for sth** als Sühne *or* Buße für etw

A to Z® N Stadtplan *m* (*mit Straßenverzeichnis, meist in Buchform*)

at-risk ['ætˌrɪsk] ADJ Risiko-; **~ register** (*Social Work*) Register *nt* gefährdeter Kinder

atrocious ADJ, **atrociously** ADV [ə'trəʊʃəs, -lɪ] grauenhaft

atrocity [ə'trɒsɪtɪ] N Grausamkeit *f*

atrophy ['ætrəfɪ] **1** N Schwund *m* **2** VI verkümmern, schwinden

att ABBR *of* **attorney**

attaboy ['ætəbɔɪ] INTERJ (*esp US inf*) gut gemacht!

attach [ə'tætʃ] **1** VT **(a)** (= *join*) befestigen (*to* an +*dat*); **document to a letter etc** beiheften; **please find ...ed ...** beigeheftet ...; **to ~ conditions to sth** Bedingungen an etw (*acc*) knüpfen **(b) to be ~ed to sb/sth** (= *be fond of*) an jdm/etw hängen **(c)** (= *attribute*) **importance** beimessen (*to* +*dat*) **(d)** (*Mil etc*) **personnel** zuteilen (*to* +*dat*) **2** VI **no blame ~es to him** ihn trifft keine Schuld

attaché [ə'tæʃeɪ] N Attaché *m*

attaché case N Aktenkoffer *m*

attachment [ə'tætʃmənt] N **(a)** (= *accessory: for tool etc*) Zusatzteil *nt* **(b)** (*fig*: = *affection*) Zuneigung *f* (*to* zu) **(c)** (*Mil etc*: = *temporary transfer*) Zuordnung *f* **(d)** (*Comput*) Attachment *nt*

attack [ə'tæk] **1** N **(a)** (*Mil, Sport, fig*) Angriff *m* (*on* auf +*acc*); **to be under ~** angegriffen werden; (*fig also*) unter Beschuss stehen; **to go on to the ~** zum Angriff übergehen **(b)** (*Med etc*) Anfall *m*; **to have an ~ of nerves** plötzlich Nerven bekommen **2** VT **(a)** (*Mil, Sport, fig*) angreifen; (*from ambush, in robbery etc*) überfallen **(b) task, problem** in Angriff nehmen **3** VI angreifen; **an ~ing side** eine offensive Mannschaft

attacker [ə'tækə'] N Angreifer(in) *m(f)*

attagirl ['ætəgɜːl] INTERJ (*esp US inf*) gut gemacht!

attain [ə'teɪn] VT **aim, rank** erreichen; **knowledge, independence** erlangen; **happiness, prosperity, power** gelangen zu

attainable [ə'teɪnəbl] ADJ erreichbar; **knowledge, happiness, power** zu erlangen

attainment [ə'teɪnmənt] N **(a)** (*of knowledge, happiness, prosperity, power*) Erlangen *nt* **(b)** (*usu pl*: = *accomplishment*) Fertigkeit *f*

attempt [ə'tempt] **1** VT versuchen; **smile, conversation** den Versuch machen zu; **task** sich versuchen an (+*dat*); **~ed murder** Mordversuch *m* **2** N Versuch *m*; (*on sb's life*) (Mord)anschlag *m* (*on* auf +*acc*); **an ~ on the record** ein Versuch, den Rekord zu brechen; **to make an ~ at doing sth** *or* **to do sth** versuchen, etw zu tun; **at the first ~** beim ersten Versuch; **in the ~** dabei

attend [ə'tend] **1** VT **church, meeting, school etc** besuchen; **wedding, funeral** anwesend sein bei; **the wedding was well ~ed** die Hochzeit war gut besucht **2** VI (= *be present*) anwesend sein; **are you going to ~?** gehen Sie hin?

➤ **attend to** VI +PREP OBJ (= *see to*) sich kümmern um; (= *pay attention to*) **work etc** Aufmerksamkeit widmen (+*dat*); (= *listen to*) **teacher, sb's remark** zuhören (+*dat*); (= *heed*) **advice, warning** hören auf (+*acc*); (= *serve*) **customers etc** bedienen; **are you being attended to?** werden Sie schon bedient?; **that's being attended to** das wird (bereits) erledigt

attendance [ə'tendəns] N **(a)** (= *being present*) Anwesenheit *f* (*at* bei); **to be in ~ at sth** bei etw anwesend sein **(b)** (= *number of people present*) Teilnehmerzahl *f*

attendance: **attendance allowance** N (*Brit*) Pflegegeld *nt*; **attendance centre** N (*Brit*) Heim *nt* für jugendliche Straftäter; **attendance record** N **he doesn't have a very good ~** er fehlt oft

attendant [ə'tendənt] **1** N (*in public toilets*) Toilettenwart *m*, Toilettenfrau *f*; (*in swimming baths*) Bademeister(in) *m(f)*; (*in art galleries, museums*) Aufseher(in) *m(f)* **2** ADJ **problems etc** (da)zugehörig; **~ circumstances** Begleitumstände *pl*; **to be ~ (up)on sth** mit etw zusammenhängen

attendee [ˌæten'diː] N (*esp US*) Teilnehmer(in) *m(f)*

attention [ə'tenʃən] N **(a)** NO PL (= *consideration*) Aufmerksamkeit *f*; **to call** *or* **draw sb's ~ to sth, to call** *or* **draw sth to sb's ~** jdn auf etw (*acc*) aufmerksam machen; **to turn one's ~ to sb/sth** seine Aufmerksamkeit auf jdn/etw richten; **to pay ~/no ~ to sb/sth** jdn/etw beachten/nicht beachten; **to pay ~ to the teacher** dem Lehrer zuhören; **to hold sb's ~** jdn fesseln; **~!** Achtung!; **your ~, please** ich bitte um Aufmerksamkeit; (*official announcement*) Achtung, Achtung!; **it has come to my ~ that ...** ich bin darauf aufmerksam geworden, dass ...

(b) (*Comm*) **~ Miss Smith, for the ~ of Miss Smith** zu Händen von Frau Smith; **your letter will receive our earliest ~** Ihr Brief wird baldmöglichst bearbeitet; **for your ~** zur gefälligen Beachtung

(c) (*Mil*) **to stand to** *or* **at ~, to come to ~** stillstehen; **~!** stillgestanden!

Attention Deficit Disorder N (*Med*) Aufmerksamkeits-Defizit-Störung *f*

attentive [ə'tentɪv] ADJ aufmerksam; **to be ~ to sb** sich jdm gegenüber aufmerksam verhalten; **to be ~ to sth** einer Sache (*dat*) Beachtung schenken; **to be ~ to sb's needs** sich um jds Bedürfnisse kümmern

attentively [ə'tentɪvlɪ] ADV aufmerksam

attenuate [ə'tenjʊeɪt] VT (= *weaken*) abschwächen; **attenuating circumstances** mildernde Umstände

attest [ə'test] VT **(a)** (= *testify to*) **sb's innocence, authenticity** bescheinigen; **signature** beglaubigen; (*on oath*) beschwören **(b)** (= *be proof of*) beweisen, bezeugen

➤ **attest to** VI +PREP OBJ bezeugen

attestation [ˌætes'teɪʃən] N (= *document*) Bescheinigung *f*

attic ['ætɪk] N Dachboden *m*; (*lived-in*) Mansarde *f*; **~ room** Dachkammer *f*; **in the ~** auf dem (Dach)boden

attire [ə'taɪə'] **1** VT kleiden (*in* in +*acc*) **2** N, NO PL Kleidung *f*; **ceremonial ~** Festtracht *f*

attitude ['ætɪtjuːd] N (= *way of thinking*) Einstellung *f* (*to, towards* zu); (= *way of acting, manner*) Haltung *f* (*to, towards* gegenüber); **women with ~** kämpferische Frauen

attn ABBR *of* **attention** z. Hd(n) von

attorney [ə'tɜːnɪ] N **(a)** (*Comm, Jur*: = *representative*) Bevollmächtigte(r) *mf*; **letter of ~** (schriftliche) Vollmacht **(b)** (*US*: = *lawyer*) (Rechts)anwalt *m*/-anwältin *f*

Attorney General N, *pl* **Attorneys General** *or* **Attorney Generals** (*US*: = *public prosecutor*) (*of state government*) Generalstaatsanwalt *m*/-anwältin *f*; (*of federal government*) ≈ Generalbundesanwalt *m*/-anwältin *f*; (*Brit*) ≈ Justiz-minister(in) *m(f)*

attract [ə'trækt] VT **(a)** (*Phys*) anziehen **(b)** (*fig*: = *appeal to*) (*person*) anziehen; (*idea, place etc*) ansprechen; **she feels ~ed to him** sie fühlt sich von ihm angezogen **(c)** (*fig*: = *win*) **attention etc** auf sich (*acc*) ziehen; **new members etc** anziehen; **to ~ publicity** (öffentliches) Aufsehen erregen

attraction [ə'trækʃən] N **(a)** (*Phys, fig*) Anziehungskraft *f*; (*esp of big city etc*) Reiz *m* **(b)** (= *attractive thing*) Attraktion *f*

attractive [ə'træktɪv] ADJ attraktiv; **personality, smile** anziehend; **house, dress** reizvoll

attractively [ə'træktɪvlɪ] ADV attraktiv; **dress, furnish, paint** reizvoll; **~ priced** zum attraktiven Preis (*at* von)

attractiveness [ə'træktɪvnɪs] N Attraktivität *f*; (*of house, view etc*) Reiz *m*

attributable [ə'trɪbjʊtəbl] ADJ **to be ~ to sb/sth** jdm/einer Sache zuzuschreiben sein

attribute [ə'trɪbjuːt] **1** VT **to ~ sth to sb** **play, remark etc** jdm etw zuschreiben; **to ~ sth to sth** **success, accident etc** etw auf etw

(acc) zurückführen; (= *attach*) *importance etc* einer Sache (*dat*) etw beimessen **2** [ˈætrɪbjuːt] N Attribut *nt*

attributive [əˈtrɪbjʊtɪv] (*Gram*) **1** ADJ attributiv **2** N Attributiv *nt*

attributively [əˈtrɪbjʊtɪvlɪ] ADV attributiv

attrition [əˈtrɪʃən] N (*fig*) Zermürbung *f*; **war of ~** (*Mil*) Zermürbungskrieg *m*

attune [əˈtjuːn] VT (*fig*) abstimmen (*to* auf +*acc*); **to become ~d to sth** sich an etw (*acc*) gewöhnen

atypical [ˌeɪˈtɪpɪkəl] ADJ atypisch

aubergine [ˈəʊbəʒiːn] **1** N (= *vegetable*) Aubergine *f*; (= *colour*) Aubergine *nt* **2** ADJ aubergine(farben)

auburn [ˈɔːbən] ADJ *hair* rotbraun

auction [ˈɔːkʃən] **1** N Auktion *f*; **to sell sth by ~** etw versteigern; **to put sth up for ~** etw zur Versteigerung anbieten **2** VT (*also ~ off*) versteigern

auctioneer [ˌɔːkʃəˈnɪəʳ] N Auktionator(in) *m(f)*

auction: auction house N Auktionshaus *nt*; **auction room(s)** N(PL) Auktionshalle *f*; **auction sale** N Auktion *f*

audacious ADJ, **audaciously** ADV [ɔːˈdeɪʃəs, -lɪ] **(a)** (= *impudent*) dreist **(b)** (= *bold*) kühn, verwegen

audacity [ɔːˈdæsɪtɪ], **audaciousness** [ɔːˈdeɪʃəsnɪs] N **(a)** (= *impudence*) Dreistigkeit *f*; **to have the ~ to do sth** die Dreistigkeit besitzen, etw zu tun **(b)** (= *boldness*) Kühnheit *f*, Verwegenheit *f*

audible ADJ, **audibly** ADV [ˈɔːdɪbl, -ɪ] hörbar

audience [ˈɔːdɪəns] N **(a)** Publikum *nt no pl*; (*of writer, book*) Leserschaft *f*; (*Rad*) Zuhörerschaft *f* **(b)** (= *formal interview*) Audienz *f* (*with* bei)

audio [ˈɔːdɪəʊ] IN CPDS Audio-; **audio book** N Hörbuch *nt*; **audio cassette** N Audiokassette *f*; **audio equipment** N (*in recording studio*) Audiogeräte *pl*; (= *hi-fi*) Stereoanlage *f*

audiotape 1 N **(a)** (Ton)band *m* **(b)** (*US*: = *cassette*) Kassette *f* **2** VT auf (Ton)band/Kassette aufnehmen; **audio typist** N Phonotypistin *f*; **audiovisual** ADJ audiovisuell

audit [ˈɔːdɪt] **1** N Buchprüfung *f* **2** VT **(a)** *accounts, company* prüfen **(b)** (*US Univ*) Gasthörer sein bei

audition [ɔːˈdɪʃən] **1** N (*Theat*) Vorsprechprobe *f*; (*of musician*) Probespiel *nt*; (*of singer*) Vorsingen *nt* **2** VT vorsprechen/vorspielen/vorsingen lassen **3** VI vorsprechen/vorspielen/vorsingen

auditor [ˈɔːdɪtəʳ] N **(a)** (*Comm*) Buchprüfer(in) *m(f)*; **~'s report** Prüfungsbericht *m* des Wirtschaftsprüfers **(b)** (*US Univ*) Gasthörer(in) *m(f)*

auditorium [ˌɔːdɪˈtɔːrɪəm] N Auditorium *nt*

au fait [əʊˈfeɪ] ADJ **to be ~ with sth** mit etw vertraut sein

Aug ABBR *of* **August** Aug

augment [ɔːgˈment] **1** VT vermehren **2** VI zunehmen

augmentation [ˌɔːgmənˈteɪʃən] N Vermehrung *f*; (*in numbers*) Zunahme *f*; (*Mus*) Augmentation *f*; **breast ~** Brustvergrößerung *f*

augur [ˈɔːgəʳ] VI **to ~ well/ill** etwas Gutes/nichts Gutes verheißen

August [ˈɔːgəst] N August *m*; *see also* **September**

august [ɔːˈgʌst] ADJ illuster; *occasion, spectacle* erhaben

auk [ɔːk] N (*Zool*) Alk *m*

auld [ɔːld] ADJ (+ER) (*Scot*) alt; **for ~ lang syne** um der alten Zeiten willen

aunt [ɑːnt] N Tante *f*

auntie, aunty [ˈɑːntɪ] N (*esp Brit inf*) Tante *f*; **~!** Tantchen!

Aunt Sally [ˌɑːntˈsælɪ] N (*Brit fig*) Zielscheibe *f*

au pair [əʊˈpeəʳ] N, *pl* **- -s** (*also* **~ girl**) Aupair(mädchen *nt*) *nt*

aura [ˈɔːrə] N Aura *f* (*geh*); **she has an ~ of mystery about her** eine geheimnisvolle Aura umgibt sie

aural [ˈɔːrəl] ADJ Gehör-; **~ examination** Hörtest *m*

auspices [ˈɔːspɪsɪz] PL (= *sponsorship*) **under the ~ of** unter der Schirmherrschaft (+*gen*), unter den Auspizien (+*gen*) (*geh*)

auspicious [ɔːsˈpɪʃəs] ADJ günstig; *start* viel versprechend

auspiciously [ɔːsˈpɪʃəslɪ] ADV viel versprechend

Aussie [ˈɒzɪ] (*inf*) **1** N (= *person*) Australier(in) *m(f)* **2** ADJ australisch

austere [ɒsˈtɪəʳ] ADJ streng; *room* karg

austerely [ɒsˈtɪəlɪ] ADV streng; *furnish* karg; *live* asketisch

austerity [ɒsˈterɪtɪ] N **(a)** (= *severity*) Strenge *f*; (= *simplicity*) Schmucklosigkeit *f* **(b)** (= *hardship, shortage*) **after the ~ of the war years** nach den Entbehrungen der Kriegsjahre; **~ budget** Sparhaushalt *m*; **~ measures** Sparmaßnahmen *pl*

Australasia [ˌɒstrəˈleɪsjə] N Australien und Ozeanien *nt*

Australasian [ˌɒstrəˈleɪsjən] **1** N Ozeanier(in) *m(f)* **2** ADJ ozeanisch

Australia [ɒsˈtreɪlɪə] N Australien *nt*

Australian [ɒsˈtreɪlɪən] **1** N Australier(in) *m(f)*; (= *accent*) australisches Englisch **2** ADJ australisch

Austria [ˈɒstrɪə] N Österreich *nt*

Austrian [ˈɒstrɪən] **1** N Österreicher(in) *m(f)*; (= *dialect*) Österreichisch *nt* **2** ADJ österreichisch

Austro- [ˈɒstrəʊ-] PREF österreichisch-

authentic [ɔːˈθentɪk] ADJ *signature, manuscript* authentisch; *accent, antique, tears* echt

authentically [ɔːˈθentɪkəlɪ] ADV echt; *restored* authentisch

authenticate [ɔːˈθentɪkeɪt] VT bestätigen; *signature, document* beglaubigen; *work of art* für echt befinden

authentication [ɔːˌθentɪˈkeɪʃən] N Bestätigung *f*; (*of signature, document*) Beglaubigung *f*; (*of work of art*) Echtheitserklärung *f*

authenticity [ˌɔːθenˈtɪsɪtɪ] N Echtheit *f*; (*of claim*) Berechtigung *f*

author [ˈɔːθəʳ] N (*profession*) Autor(in) *m(f)*; (*of report*) Verfasser(in) *m(f)*; (*fig*) Urheber(in) *m(f)*; (*of plan*) Initiator(in) *m(f)*

authoress [ˈɔːθərɪs] N Autorin *f*

authoritarian [ˌɔːθɒrɪˈteərɪən] **1** ADJ autoritär **2** N autoritärer Mensch; **to be an ~** autoritär sein

authoritarianism [ˌɔːθɒrɪˈteərɪənɪzəm] N Autoritarismus *m*

authoritative [ɔːˈθɒrɪtətɪv] ADJ **(a)** (= *commanding*) bestimmt; *manner* respekteinflößend **(b)** (= *reliable*) zuverlässig; (= *definitive*) maßgeblich

authoritatively [ɔːˈθɒrɪtətɪvlɪ] ADV (= *with authority*) bestimmt; (= *definitively*) maßgeblich; (= *reliably*) zuverlässig

authority [ɔːˈθɒrɪtɪ] N **(a)** (= *power, influence*) Autorität *f*; (= *right*) Befugnis *f*; (= *specifically delegated power*) Vollmacht *f*; (*Mil*) Befehlsgewalt *f*; **who's in ~ here?** wer ist hier der Verantwortliche?; **parental ~** Autorität der Eltern; (*Jur*) elterliche Gewalt; **to be in** *or* **have ~ over sb** Weisungsbefugnis gegenüber jdm haben (*form*); (*describing hierarchy*) jdm übergeordnet sein; **on one's own ~** auf eigene Verantwortung; **to have the ~ to do sth** berechtigt sein, etw zu tun; **to give sb the ~ to do sth** jdm die Vollmacht erteilen, etw zu tun; **I can speak with ~ on this matter** darüber kann ich mich kompetent äußern
(b) (*also pl*: = *ruling body*) Behörde *f*; (= *body of people*) Verwaltung *f*; (= *power of ruler*) (Staats)gewalt *f*; **the local ~** *or* **authorities** die Gemeindeverwaltung; **this will have to be decided by a higher ~** das muss an höherer Stelle entschieden werden; **you must have respect for ~** du musst Achtung gegenüber Respektspersonen haben
(c) (= *expert, definitive book etc*) (anerkannte) Autorität *f*; (= *source*) Quelle *f*; **to have sth on good ~** etw aus zuverlässiger Quelle wissen

authorization [ˌɔːθəraɪˈzeɪʃən] N Genehmigung *f*; (= *right*) Recht *nt*

authorize [ˈɔːθəraɪz] VT **(a)** (= *empower*) ermächtigen, autorisieren (*geh*); **to be ~d to do sth** (= *have right*) das Recht haben, etw zu tun **(b)** (= *permit*) genehmigen; *biography etc* autorisieren

authorized [ˈɔːθəraɪzd] ADJ *overdraft* bewilligt; *person, bank* autorisiert, bevollmächtigt; *biography* autorisiert; **"~ personnel only"** „Zutritt nur für Befugte"; **duly ~** (*Jur, Fin*) ordnungsgemäß bevollmächtigt; **~ dealer** Vertragshändler(in) *m(f)*; **~ signatory** Zeichnungsberechtigte(r) *mf*; **~ signature** Unterschrift *f* eines bevollmächtigten Vertreters

authorized capital N autorisiertes Kapital

Authorized Version N *die englische Bibelfassung von 1611*

autism [ˈɔːtɪzəm] N Autismus *m*

autistic [ɔːˈtɪstɪk] ADJ autistisch

auto [ˈɔːtəʊ] N (*US*) Auto *nt*

autobiographical [ˈɔːtəʊˌbaɪəʊˈgræfɪkəl] ADJ autobiografisch

autobiography [ɔːtəʊbaɪˈɒɡrəfɪ] N Autobiografie f

autocade [ˈɔːtəʊkeɪd] N (US) Wagenkolonne f

autocracy [ɔːˈtɒkrəsɪ] N Autokratie f

autocrat [ˈɔːtəʊkræt] N Autokrat(in) m(f)

autocratic [ɔːtəʊˈkrætɪk] ADJ autokratisch

Autocue® [ˈɔːtəʊkjuː] N (Brit TV) Teleprompter m

autofocus [ˈɔːtəʊfəʊkəs] N (Phot) Autofokus m

autograph [ˈɔːtəɡrɑːf] ◼ N (= signature) Autogramm nt ◼ VT signieren

autograph album N Autogrammalbum nt

automat [ˈɔːtəmæt] N (US) Automatenrestaurant nt

automate [ˈɔːtəmeɪt] VT automatisieren; **~d telling machine** Geldautomat m

automatic [ɔːtəˈmætɪk] ◼ ADJ (lit, fig) automatisch; **he has the ~ right ...** er hat automatisch das Recht ...; **~ camera** Automatikkamera f; **~ data processing** automatische Datenverarbeitung; **~ gearbox** or **transmission** (Aut) Automatikgetriebe nt; **~ rifle** or **weapon** Schnellfeuergewehr nt ◼ N (= car) Automatikwagen m; (= gun) automatische Waffe; (= washing machine) Waschautomat m

automatically [ɔːtəˈmætɪkəlɪ] ADV automatisch

automation [ɔːtəˈmeɪʃən] N Automatisierung f

automobile [ˈɔːtəməbiːl] N Auto(mobil) nt

automotive [ɔːtəˈməʊtɪv] ADJ vehicle selbstfahrend; **the ~ industry** die Automobilindustrie

automotive engineering N Kfz-Technik f

autonomous ADJ, **autonomously** ADV [ɔːˈtɒnəməs, -lɪ] autonom

autonomy [ɔːˈtɒnəmɪ] N Autonomie f

autopilot [ˈɔːtəʊpaɪlət] N Autopilot m; **on ~** (lit) mit Autopilot; **he was on ~** (fig) er funktionierte wie ferngesteuert

autopsy [ˈɔːtɒpsɪ] N Autopsie f

autotimer [ˈɔːtəʊtaɪməʳ] N (on cooker etc) Ein-/ Abschaltautomatik f

autumn [ˈɔːtəm] (esp Brit) ◼ N (lit, fig) Herbst m; **in (the) ~** im Herbst ◼ ADJ ATTR Herbst-, herbstlich; **~ leaves** bunte (Herbst)blätter pl

autumnal [ɔːˈtʌmnəl] ADJ herbstlich, Herbst-; **~ weather** Herbstwetter nt

auxiliary [ɔːɡˈzɪlɪərɪ] ◼ ADJ Hilfs- (also Comput); (= additional) generator etc zusätzlich; **~ nurse** Schwesternhelferin f; **~ program** (Comput) Hilfsprogramm nt; **~ verb** Hilfsverb nt ◼ N (a) (Mil: esp pl) Soldat(in) m(f) der Hilfstruppe; **auxiliaries** pl Hilfstruppen pl
(b) (general: = assistant) Hilfskraft f; **teaching ~** (Aus)hilfslehrer(in) m(f); **nursing ~** Schwesternhelferin f
(c) (= ~ verb) Hilfsverb nt

Av ABBR of **avenue**

avail [əˈveɪl] ◼ VR **to ~ oneself of sth** von etw Gebrauch machen; **to ~ oneself of the opportunity of doing sth** die Gelegenheit nutzen, etw zu tun ◼ N **of no ~** erfolglos, ohne Erfolg, vergeblich; **to no ~** vergebens, vergeblich

availability [əveɪləˈbɪlɪtɪ] N (of object) Erhältlichkeit f; (Comm: of stock) Vorrätigkeit f; (of means, resources) Verfügbarkeit f; **offer subject to ~ while stocks last** (das Angebot gilt) nur solange der Vorrat reicht; **because of the limited ~ of seats** weil nur eine begrenzte Anzahl an Plätzen zur Verfügung steht

available [əˈveɪləbl] ADJ object erhältlich; (Comm: = in stock) vorrätig; (= free) time, post, seats etc frei; (= at one's disposal) means, resources etc verfügbar; **to be ~** vorhanden sein; (= at one's disposal) zur Verfügung stehen; (person) (= not otherwise occupied) frei sein; (for discussion) zu sprechen sein; **to make sth ~ to sb** jdm etw zur Verfügung stellen; (= accessible) information jdm etw zugänglich machen; **to make oneself ~ to sb** sich jdm zur Verfügung stellen; **the best dictionary ~**, **the best ~ dictionary** das beste Wörterbuch, das es gibt; **he caught the next ~ flight home** er nahm den nächsten Flug nach Hause; **to try every ~ means** nichts unversucht lassen; **when will you be ~ to start in the new job?** wann können Sie die Stelle antreten?

avalanche [ˈævəlɑːnʃ] N (lit, fig) Lawine f

avant-garde [ævɒŋˈɡɑːd] ◼ N Avantgarde f ◼ ADJ avantgardistisch

avarice [ˈævərɪs] N Habgier f

avaricious [ævəˈrɪʃəs] ADJ habgierig, habsüchtig

Ave ABBR of **avenue**

avenge [əˈvendʒ] VT rächen; **to ~ oneself on sb (for sth)** sich an jdm (für etw) rächen

avenue [ˈævənjuː] N (a) (tree-lined) Allee f; (= broad street) Boulevard m (b) (fig: = method) Weg m; **to explore every ~** alle sich bietenden Wege prüfen

aver [əˈvɜː] VT (form) mit Nachdruck betonen; love, innocence beteuern

average [ˈævərɪdʒ] ◼ N (a) Durchschnitt m; **to do an ~ of 50 miles a day/3% a week** durchschnittlich 50 Meilen pro Tag fahren/3% pro Woche erledigen; **on ~** durchschnittlich; (= normally) normalerweise; **above ~** überdurchschnittlich; **below ~** unterdurchschnittlich; **by the law of ~s** aller Wahrscheinlichkeit nach
(b) (Naut) Havarie f, Seeschaden m
◼ ADJ durchschnittlich; (= ordinary) Durchschnitts-; (= not good or bad) mittelmäßig; **above/below ~** über-/ unterdurchschnittlich; **the ~ man**, **Mr Average** der Durchschnittsbürger; **he's a man of ~ height** er ist von mittlerer Größe
◼ VT (a) (= do etc on ~) auf einen Schnitt von ... kommen; **we ~d 80 km/h** wir kamen auf einen Schnitt von 80 km/h, wir sind durchschnittlich 80 km/h gefahren
(b) (= ~ out at) **sales are averaging 10,000 copies per day** der Absatz beträgt durchschnittlich 10.000 Exemplare pro Tag

➤ **average out** ◼ VT SEP **if you average it out** im Durchschnitt; **it'll average itself out** es wird sich ausgleichen ◼ VI durchschnittlich ausmachen (at, to +acc); (= balance out) sich ausgleichen; **how does it average out on a weekly basis?** wie viel ist das durchschnittlich pro Woche?

averse [əˈvɜːs] ADJ PRED abgeneigt; **I am not ~ to a glass of wine** einem Glas Wein bin ich nicht abgeneigt; **I am rather ~ to doing that** es widerstrebt mir, das zu tun

aversion [əˈvɜːʃən] N (= strong dislike) Abneigung f, Aversion f (geh, Psych) (to gegen); **he has an ~ to getting wet** er hat eine Abscheu davor, nass zu werden

avert [əˈvɜːt] VT abwenden; suspicion ablenken; blow etc abwehren; accident verhüten

aviary [ˈeɪvɪərɪ] N Vogelhaus nt

aviation [eɪvɪˈeɪʃən] N die Luftfahrt

aviator [ˈeɪvɪeɪtəʳ] N Flieger(in) m(f)

avid [ˈævɪd] ADJ (a) (= desirous) gierig (for nach); (esp for fame, praise) süchtig (for nach) (b) (= keen) begeistert; interest lebhaft; **I am an ~ reader** ich lese leidenschaftlich gern

avidly [ˈævɪdlɪ] ADV (a) (= eagerly) begierig; (pej) gierig (b) (= keenly) eifrig; read leidenschaftlich gern

avocado [ævəˈkɑːdəʊ] N, pl **-s** (also **~ pear**) Avocado(birne) f

avoid [əˈvɔɪd] VT vermeiden; person meiden, aus dem Weg gehen (+dat); obstacle ausweichen (+dat); difficulty, duty, truth umgehen; **in order to ~ being seen** um nicht gesehen zu werden; **I'm not going if I can possibly ~ it** wenn es sich irgendwie vermeiden lässt, gehe ich nicht; **to ~ sb's eye** jds Blick (dat) ausweichen

avoidable [əˈvɔɪdəbl] ADJ vermeidbar

avoidance [əˈvɔɪdəns] N Vermeidung f; **the ~ of inheritance tax** die Umgehung der Erbschaftssteuer

avow [əˈvaʊ] VT (liter) erklären; faith bekennen; **he ~ed himself to be a royalist** er bekannte (offen), Royalist zu sein

avowal [əˈvaʊəl] N Erklärung f; (of faith) Bekenntnis nt; (of belief, interest) Bekundung f

avowed [əˈvaʊd] ADJ erklärt

AWACS, Awacs [ˈeɪwæks] ABBR of **airborne warning and control system** Awacs-Flugzeug nt, mit Frühwarnsystem ausgestattetes Aufklärungsflugzeug der US-Luftwaffe

await [əˈweɪt] VT erwarten; future events, decision etc entgegensehen (+dat); **the long ~ed day** der lang ersehnte Tag; **he is ~ing trial** sein Fall steht noch zur Verhandlung an

awake [əˈweɪk], pret **awoke**, ptp **awoken** or **awaked** [əˈweɪkt] ◼ VI (lit, fig) erwachen ◼ VT wecken ◼ ADJ PRED (lit, fig) wach; **to be/lie/stay ~** wach sein/liegen/bleiben; **to keep sb ~** jdn wach halten; **wide ~** (lit, fig) hellwach

awaken [əˈweɪkən] VTI = **awake**

awakening [əˈweɪknɪŋ] N (lit, fig) Erwachen nt; **a rude ~** (lit, fig) ein böses Erwachen

award [əˈwɔːd] **1** VT *prize, penalty etc* zuerkennen (*to sb* jdm); (= *present*) *prize, degree etc* verleihen (*to sb* jdm); **to be ~ed damages** Schadenersatz zugesprochen bekommen **2** N (= *prize*) Preis *m*; (*for bravery etc*) Auszeichnung *f*; (*Jur*) Zuerkennung *f*; **to make an ~** (*to sb*) einen Preis (an jdn) vergeben

award: **award(s) ceremony** N (*Film, Theat, TV*) Preisverleihung *f*; **award-winning** ADJ preisgekrönt

aware [əˈwɛəʳ] ADJ ESP PRED bewusst; **to be/become ~ of sb/sth** sich (*dat*) jds/einer Sache bewusst sein/werden; **I was not ~ (of the fact) that ...** es war mir nicht bewusst, dass ...; **not that I am ~ (of)** nicht dass ich wüsste; **as far as I am ~** so viel ich weiß; **to make sb ~ of sth** jdm etw bewusst machen

awareness [əˈwɛənɪs] N Bewusstsein *nt*; **he showed no ~ of the urgency of the problem** er schien sich der Dringlichkeit des Problems nicht bewusst zu sein

awash [əˈwɒʃ] ADJ PRED überspült; *cellar* unter Wasser; **to be ~ with blood/money** im Blut/Geld schwimmen

away [əˈweɪ] **1** ADV (**a**) weg; **three miles ~ (from here)** drei Meilen von hier; **lunch seemed a long time ~** es schien noch lange bis zum Mittagessen zu sein; **but he was ~ before I could say a word** aber er war fort *or* weg, bevor ich den Mund auftun konnte; **to look ~** wegsehen; **~ we go!** los (gehts)!; **they're ~!** (*horses, runners etc*) sie sind gestartet; **to put/give ~** weglegen/weggeben; **to gamble/die ~** verspielen/verhallen (**b**) (= *absent*) fort, weg; **he's ~ in London** er ist in London (**c**) (*Sport*) **to play ~** auswärts spielen; **they're ~ to Arsenal** sie haben ein Auswärtsspiel bei Arsenal (**d**) (= *continuously*) **to work/knit** *etc* **~** vor sich (*acc*) hin arbeiten/stricken *etc* (**e**) (= *forthwith*) **ask ~!** frag nur!; **right** *or* **straight ~** sofort (**f**) (*inf*) **he's ~ again** (*giggling, drunk etc*) es geht wieder los; **~ with you!** ach wo! **2** ADJ ATTR (*Sport*) Auswärts-; **~ match** Auswärtsspiel *nt*; **~ team** Gastmannschaft *f*

AWB ABBR *of* **air waybill**

awe [ɔː] **1** N Ehrfurcht *f*; **to be** *or* **stand in ~ of sb** Ehrfurcht vor jdm haben **2** VT Ehrfurcht einflößen (+*dat*)

awe-inspiring [ˈɔːɪnˌspaɪərɪŋ] ADJ Ehrfurcht gebietend

awesome [ˈɔːsəm] ADJ (= *frightening*) beängstigend; (= *impressive*) beeindruckend; (*esp US inf*: = *excellent*) irre (*inf*)

awe-stricken [ˈɔːˌstrɪkən], **awe-struck** [ˈɔːˌstrʌk] ADJ von Ehrfurcht ergriffen

awful [ˈɔːfəl] ADJ (*inf*) schrecklich; **you are ~!** du bist wirklich schrecklich!; **an ~ lot of money** furchtbar viel Geld

awfully [ˈɔːflɪ] ADV (*inf*) schrecklich (*inf*); **thanks ~** (*Brit*) vielen, vielen Dank!

awfulness [ˈɔːfʊlnɪs] N (*of situation*) Schrecklichkeit *f*

awhile [əˈwaɪl] ADV (*liter*) eine Weile

awkward [ˈɔːkwəd] ADJ (**a**) (= *difficult*) schwierig; *time, angle, shape* ungünstig; **to make things ~ for sb** jdm Schwierigkeiten machen; **~ customer** übler Bursche (*inf*) (**b**) (= *embarrassing*) peinlich (**c**) (= *embarrassed*) verlegen; *silence* betreten; **I feel ~ about doing that** es ist mir unangenehm, das zu tun; **to feel ~ in sb's company** sich in jds Gesellschaft (*dat*) nicht wohl fühlen (**d**) (= *clumsy*) unbeholfen

awkwardly [ˈɔːkwədlɪ] ADV (**a**) (= *clumsily*) ungeschickt, unbeholfen; *lie* unbequem (**b**) (= *embarrassingly*) peinlich (**c**) (= *embarrassedly*) verlegen

awkwardness [ˈɔːkwədnɪs] N (**a**) (= *difficulty*) Schwierigkeit *f*; (*of time, angle, shape*) Ungünstigkeit *f* (**b**) (= *discomfort*) Peinlichkeit *f* (**c**) (= *embarrassment*) Verlegenheit *f* (**d**) (= *clumsiness*) Unbeholfenheit *f*

awning [ˈɔːnɪŋ] N (*on window, of shop*) Markise *f*; (= *caravan ~*) Vordach *nt*

awoke [əˈwəʊk] PRET *of* **awake**

awoken [əˈwəʊkən] PTP *of* **awake**

AWOL [ˈeɪwɒl] (*Mil*) ABBR *of* **absent without leave**

awry [əˈraɪ] ADJ PRED, ADV **to go ~** schief gehen

axe, (*US*) **ax** [æks] **1** N Axt *f*, Beil *nt*; **to get** *or* **be given the ~** (*employee*) abgesägt werden; (*project*) eingestellt werden; **to have an/no ~ to grind** (*fig*) ein/kein persönliches Interesse haben **2** VT streichen; *person* entlassen

axiom [ˈæksɪəm] N Axiom *nt*

axiomatic [ˌæksɪəʊˈmætɪk] ADJ axiomatisch

axis [ˈæksɪs] N, *pl* **axes** [ˈæksiːz] Achse *f*

axle [ˈæksl] N Achse *f*

ayatollah [ˌaɪəˈtɒlə] N Ajatollah *m*

aye [aɪ] **1** INTERJ (*esp Scot, dial*) ja; **~, ~, Sir** (*Naut*) jawohl, Herr Admiral *etc* **2** N (*esp Parl*) **the ~s have it** die Mehrheit ist dafür

azalea [əˈzeɪlɪə] N Azalee *f*

Azerbaijani [ˌæzəbaɪˈdʒɑːnɪ] **1** ADJ aserbaidschanisch **2** N Aserbaidschaner(in) *m(f)*

Azores [əˈzɔːz] PL Azoren *pl*

Aztec [ˈæztek] **1** N Azteke *m*, Aztekin *f* **2** ADJ aztekisch

azure [ˈæʒəʳ] ADJ azurblau; **~ blue** azurblau

Bb

B, b [biː] N B *nt*, b *nt*; (*Sch: as a mark*) zwei, gut; (*Mus*) H *nt*, h *nt*; **B flat** B *nt*, b *nt*; **B sharp** His *nt*, his *nt*

b ABBR *of* **born** geb.

BA ABBR *of* **Bachelor of Arts**

baa [baː] VI mäh machen (*baby-talk*)

babble ['bæbl] **1** N Gemurmel *nt*; (*of baby, excited person etc*) Geplapper *nt*; **~ (of voices)** Stimmengewirr *nt* **2** VI (*person, baby*) plappern (inf)

babe [beɪb] N **(a)** (*esp US inf*) Baby *nt* (inf); **hey Mike ~!** he du, Mike!; *see also* **baby (b)** (*inf: = girl*) Tussi *f* (sl), Braut *f* (sl)

baboon [bə'buːn] N Pavian *m*

baby ['beɪbɪ] **1** N **(a)** Baby *nt*; (*esp in weeks after birth*) Säugling *m*; (*of animal*) Junge(s) *nt*; **to have a ~** ein Baby bekommen; **I've known him since he was a ~** ich kenne ihn von klein auf; **don't be such a ~!** stell dich nicht so an! (inf); **to be left holding the ~** (*Brit inf*) der Dumme sein (inf); **to throw out the ~ with the bathwater** das Kind mit dem Bade ausschütten **(b)** (*= small object of its type*) Pikkolo *m* (hum) **(c)** (*inf: = thing for which one is responsible*) **that's a costing problem, that's Harrison's** ~ das ist eine Kostenfrage, das ist Harrisons Problem **(d)** (*inf: = girlfriend, boyfriend*) Schatz *m* **(e)** (*esp US inf*) (*as address*) Schätzchen *nt* (inf); (*man to man*) mein Freund; **Mike ~, listen** du, Mike, hör mal her! **2** VT (inf) wie einen Säugling behandeln

baby: baby-battering N Kindesmisshandlung *f*; **baby blue** N Himmelblau *nt*; **baby-blue** ADJ himmelblau; **baby boom** N Babyboom *m*; **Baby-bouncer®** N Babywippe *f*; **baby boy** N kleiner Junge; (*= son*) Sohn *m*; **baby brother** N kleiner Bruder; **baby buggy®** N (*Brit*) Sportwagen *m*; **baby carriage** N (*US*) Kinderwagen *m*; **baby clothes** PL Babywäsche *f*; **baby-faced** ADJ milchgesichtig; **baby fat** N (*US*) Babyspeck *m* (inf); **baby food** N Babynahrung *f*; **baby girl** N kleines Mädchen; (*= daughter*) Töchterchen *nt*; **baby grand (piano)** N Stutzflügel *m*

babyish ['beɪbɪɪʃ] ADJ kindisch

Babylon ['bæbɪlən] N Babylon *nt*

baby: baby-minder N Kinderpfleger(in) *m(f)*; **baby seat** N (*in car*) Baby(sicherheits)sitz *m*; **baby sister** N kleine Schwester; **baby-sit** *pret, ptp* **baby-sat** VI babysitten; **she ~s for them** sie geht bei ihnen babysitten; **baby-sitter** N Babysitter(in) *m(f)*; **baby-sitting** N Babysitting *nt*; **baby-snatching** N Kindesentführung *f*; **baby stroller** N (*US*) Sportwagen *m*; **baby tooth** N Milchzahn *m*; **baby-walker** N Laufstuhl *m*

baccy ['bækɪ] N (inf) Tabak *m*

bachelor ['bætʃələʳ] N **(a)** Junggeselle *m* **(b)** (*Univ*) **Bachelor of Arts/Science** ≈ Magister *m* (der philosophischen/ naturwissenschaftlichen Fakultät)

bachelor flat N Junggesellenwohnung *f*

bacilli [bə'sɪləs] N, *pl* **bacilli** [bə'sɪlaɪ] Bazillus *m*

back [bæk] **1** N **(a)** (*of person, animal, book*) Rücken *m*; (*of chair*) (Rücken)lehne *f*; **to break one's ~** (*lit*) sich (*dat*) das Rückgrat brechen; (*fig*) sich abrackern; **behind sb's ~** (*fig*) hinter jds Rücken (*dat*); **to put** *or* **get sb's ~ up** (*fig*) sich bei etw anstrengen; **to put** *or* **get sb's ~ up** jdn gegen sich aufbringen; **to turn one's ~ on sb** (*lit*) jdm den Rücken zuwenden; (*fig*) sich von jdm abwenden; **get off my ~!** (inf) lass mich endlich in Ruhe!; **he's got the boss on his ~ all the time** er hat dauernd seinen Chef auf dem Hals; **to have one's ~ to the wall** (*fig*) in die Enge getrieben sein/werden; **I was pleased to see the ~ of them** (inf) ich war froh, sie endlich los zu sein (inf) **(b)** (*as opposed to front*) Rückseite *f*; (*of hand, dress*) Rücken *m*; (*of material*) linke Seite; **I know London like the ~ of my hand** ich kenne London wie meine Westentasche; **at the ~ of the book/cupboard** hinten im Buch/Schrank; **he drove into the ~ of me** er ist mir hinten reingefahren (inf); **at/on the ~ of the bus** hinten im/am Bus; **in the ~ (of a car)** hinten (im Auto); **there's one other worry at the ~ of my mind** da ist noch etwas, das mich beschäftigt; **right at the ~ of the cupboard** ganz hinten im Schrank; **at the ~ of beyond** am Ende der Welt; **in ~** (*US*) hinten

(c) (*Ftbl*) Verteidiger(in) *m(f)*; (*Rugby*) Hinterspieler(in) *m(f)* **2** ADJ Hinter-; **rent** ausstehend **3** ADV **(a)** zurück; **(stand) ~!** zurück(treten)!; **~ and forth** hin und her; **to pay sth ~** etw zurückzahlen; **to come ~** zurückkommen; **there and ~** hin und zurück

(b) (*= again*) wieder; **I'll never go ~** da gehe ich nie wieder hin; **~ in London** zurück in London

(c) (*= ago*) **a week ~** vor einer Woche; **as far ~ as the 18th century** (*= dating ~*) bis ins 18. Jahrhundert zurück; (*point in time*) schon im 18. Jahrhundert; **~ in March, 1997** im März 1997

4 PREP (*US*) **~ of** hinter **5** VT **(a)** (*= support*) unterstützen; **if the bank won't ~ us** wenn die Bank nicht mitmacht; **to ~ a bill** (*Fin*) einen Wechsel indossieren

(b) (*Betting*) setzen *or* wetten auf (+*acc*)

(c) (*= cause to move*) *car* zurückfahren *or* -setzen; **he ~ed his car into the tree/garage** er fuhr rückwärts gegen den Baum/ in die Garage

(d) (*Mus*) *singer* begleiten

(e) (*= put sth behind*) *picture* mit einem Rücken versehen **6** VI (*= move backwards: car, train*) zurücksetzen; **she ~ed into me** sie fuhr rückwärts in mein Auto

▶ **back away** VI zurückweichen (*from* vor +*dat*)

▶ **back down** VI (*fig*) nachgeben

▶ **back off** VI (*= step back*) zurückweichen; (*crowd*) zurücktreten; (*= stop harassing*) sich zurückhalten; **back off!** verschwinde!

▶ **back on to** VI +PREP OBJ hinten angrenzen an (+*acc*)

▶ **back out** VI **(a)** (*car etc*) rückwärts herausfahren **(b)** (*fig: of deal etc*) aussteigen (*of, from* aus) (inf)

▶ **back up** VI **1** **(a)** (*car etc*) zurücksetzen **(b)** (*traffic*) sich stauen; (*US: drain*) verstopfen **(c)** (*Comput*) sichern **2** VT SEP **(a)** (*= support*) unterstützen; (*= confirm*) *story* bestätigen; *claim, theory* untermauern; **he can back me up in this** er kann das bestätigen **(b)** *car etc* zurückfahren **(c)** (*Comput*) sichern

back: backache N Rückenschmerzen *pl*; **back alley** N Gasse *f*; **back bench** N (*esp Brit*) **the ~es** das Plenum; **backbench** ADJ (*Parl: Brit, Austral*) auf den hinteren Reihen des Parlaments; **~ MP** Abgeordnete(r) *mf* ohne Partei- und Regierungsamt; **backbencher** N (*esp Brit*) Abgeordnete(r) *mf* (auf den hinteren Reihen im britischen Parlament)

BACKBENCHER

*Alle britischen Unterhausabgeordneten, die weder in der Regierung noch im Schattenkabinett der Opposition sind, werden als **backbenchers** bezeichnet, da sie nicht in den vorderen Rängen, den **front benches**, des Unterhauses neben dem Premierminister bzw. dem Oppositionsführer sitzen. Da sie kein offizielles Amt innehaben, ist es für die **backbenchers** oft einfacher, sich entgegen der offiziellen Parteilinie zu äußern oder gegen sie zu stimmen. Mit the **back benches** werden generell alle Abgeordneten beider Seiten im Unterhaus bezeichnet, die keine wichtige Stellung innehaben.*

---

back: backbiting N Lästern *nt*; **backbone** N (*lit, fig*) Rückgrat *nt*; **backbreaking** ['bækbreɪkɪŋ] ADJ erschöpfend; **back burner** N (*lit*) hintere Kochplatte; **to put sth on the ~** (*fig inf*) etw zurückstellen; **back catalogue** N (*Mus*) ältere Aufnahmen *pl*, Back-Katalog *m*; **backchat** N, NO PL (inf) Widerrede *f*; **back copy** N alte Ausgabe; **back country, backcountry** (*US*) **1** N **the ~** das Hinterland **2** ADJ *road* Land-; **back cover** N Rückseite *f*; **backdate** VT (zu)rückdatieren; **salary increase ~d to May** Gehaltserhöhung rückwirkend ab Mai; **back door** N (*lit*) Hintertür *f*; **by the ~** (*fig*) durch die Hintertür; **backdrop** N Hintergrund *m*

-backed [-bækt] ADJ SUF **low/high/straight-backed** *chair* mit niedriger/hoher/gerader Rückenlehne; **a low-backed dress** ein Kleid mit tiefem Rückenausschnitt

back end N (*= rear*) hinteres Ende; **at the ~ of the year** gegen Ende des Jahres

backer ['bækəʳ] N **(a)** (*= supporter*) **his ~s** (diejenigen,) die ihn unterstützen **(b)** (*Betting*) Wettende(r) *mf* **(c)** (*Comm*) Geldgeber(in) *m(f)*

back: **backfile** N alte Akte; **backfire 1** N (*US*) Gegenfeuer *nt* **2** VI **(a)** (*Aut*) Fehlzündungen haben **(b)** (*inf*: *plan etc*) ins Auge gehen (*inf*); **it ~d on us** der Schuss ging nach hinten los (*inf*); **backgammon** N Backgammon *nt*; **back garden** N Garten *m* (hinterm Haus)

background [ˈbækɡraʊnd] **1** N **(a)** (*of painting etc, fig*) Hintergrund *m*; **to stay in the ~** im Hintergrund bleiben, sich im Hintergrund halten **(b)** (*of person*) (*educational etc*) Werdegang *m*; (*social*) Verhältnisse *pl*; (= *family ~*) Herkunft *f no pl*; **children from all ~s** Kinder aus allen Schichten **(c)** (*of case, problem etc*) Hintergründe *pl* **2** ADJ Hintergrund-; *reading* vertiefend; **~ music** Hintergrundmusik *f*, Musikuntermalung *f*; **~ information** Hintergrundinformationen *pl*

background program N (*Comput*) Hintergrundprogramm *nt*

back: **backhand 1** N (*Sport*) Rückhand *f no pl*; (*one stroke*) Rückhandschlag *m* **2** ADJ **~ stroke** Rückhandschlag *m* **3** ADV mit der Rückhand; **backhanded** ADJ *compliment* zweifelhaft; **backhander** N **(a)** (*Sport*) Rückhandschlag *m* **(b)** (*inf*: = *bribe*) Schmiergeld *nt*; **to give sb a ~** jdn schmieren (*inf*)

backing [ˈbækɪŋ] N **(a)** (= *support*) Unterstützung *f* **(b)** (*Mus*) Begleitung *f*; **~ group** Begleitband *f*; **~ singer** Begleitsänger(in) *m(f)*; **~ vocals** Begleitung *f* **(c)** (*for strengthening*) Rücken *m*

back: **backlash** N (*fig*) Gegenreaktion *f*; **backless** ADJ *dress* rückenfrei; **backlog** N Rückstände *pl*; **I have a ~ of work** ich bin mit der Arbeit im Rückstand; **back marker** N (*Sport*) Schlusslicht *nt*; **the ~s** die Nachhut; **back number** N (*of paper*) alte Ausgabe; **backpack** N Rucksack *m*; **backpacker** N Wanderer *m*, Wanderin *f*; (= *hitch-hiker*) Rucksacktourist(in) *m(f)*; **backpacking** N Wandern *nt*; (= *hitch-hiking*) Trampen *nt*; **to go ~** auf (Berg)tour gehen; trampen; **back pay** N Nachzahlung *f*; **back-pedal** VI (*lit*) rückwärts treten; (*fig inf*) einen Rückzieher machen (*inf*) (*on* bei); **back pocket** N Gesäßtasche *f*; **back rest** N Rückenstütze *f*; **back road** N kleine Landstraße; **backscratching** N, NO PL gegenseitige Begünstigung; **back seat** N Rücksitz *m*; **to take a ~** (*fig*) sich zurückhalten; **back-seat driver** N **she is a terrible ~** sie redet beim Fahren immer rein; **backside** N (*Brit inf*) Hintern *m* (*inf*), **backslash** N (*Comput*) Backslash *m*; **backslide** VI (*fig*) rückfällig werden; **backspace** VTI (*Typing*) zurücksetzen; **backspace key** N Rücktaste *f*; **backstage** ADV, ADJ hinter den Kulissen; **backstreet** N Seitensträßchen *nt*; **backstreet abortion** N illegale Abtreibung; **backstreet abortionist** N Engelmacher(in) *m(f)* (*inf*); **backstroke** N (*Swimming*) Rückenschwimmen *nt*; **can you do the ~?** können Sie rückenschwimmen?; **back to back** ADV Rücken an Rücken; (*things*) mit den Rückseiten aneinander; **back-to-back** ADJ direkt aufeinander folgend *attr*; **back to front** ADV verkehrt herum; *read* von hinten nach vorne; **back tooth** N Backenzahn *m*; **backtrack** VI (*over ground*) denselben Weg zurückgehen; (*on policy etc*) einen Rückzieher machen (*on sth* bei etw); **backup 1** N **(a)** Unterstützung *f* **(b)** (*Comput*) Sicherungskopie *f*, Backup *nt* **2** ADJ **(a)** *services* zur Unterstützung; **~ troops** Unterstützungstruppen *pl*; **~ plan** Ausweichplan *m* **(b)** (*Comput*) **~ copy** Sicherungs- *or* Backupkopie *f*; **back-up light** N (*US Aut*) Rückfahrscheinwerfer *m*

backward [ˈbækwəd] **1** ADJ **(a)** **a ~ glance** ein Blick zurück; **a ~ step** (*fig*) ein Schritt *m* zurück **(b)** (*fig*) *economy, region* rückständig; (*pej*: = *retarded*) *child* zurückgeblieben **2** ADV **backwards**

backwardness [ˈbækwədnɪs] N (*mental*) Zurückgebliebenheit *f*; (*of region*) Rückständigkeit *f*

backwards [ˈbækwədz] ADV **(a)** rückwärts; **to fall ~** nach hinten fallen; **to walk ~ and forwards** hin und her gehen; **to lean** *or* **bend over ~ to do sth** (*inf*) sich (*dat*) ein Bein ausreißen, um etw zu tun (*inf*); **I know it ~** (*Brit*) *or* **~ and forwards** (*US*) das kenne ich in- und auswendig **(b)** (= *towards the past*) zurück

backwards-compatible [ˌbækwədzkəmˈpætɪbl] ADJ (*Comput, Hi-Fi etc*) abwärtskompatibel

back: **backwater** N (*fig*) rückständiges Nest; **this town is a cultural ~** kulturell ist diese Stadt tiefste Provinz; **backwoods** PL unterschlossene (Wald)gebiete *pl*; **backwoodsman** N Waldsiedler *m*; (*fig inf*) Hinterwäldler *m*; **back yard** N Hinterhof *m*; **in one's own ~** (*fig*) vor der eigenen Haustür

bacon [ˈbeɪkən] N durchwachsener Speck; **~ and eggs** Eier mit Speck; **to save sb's ~** (*inf*) jds Rettung sein; **to bring home the ~** (*inf*: = *earn a living*) die Brötchen verdienen (*inf*)

bacteria [bækˈtɪərɪə] PL *of* **bacterium**

bacterial [bækˈtɪərɪəl] ADJ bakteriell

bacteriological [bækˌtɪərɪəˈlɒdʒɪkəl] ADJ bakteriologisch

bacteriologist [bækˌtɪərɪˈɒlədʒɪst] N Bakteriologe *m*, Bakteriologin *f*

bacterium [bækˈtɪərɪəm] N, *pl* **bacteria** [bækˈtɪərɪə] Bakterie *f*

bad¹ [bæd] **1** ADJ, *comp* **worse**, *superl* **worst** **(a)** schlecht; *smell* übel; *risk* hoch; *word* unanständig; (= *immoral, wicked*) böse; (= *naughty, misbehaved*) unartig, ungezogen; **it was a ~ thing to do** das hättest du/hätte er *etc* nicht tun sollen; **he went through a ~ time** er hat eine schlimme Zeit durchgemacht; **I've had a really ~ day** ich hatte einen furchtbaren Tag; **it's a ~ business** das ist eine üble Sache; **to go ~** schlecht werden; **he's gone ~** (*US*) er ist auf die schiefe Bahn geraten; **he's ~ at French** er ist schlecht in Französisch; **that's not a ~ idea!** das ist keine schlechte Idee!; **too ~ you couldn't make it** (es ist) wirklich schade, dass Sie nicht kommen konnten; **to have a ~ hair day** (*inf*) Probleme mit der Frisur haben; (*fig*) total durch den Wind sein (*inf*); **to be in ~ with sb** (*US*) bei jdm schlecht angeschrieben sein **(b)** (= *serious*) *wound, sprain* schlimm; *accident, mistake, cold* schwer; *headache* stark; **he's got it ~** (*inf*) ihn hats schwer erwischt (*inf*) **(c)** (= *unfavourable*) *time* ungünstig **(d)** (= *in poor health*) *stomach* krank; *leg, knee, hand* schlimm; **he/the economy is in a ~ way** (*Brit*) es geht ihm schlecht/es steht schlecht um die *or* mit der Wirtschaft; **I feel ~** mir geht es nicht gut, mir ist nicht gut; **how is he? – he's not so ~** wie geht es ihm? – nicht schlecht **(e)** (= *regretful*) **I feel really ~ about not having told him** es tut mir wirklich Leid, dass ich ihm das nicht gesagt habe; **don't feel ~ about it** machen Sie sich (*dat*) keine Gedanken (darüber) **(f)** *debt* uneinbringlich **2** N, NO PL **(a)** **to take the good with the ~** (auch) die schlechten Seiten in Kauf nehmen **(b)** **he's gone to the ~** (*Brit*) er ist auf die schiefe Bahn geraten

bad² PRET *of* **bid**

bad: **bad-ass** [ˈbædæs] (*US sl*) **1** N knallharter Typ (*inf*) **2** ADJ knallhart (*inf*); **bad blood** N böses Blut; **there is ~ between them** sie haben ein gestörtes Verhältnis; **bad cheque**, (*US*) **bad check** N (*not covered by funds*) ungedeckter Scheck

baddie [ˈbædɪ] N (*inf*) Bösewicht *m*

bade [beɪd] PRET *of* **bid**

badge [bædʒ] N **(a)** Abzeichen *nt*; (*made of metal*) Button *m*; (*on car etc*) Plakette *f*; (= *sticker*) Aufkleber *m* **(b)** (*fig*: = *symbol*) Merkmal *nt*

badger [ˈbædʒə] **1** N Dachs *m* **2** VT zusetzen (+*dat*), bearbeiten (*inf*); **to ~ sb for sth** jdm mit etw in den Ohren liegen

badly [ˈbædlɪ] ADV **(a)** schlecht; **to do ~** (*in election, exam etc*) schlecht abschneiden; (*Fin*) schlecht stehen; (*Comm*) schlecht gehen; **to go ~** schlecht laufen; **to be ~ off** schlecht dran sein; **to reflect ~ on sb** ein schlechtes Licht auf jdn werfen; **to think ~ of sb** schlecht von jdm denken **(b)** *wounded, mistaken* schwer; **~ beaten** *person* schwer verprügelt **(c)** (= *very much*) sehr; *in debt* hoch; **to want sth ~** etw unbedingt wollen; **I need it ~** ich brauche es dringend

bad-mannered [ˌbædˈmænəd] ADJ unhöflich

badminton [ˈbædmɪntən] N Federball *nt*; (*on court*) Badminton *nt*

bad-mouth [ˈbædmaʊθ] VT (*inf*) herziehen über (+*acc*) (*inf*)

bad-tempered [ˌbædˈtempəd] ADJ schlecht gelaunt; **to be ~** schlechte Laune haben; (*as characteristic*) ein übellauniger Mensch sein

baffle [ˈbæfl] VT (= *confound, amaze*) verblüffen; (= *cause incomprehension*) vor ein Rätsel stellen; **it really ~s me how ...** es ist mir wirklich ein Rätsel, wie ...

baffling [ˈbæflɪŋ] ADJ *case* rätselhaft; *mystery* unergründlich; **I find it ~** es ist mir ein Rätsel

bag [bæɡ] **1** N **(a)** Tasche *f*; (*with drawstrings, pouch*) Beutel *m*; (*for school*) Schultasche *f*; (*made of paper, plastic*) Tüte *f*;

(= *sack*) Sack *m*; (= *suitcase*) Reisetasche *f*; **~s** (Reise)gepäck *nt*; **to pack one's ~s** seine Sachen packen; **to be left holding the ~** (*US inf*) die Sache ausbaden müssen (*inf*)
(b) it's in the ~ (*fig inf*) das ist gelaufen (*inf*)
(c) ~s under the eyes (*black*) Ringe *pl* unter den Augen; (*of skin*) Tränensäcke *pl*
(d) (*inf*: = *a lot*) **~s of** jede Menge (*inf*)
(e) (*pej inf*: = *woman*) (**old**) **~** Schachtel *f* (*pej inf*); **ugly old ~** Schreckschraube *f* (*inf*)
2 VT in Tüten/Säcke verpacken

bagel ['beɪgəl] N Bagel *m*, *kleines, rundes Brötchen*

bagful ['bægfʊl] N **a ~ of groceries** eine Tasche voll Lebensmittel

baggage ['bægɪdʒ] N (= *luggage*) (Reise)gepäck *nt*

baggage (*esp US*): **baggage allowance** N Freigepäck *nt*; **baggage car** N Gepäckwagen *m*; **baggage check** N Gepäckkontrolle *f*; **baggage claim** N Gepäckausgabe *f*; **baggage handler** N Gepäckmann *m*; **baggage locker** N Gepäckschließfach *nt*; **baggage reclaim** N Gepäckausgabe *f*

baggy ['bægɪ] ADJ (+ER) (= *ill-fitting*) zu weit; *dress* sackartig; (= *out of shape*) *trousers* ausgebeult; *jumper* ausgeleiert

bag lady N Stadtstreicherin *f* (*die ihre gesamte Habe in Einkaufstaschen mit sich führt*)

bagpipe(s) ['bægpaɪp(s)] N(PL) Dudelsack *m*

bags [bægz] PL *see* **bag**

bag-snatcher ['bæg,snætʃəʳ] N Handtaschendieb(in) *m(f)*

baguette [bæ'get] N Baguette *f or nt*

Bahamas [bə'hɑːməz] PL **the ~** die Bahamas *pl*

Bahrain, Bahrein [bɑːreɪn] N Bahrain *nt*

bail[1] [beɪl] N (*Jur*) Kaution *f*; **to stand** *or* **put up ~ for sb** für jdn (die) Kaution stellen
► **bail out** VT SEP **(a)** (*fig*) aus der Patsche helfen (+*dat*) (*inf*)
(b) *boat* = **bale out**

bail[2] VI = **bale**[2]

bail (*US Jur*): **bail bond** N (= *document*) Verpflichtungserklärung *f*; (= *money*) Kaution *f*; **bail bondsman** N Kautionsbürge *m*

bailee [beɪ'liː] N Pfandgläubiger(in) *m(f)*

bailiff ['beɪlɪf] N (*Jur*) (*Brit: also* **sheriff's ~**) Amtsdiener(in) *m(f)*; (*Brit: for property*) Gerichtsvollzieher(in) *m(f)*; (*US: in court*) Gerichtsdiener(in) *m(f)*

bait [beɪt] **1** N (*lit, fig*) Köder *m*; **to take** *or* **swallow the ~, to rise to the ~** (*lit, fig*) anbeißen; (*fig*: = *be trapped*) sich ködern lassen **2** VT **(a)** *hook, trap* mit einem Köder versehen **(b)** (= *torment*) *animal* (mit Hunden) hetzen; *person* quälen

baize [beɪz] N Fries *m*, Flaus *m*; **green ~** Billardtuch *nt*

bake [beɪk] **1** VT **(a)** (*Cook*) backen; **~d apples** *pl* Bratäpfel *pl*; **~d potatoes** *pl* in der Schale gebackene Kartoffeln *pl* **(b)** *clay* brennen; (*sun*) *earth* ausdörren **2** VI (*Cook*) backen; (*cake*) im (Back)ofen sein

baker ['beɪkəʳ] N Bäcker(in) *m(f)*; **~'s (shop)** Bäckerei *f*, Bäckerladen *m*

baker's dozen ['beɪkəz'dʌzn] N 13 (Stück)

bakery ['beɪkərɪ] N Bäckerei *f*

baking ['beɪkɪŋ] **1** N (*act*) (*Cook*) Backen *nt*; (*of earthenware*) Brennen *nt* **2** ADJ (*inf*: = *stifling*) **I'm ~** ich komme um vor Hitze; **it's ~ (hot) today** es ist eine Affenhitze heute (*inf*)

baking: **baking dish** N Backform *f*; **baking mitt** N (*US*) Topfhandschuh *m*; **baking pan** N (*US*) Backblech *nt*; **baking powder** N Backpulver *nt*; **baking sheet** N Backblech *nt*; **baking soda** N ≈ Backpulver *nt*; **baking tin** N (*Brit*) Backform *f*; **baking tray** N (*Brit*) Kuchenblech *nt*

Balaclava [,bælə'klɑːvə] N Kapuzenmütze *f*

balance ['bæləns] **1** N **(a)** (= *apparatus*) Waage *f*; **to be** *or* **hang in the ~** (*fig*) in der Schwebe sein
(b) (= *counterpoise*) Gegengewicht *nt* (*to* zu); (*fig*) Ausgleich *m* (*to* für)
(c) (*lit, fig*: = *equilibrium*) Gleichgewicht *nt*; **to keep/lose one's ~** das Gleichgewicht (be)halten/verlieren; **to throw sb off (his) ~** jdn aus dem Gleichgewicht bringen; **the right ~ of personalities in the team** eine ausgewogene Mischung verschiedener Charaktere in der Mannschaft; **the ~ of power** das Gleichgewicht der Kräfte; **on ~** (*fig*) alles in allem
(d) (*Comm, Fin*: = *state of account*) Saldo *m*; (*with bank*) Kontostand *m*, Saldo *m*; (*of company*) Bilanz *f*; **~ in hand**

(*Comm*) Kassen(be)stand *m*; **~ carried forward** Saldoübertrag *m*; **~ due** (*Fin*) Debetsaldo *m*, Soll *nt*; (*Comm*) Rechnungsbetrag *m*; **~ in your favour** (*Brit*) *or* **favor** (*US*) Saldoguthaben *nt*; **~ of current account** (*Comm*) Leistungsbilanz *f*; **~ of capital movements** Kapitalverkehrsbilanz *f*; **~ of payments/trade** Zahlungs-/Handelsbilanz *f*; **~ of trade surplus/deficit** Handelsbilanzüberschuss *m*/-defizit *nt*; **~ of invisible trade** Dienstleistungsbilanz *f*
(e) (= *remainder*) Rest *m*; **to pay off the ~** den Rest bezahlen; **my father has promised to make up the ~** mein Vater hat versprochen, die Differenz zu (be)zahlen
2 VT **(a)** (= *keep level, in equilibrium*) im Gleichgewicht halten; (= *bring into equilibrium*) ins Gleichgewicht bringen; **the seal ~s a ball on its nose** der Seehund balanciert einen Ball auf der Nase
(b) (*in the mind*) *needs* abwägen (*against* gegen); **to ~ sth against sth** etw einer Sache (*dat*) gegenüberstellen
(c) (= *equal, make up for*) ausgleichen
(d) (*Comm, Fin*) *account* (= *add up*) saldieren, abschließen; (= *make equal*) ausgleichen; (= *pay off*) begleichen; *budget* ausgleichen; **~d budget** ausgeglichener Haushalt; **to ~ the books** die Bilanz ziehen *or* machen
3 VI **(a)** (= *be in equilibrium*) Gleichgewicht halten; (*scales*) sich ausbalancieren; **he ~d on one foot** er balancierte auf einem Bein
(b) (*Comm, Fin: accounts*) ausgeglichen sein; **the books don't ~** die Abrechnung stimmt nicht; **to make the books ~** die Abrechnung ausgleichen
► **balance out** **1** VT SEP ausgleichen; **they balance each other out** sie halten sich die Waage; (*personalities*) sie gleichen sich aus **2** VI sich ausgleichen

balanced ['bælənst] ADJ ausgewogen; **~ budget** ausgeglichener Haushalt

balance sheet N (*Fin*) Bilanz *f*; (= *document*) Bilanzaufstellung *f*

balancing act ['bælənsɪŋækt] N (*lit, fig*) Balanceakt *m*

balcony ['bælkənɪ] N **(a)** Balkon *m* **(b)** (*Theat*) oberster Rang

bald [bɔːld] ADJ (+ER) **(a)** kahl; *bird* federlos; **he is ~** er hat eine Glatze; **to go ~** eine Glatze bekommen, kahl werden; **~ patch** kahle Stelle **(b)** (*Aut*: = *worn*) *tyre* abgefahren **(c)** *style, statement* knapp

---

Be careful! **bald** *is not translated by the German word* **bald**.

---

bald: **bald eagle** N weißköpfiger Seeadler; **bald-faced** ADJ (*US*) *lie* unverfroren, unverschämt; **baldheaded** ADJ kahl- *or* glatzköpfig

balding ['bɔːldɪŋ] ADJ **he is ~** er bekommt langsam eine Glatze

baldly ['bɔːldlɪ] ADV (*fig*) (= *bluntly*) unverblümt; (= *roughly*) grob

baldness ['bɔːldnɪs] N **(a)** Kahlheit *f* **(b)** (*of style, statement*) Knappheit *f*

baldy ['bɔːldɪ] N (*inf*) Glatzkopf *m*

bale[1] [beɪl] N (*of hay etc*) Bündel *nt*; (*out of combine harvester, of cotton*) Ballen *m*; (*of paper etc*) Pack *m*

bale[2] VI (*Naut*) schöpfen
► **bale out** **1** VI **(a)** (*Aviat*) abspringen (*of* aus) **(b)** (*Naut*) schöpfen **2** VT SEP (*Naut*) *water* schöpfen; *ship* ausschöpfen

Balearic [,bælɪ'ærɪk] ADJ **the ~ Islands** die Balearen *pl*

baleful ['beɪlfʊl] ADJ (= *evil*) böse

balk, baulk [bɔːk] VI zurückschrecken (*at* vor +*dat*)

Balkan ['bɔːlkən] **1** ADJ Balkan- **2** N **the ~s** der Balkan

ball[1] [bɔːl] **1** N **(a)** Ball *m*; (= *sphere*) Kugel *f*; (*of wool, string*) Knäuel *m*; (*Billiards, Croquet*) Kugel *f*; (*US*: = *baseball*) Baseball *nt*; **to play ~** Ball/Baseball spielen; **the cat lay curled up in a ~** die Katze hatte sich zusammengerollt; **~ and chain** Fußfessel *f* (mit Gewicht)
(b) (= *delivery of a ~*) Ball *m*; (*Tennis, Golf*) Schlag *m*; (*Ftbl, Hockey*) Schuss *m*; (*Ftbl*: = *pass*) Pass *m*; (*Cricket*) Wurf *m*
(c) (*fig phrases*) **to keep the ~ rolling** das Gespräch in Gang halten; **to start** *or* **set** *or* **get the ~ rolling** den Stein ins Rollen bringen; **the ~ is in your court** Sie sind am Ball (*inf*); **to be on the ~** (*inf*) am Ball sein (*inf*); **to run with the ~** (*US inf*) die Sache mit Volldampf vorantreiben (*inf*)
(d) (*Anat*) **~ of the foot** Fußballen *m*
(e) (*sl*: = *testicle*) Ei *nt usu pl* (*sl*); (*pl*) Eier *pl* (*sl*); **~s!**

(= *nonsense*) red keinen Scheiß (*inf*); **~s** (*inf*: = *courage*) Schneid *m* (*inf*)
2 VTI (*dated US vulg*) ficken (*vulg*)

ball² N **(a)** (= *dance*) Ball *m* **(b)** (*inf*: = *good time*) **to have a ~** sich prima amüsieren (*inf*)

ballad ['bæləd] N (*Mus, Liter*) Ballade *f*

ball-and-socket joint [bɔːlən'sɒkɪtdʒɔɪnt] N Kugelgelenk *nt*

ballast ['bæləst] N (*Naut, Aviat, fig*) Ballast *m*

ball: ball bearing N Kugellager *nt*; (= *ball*) Kugellagerkugel *f*; **ball boy** N Balljunge *m*; **ball cock** N Schwimmerhahn *m*; **ball control** N Ballführung *f*

ballerina [bælə'riːnə] N Ballerina *f*; (*principal*) Primaballerina *f*

ballet ['bæleɪ] N Ballett *nt*

ballet: ballet dancer N Balletttänzer(in) *m(f)*; **ballet pump, ballet shoe** N Ballettschuh *m*; **ballet skirt** N Ballettröckchen *nt*

ball: ball game N Ballspiel *nt*; **it's a whole new/different ~** (*fig inf*) das ist eine ganz andere Chose (*inf*); **ball girl** N Ballmädchen *nt*

ballistic [bə'lɪstɪk] ADJ ballistisch; **to go ~** (*inf*) an die Decke gehen (*inf*)

ballistic missile N Raketengeschoss *nt*

ballistics [bə'lɪstɪks] N SING Ballistik *f*; **~ expert** Schusswaffenfachmann *m*

balloon [bə'luːn] N **(a)** (*Aviat*) (Frei)ballon *m*; (*toy*) (Luft)ballon *m*; (*Met*) (Wetter)ballon *m*; **the ~ went up** (*fig inf*) da ist die Bombe geplatzt (*inf*); **that went down like a lead ~** (*inf*) das kam überhaupt nicht an (*inf*) **(b)** (*in cartoons*) Sprechblase *f* **2** VI **(a)** **to go ~ing** auf Ballonfahrt gehen **(b)** (= *swell out*) sich blähen

ballot ['bælət] N **1** N **(a)** (= *method of voting*) (geheime) Abstimmung; (= *election*) Geheimwahl *f* **(b)** (= *vote*) Abstimmung *f*; (= *election*) Wahl *f*; **first/second ~** erster/zweiter Wahlgang; **to take** *or* **hold a ~** abstimmen **2** VI abstimmen; (= *elect*) eine (geheime) Wahl abhalten **3** VT *members* abstimmen lassen

ballot: ballot box N Wahlurne *f*; **ballot paper** N Stimmzettel *m*

ball: ballpark N **(a)** (*US*) Baseballstadion *nt* **(b)** **~ figure** Richtzahl *f*; **ballplayer** N (*US*) Baseballspieler(in) *m(f)*; **ballpoint (pen)** N Kugelschreiber *m*; **ballroom** N Ballsaal *m*; **ballroom dancing** N Gesellschaftstänze *pl*

balls-up ['bɔːlzʌp], (*esp US*) **ball up** N (*inf*) Durcheinander *nt*; **he made a complete ~ of the job** er hat bei der Arbeit totale Scheiße gebaut (*sl*)
➤ **balls up**, (*esp US*) **ball up** VT SEP (*inf*) verhunzen (*inf*)

ballyhoo [bælɪ'huː] (*inf*) N Tamtam *nt* (*inf*)

balm [bɑːm] N (*lit, fig*) Balsam *m*

balmy ['bɑːmɪ] ADJ (+ER) (= *mild*) sanft

baloney [bə'ləʊnɪ] N **(a)** (*inf*) Quatsch *m* (*inf*) **(b)** (*US*: = *sausage*) Mortadella *f*

balsa ['bɔːlsə] N (*also* **~ wood**) Balsa(holz) *nt*

Baltic ['bɔːltɪk] **1** ADJ Ostsee-; *language* (= *of ~ States*) baltisch; **the ~ States** die baltischen Staaten **2** N **the ~** die Ostsee

Baltic Sea N Ostsee *f*

balustrade [bælə'streɪd] N Balustrade *f*

bamboo [bæm'buː] **1** N Bambus *m* **2** ATTR Bambus-; **~ shoots** *pl* Bambussprossen *pl*

ban [bæn] **1** N Verbot *nt*; (*Comm*) Embargo *nt*; **to put a ~ on sth** etw verbieten; **a ~ on smoking** Rauchverbot *nt* **2** VT (= *prohibit*) verbieten; *footballer etc* sperren; **to ~ sb from doing sth** jdm verbieten, etw zu tun; **she was ~ned from driving** ihr wurde Fahrverbot erteilt

banal [bə'nɑːl] ADJ banal

banality [bə'nælɪtɪ] N Banalität *f*

banana [bə'nɑːnə] N Banane *f*

banana peel N Bananenschale *f*

bananas [bə'nɑːnəz] ADJ PRED (*inf*: = *crazy*) bescheuert (*inf*); **the whole place went ~** der ganze Saal drehte durch (*inf*)

banana: banana skin N Bananenschale *f*; **to slip on a ~** (*fig*) über eine Kleinigkeit stolpern; **banana split** N (*Cook*) Bananensplit *nt*

band¹ [bænd] N **(a)** (*of cloth, iron, also Rad*) Band *nt*; (*of leather*) Band *nt*, Riemen *m*; (= *waistband*) Bund *m*; (= *ring*) Ring *m*; (*on machine*) Riemen *m* **(b)** (= *stripe*) Streifen *m*

band² N **(a)** Schar *f*; (*of robbers etc*) Bande *f*; (*of workers*) Kolonne *f* **(b)** (*Mus*) Band *f*; (= *dance ~*) Tanzkapelle *f*; (*brass ~*) (Musik)kapelle *f*
➤ **band together** VI sich zusammenschließen

bandage ['bændɪdʒ] **1** N Verband *m*; (= *strip of cloth*) Binde *f* **2** VT (*also* **~ up**) *cut* verbinden; *broken limb* bandagieren

Band-Aid® ['bændeɪd] (*US*) **1** N Heftpflaster *nt* **2** ADJ (*also* **band-aid**) (*inf*: = *makeshift*) behelfsmäßig

bandan(n)a [bæn'dænə] N großes Schnupftuch; (*round neck*) Halstuch *nt*

B & B [biːən'biː] N ABBR *of* **bed and breakfast**

bandit ['bændɪt] N Bandit(in) *m(f)*

band: band leader N Bandleader(in) *m(f)*; **bandmaster** N Kapellmeister *m*

bandsman ['bændzmən] N, *pl* **-men** [-mən] Musiker *m*; **military ~** Mitglied *nt* eines Musikkorps

band: bandstand N Musikpavillon *m*; **bandwagon** N (*US*) (Fest)wagen *m* der Musikkapelle; **to jump** *or* **climb on the ~** (*also Brit*: *fig inf*) auf den fahrenden Zug aufspringen

bandy¹ ['bændɪ] ADJ **~ legs** O-Beine

bandy² VT *jokes* sich (*dat*) erzählen
➤ **bandy about** (*Brit*) *or* **around** VT SEP *sb's name* immer wieder nennen; *ideas* verbreiten; *figures, words, technical expressions* um sich werfen mit

bane [beɪn] N (= *cause of distress*) Fluch *m*; **he's/it's the ~ of my life** er/das ist noch mal mein Ende (*inf*)

bang¹ [bæŋ] **1** N **(a)** (= *noise*) Knall *m*; (*of sth falling*) Plumps *m*; **there was a ~ outside** draußen hat es geknallt **(b)** (= *violent blow*) Schlag *m*; **he gave himself a ~ on the shins** er hat sich (*dat*) die Schienbeine angeschlagen **2** ADV **(a)** **to go ~** knallen; (*balloon*) zerplatzen **(b)** (*inf*: = *exactly etc*) voll (*inf*), genau; **his answer was ~ on** seine Antwort war genau richtig; **she came ~ on time** sie war auf die Sekunde pünktlich; **~ up to date** brandaktuell (*inf*) **3** INTERJ peng; (*of hammer*) klopf; **~ goes my chance of promotion** (*inf*) und das wars dann mit der Beförderung (*inf*) **4** VT **(a)** (= *thump*) schlagen; **he ~ed his fist on the table** er schlug mit der Faust auf den Tisch **(b)** (= *shut noisily*) *door* zuschlagen **(c)** (= *hit*) *head, shin* sich (*dat*) anschlagen (*on an* +*dat*); **to ~ one's head** *etc* **on sth** sich (*dat*) den Kopf *etc* an etw (*dat*) anschlagen, mit dem Kopf *etc* gegen etw knallen (*inf*) **5** VI **(a)** (*door*: = *shut*) zuschlagen; (*fireworks, gun*) knallen **(b)** **to ~ on** *or* **at sth** gegen *or* an etw (*acc*) schlagen
➤ **bang about** (*Brit*) *or* **around 1** VI Krach machen **2** VT SEP Krach machen mit
➤ **bang down** VT SEP (hin)knallen (*inf*); *lid* zuschlagen, zuknallen (*inf*); **to bang down the receiver** den Hörer aufknallen (*inf*)
➤ **bang into** VI +PREP OBJ (= *collide with*) prallen auf (+*acc*)
➤ **bang on** VI +PREP OBJ (*Brit inf*) schwafeln von (*inf*)
➤ **bang out** VT SEP **to bang out a tune on the piano** eine Melodie auf dem Klavier hämmern (*inf*); **to bang out a letter on the typewriter** einen Brief auf der Schreibmaschine herunterhauen (*inf*)
➤ **bang up** VT SEP (*sl*) *prisoner* einbuchten (*inf*)

bang² N (*US*: = *fringe*) Pony *m*; **~s** Ponyfrisur *f*

banger ['bæŋəʳ] N **(a)** (*Brit inf*: = *sausage*) Wurst *f* **(b)** (*inf*: = *old car*) Klapperkiste *f* (*inf*) **(c)** (*Brit*: = *firework*) Knallkörper *m*

Bangladesh ['bæŋgləˈdeʃ] N Bangladesch *nt*

Bangladeshi [bæŋgləˈdeʃɪ] **1** N Einwohner(in) *m(f)* von Bangladesch, Bangladeshi *mf* **2** ADJ aus Bangladesch

bangle ['bæŋgl] N Armreif(en) *m*

banish ['bænɪʃ] VT *person* verbannen; *cares, fear* vertreiben

banishment ['bænɪʃmənt] N Verbannung *f*

banister, bannister ['bænɪstəʳ] N (*also* **~s**) Geländer *nt*

banjo ['bændʒəʊ] N, *pl* **-es** *or* (*US*) **-s** Banjo *nt*

bank¹ [bæŋk] **1** N **(a)** (*of earth, sand*) Damm *m*; (*Rail*) (Bahn)damm *m*; (= *slope*) Böschung *f*; **~ of snow** Schneeverwehung *f* **(b)** (*of river, lake*) Ufer *nt*; **we sat on the ~s of a river/lake** wir saßen an einem Fluss-/Seeufer **(c)** (*in* *sea, river*) (Sand)bank *f* **(d)** (*of clouds*) Bank *f* **2** VI (*Aviat*) in die Querlage gehen

➤ **bank up** VT SEP *fire* mit Kohlestaub bedecken (*damit es langsam brennt*)

bank² **1** N Bank *f*; **to keep** *or* **be the ~** die Bank halten **2** VT *money* zur Bank bringen **3** VI **where do you ~?** bei welcher Bank haben Sie Ihr Konto?

➤ **bank on** VI +PREP OBJ sich verlassen auf (+*acc*), rechnen mit; **I was banking on your coming** ich hatte fest damit gerechnet, dass du kommst

bank³ N (= *row of objects, oars*) Reihe *f*

bankable ['bæŋkəbl] ADJ *cheque* einzahlbar; **a very ~ film star** (*fig inf*) ein Filmstar, der viel Geld einbringt

bank: bank account N Bankkonto *nt*; **bank advance** N Bankdarlehen *nt*; **bank balance** N Kontostand *m*; **bankbook** N Sparbuch *nt*; **bank charge** N Kontoführungsgebühr *f*; **bank clerk** N Bankangestellte(r) *mf*; **bank draft** N Bankwechsel *m*

banker ['bæŋkəʳ] N (*Fin*) Bankier *m*, Banker(in) *m(f)* (*inf*); (*Gambling*) Bankhalter(in) *m(f)*

banker's: banker's card N Scheckkarte *f*; **banker's cheque** (*Brit*), **banker's draft** (*US*) N Bankscheck *m*; **banker's order** N (= *standing order*) Dauerauftrag *m*; **banker's reference** N Bankauskunft *f*

bank giro N Banküberweisung *f*; **bank holiday** N (*Brit*) öffentlicher Feiertag; (*US*) Bankfeiertag *m*

banking ['bæŋkɪŋ] **1** N Bankwesen *nt*; **he wants to go into ~** er will ins Bankfach *or* Bankgewerbe gehen **2** ATTR Bank-; **~ service** Bankdienstleistungen *pl*

banking hours PL Schalterstunden *pl*

bank: bank loan N Bankkredit *m*; **bank manager** N Filialleiter(in) *m(f)* (*einer Bank*); **my ~** der Filialleiter/die Filialleiterin meiner Bank; **banknote** N Banknote *f*; **bank rate** N (*Brit*) Diskontsatz *m*; **bank robber** N Bankräuber(in) *m(f)*; **bank robbery** N Bankraub *m*

bankrupt ['bæŋkrʌpt] **1** N Konkursschuldner(in) *m(f)* (*Jur*), Bankrotteur(in) *m(f)* **2** ADJ (*Jur, fig*) bankrott; **to go ~** Bankrott machen **3** VT zugrunde richten

bankruptcy ['bæŋkrəptsɪ] N (*Jur, fig*) Bankrott *m*; (*instance*) Konkurs *m*

bankruptcy: Bankruptcy Court N Konkursgericht *nt*; **bankruptcy order** N Konkurseröffnungsbeschluss *m*; **bankruptcy proceedings** PL Konkursverfahren *nt*

bank: bank sort code N Bankleitzahl *f*; **bank statement** N Kontoauszug *m*; **bank transfer** N Banküberweisung *f*

banned substance N (*Sport*) illegale *or* verbotene Substanz

banner ['bænəʳ] N Banner *nt* (*also fig*); (*in processions*) Transparent *nt*

banner headlines ['bænəˈhedlaɪnz] N Schlagzeilen *pl*

banning ['bænɪŋ] N Verbot *nt*; **the ~ of cars from city centres** (*Brit*) *or* **centers** (*US*) das Fahrverbot in den Innenstädten

bannister ['bænɪstəʳ] N = **banister**

banns [bænz] PL (*Eccl*) Aufgebot *nt*; **to read the ~** das Aufgebot verlesen

banquet ['bæŋkwɪt] N (= *lavish feast*) Festessen *nt*; (= *ceremonial dinner also*) Bankett *nt*

banter ['bæntəʳ] N Geplänkel *nt*

bantering ['bæntərɪŋ] ADJ (= *joking*) scherzhaft; (= *teasing*) neckend

bap (bun) ['bæp(bʌn)] N (*Brit*) weiches Brötchen

baptism ['bæptɪzəm] N Taufe *f*; **~ of fire** (*fig*) Feuertaufe *f*

Baptist ['bæptɪst] N Baptist(in) *m(f)*; **the ~ Church** (= *people*) die Baptistengemeinde; (= *teaching*) der Baptismus

baptize [bæpˈtaɪz] VT taufen

bar¹ [bɑːʳ] **1** N **(a)** (*of metal, wood*) Stange *f*; (*Ftbl*) Querbalken *m*; (*of toffee etc*) Riegel *m*; **~ of gold** Goldbarren *m*; **a ~ of chocolate, a chocolate ~** (= *slab*) eine Tafel Schokolade; (*Mars® ~ etc*) ein Schokoladenriegel *m*; **a ~ of soap** ein Stück *nt* Seife; **a two-~ electric fire** ein Heizgerät *nt* mit zwei Heizstäben

(b) (*of window, grate, cage*) (Gitter)stab *m*; (*of door*) Stange *f*; **the window has ~s** das Fenster ist vergittert; **to put sb behind ~s** jdn hinter Gitter bringen

(c) (*Sport*) (*horizontal*) Reck *nt*; (*for high jump etc*) Latte *f*; **~s** *pl* (*parallel*) Barren *m*; **(wall) ~s** Sprossenwand *f*

(d) (*fig*: = *obstacle*) **to be a ~ to sth** einer Sache (*dat*) im Wege

stehen

(e) (*of colour*) Streifen *m*; (*of light*) Strahl *m*

(f) (*Jur*) **the Bar** die Anwaltschaft; **to be called** *or* (*US*) **admitted to the Bar** als Verteidiger zugelassen werden

(g) (*for prisoners*) **to stand at the ~** auf der Anklagebank sitzen

(h) (*for drinks*) Lokal *nt*; (*esp expensive*) Bar *f*; (*part of pub*) Gaststube *f*; (= *counter*) Theke *f*, Tresen *m*

(i) (*Mus*) Takt *m*; (= *~ line*) Taktstrich *m*

2 VT **(a)** (= *obstruct*) *road* blockieren; **to ~ sb's way** jdm den Weg versperren

(b) (= *fasten*) *window, door* versperren

(c) *person, possibility* ausschließen; *action, thing* untersagen; **they've been ~red from the club** sie haben Klubverbot

bar² PREP **~ none** ohne Ausnahme; **~ one** außer einem

barb [bɑːb] N **(a)** (*of hook*) Widerhaken *m*; (*of barbed wire*) Stachel *m*; (*of feather*) Fahne *f*; (*Bot, Zool*) Bart *m* **(b)** (*fig: of wit etc*) Spitze *f*

Barbados [bɑːˈbeɪdɒs] N Barbados *nt*

barbarian [bɑːˈbɛərɪən] **1** N (*Hist, fig*) Barbar(in) *m(f)* **2** ADJ (*Hist, fig*) barbarisch

barbaric [bɑːˈbærɪk] ADJ barbarisch; *guard etc* grausam; (*fig inf*) *conditions* grauenhaft

barbarism ['bɑːbərɪzəm] N (*Hist, fig*) Barbarei *f*

barbarity [bɑːˈbærɪtɪ] N Barbarei *f*; (*fig*) Primitivität *f*; (= *cruelty*) Grausamkeit *f*

barbarous ['bɑːbərəs] ADJ (*Hist*) (*fig*) barbarisch; (= *cruel*) grausam; *guard etc* roh; *accent* grauenhaft

barbecue ['bɑːbɪkjuː] **1** N **(a)** (*Cook*: = *grid*) Grill *m* **(b)** (= *occasion*) Grillparty *f*, Barbecue *nt* **2** VT *steak etc* grillen; *animal* am Spieß braten

barbed [bɑːbd] ADJ (*fig*) *wit* beißend; *remark* spitz, bissig

barbed: barbed wire N Stacheldraht *m*; **barbed-wire fence** N Stacheldrahtzaun *m*

barber ['bɑːbəʳ] N (Herren)friseur *m*, Barbier *m* (*old*); **at/to the ~'s** beim/zum Friseur

barbershop ['bɑːbəʃɒp] **1** N (*US*) (Herren)friseurgeschäft *nt* **2** ADJ **~ quartet** Barbershop-Quartett *nt*

Barbie (doll)® ['bɑːbɪ(ˌdɒl)] N Barbie-Puppe® *f*

bar billiards N (*esp Brit*) *eine Art Billard, das in Pubs gespielt wird*

barbiturate [bɑːˈbɪtjʊrɪt] N Schlafmittel *nt*, Barbiturat *nt*

bar: bar chart N Balkendiagramm *nt*; **bar code** N Strichkode *m*, Bar-Code *m*; **bar-coded** ADJ mit Strichkodierung; **bar code reader** N Strichkodeleser *m*

bard [bɑːd] N Barde *m*, Bardin *f*

bare [bɛəʳ] **1** ADJ (+ER) **(a)** (= *naked, uncovered*) nackt; *room, garden* leer; *wire* blank; **~ patch** kahle Stelle; **the ~ facts** die nackten Tatsachen; **with his ~ hands** mit bloßen Händen; **she told him the ~ bones of the story** sie erzählte ihm die Geschichte in groben Zügen

(b) (= *scanty, mere*) knapp; **a ~ ten centimetres** (*Brit*) *or* **centimeters** (*US*) knappe zehn Zentimeter; **the ~ minimum** das absolute Minimum

2 VT *breast, leg* entblößen; (*at doctor's*) freimachen; *teeth* (*in anger*) fletschen; **to ~ one's soul** seine Seele entblößen

bare: bareback ADV, ADJ ohne Sattel; **a ~ rider** ein Reiter, der/ eine Reiterin, die ohne Sattel reitet; **barefaced** ADJ (*fig*: = *shameless*) unverschämt; **barefoot(ed)** **1** ADV barfuß **2** ADJ barfüßig; **bareheaded** ADJ, ADV ohne Kopfbedeckung; **barelegged** ADJ mit bloßen Beinen

barely ['bɛəlɪ] ADV **(a)** (= *scarcely*) kaum **(b)** *furnished* spärlich

bareness ['bɛənɪs] N (*of trees, countryside*) Kahlheit *f*; (*of room, garden*) Leere *f*

bargain ['bɑːgɪn] **1** N **(a)** (= *transaction*) Handel *m*; **to make** *or* **strike a ~** sich einigen; **I'll make a ~ with you** ich mache Ihnen ein Angebot; **to keep one's side of the ~** sich an die Abmachung halten; **you drive a hard ~** Sie stellen ja harte Forderungen!; **then it started raining into the ~** dann hat es (obendrein) auch noch angefangen zu regnen

(b) (= *cheap offer*) Sonderangebot *nt*; (*thing bought*) Gelegenheitskauf *m*; **what a ~!** das ist aber günstig! **2** VI handeln (*for* um); (*in negotiations*) verhandeln

➤ **bargain for** VI +PREP OBJ (*inf*: = *expect*) rechnen mit; **I got more than I bargained for** ich habe vielleicht mein blaues Wunder erlebt! (*inf*)

➤ **bargain on** VI +PREP OBJ zählen auf (+*acc*)

bargain: **bargain basement** N *Untergeschoss eines Kaufhauses mit Sonderangeboten*; **bargain-hunting** N **to go** ~ auf Jagd nach Sonderangeboten gehen

bargaining ['bɑːgɪnɪŋ] N Handeln *nt*; (= *negotiating*) Verhandeln *nt*; ~ **position** Verhandlungsposition *f*

bargain: **bargain offer** N Sonderangebot *nt*; **bargain sale** N Ausverkauf *m*

barge [bɑːdʒ] **1** N (*for freight*) Frachtkahn *m*; (*unpowered*) Schleppkahn *m*; (= *houseboat*) Hausboot *nt* **2** VT **he ~d me out of the way** er hat mich weggestoßen; **he ~d his way into the room** er ist (ins Zimmer) hereingeplatzt (*inf*); **he ~d his way through the crowd** er hat sich durch die Menge geboxt (*inf*) **3** VI **to** ~ **into a room** (in ein Zimmer) hereinplatzen (*inf*); **to ~ out of a room** aus einem Zimmer hinausstürmen; **he ~d through the crowd** er drängte sich durch die Menge

➤ **barge in** VI (*inf*) (a) (= *enter suddenly*) hereinplatzen (*inf*) (b) (= *interrupt*) dazwischenplatzen (*inf*) (*on* bei)

➤ **barge into** VI +PREP OBJ (= *knock against*) person (hinein)rennen in (+*acc*) (*inf*); thing rennen gegen (*inf*)

bargepole ['bɑːdʒpəʊl] N **I wouldn't touch it/him with a** ~ (*Brit inf*) von so etwas/so jemandem lasse ich die Finger (*inf*); (*out of disgust*) das/den würde ich noch nicht mal mit der Kneifzange anfassen (*inf*)

bar graph N (*Comput*) Balkendiagramm *nt*

baritone ['bærɪtəʊn] **1** N Bariton *m* **2** ADJ Bariton-

barium ['bɛərɪəm] N Barium *nt*

barium meal N Bariumbrei *m*

bark¹ [bɑːk] N (*of tree*) Rinde *f*, Borke *f*

bark² [bɑːk] **1** N (*of dog*) Bellen *nt*; **his ~ is worse than his bite** (*Prov*) Hunde, die bellen, beißen nicht (*Prov*) **2** VI bellen; **to ~ at sb** jdn anbellen; (*person*) jdn anfahren; **to be ~ing up the wrong tree** (*fig inf*) auf dem Holzweg sein (*inf*)

➤ **bark out** VT SEP orders bellen

barkeep(er) ['bɑːkiːp(əʳ)] N (*US*) Gastwirt *m*; (= *bartender*) Barkeeper *m*

barking (mad) ['bɑːkɪŋ('mæd)] ADJ (*inf*) total verrückt *or* übergeschnappt (*inf*)

barley ['bɑːlɪ] N Gerste *f*

barley: **barley sugar** N Malzzucker *m*; (*sweet*) hartes Zuckerbonbon; **barley water** N Art Gerstenextrakt; **lemon ~** konzentriertes Zitronengetränk

bar: **barmaid** N Bardame *f*; **barman** N Barkeeper *m*

Bar Mitzvah [bɑːˈmɪtsvə] N Bar Mizwa *nt*

barmy ['bɑːmɪ] ADJ +ER (*Brit inf*) bekloppt (*inf*); idea etc blödsinnig (*inf*)

barn [bɑːn] N (a) Scheune *f* (b) (*US: for trucks*) Depot *nt*

barnacle ['bɑːnəkl] N (Rankenfuß)krebs *m*

barn: **barn dance** N Bauerntanz *m*; **barn owl** N Schleiereule *f*; **barnstorm** VI (*esp US*) (*Theat*) in der Provinz spielen; (*Pol*) in der Provinz Wahlreden halten; **barnstormer** N (*US Pol*) Wahlredner(in) *m(f)* in der Provinz; (*Theat*) Wanderschauspieler(in) *m(f)*; **barnstorming** ADJ (*Brit*) performance hinreißend; **barnyard** N (Bauern)hof *m*

barometer [bəˈrɒmɪtəʳ] N (*lit, fig*) Barometer *nt*

barometric pressure [bærəʊmetrɪkˈprɛʃəʳ] N Luftdruck *m*

baron ['bærən] N (a) Baron *m* (b) (*fig*) Baron *m*, Magnat *m*; **oil ~** Ölmagnat *m*; **press ~** Pressezar *m*

baroness ['bærənɪs] N Baronin *f*; (*unmarried*) Baronesse *f*

baroque [bəˈrɒk] **1** ADJ barock, Barock- **2** N (= *style*) Barock *m or nt*; **the ~ period** das *or* der Barock, die Barockzeit

barrack ['bærək] VT actor etc auspfeifen

barracking ['bærəkɪŋ] N **to get a ~** ausgepfiffen werden

barrack-room ['bærəkruːm] ADJ ATTR rau, roh; ~ **language** Landsersprache *f*

barracks ['bærəks] PL (*often with sing vb*) (*Mil*) Kaserne *f*; (*fig pej also*) Mietskaserne *f*; **to live in ~** in der Kaserne wohnen

barrage ['bærɑːʒ] N (a) (*across river*) Wehr *nt*; (*larger*) Staustufe *f* (b) (*Mil*) Sperrfeuer *nt* (c) (*fig: of questions etc*) Hagel *m*; **he faced a ~ of questions** er wurde mit Fragen beschossen

barred [bɑːd] ADJ (a) SUF **five-~ gate** Weidengatter *nt* (mit fünf Querbalken) (b) ~ **window** Gitterfenster *nt*

barrel ['bærəl] N (a) Fass *nt*; (*for oil, rainwater etc*) Tonne *f*; (= *measure: of oil*) Barrel *nt*; **they've got us over a ~** (*inf*) sie haben uns in der Zange (*inf*); **it wasn't exactly a ~ of laughs** (*inf*) es war nicht gerade komisch; **it's a ~ of laughs** (*inf*) es ist das reinste Vergnügen; **he's a ~ of laughs** (*inf*) er ist eine echte Spaßkanone (*inf*); **to pay cash on the ~** (*US*) bar auf den Tisch *or* die Kralle (*inf*) zahlen (b) (*of handgun*) Lauf *m*; (*of cannon etc*) Rohr *nt* (c) (*of fountain pen*) Tank *m*

barrel: **barrelhead** N **to pay cash on the ~** (*US*) bar auf den Tisch *or* die Kralle (*inf*) zahlen; **barrelhouse** (*US*) **1** N Kneipe *f*; (= *jazz*) Kneipenjazz *m* **2** ADJ ~ **blues** alte, in Kneipen gespielte Form des Blues; **barrel organ** N Leierkasten *m*

barren ['bærən] **1** ADJ (*lit, fig*) unfruchtbar; subject trocken **2** N **barrens** PL (*esp US*) Ödland *nt*

barrenness ['bærənɪs] N (*lit, fig*) Unfruchtbarkeit *f*

barrette [bəˈret] N (*US*) (Haar)spange *f*

barricade [bærɪˈkeɪd] **1** N Barrikade *f* **2** VT verbarrikadieren

barrier ['bærɪəʳ] N (a) (*natural*) Barriere *f*; (= *railing etc*) Schranke *f*; (= *crash ~*) (Leit)planke *f* (b) (*fig*) (= *obstacle*) Hindernis *nt*; (*of class, between people*) Schranke *f*; **trade ~s** Handelsschranken *pl*; **language ~** Sprachbarriere *f*; **a ~ to success** etc ein Hindernis für den Erfolg *etc*; **to break down ~s** Zäune niederreißen

barrier: **barrier contraceptive** N mechanisches Verhütungsmittel; **barrier cream** N Haut(schutz)creme *f*

barring ['bɑːrɪŋ] PREP ~ **accidents** falls nichts passiert; ~ **one** außer einem

barrister ['bærɪstəʳ] N (*Brit*) Rechtsanwalt *m*/-anwältin *f* (bei Gericht)

barrow ['bærəʊ] N Karre(n *m*) *f*; (= *wheel ~*) Schubkarre(n *m*) *f*; (*esp Brit: costermonger's*) (handgezogener) Obst-/Gemüsekarren *etc m*

bartender ['bɑːtendəʳ] N (*US*) Barkeeper *m*; ~**!** hallo!

barter ['bɑːtəʳ] VTI tauschen (*for* gegen)

barter: **barter economy** N Tauschwirtschaft *f*; **barter society** N Tauschgesellschaft *f*; **barter trade** N Tauschhandel *m*

base¹ [beɪs] **1** N (a) (= *lowest part*) Basis *f*; (*Archit*: = *support for statue etc*) Sockel *m*; (*of lamp, tree, mountain*) Fuß *m*; **at the ~ (of)** unten (an +*dat*) (b) (= *main ingredient*) Hauptbestandteil *m* (c) (*Mil etc, fig: for holidays, climbing etc*) Stützpunkt *m*; **to return to ~** zum Stützpunkt zurückkehren (d) (*Baseball*) Mal *nt*, Base *nt*; **at or on second ~** auf Mal *or* Base 2; **to touch ~** (*US inf*) sich melden (*with* bei); **to touch or cover all the ~s** (*US fig*) an alles denken **2** VT (a) (*fig*) opinion, hopes, theory basieren (*on* auf +*acc*); relationship bauen (*on* auf +*acc*); **to be ~d on sth** auf etw (*dat*) basieren; **to ~ one's technique on sth** in seiner Technik von etw ausgehen (b) stationieren; **the company is ~d in London** die Firma hat ihren Sitz in London; **my job is ~d in Glasgow** ich arbeite in Glasgow

base² ADJ (+ER) (a) gemein; motive, character niedrig (b) metal unedel

baseball ['beɪsbɔːl] N Baseball *m or nt*

BASEBALL

Baseball ist ein amerikanischer Nationalsport. Zwei Teams mit neun Spielern spielen auf einem Spielfeld mit vier Markierungen, die als Male (*bases*) bezeichnet werden und in Form einer Raute angeordnet sind. Ein Mitglied des schlagenden Teams (*batter*) versucht, den Ball, der vom Werfer (*pitcher*) geworfen wurde, außerhalb der Reichweite der Fänger (*fielders*) zu schlagen, damit er von Mal zu Mal laufend wieder zu dem Punkt zurückkehren kann, von dem aus er geschlagen hat.

Es gibt zwei wichtige Baseball-Ligen in den USA: die National League und die American League. Die jeweiligen Gewinner beider Ligen spielen dann in mehreren Begegnungen gegeneinander, die als *World Series* bekannt sind.

baseball cap N Baseballmütze *f*

base: **baseboard** ['beɪsbɔːd] N (*US*) Fußleiste *f*; **base camp** N Basislager *nt*

-based [-beɪst] ADJ SUF **London-based** mit Sitz in London; **to be computer-based** auf Computerbasis arbeiten

baseless ['beɪslɪs] ADJ unbegründet

baseline ['beɪslaɪn] N (*Baseball*) Verbindungslinie zwischen zwei Malen; (*of a diagram, Tennis*) Grundlinie *f*

basement ['beɪsmənt] N Untergeschoss *nt*, Untergeschoß *nt* (*Aus*); **~ flat** (*Brit*) **or apartment** Souterrainwohnung *f*

base rate N Leitzins *m*

bash [bæʃ] (*inf*) **◼ N (a)** Schlag *m*; **to give sb a ~ on the nose** jdm (eine) auf die Nase hauen (*inf*); **the door has had a ~** die Tür hat eine Delle abgekriegt (*inf*)
(b) I'll have a ~ (at it) ich probiers mal (*inf*)
◻ VT *person* verprügeln; *ball* knallen (*inf*); *car* eindellen (*inf*); **to ~ one's head (against or on sth)** sich (*dat*) den Kopf (an etw (*dat*)) anschlagen; **to ~ sb on or over the head with sth** jdm mit etw auf den Kopf hauen
➤ **bash in** VT SEP (*inf*) *door* einschlagen; *hat, car* eindellen (*inf*); **to bash sb's head in** jdm den Schädel einschlagen (*inf*)
➤ **bash up** VT SEP (*esp Brit inf*) *person* vermöbeln (*inf*); *car* demolieren (*inf*)

-basher [-bæʃəʳ] SUF (*inf*) **queer-basher** Schwulenklatscher(in) *m(f)* (*inf*)

bashful ['bæʃfʊl] ADJ, **bashfully** ['bæʃfəlɪ] ADV schüchtern; (*on particular occasion*) verlegen

-bashing SUF (*inf*) **queer-bashing** (*physical*) Überfälle *pl* auf Schwule; **Tory-bashing** (*verbal*) das Heruntermachen der Konservativen (*inf*)

Basic ['beɪsɪk] (*Comput*) ABBR *of* **beginner's all-purpose symbolic instruction code** BASIC *nt*

basic ['beɪsɪk] **◼ ADJ (a)** (= *fundamental*) Grund-; *problem also, reason, issue* Haupt-; *points* wesentlich; *intention, purpose* eigentlich; *indifference, problem* grundsätzlich; **there's no ~ difference** es besteht kein grundlegender Unterschied; **the ~ thing to remember is ...** woran man vor allem denken muss, ist ...; **his knowledge is rather ~** er hat nur ziemlich elementare Kenntnisse; **the furniture is rather ~** die Möbel sind ziemlich primitiv; **~ salary/working hours** Grundgehalt *nt*/-arbeitszeit *f*; **~ vocabulary** Grundwortschatz *m*
(b) (= *essential*) notwendig
◻ PL the ~s das Wesentliche; **to get down to (the) ~s** zum Kern der Sache kommen; **to get back to ~s** sich auf das Wesentliche besinnen

basically ['beɪsɪkəlɪ] ADV im Grunde; (= *mainly*) hauptsächlich; **is that correct? – ~ yes** stimmt das? – im Prinzip, ja; **that's ~ it** das wärs im Wesentlichen

basic: basic English N englischer Grundwortschatz; **basic rate** N (*of wage*) Grundgehalt *nt*; (*of tax*) Eingangssteuersatz *m*; **the ~ of income tax** der Eingangssteuersatz bei Lohn- und Einkommensteuer

basil ['bæzl] N (*Bot*) Basilikum *nt*

basin ['beɪsn] N **(a)** (= *vessel*) Schüssel *f*; (= *wash ~*) (Wasch)becken *nt* **(b)** (*Geog*) Becken *nt*

basis ['beɪsɪs] N, *pl* **bases** (*lit, fig*) Basis *f*; (*for assumption*) Grund *m*; **we're working on the ~ that ...** wir gehen von der Annahme aus, dass ...; **to be on a sound ~** (*business*) auf festen Füßen stehen; **on the ~ of this evidence** aufgrund dieses Beweismaterials

basis point N (*Fin*) Basispunkt *m*

bask [bɑːsk] VI (*in sun*) sich aalen (*in* in +*dat*); (*in sb's favour etc*) sich sonnen (*in* in +*dat*)

basket ['bɑːskɪt] N Korb *m*; (*for rolls, fruit etc*) Körbchen *nt*; **a ~ of currencies** ein Währungskorb *m*

basket: basketball N Basketball *m*; **basket case** N (*sl*) hoffnungsloser Fall; **basket chair** N Korbsessel *m*

Basle [bɑːl] N Basel *nt*

Basque [bæsk] **◼ N (a)** (= *person*) Baske *m*, Baskin *f* **(b)** (= *language*) Baskisch *nt* **◻ ADJ** baskisch

bass¹ [beɪs] (*Mus*) **◼ N** Bass *m* **◻ ADJ** Bass-

bass² [bæs] N, *pl* **-(es)** (= *fish*) (Wolfs)barsch *m*

bass [beɪs]: **bass clef** N Bassschlüssel *m*; **bass drum** N große Trommel

bassoon [bə'suːn] N Fagott *nt*

bastard ['bɑːstəd] **◼ N (a)** (*lit*) uneheliches Kind **(b)** (*sl*: = *person*) Scheißkerl *m* (*inf*); **poor ~** armes Schwein (*inf*) **(c)** (*sl*: = *difficult job etc*) **this question is a real ~** diese Frage ist wirklich hundsgemein (*inf*); **a ~ of a job** *etc* eine Scheißarbeit *etc* (*inf*) **◻ ADJ** *child* unehelich

bastardize ['bɑːstədaɪz] VT (*fig*) verfälschen

baste [beɪst] VT (*Cook*) (mit Fett) begießen

bastion ['bæstɪən] N (*lit, fig*) Bastion *f*; (= *person*) Stütze *f*, Säule *f*

bat¹ [bæt] N (*Zool*) Fledermaus *f*; **he drove like a ~ out of hell** er fuhr, wie wenn der Teufel hinter ihm her wäre; **(as) blind as a ~** stockblind (*inf*)

bat² (*Sport*) **◼ N** (*Baseball, Cricket*) Schlagholz *nt*; (*Table-tennis*) Schläger *m*; **off one's own ~** (*Brit inf*) auf eigene Faust (*inf*); **right off the ~** (*US*) prompt **◻ VT** (*Baseball, Cricket*) schlagen; **to ~ sth around** (*US inf*: = *discuss*) etw bekakeln (*inf*) **◼ VI** (*Baseball, Cricket*) schlagen

bat³ VT **not to ~ an eyelid** (*Brit*) **or eye** (*US*) nicht mal mit der Wimper zucken

bat⁴ N (*US sl*: = *binge*) Sauftour *f* (*inf*); **to go on a ~** auf Sauftour gehen (*inf*)

batch [bætʃ] N (*of people*) Schwung *m* (*inf*); (*of loaves*) Schub *m*; (*of things dispatched*) Sendung *f*; (*of letters, work*) Stoß *m*

batch (*Comput*): **batch command** N Batchbefehl *m*; **batch file** N Stapeldatei *f*, Batchdatei *f*; **batch job** N Stapelverarbeitung *f*; **batch processing** N Stapelverarbeitung *f*

bated ['beɪtɪd] ADJ **with ~ breath** mit angehaltenem Atem

bath [bɑːθ] **◼ N (a)** Bad *nt*; **to have or take a ~** baden; **to give sb a ~** jdn baden **(b)** (= *~tub*) (Bade)wanne *f*; **I was just in my or the ~** ich war gerade im Bad **(c) (swimming) ~s** *pl* (Schwimm)bad *nt*; **(public) ~s** *pl* Badeanstalt *f* **◻ VT** (*Brit*) baden **◼ VI** (*Brit*) (sich) baden

bathchair ['bɑːθtʃeəʳ] N Krankenstuhl *m*

bath cube N Würfel *m* Badesalz

bathe [beɪð] **◼ VT (a)** baden; (*with cotton wool etc*) waschen; **to ~ one's eyes** ein Augenbad machen; **~d in tears** tränenüberströmt; **to be ~d in sweat** schweißgebadet sein **(b)** (*US*) = **bath 2 ◻ VI** baden **◼ N** Bad *nt*; **to have or take a ~** baden

bather ['beɪðəʳ] N Badende(r) *mf*

bathing: **bathing cap** N Badekappe *f*; **bathing costume** N Badeanzug *m*; **bathing trunks** PL Badehose *f*

bathmat ['bɑːθmæt] N Badematte *f*

bathrobe ['bɑːθrəʊb] N Bademantel *m*

bathroom ['bɑːθruːm] N Bad(ezimmer) *nt*; (*euph*: = *lavatory*) Toilette *f*

bathroom: bathroom cabinet N Toilettenschrank *m*; **bathroom scales** PL Personenwaage *f*

bath: bath salts PL Badesalz *nt*; **bathtowel** N Badetuch *nt*; **bathtub** N Badewanne *f*

batik ['bætɪk] N Batik *m*; (= *cloth*) Batikdruck *m*

batman ['bætmən] N, *pl* **-men** [-mən] (*Mil*) (Offiziers)bursche *m*

baton ['bætən, (*US*) bæ'ton] N **(a)** (*Mus*) Taktstock *m*; (*Mil*) (Kommando)stab *m* **(b)** (*of policeman*) Schlagstock *m* **(c)** (*in relay race*) Staffelholz *nt*, Stab *m*

baton charge N **to make a ~** Schlagstöcke einsetzen

baton round N (*Mil*) Plastikgeschosse *pl*

batsman ['bætsmən] N, *pl* **-men** [-mən] (*Sport*) Schlagmann *m*

battalion [bə'tælɪən] N (*Mil, fig*) Bataillon *nt*

batten ['bætn] N Leiste *f*, Latte *f*
➤ **batten down** VT SEP **to batten down the hatches** (*fig*) (= *close doors, windows*) alles dicht machen; (= *prepare oneself*) sich auf etwas gefasst machen

batter¹ ['bætəʳ] N (*Cook*) Teig *m*

batter² N (*Sport*) Schlagmann *m*

batter³ **◼ VT** (= *hit*) einschlagen auf (+*acc*); (= *strike repeatedly*) *wife, baby* prügeln **◻ VI** schlagen; **to ~ at the door** an die Tür trommeln (*inf*)
➤ **batter down** VT SEP *wall* zertrümmern; *door* einschlagen

battered ['bætəd] ADJ übel zugerichtet; *wife, baby* misshandelt; *hat, car* verbeult; *furniture, reputation* ramponiert (*inf*); **~ baby syndrome** Phänomen *nt* der Kindesmisshandlung

batterer ['bætərəʳ] N **wife-~** prügelnder Ehemann; **child-~** prügelnder Vater, prügelnde Mutter

battering ['bætərɪŋ] N (*lit*) Prügel *pl*; **he/it got or took a real ~** er/es hat ganz schön was abgekriegt (*inf*)

battery ['bætərɪ] N Batterie *f*; (*fig*: *of arguments etc*) Reihe *f*

battery: **battery charger** N Ladegerät *nt*; **battery farm** N Legebatterie *f*; **battery farming** N Legebatterien *pl*; **battery hen** N (*Agr*) Batteriehuhn *nt*; **battery-powered** ADJ batteriebetrieben

battle ['bætl] **1** N (*lit*) Schlacht *f*; (*fig*) Kampf *m*; **to fight a ~** eine Schlacht schlagen; (*fig*) einen Kampf führen; **to do ~ for sb/sth** sich für jdn/etw einsetzen; **killed in ~** (im Kampf) gefallen; **~ of wits** Machtkampf *m*; **~ of words** Wortgefecht *nt*; **~ of wills** geistiger Wettstreit; **that's half the ~** damit ist schon viel gewonnen; **getting an interview is only half the ~** damit, dass man ein Interview bekommt, ist es noch nicht getan **2** VI sich schlagen; (*fig*) kämpfen **3** VT (*fig*) **to ~ one's way through four qualifying matches** sich durch vier Qualifikationsspiele durchschlagen
➤ **battle out** VT SEP **to battle it out** sich einen harten Kampf liefern

battle: **battle-axe**, (*US*) **battle-ax** N (= *weapon*) Streitaxt *f*; (*inf*: = *woman*) Drachen *m* (*inf*); **battle cry** N Schlachtruf *m*; **battlefield** N Schlachtfeld *nt*; **battleground** N Schlachtfeld *nt*

battlements ['bætlmənts] PL Zinnen *pl*

battleship N Schlachtschiff *nt*; **~s** (= *game*) Schiffeversenken *nt*

batty ['bætɪ] ADJ (+ER) (*Brit inf*) verrückt

bauble ['bɔːbl] N Flitter *m no pl*; **~s** Flitterzeug *nt*

baud [bɔːd] N (*Comput*) Baud *nt*

baulk [bɔːk] VI = **balk**

Bavaria [bəˈvɛərɪə] N Bayern *nt*

Bavarian [bəˈvɛərɪən] **1** N (a) (= *person*) Bayer(in) *m(f)* (b) (= *dialect*) Bayrisch *nt* **2** ADJ bay(e)risch

bawdy ['bɔːdɪ] ADJ (+ER) derb

bawl [bɔːl] **1** VI (a) (= *shout*) brüllen; (= *sing*) grölen (*inf*) (b) (*inf*: = *weep*) heulen (*inf*) **2** VT *order* brüllen; *song* grölen (*pej inf*)
➤ **bawl out** VT SEP (a) *order* brüllen; *song* grölen (*inf*) (b) (*inf*: = *scold*) ausschimpfen

bay¹ [beɪ] N Bucht *f*; **Hudson Bay** die Hudsonbai

bay² N (= *loading ~*) Ladeplatz *m*; (= *parking ~*) Parkbucht *f*

bay³ **1** N **to be at ~** (*fig*) in die Enge getrieben sein; **to keep** *or* **hold sb/sth at ~** jdn/etw in Schach halten **2** VI bellen; **to ~ for sb's blood** jds Kopf fordern

bay⁴ **1** ADJ *horse* (kastanien)braun **2** N (= *horse*) Braune(r) *m*

bay leaf N Lorbeerblatt *nt*

bayonet ['beɪənɪt] **1** N Bajonett *nt* **2** VT mit dem Bajonett aufspießen

bayonet fitting N (*Elec*) Bajonettfassung *f*

bay window N Erkerfenster *nt*

bazaar [bəˈzɑːʳ] N Basar *m*

BBC ABBR *of* **British Broadcasting Corporation** BBC *f*

BBQ ABBR *of* **barbecue**

BBS (*Comput*) ABBR *of* **bulletin board system** BBS *nt*

BC¹ ABBR *of* **before Christ** v. Chr

BC² ABBR *of* **British Columbia**

---

be [biː]

1 COPULATIVE VERB	**3** INTRANSITIVE VERB
2 AUXILIARY VERB	**4** IMPERSONAL VERB

pres **am, is, are**, *pret* **was, were**, *ptp* **been**

1 COPULATIVE VERB
(a) sein; **be sensible!** sei vernünftig; **who's that? – it's me/ that's Mary** wer ist das? – ich bins/das ist Mary; **he is a soldier/ a German** er ist Soldat/Deutscher; **he wants to be a doctor** er möchte Arzt werden

Note that the article is used in German only when the noun is qualified by an adjective.

he's a good student/a true Englishman er ist ein guter Student/ein echter Engländer; **he's five** er ist fünf; **two times two is** *or* **are four** zwei mal zwei ist *or* sind vier
(b) (*referring to physical, mental state*) **how are you?** wie gehts?; **she's not at all well** es geht ihr gar nicht gut; **to be hungry/ thirsty** Hunger/Durst haben; **I am hot/cold** mir ist heiß/kalt
(c) (= *cost*) kosten; **how much is that?** wie viel kostet das?
(d) (*with possessive*) gehören (+*dat*); **that book is his** das Buch

gehört ihm
(e) (*in exclamations*) **was he pleased to hear it!** er war vielleicht froh, das zu hören!

2 AUXILIARY VERB
(a) (*in continuous tenses*)

Note how German uses the simple tense.

what are you doing? was machst du da?; **they're coming tomorrow** sie kommen morgen

Note how German uses the present tense.

I have been waiting for you for half an hour ich warte schon seit einer halben Stunde auf Sie; **will you be seeing her tomorrow?** sehen *or* treffen Sie sie morgen?

Note the use of bei + infinitive.

I was packing my case when ... ich war gerade beim Kofferpacken, als ...
(b) (*in passive constructions*) werden; **he was run over** er ist überfahren worden; **it is being repaired** es wird gerade repariert; **I will not be intimidated** ich lasse mich nicht einschüchtern
✦**to be/not to be ...** (INTENTION) **they are shortly to be married** sie werden bald heiraten; **the car is to be sold** das Auto soll verkauft werden
(= OUGHT TO BE) **he is to be pitied** er ist zu bedauern; **what is to be done?** was soll geschehen?
(OBLIGATION, COMMAND) **I am to look after her** ich soll mich um sie kümmern; **I am not to be disturbed** ich möchte nicht gestört werden; **I wasn't to tell you his name** (*but I did*) ich hätte Ihnen eigentlich nicht sagen sollen, wie er heißt
(= BE DESTINED) **she was never to return** sie sollte nie zurückkehren
(POSSIBILITY) **he was not to be persuaded** er ließ sich nicht überreden; **if it were** *or* **was to snow** falls es schneien sollte; **and if I were to tell him?** und wenn ich es ihm sagen würde?
(c) (*in tag questions/short answers*) **he's always late, isn't he? – yes he is** er kommt doch immer zu spät, nicht? – ja, das stimmt; **he's never late, is he? – yes he is** er kommt nie zu spät, oder? – oh, doch; **it's all done, is it? – yes it is/no it isn't** es ist also alles erledigt? – ja/nein

3 INTRANSITIVE VERB sein; (= *remain*) bleiben; (= *be situated*: *town, papers*) liegen, sein; (= *be situated*: *car, tower, chair*) stehen, sein; **we've been here a long time** wir sind schon lange hier; **let me be** lass mich; **be that as it may** wie dem auch sei; **I've been to Paris** ich war schon (ein)mal in Paris; **the milkman has already been** der Milchmann war schon da; **he has been and gone** er war da und ist wieder gegangen
✦**here/there is...** **here is a book/are two books** hier ist ein Buch/sind zwei Bücher; **here/there you are** (= *you've arrived*) da sind Sie ja; (= *take this*) hier/da, bitte; **there he was sitting at the table** da saß er nun am Tisch; **nearby there are two churches** in der Nähe sind zwei Kirchen

4 IMPERSONAL VERB sein; **it is dark** es ist dunkel; **tomorrow is Friday/the 14th of June** morgen ist Freitag/der 14. Juni, morgen haben wir Freitag/den 14. Juni; **it is 5 km to the nearest town** es sind 5 km bis zur nächsten Stadt
✦**it was us/you** *etc* **who...** **it was us** *or* **we** (*form*) **who found it** WIR haben das gefunden
✦**were it not ...** **were it not for the fact that I am a teacher, I would ...** wenn ich kein Lehrer wäre, dann würde ich ...; **were it not for him, if it weren't** *or* **wasn't for him** wenn er nicht wäre
✦**had it not been for...** **had it not been** *or* **if it hadn't been for him** wenn er nicht gewesen wäre

B/E ABBR *of* **bill of exchange**

beach [biːtʃ] **1** N Strand *m*; **on the ~** am Strand **2** VT auf Strand setzen

beach: **beach ball** N Wasserball *m*; **beach buggy** N Strandbuggy *m*; **beach towel** N Strandtuch *nt*; **beach volleyball** N Beachvolleyball *m*

beacon ['bi:kən] N (= *fire, light*) Leuchtfeuer *nt*; (= *radio ~*) Funkfeuer *nt*

bead [bi:d] N **(a)** Perle *f*; **(string of) ~s** Perlenschnur *f*; (= *necklace*) Perlenkette *f* **(b)** (= *drop: of sweat*) Tropfen *m*

beady ['bi:dɪ] ADJ **I've got my ~ eye on you** (*inf*) ich beobachte Sie genau!

beagle ['bi:gl] N Beagle *m*

beak [bi:k] N Schnabel *m*

beaker ['bi:kə'] N Becher *m*; (*Chem etc*) Becherglas *nt*

be-all and end-all ['bi:ɔ:ländˈendɔ:l] N **the ~** das A und O; **it's not the ~** das ist auch nicht alles

beam [bi:m] **1** N **(a)** (*Build, of scales*) Balken *m* **(b)** (*of light etc*) Strahl *m*; **to be on full** *or* **high ~** das Fernlicht eingeschaltet haben **(c)** (*fig inf*) **you're way off ~** (*fig inf*) Sie haben total danebengehauen (*inf*) **2** VI (*lit, fig*) strahlen; **to ~ down** (*sun*) niederstrahlen; **she was ~ing with joy** sie strahlte übers ganze Gesicht **3** VT (*Rad, TV*) ausstrahlen

beaming ['bi:mɪŋ] ADJ strahlend

bean [bi:n] N **(a)** Bohne *f*; **he hasn't (got) a ~** (*Brit inf*) er hat keinen roten Heller (*inf*) **(b)** (*fig*) **to be full of ~s** (*inf*) putzmunter sein (*inf*)

bean: beanbag N (= *seat*) Sitzsack *m*; **beanburger** N vegetarischer Hamburger (*mit Bohnen*)

beanery ['bi:nərɪ] N (*US inf*) billiges Speiselokal

bean: beanfeast N (*inf*) Schmaus *m* (*inf*); **beanpole** N (*lit, fig*) Bohnenstange *f*; **bean sprout** N Sojabohnensprosse *f*

bear[1] [beə'], *pret* **bore**, *ptp* **borne** **1** VT **(a)** (*weight; gift, message*) mit sich führen; *mark, likeness* aufweisen; **he was borne along by the crowd** die Menge trug ihn mit (sich); **to ~ comparison** einem Vergleich standhalten; **it doesn't ~ thinking about** man darf gar nicht daran denken
(b) (= *have in heart or mind*) *love, grudge* empfinden
(c) (= *endure, tolerate*) ertragen; *pain* aushalten; *criticism, smell, noise etc* vertragen; **she can't ~ being laughed at** sie kann es nicht vertragen, wenn man über sie lacht
(d) (= *give birth to*) gebären
2 VI **(a)** (= *move*) **to ~ left/north** sich links/nach Norden halten
(b) **to bring pressure to ~ on sb/sth** Druck auf jdn/etw ausüben
3 VR sich halten
➤ **bear down** VI sich nahen (*geh*)
➤ **bear on** VI +PREP OBJ = **bear (up)on**
➤ **bear out** VT SEP bestätigen; **to bear sb out in sth** jdn in etw bestätigen
➤ **bear up** VI sich halten; **how are you? – bearing up!** wie gehts? – man lebt!
➤ **bear (up)on** VI +PREP OBJ (= *relate to*) betreffen
➤ **bear with** VI if **you would just bear with me for a couple of minutes** wenn Sie sich vielleicht zwei Minuten gedulden wollen

bear[2] N **(a)** Bär *m*; **he is like a ~ with a sore head** er ist ein richtiger Brummbär (*inf*) **(b)** (*Astron*) **the Great/Little Bear** der Große/Kleine Bär *or* Wagen **(c)** (*St Ex*) Baissespekulant *m*, Baissier *m*

bearable ['beərəbl] ADJ erträglich

bear cub N Bärenjunge(s) *nt*

beard [bɪəd] N Bart *m*; **a man with a ~** ein Mann mit Bart

bearded ['bɪədɪd] ADJ bärtig

bearer ['beərə'] N (= *carrier*) Träger(in) *m(f)*; (*of news, letter, cheque*) Überbringer *m*; (*of name, title, passport*) Inhaber(in) *m(f)*; **~ bond** Inhaberschuldverschreibung *f*; **~ cheque** (*Brit*) *or* **check** (*US*) Inhaberscheck *m*

bear hug N ungestüme Umarmung

bearing ['beərɪŋ] N **(a)** (= *posture*) Haltung *f*; (= *behaviour*) Auftreten *nt* **(b)** (= *relevance, influence*) Auswirkung *f* (*on* auf +*acc*); (= *connection*) Bezug *m* (*on* zu); **to have some/no ~ on sth** von Belang/belanglos für etw sein; (= *be/not be connected with*) einen gewissen/keinen Bezug zu etw haben **(c)** (= *direction*) **to get** *or* **find one's ~s** sich zurechtfinden; **to lose one's ~s** die Orientierung verlieren

bear: bear market N (*St Ex*) Baisse *f*; **bear position** N (*St Ex*) Baisseposition *f*; **bear raid** N (*St Ex*) Baissemanöver *nt*; **bearskin** ['beəskɪn] N (*Mil*) Bärenfellmütze *f*; **bear slide** N (*St Ex*) Kurssturz *m*; **bear squeeze** N (*St Ex*) Baissedruck *m*

beast [bi:st] N **(a)** Tier *nt* **(b)** (*inf*: = *person*) Biest *nt*

beastly ['bi:stlɪ] (*inf*) ADJ scheußlich

beat [bi:t] VB, *pret* **beat**, *ptp* **beaten** **1** N **(a)** (*of heart, drum*) (= *single ~*) Schlag *m*; (= *repeated beating*) Schlagen *nt*; **to the ~ of the drum** zum Schlag der Trommeln
(b) (*of policeman, sentry*) Runde *f*; (= *district*) Revier *nt*; **to be on** *or* **to patrol the ~** seine Runde machen
(c) (*Mus, Poet*) Takt *m*; (*of baton*) Taktschlag *m*; **on/off the ~** auf dem betonten/unbetonten Taktteil
2 VT **(a)** schlagen; *carpet* klopfen; **to ~ a/one's way through sth** einen/sich (*dat*) einen Weg durch etw bahnen; **to ~ a path to sb's door** (*fig*) jdm die Bude einrennen (*inf*); **to ~ a/ the drum** trommeln; **~ it!** (*fig inf*) hau ab! (*inf*); **the bird ~s its wings** der Vogel schlägt mit den Flügeln; **to ~ time (to the music)** den Takt schlagen
(b) (= *hammer*) *metal* hämmern
(c) (= *defeat*) schlagen; *record* brechen; *inflation* in den Griff bekommen; *disease* erfolgreich bekämpfen; **his forehand ~ me** ich war dem Vorhandschlag nicht gewachsen; **to ~ sb into second place** jdn auf den zweiten Platz verweisen; **you can't ~ real wool** es geht doch nichts über reine Wolle; **if you can't ~ them, join them** (*inf*) wenn dus nicht besser machen kannst, dann mach es genauso; **coffee ~s tea any day** Kaffee ist allemal besser als Tee; **it ~s me (how/why ...)** (*inf*) es ist mir ein Rätsel(, wie/warum ...) (*inf*)
(d) (= *be before*) *budget, crowds* zuvorkommen (+*dat*); **I'll ~ you down to the beach** ich bin vor dir am Strand; **to ~ the deadline** vor Ablauf der Frist fertig sein; **to ~ sb to it** jdm zuvorkommen
3 VI schlagen; (*rain*) trommeln; **to ~ on the door (with one's fists)** mit den Fäusten) gegen die Tür schlagen
4 ADJ **(a)** (*inf*: = *exhausted*) **to be (dead) ~** total kaputt sein (*inf*)
(b) (*inf*: = *defeated*) **to be ~(en)** aufgeben müssen (*inf*); **he doesn't know when he's ~(en)** er gibt nicht auf (*inf*); **this problem's got me ~** mit dem Problem komme ich nicht klar (*inf*)
➤ **beat back** VT SEP *flames, enemy* zurückschlagen
➤ **beat down** **1** VI (*rain*) herunterprasseln; (*sun*) herunterbrennen **2** VT SEP **(a)** (= *reduce*) **I managed to beat him down (on the price)** ich konnte den Preis herunterhandeln **(b)** (= *flatten*) *door* einrennen
➤ **beat in** VT SEP **(a)** *door* einschlagen **(b)** (*Cook*) *eggs etc* unterrühren
➤ **beat off** VT SEP abwehren
➤ **beat out** VT SEP *fire* ausschlagen; *metal, dent* aushämmern; *tune, rhythm* schlagen; (*on drum*) trommeln; **to beat sb's brains out** (*inf*: = *kill*) jdm den Schädel einschlagen (*inf*)
➤ **beat up** VT SEP *person* zusammenschlagen
➤ **beat up on** VI +PREP OBJ (*US inf*) (= *hit*) verhauen (*inf*); (= *bully*) einschüchtern; (= *criticize*) auseinander nehmen (*inf*)

beaten ['bi:tn] **1** PTP *of* **beat 2** ADJ *earth* festgetreten; *path* ausgetreten; **to be off the ~ track** (*fig*) abgelegen sein

beater ['bi:tə'] N (*carpet ~*) Klopfer *m*; (= *egg ~*) Schneebesen *m*

beating ['bi:tɪŋ] N **(a)** (= *series of blows*) Prügel *pl*; **to give sb a ~** verprügeln; **to get a ~** verprügelt werden **(b)** (*of drums, heart, wings*) Schlagen *nt* **(c)** (= *defeat*) Niederlage *f*; **to take a ~ (at the hands of sb)** (von jdm) nach allen Regeln der Kunst geschlagen werden **(d) to take some ~** nicht leicht zu übertreffen sein; (*idea, insolence etc*) seines-/ihresgleichen suchen

beat-up ['bi:tʌp] ADJ (*inf*) ramponiert (*inf*)

Beaufort scale ['bəufət,skeɪl] N Beaufortskala *f*

beautician [bju:'tɪʃən] N Kosmetiker(in) *m(f)*

beautiful ['bju:tɪfəl] ADJ schön; *idea, meal* herrlich, wunderbar; (= *good*) *swimmer, organization, piece of work* hervorragend, wunderbar

beautifully ['bju:tɪfəlɪ] ADV schön; *warm, prepared, simple* herrlich; (= *well*) *sew, swim* sehr gut

beautify ['bju:tɪfaɪ] VT verschönern

beauty ['bju:tɪ] N **(a)** Schönheit *f*; **~ is in the eye of the beholder** (*Prov*) schön ist, was (einem) gefällt **(b)** (= *good example*) Prachtexemplar *nt* **(c)** (= *pleasing feature*) **the ~ of it is that ...** das Schöne *or* Schönste daran ist, dass ...

beauty IN CPDS Schönheits-; **beauty competition, beauty contest** N Schönheitswettbewerb *m*; **beauty parlour,** (*US*)

beauty parlor N Schönheitssalon *m*; **beauty queen** N Schönheitskönigin *f*; **beauty shop** N (US) Schönheitssalon *m*; **beauty sleep** N (*hum*) Schlaf *m*; **beauty spot** N (a) Schönheitsfleck *m* (b) (= *place*) schönes *or* hübsches Fleckchen (Erde); **beauty treatment** N kosmetische Behandlung

beaver ['biːvəʳ] N (a) Biber *m* (b) (= *fur*) Biber(pelz) *m*
➤ **beaver away** VI (*inf*) schuften (*inf*) (*at* an +*dat*)

became [bɪ'keɪm] PRET *of* **become**

because [bɪ'kɒz] ❶ CONJ weil; **it was the more surprising ~ we were not expecting it** es war umso überraschender, als wir es nicht erwartet hatten; **why did you do it? – just ~** (*inf*) warum hast du das getan? – darum ❷ PREP **~ of** wegen (+*gen or* (*inf*) +*dat*); **I only did it ~ of you** ich habe es nur deinetwegen getan

beck [bek] N **to be (completely) at sb's ~ and call** jdm voll und ganz zur Verfügung stehen

beckon ['bekən] VTI winken; **he ~ed to her to follow (him)** er gab ihr ein Zeichen, ihm zu folgen; **fame ~ed** der Ruhm lockte

become [bɪ'kʌm], *pret* **became**, *ptp* **become** ❶ VI werden; **it has ~ a rule** es ist jetzt Vorschrift; **it has ~ a nuisance/habit** es ist lästig/zur Gewohnheit geworden; **to ~ interested in sb/sth** anfangen, sich für jdn/etw zu interessieren; **to ~ king/a doctor** König/Arzt werden; **what has ~ of him?** was ist aus ihm geworden?; **what's to ~ of him?** was soll aus ihm werden? ❷ VT (a) (= *suit*) stehen (+*dat*) (b) (= *befit*) sich schicken für

> *Be careful!* **to become** *is not translated by the German word* ***bekommen***.

becoming [bɪ'kʌmɪŋ] ADJ (a) (= *suitable, fitting*) schicklich; **it's not ~ (for a lady) to sit like that** es schickt sich (für eine Dame) nicht, so zu sitzen (b) (= *flattering*) vorteilhaft, kleidsam; **that dress is very ~** das Kleid steht ihr/dir *etc* sehr gut

B Ed ABBR *of* **Bachelor of Education**

bed [bed] N (a) Bett *nt*; **to go to ~** zu *or* ins Bett gehen; **to put *or* get sb to ~** jdn ins *or* zu Bett bringen; **to get into ~** sich ins Bett legen; **to get into ~ with sb** (*lit, fig*) mit jdm ins Bett steigen (*inf*); **he must have got out of ~ on the wrong side** (*inf*) er ist wohl mit dem linken Fuß zuerst aufgestanden; **to be in ~** im Bett sein; **to make the ~** das Bett machen; **can I have a ~ for the night?** kann ich hier/bei euch *etc* übernachten? (b) (*of ore, coal*) Lager *nt*; **a ~ of clay** Lehmboden *m* (c) (= *sea ~*) Grund *m*; (= *river ~*) Bett *nt* (d) (= *flower ~*) Beet *nt*
➤ **bed down** VI sein Lager aufschlagen; **to bed down for the night** sein Nachtlager aufschlagen

bed and breakfast N Übernachtung *f* mit Frühstück; (*also ~ place*) Frühstückspension *f*; "**~**" „Fremdenzimmer"
bed IN CPDS Bett-; **bed bath** N **to give sb a ~** jdn im Bett waschen; **bedbug** N Wanze *f*; **bedclothes** PL (*Brit*) Bettzeug *nt*
bedding ['bedɪŋ] N Bettzeug *nt*
bedding plant N Setzling *m*
bedeck [bɪ'dek] VT schmücken
bedevil [bɪ'devl] VT erschweren; **bedevilled** (*Brit*) *or* **bedeviled** (*US*) **by misfortune** vom Schicksal verfolgt
bed: **bedfellow** N **to be *or* make strange ~s** (*fig*) ein merkwürdiges Gespann sein; **bedhead** N Kopfteil *m* des Bettes
bedlam ['bedləm] N (*fig: = uproar*) Chaos *nt*
bed linen N Bettwäsche *f*
Bedouin ['beduɪn] ❶ N Beduine *m*, Beduinin *f* ❷ ADJ beduinisch
bedraggled [bɪ'dræɡld] ADJ (= *wet*) triefnass; (= *dirty*) verdreckt; (= *untidy*) ungepflegt
bedridden ['bedrɪdn] ADJ bettlägerig
bedroom ['bedruːm] N Schlafzimmer *nt*
bedside ['bedsaɪd] N **to be/sit at sb's ~** an jds Bett (*dat*) sein/sitzen
bedside: **bedside lamp** N Nachttischlampe *f*; **bedside manner** N **he has a good/bad ~** er kann gut/nicht gut mit den Kranken umgehen; **bedside table** N Nachttisch *m*

bed: **bedsit(ter)** ['bedsɪt(əʳ)] (*inf*), **bedsitting room** [ˌbed'sɪtɪŋruːm] N (*Brit*) möbliertes Zimmer; **bedsock** N Bettschuh *m*; **bedsore** N wund gelegene Stelle; **to get ~s** sich wund liegen; **bedspread** N Tagesdecke *f*; **bedstead** N Bettgestell *nt*; **bedtime** N Schlafenszeit *f*; **it's ~** es ist Schlafenszeit; **his ~ is 10 o'clock** er geht um 10 Uhr schlafen; **it's past your ~** du müsstest schon lange im Bett sein; **bedtime story** N Gutenachtgeschichte *f*; **bed-wetting** N Bettnässen *nt*

bee [biː] N Biene *f*; **to have a ~ in one's bonnet** (*inf*) einen Tick haben (*inf*)
Beeb [biːb] N **the ~** (*Brit inf*) die BBC
beech [biːtʃ] N (a) (= *tree*) Buche *f* (b) (= *wood*) Buche(nholz *nt*) *f*
beech tree N Buche *f*
beef [biːf] ❶ N (a) (= *meat*) Rindfleisch *nt* (b) (*inf: = muscles*) Muskeln *pl* ❷ VI (*inf: = complain*) meckern (*inf*) (*about* über +*acc*); **what are you ~ing about?** was hast du zu meckern? (*inf*)
➤ **beef up** VT SEP (= *make more powerful etc*) aufmotzen (*inf*)
beef: **beefburger** N Hamburger *m*; **beefeater** N (a) Beefeater *m* (b) (US *inf*) Engländer(in) *m(f)*; **beefsteak** N Beefsteak *nt*; **beef tea** N Kraft- *or* Fleischbrühe *f*
beefy ['biːfɪ] ADJ (+ER) fleischig
bee: **beehive** ❶ N Bienenstock *m*; (*dome-shaped*) Bienenkorb *m* ❷ ADJ **~ hairdo** toupierte Hochfrisur; **beekeeper** N Imker(in) *m(f)*; **beeline** N **to make a ~ for sb/sth** schnurstracks auf jdn/etw zugehen
been [biːn] PTP *of* **be**
beep [biːp] (*inf*) ❶ N Tut(tut) *nt* (*inf*); **leave your name and number after the ~** hinterlassen Sie Ihren Namen und Ihre Nummer nach dem Signalton ❷ VT **to ~ the *or* one's horn** hupen ❸ VI tuten (*inf*); **~ ~!** tut, tut (*inf*)
beer [bɪəʳ] N Bier *nt*; **two ~s, please** zwei Bier, bitte

BEER

*In England und Wales ist das am weitesten verbreitete Fassbier (**draught beer**) ein **bitter**, das so heißt wegen seines vollen, leicht bitteren Geschmacks. Das schottische **heavy** ähnelt dem englischen **bitter**. Außerdem werden in Großbritannien noch andere Biersorten gerne getrunken, so z. B. das **stout**, das stark und sehr dunkel ist, das **mild**, das ähnlich wie ein **bitter** schmeckt, aber mit weniger Hopfen gebraut wird, und das **lager**, ein leichtes Bier, das am ehesten einem deutschen Export entspricht.*

---

beer IN CPDS Bier-; **beer belly** N (*inf*) Bierbauch *m* (*inf*); **beer bottle** N Bierflasche *f*; **beer bust** N (US *Univ sl*) (= *party*) Bierfete *f* (*inf*); (= *drinking spree*) Saufgelage *nt* (*pej inf*); **beer garden** N (*Brit*) Biergarten *m*; **beer glass** N Bierglas *nt*; **beer gut** N (*inf*) Bierbauch *m* (*inf*); **beer mat** N (*Brit*) Bierdeckel *m*
bee sting N Bienenstich *m*
beeswax ['biːzwæks] N Bienenwachs *nt*
beet [biːt] N Rübe *f*
beetle ['biːtl] N Käfer *m*
beetroot [biːtruːt] N Rote Bete *or* Rübe
befall [bɪ'fɔːl], *pret* **befell** [bɪ'fel], *ptp* **befallen** [bɪ'fɔːlən] (*old, liter*) VT widerfahren (+*dat*) (*geh*)
befit [bɪ'fɪt] VT (*form*) **sb** sich ziemen für (*geh*); **occasion** angemessen sein (+*dat*)
before [bɪ'fɔːʳ] ❶ PREP vor (+*dat*); (*with movement*) vor (+*acc*); **the year ~ last** vorletztes Jahr, das vorletzte Jahr; **the day ~ yesterday** vorgestern; **the day/time ~ that** der Tag/die Zeit davor; **~ then** vorher; **you should have done it ~ now** das hättest du schon (eher) gemacht haben sollen; **~ long** bald; **~ everything else** zuallererst; **to come ~ sb/sth** vor jdm/etw kommen; **ladies ~ gentlemen** Damen haben den Vortritt; **my (very) eyes** vor meinen Augen; **the task ~ us** (= *with which we are confronted*) die Aufgabe, vor der wir stehen; (= *which lies ahead of us*) die uns bevorstehende Aufgabe ❷ ADV (*indicating time, order*) (= *before that*) davor; (= *before now*) vorher; **have you been to Scotland ~?** waren Sie schon einmal in Schottland?; **I have seen** *etc* **this ~** ich habe das schon einmal gesehen *etc*; **never ~** noch nie; **(on) the evening/day ~** am Abend/Tag vorher; **(in) the month/year ~** im Monat/Jahr davor; **two hours ~** zwei Stunden vorher; **two days ~** zwei Tage davor *or* zuvor; **things continued as ~** alles war wie gehabt; **life went on as ~** das Leben ging seinen gewohnten Gang; **that chapter and the one ~** dieses Kapitel

und das davor

3 CONJ bevor; ~ **doing sth** bevor man etw tut; **you can't go ~ this is done** du kannst erst gehen, wenn das gemacht ist; **it will be a long time ~ he comes back** es wird lange dauern, bis er zurückkommt

beforehand [bɪˈfɔːhænd] ADV im Voraus; **you must tell me ~** Sie müssen mir vorher Bescheid sagen

before-tax [bɪˈfɔːtæks] ADJ *income, profits* vor Steuern

befriend [bɪˈfrend] VT Umgang pflegen mit

befuddle [bɪˈfʌdl] VT **he is rather ~d** er ist ziemlich verwirrt

beg [beg] **1** VT **(a)** *money, alms* betteln um **(b)** (= *crave, ask for*) *forgiveness, a favour* bitten um; **to ~ sth of sb** jdn um etw bitten; **he ~ged to be allowed to ...** er bat darum, ... zu dürfen; **I ~ to differ** ich erlaube mir, anderer Meinung zu sein **(c)** (= *entreat*) *sb* anflehen; **I ~ you!** ich flehe dich an! **(d) to ~ the question** an der eigentlichen Frage vorbeigehen **2** VI **(a)** (*beggar*) betteln; (*dog*) Männchen machen **(b)** (*for help, time etc*) bitten (*for* um) **(c)** (= *entreat*) **I ~ of you** ich bitte Sie **(d) to go ~ging** (*inf*) noch zu haben sein; (= *be unwanted*) keine Abnehmer finden

began [bɪˈgæn] PRET *of* begin

beget [bɪˈget], *pret* **begot** *or* (*obs*) **begat** [bɪˈgæt], *ptp* **begotten** *or* **begot** VT (*fig*) *difficulties etc* zeugen (*geh*); **violence ~s violence** Gewalt erzeugt Gewalt

beggar [ˈbegəʳ] **1** N **(a)** Bettler(in) *m(f)*; **~s can't be choosers** (*prov*) in der Not frisst der Teufel Fliegen (*prov*) **(b)** (*Brit inf*) Kerl *m* (*inf*); **poor ~!** armer Kerl! (*inf*); **a lucky ~** ein Glückspilz *m* **2** VT (*fig*) **to ~ description** jeder Beschreibung (*gen*) spotten; **to ~ belief** nicht zu fassen sein

begging [ˈbegɪŋ]: **begging bowl** N Bettlerschale *f*; **to hold out a ~ (to sb)** (*fig*) (bei jdm) betteln gehen; **begging letter** N Bittbrief *m*

begin [bɪˈgɪn], *pret* **began**, *ptp* **begun** **1** VT **(a)** (= *start*) beginnen, anfangen; *rehearsals, work* anfangen mit; *task* in Angriff nehmen; **to ~ to do sth** *or* **doing sth** anfangen *or* beginnen, etw zu tun; **to ~ working** *or* **to work on sth** mit der Arbeit an etw (*dat*) anfangen *or* beginnen; **she ~s the job next week** sie fängt nächste Woche (bei der Stelle) an; **to ~ school** in die Schule kommen; **she began to feel tired** sie wurde langsam müde; **she's ~ning to understand** sie fängt langsam an zu verstehen; **I'd begun to think you weren't coming** ich habe schon gedacht, du kommst nicht mehr **(b)** (= *initiate, originate*) anfangen; *fashion, custom, policy* einführen; *society, firm, movement* gründen; (= *cause*) *war* auslösen; **he began the rumour** (*Brit*) *or* **rumor** (*US*) er hat das Gerücht in die Welt gesetzt

2 VI beginnen, anfangen; (*new play etc*) anlaufen; **to ~ by doing sth** etw zuerst (einmal) tun; **he began by saying that ...** er sagte einleitend, dass ...; **~ning from Monday** ab Montag; **~ning from page 10** von Seite 10 an; **it all/the trouble began when ...** es fing alles/der Ärger fing damit an, dass ...; **to ~ with sb/sth** mit jdm/etw anfangen; **to ~ with there were only three** anfänglich waren es nur drei; **to ~ with, this is wrong, and ...** erstens einmal ist das falsch, dann ...; **to ~ on sth** etw anfangen *or* beginnen

beginner [bɪˈgɪnəʳ] N Anfänger(in) *m(f)*; **~'s luck** Anfängerglück *nt*

beginning [bɪˈgɪnɪŋ] N Anfang *m*; (*of custom, movement*) Entstehen *nt no pl*; **at the ~** anfänglich, zuerst; **at the ~ of sth** am Anfang einer Sache (*gen*); **the wedding will be at the ~ of July** die Hochzeit findet Anfang Juli statt; **from the ~** von Anfang an; **from the ~ of the week/poem** seit Anfang der Woche/vom Anfang des Gedichtes an; **read the paragraph from the ~** lesen Sie den Paragraphen von (ganz) vorne; **from ~ to end** von vorn bis hinten; (*temporal*) von Anfang bis Ende; **to start again** at *or* **from the ~** noch einmal von vorn anfangen; **to begin at the ~** ganz vorn anfangen; **it was the ~ of the end for him** das war der Anfang vom Ende für ihn; **his humble ~s** seine einfachen Anfänge

begonia [bɪˈgəʊnɪə] N Begonie *f*

begot [bɪˈgɒt] PRET, PTP *of* beget

begotten [bɪˈgɒtn] PTP *of* beget

begrudge [bɪˈgrʌdʒ] VT **(a)** (= *be reluctant*) **to ~ doing sth** etw widerwillig tun **(b)** (= *envy*) missgönnen (*sb sth* jdm etw)

(c) (= *give unwillingly*) nicht gönnen (*sb sth* jdm etw); **I won't ~ you £5** du sollst die £ 5 haben

begrudgingly [bɪˈgrʌdʒɪŋlɪ] ADV widerwillig

beguile [bɪˈgaɪl] VT betören (*geh*); **to ~ sb into doing sth** jdn dazu verführen, etw zu tun

beguiling [bɪˈgaɪlɪŋ] ADJ betörend

begun [bɪˈgʌn] PTP *of* begin

behalf [bɪˈhɑːf] N **on** *or* **in** (*US*) **~ of** für, im Interesse von; (*as spokesman*) im Namen von; (*as authorized representative*) im Auftrag von

behave [bɪˈheɪv] **1** VI sich verhalten; (= *be good*) sich benehmen; **to ~ well/badly** sich gut/schlecht benehmen; **what a way to ~!** was für ein Benehmen!; **to ~ badly/well toward(s) sb** jdn schlecht/gut behandeln; **~! benimm dich!; can't you make your dog ~?** kannst du deinem Hund keine Manieren beibringen?; **he knows how to ~ at a cocktail party** er weiß sich bei Cocktailpartys zu benehmen **2** VR **to ~ oneself** sich benehmen; **~ yourself!** benimm dich!

behaviour, (*US*) **behavior** [bɪˈheɪvjəʳ] N **(a)** (= *manner, bearing*) Benehmen *nt*; **to be on one's best ~** sich von seiner besten Seite zeigen **(b)** (*towards others*) Verhalten *nt* (*to(wards)* gegenüber)

behavioural, (*US*) **behavioral** [bɪˈheɪvjərəl] ADJ IN CPDS Verhaltens-; **behavioural science** N Verhaltensforschung *f*; **behavioural scientist** N Verhaltensforscher(in) *m(f)*

behead [bɪˈhed] VT enthaupten, köpfen

beheld [bɪˈheld] PRET, PTP *of* behold

behind [bɪˈhaɪnd] **1** PREP **(a)** hinter (+*dat*); (*with motion*) hinter (+*acc*); **come out from ~ the door** komm hinter der Tür (her)vor; **he came up ~ me** er trat von hinten an mich heran; **walk close ~ me** gehen Sie dicht hinter mir; **put it ~ the books** stellen Sie es hinter die Bücher; **what is ~ this incident?** was steckt hinter diesem Vorfall?; **to be ~ sb** hinter jdm zurück sein

(b) (*in time*) **to be ~ time** (*train etc*) Verspätung haben; (*with work etc*) im Rückstand sein; **to be ~ schedule** im Verzug sein; **to be ~ the times** (*fig*) hinter seiner Zeit zurück(geblieben) sein; **you must put the past ~ you** Sie müssen Vergangenes vergangen sein lassen **2** ADV **(a)** (= *in or at rear*) hinten; (= ~ *this, sb etc*) dahinter; **from ~** von hinten; **to look ~** zurückblicken; **to stand ~** (= *be standing*) dahinter stehen; (= *position oneself*) sich dahinter stellen

(b) (= *late*) **to be ~ with one's studies** mit seinen Studien im Rückstand sein

3 N (*inf*) Hinterteil *nt* (*inf*)

behindhand [bɪˈhaɪndhænd] ADV, ADJ **to be ~ with sth** mit etw im Rückstand *or* Verzug sein

behold [bɪˈhəʊld], *pret*, *ptp* **beheld** VT (*liter*) erblicken (*liter*)

beige [beɪʒ] **1** ADJ beige **2** N Beige *nt*

being [ˈbiːɪŋ] N **(a)** (= *existence*) Dasein *nt*; **to come into ~** entstehen; **to bring into ~** ins Leben rufen **(b)** (= *that which exists*) (Lebe)wesen *nt*; **~s from outer space** Wesen *pl* aus dem All **(c)** (= *essence*) Wesen *nt*; **with all** *or* **every fibre** (*Brit*) *or* **fiber** (*US*) **of my ~** mit jeder Faser meines Herzens

Beirut [beɪˈruːt] N Beirut *nt*

belated ADJ, **belatedly** ADV [bɪˈleɪtɪd, -lɪ] verspätet

belch [beltʃ] **1** VI (*person*) rülpsen **2** VT (*also* ~ **forth** *or* **out**) *smoke* ausstoßen **3** N Rülpser *m* (*inf*)

beleaguer [bɪˈliːgəʳ] VT belagern; (*fig*) umgeben

beleaguered [bɪˈliːgəd] ADJ (*fig*) unter Druck stehend

belfry [ˈbelfrɪ] N Glockenstube *f*

Belgian [ˈbeldʒən] **1** N Belgier(in) *m(f)* **2** ADJ belgisch

Belgium [ˈbeldʒəm] N Belgien *nt*

Belgrade [belˈgreɪd] N Belgrad *nt*

belie [bɪˈlaɪ] VT **(a)** (= *prove false*) Lügen strafen, widerlegen **(b)** (= *give false impression of*) hinwegtäuschen über (+*acc*)

belief [bɪˈliːf] N Glaube *m* (*in* an +*acc*); (= *doctrine*) (Glaubens)lehre *f*; **it is beyond ~** es ist unglaublich; **in the ~ that ...** im Glauben, dass ...; **it is my ~ that ...** ich bin der Überzeugung, dass ...; **to have ~ in** glauben an (+*acc*)

believable [bɪˈliːvəbl] ADJ glaubwürdig

believe [bɪˈliːv] **1** VT glauben; **I don't ~ you** das glaube ich (Ihnen) nicht; **don't you ~ it** wers glaubt, wird selig (*inf*); **~ you me!** (*inf*) das können Sie mir glauben!; **~ it or not** ob Sies glauben oder nicht; **would you ~ it!** (*inf*) ist das (denn) die Möglichkeit (*inf*); **I would never have ~d it of him** das hätte ich nie von ihm geglaubt; **he could hardly ~ his eyes** er traute seinen Augen nicht; **he is ~d to be ill** es heißt, dass er krank ist; **I ~ so/not** ich glaube schon/nicht

2 VI (= *have a religious faith*) an Gott glauben

➤ **believe in** VI +PREP OBJ **(a)** glauben an (+*acc*); **he doesn't believe in doctors** er hält nicht viel von Ärzten **(b)** (= *support idea of*) **to believe in sth** (prinzipiell) für etw sein; **he believes in getting up early** er ist überzeugter Frühaufsteher; **he believes in giving people a second chance** er gibt prinzipiell jedem noch einmal eine Chance; **I don't believe in compromises** ich halte nichts von Kompromissen

believer [bɪˈliːvəʳ] N **(a)** (*Rel*) Gläubige(r) *mf* **(b) to be a (firm) ~ in sth** (grundsätzlich) für etw sein

belittle [bɪˈlɪtl] VT herabsetzen, heruntermachen (*inf*); **to ~ oneself** sich schlechter machen, als man ist

bell [bel] **1** N **(a)** Glocke *f*; (*small*) Glöckchen *nt*, Schelle *f*; (= *school ~, doorbell, of bicycle, phone*) Klingel *f*; **as clear as a ~** *voice* glasklar; *hear, sound* laut und deutlich
(b) (= *sound of ~*) **there's the ~** es klingelt *or* läutet; **he's coming up to the ~** er geht nun in die letzte Runde; **to give sb a ~** (*Brit inf*) jdn anrufen
(c) (*of flower*) Kelch *m*
2 VT eine Glocke/ein Glöckchen umhängen (+*dat*)

bell: **bell-bottomed trousers** (*esp Brit*), **bell-bottoms** PL ausgestellte Hosen; **bellboy** N (*esp US*) Page *m*; **bell captain** N (*US*) Chef(in) *m(f)* der Hotelpagen

belle [bel] N Schönheit *f*; **the ~ of the ball** die Ballkönigin

bellhop N (*US*) = **bellboy**

belligerence [bɪˈlɪdʒərəns] N (*of nation*) Kriegslust *f*; (*of person*) Streitlust *f*

belligerent [bɪˈlɪdʒərənt] ADJ *nation* kriegslustig; *person* streitlustig; *speech* aggressiv

belligerently [bɪˈlɪdʒərəntlɪ] ADV *say, act* streitlustig

bellow [ˈbeləʊ] **1** VTI brüllen; **to ~ at sb** jdn anbrüllen **2** N Brüllen *nt*

bellows [ˈbeləʊz] PL Blasebalg *m*; **a pair of ~** ein Blasebalg

bell: **bell pull** N Klingelzug *m*; **bell push** N Klingel *f*; **bell-ringer** N Glöckner *m*; **bell-ringing** N Glockenläuten *nt*; **bell rope** N Glockenstrang *m*

belly [ˈbelɪ] N Bauch *m*; (*of violin etc*) Decke *f*

belly: **bellyache** (*inf*) **1** N Bauchschmerzen *pl* **2** VI (= *complain*) murren (*about* über +*acc*); **bellybutton** N (*inf*) Bauchnabel *m*; **belly dance** N Bauchtanz *m*; **belly-dance** VI bauchtanzen; **belly dancer** N Bauchtänzerin *f*; **bellyflop** N (*inf*) Bauchklatscher *m* (*inf*); **to do a ~** einen Bauchklatscher machen (*inf*)

bellyful [ˈbelɪfʊl] N (*inf*) **I've had a ~ of him/writing these letters** ich habe die Nase voll von ihm/davon, immer diese Briefe zu schreiben (*inf*)

belly: **belly laugh** N dröhnendes Lachen; **he gave a great ~** er lachte lauthals los; **belly up** ADV **to go ~** (*inf: company*) Pleite gehen (*inf*)

belong [bɪˈlɒŋ] VI gehören (*to sb* jdm, *to sth* zu etw); **who does it ~ to?** wem gehört es?; **to ~ together** zusammengehören; **to ~ to a club** einem Klub angehören; **to feel that one doesn't ~** das Gefühl haben, dass man nicht dazugehört; **it ~s under the heading of …** das fällt in die Rubrik der …

belongings [bɪˈlɒŋɪŋz] PL Sachen *pl*, Besitz *m*; **personal ~** persönlicher Besitz; **all his ~** sein ganzes Hab und Gut

beloved [bɪˈlʌvɪd] **1** ADJ geliebt **2** N Geliebte(r) *mf*; **dearly ~** (*Rel*) liebe Brüder und Schwestern im Herrn

below [bɪˈləʊ] **1** PREP unterhalb (+*gen*); (*with level etc also*) unter (+*dat or with motion* +*acc*); **her skirt comes well ~ her knees** *or* **the knee** ihr Rock geht bis weit unters Knie; **to be ~ sb** (*in rank*) (rangmäßig) unter jdm stehen
2 ADV **(a)** (= *lower down*) unten; **the cows in the valley ~** die Kühe drunten im Tal; **they live one floor ~** sie wohnen ein Stockwerk tiefer; **the apartment/class ~** die Wohnung/Klasse darunter; (*below us*) die Wohnung/Klasse unter uns; **down ~** unten; **see ~** siehe unten
(b) (*Naut*) unter Deck; **to go ~** unter Deck gehen
(c) 15 degrees ~ 15 Grad unter null

belt [belt] **1** N **(a)** (*on clothes, of land*) Gürtel *m*; (*for holding, carrying etc, seat ~*) Gurt *m*; (*Mil etc: on uniform*) Koppel *nt*;

that was below the ~ das war ein Schlag unter die Gürtellinie; **to tighten one's ~** (*fig*) den Gürtel *or* Riemen enger schnallen; **under one's ~** (*fig inf*) auf dem Rücken (*inf*); **industrial ~** Industriegürtel *m*
(b) (*Tech*) (Treib)riemen *m*; (= *conveyor ~*) Band *nt*
(c) (*inf.*: = *hit*) Schlag *m*; **to give sb/the ball a ~** jdm eine knallen (*inf*)/den Ball knallen (*inf*)
(d) (*US*: = *ring road*) Umgehungsstraße *f*
(e) (*US*: = *drink*) Schluck *m* aus der Pulle (*inf*)
2 VT (*inf.*: = *hit*) knallen (*inf*); **she ~ed him one in the eye** sie knallte ihm eins aufs Auge (*inf*)
3 VI (*inf.*: = *rush*) rasen (*inf*); **to ~ out** hinausrasen (*inf*); **we were really ~ing along** wir sind wirklich gerast (*inf*)

➤ **belt out** VT SEP (*inf*) *tune* schmettern (*inf*); (*on piano*) hämmern (*inf*)

➤ **belt up** VI (*inf*) die Klappe halten (*inf*); (= *stop making noise*) mit dem Krach aufhören (*inf*)

belt drive N Riemenantrieb *m*

beltway [ˈbeltweɪ] N (*US*) Umgehungsstraße *f*

bemoan [bɪˈməʊn] VT beklagen

bemused [bɪˈmjuːzd] ADJ ratlos; **to be ~ by sth** einer Sache (*dat*) ratlos gegenüberstehen

bench [bentʃ] **1** N **(a)** (= *seat*) Bank *f* **(b)** (*Jur*) (= *judges generally*) Richter *pl*; (= *court*) Gericht *nt*; **to be on the ~** (= *permanent office*) Richter sein; (*when in court*) der Richter sein **(c)** (= *workbench*) Werkbank *f*; (*in lab*) Experimentiertisch *m* **(d)** (*Sport*) **on the ~** auf der Reservebank **2** VT (*US Sport*) auf die Strafbank schicken; (= *keep as substitute*) auf die Reservebank setzen

benchmark [ˈbentʃmɑːk] **1** N (*fig*) Maßstab *m* **2** ADJ ATTR **~ price** Richtpreis *m*; **~ rate** Benchmark *f*

bend [bend] VB, *pret*, *ptp* **bent** **1** N (*in river, tube, etc*) Biegung *f*; (*in road*) Kurve *f*; **there is a ~ in the road** die Straße macht (da) eine Kurve; **to go/be round the ~** (*Brit inf*) verrückt werden/sein (*inf*); **to drive sb round the ~** (*Brit inf*) jdn verrückt machen (*inf*)
2 VT **(a)** (= *curve, make angular*) biegen; *arm, knee also* beugen; *head* beugen, neigen; **to ~ sth out of shape** etw verbiegen
(b) (*fig*) *rules, truth* es nicht so genau nehmen mit; **to ~ the law** das Gesetz beugen
3 VI **(a)** sich biegen; (*person*) sich beugen; **this metal ~s easily** (*a bad thing*) dieses Metall verbiegt sich leicht; (*a good thing*) dieses Metall lässt sich leicht biegen; **my arm won't ~** ich kann den Arm nicht biegen
(b) (*river*) eine Biegung machen; (*road*) eine Kurve machen

➤ **bend back 1** VI sich zurückbiegen; (*over backwards*) sich nach hinten biegen **2** VT SEP zurückbiegen

➤ **bend down 1** VI (*person*) sich bücken; **she bent down to look at the baby** sie beugte sich hinunter, um das Baby anzusehen **2** VT SEP *edges* nach unten biegen

➤ **bend over 1** VI (*person*) sich bücken; **to bend over to look at sth** sich nach vorn beugen, um etw anzusehen **2** VT SEP umbiegen

bender [ˈbendəʳ] N (*Brit inf*) Kneipkur *f* (*hum inf*); **to go on a ~** (*Brit inf*) sich besaufen (*inf*)

beneath [bɪˈniːθ] **1** PREP **(a)** unter (+*dat or with motion* +*acc*); (*with level etc also*) unterhalb (+*gen*); **to marry ~ one** unter seinem Stand heiraten **(b)** (= *unworthy of*) **it is ~ him** das ist unter seiner Würde **2** ADV unten

Benedictine [ˌbenɪˈdɪktɪn] **1** N (*Eccl*) Benediktiner(in) *m(f)* **2** ADJ Benediktiner-

benediction [ˌbenɪˈdɪkʃən] N (= *blessing*) Segen *m*; (= *act of blessing*) Segnung *f*

benefactor [ˈbenɪfæktəʳ] N Wohltäter *m*

beneficial [ˌbenɪˈfɪʃəl] ADJ gut (*to* für); *influence also* vorteilhaft; *advice, lesson* nützlich (*to* für); (= *advantageous*) günstig

beneficiary [ˌbenɪˈfɪʃərɪ] N Nutznießer(in) *m(f)*; (*of will etc*) Begünstigte(r) *mf*

benefit [ˈbenɪfɪt] **1** N **(a)** (= *advantage*) Vorteil *m*; (= *profit*) Gewinn *m*; **to derive** *or* **get ~ from sth** aus etw Nutzen ziehen; **for the ~ of the poor** für das Wohl der Armen; **for your ~** Ihretwegen; **we should give him the ~ of the doubt** wir sollten das zu seinen Gunsten auslegen
(b) (= *allowance*) Unterstützung *f*; (= *sickness ~*) Krankengeld *nt*; (*Brit*: = *child ~*) Kindergeld *nt*; (= *social security ~*) Sozialhilfe *f*; (*Brit*: = *maternity ~*) Wochengeld *nt*; **to be on**

~(s) staatliche Unterstützung erhalten **(c)** (= *special performance*) Benefizveranstaltung *f* **2** VT gut tun (+*dat*), nützen (+*dat*); (*healthwise*) gut tun (+*dat*) **3** VI profitieren (*from, by* von); **he would ~ from a week off** eine Woche Urlaub würde ihm gut tun; **I think you'll ~ from the experience** ich glaube, diese Erfahrung wird Ihnen nützlich sein *or* von Nutzen sein

benefit: **benefit concert** N Benefizkonzert *nt*; **benefit match** N Benefizspiel *nt*; **benefit performance** N Benefizveranstaltung *f*

Benelux ['benɪlʌks] N Benelux-Wirtschaftsunion *f*; **~ countries** Beneluxstaaten *pl*

benevolence [bɪ'nevələns] N Wohlwollen *nt*; (*as character trait*) Güte *f*; (*of emperor, judge*) Milde *f*

benevolent [bɪ'nevələnt] ADJ wohlwollend; (*as character trait*) gütig; *emperor, judge* mild

Bengal [beŋ'gɔːl] N Bengalen *nt*

Bengali [beŋ'gɔːlɪ] **1** N (= *language*) Bengali *nt*; (= *person*) Bengale *m*, Bengalin *f* **2** ADJ bengalisch

benign [bɪ'naɪn] ADJ **(a)** gütig; *influence* günstig; *climate* mild; (= *harmless*) harmlos **(b)** (*Med*) *tumour* gutartig

bent [bent] **1** PRET, PTP of **bend** **2** ADJ **(a)** *metal etc* gebogen; (= *out of shape*) verbogen **(b)** (*Brit inf*: = *dishonest*) korrupt **(c) to be ~ on sth/doing sth** etw unbedingt wollen/tun wollen **3** N (= *aptitude*) Neigung *f* (*for* zu); (= *type of mind, character*) Schlag *m*; **to follow one's ~** seiner Neigung folgen; **people with** *or* **of a musical ~** Menschen mit einer musikalischen Veranlagung

Benzedrine® ['benzɪdriːn] N Benzedrin *nt*

benzene ['benziːn] N Benzol *nt*

bequeath [bɪ'kwiːð] VT (*in will*) vermachen (*to sb* jdm)

bequest [bɪ'kwest] N (= *act of bequeathing*) Vermachen *nt* (*to* an +*acc*); (= *legacy*) Nachlass *m*

berate [bɪ'reɪt] VT (*liter*) schelten

Berber ['bɜːbəʳ] **1** N Berber(in) *m(f)* **2** ADJ berberisch

bereaved [bɪ'riːvd] ADJ leidtragend; **the ~** die Hinterbliebenen *pl*

bereavement [bɪ'riːvmənt] N (= *death in family*) Trauerfall *m*; **to sympathize with sb in his ~** jds Leid teilen

bereft [bɪ'reft] ADJ **to be ~ of sth** einer Sache (*gen*) bar sein (*geh*)

beret ['bereɪ] N Baskenmütze *f*

Bering ['berɪŋ]: **Bering Sea** N Beringmeer *nt*; **Bering Strait** N Beringstraße *f*

berk [bɜːk] N (*Brit inf*) Dussel *m* (*inf*)

Berlin [bɜː'lɪn] N Berlin *nt*; **the ~ Wall** die Mauer

Bermuda [bɜː'mjuːdə] N Bermuda *nt* (*form rare*); **to go to ~** auf die Bermudas fahren

Bermuda shorts PL Bermudashorts *pl*

Berne [bɜːn] N Bern *nt*

berry ['berɪ] N Beere *f*; **as brown as a ~** (*Brit*) ganz braun gebrannt

berserk [bə'sɜːk] ADJ wild; **to go ~** wild werden; (*audience*) zu toben anfangen; (= *go mad*) überschnappen (*inf*)

berth [bɜːθ] **1** N **(a)** (*on ship*) Koje *f*; (*on train*) Schlafwagenplatz *m* **(b)** (*Naut: for ship*) Liegeplatz *m* **(c) to give sb/sth a wide ~** (*fig*) einen (weiten) Bogen um jdn/etw machen **2** VI anlegen **3** VT **where is she ~ed?** wo liegt es?

beseech [bɪ'siːtʃ] VT (*liter*) anflehen

beset [bɪ'set], *pret*, *ptp* **beset** VT (*difficulties, dangers*) bedrängen; (*doubts*) befallen; **to be ~ with difficulties/danger** voller Schwierigkeiten/Gefahren sein; **~ by doubts** von Zweifeln befallen

beside [bɪ'saɪd] PREP **(a)** (= *at the side of*) neben (+*dat or with motion* +*acc*); (= *at the edge of*) *road, river* an (+*dat or with motion* +*acc*); **~ the road** am Straßenrand **(b)** (= *compared with*) neben (+*dat*) **(c)** (= *irrelevant to*) **to be ~ the point** damit nichts zu tun haben **(d) to be ~ oneself** (*with anger*) außer sich sein (*with* vor)

besides [bɪ'saɪdz] **1** ADV **(a)** (= *in addition*) außerdem, obendrein; **many more ~** noch viele mehr; **have you got any others ~?** haben Sie noch andere? **(b)** (= *anyway, moreover*) außerdem **2** PREP außer; **others ~ ourselves** außer uns noch andere; **there were three of us ~ Mary** Mary nicht

---

mitgerechnet, waren wir zu dritt; **~ which he was unwell** außerdem fühlte er sich nicht wohl

besiege [bɪ'siːdʒ] VT **(a)** (*Mil*) belagern **(b)** (*fig*) belagern; (*with information, offers*) überhäufen; (= *pester*) bedrängen

besmirch [bɪ'smɜːtʃ] VT (*lit, fig*) besudeln

besotted [bɪ'sɒtɪd] ADJ (= *infatuated*) völlig vernarrt (*with* in +*acc*); (*with idea*) berauscht (*with* von)

bespoke [bɪ'spəʊk] ADJ *goods* nach Maß; *service, software* maßgeschneidert; **a ~ tailor** ein Maßschneider *m*

best [best] **1** ADJ SUPERL of **good** beste(r, s) *attr*; **to be ~** am besten sein; **to be ~ of all** am allerbesten sein; **that was the ~ thing about her/that could happen** das war das Beste an ihr/, was geschehen konnte; **the ~ thing to do is to wait, it's ~ to wait** das Beste ist zu warten; **may the ~ man win!** dem Besten der Sieg!; **the ~ part of the year/my money** fast das ganze Jahr/all mein Geld

2 ADV SUPERL *of* **well** am besten; *like* am liebsten; *enjoy* am meisten; **the ~ fitting dress** das am besten passende Kleid; **her ~ known novel** ihr bekanntester Roman; **he was ~ known for ...** er war vor allem bekannt für ...; **~ of all** am allerliebsten/-liebsten/-meisten; **I helped him as ~ I could** ich half ihm, so gut ich konnte; **I thought it ~ to go** ich hielt es für das Beste zu gehen; **do as you think ~** tun Sie, was Sie für richtig halten; **you know ~** Sie müssen es (am besten) wissen; **you had ~ go now** am besten gehen Sie jetzt

3 N **the ~** der/die/das Beste; **his last book was his ~** sein letztes Buch war sein bestes; **they are the ~ of friends** sie sind enge Freunde; **to do one's (very) ~** sein Bestes tun; **do the ~ you can!** machen Sie es so gut Sie können!; **it's the ~ I can do** mehr kann ich nicht tun; **to get the ~ out of sb/sth** das Beste aus jdm/etw herausholen; **to play the ~ of three** nur so lange spielen, bis eine Partei zweimal gewonnen hat; **to make the ~ of it/a bad job** das Beste daraus machen; **to make the ~ of one's opportunities** seine Chancen voll nützen; **the ~ of it is that ...** das Beste daran ist, dass ...; **it's all for the ~** es ist nur zum Guten; **to do sth for the ~** etw in bester Absicht tun; **to the ~ of my ability** so gut ich kann/konnte; **to the ~ of my knowledge** meines Wissens; **to look one's ~** besonders gut aussehen; **it's not enough (even) at the ~ of times** das ist schon normalerweise nicht genug; **at ~** bestenfalls; **all the ~ (to you)** alles Gute!

best: **best-before date** N Haltbarkeitsdatum *nt*; **best-dressed** ADJ bestgekleidet *attr*

bestial ['bestɪəl] ADJ bestialisch

bestiality [ˌbestɪ'ælɪtɪ] N **(a)** (*of behaviour*) Bestialität *f*; (*of person*) Brutalität *f* **(b)** (= *act*) Gräueltat *f*

best man N Trauzeuge *m* (*des Bräutigams*)

BEST MAN

*Bei einer traditionellen Hochzeit ist der **best man** der Trauzeuge des Bräutigams, normalerweise ein enger Freund oder Verwandter, zum Beispiel ein Bruder oder ein Cousin. Seine Pflichten umfassen so wichtige Aufgaben wie den Bräutigam pünktlich zur Kirche zu bringen, Hochzeitsgäste zu empfangen und sich um die Trauringe zu kümmern. Auf dem Hochzeitsempfang übermittelt er normalerweise die Glückwünsche all derer, die nicht kommen konnten, sagt die Redner an, hält selbst eine humorvolle Rede und bringt einen Toast auf das Brautpaar aus.*

---

bestow [bɪ'stəʊ] VT (*up*)*on sb* jdm); *gift* schenken; *honour* erweisen, zuteil werden lassen (*geh*); *title, medal* verleihen

best: **bestseller** N Verkaufsschlager *m* (= *book*) Bestseller *m*; **bestselling** ADJ *article* absatzstark; *author* Erfolgs-; **a ~ novel** ein Bestseller *m*

bet [bet], *vb*: *pret*, *ptp* **bet** **1** N Wette *f* (*on* auf +*acc*); (= *money etc staked*) Wetteinsatz *m*; **to make** *or* **have a ~ with sb** mit jdm wetten; **it's a good** *or* **safe ~ – he'll be in the bar** er ist garantiert in der Kneipe

2 VT **(a)** (*Gambling*) wetten, setzen (*against* gegen/*on* auf +*acc*); **I ~ him £5** ich habe mit ihm (um) £ 5 gewettet **(b)** (*inf*: = *wager*) wetten; **I ~ he'll come!** wetten, dass er kommt! (*inf*); **~ you I can!** wetten, dass ich das kann! (*inf*) **3** VI wetten; **to ~ on a horse** auf ein Pferd setzen *or* wetten; **don't ~ on it** darauf würde ich nicht wetten; **you ~!** (*inf*) und ob! (*inf*); **(do you) want to ~?** (wollen wir) wetten?

beta-blocker ['biːtəˌblɒkəʳ] N Betablocker *m*

bête noire [bet'nwɑːʳ] N **to be sb's ~** jdm ein Gräuel sein

betray [bɪ'treɪ] VT verraten (*to* an +*dat*); *trust* enttäuschen; (= *be unfaithful to*) untreu werden (+*dat*); **to ~ oneself** sich verraten

betrayal [bɪ'treɪəl] N (= *act*) Verrat *m* (*of* an +*dat*); **a ~ of trust** ein Vertrauensbruch *m*

betrayer [bɪ'treɪəʳ] N Verräter(in) *m(f)* (*of* an +*dat*)

betrothed [bɪ'trəʊðd] N (*obs, liter, hum*) Anverlobte(r) *mf* (*obs*)

better ◼ ADJ COMP *of* **good** besser; **he's** ~ (= *recovered*) es geht ihm wieder besser; **his foot is getting** ~ seinem Fuß geht es schon viel besser; **I hope you get ~ soon** hoffentlich sind Sie bald wieder gesund; **~ and ~** immer besser; **that's ~!** (*approval*) so ist es besser!; (*relief etc*) so!; **it couldn't be ~** es könnte gar nicht besser sein; **the ~ part of an hour/my money** fast eine Stunde/mein ganzes Geld; **it would be ~ to go early** es wäre besser, früh zu gehen; **you would be ~ to go early** Sie gehen besser früh; **to go one ~** einen Schritt weiter gehen; (*in offer*) höher gehen; **this hat has seen ~ days** dieser Hut hat auch schon bessere Tage gesehen (*inf*)
◼ ADV COMP *of* **well** besser; *like* lieber; *enjoy* mehr; **they are ~ off than we are** sie sind besser dran als wir; **he is ~ off where he is** er ist besser dran, wo er ist (*inf*); **you would do ~ to go early** Sie sollten lieber früh gehen; **to think ~ of it** es sich (*dat*) noch einmal überlegen; **I had ~ go** ich gehe jetzt wohl besser; **you'd ~ do what he says** tun Sie lieber, was er sagt; **I won't touch it – you'd ~ not!** ich fasse es nicht an – das will ich dir auch geraten haben
◼ N **that's no way to talk to your ~s** man muss immer wissen, wen man vor sich (*dat*) hat; **it's a change for the ~** es ist eine Wendung zum Guten; **all the ~, so much the ~** umso besser; **the bigger/sooner the ~** je größer/eher, desto besser; **to get the ~ of sb** (*person*) jdn unterkriegen (*inf*); (*problem etc*) jdm schwer zu schaffen machen
◼ VT (= *improve on*) verbessern; (= *surpass*) übertreffen
◼ VR (= *increase one's knowledge*) sich weiterbilden; (*in social scale*) sich verbessern

better half N (*inf*) bessere Hälfte (*inf*)

betting ['betɪŋ] N Wetten *nt*

betting: betting shop N Wettannahme *f*; **betting slip** N Wettschein *m*

between [bɪ'twiːn] ◼ PREP **(a)** zwischen (+*dat*); (*with movement*) zwischen (+*acc*); **I was sitting ~ them** ich saß zwischen ihnen; **sit down ~ those two boys** setzen Sie sich zwischen diese beiden Jungen; **in ~** zwischen (+*dat/acc*); **~ now and next week we must ...** bis nächste Woche müssen wir ...; **there's nothing ~ them** (= *they're equal*) sie sind gleich gut; (*no relationship*) zwischen ihnen ist nichts
(b) (= *amongst*) unter (+*dat/acc*); **share the sweets ~ the two children** teilen Sie die Süßigkeiten zwischen den beiden Kindern auf; **divide the sweets ~ the children** verteilen Sie die Süßigkeiten unter die Kinder; **we shared an apple ~ us** wir teilten uns (*dat*) einen Apfel; **~ ourselves** *or* **~ you and me** he is not very clever unter uns (*dat*) gesagt, er ist nicht besonders gescheit; **that's just ~ ourselves** das bleibt aber unter uns
(c) (= *jointly, showing combined effort*) **~ us/them** zusammen; **we have a car ~ the three of us** wir haben zu dritt ein Auto
◼ ADV dazwischen; **in ~** dazwischen; **the space/time ~** der Raum/die Zeit dazwischen

beverage ['bevərɪdʒ] N Getränk *nt*

bevvy ['bevɪ] N (*Brit inf*: = *drink*) **to go for a ~** einen trinken gehen

bevy ['bevɪ] N (*of girls*) Schar *f*

bewail [bɪ'weɪl] VT (= *deplore*) beklagen; (= *lament*) bejammern

beware [bɪ'weəʳ] ◼ VI IMPER AND INFIN ONLY **to ~ of sb/sth** sich vor jdm/etw hüten; **to ~ of doing sth** sich davor hüten, etw zu tun; **"~ of the dog"** „Vorsicht, bissiger Hund"; **"~ of pickpockets"** „vor Taschendieben wird gewarnt"; ◼ VT IMPER AND INFIN ONLY **to ~ sb/sth** sich vor jdm/etw hüten, sich vor jdm/etw in Acht nehmen; **to ~ doing sth** sich davor hüten, etw zu tun

bewilder [bɪ'wɪldəʳ] VT (= *confuse*) verwirren; (= *baffle*) verblüffen

bewildered [bɪ'wɪldəd] ADJ (= *confused*) verwirrt; (= *baffled*) verblüfft

bewildering [bɪ'wɪldərɪŋ] ADJ (= *confusing*) verwirrend; (= *baffling*) verblüffend

bewilderment [bɪ'wɪldəmənt] N (= *confusion*) Verwirrung *f*; (= *bafflement*) Verblüffung *f*; **in ~** verwundert

bewitch [bɪ'wɪtʃ] VT (*fig*) bezaubern

bewitching [bɪ'wɪtʃɪŋ] ADJ bezaubernd

beyond [bɪ'jɒnd] ◼ PREP **(a)** (*in space*) (= *on the other side of*) über (+*dat*), jenseits (+*gen*) (*geh*); (= *further than*) über (+*acc*) ... hinaus, weiter als; **~ the Alps** jenseits der Alpen
(b) (*in time*) **~ 6 o'clock/next week** nach 6 Uhr/nächster Woche; **~ the middle of June/the week** über Mitte Juni/der Woche hinaus
(c) (= *surpassing*) **a task ~ her abilities** eine Aufgabe, die über ihre Fähigkeiten geht; **that is ~ human understanding** das übersteigt menschliches Verständnis; **~ repair** nicht mehr zu reparieren; **it was ~ her to pass the exam** sie schaffte es nicht, das Examen zu bestehen; **that's ~ me** (= *I don't understand*) das geht über meinen Verstand
(d) (*with neg, interrog*) außer; **have you any money ~ what you have in the bank?** haben Sie außer dem, was Sie auf der Bank haben, noch Geld?; **~ this/that** sonst
◼ ADV (= *on the other side of*) jenseits davon (*geh*); (= *after that*) danach; (= *further than that*) darüber hinaus; **India and the lands ~** Indien und die Gegenden jenseits davon; **... a river, and ~ is a small field** ... ein Fluss, und danach kommt ein kleines Feld

B/F, b/f ABBR *of* **brought forward** Übertrag

biannual ADJ, **biannually** ADV [baɪ'ænjʊəl, -ɪ] zweimal jährlich; (= *half-yearly*) halbjährlich

bias ['baɪəs], *vb*: *pret, ptp* **biased** *or* (*US*) **biassed** ◼ N (= *inclination*) (*of course, newspaper etc*) (einseitige) Ausrichtung *f* (*towards* auf +*acc*); (*of person*) Vorliebe *f* (*towards* für); **to have a ~ against sth** (*course, newspaper etc*) gegen etw eingestellt sein; (*person*) eine Abneigung gegen etw haben; **to have a left-/right-wing ~** nach links/rechts ausgerichtet sein; **to be without ~** ohne Vorurteile sein ◼ VT *person* beeinflussen; **to ~ sb toward(s)/against sth** jdn für/gegen etw einnehmen

biased, (*US*) **biassed** ['baɪəst] ADJ voreingenommen, befangen; **~ in favour** (*Brit*) *or* **favor** (*US*) **of/against** voreingenommen für/gegen

bib [bɪb] N (*for baby*) Lätzchen *nt*

Bible ['baɪbl] N Bibel *f*

Bible: Bible-basher N (*inf*) aufdringlicher Bibelfritze (*sl*); **Bible class** N Bibelstunde *f*; **Bible school** N (*US*) Bibelschule *f*; **Bible story** N biblische Geschichte

biblical ['bɪblɪkəl] ADJ biblisch

bibliographer [ˌbɪblɪ'ɒɡrəfəʳ] N Bibliograf *m*

bibliography [ˌbɪblɪ'ɒɡrəfɪ] N Bibliografie *f*

bicarbonate of soda [baɪˌkɑː'bɒnɪtəv'səʊdə] N (*Cook*) ≈ Backpulver *nt*

bicentenary [ˌbaɪsen'tiːnərɪ], (*US*) **bicentennial** [ˌbaɪsen'tenɪəl] ◼ N zweihundertjähriges Jubiläum; **the ~ of Beethoven's birth/death** Beethovens zweihundertster Geburts-/Todestag ◼ ADJ zweihundertjährig; **~ celebrations** Zweihundertjahrfeier *f*

biceps ['baɪseps] PL Bizeps *m*

bicker ['bɪkəʳ] VI (= *quarrel*) sich zanken; **they are always ~ing** sie liegen sich dauernd in den Haaren

bickering ['bɪkərɪŋ] N Gezänk *nt*

bicycle ['baɪsɪkl] N Fahrrad *nt*; **to ride a ~** Fahrrad fahren

bicycle IN CPDS *see* **cycle**

bid [bɪd] ◼ VT **(a)** *pret, ptp* **bid** (*at auction*) bieten (*for* auf +*acc*)
(b) *pret, ptp* **bid** (*Cards*) reizen, bieten
(c) *pret* **bade** *or* **bad**, *ptp* **bidden** (= *say*) **to ~ farewell to sb**, **to ~ sb farewell** von jdm Abschied nehmen
◼ VI **(a)** *pret, ptp* **bid** (*at auction*) bieten
(b) *pret, ptp* **bid** (*Cards*) bieten, reizen
◼ N **(a)** (*at auction*) Gebot *nt* (*for* auf +*acc*); (*Comm*) Angebot *nt* (*for* für)
(b) (*Cards*) Ansage *f*, Gebot *nt*; **to raise the ~** höher bieten; **to make no ~** passen
(c) (= *attempt*) Versuch *m*; **to make a ~ for power** nach der Macht greifen; **to make a ~ for freedom** versuchen, die Freiheit zu erlangen; **she tried acupuncture in a ~ to stop smoking** sie versuchte es mit Akupunktur, um das Rauchen aufzugeben

bidden ['bɪdn] PTP *of* **bid**

bidder ['bɪdə'] N **to sell to the highest ~** an den Meistbietenden verkaufen; **there were no ~s** niemand hat geboten

bidding ['bɪdɪŋ] N **(a)** (*at auction*) Bieten *nt*; **how high did the ~ go?** wie hoch wurde gesteigert? **(b)** (*Cards*) Bieten *nt*, Reizen *nt* **(c)** (= *order*) **at whose ~?** auf wessen Geheiß? (*old*)

bidding war N (*Fin*) Übernahmeschlacht *f*

bide [baɪd] VT **to ~ one's time** den rechten Augenblick abwarten

bidet ['biːdeɪ] N Bidet *nt*

bidirectional [baɪdɪ'rekʃənəl] ADJ (*Comput*) printing bidirektional

bid price N (*St Ex*) Geldkurs *m*

biennial [baɪ'enɪəl] ADJ (= *every two years*) zweijährlich

biff [bɪf] VT (*esp Brit inf*) person boxen

bifocal [baɪ'fəʊkəl] **1** ADJ Bifokal- **2** N **bifocals** PL Bifokalbrille *f*

big [bɪg] **1** ADJ (+ER) **(a)** groß; **a ~ man** ein großer, schwerer Mann; **my ~ brother** mein großer Bruder **(b)** (= *important*) groß, wichtig; **to be ~ in publishing** eine Größe im Verlagswesen sein; **to be onto something ~** (*inf*) einer großen Sache auf der Spur sein **(c)** (= *conceited*) **~ talk** Angeberei *f* (*inf*); **he's getting too ~ for his boots** (*child*) er wird ein bisschen zu aufmüpfig (*inf*); (*employee*) er wird langsam größenwahnsinnig; **to have a ~ head** (*inf*) eingebildet sein **(d)** (= *generous*, *iro*) großzügig; (= *forgiving*) großmütig; **heart** groß; **he was ~ enough to admit he was wrong** er hatte die Größe zuzugeben, dass er Unrecht hatte; **that's really ~ of you** (*iro*) wirklich nobel von dir (*iro*) **(e)** (*inf:* = *fashionable*) in (*inf*) **(f)** (*fig phrases*) **to earn ~ money** das große Geld verdienen (*inf*); **to have ~ ideas** große Pläne haben; **to have a ~ mouth** (*inf*) eine große Klappe haben (*inf*); **to do things in a ~ way** alles im großen (Stil) tun; **it's no ~ deal** (*inf*) (= *nothing special*) das ist nichts Besonderes; (= *quite all right*) (das ist) schon in Ordnung; **~ deal!** (*iro inf*) na und? (*inf*); **what's the ~ idea?** (*inf*) was soll denn das? (*inf*); **our company is ~ on service** (*inf*) unsere Firma ist ganz groß in puncto Kundendienst **2** ADV **to talk ~** groß daherreden (*inf*); **to think ~** im großen Maßstab planen; **to make it ~ (as a singer)** (als Sänger(in)) ganz groß rauskommen (*inf*)

bigamist ['bɪgəmɪst] N Bigamist *m*

bigamy ['bɪgəmɪ] N Bigamie *f*

big: **Big Apple** N **the ~** (*inf*) New York *nt*; **big band** **1** N Big Band *f* **2** ADJ ATTR Bigband-; **big bang** N (*Astron*) Urknall *m*; **big board** N (*St Ex*) Anzeigentafel *f*; **Big Board** (*US*) bedeutendste New Yorker Börse; **big business** N (= *high finance*) Großkapital *nt*, Hochfinanz *f*; **to be ~** das große Geschäft sein; **big cat** N Großkatze *f*; **big dipper** N **(a)** (*Brit: at fair*) Achterbahn *f* **(b)** (*US Astron*) **Big Dipper** Großer Bär *or* Wagen; **big game** N (*Hunt*) Großwild *nt*; **bighead** N (*inf:* = *person*) Angeber(in) *m(f)* (*inf*); **bigheaded** ADJ (*inf*) eingebildet, angeberisch (*inf*); **bigmouth** N (*inf*) Angeber(in) *m(f)* (*inf*); (= *blabbermouth*) Schwätzer(in) *m(f)* (*pej*); **big name** N (*inf:* = *person*) Größe *f* (*in* + *gen*); **all the ~s were there** alles, was Rang und Namen hat, war da

bigot ['bɪgət] N Eiferer *m*

bigoted ['bɪgətɪd] ADJ eifernd; (*Rel*) bigott

bigotry ['bɪgətrɪ] N eifernde Borniertheit; (*Rel*) Bigotterie *f*

big: **big shot** N hohes Tier (*inf*); **big-ticket** ADJ (*US*) **~ item** teure Anschaffung; **big time** N (*inf*) **to make** *or* **hit the ~** groß einsteigen (*inf*); **big-time** (*inf*) **1** ADJ **a ~ politician** eine große Nummer in der Politik (*inf*) **2** ADV **they lost ~** sie haben gewaltig verloren; **big toe** N große Zehe; **big top** N (= *circus*) Zirkus *m*; (= *main tent*) Hauptzelt *nt*; **big wheel** N **(a)** (*US inf*) = **big shot (b)** (*Brit: at fair*) Riesenrad *nt*; **bigwig** N (*inf*) hohes Tier (*inf*); **the local ~s** die Honoratioren des Ortes

bike [baɪk] (*inf*) **1** N (*Fahr*)rad *nt*; (= *motorbike*) Motorrad *nt*, Maschine *f* (*inf*); **on your ~!** (*Brit inf:* = *clear off*) verschwinde! (*inf*) **2** VI radeln (*inf*)

bike IN CPDS *see* **cycle**

biker ['baɪkə'] N (*inf*) Motorradfahrer *m*; (= *gang member*) Rocker *m*

bikini [bɪ'kiːnɪ] N Bikini *m*

bikini line N Bikinilinie *f*

bilateral ADJ, **bilaterally** [baɪ'lætərəl, -ɪ] ADV bilateral

bilberry ['bɪlbərɪ] N Heidelbeere *f*, Blaubeere *f*

bile [baɪl] N **(a)** (*Med*) Galle *f* **(b)** (*fig:* = *anger*) Übellaunigkeit *f*

bilingual ADJ, **bilingually** ADV [baɪ'lɪŋgwəl, -ɪ] zweisprachig; **~ secretary** Fremdsprachensekretär(in) *m(f)*

bill[1] [bɪl] N (*of bird, turtle*) Schnabel *m*

bill[2] **1** N **(a)** (= *statement of charges*) Rechnung *f*; **could we have the ~ please?** (*esp Brit*) zahlen bitte!; **~s payable/ receivable** (*on balance sheet*) Wechselschulden *pl*/-forderungen *pl* **(b)** (*US:* = *banknote*) Banknote *f*; **five-dollar ~** Fünfdollarschein *m* **(c)** (= *poster*) Plakat *nt*; **"post no ~s"** (*Brit*) „Plakate ankleben verboten" **(d)** (*Theat:* = *programme*) Programm *nt*; **to head** *or* **top the ~, to be top of the ~** Star *m* des Abends/der Saison sein; (*act*) die Hauptattraktion sein **(e)** (*Parl*) (Gesetz)entwurf *m*, (Gesetzes)vorlage *f*; **the ~ was passed** das Gesetz wurde verabschiedet **(f)** (*esp Comm, Fin:* = *certificate, statement*) **~ of exchange** Wechsel *m*, Tratte *f*; **~ of sale** Verkaufsurkunde *f*; **to give sb a clean ~ of health** (*lit, fig*) jdm (gute) Gesundheit bescheinigen; **to fit** *or* **fill the ~** (*fig*) der/die/das Richtige sein, passen **2** VT **(a)** *customers* eine Rechnung ausstellen (+ *dat*); **we won't ~ you for that, sir** (= *not charge*) wir werden Ihnen das nicht berechnen **(b)** (*fig:* = *advertise*) anpreisen; **to ~ oneself as ...** sich anpreisen als ...

billboard ['bɪlbɔːd] N Reklametafel *f*

billet ['bɪlɪt] **1** N (*Mil:* = *accommodation*) Quartier *nt* **2** VT (*Mil*) *soldier* einquartieren (*on sb* bei jdm)

billfold ['bɪlfəʊld] N (*US*) Brieftasche *f*

billiard ['bɪljəd]: **billiard ball** N Billardkugel *f*; **billiard cue** N Queue *nt*

billiards ['bɪljədz] N Billard *nt*; **to have a game of ~** Billard spielen

billiard table N Billardtisch *m*

billion ['bɪljən] N Milliarde *f*; (*dated Brit*) Billion *f*; **~s of ...** (*inf*) tausende von ...

billionaire [bɪljə'neə'] N (*esp US*) Milliardär(in) *m(f)*

billionth ['bɪljənθ] **1** ADJ milliardste(r, s); (*dated Brit*) billionste(r, s) **2** N Milliardstel *nt*; (*dated Brit*) Billionstel *nt*

Bill of Rights N ≈ Grundgesetz *nt*

BILL OF RIGHTS

*Die **Bill of Rights** besteht aus den zehn ursprünglichen Amendments (Änderungen oder Zusätzen) zur Verfassung der Vereinigten Staaten von Amerika, die 1791 in Kraft traten. In einer Reihe von durchnummerierten Artikeln listet die **Bill of Rights** die Rechte auf, die jedem amerikanischen Bürger garantiert werden und definiert die verschiedenen Zuständigkeitsbereiche von Staat und Bundesregierung. In der **Bill of Rights** sind Religions-, Versammlungs- und Pressefreiheit (First Amendment), das Recht, eine Waffe zu tragen (Second Amendment), und das Recht auf eine faire Gerichtsverhandlung (Sixth Amendment) festgelegt. Zusatzartikel nach 1791 betreffen das Recht auf gleichen Schutz durch das Gesetz für alle Staatsbürger (Fourteenth Amendment) und das allgemeine Wahlrecht (Fifteenth Amendment).*
▶ FIFTH AMENDMENT

billow ['bɪləʊ] **1** N (*fig: of smoke*) Schwaden *m* **2** VI (*fig*) (*sail*) sich blähen; (*dress etc*) sich bauschen; (*smoke*) in Schwaden vorüberziehen

billposter ['bɪlpəʊstə'], **billsticker** ['bɪlstɪkə'] N Plakatkleber *m*

bill rate N (*Fin*) Wechseldiskontsatz *m*

billy goat ['bɪlɪgəʊt] N Ziegenbock *m*

bimbo ['bɪmbəʊ] N (*pej inf*) Häschen *nt* (*inf*)

bimonthly [baɪ'mʌnθlɪ] ADJ **(a)** (= *twice a month*) vierzehntäglich **(b)** (= *every two months*) zweimonatlich

bin [bɪn] N (*esp Brit*) (= *rubbish*) Mülleimer *m*; (= *dustbin*) Mülltonne *f*; (= *litter ~*) Abfallbehälter *m*; (*for bread*) Brotkasten *m*

binary ['baɪnərɪ] ADJ binär

binary: **binary code** N (*Comput*) Binärkode *m*; **binary number** N (*Math*) Dualzahl *f*, binäre Zahl; **binary system** N (*Math*) Dualsystem *nt*, binäres System

bind [baɪnd], *pret*, *ptp* **bound** ▮ VT (**a**) binden (*to* an +*acc*); *person* fesseln; (*fig*) verbinden (*to* mit); **bound hand and foot** an Händen und Füßen gefesselt
(**b**) (= *tie round*) *wound*, *arm etc* verbinden; *artery* abbinden
(**c**) (= *oblige*: *by contract*, *promise*) **to ~ sb to sth** jdn zu etw verpflichten; **to ~ sb to do sth** jdn verpflichten, etw zu tun
▮ VI (= *cohere*: *cement etc*) binden
▮ N (*inf*) (**a**) **in a ~** in der Klemme (*inf*)
(**b**) **to be (a bit of) a ~** (*Brit*) recht lästig sein
➤ **bind over** VT SEP (*Jur*) **he was bound over for six months** er bekam eine sechsmonatige Bewährungsfrist
➤ **bind together** VT SEP (*lit*) zusammenbinden; (*fig*) verbinden
➤ **bind up** VT SEP (**a**) *wound* verbinden (**b**) (*fig*) **to be bound up with** *or* **in sth** eng mit etw verknüpft sein

binder ['baɪndə'] N (**a**) (*Typ*: = *machine*) Bindemaschine *f* (**b**) (*for papers*) Hefter *m*

binding ['baɪndɪŋ] ▮ N (**a**) (*of book*) Einband *m*; (= *act*) Binden *nt* (**b**) (*Sew*) Band *nt* (**c**) (*on skis*) Bindung *f* ▮ ADJ *agreement* bindend (*on* für)

binge [bɪndʒ] (*inf*) ▮ N **to go on a ~** (= *drinking*) auf eine Sauftour gehen (*inf*); (= *eating*) eine Fresstour machen (*inf*); (= *spending*) groß einkaufen gehen (*inf*) ▮ VI auf eine Sauf-/Fresstour gehen (*inf*)

bingo ['bɪŋgəʊ] N Bingo *nt*

bin liner N (*Brit*) Mülltüte *f*

binoculars [bɪ'nɒkjʊləz] PL Fernglas *nt*; **a pair of ~** ein Fernglas

bio [baɪəʊ]: **biochemist** N Biochemiker(in) *m(f)*; **biochemistry** N Biochemie *f*; **biodegradable** ADJ biologisch abbaubar; **biodiversity** N Artenvielfalt *f*

biographer [baɪ'ɒgrəfə'] N Biograf(in) *m(f)*

biographic(al) [baɪəʊ'græfɪk(əl)] ADJ biografisch

biography [baɪ'ɒgrəfɪ] N Biografie *f*

biological [baɪə'lɒdʒɪkəl] ADJ biologisch; **~ detergent** Biowaschmittel *nt*

biological clock N biologische Uhr

biologically [baɪəʊ'lɒdʒɪkəlɪ] ADV biologisch

biologist [baɪ'ɒlədʒɪst] N Biologe *m*, Biologin *f*

biology [baɪ'ɒlədʒɪ] N Biologie *f*

biomass N Biomasse *f*

bionic [baɪ'ɒnɪk] ADJ bionisch

biopsy ['baɪɒpsɪ] N Biopsie *f*

biotechnology [baɪəʊtek'nɒlədʒɪ] N Biotechnik *f*

bioterrorism N Bioterrorismus *m*

bipartite [baɪ'pɑːtaɪt] ADJ zweiteilig; (= *affecting two parties*) zweiseitig

biplane ['baɪpleɪn] N Doppeldecker *m*

birch [bɜːtʃ] N (**a**) Birke *f* (**b**) (*for whipping*) Rute *f*

bird [bɜːd] N (**a**) Vogel *m*; **a little ~ told me** (*inf*) das sagt mir mein kleiner Finger; **a ~ in the hand is worth two in the bush** (*Prov*) der Spatz in der Hand ist besser als die Taube auf dem Dach (*Prov*); **to tell sb about the ~s and the bees** jdm erzählen, wo die kleinen Kinder herkommen
(**b**) (*Brit inf*: = *girl*) Tussi *f* (*sl*)
(**c**) **to give sb the ~** (*esp Brit inf*: = *boo*) jdn auspfeifen; (*US sl*: = *show the finger*) jdm den Stinkefinger zeigen; **to get the ~** (*esp Brit inf*) ausgepfiffen werden; (*US sl*) den Stinkefinger gezeigt bekommen

bird: **birdbath** N Vogelbad *nt*; **bird box** N Vogelhäuschen *nt*; **bird brain** N (*inf*) **to be a ~** ein Spatzenhirn haben (*inf*); **birdcage** N Vogelbauer *nt or* -käfig *m*; **bird call** N Vogelruf *m*; **bird dog** (*US*) ▮ N (*lit*, *fig*) Spürhund *m* ▮ VT (*inf*) beschatten (*inf*); **bird sanctuary** N Vogelschutzgebiet *nt*; **birdseed** N Vogelfutter *nt*

bird's: **bird's-eye view** N Vogelperspektive *f*; **to get a ~ of the town** die Stadt aus der Vogelperspektive sehen; **bird's nest** N Vogelnest *nt*

bird: **birdsong** N Vogelgesang *m*; **bird table** N Futterplatz *m* (*für Vögel*); **bird-watcher** N Vogelbeobachter(in) *m(f)*

Biro® ['baɪərəʊ] N (*Brit*) Kugelschreiber *m*, Kuli *m* (*inf*)

birth [bɜːθ] N (**a**) (*lit*, *fig*) Geburt *f*; (*of movement*, *fashion etc*) Aufkommen *nt*; (*of new era*) Anbruch *m*; **the town/country of his ~** seine Geburtsstadt/sein Geburtsland *nt*; **blind from** *or* **since ~** von Geburt an blind; **to give ~** gebären; **to give ~** entbinden; (*animal*) jungen
(**b**) (= *parentage*) Abstammung *f*, Herkunft *f*; **Scottish by ~** gebürtiger Schotte; **of good ~** aus gutem Hause; **of low** *or* **humble ~** von niedriger Geburt

birth: **birth certificate** N Geburtsurkunde *f*; **birth control** N Geburtenkontrolle *f*; **birth-control clinic** N Familienberatungsstelle *f*; **birthdate** N Geburtsdatum *nt*

birthday ['bɜːθdeɪ] N Geburtstag *m*; **what did you get for your ~?** was hast du zum Geburtstag bekommen?

birthday IN CPDS Geburtstags-; **birthday cake** N Geburtstagskuchen *m or* -torte *f*; **birthday card** N Geburtstagskarte *f*; **birthday party** N Geburtstagsfeier *f*; (*for child*) Kindergeburtstag *m*; **birthday suit** N (*inf*) **in one's ~** im Adams-/Evaskostüm (*inf*)

birth: **birthmark** N Muttermal *nt*; **birthplace** N Geburtsort *m*; **birth plan** N Geburtsplan *m*; **birthrate** N Geburtenrate *f*; **birthright** N Geburtsrecht *nt*

biscuit ['bɪskɪt] N (**a**) (*Brit*) Keks *m*; (= *dog ~*) Hundekuchen *m*; **that takes/you take the ~!** (*Brit inf*) das übertrifft alles (**b**) (*US*) Brötchen *nt*

bisect [baɪ'sekt] VT in zwei Teile *or* (*equal parts*) Hälften teilen; (*Math*) halbieren

bisexual [baɪ'seksjʊəl] ▮ ADJ bisexuell ▮ N (= *person*) Bisexuelle(r) *mf*

bisexuality [baɪˌseksjʊ'ælɪtɪ] N Bisexualität *f*

bishop ['bɪʃəp] N (**a**) (*Eccl*) Bischof *m* (**b**) (*Chess*) Läufer *m*

bison ['baɪsn] N (*American*) Bison *m*; (*European*) Wisent *m*

bistro ['biːstrəʊ] N Bistro *nt*

bit[1] [bɪt] N (**a**) (*for horse*) Gebissstange *f* (**b**) (*of drill*) (Bohr)einsatz *m*

bit[2] ▮ N (**a**) (= *piece*) Stück *nt*; (*smaller*) Stückchen *nt*; (*of glass*) Scherbe *f*; (= *section*: *of book etc*) Teil *m*; (*part or place in book etc*) Stelle *f*; **a few ~s of furniture** ein paar Möbelstücke; **a ~ of bread** ein Stück Brot; **I gave my ~ to my sister** ich habe meiner Schwester meinen Teil gegeben; **a ~** (= *not much*, *small amount*) ein bisschen; **a ~ of advice/luck/news** ein Rat *m*/ein Glück *nt*/eine Neuigkeit; **we had a ~ of trouble** wir hatten ein wenig Ärger; **it wasn't a ~ of help** das war überhaupt keine Hilfe; **I've experienced quite a ~ in my life** ich habe in meinem Leben schon (so) einiges erlebt; **there's quite a ~ of work left to do/bread left** es ist noch eine ganze Menge Arbeit zu erledigen/Brot da; **in ~s and pieces** (= *broken*) in tausend Stücken; (*lit*, *fig*: = *come apart*) in die Brüche gegangen; **bring all your ~s and pieces** bring deine Siebensachen; **to come** *or* **fall to ~s** kaputtgehen; **to pull** *or* **tear sth to ~s** (*lit*) etw in Stücke reißen; (*fig*) keinen guten Faden an etw (*dat*) lassen; **to go to ~s** (*fig inf*) durchdrehen (*inf*); **~ by ~** Stück für Stück; (= *gradually*) nach und nach; **he is every ~ as good as ...** es/er ist genauso gut, wie ...; **not a ~ of it** keine Spur (*inf*)
(**b**) (*with time*) **a ~** ein Weilchen *nt*; **he's gone out for a ~** er ist mal kurz weggegangen
(**c**) (*with cost*) **a ~** eine ganze Menge; **it cost quite a ~** das hat ganz schön (viel) gekostet (*inf*)
(**d**) **to do one's ~** sein(en) Teil tun
(**e**) **a ~ of a crack/bruise** *etc* ein kleiner Riss/Fleck *etc*; **he's a ~ of a rogue/an expert** er ist ein ziemlicher Schlingel/ein Fachmann; **she's a ~ of a connoisseur** sie versteht einiges davon; **it's a ~ of a nuisance** das ist schon etwas ärgerlich
(**f**) (= *coin*) (*Brit*) Münze *f*; **2/4/6 ~s** (*US*) 25/50/75 Cent(s)
▮ ADV **a ~** ein bisschen, etwas; **wasn't she a little ~ surprised?** war sie nicht etwas erstaunt?; **I'm not a (little) ~ surprised** das wundert mich überhaupt nicht; **quite a ~** ziemlich viel

bit[3] N (*Comput*) Bit *nt*

bit[4] PRET *of* **bite**

bitch [bɪtʃ] ▮ N (**a**) (*of dog*) Hündin *f*; (*of canines generally*) Weibchen *nt*; **terrier ~** weiblicher Terrier (**b**) (*sl*) (= *woman*) Miststück *nt* (*inf*); (*spiteful*) Hexe *f*; **silly ~** doofe Ziege (*inf*)
(**c**) (*inf*: = *complaint*) **to have a ~ (about sb/sth)** (über jdn/etw) meckern (*inf*) ▮ VI (*inf*: = *complain*) meckern (*inf*) (*about* über +*acc*)

bitchiness ['bɪtʃɪnɪs] N Gehässigkeit *f*

bitchy ['bɪtʃɪ] ADJ (+ER) (*inf*) *woman* gehässig

bite [baɪt], *vb: pret* **bit**, *ptp* **bitten** ◫ N **(a)** Biss *m*; (= *insect* ~) Stich *m*; **he took a ~ (out) of the apple** er biss in den Apfel; **to get a second** *or* **another ~ at the cherry** (*fig*) eine zweite Chance bekommen
(b) (*Fishing*) **I think I've got a ~** ich glaube, es hat einer angebissen
(c) (*of food*) Happen *m*; **do you fancy a ~ (to eat)?** möchten Sie etwas essen?
◩ VT **(a)** (*person, dog*) beißen; (*insect*) stechen; **to ~ one's nails** an seinen Nägeln kauen; **to ~ one's tongue/lip** (*lit, fig*) sich (*dat*) auf die Zunge/Lippen beißen; **don't worry, he won't ~ you** (*fig inf*) keine Angst, er wird dich schon nicht beißen (*inf*); **to ~ the dust** (*inf*) dran glauben müssen (*inf*); **he had been bitten by the travel bug** ihn hatte das Reisefieber erwischt (*inf*); **once bitten twice shy** (*Prov*) (ein) gebranntes Kind scheut das Feuer (*Prov*); **to ~ the hand that feeds you** (*prov*) sich (*dat*) ins eigene Fleisch schneiden
(b) (*cold, wind*) schneiden in (+*dat*)
◪ VI **(a)** (*dog etc*) beißen; (*insects*) stechen
(b) (*fish, fig inf*) anbeißen
(c) (*wheels, screw*) greifen; (*saw, anchor*) fassen
➤ **bite into** VI +PREP OBJ (*person*) (hinein)beißen in (+*acc*); (*acid, saw*) sich hineinfressen in (+*acc*)
➤ **bite off** VT SEP abbeißen; **he won't bite your head off** (*inf*) er wird dir schon nicht den Kopf abreißen; **to bite off more than one can chew** (*prov*) sich (*dat*) zu viel zumuten
bite-size(d) ['baɪtsaɪz(d)] ADJ mundgerecht
biting ['baɪtɪŋ] ADJ beißend; *wind* schneidend
bit: **bitmap** N (*Comput*) **(a)** NO PL (= *mode*) Bitmap *nt* **(b)** (*also* ~**ped image**) Bitmap-Abbildung *f*; **bitmapped** ADJ (*Comput*) Bitmap-; ~ **graphics** Bitmapgrafik *f*; **bit part** N kleine Nebenrolle
bitten ['bɪtn] PTP *of* **bite**
bitter ['bɪtəʳ] ◫ ADJ (+ER) bitter; *weather, wind* eisig; *enemy, struggle, opposition* erbittert; (= *embittered*) *person* verbittert; **it's ~ today** es ist heute bitterkalt; **to the ~ end** bis zum bitteren Ende ◩ ADV ~ **cold** bitterkalt ◪ N (*Brit*: = *beer*) halbdunkles obergäriges Bier
bitter lemon N Bitter Lemon *nt*
bitterly ['bɪtəlɪ] ADV **(a)** *reproach, disappointed, cold* bitter; *complain, weep* bitterlich; *oppose* erbittert; *criticize* scharf
(b) (= *showing embitteredness*) verbittert; *criticize* erbittert
bitterness ['bɪtənɪs] N Bitterkeit *f*; (*of weather, wind*) bittere Kälte; (*of struggle, opposition*) Erbittertheit *f*
bittersweet ['bɪtəˌswiːt] ADJ (*lit, fig*) bittersüß
bitty ['bɪtɪ] ADJ (+ER) (*Brit inf*: = *scrappy*) zusammengestückelt (*inf*)
bitumen ['bɪtjʊmɪn] N Bitumen *nt*
biweekly ['baɪ'wiːklɪ] ◫ ADJ **(a)** (= *twice a week*) ~ **meetings** Konferenzen, die zweimal wöchentlich stattfinden
(b) (= *fortnightly*) zweiwöchentlich, vierzehntäglich ◩ ADV **(a)** (= *twice a week*) zweimal in der Woche **(b)** (= *fortnightly*) alle vierzehn Tage, vierzehntäglich
biz [bɪz] (*inf*) ABBR *of* **business**
bizarre [bɪ'zɑːʳ] ADJ bizarr
BL ABBR *of* **Bachelor of Law**
B/L ABBR *of* **bill of lading**
blab [blæb] ◫ VI quatschen (*inf*); (= *talk fast, tell secret*) plappern ◩ VT (*also* ~ **out**) *secret* ausplaudern
black [blæk] ◫ ADJ (+ER) **(a)** schwarz; ~ **man/woman** Schwarze(r) *mf*; ~ **and blue** grün und blau; ~ **and white photography** Schwarzweißfotografie *f*; **the situation isn't so ~ and white as that** die Situation ist nicht so eindeutig schwarz-weiß
(b) *future, prospects, mood* düster, finster; **maybe things aren't as ~ as they seem** vielleicht ist alles gar nicht so schlimm, wie es aussieht; **this was a ~ day for ...** das war ein schwarzer Tag für ...
(c) (*fig:* = *angry*) *looks* böse
◩ N **(a)** Schwarz *nt*; **he is dressed in ~** er trägt Schwarz; **to wear ~** (*in mourning*) Trauer *or* Schwarz tragen; **it's written down in ~** *and white* es steht schwarz auf weiß geschrieben; **in the ~** (*Fin*) in den schwarzen Zahlen
(b) (= *negro*) Schwarze(r) *mf*
◪ VT (= *blacken*) **to ~ sb's eye** jdm ein blaues Auge schlagen

➤ **black out** ◫ VI das Bewusstsein verlieren ◩ VT SEP **(a)** *stage, window* verdunkeln **(b)** (*with ink, paint*) schwärzen
black: Black Africa N Schwarzafrika *nt*; **blackball** VT (= *vote against*) stimmen gegen; (*inf:* = *exclude*) ausschließen; **blackberry** N Brombeere *f*; **to go ~ing** (*Brit*) Brombeeren pflücken gehen; **blackbird** N Amsel *f*; **blackboard** N Tafel *f*; **to write sth on the ~** etw an die Tafel schreiben; **black book** N **to be in sb's ~s** bei jdm schlecht angeschrieben sein (*inf*); **black box** N (*Aviat*) Flugschreiber *m*; (= *mysterious device*) Blackbox *f*; **black cab** N (*Brit*) britisches Taxi; **blackcap** N (*US:* = *berry*) Barett *nt*; **black comedy** N schwarze Komödie; **Black Country** N Industriegebiet in den englischen Midlands; **blackcurrant** N schwarze Johannisbeere; **black economy** N Schattenwirtschaft *f*
blacken ['blækən] VT **(a)** (= *make black*) schwarz machen; *one's face* schwarz anmalen; (*US Cook*) schwärzen; **the walls were ~ed by the fire** die Wände waren vom Feuer schwarz **(b)** (*fig*) *character* verunglimpfen; **to ~ sb's name** *or* **reputation** jdn schlecht machen
black: black eye N blaues Auge; **to give sb a ~** jdm ein blaues Auge schlagen; **Black Forest** N Schwarzwald *m*; **Black Forest gateau** N (*esp Brit*) Schwarzwälder Kirschtorte *f*; **blackhead** N Mitesser *m*; **black hole** N (*Astron, fig*) schwarzes Loch; **black humour,** (*US*) **black humor** N schwarzer Humor; **black ice** N Glatteis *nt*; **blackjack** ◫ N **(a)** (*Cards:* = *pontoon*) Siebzehnundvier *nt* **(b)** (*US:* = *weapon*) Totschläger *m* ◩ VT (*US:* = *hit*) prügeln; **blackleg** (*Brit Ind*) N Streikbrecher(in) *m(f)*; **black list** N schwarze Liste; **blacklist** VT auf die schwarze Liste setzen; **black magic** N schwarze Kunst; **blackmail** ◫ N Erpressung *f* ◩ VT erpressen; **to ~ sb into doing sth** jdn durch Erpressung dazu zwingen, etw zu tun; **blackmailer** N Erpresser(in) *m(f)*; **black mark** N **that's a ~ for** *or* **against him** das ist ein Minuspunkt für ihn; **black market** ◫ N Schwarzmarkt *m* ◩ ADJ ATTR Schwarzmarkt-; **black marketeer** N Schwarzhändler(in) *m(f)*; **Black Nationalism** (*US*) schwarzer Nationalismus; **blackout** N **(a)** (*Med*) Ohnmachtsanfall *m*; **I must have had a ~** ich muss wohl in Ohnmacht gefallen sein **(b)** (= *light failure*) Stromausfall *m*; (*Theat*) Blackout *nt*; (*during war*) Verdunkelung *f* **(c)** (= *news* ~) Nachrichtensperre *f*; **black pepper** N schwarzer Pfeffer; **black pudding** N ≈ Blutwurst *f*; **Black Sea** N Schwarzes Meer; **black sheep** N (*fig*) schwarzes Schaf; **blacksmith** N Hufschmied *m*; **black spot** N (*also* **accident** ~) Gefahrenstelle *f*; **black tie** ◫ N (*on invitation*) Abendanzug *m* ◩ ADJ *function* mit Smokingzwang; **is it ~?** ist da Smokingzwang?; **blacktop** (*US*) (= *substance*) schwarzer Straßenbelag; (= *road*) geteerte Straße; (*paved with asphalt*) Asphaltstraße *f*
bladder ['blædəʳ] N (*Anat, Bot*) Blase *f*
blade [bleɪd] N **(a)** (*of knife, tool*) Klinge *f*; (*of guillotine*) Beil *nt* **(b)** (*of oar, spade, saw, propeller*) Blatt *nt*; (*of plough*) Schar *f*; (*of turbine*) Schaufel *f* **(c)** (*of grass*) Halm *m*
blag [blæg] VT (*Brit inf*) schnorren (*inf*); **to ~ one's way into a club** sich in einen Klub hineinmogeln (*inf*)
blah [blɑː] INTERJ (*inf*) ~**,** ~**,** ~ blabla (*inf*)
blame [bleɪm] ◫ VT **(a)** (= *hold responsible*) die Schuld geben (+*dat*), beschuldigen; **to ~ sb for sth/sth on sb** jdm die Schuld an etw (*dat*) geben; **to ~ sth on sb** die Schuld an etw (*dat*) auf etw (*acc*) schieben; **you only have yourself** *or* **you have no-one but yourself to ~** das hast du dir selbst zuzuschreiben; **who/what is to ~ for this accident?** wer/was ist schuld an diesem Unfall?; **to ~ oneself for sth** (= *feel responsible*) sich für etw verantwortlich fühlen
(b) (= *reproach*) Vorwürfe machen (*sb for* jdm für *or* wegen) **(c)** **he decided to turn down the offer – well, I can't say I ~ him** er entschloss sich, das Angebot abzulehnen – das kann man ihm wahrhaftig nicht verdenken
◩ N (= *responsibility*) Schuld *f*; **to put the ~ for sth on sb** jdm die Schuld an etw (*dat*) geben; **to take the ~** die Schuld auf sich (*acc*) nehmen; (*for sb's mistakes also*) den Kopf hinhalten

Be careful! **to blame** *is not translated by the German word* **blamieren**.

blameless ['bleɪmlɪs] ADJ schuldlos; *life* untadelig
blanch [blɑːntʃ] ◫ VT (*Cook*) *vegetables* blanchieren; *almonds* brühen ◩ VI (*with* vor +*dat*) (*person*) blass werden
blancmange [blə'mɒnʒ] N Pudding *m*

bland [blænd] ADJ (+ER) *food* fad; *book, film, statement* nichts
sagend; *person* langweilig

blandness ['blændnıs] N (*of food*) Fadheit *f*; (*of book, film,
statement*) Inhaltslosigkeit *f*

blank [blæŋk] **1** ADJ (+ER) **(a)** *piece of paper, page, wall* leer; **a ~
space** eine Lücke; (*on form*) ein freies Feld; **please leave ~** (*on
form*) bitte frei lassen
(b) (= *expressionless*) *face, look* ausdruckslos;
(= *uncomprehending*) verständnislos; **to look ~**
(= *uncomprehending*) verständnislos dreinschauen; **my mind
or I went ~** ich hatte ein Brett vor dem Kopf (*inf*)
2 N **(a)** (*in document*) freier Raum, leere Stelle
(b) (= *void*) Leere *f*; **I** *or* **my mind was/went a complete ~** ich
hatte totale Mattscheibe (*inf*)
(c) to draw a ~ (*fig*) kein Glück haben
(d) (= *cartridge*) Platzpatrone *f*
(e) (= *domino*) Blank *nt*
➤ **blank out** VT SEP *feeling, thought etc* ausschalten

blank cheque, (*US*) **blank check** N Blankoscheck *m*; **to give
sb a ~** (*fig*) jdm freie Hand geben

blanket ['blæŋkıt] **1** N (*lit, fig*) Decke *f*; **a ~ of snow** eine
Schneedecke **2** ADJ ATTR *statement* pauschal; *insurance,
coverage* umfassend; *ban* generell; *bombing* flächendeckend

blanket: blanket bath N **to give sb a ~** jdn im Bett waschen;
blanket insurance N kombinierte Versicherung

blankly ['blæŋklı] ADV (= *expressionlessly*) ausdruckslos;
(= *uncomprehendingly*) verständnislos; **she just looked at me
~** sie sah mich nur groß an (*inf*)

blank verse N Blankvers *m*

blare [blɛəʳ] **1** N Plärren *nt*; (*of car horn*) lautes Hupen; (*of
trumpets*) Schmettern *nt* **2** VI plärren; (*car horn*) laut hupen;
(*trumpets*) schmettern
➤ **blare out** VI (*loud voice, music*) schallen; (*trumpets*)
schmettern; (*car horn*) laut hupen

blarney ['blɑːnı] N Schmeichelei *f*

blaspheme [blæs'fiːm] VI Gott lästern; **to ~ against sb/sth** (*lit,
fig*) jdn/etw schmähen (*geh*)

blasphemous ['blæsfıməs] ADJ (*lit, fig*) blasphemisch

blasphemy ['blæsfımı] N Blasphemie *f*

blast [blɑːst] **1** N **(a)** Windstoß *m*; (*of hot air*) Schwall *m*; **a ~
of wind** ein Windstoß; **an icy ~** ein eisiger Wind; **a ~ from the
past** (*inf*) eine Erinnerung an vergangene Zeiten
(b) (= *sound*) **the ship gave a long ~ on its foghorn** das Schiff
ließ sein Nebelhorn ertönen
(c) (= *noise, explosion*) Explosion *f*; **to get the full ~ of sb's
anger** jds Wut in voller Wucht abkriegen
(d) with the heating on (at) full ~ mit der Heizung voll
aufgedreht
2 VT **(a)** (*with powder*) sprengen
(b) (= *send*) *rocket* schießen; *ball* mit Wucht schießen; *air*
blasen
3 INTERJ (*inf*) **~ (it)!** verdammt! (*inf*); **~ this car!** dieses
verdammte Auto! (*inf*)
➤ **blast away** VI (*with gun*) drauflosschießen; (*radio, rock band
etc*) dröhnen
➤ **blast off** VI (*rocket*) abheben, starten
➤ **blast out** VI (*music*) dröhnen

blasted ['blɑːstıd] ADJ, ADV (*inf*) verdammt (*inf*)

blast furnace N Hochofen *m*

blastoff ['blɑːstɒf] N Abschuss *m*

blatant ['bleıtənt] ADJ (= *very obvious*) offensichtlich; *error* krass;
liar unverfroren; *disregard* offen

blatantly ['bleıtəntlı] ADV offensichtlich; (= *openly*) offen;
(= *without respect*) unverfroren; **she ~ ignored it** sie hat das
schlicht und einfach ignoriert

blather ['blæðəʳ] N, VI (*inf*) = **blether**

blaze¹ [bleız] **1** N **(a)** (= *fire*) Feuer *nt*; (*of building etc also*)
Brand *m*; **six people died in the ~** sechs Menschen kamen in
den Flammen um
(b) a ~ of lights ein Lichtermeer *nt*; **a ~ of colour** (*Brit*) *or*
color (*US*) ein Meer *nt* von Farben; **he went out in a ~ of glory**
er trat mit Glanz und Gloria ab
2 VT **(a)** (*sun, fire*) brennen; **to ~ with anger** vor Zorn glühen
(b) (*guns*) feuern; **with all guns blazing** aus allen Rohren
feuernd

blaze² VT **to ~ a trail** (*fig*) den Weg bahnen

blazer ['bleızəʳ] N Blazer *m* (*also Sch*)

blazing ['bleızıŋ] ADJ **(a)** brennend; *fire, torch* lodernd; *sun, light*
grell **(b)** (*fig*) *row* furchtbar

bleach [bliːtʃ] **1** N Bleichmittel *nt*; (= *household* ~)
Reinigungsmittel *nt* **2** VT bleichen; (*sun*) *colour, fabric*
verbleichen lassen

bleachers ['bliːtʃəz] PL (*US*) unüberdachte Zuschauertribüne

bleak [bliːk] ADJ (+ER) **(a)** *landscape, place* öde **(b)** *weather, wind*
rau, kalt **(c)** (*fig*) trostlos; *prospects also* trüb; **his face was ~** er
sah niedergeschlagen aus

bleakness ['bliːknıs] N **(a)** (*of landscape*) Öde *f* **(b)** (*fig*)
Trostlosigkeit *f*; (*of prospects*) Trübheit *f*

bleary ['blıərı] ADJ (+ER) *eyes* trübe; (*after sleep*) verschlafen

bleary-eyed ['blıərıaıd] ADJ (*after sleep*) verschlafen

bleat [bliːt] VI **(a)** (*sheep, calf*) blöken; (*goat*) meckern **(b)** (*fig
inf*: = *complain, moan*) meckern (*inf*)

bleed [bliːd] *pret, ptp* **bled** [bled] **1** VI (= *lose blood*) bluten; **to
~ to death** verbluten; **my heart ~s for you** (*iro*) ich fang gleich
an zu weinen **2** VT **(a)** (*fig inf*) schröpfen (*inf*) (*for* um); **to ~
sb dry** jdn total ausnehmen (*inf*) **(b)** *radiator* (ent)lüften; *(Aut)*
brakes lüften

bleeding ['bliːdıŋ] **1** N (= *loss of blood*) Blutung *f*; **internal ~**
innere Blutungen *pl* **2** ADJ **(a)** blutend; (*fig*) *heart* gebrochen
(b) (*Brit inf*) verdammt (*inf*); (*in positive sense*) *miracle etc*
verdammt (*inf*); (*in positive sense*) *miracle etc*
verdammt (*inf*) **3** ADV (*Brit inf*) verdammt (*inf*); **that's ~
marvellous** das ist ja wieder toll! (*inf*), na klasse! (*inf*)

bleeding heart N (*pej*: = *person*) Sensibelchen *nt* (*inf*)

bleep [bliːp] **1** N (*Rad, TV*) Piepton *m* **2** VI (*transmitter*) piepen
3 VT (*in hospital*) *doctor* rufen

bleeper ['bliːpəʳ] N Piepser *m* (*inf*)

blemish ['blemıʃ] **1** N (*lit, fig*) Makel *m*; **without (a) ~** makellos
2 VT *reputation* beflecken; **~ed skin** unreine Haut

blend [blend] **1** N Mischung *f*; (*of whiskies also*) Blend *m*; **a ~
of tea** eine Teemischung **2** VT **(a)** *teas, colours etc*
(ver)mischen **(b)** (*Cook*) (= *stir*) einrühren; (*in blender*) *liquids*
mixen; *semisolids* pürieren **3** VI **(a)** (= *mix together: voices,
colours*) verschmelzen **(b)** (*also* ~ **in**: = *harmonize*)
harmonieren
➤ **blend in 1** VT SEP *flavouring* einrühren; *colour, tea* darunter
mischen **2** VI = **blend 3**

blended ['blendıd] ADJ ~ **whisky** Blended *m*

blender ['blendəʳ] N Mixer *m*

bless [bles] VT **(a)** segnen; **God ~ (you)** behüt dich/euch Gott;
did you buy that for me, ~ you? (*inf*) hast du das für mich
gekauft? das ist aber lieb von dir! (*inf*); **~ you!** (*to sneezer*)
Gesundheit! **(b) to be ~ed with** gesegnet sein mit

blessed ['blesıd] ADJ **(a)** (*Rel*) heilig; **the Blessed X** der selige X
(b) (*euph inf*: = *cursed*) verflixt (*inf*); **I couldn't remember a ~
thing** ich konnte mich an rein gar nichts mehr erinnern
(*inf*); **every ~ evening** aber auch JEDEN Abend

Blessed Virgin N Heilige Jungfrau (Maria)

blessing ['blesıŋ] N (*Rel, fig*) Segen *m*; **he can count his ~s** da
kann er von Glück sagen; **it was a ~ in disguise** es war
schließlich doch ein Segen

blether ['bleðəʳ] VI (*Scot inf*) quatschen (*inf*)

blew [bluː] PRET *of* **blow²**

blight [blaıt] **1** N **(a)** (*on plants*) Braunfäule *f* **(b)** (*fig*) **to be a
~ on** *or* **upon sb's life/happiness** jdm das Leben/jds Glück
vergällen; **these slums are a ~ upon the city** diese Slums sind
ein Schandfleck für die Stadt **2** VT (*fig*) *hopes* vereiteln; **to ~
sb's life** jdm das Leben verderben

blighter ['blaıtəʳ] N (*Brit inf*) Kerl *m* (*inf*); (= *boy*) ungezogener
Bengel; (= *girl*) Luder *nt* (*inf*); **what a lucky ~!** so ein
Glückspilz!

blimey ['blaımı] INTERJ (*Brit inf*) verflucht (*inf*)

blind [blaınd] **1** ADJ (+ER) **(a)** (*lit, fig*) blind; **to go ~** erblinden,
blind werden; **a ~ man/woman** ein Blinder/eine Blinde; **~ in
one eye** auf einem Auge blind; **to be ~ to sth** (*fig*) für etw
blind sein; **to turn a ~ eye to sth** (*fig*) bei etw ein Auge zudrücken;
she remained ~ to the fact that ... sie sah einfach nicht,
dass ...; **~ faith (in sth)** blindes Vertrauen (in etw *acc*)
(b) (= *vision obscured*) *corner* unübersichtlich
(c) (*Brit inf*) **he didn't take a ~ bit of notice** aber er hat sich
nicht die Spur darum gekümmert (*inf*)
2 VT **(a)** (= *make* ~: *light, sun*) blenden; **the explosion ~ed**

him er ist durch die Explosion blind geworden; **he was ~ed in the war** er ist kriegsblind
(b) (*fig*) (*love, hate etc*) blind machen (*to* für, gegen); (*wealth, beauty*) blenden; **to ~ sb with science** jdn mit Fachjargon beeindrucken (*wollen*)
⊠ N´ **(a) the ~** die Blinden *pl*
(b) (= *window shade*) (*cloth*) Rollo *nt*; (*slats*) Jalousie *f*; (*outside*) Rollladen *m*
(c) (= *cover*) Tarnung *f*; **to be a ~** zur Tarnung dienen
(d) (*US*: = *hide*) Versteck *nt*
⊡ ADV **(a)** (*Aviat*) fly blind
(b) (*Cook*) **to bake sth ~** etw vorbacken
(c) ~ drunk (*inf*) sinnlos betrunken
blind: blind alley N (*lit, fig*) Sackgasse *f*; **blind date** N Rendezvous *nt* mit einem/einer Unbekannten

blinder ['blaɪndəʳ] N **(a)** (*US*: = *blinker*) Scheuklappe *f* **(b)** (*Brit inf*) **to play a ~** (*Sport*) spitzenmäßig spielen (*inf*)

blindfold ['blaɪndfəʊld] **⊠** VT die Augen verbinden (+*dat*) **⊡** N Augenbinde *f* **⊟** ADJ **I could do it ~** (*inf*) das mach ich mit links (*inf*)

blinding ['blaɪndɪŋ] ADJ *light* blendend; *truth* ins Auge stechend; *headache, pain* furchtbar

blindingly ['blaɪndɪŋlɪ] ADV **it is ~ obvious** das sieht doch ein Blinder (*inf*)

blindly ['blaɪndlɪ] ADV (*lit, fig*) blind(lings)

blind man's buff N Blindekuh *no art*

blindness ['blaɪndnɪs] N (*lit, fig*) Blindheit *f* (*to* gegenüber)

blind: blind spot N (*Med*) blinder Fleck; (*Aut, Aviat*) toter Winkel; **to have a ~ about sth** einen blinden Fleck in Bezug auf etw (*acc*) haben; **blind summit** N (*Aut*) unübersichtliche Kuppe; **blind trust** N (*Fin*) Blind Trust *m*

blink [blɪŋk] **⊠** N Blinzeln *nt*; **in the ~ of an eye** im Nu; **to be on the ~** (*inf*) kaputt sein (*inf*) **⊡** VI **(a)** (*person*) blinzeln **(b)** (*light*) blinken **⊟** VT **to ~ one's eyes** mit den Augen zwinkern

blinker ['blɪŋkəʳ] N **(a)** (*US inf*: = *light*) Blinker *m* **(b) blinkers** PL Scheuklappen *pl*

blinkered ['blɪŋkəd] ADJ **(a)** (*fig*) engstirnig **(b)** *horse* mit Scheuklappen

blinking ['blɪŋkɪŋ] (*Brit inf*) **⊠** ADJ verflixt (*inf*), blöd (*inf*); **it's about ~ time too!** das wird aber auch Zeit! (*inf*) **⊡** ADV verflixt (*inf*)

blintz(e) [blɪnts] N (*US Cook*) dünner Pfannkuchen

blip [blɪp] N leuchtender Punkt (auf dem Radarschirm); (*fig*) kurzzeitiger Tiefpunkt

bliss [blɪs] N Glück *nt*; (*Rel*) (Glück)seligkeit *f*; **this is ~!** das ist herrlich!

blissful ['blɪsfʊl] ADJ *time, feeling* herrlich; *state, look, smile* (glück)selig; **in ~ ignorance of the fact that ...** (*iro*) in keinster Weise ahnend, dass ...

blissfully ['blɪsfʊlɪ] ADV *peaceful* herrlich; **~ happy** überglücklich; **he remained ~ ignorant of what was going on** er ahnte in keinster Weise, was eigentlich vor sich ging

blister ['blɪstəʳ] **⊠** N (*on skin, paint*) Blase *f* **⊡** VI (*skin*) Blasen bekommen; (*paintwork*) Blasen werfen

blistered ['blɪstəd] ADJ **to have ~ skin/hands** Blasen auf der Haut/an den Händen haben; **to be ~** Blasen haben; **~ paint** Blasen werfende Farbe

blistering ['blɪstərɪŋ] ADJ **(a)** *heat, sun* glühend; *pace* mörderisch **(b)** (= *scathing*) vernichtend

blister pack N (Klar)sichtpackung *f*

blithe [blaɪð] ADJ (+ER) (*pej*: = *casual*) unbekümmert

blithely ['blaɪðlɪ] ADV *carry on* so munter; *say, announce* unbekümmert; *unaware* erstaunlich

blithering ['blɪðərɪŋ] ADJ (*inf*) **a ~ idiot** ein Trottel *m* (*inf*)

B Litt ABBR *of Bachelor of Letters*

blitz [blɪts] N **(a)** (*aerial*) Luftangriff *m*; **the Blitz** *deutscher Luftangriff auf britische Städte 1940–41* **(b)** (*fig inf*) Blitzaktion *f*; **he had a ~ on his room** er machte gründlich in seinem Zimmer sauber

blizzard ['blɪzəd] N Schneesturm *m*, Blizzard *m*

bloated ['bləʊtɪd] ADJ **(a)** aufgedunsen; **I feel absolutely ~** (*inf*) ich bin zum Platzen voll (*inf*) **(b)** (*fig*: *with pride*) aufgeblasen (*with* vor +*dat*)

blob [blɒb] N (*of water, honey*) Tropfen *m*; (*of ink*) Klecks *m*; (*of paint*) Tupfer *m*; (*of ice cream, mashed potato*) Klacks *m*

bloc [blɒk] N (*Pol*) Block *m*

block [blɒk] **⊠** N **(a)** Block *m*; (*of wood, stone also*) Klotz *m*; (= *executioner's ~*) Richtblock *m*; (= *engine ~*) Motorblock *m*; **~s** (= *toys*) (Bau)klötze *pl*; **to put** *or* **lay one's head on the ~** (*fig*) Kopf und Kragen riskieren; **~ of flats** (*Brit*) Wohnblock *m*; **she lived in the next ~/three ~s from us** (*esp US*) sie wohnte im nächsten Block/drei Blocks weiter
(b) (= *obstruction*) (*in pipe, Med*) Verstopfung *f*; (*mental*) geistige Sperre (*about* in Bezug auf +*acc*), Mattscheibe *f* (*inf*); **I've a mental ~ about it** da habe ich totale Mattscheibe (*inf*)
(c) (*inf*: = *head*) **to knock sb's ~ off** jdm eins überziehen (*inf*)
(d) (*usu pl*: *also* **starting ~**) Startblock *m*
⊡ VT **(a)** blockieren; *traffic, progress* aufhalten; *pipe* verstopfen; (*Ftbl*) *one's opponent* blocken; *ball* stoppen; **to ~ sb's way/view** jdm den Weg/die Sicht versperren
(b) *credit* sperren
(c) (*Comput*) blocken
► **block in** VT SEP (= *hem in*) einkeilen
► **block off** VT SEP *street* absperren; *fireplace* abdecken
► **block out** VT SEP **(a)** (= *obscure*) *light* nicht durchlassen; **the trees are blocking out all the light** die Bäume nehmen das ganze Licht weg **(b)** (= *obliterate*) *part of picture* wegretuschieren **(c)** (= *ignore*) *pain, fact, past* verdrängen; *noise* (*double glazing etc*) unterdrücken
► **block up** VT SEP **(a)** (= *obstruct*) *gangway* blockieren; *pipe* verstopfen; **my nose is ~ed** *or* **I'm all blocked up** meine Nase ist völlig verstopft **(b)** (= *close, fill in*) *window, entrance* zumauern; *hole* zustopfen

blockade [blɒ'keɪd] **⊠** N **(a)** (*Mil*) Blockade *f*; **to break** *or* **run the ~** die Blockade brechen **(b)** (= *obstruction*) Sperre *f* **⊡** VT blockieren

blockage ['blɒkɪdʒ] N Verstopfung *f*; (*in windpipe etc*) Blockade *f*; (= *act*) Blockierung *f*

block: block booking N (= *travel booking*) Gruppenbuchung *f*; (*Theat*) Gruppenbestellung *f*; **blockbuster** N (*inf*) Knüller *m* (*inf*); (= *film*) Kinohit *m* (*inf*); **blockhead** N (*inf*) Dummkopf *m*; **block letters** PL Blockschrift *f*; **block vote** N Stimmenblock *m*

bloke [bləʊk] N (*Brit inf*) Typ *m* (*inf*)

blond [blɒnd] ADJ blond

blonde [blɒnd] **⊠** ADJ blond **⊡** N (= *woman*) Blondine *f*

blonde bombshell N (*inf*) Superblondine *f* (*inf*)

blood [blʌd] N **(a)** Blut *nt*; **to give ~** Blut spenden; **to spill** *or* **shed ~** Blut vergießen; **it makes my ~ boil** das macht mich rasend; **she's out for** *or* **after his ~** sie will ihm an den Kragen (*inf*); **his ~ ran cold** es lief ihm eiskalt über den Rücken; **this firm needs new ~** diese Firma braucht frisches Blut; **it is like trying to get ~ from a stone** (*prov*) das ist verlorene Liebesmüh
(b) (*fig*: = *lineage*) Blut *nt*, Abstammung *f*; **it's in his ~** das liegt ihm im Blut

blood IN CPDS Blut-; **blood bank** N Blutbank *f*; **blood bath** N Blutbad *nt*; **blood clot** N Blutgerinnsel *nt*; **blood count** N (*Med*) Blutbild *nt*; **bloodcurdling** ADJ Grauen erregend; **they heard a ~ cry** sie hörten einen Schrei, der ihnen das Blut in den Adern erstarren ließ (*geh*); **blood donor** N Blutspender(in) *m(f)*; **blood group** N Blutgruppe *f*; **bloodhound** N Bluthund *m*

bloodless ['blʌdlɪs] ADJ *victory, coup* unblutig

blood: bloodmobile N (*US*) Blutspendewagen *m*; **blood orange** N Blutorange *f*; **blood poisoning** N Blutvergiftung *f*; **blood pressure** N Blutdruck *m*; **to have high ~** hohen Blutdruck haben; **blood-red** ADJ blutrot; **blood relation** N Blutsverwandte(r) *mf*; **bloodshed** N Blutvergießen *nt*; **bloodshot** ADJ blutunterlaufen; **blood sports** PL Jagdsport, Hahnenkampf *etc*; **bloodstain** N Blutfleck *m*; **bloodstained** ADJ blutig, blutbefleckt; **bloodstream** N Blutkreislauf *m*; **bloodsucker** N (*Zool, fig*) Blutsauger *m*; **blood sugar** N Blutzucker *m*; **~ level** Blutzuckerspiegel *m*; **blood test** N Blutprobe *f*; **bloodthirsty** ADJ blutrünstig; **blood transfusion** N (Blut)transfusion *f*; **blood vessel** N Blutgefäß *nt*

bloody ['blʌdɪ] **⊠** ADJ (+ER) **(a)** (*lit*) blutig; **to give sb a ~ nose** (*fig*) (*in contest*) jdm eine Denkzettel verpassen
(b) (*Brit inf*: = *damned*) verdammt (*inf*); (*in positive sense*) *genius, wonder* echt (*inf*); **~ hell!** verdammt! (*inf*); (*in*

amazement) Menschenskind! *(inf)*, meine Fresse! *(sl)* **2** ADV *(Brit inf)* verdammt *(inf)*; *hot, stupid* sau- *(inf)*; *(in positive sense)* brilliant echt *(inf)*; **not ~ likely** da ist überhaupt nichts drin *(inf)*; **he can ~ well do it himself** das soll er schön alleine machen, verdammt noch mal! *(inf)* **3** VT blutig machen

bloody-minded [ˈblʌdɪˈmaɪndɪd] ADJ *(Brit inf)* stur *(inf)*

bloom [bluːm] **1** N **(a)** Blüte *f*; **to be in (full) ~** in (voller) Blüte stehen; **to come into ~** aufblühen **(b)** *(fig)* **her skin has lost its ~** ihre Haut ist welk geworden *(lit, fig)* blühen

blooming [ˈbluːmɪŋ] ADJ *(inf)* verflixt *(inf)*

blooper [ˈbluːpəʳ] N *(US inf)* Schnitzer *m* *(inf)*

blossom [ˈblɒsəm] **1** N Blüte *f*; **in ~** in Blüte **2** VI *(lit, fig)* blühen

blot [blɒt] **1** N **(a)** *(of ink)* (Tinten)klecks *m* **(b)** *(fig: on reputation)* Fleck *m* *(on* auf +*dat)*; **a ~ on the landscape** ein Schandfleck *m* in der Landschaft **2** VT **(a) to ~ one's copybook** *(fig)* sich unmöglich machen; *(with sb)* es sich *(dat)* verderben **(b)** *(= dry)* ink ablöschen

➤ **blot out** VT SEP *(fig: = hide from view)* landscape, sun verdecken; *(= obliterate)* memories auslöschen

blotch [blɒtʃ] N Fleck *m*

blotchy [ˈblɒtʃɪ] ADJ (+ER) *skin* fleckig; *drawing, paint* klecksig

blotter [ˈblɒtəʳ] N **(a)** (Tinten)löscher *m* **(b)** *(US)* *(= record book)* Kladde *f*; *(= police ~)* Polizeiregister *nt*

blotting [ˈblɒtɪŋ]: **blotting pad** N Schreibunterlage *f*; **blotting paper** N Löschpapier *nt*

blotto [ˈblɒtəʊ] ADJ PRED *(Brit inf: = drunk)* stockbesoffen *(inf)*

blouse [blaʊz] N **(a)** Bluse *f* **(b)** *(US Mil)* (Feld)bluse *f*

blouson [ˈbluːzɒn] N *(Brit)* Blouson *m or nt*

blow¹ [bləʊ] N *(lit, fig)* Schlag *m*; **to come to ~s** handgreiflich werden; **at a (single) or one ~** *(fig)* mit einem Schlag *(inf)*; **to deal sb/sth a ~** *(fig)* jdm/einer Sache einen Schlag versetzen; **to strike a ~ for sth** *(fig)* einer Sache *(dat)* einen großen Dienst erweisen

blow² *vb: pret* **blew**, *ptp* **blown 1** VI **(a)** *(wind)* wehen; **there was a draught** *(Brit)* or **draft** *(US)* **~ing in from the window** es zog vom Fenster her **(b)** *(person, horn)* blasen *(on* auf +*acc)*; **the whistle blew** *(Sport)* da kam der Pfiff **(c)** *(= move with the wind)* fliegen; **the door blew open/shut** die Tür flog auf/zu **(d)** *(fuse, light bulb)* durchbrennen; *(gasket)* platzen **2** VT **(a)** *(= move by ~ing)* *(breeze)* wehen; *(strong wind, draught, person)* blasen; *(gale etc)* treiben; **the wind blew the ship off course** der Wind trieb das Schiff vom Kurs ab; **to ~ sb a kiss** jdm eine Kusshand zuwerfen **(b)** *(= drive air into)* eggs ausblasen; **to ~ one's nose** sich *(dat)* die Nase putzen **(c)** *glass, smoke rings, trumpet* blasen; *bubbles* machen; *(Hunt, Mil)* horn blasen in (+*acc)*; **the referee blew his whistle** der Schiedsrichter pfiff; **to ~ one's own trumpet** *(Brit)* or **horn** *(US)* *(fig)* sein eigenes Lob singen **(d)** *(= burn out, ~ up)* valve, gasket platzen lassen; **I've ~n a fuse** mir ist eine Sicherung durchgebrannt; **the car blew a tyre** *(Brit)* or **tire** *(US)* an dem Auto ist ein Reifen geplatzt; **to be ~n to pieces** *(bridge, car)* in die Luft gesprengt werden; *(person)* zerfetzt werden **(e)** *(inf: = spend extravagantly)* verpulvern *(inf)* **(f)** *(Brit inf: = damn)* ~ it! Mist! *(inf)*; **~ the expense!** das ist doch wurscht, was es kostet *(inf)*; **I'll be ~ed if I'll do it** ich denke nicht im Traum dran(, das zu tun) *(inf)* **(g)** *(inf)* **to ~ one's chances of doing sth** es sich *(dat)* verscherzen, etw zu tun; **I think I've ~n it** ich glaube, ich habs versaut *(inf)*

➤ **blow away 1** VI wegfliegen **2** VT SEP **(a)** wegblasen **(b)** *(inf: = kill)* abknallen *(inf)*

➤ **blow down** VT SEP *(lit)* umwehen

➤ **blow in 1** VI *(inf: = arrive unexpectedly)* hereinschneien *(inf)* *(+prep obj, -to* in +*acc)* **2** VT SEP *window, door etc* eindrücken; *dust etc* hineinblasen *(+prep obj, -to* in +*acc)*

➤ **blow off 1** VI wegfliegen **2** VT SEP wegblasen; **to blow sb's head off** *(= kill)* jdm eine Kugel durch den Kopf jagen *(inf)*

➤ **blow out 1** VT SEP **(a)** *candle* ausblasen **(b)** *(= fill with air)* aufblasen **(c)** **to blow one's/sb's brains out** sich/jdm eine Kugel durch den Kopf jagen *(inf)* **2** VR *(wind, storm)* sich legen; *(fig: passion)* verpuffen *(inf)*

➤ **blow over 1** VI *(lit, fig: storm, dispute)* sich legen **2** VT SEP *tree etc* umstürzen

➤ **blow up 1** VI **(a)** *(= be exploded)* in die Luft fliegen; *(bomb)* explodieren **(b)** *(lit, fig: gale, crisis, row)* ausbrechen; **his allegations could blow up in his face** seine Behauptungen könnten nach hinten losgehen *(fig inf: person)* explodieren *(inf)* **2** VT SEP **(a)** *mine, bridge, person* in die Luft jagen **(b)** *tyre, balloon* aufblasen **(c)** *photo* vergrößern **(d)** *(fig: = exaggerate)* aufbauschen *(into* zu)

blow-dry [ˈbləʊdraɪ] **1** N **to have a cut and ~** sich *(dat)* die Haare schneiden und föhnen lassen **2** VT föhnen

blowlamp [ˈbləʊlæmp] N Lötlampe *f*

blown [bləʊn] PTP *of* **blow²**

blow: blowout N *(= burst tyre)* **he had a ~** ihm ist ein Reifen geplatzt; **blowtorch** N Lötlampe *f*; **blow-up** N *(Phot)* Vergrößerung *f*

blowy [ˈbləʊɪ] ADJ (+ER) windig

blubber [ˈblʌbəʳ] **1** N Walfischspeck *m* **2** VTI *(inf)* heulen *(inf)*

bludgeon [ˈblʌdʒən] VT **(a)** *(= hit)* verprügeln; **to ~ sb to death** jdn zu Tode prügeln **(b)** *(fig)* bearbeiten *(inf)*; **he ~ed me into doing it** er hat mich so lange bearbeitet, bis ich es getan habe *(inf)*

blue [bluː] **1** ADJ (+ER) **(a)** blau; **~ with cold** blau vor Kälte; **until you're ~ in the face** *(inf)* bis zum Gehtnichtmehr *(inf)*; **once in a ~ moon** alle Jubeljahre (einmal) **(b)** *(inf: = miserable)* melancholisch; **to feel ~** den Moralischen haben *(inf)* **(c)** *(inf: = obscene)* language derb; *joke* schlüpfrig; *film* Porno- **2** N **(a)** Blau *nt*; **out of the ~** *(fig inf)* aus heiterem Himmel *(inf)*; **to have the ~s** *(inf)* den Moralischen haben *(inf)* **(b)** *(Mus)* **the blues** PL der Blues; **a ~s** *sing* ein Blues

blue: bluebell N Sternhyazinthe *f*; **blue beret** N Blauhelm *m*; **blueberry** N Blau- *or* Heidelbeere *f*; **blue-blooded** ADJ blaublütig; **bluebook** *(US)* N **(a)** *(= list of prominent people)* ≈ Who's Who *nt* **(b)** *(= used-car price list)* Gebrauchtwagenpreisliste *f*, ≈ Schwacke-Liste *f*; **bluebottle** N Schmeißfliege *f*; **blue cheese** N Blauschimmelkäse *m*; **blue-chip** ADJ *company* erstklassig; *shares* Bluechip-; *investment* sicher; **blue-collar** ADJ **~ worker/union/jobs** Arbeiter *m*/Arbeitergewerkschaft *f*/Stellen *pl* für Arbeiter; **blue-eyed** ADJ blauäugig; **sb's ~ boy** *(fig)* jds Liebling(sjunge) *m*; **blue jeans** *pl* Bluejeans *pl*; **blueprint** N Blaupause *f*; *(fig)* Plan *m*; **blue rinse** N **with her ~** mit ihrem silberblau getönten Haar; **bluetit** N Blaumeise *f*

bluff¹ [blʌf] ADJ rau aber herzlich *(inf)*; *honesty, answer* aufrichtig

bluff² **1** VTI bluffen; **he ~ed his way through it** er hat sich durchgeschummelt *(inf)* **2** N Bluff *m*; **to call sb's ~** es darauf ankommen lassen; *(= make prove)* jdn auf die Probe stellen

➤ **bluff out** VT SEP **to bluff one's way out of sth** sich aus etw rausreden *(inf)*

bluish [ˈbluːɪʃ] ADJ bläulich

blunder [ˈblʌndəʳ] **1** N (dummer) Fehler; **to make a ~** einen Bock schießen *(inf)*; *(socially)* einen Fauxpas begehen **2** VI **(a)** *(= make a ~)* einen Bock schießen *(inf)*; *(socially)* sich blamieren **(b)** *(= move clumsily)* tappen *(into* gegen)

blunt [blʌnt] **1** ADJ (+ER) **(a)** stumpf **(b)** *(= outspoken)* person geradeheraus pred; *message, language* unverblümt; **he was very ~ about it** er hat sich sehr deutlich ausgedrückt **2** VT *knife etc* stumpf machen; *(fig)* palate, senses abstumpfen

bluntly [ˈblʌntlɪ] ADV *speak* geradeheraus; **he told us quite ~ what he thought** er sagte uns ganz unverblümt seine Meinung

bluntness [ˈblʌntnɪs] N *(= outspokenness)* Unverblümtheit *f*

blur [blɜːʳ] **1** N verschwommener Fleck; **the trees became a ~** man konnte die Bäume nur noch verschwommen erkennen; **a ~ of colours** *(Brit)* or **colors** *(US)* ein buntes Durcheinander von Farben **2** VT **(a)** *writing* verwischen; *outline, photograph* unscharf machen; *sound* verzerren; **to have ~red vision** nur noch verschwommen sehen; **to be/become ~red** undeutlich sein/ werden; *(image etc also)* verschwommen sein/ verschwimmen **(b)** *(fig)* senses, judgement trüben; *memory, meaning* verwischen **3** VI *(vision, image)* verschwimmen

blurb [blɜːb] N Informationen *pl*; (*on book cover*) Klappentext *m*

blurt (out) [blɜːt(ˈaʊt)] VT SEP herausplatzen mit (*inf*)

blush [blʌʃ] **1** VI **(a)** (= *go red*) erröten (*with* vor +*dat*) **(b)** (*fig:* = *be ashamed*) sich schämen (*for* für) **2** N Erröten *nt no pl*; **with a ~** errötend

blusher [ˈblʌʃəʳ] N Rouge *nt*

bluster [ˈblʌstəʳ] **1** VI (*person*) ein großes Geschrei machen **2** VT **to ~ one's way out of sth** etw lautstark abstreiten

blustery [ˈblʌstərɪ] ADJ stürmisch

Blu-Tack® [ˈbluːtæk] N Klebmasse *f*

BMA ABBR *of* **British Medical Association** *britischer Ärzteverband*

B-movie [ˈbiːˌmuːvɪ] N B-Movie *nt*

B Mus ABBR *of* **Bachelor of Music**

BMX ABBR *of* **bicycle motocross** (= *sport*) BMX-Radsport *m*; (= *bicycle*) BMX-Rad *nt*

bn ABBR *of* **billion**

BO (*inf*) ABBR *of* **body odour** Körpergeruch *m*

boa [ˈbəʊə] N Boa *f*; **~ constrictor** Boa constrictor *f*

boar [bɔːʳ] N (= *male pig*) Eber *m*; (*wild*) Keiler *m*

board [bɔːd] **1** N **(a)** Brett *nt*; (= *blackboard*) Tafel *f*; (= *notice* ~) schwarzes Brett; (= *signboard*) Schild *nt*; (= *floorboard*) Diele *f*
(b) (= *provision of meals*) Kost *f*, Verpflegung *f*; **~ and lodging** Kost und Logis; **full/half ~** Voll-/Halbpension *f*
(c) (= *group of officials*) Ausschuss *m*; (*with advisory function:* = ~ *of trustees*) Beirat *m*; (= *gas* ~ *etc*) Behörde *f*; (*of company: also* ~ **of directors**) Vorstand *m*; (*of British/American company*) Verwaltungsrat *m*; (*including shareholders, advisers*) Aufsichtsrat *m*; **to be on the ~**, **to have a seat on the ~** im Vorstand/Aufsichtsrat sein; **~ of governors** (*Brit Sch*) Verwaltungsrat *m*; **Board of Trade** (*Brit*) Handelsministerium *nt*; (*US*) Handelskammer *f*
(d) (*Naut, Aviat*) **on ~** an Bord; **to go on ~** an Bord gehen; **on ~ the ship/plane** an Bord des Schiffes/Flugzeugs; **on ~ the bus** im Bus
(e) (= *cardboard*) Pappe *f*
(f) (= ~ *of interviewers*) Gremium *nt* (zur Auswahl von Bewerbern)
(g) (*US St Ex*) Notierung *f*; (*inf:* = *stock exchange*) Börse *f*
(h) (*fig phrases*) **across the ~** allgemein; *criticize, agree, reject* pauschal; **to go by the ~** (*work, ideas*) unter den Tisch fallen; (*hopes*) zunichte werden; (*principles*) über Bord geworfen werden; **to take sth on ~** (= *understand*) etw begreifen; (= *deal with*) sich einer Sache (*gen*) annehmen
2 VT *ship, plane* besteigen, an Bord (+*gen*) gehen/kommen; *train, bus* einsteigen in (+*acc*); (*Naut: in attack*) entern
3 VI **(a)** in Pension sein (*with* bei)
(b) (*Sch*) Internatsschüler(in) *m(f)* sein
(c) (*Aviat*) die Maschine besteigen; **flight ZA173 now ~ing at gate 13** Passagiere des Fluges ZA173, bitte zum Flugsteig 13
➤ **board up** VT SEP *window* mit Brettern vernageln

boarder [ˈbɔːdəʳ] N **(a)** Pensionsgast *m*; **to take in ~s** Leute in Pension nehmen **(b)** (*Sch*) Internatsschüler(in) *m(f)*

board game N Brettspiel *nt*

boarding [ˈbɔːdɪŋ]: **boarding card** N Bordkarte *f*; **boarding house** N Pension *f*; **boarding pass** N Bordkarte *f*; **boarding school** N Internat *nt*

board: **board meeting** N Vorstandssitzung *f*; **boardroom** N Vorstandsetage *f*; **boardwalk** N (*US*) Holzsteg *m*; (*on beach*) hölzerne Uferpromenade

boast [bəʊst] **1** N Prahlerei *f* **2** VI prahlen (*about, of* mit to *sb* jdm gegenüber) **3** VT **(a)** (= *possess*) sich rühmen (+*gen*) (*geh*) **(b)** (= *say boastfully*) prahlen

boastful [ˈbəʊstfʊl] ADJ, **boastfully** [ˈbəʊstfəlɪ] ADV prahlerisch

boasting [ˈbəʊstɪŋ] N Prahlerei *f* (*about, of* mit)

boat [bəʊt] N Boot *nt*; (*seagoing:* = *passenger* ~) Schiff *nt*; (= *pleasure steamer etc*) Dampfer *m*; **by ~** mit dem Schiff; **to miss the ~** (*fig inf*) den Anschluss verpassen; **to push the ~ out** (*fig inf:* = *celebrate*) auf den Putz hauen (*inf*); **we're all in the same ~** (*fig inf*) wir sitzen alle in einem *or* im gleichen Boot

boat: **boatbuilding** N Bootsbau *m*; **boat deck** N Bootsdeck *nt*

boater [ˈbəʊtəʳ] N (= *hat*) steifer Strohhut

boat: **boat hire** N Bootsverleih *m*; **boathook** N Bootshaken *m*; **boathouse** N Bootshaus *nt*

boating [ˈbəʊtɪŋ] N Bootfahren *nt*; **to go ~** eine Bootsfahrt machen; **~ holiday/trip** Bootsferien *pl*/-fahrt *f*

boat: **boatload** N Bootsladung *f*; **boatman** N (*handling boat*) Segler *m*; Ruderer *m*; (= *hirer*) Bootsverleiher *m*; **boat people** PL Bootsflüchtlinge *pl*; **boat race** N Regatta *f*; **boat train** N Zug *m* mit Fähranschluss; **boatyard** N Bootshandlung *f*; (*as dry dock*) Liegeplatz *m*

bob¹ [bɒb] **1** VI (= *move up and down*) sich auf und ab bewegen; (*rabbit*) hoppeln; (*boxer*) tänzeln; **to ~ (up and down) in** *or* **on the water** auf dem Wasser schaukeln; (*cork etc*) sich im Wasser auf und ab bewegen; **he ~bed out of sight** er duckte sich **2** VT (= *move jerkily*) *head* nicken mit **3** N (*of head*) Nicken *nt no pl*
➤ **bob down** **1** VI sich ducken **2** VT SEP *one's head* ducken
➤ **bob up** **1** VI (*lit, fig*) auftauchen **2** VT SEP **he bobbed his head up** sein Kopf schnellte hoch

bob² N, *pl* **bob** (*dated Brit inf*) Shilling *m*; **that must have cost a ~ or two** das muss schon so einiges gekostet haben (*inf*); **that must be worth a few ~** das muss eine Stange Geld wert sein (*inf*)

bob³ N **(a)** (= *haircut*) Bubikopf *m* **(b)** **a few/various bits and ~s** so ein paar/verschiedene Dinge

bob⁴ N (= *sleigh*) Bob *m*; **two-/four-man ~** Zweier-/Viererbob *m*

Bob [bɒb] DIM *of* **Robert**; **... and ~'s your uncle!** (*inf*) ... und fertig ist der Lack! (*inf*)

bobbin [ˈbɒbɪn] N Spule *f*; (= *cotton reel*) Rolle *f*

bobble [ˈbɒbl] N **(a)** Bommel *f* **(b)** (*US inf:* = *mistake*) Schnitzer *m* (*inf*)

bobble hat N (*Brit*) Pudelmütze *f*

bobby [ˈbɒbɪ] N (*dated Brit inf:* = *policeman*) Bobby *m*, Schupo *m* (*dated*)

bobby: **bobby sox** PL (*dated US*) kurze Söckchen *pl*; **bobbysoxer** N (*dated US inf*) junges Mädchen

bob: **bobcat** N (*US*) Luchs *m*; **bobsleigh**, (*US*) **bobsled** **1** N Bob *m* **2** VI Bob fahren

bod [bɒd] N **(a)** (*Brit inf:* = *person*) Mensch *m*; **odd ~** komischer Kerl **(b)** (*sl:* = *body*) Body *m* (*sl*)

bodacious [bəʊˈdeɪʃəs] ADJ (*US inf*) toll

bode [bəʊd] VI **to ~ well/ill** ein gutes/schlechtes Zeichen sein

bodge [bɒdʒ] VT = **botch**

bodice [ˈbɒdɪs] N Mieder *nt*

bodily [ˈbɒdɪlɪ] **1** ADJ (= *physical*) körperlich; **~ needs** leibliche Bedürfnisse *pl*; **~ functions/fluids** Körperfunktionen/-flüssigkeiten *pl* **2** ADV (= *forcibly*) gewaltsam

body [ˈbɒdɪ] N **(a)** Körper *m*; **the ~ of Christ** der Leib des Herrn; **just enough to keep ~ and soul together** gerade genug, um Leib und Seele zusammenzuhalten
(b) (= *corpse*) Leiche *f*
(c) (*of plane, ship*) Rumpf *m*; (*of church, speech, army: also* **main ~**) Hauptteil *m*; **the main ~ of the students** das Gros der Studenten
(d) (*of car*) Karosserie *f*
(e) (= *group of people*) Gruppe *f*; **the student ~** die Studentenschaft; **a large ~ of people** eine große Menschenmenge; **in a ~** geschlossen
(f) (= *organization*) Organ *nt*; (= *committee*) Gremium *nt*; (= *corporation*) Körperschaft *f*
(g) (= *quantity*) **a ~ of evidence/data** Beweis-/Datenmaterial *nt*
(h) (*inf:* = *person*) Mensch *m*
(i) (*also* ~ **stocking**) Body *m*

body: **body blow** N (*fig*) Schlag *m* ins Kontor (*to, for* für); **body builder** N (= *person*) Bodybuilder(in) *m(f)*; **body building** **1** N Bodybuilding *nt* **2** ADJ muskelkräftigend; **body clock** N innere Uhr; **bodyguard** N Leibwache *f*; **body language** N Körpersprache *f*; **body lotion** N Körperlotion *f*; **body (repair) shop** N Karosseriewerkstatt *f*; **body search** N Leibesvisitation *f*; **body stocking** N Body(stocking) *m*; **body swerve** N **to give sb/sth a ~** (*fig inf*) einen weiten Bogen um jdn/etw machen; **body warmer** N Thermoweste *f*; **bodywork** N (*Aut*) Karosserie *f*

Boer [bɔːʳ] **1** N Bure *m*, Burin *f* **2** ADJ burisch; **the ~ War** der Burenkrieg

boffin [ˈbɒfɪn] N (*Brit inf*) Eierkopf *m* (*inf*)

bog [bɒg] N **(a)** Sumpf *m*; (= *peat* ~) (Torf)moor *nt* **(b)** (*Brit inf:* = *toilet*) Klo *nt* (*inf*)

➤ **bog down** VT SEP **to get bogged down** (*lit, fig*) stecken bleiben; (*in details*) sich verzetteln

bogeyman [ˈbəʊɡɪmæn], *pl* **bogeymen** [-men] schwarzer Mann

boggle [ˈbɒɡl] VI **the mind ~s** das ist kaum auszumalen (*inf*)

boggy [ˈbɒɡɪ] ADJ (+ER) sumpfig

bog paper, bog roll N (*Brit inf*) Klopapier *nt* (*inf*)

bog-standard [bɒɡˈstændəd] ADJ (*Brit inf*) stinknormal (*inf*)

bogus [ˈbəʊɡəs] ADJ *doctor, name* falsch; *document* gefälscht; *company, transaction* Schwindel-; *claim* erfunden

bohemian [bəˈhiːmɪən] **1** N Bohemien *m* **2** ADJ *lifestyle* unkonventionell; *circles, quarter* Künstler-

boil¹ [bɔɪl] N (*Med*) Furunkel *m*

boil² **1** VI (a) (*lit*) kochen; (*water also, Phys*) sieden; **the kettle was ~ing** das Wasser im Kessel kochte; **to let the kettle ~ dry** das Wasser im Kessel verkochen lassen
(b) (*fig inf*: = *be hot*) **~ing hot water** kochend heißes Wasser; **it was ~ing (hot) in the office** es war eine Affenhitze im Büro (*inf*); **I was ~ing (hot)** mir war fürchterlich heiß
(c) (*fig inf*: = *be angry*) kochen (*with* vor +*dat*)
2 VT kochen; **~ed/hard ~ed egg** weich/hart gekochtes Ei; **~ed potatoes** Salzkartoffeln *pl*
3 N **to bring sth to the** (*Brit*) or **a** (*US*) **~** etw aufkochen lassen; **to keep sth on the ~** etw kochen lassen; **to come to/ go off the ~** zu kochen anfangen/aufhören

➤ **boil away** VI (= *evaporate*) verdampfen

➤ **boil down** (*fig*) **to boil down to sth** auf etw (*acc*) hinauslaufen; **what it boils down to is that ...** das läuft darauf hinaus, dass ...

➤ **boil over** VI (a) (*lit*) überkochen (b) (*fig: situation, quarrel*) den Siedepunkt erreichen

boiled sweet N Bonbon *nt*

boiler [ˈbɔɪləʳ] N (*domestic*) Boiler *m*, Warmwasserbereiter *m*; (*in ship, engine*) (Dampf)kessel *m*

boiler: boilerplate letter N (*US*) (Brief)rumpf *m*; **boiler room** N Kesselraum *m*; **boiler suit** N (*Brit*) Overall *m*

boiling point [ˈbɔɪlɪŋpɔɪnt] N (*lit, fig*) Siedepunkt *m*; **at ~** (*lit, fig*) auf dem Siedepunkt; **to reach ~** (*lit, fig*) den Siedepunkt erreichen; (*feelings also, person*) auf dem Siedepunkt anlangen

boisterous [ˈbɔɪstərəs] ADJ ausgelassen

boisterously [ˈbɔɪstərəslɪ] ADV ausgelassen; *play* wild

bold [bəʊld] ADJ (+ER) (a) (= *brave*) kühn (*geh*), mutig
(b) (= *impudent*) dreist; **might I be so ~ as to ...?** wenn ich es mir erlauben darf, zu ...?; **as ~ as brass** (*inf*) rotzfrech (*inf*)
(c) (= *striking*) *colours, pattern* kräftig; *style* kraftvoll (d) (*Typ*) fett; (= *secondary ~*) halbfett; **~ type** Fettdruck *m*

boldly [ˈbəʊldlɪ] ADV (a) (= *bravely*) mutig (b) (= *forthrightly*) dreist (c) (= *strikingly*) auffallend

boldness [ˈbəʊldnɪs] N (a) (= *bravery*) Kühnheit *f* (*geh*), Mut *m* (b) (= *impudence*) Dreistigkeit *f* (c) (*of colours, pattern*) Kräftigkeit *f*; (*of style*) Ausdruckskraft *f*

Bolivia [bəˈlɪvɪə] N Bolivien *nt*

Bolivian [bəˈlɪvɪən] **1** N Bolivianer(in) *m(f)* **2** ADJ bolivianisch

bollard [ˈbɒləd] N Poller *m*

bollocking [ˈbɒlɒkɪŋ] N (*Brit sl*) Schimpfkanonade *f* (*inf*); **to give sb a ~** jdn zur Sau machen (*inf*)

bollocks [ˈbɒləks] PL (*sl*) (a) (= *testicles*) Eier *pl* (*sl*) (b) (= *nonsense*) (**that's**) **~!** Quatsch mit Soße! (*inf*)

Bolshevik [ˈbɒlʃəvɪk] **1** N Bolschewik *m* **2** ADJ bolschewistisch

bolshie, bolshy [ˈbɒlʃɪ] (*inf*) ADJ (+ER) (*Brit fig*) (= *uncooperative*) stur; (= *aggressive*) pampig (*inf*)

bolster [ˈbəʊlstəʳ] **1** N (*on bed*) Nackenrolle *f* **2** VT (*also* ~ **up**: *fig*) *person* Mut machen (+*dat*); *currency* stützen; *economy, confidence* Auftrieb geben (+*dat*); *profits, power* erhöhen

bolt [bəʊlt] **1** N (a) (*on door etc*) Riegel *m*
(b) (*Tech*) Bolzen *m*
(c) (*of lightning*) Blitzstrahl *m*; **it came/was like a ~ from the blue** (*fig*) das schlug ein/war wie ein Blitz aus heiterem Himmel
(d) (= *sudden dash*) **he made a ~ for the door** er machte einen Satz zur Tür; **to make a ~ for it** losrennen
2 ADV **~ upright** kerzengerade
3 VI (a) (*horse*) durchgehen; (*person*) Reißaus nehmen (*inf*)
(b) (= *move quickly*) rasen
4 VT (a) *door, window* verriegeln

(b) (*Tech*) *parts* verschrauben (*to* mit); **to ~ together** verschrauben
(c) (*also* ~ **down**) *one's food* hinunterschlingen

➤ **bolt on** VT SEP (*Tech*) festschrauben (*prep obj,-to* an +*dat*)

bolt hole N Schlupfloch *nt*

bomb [bɒm] **1** N (a) (= *device*) Bombe *f*; **to put a ~ under sb/ sth** (*Brit fig inf*) jdn/etw radikal verändern
(b) (*Brit inf*) **the car goes like a ~** das ist die reinste Rakete von Wagen (*inf*); **the car cost a ~** das Auto hat ein Bombengeld gekostet (*inf*); **to make a ~** eine Stange Geld verdienen (*inf*); **to go down a ~** Riesenanklang finden (*with* bei) (*inf*)
(c) (*US inf*) **the play was a real ~** das Stück war ein totaler Reinfall
2 VT (a) (*lit*) bombardieren
(b) (*US inf*: = *fail*) durchfallen bei
3 VI (a) (*inf*: = *go fast*) fegen (*inf*), zischen (*inf*)
(b) (*US inf*: = *fail*) durchfallen (*inf*)

➤ **bomb along** VI (*inf*: = *drive fast*) dahinrasen (*inf*)

bombard [bɒmˈbɑːd] VT (*Mil, fig*) bombardieren

bombardment [bɒmˈbɑːdmənt] N (*Mil, fig*) Bombardierung *f*

bombast [ˈbɒmbæst] N Bombast *m*

bombastic [bɒmˈbæstɪk] ADJ bombastisch

bomb: bomb attack N Bombenangriff *m*; **bomb disposal** N Bombenräumung *f*; **bomb disposal squad** N Bombenräumtrupp *m*

bomber [ˈbɒməʳ] N (a) (= *aircraft*) Bomber *m* (b) (= *terrorist*) Bombenattentäter(in) *m(f)*

bomber: bomber jacket N Fliegerjacke *f*; **bomber pilot** N Bomberpilot *m*

bombing [ˈbɒmɪŋ] **1** N Bombenangriff *m* (*of* auf +*acc*) **2** ADJ *raid, mission* Bomben-

bomb: bomb scare N Bombenalarm *m*; **bombshell** N (*fig*) **this news was a ~** die Nachricht schlug wie eine Bombe ein; **to drop a** *or* **the ~** die Bombe platzen lassen; **bomb shelter** N Luftschutzkeller *m*; (*specially built*) (Luftschutz)bunker *m*; **bomb site** N Trümmergrundstück *nt*

bona fide [ˈbəʊnəˈfaɪdɪ] ADJ bona fide; *traveller, word, antique* echt; **it's a ~ offer** es ist ein Angebot auf Treu und Glauben

bonanza [bəˈnænzə] N (*fig*) Goldgrube *f*; **the oil ~** der Ölboom

bonce [bɒns] N (*Brit inf*: = *head*) Birne *f* (*inf*)

bond [bɒnd] **1** N (a) (= *agreement*) Übereinkommen *nt*
(b) (*fig*: = *link*) Band *nt* (*geh*), Bindung *f*
(c) **bonds** PL (*lit*) (= *chains*) Fesseln *pl*; (*fig*) (= *ties*) Bande *pl* (*geh*); (*burdensome*) Fesseln *pl*
(d) (*Comm, Fin*) Pfandbrief *m*, festverzinsliches Wertpapier, Bond *m*; **government ~** Staatsanleihe *f*; **~s payable** (*Book-keeping*) Anleiheverbindlichkeiten *pl*
(e) (*Comm*: = *custody of goods*) **to put sth into ~** etw unter Zollverschluss geben; **goods in ~** Zollgut *nt*
(f) (= *adhesion between surfaces*) Haftfestigkeit *f*
(g) (*Chem*) Bindung *f*
2 VT (*Comm*) *goods* unter Zollverschluss nehmen
3 VI (a) (*glue*) binden
(b) **to ~ with one's baby** Liebe zu seinem Kind entwickeln; **we ~ed immediately** wir haben uns auf Anhieb gut verstanden

bondage [ˈbɒndɪdʒ] N (a) (*fig liter*) **in ~ to sth** einer Sache (*dat*) unterworfen (b) (*sexual*) Fesseln *nt*; **~ gear** Sadomasoausrüstung *f*

bonded [ˈbɒndɪd] ADJ *goods* unter Zollverschluss

bonded warehouse N Zolllager *nt*

bond: bondholder N Pfandbriefinhaber(in) *m(f)*; **bond indenture** N (*St Ex*) Emissionsbedingung *f*

bone [bəʊn] **1** N Knochen *m*; (*of fish*) Gräte *f*; **~s** *pl* (*of the dead*) Gebeine *pl*; **ham off the ~** Schinken *m* vom Knochen; **meat on the ~** Fleisch *nt* am Knochen; **chilled to the ~** völlig durchgefroren; **to work one's fingers to the ~** sich (*dat*) die Finger abarbeiten; **~ of contention** Zankapfel *m*; **to have a ~ to pick with sb** (*inf*) mit jdm ein Hühnchen zu rupfen haben (*inf*); **I'll make no ~s about it, you're ...** (*inf*) du bist, ehrlich gesagt, ...; **I can feel it in my ~s** das spüre ich in den Knochen
2 ADJ ATTR (= *made of* ~) beinern
3 VT die Knochen lösen aus; *fish* entgräten

➤ **bone up on** VI +PREP OBJ (*inf*) pauken (*inf*)

bone china N feines Porzellan

boned [bəʊnd] ADJ *meat* ohne Knochen; *fish* entgrätet

bone: **bone dry** ADJ PRED, **bone-dry** ADJ ATTR (*inf*) knochentrocken; **bone idle** ADJ (*Brit inf*) stinkfaul (*inf*); **boneless** ADJ *meat* ohne Knochen; *fish* ohne Gräten; **bone meal** N Knochenmehl *nt*

boner ['bəʊnəʳ] N (*US sl*) Schnitzer *m* (*inf*)

bone structure N (*of face*) Gesichtszüge *pl*

bonfire ['bɒnfaɪəʳ] N (*for burning rubbish*) Feuer *nt*; (*as beacon*) Leuchtfeuer *nt*; (*for Guy Fawkes' Night*) Guy-Fawkes-Feuer *nt*; (*for celebration*) Freudenfeuer *nt*

bonfire night N 5. November (*Jahrestag der Pulververschwörung*)

bongo ['bɒŋgəʊ] N Bongo *nt or f*

bonk [bɒŋk] (*inf*) VTI bumsen (*inf*)

bonkers ['bɒŋkəz] ADJ (*esp Brit inf*) meschugge (*inf*); **to be ~** spinnen (*inf*)

bonnet ['bɒnɪt] N (**a**) (*woman's*) Haube *f*; (*baby's*) Häubchen *nt* (**b**) (*Brit Aut*) Motorhaube *f*

bonnie, bonny ['bɒnɪ] ADJ (*esp Scot*) schön; *baby* prächtig

bonsai ['bɒnsaɪ] N, *pl* - Bonsai *nt*

bonus ['bəʊnəs] N (**a**) Prämie *f*; (= *cost-of-living ~*) Zuschlag *m*; (= *Christmas ~*) Gratifikation *f*; **~ scheme** Prämiensystem *nt*; **~ point** (*in quiz etc*) Bonuspunkt *m* (**b**) (*Fin: on shares*) Sonderausschüttung *f*; **~ issue** (*US*) Ausgabe *f* von Gratisaktien (**c**) (*inf: = sth extra*) Zugabe *f*

bony ['bəʊnɪ] ADJ (+ER) knochig

boo [buː] ■ INTERJ buh; **he wouldn't say ~ to a goose** (*inf*) er ist ein schüchternes Pflänzchen ■ VT *speaker, referee* auspfeifen ■ VI buhen ■ N Buhruf *m*

boob [buːb] ■ N (**a**) (*Brit inf: = mistake*) Schnitzer *m* (*inf*) (**b**) (*inf: woman's breast*) Brust *f*; **big ~s** große Titten *pl or* Möpse *pl* (*sl*) ■ VI (*Brit inf*) einen Schnitzer machen (*inf*)

boob job N (*inf*) Brustkorrektur *f*

boob tube N (**a**) (*Brit Tex*) Bustier *nt* (**b**) (*esp US inf*: = *television*) Glotze *f* (*inf*)

booby: **booby hatch** N (*dated US sl*) Klapsmühle *f* (*inf*); **booby prize** N Scherzpreis für den schlechtesten Teilnehmer; **booby trap** ■ N (*Mil etc*) versteckte Bombe ■ VT **the suitcase was booby-trapped** in dem Koffer war eine Bombe versteckt

booing ['buːɪŋ] N Buhrufen *nt*

book [bʊk] ■ N (**a**) Buch *nt*; (= *exercise ~*) Heft *nt*; **the Book of Genesis** die Genesis, das 1. Buch Mose; **to bring sb to ~** jdn zur Rechenschaft ziehen; **to throw the ~ at sb** (*inf*) jdn nach allen Regeln der Kunst fertig machen (*inf*); **to go by the ~** sich an die Vorschriften halten; **to be in sb's good/bad ~s** bei jdm gut/schlecht angeschrieben sein (*inf*); **I can read him like a ~** ich kann in ihm lesen wie in einem Buch; **it's a closed ~ to me** das ist ein Buch mit sieben Siegeln für mich; **he'll use every trick in the ~ to get what he wants** (*inf*) er wird alles und jedes versuchen, um zu erreichen, was er will; **that counts as cheating in my ~** (*inf*) für mich ist das Betrug (**b**) (*of tickets*) Heft *nt*; **~ of stamps** Briefmarkenheftchen *nt* (**c**) **books** PL (*Comm, Fin*) Bücher *pl*; **to keep the ~s of a firm** die Bücher einer Firma führen; **to do the ~s for sb** jdm die Bücher führen; **balance per ~s** buchmäßige Bilanz ■ VT (**a**) (= *reserve*) bestellen; *seat, room* buchen; *artiste* engagieren; **fully ~ed** (*performance*) ausverkauft; (*flight*) ausgebucht; (*hotel*) voll belegt; **to ~ sb through to Hull** (*Rail*) jdn bis Hull durchbuchen (**b**) (*Fin, Comm*) *order* aufnehmen; **to ~ goods to sb's account** jdm Waren in Rechnung stellen (**c**) (*inf*) *driver etc* aufschreiben (*inf*); *footballer* verwarnen; **to be ~ed for speeding** wegen zu schnellen Fahrens aufgeschrieben werden ■ VI bestellen; (= *reserve seat, room also*) buchen; **to ~ through to Hull** bis Hull durchlösen

➤ **book in** ■ VI (*in hotel etc*) sich eintragen; **we booked in at** *or* **into the Hilton** wir sind im Hilton abgestiegen ■ VT SEP **to book sb into a hotel** jdm ein Hotelzimmer reservieren lassen; **we're booked in at** *or* **into the Hilton** unsere Zimmer sind im Hilton reserviert

➤ **book up** VT SEP **to be (fully) booked up** (ganz) ausgebucht sein; (*performance, theatre*) ausverkauft sein

bookable ['bʊkəbl] ADJ (**a**) im Vorverkauf erhältlich (**b**) (*Sport*) **a ~ offence** (*Brit*) *or* **offense** (*US*) ein Verstoß *m*, für den es eine Verwarnung gibt

book: **bookbinder** N Buchbinder *m*; **bookbinding** N Buchbinderei *f*; **bookcase** N Bücherregal *nt*; (*with doors*) Bücherschrank *m*; **book club** N Buchgemeinschaft *f*; **book end** N Bücherstütze *f*; **book fair** N Buchmesse *f*

bookie ['bʊkɪ] N (*inf*) Buchmacher(in) *m(f)*

booking N Buchung *f*; (*of performer*) Engagement *nt*; **to make a ~** buchen; **to cancel a ~** den Tisch/die Karte *etc* abbestellen, die Reise/den Flug *etc* stornieren

booking: **booking clerk** N Fahrkartenverkäufer(in) *m(f)*; **booking fee** N Buchungsgebühr *f*; **booking office** N (*Rail*) Fahrkartenschalter *m*; (*Theat*) Vorverkaufsstelle *f*

bookish ['bʊkɪʃ] ADJ gelehrt (*pej, hum*); (= *given to reading*) lesewütig; (= *not worldly*) lebensfremd

book: **book-keeper** N Buchhalter(in) *m(f)*; **book-keeping** N Buchhaltung *f*

booklet ['bʊklɪt] N Broschüre *f*

book: **book lover** N Bücherfreund(in) *m(f)*; **bookmaker** N Buchmacher(in) *m(f)*; **bookmaking** N Buchmacherei *f*; **bookmark** ■ N Lesezeichen *nt*; (*Comput*) Bookmark *nt* ■ VT (*Comput*) ein Bookmark einrichten für, bookmarken; **bookmobile** N (*US*) Fahrbücherei *f*; **bookrest** N Lesepult *nt*; **book review** N Buchbesprechung *f*, Rezension *f*; **bookseller** N Buchhändler *m*; **bookshelf** N Bücherbord *nt*; **bookshelves** PL (= *bookcase*) Bücherregal *nt*; **bookshop** (*esp Brit*), **bookstore** (*US*) N Buchhandlung *f*; **bookstall** N Bücherstand *m*; **bookstand** N (*US*) (**a**) (= *bookrest*) Lesepult *nt* (**b**) (= *bookcase*) Bücherregal *nt* (**c**) (= *bookstall: in station, airport*) Bücherstand *m*; **book token** N Buchgutschein *m*; **book value** N (*Fin*) Buchwert *m*, Bilanzwert *m*; **bookworm** (*fig*) Bücherwurm *m*

boom[1] [buːm] N (*Naut*) Baum *m*

boom[2] ■ N (*of thunder*) Hallen *nt*; (*of guns*) Donnern *nt*; (*of organ, voice*) Dröhnen *nt* ■ VI (**a**) (*thunder*) hallen (**b**) (*organ, voice: also ~ out*) dröhnen; (*guns*) donnern ■ INTERJ bum

boom[3] ■ VI (*trade*) einen Aufschwung nehmen, boomen (*inf*); **business is ~ing** das Geschäft blüht ■ N (*of business, fig*) Boom *m*, Aufschwung *m*; (= *period of economic growth*) Hochkonjunktur *f*

boom: **boom box** N (*US inf*) Ghettoblaster *m* (*inf*); **boom-bust** ADJ (*Econ*) **~ cycle** Konjunkturzyklus *m*

boomerang ['buːməræŋ] ■ N (*lit, fig*) Bumerang *m*; **to have a ~ effect** einen Bumerangeffekt haben ■ VI (*fig inf: words, actions*) wie ein Bumerang zurückkommen (*on* zu)

booming[1] ['buːmɪŋ] ADJ *sound* dröhnend

booming[2] ADJ *town, economy, industry, business* boomend, florierend

boom town N Goldgräberstadt *f*

boon [buːn] N Segen *m*

boondockers ['buːndɒkəz] PL (*US inf: = heavy boots*) (schwere) Stiefel *pl*

boondocks ['buːndɒks] PL (*US inf: = backwoods*) Wildnis *f*; **in the ~** irgendwo, jwd (*inf*)

boondoggle ['buːndɒgl] (*US inf*) N Zeitverschwendung *f* auf Staatskosten

boondoggler ['buːndɒgləʳ] N (*US inf*) kleinkarierte Beamtenseele

boor [bʊəʳ] N Rüpel *m*

boorish ['bʊərɪʃ] ADJ, **boorishly** ADV ['bʊərɪʃ, -lɪ] rüpelhaft

boost [buːst] ■ N Auftrieb *m no pl*; (*Elec, Aut*) Verstärkung *f*; **to give sb/sth a ~** jdm/einer Sache Auftrieb geben; **to give a ~ to sb's morale** jdm Auftrieb geben; **to give a ~ to sb's confidence** jds Selbstvertrauen stärken ■ VT *production, sales, economy* ankurbeln; *profits, prices, income, chances* erhöhen; *shares* in die Höhe treiben; *confidence, sb's ego* stärken; *morale* heben

booster ['buːstəʳ] N (**a**) (= *~ rocket*) Booster *m* (**b**) (*Med: also ~ shot*) Wiederholungsimpfung *f*; **~ dose** zusätzliche Dosis

booster cushion N, **booster seat** N (*Aut*) Kindersitz *m*

boot[1] [buːt] ■ N (**a**) Stiefel *m*; **the ~ is on the other foot** (*fig*) es ist genau umgekehrt; **to give sb (the order of the ~)** (*hum*) – (*inf*) jdn rausschmeißen (*inf*); **to get the ~** (*inf*) rausgeschmissen werden (*inf*); **to quake** *or* **tremble in one's ~s** vor Angst fast umkommen; **to put the ~ into sb/sth** (*Brit fig inf*) jdn/etw niedermachen (**b**) (*Brit: of car etc*) Kofferraum *m* (**c**) (*inf: = kick*) **to give sb/sth a ~** jdm/einer Sache einen Tritt

geben
2 VT **(a)** (*inf*: = *kick*) einen (Fuß)tritt geben (+*dat*); *ball* kicken **(b)** (*Comput*) laden
3 VI (*Comput*) laden

➤ **boot out** VT SEP (*inf*: *lit*, *fig*) rausschmeißen (*inf*)

➤ **boot up** (*Comput*) **1** VT SEP booten **2** VI booten

boot² ADV (*hum*, *form*) **to ~** obendrein

boot camp N (*US Mil inf*) Armee-Ausbildungslager *nt*

bootee [buːˈtiː] N gestrickter Babyschuh

booth [buːð] N **(a)** (*at fair*) (Markt)bude *f*; (*at show*) (Messe)stand *m* **(b)** (= *telephone* ~) Zelle *f*; (= *polling* ~, *in language laboratory*) Kabine *f*; (*in restaurant*) Nische *f*

boot: **bootlace** N Schnürsenkel *m*; **bootleg** ADJ *whisky etc* schwarzgebrannt; *goods* schwarz hergestellt; *cassettes etc* schwarz mitgeschnitten; **bootlicker** N (*pej inf*) Speichellecker *m* (*pej inf*); **boot polish** N Schuhcreme *f*; **bootstrap** N **to pull oneself up by one's (own) ~s** (*inf*) sich aus eigener Kraft hocharbeiten

booty [ˈbuːtɪ] N (*lit*, *fig*) Beute *f*

booze [buːz] (*inf*) **1** N Alkohol *m*; **keep off the ~** lass das Saufen sein (*inf*); **bring some ~** bring was zu schlucken mit (*inf*) **2** VI saufen (*inf*); **to go out boozing** saufen gehen (*inf*)

boozed(-up) [ˈbuːzd(ʌp)] ADJ (*inf*) blau (*inf*)

boozer [ˈbuːzəʳ] N **(a)** (*pej inf*: = *drinker*) Säufer(in) *m(f)* (*pej inf*) **(b)** (*Brit inf*: = *pub*) Kneipe *f* (*inf*)

booze-up [ˈbuːzʌp] N (*inf*) Besäufnis *nt* (*inf*)

bop [bɒp] **1** N **(a)** (*inf*: = *dance*) Schwof *m* (*inf*) **(b)** (*inf*: = *blow*) **to give sb a ~ on the nose** jdm eins auf die Nase geben **2** VI (*inf*: = *dance*) schwofen (*inf*) **3** VT **to ~ sb on the head** jdm eins auf den Kopf geben

border [ˈbɔːdəʳ] **1** N **(a)** (= *edge*: *of woods*, *field*) Rand *m* **(b)** (= *boundary*, *frontier*) Grenze *f*; **on the French ~** an der französischen Grenze; **north/south of the ~** (*Brit*) in/nach Schottland/England
(c) (*in garden*) Rabatte *f*
(d) (= *edging*) (*on dress*) Bordüre *f*; (*of carpet*) Einfassung *f*; (*of picture*) Umrahmung *f*
2 VT **(a)** (= *line edges of*) *path* säumen; *garden*, *estate etc* begrenzen; (*on all sides*) umschließen
(b) (*land etc*: = ~ *on*) grenzen an (+*acc*)

➤ **border on** or **upon** VI +PREP OBJ (*lit*, *fig*) grenzen an (+*acc*)

border: **border dispute** N Grenzstreitigkeit *f*; **border guard** N Grenzsoldat *m*; **border incident** N Grenzzwischenfall *m*

bordering [ˈbɔːdərɪŋ] ADJ *country* angrenzend

border: **borderland** N Grenzgebiet *nt*; (*fig*) Grenzbereich *m*; **borderline** **1** N (*lit*, *fig*) Grenze *f*; **to be on the ~** an der Grenze liegen **2** ADJ (*fig*) **a ~ case** ein Grenzfall *m*; **it was a ~ pass/fail** *etc* ist ganz knapp durchgekommen/ durchgefallen; **border state** N Grenzstaat *m*; **border town** N Grenzstadt *f*

bore¹ [bɔːʳ] **1** VT *hole* bohren **2** VI bohren (*for* nach) **3** N (*of shotgun*) Kaliber *nt*; **a 12 ~ shotgun** eine Flinte vom Kaliber 12

bore² **1** N **(a)** (= *person*) Langweiler *m* **(b)** (= *thing*, *situation etc*) **to be a ~** langweilig sein **(c)** (= *nuisance*) **don't be a ~** nun sei doch nicht so (schwierig)!; **it's such a ~ having to go** es ist wirklich zu dumm, dass ich gehen muss **2** VT langweilen; **to ~ sb stiff** or **to death** or **to tears**, **to ~ the pants off sb** (*inf*) jdn zu Tode langweilen; **he is ~d with his job** seine Arbeit langweilt ihn

bore³ PRET of **bear¹**

boredom [ˈbɔːdəm] N Lang(e)weile *f*

borehole [ˈbɔːhəʊl] N Bohrloch *nt*

boring [ˈbɔːrɪŋ] ADJ langweilig

born [bɔːn] **1** PTP of **bear¹**; **to be ~** (*person*, *fig*: *idea*) geboren werden; (*fig*: *organization*) entstehen; **I was ~ in 1988** ich bin or wurde 1988 geboren; **when were you ~?** wann sind Sie geboren?; **he was ~ into a rich family** er wurde in eine reiche Familie hineingeboren; **to be ~ deaf** zur Geburt an taub sein; **the baby was ~ dead** das Baby war eine Totgeburt; **I wasn't ~ yesterday** (*inf*) ich bin nicht von gestern (*inf*); **there's one ~ every minute!** (*fig inf*) die Dummen werden nicht alle! **2** ADJ SUF (= *native of*) **he is Chicago-~** er ist ein gebürtiger Chicagoer; **his foreign-/French-~ wife** seine Frau, die Ausländerin/gebürtige Französin ist

3 ADJ geboren; **he is a ~ teacher** er ist der geborene Lehrer; **an Englishman ~ and bred** ein echter Engländer

born-again [ˈbɔːnəˌgen] ADJ *Christian etc* wieder geboren

borne [bɔːn] PTP of **bear¹**

Borneo [ˈbɔːnɪəʊ] N Borneo *nt*

borough [ˈbʌrə] N (*also* **municipal ~**) Bezirk *m*

borrow [ˈbɒrəʊ] **1** VT (*sich dat*) borgen (*from* von); *amount from bank*, *car* sich (*dat*) leihen; *library book* ausleihen; *word* entlehnen; (*fig*) *idea*, *methodology* übernehmen (*from* von); **to ~ money from the bank** Kredit bei der Bank aufnehmen **2** VI borgen; (*from bank*) Kredit ~ aufnehmen

borrower [ˈbɒrəʊəʳ] N (*of capital etc*) Kreditnehmer(in) *m(f)*

borrowing [ˈbɒrəʊɪŋ] N **~ of money from the bank** Kreditaufnahme *f* or (*short-term*) Geldaufnahme *f* bei der Bank; **government ~** staatliche Kreditaufnahme; **consumer ~** Verbraucherkredit *m*; **~s** (*Fin*) aufgenommene Schulden *pl*; **~ requirements** Kreditbedarf *m*

Bosnia [ˈbɒznɪə] N Bosnien *nt*

Bosnia-Herzegovina [ˈbɒznɪəˌhɜːtsəgəʊˈviːnə] N Bosnien-Herzegowina *nt*

Bosnian [ˈbɒznɪən] **1** ADJ bosnisch **2** N Bosnier(in) *m(f)*

bosom [ˈbʊzəm] **1** N **(a)** (*lit*, *fig*: *of person*) Busen *m* **(b)** (*fig*) **in the ~ of his family** im Schoß der Familie **2** ADJ ATTR Busen-

boss [bɒs] N Chef *m*, Boss *m* (*inf*); **his wife is the ~** seine Frau hat das Sagen; **OK, you're the ~** in Ordnung, du hast zu bestimmen

➤ **boss about** (*Brit*) or **around** VT SEP (*inf*) rumkommandieren (*inf*)

boss-eyed [ˈbɒsˌaɪd] ADJ (*Brit inf*) schielend *attr*; **to be ~** schielen

bossy [ˈbɒsɪ] ADJ (+ER) herrisch

Boston baked beans [ˌbɒstənbeɪktˈbiːnz] PL (*US*) weiße Bohnen mit gepökeltem Schweinefleisch und Melasse oder braunem Zucker

botanic(al) [bəˈtænɪk(əl)] ADJ botanisch

botanic(al) gardens [bəˌtænɪk(əl)ˈgɑːdnz] PL botanischer Garten

botanist [ˈbɒtənɪst] N Botaniker(in) *m(f)*

botany [ˈbɒtənɪ] N Botanik *f*

botch [bɒtʃ] VT (*inf*: *also* **~ up**) verpfuschen; *plans etc* vermasseln; (**a ~ed job** ein Pfusch *m* (*inf*))

botch-up [ˈbɒtʃʌp] N (*inf*) Pfusch *m* (*inf*)

both [bəʊθ] **1** ADJ beide; **~ (the) boys** beide Jungen **2** PRON beide; (*two different things*) beides; **~ of them were there**, **they were ~ there** sie waren alle beide da; **two pencils/a pencil and a picture - he took ~** zwei Bleistifte/ein Bleistift und ein Bild - er hat beide/beides genommen; **~ of these answers are wrong** beide Antworten sind falsch **3** ADV **~ ... and ...** sowohl ... als auch ...; **~ you and I** wir beide; **John and I ~ came** John und ich sind beide gekommen; **she was ~ laughing and crying** sie lachte und weinte zugleich; **is it black or white?** - **~** ist es schwarz oder weiß? – beides; **you and me ~** (*inf*) wir zwei beide (*inf*)

bother [ˈbɒðəʳ] **1** VT **(a)** stören; (= *annoy*) belästigen; (= *give trouble*: *teeth etc*) zu schaffen machen (+*dat*); (= *worry*) Sorgen machen (+*dat*); (*problem*, *question*) keine Ruhe lassen (+*dat*); **I'm sorry to ~ you but ...** es tut mir Leid, dass ich Sie damit belästigen muss, aber ...; **don't ~ your head about that** zerbrechen Sie sich (*dat*) darüber nicht den Kopf; **I shouldn't let it ~ you** machen Sie sich mal keine Sorgen; **don't ~ me!** lass mich in Frieden!
(b) **I can't be ~ed** ich habe keine Lust; **I can't be ~ed with people like him/with opera** für solche Leute/für Opern habe ich nichts übrig; **I can't be ~ed to do** or **with doing that** ich habe einfach keine Lust, das zu machen; **do you want to stay or go?** - **I'm not ~ed** willst du bleiben oder gehen? – das ist mir egal; **I'm not ~ed about him/the money** seinetwegen/ wegen des Geldes mache ich mir keine Gedanken
(c) (= *take trouble to do*) **don't ~ to do it again** das brauchen Sie nicht nochmals zu tun; **she didn't even ~ to ask** sie hat gar nicht erst gefragt; **please don't ~ getting up** or **to get up** bitte, bleiben Sie doch sitzen
2 VI sich kümmern (*about* um); (= *get worried*) sich (*dat*) Sorgen machen (*about* um); **don't ~ about me!** machen Sie sich meinetwegen keine Sorgen; (*sarcastic*) ist ja egal, was ich will; **he/it is not worth ~ing about** über ihn/darüber

brauchen wir gar nicht zu reden, er/das ist nicht der Mühe wert; **I'm not going to ~ with that** das lasse ich; **don't ~!** nicht nötig!; **really you needn't have ~ed!** das wäre aber wirklich nicht nötig gewesen!
3 N **(a)** (= *nuisance*) Plage *f*; **I know it's an awful ~ for you but ...** ich weiß, dass Ihnen das fürchterliche Umstände macht, aber ...
(b) (= *trouble, contretemps etc*) Ärger *m*; (= *difficulties*) Schwierigkeiten *pl*; **we had a spot** *or* **bit of ~ with the car** wir hatten Ärger mit dem Auto; **I didn't have any ~ getting the visa** es war kein Problem, das Visum zu bekommen; **it wasn't any ~** (= *don't mention it*) das ist gern geschehen; (= *not difficult*) das war ganz einfach; **the children were no ~ at all** wir hatten mit den Kindern überhaupt keine Probleme; **to go to a lot of ~ to do sth** sich (*dat*) mit etw viel Mühe geben

bottle ['bɒtl] **1** N **(a)** Flasche *f*; **a ~ of wine** eine Flasche Wein **(b)** (*Brit inf*: = *courage*) Mumm *m* (*inf*) **(c)** (*fig inf*: = *drink*) Flasche *f* (*inf*); **to be off the ~** nicht mehr trinken **2** VT **(a)** in Flaschen abfüllen **(b)** (*Brit inf*: = *lose nerve*) **to ~ it** die Nerven verlieren
➤ **bottle out** VI (*Brit inf*: = *lose nerve*) die Nerven verlieren
➤ **bottle up** VT SEP *emotion* in sich (*dat*) aufstauen
bottle bank N Altglascontainer *m*
bottled ['bɒtld] ADJ *wine* in Flaschen (abgefüllt); *gas* in Flaschen; *beer* Flaschen-; *fruit* eingemacht
bottle: bottle-fed ADJ **he is ~** er wird aus der Flasche ernährt; **bottle-feed** VT aus der Flasche ernähren; **bottleneck** N (*lit, fig*) Engpass *m*; **bottle-opener** N Flaschenöffner *m*; **bottle rack** N Flaschengestell *nt*
bottom ['bɒtəm] **1** N **(a)** (= *lowest part*) (*of box, glass, ship*) Boden *m*; (*of mountain, pillar*) Fuß *m*; (*of well, canyon*) Grund *m*; (*of page, screen, wall*) unteres Ende; (*of list, road*) Ende *nt*; (*of trousers*) unteres Beinteil; (*of dress*) Saum *m*; **which end is the ~?** wo ist unten?; **at the ~ of the page/league/hill** *etc* unten auf der Seite/in der Tabelle/am Berg *etc*; **at the ~ of the mountain** am Fuß des Berges; **to be (at the) ~ of the class** der/ die Letzte in der Klasse sein; **at the ~ of the garden** hinten im Garten; **~s up!** hoch die Tassen (*inf*); **from the ~ of my heart** aus tiefstem Herzen; **at ~** (*fig*) im Grunde; **the ~ dropped** *or* **fell out of the market** die Marktlage hat einen Tiefstand erreicht
(b) (= *underside*) Unterseite *f*; **on the ~ of the tin** unten an der Dose
(c) (*of sea, river*) Grund *m*, Boden *m*; **at the ~ of the sea** auf dem Meeresboden
(d) (*of chair*) Sitz *m*
(e) (*of person*) Hintern *m* (*inf*)
(f) (*fig: causally*) **to be at the ~ of sth** (*person*) hinter etw (*dat*) stecken; (*thing*) einer Sache (*dat*) zugrunde liegen; **to get to the ~ of sth** einer Sache (*dat*) auf den Grund kommen
(g) (*Brit Aut*) **~ (gear)** erster Gang; **in ~ (gear)** im ersten Gang
(h) bottoms PL (*US*: = *low land*) Ebene *f*
(i) tracksuit/pyjama (*Brit*) *or* **pajama** (*US*) **~s** Training-/ Schlafanzughose *f*; **bikini ~(s)** Bikiniunterteil *nt*
2 ADJ ATTR (= *lower*) untere(r, s); (= *lowest*) unterste(r, s); (*Fin*) Tiefst-; **~ half** (*of box*) untere Hälfte; (*of list, class*) zweite Hälfte
➤ **bottom out** VI (= *reach lowest point*) die Talsohle erreichen (*at* bei); (= *pass lowest point*) die Talsohle überwinden
bottom: bottomless ADJ (*lit*) bodenlos; (*fig*) *funds* unerschöpflich; **a ~ pit** (*fig*) ein Fass ohne Boden; **bottom line** N **(a)** (*of accounts etc*) Saldo *m* **(b)** (*fig*) **that's the ~ (of it)** (= *decisive factor*) das ist das Entscheidende (dabei); (= *what it amounts to*) darauf läuft es im Endeffekt hinaus; **bottom-line** ADJ ATTR *management* gewinnorientiert
bouffant ['buːfɒŋ] ADJ aufgebauscht
bough [baʊ] N Ast *m*
bought [bɔːt] PRET, PTP *of* **buy**
bouillon ['buːjɒŋ] N Bouillon *f*
bouillon cube N (*US*) Brühwürfel *m*
boulder ['bəʊldəʳ] N Felsblock *m*
boulevard ['buːləvɑːʳ] N Boulevard *m*
bounce [baʊns] **1** VI **(a)** (*ball etc*) springen; (*Sport: ball*) aufspringen; (*chins etc*) wackeln; **the child ~d up and down on the bed** das Kind hüpfte auf dem Bett herum
(b) (*inf: cheque*) platzen (*inf*)
2 VT *ball* aufprallen lassen; *light, radio waves* reflektieren; **he**

~d the ball against the wall er warf den Ball gegen die Wand; **he ~d the baby on his knee** er ließ das Kind auf den Knien reiten
3 N (*of ball*: = *rebound*) Aufprall *m*; **to hit a ball on the ~** den Ball beim Aufprall nehmen
➤ **bounce back** VI (*fig inf: person*) sich nicht unterkriegen lassen (*inf*)
➤ **bounce off 1** VT ALWAYS SEPARATE **to bounce sth off sth** etw von etw abprallen lassen; **to bounce an idea off sb** (*fig inf*) eine Idee an jdm testen (*inf*) **2** VI abprallen
bouncer ['baʊnsəʳ] N (*inf*) Rausschmeißer(in) *m(f)* (*inf*)
bouncy ['baʊnsɪ] ADJ (+ER) **(a)** *mattress* federnd **(b)** (*fig inf*: = *exuberant*) quietschvergnügt (*inf*)
bouncy castle® N Hüpfburg *f*
bound¹ [baʊnd] N USU PL (*lit, fig*) Grenze *f*; **to keep within ~s** innerhalb der Grenzen bleiben; **within the ~s of probability** im Bereich des Wahrscheinlichen; **his ambition knows no ~s** sein Ehrgeiz kennt keine Grenzen; **the bar is out of ~s** das Betreten des Lokals ist verboten; **this part of town is out of ~s** dieser Stadtteil ist Sperrzone
bound² **1** N Sprung *m*, Satz *m* **2** VI springen; **the dog came ~ing up** der Hund kam angesprungen
bound³ **1** PRET, PTP *of* **bind 2** ADJ **(a)** gebunden; **~ hand and foot** an Händen und Füßen gebunden **(b)** (= *sure*) **to be ~ to do sth** etw bestimmt tun; **it's ~ to happen** das muss so kommen **(c)** (= *obliged*) **but I'm ~ to say ...** (*inf*) aber ich muss schon sagen ...
bound⁴ ADJ PRED **to be ~ for London** (= *heading for*) auf dem Weg nach London sein; (= *about to start*) (*ship, lorry etc*) nach London gehen; (*person*) nach London reisen wollen; **all passengers ~ for London will ...** alle Passagiere nach London werden ...
boundary ['baʊndərɪ] N Grenze *f*
boundary line N Grenzlinie *f*; (*Sport*) Spielfeldgrenze *f*
boundless ['baʊndlɪs] ADJ (*lit, fig*) grenzenlos
bountiful ['baʊntɪfʊl] ADJ großzügig; *harvest, gifts* (über)reich
bouquet ['bʊkeɪ] N **(a)** Strauß *m* **(b)** (*of wine*) Bukett *nt*
bouquet garni ['bʊkeɪgɑːˈniː] N (*Cook*) Kräutermischung *f*
bourbon ['bɜːbən] N (*also* = *whiskey*) Bourbon *m*
bourgeois ['bʊəʒwɑː] **1** N Bürger(in) *m(f)*, Bourgeois *m* (*esp Sociol*); (*pej*) Spießbürger(in) *m(f)* **2** ADJ bürgerlich; (*pej*) spießbürgerlich
bourgeoisie [bʊəʒwɑːˈziː] N Bürgertum *nt*
bout [baʊt] N **(a)** (*of flu etc*) Anfall *m*; **a ~ of fever** ein Fieberanfall *m*; **a drinking ~** eine Zecherei **(b)** (*Boxing, Fencing*) Kampf *m*
boutique [buːˈtiːk] N Boutique *f*
bow¹ [bəʊ] N **(a)** (*weapon, for violin etc*) Bogen *m*; **a ~ and arrow** Pfeil und Bogen *pl* **(b)** (= *knot*) Schleife *f*
bow² [baʊ] **1** N (*with head, body*) Verbeugung *f*; **to take a ~** sich verbeugen **2** VI **(a)** (*person: with body*) sich verbeugen (*to sb vor* jdm); **to ~ and scrape** katzbuckeln (*pej*) **(b)** (*fig*: = *submit*) sich beugen (*before* vor +*dat*, *under* unter +*dat*, *to* +*dat*); **to ~ to the inevitable** sich in das Unvermeidliche fügen **3** VT **to ~ one's head** den Kopf senken; (*in prayer*) sich verneigen
➤ **bow down 1** VI (*lit*) sich beugen; **to bow down to** *or* **before sb** (*fig*) sich jdm beugen **2** VT SEP **bowed down with cares** mit Sorgen beladen
➤ **bow out** VI (*fig*) sich verabschieden; **to bow out of sth** sich aus etw zurückziehen
bow³ [baʊ] N OFTEN PL Bug *m*; **in the ~s** im Bug; **on the port/ starboard ~** backbord(s)/steuerbord(s) voraus; **~ doors** Bugtor *nt*
bowed¹ [bəʊd] ADJ *legs* krumm
bowed² [baʊd] ADJ *person* gebeugt; *shoulders* hängend
bowel ['baʊəl] N USU PL **(a)** (*Anat*) Eingeweide *nt usu pl*; **a ~ movement** Stuhl(gang) *m* **(b)** (*fig*) **the ~s of the earth** *etc* das Erdinnere *etc*
bowl¹ [bəʊl] N **(a)** Schüssel *f*; (*fingerbowl*) Schale *f*; (*for sugar etc*) Schälchen *nt*; (= *punch ~*) Bowle *f*; **a ~ of milk** eine Schale Milch **(b)** (*of lavatory*) Becken *nt* **(c)** (*US*: = *stadium*) Stadion *nt*
bowl² **1** N (*Sport*: = *ball*) Kugel *f*; *see also* **bowls 2** VI **(a)** (*Bowls, tenpin*) Bowling spielen **(b)** (*Cricket*) werfen **(c)** (= *travel*)

brausen (*inf*); **he came ~ing down the street** er kam auf der Straße angerauscht (*inf*) **3** VT **(a)** (= *roll*) *ball* rollen **(b)** (*Cricket*) *ball* werfen; *batsman* ausschlagen

➤ **bowl over** VT SEP (*fig*) umwerfen; **he was bowled over by the news** die Nachricht hat ihn (einfach) überwältigt

bow-legged [ˌbəʊˈlegɪd] ADJ o-beinig

bowler[1] [ˈbəʊləʳ] N (*Cricket*) Werfer *m*

bowler[2] N (*Brit: also* ~ **hat**) Melone *f*

bowling [ˈbəʊlɪŋ] N **(a)** (*Cricket*) Werfen *nt* **(b)** (= *tenpin* ~) Bowling *nt*; **to go** ~ bowlen gehen

bowling: bowling alley N Bowlingbahn *f*; **bowling green** N Rasenfläche *f* für Bowling

bowls [bəʊlz] N Bowling *nt*

bows [baʊz] PL *see* **bow**[3]

bow tie [bəʊ-] N Fliege *f*

bow window [bəʊ-] N Erkerfenster *nt*

box[1] [bɒks] **1** VTI (*Sport*) boxen; **to** ~ **sb's ears** jdn ohrfeigen **2** N a ~ **on the ears** eine Ohrfeige

box[2] N **(a)** (*made of wood or strong cardboard*) Kiste *f*; (= *cardboard* ~) Karton *m*; (*made of light cardboard, = matchbox*) Schachtel *f*; (*of chocolates etc*) Packung *f*; (= *jewellery* ~) Schatulle *f*; (= *tool* ~) (Werkzeug)kasten *m*; (= *money* ~) (*with lid and lock*) Kassette *f*; (*for saving*) Spardose *f*; (= *collection* ~) (Sammel)büchse *f* **(b)** (*on form*) Kästchen *nt*; (*on newspaper page*) Kasten *m*; (*Baseball*) Box *f*; (*Ftbl*) Strafraum *m* **(c)** (*Theat*) Loge *f* **(d)** (*Tech*: = *housing*) Gehäuse *nt* **(e)** (= *sentry* ~) Schilderhaus *nt*; (= *signal* ~) Häuschen *nt* **(f)** (*esp Brit inf*: = *TV*) Glotze *f* (*inf*); **what's on the ~?** was gibts im Fernsehen?; **I was watching the** ~ ich habe geglotzt (*inf*)

➤ **box in** VT SEP *player* in die Zange nehmen; *parked car* einklemmen; (*fig*) einengen

boxcar [ˈbɒkskɑːʳ] N (*US Rail*) (geschlossener) Güterwagen

boxer [ˈbɒksəʳ] N **(a)** (*Sport*) Boxer *m* **(b)** (= *dog*) Boxer *m*

boxer shorts PL Boxershorts *pl*

boxing [ˈbɒksɪŋ] N Boxen *nt*

boxing IN CPDS Box-; **Boxing Day** N (*Brit*) zweiter Weihnachts(feier)tag; **boxing match** N Boxkampf *m*; **boxing ring** N Boxring *m*

box: box junction N (*Mot*) gelb schraffierte Kreuzung (*in die bei Stau nicht eingefahren werden darf*); **box lunch** N (*US*) Lunchpaket *nt*; **box number** N Chiffre *f*; (*at post office*) Postfach *nt*; **box office** **1** N Kasse *f*; **to be good** ~ ein Kassenschlager sein **2** ATTR ~ **success/hit** Kassenschlager *m*; **boxroom** N (*Brit*) Abstellraum *m*

boy [bɔɪ] N **(a)** (= *male child*) Junge *m*, Bub *m* (*dial*); **the Jones** ~ der Junge von Jones; **~s will be ~s** Jungen sind nun mal so **(b)** (*inf*: = *fellow*) Knabe *m* (*inf*); **the old** ~ (= *boss*) der Alte (*inf*); (= *father*) mein *etc* alter Herr **(c)** (= *friend*) **the ~s** meine/seine Kumpels; **our ~s** (= *team*) unsere Jungs; **jobs for the ~s** Vetternwirtschaft *f* **(d) oh ~!** (*inf*) Junge, Junge! (*inf*)

boy band N (*Mus*) Boygroup *f*

boycott [ˈbɔɪkɒt] **1** N Boykott *m* **2** VT boykottieren

boy: boyfriend N Freund *m*; **boyhood** N Kindheit *f*; (*as teenager*) Jugend(zeit) *f*

boyish [ˈbɔɪɪʃ] ADJ jungenhaft; *woman* knabenhaft

boy: boy scout N Pfadfinder *m*; **Boy Scouts** N SING Pfadfinder *pl*;

bozo [ˈbəʊzəʊ] N (*US*) (primitiver) Kerl (*inf*)

bpi (*Comput*) ABBR *of* **bits per inch** Bits pro Zoll

BR (*dated*) ABBR *of* **British Rail** die britischen Eisenbahnen

bra [brɑː] N ABBR *of* **brassière** BH *m*

brace [breɪs] **1** N **(a)** (= *tool*) ~ **and bit** Bohrer *m* (mit Einsatz) **(b)** (*on teeth*) Klammer *f*; (*Med*) Stützapparat *m* **2** VR sich bereithalten; **to** ~ **oneself for sth** sich auf etw (*acc*) gefasst machen; ~ **yourself, I've got bad news for you** mach dich auf eine schlechte Nachricht gefasst

bracelet [ˈbreɪslɪt] N Armband *nt*; (= *bangle*) Armreif(en) *m*

braces [ˈbreɪsɪz] PL (*Brit*) Hosenträger *pl*; **a pair of** ~ (ein Paar) Hosenträger

bracing [ˈbreɪsɪŋ] ADJ anregend; *climate* Reiz-

bracken [ˈbrækən] N Adlerfarn *m*

bracket [ˈbrækɪt] **1** N **(a)** (= *angle* ~) Winkelträger *m*; (*for shelf*) (Regal)träger *m* **(b)** (*Typ, Mus*) Klammer *f*; **in ~s** in Klammern **(c)** (= *group*) Gruppe *f*, Klasse *f* **2** VT (*also* ~ **together**) (*fig*: = *group together*) zusammenfassen

brag [bræg] **1** VI angeben (*about, of* mit) **2** VT **to** ~ **that** damit angeben, dass

bragging [ˈbrægɪŋ] N Angeberei *f*

braid [breɪd] **1** N **(a)** (*of hair*) Zopf *m* **(b)** (= *trimming*) Borte *f* **2** VT (= *plait*) flechten

Braille [breɪl] **1** N Blindenschrift *f* **2** ADJ Blindenschrift-; ~ **books** Bücher *pl* in Blindenschrift

brain [breɪn] **1** N **(a)** (*Anat, of machine*) Gehirn *nt*; **he's got sex on the** ~ (*inf*) er hat nur Sex im Kopf **(b) brains** PL (*Anat*) Gehirn *nt*; (*Cook*) Hirn *nt* **(c)** (= *mind*) Verstand *m*; **~s** *pl* (= *intelligence*) Intelligenz *f*, Grips *m* (*inf*); **to have a good** ~ einen klaren Verstand haben; **he has ~s** er ist intelligent, er hat Grips (*inf*); **use your ~s** streng mal deinen Kopf *or* Grips (*inf*) an **2** VT den Schädel einschlagen (*sb* jdm)

brain: brainbox N (*hum inf*) Schlauberger *m* (*inf*); **brainchild** N Erfindung *f*; (= *idea*) Geistesprodukt *nt*; **brain-damaged** ADJ hirngeschädigt; **braindead** ADJ (ge)hirntot; **brain drain** N Abwanderung *f* von Wissenschaftlern, Braindrain *m*; **brainless** ADJ hirnlos, dumm; **brain scan** N Computertomografie *f* des Schädels; **brainstorm** **1** N (*US*: = *brainwave*) Geistesblitz *m* **2** VI ein Brainstorming machen **3** VT gemeinsam erarbeiten; **brainstorming** N Brainstorming *nt*; **to have a ~ session** ein Brainstorming veranstalten; **brain surgeon** N Hirnchirurg(in) *m(f)*; **brain tumour**, (*US*) **brain tumor** N Gehirntumor *m*; **brainwash** VT einer Gehirnwäsche (*dat*) unterziehen; **to ~ sb into believing** *etc* **that ...** jdm (ständig) einreden, dass ...; **brainwashing** N Gehirnwäsche *f*; **brainwave** N (*Brit*) Geistesblitz *m*

brainy [ˈbreɪnɪ] ADJ (+ER) (*inf*) gescheit

braise [breɪz] VT (*Cook*) schmoren

brake [breɪk] **1** N (*Tech*) Bremse *f*; **to put the ~s on** (*lit, fig*) bremsen **2** VI bremsen

brake IN CPDS Brems-; **brake disc** N Bremsscheibe *f*; **brake drum** N Bremstrommel *f*; **brake fluid** N Bremsflüssigkeit *f*; **brake light** N Bremslicht *nt*; **brake pad** N Bremsklotz *m*; **brake shoe** N Bremsbacke *f*

braking [ˈbreɪkɪŋ] N Bremsen *nt*

braking distance N Bremsweg *m*

bramble [ˈbræmbl] N (= *bush*) Brombeerstrauch *m*

bran [bræn] N Kleie *f*

branch [brɑːntʃ] **1** N **(a)** (*Bot*) Zweig *m*; (*growing from trunk*) Ast *m* **(b)** (*of river, pipe*) Arm *m*; (*of road*) Abzweigung *f*; (*of family, language*) Zweig *m*; (*of railway*) Abzweig *m* **(c)** (*in river, road, railway, pipe*) Gabelung *f* **(d)** (*Comm*) Zweigstelle *f*; **main** ~ Haupt(geschäfts)stelle *f*; (*of store*) Hauptgeschäft *nt* **(e)** (= *field: of subject etc*) Zweig *m* **2** VI (= *divide*) (*river, road etc*) sich gabeln; (*in more than two*) sich verzweigen

➤ **branch off** VI (*road*) abzweigen; (*driver*) abbiegen

➤ **branch out** VI (*fig: person, company*) sein Geschäft ausdehnen (*into* auf +*acc*); **to branch out on one's own** sich selbstständig machen

branch: branch line N (*Rail*) Nebenlinie *f*; **branch manager** N Filialleiter *m*; **branch office** N Zweigstelle *f*

brand [brænd] **1** N **(a)** (= *make*) Marke *f* **(b)** (= *mark: on cattle*) Brandzeichen *nt* **2** VT **(a)** *goods* mit seinem Warenzeichen versehen; **~ed goods** Markenartikel *pl* **(b)** *cattle* mit einem Brandzeichen kennzeichnen **(c)** (= *stigmatize*) *person* brandmarken

brand: brand awareness N Markenbewusstsein *nt*; **brand image** N Markenimage *nt*

branding [ˈbrændɪŋ] N Markenkennzeichnung *f*

brandish [ˈbrændɪʃ] VT schwingen

brand: brand leader N führende Marke; **brand loyalty** N Markentreue *f*; **brand name** N Markenname *m*; **brand-new** ADJ nagelneu

brandy [ˈbrændɪ] N Weinbrand *m*

brash [bræʃ] ADJ (+ER) dreist

brass [brɑːs] **1** N **(a)** Messing nt **(b) the ~** (Mus) die Blechbläser pl **(c)** (= plaque) Messingtafel f; (in church: on tomb) Grabplatte f aus Messing **(d)** (inf) **the top ~** die hohen Tiere (inf) **(e)** (inf: = money) Kohle f (inf) **2** ADJ (= made of ~) Messing-; (Mus) Blech-; **~ player** Blechbläser m; **~ section** Blechbläser pl

brass: brass band N Blaskapelle f; **brass plaque, brass plate** N Messingschild nt; (in church) Messinggedenktafel f; **brass rubbing** N (= activity) Durchpausen nt (des Bildes auf einer Messinggrabtafel); (= result) Pauszeichnung f (des Bildes auf einer Messinggrabtafel); **brass tacks** PL **to get down to ~** (inf) zur Sache kommen

brat [bræt] N (pej inf) Balg m or nt (inf); (esp girl) Göre f (inf)

bravado [brə'vɑːdəʊ] N (= showy bravery) Draufgängertum nt; (hiding fear) gespielte Tapferkeit

brave [breɪv] **1** ADJ (+ER) person, act mutig; (= showing courage, suffering pain) tapfer; **be ~!** nur Mut!; (more seriously) sei tapfer!; **new world** schöne neue Welt **2** VT die Stirn bieten (+dat); weather, elements trotzen (+dat)

> Be careful! **brave** is not translated by the German word **brav**.

bravely ['breɪvlɪ] ADV tapfer

bravery ['breɪvərɪ] N Mut m

bravo [brɑː'vəʊ] INTERJ bravo!

brawl [brɔːl] **1** VI sich schlagen **2** N Schlägerei f

brawling ['brɔːlɪŋ] N Schlägereien pl

brawn [brɔːn] N Muskelkraft f; **he's all ~ and no brains** er hat Muskeln, aber kein Gehirn

brawny ['brɔːnɪ] ADJ (+ER) muskulös

bray [breɪ] VI (ass) schreien

brazen ['breɪzn] ADJ (= impudent) dreist; lie schamlos; **to be ~ about sth** klar zu etw stehen

> **brazen out** VT SEP **to brazen it out** durchhalten; (by lying) sich durchmogeln (inf)

brazenly ['breɪznlɪ] ADV dreist; lie schamlos

Brazil [brə'zɪl] N Brasilien nt

brazil [brə'zɪl] N (also ~ nut) Paranuss f

Brazilian [brə'zɪlɪən] **1** N Brasilianer(in) m(f) **2** ADJ brasilianisch

breach [briːtʃ] **1** N **(a)** Verstoß m (of gegen); (of law) Übertretung f (of +gen), Verstoß m; **a ~ of contract/faith** ein Vertrags-/Vertrauensbruch m; **~ of duty** Pflichtverletzung f; **~ of the peace** (Jur) öffentliche Ruhestörung; **a ~ of security** ein Verstoß m gegen die Sicherheitsbestimmungen; **~ of trust** (Fin) Untreue f **(b)** (in friendship etc) Bruch m **(c)** (in wall etc, in security) Lücke f; **to step into the ~** (fig) in die Bresche springen **2** VT **(a)** wall eine Bresche schlagen in (+acc); defences, security durchbrechen **(b)** contract verletzen

bread [bred] **1** N **(a)** Brot nt; **a piece of ~ and butter** ein Butterbrot nt; **he knows which side his ~ is buttered (on)** er weiß, wo was zu holen ist **(b)** (= livelihood) **writing is his ~ and butter** er verdient sich damit seinen Lebensunterhalt mit Schreiben **(c)** (inf: = money) Kohle f (inf) **2** VT panieren

bread: bread-and-butter pudding N Brotauflauf m; **breadbin** N (Brit) Brotkasten m; **breadboard** N Brot(schneide)brett nt; **breadbox** N (US) Brotkasten m; **breadcrumbs** PL (Cook) Paniermehl nt; **in ~** paniert; **breadknife** N Brotmesser nt; **breadline** N **to be on the ~** (fig) nur das Allernotwendigste zum Leben haben; **bread roll** N Brötchen nt; **breadstick** N Knabberstange f

breadth [bretθ] N Breite f; **a hundred metres** (Brit) or **meters** (US) **in ~** hundert Meter breit

breadwinner ['bredwɪnər] N Brotverdiener(in) m(f)

---

break [breɪk]	
1 NOUN	**3** INTRANSITIVE VERB
2 TRANSITIVE VERB	**4** PHRASAL VERBS

vb: pret **broke**, ptp **broken**

1 NOUN
(a) (= fracture) (in bone, pipe, relations) Bruch m; **break in the circuit** (Elec) Stromkreisunterbrechung f
(b) (= gap) Lücke f; (in rock) Spalte f, Riss m; **row upon row of houses without a break** Häuserzeile auf Häuserzeile, ohne Lücke
(c) (= pause) (also Brit Sch) Pause f; **without a break** ohne Pause, ununterbrochen; **to take** or **have a break** (eine) Pause machen; **at break** (Sch) in der Pause; **give me a break!** (inf: expressing annoyance) nun mach mal halblang! (inf)
(d) (= change) Abwechslung f; **break in the weather** Wetterumschwung m
(e) (= respite) Erholung f
(f) (= holiday) Urlaub m
(g) at break of day bei Tagesanbruch
(h) (= escape) (inf) **they made a break for it** sie versuchten zu entkommen
(i) (= opportunity) (inf) **we had a few lucky breaks** wir haben ein paar Mal Glück gehabt; **she had her first big break in a Broadway play** sie bekam ihre erste große Chance in einem Broadwaystück
(j) (Billiards) Break nt or m

2 TRANSITIVE VERB
(a) (in pieces) (= fracture) bone sich (dat) brechen; stick zerbrechen; (= smash) kaputtschlagen; glass zerbrechen; window einschlagen; egg aufbrechen; **to break sth from sth** etw von etw abbrechen; **to break one's leg** sich (dat) das Bein brechen
(b) (= make unusable) toy, chair kaputtmachen
(c) (promise, treaty, record, spell) brechen; law, rule verletzen
(d) (= interrupt) journey, silence unterbrechen; **he couldn't break the habit of smoking** er konnte sich das Rauchen nicht abgewöhnen
(e) (= penetrate) skin ritzen; surface, shell durchbrechen
(f) (= tame) horse zureiten; person brechen
(g) (= destroy) person kleinkriegen (inf), mürbe machen; resistance, strike brechen; code entziffern; (Tennis) serve durchbrechen; **to break sb (financially)** jdn ruinieren; **37p, well that won't exactly break the bank** 37 Pence, na, davon gehe ich/gehen wir noch nicht Bankrott
(h) (= soften) fall dämpfen
(i) (= get out of) jail, one's bonds ausbrechen aus
(j) (= disclose) news mitteilen; **how can I break it to her?** wie soll ich es ihr sagen?

3 INTRANSITIVE VERB
(a) (twig, bone, voice) brechen; (rope) zerreißen; (= smash) (window) kaputtgehen; (glass) zerbrechen
(b) (= become useless) (watch, chair) kaputtgehen
(c) (= become detached) **to break from sth** von etw abbrechen
(d) (= pause) (eine) Pause machen; **to break for lunch** Mittagspause machen
(e) (= change) (weather) umschlagen
(f) (= give way) (under interrogation etc) zusammenbrechen
(g) (wave) sich brechen
(h) (day, dawn) anbrechen; (suddenly: storm) losbrechen
(i) (voice) (with emotion) brechen; **his voice is beginning to break** (boy) er kommt in den Stimmbruch
(j) (= become known) (story, news) bekannt werden, ans Licht kommen
(k) (company) **to break even** seine (Un)kosten decken
(l) (Billiards) anstoßen

4 PHRASAL VERBS
> **break away (a)** (= dash away) weglaufen; (prisoner) sich losreißen; (Ftbl) sich absetzen; **he broke away from the rest of the field** er hängte das ganze Feld ab **(b)** (= cut ties) sich trennen or lossagen; (US Sport: = start too soon) zu früh starten

➤ **break down** ◼ VI **(a)** zusammenbrechen; (*negotiations, plan, marriage*) scheitern
(b) (*vehicle*) eine Panne haben; (*machine*) versagen
(c) (= *be analysed*: *expenditure*) sich aufschlüsseln; (*theory*) sich aufgliedern (lassen); (*Chem: substance*) sich zerlegen (lassen); (= *change its composition*: *substance*) sich aufspalten (*into* in +*acc*)
◼ VT SEP **(a)** (= *smash down*) *door* einrennen; *wall* niederreißen
(b) (= *overcome*) *opposition* brechen; *hostility, reserve* überwinden
(c) (*to constituent parts*) *expenditure* aufschlüsseln; *argument* aufgliedern; (= *change composition of*) umsetzen
➤ **break in** ◼ VI **(a)** (= *interrupt*) unterbrechen (*on sb/sth* jdn/etw) **(b)** (= *enter illegally*) einbrechen ◼ VT SEP **(a)** *door* aufbrechen **(b)** *shoes* einlaufen
➤ **break into** VI +PREP OBJ **(a)** *house* einbrechen in (+*acc*); *safe, car* aufbrechen **(b)** (= *use part of*) *savings, rations* anbrechen
(c) (= *begin suddenly*) **to break into song/a run** zu singen/laufen anfangen
➤ **break off** ◼ VI **(a)** (*branch, piece*) abbrechen **(b)** (= *stop*) aufhören; (= *stop speaking*) abbrechen; (*temporarily*) unterbrechen ◼ VT SEP **(a)** *twig, piece etc* abbrechen
(b) *negotiations, relations* abbrechen; *engagement* lösen
➤ **break open** VT SEP aufbrechen
➤ **break out** VI **(a)** (*epidemic, fire, war*) ausbrechen **(b)** to **break out in a rash** einen Ausschlag bekommen; **he broke out in a sweat** ihm brach der Schweiß aus **(c)** (= *escape*) ausbrechen (*from, of* aus)
➤ **break through** ◼ VI (*Mil, sun*) durchbrechen ◼ VI +PREP OBJ *defences, crowd* durchbrechen
➤ **break up** ◼ VI **(a)** (*road, ice*) aufbrechen
(b) (*clouds*) sich lichten; (*crowd, group*) auseinander laufen; (*meeting, partnership*) sich auflösen; (*marriage, relationship*) in die Brüche gehen; (*party*) zum Ende kommen; (*friends, partners*) sich trennen; **to break up with sb** sich von jdm trennen
(c) (*Brit Sch*) aufhören; **when do you break up?** wann hört bei euch die Schule auf?
(d) (*on mobile phone*) **you're breaking up** ich kann Sie nicht verstehen
◼ VT SEP **(a)** *ground, road* aufbrechen
(b) *estate, country* aufteilen; *sentence* unterteilen
(c) *marriage, home* zerstören; *meeting* (*trouble etc*) auflösen; (*trouble-makers*) sprengen; *crowd* (*police*) zerstreuen; **he broke up the fight** er trennte die Kämpfer; **break it up!** auseinander!

breakable ['breɪkəbl] ADJ zerbrechlich
breakage ['breɪkɪdʒ] N **to pay for ~s** für zerbrochene Ware bezahlen
breakaway ['breɪkə,weɪ] ◼ N (*US Sport*: = *false start*) Fehlstart *m* ◼ ADJ *group* Splitter-
break: **break-bulk ship** N Stückgutschiff *nt*; **break command** N (*Comput*) Unterbrechungsbefehl *m*; **break dance** VI Breakdance tanzen
breakdown ['breɪkdaʊn] N **(a)** (*of machine*) Betriebsschaden *m*; (*of vehicle*) Panne *f* **(b)** (*of system, Med*) Zusammenbruch *m* **(c)** (*of figures etc*) Aufschlüsselung *f*
breakdown: **breakdown service** N Pannendienst *m*; **breakdown truck, breakdown van** N Abschleppwagen *m*
breaker ['breɪkə^r] N **(a)** (= *wave*) Brecher *m* **(b)** (*also* ~**'s** (*yard*)) **to send a vehicle to the ~'s (yard)** ein Fahrzeug abwracken
breakeven point [breɪk'iːvən,pɔɪnt] N Gewinnschwelle *f*
breakfast ['brekfəst] ◼ N Frühstück *nt*; **to have ~** frühstücken; **for ~** zum Frühstück ◼ VI frühstücken; **he ~ed on bacon and eggs** er frühstückte Eier mit Speck
breakfast IN CPDS Frühstücks-; **breakfast cereal** N Zerealien *pl*; **breakfast television** N Frühstücksfernsehen *nt*; **breakfast time** N Frühstückszeit *f*
break-in ['breɪkɪn] N Einbruch *m*; **we've had a ~** bei uns ist eingebrochen worden
breaking point N (*fig*) **she is at** *or* **has reached ~** sie ist nervlich völlig am Ende (ihrer Kräfte)
break: **breakneck** ADJ **at ~ speed** (*Brit*) mit halsbrecherischer Geschwindigkeit; **break-out** N Ausbruch *m*; **breakthrough** N (*Mil, fig*) Durchbruch *m*; **break-up** N (*of friendship*) Bruch *m*;

(*of marriage*) Zerrüttung *f*; (*of political party*) Zersplitterung *f*; (*of partnership*) Auflösung *f*; **break-up value** N (*Fin*) Liquidationswert *m*; **breakwater** N Wellenbrecher *m*
breast [brest] N Brust *f*
breastbone ['brestbəʊn] N Brustbein *nt*; (*of bird*) Brustknochen *m*
breast cancer N Brustkrebs *m*
-breasted [-'brestɪd] ADJ SUF **a double-/single-breasted jacket** ein Einreiher *m*/Zweireiher *m*
breast: **breast-fed** ADJ **to be ~** gestillt werden; **breast-feed** VTI stillen; **breast-feeding** N Stillen *nt*; **breast milk** N Muttermilch *f*; **breast pocket** N Brusttasche *f*; **breaststroke** N Brustschwimmen *nt*; **to swim** *or* **do the ~** brustschwimmen
breath [breθ] N **(a)** Atem *m*; **to take a deep ~** einmal tief Luft holen; (*before diving etc*) einmal tief einatmen; **to have bad ~** Mundgeruch haben; **out of ~** außer Atem; **short of ~** kurzatmig; **to get one's ~ back** wieder zu Atem kommen; **in the same ~** im selben Atemzug; **to take sb's ~ away** jdm den Atem verschlagen; **to say sth under one's ~** etw vor sich (*acc*) hin murmeln; **you're wasting your ~** du redest umsonst
(b) (= *slight stirring*) ~ **of wind** Lüftchen *nt*
breathalyze ['breθəlaɪz] VT blasen lassen
Breathalyzer® ['breθəlaɪzə^r] N Atem(luft)messgerät *nt*, Promillemesser *m* (*inf*); **to blow into the ~** ins Röhrchen blasen
breathe [briːð] ◼ VI (*person, fabric*) atmen; (*inf*: = *rest*) verschnaufen; **now we can ~ again** jetzt können wir wieder frei atmen; **I don't want him breathing down my neck** ich will nicht, dass er mir die Hölle heiß macht (*inf*)
◼ VT **(a)** *air* einatmen; **to ~ one's last** seinen letzten Atemzug tun
(b) (= *exhale*) atmen (*into* in +*acc*); **he ~d garlic all over me** er verströmte einen solchen Knoblauchgeruch; **he ~d new life into the firm** er brachte neues Leben in die Firma
(c) (= *utter*) **to ~ a sigh of relief** erleichtert aufatmen; **don't ~ a word of it!** sag kein Sterbenswörtchen darüber!
➤ **breathe in** VI, VT SEP einatmen
➤ **breathe out** VI, VT SEP ausatmen
breather ['briːðə^r] N (= *short rest*) Atempause *f*; **to take** *or* **have a ~** sich verschnaufen
breathing ['briːðɪŋ] N Atmung *f*
breathing: **breathing apparatus** N Sauerstoffgerät *nt*; **breathing space** N (*fig*) Atempause *f*
breathless ['breθlɪs] ADJ atemlos; ~ **with excitement** ganz atemlos vor Aufregung
breathtaking ['breθteɪkɪŋ] ADJ atemberaubend
breath test N Atemalkoholtest *m*
bred [bred] PRET, PTP *of* **breed**
-bred ADJ SUF **-erzogen**
breed [briːd] *vb: pret, ptp* **bred** ◼ N (*lit, fig*: = *species*) Art *f*; **they produced a new ~** sie haben eine neue Züchtung hervorgebracht ◼ VT **(a)** (= *raise*) *animals, flowers* züchten
(b) (*fig*: = *give rise to*) erzeugen ◼ VI **(a)** (*animals*) Junge haben; (*birds*) brüten; (*pej, hum*: *people*) sich vermehren
breeder ['briːdə^r] N (= *person*) Züchter(in) *m(f)*
breeding ['briːdɪŋ] N **(a)** (= *reproduction*) Fortpflanzung und Aufzucht *f* der Jungen **(b)** (= *rearing*) Zucht *f*
(c) (= *upbringing*: *also* **good** ~) gute Erziehung
breeding place N (*lit, fig*) Brutstätte *f*
breeze [briːz] N Brise *f*
➤ **breeze** VI fröhlich hereinschneien; **he breezed into the room** er kam fröhlich ins Zimmer geschneit
breeze: **breeze block** N (*Brit Build*) Ytong® *m*; **breezeway** N (*US*) überdachter Durchgang
breezily ['briːzɪlɪ] ADV (*fig*) frisch-fröhlich
breezy ['briːzɪ] ADJ (+*ER*) **(a)** *day, spot* windig **(b)** *manner* frisch-fröhlich
brevity ['brevɪtɪ] N Kürze *f*
brew [bruː] ◼ N **(a)** (= *beer*) Bräu *nt* **(b)** (*of tea*) Tee *m*, Gebräu *nt* (*iro*); (*of herbs*) Kräutermischung *f* ◼ VT *beer* brauen; *tea* aufbrühen ◼ VI **(a)** (*beer*) gären; (*tea*) ziehen **(b)** (*fig*) **there's trouble ~ing (up)** da braut sich ein Konflikt zusammen
brewer ['bruːə^r] N Brauer *m*
brewery ['bruːərɪ] N Brauerei *f*
briar ['braɪə^r] N = **brier**

bribe [braɪb] **1** N Bestechung *f*; **to take a ~** sich bestechen lassen; **to offer sb a ~** jdn. bestechen wollen **2** VT bestechen; **to ~ sb to do sth** jdn bestechen, damit er etw tut

bribery ['braɪbərɪ] N Bestechung *f*

bric-a-brac ['brɪkəbræk] N Nippes *m*

brick [brɪk] N **(a)** (*Build*) Backstein *m*; **~s and mortar** (= *property*) Immobilien *pl*; **he came** *or* **was down on me like a ton of ~s** (*inf*) er hat mich unheimlich fertig gemacht (*inf*) **(b)** (= *toy*) (Bau)klotz *m*; **box of (building) ~s** Baukasten *m* **(c)** **~s** (*Brit sl:* = *money*) Kohle *f* (*inf*)

➤ **brick in** *or* **up** VT SEP *window* zumauern

brickbat ['brɪkbæt] N (*fig*) Beschimpfung *f*

brick: bricklayer N Maurer *m*; **brick-red** ADJ ziegelrot; **brick wall** N (*fig inf*) **I might as well be talking to a ~** ich könnte genauso gut gegen eine Wand reden; **it's like beating** *or* **banging one's head against a ~** es ist, wie wenn man mit dem Kopf gegen die Wand rennt; **to come up against** *or* **hit a ~** plötzlich vor einer Mauer stehen; **brickwork** N Backsteinmauerwerk *nt*

bridal ['braɪdl] ADJ Braut-; *procession also, feast* Hochzeits-; **~ gown** Hochzeitskleid *nt*

bridal suite N Hochzeitssuite *f*

bride [braɪd] N Braut *f*; **the ~ and (bride)groom** das Hochzeitspaar

bridegroom ['braɪdgruːm] N Bräutigam *m*

bridesmaid ['braɪdzmeɪd] N Brautjungfer *f*

bridge¹ [brɪdʒ] **1** N Brücke *f*; (*of nose*) Sattel *m*; (*of spectacles, violin*) Steg *m*; **to build ~s** (*fig*) Brücken schlagen **2** VT (*fig*) überbrücken; **to ~ the gap** (*fig*) die Zeit überbrücken; (*between people*) die Kluft überbrücken

bridge² N (*Cards*) Bridge *nt*

bridgework ['brɪdʒwɜːk] N (*Dentistry*) Zahnbrücken *pl*; (*of individual*) Zahnbrücke *f*

bridging loan ['brɪdʒɪŋləʊn] N Überbrückungskredit *m*

bridle ['braɪdl] **1** N (*of horse*) Zaum *m* **2** VI sich entrüsten wehren (*at* gegen)

bridle path N Reitweg *m*

brief [briːf] **1** ADJ (+ER) kurz; (= *curt*) kurz angebunden; **in ~** kurz; **the news in ~** Kurznachrichten *pl*; **to be ~** um es kurz zu machen
2 N **(a)** (*Jur*) Auftrag *m* (*an einen Anwalt*); (= *document*) Unterlagen *pl* zu dem/einem Fall; (= *instructions*) Instruktionen *pl*
(b) (= *instructions*) Auftrag *m*
3 VT **(a)** (*Jur*) *lawyer* instruieren; (= *employ*) beauftragen
(b) (= *give instructions to*) instruieren (*on* über +*acc*)

briefcase ['briːfkeɪs] N (Akten)tasche *f*; (Akten)mappe *f*

briefing ['briːfɪŋ] N (= *instructions*) Instruktionen *pl*; (*also ~ session*) Einsatzbesprechung *f*

briefly ['briːflɪ] ADV kurz

briefs [briːfs] PL Slip *m*; **a pair of ~** ein Slip

brier ['braɪə'] N (= *wild rose*) wilde Rose

brigade [brɪ'geɪd] N (*Mil*) Brigade *f*

brigadier [ˌbrɪgə'dɪə'] N (*Brit*) Brigadegeneral *m*

bright [braɪt] ADJ (+ER) **(a)** *light, fire* hell; *colour* leuchtend; *sunshine, star also, eyes, gem* strahlend; *day* heiter; *metal* glänzend; **~ red** knallrot; **it was really ~ outside** es war wirklich sehr hell draußen; **~ intervals** *or* **periods** (*Met*) Aufheiterungen *pl*
(b) (= *cheerful*) fröhlich; **I wasn't feeling too ~** es ging mir nicht besonders gut; **~ and early** in aller Frühe
(c) (= *intelligent*) *person* intelligent, schlau; *child* aufgeweckt; *idea* glänzend; (*iro*) intelligent
(d) (= *favourable*) *prospects* glänzend; **things aren't looking too ~** es sieht nicht gerade rosig aus

brighten (up) ['braɪtn(ʌp)] **1** VT SEP **(a)** (= *make cheerful*) aufheitern **(b)** (= *make bright*) aufhellen **2** VI **(a)** (*weather*) sich aufklären *or* aufheitern **(b)** (*person*) fröhlicher werden; (*face*) sich aufheitern

bright-eyed ['braɪtaɪd] ADJ mit strahlenden Augen; **~ and bushy-tailed** (*hum inf*) putzmunter (*inf*)

brightly ['braɪtlɪ] ADV **(a)** *shine, burn* hell; **~ lit** hell erleuchtet **(b)** (= *cheerfully*) fröhlich

brightness ['braɪtnɪs] N (*of light, fire*) Helligkeit *f*; (*of colour*) Leuchten *nt*; (*of sunshine, star also, eyes, gem*) Strahlen *nt*; (*of metal*) Glanz *m*

brilliance ['brɪljəns] N **(a)** (= *brightness*) Strahlen *nt* **(b)** (*fig*) (= *intelligence*) Großartigkeit *f*; (*of scientist, artist, wit*) Brillanz *f*

brilliant ['brɪljənt] **1** ADJ **(a)** (*fig*) großartig (*also iro*); *scientist, artist, wit* brillant; *student* hervorragend; **he is ~ with my children** er versteht sich großartig mit meinen Kindern; **to be ~ at sth/doing sth** etw hervorragend können/tun können **(b)** *sunshine, light, colour* strahlend **2** EXCL (*inf:* = *great*) super (*inf*)

brilliantly ['brɪljəntlɪ] ADV **(a)** *shine, lit* hell; **~ coloured** (*Brit*) *or* **colored** (*US*) in kräftigen Farben **(b)** (= *superbly*) großartig; *perform* brillant; *funny, simple* herrlich

brim [brɪm] **1** N (*of cup, hat*) Rand *m*; **full to the ~ (with sth)** (*lit*) randvoll (mit etw) **2** VI strotzen (*with* von *or* vor +*dat*); **her eyes were ~ming with tears** ihre Augen schwammen in Tränen

➤ **brim over** VI (*lit, fig*) überfließen (*with* vor +*dat*)

brimful ['brɪm'fʊl] ADJ (*lit*) randvoll; (*fig*) voll (*of, with* von)

brine [braɪn] N (= *salt water*) Sole *f*; (*for pickling*) Lake *f*

bring [brɪŋ], *pret, ptp* **brought** VT bringen; (*also ~ with one*) mitbringen; **did you ~ the car** *etc***?** haben Sie den Wagen *etc* mitgebracht?; **to ~ sb across/inside** *etc* jdn herüber-/hereinbringen *etc*; **to ~ tears to sb's eyes** jdm die Tränen in die Augen treiben; **I cannot ~ myself to speak to him** ich kann es nicht über mich bringen, mit ihm zu sprechen; **to ~ sth to a close** *or* **an end** etw zu Ende bringen; **to ~ sth to sb's attention** jdn auf etw (*acc*) aufmerksam machen

➤ **bring about** VT SEP (= *cause*) herbeiführen

➤ **bring along** VT SEP (= *bring with one*) mitbringen

➤ **bring away** VT SEP *person* wegbringen; *memories, impression* mitnehmen

➤ **bring back** VT SEP **(a)** (*lit*) *person, object, memories* zurückbringen **(b)** (= *restore*) *custom* wieder einführen; **to bring sb back to life/health** jdn wieder lebendig/gesund machen

➤ **bring down** VT SEP **(a)** (= *shoot down*) herunterholen; (= *land*) *plane* herunterbringen; **you'll bring the boss down on us** da werden wir es mit dem Chef zu tun bekommen **(b)** *opponent, government* zu Fall bringen **(c)** (= *reduce*) senken; *swelling* reduzieren

➤ **bring forward** VT SEP **(a)** (*lit*) *person, chair* nach vorne bringen **(b)** (*fig:* = *present*) *evidence, proposal* unterbreiten **(c)** (= *advance time of*) *meeting* vorverlegen **(d)** (*Comm*) *amount* übertragen; **amount brought forward** Übertrag *m*

➤ **bring in** VT SEP **(a)** (*lit*) *person, object* hereinbringen (*prep obj, -to* in +*acc*); *harvest, income* einbringen; (*Comm*) *business* bringen
(b) (*fig:* = *introduce*) *fashion* einführen; (*Parl*) *bill* einbringen; **to bring sth into fashion** etw in Mode bringen
(c) (= *involve, call in*) *police etc* einschalten (*on* bei); **don't bring him into it** lass ihn aus der Sache raus; **why bring that in?** was hat das damit zu tun?
(d) (*Jur: jury*) *verdict* fällen

➤ **bring off** VT SEP (= *succeed with*) zustande bringen; **he brought it off!** er hat es geschafft! (*inf*)

➤ **bring on** VT SEP **(a)** (= *cause*) herbeiführen **(b)** (*Theat*) *person* auftreten lassen; *thing* auf die Bühne bringen; (*Sport*) *player* einsetzen **(c)** **to bring sth (up)on oneself** sich (*dat*) etw selbst aufladen; **you brought it (up)on yourself** das hast du dir selbst zuzuschreiben

➤ **bring out** VT SEP **(a)** (*lit*) (heraus)bringen (*of* aus); (*of pocket*) herausholen (*of* aus) **(b)** (= *draw out*) *person* die Hemmungen nehmen (+*dat*) **(c)** (= *elicit*) **to bring out the best/worst in sb** das Beste/Schlimmste in jdm zum Vorschein bringen **(d)** (*also bring out on strike*) *workers* auf die Straße schicken **(e)** *new product, book* herausbringen **(f)** (= *emphasize*) hervorheben **(g)** **to bring sb out in a rash** bei jdm einen Ausschlag verursachen

➤ **bring over** VT SEP (*lit*) herüberbringen

➤ **bring round** VT SEP (*esp Brit*) **(a)** (*to one's house etc*) vorbeibringen **(b)** (= *steer*) *discussion* bringen (*to* auf +*acc*) **(c)** *unconscious person* wieder zu Bewusstsein bringen **(d)** (= *convert*) herumkriegen (*inf*)

➤ **bring to** VT ALWAYS SEPARATE **to bring sb to** *unconscious person* jdn wieder zu Bewusstsein bringen
➤ **bring together** VT SEP zusammenbringen
➤ **bring up** VT SEP **(a)** (*to a higher place*) heraufbringen; (*to the front*) hinbringen
(b) (= *increase*) *amount, reserves* erhöhen (*to* auf +*acc*); *level, standards* anheben; **to bring sb up to a certain standard** jdn auf ein gewisses Niveau bringen
(c) (= *rear*) *child, animal* großziehen; (= *educate*) erziehen; **to bring sb up to do sth** jdn dazu erziehen, etw zu tun
(d) (= *vomit up*) brechen; (*esp baby, patient*) spucken (*inf*)
(e) (= *mention*) zur Sprache bringen
(f) to bring sb up short jdn innehalten lassen
➤ **bring upon** VT SEP +PREP OBJ = **bring on (c)**
bring-and-buy (sale) ['brɪŋən'baɪ(ˌseɪl)] N (*Brit*) Basar *m* (*wo mitgebrachte Sachen angeboten und verkauft werden*)
brink [brɪŋk] N (*lit, fig*) Rand *m*; **on the ~ of sth** (*lit, fig*) am Rande von etw; **on the ~ of doing sth** (*lit, fig*) nahe daran, etw zu tun
brinkmanship ['brɪŋkmənʃɪp] N (*inf*) Spiel *nt* mit dem Feuer
brisk [brɪsk] ADJ (+ER) **(a)** *person, way of speaking* forsch; *service, pace* flott; **to go for a ~ walk** einen ordentlichen Spaziergang machen **(b)** (*fig*) *trade, betting* lebhaft **(c)** *wind* frisch
briskly ['brɪsklɪ] ADV **(a)** *speak, act* forsch; *walk* flott **(b)** (*Comm etc*) *trade* lebhaft
bristle ['brɪsl] **■** N (*of brush, boar etc*) Borste *f*; (*of beard*) Stoppel *f* **2** VI **(a)** (*fig: person*) zornig werden; **to ~ with anger** vor Wut schnauben **(b)** (*fig*) **to be bristling with people** von *or* vor Leuten wimmeln
bristly ['brɪslɪ] ADJ (+ER) *chin* stoppelig; *hair, beard* borstig
Brit [brɪt] N (*inf*) Brite *m*, Britin *f*, Tommy *m* (*inf*)
Britain ['brɪtən] N Großbritannien *nt*

BRITAIN, GREAT BRITAIN, UNITED KINGDOM

Great Britain, *Großbritannien, ist der Name der britischen Hauptinsel mit England, Schottland und Wales.*

The British Isles, *die Britischen Inseln, ist die geografische Bezeichnung für Großbritannien, die Isle of Man, und die Insel Irland. Politisch gesehen umfassen sie zwei souveräne Staaten, nämlich* **the United Kingdom of Great Britain and Northern Ireland** *und die Republik Irland.*

The United Kingdom of Great Britain and Northern Ireland *oder auch* **UK**, *das Vereinigte Königreich, ist eine politische Einheit, die aus Großbritannien und Nordirland besteht.*

Um die Verwirrung komplett zu machen, wird **Britain** *sowohl als Synonym für* **United Kingdom** *als auch für* **Great Britain** *verwendet.*

British ['brɪtɪʃ] **■** ADJ britisch; **I'm ~** ich bin Brite/Britin; **~ English** britisches Englisch **2** N **the ~** *pl* die Briten *pl*
British Council N British Council *m*, *Organisation zur Förderung britischer Kultur im Ausland*
Britisher ['brɪtɪʃəʳ] N (*dated US*) Brite *m*, Britin *f*
British Isles PL **the ~** die Britischen Inseln
Briton ['brɪtən] N Brite *m*, Britin *f*
Brittany ['brɪtənɪ] N die Bretagne
brittle ['brɪtl] ADJ **(a)** spröde; **~ bones** schwache Knochen **(b)** (*fig*) *nerves* schwach; *voice, laugh* schrill
bro [brəʊ] N (*US inf*) **(a)** (= *friend*) Kumpel *m*; **hi, ~!** hallo, Kumpel! **(b)** (= *brother*) Bruder *m*
broach [brəʊtʃ] VT *subject* anschneiden
B-road ['biːrəʊd] N (*Brit*) ≈ Landstraße *f*
broad [brɔːd] **■** ADJ (+ER) **(a)** (= *wide*) breit; **to make ~er** verbreitern **(b)** (= *widely applicable*) *theory* umfassend; (= *general*) allgemein **(c)** *distinction, outline* grob; *sense* weit **(d)** (= *liberal*) tolerant **(e)** *hint* deutlich; (= *indelicate*) *humour* derb **(f)** *accent* stark **2** N (*sl: = woman*) Tussi *f* (*sl*)
broad: **broadband** (*Comput*) **■** ADJ Breitband- **2** N Breitband *nt*
broad bean N Saubohne *f*
broadcast ['brɔːdkɑːst], *vb: pret, ptp* broadcast **■** N (*Rad, TV*) Sendung *f*; (*of match etc*) Übertragung *f* **2** VT **(a)** (*Rad, TV*) senden; *event* übertragen **(b)** (*fig*) *news, rumour etc* verbreiten **3** VI (*Rad, TV*) (*station*) senden; (*person*) im Rundfunk/Fernsehen sprechen

broadcaster ['brɔːdkɑːstəʳ] N (*Rad, TV*) (= *announcer*) Rundfunk-/Fernsehsprecher(in) *m(f)*; (= *personality*) Rundfunk-/Fernsehpersönlichkeit *f*
broadcasting ['brɔːdkɑːstɪŋ] **■** N (*Rad, TV*) Sendung *f*; (*of event*) Übertragung *f*; **to work in ~** beim Rundfunk/Fernsehen arbeiten **2** ATTR (*Rad*) Rundfunk-; (*TV*) Fernseh-
broaden (out) ['brɔːdn(aʊt)] **■** VT (SEP) (*fig*) *attitudes* aufgeschlossener machen; **to broaden one's mind/one's horizons** (*fig*) seinen Horizont erweitern **2** VI breiter werden, sich verbreitern
broad jump N (*US Sport*) Weitsprung *m*
broadly ['brɔːdlɪ] ADV allgemein; *outline, describe* grob; *agree, accept* weitgehend; **~ speaking** ganz allgemein gesprochen
broad: **broad-minded** ADJ tolerant; **broadsheet** N (*Press*) großformatige Zeitung; **broadside** N (*fig*) Attacke *f*
brocade [brəʊ'keɪd] **■** N Brokat *m* **2** ATTR Brokat-
broccoli ['brɒkəlɪ] N Brokkoli *pl*
brochure ['brəʊʃjʊəʳ] N Broschüre *f*, Prospekt *m*
brogue¹ [brəʊg] N (= *shoe*) Budapester *m*
brogue² N (= *Irish accent*) irischer Akzent
broil [brɔɪl] VTI (*Cook*) grillen
broiler ['brɔɪləʳ] N (= *grill*) Grill *m*
broiling ['brɔɪlɪŋ] ADJ (*esp US*) *sun* brütend heiß
broke [brəʊk] **■** PRET *of* **break** **2** ADJ PRED (*inf*) abgebrannt (*inf*), pleite (*inf*); **to go ~** Pleite machen (*inf*); **to go for ~** alles riskieren
broken ['brəʊkən] **■** PTP *of* **break** **2** ADJ **(a)** kaputt; *twig* geknickt; *bone* gebrochen; *rope also* gerissen; (= *smashed*) *glass etc* zerbrochen, kaputt **(b)** (*fig*) *heart, man, promise, English* gebrochen; *marriage* zerrüttet; **from a ~ home** aus zerrütteten Familienverhältnissen **(c)** *surface, ground* uneben **(d)** (= *interrupted*) *journey* unterbrochen; *line* gestrichelt
broken-down ['brəʊkən'daʊn] ADJ kaputt (*inf*)
brokenhearted ['brəʊkən'hɑːtɪd] ADJ untröstlich
broker ['brəʊkəʳ] **■** N (*St Ex, Fin, real estate*) Makler *m* **2** VT *deal* aushandeln
brokerage ['brəʊkərɪdʒ] N **(a)** (= *commission*) Maklergebühr *f* **(b)** (= *trade*) Maklergeschäft *nt*
brolly ['brɒlɪ] N (*Brit inf*) (Regen)schirm *m*
bronchial ['brɒŋkɪəl] ADJ bronchial
bronchial tubes PL Bronchien *pl*
bronchitis [brɒŋ'kaɪtɪs] N Bronchitis *f*
bronco ['brɒŋkəʊ] N *wildes oder halbwildes Pferd in den USA*
Bronx cheer [brɒŋks'tʃɪəʳ] N (*US inf*) **to get a ~** ausgelacht werden; **to give sb a ~** jdn auslachen
bronze [brɒnz] **■** N Bronze *f* **2** ADJ Bronze-
Bronze Age N Bronzezeit *f*
bronzed [brɒnzd] ADJ *face, person* braun
bronzing ['brɒnzɪŋ] ADJ Bräunungs-
brooch [brəʊtʃ] N Brosche *f*
brood [bruːd] **■** N (*lit, fig*) Brut *f* **2** VI (*fig: person*) grübeln
➤ **brood over** *or* **(up)on** VI +PREP OBJ nachgrübeln über (+*acc*)
broody ['bruːdɪ] ADJ **(a) to be feeling ~** (*hum inf*) den Wunsch nach einem Kind haben **(b)** *person* grüblerisch; (= *sad, moody*) schwerblütig
brook [brʊk] N Bach *m*
broom [bruːm] N Besen *m*
broom: **broom cupboard** N Besenschrank *m*; **broomstick** N Besenstiel *m*; **a witch on her ~** eine Hexe auf ihrem Besen
Bros PL (*Comm*) ABBR *of* **Brothers** Gebr.
broth [brɒθ] N Fleischbrühe *f*; (= *thickened soup*) Suppe *f*
brothel ['brɒθl] N Bordell *nt*
brother ['brʌðəʳ] N, *pl* **-s** *or* (*obs, Eccl*) **brethren** (*also Eccl*) Bruder *m*; **they are ~ and sister** sie sind Geschwister; **my ~s and sisters** meine Geschwister; **the Clarke ~s** die Brüder Clarke; (*Comm*) die Gebrüder Clarke; **oh ~!** (*esp US inf*) Junge, Junge! (*inf*); **his ~ officers** seine Offizierskameraden
brother: **brotherhood** N **(a)** Brüderlichkeit *f* **(b)** (= *organization*) Bruderschaft *f*; **brother-in-law** N, *pl* **brothers-in-law** Schwager *m*
brotherly ['brʌðəlɪ] ADJ brüderlich
brought [brɔːt] PRET, PTP *of* **bring**

brow [braʊ] N **(a)** (= *eyebrow*) Braue *f* **(b)** (= *forehead*) Stirn *f* **(c)** (*of hill*) (Berg)kuppe *f*

browbeat ['braʊbiːt], *pret* **browbeat**, *ptp* **browbeaten** VT unter (moralischen) Druck setzen; **to ~ sb into doing sth** jdn so unter Druck setzen, dass er etw tut

brown [braʊn] **1** ADJ (+ER) braun **2** N Braun *nt* **3** VT bräunen; *meat* anbraten **4** VI braun werden

➤ **brown off** VT **to be browned off with sb/sth** (*esp Brit inf*) jdn/etw satt haben (*inf*)

brown: brown ale N Malzbier *nt*; **brown bear** N Braunbär *m*; **brown bread** N Grau- *or* Mischbrot *nt*; (*from wholemeal*) Vollkornbrot *nt*; **brownfield** ['braʊnfiːld] ADJ *site, land* Brachflächen-; **brown goods** PL braune Ware, Unterhaltungselektronik *f*

brownie ['braʊnɪ] N **(a)** (= *cake*) kleiner Schokoladenkuchen **(b)** Brownie (*in Guide Movement*) Wichtel *m*

Brownie points PL Pluspunkte *pl*; **to score ~ with sb** sich bei jdm beliebt machen

brownish ['braʊnɪʃ] ADJ bräunlich

brown: brown paper N Packpapier *nt*; **brown rice** N geschälter Reis; **brown sauce** N (*Brit Cook*) braune Soße; **brownstone** N (*US*) (= *material*) rötlich brauner Sandstein; (= *house*) (rotes) Sandsteinhaus *nt*; **brown sugar** N brauner Zucker

browse [braʊz] **1** VI **(a) to ~ through a book** in einem Buch schmökern; **to ~ (around)** sich umsehen **(b)** (*Comput*) browsen, surfen **2** VT (*Comput*) browsen **3** N **to have a ~ (around)** sich umsehen; **to have a ~ through the books** in den Büchern schmökern

browser ['braʊzə'] N (*Comput*) Browser *m*

bruise [bruːz] **1** N (*on person*) blauer Fleck; (*more serious*) Prellung *f*; (*on fruit*) Druckstelle *f* **2** VT *person* einen blauen Fleck/blaue Flecke(n) schlagen (+*dat*); (*more seriously*) eine Prellung/Prellungen beibringen (+*dat*); *fruit* beschädigen; (*fig*) *feelings* verletzen; **to ~ one's elbow** sich (*dat*) einen blauen Fleck am Ellbogen holen

bruised [bruːzd] ADJ **(a) to be ~** (*person*) einen blauen Fleck/blaue Flecke haben; (= *have severe bruising*) Prellungen haben; (*fruit*) eine Druckstelle/Druckstellen haben; **she has a ~ shoulder, her shoulder is ~** sie hat einen blauen Fleck auf der Schulter **(b)** (*fig*) *ego, feelings* verletzt

bruising ['bruːzɪŋ] N Prellungen *pl*

brunch [brʌntʃ] N Brunch *m*

brunette [bruːˈnet] **1** N Brünette *f* **2** ADJ brünett

brunt [brʌnt] N **to bear the (main) ~ of the attack** die volle Wucht des Angriffs tragen; **to bear the (main) ~ of the costs** die Hauptlast der Kosten tragen; **to bear the ~** das meiste abkriegen

brush [brʌʃ] **1** N **(a)** (= *object*) Bürste *f*; (= *paintbrush, shaving ~, pastry ~*) Pinsel *m*; (= *hearth ~*) Besen *m*; (*with dustpan*) Handbesen *or* -feger *m* **(b)** (= *action*) **to give sth a ~** etw bürsten; *jacket, shoes* etw abbürsten; **to give one's hair a ~** sich die Haare bürsten **(c)** (= *undergrowth*) Unterholz *nt* **(d)** (= *quarrel, incident*) **to have a ~ with sb** mit jdm aneinander geraten **2** VT **(a)** (= *clean*) bürsten; (*with hand*) wischen; **to ~ one's teeth** sich (*dat*) die Zähne putzen; **to ~ one's hair** sich (*dat*) das Haar bürsten **(b)** (= *sweep*) fegen, kehren; (*with hand*) wischen **(c)** (= *touch lightly*) streifen

➤ **brush against** VI +PREP OBJ streifen

➤ **brush aside** VT SEP *obstacle, person* zur Seite schieben; *objections* abtun

➤ **brush away** VT SEP verscheuchen

➤ **brush off** VT SEP **(a)** *mud* abbürsten **(b)** (*inf:* = *reject*) *person* abblitzen lassen (*inf*); *suggestion, criticism* zurückweisen

➤ **brush past** VI streifen (*prep obj* +*acc*)

➤ **brush up** VT SEP **(a)** *crumbs, dirt* auffegen, aufkehren **(b)** (*fig: also* **brush up on**) *subject* auffrischen

brush: brushoff N (*inf*) **to give sb the ~** jdn abblitzen lassen (*inf*); **brushstroke** N Pinselstrich *m*; **brushwood** N (= *cut twigs*) Reisig *nt*

brusque ADJ (+ER), **brusquely** ADV [bruːsk, -lɪ] brüsk; *reply* schroff

Brussels ['brʌslz] N Brüssel *nt*

Brussels sprouts PL Rosenkohl *m*

brutal ['bruːtl] ADJ brutal

brutality [bruːˈtælɪtɪ] N Brutalität *f*

brutalize ['bruːtəlaɪz] VT brutalisieren

brutally ['bruːtəlɪ] ADV brutal

brute [bruːt] **1** N (= *person*) brutaler Kerl **2** ADJ ATTR *strength* roh; **by ~ force** mit roher Gewalt

brutish ['bruːtɪʃ] ADJ viehisch, brutal

BSc ABBR *of* **Bachelor of Science**

BSE ABBR *of* **bovine spongiform encephalopathy** BSE *f*, Rinderwahn(sinn) *m*

B-side ['biːsaɪd] N (*of record*) B-Seite *f*

BST ABBR *of* **British Summer Time, British Standard Time**

BT ABBR *of* **British Telecom** *britisches Telekommunikationsunternehmen*

BTW (*inf*) ABBR *of* **by the way**

bub [bʌb] N (*US inf*) Alte(r) *m* (*inf*), Mann *m* (*inf*)

bubble ['bʌbl] **1** N Blase *f*; **to blow ~s** Blasen machen; **the ~ has burst** (*fig*) alles ist wie eine Seifenblase zerplatzt **2** VI **(a)** (*liquid*) sprudeln; (*wine*) perlen **(b)** (= *make bubbling noise*) blubbern (*inf*); (*cooking liquid, geyser etc*) brodeln; (*stream*) plätschern **(c)** (*fig*) **to ~ with enthusiasm** fast platzen vor Begeisterung

➤ **bubble over** VI (*lit*) überschäumen; (*fig*) übersprudeln (*with* vor +*dat*)

bubble: bubble bath N Schaumbad *nt*; **bubble gum** N Bubblegum *m*; **bubblehead** N (*esp US pej inf*) Schwachkopf *m* (*inf*); **bubble-jet printer** N (*Comput*) Bubblejet-Drucker *m*; **bubble memory** N (*Comput*) Blasenspeicher *m*; **bubble pack** N (Klar)sichtpackung *f*

bubbly ['bʌblɪ] **1** ADJ (+ER) **(a)** (*lit*) sprudelnd **(b)** (*fig inf*) *personality* temperamentvoll **2** N (*inf*) Schampus *m* (*inf*)

bubonic plague [bjuːˈbɒnɪkˈpleɪg] N Beulenpest *f*

Bucharest [bjuːkəˈrest] N Bukarest *nt*

buck [bʌk] **1** N **(a)** (= *male deer*) Bock *m*; (= *male rabbit, hare*) Rammler *m* **(b)** (*US inf:* = *dollar*) Dollar *m*; **20 ~s** 20 Dollar; **to make a ~** Geld verdienen; **to make a fast** *or* **quick ~** (*also Brit*) schnell Kohle machen (*inf*) **(c) to pass the ~** (*difficulty etc*) den schwarzen Peter weitergeben **2** VI (*horse*) bocken **3** VT **you can't ~ the market** gegen den Markt kommt man nicht an; **to ~ the trend** sich dem Trend widersetzen

➤ **buck for** VI +PREP OBJ (*US inf*) **to buck for promotion** mit aller Gewalt befördert werden wollen

➤ **buck up** (*inf*) **1** VI **(a)** (= *hurry up*) sich ranhalten (*inf*) **(b)** (= *cheer up*) aufleben; **buck up!** Kopf hoch! **2** VT SEP **(a)** (= *make hurry*) Dampf machen (+*dat*) (*inf*) **(b)** (= *make cheerful*) aufmuntern **(c) to buck one's ideas up** sich zusammenreißen (*inf*)

buckaroo [bʌkəˈruː] N (*US inf hum*) Cowboy *m*

bucket ['bʌkɪt] **1** N Eimer *m*; (*of excavator, water wheel*) Schaufel *f*; **a ~ of water** ein Eimer *m* Wasser **2** VI (*Brit inf*) **it's ~ing!, the rain is ~ing (down)!** es gießt wie aus Kübeln (*inf*)

bucketful ['bʌkɪtfʊl] N Eimer *m*; **by the ~** (*fig inf*) tonnenweise (*inf*)

bucket shop N (*Fin*) Schwindelmakler *m*; (= *travel agency*) Agentur *f* für Billigreisen

buckeye ['bʌkaɪ] N (*US*) Rosskastanie *f*; (= *seed*) Kastanie *f*

Buckingham Palace ['bʌkɪŋəmˈpælɪs] N der Buckingham-Palast

buckle ['bʌkl] **1** N (*on belt, shoe*) Schnalle *f* **2** VT **(a)** *belt, shoes* zuschnallen **(b)** *wheel, girder etc* verbiegen; (= *dent*) verbeulen **3** VI (*wheel, metal*) sich verbiegen

➤ **buckle down** VI (*inf*) sich dahinter klemmen (*inf*); **to buckle down to a task** sich hinter eine Aufgabe klemmen (*inf*)

buck: buckshot N grober Schrot; **buckskin** N Wildleder *nt*; **buckwheat** N Buchweizen *m*

bud[1] [bʌd] **1** N Knospe *f*; **to be in ~** Knospen treiben **2** VI Knospen treiben; (*tree also*) ausschlagen

bud[2] INTERJ (*US inf*) = **buddy**

Budapest [bjuːdəˈpest] N Budapest *nt*

Buddha ['bʊdə] N Buddha *m*

Buddhism ['bʊdɪzəm] N Buddhismus *m*

Buddhist ['bʊdɪst] **1** N Buddhist(in) *m(f)* **2** ADJ buddhistisch

budding ['bʌdɪŋ] ADJ (*fig*) *poet etc* angehend

buddy ['bʌdɪ] N (*US inf*) Kumpel *m*

buddy-buddy [ˈbʌdɪbʌdɪ] ADJ (*US inf*) **to be ~ with sb** mit jdm dick befreundet sein (*inf*); **to try to get ~ with sb** sich bei jdm anbiedern

budge [bʌdʒ] **1** VI (a) (= *move*) sich bewegen; **~ up** *or* **over!** mach Platz! (b) (*fig*: = *give way*) nachgeben; **I will not ~ an inch** ich werde keinen Fingerbreit nachgeben **2** VT (a) (= *move*) (von der Stelle) bewegen (b) (= *force to give way*) zum Nachgeben bewegen

budgerigar [ˈbʌdʒərɪgɑːʳ] N Wellensittich *m*

budget [ˈbʌdʒɪt] **1** N Etat *m*, Budget *nt* **2** VI haushalten **3** VT (a) *money, time* verplanen (b) *item* kostenmäßig einplanen; *costs* einplanen; **~ed costs** vorgesehene Kosten *pl*; **~ed revenue** Sollertrag *m*
➤ **budget for** VI +PREP OBJ (im Etat) einplanen

-budget SUF **low-budget** mit bescheidenen Mitteln finanziert; **big-budget** aufwändig (finanziert)

budget account N Kundenkonto *nt*

budgetary [ˈbʌdʒɪtrɪ] ADJ Etat-, Budget-; **~ constraints** finanzielle Zwänge; **~ policy** Haushaltspolitik *f*

budget: **budget day** N (*Parl*) ≈ Haushaltsdebatte *f*; **budget deficit** N Haushaltsdefizit *nt*

budgeting [ˈbʌdʒɪtɪŋ] N Budgetierung *f*

budget speech N (*Parl*) Etatrede *f*

budgie [ˈbʌdʒɪ] N (*inf*) ABBR *of* **budgerigar** Wellensittich *m*

buff[1] [bʌf] **1** N (a) **in the ~** nackt, im Adams-/Evaskostüm (*hum*) (b) (= *colour*) Gelbbraun *nt* **2** ADJ (*colour*) gelbbraun **3** VT *metal* polieren

buff[2] N (*inf*: = *movie etc* ~) Fan *m* (*inf*)

buffalo [ˈbʌfələʊ] N, *pl* **-es**, *collective pl* **-** Büffel *m*

buffer [ˈbʌfəʳ] N (*lit, fig, Comput*) Puffer *m*; (*Rail*: *at terminus*) Prellbock *m*

buffering [ˈbʌfərɪŋ] N (*Comput*) Pufferung *f*

buffer: **buffer state** N (*Pol*) Pufferstaat *m*; **buffer stock** N (*Comm*) Mindestbestand *m*

buffet[1] [ˈbʌfɪt] VT hin und her werfen; **~ed by the wind** vom Wind gerüttelt

buffet[2] [ˈbʊfeɪ] N Büffett *nt*; (*Brit Rail*) Speisewagen *m*; (= *meal*) Stehimbiss *m*; (= *cold* ~) kaltes Büffett; **~ lunch/meal** Stehimbiss *m*

buffet car [ˈbʊfeɪ-] N (*Brit Rail*) Speisewagen *m*

bug [bʌg] **1** N (a) (*also Comput*) Wanze *f*; (*inf*: = *any insect*) Käfer *m*; **~s** *pl* Ungeziefer *nt* (b) (*inf*: = *germ, virus*) Bazillus *f*; **he picked up a ~ while on holiday** (*esp Brit*) *or* **vacation** (*US*) er hat sich (*dat*) im Urlaub eine Krankheit geholt; **there must be a ~ going about** das geht zur Zeit um (c) (*inf*: = *obsession*) **she's got the travel ~** die Reiselust hat sie gepackt **2** VT (a) *room* Wanzen *pl* installieren in (+*dat*) *or* einbauen in (+*acc*) (*inf*); **this room is ~ged** das Zimmer ist verwanzt (*inf*) (b) (*inf*: = *worry*) stören; (= *annoy*) nerven (*inf*)

bugbear [ˈbʌgbɛəʳ] N Schreckgespenst *nt*

bug-free [bʌgˈfriː] ADJ (*Comput*) fehlerfrei

bugger [ˈbʌgəʳ] **1** N (*inf*) Scheißkerl *m* (*inf*); (*when not contemptible*) Kerl *m* (*inf*); (= *thing*) Scheißding *nt* (*inf*); **you lucky ~!** du hast vielleicht ein Schwein! (*inf*) **2** INTERJ (*Brit inf*) **~ (it)!** Scheiße! (*inf*); **~ this car!** dieses Scheißauto! (*inf*); **~ him** dieser Scheißkerl (*inf*); (= *he can get lost*) der kann mich mal (*inf*)
➤ **bugger about** *or* **around** (*Brit inf*) **1** VI (= *laze about etc*) rumgammeln (*inf*); (= *be ineffective*) blöd rummachen (*inf*); **to bugger about** *or* **around with sth** an etw (*dat*) rumpfuschen (*inf*) **2** VT SEP verarschen (*inf*)
➤ **bugger off** VI (*Brit inf*) abhauen (*inf*)

➤ **bugger up** VT SEP (*Brit inf*) versauen (*inf*)

bugger all [ˌbʌgərˈɔːl] N (*Brit inf*) rein gar nichts

buggered [ˈbʌgəd] ADJ (*Brit inf*) (= *broken, ruined*) im Arsch (*sl*); (= *exhausted*) *person* fix und fertig (*inf*); **I'm ~ if I'll do it** ich denke nicht im Traum daran, es zu tun

bugging device [ˈbʌgɪŋdɪˌvaɪs] N Abhörgerät *nt*, Wanze *f* (*inf*)

buggy [ˈbʌgɪ] N (**baby**) **~** (*Brit*) Sportwagen *m*; (*US*) Kinderwagen *m*

bugle [ˈbjuːgl] N Bügelhorn *nt*

build [bɪld], *vb*: *pret, ptp* **built** **1** N Körperbau *m* **2** VT (a) (*generally*) bauen; **the house is being built** das Haus ist im Bau (b) (*fig*) *relationship, career, system etc* aufbauen; *future* schaffen **3** VI bauen
➤ **build in** VT SEP (*lit, fig*) *wardrobe, proviso etc* einbauen
➤ **build on** **1** VT SEP anbauen; **to build sth onto sth** etw an etw (*acc*) anbauen **2** VI +PREP OBJ bauen auf (+*acc*)
➤ **build up** **1** VI (a) (*business*) wachsen; (*residue*) sich ablagern; (= *increase*) zunehmen; **the music builds up to a huge crescendo** die Musik steigert sich zu einem gewaltigen Crescendo (b) (*traffic*) sich verdichten; (*queue*) sich bilden **2** VT SEP (a) aufbauen (*into zu*); *finances* aufbessern; *pressure* steigern; *forces* (= *mass*) zusammenziehen; *health* kräftigen; *sb's confidence* stärken; **porridge builds you up** von Porridge wirst du groß und stark; **to build up sb's hopes** jdm Hoffnung(en) machen; **to build up a reputation** sich (*dat*) einen Namen machen (b) (= *cover with houses*) (ganz) bebauen

builder [ˈbɪldəʳ] N (= *worker*) Bauarbeiter(in) *m(f)*; (= *contractor*) Bauunternehmer *m*; **~'s merchant** Baustoffhändler *m*

building [ˈbɪldɪŋ] N (a) Gebäude *nt*; **it's the next ~ but one** das ist zwei Häuser weiter (b) (= *act of constructing*) Bauen *nt*

building: **building block** N (*in toy set*) Bauklotz *m*; (*fig*) Baustein *m*; **building contractor** N Bauunternehmer *m*; **building materials** PL Baumaterial *nt*; **building site** N Baustelle *f*; **building society** N (*Brit*) Bausparkasse *f*; **building trade** N Baugewerbe *nt*

build-up [ˈbɪldʌp] N (a) (*inf*) Werbung *f*; **the chairman gave the speaker a tremendous ~** der Vorsitzende hat den Redner ganz groß angekündigt (b) (*of pressure*) Steigerung *f*; **a traffic ~, a ~ of traffic** eine Verkehrsverdichtung

built [bɪlt] **1** PRET, PTP *of* **build** **2** ADJ **heavily/slightly ~** *person* kräftig/zierlich gebaut

built: **built-in** ADJ *cupboard etc* eingebaut, Einbau-; (*fig*: = *instinctive*) instinktmäßig; **built-up** ADJ **~ area** (= *urbanized*) bebautes Gebiet; (*Mot*) geschlossene Ortschaft

bulb [bʌlb] N (a) Zwiebel *f*; (*of garlic*) Knolle *f* (b) (*Elec*) (Glüh)birne *f*

Bulgaria [bʌlˈgɛərɪə] N Bulgarien *nt*

Bulgarian [bʌlˈgɛərɪən] **1** ADJ bulgarisch **2** N (a) Bulgare *m*, Bulgarin *f* (b) (*Ling*) Bulgarisch *nt*

bulge [bʌldʒ] **1** N Wölbung *f*; (*irregular*) Unebenheit *f*; (*in plaster, metal: accidental*) Beule *f*; (*in line*) Bogen *m*; **what's that ~ in your pocket?** was steht denn in deiner Tasche so vor? **2** VI (a) (*also* **~ out**) (= *swell*) (an)schwellen; (*metal, sides of box*) sich wölben; (= *stick out*) vorstehen; **his eyes were bulging out of his head** (*fig*) er bekam Stielaugen (*inf*) (b) (*pocket, sack*) prall gefüllt sein; (*cheek*) voll sein

bulging [ˈbʌldʒɪŋ] ADJ *stomach* prall; *pockets, suitcase* prall gefüllt

bulimia [bəˈlɪmɪə] N Bulimie *f*

bulimic [bəˈlɪmɪk] **1** ADJ bulimisch **2** N Bulimiker(in) *m(f)*

bulk [bʌlk] N (a) (= *size*) Größe *f*; (= *large shape*) (*of thing*) massige Form; (*of person, animal*) massige Gestalt (b) (*also* **great ~**) größter Teil (c) (*Comm*) **in ~** en gros

bulk: **bulk buying** N Großeinkauf *m*; **bulk cargo** N Massengut *nt*; **bulk carrier** N (*ship*) Massengutfrachter *m*

bulking N (*Comm*) Zusammenlegen *nt*; **~ of orders** Zusammenlegung *f* vieler Aufträge

bulky [ˈbʌlkɪ] ADJ (+ER) (a) *object* sperrig; *book* dick; *sweater* unförmig; **~ goods** Sperrgut *nt* (b) *person* massig, wuchtig

bull [bʊl] N (a) Stier *m*; (*for breeding*) Bulle *m*; **to take** *or* **seize the ~ by the horns** (*fig*) den Stier bei den Hörnern packen; **like a ~ in a china shop** (*inf*) wie ein Elefant im Porzellanladen (*inf*) (b) (= *male of elephant, whale etc*) Bulle *m*; **a ~ elephant** ein Elefantenbulle *m*; **~ calf** Bullenkalb *nt*

(c) (*St Ex*) Haussespekulant(in) *m(f)* **(d)** (*inf: = nonsense*) Unsinn *m*, Quatsch *m* (*inf*)

bull bars PL (*Aut*) Kuhfänger *m*

bulldog ['bʊldɒg] N Bulldogge *f*

bulldog clip N (*Brit*) Papierklammer *f*

bulldoze ['bʊldəʊz] VT (*fig: = force*) **to ~ sb into doing sth** jdn so unter Druck setzen, dass er *etc* etw tut; **to ~ a bill through parliament** eine Maßnahme im Parlament durchpeitschen

bulldozer ['bʊldəʊzə'] N Bulldozer *m*

bullet ['bʊlɪt] N Kugel *f*; **to bite the ~** in den sauren Apfel beißen (*inf*)

bullet hole N Einschuss(loch *nt*) *m*

bulletin ['bʊlɪtɪn] N Bulletin *nt*; **health ~** Krankenbericht *m*

bulletin board N (*US: = notice board*, *Comput*) schwarzes Brett

bullet: bulletproof ADJ kugelsicher; **bullet wound** N Schussverletzung *f*

bull: bullfighter N Stierkämpfer *m*; **bullfighting** N Stierkampf *m*; **bullhorn** N (*US*) Megaphon *nt*

bullion ['bʊljən] N, NO PL Gold-/Silberbarren *pl*

bullish ['bʊlɪʃ] ADJ **to be ~ about sth** in Bezug auf etw (*acc*) zuversichtlich sein

bull market N (*St Ex*) Haussemarkt *m*, Haussesituation *f*

bullock ['bʊlək] N Ochse *m*

bull: bullpen N (*US inf*) **(a)** (*Baseball*) (*= area*) Bereich in dem sich Einwechsel-Werfer aufwärmen; (*= players*) Einwechsel-Werfer *pl* **(b)** (*= office*) Großraumbüro *nt* **(c)** (*= cell*) Sammelzelle *f*; **bull position** N (*St Ex*) Hausseposition *f*; **bullring** N Stierkampfarena *f*

bull's-eye N (*of target*) Scheibenmittelpunkt *m*; (*= hit*) Schuss *m* ins Schwarze; (*in darts*) Bull's eye *nt*; (*in archery*) Mouche *f*

bull: bullshit (*sl*) **1** N (*fig*) Scheiß *m* (*inf*) **2** INTERJ ach Quatsch (*inf*) **3** VI Scheiß erzählen (*inf*) **4** VT **to ~ sb** jdm Scheiß erzählen (*inf*); **bullshitter** N (*sl*) Dummschwätzer(in) *m(f)* (*inf*); **bull terrier** N Bullterrier *m*

bully ['bʊlɪ] **1** N Tyrann *m*; **you great big ~** du Rüpel **2** VT tyrannisieren; (*using violence*) drangsalieren; (*into doing sth*) unter Druck setzen; **to ~ sb into doing sth** jdn so unter Druck setzen, dass er *etc* etw tut

bully-boy ['bʊlɪbɔɪ] ADJ ATTR **~ tactics** Einschüchterungstaktik *f*

bullying ['bʊlɪɪŋ] **1** ADJ tyrannisch **2** N Tyrannisieren *nt*; (*with violence*) Drangsalieren *nt*; (*= coercion*) Anwendung *f* von Druck (*of auf +acc*)

bulwark ['bʊlwək] N (*lit, fig*) Bollwerk *nt*

bum¹ [bʌm] N (*esp Brit inf*) Hintern *m* (*inf*); **to put ~s on seats** (*pop star etc*) ein Publikumsmagnet *m* sein

bum² (*inf*) **1** N (*esp US*) **(a)** (*= good-for-nothing*) Rumtreiber *m* (*inf*); (*young*) Gammler *m*; (*= down-and-out*) Penner *m* (*inf*), Pennbruder *m* (*inf*) **(b)** (*= despicable person*) Saukerl *m* (*inf*) **2** ADJ (*= bad*) beschissen (*inf*); (*trick*) hundsgemein (*inf*); **~ rap** (*US inf*) falsche Anklage; **to give sb a ~ steer** (*US inf*) jdn auf die falsche Fährte locken **3** VT *money, food* schnorren (*inf*) (*off sb* bei jdm); **could I ~ a lift into town?** kannst du mich in die Stadt mitnehmen?

➤ **bum about** (*Brit*) or **around** (*inf*) **1** VI rumgammeln (*inf*) **2** VI +PREP OBJ ziehen durch (*inf*)

bum bag N Gürteltasche *f*

bumblebee ['bʌmblbiː] N Hummel *f*

bumbling ['bʌmblɪŋ] ADJ (*= clumsy*) schusselig (*inf*); **some ~ idiot** irgend so ein Vollidiot (*inf*)

bumf [bʌmf] N = **bumph**

bum-fluff ['bʌmflʌf] N (*inf*) Flaumbart *m*

bummer ['bʌmə'] N (*inf*) **what a ~** (*= nuisance etc*) so 'ne Scheiße (*inf*)

bump [bʌmp] **1** N **(a)** (*= blow, noise, jolt*) Bums *m* (*inf*); (*of sth falling also*) Plumps *m* (*inf*); **to get a ~ on the head** sich (*dat*) den Kopf anschlagen; **he sat down with a ~** er ließ sich plumpsen (*inf*); **the car has had a few ~s** mit dem Auto hat es ein paar Mal gebumst (*inf*) **(b)** (*on any surface*) Unebenheit *f*; (*on head, knee etc*) Beule *f*; (*on car*) Delle *f* **2** VT stoßen (*obj* gegen); **one's own car** eine Delle fahren in (*+acc*); *another car* auffahren auf (*+acc*); **to ~ one's head** sich (*dat*) den Kopf anstoßen (*on, against* an *+dat*)

3 VI (*= move joltingly*) holpern; **he fell and went ~ing down the stairs** er stürzte und fiel polternd die Treppe hinunter

➤ **bump into** VI +PREP OBJ **(a)** (*= knock into*) stoßen gegen; (*driver, car*) fahren gegen; *another car* fahren auf (*+acc*) **(b)** (*inf: = meet*) begegnen (*+dat*), treffen

➤ **bump off** VT SEP (*inf*) abmurksen (*inf*)

➤ **bump up** VT SEP (*inf*) (*to auf +acc*) *prices, total* erhöhen; *salary* aufbessern

bumper ['bʌmpə'] **1** N (*of car*) Stoßstange *f* **2** ADJ **~ crop** Rekordernte *f*; **a special ~ edition** eine Riesensonderausgabe

bumper car N Autoskooter *m*

bumper sticker N (*Aut*) Aufkleber *m*

bumph [bʌmf] N (*Brit inf*) Papierkram *m* (*inf*)

bumpkin ['bʌmpkɪn] N (*also* **country ~**) (*= man*) (Bauern)tölpel *m*; (*= woman*) Trampel *f* vom Land

bumpy ['bʌmpɪ] ADJ (*+ER*) *surface* uneben; *road, drive* holp(e)rig; *flight* unruhig

bun [bʌn] N **(a)** (*= bread*) Brötchen *nt*; (*= iced ~ etc*) süßes Teilchen **(b)** (*= hairstyle*) Knoten *m*; **she wears her hair in a ~** sie trägt einen Knoten

bunch [bʌntʃ] **1** N **(a)** (*of flowers*) Strauß *m*; (*of bananas*) Büschel *nt*; (*of radishes, asparagus*) Bund *nt*; **a ~ of roses** ein Strauß *m* Rosen; **a ~ of flowers** ein Blumenstrauß *m*; **~ of grapes** Weintraube *f*; **~ of keys** Schlüsselbund *m*; **to wear one's hair in ~es** Zöpfchen *pl* haben; **the pick** or **best of the ~** die Allerbesten; (*things*) das Beste vom Besten **(b)** (*= of people*) Haufen *m* (*inf*); **a small ~ of tourists** eine kleine Gruppe Touristen **(c)** (*inf: = a lot*) **thanks a ~** (*esp iro*) schönen Dank **2** VI (*dress*) sich bauschen

➤ **bunch together** or **up** VI (*people*) Grüppchen bilden; **don't bunch together** or **up, spread out!** bleibt nicht alle auf einem Haufen, verteilt euch!

bundle ['bʌndl] **1** N **(a)** (*= pile*) Bündel *nt*; **to tie sth in a ~** etw bündeln **(b)** (*fig*) **a ~ of** (*= large number of*) eine ganze Menge; **he is a ~ of nerves** er ist ein Nervenbündel; **a ~ of fun** (*inf*) das reinste Vergnügen; **it cost a ~** (*inf*) das hat eine Stange Geld gekostet (*inf*) **2** VT **(a)** (*= tie in a ~*) bündeln; **~d software** (*Comput*) Softwarepaket *nt*; **it comes ~d with ...** (*Comput*) ... ist im Softwarepaket enthalten **(b)** (*= put, send hastily*) *things* stopfen; *people* verfrachten

➤ **bundle off** VT SEP *person* schaffen; **he was bundled off to Australia** er wurde nach Australien verfrachtet

➤ **bundle up** VT SEP (*= tie into bundles*) bündeln; **bundled up in his overcoat** in seinen Mantel eingehüllt

bung [bʌŋ] (*Brit*) **1** N **(a)** (*of cask*) Spund(zapfen) *m* **(b)** (*inf: = bribe*) Schmiergeld *nt* (*inf*) **2** VT (*Brit inf: = throw*) schmeißen (*inf*)

➤ **bung up** VT SEP (*inf*) *pipe* verstopfen; **I'm all bunged up** meine Nase ist verstopft

bungalow ['bʌŋgələʊ] N Bungalow *m*

bungee jumping ['bʌndʒiː'dʒʌmpɪŋ] N Bungeespringen *nt*

bungle ['bʌŋgl] verpfuschen; **it was a ~d job** die Sache war verpfuscht

bungling ['bʌŋglɪŋ] ADJ *person* trottelhaft; **some ~ idiot has ...** irgendein Trottel hat ... (*inf*)

bunion ['bʌnjən] N Ballen *m*

bunk¹ [bʌŋk] N **to do a ~** (*Brit inf*) türmen (*inf*)

➤ **bunk off** VI (*Brit Sch inf*) schwänzen

bunk² N (*inf*) Quatsch *m* (*inf*)

bunk³ N (*in ship*) Koje *f*; (*in train, dormitory*) Bett *nt*

bunk beds PL Etagenbett *nt*

bunker ['bʌŋkə'] N (*Golf, Mil*) Bunker *m*

bunkum ['bʌŋkəm] N (*inf*) Quatsch *m* (*inf*)

bunny ['bʌnɪ] N (*also* **~ rabbit**) Hase *m*

Bunsen (burner) ['bʌnsn('bɜːnə')] N Bunsenbrenner *m*

bunting ['bʌntɪŋ] N (*= flags*) Wimpel *pl*

buoy [bɔɪ] N Boje *f*

➤ **buoy up** VT SEP (*fig, Fin*) Auftrieb geben (*+dat*); *sb's hopes* beleben

buoyant ['bɔɪənt] ADJ **(a)** *ship, object* schwimmend **(b)** (*fig*) *mood* heiter **(c)** (*Fin*) *market, prices* fest; *trading* rege

burble [ˈbɜːbl] VI **(a)** (*stream*) plätschern **(b)** (*fig*) (*person*) plappern; (*baby*) gurgeln; **what's he burbling (on) about?** (*inf*) worüber quasselt er eigentlich? (*inf*)

burbs, 'burbs [bɜːbz] PL (*US inf*) = **suburbs**

burden [ˈbɜːdn] **◨** N **(a)** (*lit*) Last *f* (*fig*) Belastung *f* (*on, to* für); ~ **of taxation** Steuerlast *f*; **I don't want to be a ~ to you** ich möchte Ihnen nicht zur Last fallen; **the ~ of proof is on him** er muss den Beweis dafür liefern; (*Jur*) er trägt die Beweislast **◨** VT belasten; **to be ~ed by guilt** von Schuldgefühlen geplagt sein

burdensome [ˈbɜːdnsəm] ADJ *load* schwer; *task* mühsam; **to be ~** eine Belastung darstellen

bureau [bjʊəˈrəʊ] N **(a)** (*Brit*: = *desk*) Sekretär *m* **(b)** (*US*: = *chest of drawers*) Kommode *f* **(c)** (= *office*) Büro *nt* **(d)** (= *government department*) Behörde *f*; **Bureau of the Census** (*US*) Statistisches Amt

BUREAU OF INDIAN AFFAIRS

*Das **Bureau of Indian Affairs** ist eine Regierungsbehörde der USA, die sich um alle Belange der Nachkommen der amerikanischen Urbevölkerung kümmert. 1824 wurde sie als Teil des Kriegsministeriums eingerichtet und war ursprünglich für die Verwaltung der Indianerreservate verantwortlich. Heute ist sie dem Innenministerium unterstellt, sieht ihre Hauptaufgabe im Schutz des indianischen Landes und seiner Ressourcen und arbeitet mit der Urbevölkerung zusammen, um deren Lebensbedingungen zu verbessern. Dabei werden zum Beispiel Gesundheits- und Sozialpläne erstellt sowie Ausbildungs- und Arbeitsplätze geschaffen. Seit 1960 stellt das Büro für indianische Angelegenheiten auch technische Hilfsmittel und Schulungsmöglichkeiten auf dem Gebiet der Landwirtschaft und der Ressourcengewinnung.* ▶ NATIVE AMERICAN

bureaucracy [bjʊəˈrɒkrəsɪ] N Bürokratie *f*
bureaucrat [ˈbjʊərəʊkræt] N Bürokrat *m*
bureaucratic [ˌbjʊərəʊˈkrætɪk] ADJ bürokratisch
burgeoning [ˈbɜːdʒənɪŋ] ADJ *industry, market* boomend; *career* Erfolg versprechend; *demand* wachsend
burger [ˈbɜːgəʳ] N (*inf*) Hamburger *m*
burger bar N Imbissstube *f*
burglar [ˈbɜːgləʳ] N Einbrecher(in) *m(f)*
burglar alarm N Alarmanlage *f*
burglarize [ˈbɜːgləraɪz] VT (*US*) einbrechen in (+*acc*); **the place/he was ~d** in dem Gebäude/bei ihm wurde eingebrochen
burglary [ˈbɜːglərɪ] N Einbruch *m*; (= *offence*) (Einbruchs)diebstahl *m*
burgle [ˈbɜːgl] VT (*Brit*) einbrechen in (+*acc*); **the place/he was ~d** in dem Gebäude/bei ihm wurde eingebrochen
Burgundy [ˈbɜːgəndɪ] N (= *wine*) Burgunder *m*
burial [ˈberɪəl] N Beerdigung *f*; **Christian ~** christliches Begräbnis; **~ at sea** Seebestattung *f*
burial ground N Begräbnisstätte *f*
burly [ˈbɜːlɪ] ADJ (+ER) kräftig, stramm
Burma [ˈbɜːmə] N Birma *nt*
Burmese [bɜːˈmiːz] **◨** ADJ birmanisch **◨** N Birmane *m*, Birmanin *f*

burn [bɜːn], *vb: pret, ptp* **burnt** (*Brit*) or **burned** **◨** N (*on skin*) Brandwunde *f*; (*on material*) Brandfleck *m*; **severe ~s** schwere Verbrennungen *pl* **◨** VT (*a*) verbrennen; *incense* abbrennen; *village, building* niederbrennen; **to ~ oneself** sich verbrennen; **to be ~ed to death** verbrannt werden; (*in accident*) verbrennen; **to ~ a hole in sth** ein Loch in etw (*acc*) brennen; **to ~ one's fingers** (*lit, fig*) sich (*dat*) die Finger verbrennen; **he's got money to ~** (*fig*) er hat Geld wie Heu; **to ~ one's boats** or **bridges** (*Brit fig*) alle Brücken hinter sich (*dat*) abbrechen; **to ~ the midnight oil** (*fig*) bis tief in die Nacht arbeiten **(b)** *meat, toast etc* verbrennen lassen; (*slightly*) anbrennen lassen; (*sun*) *person, skin* verbrennen **(c)** (*acid*) ätzen; **the curry ~ed his throat** das Currygericht brannte ihm im Hals **◨** VI (*a*) brennen; **to ~ to death** verbrennen; **to be ~ing to do sth** darauf brennen, etw zu tun **(b)** *meat, pastry etc* verbrennen; (*slightly*) anbrennen; **she/her skin ~s easily** sie bekommt leicht einen Sonnenbrand
▶ **burn down** **◨** VI (*a*) (*house etc*) abbrennen **(b)** (*fire, candle*) herunterbrennen **◨** VT SEP abbrennen

▶ **burn off** VT SEP *paint etc* abbrennen
▶ **burn out** **◨** VI (*fire, candle*) ausgehen; (*fuse etc*) durchbrennen **◨** VR **(a)** (*candle*) herunterbrennen; (*fire*) ausbrennen **(b)** (*fig inf*) **to burn oneself out** sich kaputtmachen **◨** VT SEP USU PASS **burned out cars** ausgebrannte Autos; **he is burned out** (*inf*) er hat sich völlig verausgabt
▶ **burn up** **◨** VI (*rocket etc in atmosphere*) verglühen **◨** VT SEP **(a)** *fuel, energy* verbrauchen; *excess fat also* abbauen **(b)** (*US inf*: = *make angry*) zur Weißglut bringen (*inf*)
burner [ˈbɜːnəʳ] N (*of gas cooker, lamp*) Brenner *m*
burning [ˈbɜːnɪŋ] **◨** ADJ (*lit, fig*) brennend; *face, fever, passion, ambition* glühend; **I still have this ~ sensation on my skin** meine Haut brennt immer noch **◨** N **there is a smell of ~, I can smell ~** es riecht verbrannt
burns unit N (*Med*) Verbrennungsintensivstation *f*
burnt [bɜːnt] ADJ (*Brit*) verbrannt; **there's a ~ smell** es riecht verbrannt or (*Cook also*) angebrannt
burp [bɜːp] (*inf*) **◨** VI rülpsen (*inf*); (*baby*) aufstoßen **◨** N Rülpser *m* (*inf*)
burrow [ˈbʌrəʊ] **◨** N (*of rabbit etc*) Bau *m* **◨** VI (*rabbits, dogs etc*) graben; **they had ~ed under the fence** sie hatten sich (*dat*) ein Loch or (*below ground*) einen Gang unterm Zaun gegraben
bursar [ˈbɜːsəʳ] N Schatzmeister(in) *m(f)*
bursary [ˈbɜːsərɪ] N (*Brit*: = *grant*) Stipendium *nt*
burst [bɜːst], *vb: pret, ptp* **burst** **◨** N **(a)** (*of shell etc*) Explosion *f* **(b)** (*in pipe etc*) Bruch *m* **(c)** (*of anger, activity etc*) Ausbruch *m*; **~ of laughter** Lachsalve *f*; **~ of applause** Beifallssturm *m*; **~ of speed** Spurt *m*; (*of cars etc*) Riesenbeschleunigung *f* (*inf*); **a ~ of automatic gunfire** eine Maschinengewehrsalve **◨** VI **(a)** platzen; **to ~ open** (*box, door etc*) aufspringen; **to be full to ~ing** zum Platzen voll sein; **to be ~ing with health** vor Gesundheit strotzen; **to be ~ing with pride** vor Stolz platzen; **if I eat any more, I'll ~** (*inf*) wenn ich noch mehr esse, platze ich (*inf*); **I'm ~ing** (*inf*: = *need the toilet*) ich muss ganz dringend (*inf*); **he was ~ing to tell us** (*inf*) er brannte darauf, uns das zu sagen **(b)** (= *start, go suddenly*) **to ~ into tears** in Tränen ausbrechen; **to ~ into flames** in Flammen aufgehen; **he ~ into the room** er platzte ins Zimmer; **to ~ into song** lossingen **◨** VT *balloon, bubble, tyre* zum Platzen bringen; (*person*) kaputtmachen (*inf*); *boiler, pipe, dyke* sprengen; **the river has ~ its banks** der Fluss ist über die Ufer getreten
▶ **burst in** VI hineinstürzen; (*on conversation*) dazwischenplatzen (*on* bei); **he burst in on us** er platzte bei uns herein
▶ **burst out** VI **(a)** **she's bursting out of that dress** sie sprengt das Kleid fast **(b)** **to burst out of a room** aus einem Zimmer stürzen **(c)** **to burst out laughing/crying** in Gelächter/Tränen ausbrechen
bury [ˈberɪ] VT **(a)** begraben; *treasure* vergraben; (= *put in earth*) *end of post, roots* eingraben; **where is he buried?** wo liegt or ist er begraben?; **to ~ sb at sea** jdn auf See bestatten (*geh*); **that's all dead and buried** (*fig*) das ist schon lange passé (*inf*); **buried by an avalanche** von einer Lawine verschüttet; **to ~ one's head in the sand** (*fig*) den Kopf in den Sand stecken **(b)** *hands, fingers* vergraben (*in* in +*dat*); *claws, teeth* schlagen (*in* in +*acc*); **to ~ one's face in one's hands** das Gesicht in den Händen vergraben; **to ~ oneself in one's books** sich in seinen Büchern vergraben
bus¹ [bʌs] **◨** N, *pl* **-es** or (*US*) **-ses** Bus *m*; **by ~** mit dem Bus **◨** VI (*inf*) mit dem Bus fahren **◨** VT (*esp US*) mit dem Bus befördern or fahren
bus² N (*Comput*) (Daten)bus *m*
bus boy N (*US*) Bedienungshilfe *f*
bus: bus conductor N Busschaffner *m*; **bus conductress** N Busschaffnerin *f*; **bus depot** N Busdepot *nt*; **bus driver** N Busfahrer(in) *m(f)*
bush [bʊʃ] N **(a)** (= *shrub*) Busch *m*, Strauch *m*; (= *thicket*: *also* **~es**) Gebüsch *nt*; **to beat about** (*Brit*) or **around the ~** (*fig*) um den heißen Brei herumreden; (= *not act etc*) wie die Katze um den heißen Brei herumschleichen **(b)** (*in Africa, Australia*) Busch *m*; (*Austral*: = *the country*) freies or offenes Land
bushel [ˈbʊʃl] N **to hide one's light under a ~** (*prov*) sein Licht unter den Scheffel stellen (*prov*)

bush: **bushfire** N Buschfeuer nt; **bush league** N (US) Provinzliga f; **bush leaguer** N (US) Provinzspieler m; (fig) Dilettant m; **bushranger** N (US, Canada) jd, der in der Wildnis lebt

bushy [ˈbʊʃɪ] ADJ (+ER) buschig

busily [ˈbɪzɪlɪ] ADV (= actively, eagerly) eifrig

business [ˈbɪznɪs] N (a) NO PL Geschäft nt; (= line of ~) Branche f; (commercial enterprise also) Betrieb m; **to be in ~** Geschäftsmann sein; **a small ~** ein kleines Unternehmen; **a family ~** ein Familienunternehmen nt; **to go into/set up in ~ with sb** mit jdm ein Geschäft gründen; **what line of ~ is she in?** was macht sie beruflich?; **to be in the publishing/ insurance ~** im Verlagswesen/der Versicherungsbranche tätig sein; **to go out of ~** zumachen; **to do ~ with sb** Geschäfte pl mit jdm machen; **"~ as usual"** (during renovation etc) das Geschäft bleibt geöffnet; **it's ~ as usual** alles geht wie gewohnt weiter; **how's ~?** wie gehen die Geschäfte?; **~ is good** die Geschäfte gehen gut; **to go to Paris on ~** geschäftlich nach Paris fahren; **he is here/away on ~** er ist geschäftlich hier/unterwegs; **to know one's ~** seine Sache verstehen; **to get down to ~** zur Sache kommen; **you shouldn't mix ~ with pleasure** man sollte Geschäftliches und Vergnügen trennen
(b) (fig inf) **now we're in ~** jetzt kanns losgehen (inf); **to mean ~** es ernst meinen
(c) (= concern, inf: = affair) Sache f; **that's my ~** das ist meine Sache; **that's no ~ of yours, that's none of your ~** das geht dich nichts an; **to make it one's ~ to do sth** es sich (dat) zur Aufgabe machen, etw zu tun; **you've no ~ doing that** du hast kein Recht, das zu tun; **moving house can be a stressful ~** ein Umzug kann ganz schön stressig sein

business: **business activity** N Geschäftstätigkeit f; **business address** N Geschäftsadresse f; **business card** N (Visiten)karte f; **business centre**, (US) **business center** N Geschäftszentrum nt; **business class** N Businessklasse f; **business college** N Wirtschaftshochschule f; **business cycle** N Konjunkturzyklus m; **business development loan** N Investitionskredit m; **business expenses** PL Spesen pl; **business hours** PL Geschäftsstunden pl; **business letter** N Geschäftsbrief m; **business license** N (US) Gewerbeschein m

businesslike [ˈbɪznɪslaɪk] ADJ (= good at doing business) geschäftstüchtig; manner geschäftsmäßig; transaction geschäftlich; (= efficient) person nüchtern

business: **businessman** N Geschäftsmann m; **business management** N Betriebswirtschaft(slehre) f; **business manager** N (for theatre) Verwaltungsdirektor(in) m(f); (of pop star etc) Manager(in) m(f); **business organization** N Unternehmensorganisation f; **business park** N Industriegelände nt; **business people** PL Geschäftsleute pl; **business plan** N Geschäftsplan m; **business practice** N Geschäftspraxis f; **business proposition** N (= proposal) Geschäftsangebot nt; (= idea) Geschäftsvorhaben nt; **business school** N Wirtschaftsschule f; **business sector** N Geschäfts- or Unternehmensbereich m; **business sense** N Geschäftssinn m; **Business Statistics Office** N (Brit) Statistisches Amt; **business studies** PL Wirtschaftslehre f; **business suit** N Straßenanzug m; **business trip** N Geschäftsreise f; **businesswoman** N Geschäftsfrau f

busing [ˈbʌsɪŋ] N = **bussing**

busk [bʌsk] VI als Straßenmusikant vor Kinos, Theatern etc spielen

busker [ˈbʌskəʳ] N Straßenmusikant m

bus: **bus lane** N Busspur f; **busload** N a **~ of children** eine Busladung Kinder; **by the ~** (inf), **in ~s** (inf) busweise (inf); **bus pass** N Seniorenkarte f für Busse; (for the disabled) Behindertenkarte f für Busse; **bus route** N Buslinie f; **we're not on a ~** wir haben keine Busverbindung; **bus service** N Busverbindung f (= network) Busverbindungen pl; **bus shelter** N Wartehäuschen nt

bussing [ˈbʌsɪŋ] N (esp US) Busbeförderung von Schulkindern in andere Bezirke, um Rassentrennung zu verhindern

bus: **bus station** N Busbahnhof m; **bus stop** N Bushaltestelle f

bust[1] [bʌst] N Büste f; (Anat) Busen m; **~ measurement** Oberweite f

bust[2] vb: pret, ptp **bust** (inf) **11** ADJ (a) (= broken) kaputt (inf) (b) (= bankrupt) pleite (inf)
2 ADV (= bankrupt) **to go ~** pleite gehen (inf)

3 N (a) (inf: also **drugs ~**) Drogenrazzia f
(b) (US: = failure) Pleite f (inf)
4 VT (a) (= break) kaputtmachen (inf)
(b) (= catch, convict) hinter Schloss und Riegel bringen; drugs ring auffliegen lassen (inf)
(c) (US Mil: = demote) degradieren (to zu)
5 VI (= break) kaputtgehen (inf)
► **bust up** VT SEP (inf) marriage kaputtmachen (inf); meeting auffliegen lassen (inf); (by starting fights) stören

buster [ˈbʌstəʳ] N (esp US inf) (as address) Meister m (inf); (threatening) Freundchen nt (inf)

-buster SUF (inf) -brecher; **sanctions-buster** Sanktionsbrecher(in) m(f); **crime-buster** Verbrechensbekämpfer(in) m(f)

bus ticket N Busfahrschein m

bustle [bʌsl] **11** N Betrieb m (of in +dat); (of fair, streets also) reges Treiben (of in +dat) **2** VI **to ~ about** geschäftig hin und her eilen (inf); **the marketplace was bustling with activity** auf dem Markt herrschte ein reges Treiben

bust-up [ˈbʌstʌp] N (inf) Krach m (inf); **they had a ~** sie haben Krach gehabt (inf); (= split up) sie haben sich verkracht (inf)

busway [ˈbʌsweɪ] N (US) Busspur f

busy [ˈbɪzɪ] **11** ADJ (+ER) (a) (= occupied) person beschäftigt; **are you ~?** haben Sie gerade Zeit?; (in business) haben Sie viel zu tun?; **I'll come back when you're less ~** ich komme wieder, wenn Sie mehr Zeit haben; **to keep sb/oneself ~** jdn/sich selbst beschäftigen; **I was ~ studying when you called** ich war gerade beim Lernen, als Sie kamen
(b) (= active) life, time bewegt; place, street belebt; (with traffic) verkehrsreich; street stark befahren; **it's been a ~ day/week** heute/diese Woche war viel los; **have you had a ~ day?** hast du heute viel zu tun gehabt?; **he leads a very ~ life** bei ihm ist immer etwas los
(c) (esp US) telephone line besetzt
(d) pattern unruhig
2 VR **to ~ oneself doing sth** sich damit beschäftigen, etw zu tun; **to ~ oneself with sth** sich mit etw beschäftigen

busybody [ˈbɪzɪˌbɒdɪ] N Wichtigtuer m

busy signal N (esp US Telec) Besetztzeichen nt

but [bʌt] **11** CONJ (a) aber; **~ you must know that ...** Sie müssen aber wissen, dass ...; **they all went – I didn't** sie sind alle gegangen, nur ich nicht; **~ then he couldn't have known that** aber er hat das ja gar nicht wissen können; **~ then you must be my brother!** dann müssen Sie ja mein Bruder sein!; **~ then it is well paid** aber dafür wird es gut bezahlt
(b) not X **~** Y nicht X sondern Y
(c) (subordinating) ohne dass; **never a week passes ~ she is ill** keine Woche vergeht, ohne dass sie krank ist
2 ADV **I cannot (help) ~ think that ...** ich kann nicht umhin zu denken, dass ...; **one cannot (help) ~ admire him/suspect that ...** man kann ihn nur bewundern/nur annehmen, dass ...; **you can ~ try** du kannst es immerhin versuchen; **I had no alternative ~ to leave** mir blieb keine andere Wahl als zu gehen
3 PREP **no one ~ me could do it** nur ich konnte es tun; **anything ~ that!** (alles,) nur das nicht!; **it was anything ~ simple** das war alles andere als einfach; **he was nothing ~ trouble** er hat nur Schwierigkeiten gemacht; **the last house ~ one/two/three** das vorletzte/vorvorletzte/drittletzte Haus; **the first ~ one** der/die/das Zweite; **the next street ~ one/two/ three** die übernächste/überübernächste Straße/vier Straßen weiter; **~ for you I would be dead** wenn Sie nicht gewesen wären, wäre ich tot; **I could definitely live in Scotland, ~ for the weather** ich könnte ganz bestimmt in Schottland leben, wenn das Wetter nicht wäre
4 N **no ~s about it** kein Aber nt

butane [ˈbjuːteɪn] N Butan nt

butcher [ˈbʊtʃəʳ] **11** N Fleischer m; **~'s (shop)** Fleischerei f; **at the ~'s** beim Fleischer **2** VT animals schlachten; people abschlachten; (fig) play, piece of music vergewaltigen

butchery [ˈbʊtʃərɪ] N (= slaughter) Gemetzel nt

butler [ˈbʌtləʳ] N Butler m

butt[1] [bʌt] N (also **~ end**) dickes Ende; (of rifle) (Gewehr)kolben m; (of cigarette) Stummel m

butt[2] N (US inf: = cigarette) Kippe f (inf)

butt[3] N (fig: = person) Zielscheibe f; **she's always the ~ of his jokes** sie ist immer (die) Zielscheibe seines Spottes

butt⁴ VT mit dem Kopf stoßen
➤ **butt in** VI sich einmischen (*on* in +*acc*)
butt⁵ N (*US inf:* = *backside*) Arsch *m* (*vulg*); **get up off your ~** setz mal deinen Arsch in Bewegung (*sl*)
butt-cheeks [ˈbʌtʃiːks] PL (*US sl:* = *buttocks*) Pobacken *pl* (*inf*)
butter [ˈbʌtə] **1** N Butter *f*; **she looks as if ~ wouldn't melt in her mouth** sie sieht aus, als ob sie kein Wässerchen trüben könnte **2** VT *bread etc* buttern
➤ **butter up** VT SEP (*inf*) um den Bart gehen (+*dat*) (*inf*)
butter: **butterball** N (*US inf:* = *fat person*) Fettkloß *m* (*inf*); **butter bean** N Mondbohne *f*; **buttercup** N Butterblume *f*; **butter dish** N Butterdose *f*
butterfly [ˈbʌtəflaɪ] N **(a)** Schmetterling *m*; **I've got/I get butterflies (in my stomach)** mir ist/wird ganz flau im Magen (*inf*) **(b)** (*Swimming*) Butterfly *m*
butter: **buttermilk** N Buttermilch *f*; **butterscotch** **1** N ≈ Karamellbonbon *m* **2** ADJ Karamell-
buttock [ˈbʌtək] N (Hinter)backe *f*; **~s** *pl* Gesäß *nt*
button [ˈbʌtn] **1** N Knopf *m*; **his answer was right on the ~** (*inf*) seine Antwort hat voll ins Schwarze getroffen (*inf*); **to push** *or* **press the right ~s** (*fig inf*) es richtig anstellen (*inf*) **2** VT *garment* zuknöpfen **3** VI (*garment*) geknöpft werden
➤ **button up** VT SEP zuknöpfen
button-down [ˈbʌtndaʊn] ADJ **~ collar** Button-down-Kragen *m*
button: **buttonhole** **1** N **(a)** (*in garment*) Knopfloch *nt* **(b)** (= *flower*) Blume *f* im Knopfloch **2** VT (*fig*) zu fassen bekommen; **button mushroom** N junger Champignon
buttress [ˈbʌtrɪs] **1** N (*Archit*) Strebepfeiler *m* **2** VT (*fig*) stützen
buxom [ˈbʌksəm] ADJ drall
buy [baɪ], *vb: pret, ptp* **bought** **1** VT **(a)** (= *purchase*) kaufen; **to ~ and sell goods** Waren an- und verkaufen **(b)** (*fig*) *victory, fame* sich (*dat*) erkaufen; *time* gewinnen; (= *bribe*) bestechen, kaufen **(c) to ~ sth** (*inf:* = *accept*) etw akzeptieren; **I'll ~ that** das ist o.k. (*inf*); (= *believe*) ja, das glaube ich **2** VI kaufen **3** N (*inf*) Kauf *m*; **to be a good ~** ein guter Kauf sein; (*food*) preiswert sein
➤ **buy back** VT SEP zurückkaufen
➤ **buy forward** VT (*Fin*) auf Termin kaufen
➤ **buy in** VT SEP *goods* einkaufen
➤ **buy into** VI +PREP OBJ (*Comm*) sich einkaufen in (+*acc*)
➤ **buy off** VT SEP (*inf:* = *bribe*) kaufen (*inf*)
➤ **buy out** VT SEP *shareholders etc* auszahlen; *firm* aufkaufen
➤ **buy up** VT SEP aufkaufen
buy-back [ˈbaɪbæk] ADJ **~ option** Rückkaufoption *f*; **~ price** Rückkaufpreis *m*; **~ agreement** (*Fin*) Wertpapier-Pensionsgeschäft *nt*
buyer [ˈbaɪə] N Käufer *m*; (= *agent*) Einkäufer *m*; **~'s market** Käufermarkt *m*
buyout [ˈbaɪaʊt] N Aufkauf *m*
buzz [bʌz] **1** VI **(a)** (*insect, device*) summen **(b) my ears are ~ing** mir dröhnen die Ohren; **my head is ~ing** (*with ideas etc*) mir schwirrt der Kopf **(c) the city was ~ing with excitement** die Stadt war in heller Aufregung **2** VT **(a)** (= *call*) *secretary* (mit dem Summer) rufen **(b)** (*US inf:* = *telephone*) anrufen **3** N **(a)** (*of conversation*) Gemurmel *nt*; **~ of excitement/anticipation** aufgeregtes/erwartungsvolles Gemurmel **(b)** (*inf:* = *telephone call*) **to give sb a ~** jdn anrufen; (= *signal*) *secretary etc* jdn (mit dem Summer) rufen **(c)** (*inf:* = *thrill*) **driving fast gives me a ~, I get a ~ from driving fast** ich verspüre einen Kitzel, wenn ich schnell fahre
➤ **buzz off** VI (*Brit inf*) abzischen (*inf*)
buzzard [ˈbʌzəd] N Bussard *m*
buzzer [ˈbʌzə] N Summer *m*
buzz word N Modewort *nt*
b/w ABBR *of* **black and white** S/W
by [baɪ] **1** PREP **(a)** (= *close to*) bei, an (+*dat*); (*with movement*) an (+*acc*); (= *next to*) neben (+*dat*); (*with movement*) neben (+*acc*); **by the window** am *or* beim Fenster; **by the church** an *or* bei der Kirche; **a holiday** (*esp Brit*) *or* **vacation** (*US*) **by the**

sea Ferien *pl* an der See; **come and sit by me** komm, setz dich neben mich; **to keep sth by one** etw bei sich haben
(b) (= *via*) über (+*acc*)
(c) (= *past*) **to rush** *etc* **by sb/sth** an jdm/etw vorbeieilen *etc*
(d) (*time:* = *during*) **by day/night** bei Tag/Nacht
(e) (*time:* = *not later than*) bis; **can you do it by tomorrow?** kannst du es bis morgen machen?; **by tomorrow I'll be in France** morgen werde ich in Frankreich sein; **by the time I got there, he had gone** bis ich dorthin kam, war er gegangen; **but by that time** *or* **by then it will be too late** aber dann ist es schon zu spät; **by now** inzwischen
(f) (*indicating amount*) **by the kilo/hour** kilo-/stundenweise; **one by one** einer nach dem anderen; **they came in two by two** sie kamen paarweise herein; **letters came in by the hundred** hunderte von Briefen kamen
(g) (*indicating agent, cause*) von; **killed by a bullet** von einer Kugel getötet; **indicated by an asterisk** durch Sternchen gekennzeichnet
(h) (*indicating method, means, manner: see also nouns*) **by bus/car/bicycle** mit dem *or* per Bus/Auto/Fahrrad; **to pay by cheque** (*Brit*) *or* **check** (*US*) mit Scheck bezahlen; **made by hand** handgearbeitet; **to know sb by name/sight** jdn dem Namen nach/vom Sehen her kennen; **to be known by the name of ...** unter dem Namen ... bekannt sein; **to lead sb by the hand** jdn an der Hand führen; **to grab sb by the collar** jdn am Kragen packen; **he had a daughter by his first wife** von seiner ersten Frau hatte er eine Tochter; **by myself/himself** *etc* allein
(i) by saving hard he managed to ... durch eisernes Sparen gelang es ihm ...; **by turning this knob** wenn Sie an diesem Knopf drehen
(j) (*according to: see also nouns*) nach; **by my watch it is nine o'clock** nach meiner Uhr ist es neun; **to call sb/sth by his/its proper name** jdn/etw beim richtigen Namen nennen; **if it's OK by you** *etc* wenn es Ihnen *etc* recht ist; **it's all right by me** von mir aus gern *or* schon
(k) (*measuring difference*) um; **broader by a foot** um einen Fuß breiter; **it missed me by inches** es verfehlte mich um Zentimeter
(l) (*Math, Measure*) **to divide/multiply by** dividieren durch/multiplizieren mit; **a room 20 feet by 30** ein Zimmer 20 mal 30 Fuß
(m) (*points of compass*) **South by South West** Südsüdwest
(n) (*in oaths*) bei; **I swear by Almighty God** ich schwöre beim allmächtigen Gott
(o) by the way *or* **by(e)** übrigens; **all this is by the way** *or* **by(e)** (= *irrelevant*) das ist alles Nebensache
2 ADV **(a)** (= *past*) **to pass/rush** *etc* **by** vorbeikommen/-eilen *etc*
(b) (= *in reserve*) **to put** *or* **lay by** beiseite legen
(c) (*phrases*) **by and by** irgendwann; (*with past tense*) nach einiger Zeit; **by and large** im Großen und Ganzen
bye [baɪ] INTERJ (*inf*) tschüs(s); **~ for now!** bis bald!
bye-bye [ˈbaɪˈbaɪ] INTERJ (*inf*) Wiedersehen (*inf*)
by(e)-election [ˈbaɪɪlekʃən] N Nachwahl *f*
bygone [ˈbaɪɡɒn] **1** ADJ längst vergangen; **in ~ days** in früheren Zeiten **2** N **to let ~s be ~s** die Vergangenheit ruhen lassen
bylaw, bye-law [ˈbaɪlɔː] N Verordnung *f* **bylaws** PL (*US: of an incorporated company*) Satzung *f*
bypass [ˈbaɪpɑːs] **1** N (= *road*) Umgehungsstraße *f*; (*Med*) Bypass *m* **2** VT *town* umgehen; (*Med*) umgehen; (*fig*) *person* übergehen; *stage* überspringen; *difficulties* umgehen
bypass: **bypass operation** N Bypassoperation *f*; **bypass surgery** N Bypasschirurgie *f*; **to have ~** sich einer Bypassoperation unterziehen
by-product [ˈbaɪprɒdʌkt] N (*lit, fig*) Nebenprodukt *nt*
bystander [ˈbaɪstændə] N Zuschauer *m*; **innocent ~** unbeteiligter Zuschauer
byte [baɪt] N (*Comput*) Byte *nt*
byword [ˈbaɪwɜːd] N **to become a ~ for sth** gleichbedeutend mit etw werden

Cc

C, c [siː] C, c nt; **C sharp** Cis nt; **C flat** Ces nt

C ABBR of **centigrade** C

c ABBR of **cent** c, ct

cab [kæb] N **(a)** (= taxi) Taxi nt **(b)** (of railway engine, lorry) Führerhaus nt

cabaret ['kæbəreɪ] N Varietee nt; (satirical) Kabarett nt

cabbage ['kæbɪdʒ] N **(a)** Kohl m **(b)** (inf: = person) geistiger Krüppel (inf)

cabby ['kæbɪ] N (inf: of taxi) Taxifahrer(in) m(f)

cab driver N Taxifahrer(in) m(f)

cabin ['kæbɪn] N **(a)** (= hut) Hütte f **(b)** (Naut) Kajüte f; (= stateroom) Kabine f **(c)** (Aviat) (for passengers) Passagierraum m; (for pilot) Cockpit nt

cabin crew N (Aviat) Flugbegleitpersonal nt; **cabin cruiser** N Kajütboot nt

cabinet ['kæbɪnɪt] N **(a)** Schränkchen nt; (for display) Vitrine f; (for TV etc) Schrank m **(b)** (Parl) Kabinett nt

cabinet: cabinet-maker N (Möbel)tischler(in) m(f); **cabinet minister** N ≈ Mitglied nt des Kabinetts, Minister(in) m(f); **cabinet reshuffle** N (Brit Pol) Kabinettsumbildung f

cable ['keɪbl] **1** N **(a)** Tau nt; (of wire) Kabel nt **(b)** (Elec) Kabel nt, Leitung f **(c)** (= ~gram) Telegramm nt; **by** ~ per Telegramm/Kabel **(d)** (= television) Kabelfernsehen nt **2** VT information telegrafisch durchgeben; **to** ~ **sb** jdm telegrafieren/kabeln

cable: cable car N (hanging) Drahtseilbahn f; (= funicular) Standseilbahn f; **cable railway** N Bergbahn f; **cable television** N Kabelfernsehen nt

caboodle [kə'buːdl] N (inf) **the whole (kit and)** ~ das ganze Zeug(s) (inf), der ganze Kram (inf)

caboose [kə'buːs] N (US Rail) Dienstwagen m

cacao [kə'kɑːəʊ] N (= tree, bean) Kakao m

cache [kæʃ] N **(a)** Versteck nt **(b)** (Comput: also ~ **memory**) Zwischenspeicher m

cachet ['kæʃeɪ] N Gütesiegel nt; **the name has a certain** ~ **on the French market** der Name gilt auf dem französischen Markt als Gütezeichen

cack-handed ['kæk'hændəd] ADJ (Brit inf) tollpatschig (inf)

cackle ['kækl] **1** N (of hens) Gackern nt; (= laughter) (meckerndes) Lachen **2** VI (hens) gackern; (= laugh) meckernd lachen

cacophony [kæ'kɒfənɪ] N Kakophonie f (geh)

cactus ['kæktəs] N Kaktus m

CAD [kæd] ABBR of **computer-aided design** CAD

cadaver [kə'dævəʳ] N Kadaver m; (of humans) Leiche f

cadaverous [kə'dævərəs] ADJ (= gaunt) ausgezehrt; (= pale) leichenblass

CAD/CAM ['kæd'kæm] ABBR of **computer-aided design/ computer-aided manufacture** CAD/CAM

caddie ['kædɪ] (Golf) **1** N Caddie m **2** VI Caddie sein

caddy ['kædɪ] N **(a)** (= tea) Büchse f **(b)** (US: = shopping trolley) Einkaufswagen m **(c)** = **caddie 1**

cadence ['keɪdəns] N (Mus) Kadenz f; (of voice) Tonfall m; (= rhythm) Rhythmus m

cadenza [kə'denzə] N (Mus) Kadenz f

cadet [kə'det] N (Mil etc) Kadett m

cadge [kædʒ] VTI schnorren (inf) (from sb bei or von jdm); **could I ~ a lift with you?** könnten Sie mich vielleicht (ein Stück) mitnehmen?

cadre ['kædrɪ] N (Mil, fig) Kader m

Caesar ['siːzəʳ] N Cäsar m

Caesarean, (US) **Cesarean** [siː'zɛərɪən] N (Med: also ~ **section**) Kaiserschnitt m; **she had a (baby by)** ~ sie hatte einen Kaiserschnitt

Caesarian, (US) **Cesarian** [siː'zɛərɪən] N = **Caesarean**

café ['kæfeɪ] N Café nt

café bar N Cafébar f

cafeteria [kæfɪ'tɪərɪə] N Cafeteria f

cafetière [kæfə'tjeəʳ] N Kaffeebereiter m

caff [kæf] N (Brit inf) Café nt

caffein(e) ['kæfiːn] N Koffein nt

caftan ['kæftæn] N Kaftan m

cage [keɪdʒ] **1** N **(a)** Käfig m; (= small birdcage) Bauer nt or m; ~ **bird** Käfigvogel m **(b)** (of lift) Aufzug m; (Min) Förderkorb m **2** VT (also ~ **up**) in einen Käfig sperren, einsperren

cagey ['keɪdʒɪ] ADJ (inf) vorsichtig; (= evasive) ausweichend; **what are you being so ~ about?** warum tust du so geheimnisvoll?; **he was very ~ about his plans** er hat mit seinen Absichten hinterm Berg gehalten

cagily ['keɪdʒɪlɪ] ADV (inf) vorsichtig; (= evasively) ausweichend

cagoule [kə'guːl] N Windhemd nt

cahoots [kə'huːts] N (inf) **to be in ~ with sb** mit jdm unter einer Decke stecken

cairn [kɛən] N Steinpyramide f

Cairo ['kaɪərəʊ] N Kairo nt

cajole [kə'dʒəʊl] VT gut zureden (+dat); **to ~ sb into doing sth** jdn dazu bringen, etw zu tun

cake [keɪk] **1** N **(a)** Kuchen m; (= gateau) Torte f; (= bun, individual ~) Gebäckstück nt; **a piece of ~** (fig inf) ein Kinderspiel nt, ein Klacks m (inf); **to sell like hot ~s** weggehen wie warme Semmeln (inf); **you can't have your ~ and eat it** (prov) beides auf einmal geht nicht **2** VT **my shoes are ~d with** or **in mud** meine Schuhe sind völlig verdreckt or dreckverkrustet

cake: cake mix N Backmischung f; **cake mixture** N Kuchenteig m; **cake pan** N (US) Kuchenform f; **cake shop** N Konditorei f; **cake tin** N (Brit) (for baking) Kuchenform f; (for storage) Kuchenbüchse f

calamine lotion ['kæləmaɪnˌləʊʃən] N Galmeilotion f

calamitous [kə'læmɪtəs] ADJ katastrophal

calamity [kə'læmɪtɪ] N Katastrophe f

calcium ['kælsɪəm] N Kalzium nt

calculable ['kælkjʊləbl] ADJ berechenbar, kalkulierbar

calculate ['kælkjʊleɪt] **1** VT **(a)** berechnen **(b)** (fig: = estimate critically) kalkulieren, schätzen **(c)** **to be ~d to do sth** (= be intended) auf etw (acc) abzielen; (= have the effect) zu etw angetan sein **(d)** (US inf: = suppose) schätzen **2** VI (Math) rechnen

➤ **calculate on** VI +PREP OBJ rechnen mit

calculated ['kælkjʊleɪtɪd] ADJ (= deliberate) berechnet; **a ~ risk** ein kalkuliertes Risiko

calculating ['kælkjʊleɪtɪŋ] ADJ berechnend

calculation [kælkjʊ'leɪʃən] N Berechnung f, Kalkulation f; (= critical estimation) Schätzung f; **you've got this all ~s** du hast dich verrechnet; **by my ~s he will arrive on Sunday** nach meiner Schätzung müsste er Sonntag ankommen

calculator ['kælkjʊleɪtəʳ] N (= machine) Rechner m

calculus ['kælkjʊləs] N (Math) Infinitesimalrechnung f

calendar ['kæləndəʳ] N **(a)** Kalender m **(b)** (= schedule) Terminkalender m; ~ **of events** Veranstaltungskalender m

calendar month N Kalendermonat m

calf¹ [kɑːf] N, pl **calves (a)** Kalb nt; **a cow in** or **with** ~ eine trächtige Kuh **(b)** (= young elephant, seal etc) Junge(s) nt **(c)** (= leather) Kalb(s)leder nt

calf² N, pl **calves** (Anat) Wade f

calfskin ['kɑːfskɪn] N Kalb(s)leder nt

caliber (US) = **calibre**

calibration [kælɪ'breɪʃən] N (= mark) Eichung f

calibre, (US) **caliber** ['kælɪbəʳ] N (lit, fig) Kaliber nt

calico ['kælɪkəʊ] N Kattun m

California [kælɪ'fɔːnɪə] N (abbr **Cal(if)**) Kalifornien nt

Californian [kælɪ'fɔːnɪən] ADJ kalifornisch

calipers ['kælɪpəz] PL (US) = **callipers**

calisthenics [kælɪs'θenɪks] N (US) = **callisthenics**

call [kɔːl] **1** N **(a)** (= shout, cry) (of person, bird etc) Ruf m; (of bugle) Signal nt; **to give sb a** ~ jdn (herbei)rufen; (= inform sb) jdm Bescheid sagen; (= wake sb) jdn wecken; **a ~ for help** (lit, fig) ein Hilferuf m
(b) (= telephone ~) Gespräch nt; **to give sb a** ~ jdn anrufen;

to take a ~ ein Gespräch entgegennehmen; **will you take the ~?** nehmen Sie das Gespräch an?
(c) (= *summons*) (*for flight, meal etc*) Aufruf *m*; (*fig:* = *lure*) Ruf *m*; **to be on ~** Bereitschaftsdienst haben; **he acted above and beyond the ~ of duty** er handelte über die bloße Pflichterfüllung hinaus
(d) (= *visit*) Besuch *m*; **to pay a ~ on sb** jdn besuchen; **I have several ~s to make** ich muss noch einige Besuche machen
(e) (= *demand, claim*) Inanspruchnahme *f*; (*Comm*) Nachfrage *f* (*for* nach); **to have many ~s on one's purse/time** finanziell/zeitlich sehr in Anspruch genommen sein; **to have first ~ on sth** ein Vorrecht *nt* auf etw (*acc*) haben
(f) (= *need*) Grund *m*, Veranlassung *f*; **there is no ~ for you to worry** es besteht kein Grund zur Sorge, Sie brauchen sich (*dat*) keine Sorgen zu machen
(g) (*Cards*) Ansage *f*; **whose ~ is it?** wer sagt an?
(h) (*Tennis*) Entscheidung *f*; **it's our/your ~** das ist unsere/eure Entscheidung
2 VT **(a)** (= *shout out, summon*) rufen; *meeting* einberufen; *elections* ausschreiben; *strike* ausrufen; (*Jur*) *witness* aufrufen; (= *subpoena*) vorladen; (= *waken*) wecken; **the landlord ~ed time** der Wirt rief „Feierabend"; **to ~ spades** (*Cards*) Pik reizen; **the ball was ~ed out** der Ball wurde für „aus" erklärt
(b) (= *name, consider*) nennen; **to be ~ed** heißen; **what's he ~ed?** wie heißt er?; **what do you ~ your cat?** wie heißt deine Katze?; **she ~s me lazy** sie nennt mich faul; **what's this ~ed in German?** wie heißt das auf Deutsch?; **let's ~ it a day** machen wir Schluss für heute; **~ it £5** sagen wir £ 5
(c) (= *telephone*) anrufen; (= *contact by radio*) rufen
(d) (*US Sport*: ~ = *off*) abbrechen
3 VI **(a)** (= *shout: person, animal*) rufen; **to ~ for help** um Hilfe rufen; **to ~ to sb** jdm zurufen
(b) (= *visit*) vorbeikommen; **she ~ed to see her mother** sie machte einen Besuch bei ihrer Mutter; **the gasman ~ed to read the meter** der Gasmann kam, um die Gasuhr abzulesen
(c) (*Telec*) anrufen; (*by radio*) rufen; **who's ~ing, please?** wer spricht da bitte?; **thanks for ~ing** vielen Dank für den Anruf
➤ **call (a)round** VI (*inf*) vorbeikommen
➤ **call at** VI +PREP OBJ (*person*) vorbeigehen bei; (*Rail*) halten in (+*dat*); (*Naut*) anlaufen; **a train for Lisbon calling at ...** ein Zug nach Lissabon über ...
➤ **call away** VT SEP wegrufen; **I was called away on business** ich wurde geschäftlich abgerufen; **he was called away from the meeting** er wurde aus der Sitzung gerufen
➤ **call back** VTI SEP zurückrufen
➤ **call down** VT SEP **to call sb down** (*US:* = *reprimand*) jdn ausschimpfen
➤ **call for** VI +PREP OBJ **(a)** (= *send for*) *person* rufen; *food, drink* kommen lassen; (= *ask for*) verlangen (nach), fordern **(b)** (= *need*) *courage* verlangen; **that calls for a drink!** darauf muss ich/müssen wir einen trinken!; **that calls for a celebration!** das muss gefeiert werden! **(c)** (= *collect*) abholen; **"to be called for"** (*goods*) (*sent by rail*) „bahnlagernd"; (*sent by post*) „postlagernd"; (*in shop*) „wird abgeholt"
➤ **call in 1** VT SEP *doctor* zurate ziehen **2** (= *visit*) vorbeigehen (*at, on* bei)
➤ **call off** VT SEP **(a)** (= *cancel*) *appointment, holiday, strike* absagen; *deal* rückgängig machen; (= *end*) abbrechen; *engagement* lösen **(b)** *dog* zurückrufen
➤ **call on** VI +PREP OBJ **(a)** (= *visit*) besuchen **(b)** = **call upon**
➤ **call out 1** VI rufen, schreien **2** VT SEP **(a)** *names* aufrufen; (= *announce*) ansagen **(b)** *doctor* rufen; *fire brigade* alarmieren **(c)** (= *order to strike*) zum Streik aufrufen
➤ **call out for** VI +PREP OBJ *food* verlangen; *help* rufen um
➤ **call up 1** VT SEP **(a)** (*Brit Mil*) *reservist* einberufen; *reinforcements* mobilisieren **(b)** (*Sport*) berufen (*to* in +*acc*) **(c)** (*Telec*) anrufen **(d)** (*fig*) (herauf)beschwören; *memories also* wachrufen **2** VI (*Telec*) anrufen
➤ **call upon** VI +PREP OBJ **(a)** (= *ask*) **to call upon sb to do sth** jdn bitten, etw zu tun **(b)** (= *invoke*) **to call upon sb's generosity** an jds Großzügigkeit (*acc*) appellieren
call: callback N (*Comm:* = *action*) Rückrufaktion *f*; **there were 1,000 ~s** 1.000 wurden zurückbeordert; **call box** N (*Brit*) Telefonzelle *f*; **call centre** N (*Brit*) Callcenter *nt*
caller ['kɔːlər] N **(a)** (= *visitor*) Besuch *m*, Besucher(in) *m(f)* **(b)** (*Telec*) Anrufer(in) *m(f)*
call forwarding N (*Telec*) Anrufweiterschaltung *f*

callgirl ['kɔːlgɜːl] N Callgirl *nt*
calligraphy [kə'lɪɡrəfɪ] N Kalligrafie *f*
calling ['kɔːlɪŋ] N Berufung *f*
calling card N Visitenkarte *f*
callipers, (*US*) **calipers** ['kælɪpəz] PL Tastzirkel *m*
callisthenics, (*US*) **calisthenics** [ˌkælɪs'θenɪks] N SING *or* PL Gymnastik *f*
callous ADJ, **callously** ADV ['kæləs, -lɪ] herzlos
callousness ['kæləsnɪs] N Herzlosigkeit *f*
call-out charge, call-out fee ['kɔːlaʊt-] N Anfahrtkosten *pl*
callow ['kæləʊ] ADJ unreif; **a ~ youth** ein grüner Junge (*inf*)
call: call-up N (*Brit*) (*Mil*) Einberufung *f*; (*Sport*) Berufung *f* (*to* in +*acc*); **call-up papers** PL (*Brit Mil*) Einberufungsbescheid *m*
callus ['kæləs] N (*Med*) Schwiele *f*
call waiting N (*Telec*) Anklopffunktion *f*
calm [kɑːm] **1** ADJ (+ER) ruhig; **keep ~!** bleib ruhig!; **(cool,) ~ and collected** ruhig und gelassen **2** N Ruhe *f*; (*at sea*) Flaute *f*; (*of wind*) Windstille *f*; **the ~ before the storm** (*lit, fig*) die Ruhe vor dem Sturm **3** VT beruhigen; *pain* lindern; *protests* mildern; **to ~ sb's fears** jdn beruhigen
➤ **calm down 1** VT SEP beruhigen **2** VI sich beruhigen; (*wind*) abflauen
calming ['kɑːmɪŋ] ADJ beruhigend
calmly ['kɑːmlɪ] ADV ruhig
calmness ['kɑːmnɪs] N (*of person*) Ruhe *f*; (*of wind, sea*) Stille *f*
Calor Gas® ['kæləɡæs] N Butangas *nt*
calorie ['kælərɪ] N Kalorie *f*; **low on ~s** kalorienarm
calorie IN CPDS Kalorien-, kalorien-; **calorie-conscious** ADJ kalorienbewusst
calumny ['kæləmnɪ] N (*liter*) Schmähung *f* (*geh*)
calve [kɑːv] VI kalben
calves [kɑːvz] PL *of* **calf**[1], **calf**[2]
Calvinist ['kælvɪnɪst] **1** N Kalvinist(in) *m(f)* **2** ADJ kalvinistisch
calypso [kə'lɪpsəʊ] N Calypso *m*
CAM [kæm] ABBR *of* **computer-aided manufacture** CAM
camaraderie [ˌkæmə'rɑːdərɪ] N Kameradschaft *f*
Cambodia [kæm'bəʊdɪə] N Kambodscha *nt*
Cambodian [kæm'bəʊdɪən] **1** ADJ kambodschanisch **2** N Kambodschaner(in) *m(f)*
camcorder ['kæmkɔːdər] N Camcorder *m*
came [keɪm] PRET *of* **come**
camel ['kæməl] **1** N Kamel *nt* **2** ATTR (= *colour*) *coat* kamelhaarfarben
camelhair ['kæməlheər] ADJ ATTR **~ coat** Kamelhaarmantel *m*
camellia [kə'miːlɪə] N Kamelie *f*
cameo ['kæmɪəʊ] N **(a)** (= *jewellery*) Kamee *f* **(b)** (*Liter*) Miniatur *f* **(c)** (*also* ~ **part**) Miniaturrolle *f*
camera[1] ['kæmərə] N Kamera *f*; (*for stills also*) Fotoapparat *m*
camera[2] N (*Jur*) **in ~** unter Ausschluss der Öffentlichkeit
camera: camera crew N Kamerateam *nt*; **cameraman** N Kameramann *m*; **camera-shy** ADJ kamerascheu; **camerawork** N Kameraführung *f*
camisole ['kæmɪsəʊl] N Mieder *nt*, Leibchen *nt*
camomile ['kæməʊmaɪl] N Kamille *f*; **~ tea** Kamillentee *m*
camouflage ['kæməflɑːʒ] **1** N Tarnung *f*; **for ~** zur Tarnung **2** VT (*Mil, fig*) tarnen
camp[1] [kæmp] **1** N (*lit, fig*) Lager *nt*; **to be in ~** im Lager leben *or* sein; (*Mil*) im Felde leben; **to pitch ~** Zelte *or* ein Lager aufschlagen; **to strike** *or* **break ~** das Lager *or* die Zelte abbrechen; **to have a foot in both ~s** mit beiden Seiten zu tun haben **2** VI (*Tent*) zelten; (*Mil*) lagern; **to go ~ing** zelten (gehen)
➤ **camp out** VI zelten
camp[2] ADJ (= *theatrical*) maniert; (= *effeminate*) tuntenhaft (*inf*); (= *homosexual*) schwul (*inf*)
➤ **camp up** VT SEP **to camp it up** (*Theat*) es übertreiben; (= *act homosexually*) sich tuntenhaft benehmen (*inf*)
campaign [kæm'peɪn] **1** N **(a)** (*Mil*) Feldzug *m* **(b)** (*fig*) Kampagne *f* **2** VI **(a)** (*Mil*) Krieg führen **(b)** (*fig*) (*for* für, *against* gegen) sich einsetzen; (*candidate*) im Wahlkampf stehen; (*supporters*) Wahlwerbung treiben
campaigner [kæm'peɪnər] N (*for sth*) Befürworter(in) *m(f)* (*for* +*gen*); (*against sth*) Gegner(in) *m(f)* (*against* +*gen*); (*for politician*) Wahlwerber(in) *m(f)*

camp bed N (*Brit*) Campingliege *f*
camper ['kæmpə'] N **(a)** Camper(in) *m(f)* **(b)** (= *vehicle: also* ~ **van**) Wohnmobil *nt*
camper van N Wohnmobil *nt*
camp: **campfire** N Lagerfeuer *nt*; **campground** N (*US*) Campingplatz *m*
camping ['kæmpɪŋ] N Camping *nt*
camping IN CPDS Camping-; **camping gas** N (*US*) Campinggas *nt*; **camping site** N Campingplatz *m*
camp: **camp meeting** N (*US Rel*) Campmeeting *nt*; **camp site** N Campingplatz *m*
campus ['kæmpəs] N Campus *m*
camshaft ['kæmʃɑːft] N Nockenwelle *f*
can¹ [kæn], *pret* **could** MODAL AUX VB (*defective parts supplied by to be able to*) können; (= *may*) dürfen, können; ~ **you come tomorrow?** kannst du morgen kommen?; **I ~'t** *or* ~**not go to the theatre tomorrow** ich kann morgen nicht ins Theater (gehen); **he'll help you all he** ~ er wird tun, was in seinen Kräften steht; **as soon as it** ~ **be arranged** sobald es sich machen lässt; **could you tell me …** können *or* könnten Sie mir sagen, …; ~ **you speak German?** können *or* sprechen Sie Deutsch?; ~ **I come too?** kann ich mitkommen?; ~ *or* **could I take some more?** darf ich mir noch etwas nehmen?; **how ~I could you say such a thing!** wie können/konnten Sie nur *or* bloß so etwas sagen!; **where** ~ **it be?** wo kann das bloß sein?; **you** ~'**t be serious** das kann doch wohl nicht dein Ernst sein; **it could be that he's got lost** vielleicht hat er sich verlaufen; **to think he could have become a doctor** wenn man bedenkt, dass er hätte Arzt werden können; **you could try telephoning him** Sie könnten ihn ja mal anrufen; **you could have told me** das hätten Sie mir auch sagen können; **we could do with some new furniture** wir könnten neue Möbel gebrauchen; **I could do with a drink now** ich könnte jetzt etwas zu trinken vertragen; **this room could do with a coat of paint** das Zimmer könnte mal wieder gestrichen werden; **he looks as though he could do with a haircut** ich glaube, er müsste sich (*dat*) mal wieder die Haare schneiden lassen
can² N **(a)** (= *container*) Kanister *m*; (*esp US*: = *garbage* ~) (Müll)eimer *m*; **to carry the** ~ (*Brit fig inf*) die Sache ausbaden (*inf*) **(b)** (= *tin*) Dose *f*; **a** ~ **of beer** eine Dose Bier; **a beer** ~ eine Bierdose **(c)** (*US inf*: = *prison*) Knast *m* (*inf*) **(d)** (*US inf*: = *lavatory*) Klo *nt* (*inf*) **②** VT *foodstuffs* einmachen
Canada ['kænədə] N Kanada *nt*
Canadian [kə'neɪdɪən] **①** ADJ kanadisch **②** N Kanadier(in) *m(f)*
Canadian elk N Wapiti(hirsch) *m*
canal [kə'næl] N Kanal *m*
canapé ['kænəpeɪ] N Appetithappen *m*
Canaries [kə'nɛərɪz] PL = **Canary Isles**
canary [kə'nɛərɪ] N Kanarienvogel *m*
Canary Isles [kə'nɛərɪ'aɪlz] PL Kanarische Inseln *pl*
canasta [kə'næstə] N Canasta *nt*
cancan ['kænkæn] N Cancan *m*
cancel ['kænsəl] **①** VT **(a)** (= *call off*) absagen; (*officially*) stornieren; *plans* aufgeben, fallen lassen; *train, bus* streichen; **the last train has been** ~**led** (*Brit*) *or* ~**ed** (*US*) der letzte Zug fällt aus
(b) (= *revoke, annul*) rückgängig machen; *contract also* (auf)lösen; *debt* streichen; *order* stornieren; *subscription* kündigen
(c) (= *frank*) *stamp, ticket* entwerten
(d) (*Math*) kürzen; **this X ~s that one** dieses X hebt das X auf **②** VI (= *revoke order, contract*) stornieren; (= *call off appointment, holiday*) absagen
➤ **cancel out** VT SEP (*Math*) aufheben; (*fig*) zunichte machen; **to cancel each other out** (*Math*) sich aufheben; (*fig*) sich gegenseitig aufheben
cancellation [ˌkænsə'leɪʃən] N **(a)** (= *calling off*) Absage *f*; (*official*) Stornierung *f*; (*of plans*) Aufgabe *f*; (*of train, bus*) Streichung *f* **(b)** (= *annulment*) Rückgängigmachung *f*; (*of contract also*) Auflösung *f*; (*of debt*) Streichung *f*; (*of order*) Stornierung *f*; (*of subscription*) Kündigung *f*
cancer ['kænsə'] N (*Med*) Krebs *m*; (*fig*) Krebsgeschwür *nt*; ~ **of the throat** Kehlkopfkrebs *m*; **Cancer** (*Astrol*) Krebs *m*; **he's a** ~ **Cancer** er ist Krebs
cancerous ['kænsərəs] ADJ krebsartig
cancer research N Krebsforschung *f*

candelabra [ˌkændɪ'lɑːbrə] N Kandelaber *m*
candid ['kændɪd] ADJ offen, ehrlich
candidacy ['kændɪdəsɪ] N Kandidatur *f*
candidate ['kændɪdeɪt] N Kandidat(in) *m(f)*; **to stand as (a)** ~ kandidieren; **the obese are prime ~s for heart disease** Fettleibige stehen auf der Liste der Herzinfarktkandidaten ganz oben
candidature ['kændɪdətʃə'] N (*Brit*) = **candidacy**
candidly ['kændɪdlɪ] ADV offen, ehrlich; **quite ~, …** offen gestanden, …; **to speak** ~ offen *or* ehrlich sein
candied ['kændɪd] ADJ (*Cook*) kandiert; ~ **peel** (*of lemon*) Zitronat *nt*; (*of orange*) Orangeat *nt*
candle ['kændl] N Kerze *f*; **to burn the** ~ **at both ends** mit seinen Kräften Raubbau treiben; **he can't hold a** ~ **to his brother** er kann seinem Bruder nicht das Wasser reichen
candle IN CPDS Kerzen-; **candlelight** N Kerzenlicht *nt*, Kerzenschein *m*; **by** ~ im Kerzenschein; **a** ~ **dinner** ein Essen *nt* bei Kerzenlicht
candlestick ['kændlstɪk] N Kerzenhalter *m*
candour, (*US*) **candor** ['kændə'] N Offenheit *f*, Ehrlichkeit *f*
candy ['kændɪ] N (*US*) (= *sweet*) Bonbon *m or nt*; (= *sweets*) Süßigkeiten *pl*, Bonbons *pl*; (= *bar of chocolate*) (Tafel *f*) Schokolade *f*; (= *individual chocolate*) Praline *f*; **it's like taking** ~ **from a baby** das ist kinderleicht
candy: **candy-ass** N (*US sl*) Weichei *nt* (*pej inf*); **candy bar** N (*US*) Schokoladenriegel *m*; **candyfloss** N (*Brit*) Zuckerwatte *f*; **candy store** N (*US*) Süßwarenhandlung *f*
cane [keɪn] **①** N **(a)** (= *stem of bamboo, sugar etc*) Rohr *nt*; (*for supporting plants*) Stock *m*; ~ **chair** Rohrstuhl *m* **(b)** (= *walking stick*) (Spazier)stock *m*; (= *instrument of punishment*) (Rohr)stock *m*; **to get the** ~ Prügel bekommen **②** VT *schoolboy* mit dem Stock schlagen
cane IN CPDS Rohr-; **cane sugar** N Rohrzucker *m*
canine ['keɪnaɪn] **①** N **(a)** (= *animal*) Hund *m* **(b)** (*also* ~ **tooth**) Eckzahn *m* **②** ADJ Hunde-
canister ['kænɪstə'] N Behälter *m*; (*for tea etc also*) Dose *f*
canker ['kæŋkə'] N (*fig*) (Krebs)geschwür *nt*
cannabis ['kænəbɪs] N Cannabis *m*
canned [kænd] ADJ **(a)** (*US*) Dosen-, in Dosen; ~ **beer** Dosenbier *nt*; ~ **goods** Konserven *pl* **(b)** (*inf*) ~ **music** Musikberieselung *f* (*inf*); ~ **laughter** Gelächter *nt* vom Band **(c)** (*inf*: = *drunk*) blau (*inf*), voll (*sl*)
cannery ['kænərɪ] N (*US*) Konservenfabrik *f*
cannibal ['kænɪbəl] N (= *person*) Kannibale *m*, Kannibalin *f*
cannibalism ['kænɪbəlɪzəm] N (*of people*) Kannibalismus *m*
cannibalize ['kænɪbəlaɪz] VT *old car etc* ausschlachten
cannily ['kænɪlɪ] ADV clever, raffiniert
cannon ['kænən] N (*Mil*) Kanone *f*
➤ **cannon into** VI +PREP OBJ zusammenprallen mit
cannon: **cannonball** N Kanonenkugel *f*; **cannon fodder** N Kanonenfutter *nt*
cannot ['kænɒt] NEG *of* **can¹**
canny ['kænɪ] ADJ (+ER) (= *cautious*) vorsichtig; (= *shrewd also*) clever
canoe [kə'nuː] **①** N Kanu *nt* **②** VI Kanu fahren
canoeing [kə'nuːɪŋ] N Kanusport *m*
canon¹ ['kænən] N (*all senses*) Kanon *m*
canon² N (= *priest*) Kanoniker *m*
cañon (*US*) = **canyon**
canonize ['kænənaɪz] VT (*Eccl*) heilig sprechen
canon law N (*Eccl*) kanonisches Recht
canoodle [kə'nuːdl] VI (*Brit inf*) rumschmusen (*inf*)
can-opener ['kæn,əʊpnə'] N Dosenöffner *m*
canopy ['kænəpɪ] N (= *awning*) Markise *f*; (*over entrance*) Pergola *f*; (*of bed, throne*) Baldachin *m*
cant [kænt] N (= *hypocrisy*) Heuchelei *f*
can't [kɑːnt] CONTR *of* **can not**
cantaloup(e) ['kæntəluːp] N Honigmelone *f*
cantankerous [kæn'tæŋkərəs] ADJ mürrisch, knurrig
cantata [kæn'tɑːtə] N Kantate *f*
canteen [kæn'tiːn] N **(a)** (= *restaurant*) Kantine *f*; (*in university*) Mensa *f* **(b)** (*Mil*: = *flask*) Feldflasche *f* **(c)** (*Brit*: *of cutlery*) Besteckkasten *m*

canter ['kæntə^r] **1** N Kanter *m* **2** VI langsam galoppieren

canton ['kæntɒn] N Kanton *m*

Cantonese [kæntə'ni:z] **1** ADJ kantonesisch **2** N
(a) Kantonese *m*, Kantonesin *f* (b) (*Ling*) Kantonesisch *nt*

Canuck [kə'nʌk] N (*US pej inf*) (Franko)kanadier(in) *m(f)*

canvas ['kænvəs] N Leinwand *f*; (*for sails*) Segeltuch *nt*; (*for tent*)
Zeltbahn *f*; (*Art*) (= *material*) Leinwand *f*; (= *painting*)
Gemälde *nt*; **under ~** (= *in a tent*) im Zelt; **~ shoes**
Segeltuchschuhe *pl*

canvass ['kænvəs] **1** VT (a) (*Pol*) *district* Wahlwerbung machen
in (+*dat*); *person* für seine Partei zu gewinnen suchen
(b) *customers, citizens etc* ansprechen, werben; *district*
bereisen; *opinions* erforschen **2** VI (a) (*Pol*) um Stimmen
werben (b) (*Comm*) werben

canvasser ['kænvəsə^r] N (a) (*Pol*) Wahlhelfer(in) *m(f)*
(b) (*Comm*) Vertreter(in) *m(f)*

canvassing ['kænvəsɪŋ] N (a) (*Pol*) Wahlwerbung *f* (b) (*Comm*)
Klinkenputzen *nt* (*inf*)

canyon, (*US*) **cañon** ['kænjən] N Cañon *m*

CAP ABBR *of* **Common Agricultural Policy** GAP *f*

cap¹ [kæp] **1** N (a) (= *hat*) Mütze *f*; (= *soldier's ~ also*) Käppi *nt*;
(= *nurse's ~*) Haube *f*; (*Jur, Univ*) Barett *nt*; (*for swimming*)
Badekappe *f*; **~ in hand** kleinlaut; **if the ~ fits(, wear it)** (*Brit
prov*) wem die Jacke passt(, der soll sie sich (*dat*) anziehen)
(b) (*Brit Sport*) **he has won 50 ~s for Scotland** er ist 50 Mal mit
der schottischen Mannschaft angetreten
(c) (= *lid, cover*) Verschluss *m*; (*of fountain pen, valve*) Kappe *f*
(d) (= *contraceptive*) Pessar *nt*
(e) (= *explosive*) Platzpatrone *f*; (*for toy gun*) Zündplättchen *nt*
2 VT (a) **to have one's teeth ~ped** sich (*dat*) die Zähne
überkronen lassen
(b) (*Sport*) **he was ~ped four times for England** er wurde
viermal für die englische Nationalmannschaft aufgestellt
(c) (= *do or say better*) überbieten; **and then to ~ it all ...** und,
um dem Ganzen die Krone aufzusetzen ...
(d) (*in spending etc*) **they ~ped spending at £50,000** die
Ausgaben wurden bei £ 50.000 gedeckelt; **the council was
~ped** (*Brit*) dem Stadtrat wurde von der Regierung ein
Höchstsatz für die Kommunalsteuer *etc* auferlegt

cap² N (*Typ inf*) großer Buchstabe; **in ~s** in Großbuchstaben;
see also **capital**

capability [keɪpə'bɪlɪtɪ] N (a) Fähigkeit *f*; **sth is within sb's
capabilities** jd ist zu etw fähig; **sth is beyond sb's capabilities**
etw übersteigt jds Fähigkeiten (b) (*Mil*) Potenzial *nt*

capable ['keɪpəbl] ADJ (a) kompetent (b) **to be ~ of doing sth**
etw tun können; **to be ~ of sth** etw können, zu etw fähig
sein; **it's ~ of speeds of up to ...** es erreicht
Geschwindigkeiten bis zu ...

capably ['keɪpəblɪ] ADV kompetent

capacious [kə'peɪʃəs] ADJ geräumig; *dress* weit

capacity [kə'pæsɪtɪ] N (a) (= *cubic content etc*) Fassungsvermögen *nt*, (Raum)inhalt *m*; (= *maximum output*) Kapazität
f; (= *maximum weight*) Tragfähigkeit *f*; **seating ~ of 400** 400
Sitzplätze; **working at full ~** voll ausgelastet; **the Stones
played to ~ audiences** die Stones spielten vor ausverkauften
Sälen
(b) (= *ability*) Fähigkeit *f*; **his ~ for learning** seine
Aufnahmefähigkeit
(c) (= *role*) Eigenschaft *f*; **speaking in his official ~ as mayor,
he said ...** er sagte in seiner Eigenschaft als Bürgermeister ...

cape¹ [keɪp] N Cape *nt*

cape² N (*Geog*) Kap *nt*

Cape: Cape Horn N Kap *nt* Hoorn; **Cape of Good Hope** N Kap
nt der guten Hoffnung

caper¹ ['keɪpə^r] **1** VI herumtollen **2** N (a) (= *prank*) Eskapade *f*
(b) (*inf*: = *crime*) Ding *nt* (*sl*)

caper² N (*Bot, Cook*) Kaper *f*

Cape Town N Kapstadt *nt*

capful ['kæpfʊl] N **one ~ to one litre of water** eine
Verschlusskappe auf einen Liter Wasser

capillary [kə'pɪlərɪ] N Kapillare *f*

capital ['kæpɪtl] **1** N (a) (*also ~* **city**) Hauptstadt *f*; (*fig*:
= *centre*) Zentrum *nt*
(b) (*also ~* **letter**) Großbuchstabe *m*; **small ~s** Kapitälchen *pl*
(*spec*); **please write in ~s** bitte in Blockschrift schreiben!
(c) NO PL (*Fin, fig*: = *knowledge, skill*) Kapital *nt*; **to make ~ out**

of sth (*fig*) aus etw Kapital schlagen
2 ADJ (a) *letter* Groß-; **love with a ~ L** die große Liebe
(b) (= *major*) **of ~ importance** von größter Bedeutung
(c) (*Jur*) Kapital-

capital IN CPDS Kapital-; **capital allowance** N Abschreibung *f*;
capital expenditure N Kapitalaufwendungen *pl*; **capital
flight** N (*Fin*) Kapitalflucht *f*; **capital gains tax** N
Kapitalertragssteuer *f*; **capital investment** N Kapitalanlage *f*

capitalism ['kæpɪtəlɪzəm] N Kapitalismus *m*

capitalist ['kæpɪtəlɪst] **1** N Kapitalist(in) *m(f)* **2** ADJ
kapitalistisch

capitalization [kæpɪtəlaɪ'zeɪʃən] N (*Fin*) Kapitalisierung *f*; **~
issue** (*Brit St Ex*) Ausgabe *f* von Gratisaktien

capitalize ['kæpɪtəlaɪz] VT (*Fin*) kapitalisieren
➤ **capitalize on** VI +PREP (*fig*) Kapital schlagen aus

capital: capital market N Kapitalmarkt *m*; **capital offence** N
Kapitalverbrechen *nt*; **capital punishment** N die Todesstrafe;
capital spending N Kapitalaufwendungen *pl*; **capital
transfer tax** N Kapitalverkehrssteuer *f*; (*for inheritance*)
Erbschaftssteuer *f*

Capitol ['kæpɪtl] N Kapitol *nt*

capitulate [kə'pɪtjʊleɪt] VI kapitulieren (*also Mil*) (*to* vor +*dat*)

capitulation [kəpɪtjʊ'leɪʃən] N Kapitulation *f*

cappuccino [kæpʊ'tʃiːnəʊ] N Cappuccino *m*

caprice [kə'priːs] N Laune(nhaftigkeit) *f*

capricious [kə'prɪʃəs] ADJ launisch

Capricorn ['kæprɪkɔːn] N Steinbock *m*; **I'm (a) ~** ich bin
Steinbock

capsicum ['kæpsɪkəm] N Pfefferschote *f*

capsize [kæp'saɪz] **1** VI kentern **2** VT zum Kentern bringen

capsule ['kæpsjuːl] N Kapsel *f*

captain ['kæptɪn] (*abbr* **Capt**) **1** N (*Mil*) Hauptmann *m*; (*Naut,
Aviat, Sport*) Kapitän *m*; (*US: in restaurant*) Oberkellner *m*; **yes,
~!** jawohl, Herr Hauptmann/Kapitän!; **~ of industry**
Industriekapitän *m* **2** VT (*Sport*) *team* anführen; (*Naut*) *ship*
befehligen

captaincy ['kæptənsɪ] N Befehl *m*; (*Sport*) Führung *f*; **under his
~** mit ihm als Kapitän

caption ['kæpʃən] **1** N Überschrift *f*; (*under cartoon*)
Bildunterschrift *f*; (*Film*: = *subtitle*) Untertitel *m* **2** VT betiteln

captivate ['kæptɪveɪt] VT faszinieren

captivating ['kæptɪveɪtɪŋ] ADJ bezaubernd; *personality*
einnehmend

captive ['kæptɪv] **1** N Gefangene(r) *mf*; **to take sb ~** jdn
gefangen nehmen; **to hold sb ~** jdn gefangen halten; (*fig*)
jdn fesseln **2** ADJ *person* gefangen; *animal, bird* in
Gefangenschaft; **a ~ audience** ein unfreiwilliges Publikum

captive market N Monopol-Absatzmarkt *m*

captivity [kæp'tɪvɪtɪ] N Gefangenschaft *f*

captor ['kæptə^r] N **his ~s treated him kindly** er wurde nach
seiner Gefangennahme gut behandelt

capture ['kæptʃə^r] **1** VT (a) *town* einnehmen; *treasure* erobern;
person gefangen nehmen; *animal* (ein)fangen; *ship* kapern
(b) (*fig*) *votes* erringen; *atmosphere* einfangen; *attention, sb's
interest* erregen (c) (*Comput*) *data* erfassen **2** N Eroberung *f*;
(*of escapee*) Gefangennahme *f*; (*of animal*) Einfangen *nt*;
(*Comput: of data*) Erfassung *f*

car [kɑː^r] N (a) Auto *nt*; **by ~** mit dem Auto; **~ ride** Autofahrt *f*
(b) (*esp US Rail*: = *tram ~*) Wagen *m* (c) (*US: of elevator*)
Fahrkorb *m*

carafe [kə'ræf] N Karaffe *f*

car alarm N Auto-Alarmanlage *f*

caramel ['kærəməl] N (= *substance*) Karamell *m*; (= *sweet*)
Karamelle *f*

carat ['kærət] N Karat *nt*; **nine ~ gold** neunkarätiges Gold

caravan ['kærəvæn] N (a) (*Brit Aut*) Wohnwagen *m*; **~ holiday**
Ferien *pl* im Wohnwagen (b) (= *gipsy ~*) Zigeunerwagen *m*
(c) (= *desert ~*) Karawane *f*

caravanning ['kærəvænɪŋ] N Urlaub *m* im Wohnwagen; **to go
~** Urlaub im Wohnwagen machen

caravan site N Campingplatz *m* für Wohnwagen

caraway seeds ['kærəweɪsiːdz] PL Kümmel(körner *pl*) *m*

carbohydrate [kɑːbəˈhaɪdreɪt] N Kohle(n)hydrat *nt*

carbolic [kɑː'bɒlɪk] N (*also ~* **soap**) Karbolseife *f*

carbolic acid N Karbolsäure f

car bomb N Autobombe f

carbon [ˈkɑːbən] N (*Chem*) Kohlenstoff m

carbonate [ˈkɑːbənɪt] N Karbonat nt

carbonated [ˈkɑːbəˌneɪtəd] ADJ mit Kohlensäure (versetzt)

carbon: **carbon copy** N Durchschlag m; **to be a ~ of sth** das genaue Ebenbild einer Sache (*gen*) sein; **carbon dating** N Kohlenstoffdatierung f; **carbon dioxide** N Kohlendioxid nt

carbonize [ˈkɑːbənaɪz] VT karbonisieren

carbon: **carbon monoxide** N Kohlenmonoxid nt; **carbon paper** N Kohlepapier nt

---

CAR-BOOT SALE, GARAGE SALE

Car-boot sales sind in Großbritannien recht beliebte Flohmärkte, bei denen die Leute Dinge, die sie nicht mehr länger benötigen, wie Kleider, Möbel und andere Haushaltsgegenstände, aus den Kofferräumen ihrer Autos heraus verkaufen.

In den USA verkaufen Hausbesitzer überflüssigen Hausrat und Kleider, indem sie einen **garage sale** oder auch **yard sale** abhalten und alles, von dem sie sich trennen wollen, im Garten oder in der Garage zum Verkauf anbieten. Manchmal schließen sich auch mehrere Nachbarn zusammen und veranstalten einen gemeinsamen **garage sale**.

---

carbuncle [ˈkɑːbʌŋkl] N (*Med*) Karbunkel m

carburettor, (*US*) **carburetor** [ˌkɑːbəˈretə^r] N Vergaser m

carcass [ˈkɑːkəs] N **(a)** (= *corpse*) Leiche f; (*of animal*) Kadaver m **(b)** (*of ship, house*) Skelett nt; (= *remains*) Überbleibsel pl, Trümmer pl

carcinogen [kɑːˈsɪnədʒən] N Karzinogen nt

carcinogenic [ˌkɑːsɪnəˈdʒenɪk] ADJ karzinogen

car crash N (*Auto*)unfall m

card [kɑːd] N **(a)** NO PL (= *cardboard*) Pappe f **(b)** (= *greetings, business, cheque ~ etc*) Karte f **(c) cards** PL (= *employment ~s*) Papiere pl **(d)** (= *playing ~*) (Spiel)karte f; **to play ~s** Karten spielen; **game of ~s** Kartenspiel nt **(e)** (*fig*) **to put** or **lay one's ~s on the table** seine Karten aufdecken; **to play one's ~s right/badly** geschickt/ungeschickt taktieren; **to hold all the ~s** alle Trümpfe in der Hand haben; **to play** or **keep one's ~s close to one's chest** or (*US*) **close to the vest** sich (*dat*) nicht in die Karten sehen lassen; **it's on the ~s** das ist zu erwarten

cardamom [ˈkɑːdəməm] N Kardamom m or nt

card: **cardboard** ❚ N Karton m, Pappe f ❷ ATTR Papp-; (*fig*) *character* stereotyp; **cardboard box** N (Papp)karton m; **card-carrying** ADJ **a ~ member** ein eingetragenes Mitglied; **card game** N Kartenspiel nt; **card holder** N (*Fin*) Karteninhaber(in) m(f)

cardiac [ˈkɑːdɪæk] ADJ Herz-

cardiac arrest N Herzstillstand m

cardigan [ˈkɑːdɪɡən] N Strickjacke f

cardinal [ˈkɑːdɪnl] ❚ N (*Eccl*) Kardinal m ❷ ADJ (= *chief*) Haupt-

cardinal: **cardinal number** N Kardinalzahl f; **cardinal sin** N Todsünde f

card index N Kartei f; (*in library*) Katalog m

cardio- [ˈkɑːdɪəʊ-] PREF Kardio-; **~gram** Kardiogramm nt

cardiologist [ˌkɑːdɪˈɒlɪdʒɪst] N Kardiologe m, Kardiologin f

cardiology [ˌkɑːdɪˈɒlədʒɪ] N Kardiologie f

cardiovascular [ˌkɑːdɪəʊˈvæskjʊlə^r] ADJ kardiovaskulär

card: **cardphone** N Kartentelefon nt; **card player** N Kartenspieler(in) m(f); **card table** N Spieltisch m; **card trick** N Kartenkunststück nt

CARE [kɛə^r] ABBR of **Cooperative for American Relief Everywhere**; **~ packet** Carepaket nt

---

care [kɛə^r]	
❚ NOUN	❸ TRANSITIVE VERB
❷ INTRANSITIVE VERB	❹ PHRASAL VERB

❚ NOUN

(a) (= *worry*) Sorge f (*of* um); **free of care(s)** ohne Sorgen; **he hasn't a care in the world** er hat keinerlei Sorgen

(b) (= *carefulness*) Sorgfalt f; **this word should be used with care** dieses Wort sollte sorgfältig or mit Sorgfalt gebraucht werden; **paint strippers need to be used with care** Abbeizmittel müssen vorsichtig angewandt werden; **"fragile, with care"**, **"handle with care"** „Vorsicht, zerbrechlich"

✦**to take care** (= *be careful*) aufpassen, vorsichtig sein; **take care he doesn't cheat you** sehen Sie sich vor, dass er Sie nicht betrügt; **bye-bye, take care** tschüs(s), machs gut

✦**to take care to do sth** sich bemühen, etw zu tun

✦**to take care over** or **with sth/in doing sth** etw sorgfältig tun; **you should take more care with** or **over the details** Sie sollten sich sorgfältiger mit den Einzelheiten befassen

(c) (= *maintenance*) (*of teeth, car etc*) Pflege f; **to take care of sth** (= *maintain*) auf etw (*acc*) aufpassen; *one's appearance, car, furniture etc* pflegen; (= *not treat roughly*) etw schonen; **to take care of oneself** sich um sich selbst kümmern; (*as regards health*) sich schonen; (*as regards appearance*) sich pflegen

(d) (*of old people, children*) Versorgung f; **medical care** ärztliche Versorgung; **to take care of sb** sich um jdn kümmern; *patients* jdn versorgen; *one's family* für jdn sorgen **(e)** (= *protection*) Obhut f; **in care of** (*Brit*), **in care of** (*US*) bei; **in** or **under sb's care** in jds (*dat*) Obhut; **to take a child into care** ein Kind in Pflege nehmen; **to be taken into care** in Pflege gegeben werden; **the valuables in my care** die mir anvertrauten Wertsachen; **to take care of sth** *valuables etc* auf etw (*acc*) aufpassen; *plants, animals etc* sich um etw kümmern; (*over longer period*) etw versorgen

✦**to take care of sb/sth** (= *see to*) sich um jdn/etw kümmern; **that takes care of him/it** das wäre erledigt; **let me take care of that** überlassen Sie das mir; **that can take care of itself** das wird sich schon irgendwie geben

---

❷ INTRANSITIVE VERB (= *feel concern*) **I don't care** das ist mir egal; **for all I care** meinetwegen; **who cares?** na und?

✦**to care about sth** Wert auf etw (*acc*) legen; **a company that cares about its staff** eine Firma, die für ihr Personal sorgt; **that's all he cares about** alles andere ist ihm egal; **he cares deeply about her** sie liegt ihm sehr am Herzen; **he doesn't care about her** sie ist ihm gleichgültig

---

❸ TRANSITIVE VERB

(a) (= *mind*) **I don't care what people say** es ist mir egal, was die Leute sagen; **what do I care?** was geht mich das an?; **I couldn't care less what people say** es ist mir doch völlig egal, was die Leute sagen

(b) (= *like*) **to care to do sth** etw gerne tun mögen or wollen; **I wouldn't care to meet him** ich würde keinen gesteigerten Wert darauf legen, ihn kennen zu lernen

---

❹ PHRASAL VERB

➤ **care for** VI +PREP OBJ **(a)** (= *look after*) sich kümmern um; *hands, furniture etc* pflegen; **well cared-for** *person* gut versorgt; *hands, hair, house* gepflegt **(b)** (= *like*) **I don't care for that suggestion/him** dieser Vorschlag/er sagt mir nicht zu; **would you care for a cup of tea?** hätten Sie gerne eine Tasse Tee?; **I've never much cared for his films** ich habe mir noch nie viel aus seinen Filmen gemacht; **but you know I do care for you** aber du weißt doch, dass du mir viel bedeutest

---

career [kəˈrɪə^r] ❚ N Karriere f; (= *profession, job*) Beruf m; (= *working life*) Laufbahn f; **to make a ~ for oneself** Karriere machen ❷ ATTR Karriere-; *soldier, diplomat* Berufs-; **a good/bad ~ move** ein karrierefördernder/karriereschädlicher Schritt ❸ VI rasen; **the car ~ed out of control** das Auto geriet außer Kontrolle

careerist [kəˈrɪərɪst] N Karrierist(in) m(f)

careers [kəˈrɪəz]: **Careers Adviser** N *see* **Careers Officer**; **careers guidance** N Berufsberatung f; **Careers Officer** N Berufsberater(in) m(f)

career woman N Karrierefrau f

carefree [ˈkɛəfriː] ADJ sorglos, unbekümmert

careful [ˈkɛəfʊl] ADJ sorgfältig; (= *cautious*) vorsichtig; (*with money etc*) sparsam; **~!** Vorsicht!; **to be ~** aufpassen (*of* auf +*acc*); **be ~ with the glasses** sei mit den Gläsern vorsichtig; **she's very ~ about what she eats** sie achtet genau darauf, was sie isst; **to be ~ about doing sth** es sich gut überlegen, ob man etw tun soll; **be ~ (that) they don't hear you** gib Acht, damit or dass sie dich nicht hören; **be ~ not to drop it** pass auf, dass du das nicht fallen lässt; **he is very ~ with his money** er hält sein Geld gut zusammen

carefully ['kɛəfəlɪ] ADV sorgfältig; (= cautiously) vorsichtig; consider gründlich; listen gut; explain genau

carefulness ['kɛəfʊlnɪs] N Sorgfalt f; (= caution) Vorsicht f

care: **care home** N Pflegeheim nt; **care label** N Pflegeetikett nt

careless ['kɛəlɪs] ADJ person, work nachlässig; driver unvorsichtig; driving leichtsinnig; remark gedankenlos; **~ mistake** Flüchtigkeitsfehler m; **how ~ of me!** wie dumm von mir; (= clumsy) wie ungeschickt von mir

carelessly ['kɛəlɪslɪ] ADV **(a)** (= negligently) leichtsinnigerweise, unvorsichtigerweise **(b)** (= casually) say gedankenlos; throw achtlos

carelessness ['kɛəlɪsnɪs] N (of person, work) Nachlässigkeit f; (of driver) Unvorsicht(igkeit) f; (of remark) Gedankenlosigkeit f

care order N (Brit: Jur, Sociol) Fürsorgeanordnung f

carer ['kɛərəʳ] N im Sozialbereich Tätige(r) mf; **the elderly and their ~s** Senioren und ihre Fürsorgenden

caress [kə'rɛs] **1** N Liebkosung f **2** VT streicheln, liebkosen

care: **caretaker** N Hausmeister(in) m(f); **caretaker government** N geschäftsführende Regierung; **care worker** N Heimbetreuer(in) für Kinder, Geisteskranke oder alte Menschen; **careworn** ADJ von Sorgen gezeichnet

car: **carfare** N (US) Fahrpreis m; **car ferry** N Autofähre f

cargo ['kɑːgəʊ] N Fracht f, Ladung f; **~ insurance** Kargoversicherung f; **~ liner** Linienfrachter m; **general ~** (in transport) Stückgut nt

car hire N Autovermietung f

Caribbean [kærɪ'biːən, (US) kə'rɪbɪən] **1** ADJ karibisch; **~ Sea** Karibisches Meer; **a ~ island** eine Insel in der Karibik **2** N Karibik f

caricature ['kærɪkətʊəʳ] **1** N Karikatur f **2** VT karikieren

caring ['kɛərɪŋ] ADJ attitude warmherzig, mitfühlend; parent, husband liebevoll; teacher engagiert; government, society sozial, mitmenschlich; **~ profession** Sozialberuf m

car: **car insurance** N Kfz-Versicherung f; **car keys** PL Autoschlüssel pl

carnage ['kɑːnɪdʒ] N Blutbad nt

carnal ['kɑːnl] ADJ fleischlich; **~ desires** sinnliche Begierden pl

carnation [kɑː'neɪʃən] N Nelke f

carnival ['kɑːnɪvəl] **1** N Volksfest nt; (= village ~ etc) Schützenfest nt; (based on religion) Karneval m **2** ATTR Fest-, Karnevals-

carnivore ['kɑːnɪvɔːʳ] N, pl carnivora [kɑː'nɪvərə] (= animal) Fleischfresser m

carnivorous [kɑː'nɪvərəs] ADJ Fleisch fressend

carob ['kærəʊ] N (= fruit) Johannisbrot nt

carol ['kærəl] N Lied nt

carol: **carol singers** PL ≈ Sternsinger pl; **carol singing** N Weihnachtssingen nt

carousel [kærʊ'sɛl] N Karussell nt

carp[1] [kɑːp] N (= fish) Karpfen m

carp[2] VI nörgeln

car: **car park** N (Brit) (open-air) Parkplatz m; (covered) Parkhaus nt; **car parking ~ facilities are available** Parkplatz vorhanden

carpenter ['kɑːpɪntəʳ] N Zimmermann m, Zimmerfrau f; (for furniture) Tischler(in) m(f)

carpentry ['kɑːpɪntrɪ] N Zimmerhandwerk nt; (as hobby) Tischlern nt

carpet ['kɑːpɪt] **1** N (lit, fig) Teppich m; (fitted) Teppichboden m **2** VT floor (mit Teppichen/Teppichboden) auslegen

carpetbagger ['kɑːpɪtbægəʳ] N **(a)** (US Pol inf) politischer Abenteurer, politische Abenteuerin **(b)** (Fin) Spekulant(in) m(f) (der/die Geld bei vielen verschiedenen Hypothekenbanken investiert in der Hoffnung, bei Änderung der Statuten einen Gewinn zu machen)

carpeting ['kɑːpɪtɪŋ] N Teppiche pl

carpet: **carpet-sweeper** N Teppichkehrer m, Teppichkehrmaschine f; **carpet tile** N Teppichfliese f

car phone N Autotelefon nt

carping ['kɑːpɪŋ] N Nörgelei(en) f(pl)

car: **carpool** N **(a)** (= people) Fahrgemeinschaft f **(b)** (= vehicles) Fuhrpark m; **carport** N Einstellplatz m; **car radio** N Autoradio nt

carriage ['kærɪdʒ] N **(a)** (= horse-drawn vehicle) Kutsche f; (US: = baby ~) Kinderwagen m **(b)** (Brit Rail) Wagen m **(c)** (Comm: = conveyance) Beförderung f; **contract of ~** (Brit) Beförderungsvertrag m; **~ forward** Fracht zahlt Empfänger; **~ free** frachtfrei; **~ paid** frei Haus **(d)** (Typ) Wagen m **(e)** (of person: = bearing) Haltung f

carriageway ['kærɪdʒweɪ] N (Brit) Fahrbahn f

carrier ['kærɪəʳ] N **(a)** (= haulier) Spediteur m; (= passenger airline) Fluggesellschaft f **(b)** (of disease) Überträger m **(c)** (= aircraft ~) Flugzeugträger m; (= troop ~) Transportflugzeug nt/-schiff nt **(d)** (Brit: also ~ bag) Tragetasche f, Tragetüte f

carrion ['kærɪən] N Aas nt

carrot ['kærət] N Mohrrübe f; (fig) Köder m; **to dangle a ~ before sb** or **in front of sb** jdm einen Köder unter die Nase halten

carrot: **carrot-and-stick** ADJ **~ policy** Politik f von Zuckerbrot und Peitsche; **carrot cake** N Karottenkuchen m

carry ['kærɪ] **1** VT **(a)** tragen; message überbringen **(b)** (vehicle: = convey) befördern; **this coach carries 30 people** dieser Bus kann 30 Personen befördern; **the current carried them along** die Strömung trieb sie mit sich **(c)** (= have on person) money bei sich haben; gun tragen; **to ~ sth about** or **around with one** etw mit sich herumtragen **(d)** (fig) **he carried his audience (along) with him** er begeisterte das Publikum; **the loan carries 5% interest** das Darlehen wird mit 5% verzinst; **this job carries a lot of responsibility** dieser Posten bringt viel Verantwortung mit sich; **the offence carries a penalty of £50** darauf steht eine Geldstrafe von £ 50 **(e)** (Comm) goods, stock führen **(f)** (Tech: pipe) water etc führen; (wire) sound übertragen **(g)** (= extend) führen, (ver)legen; **to ~ sth too far** (fig) etw zu weit treiben **(h)** (= win) einnehmen, erobern; **to ~ the day** siegreich sein; **the motion was carried unanimously** der Antrag wurde einstimmig angenommen **(i)** **he carried himself well/like a soldier** er hat eine gute/soldatische Haltung **(j)** (Press) story bringen **(k)** (Med) **people ~ing the AIDS virus** Menschen, die das Aidsvirus in sich (dat) tragen **(l)** (= be pregnant with) **to be ~ing a child** schwanger sein **(m)** (Math) ... **and ~ 2** ... übertrage or behalte 2 **2** VI (voice, sound) tragen; **the sound of the alphorn carried for miles** der Klang des Alphorns war meilenweit zu hören

➤ **carry away** VT SEP **(a)** (lit) (hin)wegtragen; (flood) (hin)wegspülen; (tornado) hinwegfegen **(b)** (fig) **to get carried away** sich nicht mehr bremsen können (inf); **don't get carried away!** übertreibs nicht!; **to be carried away by one's feelings** sich (in seine Gefühle) hineinsteigern

➤ **carry back** VT SEP (fig) person zurückversetzen (to in +acc)

➤ **carry forward** VT SEP (Fin) vortragen

➤ **carry off** VT SEP **(a)** (= seize) wegtragen **(b)** (= win) prizes gewinnen **(c)** **to carry it off** es hinkriegen (inf)

➤ **carry on** **1** VI **(a)** (= continue) weitermachen; (life) weitergehen **(b)** (inf: = talk) reden und reden; (= make a scene) ein Theater machen (inf); **to carry on about sth** sich über etw (acc) auslassen **(c)** (= have an affair) etwas haben (inf) **2** VT SEP **(a)** (= continue) tradition, family business fortführen **(b)** (= conduct) conversation führen

➤ **carry out** VT SEP **(a)** (lit) heraustragen **(b)** (fig) order, job ausführen; promises, obligations erfüllen; plan, search, experiment durchführen; threats wahrmachen

➤ **carry over** VT SEP **(a)** (Fin) vortragen **(b)** (to next meeting etc) vertagen

➤ **carry through** VT SEP **(a)** (= carry out) zu Ende führen **(b)** (= sustain) überstehen lassen

carry: **carryall** N (US) (Einkaufs-/Reise)tasche f; **carrycot** N (Brit) Babytragetasche f

carryings-on ['kærɪŋz'ɒn] PL (inf) übles Treiben (inf)

carry: **carry-on** N (inf) Theater nt (inf); **carry-out** (US, Scot) **1** N **(a)** (= restaurant) Imbissstube f/Restaurant nt für Außer-Haus-Verkauf; (= bar) Schalter m für Außer-Haus-Verkauf **(b)** (= meal, drink) Speisen pl/Getränke pl zum Mitnehmen;

let's get a ~ kaufen wir uns etwas zum Mitnehmen **2** ADJ ATTR Außer-Haus-; **carry-over** N Überbleibsel nt; (Fin) Saldovortrag m

carsick ['kɑːsɪk] ADJ **I used to get ~** früher wurde mir beim Autofahren immer schlecht

cart [kɑːt] **1** N Wagen m, Karren m; **to put the ~ before the horse** (prov) das Pferd beim Schwanz aufzäumen (prov) **2** VT (fig inf) mit sich schleppen

➤ **cart away** or **off** VT SEP abtransportieren

carte blanche ['kɑːt'blɑːnʃ] N, NO PL **to give sb ~** jdm Carte blanche f (geh) or eine Blankovollmacht geben

cartel [kɑː'tel] N Kartell nt

carthorse ['kɑːthɔːs] N Zugpferd nt

cartilage ['kɑːtɪlɪdʒ] N Knorpel m

cartload ['kɑːtləʊd] N Wagenladung f

cartographer [kɑː'tɒɡrəfəʳ] N Kartograf(in) m(f)

cartography [kɑː'tɒɡrəfɪ] N Kartografie f

carton ['kɑːtən] N (Papp)karton m; (of cigarettes) Stange f; (of milk) Tüte f

cartoon [kɑː'tuːn] N **(a)** Cartoon m or nt; (= single picture) Karikatur f **(b)** (Film, TV) (Zeichen)trickfilm m

cartoon character N Comicfigur f

cartoonist [kɑː'tuːnɪst] N **(a)** Karikaturist(in) m(f) **(b)** (Film, TV) Trickzeichner(in) m(f)

cartoon strip N (esp Brit) Cartoon m or nt, Comic m

cartridge ['kɑːtrɪdʒ] N (for rifle, pen) Patrone f; (Phot) Kassette f; (for record player) Tonabnehmer m

cartridge belt N Patronengurt m

cartwheel ['kɑːtwiːl] N (lit) Wagenrad nt; (Sport) Rad nt; **to turn** or **do ~s** Rad schlagen

carve [kɑːv] **1** VT **(a)** (Art: = cut) wood schnitzen; stone etc (be)hauen; **~d in(to) the wood** in das Holz geschnitzt; **~d in(to) the stone** in den Stein gehauen **(b)** (Cook) tranchieren **2** VI (Cook) tranchieren

➤ **carve out** VT SEP **to carve out a career for oneself** sich (dat) eine Karriere aufbauen

➤ **carve up** VT SEP **(a)** meat aufschneiden **(b)** (fig) inheritance verteilen; country aufteilen

carvery ['kɑːvərɪ] N Buffet nt

carving ['kɑːvɪŋ] N (Art) (= thing carved) Skulptur f; (in wood also) Schnitzerei f; (= relief) Relief nt; (in wood) Holzschnitt m

carving knife N Tranchiermesser nt

carwash ['kɑːwɒʃ] N (= place) Autowaschanlage f

cascade [kæs'keɪd] **1** N Kaskade f; (fig: of sparks) Regen m **2** VI (also ~ **down**) (onto auf +acc) (in Kaskaden) herabfallen; (sparks) herabsprühen; (hair) wallend herabfallen

case¹ [keɪs] N **(a)** Fall m; **if that's the ~** wenn das der Fall ist; **is that the ~ with you?** ist das bei Ihnen der Fall?; **as the ~ may be** je nachdem; **in most ~s** meist(ens); **in ~** falls; **(just) in ~** für alle Fälle; **in ~ of emergency** im Notfall; **in any ~** sowieso; **in this/that ~** in dem Fall; **to win one's ~** (Jur) seinen Prozess gewinnen; **the ~ for the defence/prosecution** die Verteidigung/Anklage; **in the ~ Higgins v Schwarz** in der Sache Higgins gegen Schwarz; **the ~ for/against the abolition of capital punishment** die Argumente für/gegen die Abschaffung der Todesstrafe; **you haven't got a ~** das Belastungsmaterial reicht nicht für ein Verfahren; (fig) Sie haben keine Handhabe; **to have a good ~** (Jur) gute Chancen haben durchzukommen; **you/they have a good ~** es ist durchaus gerechtfertigt, was Sie/sie sagen; **there's a very good ~ for adopting this method** es spricht sehr viel dafür, diese Methode zu übernehmen; **to put one's ~** seinen Fall darlegen; **to put the ~ for sth** etw vertreten; **to be on the ~** am Ball sein
(b) (Gram) Fall m, Kasus m; **in the genitive ~** im Genitiv
(c) (inf: = person) Type f (inf); **a hopeless ~** ein hoffnungsloser Fall

case² N **(a)** (= suitcase) Koffer m; (= packing ~) Kiste f; (= display ~) Vitrine f; **a ~ of champagne** eine Kiste Champagner **(b)** (= box) Schachtel f; (for jewels) Schatulle f; (for spectacles) Etui nt; (for CD) Hülle f; (for musical instrument) Kasten m; (of watch) Gehäuse nt **(c)** (Typ) **upper/lower ~** groß-/kleingeschrieben

case: **casebook** N (Med) (Kranken)fälle pl; (in social work, Jur) Fallsammlung f; **case ending** N (Gram) Endung f; **case**

history N (Med) Krankengeschichte f; (Sociol, Psych) Vorgeschichte f

casement ['keɪsmənt] N (= window) Flügelfenster nt

case: **case-sensitive** ADJ case-sensitive, Groß-/Kleinschreibung beachtend; **case study** N Fallstudie f; **casework** N (Sociol) ≈ Sozialarbeit f; **caseworker** N (Sociol) ≈ Sozialarbeiter(in) m(f)

cash [kæʃ] **1** N **(a)** Bargeld nt; (= change also) Kleingeld nt; **~ in hand** Barbestand m; **to pay (in) ~** bar bezahlen; **how much do you have in ready ~?** wie viel Geld haben Sie verfügbar?
(b) (= immediate payment) Barzahlung f; (= not credit) Sofortzahlung f; **to pay ~ (in)** bar/sofort bezahlen; **~ in advance** Vorauszahlung f; **~ against documents** (Comm) Kasse f or Barzahlung f gegen Dokumente; **~ with order** Zahlung f bei Auftragserteilung; **~ on delivery** per Nachnahme
(c) (= money) Geld nt; **to be short of ~** knapp bei Kasse sein (inf); **I'm out of ~** ich bin blank (inf)
2 VT cheque einlösen

➤ **cash in** **1** VT SEP einlösen **2** VI **to cash in on sth** aus etw Kapital schlagen

➤ **cash up** VI (Brit) Kasse machen

cash: **cash-and-carry** N (for retailers) Cash and Carry m; (for public) Verbrauchermarkt m; **cashback** N (at supermarket) Barauszahlung f (zusätzlich zu dem Preis der gekauften Ware, wenn man mit Bankkarte bezahlt); **I'd like £10 ~, please** und ich hätte gern zusätzlich £ 10 in bar; **cash basis** N **on a ~** auf der Grundlage von Barzahlung, über Barzahlung; **cashbook** N Kassenbuch nt; **cash box** N (Geld)kassette f; **cash card** N (Geld)automatenkarte f; **cash crop** N zum Verkauf bestimmte Ernte; **cash desk** N (Brit) Kasse f; **cash discount** N Skonto m or nt; **cash dispenser** N (Brit) Geldautomat m

cashew [kæ'ʃuː] N (= nut) Cashewnuss f

cash flow **1** N Cashflow m **2** ATTR **cash-flow analysis** Cashflowanalyse f; **cash-flow problems** Liquiditätsprobleme pl; **I've got cash-flow problems** (personal) ich bin in Geldschwierigkeiten; **~ statement** Cashflowbericht m

cashier [kæ'ʃɪəʳ] N Kassierer(in) m(f)

cashier's check N (US) Bankscheck m, Banktratte f

cashless ['kæʃləs] ADJ bargeldlos

cashmere ['kæʃmɪəʳ] N Kaschmir m; **~ (wool)** Kaschmirwolle f

cash: **cash offer** N Bar(zahlungs)angebot nt; **cash payment** N Barzahlung f; **cash point** N (Brit: = ATM) Geldautomat m; **cash price** N Bar(zahlungs)preis m; **cash receipts account** N Bareingänge pl; **cash register** N Registrierkasse f; **cash sale** N Barverkauf m; **cash transaction** N Bargeldtransfer m

casing ['keɪsɪŋ] N (Tech) Gehäuse nt

casino [kə'siːnəʊ] N (Spiel)kasino nt

cask [kɑːsk] N Fass nt

casket ['kɑːskɪt] N Schatulle f; (US: = coffin) Sarg m

Caspian Sea ['kæspɪən'siː] N Kaspisches Meer

casserole ['kæsərəʊl] N (Cook) Schmortopf m; **a lamb ~, a ~ of lamb** eine Lammkasserolle

cassette [kæ'set] N Kassette f

cassette: **cassette deck** N Kassettendeck nt; **cassette player, cassette recorder** N Kassettenrekorder m

cassock ['kæsək] N Talar m

cast [kɑːst] vb: pret, ptp **cast** **1** N **(a)** (= mould) (Guss)form f; (= object moulded) Abdruck m; (in metal) (Ab)guss m
(b) (= plaster ~) Gipsverband m
(c) (Theat) Besetzung f; **~ (in order of appearance)** Darsteller pl (in der Reihenfolge ihres Auftritts); **who's in the ~?** wer spielt mit?
2 VT **(a)** (lit liter, fig: = throw) werfen; anchor, net auswerfen; **to ~ one's vote** seine Stimme abgeben; **to ~ one's eyes over sth** einen Blick auf etw (acc) werfen; **to ~ a critical eye on sth** etw kritisch begutachten; **to ~ a shadow** (lit, fig) einen Schatten werfen (on auf +acc)
(b) (= shed) **to ~ its skin** sich häuten
(c) (Tech, Art) gießen
(d) (Theat) play, parts besetzen; **he was well/badly ~** die Rolle passte gut/schlecht zu ihm; **I don't know why they ~ him as the villain** ich weiß nicht, warum sie ihm die Rolle des Schurken gegeben haben
3 VI (Fishing) die Angel auswerfen

➤ **cast about** (Brit) or **around for** VI +PREP OBJ zu finden versuchen; **he was casting about** or **around for something to say** er suchte nach Worten

➤ **cast aside** VT SEP cares, habits ablegen; person fallen lassen

➤ **cast back 1** VI (fig) **to cast back (in one's mind)** im Geiste zurückdenken (to an +acc) **2** VT SEP **to cast one's thoughts** or **mind back** seine Gedanken zurückschweifen lassen (to in +acc)

➤ **cast down** VT SEP **to be cast down** (fig) niedergeschlagen sein

➤ **cast off** VTI SEP **(a)** (Naut) losmachen **(b)** (Knitting) abketten

➤ **cast on** (Knitting) VTI SEP anschlagen

castanets [ˌkæstə'nets] PL Kastagnetten pl

castaway ['kɑːstəweɪ] N (lit, fig) Schiffbrüchige(r) mf

caste [kɑːst] **1** N Kaste f **2** ADJ ATTR Kasten-

caster ['kɑːstəʳ] N = **castor**

caster sugar N (Brit) Sandzucker m

castigate ['kæstɪgeɪt] VT (verbally) geißeln

casting ['kɑːstɪŋ] N **(a)** (Tech, Art) (= act, object) (Ab)guss m; (in plaster also) Abdruck m **(b)** (Theat) Besetzung f

casting: casting couch N (hum) Besetzungscouch f (hum inf); **casting vote** N ausschlaggebende Stimme

cast iron 1 N Gusseisen nt **2** ADJ **cast-iron (a)** (lit) gusseisern **(b)** (fig) will, constitution eisern; case, alibi hieb- und stichfest

castle ['kɑːsl] **1** N **(a)** Schloss nt; (= medieval fortress) Burg f; **to build ~s in the air** Luftschlösser bauen **(b)** (Chess) Turm m **2** VI (Chess) rochieren

castoffs ['kɑːstɒfs] PL (Brit inf) abgelegte Kleider pl; **she's one of his ~** (fig inf) sie ist eine seiner ausrangierten Freundinnen (inf)

castor ['kɑːstəʳ] N (= wheel) Rad nt

castor oil N Rizinus(öl) nt

castrate [kæs'treɪt] VT kastrieren

castration [kæs'treɪʃən] N Kastration f

casual ['kæʒjʊl] ADJ **(a)** (= not planned) zufällig; acquaintance, glance flüchtig
(b) (= careless) lässig; attitude gleichgültig; remark beiläufig; (= lacking emotion) gleichgültig; **it was just a ~ remark** das habe ich/hat er etc nur so gesagt; **he was very ~ about it** es war ihm offensichtlich gleichgültig; (in reaction) das hat ihn kalt gelassen (inf); **the ~ observer** der oberflächliche Betrachter
(c) (= informal) zwanglos; clothes leger; **a ~ shirt** ein Freizeithemd nt; **he was wearing ~ clothes** er war leger gekleidet
(d) (= irregular) work, worker Gelegenheits-; (= occasional) affair, relationship locker; **~ earnings** Nebeneinkünfte pl, Nebeneinnahmen pl

casually ['kæʒjʊlɪ] ADV (= without planning) zufällig; (= without emotion) ungerührt; (= incidentally, in an offhand manner) beiläufig; (= without seriousness) lässig; (= informally) zwanglos; dressed leger

casualty ['kæʒjʊltɪ] N **(a)** (lit, fig) Opfer nt; (injured also) Verletzte(r) mf; (killed also) Tote(r) mf; **were there many casualties?** gab es viele Opfer?; (Mil) gab es hohe Verluste? **(b)** (also = **unit**) Notaufnahme f; **to go to ~** in die Notaufnahme gehen; **to be in ~** in der Notaufnahme sein

casualty ward N Unfallstation f

cat [kæt] N Katze f; (= tiger etc) (Raub)katze f; **to let the ~ out of the bag** die Katze aus dem Sack lassen; **to play a ~-and-mouse game with sb** mit jdm Katz und Maus spielen; **there isn't room to swing a ~** (inf) man kann sich nicht rühren(, so eng ist es); **to be like a ~ on hot bricks, to be like a ~ on a hot tin roof** wie auf glühenden Kohlen sitzen; **that's put the ~ among the pigeons!** da hast du etc aber was (Schönes) angerichtet!; **he doesn't have a ~ in hell's chance of winning** er hat nicht die geringste Chance zu gewinnen; **when** or **while the ~'s away the mice will play** (Prov) wenn die Katze aus dem Haus ist, tanzen die Mäuse (Prov); **has the ~ got your tongue?** (inf) du hast wohl die Sprache verloren?

cataclysmic [ˌkætə'klɪzmɪk] ADJ (fig) umwälzend

catacombs ['kætəkuːmz] PL Katakomben pl

catalogue, (US) **catalog** ['kætəlɒg] **1** N **(a)** Katalog m **(b)** (= series) **a ~ of errors/injuries/disasters** eine Reihe or Serie von Fehlern/Verletzungen/Katastrophen **2** VT katalogisieren

catalyst ['kætəlɪst] N (lit, fig) Katalysator m

catalytic converter [ˌkætəlɪtɪkkən'vɜːtəʳ] N (Aut) Katalysator m

catamaran [ˌkætəmə'ræn] N Katamaran m

catapult ['kætəpʌlt] **1** N (Brit: = slingshot) Schleuder f **2** VT katapultieren

cataract ['kætərækt] N (Med) grauer Star

catarrh [kə'tɑːʳ] N Katarr(h) m

catastrophe [kə'tæstrəfɪ] N Katastrophe f; **to end in ~** in einer Katastrophe enden

catastrophic [ˌkætə'strɒfɪk] ADJ katastrophal

catch [kætʃ], vb: pret, ptp **caught 1** N **(a)** (of ball etc) **to make a (good) ~** (gut) fangen; **he missed an easy ~** er hat einen leichten Ball nicht gefangen
(b) (Fishing, Hunt) Fang m; **he's a good ~** (fig inf) er ist ein guter Fang
(c) (= children's game) Fangen nt
(d) (= snag) Haken m; **there's a ~ in it somewhere!** die Sache hat irgendwo einen Haken
(e) (= device for fastening) Verschluss(vorrichtung f) m; (= hook) Haken m; (= latch) Riegel m
2 VT **(a)** object, fish, mice fangen; thief fassen; escaped animal (ein)fangen; (inf: = manage to see) erwischen (inf); **to ~ sb's arm, to ~ sb by the arm** jdn am Arm fassen; **glass which ~es the light** Glas, in dem sich das Licht spiegelt; **to ~ sight/a glimpse of sb/sth** jdn/etw erblicken; **to ~ sb's attention/eye** jdn auf sich (acc) aufmerksam machen
(b) (= take by surprise) erwischen; **to ~ sb by surprise** jdn überraschen; **to be caught unprepared** nicht darauf vorbereitet sein; **to ~ sb at a bad time** jdm ungelegen kommen; **I caught him flirting with my wife** ich habe ihn (dabei) erwischt, wie er mit meiner Frau flirtete; **you won't ~ me signing any contract** (inf) ich unterschreibe doch keinen Vertrag; **caught in the act** auf frischer Tat ertappt; (sexually) in flagranti erwischt; **we were caught in a storm** wir wurden von einem Unwetter überrascht; **to ~ sb on the wrong foot** or **off balance** (fig) jdn überrumpeln
(c) (= take) bus, train etc nehmen
(d) (= be in time for) train, bus erreichen; **if I hurry I'll ~ the end of the film** wenn ich mich beeile kriege ich das Ende des Films noch mit (inf)
(e) (= become entangled) **I caught my finger in the car door** ich habe mir den Finger in der Wagentür eingeklemmt; **he caught his foot in the grating** er ist mit dem Fuß im Gitter hängen geblieben
(f) (= understand, hear) mitkriegen (inf)
(g) **to ~ an illness** sich (dat) eine Krankheit zuziehen; **he's always ~ing cold(s)** er erkältet sich leicht; **you'll ~ your death (of cold)!** du holst dir den Tod! (inf)
(h) (= portray) mood etc einfangen
(i) **to ~ one's breath** (after exercise etc) Luft holen, verschnaufen; **the blow caught him on the arm** der Schlag traf ihn am Arm; **you'll ~ it!** (Brit inf) du kannst (aber) was erleben! (inf)
3 VI **(a)** (with ball) fangen
(b) (= get stuck) klemmen; (= get entangled) sich verfangen; **her dress caught in the door** sie blieb mit ihrem Kleid in der Tür hängen

➤ **catch on** VI (inf) **(a)** (= become popular) ankommen; (fashion also) sich durchsetzen **(b)** (= understand) kapieren (inf)

➤ **catch out** VT SEP (fig) überführen; (with trick question etc) hereinlegen (inf)

➤ **catch up 1** VI aufholen; **to catch up on one's sleep** Schlaf nachholen; **to catch up on** or **with one's work** Arbeit nachholen; **to catch up with sb** (running, in work etc) jdn einholen **2** VT SEP **(a) to catch sb up** (walking, working etc) jdn einholen **(b)** (= get caught up in sth (= entangled) sich in etw (dat) verfangen; in traffic in etw (acc) kommen

catch-22 [ˌkætʃtwentɪ'tuː] N **a ~ situation** (inf) eine Zwickmühle

catchall ['kætʃɔːl] N **(a)** (US: = drawer etc) Schublade f für Krimskrams (inf) **(b)** (= phrase, clause etc) allgemeine Bezeichnung/Klausel etc

catcher ['kætʃəʳ] N Fänger m

catching ['kætʃɪŋ] ADJ (Med, fig) ansteckend

catchment area ['kætʃmənt'eərɪə] N Einzugsgebiet nt

catch phrase N Slogan m

catchup ['kætʃəp] N (US) = **ketchup**

catchword ['kætʃwɜːd] N Schlagwort nt

catchy [ˈkætʃɪ] ADJ (+ER) *tune, slogan* eingängig; *title* einprägsam

catechism [ˈkætɪkɪzəm] N (= *instruction*) Katechese *f*; (= *book*) Katechismus *m*

categorical [ˌkætɪˈɡɒrɪkəl] ADJ kategorisch; **he was quite ~ about it** er hat das mit Bestimmtheit gesagt

categorically [ˌkætɪˈɡɒrɪkəlɪ] ADV *state, deny* kategorisch; *say* mit Bestimmtheit

categorize [ˈkætɪɡəraɪz] VT kategorisieren

category [ˈkætɪɡərɪ] N Kategorie *f*

➤ **cater for** VI +PREP OBJ **(a)** (= *serve with food*) mit Speisen und Getränken versorgen; *coach party etc* (mit Speisen und Getränken) bedienen **(b)** (= *provide for*) ausgerichtet sein auf (+*acc*); (*also* **cater to**) *needs, tastes* gerecht werden (+*dat*)

cater-corner(ed) [ˈkeɪtəˈkɔːnəʳ(-əd)] ADV (*US*) diagonal

caterer [ˈkeɪtərəʳ] N (= *company*) Lieferfirma *f* für Speisen und Getränke; (*for parties etc*) Partyservice *m*

catering [ˈkeɪtərɪŋ] N Versorgung *f* mit Speisen und Getränken (*for* +*gen*); **who's doing the ~?** wer liefert das Essen und die Getränke?; **~ trade** (Hotel- und) Gaststättengewerbe *nt*

caterpillar [ˈkætəpɪləʳ] N (*Zool*) Raupe *f*

caterpillar track® N Raupenkette *f*

caterwauling [ˈkætəwɔːlɪŋ] N Gejaule *nt*

catgut [ˈkætɡʌt] N Katgut *nt*

catharsis [kəˈθɑːsɪs] N (*Liter, Philos*) Katharsis *f*

cathartic [kəˈθɑːtɪk] ADJ (*Liter, Philos*) kathartisch

cathedral [kəˈθiːdrəl] N Dom *m*; (*esp in England, France, Spain*) Kathedrale *f*; **~ town/city** Domstadt *f*

Catherine wheel [ˈkæθərɪnwiːl] N Feuerrad *nt*

catheter [ˈkæθɪtəʳ] N Katheter *m*

cathode-ray tube [ˌkæθəʊdˈreɪtjuːb] N Kat(h)odenstrahlröhre *f*

Catholic [ˈkæθəlɪk] **1** ADJ (*Eccl*) katholisch; **the ~ Church** die katholische Kirche **2** N Katholik(in) *m(f)*

catholic [ˈkæθəlɪk] ADJ (= *varied*) vielseitig; **he's a man of very ~ tastes** er ist (ein) sehr vielseitig interessiert(er Mensch)

Catholicism [kəˈθɒlɪsɪzəm] N Katholizismus *m*

cat: **catkin** N (*Bot*) Kätzchen *nt*; **cat litter** N Katzenstreu *f*; **catnap 1** N **to have a ~** ein Nickerchen *nt* machen (*inf*) **2** VI dösen

CAT scan [ˈkætˌskæn] N Computertomografie *f*

Catseye® [ˈkætsˌaɪ] N (*Brit Aut*) Katzenauge *nt*

catsuit [ˈkætsuːt] N einteiliger Hosenanzug

catsup [ˈkætsəp] N (*US*) = **ketchup**

cattail [ˈkætˌteɪl] N (*US*) Rohrkolben *m*

cattle [ˈkætl] PL Rind(vieh) *nt*; **500 head of ~** 500 Rinder; **they were treated like ~** sie wurden wie Vieh behandelt

cattle: **cattle-grid** N, **cattle guard** N (*US*) Weidenrost *m*; **cattle market** N (*lit*) Viehmarkt *m*; **cattle shed** N Viehstall *m*; **cattle truck** N (*Aut*) Viehanhänger *m*; (*Rail*) Viehwagen *m*

catty [ˈkætɪ] ADJ (+ER) gehässig

catty-corner(ed) [ˈkætɪˈkɔːnəʳ(-əd)] ADJ, ADV (*US*) = **cater-corner(ed)**

catwalk [ˈkætwɔːk] N Steg *m*; (*for models*) Laufsteg *m*

Caucasian [kɔːˈkeɪzɪən] **1** ADJ kaukasisch **2** N Kaukasier(in) *m(f)*

caucus [ˈkɔːkəs] N (= *committee*) Ausschuss *m*; (*US*: = *meeting*) Sitzung *f*

caught [kɔːt] PRET, PTP *of* **catch**

cauldron [ˈkɔːldrən] N großer Kessel

cauliflower [ˈkɒlɪflaʊəʳ] N Blumenkohl *m*

cauliflower ear N Boxerohr *nt*

causal [ˈkɔːzəl] ADJ ursächlich; **~ relationship** Kausalzusammenhang *m*

causative [ˈkɔːzətɪv] ADJ *factor* verursachend

cause [kɔːz] **1** N **(a)** Ursache *f* (*of* für); **~ and effect** Ursache und Wirkung; **what was the ~ of the fire?** wodurch ist das Feuer entstanden?
(b) (= *reason*) Grund *m*; **the ~ of his failure** der Grund für sein Versagen; **with/without (good) ~** mit (triftigem)/ohne (triftigen) Grund; **there's no ~ for alarm** es besteht kein Grund *or* Anlass zur Aufregung; **you have every ~ to be worried** du hast allen Anlass zur Sorge
(c) (= *purpose, ideal*) Sache *f*; **to work for *or* in a good ~** sich für eine gute Sache einsetzen; **he died for the ~ of peace** er

starb für den Frieden; **it's all in a good ~** es ist für eine gute Sache
2 VT verursachen; **to ~ sb grief** jdm Kummer machen; **to ~ sb to do sth** (*form*) jdn veranlassen, etw zu tun (*form*)

causeway [ˈkɔːzweɪ] N Damm *m*

caustic [ˈkɔːstɪk] ADJ (*Chem, fig*) ätzend; *remark* bissig; **he was very ~ about the project** er äußerte sich sehr bissig über das Projekt

caustically [ˈkɔːstɪklɪ] ADV *say, remark* bissig

caustic soda N Ätznatron *nt*

cauterize [ˈkɔːtəraɪz] VT (*Med*) kauterisieren

caution [ˈkɔːʃən] **1** N **(a)** (= *circumspection*) Vorsicht *f*; **"~!"** „Vorsicht!"; **to act with ~** Vorsicht walten lassen; **~ marks** (*Comm*) Sicherheitsmarkierungen *pl* **(b)** (= *warning*) Warnung *f*; (*official*) Verwarnung *f* **2** VT **to ~ sb** jdn warnen (*against* vor +*dat*); (*officially*) jdn verwarnen; **to ~ sb against doing sth** jdn davor warnen, etw zu tun

cautionary [ˈkɔːʃənərɪ] ADJ belehrend; **a ~ tale** eine Geschichte mit Moral

cautious [ˈkɔːʃəs] ADJ vorsichtig; **to give sth a ~ welcome** etw mit verhaltener Zustimmung aufnehmen

cautiously [ˈkɔːʃəslɪ] ADV vorsichtig; *welcome* verhalten; **~ optimistic** verhalten optimistisch

cavalcade [ˌkævəlˈkeɪd] N Kavalkade *f*

cavalier [ˌkævəˈlɪəʳ] ADJ (= *offhand*) unbekümmert

cavalry [ˈkævəlrɪ] N Kavallerie *f*

cavalry: **cavalryman** N Kavallerist *m*; **cavalry officer** N Kavallerieoffizier *m*

cave [keɪv] **1** N Höhle *f* **2** VI **to go caving** auf Höhlenexpedition(en) gehen

➤ **cave in** VI **(a)** (= *collapse*) einstürzen **(b)** (*inf*: = *surrender, yield*) nachgeben

caveat [ˈkævɪæt] N Vorbehalt *m*

cave: **cave dweller** N Höhlenbewohner *m*; **caveman** N Höhlenmensch *m*; **cave painting** N Höhlenmalerei *f*

caver [ˈkeɪvəʳ] N Höhlenforscher(in) *m(f)*

cavern [ˈkævən] N Höhle *f*

cavernous [ˈkævənəs] ADJ tief; *mouth* riesig

caviar(e) [ˈkævɪɑːʳ] N Kaviar *m*

cavil [ˈkævɪl] VI kritteln; **to ~ at sth** an etw (*dat*) herumkritteln

cavity [ˈkævɪtɪ] N Hohlraum *m*; (*in tooth*) Loch *nt*; **nasal/chest ~** (*Anat*) Nasen-/Brusthöhle *f*

cavity wall N Hohlwand *f*; **~ insulation** Schaumisolierung *f*

cavort [kəˈvɔːt] VI tollen, toben

cayenne pepper [ˈkeɪenˈpepəʳ] N Cayennepfeffer *m*

CB ABBR *of* **Citizens' Band** CB; **CB radio** CB-Funk *m*

CBE (*Brit*) ABBR *of* **Commander of the Order of the British Empire**

CBI (*Brit*) ABBR *of* **Confederation of British Industry** ≈ BDI

cc[1] ABBR *of* **cubic centimetre** cc, cm^3

cc[2] ABBR *of* **carbon copy 1** N Kopie *f* **2** VT eine Kopie senden an (+*acc*); **cc: ...** Kopie (an): ...

CCTV N ABBR *of* **closed-circuit television**

CD (a) ABBR *of* **compact disc** CD *f*; **CD player** CD-Spieler *m*; **CD case** CD-Hülle *f* **(b)** (*US*) ABBR *of* **Congressional District** **(c)** (*Fin*) ABBR *of* **certificate of deposit**

cd ABBR *of* **cum dividend** (*St Ex*) mit Dividende

CDC (*US*) ABBR *of* **Centers for Disease Control and Prevention**

CDC

*Die **Centers for Disease Control and Prevention**, kurz **CDC**, bilden eine US-Bundesbehörde, die für viele Aspekte der öffentlichen Gesundheit zuständig ist. Zu ihren Aufgaben gehört das Festlegen und Verschärfen von Schadstoffgrenzwerten und Sicherheitsstandards für Umwelt oder Arbeitsplätze, das Sammeln und Analysieren von Daten, die für das Gesundheitswesen relevant sind, sowie die Vorsorge gegen übertragbare Krankheiten und deren Kontrolle. Der Hauptsitz der **CDC** ist in Atlanta, Georgia. Im Ausland wurde die US-Seuchenkontrollbehörde vor allem durch ihre Vorreiterrolle bei der Beobachtung der Ausbreitung des HIV-Virus und der Identifizierung von dessen Übertragungswegen bekannt.*

CD-ROM [ˈsiːdiːˈrɒm] ABBR *of* **compact disk - read only memory** CD-ROM *f*; **~ drive** CD-ROM-Laufwerk *nt*

CDT (a) (*US*) ABBR *of* **Central Daylight Time (b)** (*Brit Sch*) ABBR *of* **Craft, Design and Technology** ≈ Arbeitslehre *f*

cease [siːs] **1** VI enden; (*noise, shouting etc*) verstummen **2** VT beenden; *fire, payments, production, trading* einstellen; **to ~ doing sth** aufhören, etw zu tun

cease-fire [ˈsiːsˈfaɪəʳ] N Feuerpause *f*; (*longer*) Waffenruhe *f*

ceaseless [ˈsiːslɪs] ADJ (= *endless*) endlos; (= *relentless*) *vigilance* unablässig

ceaselessly [ˈsiːslɪslɪ] ADV (= *endlessly*) unaufhörlich; (= *relentlessly*) unablässig

cedar [ˈsiːdəʳ] N **(a)** (= *tree*) Zeder *f* **(b)** (*also* **~wood**) Zedernholz *nt*

cede [siːd] VT *territory* abtreten (*to* an +*acc*); **to ~ a point in an argument** in einem Punkt nachgeben

cedilla [sɪˈdɪlə] N Cedille *f*

Ceefax® [ˈsiːfæks] N *Videotext der BBC*

ceiling [ˈsiːlɪŋ] N **(a)** (Zimmer)decke *f* **(b)** (*fig*: = *upper limit*) Höchstgrenze *f*; **price ~** oberste Preisgrenze; **to put a ~ on sth** etw nach oben begrenzen

celebrate [ˈselɪbreɪt] **1** VT **(a)** feiern **(b)** *mass, ritual* zelebrieren; *communion* feiern **2** VI feiern

celebrated [ˈselɪbreɪtɪd] ADJ gefeiert (*for* wegen)

celebration [ˌselɪˈbreɪʃən] N **(a)** (= *party, festival*) Feier *f*; (= *act of celebrating*) Feiern *nt*; **in ~ of** zur Feier (+*gen*) **(b)** (*of mass, ritual*) Zelebration *f*; (*of communion*) Feier *f*

celebratory [ˌselɪˈbreɪtərɪ] ADJ *meal, drink* zur Feier des Tages

celebrity [sɪˈlebrɪtɪ] N Berühmtheit *f*

celeriac [səˈlerɪæk] N (Knollen)sellerie *f*

celery [ˈselərɪ] N Stangensellerie *m or f*; **three stalks of ~** drei Stangen Sellerie

celestial [sɪˈlestɪəl] ADJ himmlisch; (*Astron*) Himmels-

celibacy [ˈselɪbəsɪ] N Zölibat *nt or m*

celibate [ˈselɪbɪt] ADJ (*Rel*) keusch, zölibatär (*spec*)

cell [sel] N (*all senses*) Zelle *f*; **~ wall** Zellwand *f*

cellar [ˈseləʳ] N Keller *m*

cellist [ˈtʃelɪst] N Cellist(in) *m(f)*

cello, 'cello [ˈtʃeləʊ] N Cello *nt*

Cellophane® [ˈseləfeɪn] N Cellophan® *nt*

cellular [ˈseljʊləʳ] ADJ zellular, Zell-

cellular phone N Mobiltelefon *nt*

cellulite [ˈseljʊˌlaɪt] N Cellulitis *f*

celluloid [ˈseljʊlɔɪd] N Zelluloid *nt*; **on ~** auf der Leinwand

cellulose [ˈseljʊləʊs] N Zellulose *f*, Zellstoff *m*

Celsius [ˈselsɪəs] ADJ Celsius-; **30 degrees ~** 30 Grad Celsius

Celt [kelt, selt] N Kelte *m*, Keltin *f*

Celtic [ˈkeltɪk, ˈseltɪk] **1** ADJ keltisch **2** N (*Ling*) Keltisch *nt*

cement [səˈment] **1** N **(a)** (*Build*) Zement *m*; (*inf*: = *concrete*) Beton *m* **(b)** (= *glue*) Leim *m* **2** VT (*Build*) zementieren; (= *glue*) leimen; (*fig*) festigen

cement mixer N Betonmischmaschine *f*

cemetery [ˈsemɪtrɪ] N Friedhof *m*

cenotaph [ˈsenətɑːf] N Mahnmal *nt*, Ehrenmal *nt*

censor [ˈsensəʳ] **1** N Zensor *m* **2** VT zensieren

censorious [senˈsɔːrɪəs] ADJ *remark, glance* strafend

censorship [ˈsensəʃɪp] N Zensur *f*; **press ~, ~ of the press** Pressezensur *f*

censure [ˈsenʃəʳ] **1** VT tadeln **2** N Tadel *m*

census [ˈsensəs] N Volkszählung *f*

cent [sent] N Cent *m*; **I haven't a ~** (*US*) ich habe keinen Cent; **to put in one's two ~s' worth** (*esp US*) seinen Senf dazugeben (*inf*)

centenarian [ˌsentɪˈnɛərɪən] N Hundertjährige(r) *mf*

centenary [senˈtiːnərɪ] N (= *anniversary*) hundertster Jahrestag; **she has just celebrated her ~** sie ist gerade hundert Jahre alt geworden

centennial [senˈtenɪəl] N (*esp US*) Hundertjahrfeier *f*

center N (*US*) = **centre**

centigrade [ˈsentɪgreɪd] ADJ Celsius-; **one degree ~** ein Grad Celsius

centilitre, (*US*) **centiliter** [ˈsentɪˌliːtəʳ] N Zentiliter *m or nt*

centimetre, (*US*) **centimeter** [ˈsentɪˌmiːtəʳ] N Zentimeter *m or nt*

centipede [ˈsentɪpiːd] N Tausendfüßler *m*

central [ˈsentrəl] **1** ADJ **(a)** zentral, Zentral-; (= *main, chief*) Haupt-; **the ~ area of the city** das Innenstadtgebiet; **~ London** das Zentrum von London **(b)** (*fig*) wesentlich; *importance, issue* zentral; **to be ~ to sth** das Wesentliche an etw (*dat*) sein **2** N (*US*: = *exchange, operator*) Fernamt *nt*

central: Central America N Mittelamerika *nt*; **Central American** ADJ mittelamerikanisch; **central bank** N (*Fin*) Zentral(noten)bank *f*; **Central Europe** N Mitteleuropa *nt*; **Central European** ADJ mitteleuropäisch; **Central European Time** N mitteleuropäische Zeit; **central government** N Zentralregierung *f*; **central heating** N Zentralheizung *f*

centralization [ˌsentrəlaɪˈzeɪʃən] N Zentralisierung *f*

centralize [ˈsentrəlaɪz] VT zentralisieren

central locking [ˌsentrəlˈlɒkɪŋ] N Zentralverriegelung *f*

centrally [ˈsentrəlɪ] ADV zentral; **~ heated** zentralbeheizt

central: central nervous system N Zentralnervensystem *nt*; **Central Office of Information** N (*Brit*) Zentrales Presseamt; **central processing unit** N (*Comput*) Zentraleinheit *f*; **central reservation** N Mittelstreifen *m*; **Central Standard Time** N Central Standard Time *f*

centre, (*US*) **center** [ˈsentəʳ] **1** N **(a)** Zentrum *nt*; (= *community ~, sports ~, shopping ~* *also*) Center *nt* **(b)** (= *middle, Pol*) Mitte *f*; (*of circle*) Mittelpunkt *m*; (= *town ~*) Stadtmitte *f*; (= *city ~*) Zentrum *nt*; **~ of gravity** Schwerpunkt *m*; **she always wants to be the ~ of attention** *or* **attraction** sie will immer im Mittelpunkt stehen; **the man at the ~ of the controversy** der Mann im Mittelpunkt der Kontroverse; **left of ~** (*Pol*) links der Mitte; **politician/party of the ~** Politiker(in) *m(f)*/Partei *f* der Mitte **(c)** (*Rugby*) mittlerer Dreiviertelspieler; (*Basketball, Netball*) Center *m* **2** VT **(a)** (*also Comput*) zentrieren **(b)** (= *concentrate*) **to be ~d on sth** sich auf etw (*acc*) konzentrieren **(c)** (*Sport*) *ball* zur Mitte (ab)spielen

▶ **centre (up)on** VI +PREP OBJ (*thoughts, problem, talk etc*) kreisen um

centre, (*US*) **center: centrefold**, (*US*) **centerfold** N *doppelseitiges Bild in der Mitte einer Zeitschrift*; (= *girl*) *weibliches Aktmodell, dessen Foto auf den Mittelseiten einer Zeitschrift abgedruckt ist*; **centre forward** N (*Sport*) Mittelstürmer(in) *m(f)*; **centre half** N (*Sport*) Stopper(in) *m(f)*; **centre party** N Partei *f* der Mitte; **centrepiece**, (*US*) **centerpiece** N (*fig*) (*of meeting, statement*) Kernstück *nt*; (*of novel, work*) Herzstück *nt*; (*of show*) Hauptattraktion *f*

centrifugal [ˌsentrɪˈfjuːgəl] ADJ **~ force** Fliehkraft *f*

century [ˈsentʃʊrɪ] N **(a)** Jahrhundert *nt*; **in the twentieth ~** im zwanzigsten Jahrhundert; (*written*) im 20. Jahrhundert **(b)** (*Cricket*) Hundert *f*

ceramic [sɪˈræmɪk] ADJ keramisch; **~ hob** Glaskeramikkochfeld *nt*

ceramics [sɪˈræmɪks] N **(a)** SING (= *art*) Keramik *f* **(b)** PL (= *articles*) Keramik(en *pl*) *f*

cereal [ˈsɪərɪəl] N **(a)** (= *crop*) Getreide *nt* **(b)** (= *food*) Cornflakes *pl*/Müsli *nt etc*

cerebral [ˈserɪbrəl] ADJ (*Physiol*) zerebral; (= *intellectual*) geistig; *person* vergeistigt; **~ palsy** zerebrale Lähmung

ceremonial [ˌserɪˈməʊnɪəl] ADJ zeremoniell

ceremoniously [ˌserɪˈməʊnɪəslɪ] ADV mit großem Zeremoniell

ceremony [ˈserɪmənɪ] N **(a)** (= *event etc*) Zeremonie *f* **(b)** (= *formality*) Förmlichkeit(en *pl*) *f*; **to stand on ~** förmlich sein

cert [sɜːt] N (*Brit inf*) **a (dead) ~** eine todsichere Sache (*inf*)

certain [ˈsɜːtən] **1** ADJ **(a)** (= *convinced*) sicher; (= *inevitable*) gewiss; **are you ~ of** *or* **about that?** sind Sie sich (*dat*) dessen sicher?; **is he ~?** weiß er das genau?; **I don't know for ~, but I think ...** ich bin mir nicht ganz sicher, aber ich glaube ...; **I can't say for ~** ich kann das nicht genau sagen; **he is ~ to come** er wird ganz bestimmt kommen; **to make ~ of sth** (= *check*) sich einer Sache (*gen*) vergewissern; (= *ensure*) für etw sorgen; **be ~ to tell him** vergessen Sie bitte nicht, ihm das zu sagen **(b)** ATTR (= *not specified*) gewiss; *reason, conditions* bestimmt; **a ~ gentleman** ein gewisser Herr; **to a ~ extent** *or* **degree** in

gewisser Hinsicht; **of a ~ age** in einem gewissen Alter
2 PRON einige; **~ of you/them** einige von euch/ihnen

certainly ['sɜːtənlɪ] ADV (= *admittedly*) sicher(lich); (= *without doubt*) bestimmt; **~ not!** ganz bestimmt nicht; **I ~ will not!** ich denke nicht daran!; **~! sicher!**

certainty ['sɜːtəntɪ] N Gewissheit *f*; **to know for a ~ that ...** mit Sicherheit wissen, dass ...; **his success is a ~** er wird mit Sicherheit Erfolg haben; **it's a ~ that ...** es ist absolut sicher, dass ...

CertEd (*Brit*) ABBR *of* **Certificate in Education**

certifiable [ˌsɜːtɪ'faɪəbl] ADJ (*Psych*) unzurechnungsfähig; (*inf*: = *mad*) nicht zurechnungsfähig

certificate [sə'tɪfɪkɪt] N Bescheinigung *f*; (*of qualifications, health*) Zeugnis *nt*; (*Film*) Freigabe *f*; **~ of deposit** (*Fin*) Einlagenzertifikat *nt*, Geldmarktzertifikat *nt*; **~ of incorporation** (*Comm*) Gründungsurkunde *f*; **~ of inspection** (*Comm*) Beschaffenheitszeugnis *nt*, Inspektionszertifikat *nt*; **~ of insurance** (*Comm*) Versicherungspolice *f*; **~ of origin** (*Comm*) Ursprungszeugnis *nt*; **~ of trading** (*Brit*) Gewerbeschein *m*

certified ['sɜːtɪfaɪd]: **certified mail** N (*US*) Einschreiben *nt*; **certified milk** N (*US*) Vorzugsmilch *f*; **certified public accountant** N (*US*) geprüfter Buchhalter, geprüfte Buchhalterin

certify ['sɜːtɪfaɪ] VT (= *confirm*) bescheinigen; (*Jur*) beglaubigen; **this is to ~ that ...** hiermit wird bescheinigt *or* bestätigt, dass ...; **she was certified dead** sie wurde für tot erklärt; **the painting has been certified (as) genuine** das Gemälde wurde als echt erklärt (b) (*Psych*) für unzurechnungsfähig erklären; **he should be certified** (*inf*) der ist doch nicht ganz zurechnungsfähig (*inf*)

cervical ['sɜːvɪkl, sə'vaɪkəl]: **cervical cancer** N Gebärmutterhalskrebs *m*; **cervical smear** N Abstrich *m*

Cesarean, Cesarian [siː'zɛərɪən] N (*US*) = **Caesarean**

cessation [se'seɪʃən] N Ende *nt*; (*of hostilities*) Einstellung *f*

cesspit ['sespɪt], **cesspool** ['sespuːl] N Jauchegrube *f*

CET ABBR *of* **Central European Time** MEZ

Ceylon [sɪ'lɒn] N Ceylon *nt*

CF (*US*) ABBR *of* **cost and freight** cf

cf ABBR *of* **confer** vgl

C/F ABBR *of* **carriage forward** (*Brit Comm*) unfrei, gegen Nachnahme

c/f ABBR *of* **carry forward**

CFC ABBR *of* **chlorofluorocarbon** FCKW *m*

CFI (*US*) ABBR *of* **cost, freight and insurance** cif

CFR ABBR *of* **cost and freight** cf

CFS (*Med*) ABBR *of* **chronic fatigue syndrome** CFS

CGA (*Comput*) ABBR *of* **colour graphics adaptor** CGA *m*

CGT (*Fin*) N ABBR *of* **capital gains tax**

cha-cha ['tʃɑːtʃɑː] N Cha-Cha-Cha *m*

chador ['tʃɑːdɔː] N Chador *m*

chafe [tʃeɪf] **1** VT (= *rub*) (auf)scheuern; **his shirt ~d his neck** sein (Hemd)kragen scheuerte (ihn) **2** VI (a) (= *rub*) sich aufscheuern; (= *cause soreness*) scheuern; **her skin ~s easily** ihre Haut wird leicht wund (b) (*fig*) sich ärgern (*at, against* über +*acc*)

chaff [tʃɑːf] N (= *husks of grain*) Spreu *f*

chaffinch ['tʃæfɪntʃ] N Buchfink *m*

chagrin ['ʃægrɪn] N Ärger *m*

chain [tʃeɪn] **1** N Kette *f*; **~s** (*lit, fig*: = *fetters*) Ketten *pl*; (*Aut*) (Schnee)ketten *pl*; (*of mountains*) (Berg)kette *f*; **~ of command** (*in management*) Weisungskette *f*; **~ of office** Amtskette *f*; **~ of shops** Ladenkette *f*; **~ of events** Kette von Ereignissen; **~ of command** (*Mil*) Befehlskette *f*; (*in management*) Weisungskette *f*
2 VT (*lit, fig*) anketten; *dog* an die Kette legen; **to ~ sb/sth to sth** jdn/etw an etw (*acc*) ketten
➤ **chain up** VT SEP *prisoner* in Ketten legen; *dog* an die Kette legen

chain IN CPDS Ketten-; **chain letter** N Kettenbrief *m*; **chain mail** N Kettenhemd *nt*; **chain reaction** N Kettenreaktion *f*; **chain saw** N Kettensäge *f*; **chain-smoke** VI eine (Zigarette) nach der anderen rauchen, kettenrauchen *infin only*; **chain store** N Kettenladen *m*

chair [tʃɛəʳ] **1** N (a) (= *seat*) Stuhl *m*; (= *armchair*) Sessel *m*; **please take a ~** bitte nehmen Sie Platz! (b) (*in committees etc*) Vorsitz *m*; **to be in/take the ~** den Vorsitz führen (c) (= *professorship*) Lehrstuhl *m* (*of* für) (d) (= *electric ~*) (elektrischer) Stuhl **2** VT *meeting* den Vorsitz führen bei

chair: **chairlift** N Sessellift *m*; **chairman** N Vorsitzende(r) *mf*; **Mr/Madam Chairman** Herr Vorsitzender/Frau Vorsitzende; **~'s statement** Geschäftsbericht *m* des Vorsitzenden; **chairmanship** N Vorsitz *m*; **chairperson** N Vorsitzende(r) *mf*; **chairwoman** N Vorsitzende *f*

chaise longue [ʃeɪz'lɒŋ] N Chaiselongue *f*

chalet ['ʃæleɪ] N Chalet *nt*; (*in motel etc*) Apartment *nt*

chalk [tʃɔːk] **1** N Kreide *f*; **not by a long ~** (*Brit inf*) bei weitem nicht; **they're as different as ~ and cheese** (*Brit*) sie sind (so verschieden) wie Tag und Nacht **2** VT *message etc* mit Kreide schreiben; *billiard cue* mit Kreide einreiben
➤ **chalk up** VT SEP (*fig*) *success, victory* verbuchen

challenge ['tʃælɪndʒ] **1** N (a) (*to duel, match etc*) Herausforderung *f* (*to an* +*acc*); (*fig*: = *demands*) Anforderung(en *pl*) *f*; **to issue a ~ to sb** jdn herausfordern; **this job is a ~** bei dieser Arbeit ist man gefordert; **I see this task as a ~** ich sehe diese Aufgabe als Herausforderung; **those who rose to the ~** diejenigen, die sich der Herausforderung stellten
(b) (= *bid*: *for leadership etc*) Griff *m* (*for* nach); **a direct ~ to his authority** eine direkte Infragestellung seiner Autorität **2** VT (a) (*to duel, race etc*) herausfordern; *world record etc* überbieten wollen; **to ~ sb to do sth** wetten, dass jd etw nicht (tun) kann; **to ~ sb to a duel** jdn zum Duell fordern; **to ~ sb to a game** jdn zu einer Partie herausfordern
(b) (*fig*: = *make demands on*) fordern
(c) (*fig*) *remarks, sb's authority* infrage stellen, anfechten
(d) (*sentry*) anrufen
(e) (*Jur*) *witnesses* ablehnen; *evidence, verdict* anfechten

-challenged [-'tʃælɪndʒd] ADJ SUF (*usu hum*) **vertically-challenged** zu kurz geraten (*hum*); **intellectually-challenged** geistig minderbemittelt (*inf*)

challenger ['tʃælɪndʒəʳ] N (*to match etc*) Herausforderer *m*, Herausforderin *f*

challenging ['tʃælɪndʒɪŋ] ADJ (= *provocative*) herausfordernd; (= *thought-provoking*) reizvoll; (= *demanding*) anspruchsvoll

chamber ['tʃeɪmbəʳ] N (a) (*old*: = *room*) Gemach *nt* (*old*); **~ of horrors** Horrorkabinett *nt* (b) (*Brit*) **~s** *pl* (*of solicitor*) Kanzlei *f*; (*of judge*) Amtszimmer *nt* (c) **Chamber of Commerce** Handelskammer *f*; **the Upper/Lower Chamber** (*Parl*) die Erste/Zweite Kammer

chamber: **chambermaid** N Zimmermädchen *nt*, Kammerzofe *f* (*old*); **chamber music** N Kammermusik *f*; **chamber orchestra** N Kammerorchester *nt*; **chamber pot** N Nachttopf *m*

chameleon [kə'miːliən] N (*Zool, fig*) Chamäleon *nt*

chamois ['ʃæmwɑː] N a ~ **(leather)** ein Fensterleder *nt*

champ¹ [tʃæmp] VT **to ~ at the bit** (*fig*) vor Ungeduld fiebern

champ² N (*inf*) Champion *m*

champagne [ʃæm'peɪn] N Sekt *m*, Schaumwein *m*; (= *French ~*) Champagner *m*; **~ glass** Sekt-/Champagnerglas *nt*

champion ['tʃæmpjən] **1** N (a) (*Sport*) Meister(in) *m(f)*, Champion *m*; **~s** (= *team*) Meister *m*; **world ~** Weltmeister(in) *m(f)*; **boxing ~** Boxchampion *m*; **heavyweight ~ of the world** Weltmeister *m* im Schwergewicht (b) (*of a cause*) Verfechter *m* **2** VT *person, cause* eintreten für

championship ['tʃæmpjənʃɪp] N (a) (*Sport*) Meisterschaft *f* (b) **championships** PL (= *event*) Meisterschaftskämpfe *pl*

Champions' League N (*Ftbl*) Champions League *f*

chance [tʃɑːns] **1** N (a) (= *coincidence*) Zufall *m*; (= *luck*) Glück *nt*; **by ~** zufällig; **would you by any ~ be able to help?** könnten Sie mir vielleicht behilflich sein?
(b) (= *possibility, opportunity*) Chance(n *pl*) *f*; (= *probability*) Möglichkeit *f*; **(the) ~s are that ...** wahrscheinlich ...; **what are the ~s of his coming?** wie groß ist die Wahrscheinlichkeit, dass er kommt?; **is there any ~ of us meeting again?** könnten wir uns vielleicht wiedersehen?; **he doesn't stand or hasn't got a ~** er hat keine(rlei) Chance(n); **he has a good ~ of winning** er hat gute Aussicht zu gewinnen; **to be in with a ~** eine Chance haben; **no ~!** (*inf*) nee! (*inf*); **you won't get another ~** das ist eine einmalige Gelegenheit; **I had**

the ~ **to go** *or* **of going** ich hatte (die) Gelegenheit, dahin zu gehen; **now's your ~!** das ist deine Chance!
(c) (= *risk*) Risiko *nt*; **to take a ~** es darauf ankommen lassen; **he's not taking any ~s** er geht kein Risiko ein
2 ATTR zufällig; ~ **meeting** zufällige Begegnung
3 VT **I'll ~ it!** (*inf*) ich versuchs mal (*inf*)
➤ **chance (up)on** VI +PREP OBJ *person* zufällig treffen; *thing* zufällig stoßen auf (+*acc*)

chancel ['tʃɑːnsəl] N Chor *m*

chancellor ['tʃɑːnsələ'] N (*Jur, Pol, Univ*) Kanzler *m*; **Chancellor (of the Exchequer)** (*Brit*) Schatzkanzler(in) *m(f)*, Finanzminister(in) *m(f)*

chancy ['tʃɑːnsɪ] ADJ (+ER) (*inf*: = *risky*) riskant

chandelier [ʃændə'lɪə'] N Kronleuchter *m*

change [tʃeɪndʒ] **1** N **(a)** (= *alteration*) Veränderung *f*; (= *modification also*) Änderung *f* (*to* +*gen*); **a ~ for the better/worse** eine Verbesserung/Verschlechterung; ~ **of address** Adressenänderung *f*; **a ~ in the weather** eine Wetterveränderung; **no ~** unverändert; **I need a ~ of scene** ich brauche Tapetenwechsel; **to make ~s (to sth)** (an etw *dat*) (Ver)änderungen *pl* vornehmen; **to make a ~ in sth** etw ändern; **I didn't have a ~ of clothes with me** ich hatte nichts zum Wechseln mit; **a ~ of job** ein Stellenwechsel *m*
(b) (= *variety*) Abwechslung *f*; **(just) for a ~** zur Abwechslung (mal); **that makes a ~** das ist mal was anderes; (*iro*) das ist ja was ganz Neues!
(c) (*of one thing for another*) Wechsel *m*; **a ~ of government** ein Regierungswechsel *m*
(d) NO PL (= *money*) Wechselgeld *nt*; (= *small ~*) Kleingeld *nt*; **can you give me ~ for a pound?** können Sie mir ein Pfund wechseln?; **I haven't got any ~** ich habe kein Kleingeld; **you won't get much ~ out of £5** von £ 5 wird wohl nicht viel übrig bleiben; **keep the ~** der Rest ist für Sie
2 VT **(a)** wechseln; *address, name* ändern; **to ~ trains/buses** *etc* umsteigen; **to ~ one's clothes** sich umziehen; **to ~ a wheel/the oil** ein Rad/das Öl wechseln; **to ~ a baby's nappy** (*Brit*) *or* **diaper** (*US*), **to ~ a baby** (bei einem Baby) die Windeln wechseln; **to ~ the sheets** *or* **the bed** die Bettwäsche wechseln; **to ~ hands** den Besitzer wechseln; **she ~d places with him** er und sie tauschten die Plätze
(b) (= *alter*) (ver)ändern; *person, ideas* ändern; (= *transform*) verwandeln; **to ~ sb/sth into sth** jdn/etw in etw (*acc*) verwandeln
(c) (= *exchange: in shop etc*) umtauschen; **she ~d the dress for one of a different colour** sie tauschte das Kleid gegen ein andersfarbiges um
(d) (*Brit Aut*) **to ~ gear** schalten
3 VI **(a)** (= *alter*) sich ändern; (*town, person also*) sich verändern; **to ~ from sth into ...** sich aus etw in ... (*acc*) verwandeln
(b) (= ~ *clothes*) sich umziehen; **she ~d into an old skirt** sie zog sich einen alten Rock an; **I'll just ~ out of these old clothes** ich muss mir noch die alten Sachen ausziehen
(c) (= ~ *trains etc*) umsteigen; **all ~!** alle aussteigen!
(d) (*Brit Aut*: = ~ *gear*) schalten; (*traffic lights*) umspringen (*to* auf +*acc*)
(e) (*from one thing to another*) **to ~ to a different system** auf ein anderes System umstellen; **I ~d to philosophy from chemistry** ich habe von Chemie zu Philosophie gewechselt
➤ **change around** VT SEP = **change round 2**
➤ **change down** VI (*Brit Aut*) in einen niedrigeren Gang schalten
➤ **change over 1** VI **(a)** (= *change to sth different*) sich umstellen (*to auf* +*acc*); **we have just changed over from gas to electricity** hier *or* bei uns ist gerade von Gas auf Strom umgestellt worden **(b)** (= *exchange places, activities etc*) wechseln **2** VT SEP austauschen
➤ **change round** (*esp Brit*) **1** VI = **change over 1 2** VT SEP *room* umräumen; *furniture* umstellen
➤ **change up** VI (*Brit Aut*) in einen höheren Gang schalten

changeable ['tʃeɪndʒəbl] ADJ *character* unbeständig; *weather* wechselhaft; *mood* wechselnd

change machine N Geldwechsler *m*

changeover ['tʃeɪndʒəʊvə'] N Umstellung *f* (*to* auf +*acc*)

changing ['tʃeɪndʒɪŋ] ADJ wechselnd

changing room N (*in store*) Ankleideraum *m*; (*Sport*) Umkleideraum *m*

channel ['tʃænl] **1** N **(a)** (= *watercourse*) (Fluss)bett *nt*; (= *strait*, *also TV, Rad*) Kanal *m*; **the (English) Channel** der Ärmelkanal
(b) (*fig, usu pl*) (*of bureaucracy etc*) Dienstweg *m*; (*of information etc*) Kanal *m*; **to go through the official ~s** den Dienstweg gehen; **you'll have to go through ~s** (*US*) Sie werden den Dienstweg einhalten müssen; ~ **of distibution** (*Comm*) Vertriebsweg *m*
(c) (= *groove*) Furche *f*
2 VT **(a)** (= *direct*) *water* (hindurch)leiten
(b) (*fig*) lenken (*into* auf +*acc*)

channel: **Channel ferry** N (*Brit*) Kanalfähre *f*; **channel-hopping** N (*Brit TV inf*) Zappen *nt* (*inf*); **Channel Islands** PL Kanalinseln *pl*; **channel-surfing** N (*esp US TV inf*) = **channel-hopping**; **Channel Tunnel** N Kanaltunnel *m*

chant [tʃɑːnt] **1** N (*Eccl, Mus*) Gesang *m*; (*of football fans etc*) Sprechchor *m* **2** VT im (Sprech)chor rufen; (*Eccl*) singen **3** VI Sprechchöre anstimmen; (*Eccl*) singen

chaos ['keɪɒs] N Chaos *nt*; **complete ~** ein totales Durcheinander

chaotic [keɪ'ɒtɪk] ADJ chaotisch

chap¹ [tʃæp] VT sspröde machen; **~ped lips** aufgesprungene *or* raue Lippen *pl*

chap² N (*Brit inf*: = *man*) Typ *m* (*inf*)

chapel ['tʃæpəl] N **(a)** Kapelle *f* **(b)** (= *nonconformist church*) Sektenkirche *f*

chaperon(e) ['ʃæpərəʊn] **1** N **(a)** (*for propriety*) Anstandsdame *f* **(b)** (= *escort*) Begleiter(in) *m(f)* **(c)** (*esp US*: = *supervisor*) Aufsichts- *or* Begleitperson *f* **2** VT **(a)** (*for propriety*) Anstandsdame spielen bei **(b)** (= *escort*) begleiten **(c)** (*esp US*: = *supervise*) beaufsichtigen

chaplain ['tʃæplɪn] N Kaplan *m*

chaplaincy ['tʃæplənsɪ] N (= *building*) Diensträume *pl* eines Kaplans

chapter ['tʃæptə'] N (*lit, fig*) Kapitel *nt*

char¹ [tʃɑː'] VT (= *burn black*) verkohlen

char² (*Brit inf*) N (*also* **~woman, ~lady**) Putzfrau *f*

character ['kærɪktə'] N **(a)** Charakter *m*; (*of people*) Wesen *nt no pl*; **it's out of ~ for him to do that** es ist eigentlich nicht seine Art, so etwas zu tun; **to be of good/bad ~** ein guter/schlechter Mensch sein; **she/it has no ~** sie/es hat keine eigene Note; **a man of ~** ein Mann von Charakter
(b) (*in novel*) (Roman)figur *f*; (*Theat*) Gestalt *f*
(c) (= *original person*) Original *nt*; (*inf*: = *person*) Typ *m* (*inf*)
(d) (*Typ, Comput*) Zeichen *nt*; (*Chinese etc also*) Schriftzeichen *nt*

characteristic [kærɪktə'rɪstɪk] **1** ADJ charakteristisch, typisch (*of* für) **2** N (*typisches*) Merkmal, Charakteristikum *nt*

characterization [kærɪktəraɪ'zeɪʃən] N (*in a novel etc*) Personenbeschreibung *f*; (*of one character*) Charakterisierung *f*

characterize ['kærɪktəraɪz] VT **(a)** (= *be characteristic of*) charakterisieren **(b)** (= *describe*) beschreiben

character: **character set** N (*Comput*) Zeichensatz *m*; **character space** N (*Comput*) Zeichenplatz *m*; **character string** N (*Comput*) Zeichenkette *f*; **character witness** N (*Jur*) Leumundszeuge *m*, Leumundszeugin *f*

charade [ʃə'rɑːd] N Scharade *f*; (*fig*) Farce *f*

char-broiled ['tʃɑːbrɔɪld] ADJ (*US*) = **char-grilled**

charcoal ['tʃɑːkəʊl] N Holzkohle *f*

charcoal drawing N Kohlezeichnung *f*

charge [tʃɑːdʒ] **1** N **(a)** (*Jur*: = *accusation*) Anklage *f* (*of* wegen); **convicted on all three ~s** in allen drei Anklagepunkten für schuldig befunden; **to bring a ~ against sb** gegen jdn Anklage erheben; **he was arrested on a ~ of murder** er wurde wegen Mordverdacht festgenommen
(b) (= *attack: of soldiers etc*) Angriff *m*
(c) (= *fee*) Gebühr *f*; **what's the ~?** was kostet das?; **to make a ~ (of £5) for sth** (£ 5 für) etw berechnen; **he made no ~ for mending my watch** er hat mir für die Reparatur der Uhr nichts berechnet; **there's an extra ~ for delivery** die Lieferung wird zusätzlich berechnet; **free of ~** kostenlos, gratis; **delivered free of ~** Lieferung frei Haus; **~ on a property** Grundpfandrecht *nt*
(d) (= *explosive*) (Spreng)ladung *f*; (*in firearm, Elec, Phys*) Ladung *f*
(e) (= *position of responsibility*) **to be in ~** die Verantwortung

haben; **who is in ~ here?** wer ist hier der Verantwortliche?; **to be in ~ of sth** für etw die Verantwortung haben; (of department) etw leiten; **to put sb in ~ of sth** jdm die Verantwortung für etw übertragen; (of department) jdm die Leitung von etw übertragen; **the children were placed in their aunt's ~** die Kinder wurden der Obhut der Tante anvertraut; **to take ~ of sth** etw übernehmen; **he took ~ of the situation** er nahm die Sache in die Hand **Ⅲ** VT **(a)** (with +gen) (Jur) anklagen; (fig) beschuldigen; **to ~ sb with doing sth** jdm vorwerfen, etw getan zu haben **(b)** (= attack) stürmen; troops angreifen; (bull etc) losgehen auf (+acc); (Sport) player angehen **(c)** (= ask in payment) berechnen; **I won't ~ you for that** ich berechne Ihnen nichts dafür **(d)** (= record as debt) in Rechnung stellen; **please ~ all these purchases to my account** bitte setzen Sie diese Einkäufe auf meine Rechnung **(e)** firearm laden; (Phys, Elec) battery (auf)laden **(f)** (form: = give as responsibility) **to ~ sb with sth** jdn mit etw beauftragen **Ⅲ** VI **(a)** (= attack) stürmen; (at people) angreifen (at sb jdn); (bull) losgehen (at sb auf jdn); **~!** vorwärts! **(b)** (inf: = rush) rennen; **he ~d into the room/upstairs** er stürmte ins Zimmer/die Treppe hoch

chargeable [ˈtʃɑːdʒəbl] ADJ **to be ~ to sb** auf jds Kosten (acc) gehen

charge: charge account N Kunden(kredit)konto nt; **charge card** N Kundenkreditkarte f

charged [tʃɑːdʒd] ADJ (lit, fig) geladen

chargé d'affaires [ˈʃɑːʒeɪdæˈfeəʳ] N Chargé d'affaires m

charger [ˈtʃɑːdʒəʳ] N (= battery ~) Ladegerät nt

char-grilled [ˈtʃɑːɡrɪld] ADJ (Brit) vom Holzkohlengrill

chariot [ˈtʃærɪət] N Streitwagen m (liter)

charisma [kæˈrɪzmə] N Charisma nt

charismatic [ˌkærɪzˈmætɪk] ADJ charismatisch

charitable [ˈtʃærɪtəbl] ADJ menschenfreundlich, gütig; organization Wohltätigkeits-, karitativ; (= financially generous, tolerant) großzügig; thought, remark etc freundlich; **to have ~ status** als gemeinnützig anerkannt sein

charity [ˈtʃærɪtɪ] N **(a)** (= tolerance, kindness) Menschenfreundlichkeit f; **~ begins at home** (Prov) man muss zuerst an seine eigene Familie/sein eigenes Land etc denken **(b)** (= alms) **to live on ~** von Almosen leben **(c)** (= charitable society) Wohltätigkeitsverein m, karitative Organisation; **to work for ~** für die Wohlfahrt arbeiten; **a collection for ~** eine Sammlung für wohltätige Zwecke

charlady [ˈtʃɑːˌleɪdɪ] N (Brit) Reinemache- or Putzfrau f

charlatan [ˈʃɑːlətən] N Scharlatan m

charley horse [ˈtʃɑːlɪhɔːs] N (US inf) steifes Bein

charm [tʃɑːm] **Ⅲ** N **(a)** (= attractiveness) Charme m no pl; (of cottage, countryside) Reiz m; **feminine ~s** (weibliche) Reize pl; **to turn on the ~** seinen (ganzen) Charme spielen lassen **(b)** (= spell) Bann m **(c)** (= amulet) Talisman m; (= trinket) Anhänger m **Ⅲ** VT (= attract, please) bezaubern; **to ~ one's way out of sth** sich mit Charme vor etw (dat) drücken

charm bracelet N Armband nt mit Anhängern

charming [ˈtʃɑːmɪŋ] ADJ reizend, charmant; **~!** (iro) wie reizend! (iro)

charm offensive N Charmeoffensive f

chart [tʃɑːt] **Ⅲ** N **(a)** Tabelle f; (= graph) Diagramm nt; (= map, weather ~) Karte f; **on a ~** in einer Tabelle/einem Diagramm **(b)** **charts** PL (= top twenty) Charts pl **Ⅲ** VT (= make a map of) kartografisch erfassen; (= record progress of) auswerten

charter [ˈtʃɑːtəʳ] **Ⅲ** N **(a)** Charta f; (= town ~, Univ also) Gründungsurkunde f; (of a society) Satzung f **(b)** (Naut, Aviat etc: = hire) **on ~** gechartert **Ⅲ** VT plane, bus etc chartern

chartered accountant [ˌtʃɑːtədəˈkaʊntənt] N (Brit) staatlich geprüfter Bilanzbuchhalter, staatlich geprüfte Bilanzbuchhalterin

charter: charter flight N Charterflug m; **charter plane** N Charterflugzeug nt

chartist [ˈtʃɑːtɪst] N (St Ex) Chartanalyst(in) m(f)

charwoman [ˈtʃɑːˌwʊmən] N (Brit) = **charlady**

chary [ˈtʃeərɪ] ADJ (+ER) (= cautious) vorsichtig; (= sparing) zurückhaltend (of mit)

chase [tʃeɪs] **Ⅲ** N Verfolgungsjagd f; (Hunt) Jagd f; **a (high-speed) car ~** eine Verfolgungsjagd im Auto; **to give ~** die Verfolgung aufnehmen; **to cut to the ~** (esp US inf) zum Kern der Sache kommen **Ⅲ** VT jagen; (= follow) verfolgen; member of opposite sex hinterherlaufen (+dat) **Ⅲ** VI **to ~ after sb** hinter jdm herrennen (inf); (in vehicle) hinter jdm herrasen (inf); **to ~ around** herumrasen (inf)

➤ **chase away** or **off** VT SEP wegjagen

➤ **chase down** VT SEP (US: = catch) aufspüren

➤ **chase up** VT SEP person rankriegen (inf); information etc ranschaffen (inf)

chaser [ˈtʃeɪsəʳ] N (= drink) **have a whisky ~** trinken Sie einen Whisky dazu

chasm [ˈkæzəm] N (Geol) Spalte f, Kluft f (also fig)

chassis [ˈʃæsɪ] N Chassis nt

chaste [tʃeɪst] ADJ (+ER) (= pure, virtuous) keusch; (= simple) style, elegance schlicht

chasten [ˈtʃeɪsn] VT **~ed by ...** durch ... zur Einsicht gelangt

chastise [tʃæsˈtaɪz] VT (verbally) schelten

chastity [ˈtʃæstɪtɪ] N (= sexual purity) Keuschheit f; (= virginity also) Unberührtheit f

chat [tʃæt] **Ⅲ** N Unterhaltung f; **could we have a ~ about it?** können wir uns mal darüber unterhalten? **Ⅲ** VI plaudern

➤ **chat up** VT SEP (Brit inf) person einreden auf (+acc); prospective girl-/boyfriend anquatschen (inf)

chat room N (Comput) Chatroom m

chat show N (Brit) Talkshow f

chatter [ˈtʃætəʳ] **Ⅲ** N (of person) Geschwätz nt **Ⅲ** VI (person) schwatzen; (teeth) klappern

chatterbox [ˈtʃætəbɒks] N Quasselstrippe f (inf)

chattering [ˈtʃætərɪŋ] **Ⅲ** N Geschwätz nt **Ⅲ** ADJ **the ~ classes** (Brit pej inf) das Bildungsbürgertum

chatty [ˈtʃætɪ] ADJ (+ER) person geschwätzig; **written in a ~ style** im Plauderton geschrieben

chauffeur [ˈʃəʊfəʳ] N Chauffeur m

chauvinist [ˈʃəʊvɪnɪst] **Ⅲ** N (= male ~) männlicher Chauvinist **Ⅲ** ADJ (male) **~ pig** Chauvinistenschwein nt (inf)

chauvinistic [ˌʃəʊvɪˈnɪstɪk] ADJ chauvinistisch

cheap [tʃiːp] **Ⅲ** ADJ (+ER) ALSO ADV billig; behaviour, appearance ordinär; **to feel ~** sich (dat) schäbig vorkommen; **it doesn't come ~** es ist nicht billig, preiswert; **it's ~ at the price** es ist spottbillig; (= poor quality) minderwertig; **~ money** (Econ) billiges Geld **Ⅲ** N **to buy sth on the ~** (inf) etw für einen Pappenstiel kaufen (inf); **to make sth on the ~** (inf) etw ganz billig produzieren

cheapen [ˈtʃiːpən] VT (fig) schlecht machen

cheaply [ˈtʃiːplɪ] ADV billig; make, eat, live günstig

cheapness [ˈtʃiːpnɪs] N **(a)** (= inexpensiveness) billiger Preis **(b)** (= poor quality) Minderwertigkeit f

cheapo [ˈtʃiːpəʊ] ADJ (inf) Billig-; **~ video** Billigvideo nt

cheapskate [ˈtʃiːpskeɪt] N (inf) Knauser m (inf)

cheat [tʃiːt] **Ⅲ** VT betrügen; **to ~ sb out of sth** jdn um etw betrügen **Ⅲ** VI betrügen; (in exam, game etc) mogeln (inf) **Ⅲ** N (= person) Betrüger(in) m(f); (in exam, game etc) Mogler(in) m(f) (inf)

➤ **cheat on** VI +PREP OBJ betrügen

cheater [ˈtʃiːtəʳ] N (US: = person) = **cheat**

cheating [ˈtʃiːtɪŋ] N Betrügen nt, Betrug m; (in exam, game etc) Mogeln m (inf)

check [tʃek] **Ⅲ** N **(a)** (= examination) Überprüfung f, Kontrolle f; **to keep a ~ on sb/sth** jdn/etw überwachen **(b)** (= restraint) **to hold** or **keep sb in ~** jdn in Schach halten; **to keep one's temper in ~** sich beherrschen **(c)** (= pattern) Karo(muster) nt; (= square) Karo nt **(d)** (Chess) Schach nt; **to be in ~** im Schach stehen **(e)** (US) (= cheque) Scheck m; (= bill) Rechnung f; **~ please** bitte (be)zahlen **(f)** (US: = room) (Rail) Gepäckaufbewahrung f; (Theat) Garderobe f; (= ticket) (Rail) (Gepäck)schein m; (Theat) (Garderoben)marke f **(g)** (US: = tick) Haken m **Ⅲ** VT **(a)** (= examine) überprüfen; tickets also kontrollieren; **to ~ whether** or **if ...** nachprüfen, ob ... **(b)** (= act as control on) kontrollieren; (= stop) enemy, advance aufhalten

(c) (*Aviat*) *luggage* einchecken; (*US*) *coat etc* abgeben; (*US Rail*) *luggage* (= *register*) aufgeben; (= *deposit*) abgeben **(d)** (*US*: = *tick*) abhaken **3** VI (= *make sure*) nachfragen (*with* bei); (= *have a look*) nachsehen; **I was just ~ing** ich wollte nur nachprüfen
▶ **check in 1** VI (*at airport*) einchecken; (*at hotel*) sich anmelden; **what time do you have to check in?** wann musst du am Flughafen sein? **2** VT SEP (*at airport*) *luggage* einchecken; (*at hotel*) *person* anmelden
▶ **check off** VT SEP (*esp US*) abhaken
▶ **check out 1** VI sich abmelden; (= *leave hotel*) abreisen; (= *sign out*) sich austragen **2** VT SEP **(a)** *figures, facts* überprüfen; **check it out with the boss** klären Sie das mit dem Chef ab **(b)** (*hotel*) *guest* abfertigen
▶ **check over** VT SEP überprüfen
▶ **check through** VT SEP **(a)** *account, proofs* durchsehen **(b) they checked my bags through to Berlin** mein Gepäck wurde nach Berlin durchgecheckt
▶ **check up** VI überprüfen
▶ **check up on** VI +PREP OBJ überprüfen; (= *keep a check on*) *sb* kontrollieren
checkbook ['tʃekbʊk] N (*US*) Scheckbuch *nt*
checked [tʃekt] ADJ (*in pattern*) kariert; **~ pattern** Karomuster *nt*
checker ['tʃekəʳ] N **(a)** (*US*: *in supermarket*) Kassierer(in) *m(f)* **(b)** (*US*: *for coats etc*) Garderobenfrau *f*/-mann *m*
checkers ['tʃekəz] N (*US*) Damespiel *nt*; **to play ~** Dame spielen
check-in (desk) ['tʃekɪn(ˌdesk)] N (*Aviat*) Abflugschalter *m*; (*US*: *in hotel*) Rezeption *f*
checking ['tʃekɪŋ] N Überprüfung *f*, Kontrolle *f*; **~ account** (*US*) Girokonto *nt*
check: check list N Checkliste *f*; **checkmate 1** N Schachmatt *nt*; **~!** matt! **2** VT matt setzen; **checkout** N (*in supermarket*) Kasse *f*; **checkpoint** N Kontrollpunkt *m*; **checkroom** N (*US*) (*Theat*) Garderobe *f*; (*Rail*) Gepäckaufbewahrung *f*; **checkup** N (*Med*) Check-up *m*; **to have a ~/go for a ~** einen Check-up machen lassen
cheddar ['tʃedəʳ] N Cheddar(käse) *m*
cheek [tʃiːk] N **(a)** Backe *f*; **to turn the other ~** die andere Wange hinhalten **(b)** (*Brit*: = *impudence*) Frechheit *f*; **to have the ~ to do sth** die Frechheit *or* Stirn haben, etw zu tun; **they gave him a lot of ~** sie waren ganz schön frech zu ihm; **enough of your ~!** jetzt reichts aber!
cheekbone ['tʃiːkbəʊn] N Wangenknochen *m*
cheekily ['tʃiːkɪlɪ] ADV frech
cheeky ['tʃiːkɪ] ADJ (+ER) (*Brit*) frech; **it's a bit ~ asking for another pay rise so soon** es ist etwas unverschämt, schon wieder eine Gehaltserhöhung zu verlangen
cheer [tʃɪəʳ] **1** N **(a)** Hurra- *or* Beifallsruf *m*; (= *cheering*) Hurrageschrei *nt*, Jubel *m*; **three ~s for Mike!** ein dreifaches Hurra für Mike!; **~s!** (*inf*: = *your health*) prost!; (*Brit inf*: = *goodbye*) tschüs(s)! (*inf*); (*Brit inf*: = *thank you*) danke schön! **(b)** (= *comfort*) Aufmunterung *f*
2 VT *person* zujubeln (+*dat*); *thing, event* bejubeln **3** VI jubeln, Hurra rufen
▶ **cheer on** VT SEP anfeuern
▶ **cheer up 1** VT SEP aufmuntern; *place* aufheitern **2** VI (*person*) vergnügter *or* fröhlicher werden; (*things*) besser werden; **cheer up!** lass den Kopf nicht hängen!
cheerful ['tʃɪəfʊl] ADJ fröhlich, vergnügt; *place, colour etc* heiter; *prospect, news* erfreulich; *tune* fröhlich; **to be ~ about sth** in Bezug auf etw optimistisch sein
cheerfully ['tʃɪəfʊlɪ] ADV fröhlich, vergnügt
cheering ['tʃɪərɪŋ] **1** N Jubel *m*, Hurrageschrei *nt* **2** ADJ *crowds* jubelnd
cheerio ['tʃɪərɪ'əʊ] INTERJ (*esp Brit*) (*inf*) (= *goodbye*) Wiedersehen (*inf*); (*to friends*) tschüs(s) (*inf*)
cheers [tʃɪəz] INTERJ *see* **cheer 1**
cheese [tʃiːz] N Käse *m*; **say ~!** (*Phot*) bitte recht freundlich
cheese IN CPDS Käse-; **cheeseboard** N Käsebrett *nt*; (= *course*) Käseplatte *f*; **cheeseburger** N Cheeseburger *m*; **cheesecake** N (*Cook*) Käsekuchen *m*; **cheesecloth** N Käseleinen *nt*
cheesed off [tʃiːzd'ɒf] ADJ (*Brit inf*) angeödet (*inf*); **I'm ~ with this job** diese Arbeit ödet mich an (*inf*)
cheesy ['tʃiːzɪ] ADJ (+ER) (*inf*: = *shoddy*) mies (*inf*)

cheetah ['tʃiːtə] N Gepard *m*
chef [ʃef] N Küchenchef *m*; (*as profession*) Koch *m*

> Be careful! **chef** is not translated by the German word **Chef**.

chemical ['kemɪkəl] **1** ADJ chemisch **2** N Chemikalie *f*
chemical: chemical engineering N Chemotechnik *f*; **chemical toilet** N Chemietoilette *f*
chemist ['kemɪst] N **(a)** (= *expert in chemistry*) Chemiker(in) *m(f)* **(b)** (*Brit*: *in shop*) Drogist(in) *m(f)*; (*dispensing*) Apotheker(in) *m(f)*; **~'s shop** Drogerie *f*; (*dispensing*) Apotheke *f*
chemistry ['kemɪstrɪ] N **(a)** Chemie *f* **(b)** (*fig*) Verträglichkeit *f*; **the ~ between us was perfect** wir haben uns sofort vertragen
chemo ['kiːməʊ] N (*inf*) Chemo *f* (*inf*)
chemotherapy [ˌkiːməʊ'θerəpɪ] N Chemotherapie *f*
cheque, (*US*) **check** [tʃek] N Scheck *m*; **a ~ for £100** ein Scheck über £ 100; **to pay by ~** mit (einem) Scheck bezahlen
chequebook, (*US*) **checkbook** ['tʃekbʊk] N Scheckbuch *nt*
cheque card N Scheckkarte *f*
chequered, (*US*) **checkered** ['tʃekəd] ADJ (*lit*) kariert; (*fig*) *history* bewegt
cherish ['tʃerɪʃ] VT **(a)** *person* liebevoll sorgen für **(b)** *feelings, hope* hegen; *idea, illusion* sich hingeben (+*dat*); **to ~ sb's memory** jds Andenken in Ehren halten
cherished ['tʃerɪʃt] ADJ *dream, belief* lang gehegt; **her most ~ possessions** die Dinge, an denen sie am meisten hängt
cherry ['tʃerɪ] **1** N Kirsche *f* **2** ADJ (*colour*) kirschrot; (*Cook*) Kirsch-
cherry IN CPDS Kirsch-; **cherry blossom** N Kirschblüte *f*; **cherry bomb** N (*US*) Knallerbse *f*; **cherry-pick** (*fig inf*) **1** VT die Rosinen herauspicken aus (*inf*) **2** VI sich (*dat*) die Rosinen herauspicken (*inf*); **cherry picker** N (= *vehicle*) Bockkran *m*
chess [tʃes] N Schach(spiel) *nt*
chess: chessboard N Schachbrett *nt*; **chessman, chesspiece** N Schachfigur *f*; **chess set** N Schachspiel *nt*
chest¹ [tʃest] N (*for tea, tools etc*) Kiste *f*; (= *piece of furniture, for clothes etc*) Truhe *f*; **~ of drawers** Kommode *f*
chest² N (*Anat*) Brust *f*; **to measure sb's ~** jds Brustumfang messen; **to get sth off one's ~** (*inf*: *dat*) etw von der Seele reden; **~ pains** Schmerzen *pl* in der Brust
chest infection N Lungeninfekt *m*
chestnut ['tʃesnʌt] **1** N **(a)** (= *nut, tree*) Kastanie *f* **(b)** (= *colour*) Kastanienbraun *nt* **(c)** (= *horse*) Fuchs *m* **2** ADJ (*colour*) kastanienbraun
chest specialist N Lungenfacharzt *m*/-ärztin *f*
chesty ['tʃestɪ] ADJ (+ER) (*Brit inf*) *cough* rau, schnarrend
chew [tʃuː] VT kauen; **that dog's been ~ing the carpet again** der Hund hat schon wieder am Teppich genagt; **don't ~ your fingernails** kaue nicht an deinen Nägeln
▶ **chew off** *or* **out** VT SEP (*US inf*) zur Schnecke machen (*inf*)
▶ **chew on** VI +PREP OBJ **(a)** (*lit*) (herum)kauen auf (+*dat*) **(b)** (*also* **chew over**: *inf*) *problem* sich (*dat*) durch den Kopf gehen lassen
chewing gum ['tʃuːɪŋgʌm] N Kaugummi *m or nt*
chewy ['tʃuːɪ] ADJ *meat* zäh; *pasta* kernig; *sweets* weich
chic [ʃiːk] ADJ (+ER) schick, elegant
chick [tʃɪk] N **(a)** (*of chicken*) Küken *nt*; (= *young bird*) Junge(s) *nt* **(b)** (*inf*: = *girl*) Mieze *f* (*inf*)
chicken ['tʃɪkɪn] **1** N Huhn *nt*; (*for roasting, frying*) Hähnchen *nt*; **~ liver** Geflügelleber *f*; **to run around like a headless ~** wie ein kopfloses Huhn herumlaufen; **don't count your ~s (before they're hatched)** (*Prov*) man soll den Tag nicht vor dem Abend loben (*Prov*) **2** ADJ (*inf*) feig; **he's ~** er ist ein Feigling
▶ **chicken out** VI (*inf*) kneifen (*inf*)
chicken IN CPDS Hühner-; **chicken farmer** N Hühnerzüchter *m*; **chicken feed** N **(a)** (*lit*) Hühnerfutter *nt* **(b)** (*inf*: = *insignificant sum*) Peanuts *pl* (*inf*); **chickenpox** N Windpocken *pl*; **chickenshit** (*US sl*) **1** N **(a)** (= *coward*) Memme *f* (*pej inf*) **(b)** NO PL **to be ~** (= *be worthless*) Scheiße sein (*sl*) **2** ADJ **(a)** (= *cowardly*) feige (*sl*) **(b)** (= *worthless*) beschissen (*sl*); **chicken wire** N Hühnerdraht *m*
chickpea ['tʃɪkpiː] N Kichererbse *f*
chicory ['tʃɪkərɪ] N Chicorée *f or m*; (*in coffee*) Zichorie *f*

chide [tʃaɪd], *pret* **chid** *(old)* *or* **chided** [tʃɪd, 'tʃaɪdɪd], *ptp* **chided** *or* **chidden** *(old)* ['tʃɪdn] VT rügen

chief [tʃiːf] **1** N, *pl* **-s** *(of organization)* Leiter(in) *m(f)*; *(of tribe)* Häuptling *m*; *(inf:* = *boss)* Chef *m*; ~ **of police** Polizeipräsident(in) *or* -chef(in) *m(f)*; ~ **of staff** *(Mil)* Stabschef(in) *m(f)*
2 ADJ **(a)** (= *most important*) Haupt-, wichtigste(r, s) **(b)** (= *most senior*) Haupt-, erste(r); ~ **accounting officer** *(US)* Leiter(in) *m(f)* des Rechnungswesens; ~ **buyer** Chefeinkäufer(in) *m(f)*; ~ **executive** leitender Direktor, leitende Direktorin; ~ **executive officer** Generaldirektor *m*; ~ **financial officer** *(US)* Finanzdirektor(in) *m(f)*; ~ **inspector** *(Comm)* Leiter(in) *m(f)* der Qualitätskontrolle; ~ **operating officer** *(US Comm)* Betriebsleiter(in) *m(f)*

chief constable N *(Brit)* Polizeipräsident(in) *m(f) or* -chef(in) *m(f)*

chiefly ['tʃiːflɪ] ADV hauptsächlich

chiffon ['ʃɪfɒn] **1** N Chiffon *m* **2** ADJ Chiffon-

child [tʃaɪld] N, *pl* **children** *(lit, fig)* Kind *nt*; **when I was a** ~ in *or* zu meiner Kindheit

child IN CPDS Kinder-; **child abuse** N Kindesmisshandlung *f*; *(sexually)* Notzucht *f* mit Kindern; **child-bearing** **1** N Mutterschaft *f* **2** ADJ **of** ~ **age** im gebärfähigen Alter; **child benefit** N *(Brit)* Kindergeld *nt*; **childbirth** N Geburt *f*; **to die in** ~ bei der Geburt sterben; **childcare** N Kinderbetreuung *f*; **childhood** N Kindheit *f*

childish ADJ, **childishly** ADV ['tʃaɪldɪʃ, -lɪ] *(pej)* kindisch

childishness ['tʃaɪldɪʃnɪs] N *(pej)* kindisches Gehabe

child: child labour, *(US)* **child labor** N Kinderarbeit *f*; **childless** ADJ kinderlos; **childlike** ADJ kindlich; **child lock** N Kindersicherung *f*; **childminder** N *(Brit)* Tagesmutter *f*; **childminding** N *(Brit)* Beaufsichtigung *f* von Kindern; **child prodigy** N Wunderkind *nt*; **childproof** ADJ kindersicher

children ['tʃɪldrən] PL *of* **child**

child: child seat N Kindersitz *m*; **child's play** N ein Kinderspiel *nt*

Chile ['tʃɪlɪ] N Chile *nt*

Chilean ['tʃɪlɪən] **1** ADJ chilenisch **2** N Chilene *m*, Chilenin *f*

chill [tʃɪl] **1** N **(a)** Frische *f*; **there's quite a** ~ **in the air** es ist ziemlich frisch; **the sun took the** ~ **off the water** die Sonne hat das Wasser ein bisschen erwärmt **(b)** *(Med)* fieberhafte Erkältung; (= *shiver*) Schauder *m*, Frösteln *nt*; **to catch a** ~ sich verkühlen **2** ADJ *(lit)* kühl, frisch **3** VT **(a)** *(lit) wine, meat* kühlen; **I was ~ed to the bone** *or* **marrow** die Kälte ging mir bis auf die Knochen **(b)** *(fig) blood* gefrieren lassen
➤ **chill out** VI *(inf)* relaxen *(sl)*

chilli, *(US)* **chili** ['tʃɪlɪ] N Peperoni *pl*; (= *spice, meal*) Chili *m*

chilling ['tʃɪlɪŋ] ADJ Schrecken erregend

chilly ['tʃɪlɪ] ADJ (+ER) *weather* kühl, frisch; *manner, smile etc* kühl, frostig; **I feel** ~ mich fröstelts

chime [tʃaɪm] **1** N Glockenspiel *nt*; *(of doorbell)* Läuten *nt no pl* **2** VI läuten
➤ **chime in** VI *(inf)* sich einschalten

chimney ['tʃɪmnɪ] N Schornstein *m*

chimney: chimneypot N Schornsteinkopf *m*; **chimney stack** N Schornstein *m*; **chimney sweep** N Schornsteinfeger *m*

chimp [tʃɪmp] *(inf)*, **chimpanzee** [ˌtʃɪmpæn'ziː] N Schimpanse *m*

chin [tʃɪn] N Kinn *nt*; **keep your** ~ **up!** Kopf hoch!; **he took it on the** ~ *(fig inf)* er hats mit Fassung getragen

China ['tʃaɪnə] N China *nt*

china ['tʃaɪnə] **1** N Porzellan *nt* **2** ADJ Porzellan-

china: china clay N Kaolin *m*; **Chinatown** N Chinesenviertel *nt*

Chinese [tʃaɪ'niːz] **1** N **(a)** (= *person*) Chinese *m*, Chinesin *f* **(b)** (= *language*) Chinesisch *nt* **(c)** *(inf)* (= *restaurant*) Chinarestaurant *nt*; (= *meal*) chinesisches Essen **2** ADJ chinesisch; ~ **restaurant** Chinarestaurant *nt*

Chinese: Chinese lantern N Lampion *m*; **Chinese leaves** N Chinakohl *m*

chink[1] [tʃɪŋk] **1** N Ritze *f*; *(in door)* Spalt *m*; **a** ~ **of light** ein dünner Lichtstreifen *or* -strahl; **the** ~ **in sb's armour** *(fig)* jds schwacher Punkt **2** VT *(US)* stopfen

chink[2] **1** VT klirren mit; *coins* klimpern mit **2** VI klirren; *(coins)* klimpern

chin: chin rest N Kinnstütze *f*; **chin strap** N Kinnriemen *m*

chip [tʃɪp] **1** N **(a)** Splitter *m*; *(of glass also)* Scherbe *f*; *(of wood)* Span *m*; **chocolate ~s** ≈ Schokoladenstreusel *pl*; **he's a ~ off the old block** er ist ganz der Vater; **to have a ~ on one's shoulder** einen Komplex haben *(about* wegen)
(b) *(Brit:* = *potato stick)* Pomme frite *m or nt usu pl*; *(US:* = *potato slice)* Chip *m usu pl*
(c) *(in crockery etc)* abgestoßene Ecke *or* Stelle; **this cup has a** ~ diese Tasse ist angeschlagen
(d) *(in poker, Comput)* Chip *m*; **to be in the ~s** *(US inf)* Kleingeld haben *(inf)*; **when the ~s are down** wenn es drauf ankommt
2 VT **(a)** *cup, stone* anschlagen; *paint* abstoßen; *wood* beschädigen
(b) *(Sport) ball* chippen
3 VI *(cup etc)* angeschlagen werden; *(paint)* abspringen; *(stone)* splittern
➤ **chip away at** VI + PREP OBJ *authority, system* unterminieren; *debts* reduzieren, verringern
➤ **chip in** VI *(inf)* **(a)** (= *interrupt*) sich einschalten **(b)** (= *contribute*) **he chipped in with £3** er steuerte £ 3 bei
➤ **chip off** VT SEP *paint etc* wegschlagen; *piece of china* abschlagen

chipboard ['tʃɪpbɔːd] N Spanholz *nt*

chipmunk ['tʃɪpmʌŋk] N Backenhörnchen *nt*

chip pan N Fritteuse *f*

chipped [tʃɪpt] ADJ **(a)** *cup, bone* angeschlagen; *paint* abgesplittert **(b)** *(Brit Cook)* ~ **potatoes** Pommes frites *pl*

chippings ['tʃɪpɪŋz] PL Splitter *pl*; *(of wood)* Späne *pl*; (= *road* ~) Schotter *m*

chippy ['tʃɪpɪ] N *(inf:* = *chip shop*) Pommesbude *f (inf)*

chip shot N *(Golf)* Chip(shot) *m*; *(Tennis)* Chip *m*

chiropodist [kɪ'rɒpədɪst] N Fußpfleger(in) *m(f)*

chiropody [kɪ'rɒpədɪ] N Fußpflege *f*

chiropractor ['kaɪərəʊˌpræktə'] N Chiropraktiker(in) *m(f)*

chirp [tʃɜːp] VI *(birds)* zwitschern; *(crickets)* zirpen

chirpy ['tʃɜːpɪ] ADJ (+ER) *(inf)* munter

chisel ['tʃɪzl] **1** N Meißel *m*; *(for wood)* Beitel *m* **2** VT meißeln; *(in wood)* stemmen

chit [tʃɪt] N *(also* = ~ **of paper)** Zettel *m*

chitchat ['tʃɪttʃæt] N *(inf)* Geschwätz *nt*

chivalrous ADJ, **chivalrously** ADV ['ʃɪvəlrəs, -lɪ] ritterlich

chives [tʃaɪvz] N Schnittlauch *m*

chivvy ['tʃɪvɪ] VT *(Brit inf: also* ~ **along** *or* **up)** antreiben; **to ~ sb into doing sth** jdn dazu antreiben, etw zu tun

chlorinate ['klɒrɪneɪt] VT *water* chloren

chlorine ['klɔːriːn] N Chlor *nt*

chlorofluorocarbon [ˌklɒrəʊfluərə'kɑːbən] N Chlorfluorkohlenwasserstoff *m*

chloroform ['klɒrəfɔːm] N Chloroform *nt*

choc-ice ['tʃɒkaɪs] N Eismohrle *nt* *(Eiscreme mit Schokoladenüberzug)*

chock [tʃɒk] N Bremsklotz *m*

chock-a-block ['tʃɒkəblɒk] ADJ *(esp Brit inf)*, **chock-full** ['tʃɒkfʊl] ADJ *(inf)* knüppelvoll *(inf)*

chocolate ['tʃɒklɪt] **1** N **(a)** Schokolade *f*; **(hot** *or* **drinking)** ~ Schokolade *f*; **a** ~ eine Praline **(b)** (= *colour*) Schokoladenbraun *nt* **2** ADJ Schokoladen-; (= ~*-coloured*) schokoladenbraun

chocolate: chocolate bar N (= *slab*) Tafel *f* Schokolade; (= *Mars® bar etc*) Schokoladenriegel *m*; **chocolate biscuit** N Schokoladenkeks *m*; **chocolate-box** ADJ Postkarten-; **chocolate cake** N Schokoladenkuchen *m*; **chocolate-flavoured** ADJ mit Schokoladengeschmack

choice [tʃɔɪs] **1** N **(a)** Wahl *f*; **it's your** ~ du hast die Wahl; **to make a** ~ eine Wahl treffen; **I didn't do it from** ~ ich habe es mir nicht ausgesucht; **he had no** *or* **little** ~ **but to obey** er hatte keine (andere) Wahl als zu gehorchen; **it was your** ~ du wolltest es ja so; **the drug/weapon of** ~ die bevorzugte Droge/Waffe **(b)** (= *variety to choose from*) Auswahl *f (of an* +*dat*, von) **2** ADJ *(Comm) goods* Qualitäts-, erstklassig

choir ['kwaɪə'] N **(a)** Chor *m* **(b)** *(Archit)* Chor(raum) *m*

choir IN CPDS Chor-; **choirboy** N Chor- *or* Sängerknabe *m*; **choir master** N Chorleiter *m*

choke [tʃəʊk] **1** VT *person* ersticken; (= *throttle*) (er)würgen; **in a voice ~d with tears/emotion** mit tränenerstickter/tief bewegter Stimme **2** VI ersticken (*on* an +*dat*) **3** N (*Aut*) Choke *m*
➤ **choke back** VT SEP *feelings, tears* unterdrücken
choker [ˈtʃəʊkəʳ] N (= *necklace*) enger Halsreif; (*of velvet etc*) Kropfband *nt*
choking [ˈtʃəʊkɪŋ] ADJ *smoke* beißend
cholera [ˈkɒlərə] N Cholera *f*
cholesterol [kɒˈlestərəl] N Cholesterin *nt*
chomp [tʃɒmp] VT laut mahlen; (*person*) mampfen (*inf*)
choose [tʃuːz], *pret* chose, *ptp* chosen **1** VT (a) (= *select*) (aus)wählen; **to ~ a team** eine Mannschaft auswählen *or* zusammenstellen; **they chose him as their leader** *or* **to be their leader** sie wählten ihn zu ihrem Anführer (b) (= *decide, elect*) **to ~ to do sth** es vorziehen, etw zu tun **2** VI **to ~ (between** *or* **among/from)** wählen (zwischen +*dat*/ aus *or* unter +*dat*); **there is nothing** *or* **little to ~ between them** sie sind gleich gut
choos(e)y [ˈtʃuːzɪ] ADJ (+ER) wählerisch
chop¹ [tʃɒp] **1** N (a) (*Cook*) Kotelett *nt* (b) (*Karate*) Karateschlag *m* (c) (*inf*) **to get the ~** (= *be axed*) dem Rotstift zum Opfer fallen; (= *be fired*) rausgeschmissen werden (*inf*); **to give sb the ~** jdn rausschmeißen (*inf*) **2** VT hacken; *meat, vegetables etc* klein schneiden
➤ **chop down** VT SEP *tree* fällen
➤ **chop off** VT SEP abschlagen
➤ **chop up** VT SEP zerhacken
chop² VI **to ~ and change (one's mind)** ständig seine Meinung ändern
chopper [ˈtʃɒpəʳ] N (a) (= *axe*) Hackbeil *nt* (b) (*inf*: = *helicopter*) Hubschrauber *m*
chopping [ˈtʃɒpɪŋ]: **chopping block** N Hackklotz *m*; (*for wood, executions etc*) Block *m*; **chopping board** N (*Brit*) Hackbrett *nt*; **chopping knife** N (*Brit*) Hackmesser *nt*; (*with rounded blade*) Wiegemesser *nt*
choppy [ˈtʃɒpɪ] ADJ (+ER) *sea* kabbelig
chop: **chopstick** N Stäbchen *nt*; **chop suey** [tʃɒpˈsuːɪ] N Chopsuey *nt*
choral [ˈkɔːrəl] ADJ Chor-; **~ society** Gesangverein *m*
chord [kɔːd] N (*Mus*) Akkord *m*; **to strike the right ~** (*fig*) den richtigen Ton treffen; **to strike a sympathetic ~** (*fig*) auf Verständnis stoßen
chore [tʃɔːʳ] N lästige Pflicht; **~s** *pl* Hausarbeit *f*; **to do the ~s** die Hausarbeit erledigen
choreographer [ˌkɒrɪˈɒgrəfəʳ] N Choreograf(in) *m(f)*
choreography [ˌkɒrɪˈɒgrəfɪ] N Choreografie *f*
chorister [ˈkɒrɪstəʳ] N (Kirchen)chormitglied *nt*; (= *boy*) Chorknabe *m*
chortle [ˈtʃɔːtl] VI gluckern
chorus [ˈkɔːrəs] N (a) (= *refrain*) Refrain *m* (b) Chor *m*; (*of opera*) Opernchor *m*; (= *dancers*) Tanzgruppe *f*; **she's in the ~** sie singt im Chor/sie ist bei der Tanzgruppe; **in ~** im Chor
chorus: **chorus girl** N Revuetänzerin *f or* -girl *nt*; **chorus line** N Revue *f*
chose [tʃəʊz] PRET *of* choose
chosen [ˈtʃəʊzn] **1** PTP *of* choose **2** ADJ **the ~ people** das auserwählte Volk; **the ~ few** die wenigen Auserwählten
choux pastry [ˈʃuːˈpeɪstrɪ] N Brandteig *m*
chow mein [tʃaʊˈmeɪn] N gebratene Nudeln mit Pilzen, Fleisch, Shrimps etc
Christ [kraɪst] **1** N Christus *m* **2** INTERJ (*sl*) Herrgott (*inf*)
christen [ˈkrɪsn] VT (a) (= *baptize*) taufen; **to ~ sb after sb** jdn nach jdm (be)nennen (b) (*inf*: = *use for first time*) einweihen
christening [ˈkrɪsnɪŋ] N Taufe *f*; **~ robe** Taufkleid *nt*
Christian [ˈkrɪstɪən] **1** N Christ *m* **2** ADJ (*lit, fig*) christlich
Christianity [ˌkrɪstɪˈænɪtɪ] N (= *religion*) Christentum *nt*; (= *body of Christians*) Christenheit *f*
Christian name N Vorname *m*
Christmas [ˈkrɪsməs] N Weihnachten *nt*; **are you going home for ~?** fährst du (über) Weihnachten nach Hause?; **what did you get for ~?** was hast du zu Weihnachten bekommen?; **merry** *or* **happy ~!** frohe *or* fröhliche Weihnachten!

Christmas: **Christmas cake** N Früchtekuchen mit Zuckerguss zu Weihnachten; **Christmas card** N Weihnachtskarte *f*; **Christmas carol** N Weihnachtslied *nt*; **Christmas Day** N der erste Weihnachtstag; **on ~** am ersten (Weihnachts)feiertag; **Christmas Eve** N Heiligabend *m*; **on ~** Heiligabend; **Christmas present** N Weihnachtsgeschenk *nt*; **Christmas pudding** N Plumpudding *m*; **Christmas tree** N Weihnachtsbaum *m*
chromatic [krəˈmætɪk] ADJ (*Art, Mus*) chromatisch
chrome [krəʊm] N Chrom *nt*
chromium [ˈkrəʊmɪəm] N Chrom *nt*
chromium-plated [ˈkrəʊmɪəmˌpleɪtɪd] ADJ verchromt
chromosome [ˈkrəʊməsəʊm] N Chromosom *nt*
chronic [ˈkrɒnɪk] ADJ (a) *disease, liar, underfunding etc* chronisch; **Chronic Fatigue Syndrome** chronisches Erschöpfungssyndrom (b) (*inf*: = *terrible*) miserabel (*inf*)
chronically [ˈkrɒnɪklɪ] ADV *ill, underfunded* chronisch
chronicle [ˈkrɒnɪkl] **1** N Chronik *f* **2** VT aufzeichnen
chronological [ˌkrɒnəˈlɒdʒɪkəl] ADJ chronologisch; **in ~ order** in chronologischer Reihenfolge
chronologically [ˌkrɒnəˈlɒdʒɪkəlɪ] ADV chronologisch; **~ arranged** in chronologischer Reihenfolge
chronology [krəˈnɒlədʒɪ] N Chronologie *f* (*form*); (= *list of dates*) Zeittafel *f*
chrysalis [ˈkrɪsəlɪs] N, *pl* -es (*Biol*) Puppe *f*
chrysanthemum [krɪˈsænθəməm] N Chrysantheme *f*
chubby [ˈtʃʌbɪ] ADJ (+ER) rundlich; **~ cheeks** Pausbacken *pl*
chuck¹ [tʃʌk] VT (*inf*) (a) (= *throw*) schmeißen (*inf*) (b) (*inf*) *girlfriend etc* Schluss machen mit; *job* hinschmeißen (*inf*); **~ it!** (= *stop it*) Schluss jetzt!
➤ **chuck away** VT SEP (*inf*) (= *throw out*) wegschmeißen (*inf*); (= *waste*) *money* aus dem Fenster schmeißen (*inf*)
➤ **chuck in** VT SEP (*Brit inf*) *job* hinschmeißen (*inf*); **to chuck it (all) in** den Laden hinschmeißen (*inf*)
➤ **chuck out** VT SEP (*inf*) rausschmeißen (*inf*); *useless articles also* wegschmeißen (*inf*); **to be chucked out** rausfliegen (*of* aus) (*inf*)
chuck² N (*dated US inf*: = *food*) Essen *nt*
chuckle [ˈtʃʌkl] VI leise in sich (*acc*) hineinlachen
chuck wagon N (*dated US inf*) Proviantwagen *m* mit fahrbarer Küche
chuffed [tʃʌft] ADJ (*Brit inf*) vergnügt und zufrieden
chug [tʃʌg] VI tuckern
➤ **chug along** VI entlangtuckern; (*fig inf*) gut vorankommen
chum [tʃʌm] N (*inf*) Kumpel *m* (*inf*)
chummy [ˈtʃʌmɪ] ADJ (+ER) (*inf*) kameradschaftlich; **to be ~ with sb** mit jdm sehr dicke sein (*inf*)
chunk [tʃʌŋk] N großes Stück, (*of meat*) Batzen *m*; (*of stone*) Brocken *m*
chunky [ˈtʃʌŋkɪ] ADJ (+ER) (*inf*) stämmig; *knitwear* dick, klobig
church [tʃɜːtʃ] N Kirche *f*; (= *service*) die Kirche; **to go to ~** in die Kirche gehen; **the Church of England** die anglikanische Kirche
church IN CPDS Kirchen-; **churchgoer** [ˈtʃɜːtʃˌgəʊəʳ] N Kirchgänger(in) *m(f)*; **church hall** N Gemeindehalle *f*; **church service** N Gottesdienst *m*; **churchyard** N Friedhof *m*
churlish ADJ, **churlishly** ADV [ˈtʃɜːlɪʃ, -lɪ] ungehobelt
churn [tʃɜːn] **1** N (*for butter*) Butterfass *nt*; (*Brit*: = *milk ~*) Milchkanne *f* **2** VT (a) **to ~ butter** buttern (b) (= *agitate*) *sea, mud etc* aufwühlen **3** VI **his stomach was ~ing** sein Magen revoltierte
➤ **churn out** VT SEP am laufenden Band produzieren
➤ **churn up** VT SEP aufwühlen
chute [ʃuːt] N (a) Rutsche *f*; (= *garbage ~*) Müllschlucker *m* (b) (*inf*: = *parachute*) Fallschirm *m*
chutney [ˈtʃʌtnɪ] N Chutney *m*
CI ABBR *of* **Channel Islands**
CIA ABBR *of* **Central Intelligence Agency** CIA *m*
CID (*Brit*) ABBR *of* **Criminal Investigation Department** ≈ Kripo *f*
cider [ˈsaɪdəʳ] N Cidre *m*; **hard ~** (*US*) Apfelwein *m* (*voll vergoren*); **sweet ~** süßer Apfelwein (*teilweise vergoren*)
cigar [sɪˈgɑːʳ] N Zigarre *f*
cigarette [ˌsɪgəˈret] N Zigarette *f*
cigarette: **cigarette case** N Zigarettenetui *nt*; **cigarette end** N Zigarettenstummel *m*; **cigarette holder** N Zigarettenspitze *f*;

cigarette lighter N Feuerzeug *nt*; **cigarette machine** N Zigarettenautomat *m*

cigar lighter N (*in car*) Zigarettenanzünder *m*

ciggy ['sɪgɪ] N (*inf*) Kippe *f* (*inf*)

CIM N ABBR *of* **computer-integrated manufacturing** computerintegrierte Fertigung

CIM consignment note N (*Comm*) CIM-Frachtbrief *m*

cinch [sɪntʃ] ◼ N **(a)** (*US: = saddle girth*) Sattelgurt *m* **(b)** (*inf*) it's a ~ (*= easy*) das ist ein Kinderspiel *or* ein Klacks (*inf*); (*esp US: = certain*) es ist todsicher (*inf*) ◼ VT (*US*) **(a) to ~ a horse** den Sattelgurt anziehen **(b)** (*inf*) deal regeln (*sl*)

cinder ['sɪndəʳ] N ~s *pl* Asche *f*; **burnt to a** ~ (*Brit fig*) verkohlt

Cinderella [ˌsɪndəˈrelə] N (*lit, fig*) Aschenputtel *nt*

cine ['sɪnɪ]: **cine camera** N (*Brit*) (Schmal)filmkamera *f*; **cine film** N (*Brit*) Schmalfilm *m*

cinema ['sɪnəmə] N (*esp Brit*) Kino *nt*; (*= films collectively also*) Film *m*; **at/to the** ~ im/ins Kino

cinemagoer ['sɪnəməgəʊəʳ] N Kinogänger(in) *m(f)*

cinematic [sɪnəˈmætɪk] ADJ filmisch; ~ **art** Filmkunst *f*

cine projector N (*Brit*) Filmprojektor *m*

cinnamon ['sɪnəmən] ◼ N Zimt *m* ◼ ADJ ATTR Zimt-

CIO (*US*) ABBR *of* **Congress of Industrial Organizations** *amerikanischer Gewerkschaftsdachverband*

CIP ABBR *of* **carriage and insurance paid** frachtfrei versichert

cipher ['saɪfəʳ] N **(a)** (*= nonentity*) Niemand *m no pl* **(b)** (*= code*) Chiffre *f*, Kode *m*; **in** ~ chiffriert

circa ['sɜːkə] PREP zirka

circle ['sɜːkl] ◼ N **(a)** Kreis *m*; **to stand in a** ~ im Kreis stehen; **to have come full** ~ (*fig*) wieder da sein, wo man angefangen hat; **we're just going round in** ~s (*fig*) wir bewegen uns nur im Kreise; **a close** ~ **of friends** ein enger Freundeskreis; **in political** ~s in politischen Kreisen; **he's moving in different** ~s **now** er verkehrt jetzt in anderen Kreisen **(b)** (*of hills etc*) Ring *m* **(c)** (*Brit Theat*) Rang *m* ◼ VT **(a)** (*= surround*) umgeben **(b)** (*= move around*) kreisen um; **the enemy** ~d **the town** der Feind kreiste die Stadt ein **(c)** (*= draw a* ~ *round*) einen Kreis machen um; ~d **in red** rot umkringelt ◼ VI (*= fly in a* ~) kreisen

➤ **circle around** VI (*birds*) Kreise ziehen; (*plane*) kreisen

circuit ['sɜːkɪt] N **(a)** (*= journey around etc*) Rundgang *m*/-fahrt *f*/-reise *f* (*of* um); **to make a** ~ **of sth** um etw herumgehen/-fahren; **three** ~s **of the racetrack** drei Runden auf der Rennbahn **(b)** (*of judges etc*) Gerichtsbezirk *m* **(c)** (*Elec*) Stromkreis *m*; (*= apparatus*) Schaltung *f* **(d)** (*Sport: = track*) Rennbahn *f* **(e)** **the professional tennis** ~ die Tennisturnierrunde (der Berufsspieler)

circuit: **circuit board** N (*Tech*) Platine *f*; **circuit breaker** N Stromkreisunterbrecher *m*; **circuit diagram** N Schaltplan *m*

circuitous [sɜːˈkjʊɪtəs] ADJ umständlich

circuitry ['sɜːkɪtrɪ] N Schaltkreise *pl*

circular ['sɜːkjʊləʳ] ◼ ADJ object kreisförmig; ~ **motion** Kreisbewegung *f*; ~ **tour** Rundfahrt *f*/-reise *f* ◼ N (*in firm*) Rundschreiben *nt*; (*= printed advertisement*) Wurfsendung *f*

circular saw N Kreissäge *f*

circulate ['sɜːkjʊleɪt] ◼ VI **(a)** (*water, blood, money*) zirkulieren; (*traffic*) fließen; (*news, rumour*) kursieren **(b)** (*person: at party*) die Runde machen ◼ VT news, rumour in Umlauf bringen; memo etc zirkulieren lassen; water pumpen

circulation [sɜːkjʊˈleɪʃən] N **(a)** (*Med*) Kreislauf *m*; (*of money*) Umlauf *m*; **to have poor** ~ Kreislaufstörungen haben; **this coin was withdrawn from** *or* **taken out of** ~ diese Münze wurde aus dem Verkehr gezogen; **to be out of** ~ (*inf*) (*person*) von der Bildfläche verschwunden sein; (*criminal, politician*) aus dem Verkehr gezogen worden sein; **in free** ~ (*goods*) frei im Umlauf befindlich **(b)** (*of newspaper etc*) Auflage(nziffer) *f*

circulatory [sɜːkjʊˈleɪtərɪ] ADJ Kreislauf-; ~ **system** Blutkreislauf *m*

circumcise ['sɜːkəmsaɪz] VT beschneiden

circumcision [sɜːkəmˈsɪʒən] N Beschneidung *f*

circumference [səˈkʌmfərəns] N Umfang *m*; **the tree is 10 ft in** ~ der Baum hat einen Umfang von 10 Fuß

circumflex ['sɜːkəmfleks] N Zirkumflex *m*

circumlocution [sɜːkəmləˈkjuːʃən] N Weitschweifigkeit *f*; (*= evasiveness*) Drumherumreden *nt* (*inf*)

circumnavigate [sɜːkəmˈnævɪgeɪt] VT umfahren

circumscribe ['sɜːkəmskraɪb] VT (*= restrict*) eingrenzen

circumspect ['sɜːkəmspekt] ADJ umsichtig

circumstance ['sɜːkəmstəns] N **(a)** Umstand *m*; **in** *or* **under the** ~**s** unter diesen Umständen; **in** *or* **under no** ~**s** unter gar keinen Umständen; **in certain** ~**s** unter Umständen **(b) circumstances** PL (*= financial condition*) Umstände *pl* (*form*)

circumstantial [sɜːkəmˈstænʃəl] ADJ (*Jur*) ~ **evidence** Indizienbeweis *m*; **the case against him is purely** ~ sein Fall beruht allein auf Indizienbeweisen

circumvent [sɜːkəmˈvent] VT umgehen

circus ['sɜːkəs] N Zirkus *m*

cirrhosis [sɪˈrəʊsɪs] N Zirrhose *f*

CIS ABBR *of* **Commonwealth of Independent States** GUS *f*

cissy ['sɪsɪ] N = **sissy**

cistern ['sɪstən] N Zisterne *f*; (*of WC*) Spülkasten *m*

citadel ['sɪtədl] N Zitadelle *f*

citation [saɪˈteɪʃən] N (*= quote*) Zitat *nt*; (*= act of quoting*) Zitieren *nt*

cite [saɪt] VT **(a)** (*= quote*) zitieren **(b)** (*Jur*) vorladen; **he was** ~**d as the co-respondent** (*= mentioned*) er wurde als der Dritte in der Scheidungssache genannt

citizen ['sɪtɪzn] N **(a)** Bürger(in) *m(f)* **(b)** (*of a state*) (Staats)bürger(in) *m(f)*; **French** ~ französischer Staatsbürger, französische Staatsbürgerin

citizen: **Citizens' Advice Bureau** N (*Brit*) ≈ Bürgerberatungsstelle *f*; **citizen's arrest** N *Festnahme durch eine Zivilperson*; **Citizens' Band** N CB-Funk *m*

citizenship ['sɪtɪznʃɪp] N Staatsbürgerschaft *f*

citric acid ['sɪtrɪkæsɪd] N Zitronensäure *f*

citrus ['sɪtrəs] N Zitrusgewächs *nt*; ~ **fruits** Zitrusfrüchte *pl*

city ['sɪtɪ] N **(a)** Stadt *f*, Großstadt *f*; **the** ~ **of Glasgow** die Stadt Glasgow **(b)** (*in London*) **the City** die City

city: **city centre**, (*US*) **city center** N Stadtmitte *f*, Stadtzentrum *nt*, Innenstadt *f*; **city dweller** N Stadtbewohner(in) *m(f)*; **city father** N Stadtverordnete(r) *m*; **the** ~**s** die Stadtväter *pl*; **city hall** N Rathaus *nt*; (*US: = municipal government*) Stadtverwaltung *f*; **city life** N (Groß)stadtleben *nt*; **city manager** N (*US*) Oberstadtdirektor(in) *m(f)*; **cityscape** N (Groß)stadtlandschaft *f*; **city state** N Stadtstaat *m*

civic ['sɪvɪk] ADJ rights, virtues Bürger-; duties als Bürger; authorities städtisch; event der Stadt

civil ['sɪvl] ADJ **(a)** (*= of society*) bürgerlich; unrest in der Bevölkerung **(b)** (*= polite*) höflich; **to be** ~ **to sb** höflich zu jdm sein **(c)** (*Jur*) zivilrechtlich

civil: **Civil Aviation Authority** N Behörde *f* für Zivilluftfahrt; **civil defence**, (*US*) **civil defense** N Zivilschutz *m*; **civil disobedience** N ziviler Ungehorsam; **civil engineer** N Bauingenieur(in) *m(f)*; **civil engineering** N Hoch- und Tiefbau *m*

civilian [sɪˈvɪljən] ◼ N Zivilist(in) *m(f)* ◼ ADJ zivil, Zivil-; **in** ~ **clothes** in Zivil; ~ **casualties** Verluste *pl* unter der Zivilbevölkerung

civilization [sɪvɪlaɪˈzeɪʃən] N **(a)** (*= civilized world*) Zivilisation *f* **(b)** (*= state: of Greeks etc*) Kultur *f*

civilize ['sɪvɪlaɪz] VT zivilisieren

civilized ['sɪvɪlaɪzd] ADJ **(a)** zivilisiert; **all** ~ **nations** alle Kulturnationen **(b)** conditions, hour zivil; (*= cultured*) lifestyle, age etc kultiviert

civil: **civil law** N bürgerliches Recht; **civil liberty** N Bürgerrecht *nt*; **civil list** N Zivilliste *f*

civilly ['sɪvɪlɪ] ADV (*= politely*) höflich

civil: **civil marriage** N standesamtliche Trauung; **civil rights** ◼ PL (staats)bürgerliche Rechte *pl* ◼ ATTR march, campaign Bürgerrechts-; **civil servant** N ≈ Staatsbeamte(r) *m*, Staatsbeamtin *f*; **civil service** N ≈ Staatsdienst *m* (*ohne Richter und Lehrer*); (*= civil servants collectively*) Beamtenschaft *f*; **civil war** N Bürgerkrieg *m*

civvies ['sɪvɪz] PL (*inf*) Zivil *nt*

CJD ABBR *of* **Creutzfeldt-Jakob disease** CJK *f*

cl ABBR *of* **centilitre(s)** cl

clad [klæd] **1** ADJ (*liter*) gekleidet **2** ADJ SUF **fur-~** in Pelze gekleidet; **steel-~** mit Stahl verkleidet

claim [kleɪm] **1** VT **(a)** (= *demand as one's own or due*) Anspruch *m* erheben auf (+*acc*); *benefits, sum of money* (= *apply for*) beantragen; (= *draw*) beanspruchen; *lost property* abholen; **to ~ sth as one's own** etw für sich beanspruchen; **territories ~ed by the Arabs** von den Arabern beanspruchte Gebiete; **the fighting ~ed many lives** die Kämpfe forderten viele Menschenleben
(b) (= *assert*) behaupten
2 VI **(a)** (*Insur*) Ansprüche geltend machen; (*for damage done by people*) Schadensersatz *m* verlangen
(b) (*for expenses etc*) **to ~ for sth** sich (*dat*) etw zurückgeben *or* -zahlen lassen; **you can ~ for your travelling expenses** Sie können sich (*dat*) Ihre Reisekosten zurückerstatten lassen
3 N **(a)** (= *demand*) Anspruch *m*; (= *pay ~*, Ind) Forderung *f*; **his ~ to the title/property** *etc* sein Anspruch auf den Titel/das Grundstück *etc*; **to lay ~ to sth** Anspruch auf etw (*acc*) erheben; **to put in a ~ (for sth)** etw beantragen; (*Insur*) Ansprüche geltend machen; **they put in a ~ for extra pay** sie forderten einen Zuschlag; **he put in an expenses ~ for £100** er reichte Spesen in Höhe von £ 100 ein; **~ for damages** Schadensersatzanspruch *m*
(b) (= *assertion*) Behauptung *f*; **to make a ~** eine Behauptung aufstellen; **I make no ~ to be a genius** ich erhebe nicht den Anspruch, ein Genie zu sein
➤ **claim back** VT SEP zurückfordern; **to claim sth back (as expenses)** sich (*dat*) etw zurückzahlen lassen

claimant ['kleɪmənt] N (*for social security etc*) Antragsteller(in) *m(f)*; (*for inheritance etc*) Anspruchsteller(in) *m(f)* (*to auf* +*acc*); (*Jur*) Kläger(in) *m(f)*

clairvoyant [kleə'vɔɪənt] N Hellseher(in) *m(f)*

clam [klæm] N Venusmuschel *f*
➤ **clam up** VI (*inf*) keinen Piep (mehr) sagen (*inf*)

clambake ['klæmbeɪk] N (*US*) Muschelessen *nt* am Strand; (*inf*: = *party*) Fete *f* (*inf*)

clamber ['klæmbə^r] VI klettern; **to ~ up a hill** auf einen Berg klettern

clammy ['klæmɪ] ADJ (+ER) feucht, klamm

clamour, (*US*) **clamor** ['klæmə^r] **1** N (= *demand*) lautstark erhobene Forderung (*for nach*) **2** VI **to ~ for sth** nach etw schreien; **the men were ~ing to go home** die Männer forderten lautstark die Heimkehr

clamp [klæmp] **1** N Schraubzwinge *f*; (*Med, Elec*) Klemme *f*; (*for illegally parked car*) Parkkralle *f* **2** VT (ein)spannen; *illegally parked car* eine Parkkralle befestigen an (+*dat*)
➤ **clamp down** VI (*fig: police, government*) rigoros durchgreifen
➤ **clamp down on** VI +PREP OBJ *person* an die Kandare nehmen; *activities* einen Riegel vorschieben (+*dat*)

clampdown ['klæmpdaʊn] N Schlag *m* (*on gegen*)

clandestine [klæn'destɪn] ADJ geheim; *meeting, society* Geheim-; *rendezvous* heimlich

clang [klæŋ] **1** N Klappern *nt* **2** VI klappern **3** VT klappern mit

clanger ['klæŋə^r] N (*Brit inf*) Schnitzer *m* (*inf*); **to drop a ~** ins Fettnäpfchen treten (*inf*)

clank [klæŋk] **1** N Klirren *nt* **2** VT klirren mit **3** VI klirren

clannish ['klænɪʃ] ADJ *group* klüngelhaft; *person* cliquenbewusst

clansman ['klænzmən] N, *pl* **-men** [-mən] Clanmitglied *nt*

clap [klæp] **1** N Klatschen *nt no pl*; **a ~ of thunder** ein Donnerschlag *m*; **give him a ~!** klatscht ihm Beifall!; **a ~ on the back** ein Schlag *m* auf die Schulter **2** VT **(a)** (= *applaud*) Beifall klatschen (+*dat*)
(b) **to ~ one's hands** in die Hände klatschen; **to ~ sb on the back** jdm auf die Schulter klopfen
(c) (= *put quickly*) **he ~ped his hand over my mouth** er hielt mir den Mund zu; **to ~ eyes on sb/sth** (*inf*) jdn/etw zu sehen kriegen (*inf*)
3 VI (Beifall) klatschen

clapboard ['klæpbɔːd] N Schindel *f*

clapped-out ['klæptaʊt] ADJ ATTR, **clapped out** ['klæpt'aʊt] ADJ PRED (*inf*) klapprig; **a ~ old car** eine Klapperkiste (*inf*)

clapper ['klæpə^r] N **to go/drive/work like the ~s** (*Brit inf*) ein Mordstempo draufhaben (*inf*)

clapping ['klæpɪŋ] N Beifall *m*

claptrap ['klæptræp] N (*inf*) Geschwafel *nt* (*inf*)

claret ['klærət] N (= *wine*) roter Bordeauxwein

clarification [ˌklærɪfɪ'keɪʃən] N (= *explanation*) Klarstellung *f*; **I'd like a little ~ on this point** ich hätte diesen Punkt gerne näher erläutert

clarify ['klærɪfaɪ] VT (= *explain*) klären; *text* erklären; *statement* näher erläutern

clarinet [ˌklærɪ'net] N Klarinette *f*

clarity ['klærɪtɪ] N Klarheit *f*

clash [klæʃ] **1** VI **(a)** (*armies, demonstrators*) zusammenstoßen; **the chairman ~ed with the committee at the last meeting** der Vorsitzende hatte auf der letzten Sitzung eine Auseinandersetzung mit dem Komitee
(b) (*colours*) sich beißen; (*interests*) kollidieren; (*programmes, films*) sich überschneiden; **our personalities** *or* **we ~ too much** wir passen einfach nicht zusammen
2 N **(a)** (*of armies, demonstrators etc*) Zusammenstoß *m*; (*between people, parties*) Konflikt *m*
(b) (*of personalities*) Unvereinbarkeit *f*; **a ~ of interests** eine Interessenkollision

clasp [klɑːsp] **1** N (*on brooch etc*) (Schnapp)verschluss *m* **2** VT (= *hold*) (er)greifen; **to ~ sb's hand** jds Hand ergreifen; **to ~ one's hands (together)** die Hände falten; **to ~ sb in one's arms** jdn in die Arme nehmen

class [klɑːs] **1** N **(a)** (= *group, also Sch, Univ*) Klasse *f*; **what ~ are you travelling?** in welcher Klasse reisen Sie?; **they're just not in the same ~** man kann sie einfach nicht vergleichen; **in a ~ by itself** *or* **of its own** weitaus das Beste; **~ of products** (*Comm*) Warengruppe *f*; **I don't like her ~es** ihr Unterricht gefällt mir nicht; **the French ~** (= *lesson*) die Französischstunde; (= *people*) die Französischklasse; **the ~ of 1980** der Jahrgang 1980, *die Schul-/Universitätsabgänger etc des Jahres 1980*
(b) (= *social rank*) gesellschaftliche Stellung; **the ruling ~** die herrschende Klasse
(c) (*Brit Univ: of degree*) Prädikat *nt*; **a first-~ degree** ein Prädikatsexamen *nt*; **second-/third-~ degree** ≈ Prädikat Gut/ Befriedigend
(d) (*inf*: = *quality, tone*) Stil *m*; **to have ~** (*person*) Format haben
2 ADJ (*inf*: = *excellent*) erstklassig
3 VT einordnen, klassifizieren

class: **class-conscious** ADJ standesbewusst, klassenbewusst; **class distinction** N Klassenunterschied *m*

classic ['klæsɪk] **1** ADJ (*lit, fig*) klassisch; **a ~ example of sth** ein klassisches Beispiel für etw **2** N Klassiker *m*

classical ['klæsɪkəl] ADJ klassisch; (= *in the style of ~ architecture*) klassizistisch; *education* humanistisch; **~ music** klassische Musik; **the ~ world** die antike Welt

classicism ['klæsɪsɪzəm] N Klassik *f*; (= *style of classic architecture*) Klassizismus *m*

classicist ['klæsɪsɪst] N Altphilologe *m*/-philologin *f*

classics ['klæsɪks] N SING (*Univ*) Altphilologie *f*

classification [ˌklæsɪfɪ'keɪʃən] N Klassifizierung *f*

classified ['klæsɪfaɪd] ADJ in Klassen eingeteilt; **~ ad(vertisement)** Kleinanzeige *f*; **~ information** (*Mil*) Verschlusssache *f*; (*Pol*) Geheimsache *f*; **~ results** (*Brit Sport*) (Spiel)ergebnisse *pl*

classify ['klæsɪfaɪ] VT klassifizieren

class: **classless** ADJ *society* klassenlos; **classmate** N Mitschüler(in) *m(f)*; **classroom** N Klassenzimmer *nt*; **classroom assistant** N Assistenzlehrkraft *f*; **class system** N Klassensystem *nt*

classy ['klɑːsɪ] ADJ (+ER) (*inf*) nobel (*inf*)

clatter ['klætə^r] **1** N Geklapper *nt* **2** VI klappern

clause [klɔːz] N **(a)** (*Gram*) Satz *m* **(b)** (*Jur etc*) Klausel *f*

claustrophobia [ˌklɔːstrə'fəʊbɪə] N Klaustrophobie *f*, Platzangst *f* (*inf*)

claustrophobic [ˌklɔːstrə'fəʊbɪk] ADJ klaustrophob(isch) (*Psych*); **it's so ~ in here** hier kriegt man Platzangst (*inf*)

claw [klɔː] **1** N Kralle *f*; (*of lobster etc*) Schere *f*, Zange *f*; **to get one's ~s into sb** (*inf*) (dauernd) auf jdm herumhacken **2** VT kratzen; **they ~ed their way out from under the rubble** sie wühlten sich aus dem Schutt hervor; **he ~ed his way to the top** (*fig*) er hat sich an die Spitze durchgeboxt **3** VI **to ~ at sth** sich an etw (*acc*) krallen

➤ **claw back** VT SEP (*taxman etc*) sich (*dat*) zurückholen

claw hammer N Tischlerhammer *m*

clay [kleɪ] N Lehm *m*; **to have feet of ~** *or* (*US*) **~ feet** einen Makel auf seiner weißen Weste haben

clay: **clay pigeon** N Tontaube *f*; **clay pigeon shooting** N Tontaubenschießen *nt*; **clay pipe** N Tonpfeife *f*

clean [kliːn] **1** ADJ (+ER) **(a)** sauber; (= *not used also*) neu; **to wash sth ~** etw abwaschen; **to wipe a disk ~** (*Comput*) alle Daten von einer Diskette löschen; **to make a ~ start** ganz von vorne anfangen; (*in life*) ein neues Leben anfangen; **he has a ~ record** gegen ihn liegt nichts vor; **~ bill of lading** (*Comm*) reines Konnossement; **a ~ driving licence** ein Führerschein *m* ohne Strafpunkte; **a ~ break** (*fig*) ein klares Ende

(b) (= *not obscene*) *joke* stubenrein; *film* anständig

(c) (= *well-shaped*) *lines* klar

(d) to make a ~ breast of sth etw gestehen

2 ADV glatt; **I ~ forgot** das habe ich glatt(weg) vergessen (*inf*); **he got ~ away** er verschwand spurlos; **to cut ~ through sth** etw ganz durchschneiden/durchschlagen *etc*; **to come ~** (*inf*) auspacken (*inf*); **to come ~ about sth** etw gestehen

3 VT sauber machen; (= *remove stains etc*) säubern; (= *dry-~*) reinigen; *nails, paintbrush, furniture also, old buildings* reinigen; *window, shoes, vegetables* putzen; *fish, wound* säubern; *chicken* ausnehmen; (= *wash*) (ab)waschen; (= *wipe*) abwischen; *car* waschen; **to ~ one's hands** (= *wash*) sich (*dat*) die Hände waschen *or* (*wipe*) abwischen; **to ~ one's teeth** sich (*dat*) die Zähne putzen; **~ the dirt off your face** wisch dir den Schmutz vom Gesicht!

4 VI reinigen

5 N **to give sth a ~** *see vt*

➤ **clean off** VT SEP (= *wash*) abwaschen; (= *wipe*) abwischen; (= *scrape, rub*) abreiben; *dirt, rust* entfernen

➤ **clean out** VT SEP **(a)** (*lit*) gründlich sauber machen **(b)** (*inf*) (= *to leave penniless*) ausnehmen (wie einen Weihnachtsgans) (*inf*); (= *to burgle*) *house* ausräumen (*inf*) **(c)** (*inf*: = *buy all stock*) **to clean sb out** jdm alles wegkaufen

➤ **clean up** **1** VT SEP **(a)** (*lit*) sauber machen; *old building, old painting* reinigen; *mess* aufräumen **(b)** (*fig*) **the new mayor cleaned up the city** der neue Bürgermeister hat für Sauberkeit in der Stadt gesorgt; **to clean up television** den Bildschirm (*von Gewalt, Sex etc*) säubern **2** VI **(a)** (*lit*) aufräumen **(b)** (*inf*) abkassieren (*inf*)

clean-cut [ˈkliːnˈkʌt] ADJ klar, klar umrissen; *sort of person* gepflegt; **~ features** klare Gesichtszüge *pl*

cleaner [ˈkliːnəʳ] N **(a)** (= *person*) Reinemachefrau *f*; **the ~s come once a week** das Reinigungspersonal kommt einmal pro Woche **(b)** (= *shop*) **~'s** Reinigung *f*; **to take sb to the ~'s** (*inf*: = *trick*) jdn reinlegen (*inf*) **(c)** (= *substance*) Reinigungsmittel *nt*

cleaning [ˈkliːnɪŋ] N **the ladies who do the ~** die Frauen, die (hier) sauber machen; **~ fluid** Reinigungsflüssigkeit *f*

cleaning lady N Reinemachefrau *f*

cleanliness [ˈklɛnlɪnɪs] N Reinlichkeit *f*

clean-living [ˈkliːnˈlɪvɪŋ] ADJ anständig

cleanly [ˈkliːnlɪ] ADV sauber; **the bone broke ~** es war ein glatter Knochenbruch

cleanness [ˈkliːnnɪs] N Sauberkeit *f*

clean-out [ˈkliːnaʊt] N **to give sth a ~** etw sauber machen

cleanse [klɛnz] VT reinigen; (*spiritually*) läutern (*of* von)

cleanser [ˈklɛnzəʳ] N (= *detergent*) Reinigungsmittel *nt*; (*for skin*) Reinigungsmilch *f*

clean-shaven [ˈkliːnˈʃeɪvn] ADJ glatt rasiert

cleansing [ˈklɛnzɪŋ] ADJ *agent* Reinigungs-

cleansing department N Stadtreinigung *f*

clear [klɪəʳ]	
1 ADJECTIVE	**4** TRANSITIVE VERB
2 NOUN	**5** INTRANSITIVE VERB
3 ADVERB	**6** PHRASAL VERBS

1 ADJECTIVE (+ER)
(a) (*generally*) klar; *complexion* rein; *photograph* scharf; **on a clear day** bei klarem Wetter; **to be clear to sb** jdm klar sein;

you weren't very clear du hast dich nicht sehr klar ausgedrückt; **is that clear?** alles klar?; **let's get this clear, I'm the boss** eins wollen wir mal klarstellen, ich bin hier der Chef; **to be clear on** *or* **about sth** (sich *dat*) über etw (*acc*) im Klaren sein

✦**to make + clear** **to make oneself** *or* **one's meaning clear** sich klar ausdrücken; **to make it clear to sb that ...** es jdm (unmissverständlich) klarmachen, dass ...

(b) (= *free*) **to be clear of sth** frei von etw sein; **we're now clear of debts** jetzt sind wir schuldenfrei

(c) (= *unobstructed*) *way* frei

✦**clear of** (= AWAY FROM) **the bottom of the door should be about 3 mm clear of the floor** zwischen Tür und Fußboden müssen etwa 3 mm Luft sein; **OK, keep going, you're clear of the wall** in Ordnung, fahr, bis zur Mauer ist noch ein ganzes Stück Platz

(= BEYOND) **the plane climbed until it was clear of the clouds** das Flugzeug stieg auf, bis es aus den Wolken heraus war; **at last we were/got clear of the prison walls** endlich hatten wir die Gefängnismauern hinter uns

(d) (= *ahead*) (*Brit*) **Rangers are now three points clear of Celtic** Rangers liegt jetzt drei Punkte vor Celtic

(e) (= *complete*) vollständig

(f) (= *net*) klar; **a clear profit** ein Reingewinn *m*; **to have a clear lead** klar führen

2 NOUN

✦**in the clear** **to be in the clear** (= *free from suspicion*) frei von jedem Verdacht sein; **we're not in the clear yet** (= *not out of difficulties*) wir sind noch nicht aus allem heraus

3 ADVERB

(a) (= *distinctly*) **loud and clear** laut und deutlich

(b) (= *completely*) **he got clear away** er verschwand spurlos

(c) (= *away*) **he kicked the ball clear** er klärte; **he leapt clear of the burning car** er rettete sich durch einen Sprung aus dem brennenden Auto

✦**to steer/keep clear** **to steer** *or* **keep clear of sb** jdm aus dem Wege gehen; **to steer** *or* **keep clear of sth** etw meiden; **to steer** *or* **keep clear of a place** um einen Ort einen großen Bogen machen; **exit, keep clear** Ausfahrt freihalten!

✦**to stand clear** zurückbleiben; **stand clear of the doors!** bitte von den Türen zurücktreten!

4 TRANSITIVE VERB

(a) (= *remove obstacles from*) *pipe* reinigen; *blockage* beseitigen; *land, road, railway line* räumen; *one's conscience* erleichtern; (*Comput*) *screen* löschen; (*Comm*) *accounts* abrechnen; **to clear the table** den Tisch abräumen; **to clear a space for sth** für etw Platz schaffen; **to clear the way for sb/ sth** den Weg für jdn/etw frei machen; **to clear a way through the crowd** sich (*dat*) Weg durch die Menge bahnen; **to clear a room** (*of people*) ein Zimmer räumen; (*of things*) ein Zimmer ausräumen; **to clear one's head** (wieder) einen klaren Kopf bekommen

(b) (= *clear away*) *snow, rubbish* räumen

(c) (= *free from guilt*) (*Jur*: = *find innocent*) *person* freisprechen; *one's/sb's name* rein waschen; **that clears him** das beweist seine Unschuld

(d) (= *get past or over*) **he cleared the bar easily** er übersprang die Latte mit Leichtigkeit; **raise the car till the wheel clears the ground** das Auto anheben, bis das Rad den Boden nicht mehr berührt

(e) (*Ftbl etc*) (*Brit*) **to clear the ball** klären

(f) (*debt*) begleichen

(g) (*stock*) räumen; **"half price, to clear"** „Restposten zum halben Preis"

(h) (= *approve*) abfertigen; *expenses, appointment* bestätigen; *goods* zollamtlich abfertigen; **to clear a cheque** *or* (*US*) **check** bestätigen, dass ein Scheck gedeckt ist; **you'll have to clear that with management** Sie müssen das mit der Firmenleitung regeln; **cleared by security** von den Sicherheitsbehörden für unbedenklich erklärt

5 INTRANSITIVE VERB (*weather*) aufklaren; (*mist, smoke*) sich auflösen

6 PHRASAL VERBS
➤ **clear away 1** VT SEP wegräumen **2** VI **(a)** (*mist etc*) sich auflösen **(b)** (= *clear away the dishes*) den Tisch abräumen
➤ **clear off 1** VT SEP *debts* begleichen **2** VI (*Brit inf*) abhauen (*inf*)
➤ **clear out 1** VT SEP *cupboard, unwanted objects* ausräumen **2** VI (*inf*) **(a)** (= *leave*) verschwinden (*inf*) **(b)** (= *leave home etc*) ausziehen
➤ **clear up 1** VT SEP **(a)** *point, matter* klären; *mystery* aufklären **(b)** (= *tidy*) aufräumen; *litter* wegräumen **2** VI **(a)** (*weather*) (sich) aufklären **(b)** (= *tidy up*) aufräumen

clearance ['klɪərəns] N **(a)** (= *act of clearing*) Beseitigung *f* **(b)** (*Ftbl etc*) **it was a good ~ by the defender** der Verteidiger hat gut geklärt **(c)** (*by customs*) Abfertigung *f*; (*by security*) Unbedenklichkeitserklärung *f*; **the despatch was sent to the Foreign Office for ~** der Bericht wurde zur Überprüfung ans Außenministerium geschickt
clearance sale N (*Comm*) Räumungsverkauf *m*
clear-cut ['klɪə'kʌt] ADJ klar; *issue, problem* klar umrissen
clearing ['klɪərɪŋ] N (*in forest*) Lichtung *f*
clearing: clearing bank N (*Brit*) Clearingbank *f*; **clearing house** N Clearingstelle *f*
clearly ['klɪəlɪ] ADV **(a)** (= *distinctly*) klar; **~ visible** klar zu sehen **(b)** (= *obviously*) eindeutig; **~ we cannot allow ...** wir können keinesfalls zulassen ...; **this ~ can't be true** das kann auf keinen Fall stimmen
clear-sighted ['klɪə'saɪtɪd] ADJ (*fig*) klar- *or* scharfsichtig
cleavage ['kliːvɪdʒ] N (*of woman's breasts*) Dekolletee *nt*
cleaver ['kliːvə'] N Hackbeil *nt*
clef [klef] N (Noten)schlüssel *m*
cleft [kleft] **1** ADJ gespalten; **a ~ chin** ein Kinn *nt* mit Grübchen **2** N Spalte *f*; (*in chin*) Grübchen *nt*
cleft palate N Wolfsrachen *m*
clematis ['klemətɪs] N Klematis *f*
clemency ['klemənsɪ] N Milde *f* (*towards sb* jdm gegenüber); **the prisoner was shown ~** dem Gefangenen wurde eine milde Behandlung zuteil
clementine ['kleməntaɪn] N (= *fruit*) Klementine *f*
clench [klentʃ] VT *fist* ballen; *teeth* zusammenbeißen; (= *grasp firmly*) packen
clergy ['klɜːdʒɪ] PL Klerus *m*
clergyman ['klɜːdʒɪmən] N, *pl* **-men** [-mən] Geistliche(r) *m*
clergywoman ['klɜːdʒɪ,wʊmən] N, *pl* **-women** [-wɪmɪn] N Geistliche *f*
cleric ['klerɪk] N Geistliche(r) *m*
clerical ['klerɪkəl] ADJ **(a)** **~ work/job** Schreib- *or* Büroarbeit *f*; **~ worker** Schreib- *or* Bürokraft *f*; **~ staff** Schreibkräfte *pl*; **~ error** Versehen *nt*; (*in wording etc*) Schreibfehler *m* **(b)** (*Eccl*) geistlich
clerk [klɑːk, (US) klɜːrk] N **(a)** (Büro)angestellte(r) *mf*; **~ typist** (*US*) Schreibkraft *f* **(b)** (= *secretary*) Schriftführer(in) *m(f)* **(c)** (*US*: = *shop assistant*) Verkäufer(in) *m(f)* **(d)** (*US*: *in hotel*) Hotelsekretär(in) *m(f)*
clever ['klevə'] ADJ **(a)** (= *mentally bright*) schlau **(b)** (= *ingenious, skilful, witty*) klug; *device* raffiniert, geschickt; **to be ~ at sth** in etw (*dat*) geschickt sein; **he is ~ at raising money** er ist geschickt, wenn es darum geht, Geld aufzubringen **(c)** (= *cunning, smart*) schlau, clever (*inf*)
cleverly ['klevəlɪ] ADV geschickt; (= *wittily*) schlau, klug
cleverness ['klevənɪs] N **(a)** (= *intelligence*) Schlauheit *f* **(b)** (= *skill, ingenuity*) Klugheit *f* **(c)** (= *cunning*) Schläue *pl*
cliché ['kliːʃeɪ] N Klischee *nt*
clichéd ['kliːʃeɪd] ADJ klischeehaft
click [klɪk] **1** N Klicken *nt*; (*of light switch*) Knipsen *nt*; (*of fingers*) Schnipsen *nt*; (*of latch, key in lock*) Schnappen *nt*; (*of tongue*) Schnalzen *nt* **2** VI **(a)** klicken; (*light switch*) knipsen; (*fingers*) schnipsen; (*latch, key in lock*) schnappen; (*high heels*) klappern **(b)** (*inf*: = *be understood*) funken (*inf*); **suddenly it all ~ed (into place)** plötzlich hatte es gefunkt (*inf*) **(c)** (*inf*: = *get on well*) funken (*inf*); **some people you ~ with straight away** mit manchen Leuten versteht man sich auf Anhieb

3 VT *fingers* schnippen mit; *tongue* schnalzen mit; **to ~ sth into place** etw einschnappen lassen
➤ **click on** VI (*Comput*) **to click on the mouse** mit der Maus klicken; **to click on an icon** ein Icon anklicken
clickable ['klɪkəbl] ADJ (*Comput*) anklickbar
client ['klaɪənt] N **(a)** Kunde *m*, Kundin *f*; (*of solicitor*) Klient(in) *m(f)*; (*of barrister*) Mandant(in) *m(f)* **(b)** (*US*: *receiving welfare*) Bezieher(in) *m(f)*
clientele [kliːɒn'tel] N Kundschaft *f*, Klientel *f*
cliff [klɪf] N Klippe *f*
cliff: cliffhanger N Superthriller *m* (*inf*); **clifftop** N Felskuppe *f*; **a house on a ~** ein Haus oben auf einem Felsen
climactic [klaɪ'mæktɪk] ADJ **a ~ scene** ein Höhepunkt
climate ['klaɪmɪt] N (*lit, fig*) Klima *nt*; **the two countries have very different ~s** die beiden Länder haben (ein) sehr unterschiedliches Klima; **to move to a warmer ~** in eine wärmere Gegend ziehen
climatic [klaɪ'mætɪk] ADJ klimatisch, Klima-
climax ['klaɪmæks] N (*all senses*) Höhepunkt *m*
climb [klaɪm] **1** VT **(a)** (*also ~ up*) klettern auf (+*acc*); *hill* steigen auf (+*acc*); *ladder, steps* hoch- *or* hinaufsteigen; *pole, cliffs* hochklettern; **my car can't ~ that hill** mein Auto schafft den Berg nicht; **to ~ a rope** an einem Seil hochklettern **(b)** (*also ~ over*) *wall etc* steigen *or* klettern über (+*acc*) **2** VI klettern; (*as mountaineer*) bergsteigen; (*into train, car etc*) steigen; (*road*) ansteigen; (*prices, aircraft*) steigen **3** N **(a)** (= *climbing*) **we're going out for a ~** wir machen eine Kletter- *or* Bergtour; (*as mountaineers*) wir gehen bergsteigen **(b)** (*of aircraft*) Steigflug *m*; **the plane went into a steep ~** das Flugzeug zog steil nach oben
➤ **climb down 1** VI **(a)** (*person*) (*from tree, wall*) herunterklettern; (*from ladder*) heruntersteigen **(b)** (= *admit error*) nachgeben **2** VI +PREP OBJ *tree, wall* herunterklettern von; *ladder* heruntersteigen
➤ **climb in** VI einsteigen
➤ **climb up 1** VI = **climb 2 2** VI +PREP OBJ *ladder etc* hinaufsteigen; *tree, wall* hochklettern
climb-down ['klaɪmdaʊn] N (*fig*) Abstieg *m*
climber ['klaɪmə'] N **(a)** (= *mountaineer*) Bergsteiger(in) *m(f)*; (= *rock ~*) Kletterer(in) *m(f)* **(b)** (= *plant*) Kletterpflanze *f*
climbing ['klaɪmɪŋ] **1** ADJ **(a)** Berg(steiger)-; (= *rock ~*) Kletter-; *accident* beim Bergsteigen; **we are going on a ~ holiday** wir gehen im Urlaub zum Bergsteigen/Klettern **(b)** *plant* Kletter- **2** N Bergsteigen *nt*; (= *rock ~*) Klettern *nt*; **to go ~** bergsteigen/klettern gehen
clinch [klɪntʃ] **1** VT *argument* zum Abschluss bringen; **to ~ the deal** den Handel perfekt machen; **that ~es it** damit ist der Fall erledigt **2** N (*Boxing, fig*) Clinch *m*; **in a ~** im Clinch (*inf*)
clincher ['klɪntʃə'] N (*inf*) **that was the ~** das gab den Ausschlag
cling [klɪŋ], *pret, ptp* **clung** VI (= *hold on tightly*) sich klammern (*to* an +*acc*); (= *remain close*) sich halten (*to* an +*acc*); (*clothes*) sich anschmiegen (*to* +*dat*); **to ~ together** sich aneinander klammern; (*lovers*) sich umschlingen; **she clung around her father's neck** sie hing ihrem Vater am Hals
clingfilm ['klɪŋfɪlm] N Frischhaltefolie *f*
clinging ['klɪŋɪŋ] ADJ *garment* sich anschmiegend; **she's the ~ sort** sie ist wie eine Klette (*inf*)
clinic ['klɪnɪk] N Klinik *f*
clinical ['klɪnɪkəl] ADJ **(a)** (*Med*) klinisch **(b)** (*fig*) (*atmosphere*) steril; (= *dispassionate*) nüchtern
clinical depression N klinische Depression
clinically ['klɪnɪkəlɪ] ADV klinisch; **~ depressed** klinisch depressiv
clink¹ [klɪŋk] **1** VT klirren lassen; (= *jingle*) klimpern mit; **to ~ glasses with sb** mit jdm anstoßen **2** VI klirren; (= *jingle*) klimpern
clink² N (*inf*: = *prison*) Knast *m* (*inf*); **in ~** im Knast
clip¹ [klɪp] **1** N (*for holding things*) Klammer *f* **2** VT **to ~ sth onto sth** etw an etw (*acc*) anklemmen **3** VI **to ~ on (to sth)** (an etw *acc*) angeklemmt werden; **to ~ together** zusammengeklemmt werden
clip² **1** VT **(a)** (= *trim*) scheren; *hedge, fingernails* schneiden **(b)** (*also ~ out*) *article* aus Papier ausschneiden; (*also ~ off*) *hair* abschneiden **(c)** (= *hit*) treffen; (= *graze*: *car, bullet*) streifen

2 N **(a)** (= *trim*) **to give the hedge a ~** die Hecke (be)schneiden; **to give one's fingernails a ~** sich (*dat*) die Fingernägel schneiden **(b)** (= *hit*) Schlag *m*; **he gave him a ~ round the ear** er gab ihm eins hinter die Ohren (*inf*) **(c)** (*from film*) Clip *m*

clip: **clip art** N (*Comput*) Clip-Art *f*; **clipboard** N Klemmbrett *nt*; **clip-on** ADJ *tie* zum Anstecken; **~ earrings** Klips *pl*; **~ sunglasses** Sonnenklip *m*

clipped [klɪpt] ADJ *accent* abgehackt

clippers ['klɪpəz] PL (*also* **pair of ~**) Schere *f*; (*for hair*) Haarschneidemaschine *f*; (*for fingernails*) Zwicker *m*, Nagelzange *f*

clipping ['klɪpɪŋ] N (= *newspaper ~*) Ausschnitt *m*; **nail ~s** abgeschnittene Nägel *pl*

clique [kliːk] N Clique *f*

clitoris ['klɪtərɪs] N Klitoris *f*

cloak [kləʊk] **1** N (*lit*) Umhang *m*; (*fig*: = *veil*: *of secrecy etc*) Schleier *m*; **under the ~ of darkness** im Schutz der Dunkelheit **2** VT (*fig*) verhüllen

cloak: **cloak-and-dagger** ADJ geheimnisumwittert; **cloakroom** N **(a)** (*Brit*: *for coats*) Garderobe *f* **(b)** (*Brit euph*) Waschraum *m* (*euph*)

clobber ['klɒbə^r] (*inf*) **1** N (*Brit*: = *belongings*) Zeug *nt* (*inf*); (= *clothes*) Klamotten *pl* (*inf*) **2** VT **(a)** (= *hit*, *defeat*) **to get ~ed** eins übergebraten kriegen (*inf*) **(b)** (= *charge a lot*) schröpfen

clock [klɒk] **1** N **(a)** Uhr *f*; **round the ~** rund um die Uhr; **against the ~** (*Sport*) nach *or* auf Zeit; **to work against the ~** gegen die Uhr arbeiten; **to beat the ~** schneller als vorgesehen fertig sein; **to put the ~ back/forward** or **on** (*lit*) die Uhr zurückstellen/vorstellen; **to put** *or* **turn the ~ back** (*fig*) die Zeit zurückdrehen; **to watch the ~** (*inf*) dauernd auf die Uhr sehen **(b)** (*inf*) (= *speedometer*, *milometer*) Tacho *m* (*inf*); (*of taxi*) Uhr *f*; **it's got 100,000 miles on the ~** es hat einen Tachostand von 100.000 Meilen **2** VT **(a)** (*Sport*) **he ~ed four minutes for the mile** er lief die Meile in vier Minuten **(b)** (*Brit inf*: = *see*) sehen

➤ **clock in** *or* **on** VI (den Arbeitsbeginn) stempeln *or* stechen

➤ **clock off** *or* **out** VI (das Arbeitsende) stempeln *or* stechen

➤ **clock up** VT SEP **(a)** *speed*, *distance* fahren **(b)** (*inf*) *success* verbuchen

clock IN CPDS Uhr(en)-; **clock face** N Zifferblatt *nt*; **clockmaker** N Uhrmacher(in) *m(f)*; **clock radio** N Radiouhr *f*; **clock tower** N Uhrenturm *m*; **clock-watching** N Auf-die-Uhr-Schauen *nt*; **clockwise** ADJ, ADV im Uhrzeigersinn; **clockwork** **1** N (*of toy*) Aufziehmechanismus *m*; **like ~** wie am Schnürchen **2** ATTR **(a)** *train*, *car* aufziehbar **(b)** **with ~ regularity** mit der Regelmäßigkeit eines Uhrwerks

clod [klɒd] N (*of earth*) Klumpen *m*

clog [klɒg] **1** N (= *shoe*) Holzschuh *m*; **~s** *pl* (*modern*) Clogs *pl* **2** VT (*also* **~ up**) *pipe etc* verstopfen; *mechanism* blockieren; **~ged with traffic** verstopft **3** VI (*also* **~ up**) (*pipe etc*) verstopfen; (*mechanism etc*) blockieren

cloister ['klɔɪstə^r] N **(a)** (= *covered walk*) Kreuzgang *m* **(b)** (= *monastery*) Kloster *nt*

cloistered ['klɔɪstəd] ADJ (*fig*) weltabgeschieden

clone [kləʊn] **1** N Klon *m* **2** VT klonen

close[1] [kləʊs] **1** ADJ (+ER) **(a)** (= *near*) in der Nähe (*to* +*gen*, *von*); **is Glasgow ~ to Edinburgh?** liegt Glasgow in der Nähe von Edinburgh?; **you're very ~** (*in guessing etc*) du bist dicht dran; **at ~ quarters** aus unmittelbarer Nähe; **we use this pub because it's the ~st** wir gehen in dieses Lokal, weil es am nächsten ist **(b)** (*in time*) nahe (bevorstehend); **nobody realized how ~ a nuclear war was** es war niemandem klar, wie nahe ein Atomkrieg bevorstand **(c)** (*fig*) *friend*, *co-operation*, *connection etc* eng; *relative* nahe; *resemblance* groß; **they were very ~ (to each other)** sie standen sich sehr nahe **(d)** (= *not spread out*) *print* eng; *ranks* geschlossen **(e)** (= *exact*) *examination* genau; *watch* scharf; **now pay ~ attention to me** jetzt hör mir gut zu; **you have to pay very ~ attention to the traffic signs** du musst genau auf die Verkehrszeichen achten

(f) (= *stuffy*) schwül; (*indoors*) stickig **(g)** (= *almost equal*) *fight*, *result* knapp; **a ~(-fought) match** ein (ganz) knappes Spiel; **a ~ finish** ein Kopf-an-Kopf-Rennen *nt*; **it was a ~ thing** *or* **call** das war knapp!; **the vote was too ~ to call** der Ausgang der Abstimmung war völlig offen **2** ADV (+ER) nahe; **~ by** in der Nähe; **~ by us** in unserer Nähe; **stay ~ to me** bleib dicht bei mir; **~ to the ground** nahe am Boden; **he followed ~ behind me** er ging dicht hinter mir; **don't stand too ~ to the fire** stell dich nicht zu nahe ans Feuer; **to be ~ to tears** den Tränen nahe sein; **~ together** nahe zusammen; **this pattern comes ~st to the sort of thing we wanted** dieses Muster kommt dem, was wir uns vorgestellt haben, am nächsten; **what does it look like (from) ~ up?** wie sieht es von nahem aus? **3** N (*of cathedral etc*) Domhof *m*

close[2] [kləʊz] **1** VT **(a)** (= *shut*) schließen; *eyes*, *door*, *shop*, *window*, *curtains also* zumachen; (*permanently*) *business etc* schließen; *factory* stilllegen; (= *block*) *opening etc* verschließen; *road* sperren; **"~d"** "geschlossen"; **sorry, we're ~d** tut uns Leid, wir haben geschlossen; **to ~ one's eyes/ears to sth** sich einer Sache gegenüber blind/taub stellen; **to ~ ranks** (*Mil*, *fig*) die Reihen schließen **(b)** (= *bring to an end*) *meeting* beenden; *bank account etc* auflösen; **the matter is ~d** der Fall ist abgeschlossen **2** VI **(a)** (= *shut*, *come together*) sich schließen; (= *can be shut*) zugehen; (*shop*, *factory*) zumachen; (*factory*: *permanently*) stillgelegt werden; **his eyes ~d** die Augen fielen ihm zu **(b)** (= *come to an end*, *St Ex*) schließen; (*Theat*: *play*) auslaufen; **the shares ~d at £5** die Aktien erreichten eine Schlussnotierung von £ 5 **(c)** (*Comm*: = *accept offer*) abschließen **3** N Ende *nt*, Schluss *m*; **to come to a ~** enden; **to draw to a ~** sich dem Ende nähern; **to bring sth to a ~** etw beenden; **at the ~ (of business)** bei Geschäfts- *or* (*St Ex*) Börsenschluss

➤ **close down** **1** VI **(a)** (*business etc*) schließen, zumachen (*inf*); (*factory*: *permanently*) stillgelegt werden **(b)** (*Rad*, *TV*) das Programm beenden **2** VT SEP *business etc* schließen; *factory* (*permanently*) stilllegen

➤ **close in** VI (*winter*) anbrechen; (*night*, *darkness*) hereinbrechen; (*days*) kürzer werden; (*enemy etc*) bedrohlich nahe kommen; **to close in on sb** (*gang*, *individual etc*) jdm auf den Leib rücken; (*the police are closing in on him* die Polizei zieht das Netz um ihn zu; (*physically*) die Polizisten umzingeln ihn

➤ **close off** VT SEP (ab)sperren; (= *separate off*) abteilen

➤ **close on** VI +PREP OBJ einholen

➤ **close up** **1** VI (*line of people*) zusammenrücken **2** VT SEP *house*, *shop* zumachen

➤ **close with** VI +PREP OBJ (= *strike bargain with*) handelseinig sein *or* werden mit

closed-circuit television [kləʊzd'sɜːkɪt'telɪvɪʒən] N interne Fernsehanlage; (*for supervision*) Fernsehüberwachungsanlage *f*

closed corporation N (*US Comm*) Gesellschaft *f* mit beschränkter Haftung

close-down ['kləʊzdaʊn] N (*Rad*, *TV*) Sendeschluss *m*

closed [kləʊzd]: **closed primary** N (*US Pol*) Vorwahl mit Fraktionszwang, bei der nur Mitglieder der eigenen Partei gewählt werden können; **closed shop** N Closedshop *m*; **we have a ~** wir haben Gewerkschaftszwang

close [kləʊs]: **close-fitting** ADJ eng anliegend; **close-knit** ADJ, *comp* **closer-knit** *community* eng *or* fest zusammengewachsen

closely ['kləʊslɪ] ADV **(a)** eng, dicht; *work*, *connect* eng; *woven* fest; *related* nah(e), eng; *follow* (*in time*) dicht; **he was ~ followed by a policeman** ein Polizist ging dicht hinter ihm; **the match was ~ contested** der Spielausgang war hart umkämpft **(b)** (= *attentively*) *watch*, *listen etc* genau; *guard* scharf; **a ~-guarded secret** ein streng gehütetes Geheimnis

closeness ['kləʊsnɪs] N **(a)** (= *nearness*, *in time*) Nähe *f* **(b)** (*fig*: *of friendship*) Innigkeit *f*; **the ~ of their relationship caused problems** ihre so enge Beziehung verursachte Probleme

close [kləʊs]: **close-run** ADJ, *comp* **closer-run** *race* mit knappem Ausgang; **it was a ~ thing** es war eine knappe Sache; **close-set** ADJ, *comp* **closer-set** *eyes* eng zusammenstehend

closet ['klɒzɪt] N (*US*) Wandschrank *m*; **to come out of the ~** (*fig*) (*man*) sich als Homosexueller outen; (*woman*) sich als Lesbe outen

close-up [ˈkləʊsʌp] N Nahaufnahme *f*; **in ~** in Nahaufnahme; *(face)* in Großaufnahme

closing [ˈkləʊzɪŋ] **1** N (= *shutting*) Schließung *f*; *(of factory: permanently)* Stilllegung *f* **2** ADJ **(a)** *remarks etc* abschließend; **~ arguments** *(Jur)* Schlussplädoyers *pl* **(b)** *(St Ex)* **~ prices** Schlusskurse *pl*

closing: **closing date** N Einsendeschluss *m*; **closing-down sale** [ˌkləʊzɪŋˈdaʊnseɪl] N *(Comm)* Räumungsverkauf *m*; **closing time** N Geschäfts- *or* Ladenschluss *m*; *(Brit: in pub)* Polizei- *or* Sperrstunde *f*

closure [ˈkləʊʒəʳ] N Schließung *f*; *(of road)* Sperrung *f*

clot [klɒt] **1** N *(of blood)* (Blut)gerinnsel *nt* **2** VI *(blood)* gerinnen

cloth [klɒθ] N **(a)** Tuch *nt*, Stoff *m* **(b)** (= *dishcloth etc*) Tuch *nt*; *(for cleaning also)* Lappen *m*; (= *tablecloth*) Tischdecke *f*

cloth cap N Schlägermütze *f*

clothe [kləʊð], *pret, ptp* **clothed** VT **(a)** (*usu pass*: = *dress*) anziehen **(b)** (= *provide clothes for*) anziehen

clothes [kləʊðz] PL **(a)** (= *garments*) Kleider *pl*; **his mother still washes his ~** seine Mutter macht ihm immer noch die Wäsche; **with one's ~ on/off** an-/ausgezogen; **to put on/take off one's ~** sich an-/ausziehen **(b)** (= *bedclothes*) Bettzeug *nt*

clothes: **clothes basket** N Wäschekorb *m*; **clothes brush** N Kleiderbürste *f*; **clothes horse** N Wäscheständer *m*; **clothes line** N Wäscheleine *f*; **clothes peg**, (*US*) **clothes pin** N Wäscheklammer *f*; **clothes shop** N Bekleidungsgeschäft *nt*

clothing [ˈkləʊðɪŋ] N Kleidung *f*; **~ industry** Bekleidungsindustrie *f*

clotted cream [ˈklɒtɪdˈkriːm] N Sahne *f* (*aus erhitzter Milch*)

cloud [klaʊd] **1** N *(in sky, of dust etc)* Wolke *f*; *(of gas, smoke from fire)* Schwaden *m*; **to have one's head in the ~s** in höheren Regionen schweben; *(momentarily)* geistesabwesend sein; **to be on ~ nine** (*inf*) im siebten Himmel schweben (*inf*); **every ~ has a silver lining** (*Prov*) kein Unglück ist so groß, es hat sein Glück im Schoß (*Prov*); **he's been under a ~ for weeks** (= *under suspicion*) seit Wochen haftet ein Verdacht an ihm; (= *in disgrace*) die Geschichte hängt ihm schon wochenlang nach **2** VT *(fig*: = *cast gloom on*) *prospect, sb's enjoyment* trüben; *face* umwölken (*geh*); (= *make less clear*) *mind, judgement* trüben; *nature of problem* verschleiern; **to ~ the issue** (= *complicate*) es unnötig kompliziert machen; (= *hide deliberately*) die Angelegenheit verschleiern

► **cloud over** VI *(sky)* sich bewölken; **his face clouded over** seine Stirn umwölkte sich (*geh*)

cloud: **cloudburst** N Wolkenbruch *m*; **cloud-cuckoo-land** N **you're living in ~ if you think …** du lebst auf dem Mond, wenn du glaubst … (*inf*)

cloudless [ˈklaʊdlɪs] ADJ wolkenlos

cloudy [ˈklaʊdɪ] ADJ (+ER) **(a)** *sky* bewölkt; *weather* grau; **it's getting ~** es bewölkt sich **(b)** *liquid, glass, eyes etc* trüb

clout [klaʊt] **1** N **(a)** (*inf*: = *blow*) Schlag *m*; **to give sb a ~** jdm eine runterhauen (*inf*); **to give sth a ~** *(acc)* schlagen *or* hauen (*inf*) **(b)** *(political, industrial)* Schlagkraft *f* **2** VT (*inf*) schlagen, hauen (*inf*); **to ~ sb one** jdm eine runterhauen (*inf*) *or* eins verpassen (*inf*)

clove [kləʊv] N **(a)** Gewürznelke *f*; **oil of ~s** Nelkenöl *nt* **(b)** **~ of garlic** Knoblauchzehe *f*

clover [ˈkləʊvəʳ] N Klee *m*; **to be/live in ~** wie Gott in Frankreich leben

clown [klaʊn] **1** N *(in circus etc)* Clown *m*; (*inf*) (*pej*) Idiot *m*, Trottel *m*; **to act the ~** den Clown spielen **2** VI *(also ~ about or around)* herumblödeln (*inf*) *or* -kaspern (*inf*)

cloying [ˈklɔɪɪŋ] ADJ (*lit*) übermäßig süß; **~ sentimentality** gefühlsduselige Sentimentalität

club [klʌb] **1** N **(a)** (= *weapon*) Knüppel *m*; (= *golf ~*) Golfschläger *m* **(b) clubs** PL *(Cards)* Kreuz *nt*; **the ace/nine of ~s** (das) Kreuzass/(die) Kreuzneun **(c)** (= *society*) Klub *m*, Verein *m*; (= *tennis ~, gentleman's ~, night ~*) Klub *m*; *(Ftbl)* Verein *m*; **join the ~!** (*inf*) gratuliere! du auch!; **the London ~ scene** das Nachtleben von London **2** VT einknüppeln auf (+*acc*) **3** VI **to go clubbing** Nachtklubs besuchen

► **club together** VI (*Brit*) zusammenlegen

club: **club class** N *(Aviat)* Clubklasse *f*, Businessklasse *f*; **club foot** N Klumpfuß *m*; **clubhouse** N Klubhaus *nt*; **club member** N Vereins- *or* Klubmitglied *nt*

cluck [klʌk] VI gackern

clue [kluː] N Anhaltspunkt *m*; *(in crosswords)* Frage *f*; **to find a/ the ~ to sth** den Schlüssel zu etw finden; **I'll give you a ~** ich gebe dir einen Tipp; **I haven't a ~!** (ich hab) keine Ahnung!

► **clue up** VT SEP (*inf*) **to be clued up on** *or* **about sth** über etw (*acc*) im Bilde sein; *(about subject)* mit etw vertraut sein

clueless [ˈkluːlɪs] ADJ (*inf*) ahnungslos

clump [klʌmp] **1** N *(of trees, flowers etc)* Gruppe *f*; *(of earth)* Klumpen *m* **2** VI trampeln; *(with adv of place)* stapfen; **to ~ about** herumtrampeln

clumsily [ˈklʌmzɪlɪ] ADV ungeschickt; (= *in an ungainly way, inelegantly*) schwerfällig

clumsiness [ˈklʌmzɪnɪs] N Ungeschicklichkeit *f*; *(of prose, translation etc, = ungainliness)* Schwerfälligkeit *f*

clumsy [ˈklʌmzɪ] ADJ (+ER) **(a)** ungeschickt; (= *ungainly, inelegant*) schwerfällig **(b)** (= *careless*) *mistake* dumm

clung [klʌŋ] PRET, PTP *of* **cling**

clunk [klʌŋk] **1** N dumpfes Geräusch **2** VI **the door ~ed shut** die Tür schloss sich mit einem dumpfen Geräusch

clunker [ˈklʌŋkəʳ] N *(US pej inf*: = *car)* Kiste *f* (*pej inf*)

cluster [ˈklʌstəʳ] **1** N *(of trees, flowers, houses)* Gruppe *f*, Haufen *m*; *(of islands)* Gruppe *f*; *(of diamonds)* Büschel *nt* **2** VI *(people)* sich drängen *or* scharen

clutch [klʌtʃ] **1** N **(a)** (= *grip*) Griff *m* **(b)** *(Aut)* Kupplung *f*; **to let in/out the ~** ein-/auskuppeln **(c)** *(fig)* **to fall into sb's ~es** jdm in die Hände fallen; **to be in sb's ~es** in jds Gewalt (*dat*) sein **2** VT (= *grab*) umklammern; (= *hold tightly*) umklammert halten

► **clutch at** VI +PREP OBJ (*lit*) schnappen nach (+*dat*); (= *hold tightly*) umklammert halten; *(fig)* sich klammern an (+*acc*)

clutter [ˈklʌtəʳ] **1** N (= *confusion*) Durcheinander *nt*; (= *disorderly articles*) Kram *m* (*inf*) **2** VT *(also ~ up)* zu voll machen (*inf*)/stellen; *painting* überladen; *mind* voll stopfen; **to be ~ed with sth** *(mind, room, drawer etc)* mit etw voll gestopft sein; *(floor, desk etc)* mit etw übersät sein

cm ABBR *of* **centimetre** cm

CMR consignment note N *(Comm)* internationaler CMR-Frachtbrief

CO ABBR *of* **Commanding Officer**

Co (a) ABBR *of* **company** KG *f* **(b)** ABBR *of* **county**

co- [kəʊ-] PREF Mit-, mit-

c/o (a) ABBR *of* **care of** bei, c/o **(b)** ABBR *of* **carried over** Übertr.

coach [kəʊtʃ] **1** N **(a)** *(horsedrawn)* Kutsche *f* **(b)** *(Rail)* (Eisenbahn)wagen *m* **(c)** *(Brit*: = *motor ~)* (Reise)bus *m*; **by ~** mit dem Bus; **~ travel/journeys** Busreisen *pl*; **~ driver** Busfahrer *m* **(d)** (= *tutor*) Nachhilfelehrer(in) *m(f)*; *(Sport)* Trainer *m* **2** VT **(a)** *(Sport)* trainieren **(b)** **to ~ sb for an exam** jdn aufs Examen vorbereiten

coaching [ˈkəʊtʃɪŋ] N *(Sport)* Trainerstunden *pl*; *(Tennis)* Training *nt*; (= *tutoring*) Nachhilfe *f*

coach: **coachload** N *(Brit)* = **busload**; **coach party** N *(Brit)* Busreisegruppe *f*; **coach station** N *(Brit)* Busbahnhof *m*; **coach trip** N *(Brit)* Busfahrt *f*

coagulate [kəʊˈægjʊleɪt] VI *(blood)* gerinnen; *(milk)* dick werden

coal [kəʊl] N Kohle *f*; **to carry** *or* **take ~s to Newcastle** *(Brit Prov)* Eulen nach Athen tragen (*Prov*); **to haul** *(Brit)* *or* **drag sb over the ~s** jdm eine Standpauke halten

coal IN CPDS Kohlen-; **coal cellar** N Kohlenkeller *m*; **coal dust** N Kohlenstaub *m*

coalesce [ˌkəʊəˈles] VI *(fig)* sich vereinigen

coal: **coalface** N *(Brit)* Streb *m*; **coalfield** N Kohlenrevier *nt*; **coal fire** N Kamin *m*; **coal-fired** ADJ Kohle(n)-; **~ power station** Kohlekraftwerk *nt*

coalition [ˌkəʊəˈlɪʃən] N Koalition *f*; **~ government** Koalitionsregierung *f*

coal: **coal mine** N Grube *f*, Zeche *f*; **coal miner** N Bergmann *m*; **coal-mining** N Kohle(n)bergbau *m*; **~ area** Kohlenrevier *nt*; **coal scuttle** N Kohleneimer *m*, Kohlenkasten *m*

coarse [kɔːs] ADJ (+ER) **(a)** (= *not delicate, in texture*) grob **(b)** (= *uncouth*) gewöhnlich; *manners also* grob; *laugh, joke* derb **(c)** (= *common*) *food* einfach; **~ red wine** einfacher (Land)rotwein

coarsely [ˈkɔːslɪ] ADV **(a)** *chop, grate* grob; **~ woven cloth** grob gewebter Stoff **(b)** (= *uncouthly*) *joke, speak* derb; *behave* ungehobelt

coarsen [ˈkɔːsn] VT *skin* gerben

coarseness [ˈkɔːsnɪs] N **(a)** *(of texture)* Grobheit *f* **(b)** *(fig:* = *vulgarity)* Gewöhnlichkeit *f*; *(of manners also)* Grobheit *f*; *(of joke also)* Unanständigkeit *f*; *(of sb's language)* Derbheit *f*

coast [kəʊst] **1** N Küste *f*; **on the ~** am Meer; **we're going to the ~** wir fahren ans Meer; **the ~ is clear** *(fig)* die Luft ist rein **2** VI **(a)** *(car, cyclist)* *(in neutral)* (im Leerlauf) fahren; (= *cruise effortlessly)* dahinrollen; *(athlete)* locker laufen; *(US: on sled)* hinunterrodeln **(b)** *(fig)* **to be ~ing along** mühelos vorankommen

coaster [ˈkəʊstəʳ] N **(a)** (= *drip mat)* Untersetzer *m* **(b)** *(US)* (= *sled)* (Rodel)schlitten *m*; (= *roller-~)* Achterbahn *f*

coaster brake N *(US)* Rücktrittbremse *f*

coast: coastguard N Küstenwache *f*; **the ~s** die Küstenwacht; **coastline** N Küste *f*

coat [kəʊt] **1** N **(a)** (= *outdoor garment)* Mantel *m*; (= *doctor's ~ etc also)* (Arzt)kittel *m* **(b)** *(Her)* **~ of arms** Wappen *nt* **(c)** *(of animal)* Fell *nt* **(d)** *(of paint etc)* (= *application)* Anstrich *m*; (= *actual layer)* Schicht *f*; **give it a second ~** *(of paint)* streich es noch einmal **2** VT *(with paint etc)* streichen; *(with icing etc)* überziehen; **to be ~ed with mud** mit einer Schmutzschicht überzogen sein

coat hanger N Kleiderbügel *m*

coating [ˈkəʊtɪŋ] N Überzug *m*; *(of paint)* Anstrich *m*

coat stand N Garderobenständer *m*

co-author [ˈkəʊˌɔːθəʳ] N Mitautor(in) *m(f)*

coax [kəʊks] VT überreden; **to ~ sb into doing sth** jdn beschwatzen, etw zu tun *(inf)*; **to ~ sth out of sb** jdm etw entlocken

cob [kɒb] N (= *corn)* (Mais)kolben *m*; **corn on the ~** Maiskolben *m*

cobble [ˈkɒbl] **1** N *(also* **~stone)** Kopfstein *m* **2** VT **a ~d street** eine Straße mit Kopfsteinpflaster

➤ **cobble together** VT SEP *(inf)* essay etc zusammenschustern

cobbler [ˈkɒbləʳ] N **(a)** Schuster *m* **(b)** *(esp US: = fruit pie)* Obst mit Teig überbacken

cobblers [ˈkɒbləz] PL *(Brit inf)* Scheiße *f* *(inf)*, Mist *m* *(inf)*; **(what a load of old) ~!** was fürn Haufen Mist! *(inf)*

cobblestone [ˈkɒblstəʊn] N Kopfstein *m*

COBOL [ˈkəʊbɒl] ABBR *of* **common business oriented language** COBOL

cobweb [ˈkɒbweb] N Spinnennetz *nt*; **a brisk walk will blow away the ~s** *(fig)* ein ordentlicher Spaziergang und man hat wieder einen klaren Kopf

cocaine [kəˈkeɪn] N Kokain *nt*

cochineal [ˌkɒtʃɪˈniːl] N Koschenille *f*

cock [kɒk] **1** N **(a)** (= *rooster)* Hahn *m* **(b)** (= *male bird)* Männchen *nt* **(c)** (= *tap)* (Wasser)hahn *m* **(d)** *(sl:* = *penis)* Schwanz *m* *(sl)* **2** VT **(a)** **to ~ the gun** den Hahn spannen **(b)** *ears* spitzen

➤ **cock up** VT SEP *(Brit inf:* = *mess up)* versauen *(inf)*

cock: cock-a-doodle-doo N Kikeriki *nt*; **cock-a-hoop** ADJ ganz aus dem Häuschen; **cock-a-leekie (soup)** N Lauchsuppe *f* mit Huhn

cockamamie [ˌkɒkəˈmeɪmɪ] ADJ *(US inf:* = *poor quality)* mies *(inf)*

cock-and-bull story [ˌkɒkənˈbʊlˌstɔːrɪ] N Lügengeschichte *f*

cockatiel [ˌkɒkəˈtiːl] N Nymphensittich *m*

cockatoo [ˌkɒkəˈtuː] N Kakadu *m*

cocker [ˈkɒkəʳ] N *(also* **~ spaniel)** Cocker(spaniel) *m*

cockerel [ˈkɒkərəl] N junger Hahn

cock: cockeyed [ˈkɒkaɪd] ADJ *(inf)* **(a)** (= *crooked)* schief **(b)** (= *absurd)* *idea* verrückt; **cockfight** N Hahnenkampf *m*

cockily [ˈkɒkɪlɪ] ADV *(inf)* großspurig

cockle [ˈkɒkl] N (= *shellfish: also* **~shell)** Herzmuschel *f*

cockney [ˈkɒknɪ] **1** N **(a)** (= *dialect)* Cockney *nt* **(b)** (= *person)* Cockney *m* **2** ADJ Cockney-

COCKNEY

Ein **Cockney** *ist jemand, der in Londons East End geboren ist. Traditionellerweise ist er nur dann ein waschechter* **Cockney***, wenn seine Geburt innerhalb der Hörweite der* **Bow Bells***, der Kirchenglocken von St Mary-le-Bow in Cheapside im Osten Londons, stattfand. Mit* **Cockney** *wird auch der Dialekt bezeichnet, der in diesem Teil Londons gesprochen wird; fälschlicherweise wird der Ausdruck oft für jeden Akzent der Londoner Arbeiterklasse verwendet.*

cockpit [ˈkɒkpɪt] N Cockpit *nt*

cockroach [ˈkɒkrəʊtʃ] N Kakerlak *m*

cocktail [ˈkɒkteɪl] N Cocktail *m*; **we're invited for ~s** wir sind zum Cocktail eingeladen

cocktail IN CPDS Cocktail-; **cocktail bar** N Cocktailbar *f*; **cocktail cabinet** N Hausbar *f*; **cocktail lounge** N Cocktailbar *f*; **cocktail stick** N Cocktailspieß *m*; **cocktail waiter** N *(esp US)* Getränkekellner *m*; **cocktail waitress** N *(esp US)* Getränkekellnerin *f*

cockup [ˈkɒkʌp] N *(Brit inf)* **to be a ~** in die Hose gehen *(inf)*; **to make a ~ of sth** bei *or* mit etw Scheiße bauen *(inf)*

cocky [ˈkɒkɪ] ADJ *(+ER)* *(inf)* großspurig

cocoa [ˈkəʊkəʊ] N Kakao *m*

coconut [ˈkəʊkənʌt] **1** N Kokosnuss *f* **2** ATTR Kokos-

coconut: coconut oil N Kokosöl *nt*; **coconut palm, coconut tree** N Kokospalme *f*

cocoon [kəˈkuːn] **1** N Kokon *m*; *(fig: of blankets etc)* Hülle *f* **2** VT einhüllen

COD ABBR *of* **cash** *(Brit)* *or* **collect** *(US)* **on delivery**

cod [kɒd] N Kabeljau *m*

coddle [ˈkɒdl] VT verhätscheln

code [kəʊd] **1** N **(a)** (= *cipher, Comput)* Kode *m*; **in ~** verschlüsselt; **to put into ~** verschlüsseln **(b)** (= *rules, principles)* Kodex *m*; **~ of conduct** Verhaltenskodex *m*; **~ of practice** Verfahrensregeln *pl* **(c)** *(Telec)* Vorwahl *f* **(d)** post *or* zip *(US)* **~** Postleitzahl *f* **2** VT verschlüsseln; *(Comput)* kodieren

coded [ˈkəʊdɪd] ADJ **(a)** (= *in code)* kodiert **(b)** (= *indirect)* *reference* versteckt; **in ~ language** in verschlüsselter *or* kodierter Sprache

codeine [ˈkəʊdiːn] N Kodein *nt*

code: code name N Deckname *m*; **code number** N Kennziffer *f*

co-dependent [ˌkəʊdɪˈpendənt] *(esp US Psych)* **1** N Koabhängige(r) *mf* **2** ADJ koabhängig

co-determination [ˌkəʊdɪtɜːmɪˈneɪʃən] N *(Ind)* Mitbestimmung *f*

code word N Kodewort *nt*; *(Comput also)* Passwort *nt*

codicil [ˈkɒdɪsɪl] N Kodizill *nt*

coding [ˈkəʊdɪŋ] N **(a)** Chiffrieren *nt*; **a new ~ system** ein neues Chiffriersystem; **I don't understand the ~** ich verstehe den Kode nicht **(b)** *(Comput:* = *codes)* Kodierung(en *pl*) *f*

cod-liver oil [ˈkɒdlɪvərˌɔɪl] N Lebertran *m*

co-ed, coed [ˈkəʊˈed] **1** N *(inf)* *(Brit:* = *school)* gemischte Schule, Koedukationsschule *f*; *(dated US:* = *girl student)* Schülerin *f or* Studentin *f* einer gemischten Schule **2** ADJ *school* gemischt, Koedukations-

coeducational [ˈkəʊˌedjʊˈkeɪʃənl] ADJ *teaching* koedukativ; *school* Koedukations-

coefficient [ˌkəʊɪˈfɪʃənt] N *(Math, Phys)* Koeffizient *m*

coerce [kəʊˈɜːs] VT zwingen; **to ~ sb into doing sth** jdn dazu zwingen, etw zu tun

coercion [kəʊˈɜːʃən] N Zwang *m*

coexist [ˌkəʊɪɡˈzɪst] VI koexistieren *(Pol, Sociol, geh)*, nebeneinander bestehen; **to ~ with** *or* **alongside sb/sth** neben jdm/etw bestehen *or* existieren

coexistence [ˌkəʊɪɡˈzɪstəns] N Koexistenz *f*

C of E ABBR *of* **Church of England**

coffee [ˈkɒfɪ] N Kaffee *m*; **two ~s, please** zwei Kaffee, bitte

coffee IN CPDS Kaffee-; **coffee bar** N Café *nt*; **coffee bean** N Kaffeebohne *f*; **coffee break** N Kaffeepause *f*; **coffee cup** N Kaffeetasse *f*; **coffee filter** N Kaffeefilter *m*; **coffee grinder** N Kaffeemühle *f*; **coffee machine** N (= *coffee maker)*

Kaffeemaschine *f*; (= *vending machine*) Kaffee-Verkaufsautomat *m*; **coffee maker** N Kaffeemaschine *f*; **coffeepot** N Kaffeekanne *f*; **coffee table** N Couchtisch *m*; **coffee-table** ADJ ~ **book** Bildband *m*

coffer [ˈkɒfəʳ] N (*fig*) **the ~s** die Schatulle; (*of state*) das Staatssäckel

coffin [ˈkɒfɪn] N Sarg *m*

cog [kɒg] N (*Tech*) Zahn *m*; (= *~wheel*) Zahnrad *nt*; **he's only a ~ in the machine** (*fig*) er ist nur ein Rädchen im Getriebe

cogent ADJ, **cogently** ADV [ˈkəʊdʒənt, -lɪ] stichhaltig

cognac [ˈkɒnjæk] N Kognak *m*; (*French*) Cognac *m*

cognate [ˈkɒgneɪt] ADJ verwandt

cognitive [ˈkɒgnɪtɪv] ADJ kognitiv

cognoscenti [ˌkɒgnəʊˈʃentiː] PL Kenner *pl*

cog: cog railway N (*US*) Zahnradbahn *f*; **cogwheel** N Zahnrad *nt*

cohabit [kəʊˈhæbɪt] VI (*esp Jur*) in nichtehelicher Lebensgemeinschaft leben, zusammenleben

coherence [kəʊˈhɪərəns] N (*of argument, style*) Kohärenz *f*; **his speech lacked ~** seiner Rede (*dat*) fehlte der Zusammenhang

coherent [kəʊˈhɪərənt] ADJ (a) (= *comprehensible*) zusammenhängend; **incapable of ~ speech** unfähig, zusammenhängend zu sprechen (b) (= *cohesive*) *logic, reasoning etc* kohärent; *case* schlüssig

coherently [kəʊˈhɪərəntlɪ] ADV (a) (= *comprehensibly*) zusammenhängend (b) (= *cohesively*) kohärent

cohesion [kəʊˈhiːʒən] N (*of group*) Zusammenhalt *m*

cohort [ˈkəʊhɔːt] N Kohorte *f*

coiffure [kwɒˈfjʊəʳ] N Haartracht *f*

coil [kɔɪl] **1** N (a) (*of rope etc*) Rolle *f*; (*in light bulb*) Glühdraht *m*; (*of smoke*) Kringel *m*; (*of hair*) Kranz *m* (b) (*Elec*) Spule *f* (c) (= *contraceptive*) Spirale *f* **2** VT aufwickeln; **to ~ sth round sth** etw um etw wickeln

coin [kɔɪn] **1** N Münze *f*; **the other side of the ~** (*fig*) die Kehrseite der Medaille; **they are two sides of the same ~** das sind zwei Seiten derselben Sache **2** VT *phrase* prägen; **..., to ~ a phrase** ..., um mich mal so auszudrücken

coinage [ˈkɔɪnɪdʒ] N (a) (= *system*) Währung *f* (b) (*fig*) Neuschöpfung *f*

coin box N (= *telephone*) Münzfernsprecher *m*; (= *box*) Geldkasten *m*; (*on telephone, meter*) Münzzähler *m*

coincide [ˌkəʊɪnˈsaɪd] VI (*in time, place*) zusammenfallen; (= *agree*) übereinstimmen; **the two concerts ~** die beiden Konzerte finden zur gleichen Zeit statt

coincidence [kəʊˈɪnsɪdəns] N Zufall *m*; **what a ~!** welch ein Zufall!

coincidental ADJ, **coincidentally** ADV [kəʊˌɪnsɪˈdentl, -təlɪ] zufällig

coin-operated [ˈkɔɪnˈɒpəreɪtɪd] ADJ Münz-; ~ **machine** Münzautomat *m*

Coke® [kəʊk] N (*inf*) (Coca-)Cola® *f*

coke¹ [kəʊk] N Koks *m*

coke² N (*inf.* = *cocaine*) Koks *m* (*inf*)

Col ABBR of **Colonel**

col ABBR of **column** Sp.

COLA [ˈkəʊlə] (*US Fin*) ABBR of **cost-of-living adjustment** Teuerungszulage *f*, Anpassung *f* an die Lebenshaltungskosten

colander [ˈkʌləndəʳ] N Sieb *nt*

cold [kəʊld] **1** ADJ (+ER) (a) kalt; ~ **meats** Aufschnitt *m*; **I am ~** mir ist kalt; **my hands are ~/are getting ~** ich habe/kriege kalte Hände; **if you get ~** wenn es dir zu kalt wird (b) (*fig*) kalt; *answer, reception* betont kühl; (= *dispassionate, not sensual*) kühl; **to be ~ to sb** jdn kühl behandeln; **that leaves me ~** das lässt mich kalt (c) (*inf*) **to be out ~** bewusstlos sein; (= *knocked out*) k. o. sein (d) (*phrases*) **in ~ blood** kaltblütig; **to get/have ~ feet** (*fig inf*) kalte Füße kriegen/haben; (*inf*) **that brought him out in a ~ sweat** dabei brach ihm der kalte Schweiß aus; **to throw ~ water on sb's plans** (*inf*) jdm eine kalte Dusche geben **2** ADV **to come to sth ~** unvorbereitet an eine Sache herangehen; **to learn/know sth ~** (*US*) etw gut lernen/können; **he stopped ~ when ...** (*US*) er hielt unvermittelt an, als ... **3** N (a) Kälte *f*; **to feel the ~** kälteempfindlich sein; **to be left**

out in the ~ (*fig*) ausgeschlossen werden (b) (*Med*) Erkältung *f*; (= *runny nose*) Schnupfen *m*; **to have a ~** erkältet sein; (= *runny nose*) einen Schnupfen haben; **to get** *or* **catch a ~** sich erkälten; **to catch ~** sich erkälten

cold: cold-blooded ADJ (*Zool, fig*) kaltblütig; **cold calling** N (*Comm*) (*on phone*) unaufgeforderte Telefonwerbung; (= *visit*) unaufgeforderter Vertreterbesuch; **cold cream** N Coldcream *f or nt*, halbfette Feuchtigkeitscreme; **cold cuts** PL (*US*) Aufschnitt *m*

coldly [ˈkəʊldlɪ] ADV (*lit, fig*) kalt; *answer, receive* betont kühl

coldness [ˈkəʊldnɪs] N (*lit, fig*) Kälte *f*; (*of answer, reception*) betonte Kühle

cold: cold shoulder N (*inf*) **to give sb the ~** jdm die kalte Schulter zeigen; **cold sore** N (*Med*) Bläschenausschlag *m*; **cold start** N (*Aut, Comput*) Kaltstart *m*; **cold storage** N Kühllagerung *f*; **to put sth into ~** (*lit*) *food* etw kühl lagern; (*fig*) *plan* etw auf Eis legen; **cold store** N Kühlhaus *nt*; **cold war** N kalter Krieg

coleslaw [ˈkəʊlslɔː] N Krautsalat *m*

collaborate [kəˈlæbəreɪt] VI (a) (= *work together*) zusammenarbeiten; **they asked him to ~** sie baten ihn mitzuarbeiten; **to ~ with sb on** *or* **in sth** mit jdm bei etw zusammenarbeiten (b) (*with enemy*) kollaborieren

collaboration [kəˌlæbəˈreɪʃən] N (a) (= *working together*) Zusammenarbeit *f*; (*of one party*) Mitarbeit *f* (b) (*with enemy*) Kollaboration *f* (c) (= *piece of work*) Gemeinschaftsproduktion *f*

collaborative [kəˈlæbərətɪv] ADJ gemeinschaftlich

collaborator [kəˈlæbəreɪtəʳ] N (a) Mitarbeiter(in) *m(f)* (b) (*with enemy*) Kollaborateur(in) *m(f)*

collapse [kəˈlæps] **1** VI (a) zusammenbrechen; (*mentally*, = *have heart attack also*) einen Kollaps erleiden *or* haben; (*building, wall, roof also*) einstürzen; (*negotiations*) scheitern; (*prices, government*) stürzen; **they all ~d with laughter** sie konnten sich alle vor Lachen nicht mehr halten; **she ~d onto her bed, exhausted** sie plumpste erschöpft aufs Bett (b) (*table, bicycle etc*) sich zusammenklappen lassen **2** VT *table, bicycle etc* zusammenklappen **3** N Zusammenbruch *m*; (= *nervous breakdown also, heart attack*) Kollaps *m*; (*of building, wall, roof also*) Einsturz *m*; (*of negotiations also*) Scheitern *nt*; (*of government*) Sturz *m*

collapsible [kəˈlæpsəbl] ADJ *table, bicycle etc* zusammenklappbar; *telescope, walking stick* zusammenschiebbar; ~ **umbrella** Knirps® *m*

collar [ˈkɒləʳ] **1** N (a) Kragen *m*; **he got hold of him by the ~** er packte ihn am Kragen (b) (*for dogs*) Halsband *nt*; (*for horses*) Kum(me)t *nt* **2** VT (= *capture*) fassen

collarbone [ˈkɒləʳbəʊn] N Schlüsselbein *nt*

collate [kɒˈleɪt] VT (a) *data* zusammentragen (b) (*Typ*) kollationieren, zusammentragen

collateral [kɒˈlætərəl] N (*Fin*) (zusätzliche) Sicherheit *f*

colleague [ˈkɒliːg] N Kollege *m*, Kollegin *f*

collect [kəˈlekt] **1** VT (a) sammeln; *empty glasses, tickets etc* einsammeln; *litter* aufsammeln; *prize* bekommen; *belongings* zusammenpacken *or* -sammeln; (= *accumulate*) ansammeln; *dust* anziehen (b) (= *pick up, fetch*) abholen (*from* bei) (c) *taxes* einziehen; *money for charity* sammeln; *rent, fares* kassieren; *debts* eintreiben **2** VI (a) (= *gather*) sich ansammeln; (*dust*) sich absetzen (b) (= ~ *money*) kassieren; (*for charity*) sammeln **3** ADV (*US*) **to pay ~** bei Empfang bezahlen; **to call ~** ein R-Gespräch führen; **to pay ~ on delivery** bei Lieferung bezahlen; (*through post*) per Nachnahme bezahlen

➤ **collect up** VT SEP einsammeln; *litter* aufsammeln; *belongings* zusammenpacken *or* -sammeln

collect cable N (*US*) vom Empfänger bezahltes Telegramm

collect call N (*US*) R-Gespräch *nt*

collected [kəˈlektɪd] ADJ (a) **the ~ works of Oscar Wilde** Oscar Wildes gesammelte Werke (b) (= *calm*) ruhig

collection [kəˈlekʃən] N (a) (= *group of people, objects*) Ansammlung *f*; (*of stamps, coins etc*) Sammlung *f* (b) (= *collecting*); (*from letter box*) Leerung *f*; (*of money for charity*) Sammlung *f*; (*in church*) Kollekte *f*; **to hold a ~ for sb/sth** für jdn/etw eine Sammlung durchführen; ~ **letter** (*for debts*) Beitreibungsschreiben *nt*

collective [kə'lektɪv] ADJ **(a)** kollektiv; ~ **advertising** Gemeinschaftswerbung f **(b)** (= *accumulated*) *experience* gesamt *attr*

collective bargaining N Tarifverhandlungen pl

collectively [kə'lektɪvlɪ] ADV gemeinsam, zusammen; (*in socialist context also*) kollektiv

collective noun N (*Gram*) Kollektivum nt

collector [kə'lektə*] N (*of stamps etc*) Sammler(in) m(f); ~'s item, price Sammler-, Liebhaber-

college ['kɒlɪdʒ] N **(a)** (= *part of university*) College nt, Institut nt; **to go to** ~ (= *university*) studieren; **to start** ~ sein Studium beginnen; **we met at** ~ wir haben uns im Studium kennen gelernt **(b)** (*of music, technology etc*) Fachhochschule f; **College of Art** Kunstakademie f

---

COLLEGE

College ist ein allgemeiner Oberbegriff für höhere Bildungsinstitute. In Großbritannien kann es auf Einrichtungen beziehen, in denen man in einzelnen Fachbereichen, wie Kunst oder Musik, einen Hochschulabschluss erwerben kann, aber ebenso auf Schulen ohne weiteren Abschluss, z. B. für Sekretärinnen oder Friseure. Einige britische Universitäten, darunter Oxford und Cambridge, setzen sich aus Colleges zusammen.

In den USA werden die Universitäten in Verwaltungseinheiten unterteilt, die als Colleges bezeichnet werden: zum Beispiel das „College of Arts and Sciences" oder das „College of Medicine". Graduate schools, die normalerweise Teil einer Universität sind, bieten auf dem bachelor aufbauende Studiengänge zur weiteren Spezialisierung an. Junior oder community colleges sind Institute, an denen man nach zweijähriger Studienzeit einen berufsbezogenen Abschluss machen kann; sie bieten auch Weiterbildungen für Berufstätige an. ▶ DEGREE, OXBRIDGE

---

collide [kə'laɪd] VI **(a)** (*lit*) zusammenstoßen *or* -prallen; (*Naut*) kollidieren; **to** ~ **with sb** mit jdm zusammenstoßen; **to** ~ **with sth** gegen etw prallen **(b)** (*fig: interest, demands*) kollidieren

colliery ['kɒlɪərɪ] N Zeche f

collision [kə'lɪʒən] N (*lit*) Zusammenstoß m; (*fig*) Konflikt m; (*Naut*) Kollision f; **on a** ~ **course** (*lit, fig*) auf Kollisionskurs

colloquial [kə'ləʊkwɪəl] ADJ umgangssprachlich

colloquialism [kə'ləʊkwɪəlɪzəm] N umgangssprachlicher Ausdruck

collude [kə'luːd] VI gemeinsame Sache machen

collusion [kə'luːʒən] N (geheime) Absprache; **they're acting in** ~ sie haben sich abgesprochen

Cologne [kə'ləʊn] N Köln nt

cologne [kə'ləʊn] N Kölnischwasser nt

colon¹ ['kəʊlən] N (*Anat*) Dickdarm m

colon² N (*Gram*) Doppelpunkt m

colonel ['kɜːnl] N Oberst m; (*as address*) Herr Oberst

colonial [kə'ləʊnɪəl] **1** ADJ Kolonial-, kolonial **2** N Bewohner(in) m(f) einer Kolonie/der Kolonien

colonialism [kə'ləʊnɪəlɪzəm] N Kolonialismus m

colonialist [kə'ləʊnɪəlɪst] **1** ADJ kolonialistisch **2** N Kolonialist(in) m(f)

colonist ['kɒlənɪst] N Kolonist(in) m(f), Siedler(in) m(f)

colonization [ˌkɒlənaɪ'zeɪʃən] N Kolonisation f

colonize ['kɒlənaɪz] VT kolonisieren

colony ['kɒlənɪ] N Kolonie f

color *etc* (*US*) = **colour** *etc*

colorant ['kʌlərənt] N (*US*) = **colourant**

colossal [kə'lɒsl] ADJ riesig, ungeheuer, gewaltig; *cheek, mistake* ungeheuer; *car, man, city* riesig

colostomy [kə'lɒstəmɪ] N (*Med*) Kolostomie f; ~ **bag** Kolostomiebeutel m

colour, (*US*) **color** ['kʌlə*] **1** N **(a)** (*lit, fig*) Farbe f; **what** ~ **is it?** welche Farbe hat es?; **red in** ~ rot; **the film was in** ~ der Film war in Farbe; ~ **illustration** farbige Illustration **(b)** (= *complexion*) (Gesichts)farbe f; **to bring the** ~ **back to sb's cheeks** jdm wieder Farbe geben; **he had gone a funny** ~ er nahm eine komische Farbe an **(c)** (*racial*) Hautfarbe f **(d)** **colours** PL (= *paints*) Farben pl **(e)** (*of place, period etc*) Atmosphäre f; **to add** ~ **to a story** einer Geschichte (*dat*) Farbe geben **(f)** **colours** PL (*Sport*) (Sport)abzeichen nt; **to nail one's ~s to**

the mast (*fig*) Farbe bekennen; **to show one's true ~s** (*fig*) sein wahres Gesicht zeigen **2** VT **(a)** (*lit*) anmalen; (*Art*) kolorieren; (= *dye*) färben **(b)** (*fig*) beeinflussen; (= *bias deliberately*) färben **3** VI (*person: also* ~ **up**) erröten

➤ **colour in** VT SEP anmalen; (*Art*) kolorieren

colourant, (*US*) **colorant** ['kʌlərənt] N Farbstoff m

colour, (*US*) **color** IN CPDS Farb-; (*racial*) Rassen-; **colour bar** N Rassenschranke f; **colour-blind** ADJ farbenblind; **colour-code** VT farbig kennzeichnen *or* kodieren

coloured, (*US*) **colored** ['kʌləd] **1** ADJ **(a)** bunt **(b)** *person, race* farbig **2** N Farbige(r) mf

-coloured, (*US*) **-colored** ADJ SUF **yellow-coloured** gelb; **straw-/dark-coloured** strohfarben/dunkel

colourfast, (*US*) **colorfast** ['kʌləfɑːst] ADJ farbecht

colourful, (*US*) **colorful** ['kʌləfʊl] ADJ **(a)** (*lit*) bunt; *spectacle* farbenfroh *or* -prächtig **(b)** (*fig*) *account etc* farbig; *life, historical period* (bunt) bewegt; *personality* (bunt) schillernd; **his** ~ **past** seine bewegte Vergangenheit **(c)** (*euph*: = *vulgar*) *language* derb

colourfully, (*US*) **colorfully** ['kʌləfəlɪ] ADV bunt

colouring, (*US*) **coloring** ['kʌlərɪŋ] N **(a)** (= *substance*) Farbstoff m **(b)** (= *colours*) Farben pl

colouring book, (*US*) **coloring book** N Malbuch nt

colourless, (*US*) **colorless** ['kʌlələs] ADJ (*lit, fig*) farblos

colour, (*US*) **color: colour photograph** N Farbfoto nt; **colour scheme** N Farbzusammenstellung f; **colour supplement** N Magazin nt; **colour television** N Farbfernsehen nt; (= *set*) Farbfernseher m

colt [kəʊlt] N Hengstfohlen nt

Co Ltd ABBR *of* **company limited** GmbH f

Columbus Day N (*US*) *amerikanischer Feiertag am zweiten Montag im Oktober, an dem die Entdeckung Amerikas durch Kolumbus gefeiert wird*

column ['kɒləm] N **(a)** (*Archit, of smoke, water etc*) Säule f **(b)** (*of names, vehicles etc*) Kolonne f; (= *division of page*) Spalte f; (= *article in newspaper*) Kolumne f

columnist ['kɒləmnɪst] N Kolumnist(in) m(f)

coma ['kəʊmə] N Koma nt; **to be in a** ~ im Koma liegen; **to go** *or* **fall into a** ~ ins Koma fallen

comb [kəʊm] **1** N **(a)** Kamm m **(b)** (= *act*) **to give one's hair a** ~ sich kämmen **2** VT **(a)** *hair* kämmen; **to** ~ **one's hair** sich kämmen **(b)** (= *search*) durchkämmen; *newspapers* durchforsten

➤ **comb out** VT SEP *hair* auskämmen

➤ **comb through** VI +PREP OBJ *files etc* durchgehen; *shops* durchstöbern

combat ['kɒmbæt] **1** N Kampf m **2** VT (*lit, fig*) bekämpfen

combatant ['kɒmbətənt] N (*lit, fig*) Kombattant m

combative ['kɒmbətɪv] ADJ (= *pugnacious*) kämpferisch; (= *competitive*) aggressiv

combat: combat jacket N Feldjacke f; **combats** ['kɒmbæts] PL (*inf*) Tarnhose f, Kampfhose f; **combat troops** PL Kampftruppen pl; **combat trousers** PL (*Brit*) Armeehosen pl

combination [ˌkɒmbɪ'neɪʃən] N Kombination f; (= *combining*) (*of organizations, people etc*) Vereinigung f; (*of events*) Verkettung f; **in** ~ zusammen, gemeinsam; **an unusual colour** ~ eine ungewöhnliche Farbzusammenstellung

combination: combination lock N Kombinationsschloss nt; **combination sandwich** N (*US*) gemischt belegtes Sandwich

combine [kəm'baɪn] **1** VT kombinieren **2** VI sich zusammenschließen; (*Chem*) sich verbinden **3** ['kɒmbaɪn] N **(a)** (*Econ*) Konzern m **(b)** (*Agr: also* ~ **harvester**) Mähdrescher m

combined [kəm'baɪnd] ADJ gemeinsam; *talents, efforts* vereint; *forces* vereinigt; ~ **with** in Kombination mit; (*esp clothes, furniture*) kombiniert mit; ~ **transport bill of lading** (*Comm*) kombiniertes Konnossement

combustible [kəm'bʌstɪbl] ADJ brennbar

combustion [kəm'bʌstʃən] N Verbrennung f

come [kʌm], *pret* **came**, *ptp* **come 1** VI **(a)** kommen; (= *reach, extend*) reichen (*to* an/in/bis *etc* +*acc*); **they came to a town/ castle** sie kamen in eine Stadt/zu einem Schloss; ~ **and get it!** (das) Essen ist fertig!; **I don't know whether I'm coming or going** ich weiß nicht (mehr), wo mir der Kopf steht (*inf*); ~

and see me soon besuchen Sie mich bald einmal; **he has ~ a long way** er hat einen weiten Weg hinter sich; *(fig)* er ist weit gekommen; **he came running into the room** er kam ins Zimmer gerannt; **he came hurrying/laughing into the room** er eilte/kam lachend ins Zimmer; **coming!** ich komme (gleich)!; **Christmas is coming** bald ist Weihnachten; **May ~s before June** Mai kommt vor Juni; **the adjective must ~ before the noun** das Adjektiv muss vor dem Substantiv stehen; **the years/weeks to ~** die kommenden *or* nächsten Jahre/Wochen; **that must ~ first** das muss an erster Stelle kommen

(b) (= *happen*) geschehen; **~ what may** ganz gleich, was geschieht; **you could see it coming** das konnte man ja kommen sehen; **she had it coming to her** *(inf)* das musste ja so kommen

(c) how ~? *(inf)* wieso?; **how ~ you're so late?**, **how do you ~ to be so late?** wieso kommst du so spät?

(d) (= *be, become*) werden; **his dreams came true** seine Träume wurden wahr; **the handle has ~ loose** der Griff hat sich gelockert

(e) *(Comm:* = *be available)* erhältlich sein; **milk now ~s in plastic bottles** es gibt jetzt Milch in Plastikflaschen

(f) (+*infin*: = *be finally in a position to*) **I have ~ to believe him** mittlerweile glaube ich ihm; **(now I) ~ to think of it** wenn ich es mir recht überlege

(g) *(inf uses)* **... ~ next week** nächste Woche ...; **I've known him for three years ~ January** im Januar kenne ich ihn drei Jahre; **~ again?** wie bitte?; **she is as vain as they ~** sie ist so eingebildet wie nur was *(inf)*

(h) *(inf:* = *have orgasm)* kommen *(inf)*

2 VT *(Brit inf:* = *act as if one were)* spielen; **don't ~ the innocent with me** spielen Sie hier bloß nicht den Unschuldigen!

➤ **come about** VI IMPERS (= *happen*) passieren; **this is why it came about** das ist so gekommen

➤ **come across 1** VI **(a)** (= *cross*) herüberkommen **(b)** (= *be understood*) verstanden werden; *(message)* ankommen **(c)** (= *make an impression*) wirken; **he wants to come across as a tough guy** er mimt gerne den starken Mann *(inf)* **2** VI +PREP OBJ (= *find or meet by chance*) treffen auf (+*acc*); **if you come across my watch ...** wenn du zufällig meine Uhr siehst

➤ **come after 1** VI +PREP OBJ **(a)** (= *follow in sequence, be of less importance than*) kommen nach; **the noun comes after the verb** das Substantiv steht nach *or* hinter dem Verb **(b)** (= *pursue*) herkommen hinter (+*dat*) **(c)** (= *follow later*) nachkommen **2** VI (= *follow later*) nachkommen

➤ **come along** VI **(a)** (= *hurry up, make an effort etc: also* **come on**) kommen **(b)** (= *attend, accompany*) mitkommen; **come along with me** kommen Sie mal (bitte) mit **(c)** (= *develop: also* **come on**) **to be coming along** sich machen; **how is your broken arm? – it's coming along nicely** was macht dein gebrochener Arm? – dem gehts ganz gut **(d)** (= *arrive, turn up*) kommen; *(chance etc)* sich ergeben

➤ **come apart** VI (= *fall to pieces*) auseinander fallen; (= *be able to be taken apart*) zerlegbar sein

➤ **come (a)round** VI **(a) the road was blocked and we had to come (a)round by the farm** die Straße war blockiert, so dass *or* sodass wir einen Umweg über den Bauernhof machen mussten **(b)** (= *call round*) vorbeikommen *or* -schauen **(c)** (= *change one's opinions*) es sich *(dat)* anders überlegen; **eventually he came (a)round to our way of thinking** schließlich machte er sich *(dat)* unsere Denkungsart zu Eigen **(d)** (= *regain consciousness*) wieder zu sich *(dat)* kommen

➤ **come at** VI +PREP OBJ (= *attack*) sb losgehen auf (+*acc*)

➤ **come away** VI **(a)** (= *leave*) (weg)gehen; **come away with me for a few days** fahr doch ein paar Tage mit mir weg!; **come away from there!** komm da weg! **(b)** (= *become detached*) abgehen

➤ **come back** VI **(a)** (= *return*) zurückkommen; (= *drive back*) zurückfahren; **can I come back to you on that one?** kann ich später darauf zurückkommen?; **the colour is coming back to her cheeks** langsam bekommt sie wieder Farbe **(b)** (= *return to one's memory*) **his name is coming back to me** langsam erinnere ich mich wieder an seinen Namen; **ah yes, it's all coming back** ach ja, jetzt fällt mir alles wieder ein **(c)** (= *become popular again*) wieder in Mode kommen **(d)** (= *make a comeback*) **they came back into the game with a**

superb goal sie fanden mit wunderbaren Tor ins Spielgeschehen zurück

➤ **come before** VT *(Jur. person)* gebracht werden vor (+*acc*)

➤ **come between** VI +PREP OBJ *people, lovers* treten zwischen (+*acc*)

➤ **come by 1** VI +PREP OBJ (= *obtain*) kriegen; *illness, bruise* sich *(dat)* holen; *idea* kommen auf (+*acc*) **2** VI (= *visit*) vorbeikommen

➤ **come close to** VI +PREP OBJ **= come near to**

➤ **come down** VI **(a)** *(from ladder, stairs)* herunterkommen; *(aircraft)* landen; *(rain)* fallen; **come down from there at once!** komm da sofort runter!

(b) (= *drop*) *(prices)* sinken; *(seller)* runtergehen *(to* auf +*acc*)

(c) (= *be a question of*) ankommen *(to* auf +*acc*); **when you come** *or* **it comes down to it** letzten Endes

(d) (= *lose social rank*) absteigen; **you've come down in the world a bit** du bist aber ganz schön tief gesunken

(e) (= *reach*) reichen *(to* bis auf +*acc*, zu*)*; **her hair comes down to her shoulders** die Haare gehen ihr bis auf die Schultern

(f) (= *be transmitted: tradition, story etc*) überliefert werden

(g) *(dated US inf:* = *be about to happen)* **there's a bank robbery coming down next week** für nächste Woche ist ein Banküberfall geplant

➤ **come down on** VI +PREP OBJ **(a)** (= *punish, rebuke*) zusammenstauchen *(inf)* **(b)** (= *decide in favour of*) **you've got to come down on one side or the other** du musst dich so oder so entscheiden

➤ **come down with** VI +PREP OBJ *illness* kriegen

➤ **come for** VI +PREP OBJ kommen wegen

➤ **come forward** VI **(a)** (= *make oneself known*) sich melden **(b) to come forward with help** Hilfe anbieten; **to come forward with a good suggestion** mit einem guten Vorschlag kommen

➤ **come from** VI +PREP OBJ kommen aus; *(suggestion)* kommen *or* stammen von; **where does he/it come from?** wo kommt er/das her?; **I know where you're coming from** *(inf)* ich weiß, was du meinst

➤ **come in** VI **(a)** (= *enter*) (he)reinkommen; **come in!** herein! **(b)** (= *arrive*) ankommen, eintreffen **(c)** *(tide)* kommen **(d)** *(report etc)* hereinkommen; **a report has just come in of ...** uns ist gerade eine Meldung über ... zugegangen **(e)** *(fashions, vogue)* aufkommen **(f)** *(in a race)* **he came in fourth** er wurde Vierter **(g)** *(Pol:* = *be elected to power)* **when the socialists came in** als die Sozialisten ans Ruder *or* an die Regierung kamen **(h)** (= *be received as income*) **he has £15,000 coming in every year** er kriegt *(inf) or* hat £ 15.000 im Jahr **(i)** (= *have a part to play*) **where do I come in?** welche Rolle spiele ich dabei?; **that will come in handy** *(inf) or* **useful** das kann ich/man noch gut gebrauchen

➤ **come in for** VI +PREP OBJ *attention, admiration* erregen; *criticism etc also* einstecken müssen

➤ **come in on** VI +PREP OBJ *venture etc* sich beteiligen an (+*dat*)

➤ **come into** VI +PREP OBJ **(a)** (= *inherit*) erben **(b)** (= *be involved*) **I don't see where I come into all this** ich verstehe nicht, was ich mit der ganzen Sache zu tun habe **(c)** *(in fixed collocations)* **to come into one's own** zeigen, was in einem steckt; **to come into being** *or* **existence** entstehen; **to come into sb's possession** in jds Besitz (*acc*) gelangen

➤ **come near to** VI +PREP OBJ **to come near to doing sth** drauf und dran sein, etw zu tun

➤ **come of** VI +PREP OBJ (= *result from*) **nothing came of it** es ist nichts daraus geworden; **that's what comes of disobeying!** das kommt davon, wenn man nicht hören will!

➤ **come off 1** VI **(a)** *(person: off bicycle etc)* runterfallen **(b)** *(button, handle, paint etc)* abgehen **(c)** *(stains)* weg- *or* rausgehen **(d)** (= *take place*) stattfinden **(e)** *(plans, attempts etc)* klappen *(inf)* **(f)** (= *acquit oneself*) abschneiden; **he came off well in comparison to his brother** im Vergleich zu seinem Bruder ist er gut weggekommen **2** VI +PREP OBJ **(a)** *bicycle etc* fallen von **(b)** *(button, paint, stain)* abgehen von **(c)** *drugs, medication* aufhören mit **(d)** *(inf)* **come off it!** nun mach mal halblang! *(inf)*

➤ **come on** ■ VI (a) (= follow) nachkommen (b) = **come along** (a); **come on!** komm! (c) (= continue to advance) zukommen (towards auf +acc) (d) (Brit: = progress) = **come along** (c) (e) (= start: storm) ausbrechen; **I've a cold coming on** ich kriege eine Erkältung (f) (Sport: player) ins Spiel kommen; (Theat) (actor) auftreten; (play) gegeben werden ■ VI +PREP OBJ = **come (up)on**

➤ **come on to** VI +PREP OBJ (esp US inf: = make advances to) anmachen (inf)

➤ **come out** VI (a) (he)rauskommen; **to come out of a room** etc aus einem Zimmer etc kommen; **do you want to come out with me?** gehst du mit mir weg?; **to come out fighting** (fig) sich kämpferisch geben; **he came out in a rash** er bekam einen Ausschlag; **to come out against/in favour of or for sth** sich gegen/für etw aussprechen; **to come out of sth badly/ well** bei etw schlecht/nicht schlecht wegkommen; **to come out on top** sich durchsetzen
(b) (= be published, marketed) (book) erscheinen; (new product) auf den Markt kommen; (film) (in den Kinos) anlaufen; (= become known) bekannt werden
(c) (Ind) **to come out (on strike)** in den Streik treten
(d) (Phot) **the photo of the hills hasn't come out very well** das Foto von den Bergen ist nicht sehr gut geworden; **all the details have come out clearly** alle Einzelheiten kommen klar (he)raus
(e) (splinter, stains etc) (he)rausgehen
(f) (= total, average) betragen; **the total comes out at £500** das Ganze beläuft sich auf (+acc) or macht (inf) £ 500
(g) (homosexual) sich outen

➤ **come out with** VI +PREP OBJ truth, facts rausrücken mit (inf); remarks, nonsense loslassen (inf)

➤ **come over** ■ VI (a) (lit) herüberkommen; **he came over to England** er kam nach England
(b) (= change one's opinions, allegiance) **he came over to our side** er trat auf unsere Seite über
(c) (inf: = become suddenly) werden; **I came over (all) queer or funny** mir wurde ganz komisch (inf)
(d) (= be understood) = **come across** 1(b)
(e) (= make an impression) = **come across** 1(c)
■ VI +PREP OBJ (feelings) überkommen; **what's come over you?** was ist denn (auf einmal) mit dir los?

➤ **come through** ■ VI (phone call, order) durchkommen; **your papers haven't come through yet** Ihre Papiere sind noch nicht fertig; **his divorce has come through** seine Scheidung ist durch (inf) ■ VI +PREP OBJ illness, danger überstehen

➤ **come to** ■ VI (= regain consciousness: also **come to oneself**) wieder zu sich kommen
■ VI +PREP OBJ (a) **that didn't come to anything** daraus ist nichts geworden
(b) IMPERS **when it comes to mathematics ...** wenn es um Mathematik geht, ...; **let's hope it never comes to a court case or to court** wollen wir hoffen, dass es nie zum Prozess kommt; **it comes to the same thing** das kommt or läuft auf dasselbe hinaus
(c) (price, bill) **how much does it come to?** wie viel macht das?; **it comes to £20** es kommt or beläuft sich auf £ 20
(d) (in certain collocations) **to come to a decision** zu einer Entscheidung kommen; **what are things or what is the world coming to!** wohin soll das noch führen!

➤ **come together** VI zusammenkommen, sich treffen

➤ **come under** VI +PREP OBJ (a) (= be subject to) **to come under sb's influence** unter jds Einfluss geraten; **this comes under another department** das ist Sache einer anderen Abteilung
(b) category kommen unter (+acc)

➤ **come up** VI (a) (lit) hochkommen; (diver) nach oben kommen; (sun, moon) aufgehen; **do you come up to town often?** kommen Sie oft in die Stadt?; **he came up to me with a smile** er kam lächelnd auf mich zu
(b) (Jur: case) verhandelt werden
(c) (plants) herauskommen
(d) (matter for discussion) aufkommen; (name) erwähnt werden; **I can't do it as I'm afraid something has come up** ich bin leider verhindert
(e) (number in lottery etc) gewinnen; **to come up for sale** zum Verkauf kommen; **my contract will soon come up for renewal** mein Vertrag muss bald verlängert werden
(f) (post, job) frei werden
(g) (exams, election) bevorstehen

➤ **come up against** VI +PREP OBJ stoßen auf (+acc); opposing team treffen auf (+acc)

➤ **come (up)on** VI +PREP OBJ (a) (fig: disaster) hereinbrechen über (+acc) (b) (= find) stoßen auf (+acc)

➤ **come up to** VI +PREP OBJ (a) (= reach up to) gehen or reichen bis zu or an (+acc) (b) expectations entsprechen (+dat) (c) (inf: = approach) **she's coming up to twenty** sie wird bald zwanzig; **it's just coming up to 10 o'clock** es ist gleich 10 Uhr

➤ **come up with** VI +PREP OBJ answer, idea haben; plan sich (dat) ausdenken; suggestion machen; **let me know if you come up with anything** sagen Sie mir Bescheid, falls Ihnen etwas einfällt

comeback ['kʌmbæk] N (a) (Theat etc, fig) Comeback nt; **to make or stage a ~** ein Comeback machen (b) (inf: = redress) Anspruch m auf Schadenersatz; **we've got no ~ in this situation** wir können da nichts machen

comedian [kə'miːdɪən] N Komiker(in) m(f)

comedienne [kə,miːdɪ'en] N Komikerin f

comedown ['kʌmdaʊn] N (inf) Abstieg m

comedy ['kɒmɪdɪ] N (a) (Theat) Komödie f (b) (fig) Komödie f, Theater nt (inf)

come-on ['kʌmɒn] N (inf: = lure) Köder m (fig); **to give sb the ~** jdn anmachen (inf)

comer ['kʌmə'] N **this competition is open to all ~s** an diesem Wettbewerb kann sich jeder beteiligen

comet ['kɒmɪt] N Komet m

comeuppance [kʌm'ʌpəns] N (inf) **to get one's ~** die Quittung kriegen (inf)

comfort ['kʌmfət] ■ N (a) Komfort m; **to live in ~** komfortabel leben; **an apartment with all modern ~s** eine Wohnung mit allem Komfort
(b) (= consolation) Trost m; **to take ~ from the fact that ...** sich mit dem Gedanken or sich damit trösten, dass ...; **your presence is/you are a great ~ to me** es beruhigt mich sehr, dass Sie da sind; **it is no ~ or of little ~ to know that ...** es ist nicht sehr tröstlich zu wissen, dass ...; **too close for ~** bedrohlich nahe
■ VT (= console) trösten

comfortable ['kʌmfətəbl] ADJ (a) bequem; room, hotel etc komfortabel; temperature angenehm; **to make sb/oneself ~** es jdm/sich bequem machen; (= make at home) es jdm/sich gemütlich machen; **the patient is ~** der Patient ist wohlauf (b) (fig) income ausreichend; life angenehm; majority, lead sicher; winner überlegen; **to feel ~ with sb/sth** sich bei jdm/ etw wohl fühlen; **I'm not very ~ about it** mir ist nicht ganz wohl bei der Sache

comfortably ['kʌmfətəblɪ] ADV (a) bequem; furnished komfortabel (b) (fig) win, lead sicher; live angenehm; afford gut und gern; **they are ~ off** es geht ihnen gut

comforter ['kʌmfətə'] N (a) (= person) Tröster(in) m(f) (b) (US: = quilt) Deckbett nt

comforting ['kʌmfətɪŋ] ADJ tröstlich

comfort station N (US) öffentliche Toilette

comfy ['kʌmfɪ] ADJ (+ER) (inf) chair bequem; hotel, room gemütlich; **are you ~?** sitzt/liegst du bequem?

comic ['kɒmɪk] ■ ADJ komisch; **~ actor** Komödiendarsteller(in) m(f); **~ verse** humoristische Gedichte pl ■ N (a) (= person) Komiker(in) m(f)
(b) (= magazine) Comicheft(chen) nt (c) (US) **~s** Comics pl

comical ADJ, **comically** ADV ['kɒmɪkəl, -ɪ] komisch

comic: comic book N Comicbuch nt; **comic opera** N komische Oper; **comic strip** N Comicstrip m

coming ['kʌmɪŋ] ■ N Kommen nt; **~(s) and going(s)** Kommen und Gehen nt; **~ of age** Erreichung f der Volljährigkeit ■ ADJ (lit, fig) kommend; **the ~ election** die bevorstehende Wahl

coming-out [kʌmɪŋ'aʊt] N (of homosexual) Coming-out nt

comma ['kɒmə] N Komma nt

command [kə'mɑːnd] ■ VT (a) (= order) befehlen
(b) army, ship kommandieren
(c) **to ~ sb's admiration/respect** jdm Bewunderung/Respekt abnötigen
■ N (a) (= order, also Comput) Befehl m; **at/by the ~ of** auf Befehl +gen; **on ~** auf Befehl or Kommando
(b) (Mil: = authority) Kommando nt, Befehlsgewalt f; **to be in ~** das Kommando or den (Ober)befehl haben (of über +acc); **to take ~** das Kommando übernehmen (of +gen); **during/**

under his ~ unter seinem Kommando; **to be second in ~** zweiter Befehlshaber sein
(c) *(fig: = mastery)* Beherrschung *f*; **his ~ of English is excellent** er beherrscht das Englische ausgezeichnet; **I am at your ~** ich stehe zu Ihrer Verfügung

commandant [ˌkɒmənˈdænt] N (*Mil*) Kommandant(in) *m(f)*

commandeer [ˌkɒmənˈdɪəʳ] VT (*Mil, fig*) beschlagnahmen

commander [kəˈmɑːndəʳ] N (*Mil, Aviat*) Kommandant(in) *m(f)*; (*Naut*) Fregattenkapitän(in) *m(f)*

commander in chief N, *pl* **commanders in chief** Oberbefehlshaber(in) *m(f)*

commanding [kəˈmɑːndɪŋ] ADJ *position* führend; *voice* Kommando- (*pej*); **to have a ~ lead** überlegen führen

commanding officer N (*Mil*) befehlshabender Offizier

commandment [kəˈmɑːndmənt] N (*Bibl*) Gebot *nt*

commando [kəˈmɑːndəʊ] N, *pl* **-s** (*Mil*) (= *soldier*) Angehörige(r) *m* eines Kommando(trupp)s; (= *unit*) Kommando(trupp *m*) *nt*

commemorate [kəˈmeməreɪt] VT gedenken (+*gen*)

commemoration [kəˌmeməˈreɪʃən] N Gedenken *nt*; **in ~ of** zum Gedenken an (+*acc*)

commemorative [kəˈmemərətɪv] ADJ Gedenk-

commence [kəˈmens] (*form*) ⬛1 VI beginnen ⬛2 VT beginnen (*obj* mit +*dat*); *legal proceedings* eröffnen; **to ~ doing** *or* **to do sth** mit etw anfangen

commencement [kəˈmensmənt] N (*form*) Beginn *m*

commend [kəˈmend] VT (= *praise*) loben; (= *recommend*) empfehlen; **it has much/little to ~ it** es ist sehr/nicht sehr empfehlenswert

commendable [kəˈmendəbl] ADJ lobenswert

commendation [ˌkɒmenˈdeɪʃən] N (= *award*) Auszeichnung *f*

commensurate [kəˈmenʃərɪt] ADJ entsprechend (*with* +*dat*); **to be ~ with sth** einer Sache (*dat*) entsprechen

comment [ˈkɒment] ⬛1 N Bemerkung *f* (*on,about* über +*acc*, zu); (*official*) Kommentar *m* (*on* zu); (*no pl:* = *talk, gossip*) Gerede *nt*; (= *textual note etc*) Anmerkung *f*; **no ~** kein Kommentar!; **to make a ~** eine Bemerkung machen ⬛2 VI sich äußern (*on* über +*acc*, zu) ⬛3 VT bemerken

commentary [ˈkɒməntəri] N Kommentar *m* (*on* zu)

commentate [ˈkɒmenteɪt] VI (*Rad, TV*) Reporter(in) *m(f)* sein (*on* bei)

commentator [ˈkɒmenteɪtəʳ] N (*Rad, TV*) Reporter(in) *m(f)*

commerce [ˈkɒmɜːs] N Handel *m*; **he is in ~** er ist Geschäftsmann

commercial [kəˈmɜːʃəl] ⬛1 ADJ Handels-; *custom also, training* kaufmännisch; *language, premises, vehicle* Geschäfts-; *production, radio, project, success, farming* kommerziell; (*pej*) *film, music etc* kommerziell; **of no ~ value** ohne Verkaufswert; **it makes good ~ sense** das lässt sich kaufmännisch durchaus vertreten; **~ invoice** Handelsrechnung *f*; **~ law** Handelsrecht *nt*; **~ rate** (*Comm*) handelsüblicher Satz ⬛2 N (*Rad, TV*) Werbespot *m*; **during the ~s** während der (Fernseh)werbung

commercial: commercial attaché N Handelsattaché *m*; **commercial bank** N Handelsbank *f*; **commercial break** N Werbepause *f*

commercialism [kəˈmɜːʃəlɪzəm] N Kommerzialisierung *f*; (*connected with art, literature also*) Kommerz *m*

commercialization [kəˌmɜːʃəlaɪˈzeɪʃən] N Kommerzialisierung *f*

commercialize [kəˈmɜːʃəlaɪz] VT kommerzialisieren

commercially [kəˈmɜːʃəli] ADV geschäftlich; *manufacture, succeed* kommerziell; **to be ~ minded** kaufmännisch veranlagt sein

commercial: commercial paper N (*Fin*) kurzfristige Schuldverschreibung; **commercial television** N kommerzielles Fernsehen; **commercial vehicle** N Nutzfahrzeug *nt*

commie [ˈkɒmɪ] (*pej inf*) ⬛1 N Rote(r) *mf* (*pej inf*) ⬛2 ADJ rot (*pej inf*)

commiserate [kəˈmɪzəreɪt] VI mitfühlen (*with* mit); **we ~ with you on the loss of your husband** wir nehmen Anteil am Tode Ihres Gatten

commiseration [kəˌmɪzəˈreɪʃən] N **my ~s** herzliches Beileid (*on* zu)

commission [kəˈmɪʃən] ⬛1 N **(a)** (*for building, painting etc*) Auftrag *m*
(b) (*Comm*) Provision *f*; **on ~, on a ~ basis** auf Provision(sbasis); **to charge ~** (*bank etc*) eine Kommission berechnen
(c) (= *special committee*) Kommission *f*; **the (EC) Commission** die EG-Kommission
⬛2 VT **(a)** *person* beauftragen; *book, painting* in Auftrag geben; **to ~ sb to do sth** jdn damit beauftragen, etw zu tun
(b) (*Mil*) *sb* zum Offizier ernennen; *officer* ernennen

commissioned officer N Offizier *m*

commissioner [kəˈmɪʃənəʳ] N (*of police*) Polizeipräsident(in) *m(f)*

commit [kəˈmɪt] ⬛1 VT **(a)** (= *perpetrate*) begehen
(b) **to ~ sb (to prison)** jdn ins Gefängnis einweisen; **to have sb ~ted (to an asylum)** jdn in eine Anstalt einweisen lassen; **to ~ sb for trial** jdn einem Gericht überstellen; **to ~ sb/sth to sb's care** jdn/etw jds Obhut (*dat*) anvertrauen
(c) (= *involve, obligate*) festlegen (*to* auf +*acc*); **to ~ resources to a project** Mittel für ein Projekt einsetzen; **that doesn't ~ you to buying the book** das verpflichtet Sie nicht zum Kauf des Buches
⬛2 VI **to ~ to sb/sth** sich jdm gegenüber/zu etw verpflichten ⬛3 VR sich festlegen (*to* auf +*acc*); **you have to ~ yourself totally to the cause** man muss sich voll und ganz für die Sache einsetzen; **the government has ~ted itself to (undertake) far-reaching reforms** die Regierung hat sich zu weitreichenden Reformen bekannt *or* verpflichtet

commitment [kəˈmɪtmənt] N (= *obligation*) Verpflichtung *f*; (= *dedication*) Engagement *nt*; **his family ~s** seine familiären Verpflichtungen *pl*; **his teaching ~s** seine Lehrverpflichtungen *pl*; **there's no ~ (to buy)** es besteht kein(erlei) Kaufzwang; **to make a ~ to do sth** (*form*) sich verpflichten, etw zu tun; **he is frightened of ~** (*in relationship*) er hat Angst davor, sich festzulegen

committal [kəˈmɪtl] N (*to prison etc*) Einweisung *f*; **his ~ for trial** seine Überstellung ans Gericht; **~ proceedings** gerichtliche Voruntersuchung

committed [kəˈmɪtɪd] ADJ (= *dedicated*) engagiert; **he is so ~ to his work that ...** er geht so in seiner Arbeit auf, dass ...; **all his life he has been ~ to this cause** er hat sich sein Leben lang für diese Sache eingesetzt

committee [kəˈmɪtɪ] N Ausschuss *m* (*also Parl*), Komitee *nt*; **to be** *or* **sit on a ~** in einem Ausschuss *or* Komitee sein *or* sitzen; **~ meeting** Ausschusssitzung *f*; **~ member** Ausschussmitglied *nt*

committeeman [kəˈmɪtɪmæn] N, *pl* **-men** [-men] (*esp US*) **(a)** (= *member of committee*) Komiteemitglied *nt* **(b)** (*Pol*) lokaler Parteiführer

committeewoman [kəˈmɪtɪwʊmən] N, *pl* **-women** [-wɪmɪn] (*esp US*) **(a)** (= *member of committee*) Komiteemitglied *nt* **(b)** (*Pol*) lokale Parteiführerin

commodity [kəˈmɒdɪtɪ] N Ware *f*; (*agricultural*) Erzeugnis *nt*; **~ market** Warenbörse *f*

common [ˈkɒmən] ⬛1 ADJ (+*ER*) **(a)** (= *shared by many*) gemeinsam; **~ land** Allmende *f*; **it is ~ knowledge that ...** es ist allgemein bekannt, dass ...; **to find ~ ground** eine gemeinsame Basis finden; **sth is ~ to everyone/sth** alle haben/etw hat etw gemein
(b) (= *frequently seen etc*) häufig; *experience also* allgemein; *animal, bird* (weit)verbreitet, häufig *pred*, häufig anzutreffend *attr*; *belief, custom* (weit)verbreitet; (= *usual*) normal; **it's quite a ~ sight** das sieht man ziemlich häufig; **it's ~ for visitors to feel ill here** Besucher fühlen sich hier häufig krank
(c) (= *ordinary, vulgar*) gewöhnlich; **the ~ man** der Normalbürger; **the ~ people** die einfachen Leute; **as ~ as muck** (*Brit inf*) stinkgewöhnlich (*inf*)
⬛2 N **(a)** (= *land*) Anger *m*
(b) **to have sth in ~ (with sb/sth)** etw (mit jdm/etw) gemein haben; **to have a lot/nothing in ~** viele/keine Gemeinsamkeiten haben; **in ~ with many other people/countries** (ebenso *or* genauso) wie viele andere (Leute)/Länder ...

common: Common Agricultural Policy N gemeinsame Agrarpolitik; **common cold** N Schnupfen *m*; **common**

denominator N (*Math, fig*) gemeinsamer Nenner; **lowest ~** (*Math, fig*) kleinster gemeinsamer Nenner

commoner [ˈkɒmənəʳ] N Bürgerliche(r) *mf*

common: **common factor** N gemeinsamer Teiler; **common law** N Gewohnheitsrecht *nt*; **common-law** ADJ **she is his ~ wife** sie lebt mit ihm in eheähnlicher Gemeinschaft

commonly [ˈkɒmənlɪ] ADV (= *often*) häufig; (= *widely*) gemeinhin; **a ~ held belief** eine weitverbreitete Ansicht; **(more) ~ known as ...** besser bekannt als ...

common: **Common Market** N Gemeinsamer Markt; **common-or-garden** ADJ (*Brit*) Feld-, Wald- und Wiesen- (*inf*); *topic etc* ganz gewöhnlich; **commonplace** ◨ ADJ alltäglich; (= *banal*) banal ◨ N Gemeinplatz *m*; **a ~** (= *frequent sight or event*) etwas Alltägliches; **common room** N Aufenthaltsraum *m*; (*for teachers*) Lehrerzimmer *nt*; (*Univ*) Dozentenzimmer *nt*

Commons [ˈkɒmənz] PL **the ~** (*Parl*) das Unterhaus

common: **common sense** N gesunder Menschenverstand; **common-sense** ADJ vernünftig; **common stock** N (*US St Ex*) Stammaktien *pl*

commonwealth [ˈkɒmənwelθ] N (*US*) *Bezeichnung für die US-Bundesstaaten Kentucky, Massachusetts, Pennsylvania und Virginia;* **the (British) Commonwealth** das Commonwealth

COMMONWEALTH

*Das **Commonwealth**, offiziell **Commonwealth of Nations**, ist ein freiwilliger Zusammenschluss souveräner Staaten, die vormals fast alle britische Kolonien waren. Im Moment gibt es 51 Mitglieder, darunter Großbritannien, Australien, Kanada, Indien, Jamaika, Neuseeland, Pakistan und Südafrika, die zusammen ein Viertel der Weltbevölkerung stellen. Alle Mitgliedstaaten erkennen den britischen Monarchen als Oberhaupt des Commonwealth an.*

commotion [kəˈməʊʃən] N Aufregung *f usu no indef art*; (= *noise*) Lärm *m*; **to cause a ~** Aufsehen erregen

communal [ˈkɒmjuːnl] ADJ (a) (= *of a community*) Gemeinde-; **~ life** Gemeinschaftsleben *nt* (b) (= *owned, used in common*) gemeinsam

communally [ˈkɒmjuːnəlɪ] ADV gemeinsam; **to be ~ owned** Gemein- *or* Gemeinschaftseigentum sein

commune¹ [kəˈmjuːn] VI (= *communicate*) Zwiesprache halten

commune² [ˈkɒmjuːn] N Kommune *f*; (= *administrative division also*) Gemeinde *f*

communicable [kəˈmjuːnɪkəbl] ADJ *disease* übertragbar

communicate [kəˈmjuːnɪkeɪt] ◨ VT *news etc* übermitteln; *ideas, feelings* vermitteln ◨ VI (a) (= *be in communication*) in Verbindung *or* Kontakt stehen (b) (= *convey or exchange thoughts*) sich verständigen

communication [kəˌmjuːnɪˈkeɪʃən] N (a) (= *communicating*) Verständigung *f*, Kommunikation *f*; (*of ideas, information*) Vermittlung *f*; (= *contact*) Verbindung *f*; **system/means of ~** Kommunikationssystem *nt*/-mittel *nt*; **to be in ~ with sb** mit jdm in Verbindung stehen (*about* wegen); **~s breakdown** gestörte Kommunikation
(b) (= *exchanging of ideas*) Verständigung *f*
(c) (= *message*) Mitteilung *f*
(d) **~s** (= *roads, telegraph lines etc*) Kommunikationsnetz *nt*; **they're trying to restore ~s** man versucht, die Verbindung wieder herzustellen
(e) **~s** (*Telec*) Telekommunikation *f*

communication: **communication cord** N (*Brit Rail*) ≈ Notbremse *f*; **communication lines** PL (*Ind*) Kommunikationsstruktur *f*; **communication skills** PL Kommunikationsfähigkeit *f*

communications [kəˌmjuːnɪˈkeɪʃənz]: **communications satellite** N Nachrichtensatellit *m*; **communications software** N Kommunikationssoftware *f*

communicative [kəˈmjuːnɪkətɪv] ADJ mitteilsam

communion [kəˈmjuːnɪən] N (a) (= *intercourse etc*) Zwiesprache *f*; **a sense of ~ with nature** ein Gefühl *nt* der Verbundenheit mit der Natur (b) (*Eccl: also* **Communion**) (*Protestant*) Abendmahl *nt*; (*Catholic*) Kommunion *f*; **to receive** *or* **take ~** die Kommunion/das Abendmahl empfangen

communiqué [kəˈmjuːnɪkeɪ] N Kommunikee *f*

communism [ˈkɒmjʊnɪzəm] N Kommunismus *m*

communist [ˈkɒmjʊnɪst] ◨ N Kommunist(in) *m(f)* ◨ ADJ kommunistisch

Communist Party N kommunistische Partei

community [kəˈmjuːnɪtɪ] N Gemeinschaft *f*; **the ~ at large** das ganze Volk; **a sense of ~** (ein) Gemeinschaftsgefühl *nt*; **to work in the ~** im Sozialbereich tätig sein

community: **community association** N (*Brit*) Bürgerverein *m*; **community care** N (*Brit Sociol*) **(a)** (= *home care*) häusliche Pflege **(b)** (*also* **~ programme**) kommunales Fürsorgeprogramm; **community centre**, (*US*) **community center** N Gemeindezentrum *nt*; **community chest** N (*US*) Wohltätigkeits- *or* Hilfsfonds *m*; **community college** N (*US*) *College zur Berufsausbildung und Vorbereitung auf ein Hochschulstudium;* **community service** N (*Jur*) Sozialdienst *m*; **community-wide** [kəˈmjuːnɪtɪˌwaɪd] ADJ (*within the EU*) EU-weit

commutation [ˌkɒmjʊˈteɪʃən] N **~ ticket** (*US*) Zeitnetzkarte *f*

commute [kəˈmjuːt] ◨ VT umwandeln ◨ VI pendeln ◨ N Pendelfahrt *f*

commuter [kəˈmjuːtəʳ] N Pendler(in) *m(f)*; **the ~ belt** das Einzugsgebiet; **~ train** Pendlerzug *m*

commuting [kəˈmjuːtɪŋ] N Pendeln *nt*; **within ~ distance** nahe genug, um zu pendeln

compact¹ [kəmˈpækt] ◨ ADJ (+ER) kompakt; *soil, snow* fest ◨ VT *snow, soil* festtreten/-fahren *etc*

compact² [ˈkɒmpækt] N **(a)** (*powder ~*) Puderdose *f* **(b)** (*US: = car*) Kompaktwagen *m*

compact camera N Kompaktkamera *f*

compact disc N Compactdisc *f*; **~ player** CD-Spieler *m*

companion [kəmˈpænjən] N **(a)** (= *person with one*) Begleiter(in) *m(f)*; **travelling ~** Reisebegleiter(in) *m(f)*; **drinking ~** Zechgenosse *m*, -genossin *f* **(b)** (= *friend*) Freund(in) *m(f)*

companionship [kəmˈpænjənʃɪp] N Gesellschaft *f*

company [ˈkʌmpənɪ] ◨ N **(a)** Gesellschaft *f*; **to keep sb ~** jdm Gesellschaft leisten; **I enjoy his ~** ich bin gern mit ihm zusammen; **he's good ~** seine Gesellschaft ist angenehm; **she has a cat, it's ~ for her** sie hält sich eine Katze, da hat sie (wenigstens) Gesellschaft; **you'll be in good ~ if ...** wenn du ..., bist du in guter Gesellschaft
(b) (= *guests*) Besuch *m*
(c) (*Comm*) Firma *f*; **Smith & Company**, **Smith & Co.** Smith & Co.; **publishing ~** Verlagshaus *nt*, Verlag *m*; **a printing/clothes ~** ein Druckerei-/Textilbetrieb *m*
(d) (*Theat*) (Schauspiel)truppe *f*
(e) (*Mil*) Kompanie *f*
◨ ATTR Firmen-

company: **company car** N Firmenwagen *m*; **company director** N Direktor(in) *m(f)*; **company law** N Gesellschaftsrecht *nt*; **company pension** N Betriebsrente *f*; **company policy** N Geschäftspolitik *f*; **company progress report** N Bericht *m* zur Unternehmenslage; **company secretary** N (*Brit Comm*) ≈ Prokurist(in) *m(f)*; **company stationery** N (*US*) Firmenbriefpapier *nt*

comparable [ˈkɒmpərəbl] ADJ vergleichbar (*with, to* mit)

comparably [ˈkɒmpərəblɪ] ADV ähnlich

comparative [kəmˈpærətɪv] ◨ ADJ **(a)** *religion etc* vergleichend **(b)** **the ~ form** (*Gram*) der Komparativ **(c)** (= *relative*) relativ; **to live in ~ luxury** relativ luxuriös leben ◨ N (*Gram*) Komparativ *m*

comparatively [kəmˈpærətɪvlɪ] ADV (= *relatively*) verhältnismäßig

compare [kəmˈpeəʳ] ◨ VT vergleichen (*with, to* mit); **~d with** *or* **to** im Vergleich zu; **to ~ notes** Eindrücke/Erfahrungen austauschen ◨ VI sich vergleichen lassen (*with* mit); **it ~s badly/well** es schneidet vergleichsweise schlecht/gut ab; **how do the two cars ~ in terms of speed?** wie sieht ein Geschwindigkeitsvergleich der beiden Wagen aus?

comparison [kəmˈpærɪsn] N Vergleich *m* (*to* mit); **in** *or* **by ~** vergleichsweise; **in** *or* **by ~ with** im Vergleich zu; **to make** *or* **draw a ~** einen Vergleich anstellen; **there's no ~** das ist gar kein Vergleich

compartment [kəmˈpɑːtmənt] N (*in fridge, desk etc*) Fach *nt*; (*Rail*) Abteil *nt*

compartmentalize [ˌkɒmpɑːˈtmentəlaɪz] VT aufspalten

compass [ˈkʌmpəs] N **(a)** Kompass *m* **(b)** **compasses** PL (*also* **pair of ~es**) Zirkel *m* **(c)** (*fig: = extent*) Rahmen *m*

compass bearing N Kompasspeilung *f*

compassion [kəmˈpæʃən] N Mitleid *nt* (*for* mit)

compassionate [kəmˈpæʃənɪt] ADJ mitfühlend; **on ~ grounds** aus familiären Gründen

compassionate leave N Beurlaubung *f* wegen einer dringenden Familienangelegenheit

compatibility [kəmˌpætəˈbɪlɪtɪ] N Vereinbarkeit *f*; (*Med*) Verträglichkeit *f*; (*Comput*) Kompatibilität *f*

compatible [kəmˈpætɪbl] ADJ vereinbar; (*Med*) verträglich; (*Comput*) kompatibel; **to be ~** (*people*) zueinander passen; (*colours*) zusammenpassen; (*plan*) vereinbar sein; **an IBM-~ computer** ein IBM-kompatibler Computer

compatriot [kəmˈpætrɪət] N Landsmann *m*, Landsmännin *f*

compel [kəmˈpel] VT **(a)** (= *force*) zwingen **(b)** *admiration, respect* abnötigen (*from sb* jdm)

compelling [kəmˈpelɪŋ] ADJ zwingend; *performance, personality, eyes* bezwingend; **to make a ~ case for sth** schlagende Beweise für etw liefern

compendium [kəmˈpendɪəm] N Handbuch *nt*; **~ of games** Spielemagazin *nt*

compensate [ˈkɒmpənseɪt] **◼** VT (= *recompense*) entschädigen; (*Mech*) ausgleichen **◼** VI (*Psych*) kompensieren

▶ **compensate for** VI +PREP OBJ (*in money etc*) ersetzen; (= *make up for*) wieder wettmachen; (*Psych*) kompensieren

compensation [ˌkɒmpənˈseɪʃən] N (= *damages*) Entschädigung *f*; (*fig*) Ausgleich *m*; **in ~** als Entschädigung/Ausgleich

compensatory [kəmˈpensətərɪ] ADJ kompensierend

compère [ˈkɒmpeə͏ʳ] (*Brit*) **◼** N Conférencier *m* **◼** VT **to ~ a show** bei einer Show der Conférencier sein

compete [kəmˈpiːt] VI **(a)** (*firm, country*) konkurrieren; **to ~ with each other** sich (gegenseitig) Konkurrenz machen; **to ~ for sth** um etw kämpfen; **his poetry can't ~ with Eliot's** seine Gedichte können sich nicht mit denen Eliots messen **(b)** (*Sport*) teilnehmen; **to ~ with/against sb** gegen jdn kämpfen

competence [ˈkɒmpɪtəns], **competency** [ˈkɒmpɪtənsɪ] N Fähigkeit *f*; (*of scientist etc also, Ling*) Kompetenz *f*; **his ~ in handling money/dealing with awkward clients** sein Geschick im Umgang mit Geld/schwierigen Kunden

competent [ˈkɒmpɪtənt] ADJ fähig; (*in a particular field*) kompetent; (= *adequate*) angemessen; **to be ~ to do sth** kompetent *or* fähig sein, etw zu tun

competently [ˈkɒmpɪtəntlɪ] ADV kompetent

competition [ˌkɒmpɪˈtɪʃən] N **(a)** NO PL Konkurrenz *f* (*for* um); **unfair ~** unlauterer Wettbewerb; **to be in ~ with sb** mit jdm wetteifern *or* (*esp Comm*) konkurrieren **(b)** (= *contest*) Wettbewerb *m*; (*in newspapers etc*) Preisausschreiben *nt*

competitive [kəmˈpetɪtɪv] ADJ *attitude* vom Konkurrenzdenken geprägt; *sport* (Wett)kampf-; **~ spirit** Konkurrenzgeist *m*; (*of team*) Kampfgeist *m*; **he's a very ~ sort of person** er genießt Wettbewerbssituationen; (*in job etc*) er ist ein sehr ehrgeiziger Mensch **(b)** (*Comm*) wettbewerbsfähig; **a highly ~ market** ein Markt mit starker Konkurrenz

competitively [kəmˈpetɪtɪvlɪ] ADV **(a) to be ~ priced** im Preis konkurrenzfähig sein **(b)** *swim, play etc* in Wettkämpfen

competitiveness [kəmˈpetɪtɪvnɪs] N (= *competitive spirit*) Konkurrenzgeist *m*; (*of product*) Wettbewerbsfähigkeit *f*

competitor [kəmˈpetɪtəʳ] N **(a)** (*Sport, in contest*) Teilnehmer(in) *m(f)*; **to be a ~** teilnehmen **(b)** (*Comm*) Konkurrent(in) *m(f)*; **our ~s** unsere Konkurrenz

compilation [ˌkɒmpɪˈleɪʃən] N Zusammenstellung *f*; (*of material*) Sammlung *f*; (*of dictionary*) Abfassung *f*

compile [kəmˈpaɪl] VT zusammenstellen; *material* sammeln; *dictionary* verfassen; (*Comput*) kompilieren

compiler [kəmˈpaɪləʳ] N (*of dictionary*) Verfasser(in) *m(f)*; (*Comput*) Compiler *m*

complacency [kəmˈpleɪsnsɪ] N Selbstzufriedenheit *f*

complacent ADJ, **complacently** ADV [kəmˈpleɪsənt, -lɪ] selbstzufrieden

complain [kəmˈpleɪn] VI sich beklagen (*about* über +*acc*); (= *to make a formal complaint*) sich beschweren (*about* über +*acc, to* bei); **to ~ that** ... sich darüber beklagen/beschweren, dass ...; **(I) can't ~** (*inf*) ich kann nicht klagen (*inf*); **to ~ of sth** über etw (*acc*) klagen; **she's always ~ing** sie muss sich immer beklagen

complaint [kəmˈpleɪnt] N **(a)** Klage *f*; (= *formal ~*) Beschwerde *f* (*to* bei); **I have no cause for ~** ich kann mich nicht beklagen; **~s department** (*Comm*) Reklamationsabteilung *f* **(b)** (= *illness*) Beschwerden *pl*; **a very rare ~** eine sehr seltene Krankheit

complement [ˈkɒmplɪmənt] **◼** N **(a)** (= *addition*) Ergänzung *f* (*to* +*gen*); (*to perfect sth*) Vervollkommnung *f* (*to* +*gen*) **(b)** (= *full number*) volle Stärke; **we've got our full ~ in the office now** unser Büro ist jetzt voll besetzt **(c)** (*Comm*) Komplementärgut *nt* **◼** [ˈkɒmplɪment] VT (= *add to*) ergänzen; (= *make perfect*) vervollkommnen; (*colour*) herausbringen; **to ~ each other** sich ergänzen; (*colours*) aufeinander abgestimmt sein

complementary [ˌkɒmplɪˈmentərɪ] ADJ *colour* Komplementär-

complete [kəmˈpliːt] **◼** ADJ **(a)** (= *entire*) ganz *attr*; *set also, wardrobe* vollständig; (= *having the required numbers*) vollzählig; **my happiness was ~** mein Glück war vollkommen; **the ~ works of Shakespeare** die gesammelten Werke Shakespeares; **~ with** komplett mit **(b)** ATTR (= *absolute*) völlig; *failure, beginner, disaster* total; *surprise, approval* voll; **we were ~ strangers** wir waren uns völlig fremd **(c)** (= *finished*) fertig **(d)** *sportsman, gardener etc* perfekt **◼** VT **(a)** (= *make whole*) *collection, set* vervollständigen; *team* vollzählig machen; *education, meal* abrunden; **that ~s my collection** damit ist meine Sammlung vollständig **(b)** (= *finish*) beenden; *building, work* fertigstellen; *prison sentence* verbüßen; **~ this phrase** ergänzen Sie diesen Ausspruch; **it's not ~d yet** es ist noch nicht fertig **(c)** *form* ausfüllen

completely [kəmˈpliːtlɪ] ADV vollkommen; **he's ~ wrong** er irrt sich gewaltig, er hat völlig Unrecht

completeness [kəmˈpliːtnɪs] N Vollständigkeit *f*

completion [kəmˈpliːʃən] N **(a)** (= *finishing*) Fertigstellung *f*; (*of project, course*) Abschluss *m*; **to be near ~** kurz vor dem Abschluss stehen; **to bring sth to ~** etw zum Abschluss bringen; **on ~ of the course** nach Abschluss des Kurses; **on ~ of the contract/sale** bei Vertrags-/Kaufabschluss; **~ date** Fertigstellungstermin *m* **(b)** (= *making whole*) Vervollständigung *f*

complex [ˈkɒmpleks] **◼** ADJ komplex; *pattern, paragraph* kompliziert **◼** N Komplex *m*; **industrial ~** Industriekomplex *m*; **he has a ~ about his ears** er hat Komplexe wegen seiner Ohren

complexion [kəmˈplekʃən] N **(a)** Teint *m*; (= *skin colour*) Gesichtsfarbe *f* **(b)** (*fig*: = *aspect*) Anstrich *m*, Aspekt *m*; **to put a new ~ etc ~ on sth** etw in einem neuen *etc* Licht erscheinen lassen

complexity [kəmˈpleksɪtɪ] N Komplexität *f*; (*pattern*) Kompliziertheit *f*

compliance [kəmˈplaɪəns] N Einverständnis *nt*; (*with rules etc*) Einhalten *nt* (*with* +*gen*); (= *submissiveness*) Fügsamkeit *f*; **in ~ with the law etc** dem Gesetz *etc* gemäß

complicate [ˈkɒmplɪkeɪt] VT komplizieren

complicated [ˈkɒmplɪkeɪtɪd] ADJ kompliziert

complication [ˌkɒmplɪˈkeɪʃən] N Komplikation *f*

complicity [kəmˈplɪsɪtɪ] N Mittäterschaft *f* (*in* bei)

compliment [ˈkɒmplɪmənt] **◼** N **(a)** Kompliment *nt* (*on* zu, *wegen*); **to pay sb a ~** jdm ein Kompliment machen; (*give*) **my ~s to the chef** mein Kompliment dem Koch/der Köchin **(b) compliments** PL (*form*) Grüße *pl*; **give him my ~s** empfehlen Sie mich ihm (*dated form*); **"with the ~s of Mr X/ the management"** „mit den besten Empfehlungen von Herrn X/der Geschäftsleitung" **◼** [ˈkɒmplɪment] VT ein Kompliment/Komplimente machen (+*dat*) (*on* wegen, zu)

complimentary [ˌkɒmplɪˈmentərɪ] ADJ **(a)** (= *praising*) schmeichelhaft; **to be ~ about sb/sth** sich schmeichelhaft über jdn/etw äußern **(b)** (= *free*) Frei-; **~ copy** Freiexemplar *nt*; (*of magazine*) Werbenummer *f*

compliments slip [ˈkɒmplɪmənts͵slɪp] N (*Comm*) Empfehlungszettel *m*

comply [kəmˈplaɪ] VI (*person*) einwilligen; (*object, system etc*) die Bedingungen erfüllen; **to ~ with sth** einer Sache (*dat*) entsprechen; (*system*) in Einklang mit etw stehen; **to ~ with a request/instructions** einer Bitte/den Anordnungen nachkommen (form); **to ~ with the rules** sich an die Regeln halten

component [kəm'pəʊnənt] **1** N Teil nt, Bestandteil m **2** ADJ a **~ part** ein (Bestand)teil m; **the ~ parts of a machine** die einzelnen Maschinenteile pl

compose [kəm'pəʊz] VT **(a)** music komponieren; letter abfassen; poem verfassen **(b)** (= constitute) bilden; **to be ~d of** sich zusammensetzen aus; **water is ~d of ...** Wasser besteht aus ... **(c) to ~ oneself** sich sammeln; **to ~ one's thoughts** Ordnung in seine Gedanken bringen

composed [kəm'pəʊzd] ADJ (= calm) gelassen

composer [kəm'pəʊzəʳ] N (Mus) Komponist(in) m(f)

composite ['kɒmpəzɪt] ADJ zusammengesetzt; **~ materials** (Ind) Verbundwerkstoffe pl; **~ structure** gegliederter Aufbau

composition [ˌkɒmpə'zɪʃən] N **(a)** (= act of composing) Komponieren nt **(b)** (= arrangement, Mus, Art) Komposition f **(c)** (Sch: = essay) Aufsatz m **(d)** (= constitution) Zusammensetzung f; (of sentence) Aufbau m

compositional [ˌkɒmpə'zɪʃənl] ADJ Kompositions-

compost ['kɒmpɒst] N Kompost m; **~ heap** Komposthaufen m

composure [kəm'pəʊʒəʳ] N Beherrschung f; **to lose one's ~** die Beherrschung verlieren; **to regain one's ~** seine Selbstbeherrschung wiederfinden

compote ['kɒmpəʊt] N Kompott nt

compound[1] ['kɒmpaʊnd] **1** N (Chem) Verbindung f; (Gram) zusammengesetztes Wort **2** ADJ (Gram) zusammengesetzt **3** [kəm'paʊnd] VT (= make worse) verschlimmern; **problem** vergrößern

compound[2] ['kɒmpaʊnd] N (= enclosed area) Lager nt; (in prison) Gefängnishof m; (= living quarters) Siedlung f; (in zoo) Gehege nt

compound: compound fracture N (Med) offener or komplizierter Bruch; **compound interest** N (Fin) Zinseszins m

comprehend [ˌkɒmprɪ'hend] VT verstehen

comprehensible [ˌkɒmprɪ'hensəbl] ADJ verständlich

comprehension [ˌkɒmprɪ'henʃən] N **(a)** (= understanding) Verständnis nt; (= ability to understand) Begriffsvermögen nt; **that is beyond my ~** das übersteigt mein Begriffsvermögen; (behaviour) das ist mir unbegreiflich **(b)** (= school exercise) Fragen pl zum Textverständnis

comprehensive [ˌkɒmprɪ'hensɪv] **1** ADJ umfassend; **(fully) ~ insurance** Vollkasko(versicherung f) nt **2** N (Brit) Gesamtschule f

comprehensively [ˌkɒmprɪ'hensɪvlɪ] ADV umfassend

comprehensive school N (Brit) Gesamtschule f

COMPREHENSIVE SCHOOL

Comprehensive schools sind in Großbritannien weiterführende Schulen, an denen alle Kinder aus einem Einzugsgebiet unterrichtet werden und alle Schulabschlüsse gemacht werden können. Diese Gesamtschulen wurden in den sechziger Jahren eingeführt, um das vorherige selektive System von *grammar schools* und *secondary modern schools* abzulösen. Auch wenn es immer noch einige *grammar schools* gibt, sind die meisten staatlichen Schulen in Großbritannien heutzutage *comprehensive schools*.

compress [kəm'pres] VT komprimieren (into auf +acc); materials zusammenpressen (into zu)

compressed air [kəmˌprest'ɛəʳ] N Druck- or Pressluft f

comprise [kəm'praɪz] VT bestehen aus

compromise ['kɒmprəmaɪz] **1** N Kompromiss m; **to come to** or **reach** or **make a ~** einen Kompromiss schließen **2** ADJ ATTR Kompromiss- **3** VI Kompromisse schließen (about in +dat); **we agreed to ~** wir einigten uns auf einen Kompromiss **4** VT sb kompromittieren; **to ~ oneself** sich kompromittieren; **to ~ one's reputation** seinem guten Ruf schaden; **to ~ one's principles** seinen Prinzipien untreu werden

compromising ['kɒmprəmaɪzɪŋ] ADJ kompromittierend

compulsion [kəm'pʌlʃən] N Zwang m; (Psych) innerer Zwang; **you are under no ~** niemand zwingt Sie

compulsive [kəm'pʌlsɪv] ADJ zwanghaft, Zwangs-; neurosis Zwangs-; behaviour zwanghaft; **he is a ~ eater** er hat die Esssucht; **he is a ~ liar** er hat einen krankhaften Trieb zu lügen; **it makes ~ reading** das muss man einfach lesen

compulsively [kəm'pʌlsɪvlɪ] ADV zwanghaft

compulsory [kəm'pʌlsərɪ] ADJ obligatorisch; measures Zwangs-; subject Pflicht-; **~ retirement** Zwangspensionierung f

compulsory: compulsory purchase order N Enteignungsbeschluss m; **compulsory service** N (US) Wehrpflicht f

compunction [kəm'pʌŋkʃən] N (liter) **without the slightest ~** ohne sich im Geringsten schuldig zu fühlen

computation [ˌkɒmpjʊ'teɪʃən] N Berechnung f

computational [ˌkɒmpjʊ'teɪʃənəl] ADJ Computer-

computer [kəm'pjuːtəʳ] N Computer m, Rechner m; **to put/have sth on ~** etw im Computer speichern/(gespeichert) haben; **it's all done by ~** das geht alles per Computer; **~ skills** Computerkenntnisse pl

computer IN CPDS Computer-; **computer-aided design** N rechnergestützter Entwurf; **computer-aided manufacturing** N computergestützte Fertigung; **computer-based** ADJ auf Computerbasis; **computer-controlled** ADJ rechnergesteuert; **computer dating** N Partnervermittlung f per Computer; **~ agency** or **bureau** Partnervermittlungsbüro nt auf Computerbasis; **computer-designed** ADJ mit Computerunterstützung entworfen; **computer error** N Computerfehler m; **computer freak** N (inf) Computerfreak m (inf); **computer game** N Computerspiel nt; **computer-generated** ADJ computergeneriert; **computer graphics** N SING Computergrafik f; **computer-integrated manufacturing** N computerintegrierte Fertigung

computerization [kəmˌpjuːtəraɪ'zeɪʃən] N (of information etc) Computerisierung f; **the ~ of the factory** die Umstellung der Fabrik auf Computer

computerize [kəm'pjuːtəraɪz] VT information computerisieren; company, methods auf Computer or EDV umstellen

computer: computer language N Computersprache f; **computer literate** ADJ **to be ~** sich mit Computern auskennen; **computer model** N Computermodell nt; **computer network** N Computernetzwerk nt; **computer-operated** ADJ computergesteuert; **computer operator** N Operator(in) m(f); **computer printout** N (Computer)ausdruck m; **computer program** N (Computer)programm nt; **computer programmer** N Programmierer(in) m(f); **computer-readable** ADJ computerlesbar; **computer science** N Informatik f; **computer studies** PL Computerwissenschaft f; **computer virus** N Computervirus m

computing [kəm'pjuːtɪŋ] **1** N (= subject) Computerwissenschaft f; **her husband's in ~** ihr Mann ist in der Computerbranche **2** ATTR rechnerisch

comrade ['kɒmrɪd] N Kamerad m; (Pol) Genosse m, Genossin f

comradeship ['kɒmrɪdʃɪp] N Kameradschaft(lichkeit) f

con[1] [kɒn] ADV, N see pro

con[2] (inf) **1** N Schwindel m; **it's a ~!** das ist alles Schwindel **2** VT hereinlegen (inf); **he ~ned her out of all her money** er hat sie um ihr ganzes Geld gebracht; **to ~ sb into doing sth** jdn durch einen faulen Trick dazu bringen, dass er etw tut (inf)

con artist N (inf) Schwindler(in) m(f)

concave ['kɒnkeɪv] ADJ konkav; mirror Konkav-

conceal [kən'siːl] VT object, emotions, thoughts verbergen; (= keep secret) verheimlichen (sth from sb jdm etw); **why did they ~ this information from us?** warum hat man uns diese Informationen vorenthalten?

concealed [kən'siːld] ADJ verborgen; lighting, entrance verdeckt; camera versteckt

concealment [kən'siːlmənt] N (of facts) Verheimlichung f; (of evidence) Unterschlagung f

concede [kən'siːd] VT **(a)** (= give up) privilege aufgeben; lands abtreten (to an +acc); **to ~ a right to sb** jdm ein Recht überlassen; **to ~ victory to sb** vor jdm kapitulieren; **to ~ a match** (= give up) aufgeben; (= lose) ein Match abgeben; **to ~ a penalty** einen Elfmeter verursachen; **to ~ a point to sb** jdm in einem Punkt Recht geben; (Sport) einen Punkt an jdn abgeben

(b) (= admit, grant) zugeben; right zugestehen (to sb jdm); **it's generally ~d that ...** es ist allgemein anerkannt, dass ...; **to ~ defeat** sich geschlagen geben

conceit [kən'siːt] N (= pride) Einbildung f

conceited [kən'siːtɪd] ADJ eingebildet

conceivable [kən'siːvəbl] ADJ denkbar; **it is hardly ~ that ...** es ist kaum denkbar, dass ...

conceivably [kən'siːvəblɪ] ADV **she may ~ be right** es ist durchaus möglich, dass sie Recht hat; **will it happen? – ~** wird das geschehen? – das ist durchaus denkbar

conceive [kən'siːv] ■ VT **(a)** child empfangen **(b)** (= imagine) sich (dat) denken or vorstellen; idea, plan haben ■ VI (woman) empfangen
➤ **conceive of** VI +PREP OBJ sich (dat) vorstellen

concentrate ['kɒnsəntreɪt] ■ VT konzentrieren (on auf +acc); **to ~ all one's energies on sth** sich (voll und) ganz auf etw (acc) konzentrieren; **to ~ one's mind on sth** sich auf etw (acc) konzentrieren; **a spell in prison will certainly ~ his mind** eine Gefängnisstrafe wird ihm sicher zu denken geben ■ VI (= give one's attention) sich konzentrieren; **to ~ on doing sth** sich darauf konzentrieren, etw zu tun

concentrated ['kɒnsəntreɪtɪd] ADJ konzentriert; **~ orange juice** Orangensaftkonzentrat nt

concentration [,kɒnsən'treɪʃən] N **(a)** (also Chem) Konzentration f; **powers of ~** Konzentrationsfähigkeit f **(b)** (= gathering) Ansammlung f

concentration camp N Konzentrationslager nt, KZ nt

concentric [kən'sentrɪk] ADJ konzentrisch

concept ['kɒnsept] N Begriff m; (= conception) Vorstellung f; **our ~ of the world** unser Weltbild nt; **his ~ of marriage** seine Vorstellungen von der Ehe

conception [kən'sepʃən] N **(a)** (= idea) Vorstellung f; (= way sth is conceived) Konzeption f; **the Buddhist ~ of life/nature** die buddhistische Auffassung vom Leben/Vorstellung von der Natur; **he has no ~ of how difficult it is** er hat keine Vorstellung, wie schwer das ist **(b)** (of child) die Empfängnis

conceptualize [kən'septjuəlaɪz] VT in Begriffe fassen

concern [kən'sɜːn] N **(a)** (= business, affair) Angelegenheit(en pl) f; (= matter of interest and importance to sb) Anliegen nt; **the day-to-day ~s of government** die täglichen Regierungsgeschäfte; **it's no ~ of his** das geht ihn nichts an **(b)** (Comm) Konzern m **(c)** (= anxiety) Sorge f; **the situation in the Middle East is causing ~** die Lage im Nahen Osten ist Besorgnis erregend; **there's some/no cause for ~** es besteht Grund/kein Grund zur Sorge; **to do sth out of ~ for sb** etw aus Sorge um jdn tun; **he showed great ~ for your safety** er war sehr um Ihre Sicherheit besorgt **(d)** (= importance) Bedeutung f; **issues of national ~** Fragen pl von nationalem Interesse; **to be of little/great ~ to sb** jdm nicht/sehr wichtig sein ■ VT **(a)** (= be about) handeln von; **it ~s the following issue** es geht um die folgende Frage; **the last chapter is ~ed with ...** das letzte Kapitel behandelt ... **(b)** (= be the business of, affect) betreffen; **that doesn't ~ you** das betrifft Sie nicht; (as snub) das geht Sie nichts an; **where money/honour is ~ed** wenn es um Geld/die Ehre geht; **as far as the money is ~ed** was das Geld betrifft; **as far as he is ~ed it's just another job, but ...** für ihn ist es nur ein anderer Job, aber ...; **as far as I'm ~ed you can do what you like** von mir aus kannst du tun und lassen, was du willst; **the department ~ed** (= relevant) die zuständige Abteilung; (= involved) die betreffende Abteilung; **the persons ~ed** die Betroffenen **(c)** (= interest) **he is only ~ed with facts** ihn interessieren nur die Fakten; (= is only dealing with) ihm geht es nur um die Fakten; **to ~ oneself with or about sth** sich für etw interessieren **(d)** (= have at heart) **we should be ~ed more with or about quality** Qualität sollte uns ein größeres Anliegen sein; **there's no need for you to ~ yourself about that** darum brauchen Sie sich nicht zu kümmern **(e)** (= worry: usu pass) **to be ~ed about sth** sich (dat) um etw Sorgen machen; **I was very ~ed to hear about your illness** ich habe mir Sorgen gemacht, als ich von Ihrer Krankheit hörte; **I am ~ed to hear that ...** es beunruhigt mich, dass ...; **~ed parents** besorgte Eltern

concerning [kən'sɜːnɪŋ] PREP bezüglich (+gen); **~ your request ...** was Ihre Anfrage betrifft ...; **~ what?** worüber?

concert ['kɒnsət] N **(a)** (Mus) Konzert nt; **were you at the ~?** waren Sie in dem Konzert?; **Madonna in ~** Madonna live

(b) (fig) **in ~** gemeinsam; **to work in ~ with sb** mit jdm zusammenarbeiten

concerted [kən'sɜːtɪd] ADJ konzertiert; **to take ~ action** gemeinsam vorgehen

concert: concertgoer N Konzertbesucher(in) m(f); **concert hall** N Konzerthalle f

concertina [,kɒnsə'tiːnə] N Konzertina f

concertmaster ['kɒnsətmæstə'] N (US) Konzertmeister m

concerto [kən'tʃɜːtəʊ] N Konzert nt

concert pianist N Pianist(in) m(f)

concession [kən'seʃən] N Zugeständnis nt (to an +acc); (Comm) Konzession f; **to make ~s to sb** jdm Zugeständnisse machen

concessionary [kən'seʃənərɪ] ADJ (Comm) Konzessions-; rates, fares verbilligt

conciliate [kən'sɪlɪeɪt] VT (= placate) besänftigen; (= win the goodwill of) versöhnlich stimmen

conciliation [kən,sɪlɪ'eɪʃən] N Schlichtung f

conciliatory [kən'sɪlɪətərɪ] ADJ (= intended to reconcile) versöhnlich; (= placatory) besänftigend

concise ADJ, **concisely** ADV [kən'saɪs, -lɪ] präzis(e)

conclude [kən'kluːd] ■ VT **(a)** (= end) beenden **(b)** treaty, deal abschließen **(c)** (= infer) folgern (from aus); **what did you ~?** was haben Sie daraus gefolgert? **(d)** (= decide) zu dem Schluss kommen ■ VI enden; **to ~ I would like to say ..., I would like to ~ by saying ...** abschließend möchte ich zu sagen ...

concluding [kən'kluːdɪŋ] ADJ remarks abschließend; **the ~ stages of the tournament** die letzten Durchgänge des Turniers

conclusion [kən'kluːʒən] N **(a)** (= end) Abschluss m; (of essay etc) Schluss m; **in ~** abschließend **(b)** Schluss(folgerung f) m; **what ~ do you draw or reach from all this?** welchen Schluss ziehen Sie daraus?

conclusive [kən'kluːsɪv] ADJ (= convincing) überzeugend; (Jur) evidence einschlägig; proof eindeutig

conclusively [kən'kluːsɪvlɪ] ADV prove eindeutig

concoct [kən'kɒkt] VT **(a)** (Cook etc) (zu)bereiten; (hum) kreieren **(b)** (fig) sich (dat) zurechtlegen

concoction [kən'kɒkʃən] N **(a)** (= food) Kreation f; (= drink) Gebräu nt

concord ['kɒŋkɔːd] N (= harmony) Eintracht f

concourse ['kɒŋkɔːs] N (= place) Eingangshalle f; (US: in park) freier Platz; **station ~** Bahnhofshalle f

concrete[1] ['kɒŋkriːt] ADJ object, evidence, measures konkret

concrete[2] ■ N (Build) Beton m; **nothing is set in ~ yet** (fig) es ist noch nichts definitiv festgelegt ■ ADJ Beton-

concrete mixer N Betonmischmaschine f

concur [kən'kɜː'] VI (= agree) übereinstimmen; (with a suggestion etc) beipflichten (with +dat); **John and I ~red** John und ich waren einer Meinung; **I ~ with that** ich pflichte dem bei

concurrence [kən'kʌrəns] N (= agreement, permission) Einverständnis nt

concurrent [kən'kʌrənt] ADJ gleichzeitig; **to be ~ with sth** mit etw zusammentreffen

concurrently [kən'kʌrəntlɪ] ADV gleichzeitig; **the two sentences to run ~** (Jur) unter gleichzeitigem Vollzug beider Freiheitsstrafen

concuss [kən'kʌs] VT (usu pass) **to be ~ed** eine Gehirnerschütterung haben

concussion [kən'kʌʃən] N Gehirnerschütterung f

condemn [kən'dem] VT **(a)** (also Jur) verurteilen; **to ~ sb to death/10 years' imprisonment** jdn zum Tode/zu 10 Jahren Gefängnis verurteilen; **the ~ed man** der zum Tode Verurteilte **(b)** (fig) verdammen (to zu) **(c)** building für abbruchreif erklären; **these houses are/should be ~ed** diese Häuser stehen auf der Abrissliste/sollten abgerissen werden **(d)** (US Jur) beschlagnahmen; land enteignen

condemnation [,kɒndem'neɪʃən] N **(a)** Verurteilung f **(b)** (US Jur) Beschlagnahme f; (of land) Enteignung f

condensation [,kɒndən'seɪʃən] N (of vapour) Kondensation f; (= liquid formed) Kondensat nt; (on window panes etc) Kondenswasser nt; **the windows are covered with ~** die Fenster sind beschlagen

condense [kən'dens] **1** VT **(a)** kondensieren **(b)** (= *shorten*) zusammenfassen **2** VI (*gas*) kondensieren

condensed milk [kən‚denst'mɪlk] N Kondensmilch *f*

condescend [‚kɒndɪ'send] VI **(a) to ~ to do sth** sich herablassen, etw zu tun **(b) to ~ to sb** jdn herablassend behandeln

condescending [‚kɒndɪ'sendɪŋ] ADJ (*pej*) herablassend; **to be ~ to** *or* **toward(s) sb** jdn herablassend behandeln

condescendingly [‚kɒndɪ'sendɪŋlɪ] ADV (*pej*) herablassend

condescension [‚kɒndɪ'senʃən] N (*pej*) Herablassung *f*; (= *attitude also*) herablassende Haltung

condiment ['kɒndɪmənt] N Würze *f*

condition [kən'dɪʃən] **1** N **(a)** (= *determining factor*) Bedingung *f* (*also Jur, Comm*); (= *prerequisite*) Voraussetzung *f*; **~s of sale** Verkaufsbedingungen *pl*; **on ~ that ...** unter der Bedingung, dass ...; **on no ~** auf keinen Fall; **he made it a ~ that ...** er machte es zur Bedingung, dass ... **(b) conditions** PL (= *circumstances*) Verhältnisse *pl*; **working ~s** Arbeitsbedingungen *pl*; **living ~s** Wohnverhältnisse *pl*; **weather ~s** die Wetterlage; **in** *or* **under (the) present ~s** bei den derzeitigen Verhältnissen **(c)** NO PL (= *state*) Zustand *m*; **he is in good ~** er ist in guter Verfassung; **it is in bad ~** es ist in schlechtem Zustand; **he is in a critical ~** sein Zustand ist kritisch; **you're in no ~ to drive** du bist nicht mehr fahrtüchtig; **to be in/out of ~** eine gute/keine Kondition haben; **to keep in/get into ~** in Form bleiben/kommen **(d)** (*Med*) Beschwerden *pl*; **heart ~** Herzdrüsenleiden *nt*; **he has a heart ~** er ist herzkrank **2** VT **(a)** (*esp pass*: = *determine*) bedingen; **to be ~ed by** bedingt sein durch **(b)** (*Psych etc*) (= *train*) konditionieren; (= *accustom*) gewöhnen; **they have become ~ed to believe it** sie sind so konditioniert, dass sie es glauben

conditional [kən'dɪʃənl] **1** ADJ **(a)** bedingt, vorbehaltlich; **to be ~ (up)on sth** von etw abhängen **(b)** (*Gram*) konditional, Konditional-; **the ~ mood/tense** der Konditional **2** N (*Gram*) Konditional *m*

conditional discharge N (*Jur*) Entlassung *f* auf Bewährung

conditioner [kən'dɪʃənəʳ] N **(a)** (*for hair*) Pflegespülung *f*; (*for washing*) Weichspüler *m*

conditioning shampoo [kən'dɪʃənɪŋʃæm'puː] N Pflegeshampoo *nt*

condo ['kɒndəʊ] N (*US inf*) = **condominium**

condolence [kən'dəʊləns] N **message of ~** Kondolenzbotschaft *fm* **please accept my ~s on the death of your mother** (meine) aufrichtige Anteilnahme zum Tode Ihrer Mutter

condom ['kɒndɒm] N Kondom *nt or m*

condominium [‚kɒndə'mɪnɪəm] N (*US*) (= *apartment house*) ≈ Haus *nt* mit Eigentumswohnungen; (= *single apartment*) ≈ Eigentumswohnung *f*

condone [kən'dəʊn] VT (= *overlook*) (stillschweigend) hinwegsehen über (+*acc*); (= *approve*) (stillschweigend) dulden

conducive [kən'djuːsɪv] ADJ förderlich (*to* +*dat*)

conduct ['kɒndʌkt] **1** N **(a)** (= *behaviour*) Benehmen *nt* (*towards* gegenüber); (*of prisoner*) Führung *f* **(b)** (= *management*) Führung *f*; (*of conference*) Leitung *f*; (*of investigation*) Durchführung *f* **2** [kən'dʌkt] VT **(a)** führen; *investigation* durchführen; *private affairs* handhaben; (= *tour* (*of*)) (*of building*) Führung *f* (*durch*); **he ~ed his own defence** er übernahm seine eigene Verteidigung **(b)** (*Mus*) dirigieren **(c)** (*Phys, Physiol*) leiten; *lightning* ableiten **3** [kən'dʌkt] VI (*Mus*) dirigieren **4** [kən'dʌkt] VR sich benehmen

conductivity [‚kɒndʌk'tɪvɪtɪ] N (*Phys, Physiol*) Leitfähigkeit *f*

conductor [kən'dʌktəʳ] N **(a)** (*Mus*) Dirigent(in) *m(f)* **(b)** (= *bus, tram ~*) Schaffner *m*; (*US Rail*: = *guard*) Zugführer *m* **(c)** (*Phys*) Leiter *m*; (= *lightning ~*) Blitzableiter *m*

conductress [kən'dʌktrɪs] N (*on bus etc*) Schaffnerin *f*

cone [kəʊn] N **(a)** Kegel *m*; (= *traffic ~*) Pylon *m* (*form*), Leitkegel *m* **(b)** (*Bot*) Zapfen *m* **(c)** (= *ice-cream ~*) (Eis)tüte *f*

confectioner [kən'fekʃənəʳ] N Süßwarenverkäufer(in) *m(f)*

confectioner's sugar N (*US*) Puderzucker *m*

confectionery [kən'fekʃənərɪ] N Süßwaren *pl*; (= *chocolates*) Konfekt *nt*

confederacy [kən'fedərəsɪ] N (*Pol*) (= *confederation*) Bündnis *nt*; (*of nations*) Konföderation *f*

confederate [kən'fedərɪt] **1** ADJ konföderiert; **the Confederate States** (*US Hist*) die Konföderierten Staaten von Amerika **2** N (*pej*: = *accomplice*) Komplize *m* (*pej*); **the Confederates** (*US Hist*) die Konföderierten *pl*

confederation [kən‚fedə'reɪʃən] N Bund *m*; (= *alliance also*) Bündnis *nt*; **the Swiss Confederation** die Schweizerische Eidgenossenschaft; **Confederation of British Industry** Verband *m* der britischen Industrie

confer [kən'fɜːʳ] **1** VT (*on, upon sb* jdm) verleihen **2** VI sich beraten

conference ['kɒnfərəns] N Konferenz *f*; (*more informal*) Besprechung *f*; **to be in a ~ (with)** eine Besprechung haben (*mit*)

conference call N (*Telec*) Konferenzschaltung *f*

conference room N Konferenzzimmer *nt*

confess [kən'fes] **1** VT **(a)** (= *acknowledge*) zugeben **(b)** (*Eccl*) *sins* bekennen; (*to priest*) beichten **2** VI **(a)** (= *admit*) gestehen (*to* +*acc*); **to ~ to sth** etw gestehen **(b)** (*Eccl*) beichten; **to ~ to sb/to sth** jdm/etw (*acc*) beichten

confessed [kən'fest] ADJ (= *self-~*) nach eigenen Angaben

confession [kən'feʃən] N **(a)** (= *admission*) Eingeständnis *nt*; (*of guilt, crime etc*) Geständnis *nt*; **I have a ~ to make** ich muss dir etwas gestehen; (*Jur*) ich möchte ein Geständnis ablegen **(b)** (*Eccl: of sins*) Beichte *f*; **to hear ~** (die) Beichte hören

> *Be careful!* **confession** *is not translated by the German word* ***Konfession***.

confessional [kən'feʃənl] N Beichtstuhl *m*

confetti [kən'fetiː] N, NO PL Konfetti *nt*

confidant [‚kɒnfɪ'dænt] N Vertraute(r) *m*

confidante [‚kɒnfɪ'dænt] N Vertraute *f*

confide [kən'faɪd] VT anvertrauen (*to sb* jdm)

➤ **confide in** VI +PREP OBJ sich anvertrauen (+*dat*); **to confide in sb about sth** jdm etw anvertrauen

confidence ['kɒnfɪdəns] N **(a)** (= *trust*) Vertrauen *nt* (*in* zu); (= *confident expectation*) Zuversicht *f*; **to have (every/no) ~ in sb/sth** volles/kein) Vertrauen zu jdm/etw haben; **I have every ~ that ...** ich bin ganz zuversichtlich, dass ...; **to put one's ~ in sb/sth** auf jdn/etw bauen; **to give a vote of ~** (*Parl*) das Vertrauen aussprechen; **motion/vote of no ~** Misstrauensantrag *m*/-votum *nt* **(b)** (= *self-~*) (Selbst)vertrauen *nt* **(c)** (= *confidential relationship*) **in (strict) ~** (streng) vertraulich; **to take sb into one's ~** jdn ins Vertrauen ziehen

confidence trick N Schwindel *m*

confident ['kɒnfɪdənt] ADJ **(a)** (= *sure*) überzeugt; *look etc* zuversichtlich; **to be ~ of success** *or* **succeeding** vom Erfolg überzeugt sein; **to be/feel ~ about sth** in Bezug auf etw zuversichtlich sein **(b)** (= *self-assured*) (selbst)sicher

confidential [‚kɒnfɪ'denʃəl] ADJ vertraulich; **to treat sth as ~** etw vertraulich behandeln

confidentiality [‚kɒnfɪ‚denʃɪ'ælɪtɪ] N Vertraulichkeit *f*

confidentially [‚kɒnfɪ'denʃəlɪ] ADV vertraulich

confidently ['kɒnfɪdəntlɪ] ADV **(a)** zuversichtlich **(b)** (= *self-~*) selbstsicher

configuration [kən‚fɪgjʊ'reɪʃən] N Konfiguration *f*

confine [kən'faɪn] **1** VT **(a)** *person, animal* (ein)sperren; **to be ~d to the house** nicht aus dem Haus können; **to be ~d to barracks/one's room** Kasernen-/Stubenarrest haben **(b)** (= *limit*) *remarks* beschränken (*to* auf +*acc*); **to ~ oneself to doing sth** sich darauf beschränken, etw zu tun **2** **confines** ['kɒnfaɪnz] PL (*of space, thing etc*) Grenzen *pl*; (*of system*) enge Grenzen *pl*

confined [kən'faɪnd] ADJ *space* begrenzt

confinement [kən'faɪnmənt] N (= *imprisonment*) (= *act*) Einsperren *nt*; (*of animals*) Gefangenhalten *nt*; (= *state*) Eingesperrtsein *nt*; (*in jail*) Haft *f*; (*of animals*) Gefangenschaft *f*; **~ to barracks** Kasernenarrest *m*

confirm [kən'fɜːm] VT **(a)** (= *verify*) bestätigen; **his new play ~s him as our leading playwright** sein neues Stück stellt wieder unter Beweis, dass er unser führender Schauspieldichter ist

(b) (= *strengthen*) bestärken **(c)** (*Eccl*) konfirmieren; *Roman Catholic* firmen

confirmation [ˌkɒnfəˈmeɪʃən] N **(a)** Bestätigung *f* **(b)** (*Eccl*) Konfirmation *f*; (*of Roman Catholics*) Firmung *f*

confirmed [kənˈfɜːmd] ADJ **(a)** erklärt; *non-smoker, atheist* überzeugt; *bachelor* eingefleischt **(b)** *booking, letter of credit* bestätigt

confiscate [ˈkɒnfɪskeɪt] VT beschlagnahmen; **to ~ sth from sb** jdm etw abnehmen

confiscation [ˌkɒnfɪsˈkeɪʃən] N Beschlagnahme *f*

conflagration [ˌkɒnfləˈgreɪʃən] N Großbrand *m*

conflate [kənˈfleɪt] VT zusammenfassen

conflation [kənˈfleɪʃən] N Zusammenfassung *f*

conflict [ˈkɒnflɪkt] **1** N Konflikt *m*; (*between two accounts etc*) Widerspruch *m*; (= *fighting*) Zusammenstoß *m*; **to be in ~ with sb/sth** mit jdm/etw im Konflikt liegen; **to come into ~ with sb/sth** mit jdm/etw in Konflikt geraten; **~ of interests** Interessenkonflikt *m*; **~ resolution** Konfliktlösung *f* **2** [kənˈflɪkt] VI im Widerspruch stehen (*with* zu)

conflicting [kənˈflɪktɪŋ] ADJ widersprüchlich

conform [kənˈfɔːm] VI (*things*: = *comply with*) entsprechen (*to* +*dat*); (*people: socially*) sich anpassen (*to* an +*acc*); (*to rules etc*) sich richten (*to* nach)

conformist [kənˈfɔːmɪst] **1** ADJ konformistisch **2** N Konformist *m*

conformity [kənˈfɔːmɪtɪ] N **(a)** (= *uniformity*) Konformismus *m* **(b)** (= *compliance*) Übereinstimmung *f*; (*socially*) Anpassung *f* (*with* an +*acc*); **to be in ~ with sth** einer Sache (*dat*) entsprechen

confound [kənˈfaʊnd] VT **(a)** (= *amaze*) verblüffen **(b)** (= *throw into confusion*) verwirren

confounded [kənˈfaʊndɪd] ADJ (*inf*) verflixt (*inf*); *noise also* Heiden- (*inf*); *nuisance* elend (*inf*)

confront [kənˈfrʌnt] VT **(a)** (= *face*) gegenübertreten (+*dat*); (*fig*) *problems, issue also* begegnen (+*dat*); (*problems, decisions*) sich stellen (+*dat*) **(b)** (= *bring face to face with*) **to ~ sb with sb/sth** jdn mit jdm/etw konfrontieren; **to be ~ed with sth** mit etw konfrontiert sein

confrontation [ˌkɒnfrənˈteɪʃən] N Konfrontation *f* (*also Pol*)

confuse [kənˈfjuːz] VT **(a)** *people* verwirren; *situation* verworren machen; **don't ~ the issue!** bring (jetzt) nicht alles durcheinander! **(b)** (= *mix up*) verwechseln

confused [kənˈfjuːzd] ADJ (= *muddled*) konfus; *person also* verwirrt; (*through old age, after anaesthetic etc*) wirr im Kopf; *sound, jumble* wirr

confusing [kənˈfjuːzɪŋ] ADJ verwirrend

confusion [kənˈfjuːʒən] N **(a)** (= *disorder*) Durcheinander *nt*; (= *jumble*) Wirrwarr *m*; **to be in ~** durcheinander sein; **to throw everything into ~** alles durcheinander bringen **(b)** (= *perplexity*) Verwirrung *f*; (*after drugs, blow on head etc*) Verwirrtheit *f*; (*through old age etc*) Wirrheit *f*

congeal [kənˈdʒiːl] VI erstarren; (*blood*) gerinnen

congenial [kənˈdʒiːnɪəl] ADJ (= *pleasant*) ansprechend; *place, job also, atmosphere* angenehm

congenital [kənˈdʒenɪtl] ADJ angeboren; **~ defect** Geburtsfehler *m*; **~ liar** (*inf*) Erzlügner(in) *m(f)* (*inf*)

congested [kənˈdʒestɪd] ADJ überfüllt; (*with traffic*) verstopft; **his lungs are ~** in seiner Lunge hat sich Blut angestaut

congestion [kənˈdʒestʃən] N Stau *m*; (*in corridors etc*) Gedränge *nt*; (*Med*) Blutstau *m*; **the ~ in the city centre is getting so bad ...** die Verstopfung in der Innenstadt nimmt derartige Ausmaße an ...

congestion charge N City-Maut *f*

conglomerate [kənˈglɒmərɪt] N (*also Geol, Comm*) Konglomerat *nt*

Congo [ˈkɒŋgəʊ] N Kongo *m*

congratulate [kənˈgrætjʊleɪt] VT gratulieren (+*dat*) (*also on birthday etc*), beglückwünschen (*on* zu)

congratulation [kənˌgrætjʊˈleɪʃən] N **message of ~** Glückwunschbotschaft *mf*

congratulations [kənˌgrætjʊˈleɪʃənz] **1** PL Glückwunsch *m*, Glückwünsche *pl*; **to offer/send one's ~** jdm gratulieren **2** INTERJ (ich) gratuliere!, herzlichen Glückwunsch!; (*iro*) gratuliere!; **~ on ...!** herzlichen Glückwunsch *or* herzliche Glückwünsche zu ...!

congratulatory [kənˈgrætjʊlətərɪ] ADJ Glückwunsch-

congregate [ˈkɒŋgrɪgeɪt] VI sich sammeln; (*on a particular occasion*) sich versammeln

congregation [ˌkɒŋgrɪˈgeɪʃən] N (*Eccl*) Gemeinde *f*

congress [ˈkɒŋgres] N **(a)** (= *meeting*) Kongress *m*; (*of political party*) Parteitag *m* **(b) Congress** (*US etc Pol*) der Kongress

congressional [kɒŋˈgreʃənl] ADJ Kongress-

Congressional district N (*US Pol*) Kongresswahlbezirk *m*

Congressional Record N (*US Pol*) Veröffentlichung *f* der Kongressdebatten

Congressman [ˈkɒŋgresmən] N, *pl* **-men** [-mən] Kongressabgeordnete(r) *m*

Congresswoman [ˈkɒŋgresˌwʊmən] N, *pl* **-women** [-wɪmɪn] Kongressabgeordnete *f*

conic [ˈkɒnɪk] ADJ (*also* ~**al**) kegelförmig

conifer [ˈkɒnɪfəʳ] N Nadelbaum *m*; ~**s** Nadelhölzer *pl*

coniferous [kəˈnɪfərəs] ADJ Nadel-

conjectural [kənˈdʒektʃərəl] ADJ auf Vermutungen beruhend; **it is entirely ~** es ist reine Vermutung

conjecture [kənˈdʒektʃəʳ] **1** VT vermuten **2** VI Vermutungen anstellen **3** N Vermutung *f*

conjugal [ˈkɒndʒʊgəl] ADJ ehelich; *state* Ehe-

conjugate [ˈkɒndʒʊgeɪt] **1** VT (*Gram*) konjugieren **2** VI (*Gram*) sich konjugieren lassen

conjugation [ˌkɒndʒʊˈgeɪʃən] N (*Gram*) Konjugation *f*

conjunction [kənˈdʒʌŋkʃən] N **(a)** (*Gram*) Konjunktion *f* **(b) in ~ with the new evidence** in Verbindung mit dem neuen Beweismaterial; **the programme was produced in ~ with the NBC** das Programm wurde in Zusammenarbeit mit NBC aufgezeichnet

conjunctivitis [kənˌdʒʌŋktɪˈvaɪtɪs] N (*Med*) Bindehautentzündung *f*

conjure [ˈkʌndʒəʳ] **1** VI zaubern; **a name to ~ with** ein Name, der Wunder wirkt **2** VT zaubern; *image, memory* heraufbeschwören; **to ~ something out of nothing** etwas aus dem Nichts herbeizaubern

▶ **conjure up** VT SEP *memories etc* heraufbeschwören; (= *provide, produce*) hervorzaubern; *meal* zusammenzaubern

conjurer [ˈkʌndʒərəʳ] N Zauberkünstler(in) *m(f)*

conjuring [ˈkʌndʒərɪŋ] N Zaubern *nt*; (= *performance*) Zauberei *f*; **~ trick** Zaubertrick *m*

conjuror [ˈkʌndʒərəʳ] N = **conjurer**

▶ **conk out** VI (*inf*) den Geist aufgeben; (*person*, = *faint*) umkippen (*inf*)

conker [ˈkɒŋkəʳ] N (*Brit inf*) (Ross)kastanie *f*

con man N, *pl* **con men** (*inf*) Schwindler *m*, Bauernfänger *m* (*inf*)

connect [kəˈnekt] **1** VT **(a)** verbinden (*to, with* mit); (*Elec etc*: *also* ~ **up**) *appliances, subscribers* anschließen (*to* an +*acc*); **I'll ~ you** (*Telec*) ich verbinde (Sie); **to be ~ed** (*two things*) miteinander verbunden sein; (*several things*) untereinander verbunden sein; (*ideas etc*) in Beziehung zueinander stehen; **to be ~ed with** (*of ideas, theories*) eine Beziehung haben zu; **he's ~ed with the university** er hat mit der der Universität zu tun

(b) (*fig*: = *associate*) in Verbindung bringen; **I always ~ Paris with springtime** ich verbinde Paris immer mit Frühling **2** VI **(a)** (= *join*) (*two rooms*) eine Verbindung haben (*to, with* zu); (*two parts etc*) Kontakt haben; **~ing rooms** angrenzende Zimmer *pl* (*mit Verbindungstür*)

(b) (*Rail, Aviat etc*) Anschluss haben (*with* an +*acc*); **~ing flight** Anschlussflug *m*

(c) (*inf*: = *hit*) (*fist etc*) landen (*inf*) (*with* auf +*dat*); (*golf club etc*) treffen (*with* +*acc*)

▶ **connect up** VT SEP (*Elec etc*) anschließen (*to, with* an +*acc*)

connection [kəˈnekʃən] N **(a)** Verbindung *f* (*to, with* zu, mit); (= *telephone line also, wire*) Leitung *f*; (*to mains*) Anschluss *m* (*to* an +*acc*); **~ charge** (*Telec*) Anschlussgebühr *f* **(b)** (*fig*: = *link*) Zusammenhang *m*; **in ~ with** in Zusammenhang mit **(c)** (= *relationship, business ~*) Beziehung *f* (*with* zu); **to have ~s** Beziehungen haben **(d)** (*Rail etc*) Anschluss *m*

connector [kəˈnektəʳ] N (= *device*) Verbindungsstück *nt*; (*Elec*) Lüsterklemme *f*

connivance [kə'naɪvəns] N (= *tacit consent*) stillschweigendes Einverständnis; (= *dishonest dealing*) Schiebung *f*; **to do sth in ~ with sb** etw mit jds Wissen tun

connive [kə'naɪv] VI **(a)** (= *conspire*) sich verschwören **(b)** (= *deliberately overlook*) **to ~ at sth** etw stillschweigend dulden

connoisseur [ˌkɒnə'sɜːʳ] N Kenner *m*; **~ of wines** Weinkenner *m*

connotation [ˌkɒnəʊ'teɪʃən] N Assoziation *f*

conquer ['kɒŋkəʳ] VT **(a)** (*lit*) *country* erobern; *enemy, nation* besiegen **(b)** (*fig*) *difficulties, feelings, disease, mountain* bezwingen

conqueror ['kɒŋkərəʳ] N (*of country*) Eroberer *m*, Eroberin *f*

conquest ['kɒŋkwest] N Eroberung *f*; (*of enemy etc*) Sieg *m* (*of* über *+acc*)

conscience ['kɒnʃəns] N Gewissen *nt*; **to have a clear/easy/bad/ guilty ~** ein reines/gutes/schlechtes/böses Gewissen haben (*about* wegen); **with an easy ~** mit ruhigem Gewissen; **she/it is on my ~** ich habe ihretwegen/deswegen Gewissensbisse; **I can't in all ~ ...** ich kann unmöglich ...

conscientious [ˌkɒnʃi'enʃəs] ADJ (= *diligent*) gewissenhaft; (= *conscious of one's duty*) pflichtbewusst

conscientiously [ˌkɒnʃi'enʃəslɪ] ADV *practise* gewissenhaft; *obey* pflichtschuldigst

conscientious objector N (*Mil*) Kriegsdienstverweigerer *m* (*aus Gewissensgründen*)

conscious ['kɒnʃəs] ADJ **(a)** (*Med*) bei Bewusstsein **(b)** (= *aware, deliberate*) bewusst (*also Psych*); **to be/become ~ of sth** sich (*dat*) einer Sache (*gen*) bewusst sein/werden; **I was/ became ~ that** es war/wurde mir bewusst, dass; **environmentally ~** umweltbewusst

-conscious ADJ SUF -bewusst

consciously ['kɒnʃəslɪ] ADV bewusst

consciousness ['kɒnʃəsnɪs] N Bewusstsein *nt*; **to lose ~** das Bewusstsein verlieren

conscript [kən'skrɪpt] **1** VT einberufen; *army* ausheben **2** ['kɒnskrɪpt] N (*Brit*) Wehrpflichtige(r) *m*

conscripted [kən'skrɪptɪd] ADJ *soldier* einberufen; *troops* aus Wehrpflichtigen bestehend

conscription [kən'skrɪpʃən] N Wehrpflicht *f*; (= *act of conscripting*) Einberufung *f*; (*of army*) Aushebung *f*

consecrate ['kɒnsɪkreɪt] VT (*lit, fig*) weihen

consecration [ˌkɒnsɪ'kreɪʃən] N Weihe *f*; (*in Mass*) Wandlung *f*

consecutive [kən'sekjʊtɪv] ADJ aufeinander folgend; *numbers* fortlaufend; **on four ~ days** vier Tage hintereinander

consecutively [kən'sekjʊtɪvlɪ] ADV nacheinander; *numbered* fortlaufend

consensus [kən'sensəs] N Übereinstimmung *f*; **what's the ~?** was ist die allgemeine Meinung?; **the ~ is that ...** man ist allgemein der Meinung, dass ...; **there's a ~ (of opinion) in favour of ...** die allgemeine Mehrheit ist für ...; **there was no ~ (among them)** sie waren sich nicht einig

consent [kən'sent] **1** VI zustimmen (*to* +*dat*); **to ~ to do sth** sich bereit erklären, etw zu tun; **to ~ to sb doing sth** damit einverstanden sein, dass jd etw tut **2** N Zustimmung *f* (*to* zu); **he is by common** *or* **general ~ ...** man hält ihn allgemein für ...

consent form N (*Med*) Einverständniserklärung *f*

consequence ['kɒnsɪkwəns] N **(a)** (= *result, effect*) Folge *f*; **in ~** folglich; **in ~ of** infolge (*+gen*); **as a ~ of ...** als Folge (*+gen*); **with the ~ that he ...** was zur Folge hatte, dass er ...; **to face** *or* **take the ~s** die Folgen tragen **(b)** (= *importance*) Wichtigkeit *f*; **it's of no ~** das spielt keine Rolle

consequent ['kɒnsɪkwənt] ADJ ATTR daraus folgend

consequently ['kɒnsɪkwəntlɪ] ADV folglich

conservation [ˌkɒnsə'veɪʃən] N Erhaltung *f*; **~ law** Umweltschutzgesetz *nt*

conservation area N Naturschutzgebiet *nt*; (*in town*) unter Denkmalschutz stehendes Gebiet

conservationist [ˌkɒnsə'veɪʃənɪst] N Umweltschützer(in) *m(f)*; (*as regards old buildings etc*) Denkmalpfleger(in) *m(f)*

conservatism [kən'sɜːvətɪzəm] N Konservatismus *m*

conservative [kən'sɜːvətɪv] **1** ADJ (*also Pol*) konservativ; (= *cautious*) vorsichtig; **at a ~ estimate** bei vorsichtiger Schätzung; **the Conservative Party** (*Brit*) die Konservative Partei **2** N (*Pol: also* **Conservative**) Konservative(r) *mf*

conservatively [kən'sɜːvətɪvlɪ] ADV konservativ; *estimate, invest* vorsichtig

conservatory [kən'sɜːvətrɪ] N Wintergarten *m*

conserve [kən'sɜːv] VT erhalten; *one's strength* schonen; *energy* sparen

consider [kən'sɪdəʳ] VT **(a)** *plan, idea, offer* nachdenken über (*+acc*); *possibilities* sich (*dat*) überlegen **(b)** (= *have in mind*) in Erwägung ziehen; **I'm ~ing going abroad** ich spiele mit dem Gedanken, ins Ausland zu gehen **(c)** (= *entertain*) in Betracht ziehen; **I won't even ~ it!** ich denke nicht daran!; **I'm sure he would never ~ doing anything criminal** ich bin überzeugt, es käme ihm nie in den Sinn, etwas Kriminelles zu tun **(d)** (= *think of, take into account*) denken an (*+acc*); *cost, difficulties, facts* bedenken, berücksichtigen; *person, feelings also* Rücksicht nehmen auf (*+acc*); **when one ~s that ...** wenn man bedenkt, dass ...; **all things ~ed** alles in allem; **~ my position** überlegen Sie sich meine Lage; **~ this case, for example** nehmen Sie zum Beispiel diesen Fall; **have you ~ed going by train?** haben Sie daran gedacht, mit dem Zug zu fahren? **(e)** (= *regard as*) betrachten als; *person* halten für; **to ~ sb to be** *or* **as ...** jdn für ... halten; **to ~ oneself lucky/honoured** sich glücklich schätzen/geehrt fühlen; **~ it (as) done!** schon so gut wie geschehen! **(f)** (= *look at*) (eingehend) betrachten

considerable [kən'sɪdərəbl] ADJ beträchtlich, erheblich; *interest, income* groß; (*used admiringly*) *number, achievement etc* beachtlich; **to a ~ extent** *or* **degree** weitgehend; **for a** *or* **some ~ time** für eine ganze Zeit

considerably [kən'sɪdərəblɪ] ADV (*in comparisons*) *older, better* beträchtlich; (= *very*) *upset, impressed* höchst

considerate [kən'sɪdərɪt] ADJ rücksichtsvoll (*to(wards)* gegenüber); (= *kind*) aufmerksam

considerately [kən'sɪdərɪtlɪ] ADV rücksichtsvoll

consideration [kənˌsɪdə'reɪʃən] N **(a)** NO PL (= *careful thought*) Überlegung *f*; **I'll give it my ~** ich werde es mir überlegen **(b)** NO PL (= *regard, account*) **to take sth into ~** etw berücksichtigen; **taking everything into ~** alles in allem; **the matter is under ~** die Sache wird zurzeit geprüft (*form*); **in ~ of** (= *in view of*) mit Rücksicht auf (*+acc*) **(c)** NO PL (= *thoughtfulness*) Rücksicht *f* (*for* auf +*acc*); **to show** *or* **have ~ for sb/sb's feelings** Rücksicht auf jdn/jds Gefühle nehmen; **his lack of ~ (for others)** seine Rücksichtslosigkeit (anderen gegenüber) **(d)** (= *sth taken into account*) Faktor *m*; **money is not a ~/his first ~** Geld spielt keine Rolle/bei ihm die größte Rolle

considered [kən'sɪdəd] ADJ *opinion* ernsthaft

considering [kən'sɪdərɪŋ] **1** PREP für (*+acc*), wenn man ... (*acc*) bedenkt **2** CONJ wenn man bedenkt **3** ADV eigentlich; **it's not too bad ~** es ist eigentlich gar nicht so schlecht

consign [kən'saɪn] VT **(a)** (*Comm*) (= *send*) versenden; (= *address*) adressieren (*to* an +*acc*); **the goods are ~ed to ...** die Waren sind für ... bestimmt **(b)** (= *commit*) übergeben (*to* +*dat*); **it was ~ed to the rubbish heap** es landete auf dem Abfallhaufen

consignment [kən'saɪnmənt] N (*Comm*) (= *goods*) Sendung *f*; (*bigger*) Ladung *f*

consignment note N (*Comm*) Frachtbrief *m*

consist [kən'sɪst] VI **(a)** (= *be composed*) **to ~ of** bestehen aus **(b)** (= *have as its essence*) **his happiness ~s in helping others** sein Glück besteht darin, anderen zu helfen

consistency [kən'sɪstənsɪ] N **(a)** NO PL Konsequenz *f*; (*of statements*) Übereinstimmung *f*; (*of argument*) Logik *f*; **his statements lack ~** seine Aussagen widersprechen sich **(b)** NO PL (= *uniformity*) (*of quality*) Beständigkeit *f*; (*of performance*) Stetigkeit *f*; (*of style*) Einheitlichkeit *f* **(c)** (*of substance*) Konsistenz *f*

consistent [kən'sɪstənt] ADJ **(a)** konsequent; *statements* übereinstimmend; (= *logical*) logisch **(b)** (= *uniform*) *quality* beständig; *performance, results* stetig; *style* einheitlich **(c)** (= *in agreement*) **to be ~ with sth** einer Sache (*dat*) entsprechen; **what you're saying now is not ~ with what you said before** was Sie jetzt sagen, widerspricht dem, was Sie davor gesagt haben

consistently [kən'sɪstəntlɪ] ADV **(a)** *argue, behave* konsequent; (= *constantly*) *fail* ständig; *oppose, reject* hartnäckig **(b)** (= *uniformly*) einheitlich

consolation [ˌkɒnsə'leɪʃən] N Trost *m no pl*; **it is some ~ to know that ...** es ist tröstlich zu wissen, dass ...; **old age has its ~s** das Alter hat auch seine guten Seiten

consolation prize N Trostpreis *m*

console[1] [kən'səʊl] VT trösten

console[2] ['kɒnsəʊl] N (= *control panel*) (Kontroll)pult *nt*

consolidate [kən'sɒlɪdeɪt] VT **(a)** (= *confirm*) festigen **(b)** (= *combine*) zusammenlegen; *companies* zusammenschließen; **~d shipment** (*US*) Sammelverkehr *m*

consolidation [kənˌsɒlɪ'deɪʃən] N **(a)** (= *strengthening*) Festigung *f* **(b)** (*US: in transport*) Sammelverkehr *m*

consommé [kɒn'sɒmeɪ] N Kraftbrühe *f*

consonant ['kɒnsənənt] N (*Phon*) Konsonant *m*, Mitlaut *m*

consort [kən'sɔːt] VI (*form*: = *associate*) verkehren (*with* mit)

consortium [kən'sɔːtɪəm] N Konsortium *nt*

conspicuous [kən'spɪkjʊəs] ADJ *person, clothes, behaviour* auffällig; *road signs* deutlich sichtbar; *lack of sympathy etc* offensichtlich; **to be/make oneself ~** auffallen; **he was ~ by his absence** er glänzte durch Abwesenheit

conspicuously [kən'spɪkjʊəslɪ] ADV (= *prominently*) gut sichtbar; *silent, uneasy* auffällig; *successful* bemerkenswert

conspiracy [kən'spɪrəsɪ] N Verschwörung *f*; (*Jur*) (strafbare) Verabredung; **a ~ of silence** ein verabredetes Schweigen

conspirator [kən'spɪrətəʳ] N Verschwörer(in) *m(f)*

conspiratorial [kənˌspɪrə'tɔːrɪəl] ADJ verschwörerisch

conspire [kən'spaɪəʳ] VI (*people*) sich verschwören (*against* gegen); **to ~ (together) to do sth** sich verabreden, etw zu tun

constable ['kʌnstəbl] N (*Brit*: = *police ~*) Polizist(in) *m(f)*; (*in address*) Herr Wachtmeister, Frau Wachtmeisterin

constabulary [kən'stæbjʊlərɪ] N (*Brit*) Polizei *f no pl*

constant ['kɒnstənt] **1** ADJ **(a)** *interruptions, noise* ständig **(b)** *temperature* konstant; **x remains ~ while y ...** x bleibt konstant, während y ... **(c)** *affection, devotion* beständig **2** N (*Math, Phys, fig*) Konstante *f*

constantly ['kɒnstəntlɪ] ADV (an)dauernd

constellation [ˌkɒnstə'leɪʃən] N Sternbild *nt*, Konstellation *f* (*also fig*)

consternation [ˌkɒnstə'neɪʃən] N (= *dismay*) Bestürzung *f*; (= *concern, worry*) Sorge *f*; (= *fear and confusion*) Aufruhr *m*; **in ~** bestürzt; **to cause ~** Grund zur Sorge geben; (*news*) Bestürzung auslösen

constipated ['kɒnstɪpeɪtɪd] ADJ *bowels* verstopft; **he is ~** er hat Verstopfung

constipation [ˌkɒnstɪ'peɪʃən] N, NO PL Verstopfung *f*

constituency [kən'stɪtjʊənsɪ] N (*Pol*) Wahlkreis *m*

constituent [kən'stɪtjʊənt] **1** ADJ **~ part** *or* **element** Bestandteil *m* **2** N **(a)** (*Pol*) Wähler(in) *m(f)* **(b)** (= *part*) Bestandteil *m*

constitute ['kɒnstɪtjuːt] VT **(a)** (= *make up*) bilden **(b)** (= *amount to*) darstellen; **that ~s a lie** das ist eine glatte Lüge

constitution [ˌkɒnstɪ'tjuːʃən] N **(a)** (*Pol*) Verfassung *f*; (*of club etc*) Satzung *f* **(b)** (*of person*) Konstitution *f*; **to have a strong ~** eine starke Konstitution haben

constitutional [ˌkɒnstɪ'tjuːʃənl] ADJ (*Pol*) Verfassungs-; *monarchy, monarch* konstitutionell

constrain [kən'streɪn] VT zwingen

constrained [kən'streɪnd] ADJ gezwungen; **to feel ~ by sth** sich durch etw eingeengt sehen; **to be/feel ~ to do sth** gezwungen sein/sich gezwungen sehen, etw zu tun

constraint [kən'streɪnt] N **(a)** (= *compulsion*) Zwang *m* **(b)** (= *restriction*) Beschränkung *f*

constrict [kən'strɪkt] VT **(a)** (= *compress*) einzwängen; *vein* verengen **(b)** (= *hamper*) *movements* behindern, einschränken (*also fig*); *breathing* behindern; (*rules, traditions etc*) einengen; *outlook etc* beschränken

constriction [kən'strɪkʃən] N (*of movements*) Behinderung *f*; (*caused by rules, traditions etc*) Einengung *f*

construct [kən'strʌkt] VT *bauen*; *sentence* bilden; *novel etc* aufbauen; *theory* entwickeln

construction [kən'strʌkʃən] N **(a)** (*of building, road*) Bau *m*; **under ~** in *or* im Bau **(b)** (= *way sth is constructed*) Struktur *f*; (*of building*) Bauweise *f*; (*of machine, bridge, also Gram*) Konstruktion *f*; **sentence ~** Satzbau *m* **(c)** (= *sth constructed*) Bau *m*; (= *bridge, machine, also Gram*) Konstruktion *f*

construction: **construction industry** N Bauindustrie *f*; **construction site** N Baustelle *f*; **construction worker** N Bauarbeiter(in) *m(f)*

constructive ADJ, **constructively** ADV [kən'strʌktɪv, -lɪ] konstruktiv

construe [kən'struː] VT auslegen

consul ['kɒnsəl] N Konsul *m*

consular ['kɒnsjʊləʳ] ADJ konsularisch; **~ invoice** Konsulatsfaktura *f*

consulate ['kɒnsjʊlɪt] N Konsulat *nt*

consult [kən'sʌlt] **1** VT (= *ask*) konsultieren; *dictionary* nachschlagen in (+*dat*); *map* nachsehen auf (+*dat*); **he did it without ~ing anyone** er hat das getan, ohne jemanden zu fragen **2** VI (= *confer*) sich beraten

consultancy [kən'sʌltənsɪ] N (= *business*) Beratungsbüro *nt*

consultant [kən'sʌltənt] **1** N (*Brit Med*) Facharzt *m*/-ärztin *f* (*am Krankenhaus*); (*other professions*) Berater(in) *m(f)* **2** ADJ ATTR beratend

consultation [ˌkɒnsəl'teɪʃən] N (= *meeting*) Beratung *f*, Besprechung *f*; (*of doctor, lawyer*) Konsultation *f* (*of* +*gen*); **in ~ with** in gemeinsamer Beratung mit; **~ committee** (*in company*) beratender Ausschuss

consultative [kən'sʌltətɪv] ADJ *document* beratend

consulting [kən'sʌltɪŋ] ADJ *engineer, psychiatrist* beratend

consulting: **consulting hours** PL (*Med*) Sprechstunde *f*; **consulting room** N (*Med*) Sprechzimmer *nt*

consumable [kən'sjuːməbl] N Konsumgut *nt*; **~s** (*Comput*) Verbrauchsmaterial *nt*

consume [kən'sjuːm] VT **(a)** *food, drink* zu sich nehmen; (*Econ*) konsumieren **(b)** (= *destroy: fire*) vernichten; *fuel* verbrauchen; *energy* aufbrauchen

consumer [kən'sjuːməʳ] N Verbraucher(in) *m(f)*

consumer IN CPDS Verbraucher-; **consumer acceptance** N Akzeptanz *f* beim Verbraucher; **consumer behaviour** (*Brit*), **consumer behavior** (*US*) N Verbraucherverhalten *nt*; **consumer borrowing** N Kreditaufnahme *f* durch Verbraucher; **consumer co-operative** N Verbraucher-genossenschaft *f*; **consumer demand** N Nachfrage *f*; **consumer goods** PL Konsumgüter *pl*; **consumer group** N Verbrauchergruppe *f*

consumerism [kən'sjuːmərɪzəm] N Konsumdenken *nt*

consumer: **consumer profile** N Verbraucherprofil *nt*; **consumer protection** N Verbraucherschutz *m*; **consumer research** N Verbraucherbefragung *f*; **consumer society** N Konsumgesellschaft *f*; **consumer spending** N Verbraucherausgaben *pl*

consuming [kən'sjuːmɪŋ] ADJ *ambition, interest* glühend

consummate [kən'sʌmɪt] **1** ADJ *skill* vollendet; *politician* unübertrefflich; **with ~ ease** mit spielender Leichtigkeit **2** ['kɒnsəmeɪt] VT *marriage* vollziehen

consumption [kən'sʌmpʃən] N (*Econ*) Konsum *m*; (*of non-edible products*) Verbrauch *m*; **not fit for human ~** zum Verzehr ungeeignet; **world ~ of oil** Weltölverbrauch *m*

contact ['kɒntækt] **1** N **(a)** Kontakt *m*; (= *touching also*) Berührung *f*; **to be in ~ with sb/sth** (= *be touching*) jdn/etw berühren; (= *in communication*) mit jdm/etw in Kontakt stehen; **to keep in ~ with sb** mit jdm in Kontakt bleiben; **to come into ~ with sb/sth** (*lit, fig*) mit jdm/etw in Berührung kommen; **he has no ~ with his family** er hat keinen Kontakt zu seiner Familie; **I'll get in ~** ich werde von mir hören lassen; **how can we get in(to) ~ with him?** wie können wir ihn erreichen?; **to make ~** (= *two things*) sich berühren; (*wires, wheels etc*) in Kontakt (miteinander) kommen; (*two people*) (= *get in touch*) sich miteinander in Verbindung setzen; (*by radio etc*) eine Verbindung herstellen; **I finally made ~ with him at his office** ich habe ihn schließlich im Büro erreicht; **to lose ~ (with sb/sth)** den Kontakt (zu jdm/etw) verlieren **(b)** (*Elec*) (= *act*) Kontakt *m*; (= *equipment*) Kontakt- *or* Schaltstück *nt* **(c)** (= *person*) Kontaktperson *f*; **~s** *pl* Kontakte *pl*, Verbindungen *pl*; **to make ~s** Kontakte herstellen **2** VT *person, lawyer* sich in Verbindung setzen mit; *police* sich wenden an (+*acc*); **I've been trying to ~ you for hours** ich versuche schon seit Stunden, Sie zu erreichen

contact lens N Kontaktlinse *f*

contagious [kən'teɪdʒəs] ADJ (*Med, fig*) ansteckend

contain [kən'teɪn] VT **(a)** (= *hold within itself*) enthalten **(b)** (*box, bottle, room*) fassen **(c)** (= *control*) emotions, oneself beherrschen; *tears* zurückhalten; *laughter* unterdrücken; *disease, inflation* in Grenzen halten; *epidemic, flood* aufhalten; **he could hardly ~ himself** er konnte kaum an sich (*acc*) halten

container [kən'teɪnəʳ] **1** N **(a)** Behälter *m* **(b)** (*Comm: for transport*) Container *m* **2** ADJ ATTR Container-; **by ~ lorry** per Container; **~ bill of lading** (*Comm*) kombiniertes Konnossement; **~ ship** Containerschiff *nt*

contaminate [kən'tæmɪneɪt] VT verschmutzen; (= *poison*) vergiften; (*radioactivity*) verseuchen

contamination [kən,tæmɪ'neɪʃən] N, NO PL Verschmutzung *f*; (*by poison*) Vergiftung *f*; (*by radioactivity*) Verseuchung *f*

contd ABBR *of* **continued** Forts., Fortsetzung *f*

contemplate ['kɒntempleɪt] VT **(a)** (= *look at*) betrachten **(b)** (= *reflect upon*) nachdenken über (+*acc*); (= *consider*) action, accepting an offer in Erwägung ziehen; **he ~d the future with some misgivings** er sah der Zukunft mit einem unguten Gefühl entgegen; **he would never ~ violence** der Gedanke an Gewalttätigkeit würde ihm nie kommen **(c)** (= *intend*) **to ~ doing sth** daran denken, etw zu tun

contemplation [,kɒntem'pleɪʃən] N, NO PL (= *act of thinking*) Nachdenken *nt* (*of* über +*acc*); (= *deep thought*) Besinnung *f*

contemporary [kən'tempərərɪ] **1** ADJ **(a)** (= *of the same time*) *events* gleichzeitig; *records, literature* zeitgenössisch; *manuscript* gleich alt **(b)** (= *of the present time*) *life* heutig; *art, design* zeitgenössisch **2** N Altersgenosse *m*/-genossin *f*; (*in history*) Zeitgenosse *m*/-genossin *f*; (*at university*) Kommilitone *m*, Kommilitonin *f*

contempt [kən'tempt] N **(a)** Verachtung *f*; **to hold in ~** verachten; **to bring into ~** in Verruf bringen; **beneath ~** unter aller Kritik **(b)** (*Jur*) **to be in ~ (of court)** das Gericht *or* die Würde des Gerichts missachten

contemptible [kən'temptəbl] ADJ verachtenswert

contemptuous [kən'temptjʊəs] ADJ verächtlich; *person* herablassend

contend [kən'tend] **1** VI **(a)** (= *compete*) kämpfen; **then you'll have me to ~ with** dann bekommst du es mit mir zu tun **(b)** (= *cope*) **to ~ with sb/sth** mit jdm/etw fertig werden **2** VT behaupten

contender [kən'tendəʳ] N Kandidat(in) *m(f)*; (*Sport*) Wettkämpfer(in) *m(f)* (*for* um)

content¹ [kən'tent] **1** ADJ PRED zufrieden; **to be/feel ~** zufrieden sein; **she's quite ~ to stay at home** sie bleibt ganz gern zu Hause **2** VT **to ~ oneself with** sich zufrieden geben mit; **to ~ oneself with doing sth** sich damit zufrieden geben, etw zu tun

content² ['kɒntent] N **(a)** **contents** PL (*of room, book etc*) Inhalt *m*; **(table of) ~s** Inhaltsverzeichnis *nt* **(b)** NO PL (= *component*) Gehalt *m*; (*of book etc also*) Inhalt *m*

contented ADJ, **contentedly** ADV [kən'tentɪd, -lɪ] zufrieden

contention [kən'tenʃən] N **(a)** (= *dispute*) **that is no longer in ~** das steht nicht mehr zur Debatte **(b)** (= *argument*) Behauptung *f*; **it is my ~ that ...** ich behaupte, dass ... **(c)** (*in contest*) **to be in ~ (for sth)** Chancen (auf etw (*acc*)) haben

contentious [kən'tenʃəs] ADJ umstritten

contentment [kən'tentmənt] N Zufriedenheit *f*

content provider ['kɒntent-] N (*Comput*) Content Provider *m*

contest ['kɒntest] **1** N (*for* um) Kampf *m*; (= *competition also*) Wettkampf *m*; (= *beauty ~ etc*) Wettbewerb *m*; **it's no ~** das ist ein ungleicher Kampf **2** [kən'test] VT **(a)** (= *fight over*) kämpfen um; (*Parl*) *election* teilnehmen an (+*dat*) **(b)** (= *dispute*) bestreiten; (*Jur*) *will, right* anfechten

contestant [kən'testənt] N (Wettbewerbs)teilnehmer(in) *m(f)*; (*in quiz*) Kandidat(in) *m(f)*; (*Sport*) (Wettkampf)teilnehmer(in) *m(f)*

context ['kɒntekst] N Zusammenhang *m*; **(taken) out of ~** aus dem Zusammenhang gerissen; **in an office ~** in einem Büro

continent ['kɒntɪnənt] N (*Geog*) Kontinent *m*, Erdteil *m*; (= *mainland*) Festland *nt*; **the Continent (of Europe)** (*Brit*)

Kontinentaleuropa *nt*; **on the Continent** in Europa, auf dem Kontinent

continental [,kɒntɪ'nentl] **1** ADJ **(a)** (*Geog*) kontinental **(b)** (*Brit:* = *European*) europäisch; *holidays* in Europa **2** N (Festlands)europäer(in) *m(f)*

continental: **continental breakfast** N kleines Frühstück; **continental quilt** N Steppdecke *f*

contingency [kən'tɪndʒənsɪ] N Eventualität *f*; **to provide for all contingencies** alle Eventualitäten berücksichtigen; **a ~ plan** ein Ausweichplan *m*

contingency fee N (*US Jur*) Erfolgshonorar *nt*

contingent [kən'tɪndʒənt] N Kontingent *nt*; (= *section*) Gruppe *f*; (*Mil*) Trupp *m*

continual [kən'tɪnjʊəl] ADJ (= *frequent*) ständig; (= *unceasing*) ununterbrochen

continually [kən'tɪnjʊəlɪ] ADV (= *repeatedly*) ständig; (= *ceaselessly*) ununterbrochen

continuation [kən,tɪnjʊ'eɪʃən] N **(a)** Fortsetzung *f* **(b)** (= *resumption*) Wiederaufnahme *f*

continue [kən'tɪnjuː] **1** VT fortsetzen; (= *carry on*) fortfahren mit; **to ~ doing** *or* **to do sth** etw weiter tun; **to ~ to read, to ~ reading** weiterlesen; **to be ~d** Fortsetzung folgt; **~d on p 10** weiter *or* Fortsetzung auf Seite 10 **2** VI (= *go on*) (*person*) weitermachen; (*crisis*) (an)dauern; (*weather*) anhalten; (*road, forest, concert etc*) weitergehen; **to ~ on one's way** weiterfahren; (*on foot*) weitergehen; **he ~d after a short pause** er redete/schrieb/las *etc* nach einer kurzen Pause weiter; **to ~ with one's work** mit seiner Arbeit weitermachen; **please ~** bitte machen Sie weiter; (*in talking*) fahren Sie fort; **he ~s to be optimistic** er ist nach wie vor optimistisch; **to ~ at university/with a company/as sb's secretary** auf der Universität/bei einer Firma/jds Sekretärin bleiben

continuity [kɒntɪ'njuːɪtɪ] N **(a)** Kontinuität *f*; **the story lacks ~** der Geschichte fehlt der rote Faden **(b)** (*Film*) Anschluss *m*

continuous [kən'tɪnjʊəs] ADJ dauernd; *line* durchgezogen; *rise, movement etc* stetig; **to be in ~ use** ständig in Benutzung sein; **~ assessment** Beurteilung *f* der Leistungen während des ganzen Jahres; **~ paper** (*Comput*) Endlospapier *nt*; (*pre-printed*) Endlosformular *nt*; **~ stocktaking** (*Comm*) permanente Inventur; **~ tense** (*Gram*) Verlaufsform *f*

continuously [kən'tɪnjʊəslɪ] ADV (= *repeatedly*) dauernd; (= *ceaselessly*) ununterbrochen; *rise, move* stetig

contort [kən'tɔːt] VT *one's features, metal* verziehen (*into* zu); *limbs* verrenken; **a face ~ed with pain** ein schmerzverzerrtes Gesicht

contortion [kən'tɔːʃən] N (*esp of acrobat*) Verrenkung *f*; (*of features*) Verzerrung *f*

contortionist [kən'tɔːʃənɪst] N Schlangenmensch *m*

contour ['kɒntʊəʳ] N **(a)** (= *outline*) Kontur *f* **(b)** **contours** PL (= *shape*) Konturen *pl* **(c)** (*Geog*) Höhenlinie *f*

contour (*Geog*): **contour line** N Höhenlinie *f*; **contour map** N Höhenlinienkarte *f*

contra- ['kɒntrə-] PREF Gegen-, Kontra-

contraband ['kɒntrəbænd] N, NO PL Schmuggelware *f*

contraception [,kɒntrə'sepʃən] N Empfängnisverhütung *f*

contraceptive [,kɒntrə'septɪv] **1** N empfängnisverhütendes Mittel **2** ADJ empfängnisverhütend; *pill* Antibaby-

contract¹ ['kɒntrækt] **1** N **(a)** (= *agreement*) Vertrag *m*; (*Comm:* = *order*) Auftrag *m*; **to enter into** *or* **make a ~** einen Vertrag eingehen; **to be under ~** unter Vertrag stehen (*to* bei, mit) **(b)** (*Bridge*) Kontrakt *m* **2** ADJ *price, date* vertraglich vereinbart; **~ work** Auftragsarbeit *f* **3** [kən'trækt] VT **(a)** *debts* machen; *illness* erkranken an (+*dat*) **(b)** *marriage, alliance* eingehen **4** [kən'trækt] VI (*Comm*) **to ~ to do sth** sich vertraglich verpflichten, etw zu tun

▶ **contract out 1** VI (= *not join*) sich nicht anschließen (*of* +*dat*); (*of insurance scheme*) nicht beitreten (*of* +*dat*) **2** VT SEP (*Comm*) *work* außer Haus machen lassen (*to* von)

contract² [kən'trækt] VI (*muscle, metal etc*) sich zusammenziehen; (*fig: influence, business*) (zusammen)schrumpfen

contract bridge ['kɒntrækt-] N Kontrakt-Bridge *nt*

contraction [kənˈtrækʃən] N **(a)** (of metal, muscles) Zusammenziehen nt **(b)** (in childbirth) ~**s** Wehen pl

contract law [ˈkɒntrækt-] N, NO PL Vertragsrecht nt

contractor [kənˈtræktəʳ] N (= individual) Auftragnehmer m; (= building ~) Bauunternehmer m; (= company) Bauunternehmen nt; **that is done by outside ~s** damit ist eine andere Firma beauftragt

contractual [kənˈtræktʃʊəl] ADJ vertraglich

contradict [ˌkɒntrəˈdɪkt] VT (person) widersprechen (+dat); **to ~ oneself** sich (dat) widersprechen

contradiction [ˌkɒntrəˈdɪkʃən] N Widerspruch m (of zu); **full of ~s** voller Widersprüchlichkeiten

contradictory [ˌkɒntrəˈdɪktərɪ] ADJ widersprüchlich

contraflow [ˈkɒntrəfləʊ] N (Mot) Gegenverkehr m

contralto [kənˈtræltəʊ] **1** N (= voice) Alt m; (= singer also) Altist(in) m(f) **2** ADJ voice Alt-; **the ~ part** der Alt

contraption [kənˈtræpʃən] N (inf) Apparat m (inf); (= vehicle also) Kiste f (inf)

contrary [ˈkɒntrərɪ] **1** ADJ (= opposite) entgegengesetzt; (= conflicting) gegensätzlich; **sth is ~ to sth** etw steht im Gegensatz zu etw; **it is ~ to our agreement** es entspricht nicht unseren Abmachungen; **to run ~ to sth** einer Sache (dat) zuwiderlaufen; **~ to what I expected** entgegen meinen Erwartungen **2** N Gegenteil nt; **on the ~** im Gegenteil; **unless you hear to the ~** sofern Sie nichts Gegenteiliges hören; **quite the ~** ganz im Gegenteil

contrast [ˈkɒntrɑːst] **1** N Gegensatz m (with, to zu); (visual, = striking difference, also TV) Kontrast m (with, to zu); **by or in ~** im Gegensatz dazu; **to be in ~ with or to sth** im Gegensatz/ in Kontrast zu etw stehen; **the ~ between the state of the £ now and last year** der Unterschied zwischen dem jetzigen Stand des Pfundes und seinem Wert im letzten Jahr; **and now, by way of ~** und nun etwas ganz anderes **2** [kənˈtrɑːst] VT gegenüberstellen (with +dat) **3** [kənˈtrɑːst] VI im Gegensatz or in Kontrast stehen (with zu); **to ~ unfavourably with sth** bei einem Vergleich mit etw schlecht abschneiden

contrasting [kənˈtrɑːstɪŋ] ADJ opinions etc gegensätzlich; colours kontrastierend

contravene [ˌkɒntrəˈviːn] VT law, custom etc verstoßen gegen

contravention [ˌkɒntrəˈvenʃən] N Verstoß m (of gegen); **to be in ~ of …** gegen … verstoßen

contribute [kənˈtrɪbjuːt] **1** VT beitragen (to zu); money, supplies beisteuern (to zu); (to charity) spenden (to für); press article also, information liefern (to für) **2** VI beitragen (to zu); (to pension fund, newspaper, society etc) einen Beitrag leisten (to zu); (to present) beisteuern (to zu); (to charity) spenden (to für); (regularly: to a magazine etc) mitwirken (to an +dat)

contribution [ˌkɒntrɪˈbjuːʃən] N Beitrag m (to zu); **to make a ~ to sth** einen Beitrag zu etw leisten

contributor [kənˈtrɪbjʊtəʳ] N (to magazine etc) Mitarbeiter(in) m(f) (to an +dat); (of goods, money) Spender(in) m(f)

contributory [kənˈtrɪbjʊtərɪ] ADJ **(a)** it's certainly a ~ factor/ cause es ist sicherlich ein Faktor, der mit eine Rolle spielt **(b)** pension scheme beitragspflichtig

con trick N (inf) Schwindel m

contrite [kənˈtraɪt] ADJ reuig

contrivance [kənˈtraɪvəns] N **(a)** (= device) Vorrichtung f; (mechanical) Apparat m **(b)** (= scheme) List f

contrive [kənˈtraɪv] VT **(a)** (= devise) entwickeln; (= make) fabrizieren; **to ~ a means of doing sth** einen Weg finden, etw zu tun **(b)** (= manage, arrange) bewerkstelligen; **to ~ to do sth** es fertig bringen (also iro), etw zu tun

contrived [kənˈtraɪvd] ADJ gestellt; style also gekünstelt

control [kənˈtrəʊl] **1** N **(a)** NO PL (= management, supervision) Aufsicht f (of über +acc); (of money) Verwaltung f (of +gen); (of situation, emotion) Beherrschung f (of +gen); (= self-~) (Selbst)beherrschung f; (over territory) Gewalt f (over über +acc); (of prices, disease, also = check) Kontrolle f (of +gen); (of traffic) Regelung f (of +gen); **his ~ of the ball** seine Ballführung; **to be in ~ of sth**, **to have ~ of sth** business, office etw leiten; money etw verwalten; **to be in ~ of sth**, **to have sth under ~** etw in der Hand haben; car, inflation, disease, pollution etw unter Kontrolle haben; **to have no ~ over sb/sth** keinen Einfluss auf jdn/etw haben; over money keine

Kontrolle über etw (acc) haben; **to lose ~ (of sth)** (etw) nicht mehr in der Hand haben; of business, car die Kontrolle (über etw acc) verlieren; **to lose ~ of oneself** die Beherrschung verlieren; **to be/get out of ~** (child, class) außer Rand und Band sein/geraten; (situation, car) außer Kontrolle sein/ geraten; (prices, disease, pollution) sich jeglicher Kontrolle (dat) entziehen; **to be under ~** unter Kontrolle sein; (children, class) sich benehmen; (car) (wieder) lenkbar sein; **everything or the situation is under ~** wir/sie etc haben die Sache im Griff (inf); **circumstances beyond our ~** nicht in unserer Hand liegende Umstände; **price ~s** Preiskontrolle f **(b)** (= knob, switch) Regler m; (of vehicle, machine) Schalter m; **to be at the ~s** (of airliner) am Kontrollpult sitzen; (of small plane) die Steuerung haben **2** VT kontrollieren; business leiten; organization in der Hand haben; animal, child, class fertig werden mit; car steuern; traffic regeln; emotions, movements beherrschen; temperature, speed regulieren; disease unter Kontrolle bringen; population eindämmen; **to ~ oneself/one's temper** sich beherrschen; **please try to ~ your children** bitte sehen Sie zu, dass sich Ihre Kinder benehmen

control: **control centre**, (US) **control center** N Kontrollzentrum nt; **control column** N Steuerknüppel m; **control freak** N (inf) most men are total ~s die meisten Männer müssen immer alles unter Kontrolle haben; **control key** N (Comput) Control-Taste f

controllable [kənˈtrəʊləbl] ADJ kontrollierbar

controlled [kənˈtrəʊld] ADJ **~ drugs** or **substances** verschreibungspflichtige Medikamente pl

controller [kənˈtrəʊləʳ] N **(a)** (= director: Rad) Intendant(in) m(f) **(b)** (= financial head) Leiter(in) m(f) des Rechnungswesens **(c)** (Ind) Kontroll- und Steuerungseinheit f

controlling [kənˈtrəʊlɪŋ] ADJ ATTR body Aufsichts-; **~ interest** Mehrheitsanteil m; **~ stake** (Comm) Mehrheitsbeteiligung f

control: **control panel** N Schalttafel f; (on aircraft, TV) Bedienungsfeld nt; **control room** N Kontrollraum m; (Mil) (Operations)zentrale f; (of police) Zentrale f; **control tower** N (Aviat) Kontrollturm m

controversial [ˌkɒntrəˈvɜːʃəl] ADJ kontrovers; (= debatable) decision also umstritten

controversy [ˈkɒntrəvɜːsɪ, kənˈtrɒvəsɪ] N Streit m

conundrum [kəˈnʌndrəm] N (lit, fig) Rätsel nt

conurbation [ˌkɒnɜːˈbeɪʃən] N Ballungsgebiet nt

convalesce [ˌkɒnvəˈles] VI genesen (from, after von)

convalescence [ˌkɒnvəˈlesəns] N Genesung f; (= period) Genesungszeit f

convalescent home N Genesungsheim nt

convection [kənˈvekʃən] N Konvektion f

convector [kənˈvektəʳ] N (also ~ **heater**) Heizlüfter m

convene [kənˈviːn] **1** VT meeting einberufen; group of people zusammenrufen **2** VI zusammenkommen; (parliament, court) zusammentreten

convenience [kənˈviːnɪəns] N **(a)** NO PL (= usefulness, amenity) Annehmlichkeit f; **for the sake of ~** aus praktischen Gründen; **a house with all modern ~s** ein Haus mit allem modernen Komfort **(b)** NO PL these chairs are for the ~ of customers diese Stühle sind für unsere Kunden gedacht; **at your own ~** wann es Ihnen passt (inf); **at your earliest ~** (Comm) möglichst bald

convenience foods PL Fertiggerichte pl

convenient [kənˈviːnɪənt] ADJ (= useful) praktisch; area günstig gelegen; time günstig; **if it is ~** wenn es Ihnen (so) passt; **is tomorrow ~ (for you)?** passt (es) Ihnen morgen?; **the trams are very ~** (= nearby) die Straßenbahnhaltestellen liegen sehr günstig; (= useful) die Straßenbahn ist sehr praktisch

conveniently [kənˈviːnɪəntlɪ] ADV günstigerweise; situated günstig

convent [ˈkɒnvənt] N (Frauen)kloster nt

convention [kənˈvenʃən] N **(a)** Brauch m; (= social rule) Konvention f; **~ requires** or **demands that …** der Brauch will es so, dass …; **it's a ~ that …** es ist so üblich, dass … **(b)** (= agreement) Abkommen nt **(c)** (= conference) Konferenz f; (Pol) Versammlung f

conventional [kən'venʃənl] ADJ konventionell; *beliefs, theory, manner* herkömmlich; *theatre, style* traditionell; ~ **medicine** konventionelle Medizin

conventionally [kən'venʃnəlɪ] ADV konventionell; *written, designed* traditionell

conventioneer [ˌkɒnvenʃəˈnɪəʳ] N (*esp US*) Konferenzteilnehmer(in) *m(f)*

converge [kən'vɜːdʒ] VI (*lines*) zusammenlaufen (*at* in *or* an +dat); (*Math, Phys*) konvergieren (*at* in +dat); (*fig: views etc*) sich aneinander annähern; **to ~ on sb/sth/New York** von überallher zu jdm/etw/nach New York strömen

convergence [kən'vɜːdʒəns] N (*fig: of views etc*) Annäherung *f*

conversant [kən'vɜːsənt] ADJ PRED ~ **with sth** mit etw vertraut

conversation [ˌkɒnvəˈseɪʃən] N Unterhaltung *f*; (*Sch*) Konversation *f*; **to make ~** Konversation machen; **to get into/be in ~ with sb** mit jdm ins Gespräch kommen/im Gespräch sein; **to have a ~ with sb (about sth)** sich mit jdm (über etw *acc*) unterhalten

conversational [ˌkɒnvəˈseɪʃənl] ADJ Unterhaltungs-, leger; ~ **German** gesprochenes Deutsch

conversationalist [ˌkɒnvəˈseɪʃnəlɪst] N guter Gesprächspartner, gute Gesprächspartnerin; **not much of a ~** nicht gerade ein Konversationsgenie

conversation mode N (*Comput*) Dialogbetrieb *m*

converse¹ [kən'vɜːs] VI (*form*) sich unterhalten

converse² ['kɒnvɜːs] N (= *opposite*) Gegenteil *nt*

conversely [kɒn'vɜːslɪ] ADV umgekehrt

conversion [kən'vɜːʃən] N **(a)** Konversion *f* (*into* in +acc); (*Fin, Sci also*) Umwandlung *f* (*into* in +acc); (*Rugby*) Verwandlung *f*; (*of van etc*) Umrüstung *f*; (*of building*) Umbau *m* (*into* zu); ~ **table** Umrechnungstabelle *f* **(b)** (*Rel, fig*) Bekehrung *f*

convert ['kɒnvɜːt] ◼ N (*lit, fig*) Bekehrte(r) *mf*; (*to another denomination*) Konvertit *m*; **to become a ~ to sth** (*lit, fig*) sich zu etw bekehren
◼ [kən'vɜːt] VT **(a)** (= *transform*) konvertieren (*into* in +acc); (*Fin, Sci also*) umwandeln (*into* in +acc); (*Rugby*) verwandeln; *van etc* umrüsten; *attic* ausbauen (*into* zu); *building* umbauen (*into* zu); **to ~ financial investments into cash** Finanzinvestitionen in Bargeld umwandeln
(b) (*Rel, fig*) bekehren (*to* zu); (*to another denomination*) konvertieren
◼ [kən'vɜːt] VI sich verwandeln lassen (*into* in +acc)

converted [kən'vɜːtɪd] ADJ umgebaut; *loft* ausgebaut

convertible [kən'vɜːtəbl] ◼ ADJ verwandelbar; *currency* konvertibel; ~ **debentures**, ~ **bonds** (*US*), ~ **loan stock** (*Brit*) Wandelschuldverschreibungen *pl* ◼ N (= *car*) Kabrio *nt*

convex [kɒn'veks] ADJ konvex, Konvex-

convey [kən'veɪ] VT **(a)** (= *transport*) befördern; *goods* spedieren; *water* leiten **(b)** *opinion, idea* vermitteln; *meaning* klarmachen; *message, best wishes* übermitteln; **what does this poem ~ to you?** was sagt Ihnen dieses Gedicht?

conveyance [kən'veɪəns] N (= *transport*) Beförderung *f*

conveyancing [kən'veɪənsɪŋ] N (*Jur*) (Eigentums)übertragung *f*

conveyor belt [kən'veɪəbelt] N Fließband *nt*; (*for transport, supply*) Förderband *nt*

convict ['kɒnvɪkt] ◼ N Sträfling *m* ◼ [kən'vɪkt] VT (*Jur*) *person* verurteilen (*of* wegen); **a ~ed criminal** ein verurteilter Verbrecher, eine verurteilte Verbrecherin

conviction [kən'vɪkʃən] N **(a)** (*Jur*) Verurteilung *f*; **five previous ~s** fünf Vorstrafen **(b)** (= *belief, act of convincing*) Überzeugung *f*; **his speech lacked ~** seine Rede klang wenig überzeugend; **his fundamental political ~s** seine politische Gesinnung

convince [kən'vɪns] VT überzeugen; **I'm trying to ~ him that ...** ich versuche, ihn davon zu überzeugen, dass ...

convinced [kən'vɪnst] ADJ überzeugt

convincing ADJ, **convincingly** ADV [kən'vɪnsɪŋ, -lɪ] überzeugend

convivial [kən'vɪvɪəl] ADJ heiter und unbeschwert; (= *sociable*) gesellig

convoluted [ˌkɒnvəˈluːtɪd] ADJ verwickelt; *theory also* kompliziert; *style* gewunden

convolution [ˌkɒnvəˈluːʃən] N USU PL (*of plot*) Verschlungenheit *f no pl*; (*of theory*) Kompliziertheit *f*

convoy ['kɒnvɔɪ] N (*fig*) Konvoi *m*; **in ~** im Konvoi

convulse [kən'vʌls] VT krampfhaft zusammenziehen; **to be ~d with laughter/in pain** sich vor Lachen schütteln/Schmerzen krümmen

convulsion [kən'vʌlʃən] N **(a)** (*Med*) Schüttelkrampf *m no pl* **(b)** (*caused by social upheaval etc*) Erschütterung *f*

convulsive [kən'vʌlsɪv] ADJ Krampf-; *movement also* krampfhaft

cony, coney ['kəʊnɪ] N (*US*) Kaninchen *nt*

COO N ABBR *of* **Chief operating officer** (*US Ind*) Betriebsleiter(in) *m(f)*

coo [kuː] VI (*pigeon, fig*) gurren

cook [kʊk] ◼ N Koch *m*, Köchin *f*; **she is a good ~** sie kocht gut; **too many ~s (spoil the broth)** (*Prov*) viele Köche verderben den Brei (*Prov*)
◼ VT *food* zubereiten; (*in water etc*) kochen; (= *fry, roast*) braten; *pie also* backen; **how are you going to ~ the duck?** wie willst du die Ente zubereiten?; **a ~ed meal** eine warme Mahlzeit; **a ~ed breakfast** ein Frühstück *nt* mit warmen Gerichten
◼ VI kochen; (= *fry, roast*) braten; (*pie*) backen; **the pie takes half an hour to ~** die Pastete ist in einer halben Stunde fertig
➤ **cook up** VT SEP (*fig inf*) excuse sich (*dat*) einfallen lassen

cookbook ['kʊkbʊk] N Kochbuch *nt*

cooker ['kʊkəʳ] N (*esp Brit*) Herd *m*

cookery ['kʊkərɪ] N Kochen *nt* (*also Sch*); **French ~** französische Küche

cookery book N Kochbuch *nt*

cookie, cooky ['kʊkɪ] N (*US*: = *biscuit*) Keks *m*; **that's the way the ~ crumbles** (*also Brit inf*) so ist das nun mal (im Leben); **to get caught with one's hands in the ~ jar** (*fig inf*) ertappt werden (*inf*)

cooking ['kʊkɪŋ] N Kochen *nt*; (= *food*) Essen *nt*; **French ~** französisches Essen; **his ~ is atrocious** er kocht miserabel

cooking IN CPDS Koch-; **cooking apple** N Kochapfel *m*; **cooking chocolate** N Blockschokolade *f*; **cooking salt** N Kochsalz *nt*

cookout ['kʊkaʊt] N (*US*) Kochen *nt* am Lagerfeuer; (*on barbeque*) Grillparty *f*

cool [kuːl] ◼ ADJ (+ER) **(a)** *water, weather, reception* kühl; *clothes* luftig; **serve ~** kalt *or* (*gut*) gekühlt servieren; **"keep in a ~ place"** „kühl aufbewahren"
(b) (= *calm*) besonnen; **to keep ~**, **to keep a ~ head** einen kühlen Kopf behalten; **keep ~!** reg dich nicht auf!
(c) (= *audacious*) kaltblütig; **a ~ customer** (*inf*) ein cooler Typ (*inf*)
(d) *colour* kalt; ~ **green** kaltes Grün
(e) (*inf: with numbers etc*) glatt (*inf*); **he earns a ~ thirty thousand a year** er verdient glatte dreißigtausend im Jahr (*inf*)
(f) (*inf.* = *great*) *idea, pub etc* stark (*inf*), cool (*sl*); **to act ~** sich cool geben (*sl*)
◼ N **(a)** Kühle *f*; **in the ~ of the evening** in der Abendkühle
(b) (*inf*) **keep your ~!** reg dich nicht auf!; **to lose one's ~** durchdrehen (*inf*)
◼ VT **(a)** kühlen; (= ~ *down*) abkühlen
(b) (*inf*) ~ **it!** (= *don't get excited*) reg dich ab! (*inf*); (= *don't cause trouble*) mach keinen Ärger! (*inf*)
◼ VI (*lit, fig*) abkühlen; (*enthusiasm*) nachlassen; **he has ~ed toward(s) her** er ist ihr gegenüber kühler geworden
➤ **cool down** ◼ VI **(a)** (*lit*) abkühlen; (*person*) sich abkühlen **(b)** (= *calm down*) sich beruhigen; **to let things cool down** die Sache etwas ruhen lassen ◼ VT SEP abkühlen; **to cool oneself down** sich abkühlen
➤ **cool off** VI sich abkühlen

coolant ['kuːlənt] N Kühlmittel *nt*

cool: cool bag N Kühltasche *f*; **cool box** N Kühlbox *f*; **cool-headed** ADJ kühl (und besonnen)

cooling-off period N **(a)** (*Ind*) Friedenspflicht *f*; (*in contract law*) Widerrufsfrist *f* nach Vertragsabschluss **(b)** (*in relationship etc*) Zeit *f* zur Abkühlung

coolly ['kuːlɪ] ADV **(a)** (= *calmly*) ruhig **(b)** (= *in an unfriendly way*) kühl **(c)** (= *audaciously*) kaltblütig

coolness ['kuːlnɪs] N **(a)** (*of water, weather, reception*) Kühle *f* **(b)** (= *calmness*) Besonnenheit *f* **(c)** (= *audacity*) Kaltblütigkeit *f*

coop [kuːp] N (*also* **hen ~**) Hühnerstall *m*

➤ **coop up** VT SEP *person* einsperren; *several people* zusammenpferchen *(inf)*

co-op [ˈkəʊˈɒp] N Genossenschaft *f*; (= *shop*) Coop *m*, Konsum *m*

cooperate [kəʊˈɒpəreɪt] VI kooperieren, zusammenarbeiten; (= *not be awkward*) mitmachen

cooperation [kəʊˌɒpəˈreɪʃən] N Kooperation *f*, Zusammenarbeit *f*; (= *help*) Mitarbeit *f*; **we produced this model in ~ with ...** wir haben dieses Modell in Gemeinschaftsarbeit ... produziert

cooperative [kəʊˈɒpərətɪv] **1** ADJ **(a)** (= *prepared to comply*) kooperativ; (= *prepared to help*) hilfsbereit **(b)** *firm* auf Genossenschaftsbasis; ~ **farm** Bauernhof *m* auf Genossenschaftsbasis **2** N Genossenschaft *f*; (*also* ~ **farm**) Bauernhof *m* auf Genossenschaftsbasis

cooperative bank N (*US*) Genossenschaftsbank *f*

coopt [kəʊˈɒpt] VT selbst (hinzu)wählen; **he was ~ed onto the committee** er wurde vom Komitee selbst dazugewählt

coordinate [kəʊˈɔːdɪnɪt] **1** N (*Math etc*) Koordinate *f*; ~**s** (= *clothes*) Kleidung *f* zum Kombinieren **2** [kəʊˈɔːdɪneɪt] VT koordinieren; **to ~ one thing with another** eine Sache auf eine andere abstimmen

coordinated [kəʊˈɔːdɪneɪtɪd] ADJ koordiniert

coordination [kəʊˌɔːdɪˈneɪʃən] N Koordination *f*; **in ~ with** in Abstimmung mit

coordinator [kəʊˈɔːdɪneɪtəʳ] N Koordinator(in) *m(f)*

cootie [ˈkuːtɪ] N (*US inf*) Laus *f*

cop [kɒp] **1** N **(a)** (*inf*: = *policeman*) Polizist(in) *m(f)*, Bulle *m* (*pej inf*) **(b)** (*Brit inf*) **it's not much ~** das ist nichts Besonderes **2** VT (*inf*: = *catch*) **when they found out he didn't have a licence he really ~ped it** (*Brit*) als sie herausfanden, dass er keinen Führerschein hatte, war er dran (*inf*)

➤ **cop off** VI +PREP OBJ (*Brit inf*) **to cop off with sb** jdn abschleppen (*inf*)

➤ **cop out** VI (*inf*) aussteigen (*inf*) (*of* aus)

cope [kəʊp] VI zurechtkommen; (*with work*) es schaffen; **to ~ with** fertig werden mit; **I can't ~ with all this work** ich bin mit all der Arbeit überfordert

Copenhagen [ˌkəʊpnˈheɪgən] N Kopenhagen *nt*

copier [ˈkɒpɪəʳ] N (= *machine*) Kopiergerät *nt*, Kopierer *m* (*inf*)

co-pilot [ˈkəʊpaɪlət] N Kopilot(in) *m(f)*

copious [ˈkəʊpɪəs] ADJ *supply* groß, reichlich; *information* zahlreich; ~ **amounts of sth** reichliche Mengen von etw

cop-out [ˈkɒpaʊt] N (*inf*) (= *going back on sth*) Rückzieher *m* (*inf*); (= *deliberate evasion*) Ausweichmanöver *nt*; **this solution is just a ~** diese Lösung weicht dem Problem nur aus

copper [ˈkɒpəʳ] N **(a)** (= *metal*) Kupfer *nt* **(b)** (= *colour*) Kupferrot *nt* **(c)** (*esp Brit inf*: = *coin*) ~**s** Kleingeld *nt* **(d)** (*inf*: = *policeman*) Polizist(in) *m(f)*, Bulle *m* (*pej inf*)

copper: copper beech N Rotbuche *f*; **copper-bottomed** ADJ (*Fin, fig*) gesund

coppice [ˈkɒpɪs] N Wäldchen *nt*

co-produce [ˌkəʊprəˈdjuːs] VT koproduzieren

copse [kɒps] N Wäldchen *nt*

copulate [ˈkɒpjʊleɪt] VI kopulieren

copulation [ˌkɒpjʊˈleɪʃən] N Kopulation *f*

copy [ˈkɒpɪ] **1** N **(a)** Kopie *f* (*also Comput*); (*typed carbon also*) Durchschlag *m*; (*handwritten carbon also*) Durchschrift *f*; (*Phot*) Abzug *m*; **to take** *or* **make a ~ of sth** eine Kopie/Zweitschrift *etc* von etw machen; **to write out a fair ~** etw ins Reine schreiben
(b) (*of book etc*) Exemplar *nt*; **have you got a ~ of today's "Times"?** hast du die „Times" von heute?
(c) (*Press etc*) = *subject matter*) Stoff *m*; (= *material to be printed*) Artikel *m*; (*Typ*) (Manu)skript *nt*; **this murder story will make good ~** aus diesem Mord kann man etwas machen **2** VI (= *imitate*) nachahmen; (*Sch etc*) abschreiben **3** VT **(a)** (= *make a ~ of*) kopieren (*also Comput*); (*typed/handwritten carbon*) einen Durchschlag/eine Durchschrift machen von; (*Phot*) abziehen; (= *write out again*) abschreiben; **to ~ sth to a disk** etw auf eine Diskette kopieren
(b) (= *imitate*) nachmachen
(c) (*Sch etc*) *sb else's work* abschreiben; (*by painting*) abmalen; **to ~ Brecht** (von) Brecht abschreiben

copy: copycat **1** N (*inf*) Nachahmer(in) *m(f)* **2** ADJ ATTR **his was a ~ crime** er war ein Nachahmungstäter; **copy editor** N (*Press*) Redakteur(in) *m(f)*; **copy-protected** ADJ (*Comput*) kopiergeschützt

copyright [ˈkɒpɪraɪt] **1** N Copyright *nt*, Urheberrecht *nt*; **out of ~** urheberrechtlich nicht mehr geschützt **2** ADJ urheberrechtlich geschützt **3** VT *book* urheberrechtlich schützen; (*author*) urheberrechtlich schützen lassen

copywriter [ˈkɒpɪraɪtəʳ] N Werbetexter(in) *m(f)*

cor [kɔːʳ] INTERJ (*Brit inf*) Mensch (*inf*), Mann (*sl*)

coral [ˈkɒrəl] N **(a)** Koralle *f* **(b)** (= *colour*) Korallenrot *nt*

coral IN CPDS Korallen-; **coral island** N Koralleninsel *f*; **coral reef** N Korallenriff *nt*

cord [kɔːd] **1** N **(a)** Schnur *f* (*also Elec*); (*for clothes*) Kordel *f* **(b) cords** PL (*also a pair of* ~**s**) Kordhosen *pl* **2** ATTR (*Brit*) Kord-

cordial [ˈkɔːdɪəl] **1** ADJ freundlich **2** N (= *drink*) Fruchtsaftkonzentrat *nt*

cordially [ˈkɔːdɪəlɪ] ADV freundlich

cordless [ˈkɔːdlɪs] ADJ schnurlos

cordon [ˈkɔːdn] N Kordon *m*, Postenkette *f*

➤ **cordon off** VT SEP absperren

cordon bleu [ˌkɔːdɒnˈblɜː] ADJ *cook* vorzüglich; *recipe, dish* exquisit

corduroy [ˈkɔːdərɔɪ] N Kordsamt *m*

CORE [kɔːʳ] (*US*) ABBR *of* **Congress of Racial Equality** Verband zur Bekämpfung von Rassendiskriminierung

core [kɔːʳ] **1** N (*lit, fig*) Kern *m*; (*of apple*) Kernhaus *nt*; (*of rock*) Innere(s) *nt*; **rotten to the ~** (*fig*) durch und durch schlecht; **shaken to the ~** zutiefst erschüttert **2** ADJ ATTR *issue* Kern-; (*Sch*) *subject* Haupt-; ~ **activity** (*Comm*) Haupttätigkeit *f*; ~ **benefit** Hauptvorteil *m*; ~ **business** (*Comm*) Hauptgeschäft *nt*; ~ **product** wichtigstes Erzeugnis, Hauptprodukt *nt* **3** VT *fruit* entkernen; *apple* das Kernhaus (+*gen*) entfernen

corer [ˈkɔːrəʳ] N (*Cook*) Apfelstecher *m*

co-respondent [ˈkəʊrɪsˈpɒndənt] N (*Jur*) Mitbeklagte(r) *or* Dritte(r) *mf* (*im Scheidungsprozess*)

core time N Kernzeit *f*

Corfu [kɔːˈfuː] N Korfu *nt*

corgi [ˈkɔːgɪ] N Corgi *m*

coriander [ˌkɒrɪˈændəʳ] N Koriander *m*

cork [kɔːk] **1** N **(a)** NO PL (= *substance*) Kork *m* **(b)** (= *stopper*) Korken *m* **2** VT zu- *or* verkorken **3** ADJ Kork-

corked [kɔːkt] ADJ **the wine is ~** der Wein schmeckt nach Kork

corkscrew [ˈkɔːskruː] N Korkenzieher *m*

corn¹ [kɔːn] N **(a)** NO PL (*Brit*: = *cereal*) Getreide *nt* **(b)** (= *seed of ~*) Korn *nt* **(c)** NO PL (*esp US*: = *maize*) Mais *m*

corn² N (*on foot*) Hühnerauge *nt*; ~ **plaster** Hühneraugenpflaster *nt*

corn: cornball N (*US inf*) **1** N Gefühlsdusel *m* (*inf*) **2** ADJ gefühlsduselig (*inf*); **corn bread** N (*US*) Maisbrot *nt*; **corncob** N Maiskolben *m*; **corncrib** N (*US*) Maisspeicher *m*; **corn dodger** N (*US*) Maisfladen *m*; **corn dog** N (*US Cook*) mit Maismehl paniertes Bratwürstchen

cornea [ˈkɔːnɪə] N Hornhaut *f*

corned beef [ˈkɔːndˈbiːf] N Cornedbeef *nt*

corner [ˈkɔːnəʳ] **1** N (*generally, Boxing, Ftbl*) Ecke *f*; (*of mouth, also* = *out-of-the-way place*) Winkel *m*; (= *in road*) Kurve *f*; (*fig*: = *awkward situation*) Klemme *f* (*inf*); **at** *or* **on the ~** an der Ecke; **it's just round the ~** (= *near*) es ist gleich um die Ecke; (*inf*: = *about to happen*) das steht kurz bevor; (*fig: recovery etc*) das wird bald eintreten; **to turn the ~** (*lit*) um die Ecke biegen; **we've turned the ~ now** (*fig*) wir sind jetzt über den Berg; **out of the ~ of one's eye** aus dem Augenwinkel (heraus); **to cut ~s** (*fig*) das Verfahren abkürzen; **to drive** *or* **force sb into a ~** (*fig*) jdn in die Enge treiben; **to fight one's ~** (*esp Brit fig*) für seine Sache kämpfen; **in every ~ of Europe/ the globe** in allen (Ecken und) Winkeln Europas/der Erde; **an attractive ~ of Britain** eine reizvolle Gegend Großbritanniens; **to take a ~** (*Ftbl*) eine Ecke ausführen; **have you got an odd ~ somewhere where I could store my books?** hast du irgendwo ein Eckchen, wo ich meine Bücher lagern könnte? **2** VT **(a)** (*lit, fig*) in die Enge treiben

(b) (*Comm*) *the market* monopolisieren
[3] VI (= *take a ~: person*) Kurven/die Kurve nehmen; **this car ~s well** dieses Auto hat eine gute Kurvenlage

-cornered [-'kɔːnəd] ADJ SUF -eckig; **three-cornered** dreieckig

corner: corner kick N (*Ftbl*) Eckstoß *m*; **corner seat** N (*Rail*) Eckplatz *m*; **corner shop** N Laden *m* an der Ecke; **cornerstone** N (*lit, fig*) Grundstein *m*; **corner store** N (*US*) = corner shop

cornet ['kɔːnɪt] N **(a)** (*Mus*) Kornett *nt* **(b)** (= *ice-cream ~*) (Eis)tüte *f*

corn: cornfield N (*Brit*) Kornfeld *nt*; (*US*) Maisfeld *nt*; **cornflakes** PL Cornflakes *pl*; **cornflour** N (*Brit*) Stärkemehl *nt*; **cornflower** N Kornblume *f*

cornice ['kɔːnɪs] N (*Archit*) (Ge)sims *nt*

Cornish ['kɔːnɪʃ] ADJ kornisch, aus Cornwall

Cornish pasty N (*Brit*) *Gebäckstück aus Blätterteig mit Fleischfüllung*

corn: cornmeal N (*US*) Maismehl *nt*; **corn pone** N (*US*) Maisbrot *nt*; **cornstarch** N (*US*) Stärkemehl *nt*; **corn syrup** N (*US*) (Mais)sirup *m*

cornucopia [ˌkɔːnjʊ'kəʊpɪə] N (*fig*) Fülle *f*

corn whisky N (*US*) Maiswhisky *m*

corny ['kɔːnɪ] ADJ (+ER) (*inf*) *joke* blöd (*inf*); (= *sentimental*) kitschig

corollary [kə'rɒlərɪ] N (logische) Folge

coronary ['kɒrənərɪ] **[1]** ADJ (*Med*) Koronar- (*spec*); **~ failure** Herzversagen *nt* (*inf*) **[2]** N Herzinfarkt *m*

coronation [ˌkɒrə'neɪʃən] N Krönung *f*

coroner ['kɒrənəʳ] N *Beamter, der Todesfälle untersucht, die nicht eindeutig eine natürliche Ursache haben*

coronet ['kɒrənɪt] N Krone *f*

corp. ABBR *of* corporation

corporal ['kɔːpərəl] N (*Mil*) Stabsunteroffizier(in) *m(f)*

corporal punishment N Prügelstrafe *f*

corporate ['kɔːpərɪt] ADJ **(a)** (= *of a group*) gemeinsam; **to take out ~ membership of another society** als geschlossene Gruppe Mitglied eines anderen Vereins werden
(b) (*of a corporation*) korporativ; (*of a company*) Firmen-; (*Jur*) Korporations-; **~ bond** (*US*) (Industrie)schuldverschreibung *f*; **~ finance** Unternehmensfinanzen *pl*; **~ identity** Corporate Identity *f*; **~ image** Firmenimage *nt*; **to move up the ~ ladder** in der Firma aufsteigen; **our ~ liabilities** unsere Verbindlichkeiten als Firma; **~ planning** Unternehmensplanung *f*

corporate: corporate hospitality N *Unterhaltung und Bewirtung von Firmenkunden*; **corporate identity** N Firmenimage *nt*; **corporate law** N Gesellschaftsrecht *nt*; **corporate lawyer** N (*working for corporation*) Firmenanwalt *m*/-anwältin *f*; (= *specialist in corporate law*) Anwalt *m*/Anwältin *f* für Gesellschaftsrecht; **corporate raider** N Firmenaufkäufer(in) *m(f)*

corporation [ˌkɔːpə'reɪʃən] N **(a)** (= *municipal ~*) Gemeinde *f*, Stadt *f*
(b) (*Brit Comm*: = *incorporated company*) Handelsgesellschaft *f*; (*US Comm*: = *limited liability company*) Gesellschaft *f* mit beschränkter Haftung; **joint-stock ~** (*US*) Aktiengesellschft *f*; **private ~** Privatunternehmen *nt*; **public ~** staatliches Unternehmen; **~ aggregate** (*Brit*) Gesellschaft *f* mit mehreren Mitgliedern; **~ sole** (*Brit*) Einpersonengesellschaft *f*

corporation tax N Körperschaftssteuer *f*

corps [kɔːʳ] N, *pl* - (*Mil*) Korps *nt*

corps de ballet N Corps de Ballet *nt*

corpse [kɔːps] N Leiche *f*, Leichnam *m* (*geh*)

corpulent ['kɔːpjʊlənt] ADJ korpulent

corpus ['kɔːpəs] N **(a)** (= *collection*) Korpus *m* **(b)** (= *main body*) Großteil *m*; **the main ~ of his work** der Hauptteil seiner Arbeit

Corpus Christi ['kɔːpəs'krɪstɪ] N (*Eccl*) Fronleichnam *m*

corpuscle ['kɔːpʌsl] N **blood ~** Blutkörperchen *nt*

corral [kə'rɑːl] N Korral *m*

correct [kə'rekt] **[1]** ADJ **(a)** (= *right*) richtig; *time also* genau; **to be ~** (*person*) Recht haben; **am I ~ in thinking that ...?** gehe ich recht in der Annahme, dass ...?; **~ money** *or* **change only** nur abgezähltes Geld
(b) (= *proper, suitable*) korrekt; **it's the ~ thing to do** das

gehört sich so; **she was ~ to reject the offer** es war richtig, dass sie das Angebot abgelehnt hat
[2] VT korrigieren; *bad habit* sich/jdm abgewöhnen; **to ~ proofs** Korrektur lesen; **~ me if I'm wrong** Sie können mich gern berichtigen; **I stand ~ed** ich nehme alles zurück

correcting fluid [kə'rektɪŋˌfluːɪd] N Korrekturflüssigkeit *f*

correction [kə'rekʃən] N Korrektur *f*; **to do one's ~s** (*Sch*) die Verbesserung machen

correctional [kə'rekʃənəl] ADJ (*US*) **~ officer** Justizvollzugsbeamte(r) *m*/-beamtin *f*; **the ~ system** das Justizvollzugssystem; **~ facility** Justizvollzugsanstalt *f*

corrective [kə'rektɪv] **[1]** ADJ korrigierend; **to take ~ action** korrigierend eingreifen; **to have ~ surgery** sich einem korrigierenden Eingriff unterziehen **[2]** N Korrektiv *nt*

correctly [kə'rektlɪ] ADV **(a)** (= *accurately*) richtig; **if I remember ~** wenn ich mich recht entsinne **(b)** *behave, speak, dress* korrekt

correctness [kə'rektnɪs] N **(a)** (= *accuracy*) Richtigkeit *f* **(b)** (*of behaviour etc*) Korrektheit *f*

correlate ['kɒrɪleɪt] **[1]** VT zueinander in Beziehung setzen **[2]** VI sich entsprechen; **to ~ with sth** mit etw in Beziehung stehen

correlation [ˌkɒrɪ'leɪʃən] N (= *correspondence*) Beziehung *f*; (= *close relationship*) enger *or* direkter Zusammenhang; (*Math*) Korrelation *f*

correspond [ˌkɒrɪs'pɒnd] VI **(a)** (= *be equivalent*) entsprechen (*to, with +dat*); (*to one another*) sich entsprechen; (= *be in accordance also*) sich decken (*with* mit) **(b)** (= *exchange letters*) korrespondieren (*with* mit)

correspondence [ˌkɒrɪs'pɒndəns] N **(a)** (= *equivalence*) Übereinstimmung *f* **(b)** (= *letter-writing*) Korrespondenz *f*; (*in newspaper*) Leserbriefe *pl*; **to be in ~ with sb** mit jdm korrespondieren; (*private*) mit jdm in Briefwechsel stehen

correspondence: correspondence column N (*Press*) Leserbriefspalte *f*; **correspondence course** N Fernkurs *m*

correspondent [ˌkɒrɪs'pɒndənt] N (*Press*) Korrespondent(in) *m(f)*

corresponding [ˌkɒrɪs'pɒndɪŋ] ADJ entsprechend

correspondingly [ˌkɒrɪs'pɒndɪŋlɪ] ADV (dem)entsprechend

corridor ['kɒrɪdɔːʳ] N Korridor *m*; (*in train, bus*) Gang *m*; **in the ~s of power** an den Schalthebeln der Macht

corridor train N D-Zug *m*

corroborate [kə'rɒbəreɪt] VT bestätigen

corroboration [kəˌrɒbə'reɪʃən] N Bestätigung *f*; **in ~ of** zur Unterstützung (*+gen*)

corroborative [kə'rɒbərətɪv] ADJ erhärtend *attr*

corrode [kə'rəʊd] **[1]** VT zerfressen **[2]** VI korrodieren

corroded [kə'rəʊdɪd] ADJ korrodiert

corrosion [kə'rəʊʒən] N Korrosion *f*

corrosive [kə'rəʊzɪv] ADJ korrosiv

corrugated ['kɒrəgeɪtɪd] ADJ gewellt; **~ cardboard** dicke Wellpappe

corrugated iron N Wellblech *nt*

corrupt [kə'rʌpt] **[1]** ADJ verdorben; (= *open to bribery*) korrupt; *text* korrumpiert; (*Comput*) *disk* nicht lesbar **[2]** VT (*morally*) verderben; (*form*: = *bribe*) bestechen; (*Comput*) *data* zerstören; **to become ~ed** (*text*) korrumpiert werden

corruptible [kə'rʌptəbl] ADJ korrumpierbar

corruption [kə'rʌpʃən] N **(a)** (= *act*) Korruption *f*; (*Comput*: *of data*) Zerstörung *f* **(b)** (= *corrupt nature*) Verdorbenheit *f*; (*by bribery*) Bestechlichkeit *f*; (*of morals*) Verfall *m*; (*of text*) Korrumpierung *f*

corruptly [kə'rʌptlɪ] ADV korrupt

corset ['kɔːsɪt] N, **corsets** PL Korsett *nt*

Corsica ['kɔːsɪkə] N Korsika *nt*

Corsican ['kɔːsɪkən] **[1]** ADJ korsisch; **she is ~** sie ist Korsin **[2]** N Korse *m*, Korsin *f*

cortège [kɔː'teɪʒ] N (= *retinue*) Gefolge *nt*; (= *procession*) Prozession *f*; (= *funeral ~*) Leichenzug *m*

cortisone ['kɔːtɪzəʊn] N Kortison *nt*

cos¹ [kɒz] ABBR *of* cosine cos

cos² [kɒs] N (*also* = **lettuce**) Romagnasalat *m*

cos³ [kəz] CONJ (*inf*) = because

cosh [kɒʃ] **[1]** VT auf den Schädel schlagen **[2]** N Totschläger *m*

cosily, (*US*) **cozily** [ˈkəʊzɪlɪ] ADV **(a)** *furnished, decorated* behaglich **(b)** *sit, settle* behaglich **(c)** *chat* gemütlich

cosine [ˈkəʊsaɪn] N Kosinus *m*

cosiness, (*US*) **coziness** [ˈkəʊzɪnɪs] N Gemütlichkeit *f*; (= *warmth*) mollige Wärme

cosmetic [kɒzˈmetɪk] **1** ADJ (*lit, fig*) kosmetisch **2** N Kosmetikum *nt*

cosmetic surgery N kosmetische Chirurgie; **she's had ~** sie hat eine Schönheitsoperation gehabt

cosmic [ˈkɒzmɪk] ADJ kosmisch

cosmology [kɒzˈmɒlədʒɪ] N Kosmologie *f*

cosmopolitan [ˌkɒzməˈpɒlɪtən] ADJ kosmopolitisch

cosmos [ˈkɒzmɒs] N Kosmos *m*

cossack [ˈkɒsæk] N Kosak(in) *m(f)*

cosset [ˈkɒsɪt] VT verwöhnen

cossie, cozzie [ˈkɒzɪ] N (*Brit inf*) Badeanzug *m*

cost [kɒst], *vb*: pret, ptp **cost 1** VT **(a)** (*lit, fig*) kosten; **how much does it ~?** wie viel kostet es?; **how much will it ~ to have it repaired?** wie viel kostet die Reparatur?; **it ~ him a lot of time** es kostete ihn viel Zeit; **that mistake could ~ you your life** der Fehler könnte dich das Leben kosten; **it'll ~ you** (*inf*) das kostet dich was (*inf*)
(b) pret, ptp **costed** (= *work out* = *of*) veranschlagen **2** N **(a)** (*lit*) Kosten *pl* (*of* für); **to bear the ~ of sth** die Kosten für etw tragen; **the ~ of petrol these days** die Benzinpreise heutzutage; **at little ~ to oneself** ohne große eigene Kosten; **~ and freight** (*Comm*) Kosten und Fracht; **~, insurance and freight** (*Comm*) Kosten, Versicherung und Fracht; **~ of sales** (*Comm*) Absatzkosten *pl*; **to buy/sell at ~** zum Selbstkostenpreis kaufen/verkaufen
(b) (*fig*) Preis *m*; **at all ~s, at any ~** um jeden Preis; **at the ~ of one's health/** *etc* auf Kosten seiner Gesundheit *etc*; **at great/ little personal ~** unter großen/geringen eigenen Kosten; **he found out to his ~ that ...** er machte die bittere Erfahrung, dass ...
(c) costs PL (*Jur*) Kosten *pl*; **to be ordered to pay ~s** zur Übernahme der Kosten verurteilt werden

➤ **cost out** VT SEP (kostenmäßig) kalkulieren

co-star [ˈkəʊstɑː*] **1** N einer der Hauptdarsteller; **Burton and Taylor were ~s** Burton und Taylor spielten die Hauptrollen **2** VT **the film ~s R. Burton** der Film zeigt R. Burton in einer der Hauptrollen **3** VI als Hauptdarsteller auftreten

Costa Rica [ˈkɒstəˈriːkə] N Costa Rica *nt*

Costa Rican [ˈkɒstəˈriːkən] N Costa-Ricaner(in) *m(f)*

cost: **cost-cutting 1** N Kostenverringerung *f* **2** ADJ ATTR **~ exercise** Kosten dämpfende Maßnahmen *pl*; **cost-effective** ADJ rentabel; **cost-effectiveness** N Rentabilität *f*

costing [ˈkɒstɪŋ] N Kalkulation *f*; **full ~** Vollkostenkalkulation *f*, Vollkostenrechnung *f*

costly [ˈkɒstlɪ] ADJ teuer

cost: **cost of living** N Lebenshaltungskosten *pl*; **cost-of-living adjustment** N (*US Fin*) Teuerungszulage *f*, Anpassung *f* an die Lebenshaltungskosten; **cost-of-living index** N Lebenshaltungsindex *m*; **cost price** N Selbstkostenpreis *m*

costume [ˈkɒstjuːm] N Kostüm *nt*; (= *bathing ~*) Badeanzug *m*

costume: **costume drama** N **(a)** (= *play*) Schauspiel *nt* in historischen Kostümen; (= *film*) Historienfilm *m*; (= *series*) Serie *f* in historischen Kostümen **(b)** (= *genre*) (*Theat*) Schauspiele *pl* in historischen Kostümen; (*Film*) Kostümfilme *pl*; (*TV*) Serien *pl* in historischen Kostümen; **costume jewellery** N Modeschmuck *m*

cosy, (*US*) **cozy** [ˈkəʊzɪ] **1** ADJ (+ER) gemütlich; (= *warm*) mollig warm; (*fig*) *chat* gemütlich; *relationship* traut **2** N (= *tea ~*) Wärmer *m*

cot [kɒt] N (*esp Brit*: = *child's bed*) Kinderbett *nt*; (*US*: = *camp bed*) Feldbett *nt*

cot death N (*Brit*) plötzlicher Kindstod

cottage [ˈkɒtɪdʒ] N Häuschen *nt*; (*US*: *in institution*) Wohneinheit *f*

cottage: **cottage cheese** N Hüttenkäse *m*; **cottage industry** N Manufaktur *f*; **cottage pie** N *Hackfleisch mit Kartoffelbrei überbacken*

cotton [ˈkɒtn] **1** N Baumwolle *f*; (= *plant*) Baumwollstrauch *m*; (= *fabric*) Baumwollstoff *m*; (= *sewing thread*) (Baumwoll)garn *nt* **2** ADJ Baumwoll-, baumwollen

➤ **cotton on** VI (*Brit inf*) es kapieren (*inf*); **to cotton on to sth** etw checken (*inf*)

➤ **cotton to** VI +PREP OBJ (*US inf*) *plan, suggestion* gut finden

cotton IN CPDS Baumwoll-; **cotton batting** N (*US*) Gaze *f*; **cotton bud** N (*Brit*) Wattestäbchen *nt*; **cotton candy** N (*US*) Zuckerwatte *f*; **cotton mill** N Baumwollspinnerei *f*; **cotton-picking** ADJ (*US inf*) verflucht (*inf*); **cottontail** N (*US*) Kaninchen *nt*; **cotton wool** N (*Brit*) Watte *f*

couch [kaʊtʃ] **1** N Sofa *nt*; (= *doctor's ~*) Liege *f*; (= *psychiatrist's ~*) Couch *f* **2** VT *request* formulieren

couchette [kuːˈʃet] N (*Rail*) Liegewagen(platz) *m*

couch potato N (*inf*) Couchpotato *f*

cough [kɒf] **1** N Husten *m*; **he has a bit of a ~** er hat etwas Husten; **to give a warning ~** sich warnend räuspern; **a smoker's ~** Raucherhusten *m* **2** VTI husten

➤ **cough up 1** VT SEP (*lit*) aushusten **2** VT INSEP (*fig inf*) *money* rausrücken (*inf*) **3** VI (*fig inf*) blechen (*inf*)

cough: **cough mixture** N Hustensaft *m*; **cough sweet** N (*Brit*) Hustenbonbon *nt*

could [kʊd] PRET *of* **can**[1]

couldn't [ˈkʊdnt] CONTR *of* **could not**

council [ˈkaʊnsl] **1** N Rat *m*; **city/town ~** Stadtrat *m*; **to be on the ~** Ratsmitglied sein; **Council of Europe** Europarat *m*; **Council of Ministers** (*Pol*) Ministerrat *m* **2** ADJ ATTR **~ meeting** Ratssitzung *f*

council (*Brit*): **council estate** N Sozialwohnungssiedlung *f*; **council flat** N Sozialwohnung *f*; **council house** N Sozialwohnung *f*; **council housing** N sozialer Wohnungsbau

councillor, (*US*) **councilor** [ˈkaʊnsələ*] N Ratsmitglied *nt*; (= *town ~*) Stadtrat *m*/-rätin *f*; **~ Smith** Herr Stadtrat/Frau Stadträtin Smith

council tax N (*Brit*) Kommunalsteuer *f*

counsel [ˈkaʊnsəl] **1** N **(a)** (*form*: = *advice*) Rat(schlag) *m*; **to keep one's own ~** seine Meinung für sich behalten **(b)** *pl* - (*Jur*) Rechtsanwalt *m*; **~ for the defence/prosecution** Verteidiger(in) *m(f)*/Vertreter(in) *m(f)* der Anklage **2** VT *person* beraten; *course of action* empfehlen; **to ~ sb to do sth** jdm raten, etw zu tun

counselling, (*US*) **counseling** [ˈkaʊnsəlɪŋ] N Beratung *f*; (*Sociol*) soziale Beratung; (*by therapist*) Therapie *f*; **to need ~** professionelle Hilfe brauchen; **to go for** *or* **have ~** zur Beratung/Therapie gehen

counsellor, (*US*) **counselor** [ˈkaʊnsələ*] N **(a)** (= *adviser*) Berater(in) *m(f)* **(b)** (*US, Ir.*: = *lawyer*) Rechtsanwalt *m*/-anwältin *f*

count[1] [kaʊnt] **1** N **(a)** (*with numbers*) Zählung *f*; (*Sport*) Auszählen *nt*; (*of votes*) (Stimmen)auszählung *f*; **she lost ~ when she was interrupted** sie kam mit dem Zählen durcheinander, als sie unterbrochen wurde; **I've lost all ~ of her boyfriends** ich habe die Übersicht über ihre Freunde vollkommen verloren; **to keep ~ (of sth)** (etw) mitzählen; (= *keep track*) die Übersicht (über etw (*acc*)) behalten; **at the last ~ there were twenty members** bei der letzten Zählung waren es zwanzig Mitglieder; **all together now, on the ~ of three** und jetzt alle zusammen, bei drei gehts los
(b) (*Jur*: = *charge*) Anklagepunkt *m*; **you're wrong on both ~s** (*fig*) Sie haben in beiden Punkten Unrecht
2 VT **(a)** (*with numbers*) (ab)zählen; (= *~ again*) nachzählen; *votes* (aus)zählen; **I only ~ed ten people** ich habe nur zehn Leute gezählt; **she'll help anyone without ~ing the cost to herself** sie hilft jedem, ohne an sich selbst zu denken
(b) (= *consider*) ansehen; (= *include*) mitrechnen; **to ~ sb (as) a friend/among one's friends** jdn als Freund ansehen/zu seinen Freunden zählen; **you should ~ yourself lucky to be alive** Sie können noch von Glück sagen, dass Sie noch leben; **ten people (not) ~ing the children** zehn Leute, die Kinder (nicht) mitgerechnet
3 VI **(a)** (*with numbers*) zählen; **to ~ to ten** bis zehn zählen; **~ing from today** von heute an (gerechnet)
(b) (= *be considered*) angesehen werden; (= *be included*) mitgerechnet werden; (= *be important*) wichtig sein; **the children don't ~** die Kinder zählen nicht; **that doesn't ~** das zählt nicht; **every minute/it all ~s** jede Minute ist/das ist alles wichtig; **to ~ against sb** jdn gegen jdn sprechen

➤ **count down** VI den Countdown durchführen; **to count down to blast-off** bis zum Abschuss (der Rakete) rückwärts zählen

➤ **count for** VI +PREP OBJ **to count for a lot** sehr viel bedeuten; **to count for nothing** nichts gelten

➤ **count in** VT SEP mitzählen; **to count sb in on sth** davon ausgehen *or* damit rechnen, dass jd bei etw mitmacht; **you can count me in!** Sie können mit mir rechnen

➤ **count on** VI +PREP OBJ rechnen mit; **to count on doing sth** die Absicht haben, etw zu tun; **you can count on him to help you** du kannst auf seine Hilfe zählen

➤ **count out** VT SEP **(a)** (*Sport*) auszählen **(b)** *money, books etc* abzählen **(c)** (*inf*: = *exclude*) **(you can) count me out (of that)!** ohne mich!

➤ **count up** VT SEP zusammenzählen

count² N Graf *m*

countable [ˈkaʊntəbl] ADJ zählbar (*Gram*)

countdown [ˈkaʊntdaʊn] N Countdown *m*

countenance [ˈkaʊntɪnəns] **◼** N Gesichtsausdruck *m* **◼** VT *behaviour, plan* gutheißen

counter [ˈkaʊntə] **◼** N **(a)** (*in shop*) Ladentisch *m*; (*in café*) Theke *f*; (*in bank, post office*) Schalter *m*; **to sell/buy sth under/ over the ~** etw unter dem/über den Ladentisch verkaufen/ bekommen; **medicines which can be bought over the ~** Medikamente, die man rezeptfrei bekommt; **under-the-~ deals** (*fig*) dunkle Geschäfte *pl*
(b) (= *small disc for games*) Spielmarke *f*
(c) (*Tech*) Zähler *m*
◼ VT antworten auf (+*acc*), kontern (*also Sport*)
◼ VI kontern (*also Sport*)
◼ ADV = gegen (+*acc*); **the results are ~ to expectations** die Ergebnisse widersprechen den Erwartungen

counter: **counteract** VT (= *make ineffective*) neutralisieren; (= *act in opposition to*) entgegenwirken (+*dat*); *disease* bekämpfen; **counterattack ◼** N Gegenangriff *m* **◼** VTI zurückschlagen; **counterbalance ◼** N Gegengewicht *nt* **◼** VT ausgleichen; **counter clerk** N (*in bank etc*) Angestellte(r) *mf* im Schalterdienst; (*in post office etc*) Schalterbeamte(r) *m*/ -beamtin *f*; **counterclockwise** ADJ, ADV (*US*) **= anticlockwise**; **counter-cyclical** ADJ (*Econ*) antizyklisch

counterfeit [ˈkaʊntəfiːt] **◼** ADJ gefälscht; **~ money/coins** Falschgeld *nt* **◼** N Fälschung *f* **◼** VT fälschen

counterfoil [ˈkaʊntəfɔɪl] N Kontrollabschnitt *m*

countermand [ˈkaʊntəmɑːnd] VT aufheben

counter: **counterpart** N (= *equivalent*) Gegenüber *nt*; (= *complement*) Gegenstück *nt*; **counterpoint** N (*Mus, fig*) Kontrapunkt *m*; **counterproductive** ADJ widersinnig; *criticism, measures* kontraproduktiv; **counter-revolutionary** ADJ konterrevolutionär; **countersign** VT *cheque etc* gegenzeichnen; **counter staff** PL (*in shop*) Verkäufer *pl*; **countersunk** ADJ *screw* Senk-; **countertop** N (*US*) Arbeitsfläche *f*; **countertrade** N (*Comm*) Kompensationshandel *m*; **counterweight** N Gegengewicht *nt*

countess [ˈkaʊntɪs] N Gräfin *f*

countless [ˈkaʊntlɪs] ADJ unzählig *attr*

country [ˈkʌntrɪ] N **(a)** (= *state*) Land *nt*; (= *people also*) Volk *nt*; **his own ~** seine Heimat; **to go to the ~** Neuwahlen ausschreiben; **~ of origin** (*Comm*) Ursprungsland *nt* **(b)** NO PL (*as opposed to town*) Land *nt*; (= *countryside also*) Landschaft *f*; **in/to the ~** auf dem/aufs Land; **this is good fishing ~** das ist eine gute Fischgegend; **this is mining ~** dies ist ein Bergbaugebiet

country IN CPDS Land-; **country and western** N Country-und-Western-Musik *f*; **country-and-western** ADJ Country- und Western-; **country club** N *Klub auf dem Lande*; **country code** N **(a)** (*Telec*) internationale Vorwahl **(b)** (*Brit*: = *set of rules*) Verhaltenskodex *m* für Besucher auf dem Lande; **country dancing** N Volkstanz *m*; **country dweller** N Landbewohner(in) *m(f)*; **country house** N Landhaus *nt*; **country life** N das Landleben; **countryman** N **(a)** (= *compatriot*) Landsmann *m*; **his fellow countrymen** seine Landsleute **(b)** (= *country dweller*) Landmann *m*; **country mile** N (*US inf*) **to miss sth by a ~** etw um Längen verpassen; **country music** N Countrymusik *f*; **country people** PL Leute *pl* vom Land(e); **country road** N Landstraße *f*; **country seat** N Landsitz *m*; **countryside** N (= *scenery*) Landschaft *f*; (= *rural*

area) Land *nt*; **country-wide** ADJ landesweit; **countrywoman** N **(a)** (= *compatriot*) Landsmännin *f* **(b)** (= *country dweller*) Landfrau *f*

county [ˈkaʊntɪ] N (*Brit*) Grafschaft *f*; (*US*) (Verwaltungs)bezirk *m*

county: **county council** N (*Brit*) Grafschaftsrat *m*; **county seat** N (*US*) Hauptstadt eines Verwaltungsbezirkes; **county town** N (*Brit*) Hauptstadt einer Grafschaft

coup [kuː] N **(a)** (= *successful action*) Coup *m* **(b)** (= ~ *d'état*) Staatsstreich *m*

coup de grâce [ˌkuːdəˈɡrɑːs] N (*lit, fig*) Gnadenstoß *m*

coup d'état [ˌkuːdeɪˈtɑː] N Staatsstreich *m*

coupé [ˈkuːpeɪ] N Coupé *nt*

couple [ˈkʌpl] **◼** N **(a)** (= *pair*) Paar *nt*; (= *married* ~) Ehepaar *nt*; **in ~s** paarweise **(b)** (*inf*) **a ~** (= *two*) zwei; (= *several*) ein paar; **a ~ of letters** *etc* ein paar Briefe *etc*; **a ~ of times** ein paar Mal; **it took a ~ of minutes/hours** es hat ein paar Minuten/ ungefähr zwei Stunden gedauert **◼** VT (= *link*) verbinden; *carriages etc* koppeln; **smoking ~d with poor diet ...** Rauchen in Verbindung mit schlechter Ernährung ...

coupler [ˈkʌplə] N (*Comput*) Koppler *m*

couplet [ˈkʌplɪt] N Verspaar *nt*

coupling [ˈkʌplɪŋ] N **(a)** (= *linking*) Verbindung *f*; (*of carriages etc*) Kopplung *f* **(b)** (= *linking device*) Kupplung *f*

coupon [ˈkuːpɒn] N Gutschein *m*; **~ yield** (*Brit*), **~ rate** (*US*) Jahreszins *m* bei festverzinslichen Papieren

courage [ˈkʌrɪdʒ] N Mut *m*; **to have/lack the ~ of one's convictions** Zivilcourage/keine Zivilcourage haben; **to take one's ~ in both hands** sein Herz in beide Hände nehmen

courageous [kəˈreɪdʒəs] ADJ mutig; (= *with courage of convictions*) couragiert

courageously [kəˈreɪdʒəslɪ] ADV *fight* mutig; *criticize* couragiert

courgette [kʊəˈʒet] N (*Brit*) Zucchini *f*

courier [ˈkʊrɪə] **◼** N **(a)** (= *messenger*) Kurier *m*; **by ~** per Kurier **(b)** (= *tourist guide*) Reiseleiter(in) *m(f)* **◼** VT per Kurier schicken

course [kɔːs] N **(a)** (*of plane, ship,* = *race*) Kurs *m*; (*of river, history*) Lauf *m*; (= *golf* ~) Platz *m*; (*fig*) (*of illness, relationship*) Verlauf *m*; (*of action etc*) Vorgehensweise *f*; **to change** *or* **alter ~** den Kurs ändern; **to be on/off ~** auf Kurs sein/vom Kurs abgekommen sein; **to be on ~ for sth** (*fig*) gute Aussichten auf etw (*acc*) haben; **to let sth take** *or* **run its ~** einer Sache (*dat*) ihren Lauf lassen; **the affair has run its ~** die Angelegenheit ist zu einem Ende gekommen; **which ~ of action did you take?** wie sind Sie vorgegangen?; **the best ~ (of action) would be ...** das Beste wäre ...; **in the ~ of the next few weeks/the meeting** *etc* während der nächsten paar Wochen/der Versammlung *etc*; **in the ~ of time** im Laufe der Zeit
(b) of **~** (= *admittedly*) natürlich; **of ~!** natürlich!; **don't you like me? – of ~ I do** magst du mich nicht? — doch, natürlich; **he's rather young, of ~, but ...** er ist natürlich ziemlich jung, aber ...
(c) (*Sch, Univ*) Studium *nt*; (= *summer ~ etc*) Kurs(us) *m*; (*at work*) Lehrgang *m*; (*Med: of treatment*) Kur *f*; **to go on a French ~** einen Französischkurs(us) besuchen; **a ~ in first aid** ein Erste-Hilfe-Kurs; **a ~ of lectures, a lecture ~** eine Vorlesungsreihe; **a ~ of pills/treatment** eine Pillenkur/eine Behandlung
(d) (*Cook*) Gang *m*; **first ~** erster Gang; **a three-~ meal** ein Essen *nt* mit drei Gängen

court [kɔːt] **◼** N **(a)** (*Jur*) (*also* **~ of justice** *or* **law**) Gericht *nt*; (= *room*) Gerichtssaal *m*; **to appear in ~** vor Gericht erscheinen; **to take sb to ~** jdn verklagen; **to go to ~ over a matter** eine Sache vor Gericht bringen
(b) (*royal*) Hof *m*
(c) (*Sport*) Platz *m*; (*for squash*) Halle *f*; (= *marked-off area*) Spielfeld *nt*; (= *service ~ etc*) Feld *nt*; **grass/hard ~** Rasen-/ Hartplatz *m*; **on ~** auf dem Platz/in der Halle
◼ VT *person's favour* werben um; *danger, defeat* herausfordern

3 VI *(dated)* **they were ~ing at the time** zu der Zeit gingen sie zusammen; **she's ~ing** sie hat einen Freund

---

COURT

In England, Wales und Nordirland werden Schwerverbrechen und Verfahren, bei denen der Angeklagte auf „nicht schuldig" plädiert, im Crown Court vor einem Richter und zwölf Geschworenen verhandelt. Weniger schwere Straftaten werden in einem magistrates' court vor einem magistrate ohne Geschworene verhandelt.

Die schottische Rechtssprechung ist anders angelegt. Hier befasst sich der High Court of Justiciary mit den Schwerverbrechen und sheriff courts mit den weniger schweren Straftaten. Der oberste Gerichtshof für Zivilrecht ist der Court of Session.

In den USA kümmern sich Bundesgerichte um Straftaten gegen das Bundesrecht; hier werden Fälle aus verschiedenen Staaten behandelt. Straftaten gegen die Gesetze eines Bundesstaates werden dagegen vor Gerichten im jeweiligen Staat verhandelt. Jeder Staat hat sein eigenes Rechtssystem und kann eigene Gesetze erlassen, mit der Einschränkung, dass diese nicht gegen die Verfassung der USA oder Bundesgesetze verstoßen dürfen. Es gibt keine unterschiedlichen Gerichte für Straf- und Zivilangelegenheiten.

Die meisten Bundesstraffälle werden in district courts verhandelt, zwölf Courts of Appeal sind zuständig für die Berufungsfälle der untergeordneten Bundesgerichte. Oberste Gerichtshöfe für sowohl Bundes- wie Staatsrecht sind die Supreme Courts, einer in jedem Staat und einer für den Bund. Im Bundesstaatsrecht sind diesen Appelate Courts (Berufungsgerichte) untergeordnet, darunter county oder city courts, die sich mit Fällen der allgemeinen Rechtsprechung befassen.

---

court: **court appearance** N Erscheinen *nt* vor Gericht; **court case** N *(Jur)* Gerichtsverfahren *nt*, Prozess *m*

courteous ADJ, **courteously** ADV ['kɜːtɪəs, -lɪ] höflich

courtesy ['kɜːtɪsɪ] N Höflichkeit *f*; **(by) ~ of** freundlicherweise zur Verfügung gestellt von

courtesy: **courtesy bus** N gebührenfreier Bus; **courtesy light** N *(Aut)* Innenleuchte *f*; **courtesy visit** N Höflichkeitsbesuch *m*

court: **court hearing** N *(Jur)* Gerichtsverhandlung *f*; **courthouse** N *(Jur)* Gerichtsgebäude *nt*; **court martial** N, *pl* **court martials** *or* **courts martial** *(Mil)* Militärgericht *nt*; **court-martial** VT vor das/ein Militärgericht stellen *(for* wegen*)*; **court order** N *(Jur)* gerichtliche Verfügung; **courtroom** N *(Jur)* Gerichtssaal *m*

courtship ['kɔːtʃɪp] N *(dated)* (Braut)werbung *f (dated) (of* um*)*; **during their ~** während er um sie warb

court: **court shoe** N Pumps *m*; **court tennis** N *(US)* Tennis *nt*; **courtyard** N Hof *m*

couscous ['kuːskuːs] N Couscous *m*

cousin ['kʌzn] N *(male)* Cousin *m*; *(female)* Cousine *f*; **Kevin and Susan are ~s** Kevin und Susan sind Cousin und Cousine

couture [kuːˈtjʊəʳ] N Couture *f*

couturier [kuːˈtjʊərɪeʳ] N Couturier *m*

cove [kəʊv] N *(Geog)* (kleine) Bucht

covenant ['kʌvɪnənt] N Schwur *m*; *(Bibl)* Bund *m*; *(Jur)* Verpflichtung *f* zu regelmäßigen Spenden

Coventry ['kɒvəntrɪ] N **to send sb to ~** *(Brit inf)* jdn schneiden *(inf)*

cover ['kʌvəʳ] **1** N **(a)** *(= lid)* Deckel *m*; *(of lens)* (Schutz)kappe *f*; *(= loose ~)* Bezug *m*; *(for typewriter, umbrella etc)* Hülle *f*; *(on lorries, tennis court)* Plane *f*; *(= blanket, quilt)* (Bett)decke *f*; **he put a ~ over it** er deckte es zu; **she pulled the ~s up to her chin** sie zog die Decke bis ans Kinn (hoch)

(b) *(of book)* Einband *m*; *(of magazine)* Umschlag *m*; *(= dust ~)* (Schutz)umschlag *m*; **to read a book from ~ to ~** ein Buch von der ersten bis zur letzten Seite lesen; **on the ~** auf dem Einband/Umschlag; *(of magazine)* auf der Titelseite

(c) *(Comm: = envelope)* **under separate ~** getrennt; **under plain ~** in neutralem Umschlag

(d) NO PL *(= protection)* Schutz *m (from* vor +*dat*, gegen*)*; *(Mil)* Deckung *f (from* vor +*dat*, gegen*)*; **to take ~** *(from rain)* sich unterstellen; *(Mil)* in Deckung gehen *(from* vor +*dat*); **the car should be kept under ~** das Auto sollte abgedeckt sein *or (under roof)* durch ein Dach geschützt sein; **under ~ of darkness** im Schutz(e) der Dunkelheit

(e) *(Brit) (Comm, Fin)* Deckung *f*; *(= insurance ~)* Versicherung

f; **to take out ~ for a car** ein Auto versichern; **to take out ~ against fire** eine Feuerversicherung abschließen; **to get ~ for sth** etw versichern (lassen); **do you have adequate ~?** sind Sie ausreichend versichert?

(f) *(= assumed identity)* Tarnung *f*; **to operate under ~** als Agent tätig sein

(g) *(Mus: also ~ version)* Coverversion *f*

2 VT **(a)** *(= put ~ on)* bedecken; *(= ~ over)* zudecken; *(with loose ~)* chair etc beziehen; **a ~ed way** ein überdachter Weg; **the mountain was ~ed with** *or* **in snow** der Berg war schneebedeckt; **you're all ~ed with dog hairs** du bist voller Hundehaare

(b) *mistake, tracks* verdecken; **to ~ one's face with one's hands** sein Gesicht in den Händen verbergen

(c) *(= protect, also Fin)* decken; *(Insur)* versichern; **will £30 ~ the drinks?** reichen £ 30 für die Getränke?; **he gave me £30 to ~ the drinks** er gab mir £ 30 für Getränke; **he only said that to ~ himself** er hat das nur gesagt, um sich abzudecken

(d) *(= point a gun at etc)* door etc sichern; *sb* decken, sichern; **to keep sb ~ed** jdn in Schach halten

(e) *(= include)* behandeln; *eventualities* vorsehen; **what does your travel insurance ~ you for?** was deckt deine Reiseversicherung ab?; **to ~ the waterfront** *(esp US)* einen weiten Bereich abdecken

(f) *(Press: = report on)* berichten über *(+acc)*

(g) *distance* zurücklegen

(h) *(Mus) song* neu interpretieren

➤ **cover for** VI +PREP OBJ **(a)** *absent person* vertreten **(b)** *(= protect)* decken

➤ **cover over** VT SEP zudecken; *(for protection)* abdecken

➤ **cover up 1** VI **to cover up for sb** jdn decken **2** VT SEP **(a)** *child* zudecken; *object also, tennis court* abdecken **(b)** *truth, facts* vertuschen

coverage ['kʌvərɪdʒ] N, NO PL *(in media)* Berichterstattung *f (of* über +*acc*); **the games got excellent TV ~** die Spiele wurden ausführlich im Fernsehen gebracht

cover: **coverall** N USU PL *(US)* Overall *m*; **cover charge** N Kosten *pl* für ein Gedeck

covered market [ˌkʌvəd ˈmɑːkɪt] N überdachter Markt

covering ['kʌvərɪŋ] N Decke *f*; **a ~ of snow** eine Schneedecke

covering letter N *(Brit)* Begleitbrief *m*

cover letter N *(US)* = covering letter

cover: **cover note** N Deckungszusage *f*; **cover price** N Einzel(exemplar)preis *m*; **cover story** N *(of paper)* Titelgeschichte *f*

covert ['kʌvət] ADJ versteckt; *surveillance* heimlich

covertly ['kʌvətlɪ] ADV heimlich

cover-up ['kʌvərʌp] N Vertuschung *f*

cover version N *(Mus)* Coverversion *f*

covet ['kʌvɪt] VT begehren

cow¹ [kaʊ] N **(a)** Kuh *f*; **a ~ elephant** eine Elefantenkuh; **till the ~s come home** *(fig inf)* bis in alle Ewigkeit *(inf)*; **to have a ~** *(US inf)* die Fassung verlieren **(b)** *(pej inf: = woman) (stupid)* Kuh *f (inf)*; *(nasty)* gemeine Ziege *(inf)*; **cheeky ~!** freches Stück! *(inf)*

cow² VT einschüchtern; **to ~ sb into submission** jdn (durch Einschüchterung) gefügig machen

coward ['kaʊəd] N Feigling *m*

cowardice ['kaʊədɪs], **cowardliness** ['kaʊədlɪnɪs] N Feigheit *f*

cowardly ['kaʊədlɪ] ADJ feig(e)

cow: **cowbell** N Kuhglocke *f*; **cowboy** N **(a)** Cowboy *m*; **to play ~s and Indians** Indianer spielen **(b)** *(fig inf) (incompetent)* Pfuscher *m*; *(dishonest)* Gauner *m (inf)*; **cowboy hat** N Cowboyhut *m*

cower ['kaʊəʳ] VI sich ducken; *(squatting)* kauern; **he stood ~ing in a corner** er stand geduckt in einer Ecke

cow: **cowgirl** N Cowgirl *nt*; **cowhand** N Hilfscowboy *m*; *(on farm)* Stallknecht *m*; **cowhide** N **(a)** *(untanned)* Kuhhaut *f*; *(no pl: = leather)* Rindsleder *nt* **(b)** *(US: = whip)* Lederpeitsche *f*

cowl [kaʊl] N Kapuze *f*

cow: **cowman** N *(US)* Viehzüchter *m*; **cowpat** N Kuhfladen *m*; **cowpoke, cowpuncher** N *(US inf)* Cowboy *m*; **cowshed** N Kuhstall *m*

cox [kɒks] N Steuermann *m*

coy [kɔɪ] ADJ *(+ER)* *(= affectedly shy)* verschämt; *(= coquettish)* neckisch; *(= evasive)* zurückhaltend; **to be ~ about sth** *(= shy)* in Bezug auf etw (*acc*) verschämt tun; (= *evasive*) sich ausweichend zu etw äußern

coyly ['kɔɪlɪ] ADV (= *shyly*) schüchtern; (= *evasively*) ausweichend

coyote [kɔɪ'əʊtɪ] N Kojote *m*

cozy ADJ (*US*) = **cosy**

cozzie ['kɒzɪ] N (*Brit inf*) = **cossie**

C/P (*Comm*) ABBR *of* **carriage paid** frachtfrei

CPA (*US*) ABBR *of* **certified public accountant**

CPI (*US*) ABBR *of* **Consumer Price Index**

CPR (*Med*) ABBR *of* **cardiopulmonary resuscitation**

CPT ABBR *of* **carriage paid to** frachtfrei

CPU ABBR *of* **central processing unit** CPU *f*

crab [kræb] N Krabbe *f*

crab apple N (= *fruit*) Holzapfel *m*; (= *tree*) Holzapfelbaum *m*

crabby ['kræbɪ] ADJ (+ER) griesgrämig

crabmeat ['kræbmiːt] N Krabbenfleisch *nt*

crack [kræk] **1** N **(a)** Riss *m*; (*between floorboards etc*) Ritze *f*; (= *wider hole etc*) Spalte *f*; (= *fine line: in pottery etc*) Sprung *m*; **leave the window open a ~** lass das Fenster einen Spalt offen; **at the ~ of dawn** in aller Frühe; **to fall** *or* **slip through the ~s** (*US fig*) durch die Maschen schlüpfen
(b) (= *sharp noise*) (*of wood etc breaking*) Knacks *m*; (*of gun, whip*) Knall(en *nt no pl*) *m*
(c) (= *sharp blow*) Schlag *m*; **to give oneself a ~ on the head** sich (*dat*) den Kopf anschlagen
(d) (*inf*) (= *gibe*) Stichelei *f*; (= *joke*) Witz *m*; **to make a ~ about sb/sth** einen Witz über jdn/etw reißen
(e) (*inf*: = *attempt*) **to have a ~ at sth** etw mal probieren (*inf*)
(f) (*Drugs*) Crack *nt*
(g) (*Brit vulg*: = *vagina*) Fotze *f* (*vulg*)
2 ADJ ATTR erstklassig; (*Mil*) Elite-; **~ shot** Meisterschütze *m*, Meisterschützin *f*
3 VT **(a)** *pottery* einen Sprung machen in (+*acc*); *ground, ice* einen Riss/Risse machen in (+*acc*)
(b) *nuts, safe* knacken; (*fig inf*) *code* knacken; *case, problem* lösen; **I've ~ed it** (= *solved it*) ich habs!
(c) *joke* reißen
(d) *whip* knallen mit; *finger* knacken mit; **to ~ the whip** (*fig*) die Peitsche schwingen
(e) (= *hit sharply*) schlagen; **he ~ed his head against the pavement** er krachte mit dem Kopf aufs Pflaster
4 VI **(a)** (*pottery*) einen Sprung/Sprünge bekommen; (*ice, road*) einen Riss/Risse bekommen; (*lips, skin*) rissig werden; (= *break*) brechen
(b) (= *make a cracking sound*) (*twigs, joints*) knacken; (*whip, gun*) knallen
(c) (*inf*) **to get ~ing** loslegen (*inf*); **to get ~ing with** *or* **on sth** mit etw loslegen (*inf*); **get ~ing!** los jetzt!
(d) = **crack up 1**; **he ~ed under the strain** er ist unter der Belastung zusammengebrochen

➤ **crack down** VI hart durchgreifen (*on* bei)

➤ **crack on** VI (*Brit inf*) weitermachen

➤ **crack open** VT SEP aufbrechen; **to crack open the champagne** die Sektkorken knallen lassen

➤ **crack up** **1** VI (*fig inf*) (*person*) durchdrehen (*inf*); (*under strain*) zusammenbrechen; (= *have a mental breakdown*) einen Nervenzusammenbruch haben; (= *lose strength: athlete etc*) abbauen; **I/he must be cracking up** (*hum*) so fängts an (*inf*)
2 VT SEP (*inf*) **it's not all it's cracked up to be** so toll ist es dann auch wieder nicht

crackdown ['krækdaʊn] N (*inf*) scharfes Durchgreifen

cracked [krækt] ADJ **(a)** *glass, plate, ice* gesprungen; *bone* angebrochen; (= *broken*) gebrochen; *surface, walls* rissig; *lips, skin* aufgesprungen **(b)** (*Brit inf*: = *mad*) übergeschnappt (*inf*)

cracker ['krækə'] N **(a)** (= *biscuit*) Kräcker *m* **(b)** (= *firecracker*) Knallkörper *m*; (= *Christmas ~*) Knallbonbon *nt* **(c)** (*Brit inf*) (= *woman*) tolle Frau (*inf*); (= *man*) toller Mann (*inf*); (= *thing*) tolles Ding (*inf*)

crackers ['krækəz] ADJ PRED (*Brit inf*) übergeschnappt (*inf*)

cracking ['krækɪŋ] ADJ (*inf*) *pace* scharf; (*dated*: = *good*) fantastisch

crackle ['krækl] **1** VI (*fire*) knistern; (*twigs, telephone line*) knacken **2** N (*crackling noise, of telephone line*) Knacken *nt*

crackling ['kræklɪŋ] N, NO PL **(a)** = **crackle (b)** (*Cook*) Kruste *f* (*des Schweinebratens*)

crackpot ['krækpɒt] (*inf*) **1** N Spinner(in) *m(f)* (*inf*) **2** ADJ verrückt

cradle ['kreɪdl] **1** N (= *cot, fig*: = *birthplace*) Wiege *f*; (*of phone*) Gabel *f*; **from the ~ to the grave** von der Wiege bis zur Bahre **2** VT (= *hold closely*) an sich (*acc*) drücken; **he was cradling his injured arm** er hielt sich (*dat*) seinen verletzten Arm; **to ~ sb/ sth in one's arms** jdn/etw fest in den Armen halten

craft [krɑːft] **1** N **(a)** (= *handicraft*) Kunsthandwerk *nt*; (*as trade*) Kunstgewerbe *nt*; (= *trade*) Handwerk *nt* **(b)** NO PL (= *skill*) Kunst *f* **(c)** *pl* **craft** (= *boat*) Boot *nt*

craft fair N Kunstgewerbemarkt *m*

craftily ['krɑːftɪlɪ] ADV schlau, clever

craftiness ['krɑːftɪnɪs] N Schlauheit *f*, Cleverness *f*

craftsman ['krɑːftsmən] N, *pl* **-men** [-mən] Kunsthandwerker *m*

craftsmanship ['krɑːftsmənʃɪp] N Handwerkskunst *f*

craftswoman ['krɑːftswʊmən] N, *pl* **-women** [-wɪmɪn] Kunsthandwerkerin *f*

crafty ['krɑːftɪ] ADJ (+ER) schlau, clever; **he's a ~ one** (*inf*) er ist ein ganz Schlauer (*inf*)

crag [kræg] N Fels *m*

craggy ['krægɪ] ADJ (+ER) (= *rocky*) felsig; (= *jagged*) zerklüftet; *face* kantig

cram [kræm] **1** VT (= *fill*) voll stopfen; (= *stuff in*) hineinstopfen (*in(to)* +*acc*); *people* hineinzwängen (*in(to)* +*acc*); **the room was ~med (with furniture)** der Raum war (mit Möbeln) voll gestopft; **we were all ~med into one room** wir waren alle in einem Zimmer zusammengepfercht **2** VI (= *swot*) pauken (*inf*)

➤ **cram in** VI (*people*) sich hinein-/hereinquetschen (*-to* in +*acc*)

cram-full [kræm'fʊl] ADJ (*inf*) voll gestopft (*of* mit)

cramp [kræmp] **1** N (*Med*) Krampf *m*; **to have ~ in one's leg** einen Krampf im Bein haben; **to have the ~s** (*US*) Krämpfe haben **2** VT (*fig*: = *hinder*) behindern; **to ~ sb's style** jdm im Weg sein

cramped [kræmpt] ADJ *space* beschränkt; *flat, room* beengt; *train, plane* überfüllt; **we are very ~ (for space)** wir sind räumlich sehr beschränkt

crampon ['kræmpən] N Steigeisen *nt*

cranberry ['krænbərɪ] N Preiselbeere *f*; **~ sauce** Preiselbeersoße *f*

crane [kreɪn] **1** N **(a)** (*Mech*) Kran *m*; **~ driver** Kranführer(in) *m(f)* **(b)** (*Orn*) Kranich *m* **2** VT **to ~ one's neck** sich (*dat*) fast den Hals verrenken (*inf*) **3** VI (*also* **~ forward**) den Hals recken

cranefly ['kreɪnflaɪ] N Schnake *f*

cranium ['kreɪnɪəm] N, *pl* **crania** ['kreɪnɪə] (*Anat*) Schädel *m*

crank¹ [kræŋk] N (= *eccentric person*) Spinner(in) *m(f)* (*inf*); (*US*: = *cross person*) Griesgram *m*

crank² **1** N (*Mech*) Kurbel *f* **2** VT (*also* **~ up**) ankurbeln

crankshaft ['kræŋkʃɑːft] N (*Aut*) Kurbelwelle *f*

cranky ['kræŋkɪ] ADJ (+ER) **(a)** (= *eccentric*) verrückt **(b)** (*esp US*: = *bad-tempered*) griesgrämig

cranny ['krænɪ] N Ritze *f*

crap [kræp] **1** N **(a)** (*sl*) Scheiße *f* (*vulg*); **to go for/have a ~** scheißen gehen (*vulg*) **(b)** (*inf*: = *rubbish*) Scheiße *f* (*inf*); **a load of ~** große Scheiße (*inf*) **2** VI (*sl*) scheißen (*vulg*) **3** ADJ ATTR (*inf*) Scheiß- (*inf*)

crap game N (*US*) Würfelspiel *nt* (*mit zwei Würfeln*)

crappy ['kræpɪ] ADJ (+ER) (*inf*) beschissen (*inf*)

craps [kræps] N (*US*) Würfelspiel *nt*; **to shoot ~** Würfel spielen

crapshooter ['kræpʃuːtə'] N Würfelspieler(in) *m(f)*

crash [kræʃ] **1** N **(a)** (= *noise*) Krach(en *nt no pl*) *m no pl*; **there was a ~ upstairs** es hat oben gekracht; **the vase fell to the ground with a ~** die Vase fiel krachend zu Boden
(b) (= *accident*) Unfall *m*; (= *collision also*) Zusammenstoß *m*; (*with several cars*) Karambolage *f*; (= *plane ~*) (Flugzeug)unglück *nt*; **to be in a (car) ~** in einen (Auto)unfall verwickelt sein; **to have a ~** einen (Auto)unfall haben; (= *cause it*) einen Unfall verursachen
(c) (*Fin*) Zusammenbruch *m*; (*St Ex*) Börsenkrach *m*
2 ADV krach; **he went ~ into a tree** er krachte gegen einen Baum
3 VT **(a)** *car, bicycle* einen Unfall haben mit; *plane* abstürzen mit; **to ~ one's car into sth** mit dem Auto gegen etw krachen
(b) (*inf*: = *gatecrash*) **to ~ a party** uneingeladen zu einer Party gehen

4 VI **(a)** einen Unfall haben; (*plane, Comput*) abstürzen; **to ~ into sth** gegen etw (*acc*) krachen
(b) (*with particle*: = *move with a* ~) krachen; **to ~ to the ground** zu Boden krachen; **the whole roof came ~ing down (on him)** das ganze Dach krachte auf ihn herunter
(c) (*Fin*) Pleite machen (*inf*); **when Wall Street ~ed** beim Börsenkrach der Wall Street
(d) (*inf: also ~ out*) (= *sleep*) knacken (*sl*); (= *fall asleep*) einknacken (*sl*)

crash: **crash barrier** N Leitplanke *f*; **crash course** N Intensivkurs *m*; **crash helmet** N Sturzhelm *m*; **crash-land** **1** VI bruchlanden **2** VT bruchlanden mit; **crash-landing** N Bruchlandung *f*

crass [krɑːs] ADJ (+ER) (= *unsubtle*) krass; (= *coarse*) unfein

crassly ['krɑːslɪ] ADV krass; *behave* unfein

crassness ['krɑːsnɪs] N (= *insensitivity*) Krassheit *f*; (= *coarseness*) Derbheit *f*

crate [kreɪt] N (*also inf*: = *car*) Kiste *f*; (= *beer* ~) Kasten *m*

crater ['kreɪtəʳ] N Krater *m*

cravat(te) [krə'væt] N Halstuch *nt*

crave [kreɪv] VT (*liter*: = *beg*) erbitten; (= *desire*) sich sehnen nach
➤ **crave for** VI +PREP OBJ sich sehnen nach

craven ['kreɪvən] (*liter*) ADJ feig(e)

craving ['kreɪvɪŋ] N Verlangen *nt*; **to have a ~ for sth** Verlangen nach etw haben

crawfish ['krɔːfɪʃ] N Languste *f*

crawl [krɔːl] **1** N (a) (= *slow speed*) **we could only go at a ~** wir kamen nur im Schneckentempo voran
(b) (= *swimming stroke*) Kraul(stil) *m*; **to do the ~** kraulen
2 VI (a) (*person, traffic*) kriechen; (*baby*) krabbeln; **he tried to ~ away** er versuchte wegzukriechen
(b) (= *be infested*) wimmeln (*with* von); **the street was ~ing with police** auf der Straße wimmelte es von Polizisten
(c) he makes my flesh *or* **skin ~** wenn ich ihn sehe, kriege ich eine Gänsehaut
(d) (*inf*: = *suck up*) kriechen (*to* vor +*dat*); **he went ~ing to teacher** er ist gleich zum Lehrer gerannt

crawler lane ['krɔːlələn] N (*Brit Aut*) Kriechspur *f*

crawl space N (*US*) niedriger Keller; (*under roof*) Zwischendecke *f*

crayfish ['kreɪfɪʃ] N (a) (*freshwater*) Flusskrebs *m* (b) (*saltwater: also* **crawfish**) Languste *f*

crayon ['kreɪən] **1** N (= *pencil*) Buntstift *m*; (= *wax* ~) Wachs(mal)stift *m*; (= *chalk* ~) Pastellstift *m* **2** VTI (mit Bunt-/Wachsmal-/Pastellstiften) zeichnen *or* malen

craze [kreɪz] **1** N Fimmel *m* (*inf*); **there's a ~ for collecting old things just now** es ist zur Zeit große Mode, alte Sachen zu sammeln **2** VT **a ~d gunman** ein Amokschütze *m*; **he had a ~d look on his face** er hatte den Gesichtsausdruck eines Wahnsinnigen

crazily ['kreɪzɪlɪ] ADV (a) *skid, whirl* wie verrückt (b) (= *madly*) verrückt

craziness ['kreɪzɪnɪs] N Verrücktheit *f*

crazy ['kreɪzɪ] ADJ (+ER) verrückt (*with* vor +*dat*); **to send** *or* **drive sb ~** jdn verrückt machen; **to go ~** verrückt werden; **like ~** (*inf*) wie verrückt (*inf*); **to be ~ about sb/sth** ganz verrückt auf jdn/etw sein (*inf*); **football-~** fußballverrückt (*inf*)

crazy: **crazy bone** N (*US*) Musikantenknochen *m*; **crazy golf** N (*Brit*) Minigolf *nt*; **crazy house** N (*US inf*) Irrenhaus *nt*; **crazy paving** N Mosaikpflaster *nt*; **crazy quilt** N (*US*) Flickendecke *f*

creak [kriːk] **1** N Knarren *nt no pl*; (*of hinges, bed springs*) Quietschen *nt no pl*; **to give a loud ~** laut knarren/quietschen **2** VI knarren; (*hinges, bed springs*) quietschen

creaky ['kriːkɪ] ADJ (+ER) (*lit*) knarrend; *hinges, bed springs* quietschend

cream [kriːm] **1** N (a) Sahne *f*; (= ~ *pudding, artificial* ~, *lotion*) Creme *f*; **~ of chicken soup** Hühnercremesuppe *f*
(b) (= *colour*) Creme(farbe *f*) *nt*
(c) (*fig*: = *best*) die Besten; **our rivals take the ~ of the applicants** unsere Konkurrenz sahnt die besten Bewerber ab; **the ~ of the crop** (= *people*) die Elite; (= *things*) das Nonplusultra
2 ADJ (a) (= *colour*) creme *inv*, cremefarben
(b) (= *made with* ~) Sahne-, Creme-
3 VT (a) *butter* cremig rühren; **~ed potatoes** Kartoffelpüree *nt*

(b) (*US inf*: = *defeat easily*) in die Pfanne hauen (*inf*)
➤ **cream off** VT SEP (*fig*) absahnen

cream: **cream cake** N Sahnetorte *f*; (*small*) Sahnetörtchen *nt*; **cream cheese** N (Doppelrahm)frischkäse *m*

creamer ['kriːməʳ] N (*US*: = *jug*) Sahnekännchen *nt*

cream: **cream puff** N Windbeutel *m*; **cream tea** N Nachmittagstee *m*

creamy ['kriːmɪ] ADJ (+ER) (= *tasting of cream*) sahnig; (= *smooth*) cremig

crease [kriːs] **1** N Falte *f*; (= *deliberate fold*) (*in material*) Kniff *m*; (*in paper also*) Falz *m*; (*ironed: in trousers etc*) (Bügel)falte *f* **2** VT (*deliberately*) *clothes* Falten/eine Falte machen in (+*acc*); *material, paper* Kniffe/einen Kniff machen in (+*acc*); *paper* falzen; (*unintentionally*) zerknittern

crease-proof ['kriːspruːf], **crease-resistant** ['kriːsrɪzɪstənt] ADJ knitterfrei

create [kriː'eɪt] **1** VT schaffen; *the world, man* erschaffen; *draught, noise* verursachen; *difficulties, impression* machen; *problems* (*person*) schaffen; (*action, event*) verursachen; (*Comput*) *file* anlegen; **to ~ a sensation** eine Sensation sein; **to ~ a fuss** Theater machen (*inf*) **2** VI (*Brit inf*) Theater machen (*inf*)

creation [kriː'eɪʃən] N (a) NO PL Schaffung *f*; (*of the world, man*) Erschaffung *f* (b) NO PL **the Creation** die Schöpfung; **all ~, the whole of ~** die Schöpfung (c) (= *created object*) (*Art*) Werk *nt*; (*Fashion*) Kreation *f*

creative [kriː'eɪtɪv] ADJ *power etc* schöpferisch; *approach, person* kreativ; **the ~ use of language** kreativer Sprachgebrauch

creative accounting N kreative Buchführung *f* (*um einen falschen Eindruck vom erzielten Gewinn zu erwecken*)

creatively [kriː'eɪtɪvlɪ] ADV kreativ

creative writing N dichterisches Schreiben

creativity [kriːeɪ'tɪvɪtɪ] N schöpferische Begabung; (*of person also, of approach*) Kreativität *f*

creator [kriː'eɪtəʳ] N Schöpfer(in) *m(f)*

creature ['kriːtʃəʳ] N Geschöpf *nt*

creature comforts PL leibliches Wohl

crèche [kreʃ] N (*Brit*: = *day nursery*) (Kinder)krippe *f*; (*esp US*: = *children's home*) Kinderheim *nt*

credence ['kriːdəns] N, NO PL **to lend** *or* **give ~ to sth** etw glaubwürdig machen; **to give** *or* **attach ~ to sth** einer Sache (*dat*) Glauben schenken

credentials [krɪ'denʃəlz] PL (= *references*) Referenzen *pl*; (= *identity papers*) (Ausweis)papiere *pl*; **to present one's ~** seine Papiere vorlegen

credibility [ˌkredə'bɪlɪtɪ] N Glaubwürdigkeit *f*

credibility gap N Glaubwürdigkeitslücke *f*

credible ['kredɪbl] ADJ glaubwürdig

credibly ['kredɪblɪ] ADV glaubwürdig

credit ['kredɪt] **1** N (a) NO PL (*Fin*) Kredit *m*; (*in pub etc*) Stundung *f*; **the bank will let me have £5,000 ~** die Bank räumt mir einen Kredit von £ 5.000 ein; **to buy on ~** auf Kredit kaufen; **his ~ is good** er ist kreditwürdig; (*in small shop*) er ist vertrauenswürdig; **to give sb (unlimited) ~** jdm (unbegrenzt) Kredit geben
(b) (*Fin*: = *money possessed by person, firm*) (Gut)haben *nt*; (*Comm*: = *sum of money*) Kreditposten *m*; **to be in ~** Geld *nt* auf dem Konto haben; **to keep one's account in ~** sein Konto nicht überziehen; **the ~s and debits** Soll und Haben *nt*; **how much have we got to our ~?** wie viel haben wir auf dem Konto?
(c) NO PL (= *honour*) Ehre *f*; (= *recognition*) Anerkennung *f*; (*Sch, Univ*: = *distinction*) Auszeichnung *f*; **he does his family ~** er macht seiner Familie Ehre; **that's to his ~** das ehrt ihn; **her generosity does her ~** ihre Großzügigkeit macht ihr alle Ehre; **to come out of sth with ~** ehrenvoll aus etw hervorgehen; **to get all the ~** die ganze Anerkennung einstecken; **to take the ~ for sth** das Verdienst für etw in Anspruch nehmen; **~ where ~ is due** (*prov*) Ehre, wem Ehre gebührt (*prov*)
(d) NO PL (= *belief*) Glaube *m*; **to give ~ to sth** etw glauben; **I gave you ~ for more sense** ich habe Sie für vernünftiger gehalten
(e) (*esp US Univ*) Schein *m*; **to take** *or* **do ~s** Scheine machen
(f) credits PL (*Film etc*) Vor-/Nachspann *m*; (*in book*)

Herausgeber- und Mitarbeiterverzeichnis *nt*
2 VT **(a)** (= *believe*) glauben; **would you ~ it!** ist das denn die Möglichkeit!
(b) (= *attribute*) zuschreiben (+*dat*); **I ~ed him with more sense** ich habe ihn für vernünftiger gehalten; **he was ~ed with having invented it** die Erfindung wurde ihm zugeschrieben
(c) (*Fin*) gutschreiben; **to ~ a sum to sb's account** jds Konto (*dat*) einen Betrag gutschreiben (lassen); **he had been ~ed with £100** ihm waren £ 100 gutgeschrieben worden
creditable ['krɛdɪtəbl] ADJ lobenswert
creditably ['krɛdɪtəblɪ] ADV löblich
credit: **credit account** N Kreditkonto *nt*; **credit balance** N Kontostand *m*; **credit card** N Kreditkarte *f*; **credit check** N Überprüfung *f* der Kreditwürdigkeit; **to run a ~ on sb** jds Kreditwürdigkeit überprüfen; **credit enquiry, credit inquiry** N Kreditauskunft *f*; **credit facilities** PL Kreditmöglichkeiten *pl*; **credit insurance** N Kreditversicherung *f*; **credit-led** ADJ (*Econ*) kreditabhängig; **credit limit, credit line** N Kreditrahmen *m*, Kreditlinie *f*; **credit note** N Gutschrift *f*
creditor ['krɛdɪtə'] N Gläubiger *m*
credit: **credit policy** N (*in banking*) Kreditvergabepolitik *f*; **credit rating** N Kreditwürdigkeit *f*; **to have a good/bad ~** als kreditwürdig/als nicht kreditwürdig eingestuft werden; **credit risk** N **to be a good/poor ~** ein geringes/großes Kreditrisiko darstellen; **credit side** N (*lit, fig*) Habenseite *f*; **on the ~ he's young** für ihn spricht, dass er jung ist; **credit standing** N Kreditwürdigkeit *f*, Bonität *f*; **credit status** N Kreditstatus *m*; **credit terms** PL Kreditbedingungen *pl*; **credit union** N Kreditgenossenschaft *f*; **creditworthiness** N Kreditwürdigkeit *f*; **creditworthy** ADJ kreditwürdig
credo ['kreɪdəʊ] N (*lit, fig*) Glaubensbekenntnis *nt*
credulity [krɪ'djuːlɪtɪ] N, NO PL Leichtgläubigkeit *f*
credulous ['krɛdjʊləs] ADJ leichtgläubig
creed [kriːd] N (*fig*) Credo *nt*
creek [kriːk] N (*esp Brit*: = *inlet*) (kleine) Bucht; (*US*: = *brook*) Bach *m*; **to be up the ~ (without a paddle)** (*inf*) in der Tinte sitzen (*inf*)
creep [kriːp] *vb: pret, ptp* **crept** **1** VI schleichen; (*with the body close to the ground, insects*) kriechen; **the water level crept higher and higher** der Wasserspiegel kletterte immer höher; **the story made my flesh ~** bei der Geschichte bekam ich eine Gänsehaut **2** N **(a)** (*inf*: = *unpleasant person*) Widerling *m* (*inf*) **(b)** (*inf*) **he gives me the ~s** er ist mir nicht geheuer; **this old house gives me the ~s** in dem alten Haus ist es mir nicht geheuer
➤ **creep in** VI (*mistakes, doubts*) sich einschleichen (*-to* in +*acc*)
➤ **creep up** VI sich heranschleichen (*on an* +*acc*); (*prices*) (in die Höhe) klettern
creeper ['kriːpə'] N **(a)** (= *plant*) (*along ground*) Kriechpflanze *f*; (*upwards*) Kletterpflanze *f* **(b)** **creepers** PL (*US*) Schuhe mit dicken Gummisohlen, Leisetreter *pl* (*inf*)
creepy ['kriːpɪ] ADJ (+ER) unheimlich
creepy-crawly ['kriːpɪ'krɔːlɪ] (*inf*) N Krabbeltier *nt*
cremate [krɪ'meɪt] VT einäschern
cremation [krɪ'meɪʃən] N Einäscherung *f*
crematorium [,krɛmə'tɔːrɪəm], (*esp US*) **crematory** ['krɛmətɔːrɪ] N Krematorium *nt*
crème de la crème ['krɛmdəlæ'krɛm] N Crème de la Crème *f*
Creole ['kriːəʊl] **1** N **(a)** (*Ling*) Kreolisch *nt* **(b)** (= *person*) Kreole *m*, Kreolin *f* **2** ADJ kreolisch; **he is ~** er ist Kreole
creosote ['krɪəsəʊt] **1** N Kreosot *nt* **2** VT mit Kreosot streichen
crêpe [kreɪp] **1** N **(a)** (*Tex*) Krepp *m* **(b)** (*Cook*) Crêpe *m* **(c)** (*also* = *rubber*) Kreppgummi *m* **2** ADJ Krepp-
crêpe: **crêpe bandage** N elastische Binde; **crêpe paper** N Krepppapier *nt*; **crêpe rubber** **1** N Kreppgummi *m* **2** ADJ Kreppgummi-; **crêpe-soled** ['kreɪp'səʊld] ADJ mit Kreppsohle(n)
crept [krɛpt] PRET, PTP *of* **creep**
crescendo [krɪ'ʃɛndəʊ] N (*Mus*) Crescendo *nt*; (*fig*) Zunahme *f*
crescent ['krɛsnt] N Halbmond *m*; (*in street names*) Weg *m* (*halbmondförmig verlaufende Straße*)
cress [krɛs] N (*Garten*)kresse *f*; (= *watercress*) Brunnenkresse *f*
crest [krɛst] N **(a)** (*of bird*) Haube *f*; (*of cock, hill, wave*) Kamm *m*; **he's riding on the ~ of a wave** (*fig*) er schwimmt im

Augenblick oben **(b)** (*Her*) Helmzierde *f*; (= *coat of arms*) Wappen *nt*
crestfallen ['krɛst,fɔːlən] ADJ geknickt, niedergeschlagen
Cretan ['kriːtən] **1** ADJ kretisch **2** N Kreter(in) *m(f)*
Crete [kriːt] N Kreta *nt*
cretin ['krɛtɪn] N (*inf*) Schwachkopf *m* (*inf*)
cretinous ['krɛtɪnəs] ADJ (*inf*) schwachsinnig
Creutzfeldt-Jakob disease [,krɔɪtsfɛlt'jækɒbdɪ,ziːz] N, NO PL Creutzfeldt-Jakob-Krankheit *f*
crevasse [krɪ'væs] N (*Gletscher*)spalte *f*
crevice ['krɛvɪs] N Spalte *f*
crew¹ [kruː] N **(a)** Mannschaft *f*; (*including officers: of ship also, of plane, tank*) Besatzung *f*; **50 passengers and 20 ~** 50 Passagiere und 20 Mann Besatzung **(b)** (*Brit inf*: = *gang*) Bande *f*
crew² (*old*) PRET *of* **crow**
crew: **crew cut** N Bürstenschnitt *m*; **crew member** N *see* **crew¹** Mitglied *nt* der Mannschaft; Besatzungsmitglied *nt*; **crew neck** N runder Halsausschnitt; (*also* **crew-neck pullover** *or* **sweater**) Pullover *m* mit rundem Halsausschnitt
crib [krɪb] **1** N **(a)** (*US*: = *cot*) Kinderbett *nt* **(b)** (= *manger*) Krippe *f* **(c)** (*US*: = *maize bin*) Trockengerüst *nt* für Maiskolben **(d)** (*esp Brit Sch*: = *cheating aid*) Spickzettel *m* (*inf*); (*inf*: = *plagiarism*) Anleihe *f* (*inf*) **2** VI (*esp Brit Sch inf*) abschreiben (*inf*); **to ~ from sb** von jdm abschreiben (*inf*) **3** VT (*esp Brit Sch inf*) abschreiben (*inf*); **to ~ sth from sb** etw von jdm abschreiben (*inf*)
cribbage ['krɪbɪdʒ] N Cribbage *nt*
crib death N (*US*) plötzlicher Kindstod
crick [krɪk] **1** N **a – in one's neck** ein steifes Genick **2** VT **to ~ one's back** sich (*dat*) einen steifen Rücken zuziehen
cricket¹ ['krɪkɪt] N (= *insect*) Grille *f*
cricket² N (*Sport*) Kricket *nt*; **that's not ~** (*fig inf*) das ist nicht fair

CRICKET

Cricket wird überwiegend im Sommer auf großen Spielfeldern im Freien gespielt. Dabei treten zwei Teams mit jeweils elf Spielern gegeneinander an. Jedes Team schlägt abwechselnd den Ball möglichst weit weg und versucht dann, mit runs Punkte zu erzielen. Die gegnerische Mannschaft, die fielders, versuchen dabei, den Ball zu fangen oder abzustoppen, damit der batsman, der Schlagmann, keinen Punkt machen kann. Wenn der Ball das Tor des Schlagmanns berührt oder gefangen wird, ohne nach dem Abschlag den Boden berührt zu haben, ist der Schlagmann draußen und muss ersetzt werden. Sind alle zehn Schlagmänner im Aus, wechseln die Mannschaften die Rollen; jetzt muss das andere Team aufschlagen. Die Mannschaft, die die meisten runs punkten konnte, gewinnt.

cricket IN CPDS Kricket-; **cricket bat** N (Kricket)schlagholz *nt*
cricketer ['krɪkɪtə'] N Kricketspieler(in) *m(f)*
cricket: **cricket match** N Kricketspiel *nt*; **cricket pitch** N Kricketfeld *nt*
crime [kraɪm] N Straftat *f*; (= *serious ~ also, fig*) Verbrechen *nt*; **it's not a ~!** das ist nicht verboten; **it's a ~ to throw away all that good food** es ist eine Schande, all das gute Essen wegzuwerfen; **~ is on the increase** die Zahl der Verbrechen nimmt zu
Crimea [kraɪ'mɪə] N (*Geog*) Krim *f*
Crimean [kraɪ'mɪən] ADJ Krim-
crime: **crime prevention** N Verbrechensverhütung *f*; **crime rate** N Verbrechensrate *f*; **crime scene** N Tatort *m*; **crime wave** N Verbrechenswelle *f*
criminal ['krɪmɪnl] **1** N Straftäter(in) *m(f)* (*form*), Kriminelle(r) *mf*; (*guilty of serious crimes also, fig*) Verbrecher(in) *m(f)* **2** ADJ **(a)** kriminell, verbrecherisch; **~ law** Strafrecht *nt*; **to have a ~ record** vorbestraft sein **(b)** (*fig*) kriminell; **it's ~ to stay in in this weather** es ist eine Schande, bei diesem Wetter drinnen zu bleiben
criminal: **criminal charge** N **she faces ~s** sie wird eines Verbrechens angeklagt; **criminal code** N Strafgesetzbuch *nt*; **criminal court** N Strafkammer *m*; **Criminal Investigation Department** N (*Brit*) Kriminalpolizei *f*

criminality [ˌkrɪmɪˈnælɪtɪ] N Kriminalität f
criminalize [ˈkrɪmɪnəlaɪz] VT kriminalisieren
criminal lawyer N Anwalt m/Anwältin f für Strafsachen; (specializing in defence) Strafverteidiger(in) m(f)
criminally [ˈkrɪmɪnəlɪ] ADV kriminell, verbrecherisch
criminal offence, (US) **criminal offense** N strafbare Handlung
criminologist [ˌkrɪmɪˈnɒlədʒɪst] N Kriminologe m, Kriminologin f
criminology [ˌkrɪmɪˈnɒlədʒɪ] N Kriminologie f
crimp [krɪmp] VT (mit der Brennschere) wellen
Crimplene® [ˈkrɪmpliːn] N ≈ knitterfreier Trevira®
crimson [ˈkrɪmzn] **1** ADJ purpurrot; (through blushing) knallrot (inf); **to turn** or **go ~** knallrot werden (inf) **2** N Purpur nt, Purpurrot nt
cringe [krɪndʒ] VI **(a)** zurückschrecken (at vor +dat); (fig) schaudern; **he ~d at the thought** er or ihn schauderte bei dem Gedanken; **he ~d when she mispronounced his name** er zuckte zusammen, als sie seinen Namen falsch aussprach **(b)** (= humble oneself) katzbuckeln (to vor +dat)
crinkle [ˈkrɪŋkl] **1** N (Knitter)falte f; (in skin) Fältchen nt **2** VT paper, dress etc (zer)knittern; edge of paper wellen **3** VI (= wrinkle) (paper, dress etc) knittern; (skin) (Lach)fältchen bekommen; (edges of paper) sich wellen
crinkled [ˈkrɪŋkld] ADJ zerknittert
crinkly [ˈkrɪŋklɪ] ADJ (+ER) paper etc zerknittert; edges wellig; hair krauselig (inf)
cripple [ˈkrɪpl] **1** N Krüppel m **2** VT person zum Krüppel machen; ship, plane aktionsunfähig machen; (fig) industry, person lähmen; **~d with rheumatism** von Rheuma praktisch gelähmt; **to be emotionally ~d** ein emotionaler Krüppel sein
crippling [ˈkrɪplɪŋ] ADJ lähmend; taxes, repayments erdrückend; strikes alles lähmend attr; **a ~ disease** ein Leiden, das einen bewegungsunfähig macht; **a ~ blow** (lit, fig) ein schwerer Schlag
crisis [ˈkraɪsɪs] N, pl **crises** [ˈkraɪsiːz] Krise f (also Med); **to reach ~ point** den Höhepunkt erreichen; **that was a ~ in his life** (= decisive moment) das war ein entscheidender Punkt in seinem Leben; (= emotional ~) das war eine Krise in seinem Leben; **in times of ~** in Krisenzeiten
crisis: **crisis centre** N Einsatzzentrum nt (für Krisenfälle); **crisis management** N Krisenmanagement nt
crisp [krɪsp] **1** ADJ (+ER) apple, lettuce knackig; biscuits, bacon knusprig; snow verharscht; leaves trocken; manner, style knapp; air frisch; ten-pound note brandneu **2** N (Brit: = potato ~) Chip m; **burned** or **blackened to a ~** völlig verbrutzelt; toast völlig verkohlt
crispbread [ˈkrɪspbred] N Knäckebrot nt
crisper [ˈkrɪspər] N (in fridge) Gemüsefach nt
crisply [ˈkrɪsplɪ] ADV knackig; baked, fried knusprig; write, speak knapp
crispy [ˈkrɪspɪ] ADJ (+ER) (inf) knusprig
crisscross [ˈkrɪskrɒs] ADJ pattern Kreuz-
criterion [kraɪˈtɪərɪən] N, pl **criteria** [kraɪˈtɪərɪə] Kriterium nt
critic [ˈkrɪtɪk] N Kritiker(in) m(f); literary ~ Literaturkritiker(in) m(f); **he's his own worst ~** er kritisiert sich selbst am meisten; **she is a constant ~ of the government** sie kritisiert die Regierung ständig
critical [ˈkrɪtɪkəl] ADJ kritisch; (= crucial also) entscheidend; (Med) person in kritischem Zustand; **the book was a ~ success** das Buch kam bei den Kritikern an; **to cast a ~ eye over sth** sich (dat) etw kritisch ansehen; **to be ~ of sb/sth** jdn/etw kritisieren; **it is ~ (for us) to understand what is happening** es ist (für uns) von entscheidender Bedeutung zu wissen, was vorgeht; **of ~ importance** von entscheidender Bedeutung
critically [ˈkrɪtɪkəlɪ] ADV **(a)** (= finding fault) kritisch **(b)** ill schwer **(c)** (= crucially) **to be ~ important** von entscheidender Bedeutung sein **(d)** (Art, Liter etc) ~ acclaimed in den Kritiken gelobt
criticism [ˈkrɪtɪsɪzəm] N Kritik f; literary ~ Literaturkritik f; **to come in for a lot of ~** schwer kritisiert werden
criticize [ˈkrɪtɪsaɪz] VTI kritisieren; **to ~ sb for sth** jdn für etw kritisieren; **I ~d her for always being late** ich kritisierte sie dafür, dass sie immer zu spät kommt
critique [krɪˈtiːk] N Kritik f

critter [ˈkrɪtər] N (US dial) = creature
croak [krəʊk] VTI (frog) quaken; (raven, person) krächzen
croaky [ˈkrəʊkɪ] ADJ (+ER) (inf) krächzend
Croat [ˈkrəʊæt] N (= person) Kroate m, Kroatin f; (Ling) Kroatisch nt
Croatia [krəʊˈeɪʃə] N Kroatien nt
Croatian [krəʊˈeɪʃən] **1** N = **Croat 2** ADJ kroatisch; **she is ~** sie ist Kroatin
crochet [ˈkrəʊʃeɪ] **1** N (also ~ **work**) Häkelei f; ~ **hook** Häkelnadel f **2** VTI häkeln
crocked [krɒkt] ADJ (US inf) breit (sl)
crockery [ˈkrɒkərɪ] N (Brit) Geschirr nt
crocodile [ˈkrɒkədaɪl] N Krokodil nt
crocus [ˈkrəʊkəs] N Krokus m
croissant [ˈkrwɑːsɒn] N Hörnchen nt
crony [ˈkrəʊnɪ] N Freund(in) m(f)
crook [krʊk] **1** N **(a)** (= dishonest person) Gauner m (inf) **(b)** (of shepherd) Hirtenstab m; (of bishop) Bischofsstab m **2** VT finger krümmen; arm beugen
crooked [ˈkrʊkɪd] ADJ (lit: = bent) krumm; smile schief; (fig inf: = dishonest) method krumm; person unehrlich
crookedly [ˈkrʊkɪdlɪ] ADV schief
croon [kruːn] **1** VT leise singen; (usu pej: sentimentally) gefühlvoll or schmalzig (pej inf) singen **2** VI leise singen; (usu pej: sentimentally) Schnulzen (pej inf) or sentimentale Lieder singen
crooner [ˈkruːnər] N Sänger m (sentimentaler Lieder)
crop [krɒp] **1** N **(a)** (= produce) Ernte f; (= species grown) (Feld)frucht f; (fig: = large number) Schwung m; **a good ~ of potatoes** eine gute Kartoffelernte; **he grows a different ~ every year** er baut jedes Jahr etwas anderes an; **to bring the ~s in** die Ernte einbringen; **a ~ of problems** (inf) eine Reihe von Problemen **(b)** (of bird) Kropf m **(c)** (= hunting ~) Reitpeitsche f **(d)** (= hairstyle) Kurzhaarschnitt m; **to give sb a close ~** jdm die Haare gehörig stutzen **2** VT hair, tail stutzen; **the goat ~ped the grass** die Ziege fraß das Gras ab; **~ped hair, hair ~ped short** kurz geschnittenes Haar

➤ **crop up** VI aufkommen; **something's cropped up** es ist etwas dazwischengekommen

cropper [ˈkrɒpər] N (Brit inf) **to come a ~** (lit: = fall) hinfliegen (inf); (fig: = fail) auf die Nase fallen
croquet [ˈkrəʊkeɪ] N Krocket(spiel) nt
croquette [krəʊˈket] N Krokette f
cross¹ [krɒs] **1** N **(a)** Kreuz nt; **to make the sign of the Cross** das Kreuzzeichen machen; **we all have our ~ to bear** wir haben alle unser Kreuz zu tragen **(b)** (= hybrid) Kreuzung f; (fig) Mittelding nt; **a ~ between a laugh and a bark** eine Mischung aus Lachen und Bellen **(c)** (Ftbl) Flanke f; **to hit a ~ to sb** jdm zuflanken **2** ATTR street, line etc Quer- **3** VT **(a)** road, river, mountains überqueren; picket line etc überschreiten; country, desert, room durchqueren; **to ~ the road** die Straße überqueren; **to ~ sb's path** (fig) jdm über den Weg laufen; **it ~ed my mind that ...** es fiel mir ein, dass ...; **we'll ~ that bridge when we come to it** lassen wir das Problem mal auf uns zukommen **(b)** (= intersect, create hybrids of) kreuzen; **to ~ one's legs** die Beine übereinander schlagen; **to ~ one's arms** die Arme verschränken; **the lines are ~ed, we have a ~ed line** (Telec) die Leitungen überschneiden sich; **line AB ~es line CD at point E** AB schneidet CD in E; **I'm keeping my fingers ~ed (for you)** (inf) ich drücke (dir) die Daumen (inf) **(c)** (= put a line across) letter, t einen Querstrich machen durch; (Brit) cheque ≈ zur Verrechnung ausstellen; **a ~ed cheque** ein Verrechnungsscheck m; **to ~ sth through** etw durchstreichen **(d)** (= make the sign of the Cross) **to ~ oneself** sich bekreuzigen **(e)** (= go against) **to ~ sb** jdn verärgern **4** VI **(a)** (across road) die Straße überqueren; (across Channel etc) hinüberfahren **(b)** (paths, letters) sich kreuzen; **our paths have ~ed several times** (fig) unsere Wege haben sich öfters gekreuzt

➤ **cross off** VT SEP streichen (prep obj aus, von)

➤ **cross out** VT SEP ausstreichen

➤ **cross over** VI **(a)** (= *cross the road*) die Straße überqueren **(b)** (= *change sides*) überwechseln (*to* zu)

cross² ADJ (+ER) böse; **to be ~ with sb** mit jdm *or* auf jdn böse sein

cross: **crossbar** N (*of bicycle*) Stange *f*; (*Sport*) Querlatte *f*; **cross-border** ADJ (*Comm*) grenzüberschreitend; **crossbow** N (Stand)armbrust *f*; **crossbred** ADJ (*Zool, Biol*) gekreuzt; **crossbreed** (*Zool, Biol*) **1** N Kreuzung *f* **2** VT kreuzen; **cross-Channel** ADJ ATTR Kanal-; **crosscheck** VT überprüfen; **cross-country 1** ADJ Querfeldein-; **~ skiing** Langlauf *m* **2** ADV querfeldein **3** N (= *race*) Querfeldeinrennen *nt*; **crosscurrent** N Gegenströmung *f*; **cross-dress** VI sich als Transvestit kleiden; **cross-dresser** N Transvestit *m*; **cross-dressing** N Transvestismus *m*; **cross-examination** N Kreuzverhör *nt* (*of* über +*acc*); **cross-examine** VT ins Kreuzverhör nehmen; **cross-eyed** ADJ schielend; **to be ~** schielen; **cross-fertilization** N, NO PL (*Bot*) Kreuzbefruchtung *f*; (*fig*) gegenseitige Befruchtung; **cross-fertilize** VT (*Bot*) kreuzbefruchten; **crossfire** N Kreuzfeuer *nt*; **to be caught in the ~** (*lit, fig*) ins Kreuzfeuer geraten

crossing ['krɒsɪŋ] N **(a)** (= *act*) Überquerung *f*; (= *sea ~*) Überfahrt *f* **(b)** (= *~ place*) Übergang *m*; (= *crossroads*) Kreuzung *f*

cross-legged [ˌkrɒs'leg(ɪ)d] ADJ, ADV mit gekreuzten Beinen; (*on ground*) im Schneidersitz

crossly ['krɒslɪ] ADV böse

cross: **crossover** N (*Mus*) **a jazz-rap** = ein Jazz-Rap-Crossover *m*; **cross-party** ADJ (*Pol*) **talks** parteienübergreifend; **support** überparteilich; **cross-ply** ADJ Diagonal-; **cross-purposes** PL **to be** *or* **talk at ~** aneinander vorbeireden; **cross-question** VT = **cross-examine**; **cross-refer** VT verweisen (*to* auf +*acc*); **cross-reference 1** N (Quer)verweis *m* (*to* auf +*acc*) **2** VT = **cross-refer**; **crossroads** N SING *or* PL (*lit*) Kreuzung *f*; (*fig*) Scheideweg *m*; **cross section** N Querschnitt *m*; **a ~ of the population** ein Querschnitt durch die Bevölkerung; **cross-stitch** N (*Sew*) Kreuzstich *m*; **cross-town** ADJ (*US*) quer durch die Stadt; **crosswalk** N (*US*) Fußgängerüberweg *m*; **crosswise** ADV quer; **crossword (puzzle)** N Kreuzworträtsel *nt*

crotch [krɒtʃ] N (*of trousers*) Schritt *m*; (*Anat*) Unterleib *m*; **a kick in the ~** ein Tritt zwischen die Beine

crotchet ['krɒtʃɪt] N (*Brit Mus*) Viertelnote *f*; **~ rest** Viertelpause *f*

crotchety ['krɒtʃɪtɪ] ADJ (*inf*) miesepetrig (*inf*)

crouch [kraʊtʃ] VI sich zusammenkauern; **to ~ down** sich niederkauern

croupier ['kruːpɪeɪ] N Croupier *m*

crouton ['kruːtɒn] N Croûton *m*

crow¹ [krəʊ] N (*Orn*) Krähe *f*; **as the ~ flies** (in der) Luftlinie; **to eat ~** (*US inf*) zu Kreuze kriechen

crow² **1** N (*of cock*) Krähen *nt no pl* **2** VI **(a)** *pret* **crowed** *or* (*old*) **crew**, *ptp* **crowed** (*cock*) krähen **(b)** *pret, ptp* **crowed** (*fig*) (= *boast*) angeben (*about* mit); (= *exult*) hämisch frohlocken (*over* über +*acc*)

crowbar ['krəʊbaː'] N Brecheisen *nt*

crowd [kraʊd] **1** N **(a)** Menschenmenge *f*; (*Sport, Theat*) Zuschauermenge *f*; **to get lost in the ~(s)** in der Menge verloren gehen; **~s of people** Menschenmassen *pl*; **to get a good ~ at a match** bei einem Spiel eine Menge Zuschauer haben; **there was quite a ~** es waren eine ganze Menge Leute da; **a whole ~ of us** ein ganzer Haufen von uns (*inf*) **(b)** (= *clique*) Clique *f*; **the university ~** die Uni-Clique; **the usual ~** die üblichen Leute **(c)** NO PL (= *the masses*) **to go with** *or* **follow the ~** mit der Herde laufen; **she hates to be just one of the ~** sie geht nicht gern in der Masse unter **2** VI (*sich*) drängen; **to ~ (a)round** sich herumdrängen; **to ~ in** (*sich*) hereindrängen; **to ~ (a)round sb/sth** (*sich*) um jdn/etw herumdrängen **3** VT **(a)** **to ~ the streets** die Straßen bevölkern **(b)** (*inf*: = *harass*) **to ~ sb** jdn drängeln

➤ **crowd out** VT SEP (= *not let in*) wegdrängen; (= *make leave*) herausdrängen; **the pub was crowded out** das Lokal war gerammelt voll (*inf*)

crowded ['kraʊdɪd] ADJ **(a)** *train, shop etc* überfüllt; **the streets/shops/trains are ~** es ist voll auf den Straßen/in den

Geschäften/in den Zügen; **~ with people** voller Menschen **(b)** *city, district* überbevölkert; *conditions* beengt

crowd: **crowd pleaser** ['kraʊdpliːzə'] N (= *person*) Publikumsliebling *m*; (= *event etc*) Publikumserfolg *m*; **crowd puller** ['kraʊdpʊlə'] N Kassenmagnet *m*

crown [kraʊn] **1** N **(a)** Krone *f*; **the Crown** die Krone; **to be heir to the ~** Thronfolger(in) *m(f)* sein **(b)** (*of head*) Wirbel *m*; (*of hat*) Kopf *m*; (*of hill*) Kuppe *f* **2** VT (*also*) krönen; **he was ~ed king** er ist zum König gekrönt worden; **to be ~ed with success** von Erfolg gekrönt sein; **to ~ it all** it began to snow (*inf*) zur Krönung des Ganzen begann es zu schneien **(b)** *tooth* eine Krone machen für

crown court N *Bezirksgericht für Strafsachen*

crowning ['kraʊnɪŋ] ADJ krönend; **that symphony was his ~ glory** diese Sinfonie war die Krönung seines Werkes

crown: **crown jewels** PL Kronjuwelen *pl*; **crown prince** N Kronprinz *m*; **crown princess** N Kronprinzessin *f*

crow's: **crow's feet** PL Krähenfüße *pl*; **crow's nest** N (*Naut*) Mastkorb *m*; (*on foremast*) Krähennest *nt*

crucial ['kruːʃəl] ADJ **(a)** (= *decisive*) entscheidend (*to* für) **(b)** (= *very important*) äußerst wichtig

crucially ['kruːʃəlɪ] ADV ausschlaggebend; *different* bedeutend; **~ important** von entscheidender Bedeutung; **~, he is 10 years older than she is** von entscheidender Bedeutung ist, dass er 10 Jahre älter ist als sie

crucible ['kruːsɪbl] N (Schmelz)tiegel *m*

crucifix ['kruːsɪfɪks] N Kruzifix *nt*

crucifixion [ˌkruːsɪ'fɪkʃən] N Kreuzigung *f*

crucify ['kruːsɪfaɪ] VT **(a)** (*lit*) kreuzigen **(b)** (*fig inf*) *author* verreißen; *person* in der Luft zerreißen (*inf*)

crude [kruːd] **1** ADJ (+ER) **(a)** (= *unprocessed*) Roh-, roh **(b)** (= *vulgar*) derb **(c)** (= *unsophisticated*) primitiv; *sketch, manners* grob; *attempt* unbeholfen **2** N Rohöl *nt*

crudely ['kruːdlɪ] ADV **(a)** (= *vulgarly*) derb **(b)** (= *unsophisticatedly*) primitiv; *behave* ungehobelt; (= *approximately*) grob; **to put it ~** um es ganz grob auszudrücken

crudeness ['kruːdnɪs], **crudity** ['kruːdɪtɪ] N **(a)** (= *vulgarity*) Derbheit *f* **(b)** (= *lack of sophistication*) Primitivität *f*

crude oil N Rohöl *nt*

crudités ['kruːdɪteɪz] PL *rohes Gemüse, serviert mit Dips*

cruel ['kruːəl] ADJ grausam (*to* zu); **to be ~ to animals** ein Tierquäler sein; **to be ~ to one's dog** seinen Hund quälen; **don't be ~!** sei nicht so gemein!

cruelly ['kruːəlɪ] ADV grausam

cruelty ['kruːəltɪ] N Grausamkeit *f* (*to* gegenüber); **~ to children** Kindesmisshandlung *f*; **~ to animals** Tierquälerei *f*; **mental ~** seelische Grausamkeit

cruet ['kruːɪt] N Gewürzständer *m*

cruise [kruːz] **1** VI **(a)** (*person*) eine Kreuzfahrt machen **(b)** (*car*) Dauergeschwindigkeit fahren; (*aircraft*) (mit Reisegeschwindigkeit) fliegen; (= *drive around*) herumfahren; **we were cruising along the road** wir fuhren (gemächlich) die Straße entlang; **we are now cruising at a height/speed of ...** wir fliegen nun in einer Flughöhe/mit einer Reisegeschwindigkeit von ... **(c)** (*fig*) **to ~ to victory** einen leichten Sieg erringen **2** VT (*ship*) befahren; (*car*) *streets* fahren auf (+*dat*); *area* abfahren **3** N Kreuzfahrt *f*; **to go on** *or* **for a ~** eine Kreuzfahrt machen

cruise missile N Marschflugkörper *m*

cruiser ['kruːzə'] N (*Naut*) Kreuzer *m*; (= *pleasure ~*) Vergnügungsjacht *f*

cruller ['krʌlə'] N (*US Cook*) *eine Art Berliner*

crumb [krʌm] N Krümel *m*; **a few ~s of information** ein paar Informationsbrocken; **that's one ~ of comfort** das ist (wenigstens) ein winziger Trost

crumble ['krʌmbl] **1** VT zerkrümeln; **to ~ sth into/onto sth** etw in/auf etw (*acc*) krümeln **2** VI (*brick*) bröckeln; (*cake etc*) krümeln; (*also ~ away*) (*earth, building*) zerbröckeln; (*fig: resistance*) sich auflösen **3** N (*Brit Cook*) Obst *nt* mit Streusel; (= *topping*) Streusel *pl*; **rhubarb ~** mit Streuseln bestreutes, überbackenes Rhabarberdessert

crumbly ['krʌmblɪ] ADJ (+ER) *stone, earth* bröckelig; *cake* krümelig

crummy ['krʌmɪ] ADJ (+ER) (inf) mies (inf)

crumpet ['krʌmpɪt] N (Cook) süßes, pfannkuchenartiges Gebäck

crumple ['krʌmpl] **1** VT (also ~ **up**) (= crease) zer- or verknittern; (= screw up) zusammenknüllen; metal eindrücken **2** VI (lit, fig) zusammenbrechen; (car, metal) zusammengedrückt werden

crunch [krʌntʃ] **1** VT (a) biscuit etc mampfen (inf); **he ~ed the beetle/ice underfoot** der Käfer zerknackte/das Eis zersplitterte unter seinen Füßen; **to ~ the gears** (Aut) die Gänge reinwürgen (inf) **(b)** (Comput) verarbeiten **2** VI (gravel, snow etc) knirschen; (gears) krachen; **he ~ed across the gravel** er ging mit knirschenden Schritten über den Kies; **he was ~ing on a carrot** er mampfte eine Möhre (inf) **3** N **(a)** (= sound) Krachen nt; (of footsteps, gravel etc) Knirschen nt **(b)** (inf) **the ~** der große Krach; **when it comes to the ~** wenn der entscheidende Moment kommt

crunchy ['krʌntʃɪ] ADJ (+ER) apple knackig; biscuit knusprig

crusade [kruːˈseɪd] **1** N (Hist, fig) Kreuzzug m **2** VI (Hist, fig) einen Kreuzzug/Kreuzzüge führen

crusader [kruːˈseɪdə^r] N (Hist) Kreuzfahrer m; (fig) Apostel m

crush [krʌʃ] **1** N **(a)** (= crowd) Gedrängel nt; **it'll be a bit of a ~** es wird ein bisschen eng werden **(b)** (inf) **to have a ~ on sb** in jdn verschossen sein (inf); **schoolgirl ~** Schulmädchenschwärmerei f **(c)** (= drink) Saftgetränk nt **2** VT **(a)** quetschen; (= damage) soft fruit etc zerdrücken; (rock, car etc) sb zerquetschen; (= kill) zu Tode quetschen; spices, garlic (zer)stoßen; ice stoßen; ore, stone zerstampfen; scrap metal zusammenpressen; clothes, paper zerknittern; **I was ~ed between two enormous men in the plane** ich war im Flugzeug zwischen zwei fetten Männern eingequetscht; **to ~ sb into sth** jdn in etw (acc) quetschen; **to ~ sth into sth** etw in etw (acc) stopfen **(b)** (fig) enemy vernichten; revolution, opposition niederschlagen; **to ~ sb's spirit** jdn brechen

➤ **crush up** VT SEP **(a)** (= pulverize) zerstoßen **(b)** (= pack tightly together) zusammendrücken; **we were (sitting) all crushed up** wir saßen alle zusammengequetscht

crushing ['krʌʃɪŋ] ADJ defeat zerschmetternd; blow, reply vernichtend

crust [krʌst] N (all senses) Kruste f; **the earth's ~** die Erdkruste; **to earn a ~** (inf) seinen Lebensunterhalt verdienen

crustacean [krʌsˈteɪʃən] N Schalentier nt

crusty ['krʌstɪ] ADJ (+ER) knusprig

crutch [krʌtʃ] N **(a)** (for walking) Krücke f; **to use sb/sth as a ~** (fig) sich an jdn/etw klammern **(b)** = **crotch**

crux [krʌks] N Kern m

cry [kraɪ] **1** N **(a)** Schrei m; (= call) Ruf m; (Hunt: of hounds) Geheul nt; **to be in full ~** (fig) voll in Aktion sein (inf); **to give or utter a ~** (auf)schreien; **a ~ of fear/pain** ein Angst-/Schmerzensschrei m; **a ~ for help** ein Hilferuf m; **he gave a ~ for help** er rief um Hilfe **(b)** (= slogan) Parole f; (= battle ~) Schlachtruf m **(c)** (= outcry) **a ~ for sth** ein Ruf m nach etw; **a ~ against sth** ein Protest m gegen etw **(d)** (= weep) **to have a good ~** sich einmal richtig ausweinen **2** VI **(a)** (= weep) weinen; (baby) schreien; **she was ~ing for her teddy bear** sie weinte nach ihrem Teddy **(b)** (= call) rufen; (louder) schreien; **to ~ for help** um Hilfe rufen/schreien; **she cried for somebody to come** sie rief/schrie nach jemandem **3** VT **(a)** (= shout out) rufen; (louder) schreien; **he cried to me to go away** er rief mir zu, dass ich verschwinden sollte **(b)** (= weep) weinen; **to ~ one's eyes out** sich (dat) die Augen ausweinen; **to ~ oneself to sleep** sich in den Schlaf weinen

➤ **cry off** VI (Brit) einen Rückzieher machen

➤ **cry out** VI **(a)** aufschreien; **to cry out to sb** jdm etwas zuschreien; **well, for crying out loud!** (inf) na, das darf doch wohl nicht wahr sein! (inf) **(b)** (fig) **to be crying out for sth** nach etw schreien

crybaby ['kraɪbeɪbɪ] N (inf) Heulsuse f (inf)

crying ['kraɪɪŋ] **1** ADJ (fig) need dringend; **it is a ~ shame** es ist jammerschade **2** N (= weeping) Weinen nt; (of baby) Schreien nt

crypt [krɪpt] N Krypta f; (= burial ~) Gruft f

cryptic ['krɪptɪk] ADJ remark etc hintergründig; clue etc verschlüsselt

cryptically ['krɪptɪkəlɪ] ADV hintergründig

crystal ['krɪstl] **1** N Kristall m; (= quartz) (Quarz)kristall m **2** ADJ Kristall-; (= like a ~) kristallartig; (= quartz) Quarzkristall-

crystal: **crystal ball** N Glaskugel f; **crystal-clear** ADJ (lit, fig) glasklar

crystallize ['krɪstəlaɪz] **1** VT (lit) zum Kristallisieren bringen; (= separating out) auskristallisieren; (fig) (feste) Form geben (+dat) **2** VI (lit) kristallisieren; (= separate out) (sich) auskristallisieren; (fig) feste Form annehmen; **this theory ~d out of many years' research** diese Theorie hat sich nach jahrelanger Forschung herauskristallisiert

crystallized ['krɪstəlaɪzd] ADJ kristallisiert; fruit kandiert

CS gas N ≈ Tränengas nt

CST ABBR of **Central Standard Time**

ct (a) ABBR of **cent (b)** ABBR of **carat**

C term N C-Klausel f

CTT N ABBR of **capital transfer tax**

cub [kʌb] N **(a)** (of animal) Junge(s) nt **(b)** **Cub** (= Cub Scout) Wölfling m

Cuba ['kjuːbə] N Kuba nt

Cuban ['kjuːbən] **1** ADJ kubanisch **2** N Kubaner(in) m(f)

cubbyhole ['kʌbɪhəʊl] N Kabuff nt

cube [kjuːb] **1** N **(a)** Würfel m **(b)** (Math) dritte Potenz; **the ~ of 3 is 27** 3 hoch 3 ist 27 **2** VT **(a)** (Math) hoch 3 nehmen; **four ~d** vier hoch drei **(b)** (Cook) in Würfel schneiden

cube: **cube root** N Kubikwurzel f; **cube sugar** N Würfelzucker m

cubic ['kjuːbɪk] ADJ Kubik-; **~ metre/foot** Kubikmeter m or nt/Kubikfuß m

cubic capacity N Fassungsvermögen nt; (of engine) Hubraum m

cubicle ['kjuːbɪkəl] N Kabine f; (in toilets) (Einzel)toilette f

cubism ['kjuːbɪzəm] N Kubismus m

cubist ['kjuːbɪst] **1** N Kubist(in) m(f) **2** ADJ kubistisch

Cub Scout N Wölfling m

cuckoo ['kʊkuː] N Kuckuck m

cuckoo clock N Kuckucksuhr f

cucumber ['kjuːkʌmbə^r] N (Salat)gurke f; **as cool as a ~** seelenruhig

cud [kʌd] N **to chew the ~** (lit) wiederkäuen

cuddle ['kʌdl] **1** N Liebkosung f; **to give sb a ~** jdn in den Arm nehmen; **to have a ~** schmusen **2** VT in den Arm nehmen **3** VI schmusen

➤ **cuddle up** VI sich kuscheln (to, against an +acc); **to cuddle up in bed** sich im Bett zusammenkuscheln

cuddly ['kʌdlɪ] ADJ (+ER) knuddelig (inf)

cuddly toy N Schmusetier nt (inf)

cudgel ['kʌdʒəl] N (Brit) Knüppel m; **to take up the ~s for or on behalf of sb/sth** (fig) für jdn/etw eintreten

cue [kjuː] **1** N **(a)** (Theat, fig) Stichwort nt; (action) (Einsatz)zeichen nt; (Film, TV) Zeichen nt zum Aufnahmebeginn; (Mus) Einsatz m; **to give sb his ~** (Theat) jdm das or sein Stichwort geben; (action) jdm das (Einsatz)zeichen geben; (Mus) jdm den Einsatz geben; **to take one's ~ from sb** sich nach jdm richten **(b)** (Billiards) Queue nt **2** VT (Theat) das Stichwort geben (+dat); (with gesture etc) das Einsatzzeichen geben (+dat); (Film, TV) scene abfahren lassen; (Mus) player den Einsatz geben (+dat); trumpet flourish etc den Einsatz geben für

➤ **cue in** VT SEP den Einsatz geben (+dat); (Film, TV) scene abfahren lassen; tape etc (zur rechten Zeit) einspielen

cue ball N Spielball m

cuff[1] [kʌf] N **(a)** Manschette f; **off the ~** aus dem Stegreif **(b)** (US: of trousers) (Hosen)aufschlag m **(c)** US PL (inf: = handcuff) Handschelle f **(d)** (dated US inf: = credit) **on the ~** auf Stottern (inf)

cuff[2] VT (= strike) einen Klaps geben (+dat) **2** N (= blow) Klaps m

cuff link N Manschettenknopf m

cuisine [kwɪˈziːn] N Küche f

cul-de-sac [ˈkʌldəsæk] N Sackgasse f

culinary [ˈkʌlɪnərɪ] ADJ kulinarisch; *skill etc* im Kochen

cull [kʌl] **1** N *Erlegen überschüssiger Tierbestände,* *Reduktionsabschuss m;* **~ of seals** Robbenschlag *m* **2** VT **(a)** (= *collect*) entnehmen *(from +dat)* **(b)** (= *kill as surplus*) (als überschüssig) erlegen; **to ~ seals** Robbenschlag *m* betreiben

culminate [ˈkʌlmɪneɪt] **1** VI *(fig)* (= *reach a climax*) gipfeln *(in* in *+dat)*; (= *end*) herauslaufen *(in* auf *+acc)* **2** VT *(US)* den Höhepunkt *(+gen)* darstellen

culmination [ˌkʌlmɪˈneɪʃən] N *(fig)* (= *high point*) Höhepunkt *m*; (= *end*) Ende *nt*

culottes [kjuːˈlɒts] PL Hosenrock *m*; **a pair of ~** ein Hosenrock

culpability [ˌkʌlpəˈbɪlɪtɪ] N *(form)* Schuld f

culpable [ˈkʌlpəbl] ADJ *(form)* schuldig

culprit [ˈkʌlprɪt] N Schuldige(r) *mf*; *(Jur)* Täter(in) *m(f)*; *(inf)* (= *person causing trouble*) Übeltäter(in) *m(f)*; (= *thing causing trouble*) Übeltäter *m*

cult [kʌlt] **1** N *(Rel, fig)* Kult *m*; **to make a ~ of sth** (einen) Kult mit etw treiben **2** ATTR Kult-

cultivate [ˈkʌltɪveɪt] VT **(a)** *(lit)* kultivieren; *crop etc* anbauen; *beard* wachsen lassen **(b)** *(fig) friendship, links etc* pflegen; *skill, taste* entwickeln; *sb* die Beziehung zu ... pflegen; **to ~ one's mind** sich bilden

cultivated [ˈkʌltɪveɪtɪd] ADJ *(Agr, fig)* kultiviert

cultivation [ˌkʌltɪˈveɪʃən] N **(a)** *(lit)* Kultivieren *nt*; *(of crop etc)* Anbau *m*; **to be under ~** bebaut werden **(b)** *(fig) (of friendship, links etc)* Pflege f *(of* von); *(of skill)* Entwicklung f

cultivator [ˈkʌltɪveɪtə] N (= *machine*) Grubber *m*

cult movie N Kultfilm *m*

cultural [ˈkʌltʃərəl] ADJ Kultur-; *similarities, events* kulturell; **~ differences** kulturelle Unterschiede *pl*; **what sort of ~ activities are there?** was wird kulturell geboten?; **we enjoyed a very ~ evening** wir hatten einen kulturell sehr anspruchsvollen Abend

culturally [ˈkʌltʃərəlɪ] ADV kulturell

culture [ˈkʌltʃə] N Kultur f; *(of animals)* Zucht f; **a man of ~/of no ~** ein Mann mit/ohne Kultur; **to study German ~** die deutsche Kultur studieren

cultured [ˈkʌltʃəd] ADJ kultiviert

cultured pearl N Zuchtperle f

culture: culture shock N Kulturschock *m*; **culture vulture** N *(hum)* Kulturfanatiker(in) *m(f)*

cum [kʌm] PREP in einem; **a sort of sofa-~-bed** eine Art von Sofa und Bett in einem; **~ dividend** *(Fin)* mit Dividende

cumbersome [ˈkʌmbəsəm] ADJ *clothing* (be)hinderlich; *spacesuit, style* schwerfällig; *vehicle* unhandlich *(inf)*; *suitcases, parcels* sperrig; *procedure* beschwerlich

cumin [ˈkʌmɪn] N Kreuzkümmel *m*

cummerbund [ˈkʌməbʌnd] N Kummerbund *m*

cumulative [ˈkjuːmjʊlətɪv] ADJ gesamt

cumulative interest N *(Fin)* Zins und Zinseszins

cumulatively [ˈkjuːmjʊlətɪvlɪ] ADV kumulativ

cunnilingus [ˌkʌnɪˈlɪŋɡəs] N Cunnilingus *m*

cunning [ˈkʌnɪŋ] **1** N Schlauheit f **2** ADJ **(a)** *plan, person* schlau; *smile, expression* verschmitzt; (= *ingenious*) *gadget* clever ausgedacht *(inf)* **(b)** *(US inf)* drollig

cunningly [ˈkʌnɪŋlɪ] ADV schlau; **a ~ designed little gadget** ein clever ausgedachtes Ding

cunt [kʌnt] N *(vulg)* (= *vagina*) Fotze f *(vulg)*; *(term of abuse)* Arsch *m (vulg)*

cup [kʌp] **1** N **(a)** Tasse f; (= *goblet, football ~ etc*) Pokal *m*; (= *mug*) Becher *m*; *(Eccl)* Kelch *m*; *(Cook: standard measure)* 8 fl oz = 0,22 l; **a ~ of tea/water** eine Tasse Tee/Wasser; **that's not my ~ of tea** *(fig inf)* das ist nicht mein Fall; **they're out of the Cup** sie sind aus dem Pokal(wettbewerb) ausgeschieden **(b)** (= *drink*) Mix *m* **(c)** *(of bra)* Körbchen *nt* **2** VT *hands* hohl machen; **to ~ one's** *or* **a hand to one's ear** die Hand ans Ohr halten

cupboard [ˈkʌbəd] N Schrank *m*

cup: cupcake N *kleiner, runder Kuchen*; **Cup Final** N Pokalendspiel *nt*; **cupful** N, *pl* cupsful, cupfuls Tasse f *(voll)*

cupid [ˈkjuːpɪd] N Amorette f; **Cupid** Amor *m*

cupola [ˈkjuːpələ] N *(Archit)* Kuppel f

cuppa [ˈkʌpə] N *(Brit inf)* Tasse Tee f

cup: cup size N *(of bra)* Körbchengröße f; **cup tie** N Pokalspiel *nt*; **Cup Winners' Cup** N *(Ftbl)* Europapokal *m* der Pokalsieger

cur [kɜːʳ] N *(pej)* Köter *m (pej)*

curable [ˈkjʊərəbl] ADJ heilbar

curate [ˈkjʊərɪt] N *(Catholic)* Kurat *m*; *(Protestant)* Vikar(in) *m(f)*

curator [kjʊəˈreɪtəʳ] N *(of museum etc)* Kustos *m*

curb [kɜːb] **1** N **(a)** *(fig)* Behinderung f; **to put a ~ on sth** etw einschränken **(b)** *(esp US:* = *curbstone)* = **kerb 2** VT *(fig)* zügeln; *public spending* dämpfen; *immigration, investment etc* bremsen *(inf)*

curb: curb market N *(US St Ex)* Freiverkehr *m*; **curb service** N *(US)* Bedienung f am Fahrzeug; **curbstone** N *(esp US)* = **kerbstone**

curd [kɜːd] N *(often pl)* Quark *m*

curd cheese N Weißkäse *m*

curdle [ˈkɜːdl] **1** VT *(lit, fig)* gerinnen lassen **2** VI gerinnen; **his blood ~d** das Blut gerann ihm in den Adern

cure [kjʊəʳ] **1** VT **(a)** *(Med)* heilen; **to be/get ~d (of sth)** (von etw) geheilt sein/werden **(b)** *(fig) inflation, ill etc* abhelfen *(+dat)*; **to ~ sb of sth** jdm etw austreiben **(c)** *food* haltbar machen; (= *salt*) pökeln; (= *smoke*) räuchern; (= *dry*) trocknen **2** VI *(food)* **it is left to ~** (= *to salt*) es wird zum Pökeln eingelegt; (= *to smoke*) es wird zum Räuchern aufgehängt; (= *to dry*) es wird zum Trocknen ausgebreitet **3** N *(Med)* (= *remedy*) (Heil)mittel *nt (for* gegen); (= *treatment*) Heilverfahren *nt (for sb* für jdn, *for sth* gegen etw); (= *recovery*) Heilung f; (= *health ~*) Kur f; *(fig:* = *remedy)* Mittel *nt (for* gegen); **there's no ~ for that** *(lit)* das ist unheilbar; *(fig)* dagegen kann man nichts machen

cure-all [ˈkjʊərɔːl] N *(lit, fig)* Allheilmittel *nt*

curfew [ˈkɜːfjuː] N Ausgangssperre f; **to be under ~** unter Ausgangssperre stehen

curio [ˈkjʊərɪəʊ] N Kuriosität f

curiosity [ˌkjʊərɪˈɒsɪtɪ] N **(a)** NO PL (= *inquisitiveness*) Neugier f; *(for knowledge)* Wissbegier(de) f; **out of** *or* **from ~** aus Neugier **(b)** (= *odd*, *person*) Kuriosität f

curious [ˈkjʊərɪəs] ADJ **(a)** (= *inquisitive*) neugierig; **I'm ~ to know what he'll do** ich bin mal gespannt, was er macht; **I'm ~ to know how he did it** ich bin neugierig zu erfahren, wie er das gemacht hat; **why do you ask? – I'm just ~** warum fragst du? – nur so **(b)** (= *odd*) sonderbar; **how ~!** wie seltsam!; **it's ~ the way he already knew that** sonderbar, dass er das schon gewusst hat

> *Be careful!* **curious** *is not translated by the German word* **kurios**.

curiously [ˈkjʊərɪəslɪ] ADV **(a)** (= *inquisitively*) neugierig **(b)** (= *oddly*) seltsam; **they are ~ similar** sie ähneln sich auf seltsame Weise; **~ (enough), he didn't object** merkwürdigerweise hatte er nichts dagegen

curl [kɜːl] **1** N *(of hair)* Locke f; **in ~s** in Locken, gelockt; *(tight)* kraus **2** VT *hair* locken; *(with curlers)* in Locken legen; *(in tight ~s)* kräuseln; *edges* umbiegen **3** VI *(hair)* sich locken; *(tightly ~s)* sich kräuseln; *(naturally)* lockig sein; *(paper)* sich wellen

➤ **curl up 1** VI *(animal, person)* sich zusammenrollen; *(hedgehog)* sich einigeln; *(paper)* sich wellen; *(leaf)* sich hochbiegen; **to curl up in bed/in an armchair** sich ins Bett/in einen Sessel kuscheln; **to curl up with a good book** es sich *(dat)* mit einem guten Buch gemütlich machen **2** VT SEP *moustache, piece of paper etc* wellen; *edges* hochbiegen; **to curl oneself/itself up** sich zusammenkugeln

curler [ˈkɜːləʳ] N *(hair ~)* Lockenwickel *m*; **to put one's ~s in** sich *(dat)* die Haare eindrehen; **my hair was in ~s, I had my ~s in** ich hatte Lockenwickel im Haar

curlew [ˈkɜːljuː] N Brachvogel *m*

curling [ˈkɜːlɪŋ] N *(Sport)* Curling *nt*

curling tongs, *(US)* **curling iron** PL Lockenschere f; *(electric)* Lockenstab *m*

curly [ˈkɜːlɪ] ADJ (+ER) *hair* lockig; *(tighter)* kraus; *tail* geringelt; *lettuce* kraus; *pattern, writing* verschnörkelt

curly-haired [ˈkɜːlɪˈhɛəd] ADJ lockig; *(tighter)* krausköpfig

currant [ˈkʌrənt] N **(a)** (= *dried fruit*) Korinthe *f* **(b)** (*Bot*) Johannisbeere *f*; **~ bush** Johannisbeerstrauch *m*

currant bun N Rosinenbrötchen *nt*

currency [ˈkʌrənsɪ] N **(a)** (*Fin*) Währung *f*; **foreign ~** Devisen *pl* **(b)** (*of word, expression*) Gebräuchlichkeit *f*; **to gain ~** sich verbreiten

currency market N Devisenmarkt *m*

currency outflow N (*Comm, Fin*) Devisenabfluss *m*

current [ˈkʌrənt] **1** ADJ (= *present*) gegenwärtig; *policy, price* aktuell; *research, month, week etc* laufend; *edition* letzte(r, s); *opinion* verbreitet; **to be no longer ~** nicht mehr aktuell sein; **~ affairs** aktuelle Fragen *pl*; **in ~ use** allgemein gebräuchlich; **~ yield** (*Fin*) laufende Rendite **2** N **(a)** (*of water*) Strömung *f*; (*of air*) Luftströmung *f*; **with/against the ~** mit dem/gegen den Strom **(b)** (*Elec*) Strom *m* **(c)** (*fig: of events etc*) Trend *m*; **to go against the ~ of popular opinion** gegen den Strom der öffentlichen Meinung anschwimmen; **to go with the ~ of popular opinion** mit dem Strom der öffentlichen Meinung schwimmen

current: **current account** N Girokonto *nt*; **current assets** PL Umlaufvermögen *nt*; **current capital** N (*US*) Betriebskapital *nt*; **current expenses** PL laufende Ausgaben *pl*; **current liabilities** PL kurzfristige Verbindlichkeiten *pl*

currently [ˈkʌrəntlɪ] ADV gegenwärtig

current ratio N (*Fin*) *Verhältnis des gesamten Umlaufvermögens zu kurzfristigen Verbindlichkeiten*

curricula [kəˈrɪkjʊlə] PL *of* **curriculum**

curricular [kəˈrɪkjʊləʳ] ADJ lehrplanmäßig

curriculum [kəˈrɪkjʊləm] N, *pl* **curricula** Lehrplan *m*; **to be on the ~** auf dem Lehrplan stehen

curriculum vitae [kəˈrɪkjʊləmˈviːtaɪ] N (*Brit*) Lebenslauf *m*

curry[1] [ˈkʌrɪ] (*Cook*) **1** N (= *spice*) Curry *m or nt*; (= *dish*) Curry *nt*; **~ sauce** Currysauce *f* **2** VT mit Curry zubereiten

curry[2] VT **to ~ favour (with sb)** sich (bei jdm) einschmeicheln

curry powder N Currypulver *nt*

curse [kɜːs] **1** N Fluch *m*; (*inf: = nuisance*) Plage *f* (*inf*); **the ~ of drunkenness** der Fluch des Alkohols; **to be under a ~** unter einem Fluch stehen; **to put sb under a ~** jdn mit einem Fluch belegen **2** VT **(a)** (= *put a ~ on*) verfluchen; **~ you/it!** (*inf*) verflucht! (*inf*); **where is he now, ~ him!** (*inf*) wo steckt er jetzt, der verfluchte Kerl! (*inf*) **(b)** (= *swear at or about*) fluchen über (+*acc*) **(c)** (*fig: = afflict*) **to be ~d with sb/sth** mit jdm/etw geschlagen sein **3** VI fluchen

cursed [ˈkɜːsɪd] ADJ (*inf*) verflucht (*inf*)

cursor [ˈkɜːsəʳ] N (*Comput*) Cursor *m*

cursorily [ˈkɜːsərɪlɪ] ADV flüchtig

cursory [ˈkɜːsərɪ] ADJ flüchtig

curt [kɜːt] ADJ (+ER) *person* kurz angebunden; *letter, refusal* kurz, knapp; **to be ~ with sb** zu jdm kurz angebunden sein

curtail [kɜːˈteɪl] VT kürzen

curtain [ˈkɜːtn] N **(a)** Vorhang *m* (*also Theat*); (= *net ~*) Gardine *f*; **to draw or pull the ~s** (= *open*) den Vorhang/die Vorhänge aufziehen; (= *close*) den Vorhang/die Vorhänge zuziehen; **the ~ rises/falls** der Vorhang hebt sich/fällt; **to bring the ~ down on sth** (*fig*) den Vorhang endgültig über etw (*acc*) fallen lassen **(b)** (*fig: of mystery*) Schleier *m*; **a ~ of smoke/rain** eine Rauch-/Regenwand; **if you get caught it'll be ~s for you** (*inf*) wenn sie dich erwischen, bist du weg vom Fenster (*inf*)

➤ **curtain off** VT SEP durch einen Vorhang/Vorhänge abtrennen

curtain: **curtain call** N (*Theat*) Vorhang *m*; **to take a ~** vor den Vorhang treten; **curtain hook** N Gardinengleithaken *m*; **curtain pole** N Vorhangstange *f*; **curtain rail** N Vorhangschiene *f*; **curtain-raiser** N (*Theat*) kurzes Vorspiel; **curtain ring** N Gardinenring *m*

curtly [ˈkɜːtlɪ] ADV *reply* kurz, knapp; *refuse* kurzerhand

curtsey, (*US*) **curtsy** [ˈkɜːtsɪ] **1** N Knicks *m*; (*to royalty*) Hofknicks *m* **2** VI knicksen (*to* vor +*dat*)

curvaceous [kɜːˈveɪʃəs] ADJ üppig

curvature [ˈkɜːvətʃəʳ] N Krümmung *f*; (*misshapen*) Verkrümmung *f*; **~ of the spine** (*normal*) Rückgratkrümmung *f*; (*abnormal*) Rückgratverkrümmung *f*

curve [kɜːv] **1** N Kurve *f*; (*of body, vase etc*) Rundung *f*; (*of river*) Biegung *f*; (*of archway*) Bogen *m*; **there's a ~ in the road** die Straße macht einen Bogen; **her ~s** (*inf*) ihre Rundungen *pl* (*inf*) **2** VT biegen; (= *build with a ~*) wölben; **he ~d the ball around the wall** er zirkelte den Ball um die Mauer herum **3** VI **(a)** (*line, road*) einen Bogen machen; (*river*) eine Biegung machen **(b)** (= *be curved*) sich wölben; (*metal strip etc*) sich biegen

curve ball N **(a)** (*US Baseball*) Ball, der bogenförmig vom Werfer zum Schlagmann geworfen wird **(b)** (= *tricky problem*) böse Überraschung; **to throw sb a ~** jdn mit einem Problem konfrontieren

curved [kɜːvd] ADJ *line* gebogen; *surface, arch* gewölbt

cushion [ˈkʊʃən] **1** N Kissen *nt*; (= *pad, fig: = buffer*) Polster *nt*; (*Billiards*) Bande *f*; **a ~ of air** ein Luftkissen *nt*; **~ cover** Kissenbezug *m* **2** VT **(a)** *fall, blow, disappointment* dämpfen **(b)** (*fig: = protect*) **to ~ sb against sth** jdn gegen etw abschirmen

cushy [ˈkʊʃɪ] ADJ (+ER) (*inf*) bequem; **to have a ~ time of it, to be onto a ~ number** eine ruhige Kugel schieben (*inf*); **a ~ job** ein ruhiger Job

cusp [kʌsp] N **on the ~ of** (*fig*) an der Schwelle zu

cuspidor [ˈkʌspɪdɔːʳ] N (*US*) Spucknapf *m*

cussed [ˈkʌsɪd] ADJ stur

cussedness [ˈkʌsɪdnɪs] N (*inf*) Sturheit *f*

cussword [ˈkʌswɜːd] N (*US inf*) Kraftausdruck *m*

custard [ˈkʌstəd] N (= *pouring*) ≈ Vanillesoße *f*; (= *set ~*) ≈ Vanillepudding *m*

custard pie N (*in slapstick*) Sahnetorte *f*

custodial [kʌsˈtəʊdɪəl] ADJ (*form*) **~ sentence** Gefängnisstrafe *f*

custodian [kʌsˈtəʊdɪən] N (*of park, museum*) Aufseher(in) *m(f)*; (*of treasure, tradition, world peace etc*) Hüter(in) *m(f)*

custody [ˈkʌstədɪ] N **(a)** (= *keeping*) Obhut *f*; (*Jur*) (*of children*) Sorgerecht *nt* (*of* für, über +*acc*); (= *guardianship*) Vormundschaft *f* (*of* für, über +*acc*); **to put or place sth in sb's ~** etw jdm zur Aufbewahrung anvertrauen; **the mother was awarded ~ of the children after the divorce** der Mutter wurde bei der Scheidung das Sorgerecht über die Kinder zugesprochen; **he is in the ~ of his aunt** seine Tante hat die Vormundschaft über ihn **(b)** (= *police detention*) (polizeilicher) Gewahrsam; **to take sb into ~** jdn verhaften

custom [ˈkʌstəm] **1** N **(a)** (= *convention*) Sitte *f*, Brauch *m*; **~ demands ...** es ist Sitte *or* Brauch ... **(b)** (= *habit*) (An)gewohnheit *f*; **it was his ~ to rest each afternoon** er pflegte am Nachmittag zu ruhen (*geh*) **(c)** NO PL (*Comm: = patronage*) Kundschaft *f*; **to get sb's ~** jdn als Kunden gewinnen; **to take one's ~ elsewhere** woanders Kunde werden **(d)** **customs** PL (*the*) Customs der Zoll; **the Customs and Excise Department** die britische Zollbehörde; **to go through ~s** durch den Zoll gehen; **to get sth through the ~s** etw durch den Zoll bekommen **2** ADJ (*US*) *suit, shoes* maßgefertigt; *carpenter* auf Bestellung arbeitend; **~ tailor** Maßschneider(in) *m(f)*

customarily [ˈkʌstəmərəlɪ] ADV üblicherweise

customary [ˈkʌstəmərɪ] ADJ (= *conventional*) üblich; (= *habitual*) gewohnt; **it's ~ to wear a tie** man trägt normalerweise *or* gewöhnlich eine Krawatte

custom-built [ˈkʌstəmˈbɪlt] ADJ speziell angefertigt

customer [ˈkʌstəməʳ] N **(a)** (*Comm*) Kunde *m*, Kundin *f*; **our ~s** unsere Kundschaft; **~ satisfaction** Zufriedenheit *f* des Kunden **(b)** (*inf: = person*) Kunde *m* (*inf*)

customer base N Kundenstamm *m*

customer service(s) N Kundendienst *m*; **~ department** Kundendienstabteilung *f*

customize [ˈkʌstəmaɪz] VT auf Bestellung fertigen; **~d peripheral equipment** Peripherieausstattung nach Wunsch

custom-made [ˈkʌstəmmeɪd] ADJ *clothes, shoes* maßgefertigt; *furniture, car* speziell angefertigt

customs: **customs authorities** PL Zollbehörden *pl*; **customs clearance** N Zollabfertigung *f*; **to get ~ for sth** etw zollamtlich abfertigen lassen; **customs declaration** N Zollerklärung f; **customs duty** N Zoll m; **customs house** N Zollamt nt; **customs inspection** N Zollkontrolle f; **customs officer** N Zollbeamte(r) m, Zollbeamtin f; **customs specification** N Zollbestimmung f

cut [kʌt]

1 NOUN	**4** INTRANSITIVE VERB
2 ADJECTIVE	**5** PHRASAL VERBS
3 TRANSITIVE VERB	

vb: pret, ptp **cut**

1 NOUN
(a) Schnitt m; (= wound) Schnittwunde f; **to make a cut in sth** in etw (acc) einen Einschnitt machen; **his hair could do with a cut** seine Haare könnten mal wieder geschnitten werden; **it's a cut above the rest of them** es ist den anderen um einiges überlegen; **the cut and thrust of politics** das Spannungsfeld der Politik; **the cut and thrust of the debate** die Hitze der Debatte
(b) (= reduction) (in prices) Senkung f; (in salaries, expenditure, text, film etc) Kürzung f; (in working hours, holidays) (Ver)kürzung f; (in production, output) Einschränkung f; **a cut in prices/taxes** eine Preis-/Steuersenkung; **a 1% cut in interest rates** eine 1%ige Senkung des Zinssatzes; **he had to take a cut in (his) salary** er musste eine Gehaltskürzung hinnehmen; **the censor had made so many cuts** die Zensur hatte so viel gestrichen
(c) (of meat) Stück nt
(d) (= share) (inf) Anteil m, Teil m; **to take one's cut** sich (dat) seinen Teil or Anteil nehmen
(e) (Elec) Unterbrechung f (in +gen); (planned) Sperre f; **power/electricity cut** Stromausfall m; (planned) Stromsperre f
(f) (Cards) Abheben nt; **it's your cut** du hebst ab

2 ADJECTIVE geschnitten; grass gemäht; prices herabgesetzt; **to have a cut finger/lip** eine Schnittwunde am Finger/an der Lippe haben; **a well-cut dress** ein gut geschnittenes Kleid; **cut flowers** Schnittblumen pl; **hand-cut crystal** handgeschliffenes Kristall; **the cut version of a film** die gekürzte Fassung eines Films

3 TRANSITIVE VERB
(a) (= make cut in) schneiden; cake anschneiden; rope durchschneiden; grass mähen; **to cut one's finger** sich (dat) am Finger schneiden; **to cut one's nails** sich (dat) die Nägel schneiden; **to cut oneself (shaving)** sich (beim Rasieren) schneiden; **to cut sth in half/three** sie halbieren/dritteln; **to cut a hole in sth** ein Loch in etw (acc) schneiden; **to cut to pieces** zerstückeln; **to cut open** aufschneiden; **he cut his head open** er hat sich (dat) den Kopf aufgeschlagen; **to have or get one's hair cut** sich (dat) die Haare schneiden lassen; **to cut sb free/loose** jdn losschneiden
(b) (= shape) steps schlagen; channel ausheben; glass, crystal, diamond schleifen; fabric, suit, dress zuschneiden; key anfertigen; **to cut a fine/sorry figure** eine gute/schlechte Figur machen
(c) (= break off) ties, links abbrechen
(d) (= reduce) prices herabsetzen; quantity reduzieren; working hours, holidays, expenses, salary, text, programme, film kürzen; production, output verringern
(e) (= remove) part of programme, text, film streichen; **to cut and paste text** (Comput) Text ausschneiden und einfügen
(f) (= censor) film Teile streichen aus
(g) (Cards) **to cut the cards/the pack** abheben
(h) (= edit) film schneiden
(i) (Mus) record pressen; (singer) machen
(j) (= stop) engine abstellen
(k) (set structures)

✦**to cut sb/sth short** **to cut sb short** jdm das Wort abschneiden; **to cut sth short** etw vorzeitig abbrechen; **to cut a long story short** der langen Rede kurzer Sinn
✦**to cut sb dead** (Brit) jdn wie Luft behandeln
✦**to cut a tooth** zahnen

✦**to cut it fine** (Brit) **2.20 would be cutting it a bit fine** 2.20 Uhr wäre ein bisschen knapp; **aren't you cutting it a bit fine?** ist das nicht ein bisschen knapp?
✦**to cut one's losses** eine Sache abschließen, ehe der Schaden (noch) größer wird

4 INTRANSITIVE VERB
(a) (instrument) (knife, scissors) schneiden; (lawn mower) mähen; **to cut loose** (fig) sich losmachen; (US inf) loslegen (inf)
✦**to cut both ways** (fig) ein zweischneidiges Schwert sein
✦**to cut and run** abhauen (inf)
(b) (= intersect) sich schneiden
(c) (Film) (= change scenes) überblenden (to zu); (= stop filming) abbrechen; **cut!** Schnitt!
(d) (Cards) abheben

5 PHRASAL VERBS
➤ **cut across** VI +PREP OBJ **(a)** (lit) hinübergehen/-fahren etc (prep obj über +acc); **if you cut across the fields** wenn Sie über die Felder gehen **(b)** (fig) **this problem cuts across all ages** dieses Problem betrifft alle Altersgruppen
➤ **cut back** **1** VI **(a)** (= go back) zurückgehen/-fahren; (Film) zurückblenden **(b)** (= reduce expenditure etc) sich einschränken; **to cut back on expenses** etc die Ausgaben etc einschränken; **to cut back on smoking/sweets** weniger rauchen/Süßigkeiten essen **2** VT SEP **(a)** plants zurückschneiden **(b)** production zurückschrauben; outgoings einschränken
➤ **cut down** **1** VT SEP **(a)** tree fällen; corn schneiden **(b)** number, expenses einschränken; text zusammenstreichen (to auf +acc); **to cut sb down to size** jdn auf seinen Platz verweisen **(c)** USU PASS (= kill) dahinraffen (geh) **2** VI sich einschränken; **to cut down on sth** etw einschränken; **to cut down on sweets** weniger Süßigkeiten essen
➤ **cut in** VI **(a)** (= interrupt) sich einschalten (on in +acc); **to cut in on sb** jdn unterbrechen **(b)** (Aut) sich direkt vor ein anderes/das andere Auto hineindrängen; **to cut in in front of sb** jdn schneiden
➤ **cut into** VI +PREP OBJ **(a)** cake, meat anschneiden **(b)** (fig) savings ein Loch reißen in (+acc); holidays verkürzen
➤ **cut off** VT SEP **(a)** abschneiden; allowance sperren; **we're very cut off out here** wir leben hier draußen sehr abgeschieden; **to cut sb off in the middle of a sentence** jdn mitten im Satz unterbrechen **(b)** (= disinherit) enterben **(c)** gas, telephone etc abstellen; **we've been cut off** (Telec) wir sind unterbrochen worden
➤ **cut out** **1** VI (engine) aussetzen **2** VT SEP **(a)** ausschneiden; malignant growth herausschneiden **(b)** coat, dress zuschneiden **(c)** (= delete) (heraus)streichen; (= not bother with) verzichten auf (+acc), sich (dat) schenken; smoking, swearing etc aufhören mit; **double glazing cuts out the noise** Doppelfenster verhindern, dass der Lärm hereindringt; **cut it out!** (inf) lass das (sein)! (inf); **and you can cut out the self-pity for a start!** und mit Selbstmitleid brauchst du gar nicht erst zu kommen!
(d) (fig) **to be cut out for sth** zu etw geeignet sein; **he's not cut out to be a doctor** er ist nicht zum Arzt geeignet **(e)** **to have one's work cut out** alle Hände voll zu tun haben
➤ **cut through** VT SEP **we cut through the housing estate** wir gingen/fuhren durch die Siedlung
➤ **cut up** VT SEP **(a)** meat aufschneiden; wood spalten **(b)** (Aut) **to cut sb up** jdn schneiden

cut-and-dried [ˌkʌtənˈdraɪd] ADJ (fig) festgelegt; **as far as he's concerned the whole issue is now ~** für ihn ist die ganze Angelegenheit erledigt
cut-and-paste [ˌkʌtənˈpeɪst] ADJ (US) **a ~ job** eine zusammengestückelte Arbeit (usu pej)
cutaway [ˈkʌtəweɪ] ADJ **~ drawing** Schnittdiagramm nt
cutback [ˈkʌtbæk] N Kürzung f
cute [kjuːt] ADJ (+ER) **(a)** (inf: = sweet) süß **(b)** (esp US inf: = clever) prima (inf); (= shrewd) schlau, clever (inf)
cutesy [ˈkjuːtsɪ] ADJ (pej inf) person zuckersüß; painting, clothes kitschig

cut glass N geschliffenes Glas
cut-glass [ˈkʌtglɑːs] ADJ (*lit*) aus geschliffenem Glas
cuticle [ˈkjuːtɪkl] N (*of nail*) Nagelhaut *f*
cutie [ˈkjuːtɪ] N (*esp US inf*) flotter Käfer (*inf*); (= *child*) süßer Fratz (*inf*); (= *shrewd person*) gewitzter Typ
cutie-pie [ˈkjuːtɪpaɪ] N (*esp US inf*) süßer Fratz (*inf*)
cutlery [ˈkʌtlərɪ] N, NO PL (*esp Brit*) Besteck *nt*
cutlet [ˈkʌtlɪt] N Schnitzel *nt*
cut: **cut loaf** N aufgeschnittenes Brot; **cutoff** N (**a**) (*Tech: device*) Ausschaltmechanismus *m* (**b**) (*also* ~ **point**) Trennlinie *f*; **cutout** ◫ N (**a**) (= *model*) Ausschneidemodell *nt*; (= *figure, doll*) Ausschneidepuppe *f*; **his characters are just cardboard** ~**s** seine Figuren sind einfach nur oberflächlich (**b**) (*Elec*) Sperre *f* ◫ ADJ (**a**) **model etc zum Ausschneiden** (**b**) (*Elec*) Abschalt-; ~ **device** Abschaltautomatik *f*; **cut-price** ADJ zu Schleuderpreisen; ~ **offer** Billigangebot *nt*; **cut-rate** ADJ zu verbilligtem Tarif; **cut sheet feed** N (*Comput*) Einzelblatteinzug *m*
cutter [ˈkʌtə] N (**a**) Messer *nt*; **a pair of (wire)** ~**s** eine Drahtschere (**b**) (= *boat*) Kutter *m*; (*US*: = *coastguard's boat*) Boot *nt* der Küstenwache
cut-throat [ˈkʌtθrəut] ADJ *competition* mörderisch
cutting [ˈkʌtɪŋ] ◫ N (**a**) Schneiden *nt*; (*of grass*) Mähen *nt*; (*of cake*) Anschneiden *nt*
(**b**) (*of glass, jewel*) Schliff *m*; (*of key*) Anfertigung *f*; (*of record*) Pressen *nt*
(**c**) (*of prices*) Herabsetzung *f*; (*of quantity*) Reduzierung *f*; (*of working hours*) Verkürzung *f*; (*of expenses, salary*) Kürzung *f*
(**d**) (= *editing*) (*Film*) Schnitt *m*; (*of part of text*) Streichung *f*
(**e**) (*Brit*: = *road* ~, *railway* ~) Durchstich *m*
(**f**) (*Brit*: *from newspaper*) Ausschnitt *m*
(**g**) (*Hort*) Ableger *m*; **to take a** ~ einen Ableger nehmen
◫ ADJ (**a**) scharf; **to be at the** ~ **edge of sth** in etw (*dat*) führend sein
(**b**) (*fig*) *wind, cold* schneidend; *remark* spitz
cutting: **cutting board** N (*US*) = **chopping board**; **cutting room** N (*Film*) Schneideraum *m*; **to end up on the** ~ **floor** (*fig*) im Papierkorb enden
cuttlefish [ˈkʌtlfɪʃ] N Sepie *f*
cut up ADJ (*inf*) **he was very** ~ **about it** das hat ihn schwer getroffen
CV ABBR *of* **curriculum vitae**
CWO ABBR *of* **cash with order** Zahlung bei Auftragserteilung
cwt ABBR *of* **hundredweight**

cyanide [ˈsaɪənaɪd] N Zyanid *nt*
cyber- [ˈsaɪbə-]: **cybercafé** N Internetcafé *nt*; **cybernetics** N SING Kybernetik *f*; **cyberspace** N Cyberspace *m*
cycle [ˈsaɪkl] ◫ N (**a**) Zyklus *m*; (*of events*) Gang *m*; **business** ~ Konjunkturzyklus *m* (**b**) (= *bicycle*) (Fahr)rad *nt* ◫ VI mit dem (Fahr)rad fahren
cycle: **cycle lane** N (Fahr)radweg *m*; **cycle path** N (Fahr)radweg *m*
cycler [ˈsaɪklə] N (*US*) = **cyclist**
cycle: **cycle race** N Radrennen *nt*; **cycle rack** N Fahrradständer *m*; **cycle shed** N Fahrradstand *m*; **cycle track** N (= *path*) (Fahr)radweg *m*; (*for racing*) Radrennbahn *f*
cyclic(al) [ˈsaɪklɪk(əl)] ADJ zyklisch; (*Econ*) konjunkturbedingt
cycling [ˈsaɪklɪŋ] N Radfahren *nt*; **I enjoy** ~ ich fahre gern Rad
cycling: **cycling holiday** N Urlaub *m* mit dem Fahrrad; **cycling shorts** PL Radlerhose *f*; **cycling tour** N Radtour *f*
cyclist [ˈsaɪklɪst] N (Fahr)radfahrer(in) *m(f)*
cyclone [ˈsaɪkləun] N Zyklon *m*; ~ **cellar** (*US*) tiefer Keller zum Schutz vor Zyklonen
cygnet [ˈsɪgnɪt] N Schwanjunge(s) *nt*
cylinder [ˈsɪlɪndə] N (*Math, Aut*) Zylinder *m*; (*of revolver, typewriter*) Walze *f*; **a four-** ~ **car** ein vierzylindriges Auto; **to be firing on all** ~**s** (*fig*) in Fahrt sein
cylinder: **cylinder capacity** N (*Aut*) Hubraum *m*; **cylinder head** N (*Aut*) Zylinderkopf *m*
cylindrical [sɪˈlɪndrɪkəl] ADJ zylindrisch
cymbal [ˈsɪmbəl] N Beckenteller *m*; ~**s** Becken *nt*
cynic [ˈsɪnɪk] N Zyniker(in) *m(f)*
cynical ADJ, **cynically** ADV [ˈsɪnɪkəl, -klɪ] zynisch; **he was very** ~ **about it** er äußerte sich sehr zynisch dazu
cynicism [ˈsɪnɪsɪzəm] N Zynismus *m*
cypher N, VT = **cipher**
Cypriot [ˈsɪprɪət] ◫ ADJ zypriotisch ◫ N Zypriot(in) *m(f)*
Cyprus [ˈsaɪprəs] N Zypern *nt*
Cyrillic [sɪˈrɪlɪk] ADJ kyrillisch
cyst [sɪst] N Zyste *f*
cystic fibrosis [sɪstɪkfaɪˈbrəusɪs] N zystische Fibrose
czar [zɑːˈ] N Zar *m*
Czech [tʃek] ◫ ADJ tschechisch ◫ N (**a**) Tscheche *m*, Tschechin *f* (**b**) (*Ling*) Tschechisch *nt*
Czechoslovakia [tʃekəusləˈvækɪə] N die Tschechoslowakei
Czech Republic N Tschechien *nt*

Dd

D, d [di:] N D *nt*, d *nt*; (*Sch: as a mark*) ausreichend; **D sharp** Dis *nt*, dis *nt*; **D flat** Des *nt*, des *nt*

'd = had, would

DA (*US*) ABBR *of* **District Attorney**

dab¹ [dæb] **1** N Klecks *m*; (*of cream, powder etc*) Tupfer *m*; (*of liquid, perfume, glue etc*) Tropfen *m*; **a ~ of powder/ointment** *etc* ein bisschen Puder/Salbe *etc*; **to give sth a ~ of paint** etw überstreichen **2** VT (*with powder etc*) betupfen; (*with towel etc*) tupfen; **to ~ one's eyes** sich (*dat*) die Augen tupfen; **she ~bed ointment on the wound** sie betupfte sich (*dat*) die Wunde mit Salbe

dab² ADJ (*inf*) **to be a ~ hand at sth** gut in etw (*dat*) sein; **to be a ~ hand at doing sth** sich darauf verstehen, etw zu tun

dabble ['dæbl] VI (*fig*) **to ~ in/at sth** sich (nebenbei) mit etw beschäftigen; **he ~s in stocks and shares/antiques** er versucht sich an der Börse/in Antiquitäten

dacha ['dætʃə] N Datsche *f*

dachshund ['dækshʊnd] N Dackel *m*

Dacron® ['dækrɒn] N (*US*) Dacron® *nt*

dad [dæd], **daddy** ['dædɪ] N (*inf*) Papa *m* (*inf*), Vati *m* (*inf*)

daddy-longlegs [dædɪ'lɒŋlegz] N, *pl* - (*Brit*) Schnake *f*; (*US*) Weberknecht *m*

dado ['deɪdəʊ] N (*of wall*) Paneel *nt*

DAF (*Comm*) ABBR *of* **delivered at frontier** geliefert Grenze

daffodil ['dæfədɪl] N Narzisse *f*

daft [dɑːft] ADJ (+ER) doof (*inf*); **what a ~ thing to do** so was Doofes (*inf*); **he's ~ about football** (*inf*) er ist verrückt nach Fußball (*inf*)

dagger ['dægə'] N Dolch *m*; **to be at ~s drawn with sb** (*fig*) mit jdm auf (dem) Kriegsfuß stehen; **to look ~s at sb** (*Brit*) jdn mit Blicken durchbohren

dahlia ['deɪlɪə] N Dahlie *f*

daily ['deɪlɪ] **1** ADJ, ADV täglich; **~ newspaper** Tageszeitung *f*; **~ wage** Tageslohn *m*; **~ grind** täglicher Trott; **~ life** der Alltag; **he is employed on a ~ basis** er ist tageweise angestellt; (*labourer*) er steht im Tagelohn **2** N **(a)** (= *newspaper*) Tageszeitung *f* **(b)** (*also* ~ **help, ~ woman**) Putzfrau *f*

daily bread N (*fig*) **to earn one's ~** sich (*dat*) sein Brot verdienen

daintily ['deɪntɪlɪ] ADV zierlich; *hold, move* anmutig

dainty ['deɪntɪ] ADJ (+ER) **(a)** zierlich; *handkerchief* fein; *movement* anmutig **(b)** (= *refined*) geziert

dairy ['dɛərɪ] N Molkerei *f*; (*on farm*) Milchkammer *f*; (= *shop*) Milchgeschäft *nt*

dairy: **dairy cattle** PL Milchvieh *nt*; **dairy cow** N Milchkuh *f*; **dairy farm** N auf Milchviehhaltung spezialisierter Bauernhof; **dairy farming** N Milchviehhaltung *f*; **dairy produce** N, **dairy products** PL Milchprodukte *pl*

dais ['deɪs] N Podium *nt*

daisy ['deɪzɪ] N Gänseblümchen *nt*; **to be pushing up the daisies** (*inf*) sich (*dat*) die Radieschen von unten besehen (*hum*)

daisywheel ['deɪzɪwiːl] N (*Typ, Comput*) Typenrad *m*

daisywheel printer N Typenraddrucker *m*

dale [deɪl] N (*N Engl, liter*) Tal *nt*

Dalmatian [dæl'meɪʃən] N (= *dog*) Dalmatiner *m*

dam [dæm] **1** N Damm *m* **2** VT (*also* ~ **up**) (auf)stauen; *valley* eindämmen

damage ['dæmɪdʒ] **1** N **(a)** Schaden *m* (*to* an +*dat*); **to do a lot of ~** großen Schaden anrichten; **to do sb/sth a lot of ~** jdm/ einer Sache (*dat*) großen Schaden zufügen; **it did no ~ to his reputation** das hat seinem Ruf nicht geschadet; **the ~ is done** (*fig*) es ist passiert
(b) **damages** PL (*Jur*) Schaden(s)ersatz *m*
(c) (*inf*: = *cost*) **what's the ~?** was kostet der Spaß? (*inf*)
2 VT schaden (*+dat*); *machine, car, furniture, fruit, tree* beschädigen; **to ~ one's eyesight** sich (*dat*) die Augen verderben; **to ~ one's chances** sich (*dat*) die Chancen verderben

damage limitation N Schadensbegrenzung *f*

damaging ['dæmɪdʒɪŋ] ADJ schädlich; *remarks* abträglich; **to be ~ to sb/sth** schädlich für jdn/etw sein

dame [deɪm] N **(a)** Dame (*Brit*) Titel der weiblichen Träger des „Order of the British Empire" **(b)** (*Theat*) (komische) Alte **(c)** (*US inf*) Weib *nt* (*inf*)

dammit ['dæmɪt] INTERJ (*inf*) verdammt (*inf*); **it weighs 2 kilos as near as ~** es wiegt so gut wie 2 Kilo

damn [dæm] **1** INTERJ (*inf*) verdammt (*inf*)
2 N (*inf*) **he doesn't care** *or* **give a ~** er schert sich einen Dreck (darum) (*inf*); **I don't give a ~** das ist mir piepegal (*inf*)
3 ADJ ATTR (*inf*) verdammt; **it's a ~ nuisance** das ist ein verdammter Mist (*inf*); **a ~ sight better/worse** verdammt viel besser/schlechter (*inf*); **I can't see a ~ thing** verdammt (noch mal), ich kann überhaupt nichts sehen (*inf*)
4 ADV (*inf*) verdammt; **I should ~ well hope/think so** das will ich aber auch stark hoffen/ich doch stark annehmen; **pretty ~ good/quick** verdammt gut/schnell (*inf*); **you're ~ right** du hast völlig recht
5 VT **(a)** (*Rel*) verdammen
(b) (= *bring condemnation, ruin on*) das Genick brechen (+*dat*); (*evidence*) überführen
(c) (= *judge and condemn*) verurteilen; *book etc* verreißen; **to ~ sb/sth with faint praise** jdn/etw auf eine Weise loben, die ihn/es bloßstellt
(d) (*inf*) **~ him/you!** (*annoyed*) verdammt! (*inf*); (*indifferent*) der kann/du kannst mich mal! (*inf*); **~ it!** verdammt (noch mal)! (*inf*); **well, I'll be ~ed!** Donnerwetter! (*inf*); **I'll be ~ed if I'll go there** ich denk nicht (im Schlaf) dran, da hinzugehen (*inf*); **I'll be ~ed if I know** weiß der Teufel (*inf*)

damnation [dæm'neɪʃən] **1** N (*Eccl*) (= *act*) Verdammung *f*; (= *state of* ~) Verdammnis *f* **2** INTERJ (*inf*) verdammt (*inf*)

damned [dæmd] **1** ADJ **(a)** *soul* verdammt **(b)** (*inf*) = **damn 3 2** ADV = **damn 4 3** N (*Eccl, liter*) **the ~** *pl* die Verdammten *pl*

damnedest ['dæmdɪst] N **to do** *or* **try one's ~** (*inf*) verdammt noch mal sein Möglichstes tun (*inf*)

damning ['dæmɪŋ] ADJ vernichtend; *evidence* belastend

damp [dæmp] **1** ADJ (+ER) feucht; **a ~ squib** (*fig*) ein Reinfall *m* **2** N (= *dampness*) Feuchtigkeit *f* **3** VT **(a)** anfeuchten **(b)** *sounds, enthusiasm* dämpfen; (*also* ~ **down**) *fire* ersticken

damp course N Dämmschicht *f*

dampen ['dæmpən] VT = **damp 3**

damper ['dæmpə'] N **to put a ~ on sth** einer Sache (*dat*) einen Dämpfer aufsetzen

dampness ['dæmpnɪs] N Feuchtigkeit *f*

damp-proof ['dæmpruːf] ADJ **~ course** Dämmschicht *f*

damson ['dæmzən] N (= *fruit*) Damaszenerpflaume *f*

dance [dɑːns] **1** N Tanz *m*; **~ class** Tanzstunde *f*; **may I have the next ~?** darf ich um den nächsten Tanz bitten?; **she's led him a merry ~** sie hat ihn ja ganz schön an der Nase herumgeführt; (= *caused a lot of trouble*) ihretwegen hat er sich (*dat*) die Hacken abgelaufen; **to give** *or* **hold a ~** einen Tanz veranstalten; (*privately*) eine Tanzparty geben; **to go to a ~** tanzen gehen
2 VT tanzen
3 VI **(a)** tanzen; **would you like to ~?** möchten Sie tanzen? **(b)** (= *move here and there*) **to ~ about** (herum)tänzeln; **to ~ up and down** auf- und abhüpfen; **to ~ for joy** einen Freudentanz aufführen

dance IN CPDS Tanz-; **dance band** N Tanzkapelle *f*; **dance floor** N Tanzboden *m*; (*in restaurant*) Tanzfläche *f*; **dance hall** N Tanzsaal *m*; **dance music** N Tanzmusik *f*

dancer ['dɑːnsə'] N Tänzer(in) *m(f)*

dancing ['dɑːnsɪŋ] **1** N Tanzen *nt* **2** ATTR Tanz-

dancing girl N Tänzerin *f*

dandelion ['dændɪlaɪən] N Löwenzahn *m*

dandruff ['dændrəf] N Schuppen *pl*

Dane [deɪn] N Däne *m*, Dänin *f*

danger ['deɪndʒə'] N **(a)** Gefahr *f*; **he loves ~** er liebt die Gefahr; **the ~s of smoking** die mit dem Rauchen verbundenen Gefahren; **to put sb/sth in ~** jdn/etw gefährden; **to be in ~ of doing sth** Gefahr laufen, etw zu tun; **the species is in ~ of**

extinction die Art ist vom Aussterben bedroht; **out of ~** außer Gefahr; **there is a ~ of fire** es besteht Feuergefahr; **there is a ~ of his getting lost** es besteht die Gefahr, dass er sich verirrt; **to be a ~ to sb/sth** für jdn/etw eine Gefahr bedeuten; **he's a ~ to himself** er bringt sich selbst in Gefahr **(b)** „~" „Achtung, Lebensgefahr!"; (*Mot*) „Gefahrenstelle"; **"~, keep out"** „Zutritt verboten, Lebensgefahr!"

danger money N Gefahrenzulage *f*

dangerous ['deɪndʒrəs] ADJ gefährlich; *driving* rücksichtslos; **the Bronx can be a ~ place** die Bronx kann gefährlich sein; **this is a ~ game we're playing** wir spielen hier gefährlich

dangerously ['deɪndʒrəslɪ] ADV gefährlich; *low, high* bedenklich; *drive* rücksichtslos; **the deadline is getting ~ close** der Termin rückt bedenklich nahe; **she was ~ ill** sie war todkrank; **let's live ~ for once** lass uns einmal etwas riskieren

danger signal N (*lit, fig*) Warnsignal *nt*

dangle ['dæŋgl] **1** VT baumeln lassen **2** VI baumeln

Danish ['deɪnɪʃ] **1** ADJ dänisch **2** N (= *language*) Dänisch *nt*

Danish blue (cheese) N Blauschimmelkäse *m*

Danish pastry N Plundergebäck *nt*

Danube ['dænjuːb] N Donau *f*

dappled ['dæpld] ADJ **(a)** *light* gefleckt **(b)** *horse* scheckig

Dardanelles [ˌdɑːdə'nelz] PL Dardanellen *pl*

dare [dɛəʳ] **1** VI (= *be bold enough*) es wagen; (= *have the confidence*) sich trauen; **he wouldn't ~!** er wird sich schwer hüten; **you ~!** unterstehe dich!; **how ~ you!** was fällt dir ein! **2** VT **(a)** **to ~ (to) do sth** (es) wagen, etw zu tun; **he wouldn't ~ say anything bad about his boss** er wird sich hüten, etwas Schlechtes über seinen Chef zu sagen; **he ~ not** *or* **~n't do it** das wagt er nicht!; **how ~ you say such things?** wie kannst du es wagen, so etwas zu sagen?; **~ you do it?** trauen Sie sich? **(b)** (= *challenge*) **go on, I ~ you!** (trau dich doch, du) Feigling!; **are you daring me?** wetten, dass? (*inf*); **(I) ~ you to jump off** spring doch, du Feigling! **3** N Mutprobe *f*; **to do sth for a ~** etw als Mutprobe tun

daredevil ['dɛəˌdevl] **1** N Waghals *m* **2** ADJ waghalsig

daring ['dɛərɪŋ] **1** ADJ **(a)** (= *courageous*) mutig, kühn (*geh*); *attempt* kühn (*geh*); *escape* waghalsig **(b)** (= *audacious*) *person* wagemutig; *writer, clothes, film, book* gewagt **2** N Wagemut *m*, Kühnheit *f* (*geh*)

daringly ['dɛərɪŋlɪ] ADV mutig, kühn (*geh*)

dark [dɑːk] **1** ADJ (+ER) (*lit, fig*) dunkel; *forces, look, threat* finster; **it's getting ~** es wird dunkel; **a ~ blue** ein dunkles Blau; **the ~ side** of the Schattenseite einer Sache (*gen*); **to drop ~ hints** dunkle Andeutungen machen **2** N **(a)** **the ~** die Dunkelheit; **they aren't afraid of the ~** sie haben keine Angst vor der Dunkelheit; **after/before ~** nach/ vor Einbruch der Dunkelheit; **we'll be back after ~** wir kommen wieder, wenn es dunkel ist **(b)** (*fig*) **to be in the ~ (about sth)** keine Ahnung (von etw) haben; **to keep** *or* **leave sb in the ~ (about sth)** jdn (über etw *acc*) im Dunkeln lassen

dark: dark age N **the Dark Ages** das frühe Mittelalter; **to be living in the ~s** (*pej*) im finstersten Mittelalter leben; **dark chocolate** N Zartbitterschokolade *f*

darken ['dɑːkən] **1** VT (*lit*) dunkel machen; *sky* verdunkeln; (*before storm*) verfinstern **2** VI **(a)** (*lit*) dunkel werden; (*sky*) sich verdunkeln; (*before storm*) sich verfinstern **(b)** (*fig*) (*atmosphere*) sich verdüstern; (*face*) sich verfinstern

dark: dark-eyed ADJ dunkeläugig; **dark glasses** PL Sonnenbrille *f*; (*of blind person*) dunkle Brille; **dark horse** N (*fig*) stilles Wasser; (= *unexpected winner*) unbekannte Größe

darkly ['dɑːklɪ] ADV (+ *vb*) finster; (+ *adj*) auf finstere Weise; **a ~ comic novel** ein finster-komischer Roman

darkness ['dɑːknɪs] N (*lit*) Dunkelheit *f*; **in total ~** in völliger Dunkelheit, in tiefem Dunkel (*geh*); **the house was in ~** das Haus lag im Dunkeln

dark: darkroom N (*Phot*) Dunkelkammer *f*; **dark-skinned** ADJ dunkelhäutig

darling ['dɑːlɪŋ] N **(a)** Schatz *m*; (*esp child*) Schätzchen *nt*; **he is the ~ of the crowds** er ist der Publikumsliebling; **be a ~ and ...** sei ein Schatz und ... **(b)** (*form of address*) Liebling *m*

darn¹ [dɑːn] (*Sew*) VT stopfen

darn² (*also* **~ed**) (*inf*) **1** ADJ verdammt (*inf*); **a ~ sight better** ein ganzes Ende besser (*inf*) **2** ADV verdammt (*inf*), verflixt (*inf*); **you're ~ right** du hast völlig Recht; **we'll do just as we ~**

well please wir machen genau das, was wir wollen; **~ near impossible** so gut wie unmöglich **3** VT **~ it!** verflixt noch mal! (*inf*)

darned [dɑːnd] ADJ, ADV (*inf*) = **darn²**

dart [dɑːt] **1** N **(a)** (*movement*) Satz *m* **(b)** (*Sport*) (Wurf)pfeil *m* **2** VI flitzen; (*fish*) schnellen; **to ~ out** (*person*) hinausflitzen; (*fish, tongue*) herausschnellen; **to ~ in** (*person*) hereinstürzen; **he ~ed behind a bush** er hechtete hinter einen Busch; **he ~ed off** *or* **away** er flitzte davon **3** VT *look* werfen; **to ~ a glance at sb** jdm einen Blick zuwerfen; **to ~ a glance at sth** einen Blick auf etw (*acc*) werfen

dart board N Dartscheibe *f*

darts [dɑːts] N SING Darts *nt*

dash [dæʃ] **1** N **(a)** Jagd *f*; **he made a ~ for the door** er stürzte auf die Tür zu; **she made a ~ for it** sie rannte, so schnell sie konnte; **to make a ~ for freedom** versuchen, in die Freiheit zu entkommen; **it was a mad ~ to the hospital** wir/sie *etc* eilten Hals über Kopf zum Krankenhaus **(b)** (= *small amount*) **a ~ of** etwas; (*of lemon*) ein Spritzer *m*; **a ~ of colour** (*Brit*) *or* **color** (*US*) ein Farbtupfer *m* **(c)** (*Typ*) Gedankenstrich *m* **2** VT **(a)** (= *throw violently*) schleudern; **to ~ sth to pieces** etw in tausend Stücke zerschlagen **(b)** *sb's hopes* zunichte machen **(c)** (*inf*) = **darn²** **3** **3** VI **(a)** sausen (*inf*); **to ~ into/across a room** in ein Zimmer/ quer durch ein Zimmer stürzen *or* stürmen; **to ~ away/back/ up** fort-/zurück-/hinaufstürzen **(b)** (= *knock, be hurled*) schlagen; (*waves*) peitschen

► **dash off 1** VI losstürzen; **sorry to have to dash off like this** es tut mir Leid, dass ich so forthetzen muss **2** VT SEP *letter* hinwerfen

dashboard ['dæʃbɔːd] N Armaturenbrett *nt*

DAT N ABBR *of* **digital audio tape** DAT *nt*

data ['deɪtə] PL USU WITH SING VB Daten *pl*

data: data bank N Datenbank *f*; **database** N Datenbank *f*; **~ manager** Datenbankmanager(in) *m(f)*; **data capture** N Datenerfassung *f*; **data processing** N Datenverarbeitung *f*; **data protection** N Datenschutz *m*; **data retrieval** N Datenabruf *m*; **data transfer** N Datentransfer *m*

date¹ [deɪt] N (= *fruit*) Dattel *f*; (= *tree*) Dattelpalme *f*

date² [deɪt] **1** N **(a)** Datum *nt*; (= *historical ~*) Geschichts- *or* Jahreszahl *f*; (*for appointment*) Termin *m*; **~ of birth** Geburtsdatum *nt*; **~ of order** (*Comm*) Bestelldatum *nt*; **what's the ~ today?** welches Datum haben wir heute?; **what is the ~ of that letter?** von wann ist der Brief datiert?; **to ~** bis heute; **the band's UK tour ~s are: ...** die Band tritt an den folgenden Daten in Großbritannien auf: ... **(b)** (= *appointment*) Verabredung *f*; (*with girlfriend etc*) Rendezvous *nt*; **who's his ~?** mit wem trifft er sich?; **his ~ didn't show up** diejenige, mit der er ausgehen wollte, hat ihn versetzt (*inf*); **to make a ~ with sb** sich mit jdm verabreden; **I've got a lunch ~ today** (*with friend*) ich habe mich heute zum Mittagessen verabredet **2** VT **(a)** mit dem Datum versehen; *letter etc* datieren; **a letter ~d the seventh of August** ein vom siebten August datierter Brief **(b)** (= *establish age of*) *work of art etc* datieren **(c)** *girlfriend etc* ausgehen mit; (*regularly*) gehen mit (*inf*) **3** VI **(a)** **to ~ back to** zurückdatieren auf (+*acc*); **to ~ from** zurückgehen auf (+*acc*); (*antique etc*) stammen aus **(b)** (*couple*) miteinander gehen

dated ['deɪtɪd] ADJ altmodisch

date: dateless ADJ (= *never old-fashioned*) zeitlos; **date marking** N (*Brit Comm*) Datumskennzeichnung *f*; **date rape** N Vergewaltigung nach einem Rendezvous; **date-rape drug** N Date-Rape-Droge *f*, Vergewaltigungsdroge *f*; **date stamp** N Datumsstempel *m*

dative ['deɪtɪv] **1** N Dativ *m*; **in the ~** im Dativ **2** ADJ **~ object** Dativobjekt *nt*; **the ~ case** der Dativ

daub [dɔːb] VT *walls* beschmieren; *paint, slogans* schmieren; *axle* einschmieren; *grease, mud* streichen

daughter ['dɔːtəʳ] N (*lit, fig*) Tochter *f*

daughter-in-law ['dɔːtərɪnlɔː] N, *pl* **daughters-in-law** Schwiegertochter *f*

daunt [dɔːnt] VT **to be ~ed by sth** sich von etw entmutigen lassen

daunting ['dɔːntɪŋ] ADJ entmutigend

dawdle ['dɔːdl] VI trödeln; (= *stroll*) bummeln

dawdler ['dɔːdləʳ] N Trödler(in) *m(f)*

dawn [dɔːn] **1** N (*lit, fig*) (Morgen)dämmerung *f*; (*no art: time of day*) Tagesanbruch *m*; **at ~** bei Tagesanbruch; **it's almost ~** es ist fast Morgen; **from ~ to dusk** von morgens bis abends **2** VI **(a) day was already ~ing** es dämmerte schon **(b)** (*fig: new age etc*) anbrechen **(c)** (*inf*) **to ~ (up)on sb** jdm zum Bewusstsein kommen; **it ~ed on him that ...** es wurde ihm langsam klar, dass ...

dawn: dawn chorus N Morgenkonzert *nt* der Vögel; **dawn raid** N (*by police*) Razzia *f* (*in den frühen Morgenstunden*)

day [deɪ] N **(a)** Tag *m*; **it will arrive any ~ now** es muss jeden Tag kommen; **what ~ is it today?** welcher Tag ist heute?, was haben wir heute?; **twice a ~** zweimal täglich; **the ~ before yesterday** vorgestern; **the ~ after/before, the following/previous ~** am Tag danach/zuvor; **the ~ after tomorrow** übermorgen; **from that ~ on(wards)** von dem Tag an; **two years ago to the ~** auf den Tag genau vor zwei Jahren; **one ~** eines Tages; **one ~ we went swimming, and the next ...** einen Tag gingen wir schwimmen, und den nächsten ...; **one of these ~s** irgendwann (einmal); **~ in, ~ out** tagein, tagaus; **they went to London for the ~** sie machten einen Tagesausflug nach London; **for ~s on end** tagelang; **~ after ~** Tag für Tag; **by ~** jeden Tag; **the other ~** neulich; **at the end of the ~** (*fig*) letzten Endes; **to live from ~ to ~** von einem Tag auf den andern leben; **today of all ~s** ausgerechnet heute; **some ~ soon** demnächst; **I remember it to this ~** daran erinnere ich mich noch heute; **all ~** den ganzen Tag; **to travel during the ~ or by ~** tagsüber *or* während des Tages reisen; **at that time of ~** zu der Tageszeit; **to be paid by the ~** tageweise bezahlt werden; **let's call it a ~** machen wir Schluss; **some time during the ~** irgendwann im Laufe des Tages; **to have a nice ~** einen schönen Tag verbringen; **to have a lazy ~** einen Tag faulenzen; **have a nice ~!** viel Spaß!; (*esp US: said by storekeeper etc*) schönen Tag noch!; **did you have a nice ~?** wars schön?; **did you have a good ~ at the office?** wars im Büro?; **what a ~!** (*terrible*) so ein fürchterlicher Tag!; **to work an eight-hour ~** einen Achtstundentag haben; **it's all in the or a ~'s work!** das ist (doch) selbstverständlich; **that'll be the ~** das möcht ich sehen **(b)** (*period of time: often pl*) **these ~s** heutzutage; **what are you doing these ~s?** was machst du denn so?; **in this ~ and age** heutzutage; **in ~s to come** künftig; **in his younger ~s** als er noch jünger war; **the happiest ~s of my life** die glücklichste Zeit meines Lebens; **those were the ~s** das waren noch Zeiten; **in the old ~s** früher; **in the good old ~s** in der guten alten Zeit; **it's early ~s yet** es ist noch zu früh; **this material has seen better ~s** dieser Stoff hat (auch) schon bessere Tage gesehen; **famous in her ~** in ihrer Zeit berühmt; **it has had its ~** das hat seine Glanzzeit überschritten; **his ~ will come** sein Tag wird kommen **(c)** NO PL (= *contest, battle*) **to win or carry the ~** den Sieg bringen; **to save the ~** den Kampf retten

day: daybook N (*Comm*) Tagebuch *nt*; **daybreak** N Tagesanbruch *m*; **at ~** bei Tagesanbruch; **daycare** N **to be in ~** (*child*) in einer Tagesstätte untergebracht sein; **day(care) centre,** (*US*) **day(care) center** N (*for children*) Tagesstätte *f*; (*for old people*) Altentagesstätte *f*; **daydream** N Tagtraum *m* **2** VI (*mit offenen Augen*) träumen; **day job** N Hauptberuf *m*; **don't give up the ~** (*hum*) häng deinen Beruf nicht gleich an den Nagel (*inf*); **day labourer,** (*US*) **day laborer** N Tagelöhner(in) *m(f)*

daylight ['deɪlaɪt] N Tageslicht *nt*; **in broad ~** am helllichten Tage; **to scare the living ~s out of sb** (*inf*) jdm einen fürchterlichen Schreck einjagen (*inf*)

daylight: daylight robbery N (*Brit inf*) Halsabschneiderei *f* (*inf*); **daylight saving time** N (*esp US*) Sommerzeit *f*

day: day nursery N Kindertagesstätte *f*; **day-old** ADJ *strike, ceasefire* seit einem Tag andauernd; *food, newspaper* vom Vortag; **day pupil** N (*Sch*) Externe(r) *mf*; **day release** N (*Brit*) tageweise Freistellung von Angestellten zur Weiterbildung; **day return (ticket)** N (*Brit Rail*) Tagesrückfahrkarte *f*; **day shift** N Tagschicht *f*

daytime ['deɪtaɪm] **1** N Tag *m*; **in the ~** tagsüber **2** ATTR am Tage; *raid* am helllichten Tage; **what's your ~ phone number?**

unter welcher Nummer sind Sie tagsüber erreichbar?; **~ television** Vor- und Nachmittagsprogramm *nt*

day: day-to-day ADJ täglich; *occurrence* alltäglich; **on a ~ basis** tageweise; **~ operations** (*Comm*) Tagesgeschäft *nt*; **day trader** N (*St Ex*) Daytrader(in) *m(f)*, Tageshändler(in) *m(f)*; **day trading** N (*St Ex*) Tagesspekulation *f*, Daytrading *nt*; **day trip** N Tagesausflug *m*; **day-tripper** N Tagesausflügler(in) *m(f)*

daze [deɪz] N Benommenheit *f*; **in a ~** ganz benommen

dazed [deɪzd] ADJ benommen

dazzle ['dæzl] VT (*lit, fig*) blenden

dazzling ['dæzlɪŋ] ADJ (*lit*) blendend

dazzlingly ['dæzlɪŋlɪ] ADV (*lit, fig*) blendend; **~ beautiful** strahlend schön

DC (a) ABBR *of* **direct current (b)** ABBR *of* **District of Columbia**

D/C ABBR *of* **documentary credit** Dokumentenakkreditiv *nt*

D/D ABBR *of* **direct debit**

D-day ['diːdeɪ] N (*Hist, fig*) der Tag X

DDP ABBR *of* **delivered duty paid** geliefert verzollt

DDT ABBR *of* **dichloro-diphenyl-trichloroethane** DDT *nt*

DDU ABBR *of* **delivered duty unpaid** geliefert unverzollt

deactivate [diːˈæktɪveɪt] VT entschärfen

dead [ded] **1** ADJ **(a)** (*lit, fig*) tot; **he has been ~ for two years** er ist seit zwei Jahren tot; **to shoot sb ~** jdn erschießen; **over my ~ body** (*inf*) nur über meine Leiche (*inf*); **to be ~ and buried,** **to be ~ in the water** tot und begraben sein **(b)** *limbs* abgestorben; **my hand's gone ~** ich habe kein Gefühl in meiner Hand; **to be ~ to the world** tief und fest schlafen **(c)** (*Elec*) *cable* stromlos; (*Telec*) tot; **to go ~** ausfallen **(d)** (= *absolute, exact*) total, völlig; **~ silence** Totenstille *f*; **to come to a ~ stop** völlig zum Stillstand kommen **(e)** (*inf: = exhausted*) völlig kaputt (*inf*); **she looked half ~** sie sah völlig kaputt aus (*inf*); **I'm ~ on my feet** ich bin zum Umfallen kaputt (*inf*) **2** ADV **(a)** (= *exactly*) genau; **~ straight** schnurgerade; **to be ~ on time** auf die Minute pünktlich kommen **(b)** (*Brit inf*: = *very*) total (*inf*); **~ drunk** total betrunken; **~ tired** totmüde; **you're ~ right** Sie haben völlig Recht; **he was ~ lucky** er hat irrsinnig Glück gehabt; **~ slow** ganz langsam; **to be ~ certain about sth** (*inf*) bei etw todsicher sein; **he's ~ against it** er ist total dagegen **(c) to stop ~** abrupt stehen bleiben **3** N **(a) the ~** *pl* die Toten *pl* **(b) in the or at ~ of night** mitten in der Nacht

dead: dead beat ADJ (*Brit inf*) völlig kaputt (*inf*); **dead duck** N **to be a ~** passé sein

deaden ['dedn] VT *pain* mildern; *force, blow* abschwächen; *nerve* abtöten; *sound* dämpfen; *feeling* abstumpfen

dead: dead end N Sackgasse *f*; **to come to a ~** (*lit*) (*road*) in einer Sackgasse enden; (*driver*) an eine Sackgasse kommen; (*fig*) in eine Sackgasse geraten; **dead-end** ADJ ATTR **~ street** (*esp US*) Sackgasse *f*; **a ~ job** ein Job *m* ohne Aufstiegsmöglichkeiten; **dead heat** N totes Rennen; **deadline** N (letzter) Termin; **to fix or set a ~** eine Frist setzen; **to work to a ~** auf einen Termin hinarbeiten; **deadlock** N **to reach (a) ~** in eine Sackgasse geraten; **to end in ~** sich festfahren; **to break the ~** aus der Sackgasse herauskommen

deadly ['dedlɪ] **1** ADJ (+ER) **(a)** tödlich; *striker* treffsicher; **assault with a ~ weapon** (*Jur*) Körperverletzung *f* mit einer gefährlichen Waffe; **their ~ enemy** ihr Todfeind *m* **(b)** *logic, look* vernichtend **2** ADV **~ dull** todlangweilig (*inf*); **he was ~ serious** er meinte es todernst; **~ poisonous** tödlich

dead: Dead Sea N Totes Meer; **dead weight** N (*Tech*) Eigengewicht *nt*

deaf [def] **1** ADJ (+ER) (*lit, fig*) taub; **as ~ as a (door)post** stocktaub; **our pleas fell on ~ ears** unsere Bitten fanden kein Gehör **2** N **the ~** *pl* die Tauben *pl*

deaf-and-dumb [defənˈdʌm] ADJ taubstumm

deafen ['defn] VT (*lit*) taub machen; (*fig*) betäuben

deafening ['defnɪŋ] ADJ *noise* ohrenbetäubend; *row* lautstark; **a ~ silence** ein eisiges Schweigen

deafness ['defnɪs] N (*lit, fig*) Taubheit *f* (*to* gegenüber)

deal¹ [diːl] **1** N (= *amount*) Menge *f*; **a good or great ~ of** eine Menge; **not a great ~ of** nicht (besonders) viel; **there's a good or great ~ of truth in what he says** es ist schon ziemlich viel Wahres an dem, was er sagt; **and that's saying a great ~** und damit ist schon viel gesagt; **to mean a great ~ to sb** jdm viel bedeuten **2** ADV **a good** or **great ~** viel

deal² *vb: pret, ptp* **dealt 1** N (a) (*also* **business ~**) Geschäft *nt*; (= *arrangement*) Handel *m*; **to do** or **make a ~ with sb** mit jdm ein Geschäft machen; **it's a ~** abgemacht!; **it's a done ~** (*US*) es ist beschlossene Sache
(b) (*inf*) **to give sb a fair ~** jdn anständig behandeln; **the workers have always had a bad ~** die Arbeiter sind immer schlecht behandelt worden
2 VT **(a)** (*also* **~ out**) *cards* geben
(b) *drugs* dealen (*inf*)
3 VI **(a)** (*Cards*) geben
(b) (*in drugs*) dealen (*inf*)
➤ **deal in** VI +PREP OBJ (*Comm*) *goods* handeln mit
➤ **deal out** VT SEP verteilen (*to* an +*acc*); *cards* (aus)geben (*to* +*dat*); **to deal out punishment** Strafen verhängen
➤ **deal with** VI +PREP OBJ **(a)** (= *do business with*) verhandeln mit
(b) (= *manage, handle*) sich kümmern um; *job* sich befassen mit; *emotions* umgehen mit; (*successfully*) fertig werden mit; (*Comm*) *orders* erledigen; (= *be responsible for*) zuständig sein für; **let's deal with the adjectives first** behandeln wir zuerst die Adjektive; **you bad boy, I'll deal with you later** (*inf*) dich nehm ich mir später vor, du Lausebengel! (*inf*)
(c) (*book, film etc*) handeln von; (*author*) sich befassen mit

dealer ['diːlə'] N **(a)** (*Comm*) Händler(in) *m(f)*; (= *wholesaler*) Großhändler(in) *m(f)* **(b)** (*in drugs*) Dealer(in) *m(f)* (*inf*)
(c) (*Cards*) Kartengeber *m*

dealing ['diːlɪŋ] N **(a)** (= *trading*) Handel *m*; (*in drugs*) Dealen *nt*
(b) dealings PL (*Comm*) Geschäfte *pl*; (*generally*) Umgang *m*; **to have ~s with sb** mit jdm zu tun haben; (*Comm*) Geschäftsbeziehungen zu jdm haben

dealing room N (*Fin*) Geschäftsraum *m* für Devisengeschäfte

dealt [delt] PRET, PTP *of* **deal²**

dean [diːn] N (*Eccl, Univ*) Dekan(in) *m(f)*

dear [dɪə'] **1** ADJ (+ER) **(a)** lieb; **she is a ~ friend of mine** sie ist eine sehr gute Freundin von mir; **that is my ~est wish** das ist mein sehnlichster Wunsch; **these memories are very ~ to him** diese Erinnerungen sind ihm teuer
(b) (= *lovable, sweet*) *child, thing* süß, reizend
(c) (*in letter-writing etc*) **~ Daddy/John** lieber Vati/John!; **~ Sir** sehr geehrter Herr X!; **~ Madam** sehr geehrte Frau X!; **~ Sir or Madam** sehr geehrte Damen und Herren!; **~ Mr Kemp** sehr geehrter Herr Kemp!; (*less formal*) lieber Herr Kemp!
(d) (= *expensive*) teuer; *prices* hoch; **~ money** (*Econ*) teures or knappes Geld
2 INTERJ **oh ~!** oje!, ach du meine Güte or du liebe Zeit!
3 N **hello/thank you ~** hallo/vielen Dank; **Robert ~** (mein lieber) Robert; **yes, ~** (*husband to wife etc*) ja, Schätzchen or Liebling; **are you being served, ~?** (*inf*) werden Sie schon bedient?
4 ADV (*lit, fig*) teuer; **this will cost them ~** das wird sie teuer zu stehen kommen

dearly ['dɪəlɪ] ADV **(a)** *love* von ganzem Herzen; *hope* sehr; **I would ~ love to marry** ich würde liebend gern heiraten
(b) (*fig*) **he paid ~ (for it)** er hat es teuer bezahlt

death [deθ] N Tod *m*; **~ by drowning** Tod durch Ertrinken; **in ~ as in life** im Tod wie im Leben; **to be afraid of ~** sich vor dem Tod fürchten; **to be burned to ~** verbrennen; (*at stake*) verbrannt werden; **to starve to ~** verhungern; **to bleed to ~** verbluten; **to freeze to ~** erfrieren; **a fight to the ~** ein Kampf auf Leben und Tod; **to put sb to ~** jdn hinrichten; **to drink oneself to ~** sich zu Tode trinken; **he works his men to ~** er schindet seine Leute zu Tode; **to be at ~'s door** an der Schwelle des Todes stehen; **it will be the ~ of you** (*inf*) das wird dein Tod sein; **he will be the ~ of me** (*inf.* = *he's annoying*) er bringt mich noch ins Grab; **to catch one's ~ (of cold)** (*inf*) sich (*dat*) den Tod holen; **I am sick to ~ of all this** (*inf*) ich bin das alles gründlich satt; **he looked like ~ warmed up** (*Brit inf*) or **over** (*US inf*) er sah wie der Tod auf Urlaub aus (*inf*)

death: deathbed N Sterbebett *nt*; **to be on one's ~** auf dem Sterbebett liegen; **death benefit** N (*Insur*) Versicherungsprämie *f* im Todesfall; **death camp** N Vernichtungslager *nt*; **death certificate** N Totenschein *m*; **death duties** PL (*Brit*) Erbschaftssteuern *pl*

deathly ['deθlɪ] **1** ADJ **~ hush** or **silence** Totenstille *f* **2** ADV **~ pale** totenblass; **~ quiet** totenstill

death: death penalty N Todesstrafe *f*; **death rate** N Sterbeziffer *f*; **death row** N Todestrakt *m*; **death sentence** N Todesurteil *nt*; **death squad** N Todeskommando *nt*; **death taxes** PL (*US*) Erbschaftssteuern *pl*; **death threat** N Morddrohung *f*; **death toll** N Zahl *f* der (Todes)opfer; **deathtrap** N Todesfalle *f*; **death warrant** N **to sign one's own ~** (*fig*) sein eigenes Todesurteil unterschreiben

débâcle [deˈbɑːkl] N Debakel *nt* (*over* bei)

debatable [dɪˈbeɪtəbl] ADJ fraglich

debate [dɪˈbeɪt] **1** VTI debattieren (*with* mit, *about* über *acc*); **he was debating with himself whether or not to go** er überlegte hin und her, ob er gehen sollte **2** N Debatte *f*; **to be open to ~** zur Debatte stehen

debenture: debenture bond N Obligation *f*; **debenture holder** N Obligationär(in) *m(f)*; **debenture stock** N Obligationen *pl*

debilitating [dɪˈbɪlɪteɪtɪŋ] ADJ schwächend; *lack of funds, war, depression etc* lähmend

debit ['debɪt] **1** N Debet *nt*; (*with bank*) Sollsaldo *nt*; **~ account** Debetkonto *nt*; **to enter sth to the ~ side of an account** etw auf der Sollseite verbuchen **2** VT **to ~ sb/sb's account (with a sum),** to **~ (a sum) to sb/sb's account** jdn/jds Konto (mit einer Summe) belasten

debit: debit card N Kundenkarte *f*; **debit entry** N Abbuchung *f*; **debit note** N Lastschrift(anzeige) *f*

deboard [dɪˈbɔːd] (*US*) **1** VI aussteigen; (*from boat*) ausschiffen **2** VT aussteigen aus; *boat* ausschiffen aus

debris ['debriː] N Trümmer *pl*; (*Geol*) Geröll *nt*

debt [det] N (= *obligation*) Schuld *f*; (= *money owed*) Schulden *pl*; **to be in ~** verschuldet sein (*to* gegenüber); **to be £5 in ~** £ 5 Schulden haben (*to* bei); **he is in my ~** (*for money*) er hat Schulden bei mir; (*for help etc*) er steht in meiner Schuld; **to run** or **get into ~** Schulden machen, sich verschulden; **to get out of ~** aus den Schulden herauskommen; **to repay a ~** (*lit, fig*) eine Schuld begleichen

debt: debt burden N Schuldenlast *f*; **debt collector** N Inkassobeauftragte(r) *mf*, Schuldeneintreiber(in) *m(f)* (*inf*); **debt crisis** N Schuldenkrise *f*; **debt forgiveness** N Schuldenerlass *m*

debtor ['detə'] N Schuldner(in) *m(f)*; **~ turnover** (*Fin*) Debitorenumsatz *m*

debt: debt relief N Schuldenerleichterung *m*; **debt service** N (*Econ*) Schuldendienst *m*

debug [diːˈbʌg] VT (*Comput*) entwanzen; **~ging program** Fehlerkorrekturprogramm *nt*

debugger [diːˈbʌgə'] N (*Comput*) Debugger *m*

début ['deɪbjuː] **1** N (*lit, fig*) Debüt *nt*; **to make one's ~** (*Theat*) debütieren; (*fig*) sein Debüt geben; **~ album** Debütalbum *nt* **2** VI (*Theat*) debütieren, sein Debüt geben; (*fig*) sein Debüt geben

decade ['dekeɪd] N Jahrzehnt *nt*

decadence ['dekədəns] N Dekadenz *f*

decadent ['dekədənt] ADJ dekadent

decaff ['diːkæf] N ABBR *of* **decaffeinated** (*inf*) Koffeinfreie(r) *m* (*inf*)

decaffeinated [ˌdiːˈkæfɪneɪtɪd] ADJ koffeinfrei

decanter [dɪˈkæntə'] N Karaffe *f*

decapitate [dɪˈkæpɪteɪt] VT enthaupten (*geh*), köpfen, dekapitieren (*form*)

decathlon [dɪˈkæθlən] N Zehnkampf *m*

decay [dɪˈkeɪ] **1** VI (*lit, fig*) verfallen; (*Phys*) zerfallen; (*flesh, vegetable matter*) verwesen; (*tooth*) faulen **2** N Verfall *m*; (*Phys*) Zerfall *m*; (*of flesh, vegetable matter*) Verwesung *f*; (*of bones, wood*) Morschwerden *nt*; **tooth ~** Zahnfäule *f*; **to fall into ~** verfallen

decayed [dɪˈkeɪd] ADJ *wood etc* morsch; *tooth* faul; *body, vegetable matter* verwest

deceased [dɪˈsiːst] (*Jur, form*) **1** ADJ verstorben **2 the ~** der/die Tote or Verstorbene; (*pl*) die Verstorbenen *pl*

deceit [dɪˈsiːt] N Täuschung *f*

deceitful [dɪˈsiːtfʊl] ADJ betrügerisch

deceitfully [dɪˈsiːtfəlɪ] ADV betrügerischerweise; *behave* betrügerisch

deceitfulness [dɪˈsiːtfʊlnɪs] N Falschheit f

deceive [dɪˈsiːv] **1** VT täuschen; *one's wife, husband* betrügen; **to ~ sb into doing sth** jdn durch Täuschung dazu bringen, etw zu tun; **to ~ oneself** sich (*dat*) selbst etwas vormachen **2** VI täuschen

decelerate [diːˈseləreɪt] VI (*car, train*) langsamer werden; (*driver*) die Geschwindigkeit herabsetzen

December [dɪˈsembə^r] N Dezember m; *see also* **September**

decency [ˈdiːsənsɪ] N Anstand m; (*of dress etc*) Anständigkeit f; (*of behaviour*) Schicklichkeit f; **it's only common ~ to ...** es gehört sich einfach, zu ...; **he could have had the ~ to tell me** er hätte es mir anständigerweise auch sagen können; **I hope you'll have the ~ to tell me** ich hoffe, du wirst die Anständigkeit besitzen, es mir zu sagen

decent [ˈdiːsənt] ADJ anständig; **are you ~?** (*inf*) bist du schon salonfähig? (*inf*); **to do the ~ thing** das einzig Anständige tun

> *Be careful!* **decent** *is not translated by the German word* **dezent***.*

decently [ˈdiːsəntlɪ] ADV anständig

decentralize [diːˈsentrəlaɪz] VTI dezentralisieren

decentralized [diːˈsentrəlaɪzd] ADJ dezentral

deception [dɪˈsepʃən] N (= *act of deceiving*) Täuschung f; (*of wife etc*) Betrug m

deceptive [dɪˈseptɪv] ADJ irreführend; *similarity* täuschend; *simplicity* trügerisch; **to be ~** täuschen; **appearances are** *or* **can be ~** der Schein trügt

deceptively [dɪˈseptɪvlɪ] ADV *easy* täuschend; *powerful* überraschend; *mild* trügerisch; **to look ~ like sb/sth** jdm/einer Sache täuschend ähnlich sehen

decide [dɪˈsaɪd] **1** VT entscheiden; (= *take it into one's head*) beschließen; **what did you ~?** (*yes or no*) wie habt ihr euch entschieden?; (*what measures*) was habt ihr beschlossen?; **did you ~ anything?** habt ihr irgendwelche Entscheidungen getroffen?; **I have ~d we are making a big mistake** ich bin zu der Ansicht gekommen, dass wir einen großen Fehler machen; **I'll ~ what we do!** ich bestimme, was wir tun! **2** VI (sich) entscheiden; **to ~ for/ against sth** (sich) für/gegen etw entscheiden

➤ **decide on** VI +PREP OBJ sich entscheiden für

decided [dɪˈsaɪdɪd] ADJ *improvement* entschieden; *advantage* deutlich

decidedly [dɪˈsaɪdɪdlɪ] ADV entschieden; **he's ~ uncomfortable about it** es ist ihm gar nicht wohl dabei; **~ dangerous** ausgesprochen gefährlich

decider [dɪˈsaɪdə^r] N (*Brit*) (= *game*) Entscheidungsspiel nt; (= *goal*) Entscheidungstreffer m

deciding [dɪˈsaɪdɪŋ] ADJ entscheidend; *factor also* ausschlaggebend

deciduous [dɪˈsɪdjʊəs] ADJ **~ tree/forest** Laubbaum m/-wald m

decimal [ˈdesɪməl] **1** ADJ Dezimal- **2** N Dezimalzahl f

decimal point N Komma nt

decimate [ˈdesɪmeɪt] VT dezimieren

decision [dɪˈsɪʒən] N Entscheidung f (*on* über +acc), Entschluss m; (*esp of committee etc*) Beschluss m; **to make a ~** eine Entscheidung treffen; **it's your ~** das musst du entscheiden; **to come to a ~** zu einer Entscheidung kommen; **I've come to the ~ that it's a waste of time** ich bin zu dem Schluss gekommen, dass es Zeitverschwendung ist; **~s, ~s!** immer diese Entscheidungen!

decision-making **1** N Entscheidungsfindung f **2** ADJ ATTR **~ skills** *or* **abilities** Entscheidungskraft f; **the ~ process** der Entscheidungsprozess

decisive [dɪˈsaɪsɪv] ADJ (a) (= *crucial*) entscheidend (b) *manner, answer* entschlossen; *person* entschlussfreudig

decisively [dɪˈsaɪsɪvlɪ] ADV *change, influence* entscheidend; *defeat* deutlich

decisiveness [dɪˈsaɪsɪvnɪs] N Entschlossenheit f

deck [dek] N (a) (*of bus, ship*) Deck nt; **on ~** auf Deck; **to go up on ~** an Deck gehen; **top** *or* **upper ~** Oberdeck nt (b) (*US:* = *verandah*) Veranda f (c) (*Cards*) **a ~ of cards** ein Kartenspiel nt

deck chair N Liegestuhl m

-decker [-ˈdekə^r] N SUF -decker m

declaration [dekləˈreɪʃən] N Erklärung f; (*Customs*) Deklaration f (*form*); **~ of love** Liebeserklärung f; **~ of bankruptcy** Konkursanmeldung f; **to make a ~** eine Erklärung abgeben; **~ of war** Kriegserklärung f

declare [dɪˈkleə^r] VT *intentions* erklären; *results* bekannt geben; *goods* angeben; **have you anything to ~?** haben Sie etwas zu verzollen?; **to ~ one's income** sein Einkommen angeben; **to ~ one's support** seine Unterstützung zum Ausdruck bringen; **to ~ war (on sb)** (jdm) den Krieg erklären; **to ~ a state of emergency** den Notstand ausrufen; **to ~ independence** sich für unabhängig erklären; **to ~ sb bankrupt** jdn für bankrott erklären; **he ~d the meeting closed** er erklärte die Sitzung für geschlossen; **to ~ sb the winner** jdn zum Sieger erklären; **he ~d himself fit to play** er erklärte sich für spielfähig; (= *assert*) versichern

declared [dɪˈkleəd] ADJ erklärt

declension [dɪˈklenʃən] N (*Gram*) Deklination f

declinable [dɪˈklaɪnəbl] ADJ (*Gram*) deklinierbar

decline [dɪˈklaɪn] **1** N Rückgang m; (*of empire, a party's supremacy*) Niedergang m; (*of product*) Degeneration f; **to be on the** *or* **in ~, to go** *or* **fall into ~** (*business*) zurückgehen; (*empire*) verfallen **2** VT (a) *invitation, honour* ablehnen (b) (*Gram*) deklinieren **3** VI (a) (*health*) sich verschlechtern; (*prices, business*) zurückgehen; (*significance, value*) geringer werden; (*popularity, interest, population, influence*) abnehmen; **declining demand** (*Comm*) sinkende Nachfrage (b) (*Gram*) dekliniert werden

declining-balance [dɪˈklaɪnɪŋbæləns] ADJ (*Fin*) degressiv

decode [diːˈkəʊd] VT dekodieren

decoder [diːˈkəʊdə^r] N Dekoder m

decompose [diːkəmˈpəʊz] VI zerlegt werden; (= *rot*) sich zersetzen

decomposition [diːkɒmpəˈzɪʃən] N (= *rotting*) Zersetzung f, Verfaulen nt

decongestant [diːkənˈdʒestənt] N abschwellendes Mittel; (*drops etc*) Nasentropfen pl/-spray nt

decontaminate [diːkənˈtæmɪneɪt] VT entgiften; (*from radioactivity*) entseuchen

decontamination [diːkənˌtæmɪˈneɪʃən] N Entgiftung f; (*from radioactivity*) Entseuchung f

decontrol [diːkənˈtrəʊl] VT (*Comm*) freigeben

décor [ˈdeɪkɔː^r] N Ausstattung f

decorate [ˈdekəreɪt] VT *cake* verzieren; *street, building, Christmas tree* schmücken; *room* tapezieren; (= *paint*) (an)streichen; (*for special occasion*) dekorieren

decorating [ˈdekəreɪtɪŋ] N Tapezieren nt; (= *painting*) Streichen nt

decoration [dekəˈreɪʃən] N (*on cake, hat etc*) Verzierung f; (*on Christmas tree, building, in street*) Schmuck m no pl; **Christmas ~s** Weihnachtsdekorationen pl *or* -schmuck m; **interior ~** Innenausstattung f

decorative [ˈdekərətɪv] ADJ dekorativ

decorator [ˈdekəreɪtə^r] N (*Brit*) Maler(in) m(f)

decrease [diːˈkriːs] **1** VI abnehmen; (*strength, enthusiasm, intensity*) nachlassen **2** VT reduzieren **3** [ˈdiːkriːs] N Abnahme f; (*in figures, birth rate, production*) Rückgang m; (*in strength, enthusiasm, intensity*) Nachlassen nt

decreasingly [diːˈkriːsɪŋlɪ] ADV immer weniger

decree [dɪˈkriː] **1** N Anordnung f; (*Pol: of king etc*) Erlass m; (*Jur*) Verfügung f; (*of tribunal, court*) Entscheid m; **by royal ~** auf königlichen Erlass; **to issue a ~** einen Erlass herausgeben **2** VT verordnen, verfügen; **he ~d an annual holiday on 1st April** er erklärte den 1. April zum Feiertag

decree absolute N (*Jur*) endgültiges Scheidungsurteil

decree nisi [dɪˌkriːˈnaɪsaɪ] N (*Jur*) vorläufiges Scheidungsurteil

decrepit [dɪˈkrepɪt] ADJ altersschwach; *building* baufällig

dedicate [ˈdedɪkeɪt] VT widmen (*to sb* jdm); (*US Ind*) *plant, power station* in Dienst stellen; **to ~ oneself** *or* **one's life to sb/ sth** sich *or* sein Leben jdm/einer Sache widmen; **~d to the memory of ...** zum Gedenken an ...

dedicated [ˈdedɪkeɪtɪd] ADJ (a) *attitude* hingebungsvoll; *service, fans* treu; (*in one's work*) engagiert; **a ~ nurse** eine Krankenschwester, die mit Leib und Seele bei der Sache ist;

he is completely ~, he thinks of nothing but his work er hat sich völlig seiner Arbeit verschrieben, er denkt an nichts anderes; **she's ~ to her students** sie engagiert sich sehr für ihre Studenten **(b)** (*in book*) ~ **word processor** dediziertes Textverarbeitungssystem

dedication [ˌdedɪˈkeɪʃən] N **(a)** (= *quality*) Hingabe *f* (*to* an +*acc*) **(b)** (*in book*) Widmung *f*

deduce [dɪˈdjuːs] VT folgern, schließen (*from* aus)

deduct [dɪˈdʌkt] VT abziehen (*from* von); **to ~ sth from the price** etw vom Preis ablassen; **to ~ income tax at source** Einkommensteuer einbehalten; **after ~ing 5%** nach Abzug von 5%

deductible [dɪˈdʌktəbl] **1** ADJ abziehbar; (= *tax ~*) absetzbar **2** N (*Insur*) Selbstbeteiligung *f* (*on* bei)

deduction [dɪˈdʌkʃən] N **(a)** Abzug *m*; (*from price*) Nachlass *m* (*from* für, auf +*acc*) **(b) by a process of** ~ durch Folgern

deed [diːd] N **(a)** Tat *f*; **good ~** gute Tat; **evil ~** Übeltat *f*; **in ~** tatsächlich, in der Tat **(b)** (*Jur*) Übertragungsurkunde *f*; ~ **of covenant** Vertragsurkunde *f*; ~ **of partnership** (*Comm*) Gesellschaftsvertrag *m* **2** VT (*US*) überschreiben (*to* auf +*acc*)

deep [diːp] **1** ADJ (+ER) tief; (= *wide*) border, edge breit; (= *profound*) tiefsinnig; *concern, relief* groß; *sorrow* tief (*empfunden*); **the pond/snow was 4 feet ~** der Teich war/der Schnee lag 4 Fuß tief; **two feet ~ in snow** mit zwei Fuß Schnee bedeckt; **two feet ~ in water** zwei Fuß tief unter Wasser; **the ~ end** (*of swimming pool*) das Tiefe; **to go off (at) the ~ end** (*fig inf*) auf die Palme gehen (*inf*); **to go** or **jump in at the ~ end** (*fig*) sich kopfüber in die Sache stürzen; **to be thrown in at the ~ end** (*fig*) gleich zu Anfang richtig ranmüssen (*inf*); **the spectators stood ten ~** die Zuschauer standen zu zehnt hintereinander; **~est sympathy** aufrichtiges Beileid; ~ **down, she knew he was right** im Innersten wusste sie, dass er Recht hatte; ~ **in conversation** ins Gespräch vertieft; ~ **in debt** hoch verschuldet; ~ **in recession** mitten in einer Rezession; **we had a ~ and meaningful relationship** wir hatten eine tiefer gehende und sinnvolle Beziehung; **to be in ~ trouble** in großen Schwierigkeiten sein **2** ADV (+ER) tief; ~ **into the night** bis tief in die Nacht hinein; **he's in it pretty ~** (*inf*) er steckt ganz schön tief da drin (*inf*)

deepen [ˈdiːpən] **1** VT (*lit, fig*) vertiefen; *mystery* vergrößern; *crisis, recession* verschärfen **2** VI (*lit, fig*) tiefer werden; (*sorrow, concern, interest*) zunehmen; (*mystery*) größer werden; (*rift, divisions*) sich vertiefen; (*crisis, recession*) sich verschärfen

deepening [ˈdiːpənɪŋ] ADJ *sorrow, concern etc* zunehmend; *crisis, recession* sich verschärfend; *mystery* sich vertiefend

deep: deep-fat fryer N Fritteuse *f*; **deepfreeze** N Tiefkühltruhe *f*; (*upright*) Gefrierschrank *m*; **deep-frozen** ADJ ~ **foods** Tiefkühlkost *f*; **deep-fry** VT frittieren

deeply [ˈdiːplɪ] ADV (*lit, fig*) tief; *worried, unhappy, suspicious* äußerst; *regret, move, shock, grateful* zutiefst; *love* sehr; ~ **committed** stark engagiert; **they are ~ embarrassed by it** es ist ihnen äußerst peinlich; **to fall ~ in love** sich sehr verlieben; **a ~ ingrained prejudice** ein fest verwurzeltes Vorurteil

deep: deep-pan pizza N Pfannenpizza *f*; **deep-rooted** ADJ, *comp* **deeper-rooted** (*fig*) tief verwurzelt; **deep-sea** ADJ Tiefsee-; **deep-seated** ADJ, *comp* **deeper-seated** tief sitzend; **deep-set** ADJ, *comp* **deeper-set** tief liegend; **deep space** N der äußere Weltraum

deer [dɪəʳ] N, *pl* - (= *roe* ~) Reh *nt*; (= *stag*) Hirsch *m*; (*collectively*) Rotwild *nt*

defamatory [dɪˈfæmətərɪ] ADJ diffamierend

default [dɪˈfɔːlt] **1** N **(a) to win by** ~ kampflos gewinnen **(b)** [ˈdiːfɔːlt] (*Comput*) Default *m*, Voreinstellung *f* **2** [ˈdiːfɔːlt] ATTR (*Comput*) *parameter* voreingestellt; ~ **drive** Standardlaufwerk *nt* **3** VI (= *not perform duty, not pay*) säumig sein; (*Fin*: = *go bankrupt*) zahlungsunfähig werden; **to ~ in one's payments** seinen Zahlungsverpflichtungen nicht nachkommen

default interest N (*Fin*) Verzugszinsen *pl*

default summons N Mahnbescheid *m*

defeat [dɪˈfiːt] **1** N Niederlage *f*; (*of motion, bill*) Ablehnung *f*; **their ~ of the enemy** ihr Sieg über den Feind; **to admit ~** sich geschlagen geben; **to suffer a ~** eine Niederlage erleiden **2** VT *army, team* besiegen, schlagen; *government* eine Niederlage beibringen (+*dat*); *motion, bill* ablehnen; **that**

---

would be ~ing the purpose of the exercise dann verliert die Übung ihren Sinn

defect[1] [ˈdiːfekt] N Fehler *m*; (*in mechanism*) Defekt *m*

defect[2] [dɪˈfekt] VI (*Pol*) sich absetzen; **to ~ to the enemy** zum Feind überlaufen

defection [dɪˈfekʃən] N (*Pol*) Überlaufen *nt*

defective [dɪˈfektɪv] ADJ (*lit, fig*) fehlerhaft; *machine, gene* defekt

defence, (US) defense [dɪˈfens] N **(a)** NO PL (*also Jur, Sport*) Verteidigung *f no pl*; **in his ~** zu seiner Verteidigung; **to come to sb's ~** jdn verteidigen; **to put up** or **make a spirited ~ of sb/sth** jdn/etw mutig verteidigen; **his only ~ was ...** seine einzige Rechtfertigung war ... **(b)** (= *form of protection*) Abwehrmaßnahme *f*; (*Mil*: = *fortification etc*) Befestigung *f*, Verteidigungsanlage *f*; **as a ~ against** als Schutz gegen; **his ~s were down** er war wehrlos

defence, (US) defense: defence counsel N Verteidiger(in) *m(f)*; **defenceless, (US) defenseless** ADJ schutzlos; **defence mechanism** N (*Physiol, Psych*) Abwehrmechanismus *m*; **defence minister** N Verteidigungsminister(in) *m(f)*

defend [dɪˈfend] VT verteidigen (*also Jur*) (*against* gegen)

defendant [dɪˈfendənt] N Angeklagte(r) *mf*; (*in civil cases*) Beklagte(r) *mf*

defender [dɪˈfendəʳ] N Verteidiger(in) *m(f)*

defending [dɪˈfendɪŋ] ADJ **the ~ champions** die Titelverteidiger *pl*

defense *etc* (*US*) = **defence** *etc*

defensive [dɪˈfensɪv] **1** ADJ defensiv (*also fig*); **a good ~ player** ein guter Verteidiger **2** N (*Mil*) Abwehraktion *f*; **to be on the ~** (*Mil, fig*) in der Defensive sein

defensively [dɪˈfensɪvlɪ] ADV (*also Sport*) defensiv

defer [dɪˈfɜːʳ] VT (= *delay*) verschieben; **to ~ doing sth** es verschieben, etw zu tun

deference [ˈdefərəns] N Achtung *f*; **out of** or **in ~ to** aus Achtung (*dat*) vor

deferential [ˌdefəˈrenʃəl] ADJ respektvoll

deferred [dɪˈfɜːd]: **deferred annuity** N nach bestimmter Zeit fällige Rente; **deferred pay** N (*Mil*) einbehaltener Sold; (*Naut*) einbehaltene Heuer; **deferred payment** N Zahlungsaufschub *m*; (*US: by instalments*) Ratenzahlung *f*; **deferred shares** PL Nachzugsaktien *pl*; **deferred taxation** N Steuerrückstellung *f*

defiance [dɪˈfaɪəns] N Trotz *m* (*of sb* jdm gegenüber); (*of order, law, danger*) Missachtung *f* (*of* +*gen*); **an act of ~** eine Trotzhandlung; **in ~ of sb/sth** jdm/etw zum Trotz

defiant [dɪˈfaɪənt] ADJ trotzig; (= *rebellious*) aufsässig; (= *challenging*) *attitude* herausfordernd

defiantly [dɪˈfaɪəntlɪ] ADV trotzig; *resist* standhaft

deficiency [dɪˈfɪʃənsɪ] N Mangel *m*; (*Fin*) Defizit *nt*; (= *defect: in character, system*) Schwäche *f*; **iron ~** Eisenmangel *m*

deficient [dɪˈfɪʃənt] ADJ unzulänglich; (*Comm*) *goods* fehlerhaft, mangelhaft; **sb/sth is ~ in sth** jdm/einer Sache fehlt es an etw (*dat*)

deficit [ˈdefɪsɪt] N Defizit *nt*

definable [dɪˈfaɪnəbl] ADJ definierbar; *conditions, boundaries, duties etc* bestimmbar

define [dɪˈfaɪn] VT definieren; *conditions, powers, duties etc* festlegen

definite [ˈdefɪnɪt] ADJ **(a)** definitiv; *answer, decision* klar; *agreement, date, plan, intention, wish* fest; *command, request* bestimmt; **is that ~?** ist das sicher?; **for ~** say, know mit Bestimmtheit **(b)** *mark, stain, lisp* deutlich; *advantage, improvement* eindeutig; *problem, possibility* echt **(c)** *tone, manner* bestimmt; **she was very ~ about it** sie war sich (*dat*) sehr sicher

definite article N (*Gram*) bestimmter Artikel

definitely [ˈdefɪnɪtlɪ] ADV **(a)** *decide, say* endgültig; **it's not ~ arranged/agreed yet** es steht noch nicht fest **(b)** (= *clearly*) eindeutig; (= *certainly*) bestimmt; (= *whatever happens*) auf jeden Fall; **~ not** auf keinen Fall; **he ~ wanted to come** er wollte bestimmt kommen **(c)** (= *emphatically*) nachdrücklich

definition [ˌdefɪˈnɪʃən] N **(a)** (*of word, concept*) Definition *f*; **by ~** per definitionem, definitionsgemäß **(b)** (*of powers, duties, boundaries*) Festlegung *f* **(c)** (*Phot, TV*) Bildschärfe *f*

definitive [dɪˈfɪnɪtɪv] ADJ *victory, answer* entschieden; *book* maßgeblich (*on* für); *term* beschreibend

deflate [diːˈfleɪt] **1** VT die Luft ablassen aus; **to ~ the currency** (*Fin*) eine Deflation herbeiführen; **he felt a bit ~d when ...** es war ein ziemlicher Dämpfer für ihn, dass ... **2** VI (*Fin*) eine Deflation herbeiführen

deflation [diːˈfleɪʃən] N (*Fin*) Deflation *f*

deflationary [diːˈfleɪʃənərɪ] ADJ (*Fin*) deflationistisch; **~ policy** Deflationspolitik *f*

deflect [dɪˈflekt] VT ablenken; *ball* abfälschen; (*Phys*) *light* beugen

deflection [dɪˈflekʃən] N Ablenkung *f*; (*of ball*) Abfälschung *f*; (*Phys: of light*) Beugung *f*

deforestation [diːˌfɒrɪˈsteɪʃən] N Entwaldung *f*

deformed [dɪˈfɔːmd] ADJ deformiert; (*Tech*) verformt

deformity [dɪˈfɔːmɪtɪ] N Deformität *f*

defraud [dɪˈfrɔːd] VT betrügen; **to ~ sb of sth** jdn um etw betrügen

defrost [diːˈfrɒst] **1** VT *fridge* abtauen; *food* auftauen **2** VI (*fridge*) abtauen; (*food*) auftauen

deft ADJ (+ER), **deftly** ADV [deft, -lɪ] geschickt

deftly ADV geschickt

defunct [dɪˈfʌŋkt] ADJ (*fig*) *institution etc* eingegangen; *idea* untergegangen; *industry* nicht mehr existent; *law* außer Kraft

defuse [diːˈfjuːz] VT (*lit, fig*) entschärfen

defy [dɪˈfaɪ] VT (a) *person* sich widersetzen (+*dat*); *orders, law, death, danger* trotzen (+*dat*) (b) (*fig: = make impossible*) widerstehen (+*dat*); **to ~ description** jeder Beschreibung spotten; **that defies belief!** das ist ja unglaublich!; **to ~ gravity/logic** den Gesetzen der Schwerkraft/Logik widersprechen

degenerate [dɪˈdʒenəreɪt] VI degenerieren; (*people, morals*) entarten; **the demonstration ~d into violence** die Demonstration artete in Gewalttätigkeiten aus

degradation [ˌdegrəˈdeɪʃən] N Erniedrigung *f*; (*Geol*) Erosion *f*; (*Chem*) Abbau *m*

degrade [dɪˈgreɪd] **1** VT erniedrigen; (*Geol*) erodieren; (*Chem*) abbauen; **to ~ oneself** sich erniedrigen **2** VI (*Chem*) sich abbauen

degrading [dɪˈgreɪdɪŋ] ADJ erniedrigend

degree [dɪˈgriː] N (a) Grad *m no pl*; **an angle of 90 ~s** ein Winkel *m* von 90 Grad; **first ~ murder** (*Jur*) Mord *m*; **second ~ murder** (*Jur*) Totschlag *m*

(b) (*of risk, uncertainty etc*) Maß *nt*; **some or a certain ~ of** ein gewisses Maß an (+*dat*); **to some ~, to a (certain) ~** in gewissem Maße; **to a high ~** in hohem Maße; **to such a ~ that ...** so sehr *or* in solchem Maße, dass ...

(c) (*Univ*) akademischer Grad; **first ~** erster akademischer Grad; **to get one's ~** seinen akademischen Grad erhalten; **to do a ~** studieren; **when did you do your ~?** wann haben Sie das Examen gemacht?; **I'm taking *or* doing a language ~ *or* a ~ in languages** ich studiere Sprachwissenschaften; **I've got a ~ in Business Studies** ich habe einen Hochschulabschluss in Wirtschaftslehre

degree course N *Universitätskurs, der mit dem ersten akademischen Grad abschließt*

dehumidifier [ˌdiːhjuːˈmɪdɪfaɪəʳ] N Luftentfeuchter *m*

dehydrated [ˌdiːhaɪˈdreɪtɪd] ADJ dehydriert; *foods* getrocknet; *person, skin* ausgetrocknet

dehydration [ˌdiːhaɪˈdreɪʃən] N Austrocknung *f*

de-icer [diːˈaɪsəʳ] N Enteiser *m*; (= *spray for cars*) Defroster *m*

deign [deɪn] VT **to ~ to do sth** sich herablassen, etw zu tun

deity [ˈdiːɪtɪ] N Gottheit *f*; **the Deity** Gott *m*

déjà vu [ˈdeɪʒɑːˈvuː] N Déjà-vu-Erlebnis *nt*; **a feeling or sense of ~** das Gefühl, das schon einmal gesehen zu haben

dejected ADJ, **dejectedly** ADV [dɪˈdʒektɪd, -lɪ] deprimiert

dejection [dɪˈdʒekʃən] N Depression *f*

delay [dɪˈleɪ] **1** VT (a) (= *postpone*) verschieben; **to ~ doing sth** es verschieben, etw zu tun; **he ~ed paying until ...** er wartete so lange mit dem Zahlen, bis ...; **rain ~ed play** der Beginn des Spiels verzögerte sich wegen Regens; **~ed delivery** (*Comm*) Lieferverzug *m*

(b) (= *hold up*) *person, train, traffic* aufhalten

2 VI warten; **to ~ in doing sth** es verschieben, etw zu tun; **he ~ed in paying the bill** er schob die Zahlung der Rechnung hinaus

3 N (= *hold-up*) Aufenthalt *m*; (*to traffic*) Stockung *f*; (*to train, plane*) Verspätung *f*; (= *time lapse*) Verzögerung *f*; **roadworks are causing ~s of up to 1 hour** Straßenbauarbeiten verursachen Staus bis zu 1 Stunde; **"~s possible (until ...)"** „Staugefahr! (bis ...)"; **there are ~s to all flights** alle Flüge haben Verspätung; **without ~** unverzüglich; **without further ~** ohne weitere Verzögerung

delaying [dɪˈleɪɪŋ] ADJ verzögernd, hinhaltend; **~ tactics** Verzögerungstaktik *f*

del credere ADJ (*Comm*) Delkredere-

delegate [ˈdelɪgeɪt] **1** VT delegieren; *authority* übertragen (*to sb* jdm); **to ~ sb to do sth** jdn damit beauftragen, etw zu tun **2** VI delegieren **3** [ˈdelɪgət] N Delegierte(r) *mf*

delegation [ˌdelɪˈgeɪʃən] N Delegation *f*

delete [dɪˈliːt] VT streichen; (*Comput*) löschen; **"~ where applicable"** „Nichtzutreffendes (bitte) streichen"

deletion [dɪˈliːʃən] N Streichung *f*; (*Comput*) Löschung *f*; **to make a ~** etwas streichen; **he made several ~s in the text** er strich mehrere Stellen im Text

deli [ˈdelɪ] N (*inf*) = **delicatessen**

deliberate [dɪˈlɪbərɪt] **1** ADJ (a) (= *intentional*) absichtlich; *action, attempt, insult, lie* bewusst; (*Jur, Insur*) vorsätzlich; **~ damage** mutwillige Beschädigung

(b) (= *cautious, thoughtful*) besonnen; *action, decision, judgement* (wohl) überlegt; *movement, step* bedächtig

2 [dɪˈlɪbəreɪt] VI (= *ponder*) nachdenken (*on, upon* über +*acc*); (= *discuss*) sich beraten (*on, upon* über +*acc*, *wegen*)

3 [dɪˈlɪbəreɪt] VT (= *ponder*) bedenken; (= *discuss*) beraten

deliberately [dɪˈlɪbərɪtlɪ] ADV (a) (= *intentionally*) absichtlich; *plan* vorsätzlich; **it looks as if the blaze was started ~** es sieht so aus, als sei der Brand vorsätzlich gelegt worden

(b) (= *cautiously, thoughtfully*) überlegt; *move* bedächtig

deliberation [dɪˌlɪbəˈreɪʃən] N (a) (= *consideration*) Überlegung *f* (*on* zu) (b) **deliberations** PL (= *discussions*) Beratungen *pl* (*of, on* über +*acc*)

delicacy [ˈdelɪkəsɪ] N (a) = **delicateness** (b) (= *food*) Delikatesse *f*

delicate [ˈdelɪkɪt] **1** ADJ (a) fein; *colour, health* zart; *food* delikat; *person, china* zerbrechlich; *fabric, flower, stomach* empfindlich; **she's feeling a bit ~ after the party** nach der Party fühlt sie sich etwas angeschlagen (b) *operation, subject, situation* heikel, delikat **2** **delicates** PL (= *fabrics*) Feinwäsche *f*

delicately [ˈdelɪkɪtlɪ] ADV (a) *move, touch, coloured* zart (b) *spiced, scented* fein; **~ flavoured** (*Brit*) *or* **flavored** (*US*) mit einem delikaten Geschmack (c) (= *tactfully*) taktvoll

delicateness [ˈdelɪkɪtnɪs] N (a) Zartheit *f*; (= *fragility*) Zerbrechlichkeit *f*; (*of fabric, flower, liver*) Empfindlichkeit *f* (b) (= *sensitivity: of task*) Feinheit *f* (c) (*of operation, subject, situation*) heikle Natur

delicatessen [ˌdelɪkəˈtesn] N Feinkostgeschäft *nt*

delicious [dɪˈlɪʃəs] ADJ (a) *food etc* köstlich (b) (= *delightful*) herrlich

deliciously [dɪˈlɪʃəslɪ] ADV (a) *tender, creamy* köstlich (b) *warm, fresh, fragrant* herrlich

delight [dɪˈlaɪt] **1** N Freude *f*; **to my ~** zu meiner Freude; **he takes great ~ in doing that** es bereitet ihm große Freude, das zu tun; **he's a ~ to watch, it's a ~ to watch him** es ist eine Freude, ihm zuzusehen **2** VI sich erfreuen (*in* an +*dat*)

delighted [dɪˈlaɪtɪd] ADJ (*with* über +*acc*) erfreut; **to be ~** sich sehr freuen (*at* über +*acc*, *that* dass); **absolutely ~** hocherfreut; **~ to meet you!** sehr angenehm!; **I'd be ~ to help you** ich würde Ihnen sehr gern helfen

delightful [dɪˈlaɪtfʊl] ADJ reizend; *weather, party, meal* wunderbar

delightfully [dɪˈlaɪtfəlɪ] ADV wunderbar

delinquency [dɪˈlɪŋkwənsɪ] N Kriminalität *f*

delinquent [dɪˈlɪŋkwənt] **1** ADJ (a) straffällig (b) *bill* überfällig; *account* rückständig **2** N Delinquent(in) *m(f)*

delirious [dɪˈlɪrɪəs] ADJ (*Med*) im Delirium; (*fig*) im Taumel; **to be ~ with joy** im Freudentaumel sein

deliriously [dɪˈlɪrɪəslɪ] ADV (a) *scream, cheer* ekstatisch; **~ happy** euphorisch (b) (*Med*) im Delirium

deliver [dɪˈlɪvəʳ] **1** VT (a) *goods* liefern; *note, message* überbringen; (*on regular basis*) *papers etc* zustellen; (*on foot*) austragen; (*by car*) ausfahren; **to ~ sth to sb** jdm etw liefern/überbringen/zustellen; **he ~ed the goods to the door** er lieferte die Waren ins Haus; **~ed free of charge** frei Haus (geliefert); **to ~ the goods** (*fig inf*) es bringen (*sl*) (b) *speech, sermon* halten; *ultimatum* stellen; *verdict* sprechen, verkünden; *warning* aussprechen (c) (*Med*) *baby* zur Welt bringen (d) *blow* versetzen; *ball* werfen **2** VI (*lit*) liefern

deliverer [dɪˈlɪvərəʳ] N (*Comm*) Lieferant *m*

delivery [dɪˈlɪvərɪ] N (a) (*of goods*) (Aus)lieferung *f*; (*of parcels, letters*) Zustellung *f*; **please allow 28 days for ~** die Lieferzeit kann bis zu 28 Tagen betragen (b) (*Med*) Entbindung *f* (c) (*of speaker*) Vortragsweise *f* (d) (*of blow*) Landung *f* (*inf*); (*Cricket*) Wurf *m*

delivery: **delivery boy** N Bote *m*; (*for newspapers*) Träger *m*; **delivery contract** N Liefervertrag *m*; **delivery costs** PL Versandkosten *pl*; **delivery date** N Liefertermin *m*; **delivery man** N Lieferant *m*; **delivery note** N Lieferschein *m*; **delivery period** N Lieferfrist *f*; **delivery room** N Kreißsaal *m*, Entbindungssaal *m*; **delivery service** N Zustelldienst *m*; **delivery time** N Lieferzeit *f*; **delivery van** N Lieferwagen *m*

delude [dɪˈluːd] VT täuschen; **to ~ oneself** sich (*dat*) etwas vormachen; **stop deluding yourself that ...** hör auf, dir vorzumachen, dass ...

deluded [dɪˈluːdɪd] ADJ voller Illusionen

deluge [ˈdeljuːdʒ] N (*lit*) Überschwemmung *f*; (*of rain*) Guss *m*; (*fig*: *of letters etc*) Flut *f*

delusion [dɪˈluːʒən] N Illusion *f*; (*Psych*) Wahnvorstellung *f*; **to be** *or* **labour** (*Brit*) *or* **labor** (*US*) **under a ~** in einem Wahn leben; **to have ~s of grandeur** den Größenwahn haben

de luxe [dɪˈlʌks] ADJ Luxus-; **~ model** Luxusmodell *nt*; **~ version** De-Luxe-Ausführung *f*

delve [delv] VI (*into subject*) sich eingehend befassen (*into* mit); (*into book*) sich vertiefen (*into* in +*acc*); **to ~ in(to) one's pocket** tief in die Tasche greifen; **to ~ into the past** die Vergangenheit erforschen

demand [dɪˈmɑːnd] **1** VT verlangen; *time* beanspruchen; **he ~ed money** er wollte Geld haben; **he ~ed to know what had happened** er verlangte zu wissen, was passiert war; **he ~ed to see my passport** er wollte meinen Pass sehen **2** N (a) Forderung *f*, Verlangen *nt* (*for* nach); (= *claim for better pay, of kidnapper etc*) Forderung *f* (*for* nach); **by popular ~** auf allgemeinen Wunsch; **to be available on ~** auf Wunsch erhältlich sein; **to make ~s on sb** Forderungen an jdn stellen; **final ~** (*Comm*) letzte Mahnung *or* Zahlungsaufforderung (b) NO PL (*Comm*) Nachfrage *f*; **there's no ~ for it** es besteht keine Nachfrage danach; **to be in (great) ~** sehr gefragt sein

demand curve N (*Econ*) Nachfragekurve *f*

demand deposit N (*US Fin*) Sichteinlage *f*, Tagesgeld *nt*

demanding [dɪˈmɑːndɪŋ] ADJ *child, job* anstrengend; *task also, teacher, boss* anspruchsvoll

demand management N Steuerung *f* der Nachfrage

demean [dɪˈmiːn] **1** VR sich erniedrigen; **I will not ~ myself by doing that** ich werde mich nicht dazu hergeben, das zu tun **2** VT erniedrigen

demeaning [dɪˈmiːnɪŋ] ADJ erniedrigend

demeanour, (*US*) **demeanor** [dɪˈmiːnəʳ] N (= *behaviour*) Benehmen *nt*; (= *bearing*) Haltung *f*

demented [dɪˈmentɪd] ADJ verrückt

dementia [dɪˈmenʃə] N Schwachsinn *m*

demerara (sugar) [deməˈrɛərə(ˈʃʊgəʳ)] N brauner Rohrzucker

demerge [diːˈmɜːdʒ] VT *company* entflechten

demi [ˈdemɪ] PREF Halb-, halb-

demilitarization [diːˌmɪlɪtərəˈzeɪʃən] N Entmilitarisierung *f*

demilitarize [diːˈmɪlɪtəraɪz] VT entmilitarisieren; **~d zone** entmilitarisierte Zone

demise [dɪˈmaɪz] N (= *death*) Tod *m*; (*of person also*) Ableben *nt* (*geh*); (*fig*: *of institution etc*) Ende *nt*

demo [ˈdeməʊ] **1** N ABBR *of* **demonstration** Demo(nstration) *f* **2** ADJ ATTR **~ tape** Demoband *nt*

demobilize [diːˈməʊbɪlaɪz] VT demobilisieren

democracy [dɪˈmɒkrəsɪ] N Demokratie *f*

democrat [ˈdeməkræt] N Demokrat(in) *m(f)*

democratic [deməˈkrætɪk] ADJ (a) demokratisch; **the Social Democratic Party** die Sozialdemokratische Partei; **the Christian Democratic Party** die Christlich-Demokratische Partei (b) **Democratic** (*US Pol*) *candidate, convention* der Demokratischen Partei; **the Democratic Party** die Demokratische Partei

democratically [deməˈkrætɪkəlɪ] ADV demokratisch

demolish [dɪˈmɒlɪʃ] VT *building* abbrechen; (*fig*) *opponent, theory* vernichten; (*hum*) *cake etc* vertilgen

demolition [deməˈlɪʃən] N Abbruch *m*

demolition: **demolition squad** N Abbruchkolonne *f*; **demolition work** N Abbrucharbeiten *pl*

demon [ˈdiːmən] N Dämon *m*; (*fig*) (= *person*) Dämon(in) *m(f)*; (*inf*: = *child*) Teufel *m*; **the Demon Drink** König Alkohol *m*

demonic [dɪˈmɒnɪk] ADJ dämonisch

demonize [ˈdiːmənaɪz] VT dämonisieren

demonstrate [ˈdemənstreɪt] **1** VT beweisen; (*by experiment, example*) demonstrieren; *appliance, operation* vorführen **2** VI (*Pol etc*) demonstrieren

demonstration [demənˈstreɪʃən] N Beweis *m*; (*by experiment, example*) Demonstration *f* (*also Pol etc*); (*of appliance, operation*) Vorführung *f*; **to give a ~ of sth** etw demonstrieren; *of operation, gadget* etw vorführen; **he gave us a ~** er zeigte es uns

demonstration model N Vorführmodell *m*

demonstrator [ˈdemənstreɪtəʳ] N (a) (*Comm*) Vorführer(in) *m(f)* (von technischen Geräten) (b) (*Pol*) Demonstrant(in) *m(f)*

demoralization [dɪˌmɒrəlaɪˈzeɪʃən] N Entmutigung *f*; (*of troops etc*) Demoralisierung *f*

demoralize [dɪˈmɒrəlaɪz] VT entmutigen; *troops etc* demoralisieren

demoralizing [dɪˈmɒrəlaɪzɪŋ] ADJ entmutigend; (*for troops etc*) demoralisierend

demote [dɪˈməʊt] VT (*Mil*) degradieren (*to* zu); (*in business etc*) zurückstufen; **to be ~d** (*Sport*) absteigen

demotion [dɪˈməʊʃən] N (*Mil*) Degradierung *f*; (*in business etc*) Zurückstufung *f*; (*Sport*) Abstieg *m*

demotivate [diːˈməʊtɪveɪt] VT demotivieren

demurrage [dɪˈmʌrɪdʒ] N (*Comm*) (Über)liegegeld *nt*

demutualize [diːˈmjuːtjʊəlaɪz] VI (*Fin*) demutualisieren

den [den] N (a) (*of lion, tiger etc*) Höhle *f*; (*of fox*) Bau *m* (b) **~ of thieves** Spelunke *f* (c) (= *study*) Arbeitszimmer *nt*; (= *private room*) Bude *f* (*inf*)

denazification [diːˌnætsɪfɪˈkeɪʃən] N Entnazifizierung *f*

denial [dɪˈnaɪəl] N (a) (*of accusation, guilt*) Leugnen *nt*; **the government issued an official ~** die Regierung gab ein offizielles Dementi heraus (b) (= *refusal*) Ablehnung *f*; (*official*) abschlägiger Bescheid; (*of rights*) Verweigerung *f* (c) (= *self-~*) Selbstverleugnung *f*

denim [ˈdenɪm] **1** N (a) Jeansstoff *m* (b) **denims** PL Jeans *pl* **2** ADJ ATTR Jeans-

Denmark [ˈdenmɑːk] N Dänemark *nt*

denote [dɪˈnəʊt] VT bedeuten; *symbol, word* bezeichnen

denounce [dɪˈnaʊns] VT (a) (= *accuse publicly*) anprangern; (= *inform against*) denunzieren (*sb to sb* jdn bei jdm) (b) *alcohol, habit etc* verurteilen

dense [dens] ADJ (+ER) **(a)** *fog, smoke, forest* dicht (*also Phys*); *crowd* dicht gedrängt **(b)** *language, style* (= *concentrated*) gedrängt; (= *over-complex*) überladen **(c)** (*inf*) (= *of low intellect*) beschränkt (*inf*); (= *slow*) begriffsstutzig (*inf*)

densely ['densli] ADV *populated, wooded* dicht

density ['densiti] N Dichte *f*; **population ~** Bevölkerungsdichte *f*

dent [dent] **1** N (*in metal*) Beule *f*; (*in wood*) Kerbe *f*; **that made a ~ in his savings** (*inf*) das hat ein Loch in seine Ersparnisse gerissen **2** VT *car* verbeulen; *wood* eine Delle machen in (+*acc*); (*inf*) *pride, confidence* anknacksen (*inf*)

dental ['dentl] ADJ Zahn-; *treatment* zahnärztlich

dental: dental assistant N Zahnarzthelfer(in) *m(f)*; **dental floss** N Zahnseide *f*; **dental hygiene** N Zahnpflege *f*; **dental hygienist** [,dentl'haɪdʒiːnɪst] N zahnmedizinischer Fachhelfer, zahnmedizinische Fachhelferin; **dental nurse** N Zahnarzthelfer(in) *m(f)*; **dental surgeon** N Zahnarzt *m/*-ärztin *f*

dentist ['dentɪst] N Zahnarzt *m*, Zahnärztin *f*; **at the ~('s)** beim Zahnarzt

dentistry ['dentɪstrɪ] N Zahnmedizin *f*

dentures ['dentʃəz] PL Zahnprothese *f*; (*full*) Gebiss *nt*

denunciation [dɪ,nʌnsɪ'eɪʃən] N (= *accusation*) Anprangerung *f*; (= *informing*) Denunziation *f*; (= *condemnation*) Verurteilung *f*

deny [dɪ'naɪ] VT **(a)** *accusation etc* bestreiten; *existence of God* leugnen; (*officially*) dementieren; **do you ~ having said that?** bestreiten *or* leugnen Sie, das gesagt zu haben?; **there's no ~ing it** das lässt sich nicht bestreiten; **to ~ liability** keine Haftung übernehmen **(b)** (= *refuse*) **to ~ sb's request** jdm seine Bitte abschlagen; **to ~ sb his rights** jdm seine Rechte vorenthalten; **to ~ sb aid/a privilege** jdm Hilfe/ein Privileg versagen; **to ~ sb access (to sth)** jdm den Zugang (zu etw) verwehren; **to ~ sb credit** jdm den Kredit verweigern; **I can't ~ her anything** ich kann ihr nichts abschlagen; **why should I ~ myself these little comforts?** warum sollte ich mir das bisschen Komfort nicht gönnen?

deodorant [diː'əʊdərənt] N Deodorant *nt*

dep. ABBR *of* **departs, departure** (*in timetables etc*) Abf.

depart [dɪ'pɑːt] VI weggehen; (*on journey*) abreisen; (*by bus, car etc*) wegfahren; (*train, bus etc*) abfahren; **the train at platform 6 ~ing for ...** der Zug auf Bahnsteig 6 nach ...; **to be ready to ~** (*person*) startbereit sein; **the visitors were about to ~** die Gäste waren im Begriff aufzubrechen

department [dɪ'pɑːtmənt] N **(a)** (*generally*) Abteilung *f*; (*in civil service*) Ressort *nt*; **Department of Commerce** (*US*) Handelsministerium *nt*; **Department of Employment** (*Brit*), **Department of Labor** (*US*) Arbeitsministerium *nt*; **Department of the Environment** (*Brit*) Umweltministerium *nt*; **Department of the Treasury** (*US*) Finanzministerium *nt*; **Department of Trade and Industry** (*Brit*) ≈ Handelsministerium *nt*; **Department of Transport** (*Brit*), **Department of Transportation** (*US*) Verkehrsministerium *nt*; **that's not my ~** (*fig*) dafür bin ich nicht zuständig **(b)** (*Sch, Univ*) Fachbereich *m*

departmental [,diːpɑːt'mentl] ADJ Abteilungs-; (*Sch, Univ*) Fachbereichs-; (*in civil service*) *committee* des Ressorts; **~ manager** Abteilungsleiter(in) *m(f)*; **~ head** (*Sch, Univ*) Fachbereichsleiter(in) *m(f)*

department store N Kaufhaus *nt*

departure [dɪ'pɑːtʃə'] N **(a)** (*of person*) Weggang *m*; (*on journey*) Abreise *f* (*from* aus); (*of vehicle*) Abfahrt *f*; (*of plane*) Abflug *m*; **"~s"** "Abfahrt"; (*at airport*) "Abflug" **(b)** (*fig*: = *change in policy etc*) neue Richtung *f*

departure: departure board N (*Rail*) Abfahrtstafel *f*; (*Aviat*) Abfluganzeige *f*; **departure gate** N Ausgang *m*; **departure lounge** N Abflughalle *f*; (*for single flight*) Warteraum *m*; **departure time** N (*Aviat*) Abflugzeit *f*; (*Rail, bus*) Abfahrtzeit *f*

depend [dɪ'pend] VI **(a)** abhängen (*on sb/sth* von jdm/etw); **the price ~s on the quantity you buy** der Preis hängt von der Menge ab, die Sie kaufen; **it ~s on what you mean by reasonable** es kommt darauf an, was Sie unter vernünftig verstehen; **how long are you staying? – it ~s** wie lange bleiben Sie? – das kommt darauf an; **it all ~s on ...** das kommt ganz auf ... an; **~ing on his mood** je nach seiner

Laune; **~ing on how late we arrive** je nachdem, wie spät wir ankommen **(b)** (= *rely*) sich verlassen (*on, upon* auf +*acc*); **you can ~ (up)on it!** darauf können Sie sich verlassen! **(c)** (*person*: = *be dependent on*) **to ~ on** abhängig sein von, angewiesen sein auf (+*acc*)

dependable [dɪ'pendəbl] ADJ zuverlässig

dependant, dependent [dɪ'pendənt] N Abhängige(r) *mf*; **do you have ~s?** haben Sie Angehörige?

dependence [dɪ'pendəns] N Abhängigkeit *f* (*on, upon* von); **drug/alcohol ~** Drogen-/Alkoholabhängigkeit *f*

dependency [dɪ'pendənsɪ] N = **dependence**

dependent [dɪ'pendənt] ADJ (*also Gram, Math*) abhängig; **~ on insulin** insulinabhängig; **to be ~ on** *or* **upon sb/sth** von jdm/etw abhängig sein; **to be ~ on charity/sb's goodwill** auf Almosen/jds Wohlwollen angewiesen sein; **to be ~ on** *or* **upon sb/sth for sth** für etw auf jdn/etw angewiesen sein **2** N = **dependant**

depict [dɪ'pɪkt] VT darstellen

depiction [dɪ'pɪkʃən] N Darstellung *f*

deplete [dɪ'pliːt] VT (= *exhaust*) erschöpfen; (= *reduce*) verringern

depletion [dɪ'pliːʃən] N (= *exhausting*) Erschöpfung *f*; (= *reduction*) Verringerung *f*; (*of stock, membership*) Abnahme *f*

deplorable [dɪ'plɔːrəbl] ADJ (= *dreadful*) schrecklich; (= *disgraceful*) schändlich; **it is ~ that ...** es ist eine Schande, dass ...

deplorably [dɪ'plɔːrəblɪ] ADV schrecklich; **the press are acting ~** es ist eine Schande, wie die Presse sich verhält

deplore [dɪ'plɔː'] VT (= *regret*) bedauern; (= *disapprove of*) missbilligen

deploy [dɪ'plɔɪ] **1** VT (*Mil, fig*) einsetzen; (= *position*) aufstellen; **the number of troops ~ed in Germany** die Zahl der in Deutschland stationierten Streitkräfte **2** VI (*Mil*) aufmarschieren

deployment [dɪ'plɔɪmənt] N (*Mil, fig*) Einsatz *m*; (= *positioning*) Stationierung *f*

deport [dɪ'pɔːt] VT *prisoner* deportieren; *foreign national* abschieben

deportation [,diːpɔː'teɪʃən] N (*of prisoner*) Deportation *f*; (*of foreign national*) Abschiebung *f*

depose [dɪ'pəʊz] VT absetzen

deposit [dɪ'pɒzɪt] **1** VT **(a)** (= *put down*) hinlegen; (*upright*) hinstellen **(b)** *money, valuables* deponieren (*in or with* bei); **I ~ed £500 in my account** ich zahlte £ 500 auf mein Konto ein **(c)** (*Geol*) ablagern **2** N **(a)** (*Fin: in bank*) Guthaben *nt*; **to have £500 on ~** ein Guthaben von £ 500 haben **(b)** (*Comm*) (= *part payment*) Anzahlung *f*; (= *returnable security*) Kaution *f*; (*for bottle*) Pfand *nt*; **to put down a ~ of £1000 on a car** eine Anzahlung von £ 1000 für ein Auto leisten; **to leave a ~** eine Kaution hinterlegen **(c)** (*Chem: in wine, Geol*) Ablagerung *f*; (= *of ore, coal, oil*) (Lager)stätte *f*

depositor [dɪ'pɒzɪtə'] N Einzahler(in) *m(f)*

deposit slip N Einzahlungsbeleg *m*

depot ['depəʊ] N **(a)** (= *bus garage etc*) Depot *nt*; (= *store*) Lager(haus) *nt* **(b)** (*US Rail*) Bahnhof *m*

depraved [dɪ'preɪvd] ADJ verworfen

depravity [dɪ'prævɪtɪ] N Verworfenheit *f*

depreciate [dɪ'priːʃɪeɪt] **1** VT *value* mindern; *exchange rate* abwerten; **to ~ a currency** die Kaufkraft einer Währung mindern; **to ~ a property** den Wert einer Immobilie mindern **2** VI an Wert verlieren; (*currency*) an Kaufkraft verlieren; (*exchange rate*) fallen; **the pound has ~d by 8%** das Pfund ist um 8% gefallen

depreciation [dɪ,priːʃɪ'eɪʃən] N (*of property, value*) Wertminderung *f*; (*in accounting*) Abschreibung *f*; (*of currency*) Kaufkraftverlust *m*; **~ provisions** (*Comm, Fin*) Wertberichtigung *f* auf Anlagevermögen

depress [dɪ'pres] VT *person* deprimieren; *immune system, market* schwächen; *prices* fallen lassen; *sales* zurückgehen lassen; (= *discourage*) entmutigen

depressed [dɪ'prest] ADJ **(a)** deprimiert (*about* über +*acc*); (*Med*) depressiv; **to look ~** niedergeschlagen aussehen **(b)** (*Econ*) *market* flau; *economy, industry* geschwächt; *region* Not leidend; *share prices* fallend; *sales* rückläufig; **the ~ state of the property market** die schlechte Marktlage bei Immobilien

depressing [dɪ'presɪŋ] ADJ deprimierend; **these figures make ~ reading** es ist deprimierend, diese Zahlen zu lesen

depressingly [dɪ'presɪŋlɪ] ADV deprimierend; **it all sounded ~ familiar** es hörte sich alles nur zu vertraut an

depression [dɪ'preʃən] N **(a)** Depression *f*; (*Med*) Depressionen *pl* **(b)** (*Met*) Tief(druckgebiet) *nt* **(c)** (*Econ*) Flaute *f*; (*St Ex*) Baisse *f*; **the Depression** die Weltwirtschaftskrise

deprivation [deprɪ'veɪʃən] N **(a)** (= *depriving*) Entzug *m*; (= *loss*) Verlust *m*; (*Psych*) Deprivation *f*; (*of rights*) Beraubung *f* **(b)** (= *state*) Entbehrung *f*; (= *lack of necessities*) Mangel *m*

deprive [dɪ'praɪv] VT **to ~ sb of sth** (*of sth one has*) jdn einer Sache (*gen*) berauben; (*of sth to which one has a right*) jdm etw vorenthalten; **the team was ~d of the injured Owen** die Mannschaft musste ohne den verletzten Owen auskommen; **she was ~d of sleep** sie litt an Schlafmangel

deprived [dɪ'praɪvd] ADJ *person, background, area* benachteiligt; *childhood* arm; **the ~ areas of the city** die Armenviertel der Stadt

dept ABBR *of* **department** Abt.

depth [depθ] N **(a)** Tiefe *f*; **at a ~ of 3 feet** in einer Tiefe von 3 Fuß, in 3 Fuß Tiefe; **to be out of one's ~** (*lit, fig*) den Boden unter den Füßen verlieren; **he had no idea of the ~ of feeling against him** er hatte keine Ahnung, wie abgrundtief die Abneigung gegen ihn war; **in ~** eingehend; *interview* ausführlich **(b)** **~(s)** Tiefen *pl*; **in the ~s of despair** in tiefster Verzweiflung; **in the ~s of winter/the forest** im tiefsten Winter/Wald; **in the ~s of the countryside** auf dem flachen Land; **in the ~s of recession** mitten in der Rezession; **to sink to new ~s** so tief wie nie zuvor sinken

deputize [depjʊtaɪz] VI vertreten (*for sb* jdn)

deputy ['depjʊtɪ] **1** N **(a)** Stellvertreter(in) *m(f)* **(b)** (*also ~ sheriff*) Hilfssheriff *m* **(c)** (*US: in foreign parliaments*) Abgeordnete(r) *mf* **2** ADJ ATTR stellvertretend

DEQ ABBR *of* **delivered ex quai** geliefert ab Kai

derail [dɪ'reɪl] VT entgleisen lassen; (*fig*) *plan, negotiations* scheitern lassen; **to be ~ed** entgleisen

derailment [dɪ'reɪlmənt] N Entgleisung *f*

deranged [dɪ'reɪndʒd] ADJ *mind* verwirrt; *person* geistesgestört

deregistration [dɪːredʒɪ'streɪʃən] N (*of company*) Löschung *f*; **~ from the Register of Companies** Löschung im Handelsregister

deregulate [diː'regjʊleɪt] VT deregulieren; *buses etc* dem freien Wettbewerb überlassen

deregulation [diː'regjʊ'leɪʃən] N Deregulierung *f*; (*of buses etc*) Wettbewerbsfreiheit *f* (*of* für)

derelict ['derɪlɪkt] ADJ (= *abandoned*) verlassen; (= *ruined*) verfallen

deride [dɪ'raɪd] VT verspotten

derision [dɪ'rɪʒən] N Spott *m*; **object of ~** Zielscheibe *f* des Spotts; **to be greeted with ~** mit Spott aufgenommen werden

derisive [dɪ'raɪsɪv] ADJ spöttisch; (= *malicious*) verächtlich

derisory [dɪ'raɪsərɪ] ADJ **(a)** *amount, offer* lächerlich **(b)** = **derisive**

derivative [dɪ'rɪvətɪv] **1** ADJ abgeleitet; (*fig*) *style, work etc* nachgeahmt, imitiert; **~ markets** (*Fin*) Markt *m* für Derivate; **~ products** (*Fin*) Derivate *pl* **2** N **(a)** Ableitung *f* **(b)** (*Fin*) Derivat *nt*

derive [dɪ'raɪv] **1** VT *idea, name, origins* ableiten (*from* von); *profit, benefit* ziehen (*from* aus); *satisfaction, pleasure, energy* gewinnen (*from* aus); *income* beziehen (*from* aus) **2** VI **to ~ from** sich ableiten von; (*power, fortune*) beruhen auf (+*dat*); (*ideas*) stammen von

dermatitis [dɜːmə'taɪtɪs] N Hautentzündung *f*

dermatologist [dɜːmə'tɒlədʒɪst] N Hautarzt *m*, Hautärztin *f*

dermatology [dɜːmə'tɒlədʒɪ] N Dermatologie *f*

derogatory [dɪ'rɒgətərɪ] ADJ abfällig

DES (*Comm*) ABBR *of* **delivered ex ship** geliefert ab Schiff

descend [dɪ'send] **1** VI **(a)** (*person*) hinuntergehen; (*lift, vehicle*) hinunterfahren; (*road*) hinunterführen; (*hill*) abfallen **(b)** (= *have as ancestor*) abstammen (*from* von) **(c)** (= *attack suddenly*) herfallen (*on, upon* über +*acc*); (= *come over*) (*sadness etc*) befallen (*on, upon sb* jdn); (*silence*) sich senken (*on, upon* über +*acc*) **(d)** (*inf*: = *visit*) **to ~ (up)on sb** jdn überfallen (*inf*); **thousands of fans are expected to ~ on the city** man erwartet, dass tausende von Fans die Stadt überlaufen **(e)** (= *lower oneself*) **to ~ into chaos/civil war** in Chaos/einen Bürgerkrieg versinken **2** VT **(a)** *stairs* hinuntergehen **(b)** **to be ~ed from** abstammen von

descendant [dɪ'sendənt] N Nachkomme *m*

descent [dɪ'sent] N **(a)** (*of person*) Hinuntergehen *nt*; (*from mountain, of plane, into underworld*) Abstieg *m*; (*of gymnast*) Abgang *m*; (= *slope: of road*) Abfall *m*; **~ by parachute** Fallschirmabsprung *m* **(b)** (= *ancestry*) Abstammung *f*; **of noble ~** von adliger Abstammung **(c)** (*fig*) (*into crime etc*) Absinken *nt* (*into* in +*acc*); (*into chaos, civil war, madness*) Versinken *nt* (*into* in +*acc*)

descramble [diː'skræmbl] VT (*Telec*) entschlüsseln

describe [dɪ'skraɪb] VT beschreiben; **~ him for us** beschreiben Sie ihn uns (*dat*); **to ~ oneself/sb as ...** sich/jdn als ... bezeichnen; **the police ~ him as dangerous** die Polizei bezeichnet ihn als gefährlich; **he is ~d as being tall with short fair hair** er wird als groß mit kurzen blonden Haaren beschrieben

description [dɪ'skrɪpʃən] N **(a)** Beschreibung *f*; **she gave a detailed ~ of what had happened** sie beschrieb ausführlich, was vorgefallen war; **this is beyond ~** das ist ja unbeschreiblich; **to answer (to)** *or* **fit the ~ of ...** der Beschreibung als ... entsprechen; **they answer** *or* **fit the ~ of the suspects** auf sie trifft die Beschreibung der Verdächtigen zu; **do you know anyone of this ~?** kennen Sie jemanden, auf den diese Beschreibung zutrifft? **(b)** (= *sort*) Art *f*; **vehicles of every ~** *or* **of all ~s** Fahrzeuge aller Art

descriptive [dɪ'skrɪptɪv] ADJ beschreibend; *account, adjective* anschaulich

desecrate ['desɪkreɪt] VT schänden

desecration [desɪ'kreɪʃən] N Schändung *f*

desensitize [diː'sensɪtaɪz] VT (*Med*) desensibilisieren; **to become ~d to sth** (*fig*) einer Sache (*dat*) gegenüber abstumpfen

desert[1] ['dezət] **1** N (*lit, fig*) Wüste *f* **2** ADJ ATTR Wüsten-

desert[2] [dɪ'zɜːt] **1** VT (= *leave*) verlassen; (= *abandon*) im Stich lassen; **by the time the police arrived the place was ~ed** als die Polizei eintraf, war niemand mehr da; **in winter the place is ~ed** im Winter ist der Ort verlassen **2** VI (*Mil, fig*) desertieren

deserter [dɪ'zɜːtə'] N (*Mil, fig*) Deserteur(in) *m(f)*

desertion [dɪ'zɜːʃən] N (= *act*) Verlassen *nt*; (*Jur: of wife, family*) böswilliges Verlassen; (*Mil*) Desertion *f*; (*fig*) Fahnenflucht *f*

desert island ['dezət-] N einsame Insel

deserve [dɪ'zɜːv] VT verdienen; **he ~s to win** er verdient den Sieg; **he ~s to be punished** er verdient es, bestraft zu werden; **she ~s better** sie hat etwas Besseres verdient

deservedly [dɪ'zɜːvɪdlɪ] ADV verdientermaßen; **and ~ so** und das zu Recht

deserving [dɪ'zɜːvɪŋ] ADJ verdienstvoll; *winner* verdient

design [dɪ'zaɪn] **1** N **(a)** (*of building, book, picture, dress etc*) Entwurf *m*; (*of car, machine, plane etc*) Konstruktion *f*; **it's still at the ~ stage** es befindet sich noch im Konstruktionsstadium; **it was a good/faulty ~** es war gut/schlecht konstruiert; **~ department** Abteilung *f* für Produktgestaltung **(b)** NO PL (*as subject*: = *art of designing*) Design *nt* **(c)** (= *pattern*) Muster *nt* **(d)** (= *intention*) Absicht *f*; **by ~ (rather than accident)** absichtlich (und nicht zufällig); **to have ~s on sb/sth** es auf jdn/etw abgesehen haben **2** VT **(a)** (= *plan, draw*) entwerfen; *machine* konstruieren; **a well ~ed machine** eine gut durchkonstruierte Maschine **(b)** (= *intend*) **to be ~ed for sb/sth** für jdn/etw bestimmt sein;

this magazine is ~ed to appeal to young people diese Zeitschrift soll junge Leute ansprechen

designate ['dezɪgneɪt] VT **(a)** (= *appoint*) ernennen; **to ~ sb as sth** jdn zu etw ernennen **(b)** (= *indicate, specify*) festlegen, bestimmen; **smoking is permitted in ~d areas** Rauchen ist in den dafür bestimmten Bereichen erlaubt; **to be the ~d driver** als Fahrer bestimmt sein

designer [dɪ'zaɪnəʳ] **1** N Designer(in); (= *fashion ~*) Modeschöpfer(in) *m(f)*; (*of machines etc*) Konstrukteur(in) *m(f)* **2** ADJ ATTR Designer-; **~ clothes** Designerkleider *pl*

designer baby N Designerbaby *nt*

design fault N Designfehler *m*

desirability [dɪ,zaɪərə'bɪlɪti] N Wünschbarkeit *f*; **they discussed the ~ of launching the product in July** sie erörterten, ob es wünschenswert sei, das Produkt im Juli auf den Markt zu bringen; **in his eyes this only increased her ~** das machte sie in seinen Augen umso begehrenswerter

desirable [dɪ'zaɪərəbl] ADJ **(a)** wünschenswert; *action, progress* erwünscht; *goal* erstrebenswert **(b)** *position, offer, house, area* reizvoll **(c)** *woman* begehrenswert

desire [dɪ'zaɪəʳ] **1** N Wunsch *m* (*for* nach); (= *longing*) Sehnsucht *f* (*for* nach); (*sexual*) Verlangen *nt* (*for* nach), Begehren *nt* (*for* nach); **a ~ for peace/revenge** ein Verlangen *nt* nach Frieden/Rache; **heart's ~** Herzenswunsch *m*; **I have no ~ to see him** ich habe kein Verlangen, ihn zu sehen; **I have no ~ to cause you any trouble** ich möchte Ihnen keine Unannehmlichkeiten bereiten **2** VT wünschen; *object* sich (*dat*) wünschen; *woman* begehren; *peace* verlangen nach; **if ~d** auf Wunsch; **to have the ~d effect** die gewünschte Wirkung haben; **it leaves much** *or* **a lot to be ~d** das lässt viel zu wünschen übrig; **it leaves something to be ~d** es lässt zu wünschen übrig

desk [desk] N Schreibtisch *m*; (*for pupils, master*) Pult *nt*; (*in shop, restaurant*) Kasse *f*; (*in hotel*) Empfang *m*; (*Press*) Ressort *nt*

desk: desk calendar N (*US*) Tischkalender *m*; **desk clerk** N (*US*) Empfangschef *m*, Empfangsdame *f*; **desk job** N Bürojob *m*

desktop ['desktɒp]: **desktop computer** N Desktopcomputer *m*; **desktop publishing** N Desktop-Publishing *nt*

desolate ['desəlɪt] **1** ADJ trostlos; (= *devastated*) *place* verwüstet; *feeling, cry* verzweifelt **2** ['desəleɪt] VT (*liter*) *place* verwüsten

desolation [desə'leɪʃən] N **(a)** (*of country by war*) Verwüstung *f* **(b)** (*of landscape*) (= *grief*) Trostlosigkeit *f*; (= *friendlessness*) Verlassenheit *f*

despair [dɪ'speəʳ] **1** N Verzweiflung *f* (*about, at* über +*acc*); **he was filled with ~** Verzweiflung überkam ihn; **to be in ~** verzweifelt sein; **she looked at him in ~** sie sah ihn verzweifelt *or* voller Verzweiflung an **2** VI verzweifeln; **to ~ of doing sth** alle Hoffnung aufgeben, etw zu tun; **to ~ of sth** alle Hoffnung auf etw (*acc*) aufgeben; **I ~ of you** du bringst mich zur Verzweiflung

despairing, despairingly ADJ, ADV [dɪs'peərɪŋ, -lɪ] verzweifelt

despatch [dɪs'pætʃ] VT, N (*esp Brit*) = **dispatch**

desperate ['despərɪt] ADJ **(a)** verzweifelt; *criminal* zum Äußersten entschlossen; *solution* extrem; **to get** *or* **grow ~** verzweifeln; **things are ~** die Lage ist extrem; **the company's ~ financial position** die extrem gespannte Finanzlage der Firma; **the ~ plight of the refugees** die schreckliche Not der Flüchtlinge; **to be ~ to do sth** etw unbedingt tun wollen; **to be ~ for sb to do sth** unbedingt wollen, dass jd etw tut; **to be ~ for sth** etw unbedingt brauchen; (*inf hum*) **are you going out with Jim? you must be ~!** du gehst mit Jim aus? dir muss es ja wirklich schlecht gehen!; **I'm not that ~!** so schlimm ist es auch wieder nicht!

(b) *need, shortage* dringend; **to be in ~ need of sth** etw dringend brauchen; **a building in ~ need of repair** ein Gebäude, das dringend repariert werden muss

desperately ['despərɪtlɪ] ADV **(a)** *fight, look for, hope, try* verzweifelt

(b) *need* dringend; *want* unbedingt

(c) *difficult* extrem; *important, sad* äußerst; **~ ill** schwer krank; **to be ~ worried (about sth)** sich (*dat*) (über etw *acc*) schreckliche Sorgen machen; **I'm not ~ worried** ich mache mir keine allzu großen Sorgen; **to be ~ keen to do sth** etw unbedingt tun wollen; **I'm not ~ keen on …** ich bin nicht

besonders scharf auf (*acc*) …; **~ unhappy** todunglücklich; **to try ~ hard to do sth** verzweifelt versuchen, etw zu tun

desperation [despə'reɪʃən] N Verzweiflung *f*; **an act of ~** eine Verzweiflungstat

despicable [dɪ'spɪkəbl] ADJ verabscheuungswürdig; *person* verachtenswert

despicably [dɪ'spɪkəblɪ] ADV (+*vb*) abscheulich

despise [dɪ'spaɪz] VT verachten; **to ~ oneself (for sth)** sich selbst (wegen etw) verachten

despite [dɪ'spaɪt] PREP trotz (+*gen*); **~ his warnings** seinen Warnungen zum Trotz; **~ what she says** trotz allem, was sie sagt

despondent [dɪ'spɒndənt] ADJ niedergeschlagen

despondently [dɪ'spɒndəntlɪ] ADV niedergeschlagen; *say* bedrückt

dessert [dɪ'zɜːt] N Nachtisch *m*; **for ~** zum Nachtisch

dessertspoon [dɪ'zɜːtspuːn] N Dessertlöffel *m*

destabilization [diːsteɪbɪlaɪ'zeɪʃən] N Destabilisierung *f*

destabilize [diː'steɪbɪlaɪz] VT destabilisieren

destination [destɪ'neɪʃən] N (*of person*) Reiseziel *nt*; (*of goods*) Bestimmungsort *m*

destine ['destɪn] VT **(a)** (= *set apart, predestine*) bestimmen; **to be ~d to do sth** dazu bestimmt sein, etw zu tun; **to be ~d for sth** zu etw bestimmt sein **(b)** USU PASS (= *be fated*) **we were ~d to meet** das Schicksal hat es so gewollt, dass wir uns begegnen; **I was ~d never to see them again** ich sollte sie nie (mehr) wiedersehen

destined ['destɪnd] ADJ **~ for** unterwegs nach; *goods* für

destiny ['destɪnɪ] N Schicksal *nt*; **to control one's own ~** sein Schicksal selbst in die Hand nehmen

destitute ['destɪtjuːt] ADJ mittellos

destroy [dɪ'strɔɪ] VT zerstören; *box, toy, watch etc* kaputtmachen; *documents, trace, person* vernichten; *animal* einschläfern; *hopes, chances* zunichte machen; *reputation, beauty* ruinieren; **to be ~ed by fire** durch Brand vernichtet werden

destruction [dɪ'strʌkʃən] N **(a)** (= *destroying*) Zerstörung *f*; (*of enemy, people, documents*) Vernichtung *f* **(b)** (= *damage*) Verwüstung *f*

destructive [dɪ'strʌktɪv] ADJ destruktiv; *power, nature, war, wind* zerstörerisch; *effect* zerstörend

destructively [dɪ'strʌktɪvlɪ] ADV destruktiv

destructiveness [dɪ'strʌktɪvnɪs] N Destruktivität *f*; (*of fire, war*) zerstörende Wirkung; (*of weapon*) Zerstörungskraft *f*

detach [dɪ'tætʃ] VT *rope, cart* loslösen; *section of form, document* abtrennen; *part of machine, wooden leg, hood* abnehmen (*from* von); **to ~ oneself from a group** sich von einer Gruppe trennen

detachable [dɪ'tætʃəbl] ADJ *part of machine, collar, legs* abnehmbar; *section of document* abtrennbar (*from* von); *lining* ausknöpfbar; (*with zip*) ausreißbar

detached [dɪ'tætʃt] ADJ **(a)** *manner, expression* distanziert **(b)** (*Brit*) **~ house** Einzelhaus *nt*

detail ['diːteɪl] N Detail *nt*; (*particular*) Einzelheit *f*; (= *part of painting, photo etc*) Ausschnitt *m*; **in ~** im Detail; **in great ~, in every ~** in allen Einzelheiten; **please send me further ~s** bitte schicken Sie mir nähere Einzelheiten; **to go into ~s** ins Detail gehen; **his attention to ~** seine Aufmerksamkeit für das Detail

detailed ['diːteɪld] ADJ ausführlich; *analysis* eingehend; *knowledge, work, results, map, picture* detailliert; (= *precise*) genau; **~ accounts** (*Fin*) genau geführte Geschäftsbücher; **they gave a more ~ account of what they had seen** sie beschrieben ausführlicher, was sie gesehen hatten

detain [dɪ'teɪn] VT (*police*) in Haft nehmen; **to be ~ed** (= *be arrested*) verhaftet werden; (= *be in detention*) sich in Haft befinden; **to ~ sb for questioning** jdn zur Vernehmung festhalten

detect [dɪ'tekt] VT entdecken; (= *see, make out*) ausfindig machen; *crime* aufdecken; *disease* feststellen; *sadness, movement, noise* wahrnehmen; *mine, gas* aufspüren; **do I ~ a note of irony?** höre ich da nicht eine gewisse Ironie (heraus)?

detection [dɪ'tekʃən] N **(a)** (*of crime, fault*) Entdeckung *f*; (*of disease*) Feststellung *f*; (= *detective work*) Ermittlungsarbeit *f*;

to avoid or **escape** ~ nicht entdeckt werden **(b)** (of gases, mines) Aufspürung f

detective [dɪ'tektɪv] N Detektiv(in) m(f); (= police ~) Kriminalbeamte(r) m/-beamtin f

detective: **detective agency** N Detektivbüro nt; **detective constable** N (Brit) Kriminalbeamte(r) m/-beamtin f; **detective inspector** N Kriminalinspektor(in) m(f); **detective sergeant** N Kriminalmeister(in) m(f); **detective story** N Kriminalgeschichte f, Krimi m (inf); **detective work** N kriminalistische Arbeit

detention [dɪ'tenʃən] N (= captivity) Haft f; (= act) Festnahme f; (Sch) Nachsitzen nt; **to give a pupil two hours'** ~ einen Schüler zwei Stunden nachsitzen lassen; **he's in** ~ (Sch) er sitzt nach

detention centre, (US) **detention center** N Jugendstrafanstalt f

deter [dɪ'tɜː] VT (= prevent) abhalten; (= discourage) abschrecken; **to** ~ **sb from sth** jdn von etw abhalten; **to** ~ **sb from doing sth** jdn davon abhalten, etw zu tun

detergent [dɪ'tɜːdʒənt] N Reinigungsmittel nt; (= soap powder etc) Waschmittel nt

deteriorate [dɪ'tɪərɪəreɪt] VI sich verschlechtern; (materials) verderben; (profits) zurückgehen

deterioration [dɪ,tɪərɪə'reɪʃən] N Verschlechterung f; (of materials) Verderben nt

determination [dɪ,tɜːmɪ'neɪʃən] N Entschlossenheit f; **he has great** ~ er ist ein Mensch von großer Entschlusskraft

determine [dɪ'tɜːmɪn] VT bestimmen; conditions, price festlegen

determined [dɪ'tɜːmɪnd] ADJ entschlossen; **to make a** ~ **effort** or **attempt to do sth** sein Möglichstes tun, um etw zu tun; **he is** ~ **that** ... er hat (fest) beschlossen, dass ...; **to be** ~ **to do sth** fest entschlossen sein, etw zu tun; **he's** ~ **to make me lose my temper** er legt es darauf an, dass ich wütend werde; **you seem** ~ **to exhaust yourself** du scheinst dich mit aller Gewalt kaputtmachen zu wollen

determinedly [dɪ'tɜːmɪndlɪ] ADV (+vb) entschlossen; say bestimmt; (+adj) entschieden

determining [dɪ'tɜːmɪnɪŋ] ADJ bestimmend

deterrent [dɪ'terənt] **1** N (also Mil) Abschreckungsmittel nt; **to be a** ~ abschrecken **2** ADJ abschreckend

detest [dɪ'test] VT hassen; **I** ~ **having to get up early** ich hasse es, früh aufstehen zu müssen

detonate ['detəneɪt] **1** VI (fuse) zünden; (bomb) detonieren **2** VT zur Explosion bringen

detonation [detə'neɪʃən] N Zündung f

detonator ['detəneɪtə'] N Zündkapsel f

detour ['diːtʊə'] **1** N (a) (in road, also fig) Umweg m; **to make a** ~ einen Umweg machen **(b)** (for traffic) Umleitung f **2** VI einen Umweg machen

detox [dɪ'tɒks] N (inf) Entzug m (inf); ~ **programme** (Brit) or **program** (US) Entzugsprogramm nt (inf)

detract [dɪ'trækt] VI **to** ~ **from sth** einer Sache (dat) Abbruch tun

detriment ['detrɪmənt] N Schaden m; **to the** ~ **of sth** zum Schaden von etw

detrimental [detrɪ'mentl] ADJ schädlich; (to case, cause, one's interest) abträglich (to dat); **to be** ~ **to sb/sth** jdm/einer Sache (dat) schaden; **this could have a** ~ **effect** das könnte sich nachteilig auswirken

detritus [dɪ'traɪtəs] N (Geol) Geröll nt; (fig) Müll m

deuce [djuːs] N (Tennis) Einstand m

Deutschmark ['dɔɪtʃmɑːk] N (Hist) D-Mark f

devaluation [diːvæljʊ'eɪʃən] N Abwertung f

devalue [diː'væljuː] VT abwerten

devastate ['devəsteɪt] VT **(a)** town, land verwüsten; opposition vernichten; economy zugrunde richten **(b)** (inf. = overwhelm) umhauen (inf); **I was** ~**d** das hat mich umgehauen (inf); **they were** ~**d by the news** die Nachricht hat sie tief erschüttert

devastating ['devəsteɪtɪŋ] ADJ **(a)** (= destructive) verheerend; **to be** ~ **to** or **for sth**, **to have a** ~ **effect on sth** verheerende Folgen für etw haben **(b)** (fig) effect schrecklich; news niederschmetternd; report, attack, performance unschlagbar; defeat vernichtend; **a** ~ **blow/loss** ein vernichtender Schlag/ Verlust; **to be** ~ **to** or **for sb** jdn niederschmettern; **to be in** ~ **form** in unschlagbarer Form sein

devastatingly ['devəsteɪtɪŋlɪ] ADV (lit) vernichtend; (fig) attractive, effective, funny umwerfend (inf); accurate, frank verheerend

devastation [devə'steɪʃən] N Verwüstung f

develop [dɪ'veləp] **1** VT **(a)** (also Phot) entwickeln **(b)** argument, outlines, original idea (weiter)entwickeln; plot of novel (= unfold) entfalten; (= fill out) ausbauen **(c)** natural resources, region, ground erschließen; old part of a town sanieren; business (from scratch) aufziehen; (= expand) ausbauen; cold sich (dat) zuziehen **2** VI sich entwickeln; (talent, plot etc) sich entfalten; **to** ~ **into sth** sich zu etw entwickeln

developer [dɪ'veləpə'] N **(a)** = property developer **(b)** late ~ Spätentwickler(in) m(f)

developing [dɪ'veləpɪŋ] ADJ crisis, storm aufkommend; industry neu entstehend; embryo, society, economy sich entwickelnd; **the** ~ **world** die Entwicklungsländer pl

developing country N Entwicklungsland nt

development [dɪ'veləpmənt] N **(a)** Entwicklung f; (= way subject, plot etc is developed) Ausführung f; **to await (further)** ~**s** neue Entwicklungen abwarten **(b)** (of area, new town) Erschließung f; (of old part of town) Sanierung f; (= expansion) Ausbau m; **industrial** ~ Gewerbegebiet nt; **office** ~ Bürokomplex m; **business** ~ Geschäftszentrum nt; **we live in a new** ~ wir leben in einer neuen Siedlung; ~ **aid** (Pol) Entwicklungshilfe f

developmental [dɪveləp'mentl] ADJ Entwicklungs-; ~ **stage** Entwicklungsphase f

development: **development area** N Entwicklungsgebiet nt; (in town) Erschließungsgebiet nt; (in old town) Sanierungsgebiet nt; **development capital** N (Fin, Pol) Entwicklungskapital nt; **development company** N (Wohnungs)baugesellschaft f; **development costs** PL Erschließungskosten pl; **development grant** N Entwicklungsförderung f; **development zone** N (Pol) besonders förderungsbedürftiges Gebiet

deviate ['diːvɪeɪt] VI abweichen (from von); (ship, plane, projectile) vom Kurs abweichen; (deliberately) vom Kurs abgehen

deviation [diːvɪ'eɪʃən] N Abweichung f

device [dɪ'vaɪs] N **(a)** Gerät nt; (explosive) ~ Sprengkörper m **(b)** **to leave sb to his own** ~**s** jdn sich (dat) selbst überlassen

devil ['devl] N **(a)** (lit, fig inf) Teufel m; (= object, screw etc) Plage f; (= daring person) Teufelskerl m; **you little** ~! du kleiner Satansbraten!; **shall I have another?** – **go on, be a** ~ soll ich noch einen trinken etc? – los, nur zu, riskiers! (inf)
(b) (inf) **I had a** ~ **of a job getting here** es war verdammt schwierig, hierher zu kommen (inf); **how/what/why/who the** ~ ...? wie/was/warum/wer zum Teufel ... in drei Teufels Namen ...?
(c) (in expressions) **to be between the Devil and the deep blue sea** sich in einer Zwickmühle befinden; **go to the** ~! (inf) scher dich zum Teufel! (inf); **speak** or **talk** (Brit) **of the** ~! wenn man vom Teufel spricht!; **better the** ~ **you know (than the** ~ **you don't)** (prov) von zwei Übeln wählt man besser das, was man schon kennt

devilish ['devlɪʃ] ADJ teuflisch; chuckle, grin verschmitzt

devil's advocate N **to play** ~ den Advocatus Diaboli spielen

devious ['diːvɪəs] ADJ **(a)** person verschlagen; means, method hinterhältig; business, plan, game, attempt trickreich; **by** ~ **means** auf die krumme Tour (inf); **to have a** ~ **mind** ganz schön schlau sein **(b)** (= tortuous) route, way gewunden

deviously ['diːvɪəslɪ] ADV (+vb) mit List und Tücke

deviousness ['diːvɪəsnɪs] N Verschlagenheit f

devise [dɪ'vaɪz] VT scheme, style sich (dat) ausdenken; way, means finden; plan schmieden; strategy, policy ausarbeiten

devoid [dɪ'vɔɪd] ADJ ~ **of** ohne

devolution [diːvə'luːʃən] N (of power) Übertragung f (from ... to von ... auf +acc); (Pol) Dezentralisierung f

devolve [dɪ'vɒlv] VT *duty, power etc* übertragen (*on, upon* auf +*acc*) **a ~d government** eine dezentralisierte Regierung

devote [dɪ'vəʊt] VT widmen (*to dat*); *thought* verwenden (*to* auf +*acc*); *one's energies* konzentrieren (*to* auf +*acc*); *building* verwenden (*to* für); *resources* bestimmen (*to* für)

devoted [dɪ'vəʊtɪd] ADJ *wife, father* liebend; *servant, follower, fan* treu; *admirer* eifrig; **to be ~ to sb** jdn innig lieben; (*servant, fan*) jdm treu ergeben sein; **to be ~ to a cause** sich völlig für eine Sache engagieren; **to be ~ to one's family** in seiner Familie völlig aufgehen

devotedly [dɪ'vəʊtɪdlɪ] ADV hingebungsvoll; *serve, follow* treu; *support* eifrig

devotion [dɪ'vəʊʃən] N **(a)** (*to friend, wife etc*) Ergebenheit *f* (*to* gegenüber); (*to work*) Hingabe *f* (*to* an an +*acc*); **~ to duty** Pflichteifer *m* **(b)** (*of part of building, time etc*) (*to* für) Verwendung *f*; (*of resources*) Bestimmung *f*

devour [dɪ'vaʊə*r*] VT (*lit, fig*) verschlingen; **to be ~ed by jealousy** von Eifersucht verzehrt werden

devout [dɪ'vaʊt] ADJ *person, Muslim* fromm; *Marxist, follower* überzeugt; *supporter* treu; *opponent* eingeschworen

devoutly [dɪ'vaʊtlɪ] ADV (*Rel*) (+*adj*) tief; (+*vb*) fromm; **~ religious** tiefreligiös

dew [dju:] N Tau *m*

dexterity [deks'terɪtɪ] N Geschick *nt*

DfEE (*Brit*) ABBR *of* **Department for Education and Employment** Ministerium *nt* für Bildung und Arbeit

diabetes [ˌdaɪə'bi:ti:z] N Zuckerkrankheit *f*, Diabetes *m*

diabetic [ˌdaɪə'betɪk] ▉ ADJ **(a)** zuckerkrank **(b)** *chocolate, drugs* für Diabetiker ▉ N Diabetiker(in) *m(f)*

diabolic [ˌdaɪə'bɒlɪk], **diabolical** [ˌdaɪə'bɒlɪkəl] ADJ (*inf*) entsetzlich; **diabolical weather** Sauwetter *nt* (*inf*)

diagnose ['daɪəgnəʊz] VT (*Med, fig*) diagnostizieren

diagnosis [ˌdaɪəg'nəʊsɪs] N, *pl* **diagnoses** [ˌdaɪəg'nəʊsi:z] Diagnose *f*; **to make a ~** eine Diagnose stellen

diagnostic [ˌdaɪəg'nɒstɪk] ADJ diagnostisch

diagnostics [ˌdaɪəg'nɒstɪks] N SING or PL Diagnose *f*; **~ program** (*Comput*) Diagnoseprogramm *nt*

diagonal [daɪ'ægənl] ▉ ADJ diagonal ▉ N Diagonale *f*

diagonally [daɪ'ægənəlɪ] ADV diagonal; (*loosely*: = *crossways*) schräg; **he crossed the street ~** er ging schräg über die Straße; **~ across from** or **opposite sb/sth** jdm/einer Sache (*dat*) schräg gegenüber

diagram ['daɪəgræm] N Diagramm *nt*; (= *chart: of figures etc*) grafische Darstellung; **as shown in the ~** wie das Diagramm/ die grafische Darstellung zeigt

dial ['daɪəl] ▉ N (*of clock*) Zifferblatt *nt*; (*of speedometer, pressure gauge*) Skala *f*; (*Telec*) Nummernscheibe *f*; (*on radio etc*) Einstellskala *f* ▉ VTI (*Telec*) wählen; **to ~ direct** durchwählen; **you can ~ London direct** man kann nach London durchwählen; **to ~ 999** den Notruf wählen

dialect ['daɪəlekt] ▉ N Dialekt *m*; (*local, rural also*) Mundart *f*; **the country people spoke in ~** die Landbevölkerung sprach Dialekt ▉ ATTR Dialekt-

dialling ['daɪəlɪŋ]: **dialling code** N (*Brit Telec*) Vorwahl(nummer) *f*; **dialling tone** N (*Brit Telec*) Amtszeichen *nt*

dialogue, (*US*) **dialog** ['daɪəlɒg] ▉ N Dialog *m*; **~ box** (*Comput*) Dialogfeld *nt*

dial tone N (*US Telec*) Amtszeichen *nt*

dial-up ['daɪəl'ʌp] ADJ ATTR (*Comput*) Wähl-; **~ link** Wählverbindung *f*; **~ modem** (Wähl)modem *nt*

diameter [daɪ'æmɪtə*r*] N Durchmesser *m*; **to be one foot in ~** einen Durchmesser von einem Fuß haben

diamond ['daɪəmənd] N **(a)** Diamant *m* **(b) diamonds** PL (*Cards*) Karo *nt*; **the ace/seven of ~s** das Karoass/die Karosieben **(c)** (*Baseball*) Innenfeld *nt*

diamond IN CPDS: **~ bracelet** Diamantarmband *nt*; **diamond jubilee** N 60-jähriges Jubiläum; **diamond-shaped** ADJ rautenförmig; **diamond wedding** N diamantene Hochzeit

diaper ['daɪəpə*r*] N (*US*) Windel *f*

diarrhoea, (*US*) **diarrhea** [ˌdaɪə'ri:ə] N Durchfall *m*

diary ['daɪərɪ] N (*of personal experience*) Tagebuch *nt*; (*for noting dates*) (Termin)kalender *m*; **to keep a ~** Tagebuch führen; **desk/pocket ~** Schreibtisch-/Taschenkalender *m*; **I've got it in my ~** es steht in meinem (Termin)kalender

dice [daɪs] ▉ N, *pl* - Würfel *m*; **to play ~** Würfel spielen; **to roll the ~** würfeln; **no ~** (*esp US inf*) (das) ist nicht drin (*inf*) ▉ VT (*Cook*) in Würfel schneiden

dick [dɪk] N (*sl*: = *penis*) Schwanz *m* (*sl*)

dicker ['dɪkə*r*] VI (*US*) feilschen

dickybird ['dɪkɪbɜːd] N (*Brit*) **I haven't heard a ~ from him** (*inf*) ich habe keinen Ton von ihm gehört

dictate [dɪk'teɪt] VTI (*all senses*) diktieren; **common sense ~s that ...** der gesunde Menschenverstand sagt uns, dass ...

▸ **dictate to** VI +PREP OBJ diktieren (+*dat*), Vorschriften machen (+*dat*); **I won't be dictated to** ich lasse mir keine Vorschriften machen

dictation [dɪk'teɪʃən] N (*also Sch*) Diktat *nt*; **to take (down) ~** ein Diktat aufnehmen

dictator [dɪk'teɪtə*r*] N (*Pol, fig*) Diktator(in) *m(f)*

dictatorial ADJ, **dictatorially** ADV [ˌdɪktə'tɔ:rɪəl, -ɪ] diktatorisch

dictatorship [dɪk'teɪtəʃɪp] N (*Pol, fig*) Diktatur *f*

dictionary ['dɪkʃənrɪ] N Wörterbuch *nt*

did [dɪd] PRET *of* **do**

didactic [dɪ'dæktɪk] ADJ didaktisch

diddly-squat ['dɪdlɪ'skwɒt] N (*US inf*) nix (*inf*)

didn't ['dɪdənt] = **did not**; *see* **do**

die [daɪ] ▉ VI **(a)** (*lit*) sterben; (*engine*) absterben; (*planet*) vergehen; **to ~ of** or **from hunger/pneumonia/grief** vor Hunger/an Lungenentzündung/vor or aus Kummer sterben; **he ~d from his injuries** er erlag seinen Verletzungen; **he ~d of a broken heart** er starb an einem gebrochenen Herzen; **he ~d happy/a hero** er starb glücklich/als Held; **to be dying** im Sterben liegen; **never say ~!** nur nicht aufgeben!; **to ~ laughing** (*inf*) sich totlachen (*inf*); **I'd rather** or **sooner ~!** (*inf*) lieber würde ich sterben!

(b) (*fig inf*) **to be dying to do sth** darauf brennen, etw zu tun; **I'm dying to know what happened** ich bin schrecklich gespannt zu hören, was passiert ist; **I'm dying for a cigarette** ich brauche jetzt unbedingt eine Zigarette; **I'm dying of thirst** ich verdurste fast; **I'm dying for him to visit** ich kann seinen Besuch kaum noch abwarten; **old habits ~ hard** alte Gewohnheiten legt man nur schwer ab

▉ VT **to ~ a hero's/a violent death** den Heldentod/eines gewaltsamen Todes sterben

▸ **die away** VI (*sound, voice*) schwächer werden; (*wind, anger*) sich legen

▸ **die down** VI nachlassen; (*fire*) herunterbrennen; (*flames*) kleiner werden; (*storm, wind*) sich legen, nachlassen; (*noise*) schwächer werden

▸ **die off** VI (hin)wegsterben

▸ **die out** VI aussterben

die-hard ['daɪhɑːd] ADJ zäh; (*pej*) reaktionär

diesel ['diːzəl] N (= *train*) Dieseltriebwagen *m*; (= *car, fuel*) Diesel *m*

diesel: **diesel engine** N Dieselmotor *m*; **diesel oil** N Dieselöl *nt*; **diesel train** N Dieseltriebwagen *m*

diet ['daɪət] ▉ N Nahrung *f*; (= *special ~*) Diät *f*; (= *slimming ~*) Schlankheitskur *f*; **to put sb on a ~/a special ~** jdm eine Schlankheitskur/eine Diät verordnen; **to be/go on a ~** eine Schlankheitskur machen; **high protein ~** proteinreiche Diät ▉ VI eine Schlankheitskur machen

dietary ['daɪətərɪ] ADJ Ernährungs-

dietician [ˌdaɪə'tɪʃən] N Diätist(in) *m(f)*

diet sheet N Diät-/Schlankheits(fahr)plan *m*

differ ['dɪfə*r*] VI **(a)** (= *be different*) sich unterscheiden (*from* von) **(b)** (= *disagree*) **to ~ with sb on** or **over sth** über etw (*acc*) anderer Meinung sein als jd

difference ['dɪfrəns] N **(a)** Unterschied *m* (*in, between* zwischen +*dat*); **that makes a big ~ to me** das ist für mich ein großer Unterschied; **to make a ~ to** or **in sth** einen Unterschied bei etw machen; **that makes a big** or **a lot of ~, that makes all the ~** das ändert die Sache völlig; **it makes all the ~ in the world** da liegt der entscheidende Unterschied; **what ~ does it make if ...?** was macht es schon, wenn ...?; **it makes no ~, it doesn't make any ~** es ist egal; **it makes no ~ to me** das ist mir egal; **for all the ~ it makes** obwohl es ja eigentlich egal ist; **I can't tell the ~** ich kann keinen Unterschied erkennen; **a job with a ~** (*inf*) ein Job, der mal was anderes ist

(b) (*between numbers, amounts*) Differenz *f*; **to split the ~** sich

(*dat*) die Differenz *or* den Rest(betrag) teilen
(c) (= *quarrel*) Auseinandersetzung *f*; **a ~ of opinion** eine Meinungsverschiedenheit; **to settle** *or* **resolve one's ~s** die Differenzen beilegen

different ['dɪfrənt] **1** ADJ andere(r, s), anders *pred* (*from*, *to* als); *two people, things* (= *various*) verschieden; **completely ~** völlig verschieden; (= *changed*) völlig verändert; **that's ~!** das ist was anderes!; **in what way are they ~?** wie unterscheiden sie sich?; **to feel (like) a ~ person** ein ganz anderer Mensch sein; **to do something ~** etwas anderes tun; **that's quite a ~ matter** das ist etwas völlig anderes; **he wants to be ~** er will unbedingt anders sein
2 ADV anders; **he doesn't know any ~** er kennt es nicht anders; (*with behaviour*) er weiß es nicht besser

differential [,dɪfə'renʃəl] **1** ADJ unterschiedlich; **~ pricing** (*Comm*) Preisdiskriminierung *f* **2** N Unterschied *m* (*between* zwischen)

differentiate [,dɪfə'renʃɪeɪt] VTI unterscheiden

differently ['dɪfrəntlɪ] ADV anders (*from* als); (*from one another*) unterschiedlich

difficult ['dɪfɪkəlt] ADJ schwer; *person, situation, book* schwierig; **there's nothing ~ about it** das ist doch gar nicht schwer; **the ~ thing is that ...** die Schwierigkeit liegt darin, dass ...; **it was a ~ decision to make** es war eine schwere Entscheidung; **it was ~ for him to leave her** es fiel ihm schwer, sie zu verlassen; **it's ~ for youngsters** *or* **youngsters find it ~ to get a job** junge Leute haben Schwierigkeiten, eine Stelle zu finden; **it's ~ to see what they could have done** es lässt sich schwer vorstellen, was sie hätten tun können; **he's ~ to get on with** es ist schwer, mit ihm auszukommen; **to make it ~ for sb** es jdm nicht leicht machen; **to have a ~ time (doing sth)** Schwierigkeiten haben(, etw zu tun); **to put sb in a ~ position** jdn in eine schwierige Lage bringen; **to be ~ (about sth)** (wegen etw) Schwierigkeiten machen

difficulty ['dɪfɪkəltɪ] N Schwierigkeit *f*; **with/without ~** mit/ohne Schwierigkeiten; **he had ~ (in) setting up in business** es fiel ihm nicht leicht, sich selbstständig zu machen; **she had great ~ (in) breathing** sie konnte kaum atmen; **in ~** *or* **difficulties** in Schwierigkeiten; **to get into difficulties** in Schwierigkeiten geraten

diffuse [dɪ'fjuːz] VT *tension* verringern, abbauen

dig [dɪg], *vb: pret, ptp* **dug 1** VT **(a)** graben; *garden* umgraben; *grave* ausheben
(b) (= *poke, thrust*) bohren (*sth into sth* etw in etw *acc*); **to ~ sb in the ribs** jdn in die Rippen stoßen
2 VI graben; (*Tech*) schürfen; (*Archeol*) Ausgrabungen machen; **to ~ for minerals** Erz schürfen; **to ~ deep** (*Sport, fig*) auf seine letzten Reserven zurückgreifen; (*fig:* = *investigate*) gründlich nachforschen
3 N **(a)** (*Brit: with elbow*) Stoß *m*; **to give sb a ~ in the ribs** jdm einen Rippenstoß geben
(b) (*Brit:* = *sarcastic remark*) Seitenhieb *m*; **to have a ~ at sb/sth** eine spitze Bemerkung über jdn/etw machen
► **dig around** VI (*inf*) herumsuchen
► **dig in 1** VI (*inf:* = *eat*) reinhauen (*inf*) **2** VT SEP **to dig one's heels in** (*fig*) sich auf die Hinterbeine stellen (*inf*)
► **dig into** VI +PREP OBJ *sb's past* wühlen in (+*dat*); **to dig (deep) into one's pockets** *or* **purse** (*fig*) tief in die Tasche greifen
► **dig out** VT SEP (*lit, fig*) ausgraben (*of* aus)
► **dig up** VT SEP (*lit, fig*) ausgraben; *earth* aufwühlen; *lawn, garden* umgraben; **where did you dig her up?** (*inf*) wo hast du die denn aufgegabelt? (*inf*)

digest [daɪ'dʒest] VTI (*lit, fig*) verdauen

digestible [dɪ'dʒestɪbl] ADJ verdaulich

digestion [dɪ'dʒestʃən] N Verdauung *f*

digestive system [dɪ'dʒestɪvsɪstəm] N Verdauungssystem *nt*

digger ['dɪgəʳ] N (*Tech:* = *excavator*) Bagger *m*

digicam ['dɪdʒɪkæm] N (*Comput*) Digitalkamera *f*

digit ['dɪdʒɪt] N **(a)** (= *finger*) Finger *m*; (= *toe*) Zehe *f* **(b)** (*Math*) Ziffer *f*; **a four-~ number** eine vierstellige Zahl

digital ['dɪdʒɪtəl] ADJ Digital-; **~ display** Digitalanzeige *f*; **~ technology** Digitaltechnik *f*

digital: digital audio tape N DAT-Band *nt*; **digital camera** N digitale Kamera, Digitalkamera *f*

digitally ['dɪdʒɪtəlɪ] ADV digital; **~ remastered** digital aufbereitet; **~ recorded** im Digitalverfahren aufgenommen

digital: digital radio N digitales Radio; **digital recording** N Digitalaufnahme *f*; **digital television, digital TV** N digitales Fernsehen

digitize ['dɪdʒɪtaɪz] VT (*Comput*) digitalisieren

dignified ['dɪgnɪfaɪd] ADJ *person* (ehr)würdig; *behaviour, manner, face* würdevoll

dignity ['dɪgnɪtɪ] N Würde *f*; **to die with ~** in Würde sterben; **to lose one's ~** sich blamieren

digress [daɪ'gres] VI abschweifen

dike [daɪk] N, VT = **dyke**

dilapidated [dɪ'læpɪdeɪtɪd] ADJ verfallen

dilate [daɪ'leɪt] **1** VT weiten, dehnen; **~d pupils** erweiterte Pupillen *pl* **2** VI sich weiten; (*pupils*) sich erweitern

dilemma [daɪ'lemə] N Dilemma *nt*; **to be in a ~** sich in einem Dilemma befinden; **to place sb in a ~** jdn in ein Dilemma bringen *inf*

diligence ['dɪlɪdʒəns] N Fleiß *m*

diligent ['dɪlɪdʒənt] ADJ *person* fleißig; *search, work* sorgfältig

diligently ['dɪlɪdʒəntlɪ] ADV fleißig; (= *carefully*) sorgfältig

dill [dɪl] N Dill *m*

dilute [daɪ'luːt] **1** VT verdünnen; **~ to taste** nach Geschmack verdünnen **2** ADJ verdünnt

dilution [daɪ'luːʃən] N Verdünnung *f*; (*fig*) Milderung *f*; (*of power, influence*) Schwächung *f*

dim [dɪm] **1** ADJ (+ER) **(a)** *light, lamp* schwach; *room* dunkel; **the room grew ~** im Zimmer wurde es dunkel
(b) (= *vague*) undeutlich; *memory, recollection* dunkel; **I have a ~ memory** *or* **recollection of it** ich erinnere mich nur (noch) dunkel daran
(c) (*inf:* = *stupid*) beschränkt (*inf*)
2 VT *light* dämpfen; *lamp* verdunkeln; **to ~ the lights** (*Theat*) das Licht langsam ausgehen lassen; **to ~ one's headlights** (*esp US*) abblenden
3 VI (*light*) schwach werden; (*lamp*) dunkler werden
► **dim out** VT SEP (*US*) *city* verdunkeln

dime [daɪm] N (*US*) Zehncentstück *nt*; **~ novel** Groschenroman *m*

dimension [daɪ'menʃən] N Dimension *f*; (= *measurement*) Maß *nt*

-dimensional [-daɪ'menʃənl] ADJ SUF -dimensional; **one-dimensional** eindimensional

diminish [dɪ'mɪnɪʃ] **1** VT verringern; *authority* herabsetzen; *number* verkleinern; *enthusiasm* dämpfen; *power* einschränken **2** VI sich verringern; (*speed, authority, strength*) abnehmen; (*number*) sich verkleinern; (*enthusiasm*) nachlassen; **law of ~ing returns** (*Econ*) Gesetz *nt* von der fallenden Profitrate; **to ~ in size** kleiner werden; **to ~ in value** im Wert sinken

dimly ['dɪmlɪ] ADV **(a)** *shine* schwach; **~ lit** schwach beleuchtet
(b) (= *vaguely*) undeutlich; *see* verschwommen; **I was ~ aware that ...** es war mir undeutlich bewusst, dass ...

dimmer ['dɪməʳ] N (*Elec*) Dimmer *m*; (*US Aut*) Abblendschalter *m*; **~s** *pl* (*US Aut*) Abblendlicht *nt*; (= *sidelights*) Begrenzungsleuchten *pl*

dimmer switch N Dimmer *m*

dimness ['dɪmnɪs] N **(a)** (*of light*) Schwäche *f*; **the ~ of the room** das Halbdunkel im Zimmer **(b)** (*of shape*) Undeutlichkeit *f*; (*of outline, eyesight, memory*) Schwäche *f*

dim-out ['dɪmaʊt] N (*US*) Verdunkelung *f*

dimple ['dɪmpl] N (*on cheek, chin*) Grübchen *nt*; (= *depression*) Vertiefung *f*

dim: dimwit N (*inf*) Schwachkopf *m* (*inf*); **dim-witted** ADJ (*inf*) dämlich (*inf*)

din [dɪn] N Lärm *m*; **an infernal ~** ein Höllenlärm *m*

dine [daɪn] VI speisen (*on* etw); **they ~d on caviare every night** sie aßen jeden Abend Kaviar

diner ['daɪnəʳ] N **(a)** (= *person*) Speisende(r) *mf*; (*in restaurant*) Gast *m* **(b)** (= *café etc*) Esslokal *nt*

ding-a-ling ['dɪŋə'lɪŋ] N (*US inf:* = *fool*) Depp *m* (*inf*)

ding(e)y, dinghy ['dɪŋgɪ] N Ding(h)i *nt*; (*collapsible*) Schlauchboot *nt*

dinginess ['dɪndʒɪnɪs] N Unansehnlichkeit f
dingy[1] ['dɪndʒɪ] ADJ (+ER) düster; *colour* schmutzig
dingy[2] ['dɪŋgɪ] N = **ding(e)y**
dining ['daɪnɪŋ]: **dining car** N Speisewagen m; **dining hall** N Speisesaal m; **dining room** N Esszimmer nt; (*in hotel*) Speiseraum m; **dining table** N Esstisch m
dinky ['dɪŋkɪ] ADJ (a) (*Brit inf*: = *cute*) schnuckelig (*inf*) (b) (*US inf*: = *small*) winzig
dinner ['dɪnə'] N (= *evening meal*) Abendessen nt; (*formal*) Essen nt; (= *lunch*) Mittagessen nt; **to be eating** *or* **having one's ~** zu Abend/Mittag essen; **we're having people to ~** wir haben Gäste zum Essen; **~'s ready** das Essen ist fertig; **to finish one's ~** zu Ende essen; **to go out to ~** (*in restaurant*) auswärts essen (gehen); (*at friends'*) zum Essen eingeladen sein; **a formal ~** ein offizielles Essen
dinner: **dinner-dance** N *Abendessen mit Tanz*; **dinner jacket** N Smokingjacke f; **dinner money** N (*Brit Sch*) Essensgeld nt; **dinner party** N Abendgesellschaft f (mit Essen); **to have** *or* **give a small ~** ein kleines Essen geben; **dinner plate** N Tafelteller m; **dinner service** N Tafelservice nt; **dinner table** N Tafel f; **dinner theater** N (*US*) *Restaurant mit Theatervorführung*; **dinnertime** N Essenszeit f
dinosaur ['daɪnəsɔː'] N Dinosaurier m
diocese ['daɪəsɪs] N Diözese f
dioxide [daɪ'ɒksaɪd] N Dioxid nt
Dip ABBR *of* **diploma**
dip [dɪp] **1** VT (a) (*into*) in +acc) (*into liquid*) tauchen; *hand, brush* (ein)tauchen; *bread* (ein)tunken; **to ~ sth in flour/egg** etw in Mehl/Ei wälzen
(b) (*into bag, basket*) *hand* stecken
(c) (*Brit Aut*) *headlights* abblenden; **~ped headlights** Abblendlicht nt
2 VI (*ground*) sich senken; (*temperature, pointer on scale, prices*) fallen
3 N (a) (= *swim*) **to go for a** *or* **to have a ~** kurz mal schwimmen gehen
(b) (*in ground*) (= *hollow*) Bodensenke f; (= *slope*) Abfall m
(c) (*in prices etc*) Fallen nt; **to take a ~** fallen
(d) (*Cook*) Dip m; **a garlic ~** ein Knoblauchdip
➤ **dip into** VI +PREP OBJ (a) (*lit*) **she dipped into her bag for her keys** sie griff in ihre Tasche, um ihre Schlüssel zu holen
(b) (*fig*) **to dip into one's pocket** tief in die Tasche greifen; **to dip into one's savings** an seine Ersparnisse gehen (c) *book* einen kurzen Blick werfen in (+acc)
Dip. Ed. ['dɪp'ed] (*Brit Univ*) ABBR *of* **Diploma in Education** Diplom nt in Pädagogik
diphtheria [dɪf'θɪərɪə] N Diphtherie f
diphthong ['dɪfθɒŋ] N Diphthong m
diploma [dɪ'pləʊmə] N Diplom nt; **teacher's ~** Lehrerdiplom nt; **to hold a ~ in** ein Diplom haben in (+dat)
diplomacy [dɪ'pləʊməsɪ] N (*Pol, fig*) Diplomatie f; **to use ~** diplomatisch vorgehen
diplomat ['dɪpləmæt] N (*Pol, fig*) Diplomat(in) m(f)
diplomatic [ˌdɪplə'mætɪk] ADJ (*lit, fig*) diplomatisch
diplomatically [ˌdɪplə'mætɪkəlɪ] ADV (*lit, fig*) (= *tactfully*) diplomatisch; (= *by diplomatic means*) auf diplomatischem Wege; (= *at a diplomatic level*) auf diplomatischer Ebene
diplomatic: **diplomatic bag** N (*Brit*) Diplomatenpost f; **diplomatic corps** N diplomatisches Korps; **diplomatic immunity** N Immunität f; **diplomatic pouch** N (*US*) Diplomatenpost f; **diplomatic service** N diplomatischer Dienst
dipper ['dɪpə'] N (*US Astron*) **the Big** *or* **Great/Little Dipper** der Große/Kleine Wagen *or* Bär
dippy ['dɪpɪ] ADJ (*inf*) meschugge (*inf*)
dip rod N (*US*) = **dipstick**
dipstick ['dɪpstɪk] N Ölmessstab m
DIP switch ['dɪpswɪtʃ] N (*Comput*) DIP-Schalter m
dip switch N (*Aut*) Abblendschalter m
dire [daɪə'] ADJ (a) *consequences* verheerend; *warning, prediction, threat* unheilvoll; *effects* katastrophal; *situation* miserabel; (= *desperate*) verzweifelt; **the ~ state of the property market** die miserable Lage auf dem Immobilienmarkt; **in ~ poverty** in äußerster Armut; **to be in**

~ need of sth etw dringend brauchen; **to be in ~ straits** in einer ernsten Notlage sein (b) (*inf*: = *awful*) mies (*inf*)
direct [daɪ'rekt] **1** ADJ direkt; *responsibility, cause* unmittelbar; *train* durchgehend; *opposite* genau; *refusal, denial* glatt; **~ costs** (*Fin*) direkte Kosten; **~ distribution** (*Comm*) Direktvertrieb m; **to be a ~ descendant of sb** ein direkter Nachkomme von jdm sein; **to pay by ~ debit** (*Brit*) *or* **deposit** (*US*) per Einzugsauftrag bezahlen; **avoid ~ sunlight** direkte Sonneneinstrahlung meiden; **to take a ~ hit** einen Volltreffer einstecken; **~ speech** (*Brit*) *or* **discourse** (*US*) (*Gram*) direkte Rede; **~ taxation** direkte Besteuerung
2 VT (a) *remark, letter* richten (*to* an +acc); *efforts, look* richten (*towards* auf +acc); *anger* auslassen (*towards* an +acc); **the violence was ~ed against the police** die Gewalttätigkeiten richteten sich gegen die Polizei; **to ~ sb's attention to sb/sth** jds Aufmerksamkeit auf jdn/etw lenken; **can you ~ me to the town hall?** können Sie mir den Weg zum Rathaus sagen?
(b) (= *supervise*) *person's work, business* leiten; *traffic* regeln
(c) (= *order*) anweisen (*sb to do sth* jdn, etw zu tun); **the judge ~ed the jury to ...** (*Jur*) der Richter belehrte die Schöffen darüber, dass ...
(d) *film, play* Regie führen bei; *group of actors* dirigieren; *radio/TV programme* leiten
3 ADV direkt
direct: **direct access** N (*Comput*) Direktzugriff m; **direct action** N direkte Aktion; **to take ~** direkt handeln; **direct current** N (*Elec*) Gleichstrom m; **direct flight** N Direktflug m
direction [dɪ'rekʃən] N (a) (*lit, fig*) Richtung f; **in the wrong/right ~** (*lit, fig*) in die falsche/richtige Richtung; **in the ~ of Hamburg/the hotel** in Richtung Hamburg/des Hotels; **a sense of ~** (*lit*) Orientierungssinn m
(b) (= *management*: *of company etc*) Leitung f
(c) (*of film, play, actors*) Regie f; (*of radio/TV programme*) Leitung f
(d) **directions** PL (= *instructions*) Anweisungen pl; (*to a place*) Angaben pl; (*for use*) (Gebrauchs)anweisung f
directive [dɪ'rektɪv] N Direktive f
directly [dɪ'rektlɪ] ADV direkt; *refuse, deny* glatt; (= *at once*) sofort; (= *shortly*) gleich; **he is ~ descended from X** er stammt in direkter Linie von X ab; **~ responsible** unmittelbar verantwortlich
direct: **direct marketing** N Direktmarketing nt; **direct object** N (*Gram*) direktes Objekt
director [dɪ'rektə'] N Direktor(in) m(f); (*Film, Theat*) Regisseur(in) m(f); (*Univ*) Rektor(in) m(f); **~ of Public Prosecutions** Oberstaatsanwalt m/-anwältin f; **~'s report** (*of company*) Geschäftsbericht m
directorate [daɪ'rektərɪt] N (= *board of directors*) Aufsichtsrat m
director: **director's chair** N (*Film*) Regiestuhl m; **director's cut** N (*Film*) vom Regisseur geschnittene Fassung
directorship [dɪ'rektəʃɪp] N Direktorstelle f; **under his ~** unter seiner Leitung
directory [dɪ'rektərɪ] N (a) Adressbuch nt; (= *telephone ~*) Telefonbuch nt; (= *trade ~*) Branchenverzeichnis nt; **~ inquiries** (*Brit*) *or* **assistance** (*US*) (*Telec*) (Fernsprech)auskunft f (b) (*Comput*) Directory nt
direct taxation N direkte Besteuerung
dirt [dɜːt] N (*lit, fig*) Schmutz m; (= *soil*) Erde f; (= *excrement*) Dreck m; **to be covered in ~** völlig verschmutzt sein; **to treat sb like ~** jdn wie (den letzten) Dreck behandeln (*inf*)
dirt: **dirt-cheap** ADJ, ADV (*inf*) spottbillig (*inf*); **dirt farmer** N (*US*) Kleinbauer m, Kleinbäuerin f; **dirt road** N unbefestigte Straße; **dirt track** N Feldweg m; (*Sport*) Aschenbahn f
dirty ['dɜːtɪ] **1** ADJ (+ER) (*lit, fig*) schmutzig; *player, competitor* unfair; *book, film, word* unanständig; *person* obszön; **to get sth ~** etw schmutzig machen; **~ mark** Schmutzfleck m; **~ play** Foulspiel nt; **to do the ~ deed** (*Brit usu hum*) die Übeltat vollbringen; **a ~ mind** eine schmutzige Fantasie; **~ old man** (*pej, hum*) alter Lustmolch (*inf*); **to give sb a ~ look** (*inf*) jdm einen giftigen Blick zuwerfen (*inf*)
2 VT (= *soil*) beschmutzen
dirty: **dirty bomb** N (*Mil sl*) schmutzige Bombe; **dirty trick** N gemeiner Trick; **dirty weekend** N (*hum inf*) Liebeswochenende nt; **dirty work** N **to do sb's ~** (*fig*) sich (*dat*) für jdn die Finger schmutzig machen
disability [ˌdɪsə'bɪlɪtɪ] N Behinderung f

disable [dɪsˈeɪbl] VT **(a)** *person* zum/zur Behinderten machen **(b)** *tank, gun* unbrauchbar machen; *ship* kampfunfähig machen

disabled [dɪsˈeɪbld] **◻** ADJ behindert; **severely/partially ~** schwer/leicht behindert; **physically ~** körperbehindert; **mentally ~** geistig behindert; **~ toilet** Behindertentoilette *f* **◻** PL **the ~** die Behinderten *pl*

disadvantage [ˌdɪsədˈvɑːntɪdʒ] N Nachteil *m*; (= *detriment*) Schaden *m*; **to be at a ~** im Nachteil sein; **to put sb at a ~** jdn benachteiligen

disadvantaged [ˌdɪsədˈvɑːntɪdʒd] ADJ benachteiligt

disadvantageous ADJ, **disadvantageously** ADV [ˌdɪsædvɑːnˈteɪdʒəs, -lɪ] nachteilig

disagree [ˌdɪsəˈɡriː] VI **(a)** (*with person, views*) nicht übereinstimmen; (*with plan, suggestion etc*) nicht einverstanden sein; (*two people*) sich (*dat*) nicht einig sein **(b)** (= *quarrel*) eine Meinungsverschiedenheit haben **(c)** (*climate, food*) **to ~ with sb** jdm nicht bekommen; **garlic ~s with me** ich vertrage keinen Knoblauch

disagreeable [ˌdɪsəˈɡriːəbl] ADJ unangenehm; *person* unsympathisch

disagreement [ˌdɪsəˈɡriːmənt] N **(a)** (*with opinion, between opinions*) Uneinigkeit *f*; **to be in ~ with sb** mit jdm nicht einer Meinung sein; **there is still ~** es herrscht noch Uneinigkeit **(b)** (= *quarrel*) Meinungsverschiedenheit *f*

disallow [ˌdɪsəˈlaʊ] VT nicht anerkennen; *claim* zurückweisen; *plan etc* ablehnen

disappear [ˌdɪsəˈpɪəʳ] VI verschwinden; (*memory*) schwinden; (*objections*) sich zerstreuen; **he ~ed from sight** er verschwand; **to make sth ~** etw verschwinden lassen; **to ~ into thin air** sich in Luft auflösen

disappearance [ˌdɪsəˈpɪərəns] N Verschwinden *nt*

disappoint [ˌdɪsəˈpɔɪnt] VT enttäuschen

disappointed [ˌdɪsəˈpɔɪntɪd] ADJ enttäuscht; **she was ~ to learn that ...** sie war enttäuscht, als sie erfuhr, dass ...; **to be ~ that ...** enttäuscht (darüber) sein, dass ...; **to be ~ in** *or* **with** *or* **by sb/sth** von jdm/etw enttäuscht sein

disappointing [ˌdɪsəˈpɔɪntɪŋ] ADJ enttäuschend; **how ~!** so eine Enttäuschung!

disappointingly [ˌdɪsəˈpɔɪntɪŋlɪ] ADV enttäuschend

disappointment [ˌdɪsəˈpɔɪntmənt] N Enttäuschung *f*

disapproval [ˌdɪsəˈpruːvl] N Missbilligung *f*

disapprove [ˌdɪsəˈpruːv] VI dagegen sein; **to ~ of sb** jdn ablehnen; **to ~ of sth** etw missbilligen; **he ~s of children smoking** er missbilligt es, wenn Kinder rauchen

disapproving ADJ, **disapprovingly** ADV [ˌdɪsəˈpruːvɪŋ, -lɪ] missbilligend

disarm [dɪsˈɑːm] **◻** VT (*lit, fig*) entwaffnen **◻** VI (*Mil*) abrüsten

disarmament [dɪsˈɑːməmənt] N Abrüstung *f*

disarming ADJ, **disarmingly** ADV [dɪsˈɑːmɪŋ, -lɪ] entwaffnend

disarray [ˌdɪsəˈreɪ] N Unordnung *f*; **to be in ~** (*troops*) in Auflösung (begriffen) sein; (*thoughts, organization, political party*) durcheinander sein

disassociate [ˌdɪsəˈsəʊʃɪeɪt] VT = **dissociate**

disaster [dɪˈzɑːstəʳ] N Katastrophe *f*; (= *fiasco*) Fiasko *nt*

disaster: **disaster area** N Katastrophengebiet *nt*; **disaster movie** N Katastrophenfilm *m*

disastrous [dɪˈzɑːstrəs] ADJ katastrophal; **to be ~ for sb/sth** katastrophale Folgen für jdn/etw haben

disastrously [dɪˈzɑːstrəslɪ] ADV katastrophal; **it all went ~ wrong** es was eine Katastrophe

disband [dɪsˈbænd] **◻** VT auflösen **◻** VI (*army, club*) sich auflösen; (*soldiers, club members*) auseinander gehen

disbelief [ˈdɪsbəˈliːf] N Ungläubigkeit *f*; **in ~** ungläubig

disbelieve [ˈdɪsbəˈliːv] VT nicht glauben

disbeliever [ˈdɪsbəˈliːvəʳ] N Ungläubige(r) *mf*

disc, (*esp US*) **disk** [dɪsk] N **(a)** Scheibe *f*; (*Anat*) Bandscheibe *f* **(b)** (= *record, Comput*) Platte *f*; (= *CD*) CD *f*

discard [dɪˈskɑːd] VT ausrangieren; *idea, plan* verwerfen; (= *take off*) *coat* ausziehen

discharge [dɪsˈtʃɑːdʒ] **◻** VT **(a)** *employee, prisoner, patient* entlassen; *accused* freisprechen; **he ~d himself (from hospital)** er hat das Krankenhaus auf eigene Verantwortung verlassen **(b)** (= *emit, Elec*) entladen; *liquid, gas* (*pipe etc*) ausstoßen; **the**

factory was discharging toxic gas into the atmosphere aus der Fabrik strömten giftige Gase in die Atmosphäre; **to ~ effluents into a river** Abwässer in einen Fluss einleiten **◻** [ˈdɪstʃɑːdʒ] N **(a)** (= *dismissal: of soldier*) Abschied *m* **(b)** (*Elec*) Entladung *f*; (*of gas*) Ausströmen *nt*; (*of liquid, Med*: *vaginal*) Ausfluss *m*; (*of pus*) Absonderung *f* **(c)** (*of debt*) Begleichung *f*; (*of duty, function*) Erfüllung *f*; (*of bankrupt*) Entlastung *f*

disciple [dɪˈsaɪpl] N (*lit*) Jünger *m*; (*fig*) Schüler(in) *m(f)*

disciplinary [ˌdɪsɪˈplɪnərɪ] ADJ Disziplinar-; *matters* disziplinarisch; **~ proceedings** *or* **procedures** Disziplinarverfahren *nt*; **~ measures/powers** Disziplinarmaßnahmen *pl*/-gewalt *f*; **to take ~ action** Disziplinarmaßnahmen ergreifen; **they face ~ action** gegen sie werden Disziplinarmaßnahmen ergriffen

discipline [ˈdɪsɪplɪn] **◻** N Disziplin *f*; **to maintain ~** die Disziplin aufrechterhalten **◻** VT disziplinieren; *reactions, emotions* unter Kontrolle halten

disciplined [ˈdɪsɪplɪnd] ADJ diszipliniert

disc jockey N Diskjockey *m*

disclose [dɪsˈkləʊz] VT *secret* enthüllen; *intentions, news, details, identity* bekannt geben; *income* angeben

disco [ˈdɪskəʊ] N Disko *f*, Disco *f*

discolour, (*US*) **discolor** [dɪsˈkʌləʳ] **◻** VT verfärben **◻** VI sich verfärben

discoloured, (*US*) **discolored** [dɪsˈkʌləd] ADJ verfärbt

discomfort [dɪsˈkʌmfət] N (*lit*) Beschwerden *pl*; (*fig*: = *uneasiness, embarrassment*) Unbehagen *nt*; **to feel some ~** sich nicht wohl fühlen

disconcert [ˌdɪskənˈsɜːt] VT beunruhigen

disconcerting [ˌdɪskənˈsɜːtɪŋ] ADJ beunruhigend

disconnect [ˈdɪskəˈnekt] VT *pipe etc* trennen; *TV, iron* ausschalten; *gas, electricity* abstellen

discontent [ˈdɪskənˈtent] N Unzufriedenheit *f*

discontented ADJ, **discontentedly** ADV [ˌdɪskənˈtentɪd, -lɪ] unzufrieden

discontinuation [dɪskənˌtɪnjʊˈeɪʃən] N Aufgabe *f*; (*of class, conversation, treatment*) Abbruch *m*; (*Comm*) Produktionseinstellung *f*; (*Jur: of proceedings*) Einstellung *f*

discontinue [ˈdɪskənˈtɪnjuː] VT aufgeben; *class, conversation, treatment, project* abbrechen; *use* beenden; (*Comm*) *line* auslaufen lassen; *production* einstellen; **a ~d line** (*Comm*) eine ausgelaufene Serie

discord [ˈdɪskɔːd] N Uneinigkeit *f*

discount [ˈdɪskaʊnt] **◻** N **(a)** Rabatt *m*; (*for cash*) Skonto *nt or m*; **to give a ~ on sth** Rabatt auf etw (*acc*) geben; **to give sb a 5% ~** jdm 5% Rabatt/Skonto geben; **at a ~** auf Rabatt/Skonto **(b)** (*Fin*) Abschlag *m*; **to be at a ~** unter pari sein **◻** VT (*Comm*) nachlassen; *bill, note* diskontieren; **~ed bill** Diskontwechsel *m*

discount: **discount broker** N Wechselmakler(in) *m(f)*; **discount house** N **(a)** (*Fin*) Diskontbank *f* **(b)** (= *store*) Discountladen *m*; **discount rate** N (*Fin*) Diskontsatz *m*; **discount store** N Discountgeschäft *nt*

discourage [dɪsˈkʌrɪdʒ] VT **(a)** (= *dishearten*) entmutigen **(b)** (= *dissuade*) **to ~ sb from doing sth** jdm abraten, etw zu tun; (*successfully*) jdn davon abbringen, etw zu tun **(c)** (= *deter, hinder*) abhalten; *friendship, advances, plan, speculation* zu verhindern suchen; *smoking* unterbinden

discouragement [dɪsˈkʌrɪdʒmənt] N (= *dissuasion*) Abraten *nt*; (*with success*) Abbringen *nt*

discouraging ADJ, **discouragingly** ADV [dɪsˈkʌrɪdʒɪŋ, -lɪ] entmutigend

discover [dɪsˈkʌvəʳ] VT entdecken; *culprit* finden; *secret, truth* herausfinden; *cause* feststellen; *mistake, loss* bemerken; **did you ever ~ who ...?** haben Sie jemals herausgefunden, wer ...?

discoverer [dɪsˈkʌvərəʳ] N Entdecker(in) *m(f)*

discovery [dɪsˈkʌvərɪ] N Entdeckung *f*

discredit [dɪsˈkredɪt] **◻** VT **(a)** (= *cast slur/doubt on*) diskreditieren **(b)** (= *disbelieve*) keinen Glauben schenken (+*dat*) **◻** N, NO PL Misskredit *m*; **to bring ~ (up)on sb/sth** jdn/etw in Misskredit bringen

discredited [dɪsˈkredɪtɪd] ADJ diskreditiert

discreet [dɪˈskriːt] ADJ diskret; *account* taktvoll; *jewellery, tie, dress, decoration* dezent; **at a ~ distance** in einer diskreten Entfernung; **to maintain a ~ presence** eine unauffällige Präsenz aufrechterhalten; **to be ~ about sth** etw diskret behandeln

discreetly [dɪˈskriːtlɪ] ADV diskret; *dressed, decorated* dezent

discrepancy [dɪˈskrepənsɪ] N Diskrepanz *f* (*between* zwischen +*dat*)

discretion [dɪˈskreʃən] N **(a)** Diskretion *f* **(b)** (= *freedom of decision*) Ermessen *nt*; **to leave sth to sb's ~** etw in jds Ermessen (*acc*) stellen; **use your own ~** Sie müssen nach eigenem Ermessen handeln

discriminate [dɪˈskrɪmɪneɪt] **1** VI **(a)** unterscheiden (*between* zwischen +*dat*) **(b)** (= *make unfair distinction*) Unterschiede machen (*between* zwischen +*dat*); **to ~ in favour** (*Brit*) *or* **favor** (*US*) **of/against sb** jdn bevorzugen/benachteiligen **2** VT unterscheiden

➤ **discriminate against** VI +PREP OBJ diskriminieren; **they were discriminated against** sie wurden diskriminiert

discriminating [dɪˈskrɪmɪneɪtɪŋ] ADJ **(a)** *person* anspruchsvoll; *judgement, eye* kritisch **(b)** (*Fin*) *tax, tariff* diskriminierend

discrimination [dɪˌskrɪmɪˈneɪʃən] N **(a)** Diskriminierung *f*; **racial ~** Rassendiskriminierung *f*; **sex(ual)/religious ~** Diskriminierung *f* auf Grund des Geschlechts/der Religion **(b)** (= *differentiation*) Unterscheidung *f* (*between* zwischen +*dat*)

discriminatory [dɪˈskrɪmɪnətərɪ] ADJ diskriminierend

discus [ˈdɪskəs] N Diskus *m*; **in the ~** (*Sport*) im Diskuswerfen; **~ thrower** Diskuswerfer(in) *m(f)*

discuss [dɪˈskʌs] VT besprechen; *politics, theory* diskutieren; **I am not willing to ~ it** ich bin nicht gewillt, darüber zu diskutieren

discussant [dɪˈskʌsənt] N (*US*) Diskussionsteilnehmer(in) *m(f)*

discussion [dɪˈskʌʃən] N Diskussion *f* (*of, about* über +*acc*); (= *meeting*) Besprechung *f*; **after much** *or* **a lot of ~** nach langen Diskussionen; **to be under ~** zur Diskussion stehen; **that is still under ~** das ist noch in der Diskussion; **open to ~** zur Diskussion gestellt; **a subject for ~** ein Diskussionsthema *nt*; **to come up for ~** zur Diskussion gestellt werden

disdain [dɪsˈdeɪn] **1** VT *sb* verachten; *sth also* verschmähen **2** N Verachtung *f*; **with ~** verächtlich

disdainful [dɪsˈdeɪnfʊl] ADJ, **disdainfully** [dɪsˈdeɪnfəlɪ] ADV herablassend; *look* verächtlich

disease [dɪˈziːz] N (*lit, fig*) Krankheit *f*

diseased [dɪˈziːzd] ADJ (*lit, fig*) krank; *tissue, plant* befallen

diseconomy [ˌdɪsɪˈkɒnəmɪ] N **~ of scale** (*Comm*) Größennachteil *m*

disembark [ˌdɪsɪmˈbɑːk] VI von Bord gehen

disempower [ˌdɪsɪmˈpaʊəʳ] VT machtlos machen

disenfranchise [ˈdɪsɪnˈfræntʃaɪz] VT **(a)** *person* die bürgerlichen Ehrenrechte aberkennen (+*dat*) **(b)** (*Comm*) die Konzession entziehen (+*dat*)

disengage [ˌdɪsɪnˈgeɪdʒ] VT **(a)** lösen (*from* aus) **(b)** **to ~ the clutch** (*Aut*) auskuppeln

disentangle [ˈdɪsɪnˈtæŋgl] VT (*lit, fig*) entwirren; *mystery* enträtseln; **to ~ oneself (from sth)** (*lit*) sich (aus etw) lösen; (*fig*) sich (von etw) lösen

disfigure [dɪsˈfɪgəʳ] VT verunstalten; *person also* entstellen; *city, landscape* verschandeln

disgrace [dɪsˈgreɪs] **1** N Schande *f* (*to* für); (*person*) Schandfleck *m* (*to* +*gen*); **you're a complete ~!** mit dir kann man sich wirklich nur blamieren!; **the cost of rented accommodation is a ~** es ist eine Schande, wie teuer Mietwohnungen sind; **in ~** mit Schimpf und Schande; (*as a punishment*) zur Strafe; **to bring ~ (up)on sb** jdm Schande machen; **to be in ~** in Ungnade (gefallen) sein (*with* bei) **2** VT Schande machen (+*dat*); *country, family* Schande bringen über (+*acc*); **don't ~ us!** mach uns keine Schande!; **to ~ oneself** sich blamieren

disgraceful [dɪsˈgreɪsfʊl] ADJ erbärmlich (schlecht); *behaviour, scenes, negligence* skandalös; **it's quite ~ how/that ...** es ist wirklich eine Schande, wie/dass ...

disgracefully [dɪsˈgreɪsfəlɪ] ADV schändlich

disguise [dɪsˈgaɪz] **1** VT unkenntlich machen; *voice* verstellen; *vehicle, building* tarnen; *fear, dislike* verbergen; *taste* kaschieren; *facts, mistakes* verschleiern; **to ~ oneself/sb as** sich/jdn verkleiden als **2** N (*lit*) Verkleidung *f*; (*fig*) Deckmantel *m*; **in ~** verkleidet, getarnt

disgust [dɪsˈgʌst] **1** N Ekel *m*; (*at sb's behaviour*) Empörung *f*; **in ~** voller Ekel/Empörung; **much to his ~ they left** sehr zu seiner Empörung gingen sie **2** VT (*person, sight*) anekeln; (*actions*) empören

disgusted [dɪsˈgʌstɪd] ADJ angeekelt; (*at sb's behaviour*) empört; **to be ~ with sb** empört über jdn sein; **to be ~ with sth** angewidert von etw sein; **I was ~ with myself** ich war mir selbst zuwider

disgusting [dɪsˈgʌstɪŋ] ADJ **(a)** *behaviour* widerlich; (= *physically nauseating*) ekelhaft **(b)** *book, film, photo* anstößig; (= *obscene*) obszön; **don't be ~** sei nicht so ordinär **(c)** (= *disgraceful*) unerhört

disgustingly [dɪsˈgʌstɪŋlɪ] ADV ekelhaft

dish [dɪʃ] N **(a)** Schale *f*; (*for serving*) Schüssel *f* **(b)** **dishes** PL (= *crockery*) Geschirr *nt*; **to do the ~es** abwaschen **(c)** (= *food*) Gericht *nt*; **fish/pasta ~es** Fisch-/Nudelgerichte *pl* **(d)** (*Elec*) Parabolreflektor *m*; (*also* ~ **aerial** (*Brit*) *or* **antenna** (*US*)) Parabolantenne *f*, Schüssel *f* (*inf*)

➤ **dish out** VT SEP (*inf*) austeilen

➤ **dish up** **1** VT SEP (*lit*) auf dem Teller anrichten; (*in bowls*) auftragen **2** VI anrichten

dishcloth [ˈdɪʃklɒθ] N (*for drying*) Geschirrtuch *nt*; (*for washing*) Spültuch *nt*

dishearten [dɪsˈhɑːtn] VT entmutigen

disheartening ADJ, **dishearteningly** ADV [dɪsˈhɑːtnɪŋ, -lɪ] entmutigend

dishevelled, (*US*) **disheveled** [dɪˈʃevəld] ADJ unordentlich; *hair* zerzaust; *person, appearance* ungepflegt

dishonest [dɪsˈɒnɪst] ADJ unehrlich; (= *lying*) verlogen; *plan, scheme* unlauter

dishonestly [dɪsˈɒnɪstlɪ] ADV unehrlich; *pretend, claim* unehrlicherweise; (= *deceitfully*) betrügerisch; (= *with intent to deceive*) in betrügerischer Absicht

dishonesty [dɪsˈɒnɪstɪ] N Unehrlichkeit *f*; (= *lying*) Verlogenheit *f*; (*of plan, scheme*) Unlauterkeit *f*

dishonour, (*US*) **dishonor** [dɪsˈɒnəʳ] **1** N Schande *f*; **to bring ~ (up)on sb** Schande über jdn bringen **2** VT **(a)** schänden; *family* Schande machen (+*dat*) **(b)** (*Comm, Fin*) *cheque* nicht honorieren; *bill* nicht bezahlen

dishonourable, (*US*) **dishonorable** ADJ, **dishonourably**, (*US*) **dishonorably** ADV [dɪsˈɒnərəbl, -lɪ] unehrenhaft

dish: **dishtowel** N (*US, Scot*) Geschirrtuch *nt*; **dishwasher** N (= *machine*) (Geschirr)spülmaschine *f*; **dishwasher-proof** ADJ spülmaschinenfest; **dishwater** N Spülwasser *nt*

disillusion [ˌdɪsɪˈluːʒən] VT desillusionieren

disincentive [ˌdɪsɪnˈsentɪv] N Entmutigung *f*

disinclination [dɪsɪnklɪˈneɪʃən] N Abneigung *f*

disinclined [ˈdɪsɪnˈklaɪnd] ADJ abgeneigt

disinfect [ˌdɪsɪnˈfekt] VT desinfizieren

disinfectant [ˌdɪsɪnˈfektənt] N Desinfektionsmittel *nt*

disinherit [ˈdɪsɪnˈherɪt] VT enterben

disintegrate [dɪsˈɪntɪgreɪt] **1** VI zerfallen; (*rock, cement*) auseinander bröckeln; (*road surface*) rissig werden; (*group, institution*) sich auflösen; (*marriage, society, theory*) zusammenbrechen **2** VT zerfallen lassen; *rock, cement* auseinander bröckeln lassen; *group, institution* auflösen

disintegration [dɪsˌɪntɪˈgreɪʃən] N Zerfall *m*; (*of rock, cement*) Auseinanderbröckeln *nt*; (*of road surface*) Rissigkeit *f*; (*of group, institution*) Auflösung *f*; (*of marriage, society, theory*) Zusammenbruch *m*

disinterest [dɪsˈɪntrəst] N Desinteresse *nt* (*in* an +*dat*)

disinterested [dɪsˈɪntrɪstɪd] ADJ desinteressiert

disjointed [dɪsˈdʒɔɪntɪd] ADJ unzusammenhängend

disk [dɪsk] N (*Comput*) Platte *f*; (= *floppy ~*) Diskette *f*; **on ~** auf Platte/Diskette

disk (*Comput*): **disk controller** N Plattencontroller *m*; **disk drive** N Diskettenlaufwerk *nt*; (= *hard ~*) Festplattenlaufwerk *nt*

diskette [dɪsˈket] N (*Comput*) Diskette *f*

disk (*Comput*): **disk operating system** N Betriebssystem *nt*; **disk space** N Speicherkapazität *f*

dislike [dɪsˈlaɪk] **1** VT nicht mögen; **to ~ doing sth** etw ungern tun; **I ~ him/it intensely** ich mag ihn/es überhaupt nicht; **I don't ~ it** ich habe nichts dagegen **2** N Abneigung *f (of* gegen); **to take a ~ to sb/sth** eine Abneigung gegen jdn/etw entwickeln

dislocate [ˈdɪsləʊkeɪt] VT *(Med)* verrenken; **to ~ one's shoulder** sich *(dat)* den Arm auskugeln

dislodge [dɪsˈlɒdʒ] VT *obstruction, stone* lösen; (= *prise, poke out)* herausstochern; (= *knock out)* herausschlagen; *person* verdrängen

disloyal [dɪsˈlɔɪəl] ADJ illoyal; **to be ~ to sb** jdm gegenüber nicht loyal sein

disloyalty [dɪsˈlɔɪəltɪ] N Illoyalität *f (to* gegenüber)

dismal [ˈdɪzməl] ADJ *place, building, prospect, weather* trostlos; *thought* trüb; *performance, prospects* miserabel; **it makes ~ reading** es ist bedrückend zu lesen

dismally [ˈdɪzməlɪ] ADV *say, think, look* trübselig; *grey, monotonous* trostlos; *fail* kläglich

dismantle [dɪsˈmæntl] VT auseinander nehmen; *scaffolding* abbauen

dismay [dɪsˈmeɪ] **1** N Bestürzung *f;* **in ~** bestürzt **2** VT bestürzen

dismember [dɪsˈmembəʳ] VT *(lit)* animal, body zerstückeln; *(Med)* zergliedern

dismiss [dɪsˈmɪs] VT **(a)** *(from job, presence)* entlassen; *assembly* auflösen; **~!** wegtreten!; **"class ~ed"** „ihr dürft gehen" **(b)** *objection, speculation, claims* abtun; **to ~ sth from one's mind** etw verwerfen **(c)** *(Jur)* appeal abweisen; **to ~ a case** die Klage abweisen

dismissal [dɪsˈmɪsəl] N **(a)** Entlassung *f* **(b)** *(Jur)* Abweisung *f*

dismissive [dɪsˈmɪsɪv] ADJ *remark* wegwerfend; *gesture* abweisend

dismissively [dɪsˈmɪsɪvlɪ] ADV abweisend

dismount [dɪsˈmaʊnt] VI absteigen

disobedience [ˌdɪsəˈbiːdɪəns] N Ungehorsam *m (to* gegenüber)

disobedient [ˌdɪsəˈbiːdɪənt] ADJ ungehorsam

disobey [ˌdɪsəˈbeɪ] VT nicht gehorchen (+*dat);* *officer* den Gehorsam verweigern (+*dat);* *rule, law* übertreten

disorder [dɪsˈɔːdəʳ] N **(a)** Durcheinander *nt;* **in ~** durcheinander **(b)** *(Pol:* = *rioting)* Unruhen *pl* **(c)** *(Med)* Funktionsstörung *f* ~ Störung *f* des Essverhaltens

disorderly [dɪsˈɔːdəlɪ] ADJ **(a)** *(untidy)* unordentlich; *queue, row* ungeordnet **(b)** (= *unruly)* person wild; *crowd, event* undiszipliniert; *conduct, behaviour* ungehörig

disorganized [dɪsˈɔːgənaɪzd] ADJ *systemlos; life, person* chaotisch; *filing system etc* ungeordnet; **he/the office is completely ~** bei ihm/im Büro geht alles drunter und drüber

disorient [dɪsˈɔːrɪent], **disorientate** [dɪsˈɔːrɪenteɪt] VT *(lit, fig)* verwirren, desorientieren

dispatch [dɪsˈpætʃ] **1** VT *letter, goods etc* senden, schicken; *person, troops etc* (ent)senden **2** N [dɪsˈpætʃ, ˈdɪspætʃ] **(a)** *(of letter, goods etc)* Senden *nt;* *(of person, troops etc)* Entsendung *f;* **date of ~** Absendedatum *nt* **(b)** (= *message, report)* Depesche *f;* *(Press)* Bericht *m*

dispatch: **dispatch documents** PL *(Comm)* Versandpapiere *pl;* **dispatch note** N *(in advance)* Versandanzeige *f;* *(with goods)* Begleitschein *m;* **dispatch rider** N Melder(in) *m(f),* Meldefahrer(in) *m(f)*

dispel [dɪsˈpel] VT *clouds, fog* auflösen, vertreiben; *doubts, fears, gloom* zerstreuen; *myth* zerstören; *impression, notion* ein Ende machen (+*dat)*

dispensable [dɪsˈpensəbl] ADJ entbehrlich

dispense [dɪsˈpens] VT verteilen *(to an* +*acc); advice* erteilen; *(machine)* ausgeben; **to ~ justice** Recht sprechen

➤ **dispense with** VI +PREP OBJ verzichten auf (+*acc)*

dispenser [dɪsˈpensəʳ] N (= *container)* Spender *m;* (= *slot machine)* Automat *m*

dispersal [dɪsˈpɜːsəl] N Verstreuen *nt;* *(of crowd, mist)* Auflösung *f*

disperse [dɪsˈpɜːs] **1** VT verstreuen; *(Bot)* seed verteilen; *crowd, mist, oil slick* auflösen; *(fig)* knowledge etc verbreiten **2** VI sich auflösen

dispersion [dɪsˈpɜːʃən] N = **dispersal**

displace [dɪsˈpleɪs] VT verschieben; *people* vertreiben; (= *replace)* ablösen

displaced person [dɪsˌpleɪstˈpɜːsn] N Vertriebene(r) *mf*

displacement [dɪsˈpleɪsmənt] N Verschiebung *f;* *(of people)* Vertreibung *f;* (= *replacement)* Ablösung *f*

display [dɪsˈpleɪ] **1** VT **(a)** (= *show)* object zeigen; *feelings* zur Schau stellen; *power* demonstrieren; *exam results, notice* aushängen; *(on screen)* anzeigen **(b)** *(Comm)* goods ausstellen **2** N **(a)** *(of object)* Zeigen *nt;* *(of ignorance)* Beweis *m;* *(of feelings)* Zurschaustellung *f;* *(of power)* Demonstration *f;* **to make a great ~ of sth** etw groß zur Schau stellen; **to make a great ~ of doing sth** etw betont auffällig tun; **to be/go on ~** ausgestellt sein/werden; **these are only for ~** die sind nur zur Ansicht **(b)** (= *of paintings etc)* Ausstellung *f;* (= *dancing ~ etc)* Vorführung *f;* (= *military, air ~)* Schau *f;* **firework ~** (öffentliches) Feuerwerk **(c)** *(Comm)* Auslage *f,* Display *nt*

display: **display cabinet** N Schaukasten *m;* **display case** N Vitrine *f;* **display unit** N *(Comput)* Bildschirmgerät *nt*

displease [dɪsˈpliːz] VT missfallen (+*dat);* (= *annoy)* verstimmen

displeasure [dɪsˈpleʒəʳ] N Missfallen *nt (at* über +*acc)*

disposable [dɪsˈpəʊzəbl] ADJ Wegwerf-; **~ razor** Wegwerfrasierer *m;* **~ nappy** *(Brit)* Wegwerfwindel *f;* **~ syringe/needle** Einwegspritze *f/*-nadel *f;* **~ contact lenses** Kontaktlinsen *pl* zum Wegwerfen

disposable: **disposable assets** PL *(Fin)* disponibles *(spec)* or frei verfügbares Vermögen; **disposable income** N verfügbares Einkommen

disposal [dɪsˈpəʊzəl] N **(a)** Loswerden *nt;* *(of unwanted person or goods, of litter, body)* Beseitigung *f;* *(of question, matter)* Erledigung *f* **(b)** (= *control)* Verfügungsgewalt *f;* **the means at sb's ~** die jdm zur Verfügung stehenden Mittel; **to put sth at sb's ~** jdm etw zur Verfügung stellen; **to be at sb's ~** jdm zur Verfügung stehen

➤ **dispose of** VI +PREP OBJ *furniture, unwanted person, goods* loswerden; *litter, body* beseitigen; (= *kill)* eliminieren

disposition [ˌdɪspəˈzɪʃən] N Veranlagung *f;* **her cheerful ~** ihre fröhliche Art

dispossess [ˌdɪspəˈzes] VT enteignen

disproportionate [ˌdɪsprəˈpɔːʃnɪt] ADJ **to be ~ (to sth)** in keinem Verhältnis (zu etw) stehen; **a ~ amount of money** ein unverhältnismäßig hoher Geldbetrag

disproportionately [ˌdɪsprəˈpɔːʃnɪtlɪ] ADV (+*adj)* unverhältnismäßig; *affect* unverhältnismäßig stark; **~ large numbers of ...** unverhältnismäßig viele ...

disprove [dɪsˈpruːv] VT widerlegen

dispute [dɪsˈpjuːt] **1** VT **(a)** *statement* bestreiten; *claim to sth, will* anfechten **(b)** *question, subject* sich streiten über (+*acc);* **the issue was hotly ~d** das Thema wurde hitzig diskutiert **(c)** (= *contest)* kämpfen um; *territory* beanspruchen **2** N [dɪsˈpjuːt, ˈdɪspjuːt] **(a)** NO PL (= *arguing, controversy)* Disput *m;* **to be beyond ~** außer Frage stehen; **there is some ~ about which horse won** es ist umstritten, welches Pferd gewonnen hat; **a territory in** *or* **under ~** ein umstrittenes Gebiet **(b)** (= *quarrel)* Streit *m* **(c)** *(Ind)* Auseinandersetzung *f;* **wages ~** Tarifauseinandersetzung *pl*

disqualification [dɪsˌkwɒlɪfɪˈkeɪʃən] N Ausschluss *m;* *(Sport)* Disqualifikation *f;* **~ (from driving)** Führerscheinentzug *m*

disqualify [dɪsˈkwɒlɪfaɪ] VT untauglich machen *(from* für); *(Sport etc)* disqualifizieren; **to ~ sb from driving** jdm den Führerschein entziehen

disregard [ˈdɪsrɪˈgɑːd] **1** VT ignorieren **2** N Missachtung *f (for gen);* *(for money)* Geringschätzung *f (for gen);* **to show complete ~ for sth** etw völlig außer Acht lassen

disrepair [ˈdɪsrɪˈpeəʳ] N Baufälligkeit *f;* **in a state of ~** baufällig; **to fall into ~** verfallen

disrepute [ˈdɪsrɪˈpjuːt] N schlechter Ruf; **to bring sth into ~** etw in Verruf bringen; **to fall into ~** in Verruf geraten

disrespect [ˈdɪsrɪˈspekt] N Respektlosigkeit *f (for* gegenüber); **to show ~ for sth** keinen Respekt vor etw *(dat)* haben; **I don't mean any ~, but ...** ich will nicht respektlos sein, aber ...

disrespectful [ˈdɪsrɪˈspektfʊl] ADJ, **disrespectfully** [ˈdɪsrɪˈspektfəlɪ] ADV respektlos

disrupt [dɪsˈrʌpt] VT stören

disruption [dɪsˈrʌpʃən] N Störung f

disruptive [dɪsˈrʌptɪv] ADJ störend; *effect* zerstörerisch

dissatisfaction [ˈdɪsˌsætɪsˈfækʃən] N Unzufriedenheit f

dissatisfied [dɪsˈsætɪsfaɪd] ADJ unzufrieden

dissent [dɪˈsent] N Nichtübereinstimmung f

dissenting [dɪˈsentɪŋ] ADJ ATTR abweichend; **there was not a single ~ voice** es wurde keine Gegenstimme laut

dissertation [ˌdɪsəˈteɪʃən] N wissenschaftliche Arbeit; *(for PhD)* Dissertation f

disservice [dɪsˈsɜːvɪs] N **to do oneself/sb a ~** sich/jdm einen schlechten Dienst erweisen

dissident [ˈdɪsɪdənt] **1** N Dissident(in) m(f) **2** ADJ dissident

dissimilar [dɪˈsɪmɪləʳ] ADJ unterschiedlich *(to* von); *two things* verschieden; **not ~ (to sb/sth)** (jdm/einer Sache) nicht ungleich *or (in appearance)* nicht unähnlich

dissimilarity [ˌdɪsɪmɪˈlærɪtɪ] N Unterschiedlichkeit f; *(in appearance)* Unähnlichkeit f

dissociate [dɪˈsəʊʃɪeɪt] VT trennen *(from* von); **to ~ oneself from sb/sth** sich von jdm/etw distanzieren

dissolution [ˌdɪsəˈluːʃən] N Auflösung f

dissolve [dɪˈzɒlv] **1** VT auflösen **2** VI sich (auf)lösen; **it ~s in water** es ist wasserlöslich, es löst sich in Wasser

dissuade [dɪˈsweɪd] VT **to ~ sb from sth** jdn von etw abbringen; **to ~ sb from doing sth** jdn davon abbringen, etw zu tun

distance [ˈdɪstəns] **1** N Entfernung f; *(= gap, interval)* Abstand m; *(= ~ covered)* Strecke f; **at a ~ of two feet** in zwei Fuß Entfernung; **the ~ between the railway lines** der Abstand zwischen den Eisenbahnschienen; **at an equal ~ from the middle** gleich weit von der Mitte entfernt; **what's the ~ between London and Glasgow?** wie weit ist es von London nach Glasgow?; **in the (far) ~** (ganz) in der Ferne, (ganz) weit weg; **to gaze into the ~** in die Ferne starren; **he admired her at** *or* **from a ~** *(fig)* er bewunderte sie aus der Ferne; **it's within walking ~** es ist zu Fuß erreichbar; **a short ~ away** ganz in der Nähe; **it's quite a ~ (away)** es ist ziemlich weit (entfernt); **the race is over a ~ of 3 miles** das Rennen geht über eine Distanz von 3 Meilen; **to keep one's ~** Abstand halten **2** VT **to ~ oneself/sb from sb/sth** sich/jdn von jdm/etw distanzieren

distant [ˈdɪstənt] **1** ADJ *(in space, time)* fern; *galaxies* weit entfernt; *sound, relative, resemblance, memory* entfernt; *look, mind* abwesend; **with views of the ~ mountains** mit Aussicht auf die Berge in der Ferne; **in the not too** *or* **very ~ future** in nicht allzu ferner Zukunft **2** ADV *(in time, space)* entfernt

distantly [ˈdɪstəntlɪ] ADV **~ related (to sb)** entfernt (mit jdm) verwandt

distaste [dɪsˈteɪst] N Widerwille m *(for* gegen)

distasteful [dɪsˈteɪstfʊl] ADJ *task* unangenehm; *photo, magazine* geschmacklos

distil, *(US)* **distill** [dɪsˈtɪl] VT *(Chem)* destillieren; *whisky etc* brennen

distillery [dɪsˈtɪlərɪ] N Destillerie f, Brennerei f

distinct [dɪsˈtɪŋkt] ADJ **(a)** *parts, types* verschieden; **as ~ from** im Unterschied zu **(b)** *(= definite)* deutlich; *flavour* bestimmt; **to have ~ memories of sb/sth** sich deutlich an jdn/etw erinnern; **to get the ~ idea** *or* **impression that ...** den deutlichen Eindruck bekommen, dass ...; **to have the ~ feeling that ... das** bestimmte Gefühl haben, dass ...; **to have a ~ advantage (over sb)** (jdm gegenüber) deutlich im Vorteil sein; **there is a ~ possibility that ...** es besteht eindeutig die Möglichkeit, dass ...

distinction [dɪsˈtɪŋkʃən] N **(a)** *(= difference)* Unterschied m; *(= act of distinguishing)* Unterscheidung f; **to make** *or* **draw a ~ (between two things)** (zwischen zwei Dingen) unterscheiden **(b)** *(Sch, Univ)* Auszeichnung f; **he got a ~ in French** er hat das Französischexamen mit Auszeichnung bestanden

distinctive [dɪsˈtɪŋktɪv] ADJ unverwechselbar; *feature, pattern, sound* unverkennbar; *voice, dress (= characteristic)* charakteristisch; *(= striking)* auffällig; **~ features** *(of person)* besondere Kennzeichen; **with his ~ irony** mit der ihm eigenen Ironie

distinctively [dɪsˈtɪŋktɪvlɪ] ADV unverwechselbar; **music which is ~ American** Musik mit ausgeprägt amerikanischen Zügen

distinctly [dɪsˈtɪŋktlɪ] ADV **(a)** *(= clearly)* deutlich **(b)** *(= decidedly)* entschieden, eindeutig; *American, modern* ausgeprägt; *odd, uneasy* ausgesprochen; *cool, unhappy* eindeutig

distinguish [dɪsˈtɪŋgwɪʃ] **1** VT **(a)** unterscheiden **(b)** *(= make out) landmark, shape* erkennen **2** VI **to ~ between** unterscheiden zwischen (*+dat*) **3** VR sich auszeichnen

distinguishable [dɪsˈtɪŋgwɪʃəbl] ADJ **(a)** unterscheidbar; **to be (barely) ~ from sth** (kaum) von etw zu unterscheiden sein; **to be ~ by sth** an etw *(dat)* erkennbar sein **(b)** *(= discernible) shape, words* erkennbar

distinguished [dɪsˈtɪŋgwɪʃt] ADJ *guest, professor* angesehen; *scholar, writer* namhaft, angesehen; *career* glänzend

distinguishing [dɪsˈtɪŋgwɪʃɪŋ] ADJ kennzeichnend; **he has no ~ features** er hat keine besonderen Kennzeichen; **the ~ feature of his work is ...** was seine Arbeit kennzeichnet, ist ...

distort [dɪsˈtɔːt] VT verzerren *(also Phys)*; *truth, words, facts* verdrehen; *reality, history* verzerrt darstellen

distorted [dɪsˈtɔːtɪd] ADJ verzerrt; *joints, bones, plants* verformt; *mouth, face* entstellt

distortion [dɪsˈtɔːʃən] N Verzerrung f *(also Phys)*; *(of truth, words, facts)* Verdrehung f; *(of reality, history)* verzerrte Darstellung

distract [dɪsˈtrækt] VT ablenken; **to ~ sb's attention** jdn ablenken

distracted [dɪsˈtræktɪd] ADJ *(= preoccupied)* zerstreut; *(= worried)* beunruhigt

distraction [dɪsˈtrækʃən] N **(a)** NO PL *(= lack of attention)* Unaufmerksamkeit f **(b)** *(= interruption)* Ablenkung f **(c)** *(= entertainment)* Zerstreuung f **(d)** *(= distraught state)* **to drive sb to ~** jdn zur Verzweiflung treiben

distraught [dɪsˈtrɔːt] ADJ verzweifelt

distress [dɪsˈtres] **1** N **(a)** Verzweiflung f; *(physical)* Leiden nt; *(mental, cause of ~)* Kummer m; **to be in great ~** sehr leiden **(b)** *(= danger)* Not f; **to be in ~** *(ship)* in Seenot sein; *(plane)* in Not sein; **~ call** Notsignal nt **2** VT Kummer machen (*+dat*); **don't ~ yourself** machen Sie sich *(dat)* keine Sorgen!

distressed [dɪsˈtrest] ADJ bekümmert; *(= grief-stricken)* erschüttert *(about* von)

distressing [dɪsˈtresɪŋ] ADJ Besorgnis erregend; *(stronger)* erschreckend

distress signal N Notsignal nt

distributable [dɪsˈtrɪbjʊtəbl] ADJ *(Fin)* ausschüttungsfähig

distribute [dɪsˈtrɪbjuːt] VT verteilen *(to an +acc)*; *(Comm) goods* vertreiben *(to, among* an *+acc)*; *drugs* handeln mit *(to* bei); *films* verleihen *(to* an *+acc)*; *dividends* ausschütten *(to* an *+acc)*

distribution [ˌdɪstrɪˈbjuːʃən] N *(= act)* Verteilung f; *(of information, = spread)* Verbreitung f; *(Comm: of goods)* Vertrieb m; *(= dealing: of drugs)* Handel m *(of* mit) *(of films)* Verleih m; *(of dividends)* Ausschüttung f; **~ network** Vertriebsnetz nt; **~ rights** Vertriebsrechte pl; **~ system** Vertriebssystem nt

distributor [dɪsˈtrɪbjʊtəʳ] N Verteiler(in) m(f); *(Comm) (= wholesaler)* Großhändler m; *(= retailer)* Händler(in) m(f); *(of films)* Verleih(er) m; **~ discount** Händlerrabatt m

distributorship [dɪsˈtrɪbjʊtəʃɪp] N *(Comm) (= company)* Vertriebsgesellschaft f; *(= right to supply)* Vertrieb m

district [ˈdɪstrɪkt] N *(of country)* Gebiet nt; *(of town)* Viertel nt; *(= geographical area)* Gegend f; *(= administrative area)* (Verwaltungs)bezirk m; **shopping/business ~** Geschäftsviertel nt

---

DISTRICT OF COLUMBIA

*Der **District of Columbia** ist der Sitz der Regierung der Vereinigten Staaten von Amerika. Er gehört zu keinem Staat, sondern ist ein vollständig autonomer Bezirk im Osten des Landes. Er umfasst ungefähr 180 km², genau die Fläche, über die sich die Landeshauptstadt Washington erstreckt. Die Abkürzung DC wird daher hinter den Namen den Hauptstadt gestellt: Washington, DC.*

---

district: **district attorney** N *(US)* Bezirksstaatsanwalt m/ -anwältin f; **district council** N *(Brit)* Bezirksregierung f; **district court** N *(US Jur)* Bezirksgericht nt; **district manager** N *(Comm)* Bezirksdirektor(in) m(f)

distrust [dɪsˈtrʌst] **1** VT misstrauen (+dat) **2** N Misstrauen nt (of gegenüber)

distrustful [dɪsˈtrʌstfʊl] ADJ misstrauisch (of gegenüber)

disturb [dɪˈstɜːb] **1** VT (lit, fig) stören; (= alarm) beunruhigen; **sorry to ~ you** entschuldigen Sie bitte die Störung; **to ~ the peace** die Ruhe stören **2** VI stören; **"please do not ~"** „bitte nicht stören"

disturbance [dɪˈstɜːbəns] N (a) (political, social) Unruhe f; (in house, street) (Ruhe)störung f; **to cause** or **create a ~** Unruhe/ eine Ruhestörung verursachen (b) (= interruption) Störung f

disturbed [dɪˈstɜːbd] ADJ (a) (= interrupted, turbulent) unruhig (b) (Psych) gestört (c) (= worried) beunruhigt (about, at, by über +acc)

disturbing [dɪˈstɜːbɪŋ] ADJ beunruhigend; (= distracting) störend; **some viewers may find these scenes ~** einige Zuschauer könnten an diesen Szenen Anstoß nehmen

disturbingly [dɪˈstɜːbɪŋlɪ] ADV beunruhigend

disused [ˈdɪsˈjuːzd] ADJ building leer stehend; mine, railway line stillgelegt

ditch [dɪtʃ] **1** N Graben m **2** VT (inf) person abhängen (inf); employee, boyfriend abservieren (inf); plan, project baden gehen lassen (inf); unwanted object wegschmeißen (inf)

dither [ˈdɪðər] VI zaudern, schwanken; **to ~ over sth** mit etw zaudern; **to ~ over how/whether ...** schwanken, wie/ob ...; **stop ~ing (about) and get on with it!** jetzt lass doch dieses ewige Hin und Her und fang endlich mal an!

ditsy, ditzy [ˈdɪtsɪ] ADJ (esp US inf) albern; blonde doof (inf)

dive [daɪv], vb: pret **dived** or (US) **dove**, ptp **dived 1** N (a) Sprung m; (by plane) Sturzflug m; **to make a ~ for sth** (fig inf) sich auf etw (acc) stürzen; **to take a ~** (inf) (dollar etc) absacken (inf); (confidence, hopes) sich in nichts auflösen (b) (pej inf: = club etc) Spelunke f (inf)
2 VI (a) springen; (under water) tauchen; (submarine) untertauchen; (plane, bird) einen Sturzflug machen; (prices) stürzen; **the goalkeeper ~d for the ball** der Torwart hechtete nach dem Ball
(b) (inf) **he ~d under the table** er verschwand blitzschnell unter dem Tisch; **to ~ for cover** eilig in Deckung gehen; **he ~d into a taxi** er stürzte (sich) in ein Taxi
➤ **dive in** VI (a) (swimmer) hineinspringen (b) (inf: = start to eat) **dive in!** hau(t) rein! (inf)

diver [ˈdaɪvər] N Taucher(in) m(f); (off high board) Turmspringer(in) m(f); (off springboard) Kunstspringer(in) m(f)

diverge [daɪˈvɜːdʒ] VI abweichen (from von); (two things) voneinander abweichen

diverse [daɪˈvɜːs] ADJ (a) (with singular noun) gemischt; range, selection breit (b) (with plural noun) unterschiedlich; interests vielfältig

diversification [daɪˌvɜːsɪfɪˈkeɪʃən] N Abwechslung f; (of business etc) Diversifikation f

diversify [daɪˈvɜːsɪfaɪ] **1** VT abwechslungsreich(er) gestalten; business etc diversifizieren **2** VI (Comm) diversifizieren; **to ~ into new products** sich auf neue Produkte umstellen

diversion [daɪˈvɜːʃən] N (a) (of traffic, stream) Umleitung f (b) (= relaxation) Unterhaltung f (c) (Mil, fig) Ablenkung f; **to create a ~** ablenken; **as a ~** um abzulenken

diversity [daɪˈvɜːsɪtɪ] N Vielfalt f

divert [daɪˈvɜːt] VT traffic, stream umleiten; attention ablenken; conversation in eine andere Richtung lenken; blow abwenden; money abzweigen; resources, investment umlenken

divide [dɪˈvaɪd] **1** VT (a) (= separate) trennen
(b) (= split into parts, Math) teilen (into in +acc); (in order to distribute) aufteilen; **the river ~s the city into two** der Fluss teilt die Stadt; **to ~ 6 into 36, to ~ 36 by 6** 36 durch 6 teilen
(c) (= share out) verteilen
(d) (= cause disagreement among) entzweien
2 VI (a) sich teilen; **to ~ into groups** sich in Gruppen aufteilen
(b) (Math: number) sich teilen lassen (by durch)
3 N **the cultural ~** die Kluft zwischen den Kulturen
➤ **divide off** VT SEP (ab)trennen **2** VT SEP (ab)trennen
➤ **divide out** VT SEP aufteilen (among unter +acc or dat)
➤ **divide up 1** VI = divide 2(a) **2** VT SEP = divide 1(b, c)

divided [dɪˈvaɪdɪd] ADJ geteilt; government, opposition zerstritten; **to have ~ loyalties** nicht zu vereinbarende Pflichten haben; **to be ~ on** or **over sth** sich in etw (dat) nicht einig sein

divided highway N (US) ≈ Schnellstraße f

dividend [ˈdɪvɪdend] N (Fin) Dividende f; **~ cover** Verhältnis nt von Gewinn zu Dividende; **~ yield** Dividendenrendite f; **ex ~** nach Dividendenausschüttung, ex Dividende; **cum** or **with ~** mit Dividende; **to pay ~s** (fig) sich bezahlt machen

dividing [dɪˈvaɪdɪŋ] ADJ (ab)trennend

dividing line N (lit, fig) Trennlinie f

divine [dɪˈvaɪn] ADJ (Rel, fig inf) göttlich

diving [ˈdaɪvɪŋ] N: **diving board** N (Sprung)brett nt; **diving suit** N Taucheranzug m

division [dɪˈvɪʒən] N (a) Teilung f; (Math) Teilen nt; **~ of costs** (Comm) Kostenteilung f (b) (in administration) Abteilung f; (in company) Geschäftsbereich m (c) (fig: between social classes etc) Schranke f; (= dividing line: lit, fig) Trennungslinie f (d) (fig: = discord) Uneinigkeit f (e) (Sport) Liga f

divorce [dɪˈvɔːs] **1** N (Jur) Scheidung f (from von); **he wants a ~** er will sich scheiden lassen; **to get a ~ (from sb)** sich (von jdm) scheiden lassen **2** VT sich scheiden lassen von; **to get ~d** sich scheiden lassen **3** VI sich scheiden lassen

divorced [dɪˈvɔːst] ADJ (Jur) geschieden (from von)

divorcee [dɪˌvɔːˈsiː] N Geschiedene(r) mf; **she is a ~** sie ist geschieden

Diwali [dɪˈwɑːlɪ] N Diwali nt

Dixie [ˈdɪksɪ] **1** N (also **~land**) Dixie(land) m **2** ADJ der Südstaaten

---

DIY [diːaɪˈwaɪ] (Brit) ABBR of **do-it-yourself 1** N Heimwerken nt; **she was doing some ~ over the weekend** sie machte am Wochenende einige Heimwerkerarbeiten **2** ADJ product für Heimwerker; **~ fan** or **enthusiast** Heimwerker(in) m(f)

DIY shop, DIY store N Baumarkt m

dizzily [ˈdɪzɪlɪ] ADV benommen

dizziness [ˈdɪzɪnɪs] N Schwindel m

dizzy [ˈdɪzɪ] ADJ (+ER) (a) schwindelig; **I'm (feeling) ~** mir ist schwindelig (from von); **~ spell** Schwindelanfall m; **it makes me ~ to think of it** mir wird ganz schwindelig bei dem Gedanken (b) (fig) height, speed Schwindel erregend

DJ ABBR of **disc jockey**

---

do [duː]

1 AUXILIARY VERB	**4** NOUN
2 TRANSITIVE VERB	**5** PHRASAL VERBS
3 INTRANSITIVE VERB	

vb: pret **did**, ptp **done**

1 AUXILIARY VERB

*There is no equivalent in German to the use of **do** in questions, negative statements and negative commands.*

(a) (interrogative, negative) **do you understand?** verstehen Sie?; **I don't** or **do not understand** ich verstehe nicht; **what did he say?** was hat er gesagt?; **didn't you** or **did you not know?** haben Sie das nicht gewusst?; **don't be silly!** sei nicht albern!
(b) (in question tags) oder; **you know him, don't you?** Sie kennen ihn (doch), oder?; **you don't know him, do you?** Sie

kennen ihn also nicht, oder?; **so you know them, do you?** (*in surprise*) Sie kennen sie also wirklich!; **he does understand, doesn't he?** das versteht er doch, oder?
(c) (*substitute for another verb*) **you speak better German than I do** Sie sprechen besser Deutsch als ich; **he likes cheese and so do I** er isst gern Käse und ich auch; **he doesn't like cheese and neither do I** er mag keinen Käse und ich auch nicht; **I don't like cheese but he does** ich mag keinen Käse, aber er schon; **they said he would go and he did** sie sagten, er würde gehen und das tat er (dann) auch
(d) (*in tag responses*) **do you see them often? – yes, I do/no, I don't** sehen Sie sie oft? – ja/nein; **you didn't go, did you? – yes, I did** Sie sind nicht gegangen, oder? – doch; **they speak French – oh, do they?** sie sprechen Französisch – ja?, ach, wirklich?; **they speak German – do they really?** sie sprechen Deutsch – wirklich?; **may I come in? – do!** darf ich hereinkommen? – ja, bitte; **shall I open the window? – no, don't!** soll ich das Fenster öffnen? – nein, bitte nicht!; **who broke the window? – I did** wer hat das Fenster eingeschlagen? – ich
(e) (*for emphasis*) **DO come!** (*esp Brit*) kommen Sie doch (bitte)!; **DO shut up!** (*esp Brit*) sei doch (endlich) ruhig!; **it's very expensive, but I DO like it** es ist zwar sehr teuer, aber es gefällt mir nun mal; **so you DO know them!** Sie kennen sie also doch!

2 TRANSITIVE VERB
(a) tun, machen; **I've done a stupid thing** ich habe da was Dummes gemacht; **sorry, it's impossible, it can't be done** tut mir Leid, (ist) ausgeschlossen, es lässt sich nicht machen; **can you do it by yourself?** schaffst du das allein?
◆**do +noun phrase to do the housework/one's homework** die Hausarbeit/seine Hausaufgaben machen

> *Note that a more specific verb may be required in German.*

could you do this letter please tippen Sie bitte diesen Brief; **you do the painting and I'll do the papering** du streichst an und ich tapeziere; **to do one's make-up** sich schminken; **to do one's hair** sich frisieren; **to do one's teeth** (*Brit*) sich (*dat*) die Zähne putzen; **to do the dishes** spülen; **to do the washing** Wäsche waschen; **to do the ironing** bügeln
◆**do + anything/something he knows it's a mistake but he can't do anything about it** er weiß, dass es ein Fehler ist, aber er kann nichts daran ändern; **are you doing anything this evening?** haben Sie heute Abend schon etwas vor?; **we'll have to do something about this** wir müssen da etwas unternehmen; **does that do anything for you?** macht dich das an? (*inf*); **Brecht doesn't do anything for me** Brecht sagt mir nichts
◆**do + everything I've done everything I can** ich habe alles getan, was ich kann
◆**do + nothing I've got nothing to do** ich habe nichts zu tun; **I shall do nothing of the sort** ich werde nichts dergleichen tun; **he does nothing but complain** er nörgelt immer nur
◆**do with wh- phrase what's to be done?** was ist da zu tun?; **but what can you do?** aber was kann man da machen?; **what do you want me to do (about it)?** und was soll ich da machen?; **well, do what you can** mach, was du kannst; **what have you done to him?** was haben Sie mit ihm gemacht?; **now what have you done!** was hast du jetzt bloß wieder angestellt *or* gemacht?; **what are you doing on Saturday?** was machen Sie am Sonnabend?; **how do you do it?** wie macht man das?; (*in amazement*) wie machen Sie das bloß?; **what does your father do?** was macht Ihr Vater (beruflich)?
◆**that's done it** (*inf*) da haben wir die Bescherung! (*inf*)
◆**that does it!** jetzt reichts mir!
(b) (= *provide service, product*) **what can I do for you?** was kann ich für Sie tun?; **sorry, we don't do lunches** wir haben leider keinen Mittagstisch; **we do a wide range of herbal teas** wir führen eine große Auswahl an Kräutertees; **who did the food for your reception?** wer hat bei Ihrem Empfang für das Essen gesorgt?
(c) (= *complete, finish*) (*in pret, ptp only*) **the work's done now** die Arbeit ist gemacht *or* fertig; **I haven't done** (*Brit*) *or* **I'm not done telling you what I think of you** mit dir bin ich noch lange nicht fertig; **done!** (= *agreed*) abgemacht!; **are you done?** (*inf*) bist du endlich fertig?

◆**over and done with it's all over and done with** (= *is finished*) das ist alles erledigt; (= *has happened*) das ist alles vorbei
(d) (= *study, cover*) durchnehmen; **I've never done any German** ich habe nie Deutsch gelernt
(e) (*Cook*) machen (*inf*); **to do the cooking** kochen; **how do you like your steak done?** wie möchten Sie Ihr Steak?; **well done** durch(gebraten); **is the meat done?** ist das Fleisch durch?
(f) (= *solve*) lösen
(g) (*Theat, Film*) **part** spielen; **to do a play** (= *put on*) ein Stück aufführen; **to do a film** (= *produce*) einen Film machen
(h) (= *take off, mimic*) nachmachen
(i) (= *visit, see sights of*) besuchen
(j) (*inf*) (= *take*) **heroin, cocaine etc** nehmen
(k) (*Aut etc*) fahren; **this car does** *or* **can do 100** das Auto fährt 100
(l) (= *be suitable for*) (*inf*) passen (*sb* jdm); (= *be sufficient for*) reichen (*sb* jdm); **that will do me nicely** das reicht allemal
(m) (= *cheat*) (*inf*) reinlegen (*inf*); **you've been done!** du bist reingelegt worden (*inf*)
(n) (*in prison*) (*inf*) **6 years etc** sitzen

3 INTRANSITIVE VERB
(a) (= *act*) **do as I do** mach es wie ich; **he did well to take advice** er tat gut daran, sich beraten zu lassen; **he did right** es war richtig von ihm; **he did right/well to go** es war richtig/gut, dass er gegangen ist
(b) (= *get on, fare*) **how are you doing?** wie gehts (Ihnen)?; **I'm not doing so badly** es geht mir gar nicht so schlecht; **he's doing well at school** er ist gut in der Schule; **his business is doing well** sein Geschäft geht gut
◆**how do you do?** (*on introduction*) guten Tag!
(c) (= *be suitable*) gehen; **that will never do!** das geht nicht!; **this room will do** das Zimmer ist in Ordnung
(d) (= *be sufficient*) reichen; **will £10 do?** reichen £ 10?
◆**to make do you'll have to make do with £10** £ 10 müssen Ihnen reichen
◆**that'll do!** jetzt reichts aber!

4 NOUN (*Brit inf*) (= *event*) Veranstaltung *f*; (= *party*) Fete *f* (*inf*)

5 PHRASAL VERBS
► **do away with** VI +PREP OBJ **(a)** abschaffen; *building* abreißen; **to do away with the need for sth** etw unnötig machen **(b)** (*inf*: = *kill*) umbringen
► **do for** VI +PREP OBJ (*inf*: = *finish off*) *person* fertig machen (*inf*); *project* zunichte machen; **to be done for** (*person*) erledigt sein (*inf*); (*project*) gestorben sein (*inf*)
► **do in** VT SEP (*inf*) **(a)** (= *kill*) um die Ecke bringen (*inf*) **(b)** (*usu pass:* = *exhaust*) **to be** *or* **feel done in** fertig sein (*inf*)
► **do over** VT SEP (*US: = do again*) noch einmal machen
► **do up 1** VI (*dress etc*) zugemacht werden **2** VT SEP **(a)** (= *fasten*) zumachen; *tie* binden **(b)** *house, room* (neu) herrichten
► **do with** VI +PREP OBJ **(a)** brauchen; **I could do with a cup of tea** ich könnte eine Tasse Tee vertragen (*inf*); **it could do with a clean** es müsste mal sauber gemacht werden **(b)** (*inf*: = *tolerate*) ausstehen **(c)** **he has to do with the steel industry** er hat mit der Stahlindustrie zu tun; **what has that got to do with it?** was hat das damit zu tun?; **that has** *or* **is nothing to do with you!** das geht Sie gar nichts an!; **it has something to do with her being adopted** es hat etwas damit zu tun, dass sie adoptiert wurde; **it has to do with …** dabei geht es um …; **money has a lot to do with it** Geld spielt eine große Rolle dabei **(d)** **what have you done with my gloves/your hair?** was hast du mit meinen Handschuhen/deinem Haar gemacht? **(e)** **he doesn't know what to do with himself** er weiß nicht, was er mit sich anfangen soll **(f)** **to be done with sb/sth** mit jdm/etw fertig sein
► **do without** VI +PREP OBJ **I can do without your advice** Sie können sich Ihren Rat sparen; **I could have done without that!** das hätte mir (wirklich) erspart bleiben können

doable ['duːəbl] ADJ (*inf*) machbar
d.o.b. ABBR *of* **date of birth**

doc [dɒk] N (*inf*) ABBR *of* **doctor**
docile ['dəʊsaɪl] ADJ sanftmütig; *animal* fromm
dock[1] [dɒk] N Dock *nt*; (*for berthing*) Kai *m*; **~s** *pl* Hafen *m*
dock[2] N (*Jur*) Anklagebank *f*; **to stand in the ~** auf der Anklagebank sitzen
dock[3] VT *wages* kürzen; *points* abziehen; **to ~ £100 off sb's wages** jds Lohn um £ 100 kürzen
docket ['dɒkɪt] N (a) (*on document, parcel etc*) Warenbegleitschein *m* (b) (= *customs certificate*) Zollinhaltserklärung *f*
dock: **dockland** N Hafenviertel *nt*; **dockyard** N Werft *f*
doctor ['dɒktə[r]] N (a) (*Med*) Arzt *m*, Ärztin *f*; **the ~'s** (= *surgery*) der Arzt; **to go to the ~** zum Arzt gehen; **to send for the ~** den Arzt holen; **he is a ~** er ist Arzt; **a woman ~** eine Ärztin; **to be under ~'s orders** in ärztlicher Behandlung sein; **it's just what the ~ ordered** (*fig inf*) das ist genau das Richtige (b) (*Univ etc*) Doktor *m*; **to get one's ~'s degree** promovieren, seinen Doktor machen; **Dear Doctor Smith** Sehr geehrter Herr Dr./Sehr geehrte Frau Dr. Smith
doctorate ['dɒktərɪt] N Doktorwürde *f*; **he's still doing his ~** er sitzt immer noch an seiner Doktorarbeit
document ['dɒkjʊmənt] **1** N Dokument *nt*; **~s against acceptance/payment** (*Fin*) Dokumente gegen Akzept/ Zahlung **2** VT dokumentieren; *case* beurkunden
documentary [ˌdɒkjʊ'mentərɪ] **1** ADJ dokumentarisch **2** N (*Film, TV*) Dokumentarfilm *m*
documentary credit N (*Fin*) Dokumentenakkreditiv *nt*
documentation [ˌdɒkjʊmən'teɪʃən] N Dokumentation *f*
docusoap ['dɒkjʊsəʊp] N (*TV*) Dokusoap *f*
doddle ['dɒdl] N (*Brit inf*) **it was a ~** es war ein Kinderspiel
dodge [dɒdʒ] **1** VT ausweichen (+*dat*); *tax* umgehen; (= *shirk*) *work, military service* sich drücken vor (+*dat*) **2** VI ausweichen; **to ~ out of the way** zur Seite springen; **to ~ behind a tree** hinter einen Baum springen
dodgy ['dɒdʒɪ] ADJ (*Brit inf*) (a) *person, business, practices* zwielichtig; *area, loan* zweifelhaft; *plan* unsicher; *situation* verzwickt (*inf*); **there's something ~ about him** er ist nicht ganz koscher (*inf*); **he's on ~ ground** er befindet sich auf unsicherem Boden (b) *back, heart* schwach; *tyre, car/boat etc part* defekt; **he has a ~ stomach from eating oysters** er hat Austern gegessen und sich damit den Magen verdorben
doe [dəʊ] N (*roe deer*) Reh *nt*; (*red deer*) Hirschkuh *f*
does [dʌz] 3RD PERS SING *of* **do**
doesn't ['dʌznt] CONTR *of* **does not**
dog [dɒg] **1** N (a) Hund *m* (b) (*fig*) **it's a ~'s life** es ist ein Hundeleben; **it's (a case of) ~ eat ~** es ist ein Kampf aller gegen alle; **you can't teach an old ~ new tricks** der Mensch ist ein Gewohnheitstier; **~'s dinner** *or* **breakfast** (*inf*) Schlamassel *m* (*inf*); **to work like a ~** (*inf*) wie ein Pferd arbeiten (*inf*) **2** VT verfolgen; **~ged by controversy/injury** von Kontroversen/Verletzungen verfolgt
dog: **dog biscuit** N Hundekuchen *m*; **dog breeder** N Hundezüchter(in) *m(f)*; **dog collar** N (*lit*) Hundehalsband *nt*; (*vicar's*) Kollar *nt*; **dog-eared** ['dɒgɪəd] ADJ mit Eselsohren; **dog food** N Hundefutter *nt*
dogged ['dɒgɪd] ADJ *person* zäh, beharrlich; *determination, resistance, pursuit* hartnäckig; *persistence* zäh
doggedly ['dɒgɪdlɪ] ADV beharrlich
doggie, doggy ['dɒgɪ] N (*inf*) Hündchen *nt*
doggone [dɒg'gɒn] INTERJ (*US inf*) **~ (it)!** verdammt noch mal! (*inf*)
doggoned [dɒg'gɒn(d)] ADJ (*US inf*) verdammt (*inf*)
doggy N (*inf*) = **doggie**
dog: **dog handler** N Hundeführer(in) *m(f)*; **dog licence**, (*US*) **dog license** N Hundemarke *f*
dogmatic [dɒg'mætɪk] ADJ dogmatisch; **to be very ~ about sth** in etw (*dat*) sehr dogmatisch sein
dog: **dog show** N Hundeausstellung *f*; **dog-tired** ADJ hundemüde
doing ['duːɪŋ] N (a) Tun *nt*; **this is your ~** das ist dein Werk; **it was none of my ~** ich hatte nichts damit zu tun; **that takes some ~** da gehört (schon) etwas dazu (b) **doings** PL (*inf*) Taten *pl*
do-it-yourself [ˌduːɪtjə'self] ADJ, N = **DIY**
dol ABBR *of* **dollar**

doldrums ['dɒldrəmz] PL **to be in the ~** (*people*) Trübsal blasen; (*business etc*) in einer Flaute stecken
dole [dəʊl] N (*Brit inf*) Arbeitslosenunterstützung *f*, Alu *f* (*inf*); **to go/be on the ~** stempeln (gehen)
➤ dole out VT SEP austeilen
doll [dɒl] N Puppe *f*
dollar ['dɒlə[r]] N Dollar *m*
dollar: **dollar area** N Dollarraum *m*; **dollar bill** N Dollarnote *f*; **dollar diplomacy** N Finanzdiplomatie *f*; **dollar gap** N Dollarlücke *f*; **dollar rate** N Dollarkurs *m*; **dollar sign** N Dollarzeichen *nt*
doll's house, (*US*) **doll house** N Puppenhaus *nt*
dolly ['dɒlɪ] N (*inf*) Püppchen *nt*
dolomite ['dɒləmaɪt] N Dolomit *m*; **the Dolomites** die Dolomiten *pl*
dolphin ['dɒlfɪn] N Delphin *m*
domain [də'meɪn] N (*fig*) Domäne *f*; (*Comput*) Domain *nt*
domain name N (*Comput*) Domainname *m*
dome [dəʊm] N (*Archit: on building*) Kuppel *f*

> Be careful! **dome** is not translated by the German word **Dom**.

domestic [də'mestɪk] ADJ (a) häuslich; **the ~ arrangements** die häusliche Situation; **~ quarrel** Ehekrach *m*; **~ appliances** Haushaltsgeräte *pl*; **for ~ use** für den Hausgebrauch (b) (*esp Pol, Comm*) inländisch; *problems* im Inland; *news* aus dem Inland; *issues* innenpolitisch; **~ trade** Binnenhandel *m*
domestically [də'mestɪkəlɪ] ADV (*esp Pol, Comm*) inländisch; *grown, produced* im Inland
domesticate [də'mestɪkeɪt] VT domestizieren
domesticated [də'mestɪkeɪtɪd] ADJ domestiziert; *person* häuslich
domestic: **domestic economy** N (*Pol*) Binnenwirtschaft *f*; **domestic flight** N Inlandflug *m*; **domestic market** N (*Pol, Comm*) Binnenmarkt *m*; **domestic policy, domestic politics** N Innenpolitik *f*; **domestic rates** PL (*Brit Econ, Hist*) Kommunalabgaben *pl*; **domestic servant** N Hausangestellte(r) *mf*; **domestic violence** N Gewalt *f* in der Familie
domicile ['dɒmɪsaɪl] (*form*) **1** N (*Fin*) Erfüllungsort *m* **2** VT (*Fin*) domizilieren (*at* bei)
dominance ['dɒmɪnəns] N Vorherrschaft *f* (*over* über +*acc*); (*Biol*) Dominanz *f*
dominant ['dɒmɪnənt] ADJ dominierend; *gene* dominant; **to be ~** *or* **the ~ force in sth** etw dominieren
dominate ['dɒmɪneɪt] VTI dominieren
domination [ˌdɒmɪ'neɪʃən] N (Vor)herrschaft *f*
domineering [ˌdɒmɪ'nɪərɪŋ] ADJ herrisch; *mother-in-law etc also* herrschsüchtig
Dominican [də'mɪnɪkən] (*Geog*) **1** ADJ dominikanisch **2** N Dominikaner(in) *m(f)*
Dominican Republic N Dominikanische Republik
domino ['dɒmɪnəʊ] N, *pl* **-es** Domino(stein) *m*; **a game of ~es** ein Dominospiel *nt*
donate [dəʊ'neɪt] **1** VT spenden; *time* zur Verfügung stellen **2** VI spenden
donation [dəʊ'neɪʃən] N (= *act of giving*) Spenden *nt*; (= *gift*) Spende *f*; **to make a ~ of £10,000 £** 10.000 spenden
done [dʌn] **1** PTP *of* **do 2** ADJ (a) *work* erledigt; *vegetables* gar; *meat* durch; *cake* durchgebacken; **to get sth ~** etw fertig kriegen; **is it ~ yet?** ist es schon erledigt?; **~!** (= *agreed*) abgemacht!; (*inf*) **the butter is (all) ~** die Butter ist alle (b) (*Brit inf*) **I'm ~ (in)** ich bin geschafft (*inf*) (c) **it's not the ~ thing, that's not ~** das tut man nicht
donkey ['dɒŋkɪ] N Esel *m*
donkey's years ['dɒŋkɪzjɪəz] PL (*inf*) **she's been here for ~** (*inf*) sie ist schon eine Ewigkeit hier
donor ['dəʊnə[r]] N (*Med, to charity*) Spender(in) *m(f)*
donor card N Organspenderausweis *m*
don't [dəʊnt] CONTR *of* **do not**
donut ['dəʊnʌt] N (*esp US*) = **doughnut**
doodle ['duːdl] **1** VI Männchen malen **2** VT kritzeln **3** N Gekritzel *nt*

doom [duːm] ◼1 N (= *fate*) Schicksal *nt*; (= *ruin*) Verhängnis *nt*; **to send sb to his ~** jdn ins Verhängnis stürzen; **it's not all gloom and ~** so schlimm ist es ja alles gar nicht ◼2 VT verdammen; **to be ~ed** verloren sein; **~ed to failure** zum Scheitern verurteilt

door [dɔːʳ] N (a) Tür *f*; (= *entrance: to cinema etc*) Eingang *m*; **there's someone at the ~** da ist jemand an der Tür; **was that the ~?** hat es geklingelt/geklopft?; **to answer the ~** die Tür aufmachen; **to see sb to the ~** jdn zur Tür bringen; **to pay at the ~** (*Theat etc*) an der (Abend)kasse zahlen; **"~s open 2.20"** „Einlass 14.20 Uhr"; **three ~s away** drei Häuser weiter **(b)** (*phrases*) **by** *or* **through the back ~** durch ein Hintertürchen; **to have a foot** *or* **toe in the ~** mit einem Fuß drin sein; **to be at death's ~** an der Schwelle des Todes stehen (*geh*); **to show sb the ~** jdm die Tür weisen; **to shut** *or* **slam the ~ in sb's face** jdm die Tür vor der Nase zumachen; **out of ~s** im Freien; **behind closed ~s** hinter verschlossenen Türen

door IN CPDS Tür-; **doorbell** N Türklingel *f*; **there's the ~** es hat geklingelt; **doorhandle** N Türklinke *f*; (= *knob*) Türknauf *m*; **doorknob** N Türknauf *m*; **doorknocker** N Türklopfer *m*; **doorman** N (*of hotel*) Portier *m*; (*of nightclub etc*) Rausschmeißer *m*; **doormat** N Fußmatte *f*, (*fig*) Fußabtreter *m*; **doorstep** N Eingangsstufe *f*; **the bus stop is just on my ~** (*fig*) die Bushaltestelle ist direkt vor meiner Tür; **doorstep selling** N (*Brit*) Haustürverkauf *m*; **door-to-door** ADJ ATTR, **door to door** ADJ PRED **(a) ~ salesman** Vertreter *m*; **~ selling** Haustürverkauf *m* **(b)** *delivery* von Haus zu Haus; **police are carrying out ~ inquiries** die Polizei befragt alle Anwohner; **doorway** N (*of room*) Tür *f*; (*of building, shop*) Eingang *m*

dope [dəʊp] ◼1 N, NO PL (*inf*) Stoff *m* (*inf*), Drogen *pl*; (*Sport*) Aufputschmittel *nt* ◼2 VT dopen

dopehead [ˈdəʊphed] N (*inf*) Junkie *m* (*inf*)

dopey, dopy [ˈdəʊpɪ] ADJ (+ER) (*inf*) (= *stupid*) bekloppt (*inf*); (= *sleepy, half-drugged*) benebelt (*inf*)

dormant [ˈdɔːmənt] ADJ *volcano* untätig; *animal, plant, bank account* ruhend; *passion* schlummernd; **~ state** Ruhezustand *m*; **to remain ~** ruhen; (*disease, virus*) schlummern; **to lie ~** (*project, idea*) brachliegen; **~ partner** (*Comm*) stiller Partner

dormice [ˈdɔːmaɪs] PL *of* **dormouse**

dormitory [ˈdɔːmɪtrɪ] N Schlafsaal *m*; (*US: = building*) Wohnheim *nt*; **~ suburb** *or* **town** Schlafstadt *f*

dormouse [ˈdɔːmaʊs] N, *pl* **dormice** Haselmaus *f*

DOS [dɒs] (*Comput*) ABBR *of* **disk operating system** DOS *nt*

dosage [ˈdəʊsɪdʒ] N Dosis *f*

dose [dəʊs] ◼1 N (a) (*Med*) Dosis *f*; (*fig*) Ration *f*; **give him a ~ of medicine** gib ihm Medizin; **he needs a ~ of his own medicine** (*fig*) man sollte es ihm mit gleicher Münze heimzahlen; **in small/large ~s** (*fig*) in kleinen/großen Mengen; **she's all right in small ~s** sie ist nur (für) kurze Zeit zu ertragen **(b)** (*inf: = bout of illness*) Anfall *m*; **she's just had a ~ of the flu** sie hat gerade Grippe gehabt ◼2 VT *person* Arznei geben (+*dat*); **I've tried dosing myself with cough mixture** ich habe versucht, mich mit Hustensaft zu kurieren

Be careful! **dose** *is not translated by the German word* **Dose**.

dosser [ˈdɒsəʳ] N (*Brit inf*) Penner(in) *m(f)* (*inf*)

dot [dɒt] ◼1 N (a) Punkt *m* (b) **to arrive on the ~** auf die Minute pünktlich (an)kommen; **at 3 o'clock on the ~** haargenau um 3 Uhr ◼2 VT **to ~ted line** punktierte Linie; **to tear along the ~ted line** entlang der punktierten Linie abtrennen; **to sign on the ~ted line** (*fig*) formell zustimmen **(b)** (= *sprinkle*) verstreuen; **pictures ~ted around the room** im Zimmer verteilte Bilder

dotcom, dot.com [dɒtˈkɒm] N (*Comput*) Internetfirma *f*, Dotcom-Firma *f*

dot command N (*Comput*) Punktbefehl *m*

dote on [ˈdəʊtɒn] VI +PREP OBJ abgöttisch lieben

doting [ˈdəʊtɪŋ] ADJ **her ~ parents** ihre sie abgöttisch liebenden Eltern

dot matrix (printer) N Matrixdrucker *m*

dotty [ˈdɒtɪ] ADJ (+ER) (*Brit inf*) kauzig

double [ˈdʌbl] ◼1 ADV (a) doppelt so viel; *count* doppelt; **~ the size (of)** doppelt so groß (wie); **~ the amount** doppelt so viel; **we paid her ~ what she was getting before** wir zahlten ihr das Doppelte von dem, was sie vorher bekam **(b) to bend ~** sich krümmen; **she was bent ~ with laughter** sie krümmte sich vor Lachen; **to fold sth ~** etw einmal falten ◼2 ADJ (a) (= *twice as much*) doppelt; **~ taxation** Doppelbesteuerung *f* **(b)** (= *having two similar parts, in pairs*) Doppel-; **it is spelled with a ~ `p'** es wird mit zwei p geschrieben; **my phone number is 9, ~ 3, 2, 4** meine Telefonnummer ist neun drei drei zwei vier ◼3 N (a) (*twice*) das Doppelte **(b)** (= *person*) Doppelgänger(in) *m(f)*; (*Film, Theat*) Double *nt* **(c)** at the ~ (= *also Mil*) im Laufschritt; (*fig*) im Eiltempo; **on the ~** (*fig*) auf der Stelle ◼4 VT verdoppeln ◼5 VI (a) sich verdoppeln **(b)** (= *have two roles*) **this bedroom ~s as a study** dieses Schlafzimmer dient auch als Arbeitszimmer

▸ **double back** VI kehrtmachen

▸ **double over** VI = **double up**

▸ **double up** VI (= *bend over*) sich krümmen; (*with laughter*) sich biegen

double: **double act** N (*esp Theat*) (= *performers*) Zweigespann *nt*; (= *performance*) Zweiershow *f*; **double agent** N Doppelagent(in) *m(f)*; **double-barrelled name**, (*US*) **double-barreled name** N Doppelname *m*; **double-barrelled shotgun**, (*US*) **double-barreled shotgun** N doppelläufiges Gewehr; **double bass** N Kontrabass *m*; **double bed** N Doppelbett *nt*; **double-book** VT *room, seat* zweimal reservieren; *flight* zweimal buchen; **double check** N doppelte Überprüfung; **double-check** VTI noch einmal (über)prüfen; **double chin** N Doppelkinn *nt*; **double-click** (*Comput*) VTI doppelklicken (*on* auf +*acc*); **double cream** N Schlagsahne *f*; **double-decker** N Doppeldecker *m*; **double density** ADJ (*Comput*) mit doppelter Dichte; **double doors** PL Flügeltür *f*; **double Dutch** N (*esp Brit*) Kauderwelsch *nt*; **it was ~ to me** das waren für mich böhmische Dörfer; **double-edged** ADJ (*lit, fig*) zweischneidig; **tourism is ~ or is a ~ sword** der Tourismus ist ein zweischneidiges Schwert; **double entendre** [ˈduːblɒnˈtɒndrə] N (*esp Brit*) Zweideutigkeit *f*; **double figures** PL zweistellige Zahlen *pl*; **double glazing** N Doppelfenster *pl*; **double-header** N (*US Sport*) Doppelspieltag *m*; **double indemnity** N (*US Insur*) Verdoppelung der Lebensversicherungssumme bei Unfalltod; **double knot** N Doppelknoten *m*; **double life** N Doppelleben *nt*; **double meaning** N **it has a ~** es ist doppeldeutig; **double-park** VI in der zweiten Reihe parken; **double-quick** (*inf*) ◼1 ADV im Nu ◼2 ADJ **in ~ time** im Nu; **double room** N Doppelzimmer *nt*

doubles [ˈdʌblz] N SING *or* PL (*Sport*) Doppel *nt*; **to play ~** im Doppel spielen

double: **double-sided** ADJ (*Comput*) zweiseitig; **double-space** VT (*Typ*) mit doppeltem Zeilenabstand drucken; **double spacing** N doppelter Zeilenabstand; **double take** N **he did a ~** er musste zweimal hingucken; **double whammy** N Doppelschlag *m*; **double yellow lines** PL *gelbe Doppellinie am Fahrbahnrand zur Kennzeichnung des absoluten Halteverbots*

doubly [ˈdʌblɪ] ADV doppelt; **to work ~ hard** doppelt so hart arbeiten; **to make ~ sure (that ...)** ganz sichergehen(, dass ...); **~ so** umso mehr

doubt [daʊt] ◼1 N Zweifel *m*; **to have one's ~s as to** *or* **about sth** (so) seine Bedenken hinsichtlich einer Sache (*gen*) haben; **I have my ~s about her** ich habe bei ihr (so) meine Bedenken; **I have no ~s about taking the job** ich habe keine Bedenken, die Stelle anzunehmen; **there's no ~ about it** daran gibt es keinen Zweifel; **I have no ~ about it** ich bezweifle das nicht; **to cast ~ on sth** etw in Zweifel ziehen; **there is room for ~** es ist durchaus nicht sicher; **his reputation is in ~** sein Ruf wird infrage gestellt; **to be in little ~ as to sth** keine Bedenken hinsichtlich einer Sache (*gen*) haben; **I am in no ~ as to what** *or* **about what he means** ich bin mir völlig im Klaren darüber, was er meint; **the outcome is still in ~** das Ergebnis ist noch ungewiss; **when in ~** im Zweifelsfall; **no ~ he will come tomorrow** höchstwahrscheinlich kommt er morgen; **without (a) ~** ohne Zweifel ◼2 VT bezweifeln; *sb's honesty, truth of statement* anzweifeln; **to ~ sb's word** jds Wort anzweifeln; **I'm sorry I ~ed you** (*what* you said) es tut mir Leid, dass ich dir nicht geglaubt habe; (your loyalty etc) es tut mir Leid, dass ich an dir gezweifelt habe; **I don't ~ it** das bezweifle ich (auch gar) nicht; **I ~ whether he will come** ich bezweifle, dass er kommen wird

doubtful ['daʊtfʊl] ADJ **(a)** (usu pred: = unconvinced) unsicher; **I'm still ~** ich habe noch Bedenken; **to be ~ about sth** an etw (dat) zweifeln; **to be ~ about doing sth** Bedenken haben, ob man etw tun soll; **I was ~ whether I could ever manage it** ich bezweifelte, ob ich es je schaffen könnte **(b)** (= unlikely) unwahrscheinlich; **it is ~ that…** es ist unsicher or zweifelhaft, ob … **(c)** (= questionable) reputation fragwürdig; future, outcome ungewiss; taste, quality zweifelhaft; **information of ~ origin** zweifelhafte Informationen; **it is ~ whether this could be managed** es ist fraglich, ob das zu schaffen wäre; **~ account** (Fin) zweifelhafte Forderungen

doubtfully ['daʊtfəlɪ] ADV (= uncertainly) unsicher

dough [dəʊ] N **(a)** Teig m **(b)** (inf: = money) Kohle f (inf)

doughnut ['dəʊnʌt] N (Brit) Berliner (Pfannkuchen) m

dour ['dʊəʳ] ADJ verdrießlich

douse [daʊs] VT Wasser schütten über (+acc); **to ~ sb/sth in** or **with petrol** jdn/etw mit Benzin übergießen

dove¹ [dʌv] N (lit, fig) Taube f

dove² [dəʊv] (US) PRET of dive

dowdy ['daʊdɪ] ADJ (+ER) ohne jeden Schick

Dow-Jones average [daʊ'dʒəʊnz'ævəndʒ] N Dow-Jones-Index m

---

down [daʊn]

1 ADVERB	**3** ADJECTIVE
2 PREPOSITION	**4** TRANSITIVE VERB

1 ADVERB

> When **down** is an element in a phrasal verb, eg **get down, sit down, stand down, write down**, look up the verb.

(a) (indicating movement) (towards speaker) herunter; (away from speaker) hinunter; (downstairs) nach unten; **to jump down** herunter-/hinunterspringen; **on his way down from the summit** auf seinem Weg vom Gipfel herab/hinab; **on the way down to London** auf dem Weg nach London runter (inf); **all the way down to the bottom** bis ganz nach unten; **down!** (to dog) Platz!

◆**down with …!** nieder mit …!

(b) (indicating static position) unten; **down there** da unten; **I'll stay down here** ich bleibe hier unten; **don't kick a man when he's down** (fig) man soll jemanden nicht fertig machen, wenn er schon angeschlagen ist; **head down** mit dem Kopf nach unten; **I'll be down in a minute** ich komme sofort runter; **I've been down with flu** ich habe mit Grippe (im Bett) gelegen

(c) (= to or in another place) **he came down from London yesterday** er kam gestern aus London; **he's down at his brother's** er ist bei seinem Bruder; **he lives down South** er wohnt im Süden

(d) (= below previous level) **his temperature is down** sein Fieber ist zurückgegangen; **interest rates are down to/by 3%** der Zinssatz ist auf/um 3% gefallen; **he's down to his last £10** er hat nur noch £ 10; **they're still three goals down** sie liegen immer noch mit drei Toren zurück

(e) (in writing) **I've got it down in my diary** ich habe es in meinem Kalender notiert; **let's get it down on paper** schreiben wir es auf, halten wir es schriftlich fest; **to be down for the next race** für das nächste Rennen gemeldet sein; **it's down for next month** es steht für nächsten Monat auf dem Programm

(f) (indicating range or succession) **from the biggest down** vom Größten angefangen; **down through the ages** von jeher

◆**down to** (= until) bis zu; **from 1700 down to the present** von 1700 bis zur Gegenwart; **from the chairman (all the way) down to the doorman** vom Vorsitzenden bis (herunter) zum Pförtner

(g) (indicating responsibility)

◆**to be down to sb/sth** an jdm/etw liegen; **it's down to you to decide** die Entscheidung liegt bei Ihnen

(h) (as deposit) **I've put down a deposit on a new bike** ich habe eine Anzahlung für ein neues Fahrrad gemacht

2 PREPOSITION

(a) (indicating movement downwards) **to go down the hill** etc den Berg etc hinuntergehen; **he ran his finger down the list** er ging (mit dem Finger) die Liste durch

(b) (at a lower part of) **he's already halfway down the hill** er ist schon auf halbem Wege nach unten; **the other skiers were further down the slope** die anderen Skifahrer waren weiter unten; **she lives just down the street** sie wohnt ein Stückchen weiter die Straße entlang

(c) (= along) **he was walking down the street** er ging die Straße entlang; **if you look down this road, you can see …** wenn Sie diese Straße hinunterblicken, können Sie … sehen

(d) (Brit inf) **he's gone down the pub** er ist in die Kneipe gegangen; **she's down the shops** sie ist einkaufen gegangen

3 ADJECTIVE (inf)

(a) (= depressed) **he was (feeling) a bit down** er fühlte sich ein wenig down (inf) or niedergeschlagen

(b) (= not working) **to be down** außer Betrieb sein; (Comput) abgestürzt sein

4 TRANSITIVE VERB beer etc runterkippen (inf); **to down tools** die Arbeit niederlegen

down: down-and-out N Penner(in) m(f) (inf); **down arrow** N (Comput) Abwärtspfeil m; **downcast** ADJ entmutigt; **downfall** N Sturz m; (of empire) Fall m; (= cause of ruin: drink etc) Ruin m; **downgrade** VT hotel, job herunterstufen; person degradieren; **down-hearted** ADJ entmutigt

downhill 1 ADV (lit, fig) bergab; **to go ~** heruntergehen/ -fahren; (road) bergab gehen; **the economy is going ~** mit der Wirtschaft geht es bergab; **things just went steadily ~** es ging immer mehr bergab **2** ADJ **(a)** road bergab führend; **~ slope** Abhang m; **the path is ~ for two miles** der Weg führt zwei Meilen bergab; **it's all ~ (after thirty)** es geht (ab dreißig) nur noch bergab; **it was ~ all the way** or **all ~ after that** danach wurde alles viel einfacher **(b)** (Ski) **~ skiing** Abfahrtslauf m **3** N (Ski) Abfahrtslauf m

Downing Street ['daʊnɪŋ,striːt] N die Downing Street; (= the government) die britische Regierung

---

DOWNING STREET

Downing Street ist die Straße in London, in der sich der offizielle Wohnsitz des britischen Premierministers (Nr. 10) und der des Finanzministers (Nr. 11) befinden. Downing Street, oder auch Number Ten oder Ten Downing Street wird in den Medien häufig als Synonym für den Premierminister, die Regierung oder das Kabinett verwendet: „Downing Street has strenuously denied these allegations", „A statement from Number Ten is expected later this afternoon".

---

down: download (Comput) **1** VT (herunter)laden **2** VI **it won't ~** Runterladen ist nicht möglich **3** ATTR font, character ladbar; **downloadable** ADJ (Comput) herunterladbar; **down-market 1** ADJ product für den Massenmarkt; service weniger anspruchsvoll; **this restaurant is more ~** dieses Restaurant ist weniger exklusiv **2** ADV **to go ~** sich auf den Massenmarkt ausrichten; **down payment** N (Fin) Anzahlung f; **downpour** N Wolkenbruch m; **downright 1** ADV ausgesprochen; rude, disgusting geradezu **2** ADJ **a ~ lie** eine glatte Lüge; **downriver** ADV flussabwärts (from von); **~ from Bonn** unterhalb von Bonn; **downshift** VI in eine schlechter bezahlte Stelle überwechseln, runterschalten (inf); **downsize** ['daʊnsaɪz] **1** VT verkleinern; **~d economy** durch Rationalisierung und Stellenabbau gekennzeichnete wirtschaftliche Lage **2** VI sich verkleinern; **downsizing** (Comm, Comput) N Downsizing nt

Down's syndrome ['daʊnz'sɪndrəʊm] (Med) **1** N Downsyndrom nt **2** ATTR **a ~ baby** ein an Downsyndrom leidendes Kind

down: downstairs 1 ADV go, come nach unten; fall die Treppe hinunter; be, sleep, eat etc unten **2** ['daʊnsteəz] ADJ **the ~ phone** das Telefon unten; **~ flat** (Brit) or **apartment** Parterrewohnung f; **our ~ neighbours** (Brit) or **neighbors** (US) die Nachbarn unter uns; **the woman ~** die Frau von unten **3** N **the ~** das Erdgeschoss; **downstate** (*US*) **1** ADJ im Süden (des Bundesstaates); **in ~ Illinois** im Süden von Illinois **2** ADV *move, go* in den Süden (des Bundesstaates); *live, be situated* im Süden (des Bundesstaates); **downstream** ADV flussabwärts, stromabwärts (*from* von); **down-to-earth** ADJ nüchtern; **he's very ~** er steht mit beiden Füßen auf der Erde; **downtown** (*esp US*) **1** ADV *go* in die (Innen)stadt; *live, be situated* in der (Innen)stadt **2** ADJ **~ Chicago** die Innenstadt von Chicago; **the ~ area** das Stadtzentrum; **downtrend** N (*Econ*) Abwärtstrend *m*; **to be in** *or* **on a ~** sich im Abwärtstrend befinden; **downtrodden** ADJ unterdrückt; **downturn** N (*in prices, business*) Rückgang *m*; **to take a ~** zurückgehen; **his fortunes took a ~** sein Glücksstern sank; **down under** (*inf*) **1** N (= *Australia*) Australien *nt*; (= *New Zealand*) Neuseeland *nt* **2** ADV *be, live* in Australien/Neuseeland; *go* nach Australien/Neuseeland

downward ['daʊnwəd] **1** ADV (*also* **~s**) nach unten; **to work ~(s)** sich nach unten vorarbeiten; **to slope gently ~(s)** sanft abfallen; **face ~(s)** (*person*) mit dem Gesicht nach unten; (*book*) mit der aufgeschlagenen Seite nach unten; **everyone from the Queen ~(s)** jeder, bei der Königin angefangen **2** ADJ *stroke* nach unten; **~ movement** Abwärtsbewegung *f*; **~ slope** Abhang *m*; **~ gradient** (*Brit*) *or* **grade** (*US*) Gefälle *nt*; **~ trend** Abwärtstrend *m*; **~ spiral** stetiger stetiger Rückgang; **the dollar resumed its ~ path** *or* **slide against the yen** der Dollar fiel weiter gegen den Yen; **a ~ slide in prices** ein Preisrutsch *m*; **to take a ~ turn** sich zum Schlechteren wenden

downwind ['daʊnwɪnd] ADV in Windrichtung (*of, from* +*gen*)

dowry ['daʊrɪ] N Mitgift *f*

dowse [daʊs] VT = **douse**

doz ABBR *of* **dozen**

doze [dəʊz] **1** N Nickerchen *nt*; **to have a ~** dösen **2** VI (vor sich hin) dösen

➤ **doze off** VI einnicken

dozen ['dʌzn] N Dutzend *nt*; **80p a ~** 80 Pence das Dutzend; **two ~ eggs** zwei Dutzend Eier; **half a ~** sechs, ein halbes Dutzend; **~s** jede Menge; (*fig inf*) eine ganze Menge; **~s of times** (*inf*) x-mal (*inf*); **there were ~s of incidents like this one** (*inf*) es gab dutzende solcher Vorfälle; **~s of people came** (*inf*) dutzende von Leuten kamen

D/P ABBR *of* **documents against payment**

dpi (*Comput*) ABBR *of* **dots per inch** dpi

dpt ABBR *of* **department** Abt.

Dr ABBR *of* **doctor** Dr.

drab [dræb] ADJ (+ER) trist; *life, activities* eintönig

drably ['dræblɪ] ADV *dressed* trist; *painted* in tristen Farben

draft [drɑːft] **1** N **(a)** Entwurf *m* **(b)** (*Fin, Comm*) Wechsel *m* **(c)** (*US Mil*: = *conscription*) Einberufung *f* (zum Wehrdienst) **(d)** (*US*) = **draught** **(e)** (*Comput*) Draft(druck) *m* **2** VT **(a)** entwerfen **(b)** (*US Mil*) einziehen, einberufen (*into* zu); **he was ~ed into the England squad** er wurde für die englische Nationalmannschaft aufgestellt **3** ATTR (*Comput*) **~ mode** Draft-Modus *m*

draft: draft budget N Haushaltsentwurf *m*; **draft letter** N Entwurf *m* eines/des Briefes; **draft version** N Entwurf *m*

drag [dræg] **1** N **(a)** **it was a long ~ up to the top of the hill** es war ein langer, mühseliger Aufstieg zum Gipfel **(b)** (*inf*) **what a ~!** (*boring*) Mann, ist der/die/das langweilig! (*inf*); (*nuisance*) so'n Mist (*inf*) **(c)** (*inf*: = *pull on cigarette*) Zug *m* (*on, at* an +*dat*); **give me a ~** lass mich mal ziehen **(d)** (*inf*: = *women's clothing worn by men*) (von Männern getragene) Frauenkleidung *f*; **in ~** in Frauenkleidung **(e)** (*US inf*: = *street*) **the main ~** die Hauptstraße **2** VT schleppen; **he ~ged her out of/into the car** er zerrte sie aus dem/in das Auto; **she ~ged me to the library every Friday** sie schleppte mich jeden Freitag in die Bücherei; **the dog was ~ging its broken leg (behind it)** der Hund schleifte sein gebrochenes Bein hinter sich her; **to ~ one's feet** *or* **heels** (*fig*) die Sache schleifen lassen **3** VI **(a)** (= *trail along*) schleifen; (*feet*) schlurfen **(b)** (*fig*) (*time, work*) sich hinziehen; (*play, book*) sich in die Länge ziehen; (*conversation*) sich (mühsam) hinschleppen

➤ **drag along** VT SEP mitschleppen

➤ **drag apart** VT SEP auseinander zerren

➤ **drag away** VT SEP (*lit, fig*) wegschleppen; **if you can drag yourself away from the television for a second ...** wenn du dich vielleicht mal für eine Sekunde vom Fernsehen losreißen könntest ...

➤ **drag behind 1** VT +PREP OBJ **to drag sb/sth behind one** jdn/etw hinter sich (*dat*) herschleppen **2** VI (*fig*) zurückbleiben

➤ **drag down** VT SEP (*lit*) herunterziehen; (*fig*) mit sich ziehen

➤ **drag in** VT SEP (*lit*) hineinziehen; **look what the cat's dragged in** (*fig inf*) sieh mal, wer da kommt

➤ **drag off** VT SEP (*lit*) wegzerren; (*fig*) wegschleppen; **to drag sb off to a concert** jdn in ein Konzert schleppen

➤ **drag on** VI sich in die Länge ziehen; (*meeting, lecture also*) sich hinziehen; (*conversation*) sich hinschleppen

➤ **drag out** VT SEP **(a)** *meeting, discussion etc* in die Länge ziehen **(b)** **eventually I had to drag it out of him** schließlich musste ich es ihm aus der Nase ziehen (*inf*)

➤ **drag up** VT SEP *scandal, story* ausgraben

drag: drag and drop N (*Comput*) Drag-and-Drop *nt*; **drag artist** N (*inf*) Travestiekünstler(in) *m(f)*; **drag lift** N (*Ski*) Schlepplift *m*

dragon ['drægən] N (*lit, fig inf*) Drache *m*

dragonfly ['drægən,flaɪ] N Libelle *f*

drag queen N (*inf*) Tunte *f* (*inf*)

drain [dreɪn] **1** N **(a)** (= *pipe*) Rohr *nt*; (*under sink etc*) Abfluss *m*; (*under the ground*) Kanalisationsrohr *nt*; (= *cover*) Rost *m*; **open ~** (Abfluss)rinne *f*; **to pour money down the ~** (*fig inf*) das Geld zum Fenster hinauswerfen; **I had to watch all our efforts go down the ~** ich musste zusehen, wie alle unsere Bemühungen zunichte (gemacht) wurden **(b)** (*on resources etc*) Belastung *f* (*on* +*gen*) **2** VT **(a)** (*lit*) drainieren; *land* entwässern; *vegetables* abgießen; (= *let ~*) abtropfen lassen; *boiler, radiator* das Wasser ablassen aus **(b)** (*fig*) **to feel ~ed** sich ausgelaugt fühlen **(c)** (= *empty*) *glass* leeren **3** VI **(a)** (*vegetables, dishes*) abtropfen **(b)** (*fig*) **the blood/colour** (*Brit*) **or color** (*US*) **~ed from his face** das Blut/die Farbe wich aus seinem Gesicht

➤ **drain away** VI (*liquid*) ablaufen; (*strength*) dahinschwinden; (*tension*) sich lösen

➤ **drain off** VT SEP abgießen; (= *let drain*) abtropfen lassen

drain: draining board, (*US*) **drain board** N Ablauf *m*; **drainpipe** N Abflussrohr *nt*

drama ['drɑːmə] N Drama *nt*; (*no pl*: = *quality of being dramatic*) Dramatik *f*; **to make a ~ out of a crisis** eine Krise dramatisieren

drama: drama queen N (*pej inf*) Schauspielerin *f* (*pej inf*); **drama school** N Schauspielschule *f*

dramatic [drəˈmætɪk] ADJ dramatisch

dramatically [drəˈmætɪkəlɪ] ADV dramatisch; *different* radikal; *effective* extrem

dramatize ['dræmətaɪz] VT dramatisieren

drank [dræŋk] PRET *of* **drink**

drape [dreɪp] **1** VT drapieren; *person* hüllen; **to ~ sth over sth** etw über etw (*acc*) drapieren **2** N **drapes** PL (*US*) Gardinen *pl*

drastic ['dræstɪk] ADJ drastisch; *consequences* schwerwiegend; *change, improvement* einschneidend; **to take ~ action** *or* **measures** drastische Maßnahmen ergreifen

drastically ['dræstɪkəlɪ] ADV drastisch; *change, different* radikal; **to go ~ wrong** total schief gehen

draught, (*US*) **draft** [drɑːft] N **(a)** (*Luft*)zug *m*; (= *through ~*) Durchzug *m*; (*for fire*) Zug *m*; **there's a terrible ~ in here** hier zieht es fürchterlich **(b)** (= *~ beer*) Fassbier *nt*; **on ~** vom Fass **(c)** **draughts** PL (*Brit*) (= *game*) Damespiel *nt*; (+*pl vb*: = *pieces*) Damesteine *pl* **(d)** (= *rough sketch*) = **draft**

draught: draught beer, (*US*) **draft beer** N Fassbier *nt*; **draughtboard** ['drɑːftbɔːd] N (*Brit*) Damebrett *nt*

draughty, (*US*) **drafty** ['drɑːftɪ] ADJ (+ER) zugig; **it's ~ in here** hier zieht es

draw¹ [drɔː], *pret* **drew**, *ptp* **drawn 1** VT (*lit, fig*) zeichnen; *line* ziehen; **we must ~ the line somewhere** (*fig*) irgendwo muss Schluss sein; **I ~ the line at cheating** (*personally*) Mogeln kommt für mich nicht in Frage; (*in others*) beim Mogeln hörts bei mir auf **2** VI zeichnen

draw² [drɔː]

1 TRANSITIVE VERB	**3** NOUN
2 INTRANSITIVE VERB	**4** PHRASAL VERBS

vb: pret **drew**, *ptp* **drawn**

1 TRANSITIVE VERB
(a) (*lit, fig*) ziehen; *bolt* zurückschieben; *curtains* (= *open*) aufziehen; (= *shut*) zuziehen; **he drew his chair nearer the fire** er rückte seinen Stuhl näher an den Kamin heran
(b) (= *bring*) bringen
(c) (= *take*) holen; **to draw inspiration from sb/sth/somewhere** sich von jdm/von etw/von irgendwas inspirieren lassen; **to draw strength from sth** Kraft aus etw schöpfen; **to draw comfort from sth** sich mit etw trösten
✦**to draw money/a salary/a pension to draw money from the bank** Geld (vom Konto) abheben; **to draw the dole/a big salary** Arbeitslosenunterstützung/ein großes Gehalt beziehen; **to draw one's pension** seine Rente bekommen
(d) (= *elicit*) **the play has drawn a lot of criticism** das Theaterstück hat viel Kritik auf sich (*acc*) gezogen
✦**to be drawn he refuses to be drawn** (= *will not speak*) aus ihm ist nichts herauszubringen; (= *will not be provoked*) er lässt sich auf nichts ein
(e) (= *attract*) *interest* erregen; *customer, crowd* anlocken; **to feel drawn toward(s) sb** sich zu jdm hingezogen fühlen
(f) (= *formulate*) *conclusion, comparison* ziehen; *distinction* treffen
(g) (= *tie*) (*Sport*) **to draw a match** unentschieden spielen
(h) (= *choose at random*) ziehen; **we've been drawn (to play) away** wir sind für ein Auswärtsspiel gezogen worden

2 INTRANSITIVE VERB
(a) (*person, time, event*) kommen; **he drew to one side** er ging/fuhr zur Seite; **to draw to an end** *or* **to a close** zu Ende gehen; **the two horses drew level** die beiden Pferde zogen gleich
✦**to draw near** herankommen (*to an +acc*); **he drew nearer** *or* **closer (to it)** er kam (immer) näher (heran); **Christmas is drawing nearer** Weihnachten rückt näher
(b) (*Sport*) unentschieden spielen; **they drew 2-2** sie trennten sich 2:2 unentschieden

3 NOUN
(a) (= *lottery*) Ziehung *f*; (*for sports competitions*) Auslosung *f*
(b) (= *tie*) Unentschieden *nt*; **the match ended in a draw** das Spiel endete unentschieden

4 PHRASAL VERBS
➤ **draw alongside** VI heranfahren/-kommen (*+prep obj* an *+acc*)
➤ **draw apart** VI (= *move away*) sich lösen
➤ **draw aside** VT SEP *person* beiseite nehmen; *curtains* zur Seite ziehen
➤ **draw away** VI **(a)** (= *move off*: *car etc*) losfahren; (*procession*) sich entfernen **(b)** (= *move ahead*: *runner etc*) davonziehen (*from sb* jdm) **(c)** (= *move away*: *person*) sich entfernen; **she drew away from him when he put his arm around her** sie rückte von ihm ab, als er den Arm um sie legte
➤ **draw back** **1** VI zurückweichen **2** VT SEP zurückziehen; *curtains* aufziehen
➤ **draw in** **1** VI (*train*) einfahren; (*car*) anhalten **2** VT SEP **(a)** *breath, air* einziehen **(b)** *crowds* anziehen
➤ **draw into** VT SEP (= *involve*) hineinziehen
➤ **draw off** **1** VI (*car*) losfahren **2** VT SEP *excess liquid* abgießen
➤ **draw on** **1** VI **as the night drew on** mit fortschreitender Nacht **2** VI +PREP OBJ (*also* **draw upon**) sich stützen auf (*+acc*); **the author draws on his experiences in the desert** der Autor schöpft aus seinen Erfahrungen in der Wüste
➤ **draw out** **1** VI (*train*) ausfahren; (*car*) herausfahren (*of* aus) **2** VT SEP **(a)** (= *take out*) herausziehen; *money* abheben **(b)** (= *prolong*) in die Länge ziehen **(c)** (*Fin*) *bill of exchange* ziehen auf (*+acc*)
➤ **draw together** VT SEP (*lit, fig*) miteinander verknüpfen

➤ **draw up** **1** VI (= *stop*: *car*) (an)halten **2** VT SEP **(a)** (= *formulate*) entwerfen; *will* aufsetzen; *list* aufstellen; (*Fin*) *bill of exchange* ausstellen **(b)** *chair* heranziehen
➤ **draw upon** VI +PREP OBJ = **draw on 2**

drawback ['drɔːbæk] N **(a)** Nachteil *m* **(b)** (*Comm*) Zollvergütung *f*
drawee [drɔːˈiː] N (*Fin*) Bezogene(r) *mf*
drawer N **(a)** [drɔːˈ] (*in desk etc*) Schublade *f* **(b)** ['drɔːəʳ] (*of cheque etc*) Aussteller(in) *m(f)*
drawing ['drɔːɪŋ] N Zeichnung *f*; **I'm no good at ~** ich bin nicht gut im Zeichnen, ich kann nicht gut zeichnen
drawing: **drawing board** N Reißbrett *nt*; **it's back to the ~** (*fig*) das muss noch einmal ganz neu überdacht werden; **drawing paper** N Zeichenpapier *nt*; **drawing pin** N (*Brit*) Reißzwecke *f*
drawl [drɔːl] **1** VI schleppend sprechen **2** VT schleppend aussprechen **3** N schleppende Sprache; **a southern ~** ein schleppender südlicher Dialekt
drawn [drɔːn] **1** PTP *of* **draw¹**, **draw²** **2** ADJ **(a)** *curtains* zugezogen; *blinds* heruntergezogen **(b)** (*from tiredness*) abgespannt; (*from worry*) abgehärmt **(c)** *match* unentschieden
dread [dred] **1** VT sich fürchten vor (*+dat*); **I'm ~ing Christmas this year** dieses Jahr graut es mir schon vor Weihnachten; **I ~ to think what may happen** ich wage nicht daran zu denken, was passieren könnte; **I ~** *or* **I'm ~ing seeing her again** ich denke mit Schrecken an ein Wiedersehen mit ihr; **he ~s going to the dentist** er hat schreckliche Angst davor, zum Zahnarzt zu gehen
2 N **a sense of ~** ein Angstgefühl *nt*; **the thought filled me with ~** bei dem Gedanken wurde mir angst und bange; **to live in ~ of being found out** in ständiger Angst davor leben, entdeckt zu werden
dreadful ['dredfʊl] ADJ schrecklich; *weather* furchtbar; **what a ~ thing to happen** wie furchtbar, dass das passieren musste; **to feel ~** (= *ill*) sich elend fühlen; **I feel ~ (about it)** (= *mortified*) es ist mir schrecklich peinlich
dreadfully ['dredfəlɪ] ADV schrecklich
dream [driːm], *vb: pret, ptp* **dreamt** (*Brit*) *or* **dreamed** **1** N Traum *m*; **to have a bad ~** schlecht träumen; **the whole business was like a bad ~** die ganze Angelegenheit war wie ein böser Traum; **sweet ~s!** träum was Schönes!, träume süß!; **to have a ~ about sb/sth** von jdm/etw träumen; **it worked like a ~** (*inf*) das ging wie im Traum; **she goes round in a ~** sie lebt wie im Traum; **to be in a ~** (*when awake*) (mit offenen Augen) träumen; **the woman of his ~s** die Frau seiner Träume, seine Traumfrau; **never in my wildest ~s did I think I'd win** ich hätte in meinen kühnsten Träumen nicht gedacht, dass ich gewinnen würde; **in your ~s!** (*inf*) das hättest du wohl gern!; **all his ~s came true** all seine Träume gingen in Erfüllung; **it was a ~ come true** es war ein Traum, der wahrgeworden war
2 VI (*lit, fig*) träumen (*about, of* von); **~ on!** (*inf*) träum du nur weiter!
3 VT (*lit, fig*) träumen; *dream* haben; **he ~s of being free one day** er träumt davon, eines Tages frei zu sein; **I would never have ~ed of doing such a thing** ich hätte nicht im Traum daran gedacht, so etwas zu tun; **I wouldn't ~ of it** das würde mir nicht im Traum einfallen; **I never ~ed (that) he would come** ich hätte mir nie träumen lassen, dass er kommen würde
4 ADJ ATTR Traum-
➤ **dream up** VT SEP (*inf*) sich (*dat*) ausdenken; **where did you dream that up?** wie bist du denn bloß darauf gekommen?
dreamer ['driːməʳ] N Träumer(in) *m(f)*
dreamily ['driːmɪlɪ] ADV verträumt
dreamt [dremt] (*Brit*) PRET, PTP *of* **dream**
dreamy ['driːmɪ] ADJ (+ER) verträumt
dreariness ['drɪərɪnɪs] N Trostlosigkeit *f*; (*of job, life*) Eintönigkeit *f*
dreary ['drɪərɪ] ADJ (+ER) trostlos; *job, life* eintönig; *play, book* langweilig
drench [drentʃ] VT durchnässen; **I'm absolutely ~ed** ich bin durch und durch nass; **to be ~ed in sweat** schweißgebadet sein

dress [dres] **1** N (*for woman*) Kleid *nt*
2 VT (a) *child* anziehen; *family* kleiden; **to get ~ed** sich anziehen; **to ~ sb in sth** jdm etw anziehen; **~ed in black** schwarz gekleidet; **~ed in a sailor's uniform** im Matrosenanzug; **he was ~ed in a suit** er trug einen Anzug (b) (*Cook*) *salad* anmachen; *food for table* anrichten; *chicken* bratfertig machen; **~ed crab** farcierter Krebs (c) *wound* verbinden **3** VI sich anziehen; **to ~ in black** sich schwarz kleiden; **to ~ for dinner** sich zum Essen umziehen
➤ **dress up 1** VI (a) (*in smart clothes*) sich fein machen (b) (*in fancy dress*) sich verkleiden; **he came dressed up as Santa Claus** er kam als Weihnachtsmann (verkleidet)

dress circle N erster Rang

dresser[1] ['dresə'] N **she's a stylish ~** sie kleidet sich stilvoll

dresser[2] N (a) Anrichte *f* (b) (*US*: = *dressing table*) Frisierkommode *f*

dressing ['dresɪŋ] N (a) (*Med*) Verband *m* (b) (*Cook*) Soße *f*, Dressing *nt*

dressing: dressing gown N Morgenmantel *m*; (*in towelling*) Bademantel *m*; **dressing room** N (*Theat*) (Künstler)garderobe *f*; (*Sport*) Umkleidekabine *f*; **dressing table** N Frisierkommode *f*

dress: dressmaker N (Damen)schneider(in) *m(f)*; **dressmaking** N Schneidern *nt*; **dress rehearsal** N (*lit, fig*) Generalprobe *f*; **dress sense** N **her ~ is appalling** sie zieht sich fürchterlich an

drew [dru:] PRET *of* **draw**[1], **draw**[2]

dribble ['drɪbl] **1** VI (a) (*liquids*) tropfen (b) (*baby, person*) sabbern; (*animal*) geifern (c) (*Sport*) dribbeln **2** VT (a) (*Sport*) **to ~ the ball** mit dem Ball dribbeln (b) (*baby etc*) kleckern; **he ~d milk down his chin** er kleckerte sich (*dat*) Milch übers Kinn **3** N (a) (*of water*) ein paar Tropfen (b) (*of saliva*) Tropfen *m*

dribs and drabs ['drɪbzən'dræbz] PL **in ~** kleckerweise (*inf*)

dried [draɪd] **1** PRET, PTP *of* **dry 2** ADJ getrocknet; *blood* eingetrocknet; **~ yeast** Trockenhefe *f*

dried: dried flowers PL Trockenblumen *pl*; **dried fruit** N Dörrobst *nt*

drier N = **dryer**

drift [drɪft] **1** VI (a) (*Naut, Aviat, snow*) treiben; (*sand*) wehen; **to ~ off course** abtreiben (b) (*fig: person*) sich treiben lassen; **to let things ~** die Dinge treiben lassen; **he was ~ing aimlessly along** (*in life etc*) er lebte planlos in den Tag hinein; **young people are ~ing away from the villages** junge Leute wandern aus den Dörfern ab; **the audience started ~ing away** das Publikum begann wegzugehen **2** VT treiben; (*wind*) *snow also* vor sich her treiben **3** N (a) (*of sand, snow*) Verwehung *f* (b) (= *tendency*) **the ~ of policy away from this reform** das grundsätzliche Abrücken von dieser Reform; **the ~ of support away from him** die nachlassende Unterstützung für ihn (c) (= *general meaning*) Tendenz *f*; **I caught the ~ of what he said** ich verstand, worauf er hinauswollte; **if you get my ~** wenn Sie mich richtig verstehen
➤ **drift off** VI **to drift off (to sleep)** einschlafen; (= *doze*) eindämmern

drill[1] [drɪl] **1** N Bohrer *m* **2** VT bohren; *teeth* anbohren **3** VI bohren; **to ~ for oil** nach Öl bohren

drill[2] N (*inf*: = *procedure*) **they all knew the ~** sie wussten alle, was sie tun mussten

drily ['draɪlɪ] ADV (= *with dry humour*) trocken; (= *unemotionally*) nüchtern

drink [drɪŋk], *vb*: *pret* **drank**, *ptp* **drunk 1** N (a) Getränk *nt*; **food and ~** Essen und Getränke; **may I have a ~?** kann ich etwas zu trinken haben?; **would you like a ~ of water?** möchten Sie etwas Wasser? (b) (*alcoholic*) Drink *m*; **have a ~!** trink doch was!; **can I get you a ~?** kann ich Ihnen etwas zu trinken holen?; **I need a ~!** ich brauche was zu trinken!; **he likes a ~** er trinkt gern (einen); **the ~s are on me** die Getränke zahle ich; **the ~s are on the house** die Getränke gehen auf Kosten des Hauses (c) NO PL (= *alcoholic liquor*) Alkohol *m*; **he has a ~ problem** er trinkt; **to be the worse for ~** betrunken sein; **to take to ~** zu trinken anfangen; **his worries drove him to ~** vor lauter

Sorgen fing er an zu trinken; **it's enough to drive you to ~!** da könnte man wirklich zum Trinker werden **2** VT trinken; **is the water fit to ~?** ist das Trinkwasser?, kann man das Wasser trinken?; **to ~ oneself into a stupor** sich sinnlos besaufen (*inf*) **3** VI trinken; **he doesn't ~** er trinkt nicht; **his father drank** sein Vater war Trinker; **to go out ~ing** einen trinken gehen; **one shouldn't ~ and drive** man soll nach dem Trinken nicht mehr fahren; **~ing and driving** Alkohol am Steuer; **to ~ to sb** auf jdn trinken; **to ~ to sth** auf etw (*acc*) trinken); **I'll ~ to that** darauf trinke ich
➤ **drink in** VT SEP (*fig*) (begierig) in sich aufnehmen
➤ **drink up** VI, VT SEP austrinken; **drink up!** trink aus!

drinkable ['drɪŋkəbl] ADJ trinkbar

drink: drink-driver N (*Brit*) angetrunkener Autofahrer, angetrunkene Autofahrerin; **drink-driving** (*Brit*) **1** N Trunkenheit *f* am Steuer **2** ATTR *charge, conviction* wegen Trunkenheit am Steuer; *campaign* gegen Trunkenheit am Steuer

drinker ['drɪŋkə'] N Trinker(in) *m(f)*; **he's a heavy ~** er ist ein starker Trinker

drinking ['drɪŋkɪŋ] **1** N Trinken *nt*; **there had been some heavy ~ at the party** auf der Party war viel getrunken worden; **his ~ caused his marriage to break up** an seiner Trunksucht ging seine Ehe in die Brüche; **underage ~** der Alkoholkonsum von Minderjährigen **2** ADJ Trink-; **~ habits** Trinkgewohnheiten *pl*; **~ bout** *or* **spree** Sauftour *f* (*inf*)

drinking: drinking chocolate N Trinkschokolade *f*; **drinking fountain** N Trinkwasserbrunnen *m*; **drinking glass** N Trinkglas *nt*; **drinking problem** N Alkoholproblem *nt*; **drinking water** N Trinkwasser *nt*

drip [drɪp] **1** VI tropfen; **to be ~ping with sweat** schweißgebadet sein; **to be ~ping with blood** vor Blut triefen; **sweat was ~ping off his forehead** der Schweiß triefte ihm von der Stirn **2** VT tropfen; **he was ~ping water all over the carpet** Wasser tropfte überall auf den Teppich **3** N (a) (= *sound*) Tropfen *nt* (b) (= *drop*) Tropfen *m* (c) (*Med*) Tropf *m*; **to be on a ~** am Tropf hängen (d) (*inf: person*) Waschlappen *m* (*inf*)

dripping ['drɪpɪŋ] **1** ADJ (a) **~ (wet)** tropfnass (b) *tap* tropfend; *gutter* undicht **2** N Tropfen *nt*

drippy ['drɪpɪ] ADJ (+ER) (*US inf*: = *rainy*) regnerisch

drive [draɪv], *vb*: *pret* **drove**, *ptp* **driven 1** N (a) (*Aut*) (Auto)fahrt *f*; **to go for a ~** ein bisschen (raus)fahren; **he took her for a ~ in his new car** er machte mit ihr eine Spazierfahrt in seinem neuen Auto; **it's about one hour's ~ from London** es ist etwa eine Stunde Fahrt von London (entfernt) (b) (*also* **~way**) Einfahrt *f*; (*longer*) Auffahrt *f* (c) (*Psych etc*) Trieb *m*; **sex ~** Sexualtrieb *m* (d) (= *energy*) Schwung *m*, Elan *m* (e) (*Comm, Pol etc*) Aktion *f*; **recruitment ~** Anwerbungskampagne *f* (f) (*Mech*) Antrieb *m*; **front-wheel/rear-wheel ~** Vorderrad-/Hinterradantrieb *m* (g) (*Aut*) Steuerung *f*; **left-hand ~** Linkssteuerung *f* (h) (*Comput*) Laufwerk *nt* **2** VT (a) treiben; **to ~ sb out of the country** jdn aus dem Land (ver)treiben; **to ~ a nail into sth** einen Nagel in etw (*acc*) treiben; **to ~ sb round the bend** (*Brit inf*) *or* **mad** jdn verrückt machen; **to ~ sb to murder** jdn zum Mord treiben (b) *vehicle, passenger* fahren; **he ~s a taxi (for a living)** er ist Taxifahrer; **I'll ~ you home** ich fahre Sie nach Hause (c) *motor* (*belt, shaft*) antreiben; (*electricity, fuel*) betreiben; (*Comput*) steuern (d) (= *force to work hard*) hart herannehmen **3** VI (a) fahren; **can you** *or* **do you ~?** fahren Sie Auto?; **he's learning to ~** er lernt Auto fahren; **to ~ at 50 km an hour** mit 50 km in der Stunde fahren; **did you come by train? – no, we drove** sind Sie mit der Bahn gekommen? – nein, wir sind mit dem Auto gefahren; **it's cheaper to ~** mit dem Auto ist es billiger (b) (= *move violently*) schlagen, peitschen; **the rain was driving into our faces** der Regen peitschte uns (*dat*) ins Gesicht
➤ **drive along 1** VI (*vehicle, person*) dahinfahren **2** VT SEP (*wind, current*) (voran)treiben
➤ **drive at** VI +PREP OBJ (*fig*: = *mean*) hinauswollen auf (+*acc*)

➤ drive away 1 VI (*car, person*) wegfahren **2** VT SEP (*lit, fig*) *person, cares* vertreiben

➤ drive back 1 VI (*car, person*) zurückfahren **2** VT SEP **(a)** (= *cause to retreat*) zurückdrängen **(b)** (= *convey back in vehicle*) zurückfahren

➤ drive home VT SEP *nail* einschlagen; *argument* einhämmern

➤ drive in 1 VI (hinein)fahren; **he drove into the garage** er fuhr in die Garage **2** VT SEP *nail* (hin)einschlagen; *screw* (r)eindrehen

➤ drive off 1 VI abfahren **2** VT SEP **(a)** *person, enemy* vertreiben **(b) he was driven off in an ambulance** er wurde in einem Krankenwagen weggebracht *or* abtransportiert

➤ drive on VI weiterfahren

➤ drive out 1 VI hinausfahren **2** VT SEP *person* hinaustreiben

➤ drive over 1 VI hinüberfahren **2** VT ALWAYS SEPARATE (*in car*) hinüberfahren

➤ drive up 1 VI vorfahren **2** VT *prices* in die Höhe treiben

drive: **drive-in 1** ADJ ~ **cinema** (*esp Brit*) Autokino *nt*; ~ **bank** Bank *f* mit Autoschalter; ~ **restaurant** Drive-in-Restaurant *nt*; **to watch a ~ movie** sich (*dat*) einen Film im Autokino ansehen **2** N (= *restaurant*) Drive-in *m*

drivel ['drɪvl] N (*pej*) Blödsinn *m*

driven ['drɪvn] PTP *of* **drive**

-driven ['drɪvn] ADJ -betrieben; **battery-driven** batteriebetrieben; **computer-driven** computergesteuert; **steam-driven train** Zug *m* mit Dampflokomotive

driver ['draɪvəʳ] N **(a)** Fahrer(in) *m(f)*; (*Brit: of locomotive*) Führer(in) *m(f)*; ~**'s seat** (*lit*) Fahrersitz *m* **(b)** (*Comput*) Treiber *m*

driver's license N (*US*) Führerschein *m*; *see also* **driving licence**

drive: **drive-through**, (*esp US*) **drive-thru 1** N Drive-in *m* **2** ADJ *restaurant* Drive-in-; *drugstore* mit Autoschalter; **driveway** N Auffahrt *f*; (*longer*) Zufahrtsstraße *f*

driving ['draɪvɪŋ] **1** N Fahren *nt*; **I don't like ~** ich fahre nicht gern (Auto) **2** ADJ *ambition* brennend; **to be the ~ force behind sth** die treibende Kraft bei etw sein **(b)** ~ **rain** peitschender Regen; ~ **snow** Schneetreiben *nt*

driving: **driving conditions** PL Straßenverhältnisse *pl*; **driving instructor** N Fahrlehrer(in) *m(f)*; **driving lesson** N Fahrstunde *f*; **driving licence** N (*Brit*) Führerschein *m*

driving: **driving mirror** N Rückspiegel *m*; **driving offence**, (*US*) **driving offense** N Verkehrsdelikt *nt*; **driving school** N Fahrschule *f*; **driving seat** N Fahrersitz *m*; **to be in the ~** (*fig*) die Zügel in der Hand haben; **driving test** N Fahrprüfung *f*

drizzle ['drɪzl] **1** N Nieselregen *m* **2** VI nieseln **3** VT (*pour over*) träufeln; ~ **oil over the salad** Öl auf den Salat träufeln

drizzly ['drɪzlɪ] ADJ **it's ~** es nieselt

drone [drəʊn] **1** N (*of bees*) Summen *nt*; (*of engine, aircraft*) Brummen *nt* **2** VI **(a)** (*bee*) summen; (*engine, aircraft*) brummen **(b)** (*also ~ away or on*) eintönig sprechen; **he ~d on and on for hours** er redete stundenlang in seinem monotonen Tonfall

drool [druːl] VI sabbern; (*animal*) geifern

➤ drool over VI +PREP OBJ richtig verliebt sein in (+*acc*); **he sat there drooling over a copy of Playboy** er geilte sich an einem Playboyheft auf (*sl*)

droop [druːp] VI **(a)** (*lit*) (*shoulders*) hängen; (*head*) herunterfallen; (*eyelids*) herunterhängen; (*with sleepiness*) zufallen; (*flowers*) die Köpfe hängen lassen **(b)** (*fig*) erlahmen; **his spirits were beginning to ~** sein Mut begann zu schwinden

drooping ['druːpɪŋ] ADJ *shoulders, breasts, leaves, tail* hängend; *hand, branches, eyelids* herunterhängend; *moustache* nach unten hängend; *flowers* welk

droopy ['druːpɪ] ADJ schlaff; *tail* herabhängend; *moustache* nach unten hängend; *eyelids* herunterhängend

---

drop [drɒp]

1 NOUN	**3** INTRANSITIVE VERB
2 TRANSITIVE VERB	**4** PHRASAL VERBS

1 NOUN
(a) (*of liquid*) Tropfen *m*; **a drop of blood** ein Tropfen *m* Blut; **just a drop for me** für mich nur einen Tropfen; **a drop of wine?** ein Schlückchen *nt* Wein?; **it's a drop in the ocean** *or* **bucket** (*fig*) das ist ein Tropfen auf den heißen Stein
(b) (*in temperature, prices*) Rückgang *m* (*in gen*); (*sudden*) Sturz *m* (*in gen*); (*in blood pressure*) Absinken *nt* (*in gen*); **a drop in prices** ein Preisrückgang *m*/-sturz *m*; **20% is quite a drop** 20%, das ist stark gefallen; **a sudden drop in temperature** ein plötzlicher Temperaturabfall
(c) (= *difference in level*) Höhenunterschied *m*; **there's a drop of ten feet down to the ledge** bis zu dem Felsvorsprung geht es zehn Fuß hinunter; **it was a sheer drop from the top of the cliff into the sea** die Klippen fielen schroff zum Meer ab
(d) (*of supplies, arms*) Abwurf *m*

2 TRANSITIVE VERB
(a) (= *cause to fall in drops*) *liquid* tropfen
(b) (= *allow to fall*) fallen lassen; *bomb, supplies, pamphlets* abwerfen; **I dropped my watch** meine Uhr ist runtergefallen; **don't drop it!** lass es nicht fallen!; **he dropped his heavy cases on the floor** er setzte *or* stellte seine schweren Koffer auf dem Boden ab
(c) (= *set down*) (*from car*) *person* absetzen; *thing* abliefern
(d) (= *utter casually*) *remark, name* fallen lassen; *clue* geben; *hint* machen; **he let drop that he was going to get married** (*by mistake*) es rutschte ihm raus, dass er heiraten wollte (*inf*); (*deliberately*) er erwähnte so nebenbei, dass er heiraten wollte
(e) (= *send*) schreiben; **to drop sb a note** *or* **a line** jdm ein paar Zeilen schreiben
(f) (= *omit*) auslassen; (*deliberately*) weglassen (*from* in +*dat*); *programme* absetzen; **the paper refused to drop the story** die Zeitung weigerte sich, die Geschichte fallen zu lassen
(g) (= *abandon*) aufgeben; *idea, plan, candidate, friend* fallen lassen; *conversation* abbrechen; *boyfriend* Schluss machen mit; (*Jur*) *case* niederschlagen; **you'd better drop the idea** schlagen Sie sich (*dat*) das aus dem Kopf; **to drop sb from a team** jdn aus einer Mannschaft nehmen; **let's drop the subject** lassen wir das Thema; **drop it!** (*inf*) hör auf (damit)!; **drop everything (and come here immediately)!** (*inf*) lass alles stehen und liegen (und komm sofort her)!

3 INTRANSITIVE VERB
(a) (= *drip*) (herunter)tropfen
(b) (= *fall*) (*object*) (herunter)fallen; (*rate, temperature etc*) sinken; (*wind*) sich legen; (*prices*) fallen
(c) (*to the ground*) (*person*) fallen; **to drop to the ground** sich zu Boden fallen lassen; **I'm ready to drop** (*inf*) ich bin zum Umfallen müde (*inf*); **she danced till she dropped** (*inf*) sie tanzte bis zum Umfallen; **to drop dead** tot umfallen; **drop dead!** (*inf*) geh zum Teufel! (*inf*)
(d) (= *end*) (*conversation etc*) aufhören; **to let sth drop** etw auf sich beruhen lassen; **shall we let it drop?** sollen wir es darauf beruhen lassen?

4 PHRASAL VERBS
➤ drop back VI zurückfallen
➤ drop behind VI zurückfallen; **to drop behind sb** hinter jdn zurückfallen
➤ drop by VI (*inf*) vorbeikommen
➤ drop down 1 VI herunterfallen; **he dropped down behind the hedge** er duckte sich hinter die Hecke; **to drop down dead** tot umfallen; **he has dropped down to eighth overall** er ist insgesamt auf den achten Platz zurückgefallen **2** VT SEP fallen lassen

➤ **drop in** VI (*inf*) vorbeikommen; **I've just dropped in for a minute** ich wollte nur mal kurz hereinschauen

➤ **drop off** **1** VI **(a)** (= *fall down*) abfallen; (= *come off: handle etc*) abgehen **(b)** (= *fall asleep*) einschlafen; (*for brief while*) einnicken **(c)** (*sales*) zurückgehen; (*speed, interest, popularity*) nachlassen **2** VT SEP *person* absetzen; *parcel* abliefern

➤ **drop out** VI **(a)** (*of box etc*) herausfallen (*of* aus) **(b)** (*from competition etc*) ausscheiden (*of* aus); **to drop out of a race** (*before it*) an einem Rennen nicht teilnehmen; (*during it*) aus dem Rennen ausscheiden; **he dropped out of the philosophy course** er gab den Kurs in Philosophie auf; **to drop out of society** aus der Gesellschaft aussteigen (*inf*); **to drop out of school** (*Brit*) die Schule vorzeitig verlassen; (*US: out of university*) die Universität vorzeitig verlassen

➤ **drop over** VI (*inf*) vorbeikommen

---

drop: **drop-in centre** N (*Brit*) Tagesstätte *f*; **dropout** N (*from society*) Aussteiger(in) *m(f)* (*inf*); (*pej*) Asoziale(r) *mf*; (= *university ~*) Studienabbrecher(in) *m(f)*

droppings [ˈdrɒpɪŋz] PL Kot *m*

drought [draʊt] N Dürre *f*

drove¹ [drəʊv] N (*of people*) Schar *f*; **they came in ~s** sie kamen in hellen Scharen

drove² PRET *of* **drive**

drown [draʊn] **1** VI ertrinken **2** VT **(a)** ertränken; **to be ~ed** ertrinken; **to ~ one's sorrows (in drink)** seine Sorgen (im Alkohol) ertränken **(b)** (*also ~ out*) *noise, voice* übertönen; *speaker* niederschreien

drowning [ˈdraʊnɪŋ] ADJ ertrinkend

drowse [draʊz] VI (vor sich (*acc*) hin) dösen

drowsily [ˈdraʊzɪlɪ] ADV schläfrig; (*after sleep*) verschlafen

drowsiness [ˈdraʊzɪnɪs] N Schläfrigkeit *f*; (*after sleep*) Verschlafenheit *f*; **to cause ~** schläfrig machen

drowsy [ˈdraʊzɪ] ADJ (+ER) schläfrig; (*after sleep*) verschlafen; *voice* verschlafen

drudgery [ˈdrʌdʒərɪ] N stumpfsinnige Plackerei; **it's sheer ~** es ist eine einzige Plackerei

drug [drʌg] **1** N **(a)** (*Med, Pharm*) Medikament *nt*; (*inducing unconsciousness*) Betäubungsmittel *nt*; (*Sport*) Dopingmittel *nt*; **he's on ~s** (*Med*) er muss Medikamente nehmen; **to put sb on ~s** jdm Medikamente verordnen **(b)** (= *addictive substance*) Droge *f*; **to be on ~s** drogensüchtig sein; **to take ~s** Drogen nehmen **2** VT (*Med*) *patient* Medikamente geben (+*dat*); (= *render unconscious*) betäuben

drug: **drug abuse** N Drogenmissbrauch *m*; **drug addict** N Drogensüchtige(r) *mf*; **drug addiction** N Drogensucht *f*; **drug dealer** N Drogenhändler(in) *m(f)*, Dealer(in) *m(f)* (*inf*)

drugged [drʌgd] ADJ **to be ~** unter Beruhigungsmitteln stehen; **he seemed ~** er schien wie betäubt

druggist [ˈdrʌgɪst] N (*US*) Drogist(in) *m(f)*

drug pusher N Dealer(in) *m(f)* (*inf*)

drugs: **drugs raid** N Drogenrazzia *f*; **drugs ring** N Drogen(händler)ring *m*; **drugs test** N Dopingtest *m*; **drugs testing** N Dopingkontrolle *f*

drug: **drugstore** N (*US*) Drugstore *m*; **drug taking** N Einnehmen *nt* von Drogen; **drug traffic, drug trafficking** N Drogenhandel *m*; **drug trafficker** N Drogenschieber(in) *m(f)*; **drug user** N Drogenbenutzer(in) *m(f)*

drum [drʌm] **1** N **(a)** (*Mus*) Trommel *f*; **Joe Jones on ~s** am Schlagzeug: Joe Jones; **the ~s** die Trommeln *pl*; (*pop, jazz*) das Schlagzeug **(b)** (*for oil*) Tonne *f* **(c)** (*Anat: also* **ear ~**) Trommelfell *nt* **2** VI (*Mus, fig*) trommeln **3** VT **to ~ one's fingers on the table** mit den Fingern auf den Tisch trommeln

➤ **drum into** VT *always separate* **to drum sth into sb** jdm etw eintrichtern (*inf*)

➤ **drum up** VT SEP *enthusiasm, interest* wecken; *support, customers* auftreiben

drummer [ˈdrʌmər] N **(a)** (*in band*) Schlagzeuger(in) *m(f)* **(b)** (*US inf*) Vertreter(in) *m(f)*

drunk [drʌŋk] **1** PTP *of* **drink** **2** ADJ (+ER) **(a)** betrunken; **he was slightly ~** er war leicht betrunken; **to get ~** betrunken werden (*on* von); (*on purpose*) sich betrinken (*on* mit); **to be as ~ as a lord** *or* **skunk** (*inf*) blau wie ein Veilchen sein (*inf*)

(b) (*fig*) **to be ~ with** *or* **on success** vom Erfolg berauscht sein; **to be ~ with** *or* **on power** im Machtrausch sein **3** N Betrunkene(r) *mf*; (*habitual*) Trinker(in) *m(f)*

drunkard [ˈdrʌŋkəd] N Trinker(in) *m(f)*

drunk: **drunk driver** N (*esp US*) angetrunkener Autofahrer, angetrunkene Autofahrerin; **drunk driving, drunken driving** N (*esp US*) Trunkenheit *f* am Steuer

drunken [ˈdrʌŋkən] ADJ betrunken; (*habitually*) versoffen (*inf*); *evening, party* feuchtfröhlich; **in a ~ rage** *or* **fury** in einem Wutanfall im Vollrausch; **in a ~ stupor** im Vollrausch

drunkenly [ˈdrʌŋkənlɪ] ADV betrunken; *behave* wie ein Betrunkener/eine Betrunkene

drunkenness [ˈdrʌŋkənnɪs] N (= *state*) Betrunkenheit *f*; (= *habit, problem*) Trunksucht *f*

drunkometer [drʌŋˈkɒmɪtər] N (*US*) = **Breathalyzer®**

dry [draɪ] **1** VT, *pret, ptp* **dried** trocknen; **to ~ oneself** sich abtrocknen; **he dried his hands** er trocknete sich (*dat*) die Hände ab, er trocknete seine Hände ab; **to ~ the dishes** das Geschirr abtrocknen; **to ~ one's eyes** sich (*dat*) die Tränen abwischen **2** VI **(a)** (= *become ~*) trocknen; **the washing was hanging up to ~ in the sun** die Wäsche trocknete in der Sonne **(b)** (= *~ dishes*) abtrocknen **3** ADJ trocken; *soil, river* ausgetrocknet; **to run ~** (*river*) austrocknen; **~ period** *or* **spell** Trockenperiode *f*; **the ~ season** die Trockenzeit; **to rub oneself ~** sich abrubbeln; **as ~ as a bone** *or* **as dust** knochentrocken (*inf*); **~ bread** trocken Brot **4** N **in the ~** im Trockenen; **to give sth a ~** etw trocknen

➤ **dry off** **1** VI trocknen **2** VT SEP abtrocknen

➤ **dry out** **1** VI **(a)** (*clothes*) trocknen; (*ground, skin etc*) austrocknen **(b)** (*inf: alcoholic*) eine Entziehungskur machen **2** VT SEP *clothes* trocknen; *ground, skin* austrocknen

➤ **dry up** **1** VI **(a)** (*stream, well*) austrocknen; (*moisture*) trocknen; (*inspiration, source of income*) versiegen **(b)** (= *dry dishes*) abtrocknen **2** VT SEP *mess* aufwischen; *dishes* abtrocknen; (*sun*) *well, river bed* austrocknen

dry: **dry-clean** VT chemisch reinigen; **to have a dress ~ed** ein Kleid chemisch reinigen lassen; **dry-cleaner's** N chemische Reinigung; **dry-cleaning** N chemische Reinigung

dryer [ˈdraɪər] N (*for clothes*) Wäschetrockner *m*; (= *spin ~*) Wäscheschleuder *f*; (*for hands*) Händetrockner *m*; (*for hair*) Föhn *m*; (*over head*) Trockenhaube *f*

dry goods PL (*Comm*) Kurzwaren *pl*

drying-up N Abtrocknen *nt*; **to do the ~** abtrocknen

dryly [ˈdraɪlɪ] ADV = **drily**

dryness [ˈdraɪnɪs] N Trockenheit *f*

dry: **dry-roasted** ADJ trocken geröstet; **dry rot** N (Haus)schwamm *m*; **dry run** N Probe *f*; **dry ski slope** N Trockenskipiste *f*

DST (*esp US*) ABBR *of* **daylight saving time**

D term N (*Comm*) D-Klausel *f*

DTI (*Brit*) ABBR *of* **Department of Trade and Industry** ≈ Handelsministerium *nt*

dual [ˈdjʊəl] ADJ (= *double*) doppelt; (= *two kinds of*) zweierlei

dual: **dual carriageway** N (*Brit*) ≈ Schnellstraße *f*; **dual economy** N duale Volkswirtschaft; **dual nationality** N doppelte Staatsangehörigkeit; **dual pricing** N deglomerative Preisdifferenzierung; **dual-purpose** ADJ zweifach verwendbar

dub [dʌb] VT *film* synchronisieren; **the film was ~bed into French** der Film war französisch synchronisiert

Dubai [duːˈbaɪ] N Dubai *nt*

dubbing [ˈdʌbɪŋ] N (*Film*) Synchronisation *f*

dubious [ˈdjuːbɪəs] ADJ **(a)** (= *questionable*) zweifelhaft; *idea, claim, statement, basis* fragwürdig; **of ~ quality** von zweifelhafter Qualität; **it sounds ~ to me** ich habe da meine Zweifel; **to have the ~ honour** (*Brit*) *or* **honor** (*US*) **of doing sth** (*usu iro*) die zweifelhafte Ehre haben, etw zu tun **(b)** (= *uncertain*) unsicher; **I was ~ at first, but he convinced me** ich hatte zuerst Bedenken, aber er überzeugte mich; **to be ~ about sth** etw anzweifeln; **he sounded ~** er klang skeptisch

dubiously [ˈdjuːbɪəslɪ] ADV **(a)** (= *questionably*) (+*vb*) fraglicherweise; (+*adj*) fragwürdig **(b)** (= *uncertainly*) *look* skeptisch; *say, suggest* zweifelnd

dubiousness [ˈdjuːbɪəsnɪs] N Fragwürdigkeit f
duchess [ˈdʌtʃɪs] N Herzogin f
duchy [ˈdʌtʃɪ] N Herzogtum nt
duck [dʌk] **1** N Ente f; **to take to sth like a ~ to water** bei etw gleich in seinem Element sein; **it's (like) water off a ~'s back to him** das prallt alles an ihm ab **2** VI (a) (also ~ **down**) sich ducken (b) **he ~ed out of the room** er verschwand aus dem Zimmer **3** VT (a) (= push under water) untertauchen (b) **to ~ one's head** den Kopf einziehen (c) difficult question, blow ausweichen (+dat)
duckling [ˈdʌklɪŋ] N Entenküken nt; **roast ~** gebratene junge Ente
dud [dʌd] (inf) **1** ADJ (a) nutzlos; person unfähig; **~ batteries** Batterien, die nichts taugen (b) (= counterfeit) note, coin, antique gefälscht; cheque, loan ungedeckt **2** N (= bomb, shell) Blindgänger m; (= coin) Fälschung f; (= note) Blüte f (inf); (= person) Niete f (inf); **this battery is a ~** diese Batterie taugt nichts
dude [djuːd] N (US inf) Kerl m (inf)
dude ranch N (US) Ferienranch f

*Eine **dude ranch** ist eine Ranch im Westen der USA, auf der man als Tourist den Wilden Westen hautnah erleben kann. Die Ranch kann noch wirklich bewirtschaftet werden, es kann sich aber auch um ein reines Freizeitunternehmen handeln. Wer echte Cowboyluft schnuppern möchte, kann zu Pferde durch die Prärie reiten, bei der Rancharbeit helfen und am Lagerfeuer deftige Mahlzeiten einnehmen.*

due [djuː] **1** ADJ (a) (= expected, scheduled) fällig; **to be ~** (plane, train, bus) ankommen sollen; (elections, results) anstehen; **the train was ~ ten minutes ago** der Zug sollte vor 10 Minuten ankommen; **when is the baby ~?** wann soll das Baby kommen?; **the results are ~ at the end of the month** die Ergebnisse sind Ende des Monats fällig; **he is ~ back in London tomorrow** er soll morgen nach London zurückkommen; **to be ~ out** (magazine, CD) herauskommen sollen; **he is ~ to speak about now** er müsste jetzt gerade seine Rede halten; **the building is ~ to be demolished** das Gebäude soll demnächst abgerissen werden; **he is ~ for a rise** (Brit) or **raise** (US) ihm steht eine Gehaltserhöhung zu; **she is ~ for promotion** sie ist mit einer Beförderung an der Reihe; **the prisoner is ~ for release** or **~ to be released** der Gefangene soll jetzt entlassen werden; **the car is ~ for a service** das Auto muss zur Inspektion; **~ date** (Fin) Fälligkeitstermin m (b) attention, consideration gebührend; care nötig; **in ~ course** or **time** (= eventually) zu gegebener Zeit; **with (all) ~ respect** bei allem Respekt (to für) (c) (= owed) **to be ~** (money) ausstehen; **to be ~ to sb** (money, leave, respect) jdm zustehen; **to fall ~** (Fin: loan, debt) fällig werden; **to be ~ a couple of days off** ein paar freie Tage verdient haben (d) **~ to** (= owing to) auf Grund +gen; (= caused by) durch; **his death was ~ to natural causes** er ist eines natürlichen Todes gestorben **2** N (a) **dues** PL (= subscription, fees) (Mitglieds)beitrag m; **harbour ~s** Hafengebühren pl (b) **to give him his ~, he did at least try** eins muss man ihm lassen, er hat es wenigstens versucht **3** ADV **~ north** direkt nach Norden; **~ east of the village** in Richtung Osten des Dorfes
duet [djuːˈet] N Duo nt; (for voices) Duett nt
duff ADJ (Brit) (inf) (= useless) nutzlos; (= broken) kaputt (inf)
➤ **duff up** VT SEP (Brit inf) zusammenschlagen (inf)
duffel [ˈdʌfl]: **duffel bag** N Matchbeutel m; **duffel coat** N Dufflecoat m
dug PRET, PTP of **dig**
duke [djuːk] N Herzog m
dukedom [ˈdjuːkdəm] N (= territory) Herzogtum nt; (= title) Herzogswürde f
dull [dʌl] **1** ADJ (+ER) (a) light, weather, day trüb; glow schwach; colour, eyes, hair, skin, metal, paintwork matt; sky bedeckt; **it will be ~ at first** (weather forecast) es wird anfangs bewölkt (b) (= boring) langweilig; **there's never a ~ moment** man langweilt sich keinen Augenblick (c) sound, ache dumpf

(d) (= listless) person, mood träge; gaze, expression lustlos; (St Ex, Comm) market flau; trading schleppend **2** VT (a) pain betäuben; senses, mind abstumpfen; vision, hearing trüben (b) light, colour dämpfen; metal, paintwork stumpf werden lassen (c) sound dämpfen
dullness [ˈdʌlnɪs] N (a) (of light) Trübheit f; (of colours, eyes, hair, paintwork, metal) Mattheit f; (of weather, day) Trübheit f; (of sky) Bedecktheit f (b) (= boring nature) Langweiligkeit f (c) (= listlessness, St Ex, Comm: of market) Flauheit f
dully [ˈdʌlɪ] ADV (a) (= dimly) matt, schwach (b) throb, ache, feel dumpf
duly [ˈdjuːlɪ] ADV (a) elect, note, sign ordnungsgemäß; **to be ~ impressed** gebührend beeindruckt sein (b) (= as expected) wie erwartet; (= in due course) dann auch; **he ~ obliged** wie erwartet tat er es auch; er tat es dann auch
dumb [dʌm] ADJ (+ER) (a) stumm; (= silent, speechless) sprachlos; **she was struck ~ with fear/shock** die Angst/der Schock verschlug ihr die Sprache (b) (esp US inf) doof (inf); **that was a ~ thing to do/say** wie kann man nur so etwas Dummes machen/sagen!; **to act** or **play ~** sich dumm stellen
➤ **dumb down** VT SEP anspruchsloser machen
dumbbell [ˈdʌmbel] N (Sport) Hantel f
dumbfound [ˈdʌmfaʊnd] VT verblüffen; **I'm ~ed!** ich bin sprachlos!
dumbo [ˈdʌmbəʊ] N (inf: = stupid person) Doofkopp m (inf)
dumb waiter N Speiseaufzug m; (= trolley) Serviertisch m, stummer Diener
dummy [ˈdʌmɪ] **1** N (a) (= sham object, Comm) Attrappe f; (for clothes) (Schaufenster- or Kleider)puppe f (b) (Brit: = baby's teat) Schnuller m (c) (Cards) Tisch m (d) (inf: = fool) Idiot m (inf) **2** ADJ ATTR unecht; **a ~ company** eine Scheinfirma; **a ~ bomb/weapon** eine Bomben-/Waffenattrappe
dummy run N Probe f; (of air attack) Übung f
dump [dʌmp] **1** N (a) (Brit: for rubbish) Müllkippe f (b) (Mil) Depot nt (c) (pej inf) (= town) Kaff nt (inf); (= house, building) Dreckloch nt (pej inf); (= school etc) Sauladen m (pej inf) (d) (inf) **to be (down) in the ~s** deprimiert or down (inf) sein **2** VT (a) (= get rid of, let fall) abladen; bags, books etc (= drop) fallen lassen; (= leave) lassen; (inf) person, boyfriend abschieben; car abstellen; **to ~ sb/sth on sb** jdn/etw bei jdm abladen (b) (Comm) goods zu Dumpingpreisen verkaufen (c) (Comput) dumpen
➤ **dump on** VI +PREP OBJ (inf) **to dump on sb** (= mistreat) jdn von oben herab behandeln
dumper [ˈdʌmpəʳ] N (= dump truck) Kipper m
dumping [ˈdʌmpɪŋ] N (a) (of load, rubbish) Abladen nt; **"no ~"** (Brit) „Schuttabladen verboten!" (b) (Comm) Dumping nt
dumping ground N (fig) Abladeplatz m
dumpling [ˈdʌmplɪŋ] N (Cook) Kloß m
Dumpster® [ˈdʌmpstəʳ] N (US) (Müll)container m
dump truck N Kipper m
dumpy [ˈdʌmpɪ] ADJ pummelig
dunce [dʌns] N (Sch) langsamer Lerner or Schüler; (= stupid person) Dummkopf m; **to be a ~ at maths** eine Niete in Mathe sein (inf)
dune [djuːn] N Düne f
dung [dʌŋ] N Dung m; (Agr.: = manure) Mist m
dungarees [ˌdʌŋɡəˈriːz] (esp Brit) PL Latzhose f; **a pair of ~** eine Latzhose
dungeon [ˈdʌndʒən] N Verlies nt
dunk [dʌŋk] VT (ein)tunken
dunno [ˈdʌnəʊ] = (I) don't know
duo [ˈdjuːəʊ] N Duo nt
dupe [djuːp] VT überlisten; **he was ~d into believing it** er fiel darauf rein
duplex [ˈdjuːpleks] N (esp US) = **duplex apartment/house**
duplex: **duplex apartment** N (esp US) zweistöckige Wohnung; **duplex house** N (US) Zweifamilienhaus nt
duplicate [ˈdjuːplɪkeɪt] **1** VT (a) (on machine) kopieren (b) (= repeat) action, success etc wiederholen; (wastefully) zweimal machen **2** [ˈdjuːplɪkɪt] N (of document, work of art)

Kopie f; (of key) Zweitschlüssel m; **in** ~ in doppelter Ausfertigung **3** [ˈdjuːplɪkɪt] ADJ zweifach; **a ~ copy of the text** eine Kopie des Textes; **a ~ key** ein Zweitschlüssel m

duplication [djuːplɪˈkeɪʃən] N (of documents) Vervielfältigung f; (of efforts, work) Wiederholung f

duplicity [djuːˈplɪsɪtɪ] N Doppelspiel nt

durability [ˌdjʊərəˈbɪlɪtɪ] N **(a)** (of product, material) Strapazierfähigkeit f **(b)** (of peace, relationship) Dauerhaftigkeit f

durable [ˈdjʊərəbl] ADJ **(a)** product, material strapazierfähig; **CDs are more ~ than tapes** CDs halten länger als Kassetten **(b)** peace, relationship dauerhaft

durable goods PL langlebige Güter pl

duration [djʊəˈreɪʃən] N Länge f, Dauer f; **for the ~ of** für die Dauer (+gen); **of long/short ~** von langer/kurzer Dauer; **it looks as though we are here for the ~** (inf) es sieht so aus, als ob wir bis zum Ende hier sind

duress [djʊəˈres] N **under ~** unter Zwang

Durex® [ˈdjʊəreks] N Gummi m (inf)

during [ˈdjʊərɪŋ] PREP während (+gen)

dusk [dʌsk] N (= twilight) (Abend)dämmerung f; (= gloom) Finsternis f; **at ~** bei Einbruch der Dunkelheit

dusky [ˈdʌskɪ] ADJ (+ER) skin, colour dunkel; person dunkelhäutig; **~ pink** altrosa

dust [dʌst] **1** N, NO PL Staub m; **covered in ~** staubbedeckt; **to gather ~** (lit, fig) verstauben; **we'll let the ~ settle first** (fig) wir warten, bis sich die Wogen geglättet haben; **to give sth a ~** etw abstauben **2** VT **(a)** furniture abstauben; room Staub wischen in (+dat); **it's (all) done and ~ed** (Brit fig inf) das ist (alles) unter Dach und Fach **(b)** (Cook) bestäuben **3** VI (cleaner etc) Staub wischen

➤ **dust down** VT SEP (with brush) abbürsten; (with hand) abklopfen; **to dust oneself down** (fig) sich rein waschen

➤ **dust off** VT SEP dirt wegwischen; **to dust oneself off** (fig) sich rein waschen

dust: **dustbin** N (Brit) Mülltonne f; **dustbin man** N (Brit) = dustman; **dustcart** N (Brit) Müllwagen m; **dust cover** N (on book) (Schutz)umschlag m; (on furniture) Schonbezug m

duster [ˈdʌstəʳ] N Staubtuch nt; (Sch) (Tafel)schwamm m

dusting [ˈdʌstɪŋ] N **(a)** Staubwischen nt; **to do the ~** Staub wischen **(b)** **a ~ of snow** eine dünne Schneedecke

dust: **dust jacket** N (Schutz)umschlag m; **dustman** N (Brit) Müllmann m; **the dustmen come on Fridays** freitags ist Müllabfuhr; **dustpan** N Kehr- or Müllschaufel f; **dustsheet** N (Brit) Tuch nt (zum Abdecken von Möbeln)

dusty [ˈdʌstɪ] ADJ (+ER) staubig; furniture, book, photograph verstaubt

Dutch [dʌtʃ] **1** ADJ holländisch; **~ cheese** Holländer Käse; **a ~ man** ein Holländer m; **a ~ woman** eine Holländerin; **he is ~** er ist Holländer **2** N **(a)** (= people) **the ~** die Holländer pl **(b)** (= language) Holländisch nt; **to be in ~ (with sb)** (US inf) (bei jdm) schlecht angeschrieben sein **3** ADV **to go ~ (with sb)** (inf) (mit jdm) getrennte Kasse machen

Dutch: **Dutch cap** N (= diaphragm) Pessar nt; **Dutch courage** N (inf) **to get or give oneself ~** sich (dat) Mut antrinken (from mit); **Dutch door** N (US) quer geteilte Tür; **Dutch elm disease** N Ulmensterben nt; **Dutchman** N Holländer m; **Dutchwoman** N Holländerin f

dutiable [ˈdjuːtɪəbl] (= taxable) zu versteuern

dutiful [ˈdjuːtɪfʊl] ADJ child gehorsam; husband, employee pflichtbewusst

dutifully [ˈdjuːtɪfʊlɪ] ADV pflichtbewusst; (= obediently) treu und brav; **we all laughed ~** wir alle lachten brav

duty [ˈdjuːtɪ] N **(a)** Pflicht f; **to do one's ~ (by sb)** seine Pflicht (gegenüber jdm) tun; **it is my ~ to say or I am (in) ~ bound to say that ...** es ist meine Pflicht zu sagen, dass ...; **to make it**

one's ~ to do sth es sich (dat) zur Pflicht machen, etw zu tun; **contractual duties** vertragliche Verpflichtungen; **to take up one's duties** seine Pflichten aufnehmen; **to report for ~** sich zum Dienst melden; **to be on ~** (doctor etc) im Dienst sein; (Sch etc) Aufsicht haben; **who's on ~ tomorrow?** wer hat morgen Dienst/Aufsicht?; **he went on ~ at 9** sein Dienst fing um 9 an; **to be off ~** nicht im Dienst sein; **he comes off ~ at 9** sein Dienst endet um 9; **night ~** Nachtdienst m **(b)** (Fin) Zoll m; **to pay ~ on sth** Zoll auf etw (acc) zahlen

duty-free [djuːtɪˈfriː] ADJ, ADV zollfrei

duty-free: **duty-free allowance** N Zollkontingent nt, Freimenge f; **duty-free shop** N Duty-free-Shop m

duty: **duty officer** N Offizier m vom Dienst; **duty-paid** [djuːtɪˈpeɪd] ADJ verzollt; **duty roster** N Dienstplan m

duvet [ˈdjuːveɪ] N Steppdecke f

DVD N ABBR of digital versatile or video disc DVD f

DVD: **DVD player** N DVD-Player m; **DVD-Rom** N DVD-Rom f

dwarf [dwɔːf] **1** N, pl **dwarves** [dwɔːvz] Zwerg m; (= star) Zwerg(stern) m **2** ADJ **~ shrubs** Zwergsträucher pl **3** VT (skyscraper, person) klein erscheinen lassen; (through achievements, ability etc) in den Schatten stellen; **to be ~ed by sb/sth** neben jdm/etw klein erscheinen

dweeb [dwiːb] N (esp US inf) mickeriger Typ (inf)

dwell [dwel], pret, ptp **dwelt** VI (liter. = live) weilen (geh)

➤ **dwell (up)on** VI +PREP OBJ verweilen bei; **to dwell (up)on the past** sich ständig mit der Vergangenheit befassen; **let's not dwell (up)on it** wir wollen uns nicht (länger) damit aufhalten

dwelt [dwelt] PRET, PTP of **dwell**

dwindle [ˈdwɪndl] VI (interest) nachlassen; (numbers, audiences) zurückgehen; (supplies) schrumpfen

dwindling [ˈdwɪndlɪŋ] ADJ interest nachlassend; numbers, audiences zurückgehend; supplies schwindend

dye [daɪ] **1** N Farbstoff m; **hair ~** Haarfärbmittel nt; **food ~** Lebensmittelfarbe f **2** VT färben; **~d blonde hair** blond gefärbtes Haar

dyed-in-the-wool [ˈdaɪdɪnðəˌwʊl] ADJ Erz-; attitude eingefleischt

dying [ˈdaɪɪŋ] **1** PRP of **die** **2** ADJ **(a)** (lit) sterbend; plant eingehend; breath, wish, words letzte(r, s); **until or till or to one's ~ day** bis an sein Lebensende **(b)** (fig) industry, art aussterbend; days, minutes letzte(r, s); **regular customers are a ~ breed** regelmäßige Kunden gibt es fast nicht mehr **3** N **the ~ pl** die Sterbenden

dyke, (US) **dike** [daɪk] N **(a)** Deich m **(b)** (sl: = lesbian) Lesbe f (inf)

dynamic [daɪˈnæmɪk] **1** ADJ (also Phys) dynamisch **2** N Dynamik f

dynamically [daɪˈnæmɪkəlɪ] ADV (also Phys) dynamisch

dynamics [daɪˈnæmɪks] N SING or PL Dynamik f

dynamism [ˈdaɪnəmɪzəm] N Dynamismus m; (of person) Dynamik f

dynamite [ˈdaɪnəmaɪt] N (lit) Dynamit nt; (fig) Zünd- or Sprengstoff m; **she is ~** sie ist eine Wucht (inf)

dynamo [ˈdaɪnəməʊ] N Dynamo m; (Aut) Lichtmaschine f

dynasty [ˈdɪnəstɪ] N Dynastie f

dysentery [ˈdɪsɪntrɪ] N Ruhr f

dysfunction [dɪsˈfʌŋkʃən] N Fehlfunktion f; **liver ~** Funktionsstörung f der Leber

dysfunctional [dɪsˈfʌŋkʃənəl] ADJ dysfunktional

dyslexia [dɪsˈleksɪə] N Legasthenie f

dyslexic [dɪsˈleksɪk] **1** ADJ legasthenisch; **she is ~** sie ist Legasthenikerin **2** N Legastheniker(in) m(f)

dyspepsia [dɪsˈpepsɪə] N Verdauungsstörung f

Ee

E, e [iː] N E nt, e nt; (Mus) E nt, e nt; **E flat** Es nt, es nt; **E sharp** Eis nt, eis nt

E ABBR of east O

e- [iː] PREF (= *electronic*) E-, elektronisch

each [iːtʃ] **1** ADJ jede(r, s); **~ one of us** jeder von uns; **~ and every one of us** jeder Einzelne von uns
2 PRON **(a)** jede(r, s); **~ of them gave their** or **his opinion** sie sagten alle ihre Meinung, jeder (von ihnen) sagte seine Meinung
(b) ~ other sich, einander (*geh*); **they haven't seen ~ other for a long time** sie haben sich lange nicht gesehen; **they wrote (to) ~ other** sie haben sich (*dat*) geschrieben; **you must help ~ other** ihr müsst euch gegenseitig helfen; **on top of ~ other** aufeinander; **next to ~ other** nebeneinander; **they went to ~ other's house(s)** sie besuchten einander zu Hause
3 ADV je; **we gave them one apple ~** wir haben ihnen je einen Apfel gegeben; **the books are £10 ~** die Bücher kosten je £ 10; **carnations at 50p ~** Nelken zu 50 Pence das Stück

each way ADV (*Brit Horseracing etc*) **I had £10 ~ on Black Velvet** ich hatte £ 10 auf Black Velvet auf allen drei Gewinnplätzen gesetzt

eager [ˈiːɡəʳ] ADJ eifrig; *face* erwartungsvoll; *response* begeistert; **in ~ anticipation** voll gespannter Erwartung; **to be ~ to do sth** etw unbedingt tun wollen; **she is ~ to please** sie ist darum bemüht, alles richtig zu machen; **to be ~ for sth** auf etw (*acc*) aus sein

eagerly [ˈiːɡəlɪ] ADV eifrig; *await, anticipate* gespannt; *accept, agree* bereitwillig; **~ awaited** mit Spannung erwartet

eagerness [ˈiːɡənɪs] N Eifer m

eagle [ˈiːɡl] N Adler m; **to keep an ~ eye on sb/sth** ein wachsames Auge auf jdn/etw werfen; **under the ~ eye of ...** unter dem wachsamen Blick (+*gen*) ...

E & OE ABBR of errors and omissions excepted

ear[1] [ɪəʳ] N **(a)** (*Anat, fig*) Ohr nt; **to keep one's ~s open, to keep an ~ to the ground** die Ohren offen halten; **to be all ~s** ganz Ohr sein; **she was listening with only half an ~** sie hörte nur mit halbem Ohr zu; **to lend an ~** zuhören; **to find a sympathetic ~** ein offenes Ohr finden; **he has the ~ of the prime minister** der Premierminister hört auf ihn; **it goes in one ~ and out the other** das geht zum einen Ohr hinein und zum zweiten wieder hinaus; **to be up to one's ~s in work** bis über beide Ohren in Arbeit stecken; **he's got money** *etc* **coming out of his ~s** (*inf*) er hat Geld *etc* ohne Ende (*inf*); **he'll be out on his ~** (*inf*) dann fliegt er raus (*inf*); **to bend sb's ~** (*inf*) jdn voll quatschen (*inf*)
(b) (= *sense of hearing*) **to have a good ~ for music** ein feines Gehör für Musik haben; **to play by ~** (*lit*) nach (dem) Gehör spielen; **to play it by ~** (*fig*) improvisieren

ear[2] N (*of grain, plant*) Ähre f

ear: **earache** N Ohrenschmerzen pl; **eardrum** N Trommelfell nt; **earful** N (*inf*) **to get an ~** mit einer Flut von Beschimpfungen überschüttet werden; **to give sb an ~** jdn zusammenstauchen (*inf*); **earhole** N (*Brit inf*) Ohr nt, Löffel m (*inf*)

earl [ɜːl] N Graf m

earlier [ˈɜːlɪə] **1** ADJ COMP of early früher; **in ~ times** früher; **at an ~ date** früher **2** ADV **~ (on)** früher; (= *just now*) vorhin; **~ (on) in the novel** an einer früheren Stelle in dem Roman; **~ (on) today** heute (vor einigen Stunden); **~ (on) this month/year** früher in diesem Monat/Jahr; **I cannot do it ~ than Thursday** ich kann es nicht eher als Donnerstag machen

ear lobe N Ohrläppchen nt

early [ˈɜːlɪ] **1** ADV **(a) ~ (on)** früh; **~ in 1915/in February** Anfang 1915/Februar; **~ (on) in the year** Anfang des Jahres; **~ (on) in his/her/their** *etc* **life** im jungen Jahren; **~ in the race** zu Anfang des Rennens; **~ (on) in the evening** am frühen Abend; **as ~ as** (= *already*) schon; **~ this month/year** Anfang des Monats/Jahres; **~ today/this morning** heute früh; **the earliest he can come is tomorrow** er kann frühestens morgen kommen
(b) (= *before the expected time*) früher (als erwartet); (= *too ~*) zu früh; (= *earlier than usual*) früh; **she left ten minutes ~** sie

ist zehn Minuten früher gegangen; **to be five minutes ~** fünf Minuten zu früh kommen; **he left school ~** (*went home*) er ging früher von der Schule nach Hause; (*finished education*) er ging vorzeitig von der Schule ab; **to get up/go to bed ~** früh aufstehen/ins Bett gehen
2 ADJ (+ER) **(a)** früh; *death* vorzeitig; **it was ~ evening when we finished** wir waren am frühen Abend fertig; **we went for an ~ morning drive** wir machten eine Spritztour am frühen Morgen; **we had an ~ lunch** wir aßen früh zu Mittag; **in ~ spring/winter** zu Frühlings-/Winteranfang; **the ~ years/days** die ersten Jahre/Tage; **~ January** Anfang Januar; **in the ~ 1980s** Anfang der achtziger Jahre; **to have an ~ night** früh ins Bett gehen; **until** *or* **into the ~ hours** bis in die frühen Morgenstunden; **her ~ life** ihre jungen Jahre; **his ~ work** seine frühen Werke; **at an ~ age** in jungen Jahren; **from an ~ age** von klein auf; **to be in one's ~ thirties** Anfang dreißig sein; **it is too ~ to know what his motives are** man weiß noch nicht, welche Motive er hat; **it's ~ days (yet)** (*esp Brit*) wir/sie *etc* sind noch im Anfangsstadium
(b) *settlers, man* frühgeschichtlich; **an ~ form of hypnotherapy** eine Frühform der Hypnotherapie; **~ baroque** Frühbarock m
(c) (= *soon*) **at an ~ date** bald; **at the earliest possible moment** so bald wie irgend möglich

early: **early bird** N (*in morning*) Frühaufsteher(in) m(f); (*arriving etc*) Frühankömmling m; **early closing** N **it's ~ today** die Geschäfte sind heute nachmittag geschlossen; **early retirement** N **to take ~** vorzeitig in den Ruhestand gehen; **early riser** N Frühaufsteher(in) m(f); **early warning system** N Frühwarnsystem nt

ear: **earmark** VT (*fig*) vorsehen; **earmuffs** PL Ohrenschützer pl

earn [ɜːn] VT verdienen; (*Fin*) *interest* bringen; **to ~ one's keep/a living** Kost und Logis/seinen Lebensunterhalt verdienen; **to ~ a** *or* **one's crust** (*Brit*) seine Brötchen verdienen (*inf*); **this ~ed him a lot of money/respect** das trug ihm viel Geld/große Achtung ein; **he's ~ed it** das hat er sich (*dat*) verdient

earned income [ˈɜːndˈɪnkʌm] N Einkünfte pl aus selbstständiger und nichtselbstständiger Arbeit

earner [ˈɜːnə] N **(a)** (= *person*) Verdiener(in) m(f); **big ~s** Großverdiener pl **(b)** (*Brit inf*) **that video shop is a nice little ~** der Videoladen wirft ganz schön was ab (*inf*)

earnest [ˈɜːnɪst] **1** ADJ *person* ernst; *hope, desire* innig; *discussion* ernsthaft **2** N **in ~** (= *for real*) richtig; **to be in ~ about sth** (= *serious*) etw ernst meinen; **this time I'm in ~** diesmal meine ich es ernst

earnestly [ˈɜːnɪstlɪ] ADV *say, ask* ernst; *discuss, try, explain* ernsthaft; *hope* innig

earnings [ˈɜːnɪŋz] PL (*of person*) Verdienst m; (*of a business*) Einkünfte pl; **~ per share** Gewinn m je Aktie

ear: **ear, nose and throat** ADJ ATTR Hals-Nasen-Ohren-; **~ specialist** Hals-Nasen-Ohren-Facharzt m/-ärztin f; **earphones** PL Kopfhörer pl; **earpiece** N Hörer m; **ear piercing** N Durchstechen nt der Ohrläppchen; **earplug** N Ohropax® nt; **earring** N Ohrring m; **earshot** N **out of/within ~** außer/in Hörweite; **ear-splitting** ADJ ohrenbetäubend

earth [ɜːθ] **1** N **(a)** (*also Brit Elec*) Erde f; **the ~, Earth** die Erde; **on ~** auf der Erde; **the ~** die *or* **~** bis ans Ende der Welt; **where/who** *etc* **on ~ ...?** (*inf*) wo/wer *etc* ... bloß?; **what on ~ ...?** (*inf*) was in aller Welt ...? (*inf*); **nothing on ~ will stop me now** keine Macht der Welt hält mich jetzt noch auf; **there's no reason on ~ why ...** es gibt keinen erdenklichen Grund, warum ...; **it cost the ~** (*Brit inf*) das hat eine schöne Stange Geld gekostet (*inf*); **it won't cost the ~** (*Brit inf*) es wird schon nicht die Welt kosten (*inf*); **to fall to ~** zur Erde fallen; **to come back** *or* **down to ~ (again)** (*fig*) wieder auf den Boden der Tatsachen (zurück)kommen; **to bring sb down to ~ (with a bump)** (*fig*) jdn (unsanft) wieder auf den Boden der Tatsachen zurückholen
(b) (*of fox, badger etc*) Bau m; **to go to ~** (*Brit: criminal etc*) untertauchen; **to run sb/sth to ~** (*Brit fig*) jdn/etw aufstöbern **2** VT (*Brit Elec*) erden

earthen [ˈɜːθən] ADJ irden

earthenware ['ɜ:θənweə'] **1** N (= *material*) Ton *m*; (= *dishes etc*) Tongeschirr *nt* **2** ADJ aus Ton, Ton-; ~ **crockery** Tongeschirr *nt*

earthly ['ɜ:θlɪ] **1** ADJ **(a)** irdisch **(b)** there's no ~ **reason why ...** es gibt nicht den geringsten Grund, warum ... **2** N (*inf*) **she doesn't stand an** ~ sie hat nicht die geringste Chance

earth: **earthquake** N Erdbeben *nt*; **earth-shattering** ADJ (*fig*) welterschütternd; **earthworm** N Regenwurm *m*

earthy ['ɜ:θɪ] ADJ **(a)** *colour* erdfarben; *flavour, smell* erdig **(b)** (*fig*) *person* urtümlich; *humour, language, book* derb; *approach* robust

ear: **earwax** N Ohrenschmalz *nt*; **earwig** N Ohrwurm *m*

ease [i:z] **1** N **(a)** **I am never at** ~ **in his company** in seiner Gesellschaft fühle ich mich immer befangen; **to be** *or* **feel at** ~ **with oneself** sich (in seiner Haut) wohl fühlen; **to put sb at (his/her)** ~ jdm die Befangenheit nehmen; **to put** *or* **set sb's mind at** ~ jdn beruhigen; **(stand) at** ~! (*Mil*) rührt euch! **(b)** (= *absence of difficulty*) Leichtigkeit *f*; **with (the greatest of)** ~ mit (größter) Leichtigkeit; **for** ~ **of use/reference** um die Benutzung/das Nachschlagen zu erleichtern **(c)** (= *absence of work*) Muße *f*
2 VT **(a)** *pain* lindern; *mind* erleichtern; **to** ~ **the burden on sb** jdm eine Last abnehmen
(b) *rope, strap* lockern; *pressure, tension* verringern; *situation* entspannen; **he** ~**d the lid off** er löste den Deckel behutsam ab; **he** ~**d his broken leg up onto the stretcher** er hob sein gebrochenes Bein behutsam auf die Trage; **he** ~**d his way through the hole** er schob sich vorsichtig durch das Loch
3 VI nachlassen; (*situation*) sich entspannen
➤ **ease off** *or* **up** VI **(a)** (= *slow down, relax*) langsamer werden; (*driver*) verlangsamen; (*situation*) sich entspannen; **the doctor told him to ease up a bit at work** der Arzt riet ihm, bei der Arbeit etwas kürzer zu treten; **things usually ease up a little just after Christmas** nach Weihnachten wird es normalerweise etwas ruhiger **(b)** (*pain, rain*) nachlassen

easel ['i:zl] N Staffelei *f*

easily ['i:zɪlɪ] ADV **(a)** leicht; ~ **accessible** (*place*) leicht zu erreichen; **he learnt to swim** ~ er lernte mühelos schwimmen; **dishwashers can** ~ **ruin hand-painted china** Spülmaschinen können handbemaltes Porzellan leicht ruinieren; **it could just as** ~ **happen here** es könnte genauso gut hier passieren
(b) (= *unquestionably*) (*with figures*) gut und gerne; (+ *superl*) mit Abstand; **it's** ~ **25 miles** es sind gut und gerne 25 Meilen; **they are** ~ **the best** sie sind mit Abstand die Besten **(c)** *talk, breathe* ganz entspannt

east [i:st] **1** N **the** ~, **the East** (*also Pol*) der Osten; **in the** ~ im Osten; **to the** ~ nach *or* gen (*liter*) Osten; **to the** ~ **of** östlich von; **the wind is coming from the** ~ der Wind kommt von Ost(en); **the** ~ **of France** der Osten Frankreichs; **East-West relations** Ost-West-Beziehungen *pl*; **between East and West** zwischen Osten und Westen
2 ADV (= *eastward*) nach Osten; **the kitchen faces** ~ die Küche liegt nach Osten; ~ **of Paris/the river** östlich von Paris/des Flusses
3 ADJ Ost-; ~ **coast** Ostküste *f*; ~ **wind** Ostwind *m*

east: **East Africa** N Ostafrika *nt*; **East Berlin** N Ostberlin *nt*; **eastbound** ADJ (in) Richtung Osten; **the** ~ **carriageway of the M4** (*Brit*) die M4 in Richtung Osten; **to be** ~ nach Osten unterwegs sein

Easter ['i:stə'] **1** N Ostern *nt*; **at** ~ an *or* zu Ostern **2** ADJ ATTR Oster-

Easter: **Easter bunny** N Osterhase *m*; **Easter egg** N Osterei *nt*

easterly ['i:stəlɪ] ADJ östlich, Ost-; **an** ~ **wind** ein Ostwind *m*; **in an** ~ **direction** in östlicher Richtung

Easter Monday N Ostermontag *m*

eastern ['i:stən] ADJ Ost-, östlich; **Eastern Europe** Osteuropa *nt*

easterner ['i:stənə'] N (*esp US*) Oststaatler(in) *m(f)*; **he's an** ~ er kommt aus dem Osten

easternmost ['i:stənməʊst] ADJ östlichste(r, s)

Easter Sunday N Ostersonntag *m*

east: **East Europe** N (*esp US*) Osteuropa *nt*; **East European 1** ADJ osteuropäisch **2** N Osteuropäer(in) *m(f)*; **East German 1** ADJ ostdeutsch; **the** ~ **government** (*Hist*) die Regierung der DDR **2** N Ostdeutsche(r) *mf*; **East Germany** N Ostdeutschland *nt*; (= *GDR*) die DDR; **East Indies** PL Ostindien *nt* (*old*), die Malaiische Archipel; **East Timor** N

Osttimor *nt*; **eastward 1** ADV (*also* ~**s**) nach Osten **2** ADJ *direction* östlich; *route* nach Osten; **eastwardly** ADV, ADJ = **eastward**

easy ['i:zɪ] **1** ADJ (+ER) leicht; *option, solution, answer* einfach; **it's** ~ **to forget that ...** man vergisst leicht, dass ...; **it's** ~ **for her** sie hat es leicht; **that's** ~ **for you to say** du hast gut reden; **he was an** ~ **winner** er hat mühelos gewonnen; **that's the** ~ **part** das ist das Einfache; **it's an** ~ (= **enough**) **mistake to make** den Fehler kann man leicht machen; **to be within** ~ **reach of sth** etw leicht erreichen können; **as** ~ **as pie** *or* **as ABC** *or* **as falling off a log** kinderleicht; **easier said than done** leichter gesagt als getan; **on** ~ **terms** (*Comm*) zu günstigen Bedingungen; **to go for the** ~ **option, to take the** ~ **way out** es sich (*dat*) leicht machen; **she is** ~ **to work with/get on with** mit ihr kann man gut arbeiten/auskommen; **she opted for the** ~ **life** sie machte sich (*dat*) das Leben leicht; **to have it** ~, **to have an** ~ **time (of it)** es leicht haben; **he will not be given an** ~ **ride** man wird es ihm nicht leicht machen; ~ **prey** eine leichte Beute; **to be** ~ **on the eye/ear** angenehm anzusehen/anzuhören sein; **at an** ~ **pace** in gemütlichem Tempo; **I'm** ~ (*Brit inf*) ist mir egal (*inf*); **I don't feel** ~ **about it** es ist mir nicht recht; (*pej inf*) **she's** ~ sie ist immer zu haben
2 ADV (*inf*) **to go** ~ **on sb** nicht so streng mit jdm sein; **to go** ~ **on sth** mit etw sparsam umgehen; **to take it** ~, **to take things** ~ (= *rest*) sich schonen; **take it** ~! (= *calm down*) immer mit der Ruhe!; (*esp US: when saying goodbye*) machs gut!; ~ **does it** immer sachte

easy: **easy chair** N Sessel *m*; **easy-going** ADJ gelassen; **easy listening** N leichte Musik, Unterhaltungsmusik *f*; **easy money** N leicht verdientes Geld; **you can make** ~ Sie können leicht Geld machen; **easy touch** N **to be an** ~ (*inf*) nicht nein sagen können

eat [i:t], *vb*: *pret* **ate**, *ptp* **eaten** VTI (*person*) essen; (*animal*) fressen; **to** ~ **one's breakfast** frühstücken; **to** ~ **one's lunch/ dinner** zu Mittag/Abend essen; **he was forced to** ~ **his words** er musste alles zurücknehmen; **he won't** ~ **you** (*inf*) er wird dich schon nicht fressen (*inf*); **what's** ~**ing you?** (*inf*) was hast du denn?; **I haven't** ~**en for ages** ich habe schon ewig nichts mehr gegessen
➤ **eat away at** VI +PREP OBJ **(a)** (*acid, rust, pest*) anfressen; (*rot, damp*) angreifen **(b)** (*fig*) *revenue* auffressen; *finances* angreifen
➤ **eat into** VI +PREP OBJ *metal* anfressen; *capital* angreifen; *market share, profits* verringern; *time* verkürzen
➤ **eat out 1** VI zum Essen ausgehen **2** VT SEP **Elvis Presley, eat your heart out** Elvis Presley, da kannst du vor Neid erblassen
➤ **eat out of** VI +PREP OBJ **she had them eating out of her hand** (*fig*) sie fraßen ihr aus der Hand
➤ **eat up 1** VT SEP **(a)** (*lit*) aufessen; (*animal*) auffressen **(b)** (*fig*) verbrauchen **2** VI aufessen

eaten ['i:tn] PTP *of* **eat**

eater ['i:tə'] N Esser(in) *m(f)*

eating ['i:tɪŋ] N Essen *nt*

eating apple N Essapfel *m*

eau de Cologne [ˌəʊdəkə'ləʊn] N Kölnischwasser *nt*

eaves ['i:vz] PL Dachvorsprung *m*

eavesdrop ['i:vzdrɒp] VI (heimlich) lauschen; **to** ~ **on a conversation** ein Gespräch belauschen

ebb [eb] **1** N Ebbe *f*; ~ **and flow** (*fig*) Auf und Ab *nt*; **at a low** ~ (*fig*) auf einem Tiefstand; **their popularity is at its lowest** ~ ihre Beliebtheit hat einen absoluten Tiefpunkt erreicht **2** VI **(a)** (*tide*) zurückgehen **(b)** (*fig: also* ~ **away**) (*enthusiasm etc*) verebben; (*life*) zu Ende gehen

ebb tide N Ebbe *f*

ebony ['ebənɪ] N Ebenholz *nt*

e-book ['i:bʊk] N Onlinebuch *nt*

ebullience [ɪ'bʌlɪəns] N Überschwänglichkeit *f*

ebullient [ɪ'bʌlɪənt] ADJ *person* überschwänglich; *spirits, mood* übersprudelnd

e-business [ˌi:'bɪznɪs] N **(a)** (= *company*) Internetfirma *f* **(b)** (= *commerce*) E-Business *nt*, elektronischer Geschäftsverkehr

EC ABBR *of* **European Community** EG *f*

eccentric [ik'sentrik] **1** ADJ exzentrisch; *taste* ausgefallen **2** N Exzentriker(in) *m(f)*

eccentricity [ˌeksən'trɪsɪtɪ] N Exzentrizität *f*

ecclesiastical [ɪˌkliːzɪˈæstɪkəl] ADJ kirchlich

ECG ABBR of **electrocardiogram** EKG nt

ECGD N ABBR of **Export Credit Guarantees Department** staatliche Exportkreditversicherung

echelon [ˈeʃəlɒn] N the higher ~s die höheren Ränge pl

echo [ˈekəʊ] **1** N Echo nt; (fig) Anklang m (of an +acc) **2** VT (fig) wiedergeben **3** VI (sounds) widerhallen; (room, footsteps) hallen; **to ~ with sth** von etw widerhallen; **her words ~ed in his ears** ihre Worte hallten ihm in den Ohren

éclair [erˈkleəʳ] N Liebesknochen m

eclectic [ɪˈklektɪk] ADJ eklektisch

eclipse [ɪˈklɪps] **1** N (Astron) Finsternis f; ~ **of the sun/moon** Sonnen-/Mondfinsternis f **2** VT (fig) in den Schatten stellen

eco- [ˈiːkəʊ-] PREF Öko-, öko-

ecofriendly [ˌiːkəʊˈfrendlɪ] ADJ (Brit) umweltfreundlich

ecological [ˌiːkəˈlɒdʒɪkəl] ADJ ökologisch; ~ **disaster** Umweltkatastrophe f; ~ **damage** Umweltschäden pl

ecologically [ˌiːkəʊˈlɒdʒɪkəlɪ] ADV ökologisch; ~ **harmful** umweltschädlich; ~ **aware** umweltbewusst

ecologist [ɪˈkɒlədʒɪst] N Ökologe m, Ökologin f

ecology [ɪˈkɒlədʒɪ] N Ökologie f

e-commerce [ˈiːkɒmɜːs] N elektronischer Handel, E-Commerce m

economic [ˌiːkəˈnɒmɪk] ADJ **(a)** Wirtschafts-; ~ **climate** Wirtschaftsklima nt; ~ **growth** Wirtschaftswachstum nt; ~ **recovery** Wirtschaftsaufschwung m **(b)** (= cost-effective) price, rent wirtschaftlich; **it is not ~ to do this** es ist nicht rentabel, das zu tun

economical [ˌiːkəˈnɒmɪkəl] ADJ sparsam; **to be ~ with sth** mit etw haushalten; **they were ~ with the truth** sie haben es mit der Wahrheit nicht so genau genommen; **an ~ style** (Liter) ein prägnanter Stil

economically [ˌiːkəˈnɒmɪkəlɪ] ADV **(a)** wirtschaftlich; **after the war, the country suffered ~** nach dem Krieg litt die Wirtschaft des Landes **(b)** (= thriftily) sparsam; **to use sth ~** mit etw sparsam umgehen **(c)** (= in few words) prägnant

economic migrant, economic refugee N Wirtschaftsflüchtling m

economics [ˌiːkəˈnɒmɪks] N **(a)** SING or PL Volkswirtschaft f, Wirtschaftswissenschaften pl **(b)** PL (= economic aspect) **the ~ of the situation** die wirtschaftliche Seite der Situation

economist [ɪˈkɒnəmɪst] N Wirtschaftswissenschaftler(in) m(f)

economize [ɪˈkɒnəmaɪz] VI sparen
➤ **economize on** VI +PREP OBJ sparen

economy [ɪˈkɒnəmɪ] N **(a)** (system) Wirtschaft f no pl; (from a monetary aspect) Konjunktur f **(b)** (= saving) Einsparung f; **a false ~** falsche Sparsamkeit; **economies of scale** Einsparungen pl durch erhöhte Produktion; **to make economies** zu Sparmaßnahmen greifen **(c)** (= thrift) Sparsamkeit f; ~ **of language/expression** knappe Sprache/Ausdrucksweise

economy: **economy class** N Touristenklasse f; **economy drive** N Sparmaßnahmen pl; **economy size** N Sparpackung f

eco: **ecosystem** N Ökosystem nt; **ecotourism** N Ökotourismus m; **eco-warrior** n (inf) Ökokämpfer(in) m(f)

ecru [eˈkruː] ADJ naturfarben, ekrü

ecstasy [ˈekstəsɪ] N **(a)** Ekstase f; **to be in ~** ekstatisch sein; **to go into ecstasies over sth** über etw (acc) in Ekstase geraten **(b)** (= drug) Ecstasy nt

ecstatic ADJ [eksˈtætɪk] ekstatisch

ecstatically [eksˈtætɪkəlɪ] ADV ~ **happy** überglücklich

ECT ABBR of **electroconvulsive therapy** Elektrokrampftherapie f

Ecuador [ˈekwədɔːʳ] N Ecuador nt

ecumenical [ˌiːkjʊˈmenɪkəl] ADJ (form) ökumenisch

eczema [ˈeksɪmə] N Ekzem nt

ed (a) ABBR of **editor** Hrsg. **(b)** ABBR of **edition** Ausg.

eddy [ˈedɪ] **1** N Wirbel m **2** VI wirbeln

Eden [ˈiːdn] N (also fig) **Garden of ~** Garten m Eden

edge [edʒ] **1** N **(a)** (of knife) Schneide f; **to take the ~ off sth** (fig) sensation etw der Wirkung (gen) berauben; pain etw lindern; **the noise sets my teeth on ~** das Geräusch geht mir durch und durch; **his arrogance sets my teeth on ~** seine Arroganz bringt mich auf die Palme (inf); **to be on ~** nervös sein; **my nerves are on ~** ich bin schrecklich nervös; **there was**

an ~ to his voice seine Stimme klang ärgerlich; **to have the ~ on sb/sth** jdm/etw überlegen sein; **it gives her/it that extra ~** darin besteht eben der kleine Unterschied **(b)** (= outer limit) Rand m; (of brick, cube) Kante f; (of lake, river, sea) Ufer nt; (of estates etc) Grenze f; **the trees at the ~ of the road** die Bäume am Straßenrand; **the film had us on the ~ of our seats** der Film war unheimlich spannend **2** VT **(a)** (= put a border on) einfassen; ~**d in black** mit einem schwarzen Rand **(b) to ~ one's way toward(s) sth** (slowly) sich allmählich auf etw (acc) zubewegen; (carefully) sich vorsichtig auf etw (acc) zubewegen; **she ~d her way through the crowd** sie schlängelte sich durch die Menge **3** VI sich schieben; **to ~ toward(s) the door** sich zur Tür stehlen; **he ~d past me** er schob sich an mir vorbei
➤ **edge out** **1** VT SEP beiseite drängen; **Germany edged England out of the final** Deutschland verdrängte England aus dem Endspiel **2** VI **the driver edged out onto the main road** der Fahrer fuhr vorsichtig auf die Hauptstraße
➤ **edge up** **1** VT SEP prices etc hoch drücken **2** VI (prices etc) hoch gehen

edgeways [ˈedʒweɪz] ADV **I couldn't get a word in ~** ich bin überhaupt nicht zu Wort gekommen

edging [ˈedʒɪŋ] N Einfassung f

edging shears PL Rasenschere f

edgy [ˈedʒɪ] ADJ (+ER) nervös

EDI ABBR of **electronic data interchange** elektronischer Datenaustausch

edible [ˈedɪbl] ADJ essbar

edict [ˈiːdɪkt] N Erlass m

edification [ˌedɪfɪˈkeɪʃən] N **for the ~ of ...** zur Erbauung des/der ...

edifice [ˈedɪfɪs] N (lit, fig) Gebäude nt

edifying [ˈedɪfaɪɪŋ] ADJ erbaulich

edit [ˈedɪt] VT series, newspaper, magazine herausgeben; newspaper story, book, text redigieren; film, tape schneiden; (Comput) editieren
➤ **edit out** VT SEP herausnehmen; (from film, tape) herausschneiden; character (from story) herausstreichen

editable [ˈedɪtəbl] ADJ (Comput) file editierbar

editing [ˈedɪtɪŋ] N (of series, newspaper, magazine) Herausgabe f; (of newspaper story, book, text) Redaktion f; (of film, tape) Schnitt m; (Comput) Editieren nt

edition [ɪˈdɪʃən] N Ausgabe f; (= impression) Auflage f

editor [ˈedɪtəʳ] N Herausgeber(in) m(f); (publisher's) (Verlags)lektor(in) m(f); (Film) Cutter(in) m(f); (Comput) Editor m; **political ~** politischer Redakteur m, politische Redakteurin f; **sports ~** Sportredakteur(in) m(f)

editorial [ˌedɪˈtɔːrɪəl] **1** ADJ redaktionell; ~ **department** or **office** Redaktion f; ~ **page** Kommentarseite f; **the paper's ~ policy** die redaktionelle Linie der Zeitung **2** N Leitartikel m

EDP ABBR of **electronic data processing** EDV f

educate [ˈedjʊkeɪt] VT **(a)** (Sch, Univ) erziehen; **he was ~d at Eton** er ist in Eton zur Schule gegangen **(b)** public informieren; **we need to ~ our children about drugs** wir müssen dafür sorgen, dass unsere Kinder über Drogen Bescheid wissen

educated [ˈedjʊkeɪtɪd] ADJ gebildet; **to make an ~ guess** eine fundierte or wohl begründete Vermutung anstellen

education [ˌedjʊˈkeɪʃən] N Erziehung f; (= studies, training) Ausbildung f; (= knowledge, culture) Bildung f; **Ministry of Education** Ministerium nt für Erziehung und Unterricht; **lecturer in ~** Dozent(in) m(f) für Pädagogik; **College of Education** pädagogische Hochschule f; (for graduates) Studienseminar nt; (local) ~ **authority** Schulbehörde f; ~ **is free** die Schulausbildung ist kostenlos; **to get an ~** eine Ausbildung bekommen; **she had a university ~** sie hatte eine Universitätsausbildung; **she had little ~** sie war ziemlich ungebildet

educational [ˌedjʊˈkeɪʃənl] ADJ **(a)** (= academic) needs erzieherisch; (at school level) needs, achievement schulisch; ~ **system** (= institutions) Bildungswesen nt; (= structure) Bildungssystem nt; ~ **opportunities** Ausbildungschancen pl; ~ **standards** (in schools) Unterrichtsniveau nt; (of country) Bildungsniveau nt **(b)** (= teaching) issue pädagogisch; ~ **theory** Pädagogik f; ~

supplies Unterrichtsmaterial *nt*
(c) *experience, video* lehrreich; ~ **trip** (= *school trip*)
Klassenfahrt *f*; (*for adults*) Bildungsreise *f*; ~ **film** Lehrfilm *m*;
~ **toy** pädagogisch wertvolles Spielzeug; ~ **game** Lernspiel *nt*
educationalist [ˌedjʊˈkeɪʃnəlɪst] N Pädagoge *m*, Pädagogin *f*
educationally [ˌedjʊˈkeɪʃnəlɪ] ADV ~ **subnormal** lernbehindert
educational park N (*US*) Gesamtschulanlage *f*
educationist [ˌedjʊˈkeɪʃnɪst] N = **educationalist**
educative [ˈedjʊkətɪv] ADJ erzieherisch
Edwardian [edˈwɔːdɪən] ADJ Edwardianisch; ~ **England** England
in der Zeit Eduards VII.
EEC N (*dated*) ABBR *of* **European Economic Community** EG *f*,
EWG *f* (*dated*)
eel [iːl] N Aal *m*
EENT (*US Med*) ABBR *of* **eye, ear, nose and throat;** ~ **specialist**
Augen- und HNO-Arzt *m*/-Ärztin *f*
eerie, eery [ˈɪərɪ] ADJ (+ER) unheimlich
eerily [ˈɪərɪlɪ] ADV (+*vb*) unheimlich; (+*adj*) auf unheimliche
Weise; **the whole town was ~ quiet** in der ganzen Stadt
herrschte eine unheimliche Stille
efface [ɪˈfeɪs] VT auslöschen

effect [ɪˈfekt] 🔳 N **(a)** Wirkung *f*, Effekt *m*; (= *repercussion*)
Auswirkung *f*; **alcohol has the ~ of dulling your senses**
Alkohol bewirkt eine Abstumpfung der Sinne; **the ~ of this
is that ...** das hat zur Folge, dass ...; **to feel the ~s of the drugs**
die Wirkung der Drogen spüren; **to no ~** erfolglos; **to have
an ~ on sb/sth** eine Wirkung auf jdn/etw haben; **to have a
good ~ (on sb/sth)** eine gute Wirkung (auf jdn/etw) haben;
to have no ~ keine Wirkung haben; **to take ~** (*drug*) wirken;
with immediate ~ mit sofortiger Wirkung; **with ~ from 3
March** mit Wirkung vom 3. März; **to create an ~** eine
Wirkung *or* einen Effekt erzielen; **the sword was only for ~**
der Degen war nur zum Effekt da
(b) (= *meaning*) **we received a letter to the ~ that ...** wir
erhielten ein Schreiben des Inhalts, dass ...; **... or words to
that ~ ...** oder etwas in diesem Sinne
(c) **effects** PL (= *property*) Effekten *pl*
(d) (= *reality*) **in ~** in Wirklichkeit
(e) (*of laws*) **to be in ~** gültig *or* in Kraft sein; **to come into** *or*
take ~ in Kraft treten; **to put sth into ~** etw in Kraft setzen
🔳 VT bewirken; **to ~ a change** Veränderungen herbeiführen

effective [ɪˈfektɪv] ADJ **(a)** *way, measures, government, politician*
effektiv; *means, treatment, vaccine, deterrent* wirksam; **to be ~
in doing sth** bewirken, dass etw geschieht; **to be ~ against sth**
(*drug*) gegen etw wirken
(b) *pattern, combination* wirkungsvoll
(c) (= *actual, also Econ, Fin*) effektiv, tatsächlich; *leader*
eigentlich
(d) (= *operative*) wirksam, in Kraft; **a new law, ~ from** *or*
becoming ~ on 1 August ein neues Gesetz, das am 1. August
in Kraft tritt; ~ **date** In-Kraft-Treten *nt*
effectively [ɪˈfektɪvlɪ] ADV **(a)** (= *successfully*) wirksam; *function,
work, teach* effektiv **(b)** (= *in effect*) effektiv, praktisch
effectiveness [ɪˈfektɪvnɪs] N Wirksamkeit *f*; (*of strategy,
government, politician*) Effektivität *f*
effeminate [ɪˈfemɪnɪt] ADJ feminin
effervescent [ˌefəˈvesnt] ADJ sprudelnd; (*fig*) überschäumend
effete [ɪˈfiːt] ADJ schwach; *person* saft- und kraftlos
efficacy [ˈefɪkəsɪ] N Wirksamkeit *f*
efficiency [ɪˈfɪʃənsɪ] N (*of person*) Fähigkeit *f*; (*of machine,
factory, organization, system*) Leistungsfähigkeit *f*; (*of method*)
Wirksamkeit *f*; (*of engine*) Sparsamkeit *f*; (*of service*) Effizienz
f (*geh*); **jobs were lost as part of an ~ drive** Stellen wurden
wegrationalisiert
efficient [ɪˈfɪʃənt] ADJ *person* fähig; *system, machine, company,
organization* leistungsfähig; *car, engine* (= *economical*)
sparsam; *service* gut; *method* wirksam; *way, use* rationell; **to
be ~ at (doing) sth** etw gut können
efficiently [ɪˈfɪʃəntlɪ] ADV effektiv; **to work more ~** rationeller
arbeiten
effigy [ˈefɪdʒɪ] N Bildnis *nt*
effing [ˈefɪŋ] (*euph sl*) 🔳 ADJ *person* Scheiß- (*inf*) 🔳 N ~ **and blinding**
Fluchen *nt* 🔳 VI (*only in -ing form*) **he was ~ and blinding** er
erging sich in wüsten Schimpfereien
effluent [ˈeflʊənt] N Abwasser *nt*

effort [ˈefət] N **(a)** (= *attempt*) Versuch *m*; (= *strain, hard work*)
Anstrengung *f*, Mühe *f*; **to make an ~ to do sth** sich
bemühen, etw zu tun; **to make the ~ to do sth** sich (*dat*) die
Mühe machen, etw zu tun; **to make every ~** *or* **a great ~ to
do sth** sich sehr bemühen, etw zu tun; **he made no ~ to be
polite** er machte sich (*dat*) nicht die Mühe, höflich zu sein;
it's an ~ (to get up in the morning) es kostet einige
Mühe(, morgens aufzustehen); **come on, make an ~** komm,
streng dich an; **it's well worth the ~** die Mühe lohnt sich
wirklich
(b) (= *campaign*) Aktion *f*; **the famine relief ~** die Hilfsaktion
gegen die Hungersnot
(c) (*inf*) Unternehmen *nt*; **it was a pretty poor ~** das war eine
ziemlich schwache Leistung; **it's not bad for a first ~** das ist
nicht schlecht für den Anfang
effortless [ˈefətlɪs] ADJ mühelos; *charm, elegance* natürlich
effortlessly [ˈefətlɪslɪ] ADV mühelos
effrontery [ɪˈfrʌntərɪ] N Unverschämtheit *f*
effusion [ɪˈfjuːʒən] N (*lit, fig*) Erguss *m*
effusive [ɪˈfjuːsɪv] ADJ überschwänglich; (= *gushing*) exaltiert;
to be ~ in one's praise *of* **or for sb** jdn überschwänglich loben
E-fit [ˈiːfɪt] N elektronisch erstelltes Fahndungsfoto
EFL ABBR *of* **English as a Foreign Language** Englisch als
Fremdsprache; ~ **teacher** Lehrer(in) *m(f)* für Englisch als
Fremdsprache
EFTA [ˈeftə] ABBR *of* **European Free Trade Association** EFTA *f*
eg ABBR *of* **exempli gratia** (= *for example*) z. B.
EGA (*Comput*) ABBR *of* **enhanced graphics adapter** EGA *m*
egalitarian [ɪˌgælɪˈteərɪən] ADJ egalitär
egalitarianism [ɪˌgælɪˈteərɪənɪzəm] N Egalitarismus *m*
egg [eg] N Ei *nt*; **to put all one's ~s in one basket** (*prov*) alles
auf eine Karte setzen; **to have ~ on** *or* **all over one's face** (*fig
inf*) dumm dastehen (*inf*)
➤ **egg on** VT SEP anstacheln
egg: egg-and-spoon race N Eierlauf *m*; **egg cup** N Eierbecher
m; **egg custard** N Eiercreme *f*; **egghead** N (*pej inf*) Eierkopf *m*
(*inf*); **eggplant** N (*esp US*) Aubergine *f*; **eggshell** N Eierschale
f; **egg timer** N Eieruhr *f*; **egg white** N Eiweiß *nt*; **egg yolk** N
Eigelb *nt*
egis [ˈiːdʒɪs] N (*US*) = **aegis**
ego [ˈiːgəʊ] N (*Psych*) Ego *nt*, Ich *nt*; (= *self-esteem*)
Selbstbewusstsein *nt*; (= *conceit*) Einbildung *f*; **his ~ won't
allow him to admit he is wrong** sein Stolz lässt ihn nie
zugeben, dass er Unrecht hat
egocentric [ˌegəʊˈsentrɪk] ADJ egozentrisch
egoism [ˈegəʊɪzəm] N Egoismus *m*
egoist [ˈegəʊɪst] N Egoist(in) *m(f)*
egoistical [ˌegəʊˈɪstɪkəl] ADJ egoistisch
egomaniac [ˌiːgəʊˈmeɪnɪæk] N Egomane *m*, Egomanin *f*
egotism [ˈegəʊtɪzəm] N Ichbezogenheit *f*
egotist [ˈegəʊtɪst] N ichbezogener Mensch
egotistic(al) [ˌegəʊˈtɪstɪk(əl)] ADJ ichbezogen
ego trip N (*inf*) Egotrip *m* (*inf*)
Egypt [ˈiːdʒɪpt] N Ägypten *nt*
Egyptian [ɪˈdʒɪpʃən] 🔳 ADJ ägyptisch 🔳 N Ägypter(in) *m(f)*
Egyptology [ˌiːdʒɪpˈtɒlədʒɪ] N Ägyptologie *f*
eh [eɪ] INTERJ **(a)** (*inviting repetition*) **I've found a gold mine – eh?**
ich habe eine Goldmine entdeckt – was? **(b)** (*inviting
agreement*) **it's good, eh?** gut, nicht?
EIB ABBR *of* **European Investment Bank** Europäische
Investitionsbank
eiderdown [ˈaɪdədaʊn] N (= *quilt*) Federbett *nt*, Daunendecke *f*
eight [eɪt] 🔳 ADJ acht; **to be behind the ~ ball** (*US inf*) in der
Patsche sitzen (*inf*); *see* **six** 🔳 N Acht *f*; *see* **six**; **to have had one
over the ~** (*inf*) einen über den Durst getrunken haben (*inf*)
eighteen [ˈeɪˈtiːn] 🔳 ADJ achtzehn 🔳 N Achtzehn *f*
eighteenth [ˈeɪˈtiːnθ] 🔳 ADJ achtzehnte(r, s) 🔳 N (= *fraction*)
Achtzehntel *nt*; (*of series*) Achtzehnte(r, s); *see* **sixteenth**
eighth [eɪtθ] 🔳 ADJ achte(r, s) 🔳 N (= *fraction*) Achtel *nt*; (*of
series*) Achte(r, s); *see* **sixth**
eighth note N (*US Mus*) Achtelnote *f*
eightieth [ˈeɪtɪəθ] 🔳 ADJ achtzigste(r, s) 🔳 N (= *fraction*)
Achtzigstel *nt*; (*of series*) Achtzigste(r, s); *see* **sixtieth**
eighty [ˈeɪtɪ] 🔳 ADJ achtzig 🔳 N Achtzig *f*; *see* **sixty**

Eire [ˈɛərə] N Irland nt

either [ˈaɪðəʳ, ˈiːðəʳ] **1** ADJ, PRON **(a)** (= one or other) eine(r, s) (von beiden); **there are two boxes on the table, take ~ (of them)** auf dem Tisch liegen zwei Schachteln, nimm eine davon; **if on ~ side of the road there is a line of trees** wenn eine Straßenseite mit Bäumen bestanden ist **(b)** (= each, both) jede(r, s), beide pl; **~ day would suit me** beide Tage passen mir; **which bus will you take? – ~ (will do)** welchen Bus wollen Sie nehmen? – das ist egal; **on ~ side of the street** auf beiden Seiten der Straße; **it wasn't in ~ (box)** es war in keiner der beiden (Kisten) **2** ADV, CONJ **(a)** (after neg statement) auch nicht; **I have never heard of him – no, I haven't ~** ich habe noch nie von ihm gehört – ich auch nicht **(b)** **~ ... or** entweder ... oder; (after a negative) weder ... noch; **he must be ~ lazy or stupid** er muss entweder faul oder dumm sein; **I have never been to ~ Paris or Rome** ich bin weder in Paris noch in Rom gewesen **(c)** (= moreover) **she inherited some money and not an insignificant amount ~** sie hat Geld geerbt, und (zwar) gar nicht so wenig

ejaculate [ɪˈdʒækjʊleɪt] VI (Physiol) ejakulieren

ejaculation [ɪˌdʒækjʊˈleɪʃən] N (Physiol) Ejakulation f, Samenerguss m

eject [ɪˈdʒekt] **1** VT **(a)** heckler, tenant hinauswerfen **(b)** cartridge auswerfen **2** VI (pilot) den Schleudersitz betätigen

ejection [ɪˈdʒekʃən] N Hinauswurf m; (of cartridge) Auswerfen nt

ejector seat [ɪˈdʒektəsiːt], (US) **ejection seat** N (Aviat) Schleudersitz m

eke out [ˈiːkaʊt] VT SEP food, supplies strecken; money aufbessern; **to ~ a living** sich (recht und schlecht) durchschlagen

EKG N (US) = ECG

el [el] N (US) ABBR of **elevated railroad** Hochbahn f

elaborate [ɪˈlæbərɪt] **1** ADJ **(a)** (= complex, over-complex) kompliziert; (= sophisticated) ausgeklügelt; scheme groß angelegt; precautions, plans umfangreich; preparations ausführlich; cooking, ceremony, design aufwändig; **an ~ meal** ein großes Menü **(b)** (= lavish, ornate) kunstvoll **2** VT [ɪˈlæbəreɪt] (= develop) ausarbeiten; (= refine) verfeinern **3** VI [ɪˈlæbəreɪt] **would you care to or could you ~ on that?** könnten Sie darauf näher eingehen?

elaborately [ɪˈlæbərɪtlɪ] ADV **(a)** (= in detail) ausführlich; (= complexly) kompliziert; **an ~ staged press conference** eine mit großem Aufwand veranstaltete Pressekonferenz **(b)** (= ornately, lavishly) kunstvoll

elaboration [ɪˌlæbəˈreɪʃən] N (= working out) Ausarbeitung f; (= refinement) Verfeinerung f

élan [eɪˈlæn] N Elan m

elapse [ɪˈlæps] VI vergehen

elastic [ɪˈlæstɪk] **1** ADJ (lit, fig) elastisch; **~ waist** Taille f mit Gummizug **2** N Gummi(band nt) m; (US: = rubber band) Gummi m; **a piece of ~** ein Gummiband nt

elasticated [ɪˈlæstɪkeɪtɪd] ADJ elastisch; **~ waist** (of garment) Taille f mit Gummizug

elastic band N (esp Brit) Gummiband nt

elasticity [iːlæsˈtɪsɪtɪ] N Elastizität f

Elastoplast® [ɪˈlæstəʊplɑːst] N (Brit) Hansaplast® nt

elated [ɪˈleɪtɪd] ADJ begeistert

elation [ɪˈleɪʃən] N Begeisterung (at über +acc), Hochstimmung f

elbow [ˈelbəʊ] **1** N Ellbogen m; **since he's been rubbing ~s with senators** (esp US) seit er sich in Senatorenkreisen bewegt **2** VT **he ~ed his way through the crowd** er boxte sich durch die Menge; **to ~ sb aside** jdn beiseite stoßen; **he ~ed me in the stomach** er stieß mir or mich mit dem Ellbogen in den Magen

elbow: **elbow grease** N (inf) Muskelkraft f; **elbowroom** N (inf: lit, fig) Ellbogenfreiheit f (inf)

elder¹ [ˈeldəʳ] **1** ADJ ATTR COMP of **old** **(a)** (= older) brother etc ältere(r, s) **(b)** (= senior) **Pliny the ~** Plinius der Ältere **2** N **(a) respect your ~s and betters** du musst Respekt vor Älteren haben **(b)** (of tribe, Church) Älteste(r) m

elder² N (Bot) Holunder m

elderberry [ˈeldəˌberɪ] N Holunderbeere f; **~ wine** Holunderwein m

elderly [ˈeldəlɪ] ADJ ältlich, ältere(r, s) attr

elder statesman N (alt)erfahrener Staatsmann

eldest [ˈeldɪst] **1** ADJ ATTR SUPERL of **old** älteste(r, s) **2** N **the ~** der/die/das Älteste; (pl) die Ältesten pl; **the ~ of four children** das älteste von vier Kindern; **my ~** (inf) mein Ältester, meine Älteste

elect [ɪˈlekt] **1** VT **(a)** wählen; **he was ~ed chairman/MP** er wurde zum Vorsitzenden/Abgeordneten gewählt; **to ~ sb to the Senate** jdn in den Senat wählen **(b)** (= choose) sich entscheiden für; **to ~ to do sth** sich dafür entscheiden, etw zu tun **2** ADJ **the president ~** der designierte Präsident

election [ɪˈlekʃən] N Wahl f

election IN CPDS Wahl-; **election campaign** N Wahlkampf m

electioneering [ɪˌlekʃəˈnɪərɪŋ] N (= campaign) Wahlkampf m; (= propaganda) Wahlpropaganda f

elective [ɪˈlektɪv] N (US: Sch, Univ) Wahlfach nt

elector [ɪˈlektəʳ] N Wähler(in) m(f)

electoral [ɪˈlektərəl] ADJ Wahl-; **~ process** Wahlverfahren nt; **~ system** Wahlsystem nt

electoral register, electoral roll N Wählerverzeichnis nt

electorate [ɪˈlektərɪt] N Wähler pl, Wählerschaft f

electric [ɪˈlektrɪk] **1** ADJ **(a)** (lit) (= powered by electricity) elektrisch; (= carrying electricity) Strom-; **~ car/vehicle** Elektroauto nt; **~ razor** Elektrorasierer m; **~ kettle** elektrischer Wasserkocher **(b)** (fig: = exciting) wie elektrisiert; **the effect was ~** das hatte eine tolle Wirkung **2** N **(a)** (inf: = electricity) Elektrizität f **(b) electrics** PL Strom m; (Aut) Elektrik f

electrical [ɪˈlektrɪkəl] ADJ elektrisch; **~ appliance** Elektrogerät nt; **~ system** Elektrik f

electrical: **electrical engineer** N Elektrotechniker(in) m(f); (with degree) Elektroingenieur(in) m(f); **electrical engineering** N Elektrotechnik f

electrically [ɪˈlektrɪkəlɪ] ADV elektrisch; **an ~ powered car** ein Wagen m mit Elektroantrieb

electric: **electric bill** N (inf) Stromrechnung f; **electric blanket** N Heizdecke f; **electric chair** N elektrischer Stuhl; **electric cooker** N Elektroherd m; **electric eye** N Fotozelle f; **electric fence** N Elektrozaun m; **electric fire** N elektrisches Heizgerät; **electric guitar** N E-Gitarre f; **electric heater** N elektrisches Heizgerät

electrician [ɪlekˈtrɪʃən] N Elektriker(in) m(f)

electricity [ɪlekˈtrɪsɪtɪ] N Elektrizität f; (= electric power for use) (elektrischer) Strom

electricity meter N Stromzähler m

electric: **electric light** N elektrisches Licht; **electric organ** N elektrische Orgel; **electric shock** N Stromschlag m; (Med) Elektroschock m; **electric toothbrush** N elektrische Zahnbürste; **electric train** N Elektrozug m; (= model train set) elektrische Eisenbahn

electrification [ɪˌlektrɪfɪˈkeɪʃən] N Elektrifizierung f

electrify [ɪˈlektrɪfaɪ] VT **(a)** (Rail) elektrifizieren **(b)** (fig) elektrisieren

electrifying [ɪˈlektrɪfaɪɪŋ] ADJ (fig) elektrisierend

electro- [ɪˈlektrəʊ-] PREF Elektro-

electrocardiogram [ɪˌlektrəʊˈkɑːdɪəʊɡræm] N Elektrokardiogramm nt

electrocute [ɪˈlektrəkjuːt] VT durch einen (Strom)schlag töten; (= execute) durch den or auf dem elektrischen Stuhl hinrichten

electrocution [ɪˌlektrəˈkjuːʃən] N (= execution) Hinrichtung f durch den elektrischen Stuhl

electrode [ɪˈlektrəʊd] N Elektrode f

electrolysis [ɪlekˈtrɒlɪsɪs] N Elektrolyse f

electromagnetic [ɪˌlektrəʊmæɡˈnetɪk] ADJ elektromagnetisch

electron [ɪˈlektrɒn] N Elektron nt

electronic ADJ, **electronically** ADV [ɪlekˈtrɒnɪk, -əlɪ] elektronisch

electronic: **electronic banking** N elektronischer Zahlungsverkehr; **electronic data interchange** N (Comput) elektronischer Datenaustausch; **electronic data processing**

N (*Comput*) elektronische Datenverarbeitung; **electronic engineering** N Elektronik *f*; **electronic funds transfer** N ~ **at point of sale** elektronische Abbuchung am Verkaufsterminal; **electronic keyboard** N (*Mus*) elektronisches Keyboard; **electronic mail** N E-Mail *f*; **electronic music** N elektronische Musik

electronics [ɪlek'trɒnɪks] N **(a)** SING (*subject*) Elektronik *f* **(b)** PL (*of machine etc*) Elektronik *f*

electronic: electronic surveillance N elektronische Überwachung; **electronic tagging** N elektronische Fußfesseln *pl*

electroplated [ɪ'lektrəupleɪtɪd] ADJ (galvanisch) versilbert/verchromt *etc*

electroshock therapy [ɪ'lektrəuʃɒk'θerəpɪ] N Elektroschocktherapie *f*

elegance ['elɪɡəns] N Eleganz *f*

elegant ADJ, **elegantly** ADV ['elɪɡənt, -lɪ] elegant

elegiac [ˌelɪ'dʒaɪək] ADJ elegisch

elegy ['elɪdʒɪ] N Elegie *f*

element ['elɪmənt] N (*all senses*) Element *nt*; **one of the key ~s of the peace plan** einer der grundlegenden Bestandteile des Friedensplans; **an ~ of danger** ein Gefahrenelement *nt*; **an ~ of truth** eine Spur von Wahrheit; **a hooligan/criminal ~** ein paar Rowdys/Kriminelle; **the (four) ~s** die (vier) Elemente; **to be in one's ~** in seinem Element sein

elemental [ˌelɪ'mentl] ADJ (*liter*) elementar; **~ force** Naturgewalt *f*

elementary [ˌelɪ'mentərɪ] ADJ **(a)** *rules* einfach, elementar; *idea, fact, precautions* grundlegend; **~ mistake** Grundfehler *m* **(b)** (*pej:* = *rudimentary*) primitiv **(c)** (*Sch*) *level* elementar; **~ skills/knowledge** Grundkenntnisse *pl*; **~ maths** Elementarmathematik *f*

elementary school N (*US*) Grundschule *f*

elephant ['elɪfənt] N Elefant *m*

elevate ['elɪveɪt] VT **(a)** heben; (= *increase*) *blood pressure etc* erhöhen **(b)** (*fig*) *mind* erbauen **(c) to ~ sb to the peerage** jdn in den Adelsstand erheben

elevated ['elɪveɪtɪd] ADJ **(a)** (= *raised*) erhöht; **~ train, ~ railway** (*Brit*) *or* **railroad** (*US*) Hochbahn *f*; **the ~ section of the M4** die als Hochstraße gebaute Strecke der M4 **(b)** *status, tone, style, language* gehoben; *thoughts* erhaben

elevation [ˌelɪ'veɪʃən] N **(a)** (*above sea level*) Höhe *f* über dem Meeresspiegel *or* über N.N.; (*hill etc*) Anhöhe *f* **(b)** (*Archit:* = *drawing*) Aufriss *m*; **front ~** Fassadenaufriss *m*

elevator ['elɪveɪtə^r] N (*US*) Fahrstuhl *m*

eleven [ɪ'levn] **1** N (*also Sport*) Elf *f*; **the German ~** die deutsche (National)elf; **the second ~** die zweite Mannschaft **2** ADJ elf; *see also* **six**

elevenses [ɪ'levnzɪz] N SING *or* PL (*Brit*) zweites Frühstück

eleventh [ɪ'levnθ] **1** ADJ elfte(r, s); **at the ~ hour** (*fig*) fünf Minuten vor zwölf **2** N (= *fraction*) Elftel *nt*; (*of series*) Elfte(r, s); *see also* **sixth**

elf [elf] N, *pl* **elves** Kobold *m*

elicit [ɪ'lɪsɪt] VT entlocken (*from sb* jdm); *support* gewinnen (*from sb* jds)

elide [ɪ'laɪd] VT auslassen

eligibility [ˌelɪdʒə'bɪlɪtɪ] N Berechtigung *f*; **because of his undoubted ~ for the post** da er für die Stelle zweifelsohne in Frage kommt/kam

eligible ['elɪdʒəbl] ADJ in Frage kommend; (*for competition etc*) teilnahmeberechtigt; (*for student flights, grants etc*) berechtigt; (*for membership*) aufnahmeberechtigt; **to be ~ for a job** für einen Posten infrage *or* in Frage kommen; **to be ~ for a pension** pensionsberechtigt sein; **to be ~ to contract** vertragsberechtigt sein; **an ~ bachelor** ein begehrter Junggeselle

eliminate [ɪ'lɪmɪneɪt] VT **(a)** ausschließen; *competitor* ausschalten; *inflation, poverty, waste* ein Ende machen (+*dat*); *danger, problem* beseitigen; **our team was ~d in the second round** unsere Mannschaft schied in der zweiten Runde aus **(b)** (= *kill*) eliminieren

elimination [ɪˌlɪmɪ'neɪʃən] N **(a)** Ausschluss *m*; (*of competitor*) Ausschaltung *f*; (*of inflation, poverty, waste*) Beendung *f*; (*of danger, problem*) Beseitigung *f*; **by (a) process of ~** durch negative Auslese **(b)** (= *killing*) Eliminierung *f*

elision [ɪ'lɪʒən] N Elision *f*

elite [eɪ'liːt] **1** N (*often pej*) Elite *f* **2** ADJ Elite-; **~ group** Elitegruppe *f*, Elite *f*

elitism [eɪ'liːtɪzəm] N Elitedenken *nt*

elitist [eɪ'liːtɪst] **1** ADJ elitär **2** N elitär Denkende(r) *mf*; **he's an ~** er denkt elitär

elixir [ɪ'lɪksə^r] N Elixier *nt*; **~ of life** Lebenselixier *nt*

Elizabethan [ɪˌlɪzə'biːθən] **1** ADJ elisabethanisch **2** N Elisabethaner(in) *m(f)*

elk [elk] N Elch *m*

ellipse [ɪ'lɪps] N Ellipse *f*

elliptic(al) [ɪ'lɪptɪk(əl)] ADJ **(a)** (*Math etc*) elliptisch **(b)** (*fig*) *account* andeutungsweise; *style* unklar

elm [elm] N Ulme *f*

elocution [ˌelə'kjuːʃən] N Sprechtechnik *f*; **~ lessons** Sprechunterricht *m*

elongate ['iːlɒŋɡeɪt] VT verlängern; (= *stretch out*) strecken

elongated ['iːlɒŋɡeɪtɪd] ADJ verlängert; (= *stretched*) *neck* ausgestreckt; *shape* länglich

elope [ɪ'ləup] VI durchbrennen (*inf*), um zu heiraten

eloquence ['eləkwəns] N (*of person*) Redegewandtheit *f*; (*of speech, words*) Gewandtheit *f*; (*of statement, tribute, plea*) Wortgewandtheit *f*

eloquent ['eləkwənt] ADJ *speech, words* gewandt; *statement, tribute, plea* wortgewandt; *person* redegewandt; **to be ~ about sth** *or* **on sth** mit schönen Worten über etw (*acc*) reden; **to wax ~ (about** *or* **on sth)** (von etw) schwärmen

eloquently ['eləkwəntlɪ] ADV *express* mit beredten Worten; *demonstrate* deutlich

else [els] ADV **(a)** (*after pron*) andere(r, s); **anybody ~ would have done it** jeder andere hätte es gemacht; **is there anybody ~ there?** (*in addition*) ist sonst (noch) jemand da?; **since John doesn't want it, does anybody ~ want it?** da John es nicht will, will jemand anders es haben?; **somebody ~** sonst jemand; **I'd prefer something ~** ich möchte lieber etwas anderes; **have you anything ~ to say?** haben Sie sonst noch etwas zu sagen?; **do you find this species anywhere ~?** findet man die Gattung sonst wo *or* auch anderswo?; **but they haven't got anywhere ~ to go** aber sie können sonst nirgends anders hingehen; **this is somebody ~'s umbrella** dieser Schirm gehört jemand anders; **something ~** sonst etwas; **that car is something ~** (*inf*) das Auto ist einfach Spitze (*inf*); **if all ~ fails** wenn alle Stricke reißen; **above all ~** vor allen Dingen; **will there be anything ~, sir?** (*in shop*) darf es sonst noch etwas sein?; **everyone/everything ~** alle anderen/alles andere; **everywhere ~** überall sonst; **somewhere** *or* **someplace ~** woanders; (*with motion*) woandershin; **from somewhere ~** woandersher

(b) (*after pron, neg*) **nobody ~, no one ~** sonst niemand; **nothing ~** sonst nichts; **what do you want? – nothing ~, thank you** was möchten Sie? – danke, nichts weiter; **if nothing ~, you'll enjoy it** auf jeden Fall wird es dir Spaß machen; **there's nothing ~ for it but to …** da gibt es keinen anderen Ausweg, als zu …; **nowhere ~** sonst nirgends *or* nirgendwo; (*with motion*) sonst nirgendwohin; **there's not much ~ we can do** wir können kaum etwas anderes tun

(c) (*after interrog*) **where ~?** wo sonst?; **who ~?** wer sonst?; **who ~ but John could have done a thing like that?** wer anders als John hätte so etwas tun können?; **what ~?** was sonst?; **how ~ can I do it?** wie kann ich es denn sonst machen?; **what ~ could I have done?** was hätte ich sonst tun können?

(d) (= *otherwise, if not*) sonst, andernfalls; **do it now (or) ~ you'll be punished** tu es jetzt, sonst setzt es Strafe; **do it or ~ …!** mach das, sonst …!; **he's either a genius or ~ he's completely mad** er ist entweder ein Genie oder aber völlig verrückt

elsewhere [ˌels'wɛə^r] ADV woanders; **to go ~** woandershin gehen; **her thoughts were ~** sie war mit ihren Gedanken woanders

ELT ABBR *of* **English Language Teaching**

elucidate [ɪ'luːsɪdeɪt] VT *text* erklären; *issue, situation* erhellen; *point* näher ausführen

elude [ɪ'luːd] VT *observation, justice* sich entziehen (+*dat*); *sb's gaze* ausweichen (+*dat*); *police, enemy* entkommen (+*dat*); **to ~ capture** entkommen; **sleep ~d her** sie konnte keinen Schlaf finden; **the name ~s me** der Name ist mir entfallen

elusive [ɪˈluːsɪv] ADJ **(a)** *truth* schwer fassbar; *goal, target, success* schwer erreichbar; (= *unattainable*) unerreichbar; **financial success proved ~** der finanzielle Erfolg wollte sich nicht einstellen **(b)** *person* schwer zu erreichen; *prey* schwer zu fangen

elves [elvz] PL *of* **elf**

emaciated [ɪˈmeɪsɪeɪtɪd] ADJ ausgezehrt

E-mail, e-mail [ˈiːmeɪl] ◼ N E-Mail *f* ◼ VT **to ~ sb** jdm eine E-Mail schicken; **to ~ sth** etw per E-Mail schicken

emanate [ˈeməneɪt] VI ausgehen (*from* von); (*odour*) ausströmen (*from* von); (*documents, instructions*) stammen (*from* aus)

emancipate [ɪˈmænsɪpeɪt] VT *women* emanzipieren; *slaves* freilassen; *country, people* befreien

emancipated [ɪˈmænsɪpeɪtɪd] ADJ *woman, outlook* emanzipiert

emancipation [ɪˌmænsɪˈpeɪʃən] N Emanzipation *f*; (*of slave*) Freilassung *f*; (*of country, people*) Befreiung *f*

emasculate [ɪˈmæskjʊleɪt] VT (= *weaken*) entkräften

embalm [ɪmˈbɑːm] VT einbalsamieren

embankment [ɪmˈbæŋkmənt] N (Ufer)böschung *f*; (*along path, road*) Böschung *f*; (*for railway*) Bahndamm *m*; (*holding back water*) (Ufer)damm *m*

embargo [ɪmˈbɑːgəʊ] N, *pl* **-es (a)** Embargo *nt*; **oil/arms/trade ~** Öl-/Waffen-/Handelsembargo *nt*; **to impose** *or* **place** *or* **put an ~ on sth** ein Embargo über etw (*acc*) verhängen; **to lift an ~ on sth** ein Embargo über etw (*acc*) aufheben **(b)** (*fig*) Sperre *f*; **to put an ~ on further spending** alle weiteren Ausgaben sperren

embark [ɪmˈbɑːk] VI **(a)** (*Naut*) sich einschiffen; (*troops*) eingeschifft werden **(b)** (*fig*) **to ~ up(on) sth** etw beginnen

embarkation [embɑːˈkeɪʃən] N Einschiffung *f*

embarkation papers PL Bordpapiere *pl*

embarrass [ɪmˈbærəs] VT in Verlegenheit bringen; (*generosity etc*) beschämen; **she was ~ed by the question** die Frage war ihr peinlich

embarrassed [ɪmˈbærəst] ADJ verlegen; **I am/feel so ~ (about it)** es ist mir so peinlich; **she was ~ to be seen with him** *or* **about being seen with him** es war ihr peinlich, mit ihm gesehen zu werden

embarrassing [ɪmˈbærəsɪŋ] ADJ peinlich; *generosity etc* beschämend

embarrassingly [ɪmˈbærəsɪŋlɪ] ADV auf peinliche Weise; (*introducing sentence*) peinlicherweise; **it was ~ bad** es war so schlecht, dass es schon peinlich war

embarrassment [ɪmˈbærəsmənt] N Verlegenheit *f*; **to cause ~ to sb** jdn in Verlegenheit bringen; **to my great ~ she ...** sie ..., was mir sehr peinlich war; **she's an ~ to her family** sie blamiert die ganze Familie (*inf*)

embassy [ˈembəsɪ] N Botschaft *f*

embattled [ɪmˈbætld] ADJ **(a)** (= *besieged*) belagert; (= *fought over*) umkämpft; (= *fighting*) kämpfend **(b)** (*fig*) *person, government* bedrängt

embed [ɪmˈbed] VT **(a)** einlassen; **the car was firmly ~ded in the mud** das Auto steckte im Schlamm fest; **the bullet ~ded itself in the wall** die Kugel bohrte sich in die Wand; **to be (deeply) ~ded in sth** (*fig*) (tief) in etw (*dat*) verwurzelt sein **(b)** (*Comput*) **~ded commands** eingebettete Befehle

embellish [ɪmˈbelɪʃ] VT schmücken; (*fig*) *tale, account* ausschmücken; *truth* beschönigen

embellishment [ɪmˈbelɪʃmənt] N Schmuck *m*

embers [ˈembəz] PL Glut *f*

embezzle [ɪmˈbezl] VT unterschlagen, veruntreuen (*from* +*dat*)

embezzlement [ɪmˈbezlmənt] N Unterschlagung *f*, Veruntreuung *f*

embitter [ɪmˈbɪtə'] VT verbittern

emblazon [ɪmˈbleɪzən] VT *name* stolz hervorheben; **the name "Jones" was ~ed on the cover** der Name „Jones" prangte auf dem Umschlag

emblem [ˈembləm] N Emblem *nt*

emblematic [ˌembləˈmætɪk] ADJ emblematisch (*of* für)

embodiment [ɪmˈbɒdɪmənt] N Verkörperung *f*; **to be the ~ of evil** das Böse in Person sein

embody [ɪmˈbɒdɪ] VT **(a)** *ideal etc* verkörpern **(b)** (= *include*) enthalten

emboss [ɪmˈbɒs] VT *metal, leather* prägen; **the cover is ~ed with his name** sein Name ist auf den Einband aufgeprägt

embossed [ɪmˈbɒst] ADJ geprägt; *design* erhaben; **~ wallpaper** Prägetapete *f*

embrace [ɪmˈbreɪs] ◼ VT **(a)** umarmen; **they ~d each other** sie umarmten sich **(b)** *religion* annehmen; *cause* sich annehmen (+*gen*); **he ~d the idea of an integrated Europe** er machte sich (*dat*) den Gedanken eines integrierten Europas zu eigen **(c)** (= *include*) umfassen ◼ VI sich umarmen ◼ N Umarmung *f*

embroider [ɪmˈbrɔɪdə'] ◼ VT *cloth* besticken; *pattern* sticken; (*fig*) *truth* ausschmücken; **to ~ a design on sth** ein Muster auf etw (*acc*) (auf)sticken ◼ VI sticken

embroidered [ɪmˈbrɔɪdəd] ADJ *material etc* bestickt; *design* (auf)gestickt (*on* auf +*acc*)

embroidery [ɪmˈbrɔɪdərɪ] N Stickerei *f*

embroil [ɪmˈbrɔɪl] VT **to become ~ed in a dispute** in einen Streit verwickelt werden

embryo [ˈembrɪəʊ] N Embryo *m*; (*esp fig*) Keim *m*; **in ~** (*lit, fig*) im Keim

embryonic [ˌembrɪˈɒnɪk] ADJ (*esp fig*) keimhaft

emcee [ˈemˈsiː] N Conférencier *m*; (*at private functions*) Zeremonienmeister(in) *m(f)*

emerald [ˈemərəld] ◼ N **(a)** (= *stone*) Smaragd *m* **(b)** (= *colour*) Smaragdgrün *nt* ◼ ADJ smaragden; **~ ring** Smaragdring *m*

Emerald Isle N **the ~** die Grüne Insel

emerge [ɪˈmɜːdʒ] VI **(a)** auftauchen; **one arm ~d from beneath the blanket** ein Arm tauchte unter der Decke hervor; **he ~d from the house/a meeting** er kam aus dem Haus/aus einer Besprechung; **the economy is starting to ~ from the recession** die Wirtschaft beginnt sich von der Rezession zu erholen; **he ~d (as) the winner** er ging als Sieger hervor **(b)** (= *come into being*: *life, new nation*) entstehen **(c)** (*truth, facts etc*) sich herausstellen

emergency [ɪˈmɜːdʒənsɪ] ◼ N Notfall *m*; (*particular situation*) Notlage *f*; **in an ~, in case of ~** im Notfall; **to declare a state of ~** den Notstand erklären; **the doctor's been called out on an ~** der Arzt ist zu einem Notfall gerufen worden ◼ ADJ **(a)** (= *in/for an ~*) Not-; *meeting, talks* außerordentlich; *repair* notdürftig; **~ regulations** Notverordnung *f*; **to undergo ~ surgery** sich einer Notoperation unterziehen; **~ plan/procedure** Plan *m*/Maßnahmen *pl* für den Notfall; **for ~ use only** nur für den Notfall **(b)** (= *for a disaster*) Katastrophen-; **~ aid** *or* **relief** Katastrophenhilfe *f* **(c)** (= *for state of ~*) Notstands-; **~ powers** Notstandsvollmachten *pl*

emergency IN CPDS Not-; **emergency brake** N Notbremse *f*; **emergency call** N Notruf *m*; **emergency cord** N (*Rail*) Notbremse *f*; **emergency exit** N Notausgang *m*; **emergency landing** N Notlandung *f*; **emergency room** N (*US*) Unfallstation *f*; **emergency services** PL Notdienst *m*, Notdienste *pl*; **emergency stop** N (*Aut*) Vollbremsung *f*; **emergency ward** N Unfallstation *f*

emergent [ɪˈmɜːdʒənt] ADJ (*form*) *nation etc* aufstrebend

emeritus [ɪˈmerɪtəs] ADJ emeritiert; **~ professor, professor ~** Professor emeritus *m*

emetic [ɪˈmetɪk] N Brechmittel *nt*

emigrant [ˈemɪgrənt] N Auswanderer *m*, Auswanderin *f*; (*esp for political reasons*) Emigrant(in) *m(f)*

emigrate [ˈemɪgreɪt] VI auswandern; (*esp for political reasons*) emigrieren

emigration [ˌemɪˈgreɪʃən] N Auswanderung *f*; (*esp for political reasons*) Emigration *f*

émigré [ˈemɪgreɪ] N Emigrant(in) *m(f)*

eminence [ˈemɪnəns] N (= *distinction*) hohes Ansehen

eminent [ˈemɪnənt] ADJ *person* angesehen; **to be ~ in a particular field** auf einem bestimmten Gebiet führend sein

eminently [ˈemɪnəntlɪ] ADV *sensible, readable* ausgesprochen; *practical* äußerst; *desirable* überaus; **~ suitable** *or* **suited** vorzüglich geeignet; **to be ~ capable of sth** eindeutig zu etw fähig sein

emir [eˈmɪə'] N Emir *m*

emirate [ˈemɪrɪt] N Emirat *nt*

emissary [ˈemɪsərɪ] N Emissär *m*, Abgesandte(r) *mf*

emission [ɪ'mɪʃən] N Ausstrahlung *f*; (*of fumes, X-rays*) Emission *f* (*spec*); (*of gas*) Ausströmen *nt*; (*of vapour, smoke: continuous*) Abgabe *f*

emit [ɪ'mɪt] VT *light* ausstrahlen; *radiation* emittieren (*spec*); *sound* abgeben; *gas* ausströmen; *vapour, smoke* (*continuously*) abgeben

emolument [ɪ'mɒljʊmənt] N USU PL (*form*) Vergütung *f*; (= *fee*) Honorar *nt*; (= *salary*) Bezüge *pl*

emotion [ɪ'məʊʃən] N (**a**) Gefühl *nt* (**b**) NO PL (= *state of being moved*) (Gemüts)bewegung *f*; **to show no ~** unbewegt bleiben

emotional [ɪ'məʊʃənl] ADJ emotional; *problem, trauma, abuse* seelisch; *support, development* psychologisch; *decision* gefühlsmäßig; *farewell* gefühlvoll; **to become** *or* **get ~** sich aufregen; **~ outburst** Gefühlsausbruch *m*; **~ state** Gemütszustand *m*; **~ life** Seelenleben *nt*

emotional blackmail N psychologische Erpressung

emotionally [ɪ'məʊʃnəlɪ] ADV (**a**) (= *psychologically*) seelisch; **I don't want to get ~ involved (with her)** ich will mich (bei ihr) nicht ernsthaft engagieren; **~ disturbed** seelisch gestört (**b**) (= *emotively, in an emotional manner*) emotional; **~ charged** spannungsgeladen

emotionless [ɪ'məʊʃənlɪs] ADJ *face, voice etc* ausdruckslos; *person* emotionslos

emotive [ɪ'məʊtɪv] ADJ *issue* emotional; *language, word* emotional gefärbt

empathize ['empəθaɪz] VI sich hineinversetzen *or* einfühlen (*with* in +*acc*)

empathy ['empəθɪ] N Einfühlungsvermögen *nt*

emperor ['empərə'] N Kaiser *m*

emphasis ['emfəsɪs] N Betonung *f*; **to put ~ on a word** ein Wort betonen; **to say sth with ~** etw nachdrücklich betonen; **to lay ~** *or* **place** *or* **put the ~ on sth** etw betonen; **to lay ~** *or* **place** *or* **put the ~ on doing sth** Wert darauf legen, etw zu tun; **there is too much ~ on research** die Forschung steht zu sehr im Vordergrund

emphasize ['emfəsaɪz] VT betonen; *point, importance, difference, need also* hervorheben

emphatic [ɪm'fætɪk] ADJ (**a**) (= *forceful*) entschieden; *denial* energisch; **to be ~ (that ...)** (*person*) darauf bestehen(, dass ...); **to be ~ about sth** auf etw (*dat*) bestehen (**b**) *victory, winner* klar, überzeugend; *defeat* schwer

emphatically [ɪm'fætɪkəlɪ] ADV (**a**) *say* nachdrücklich; *reply, reject, deny* entschieden; **most ~** mit allem Nachdruck (**b**) (= *definitely*) eindeutig; **~ not** auf (gar) keinen Fall

empire ['empaɪə'] N (**a**) Reich *nt*; (*worldwide*) Weltreich *nt*; **the Holy Roman Empire** das Heilige Römische Reich (deutscher Nation); **the British Empire** das Britische Weltreich (**b**) (*fig, esp Comm*) Imperium *nt*; **his business ~** sein Geschäftsimperium *nt*

empirical [em'pɪrɪkəl] ADJ empirisch

employ [ɪm'plɔɪ] **1** VT (**a**) *person* beschäftigen; (= *take on*) anstellen; *private detective* beauftragen; **he has been ~ed with us for 15 years** er ist schon seit 15 Jahren bei uns; **to be ~ed in doing sth** damit beschäftigt sein, etw zu tun (**b**) *method, skill etc* anwenden, einsetzen; *word, concept* verwenden; *time* verbringen; **they ~ed the services of a chemist to help them** sie zogen einen Chemiker heran, um ihnen zu helfen **2** N **to be in the ~ of sb** (*form*) in jds Diensten stehen (*geh*)

employable [ɪm'plɔɪəbl] ADJ *person* anstellbar

employee [ˌɪmplɔɪ'iː] N Angestellte(r) *mf*; **~s and employers** Arbeitnehmer und Arbeitgeber; **the ~s** (*of one firm*) die Belegschaft

employer [ɪm'plɔɪə'] N Arbeitgeber(in) *m(f)*; (*of servants, civil servants*) Dienstherr(in) *m(f)*; **~s' federation** Arbeitgeberverband *m*; **~'s liability insurance plan** Betriebshaftpflichtversicherung *f*

employment [ɪm'plɔɪmənt] N (**a**) (An)stellung *f*, Arbeit *f*; **to seek ~** Arbeit *or* eine Stelle suchen; **how long is it since you were last in ~?** wann hatten Sie Ihre letzte Stellung?; **conditions/contract of ~** Arbeitsbedingungen *pl*/-vertrag *m* (**b**) (= *act of employing*) Beschäftigung *f*; (= *taking on*) Einstellen *nt* (**c**) (*of method, skill*) Anwendung *f*

employment agency N Stellenvermittlung *f*

emporium [em'pɔːrɪəm] N Warenhaus *nt*

empower [ɪm'paʊə'] VT (**a**) **to ~ sb to do sth** jdn ermächtigen, etw zu tun; (*Jur*) jdm (die) Vollmacht erteilen, etw zu tun (**b**) *women, minorities etc* stärken

empress ['emprɪs] N Kaiserin *f*

emptiness ['emptɪnɪs] N Leere *f*

empty ['emptɪ] **1** ADJ (+ER) (*lit, fig*) leer; *house* leer stehend *attr*; *seat, place* frei; *life, days* unausgefüllt; *expression, eyes* ausdruckslos; **to feel ~** (*fig*) ein Gefühl der Leere haben; **there were no ~ seats on the bus** im Bus waren keine Plätze frei; **on an ~ stomach** mit leerem Magen; *take drug, drink alcohol* auf leeren Magen **2** N USU PL **empties** Leergut *nt* **3** VT (**a**) leeren; *box, room* ausräumen; *house* räumen; *pond, tank* ablassen; *lorry* abladen; **her singing emptied the hall in ten minutes flat** mit ihrem Singen schaffte sie es, dass der Saal innerhalb von zehn Minuten leer war (**b**) (= *pour*) *liquid, contents* ausgießen **4** VI (*rivers*) münden (*into* in +*acc*); (*theatre, streets*) sich leeren

➤ **empty out** VT SEP ausleeren

empty: **empty-handed** ADJ **to return ~** mit leeren Händen zurückkehren; **empty-headed** ADJ strohdumm

EMS ABBR *of* **European Monetary System** EWS *nt*

EMU ABBR *of* **European Monetary Union** EWU *nt*

emu ['iːmjuː] N Emu *m*

emulate ['emjʊleɪt] VT (**a**) nacheifern (+*dat*); **I tried to ~ his success** ich versuchte, es ihm gleichzutun (**b**) (*Comput*) emulieren

emulsion [ɪ'mʌlʃən] N (*also* **~ paint**) Emulsionsfarbe *f*

enable [ɪ'neɪbl] VT **to ~ sb to do sth** es jdm ermöglichen *or* möglich machen, etw zu tun

enact [ɪ'nækt] VT (*Pol*) *law* erlassen

enamel [ɪ'næməl] **1** N Email *nt*, Emaille *f* (*inf*); (= *paint*) Email(le)lack *m*; (*of teeth*) Zahnschmelz *m* **2** ADJ Email(le)-; **~ paint** Email(le)lack *m*

enamelled, (*US*) **enameled** [ɪ'næməld] ADJ emailliert; **~ jewellery** (*Brit*), **enameled jewelry** (*US*) Email(le)schmuck *m*

enamour, (*US*) **enamor** [ɪ'næmə'] VT **to be ~ed of sb** in jdn verliebt sein; **to be ~ed of sth** von etw angetan *or* entzückt sein; **she was not exactly ~ed of the idea** sie war von der Idee nicht gerade begeistert

en bloc [ɑ̃'blɒk] ADV en bloc

encapsulate [ɪn'kæpsjʊleɪt] VT (*fig*) zusammenfassen

encase [ɪn'keɪs] VT verkleiden (*in* mit); *wires* umgeben (*in* mit); **her arms were ~d in plaster** ihre Arme waren in einem Gipsverband

enchant [ɪn'tʃɑːnt] VT entzücken; **to be ~ed by sth** von etw *or* über etw (*acc*) entzückt sein

enchanting [ɪn'tʃɑːntɪŋ] ADJ entzückend

encircle [ɪn'sɜːkl] VT umgeben; (*troops*) einkreisen; *building* umstellen

enc(l) ABBR *of* **enclosure(s)** Anl.

enclave ['enkleɪv] N Enklave *f*

enclose [ɪn'kləʊz] VT (**a**) (= *shut in*) einschließen; (= *surround*) umgeben; (*with fence etc*) *ground* einzäunen (**b**) (*in a parcel, envelope*) beilegen (*in, with dat*); **I am enclosing the original with the translation** anbei die Übersetzung sowie der Originaltext

enclosed [ɪn'kləʊzd] ADJ (**a**) *space, area* geschlossen; *garden* abgeschlossen (**b**) (*in letter, parcel*) beiliegend; **a photo was ~ in the letter** dem Brief lag ein Foto bei; **please find ~ a cheque for the sum of £25** (*Brit*) *or* **a check for the sum of 25 dollars** (*US*) in der Anlage *or* beiliegend finden Sie einen Scheck über £ 25/25 dollars

enclosure [ɪn'kləʊʒə'] N (= *ground enclosed*) eingezäuntes Grundstück *or* Feld; (*for animals*) Gehege *nt* (**b**) (= *document etc enclosed*) Anlage *f*

encode [ɪn'kəʊd] VT (*also Comput*) kodieren

encompass [ɪn'kʌmpəs] VT umfassen

encore ['ɒŋkɔː'] **1** INTERJ da capo, Zugabe **2** N Zugabe *f*; **to call for/give an ~** eine Zugabe verlangen/geben

encounter [ɪn'kaʊntə'] **1** VT *enemy, opposition* treffen auf (+*acc*); *difficulties, resistance* stoßen auf (+*acc*); *danger* geraten in (+*acc*); (*liter*) *person* begegnen (+*dat*) **2** N Begegnung *f*; (*in battle*) Zusammenstoß *m*; **sexual ~** sexuelle Erfahrung

encourage [ɪnˈkʌrɪdʒ] VT *person* ermutigen; (= *motivate*) anregen; (= *give confidence*) Mut machen (+*dat*); *industry, projects, investments* fördern; (*Sport*) *team, competitor* anfeuern; *bad habits* unterstützen; **to be ~d by sth** durch etw neuen Mut schöpfen; **to ~ sb to do sth** jdn ermutigen, etw zu tun

encouragement [ɪnˈkʌrɪdʒmənt] N Ermutigung *f*; (= *motivation*) Anregung *f*; (= *support*) Unterstützung *f*; **to give sb (a lot of) ~** jdn (sehr) ermuntern

encouraging [ɪnˈkʌrɪdʒɪŋ] ADJ ermutigend; **I found him very ~** er hat mir sehr viel Mut gemacht

encouragingly [ɪnˈkʌrɪdʒɪŋlɪ] ADV ermutigend; (+*adj*) erfreulich; (*introducing sentence*) erfreulicherweise

encroach [ɪnˈkrəʊtʃ] VI **to ~ (up)on** *land* vordringen in (+*acc*); *sphere, rights* eingreifen in (+*acc*); *time* in Anspruch nehmen

encrust [ɪnˈkrʌst] VT **~ed with earth** erdverkrustet; **a jewel-~ed brooch** eine juwelenbesetzte Brosche

encryption [ɪnˈkrɪpʃən] N (*Comput, Telec, TV*) Verschlüsselung *f*

encumbrance [ɪnˈkʌmbrəns] N (*also Jur*) Belastung *f*; (*person*) Last *f*; **to be an ~ to sb** (*luggage*) jdn behindern; (*person*) eine Last für jdn sein

encyclop(a)edia [ɪnˌsaɪkləʊˈpiːdɪə] N Lexikon *nt*

encyclop(a)edic [ɪnˌsaɪkləʊˈpiːdɪk] ADJ enzyklopädisch

end [end] **1** N **(a)** Ende *nt*; (*of finger*) Spitze *f*; **our house is the fourth from the ~** unser Haus ist das viertletzte; **to the ~s of the earth** bis ans Ende der Welt; **from ~ to ~** von einem Ende zum anderen; **who'll meet you at the other ~?** wer holt dich ab, wenn du ankommst?; **Lisa's on the other ~ (of the phone)** Lisa ist am Telefon; **for hours on ~** stundenlang ununterbrochen; **~ to ~** mit den Enden aneinander; **to change ~s** (*Sport*) die Seiten wechseln; **to make (both) ~s meet** (*fig*) zurechtkommen (*inf*); **to see no further than the ~ of one's nose** nicht weiter sehen als seine Nase (reicht); **at our/your ~** bei uns/Ihnen; **how are things at your ~?** wie sieht es bei Ihnen aus?; **at the ~** (= *to conclude*) schließlich; **at/ toward(s) the ~ of December** Ende/gegen Ende Dezember; **at the ~ of (the) winter/the war** am Ende des Winters/des Krieges; **at the ~ of the opera/the book** am Schluss der Oper/ des Buches; **at the ~ of the day** (*fig*) letzten Endes; **as far as I'm concerned, that's the ~ of the matter!** für mich ist die Sache erledigt; **we shall never hear the ~ of it** das werden wir noch lange zu hören kriegen; **to be at an ~** zu Ende sein; **to be at the ~ of one's patience/strength** mit seiner Geduld/ seinen Kräften am Ende sein; **to watch a film to the ~** einen Film bis zu Ende ansehen; **that's the ~ of him** er ist erledigt; **that's the ~ of that** das ist damit erledigt; **to bring to an ~** zu Ende bringen; *relations* ein Ende setzen (+*dat*); **to come to an ~** zu Ende gehen; **to get to the ~ of the road/book** ans Ende der Straße/zum Schluss des Buches kommen; **in the ~** schließlich; **to put an ~ to sth** einer Sache (*dat*) ein Ende setzen; **he met a violent ~** er starb einen gewaltsamen Tod **(b)** (*of candle, cigarette*) Stummel *m*; **just a few odd ~s left** nur noch ein paar Reste

(c) (*inf phrases*) **we met no ~ of famous people** (*esp Brit*) wir trafen viele berühmte Leute; **it pleased her no ~** (*esp Brit*) das hat ihr irrsinnig gefallen (*inf*)

(d) (= *purpose*) Ziel *nt*, Zweck *m*; **with this ~ in view** mit diesem Ziel vor Augen; **to what ~?** (*form*) zu welchem Zweck?; **an ~ in itself** Selbstzweck *no art*; **the ~ justifies the means** (*prov*) der Zweck heiligt die Mittel (*prov*)

2 ADJ ATTR letzte(r, s); **the ~ house** das letzte Haus

3 VT beenden; **to ~ it all** (= *commit suicide*) Schluss machen

4 VI enden; **we ~ed with a song** zum Schluss sangen wir ein Lied; **to be ~ing** zu Ende gehen; **to ~ by doing sth** schließlich etw tun; **to ~ in an "s"** auf „s" enden; **an argument which ~ed in a fight** ein Streit, der mit einer Schlägerei endete

➤ end up VI enden; **to end up doing sth** schließlich etw tun; **to end up (as) a lawyer** schließlich Rechtsanwalt werden; **to end up (as) an alcoholic** als Alkoholiker enden; **we ended up at Joe's** wir landeten schließlich bei Joe (*inf*); **you'll end up in trouble** Sie werden noch Ärger bekommen

endanger [ɪnˈdeɪndʒəʳ] VT gefährden

endangered [ɪnˈdeɪndʒəd] ADJ vom Aussterben bedroht

endear [ɪnˈdɪəʳ] VT beliebt machen (*to* bei); **to ~ oneself to sb** sich bei jdm beliebt machen

endearing [ɪnˈdɪərɪŋ] ADJ liebenswert

endearment [ɪnˈdɪəmənt] N **term of ~** Kosename *m*, Kosewort *nt*

endeavour, (*US*) **endeavor** [ɪnˈdevəʳ] **1** N (= *attempt*) Anstrengung *f*; **in an ~ to please her** um ihr eine Freude zu machen **2** VT sich anstrengen

endemic [enˈdemɪk] ADJ (*lit, fig*) endemisch; **~ to** endemisch in (*dat*)

endgame [ˈendɡeɪm] N Endspiel *nt*

ending [ˈendɪŋ] N (*of story, events*) Ausgang *m*; (= *last part*) Ende *nt*, Schluss *m*; (*of word*) Endung *f*; **a story with a happy ~** eine Geschichte mit einem Happy End; **the dispute had a happy ~** der Streit ging gut aus

endive [ˈendaɪv] N Endiviensalat *m*

endless [ˈendlɪs] ADJ **(a)** endlos; *variety* unendlich; *supply* unbegrenzt; **the list is ~** die Liste nimmt kein Ende **(b)** (= *countless*) unzählig; **the possibilities are ~** es gibt unendlich viele Möglichkeiten **(c)** *road, stretch* endlos (lang); *queue* endlos lang

endlessly [ˈendlɪslɪ] ADV endlos

endorse [ɪnˈdɔːs] VT **(a)** *document, cheque* indossieren **(b)** (*Brit Jur*) **I had my licence ~d** ich bekam einen Strafvermerk auf meinem Führerschein **(c)** (= *approve*) billigen; *product, company* empfehlen

endorsement [ɪnˈdɔːsmənt] N **(a)** (*Brit Jur: on driving licence*) Strafvermerk *m* auf dem Führerschein **(b)** (*of opinion*) Billigung *f*; (*for product, company*) Empfehlung *f*

endow [ɪnˈdaʊ] VT **(a)** *institution, church* eine Stiftung machen an (+*acc*); (*Univ, Sch*) *prize, chair* stiften **(b)** (*fig*) **to be ~ed with a natural talent for singing** ein sängerisches Naturtalent sein; **she's well ~ed** (*hum*) sie ist von der Natur reichlich ausgestattet (worden)

endowment [ɪnˈdaʊmənt] N Stiftung *f*

endowment: **endowment mortgage** N Hypothek *f* mit Lebensversicherung; **endowment policy** N Kapitallebensversicherung *f*, Erlebensfallversicherung *f*

end: **endpapers** PL Vorsatzblätter *pl*; **end product** N Endprodukt *nt*; (*fig*) Produkt *nt*; **end result** N Endergebnis *nt*

endurance [ɪnˈdjʊərəns] N Durchhaltevermögen *nt*; **he was tried beyond ~** er wurde über die Maßen gereizt

endurance test N Belastungsprobe *f*; (*fig*) Durchhaltetest *m*

endure [ɪnˈdjʊəʳ] **1** VT **(a)** (= *undergo*) *pain* erleiden **(b)** (= *put up with*) ertragen; **she can't ~ being laughed at** sie kann es nicht vertragen, wenn man über sie lacht **2** VI bestehen

enduring [ɪnˈdjʊərɪŋ] ADJ dauerhaft; *love, belief* beständig; *popularity* bleibend

end user N Endverbraucher(in) *m(f)*; (*Comput*) Endbenutzer *m*

endways [ˈendweɪz], **endwise** [ˈendwaɪz] ADV mit dem Ende zuerst; (= *end to end*) mit den Enden aneinander; **put it ~ on** legen Sie es mit dem Ende an

end zone N (*US Sport*) Endzone *f*

enema [ˈenɪmə] N Einlauf *m*

enemy [ˈenəmɪ] **1** N (*lit, fig*) Feind(in) *m(f)*; **to make enemies** sich (*dat*) Feinde machen; **he is his own worst ~** er schadet sich (*dat*) selbst am meisten **2** ADJ ATTR feindlich; *position, advance* des Feindes

energetic [ˌenəˈdʒetɪk] ADJ energiegeladen; (= *active*) aktiv; (= *strenuous*) anstrengend; *performance* schwungvoll; **to be more/very ~** mehr/viel Energie haben

energetically [ˌenəˈdʒetɪkəlɪ] ADV *protest, work* energisch; *run, dance* voller Energie

energize [ˈenədʒaɪz] VT (*fig*) *person* neue Energie geben (+*dat*); *economy* ankurbeln

energy [ˈenədʒɪ] N Energie *f*; **chocolate gives you ~** Schokolade gibt neue Energie; **to concentrate one's energies on doing sth** seine ganze Kraft dafür aufbieten, etw zu tun; **to save one's ~ for sth** seine Kräfte für etw aufsparen

energy: **energy conservation** N Energieeinsparung *f*; **energy crisis** N Energiekrise *f*; **energy-efficient** ADJ Energie sparend; **energy-saving** ADJ Energie sparend; **~ measures** Energiesparmaßnahmen *pl*; **energy tax** N Energiesteuer *f*

enervating [ˈenəveɪtɪŋ] ADJ strapazierend

enforce [ɪnˈfɔːs] VT durchführen; *one's claims, rights* geltend machen; *discipline* sorgen für; *decision, policy, ban, ruling* durchsetzen; *sanctions* verhängen; **the police ~ the law** die Polizei sorgt für die Einhaltung der Gesetze

enforcement [ɪnˈfɔːsmənt] N Durchführung *f*

engage [ɪnˈgeɪdʒ] **1** VT **(a)** *worker* anstellen; *performer* engagieren; *lawyer* sich (*dat*) nehmen; **to ~ the services of sb** jdn anstellen/engagieren; *of lawyer* sich (*dat*) jdn nehmen **(b)** *attention, interest* in Anspruch nehmen; **to ~ sb in conversation** jdn in ein Gespräch verwickeln **(c)** (*Aut*) **to ~ a gear** einen Gang einlegen; **to ~ the clutch** (ein)kuppeln

2 VI **(a)** (*gear wheels*) ineinander greifen; (*clutch*) fassen **(b) to ~ in sth** sich an etw (*dat*) beteiligen; **to ~ in conversation** sich unterhalten; (*Mil*) **to ~ with the enemy** den Feind angreifen

engaged [ɪnˈgeɪdʒd] ADJ **(a) ~ (to be married)** verlobt (*to* mit); **to get** *or* **become ~ (to sb)** sich (mit jdm) verloben **(b)** *toilet, seat* besetzt (*also Brit Telec*) **(c)** (*form:* = *busy*) **to be otherwise ~** (*at future time*) etwas anderes vorhaben; (*at present*) anderweitig beschäftigt sein; **to be ~ in sth** mit etw beschäftigt sein; **to be ~ in doing sth** dabei sein, etw zu tun

engaged tone N (*Telec*) Besetztzeichen *nt*

engagement [ɪnˈgeɪdʒmənt] N **(a)** (= *appointment*) Verabredung *f*; **a dinner ~** eine Verabredung zum Essen **(b)** (= *betrothal*) Verlobung *f*

engagement ring N Verlobungsring *m*

engaging [ɪnˈgeɪdʒɪŋ] ADJ *person* angenehm; *smile* gewinnend; *character, manner* einnehmend

engender [ɪnˈdʒendə**ʳ**] VT (*fig*) erzeugen

engine [ˈendʒɪn] N **(a)** Maschine *f*; (*of car, plane etc*) Motor *m* **(b)** (*Rail*) Lokomotive *f*, Lok *f* **(c)** (*Comput:* = *search ~*) Suchmaschine *f*

-engined [-ˈendʒɪnd] ADJ SUF -motorig; **single-/twin-engined** ein-/zweimotorig

engine driver N (*Brit*) Lok(omotiv)führer(in) *m(f)*

engineer [ˌendʒɪˈnɪə**ʳ**] **1** N **(a)** (*Tech*) Techniker(in) *m(f)*; (*with university degree etc*) Ingenieur(in) *m(f)* **(b)** (*Naut*) (*on merchant ships*) Maschinist(in) *m(f)*; (*in Navy*) (Schiffs)ingenieur(in) *m(f)* **(c)** (*US Rail*) Lokführer(in) *m(f)* **2** VT **(a)** (*Tech*) konstruieren **(b)** (*fig*) *election, campaign, coup* organisieren; *downfall, plot* einfädeln; *success, victory* in die Wege leiten

engineering [ˌendʒɪˈnɪərɪŋ] N (*Tech*) Technik *f*; (= *mechanical ~*) Maschinenbau *m*; (= ~ *profession*) Ingenieurwesen *nt*; **a brilliant piece of ~** eine Meisterkonstruktion

England [ˈɪŋglənd] **1** N England *nt* **2** ADJ ATTR **the ~ team** die englische Mannschaft

English [ˈɪŋglɪʃ] **1** ADJ englisch; **he is ~** er ist Engländer; **he's an ~ teacher** er ist Englischlehrer; **(full) ~ breakfast** englisches Frühstück

2 N **(a) the ~** *pl* die Engländer *pl* **(b)** (*Ling*) Englisch *nt*; (*as university subject*) Anglistik *f*; **can you speak ~?** können Sie Englisch?; **he doesn't speak ~** er spricht kein Englisch; **"~ spoken"** „hier wird Englisch gesprochen"; **they were speaking ~** sie unterhielten sich auf Englisch; **he speaks very good ~** er spricht ein sehr gutes Englisch; **in ~** auf Englisch; **to translate sth into/from ~** etw ins Englische/aus dem Englischen übersetzen

English: English Channel N Ärmelkanal *m*; **Englishman** N Engländer *m*; **English muffin** N (*US Cook*) flaches Milchbrötchen, *das meist getoastet gegessen wird*; **English speaker** N Englischsprachige(r) *mf*; **English-speaking** ADJ englischsprachig; **Englishwoman** N Engländerin *f*

engrave [ɪnˈgreɪv] VT *glass, metal etc* gravieren; *design, letter* eingravieren

engraved [ɪnˈgreɪvd] ADJ *glass, metal* graviert; *design, letter* eingraviert

engraving [ɪnˈgreɪvɪŋ] N (= *copy*) (Kupfer-/Stahl)stich *m*; (*from wood*) Holzschnitt *m*; (= *design*) Gravierung *f*; (*on wood, stone*) eingemeißelte Verzierung/Schrift *etc*

engross [ɪnˈgrəʊs] VT **to become ~ed in one's work** sich in seine Arbeit vertiefen; **to be ~ed in one's (own) thoughts/in conversation** in Gedanken/ins Gespräch vertieft sein

engrossing [ɪnˈgrəʊsɪŋ] ADJ fesselnd

engulf [ɪnˈgʌlf] VT verschlingen; **to be ~ed by flames** in Flammen stehen

enhance [ɪnˈhɑːns] VT verbessern; *price, value, chances* erhöhen

enigma [ɪˈnɪgmə] N Rätsel *nt*

enigmatic ADJ, **enigmatically** ADV [ˌenɪgˈmætɪk, -əlɪ] rätselhaft

enjoy [ɪnˈdʒɔɪ] **1** VT *also rights, freedom* genießen; *income, success* haben; *good health, reputation, support* sich erfreuen (+*gen*) (*geh*); **he ~s swimming** er schwimmt gern; **he ~ed writing the book** es hat ihm Freude gemacht, das Buch zu schreiben; **I ~ed the concert** das Konzert hat mir gefallen; **he ~ed the meal** das Essen hat ihm gut geschmeckt; **I didn't ~ it at all** es hat mir überhaupt keinen Spaß gemacht; **to ~ life** das Leben genießen; **did you ~ your meal?** hat Ihnen das Essen gefallen? **2** VR **to ~ oneself** sich amüsieren; **~ yourself!** viel Spaß!

enjoyable [ɪnˈdʒɔɪəbl] ADJ nett; *film, book* unterhaltsam; *evening, meal* angenehm

enjoyment [ɪnˈdʒɔɪmənt] N Vergnügen *nt*, Spaß *m* (*of* an +*dat*); **she gets a lot of ~ from reading** Lesen macht ihr großen Spaß

enlarge [ɪnˈlɑːdʒ] **1** VT vergrößern; *hole, field of knowledge* erweitern **2** VI **to ~ (up)on sth** auf etw (*acc*) näher eingehen

enlargement [ɪnˈlɑːdʒmənt] N (*Phot*) Vergrößerung *f*

enlighten [ɪnˈlaɪtn] VT aufklären (*on, as to, about* über +*acc*); **let me ~ you** darf ich es Ihnen erklären?

enlightened [ɪnˈlaɪtnd] ADJ *person, society* aufgeklärt; (= *progressive*) fortschrittlich

enlightening [ɪnˈlaɪtnɪŋ] ADJ aufschlussreich

enlightenment [ɪnˈlaɪtnmənt] N **the Enlightenment** die Aufklärung

enlist [ɪnˈlɪst] **1** VI (*Mil etc*) sich melden (*in* zu) **2** VT *recruits* einziehen; *support, supporters* gewinnen; **I had to ~ his help** ich musste seine Hilfe in Anspruch nehmen

enlisted man [ɪnˈlɪstɪdˈmæn], *pl* **enlisted men** N (*US*) gemeiner Soldat

enlistment [ɪnˈlɪstmənt] N (*of recruits*) (= *enlisting*) Meldung *f*; (= *being enlisted*) Einziehung *f*

enliven [ɪnˈlaɪvn] VT beleben

en masse [ɑ̃ˈmæs] ADV alle zusammen

enmesh [ɪnˈmeʃ] VT (*fig*) **to get ~ed in sth** in etw (*acc*) verstrickt werden

enmity [ˈenmɪtɪ] N Feindschaft *f*

enormity [ɪˈnɔːmɪtɪ] N **(a)** NO PL (*of action, offence*) ungeheures Ausmaß **(b)** (*of crime*) Ungeheuerlichkeit *f*

enormous [ɪˈnɔːməs] ADJ riesig; *person* (= *fat*) ungeheuer dick; (= *tall*) riesig groß; *quantity, variety, effort, relief* ungeheuer; **he has ~ talent** er hat enorm viel Talent; **~ amounts** *or* **sums of money** Unsummen *pl*; **an ~ amount of work** eine Unmenge Arbeit

enormously [ɪˈnɔːməslɪ] ADV (+*vb*) enorm; (+*adj*) ungeheuer

enough [ɪˈnʌf] **1** ADJ genug; **~ sugar/apples** genug *or* genügend Zucker/Äpfel; **~ trouble/problems** genug Ärger/Probleme; **proof ~** Beweis genug

2 PRON genug (*of* von); **I had not seen ~ of his work** ich hatte noch nicht genug von seiner Arbeit gesehen; **I hope it's ~** ich hoffe, es reicht *or* genügt; **two years was ~** zwei Jahre reichten; **this noise is ~ to drive me mad** dieser Lärm macht mich noch ganz verrückt; **one song was ~ to show he couldn't sing** ein Lied genügte, um zu zeigen, dass er nicht singen konnte; **it is ~ for us to know that ...** es genügt uns zu wissen, dass ...; **I've got ~ to worry about** ich habe genug Sorgen; **~ is ~** was zu viel ist, ist zu viel; **~ said** mehr braucht man nicht zu sagen; **I've had ~** ich habe genug; (*in exasperation*) jetzt reichts mir aber (*inf*); **that's ~!** jetzt reicht es aber!

3 ADV **(a)** (= *sufficiently*) genug; **to be punished ~** genug bestraft sein; **he knows well ~ what I said** er weiß ganz genau, was ich gesagt habe

(b) (= *reasonably, fairly*) **to be happy ~** einigermaßen zufrieden sein; **to be happy ~ to do sth** etw so weit ganz gern tun; **she sounded sincere ~** sie schien so weit ganz ehrlich; **it is easy ~ to make them yourself** man kann sie ohne weiteres selbst machen; **easily ~** ohne größere Schwierigkeiten

(c) oddly *or* funnily ~ komischerweise; **interestingly ~** interessanterweise

enquire *etc* [ɪnˈkwaɪəʳ] = **inquire** *etc*

enquiring [ɪnˈkwaɪərɪŋ] ADJ = **inquiring**

enquiry [ɪnˈkwaɪərɪ] N = **inquiry**

enrage [ɪnˈreɪdʒ] VT wütend machen

enrich [ɪnˈrɪtʃ] VT bereichern; *soil, food* anreichern
enriched [ɪnˈrɪtʃt] ADJ ~ **with vitamins** mit Vitaminen angereichert
enrol, *(US)* **enroll** [ɪnˈrəʊl] **1** VT einschreiben; *members* aufnehmen; *schoolchild (school, headmaster)* aufnehmen; *(parents)* anmelden; *(Univ)* immatrikulieren **2** VI sich einschreiben; *(for course, at school)* sich anmelden; *(Univ)* sich immatrikulieren
enrolment, *(US)* **enrollment** [ɪnˈrəʊlmənt] N Einschreibung *f*; *(for course, at school)* Anmeldung *f*; *(Univ)* Immatrikulation *f*
en route [ɒnˈruːt] ADV unterwegs; ~ **to/for/from** auf dem Weg zu/nach/von
ensemble [ɑ:nˈsɑ̃:mbl] N **(a)** *(Mus, Theat, Fashion)* Ensemble *nt* **(b)** *(= collection)* Ansammlung *f*
enshrine [ɪnˈʃraɪn] VT *(fig)* bewahren
ensign [ˈensaɪn] N **(a)** *(= flag)* Nationalflagge *f* **(b)** *(US Naut)* Fähnrich *m* zur See
enslave [ɪnˈsleɪv] VT zum Sklaven machen
ensnare [ɪnˈsnɛəʳ] VT *(lit)* fangen; *(fig: woman)* umgarnen; **his leg became ~d in the ropes** sein Bein verfing sich in den Seilen
ensue [ɪnˈsjuː] VI folgen *(from aus)*
ensuing [ɪnˈsjuːɪŋ] ADJ darauf folgend *attr*
en suite [ˈɒnˈswiːt] ADJ **room with ~ bathroom, ~ room** Zimmer *nt* mit eigenem Bad
ensure [ɪnˈʃʊəʳ] VT sicherstellen; *(= secure)* sichern; **will you ~ that I get a seat?** sorgen Sie dafür, dass ich einen Platz bekomme?
ENT ABBR *of* **ear, nose and throat**; ~ **department** HNO-Abteilung *f*
entail [ɪnˈteɪl] VT *expense, difficulty, loss* mit sich bringen; *work* erforderlich machen; **what is ~ed in buying a house?** was ist zum Hauskauf alles erforderlich?; **this will ~ (my) buying a new car** das bringt mit sich *or* macht es erforderlich, dass ich mir ein neues Auto kaufen muss
entangle [ɪnˈtæŋl] VT **(a) to become ~d in sth** sich in etw *(dat)* verfangen **(b)** *(= get into a tangle)* **to become ~d** sich verwirren **(c)** *(fig: in affair etc)* verwickeln *(in* in *+acc)*
entanglement [ɪnˈtæŋlmənt] N *(fig: in affair etc)* Verwicklung *f*; **she didn't want any romantic ~** sie wollte nicht in eine Romanze verwickelt werden
enter [ˈentəʳ] **1** VT **(a)** *(towards speaker)* hereinkommen in *(+acc)*; *(away from speaker)* hineingehen in *(+acc)*; *building etc* betreten; *(= drive into)* car park etc einfahren in *(+acc)*; *(= flow into)* münden in *(+acc)*; *(= penetrate: bullet etc)* eindringen in *(+acc)*; *country* einreisen in *(+acc)*; **the dispute is ~ing its fifth year** die Auseinandersetzung zieht sich jetzt schon ins fünfte Jahr hin; **the thought never ~ed my head** *or* **mind** so etwas wäre mir nie eingefallen
(b) *(= become a member of)* eintreten in *(+acc)*; **to ~ the Church** Geistlicher werden; **to ~ a profession** einen Beruf ergreifen
(c) *(= record)* eintragen *(in* in *+acc)*; *(Comput)* eingeben; **to ~ sb's/one's name** jdn/sich eintragen; ~ **these purchases under my name** *(Comm)* tragen Sie diese Käufe auf meinen Namen
(d) *(= enrol, for school, exam, contest etc)* anmelden
(e) *(= go in for)* race, contest sich beteiligen an *(+dat)*
(f) *appeal, plea* einlegen
2 VI **(a)** *(towards speaker)* hereinkommen; *(away from speaker)* hineingehen; *(= walk in)* eintreten; *(= drive in)* einfahren; *(= into country)* einreisen
(b) *(Theat)* auftreten
(c) *(for race, exam etc)* sich melden *(for* zu*)*
3 N *(Comput)* **hit ~ Enter** drücken
➤ **enter into** VI +PREP OBJ **(a)** *relations, negotiations* aufnehmen; *contract, alliance* schließen; **to enter into conversation with sb** ein Gespräch mit jdm anknüpfen; **to enter into correspondence with sb** mit jdm in Briefwechsel treten **(b)** *(= figure in)* eine Rolle spielen bei
enter key N *(Comput)* Enter-Taste *f*
enterprise [ˈentəpraɪz] N **(a)** NO PL *(= initiative)* Initiative *f*; *(= adventurousness)* Unternehmungsgeist *m*
(b) *(= undertaking, Comm: = firm)* Unternehmen *nt*; **free/public/private ~** *(= system)* freies/öffentliches/privates Unternehmertum

enterprising [ˈentəpraɪzɪŋ] ADJ *person (= adventurous)* unternehmungslustig; *(= resourceful)* einfallsreich; *company* geschäftstüchtig
entertain [ˌentəˈteɪn] **1** VT **(a)** *(= offer hospitality to)* einladen; *(to meal)* bewirten **(b)** *(= amuse)* unterhalten; *(humorously)* belustigen **(c)** *thought, intention* sich tragen mit; *suspicion, doubt* hegen; *hope* nähren; *suggestion, possibility* in Erwägung ziehen **2** VI Gäste haben
entertainer [ˌentəˈteɪnəʳ] N Unterhalter(in) *m(f)*, Entertainer(in) *m(f)*
entertaining [ˌentəˈteɪnɪŋ] **1** ADJ *(= fun)* unterhaltsam; *(= amusing)* amüsant **2** N die Bewirtung von Gästen; **she does a lot of ~** sie hat oft Gäste; **business ~** die Bewirtung von Geschäftspartnern
entertainment [ˌentəˈteɪnmənt] N **(a)** *(= amusement)* Unterhaltung *f*; *(professional)* Entertainment *nt*; **for my own ~** nur so zum Vergnügen **(b)** *(= performance)* Darbietung *f*
entertainment: entertainment allowance N ≈ Aufwandspauschale *f*; **entertainment industry** N Unterhaltungsindustrie *f*
enthral, *(US)* **enthrall** [ɪnˈθrɔːl] VT begeistern
enthralling [ɪnˈθrɔːlɪŋ] ADJ spannend
enthuse [ɪnˈθjuːz] VI schwärmen *(over* von*)*
enthusiasm [ɪnˈθjuːzɪæzəm] N **(a)** Begeisterung *f*, Enthusiasmus *m* *(for* für*)*; **she showed little ~ for the scheme** sie zeigte sich von dem Plan nicht sehr begeistert; **I can't work up any ~ for the idea** ich kann mich für die Idee nicht begeistern **(b)** *(= interest)* Interesse *nt*; *(= passion)* Leidenschaft *f*
enthusiast [ɪnˈθjuːzɪæst] N Enthusiast(in) *m(f)*; **he's a football/rock-and-roll ~** er ist begeisterter Fußballfreund/Rock 'n' Roll-Anhänger
enthusiastic [ɪnˌθjuːzɪˈæstɪk] ADJ begeistert, enthusiastisch; **he was very ~ about the plan** er war von dem Plan äußerst begeistert; **to be ~ about doing sth** etw mit Begeisterung tun; *(in future)* sich darauf freuen, etw zu tun
enthusiastically [ɪnˌθjuːzɪˈæstɪkəlɪ] ADV begeistert
entice [ɪnˈtaɪs] VT locken; **to ~ sb to do sth** *or* **into doing sth** jdn dazu verführen *or* verleiten, etw zu tun; **to ~ sb away** jdn weglocken
enticement [ɪnˈtaɪsmənt] N *(fig)* Verlockung *f*
enticing [ɪnˈtaɪsɪŋ] ADJ verlockend
entire [ɪnˈtaɪəʳ] ADJ ganz; *cost, career* gesamt
entirely [ɪnˈtaɪəlɪ] ADV **(a)** ganz, ausschließlich; **the accident was ~ the fault of the other driver** der andere Fahrer hatte die ganze Schuld an dem Unfall; **that is ~ a matter for the police** dafür ist allein die Polizei zuständig **(b)** *(emph: = totally)* völlig; **I agree ~** ich stimme voll und ganz zu; **to be another matter ~** *or* **an ~ different matter** etwas ganz *or* völlig anderes sein
entirety [ɪnˈtaɪərətɪ] N **in its ~** in seiner Gesamtheit
entitle [ɪnˈtaɪtl] VT **(a) it is ~d ...** es hat den Titel ... **(b)** *(= give the right)* **to ~ sb to sth** jdn zu etw berechtigen; *compensation, legal aid etc* jdm den Anspruch auf etw *(acc)* geben; **to ~ sb to do sth** jdn dazu berechtigen, etw zu tun; **to be ~d to sth** das Recht auf etw *(acc)* haben; *to compensation, legal aid etc* Anspruch auf etw *(acc)* haben; **to be ~d to do sth** das Recht haben, etw zu tun; **I'm ~d to my own opinion** ich kann mir meine eigene Meinung bilden
entitlement [ɪnˈtaɪtlmənt] N Berechtigung *f* *(to* zu*)*; *(to compensation, legal aid etc)* Anspruch *m* *(to* auf *+acc)*; **what is your holiday ~?** *(Brit)* wie viel Urlaub steht Ihnen zu?
entity [ˈentɪtɪ] N Wesen *nt*; **legal ~** juristische Person
entomologist [ˌentəˈmɒlədʒɪst] N Entomologe *m*, Entomologin *f*
entomology [ˌentəˈmɒlədʒɪ] N Entomologie *f*
entourage [ˌɒntʊˈrɑ:ʒ] N Entourage *f*
entrails [ˈentreɪlz] PL *(lit)* Eingeweide *pl*
entrance[1] [ɪnˈtrɑ:ns] VT in Entzücken versetzen; **to be ~d** verzückt sein; **to be ~d by/with sth** von etw entzückt sein
entrance[2] [ˈentrəns] N **(a)** *(= way in)* Eingang *m*; *(for vehicles)* Einfahrt *f*
(b) *(= entering, admission)* Eintritt *m* *(to* in *+acc)*; *(Theat)* Auftritt *m*; *(to club etc)* Zutritt *m* *(to* zu*)*; *(to school)* Aufnahme *f* *(to* in *+acc)*; **on his ~** bei seinem Eintritt/Auftritt; **he likes to**

make an ~ er setzt sich gern in Szene; **to make one's ~** (*Theat*) auftreten; (*fig*) erscheinen; **to gain ~ to a university** die Zulassung zu einer Universität erhalten

entrance: **entrance examination** N Aufnahmeprüfung *f*; **entrance fee** N (*for museum etc*) Eintrittsgeld *nt*; (*for competition*) Teilnahmegebühr *f*; (*for club membership*) Aufnahmegebühr *f*; **entrance hall** N Eingangshalle *f*; **entrance qualifications** PL Zulassungsanforderungen *pl*

entrant ['entrənt] N (*to profession*) Berufsanfänger(in) *m(f)* (*to* in +*dat*); (*in contest*) Teilnehmer(in) *m(f)*; (*in exam*) Prüfling *m*

entreat [ɪn'triːt] VT anflehen

entreaty [ɪn'triːtɪ] N dringende *or* flehentliche Bitte

entrée ['ɒntreɪ] N (*Brit*: = *starter*) Vorspeise *f*; (*esp US*: = *main course*) Hauptgericht *nt*

entrenched [ɪn'trentʃd] ADJ *position* unbeugsam; *ideas* festgefügt; *belief, attitude* fest verwurzelt; **you're too ~ in the past** Sie sind zu sehr in der Vergangenheit verhaftet

entrepreneur [ˌɒntrəprə'nɜːʳ] N Unternehmer(in) *m(f)*

entrepreneurial [ˌɒntrəprə'nɜːrɪəl] ADJ unternehmerisch

entrust [ɪn'trʌst] VT anvertrauen (*to sb* jdm); **to ~ a child to sb's care** ein Kind jds Obhut anvertrauen; **to ~ sb with a task** jdn mit einer Aufgabe betrauen; **to ~ sb with money/a secret** jdm Geld/ein Geheimnis anvertrauen

entry ['entrɪ] N **(a)** (*into* in +*acc*) Eintritt *m*; (*by car etc*) Einfahrt *f*; (*into country*) Einreise *f*; **port of ~** Einreisehafen *m*; (= *airport*) Landeflughafen *m*; **"no ~"** (*on door etc*) „Zutritt verboten"; (*on one-way street*) „keine Einfahrt" **(b)** (= *way in*) Eingang *m*; (*for vehicles*) Einfahrt *f* **(c)** (*in diary, dictionary etc*) Eintrag *m*; **the dictionary has 30,000 entries** das Wörterbuch enthält 30.000 Stichwörter **(d)** (*of competitor*) Meldung *f*; (*of piece of work*) Einsendung *f*; **there is a large ~ for the 200m** für die 200 m sind viele Meldungen eingegangen; **the closing date for entries is Friday** der Einsendeschluss ist Freitag

entry: **entry form** N Anmeldeformular *nt*; **entry permit** N Passierschein *m*; (*into country*) Einreiseerlaubnis *f*; **entry phone** N Türsprechanlage *f*; **entry visa** N Einreisevisum *nt*; **entryway** N (*US*) Eingang *m*; (*for vehicles*) Einfahrt *f*

entwine [ɪn'twaɪn] VT ineinander schlingen; **to be ~d with sth** (*fig*) mit etw verflochten sein

E number N E-Nummer *f*

enumerate [ɪ'njuːməreɪt] VT aufzählen

enunciate [ɪ'nʌnsɪeɪt] VTI artikulieren

envelop [ɪn'veləp] VT einhüllen; **flames ~ed the house** das Haus war von Flammen eingehüllt

envelope ['envələʊp] N (*Brief*)umschlag *m*; (*large*) Umschlag *m*

enviable ['envɪəbl] ADJ beneidenswert

envious ['envɪəs] ADJ neidisch; **to be ~ of sb/sth** auf jdn/etw neidisch sein

enviously ['envɪəslɪ] ADV neidisch

environment [ɪn'vaɪərənmənt] N Umwelt *f*; (*of town etc, physical surroundings*) Umgebung *f*; (= *social, cultural surroundings*) Milieu *nt*; **working-class ~** Arbeitermilieu *nt*; **Department of the Environment** (*Brit*) Umweltministerium *nt*; **Secretary** (*US*) *or* **Minister** (*Brit*) **of the Environment** Umweltminister(in) *m(f)*

Environment Agency N (*Brit*) Umweltbehörde *f*

environmental [ɪnˌvaɪərən'mentl] ADJ **(a)** Umwelt-; **~ concerns** Sorgen *pl* um die Umwelt; **~ disaster** Umweltkatastrophe *f*; **~ effects/impact** Auswirkungen *pl*/Auswirkung *f* auf die Umwelt **(b)** (= *protecting the environment*) Umweltschutz-; **~ group** Umweltschutzorganisation *f* **(c)** (= *relating to surroundings*) umgebungsbedingt; **~ change** eine Veränderung in der Umgebung

environmentalism [ɪnˌvaɪərən'mentəlɪzəm] N Umweltbewusstsein *nt*

environmentalist [ɪnˌvaɪərən'mentəlɪst] N Umweltschützer(in) *m(f)*

environmentally [ɪnˌvaɪərən'mentəlɪ] ADV im Hinblick auf die Umwelt, umwelt-; **~ correct/sound** umweltgerecht; **~ conscious** *or* **aware** umweltbewusst; **~ harmful** umweltschädlich; **~ friendly/unfriendly** umweltfreundlich/-feindlich

Environmental Protection Agency N (*US Admin*) ≈ Umweltministerium *nt*

environs [ɪn'vaɪərənz] PL Umgebung *f*; **Rome and its ~** Rom und Umgebung

envisage [ɪn'vɪzɪdʒ] VT sich (*dat*) vorstellen; **do you ~ any price rises in the near future?** halten Sie Preisanstiege in nächster Zukunft für wahrscheinlich?

envoy ['envɔɪ] N Bote *m*, Botin *f*; (= *diplomat*) Gesandte(r) *mf*

envy ['envɪ] **1** N Neid *m*; **his car was the ~ of his friends** seine Freunde beneideten ihn um sein Auto **2** VT beneiden; **to ~ sb sth** jdn um etw beneiden

enzyme ['enzaɪm] N Enzym *nt*

eon ['iːɒn] N (*US*) = **aeon**

EPA (*US*) ABBR *of* **Environmental Protection Agency**

epaulette ['epɔːlet] N Schulterstück *nt*

ephemeral [ɪ'femərəl] ADJ kurzlebig, ephemer (*geh, Zool*); *happiness* flüchtig

epic ['epɪk] **1** ADJ *poetry* episch; *novel* monumental; *performance, struggle* gewaltig; *journey* lang und abenteuerlich; **~ film** Monumentalfilm *m* **2** N Epos *nt*

epicentre, (*US*) **epicenter** ['epɪsentəʳ] N Epizentrum *nt*

epidemic [ˌepɪ'demɪk] N Epidemie *f* (*also fig*)

epidural [epɪ'djʊərəl] N Epiduralanästhesie *f*

epigram ['epɪgræm] N Epigramm *nt*

epilepsy ['epɪlepsɪ] N Epilepsie *f*

epileptic [ˌepɪ'leptɪk] **1** ADJ epileptisch; **~ fit** epileptischer Anfall; **he is ~** er ist Epileptiker **2** N Epileptiker(in) *m(f)*

epilogue, (*US*) **epilog** ['epɪlɒg] N Epilog *m*, Nachwort *nt*

Epiphany [ɪ'pɪfənɪ] N das Dreikönigsfest

episcopal [ɪ'pɪskəpəl] ADJ bischöflich

episode ['epɪsəʊd] N Episode *f*; (*of story, TV, Rad*) Fortsetzung *f*; (= *incident*) Vorfall *m*

episodic [epɪ'sɒdɪk] ADJ episodenhaft

epistle [ɪ'pɪsl] N (*old, iro*) Epistel *f*; (*Bibl*) Brief *m* (*to* an +*acc*)

epitaph ['epɪtɑːf] N Epitaph *nt*

epithet ['epɪθet] N Beiname *m*; (= *insulting name*) Schimpfname *m*

epitome [ɪ'pɪtəmɪ] N Inbegriff *m* (*of* +*gen*, an +*dat*)

epitomize [ɪ'pɪtəmaɪz] VT verkörpern

epoch ['iːpɒk] N Zeitalter *nt* (*also Geol*), Epoche *f*

equable ['ekwəbl] ADJ *climate* gleichmäßig; *person, temperament* ausgeglichen; (= *placid*) gleichmütig

equably ['ekwəblɪ] ADV ausgeglichen; (= *placidly*) gleichmütig

equal ['iːkwəl] **1** ADJ gleich; **an ~ amount of land** gleich viel Land; **~ numbers of men and women** gleich viele Männer und Frauen; **to be ~ in size (to)** gleich groß sein (wie); **a is ~ to b** a ist gleich b; **an amount ~ to the purchase price** eine dem Kaufpreis entsprechende Summe; **other things being ~** wenn nichts dazwischenkommt; **~ opportunities (for men and women)** Chancengleichheit *f* (für Männer und Frauen); **~ rights for women** die Gleichberechtigung der Frau; **to be on ~ terms (with sb)** (mit jdm) gleichgestellt sein; **to put sb on an ~ footing** jdn gleichstellen; **to be ~ to the task** der Aufgabe gewachsen sein; **to feel ~ to sth** sich zu etw imstande fühlen **2** N (*in rank*) Gleichgestellte(r) *mf*; **she is his ~** sie ist ihm ebenbürtig; **our ~s** unseresgleichen; **to treat sb as an ~** jdn als ebenbürtig behandeln; **to have no ~** nicht seinesgleichen haben; (= *be unsurpassed*) unübertroffen sein **3** VI **three times three ~s nine** drei mal drei (ist) gleich neun; **let x ~ 3** x sei (gleich) 3 **4** VT (= *match, rival*) gleichkommen (+*dat*); **there is nothing to ~ it** nichts kommt dem gleich

equality [ɪ'kwɒlɪtɪ] N Gleichheit *f*

equalize ['iːkwəlaɪz] VI (*Sport*) ausgleichen

equalizer ['iːkwəlaɪzəʳ] N **(a)** (*Brit Sport*) Ausgleich *m*; (*Ftbl etc*) Ausgleichstreffer *m*; **to score** *or* **get the ~** den Ausgleich erzielen **(b)** (*US hum inf*: = *gun*) Kanone *f* (*sl*)

equally ['iːkwəlɪ] ADV **(a)** *divide, share* gleichmäßig; **~ spaced** in gleichmäßigen Abständen; (*in time*) in regelmäßigen Abständen **(b)** (= *to the same extent, in the same way*) (+*adj*) ebenso, genauso; **all foreigners should be treated ~** alle Ausländer sollten gleich behandelt werden; **to apply ~** gleichermaßen gelten **(c)** (*introducing sentence*: = *by the same token*) ebenso

equals sign ['iːkwəlz'saɪn] N Gleichheitszeichen *nt*

equanimity [ˌekwəˈnɪmɪtɪ] N Gleichmut *m*, Gelassenheit *f*; **with ~** gleichmütig, gelassen

equate [ɪˈkweɪt] VT (= *identify*) gleichsetzen, identifizieren; (= *compare, treat as the same*) auf die gleiche Stufe stellen

equation [ɪˈkweɪʒən] N (*Math, fig*) Gleichung *f*; **that doesn't even enter the ~** das steht doch überhaupt nicht zur Debatte

equator [ɪˈkweɪtəʳ] N Äquator *m*; **at the ~** am Äquator

equatorial [ˌekwəˈtɔːrɪəl] ADJ äquatorial, Äquatorial-

equestrian [ɪˈkwestrɪən] ADJ Reit-, Reiter-; **~ events** Reitveranstaltung *f*; (*tournament*) Reitturnier *nt*

equidistant [ˈiːkwɪˈdɪstənt] ADJ gleich weit entfernt (*from* von)

equilateral [ˈiːkwɪˈlætərəl] ADJ gleichseitig

equilibrium [ˌiːkwɪˈlɪbrɪəm] N Gleichgewicht *nt*; **to keep/lose one's ~** das Gleichgewicht halten/verlieren

equine [ˈekwaɪn] ADJ Pferde-

equinox [ˈiːkwɪnɒks] N Tagundnachtgleiche *f*; **the spring/ autumn ~** die Frühjahrs-/Herbst-Tagundnachtgleiche

equip [ɪˈkwɪp] VT *ship, army, person* ausrüsten; *household, kitchen* ausstatten; **he is well ~ped for the job** (*fig*) er hat die nötigen Kenntnisse *or* das nötige Rüstzeug für die Stelle

equipment [ɪˈkwɪpmənt] N, NO PL (*of person*) Ausrüstung *f*; **laboratory ~** Laborausstattung *f*; **office ~** Büroeinrichtung *f*; **electrical ~** Elektrogeräte *pl*; **kitchen ~** Küchengeräte *pl*

equitable ADJ, **equitably** ADV [ˈekwɪtəbl, -ɪ] gerecht

equity [ˈekwɪtɪ] N **(a)** Fairness *f*, Billigkeit *f* **(b) equities** PL (*Fin*) Stammaktien *pl*, Dividendenpapiere *pl*; **equities market** Aktienmarkt *m*

equivalent [ɪˈkwɪvələnt] **1** ADJ **(a)** (= *equal*) gleichwertig, äquivalent; **that's ~ to saying ...** das ist gleichbedeutend damit, zu sagen ...
(b) (= *corresponding*) entsprechend, äquivalent; **it is ~ to £30** das entspricht £ 30; **... or the ~ value in francs ...** oder der Gegenwert in Francs
2 N Äquivalent *nt*; (= *counterpart*) Gegenstück *nt*, Pendant *nt*; (= *person*) Pendant *nt*; **that is the ~ of ...** das entspricht ... (*dat*); **what is the ~ in euros?** was ist der Gegenwert in Euro?; **the American ~ of the British public school** das amerikanische Pendant zur britischen Public School

equivocal [ɪˈkwɪvəkəl] ADJ (*form*) **(a)** (= *ambiguous*) *reply, response* zweideutig; *statement, comment* vage; *position, results, research* unklar; *evidence* nicht schlüssig; **she was ~** sie legte sich nicht fest **(b)** (= *ambivalent*) *attitude* zwiespältig; *person* ambivalent; (= *undecided*) unentschieden; **to be ~ about sth** keine klare Meinung zu etw haben

equivocally [ɪˈkwɪvəkəlɪ] ADV **(a)** (= *ambiguously*) zweideutig **(b)** (= *unclearly*) unklar

equivocate [ɪˈkwɪvəkeɪt] VI ausweichen

equivocation [ɪˌkwɪvəˈkeɪʃən] N Ausflucht *f*, ausweichende Formulierung; **without ~** ohne Ausflüchte

ER (*US*) ABBR *of* **emergency room**

ERA (*US*) ABBR *of* **Equal Rights Amendment** *Verfassungsartikel zur Gleichberechtigung*

era [ˈɪərə] N Ära *f*; (*Geol*) Erdzeitalter *nt*; **the Christian ~** (die) christliche Zeitrechnung

eradicate [ɪˈrædɪkeɪt] VT ausrotten

eradication [ɪˌrædɪˈkeɪʃən] N Ausrottung *f*

erase [ɪˈreɪz] VT ausradieren; (*from tape, Comput*) löschen; (*from mind*) streichen (*from* aus)

eraser [ɪˈreɪzəʳ] N Radiergummi *nt or m*

erasure [ɪˈreɪʒəʳ] N Auslöschen *nt*; (*from tape*) Löschen *nt*

ERDF ABBR *of* **European Regional Development Fund** EFRE *m*

erect [ɪˈrekt] **1** VT *wall, building* bauen; *statue, memorial, altar* errichten (*to sb* jdm); *machinery, furniture, scaffolding* aufstellen; *tent* aufschlagen; *mast* aufrichten; (*fig*) *barrier* errichten **2** ADJ **(a)** *person, posture, plant* aufrecht; *head* hoch erhoben; *tail* erhoben; **to stand ~** gerade stehen; **to walk ~** aufrecht gehen **(b)** (*Physiol*) *penis* steif; *nipples* aufgerichtet

erection [ɪˈrekʃən] N **(a)** (*of wall, building*) (Er)bauen *nt*; (*of statue, memorial, altar, also fig: of barrier*) Errichten *nt* **(b)** (*Physiol*) Erektion *f*

ergonomic [ˌɜːɡəʊˈnɒmɪk] ADJ ergonomisch

ERM N ABBR *of* **exchange rate mechanism**

ermine [ˈɜːmɪn] N Hermelin *m*

erode [ɪˈrəʊd] **1** VT auswaschen, erodieren (*spec*); (*fig*) *confidence, power, beliefs* untergraben; *authority* unterminieren; *value* abtragen **2** VI (*value*) abgetragen werden

erogenous [ɪˈrɒdʒənəs] ADJ erogen

erosion [ɪˈrəʊʒən] N Erosion *f*; (*fig*) (*of authority*) Unterminierung *f*; (*of value*) Abtragung *f*

erotic ADJ, **erotically** ADV [ɪˈrɒtɪk, -əlɪ] erotisch

eroticism [ɪˈrɒtɪsɪzəm] N Erotik *f*

err [ɜːʳ] VI sich irren; **to ~ in one's judgement** sich in seinem Urteil irren; **it is better to ~ on the side of caution** man sollte im Zweifelsfall lieber zu vorsichtig sein

errand [ˈerənd] N (= *shopping etc*) Besorgung *f*; (*to give a message etc*) Botengang *m*; (= *task*) Auftrag *m*; **to send sb on an ~** jdn auf Besorgungen/einen Botengang schicken

errant [ˈerənt] ADJ *ways* sündig; *husband etc* untreu

erratic [ɪˈrætɪk] ADJ unberechenbar; *progress, pattern, rhythm, pulse* ungleichmäßig; *performance* variabel; *movement* unkontrolliert; **to be (very) ~** (*sales, figures*) (stark) schwanken; **~ mood swings** starke Stimmungsschwankungen *pl*; **his ~ driving** sein unberechenbarer Fahrstil

erratically [ɪˈrætɪkəlɪ] ADV unberechenbar

erroneous [ɪˈrəʊnɪəs] ADJ falsch; *assumption, belief* irrig

erroneously [ɪˈrəʊnɪəslɪ] ADV fälschlicherweise

error [ˈerəʳ] N **(a)** (= *mistake*) Fehler *m* **(b)** (= *wrongness*) Irrtum *m*; **in ~** irrtümlicherweise; **to see the ~ of one's ways** seine Fehler einsehen

error message N (*Comput*) Fehlermeldung *f*

ersatz [ˈeəzæts] ADJ Ersatz-; **~ coffee** Kaffee-Ersatz *m*

erudite [ˈerʊdaɪt] ADJ gelehrt

erudition [erʊˈdɪʃən] N Gelehrsamkeit *f*

erupt [ɪˈrʌpt] VI ausbrechen; (*fig: person*) explodieren; **the crowd ~ed into applause** die Menge brach in Applaus aus; **her face had ~ed in spots** sie hatte im ganzen Gesicht Pickel bekommen

eruption [ɪˈrʌpʃən] N Ausbruch *m*

escalate [ˈeskəleɪt] **1** VT *war* ausweiten **2** VI sich ausweiten, eskalieren; (*costs*) in die Höhe schnellen

escalation [eskəˈleɪʃən] N Eskalation *f*

escalator [ˈeskəleɪtəʳ] N Rolltreppe *f*

escapade [eskəˈpeɪd] N Eskapade *f*

escape [ɪˈskeɪp] **1** VI **(a)** flüchten, fliehen (*from* aus); (*from pursuers, captivity*) entkommen (*from +dat*); (*from prison, cage etc*) ausbrechen (*from* aus); (*bird*) entfliegen (*from +dat*); (*water*) auslaufen (*from* aus); (*gas*) ausströmen (*from* aus); **an ~d prisoner/tiger** ein entflohener Häftling/entsprungener Tiger; **he ~d from the fire** er ist dem Feuer entkommen; **a room which I can ~ to** ein Zimmer, in das ich mich zurückziehen kann; **to ~ from reality** der Wirklichkeit entfliehen (*geh*); **to ~ from poverty** der Armut entkommen **(b)** (= *get off, be spared*) davonkommen; **these cuts will affect everyone, nobody will ~** diese Kürzungen betreffen alle, keiner wird ungeschoren davonkommen
2 VT **(a)** *pursuers* entkommen (+*dat*)
(b) *consequences, disaster, detection* entgehen (+*dat*); **no department will ~ these cuts** keine Abteilung wird von diesen Kürzungen verschont bleiben; **he narrowly ~d injury** er ist gerade noch unverletzt davongekommen; **he narrowly ~d being run over** er wäre um ein Haar überfahren worden; **but you can't ~ the fact that ...** aber du kannst nicht abstreiten, dass ...
(c) *his name ~s me* sein Name ist mir entfallen; **nothing ~s him** ihm entgeht nichts; **to ~ notice** unbemerkt bleiben
3 N **(a)** (*from prison etc*) Ausbruch *m*; (= *attempted ~*) Ausbruchsversuch *m*; (*from a country*) Flucht *f* (*from* aus); (*fig: from reality etc*) Flucht *f* (*from* vor); **to make one's ~** ausbrechen; **to have a miraculous ~** auf wunderbare Weise davonkommen; **there's no ~** (*fig*) es gibt keinen Ausweg **(b)** (*of gas*) Ausströmen *nt*; **due to an ~ of gas** aufgrund ausströmenden Gases
(c) (*Comput*) **hit ~** Escape drücken

escape: escape attempt, escape bid N Fluchtversuch *m*; **escape clause** N (*Jur*) Rücktrittsklausel *f*; **escape key** N (*Comput*) Escape-Taste *f*; **escape route** N Fluchtweg *m*

escapism [ɪˈskeɪpɪzəm] N Wirklichkeitsflucht *f*

escapist [ɪ'skeɪpɪst] ADJ eskapistisch; ~ **fantasy** unrealistische Fantasien *pl*

escapologist [ˌeskə'pɒlədʒɪst] N Entfesselungskünstler(in) *m(f)*

eschew [ɪs'tʃuː] VT (*old, liter*) scheuen, (ver)meiden

escort ['eskɔːt] ◼ N **(a)** Geleitschutz *m*; (*vehicles, ships etc*) Eskorte *f*; **under ~** unter Bewachung; **motorcycle ~** Motorradeskorte *f* **(b)** (= *male companion*) Begleiter *m*; (= *hired female*) Hostess *f* ◼ [ɪ'skɔːt] VT begleiten

escort agency N Hostessenagentur *f*

Eskimo ['eskɪməʊ] (*pej*) ◼ ADJ Eskimo-, eskimoisch ◼ N Eskimo *m*, Eskimofrau *f*

ESL ABBR *of* **English as a Second Language**

esophagus N (*esp US*) = **oesophagus**

esoteric [ˌesəʊ'terɪk] ADJ esoterisch

ESP ABBR *of* **extrasensory perception** ASW *f*

espadrille [ˌespə'drɪl] N Espadrille *f*

especial [ɪ'speʃəl] ADJ besondere(r, s)

especially [ɪ'speʃəlɪ] ADV **(a)** (= *particularly*) besonders; **not ~** nicht besonders; **(more) ~ as ...** besonders *or* vor allem, weil ...; **~ in summer** vor allem im Sommer; **why Jim ~?** warum ausgerechnet *or* gerade Jim? **(b)** (= *specifically*) speziell, eigens; **I came ~ to see you** ich bin eigens gekommen, um dich zu sehen; **to do sth ~ for sb/sth** etw speziell *or* extra für jdn/etw tun; **~ built** (*US*) speziell angefertigt

Esperanto [ˌespə'ræntəʊ] N Esperanto *nt*

espionage [ˌespɪə'nɑːʒ] N Spionage *f*

esplanade [ˌesplə'neɪd] N (Strand)promenade *f*

espouse [ɪ'spaʊz] VT (*fig*) *cause, views* eintreten für; *violence* befürworten

espresso [e'spresəʊ] N **~ (coffee)** Espresso *m*; **~ bar** Espresso(bar *f*) *nt*

esquire [ɪ'skwaɪəʳ] N (*abbr* **Esq**) (*Brit*) **James Jones, Esq** Herrn James Jones

essay ['eseɪ] N Essay *m or nt*; (*esp Sch*) Aufsatz *m*

essence ['esəns] N **(a)** Wesen *nt*; **in ~ the theories are very similar** die Theorien sind im Wesentlichen sehr ähnlich; **time is of the ~** Zeit ist von entscheidender Bedeutung; **the novel captures the ~ of life in the city** der Roman fängt das Leben in der Stadt perfekt ein **(b)** (*Chem, Cook*) Essenz *f*

essential [ɪ'senʃəl] ◼ ADJ **(a)** (= *vital*) (unbedingt) erforderlich *or* notwendig; *services, supplies* lebenswichtig; **it is ~ to act quickly** schnelles Handeln ist unbedingt erforderlich; **it is ~ that you understand this** du musst das unbedingt verstehen; **certain vitamins are ~ for good health** bestimmte Vitamine sind für die Gesundheit unerlässlich

(b) (= *basic*) wesentlich; *question, role* entscheidend; **I don't doubt his ~ goodness** ich zweifle nicht an, dass er im Grunde ein guter Mensch ist

◼ N **(a) just bring the ~s** bring nur das Allernotwendigste mit; **with only the bare ~s** nur mit dem Allernotwendigsten ausgestattet

(b) essentials PL (= *most important points*) wichtige Punkte *pl*; **the ~s of German grammar** die Grundlagen *pl* der deutschen Grammatik

essentially [ɪ'senʃəlɪ] ADV (= *fundamentally*) im Wesentlichen; (= *basically*) im Grunde genommen

EST (*US*) ABBR *of* **Eastern Standard Time** Ostküstenzeit *f*

establish [ɪ'stæblɪʃ] ◼ VT **(a)** (= *found, set up*) gründen; *new procedure* einführen; *relations* aufnehmen; *links* anknüpfen; *post* einrichten; *peace* stiften; *order* (wieder) herstellen; *reputation* sich (*dat*) verschaffen; *precedent* setzen; **to ~ one's reputation as a scholar** sich (*dat*) einen Namen als Wissenschaftler(in) machen

(b) (= *prove*) *fact, innocence* beweisen; *claim* unter Beweis stellen; **we have ~ed that ...** wir haben bewiesen *or* gezeigt, dass ...

(c) (= *determine*) *identity, facts* ermitteln

◼ VR sich etablieren; **he has now firmly ~ed himself in the company** er ist jetzt in der Firma fest etabliert

established [ɪ'stæblɪʃt] ADJ *order, company, name* etabliert; *clientele* fest; *reputation* gesichert; *tradition* althergebracht; **it's an ~ practice** *or* **custom** es ist allgemein üblich; **well** *or* **firmly ~ as sth** (= *recognized*) allgemein als etw anerkannt; **it's an ~ fact that ...** es steht fest, dass ...; **~ 1850** (*Comm etc*) gegründet 1850

establishment [ɪ'stæblɪʃmənt] N **(a)** (= *setting up*) (*of relations, links*) Aufnahme *f*; (*of post*) Einrichtung *f*; (*of company*) Gründung *f* **(b)** (= *institution etc*) Institution *f*; (= *hospital, school etc*) Anstalt *f*; **commercial ~** kommerzielles Unternehmen **(c) the Establishment** das Establishment

estate [ɪ'steɪt] N **(a)** (= *land*) Gut *nt*; **country ~** Landgut *nt*; **family ~** Familienbesitz *m* **(b)** (*Jur*: = *possessions of deceased*) Nachlass *m*; **to leave one's ~ to sb** jdm seinen ganzen Besitz vermachen *or* hinterlassen **(c)** (*esp Brit*) (= *housing ~*) Siedlung *f*; (= *trading ~*) Industriegelände *nt* **(d)** (*Brit*) = **estate car**

estate: **estate agent** N (*Brit*) Immobilienmakler(in) *m(f)*; **estate car** N (*Brit*) Kombi(wagen) *m*

esteem [ɪ'stiːm] ◼ VT *person* hoch schätzen; *qualities* schätzen ◼ N Wertschätzung *f*; **to hold sb/sth in (high) ~** jdn/etw (hoch) schätzen; **to be held in low/great ~** wenig/sehr geschätzt werden; **he went down in my ~** er ist in meiner Achtung gesunken

esthete *etc* (*esp US*) N = **aesthete** *etc*

estimable ['estɪməbl] ADJ schätzenswert

estimate ['estɪmɪt] ◼ N **(a)** Schätzung *f*; (= *valuation*) Taxierung *f*; **£100/it is just an ~** £ 100/das ist nur geschätzt; **at a rough ~** grob geschätzt **(b)** (*Comm*: *of cost*) (Kosten)voranschlag *m*; **to get an ~** einen (Kosten)voranschlag einholen ◼ ['estɪmeɪt] VT schätzen; **his wealth is ~d at ...** sein Vermögen wird auf ... geschätzt; **I ~ she must be 40** ich schätze sie auf 40

estimation [ˌestɪ'meɪʃən] N **(a)** Einschätzung *f* **(b)** (= *esteem*) Achtung *f*; **he went up/down in my ~** er ist in meiner Achtung gestiegen/gesunken

Estonia [e'stəʊnɪə] N Estland *nt*

Estonian [e'stəʊnɪən] ◼ ADJ estnisch ◼ N **(a)** Este *m*, Estin *f* **(b)** (*Ling*) Estnisch *nt*

estrange [ɪ'streɪndʒ] VT **to be/become ~d from sb/sth** sich jdm/etw entfremdet haben/entfremden; **they are ~d** (*married couple*) sie haben sich auseinander gelebt; **his ~d wife** seine von ihm getrennt lebende Frau

estuary ['estjʊərɪ] N Mündung *f*

ET (*US*) ABBR *of* **Eastern Time** Ostküstenzeit *f*

etcetera [ɪt'setərə] ADV (*abbr* **etc**) und so weiter, et cetera

etch [etʃ] ◼ VI ätzen; (*in copper*) in Kupfer stechen; (*in other metals*) radieren ◼ VT ätzen; (*in copper*) in Kupfer stechen; (*in other metals*) radieren; **the windows were ~ed with the vehicle registration number** das Autokennzeichen war in die Scheiben eingeätzt; **the event was ~ed on her mind** das Ereignis hatte sich ihr ins Gedächtnis eingegraben

etching ['etʃɪŋ] N Ätzung *f*; (*in copper*) Kupferstich *m*; (*in other metals*) Radierung *f*

E term N (*Comm*) E-Klausel *f*

eternal [ɪ'tɜːnl] ADJ **(a)** (= *everlasting*) ewig; **the Eternal City** die Ewige Stadt; **the ~ triangle** das Dreiecksverhältnis **(b)** (= *incessant*) endlos

eternally [ɪ'tɜːnəlɪ] ADV ewig; *optimistic* immer; **to be ~ grateful (to sb/for sth)** (jdm/für etw) ewig dankbar sein

eternity [ɪ'tɜːnɪtɪ] N (*lit, fig*: *inf*) Ewigkeit *f*; (*Rel*) das ewige Leben; **it seemed an ~** es kam mir wie eine Ewigkeit vor

ether ['iːθəʳ] N (*Chem, poet*) Äther *m*

ethereal [ɪ'θɪərɪəl] ADJ ätherisch

ethic ['eθɪk] N Ethik *f*

ethical ['eθɪkəl] ADJ (= *morally right*) ethisch *attr*; (*of ethics*) Moral-; **it is not ~ to ...** es ist unethisch *or* unmoralisch, zu ...; **~ behaviour** (*Brit*) *or* **behavior** (*US*) ethisch einwandfreies Verhalten

ethically ['eθɪkəlɪ] ADV ethisch; (= *with correct ethics*) ethisch einwandfrei

ethics ['eθɪks] N **(a)** SING (= *system*) Ethik *f* **(b)** PL (= *morality*) Moral *f*; **the ~ of abortion** die moralischen *or* ethischen Aspekte *pl* der Abtreibung

Ethiopia [ˌiːθɪ'əʊpɪə] N Äthiopien *nt*

Ethiopian [ˌiːθɪ'əʊpɪən] ◼ ADJ äthiopisch ◼ N Äthiopier(in) *m(f)*

ethnic ['eθnɪk] ADJ **(a)** (= *racial*) ethnisch; **~ violence** Rassenkrawalle *pl*; **~ Germans** Volksdeutsche *pl* **(b)** (= *traditional*) *atmosphere* urtümlich; *clothes* folkloristisch; **~ music** Folklore *f*

ethnically [ˈeθnɪklɪ] ADV ethnisch

ethnic cleansing N (euph) ethnische Säuberung

ethos [ˈiːθɒs] N Gesinnung f, Ethos nt

etiquette [ˈetɪket] N Etikette f; **a breach of** ~ ein Verstoß m gegen die Etikette

ETV (US) ABBR of **Educational Television** ≈ Schulfernsehen nt

etymological ADJ, **etymologically** ADV [etɪməˈlɒdʒɪkəl, -ɪ] etymologisch

etymology [etɪˈmɒlədʒɪ] N Etymologie f

EU ABBR of **European Union** EU f

eucalyptus [juːkəˈlɪptəs] N Eukalyptus m

Eucharist [ˈjuːkərɪst] N (Eccl) Abendmahlsgottesdienst m; **the** ~ das (heilige) Abendmahl

eulogy [ˈjuːlədʒɪ] N Lobesrede f

eunuch [ˈjuːnək] N Eunuch m

euphemism [ˈjuːfəmɪzəm] N Euphemismus m, Hüllwort nt

euphemistic [juːfəˈmɪstɪk] ADJ euphemistisch, verhüllend

euphemistically [juːfəˈmɪstɪkəlɪ] ADV euphemistisch, verhüllend; **to be** ~ **described/known as ...** beschönigend als ... bezeichnet werden/bekannt sein

euphoria [juːˈfɔːrɪə] N Euphorie f

euphoric [juːˈfɒrɪk] ADJ euphorisch

Eurasian [jʊəˈreɪʃn] **1** ADJ eurasisch **2** N Eurasier(in) m(f)

eureka [jʊəˈriːkə] INTERJ heureka

euro [ˈjʊərəʊ] N Euro m

Euro-, euro- [ˈjʊərəʊ] PREF Euro-, euro-; **eurocentric** ADJ eurozentrisch; **Eurocheque**, (US) **Eurocheck** [ˈjʊərəʊtʃek] N Euroscheck m; **eurocurrency** [ˈjʊərəʊˈkʌrənsɪ] N Eurowährung f; **Euroland** [ˈjʊərəʊlænd] N (inf) Eurozone f, Euroland nt (inf); **Euro MP** N (inf) Europaabgeordnete(r) mf

Europe [ˈjʊərəp] N Europa nt

European [jʊərəˈpiːən] **1** ADJ europäisch; ~ **standard** (Ind) europäische Norm **2** N Europäer(in) m(f)

European: **European Central Bank** N Europäische Zentralbank; **European Commission** N Europäische Kommission; **European Community** N Europäische Gemeinschaft; **European Council** N Europäischer Rat; **European Court of Justice** N Europäischer Gerichtshof; **European Economic Community** N Europäische Wirtschaftsgemeinschaft; **European Free Trade Association** N Europäische Freihandelszone; **European Investment Bank** N Europäische Investitionsbank; **European Monetary System** N Europäisches Währungssystem; **European Monetary Union** N Europäische Währungsunion; **European Parliament** N Europäisches Parlament; **European Regional Development Fund** N Europäischer Fonds für regionale Entwicklung; **European Union** N Europäische Union

Euro-sceptic [ˈjʊərəʊskeptɪk] N Euroskeptiker(in) m(f)

euthanasia [juːθəˈneɪzɪə] N Euthanasie f

evacuate [ɪˈvækjʊeɪt] VT räumen; women, children evakuieren (from aus, to nach)

evacuation [ɪvækjʊˈeɪʃən] N Räumung f; (of women, children) Evakuierung f

evacuee [ɪvækjʊˈiː] N Evakuierte(r) mf

evade [ɪˈveɪd] VT blow, question, sb's eyes ausweichen (+dat); pursuit, pursuers entkommen (+dat); obligation, justice, capture sich entziehen (+dat); military service umgehen; **to** ~ **taxes** Steuern hinterziehen; **if you try to** ~ **paying import duty** wenn Sie versuchen, den Einfuhrzoll zu umgehen

evaluate [ɪˈvæljʊeɪt] VT house, worth etc schätzen (at auf +acc); damages festsetzen (at auf +acc); chances, effectiveness, achievement, performance beurteilen; evidence, results auswerten; pros and cons (gegeneinander) abwägen

evaluation [ɪvæljʊˈeɪʃən] N (of house, worth etc) Schätzung f; (of chances, effectiveness, achievement, performance) Beurteilung f; (of evidence, results) Auswertung f; (of pros and cons) Abwägung f

evangelic(al) [iːvænˈdʒelɪk(əl)] ADJ evangelikal

evangelist [ɪˈvændʒəlɪst] N (= preacher) Prediger(in) m(f); (= itinerant) Wanderprediger(in) m(f)

evaporate [ɪˈvæpəreɪt] VI (a) (liquid) verdunsten (b) (fig) sich in Luft auflösen; (hopes) sich zerschlagen

evaporated milk [ɪˈvæpəreɪtɪdˈmɪlk] N Kondens- or Büchsenmilch f

evasion [ɪˈveɪʒən] N (of question etc) Ausweichen nt (of vor +dat); (of tax) Hinterziehung f

evasive [ɪˈveɪzɪv] ADJ ausweichend; **they were** ~ **about it** sie redeten drum herum; **to take** ~ **action** ein Ausweichmanöver machen

evasively [ɪˈveɪzɪvlɪ] ADV ausweichend

eve [iːv] N Vorabend m; **on the** ~ **of** am Vorabend von or +gen

even [ˈiːvən] **1** ADJ (a) surface, ground eben; **to make sth** ~ ground etw ebnen

(b) (= regular) gleichmäßig

(c) quantities, distances, values gleich; **they are an** ~ **match** sie sind einander ebenbürtig; **I will get** ~ **with you for that** das werde ich dir heimzahlen; **that makes us** ~ (in game) damit steht es unentschieden; (fig) damit sind wir quitt; **he has an** ~ **chance of winning** seine Gewinnchancen stehen fifty-fifty (inf); **to break** ~ die Kosten decken; **to give sb an** ~ **break** (esp US) jdm eine Chance geben

(d) number gerade

(e) (= exact) genau; **let's make it an** ~ **hundred** nehmen wir eine runde Zahl und sagen 100

2 ADV (a) sogar, selbst; **it'll be difficult, impossible** ~ das wird schwierig sein, wenn nicht (so)gar unmöglich

(b) (with comp adj) sogar noch; **that's** ~ **better/more beautiful** das ist sogar (noch) besser/schöner

(c) (with neg) **not** ~ nicht einmal; **without** ~ **a smile** ohne auch nur zu lächeln

(d) ~ **if** selbst wenn; ~ **though** obwohl; **but** ~ **then** aber sogar dann; ~ **as I spoke someone knocked at the door** noch während ich redete, klopfte es an der Tür; ~ **so** (aber) trotzdem

▶ **even out** **1** VI (prices) sich einpendeln **2** VT SEP tax burden, wealth gleichmäßig verteilen; **that should even things out a bit** dadurch müsste ein gewisser Ausgleich erzielt werden

▶ **even up** **1** VT SEP **that will even things up** das wird die Sache etwas ausgleichen **2** VI (= pay off debt) Schulden begleichen (with bei); **can we even up later?** können wir später abrechnen?

even-handed ADJ, **even-handedly** ADV [iːvnˈhændɪd, -lɪ] gerecht, fair

evening [ˈiːvnɪŋ] N Abend m; **in the** ~ abends, am Abend; **this/tomorrow/yesterday** ~ heute/morgen/gestern Abend; **that** ~ an jenem Abend; **on the** ~ **of the twenty-ninth** am Abend des 29.; **one** ~ **as I ...** eines Abends, als ich ...; **every Monday** ~ jeden Montagabend; **all** ~ den ganzen Abend (lang)

evening: **evening class** N Abendkurs m; **to go to** or **take** ~**es** or **an** ~ **in French** einen Abendkurs in Französisch besuchen; **evening dress** N (men's) Abendanzug m; (women's) Abendkleid nt; **evening gown** N Abendkleid nt

evenly [ˈiːvənlɪ] ADV gleichmäßig; divide in gleiche Teile; **the contestants were** ~ **matched** die Gegner waren einander ebenbürtig; **your weight should be** ~ **balanced (between your two feet)** Sie sollten Ihr Gewicht gleichmäßig (auf beide Füße) verteilen; **public opinion seems to be** ~ **divided** die öffentliche Meinung scheint in zwei gleich große Lager gespalten zu sein

evenness [ˈiːvənnɪs] N (a) (of ground) Ebenheit f

(b) (= regularity) Gleichmäßigkeit f

evensong [ˈiːvənsɒŋ] N Abendgottesdienst m

event [ɪˈvent] N (a) (= happening) Ereignis nt; **in the normal course of** ~**s** normalerweise; **it's easy to be wise after the** ~ hinterher ist man immer klüger

(b) (= organized function) Veranstaltung f; (Sport) Wettkampf m

(c) (= case) **in the** ~ **of her death** im Falle ihres Todes; **in the** ~ **of war/fire** im Kriegs-/Brandfall; **in the** ~ **of my not returning, ...** sollte ich nicht wiederkommen, ...; **in the unlikely** ~ **that ...** falls, was sehr unwahrscheinlich ist, ...; **he said he wouldn't come, but in the** ~ **he did** er sagte, er würde nicht kommen, aber er kam dann schließlich doch; **but in any** ~ **I can't give you my permission** aber ich kann dir jedenfalls nicht meine Erlaubnis geben; **but in any** ~ **you have my permission** aber Sie haben auf alle Fälle meine Erlaubnis; **at all** ~**s** auf jeden Fall

eventful [ɪˈventfʊl] ADJ ereignisreich

eventual [ɪˈventjʊəl] ADJ **he predicted the** ~ **fall of the government** er hat vorausgesagt, dass die Regierung am Ende or schließlich zu Fall kommen würde; **the** ~ **success of the**

project is not in doubt es besteht kein Zweifel, dass das Vorhaben letzten Endes Erfolg haben wird; **he lost to the ~ winner** er verlor gegen den späteren Gewinner

> *Be careful!* **eventual** *is not translated by the German word* *eventuell.*

eventuality [ɪˌventʃʊˈælɪtɪ] N Eventualität *f*; **be ready for any ~** sei auf alle Eventualitäten gefasst

eventually [ɪˈventʃʊəlɪ] ADV schließlich; (= *one day*) eines Tages; (= *in the long term*) auf lange Sicht

ever [ˈevəʳ] ADV **(a)** je(mals); **not ~** nie; **nothing ~ happens** es passiert nie etwas; **it hardly ~ snows here** hier schneit es kaum (jemals); **if I ~ catch you doing that again** wenn ich dich noch einmal dabei erwische; **seldom, if ~** selten, wenn überhaupt; **he's a rascal if ~ there was one** er ist ein richtiggehender kleiner Halunke; **don't you ~ say that again!** sag das ja nie mehr!; **have you ~ been to Glasgow?** bist du schon einmal in Glasgow gewesen?; **did you ~ see** *or* **have you ~ seen anything so strange?** hast du schon jemals so etwas Merkwürdiges gesehen?; **more beautiful than ~ (before)** schöner denn je (zuvor); **the first ... ~** der *etc* allererste ...; **I'll never, ~ forgive myself** das werde ich mir nie im Leben verzeihen
(b) (= *at all times*) **~ since I was a boy** seit ich ein Junge war; **~ since I have lived here ...** seitdem ich hier lebe ...; **~ since (then)** seitdem; **for ~** für immer; **it seemed to go on for ~ (and ~)** es schien ewig zu dauern; **~ increasing power** ständig wachsende Macht; **an ~ present feeling** ein ständiges Gefühl; **all she ~ does is complain** sie tut nichts anderes als sich ständig zu beschweren
(c) (*intensive*) **she's the best grandmother ~** sie ist die beste Großmutter, die es gibt; **what ~ shall we do?** was sollen wir bloß machen?; **when ~ will they come?** wann kommen sie denn bloß *or* endlich?; **why ~ not?** warum denn bloß nicht?
(d) (*inf*) **~ so/such** unheimlich; **~ so slightly drunk** ein ganz klein wenig betrunken; **he's ~ such a nice man** er ist ein ungemein netter Mensch; **I am ~ so sorry** es tut mir schrecklich Leid; **thank you ~ so much** ganz herzlichen Dank

Everest [ˈevarest] N **(Mount)** ~ der (Mount) Everest

evergreen [ˈevəɡriːn] **1** ADJ immergrün **2** N Nadelbaum *m*

everlasting [ˌevəˈlɑːstɪŋ] ADJ ewig; *gratitude* immer während; *glory* unvergänglich; **to his ~ shame** zu seiner ewigen Schande

evermore [ˌevəˈmɔːʳ] ADV (*liter*) auf immer und ewig; **for ~** in alle Ewigkeit

every [ˈevrɪ] ADJ **(a)** jede(r, s); **you must examine ~ one** Sie müssen jeden (Einzelnen) untersuchen; **~ man for himself** jeder für sich; **in ~ way** (= *in all respects*) in jeder Hinsicht; (= *by ~ means*) mit allen Mitteln; **he is ~ bit as clever as his brother** er ist ganz genauso schlau wie sein Bruder; **~ single time I ...** immer wenn ich ...; **~ fifth day**, **~ five days** alle fünf Tage; **write on ~ other page** bitte jede zweite Seite beschreiben; **once ~ week** einmal pro Woche; **one in ~ twenty people** jeder zwanzigste Mensch; **~ so often**, **~ once in a while**, **~ now and then** *or* **again** hin und wieder, ab und zu; **they catered to his ~ whim** sie erfüllten ihm jeden Wunsch; **his ~ word** jedes Wort, das er sagte
(b) (= *all possible*) **I have ~ confidence in him** ich habe unbedingtes *or* uneingeschränktes Vertrauen zu ihm; **I have/ there is ~ hope that ...** ich habe allen Grund/es besteht aller Grund zu der Hoffnung, dass ...; **we wish you ~ success/ happiness** wir wünschen Ihnen alles (nur erdenklich) Gute/ viel Glück und Zufriedenheit; **there was ~ prospect of success** es bestand alle Aussicht auf Erfolg

everybody [ˈevrɪbɒdɪ] PRON jeder(mann), alle *pl*; **~ has finished** alle sind fertig; **it's not ~ who can afford a video recorder** nicht jeder kann sich (*dat*) einen Videorekorder leisten

everyday [ˈevrɪdeɪ] ADJ alltäglich; *reality* täglich; **~ clothes** Alltagskleidung *f*; **to be an ~ occurrence** (all)täglich vorkommen; **for ~ use** für den täglichen Gebrauch; **~ life** der Alltag

everyone [ˈevrɪwʌn] PRON = **everybody**

everything [ˈevrɪθɪŋ] N alles; **~ possible** alles Mögliche/ Alte; **~ you have** alles, was du hast; **is ~ all right?** ist alles in Ordnung?; **time is ~** Zeit ist kostbar; **money isn't ~** Geld ist nicht alles

everywhere [ˈevrɪwɛəʳ] ADV überall; (*with direction*) überallhin; **from ~** von überallher; **~ you look there's a mistake** wo man auch hinsieht, findet man Fehler

evict [ɪˈvɪkt] VT zur Räumung zwingen (*from* +*gen*); **they were ~ed** sie wurden zum Verlassen ihrer Wohnung gezwungen

eviction [ɪˈvɪkʃən] N Ausweisung *f*

eviction order N Räumungsbefehl *m*

evidence [ˈevɪdəns] N **(a)** Beweis *m*, Beweise *pl*; **what ~ is there to support this theory?** welche Anhaltspunkte gibt es, die diese Theorie untermauern?; **there is no ~ that ...** es deutet nichts darauf hin, dass ...
(b) (*Jur*) Beweismaterial *nt*; (*object etc*) Beweisstück *nt*; (= *testimony*) Aussage *f*; **we haven't got any ~** wir haben keinerlei Beweise; **for lack of ~** aus Mangel an Beweisen; **not admissible as ~** als Beweismittel nicht zulässig; **all the ~ was against him** alles sprach *or* die Tatsachen sprachen gegen ihn; **to give ~** aussagen; **to give ~ for the defence** (*Brit*) *or* **defense** (*US*)**/prosecution** für die Verteidigung/die Anklage aussagen
(c) **to be in ~** sichtbar sein; **poverty was still (very) much in ~** es gab immer noch sichtlich viel Armut

evident ADJ, **evidently** ADV [ˈevɪdənt, -lɪ] offensichtlich

evil [ˈiːvl] **1** N **(a)** Böse(s) *nt*; **good and ~ in Victorian England** das Gute und das Böse im viktorianischen England
(b) (= *bad thing or activity*) Übel *nt*; **the lesser/greater of two ~s** das kleinere/größere Übel; **a sermon on the ~s of drink** eine Predigt über das Laster des Trinkens
2 ADJ **(a)** *person, spell* böse; *influence, reputation* schlecht; *place* verhext; **~ deed** Übeltat *f*; **with ~ intent** mit *or* aus böser Absicht
(b) *smell, taste* übel

evocation [ˌevəˈkeɪʃən] N Heraufbeschwören *nt*

evocative [ɪˈvɒkətɪv] ADJ atmosphärisch; *name* wohlklingend; **to be ~ of sth** etw heraufbeschwören

evoke [ɪˈvəʊk] VT heraufbeschwören; *admiration, response* hervorrufen

evolution [ˌiːvəˈluːʃən] N (= *development, Biol*) Evolution *f*; **theory of ~** Evolutionstheorie *f*

evolutionary [ˌiːvəˈluːʃnərɪ] ADJ evolutionär; **~ theory** Evolutionstheorie *f*

evolutionism [ˌiːvəˈluːʃənɪzəm] N Evolutionismus *m*

evolutionist [ˌiːvəˈluːʃənɪst] **1** N Evolutionist(in) *m(f)* **2** ADJ evolutionistisch

evolve [ɪˈvɒlv] **1** VT entwickeln **2** VI sich entwickeln

ewe [juː] N Mutterschaf *nt*

ex [eks] N (*inf*) Verflossene(r) *mf* (*inf*)

ex- [eks-] PREF **(a)** ehemalig, Ex-; **ex-wife** Exfrau *f* **(b) ex-factory** ab Werk

exacerbate [ekˈsæsəbeɪt] VT *pain, disease, problem* verschlimmern; *situation, crisis, tensions* verschärfen

exact [ɪɡˈzækt] **1** ADJ **(a)** genau; *translation* wörtlich; **to be ~ about sth** etw genau darlegen; **do you have the ~ amount?** haben Sie es passend?; **until this ~ moment** bis genau zu diesem Augenblick; **the ~ same thing** genau das gleiche; **he's 47 to be ~** er ist 47, um genau zu sein; **they evolved from reptiles, dinosaurs to be ~** sie stammen von Reptilien ab, genau(er) gesagt, von Dinosauriern
(b) (= *meticulous*) genau, exakt; **to be very ~ in one's work** peinlich genau arbeiten; **~ science** (*lit, fig*) exakte Wissenschaft
2 VT (*form*) *money, obedience, revenge* fordern; *payment* eintreiben; *promise* abverlangen (*from sb* jdm); *guarantee* verlangen (*from* von); **to ~ a high price** (*fig*) einen hohen Preis fordern

exacting [ɪɡˈzæktɪŋ] ADJ *person, work, task* anspruchsvoll; *standards, demands* hoch

exactly [ɪɡˈzæktlɪ] ADV genau; **I wanted to know ~ where my mother was buried** ich wollte genau wissen, wo meine Mutter begraben war; **that's ~ what I was thinking** genau das habe ich auch gedacht; **at ~ five o'clock** um Punkt fünf Uhr; **at ~ 9.43 a.m./the right time** genau um 9.43 Uhr/zur richtigen Zeit; **I want to get things ~ right** ich will es ganz richtig machen; **who ~ will be in charge?** wer wird eigentlich die Verantwortung haben?; **you mean we are stuck?** – **~** wir sitzen also fest? – stimmt genau; **is she sick?** – **not ~** ist sie krank? – eigentlich nicht; **not ~** (*iro*: = *hardly*) nicht gerade

exactness [ɪgˈzæktnɪs] N Genauigkeit f
exaggerate [ɪgˈzædʒəreɪt] **1** VT **(a)** übertreiben; **he ~d what really happened** er hat das, was wirklich geschehen war, übertrieben dargestellt **(b)** *effect* verstärken; *similarity* hervorheben **2** VI übertreiben
exaggerated [ɪgˈzædʒəreɪtɪd] ADJ übertrieben
exaggeration [ɪgˌzædʒəˈreɪʃən] N Übertreibung f; **a bit of an ~** leicht übertrieben
exalt [ɪgˈzɔːlt] VT preisen
exaltation [ˌegzɔːlˈteɪʃən] N (= *feeling*) Begeisterung f
exalted [ɪgˈzɔːltɪd] ADJ *position, style* hoch; **she moves only in the most ~ circles** sie bewegt sich nur in den besten Kreisen
exam [ɪgˈzæm] N Prüfung f
examination [ɪgˌzæmɪˈneɪʃən] N **(a)** (*Sch, Univ etc*) Prüfung f; **geography ~** Geografieprüfung f
(b) (= *inspection, also Med*) Untersuchung f; (*of machine, premises, passports*) Kontrolle f; (*of accounts*) Prüfung f; **the matter is still under ~** die Angelegenheit wird noch geprüft *or* untersucht; **she underwent a thorough ~** sie wurde gründlich untersucht
(c) (*Jur*) (*of suspect, witness*) Verhör nt; (*of case, documents*) Untersuchung f
examine [ɪgˈzæmɪn] VT **(a)** (*for* auf +*acc*) untersuchen (*also Med*); *documents, accounts* prüfen; *machine, passports, luggage* kontrollieren; **you need (to have) your head ~d** (*inf*) du solltest dich mal auf deinen Geisteszustand untersuchen lassen **(b)** *pupil, candidate* prüfen (*in* in +*dat*, *on* über +*acc*)
(c) (*Jur*) *suspect, witness* verhören
examiner [ɪgˈzæmɪnəʳ] N (*Sch, Univ*) Prüfer(in) m(f); **board of ~s** Prüfungsausschuss m
example [ɪgˈzɑːmpl] N Beispiel nt; **for ~** zum Beispiel; **to set a good/bad ~** ein gutes/schlechtes Beispiel geben; **a leader who is an ~ to his men** ein Führer, der seinen Männern als Beispiel dient; **to follow sb's ~** jds Beispiel folgen; **to take sth as an ~** sich (*dat*) an etw ein Beispiel nehmen; **to make an ~ of sb** an jdm ein Exempel statuieren
exasperate [ɪgˈzɑːspəreɪt] VT zur Verzweiflung bringen; **to become** *or* **get ~d** sich verzweifeln (*with* an +*dat*)
exasperating [ɪgˈzɑːspəreɪtɪŋ] ADJ ärgerlich; *delay, difficulty, job* leidig *attr*; *person* nervig (*inf*); **it's so ~ not to be able to buy a newspaper** es ist wirklich zum Verzweifeln, dass man keine Zeitung bekommen kann
exasperation [ɪgˌzɑːspəˈreɪʃən] N Verzweiflung f (*with* über +*acc*)
excavate [ˈekskəveɪt] **1** VT *ground* ausschachten; (*machine*) ausbaggern; (*Archeol*) *remains* ausgraben; *site* Ausgrabungen machen auf (+*dat*); *trench, graves* ausheben **2** VI (*Archeol*) Ausgrabungen machen
excavation [ˌekskəˈveɪʃən] N **(a)** (*Archeol*) (Aus)grabung f; **~s** (= *site*) Ausgrabungsstätte f **(b)** (*of tunnel etc*) Graben nt
excavator [ˈekskəveɪtəʳ] N (= *machine*) Bagger m
exceed [ɪkˈsiːd] VT **(a)** (*in value, amount, length of time*) übersteigen (*by* um); **to ~ 5 kilos in weight** das Gewicht von 5 kg übersteigen; **a fine not ~ing £500** eine Geldstrafe bis zu £ 500 **(b)** (= *go beyond*) hinausgehen über (+*acc*); *expectations, desires* übertreffen; *limits, powers* überschreiten
exceedingly [ɪkˈsiːdɪŋlɪ] ADV (+*adj, adv*) äußerst, ausgesprochen
excel [ɪkˈsel] **1** VI sich auszeichnen **2** VT **to ~ oneself** (*often iro*) sich selbst übertreffen
excellence [ˈeksələns] N hervorragende Qualität; **artistic/academic ~** höchste künstlerische/wissenschaftliche Qualität
Excellency [ˈeksələnsɪ] N **Your/His ~** Eure/Seine Exzellenz
excellent ADJ, **excellently** ADV [ˈeksələnt, -lɪ] ausgezeichnet, hervorragend
excelsior [ekˈselsɪɔːʳ] N (*US: = shavings*) Holzwolle f
except [ɪkˈsept] **1** PREP außer (+*dat*); **what can they do ~ wait?** was können sie (anders) tun als warten?; **~ for** abgesehen von; **~ that ...** außer *or* nur dass ...; **~ for the fact that** abgesehen davon, dass ...; **~ if** es sei denn(, dass); **~ when** außer wenn **2** CONJ (= *only*) doch **3** VT ausnehmen; **none ~ed** ohne Ausnahme
excepting [ɪkˈseptɪŋ] PREP außer; **not ~ X** X nicht ausgenommen

exception [ɪkˈsepʃən] N **(a)** Ausnahme f; **to make an ~ (of/for sb)** eine Ausnahme (bei jdm/für jdn) machen; **with the ~ of** mit Ausnahme von; **this case is an ~ to the rule** dieser Fall ist eine Ausnahme; **the ~ proves the rule, this is the ~ that proves the rule** (*prov*) Ausnahmen bestätigen die Regel (*prov*); **sb/sth is no ~** jd/etw ist keine Ausnahme **(b)** **to take ~ to sth** Anstoß m an etw (*dat*) nehmen
exceptional [ɪkˈsepʃənl] ADJ außergewöhnlich; **of ~ quality/ talent** außergewöhnlich gut/talentiert; **~ case** Ausnahmefall m; **in ~ cases, in** *or* **under ~ circumstances** in Ausnahmefällen; **~ child** (*US Sch*) hoch begabtes Kind
exceptionally [ɪkˈsepʃənlɪ] ADV außergewöhnlich
excerpt [ˈeksɜːpt] N Auszug m
excess [ɪkˈses] **1** N **(a)** Übermaß nt (*of* an +*dat*); **to eat/drink to ~** übermäßig essen/trinken; **he does everything to ~** er übertreibt bei allem; **to be in ~ of** hinausgehen über (+*acc*); **a figure in ~ of ...** eine Zahl über (+*dat*) ...
(b) excesses PL Exzesse *pl*; (*drinking, sex etc*) Ausschweifungen *pl*; (*brutalities*) Ausschreitungen *pl*
(c) (= *amount left over*) Überschuss m
(d) (*esp Brit Insur*) Selbstbeteiligung f
2 ADJ überschüssig; **~ fat** Fettpolster nt
excess: **excess baggage** N Übergewicht nt; **excess cost** N Kostenüberschreitung f
excessive [ɪkˈsesɪv] ADJ übermäßig; *price, profits, speed* überhöht; *demands* übertrieben; **an ~ amount of, ~ amounts of** übermäßig viel; **~ drinking** übermäßiger Alkoholgenuss; **~ inventories** (*Ind*) Überbestand m
excessively [ɪkˈsesɪvlɪ] ADV (+*vb*) übermäßig; *drink, eat* zu viel; (+*adj*) allzu; **~ so** allzu sehr
excess: **excess postage** N Nachgebühr f; **excess profit** N Übergewinn m; **excess supply** N Überangebot nt; **excess weight** N Übergewicht nt
exchange [ɪksˈtʃeɪndʒ] **1** VT *books, glances, seats* tauschen; *foreign currency* wechseln (*for* in +*acc*); *information, views, hostages, phone numbers* austauschen; **to ~ words** einen Wortwechsel haben; **to ~ letters** einen Briefwechsel führen; **to ~ greetings** sich grüßen; **to ~ insults** sich gegenseitig beleidigen; **to ~ one thing for another** eine Sache gegen eine andere austauschen *or* (*in shop*) umtauschen **2** N **(a)** (*of prisoners, views, secrets*) Austausch m; (*of one bought item for another*) Umtausch m; **in ~** dafür; **in ~ for money** gegen Geld; **in ~ for lending me your car** dafür, dass Sie mir Ihr Auto geliehen haben
(b) (*St Ex*) Börse f
(c) (telephone) ~ Fernamt nt; (*in office etc*) (Telefon)zentrale f
(d) (= *altercation*) Wortwechsel m
exchangeable [ɪksˈtʃeɪndʒəbl] ADJ austauschbar (*for* gegen); *goods bought* umtauschbar (*for* gegen)
exchange: **exchange control** N (*Fin*) Devisenkontrolle f; **exchange market** N (*Fin*) Devisenmarkt m; **exchange rate** N Wechselkurs m; **Exchange Rate Mechanism** N (*Fin*) Wechselkursmechanismus m; **exchange student** N Austauschstudent(in) m(f)
exchequer [ɪksˈtʃekəʳ] N Finanzministerium nt
excise[1] [ˈeksaɪz] N Verbrauchssteuer f (*on* auf +*acc*, für); **~ on beer/tobacco** Bier-/Tabaksteuer f
excise[2] [ekˈsaɪz] VT (*Med*) herausschneiden, entfernen (*also fig*)
excise duties [ˈeksaɪz-] PL (*Brit*), **excise tax** N (*US*) Verbrauchssteuern *pl*
excitable [ɪkˈsaɪtəbl] ADJ leicht erregbar; **in an ~ state** erregt
excite [ɪkˈsaɪt] VT **(a)** aufregen; (= *rouse enthusiasm in*) begeistern; **the whole village was ~d by the news** das ganze Dorf war über die Nachricht in Aufregung **(b)** *sentiments, passion, sexual desire* erregen; *interest, curiosity* wecken
excited [ɪkˈsaɪtɪd] ADJ aufgeregt; (= *agitated*) erregt; (= *enthusiastic*) begeistert; **to be ~ that...** begeistert darüber sein, dass ...; **to be ~ about sth** von etw begeistert sein; (= *looking forward*) sich auf etw (*acc*) freuen; **to become** *or* **get ~ (about sth)** sich (über etw *acc*) aufregen; (= *enthuse*) sich (über etw *acc*) begeistern; **to get ~** (= *sexually*) erregt werden; **it was nothing to get ~ about** es war nichts Besonderes
excitedly [ɪkˈsaɪtɪdlɪ] ADV aufgeregt
excitement [ɪkˈsaɪtmənt] N Aufregung f; **there was great ~ when ...** es herrschte große Aufregung, als ...; **what's all the ~**

about? wozu die ganze Aufregung?; **his novel has caused great ~** sein Roman hat große Begeisterung ausgelöst

exciting [ɪk'saɪtɪŋ] ADJ aufregend; *player, artist* sensationell; *prospect* reizvoll; (= *full of suspense*) spannend; (*sexually*) erregend

excl (a) ABBR *of* **excluding (b)** ABBR *of* **exclusive** exkl.

exclaim [ɪk'skleɪm] **1** VI **he ~ed in surprise when he saw it** er schrie überrascht auf, als er es sah **2** VT ausrufen

exclamation [ˌekskləˈmeɪʃən] N Ausruf *m*

exclamation mark, (*US*) **exclamation point** N Ausrufezeichen *nt*

exclude [ɪk'sklu:d] VT ausschließen; **to ~ sb from the team/an occupation** jdn aus der Mannschaft/von einer Beschäftigung ausschließen; **to ~ a child from school** ein Kind vom Schulunterricht ausschließen; **to ~ sb from doing sth** jdn davon ausschließen, etw zu tun; **£200 excluding VAT** (*Brit*) £ 200 ohne Mehrwertsteuer; **the meal costs £15 excluding wine** das Essen kostet £ 15 ohne Wein; **everything excluding the house** alles außer *or* ausgenommen das Haus

exclusion [ɪk'sklu:ʒən] N Ausschluss *m* (*from* von); (*from school*) Ausschluss *m* von Unterricht; **she thought about her job to the ~ of everything else** sie dachte ausschließlich an ihre Arbeit

exclusion: exclusion clause N (*Insur*) Haftungsausschlussklausel *f*; **exclusion order** N (*Jur*) Einreiseverbot *nt*

exclusive [ɪk'sklu:sɪv] **1** ADJ **(a)** exklusiv; *use, control* alleinig; **~ interview** Exklusivinterview *nt*; **~ offer** Exklusivangebot *nt*; **~ rights to sth** Alleinrechte *pl* an etw (*dat*); (*Press*) Exklusivrechte *pl* an etw (*dat*)
(b) (= *not inclusive*) exklusive *inv*; **our terms are ~** unsere Bedingungen verstehen sich exklusive; **~ of taxes/postage and packing** (*Comm*) exklusive Steuern/Porto und Verpackung; **they are mutually ~** sie schließen einander aus **2** N (*Press*) (= *story*) Exklusivbericht *m*; (= *interview*) Exklusivinterview *nt*

exclusively [ɪk'sklu:sɪvlɪ] ADV ausschließlich; (*Press*) exklusiv

excommunicate [ˌekskəˈmju:nɪkeɪt] VT exkommunizieren

excommunication [ˈekskəˌmju:nɪˈkeɪʃən] N Exkommunikation *f*

excrement [ˈekskrɪmənt] N Kot *m*

excrete [ɪk'skri:t] VT ausscheiden

excruciating [ɪk'skru:ʃɪeɪtɪŋ] ADJ (*lit, fig*) unerträglich; *cramp, sight, experience* fürchterlich; *joke* entsetzlich; **I was in ~ pain** ich hatte unerträgliche Schmerzen

excruciatingly [ɪk'skru:ʃɪeɪtɪŋlɪ] ADV **(a)** (*lit*) **walking was ~ painful** das Gehen bereitete unerträgliche Schmerzen **(b)** (*fig*) fürchterlich; **~ funny** urkomisch

excursion [ɪk'skɜ:ʃən] N Ausflug *m*; **to go on an ~** einen Ausflug machen

excusable [ɪk'skju:zəbl] ADJ verzeihlich

excuse [ɪk'skju:z] **1** VT **(a)** (= *seek to justify*) entschuldigen; **he ~d himself for being late** er entschuldigte sich, dass er zu spät kam
(b) (= *pardon*) **to ~ sb** jdm verzeihen; **to ~ sb for having done sth** jdm verzeihen, dass er etw getan hat; **~ me for interrupting** entschuldigen Sie bitte die Störung; **~ me!** Entschuldigung!; (*indignant*) erlauben Sie mal!
(c) (= *set free from obligation*) **to ~ sb from (doing) sth** jdm etw erlassen; **you are ~d** (*to children*) ihr könnt gehen; **can I be ~d?** darf ich mal verschwinden (*inf*)?; **and now if you will ~ me I have work to do** und nun entschuldigen Sie mich bitte, ich habe zu arbeiten
2 [ɪks'kju:s] N **(a)** (= *justification*) Entschuldigung *f*; **they had no ~ for attacking him** sie hatten keinen Grund, ihn anzugreifen; **to give sth as an ~** etw zu seiner Entschuldigung vorbringen
(b) (= *pretext*) Ausrede *f*; **to make ~s for sb/sth** jdn/etw entschuldigen; **I have a good ~ for not going** ich habe eine gute Ausrede, warum ich nicht hingehen kann; **he's only making ~s** er sucht nur nach einer Ausrede; **a good ~ for a party** ein guter Grund, ein Party zu feiern

exd ABBR *of* **ex dividend** nach Dividendenausschüttung, ex Dividende

ex-directory [ˌeksdaɪˈrektərɪ] ADJ (*Brit*) **to be ~** nicht im Telefonbuch stehen

exec [ɪg'zek] N (*inf*) Manager(in) *m(f)*

execrable [ˈeksɪkrəbl] ADJ scheußlich, abscheulich

executable [ˈeksɪkju:təbl] ADJ **~ file** (*Comput*) Programmdatei *f*

execute [ˈeksɪkju:t] VT **(a)** *plan, order, movement* ausführen; *duties* erfüllen **(b)** (*Comput*) *command* ausführen **(c)** (*Mus: = perform*) vortragen **(d)** *criminal* hinrichten

execution [ˌeksɪˈkju:ʃən] N **(a)** (*of duties*) Erfüllung *f*; **in the ~ of his duties** bei der Ausübung seines Amtes **(b)** (*Mus*) Vortrag *m*; (= *musician's skill*) Ausführung *f* **(c)** (*as punishment*) Hinrichtung *f*

executioner [ˌeksɪˈkju:ʃnər] N Henker *m*

executive [ɪg'zekjʊtɪv] **1** N **(a)** (*Admin, Comm: = person*) leitender Angestellter, leitende Angestellte, Manager(in) *m(f)*; **junior ~** leitender Angestellter, leitende Angestellte; **senior ~** Geschäftsführer(in) *m(f)*
(b) (*Comm, Pol: = managing group*) Vorstand *m*; **the party's/union's National Executive (Committee)** der Partei-/Gewerkschaftsvorstand; **to be on the ~** Vorstandsmitglied *or* im Vorstand sein
(c) the ~ (*Pol: part of government*) die Exekutive
2 ADJ **(a)** *position, post* leitend; **~ power** Exekutivgewalt *f*; **~ decision** Managemententscheidung *f*; **~ pay** *or* **salaries** Gehälter *pl* der leitenden Angestellten
(b) (= *luxury, for ~s*) für gehobene Ansprüche

executive: executive board N (*Admin, Comm*) Vorstand *m*; **executive car** N Wagen *m* der gehobenen Mittelklasse; **executive committee** N Vorstand *m*; **executive council** N Vorstand *m*; **executive director** N geschäftsführender Direktor, geschäftsführende Direktorin; **executive jet** N Privatjet *m* (für Manager); **executive lounge** N (*at airport*) VIP-Lounge *f*; **executive member** N Vorstandsmitglied *nt*; **executive order** N (*US*) Rechtsverordnung *f*; **executive producer** N (*Film, Theat*) geschäftsführender Produzent, geschäftsführende Produzentin; **executive session** N (*US Parl*) Senatssitzung *f* (unter Ausschluss der Öffentlichkeit)

executor [ɪg'zekjʊtər] N (*of will*) Testamentsvollstrecker *m*

exemplary [ɪg'zemplərɪ] ADJ vorbildlich, beispielhaft (*in sth* in etw *dat*)

exemplify [ɪg'zemplɪfaɪ] VT erläutern, veranschaulichen

exempt [ɪg'zempt] **1** ADJ befreit (*from* von); **diplomats are ~** Diplomaten sind ausgenommen **2** VT *person, business* befreien; **to ~ sb from doing sth** jdn davon befreien, etw zu tun; **to ~ sth from a ban** etw von einem Verbot ausnehmen

exemption [ɪg'zempʃən] N Befreiung *f*; **~ from taxes** Steuerfreiheit *f*

exercise [ˈeksəsaɪz] **1** N **(a)** Übung *f*; **to do one's ~s in the morning** Morgengymnastik machen; **to go on ~s** (*Mil*) eine Übung machen
(b) NO PL (*physical*) Bewegung *f*; **physical ~** (körperliche) Bewegung
(c) (= *activity*) **it was a pointless ~** es war völlig sinnlos; **it was a useful ~ in public relations** für die Publicrelations war es nützlich
(d) exercises PL (*US*: = *ceremonies*) Feierlichkeiten *pl*
2 VT *body, mind, patience* üben, trainieren; *horse* bewegen; *dog* spazieren führen; *authority, power, right* ausüben
3 VI **if you ~ regularly ...** wenn Sie sich so viel bewegen ...; **you don't ~ enough** du hast zu wenig Bewegung

exercise: exercise bike N Heimtrainer *m*; **exercise book** N Heft *nt*

exerciser [ˈeksəsaɪzər] N (= *machine*) Trainingsgerät *nt*; (*bigger*) Fitness-Center *nt*

exert [ɪg'zɜ:t] **1** VT *pressure, power* ausüben (*on* auf +*acc*); *authority* aufbieten; *force* anwenden **2** VR sich anstrengen

exertion [ɪg'zɜ:ʃən] N (= *effort*) Anstrengung *f*; **rugby requires strenuous physical ~** Rugby fordert unermüdlichen körperlichen Einsatz; **after the day's ~s** nach des Tages Mühen

exhale [eks'heɪl] VI ausatmen

exhaust [ɪg'zɔ:st] **1** VT erschöpfen; **we have ~ed the subject** wir haben das Thema erschöpfend behandelt; **the children are/this job is ~ing me** die Kinder sind/diese Arbeit ist eine Strapaze für mich **2** N (*esp Brit Aut etc*) Auspuff *m*

exhausted [ɪg'zɔ:stɪd] ADJ erschöpft; *ammunition, savings* aufgebraucht; **she was ~ from digging the garden** sie war erschöpft, weil sie den Garten umgegraben hatte; **his patience was ~** er war mit seiner Geduld am Ende

exhaust fumes PL Auspuffgase pl
exhausting [ɪgˈzɔːstɪŋ] ADJ anstrengend
exhaustion [ɪgˈzɔːstʃən] N Erschöpfung f
exhaustive [ɪgˈzɔːstɪv] ADJ erschöpfend; list vollständig; search gründlich
exhaustively [ɪgˈzɔːstɪvlɪ] ADV ausführlich
exhaust: **exhaust pipe** N (esp Brit) Auspuffrohr nt; **exhaust system** N (esp Brit) Auspuff m
exhibit [ɪgˈzɪbɪt] **1** VT (a) paintings etc, goods ausstellen (b) skill, ingenuity zeigen, beweisen **2** VI ausstellen **3** N (a) (in exhibition) Ausstellungsstück nt (b) (Jur) Beweisstück nt
exhibition [ˌeksɪˈbɪʃən] N (a) (of paintings etc) Ausstellung f; ~ space Ausstellungsfläche f (b) what an ~ of bad manners! was für schlechte Manieren!; **to make an ~ of oneself** ein Theater machen (inf)
exhibition centre, (US) **exhibition center** N Ausstellungszentrum nt; (for trade fair) Messegelände nt
exhibitionism [ˌeksɪˈbɪʃənɪzəm] N Exhibitionismus m
exhibitionist [ˌeksɪˈbɪʃənɪst] N Exhibitionist(in) m(f)
exhibitor [ɪgˈzɪbɪtəʳ] N Aussteller(in) m(f)
exhilarate [ɪgˈzɪləreɪt] VT in Hochstimmung versetzen
exhilarated [ɪgˈzɪləreɪtɪd] ADJ **to feel ~** in Hochstimmung sein
exhilarating [ɪgˈzɪləreɪtɪŋ] ADJ experience aufregend; feeling berauschend
exhilaration [ɪgˌzɪləˈreɪʃən] N Hochgefühl nt
exhort [ɪgˈzɔːt] VT ermahnen
exhortation [ˌegzɔːˈteɪʃən] N Ermahnung f
exhumation [ˌekshjuːˈmeɪʃən] N Exhumierung f
exhume [eksˈhjuːm] VT exhumieren
exile [ˈeksaɪl] **1** N (a) (= person) Verbannte(r) mf (b) (= banishment) Verbannung f; **to go into ~** ins Exil gehen; **in ~** im Exil **2** VT verbannen (from aus)
Eximbank [ˈeksɪmbæŋk] N (US) Export-Import-Bank f
exist [ɪgˈzɪst] VI (a) (= to be) existieren, bestehen; **does God ~?** existiert Gott?; **it doesn't ~** das gibt es nicht; **doubts still ~** noch bestehen Zweifel; **the understanding which ~s between the two countries** das Einvernehmen zwischen den beiden Ländern; **the possibility ~s that …** es besteht die Möglichkeit, dass … (b) (= live) existieren, leben (on von); **she ~s on very little** sie kommt mit sehr wenig aus
existence [ɪgˈzɪstəns] N (a) Existenz f; **to be in ~** existieren, bestehen; **to come into ~** entstehen; **the only one in ~** der Einzige, den es gibt (b) (= life) Leben nt; **means of ~** Lebensunterhalt m
existent [ɪgˈzɪstənt] ADJ existent
existentialism [ˌegzɪsˈtenʃəlɪzəm] N Existentialismus m
existentialist [ˌegzɪsˈtenʃəlɪst] N Existentialist(in) m(f)
existing [ɪgˈzɪstɪŋ] ADJ bestehend; circumstances gegenwärtig
exit [ˈeksɪt] **1** N (a) (from stage) Abgang m; (from competition) Ausscheiden nt; **to make an/one's ~** (from stage) abgehen; (from room) hinausgehen (b) (= way out) Ausgang m; (for vehicles) Ausfahrt f **2** VI hinausgehen; (from stage) abgehen; (from competition) ausscheiden; (Comput) das Programm/die Datei etc verlassen **3** VT (a) (US) train aussteigen aus; place hinausgehen aus (b) (Comput) program, file verlassen
exit: **exit permit** N Ausreisegenehmigung f; **exit poll** N bei Wahlen unmittelbar nach Verlassen der Wahllokale durchgeführte Umfrage; **exit visa** N Ausreisevisum nt
exodus [ˈeksədəs] N (from country) Abwanderung f; (Bibl, also fig) Exodus m; **general ~** allgemeiner Aufbruch
exonerate [ɪgˈzɒnəreɪt] VT entlasten (from von)
exorbitant [ɪgˈzɔːbɪtənt] ADJ überhöht; demand übertrieben
exorbitantly [ɪgˈzɔːbɪtəntlɪ] ADV **~ priced** or **expensive** maßlos teuer
exorcism [ˈeksɔːsɪzəm] N Exorzismus m
exorcize [ˈeksɔːsaɪz] VT exorzieren
exotic [ɪgˈzɒtɪk] ADJ exotisch; **~ dancer** exotischer Tänzer, exotische Tänzerin; **~ holidays** (esp Brit) or **vacation** (US) Urlaub m in exotischen Ländern
exoticism [ɪgˈzɒtɪsɪzəm] N Exotik f
expand [ɪkˈspænd] **1** VT ausdehnen; business, production, knowledge erweitern; influence, experience vergrößern;

summary, notes weiter ausführen; ideas entwickeln **2** VI (Chem, Phys) sich ausdehnen; (business, economy, empire, knowledge, influence) wachsen; (trade, exports, production) zunehmen; (horizons) sich erweitern; **we want to ~** wir wollen expandieren or (uns) vergrößern; **the market is ~ing** der Markt wächst
➤ expand (up)on VT subject weiter ausführen
expanse [ɪkˈspæns] N Fläche f; (of ocean etc) Weite f no pl; **a vast ~ of grass** eine riesige Grasfläche; **an ~ of woodland** ein Waldgebiet nt
expansion [ɪkˈspænʃən] N (Chem, Phys) Ausdehnung f; (of business, trade, production) Erweiterung f; (territorial, economic) Expansion f
expansion (Comput): **expansion board** N Erweiterungsplatine f; **expansion card** N Erweiterungskarte f
expansionist [ɪkˈspænʃənɪst] ADJ expansionistisch, Expansions-; **~ policy** Expansionspolitik f
expansion slot N (Comput) Erweiterungssteckplatz m
expansive [ɪkˈspænsɪv] ADJ person mitteilsam; **to be in an ~ mood** in gesprächiger Stimmung sein
expat [ˈekspæt] N, ADJ = **expatriate**
expatriate [eksˈpætrɪət] **1** N im Ausland Lebende(r) mf; **British ~s** im Ausland lebende Briten **2** ADJ im Ausland lebend; **~ community** Ausländergemeinde f
expect [ɪkˈspekt] **1** VT (a) erwarten; esp sth bad rechnen mit; **that was to be ~ed** das war zu erwarten; **I know what to ~** ich weiß, was mich erwartet; **I ~ed as much** das habe ich erwartet; **he failed as (we had) ~ed** er fiel, wie erwartet, durch; **to ~ to do sth** erwarten or damit rechnen, etw zu tun; **it is hardly to be ~ed that …** es ist kaum zu erwarten or damit zu rechnen, dass …; **the talks are ~ed to last two days** die Gespräche sollen zwei Tage dauern; **she is ~ed to resign tomorrow** es wird erwartet, dass sie morgen zurücktritt; **you can't ~ me to agree to that!** Sie erwarten doch wohl nicht, dass ich dem zustimme!; **to ~ sth of** or **from sb** etw von jdm erwarten; **to ~ sb to do sth** erwarten, dass jd etw tut; **what do you ~ me to do about it?** was soll ich da tun?; **are we ~ed to tip the waiter?** müssen wir dem Kellner Trinkgeld geben?; **I will be ~ing you tomorrow** ich erwarte dich morgen; **we'll ~ you when we see you** (inf) wenn ihr kommt, dann kommt ihr (inf)
(b) (= suppose) denken, glauben; **will they be on time? – yes, I ~ so/no, I ~ not** kommen sie pünktlich? – ja, ich glaube schon/nein, ich glaube nicht; **I ~ it will rain** es wird wohl regnen; **I ~ you're tired** Sie werden sicher müde sein; **I ~ he turned it down** ich nehme an, er hat abgelehnt; **well, I ~ he's right** er wird schon Recht haben
2 VI **she's ~ing** sie bekommt or erwartet ein Kind
expectancy [ɪkˈspektənsɪ] N Erwartung f
expectant [ɪkˈspektənt] ADJ (a) (= eagerly waiting) erwartungsvoll (b) (= future) werdend
expectantly [ɪkˈspektəntlɪ] ADV erwartungsvoll; wait gespannt
expectation [ˌekspekˈteɪʃən] N Erwartung f; **in ~ of** in Erwartung (+gen); **against** or **contrary to all ~(s)** wider Erwarten; **to exceed all ~(s)** alle Erwartungen übertreffen
expected [ɪkˈspektɪd] ADJ erwartet
expedience [ɪkˈspiːdɪəns], **expediency** [ɪkˈspiːdɪənsɪ] N (of measure etc) (= politic nature) Zweckdienlichkeit f; (= advisability) Ratsamkeit f
expedient [ɪkˈspiːdɪənt] **1** ADJ (= politic) zweckdienlich; (= advisable) ratsam **2** N Notbehelf m
expedite [ˈekspɪdaɪt] VT beschleunigen
expedition [ˌekspɪˈdɪʃən] N Expedition f; **shopping ~** Einkaufstour f; **to go on an ~** auf (eine) Expedition gehen; **to go on a shopping ~** eine Einkaufstour machen
expel [ɪkˈspel] VT (a) person vertreiben; (officially) (from country) ausweisen (from aus); (from school) verweisen (from von, +gen) (b) gas, liquid ausstoßen
expend [ɪkˈspend] VT verwenden (on auf +acc, on doing sth darauf, etw zu tun)
expendable [ɪkˈspendəbl] ADJ (form) entbehrlich
expenditure [ɪkˈspendɪtʃəʳ] N (a) (= money spent) Ausgaben pl **expenditures** PL (US Comm: = outgoings) Ausgänge pl (b) (= spending, of money) Ausgabe f; **~ of time/energy** Zeit-/Energieaufwand m

expense [ɪkˈspens] N **(a)** Kosten pl; **at my ~** auf meine Kosten; **at great ~** mit hohen Kosten; **it's a big ~** es ist eine große Ausgabe; **they went to the ~ of installing a lift** sie gaben viel Geld dafür aus, einen Lift einzubauen; **at sb's ~**, **at the ~ of sb** auf jds Kosten (acc); **at the ~ of sth** auf Kosten einer Sache (gen)
(b) (Comm: usu pl) Spesen pl; **to incur ~s** Unkosten haben; **put it on ~s** schreiben Sie es auf die Spesenrechnung; **it's all on ~s** das geht alles auf Spesen
expense: expense account N Spesenkonto nt; **this will go on his ~** das geht auf Spesen; **expenses-paid** ADJ auf Geschäftskosten; **an all-~ holiday** ein Gratisurlaub m

expensive [ɪkˈspensɪv] ADJ teuer; **the least ~ seats** die billigsten Plätze; **they were too ~ for most people** die meisten Leute konnten sie sich nicht leisten

expensively [ɪkˈspensɪvlɪ] ADV teuer

experience [ɪkˈspɪərɪəns] **1** N **(a)** Erfahrung f; **~ of life** Lebenserfahrung f; **to know sth from ~** etw aus Erfahrung wissen; **to learn/speak from ~** aus eigener Erfahrung lernen/ sprechen; **he has no ~ of living in the country** er kennt das Landleben nicht; **I gained a lot of useful ~** ich habe viele nützliche Erfahrungen gemacht; **have you had any ~ of driving a bus?** haben Sie Erfahrung im Busfahren?; **~ in a job/ in business** Berufs-/Geschäftserfahrung f; **to have a lot of teaching ~** große Erfahrung als Lehrer(in) haben; **he is working in a factory to gain ~** er arbeitet in einer Fabrik, um praktische Erfahrungen zu sammeln
(b) (= event experienced) Erlebnis nt; **I had a nasty ~** mir ist etwas Unangenehmes passiert; **it was a painful ~** es war schmerzlich (geh); **it was a new ~ for me** es war völlig neu für mich
2 VT **(a)** pain, grief, hunger erfahren; difficult times, recession durchmachen; problems haben
(b) (= feel) fühlen

experienced [ɪkˈspɪərɪənst] ADJ erfahren; **we need someone more ~** wir brauchen jemanden, der mehr Erfahrung hat; **to be ~ in sth** in etw (dat) Erfahrung haben

experiment [ɪkˈsperɪmənt] **1** N (Chem, Phys, fig) Versuch m; **to do an ~** einen Versuch machen; **as an ~** versuchsweise, als Versuch **2** VI (Chem, Phys, fig) experimentieren (on, with mit)

experimental [ɪkˌsperɪˈmentl] ADJ (also Sci, Med, Tech etc) experimentell; **~ theatre** (Brit) or **theater** (US)**/cinema** Experimentiertheater nt/-kino nt; **to be at an** or **in the ~ stage** sich im Versuchsstadium befinden; **on an ~ basis** versuchsweise

experimentation [ɪkˌsperɪmenˈteɪʃən] N Experimentieren nt

expert [ˈekspɜːt] **1** N Experte m, Expertin f; (= professional) Fachmann m, Fachfrau f; (Jur) Sachverständige(r) mf; **he is an ~ on the subject/at that sort of negotiation** er ist Fachmann auf diesem Gebiet/für solche Verhandlungen; **~ in geology** Geologieexperte m/-expertin f; **OK, you do it, you're the ~** gut, machen Sies, Sie sind der Fachmann **2** ADJ **(a)** driver, accountant etc meisterhaft; **she's an ~ typist** sie ist perfekt im Maschinenschreiben; **to be ~ at** or **in doing sth** es hervorragend verstehen, etw zu tun
(b) advice, help, attention fachmännisch; **to run** or **cast an ~ eye over sth** etw fachmännisch begutachten; **an ~ opinion** ein Gutachten nt

expertise [ˌekspɜːˈtiːz] N Sachverstand m (in in +dat, auf dem Gebiet +gen); (= manual skills) Geschick nt (in bei)

expertly [ˈekspɜːtlɪ] ADV meisterhaft; drive, manoeuvre geschickt; repair fachmännisch

expert witness N Sachverständige(r) mf

expiate [ˈekspɪeɪt] VT sühnen

expire [ɪkˈspaɪəʳ] VI (lease, passport etc) ablaufen

expiry [ɪkˈspaɪərɪ] N Ablauf m; **date of ~**, **~ date** Ablauftermin m; (of voucher, special offer) Verfallsdatum nt

explain [ɪkˈspleɪn] **1** VT erklären (to sb jdm); mystery aufklären; **that is easy to ~**, **that is easily ~ed** das lässt sich leicht erklären; **he wanted to see me but wouldn't ~ why** er wollte mich sehen, sagte aber nicht, warum **2** VR sich rechtfertigen; **~ yourself!** was soll das? **3** VI es erklären; **please ~** bitte erklären Sie das
➤ **explain away** VT SEP eine Erklärung finden für

explanation [ˌekspləˈneɪʃən] N Erklärung f; (of mystery) Aufklärung f; **it needs some/a little ~** es bedarf einer

Erklärung/einer kurzen Erklärung; **what is the ~ of this?** wie ist das zu erklären?

explanatory [ɪkˈsplænətərɪ] ADJ erklärend; **a few ~ notes** ein paar Anmerkungen zur Erklärung

expletive [ɪkˈspliːtɪv] N Kraftausdruck m

explicable [ɪkˈsplɪkəbl] ADJ erklärbar

explicit [ɪkˈsplɪsɪt] ADJ person, statement, description (klar und) deutlich; instructions, agreement, reference ausdrücklich; (esp sexually) details, picture eindeutig; **sexually ~** sexuell explizit; **there is no ~ mention of it** es wird nicht ausdrücklich erwähnt; **he was ~ about his intentions** er machte seine Absichten ganz deutlich

explicitly [ɪkˈsplɪsɪtlɪ] ADV **(a)** state deutlich **(b)** forbid, reject, mention, acknowledge ausdrücklich; (+adj) eindeutig

explode [ɪkˈspləʊd] **1** VI (lit, fig) explodieren; **to ~ with anger** vor Wut platzen (inf); **to ~ with laughter** in schallendes Gelächter ausbrechen **2** VT **(a)** bomb, plane sprengen
(b) (fig) theory zu Fall bringen; **to ~ a myth** einen Mythos entlarven

exploit [ˈeksplɔɪt] **1** N (heroic) Heldentat f; **~s** Abenteuer pl **2** [ɪksˈplɔɪt] VT workers ausbeuten; friend, weakness, talent, opportunity ausnutzen; land, natural resources, technology nutzen

exploitation [ˌeksplɔɪˈteɪʃən] N (of workers) Ausbeutung f; (of friend, weakness) Ausnutzung f

exploration [ˌeksplɔːˈreɪʃən] N (of country, area) Erforschung f; (of small area, town) Erkundung f

exploratory [ɪkˈsplɔrətərɪ] ADJ exploratorisch; **~ talks** or **discussions/meeting** Sondierungsgespräche pl/-gespräch nt; **~ trip/expedition** Erkundungsfahrt f/-expedition f; **~ digging/drilling** Probegrabungen pl/-bohrungen pl; **~ surgery, an ~ operation** (Med) eine Explorationsoperation

explore [ɪkˈsplɔːʳ] **1** VT country, unknown territory erforschen; question, implications, prospects untersuchen (also Med); possibilities, options prüfen **2** VI **to go exploring** auf Entdeckungsreise gehen; **he went off into the village to ~** er ging auf Entdeckungsreise ins Dorf

explorer [ɪkˈsplɔːrəʳ] N Forscher(in) m(f)

explosion [ɪkˈspləʊʒən] N (lit, fig) Explosion f

explosive [ɪkˈspləʊzɪv] **1** N Sprengstoff m **2** ADJ (lit, fig) explosiv; argument, reaction heftig; person, temper aufbrausend; **~ device** Sprengsatz m; **~ charge** Sprengladung f

exponent [ɪkˈspəʊnənt] N (of theory) Vertreter(in) m(f)

export [ɪkˈspɔːt] **1** VTI exportieren (also Comput), ausführen **2** [ˈekspɔːt] N Export m, Ausfuhr f **3** [ˈekspɔːt] ADJ ATTR Export-, Ausfuhr-

export [ˈekspɔːt]: **export company** N Exportfirma f; **Export Credit Guarantees Department** N staatliche Exportkreditversicherung; **export drive** N Exportkampagne f; **export duty** N Export- or Ausfuhrzoll m

exporter [ɪkˈspɔːtəʳ] N Exporteur m (of von); (= country) Exportland nt (of für)

export [ˈekspɔːt]: **export firm**, **export house** N = **export company**; **export licence**, (US) **export license** N Exportgenehmigung f; **export trade** N Exporthandel m

expose [ɪkˈspəʊz] VT **(a)** rocks, remains, wire freilegen **(b)** (to danger, rain, radiation etc) aussetzen (to dat); **not to be ~d to heat** vor Hitze (zu) schützen; **to ~ oneself to criticism** sich der Kritik aussetzen **(c)** (= display) one's ignorance offenbaren; **to ~ oneself** (indecently) sich entblößen **(d)** abuse, treachery aufdecken; scandal, plot enthüllen; person, thief entlarven **(e)** (Phot) belichten

exposé [ekˈspəʊzeɪ] N Exposé nt; (of scandal etc) Aufdeckung f

exposed [ɪkˈspəʊzd] ADJ **(a)** position, hillside, garden ungeschützt; (Mil) troops, flank ungedeckt; (Mil, fig) position exponiert; **to feel ~** sich verletzlich fühlen; **to be ~ to sth** (person) einer Sache (dat) ausgesetzt sein **(b)** skin, part of body unbedeckt; wiring, engine parts frei liegend; **to feel ~** (fig: = insecure) sich allen Blicken ausgesetzt fühlen

exposition [ˌekspəˈzɪʃən] N (of facts, theory) Darlegung f; (explanatory) Erklärung f

expostulate [ɪkˈspɒstjʊleɪt] VI protestieren

exposure [ɪkˈspəʊʒəʳ] N **(a)** (to sunlight, air, danger) Aussetzung f (to +dat); **to be suffering from ~** (Med) an Unterkühlung leiden; **to die of ~** (Med) erfrieren **(b)** (of person, thief)

Entlarvung f; (of abuses, plots, scandals, crime) Aufdeckung f
(c) (Phot) Belichtung(szeit) f **(d)** (Media) Publicity f

expound [ɪk'spaʊnd] VT theory darlegen

express [ɪk'spres] ◼ VT ausdrücken; **to ~ oneself** sich
ausdrücken; **if I may ~ my opinion** wenn ich meine Meinung
äußern darf; **the feeling which is ~ed here** das Gefühl, das
hier zum Ausdruck kommt
◼ ADJ **(a)** order, permission ausdrücklich; purpose, intention
bestimmt
(b) by ~ mail per Eilzustellung; **~ service** Express- or
Schnelldienst m
◼ ADV **to send a letter/package ~** einen Brief/ein Paket als
Eilsendung or per Express schicken
◼ N **(a)** (= train) Schnellzug m; **to send goods by ~** Waren als
Eilgut schicken
(b) (= bus, coach) Schnellbus m

express: **express company** N (US) Spedition f (für
Expressgut); **express delivery** N Eilzustellung f

expression [ɪk'spreʃən] N Ausdruck m; (of face)
(Gesichts)ausdruck m; **as an ~ of our gratitude** zum Ausdruck
unserer Dankbarkeit; **to give ~ to sth** etw zum Ausdruck
bringen

expressionism [ɪk'spreʃənɪzəm] N Expressionismus m

expressionist [ɪk'spreʃənɪst] ◼ N Expressionist(in) m(f) ◼ ADJ
expressionistisch

expressionless [ɪk'spreʃənlɪs] ADJ ausdruckslos

expressive [ɪk'spresɪv] ADJ ausdrucksvoll; glance, look viel
sagend; language ausdrucksstark

expressly [ɪk'spreslɪ] ADV **(a)** forbid, state, allow ausdrücklich
(b) design, write, make speziell; **he did it ~ to annoy me**
(= intentionally) er hat es absichtlich or bewusst getan, um
mich zu ärgern

express: **express train** N Schnellzug m; **expressway** N
Schnellstraße f

expropriate [eks'prəʊprɪeɪt] VT enteignen

expropriation [eks,prəʊprɪ'eɪʃən] N Enteignung f

expulsion [ɪk'spʌlʃən] N (from a country) Ausweisung f (from
aus); (driving out) Vertreibung f (from aus); (from school)
Verweisung f (von der Schule)

expunge [ɪk'spʌndʒ] VT (form) ausstreichen (from aus)

expurgate [ˈekspɜːgeɪt] VT die anstößigen Stellen entfernen
aus; **~d edition** gereinigte Fassung

exquisite [ɪk'skwɪzɪt] ADJ erlesen; food, wine, humour köstlich;
features, building, town, view bezaubernd

exquisitely [ɪk'skwɪzɪtlɪ] ADV dress erlesen; carved, crafted aufs
kunstvollste; decorate mit erlesenem Geschmack; **she
danced ~** sie tanzte ganz hervorragend

ex-serviceman [eks'sɜːvɪsmən] N, pl **-men** [-mən] Exsoldat m

ex-servicewoman [eks'sɜːvɪswʊmən] N, pl **-women** [-wɪmɪn]
Exsoldatin f

ext ABBR of **extension** App.

extant [ek'stænt] ADJ (noch) vorhanden or existent

extemporize [ɪk'stempəraɪz] VTI aus dem Stegreif sprechen;
(Mus) improvisieren

extend [ɪk'stend] ◼ VT **(a)** arms ausstrecken; **to ~ one's hand to
sb** jdm die Hand reichen
(b) (= prolong) line, visit, passport, deadline verlängern
(c) research, powers, franchise, frontier ausdehnen; knowledge,
limits erweitern; influence ausbauen; scheme ausweiten; house
anbauen an (+acc); property vergrößern; **to ~ one's lead** seine
Führung ausbauen
(d) (= offer) (to sb jdm) help gewähren; hospitality, friendship
erweisen; invitation, thanks, condolences etc aussprechen; **to ~
a welcome to sb** jdn willkommen heißen
◼ VI **(a)** (wall, estate, garden) sich erstrecken (to, as far as bis);
(ladder, table) sich ausziehen lassen; (meetings etc) sich
ausdehnen or hinziehen; **a career that ~ed from 1974 to 1990**
eine Laufbahn, die sich von 1974 bis 1990 erstreckte
(b) enthusiasm which ~s even to the children Begeisterung,
die sich sogar auf die Kinder überträgt

extended [ɪk'stendɪd]: **extended family** N Großfamilie f;
extended memory N (Comput) erweiterter Arbeitsspeicher

extension [ɪk'stenʃən] N **(a)** Verlängerung f; (of house) Anbau
m **(b)** (Telec) (Neben)anschluss m; **~ 3714** Apparat 3714

extension: **extension cable** N Verlängerungskabel nt;
extension course N (Univ) weiterführender Kurs; **extension
lead** N Verlängerungsschnur f

extensive [ɪk'stensɪv] ADJ area, tour ausgedehnt; plans, powers,
rights weit reichend; research, range, collection, repairs, surgery,
knowledge umfangreich; burns, rash großflächig; damage
beträchtlich; experience reich; network weit verzweigt; view
weit; **the facilities available are very ~** es steht eine Vielzahl
von Einrichtungen zur Verfügung; **we had fairly ~
discussions** wir haben es ziemlich ausführlich diskutiert; **to
make ~ use of sth** etw häufig or viel benutzen

extensively [ɪk'stensɪvlɪ] ADV travel, write, work viel; use häufig;
research, report, discuss, quote ausführlich; alter beträchtlich;
restore zum großen Teil; **the clubhouse was ~ damaged** an
dem Klubhaus entstand ein beträchtlicher Schaden; **this
edition has been ~ revised** diese Ausgabe ist grundlegend
überarbeitet worden

extent [ɪk'stent] N **(a)** (= length) Länge f; (= size) Ausdehnung
f **(b)** (of knowledge, alterations, power, activities) Umfang m; (of
damage, losses) Ausmaß nt **(c)** (= degree) Grad m, Maß nt; **to
some ~** bis zu einem gewissen Grade; **to what ~** inwieweit; **to
a certain ~** in gewissem Maße; **to a large/lesser ~** in hohem/
geringerem Maße; **to such an ~ that ...** dermaßen, dass ...

extenuate [ɪk'stenjʊeɪt] VT **extenuating circumstances**
mildernde Umstände

exterior [ɪk'stɪərɪəʳ] ◼ N Äußere(s) nt; **on the ~** außen ◼ ADJ
Außen-; **~ wall** Außenwand f; **~ decoration/paintwork**
Außenanstrich m

exterminate [ɪk'stɜːmɪneɪt] VT ausrotten

extermination [ɪk,stɜːmɪ'neɪʃən] N Ausrottung f

external [ek'stɜːnl] ◼ ADJ **(a)** (lit, fig) äußere(r, s); dimensions,
angle, diameter Außen-; injury äußerlich; **the ~ walls of the
house** die Außenwände des Hauses; **~ appearance** Aussehen
nt; **for ~ use** (Pharm) zur äußerlichen Anwendung; **~
pressures** Druck m von außen; **~ call** (Telec) externes
Gespräch **(b)** affairs, relations, policy auswärtig **(c)** examiner,
auditor extern ◼ N **externals** PL (form) Äußerlichkeiten pl

external: **external borders** PL (of country) Landesgrenzen pl;
external debt N Auslandsverschuldung f; **external degree** N
(Brit Univ) Abschluss nach einem Fernstudium

externalize [ek'stɜːnəlaɪz] VT externalisieren

externally [ek'stɜːnəlɪ] ADV **(a)** apply, use (of person, appearance)
äußerlich; (= on the outside) außen; (= to the outside) nach
außen; (= from the outside) von außen; (Comm) außer Haus;
he remained ~ calm er blieb äußerlich ruhig **(b)** (Pol: = in
foreign policy) außenpolitisch

external trade N Außenhandel m

extinct [ɪk'stɪŋkt] ADJ ausgestorben; volcano erloschen; (fig) way
of life, empire untergegangen; language tot; **to become ~** (also
fig) aussterben

extinction [ɪk'stɪŋkʃən] N Aussterben nt; **this animal was hunted
to ~** diese Tierart wurde durch Jagen ausgerottet

extinguish [ɪk'stɪŋgwɪʃ] VT fire, candle (aus)löschen; cigarette
ausmachen; light löschen

extinguisher [ɪk'stɪŋgwɪʃəʳ] N Feuerlöscher m

extol [ɪk'stəʊl] VT preisen, rühmen

extort [ɪk'stɔːt] VT money erpressen (from von); confession
erzwingen (from von)

extortion [ɪk'stɔːʃən] N (of money) Erpressung f; **this is sheer ~!**
(inf) das ist ja Wucher!

extortionate [ɪk'stɔːʃənɪt] ADJ charge, rate, amount horrend; tax,
rent, bill maßlos hoch; **~ prices** Wucherpreise pl

extra [ˈekstrə] ◼ ADJ zusätzlich; **we need an ~ chair** wir
brauchen noch einen Stuhl; **to work ~ hours** Überstunden
machen; **to make an ~ effort** sich besonders anstrengen; **~
police/troops were called in** es wurde Verstärkung gerufen;
take ~ care! sei besonders vorsichtig!; **an ~ £3 a week** £ 3
mehr pro Woche; **send 75p ~ for postage and packing**
schicken Sie zusätzlich 75 Pence für Porto und Verpackung;
there is an ~ charge/no ~ charge for breakfast das Frühstück
wird zusätzlich/nicht zusätzlich berechnet; **available at ~
cost/at no ~ cost** gegen einen Aufpreis/ohne Aufpreis
erhältlich
◼ ADV **(a)** pay, cost, charge mehr; **you have to pay ~ for
breakfast, breakfast costs ~** das Frühstück wird zusätzlich
berechnet; **post and packing ~** zuzüglich Porto und

Verpackung
(b) (= *especially*) besonders
3 N **(a)** (= *special request*) Sonderwunsch *m*
(b) extras PL (= ~ *expenses*) zusätzliche Kosten *pl*; (*in restaurant*) zusätzliche Beilagen *pl*; (*for machine*) Zubehör *nt*; (*for car*) Extras *pl*
(c) (*Film, Theat*) Statist(in) *m(f)*
(d) (= *remainder*) **what shall we do with the ~?** was sollen wir mit dem Rest machen?

extra- PREF **(a)** (= *outside*) außer-; **~-parliamentary** außerparlamentarisch **(b)** (= *especially*) besonders, extra; **~-dry** wine herb; *champagne* extra dry; **~-large** *eggs, tomatoes* besonders *or* extra groß; *T-shirt, underpants* übergroß

extract [ɪkˈstrækt] **1** VT **(a)** herausnehmen; *cork etc* (heraus)ziehen (*from* aus); *juice, minerals, oil, DNA, energy* gewinnen (*from* aus); *tooth* ziehen; *bullet, foreign body* entfernen
(b) (*fig*) *information, secrets* entlocken (*from +dat*); *confession, money* herausholen (*from* aus); *permission, promise, concession* abringen (*from +dat*)
(c) *quotation, passage* herausziehen
2 [ˈekstrækt] N **(a)** (*from book etc*) Auszug *m*
(b) (*Med, Cook*) Extrakt *m*

extraction [ɪkˈstrækʃən] N **(a)** (*minerals, oil, DNA, energy*) Gewinnung *f* **(b)** (*Dentistry*) **he had to have an ~** ihm musste ein Zahn gezogen werden **(c)** (= *descent*) Herkunft *f*

extractive [ɪkˈstræktɪv] ADJ *industries* Grundstoff-; *farming* zur Grundstoffgewinnung; *reserves* Abbau-

extractor [ɪkˈstræktə‍ʳ] N (*for juice*) Entsafter *m*

extractor fan N Sauglüfter *m*

extracurricular [ˈekstrəkəˈrɪkjʊləʳ] ADJ außerhalb des Stundenplans; **~ activity** (*esp hum*) Freizeitaktivität *f* (*hum*)

extradite [ˈekstrədaɪt] VT ausliefern

extradition [ekstrəˈdɪʃən] N Auslieferung *f*

extramarital [ˈekstrəˈmærɪtl] ADJ außerehelich

extramural [ˈekstrəˈmjʊərəl] ADJ (*Brit Univ*) **~ department** selbstständige Abteilung für Teilzeitkurse, die allen zugänglich sind; **I took an ~ course at the university** ich besuchte einen Teilzeitkurs an der Universität

extraneous [ɪkˈstreɪnɪəs] ADJ (*form*) unwesentlich; **~ to sth** für etw irrelevant

extraordinarily [ɪkˈstrɔːdnrɪlɪ] ADV außerordentlich; *high, good, well etc* ungemein; (*introducing sentence*) erstaunlicherweise

extraordinary [ɪkˈstrɔːdnrɪ] ADJ **(a)** *person, career, quality* außergewöhnlich; *success, courage, skill* außerordentlich; *behaviour, appearance, speech* eigenartig; *tale, adventure* seltsam; *insults, violence* erstaunlich; **it's ~ to think that ...** es ist (schon) eigenartig, wenn man denkt, dass ...; **what an ~ thing to say!** wie kann man nur so etwas sagen!; **it's ~ how much he resembles his brother** es ist erstaunlich, wie sehr er seinem Bruder ähnelt
(b) (*Brit form*) *measure, congress* außerordentlich; **~ meeting** Sondersitzung *f*

extraordinary general meeting N außerordentliche Hauptversammlung

extrapolate [ekˈstræpəleɪt] VTI extrapolieren (*from* aus)

extrasensory [ˈekstrəˈsensərɪ] ADJ außersinnlich; **~ perception** außersinnliche Wahrnehmung

extra-special [ˈekstrəˈspeʃəl] ADJ ganz besondere(r, s); **to take ~ care over sth** sich (*dat*) besonders viel Mühe mit etw geben

extraterrestrial [ˈekstrətɪˈrestrɪəl] **1** ADJ außerirdisch **2** N außerirdisches Lebewesen

extra time N (*Sport*) Verlängerung *f*; **we had to play ~** der Schiedsrichter ließ nachspielen

extravagance [ɪkˈstrævəgəns] N Luxus *m no pl*; (= *wastefulness*) Verschwendung *f*; **if you can't forgive her little ~s** wenn Sie es ihr nicht verzeihen können, dass sie sich ab und zu einen kleinen Luxus leistet; **the ~ of a big wedding** der Aufwand einer großen Hochzeitsfeier

extravagant [ɪkˈstrævəgənt] ADJ **(a)** (= *wasteful*) *person* verschwenderisch; *taste, habit* teuer; **your ~ spending habits** deine Angewohnheit, das Geld mit vollen Händen auszugeben **(b)** (= *lavish*) *gift, luxury* luxuriös; *lifestyle, party* aufwändig; *designs, dress* ausgefallen **(c)** (= *flamboyant*) *person* extravagant; *behaviour, gesture, praise, claim* übertrieben; (= *absurd*) *theory* abwegig

extravagantly [ɪkˈstrævəgəntlɪ] ADV **(a)** (= *lavishly*) *entertain* aufwändig; *live* luxuriös; **~ expensive** maßlos teuer
(b) (= *extremely*) übertrieben **(c)** (= *flamboyantly*) extravagant

extravaganza [ɪkˌstrævəˈgænzə] N Ausstattungsstück *nt*

extreme [ɪkˈstriːm] **1** ADJ äußerste(r, s); *discomfort, sensitivity, concern, joy, danger* größte(r, s); *example, conditions, behaviour* extrem (*also Pol*); *measures, method* drastisch; *difficulty, pressure* ungeheuer; *rudeness* maßlos; *poverty* bitterste(r, s); **of ~ importance/urgency** äußerst wichtig/dringend; **~ case** Extremfall *m*; **fascists of the ~ right** extrem rechts stehende Faschisten; **at the ~ left of the picture** ganz links im Bild
2 N Extrem *nt*; **the ~s of happiness and despair** höchstes Glück und tiefste Verzweiflung; **~s of temperature** extreme Temperaturen *pl*; **in the ~** im höchsten Grade; **to go from one ~ to the other** von einem Extrem ins andere fallen; **to go to ~s** es übertreiben; **to take *or* carry sth to ~s** etw bis zum Extrem treiben

extremely [ɪkˈstriːmlɪ] ADV äußerst; *important, high, low* extrem; **was it difficult? – ~!** war es schwierig? – sehr!

extremism [ɪkˈstriːmɪzəm] N Extremismus *m*

extremist [ɪkˈstriːmɪst] **1** N Extremist(in) *m(f)* **2** ADJ extremistisch; *violence* von Extremisten; **~ group** Extremistengruppe *f*

extremity [ɪkˈstremɪtɪ] N **(a)** äußerstes Ende; **at the northerly ~ of the continent** am nördlichsten Zipfel des Kontinents
(b) extremities PL (= *hands and feet*) Extremitäten *pl*

extricate [ˈekstrɪkeɪt] VT befreien; (*fig*) retten; **to ~ oneself from sth** (*lit, fig*) sich aus etw befreien

extrinsic [ekˈstrɪnsɪk] ADJ äußerlich; *factor, reason* äußere(r, s); *considerations* nicht hereinspielend

extrovert [ˈekstrəʊvɜːt] **1** ADJ extravertiert **2** N extravertierter Mensch

extroverted [ˈekstrəʊˌvɜːtɪd] ADJ (*esp US*) extravertiert

extrude [ɪkˈstruːd] VT ausstoßen

exuberance [ɪgˈzuːbərəns] N (*of person*) Überschwänglichkeit *f*; (*of prose, style*) Vitalität *f*

exuberant [ɪgˈzuːbərənt] ADJ *person, personality* überschwänglich; *esp child* übermütig; *mood* überschäumend; *style* übersprudelnd; *painting* lebhaft; *film, music, show* mitreißend; **he was/felt ~ (about his success)** er freute sich unbändig (über seinen Erfolg)

exuberantly [ɪgˈzjuːbərəntlɪ] ADV überschwänglich; (*esp of child*) übermütig

exude [ɪgˈzjuːd] **1** VI (*liquid*) austreten (*from* aus); (*blood, pus etc*) abgesondert werden (*from* von) **2** VT **(a)** *liquid* ausscheiden; *smell* ausströmen **(b)** (*fig*) *confidence, charisma* ausstrahlen; *optimism* verströmen; *enthusiasm* verbreiten; (*pej*) *charm* triefen vor

exult [ɪgˈzʌlt] VI frohlocken; **~ing in his freedom** seine Freiheit genießend

exultant [ɪgˈzʌltənt] ADJ *person, tone* jubelnd; *expression, smile, cry* triumphierend; **he was ~** er jubelte; **~ mood** Jubelstimmung *f*

EXW (*Brit*) ABBR *of* **ex works**

ex works ADV (*Brit*) ab Werk

eye [aɪ] **1** N Auge *nt*; (*of needle*) Öhr *nt*; **with tears in her ~s** mit Tränen in den Augen; **with one's ~s closed/open** (*lit, fig*) mit geschlossenen/offenen Augen; **as far as the ~ can see** so weit das Auge reicht; **that's one in the ~ for him** (*inf*) das ist er eins aufs Dach gekriegt; **to cast *or* run one's ~ over sth** etw überfliegen; **to look sb (straight) in the ~** jdm in die Augen sehen; **to set *or* clap** (*inf*) **~s on sb/sth** jdn/etw zu Gesicht bekommen; **a strange sight met our ~s** ein seltsamer Anblick bot sich uns; **(why don't you) use your ~s!** hast du keine Augen im Kopf?; **with one's own ~s** mit eigenen Augen; **before my very ~s** (*direkt*) vor meinen Augen; **it was there all the time right in front of my ~s** es lag schon die ganze Zeit da, direkt vor meiner Nase; **I don't have ~s in the back of my head** ich hab doch hinten keine Augen; **to keep an ~ on sb/sth** (= *look after*) auf jdn/etw aufpassen; **the police are keeping an ~ on him** (= *have him under surveillance*) die Polizei beobachtet ihn; **to take one's ~s off sb/sth** die Augen *or* den Blick von jdm/etw abwenden; **to keep one's ~s open** *or* **peeled** (*inf*) die Augen offen halten; **to keep an ~ open** *or* **out for sth** nach etw Ausschau halten; **to keep an ~ on expenditure** auf die Ausgaben achten *or* aufpassen; **to open**

sb's ~s to sb/sth jdm die Augen über jdn/etw öffnen; **to close** or **shut one's ~s to sth** die Augen vor etw (dat) verschließen; **to see ~ to ~ with sb** mit jdm einer Meinung sein; **to make ~s at sb** jdm schöne Augen machen; **to catch sb's ~** jds Aufmerksamkeit erregen; **the dress caught my ~** das Kleid fiel or stach mir ins Auge; **in the ~s of the law** in den Augen des Gesetzes; **with a critical ~** mit kritischem Blick; **with an ~ to the future** im Hinblick auf die Zukunft; **with an ~ to buying sth** in der Absicht, etw zu kaufen; **I've got my ~ on you** ich beobachte dich genau; **to have one's ~ on sth** (= want) auf etw (acc) ein Auge geworfen haben; **to have a keen ~ for sth** einen scharfen Blick für etw haben; **he has a good ~ for colour** er hat ein Auge für Farbe; **you need an ~ for detail** man muss einen Blick fürs Detail haben; **to be up to one's ~s in work** (Brit inf) in Arbeit ersticken (inf); **to be up to one's ~s in debt** (Brit inf) bis über beide Ohren verschuldet sein (inf)
2 VT anstarren

➤ **eye up** VT SEP mustern

eye: **eyeball** N Augapfel m; **to be ~ to ~** sich Auge in Auge gegenüberstehen; **drugged up to the ~s** (esp Brit inf) total zugedröhnt (inf); **eyebath** N Augenbadewanne f; **eyebrow** N Augenbraue f; **that will raise a few ~s, there will be a few**

raised ~s (at that) da werden sich einige wundern; **eyebrow pencil** N Augenbrauenstift m; **eye-catching** ADJ auffallend; publicity, poster auffällig; **eye contact** N **to make/avoid ~ with sb** Blickkontakt mit jdm aufnehmen/vermeiden; **eyecup** N (US) Augenbadewanne f

-eyed [-aɪd] ADJ SUF -äugig; **green-eyed** grünäugig

eyedrops ['aɪdrɒps] PL Augentropfen pl

eye: **eyeglasses** PL (US) Brille f; **eyelash** N Augenwimper f; **eyelet** ['aɪlɪt] N Öse f; **eyelid** N Augenlid nt; **eyeliner** ['aɪlaɪnə'] N Eyeliner m; **eye-opener** N (a) that was a real ~ to me das hat mir die Augen geöffnet (b) (US inf: = drink) (alkoholischer) Muntermacher; **eye patch** N Augenklappe f; **eyepiece** N Okular nt; **eye shadow** N Lidschatten m; **eyesight** N Sehkraft f; **to have good/poor ~** gute/schlechte Augen haben; **his ~ is failing** seine Augen lassen nach; **eyesore** N Schandfleck m; **eyestrain** N Überanstrengung f der Augen; **eye test** N Augentest m; **eyewash** N (fig inf) Gewäsch nt (inf); (= deception) Augenwischerei f; **eyewitness** N Augenzeuge m/-zeugin f

e-zine ['iːziːn] N (Comput) Onlinemagazin nt, Internetmagazin nt

Ff

F, f [ef] N F *nt*, f *nt*; **F sharp** Fis *nt*, fis *nt*; **F flat** Fes *nt*, fes *nt*

F ABBR *of* **Fahrenheit** F

f ABBR *of* **feminine** f

FA ABBR *of* **Football Association**

FAA N ABBR *of* **Federal Aviation Authority** (*US*) Luftfahrtbehörde *f*

fable ['feɪbl] N Fabel *f*

fabric ['fæbrɪk] N **(a)** (*Tex*) Stoff *m* **(b)** (*of building*) Bausubstanz *f* **(c)** (*fig: of society etc*) Gefüge *nt*

> *Be careful!* **fabric** *is not translated by the German word* **Fabrik**.

fabricate ['fæbrɪkeɪt] VT *story* erfinden; *evidence, confession* fälschen

fabrication [ˌfæbrɪ'keɪʃən] N Erfindung *f*; **it's (a) pure ~** das ist ein reines Märchen *or* (eine) reine Erfindung

Fabrikoid® ['fæbrɪkɔɪd] N (*US*) Kunstleder *nt*

fabulous ['fæbjʊləs] ADJ sagenhaft (*inf*); (*inf: = wonderful also*) toll (*inf*)

fabulously ['fæbjʊləslɪ] ADV *wealthy, expensive* sagenhaft (*inf*); (*inf: = wonderfully*) fantastisch (*inf*)

façade [fə'sɑːd] N (*lit, fig*) Fassade *f*

face [feɪs] **■** N **(a)** Gesicht *nt*; (*of clock*) Zifferblatt *nt*; (*= rock ~*) (Steil)wand *f*; (*of playing card*) Bildseite *f*; **we were standing ~ to ~** wir standen einander Auge in Auge gegenüber; **to bring sb ~ to ~ with sb/sth** jdn mit jdm/etw konfrontieren; **to come ~ to ~ with sb** jdn treffen; **he told him so to his ~** er sagte ihm das (offen) ins Gesicht; **he shut the door in my ~** er schlug mir die Tür vor der Nase zu; **he laughed in my ~** er lachte mir ins Gesicht; **to be able to look sb in the ~** jdm in die Augen sehen können; **to throw sth back in sb's ~** jdm etw wieder vorhalten; **in the ~ of great difficulties** *etc* angesichts *or* (= *despite*) trotz größter Schwierigkeiten *etc*; **to save (one's) ~** das Gesicht wahren; **to lose ~** das Gesicht verlieren; **to put sth ~ up(wards)/down(wards)** etw mit der Vorderseite nach oben/unten legen; **to be ~ up(wards)/down(wards)** (*person*) mit dem Gesicht nach oben/unten liegen; (*thing*) mit der Vorderseite nach oben/unten liegen; (*book*) mit der aufgeschlagenen Seite nach oben/unten liegen; **to work at the (coal) ~** vor Ort arbeiten; **the changing ~ of politics** das sich wandelnde Gesicht der Politik; **he/it vanished off the ~ of the earth** (*inf*) er/es war wie vom Erdboden verschwunden; **on the ~ of it** so, wie es aussieht

(b) (= *expression*) Gesicht(sausdruck *m*) *nt*; **to make** *or* **pull a ~** das Gesicht verziehen; **to make** *or* **pull ~s/a funny ~** Grimassen/eine Grimasse machen *or* schneiden (*at sb* jdm); **to put a brave ~ on it** sich (*dat*) nichts anmerken lassen; (= *do sth one dislikes*) (wohl oder übel) in den sauren Apfel beißen; **he has set his ~ against that** er stemmt sich dagegen

■ VT **(a)** gegenüber sein (+*dat*), gegenüberstehen/-liegen *etc* (+*dat*); (*window, door*) north, south gehen nach; *street, garden etc* liegen zu; (*building, room*) north, south liegen nach; *park, street* liegen zu; **to ~ the wall/light** zur Wand gekehrt/dem Licht zugekehrt sein; (*person*) mit dem Gesicht zur Wand/ zum Licht stehen/sitzen *etc*; **sit down and ~ the front!** setz dich und sieh nach vorn!; **~ this way!** bitte sehen Sie hierher!; **the wall facing you** die Wand Ihnen gegenüber **(b)** (*fig*) *possibility, prospect* rechnen müssen mit; **to ~ death** dem Tod ins Auge sehen; **to ~ financial ruin** vor dem finanziellen Ruin stehen; **to be ~d with sth** sich einer Sache (*dat*) gegenübersehen; **the problem facing us** das Problem, mit dem wir konfrontiert sind; **to be ~d with a bill for £100** eine Rechnung über £ 100 präsentiert bekommen **(c)** (= *meet confidently*) *situation, danger, criticism* sich stellen (+*dat*); *person, enemy* gegenübertreten (+*dat*); **to ~ (the) facts** den Tatsachen ins Auge sehen; **let's ~ it** machen wir uns doch nichts vor

(d) (*inf: = put up with*) verkraften (*inf*); *another drink, cake etc* runterkriegen (*inf*); **I can't ~ seeing anyone** ich kann einfach niemanden sehen; **I can't ~ it** (*inf*) ich bringe es einfach nicht über mich

■ VI (*house, room*) liegen (*towards park* dem Park zu, *onto road*

---

zur Straße, *away from road* nicht zur Straße); (*window*) gehen (*onto, towards* auf +*acc*, zu, *away from* nicht auf +*acc*); **he was sitting facing away from me** er saß mit dem Rücken zu mir; **they were all facing toward(s) the window** sie saßen alle mit dem Gesicht zum Fenster (hin); **the house ~s south/ toward(s) the sea** das Haus liegt nach Süden/zum Meer hin

> **face up to** VI +PREP OBJ *fact, truth* ins Gesicht sehen (+*dat*); *possibility* sich abfinden mit; *reality, problems* sich auseinander setzen mit; *responsibility* auf sich (*acc*) nehmen; **he won't face up to the fact that ...** er will es nicht wahrhaben, dass ...

face: **face cloth** N Waschlappen *m*; **face cream** N Gesichtscreme *f*; **faceless** ADJ (*fig*) anonym; **face-lift** N (*lit*) Facelift(ing) *nt*; (*fig: for building etc*) Verschönerung *f*; **to have a ~** sich (*dat*) das Gesicht liften lassen; (*fig*) ein neues Aussehen bekommen; **face mask** N (*Cosmetics*) Gesichtsmaske *f*; **face pack** N Gesichtspackung *f*; **face powder** N Gesichtspuder *m*; **face-saving** ADJ **a ~ measure** eine Maßnahme, die dazu dient, das Gesicht zu wahren

facet ['fæsɪt] N (*lit*) Facette *f*; (*fig*) Seite *f*

facetious [fə'siːʃəs] ADJ spöttisch; **to be ~ (about sth)** sich (über etw (*acc*)) mokieren

face: **face-to-face** ADJ persönlich; *confrontation, contact* direkt; **face value** N (*Fin*) Nennwert *m*; (*Insur*) Versicherungssumme *f*; **to take sth at (its) ~** (*fig*) etw für bare Münze nehmen

facial ['feɪʃəl] ADJ Gesichts-; **~ hair** Gesichtsbehaarung *f*; **~ expression** Gesichtsausdruck *m*

facile ['fæsaɪl] ADJ (*pej*) *person, mind, work of art* oberflächlich; *question* vordergründig; *comparison, answer* billig; *solution* simpel; *remark* nichts sagend

facilitate [fə'sɪlɪteɪt] VT erleichtern; (= *make possible*) ermöglichen

facility [fə'sɪlɪtɪ] N **(a)** Einrichtung *f*; **we have no ~ or facilities for disposing of toxic waste** wir haben keine Möglichkeit zur Beseitigung von Giftmüll; **a large hotel with all facilities** ein großes Hotel mit allem Komfort; **facilities for the disabled** Einrichtungen *pl* für Behinderte; **cooking facilities** Kochgelegenheit *f*; **toilet facilities** Toiletten *pl*; **overdraft facilities** Überziehungsmöglichkeiten *pl*; **credit ~** Kredit *m* **(b)** NO PL (= *ease*) Leichtigkeit *f*; (= *dexterity*) Gewandtheit *f*; **he has a great ~ for languages** Sprachen fallen ihm sehr leicht

facility fee N (*Fin*) Bereitstellungsprovision *f*

facing ['feɪsɪŋ] ADJ **on the ~ page** auf der gegenüberliegenden Seite

facsimile [fæk'sɪmɪlɪ] N Faksimile *nt*

fact [fækt] N **(a)** Tatsache *f*; (*historical, geographical etc*) Faktum *nt*; **hard ~s** nackte Tatsachen *pl*; **~s and figures** Fakten und Zahlen; **in view of the ~ that ...** angesichts der Tatsache, dass ...; **despite the ~ that ...** der Tatsache zum Trotz, dass ...; **to know for a ~ that** (es) ganz genau *or* sicher wissen, dass; **the ~ (of the matter) is that ...** die Sache ist die, dass ...; **... and that's a ~ ...** darüber besteht kein Zweifel!; **is that a ~?** tatsächlich?

(b) NO PL (= *reality*) Wirklichkeit *f*; **~ and fiction** Dichtung und Wahrheit; **based/founded on ~** auf Tatsachen beruhend

(c) **in (point of) ~, in actual ~** eigentlich; (= *in reality*) tatsächlich; (= *after all*) (dann) doch; (*to make previous statement more precise*) nämlich; **in ~, as a matter of ~** eigentlich; (*to intensify previous statement*) sogar; **I don't suppose you know him? – in (actual) ~** *or* **as a matter of ~ I do** Sie kennen ihn nicht zufällig? – doch, eigentlich schon; **do you know him? – in (actual) ~** *or* **as a matter of ~ I do** kennen Sie ihn? – jawohl; **it won't be easy, in ~** *or* **as a matter of ~ it'll be very difficult** es wird nicht einfach sein, es wird sogar sehr schwierig sein; **as a matter of ~ we were just talking about you** wir haben (nämlich) eben von Ihnen geredet

fact-finding ['fæktfaɪndɪŋ] ADJ **~ mission** Erkundungsmission *f*

faction ['fækʃən] N (= *group*) (Partei)gruppe *f*; (*Pol*) Fraktion *f*; (= *splinter group*) Splittergruppe *f*

fact of life N (a) (= *reality*) harte Tatsache; **that's just a ~** so ist es nun mal im Leben (b) **facts of life** PL (*sexual*) **to tell** *or* **teach sb the facts of life** jdn aufklären; **to know the facts of life** aufgeklärt sein

factor [ˈfæktəʳ] N Faktor *m*; **to be a ~ in determining/deciding sth** etw mitbestimmen/mitentscheiden; **~ of production** (*Ind*) Produktionsfaktor *m*; **by a ~ of two/three** *etc* mit einem Faktor von zwei/drei *etc*

➤ **factor in** VT SEP (*esp US*) berücksichtigen; **to factor sth into sth** etw in etw (*acc*) mit einbeziehen

factoring [ˈfæktərɪŋ] N (*Fin*) Factoring *nt*, Factoringgeschäft *nt*

factor mobility N (*Ind*) Faktormobilität *f*

factory [ˈfæktərɪ] N Fabrik *f*

factory: factory farming N industriell betriebene Viehzucht; **factory floor** N Produktionsstätte *f*; **factory worker** N Fabrikarbeiter(in) *m(f)*

factsheet [ˈfæktʃiːt] N Informationsblatt *nt*

factual [ˈfæktjʊəl] ADJ *evidence* auf Tatsachen beruhend; *account* sachlich; **~ information** Sachinformationen *pl*; (= *facts*) Fakten *pl*; **~ error** Sachfehler *m*; **the book is largely ~** das Buch beruht zum größten Teil auf Tatsachen

faculty [ˈfækəltɪ] N (a) (= *power of mind*) Fähigkeit *f*; (= *ability, aptitude*) Talent *nt*; **mental faculties** geistige Fähigkeiten *pl*; **~ of hearing/sight** Hör-/Sehvermögen *nt*; **to be in (full) possession of (all) one's faculties** im Vollbesitz seiner Kräfte sein (b) (*Univ*) Fakultät *f*; **the medical ~, the ~ of medicine** die medizinische Fakultät; **the Faculty** (= *staff*) der Lehrkörper

fad [fæd] N Tick *m* (*inf*); (= *fashion*) Masche *f* (*inf*); **it's just a ~** das ist nur ein momentaner Tick (*inf*)

faddish [ˈfædɪʃ], **faddy** [ˈfædɪ] (*inf*) ADJ wählerisch

fade [feɪd] **1** VI (a) (*lit, fig*) verblassen; (*on exposure to light*) verschießen; (*flower, beauty*) verblühen; (= *lose shine*) seinen Glanz verlieren; (*sight, strength, inspiration, feeling*) schwinden (*geh*); (*hopes*) zerrinnen; (*sound*) verklingen; (*radio signal*) schwächer werden; **hopes are fading of finding any more survivors** die Hoffnung, noch weitere Überlebende zu finden, wird immer geringer; **to ~ into the background** (*person*) sich im Hintergrund halten (b) (*Rad, TV, Film*) **to ~ to another scene** (allmählich) zu einer anderen Szene überblenden **2** VT (a) ausbleichen (b) (*Rad, TV, Film*) ausblenden; **to ~ one scene (in)to another** von einer Szene (allmählich) in eine andere überblenden

➤ **fade away** VI (*sound*) verklingen; (*person*) immer schwächer werden

➤ **fade in** VT SEP (*Rad, TV, Film*) allmählich einblenden

➤ **fade out** VT SEP (*Rad, TV, Film*) abblenden

faded [ˈfeɪdɪd] ADJ verblasst; (*after exposure to light*) verschossen; *flowers, beauty* verblüht; **a pair of ~ jeans** verblichene Jeans *pl*

faeces, (*US*) **feces** [ˈfiːsiːz] PL Kot *m*

faff about [ˈfæfəˌbaʊt], **faff around** [ˈfæfəˌraʊnd] VI (*Brit inf*) herumbosseln (*inf*)

fag [fæg] N (a) (*Brit inf*: = *cigarette*) Kippe *f* (*inf*) (b) (*esp US sl*: = *homosexual*) Schwule(r) *m* (*inf*)

fag end N (*Brit*) (a) (*inf*: = *cigarette end*) Kippe *f* (*inf*) (b) (*inf*: = *last part*) letztes Ende

fagot [ˈfægət] N (*esp US sl*: = *homosexual*) Schwule(r) *m* (*inf*)

Fahrenheit [ˈfærənhaɪt] N Fahrenheit *nt*

fail [feɪl] **1** VI (a) keinen Erfolg haben; (*in mission, life etc*) versagen; (*campaign, efforts, plan, experiment, marriage*) scheitern; (*undertaking, attempt*) fehlschlagen; (*applicant, application*) nicht angenommen werden; (*election/exam candidate, Theat: play*) durchfallen; (*business*) eingehen; (*charm, attempts at persuasion etc*) vergeblich *or* umsonst sein; **he ~ed in his attempt to take control of the company** sein Versuch, die Leitung der Firma zu übernehmen, schlug fehl; **to ~ in one's duty** seine Pflicht nicht tun; **if all else ~s** wenn alle Stricke reißen; **to ~ miserably** *or* **dismally** kläglich scheitern (b) (= *fall short*) **where he/the essay ~s is in not being detailed enough** sein Fehler/der Fehler des Aufsatzes ist, dass er nicht ausführlich genug ist (c) (*health*) sich verschlechtern; (*hearing, eyesight*) nachlassen; (*invalid*) schwächer werden (d) (*battery, radio, electricity, engine*) ausfallen; (*brakes, heart etc*) versagen; **the crops ~ed** es gab ein Missernte; (*completely*) die Ernte fiel aus **2** VT (a) *candidate* durchfallen lassen; *subject* durchfallen in (+*dat*); **to ~ an exam** eine Prüfung nicht bestehen (b) (= *let down*) im Stich lassen; (= *not live up to sb's expectations*) enttäuschen; **words ~ me** mir fehlen die Worte (c) **to ~ to do sth** etw nicht tun; (= *neglect*) (es) versäumen, etw zu tun; **she ~ed to lose weight** es gelang ihr nicht abzunehmen; **she never ~s to amaze me** sie versetzt mich immer wieder in Erstaunen; **I ~ to see why** es ist mir völlig unklar, warum; (*indignantly*) ich sehe gar nicht ein, warum **3** N **without ~** auf jeden Fall; (= *inevitably*) garantiert

failed [feɪld] ADJ gescheitert; *bank, company* bankrott; *writer, actor* verhindert

failing [ˈfeɪlɪŋ] **1** N Schwäche *f*, Fehler *m* **2** PREP **~ this/that** (oder) sonst, und wenn das nicht möglich ist; **~ which** ansonsten

fail-safe [ˈfeɪlseɪf] ADJ (ab)gesichert; *method* hundertprozentig sicher; *mechanism, system* störungssicher

failure [ˈfeɪljəʳ] N (a) Misserfolg *m*; (*of campaign, efforts, plan, experiment, marriage*) Scheitern *nt*; (*of undertaking, attempt*) Fehlschlag *m*; (*of application*) Ablehnung *f*; (*of business*) Eingehen *nt*; (= *unsuccessful person*) Versager(in) *m(f)* (*at in* +*dat*); **because of his ~ to reply/act** weil er nicht geantwortet/gehandelt hat (b) (*of generator, electricity, engine*) Ausfall *m*; (*of brakes*) Versagen *nt*; **heart/kidney/liver ~** Herz-/Nieren-/Leberversagen *nt*

faint [feɪnt] **1** ADJ (+ER) (a) schwach; *tracks, line, outline* undeutlich; *mark, stain, photocopy* blass; *colour* verblasst; *sound, suspicion, hope, smile* leise; *resemblance* entfernt; *chance* gering; **your voice is very ~** (*on telephone*) man hört dich kaum; **I have a ~ memory** *or* **recollection of that day** ich kann mich schwach an den Tag erinnern; **I haven't the ~est idea** (*emph*) ich habe nicht die leiseste *or* geringste Ahnung (b) PRED (*Med*) **she was** *or* **felt ~** sie war einer Ohnmacht nahe **2** VI (*Med*) in Ohnmacht fallen (*with, from* vor +*dat*) **3** N (*Med*) **she fell to the ground in a (dead) ~** sie fiel ohnmächtig zu Boden

faint-hearted [feɪntˈhɑːtɪd] ADJ zaghaft; **it's not for the ~** es ist nichts für ängstliche Gemüter

faintly [ˈfeɪntlɪ] ADV *glow, shine, burn* schwach; *smell, smile, absurd, suspicious* leicht; *sound, say* leise; **the words are just ~ visible** die Worte sind gerade noch sichtbar; **I could hear the siren ~** ich konnte die Sirene gerade noch hören

fair[1] [feəʳ] **1** ADJ (+ER) (a) fair (*to* *or* *on sb* jdm gegenüber, gegen jdn); *trial, conclusion* gerecht; **he tried to be ~ to everybody** er versuchte, allen gegenüber gerecht zu sein *or* (*give everybody their due*) allen gerecht zu werden; **that is a (very) ~ point** *or* **comment** das lässt sich (natürlich) nicht abstreiten; **it is ~ to say that ...** man kann wohl sagen, dass ...; **to be ~,** man muss (fairerweise) dazusagen, dass ...; **it's only ~ to ask him** man sollte ihn fairerweise fragen; **~ enough!** na gut (b) *sum* ziemlich groß; **a ~ amount of money** ziemlich viel Geld; **it's a ~ distance** *or* **way** es ist ziemlich weit; **a ~ number of students** ziemlich viele Studenten; **a ~ chance of success** ziemlich gute Erfolgsaussichten (c) *guess, assessment, idea* ziemlich gut; **I've a ~ idea that he's going to resign** ich bin mir ziemlich sicher, dass er zurücktreten wird (d) (= *average*) mittelmäßig; **~ average quality** (*Comm*) Durchschnittsqualität *f*; **~ wear and tear** normaler Verschleiß (e) (= *~-haired*) *person, hair* blond; (= *~-skinned*) *person* hellhäutig; *skin* hell (f) **the ~ sex** (*dated, hum*) das schöne Geschlecht (g) *weather* heiter **2** ADV **to play ~** fair sein; (*Sport*) fair spielen; **to play ~ with** *or* **by sb** sich jdm gegenüber fair verhalten; **~ and square** ganz klar; **they beat us ~ and square** sie haben uns deutlich geschlagen

fair[2] N (Jahr)markt *m*; (= *funfair*) Volksfest *nt*; (*Comm*) Messe *f*; **~ promoter** (*Comm*) Messeveranstalter(in) *m(f)*

fair: fair copy N Reinschrift *f*; **to write out a ~ of sth** etw ins Reine schreiben; **fair game** N (*fig*) Freiwild *nt*; **fairground** N Festplatz *m*; **fair-haired** ADJ blond

fairly [ˈfeəlɪ] ADV (a) (= *moderately*) ziemlich; **~ recently** erst kürzlich (b) *treat, share* gerecht; *claim* zu Recht; *describe,* *blame* gerechterweise **(c)** (= *positively, really*) geradezu; **we ~ flew along** wir sausten nur so dahin

fair-minded [ˈfɛəmaɪndɪd] ADJ gerecht

fairness [ˈfɛənɪs] N Gerechtigkeit *f*, Fairness *f*; **in all ~** gerechterweise

fair: **fair play** N (*Sport, fig*) Fairplay *nt*; **fairway** N (*Golf*) Fairway *nt*

fairy [ˈfɛərɪ] N Fee *f*; **good ~** gute Fee

fairy: **fairy godmother** N (*lit, fig*) gute Fee; **fairy lights** PL bunte Lichter *pl*; **fairy story, fairy tale** N (*lit, fig*) Märchen *nt*; **fairytale** ADJ (*fig*) märchenhaft

fait accompli [ˌfeɪtaˈkɒmpliː] N vollendete Tatsache; **to present sb with a ~** jdn vor vollendete Tatsachen stellen

faith [feɪθ] N **(a)** (= *trust*) Vertrauen *nt* (*in* zu); (*in human nature, science etc, religious ~*) Glaube *m* (*in* an +*acc*); **to have ~ in sb** jdm (ver)trauen; **to have ~ in sth** Vertrauen in etw (*acc*) haben **(b)** (= *religion*) Glaube *m no pl* **(c)** (= *promise*) **to keep ~ with sb** jdm treu bleiben, jdm die Treue halten (*geh*) **(d)** (= *sincerity, loyalty*) **to act in good/bad ~** in gutem Glauben/böser Absicht handeln

faithful [ˈfeɪθfʊl] ADJ **(a)** *person, animal, service* treu; **to be/ remain ~ to sb/sth** jdm/einer Sache treu sein/bleiben **(b)** *adaptation, copy* originalgetreu; *translation* genau

faithfully [ˈfeɪθfəlɪ] ADV **(a)** (*Brit*: *on letter*) hochachtungsvoll **(b)** *restore* originalgetreu; *report, reflect, translate, reproduce* genau

faith: **faith healer** N Gesundbeter(in) *m(f)*; **faith healing** N Gesundbeten *nt*

fake [feɪk] **1** ADJ unecht; *certificate, banknote, painting* gefälscht; **~ fur** Pelzimitation *f*; **a ~ suntan** Bräune *f* aus der Flasche **2** N (= *object*) Fälschung *f*; (*jewellery*) Imitation *f*; (= *person*) (*trickster*) Schwindler(in) *m(f)*; (*feigning illness*) Simulant(in) *m(f)*; **the painting was a ~** das Gemälde war gefälscht **3** VT vortäuschen; *picture, document, results etc* fälschen; *burglary, crash* fingieren

falcon [ˈfɔːlkən] N Falke *m*

fall [fɔːl], *vb*: *pret* **fell**, *ptp* **fallen** **1** N **(a)** (*lit, fig*) Fall *m, no pl*, Sturz *m*; **to break sb's ~** jds Fall auffangen; **to have a ~** (hin)fallen, stürzen; **she had a bad ~** sie ist schwer gestürzt; **~ of rain/snow** Regen-/Schneefall *m*; **there was another heavy ~ (of snow) last night** es hat heute Nacht wieder viel geschneit

(b) (*of town, fortress etc*) Einnahme *f*; (*of country*) Zusammenbruch *m*; (*of government*) Sturz *m*
(c) (= *lowering*) Sinken *nt*; (*sudden*) Sturz *m*; (*in temperature*) Abfall *m*; (*of barometer*) Fallen *nt*; (*in population, membership*) Abnahme *f*
(d) (= *waterfall*: *also* **~s**) Wasserfall *m*; **Niagara Falls** die Niagarafälle
(e) (*US*: = *autumn*) Herbst *m*; **in the ~** im Herbst

2 VI **(a)** (*lit, fig*) fallen; (*Sport, from a height, badly*) stürzen; (*object*) (*to the ground*) herunterfallen; (*population, membership etc*) abnehmen; (*voice*) sich senken; **to ~ to one's death** tödlich abstürzen; **to ~ into a trap** in die Falle gehen; **his face fell** er machte ein langes Gesicht; **to ~ in battle** fallen; (*fig*) **her eyes fell on a strange object** ihr Blick fiel auf einen merkwürdigen Gegenstand
(b) (*country, city, fortress*) eingenommen werden; (*government, ruler*) gestürzt werden
(c) (*night*) hereinbrechen
(d) (*birthday, Easter etc*) fallen (*on* auf +*acc*); (*accent*) liegen (*on* auf +*dat*); (= *be classified*) gehören (*under* in +*acc*), fallen (*under* unter +*acc*); **that ~s within/outside the scope of ...** das fällt in/nicht in den Bereich ...
(e) (= *be naturally divisible*) sich gliedern (*into* in +*acc*); **to ~ into categories** sich in Kategorien gliedern lassen
(f) (= *become*) werden; **to ~ asleep** einschlafen; **to ~ ill** krank werden; **to ~ in love with sb** sich in jdn verlieben
(g) to ~ into decline (*building*) verkommen; (*economy*) schlechter werden; **to ~ into a deep sleep** in tiefen Schlaf fallen; **to ~ into bad habits** in schlechte Gewohnheiten verfallen; **to ~ apart** or **to pieces** (*chairs, cars, book etc*) aus dem Leim gehen (*inf*); (*clothes, curtains*) sich in Wohlgefallen auflösen (*inf*); (*house*) verfallen; (*system, company, sb's life*) aus den Fugen geraten; **I fell apart when he left me** meine Welt brach zusammen, als er mich verließ

➤ **fall about** (*also* **fall about laughing**) VI (*Brit inf*) sich kranklachen (*inf*)
➤ **fall away** VI **(a)** (*ground*) abfallen **(b)** = **fall off**
➤ **fall back** VI zurückweichen (*also Mil*)
➤ **fall back (up)on** VI +PREP OBJ zurückgreifen auf (+*acc*)
➤ **fall behind** VI **(a)** (*in race, at school etc*) zurückfallen (*prep obj* hinter +*acc*) **(b)** (*with rent, work etc*) in Rückstand *or* Verzug geraten
➤ **fall down** VI **(a)** (*person*) hinfallen; (*object*) herunterfallen; (= *collapse*: *house etc*) einstürzen **(b)** (*down stairs, cliff*) hinunterfallen (*prep obj* +*acc*) **(c)** (*fig*: *person, theory, plan*) versagen; **where he/the plan falls down is ...** woran es ihm/ dem Plan fehlt, ist ...
➤ **fall for** VI +PREP OBJ **(a) I really fell for him/it** er/es hatte es mir angetan **(b)** *sales talk, propaganda* hereinfallen auf (+*acc*)
➤ **fall in** VI **(a)** (*into water etc*) hineinfallen **(b)** (= *collapse*) einstürzen **(c)** (*Mil*) **fall in!** antreten!
➤ **fall in with** VI +PREP OBJ **(a)** (= *meet, join up with*) sich anschließen (+*dat*); *bad company* geraten in (+*acc*) **(b)** (= *agree to*) mitmachen bei; *request* unterstützen
➤ **fall off** VI **(a)** (*lit*) herunterfallen (*prep obj* von) **(b)** (= *decrease*) abnehmen; (*supporters*) abfallen; (*speed*) sich verringern; (*support, enthusiasm*) nachlassen
➤ **fall on** VI +PREP OBJ **(a)** (*trip on*) fallen über (+*acc*) **(b)** (*duty, decision, task*) zufallen (+*dat*); (*blame*) treffen (+*acc*); **the responsibility falls on your shoulders** Sie tragen *or* haben die Verantwortung **(c)** (= *attack*) herfallen über (+*acc*)
➤ **fall out** VI **(a)** herausfallen; **to fall out of sth** aus etw fallen **(b)** (*quarrel*) sich (zer)streiten **(c)** (*Mil*) wegtreten
➤ **fall over** **1** VI (*person*) hinfallen; (*object, = collapse*) umfallen **2** VI +PREP OBJ (= *trip over*) fallen über (+*acc*); **they were falling over each other to get the book** sie drängelten sich, um das Buch zu bekommen **(b) to fall over oneself to do sth** sich (*dat*) die größte Mühe geben, etw zu tun
➤ **fall through** VI (*plan*) ins Wasser fallen
➤ **fall to** VI (= *be responsibility of*) zufallen (+*dat*)

fallacious [fəˈleɪʃəs] ADJ irrig; *argument* trugschlüssig

fallacy [ˈfæləsɪ] N Irrtum *m*

fallen [ˈfɔːlən] PTP *of* **fall**

fall guy N (*esp US inf*: = *victim*) Angeschmierte(r) *mf* (*inf*); (= *scapegoat*) Sündenbock *m*

fallibility [ˌfælɪˈbɪlɪtɪ] N Fehlbarkeit *f*

fallible [ˈfælɪbl] ADJ fehlbar

falling [ˈfɔːlɪŋ] ADJ fallend; *population, membership* abnehmend

falling: **falling-off** N = **fall-off**; **falling-out** N (= *quarrel*) Streit *m*

fall-off N Abnahme *f*; (*in numbers, attendances*) Abfall *m*; (*in enthusiasm, support*) Nachlassen *nt*

fallout [ˈfɔːlaʊt] N radioaktiver Niederschlag; (*fig*) Auswirkungen *pl* (*from* +*gen*)

fallow [ˈfæləʊ] ADJ **(a)** (*Agr*) brachliegend; **most of the fields are (lying) ~** die meisten Felder liegen brach **(b)** (*fig*) *period* unproduktiv

false [fɔːls] ADJ (+ER) falsch; *eyelashes* künstlich; *papers* gefälscht; *laughter, enthusiasm* gekünstelt; **that's a ~ economy** das ist am falschen Ort gespart; **~ imprisonment/arrest** willkürliche Inhaftierung/Festnahme; **~ statement** Falschaussage *f*; **under** *or* **by ~ pretences** (*Brit*) *or* **pretenses** (*US*) unter Vorspiegelung falscher Tatsachen; **~ ceiling** Zwischendecke *f*; **~ modesty** falsche Bescheidenheit; **to ring ~** nicht echt klingen

false: **false alarm** N falscher *or* blinder Alarm; **false beginner** N falscher Anfänger, falsche Anfängerin; **false friend** N (*Ling*) falscher Freund

falsehood [ˈfɔːlshʊd] N Unwahrheit *f*

falsely [ˈfɔːlslɪ] ADV *accused, convicted* zu Unrecht; *claim, report, think* fälschlicherweise

false move N **one ~, and ...** (*fig*) ein kleiner Fehler und ...

false: **false start** N Fehlstart *m*; **false teeth** PL (künstliches) Gebiss

falsetto [fɔːlˈsetəʊ] N (= *voice*) Fistelstimme *f*; (*Mus*) Falsett *nt*; (= *person*) Falsettist *m*

falsification [ˌfɔːlsɪfɪˈkeɪʃən] N (Ver)fälschung *f*

falsify [ˈfɔːlsɪfaɪ] VT fälschen; *report* entstellen; *results, tests* verfälschen

falter [ˈfɔːltəʳ] VI (*speaker*) stocken; (*steps, horse*) zögern

faltering [ˈfɔːltərɪŋ] ADJ *voice* stockend; (= *hesitating, wavering*) zögernd; (= *unsteady*) taumelnd; *economy* geschwächt

fame [feɪm] N Ruhm *m*; ~ **and fortune** Ruhm und Reichtum; **to come to** ~ zu Ruhm kommen; **Borg of Wimbledon 1979** ~ Borg, der sich 1979 in Wimbledon einen Namen gemacht hat

famed [feɪmd] ADJ berühmt

familial [fəˈmɪliəl] ADJ familiär

familiar [fəˈmɪljəʳ] ADJ **(a)** *surroundings, sight* gewohnt; *figure, voice* vertraut; *street, person, feeling* bekannt; *phrase, title, song* geläufig; *complaint* häufig; (= *customary*) *form, course, pattern* üblich; **his face is** ~ das Gesicht ist mir bekannt; **to be/seem** ~ **to sb** jdm bekannt sein/vorkommen; **it looks very** ~ es kommt mir sehr bekannt vor; **that sounds** ~ das habe ich doch schon mal gehört; **I am** ~ **with the word/the town** das Wort/die Stadt ist mir bekannt *or* (*more closely*) vertraut; **are you** ~ **with these modern techniques?** wissen Sie über diese modernen Techniken Bescheid?

(b) (= *friendly*) *tone* familiär; *greeting* freundschaftlich; (= *overfriendly*) plumpvertraulich; **to be on** ~ **terms with sb** mit jdm auf vertrautem Fuß stehen; **they're not the kind of people one wishes to become too** ~ **with** mit solchen Leuten möchte man sich nicht unbedingt näher einlassen

Be careful! The German word **familiär** *is not the most common translation for* **familiar***.*

familiarity [fəˌmɪliˈærɪti] N **(a)** NO PL Vertrautheit *f* **(b)** (*between people*) vertrautes Verhältnis; (*between colleagues etc*) ungezwungenes Verhältnis; (*pej*: = *overfriendliness*) plumpe Vertraulichkeit

familiarize [fəˈmɪliəraɪz] VT **to** ~ **sb/oneself with sth** jdn/sich mit etw vertraut machen

familiarly [fəˈmɪljəli] ADV ~ **known as** *or* **called X** von Freunden und Verwandten X genannt

family [ˈfæmɪli] **1** N Familie *f*; (*including cousins, aunts etc*) Verwandtschaft *f*; **to start a** ~ eine Familie gründen; **has he any** ~? hat er Familie?; **it runs in the** ~ das liegt in der Familie; **he's one of the** ~ er gehört zur Familie **2** ATTR Familien-; ~ **business** Familienunternehmen *nt*; **a** ~ **friend** ein Freund/ eine Freundin des Hauses *or* der Familie; **she's in the** ~ **way** (*inf*) sie ist in anderen Umständen

family: family circle N Familienkreis *m*; **family doctor** N Hausarzt *m*/-ärztin *f*; **family man** N (*home-loving*) häuslich veranlagter Mann; (*with a family*) Familienvater *m*; **family name** N Familienname *m*; **family planning** N Familienplanung *f*; **family planning clinic** N Familienberatungsstelle *f*; **family room** N **(a)** (*esp US: in house*) Wohnraum *nt* **(b)** (*Brit: in pub*) für Kinder zugelassener Raum in einem Lokal; **family-size** ADJ in Haushaltsgröße; *car, packet* Familien-; **family tree** N Stammbaum *m*; **family values** PL traditionelle (Familien)werte *pl*

famine [ˈfæmɪn] N Hungersnot *f*

famine relief N Hungerhilfe *f*

famished [ˈfæmɪʃt] ADJ (*inf*) ausgehungert; **I'm absolutely** ~ ich sterbe vor Hunger (*inf*)

famous [ˈfeɪməs] ADJ berühmt (*for* durch, für)

famously [ˈfeɪməsli] ADV (= *notoriously*) bekanntermaßen; **as X** ~ **declared** in den berühmten Worten von X

fan¹ [fæn] **1** N (*hand-held*) Fächer *m*; (*mechanical*, = *extractor* ~) Ventilator *m* **2** VT **(a) to** ~ **sb/oneself** jdm/sich (Luft) zufächeln; **to** ~ **the flames** (*lit*) das Feuer anfachen; (*fig*) Öl ins Feuer gießen **(b)** *cards* fächerförmig ausbreiten

➤ **fan out** **1** VI (*searchers etc*) ausschwärmen **2** VT SEP *cards* fächerförmig ausbreiten

fan² N (= *supporter*) Fan *m*; **I'm quite a** ~ **of yours** ich bin ein richtiger Verehrer von Ihnen

fan-assisted [ˈfænəˌsɪstɪd] ADJ ~ **oven** Umluftherd *m*

fanatic [fəˈnætɪk] N Fanatiker(in) *m(f)*

fanatical [fəˈnætɪkəl] ADJ fanatisch; **he is** ~ **about it/them** es geht/sie gehen ihm über alles; **I'm** ~ **about fitness** ich bin ein Fitnessfanatiker

fanaticism [fəˈnætɪsɪzəm] N Fanatismus *m*

fan belt N Keilriemen *m*

fancied [ˈfænsɪd] ADJ (= *imaginary*) eingebildet

fanciful [ˈfænsɪfʊl] ADJ *story, idea* fantastisch; (= *fancy*) *pattern* fantasievoll; (= *unrealistic*) *plan etc* unrealistisch; *visions* überspannt; **I think you're being somewhat** ~ ich glaube, das ist etwas weit hergeholt

fan club N Fanklub *m*

fancy [ˈfænsi] **1** VT **(a)** (= *like, be attracted by*) **I** ~ **that car/the idea** das Auto/die Idee gefällt mir; **he fancies a house on Crete** (= *would like to have*) er hätte gern ein Haus auf Kreta; **I didn't** ~ **that job** die Stelle hat mich nicht gereizt; **do you** ~ **a walk/beer?** hast du Lust zu einem Spaziergang/auf ein Bier?; **she fancies (the idea of) doing that** (= *would like to*) sie würde *or* möchte das gern tun; (= *feels like it*) sie hätte Lust, das zu tun; **I don't** ~ **him** (*sexually*) ich finde ihn nicht attraktiv; **I don't** ~ **my chances of getting that job** ich rechne mir keine großen Chancen aus, die Stelle zu bekommen **(b)** (= *imagine*) sich (*dat*) einbilden; (= *think*) glauben **(c)** (*in exclamations*) ~ **doing that!** so was(, das) zu tun!; ~ **that!** (*inf*), **(just)** ~! (*inf*) (nein) so was!; ~ **him winning!** wer hätte gedacht, dass er gewinnt!

2 VR von sich eingenommen sein; **he fancies himself as an actor/expert** er hält sich für einen (guten) Schauspieler/ einen Experten

3 N **(a)** (= *liking*) **a passing** ~ nur so eine Laune; **he's taken a** ~ **to her/the idea** sie/die Idee hat es ihm angetan; **to take** *or* **catch sb's** ~ jdm gefallen **(b)** NO PL (= *imagination*) Fantasie *f*; **that was just his** ~ das hat er sich (*dat*) nur eingebildet

4 ADJ (+ER) **(a)** (*inf*) *clothes, shoes* ausgefallen; *pattern, hairdo, manoeuvre* kunstvoll; *food, gadget* raffiniert; *word, language* hochtrabend; **nothing** ~ nichts Ausgefallenes; **you won't get anything** ~ **there** dort bekommst du nur etwas ganz Einfaches **(b)** (*often pej inf*: = *smart*) *house, car, shop* schick (*inf*); *school, restaurant* nobel

fancy: fancy dress N (Masken)kostüm *nt*; **is it** ~? geht man da verkleidet hin?; **they came in** ~ sie kamen verkleidet; **fancy-dress party** Kostümfest *nt*; **fancy-free** ADJ *see* **footloose**; **fancy goods** PL Geschenkartikel *pl*

fanfare [ˈfænfeəʳ] N Fanfare *f*; **trumpet** ~ Trompetenstoß *m*

fanfold paper [ˈfænfəʊldˈpeɪpəʳ] N (*Comput*) Endlospapier *nt*

fang [fæŋ] N (*of snake*) Giftzahn *m*; (*of wolf, dog*) Fang *m*

fan heater N Heizlüfter *m*

fan mail N Verehrerpost *f*

fanny [ˈfæni] N **(a)** (*esp US inf*) Po *m* (*inf*) **(b)** (*Brit sl*) Möse *f* (*vulg*)

fantasize [ˈfæntəsaɪz] VI fantasieren; (= *dream*) Fantasievorstellungen haben (*about* von)

fantastic [fænˈtæstɪk] **1** INTERJ (*inf*) fantastisch!, toll! (*inf*) **2** ADJ (*inf*) fantastisch; **a** ~ **amount of**, ~ **amounts of** wahnsinnig viel (*inf*)

fantastically [fænˈtæstɪkəli] ADV (*inf*) wahnsinnig (*inf*)

fantasy [ˈfæntəsi] N **(a)** (= *imagination*) Fantasie *f* **(b)** (= *illusion*) Hirngespinst *nt* (*pej*)

fanzine [ˈfænziːn] N Fanmagazin *nt*

FAQ N (*Comput*) ABBR *of* **frequently asked questions** häufig gestellte Fragen *pl*

faq ABBR *of* **fair average quality**

far [fɑːʳ], *comp* **further, farther**, *superl* **furthest, farthest** **1** ADV **(a)** weit; **we don't live** ~ *or* **we live not** ~ **from here** wir wohnen nicht weit von hier; **I'll go with you as** ~ **as the gate** ich begleite dich bis zum Tor; ~ **and wide** weit und breit; **from** ~ **and near** *or* **wide** von nah und fern; ~ **away** weit weg; **I won't be** ~ **off** *or* **away** ich bin ganz in der Nähe; **have you come** ~? kommen Sie von weit her?; **how** ~ **have you got with your plans?** wie weit sind Sie mit Ihren Plänen (gekommen)?; ~ **longer/better** weit länger/besser

(b) (*in time*) **as** ~ **back as 1945** schon (im Jahr) 1945; ~ **into the night** bis spät in die Nacht

(c) (*in set phrases*) **as** *or* **so** ~ **as I'm concerned** was mich betrifft; **it's all right as** ~ **as it goes** das ist so weit ganz gut; **in so** ~ **as** insofern als; ~ **and away the best**, **by** ~ **the best**, **the best by** ~ bei weitem *or* mit Abstand der/die/das Beste; ~ **from satisfactory** alles andere als befriedigend; ~ **from liking him I find him quite unpleasant** ich mag ihn nicht, ich finde ihn (im Gegenteil) sogar ausgesprochen unsympathisch; ~ **from it!** (ganz) im Gegenteil; ~ **be it from me to ...** es sei mir ferne, zu ...; **so ~** (= *up to now*) bisher; (= *up to this point*) so weit; **so ~ so good** so weit, so gut; **to go ~** (*money, supplies, measures etc*) weit reichen; (= *last a long time also*) lange reichen; (*person*: = *succeed*) es weit bringen; **I would go so ~ as to say ...** ich würde so weit gehen zu sagen ...; **that's going too ~** das geht zu weit; **not ~ out** (*in guess*) nicht schlecht; **~ out** *ideas* ausgefallen; (*inf*: = *fantastic*) echt geil (*sl*); **not ~ off** (*in space*) nicht weit; (*in guess, aim*) fast (getroffen); (= *almost*) nicht viel weniger; **the weekend isn't ~ off now** es ist nicht mehr lang bis zum Wochenende

2 ADJ **(a)** (= *more distant*) weiter entfernt, hintere(r, s); **the ~ end of the room** das andere Ende des Zimmers; **the ~ window/ door** das Fenster/die Tür am anderen Ende des Zimmers; **on the ~ side of** auf der anderen Seite von

(b) (= *~-off*) **in the ~ distance** in weiter Ferne; **it's a ~ cry from ...** (*fig*) das ist etwas ganz anderes als ...

faraway, far-away ['fɑːrəweɪ] ADJ **(a)** *place* entlegen; *town, region, country* fern; *sound, voice, person* weit entfernt **(b)** *look* verträumt

farce [fɑːs] N (*Theat, fig*) Farce *f*

farcical ['fɑːsɪkl] ADJ (*fig*) absurd

fare [feəʳ] **1** N **(a)** Fahrpreis *m*; (*on plane*) Flugpreis *m*; (*on boat*) Preis *m* für die Überfahrt; (= *money*) Fahrgeld *nt*; **what is the ~?** was kostet die Fahrt/der Flug/die Überfahrt?
(b) (= *passenger*) Fahrgast *m* **(c)** (*old, form*: = *food*) Kost *f*; **traditional Christmas ~** ein traditionelles Weihnachtsessen **2** VI **he ~d well** es ging ihm gut; **the dollar ~d well on the stock exchange today** der Dollar schnitt heute an der Börse gut ab

Far East N **the ~** der Ferne Osten

Far Eastern ADJ fernöstlich; **~ travel** Fernostreisen *pl*

fare: **fare-dodger** N Schwarzfahrer(in) *m(f)*; **fare stage** N Tarifgrenze *f*

farewell [feəˈwel] N Abschied *m*; **to say** *or* **make one's ~s** sich verabschieden; (*before a longer absence*) Abschied nehmen; **to bid sb ~** jdm Auf Wiedersehen sagen

farewell IN CPDS Abschieds-; **~ speech** Abschiedsrede *f*

far: **far-fetched** ADJ weit hergeholt; **far-flung** ADJ **(a)** (= *distant*) abgelegen **(b)** (= *widely spread*) weit auseinander gezogen

farm [fɑːm] **1** N Bauernhof *m*; (*bigger*) Gutshof *m*; (*in US, Australia*) Farm *f*; **pig/chicken ~** Schweine-/Hühnerfarm *f*; **trout ~** Forellenzucht *f* **2** ATTR landwirtschaftlich; **~ labourer** (*Brit*) *or* **laborer** (*US*) Landarbeiter(in) *m(f)*; **~ animals** Tiere *pl* auf dem Bauernhof **3** VT *land* bebauen; *livestock* halten; *trout, mink etc* züchten **4** VI Landwirtschaft betreiben

➤ **farm out** VT SEP *work* vergeben (*on, to* an +*acc*)

farmer ['fɑːməʳ] N Bauer *m*, Bäuerin *f*, Landwirt(in) *m(f)*; (*in US, Australia*) Farmer(in) *m(f)*; **~'s wife** Bäuerin *f*

farm: **farmhand** N Landarbeiter(in) *m(f)*; **farmhouse** N Bauernhaus *nt*

farming ['fɑːmɪŋ] N Landwirtschaft *f*

farm: **farmland** N Ackerland *nt*; **farm produce** N landwirtschaftliches Erzeugnis; **farmyard** N Hof *m*

far-off ['fɑːrɒf] ADJ **(a)** (*in the past*) weit zurückliegend; (*in the future*) weit entfernt **(b)** *place, country* fern

farrago [fəˈrɑːgəʊ] N Allerlei *nt*

far: **far-reaching** ADJ weit reichend; **far-sighted** ADJ **(a)** (*lit*) weitsichtig **(b)** (*fig*) *person, policy* weit blickend; (= *taking precautionary measures*) umsichtig; *measures* auf weite Sicht geplant

fart [fɑːt] (*inf*) **1** N **(a)** Furz *m* (*inf*) **(b)** **he's a boring old ~** er ist ein langweiliger alter Knacker (*inf*)

➤ **fart about** (*Brit*) *or* **around** VI (*inf*: = *mess around*) herumalbern (*inf*); **to fart about** *or* **around with sth** an etw (*dat*) herumfummeln (*inf*)

farther ['fɑːðəʳ] COMP *of* **far 1** ADV = **further 1** **2** ADJ weiter entfernt; **at the ~ end** am anderen Ende

farthermost ['fɑːðəməʊst] ADJ = **furthermost**

farthest ['fɑːðɪst] ADJ, ADV SUPERL *of* **far**; **the ~ point of the island** der am weitesten entfernte Punkt der Insel

FAS ABBR *of* **free alongside ship** frei Längsseite Schiff

fascia ['feɪʃə] N (*for mobile phone*) Oberschale *f*

fascinate ['fæsɪneɪt] VT faszinieren; (= *enchant*: *skill, beauty etc also*) begeistern; **this subject ~s me** ich finde dieses Gebiet faszinierend

fascinating ['fæsɪneɪtɪŋ] ADJ faszinierend

fascinatingly ['fæsɪneɪtɪŋlɪ] ADV faszinierend; *talk, describe* hochinteressant

fascination [ˌfæsɪˈneɪʃən] N Faszination *f*; **to listen/watch in ~** gebannt zuhören/zusehen; **his ~ with the cinema** die Faszination, die das Kino auf ihn ausübt; **I don't understand the ~ of this book** ich verstehe nicht, was an diesem Buch so faszinierend ist

fascism ['fæʃɪzəm] N Faschismus *m*

fascist ['fæʃɪst] **1** N Faschist(in) *m(f)* **2** ADJ faschistisch

fashion ['fæʃən] **1** N NO PL **(a)** (= *manner*) Weise *f*; (**in the**) **Indian ~** auf Indianerart; **in the usual ~** wie üblich; **in a similar ~** auf ähnliche Weise; **to do sth after** *or* **in a ~** etw recht und schlecht machen; **I can cook after a ~** ich kann so einigermaßen kochen; **in this ~** auf diese Weise, so

(b) (*in clothing*) Mode *f*; (**back**) **in ~** (wieder) modern; **it's the/all the ~** es ist Mode/große Mode; **to come into/go out of ~** in Mode/aus der Mode kommen; **she always wears the latest ~s** sie ist immer nach der neuesten Mode gekleidet; **to set a ~** eine Mode aufbringen

(c) (= *custom*) (*of society*) Sitte *f*, Brauch *m*; (*of individual*) Gewohnheit *f*

2 VT formen

fashionable ['fæʃnəbl] ADJ *clothes, look, person* modisch; *restaurant, shop, area* schick; *idea, artist* zurzeit beliebt; **~ writer** Modeschriftsteller(in) *m(f)*; **to become ~** in Mode kommen; **it's ~ to do that** es ist modern *or* (in) Mode, das zu tun

fashionably ['fæʃnəblɪ] ADV modisch

fashion: **fashion-conscious** ADJ modebewusst; **fashion designer** N Modezeichner(in) *m(f)*; **fashion magazine** N Modezeitschrift *f*; **fashion parade** N Mode(n)schau *f*; **fashion show** N Mode(n)schau *f*

fast[1] [fɑːst] ADJ (+ER), ADV schnell; **she's a ~ runner/reader** sie kann schnell laufen/lesen; **he's a ~ worker** (*lit*) er arbeitet schnell; (*fig*) er geht mächtig ran (*inf*); **to pull a ~ one (on sb)** (*inf*) jdn übers Ohr hauen (*inf*); **to be ~** (*clock, watch*) vorgehen; **to be five minutes ~** fünf Minuten vorgehen

fast[2] **1** ADJ **(a)** (= *firm, secure*) fest; **to make a boat ~** ein Boot festmachen **(b)** *colour, dye* farbecht **2** ADV **(a)** (= *firmly, securely*) fest; **to stick ~** festsitzen; (*with glue*) festkleben; **to stand ~** standhaft bleiben; **to hold ~ to sth** an etw (*dat*) festhalten **(b)** **to be ~ asleep** fest schlafen

fast[3] **1** VI (= *not eat*) fasten **2** N Fasten *nt*; (= *period of fasting*) Fastenzeit *f*

> *Be careful!* **fast** *is not translated by the German word* **fast**.

fasten ['fɑːsn] **1** VT **(a)** (= *attach*) festmachen, befestigen (*to, onto* an +*dat*); (= *do up*) *parcel etc* zuschnüren; *buttons, buckle, dress etc* zumachen; (= *tighten*) *screw etc* anziehen; (= *lock*) *door* abschließen; **to ~ one's seat belt** sich anschnallen; **to ~ two things together** zwei Dinge aneinander befestigen

(b) (*fig*) *thoughts, attention* zuwenden (*on sb* jdm) **2** VI sich schließen lassen; **the dress ~s at the back** das Kleid wird hinten zugemacht; **these two pieces ~ together** diese zwei Teile werden miteinander verbunden

> *Be careful!* **to fasten** *is not translated by the German word* **fasten**.

➤ **fasten on 1** VT SEP befestigen, festmachen (+*prep obj, -to* an +*dat*); *flower, badge* anheften (+*prep obj, -to* an +*dat*) **2** VI +PREP OBJ (= *concentrate on*) *person, subject* herumhacken auf (+*dat*) (*inf*)

➤ **fasten onto** VI +PREP OBJ (*fig*) **to fasten onto sth** sich in etw (*acc*) verbeißen

➤ **fasten up** VT SEP *dress etc* zumachen; **could you fasten me up?** (*inf*) kannst du mir zumachen? (*inf*)

fastener ['fɑːsnəʳ], **fastening** ['fɑːsnɪŋ] N Verschluss *m*

fast: **fast food** N Fastfood *nt*; **fast-food restaurant** N Fastfoodrestaurant *nt*; **fast-forward** VTI vorspulen

fastidious [fæsˈtɪdɪəs] ADJ genau (*about* in Bezug auf +*acc*); (*pej*) pingelig (*inf*) (*about* in Bezug auf +*acc*)

fastidiously [fæs'tɪdɪəslɪ] ADV (= *meticulously*) mit äußerster Sorgfalt; (*pej*: = *fussily*) pingelig (*inf*)

fast: fast lane N Überholspur *f*; **life in the ~** (*fig*) das hektische Leben; **fast-selling** ADJ leicht verkäuflich; **fast-track** VT *process, procedure* im Schnellverfahren durchführen

fat [fæt] ADJ (+ER) **(a)** (*lit, fig*) dick; (*inf*) *profit, fee, salary* üppig; **to get** *or* **become ~** dick werden; **to grow ~ (on sth)** (*fig*) (durch etw) reich werden
(b) (*iro inf*) **that's a ~ lot of good** *or* **use** das bringt doch überhaupt nichts; **~ lot of help she was** sie war 'ne schöne Hilfe! (*iro inf*); **~ chance!** schön wärs!
2 N (*Anat, Cook, Chem*) Fett *nt*; **reduce the ~ in your diet** reduzieren Sie den Fettgehalt Ihrer Ernährung

fatal ['feɪtl] ADJ **(a)** tödlich (*to, for* für); **he had a ~ accident** er ist tödlich verunglückt **(b)** *mistake, flaw, consequences, decision* verhängnisvoll; **to be** *or* **prove ~ to** *or* **for sb/sth** das Ende für jdn/etw bedeuten *or* sein; **it would be ~ to do that** es wäre verhängnisvoll, das zu tun

fatalistic [ˌfeɪtə'lɪstɪk] ADJ fatalistisch

fatality [fə'tælɪtɪ] N Todesfall *m*; (*in accident, war etc*) (Todes)opfer *nt*; **there were no fatalities** es gab keine Todesopfer

fatally ['feɪtəlɪ] ADV **(a)** *wounded, injured* tödlich **(b)** *undermine, damage, weaken* unwiderruflich; (= *disastrously*) verheerend; **to be ~ flawed** fatale Mängel aufweisen

fat cat N (*fig inf*) fette Katze (*inf*)

fate [feɪt] N Schicksal *nt*; **to leave sth to ~** etw dem Schicksal überlassen; **to leave sb to his ~** jdn seinem Schicksal überlassen; **to meet one's ~** vom Schicksal heimgesucht werden

fated ['feɪtɪd] ADJ **to be ~ to fail** *or* **to be unsuccessful** zum Scheitern verurteilt sein; **they were ~ never to meet again** es war ihnen bestimmt, sich nie wiederzusehen

fateful ['feɪtfʊl] ADJ *day, meeting, journey* schicksalhaft; *decision, consequence* verhängnisvoll; *words* schicksalsschwer

father ['fɑːðəʳ] **1** N **(a)** (*lit, fig*) Vater *m* (*to sb* jdm); (= *leader*) Führer *m*; (= *priest*) Pater *m*; **like ~ like son** der Apfel fällt nicht weit vom Stamm; **(our) Father** Vater *m* (unser); **the Holy Father** der Heilige Vater **(b)** **~s** *pl* (= *ancestors*) Väter *pl* **2** VT *child, cub etc* zeugen

father: Father Christmas N (*Brit*) der Weihnachtsmann; **father figure** N Vaterfigur *f*; **fatherhood** N Vaterschaft *f*; **father-in-law** N, *pl* **fathers-in-law** Schwiegervater *m*; **fatherland** N Vaterland *nt*

Father's Day N Vatertag *m*

fathom ['fæðəm] **1** N Faden *m* **2** VT (*inf: also ~* **out**) verstehen; **I just can't ~ him (out)** er ist mir ein Rätsel; **I couldn't ~ it (out)** ich kam der Sache nicht auf den Grund

fatigue [fə'tiːg] N **(a)** Erschöpfung *f*; **battle ~** Kampfmüdigkeit *f* **(b)** (*Tech*: = *metal ~*) Ermüdung *f* **(c)** **fatigues** PL (*Mil*) Arbeitsanzug *m*

fatness ['fætnɪs] N Dicke *f*

fatten ['fætn] **1** VT (*also ~* **up**) *animals* mästen; *people* herausfüttern (*inf*) **2** VI (*also ~* **up** or **out**) (*animal*) fett werden; (*person*) dick werden; (*through overeating*) sich mästen (*inf*)

fattening ['fætnɪŋ] ADJ *food* dick machend; **chocolate is ~** Schokolade macht dick

fatty ['fætɪ] **1** ADJ (+ER) fett; (= *greasy*) fettig; **they have a fattier diet than us** sie ernähren sich fettreicher als wir **2** N (*inf*) Dickerchen *nt* (*inf*)

fatuous ['fætjʊəs] ADJ albern

faucet ['fɔːsɪt] N (*US*) Hahn *m*

fault [fɔːlt] **1** N **(a)** Fehler *m* (*also Tennis, Horseriding*); (*Tech*) Defekt *m*; **generous to a ~** übermäßig großzügig; **to find ~ with sb/sth** etwas an jdm/etw auszusetzen haben; **he was at ~** er war im Unrecht **(b)** NO PL **it won't be my ~ if ...** es ist nicht meine Schuld, wenn ...; **whose ~ is it?** wer ist schuld (daran)? **(c)** (*Geol*) Verwerfung *f* **2** VT etwas auszusetzen haben an (+*dat*); **I can't ~ it/him** ich habe nichts daran/an ihm auszusetzen

faultless ['fɔːltlɪs] ADJ fehlerlos; *English* fehlerfrei

faultlessly ['fɔːltlɪslɪ] ADV **(a)** *speak, copy, translate* fehlerfrei **(b)** *dressed, executed* tadellos; *perform* einwandfrei

fault line N (*Geol*) Verwerfungslinie *f*

faulty ['fɔːltɪ] ADJ (+ER) (*Tech*) defekt; (*Comm*) fehlerhaft; *reasoning, logic* falsch

fauna ['fɔːnə] N Fauna *f*

faux pas [fəʊ'pɑː] N Fauxpas *m*

fava bean ['fɑːvəbiːn] N (*US*) dicke Bohne

favour, (*US*) **favor** ['feɪvəʳ] **1** N **(a)** NO PL (= *goodwill*) Gunst *f*; **to find ~ with sb** bei jdm Anklang finden; **to be in ~ with sb** bei jdm gut angeschrieben sein; (*fashion, writer etc*) bei jdm beliebt sein; **to be/fall out of ~** in Ungnade (gefallen) sein/fallen; (*fashion, writer etc*) nicht mehr ankommen (*with* bei) **(b)** **to be in ~ of sth** für etw sein; **to be in ~ of doing sth** dafür sein, etw zu tun; **a point in his ~** ein Punkt zu seinen Gunsten; **the judge ruled in his ~** der Richter entschied zu seinen Gunsten; **all those in ~ raise their hands** alle, die dafür sind, Hand hoch; **he rejected socialism in ~ of the market economy** er lehnte den Sozialismus ab und bevorzugte statt dessen die Marktwirtschaft **(c)** (= *partiality*) Vergünstigung *f*; **to show ~ to sb** jdn bevorzugen **(d)** (= *act of kindness*) Gefallen *m*; **to ask a ~ of sb** jdn um einen Gefallen bitten; **to do sb a ~** jdm einen Gefallen tun; **would you do me the ~ of returning my library books?** wären Sie bitte so freundlich und würden meine Bücher in die Bücherei zurückbringen?; **as a ~ to him** ihm zuliebe **2** VT **(a)** *idea* (= *be in favour of*) für gut halten; (= *prefer*) bevorzugen **(b)** (= *be favourable for*) begünstigen **(c)** (*US:* = *resemble*) ähneln (+*dat*)

favourable, (*US*) **favorable** ['feɪvərəbl] ADJ **(a)** (= *positive*) positiv; **her request met with a ~ response** ihre Bitte stieß auf Zustimmung; **most people were ~ to the idea** die meisten Leute standen der Idee positiv gegenüber **(b)** (= *beneficial*) günstig (*to* für); *comparison* vorteilhaft; **to show sth in a ~ light** etw in einem günstigen Licht zeigen; **on ~ terms** zu günstigen Bedingungen; **conditions are ~ for development** für die Entwicklung herrschen günstige Bedingungen

favourably, (*US*) **favorably** ['feɪvərəblɪ] ADV **(a)** *respond* positiv; *receive, regard, think, judge* wohlwollend; **he was ~ impressed by it** er war davon sehr angetan; **to be ~ disposed** *or* **inclined to(wards) sb/sth** jdm/einer Sache gewogen sein (*geh*) **(b)** (= *advantageously*) günstig; **to compare ~** im Vergleich gut abschneiden

favoured, (*US*) **favored** ['feɪvəd] ADJ **a ~ few** einige (wenige) Auserwählte

favourite, (*US*) **favorite** ['feɪvərɪt] **1** N **(a)** (= *person*) Liebling *m*; (*Hist, pej*) Günstling *m* **(b)** (= *thing*) **this one is my ~** das habe ich am liebsten; **this book/dress is my ~** das ist mein Lieblingsbuch/-kleid; **we sang all the old ~s** wir haben all die alten Lieder gesungen **(c)** (*Sport*) Favorit(in) *m(f)*; **Chelsea are the ~s** Chelsea ist (der) Favorit **2** ADJ ATTR Lieblings-; **my ~ book/film** mein Lieblingsbuch *nt*/-film *m*

favouritism, (*US*) **favoritism** ['feɪvərɪtɪzəm] N Vetternwirtschaft *f* (*inf*); (*in school*) Schätzchenwirtschaft *f* (*inf*)

fawn[1] [fɔːn] **1** N **(a)** Hirschkalb *nt*; (*of roe deer*) Rehkitz *nt* **(b)** (= *colour*) Beige *nt* **2** ADJ (*colour*) beige

fawn[2] VI (*fig: person*) katzbuckeln (*on, upon* or *over* vor +*dat*)

fax [fæks] **1** N (= *machine, document*) Fax *nt*; **to send sth by ~** etw faxen **2** VT faxen; **can you ~ us?** können Sie uns (*dat*) faxen?

fax: fax machine N = **fax** 1; **fax number** N (*Tele*)faxnummer *f*

faze [feɪz] VT (*inf:* = *take aback*) verdattern (*inf*); **the question didn't ~ me at all** die Frage brachte mich keineswegs aus der Fassung

FBI (*US*) ABBR *of* **Federal Bureau of Investigation** FBI *nt*

FCA (*Comm*) ABBR *of* **free carrier** frei Frachtführer

FCR (*Comm*) ABBR *of* **forwarding agent's certificate of receipt**

FDA

*Die **Food and Drug Administration**, kurz **FDA**, ist die älteste Verbraucherschutzbehörde in den USA. In ihren Aufgabenbereich fällt die Kontrolle von Nahrungsmitteln, Lebensmittelzusätzen, Medikamenten und Kosmetikartikeln sowie die Entscheidung darüber, ob deren Verzehr bzw. Gebrauch ungefährlich für den Verbraucher ist. Im Ausland ist die **FDA** besonders für ihre Vorreiterrolle bei der Prüfung von Ungefährlichkeit und Wirksamkeit neuer Arzneimittel bekannt, aber auch für die kontinuierliche Überwachung der Anwendung nach der Markteinführung.*

fear [fɪəʳ] **1** N **(a)** Angst f, Furcht f (for vor +dat); **~ of death/ failure** Todes-/Versagensangst f; **~ of flying** Flugangst f; **he has ~s for his sister's safety** er fürchtet für or um die Sicherheit seiner Schwester; **there are ~s that ...** es wird befürchtet, dass ...; **have no ~** (old, hum) fürchte dich nicht (old, hum); **to be in ~ of sb/sth** Angst vor jdm/etw haben; **she talked quietly for ~ of waking the baby** sie sprach leise, um das Baby nicht aufzuwecken
(b) NO PL **no ~!** (inf) nie im Leben! (inf); **there's no ~ of that happening again** keine Angst, das passiert so leicht nicht wieder
2 VT (be)fürchten; **he's a man to be ~ed** er ist ein Mann, den man fürchten muss; **many women ~ to go out at night** viele Frauen haben Angst davor, abends auszugehen
3 VI **to ~ for** fürchten für or um; **never ~!** keine Angst!

fearful [ˈfɪəfʊl] ADJ **(a)** (= apprehensive) ängstlich; **to be ~ of sb/ sth** Angst vor jdm/etw haben; **I was ~ of waking her** ich befürchtete, dass ich sie aufwecken würde **(b)** (= frightening) furchtbar

fearless ADJ, **fearlessly** ADV [ˈfɪəlɪs, -lɪ] furchtlos

fearsome [ˈfɪəsəm] ADJ Furcht erregend

feasibility [ˌfiːzəˈbɪlɪtɪ] N **(a)** (of plan etc) Durchführbarkeit f; **the ~ of doing sth** die Möglichkeit, etw zu tun
(b) (= plausibility: of story etc) Wahrscheinlichkeit f

feasibility study N Machbarkeitsstudie f

feasible [ˈfiːzəbl] ADJ **(a)** (= practicable) möglich; plan, proposition, alternative durchführbar **(b)** (= plausible) plausibel

feast [fiːst] **1** N **(a)** (= banquet) Festessen nt; **a wedding ~** ein Hochzeitsmahl nt (geh); **a ~ for the eyes** eine Augenweide **(b)** (Eccl, Rel) Fest nt; **~ day** Feiertag m **2** VI (lit) Festgelage pl/ ein Festgelage halten; **to ~ on sth** sich an etw (dat) gütlich tun **3** VT **to ~ one's eyes on sb/sth** seine Augen an jdm/etw weiden

feat [fiːt] N Leistung f; (heroic, courageous etc) Heldentat f; (skilful) Kunststück nt

feather [ˈfeðəʳ] **1** N Feder f; **~s** (= plumage) Gefieder nt; **as light as a ~** federleicht; **that's a ~ in his cap** das ist ein Ruhmesblatt nt für ihn; **they are birds of a ~** sie sind vom gleichen Schlag **2** VT **to ~ one's nest** (fig) sein Schäfchen ins Trockene bringen

feather: feather bed N mit Federn gefüllte Matratze; **feather duster** N Staubwedel m; **featherweight** N (Boxing) Federgewicht nt

feature [ˈfiːtʃəʳ] **1** N **(a)** (facial) (Gesichts)zug m
(b) (= characteristic) Merkmal nt; (of sb's character) Grundzug m; **a ~ of this book is ...** das Buch zeichnet sich durch ... aus; **special ~** Besonderheit f; **new ~** Neuheit f
(c) (of room, building etc) besonderes or herausragendes Merkmal; **to make a ~ of sth** etw besonders betonen; **the main ~ of the new shopping mall** die Hauptattraktion des neuen Einkaufszentrums
(d) (Press, Rad, TV) Feature nt
(e) (= film) Spielfilm m
2 VT **(a)** (Press) story, picture bringen
(b) **this film ~s an English actress** in diesem Film spielt eine englische Schauspielerin mit; **the album ~s their latest hit single** auf dem Album ist auch ihre neueste Hitsingle
3 VI (= occur) vorkommen; **the story ~d on all today's front pages** die Geschichte war heute auf allen Titelseiten

feature: feature film N Spielfilm m; **feature-length** ADJ film mit Spielfilmlänge; **featureless** ADJ ohne besondere Merkmale

Feb ABBR of **February** Febr.

February [ˈfebrʊərɪ] N Februar m; see **September**

feces [ˈfiːsiːz] PL (US) = **faeces**

feckless [ˈfeklɪs] ADJ nutzlos

Fed N (US) Zentralbank f der USA

fed¹ [fed] PRET, PTP of **feed**

fed² N (US inf) FBI-Agent(in) m(f)

federal [ˈfedərəl] **1** ADJ Bundes-; system etc föderalistisch (also US Hist); **~ holiday** gesetzlicher Feiertag; **~ state** Bundesstaat m; **the Federal Republic of Germany** die Bundesrepublik Deutschland; **Federal Aviation Administration** (US) Luftfahrtbehörde f; **Federal Motor Fuels Excise Tax** (US) Mineralölsteuer f; **Federal Reserve (Bank)** (US) Zentralbank f;

Federal Trade Commission (US) Kartellamt nt
2 N (US) **(a)** (Hist) Föderalist m
(b) (inf: in FBI) FBI-Agent(in) m(f)

federation [ˌfedəˈreɪʃən] N Föderation f, Bund m

fed up ADJ (inf) **I'm ~** ich habe die Nase voll (inf); **I'm ~ with him/ it** ich habe ihn/es satt; **I'm ~ waiting for him** ich habe es satt, auf ihn zu warten

fee [fiː] N Gebühr f; (of doctor, lawyer, artist, tutor) Honorar nt; (of stage performer) Gage f; (of director, administrator etc) Bezüge pl; (= membership ~) Beitrag m; **(school) ~s** Schulgeld nt

feeble [ˈfiːbl] ADJ (+ER) schwach; attempt, performance kläglich; explanation, argument, idea wenig überzeugend; excuse faul (inf); joke lahm (inf); response halbherzig

feebly [ˈfiːblɪ] ADV schwach; smile kläglich; say, explain wenig überzeugend

feed [fiːd], vb: pret, ptp **fed** **1** N **(a)** (= meal) (of animals) Fütterung f; (of baby) Mahlzeit f; (= food, of animals) Futter nt; **when is the baby's next ~?** wann wird das Baby wieder gefüttert?
(b) (Tech: to computer) Eingabe f (into in +acc)
2 VT **(a)** (= provide food for) person, army verpflegen; family ernähren
(b) (= give food to) baby, invalid, animal füttern; plant düngen; **to ~ sth to sb/an animal** jdm etw zu essen/einem Tier etw zu fressen geben
(c) (= supply) machine versorgen; furnace beschicken; meter Geld einwerfen in (+acc); fire etwas legen auf (+acc); (fig) hope, imagination, rumour nähren; **two rivers ~ this reservoir** dieses Reservoir wird von zwei Flüssen gespeist; **he steals to ~ his heroin habit** er stiehlt, um sich mit Heroin zu versorgen; **to ~ sth into a machine** etw in eine Maschine geben; **to ~ information (in)to a computer** Informationen in einen Computer eingeben; **to ~ information to sb, to ~ sb (with) information** jdn mit Informationen versorgen
(d) (Tech: = insert) führen
3 VI (animal) fressen; (baby) gefüttert werden
➤ **feed in** VT SEP tape, wire etc einführen (prep obj in +acc); facts, information eingeben (prep obj in +acc)
➤ **feed on** **1** VI +PREP OBJ sich (er)nähren von; (fig) sich nähren von **2** VT SEP +PREP OBJ **to feed sb on sth** animal, baby jdn mit etw füttern; person jdn mit etw ernähren

feed: feedback N (fig) Feedback nt; **to provide more ~ on sth** ausführlicher über etw (acc) berichten; **feedbag** N (US) Futtersack m; **to put on the ~** (inf) eine Mahlzeit einlegen

feeder [ˈfiːdəʳ] **1** N **(a)** (for birds) Futterhalter m **(b)** (= river) Zu(bringer)fluss m; (= road) Zubringer(straße f) m; (= air, bus, rail service) Zubringerlinie f **2** ATTR Zubringer-; **~ road** Zubringerstraße f; **~ pipe** Zuleitungsrohr nt

feeding [ˈfiːdɪŋ]: **feeding bottle** N Flasche f; **feeding time** N (for animal) Fütterungszeit f; (for baby) Zeit f für die Mahlzeit

feel [fiːl], vb: pret, ptp **felt** **1** VT **(a)** (= touch) fühlen; (examining) befühlen; **to ~ one's way** sich vortasten; **I'm still ~ing my way (in my new job)** ich versuche noch, mich (in meiner neuen Stelle) zurechtzufinden
(b) (= be aware of) prick, sun etc spüren; **I can't ~ anything in my left leg** ich habe kein Gefühl im linken Bein; **I felt it move** ich spürte, wie es sich bewegte
(c) regret, joy, fear etc empfinden; effects spüren; **he felt a sense of regret** er empfand Bedauern
(d) (= be affected by) heat, cold, insult, loss leiden unter (+dat); **I felt that!** (pain) das hat wehgetan!
(e) (= think) glauben; **what do you ~ about him/it?** was halten Sie von ihm/davon?; **it was felt that ...** man war der Meinung, dass ...; **he felt it necessary** er hielt es für notwendig
2 VI **(a)** (person) sich fühlen; **I ~ sick** mir ist schlecht; **to ~ convinced/certain** überzeugt/sicher sein; **to ~ hungry/sleepy**

hungrig/müde sein; **I ~ hot/cold** mir ist heiß/kalt; **he doesn't ~ quite himself today** er ist heute nicht ganz auf der Höhe; **I felt sad/strange** mir war traurig/komisch zumute; **I felt as though I'd never been away** mir war, als ob ich nie weg gewesen wäre; **I felt as if I was going to be sick** ich dachte, mir würde schlecht werden; **how do you ~ about him?** (*emotionally*) was empfinden Sie für ihn?; **you can imagine what I felt like** *or* **how I felt** Sie können sich (*dat*) vorstellen, wie mir zumute war; **what does it ~ like** *or* **how does it ~ to be all alone?** wie fühlt man sich so ganz allein?; **what does it ~ like** *or* **how does it ~ to be the boss?** wie fühlt man sich als Chef?

(b) (= ~ *to the touch*) sich anfühlen; **the room/air ~s warm** das Zimmer/die Luft kommt einem warm vor

(c) (= *think*) meinen; **how do you ~ about him/going for a walk?** was halten Sie von ihm/von einem Spaziergang?; **that's just how I ~** das meine ich auch

(d) to ~ like (= *have desire for*) Lust haben auf (+*acc*); **I ~ like something to eat** ich möchte jetzt gern etwas essen; **I ~ like going for a walk** ich habe Lust spazieren zu gehen; **I felt like screaming/giving up** ich hätte am liebsten geschrien/aufgegeben

3 N, NO PL **let me have a ~ (of it)!** lass (mich) mal fühlen!; **it has a velvety/papery ~** es fühlt sich samten/wie Papier an; **the room has a cosy ~** das Zimmer hat eine gemütliche Atmosphäre; (*fig*) **to get/have a ~ for sth** ein Gefühl *nt* für etw bekommen/haben

➤ **feel for** VI +PREP OBJ **(a)** (= *sympathize with*) Mitgefühl haben mit; **I feel for you** Sie tun mir Leid **(b)** (= *search or grope for*) tasten nach; (*in pocket, bag etc*) kramen nach

➤ **feel up to** VI +PREP OBJ sich gewachsen fühlen (+*dat*)

feeler [ˈfiːləʳ] N **(a)** (*Zool*) Fühler *m* **(b)** (*fig*) **to put out ~s** seine Fühler ausstrecken

feelgood [ˈfiːlɡʊd] ADJ Feelgood-

feelgood factor N (*Pol*) Feelgoodfaktor *m*

feeling [ˈfiːlɪŋ] N **(a)** Gefühl *nt*; **I've lost all ~ in my right arm** ich habe kein Gefühl mehr im rechten Arm; **I had a ~ of isolation** ich kam mir ganz isoliert vor; **I know the ~** ich weiß, wie das ist

(b) (= *presentiment*) (Vor)gefühl *nt*; **I've a funny ~ she won't come** ich habe so das Gefühl, dass sie nicht kommt

(c) (= *opinion: also* ~s) Meinung *f* (*on* zu); **there was a general ~ that ...** man war allgemein der Ansicht, dass ...; **there's been a lot of bad ~ about this decision** wegen dieser Entscheidung hat es viel böses Blut gegeben

(d) ~s Gefühle *pl*; **to have ~s for sb** Gefühle für jdn haben; **you've hurt his ~s** Sie haben ihn verletzt; **no hard ~s?** nimm es mir nicht übel

fee-paying [ˈfiːpeɪɪŋ] ADJ *school* gebührenpflichtig; *student* Gebühren zahlend

feet [fiːt] PL *of* **foot**

feign [feɪn] VT vortäuschen; **to ~ illness/madness** sich krank/verrückt stellen

feigned [feɪnd] ADJ vorgeblich *attr; illness also* simuliert; *interest, sympathy etc also* vorgetäuscht

feint [feɪnt] **1** N (*Sport*) Finte *f* **2** VI (*Sport*) eine Finte anwenden (*also fig*)

feisty [ˈfaɪstɪ] ADJ (+ER) robust

feline [ˈfiːlaɪn] ADJ (*lit*) Katzen-; *species* der Katzen; (*fig*) *grace* katzenhaft

fell¹ [fel] PRET *of* **fall**

fell² N (= *skin*) Fell *nt*

fell³ VT *tree* fällen; *person* niederstrecken; *animal* zur Strecke bringen

fellatio [frˈleɪʃɪəʊ] N Fellatio *f*

fellow¹ [ˈfeləʊ] N **(a)** Mann *m*, Typ *m* (*inf*); **poor ~!** der Arme!; **listen to me, ~** (*US inf*) hör mal her, Mann (*inf*); **this journalist ~** dieser komische Journalist **(b)** (= *comrade*) Kamerad *m*, Kumpel *m* (*inf*); (= *colleague*) Kollege *m*, Kollegin *f* **(c)** (*Univ*) Fellow *m* **(d)** (*of a society*) Mitglied *nt*

fellow² PREF **our ~ bankers/doctors** unsere Berufskollegen *pl*; **~ student** Kommilitone *m*, Kommilitonin *f*; **~ member** (*in club*) Klubkamerad(in) *m(f)*; (*in party*) Parteigenosse *m*/-genossin *f*; **~ sufferer** Leidensgenosse *m*/-genossin *f*; **~ worker** Kollege *m*, Kollegin *f*; **he is a ~ lexicographer** er ist auch Lexikograf; **"~ Americans..."** „meine lieben amerikanischen Mitbürger..."

fellow: fellow citizen N Mitbürger(in) *m(f)*; **fellow countrymen** PL Landsleute *pl*; **fellow feeling** N Mitgefühl *nt*; (= *togetherness*) Zusammengehörigkeitsgefühl *nt*; **fellow men** PL Mitmenschen *pl*

fellowship [ˈfeləʊʃɪp] N **(a)** NO PL Kameradschaft *f* **(b)** (*Univ*) (= *scholarship*) Forschungsstipendium *nt*; (= *job*) Position eines Fellow

fellow traveller, (*US*) **fellow traveler** N **(a)** (*lit*) Mitreisende(r) *mf* **(b)** (*Pol*) Sympathisant(in) *m(f)*

felon [ˈfelən] N (Schwer)verbrecher(in) *m(f)*

felony [ˈfelənɪ] N (schweres) Verbrechen

felt¹ [felt] PRET, PTP *of* **feel**

felt² **1** N Filz *m* **2** ADJ ATTR Filz-; **~ hat** Filzhut *m*

felt-tip (pen) [ˈfelttɪp(ˈpen)] N Filzstift *m*

female [ˈfiːmeɪl] **1** ADJ weiblich; *labour, rights* Frauen-; **a ~ doctor/student/dog** eine Ärztin/Studentin/Hündin; **a ~ companion** eine Gesellschafterin; **a ~ football team** eine Damenfußballmannschaft **2** N **(a)** (*animal*) Weibchen *nt* **(b)** (*inf:* = *woman*) Frau *f*; (*pej*) Weib *nt* (*pej*)

female condom N Femidom® *nt*

feminine [ˈfemɪnɪn] **1** ADJ **(a)** *person, clothes, perfume, voice* feminin; *beauty, qualities, nature* weiblich (*also Anat, Biol*); **his ~ side** seine feminine Seite **(b)** (*Gram*) weiblich, feminin (*spec*) **2** N (*Gram*) Femininum *nt*

feminine hygiene N Monatshygiene *f*; **~ products** Monatshygieneartikel *pl*

femininity [ˌfemɪˈnɪnɪtɪ] N Weiblichkeit *f*

feminism [ˈfemɪnɪzəm] N Feminismus *m*

feminist [ˈfemɪnɪst] **1** N Feminist(in) *m(f)* **2** ADJ feministisch; **the ~ movement** die Frauenbewegung

fence [fens] **1** N Zaun *m*; (*Sport*) Hindernis *nt*; **to sit on the ~** (*fig*) (= *be neutral*) neutral bleiben; (= *be irresolute*) zaudern; **to mend ~s** (*fig*) die Dinge bereinigen **2** VT (*also* ~ **in**) einzäunen **3** VI (*Sport*) fechten

➤ **fence in** VT SEP **(a)** (*lit*) einzäunen **(b)** (*fig*) **to fence sb in** jdn in seiner Freiheit beschränken

➤ **fence off** VT SEP abzäunen

fencer [ˈfensəʳ] N Fechter(in) *m(f)*

fencing [ˈfensɪŋ] N **(a)** (*Sport*) Fechten *nt*; **~ instructor** Fechtlehrer(in) *m(f)* **(b)** (= *fences, material*) Zaun *m*

fend [fend] VI **to ~ for oneself** (= *provide*) für sich (selbst) sorgen; (= *defend*) sich (selbst) verteidigen

➤ **fend off** VT SEP abwehren; *criticism* zurückweisen; *competition* ausschalten

fender [ˈfendəʳ] N **(a)** (*in front of fire*) Kamingitter *nt* **(b)** (*US*) (*on car*) Kotflügel *m*; (*on bicycle etc*) Schutzblech *nt* **(c)** (*US: on train, streetcar*) Puffer *m*

feng shui [fenˈfuːɪ] N Feng Shui *nt*

fennel [ˈfenl] N (*Bot*) Fenchel *m*

feral [ˈferəl] ADJ ATTR verwildert; **~ cat** Wildkatze *f*

ferment [ˈfɜːment] **1** N (*fig*) Unruhe *f*; **the city was in ~** es brodelte in der Stadt **2** [fəˈment] VI gären **3** [fəˈment] VT (*lit*) fermentieren

fermentation [ˌfɜːmenˈteɪʃən] N Gärung *f*

fern [fɜːn] N Farn(kraut *nt*) *m*

ferocious [fəˈrəʊʃəs] ADJ **(a)** *animal, person, appearance* wild; *dog* äußerst bissig; *look, glare* grimmig; *battle* erbittert; *debate, argument* heftig; *attack* brutal; *competition, criticism* scharf **(b)** *knife, teeth* Furcht erregend

ferociously [fəˈrəʊʃəslɪ] ADV *hit, fight, resist, argue* heftig; *criticize, attack* aufs schärfste; *glare* grimmig; *bark, roar* wütend

ferocity [fəˈrɒsɪtɪ] N (*of animal*) Wildheit *f*; (*of dog*) Bissigkeit *f*; (*of battle, argument, criticism*) Heftigkeit *f*; (*of attack*) Brutalität *f*

ferret [ˈferɪt] **1** N Frettchen *nt* **2** VI (*also* ~ **about** *or* **around**) herumstöbern

➤ **ferret out** VT SEP (*Brit inf*) aufstöbern

Ferris wheel [ˈferɪsˌwiːl] N Riesenrad *nt*

ferrous [ˈferəs] ADJ Eisen-; **~ chloride** Eisenchlorid *nt*

ferry [ˈferɪ] **1** N Fähre *f* **2** VT (*also* ~ **across** *or* **over**) (*by boat*) übersetzen; (*by plane, car etc*) transportieren; **to ~ sb across** *or* **over a river** jdn über einen Fluss setzen; **to ~ sb/sth back and forth** jdn/etw hin- und herbringen

fertile ['fɜːtaɪl] ADJ (*lit, fig*) fruchtbar; *soil* ergiebig; *egg, ovum* befruchtungsfähig; *mind* produktiv; **this is ~ ground for racists/ethnic hatred** das ist fruchtbarer Boden für Rassisten/ Rassenhass

fertility [fə'tɪlɪtɪ] N (*lit, fig*) Fruchtbarkeit *f*

fertilization [ˌfɜːtɪlaɪ'zeɪʃən] N Befruchtung *f*

fertilize ['fɜːtɪlaɪz] VT befruchten; *land, soil* düngen

fertilizer ['fɜːtɪlaɪzəᵣ] N Dünger *m*; **artificial ~** Kunstdünger *m*

fervent ['fɜːvənt] ADJ leidenschaftlich; *admirer* glühend; *hope, prayer, wish* inbrünstig (*geh*); **she is a ~ believer in free trade** sie glaubt leidenschaftlich an den freien Handel

fervently ['fɜːvəntlɪ] ADV leidenschaftlich; *hope, wish, pray* inbrünstig (*geh*)

fervour, (*US*) **fervor** ['fɜːvəᵣ] N Leidenschaftlichkeit *f*; (*of public speaker*) Leidenschaft *f*

fest [fest] N (*inf*) **film/jazz ~** Film-/Jazzfestival *nt*

fester ['festəᵣ] VI eitern; (*fig: resentment etc*) nagen

festival ['festɪvəl] N (a) (*Eccl etc*) Fest *nt* (b) (*cultural*) Festspiele *pl*, Festival *nt*

festive ['festɪv] ADJ festlich; *food, decorations* weihnachtlich; **the ~ season** die Festzeit

festivity [fe'stɪvɪtɪ] N (a) (= *gaiety*) Feststimmung *f* (b) (= *celebration*) Feier *f*; **festivities** *pl* Feierlichkeiten *pl*

festoon [fe'stuːn] VT **to ~ sth with sth** etw mit etw schmücken; **to be ~ed with sth** mit etw behängt sein

feta (cheese) ['fetə('tʃiːz)] N Feta(käse) *m*

fetal ['fiːtl] ADJ (*esp US*) = **foetal**

fetch [fetʃ] **1** VT (a) (= *bring*) holen; (= *collect*) abholen; **would you ~ a handkerchief for me** *or* **~ me a handkerchief?** kannst du mir ein Taschentuch holen (gehen)?; **she ~ed in the washing** sie holte die Wäsche herein (b) (= *bring in*) £10 *etc* (ein)bringen **2** VI **to ~ and carry for sb** bei jdm Mädchen für alles sein

fetching ['fetʃɪŋ] ADJ attraktiv; *smile* einnehmend

fête [feɪt] **1** N Fest *nt* **2** VT *sb, sb's success* feiern

fetid ['fetɪd] ADJ übel riechend

fetish ['fetɪʃ] N Fetisch *m*; **to have a ~ for leather/cleanliness** einen Leder-/Sauberkeitstick haben (*inf*)

fetter ['fetəᵣ] **1** VT (*fig*) in Fesseln legen **2** N **~s** *pl* (Fuß)fesseln *pl*; (*fig*) Fesseln *pl*

fettle ['fetl] N **to be in fine** *or* **good ~** in bester Form sein; (*as regards health also*) in bester Verfassung sein (*inf*)

fetus ['fiːtəs] N (*US*) = **foetus**

feud [fjuːd] (*lit, fig*) **1** N Fehde *f* **2** VI sich befehden

feudal ['fjuːdl] ADJ Feudal-, feudal; **~ system** Feudalsystem *nt*

feudalism ['fjuːdəlɪzəm] N Feudalismus *m*

fever ['fiːvəᵣ] N (a) Fieber *nt no pl*; **to have a ~** Fieber haben (b) (*fig*) Aufregung *f*; **election ~** Wahlfieber *nt*; **in a ~ of excitement** in fieberhafter Erregung

fever blister N (*US*) Bläschenausschlag *m*

feverish ['fiːvərɪʃ] ADJ (a) (= *frantic*) fieberhaft; *speculation* wild; *atmosphere* fiebrig (b) (*Med*) **to be ~** Fieber haben

feverishly ['fiːvərɪʃlɪ] ADV *work, try* fieberhaft

fever pitch N **to reach ~** am Siedepunkt angelangt sein, den Siedepunkt erreichen

few [fjuː] ADJ (+ER), PRON (a) (= *not many*) wenige; **~ people come to see him** nur wenige Leute besuchen ihn; **~ and far between** dünn gesät; **as ~ as ten cigarettes a day can be harmful** schon zehn Zigaretten am Tag können schädlich sein; **there were 3 too ~** es waren 3 zu wenig da; **he is one of the ~ people who ...** er ist einer der wenigen, die ...; **such occasions are ~** solche Gelegenheiten sind selten; **~ of them came** wenige von ihnen kamen; **the lucky ~** die wenigen Glücklichen; **however ~ there may be** wie wenig auch immer da ist; **there are too ~ of you** ihr seid zu wenige

(b) **a ~** ein paar; **a ~ more days** noch ein paar Tage; **a ~ times** ein paar Male; **there were quite a ~ waiting** ziemlich viele warteten; **he's had a ~ (too many)** er hat einen über den Durst getrunken; **quite a ~ books** ziemlich viele Bücher; **I saw a good ~** *or* **quite a ~ people** ich habe ziemlich viele Leute gesehen; **in the next/past ~ days** in den nächsten/ letzten paar Tagen; **every ~ days** alle paar Tage; **a ~ more** ein paar mehr; **quite a ~** eine ganze Menge; **quite a ~ did not believe him** ziemlich viele Leute glaubten ihm nicht; **the ~ who knew him** die wenigen, die ihn kannten

fewer ['fjuːəᵣ] ADJ, PRON COMP *of* **few** weniger; **no ~ than** nicht weniger als

fewest ['fjuːɪst] SUPERL *of* **few 1** ADJ die wenigsten **2** PRON die wenigsten, am wenigsten

ff ABBR *of* **following** ff

fiancé [fɪ'ɒnseɪ] N Verlobte(r) *m*

fiancée [fɪ'ɒnseɪ] N Verlobte *f*

fiasco [fɪ'æskəʊ] N, *pl* **-s**, (*US also*) **-es** Fiasko *nt*

fib [fɪb] (*inf*) **1** N Flunkerei *f* (*inf*); **that's a ~!** das ist geflunkert! (*inf*); **don't tell ~s** flunker nicht! (*inf*) **2** VI flunkern (*inf*)

fibbing ['fɪbɪŋ] N (*inf*) Flunkerei *f* (*inf*)

fibre, (*US*) **fiber** ['faɪbəᵣ] N (a) Faser *f* (b) (= *roughage*) Ballaststoffe *pl* (c) (*fig*) **moral ~** Charakterstärke *f*; **he has no moral ~** er hat keinen inneren Halt; **with every ~ of one's being** mit jeder Faser seines Herzens

fibre, (*US*) **fiber: fibreglass**, (*US*) **fiberglass 1** N Glasfaser *f* **2** ADJ aus Glasfaser; **fibre-tip pen** N (*Brit*) Faserschreiber *m*

fibrous ['faɪbrəs] ADJ faserig

FICA (*US*) ABBR *of* **Federal Insurance Contributions Act** (*Jur*) Gesetz über die Einbehaltung von Sozialversicherungsbeiträgen; **a third of Jack's salary went to ~** ein Drittel von Jacks Gehalt ging an die Sozialversicherung

fickle ['fɪkl] ADJ launenhaft

fiction ['fɪkʃən] N NO PL (*Liter*) Prosaliteratur *f*; **you'll find that under ~** das finden Sie unter Belletristik; **work of ~** Erzählung *f*; (*longer*) Roman *m* (b) (= *invention*) (freie) Erfindung, Fiktion *f*; **that's pure ~** das ist frei erfunden

fictional ['fɪkʃənl] ADJ (a) (= *invented*) erfunden; *film, drama* fiktional (b) (= *relating to fiction*) erzählerisch; **his ~ writing** seine erzählenden Schriften

fictitious [fɪk'tɪʃəs] ADJ (a) *name, address* falsch; *case* fingiert (b) (*Liter*) *character, event* erfunden

fiddle ['fɪdl] **1** N (a) (*Mus inf*) Fiedel *f* (*inf*), Geige *f*; **to play second ~ to sb** (*fig*) in jds Schatten (*dat*) stehen; **as fit as a ~** kerngesund

(b) (*Brit inf*) (= *cheat, swindle*) Schiebung *f*; (*with money*) faule Geschäfte *pl* (*inf*); **it's a ~** das ist Schiebung!; **tax ~** Steuermanipulation *f*; **to be on the ~** krumme Dinger machen (*inf*) **2** VI (*Mus inf*) fiedeln (*inf*), geigen **3** VT (*Brit inf*) *accounts, results* frisieren (*inf*); **he ~d it so that ...** er hat es so hingebogen, dass ...

▶ **fiddle about** (*Brit*) *or* **around** VI **to fiddle about** *or* **around with sth** an etw (*dat*) herumspielen; (= *fidget with*) mit etw herumspielen

fiddler ['fɪdləᵣ] N (*Mus inf*) Geiger(in) *m(f)*

fiddly ['fɪdlɪ] ADJ (+ER) (*Brit*) *job, task* knifflig (*inf*); *object, controls etc* umständlich

fidelity [fɪ'delɪtɪ] N Treue *f* (*to* zu); **~ guarantee** (*Brit*), **~ insurance** (*US Insur*) Vertrauensschadenversicherung *f*

fidget ['fɪdʒɪt] **1** VI (*also* **~ about** *or* **around**) zappeln; **don't ~** zappel nicht so rum **2** N (= *person*) Zappelphilipp *m* (*inf*)

fidgety ['fɪdʒɪtɪ] ADJ zappelig; *audience* unruhig

field [fiːld] **1** N (a) (*lit, fig*) Feld *nt*; (= *area of grass*) Wiese *f*; (*for cows, horses etc*) Weide *f*; **corn/wheat ~** Getreide-/Weizenfeld *nt*; **potato ~** Kartoffelacker *m*; **he's working in the ~s** er arbeitet auf dem Feld; **~ of battle** Schlachtfeld *nt*; **~ of vision** Blickfeld *nt*; **magnetic ~** Magnetfeld *nt*; **there's quite a strong ~ for the race** das Teilnehmerfeld für das Rennen ist ziemlich stark

(b) (*for football etc*) Platz *m*; **sports** *or* **games ~** Sportplatz *m* (c) (*of study, work etc*) Gebiet *nt*; **to lead the ~ (in sth)** (in etw *dat*) das Feld anführen; **what ~ are you in?** auf welchem Gebiet arbeiten Sie?; **his ~ is Renaissance painting** sein Spezialgebiet ist die Malerei der Renaissance

(d) (= *practical observation or operation*) Praxis *f*; **work in the ~** Feldforschung *f*; (*of sales rep*) Außendienst *m* (e) (*Comput*) Datenfeld *nt* **2** VT (a) *ball* auffangen und zurückwerfen; (*fig*) *question etc* abblocken; **he had to ~ calls from irate customers** er musste wütende Kunden am Telefon abwimmeln (*inf*)

(b) *team, side* aufs Feld *or* auf den Platz schicken (c) (*Pol*) *candidate* aufstellen **3** VI (*Cricket, Baseball etc*) als Fänger spielen

field day N (*fig*) **I had a ~** ich hatte meinen großen Tag

fielder [ˈfiːldəʳ] N (*Cricket, Baseball etc*) Fänger(in) *m(f)*
field: **field event** N (*Athletics*) Disziplin, die nicht auf der Aschenbahn ausgetragen wird; **field goal** N (*US*) (*Basketball*) Korbwurf *m* aus dem Spielgeschehen; (*Ftbl*) Fieldgoal *nt*; **field hockey** N (*US*) Hockey *nt*; **fieldmouse** N Feldmaus *f*; **field sports** PL Sport *m* im Freien (*Jagen und Fischen*); **field study** N Feldstudie *f*; **field test** N Feldversuch *m*; **field-test** VT in einem Feldversuch/in Feldversuchen testen; **field work** N (*of surveyor etc*) Arbeit *f* im Gelände; (*of sociologist etc*) Feldforschung *f*; **field worker** N Praktiker(in) *m(f)*
fiend [fiːnd] N (a) (= *evil spirit*) Dämon *m*; (= *person*) Teufel *m* (b) (*inf*: = *addict*) Fanatiker(in) *m(f)*; **tennis ~** Tennisnarr *m*; **she's a fresh-air ~** sie ist Frischluftfanatikerin
fiendish [ˈfiːndɪʃ] ADJ (a) (= *cruel*) teuflisch; *laughter* hämisch; **he took a ~ delight in doing it** es machte ihm eine höllische Freude, es zu tun (b) (*inf*) *plan, device* höllisch raffiniert *or* clever (*inf*) (c) (*inf*) *problem* verzwickt (*inf*)
fiendishly [ˈfiːndɪʃlɪ] ADV (*inf*) *difficult, clever* höllisch (*inf*)
fierce [fɪəs] ADJ (+ER) *animal* wild, aggressiv; *dog* böse; *person, look, appearance* grimmig; *fighting, resistance, critic, rivals* erbittert; *debate, argument, storm* heftig; *attack, competition, criticism* scharf; *pride, ambition, independence* leidenschaftlich; *heat, sun* glühend; **he has a ~ temper** er braust schnell auf
fiercely [ˈfɪəslɪ] ADV *oppose, fight, deny* heftig; *criticize* scharf; *defend, argue* leidenschaftlich; *say* böse; *independent, competitive, proud, loyal* äußerst; **the fire was burning ~** es brannte lichterloh
fiery [ˈfaɪərɪ] ADJ (+ER) *inferno, furnace, heat* glühend; *colour, orange* leuchtend; *sunset* rot glühend; *temperament, character* hitzig; *person* hitzköpfig; *speech, performance* feurig (*also Cook*); **~ red** feuerrot; **to have a ~ temper** ein Hitzkopf *m* sein
fiesta [fɪˈestə] N Fiesta *f*
FIFA [ˈfiːfə] ABBR *of* **Federation of International Football Associations** FIFA *f*
FIFO (*Comm*) ABBR *of* **first-in-first-out** Fifo; **~ costing** Fifo-Kostenerfassung *f*
fifteen [ˈfɪfˈtiːn] **1** ADJ fünfzehn **2** N (a) Fünfzehn *f* (b) a **rugby ~** eine Rugbymannschaft
fifteenth [ˈfɪfˈtiːnθ] **1** ADJ fünfzehnte(r, s) **2** N Fünfzehnte(r, s); (= *part, fraction*) Fünfzehntel *nt*; *see also* **sixteenth**
fifth [fɪfθ] **1** ADJ fünfte(r, s) **2** N Fünfte(r, s); (= *part, fraction*) Fünftel *nt*; (*Mus*) Quinte *f*; **to take the ~** (*US inf*) die Aussage verweigern; *see also* **sixth**

FIFTH AMENDMENT

Im **Fifth Amendment**, dem fünften Zusatz zur Verfassung der USA, wurden verschiedene Grundrechte zum Schutz der Bürger vor Übergriffen des Staates festgeschrieben. Es besagt unter anderem, dass niemand gegen sich selbst aussagen muss. Wenn jemand die Aussage verweigert, um sich nicht selbst zu belasten, so nennt man das auch „he/she is taking the Fifth". ▶ BILL OF RIGHTS

fiftieth [ˈfɪftɪɪθ] **1** ADJ fünfzigste(r, s) **2** N Fünfzigste(r, s); (= *part, fraction*) Fünfzigstel *nt*; *see also* **sixth**
fifty [ˈfɪftɪ] **1** ADJ fünfzig **2** N Fünfzig *f*; *see also* **sixty**
fifty-fifty [ˈfɪftɪˈfɪftɪ] **1** ADV fifty-fifty (*inf*); **to go ~ (with sb)** (mit jdm) fifty-fifty machen (*inf*) **2** ADJ **he has a ~ chance of survival/victory** er hat eine fünfzigprozentige Überlebens-/Gewinnchance
fig [fɪg] N Feige *f*
fig. ABBR *of* **figure(s)** Abb.
fight [faɪt] *vb: pret, ptp* **fought** **1** N (a) (*lit, fig*) Kampf *m*; (= *fist ~*) Schlägerei *f*; (*Mil*) Gefecht *nt*; (= *argument*) Streit *m*; **to have a ~ with sb** sich mit jdm schlagen; (= *argue*) sich mit jdm streiten; **to put up a good ~** (*lit, fig*) sich tapfer schlagen; **do you want a ~?** du willst dich wohl mit mir anlegen?; **he won't give in without a ~** er ergibt sich nicht kampflos; **the ~ for survival** der Kampf ums Überleben
(b) (= *fighting spirit*) Kampfgeist *m*; **there was no ~ left in him** sein Kampfgeist war erloschen
2 VI kämpfen; (= *have punch-up etc*) sich schlagen; (= *argue*) sich streiten; **to ~ against disease** Krankheiten bekämpfen; **to ~ for sb/sth** um jdn/etw kämpfen; **to ~ for breath** nach Atem ringen; **to ~ shy of sth** einer Sache (*dat*) aus dem Weg gehen
3 VT *person* kämpfen mit *or* gegen; (= *have punch-up with*)

sich schlagen mit; *fire, disease, cuts, crime, inflation* bekämpfen; *decision* ankämpfen gegen; *corruption* angehen gegen; **to ~ a duel** sich duellieren; **to ~ an action** (*Jur*) einen Prozess durchkämpfen *or* durchfechten; **to ~ one's way through the crowd** sich durch die Menge kämpfen; **I'm prepared to ~ him/the government** (= *argue with, take on*) ich bin bereit, das mit ihm/der Regierung durchzukämpfen
▶ **fight back** **1** VI (*in fight*) zurückschlagen; (*Mil*) Widerstand leisten; (*in argument*) sich wehren; (*Sport*) zurückkämpfen **2** VT SEP *tears, doubts etc* unterdrücken
▶ **fight off** VT SEP (*Mil, fig*) abwehren; **I'm still trying to fight off this cold** ich kämpfe immer noch mit dieser Erkältung
▶ **fight out** VT SEP **to fight it out** es untereinander ausfechten
fighter [ˈfaɪtəʳ] N (a) Kämpfer(in) *m(f)*; (*Boxing*) Fighter *m*; **he's a ~** (*fig*) er ist eine Kämpfernatur (b) (*Aviat*: = *plane*) Jagdflugzeug *nt*
fighter pilot N Jagdflieger *m*
fighting [ˈfaɪtɪŋ] N (*Mil*) Gefecht *nt*; (= *punch-ups etc*) Prügeleien *pl*; (= *arguments*) Streit *m*; **~ broke out** Kämpfe brachen aus
fighting: **fighting chance** N **he's in with** *or* **he has a ~ (of winning)** er hat eine Chance (zu gewinnen), wenn er sich anstrengt; **fighting fit** ADJ (*Brit inf*) topfit (*inf*); **fighting spirit** N Kampfgeist *m*
fig leaf N (*lit, fig*) Feigenblatt *nt*
figment [ˈfɪgmənt] N **it's all a ~ of his imagination** das ist alles eine Ausgeburt seiner Fantasie
figurative [ˈfɪgjʊrətɪv] ADJ *language* bildlich; *use, sense* übertragen
figuratively [ˈfɪgjʊrətɪvlɪ] ADV im übertragenen Sinn
figure [ˈfɪgəʳ] **1** N (a) (= *number*) Zahl *f*; (= *digit*) Ziffer *f*; (= *sum*) Summe *f*; **he didn't want to put a ~ on it** er wollte keine Zahlen nennen; **he's good at ~s** er ist ein guter Rechner; **to reach double ~s** in die zweistelligen Zahlen gehen; **a three-~ sum** eine dreistellige Summe
(b) (*in geometry, dancing, = shapeliness, statuette*) Figur *f*; **~ (of) eight** Acht *f*; **to lose one's ~** seine Figur verlieren; **she's a fine ~ of a woman** sie ist eine stattliche Frau; **he's a fine ~ of a man** er ist ein Bild von einem Mann
(c) (= *human form*) Gestalt *f*
(d) (= *personality*) Persönlichkeit *f*; (= *character in novel etc*) Gestalt *f*; **the great ~s of history** die Großen der Geschichte; **a key public ~** eine Schlüsselfigur des öffentlichen Lebens; **~ of fun** Witzfigur *f*
(e) (*Liter*) **~ of speech** Redensart *f*; **it's just a ~ of speech** das sagt man doch nur so
(f) (= *illustration*) Abbildung *f*
2 VT (a) (*esp US inf*: = *think, reckon*) glauben
(b) (*US inf*: = **~ out**) begreifen
3 VI (a) (= *appear*) erscheinen; **he ~d prominently in my plans** er spielte eine bedeutende Rolle in meinen Plänen
(b) (*inf*: = *make sense*) **that ~s** das hätte ich mir denken können
▶ **figure on** VI +PREP OBJ (*esp US*) rechnen mit
▶ **figure out** VT SEP (a) (= *understand*) begreifen (b) (= *work out*) ausrechnen; *answer, how to do sth* herausbekommen; *solution* finden
figure: **figurehead** N (*Naut, fig*) Galionsfigur *f*; **figure skating** N Eiskunstlaufen *nt*
figurine [fɪgəˈriːn] N Figurine *f*
Fiji [ˈfiːdʒiː] N Fidschiinseln *pl*
filament [ˈfɪləmənt] N (*Elec*) (Glüh- *or* Heiz)faden *m*
filch [fɪltʃ] VT (*inf*) mopsen (*inf*)
file¹ [faɪl] **1** N Feile *f* **2** VT feilen; **to ~ one's (finger)nails** sich (*dat*) die Fingernägel feilen
file² **1** N (a) (= *holder*) Aktenordner *m*; (*for card index*) Karteikasten *m*; **would you fetch it from the ~s** könnten Sie es bitte aus der Ablage holen; **it's in the ~s somewhere** das muss irgendwo bei den Akten sein
(b) (= *documents, information*) Akte *f* (*on sb* über jdn, *on sth* über etw); **have we got that on ~?** haben wir das bei den Akten?; **to open** *or* **start a ~ on sb/sth** eine Akte über jdn/zu etw anlegen; **to keep sb/sth on ~** jds Unterlagen/die Unterlagen über etw (*acc*) zurückbehalten; **the Kowalski ~** die Akte Kowalski
(c) (*Comput*) Datei *f*; **to have sth on ~** etw im Computer gespeichert haben

2 VT **(a)** *letters, documents* ablegen
(b) (*Press*) *report* einsenden
(c) (*Jur*) *complaint* erheben; *(law)suit* anstrengen
3 VI **to ~ for divorce** die Scheidung einreichen; **to ~ for bankruptcy** Konkurs anmelden

file³ **1** N (= *row*) Reihe *f*; **in single ~** im Gänsemarsch; (*Mil*) in Reihe **2** VI **to ~ in** hereinmarschieren; **they ~d out of the classroom** sie gingen hintereinander *or* nacheinander aus dem Klassenzimmer; **the troops ~d past the general** die Truppen marschierten am General vorbei

file: file cabinet N (*US*) Aktenschrank *m*; **file management** N (*Comput*) Dateiverwaltung *f*; **file manager** N (*Comput*) Dateimanager *m*; **filename** N (*Comput*) Dateiname *m*

filet [fɪˈleɪ] N (*US*) = **fillet**

filial [ˈfɪlɪəl] ADJ *duties* des Kindes; *affection* kindlich

filibuster [ˈfɪlɪbʌstəʳ] VI (*esp US*) filibustern

filigree [ˈfɪlɪgriː] **1** N Filigran *nt* **2** ADJ Filigran-

filing [ˈfaɪlɪŋ] N (*of documents*) Ablegen *nt*; **have you done the ~?** haben Sie die Akten schon abgelegt?

filing cabinet N Aktenschrank *m*

filings [ˈfaɪlɪŋz] PL Späne *pl*

filing: filing system N Ablagesystem *nt*; **filing tray** N Ablagekorb *m*

Filipino [fɪlɪˈpiːnəʊ] **1** N Filipino *m*, Filipina *f* **2** ADJ philippinisch

fill [fɪl] **1** VT **(a)** füllen; *pipe* stopfen; *teeth* plombieren; (*wind*) *sails* blähen; (*fig*) (aus)füllen; **I had three teeth ~ed** ich bekam drei Zähne plombiert *or* gefüllt
(b) (= *permeate*) erfüllen; **~ed with anger/admiration** voller Zorn/Bewunderung; **~ed with emotion** gefühlsgeladen
(c) *post, position* (*employer*) besetzen; (*employee*) (= *take up*) einnehmen; (= *be in*) innehaben; *need* entsprechen (+*dat*); *role* übernehmen; **the position is already ~ed** die Stelle ist schon besetzt
2 VI sich füllen
3 N **to drink one's ~** seinen Durst löschen; **to eat one's ~** sich satt essen; **I've had my ~ of him/it** (*inf*) ich habe von ihm/davon die Nase voll (*inf*)
➤ **fill in** **1** VI **to fill in for sb** für jdn einspringen **2** VT SEP **(a)** *hole* auffüllen; *door, fireplace* zumauern; **he's just filling in time until he gets another job** er eine andere Stelle bekommt **(b)** *form* ausfüllen; *name, missing word* eintragen **(c) to fill sb in (on sth)** jdn (über etw *acc*) aufklären *or* ins Bild setzen
➤ **fill out** **1** VI (*person*) fülliger werden; (*cheeks, face*) runder *or* voller werden **2** VT SEP *form* ausfüllen
➤ **fill up** **1** VI **(a)** (*Aut*) (auf)tanken **(b)** (*hall, barrel etc*) sich füllen **2** VT SEP *tank, cup* voll füllen; (*driver*) voll tanken; *hole* füllen; **that pie has really filled me up** ich fühle mich wirklich voll nach dieser Pastete; **you need something to fill you up** du brauchst was Sättigendes

filler [ˈfɪləʳ] N **(a)** (*Build*) Spachtelmasse *f* **(b)** (*Press, TV*) (Lücken)füller *m*

fillet [ˈfɪlɪt] **1** N (*Cook*) Filet *nt*; **~ of beef/lamb** Rinder-/Lammfilet *nt* **2** VT (*Cook*) filetieren

fillet steak N Filetsteak *nt*

filling [ˈfɪlɪŋ] **1** N (*in tooth, pie etc*) Füllung *f*; **I had to have three ~s** ich musste mir drei Zähne plombieren *or* füllen lassen **2** ADJ *food* sättigend

filling station N Tankstelle *f*

fillip [ˈfɪlɪp] N (*fig*) **to give sb a ~** jdn aufmuntern *or* anspornen; **to give sth a ~** einer Sache (*dat*) (neuen) Schwung geben

filly [ˈfɪlɪ] N Stutfohlen *nt*

film [fɪlm] **1** N Film *m*; (*of dust*) Schicht *f*; **to make** *or* **shoot a ~** einen Film drehen *or* machen; **to make a ~** (*actor*) einen Film machen; **to go to (see) a ~** ins Kino gehen **2** VT *play* verfilmen; *scene* filmen; *people* einen Film machen von **3** VI filmen; **we start ~ing** *or* **~ing starts tomorrow** die Dreharbeiten fangen morgen an
➤ **film over** *or* **up** VI (*mirror, glass*) anlaufen

film: film clip N Filmausschnitt *m*; **film festival** N Filmfestspiele *pl*; **film industry** N Filmindustrie *f*; **film maker** N Filmemacher(in) *m(f)*; **film script** N Drehbuch *nt*; **film star** N Filmstar *m*; **film studio** N Filmstudio *nt*; **film version** N Verfilmung *f*

Filofax® [ˈfaɪləʊfæks] N Filofax® *m*

filter [ˈfɪltəʳ] **1** N **(a)** Filter *m*; (*Phot, Rad, Mech*) Filter *nt or m* **(b)** (*Brit: for traffic*) grüner Pfeil (*für Abbieger*) **2** VT *liquids, air* filtern **3** VI **(a)** (*light*) durchscheinen; (*liquid, sound*) durchsickern **(b)** (*Brit Aut*) **to ~ to the left** sich links einordnen
➤ **filter in** VI (*people*) langsam *or* allmählich eindringen; (*news*) durchsickern
➤ **filter out** **1** VI (*people*) einer nach dem anderen herausgehen; (*news*) durchsickern **2** VT SEP (*lit*) herausfiltern

filter: filter lane N (*Brit*) Abbiegespur *f*; **filter paper** N Filterpapier *nt*; **filter tip** N Filter *m*

filth [fɪlθ] N (*lit*) Schmutz *m*; (*fig*) Schweinerei *f* (*inf*); (= *people*) Dreckspack *nt* (*inf*); **all the ~ they wrote about him in the papers** all der Unflat, der über ihn in der Zeitung geschrieben wurde

filthy [ˈfɪlθɪ] ADJ (+ER) (*lit, fig*) dreckig; *habit* ekelhaft; *language, expression* zotig; *book, magazine* obszön; **to live in ~ conditions** im Dreck leben; **you ~ little slut!** (*sl*) du dreckige kleine Schlampe!; **you've got a ~ mind!** du hast eine schmutzige Fantasie!

fin [fɪn] N **(a)** (*of fish*) Flosse *f* **(b)** (*Aviat*) Seitenleitwerk *nt*; (*of bomb, rocket*) Stabilisierungsfläche *f*

finagle [fɪˈneɪgəl] VT (*inf*) deichseln (*inf*); **to ~ sth out of sb** jdm etw abluchsen; **to ~ one's way out of sth** sich aus einer Sache herausmogeln

final [ˈfaɪnl] **1** ADJ **(a)** (= *last*) letzte(r, s); **~ round/match** letzte Runde/letztes Spiel; (*in a tournament*) Endrunde *f*/-spiel *nt*; **~ stage(s)** Endstadium *nt*; **~ act/chapter** Schlussakt *m*/-kapitel *nt*
(b) (= *definitive*) *result, decision, version* endgültig; **~ verdict** Endurteil *nt*; **~ score** Endergebnis *nt*; **that's my ~ offer** das ist mein letztes Angebot; **the judges' decision is ~** die Preisrichter haben das letzte Wort; **... and that's ~!** ... und damit basta! (*inf*)
2 N **(a)** (*esp Sport*) Finale *nt*; (*of quiz, field event*) Endrunde *f*; (= *game*) Endspiel *nt*; (= *race*) Endlauf *m*; **to get to the ~** ins Finale kommen; **World Cup Final** (*Ftbl*) Endspiel *nt* der Fußballweltmeisterschaft; **the ~s** das Finale; die Endrunde **(b) finals** PL (*Brit Univ*: = *examinations*) Abschlussprüfung *f*

final: final copy N (*US*) Reinschrift *f*; **final demand** N letzte Mahnung *or* Zahlungsaufforderung *f*; **final dividend** N (*Fin*) Abschlussdividende *f*

finale [fɪˈnɑːlɪ] N (*Mus, in opera, fig*) Finale *nt*; (*Theat*) Schlussszene *f*

finalist [ˈfaɪnəlɪst] N (*Sport*) Finalist(in) *m(f)*

finalize [ˈfaɪnəlaɪz] VT *plans, arrangements, details* endgültig festlegen; *deal, negotiations* zum Abschluss bringen

finally [ˈfaɪnəlɪ] ADV **(a)** (= *eventually*) schließlich; (= *at last, expressing relief*) endlich **(b)** (= *lastly*) zum Schluss; (= *introducing a final point*) abschließend **(c)** *decide, settle* endgültig

final whistle N (*Ftbl*) Schlusspfiff *m*; **to blow the ~** das Spiel abpfeifen

finance [faɪˈnæns] **1** N **(a)** Finanzen *pl*; **high ~** Hochfinanz *f* **(b)** (= *money*) Geld *nt*; **it's a question of ~** das ist eine Geldfrage; **~s** Finanzen *pl* **2** VT finanzieren

finance: finance bill N (*Fin*) Finanzwechsel *m*; **finance company** N Finanz(ierungs)gesellschaft *f*; **finance director** N Leiter(in) der Finanzabteilung

financial [faɪˈnænʃəl] ADJ **(a)** *problems, support* finanziell; **~ resources** Geldmittel *pl* **(b)** (*St Ex, Econ*) Finanz-; **on the ~ markets** auf den Finanzmärkten; **~ news** Wirtschaftsnachrichten *pl*; **~ investment** Geldanlage *f*; (*of a company*) Finanzinvestition *f*; **~ ratio** (*Comm, Fin*) finanzwirtschaftliche Kennzahl *or* Kennziffer; **Financial Times Industrial Ordinary Share Index** Aktienindex *m* der Financial Times

financial: financial accountant N Finanzbuchhalter(in) *m(f)*; **financial adviser, financial consultant** N Finanzberater(in) *m(f)*; **financial controller** N Leiter(in) *m(f)* des Rechnungswesens *or* der Buchhaltung; **financial director** N (*Comm*) Leiter(in) *m(f)* der Finanzabteilung; **financial institution** N Geldinstitut *nt*

financially [faɪˈnænʃəlɪ] ADV finanziell; (*introducing sentence*) finanziell gesehen; **the company is ~ sound** die Finanzlage der Firma ist gesund; **~ viable** rentabel

financial: financial services PL Finanzdienstleistungen *pl*; **financial statement** N (*Comm*) Abschluss *m*; (*annual*)

Jahresabschluss *m*; **financial year** N (*Brit*) Geschäftsjahr *nt*

financier [faɪˈnænsɪə^r] N Finanzier *m*

finch [fɪntʃ] N Fink *m*

find [faɪnd], *vb: pret, ptp* **found** ◼ VT **(a)** finden; **it's nowhere to be found** es lässt sich nirgendwo finden *or* auftreiben (*inf*); **to ~ pleasure in sth** Freude an etw (*dat*) haben; **he was found dead in bed** er wurde tot im Bett aufgefunden; **where am I going to ~ the money/time?** wo nehme ich nur das Geld/die Zeit her?; **I don't ~ it easy to tell you this** es fällt mir nicht leicht, Ihnen das zu sagen; **he always found languages easy/hard** ihm fielen Sprachen immer leicht/schwer; **I ~ it impossible to understand him** ich kann ihn einfach nicht verstehen; **I found myself smiling** ich musste unwillkürlich lächeln; **I ~ myself in an impossible situation/in financial difficulties** ich befinde mich in einer unmöglichen Situation/in finanziellen Schwierigkeiten; **one day he suddenly found himself out of a job** eines Tages war er plötzlich arbeitslos; **this flower is found all over England** diese Blume findet man in ganz England

(b) (= *supply*) besorgen (*sb sth* jdm etw); **go and ~ me a needle** hol mir doch mal eine Nadel; **we'll have to ~ him a desk** wir müssen einen Schreibtisch für ihn finden

(c) (= *discover, ascertain; cause*) herausfinden; **we found the car wouldn't start** es stellte sich heraus, dass das Auto nicht ansprang; **you will ~ that I am right** Sie werden sehen, dass ich Recht habe

(d) (*Jur*) **to ~ sb guilty/not guilty** jdn schuldig sprechen/freisprechen; **how do you ~ the accused?** wie lautet Ihr Urteil?

(e) (*Comput*) suchen; **~ and replace** suchen und ersetzen

◼ VI (*Jur*) **to ~ for/against the accused** den Angeklagten freisprechen/verurteilen

◼ N Fund *m*

➤ **find out** ◼ VT SEP herausfinden; (= *discover the misdeeds etc of*) *person* erwischen; (= *come to know about*) auf die Schliche kommen (+*dat*) (*inf*); **you've been found out** du bist entdeckt *or* ertappt (*inf*) ◼ VI es herausfinden; **to find out about sb/sth** (= *discover existence of*) jdn/etw entdecken; **to help children find out about other countries** Kindern dabei helfen, etwas über andere Länder herauszufinden

finder [ˈfaɪndə^r] N Finder(in) *m(f)*

finding [ˈfaɪndɪŋ] N **~s** *pl* Ergebnis(se) *nt(pl)*; (*medical*) Befund *m*

fine[1] [faɪn] ◼ N (*Jur*) Geldstrafe *f*; (*driving*) Bußgeld *nt*; (*for minor traffic offences*) (gebührenpflichtige) Verwarnung ◼ VT (*Jur*) zu einer Geldstrafe verurteilen; (*for driving offences also*) Bußgeld verhängen gegen; (*for minor traffic offences*) eine (gebührenpflichtige) Verwarnung erteilen (+*dat*); **he was ~d £100** er musste £ 100 Strafe bezahlen; **he was ~d for speeding** er hat einen Strafzettel für zu schnelles Fahren bekommen

fine[2] ◼ ADJ (+ER) **(a)** (= *excellent*) ausgezeichnet; *building, town, view* herrlich; *person* fein; *performance, performer, player* großartig; **you're doing a ~ job** Sie machen Ihre Sache ganz ausgezeichnet; **she's a ~ woman** sie ist eine bewundernswerte *or* (*in stature*) stattliche Frau

(b) (= *acceptable*) in Ordnung; **my coffee was ~** mein Kaffee war in Ordnung; **any more? – no, that's ~** *or* **it'll be ~** noch etwas? – nein, danke; **everything's going to be just ~** es wird schon alles gut gehen; **these apples are ~ for cooking** diese Äpfel eignen sich (gut) zum Kochen; **the doctor said it was ~ for me to play** der Arzt sagte, ich dürfte ohne weiteres spielen; **you look/the wallpaper looks ~ (to me)** (ich finde,) du siehst/die Tapete sieht gut aus; **your idea sounds ~** Ihre Idee hört sich gut an; **he/she is ~** (= *managing OK*) er/sie kommt gut zurecht; (= *in good health*) es geht ihm/ihr gut; (= *things are going well*) mit ihm/ihr ist alles in Ordnung; **how are you? – ~, thanks** wie geht es Ihnen? – danke, gut; **a glass of water and I'll be ~** nach einem Glas Wasser wird es mir wieder gut gehen; **that's ~ with** *or* **by me** ich habe nichts dagegen

(c) (= *high-quality, delicate*) fein; *wine, china, fabric* erlesen; *furniture, jewellery, clothes* ausgesucht; *material* dünn; *handwriting* zierlich; *mesh, weave* fein(maschig); *house* vornehm; *features* zart; **the ~st** die erlesensten Zutaten; **~ nib** spitze Feder; **a ~ rain** Nieselregen *m*; **to read the ~ print** das Kleingedruckte lesen; **not to put too ~ a point on it** um ganz offen zu sein; **there's a ~ line between genius and madness** es besteht ein feiner Unterschied zwischen Genie und Wahnsinn

(d) *weather, day* schön; **when it is/was ~** bei schönem Wetter; **one ~ day** eines schönen Tages

(e) (*iro*) *excuse, state, friend etc* schön (*iro*); **that's ~ for you to say** du hast gut reden; **you're a ~ one to talk!** du kannst gerade reden!

◼ ADV **(a)** (= *well*) tadellos; **you're doing ~** Sie machen Ihre Sache gut; (*healthwise*) Sie machen gute Fortschritte; **we get on ~** wir kommen ausgezeichnet miteinander aus

(b) *cut, slice* dünn

fine art N **(a)** USU PL schöne Künste *pl* **(b)** (= *skill*) **he's got it down to a ~** er hat den Bogen heraus (*inf*)

finely [ˈfaɪnlɪ] ADV fein; *slice* dünn; **~ ground coffee** fein gemahlener Kaffee; **~ sliced** in dünne Scheiben geschnitten; **the case is ~ balanced** der Fall kann sich so oder so entscheiden; **~ tuned** *engine, machine* genau eingestellt

finery [ˈfaɪnərɪ] N **wedding guests in all their ~** Hochzeitsgäste in vollem Staat

finesse [fɪˈnes] N Gewandtheit *f*

fine: **fine-tooth comb** N **to go over sth with a ~** etw genau unter die Lupe nehmen; *area* etw durchkämmen; *room* etw gründlich durchsuchen; **fine-tune** VT (*lit, fig*) fein abstimmen; **fine-tuning** N (*lit, fig*) Feinabstimmung *f*

finger [ˈfɪŋgə^r] ◼ N Finger *m*; **she can twist him round her little ~** sie kann ihn um den (kleinen) Finger wickeln; **to have a ~ in every pie** überall die Finger drin *or* im Spiel haben (*inf*); **I didn't lay a ~ on her** ich habe sie nicht angerührt; **he wouldn't lift a ~ to help me** er würde keinen Finger rühren, um mir zu helfen; **to point one's ~ at sb** mit dem Finger auf jdn zeigen; **I can't put my ~ on it, but …** ich kann es nicht genau ausmachen, aber …; **you've put your ~ on it there** da haben Sie den kritischen Punkt berührt; **pull your ~ out!** (*Brit inf*) es wird Zeit, dass du Nägel mit Köpfen machst! (*inf*); **to give sb the ~** (*esp US inf*) jdm den Stinkefinger zeigen (*inf*) ◼ VT (= *touch*) anfassen; (= *toy, meddle with*) befingern

finger: **fingerboard** N Griffbrett *nt*; **finger bowl** N Fingerschale *f*; **finger buffet** N Buffet *nt* mit Happethappen

fingering [ˈfɪŋgərɪŋ] N (*Mus*) **the ~ is very difficult** die Griffe sind sehr schwierig

finger: **fingermark** N Fingerabdruck *m*; **fingernail** N Fingernagel *m*; **fingerprint** ◼ N Fingerabdruck *m*; **to take sb's ~s** jdm Fingerabdrücke abnehmen ◼ VT **to ~ sb** jdm Fingerabdrücke nehmen; **fingertip** N Fingerspitze *f*; **to have sth at one's ~s** (*fig*) (= *know very well*) etw aus dem Effeff kennen (*inf*); (= *at sb's immediate disposal*) etw parat haben *inf*; **fingertip search** N Durchkämmungsaktion *f*

finicky [ˈfɪnɪkɪ] ADJ pingelig (*inf*); (*about food, clothes etc*) wählerisch; **he's a ~ eater** er ist beim Essen sehr wählerisch

finish [ˈfɪnɪʃ] ◼ N **(a)** (= *end*) Schluss *m*, Ende *nt*; (*of race*) Finish *nt*; (= *finishing line*) Ziel *nt*; **from start to ~** von Anfang bis Ende; **to fight to the ~** (*fig*) bis zum letzten Augenblick kämpfen

(b) (= *perfection: of things*) Verarbeitung *f*

(c) (*of industrial products*) Finish *nt*; (= *final coat of paint*) Deckanstrich *m*; (*of pottery*) Oberfläche *f*; (= *ornamental work*) Verzierung *f*

◼ VT **(a)** beenden; *education, course* abschließen; *piece of work, business* erledigen; **he's ~ed the painting/job** er ist mit dem Bild/der Arbeit fertig; **to have ~ed doing sth** damit fertig sein, etw zu tun; **when I ~ eating …** wenn ich mit dem Essen fertig bin, …; **to ~ writing/reading sth** etw zu Ende schreiben/lesen; **when do you ~ work?** wann machen Sie Feierabend?; **she never lets him ~ (what he's saying)** sie lässt ihn nie ausreden; **give me time to ~ my drink** lass mich austrinken; **~ what you're doing and we'll go** mach fertig, was du angefangen hast, und dann gehen wir

(b) (= *ruin*) ruinieren; (= *kill, inf: = exhaust*) den Rest geben (+*dat*) (*inf*); **another strike could ~ the firm** noch ein Streik könnte das Ende für die Firma bedeuten

(c) *surface, industrial product* fertig bearbeiten; (= *paint*) anstreichen; *car etc* lackieren; **the paintwork isn't very well ~ed** die Malerarbeiten wurden nicht sehr gut ausgeführt

◼ VI **(a)** zu Ende *or* aus sein; (*person: with task etc*) fertig sein; (= *come to an end, ~ work*) aufhören; (*piece of music, story etc*) enden; **my course ~es this week** mein Kurs geht diese Woche zu Ende; **we'll ~ by singing a song** wir wollen mit einem Lied schließen; **I've ~ed** ich bin fertig

(b) (*Sport*) das Ziel erreichen; **to ~ first/second** als erster/zweiter durchs Ziel gehen

➤ **finish off** VT SEP **(a)** *piece of work* fertig machen; *job* erledigen; **to finish off a letter** einen Brief zu Ende schreiben **(b)** *food, meal* aufessen; *drink* austrinken **(c)** (= *kill*) den Gnadenstoß geben (+*dat*); (*by shooting*) den Gnadenschuss geben (+*dat*) **(d)** (= *do for*) *person* den Rest geben (+*dat*) (*inf*)

➤ **finish up** VI (*in a place*) landen (*inf*); **he finished up a nervous wreck** er war zum Schluss ein Nervenbündel; **you'll finish up wishing you'd never started** du wünschst dir bestimmt noch, du hättest gar nicht erst angefangen

➤ **finish with** VI +PREP OBJ **(a)** (= *no longer need*) nicht mehr brauchen; **I've finished with the paper** ich bin mit der Zeitung fertig **(b)** (= *want no more to do with*) **I've finished with him** ich bin fertig mit ihm (*inf*); (*with boyfriend*) ich habe mit ihm Schluss gemacht

finished ['fɪnɪʃt] ADJ **(a)** fertig; **I'm nearly ~** ich bin fast fertig *or* so weit; **to be ~ doing sth** (*US*) damit fertig sein, etw zu tun; **to be ~ with sb/sth** mit jdm/etw fertig sein; (= *fed up*) von jdm/etw nichts mehr wissen wollen; **I'm ~ with politics** mit der Politik ist es für mich vorbei; **~ goods/products** Fertigprodukte *pl*; **the ~ article** (= *object*) das fertige Produkt; (= *piece of writing, work of art*) die endgültige Version **(b)** (= *used up*) *things* aufgebraucht; (= *over*) zu Ende; **the wine is ~** es ist kein Wein mehr da **(c)** (*inf*) **to be ~** (*politician, sportsperson etc*) erledigt sein (*inf*) (*as als*); **we're ~, it's ~ between us** es ist aus zwischen uns **(d)** (= *treated*) *product* fertig bearbeitet; (*with paint*) gestrichen; *clothing* verarbeitet; **beautifully ~ wood** wunderschön verarbeitetes Holz

finishing ['fɪnɪʃɪŋ]: **finishing line** N Ziellinie *f*; **finishing school** N (Mädchen)pensionat *nt*

finite ['faɪnaɪt] ADJ begrenzt; *universe* endlich; **a ~ number** eine begrenzte Zahl; (*Math*) eine endliche Zahl; **coal and oil are ~ resources** Kohle und Öl sind nicht erneuerbare Ressourcen

Finland ['fɪnlənd] N Finnland *nt*

Finn [fɪn] N Finne *m*, Finnin *f*

Finnish ['fɪnɪʃ] **1** ADJ finnisch; **he is ~** er ist Finne; **she is ~** sie ist Finnin **2** N (*Ling*) Finnisch *nt*

fiord [fjɔːd] N Fjord *m*

fir [fɜː^r] N Tanne *f*

fire [faɪə^r] **1** N **(a)** Feuer *nt*; **the house was on ~** das Haus brannte; **to set ~ to sth, to set sth on ~** etw anzünden; (*so as to destroy*) etw in Brand stecken; **to catch ~** Feuer fangen (*also fig*); (*building, forest etc also*) in Brand geraten; **you're playing with ~** (*fig*) du spielst mit dem Feuer; **fire!** (*Mil*) Feuer!; **to open ~ on sb** das Feuer auf jdn eröffnen; **small-arms/cannon ~** Pistolen-/Kanonenschüsse *pl*; **to come under ~** (*lit, fig*) unter Beschuss geraten **(b)** (= *house ~, forest ~ etc*) Brand *m*; **there was a ~ next door** nebenan hat es gebrannt; **fire!** Feuer! **(c)** (*in grate*) (Kamin)feuer *nt*; (= *electric ~, gas ~*) Ofen *m* **2** VT **(a)** *pottery* brennen **(b)** (*fig*) *imagination* beflügeln; *passions* entfachen (*geh*); *enthusiasm* befeuern; **to ~ sb with enthusiasm** jdn begeistern **(c)** *gun, arrow* abschießen; *shot* abgeben; *rocket* zünden; **to ~ a gun at sb** auf jdn schießen; **to ~ questions at sb** Fragen auf jdn abfeuern **(d)** (*inf*: = *dismiss*) feuern (*inf*) **3** VI **(a)** (= *shoot*) feuern, schießen (*at* auf +*acc*); **~!** (gebt) Feuer! **(b)** (*engine*) zünden; **the engine is only firing on three cylinders** der Motor läuft nur auf drei Zylindern

➤ **fire away** VI (*inf*) losschießen (*inf*)

➤ **fire off** VT SEP *letter* loslassen

➤ **fire up** VT SEP (*fig*) anfeuern; *imagination* beflügeln

fire: **fire alarm** N Feueralarm *m*; (= *apparatus*) Feuermelder *m*; **firearm** N Feuer- *or* Schusswaffe *f*; **firebrand** N (= *mischief-maker*) Unruhestifter(in) *m(f)*; **fire brigade** N (*Brit*) Feuerwehr *f*; **firecracker** N Knallkörper *m*; **fire department** N (*US*) Feuerwehr *f*; **fire door** N Feuertür *f*; **fire drill** N Probealarm *m*; (*for firemen*) Feuerwehrübung *f*; **fire engine** N Feuerwehrauto *nt*; **fire escape** N (= *staircase*) Feuertreppe *f*; (= *ladder*) Feuerleiter *f*; **fire exit** N Notausgang *m*; (= *external stairs*) Feuertreppe *f*; **fire-extinguisher** N Feuerlöscher *m*; **firefighter** N Feuerwehrmann *m*/-frau *f*; **firefighting** ADJ ATTR *techniques, team* zur Feuerbekämpfung; **~ equipment** Feuerlöschgeräte

pl; **firefly** N Leuchtkäfer *m*; **fireguard** N (Schutz)gitter *nt* (*vor dem Kamin*); **fire hazard** N **to be a ~** feuergefährlich sein; **these old houses are a ~** bei diesen alten Häusern besteht Brandgefahr; **firehouse** N (*US*) Feuerwache *f*; **fire hydrant** N Hydrant *m*; **firelight** N Schein *m* des Feuers; **firelighter** N Feueranzünder *m*; **fireman** N Feuerwehrmann *m*; **fireplace** N Kamin *m*; **fireplug** N (*dated US*) Hydrant *m*; **firepower** N Feuerkraft *f*; **fire prevention** N Brandschutz *m*; **fireproof** ADJ feuerfest; **fire regulations** PL Brandschutzbestimmungen *pl*; **fire retardant** ADJ feuerhemmend; **fireside** N **to sit by the ~** am Kamin sitzen; **fire station** N Feuerwache *f*, Feuerwehrzentrale *f*; **fire truck** N (*US*) = **fire engine**; **firewall** N (*Comput*) Firewall *f*; **firewoman** N Feuerwehrfrau *f*; **firewood** N Brennholz *nt*; **fireworks** PL Feuerwerkskörper *pl*; (= *display*) Feuerwerk *nt*

firing ['faɪrɪŋ] N **(a)** (*of pottery*) Brennen *nt* **(b)** (*Mil*) Feuer *nt*; (*of gun, shot, rocket*) Abfeuern *nt*

firing: **firing line** N (*Mil, fig*) Schusslinie *f*; **to be in the ~** (*lit, fig*) in der Schusslinie stehen; **firing squad** N Exekutionskommando *nt*

firm[1] [fɜːm] N Firma *f*; **~ of lawyers** Rechtsanwaltsbüro *nt*

firm[2] **1** ADJ (+ER) (*lit, fig*) fest; *stomach, thighs* straff; *hold, grip, evidence* sicher; *support, chair, ladder* stabil; *decision* endgültig; *news* bestätigt; *leader, father* stark; *manner, action* entschlossen; *measure* durchgreifend; **to get** *or* **take a ~ hold on sth** etw festhalten; **to keep a ~ grip** *or* **hold on sth/oneself** (*fig*) etw fest/sich gut im Griff haben; **to have a ~ grasp/understanding of sth** etw gut beherrschen/verstehen; **to set a ~ date for sth** einen festen Termin für etw vereinbaren; **to be ~ about sth** auf etw (*dat*) bestehen; **to be ~ with sb** jdm gegenüber bestimmt auftreten; **she's ~ with the children** sie ist streng mit den Kindern; **to take a ~ stand** *or* **line against sth** energisch gegen etw vorgehen; **they are ~ friends** sie sind eng befreundet; **to be a ~ favourite** (*Brit*) *or* **favorite** (*US*) (**with sb**) (bei jdm) sehr beliebt sein **2** ADV **to hold sth ~** etw festhalten; **to hold ~** (*Fin*) stabil bleiben; **to stand** *or* **hold ~** (= *not give up*) fest *or* standhaft bleiben

➤ **firm up** VT SEP *muscles* kräftigen; *thighs* straffen; *deal etc* unter Dach und Fach bringen

firmly ['fɜːmlɪ] ADV **(a)** (= *securely*) fest; *fix* sicher; **it was held ~ in place with a pin** es wurde von einer Nadel festgehalten; **to be ~ in control of sth** etw fest in der Hand haben; **to be committed to sth/to doing sth** sich voll für etw einsetzen/dafür einsetzen, etw zu tun **(b)** *say, tell* bestimmt; *reject* entschieden; **I shall tell her quite ~ that ...** ich werde ihr klipp und klar sagen, dass ...

firmness ['fɜːmnɪs] N (*of person, action, manner*) Entschlossenheit *f*; (= *strictness*) Strenge *f*

first [fɜːst] **1** ADJ erste(r, s); **his ~ novel** sein Erstlingsroman *m*; **he was ~ in the queue** (*Brit*) *or* **in line** (*US*) er war der Erste in der Schlange; **he was ~ in Latin** er war der Beste in Latein; **who's ~?** wer ist der Erste?; **the ~ time I saw her ...** als ich sie zum ersten Mal sah, ...; **in ~ place** (*Sport etc*) an erster Stelle; **in the ~ place** zunächst einmal; **why didn't you say so in the ~ place?** warum hast du denn das nicht gleich gesagt? **2** ADV **(a)** zuerst; *arrive, leave* als erste(r, s); **~ come ~ served** (*prov*) wer zuerst kommt, mahlt zuerst (*Prov*); **ladies ~** Ladies first!; **you** (**go**) **~** nach Ihnen; **he says ~ one thing then another** er sagt mal so, mal so; **he always puts his job ~** seine Arbeit kommt bei ihm immer vor allen anderen Dingen **(b)** (= *before all else*) als Erstes, zunächst; (*in listing*) erstens; **~ of all** (= *before all else, mainly*) vor allem; **~ and foremost, he is a writer** zuallererst ist er Schriftsteller **(c)** (= *for the ~ time*) zum ersten Mal; **when this model was ~ introduced** zu Anfang, als das Modell herauskam; **when it ~ became known that ...** als erstmals bekannt wurde, dass ...; **this work was ~ performed/published in 1997** dieses Werk wurde 1997 uraufgeführt/erstveröffentlicht **(d)** (= *before: in time*) (zu)erst; **I must finish this ~** ich muss das erst fertig machen **(e)** (*in preference*) eher, lieber; **I'd die ~!** eher *or* lieber würde ich sterben! **(f)** (*Naut, Rail*) **to travel ~** erster Klasse reisen **3** N **(a)** **the ~** der/die/das Erste; (= *former*) der/die/das Erstere; **he was among the (very) ~ to arrive** er war unter den Ersten, die ankamen; **he was the ~ home/to finish** er war als Erster zu Hause/fertig; (*in race*) er ging als Erster durchs Ziel;

this is the ~ I've heard of it das ist mir ja ganz neu; **the ~ he knew about it was when he saw it in the paper** er hat erst davon erfahren, als er es in der Zeitung las; **at ~** zuerst, zunächst; **from the ~** von Anfang an; **it's a ~** (= ~ *time ever done*) es ist das allererste Mal(, das so was gemacht wird); **it's a ~ for me/the firm** (= *new experience*) ich habe/die Firma hat noch nie so etwas gemacht
(b) (*Brit Univ*) Eins *f*; **he got a ~** er bestand (sein Examen) mit „Eins" *or* „sehr gut"
(c) (*Aut*) ~ **(gear)** der erste (Gang); **in ~** im ersten (Gang)
(d) (*US Baseball*) erstes Base *or* Mal

first: **first aid** N erste Hilfe; **first-aid kit** N Verband(s)kasten *m*; **first-born 1** ADJ erstgeboren **2** N Erstgeborene(r) *mf*; **first class 1** N erste Klasse **2** ADJ PRED **that's absolutely ~!** das ist einfach Spitze! (*inf*); **first-class 1** ADJ ATTR **(a)** (= *excellent*) erstklassig; **he's a ~ cook** er ist ein erstklassiger Koch **(b)** *flight, train, ticket* erster Klasse; **a ~ compartment** ein Erste-Klasse-Abteil *nt*; **~ passengers** Reisende *pl* in der ersten Klasse **(c)** (*Post*) ~ **postage/stamp** *Porto/Briefmarke für die bevorzugt beförderte Post*; **~ letter** *bevorzugt beförderter Brief* **(d)** (*Brit Univ*) ~ **(honours) degree** Examen *nt* mit „Eins" *or* „sehr gut"; **he graduated with ~ honours** er machte sein Examen mit „Eins" *or* „sehr gut" **2** ADV **(a)** *travel, fly* erster Klasse **(b)** (*Post*) **to send sth ~** etw mit der bevorzugt beförderten Post schicken; **first cousin** N Cousin *m*/Cousine *f* ersten Grades; **first edition** N Erstausgabe *f*; **first form** N (*Brit Sch*) erste Klasse; **first-former** N (*Brit Sch*) Erstklässler(in) *m(f)*; **first-hand 1** ADJ aus erster Hand; **to have ~ knowledge of sth** etw aus eigener Erfahrung kennen; **they have ~ experience of charitable organizations** sie haben persönlich Erfahrungen mit Wohlfahrtsverbänden gemacht **2** ADV *hear, experience, witness* persönlich; *see* mit eigenen Augen; **first-in-first-out costing** N Fifo-Kostenerfassung *f*; **First Lady** N First Lady *f*; **first language** N Muttersprache *f*; **first-line management** N unterste Führungsebene, unteres Management

firstly ['fɜːstlɪ] ADV zuerst; **why can't I? – well, ~ it's not yours and secondly …** warum denn nicht? – nun, zunächst *or* erstens einmal gehört es nicht dir und zweitens …

first: **First Minister** N (*Brit Pol*) Erster Minister, Erste Ministerin; **first name** N Vorname *m*; **they're on ~ terms** sie reden sich mit Vornamen an; **first night** N (*Theat*) Premiere *f*; **first person** N erste Person; **the ~ plural** die erste Person Plural; **the ~ story is in the** = die Geschichte wird von einem Icherzähler/einer Icherzählerin erzählt; **first-rate** ADJ erstklassig; **first thing 1** N she just says the ~ that comes into her head sie sagt einfach das, was ihr zuerst einfällt; **the ~ (to do) is to** … als Erstes muss man …; **the ~ to remember is that she hates formality** man muss vor allem daran denken, dass sie Förmlichkeit nicht mag; **~s first** eins nach dem anderen; (= *most important first*) das Wichtigste zuerst; **he doesn't know the ~ about it/cars** davon/von Autos hat er nicht die geringste Ahnung **2** ADV gleich; **I'll go ~ in the morning** ich gehe gleich morgen früh; **I'm not at my best ~ (in the morning)** früh am Morgen bin ich nicht gerade in Hochform; **first-time buyer** N *jd, der zum ersten Mal ein Haus/ eine Wohnung kauft*, Erstkäufer(in) *m(f)*; **First World War** N **the ~** der Erste Weltkrieg

fir tree N Tannenbaum *m*

fiscal ['fɪskəl] ADJ finanziell; *measures* finanzpolitisch; **~ crisis/ policy** Finanzkrise/-politik *f*; **~ reform** Steuerreform *f*

fiscal year N (*Fin*) Geschäftsjahr *nt*

fish [fɪʃ] **1** N, *pl* - *or* (*esp for different types*) -es Fisch *m*; **to drink like a ~** (*inf*) wie ein Loch saufen (*inf*); **like a ~ out of water** wie ein Fisch auf dem Trockenen; **there are plenty more ~ in the sea** (*fig inf*) es gibt noch mehr (davon) auf der Welt **2** VI fischen; (*with rod*) angeln; **to go ~ing** fischen/angeln gehen

➤ **fish for** VI +PREP OBJ **(a)** (*lit*) fischen; (*with rod*) angeln **(b)** (*fig*) *compliments* fischen nach; **they were fishing for information** sie waren auf Informationen aus

➤ **fish out** VT SEP herausfischen *or* -angeln (*of or from sth* aus etw)

fish: **fishbone** N (Fisch)gräte *f*; **fish cake** N Fischfrikadelle *f*

fisherman ['fɪʃəmən] N, *pl* -**men** [-mən] Fischer *m*; (*amateur*) Angler *m*

fish: **fish farm** N Fischzucht(anlage) *f*; **fishfinger** N Fischstäbchen *nt*; **fish-hook** N Angelhaken *m*

---

fishing ['fɪʃɪŋ] N Fischen *nt*; (*with rod*) Angeln *nt*; (*as industry*) Fischerei *f*

fishing: **fishing boat** N Fischerboot *nt*; **fishing net** N Fischnetz *nt*; **fishing rod** N Angelrute *f*; **fishing tackle** N (*for sport*) Angelgeräte *pl*

fish: **fish knife** N Fischmesser *nt*; **fishmonger** ['fɪʃmʌŋɡəʳ] N (*Brit*) Fischhändler(in) *m(f)*; **fishmonger's** N (*Brit*) Fischgeschäft *nt*; **fishnet stockings** PL Netzstrümpfe *pl*; **fish pond** N Fischteich *m*; **fish slice** N (*for serving*) Fischvorlegemesser *nt*; **fish stick** N (*US*) = **fishfinger**; **fish tank** N (*in house*) Aquarium *nt*

fishy ['fɪʃɪ] ADJ (+ER) **(a)** ~ **smell** Fischgeruch *m* **(b)** (*inf*) verdächtig; *excuse, story* faul (*inf*); **something ~ is going on here** ist was faul (*inf*)

fission ['fɪʃən] N (*Phys*) Spaltung *f*

fissure ['fɪʃəʳ] N Riss *m*; (*deep*) Kluft *f*; (*narrow*) Spalt *m*

fist [fɪst] N Faust *f*

fistful ['fɪstfʊl] N Hand *f* voll; **a ~ of pound coins** eine Hand voll Pfundmünzen

fit¹ [fɪt] **1** ADJ (+ER) **(a)** (= *suitable*) geeignet; **~ to eat** essbar; **~ to drink** trinkbar; **~ for habitation** *or* **to live in** bewohnbar; **she's not ~ to be a mother** sie ist als Mutter völlig ungeeignet **(b)** (= *right and proper*) richtig, angebracht; **I'll do as I think** *or* **see ~** wie ich es für richtig halte; **to see ~ to do sth** es für richtig *or* angebracht halten, etw zu tun; **he did not see ~ to cooperate** er hat es nicht für nötig gehalten zu kooperieren **(c)** (*in health*) gesund; *sportsman etc* fit, in Form; **she is not yet ~ to travel** sie ist noch nicht reisefähig **(d)** **to be ~ to drop** (*Brit*) zum Umfallen müde sein **2** N (*of clothes*) Passform *f*; **it is a very good/bad ~** es sitzt *or* passt wie angegossen/nicht gut; **it's a bit of a tight ~** (*clothes*) es ist etwas eng; (*timing, parking*) es geht gerade (noch) **3** VT **(a)** (*cover, sheet etc*) passen auf (+*acc*); (*clothes etc*) passen in (+*acc*); (*key etc*) passen in (+*acc*); **"one size ~s all"** „Einheitsgröße"; **that part won't ~ this machine** das Teil passt nicht für diese Maschine; **she was ~ted for her wedding dress** ihr Hochzeitskleid wurde ihr angepasst **(b)** *sb's plans, a theory etc* passen in (+*acc*); *needs* erfüllen; *mood* passen zu **(c)** (= *put on, attach*) anbringen (*to an* +*dat*); *double glazing* einsetzen; (= *put in*) einbauen (*in in* +*acc*); (= *furnish, provide with*) ausstatten; **to ~ a car with an alarm** eine Alarmanlage in ein Auto einbauen; **to have a new kitchen ~ted** eine neue Küche einbauen lassen **(d)** *facts, circumstances* entsprechen (+*dat*); **to make the punishment ~ the crime** eine dem Vergehen angemessene Strafe verhängen **4** VI **(a)** (*dress etc, key*) passen **(b)** (= *correspond*) zusammenstimmen *or* -passen; **the facts don't ~** die Fakten sind widersprüchlich; **it all ~s** es passt alles zusammen

➤ **fit in 1** VT SEP **(a)** (= *find space for*) unterbringen; **you can fit five people into this car** in diesem Auto haben fünf Personen Platz **(b)** (= *find time for*) *person* einen Termin geben (+*dat*); *meeting* unterbringen; (= *squeeze in*) einschieben; **Sir Charles could fit you in at 3 o'clock** um 3 Uhr hätte Sir Charles Zeit für Sie **(c)** (= *make harmonize*) **to fit sth in with sth** etw mit etw in Einklang bringen **(d)** (= *fit, put in*) einbauen **2** VI **(a)** (= *go into place*) hineinpassen; **the clothes won't fit in(to) the case** die Sachen passen nicht in den Koffer **(b)** (*plans, ideas, word*) passen; (*facts etc*) übereinstimmen; (= *match*) dazupassen; **how does this fit in?** wie passt das ins Ganze?; **to fit in with** (*plans, ideas*) in etw (*acc*) passen; (*facts*) mit etw übereinstimmen; (= *match*) zu etw passen; **he doesn't fit in here/with the others/with such a firm** er passt nicht hierhin/zu den anderen/in eine solche Firma

➤ **fit on 1** VI **(a)** (= *be right size, shape*) passen **(b)** (= *be fixed*) befestigt *or* angebracht sein **2** VT SEP (= *put in place, fix on*) anbringen

➤ **fit out** VT SEP *ship* ausstatten; *person (for an expedition)* ausrüsten; (*with clothes etc*) ausstatten; **they've fitted one room out as an office** sie haben eines der Zimmer als Büro eingerichtet

➤ **fit up** VT SEP **to fit sb/sth up with sth** jdn/etw mit etw versehen *or* ausstatten

fit² N (*Med, fig*) Anfall *m*; ~ **of coughing** Hustenanfall *m*; **in a ~ of anger** in einem Anfall von Wut; **in** *or* **by ~s and starts** stoßweise; **to be in ~s (of laughter)** sich vor Lachen biegen *or* kugeln (*inf*); **he'd have a ~** (*fig inf*) er würde (ja) einen Anfall kriegen (*inf*)

fitful ['fɪtfʊl] ADJ unbeständig; *working, progress* stoßweise; *sleep* unruhig

fitfully ['fɪtfəlɪ] ADV *sleep* unruhig; *work* sporadisch

fitness ['fɪtnɪs] N (= *health*) Gesundheit *f*; (= *condition*) Fitness *f*

fitted ['fɪtɪd] ADJ **(a) to be ~ with sth** (*room, vehicle*) mit etw ausgestattet sein **(b)** (= *built-in*) Einbau-; *bedroom, bathroom* mit Einbauelementen; ~ **wardrobe/cupboard** Einbauschrank *m*; ~ **units** Einbauelemente *pl*; ~ **kitchen** Einbauküche *f* **(c)** *jacket, shirt* tailliert; ~ **carpet** (*Brit*) Teppichboden *m*; ~ **sheet** Spannbetttuch *nt* **(d)** (*form:* = *suited*) **to be ~ to do sth** sich dazu eignen, etw zu tun

fitter ['fɪtə'] N (*Tech: for machines*) (Maschinen)schlosser(in) *m(f)*

fitting ['fɪtɪŋ] ❶ ADJ passend; *punishment, reward* angemessen ❷ N **(a)** Anprobe *f*; (= *putting on*) Anbringen *nt*; (*of tyre, lock*) Montage *f*; (= *putting in*) Einbau *m*; (= *furnishing*) Ausstatten *nt* **(b)** (= *part*) Zubehörteil *nt*; ~**s** Ausstattung *f*; = *furniture also*) Einrichtung *f*; (= *pipes*) Installation *f*; **bathroom/office ~s** Badezimmer-/Büroeinrichtung *f*; **electrical ~s** Elektroinstallationen *pl*

fittingly ['fɪtɪŋlɪ] ADV (+*adj*) angemessen; *name* passend

fitting room N Anproberaum *m*; (= *cubicle*) Anprobekabine *f*

five [faɪv] ❶ ADJ fünf ❷ N Fünf *f*; *see also* **six**

five: five-and-dime, five-and-ten N (*US*) billiges Kaufhaus; **five-a-side** ADJ *football* mit fünf Spielern pro Mannschaft; **fivefold** ❶ ADJ fünffach ❷ ADV um das Fünffache

fiver ['faɪvə'] N (*inf*) Fünfpfund-/Fünfdollarschein *m*

five: five-spot N (*US inf*) Fünfdollarschein *m*; **five-star hotel** N Fünf-Sterne-Hotel *nt*

fix [fɪks] ❶ VT **(a)** (= *make firm*) befestigen, festmachen (*sth to sth* etw an/auf etw *dat*); (*fig*) *ideas, images* verankern; **to ~ sth in one's mind** sich (*dat*) etw fest einprägen **(b)** *eyes, attention* richten (*on, upon* auf +*acc*); *gun, camera, radar* richten (*on* auf +*acc*); **all eyes were/everybody's attention was ~ed on her** alle sahen sie wie gebannt an **(c)** *date, price, limit, risk* festlegen; (= *agree on*) ausmachen; **nothing has been ~ed yet** es ist noch nichts festgelegt (ausgemacht *or* beschlossen worden) **(d)** (= *arrange*) arrangieren; *tickets, taxi etc* besorgen, organisieren (*inf*); **have you got anything ~ed for tonight?** haben Sie (für) heute Abend schon etwas vor? **(e)** (*inf:* = *get even with, sort out*) **I'll ~ him** dem werd ichs besorgen (*inf*) **(f)** (= *repair, sort out*) in Ordnung bringen; (= *put in good order, adjust*) machen (*inf*) **(g)** *drink, meal* machen; **to ~ one's hair/face** sich frisieren/ schminken **(h)** (*inf*) *race, fight, jury* manipulieren; *prices* absprechen; **the whole thing was ~ed** das war eine abgekartete Sache (*inf*) ❷ VI (*US inf:* = *intend*) **I'm ~ing to get married soon** ich habe vor, bald zu heiraten ❸ N **(a)** (*inf*) **to be in a ~** in der Patsche *or* Klemme sitzen (*inf*) **(b)** (*inf: of drugs*) Druck *m* (*sl*); **I need my daily ~ of chocolate** (*inf*) ich brauche meine tägliche Schokoladenration **(c)** (*inf*) **the fight/competition was a ~** der Kampf/ Wettbewerb war eine abgekartete Sache (*inf*)

➤ **fix on** ❶ VT SEP festmachen (*prep obj* auf +*dat*); (= *fit on*) anbringen ❷ VI +PREP OBJ (= *decide on*) sich entscheiden für

➤ **fix together** VT SEP zusammenmachen (*inf*)

➤ **fix up** VT SEP **(a)** (= *arrange*) arrangieren; *holidays etc* festmachen; (= *book*) buchen; **have you got anything fixed up for this evening?** haben Sie (für) heute Abend schon etwas vor? **(b) to fix sb up with sth** jdm etw besorgen *or* verschaffen **(c)** *room, house* einrichten

fixation [fɪk'seɪʃən] N (*Psych*) Fixierung *f*; **she has a ~ about** *or* **on cleanliness** sie hat einen Sauberkeitsfimmel (*inf*)

fixative ['fɪksətɪv] N Fixativ *nt*

fixed [fɪkst] ADJ **(a)** *amount, time* fest(gesetzt); *position* unveränderlich; *debenture* festverzinslich; **there's no ~ agenda** es gibt keine feste Tagesordnung; **of no ~ abode** *or* **address** (*Jur*) ohne festen Wohnsitz; ~ **assets** (*Econ*) Anlagevermögen *nt*; ~ **exchange rate** (*Econ*) fester

Wechselkurs; ~ **interest loan** festverzinsliches Darlehen; ~ **period loan** Kredit *m* mit fester Laufzeit; ~ **price** Festpreis *m*; ~ **rate** (*Fin*) fester Zinssatz, Festzins *m*; ~ **mortgage rate** festverzinsliches Hypothekendarlehen; ~ **penalty (fine)** pauschale Geldbuße **(b)** *idea* fest; *smile, grin* starr; **a ~ stare** ein starrer Blick **(c)** (= *rigged*) *election, game* manipuliert; **the whole thing was ~** das war eine abgekartete Sache (*inf*) **(d)** (*inf*) **how are we ~ for time?** wie siehts mit der Zeit aus?; **how are you ~ for food/money etc?** wie siehts bei dir mit Essen/Geld etc aus?

fixed: fixed assets PL (*Comm*) feste Anlagen *pl*; **fixed costs** PL (*Comm*) Fixkosten *pl*; **fixed-interest** ADJ ~ **loan** Festzinsanleihe *f*

fixedly ['fɪksɪdlɪ] ADV starr

fixed-rate ['fɪkstreɪt] ADJ Festzins-; ~ **mortgage** Festzinshypothek *f*

fixer ['fɪksə'] N (*Phot*) Fixiermittel *nt*

fixings ['fɪksɪŋz] PL (*US Cook*) Beilagen *pl*

fixture ['fɪkstʃə'] N **(a)** ~**s** Ausstattung *f*; ~**s and fittings** Anschlüsse und unbewegliches Inventar (*form*) **(b)** (*Brit Sport*) Spiel *nt*

fizz [fɪz] VI perlen

fizzle ['fɪzl] VI zischen

➤ **fizzle out** VI (*firework, enthusiasm*) verpuffen; (*rocket*) vorzeitig verglühen; (*plan*) im Sande verlaufen

fizzy ['fɪzɪ] ADJ (+ER) sprudelnd; **to be ~** sprudeln; **a ~ drink** eine Brause

fjord [fjɔːd] N Fjord *m*

F key N (*Comput*) Funktionstaste *f*

flab [flæb] N (*inf*) Speck *m*; **to fight the ~** (*hum*) etwas für die schlanke Linie tun

flabbergast ['flæbəgɑːst] VT (*inf*) verblüffen; **I was ~ed to see him/at the price** ich war platt *or* von den Socken, als ich ihn sah/als ich den Preis erfuhr (*inf*)

flabby ['flæbɪ] ADJ (+ER) schlaff; **he's getting ~ (round the middle)** er setzt (um die Taille) Speck an

flag¹ [flæg] N Fahne *f*; (*small, on map, for charity etc*) Fähnchen *nt*; (*Naut*) Flagge *f*; **to fly the ~ (for)** (*fig*) die Fahne hochhalten (für)

➤ **flag down** VT SEP *taxi etc, person* anhalten

➤ **flag up** VT SEP (*inf*) markieren

flag² VI erlahmen; (*interest, strength etc also*) nachlassen; **he's ~ging** er lässt nach; (= *he is tiring*) er wird müde

flag³ N (*also* ~**stone**) Steinplatte *f*

flag day N **(a)** (*Brit*) Tag, an dem eine Straßensammlung für einen wohltätigen Zweck durchgeführt wird **(b) Flag Day** (*US*) 14. Juni, Gedenktag der Einführung der amerikanischen Nationalflagge

flagged [flægd] ADJ *floor* gefliest

flagon ['flægən] N (= *bottle*) Flasche *f*; (= *jug*) Krug *m*

flagpole ['flægpəʊl] N Fahnenstange *f*

flagrant ['fleɪgrənt] ADJ eklatant; *injustice, crime also* himmelschreiend; *disregard* unverhohlen

flagrantly ['fleɪgrəntlɪ] ADV ganz eindeutig *or* offensichtlich

flag: flagship ❶ N (*lit, fig*) Flaggschiff *nt* ❷ ADJ ATTR Vorzeige-; ~ **store** Vorzeigeladen *m*; **flagstaff** N Fahnenmast *m*; **flagstone** N (Stein)platte *f*; (*on floor also*) Fliese *f*; **flag-waving** N Hurrapatriotismus *m*

flail [fleɪl] ❶ VT **he ~ed his arms about** *or* **around wildly** er schlug wild (mit den Armen) um sich ❷ VI **to ~ (about)** herumfuchteln

flair [fleə'] N (*for selecting the best etc*) Gespür *nt*; (= *talent*) Talent *nt*; (= *stylishness*) Flair *nt*; **his great ~ for business** sein großes Geschäftstalent

flak [flæk] N (*fig*) **he's been getting a lot of ~ (for it)** er ist (dafür) mächtig unter Beschuss geraten (*inf*)

flake [fleɪk] ❶ N (*of snow, soap*) Flocke *f*; (*of paint, rust*) Splitter *m*; (*of plaster*) abgebröckeltes Stückchen; (*of skin*) Schuppe *f*; (*of fish*) Stückchen *nt* Fischfleisch; (*of chocolate*) Raspel *m* ❷ VI (*stone, plaster etc*) abbröckeln; (*paint*) abblättern

➤ **flake off** VI (*plaster*) abbröckeln; (*paint, rust etc*) abblättern; (*skin*) sich schälen

➤ **flake out** VI (*inf*) (= *become exhausted*) abschlaffen (*inf*); (= *pass out*) umkippen; (= *fall asleep*) einpennen (*inf*)

flak jacket N kugelsichere Weste

flaky [ˈfleɪkɪ] ADJ (+ER) **(a)** *paint, plaster etc* brüchig; *crust* blättrig; *skin* schuppig **(b)** (*esp US:* = *mad, eccentric*) verrückt

flaky pastry N Blätterteig *m*

flamboyance [flæmˈbɔɪəns] N Extravaganz *f*

flamboyant [flæmˈbɔɪənt] ADJ extravagant; *gesture* großartig

flamboyantly [flæmˈbɔɪəntlɪ] ADV extravagant

flame [fleɪm] **1** N **(a)** Flamme *f*; **the house was in ~s** das Haus stand in Flammen **(b)** (*Comput*) Flame *f*, (persönlicher) Angriff **2** VT (*Comput*) **to ~ sb** jdm eine Flame schicken

➤ **flame up** VI **(a)** (*fire*) auflodern **(b)** (*fig: anger etc*) aufflammen

flamenco [fləˈmeŋkəʊ] **1** N Flamenco *m* **2** ADJ Flamenco-; **~ dancer** Flamencotänzer(in) *m(f)*

flame retardant [ˈfleɪmrɪˈtɑːdənt] ADJ feuerhemmend

flaming [ˈfleɪmɪŋ] ADJ **(a)** lodernd; **he has ~ red hair** er hat feuerrotes Haar; **to have a ~ row (with sb)** sich (mit jdm) streiten, dass die Fetzen fliegen (*inf*) **(b)** (*Brit inf:* = *bloody*) verdammt (*inf*); **it's a ~ nuisance** Mensch, das ist vielleicht ein Mist (*inf*)

flamingo [fləˈmɪŋgəʊ] N, *pl* **-(e)s** Flamingo *m*

flammable [ˈflæməbl] ADJ feuergefährlich

flan [flæn] N Kuchen *m*; **fruit ~** Obstkuchen *m*

flan case N Tortenboden *m*

flank [flæŋk] **1** N (*of animal, Mil*) Flanke *f*; (*of mountain, building*) Seite *f* **2** VT flankieren

flannel [ˈflænl] **1** N **(a)** Flanell *m* **(b)** (*Brit:* = *face ~*) Waschlappen *m* **(c)** (*Brit inf:* = *waffle*) Geschwafel *nt* (*inf*) **(d) flannels** PL (= *trousers*) Flanellhose *f* **2** ADJ Flanell-

flannelette [flænəˈlet] N (*Brit*) Baumwollflanell *m*; **~ sheet** Biberbetttuch *nt*

flap [flæp] **1** N **(a)** (*of pocket*) Klappe *f*; (*of table*) ausziehbarer Teil; (*of tent*) Eingang *m*; (*Aviat*) (Lande)klappe *f* **(b)** (*Brit inf*) helle Aufregung; **to get in(to) a ~** in helle Aufregung geraten **2** VI **(a)** (*wings, shutters*) schlagen; (*sails, tarpaulin etc*) flattern; **his coat ~ped about his legs** der Mantel schlackerte ihm um die Beine (*inf*) **(b)** (*Brit inf*) in heller Aufregung sein; **don't ~** reg dich nicht auf **3** VT **to ~ its wings** mit den Flügeln schlagen; **to ~ one's arms** mit den Armen rudern

flapjack [ˈflæpdʒæk] N (*US*) Pfannkuchen *m*; (*Brit*) Haferkeks *m*

flare [fleə] **1** N **(a)** (= *signal*) Leuchtsignal *nt*; (*from pistol etc*) Leuchtrakete *f*; (= *fire, landing ~*) Leuchtfeuer *nt* **(b)** (*Fashion*) **a skirt with a slight ~** ein leicht ausgestellter Rock; **(a pair of) ~s** (*Brit inf*) eine Hose mit Schlag, eine Schlaghose *f* **2** VI **(a)** (*match*) aufleuchten **(b)** (*trousers, skirts*) ausgestellt sein **(c)** (*fig: trouble, violence*) aufflammen; **tempers ~d** die Gemüter erhitzten sich

➤ **flare up** VI (*lit, fig: situation, affair*) aufflackern; (*fig*) (*person*) aufbrausen, auffahren; (*injury*) wieder Schwierigkeiten machen; (*fighting, epidemic*) ausbrechen; **his acne flared up** seine Akne trat wieder auf; **she flared up at me** sie fuhr mich an

flared [fleəd] ADJ *trousers, skirt* ausgestellt

flash [flæʃ] **1** N **(a)** (*of light*) Aufblinken *nt no pl*; (*very bright*) Aufblitzen *nt no pl*; (*of metal, jewels etc*) Blitzen *nt no pl*; **there was a sudden ~ of light** plötzlich blitzte es hell auf; **~ of lightning** Blitz *m*; **three short ~es is the Morse sign for S** dreimal kurz blinken ist *or* drei kurze Blinkzeichen sind das Morsezeichen für S **(b)** (*fig:* = *newsflash*) Kurzmeldung *f*; **~ of colour** (*Brit*) *or* **color** (*US*) Farbtupfer *m*; **~ of wit/inspiration** Geistesblitz *m*; **in a ~** wie der Blitz; **as quick as a ~** blitzschnell; **a ~ in the pan** (*inf*) ein Strohfeuer *nt* **(c)** (*Mil: on uniform*) Abzeichen *nt* **(d)** (*Phot*) Blitz(licht *nt*) *m*; **to use a ~** Blitzlicht benutzen **(e)** (*US inf:* = *torch*) Taschenlampe *f* **2** VI **(a)** (*light*) aufblinken; (*very brightly*) aufblitzen; (*repeatedly*) blinken; (*metal, jewels, teeth*) blitzen; (*Mot*) die Lichthupe benutzen; **to ~ on and off** immer wieder aufblinken **(b)** (= *move quickly*) **to ~ past** *or* **by** vorbeisausen *etc*; (*holidays etc*) vorbeifliegen; **the thought ~ed through my mind that ...** mir kam plötzlich der Gedanke, dass ..., es schoss mir durch

den Kopf, dass ... **3** VT **(a)** *light* aufblitzen *or* aufleuchten lassen; *SOS, message* blinken; **to ~ a torch on sb** jdn mit der Taschenlampe anleuchten; **to ~ one's headlights at sb**, **to ~ sb** jdn mit der Lichthupe anblinken; **she ~ed him a look of contempt/gratitude** sie blitzte ihn verächtlich/dankbar an **(b)** (*inf:* = *show, wave: also* **~ around**) protzen mit; *diamond ring* blitzen lassen; *identity card* kurz vorzeigen; **don't ~ all that money around** wedel nicht so mit dem vielen Geld herum (*inf*) **4** ADJ (*inf*) (= *showy*) protzig (*pej*); (= *smart*) schick

➤ **flash back** VI (*Film*) zurückblenden (*to auf +acc*); **his mind flashed back to the events of the last year** er erinnerte sich plötzlich an die Ereignisse des letzten Jahres

flash: flashback N (*Film*) Rückblende *f*; **flash card** N (*Sch*) Leselernkarte *f*

flasher [ˈflæʃə] N (*inf*) Exhibitionist(in) *m(f)*

flash: flash flood N flutartige Überschwemmung; **flash gun** N Elektronenblitzgerät *nt*; **flashlight** N (*esp US*) Taschenlampe *f*; **flash point** N (*fig*) Siedepunkt *m*

flashy [ˈflæʃɪ] ADJ (+ER) auffallend, auffällig

flask [flɑːsk] N (*Chem*) Glaskolben *m*; (= *hip ~*) Flachmann *m* (*inf*); (= *vacuum ~*) Thermosflasche *f*

flat¹ [flæt] **1** ADJ (+ER) **(a)** flach; *tyre, nose, feet* platt; *surface* eben; **he stood ~ against the wall** er stand platt gegen die Wand gedrückt; **as ~ as a pancake** (*inf*) (*tyre*) total platt; (*countryside*) total flach; **~ roof** Flachdach *nt*; **to fall ~ on one's face** auf die Nase fallen; **to lie ~** flach *or* platt liegen **(b)** (*fig*) fade; *joke* abgedroschen; *trade, market* lustlos; *battery* leer; *beer* schal; **to fall ~** (*joke*) nicht ankommen; (*play etc*) durchfallen **(c)** *refusal, denial* deutlich **(d)** (*Mus*) *instrument* zu tief (gestimmt); *voice* zu tief **(e)** (*Comm*) Pauschal-; **~ rate** Pauschale *f*; **to get a ~ rate of pay** pauschal bezahlt werden; **~ rate allowance** (*in taxation*) Grundfreibetrag *m* **2** ADV **(a)** *turn down, refuse* kategorisch; **he told me ~ (out) that ...** er sagte mir klipp und klar, dass ...; **in ten seconds ~** in sage und schreibe (nur) zehn Sekunden; **~ broke** (*inf*) total pleite (*inf*); **to go ~ out** voll aufdrehen (*inf*); **to work** *or* **go ~ out** auf Hochtouren arbeiten **(b)** (*Mus*) **to sing/play ~** zu tief singen/spielen **3** N **(a)** (*of hand*) Fläche *f*; (*of blade*) flache Seite **(b)** (*Mus*) Erniedrigungszeichen *nt*, b *nt* **(c)** (*Aut*) Platte(r) *m* (*inf*)

flat² N (*esp Brit*) Wohnung *f*

flat: flat-chested ADJ flachbrüstig; **flat feet** PL Plattfüße *pl*; **flatfish** N Plattfisch *m*; **flat-hunting** N (*Brit*) Wohnungssuche *f*; **to go/be ~** auf Wohnungssuche gehen/sein

flatly [ˈflætlɪ] ADV *refuse, deny, reject* kategorisch; *contradict* aufs Schärfste; **to be ~ against** *or* **opposed to sth** etw rundweg ablehnen; (*in principle*) kategorisch gegen etw sein

flatmate [ˈflætmeɪt] N (*Brit*) Mitbewohner(in) *m(f)*

flatness [ˈflætnɪs] N (*of surface*) Ebenheit *f*

flat: flat-pack ADJ **~ furniture** Möbel *pl* zur Selbstmontage; **flat racing** N Flachrennen *nt*; **flat screen** N (*Comput*) Flachbildschirm *m*

flatten [ˈflætn] **1** VT **(a)** *path, field* ebnen; *metal* flach *or* platt hämmern; (*storm etc*) *crops* niederdrücken; *trees* umwerfen; *town* dem Erdboden gleichmachen **(b)** (*fig*) (= *defeat*) vernichtend schlagen; (= *knock down*) niederschlagen **2** VR **to ~ oneself against sth** sich platt gegen *or* an etw drücken

➤ **flatten out 1** VI (*countryside*) flach(er) werden; (*road*) eben(er) werden; (*fig*) (*inflation, demand*) abflachen; (*prices*) nicht mehr so stark steigen **2** VT SEP *path* ebnen; *paper, fabric* glätten

flatter [ˈflætə] VT schmeicheln (+*dat*); **I was very ~ed by his remark** ich fühlte mich von seiner Bemerkung sehr geschmeichelt; **don't ~ yourself!** bilde dir ja nichts ein!

flatterer [ˈflætərə] N Schmeichler(in) *m(f)*

flattering [ˈflætərɪŋ] ADJ schmeichelhaft; *clothes, colour* vorteilhaft

flattery [ˈflætərɪ] N Schmeicheleien *pl*

flatulence [ˈflætjʊləns] N Blähung(en) *f(pl)*; **to cause ~** Blähungen verursachen

flatware ['flætweə'] N (*US*) (= *cutlery*) Besteck *nt*; (= *plates etc*) Geschirr *nt*

flaunt [flɔːnt] VT zur Schau stellen; **to ~ oneself** sich groß in Szene setzen

flautist ['flɔːtɪst] N Flötist(in) *m(f)*

flavour, (*US*) **flavor** ['fleɪvə'] **1** N (= *taste*) Geschmack *m*; (= *flavouring*) Aroma *nt*; (*fig*) Beigeschmack *m*; **strawberry-~ice cream** Eis *nt* mit Erdbeergeschmack; **the film gives the ~ of Paris in the twenties** der Film vermittelt die Atmosphäre des Paris der zwanziger Jahre; **he/it is ~ of the month** (*inf*) er/es ist diesen Monat in (*inf*) **2** VT Geschmack verleihen (+*dat*) or geben (+*dat*); **pineapple-~ed** mit Ananasgeschmack

flavouring, (*US*) **flavoring** ['fleɪvərɪŋ] N (*Cook*) Aroma(stoff *m*) *nt*; **vanilla/rum ~** Vanille-/Rumaroma *nt*

flavourless, (*US*) **flavorless** ['fleɪvəlɪs] ADJ geschmacklos

flaw [flɔː] **1** N (*lit*) Fehler *m*; (*in sb's character also*) Mangel *m* **2** VT **her argument was ~ed by lack of evidence** ihr Argument wurde durch Mangel an Beweisen entkräftet

flawed [flɔːd] ADJ fehlerhaft; **his logic was ~** seine Logik enthielt Fehler

flawless ['flɔːlɪs] ADJ *performance* fehlerlos; *behaviour* tadellos; *complexion* makellos; **~ English** fehlerloses Englisch

flax [flæks] N (*Bot*) Flachs *m*

flay [fleɪ] VT (a) (= *skin*) häuten; (= *whip*) auspeitschen; **to ~ sb alive** jdn gründlich verdreschen (b) (*fig*: = *criticize*) kein gutes Haar lassen an (+*dat*)

flea [fliː] N Floh *m*

flea: **flea-bitten** ADJ (*inf*) vergammelt (*inf*); **flea collar** N Flohhalsband *nt*; **flea market** N Flohmarkt *m*; **fleapit** N (*Brit inf*) Flohkino *nt* (*inf*)

fleck [flek] **1** N (*of red etc*) Tupfen *m*; (*of mud, paint*) (= *blotch*) Fleck(en) *m*; (= *speckle*) Spritzer *m*; (*of fluff, dust*) Teilchen *nt* **2** VT **~ed wool** melierte Wolle; **blue ~ed with white** blau mit weißen Tupfen or Punkten

fled [fled] PRET, PTP *of* **flee**

fledgling ['fledʒlɪŋ] **1** N (*Orn*) Jungvogel *m* **2** ADJ *democracy, organization* jung; *person* frisch gebacken (*inf*); **~ artist** Nachwuchskünstler(in) *m(f)*; **~ teacher/writer** Junglehrer(in) *m(f)*/-autor(in) *m(f)*

flee [fliː], pret, ptp **fled 1** VI fliehen (*from* vor +*dat*) **2** VT *town, country* fliehen aus; *temptation, danger* entfliehen (+*dat*)

fleece [fliːs] **1** N Vlies *nt*; (= *fabric, natural, artificial*) Webpelz *m* **2** VT (*fig inf*) **to ~ sb** (*out of his/her money*) jdn schröpfen

fleecy ['fliːsɪ] ADJ flauschig

fleet [fliːt] N (a) (*Naut*) Geschwader *nt*; (= *entire naval force*) Flotte *f* (b) (*of cars etc*) (Fuhr)park *m*; **he owns a ~ of trucks/taxis** er hat einen Lastwagenpark/ein Taxiunternehmen; **~ policy** (*Insur*) Flottenpolice *f*

fleeting ['fliːtɪŋ] ADJ flüchtig; **a ~ visit** eine Stippvisite (*inf*); **to catch or get a ~ glimpse of sb/sth** einen flüchtigen Blick auf jdn/etw werfen können

Flemish ['flemɪʃ] **1** ADJ flämisch **2** N (*Ling*) Flämisch *nt*

flesh [fleʃ] N (*lit, fig*) Fleisch *nt*; (*of fruit*) (Frucht)fleisch *nt*; (*of vegetable*) Mark *nt*; **to put on ~** zunehmen; **one's own ~ and blood** sein eigen(es) Fleisch und Blut; **I'm only ~ and blood** ich bin auch nur aus Fleisch und Blut; **in the ~** in Person; **to put ~ on an idea** eine Idee ausgestalten

➤ **flesh out** VT SEP ausgestalten; *details* eingehen auf (+*acc*)

flesh: **flesh-coloured**, (*US*) **flesh-colored** ADJ fleischfarben; **flesh wound** N Fleischwunde *f*

fleshy ['fleʃɪ] ADJ (+ER) *face, cheeks* fleischig; *person* füllig

flew [fluː] PRET *of* **fly²**

flex [fleks] **1** N (*Brit*) Schnur *f*; (*heavy duty*) Kabel *nt* **2** VT *body, knees, arm etc* beugen; **to ~ one's muscles** (*lit, fig*) seine Muskeln spielen lassen

flexibility [ˌfleksɪ'bɪlɪtɪ] N (a) (*lit*) Biegsamkeit *f* (b) (*fig*) Flexibilität *f*

flexible ['fleksəbl] ADJ (a) (*lit*) biegsam (b) (*fig*) flexibel; **to work ~ hours** Gleitzeit arbeiten; **to be ~ about sth** in Bezug auf etw (*acc*) flexibel sein

flex(i)time ['fleks(ɪ)taɪm] N Gleitzeit *f*

flick [flɪk] **1** N (*with finger*) Schnipsen *nt no pl*; **with a ~ of his fingers/the whip** mit einem Finger-/Peitschenschnalzen; **a ~ of the wrist** eine schnelle Drehung des Handgelenks **2** VT *whip* knallen mit; *fingers* schnalzen mit; (*with fingers*)

switch anknipsen; *dust, ash* wegschnipsen; (*with cloth*) wegwedeln; **she ~ed her hair out of her eyes** sie strich sich (*dat*) die Haare aus den Augen; **he ~ed the piece of paper onto the floor** er schnipste das Papier auf den Fußboden

➤ **flick through** VI +PREP OBJ *book* (schnell) durchblättern; *pages* (schnell) umblättern; *TV channels* (schnell) wechseln

flicker ['flɪkə'] **1** VI (*flame, candle, light*) flackern; (*TV*) flimmern; (*needle on dial*) zittern; (*eyelid*) zucken; **a smile ~ed across his face** ein Lächeln huschte über sein Gesicht **2** N (*of flame, candle, light*) Flackern *nt*; (*of TV*) Flimmern *nt*

flick knife N (*Brit*) Klappmesser *nt*

flicks [flɪks] PL (*inf*) Kintopp *m* (*inf*); **to/at the ~** in den/im Kintopp (*inf*)

flier ['flaɪə'] N (a) (*Aviat*: = *pilot*) Flieger(in) *m(f)*; **to be a good/bad ~** (*person*) Fliegen gut/nicht vertragen (b) (*dated US*) (= *train*) Schnellzug *m*; (= *fast coach*) Expressbus *m* (c) (= *leaflet*) Flugblatt *nt*

flies [flaɪz] PL (*Brit*: *on trousers*) (Hosen)schlitz *m*

flight¹ [flaɪt] N (a) Flug *m*; **in ~** (*bird*) im Flug; (*Aviat*) in der Luft (b) (*group*) (*of birds*) Schwarm *m*; (*of aeroplanes*) Geschwader *nt*; **to be in the top ~** (*fig*) zur Spitze gehören (c) (*of imagination*) Höhenflug *m*; **~ of fancy** geistiger Höhenflug (d) **~ (of stairs)** Treppe *f* (e) (*on dart, arrow*) Steuerfeder *f*

flight² [flaɪt] N Flucht *f*; **to put the enemy to ~** den Feind in die Flucht schlagen; **to take (to) ~** die Flucht ergreifen

flight: **flight attendant** N Flugbegleiter(in) *m(f)*; **flight bag** N Schultertasche *f*; **flight deck** N (a) (*Naut*) Flugdeck *nt* (b) (*Aviat*) Cockpit *nt*; **flight number** N Flugnummer *f*; **flight path** N Flugbahn *f*; (= *route*) Flugroute *f*; **flight recorder** N Flugschreiber *m*; **flight simulator** N Simulator *m*

flighty ['flaɪtɪ] ADJ (+ER) (= *fickle*) unbeständig; (= *empty-headed*) gedankenlos

flimsily ['flɪmzɪlɪ] ADV *constructed* leicht

flimsy ['flɪmzɪ] ADJ (+ER) (a) *structure* leicht gebaut; *material, paper* dünn; *box* instabil; **a ~ dress** ein Fähnchen *nt* (b) (*fig*) *evidence* fadenscheinig; *excuse* fadenscheinig; *reason* wenig stichhaltig

flinch [flɪntʃ] VI (a) zurückzucken; **without ~ing** ohne mit der Wimper zu zucken (b) (*fig*) **to ~ from sth** vor etw (*dat*) zurückschrecken; **he ~ed from telling her the truth** er scheute sich, ihr die Wahrheit zu sagen

fling [flɪŋ], *vb*: pret, ptp **flung 1** N (a) (*fig inf*) **to have a ~** (= *enjoy oneself*) sich austoben; **to have a last or final ~** sich noch einmal richtig austoben (b) (*inf*: = *relationship*) **to have a ~ (with sb)** eine Affäre (mit jdm) haben **2** VT (*lit, fig*) schleudern; **to ~ the window open** das Fenster aufstoßen; **the door was flung open** die Tür flog auf; **to ~ one's arms round sb's neck** jdm die Arme um den Hals werfen; **to ~ oneself into a chair/to the ground** sich in einen Sessel/auf den Boden werfen

➤ **fling off** VT SEP (*lit*) *coat* abwerfen

➤ **fling out** VT SEP *unwanted object* wegwerfen; *person* hinauswerfen

➤ **fling up** VT SEP **to fling one's arms up in horror** entsetzt die Hände über dem Kopf zusammenschlagen

flint [flɪnt] N Feuerstein *m*

flip [flɪp] **1** N Schnipser *m*; **by the ~ of a coin** durch Hochwerfen einer Münze **2** ADJ (*inf*: = *flippant*) schnodd(e)rig (*inf*) **3** VT schnippen; *switch* knipsen; **to ~ a coin** eine Münze werfen **4** VI (*inf*) durchdrehen (*inf*)

➤ **flip over 1** VT SEP umdrehen **2** VI (*plane*) sich in der Luft (um)drehen

➤ **flip through** VI +PREP OBJ *book* durchblättern; *pages* umblättern

flip: **flip chart** N Flipchart *f*; **flip-flop** N (*Brit*) Gummilatsche *f* (*inf*)

flippant ['flɪpənt] ADJ leichtfertig; (= *disrespectful*) schnodd(e)rig (*inf*)

flipper ['flɪpə'] N Flosse *f*

flipping ['flɪpɪŋ] ADJ, ADV (*Brit inf emph*) verdammt (*inf*)

flip side N (*of record*) B-Seite *f*

flirt [flɜːt] **1** VI flirten; **to ~ with an idea** mit einem Gedanken spielen; **to ~ with danger/disaster** die Gefahr/das Unglück herausfordern **2** N **he/she is just a ~** er/sie will nur flirten

flirtatious [flɜːˈteɪʃəs] ADJ kokett

flirty [ˈflɜːtɪ] ADJ kokett

flit [flɪt] **1** VI (*bats, butterflies etc*) flattern; (*ghost, person, image*) huschen; **to ~ in and out** (*person*) rein- und rausflitzen **2** N (*Brit*) **to do a (moonlight) ~** bei Nacht und Nebel umziehen

float [fləʊt] **1** N **(a)** (*on fishing line, in cistern, on aeroplane*) Schwimmer *m*; (*as swimming aid*) Schwimmkork *m* **(b)** (= *vehicle: in procession*) Festwagen *m* **(c)** (= *ready cash: in till*) Wechselgeld *nt no indef art* (*zu Geschäftsbeginn*) **2** VI **(a)** (*on water*) schwimmen; (= *move gently*) treiben; (*in air*) schweben; **the body ~ed (up) to the surface** die Leiche kam an die Wasseroberfläche **(b)** (*Comm: currency*) floaten **3** VT (*Comm, Fin*) company gründen; *shares* auf den Markt bringen; *currency* floaten lassen; (*fig*) *ideas, suggestion* in den Raum stellen

floating [ˈfləʊtɪŋ] **1** ADJ **(a)** *raft, logs* treibend **(b)** (*fig*) *population* wandernd; **~ voter** Wechselwähler *m* **(c)** (*Fin*) *currency* freigegeben; *debenture* variabel; **~ capital** Umlauf- *or* Betriebskapital *nt*; **~ charge** schwebende Belastung; **~ debt** schwebende Schuld; **~ policy** (*Insur*) Abschreibepolice *f*; **~ exchange rate** floatender *or* flexibler Wechselkurs **2** N (*of currency*) Freigabe *f*, Floating *nt*

floating voter [ˌfləʊtɪŋˈvəʊtəʳ] N (*fig*) Wechselwähler *m*

flock [flɒk] **1** N **(a)** (*of sheep, geese, also Eccl*) Herde *f*; (*of birds*) Schwarm *m* **(b)** (*of people*) Haufen *m* (*inf*) **2** VI in Scharen kommen; **to ~ around sb** sich um jdn scharen *or* drängen

flog [flɒg] VT **(a)** prügeln; *thief, mutineer* auspeitschen; **you're ~ging a dead horse** (*esp Brit inf*) Sie verschwenden Ihre Zeit **(b)** (*Brit inf:* = *sell*) verscherbeln (*inf*)

flogging [ˈflɒgɪŋ] N Tracht *f* Prügel; (*Jur*) Prügelstrafe *f*; (*of thief, mutineer*) Auspeitschen *nt*

flood [flʌd] **1** N (*lit, fig*) Flut *f*; **~s** Überschwemmung *f*; (*in several places*) Überschwemmungen *pl*; **the river is in ~** der Fluss führt Hochwasser; **she was in ~s of tears** sie war in Tränen gebadet **2** VT (*lit, fig*) überschwemmen; **the village/cellar was ~ed** das Dorf/der Keller war überschwemmt *or* stand unter Wasser; **to ~ the engine** den Motor absaufen lassen (*inf*); **~ed with calls/complaints** mit Anrufen/Beschwerden überhäuft; **~ed with light** lichtdurchflutet **3** VI **(a)** (*river*) über die Ufer treten; (*bath etc*) überlaufen; (*cellar*) unter Wasser stehen; (*garden, land*) überschwemmt werden **(b)** (*people*) strömen
➤ **flood back** VI (*memories, feelings*) wieder aufwallen
➤ **flood in** VI **the letters just flooded in** wir/sie *etc* hatten eine Flut von Briefen

floodgate [ˈflʌdgeɪt] N Schleusentor *nt*; **to open the ~s** (*fig*) Tür und Tor öffnen (*to +dat*)

flooding [ˈflʌdɪŋ] N Überschwemmung *f*

flood: floodlight N (= *device*) Scheinwerfer *m*; (= *light*) Flutlicht *nt*; **floodlighting** N Flutlicht(anlage *f*) *nt*; **floodlit** ADJ **~ football match** Fußballspiel *nt* bei *or* unter Flutlicht; **flood tide** N Flut *f*

floor [flɔːʳ] **1** N **(a)** Boden *m*; (*of room*) (Fuß)boden *m*; (= *dance ~*) Tanzfläche *f*; *ocean* ~ Meeresgrund *m*; **stone/tiled ~** Stein-/Fliesenboden *m*; **to take to the ~** (= *dance*) aufs Parkett gehen; **to hold** *or* **have the ~** (*speaker*) das Wort haben **(b)** (= *storey*) Stock *m*, Stockwerk *nt*; **first ~** (*Brit*) erster Stock; (*US*) Erdgeschoss *nt*, Erdgeschoß *nt* (*Aus*); **on the second ~** (*Brit*) im zweiten Stock; (*US*) im ersten Stock **(c)** (*of prices etc*) Minimum *nt*; **property prices have fallen** *or* **dropped through the ~** die Immobilienpreise sind in den Keller gefallen (*inf*) **(d)** (= *main part of chamber*) Plenar- *or* Sitzungssaal *m* (*also Parl*); (*of stock exchange*) Parkett *nt*; **a question from the ~** eine Frage aus der Zuhörerschaft; (*Brit Parl*) eine Frage aus dem Haus **2** VT **(a)** (= *knock down*) zu Boden schlagen **(b)** (= *bewilder*) verblüffen; (= *defeat*) schaffen (*inf*)

Be careful! **floor** *is not translated by the German word* **Flur**.

floor: floor area N Bodenfläche *f*; **floorboard** N Diele *f*; **floor cloth** N Scheuer- *or* Putzlappen *m*; **floor plan** N Grundriss *m* (*eines Stockwerkes*); **floor polish** N Bohnerwachs *nt*; **floor show** N Show *f* (*im Nachtklub oder Kabarett*); **floor space** N Stellraum *m*; **if you've got a sleeping bag we have plenty of ~** wenn du einen Schlafsack hast, wir haben viel Platz auf dem Fußboden; **floor trader** N (*St Ex*) Parketthändler(in) *m(f)*; **floor trading** N (*St Ex*) Parkethandel *m*; **floorwalker** N (*US Comm*) Ladenaufsicht *f*

floozie, floozy [ˈfluːzɪ] N (*inf*) Flittchen *nt* (*inf*)

flop [flɒp] **1** VI **(a)** (*person:* = *collapse*) sich fallen lassen; (*heavily*) sich hinplumpsen lassen (*inf*) **(b)** (*thing:* = *fall*) fallen; (*heavily*) plumpsen **(c)** (*inf*) (*scheme, plan*) ein Reinfall *nt* sein (*inf*); (*play, book*) durchfallen **2** N (*inf*) Flop *m* (*inf*)

floppy [ˈflɒpɪ] **1** ADJ (+*ER*) schlaff; *clothes* weit; *hair* wallend; **~ hat** Schlapphut *m* **2** N (= *disk*) Diskette *f*

floppy disk N (*Comput*) Floppydisk *f*; **~ drive** Diskettenlaufwerk *nt*

flora [ˈflɔːrə] N Flora *f*

floral [ˈflɔːrəl] ADJ **(a)** *wallpaper etc* geblümt; **~ design** *or* **pattern** Blumenmuster *nt* **(b)** (= *made of flowers*) Blumen-

florid [ˈflɒrɪd] ADJ (*usu pej*) *language* schwülstig (*pej*); *wallpaper, tie* überladen; *music, architecture* reich verziert

florist [ˈflɒrɪst] N Blumenhändler(in) *m(f)*, Florist(in) *m(f)*; **~'s (shop)** Blumengeschäft *nt*

floss [flɒs] **1** N (= *dental ~*) Zahnseide *f* **2** VT mit Zahnseide reinigen **3** VI sich (*dat*) die Zähne mit Zahnseide reinigen

flotation [fləʊˈteɪʃən] N (*Comm: of firm*) Gründung *f*; (*St Ex*) Börseneinführung *f*; (*of shares*) Emission *f*

flotilla [fləʊˈtɪlə] N Flotille *f*

flotsam [ˈflɒtsəm] N Treibgut *nt*; **~ and jetsam** (*floating*) Treibgut *nt*; (*washed ashore*) Strandgut *nt*; **the ~ and jetsam of our society** die Gestrandeten *pl* unserer Gesellschaft

flounce¹ [flaʊns] VI stolzieren; **to ~ in/out/around** herein-/heraus-/herumstolzieren

flounce² N (= *frill*) Volant *m*

flounder¹ [ˈflaʊndəʳ] N (= *fish*) Flunder *f*

flounder² VI (*lit, fig*) sich abstrampeln; **we ~ed about in the mud** wir quälten uns mühselig im Schlamm; **the company/economy was ~ing** der Firma/Wirtschaft ging es schlecht; **his career ~ed** mit seiner Karriere ging es abwärts

flour [ˈflaʊəʳ] **1** N Mehl *nt* **2** VT (*Cook*) mit Mehl bestäuben

flourish [ˈflʌrɪʃ] **1** VI (*plants etc, person*) (prächtig) gedeihen; (*business*) florieren; (*writer, artist etc*) großen Erfolg haben; **crime ~ed in poor areas** in den armen Gegenden gedieh das Verbrechen **2** VT *stick, book etc* herumwedeln *or* -fuchteln mit **3** N **(a)** (= *decoration etc*) Schnörkel *m* **(b)** (= *movement*) eleganter Schwung; **with a ~ of his stick** seinen Stock schwenkend

flourishing [ˈflʌrɪʃɪŋ] ADJ florierend *attr*; *career* erfolgreich; *garden, plant* prächtig gedeihend *attr*

floury [ˈflaʊərɪ] ADJ mehlig

flout [flaʊt] VT sich hinwegsetzen über (+*acc*); *convention* pfeifen auf (+*acc*)

flow [fləʊ] **1** VI **(a)** (*lit, fig*) fließen; (*prose*) flüssig sein; **where the river ~s into the sea** wo der Fluss ins Meer mündet; **the wine ~ed freely all evening** der Wein floss den ganzen Abend in Strömen; **to keep the traffic ~ing** den Verkehr nicht ins Stocken kommen lassen **(b)** (*dress, hair etc*) wallen **2** N Fluss *m*; (*of people*) Strom *m*; **the ~ of blood/traffic/information** der Blut-/Verkehrs-/Informationsfluss; **to go with the ~** (*fig*) mit dem Strom schwimmen; **he was in full ~** er war richtig in Fahrt

flow chart N Flussdiagramm *nt*

flower [ˈflaʊəʳ] **1** N Blume *f*; (= *blossom*) Blüte *f*; **to be in ~** in Blüte stehen **2** VI (*lit, fig*) blühen

flower: flower arrangement N Blumengesteck *nt*; **flower arranging** N Blumenstecken *nt*; **flowerbed** N Blumenbeet *nt*

flowered [ˈflaʊəd] ADJ *shirt, wallpaper* geblümt

flowering [ˈflaʊərɪŋ] ADJ Blüten-; **~ plant** Blütenpflanze *f*; **~ shrub** Zierstrauch *m*

flower: flowerpot N Blumentopf *m*; **flower-seller** N Blumenverkäufer(in) *m(f)*; **flower shop** N Blumenladen *m*; **flower show** N Blumenschau *f*

flowery ['flaʊərɪ] ADJ **(a)** *wallpaper etc* geblümt **(b)** *(fig: = elaborate)* blumig

flowing ['fləʊɪŋ] ADJ fließend; *hair, gown* wallend; *movement, style, football* flüssig

flown [fləʊn] PTP *of* **fly²**

flu, 'flu [fluː] N Grippe *f*; **to get** *or* **catch/have (the) ~** (die *or* eine) Grippe bekommen/haben

fluctuate ['flʌktjʊeɪt] VI schwanken

fluctuation [flʌktjʊ'eɪʃən] N Schwankung *f*

flue [fluː] N Rauchfang *m*

fluency ['fluːənsɪ] N *(in a foreign language)* fließendes Sprechen; **this job requires ~ in German** für diese Stelle ist fließendes Deutsch Voraussetzung; **~ in two foreign languages is a requirement** die Beherrschung von zwei Fremdsprachen ist Voraussetzung **(b)** *(in one's native language, of speaker, writer)* Gewandtheit *f*

fluent ['fluːənt] ADJ **(a)** *(in a foreign language)* **to be ~** die Sprache fließend sprechen; **to be ~ in German, to speak ~ German** fließend Deutsch sprechen; **she is ~ in six languages** sie beherrscht sechs Sprachen fließend **(b)** *(in one's native language)* *writer, talker* gewandt; *reader* fließend **(c)** *movement, action* flüssig

fluently ['fluːəntlɪ] ADV *speak, write (in a foreign language)* fließend; *(in one's native language)* flüssig

fluff [flʌf] **1** N, NO PL *(on birds, young animals)* Flaum *m*; *(from material)* Fusseln *pl*; (= dust) Staubflocken *pl*; **a bit of ~** eine Fussel/eine Staubflocke **2** VT **(a)** *(also ~ out)* *pillow* aufschütteln **(b)** *opportunity, entrance* vermasseln *(inf)*

➤ **fluff up** VT SEP *pillow etc* aufschütteln

fluffy ['flʌfɪ] ADJ (+ER) **(a)** *slippers, towel* flauschig; *hair* locker; *kitten, rabbit* flaumweich; **~ white clouds** weiße Schäfchenwolken; **~ animal** *or* **toy** (= soft toy) Kuscheltier *nt* **(b)** *omelette, rice* locker; *egg, cake mixture* schaumig

fluid ['fluːɪd] **1** N Flüssigkeit *f*; **she can only take ~s** sie kann nur flüssige Nahrung zu sich *(dat)* nehmen **2** ADJ *(lit, fig)* flüssig; *shape, painting* fließend; *situation* ungewiss

fluke [fluːk] N *(inf)* **by a ~** durch Dusel *(inf)*; **it was a (pure) ~** das war (einfach) Dusel *(inf)*

flummox ['flʌməks] VT *(inf)* durcheinander bringen; **to be ~ed by sth** durch etw aus dem Konzept gebracht werden *(inf)*

flung [flʌŋ] PRET, PTP *of* **fling**

flunk [flʌŋk] VT *(inf)* *test* verhauen *(inf)*; **to ~ German/an exam** in Deutsch/bei einer Prüfung durchfallen *(inf)*

flunk(e)y ['flʌŋkɪ] N Lakai *m*; (= flatterer) Radfahrer(in) *m(f)* *(inf)*

fluorescent [flʊə'resənt] ADJ *colour* leuchtend; *dye, paint, clothes* fluoreszierend; **~ display/screen** Leuchtanzeige *f*/-schirm *m*

fluorescent: fluorescent light N Neonlampe *f*; **fluorescent lighting** N Neonbeleuchtung *f*

fluoride ['flʊəraɪd] N Fluorid *nt*; **~ toothpaste** Fluorzahnpasta *f*

flurry ['flʌrɪ] N **(a)** *(of snow)* Gestöber *nt* **(b)** *(fig)* **a ~ of activity** eine Hektik; **a ~ of excitement** hektische Aufregung

flush¹ [flʌʃ] **1** N **(a)** (= lavatory ~) (Wasser)spülung *f* **(b)** (= blush) Röte *f* **(c)** *(of excitement, panic)* Welle *f*; **in the first ~ of youth** in der ersten Jugendblüte **2** VI **(a)** *(person, face)* rot werden *(with* vor *+dat)* **(b)** *(lavatory)* spülen **3** VT spülen; *(also ~ out)* *drain* durch- *or* ausspülen; **to ~ the lavatory** *or* **toilet** spülen; **to ~ sth down the toilet** etw die Toilette hinunterspülen

➤ **flush away** VT SEP wegspülen

➤ **flush out** VT SEP **(a)** *sink, bottle* ausspülen **(b)** *thieves, spies* aufspüren

flush² ADJ PRED **(a)** bündig; **cupboards ~ with the wall** Schränke, die mit der Wand abschließen **(b)** *(inf)* **to be ~** gut bei Kasse sein *(inf)*

flushed ['flʌʃt] ADJ **to be ~ with success/happiness** über seinen Erfolg/vor Glück strahlen

fluster ['flʌstər] VT nervös machen; (= confuse) durcheinander bringen; **to be ~ed** nervös *or* aufgeregt sein; (= confused) durcheinander sein

flute [fluːt] N *(Mus)* Querflöte *f*

flutist ['fluːtɪst] N *(US)* = **flautist**

flutter ['flʌtər] **1** VI **(a)** *(flag, bird etc)* flattern *(also Med)*; **to ~ away** *or* **off** davonflattern **(b)** *(person)* tänzeln; *(nervously)* flatterig sein **2** VT *fan, piece of paper* wedeln mit; *(birds)* *wings*

flattern mit; **to ~ one's eyelashes at sb** mit den Wimpern klimpern *(hum)* **3** N **(a)** (all) in *or* of a ~ in heller Aufregung **(b)** *(Brit inf)* **to have a ~** (= gamble) sein Glück (beim Wetten) versuchen

flux [flʌks] N Fluss *m*; **things are in a state of ~** die Dinge sind im Fluss

fly¹ [flaɪ] N Fliege *f*; **he wouldn't hurt** *or* **harm a ~** er könnte keiner Fliege etwas zuleide tun; **that's the only ~ in the ointment** *(inf)* das ist das einzige Haar in der Suppe; **there are no flies on him** *(Brit inf)* ihn legt man nicht so leicht rein *(inf)*

fly² vb: pret **flew**, ptp **flown 1** VI *(lit, fig)* fliegen; *(time)* (ver)fliegen; *(flag, hair)* wehen; **time flies!** wie die Zeit vergeht!; **the door flew open** die Tür flog auf; **to ~ into a rage** einen Wutanfall bekommen; **to ~ at sb** *(inf)* auf jdn losgehen; **he really let ~** er legte kräftig los; **to knock** *or* **send sb/sth ~ing** jdn/etw umwerfen *inf* **to go ~ing** *(person)* hinfallen; *(object)* runterfallen; **to ~ in the face of authority/tradition** sich über jede Autorität/alle Traditionen hinwegsetzen **2** VT fliegen; *kite* steigen lassen; *Atlantic* überfliegen; *flag* führen, wehen lassen

➤ **fly away** VI *(bird)* weg- *or* fortfliegen

➤ **fly in** VTI einfliegen; **she flew in from New York this morning** sie ist heute Morgen mit dem Flugzeug aus New York angekommen

➤ **fly off** VI **(a)** *(plane, person)* abfliegen; *(bird)* wegfliegen; **to fly off to the south** nach Süden fliegen **(b)** (= come off) *(hat, lid etc)* wegfliegen; *(button)* abspringen

➤ **fly out 1** VI ausfliegen; **I'll fly out and come back by ship** ich werde hin fliegen und mit dem Schiff zurückkommen **2** VT SEP *(to an area)* hinfliegen; *(out of an area)* ausfliegen

➤ **fly past 1** VI **(a)** *(ceremonially)* vorbeifliegen **(b)** *(time)* verfliegen **2** VI +PREP OBJ **to fly past sth** an etw *(dat)* vorbeifliegen

fly³ N *(on trousers)* (Hosen)schlitz *m*

fly: fly-by-night ADJ *(Fin, Comm)* operation windig *(inf)*; **fly-fishing** N Fliegenfischen *nt*

flying ['flaɪɪŋ] **1** ADJ *glass, debris* herumfliegend **2** N Fliegen *nt*; **he likes ~** er fliegt gerne; **he's afraid of ~** er hat Angst vorm Fliegen *or* Flugangst

flying: flying boat N Flugboot *nt*; **flying buttress** N *(Archit)* Strebebogen *m*; **flying colours**, *(US)* **flying colors** PL **to pass with ~** glänzend abschneiden; **flying doctor** N fliegender Arzt *(esp in Australien)*; **flying fish** N Fliegender Fisch; **flying leap** N **to take a ~** einen großen Satz machen; **flying saucer** N fliegende Untertasse; **flying start** N **to get off to a ~** *(Sport)* hervorragend wegkommen *(inf)*; *(fig)* einen glänzenden Start haben; **flying visit** N Stippvisite *f*

fly: flyleaf N Vorsatzblatt *nt*; **flyover** N Überführung *f*; *(US: = fly-past)* Luftparade *f*; **flypaper** N Fliegenfänger *m*; **fly-past** N *(Brit)* Luftparade *f*; **fly sheet** N (= entrance) Überdach *nt*; (= outer tent) Überzelt *nt*; **fly spray** N Fliegenspray *m*; **fly swat(ter)** N Fliegenklatsche *f*; **fly-tipping** N illegales Müllabladen; **flywheel** N Schwungrad *nt*

FM ABBR *of* **frequency modulation** FM

foal [fəʊl] **1** N Fohlen *nt* **2** VI fohlen

foam [fəʊm] **1** N Schaum *m* **2** VI schäumen; **to ~ at the mouth** *(lit)* Schaum vorm Mund *or* *(animal)* Maul haben; *(fig: person)* schäumen

foam rubber N Schaumgummi *m*

foamy ['fəʊmɪ] ADJ (+ER) schäumend

fob¹, FOB ['efəʊbiː] ABBR *of* **free on board**

fob² [fɒb] VT *(esp Brit)* **to ~ sb off (with promises)** jdn (mit leeren Versprechungen) abspeisen; **to ~ sth off on sb, to ~ sb off with sth** jdm etw andrehen

focal point ['fəʊkəlpɔɪnt] N *(lit, fig)* Brennpunkt *m*; **his family is the ~ of his life** seine Familie ist der Mittelpunkt seines Lebens

focus ['fəʊkəs] **1** N, pl **foci** ['fəʊkaɪ] *(Phys, Math, fig)* Brennpunkt *m*; **in ~** *camera* (scharf) eingestellt; *photo* scharf; **out of ~** *(lit)* *camera* unscharf eingestellt; *photo* unscharf; *(fig)* *ideas* vage; **to keep sth in ~** *(fig)* etw im Blickfeld behalten; **he/the new proposal was the ~ of attention** er/der neue Vorschlag stand im Mittelpunkt **2** VT *instrument* einstellen *(on* auf *+acc)*; *light, heat rays* bündeln; *(fig)* *one's efforts, resources* konzentrieren *(on* auf

+*acc*); **to ~ one's mind** sich konzentrieren; **I should like to ~ your attention (up)on a new problem** ich möchte Ihre Aufmerksamkeit auf ein neues Problem lenken

3 VI **to ~ on sth** sich auf etw (*acc*) konzentrieren; **I can't ~ properly** ich kann nicht mehr klar sehen

focus group N Fokusgruppe *f*

focus(s)ed ['fəʊkəst] ADJ (*fig*) fokussiert

fodder ['fɒdəʳ] N (*lit, fig*) Futter *nt*

foe [fəʊ] N (*liter*) Widersacher(in) *m(f)* (*geh*)

foetal, (*esp US*) **fetal** ['fiːtl] ADJ fötal

foetus, (*esp US*) **fetus** ['fiːtəs] N Fötus *m*

fog [fɒg] **1** N Nebel *m* **2** VTI (*also ~ up or over*) beschlagen

fogbound ['fɒgbaʊnd] ADJ *ship, plane* durch Nebel festgehalten; *airport* wegen Nebel(s) geschlossen; **the main road to Edinburgh is ~** auf der Hauptstraße nach Edinburgh herrscht dichter Nebel

fogey ['fəʊgɪ] N (*inf*) **old ~** alter Kauz (*inf*); (= *woman*) Schrulle *f* (*inf*)

foggy ['fɒgɪ] ADJ (+ER) (a) *day, weather* neb(e)lig (b) (*fig*) **I haven't the foggiest (idea)** (*inf*) ich habe keinen blassen Schimmer (*inf*)

fog: **foghorn** N (*Naut*) Nebelhorn *nt*; **fog lamp, fog light** N (*Aut*) Nebelscheinwerfer *m*; **rear ~** Nebelschlussleuchte *f*

foible ['fɔɪbl] N Eigenheit *f*

foil¹ [fɔɪl] N (= *metal sheet*) Folie *f*

foil² N (*Fencing*) Florett *nt*

foil³ VT *plans* durchkreuzen; *attempts* vereiteln; *person* einen Strich durch die Rechnung machen (+*dat*); **~ed again!** (*hum*) wieder nichts!

foist [fɔɪst] VT (a) **to ~ sth (off) on sb** *goods* jdm etw andrehen; *task, responsibility* etw auf jdn abschieben; *opinions* jdm etw aufdrängen (b) **to ~ oneself on(to) sb** sich jdm aufdrängen

fold [fəʊld] **1** N Falte *f*; **~s of skin** Hautfalten *pl*; **~s of fat** Fettwülste *pl*

2 VT (a) *paper* (zusammen)falten; *blanket* zusammenlegen *or* -falten; **to ~ a newspaper in two** eine Zeitung falten; **to ~ one's arms** die Arme verschränken; **she ~ed her hands in her lap** sie faltete die Hände im Schoß zusammen

(b) (= *wrap up*) einwickeln (*in* in +*acc*)

(c) (*Cook*) **to ~ sth into sth** etw unter etw (*acc*) heben **3** VI (a) (*chair, table*) sich zusammenklappen lassen; (*accidentally*) zusammenklappen

(b) (= *close down: business*) eingehen

➤ **fold away** VI (*table, bed*) zusammenklappbar sein

➤ **fold back** VT SEP *shutters* zurückfalten; *bedclothes* auf- *or* zurückschlagen

➤ **fold down** VT SEP *corner* kniffen

➤ **fold up** VT SEP *paper* zusammenfalten

folder ['fəʊldəʳ] N (a) (*for papers*) Aktenmappe *f* (b) (*Comput*) Ordner *m*

folding ['fəʊldɪŋ] ADJ ATTR Klapp-; **~ chair** Klappstuhl *m*

folding doors PL Falttür *f*

foldout ['fəʊldaʊt] ADJ ATTR ausklappbar

foliage ['fəʊlɪdʒ] N Blätter *pl*

folk [fəʊk] PL (*also ~s: inf*) (= *people*) Leute *pl*; (= *people in general*) die Leute, man; **a lot of ~(s) believe** ... viele (Leute) glauben ...; **old ~ can't** ... alte Menschen können nicht ...; **my ~s** meine Leute (*inf*)

folk: **folk dance** N Volkstanz *m*; **folklore** N Folklore *f*; **folk music** N Volksmusik *f*; **folk singer** N Sänger(in) *m(f)* (*of* von Volksliedern; (*modern songs*) Folksänger(in) *m(f)*; **folk song** N Volkslied *nt*; (*modern*) Folksong *m*

folksy ['fəʊksɪ] ADJ (*US*) *person, manner* herzlich; *speech, comment* volkstümlich

folk tale N Volksmärchen *nt*

follicle ['fɒlɪkl] N Follikel *nt*

follow ['fɒləʊ] **1** VT (= *understand also*) folgen (+*dat*); *person, car, road also* nachgehen/-fahren *etc* (+*dat*); (= *pursue also*) verfolgen; *course of study, career, serial, news* verfolgen; *fashion* mitmachen; *advice, instructions* befolgen; *athletics, swimming etc* sich interessieren für; *speech* (genau) verfolgen; **he ~ed me about** *or* folgte mir überallhin; **he ~ed me out** *or* folgte mir nach draußen; **we're being ~ed** wir werden verfolgt; **he arrived first, ~ed by the ambassador** er kam als Erster, gefolgt vom Botschafter; **the dinner will be ~ed by a** concert im Anschluss an das Essen findet ein Konzert statt; **how do you ~ that?** das ist kaum zu überbieten; **I love lasagne ~ed by ice cream** besonders gern mag ich Lasagne und danach Eis; **do you ~ me?** können Sie mir folgen?; **to ~ one's heart/conscience** auf die Stimme seines Herzens/Gewissens hören; **which team do you ~?** für welche Mannschaft sind Sie?

2 VI folgen; **his argument was as ~s** er argumentierte folgendermaßen; **to ~ in sb's footsteps** (*fig*) in jds Fußstapfen (*acc*) treten; **it doesn't ~ that ...** daraus folgt nicht, dass ...; **that doesn't ~** nicht unbedingt!; **I don't ~** das verstehe ich nicht

➤ **follow on** VI nachkommen

➤ **follow through** **1** VT SEP *idea, undertaking* (zu Ende) verfolgen, durchziehen **2** VI **to follow through with sth** (*with plan*) etw zu Ende verfolgen; (*with threat*) etw wahr machen

➤ **follow up** **1** VT SEP (a) (= *pursue, take further action on*) *request* nachgehen (+*dat*); *offer, suggestion* aufgreifen (b) (= *investigate further*) sich näher beschäftigen mit; *matter* weiterverfolgen; *rumour* nachgehen (+*dat*) (c) *success, victory* fortsetzen, ausbauen; *advantage* ausnutzen **2** VI **to follow up with sth** etw folgen lassen

follower ['fɒləʊəʳ] N Anhänger(in) *m(f)*; **to be a ~ of fashion** sehr modebewusst sein; **he's a ~ of Blair** er ist Blair-Anhänger *or* ein Anhänger von Blair

following ['fɒləʊɪŋ] **1** ADJ (a) folgend; **the ~ day** der nächste *or* (darauf) folgende Tag (b) **a ~ wind** Rückenwind *m* **2** N (a) (= *followers*) Anhängerschaft *f*, Gefolgschaft *f* (b) **he said the ~** er sagte Folgendes **3** PREP nach

follow-up ['fɒləʊˌʌp] N Fortsetzung *f* (*to* +*gen*)

folly ['fɒlɪ] N Verrücktheit *f*; (= *building*) exzentrischer, meist völlig nutzloser Prachtbau; **it is sheer ~ (to do that)** es ist der reinste Wahnsinn(, das zu tun)

foment [fəʊ'ment] VT schüren

fond [fɒnd] ADJ (+ER) (a) **to be ~ of sb** jdn gern haben *or* mögen; **to be ~ of sth** etw mögen; **she is very ~ of animals** sie ist sehr tierlieb(end); **to become** *or* **grow ~ of sb/sth** jdn/etw lieb gewinnen; **to be ~ of doing sth** etw gern tun (b) *husband, parent, look, smile* liebevoll; *friend* lieb; **to have ~ memories of sth** schöne Erinnerungen an etw (*acc*) haben (c) *hope, dream, wish* sehnlich (d) (= *foolish, vain*) **in the ~ hope/belief that ...** in der vergeblichen Hoffnung, dass ...

fondant ['fɒndənt] N Fondant *m*

fondle ['fɒndl] VT (zärtlich) spielen mit; (= *stroke*) streicheln; *person* schmusen mit

fondly ['fɒndlɪ] ADV (a) liebevoll; **to remember sb ~** jdn in bester Erinnerung behalten; **to remember sth ~** sich gern an etw (*acc*) erinnern (b) (= *naively*) *imagine, believe* naiverweise; *hope* törichterweise (*geh*)

fondness ['fɒndnɪs] N (*for people*) Zuneigung *f*, Liebe *f* (*for* zu); (*for food, place, writer etc*) Vorliebe *f* (*for* für)

fondue ['fɒnduː] N Fondue *nt*; **~ set** Fondueset *nt*

font [fɒnt] N (*Typ*) Schrift *f*

food [fuːd] N Essen *nt*; (*for animals*) Futter *nt*; (= *nourishment, also fig*) Nahrung *f*; (= *foodstuff*) Nahrungsmittel *nt*; (= *groceries*) Lebensmittel *pl*; **dog and cat ~** Hunde- und Katzenfutter; **~ and drink** Essen und Trinken; **I haven't any ~ in the house** ich habe nichts zu essen im Haus; **~ for thought** Stoff *m* zum Nachdenken

food chain N Nahrungskette *f*

foodie ['fuːdɪ] N Kochfreak *m* (*inf*)

food: **food parcel** N Lebensmittelpaket *nt*; **food poisoning** N Lebensmittelvergiftung *f*; **food processing** N Nahrungsmittelverarbeitung *f*; **food processor** N Küchenmaschine *f*; **food stamp** N (*US*) Lebensmittelmarke *f*; **foodstuff** N Nahrungsmittel *nt*; **food technology** N (*also Brit Sch*) Lebensmitteltechnologie *f*

fool [fuːl] **1** N Dummkopf *m*; **don't be a ~!** sei nicht (so) dumm!; **he was a ~ not to accept** es war dumm von ihm, nicht anzunehmen; **to be ~ enough to ...** so dumm *or* blöd (*inf*) sein, zu ...; **to play** *or* **act the ~** herumalbern; **to make a ~ of sb** (*with ridicule*) jdn lächerlich machen; (*with a trick*) jdn zum Besten *or* zum Narren halten; **he made a ~ of himself at the party** er hat sich bei der Party blamiert

2 ADJ (*esp US inf*) doof (*inf*), schwachsinnig (*inf*)

3 VI herumalbern; **to ~ with sb/sth** mit jdm/etw spielen;

stop ~ing (around)! lass den Blödsinn!; **I was only ~ing** das war doch nur Spaß

4 VT zum Narren halten; (= *trick*) hereinlegen (*inf*); (*disguise, phoney accent etc*) täuschen; **I was completely ~ed** ich bin vollkommen darauf hereingefallen; **you had me ~ed** ich habe das tatsächlich geglaubt; **they ~ed him into believing that ...** sie haben ihm weisgemacht, dass ...

➤ **fool about** (*Brit*) **or fool around** VI **(a)** (= *waste time*) herumtrödeln **(b)** (= *play the fool*) herumalbern; **to fool about** or **around with sth** mit etw Blödsinn machen **(c)** (*sexually*) **he's fooling around with my wife** er treibt seine Spielchen mit meiner Frau

foolhardy ['fuːlˌhɑːdɪ] ADJ tollkühn

foolish ['fuːlɪʃ] ADJ dumm; **don't do anything ~** mach keinen Unsinn; **what a ~ thing to do** wie kann man nur so dumm sein; **it made him look ~** dadurch kar er sich blamiert

foolishly ['fuːlɪʃlɪ] ADV *behave, act* unklug; *say* dummerweise; (*introducing sentence*) unklugerweise

foolishness ['fuːlɪʃnɪs] N Dummheit *f*; **enough of this ~** lassen wir diese Dummheiten

foolproof ['fuːlpruːf] ADJ *method, system, test* unfehlbar; *camera, recipe* idiotensicher (*inf*)

foolscap ['fuːlskæp] N (*also ~ paper*) ≈ Kanzleipapier *nt*, britisches Papierformat (13 1/4   16 1/2 Zoll)

foot [fʊt] **1** N, *pl* **feet** (*also bottom, measure*) Fuß *m*; (*of bed*) Fußende *nt*; **to be on one's feet** (*lit, fig*) auf den Beinen sein; **to get back on one's feet** (*lit, fig*) wieder auf die Beine kommen; **on ~** zu Fuß; **I'll never set ~ here again!** hier kriegen mich keine zehn Pferde mehr her! (*inf*); **the first time he set ~ in the office** als er das erste Mal das Büro betrat; **to get or rise to one's feet** aufstehen; **to jump to one's feet** aufspringen; **to put one's feet up** (*lit*) die Füße hochlegen; (*fig*) es sich (*dat*) bequem machen; **he never puts a ~ wrong** (*fig*) er macht nie einen Fehler; **3 ~ or feet wide/long** 3 Fuß breit/lang; **he's 6 ~ 3 ~** er ist 1,90 m; (*fig uses*) **to put one's ~ down** (= *act with decision or authority*) ein Machtwort sprechen; (= *forbid, refuse*) es strikt verbieten; (*Aut*) Gas geben; **to put one's ~ in it** ins Fettnäpfchen treten; **to find one's feet** sich eingewöhnen; **to fall on one's feet** auf die Beine fallen; **to have one's** or **both feet (firmly) on the ground** mit beiden Beinen (fest) auf der Erde stehen; **to have one ~ in the grave** mit einem Bein im Grabe stehen; **to get/be under sb's feet** jdm im Wege stehen or sein; **to get off on the right/wrong ~** einen guten/schlechten Start haben; **to stand on one's own two feet** auf eigenen Füßen or Beinen stehen; **a nice area, my ~!** (*inf*) und das soll eine schöne Gegend sein! **2** VT *bill* bezahlen, begleichen

foot-and-mouth (disease) ['fʊtənˈmaʊθ(dɪ,ziːz)] N (*Brit*) Maul- und Klauenseuche *f*

football ['fʊtbɔːl] N (*also ball*) Fußball *m*; (= *American ~*) (American) Football *m*

football boot N Fußballschuh *m*, Fußballstiefel *m*

footballer ['fʊtbɔːləʳ] N **(a)** (*Brit*) Fußball(spiel)er(in) *m(f)* **(b)** (*in American football*) Footballspieler *m*

football: football hooligan N Fußballrowdy or -hooligan *m*; **football pools** PL Fußballtoto *nt or m*

foot: foot bath N Fußbad *nt*; **foot brake** N Fußbremse *f*; **footbridge** N Fußgängerbrücke *f*

-footed [-fʊtɪd] ADJ SUF -füßig; **four-footed** vierfüßig

footer ['fʊtəʳ] N (*Comput*) Fußzeile *f*

foot: foothills PL (Gebirgs)ausläufer *pl*; **foothold** N Stand *m*, Halt *m*; (*fig*) sichere (Ausgangs)position; **to establish** or **gain a ~** (*fig*) Fuß fassen; **to lose one's ~** (*lit, fig*) den Halt verlieren

footie ['fʊtɪ] N (*Brit inf*) = **football**

footing ['fʊtɪŋ] N **(a)** (*lit*) **to lose one's ~** den Halt verlieren; **to miss one's ~** danebentreten **(b)** (*fig*) (= *foundation*) Basis *f*; (= *relationship*) Beziehung *f*; **we are trying to put training on a more scientific ~** wir versuchen, die Ausbildung wissenschaftlicher zu fundieren; **to be on a friendly ~ with sb** mit jdm auf freundschaftlichem Fuße stehen; **on an equal ~ (with each other)** auf gleicher Basis; **to be on a war ~** sich im Kriegszustand befinden

foot: footlights PL (*Theat*) Rampenlicht *nt*; **footloose** ADJ unbeschwert; **~ and fancy-free** frei und ungebunden; **footman** N Lakai *m*; **footnote** N Fußnote *f*; (*fig*) Anmerkung *f*; **footpath** N Fußweg *m*; **footprint** N Fußabdruck *m*;

footprints PL Fußspuren *pl*; **foot pump** N Fußpumpe *f*; **footrest** N Fußstütze *f*

Footsie ['fʊtsɪ] N (*Fin inf*) Footsie(-Index) *m* (*inf*)

foot: footsore ADJ **to be ~** wunde Füße haben; **footstep** N Schritt *m*; **footstool** N Fußbank *f*; **footwear** N Schuhe *pl*; **footwork** N, NO PL (*Sport*) Beinarbeit *f*

footy ['fʊtɪ] N (*Brit inf*) Fußball *m*

for [fɔːʳ] **1** PREP **(a)** für; (*purpose*) zu, für; (*destination*) nach; **a letter ~ me** ein Brief für mich; **destined ~ greatness** zu Höherem bestimmt; **what ~?** wofür?, wozu?; **what is this knife ~?** wozu dient dieses Messer?; **he does it ~ pleasure** er macht es zum or aus Vergnügen; **what did you do that ~?** warum or wozu haben Sie das getan?; **a bag ~ carrying books (in)** eine Tasche, um Bücher zu tragen; **to go to Spain ~ one's holidays** nach Spanien in Urlaub fahren; **the train ~ Stuttgart** der Zug nach Stuttgart; **to leave ~ the USA** in die USA or nach Amerika abreisen; **it's not ~ me to say** es steht mir nicht zu, mich dazu zu äußern; **married life is not ~ me** das Eheleben ist nichts für mich; **I'll speak to her ~ you if you like** wenn Sie wollen, rede ich an Ihrer Stelle or für Sie mit ihr; **to act ~ sb** für jdn handeln; **D ~ Daniel** D wie Daniel; **she works ~ a bank** (*in the bank*) sie arbeitet bei or in einer Bank; (*outside the bank*) sie arbeitet für eine Bank; **are you ~ or against it?** sind Sie dafür oder dagegen?; **I'm all ~ helping him** ich bin sehr dafür, ihm zu helfen; **I'm very happy ~ you** ich freue mich sehr für euch; **~ my part** was mich betrifft; **as ~ him/that** was ihn/das betrifft; **warm/cold ~ the time of year** warm/kalt für die Jahreszeit; **he is tall ~ his age** er ist groß für sein Alter; **what do you want ~ your birthday?** was wünschst du dir zum Geburtstag?; **it's all right** or **all very well ~ you (to talk)** Sie haben gut reden; **~ further information see page 77** weitere Informationen finden Sie auf Seite 77; **to pay ~ty pounds ~ a concert ticket** vierzig Pfund für eine Konzertkarte zahlen; **~ every job that is created, two are lost** für jede Stelle, die neu geschaffen wird, gehen zwei verloren; **his knack ~ saying the wrong thing** sein Talent, das Falsche zu sagen **(b)** (= *because of*) aus; **~ this reason** aus diesem Grund; **he did it ~ fear of being left** er tat es aus Angst, zurückgelassen zu werden; **to go to prison ~ theft** wegen Diebstahls ins Gefängnis wandern; **to choose sb ~ his ability** jdn wegen seiner Fähigkeiten wählen; **if it were not ~ him** wenn er nicht wäre; **do it ~ me** tu es für mich **(c)** (= *in spite of*) trotz (+*gen* or (*inf*) +*dat*) **(d)** (*in time*) seit; (*with future tense*) für; **I have not seen her ~ two years** ich habe sie seit zwei Jahren nicht gesehen; **he's been here ~ ten days** er ist seit zehn Tagen hier; **he walked ~ two hours** er ist zwei Stunden lang marschiert; **I am going away ~ a few days** ich werde (für or auf) ein paar Tage wegfahren; **I shall be away ~ a month** ich werde einen Monat (lang) weg sein; **he won't be back ~ a week** er wird erst in einer Woche zurück sein; **I'll be back home ~ Christmas** Weihnachten bin ich wieder zu Hause; **can you get it done ~ Monday?** können Sie es bis or für Montag fertig haben?; **~ a while/time** (für) eine Weile/einige Zeit; **the meeting was scheduled ~ 9 o'clock** die Besprechung sollte um 9 Uhr stattfinden **(e)** (*distance*) **we walked ~ two miles** wir sind zwei Meilen weit gelaufen; **there are roadworks on the M8 ~ two miles** auf der M8 ist es eine zwei Meilen lange Baustelle; **~ miles** meilenweit **(f)** (*with infin clauses*) **~ this to be possible** damit dies möglich wird; **it's easy ~ him to do it** er kann das leicht tun; **I brought it ~ you to see** ich habe es mitgebracht, damit Sie es sich (*dat*) ansehen können; **the best thing would be ~ you to leave** das Beste wäre, wenn Sie weggingen; **there's still time ~ him to come** er kann immer noch kommen **(g)** (*phrases*) **you're (in) ~ it!** (*inf*) jetzt bist du dran! (*inf*); **oh ~ a cup a tea!** jetzt eine Tasse Tee - das wäre schön! **2** CONJ denn **3** ADJ PRED (= *in favour*) dafür

forage ['fɒrɪdʒ] VI nach Futter suchen; (*fig*: = *rummage*) herumstöbern (*for* nach)

foray ['fɒreɪ] N (Raub)überfall *m*; (*Mil*) Ausfall *m*; (*fig*) Ausflug *m* (*into* in +*acc*); **to make a ~ into the European market** sich auf den europäischen Markt vorwagen

forbad(e) [fəˈbæd] PRET *of* **forbid**

forbear [fɔːˈbɛəʳ] , *pret* **forbore** , *ptp* **forborne** (*form*) **1** VI **I forbore from expressing my opinion** ich verzichtete darauf, meine Meinung zu äußern **2** VT **he forbore to make any comment** er enthielt sich jeden Kommentars

forbearance [fɔːˈbɛərəns] N Nachsicht *f*

forbid [fəˈbɪd], *pret* **forbad(e)**, *ptp* **forbidden** VT **(a)** (= *not allow*) verbieten; **to ~ sb to do sth** jdm verbieten, etw zu tun **(b)** (= *prevent*) verhindern; **God** *or* **Heaven ~!** Gott behüte *or* bewahre!

forbidden [fəˈbɪdn] ADJ **(a)** (= *prohibited*) *love, food, goods* verboten; **they are ~ to enter** sie dürfen nicht hereinkommen; **smoking is (strictly) ~** Rauchen ist (streng) verboten **(b)** (= *taboo*) **~ subject/word** Tabuthema *nt*/-wort *nt*; **that's ~ territory** (*fig*) das ist tabu

forbidding [fəˈbɪdɪŋ] ADJ *person, expression* Furcht einflößend; *place, terrain* unwirtlich; *building, rocks, cliffs* bedrohlich; *task* (= *uninviting*) wenig einladend; (= *overwhelming*) überwältigend; *prospect* düster

forbore [fɔːˈbɔːʳ] PRET *of* **forbear**

forborne [fɔːˈbɔːn] PTP *of* **forbear**

force [fɔːs] **1** N **(a)** NO PL (= *physical strength, power, Phys*) Kraft *f*; (*of blow, impact*) Wucht *f*; (= *physical coercion*) Gewalt *f*; **to resort to ~** Gewalt anwenden; **by** *or* **through sheer ~ of numbers** aufgrund zahlenmäßiger Überlegenheit; **there is a ~ 5 wind blowing** es herrscht Windstärke 5; **they were there in ~** sie waren in großer Zahl da; **to come into/be in ~** in Kraft treten/sein **(b)** NO PL (*fig*) (*of argument*) Überzeugungskraft *f*; (*of character*) Stärke *f*; (*of words*) Macht *f*; **by** *or* **from ~ of habit** aus Gewohnheit; **the ~ of circumstances** der Druck der Verhältnisse **(c)** (= *powerful thing, person*) Macht *f*; **there are various ~s at work here** hier sind verschiedene Kräfte am Werk; **he is a powerful ~ in the reform movement** er ist ein einflussreicher Mann in der Reformbewegung **(d)** (= *body of men*) **the ~s** (*Mil*) die Streitkräfte *pl*; **the (police) ~** die Polizei; **to join ~s** sich zusammentun **2** VT **(a)** (= *compel*) zwingen; **to ~ sb/oneself to do sth** jdn/ sich zwingen, etw zu tun; **he was ~d to conclude that ...** er sah sich zu der Folgerung gezwungen *or* gedrängt, dass ...; **to ~ sth (up)on sb** *present, one's company* jdm etw aufdrängen; *conditions, obedience* jdm etw auferlegen; *decision, war* jdm etw aufzwingen; **he ~d himself on her** (*sexually*) er tat ihr Gewalt an; **don't ~ it** erzwingen Sie es nicht **(b)** (= *extort, obtain by ~*) erzwingen; **he ~d a confession out of** *or* **from me** er erzwang ein Geständnis von mir; **to ~ an error** (*Sport*) einen Fehler erzwingen **(c)** (= *break open*) aufbrechen **(d)** (= *push, squeeze*) **to ~ books into a box** Bücher in eine Kiste zwängen; **if it won't open/go in, don't ~ it** wenn es nicht aufgeht/passt, wende keine Gewalt an; **to ~ one's way into sth** sich (*dat*) gewaltsam Zugang zu etw *or* in etw (*acc*) verschaffen; **to ~ a car off the road** ein Auto von der Fahrbahn drängen

➤ **force back** VT SEP *tears* unterdrücken
➤ **force down** VT SEP *food* sich (*dat*) hinunterquälen
➤ **force off** VT SEP *lid* mit Gewalt abmachen

forced [fɔːst] ADJ **(a)** (= *imposed*) Zwangs-; *repatriation* gewaltsam; *marriage, resignation, withdrawal* erzwungen **(b)** *smile, laughter, conversation* gezwungen; *behaviour* gekünstelt

forced: **forced labour**, (*US*) **forced labor** N Zwangsarbeit *f*; **forced landing** N (*Aviat*) Notlandung *f*

force-feed [ˈfɔːsfiːd], *vb*: *pret, ptp* **force-fed** VT zwangsernähren

forceful [ˈfɔːsfʊl] ADJ **(a)** *blow, kick* kräftig **(b)** *person, manner, action* energisch; *character, personality* stark; *criticism, denial* entschieden; *statement, style, reminder* eindringlich; *argument* (= *strong*) eindringlich; (= *convincing*) überzeugend

forcefully [ˈfɔːsfəlɪ] ADV **(a)** *remove, move* gewaltsam; (= *violently*) *push, knock* heftig **(b)** *act, intervene* entschlossen; *argue* eindringlich

forcefulness [ˈfɔːsfʊlnɪs] N (*of person, manner, action*) energische *or* entschlossene Art; (*of character, personality*) Stärke *f*; (*of argument*) (= *strength*) Eindringlichkeit *f*; (= *conviction*) Überzeugungskraft *f*

forceps [ˈfɔːseps] PL (*also pair of ~*) Zange *f*

forcible ADJ, **forcibly** ADV [ˈfɔːsəbl, -ɪ] gewaltsam

ford [fɔːd] **1** N Furt *f* **2** VT durchqueren

fore [fɔːʳ] **1** N **to the ~** im Vordergrund; **to come to the ~** ins Blickfeld geraten **2** ADJ ATTR (*Zool, Naut, Aviat*) vordere(r, s) **3** ADV (*Naut*) vorn

forearm [ˈfɔːrɑːm] N Unterarm *m*

foreboding [fɔːˈbəʊdɪŋ] N (= *presentiment*) (Vor)ahnung *f*; (= *feeling of disquiet*) ungutes Gefühl

forecast [ˈfɔːkɑːst] **1** VT vorhersehen, voraussagen **2** N Voraussage *f*, Vorhersage *f*

forecaster [ˈfɔːkɑːstəʳ] N (*Met*) Meteorologe *m*, Meteorologin *f*; **economic ~** Wirtschaftsprognostiker(in) *m(f)*

foreclose [fɔːˈkləʊz] VI **to ~ on a loan/mortgage** ein Darlehen/ eine Hypothek kündigen

forecourt [ˈfɔːkɔːt] N Vorhof *m*

forefinger [ˈfɔːfɪŋgəʳ] N Zeigefinger *m*

forefront [ˈfɔːfrʌnt] N **in** *or* **at the ~ of** an der Spitze (+*gen*)

forego [fɔːˈgəʊ], *pret* **forewent**, *ptp* **foregone** VT verzichten auf (+*acc*)

foregone [fɔːˈgɒn] **1** PTP *of* **forego** **2** [ˈfɔːgɒn] ADJ **it was a ~ conclusion** es stand von vornherein fest

foreground [ˈfɔːgraʊnd] N (*Art, Phot*) Vordergrund *m*; **in the ~** im Vordergrund

forehand [ˈfɔːhænd] (*Sport*) **1** N Vorhand *f* **2** ATTR Vorhand-; **~ volley** Vorhandvolley *m*

forehead [ˈfɔːhed, ˈfɒrɪd] N Stirn *f*

foreign [ˈfɒrən] ADJ **(a)** *person, product* ausländisch; *food, customs, appearance* fremdländisch; **to be ~** (*person*) Ausländer(in) *m(f)* sein; **~ countries** das Ausland; **~ travel** Auslandsreisen *pl*; **~ debt** Auslandsverschuldung *f*; **~ investment** Auslandsinvestition *f*; **~ news** Auslandsnachrichten *pl*; **~ trade delegation** fremde Handelsdelegation **(b)** (= *alien*) Fremd-; **~ body** *or* **object** Fremdkörper *m*; **to be ~ to sb** jdm fremd sein

foreign: **foreign affairs** PL Außenpolitik *f*; **foreign agent** N (*in espionage*) ausländischer Agent; **foreign aid** N Entwicklungshilfe *f*; **foreign correspondent** N Auslandskorrespondent(in) *m(f)*; **foreign currency** N Devisen *pl*

foreigner [ˈfɒrənəʳ] N Ausländer(in) *m(f)*

foreign: **foreign exchange** N (= *system, trading*) Devisenhandel *m*; **on the ~s** an den Devisenbörsen; **foreign language** **1** N Fremdsprache *f*; **it was like a ~ to me** (*fig*) das waren böhmische Dörfer für mich (*inf*) **2** ATTR *film* fremdsprachig; **~ assistant** Fremdsprachenassistent(in) *m(f)*; **foreign legion** N Fremdenlegion *f*; **Foreign Minister** N Außenminister(in) *m(f)*; **Foreign Office** N (*Brit*) Auswärtiges Amt; **foreign policy** N (*Pol*) Außenpolitik *f*; **Foreign Secretary** N (*Brit*) Außenminister(in) *m(f)*; **foreign trade** N Außenhandel *m*

foreknowledge [fɔːˈnɒlɪdʒ] N vorherige Kenntnis

foreleg [ˈfɔːleg] N Vorderbein *nt*

foreman [ˈfɔːmən] N, *pl* **-men** [-mən] (*in factory*) Vorarbeiter *m*; (*on building site*) Polier *m*; (*Jur: of jury*) Obmann *m*

foremost [ˈfɔːməʊst] **1** ADJ führend; **to be ~ in sth/in a field** in etw (*dat*)/auf einem Gebiet führend sein; **~ among them was John** John führte mit ihnen **2** ADV vor allem

forename [ˈfɔːneɪm] N Vorname *m*

forensic [fəˈrensɪk] ADJ forensisch; (*Med*) gerichtsmedizinisch

forensic: **forensic medicine** N Gerichtsmedizin *f*; **forensic science** N Kriminaltechnik *f*; **forensic scientist** N Kriminaltechniker(in) *m(f)*

foreplay [ˈfɔːpleɪ] N Vorspiel *nt*

forerunner [ˈfɔːrʌnəʳ] N Vorläufer *m*

foresee [fɔːˈsiː], *pret* **foresaw** [fɔːˈsɔː], *ptp* **foreseen** [fɔːˈsiːn] VT vorhersehen, voraussehen

foreseeable [fɔːˈsiːəbl] ADJ voraussehbar; **in the ~ future** in absehbarer Zeit

foreshadow [fɔːˈʃædəʊ] VT ahnen lassen

foresight [ˈfɔːsaɪt] N Weitblick *m*

foreskin [ˈfɔːskɪn] N Vorhaut *f*

forest [ˈfɒrɪst] N Wald *m*; (*for lumber etc*) Forst *m*

forestall [fɔːˈstɔːl] VT *sb, rival* zuvorkommen (+*dat*); *accident, eventuality* vorbeugen (+*dat*); *crisis, danger, disaster* abwenden; *wish, desire* im Keim ersticken; *objection* vorwegnehmen

Forest Enterprise N (Brit) Landverwaltungsabteilung der Forstbehörde

forester ['fɒrɪstə'] N Förster(in) m(f)

forest ranger N (US) Förster(in) m(f)

forestry ['fɒrɪstrɪ] N Forstwirtschaft f

foretaste ['fɔːteɪst] N Vorgeschmack m; **to give sb a ~ of sth** jdm einen Vorgeschmack von etw geben

foretell [fɔː'tel], pret, ptp **foretold** [fɔː'təʊld] VT vorhersagen

forethought ['fɔːθɔːt] N Vorbedacht m

forever [fər'evə'] ADV (a) ewig; remember, go on immer; **Scotland ~!** ein Hoch auf Schottland!; **it takes ~** (inf) es dauert ewig (inf); **these old slate roofs go on** or **last ~** (inf) diese alten Schieferdächer halten ewig (b) (= irrevocably) disappear, change unwiderruflich; **the old social order was gone** = das alte Gesellschaftssystem war für immer verschwunden (c) (inf: = constantly) **to be ~ doing sth** (an)dauernd or ständig etw tun

forewarn [fɔː'wɔːn] VT vorher warnen

forewent [fɔː'went] PRET of **forego**

foreword ['fɔːwɜːd] N Vorwort nt

forfeit ['fɔːfɪt] 1 (a) (esp Jur) verwirken (b) (fig) one's life, health, honour einbüßen; chance verpassen; right, place verlieren 2 N (esp Jur) Strafe f; (fig) Einbuße f; (in game) Pfand nt

forgave [fə'geɪv] PRET of **forgive**

forge [fɔːdʒ] 1 N Schmiede f 2 VT (a) metal, plan schmieden; friendship, alliance schließen; relationship aufbauen (b) signature, banknote fälschen 3 VI **to ~ ahead** vorwärts kommen

forger ['fɔːdʒə'] N Fälscher(in) m(f)

forgery ['fɔːdʒərɪ] N (a) (= act) **to be prosecuted for ~** wegen Fälschung angeklagt sein (b) (= thing) Fälschung f; **the signature was a ~** die Unterschrift war gefälscht

forget [fə'get], pret **forgot**, ptp **forgotten** 1 VT vergessen; ability, language verlernen; **and don't you ~ it!** und dass du das ja nicht vergisst!; **to ~ to do sth** vergessen, etw zu tun; **I ~ his name** sein Name ist mir entfallen; **to ~ one's differences** seine Meinungsverschiedenheiten ruhen lassen; **not ~ting ...** nicht zu vergessen ...; **~ it!** schon gut!; **you might as well ~ it** (inf) das kannst du vergessen (inf) 2 VI es vergessen; **don't ~!** vergiss (es) nicht!; **I never ~** ich vergesse nie etwas 3 VR (= behave improperly) sich vergessen

➤ **forget about** VI +PREP OBJ vergessen

forgetful [fə'getfʊl] ADJ vergesslich; (of one's duties etc) nachlässig (of gegenüber)

forgetfulness [fə'getfʊlnɪs] N Vergesslichkeit f

forget-me-not [fə'getmɪnɒt] N (Bot) Vergissmeinnicht nt

forgettable [fə'getəbl] ADJ **it was an instantly ~ game** es war ein Spiel, das man sofort vergessen konnte

forgivable [fə'gɪvəbl] ADJ verzeihlich, verzeihbar

forgive [fə'gɪv], pret **forgave**, ptp **forgiven** [fə'gɪvn] VT verzeihen; (esp Eccl) sin vergeben; **to ~ sb sth, to ~ sb for sth** jdm etw verzeihen; **to ~ sb for doing sth** jdm verzeihen, dass er/sie etw getan hat; **you could be ~n for thinking that ...** es ist durchaus verständlich, wenn Sie denken, dass ...; **I'll never ~ myself if anything happens to him** ich werde es mir nie verzeihen, wenn ihm etwas zustößt

forgiveness [fə'gɪvnɪs] N, NO PL (= willingness to forgive) Versöhnlichkeit f; **to ask/beg (sb's) ~** (jdn) um Verzeihung or Vergebung (esp Eccl) bitten

forgiving [fə'gɪvɪn] ADJ versöhnlich

forgo [fɔː'gəʊ], pret **forwent**, ptp **forgone** VT = **forego**

forgot [fə'gɒt] PRET of **forget**

forgotten [fə'gɒtn] PTP of **forget**

fork [fɔːk] 1 N (a) Gabel f (b) (in tree) Astgabel f; (in road, railway) Gabelung f; **take the left ~** nehmen Sie die linke Abzweigung 2 VI (road, branch) sich gabeln; **to ~ (to the) right** (road) nach rechts abzweigen; (driver) nach rechts abbiegen

➤ **fork out** (inf) VI, VT SEP blechen (inf)

forked [fɔːkt] ADJ gegabelt; tongue gespalten

fork-lift (truck) ['fɔːklɪft('trʌk)] (inf) N Gabelstapler m

forlorn [fə'lɔːn] ADJ (a) (= desolate) verlassen; (= miserable) trostlos; **a ~ figure** eine einsame Gestalt; **the palaces stood**

empty and **~** die Paläste standen leer und verlassen da (b) attempt, effort verzweifelt; **in the ~ hope of finding a better life** in der verzweifelten Hoffnung auf ein besseres Leben

forlornly [fə'lɔːnlɪ] ADV (a) stand, wait einsam und verlassen; stare verloren (b) hope, try verzweifelt; (= vainly) vergeblich

form [fɔːm] 1 N (a) Form f; (= shape: of person) Gestalt f; **~ of address** Anrede f; **a ~ of apology** eine Art der Entschuldigung; **in the ~ of** in Form von or +gen; (with reference to people) in Gestalt von +gen; **medicine in tablet ~** Arznei in Tablettenform; **the first prize will take the ~ of a trip to Rome** der erste Preis ist eine Reise nach Rom; **to take ~** (lit, fig) Form or Gestalt annehmen; **to be in fine** or **good ~** in guter Form sein; **to be on/off ~** in/nicht in or außer Form sein; **he was in great ~ that evening** er war an dem Abend in Hochform; **on past ~** auf dem Papier (b) (= document) Formular nt; **printed ~** vorgedrucktes Formular (c) (Brit Sch) Klasse f 2 VT (a) (= shape, mould) object, character formen (into zu) (b) liking, desire, idea, habit entwickeln; friendship schließen; opinion sich (dat) bilden; impression gewinnen; plan entwerfen (c) government, committee, part, circle bilden; company, society, political party gründen; **to ~ a queue** (Brit) or **line** (US) eine Schlange bilden 3 VI (a) (= take shape) Gestalt annehmen (b) **to ~ into a queue** (Brit) or **line** (US)/**into two lines** eine Schlange/zwei Reihen bilden

formal ['fɔːməl] ADJ (a) person, letter, language förmlich; (= official) talks, statement etc formell; occasion, reception feierlich; **to make a ~ apology** sich in aller Form entschuldigen; **~ clothes** or **dress** (for smart occasions) Gesellschaftskleidung f (b) (= ordered) style, approach formal; garden, borders regelmäßig angelegt; room formal eingerichtet; **~ gardens** formal angelegte Gartenanlagen pl (c) (= proper) education, training ordentlich

formality [fɔː'mælɪtɪ] N NO PL (of person, dress, language, ceremony etc) Förmlichkeit f (b) (= matter of form) Formalität f

formalize ['fɔːməlaɪz] VT rules formalisieren; agreement, arrangement formell bekräftigen; relationship formell machen

formally ['fɔːməlɪ] ADV (a) speak, behave, dress förmlich; (= officially) announce, agree etc offiziell; apologize in aller Form; **~ charged** (Jur) offiziell angeklagt (b) (= academically) **he is ~ trained** er hat eine ordentliche Ausbildung

format ['fɔːmæt] 1 N (as regards size, also of computer data, recording) Format nt; (as regards content) Aufmachung f; (Rad, TV: of programme) Struktur f; **page ~** Seitenformat nt 2 VT (Comput) formatieren

formation [fɔː'meɪʃən] N (a) (= act of forming) Formung f; (of government, committee, Gram) Bildung f; (of company, society) Gründung f (b) (of aircraft, dancers) Formation f; **battle ~** Gefechtsaufstellung f

formative ['fɔːmətɪv] ADJ prägend; **her ~ years** die charakterbildenden Jahre in ihrem Leben

former ['fɔːmə'] 1 ADJ (a) president, employee, home, hospital ehemalig; country, place, strength, authority etc früher; times, years, days vergangen; **his ~ wife** seine Exfrau; **in ~ years** or **times** or **days** in früheren Zeiten (b) (as opposed to latter) **the ~ option/alternative** etc die erstere Möglichkeit/Alternative etc 2 N **the ~** der/die/das erstere; (more than one) die ersteren pl

-former [-fɔːmə'] N SUF (Brit Sch) -klässler(in) m(f); **fifth-former** Fünftklässler(in) m(f)

formerly ['fɔːməlɪ] ADV früher; **the ~ communist countries** die ehemals kommunistischen Länder; **we had ~ agreed that ...** wir hatten uns seinerzeit darauf geeinigt, dass ...

form feed N (Comput) Papiervorschub m

Formica® [fɔː'maɪkə] N Resopal® nt

formidable ['fɔːmɪdəbl] ADJ (= commanding respect) person Achtung gebietend; intellect überragend; (= powerful, impressive) challenge, achievement, strength, height gewaltig; person, reputation beeindruckend; opponent mächtig; sight überwältigend; *talents* außerordentlich; *team, combination* außerordentlich stark

formidably ['fɔːmɪdəblɪ] ADV hervorragend; ~ **gifted** *or* **talented** außerordentlich begabt *or* talentiert

formless ['fɔːmlɪs] ADJ formlos

form letter N (*Comput*) Formbrief *m*

formula ['fɔːmjʊlə] N, *pl* **-s** *or* **-e** ['fɔːmjʊliː] **(a)** Formel *f* (*also Sci*); (*for lotion, medicine etc*) Rezeptur *f*; **there's no sure ~ for success** es gibt kein Patentrezept für Erfolg; **all his books follow the same ~** alle seine Bücher sind nach demselben Rezept geschrieben **(b)** NO PL (*also* **formula milk**) Säuglingsmilch *f*

Formula One N (*Motor Racing*) Formel 1

formulate ['fɔːmjʊleɪt] VT formulieren

formulation [,fɔːmjʊ'leɪʃən] N Formulierung *f*

forsake [fə'seɪk], *pret* **forsook** [fə'sʊk], *ptp* **forsaken** [fə'seɪkn] VT verlassen; *bad habits* aufgeben

forswear [fɔː'sweəʳ], *pret* **forswore** [fɔː'swɔːʳ], *ptp* **forsworn** [fɔː'swɔːn] VT abschwören (+*dat*); **he has forsworn smoking** er hat hoch und heilig versprochen, nicht mehr zu rauchen

fort [fɔːt] N (*Mil*) Fort *nt*; **to hold the ~** (*fig*) die Stellung halten

forte¹ ['fɔːteɪ] N (= *strong point*) Stärke *f*

forte² (*Mus*) ADV forte

forth [fɔːθ] ADV (*form, dated*) **(a)** (= *out*) heraus-; (= *forward*) hervor-; **to come ~** herauskommen **(b)** (= *onwards*) **and so ~** und so weiter

forthcoming [fɔːθ'kʌmɪŋ] ADJ (*form*) **(a)** ATTR *event, visit* bevorstehend; *album, book* in Kürze erscheinend; *film, play* in Kürze anlaufend
(b) (= *available*) **to be ~** (*money, funds*) zur Verfügung gestellt werden; (*evidence*) geliefert werden; (*aid, support*) geleistet werden; (*details*) bekannt werden; **not to be ~** ausbleiben
(c) (= *communicative*) *person* mitteilsam; **to be ~ on** *or* **about sth** offen über etw (*acc*) reden; **not to be ~ on** *or* **about sth** sich über etw (*acc*) zurückhalten

forthright ['fɔːθraɪt] ADJ *person, manner* (= *direct*) direkt; (= *frank*) offen; *statement* unverblümt; *language* deutlich

fortieth ['fɔːtɪɪθ] **1** ADJ vierzigste(r, s) **2** N (= *fraction*) Vierzigstel *nt*; (*in series*) Vierzigste(r, s); *see also* **sixth**

fortifications [,fɔːtɪfɪ'keɪʃənz] PL (*Mil*) Befestigungen *pl*

fortified wine [,fɔːtɪfaɪd'waɪn] N weinhaltiges Getränk

fortify ['fɔːtɪfaɪ] VT (*Mil*) *town* befestigen; *wine* mit zuckerreichem Most vergären; *person* bestärken; (*food, drink*) stärken

fortissimo [fɔː'tɪsɪməʊ] (*Mus*) ADV fortissimo

fortitude ['fɔːtɪtjuːd] N (innere) Kraft *or* Stärke

fortnight ['fɔːtnaɪt] N (*esp Brit*) vierzehn Tage

fortnightly ['fɔːtnaɪtlɪ] (*esp Brit*) **1** ADJ vierzehntäglich; *newspaper, magazine* alle zwei Wochen erscheinend; ~ **visits** Besuche *pl* alle vierzehn Tage **2** ADV alle vierzehn Tage

fortress ['fɔːtrɪs] N Festung *f*

fortuitous ADJ, **fortuitously** ADV [fɔː'tjuːɪtəs, -lɪ] zufällig

fortunate ['fɔːtʃənɪt] ADJ glücklich; **we are ~ that/because ...** wir können so von Glück reden, dass/weil ...; **it is ~ that ...** es ist ein Glück, dass ...; **it was ~ for him/Mr Fox that...** es war sein Glück/ein Glück für Mr Fox, dass ...

fortunately ['fɔːtʃənɪtlɪ] ADV zum Glück; ~ **for me, my friend noticed it** zu meinem Glück hat mein Freund es bemerkt

fortune ['fɔːtʃuːn] N **(a)** (= *fate*) Schicksal *nt*; (= *chance*) Zufall *m*; **she followed his ~s with interest** sie verfolgte sein Geschick mit Interesse; **he had the good ~ to have rich parents** er hatte das Glück, reiche Eltern zu haben; **to tell sb's ~** jdm wahrsagen **(b)** (= *money*) Vermögen *nt*; **to come into/make a ~** ein Vermögen erben/machen; **to seek/make one's ~** sein Glück versuchen/machen; **it costs a ~** es kostet ein Vermögen

fortune-teller ['fɔːtʃuːnteləʳ] N Wahrsager(in) *m(f)*

forty ['fɔːtɪ] **1** ADJ vierzig; **to have ~ winks** (*inf*) ein Nickerchen machen (*inf*) **2** N Vierzig *f*; *see also* **sixty**

forum ['fɔːrəm] N Forum *nt*

forward ['fɔːwəd] **1** ADV **(a)** (*also* ~**s**) (= *onwards, ahead*) vorwärts; (= *to the front, to particular point, out of line*) nach vorn; **to take two steps ~** zwei Schritte vortreten; **to rush ~** sich vorstürzen; **to go straight ~** geradeaus gehen; **he drove backward(s) and ~(s) between the station and the house** er fuhr zwischen Haus und Bahnhof hin und her
(b) (*in time*) **from this time ~** (= *from then*) seitdem; (= *from now*) von jetzt an; **to sell ~** (*Comm*) am Terminmarkt verkaufen
(c) (= *into prominence*) **to come ~** sich melden; **to bring ~ new evidence** neue Beweise *pl* vorlegen
2 ADJ **(a)** (*in place*) vordere(r, s); (*in direction*) Vorwärts-; **this seat is too far ~** dieser Sitz ist zu weit vorn
(b) (*in time*) *planning* Voraus-; (*Comm*) *buying, price* Termin-
(c) (= *presumptuous, pert*) dreist
3 N (*Sport*) Stürmer(in) *m(f)*
4 VT **(a)** *plans etc* vorantreiben; *career* voranbringen
(b) (= *dispatch*) *goods* senden; (= *send on*) *letter, parcel* nachsenden; *information* weiterleiten

forward (*St Ex*): **forward contract** N Terminkontrakt *m*; **forward dealing** N Terminhandel *m*

forwarder N (*Comm*) Spediteur(in) *m(f)*

forward exchange N (*Fin*) Termindevisen *pl*

forwarding address [,fɔːwədɪŋə'dres] N Nachsendeadresse *f*

forward-looking ['fɔːwədlʊkɪŋ] ADJ *person, attitude* fortschrittlich; *plan, vision* vorausblickend

forward risk N (*Comm*) Terminrisiko *nt*

forwards ['fɔːwədz] ADV = **forward 1(a)**

forward slash N (*Typ*) Slash *m*, (Vorwärts-)Schrägstrich *m*

forwent [fɔː'went] PRET *of* **forgo**

fossil ['fɒsl] N (*lit*) Fossil *nt*

fossil fuel N fossiler Brennstoff *m*

fossilized ['fɒsɪlaɪzd] ADJ versteinert; (*fig*) *person* verknöchert; *customs* verkrustet

foster ['fɒstəʳ] **1** ADJ ATTR (*Admin*) Pflege-; **their children are in ~ care** ihre Kinder sind in Pflege **2** VT **(a)** *child* in Pflege nehmen **(b)** *music, drama, development* fördern; *image, friendship* pflegen

foster: **foster child** N Pflegekind *nt*; **foster family** N Pflegefamilie *f*; **foster home** N Pflegestelle *f*; **foster parents** PL Pflegeeltern *pl*

fought [fɔːt] PRET, PTP *of* **fight**

foul [faʊl] **1** ADJ **(a)** *place, food, taste, breath* widerlich; *water* faulig; *air* stickig; *smell* ekelhaft
(b) *behaviour, crime* abscheulich; *temper* übel; *day* scheußlich (*inf*); **he was really ~ to her** er war wirklich gemein *or* fies (*inf*) zu ihr; **she has a ~ temper** sie ist ein ganz übellauniger Mensch; **to be in a ~ mood** *or* **temper** eine ganz miese Laune haben (*inf*); ~ **weather** scheußliches Wetter
(c) (= *offensive*) anstößig; ~ **language** Schimpfwörter *pl*
(d) **to fall** *or* **run ~ of the law/authorities** mit dem Gesetz/den Behörden in Konflikt geraten; **to fall** *or* **run ~ of sb** es sich (*dat*) mit jdm verderben
(e) (*Comm*) ~ **bill of lading** unreines Konnossement
2 VT **(a)** *air* verpesten; *beach* verschmutzen; (*dog*) *pavement* verunreinigen
(b) (= *become entangled in*) *mechanism, device* sich verfangen in (+*dat*); *net, fishing line* verheddern
(c) (*Sport*) foulen
3 N (*Sport*) Foul *nt*

foul: **foul-mouthed** ADJ unflätig; **foul play** N **(a)** (*Sport*) unfaires Spiel; (= *fouls*) Fouls *pl* **(b)** (*fig*) Unredlichkeiten *pl*; **the police do not suspect ~** die Polizei hat keinen Verdacht auf einen unnatürlichen Tod

found¹ [faʊnd] PRET, PTP *of* **find**

found² VT (= *set up, base*) gründen; **to ~ sth (up)on sth** *opinion, belief* etw auf etw (*dat*) gründen; **our society is ~ed on this** das ist die Grundlage unserer Gesellschaft; **the novel is ~ed on fact** der Roman basiert auf Tatsachen

foundation [faʊn'deɪʃən] N **(a)** (= *institution*) Stiftung *f*; **research ~** Forschungsstiftung *f* **(b)** ~**s** *pl* (*of house etc*) Fundament *nt* **(c)** (*fig*: = *basis*) Grundlage *f*; **to be without ~** (*rumours, allegations*) jeder Grundlage entbehren; (*fears*) unbegründet sein **(d)** (= *make-up*) Grundierungscreme *f*

founder¹ ['faʊndəʳ] N Gründer(in) *m(f)*; (*of charity, museum*) Stifter(in) *m(f)*; ~**'s share** (*St Ex*) Gründeraktie *f*

founder² VI (= *sink*) (*ship*) sinken **(b)** (*fig*: *plan, project*) scheitern

founder member N Gründungsmitglied *nt*

Founding Fathers ['faʊndɪŋ'fɑːðəz] PL (*US*) Väter *pl*

foundry ['faʊndrɪ] N Gießerei *f*

fount [faʊnt] N **(a)** (*fig*: = *source*) Quelle *f* **(b)** (*Typ*) Schrift *f*

fountain ['faʊntɪn] N Brunnen m; (with upward jets also) Springbrunnen m; (fig: = source) Quelle f

fountain pen N Füllfederhalter m

four [fɔː] **1** ADJ vier; **the Four Hundred** (US) die oberen zehntausend **2** N Vier f; **on all ~s** auf allen vieren; see also **six**

four: **four-door** ADJ ATTR viertürig; **four-figure** ADJ ATTR vierstellig; **fourfold** **1** ADJ vierfach **2** ADV increase um das Vierfache; **four-legged** ADJ vierbeinig; **four-letter word** N Vulgärausdruck m; **four-part** ADJ ATTR series, programme vierteilig; plan aus vier Teilen bestehend; (Mus) für vier Stimmen; harmony, choir vierstimmig; **four-poster (bed)** N Himmelbett nt; **four-seater** **1** ADJ viersitzig **2** N Viersitzer m; **foursome** N Quartett nt; (Sport) Viererspiel nt; **foursquare** ADV (fig) stand fest; **four-star** ADJ Vier-Sterne-; ~ **hotel/restaurant** Vier-Sterne-Hotel/-Restaurant nt; **four-star petrol** N (Brit) Super(benzin) nt

fourteen [fɔː'tiːn] **1** ADJ vierzehn **2** N Vierzehn f; see also **sixteen**

fourteenth [fɔː'tiːnθ] **1** ADJ vierzehnte(r, s) **2** N (= fraction) Vierzehntel nt; (of series) Vierzehnte(r, s); see also **sixteenth**

fourth [fɔːθ] **1** ADJ vierte(r, s) **2** N (= fraction) Viertel nt; (in series) Vierte(r, s); **to drive in ~** (Aut) im vierten Gang fahren; see also **sixth**

FOURTH OF JULY

Der **Fourth of July** (oder auch **Independence Day**) ist der wichtigste Feiertag in den Vereinigten Staaten, an dem der Unterzeichnung der Unabhängigkeitserklärung am 4. Juli 1776 gedacht wird, was als eigentliche Geburtsstunde der USA gilt. Daher sind die Feierlichkeiten recht patriotisch. Viele Bürger hissen die amerikanische Flagge vor ihrem Haus, und im ganzen Land wird mit öffentlichen Veranstaltungen gefeiert: Paraden, Picknicks und nicht zu vergessen das große Feuerwerk am Abend.

fourthly ['fɔːθlɪ] ADV viertens

four: **four-way stop** N (US Aut) Kreuzung, an der alle Verkehrsteilnehmer Vorfahrt gewähren müssen; **four-wheel drive** N Vierradantrieb m

fowl [faʊl] N (= poultry) Geflügel nt; (= one bird) Huhn nt/Gans f/Truthahn m etc

fox [fɒks] **1** N (a) (lit, fig) Fuchs m; **he's a sly ~** (fig) er ist ein schlauer Fuchs (b) (= fur) Fuchs(pelz) m **2** VT (= bewilder) verblüffen

fox: **fox cub** N Fuchsjunge(s) nt; **foxglove** N (Bot) Fingerhut m; **foxhound** N Fuchshund m; **fox-hunting** N Fuchsjagd f; **to go ~** auf die or zur Fuchsjagd gehen; **foxtrot** N Foxtrott m

foyer ['fɔɪeɪ] N (in theatre) Foyer nt; (esp US: in apartment house) Diele f

F.P.A. (Insur) ABBR of **free of particular average** F.P.A., Versicherung gegen Elementarschadenereignisse wie Schiffsuntergang, Feuer, Explosion etc

fracas ['frækɑː] N Tumult m

fraction ['frækʃən] N (a) (Math) Bruch m (b) (fig) Bruchteil m; **move it just a ~ (of an inch)** verrücke es (um) eine Spur; **for a ~ of a second** einen Augenblick lang

Be careful! **fraction** is not translated by the German word **Fraktion**.

fractionally ['frækʃənəlɪ] ADV less, slower geringfügig; ahead um eine Nasenlänge; behind knapp; rise, drop um einen Bruchteil

fractious ['frækʃəs] ADJ verdrießlich; child aufsässig

fracture ['fræktʃə] **1** N Bruch m **2** VTI brechen; **he ~d his shoulder** er hat sich (dat) die Schulter gebrochen; **~d skull** Schädelbruch m

fragile ['frædʒaɪl] ADJ glass, china, object zerbrechlich; structure fragil; fabric fein; beauty, skin, child, health zart; elderly person gebrechlich; ceasefire, peace brüchig; mental state, ego, economy labil; "~ (handle) with care" „Vorsicht, zerbrechlich!"; **to feel ~** (inf) sich angeschlagen fühlen

fragility [frə'dʒɪlɪtɪ] N (of glass, china, object) Zerbrechlichkeit f; (of fabric) Feinheit f; (of health) Zartheit f; (of peace, ceasefire) Brüchigkeit f; (of mental state, economy) Labilität f

fragment ['frægmənt] **1** N Bruchstück nt; (of china, glass) Scherbe f; (of shell, food) Stückchen nt; (of paper, letter) Schnipsel m; (of programme, opera etc) Bruchteil m

2 [fræg'ment] VI (rock, glass) (zer)brechen, in Stücke brechen; (fig: society) zerfallen

fragmentary ['frægməntərɪ] ADJ (lit, fig) fragmentarisch, bruchstückhaft

fragmentation [ˌfrægmen'teɪʃən] N (of society) Zerfall m

fragmented [fræg'mentɪd] ADJ bruchstückhaft; (= broken up) unzusammenhängend

fragrance ['freɪgrəns] N Duft m

fragrant ['freɪgrənt] ADJ duftend; ~ **smell** Duft m; **the air was ~ with the scent of roses** der Duft von Rosen hing in der Luft

frail [freɪl] ADJ (+ER) person gebrechlich; health zart; structure fragil; boat, aircraft leicht gebaut; **to look ~** (of person) schwach aussehen

frailty ['freɪltɪ] N (of person) Gebrechlichkeit f

frame [freɪm] **1** N (a) (= basic structure, of picture) Rahmen m; (of building, ship) Gerippe nt; (of spectacles: also ~s) Gestell nt (b) (of human, animal) Gestalt f (c) ~ **of mind** (= mental state) Verfassung f; (= mood) Stimmung f; **in a cheerful ~ of mind** in fröhlicher Stimmung (d) (fig: framework, system) grundlegende Struktur; **within the ~ of ...** im Rahmen (+gen) ... (e) (Film, Phot) (Einzel)bild nt; (in comic strip) Bild(chen) nt **2** VT (a) picture rahmen; (fig) face etc ein- or umrahmen (b) (= draw up) constitution, plan entwerfen; (= express) answer, question formulieren (c) (inf) **he said he had been ~d** er sagte, man habe ihm die Sache angehängt (inf)

frame: **frame tent** N Steilwandzelt nt; **framework** N (lit) Grundgerüst nt; (fig) (of essay, novel etc) Gerippe nt; (of society, government etc) grundlegende Struktur; **within the ~ of ...** im Rahmen (+gen) ...

franc [fræŋk] N Franc m

France [frɑːns] N Frankreich nt

franchise ['fræntʃaɪz] **1** N (a) (Pol) Wahlrecht nt (b) (Comm) Franchise f **2** VT (Comm) auf Lizenz vergeben

franchising ['fræntʃaɪzɪŋ] N Franchising nt

Franco- ['fræŋkəʊ-] IN CPDS Französisch-, Franko-; **Franco-British** ADJ französisch-britisch; **franco domicile** [ˌfræŋkəʊ'dɒmɪsaɪl] ADV (Comm) frei Haus; **Franco-German** ADJ deutsch-französisch; **francophile** N Franzosenfreund(in) m(f); **he is a ~** er ist frankophil; **Francophone** N Frankophone(r) mf

frank[1] [fræŋk] ADJ (+ER) offen; **to be ~ with sb** offen mit or zu jdm sein; **to be (perfectly) ~ (with you)** um (ganz) ehrlich zu sein

frank[2] VT letter frankieren; (= postmark) letter stempeln

frankfurter ['fræŋkfɜːtə] N (= sausage) (Frankfurter) Würstchen nt

franking machine ['fræŋkɪŋməʃiːn] N Frankiermaschine f

frankly ['fræŋklɪ] ADV (a) say, talk offen (b) (= to be frank) offen or ehrlich gesagt; **quite ~, I don't care** um ganz ehrlich zu sein, es ist mir egal

frankness ['fræŋknɪs] N Offenheit f

frantic ['fræntɪk] ADJ (a) person, phone call, search verzweifelt; **I was ~ with worry** ich war außer mir; **to drive sb ~** jdn zur Verzweiflung treiben (b) week, day hektisch; ~ **activity** (generally) hektisches Treiben; (particular instance) fieberhafte Tätigkeit

frantically ['fræntɪkəlɪ] ADV (a) try, search verzweifelt (b) work, run around hektisch; wave, scribble, run wie wild

frat [fræt] N (US Univ inf) ABBR of **fraternity**

fraternal [frə'tɜːnl] ADJ brüderlich

fraternity [frə'tɜːnɪtɪ] N (= community) Vereinigung f; (US Univ) Verbindung f; **the legal/medical/teaching ~** die Juristen pl/Mediziner pl/Lehrer pl; **the hunting/sailing ~** die Jagd-/Segelfans pl; **the criminal ~** die Kriminellen pl

fraternize ['frætənaɪz] VI (freundschaftlichen) Umgang haben (with mit); (Mil also) fraternisieren (with mit)

fraud [frɔːd] N (a) (no pl) Betrug m; (= trick) Schwindel m; ~s Betrügereien pl (b) (= person) Betrüger(in) m(f); (feigning illness) Simulant(in) m(f); (= fraudulent thing) fauler Zauber (inf)

Fraud Squad N (Brit Police) Betrugsdezernat nt

fraudulent ['frɔːdjʊlənt] ADJ betrügerisch

fraudulently ['frɔːdjʊləntlɪ] ADV act betrügerisch; obtain auf betrügerische Weise

fraught [frɔːt] ADJ **(a)** ~ **with difficulty** voller Schwierigkeiten; ~ **with danger** gefahrvoll; ~ **with tension** spannungsgeladen **(b)** *situation, atmosphere etc* gespannt; *person* angespannt

fray¹ [freɪ] N **ready for the** ~ *(lit, fig)* kampfbereit; **to enter the** ~ *(fig)* sich in den Kampf *or* Streit einschalten

fray² VI *(cloth)* (aus)fransen; *(cuff, rope)* sich durchscheuern; **tempers began to** ~ die Gemüter begannen sich zu erhitzen; **to be** ~**ing at** *or* **around the edges** *(inf: alliance etc)* zu bröckeln beginnen

frayed [freɪd] ADJ *jeans etc* ausgefranst; **tempers were** ~ die Gemüter waren erhitzt

frazzle [ˈfrӕzl] ◼ N *(inf)* **burnt to a** ~ *(Brit)* völlig verkohlt; **worn to a** ~ (= *exhausted*) total kaputt *(inf)* ◼ VT *(US inf: = fray)* ausfransen

freak [friːk] ◼ N **(a)** (= *plant*) Missbildung *f*; (= *person, animal*) Missgeburt *f*; ~ **of nature** Laune *f* der Natur **(b)** (= *event*) außergewöhnlicher Zufall; (= *snowstorm etc*) Anomalie *f* **(c)** *(inf)* jazz/health ~ Jazz-/Gesundheitsfreak *m (inf)* **(d)** *(inf: = weird person)* Irre(r) *mf* ◼ ADJ *weather, conditions* anormal; *wave* ungewöhnlich hoch; *storm* ungewöhnlich stark; *accident* verrückt; *victory, goal* überraschend ◼ VI *(inf)* ausflippen *(inf)*

➤ **freak out** *(inf)* ◼ VI ausflippen *(inf)* ◼ VT SEP **it freaked me out** dabei bin ich ausgeflippt *(inf)*

freakish [ˈfriːkɪʃ] ADJ *weather* launisch

freckle [ˈfrekl] N Sommersprosse *f*

freckled [ˈfrekld], **freckly** [ˈfreklɪ] ADJ sommersprossig

free [friː] ◼ ADJ (+ER) **(a)** frei; **as** ~ **as a bird** *or* **(the) air** frei wie ein Vogel; **to go** ~ (= *not be imprisoned*) frei ausgehen; (= *be set* ~) freigelassen werden; **you're** ~ **to choose** die Wahl steht Ihnen frei; **you're** ~ **to go now** Sie können jetzt gehen(, wenn Sie wollen); **(do) feel** ~ **to help yourself/ask questions** nehmen Sie sich/fragen Sie ruhig; **feel** ~! *(inf)* bitte, gern(e)!; **to give sb a** ~ **hand** jdm freie Hand lassen; **his arms were left** ~ (= *not tied*) seine Arme waren frei (gelassen); ~ **elections** freie Wahlen *pl*; ~ **from worry** sorgenfrei; ~ **from blame/responsibility** frei von Schuld/Verantwortung; ~ **of sth** frei von etw; ~ **of fear** ohne Angst; **a world** ~ **of nuclear weapons** eine Welt ohne Atomwaffen; **at last I was** ~ **of her** endlich war ich sie los; **I wasn't** ~ **earlier** (= *was occupied*) ich hatte nicht eher Zeit **(b)** (= *costing nothing*) kostenlos; *(Comm)* gratis; **it's** ~ das kostet nichts; **admission** ~ Eintritt frei; **to get sth** ~ etw umsonst bekommen; **we got in** ~ *or* **for** ~ *(inf)* wir kamen umsonst rein; ~ **delivery** (porto)freier Versand; ~ **carrier** frei Frachtführer; ~ **entry** *(at customs)* zollfreie Einfuhr; ~ **on board** frei an Bord **(c) to be** ~ **with one's money** großzügig mit seinem Geld umgehen; **to be** ~ **with one's advice** Ratschläge erteilen ◼ VT (= *release*) freilassen; (= *help escape*) *nation* befreien; (= *untie*) losbinden; *caught fabric* lösen; **to** ~ **sb from pain** jdn von seinen Schmerzen befreien; **to** ~ **oneself from sth** sich von etw freimachen

➤ **free up** VT *person, time* freimachen; *money, resources* verfügbar machen

-free ADJ SUF -frei; **alcohol-/tax-free** alkohol-/steuerfrei

free-and-easy [ˈfriːənˈiːzɪ] ADJ ATTR, **free and easy** ADJ PRED ungezwungen; *(morally)* locker

freebie, freebee [ˈfriːbiː] N *(inf)* Werbegeschenk *nt*; **I got it as a** ~ ich habe es gratis bekommen

freedom [ˈfriːdəm] N Freiheit *f*; ~ **of action/speech/worship** Handlungs-/Rede-/Religionsfreiheit *f*; ~ **of choice** Wahlfreiheit *f*; ~ **of the press** Pressefreiheit *f*; **to give sb (the)** ~ **to do sth** jdm (die) Freiheit lassen, etw zu tun; ~ **from sth** Freiheit *f* von etw

freedom fighter N Freiheitskämpfer(in) *m(f)*

free: **free enterprise** N freies Unternehmertum; **free fall** N **to go into** ~ *(economy etc)* sich auf eine rasante Talfahrt begeben

Freefone® [ˈfriːfəʊn] N *(Brit)* **call** ~ **0800** rufen Sie gebührenfrei unter 0800 an

free: **free-for-all** N Gerangel *nt (inf)*; (= *fight*) allgemeine Schlägerei; **free gift** N (Gratis)geschenk *nt*; **freehand** ◼ ADJ ~ **drawing** Freihandzeichnung *f* ◼ ADV aus freier Hand; **freehold** ◼ N Besitzrecht *nt*; **he bought the** ~ **of the house** er hat das Haus gekauft ◼ ADJ ~ **property** freier Grundbesitz; ~ **apartment** Eigentumswohnung *f*; ~ **house** Eigenheim *nt*; **free house** N *(Brit)* Wirtshaus, das nicht an eine bestimmte Brauerei gebunden ist; **free kick** N *(Sport)* Freistoß *m*; **freelance** ◼ ADJ *journalist, writer* frei(schaffend); *work* freiberuflich; **I do a bit of** ~ **journalism** ich arbeite gelegentlich als freier Journalist ◼ ADV freiberuflich ◼ N Freiberufler(in) *m(f)*; *(with particular item)* freier Mitarbeiter, freie Mitarbeiterin; **freeloader** N *(inf)* Schmarotzer(in) *m(f)*

freely [ˈfriːlɪ] ADV **(a)** *spend, give* (= *liberally*) großzügig; (= *willingly*) bereitwillig; *perspire* stark; **to use sth** ~ reichlich von etw Gebrauch machen; **I** ~ **admit that ...** ich gebe gern zu, dass ... **(b)** *move, operate, talk* frei; *elected, contested* in freien Wahlen; *flow, travel* ungehindert; **to be** ~ **available** ohne Schwierigkeiten zu haben sein

free: **free-market economy** N freie Marktwirtschaft; **Freemason** N Freimaurer *m*; **freemasonry** N Freimaurerei *f*; **free-port trade** N Wiederausfuhrhandel *m*; **Freepost®** N "~" ≈ „Gebühr zahlt Empfänger"; **free-range** ADJ *(Brit)* hen frei laufend; *chicken, pig etc* aus Freilandhaltung; ~ **eggs** Eier *pl* von frei laufenden Hühnern; **free sample** N Gratisprobe *f*

freesia [ˈfriːzɪə] N *(Bot)* Freesie *f*

free: **free speech** N Redefreiheit *f*; **freestanding** ADJ frei stehend; **freestyle** N (= *section*) Kür *f*; *(Swimming)* Freistil *m*; **the 200 metres** *(Brit)* or **meters** *(US)* ~ die 200 Meter Freistil; **freethinker** N Freidenker(in) *m(f)*; **free time** N freie Zeit; (= *leisure*) Freizeit *f*; **free trade** N Freihandel *m*; **free verse** N freie Verse *pl*; **freeware** N *(Comput)* Freeware *f*, freie Software; **freeway** N *(US)* Autobahn *f*; **freewheel** VI im Freilauf fahren; **freewheeling, free-wheeling** ADJ *style, atmosphere etc* ungezwungen; **free will** N **he did it of his own** ~ er hat es aus freien Stücken getan

freeze [friːz] *vb*: *pret* **froze**, *ptp* **frozen** ◼ VI **(a)** *(Met)* frieren; *(water, liquids)* gefrieren; *(lakes, rivers)* zufrieren; *(pipes)* einfrieren; **to** ~ **to death** *(lit)* erfrieren; *(fig)* sich zu Tode frieren; **meat** ~**s well** Fleisch lässt sich gut einfrieren **(b)** *(fig: blood, smile)* erstarren **(c)** (= *keep still*) in der Bewegung verharren; ~! keine Bewegung! ◼ VT **(a)** *water* gefrieren; *(Med, Cook)* einfrieren **(b)** *(Econ)* *assets* festlegen; *credit, wages, prices, bank account* einfrieren; (= *stop*) *film* anhalten ◼ N **(a)** *(Met)* Frost *m*; **the big** ~ der harte Frost **(b)** *(Econ)* Stopp *m*; **a wage(s)** ~, **a** ~ **on wages** ein Lohnstopp *m*; **a** ~ **on nuclear weapons testing** ein Atomwaffenteststopp *m*

➤ **freeze onto** VI +PREP OBJ *(US inf)* **to freeze onto sb** sich wie eine Klette an jdn hängen

➤ **freeze over** VI *(lake, river)* überfrieren; *(windscreen, windows)* vereisen

➤ **freeze up** VI zufrieren; *(pipes)* einfrieren; *(windscreen, windows)* vereisen

freeze-dry ['friːzdraɪ] VT gefriertrocknen

freezer ['friːzəʳ] N Tiefkühltruhe f; (upright) Gefrierschrank m; (Brit: = ice compartment of fridge) Gefrierfach nt

freeze-up ['friːzʌp] N (esp US: of lakes, rivers etc) **during the ~ a lot of birds perish** während Seen und Flüsse zugefroren sind, kommen viele Vögel ums Leben

freezing ['friːzɪŋ] **1** ADJ **(a)** (lit) temperature unter Null; ~ **conditions** Temperaturen pl unter null; ~ **weather** Frostwetter nt **(b)** (= extremely cold) eisig; wind eisig; **in the ~ cold** bei klirrender Kälte; **it's ~ (cold)** es ist eiskalt; **I'm ~** mir ist eiskalt; **my hands/feet are ~** meine Hände/Füße sind eiskalt **2** N **(a)** (Cook) Einfrieren nt **(b)** (= ~ point) der Gefrierpunkt; **above/below** ~ über/unter null

freezing point N Gefrierpunkt m; **below** ~ unter null

freight [freɪt] **1** N Fracht f; ~ **forward** (US) unfrei; ~ **in/out** Eingangs-/Ausgangsfracht f **2** ADV **to send sth ~/air** = etw als Frachtgut/per Luftfracht senden **3** VT goods verfrachten

freight: freight car N (US Rail) Güterwagen m; **freight depot** N (US) Güterbahnhof m

freighter ['freɪtəʳ] N (Naut) Frachter m; (Aviat) Frachtflugzeug nt

freight: freight insurance N Frachtkostenversicherung f; **freight note** N Frachtrechnung f; **freight rate** N (Comm) Frachtrate f; **freight terminal** N Fracht- or Güterterminal nt; **freight train** N Güterzug m

French [frentʃ] **1** ADJ französisch; ~ **teacher** Französischlehrer(in) m(f); **a ~ dictionary** ein Französischwörterbuch nt; **he is ~** er ist Franzose **2** N **(a)** (Ling) Französisch nt; **in ~** auf französisch; **to speak ~** Französisch sprechen; **excuse my ~** (hum inf) entschuldigen Sie die Ausdrucksweise **(b) the ~** pl die Franzosen pl

French: French bean N grüne Bohne; **French bread** N Baguette nt; **French-Canadian 1** ADJ person frankokanadisch; **she is ~** sie ist Frankokanadierin **2** N Frankokanadier(in) m(f); **French doors** PL Verandatür f; **French dressing** N (Cook) **(a)** (Brit: = oil and vinegar) Vinaigrette f **(b)** (US: = sweet, tomato-flavoured dressing) French Dressing nt; **French fried potatoes, French fries** PL Pommes frites pl; **French horn** N (Mus) (Wald)horn nt; **French kiss** N Zungenkuss m; **French loaf** N Baguette f; **Frenchman** N Franzose m; **French Revolution** N **the ~** die Französische Revolution; **French Riviera** N **the ~** die französische Riviera; **French stick** N Baguette f; **French toast** N in Ei getunktes gebratenes Brot; **French windows** PL Verandatür f; **Frenchwoman** N Französin f

frenetic [frə'netɪk] ADJ hektisch; dance wild; effort verzweifelt

frenetically [frə'netɪklɪ] ADV (+vb) wie wild; work fieberhaft; dance frenetisch

frenzied ['frenzɪd] ADJ activity, efforts fieberhaft; attack, passion, shouts wild; atmosphere überreizt; applause, crowd, haste rasend

frenzy ['frenzɪ] N Raserei f; **in a ~** in heller or wilder Aufregung; **he worked himself up into a ~** er steigerte sich in eine Raserei (hinein); ~ **of activity** hektische Betriebsamkeit; ~ **of excitement** helle Aufregung

frequency ['friːkwənsɪ] N Häufigkeit f; (Phys) Frequenz f; **high/low ~** Hoch-/Niederfrequenz f

frequency band N Frequenzband nt

frequent ['friːkwənt] **1** ADJ häufig; reports zahlreich; complaint, criticism häufig geäußert; **there are ~ trains** es verkehren viele Züge; **violent clashes were a ~ occurrence** es kam häufig or oft zu gewalttätigen Zusammenstößen **2** [frɪ'kwent] VT (form) place (oft or häufig) besuchen; **he liked to ~ the bars** er hielt sich gern in den Bars auf

frequently ['friːkwəntlɪ] ADV oft, häufig; **all too ~, ...** es kommt allzu oft or häufig vor, dass ...

fresco ['freskəʊ] N Fresko(gemälde) nt

fresh [freʃ] **1** ADJ frisch; instructions, news, wallpaper neu; allegations, reports, inquiries weitere(r, s); fighting, attack erneut; approach, style, writing erfrischend; **he has ~ ideas** er hat erfrischend neue Ideen; ~ **supplies** Nachschub m; **a ~ pot of tea** eine Kanne frisch aufgegossener Tee; **to make a ~ start** neu anfangen; ~ **milk** (not UHT) Frischmilch f; ~ **meat** (not frozen) Frischfleisch nt; ~ **orange juice** frisch gepresster Orangensaft; **as ~ as a daisy** taufrisch **2** ADV **(a)** (= straight) **young men ~ from** or **out of university** junge Männer, die frisch von der Universität kommen;

cakes ~ from the oven ofenfrische Kuchen **(b)** (inf) **we're ~ out of cheese** uns ist gerade der Käse ausgegangen; **they are ~ out of ideas** ihnen sind die Ideen ausgegangen

fresh air N frische Luft; **to go out into the ~** an die frische Luft gehen; **to go for a breath of ~** frische Luft schnappen gehen; **to be (like) a breath of ~** (fig) wirklich erfrischend sein

freshen ['freʃn] **1** VI (wind) auffrischen; (weather, air) frisch werden **2** VT **chewing gum to ~ the breath** Kaugummi, um den Atem zu erfrischen

➤ **freshen up 1** VIR (person) sich frisch machen **2** VT SEP **(a)** child, invalid etc frisch machen **(b)** room etc frischer aussehen lassen; team, image aufmöbeln (inf)

fresher ['freʃəʳ] N (Brit Univ inf) Erstsemester nt (inf)

freshly ['freʃlɪ] ADV frisch; **a ~ baked cake** ein frisch gebackener Kuchen; **the ~ dug grave** das frische Grab

freshman ['freʃmən] N, pl **-men** [-mən] (US) (Univ) Erstsemester nt (inf); (Sch) Frischling m (inf)

freshness ['freʃnɪs] N Frische f; (of outlook) Neuheit f

freshwater ['freʃwɔːtəʳ] ADJ ATTR ~ **fish/eel** Süßwasserfisch m/-aal m

fret¹ [fret] VI sich (dat) Sorgen machen (about um); (baby) unruhig sein; **don't ~** beruhige dich

fret² N (on guitar etc) Bund m

fretful ['fretful] ADJ child quengelig; adult, behaviour wehleidig; (= irritable, on edge) genervt (inf)

fret: fret saw N Laubsäge f; **fretwork** N (in wood) Laubsägearbeit f

Freudian ['frɔɪdɪən] ADJ (Psych, fig) Freudsch attr

Freudian slip N freudsche Fehlleistung; (spoken) freudscher Versprecher

FRG ABBR of **Federal Republic of Germany** BRD f

Fri ABBR of **Friday** Fr.

friar ['fraɪəʳ] N Mönch m; **Friar John** Bruder John

fricassee ['frɪkəsiː] **1** N Frikassee nt **2** VT frikassieren

friction ['frɪkʃən] N **(a)** Reibung f **(b)** (fig) Reibereien pl; **there is constant ~ between them** sie reiben sich ständig aneinander

frictional ['frɪkʃənəl] ADJ loss, heat, effect Reibungs-; unemployment Fluktuations-

friction tape N (US) Isolierband nt

Friday ['fraɪdɪ] N Freitag m; see also **Tuesday**

fridge [frɪdʒ] N Kühlschrank m

fridge-freezer ['frɪdʒ'friːzəʳ] N Kühl-Gefrierkombination f

fried [fraɪd] **1** PRET, PTP of **fry²** **2** ADJ gebraten; ~ **egg** Spiegelei nt; ~ **potatoes** Bratkartoffeln pl

friend [frend] N Freund(in) m(f); (less intimate) Bekannte(r) mf; **to become** or **make ~s with sb** mit jdm Freundschaft schließen; **he makes ~s easily** er findet leicht Freunde; **he's no ~ of mine** er ist nicht mein Freund; **to be ~s with sb** mit jdm befreundet sein; **be a ~** sei so lieb; **we're just (good) ~s** da ist nichts, wir sind nur gut befreundet; **my honourable ~** (Brit Parl)/**learned ~** (Jur) ~ mein verehrter (Herr) Kollege, meine verehrte (Frau) Kollegin; **he's a ~ of the arts** er ist Förderer der schönen Künste

friendly ['frendlɪ] **1** ADJ (+ER) **(a)** person freundlich (also Econ, Fin); argument, advice, attitude freundschaftlich; cat, dog zutraulich; **to be ~ to sb** freundlich or nett zu jdm sein; **to be ~ (with sb)** (= to be friends) (mit jdm) befreundet sein; ~ **relations** freundschaftliche Beziehungen pl; **to be on ~ terms with sb** mit jdm auf freundschaftlichem Fuße stehen; **to become** or **get ~ with sb** sich mit jdm anfreunden **(b)** (Pol) country, nation befreundet; government, corporation freundlich gesinnt (to +dat) **2** N (Sport: = match) Freundschaftsspiel nt

friendly society N (Brit) Versicherungsverein m auf Gegenseitigkeit

friendship ['frendʃɪp] N Freundschaft f

frier ['fraɪəʳ] N (Cook) Fritteuse f

fries [fraɪz] PL (esp US inf) Pommes pl (inf)

Friesian ['friːʒən] (= cow) Deutsche Schwarzbunte f

frieze [friːz] N (Archit) (= picture) Fries m; (= thin band) Zierstreifen m

frigate ['frɪgɪt] N (Naut) Fregatte f

frigging ['frɪgɪŋ] (*sl*) ADJ verdammt (*inf*); **that ~ bus** der verdammte Bus (*inf*)

fright [fraɪt] N Schreck(en) *m*; **to get** *or* **have a ~** sich erschrecken; **to give sb a ~** jdm einen Schreck(en) einjagen; **to take ~** es mit der Angst zu tun bekommen

frighten ['fraɪtn] VT (= *give a sudden fright*) erschrecken; (= *make scared*) Angst machen (+*dat*); (*idea, thought*) Angst *or* Furcht einflößen (+*dat*); **to be ~ed by sth** vor etw (*dat*) erschrecken; **to ~ sb into agreeing to sth** jdm solche Angst machen, dass er/sie einer Sache (*dat*) zustimmt; **to ~ the life out of sb** jdn zu Tode erschrecken

➤ **frighten away** *or* **off** VT SEP abschrecken; (*deliberately*) verscheuchen

frightened ['fraɪtnd] ADJ *person, animal* ängstlich; *voice, look* angsterfüllt; **to be ~ (of sb/sth)** (vor jdm/etw) Angst haben; **don't be ~** hab keine Angst; **they were ~ (that) there would be another earthquake** sie hatten Angst (davor), dass es noch ein Erdbeben geben könnte; **to be ~ to do sth** Angst (davor) haben, etw zu tun; **to be ~ about** *or* **of doing sth** Angst davor haben, etw zu tun

frightening ['fraɪtnɪŋ] ADJ **(a)** (= *alarming*) *experience, incident* Furcht erregend; *situation, sight, prospect, feeling, thought, story* erschreckend; **to look ~** zum Fürchten aussehen **(b)** (= *scary*) beängstigend; **it is ~ to think what could happen** es ist beängstigend, wenn man denkt, was alles passieren könnte

frightful ['fraɪtfʊl] ADJ (*inf*) schrecklich, furchtbar; **to look ~** zum Fürchten aussehen

frightfully ['fraɪtfʊlɪ] ADV (*inf*) schrecklich, furchtbar

frigid ['frɪdʒɪd] ADJ **(a)** (*sexually*) frigide **(b)** (*form*) *atmosphere, manner, smile* frostig

frigidity [frɪ'dʒɪdɪtɪ] N (*sexual*) Frigidität *f*

frill [frɪl] N **(a)** (*on dress, shirt etc*) Rüsche *f*; (*round meat, on plant pot etc*) Manschette *f* **(b)** **~s** *pl* (*fig*: = *ornaments*) Verzierungen *pl*; **with all the ~s** mit allem Drum und Dran (*inf*); **a simple meal without ~s** ein schlichtes Essen

frilly ['frɪlɪ] ADJ (+ER) *cushion, clothing* mit Rüschen; **to be ~** Rüschen haben; **~ dress/underwear** Rüschenkleid *nt*/ -unterwäsche *f*

fringe [frɪndʒ] N **(a)** (*on shawl*) Fransen *pl* **(b)** (*Brit*: = *hair*) Pony *m* **(c)** (*fig*: = *periphery*) Rand *m*; **on the ~ of the forest** am Waldrand; **the ~s of a city** die Randbezirke *pl* einer Stadt

fringe benefits PL zusätzliche Leistungen *pl*

fringed [frɪndʒd] ADJ *skirt, shawl* mit Fransen; *lampshade* mit Fransenkante

fringe: fringe group N Randgruppe *f*; **fringe theatre**, (*US*) **fringe theater** N avantgardistisches Theater

frippery ['frɪpərɪ] N (*pej*) (= *cheap ornament*) Kinkerlitzchen *pl* (*inf*); (= *trivialities*) belanglose Kleinigkeiten *pl*

Frisbee® ['frɪzbɪ] N Frisbee® *nt*

frisk [frɪsk] 🛈 VI (= *leap about*) umhertollen 🔢 VT *suspect etc* filzen (*inf*)

frisky ['frɪskɪ] ADJ (+ER) verspielt

frisson ['friːsɒn] N Schauer *m*

fritter¹ ['frɪtə'] VT (*Brit*: *also* ~ **away**) vergeuden

fritter² N (*Cook*) Beignet *m*; **apple ~** Apfelbeignet *m*

frivolity [frɪ'vɒlɪtɪ] N Frivolität *f*; (*of appearance, writer*) unseriöse Art

frivolous ['frɪvələs] ADJ *person, attitude, remark* frivol; *appearance, writer, scientist* unseriös; *object, activity* albern

frizz [frɪz] 🛈 VT *hair* kräuseln 🔢 VI sich kräuseln

frizz(l)y ['frɪz(l)ɪ] ADJ (+ER) *hair* kraus

fro [frəʊ] ADV *see* **to**, **to-ing and fro-ing**

frock [frɒk] N Kleid *nt*

frog [frɒg] N **(a)** Frosch *m*; **to have a ~ in one's throat** einen Frosch im Hals haben; **he's a big ~ in a small pond** (*US*) er ist ein großes Tier am Ort (*inf*) **(b)** **Frog** (*Brit pej inf*: = *French person*) Franzmann *m* (*dated inf*)

frog: frogman N Froschmann *m*; **frogmarch** VT (*Brit*) (*weg*)schleifen; (= *carry*) zu viert wegtragen; **frogspawn** N Froschlaich *m*

frolic ['frɒlɪk] *vb*: pret, ptp **frolicked** 🛈 VI (*also* ~ **about** *or* **around**) herumtoben 🔢 N Herumtoben *nt*

from [frɒm] PREP **(a)** (*indicating starting place, source, removal*) von (+*dat*); (*indicating place of origin*, = *out of*) aus (+*dat*); **he/**

the **train has come ~ London** er/der Zug ist von London gekommen; **he/it comes** *or* **is ~ Germany** er/es kommt *or* ist aus Deutschland; **where does he come ~?, where is he ~?** woher kommt *or* stammt er?; **the train ~ Manchester** der Zug aus Manchester; **the train ~ Manchester to London** der Zug von Manchester nach London; **~ house to house** von Haus zu Haus; **a representative ~ the company** ein Vertreter/eine Vertreterin der Firma; **tell him ~ me** richten Sie ihm von mir aus; **"~ ..."** (*on envelope, parcel*) „Absender ...", „Abs. ..."; **to take/grab etc sth ~ sb** jdm etw wegnehmen/wegreißen *etc*; **to steal sth ~ sb** jdm etw stehlen; **where did you get that ~?** wo hast du das her?; **I got it ~ the supermarket/Kathy** ich habe es aus dem Supermarkt/von Kathy; **to drink ~ a glass** aus einem Glas trinken; **quotation ~ "Hamlet"/the Bible/Shakespeare** Zitat *nt* aus „Hamlet"/aus der Bibel/nach Shakespeare; **translated ~ the English** aus dem Englischen übersetzt; **made ~ ...** aus ... hergestellt; **he got away ~ his pursuers** er entkam seinen Verfolgern; **he ran away ~ home** er rannte von zu Hause weg; **he escaped ~ prison** er entkam aus dem Gefängnis; **~ inside/underneath** von innen/unten

(b) (*indicating time*) (*in past*) seit (+*dat*); (*in future*) ab (+*dat*), von (+*dat*) ... an; **~ last week until** *or* **to yesterday** von letzter Woche bis gestern; **~ now on** von jetzt an, ab jetzt; **~ then on** von da an; **his childhood** von Kindheit an; **he comes ~ time to time** er kommt von Zeit zu Zeit; **as ~ the 6th May** vom 6. Mai an, ab (dem) 6. Mai; **5 years ~ now** in 5 Jahren

(c) (*indicating distance*) von (+*dat*) (... weg); (~ *town etc*) von (+*dat*) ... (entfernt); **the house is 10 km ~ the coast** das Haus ist 10 km von der Küste entfernt; **to work away ~ home** außer Haus arbeiten

(d) (*indicating lowest amount*) ab (+*dat*); **~ £2/the age of 16 (upwards)** ab £ 2/16 Jahren (aufwärts); **dresses (ranging) ~ £60 to £80** Kleider *pl* zwischen £ 60 und £ 80

(e) (*indicating change*) **things went ~ bad to worse** es wurde immer schlimmer; **he went ~ office boy to director** er stieg vom Laufjungen zum Direktor auf; **a price increase ~ £1 to £1.50 marks** eine Preiserhöhung von £ 1 auf £ 1,50

(f) (*indicating difference*) **he is quite different ~ the others** er ist ganz anders als die andern; **to tell black ~ white** Schwarz und Weiß auseinander halten

(g) (= *because of, due to*) **to act ~ compassion** aus Mitleid handeln; **to die ~ cancer** an Krebs sterben; **weak ~ hunger** schwach vor Hunger; **to suffer ~ sth** an etw (*dat*) leiden; **to shelter ~ the rain** sich vor dem Regen unterstellen; **to protect sb ~ sth** jdn vor etw (*dat*) schützen

(h) (= *on the basis of*) **~ experience** aus Erfahrung; **to judge ~ recent reports ...** nach neueren Berichten zu urteilen ...; **~ your point of view** von Ihrem Standpunkt aus (gesehen); **~ what I heard** nach dem, was ich gehört habe; **~ the look of things ...** (so) wie die Sache aussieht ...

(i) (*Math*) **3 ~ 8 leaves 5** 8 weniger 3 ist 5; **take 12 ~ 18** nimm 12 von 18 weg; **£10 will be deducted ~ your account** £ 10 werden von Ihrem Konto abgebucht

(j) to prevent/stop sb ~ doing sth jdn daran hindern/davon zurückhalten, etw zu tun

(k) +PREP **~ above** *or* **over/across sth** über etw (*acc*) hinweg; **~ beneath** *or* **underneath sth** unter etw (*dat*) hervor; **~ out of sth** aus etw heraus; **~ among the trees** zwischen den Bäumen hervor; **~ inside the house** von drinnen

fromage frais [fromɑːʒ'freɪ] N Quark *m*

frond [frɒnd] N (*of fern*) Farnwedel *m*; (*of palm*) Palmwedel *m*

front [frʌnt] 🛈 N **(a)** (= *forward side, exterior*) Vorderseite *f*; (= *forward part, of building, shirt etc*) Vorderteil *nt*; (= *façade*) Vorderfront *f*; **in ~** vorne; **in ~ of sb/sth** vor jdm/etw; **at the ~ of** (*inside*) vorne in (+*dat*); (*outside*) vor (+*dat*); (= *at the head of*) an der Spitze (+*gen*); **look in ~ of you** blicken Sie nach vorne; **he reached the ~ of the queue** (*Brit*) *or* **line** (*US*) er erreichte die Spitze der Schlange; **she spilled tea down the ~ of her dress** sie verschüttete Tee vorn über ihr Kleid

(b) (*Mil, Pol, Met*) Front *f*; **cold ~** (*Met*) Kalt(luft)front *f*; **we must present a united ~** wir müssen eine geschlossene Front bieten; **on the wages ~** was die Löhne betrifft

(c) (*Brit*: *of sea*) Strandpromenade *f*

(d) (= *outward appearance*) Fassade *f*; **to put on a bold ~** eine tapfere Miene zur Schau stellen; **it's just a ~** das ist nur Fassade

(e) (= *cover for illicit activity*) Tarnung *f*

(f) (*US*: = *figurehead of organization*) Galionsfigur *f*

(g) NO PL (= *effrontery*) Stirn *f*; **to have the ~ to do sth** die

Frechheit besitzen *or* die Stirn haben, etw zu tun **2** ADV **up** ~ vorne; **to move up** ~ nach vorne rücken; **50% up** ~ 50% Vorschuss

3 VI **the houses/windows ~ onto the street** die Häuser liegen/ die Fenster gehen auf die Straße hinaus **4** VT *organization, band* leiten **5** ADJ vorderste(r, s), Vorder-; *page* erste(r, s); ~ **tooth/wheel/ room** Vorderzahn *m*/-rad *nt*/-zimmer *nt*; ~ **row** erste *or* vorderste Reihe

frontage ['frʌntɪdʒ] N (*of building*) Front *f*; (= *ground in front of house*) Grundstück *or* Gelände *nt* vor dem Haus

frontal ['frʌntl] ADJ ATTR ~ **assault** *or* **attack** Frontalangriff *m*

front: front bench N (*Parl*) vorderste *or* erste Reihe (*wo die führenden Politiker sitzen*); **front door** N Haustür *f*; **front garden** N Vorgarten *m*

frontier ['frʌn'tɪəʳ] N (*lit, fig*) Grenze *f*; (= *boundary area*) Grenzgebiet *nt*; **to push back the ~s of science** auf wissenschaftliches Neuland vorstoßen

frontispiece ['frʌntɪspiːs] N zweite Titelseite

front: front line N Front(linie) *f*; **frontline** ADJ (*Mil*) Front-; ~ **states** Anliegerstaaten *pl* (*an einen Kriegsschauplatz*); ~ **troops** Fronttruppen *pl*; **front man** N Mann *m* an der Spitze; (*pej*) Strohmann *m*; **front money** N (*US: paid upfront*) Vorschuss *m*; **front office** N (*US Comm*) Verwaltung *f*; **front page** N Titelseite *f*; **front-page** ADJ ATTR *news* auf der ersten Seite; **to be** *or* **make ~ news** Schlagzeilen machen; **front rank** N **to be in the ~** (*fig*) zur Spitze zählen; **frontrunner** N (*fig*) Spitzenreiter(in) *m(f)*; **front seat** N Platz *m* in der ersten Reihe; (*Aut*) Vordersitz *m*; (*fig*) Logenplatz *m*

frost [frɒst] **1** N Frost *m*; (*on leaves etc*) Raureif *m*; **ten degrees of ~** zehn Grad Kälte **2** VT (*esp US*) *cake* mit Zuckerguss überziehen

frost: frostbite N Frostbeulen *pl*; (*more serious*) Erfrierungen *pl*; **to suffer (from) ~** Frostbeulen/Erfrierungen haben; **frostbitten** ADJ *fingers, toes* erfroren; **he was badly ~** er hatte sehr starke Erfrierungen

frosted ['frɒstɪd] ADJ (a) (*fig*) *eye shadow* metallisch (b) (*esp US*: = *iced*) mit Zuckerguss überzogen

frosted glass N Milchglas *nt*

frostily ['frɒstɪlɪ] ADV *say* frostig; *smile* kühl

frosting ['frɒstɪŋ] N (*esp US*) Zuckerguss *m*

frosty ['frɒstɪ] ADJ (+ER) (*lit, fig*) frostig; (= *frost-covered*) *ground, grass* von Raureif bedeckt; *look* eisig; *relations* unterkühlt; ~ **night** Frostnacht *f*; ~ **weather** Frostwetter *nt*

froth [frɒθ] **1** N (a) (*on liquids, Med*) Schaum *m* (b) (= *light conversation, frivolities*) Firlefanz *m* **2** VI schäumen; **a cup of ~ing coffee** eine Tasse Kaffee mit Schaum; **the dog was ~ing at the mouth** der Hund hatte Schaum vor dem Maul; **he was ~ing at the mouth (with rage)** er schäumte vor Wut

frothy ['frɒθɪ] ADJ (+ER) *beer, coffee, sea etc* schäumend; *mixture, cream* schaumig

frown [fraʊn] **1** N Stirnrunzeln *nt no pl*; **to give a ~** die Stirn(e) runzeln; **angry ~** finsterer Blick **2** VI (*lit, fig*) die Stirn(e) runzeln (*at* über +*acc*)

➤ **frown (up)on** VI +PREP OBJ (*fig*) missbilligen; **this practice is frowned (up)on** diese Gewohnheit ist verpönt

froze [frəʊz] PRET *of* **freeze**

frozen ['frəʊzn] **1** PTP *of* **freeze**

2 ADJ (a) *ground* gefroren; *pipe* eingefroren (*also Econ, Fin, Med*); *lock* zugefroren; ~ **hard** hart gefroren; ~ **(over)** *lake, river* zugefroren; ~ **solid** ganz zugefroren (b) *vegetables, meat* tiefgekühlt; ~ **peas** gefrorene Erbsen (c) (*inf*) *person, part of body* eiskalt; **I'm ~** mir ist eiskalt; **to be ~ stiff** steif gefroren sein (d) (= *rigid*) starr; ~ **in horror/with fear** starr *or* steif vor Schreck/vor Angst

frozen: frozen assets PL (*Fin*) festliegendes Kapital; **frozen food** N Tiefkühlkost *f*; ~ **compartment** Gefrierfach *nt*

frugal ['fruːgəl] ADJ *person, life* genügsam; *meal* karg; *food, diet* bescheiden

frugally ['fruːgəlɪ] ADV *live* genügsam; *use* sparsam; *eat* sehr wenig

fruit [fruːt] N (*as collective*) Obst *nt*; (*Bot, fig*) Frucht *f*; **is it a ~ or a vegetable?** ist es Obst oder Gemüse?; **would you like some** *or* **a piece of ~?** möchten Sie etwas Obst?; **to bear ~** (*lit, fig*) Früchte tragen

fruit: fruit bowl N Obstschale *f*; **fruitcake** N englischer Kuchen *m*; **fruit cocktail** N Obstsalat *m*; **fruit drop** N Drops *m*

fruiterer ['fruːtərəʳ] N (*esp Brit*) Obsthändler(in) *m(f)*

fruitful ['fruːtfʊl] ADJ *talks, meeting* fruchtbar; *life, career* produktiv; (= *successful*) *attempt, inquiries* erfolgreich; **it would be more ~ to wait until January** man hätte mehr davon, den Januar abzuwarten

fruitfully ['fruːtfəlɪ] ADV (= *usefully*) nutzbringend; (= *advantageously*) vorteilhaft

fruition [fruːˈɪʃən] N **to come to ~** sich verwirklichen

fruitless ['fruːtlɪs] ADJ fruchtlos, erfolglos; *attempt* vergeblich; **it is ~ to try** es ist zwecklos *or* sinnlos, es zu versuchen

fruit: fruit machine N (*Brit*) Spielautomat *m*; **fruit salad** N Obstsalat *m*; **fruit tree** N Obstbaum *m*

fruity ['fruːtɪ] ADJ (+ER) (a) *taste, wine* fruchtig (b) *voice* volltönend

frump [frʌmp] N (*pej*) Vogelscheuche *f* (*inf*)

frumpy ['frʌmpɪ] ADJ (*pej*) ohne jeden Schick

frustrate [frʌˈstreɪt] VT *person* frustrieren; *hopes* zunichte machen; *plans, plot* durchkreuzen; **he was ~d in his efforts** seine Anstrengungen waren vergebens

frustrated [frʌˈstreɪtɪd] ADJ frustriert; **I get ~ when people criticize my work** es frustriert mich, wenn meine Arbeit kritisiert wird; **he's a ~ poet** er wäre gern ein Dichter

frustrating [frʌˈstreɪtɪŋ] ADJ frustrierend

frustration [frʌˈstreɪʃən] N Frustration *f no pl*

fry¹ [fraɪ] PL (= *fish*) kleine Fische *pl*

fry² **1** VT (a) *meat etc* (in der Pfanne) braten; **to ~ an egg** ein Ei in die Pfanne schlagen (b) (*US inf*: = *electrocute*) auf dem elektrischen Stuhl hinrichten **2** VI (a) (*meat etc*) braten (b) (*US inf*) auf dem elektrischen Stuhl hingerichtet werden **3** N (*US*) Barbecue *nt*

fryer ['fraɪəʳ] N (*Cook*) Fritteuse *f*

frying pan ['fraɪɪŋpæn] N Bratpfanne *f*; **to jump out of the ~ into the fire** (*Prov*) vom Regen in die Traufe kommen (*Prov*)

fry-up ['fraɪʌp] N Pfannengericht *nt*; **to have a ~** sich (*dat*) etwas zusammenbrutzeln (*inf*)

FT ABBR *of* **Financial Times**

ft ABBR *of* **foot/feet** ft

F term N (*Comm*) F-Klausel *f*

fuchsia ['fjuːʃə] N Fuchsie *f*

fuck [fʌk] (*vulg*) **1** VT (a) (*lit*) ficken (*vulg*) (b) **you can get ~ed!, ~ you!** leck mich am Arsch (*vulg*); ~ **him!** der kann mich doch am Arsch lecken (*vulg*); ~ **this car!** dieses Scheißauto! (*inf*) **2** VI ficken (*vulg*) **3** N (a) (*lit*) Fick *m* (*vulg*); **to have a ~** ficken (*vulg*); **he's a good ~** er fickt gut (*vulg*) (b) **I don't give a ~** ich kümmere mich einen Scheiß darum (*inf*); **who/what/where the ~ is that?** wer/was/wo ist denn das, verdammt noch mal? (*inf*) **4** INTERJ (verdammte) Scheiße (*inf*)

➤ **fuck about** *or* **around** (*Brit vulg*) **1** VI rumgammeln (*inf*) **2** VT SEP verarschen (*inf*)

➤ **fuck off** VI (*vulg*) sich verpissen (*sl*); **fuck off!** verpiss dich! (*sl*)

➤ **fuck up** (*vulg*) **1** VT SEP versauen (*inf*); *piece of work, life* verpfuschen (*inf*); **she is really fucked up** (*psychologically*) sie ist total verkorkst (*inf*); **heroin will really fuck you up** Heroin macht dich echt kaputt (*inf*) **2** VI Scheiß machen (*inf*)

fuck-all ['fʌkˈɔːl] N einen Scheiß (*sl*); **he knows ~ about it** er hat null Ahnung (*inf*); **I've done ~ all day** ich hab den ganzen Tag nichts geschafft gekriegt (*inf*)

fucker ['fʌkəʳ] N (*vulg*) Arsch *m* (*vulg*), Arschloch *nt* (*vulg*)

fucking ['fʌkɪŋ] (*vulg*) **1** ADJ Scheiß- (*inf*); **this ~ machine** diese Scheißmaschine (*inf*); ~ **hell!** verdammte Scheiße! (*inf*) **2** ADV (*intensifying*) **it's ~ cold** es ist arschkalt (*inf*); **a ~ awful film** ein total beschissener Film (*inf*)

fuddled ['fʌdld] ADJ (= *muddled*) verwirrt; (= *tipsy*) beschwipst

fuddy-duddy ['fʌdɪˌdʌdɪ] N (*inf*) komischer Kauz (*inf*); **an old ~** ein alter Kauz

fudge [fʌdʒ] **1** N (a) (*Cook*) Fondant *m* (b) **her answer was a ~** ihre Antwort war ein Ausweichmanöver **2** VT *question, issue* ausweichen (+*dat*)

fuel [fjʊəl] **1** N Brennstoff *m*; (*for vehicle*) Kraftstoff *m*; (= *petrol*) Benzin *nt*; (*Aviat, Space*) Treibstoff *m*; (*fig*) Nahrung *f*; **to add ~ to the flames** *or* **fire** (*fig*) Öl in die Flammen *or* ins Feuer gießen

2 VT (= *fill*) *stove etc* mit Brennstoff versorgen; *ships etc* auftanken; (= *drive, propel*) antreiben; (*fig*) *conflict* schüren; *debate* anfachen; *inflation* anheizen; *speculation* Nahrung geben (*+dat*); **power stations fuelled** (*Brit*) *or* **fueled** (*US*) **by oil** mit Öl befeuerte Kraftwerke

fuel gauge N Benzinuhr *f*

fueling station [ˈfjʊəlɪnˌsteɪʃən] N (*US*) Tankstelle *f*

fuel: fuel-injected ADJ ~ **engine** Einspritzmotor *m*; **fuel injection** N (Benzin)einspritzung *f*; **fuel oil** N Gasöl *nt*; **fuel pump** N Benzinpumpe *f*; **fuel shortage** N Brennstoffknappheit *f*; **fuel tank** N Öltank *m*

fugitive [ˈfjuːdʒɪtɪv] **1** N Flüchtling *m* (*from* vor *+dat*); **he is a ~ from justice** er ist auf der Flucht vor der Justiz **2** ADJ flüchtig

fulcrum [ˈfʌlkrəm] N Dreh- *or* Stützpunkt *m*; (*fig*) Angelpunkt *m*

fulfil, (*US*) **fulfill** [fʊlˈfɪl] VT erfüllen; *task, order* ausführen; *ambition* verwirklichen; **the prophecy was ~led** die Prophezeiung erfüllte sich; **to be** *or* **feel ~led** Erfüllung finden

fulfilling [fʊlˈfɪlɪn] ADJ **a ~ job** ein Beruf, in dem man Erfüllung findet

fulfilment, (*US*) **fulfillment** [fʊlˈfɪlmənt] N Erfüllung *f*

full [fʊl] **1** ADJ (+ER) voll; *figure, skirt* füllig; *description, report* vollständig; *understanding, sympathy* vollste(r, s); **to be ~ of ...** voller (*+gen*) *or* voll von ... sein; **he's ~ of good ideas** er steckt voll(er) guter Ideen; **don't talk with your mouth ~** sprich nicht mit vollem Mund; **with his arms ~** mit voll geladenen Armen; **I have a ~ day ahead of me** ich habe einen ausgefüllten Tag vor mir; **I am ~ (up)** (*inf*) ich bin voll (bis obenhin) (*inf*); **we are ~ up for July** wir sind für Juli völlig ausgebucht; **at ~ speed** in voller Fahrt; **to make ~ use of sth** etw voll ausnutzen; **that's a ~ day's work** damit habe ich *etc* den ganzen Tag zu tun; **I waited two ~ hours** ich habe zwei ganze Stunden gewartet; **the ~ details** die genauen *or* alle Einzelheiten; **shots of the Rocky Mountains in ~ colour** (*Brit*) *or* **color** (*US*) schöne Farbaufnahmen von den Rocky Mountains; **to be ~ of oneself** von sich (selbst) eingenommen sein; **she was ~ of it** sie hat gar nicht mehr aufgehört, davon zu reden; **the papers were ~ of it for weeks** die Zeitungen waren wochenlang voll davon

2 ADV **it is a ~ five miles from here** es sind volle *or* gute fünf Meilen von hier; **I know ~ well that ...** ich weiß sehr wohl, dass ...; **to hit sb ~ in the face** jdn voll ins Gesicht schlagen; **to look sb ~ in the face** jdm voll in die Augen sehen **3** N **in ~** ganz, vollständig; **to write one's name in ~** seinen Namen ausschreiben; **to pay in ~** den vollen Betrag bezahlen

full: full beam N (*Brit Aut*) Fernlicht *nt*; **to drive (with one's headlights) on ~** mit Fernlicht fahren; **full-blooded** [fʊlˈblʌdɪd] ADJ (= *vigorous*) kräftig; **he's a ~ German/Scot** er ist Vollblutdeutscher/-schotte; **full-blown** ADJ *crisis, love affair, war* richtiggehend; *scandal* ausgewachsen; *investigation* gründlich; *heart attack* richtig; **~ Aids** Vollbild-Aids *nt*; **full-bodied** [fʊlˈbɒdɪd] ADJ *wine* vollmundig; **full costing** N (*Comm*) Vollkostenkalkulation *f*, Vollkostenrechnung *f*; **full-court press** N (*US fig inf*) **to give sb the ~** jdn stark unter Druck setzen; **full-cream milk** N Vollmilch *f*; **full-dress** [ˈfʊldres] ADJ ~ **uniform** Galauniform *f*; **full employment** N Vollbeschäftigung *f*; **full-face** ADJ *portrait* mit zugewandtem Gesicht; **~ photograph** En-Face-Foto *nt* (*spec*); **full-flavoured**, (*US*) **full-flavored** ADJ vollmundig; **full-fledged** ADJ (*US*) = **fully fledged**; **full-frontal** ADJ Nackt-; (*fig*) *assault* direkt; **the ~ nudity in this play** die völlig nackten Schauspieler in diesem Stück; **full-grown** ADJ ausgewachsen; **full house** N (*bei Konzert etc*) volles Haus; **each night they played to a ~** sie spielten jeden Abend vor vollem Haus; **full insurance** N Voll(wert)versicherung *f*; **full-length** **1** ADJ (a) *play, film* abendfüllend; *novel, album* vollständig **(b)** *coat, dress* (boden)lang; *boots* hoch; *curtains* bodenlang; **~ mirror** großer Spiegel(, in dem man sich ganz sehen kann); **~ portrait** Ganzporträt *nt* **2** ADV *lie* (lang) ausgestreckt; **full member** N Vollmitglied *nt*; **full moon** N Vollmond *m*; **full name** N Vor- und Zuname *m*

fullness [ˈfʊlnɪs] N **in the ~ of time** (= *eventually*) zu gegebener Zeit; (= *at predestined time*) da *or* als die Zeit gekommen war

full: full-on ADJ (*inf*: = *complete, out-and-out*) total (*inf*); **they had a ~ traditional wedding** sie feierten eine traditionelle Hochzeit mit allem Drum und Dran; **full-page** ADJ ganzseitig; **full pay** N **to be suspended on ~** unter Fortzahlung der vollen Bezüge suspendiert sein; **full-scale** ADJ **(a)** *war, riot, offensive* richtiggehend; *investigation, review* gründlich; *search* groß angelegt; *production* serienmäßig; *debate, negotiations, report* umfassend **(b)** *drawing, model* in Originalgröße; **full-size(d)** ADJ *bicycle etc* richtig (groß); *violin* ganz; **full-sized** ADJ *model, drawing* lebensgroß; **full stop** N (*esp Brit Gram*) Punkt *m*; **to come to a ~** zum völligen Stillstand kommen; **I'm not going, ~!** (*inf*) ich gehe nicht und damit basta (*inf*); **full time** **1** N (*Sport*) reguläre Spielzeit; **at ~** nach Ablauf der regulären Spielzeit; **the whistle blew for ~** das Spiel wurde abgepfiffen **2** ADV *work* ganztags; *study* voll; **full-time** ADJ **(a)** *worker* ganztags angestellt; **~ job** Ganztagsstelle *f*; **it's a ~ job** (*fig inf*) es hält einen ganz schön auf Trab (*inf*); **~ work** Ganztagsarbeit *f*; **~ student** Vollstudent(in) *m(f)* **(b)** (*Sport*) **the ~ score** der Schlussstand

fully [ˈfʊlɪ] ADV **(a)** *fit, aware, conscious* völlig; *developed, operational, qualified* voll; *understand, recover* voll und ganz; *comply, participate* uneingeschränkt; *discuss, describe, answer* ausführlich; **~ automatic** vollautomatisch; **~ booked** (ganz *or* völlig) ausgebucht; **~ clothed** (ganz) angezogen; **~ comprehensive insurance** Vollkaskoversicherung *f*; **a ~- equipped kitchen** eine komplett ausgestattete Küche; **~ illustrated** vollständig illustriert **(b)** (= *at least*) **~ 200 years** gute 200 Jahre; **~ one-quarter of the workers** ein gutes Viertel der Arbeiter

fully: **fully fledged** ADJ *member, citizen* richtig; *doctor, teacher etc* vollqualifiziert; **fully paid-up** ADJ *member* (*lit*) ohne Beitragsrückstände; (*fig*) eingeschrieben; **fully qualified** ADJ vollqualifiziert *attr*

fulminate [ˈfʊlmɪneɪt] VI (*fig*) wettern

fulsome [ˈfʊlsəm] ADJ (= *effusive*) überschwänglich; (= *exaggerated*) übertrieben

fumble [ˈfʌmbl] **1** VI (*also* ~ **about** *or* **around**) umhertasten; **to ~ (about) for sth** nach etw suchen *or* tasten; (*in case, pocket, drawer*) nach etw wühlen; **to ~ with sth** an etw (*dat*) herumfummeln **2** VT vermasseln (*inf*); **to ~ the ball** den Ball nicht sicher fangen

fume [fjuːm] VI (*fig inf: person*) wütend sein

fumes [fjuːmz] PL Dämpfe *pl*; (*of car*) Abgase *pl*; **petrol** (*Brit*) *or* **gas** (*US*) **~** Benzindämpfe *pl*

fumigate [ˈfjuːmɪgeɪt] VT ausräuchern

fun [fʌn] **1** N Spaß *m*; **to have great ~ doing sth** viel Spaß daran haben, etw zu tun; **in ~** (= *as a joke*) im *or* als Scherz; **this is ~!** das macht Spaß *or* Freude!; **we just did it for ~** wir haben das nur aus *or* zum Spaß gemacht; **to spoil the ~** den Spaß verderben; **it's ~ doing this** es macht Spaß, das zu tun; **it's no ~ living on your own/being broke** es macht nicht gerade Spaß, allein zu leben/pleite (*inf*) zu sein; **he is great ~** man kriegt mit ihm viel Spaß (*inf*); **the party was good ~** die Party hat viel Spaß gemacht; **that sounds like ~** das klingt gut; **I wasn't serious, I was just having a bit of ~** das hab ich nicht ernst gemeint, ich hab doch nur Spaß gemacht; **to make ~ of** *or* **poke ~ at sb/sth** sich über jdn/etw lustig machen; **like ~** (*US inf*) (ja,) Pustekuchen! (*inf*) **2** ADJ ATTR (*inf*) **squash is a ~ game** Squash macht Spaß; **he's a real ~ person** er ist wirklich ein lustiger Kerl

function [ˈfʌŋkʃən] **1** N **(a)** (*of heart, tool, word etc*) Funktion *f* (*also Math*); (*of person*) Aufgaben *pl*, Pflichten *pl* **(b)** (= *meeting*) Veranstaltung *f*; (= *reception*) Empfang *m*; (= *official ceremony*) Feier *f* **2** VI funktionieren; **to ~ as** fungieren als

functional [ˈfʌŋkʃənəl] ADJ **(a)** (= *able to operate*) funktionsfähig **(b)** (= *utilitarian*) zweckmäßig

functionary [ˈfʌŋkʃənərɪ] N Funktionär(in) *m(f)*

function key N (*Comput*) Funktionstaste *f*

fund [fʌnd] **1** N **(a)** (*Fin*) Fonds *m* **(b)** **funds** PL Mittel *pl*, Gelder *pl*; **public ~s** öffentliche Mittel *pl*; **~s flow statement** (*Comm, Fin*) Kapitalflussrechnung *f*; **to be pressed for ~s, to be short of ~s** knapp bei Kasse sein (*inf*) **(c)** (*of wisdom, humour etc*) Schatz *m* (*of* von *+gen*) **2** VT finanzieren

fundamental [ˌfʌndəˈmentl] **1** ADJ **(a)** (= *essential*) *issue, question* grundlegend; *reason* eigentlich; *point* zentral; *feature, part* wesentlich; **~ principle/right/beliefs**

Grundprinzip *nt*/**-recht** *nt*/**-überzeugungen** *pl*; **of ~ importance** von grundlegender Bedeutung; **carbon is ~ to life** Kohlenstoff ist für alles Leben grundlegend **(b)** (= *basic*) *problem, difference, contradiction* grundsätzlich; *change, revolution, shift* grundlegend; *mistake, flaw* fundamental; **I don't doubt his ~ goodness** ich zweifle nicht daran, dass er im Grunde ein guter Mensch ist; **~ structure/ form** Grundstruktur *f*/-form *f* **2** PL **~s** (*of subject*) Grundbegriffe *pl*; (*of problem*) Grundlagen *pl*; **to get down to (the) ~s** bis zu den Grundlagen vordringen

fundamentalism [ˌfʌndə'mentəlɪzəm] N Fundamentalismus *m*

fundamentally [ˌfʌndə'mentəlɪ] ADV im Grunde (genommen); *different, wrong, flawed, change, affect* grundlegend; *disagree* grundsätzlich; **~ different views** grundlegend unterschiedliche Ansichten; **the treaty is ~ flawed** der Vertrag enthält grundlegende Fehler

fundholding ['fʌndhəʊldɪŋ] ADJ (*Brit*) **~ doctor** *or* **GP** Arzt, der die Finanzen seiner Praxis selbst verwaltet

funding ['fʌndɪŋ] N Finanzierung *f*

fund: fund manager N (*Fin*) Fondsverwalter(in) *m(f)*; **fundraiser** N Spendensammler(in) *m(f)*; **fundraising** N Geldbeschaffung *f*; **~ campaign** Aktion *f* zur Geldbeschaffung; (*for donations*) Spendenaktion *f*

funeral ['fjuːnərəl] N Beerdigung *f*; **were you at his ~?** waren Sie auf seiner Beerdigung?; **well, that's your ~** (*inf*) das ist dein Problem (*inf*)

funeral: funeral director N Beerdigungsunternehmer(in) *m(f)*; **funeral home** N (*US*) Leichenhalle *f*; **funeral march** N Trauermarsch *m*; **funeral parlour** N (*Brit*) Leichenhalle *f*; **funeral service** N Trauergottesdienst *m*

funereal [fjuː'nɪərɪəl] ADJ trübselig

funfair ['fʌnfɛəʳ] N Kirmes *f*

fungal ['fʌŋgəl] ADJ Pilz-; **~ infection** Pilzinfektion *f*

fungi ['fʌŋgaɪ] PL *of* **fungus**

fungicide ['fʌŋgɪsaɪd] N Fungizid *nt*

fungus ['fʌŋgəs] N, *pl* **fungi** (*Bot, Med*) Pilz *m*

funicular (railway) [fjuː'nɪkjʊlə('reɪlweɪ)] N Seilbahn *f*

funk [fʌŋk] **1** N **(a)** (*esp Brit inf*: = *fear*) Schiss *m* (*inf*); **to be in a (blue) ~** (vor Angst) die Hosen voll haben (*inf*) **(b)** (*Mus*) Funk *m* **2** VT kneifen vor (+*dat*) (*inf*); **he ~ed it** er hat (davor) gekniffen (*inf*)

funky ['fʌŋkɪ] ADJ (+ER) (*inf*) geil (*sl*), funky (*sl*); **~ beat** (*inf*) Funkrhythmus *m*

fun-loving ['fʌnlʌvɪŋ] ADJ lebenslustig

funnel ['fʌnl] **1** N **(a)** (*for pouring*) Trichter *m* **(b)** (*Naut, Rail*) Schornstein *m* **2** VT (*fig*) schleusen

funnily ['fʌnɪlɪ] ADV **(a)** (= *strangely*) komisch, merkwürdig **(b)** (= *amusingly*) amüsant

funny ['fʌnɪ] **1** ADJ (+ER) **(a)** (= *comical, odd*) komisch; (= *witty*) *person* witzig; **don't try to be ~** (*inf*) mach keine Witze!; **to see the ~ side of sth** das Lustige an etw (*dat*) sehen; **it's not ~!** das ist überhaupt nicht komisch *or* zum Lachen!; **to have ~ ideas about sth** merkwürdige Vorstellungen von etw haben; **there's something ~ about that place** der Ort ist irgendwie merkwürdig *or* seltsam; **(it's) ~ (that) you should say that** komisch, dass Sie das sagen; **I just feel a bit ~** (*inf*) mir ist ein bisschen komisch *or* mulmig (*inf*); **I feel ~ about seeing her again** (*inf*) mir ist komisch dabei zumute, sie wiederzusehen **(b)** (*inf*: = *mad*) *person* merkwürdig; **she's a bit ~ (in the head)** sie spinnt ein bisschen (*inf*) **(c)** (*inf*: = *suspicious*) **~ business** *or* **tricks** faule Sachen *pl or* Tricks *pl* (*inf*); **there's something ~ going on here** hier ist doch was faul (*inf*); **don't try anything ~** keine faulen Tricks! (*inf*) **2** PL **the funnies** (*US Press inf*) die Comicstrips *pl*

funny: funny bone N Musikantenknochen *m*; **funny man** N (*inf*) Komiker *m*

fun run N Volkslauf *m* (*oft für wohltätige Zwecke durchgeführt*)

fur [fɜːʳ] **1** N **(a)** (*on animal*) Fell *nt*; (*for clothing*) Pelz *m*; **the cat has beautiful ~** die Katze hat ein wunderschönes Fell; **a ~-lined coat** ein pelzgefütterter Mantel **(b) furs** PL Pelze *pl* **(c)** (*in kettle etc*) Kesselstein *m*; (*Med*: *on tongue*) Belag *m* **2** ATTR Pelz-; **~ coat/collar** Pelzmantel *m*/-kragen *m*

▸ **fur up 1** VI (*kettle, boiler*) verkalken; (*tongue*) pelzig werden **2** VT **to be furred up** (*tongue*) pelzig sein; (*kettle, boiler*) verkalkt sein

furious ['fjʊərɪəs] ADJ **(a)** wütend; *debate, attack, battle* heftig; **he was ~ that they had ignored him** er war wütend darüber, dass sie ihn ignoriert hatten; **to be ~ about** *or* **at** *or* **over sth** wütend über etw (*acc*) sein; **to be ~ at** *or* **with sb (for doing sth)** wütend auf jdn sein(, weil er/sie etw getan hat) **(b)** *pace, speed* rasend; **at a ~ pace** in rasendem Tempo; **the jokes came fast and ~** die Witze kamen Schlag auf Schlag

furiously ['fjʊərɪəslɪ] ADV **(a)** *react, say* wütend **(b)** *work, scribble, search* wie wild

furl [fɜːl] VT *sail, flag* einrollen; *umbrella* zusammenrollen

furlong ['fɜːlɒŋ] N Achtelmeile *f*

furnace ['fɜːnɪs] N Hochofen *m*; (*Metal*) Schmelzofen *m*; **this room is like a ~** dieses Zimmer ist ja das reinste Treibhaus

furnish ['fɜːnɪʃ] VT **(a)** *house* einrichten; **~ed room** möbliertes Zimmer; **~ed flat** (*esp Brit*) *or* **apartment** möblierte Wohnung; **to live in ~ed accommodation** zur Miete wohnen (*in einer möblierten Wohnung*) **(b)** *information, reason, excuse* liefern; **to ~ sb with sth** jdm etw liefern

furnishings ['fɜːnɪʃɪŋz] PL Mobiliar *nt*; (*with carpets etc*) Einrichtung *f*; **with ~ and fittings** voll eingerichtet

furniture ['fɜːnɪtʃəʳ] N Möbel *pl*; **a piece of ~** ein Möbelstück *nt*; **I must buy some ~** ich muss Möbel kaufen; **if I stay here much longer, I'll become a part of the ~** wenn ich noch viel länger hier bleibe, gehöre ich bald zum Inventar

furore [fjʊə'rɔːrɪ], (*US*) **furor** ['fjɔːrɔːʳ] N Protest(e) *m(pl)*; **to cause a ~** einen Skandal verursachen

furred [fɜːd] ADJ *tongue* belegt, pelzig

furrier ['fʌrɪəʳ] N Kürschner(in) *m(f)*

furrow ['fʌrəʊ] **1** N (*Agr*) Furche *f*; (*on brow*) Runzel *f* **2** VT *brow* runzeln

furry ['fɜːrɪ] ADJ (+ER) **(a)** *body, belly* haarig; *tail* buschig; **~ animal** Tier *nt* mit Pelz; **the kitten is so soft and ~** das Kätzchen ist so weich und kuschelig **(b)** *slippers, material* flauschig; **~ toy** Plüschtier *nt* **(c)** *tongue* belegt

further ['fɜːðəʳ] **1** ADV COMP *of* **far** weiter; **~ on** weiter entfernt; **~ back** (*in place, time*) weiter zurück; (= *in the past*) früher; **nothing could be ~ from the truth** nichts könnte weiter von der Wahrheit entfernt sein; **nothing is ~ from my thoughts** nichts liegt mir ferner; **to get ~ and ~ away** sich immer weiter entfernen; **he has decided not to take the matter any ~** er hat beschlossen, die Angelegenheit auf sich beruhen zu lassen; **in order to make the soup go ~** um die Suppe zu strecken; **he didn't question me ~** er hat mich nicht weiter gefragt; **~, I would like to say that ...** darüber hinaus möchte ich sagen, dass ...; **~ to your letter of ...** (*Comm*) Bezug nehmend auf Ihren Brief vom ... (*form*) **2** ADJ **(a) = farther (b)** (= *additional*) weiter; **will there be anything ~?** kann ich sonst noch etwas für Sie tun?; **~ details** nähere *or* weitere Einzelheiten *pl* **3** VT *one's interests, a cause* fördern; *process* voranbringen; **to ~ one's education** sich weiterbilden; **to ~ one's career** beruflich vorankommen

further education N Weiterbildung *f*

furthermore ['fɜːðəmɔːʳ] ADV überdies, außerdem

furthermost ['fɜːðəməʊst] ADJ äußerste(r, s)

furthest ['fɜːðɪst] **1** ADV am weitesten; **these fields are ~ (away) from his farm** diese Felder liegen am weitesten von seinem Hof entfernt; **this is the ~ north you can go** dies ist der nördlichste Punkt, den man erreichen kann; **it was the ~ the Irish team had ever got** so weit war die irische Mannschaft noch nie gekommen **2** ADJ am weitesten entfernt; **the ~ of the three villages** das entfernteste von den drei Dörfern; **5 km at the ~** höchstens 5 km

furtive ['fɜːtɪv] ADJ *action* heimlich; *behaviour, person* heimlichtuerisch; (= *suspicious*) verdächtig; *look* verstohlen

furtively ['fɜːtɪvlɪ] ADV *look, glance* verstohlen; *behave* verdächtig

fury ['fjʊərɪ] N Wut *f*; **in a ~** wütend

fuse, (*US*) **fuze** [fjuːz] **1** VT **(a)** *metals* verschmelzen **(b)** (*Brit Elec*) **to ~ the lights** die Sicherung durchbrennen lassen; **I've ~d the lights** die Sicherung ist durchgebrannt **(c)** (*fig*) vereinigen; (*Comm*) fusionieren **2** VI **(a)** (*metals*) sich verbinden; (*bones*) zusammenwachsen **(b)** (*Brit Elec*) durchbrennen; **the lights ~d** die Sicherung war durchgebrannt

(c) (fig: also ~ **together**) sich vereinigen

3 N **(a)** (Elec) Sicherung f; **to blow the ~s** die Sicherung durchbrennen lassen; **he'll blow a ~** (fig inf) bei dem brennen die Sicherungen durch (inf)

(b) (in bombs etc, Min) Zündschnur f; **to light the ~** die Zündschnur anzünden; **she has got** or **is on a short ~** (fig inf) sie explodiert schnell or leicht

fuse box N Sicherungskasten m

fused ['fjuːzd] ADJ plug etc gesichert

fuselage ['fjuːzəlɑːʒ] N (Flugzeug)rumpf m

fusillade [ˌfjuːzɪˈleɪd] N Salve f

fusion ['fjuːʒən] N (of metal, fig) Verschmelzung f; (Phys: also **nuclear ~**) (Kern)fusion f

fuss [fʌs] **3** N Theater nt (inf); (= bother also) Aufheben(s) nt; (= lavish attention) Wirbel m (inf) (of um); **I don't know what all the ~ is about** ich weiß wirklich nicht, was der ganze Wirbel soll (inf); **without (any) ~** ohne großes Theater (inf); **to cause a ~** Theater machen (inf); **to make a ~, to kick up a ~** Krach schlagen (inf); **to make a ~ about** or **over sth** viel Aufhebens or Wirbel (inf) um etw machen; **to make a ~ of sb** um jdn viel Wirbel machen (inf)

2 VI sich (unnötig) aufregen; (= get into a ~) Umstände pl machen; **don't ~, mother!** ist ja gut, Mutter!

➤ **fuss over** VI +PREP OBJ details Theater machen um; person bemuttern; guests, food sich (dat) große Umstände machen mit

fussbudget ['fʌsbʌdʒɪt] N (US inf) = fusspot

fussed [fʌst] ADJ (Brit inf) **I'm not ~ (about it)** es ist mir egal

fussily ['fʌsɪlɪ] ADV (pej) **(a)** adjust, check übertrieben sorgfältig **(b)** (= ornately) überladen; **~ dressed** verspielt gekleidet

fusspot ['fʌspɒt] N (Brit inf) Umstandskrämer(in) m(f) (inf)

fussy ['fʌsɪ] ADJ (+ER) **(a)** (= choosy) wählerisch; (= petty) kleinlich; (= precise) genau; **to be ~ about one's appearance** großen Wert auf sein Äußeres legen; **she is not ~ about her food** sie ist beim Essen nicht wählerisch; **the child is a ~ eater** das Kind ist beim Essen wählerisch; **I'm not ~** (inf) das ist mir egal **(b)** (pej) design, style überladen; furnishings, dress verspielt

fusty ['fʌstɪ] ADJ (+ER) **(a)** (pej: = old-fashioned) verstaubt **(b)** (= musty) muffig

futile ['fjuːtaɪl] ADJ sinnlos; plan, idea nutzlos; effort, attempt (usu attr: = in vain) vergeblich; (usu pred: = pointless) nutzlos

futility [fjuːˈtɪlɪtɪ] N Sinnlosigkeit f

futon ['fuːtɒn] N Futon m

future ['fjuːtʃə'] **1** N **(a)** Zukunft f; **in ~** in Zukunft; **it won't happen in the foreseeable/near ~** es wird in absehbarer/ nächster Zeit nicht passieren; **in the distant/not too distant ~** in ferner/nicht allzu ferner Zukunft; **what plans do you have for the ~?** was für Zukunftspläne haben Sie?; **to have a/ any ~** eine Zukunft haben; (Gram) **the ~** das Futur, die Zukunft

(b) (St Ex) **futures** PL Termingeschäfte pl; **~s contract** Terminkontrakt m; **~s trading** Börsenterminhandel m; **coffee ~s** Terminkontrakte pl in Kaffee; **~s market** Terminbörse f

2 ADJ ATTR **(a)** (zu)künftig; **at a** or **some ~ date** zu einem späteren Zeitpunkt; **his ~ prospects/plans** seine Zukunftsaussichten/-pläne; **in ~ years** in den kommenden Jahren; **you can keep it for ~ reference** Sie können es behalten, um später darauf Bezug zu nehmen

(b) (Gram) **the ~ tense** das Futur, die Zukunft; **the ~ perfect** die vollendete Zukunft

futuristic [ˌfjuːtʃəˈrɪstɪk] ADJ futuristisch

fuze N, VTI (US) = fuse

fuzz [fʌz] N Flaum m

fuzzy ['fʌzɪ] ADJ (+ER) **(a)** material, sweater flauschig; (= frizzy) hair kraus **(b)** sound, writing undeutlich; picture, idea, memory, distinction verschwommen; details unklar; **I'm a little ~ on what happened** ich weiß nicht so genau, was passiert ist

fwd ABBR of forward

f-word ['ef,wɜːd] N (inf) **I try not to use the ~ in front of the children** ich versuche, vor den Kindern möglichst keine schlimmen Flüche zu gebrauchen

FX [ef'eks] PL (Film inf) Spezialeffekte pl

FYI ABBR of for your information zu Ihrer Information

Gg

G, g [dʒiː] N **(a)** G nt, g nt **(b) g's** PL (= *gravitational force*) g nt **(c) G** (*US inf*: = *one thousand dollars*) tausend Dollar pl **(d)** (*Mus*) G nt, g nt; **G sharp** Gis nt, gis nt; **G flat** Ges nt, ges nt

G (*US*) ABBR *of* **general audience** (*Film*) jugendfrei

g ABBR *of* **gram(s), gramme(s)** g

gab [gæb] (*inf*) ■ N **to have the gift of the ~** (= *talk a lot*) wie ein Wasserfall reden (*inf*); (= *be persuasive*) nicht auf den Mund gefallen sein ■ VI quasseln (*inf*)

gabardine, gaberdine [gæbəˈdiːn] N Gabardine m

gabble [ˈgæbl] (*Brit*) ■ VI brabbeln (*inf*) ■ VT *poem, prayer* herunterrasseln (*inf*); *excuse, explanation* brabbeln (*inf*)

gaberdine N = **gabardine**

gable [ˈgeɪbl] N Giebel m

gabled [ˈgeɪbld] ADJ **~ house/roof** Giebelhaus/-dach nt

gadabout [ˈgædəbaʊt] N rastloser Geist; (*who likes travelling*) Reiseonkel m/-tante f

➤ **gad about** (*Brit*) *or* **around** VI herumziehen (*prep obj* in +*dat*); **he's always gadding about** er ist ständig auf Achse (*inf*)

gadget [ˈgædʒɪt] N Gerät nt, Apparat m; **the latest electronic ~** die neueste elektronische Spielerei

gadgetry [ˈgædʒɪtrɪ] N Geräte pl; (= *superfluous equipment*) technische Spielereien pl

Gaelic [ˈgeɪlɪk] ■ ADJ gälisch ■ N (*Ling*) Gälisch nt

gaff [gæf] N **to blow the ~** (*inf*) nicht dichthalten (*inf*)

gaffe [gæf] N Fauxpas m; (*verbal*) taktlose Bemerkung; **to make a ~** einen Fauxpas begehen; (*by saying sth*) ins Fettnäpfchen treten (*inf*)

gaffer [ˈgæfəʳ] N (*Brit inf*) (= *foreman*) Vorarbeiter m; (= *boss*) Boss m (*inf*)

gag [gæg] ■ N **(a)** Knebel m **(b)** (= *joke*) Gag m ■ VT knebeln; (*fig*) *person* zum Schweigen bringen; *press etc* mundtot machen ■ VI **(a)** (= *joke*) Witze machen; (*comedian*) Gags machen **(b)** (= *retch*) würgen (*on* an +*dat*) **(c) to be ~ging for sth** (*inf*) scharf auf etw (*acc*) sein

gaga [ˈgɑːgɑː] ADJ (*Brit inf*) plemplem (*inf*); *old person* verkalkt (*inf*); **to go ~** verkalken (*inf*)

gage N, VT (*US*) = **gauge**

gaggle [ˈgægl] N (*of geese*) Herde f; (*hum: of people*) Horde f

gaily [ˈgeɪlɪ] ADV (= *happily*) fröhlich; (= *brightly*) *painted, dressed* farbenfroh; **~ coloured** (*Brit*) *or* **colored** (*US*) farbenprächtig

gain [geɪn] ■ N **(a)** (= *advantage*) Vorteil m; (= *profit*) Profit m; **to do sth for ~** etw zum eigenen Vorteil tun; (*for money*) etw des Geldes wegen tun; **his loss is our ~** sein Verlust ist unser Gewinn

(b) gains PL (= *winnings*) Gewinn m; (= *profits*) Gewinne pl **(c)** (= *increase*) (in +*gen*) Zunahme f; (*in speed*) Erhöhung f; **~ in weight, weight ~** Gewichtszunahme f

■ VT gewinnen; *knowledge, wealth* erwerben; *advantage, respect, access* sich (*dat*) verschaffen; *control, the lead* übernehmen; *marks, points* erzielen; *sum of money* verdienen; *liberty* erlangen; (= *achieve*) *nothing, a little etc* erreichen; **what does he hope to ~ by it?** was verspricht er sich (*dat*) davon?; **to ~ independence** unabhängig werden; **to ~ sb's confidence** jds Vertrauen erlangen; **to ~ experience** Erfahrungen sammeln; **to ~ ground** (an) Boden gewinnen; (*rumours*) sich verbreiten; **to ~ time** Zeit gewinnen; **he ~ed a reputation as ...** er hat sich (*dat*) einen Namen als ... gemacht; **to ~ height** (an) Höhe gewinnen; **to ~ speed** schneller werden; **to ~ strength** stärker werden; **she has ~ed weight/3 kilos** sie hat zugenommen/3 Kilo zugenommen; **as he ~ed confidence** als seine Selbstsicherheit zunahm; **to ~ popularity** an Beliebtheit (*dat*) gewinnen; **my watch ~s five minutes each day** meine Uhr geht fünf Minuten pro Tag vor

■ VI **(a)** (*watch*) vorgehen

(b) (= *close gap*) aufholen

(c) (= *profit: person*) profitieren (*by* von); **society would ~ from that** das wäre für die Gesellschaft von Vorteil; **we stood to ~ from the decision** die Entscheidung war für uns von Vorteil

(d) to ~ in confidence mehr Selbstvertrauen bekommen; **to ~ in popularity** an Beliebtheit (*dat*) gewinnen

➤ **gain on** VI +PREP OBJ (= *close gap*) einholen

gainer [ˈgeɪnəʳ] N **there were more losers than ~s** es gab mehr Verlierer als Gewinner; **the biggest ~ was the government** die Regierung hat am meisten (davon) profitiert

gainful [ˈgeɪnfʊl] ADJ einträglich; **to be in ~ employment** erwerbstätig sein

gainfully [ˈgeɪnfʊlɪ] ADV nutzbringend; **~ employed** erwerbstätig

gainsay [geɪnˈseɪ] VT, *pret, ptp* **gainsaid** [geɪnˈsed] (ab)leugnen; **there is no ~ing his honesty** seine Ehrlichkeit lässt sich nicht leugnen

gait [geɪt] N Gang m; (*of horse*) Gangart f; **with an unsteady ~** mit unsicheren Schritten

gala [ˈgɑːlə] N großes Fest; (*Theat, Film,* = *ball*) Galaveranstaltung f; **swimming/sports ~** großes Schwimm-/Sportfest

galactic [gəˈlæktɪk] ADJ galaktisch

gala performance N Galavorstellung f

galaxy [ˈgæləksɪ] N **(a)** (*Astron*) Sternsystem nt; **the Galaxy** die Milchstraße **(b)** (*fig*) Schar f

gale [geɪl] N **(a)** Sturm m; **it was blowing a ~** ein Sturm tobte *or* wütete; **~ force 8** Sturmstärke 8 **(b)** (*fig*) **~s of laughter** Lachsalven pl

gale: gale-force winds PL orkanartige Winde; **gale warning** N Sturmwarnung f

gall [gɔːl] ■ N (*inf*) Frechheit f; **to have the ~ to do sth** die Frechheit haben *or* besitzen, etw zu tun ■ VT (*fig*) maßlos ärgern

gallant [ˈgælənt] ADJ **(a)** (= *courageous*) tapfer **(b)** (= *chivalrous*) ritterlich

gallantly [ˈgæləntlɪ] ADV **(a)** (= *courageously*) tapfer **(b)** (= *chivalrously*) ritterlich

gallantry [ˈgæləntrɪ] N **(a)** (= *bravery*) Tapferkeit f **(b)** (= *attentiveness to women*) Galanterie f

gall bladder N Gallenblase f

galleon [ˈgælɪən] N Galeone f

gallery [ˈgælərɪ] N **(a)** (= *balcony, corridor*) Galerie f; (*Theat*) Balkon m; **to play to the ~** (*fig*) sich in Szene setzen **(b)** (*Art*) (Kunst)galerie f

galley [ˈgælɪ] N (*Naut*) (= *ship*) Galeere f; (= *kitchen*) Kombüse f

Gallic [ˈgælɪk] ADJ gallisch; **the ~ Wars** der Gallische Krieg

galling [ˈgɔːlɪŋ] ADJ äußerst ärgerlich; *experience* äußerst unangenehm

gallivant [ˌgælɪˈvænt] VI sich amüsieren; **to ~ about** *or* **around** sich herumtreiben

gallon [ˈgælən] N Gallone f

gallop [ˈgæləp] ■ N Galopp m; **at a ~** im Galopp; **at full ~** im gestreckten Galopp; **to go for a ~** ausreiten ■ VI galoppieren; **to ~ away** davongaloppieren

galloping [ˈgæləpɪŋ] ADJ **~ inflation** galoppierende Inflation

gallows [ˈgæləʊz] N Galgen m; **to send/bring sb to the ~** jdn an den Galgen bringen

gallstone [ˈgɔːlstəʊn] N Gallenstein m

Gallup poll [ˈgæləpˌpəʊl] N Meinungsumfrage f

galore [gəˈlɔːʳ] ADV in Hülle und Fülle

galoshes [gəˈlɒʃɪz] PL Galoschen pl

galvanize [ˈgælvənaɪz] VT (*fig*) elektrisieren; **to ~ sb into action** jdn plötzlich aktiv werden lassen; **to ~ sb into doing** *or* **to do sth** jdm einen Stoß geben, etw sofort zu tun

galvanized [ˈgælvənaɪzd] ADJ *iron, steel* galvanisiert

Gambia [ˈgæmbɪə] N **(the) ~** Gambia nt

gambit [ˈgæmbɪt] N **(a)** (*Chess*) Gambit nt **(b)** (*fig*) (Schach)zug m; **his favourite** (*Brit*) *or* **favorite** (*US*) **~ was to ...** was er am liebsten machte, war ...

gamble [ˈgæmbl] ■ N (*fig*) Risiko nt; **a political ~** ein politisches Wagnis; **it's a ~** es ist riskant *or* eine riskante Sache; **I'll take a ~ on it/him** ich riskiere es/es mit ihm; **he took a ~ in buying the house** beim Kauf des Hauses ist er ein Risiko eingegangen

■ VI **(a)** (*lit*) (um Geld) spielen (*with* mit); (*on horses etc*)

wetten; **to ~ on the stock exchange** an der Börse spekulieren **(b)** *(fig)* **to ~ on sth** sich auf etw *(acc)* verlassen; **she was gambling on his being late** sie hat sich darauf verlassen, dass er sich verspäten würde; **to ~ with sth** etw aufs Spiel setzen 🔳 VT **(a)** *money, fortune* einsetzen; **to ~ sth on sth** etw auf etw *(acc)* setzen

(b) *(fig)* aufs Spiel setzen

➤ **gamble away** VT SEP verspielen

gambler ['gæmblə^r] N *(lit, fig)* Spieler(in) *m(f)*

gambling ['gæmblɪŋ] N Spielen *nt* (um Geld); *(on horses etc)* Wetten *nt*

gambol ['gæmbəl] VI herumtollen; *(lambs)* herumspringen

game[1] [geɪm] N **(a)** *(lit, fig)* Spiel *nt*; *(= sport)* Sport(art *f) m*; *(= scheme, plan)* Absicht *f*, Vorhaben *nt*; *(of table tennis)* Satz *m*; *(of billiards, board ~s etc, informal tennis match)* Partie *f*; **to have *or* play a ~ of football/tennis/chess** *etc* Fußball/Tennis/Schach *etc* spielen; **do you fancy a quick ~ of tennis/chess?** hättest du Lust, ein bisschen Tennis/Schach zu spielen?; **to have a ~ with sb, to give sb a ~** mit jdm spielen; **he had a good ~** er spielte gut; **~ of chance** Glücksspiel *nt*; **~ of skill** Geschicklichkeitsspiel *nt*; **~ set and match to X** Satz und Spiel (geht an) X; **~ to X** Spiel X; **one ~ all** eins beide; **to play the ~** *(fig)* sich an die Spielregeln halten; **to play ~s with sb** *(fig)* mit jdm spielen; **the ~ is up** das Spiel ist aus; **two can play at that ~, that's a ~ (that) two can play** wie du mir, so ich dir *(inf)*; **to beat sb at his own ~** jdn mit den eigenen Waffen schlagen; **to give the ~ away** alles verderben; **to spoil sb's little ~** jdm die Suppe versalzen *(inf)*; **I wonder what his ~ is?** ich frage mich, was er im Schilde führt; **to be/keep ahead of the ~** *(fig)* um eine Nasenlänge voraus sein/bleiben

(b) games PL *(= sports event)* Spiele *pl*

(c) games SING *(Sch)* Sport *m*

(d) *(inf)* Branche *f*; **how long have you been in this ~?** wie lange machen Sie das schon?

(e) *(Hunt, Cook)* Wild *nt*

game[2] ADJ *(= brave)* mutig; **to be ~** *(= willing)* mitmachen; **to be ~ for sth** für etw bereit sein; **to be ~ for anything** für alles zu haben sein; **to be ~ for a laugh** jeden Spaß mitmachen

game bird N Federwild *nt no pl*; **the pheasant is a ~** der Fasan gehört zum Federwild

Gameboy® ['geɪmbɔɪ] N Gameboy® *m*

gamekeeper ['geɪmkiːpə^r] N Wildhüter(in) *m(f)*

gamely ['geɪmlɪ] ADV *(= bravely)* mutig

game: game reserve N Wildschutzgebiet *nt* or -reservat *nt*; **game show** N *(TV)* Spielshow *f*

gamesmanship ['geɪmzmənʃɪp] N Ablenkungsmanöver *pl*; **political/diplomatic ~** politische/diplomatische Schläue

games [geɪmz] *(Comput)*: **games port** N Spieleport *nt or m*; **games software** N Software *f* für Computerspiele

game warden N Jagdaufseher *m*

gaming ['geɪmɪŋ] N = **gambling**

gammon ['gæmən] N *(= bacon)* leicht geräucherter Vorderschinken; *(= ham)* (gekochter) Schinken; **~ steak** *dicke Scheibe Vorderschinken zum Braten oder Grillen*

gammy ['gæmɪ] ADJ *(Brit inf)* lahm

gamut ['gæmət] N *(fig)* Skala *f*

gander ['gændə^r] N **(a)** Gänserich *m* **(b)** *(inf)* **to have *or* take a ~ at sth** sich etw *(acc)* einen Blick werfen

G and T, G&T [dʒiːən'tiː] N ABBR *of* gin and tonic Gin Tonic *m*

gang [gæŋ] N Haufen *m*; *(of workers, prisoners)* Trupp *m*; *(of criminals, youths)* Bande *f*; *(of friends etc: = clique)* Clique *f*; **there was a whole ~ of them** es war ein ganzer Haufen

➤ **gang up** VI sich zusammentun; **to gang up against *or* on sb** sich gegen jdn verbünden; *(to fight)* geschlossen auf jdn *or* gegen jdn losgehen

gangbanger ['gæŋbæŋə^r] N *(US inf: = gang member)* Bandenmitglied *nt*

gangbuster ['gæŋbʌstə^r] N *(US inf)* **to be going ~s** voll im Rollen sein *(inf)*; **to do sth like ~s** bei etw voll durchstarten *(inf)*

gangland ['gæŋlænd] ADJ Unterwelt-; **a ~ boss** ein Unterweltboss *m*

gangling ['gæŋglɪŋ] ADJ schlaksig

gangplank ['gæŋplæŋk] N Laufplanke *f*

gangrene ['gæŋgriːn] N Brand *m*

gangrenous ['gæŋgrɪnəs] ADJ brandig

gangster ['gæŋstə^r] N Gangster(in) *m(f)*

gangway ['gæŋweɪ] N **(a)** *(Naut)* Landungsbrücke *f* **(b)** *(= passage)* Gang *m*

gannet ['gænɪt] N *(Zool)* Tölpel *m*; **she's a real ~** *(inf)* sie ist ein richtiger Vielfraß

gantry ['gæntrɪ] N *(for crane)* Portal *nt*; *(on motorway)* Schilderbrücke *f*; *(Rail)* Signalbrücke *f*

gaol [dʒeɪl] N, VT = **jail**

gaoler ['dʒeɪlə^r] N = **jailer**

gap [gæp] N *(lit, fig)* Lücke *f*; *(= chink)* Spalt *m*; *(in surface)* Riss *m*; *(fig)* *(in conversation, narrative)* Pause *f*; *(= gulf)* Kluft *f*; **to close the ~** *(in race)* (den Abstand) aufholen; **a ~ in one's knowledge** eine Bildungslücke; **a four-year ~, a ~ of four years** ein Abstand *m* von vier Jahren

gape [geɪp] VI **(a)** *(chasm etc)* klaffen **(b)** *(= stare)* gaffen; **to ~ at sb/sth** jdn/etw (mit offenem Mund) anstarren

gaping ['geɪpɪŋ] ADJ *hole* riesig; *wound, chasm* klaffend

gap year N *(Brit Sch)* Überbrückungsjahr *nt*

garage ['gærɑːʒ, *(US)* gə'rɑːʒ] 🔳 N *(for parking)* Garage *f*; *(Brit)* *(for petrol)* Tankstelle *f*; *(for repairs etc)* (Reparatur)werkstatt *f* 🔳 VT (in einer Garage) ab- *or* unterstellen; **the car is kept ~d** das Auto wird in einer Garage aufbewahrt

garage sale N *meist in einer Garage durchgeführter Verkauf von Haushaltsgegenständen und Trödel*

garb [gɑːb] N Gewand *nt*

garbage ['gɑːbɪdʒ] N *(lit: esp US)* Müll *m*; *(fig)* *(= useless things)* Schund *m*; *(= nonsense)* Quatsch *m* *(inf)*; *(Comput)* Garbage *m*

garbage: garbage can N *(US)* Mülleimer *m*; *(outside)* Mülltonne *f*; **garbage collector** N *(US)* Müllarbeiter *m*; **the ~s** die Müllabfuhr; **garbage disposal unit** N *(esp US)* Müllschlucker *m*; **garbage man** N *(US)* = **garbage collector**

garble ['gɑːbl] VT **to ~ one's words** sich beim Sprechen überschlagen

garbled ['gɑːbld] ADJ *version, story* entstellt; *message, instructions* konfus; *words, speech, account* wirr; **the facts got a little ~** die Tatsachen sind etwas durcheinander geraten

garden ['gɑːdn] 🔳 N Garten *m*; **the Garden of Eden** der Garten Eden 🔳 VI im Garten arbeiten

garden IN CPDS Garten-; **garden apartment** N *(US)* Souterrainwohnung *f*; **garden centre**, *(US)* **garden center** N Gartencenter *nt*

gardener ['gɑːdnə^r] N Gärtner(in) *m(f)*

garden flat N *(Brit)* Souterrainwohnung *f*

gardening ['gɑːdnɪŋ] N Gartenarbeit *f*; **she loves ~** sie arbeitet gerne im Garten; **~ tools** Gartengeräte *pl*

garden: garden party N Gartenparty *f or* -fest *nt*; **garden path** N **to lead sb up** *(esp Brit)* or **down** *(esp US)* **the ~** *(fig)* jdn an der Nase herumführen *(inf)*; **garden-variety** ADJ *(US)* *(= ordinary)* gewöhnlich; *(= standard)* durchschnittlich

gargantuan [gɑːˈgæntjʊən] ADJ gewaltig, enorm

gargle ['gɑːgl] 🔳 VI gurgeln 🔳 N *(= liquid)* Gurgelwasser *nt*

gargoyle ['gɑːgɔɪl] N Wasserspeier *m*

garish ['gɛərɪʃ] ADJ *(pej)* *colours, neon sign* grell; *clothes* knallbunt

garishly ['gɛərɪʃlɪ] ADV *(pej)* *dressed* in grellen Farben; *illuminated* grell; **~ coloured** *(Brit)* or **colored** *(US)* knallbunt

garland ['gɑːlənd] N Kranz *m*; *(= festoon)* Girlande *f*; **a ~ of flowers** eine Blumengirlande

garlic ['gɑːlɪk] N Knoblauch *m*

garlic: garlic bread N Knoblauchbrot *nt*; **garlic mushrooms** PL *fritierte Pilze mit Knoblauch*; **garlic press** N Knoblauchpresse *f*; **garlic salt** N Knoblauchsalz *nt*

garment ['gɑːmənt] N Kleidungsstück *nt*; *(= robe)* Gewand *nt* *(liter)*

garner ['gɑːnə^r] VT *(lit, fig)* sammeln; *support* gewinnen

garnet ['gɑːnɪt] N Granat *m*

garnish ['gɑːnɪʃ] 🔳 VT garnieren 🔳 N Garnierung *f*

garret ['gærət] N Mansarde *f*

garrison ['gærɪsən] 🔳 N Garnison *f* 🔳 VT *troops* in Garnison legen; **to be ~ed** in Garnison liegen

garrotte [gə'rɒt] 🔳 VT mit der Garrotte hinrichten 🔳 N Garrotte *f*

garrulous ['gærʊləs] ADJ geschwätzig

garter ['gɑːtəʳ] N Strumpfband *nt*; (*US*: = *strap for stocking*) Strumpfhalter *m*

garter belt N (*US*) Strumpfgürtel *m*

gas [gæs] **1** N (a) Gas *nt*; **to cook with ~** mit Gas kochen **(b)** (= *petrol*) Benzin *nt*; **to step on the ~** Gas geben **(c)** (= *anaesthetic*) Lachgas *nt*; **to have** (*Brit*) *or* **get** (*US*) **~** Lachgas bekommen **(d)** (*Mil*) (Gift)gas *nt* **(e)** (*US Med*: = *wind*) Blähungen *pl* **(f)** (*inf*) **it's/he's a ~** (= *fantastic*) es/er ist Klasse (*inf*); (= *hilarious*) es/er ist zum Schreien (*inf*) **2** VT vergasen; **to ~ oneself** sich mit Gas vergiften

gas IN CPDS Gas-; **gasbag** N (*inf*) Quasselstrippe *f* (*inf*); **gas chamber** N Gaskammer *f*; **gas cooker** N Gasherd *m*

gaseous ['gæsɪəs] ADJ gasförmig

gas: **gas fire** N Gasofen *m*; **gasfired** ADJ gasbefeuert (*form*); **~ power station** Gaskraftwerk *nt*; **gas guzzler** N (*esp US inf*) Benzinschlucker *m* (*inf*)

gash [gæʃ] **1** N (= *wound*) klaffende Wunde; (= *slash*) tiefe Kerbe; (*in upholstery*) tiefer Schlitz **2** VT aufschlitzen; *furniture, wood* tief einkerben; **he fell and ~ed his head/knee** er ist gestürzt und hat sich (*dat*) dabei den Kopf/das Knie aufgeschlagen

gas: **gas heater** N Gasofen *m*; **gas jet** N Gasdüse *f*

gasket ['gæskɪt] N (*Tech*) Dichtung *f*

gas: **gas lamp** N Gaslampe *f*; (*in streets*) Gaslaterne *f*; **gas lighter** N (a) Gasanzünder *m* **(b)** (*for cigarettes etc*) Gasfeuerzeug *nt*; **gas main** N Gasleitung *f*; **gasman** N Gasmann *m* (*inf*); **gas mask** N Gasmaske *f*; **gas meter** N Gasuhr *f*

gasoline ['gæsəʊliːn] N (*US*) Benzin *nt*

gasometer [gæ'sɒmɪtəʳ] N Gasometer *m*

gas oven N Gasherd *m*

gasp [gɑːsp] **1** N (*for breath*) tiefer Atemzug; **to give a ~ (of** **surprise/fear** *etc*) (vor Überraschung/Angst *etc*) nach Luft schnappen (*inf*); **this was the last ~ of the reform movement** das war das letzte Aufbäumen der Reformbewegung **2** VI (*continually*) keuchen; (*once*) tief einatmen; (*with surprise etc*) nach Luft schnappen (*inf*); **to ~ for breath** *or* **air** nach Atem ringen; **he ~ed with astonishment** er war so erstaunt, dass es ihm den Atem verschlug; **I'm ~ing for a cup of tea** (*inf*) ich lechze nach einer Tasse Tee (*inf*)

gas: **gas pipe** N Gasleitung *f*; **gas pump** N (*US*) Zapfsäule *f*; **gas ring** N Gasbrenner *m*; (*portable*) Gaskocher *m*; **gas station** N (*US*) Tankstelle *f*; **gas stove** N Gasherd *m*; (*portable*) Gaskocher *m*

gassy ['gæsɪ] ADJ (+ER) *drink* kohlensäurehaltig

gas: **gas tank** N (*US*) Benzintank *m*; **gas tap** N Gashahn *m*

gastric ['gæstrɪk] ADJ Magen-, gastrisch (*spec*)

gastric: **gastric flu** N Darmgrippe *f*; **gastric juices** PL Magensäfte *pl*; **gastric ulcer** N Magengeschwür *nt*

gastroenteritis [ˌgæstrəʊˌentə'raɪtɪs] N Magen-Darm-Entzündung *f*

gastronomic [ˌgæstrə'nɒmɪk] ADJ gastronomisch

gastronomy [gæs'trɒnəmɪ] N Gastronomie *f*

gasworks ['gæswɜːks] N SING *or* PL Gaswerk *nt*

gate [geɪt] N (a) Tor *nt*; (*small*) (= *garden ~*) Pforte *f*; (= *five-barred ~*) Gatter *nt*; (*in station*) Sperre *f*; (*in airport*) Flugsteig *m*; (*of level crossing*) Schranke *f*; (*Sport*) (= *starting ~*) Startmaschine *f*; (= *sports ground entrance*) Eingang *m*; **to open/shut the ~(s)** das Tor *etc* öffnen/schließen **(b)** (*Sport*) (= *attendance*) Zuschauerzahl *f*; (= *entrance money*) Einnahmen *pl*

gateau ['gætəʊ] N, *pl* **gateaux** ['gætəʊz] (*esp Brit*) Torte *f*

gate: **gate-crash** VT (*inf*) **to ~ a party** in eine Party reinplatzen (*inf*); **gate-crasher** N ungeladener Gast; (*at meeting*) Eindringling *m*; **gatehouse** N Pförtnerhaus *nt*; **gate money** N (*Sport*) Einnahmen *pl*; **gatepost** N Torpfosten *m*; **gateway** N (*lit, fig*) Tor *nt* (*to zu*)

gather ['gæðəʳ] **1** VT (a) (= *collect, bring together*) sammeln; *crowd, people* versammeln; *flowers, fruit* pflücken; *potatoes, corn etc* ernten; *harvest* einbringen; *support* gewinnen; (= *collect up*) *broken glass, pins etc* aufsammeln; *one's belongings, books* (zusammen)packen; **to ~ one's strength** Kräfte sammeln; **to ~ one's thoughts** seine Gedanken ordnen; **it just sat there ~ing dust** es stand nur da und verstaubte

(b) (= *increase*) **to ~ speed** schneller werden; **to ~ strength** stärker werden

(c) (= *infer*) schließen (*from* aus); **I ~ed that** das dachte ich mir; **from what** *or* **as far as I can ~** (so) wie ich es sehe; **I ~ she won't be coming** ich nehme an, dass sie nicht kommt; **as you will have/might have ~ed ...** wie Sie bestimmt/vielleicht bemerkt haben ...

(d) (*Sew*) raffen; (*at seam*) fassen **2** VI (*people*) sich versammeln; (*objects, dust etc*) sich (an)sammeln; (*clouds*) sich zusammenziehen; (*storm*) sich zusammenbrauen

➤ **gather (a)round** VI zusammenkommen; **come on, children, gather (a)round!** kommt alle her, Kinder!

➤ **gather together** **1** VI sich versammeln **2** VT SEP einsammeln; *one's belongings, books* zusammenpacken; *people* versammeln; *team* zusammenstellen; *animals* zusammentreiben

➤ **gather up** VT SEP aufsammeln; *one's belongings* zusammenpacken; *hair* hochstecken; *skirts* (hoch)raffen

gathering ['gæðərɪŋ] **1** N (= *group*) Gruppe *f*; (= *assembly*) Versammlung *f*; *family ~* Familientreffen *nt*; **a social ~** ein geselliges Beisammensein **2** ADJ *darkness* zunehmend; *storm, clouds* aufziehend

gator, 'gator ['geɪtəʳ] N (*US inf*) = **alligator**

gauche [gəʊʃ] ADJ (*socially*) unbeholfen

gaudily ['gɔːdɪlɪ] ADV knallbunt

gaudy ['gɔːdɪ] ADJ (+ER) knallig (*inf*)

gauge [geɪdʒ] **1** N (a) (= *instrument*) Messgerät *nt*; (*to measure diameter, width etc*) (Mess)lehre *f*; **pressure/wind ~** Druck-/Windmesser *m*

(b) (= *thickness, width*) Stärke *f*; (*Rail*) Spurweite *f*

(c) (*fig*) Maßstab *m* (*of* für) **2** VT (*fig*) *person's capacities, character, progress* beurteilen; *reaction, course of events* abschätzen; *situation* abwägen; *mood* einschätzen; (= *guess*) schätzen; **I tried to ~ whether she was pleased or not** ich versuchte zu beurteilen, ob sie sich freute oder nicht

gaunt [gɔːnt] ADJ (a) (= *haggard*) hager; (= *emaciated*) abgezehrt **(b)** (*liter*) *building* trist; *landscape* öde

gauntlet[1] ['gɔːntlɪt] N **to throw down/pick up** *or* **take up the ~** (*fig*) den Fehdehandschuh hinwerfen/aufnehmen

gauntlet[2] N **to (have to) run the ~ of sth** einer Sache (*dat*) ausgesetzt sein

gauze [gɔːz] N Gaze *f*

gave [geɪv] PRET *of* **give**

gawk [gɔːk] (*inf*) VI = **gawp**

gawky ['gɔːkɪ] ADJ schlaksig

gawp [gɔːp] VI (*Brit inf*) glotzen (*inf*); **to ~ at sb/sth** jdn/etw anglotzen (*inf*)

gay [geɪ] **1** ADJ (+ER) *person* schwul (*inf*); *rights* für Schwule; *sex* unter Schwulen; **~ men and women** Schwule und Lesben *pl* (*inf*); **~ movement** Schwulenbewegung *f*; **~ bar** Schwulenkneipe *f*; **the ~ community** die Schwulen *pl* **2** N Schwule(r) *mf*

gaze [geɪz] **1** N Blick *m*; **in the public ~** im Blickpunkt der Öffentlichkeit **2** VI starren; **to ~ at sb/sth** jdn/etw anstarren; **they ~d into each other's eyes** sie blickten sich tief in die Augen

gazebo [gə'ziːbəʊ] N Gartenlaube *f*

gazelle [gə'zel] N Gazelle *f*

gazetteer [ˌgæzɪ'tɪəʳ] N alphabetisches Ortsverzeichnis (*mit Ortsbeschreibung*)

gazump [gə'zʌmp] VT (*Brit*) entgegen mündlicher Zusage ein Haus an einen Höherbietenden verkaufen

GB ABBR *of* **Great Britain** GB *nt*, Großbritannien *nt*

gbh ABBR *of* **grievous bodily harm**

GCSE (*Brit*) ABBR *of* General Certificate of Secondary Education

GCSE

Das **General Certificate of Secondary Education** *oder auch* **GCSE** *ist ein der mittleren Reife vergleichbarer Schulabschluss, den die meisten britischen Oberschüler mit sechzehn Jahren in einer Reihe von Fächern ablegen. Danach steigen sie entweder ins Berufsleben ein oder setzen ihre Schulausbildung bis zum A-Level-Abschluss fort. Das schottische Äquivalent ist der* **Standard Grade.** ▶ A LEVEL

GDP ABBR *of* **gross domestic product** Bruttoinlandsprodukt *nt*

GDR (*Hist*) ABBR *of* **German Democratic Republic** DDR *f*

gear [gɪəˀ] **1** N (a) (*Aut etc*) Gang *m*; ~s *pl* (= *mechanism*) Getriebe *nt*; (*on bicycle*) Gangschaltung *f*; **a bicycle with three ~s** ein Fahrrad *nt* mit Dreigangschaltung; **the car is/you're in ~** der Gang ist eingelegt; **the car is/you're not in ~** das Auto ist im Leerlauf; **to change** (*esp Brit*) *or* **shift** (*US*) **~** schalten; **to change** (*esp Brit*) *or* **shift** (*US*) **into third ~** in den dritten Gang schalten; **to move up/down through the ~s** (durch die einzelnen Gänge) herauf-/herunterschalten; **to move up a ~** (*fig*) einen Gang zulegen (*inf*); **to get one's brain in(to) ~** (*inf*) seine Gehirnwindungen in Gang setzen
(b) (*inf*) (= *equipment*) Ausrüstung *f*, Zeug *nt* (*inf*); (= *tools*) Gerät *nt*; (= *belongings, clothing*) Sachen *pl* (*inf*)
2 VT (*fig*) abstellen, ausrichten (*to* auf +*acc*); **to be ~ed to(wards) sb/sth** auf jdn/etw abgestellt sein; (*person, needs, ambition*) auf jdn/etw ausgerichtet sein; (= *have facilities for*) auf jdn/etw eingerichtet sein
➤ **gear up** VT SEP **to gear oneself up for sth** (*fig*) sich auf etw (*acc*) einstellen

gear: **gearbox** N Getriebe *nt*; **gear lever**, (*US*) **gear shift**, **gear stick** N Schaltknüppel *m*; (*column-mounted*) Schalthebel *m*

gee [dʒiː] INTERJ (a) (*esp US inf*) Mensch (*inf*), Mann (*inf*) (b) (*to horse*) ~ **up!** hü!
➤ **gee up** VT SEP (*inf*) **to gee sb up** jdn aufmuntern

geek [giːk] N (*esp US inf*) Waschlappen *m* (*inf*)

geese [giːs] PL *of* **goose**

geezer [ˈgiːzəˀ] N (*inf*) Kerl *m* (*inf*); **old ~** Opa *m* (*inf*)

Geiger counter [ˈgaɪgəˌkaʊntəˀ] N Geigerzähler *m*

geisha (girl) [ˈgeɪʃə(gɜːl)] N Geisha *f*

gel [dʒel] **1** N Gel *nt* **2** VI gelieren; (*fig*) (*plan, idea*) Gestalt annehmen; (*people*) sich verstehen

gelatin(e) [ˈdʒelətiːn] N Gelatine *f*

gelignite [ˈdʒelɪgnaɪt] N Plastiksprengstoff *m*

gem [dʒem] N Edelstein *m*; (*fig*) (= *person*) Juwel *nt*; (*of collection etc*) Prachtstück *nt*; **thanks Pat, you're a ~** danke, Pat, du bist ein Schatz; **a ~ of a book** ein meisterhaftes Buch

Gemini [ˈdʒemɪnaɪ] N Zwillinge *pl*; **he's (a) ~** er ist Zwilling

gemstone [ˈdʒemstəʊn] N Edelstein *m*

gen [dʒen] N (*Brit inf*) Informationen *pl*; **to give sb the ~ on** *or* **about sth** jdn über etw (*acc*) informieren; **to have some ~ on sth** Informationen über etw (*acc*) haben
➤ **gen up** VI (*Brit inf*) **to gen up on sth** sich über etw (*acc*) informieren

gender [ˈdʒendəˀ] N Geschlecht *nt*; **what ~ is this word?** welches Geschlecht hat dieses Wort?; **the feminine/masculine/neuter ~** das Femininum/Maskulinum/Neutrum

gene [dʒiːn] N Gen *nt*

genealogical [ˌdʒiːnɪəˈlɒdʒɪkəl] ADJ genealogisch

genealogy [ˌdʒiːnɪˈælədʒɪ] N Genealogie *f*; (= *ancestry*) Stammbaum *m*

genera [ˈdʒenərə] PL *of* **genus**

general [ˈdʒenərəl] **1** ADJ allgemein; **to be ~** (*wording, proposals*) allgemein gehalten sein; (= *vague*) unbestimmt *or* vage sein; (*promises, clause*) unverbindlich sein; (*custom, weather etc*) weit verbreitet sein; **his ~ appearance** sein Aussehen im Allgemeinen; **there was ~ agreement among the two groups** die beiden Gruppen waren sich grundsätzlich einig; **it met with ~ approval** es wurde allgemein gebilligt; **I've got the ~ idea (of it)** ich habe eine Vorstellung, worum es geht; **to give sb a ~ idea of a subject** jdm eine ungefähre Vorstellung von einem Thema geben; **in ~ terms, in a ~ sense** generell; **in the ~ direction of the village** ungefähr in Richtung des Dorfes; **as a ~ rule** im Allgemeinen
2 N (a) **in ~** im Allgemeinen
(b) (*Mil*) General(in) *m(f)*

general: **general anaesthetic**, (*US*) **general anesthetic** N Vollnarkose *f*; **General Certificate of Secondary Education** N (*Brit*) Abschluss *m* der Sekundarstufe, ≈ mittlere Reife; **general dealer** N (*US*) = **general store**; **general delivery** ADV (*US, Canada Post*: = *poste restante*) postlagernd; **general election** N Parlamentswahlen *pl*; **general headquarters** N SING or PL (*Mil*) Generalkommando *nt*

generality [ˌdʒenəˈrælɪtɪ] N **to talk in generalities** ganz allgemein sprechen

generalization [ˌdʒenərəlaɪˈzeɪʃən] N Verallgemeinerung *f*

generalize [ˈdʒenərəlaɪz] VTI verallgemeinern; **to ~ about sth** etw verallgemeinern; **Generalized System of Preferences** (*Comm*) Allgemeines Präferenzzollsystem

general knowledge N Allgemeinwissen *nt*

generally [ˈdʒenərəlɪ] ADV (a) (= *on the whole*) im Großen und Ganzen (b) (= *usually, in general*) im Allgemeinen; **they are ~ cheapest** sie sind in der Regel am billigsten; **~ speaking** im Allgemeinen (c) (= *widely*) *accepted, recognized* allgemein; *available* überall

general: **general manager** N Hauptgeschäftsführer(in) *m(f)*; **general meeting** N Vollversammlung *f*; (*of shareholders etc*) Hauptversammlung *f*; **general partner** N persönlich haftender Gesellschafter, persönlich haftende Gesellschafterin; **general practice** N (*Brit Med*) (a) (= *work*) Allgemeinmedizin *f*; **to be in ~** praktischer Arzt/praktische Ärztin sein (b) (= *place*) allgemeinärztliche Praxis; **general practitioner** N Arzt *m*/Ärztin *f* für Allgemeinmedizin; **general public** N Öffentlichkeit *f*; **general-purpose** ADJ Universal-; **~ cleaner** Universalreiniger *m*; **General Secretary** N Generalsekretär(in) *m(f)*; **general store** N Gemischtwarenhandlung *f*; **general strike** N Generalstreik *m*

generate [ˈdʒenəreɪt] VT (*lit, fig*) erzeugen; *jobs* schaffen; *income* einbringen; *interest* wecken; *excitement* hervorrufen

generation [ˌdʒenəˈreɪʃən] N (a) (*lit, fig*) Generation *f*; **within a ~** in einer Generation (b) (= *act of generating*) Erzeugung *f*; (*of jobs*) Schaffung *f*

generational [ˌdʒenəˈreɪʃənl] ADJ der/einer Generation; **~ differences** Generationsunterschied *m*

generation gap N **the ~** Generationsunterschied *m*; (*as an issue*) Generationskonflikt *m*

generator [ˈdʒenəreɪtəˀ] N Generator *m*

generic [dʒɪˈnerɪk] ADJ artmäßig; **~ name** *or* **term** Oberbegriff *m*; **~ advertising** Gemeinschaftswerbung *f*; **~ brand** (*US*) Hausmarke *f*, Eigenmarke *f*

generic drug N Generikum *nt*

generosity [ˌdʒenəˈrɒsɪtɪ] N Großzügigkeit *f*

generous [ˈdʒenərəs] ADJ (a) großzügig; *terms* günstig; *portion, supply* reichlich; **to be ~ in one's praise** mit Lob nicht geizen; **to be ~ with one's time** großzügig mit seiner Zeit umgehen; **with the ~ support of ...** mit großzügiger Unterstützung von ... (b) (= *kind*) *person, gesture, spirit* großmütig; *remarks* wohlwollend

generously [ˈdʒenərəslɪ] ADV (a) *give, donate, provide* großzügigerweise; *reward, sized, equipped* großzügig; **please give ~ (to ...)** wir bitten um großzügige Spenden (für ...) (b) (= *kindly*) *offer, agree* großmütigerweise

genesis [ˈdʒenɪsɪs] N, *pl* **geneses** [ˈdʒenɪsiːz] Entstehung *f*

genetic [dʒɪˈnetɪk] ADJ genetisch; **~ information** Erbinformation *f*

genetically [dʒɪˈnetɪkəlɪ] ADV genetisch; **~ engineered** genmanipuliert; **~ modified** gentechnisch verändert

genetic engineering N Gentechnologie *f*

geneticist [dʒɪˈnetɪsɪst] N Genetiker(in) *m(f)*

genetics [dʒɪˈnetɪks] N SING Genetik *f*

Geneva [dʒɪˈniːvə] N Genf *nt*; **Lake ~** der Genfer See

genial [ˈdʒiːnɪəl] ADJ *person* (= *affable, cordial*) herzlich; (= *jovial*) leutselig; (= *sociable*) gesellig; *company, atmosphere* angenehm; **a ~ host** ein warmherziger Gastgeber; **in a ~ mood** gut aufgelegt

Be careful! **genial** *is not translated by the German word* ~~genial~~.

genie ['dʒi:nɪ] N dienstbarer Geist; **the ~ is out of the bottle** (fig) der Geist ist aus der Flasche; **to let the ~ out of the bottle** (fig) den Geist aus der Flasche lassen

genii ['dʒi:nɪaɪ] PL of **genius**

genital ['dʒenɪtl] ADJ Geschlechts-, Genital-; **~ organs** Geschlechts- or Genitalorgane pl

genitals ['dʒenɪtlz] PL Geschlechtsteile pl, Genitalien pl

genitive ['dʒenɪtɪv] **1** N (Gram) Genitiv m; **in the ~** im Genitiv **2** ADJ Genitiv-; **~ case** Genitiv m

genius ['dʒi:nɪəs] N, pl **-es** or **genii** Genie nt; (= mental or creative capacity) Schöpferkraft f; **a man of ~** ein Genie nt; **to have a ~ for sth/doing sth** (= talent) eine besondere Gabe für etw haben/dafür haben, etw zu tun; **a flash of ~** eine geniale Eingebung

genocide ['dʒenəʊsaɪd] N Völkermord m, Genozid nt (geh)

genre ['ʒɑ̃:ŋrə] N Genre nt (geh), Gattung f

gent [dʒent] N (inf) ABBR of **gentleman** Herr m; **"Gents"** (Brit: = lavatory) „Herren"; **where is the ~s?** wo ist die Herrentoilette?

genteel [dʒen'ti:l] ADJ (a) (= refined) vornehm (b) (= overpolite) geziert

gentility [dʒen'tɪlɪtɪ] N Vornehmheit f

gentle ['dʒentl] ADJ (+ER) (a) sanft; animal zahm; treatment schonend; pressure, breeze, rain leicht; sound leise; pace, stroll, exercise gemächlich; **cook over a ~ heat** bei geringer Hitze kochen; **to be ~ with sb** (physically) sanft or behutsam mit jdm umgehen; (mentally) sanft or einfühlsam mit jdm umgehen; **to be ~ with sth** vorsichtig or behutsam mit etw umgehen

(b) (= mild, discreet) mild; persuasion freundlich; **this detergent is ~ on the skin** dieses Putzmittel schont die Haut; **a ~ hint** eine zarte Andeutung; **a ~ reminder** ein zarter Wink; **to poke ~ fun at sb, to have a ~ dig at sb** jdn freundlich necken

gentleman ['dʒentlmən] N, pl **-men** [-mən] (a) (well-mannered, well-born) Gentleman m; (trustworthy) Ehrenmann m; **he's a real ~** er ist ein richtiger Gentleman (b) (= man) Herr m; **gentlemen!** meine Herren!

gentlemanly ['dʒentlmənlɪ] ADJ ritterlich, gentlemanlike pred; **that is hardly ~ conduct** dieses Verhalten gehört sich nicht für einen Gentleman

gentlemen's agreement ['dʒentlmənzə'gri:mənt] N Gentlemen's Agreement nt; (esp in business) Vereinbarung f auf Treu und Glauben

gentleness ['dʒentlnɪs] N Sanftheit f; (of treatment) Behutsamkeit f; (of touch) Zartheit f

gently ['dʒentlɪ] ADV sanft; simmer, cook langsam; treat schonend; **you must tell him ~** du musst es ihm schonend beibringen; **it needs to be handled ~** damit/mit ihr muss man behutsam umgehen; **~ does it!** sachte, sachte!

gentry ['dʒentrɪ] PL Gentry f, niederer Adel

genuflect ['dʒenjʊflekt] VI (Rel) eine Kniebeuge machen

genuine ['dʒenjʊm] ADJ (a) (= authentic, not fake) echt; **the picture is ~** or **the ~ article** das Bild ist echt (b) (= sincere) aufrichtig; concern, interest, buyer ernsthaft; offer, friendship ernst gemeint; Christian etc überzeugt; love, enthusiasm, difficulty echt; mistake wirklich; **she looked at me in ~ astonishment** sie sah mich aufrichtig erstaunt an (c) (= natural, not affected) person natürlich

genuinely ['dʒenjʊmlɪ] ADV wirklich; **they are ~ concerned** sie machen sich ernsthafte Sorgen

genuineness ['dʒenjʊmnɪs] N (a) (= authenticity) Echtheit f (b) (= honesty, sincerity) Aufrichtigkeit f

genus ['dʒenəs] N, pl **genera** (Biol) Gattung f

geographer [dʒɪ'ɒgrəfəʳ] N Geograf(in) m(f)

geographic(al) [dʒɪə'græfɪk(əl)] ADJ geografisch

geographically [dʒɪə'græfɪkəlɪ] ADV geografisch; (introducing sentence) geografisch gesehen

geography [dʒɪ'ɒgrəfɪ] N Geografie f

geological [dʒɪəʊ'lɒdʒɪkəl] ADJ geologisch

geologist [dʒɪ'ɒlədʒɪst] N Geologe m, Geologin f

geology [dʒɪ'ɒlədʒɪ] N Geologie f

geometric(al) [dʒɪəʊ'metrɪk(əl)] ADJ geometrisch

geometry [dʒɪ'ɒmɪtrɪ] N (Math) Geometrie f; **~ set** (Zirkelkasten m mit) Zeichengarnitur f

Georgian ['dʒɔ:dʒɪən] ADJ (Brit) georgianisch; **the ~-style library** die Bibliothek im georgianischen Stil

geranium [dʒɪ'reɪnɪəm] N Geranie f

gerbil ['dʒɜ:bɪl] N Wüstenspringmaus f

geriatric [,dʒerɪ'ætrɪk] **1** ADJ (a) (Med) geriatrisch (b) (pej inf) altersschwach **2** N (a) (Med) alter Mensch (b) (pej inf: = senile person) Tattergreis(in) m(f) (pej inf)

geriatric: **geriatric care** N Altenpflege f; **geriatric hospital** N geriatrische Klinik

geriatrics [,dʒerɪ'ætrɪks] N SING Geriatrie f

germ [dʒɜ:m] N (lit, fig) Keim m; (esp of cold) Bazillus m

German ['dʒɜ:mən] **1** ADJ deutsch; **he is ~** er ist Deutscher; **she is ~** sie ist Deutsche **2** N (a) (= person) Deutsche(r) mf; **the ~s** die Deutschen (b) (Ling) Deutsch nt; **~ lessons** Deutschunterricht m; **in ~** auf Deutsch; **to speak ~** Deutsch sprechen

German Democratic Republic N (Hist) Deutsche Demokratische Republik

Germanic [dʒɜ:'mænɪk] ADJ (a) voice, accent deutsch klingend; trait, style (typisch) deutsch (b) (Hist, Ling) germanisch

German: **German measles** N SING Röteln pl; **German shepherd (dog)**, (US) **German sheep dog** N Deutscher Schäferhund; **German-speaking** ADJ deutschsprachig; **~ Switzerland** die Deutschschweiz

Germany ['dʒɜ:mənɪ] N Deutschland nt

germinate ['dʒɜ:mɪneɪt] **1** VI keimen; (fig) aufkeimen (geh); **he let the idea ~ in his mind** er ließ die Idee in sich (dat) keimen **2** VT (lit, fig) keimen lassen

germination [,dʒɜ:mɪ'neɪʃən] N (lit) Keimung f

germ warfare N bakteriologische Kriegsführung

gerund ['dʒerənd] N Gerundium nt

gestation [dʒe'steɪʃən] N (lit) (of animals) Trächtigkeit f; (of humans) Schwangerschaft f; (fig) Reifwerden nt; **his book was 10 years in ~** der Reifungsprozess seines Buches dauerte 10 Jahre

gesticulate [dʒe'stɪkjʊleɪt] VI gestikulieren; **to ~ at sb/sth** auf jdn/etw deuten

gesticulation [dʒe,stɪkjʊ'leɪʃən] N (= act) Gestikulieren nt

gesture ['dʒestʃəʳ] **1** N (lit, fig) Geste f; **to make a ~** eine Geste machen; **a ~ of defiance/approval** eine herausfordernde/zustimmende Geste; **as a ~ of support/goodwill** als Zeichen der Unterstützung/des guten Willens **2** VI gestikulieren; **to ~ at sb/sth** auf jdn/etw deuten; **he ~d with his head toward(s) the safe** er deutete mit dem Kopf auf den Safe

---

get [get]

1 TRANSITIVE VERB	**3** REFLEXIVE VERB
2 INTRANSITIVE VERB	**4** PHRASAL VERBS

---

pret **got**, ptp **got** or (US) **gotten**

1 TRANSITIVE VERB

---

*When **get** is part of a set combination, eg. **get the sack**, **get hold of**, **get it right**, look up the other word.*

(a) (= receive) bekommen, kriegen (inf); sun, light, full force of blow abbekommen; wound sich (dat) zuziehen; time, personal characteristics haben (from von); (in children's game) fangen; (= take) train, bus fahren mit; **where did you get it (from)?** woher hast du das?; **he got the idea for his book while he was abroad/from an old document** die Idee zu dem Buch kam ihm, als er im Ausland war/hatte er von einem alten Dokument; **I get quite a surprise** ich war ziemlich überrascht; **I get the feeling that ...** ich habe das Gefühl, dass ...; **to get sb by the arm/leg** jdn am Arm/Bein packen; **get him/it!** (to dog) fass!; **(I've) got him!** (inf) ich hab ihn!; **(I've) got it!** (inf) ich hab's!; **I'll get you for that!** (inf) das wirst du mir büßen!; **you've got me there!** (inf) da bin ich überfragt; **he couldn't get himself out of bed** er kam nicht aus dem Bett; **what do you get from it?** was hast du davon?; **I don't get much from his lectures** seine Vorlesungen geben mir nicht viel

(b) (= obtain by one's own efforts) object sich (dat) besorgen;

staff, finance, partner, job finden; (= buy) kaufen; (= buy and keep) car, cat sich (dat) anschaffen; **to get sb/oneself sth, to get sth for sb/oneself** jdm/sich etw besorgen; job jdm/sich etw verschaffen; **to need to get sth** etw brauchen; **to get a glimpse of sb/sth** jdn/etw kurz zu sehen bekommen; **he got himself a wife** er hat sich (dat) eine Frau zugelegt (inf); **we could get a taxi** wir könnten (uns dat) ein Taxi nehmen; **could you get me a taxi?** könnten Sie mir ein Taxi rufen?

(c) (= fetch) person, object holen; **to get sb from the station** jdn vom Bahnhof abholen; **can I get you a drink?** möchten Sie etwas zu trinken?; **I got him/myself a drink** ich habe ihm/mir etwas zu trinken geholt

(d) (= hit) treffen, erwischen (inf)

(e) (Telec) (= contact) erreichen; number bekommen; (= put through to, get for sb) geben; **get me 339/Mr Johnston please** (to secretary) geben Sie mir bitte 339/Herrn Johnston; (to switchboard) verbinden Sie mich bitte mit 339/Herrn Johnston; **you've got the wrong number** Sie sind falsch verbunden

(f) (meal) machen; **I'll get you/myself some breakfast** ich mache dir/mir etwas zum Frühstück

(g) (= eat) essen; **to get breakfast** frühstücken; **to get lunch** zu Mittag essen; **to get a snack** eine Kleinigkeit essen

(h) (= send, take) bringen; **to get sb to hospital** jdn ins Krankenhaus bringen; **they managed to get him home** sie schafften ihn nach Hause; **where does that get us?** (inf) was bringt uns (dat) das? (inf); **this discussion isn't getting us anywhere** diese Diskussion führt zu nichts; **to get sth to sb** jdm etw zukommen lassen; (= take it oneself) jdm etw bringen

(i) (= understand) kapieren (inf), mitbekommen (also = hear); (= make a note of) notieren; **I don't get it** (inf) da komme ich nicht mit (inf); **I don't get you** or **your meaning** ich verstehe nicht, was du meinst; **get it?** (inf) kapiert? (inf)

(j) (in exclamations) (inf) **get (a load of) that!** hat man Töne! (inf)

(k) (person) (inf) (= annoy) ärgern, aufregen; (= upset) an die Nieren gehen (+dat) (inf)

(l) (to form passive) (inf) werden; **when did it last get painted?** wann ist es zuletzt gestrichen worden?; **I got paid** ich wurde bezahlt

(m) (set structures)

✦**to get sb to do sth** (= have sth done by sb) etw von jdm machen lassen; (= persuade sb) jdn dazu bringen, etw zu tun; **I'll get him to phone you back** ich sage ihm, er soll zurückrufen; (= make him) ich werde zusehen, dass er zurückruft; **you'll never get him to understand** du wirst es nie schaffen, dass er das versteht

✦**to get sb + participle** **you'll get yourself thrown out** du bringst es so weit, dass du hinausgeworfen wirst; **has she got the baby dressed yet?** hat sie das Baby schon angezogen?

✦**to get sth done/made** etc **to get the washing done** die Wäsche waschen; **to get some work done** Arbeit erledigen; **to get things done** was fertig kriegen (inf); **to get sth made for sb/oneself** jdm/sich etw machen lassen; **I'll get the house painted soon** (by sb else) ich lasse bald das Haus streichen; **did you get your expenses paid/your question answered?** haben Sie Ihre Spesen erstattet/eine Antwort auf Ihre Frage bekommen?

✦**to get sth/sb + adjective** **to get sb/sth/oneself ready** jdn/etw/sich fertig machen; **to get sth clean/open/shut** (person) etw sauber kriegen/aufkriegen/zukriegen (inf); **that'll get it clean** damit wird es sauber; **to get sb drunk** jdn betrunken machen; **to get one's hands dirty** (lit, fig) sich (dat) die Hände schmutzig machen

✦**to get sth to do sth** he can't get the lid to stay open er kriegt es nicht hin, dass der Deckel aufbleibt (inf); **can you get these two pieces to fit together?** kriegen Sie die beiden Teile zusammen?; **can you get the wound to stop bleeding?** können Sie etwas machen, dass die Wunde nicht mehr blutet?

✦**to get sth/sb doing sth** **to get sth going** car, machine etw in Gang bringen; party etw in Fahrt bringen; **to get sb talking** jdn zum Sprechen bringen

✦**to have got sth** (Brit: = have) etw haben

▣ INTRANSITIVE VERB

(a) (= arrive) kommen; **to get home** nach Hause kommen; **to**

get here hier ankommen; **can you get to work by bus?** kannst du mit dem Bus zur Arbeit fahren?; **I've got as far as page 16** ich bin auf Seite 16

✦**to get there** (fig inf: = succeed) es schaffen (inf); **how's the work going?** – **we're getting there!** wie geht die Arbeit voran? – langsam wird's was! (inf)

✦**to get somewhere/nowhere** (in job, career etc) es zu etwas/nichts bringen; (with work, in discussion etc) weiterkommen/nicht weiterkommen; **to get somewhere/nowhere (with sb)** (bei jdm) etwas/nichts erreichen

✦**to get far** (lit) weit kommen; (fig) es weit bringen; **you won't get far on £10** mit £ 10 kommst du nicht weit

(b) (= become) werden; **I'm getting cold/warm** mir wird es kalt/warm; **to get dressed/shaved/washed** etc sich anziehen/rasieren/waschen etc; **to get married** heiraten; **I'm getting bored** ich langweile mich langsam; **how stupid can you get?** wie kann man nur so dumm sein?

✦**to get started** anfangen

✦**to get + infinitive** **to get to know sb/sth** jdn/etw kennen lernen; **how did you get to know about that?** wie hast du davon erfahren?; **to get to like sth** an etw (dat) Gefallen finden; **to get to do sth** die Möglichkeit haben, etw zu tun; **to get to see sb/sth** jdn/etw zu sehen bekommen; **to get to work** sich an die Arbeit machen

✦**to get + -ing** **to get working/scrubbing** etc anfangen zu arbeiten/schrubben etc; **I got talking to him** ich kam mit ihm ins Gespräch; **to get going** (person) (= leave) aufbrechen; (= start working) sich daranmachen; (= start talking) loslegen (inf); (party etc) in Schwung kommen; (machine, fire etc) in Gang kommen

✦**to have got to do sth** (= be obliged to) etw tun müssen; **I've got to** ich muss

▣ REFLEXIVE VERB

✦**to get oneself ...** (= CONVEY ONESELF) gehen; (= come) kommen; **I had to get myself to the hospital** ich musste ins Krankenhaus (gehen)

(WITH ADJECTIVE) sich ... machen; **to get oneself pregnant/fit** schwanger/fit werden

(+ PAST PARTICIPLE) **to get oneself washed/dressed** sich waschen/anziehen; **you'll get yourself killed if you go on driving like that** du bringst dich noch um, wenn du weiter so fährst

▣ PHRASAL VERBS

▶ **get about** VI (Brit) (prep obj in +dat) **(a)** (person) sich bewegen können; (to different places) herumkommen **(b)** (news) sich herumsprechen; (rumour) sich verbreiten

▶ **get across** ▣ VI **(a)** (= cross) hinüberkommen; (+prep obj) road, river kommen über (+acc) **(b)** (play, joke) ankommen (to bei); (idea, meaning) klar werden (to +dat) ▣ VT ALWAYS SEPARATE **(a)** (= transport) herüberbringen; (+prep obj) (herüber)bringen/-bekommen über (+acc) **(b)** one's ideas, concepts verständlich machen (to sb jdm)

▶ **get ahead** VI vorankommen (in in +dat); (in race) sich (dat) einen Vorsprung verschaffen; (from behind) nach vorn kommen; **to get ahead of sb** jdn überflügeln; (in race) einen Vorsprung zu jdm gewinnen; (= overtake) jdn überholen

▶ **get along** VI **(a)** (= go) gehen; **I must be getting along** ich muss jetzt gehen **(b)** (= manage) zurechtkommen **(c)** (= progress) vorankommen; (work, patient etc) sich machen **(d)** (= be on good terms) auskommen (with mit); **they get along quite well** sie kommen ganz gut miteinander aus

▶ **get around** ▣ VI = **get about** ▣ VTI +PREP OBJ = **get round**

▶ **get around to** VI +PREP OBJ = **get round to**

▶ **get at** VI +PREP OBJ **(a)** (= gain access to, reach) herankommen an (+acc); food, money gehen an (+acc); **don't let him get at the whisky** lass ihn nicht an den Whisky (ran); **the moths had got at the carpets** die Motten hatten sich an den Teppichen zu schaffen gemacht **(b)** truth herausbekommen; facts kommen an (+acc) **(c)** (inf: = mean) hinauswollen auf (+acc); **what are you getting at?** worauf willst du hinaus? **(d)** **to get at sb** (inf) (= criticize) an jdm etwas auszusetzen haben (inf); (= nag) an jdm herumnörgeln (inf)

➤ **get away** ◼ VI wegkommen; (*prisoner, thief*) entkommen (*from sb* jdm); **I'd like to get away early today** ich würde heute gern früher gehen; **you can't get away** *or* **there's no getting away from the fact that ...** man kommt nicht um die Tatsache herum, dass ...; **to get away from it all** sich von allem frei machen *or* losmachen

◼ VT ALWAYS SEPARATE (= *remove*) wegbekommen; (= *move physically*) person weg- *or* fortbringen; *objects* wegschaffen; **get her away from here/him** sehen Sie zu, dass sie hier/von ihm wegkommt; **get him/that dog away from me** schaff ihn mir/schaff mir den Hund vom Leib

➤ **get away with** VI +PREP OBJ (*inf*) **you'll/he'll** *etc* **never get away with that** das wird nicht gut gehen; **he got away with it** er ist ungestraft *or* ungeschoren (*inf*) davongekommen

➤ **get back** ◼ VI (= *come back*) zurückkommen; (= *go back, move backwards*) zurückgehen; **to get back (home)** nach Hause kommen; **to get back to bed/sleep** wieder ins Bett gehen/einschlafen; **to get back to work** (*after interruption etc*) wieder arbeiten können; (*after break*) wieder arbeiten gehen; **get back!** zurück(treten)!

◼ VT SEP **(a)** (= *recover*) zurückbekommen; *strength* zurückgewinnen

(b) (= *bring back*) zurückbringen; (= *put back in place*) zurücktun

(c) (= *pay back*) **I'll get you back for that** das werde ich dir heimzahlen

➤ **get back at** VI +PREP OBJ (*inf*) sich rächen an (+*dat*); **to get back at sb for sth** jdm etw heimzahlen (*inf*)

➤ **get back to** VI +PREP OBJ (*esp Comm*: = *contact again*) sich wieder in Verbindung setzen mit; **I'll get back to you on that** ich werde darauf zurückkommen

➤ **get behind** VI **(a)** (+*prep obj*) *tree, person* sich stellen hinter (+*acc*); *desk* sich setzen an (+*acc*); **to get behind the wheel** sich ans *or* hinter das Steuer setzen **(b)** (*fig*) zurückbleiben; (*person*) ins Hintertreffen geraten; (*with schedule*) in Rückstand kommen

➤ **get by** VI **(a)** *to let sb/a vehicle get by* jdn/ein Fahrzeug vorbeilassen **(b)** (*inf*) **she could just about get by in German** mit ihren Deutschkenntnissen könnte sie gerade so durchkommen (*inf*) **(c)** (*inf*: = *manage*) durchkommen (*inf*); **she gets by on very little money** sie kommt mit sehr wenig Geld aus

➤ **get down** ◼ VI **(a)** (= *descend*) heruntersteigen (*prep obj, from* von); (= *manage to get down, in commands*) herunterkommen (*prep obj, from* +*acc*); (*from horse, bicycle*) absteigen (*from* von); **to get down the stairs** die Treppe hinuntergehen

(b) (= *bend down*) sich bücken; (*to hide*) sich ducken; **to get down on all fours** sich auf alle Viere begeben

◼ VT SEP **(a)** (= *take down*) herunternehmen; (= *lift down*) herunterholen; (= *carry down, manage to get down*) herunterbringen

(b) (= *swallow*) *food* hinunterbringen; **get this down (you)!** (*inf*) iss/trink das!

(c) (*inf*: = *depress*) fertig machen (*inf*)

➤ **get down to** VI +PREP OBJ sich machen an (+*acc*); **to get down to business** zur Sache kommen

➤ **get in** ◼ VI **(a)** (= *enter*) hereinkommen (*prep obj, -to* in +*acc*); (*into car, train etc*) einsteigen (*prep obj, -to* in +*acc*); **the smoke got in(to) my eyes** ich habe Rauch in die Augen bekommen *inf*

(b) (= *arrive*) (*train, bus*) ankommen (-*to* in +*dat*); (*plane*) landen

(c) (*Pol*: = *be elected*) gewählt werden (-*to* in +*acc*)

(d) (= *get home*) nach Hause kommen

◼ VT **(a)** SEP (= *bring in*) hereinbringen (*prep obj, -to* in +*acc*); *crops, harvest* einbringen

(b) SEP (= *fit, insert into, find room for*) hineinbringen *or* -kriegen (*inf*) (-*to* in +*acc*); (*fig*) *punch, request* anbringen

(c) SEP *groceries, coal* holen; **to get in supplies** sich (*dat*) Vorräte zulegen

(d) SEP *doctor, plumber* kommen lassen; *specialist, consultant etc* zuziehen

➤ **get in on** VI +PREP OBJ (*inf*) mitmachen bei (*inf*); **to get in on the act** mitmischen (*inf*)

➤ **get into** ◼ VI +PREP OBJ *see also* **get in** 1(a) **(a)** *rage, debt, trouble, difficulties etc* geraten in (+*acc*); *fight* verwickelt werden in (+*acc*); **to get into bed** sich ins Bett legen; **what's**

got into him? (*inf*) was ist bloß in ihn gefahren? (*inf*)

(b) (= *get involved in*) *book* sich einlesen bei; *work* sich einarbeiten in (+*acc*)

(c) (= *put on*) anziehen; (= *fit into*) hineinkommen in (+*acc*)

◼ VT +PREP OBJ ALWAYS SEPARATE *debt, situation etc* bringen in (+*acc*); **to get sb/oneself into trouble** jdn/sich in Schwierigkeiten (*acc*) bringen (*also euph*)

➤ **get in with** VI +PREP OBJ (= *associate with*) Anschluss finden an (+*acc*); (= *ingratiate oneself with*) sich gut stellen mit

➤ **get off** ◼ VI **(a)** (*from bus, train etc*) aussteigen (*prep obj* aus); (*from bicycle, horse*) absteigen (*prep obj* von); **to tell sb where to get off** (*inf*) jdm gründlich die Meinung sagen (*inf*)

(b) (*from lawn, ladder, sb's toes, furniture*) heruntergehen (*prep obj* von); **get off!** (= *let me go*) lass (mich) los!

(c) (= *leave*) weg- *or* loskommen; **it's time you got off to school** es ist Zeit, dass ihr in die Schule geht; **I'll see if I can get off (work) early** ich werde mal sehen, ob ich früher (von der Arbeit) wegkann (*inf*); **what time do you get off work?** wann hören Sie mit der Arbeit auf?

(d) +PREP OBJ (= *be excused*) *homework, task etc* nicht machen müssen; **he got off tidying up his room** er kam darum herum, sein Zimmer aufräumen zu müssen (*inf*)

(e) (*fig*: = *escape, be let off*) davonkommen (*inf*)

◼ VT **(a)** SEP (= *remove*) wegbekommen *or* -kriegen (*inf*) (*prep obj* von); *clothes, shoes* ausziehen; *cover, lid* heruntertun (*prep obj* von); *stains* herausmachen (*prep obj* aus); (= *take away from*) abnehmen (*prep obj* +*dat*); **get your dirty hands off my clean shirt** nimm deine schmutzigen Hände von meinem sauberen Hemd; **get him off my property!** schaffen Sie ihn von meinem Grundstück!

(b) +PREP OBJ ALWAYS SEPARATE (*inf*: = *obtain*) bekommen, kriegen (*inf*) (*prep obj* von); **I got that idea off John** ich habe die Idee von John

(c) SEP *mail, children* losschicken; **to get sb off to school** jdn für die Schule fertig machen

(d) SEP *accused* (*lawyer*) freibekommen; (*evidence etc*) entlasten

(e) SEP *day, afternoon* freibekommen

➤ **get off with** VI +PREP OBJ (*inf*) aufreißen (*inf*)

➤ **get on** ◼ VI **(a)** (= *climb on*) hinaufsteigen; (+*prep obj*) (hinauf)steigen auf (+*acc*); (*on bus, train etc*) einsteigen (*prep obj, -to* in +*acc*); (*on bicycle, horse etc*) aufsteigen (*prep obj, -to* auf +*acc*)

(b) (= *continue*) weitermachen; (= *manage to get on*) weiterkommen

(c) **time is getting on** es wird langsam spät; **he is getting on (in years)** er wird langsam alt

(d) (= *progress*) vorankommen; (*work, patient, pupil*) Fortschritte machen; (= *succeed*) Erfolg haben; **to get on in the world** es zu etwas bringen

(e) (= *fare, cope*) zurechtkommen; **how did you get on in the exam?** wie gings (dir) in der Prüfung?; **how are you getting on?** wie gehts?

(f) (= *have a good relationship*) sich verstehen, auskommen (*with* mit)

◼ VT SEP (*prep obj* auf +*acc*) *clothes, shoes* anziehen; *hat* aufsetzen; *lid, cover* drauftun; *load* (*onto cart etc*) hinauftun

➤ **get on for** VI +PREP OBJ (*time, person in age*) zugehen auf (+*acc*); **he's getting on for 40** er geht auf die 40 zu; **there were getting on for 60 people there** es waren fast 60 Leute da

➤ **get on to** VI +PREP OBJ (*inf*) **(a)** (= *get on track of*) *person* auf die Spur *or* Schliche kommen (+*dat*) (*inf*); *dubious activity* aufdecken **(b)** (= *contact*) sich in Verbindung setzen mit; **I'll get on to him about it** ich werde ihn daraufhin ansprechen

➤ **get onto** VTI +PREP OBJ *see* **get on** 1(a), **2**

➤ **get on with** VI +PREP OBJ (= *continue*) weitermachen mit; (= *manage to get on with*) weiterkommen mit; **get on with it!** nun mach schon! (*inf*); **to let sb get on with sth** jdn etw machen lassen; **this will do to be getting on with** das tuts wohl für den Anfang (*inf*)

➤ **get out** ◼ VI **(a)** (*lit, fig*) herauskommen (*of* aus); (= *climb out*) herausklettern *or* -steigen (*of* aus); (*of bus, train, car, scheme, contract*) aussteigen (*of* aus); (= *leave*) weggehen (*of* aus); (*of job*) wegkommen (*of* von); (*animal, prisoner*) entkommen; (*poisonous liquid, gas*) entweichen; (*news*) an die Öffentlichkeit dringen; **he has to get out of the country** er muss das Land verlassen; **get out!** raus! (*inf*); **get out of my house!** verlassen Sie mein Haus!, raus aus meinem Haus!

(*inf*); **to get out of bed** aufstehen
(b) (= *go walking, shopping etc*) weggehen; **you ought to get out (of the house) more** Sie müssten mehr rauskommen (*inf*); **to get out and about** herumkommen

2 VT SEP **(a)** (= *remove*) (*of* aus) herausmachen; *people* hinausbringen; (= *manage to get out*) hinausbekommen *or* -kriegen (*inf*); **I couldn't get him/it out of my head** *or* **mind** ich konnte ihn/es nicht vergessen
(b) (= *bring, take out*) herausholen *or* -nehmen (*of* aus); *car, boat, horse* herausholen (*of* aus)
(c) (= *withdraw*) *money* abheben (*of* von)
(d) (= *borrow from library*) ausleihen (*of* aus)

➤ **get out of** **1** VI +PREP OBJ *see also* **get out 1** *obligation, punishment* herumkommen um; *difficulty* herauskommen aus; **you can't get out of it now** jetzt kannst du nicht mehr anders; **I'll get out of practice** ich verlerne es; **to get out of the habit of doing sth** sich (*dat*) abgewöhnen, etw zu tun **2** VT +PREP OBJ ALWAYS SEPARATE *see also* **get out 2** *confession, truth* herausbekommen *or* -kriegen (*inf*) aus; *profit* machen bei; *money* herausholen aus; *pleasure* haben an (+*dat*); **to get the best/most out of sb/sth** das Beste aus jdm herausholen/etw machen

➤ **get over** **1** VI **(a)** (= *cross*) hinübergehen (*prep obj* über +*acc*); (= *climb over*) hinübersteigen *or* -klettern; (+*prep obj*) steigen *or* klettern über (+*acc*)
(b) +PREP OBJ (*lit, fig*) *disappointment, loss, experience* (hin)wegkommen über (+*acc*); *shock, surprise, illness* sich erholen von; **I can't get over it** (*inf*) da komm ich nicht drüber weg (*inf*)
(c) +PREP OBJ (= *overcome*) *fear, obstacle* überwinden **2** VT SEP *information, ideas etc* verständlich machen (*to dat*); (= *impress upon*) klarmachen (*to dat*) = **get over with**

➤ **get over with** VT ALWAYS SEPARATE hinter sich (*acc*) bringen; **let's get it over with** bringen wirs hinter uns

➤ **get past** VI = **get by (a)**

➤ **get round** (*esp Brit*) **1** VI herumkommen (*prep obj* um); *difficulty, law, regulations* umgehen **2** VT ALWAYS SEPARATE +PREP OBJ **I still can't get my head round it** (*inf*) ich kann es immer noch nicht begreifen

➤ **get round to** VI +PREP OBJ (*esp Brit inf*) **to get round to sth** zu etw kommen; **to get round to doing sth** dazu kommen, etw zu tun

➤ **get through** **1** VI **(a)** (*through gap, snow etc*) durchkommen (*prep obj* durch)
(b) (= *be accepted, pass*) durchkommen (*prep obj* bei); **to get through to the final** in die Endrunde kommen
(c) (*Telec*) durchkommen (*inf*) (*to sb* zu jdm, *to London/Germany* nach London/Deutschland)
(d) (= *communicate, be understood*) **he has finally got through to her** endlich hat er es geschafft, dass sie es begreift
(e) +PREP OBJ *work* erledigen; *book* fertig- *or* auslesen; *bottle* leer machen
(f) +PREP OBJ *days, time* herumbekommen *or* -kriegen (*inf*)
(g) +PREP OBJ (= *consume, use up*) verbrauchen; *food* aufessen; *fortune* durchbringen (*inf*) **2** VT ALWAYS SEPARATE **(a)** *candidate, proposal, bill* durchbekommen *or* -bringen (*prep obj* durch); **to get sb through an exam** (*teacher*) jdn durchs Examen bringen
(b) (= *send*) *message* durchgeben (*to* +*dat*); *supplies* durchbringen
(c) (= *make understand*) **to get sth through (to sb)** (jdm) etw klarmachen

➤ **get to** VI +PREP OBJ **(a)** (*lit, fig*: = *arrive at*) kommen zu; *hotel, town etc* ankommen in (+*dat*); **where did you get to last night?** (*inf*) wo bist du gestern Abend abgeblieben? (*inf*) **(b)** (*inf*) **I got to thinking/wondering** ich hab mir überlegt/mich gefragt **(c)** (*inf*: = *annoy, upset*) aufregen; **don't let them get to you** ärgere dich nicht über sie

➤ **get together** **1** VI zusammenkommen; (*estranged couple*) sich versöhnen; (= *combine forces*) sich zusammenschließen; **why don't we get together later and have a drink?** warum treffen wir uns nicht später und trinken einen? **2** VT SEP *people, collection* zusammenbringen; *documents* zusammentun *or* -suchen; *thoughts, ideas* sammeln; *band* gründen; *money* zusammenbekommen; **to get one's things together** seine Sachen zusammenpacken

➤ **get under** VI darunter kriechen; (*under umbrella etc*) darunter kommen; (+*prep obj*) kriechen/kommen unter (+*acc*)

➤ **get up** **1** VI **(a)** (= *stand up, get out of bed*) aufstehen **(b)** (= *climb up*) hinaufsteigen *or* -klettern (*prep obj* auf +*acc*); (*on horse*) aufsteigen (*prep obj, on* auf +*acc*); (*vehicle*) hinaufkommen (*prep obj* +*acc*); **he couldn't get up the stairs** er kam nicht die Treppe hinauf **2** VT **(a)** ALWAYS SEPARATE (= *get out of bed*) aus dem Bett holen; (= *help to stand up*) aufhelfen (+*dat*)
(b) SEP (= *gather*) *steam* aufbauen; **to get up speed** sich beschleunigen; **to get up one's strength up, to get up one's strength** wieder neue Kräfte sammeln; **to get up an appetite** (*inf*) Hunger bekommen *inf*
(c) ALWAYS SEPARATE (= *dress up, make attractive*) zurechtmachen; **to get oneself up as sb/sth** sich als jd/etw verkleiden

➤ **get up to** VI +PREP OBJ **(a)** (*lit, fig*: = *reach*) erreichen; *standard* herankommen an (+*acc*); *page* kommen bis; **as soon as he got up to me** sobald er neben mir stand **(b)** (= *be involved in*) anstellen (*inf*); **what have you been getting up to?** was hast du getrieben? (*inf*)

get: **getaway** **1** N Flucht *f*; **to make one's ~** sich davonmachen (*inf*) **2** ADJ ATTR **~ car** Fluchtauto *nt*; **get-together** N (*inf*) Treffen *nt*; **family ~** Familientreffen *nt*; **get-up** N (*inf*) Aufmachung *f* (*inf*); **get-well card** N Karte *f* mit Genesungswünschen

geyser [ˈgiːzəʳ] N (*Geol*) Geysir *m*

Ghana [ˈgɑːnə] N Ghana *nt*

ghastly [ˈgɑːstlɪ] ADJ (+ER) **(a)** (*inf*: = *dreadful*) schrecklich; *person* grässlich (*inf*); *object* scheußlich (*inf*) **(b)** (= *grim, gruesome*) *crime, murder* grausig

gherkin [ˈgɜːkɪn] N Gewürzgurke *f*

ghetto [ˈgetəʊ] N (*lit, fig*) G(h)etto *nt*

ghetto blaster [ˈgetəʊblɑːstəʳ] N (*inf*) Ghettoblaster *m* (*inf*)

ghost [gəʊst] N (*a*) Gespenst *nt*; (*of sb*) Geist *m* **(b)** (*fig*) **I don't have** *or* **stand the ~ of a chance** ich habe nicht die geringste Chance; **to give up the ~** (*dated inf*) seinen *or* den Geist aufgeben

ghostly [ˈgəʊstlɪ] ADJ (+ER) gespenstisch

ghost IN CPDS Geister-; **ghost story** N Geister- *or* Gespenstergeschichte *f*; **ghost town** N Geisterstadt *f*; **ghostwriter** N Ghostwriter *m*

ghoul [guːl] N Ghul *m*

ghoulish [ˈguːlɪʃ] ADJ makaber; *description* schaurig

GHQ ABBR *of* **General Headquarters**

GHz ABBR *of* **gigahertz** GHz

GI (*US*) ABBR *of* **government issue** N GI *m*

giant [ˈdʒaɪənt] **1** N Riese *m*; (*fig*) (führende) Größe; (= *company*) Gigant *m*; **a ~ of a man** ein Riese (von einem Mann); **insurance/publishing ~** Großversicherung *f*/-verlag *m* **2** ADJ riesig; (*in animal names*) Riesen-; **~ panda** N Riesenpanda *m*

gibber [ˈdʒɪbəʳ] VI (*ape*) schnattern; (*foreigner*) plappern; **a ~ing idiot** ein daherplappernder Idiot; **I was a ~ing wreck by this stage** da war ich schon so nervös, dass ich nur noch Kauderwelsch herausbrachte

gibberish [ˈdʒɪbərɪʃ] N Quatsch *m* (*inf*); (= *foreign language, baby's ~*) Kauderwelsch *nt*

gibe [dʒaɪb] N Spöttelei *f*

giblets [ˈdʒɪblɪts] PL Geflügelinnereien *pl*

Gibraltar [dʒɪˈbrɔːltəʳ] N Gibraltar *nt*

giddiness [ˈgɪdɪnɪs] N Schwindelgefühl *nt*

giddy [ˈgɪdɪ] ADJ (+ER) **(a)** (*lit*) schwind(e)lig; **~ spells** Schwindelanfälle *pl*; **I feel ~** mir ist schwind(e)lig **(b)** *speed* Schwindel erregend; *heights* schwindelnd (*also fig*) **(c)** (*fig*: = *excited*) ausgelassen; **she was ~ with excitement** sie war vor Aufregung ganz aus dem Häuschen (*inf*)

gift [gɪft] N **(a)** Geschenk *nt*; (= *donation to charity*) Spende *f*; **there is a free ~ with every purchase over £10** bei jedem Kauf im Wert von über £ 10 erhalten Sie ein Geschenk; **that question was a ~** (*inf*) die Frage war ja geschenkt (*inf*) **(b)** (= *talent*) Gabe *f*; **to have a ~ for sth** ein Talent *nt* für etw haben; **she has a ~ for teaching** sie hat eine Begabung zur

Lehrerin; **he has a ~ for languages/music** er ist sprachbegabt/
musikalisch begabt

Be careful! **gift** *is not translated by the German word* **Gift**.

gift certificate N (*US*) Geschenkgutschein *m*
gifted [ˈɡɪftɪd] ADJ begabt (*in* für)
gift: gift token, gift voucher N Geschenkgutschein *m*;
giftwrap ◧ VT *in or* mit Geschenkpapier einwickeln ◪ N
Geschenkpapier *nt*

gig [ɡɪɡ] N **(a)** (*inf*) (= *concert*) Konzert *nt*, Gig *m* (*inf*); (*of
comedian, singer, group*) Auftritt *m*; **to do a ~** ein Konzert
geben, auftreten **(b)** (*US*: = *temporary job*) Job *m*
gigantic [dʒaɪˈɡæntɪk] ADJ riesig; *building, man, task also*
gigantisch; *appetite, mistake* gewaltig; *amount* enorm
giggle [ˈɡɪɡl] ◧ N Gekicher *nt no pl*; **it was a bit of a ~** (*inf*) es
war ganz lustig; **to get the ~s** anfangen herumzukichern
◪ VI kichern
giggly [ˈɡɪɡlɪ] ADJ (+ER) albern
gild [ɡɪld], *pret* **gilded**, *ptp* **gilded** *or* **gilt** VT vergolden
gilding [ˈɡɪldɪŋ] N Vergoldung *f*
gill [ɡɪl] N (*of fish*) Kieme *f*
gilt [ɡɪlt] ◧ PTP *of* **gild** ◪ N **(a)** (= *material*) Vergoldung *f*
(b) (*Fin*) **~s** mündelsichere Wertpapiere *pl* ◨ ADJ vergoldet
gilt-edged [ɡɪltˈedʒd] ADJ (*Fin*) mündelsicher
gimlet [ˈɡɪmlɪt] N Hand- *or* Vorbohrer *m*
gimmick [ˈɡɪmɪk] N Gag *m* (*inf*); (*in film etc*) effekthaschender
Gag; (= *gadget*) Spielerei *f*; (*Comm*) verkaufsfördernde
Maßnahme; **an election ~** ein Wahltrick *m*
gimmickry [ˈɡɪmɪkrɪ] N Effekthascherei *f*; (*in advertising, sales*)
Gags *pl*; (= *gadgetry*) Spielereien *pl*
gimmicky [ˈɡɪmɪkɪ] ADJ effekthascherisch
gin [dʒɪn] N (= *drink*) Gin *m*; **~ and tonic** Gin Tonic *m*
ginger [ˈdʒɪndʒəʳ] ◧ N Ingwer *m* ◪ ADJ **(a)** (*Cook*) Ingwer-
(b) *hair* kupferrot; *cat* rötlich gelb
ginger: ginger ale N Gingerale *nt*; **ginger beer** N
Ingwerlimonade *f*; (*alcoholic*) Ingwerbier *nt*; **gingerbread**
◧ N Lebkuchen *m* mit Ingwergeschmack ◪ ADJ ATTR
Lebkuchen-; **~ man/house** Lebkuchenmann *m*/-haus *nt*
gingerly [ˈdʒɪndʒəlɪ] ADV vorsichtig; *pick up, handle* (*sth dirty*)
mit spitzen Fingern; (*sth cold or hot*) zaghaft
gingery [ˈdʒɪndʒərɪ] ADJ *hair, colour* rötlich
gingham [ˈɡɪŋəm] N Gingan *m*
gipsy, gypsy [ˈdʒɪpsɪ] ◧ N Zigeuner(in) *m(f)* ◪ ADJ ATTR
Zigeuner-; **~ music** Zigeunermusik *f*
giraffe [dʒɪˈrɑːf] N Giraffe *f*
girder [ˈɡɜːdəʳ] N Träger *m*
girdle [ˈɡɜːdl] N Hüftgürtel *or* -halter *m*
girl [ɡɜːl] N Mädchen *nt*; (= *daughter*) Tochter *f*; (= *girlfriend*)
Freundin *f*; (*in shop*) Verkäuferin *f*; (*in factory*) Arbeiterin *f*; **an
English ~** eine Engländerin; **the Smith ~s** die Smith-
Mädchen; **I'm going out with the ~s tonight** ich gehe heute
Abend mit meinen Freundinnen aus
girl: girl band N (*Mus*) Girlband *f*; **girl Friday** N
Allroundsekretärin *f*; **girlfriend** N Freundin *f*; **Girl Guide** N
(*Brit*) Pfadfinderin *f*; **girlhood** N Mädchenzeit *f*, Jugend *f*; **in
her ~** in ihrer Jugend
girlie, girly [ˈɡɜːlɪ] ADJ ATTR (*inf*) girliehaft; *magazine* Girlie-
girlish [ˈɡɜːlɪʃ] ADJ mädchenhaft; **she still looked ~** sie sah
immer noch wie ein Mädchen aus
Girl Scout N (*US*) Pfadfinderin *f*
girly [ˈɡɜːlɪ] ADJ ATTR (*inf*) = **girlie**
giro [ˈdʒaɪrəʊ] N (*Brit*) (= *bank ~*) Giro(verkehr *m*) *nt*; (= *post-
office ~*) Postscheckverkehr *or* -dienst *m*; **~** (*cheque*) (*Social
Security*) Sozialhilfeüberweisung *f*; **~ cheque** (*for paying*)
Postscheck *m*; **to pay a bill by ~** eine Rechnung durch
Überweisung bezahlen
girth [ɡɜːθ] N Umfang *m*
gismo N (*inf*) = **gizmo**
gist [dʒɪst] N, NO PL Wesentliche(s) *nt*; **that was the ~ of what
he said** das war im Wesentlichen, was er gesagt hat; **to give
sb the ~ of sth** jdm sagen, worum es bei etw geht; **I got the
~ of it** das Wesentliche habe ich verstanden
git [ɡɪt] N (*inf*) Schwachkopf *m*

---

give [ɡɪv]

◧ TRANSITIVE VERB	◨ NOUN
◪ INTRANSITIVE VERB	◫ PHRASAL VERBS

vb: pret **gave**, *ptp* **given**

◧ TRANSITIVE VERB

When **give** *is part of a set combination, eg.* **give evidence**,
give chase, *look up the other word.*

(a) geben; **to give sb sth** *or* **sth to sb** jdm etw geben; **the
teacher gave us three exercises** der Lehrer hat uns drei
Übungen gegeben *or* (*as homework*) aufgegeben; **they gave us
roast beef for lunch** sie servierten uns Roastbeef zum
(Mittag)essen; **I'd give anything to know ...** ich würde alles
darum geben, wenn ich wüsste, ...; **to give sb one's cold** (*inf*)
jdn mit seiner Erkältung anstecken

✦**to give sth for sth** (= *pay*) etw für etw ausgeben;
(= *exchange*) etw gegen etw tauschen; **what will you give me
for it?** was gibst du mir dafür?; **how much did you give for it?**
wie viel hast du dafür bezahlt?

✦**give or take** 11 o'clock, give or take a few minutes so gegen
11 Uhr; **six foot, give or take a few inches** ungefähr sechs Fuß
(b) (*as present*) schenken; (= *donate*) spenden; **to give sb sth**
or **sth to sb** jdm etw schenken; **it was given to me by my
uncle, I was given it by my uncle** ich habe es von meinem
Onkel geschenkt bekommen
(c) (*with abstract nouns*) *trouble* machen; *pleasure, joy also*
bereiten; *one's love, attention* schenken; **to give sb help** jdm
helfen; **to give sb support** jdn unterstützen; **give me
strength/patience!** großer Gott! (*inf*); **to be given a choice** die
Wahl haben; **to give sb a look/smile** jdn ansehen/anlächeln;
to give sb a push/kick jdm einen Stoß/Tritt geben; **to give
one's hair a brush/wash** sich (*dat*) die Haare bürsten/
waschen; **who gave you that idea?** wer hat dich denn auf die
Idee gebracht?; **what gives you that idea?** wie kommst du
denn auf die Idee?; **give me Spain (every time)!** (*inf*) es geht
doch nichts über Spanien!; **it gives me great pleasure to ...** es
ist mir eine große Freude ...; **to give sb a shock** jdm einen
Schock versetzen; **to give a cry/groan/laugh/sigh** aufschreien/
-stöhnen/-lachen/-seufzen

✦**to give way** (= YIELD) nachgeben (*to* +*dat*); **don't give way to
despair** überlass dich nicht der Verzweiflung
(= BE SUPERSEDED) **to give way to sth** von etw abgelöst werden
(ON ROAD) (*Brit*) **give way to oncoming traffic** der
Gegenverkehr hat Vorfahrt; **I was expecting him to give way**
ich nahm an, er würde mir die Vorfahrt lassen; **"give way"**
„Vorfahrt (gewähren)"

✦**to give sb to understand that ...** jdm zu verstehen geben,
dass ...
(d) (= *punish with*) erteilen; **he gave the child a smack** er gab
dem Kind einen Klaps; **he gave her 100 lines** (*Brit*) *or*
sentences (*US*) er gab ihr 100 Zeilen als Strafarbeit auf; **to
give sb five years** jdn zu fünf Jahren verurteilen
(e) (= *yield, produce*) *milk, warmth, light etc* geben; *results*
(er)bringen; *answer* liefern
(f) (= *allow*) *time* geben; **give yourself time to recover** lassen
Sie sich Zeit, um sich zu erholen; **give yourself half an hour**
rechnen Sie mit einer halben Stunde; **how long do you give
that marriage?** (*inf*) wie lange gibst du dieser Ehe? (*inf*)

✦**I'll give you that** (= *concede*) **it's an improvement, I'll give you
that** es ist eine Verbesserung, das gestehe ich (dir) ein; **he's a
good worker, I'll give him that** eines muss man ihm lassen, er
arbeitet gut
(g) (= *report, tell*) *information, details, description, answer, advice*
geben; *one's name, particulars* angeben; *suggestion* machen;
(= *let sb know by letter, phone etc*) *decision, opinion, results*
mitteilen; **the court hasn't given a decision yet** das Gericht
hat noch kein Urteil gefällt; **give him my regards** richten Sie
ihm (schöne) Grüße von mir aus; **to give no/the right answer**
nicht/richtig antworten; **to give sb a warning** jdn warnen; **he
forgot to give us the date** er hat vergessen, uns das Datum
mitzuteilen
(h) (= *hold, perform*) *party, dinner* geben; *speech* halten; *toast*
ausbringen (*to sb* auf jdn); **give us a song** sing uns was vor

(i) (= do) **the child gave a little jump of excitement** das Kind machte vor Aufregung einen Luftsprung; **he gave a shrug of his shoulders** er zuckte mit den Schultern
(j) (= devote) widmen (to +dat)

2 INTRANSITIVE VERB
(a) (lit, fig) (= collapse, yield, bend) nachgeben; (= break, rope, cable) reißen
(b) (= give money etc) spenden; **you have to be prepared to give and take** (fig) man muss zu Kompromissen bereit sein
(c) (esp US) **what gives?** (inf) was gibts? (inf); **what gives with him?** (inf) was ist los mit ihm? (inf)
(d) (= tell) (US inf) **OK, now give!** also, raus mit der Sprache! (inf)

3 NOUN Nachgiebigkeit f; (of floor, bed, chair) Federung f; **it has a lot of give** es gibt sehr stark nach

4 PHRASAL VERBS
▶ **give away** VT SEP **(a)** weggeben; gift, advantage, goal verschenken **(b)** bride zum Altar führen (als Brautvater etc) **(c)** (= hand out) prizes etc vergeben, verteilen **(d)** (fig: = betray) verraten (to sb an jdn); **to give the game away** (inf) alles verraten
▶ **give back** VT SEP zurück- or wiedergeben
▶ **give in** **1** VI (= surrender) sich ergeben (to sb jdm); (in guessing game etc) aufgeben; (= back down) nachgeben (to +dat); **to give in to temptation** der Versuchung erliegen **2** VT SEP document, essay einreichen
▶ **give off** VT INSEP heat, gas abgeben; smell verbreiten
▶ **give out** **1** VI (supplies, patience, strength) zu Ende gehen or (in past tense) sein; (engine, feet) versagen; **my voice gave out** mir versagte die Stimme **2** VT SEP **(a)** (= distribute) aus- or verteilen **(b)** (= announce) bekannt geben **3** VT INSEP = **give off**
▶ **give over** **1** VT SEP **(a)** (= hand over) übergeben (to +dat) **(b)** **to be given over to sth** für etw beansprucht werden **2** VI (dial inf: = stop) aufhören **3** VI +PREP OBJ aufhören; **give over tickling me!** hör auf, mich zu kitzeln!
▶ **give up** **1** VI aufgeben
2 VT SEP **(a)** aufgeben; **to give up doing sth** aufhören or es aufgeben, etw zu tun; **I'm trying to give up smoking** ich versuche, das Rauchen aufzugeben; **to give sb/sth up as lost** jdn/etw verloren geben; **to give sb up for dead** jdn für tot halten
(b) (= surrender) land, territory abtreten (to +dat); seat, place freimachen (to für); ticket abgeben (to bei)
(c) (= hand over to authorities) übergeben (to dat); **to give oneself up** sich stellen; (after siege etc) sich ergeben
(d) (= devote) widmen
▶ **give up on** VI +PREP OBJ abschreiben

give: **give-and-take** N Entgegenkommen nt; (in personal relationships) (gegenseitiges) Geben und Nehmen; **giveaway** N **(a)** **it was a real ~ when he said ...** er verriet sich, als er sagte ... **(b)** (US Comm: = gift) Geschenk nt **(c)** (US: Rad, TV) Preisraten nt
given ['gɪvn] **1** PTP of give
2 ADJ **(a)** (with indef art) bestimmt; (with def art) angegeben; **in a ~ period** in einem bestimmten Zeitraum; **within the ~ period** im angegebenen Zeitraum
(b) **~ name** (esp US) Vorname m
(c) **to be ~ to sth** zu etw neigen; **I'm not ~ to drinking on my own** ich habe nicht die Angewohnheit, allein zu trinken **3** CONJ **~ that he ...** (= in view of the fact) angesichts der Tatsache, dass er ...; (= assuming) angenommen, (dass) er ...; **~ time, we can do it** wenn wir genug Zeit haben, können wir es schaffen; **~ the chance, I would ...** wenn ich die Gelegenheit hätte, würde ich ...; **~ these circumstances/conditions** unter diesen Umständen/Voraussetzungen
gizmo ['gɪzməʊ] N (inf) Ding nt (inf)
glacé ['glæseɪ] ADJ kandiert
glacial ['gleɪsɪəl] ADJ look, wind eisig; (fig) atmosphere, smile frostig
glacier ['glæsɪə^r] N Gletscher m
glad [glæd] ADJ (+ER) PRED froh; **to be ~ about sth** sich über etw (acc) freuen; **I'm ~ (about that)** das freut mich; **to be ~ of sth**

froh über etw (acc) sein; **we'd be ~ of your help** wir wären froh, wenn Sie uns helfen könnten; **I'd be ~ of your opinion on this** ich würde gerne Ihre Meinung dazu hören; **to be ~ (that)...** sich freuen, dass ...; (= relieved) froh sein, dass ...; **I'm ~ you like it** ich freue mich, dass es Ihnen gefällt; **I'll be ~ to show you everything** ich zeige Ihnen gerne alles; **to be only too ~ to do sth** etw sehr gern tun
gladden ['glædn] VT erfreuen
glade [gleɪd] N Lichtung f
gladiator ['glædɪeɪtə^r] N Gladiator m
gladly ['glædlɪ] ADV gern(e)
glad rags PL (inf) beste Klamotten pl (inf), Sonntagsstaat m (inf)
glamor N (US) = **glamour**
glamorize ['glæməraɪz] VT idealisieren, einen glamourösen Anstrich geben (+dat); (author) war, violence verherrlichen
glamorous ['glæmərəs] ADJ person, job, life glamourös; place, clothes mondän; occasion glanzvoll; **there's nothing ~ about the job** der Job ist überhaupt nicht reizvoll
glamour, (US) **glamor** ['glæmə^r] N Glamour m; (of occasion, situation) Glanz m
glance [glɑːns] **1** N Blick m; **at a ~** auf einen Blick; **at first ~** auf den ersten Blick; **to take a quick ~ at sth** einen kurzen Blick auf etw (acc) werfen; **we exchanged ~s** wir sahen uns kurz an **2** VI sehen, blicken; **to ~ at sb/sth** jdn/etw kurz ansehen; **to ~ at or through a report** einen kurzen Blick in einen Bericht werfen; **to ~ over sth** etw überfliegen
▶ **glance off** VI (prep obj von) (bullet etc) abprallen; (light) reflektiert werden
glancing ['glɑːnsɪŋ] ADJ **to strike sth a ~ blow** etw streifen
gland [glænd] N Drüse f; (= lymph ~) Lymphknoten m
glandular ['glændjʊlə^r] ADJ **~ fever** Drüsenfieber nt
glare [gleə^r] **1** N **(a)** greller Schein; **the ~ of the sun** das grelle Sonnenlicht; **to escape the ~ of publicity** dem grellen Licht der Öffentlichkeit entkommen **(b)** (= stare) wütender or stechender Blick **2** VI **(a)** (light, sun) grell scheinen; (headlights) grell leuchten; (bulb) grell brennen **(b)** (= stare) (zornig) starren; **to ~ at sb/sth** jdn/etw zornig anstarren
glaring ['gleərɪŋ] ADJ **(a)** sun, light grell, gleißend (geh) **(b)** example, omission eklatant; error offensichtlich, grob; contradiction, inconsistency krass; injustice (himmel)schreiend
glaringly ['gleərɪŋlɪ] ADV **~ obvious** fact, statement überdeutlich; **it was ~ obvious that he had no idea** es war nur zu ersichtlich, dass er keine Ahnung hatte
glasnost ['glæznɒst] N Glasnost f
glass [glɑːs] **1** N **(a)** Glas nt; (= a pane of ~) eine Glasscheibe; **a ~ of wine** ein Glas Wein **(b)** (= spectacles) ~es pl, **pair of ~es** Brille f **2** ADJ ATTR Glas-; **~ bottle** Glasflasche f
glass IN CPDS Glas-; **glass-blowing** N Glasbläserei f; **glass fibre**, (US) **glass fiber** N Glasfaser f; **glassful** N Glas nt; **glasshouse** N (Brit Hort) Gewächshaus nt; **glassware** N Glaswaren pl
glaucoma [glɔːˈkəʊmə] N grüner Star
glaze [gleɪz] **1** N Glasur f **2** VT **(a)** door, window verglasen **(b)** pottery, tiles, cake glasieren; fruit kandieren; **~d tile** Kachel f **3** VI (eyes: also ~ over) glasig werden; **she had a ~d look in her eyes** sie hatte einen glasigen Blick
glazier ['gleɪzɪə^r] N Glaser(in) m(f)
glazing ['gleɪzɪŋ] N Glasur f
gleam [gliːm] **1** N **(a)** Schimmer m; (of metal, water) Schimmern nt; **a ~ of light** ein Lichtschimmer m **(b)** (fig) **a ~ of hope** ein Hoffnungsschimmer m; **he had a (dangerous) ~ in his eye** seine Augen funkelten (gefährlich) **2** VI schimmern; (eyes) funkeln
gleaming ['gliːmɪŋ] ADJ schimmernd; eyes funkelnd; **~ white teeth** blendend weiße Zähne
glean [gliːn] VT (fig) herausbekommen; **to ~ sth from sb/sth** etw von jdm erfahren/einer Sache (dat) entnehmen
glee [gliː] N Freude f; (malicious) Schadenfreude f; **he shouted with ~** er stieß einen Freudenschrei aus; **they were rubbing their hands in ~** (also fig) sie rieben sich (dat) schadenfroh die Hände
gleeful ['gliːfʊl] ADJ fröhlich, vergnügt; (maliciously) hämisch, schadenfroh
gleefully ['gliːfəlɪ] ADV fröhlich, vergnügt; (= maliciously) hämisch, schadenfroh

glen [glen] N Tal *nt*

glib [glɪb] ADJ (+ER) *person* zungenfertig; *excuse, reply* leichtzüngig; *attitude, ideas* leichtfertig; *promise, generalization* vorschnell; **~ talk** leichtfertiges Gerede; **~ phrases** schön klingende Phrasen *pl*

glibly ['glɪblɪ] ADV *talk* leichthin; *promise, generalize* vorschnell; *reply* leichtzüngig

glide [glaɪd] VI gleiten; *(through the air)* schweben; *(plane)* im Gleitflug fliegen; **I would like to learn to ~** ich möchte Segelfliegen lernen; **to ~ in** hereinschweben

glider ['glaɪdə'] N *(Aviat)* Segelflugzeug *nt*; **~ pilot** Segelflieger(in) *m(f)*

gliding ['glaɪdɪŋ] N *(Aviat)* Segelfliegen *nt*; **~ club** Segelfliegerklub *m*

glimmer ['glɪmə'] ■ N **(a)** *(of light, candle etc)* Schimmer *m*; *(of fire)* Glimmen *nt*; **the faint ~ of dawn** der schwache Schein der Morgendämmerung **(b)** *(fig)* **= gleam 1** ■ VI *(light, water)* schimmern; *(flame, fire)* glimmen

glimpse [glɪmps] ■ N Blick *m*; **a ~ of life in 18th-century London** ein (Ein)blick in das Leben im London des 18. Jahrhunderts; **to catch a ~ of sb/sth** einen flüchtigen Blick auf jdn/etw werfen können; *(fig)* eine Ahnung von etw bekommen ■ VT kurz sehen, einen Blick erhaschen von

glint [glɪnt] ■ N *(of light, metal)* Glitzern *nt no pl*; **a ~ of light** ein glitzernder Lichtstrahl; **he has a wicked/merry ~ in his eyes** seine Augen funkeln böse/lustig ■ VI glitzern; *(eyes)* funkeln

glisten ['glɪsn] VI glänzen; *(dewdrops, tears)* glitzern

glitch [glɪtʃ] N *(Comput)* Funktionsstörung *f*; **a technical ~** eine technische Panne

glitter ['glɪtə'] ■ N Glitzern *nt*; *(of eyes, diamonds)* Funkeln *nt*; *(for decoration)* Glitzerstaub *m*; *(fig)* Glanz *m* ■ VI glitzern; *(eyes, diamonds)* funkeln

glittering ['glɪtərɪŋ] ADJ glitzernd; *eyes, diamonds* funkelnd; *occasion* glanzvoll; *career* glänzend; *prizes* verlockend

glittery ['glɪtərɪ] ADJ *(inf)* glitzernd

glitz [glɪts] N *(inf)* Glanz *m*

glitzy ['glɪtsɪ] ADJ (+ER) *(inf)* *occasion* glanzvoll, schillernd; *dress* schick

gloat [gləʊt] VI *(with pride at oneself)* sich großtun *(over, about* mit); *(over sb's misfortune or failure)* sich hämisch freuen *(over, about* über *+acc)*; **there's no need to ~ (over me)!** das ist kein Grund zur Schadenfreude!

gloating ['gləʊtɪŋ] ■ N Selbstgefälligkeit *f*; *(over sb's misfortune or failure)* Schadenfreude *f* ■ ADJ *(= self-satisfied)* selbstgefällig; *(= malicious)* hämisch, schadenfroh

glob [glɒb] N *(inf)* Klacks *m (inf)*; *(of mud)* Klümpchen *nt*

global ['gləʊbl] ADJ global; *recession, problem* weltweit; **a ~ figure of £2 million** eine Gesamtsumme von £ 2 Millionen; **~ peace/war** Weltfrieden/-krieg *m*

global economy N Weltwirtschaft *f*

globalize ['gləʊbəlaɪz] VTI globalisieren

globally ['gləʊbəlɪ] ADV **(a)** *(= worldwide)* global **(b)** *(= universally) accepted, recognized* allgemein

global: global trade N Welthandel *m*; **global village** N Weltdorf *nt*; **global warming** N Erwärmung *f* der Erdatmosphäre

globe [gləʊb] N *(= sphere)* Kugel *f*; *(= map)* Globus *m*; *(= fish bowl)* Glaskugel *f*; **the ~** *(= the world)* der Globus; **all over the ~** auf der ganzen Erde *or* Welt

globe: globe artichoke N Artischocke *f*; **globetrotter** N Globetrotter(in) *m(f)*; **globetrotting** ■ N Globetrotten *nt* ■ ATTR globetrottend

globule ['glɒbjuːl] N Kügelchen *nt*; *(of oil, water)* Tröpfchen *nt*

gloom [gluːm] N **(a)** *(= darkness)* Düsterkeit *f* **(b)** *(= sadness)* düstere Stimmung; **economic ~** depressive Wirtschaftslage; **he was filled with ~** er war sehr bedrückt *or* niedergeschlagen

gloomily ['gluːmɪlɪ] ADV niedergeschlagen; *(= pessimistically)* pessimistisch

gloomy ['gluːmɪ] ADJ (+ER) düster; *day, weather, light* trüb; *person, mood* niedergeschlagen; *voice* traurig; *(= pessimistic)* pessimistisch *(about* über *+acc)*; *news* bedrückend; *outlook, prospects* trübe; **he is very ~ about his chances of success** er beurteilt seine Erfolgschancen sehr pessimistisch

glorification [glɔːrɪfɪ'keɪʃən] N Verherrlichung *f*

glorified ['glɔːrɪfaɪd] ADJ **this restaurant is just a ~ snack bar** dieses Restaurant ist nur eine bessere Imbissstube; **I'm just a ~ secretary** ich bin nur eine bessere Sekretärin

glorify ['glɔːrɪfaɪ] VT verherrlichen

glorious ['glɔːrɪəs] ADJ **(a)** *(= splendid)* herrlich **(b)** *(= illustrious) career, future* glanzvoll; *years, era, victory, history* ruhmreich

gloriously ['glɔːrɪəslɪ] ADV herrlich; **~ happy** überglücklich

glory ['glɔːrɪ] ■ N **(a)** *(= honour, fame)* Ruhm *m*; **moment of ~** Ruhmesstunde *f*; **covered in ~** ruhmbedeckt **(b)** *(= beauty, magnificence)* Herrlichkeit *f*; **the glories of the past, past glories** vergangene Herrlichkeiten *pl*; **they restored the car to its former ~** sie restaurierten das Auto, bis es seine frühere Schönheit wiedererlangt hatte **(c)** *(= source of pride)* Stolz *m* ■ VI **to ~ in one's/sb's success** sich in seinem/jds Erfolg sonnen; **to ~ in the knowledge/fact that ...** das Wissen/die Tatsache, dass ..., voll auskosten

gloss¹ [glɒs] N Glanz *m*; *(fig: of respectability etc)* Schein *m*; **to take the ~ off sth** *(fig)* einer Sache *(dat)* den Glanz nehmen; **~ finish** *(Phot: on paper)* Glanz(beschichtung *f)* *m*; *(of paint)* Lackanstrich *m*

▶ **gloss over** VT SEP *(= try to conceal)* vertuschen; *(= make light of)* beschönigen

gloss² N *(= explanation)* Erläuterung *f*; *(= note also)* Anmerkung *f*; **to put a ~ on sth** etw interpretieren

glossary ['glɒsərɪ] N Glossar *nt*

gloss (paint) N Glanzlack(farbe *f)* *m*

glossy ['glɒsɪ] ■ ADJ (+ER) glänzend; **to be ~** glänzen; **~ brochure** Hochglanzbroschüre *f*; **~ magazine** (Hochglanz)magazin *nt*; **~ paper/paint** Glanzpapier *nt*/-lack *m*; **~ print** *(Phot)* Hochglanzbild *nt* ■ N *(inf)* (Hochglanz)magazin *nt*

glove [glʌv] N (Finger)handschuh *m*; *(Sport)* Handschuh *m*; **to fit (sb) like a ~** (jdm) wie angegossen passen

glove: glove box, glove compartment N *(Aut)* Handschuhfach *nt*; **glove puppet** N *(Brit)* Handpuppe *f*

glow [gləʊ] ■ VI glühen; *(colour, hands of clock)* leuchten; *(lamp, candle)* scheinen; **she/her cheeks ~ed with health** sie hatte ein blühendes Aussehen; **to ~ with pride** vor Stolz glühen ■ N Glühen *nt*; *(of lamp, candle)* Schein *m*; *(of fire, sunset, passion)* Glut *f*; **her face had a healthy ~** ihr Gesicht hatte eine blühende Farbe

glower ['glaʊə'] VI ein finsteres Gesicht machen; **to ~ at sb** jdn finster ansehen

glowing ['gləʊɪŋ] ADJ *account, description* begeistert; *report* überschwänglich; **to speak of sb/sth in ~ terms** voller Begeisterung von jdm/etw sprechen

glowingly ['gləʊɪŋlɪ] ADV *(fig)* begeistert; *describe* in glühenden Farben

glow-worm ['gləʊˌwɜːm] N Glühwürmchen *nt*

glucose ['gluːkəʊs] N Glukose *f*, Traubenzucker *m*

glue [gluː] ■ N Klebstoff *m*, Leim *m* ■ VT kleben, leimen; **to ~ sth down/on** etw fest-/ankleben; **to ~ sth to sth** etw an etw *(dat)* festkleben; **to keep one's eyes ~d to sb/sth** jdn/etw nicht aus den Augen lassen; **he's been ~d to the TV all evening** er hängt schon den ganzen Abend vorm Fernseher *(inf)*; **we were ~d to our seats** wir saßen wie gebannt auf unseren Plätzen

glue-sniffing ['gluːˌsnɪfɪŋ] N (Klebstoff)schnüffeln *nt*

glum [glʌm] ADJ (+ER) niedergeschlagen; *atmosphere* gedrückt; *thoughts* schwarz

glumly ['glʌmlɪ] ADV niedergeschlagen

glut [glʌt] ■ VT *(Comm)* überschwemmen ■ N Schwemme *f*

gluten ['gluːtən] N Gluten *nt*

glutton ['glʌtn] N Vielfraß *m*; **she's a ~ for punishment** sie ist die reinste Masochistin *(inf)*

gluttonous ['glʌtənəs] ADJ *(lit, fig)* unersättlich; *person* gefräßig

gluttony ['glʌtənɪ] N Völlerei *f*

glycerin(e) ['glɪsəriːn] N Glyzerin *nt*

GM ABBR *of* **genetically modified**

gm ABBR *of* **gram(s), gramme(s)** g

GMO N ABBR *of* **genetically modified organism** genetisch veränderter Organismus, GVO *m*

GMT ABBR *of* **Greenwich Mean Time** WEZ

gnarled [nɑːld] ADJ *tree* knorrig; *hands, fingers* knotig; *person* verhutzelt; (= *bent*) krumm

gnash [næʃ] VT **to ~ one's teeth** mit den Zähnen knirschen

gnat [næt] N (Stech)mücke *f*

gnaw [nɔː] 🅱 VT nagen an (+*dat*); *fingernails also* kauen an (+*dat*); *hole* nagen; **the box had been ~ed by the rats** die Ratten hatten die Kiste angenagt 🅱 VI nagen; **to ~ at or on sth** an etw (*dat*) nagen; **to ~ at sb** (*fig*) jdn quälen; **to ~ through sth** etw durchnagen

gnawing [ˈnɔːɪŋ] ADJ *doubt, hunger, pain* nagend; *fear, guilt, remorse* quälend

gnome [nəʊm] N Gnom *m*; (*in garden*) Gartenzwerg *m*

GNP ABBR *of* **gross national product**

GNVQ (*Brit Sch*) ABBR *of* **General National Vocational Qualification** ≈ Berufsschulabschluss *m*

go [gəʊ]

🅱 INTRANSITIVE VERB	🅸 NOUN
🅱 AUXILIARY VERB	🅵 PHRASAL VERBS
🅱 TRANSITIVE VERB	

vb: pret **went**, *ptp* **gone**

When **go** *is part of a set combination, e.g.* **go crazy, go unheard, go ballistic,** *look up the other word.*

🅱 INTRANSITIVE VERB

(a) gehen; (*vehicle, person in vehicle*) fahren; (*plane*) fliegen; (= *travel*) reisen; (*road*) führen; **the doll goes everywhere with her** sie nimmt die Puppe überallhin mit; **you go first** geh du zuerst!; **you go next** du bist der Nächste; **there you go** (*giving sth*) bitte; (= *I told you so*) na bitte; **here we go again!** (*inf*) jetzt geht das schon wieder los! (*inf*); **where do we go from here?** (*lit*) wo gehen wir anschließend hin?; (*fig*) und was (wird) jetzt?; **to go to church** in die Kirche gehen; **to go to evening classes** Abendkurse besuchen; **to go to work** zur Arbeit gehen; **he's going as a pirate** er geht als Pirat; **what shall I go in?** was soll ich anziehen?; **the garden goes down to the river** der Garten geht bis zum Fluss hinunter

✦**to go to ...** **to go to France** nach Frankreich fahren; **I have to go to the doctor/to London** ich muss zum Arzt (gehen)/nach London; **to go to sb for sth** (= *ask sb*) jdn wegen etw fragen; (= *fetch from sb*) bei jdm etw holen

✦**to go on ...** **to go on a journey** eine Reise machen; **to go on a course** einen Kurs machen; **to go on holiday** (*Brit*) *or* **vacation** (*US*) in Urlaub gehen

✦**to go for ...** **to go for a walk/swim** spazieren/schwimmen gehen; **to go for a doctor/newspaper** einen Arzt/eine Zeitung holen

✦**to go and ...** **go and shut the door** mach mal die Tür zu; **go and tell him** sags ihm; **he's gone and lost his new watch** (*inf*) er hat seine neue Uhr verloren; **now you've gone and done it!** (*inf*) na, jetzt hast du es geschafft!

✦**to go + -ing** **to go fishing/shopping/shooting** angeln/ einkaufen/auf die Jagd gehen; **to go looking for sb/sth** nach jdm/etw suchen

(b) (= *depart*) gehen; (*vehicle, person in vehicle*) (ab)fahren; (*plane, person in plane*) (ab)fliegen; (= *die*) sterben; **has he gone yet?** ist er schon weg?; **when I have gone** *or* **am gone** (= *leave*) wenn ich weg bin; (= *die*) wenn ich (einmal) nicht mehr (da) bin; **we must go** *or* **be going** *or* **get going** (*inf*) wir müssen gehen *or* uns langsam auf den Weg machen (*inf*); **go!** (*Sport*) los!; **here goes!** jetzt gehts los! (*inf*)

(c) (= *disappear, vanish*) verschwinden; (= *be used up*) aufgebraucht werden; (*time*) vergehen; **it is** *or* **has gone** (= *disappeared*) es ist weg; (= *used up, eaten etc*) es ist alle (*inf*); **where has it gone?** wo ist es hin *or* geblieben?; **gone are the days when ...** die Zeiten sind vorbei, wo ...; **all his money goes on computer games** er gibt sein ganzes Geld für Computerspiele aus; **£75 a week goes** *in* *or* **on rent** £ 75 die Woche sind für die Miete (weg); **it's just gone three** es ist kurz nach drei

✦**... to go** **two days to go till ...** noch zwei Tage bis ...; **two exams down and one to go** zwei Prüfungen geschafft und

eine kommt noch

(d) (= *be got rid of*) verschwinden; (= *be abolished*) abgeschafft werden; **that old settee will have to go** das alte Sofa muss weg; **hundreds of jobs will go** hunderte von Stellen werden verloren gehen

(e) (= *be sold*) **the hats aren't going very well** die Hüte gehen nicht sehr gut (weg); **it went for £5** es ging für £ 5 weg; **how much did the house go for?** für wie viel wurde das Haus verkauft?; **going, going, gone!** zum Ersten, zum Zweiten, und zum Dritten!

(f) (= *have recourse to*) **to go to the country** (*Brit Parl*) Wahlen ausrufen; **to go to war** Krieg führen (*over* wegen); **he has gone so far as to accuse me** er ist so weit gegangen, mich zu beschuldigen

(g) (= *be awarded*) (*prize, job etc*) gehen (*to* an +*acc*); (*inheritance*) zufallen (*to sb* jdm)

(h) (= *function*) (*watch*) gehen; (*car, machine*) laufen; **to make sth go** etw in Gang bringen; **to go slow** (*workers*) im Bummelstreik sein

✦**to get going** in Schwung *or* Fahrt kommen

✦**to get going on** *or* **with sth** etw in Angriff nehmen

✦**to get sth going** etw in Gang bringen; *party* etw in Fahrt bringen; *business* etw auf Vordermann bringen

✦**to keep going** (*person*) weitermachen; (*business, machine, engine etc*) weiterlaufen; (*car*) weiterfahren; **keep going!** weiter!

✦**to keep sth/sb going** **to keep the fire going** das Feuer anbehalten; **this medicine/prospect kept her going** dieses Medikament/diese Aussicht hat sie durchhalten lassen; **here's £50/some work to keep you going** hier hast du erst mal £ 50/etwas Arbeit

(i) (= *turn out*) (*event, evening*) verlaufen; (*voting, election*) ausgehen; **how does the story/tune go?** wie war die Geschichte/Melodie noch mal?; **the election/decision went in his favour** (*Brit*) *or* **favor** (*US*) die Wahl/Entscheidung fiel zu seinen Gunsten aus; **we'll see how things go** (*inf*) wir werden sehen, wie es läuft (*inf*); **the way things are going I'll ...** so wie es aussieht, werde ich ...; **she has a lot going for her** sie ist gut dran; **how's it going?, how goes it?** (*inf*) wie gehts (denn so)? (*inf*); **how did it go?** wie wars?; **how's the essay going?** was macht der Aufsatz?

✦**to go well/badly** **things have gone well/badly** es ist gut/ schlecht gelaufen; **everything is going well** alles läuft gut; **everything is going well (with us)** bei uns läuft alles gut; **if everything goes well** wenn alles gut geht

(j) (= *fail, wear out*) kaputtgehen; (*health, strength, eyesight etc*) nachlassen; (*brakes, steering*) versagen; (*button*) abgehen; **the sweater has gone at the elbows** der Pullover ist an den Ärmeln durch (*inf*); **his mind is going** er lässt geistig sehr nach

(k) (= *be accepted*) **anything goes!** alles ist erlaubt; **what I say goes!** was ich sage, gilt *or* wird gemacht!; **that goes for me too** (= *that applies to me*) das gilt auch für mich; (= *I agree with that*) das meine ich auch

(l) (= *be available*) **there are several jobs going** es sind mehrere Stellen zu haben; **is there any tea going?** gibt es Tee?

(m) (= *become*) werden; **to go deaf/grey** (*Brit*) *or* **gray** (*US*) taub/grau werden; **to go hungry** hungern; **I went cold** mir wurde kalt; **to go to sleep** einschlafen; **to go Japanese/ethnic** auf japanisch/auf Folklore machen (*inf*)

(n) (= *be contained, fit*) gehen, passen; (= *belong*) hin- gehören; (*in drawer, cupboard etc*) (hin)kommen; **it won't go in the box** es geht *or* passt nicht in die Kiste; **4 into 12 goes 3** 4 geht in 12 dreimal; **4 into 3 won't go** 3 durch 4 geht nicht

(o) (= *match*) dazu passen; **to go with sth** zu etw passen

(p) (= *contribute*) **the money goes to help the poor** das Geld soll den Armen helfen; **the money will go toward(s) a new car** das ist Geld für ein neues Auto

(q) (= *make a sound or movement*) machen; **to go bang/shh/ ticktock** peng/pst/ticktack machen; **there goes the bell** es klingelt

(r) (= *take away*) (*US*) **large fries to go** eine große Portion Pommes zum Mitnehmen

(s) (*comparison*)

✦**as ... go** **as things go today that's not very expensive** für heutige Verhältnisse ist das nicht teuer; **he's not bad as** bosses **go** verglichen mit anderen Chefs ist er nicht übel

2 AUXILIARY VERB *(forming future tense)*
✦**to be going to ...** I'm/I was going to do it ich werde/wollte es tun; **I had been going to do it** ich habe es tun wollen; **it's going to rain** es wird wohl regnen; **there's going to be trouble** es wird Ärger geben

3 TRANSITIVE VERB
(a) *(route, way)* gehen; *(vehicle, person in vehicle)* fahren
✦**to go it** **to go it alone** sich selbstständig machen
(b) *(= become)* **my mind went a complete blank** ich hatte ein Brett vor dem Kopf *(inf)*
(c) *(= say) (inf)* sagen

4 NOUN, *pl* **goes**
(a) *(= energy) (inf)* Schwung *m*; **to be full of go** unternehmungslustig sein
✦**on the go** **to be on the go** auf Trab sein *(inf)*; **he's got two women/books on the go** er hat zwei Frauen/schreibt an zwei Büchern gleichzeitig
✦**it's all go** es ist immer was los *(inf)*
(b) *(= attempt)* Versuch *m*; **at the first go** auf Anhieb *(inf)*; **at the second go** beim zweiten Versuch
✦**at** *or* **in one go** auf einen Schlag *(inf)*; *(drink)* in einem Zug *(inf)*
✦**to have a go** *(Brit)* es versuchen, es probieren; **to have a go at doing sth** versuchen *or* probieren, etw zu tun; **have a go!** versuchs *or* probiers *(inf)* doch mal!
✦**to have a go at sb** *(inf)* *(= criticize)* jdn runterputzen *(inf)*; *(= fight)* es mit jdm aufnehmen
(c) *(= turn)* **it's your go** du bist dran *(inf)* *or* an der Reihe; **miss one go** *(Brit)* einmal aussetzen; **can I have a go?** darf ich mal?
(d) *(other set structures)*
✦**(it's) no go** *(inf)* da ist nichts zu machen
✦**to make a go of sth** in etw *(dat)* Erfolg haben
✦**from the word go** von Anfang an

5 PHRASAL VERBS
➤ **go about** **1** VI **(a)** *(Brit)* herumgehen, herumlaufen *(inf)*; *(by vehicle)* herumfahren; *(in old clothes etc)* herumlaufen; **to go about with sb** mit jdm zusammen sein **(b)** *(rumour, flu etc)* umgehen **2** VI +PREP OBJ **(a)** task, problem anpacken; **how does one go about getting seats/finding a job?** wie bekommt man Plätze/eine Stelle? **(b)** *(= be occupied with)* work erledigen; **to go about one's business** sich um seine eigenen Geschäfte kümmern
➤ **go across** **1** VI +PREP OBJ überqueren **2** VI hinübergehen; *(by vehicle)* hinüberfahren; *(by plane)* hinüberfliegen; *(to the enemy etc)* überlaufen *(to* zu*)*
➤ **go after** VI +PREP OBJ **(a)** *(= follow)* nachgehen *(+dat)*, nachlaufen *(+dat)*; *(in vehicle)* nachfahren *(+dat)*; **the police went after the escaped criminal** die Polizei hat den entkommenen Verbrecher gejagt **(b)** *(= try to win or obtain)* anstreben; job, girl sich bemühen um; *(Sport)* record einstellen wollen
➤ **go against** VI +PREP OBJ **(a)** *(= be unfavourable to)* *(luck)* sein gegen; *(events)* ungünstig verlaufen für; *(evidence, appearance)* sprechen gegen; **the verdict went against her** das Urteil fiel zu ihren Ungunsten aus; **the vote went against her** sie verlor die Abstimmung **(b)** *(= be contrary to)* im Widerspruch stehen zu; principles, trend gehen gegen; *(= oppose)* person sich widersetzen *(+dat)*; wishes, orders zuwiderhandeln *(+dat)*
➤ **go ahead** VI **(a)** *(= go in front)* vorangehen; *(in race)* sich an die Spitze setzen; *(= go earlier)* vorausgehen; *(in vehicle)* vorausfahren; **to go ahead of sb** vor jdm gehen; sich vor jdn setzen; jdm vorausgehen/-fahren **(b)** *(= proceed)* *(person)* es machen; *(work, project)* vorangehen; *(event)* stattfinden; **go ahead!** nur zu!; **to go ahead with sth** etw durchführen
➤ **go along** VI **(a)** *(= walk along)* entlanggehen; *(to an event)* hingehen; **to go along to sth** zu etw gehen; **as one goes along** *(= bit by bit)* nach und nach; *(= at the same time)* nebenbei; **I made the story up as I went along** ich habe mir die Geschichte beim Erzählen ausgedacht **(b)** *(= accompany)* mitgehen, mitkommen *(with* mit*)* **(c)** *(= agree)* zustimmen *(with +dat)*; *(= not object)* sich anschließen *(with +dat)*
➤ **go around** VI = **go about 1**, **go round**

➤ **go at** VI +PREP OBJ task sich machen an *(+acc)*
➤ **go away** VI (weg)gehen; *(for a holiday)* wegfahren; **"gone away"** *(on letter)* „verzogen"
➤ **go back** VI **(a)** *(= return)* zurückgehen; *(to a subject)* zurückkommen *(to auf +acc)*; *(= revert: to habits, methods etc)* zurückkehren *(to zu)*; **they have to go back to Germany/ school next week** nächste Woche müssen sie wieder nach Deutschland zurück/wieder zur Schule; **when do the schools go back?** wann fängt die Schule wieder an?; **to go back to the beginning** wieder von vorn anfangen; **there's no going back now** jetzt gibt es kein Zurück mehr
(b) *(= date back)* zurückgehen, zurückreichen *(to bis zu)*; **we go back a long way** wir kennen uns schon ewig
(c) *(clock: = be put back)* zurückgestellt werden
➤ **go back on** VI +PREP OBJ zurücknehmen; decision rückgängig machen; **I never go back on my word** was ich versprochen habe, halte ich auch
➤ **go before** **1** VI *(= happen before)* vorangehen; **everything that had gone before** alles Vorhergehende **2** VI +PREP OBJ **to go before the court** vor Gericht erscheinen
➤ **go beyond** VI +PREP OBJ hinausgehen über *(+acc)*; **he went beyond the bounds of decency** er hat den Anstand nicht gewahrt
➤ **go by** **1** VI *(person, opportunity)* vorbeigehen *(prep obj an +dat)*; *(procession)* vorbeiziehen *(prep obj an +dat)*; *(vehicle)* vorbeifahren *(prep obj an +dat)*; *(time)* vergehen; **as time went by** mit der Zeit; **in days gone by** in längst vergangenen Tagen **2** VI +PREP OBJ **(a)** *(= base judgement or decision on)* gehen nach; compass, stars, watch etc, sb's example sich richten nach; rules sich halten an *(+acc)*; **if that's anything to go by** wenn man danach gehen kann; **going by what he said** nach dem, was er sagte
(b) **to go by the name of Smith** Smith heißen
➤ **go down** VI **(a)** hinuntergehen *(prep obj +acc)*; *(by vehicle, lift)* hinunterfahren *(prep obj +acc)*; *(sun, moon, ship)* untergehen; *(plane)* abstürzen; *(= be defeated)* geschlagen werden *(to von)*; *(Theat: curtain)* fallen; *(= fall)* *(boxer etc)* zu Boden gehen; *(horse)* stürzen; **to go down on one's knees** sich hinknien; *(to apologize)* auf die Knie fallen
(b) *(= be accepted, approved)* ankommen *(with bei)*; **that won't go down well with me** das wird er nicht gut finden
(c) *(floods, temperature, supplies, swelling)* zurückgehen; *(taxes, value)* sich verringern; *(prices)* sinken; *(balloon, tyre)* Luft verlieren; **he has gone down in my estimation** er ist in meiner Achtung gesunken
(d) *(= go as far as)* gehen *(to bis)*; **I'll go down to the bottom of the page** ich werde die Seite noch fertig machen
(e) *(= be noted, remembered)* vermerkt werden; **to go down in history** in die Geschichte eingehen
(f) *(= become ill)* **to go down with a cold** eine Erkältung bekommen
(g) *(Comput)* ausfallen
(h) *(Sport)* *(= be relegated)* absteigen; *(= be defeated)* verlieren; **they went down 2-1 to Rangers** sie verloren 2:1 gegen Rangers
➤ **go for** VI +PREP OBJ **(a)** *(inf: = attack)* person losgehen auf *(+acc)* *(inf)*; *(verbally)* herziehen über *(+acc)* **(b)** *(inf)* *(= like)* gut finden; *(= choose)* nehmen **(c)** *(= aim at)* zielen auf *(+acc)*; *(fig)* aus sein auf *(+acc)* *(inf)*; *(in claim etc)* fordern; **go for it!** nichts wie ran! *(inf)*; **he was obviously going for the ball** er hatte es offensichtlich auf den Ball abgesehen
➤ **go forward** VI **(a)** *(= make progress)* vorangehen
(b) *(= proceed, go ahead)* **to go forward with sth** etw durchführen, etw in die Tat umsetzen
➤ **go in** VI **(a)** *(= enter)* hineingehen **(b)** *(sun, moon)* verschwinden **(c)** *(= fit in)* hineinpassen
➤ **go in for** VI +PREP OBJ **(a)** *(competition, race)* teilnehmen an *(+dat)* **(b)** *(= be interested in, practise)* zu haben sein für; *(as career)* sich entschieden haben für; **to go in for sports/tennis** *(= play oneself)* Sport treiben/Tennis spielen; *(= be interested in)* sich für Sport/Tennis interessieren
➤ **go into** VI +PREP OBJ **(a)** building, politics, the grocery trade gehen in *(+acc)*; the army, navy etc gehen zu; **to go into teaching/parliament/the Church** Lehrer(in)/Abgeordnete(r)/ Geistliche(r) werden
(b) *(= crash into)* car (hinein)fahren in *(+acc)*; wall fahren gegen
(c) explanation, description etc von sich *(dat)* geben; routine

verfallen in (+*acc*)

(d) *trance, coma* fallen in (+*acc*); *convulsions, fit* bekommen; **to go into hysterics** hysterisch werden

(e) (= *look into*) sich befassen mit; (= *treat, explain at length*) abhandeln; **to go into detail** auf Einzelheiten eingehen

(f) a lot of time/money/effort has gone into it da steckt viel Zeit/Geld/Mühe drin

➤ **go off 1** VI **(a)** (= *leave*) weggehen; (*by vehicle*) wegfahren (*on* mit); (*Theat*) abgehen; **he went off to the States** er fuhr in die Staaten; **to go off with sb/sth** (*illicitly*) mit jdm/etw auf und davon gehen (*inf*)

(b) (*light*) ausgehen; (*water, electricity, gas*) wegbleiben

(c) (*gun, bomb, alarm*) losgehen; (*alarm clock*) klingeln

(d) (*Brit*) (*food*) schlecht werden; (*milk*) sauer werden; (*butter*) ranzig werden

(e) (*inf:* = *go to sleep*) einschlafen

(f) (= *take place*) verlaufen; **to go off well/badly** gut/schlecht gehen **2** VI +PREP OBJ (*Brit:* = *lose liking for*) nicht mehr mögen; *hobby* das Interesse verlieren an (+*dat*); **I've gone off him/that** ich mache mir nichts mehr aus ihm/daraus

➤ **go on 1** VI **(a)** (= *fit*) passen (*prep obj* auf +*acc*)

(b) (*light, power*) angehen

(c) (= *walk on, carry on*) weitergehen; (*by vehicle*) weiterfahren; (= *move ahead of others*) vorausgehen; **to go on with sth** mit etw weitermachen; **to go on trying** es weiter(hin) versuchen; **go on with your work** arbeitet *or* macht weiter; **to go on speaking** weitersprechen; (*after a pause*) fortfahren; **go on, tell me!** na, sag schon!; **to have enough/something to be going on with** fürs Erste genug haben/schon mal etwas haben; **he went on to say that ...** dann sagte er, dass ...; **I can't go on** ich kann nicht mehr

(d) (= *talk incessantly*) unaufhörlich reden; (= *nag, harp on*) darauf herumhacken (*inf*); **don't go on (about it)** nun hör aber (damit) auf; **to go on about sb/sth** (= *talk a lot*) stundenlang von jdm/etw erzählen; (= *complain*) dauernd über jdn/etw klagen

(e) (= *happen*) passieren; (*party, argument etc*) im Gange sein; **this has been going on for a long time** das geht schon lange so; **what's going on here?** was geht hier vor?

(f) (*time:* = *pass*) vergehen; **as time goes on** im Laufe der Zeit

(g) (*pej:* = *behave*) sich aufführen

(h) (*Theat*) auftreten; (*Sport*) an der Reihe sein **2** VI +PREP OBJ **(a)** *bus, bike, roundabout etc* fahren mit; *tour* machen; *horse etc* reiten auf (+*dat*); **to go on the swings** auf die Schaukel gehen

(b) (= *be guided by*) gehen nach; *evidence* sich stützen auf (+*acc*); **we've got nothing to go on** wir haben keine Anhaltspunkte

(c) **to go on the dole** (*Brit*) stempeln gehen (*inf*); **to go on a diet** eine Schlankheitskur machen; **to go on the pill** die Pille nehmen; **to go on television** im Fernsehen auftreten

(d) (= *approach*) fifty etc zugehen auf (+*acc*)

➤ **go on for** VI +PREP OBJ *fifty, one o'clock* zugehen auf (+*acc*); **there were going on for twenty people there** es waren fast zwanzig Leute da

➤ **go out** VI **(a)** (= *leave*) hinausgehen; **to go out of a room** aus einem Zimmer gehen

(b) (*shopping etc*) weggehen; (*socially, to theatre etc,* = *be extinguished: fire*) ausgehen; (*with girl-/boyfriend*) gehen; **to go out for a meal** essen gehen; **to go out to work** arbeiten gehen; **to go out on strike** in den Streik treten

(c) (= *become outmoded*) unmodern werden

(d) (*tide*) zurückgehen

(e) **my heart went out to him** ich fühlte mit ihm mit; **all our sympathy goes out to you** wir teilen Ihr Leid; **the fun had gone out of it** es machte keinen Spaß mehr

(f) (*Sport:* = *be defeated*) ausscheiden

(g) (= *strive*) **to go all out** sich ins Zeug legen (*for* für)

(h) (*pamphlet, circular*) (hinaus)gehen; (*Rad, TV: programme*) ausgestrahlt werden; (*message*) verbreitet werden

➤ **go over 1** VI **(a)** (= *cross*) hinübergehen; (*by vehicle*) hinüberfahren **(b)** (= *change allegiance, habit, diet etc*) übergehen (*to* zu); (*to another party*) überwechseln (*to* zu)

(c) (*TV, Rad:* *to another studio etc*) umschalten **(d)** (= *be received: play, remarks etc*) ankommen **2** VI +PREP OBJ durchgehen; (= *examine*) *house* durchsuchen; (= *see over*) *house etc* sich (*dat*) ansehen; **to go over sth in one's mind** etw überdenken

➤ **go past** VI vorbeigehen (*prep obj* an +*dat*); (*vehicle*) vorbeifahren (*prep obj* an +*dat*); (*procession*) vorbeiziehen (*prep obj* an +*dat*); (*time*) vergehen

➤ **go round** VI **(a)** (*esp Brit*) (= *turn, spin*) sich drehen **(b)** (= *make a detour*) außen herumgehen; (*by vehicle*) außen herumfahren; **to go round sth** um etw herumgehen/-fahren; **to go round the long way** ganz außen herumgehen/-fahren **(c)** (= *visit*) vorbeigehen (*to* bei)

(d) (= *tour: round museum etc*) herumgehen (*prep obj* in +*dat*)

(e) (= *be sufficient*) (aus)reichen; **there's enough food to go round (all these people)** es ist (für all diese Leute) genügend zu essen da

(f) +PREP OBJ (= *encircle, reach round*) herumgehen um

(g) = **go about 1**

➤ **go through 1** VI (*lit, fig*) durchgehen; (*business deal*) abgeschlossen werden; (*divorce, law, bill*) durchkommen; (*Sport*) sich qualifizieren (*to* für) **2** VI +PREP OBJ **(a)** *hole, door, customs etc* gehen durch **(b)** *torture, initiation, formalities* durchmachen **(c)** *list, play, mail, lesson* durchgehen **(d)** *pocket, suitcase* durchsuchen **(e)** (= *use up*) aufbrauchen; *money* ausgeben; *food* aufessen

➤ **go through with** VI +PREP OBJ *plan* durchziehen (*inf*); *crime* ausführen; **she couldn't go through with it** sie brachte es nicht fertig

➤ **go together** VI (= *harmonize*) zusammenpassen; (*events, conditions*) zusammen auftreten

➤ **go under 1** VI (*ship, person*) untergehen; (= *fail*) (*businessman*) scheitern (*because of* an +*dat*); (*company*) eingehen (*inf*) **2** VI +PREP OBJ **(a)** (= *pass under*) durchgehen unter (+*dat*); **to go under the name of Jones** als Jones bekannt sein

➤ **go up** VI **(a)** (*price, temperature etc*) steigen; **to go up (and up) in price** (immer) teurer werden **(b)** (= *climb*) hinaufsteigen (*prep obj* +*acc*); **to go up to bed** nach oben gehen **(c)** (*lift,* = *travel north*) hochfahren; (*balloon*) aufsteigen; (*Theat: curtain*) hochgehen; (= *be built*) gebaut werden **(d)** (= *explode*) hochgehen (*inf*); **to go up in flames** in Flammen aufgehen **(e)** (*cheer, shout*) ertönen

➤ **go with** VI +PREP OBJ **(a)** *sb* gehen mit **(b)** (= *go hand in hand with*) Hand in Hand gehen mit **(c)** (= *be included or sold with*) gehören zu **(d)** (= *harmonize with*) passen zu

➤ **go without 1** VI +PREP OBJ nicht haben; **to go without food** nichts essen; **to go without breakfast** nicht frühstücken; **to have to go without sth** auf etw (*acc*) verzichten müssen **2** VI darauf verzichten

goad [gəʊd] **1** N (*fig:* = *spur*) Ansporn *m*; (= *taunt*) aufstachelnde Bemerkung **2** VT aufreizen; **to ~ sb into sth** jdn zu etw anstacheln *or* treiben

go-ahead ['gəʊəhed] **1** ADJ fortschrittlich **2** N **to give sb/sth the ~** jdm/für etw grünes Licht geben

goal [gəʊl] N **(a)** (*Sport*) Tor *nt*; **to score/kick a ~** ein Tor erzielen/schießen **(b)** (= *aim*) Ziel *nt*; **to set (oneself) a ~** (sich *dat*) ein Ziel setzen

goal definition N Zielfestsetzung *f*, Zielbestimmung *f*

goalie ['gəʊlɪ] N (*inf*) Tormann *m*/-frau *f*

goal: **goalkeeper** N Torwart *m*, Torhüter(in) *m(f)*; **goal kick** N Abstoß *m* (vom Tor); **goal line** N Torlinie *f*; **goalmouth** N unmittelbarer Torbereich; **goalpost** N Torpfosten *m*; **to move the ~s** (*fig inf*) die Spielregeln (ver)ändern

goat [gəʊt] N Ziege *f*; **to act the ~** (*inf*) herumalbern; **to get sb's ~** (*inf*) jdn auf die Palme bringen (*inf*)

goat cheese N Ziegenkäse *m*

goatee (beard) [gəʊˈtiː(ˌbɪəd)] N Spitzbart *m*

goat's cheese N Ziegenkäse *m*

gob¹ [gɒb] VI (*Brit inf*) spucken; **to ~ at sb** jdn anspucken

gob² N (*Brit inf:* = *mouth*) Schnauze *f* (*inf*); **shut your ~!** halt die Schnauze! (*inf*)

gobble ['gɒbl] **1** VT verschlingen **2** VI (= *eat noisily*) schmatzen

➤ **gobble down** VT SEP hinunterschlingen

➤ **gobble up** VT SEP (*lit, fig*) verschlingen; (*company*) schlucken

gobbledegook, gobbledygook ['gɒbldɪˌguːk] N (*inf*) Kauderwelsch *nt*

go-between ['gəʊbɪˌtwiːn] N, *pl* **-s** Vermittler(in) *m(f)*

goblet ['gɒblɪt] N Pokal *m*; (*esp of glass*) Kelchglas *nt*

gobsmacked ['gɒbsmækt] ADJ (*inf*) platt (*inf*)

go-cart ['gəʊkɑːt] N (= *child's cart*) Seifenkiste *f*; (*Sport*) Gokart *m*; (*US*) (= *walker*) Laufstuhl *m*; (= *pushchair*) Sportwagen *m*

god [gɒd] N Gott *m*; **God willing** so Gott will; **God (only) knows** (*inf*) wer weiß; **for God's sake!** (*inf*) um Gottes *or* Himmels willen (*inf*); **what/why in God's name ...?** um Himmels willen, was/warum ...?; **money is his ~** das Geld ist sein Gott *or* Götze

god: god-awful ADJ (*inf*) beschissen (*inf*); **godchild** N Patenkind *nt*; **goddamn, goddam** (*esp US inf*) ☒ ADJ (*emph*) gottverdammt (*inf*); **it's no ~ use!** es hat überhaupt keinen Zweck, verdammt noch mal! (*inf*) ☒ ADV (*emph*) verdammt (*inf*); **goddamned** ADJ, ADV = **goddamn**; **goddaughter** N Patentochter *f*

goddess ['gɒdɪs] N Göttin *f*

god: godfather N (*lit, fig*) Pate *m*; **my ~** mein Patenonkel *m*; **godforsaken** ADJ (*inf*) gottverlassen; **godless** ADJ gottlos; **godlike** ADJ göttergleich; *characteristics* gottähnlich

godly ['gɒdlɪ] ADJ (+ER) gottesfürchtig

god: godmother N Patin *f*; **my ~** meine Patentante *f*; **godparent** N Pate *m*, Patin *f*; **godsend** N Geschenk *nt* des Himmels; **godson** N Patensohn *m*

-goer N SUF -gänger(in) *m(f)*; **cinemagoer** Kinogänger(in) *m(f)*

goes [gəʊz] 3RD PERS SING PRESENT *of* go

go-getter ['gəʊgetəʳ] N (*inf*) Ellbogentyp *m* (*pej inf*)

goggle ['gɒgl] VI starren; **to ~ at sb/sth** jdn/etw anstarren

goggle-eyed ADJ **he stared at him/it ~** er starrte ihn/es an

goggles ['gɒglz] PL Schutzbrille *f*

go-go dancer N Go-go-Tänzerin *f*

going ['gəʊɪŋ] ☒ PRP *of* go

☒ N (a) (= *departure*) Weggang *m*

(b) **it's slow ~** es geht nur langsam voran; **that's good ~** das ist ein flottes Tempo; **the ~ is good/soft/hard** (*Horse-racing*) die Bahn ist gut/weich/hart; **it's heavy ~ talking to him** es ist sehr mühsam, sich mit ihm zu unterhalten; **to get out while the ~ is good** sich rechtzeitig absetzen

☒ ADJ (a) *rate, price* üblich

(b) (*after superl*: = *best*) **the best thing ~** das Beste überhaupt (c) **a ~ concern** (*Comm*) ein gut gehendes Unternehmen; **to sell a business as a ~ concern** ein bestehendes Unternehmen verkaufen

going-over [gəʊɪŋ'əʊvəʳ] N (a) Untersuchung *f*; **to give sth a good ~** *contract* etw gründlich prüfen; *house* etw gründlich durchsuchen (b) (*inf*: = *beating-up*) Abreibung *f* (*inf*); **to give sb a good ~** jdm eine tüchtige Abreibung verpassen (*inf*)

goings-on [gəʊɪŋz'ɒn] PL (*inf*) Dinge *pl*

go-kart ['gəʊkɑːt] N Gokart *m*

gold [gəʊld] ☒ N (a) Gold *nt* (b) (*Sport inf*: = ~ **medal**) Goldmedaille *f* ☒ ADJ golden; ~ **jewellery** (*Brit*) *or* **jewelry** (*US*) Goldschmuck *m*; ~ **coin** Goldmünze *f*; = **bullion** *or* **bars** Goldbarren *pl*; ~ **tooth** Goldzahn *m*; ~ **braid** Goldtressen *pl*

gold: gold-coloured, (*US*) **gold-colored** ADJ goldfarben; **gold disc** N goldene Schallplatte; **gold dust** N Goldstaub *m*; **to be (like) ~** (*fig*) sehr schwer zu finden sein

golden ['gəʊldən] ADJ (*lit, fig*) golden; *hair* goldblond; *suntan* goldbraun; *sand* goldgelb; **fry until ~** anbräunen; **a ~ opportunity/chance** eine einmalige Gelegenheit/Chance

golden: golden age N (*fig*) Blütezeit *f*; **golden eagle** N Steinadler *m*; **golden goal** N (*Ftbl*) Golden Goal *nt*; **golden handshake** N (*Brit inf*) goldener Handschlag; **golden jubilee** N goldenes Jubiläum; **golden mean** N **the ~** (= *form*) der goldene Mittelweg; **golden oldie** N (*inf*) (Golden) Oldie *m* (*inf*); **golden parachute** N (*US inf*) goldener Handschlag, hohe Abfindung; **golden rule** N **my ~ is never to ...** ich mache es mir zu Regel, niemals zu ...; **golden share** N (*St Ex*) Sperraktie *f*, Aktie *f* mit Vetorecht (*der Regierung*); **golden syrup** N (*Brit*) (gelber) Sirup; **golden wedding (anniversary)** N goldene Hochzeit

gold: goldfish N Goldfisch *m*; **goldfish bowl** N Goldfischglas *nt*; **gold leaf** N Blattgold *nt*; **gold medal** N Goldmedaille *f*; **gold mine** N Goldgrube *f* (*also fig*); **gold-plate** VT vergolden; **gold record** N goldene Schallplatte; **gold reserves** PL Goldreserven *pl*; **gold rush** N Goldrausch *m*; **goldsmith** N Goldschmied(in) *m(f)*; **gold standard** N Goldstandard *m*

golf [gɒlf] N Golf *nt*

golf: golf bag N Golftasche *f*; **golf ball** N Golfball *m*; **golf club** N (= *instrument*) Golfschläger *m*; (= *association*) Golfklub *m*; **golf course** N Golfplatz *m*

golfer ['gɒlfəʳ] N Golfer(in) *m(f)*

golliwog ['gɒlɪwɒg] N Negerpuppe *f*

gondola ['gɒndələ] N (a) Gondel *f* (b) (*US Rail*: *also* ~ **car**) offener Güterwagen

gone [gɒn] ☒ PTP *of* go ☒ ADJ PRED (a) (*inf*: = *enthusiastic*) **to be ~ on sb/sth** von jdm/etw (ganz) weg sein (*inf*) (b) (*inf*: = *pregnant*) **she was 6 months ~** sie war im 7. Monat ☒ PREP **it's just ~ three** es ist gerade drei Uhr vorbei

goner ['gɒnəʳ] N (*inf*) **to be a ~** (*patient*) es nicht mehr lange machen; (*socially, professionally*) weg vom Fenster sein (*inf*)

gonna ['gɒnə] (*incorrect*) = **going to**; **I'm not ~ tell you** das sage ich dir nicht

goo [guː] N (*inf*) Schmiere *f* (*inf*)

---

good [gʊd]

☒ ADJECTIVE	☒ NOUN
☒ ADVERB	

☒ **ADJECTIVE**, *comp* **better**, *superl* **best**

(a) gut; *moment, opportunity also* günstig; (= *kind also*) lieb; *legs, body* schön; **good weather** gutes Wetter; **that's a good one!** (*joke*) das ist ein guter Witz; (*usu iro*: *excuse*) wers glaubt, wird selig! (*inf*); **you've done a good day's work** du hast gute Arbeit (für einen Tag) geleistet; **all I need is a good meal** ich brauche nur eine ordentliche *or* anständige Mahlzeit; **to be good with people** gut mit Menschen umgehen können; **you've never had it so good!** ihr habt es noch nie so gut gehabt; **it's too good to be true** es ist zu schön, um wahr zu sein; **to be good for sb** gut für jdn sein; (= *be healthy*) gesund für jdn sein; **to drink more than is good for one** mehr trinken, als einem gut tut; **it's a good thing** *or* **job I was there** (nur) gut, dass ich dort war; **good nature** Gutmütigkeit *f*; **to be good to sb** gut zu jdm sein; **that's very good of you** das ist sehr lieb *or* nett von Ihnen; **(it was) good of you to come** nett, dass Sie gekommen sind; **would you be good enough to tell me ...** wären Sie so nett, mir zu sagen ... (*also iro*); **good man!** gut gemacht!; **good old Charles!** der gute alte Charles!

✦**to be good at sth** gut in etw (*dat*) sein; **to be good at sport/languages** gut im Sport/in Sprachen sein; **to be good at sewing/typing** gut nähen/tippen können; **I'm not very good at it** ich kann es nicht besonders gut

✦**good enough that's (not) good enough** das reicht (nicht); **if he gives his word, that's good enough for me** wenn er sein Wort gibt, reicht mir das; **it's just not good enough!** so geht das nicht!

✦**to feel good** sich wohl fühlen; **I don't feel too good about it** mir ist nicht ganz wohl dabei

✦**to look good you look good in that** das steht dir gut

✦**to make good** *mistake, damage* wieder gutmachen; *threat* wahr machen; *promise* erfüllen; **to make good one's losses** seine Verluste wettmachen; **to make good sb's losses** jdm seine Verluste ersetzen

✦**as good as** so gut wie; **as good as new** so gut wie neu; **he was as good as his word** er hat sein Wort gehalten; **he as good as called me a liar/invited me** to come er nannte mich praktisch einen Lügner/hat mich praktisch eingeladen (b) (= *enjoyable*) *holiday, evening* schön; **did you have a good day?** wie wars heute?

✦**a good time to have a good time** sich gut amüsieren; **have a good time!** viel Spaß *or* Vergnügen!

(c) (= *well-behaved*) artig, brav (*inf*); **(as) good as gold** mustergültig; **be a good girl/boy and ...** sei so lieb und ...; **good girl/boy!** (= *well done*) gut!; **that's a good dog!** guter Hund!

(d) (= *valid*) *advice, excuse, reason* gut; *ticket* gültig; **is his credit good?** ist er kreditfähig?

✦**good for he's good for £10,000** (= *will give us*) bei ihm kannst du mit £ 10.000 rechnen; (= *has got*) er hat gut und gern £ 10.000; **the car is good for another few years** das Auto hält noch ein paar Jahre; **she's good for nothing** sie ist ein Nichtsnutz *or* Taugenichts; **that's always good for a laugh** darüber kann man immer lachen

(e) (= *uninjured*) *eye, leg* gesund
(f) (= *thorough*) gut, gründlich; **to have a good cry** sich ausweinen; **to have a good laugh** ordentlich *or* so richtig lachen (*inf*); **to take a good look at sth** sich (*dat*) etw gut ansehen
(g) (= *considerable*) *hour, while* gut; *amount, distance, way* gut; **it's a good 8 km** es sind gute 8 km; **a good many/few people** ziemlich viele/nicht gerade wenig Leute
(h) (*in greetings*) gut; **good morning** guten Morgen
(i) (*in exclamations*) gut, prima; **(it's) good to see you/to be here** (es ist) schön, dich zu sehen/hier zu sein; **good grief** *or* **gracious!** ach du liebe *or* meine Güte! (*inf*); **very good, sir** sehr wohl (*old*); **good for you/him** *etc*! gut!, prima!
(j) (*emphatic use*) schön; **a good strong stick** ein schön(er) starker Stock

✦**good and ...** ganz; **good and hard/strong** (*inf*) ganz schön fest/stark (*inf*); **good and proper** (*inf*) ganz anständig (*inf*)

2 ADVERB gut; **how are you? – good!** wie gehts? – gut!

3 NOUN
(a) (= *what is morally right*) Gute(s) *nt*; **good and evil** Gut und Böse; **to do good** Gutes tun; **to be up to no good** (*inf*) nichts Gutes im Schilde führen (*inf*)
(b) (= *advantage, benefit*) Wohl *nt*; **for the good of the nation** zum Wohl(e) der Nation; **I did it for your own good** ich habe es nur gut mit dir gemeint; **for the good of one's health** *etc* seiner Gesundheit *etc* zuliebe; **he'll come to no good** mit ihm wird es noch ein böses Ende nehmen; **what's the good of hurrying?** wozu eigentlich die Eile?; **if that is any good to you** wenn es dir hilft

✦**to do good** to do (some) good (etwas) helfen *or* nützen; **to do sb good** jdm helfen; (*rest, drink, medicine etc*) jdm gut tun; **what good will that do you?** was hast du davon?; **a (fat) lot of good that will do you!** (*iro inf*) und wie dir das gut tun wird! (*iro inf*)

✦**no/not any good** that's no good das ist nichts; **he's no good to us** er nützt uns (*dat*) nichts; **it's no good doing it like that** es hat keinen Sinn, das so zu machen; **he's no good at it** er kann es nicht; **he wasn't any good for the job** er eignete sich nicht für die Arbeit
(c) (*set structures*)

✦**for good** for good (and all) für immer (und ewig)

✦**to the good** we were 5 points/£5 **to the good** wir hatten 5 Punkte zu viel/£ 5 plus; **that's all to the good** auch gut!

goodbye [gʊdˈbaɪ] **1** N Abschied *m*, Lebewohl *nt* (*geh*); **to say ~**, **to say** *or* **make one's ~** sich verabschieden; **to wish sb ~**, **to say ~ to sb** sich von jdm verabschieden; **to say ~ to sth** einer Sache (*dat*) Lebewohl sagen **2** INTERJ auf Wiedersehen **3** ADJ ATTR Abschieds-

good: good-for-nothing 1 N Nichtsnutz *m*, Taugenichts *m* **2** ADJ nichtsnutzig; **his ~ brother** sein Nichtsnutz von Bruder; **Good Friday** N Karfreitag *m*; **good-humoured**, (*US*) **good-humored** ADJ *person* (*by nature*) gutmütig (*also rivalry*); (*on a certain occasion*) gut gelaunt; *atmosphere* freundlich; *event, demonstration* friedlich; **good-looking** ADJ gut aussehend; **good-natured** ADJ *person* (*by nature*) gutmütig; (*on a certain occasion*) gut gelaunt; *demonstration* friedlich; *atmosphere* freundlich; *fun* harmlos

goodness [ˈgʊdnɪs] N Güte *f*; **out of the ~ of his/her heart** aus reiner Herzensgüte; **~ knows** weiß der Himmel (*inf*); **for ~' sake** um Himmels willen (*inf*); **(my) ~!** meine Güte! (*inf*)

goodnight [gʊdˈnaɪt] ADJ ATTR **~ kiss** Gutenachtkuss *m*

goods [gʊdz] PL Güter *pl* (*also Comm*); (= *merchandise also*) Waren *pl*; (= *possessions also*) Habe *f* (*geh, liter*); **leather/manufactured ~** Leder-/Fertigwaren *pl*; **stolen ~** Diebesgut *nt*; **~ depot/train/yard** Güterdepot *nt*/-zug *m*/-bahnhof *m*; **~ receiving department** Warenannahme(abteilung) *f*; **~ wagon** (*Brit*) Güterwagen *m*; **it's the ~** (*esp US inf*) das ist große Klasse (*inf*); **if we don't come up with the ~ on time** (*inf*) wenn wir es nicht rechtzeitig schaffen

good: good-sized ADJ ziemlich groß; **goodwill** N Wohlwollen *nt*; (*between nations*) Goodwill *m*; (*Comm*) Firmenwert *m*, Geschäftswert *m*; **a gesture of ~** ein Zeichen seines/ihres *etc* guten Willens; **~ ambassador** (*for UNICEF etc*) Botschafter(in) *m(f)* des guten Willens; **~ mission/tour** Goodwillreise *f*/-tour *f*

goody [ˈgʊdɪ] (*inf*) N **(a)** (= *person*) Gute(r) *m* **(b)** (= *delicacy*) Leckerbissen *m*; (= *sweet*) Süßigkeit *f*

goody: goody bag N (*inf*) Tüte *f* mit Leckereien; (*Comm*) (*with gifts*) Tüte *f* mit Geschenken; (*with free samples*) Tüte *f* mit Probepackungen; **goody-goody** (*inf*) N Musterkind *nt* (*inf*)

gooey [ˈguːɪ] ADJ (+ER) (*inf*) (= *sticky*) klebrig; (= *slushy*) breiig

goof [guːf] (*inf*) **1** N **(a)** (*esp US*: = *idiot*) Dussel *m* (*inf*) **(b)** (= *mistake*) Schnitzer *m* (*inf*) **2** VI **(a)** (= *blunder*) danebenhauen (*inf*) **(b)** (*US*: = *loiter*: *also* **~ around**) (herum)trödeln (*inf*); **to ~ off** abzwitschern (*inf*)

goofball [ˈguːbɔːl] N (*esp US inf*) Doofkopp *m* (*sl*)

goofy [ˈguːfɪ] ADJ (+ER) (*inf*) doof (*inf*)

goon [guːn] N (*inf*) Idiot *m*

goose [guːs] N, *pl* **geese** (*lit, inf*) Gans *f*

gooseberry [ˈgʊzbərɪ] N Stachelbeere *f*; **~ bush** Stachelbeerstrauch *m*

goose: goose bumps PL, **goose flesh** N Gänsehaut *f*; **goose pimples** PL (*Brit*) Gänsehaut *f*; **goose-step** VI im Stechschritt marschieren

gopher [ˈgəʊfəʳ] N Taschenratte *f*

gore¹ [gɔːʳ] N (*liter*) Blut *nt*

gore² VT durchbohren; **~d to death by a bull** durch die Hörner eines Stiers tödlich verletzt

gorge [gɔːdʒ] **1** N (*Geog*) Schlucht *f* **2** VR schlemmen; **to ~ (oneself) on sth** (*also fig*) etw verschlingen

gorgeous [ˈgɔːdʒəs] ADJ **(a)** (= *lovely*) herrlich, fantastisch **(b)** (*inf*: = *beautiful*) hinreißend; *present* toll (*inf*) **(c)** (= *sumptuous, magnificent*) prächtig

gorilla [gəˈrɪlə] N Gorilla *m*

gormless [ˈgɔːmlɪs] ADJ (*Brit inf*) doof (*inf*)

gory [ˈgɔːrɪ] ADJ blutrünstig; *murder, detail* blutig

gosh [gɒʃ] INTERJ Mensch (*inf*), Mann (*inf*)

go-slow [ˈgəʊsləʊ] N (*Brit*) Bummelstreik *m*

gospel [ˈgɒspəl] N **(a)** (*Bibl*) Evangelium *nt*; **the Gospels** die Evangelien *pl* **(b)** (*fig*) Prinzipien *pl*; (*of ideology, religion*) Lehre *f*; **to take sth for** *or* **as ~** etw für bare Münze nehmen (*inf*) **(c)** (*Mus*) Gospel *m*

gospel truth N (*inf*) reine Wahrheit

gossip [ˈgɒsɪp] **1** N **(a)** Klatsch *m*; (= *chat*) Schwatz *m*; **to have a ~ with sb** mit jdm schwatzen **(b)** (= *person*) Klatschbase *f* **2** VI schwatzen; (*maliciously*) klatschen

gossip column N Klatschkolumne *or* -spalte *f*

gossipy [ˈgɒsɪpɪ] ADJ *person* geschwätzig; *book, letter* im Plauderton geschrieben

got [gɒt] PRET, PTP of **get**

Gothic [ˈgɒθɪk] **1** ADJ **(a)** gotisch **(b)** (*Liter*: = *horror*) schaurig; **~ (horror) novel** Schauerroman *m* **2** N **(a)** (*Archit*) Gotik *f* **(b)** (*Typ*) Gotisch *nt*; (*US*) Grotesk *f*

gotten [ˈgɒtn] (*esp US*) PTP of **get**

gouge [gaʊdʒ] **1** N (= *tool*) Hohlmeißel *m* **2** VT bohren; **the river ~d a channel in the mountainside** der Fluss grub sich (*dat*) sein Bett in den Berg

➤ **gouge out** VT SEP herausbohren; **to gouge sb's eyes out** jdm die Augen ausstechen

gourd [gʊəd] N Flaschenkürbis *m*; (*dried*) Kürbisflasche *f*

gourmet [ˈgʊəmeɪ] N Feinschmecker(in) *m(f)*

gout [gaʊt] N (*Med*) Gicht *f*

Gov ABBR of **governor**

govern [ˈgʌvən] **1** VT **(a)** *country* regieren; *province, colony, school etc* verwalten **(b)** (*rules, laws etc*) bestimmen; (*legislation*) regeln; *choice, decision, development, actions* beeinflussen; *life* beherrschen **2** VI (*Pol*) regieren

governess [ˈgʌvənɪs] N Gouvernante *f*

governing body N (*of sport, professional association*) leitendes Gremium; (*of school*) ≈ Schulbeirat *m*; (*of university*) Senat *m*

government [ˈgʌvənmənt] **1** N **(a)** Regierung *f* **(b)** (= *system*) Regierungsform *f* **2** ATTR Regierungs-, Staats-; **~ official** Regierungsbeamter *m*/-beamtin *f*; **~ action** Maßnahmen *pl* der Regierung; (= *intervention*) staatlicher Eingriff; **~ backing** staatliche Unterstützung; **~ intervention** staatlicher Eingriff

governmental [ˌgʌvənˈmentl] ADJ Regierungs-

government: government bond N Staatsanleihe *f*; **government broker** N *Broker, der im Regierungsauftrag kauft* *und verkauft*; **government department** N Ministerium *nt*; **government-funded** ADJ mit staatlichen Mitteln finanziert; **government spending** N öffentliche Ausgaben *pl*

governor [ˈgʌvənəʳ] N **(a)** *(of colony, state etc)* Gouverneur(in) *m(f)* **(b)** *(esp Brit) (of bank, prison)* Direktor(in) *m(f)*; *(of school)* ≈ Mitglied *nt* des Schulbeirats; **the (board of) ~s** der Vorstand; *(of school)* ≈ der Schulbeirat **(c)** *(Brit inf: = boss)* Chef *m* *(inf)*

governor general N Generalgouverneur(in) *m(f)*

govt ABBR *of* **government** Reg.

gown [gaʊn] N Kleid *nt*; (= *evening ~, academic ~*) Robe *f*; *(in hospital)* Kittel *m*; *(of clergyman, judge)* Talar *m*; **wedding ~** Hochzeitskleid *nt*

GP *(Brit)* ABBR *of* **general practitioner** praktischer Arzt, praktische Ärztin; **to go to one's GP** zu seinem Hausarzt/ seiner Hausärztin gehen

grab [græb] **1** N **(a) to make a ~ at** *or* **for sth** nach etw greifen *or* schnappen *(inf)* **(b)** *(inf)* **to be up for ~s** zu haben sein *(inf)*; **~ bag** *(US)* Glücksbeutel *m* **2** VT **(a)** packen; (= *take, obtain*) wegschnappen *(inf)*; *money* raffen; *(inf: = catch) person* schnappen *(inf)*; *chance* beim Schopf ergreifen *(inf)*; *attention* auf sich *(acc)* ziehen; **he ~bed (hold of) my sleeve** er packte mich am Ärmel; **I'll just ~ a sandwich** *(inf)* ich esse nur schnell ein Sandwich **(b)** *(inf: = appeal to)* anmachen *(inf)*; **how does that ~ you?** wie findest du das? **3** VI **to ~ at** greifen nach; **he ~bed at the chance of promotion** er ließ sich die Chance, befördert zu werden, nicht entgehen

grace [greɪs] **1** N **(a)** NO PL Anmut *f*; **to do sth with (a) good/ bad ~** etw anstandslos/widerwillig *or* unwillig tun; **he had/ didn't even have the (good) ~ to apologize** er war so anständig/brachte es nicht einmal fertig, sich zu entschuldigen **(b)** (= *respite*) Zahlungsfrist *f*; **a day's ~** ein Tag *m* Aufschub; **to give sb a few days' ~** jdm ein paar Tage Zeit lassen; **days of ~** *(Brit Comm)*, **~ period** *(US)* *(Comm)* Zahlungsfrist *f*; *(Insur)* Nachfrist *f*; *(for bill of exchange)* Respekttage *pl* **(c)** (= *prayer*) **to say ~** das Tischgebet sprechen **(d)** (= *mercy*) Gnade *f*; **by the ~ of God** durch die Gnade Gottes; **to fall from ~** in Ungnade fallen **2** VT **(a)** (= *adorn*) zieren *(geh)* **(b)** (= *honour*) beehren *(with* mit); *event etc* sich *(dat)* die Ehre geben bei *(+dat)*

graceful [ˈgreɪsfʊl] ADJ anmutig; *bow, manner, way of doing sth* elegant

gracefully [ˈgreɪsfəlɪ] ADV **(a)** anmutig **(b)** *retire, accept, withdraw* anstandslos; **to grow old ~** in Würde alt werden

gracious [ˈgreɪʃəs] **1** ADJ *(form)* (= *courteous, kind*) liebenswürdig; *(condescendingly)* gnädig **2** INTERJ *(dated)* **good** *or* **goodness ~ (me)!** *(expressing surprise or interest)* ach du meine Güte!; *(expressing annoyance)* um Gottes willen!

gradation [grəˈdeɪʃən] N Abstufung *f*; (= *mark on thermometer etc*) Gradeinteilung *f*

grade [greɪd] **1** N **(a)** (= *level, standard*) Niveau *nt*; *(of goods)* (Güte)klasse *f*; **to make the ~** *(fig inf)* es schaffen *(inf)* **(b)** (= *job ~*) Position *f*; *(Mil)* (Dienst)grad *m* *(auch von Beamten)*; (= *salary ~*) Gehaltsgruppe *f*, Gehaltsstufe *f*; **to go up a ~** *(in salary)* in die nächste Gehaltsgruppe *or* Gehaltsstufe vorrücken **(c)** *(Sch)* (= *mark*) Note *f*; *(esp US: = class)* Klasse *f*; **to get good/poor ~s** gute/schlechte Noten bekommen **(d)** *(esp US)* = **gradient 2** VT **(a)** *goods, animals* klassifizieren; *students etc* einstufen **(b)** *(US Sch: = mark)* benoten

grade crossing N *(US)* Bahnübergang *m*

-grader [-ˈgreɪdəʳ] N SUF *(US Sch)* -klässler(in) *m(f)*; **sixth-grader** Sechstklässler(in) *m(f)*

grade school N *(US)* ≈ Grundschule *f*

gradient [ˈgreɪdɪənt] N *(esp Brit)* Neigung *f*; *(upward also)* Steigung *f*; *(downward also)* Gefälle *nt*; **a ~ of 1 in 10** eine Steigung/ein Gefälle von 10%

gradual [ˈgrædjʊəl] ADJ allmählich; *decline, recovery, progress* langsam; *slope* sanft

gradually [ˈgrædjʊəlɪ] ADV allmählich; *slope* sanft

graduate [ˈgrædjʊɪt] **1** N *(Brit Univ)* (Hochschul)absolvent(in) *m(f)*; (= *person with degree*) Akademiker(in) *m(f)*; *(US Sch)* Schulabgänger(in) *m(f)*; **high-school ~** *(US)* ≈ Abiturient(in) *m(f)* **2** [ˈgrædjʊeɪt] VT *(US: Sch, Univ)* als Absolventen haben **3** [ˈgrædjʊeɪt] VI *(Univ)* graduieren; *(US Sch)* die Abschlussprüfung bestehen *(from an +dat)*; **to ~ in English** einen Hochschulabschluss in Englisch machen; **she ~d to television from radio** sie arbeitete sich vom Radio zum Fernsehen hoch

graduate [ˈgrædjʊɪt-] IN CPDS *(Brit)* für Akademiker; *unemployment* unter den Akademikern

graduated [ˈgrædjʊeɪtɪd] ADJ **(a)** (= *rising*) stufenweise zunehmend; *(Fin)* gestaffelt **(b)** (= *calibrated*) mit Maßeinteilung, graduiert *(form)*; **~ tube/measure/flask** Messglas *nt*

graduate [ˈgrædjʊɪt]: **graduate school** N *(US)* *Hochschulabteilung für Studenten mit abgeschlossenem Studium*; **graduate student** N *(US)* Student(in) mit abgeschlossenem Studium, Jungakademiker(in) *m(f)*

graduation [ˌgrædjʊˈeɪʃən] N *(Univ, US Sch)* (Ab)schlussfeier *f* *(mit feierlicher Überreichung der Zeugnisse)*

graffiti [grəˈfiːtɪ] PL Graffiti *pl*

graffiti artist N Graffitikünstler(in) *m(f)*

graft [grɑːft] **1** N **(a)** *(Med)* Transplantat *nt* **(b)** *(esp US inf: = corruption)* Mauschelei *f* *(inf)* **(c)** *(Brit inf: = hard work)* Schufterei *f* *(inf)* **2** VT *(Med)* übertragen *(on* auf *+acc)*; *(fig: = incorporate)* einbauen *(onto* in *+acc)* **3** VI *(inf: = work hard)* schuften *(at an +dat)* *(inf)*

grail [greɪl] N Gral *m*

grain [greɪn] N **(a)** NO PL Getreide *nt* **(b)** *(of corn, sand etc)* Korn *nt*; *(fig: of truth)* Körnchen *nt* **(c)** *(of wood, marble)* Maserung *f*; **it goes against the** *(Brit)* *or* **my** *(US)* **~** *(fig)* es geht einem gegen den Strich

grainy [ˈgreɪnɪ] ADJ (+ER) **(a)** *texture* körnig; *surface* gekörnt **(b)** *leather* genarbt; *wood* gemasert **(c)** *photograph, video* unscharf

gram, gramme [græm] N Gramm *nt*

grammar [ˈgræməʳ] N Grammatik *f*; **his ~ is excellent** seine Grammatik ist fehlerfrei; **that is bad ~** das ist grammatik(al)isch falsch

grammar school N *(Brit)* ≈ Gymnasium *nt*; *(US)* ≈ Mittelschule *f* *(Stufe zwischen Grundschule und Höherer Schule)*

grammatical [grəˈmætɪkəl] ADJ **(a)** grammatisch; **~ error/rule** Grammatikfehler *m*/-regel *f* **(b)** (= *correct*) grammatik(al)isch richtig; **his English is not ~** sein Englisch ist grammatikalisch falsch

grammatically [grəˈmætɪkəlɪ] ADV grammat(ikal)isch richtig; **~ correct** grammat(ikal)isch richtig

gramme N = **gram**

gramophone [ˈgræməfəʊn] N *(Brit old)* Grammofon *nt*; **~ record** Schallplatte *f*

gramps [græmps] N *(US inf)* Opa *m* *(inf)*

gran [græn] N *(inf)* Oma *f* *(inf)*

granary [ˈgrænərɪ] N Kornkammer *f* *(also fig)*

grand [grænd] **1** ADJ (+ER) (= *imposing*) grandios; *architecture, building* prachtvoll; *scheme, strategy* groß angelegt; *gesture* großartig; *ideas* hochfliegend; *person, clothes, manner* vornehm; *job* bedeutend; **on a ~ scale** im großen Rahmen; **~ occasion** großer *or* feierlicher Anlass; **the ~ opening** die große Eröffnung **2** N **(a)** *(Fin inf: = thousand pounds or dollars)* Riese *m* *(inf)*; **ten ~** zehn Riesen *(inf)* **(b)** *(Mus inf: = ~ piano)* Flügel *m*

grand: **Grand Canyon** N Grand Canyon m; **grandchild** N Enkel(kind nt) m; **grand(d)ad** N (inf) Opa m (inf); **granddaughter** N Enkelin f

grandeur ['grændjə'] N Größe f

grandfather ['grændfɑːðə'] N Großvater m

grandfather clock N Standuhr f

grand finale N großes Finale

grandiloquent [græn'dɪləkwənt] ADJ (form) hochtrabend

grandiose ['grændɪəuz] ADJ (pej) person, style schwülstig; idea, plan hochfliegend; claim großspurig

grand jury N (US Jur) Großes Geschworenengericht

grandly ['grændlɪ] ADV (a) (= impressively) eindrucksvoll; named grandios; **it is ~ described as/called/titled ...** es trägt die grandiose Bezeichnung ... (b) (= pompously) großspurig; say hochtrabend

grand: **grandma** N (inf) Oma f (inf); **grand master, grandmaster** N (Chess) Großmeister(in) m(f); **grandmother** N Großmutter f; **grandpa** N (inf) Opa m (inf); **grandparent** N Großvater m/ -mutter f; **grandparents** PL Großeltern pl; **grand piano** N Flügel m; **Grand Prix** N Grand Prix m; **grand slam** N **to win the ~** (Sport) alle Wettbewerbe gewinnen; **grandson** N Enkel(sohn) m; **grandstand** N Haupttribüne f; **grand-standing** N (esp US fig) Großtuerei f; **grand total** N Gesamtsumme f; **a ~ of £50** insgesamt £ 50

granite ['grænɪt] N Granit m

granny, grannie ['grænɪ] N (inf) Oma f (inf)

granny flat N (Brit) Einliegerwohnung f

grant [grɑːnt] **1** VT (a) gewähren (sb jdm); permission, licence, visa erteilen (sb jdm); request stattgeben (+dat) (form); land, pension bewilligen (sb jdm); wish (= fulfil) erfüllen; **to ~ an amnesty to sb** jdn amnestieren
(b) (= admit, agree) zugeben, zugestehen; **to take sb/sth for ~ed** jdn/etw als selbstverständlich hinnehmen; **to take it for ~ed that ...** es selbstverständlich finden, dass ... **2** N (of money) Subvention f; (for studying etc) Stipendium nt

grant: **grant-aided** ADJ student gefördert; group, school, programme subventioniert; **grant-maintained** ADJ staatlich finanziert

granulated sugar ['grænjuleɪtɪd'fugə'] N Zuckerraffinade f

granule ['grænjuːl] N Körnchen nt

grape [greɪp] N (Wein)traube f; **a pound of ~s** ein Pfund (Wein)trauben; **a bunch of ~s** eine (ganze) Weintraube

grape: **grapefruit** N Grapefruit f, Pampelmuse f; **grapefruit juice** N Grapefruitsaft m; **grape juice** N Traubensaft m; **grapevine** N Weinstock m; **I heard it on or through the ~** es ist mir zu Ohren gekommen

graph [grɑːf] N Diagramm nt

graphic ['græfɪk] ADJ (a) account, description anschaulich; (= unpleasantly realistic) drastisch; **to describe sth in ~ detail** etw in allen Einzelheiten anschaulich darstellen (b) (Art) grafisch; **~ work** Grafiken pl

graphically ['græfɪkəlɪ] ADV describe, portray anschaulich; (= in unpleasantly realistic way) auf drastische Art

graphic: **graphic artist** N Grafiker(in) m(f); **graphic arts** PL, **graphic design** N Grafik f; **graphic designer** N Grafiker(in) m(f); **graphic equalizer** N (Graphic) Equalizer m

graphics ['græfɪks] **1** N (a) SING (= subject) Zeichnen nt (b) PL (= drawings) Zeichnungen pl (c) PL (Comput) Grafik f **2** ADJ ATTR (Comput) Grafik-

graphite ['græfaɪt] N Grafit m

graph paper N Millimeterpapier nt

grapple ['græpl] VI (lit) ringen, kämpfen; **to ~ with a problem** sich mit einem Problem herumschlagen

grasp [grɑːsp] **1** N (a) (= hold) Griff m; **he held my arm firmly in his ~** er hielt meinen Arm mit festem Griff; **the knife slipped from her ~** das Messer rutschte ihr aus der Hand; **just when fame was within their ~** gerade als Ruhm in greifbare Nähe gerückt war
(b) (fig: = understanding) Verständnis nt; **to have a good ~ of sth** etw gut beherrschen
2 VT (a) (= catch hold of) ergreifen; (= hold tightly) festhalten; **he ~ed the bundle in his arms** er hielt das Bündel in den Armen
(b) (fig: = understand) begreifen

3 VI **to ~ at sth** (lit) nach etw greifen; (fig) sich auf etw (acc) stürzen

grasping ['grɑːspɪŋ] ADJ (fig) habgierig

grass [grɑːs] **1** N (a) Gras nt; **blade of ~** Grashalm m; **~ seed** Grassamen m
(b) NO PL (= lawn) Rasen m; (= pasture) Weide(land nt) f; **to play on ~** (Sport) auf (dem) Rasen spielen; **to put or turn out to ~** (Brit) cattle auf die Weide treiben; old horses das Gnadenbrot geben (+dat); (inf) employee aufs Abstellgleis schieben (inf)
(c) (inf: = marijuana) Gras(s) nt (inf)
2 VT (also ~ over) ground mit Gras bepflanzen
3 VI (Brit inf) singen (inf) (to bei); **to ~ on sb** jdn verpfeifen (inf)

grass: **grasshopper** N Heuschrecke f, Grashüpfer m (inf); **grassland** N Grasland nt; **grass roots** PL Volk nt; (of a party) Basis f; **grass-roots** ADJ ATTR Basis-, an der Basis; **a ~ level** an der Basis; **a ~ movement** eine Bürgerinitiative; **grass snake** N Ringelnatter f

grassy ['grɑːsɪ] ADJ (+ER) grasig; **~ slope** Grashang m

grate[1] [greɪt] N (= grid) Gitter nt; (in fire) (Feuer)rost m; (= fireplace) Kamin m

grate[2] **1** VT (Cook) reiben **2** VI (= scrape) streifen (against +acc); (= make a noise) kratzen; (fig) wehtun (on sb jdm); **to ~ on sb's nerves** jdm auf die Nerven gehen

grateful ['greɪtful] ADJ dankbar; **I'm ~ to you for buying or having bought the tickets** ich bin dir dankbar (dafür), dass du die Karten gekauft hast

gratefully ['greɪtfəlɪ] ADV dankbar

grater ['greɪtə'] N Reibe f

gratification [grætɪfɪ'keɪʃən] N Genugtuung f

gratify ['grætɪfaɪ] VT (a) (= give pleasure) erfreuen; **I was gratified to hear that ...** ich habe mit Genugtuung gehört, dass ... (b) (= satisfy) zufrieden stellen

gratifying ['grætɪfaɪɪŋ] ADJ (sehr) erfreulich; **it is ~ to learn that ...** es ist erfreulich zu erfahren, dass ...

grating[1] ['greɪtɪŋ] N Gitter nt

grating[2] ADJ kratzend; sound quietschend; (= rasping) knirschend; voice schrill

gratis ['grætɪs] ADJ, ADV gratis, umsonst

gratitude ['grætɪtjuːd] N Dankbarkeit f (to gegenüber)

gratuitous [grə'tjuːɪtəs] ADJ überflüssig; (= unasked-for) unerwünscht

gratuity [grə'tjuːɪtɪ] N Gratifikation f; (form: = tip) Trinkgeld nt

grave[1] [greɪv] N (lit, fig) Grab nt; **to turn in one's ~** sich im Grabe herumdrehen; **to dig one's own ~** (fig) sein eigenes Grab graben or schaufeln

grave[2] ADJ (+ER) concern, danger, problem, difficulty groß; consequences schwerwiegend; threat, situation, matter, expression, person ernst; mistake, illness, crime schwer; news schlimm; suspicion, doubt stark

grave[3] [grɑːv] ADJ **~ accent** Gravis m, Accent grave m; **e ~, ~ e** e Accent grave

grave digger N Totengräber(in) m(f)

gravel ['grævəl] **1** N Kies m; (= large chippings) Schotter m **2** ADJ ATTR Kies-; road, drive mit Kies bedeckt; **~ path** Kiesweg m

gravelled, (US) **graveled** ['grævəld] ADJ mit Kies bedeckt; **~ path** Kiesweg m

gravely ['greɪvlɪ] ADV (a) ill, wounded schwer; **~ concerned** ernstlich besorgt (b) say, nod ernst

grave: **graveside** N **at the ~** am Grabe; **gravestone** N Grabstein m; **graveyard** N Friedhof m

gravitate ['grævɪteɪt] VI (lit) angezogen werden (to(wards) von); (fig) hingezogen werden (to(wards) zu)

gravity ['grævɪtɪ] N (a) (Phys) Schwerkraft f; **centre** (Brit) or **center** (US) **of ~** Schwerpunkt m (b) (of person, expression, situation, threat) Ernst m; (of mistake, illness, crime) Schwere f; (of danger, problem, difficulty) Größe f; (of consequences) schwerwiegende Art; **the ~ of the news** die schlimmen Nachrichten

gravy ['greɪvɪ] N (Cook) (= juice) Bratensaft m; (= sauce) Soße f

gravy boat N Sauciere f

gray N, ADJ, VI (US) = **grey**

graze[1] [greɪz] **1** VI (cattle etc) weiden **2** VT cattle weiden lassen

graze² ■ VT (= *touch lightly*) streifen; (= *scrape skin off*) aufschürfen; **to ~ one's knees** sich (*dat*) die Knie aufschürfen; **to ~ oneself** sich (*dat*) die Haut aufschürfen ■ N Abschürfung *f*

GRE (*US Univ*) ABBR **of Graduate Record Examination** *Zulassungsprüfung für ein weiterführendes Studium*

grease [griːs] ■ N Fett *nt*; (= *lubricant*) Schmiere *f* ■ VT fetten; *skin* einfetten; (*Aut, Tech*) schmieren; **to ~ back one's hair** sich (*dat*) die Haare mit Pomade nach hinten frisieren; **to ~ sb's palm** (*inf*) jdn schmieren (*inf*); **like ~d lightning** (*inf*) wie ein geölter Blitz

grease: grease mark N Fettfleck *m*; **greasepaint** N (*Theat*) (Fett)schminke *f*; **greaseproof** ADJ **~ paper** Pergamentpapier *nt*

greasy [griːsɪ] ADJ (+ER) (a) *food* fett; *hair, skin, complexion* fettig; *clothes* schmierig; *surface* rutschig (b) (*pej:* = *smarmy*) schmierig (*pej inf*)

greasy spoon (café) N (*pej inf*) billiges Fresslokal (*pej inf*)

great [greɪt] ■ ADJ (+ER) (a) groß; (= *very large*) sehr groß; (= *huge*) riesig; **there is a ~ need for economic development** wirtschaftliche Entwicklung ist dringend nötig; **of no ~ importance** ziemlich unwichtig; **in ~ detail** ganz ausführlich; **to take a ~ interest in sth** sich sehr für etw interessieren; **he did not live to a ~ age** er erreichte kein hohes Alter; **with ~ difficulty** mit großen Schwierigkeiten; **to a ~ extent** in hohem Maße; **it was a ~ fun** es hat großen Spaß gemacht; **a ~ many, a ~ number of** sehr viele; **his ~est work** sein Hauptwerk *nt*; **to think ~ thoughts** geniale Gedanken haben; **he was a ~ friend of my father** er war mit meinem Vater sehr gut befreundet; **he is a ~ admirer of British orchestras** er bewundert britische Orchester sehr; **to be a ~ believer in sth** sehr viel von etw halten; **to be a ~ believer in doing sth** grundsätzlich dafür sein, etw zu tun (b) (*inf:* = *terrific*) toll (*inf*), prima (*inf*); **this whisk is ~ for sauces** dieser Schneebesen eignet sich besonders gut für Soßen; **to be ~ at football/at singing** ein großer Fußballspieler/Sänger sein; **to feel ~** sich toll *or* prima fühlen (*inf*); **my wife isn't feeling so ~** meiner Frau geht es nicht besonders gut (c) (= *excellent, outstanding*) ausgezeichnet, großartig; **one of the ~ footballers of our generation** einer der großen Fußballspieler unserer Generation ■ INTERJ (*inf*) toll (*inf*), super (*inf*); **oh ~** (*iro*) na wunderbar ■ ADV (a) (*inf:* = *well*) **she's doing ~** (*in job*) sie macht sich hervorragend; (*healthwise*) sie macht große Fortschritte; **everything's going ~** alles läuft nach Plan (b) **~ big** (*emph inf*) riesengroß ■ N (a) PL **the ~** die Großen *pl* (b) USU PL (= *person*) Größe *f*; **the ~s** (= *stars*) die Größen *pl*

great: great ape N Menschenaffe *m*; **great-aunt** N Großtante *f*; **Great Britain** N Großbritannien *nt*; **greatcoat** N Überzieher *m*; **Great Dane** N Deutsche Dogge

greater [ˈgreɪtəʳ] ADJ COMP of **great** größer; **to pay ~ attention** besser aufpassen; **of ~ importance is ...** noch wichtiger ist ...

Greater London N Groß-London *nt*

greatest [ˈgreɪtɪst] ■ ADJ SUPERL of **great** größte(r, s); **with the ~ (of) pleasure** mit dem größten Vergnügen ■ N **he's the ~** (*inf*) er ist der Größte

great: great-grandchild N Urenkel(in) *m(f)*; **great-grandparents** PL Urgroßeltern *pl*; **Great Lakes** PL **the ~** die Großen Seen *pl*

greatly [ˈgreɪtlɪ] ADV *increase, influence, exaggerated* stark; *admire, surprise* sehr; **he was not ~ surprised** er war nicht besonders überrascht

great-nephew [ˈgreɪtˌnefjuː] N Großneffe *m*

greatness [ˈgreɪtnɪs] N Größe *f*; (= *importance also*) Bedeutung *f*

great: great-niece N Großnichte *f*; **great-uncle** N Großonkel *m*; **Great Wall of China** N Chinesische Mauer

Grecian [ˈgriːʃən] ADJ griechisch

Greece [griːs] N Griechenland *nt*

greed [griːd] N Gier *f* (*for* nach +*dat*); (*for material wealth also*) Habgier *f*; (= *gluttony*) Gefräßigkeit *f*; **~ for money/power** Geld-/Machtgier *f*

greedily [ˈgriːdɪlɪ] ADV gierig

greedy [ˈgriːdɪ] ADJ (+ER) gierig (*for* auf +*acc*, nach); (*for material wealth also*) habgierig; (= *gluttonous*) gefräßig; **~ for power/**

money macht-/geldgierig; **don't be so ~!** sei nicht so unbescheiden

greedy guts [ˈgriːdɪɡʌts] N SING (*Brit inf*) Fresssack *m* (*inf*)

Greek [griːk] ■ ADJ griechisch; **he is ~** er ist Grieche ■ N (a) (*Ling*) Griechisch *nt*; **Modern ~** Neugriechisch *nt*; **Ancient ~** Altgriechisch *nt*; **it's all ~ to me** (*inf*) das sind böhmische Dörfer für mich (*inf*) (b) (= *person*) Grieche *m*, Griechin *f*

green [griːn] ■ ADJ (+ER) grün (*also Pol*); *consumer, company* umweltbewusst; *policy, measures, product, technology* umweltfreundlich; **~ space** Grünfläche *f*; **to be/turn ~ with envy** blass *or* grün *or* gelb vor Neid sein/werden; **~ salad** grüner Salat ■ N (a) (= *colour, putting ~*) Grün *nt* (b) (= *area of grass*) Grünfläche *f*; **(village) ~** Dorfwiese *f* (c) **greens** PL (= *vegetables*) Grüngemüse *nt* (d) (*Pol*) **the Greens** die Grünen *pl* ■ ADV (*Pol*) grün

green: greenback N (*US inf*) Lappen *m* (*sl*), Geldschein *m*; **green bean** N grüne Bohne; **green belt** N Grüngürtel *m*; **green card** N (a) (*US:* = *residence permit*) Aufenthaltsgenehmigung *f* (b) (*Brit Insur*) grüne Versicherungskarte

greenery [ˈgriːnərɪ] N Grün *nt*; (= *foliage*) grünes Laub

green: greenfield ADJ **~ site** Bauplatz *m* im Grünen; **green fingers** PL (*Brit*) **to have ~** eine Hand für Pflanzen haben; **greenfly** N Blattlaus *f*; **greengrocer** N (*esp Brit*) (Obst- und) Gemüsehändler(in) *m(f)*; **at the ~'s (shop)** im Gemüseladen; **greenhouse** N Gewächshaus *nt*; **greenhouse effect** N Treibhauseffekt *m*; **greenhouse gas** N Treibhausgas *nt*

greenish [ˈgriːnɪʃ] ADJ grünlich

Greenland [ˈgriːnlənd] N Grönland *nt*

green: green light N grünes Licht; **to give sb/sth the ~** jdm/ einer Sache grünes Licht geben; **greenmail** N (*US*), **greenmailing** N (*Brit*) (*St Ex*) räuberischer Aktienkauf; **green man** N (*at street crossing*) grünes Licht; (*as said to children*) grünes Männchen; **green onion** N (*US*) Frühlingszwiebel *f*; **Green Paper** N (*Brit Pol*) Vorlage *f* für eine Parlamentsdebatte; **Green Party** N **the ~** die Grünen *pl*; **green pepper** N (grüne) Paprikaschote *f*; **greenroom** N (*Theat*) ≈ Garderobe *f*; **green tea** N grüner Tee *m*; **green thumb** N (*US*) = **green fingers**

Greenwich (Mean) Time [ˈgrenɪtʃˈmiːnˌtaɪm] N westeuropäische Zeit *f*

greet [griːt] VT (= *welcome*) begrüßen; (= *receive, meet*) empfangen; (= *say hallo to*) grüßen; *news, decision* aufnehmen; **a terrible sight ~ed him** ihm bot sich ein fürchterlicher Anblick

greeting [ˈgriːtɪŋ] N Gruß *m*; **~s** Grüße *pl*; (= *congratulations*) Glückwünsche *pl*; **to send ~s to sb** Grüße an jdn senden; (*through sb else*) jdn grüßen lassen

greetings card N Grußkarte *f*

gregarious [grɪˈgɛərɪəs] ADJ gesellig; **~ animal/instinct** Herdentier *nt*/-trieb *or* -instinkt *m*

gremlin [ˈgremlɪn] N (*hum*) Maschinenteufel *m* (*hum*)

grenade [grɪˈneɪd] N Granate *f*

grew [gruː] PRET of **grow**

grey, (*US*) **gray** [greɪ] ■ ADJ (+ER) (a) grau; (= *bleak also*) öde; (= *ashen*) *person, face* fahl; *weather, sky, day* trüb; **to go** *or* **turn ~** (*person, hair*) grau werden (b) *vote, market* Senioren- ■ N (= *colour*) Grau *nt* ■ VI (*person, hair*) grau werden

grey, (*US*) **gray: grey area** N (*fig*) Grauzone *f*; **grey-haired** ADJ grauhaarig

greyhound [ˈgreɪhaʊnd] N Windhund *m*

Die Greyhound-Gesellschaft betreibt ein Netz von Langstreckenbussen in den gesamten Vereinigten Staaten. Die Gesellschaft bietet auch ein Ticket an, mit dem man unbegrenzt durch die USA reisen kann, den so genannten „Ameripass".

greyhound racing N Windhundrennen *nt*

greyish, (*US*) **grayish** [ˈgreɪɪʃ] ADJ gräulich

grey, (*US*) **gray: grey market** N (*Comm*) grauer Markt; **grey matter** N (*Med inf*) graue Zellen *pl*; **grey squirrel** N Grauhörnchen *nt*

grid [grɪd] N **(a)** (= *grating, on map*) Gitter *nt*; (*in fireplace, on barbecue*) Rost *m* **(b)** (= *electricity, gas network*) Verteilernetz *nt*; **the (national) ~** (*Elec*) das Überland(leitungs)netz **(c)** (*Motor-racing*: = *starting ~*) Start(platz) *m*; (*US Ftbl*) Spielfeld *nt*

griddle [ˈgrɪdl] N (*Cook*) gusseiserne Platte zum *Pfannkuchenbacken*

gridiron [ˈgrɪd.aɪən] N **(a)** (*Cook*) (Brat)rost *m* **(b)** (*US Ftbl*) Spielfeld *nt*

gridlock [ˈgrɪdlɒk] N (*Mot*) totaler Stau; (*fig*) festgefahrene Situation; **total ~** (*Mot*) Verkehrskollaps *m*

gridlocked [ˈgrɪdlɒkt] ADJ **(a)** *road* völlig verstopft **(b)** (*fig*) *talks, negotiations* festgefahren

grief [griːf] N Leid *nt*, Kummer *m*; (*because of loss*) große Trauer; **to come to ~** Schaden erleiden; (= *be hurt, damaged*) zu Schaden kommen; (= *fail*) scheitern

grief-stricken [ˈgriːfˌstrɪkən] ADJ tieftraurig; *look, voice* schmerzerfüllt

grievance [ˈgriːvəns] N Klage *f*; (= *resentment*) Groll *m*; **to have a ~ against sb for sth** jdm etw übel nehmen; **to air one's ~s** seine Beschwerden vorbringen

grieve [griːv] **1** VT Kummer bereiten (+*dat*), betrüben; **it ~s me to see that ...** ich sehe mit Schmerz or Kummer, dass ... **2** VI trauern (*at, about* über +*acc*); **to ~ for sb/sth** um jdn/etw trauern; **to ~ over sb/sth** über jdn/etw zutiefst bekümmert sein

grievous [ˈgriːvəs] ADJ (*form*) schwer; *error* schwer wiegend; *injustice, wrong* schreiend; **~ bodily harm** (*Jur*) schwere Körperverletzung

grill [grɪl] **1** N **(a)** (*Cook*) (*on cooker etc*) Grill *m*; (= *gridiron*) (Brat)rost *m*; (= *food*) Grillgericht *nt* **(b)** = **grille 2** VT **(a)** (*Cook*) grillen **(b)** (*inf*: = *interrogate*) in die Zange nehmen (*inf*); **to ~ sb about sth** jdn über etw (*acc*) ausquetschen (*inf*)

grille [grɪl] N Gitter *nt*; (*on window*) Fenstergitter *nt*; (*to speak through*) Sprechgitter *nt*; (*Aut*) Kühlergrill *m*

grilling [ˈgrɪlɪŋ] N **(a)** (*Cook*) Grillen *nt* **(b)** (= *interrogation*) strenges Verhör; **to give sb a ~** jdn in die Zange nehmen (*inf*); **to give sb a ~ about sth** jdn über etw (*acc*) ausquetschen (*inf*)

grill pan N (*Brit*) Grillpfanne *f*

grim [grɪm] ADJ (+ER) **(a)** (= *terrible*) grauenvoll; *joke, warning, reminder* grauenhaft; *situation* ernst; *necessity, truth* bitter; (= *depressing*) trostlos; *prospect* düster; (= *stern*) grimmig; *battle, struggle* unerbittlich; **to look ~** (*situation, future*) trostlos aussehen; (*person*) ein grimmiges Gesicht machen; **the Grim Reaper** der Sensenmann **(b)** (*inf*: = *lousy*) fürchterlich (*inf*); **to feel ~** (= *unwell*) sich elend or mies (*inf*) fühlen

grimace [ˈgrɪməs] **1** N Grimasse *f* **2** VI Grimassen schneiden; (*with disgust, pain etc also*) das Gesicht verziehen

grime [graɪm] N Dreck *m*, Schmutz *m*; (*sooty*) Ruß *m*

grimly [ˈgrɪmlɪ] ADV *struggle, hold on* verbissen; (= *sternly*) mit grimmiger Miene; **~ determined** verbissen

grimy [ˈgraɪmɪ] ADJ schmutzig, dreckig; (= *greasy*) schmierig; (= *blackened with soot*) verrußt

grin [grɪn] **1** N (*showing pleasure*) Lächeln *nt*; (*showing scorn, stupidity, impudence*) Grinsen *nt* **2** VI (*with pleasure*) lächeln; (*in scorn, stupidly, cheekily*) grinsen; **to ~ and bear it** gute Miene zum bösen Spiel machen; (= *tolerate pain*) die Zähne zusammenbeißen; **to ~ at sb** jdn anlächeln/angrinsen

grind [graɪnd], *vb*: *pret, ptp* **ground 1** VT **(a)** (= *crush*) zermahlen; *corn, coffee, pepper, flour* mahlen; (*in mortar*) zerstoßen; **to ~ one's teeth** mit den Zähnen knirschen **(b)** *gem, lens, knife* schleifen **2** VI **to ~ to a halt** or **standstill** (*lit*) quietschend zum Stehen kommen; (*fig*) stocken; (*production etc*) zum Erliegen kommen; (*negotiations*) sich festfahren **3** N (*fig inf*: = *drudgery*) Schufterei *f* (*inf*); (*US inf*: = *swot*) Streber(in) *m(f)* (*inf*); **the daily ~** der tägliche Trott; **it's a real ~** das ist ganz schön mühsam (*inf*)

▶ **grind down** VT SEP (*fig*) zermürben; **ground down by poverty** von Armut niedergedrückt

▶ **grind out** VT SEP *article, essay* sich (*dat*) abquälen; *propaganda* ausspucken (*inf*)

▶ **grind up** VT SEP zermahlen

grinder [ˈgraɪndə^r] N (= *meat ~*) Fleischwolf *m*; (= *coffee ~*) Kaffeemühle *f*; (*for sharpening*) Schleifmaschine *f*; (= *stone*) Schleifstein *m*

grinding [ˈgraɪndɪŋ] ADJ **(a)** **to come to a ~ halt** (*lit, fig*) völlig zum Stillstand kommen; (*vehicle*) plötzlich stehen bleiben **(b)** *poverty* (er)drückend; *tedium, work* zermürbend

grindstone [ˈgraɪndstəʊn] N **to keep one's nose to the ~** hart arbeiten; **back to the ~** wieder in die Tretmühle (*hum*)

grip [grɪp] **1** N **(a)** Griff *m* (*also* = *handle*); (*on rope, on road*) Halt *m*; **to get a ~ on the road/rope** Halt finden; **these shoes/tyres** (*Brit*) or **tires** (*US*) **have got a good ~** diese Schuhe/Reifen greifen gut; **to get a ~ on sth** (*on situation, inflation etc*) etw in den Griff bekommen; **to get a ~ on oneself** (*inf*) sich zusammenreißen (*inf*); **to let go** or **release one's ~** loslassen (*on sth* etw); **to lose one's ~** (*lit*) den Halt verlieren; (*fig*) nachlassen; **the chairman is losing his ~ (on the company)** der Vorsitzende hat die Firma nicht mehr richtig im Griff; **I must be losing my ~** mit mir gehts bergab; **to lose one's ~ on reality** den Bezug zur Wirklichkeit verlieren; **the country is in the ~ of a general strike** das Land ist von einem Generalstreik lahm gelegt; **to get** or **come to ~s with sth** etw in den Griff bekommen **(b)** (*esp Brit*: = *hair ~*) Klemmchen *nt* **2** VT packen; (*fig*) (*fear etc also*) ergreifen; (*film, story etc also*) fesseln; **the tyre** (*Brit*) or **tire** (*US*) **~s the road well** der Reifen greift gut **3** VI greifen

gripe [graɪp] **1** VI (*inf*) meckern (*inf*) **2** N (*inf*) Meckerei *f* (*inf*)

gripping [ˈgrɪpɪŋ] ADJ packend

grisly [ˈgrɪzlɪ] ADJ (+ER) grausig

grist [grɪst] N **it's all ~ to his/the mill** das kann er/man alles verwerten; (*for complaint*) das ist Wasser auf seine Mühle

gristle [ˈgrɪsl] N Knorpel *m*

gristly [ˈgrɪslɪ] ADJ (+ER) knorpelig

grit [grɪt] **1** N **(a)** (= *dust, in eye*) Staub *m*; (= *gravel*) Splitt *m*; (*for roads in winter*) Streusand *m* **(b)** (= *courage*) Mut *m* **(c) grits** PL (*US*) Grütze *f* **2** VT **a** *road etc* streuen **(b) to ~ one's teeth** (*lit, fig*) die Zähne zusammenbeißen

gritty [ˈgrɪtɪ] ADJ (+ER) **(a)** (*fig*) *person* mutig; *determination* zäh **(b)** (*fig*) *realism* hart; *drama, film* wirklichkeitsnah; *portrayal, account* ungeschminkt

grizzly [ˈgrɪzlɪ] N (*also* **~ bear**) Grizzly(bär) *m*

groan [grəʊn] **1** N Stöhnen *nt*, *no pl*; **to let out** or **give a ~** (auf)stöhnen **2** VI stöhnen (*with* vor +*dat*); (*gate, planks*) ächzen (*with* vor +*dat*); **the table ~ed under the weight** der Tisch ächzte unter der Last

grocer [ˈgrəʊsə^r] N Lebensmittelhändler(in) *m(f)*; **at the ~'s** im Lebensmittelladen

grocery [ˈgrəʊsərɪ] N **(a)** Lebensmittelgeschäft *nt* **(b) groceries** PL Lebensmittel *pl*

groggy [ˈgrɒgɪ] ADJ (+ER) (*inf*) angeschlagen (*inf*), groggy *pred inv* (*inf*)

groin [grɔɪn] N (*Anat*) Leiste *f*; **to kick sb in the ~** jdn in den Unterleib treten

groom [gruːm] **1** N **(a)** (*in stables*) Stallbursche *m* **(b)** (= *bridegroom*) Bräutigam *m* **2** VT **(a)** *horse* striegeln; **to ~ oneself** (*birds, animals*) sich putzen; (*people*) sich pflegen; **well ~ed** gepflegt **(b) he's being ~ed for the job of chairman/ for the Presidency** er wird als zukünftiger Vorsitzender/ Präsidentschaftskandidat aufgebaut

groove [gruːv] N Rille *f*; (*in face*) Furche *f*

groovy [ˈgruːvɪ] ADJ (+ER) (*inf*) irr (*sl*), stark (*sl*)

grope [grəʊp] **1** VI (*also* **~ around** or **about**) (herum)tasten (*for* nach); (*for words, solution*) suchen (*for* nach); **to be groping in the dark** im Dunkeln tappen; (= *try things at random*) vor sich (*acc*) hin wursteln (*inf*) **2** VT (*inf*) *girlfriend* befummeln (*inf*); **to ~ one's way** sich vorwärts tasten **3** N (*inf*) **to have a ~** fummeln (*inf*)

gross¹ [grəʊs] N, NO PL Gros *nt*

gross² **1** ADJ (+ER) **(a)** *exaggeration, simplification, error, insult* grob; *inequality, violation* krass; *injustice* schreiend; **that is a ~ understatement** das ist stark untertrieben **(b)** (= *fat*) fett **(c)** (*inf*) (= *disgusting*) abstoßend; (= *tasteless*) ordinär **(d)** (= *total*) Gesamt-; (= *before deductions*) Brutto-; **~ amount** Gesamtbetrag *m*; **~ income** Bruttoeinkommen *nt*; **~ selling**

price Bruttoverkaufspreis *m*; **~ weight** Bruttogewicht *nt* **2** ADV *earn, pay, weigh* brutto; **the yield is 10% ~** der Bruttoertrag ist 10% **3** VT brutto verdienen

gross domestic product N (*Econ*) Bruttoinlandsprodukt *nt*

grossly ['grəʊslɪ] ADV *unfair, inadequate, inaccurate, irresponsible* äußerst; *overweight, exaggerate, underestimate* stark; *mislead* grob; *underpaid, underfunded, overpaid* extrem; **to be ~ negligent** grob fahrlässig handeln

grotesque [grəʊ'tesk] ADJ **(a)** *sight, spectacle, shape* grotesk; *idea, proposal, allegation* absurd **(b)** (= *distorted*) *grimace* verzerrt

grotesquely [grəʊ'tesklɪ] ADV auf groteske Art; *swollen, deformed* grauenhaft

grotto ['grɒtəʊ] N, *pl* **-(e)s** Grotte *f*

grotty ['grɒtɪ] ADJ (+ER) (*inf*) **(a)** (= *foul*) grausig (*inf*); (= *filthy*) verdreckt (*inf*) **(b)** (= *awful, lousy*) mies (*inf*); (= *dilapidated*) heruntergekommen; (= *tacky*) geschmacklos; **to feel ~** sich mies fühlen (*inf*)

grouch [graʊtʃ] N **(a)** (= *complaint*) Klage *f*; **to have a ~** schimpfen (*about über +acc*) **(b)** (*inf*: = *person*) Muffel *m* (*inf*)

grouchy [graʊtʃɪ] ADJ (+ER) griesgrämig

ground¹ [graʊnd] **1** N **(a)** (= *soil, terrain, surface, fig*) Boden *m*; **hilly ~** hügeliges Gelände; **there is common ~ between us** uns verbindet einiges; **to be on dangerous/firm** *or* **sure ~** (*fig*) sich auf gefährlichem/sicherem Boden bewegen; **on familiar ~** auf vertrautem Boden; **to cut the ~ from under sb** *or* **sb's feet** jdm den Boden unter den Füßen wegziehen; **to gain/lose ~** Boden gewinnen/verlieren; (*disease, rumour*) um sich greifen/im Schwinden begriffen sein; **to lose ~ to sb/sth** gegenüber jdm/etw an Boden verlieren; **to give ~ to sb/sth** vor jdm/etw zurückweichen; **to break new ~** (*lit, fig*) neue Gebiete erschließen; (*person*) sich auf ein neues *or* unbekanntes Gebiet begeben; **to prepare the ~ for sth** den Boden für etw vorbereiten; **to cover the/a lot of ~** (*fig*) das Thema/eine Menge Dinge behandeln; **to hold** *or* **stand one's ~** (*lit*) nicht von der Stelle weichen; (*fig*) seinen Mann stehen; **to shift** *or* **change one's ~** (*fig*) seine Haltung ändern; **above/below ~** über/unter der Erde; **to fall to the ~** (*lit*) zu Boden fallen; **to burn sth to the ~** etw niederbrennen; **it suits me down to the ~** das ist ideal für mich; **to get off the ~** (*plane etc*) abheben; (*fig: plans, project etc*) sich realisieren; **to go to ~** (*person*) untertauchen (*inf*) **(b)** (= *pitch*) Feld *nt*, Platz *m*; (= *parade ~, drill ~*) Platz *m* **(c) grounds** PL (= *premises, land*) Gelände *nt*; (= *gardens*) Anlagen *pl* **(d) grounds** PL (= *sediment*) Satz *m* **(e)** (*US Elec*) Erde *f* **(f)** (= *reason*) Grund *m*; **to have ~(s) for sth** Grund zu etw haben; **to be ~(s) for sth** Grund für *or* zu etw sein; **~s for dismissal** Entlassungsgrund *m*/-gründe *pl*; **on the ~s of...** aufgrund ... (*gen*); **on the ~s that ...** mit der Begründung, dass ...; **on health ~s** aus gesundheitlichen Gründen **2** VT **(a)** (*Aviat*) *plane* aus dem Verkehr ziehen; *pilot* sperren; **to be ~ed by bad weather/a strike** wegen schlechten Wetters/eines Streiks nicht starten können **(b)** *child* Hausarrest erteilen (+*dat*); **she was ~ed for a week** sie hatte eine Woche Hausarrest **(c)** (*US Elec*) erden **(d)** (= *base*) **to be ~ed on sth** sich auf etw (*acc*) gründen

ground² **1** PRET, PTP of **grind** **2** ADJ *glass* matt; *coffee* gemahlen; **~ rice** Reismehl *nt*; **freshly ~ black pepper** frisch gemahlener schwarzer Pfeffer; **~ meat** (*US*) Hackfleisch *nt*

ground: ground-breaking ADJ umwälzend; *research etc* bahnbrechend; **ground control** N (*Aviat*) Bodenkontrolle *f*; **ground crew** N Bodenpersonal *nt*; **ground floor** N Erdgeschoss *nt*, Erdgeschoß *nt* (*Aus*); **ground frost** N Bodenfrost *m*

grounding ['graʊndɪŋ] N Grundwissen *nt*; **to give sb a ~ in English** jdm die Grundlagen *pl* des Englischen beibringen

ground: groundkeeper N (*US*) = **groundsman**; **groundless** ADJ grundlos, unbegründet; **ground level** N Boden *m*; **below ~** unter dem Boden; **groundnut** N Erdnuss *f*; **ground plan** N Grundriss *m*; **ground rent** N Grundrente *f*; **ground rules** PL Grundregeln *pl*; **groundsheet** N Zeltboden(plane *f*) *m*

groundsman ['graʊndzmən] N, *pl* **-men** [-mən] (*esp Brit*) Platzwart *m*

ground: ground staff N (*Aviat*) Bodenpersonal *nt*; (*Sport*) Platzwarte *pl*; **groundswell** N (*fig*) Anschwellen *nt*, Zunahme *f*; **there was a growing ~ of public opinion against him** die Öffentlichkeit wandte sich zunehmend gegen ihn; **ground water** N Grundwasser *nt*; **groundwork** N Vorarbeit *f*; **to do the ~ for sth** die Vorarbeit für etw leisten

group [gruːp] **1** N Gruppe *f*; (= *theatre ~ also*) Ensemble *nt*; **a ~ of people** eine Gruppe Menschen; **a ~ of houses/trees** eine Häuser-/Baumgruppe **2** ATTR Gruppen-; *living, activities* in der Gruppe; **~ discussion** Gruppendiskussion *f* **3** VT gruppieren; **to ~ together** (*in one ~*) zusammentun; (*in several ~s*) in Gruppen einteilen; **it's wrong to ~ all criminals together** es ist nicht richtig, alle Verbrecher über einen Kamm zu scheren (*inf*); **~ed consignment** (*Brit Comm*) Sammelladung *f*

groupage ['gruːpɪdʒ] N (*Brit: in transport*) Sammelverkehr *m*

group booking N Gruppenbuchung *f*

groupie ['gruːpɪ] N Groupie *nt*

grouping ['gruːpɪŋ] N Gruppierung *f*; (= *group of things also*) Anordnung *f*

group: group insurance N Gruppenversicherung *f*; **group therapy** N Gruppentherapie *f*

grouse¹ [graʊs] N, *pl* **-** Waldhuhn *nt*; (= *red ~*) Schottisches Moor(schnee)huhn; **~ shooting** Moorhuhnjagd *f*

grouse² (*Brit inf*) **1** N (= *complaint*) Klage *f* **2** VI meckern (*inf*) (*about über +acc*)

grove [grəʊv] N Hain *m*

grovel ['grɒvl] VI kriechen; **to ~ to** *or* **before sb** (*fig*) vor jdm kriechen; (*in apology*) vor jdm zu Kreuze kriechen

grovelling, (*US*) **groveling** ['grɒvəlɪŋ] **1** ADJ kriecherisch (*inf*) **2** N Kriecherei *f* (*inf*)

grow [grəʊ], *pret* **grew**, *ptp* **grown** **1** VT **(a)** *plants* ziehen; (*commercially*) anbauen; (= *cultivate*) *flowers* züchten **(b)** **to ~ a beard/one's hair** sich (*dat*) einen Bart/die Haare wachsen lassen **2** VI **(a)** wachsen; (*in numbers*) zunehmen; (*in size*) sich vergrößern; (*fig*: = *become more mature*) sich weiterentwickeln; **to ~ in popularity** immer beliebter werden; **my, how you've** *or* **haven't you ~n!** du bist aber groß geworden!; **fears were ~ing for her safety** man machte sich zunehmend Sorgen um ihre Sicherheit; **the economy/population is ~ing by 2% a year** die Wirtschaft/Bevölkerung wächst um 2% pro Jahr; **pressure is ~ing for him to resign** er gerät zunehmend unter Druck zurückzutreten **(b)** (= *become*) werden; **to ~ to do/be sth** allmählich etw tun/sein; **to ~ to hate/love sb** jdn hassen/lieben lernen; **to ~ to enjoy sth** langsam Gefallen an etw (*dat*) finden; **I've ~n to like him** ich habe ihn mit der Zeit lieb gewonnen; **to ~ used to sth** sich an etw (*acc*) gewöhnen

➤ **grow apart** VI (*fig*) sich auseinander entwickeln

➤ **grow from** VI +PREP OBJ (= *arise from*) entstehen aus

➤ **grow into** VI +PREP OBJ **(a)** *clothes, job* hineinwachsen in (+*acc*) **(b)** (= *become*) sich entwickeln zu; **to grow into a man/woman** zum Mann/zur Frau heranwachsen

➤ **grow on** VI +PREP OBJ **it'll grow on you** das wird dir mit der Zeit gefallen

➤ **grow out** VI (*perm, colour*) herauswachsen

➤ **grow out of** VI +PREP OBJ **(a)** *clothes* herauswachsen aus; **to grow out of a habit** eine Angewohnheit ablegen **(b)** (= *arise from*) entstehen aus

➤ **grow up** VI (= *spend childhood*) aufwachsen; (= *become adult*) erwachsen werden; (*fig*) (*custom, hatred*) aufkommen; (*city*) entstehen; **what are you going to do when you grow up?** was willst du mal werden, wenn du groß bist?; **grow up!**, **when are you going to grow up?** werde endlich erwachsen!

grower ['grəʊə'] N (*of fruit, vegetables*) Anbauer(in) *m(f)*; (*of flowers*) Züchter(in) *m(f)*; (*of tobacco, tea*) Pflanzer(in) *m(f)*

growing ['grəʊɪŋ] ADJ (*lit, fig*) wachsend; *child* heranwachsend; *importance, interest, number etc* zunehmend; **he's still a ~ boy** er steckt noch (*inf*) *or* befindet sich noch im Wachstum

growing pains PL (*Med*) Wachstumsschmerzen *pl*; (*fig*) Kinderkrankheiten *pl*

growl [graʊl] **1** N Knurren *nt no pl*; (*of bear*) (*böses*) Brummen *no pl* **2** VI knurren; (*bear*) böse brummen; **to ~ at sb** jdn anknurren/anbrummen **3** VT *answer* knurren

grown [grəʊn] **1** PTP *of* **grow 2** ADJ erwachsen; **fully ~** ausgewachsen

grown-up ['grəʊnʌp] **1** ADJ erwachsen; *clothes, book* für Erwachsene; **they have a ~ family** sie haben schon erwachsene Kinder **2** N Erwachsene(r) *mf*

growth [grəʊθ] N **(a)** Wachstum *nt*; (= *increase in quantity, fig*: *of love, interest etc*) Zunahme *f*; (= *increase in size*) Vergrößerung *f*; (*of capital etc*) Zuwachs *m*; **~ industry** Wachstumsindustrie *f*; **~ rate** (*Econ*) Wachstumsrate *f*; **~ stock** Wachstumsaktien *pl* **(b)** (= *plants*) Vegetation *f*; (*of one plant*) Triebe *pl*; **covered with a thick ~ of ivy** von Efeu überwuchert *or* überwachsen; **with two days' ~ (of beard) on his face** mit zwei Tage alten Bartstoppeln **(c)** (*Med*) Wucherung *f*

grub [grʌb] **1** N **(a)** (= *larva*) Larve *f* **(b)** (*inf*: = *food*) Fressalien *pl* (*hum inf*); **~('s) up!** antreten zum Essenfassen (*inf*) **2** VI (*also ~ about or around*) (*pig*) wühlen (*in* in +*dat*); (*person*) (herum)wühlen (*in* in +*dat, for* nach)

grubby ['grʌbɪ] ADJ (+ER) **(a)** (= *dirty*) dreckig; *person, clothes, house* schmuddelig (*inf*) **(b)** (*fig*) *business, corruption* schmutzig

grudge [grʌdʒ] **1** N Groll *m* (*against* gegen); **to bear sb a ~, to have a ~ against sb** jdm böse sein, jdm grollen; **I bear him no ~** ich trage ihm das nicht nach **2** VT **to ~ sb sth** jdm etw nicht gönnen; **I don't ~ you your success** ich gönne Ihnen Ihren Erfolg; **to ~ doing sth** etw äußerst ungern tun; **I don't ~ doing it** es macht mir nichts aus, das zu tun

grudging ['grʌdʒɪŋ] ADJ widerwillig; *applause* sparsam; *apology* widerwillig gegeben

grudgingly ['grʌdʒɪŋlɪ] ADV widerwillig

gruelling, (*US*) **grueling** ['grʊəlɪŋ] ADJ *schedule, journey, day* (äußerst) anstrengend; *pace, conditions* mörderisch (*inf*); *race, match, event* (äußerst) strapaziös; *talks, negotiations* aufreibend

gruesome ['gruːsəm] ADJ grausig

gruff ADJ, **gruffly** ADV ['grʌf, -lɪ] barsch

grumble ['grʌmbl] **1** N Murren *nt no pl*; **his only ~ is that ...** das Einzige, was er auszusetzen hat, ist, dass ... **2** VI murren (*about, over* über +*acc*)

grumpily ['grʌmpɪlɪ] ADV (*inf*) mürrisch

grumpy ['grʌmpɪ] ADJ (+ER) (*inf*) mürrisch; *child* quengelig (*inf*)

grunge [grʌndʒ] N Grunge *nt*

grungy ['grʌndʒɪ] ADJ (*inf*) mies (*inf*)

grunt [grʌnt] **1** N (*of animal, person*) Grunzen *nt no pl*; (*of pain, in exertion*) Ächzen *nt no pl* **2** VI (*animal, person*) grunzen; (*with pain, exertion*) ächzen; (*in irritation*) knurren **3** VT *reply* knurren

GSM (*Telec*) ABBR *of* **Global System for Mobile Communications** GSM

GSP (*Comm*) ABBR *of* **Generalized System of Preferences**

G-string ['dʒiːstrɪŋ] N Tangahöschen *nt*

guarantee [ˌgærən'tiː] **1** N Garantie *f* (*of* für) (*also Comm*); (= ~ *slip*) Garantie(schein *m*) *f*; **to have *or* carry a 6-month ~** 6 Monate Garantie haben; **there is a year's ~ on this watch** auf der Uhr ist ein Jahr Garantie; **while it is still under ~** solange noch Garantie darauf ist; **to sell with a money-back ~** volles Rückgaberecht beim Verkauf von etw garantieren; **that's no ~ that ...** das heißt noch lange nicht, dass ... **2** VT garantieren (*sb sth* jdm etw) (*also Comm*); (= *take responsibility for*) garantieren für; **I can't ~ (that) he will be any good** ich kann nicht dafür garantieren, dass er gut ist

guaranteed [ˌgærən'tiːd] ADJ garantiert; **to be ~ for three months** (*goods*) drei Monate Garantie haben; (*prices*) für drei Monate garantiert sein; **such reports are ~ to cause anxiety** solche Berichte machen den Leuten garantiert Angst

guard [gɑːd] **1** N **(a)** (= *soldier, watch*) Wache *f*; **~ of honour** (*Brit*), **honor ~** (*US*) Ehrenwache *f*; **to change ~** Wachablösung machen; **to be under ~** bewacht werden; **to keep sb/sth under ~** jdn/etw bewachen; **to be on ~, to stand *or* keep ~** Wache halten *or* stehen; **to keep *or* stand ~ over sth** etw bewachen **(b)** (= *security* ~) Sicherheitsbeamte(r) *m*/-beamtin *f*; (*at factory gates, in park etc*) Wächter(in) *m(f)*; (*esp US:* = *prison* ~) Gefängniswärter(in) *m(f)*; (*Brit Rail*) Zugbegleiter(in) *m(f)* **(c)** (*Boxing, Fencing*) Deckung *f*; **on ~!** (*Fencing*) en garde!; **to**

drop *or* **lower one's ~** (*lit*) seine Deckung vernachlässigen; (*fig*) seine Reserve aufgeben; **the invitation caught me off ~** ich war auf die Einladung nicht vorbereitet; **to be on one's ~ (against sth)** (*fig*) (vor etw *dat*) auf der Hut sein; **to put sb on his ~ (against sth)** jdn (vor etw *dat*) warnen **(d)** (= *safety device, for protection*) Schutz *m* (*against* gegen); (*on machinery*) Schutz(vorrichtung *f*) *m*; (= *fire ~*) Schutzgitter *nt* **2** VT *prisoner, place, valuables* bewachen; *treasure, secret, tongue* hüten; *machinery* beaufsichtigen; *luggage* aufpassen auf (+*acc*); (= *protect*) (*lit*) *person, place* schützen (*from, against* vor +*dat*); *one's reputation* achten auf (+*acc*); (*fig*) *child etc* beschützen (*from, against* vor +*dat*); **a closely ~ed secret** ein gut *or* streng gehütetes Geheimnis

▶ **guard against** VI +PREP OBJ *suspicion, being cheated, scandal etc* sich in Acht nehmen vor (+*dat*); *illness, attack, danger, misunderstandings* vorbeugen (+*dat*); *accidents* verhüten; **you must guard against catching cold** Sie müssen aufpassen, dass Sie sich nicht erkälten

guard: **guard dog** N Wachhund *m*; **guard duty** N **to be on ~** auf Wache sein

guarded ['gɑːdɪd] ADJ *response etc* vorsichtig; **to be ~ about sth** sich über etw (*acc*) zurückhalten

guardedly ['gɑːdɪdlɪ] ADV vorsichtig

guardian ['gɑːdɪən] N Hüter(in), Wächter(in) *m(f)*; (*Jur*) Vormund *m*

guardrail ['gɑːdreɪl] N Schutzgeländer *nt*; (*around machinery*) Schutzleiste *f*

guardsman ['gɑːdzmən] N, *pl* **-men** [-mən] Wache *f*; (= *member of guards regiment*) Gardist *m*; (*US: in National Guard*) Nationalgardist *m*

guard's van N (*Brit Rail*) Dienstwagen *m*

gubernatorial [ˌguːbənə'tɔːrɪəl] ADJ (*esp US Pol*) Gouverneurs-; *candidate, campaign* für das Gouverneursamt; **~ election** Gouverneurswahl *f*

Guernsey ['gɜːnzɪ] N Guernsey *nt*

guer(r)illa [gə'rɪlə] **1** N Guerillero *m*, Guerillera *f*; **Palestinian ~s** palästinensische Freischärler *or* Guerillas *pl* **2** ATTR Guerilla-

guer(r)illa war, guer(r)illa warfare N Guerillakrieg *m*

guess [ges] **1** N Vermutung *f*; (= *estimate*) Schätzung *f*; **to have *or* make a ~ (at sth)** (etw) raten; (= *estimate*) (etw) schätzen; **it's a good ~** gut geschätzt; **it was just a lucky ~** das war ein Zufallstreffer *m*; **I'll give you three ~es** dreimal darfst du raten; **at a rough ~** grob geschätzt; **your ~ is as good as mine!** (*inf*) da kann ich auch nur raten!; **it's anybody's ~** (*inf*) das wissen die Götter (*inf*) **2** VI **(a)** raten; **how did you ~?** wie hast du das bloß erraten?; (*iro*) du merkst auch alles!; **to keep sb ~ing** jdn im Ungewissen lassen; **you'll never ~!** das wirst du nie erraten; **to ~ at sth** etw raten **(b)** (*esp US:* = *suppose*) **I ~ not** wohl nicht; **he's right, I ~** er hat wohl Recht; **I think he's right – I ~ so** ich glaube, er hat Recht – ja, das hat er wohl **3** VT **(a)** (= *surmise*) raten; (= *surmise correctly*) erraten; (= *estimate*) schätzen; **I ~ed as much** das habe ich mir schon gedacht; **you'll never ~ who/what** ... das errätst du nie, wer/ was ...; **~ what!** (*inf*) stell dir vor! (*inf*) **(b)** (*esp US:* = *suppose*) **I ~ we'll just have to wait and see** wir werden wohl abwarten müssen

guesstimate ['gestɪmɪt] N grobe Schätzung

guesswork ['geswɜːk] N (reine) Vermutung

guest [gest] **1** N Gast *m*; **~ of honour** (*Brit*) *or* **honor** (*US*) Ehrengast *m*; **be my ~** (*inf*) nur zu! (*inf*) **2** VI **to ~ on sth** einen Gastauftritt in etw (*dat*) haben

guest IN CPDS Gast-; **guest appearance** N Gastauftritt *m*; **to make a ~** als Gast auftreten; **guest artist** N Gast(star) *m*; (*Theat*) Gastspieler(in) *m(f)*; **guesthouse** N Gästehaus *nt*; (= *boarding house*) (Fremden)pension *f*; **guest list** N Gästeliste *f*; **guest room** N Gästezimmer *nt*; **guest speaker** N Gastredner(in) *m(f)*

guff [gʌf] N (*inf*) Quark *m* (*inf*)

guffaw [gʌ'fɔː] **1** N schallendes Lachen *no pl* **2** VI schallend (los)lachen

Guiana [gaɪ'ænə] N Guayana *nt*

guidance ['gaɪdəns] N (= *direction*) Führung *f*, Leitung *f*; (= *counselling*) Beratung *f* (*on* über +*acc*); (*from superior, parents, teacher etc*) Anleitung *f*; **spiritual ~** geistiger Rat; **to give sb ~ on sth** jdn bei etw beraten

guide [gaɪd] **1** N **(a)** Führer(in) *m(f)*; (*fig*) (= *indication, pointer*) Anhaltspunkt *m* (*to* für); (= *model*) Leitbild *nt*; **let reason/ your conscience be your ~** lassen Sie sich von der Vernunft/ Ihrem Gewissen leiten
(b) (*Brit*: = *Girl Guide*) Pfadfinderin *f*
(c) (= *instructions*) Anleitung *f*; (= *manual*) Handbuch *nt* (*to* +*gen*); (= *travel ~*) Führer *m*; **as a rough ~** als Faustregel **2** VT *people, blind man etc* führen; *discussion* leiten; *missile, sb's behaviour, studies* lenken; **to be ~d by sb/sth** (*person*) sich von jdm/etw leiten lassen

guidebook ['gaɪdbʊk] N (Reise)führer *m* (*to* von)

guided missile [gaɪdɪd'mɪsaɪl] N ferngelenktes Geschoss

guide dog N Blindenhund *m*

guided tour [gaɪdɪd'tʊəʳ] N Führung *f* (*of* durch)

guideline ['gaɪdlaɪn] N Richtlinie *f*; **safety ~s** Sicherheitshinweise *pl*; **I gave her a few ~s on looking after a kitten** ich gab ihr ein paar Hinweise, wie man eine junge Katze versorgt

guiding ['gaɪdɪŋ] ATTR **~ force** leitende Kraft; **~ hand** leitende Hand; **~ principle** Leitmotiv *nt*; **~ star** Leitstern *m*

guild [gɪld] N (*Hist*) Zunft *f*; (= *association*) Verein *m*

guilder ['gɪldəʳ] N Gulden *m*

guile [gaɪl] N Tücke *f*, (Arg)list *f*

guileless ['gaɪllɪs] ADJ arglos

guillotine [gɪlə'tiːn] **1** N **(a)** Guillotine *f* **(b)** (*for paper*) (Papier)schneidemaschine *f* **2** VT mit der Guillotine hinrichten

guilt [gɪlt] N Schuld *f* (*for, of* an +*dat*); **feelings of ~** Schuldgefühle *pl*; **~ complex** Schuldkomplex *m*

guiltily ['gɪltɪlɪ] ADV schuldbewusst

guilty ['gɪltɪ] ADJ (+ER) **(a)** *smile, look, silence* schuldbewusst; *secret, pleasure* mit Schuldgefühlen verbunden; **~ conscience** schlechtes Gewissen; **~ feelings** Schuldgefühle *pl*; **to feel ~ (about doing sth)** ein schlechtes Gewissen haben(, weil man etw tut/getan hat); **to make sb feel ~** jdm ein schlechtes Gewissen einreden
(b) (= *to blame*) schuldig (*of sth* einer Sache *gen*); **the ~ person** der/die Schuldige; **the ~ party** die schuldige Partei; **to find sb ~/not ~ (of sth)** jdn (einer Sache *gen*) für schuldig/ nicht schuldig befinden; **they were found not ~ of killing him** sie wurden für nicht schuldig befunden, ihn getötet zu haben; **to plead (not) ~ to a crime** sich eines Verbrechens (nicht) schuldig bekennen; **a ~ verdict, a verdict of ~** ein Schuldspruch *m*; **a not ~ verdict, a verdict of not ~** ein Freispruch *m*; **their parents are ~ of gross neglect** ihre Eltern haben sich grobe Fahrlässigkeit zuschulden kommen lassen; **we're all ~ of neglecting the problem** uns trifft alle die Schuld, dass das Problem vernachlässigt wurde

guinea pig N Meerschweinchen *nt*; (*fig*) Versuchskaninchen *nt*

guise [gaɪz] N (= *disguise*) Gestalt *f*; (= *pretence*) Vorwand *m*; **in the ~ of a clown** als Clown verkleidet; **under the ~ of scientific research** unter dem Deckmantel der wissenschaftlichen Forschung; **under the ~ of doing sth** unter dem Vorwand, etw zu tun

guitar [gɪ'tɑːʳ] N Gitarre *f*

guitarist [gɪ'tɑːrɪst] N Gitarrist(in) *m(f)*

gulch [gʌlʃ] N (*US*) Schlucht *f*

gulf [gʌlf] N **(a)** (= *bay*) Golf *m*; **the Gulf of Mexico** der Golf von Mexiko; **the (Persian) Gulf** der (Persische) Golf **(b)** (*lit, fig*: = *chasm*) tiefe Kluft

Gulf: Gulf States PL **the ~** die Golfstaaten *pl*; **Gulf Stream** N Golfstrom *m*

gull [gʌl] N Möwe *f*

gullet ['gʌlɪt] N Speiseröhre *f*; **that really stuck in my ~** (*fig*) das ging mir sehr gegen den Strich (*inf*)

gullible ['gʌlɪbl] ADJ leichtgläubig

gully ['gʌlɪ] N (= *ravine*) Schlucht *f*; (= *narrow channel*) Rinne *f*

gulp [gʌlp] **1** N Schluck *m*; **at a ~, in one** ~ auf einen Schluck **2** VT (*also ~ down*) *drink* runterstürzen; *food* runterschlingen; **to ~ back one's tears** die Tränen hinunterschlucken **3** VI (= *try to swallow*) würgen; (= *eat fast*) schlingen; (= *drink fast*) hastig trinken; (*from emotion*) trocken schlucken

gum¹ [gʌm] N (*Anat*) Zahnfleisch *nt no pl*

gum² [gʌm] **1** N **(a)** Gummi *nt*; (= *glue*) Klebstoff *m* **(b)** (= *chewing ~*) Kaugummi *m*; (= *sweet*) Weingummi *m* **2** VT (= *stick together*) kleben; (= *spread ~ on*) gummieren
➤ **gum up** VT SEP **to gum up the works** (*inf*) alles verkleben; (*fig*) die Sache vermasseln (*inf*)

gummy ['gʌmɪ] ADJ (+ER) klebrig; *eyes* verklebt

gumption ['gʌmpʃən] N (*inf*) Grips *m* (*inf*); **to have the ~ to do sth** geistesgegenwärtig genug sein, etw zu tun

gum: gumshield N Zahnschutz *m*; **gumshoe** (*US*) **1** N **(a)** (= *overshoe*) Galosche *f*; (= *gym shoe*) Turnschuh *m* **(b)** (*sl*: = *detective*) Schnüffler(in) *m(f)* (*inf*) **2** VI (*sl*: = *move stealthily*) schleichen

gun [gʌn] **1** N **(a)** (= *cannon etc*) Kanone *f*; (= *rifle*) Gewehr *nt*; (= *pistol etc, spray ~*) Pistole *f*; **to carry a ~** (mit einer Schusswaffe) bewaffnet sein; **to draw a ~ on sb** jdn mit einer Schusswaffe bedrohen; **big ~** (*fig inf*) hohes *or* großes Tier (*inf*) (*in* in +*dat*); **to hold** *or* **put a ~ to sb's head** (*fig*) jdm die Pistole auf die Brust setzen; **to stick to one's ~s** nicht nachgeben; **to jump the ~** (*Sport*) Frühstart machen; (*fig*) voreilig sein *or* handeln; **to be going great ~s** (*Brit inf*) (*team, person*) toll in Schwung *or* Fahrt sein (*inf*); (*car*) wie geschmiert laufen (*inf*); (*business*) gut in Schuss sein (*inf*)
(b) (*esp US inf*: = *gunman*) Pistolenheld *m* (*inf*); **he's the fastest ~ in the West** (*inf*) er zieht am schnellsten im ganzen Westen (*inf*)
2 VT (= *kill: also ~ down*) *person* erschießen; *pilot, plane* abschießen
3 VI (*inf*) **to be ~ning for sb** (*fig*) jdn auf dem Kieker haben (*inf*); *for opponent* jdn auf die Abschussliste gesetzt haben

gunboat N Kanonenboot *nt*

In den USA ist **gun control**, *also die Frage, ob und wie der Schusswaffenverkauf kontrolliert werden soll, ein kontrovers diskutiertes Thema. Das Recht aller Bürger, eine Waffe zu tragen, ist in der US-Verfassung festgeschrieben. Dennoch ist man besorgt über eine alarmierend hohe Zahl von Unfällen mit Schusswaffen und über den weit verbreiteten illegalen Waffengebrauch sowie eine ständig steigende Zahl von Verletzten und Todesopfern. Durch eine strengere Gesetzgebung wurden daher Verkauf und Besitz von Schusswaffen eingeschränkt und viele Typen halbautomatischer Waffen wurden verboten.*

gun: gunfight N Schießerei *f*; **gunfighter** N Revolverheld *m*; **gunfire** N Schießerei *f*; (*Mil*) Geschützfeuer *nt*

gunge [gʌndʒ] N (*Brit inf*) klebriges *or* schmieriges Zeug (*inf*)

gung ho ['gʌŋ'həʊ] ADJ (*inf*) übereifrig

gunk [gʌŋk] N (*esp US inf*) = **gunge**

gunman ['gʌnmən] N (mit einer Schusswaffe) Bewaffnete(r) *m*; **they saw the ~** sie haben den Schützen gesehen

gunner ['gʌnəʳ] N (*Mil*) Artillerist *m*; (= *title*) Kanonier *m*; (*Naut*) Geschützführer *m*; (*in plane*) Bordschütze *m*

gun: gunpoint N **to hold sb at ~** jdn mit einer Schusswaffe bedrohen; **gunpowder** N Schießpulver *nt*; **gunrunner** N Waffenschmuggler(in) *or* -schieber(in) *m(f)*; **gunrunning** N Waffenschmuggel *m*; **gunshot** N Schuss *m*; **~ wound** Schusswunde *f*; **gunslinger** ['gʌnslɪŋəʳ] N (*inf*) Pistolenheld *m* (*inf*); **gunsmith** N Büchsenmacher(in) *m(f)*

guppy ['gʌpɪ] N Guppy *m*, Millionenfisch *m*

gurgle ['gɜːgl] **1** N (*of liquid*) Gluckern *nt no pl*; (*of baby*) Glucksen *nt no pl* **2** VI (*liquid*) gluckern; (*person*) glucksen (*with* vor +*dat*)

gurney ['gɜːnɪ] N (*US*) (Trag)bahre *f*

guru ['gʊruː] N (*lit, fig*) Guru *m*

gush [gʌʃ] **1** N (*of liquid*) Strahl *m*; (*of words*) Schwall *m*; (*of emotion, enthusiasm*) Ausbruch *m* **2** VI **(a)** (*also ~ out*) (*water*) herausschießen; (*blood, tears*) hervorquellen **(b)** (*inf*: = *talk*) schwärmen (*inf*) (*about, over* von); (*insincerely*) sich ergehen (*about, over* +*acc*)

gushing ['gʌʃɪŋ] ADJ **(a)** *water* (heraus)schießend **(b)** (*fig*) überschwänglich

gushingly ['gʌʃɪŋlɪ] ADV überschwänglich

gushy ['gʌʃɪ] ADJ (*pej inf*) schwärmerisch

gusset [ˈgʌsɪt] N Zwickel *m*

gust [gʌst] **1** N (*of wind*) Bö(e) *f*; (*of rain*) Böe *f*; **a ~ of cold/hot air** ein Schwall *m* kalte/heiße Luft; **~s of up to 100 km/h** Böen von bis zu 100 km/h **2** VI böig *or* stürmisch wehen

gusto [ˈgʌstəʊ] N Begeisterung *f*; **to do sth with ~** etw mit Genuss tun

gusty [ˈgʌstɪ] ADJ (+ER) böig, stürmisch

gut [gʌt] **1** N (a) (= *alimentary canal*) Darm *m*; (= *paunch*) Bauch *m*
(b) USU PL (*inf*: = *stomach*) Eingeweide *nt*; (*fig*) (*of problem, matter*) Kern *m*; (= *contents*) Substanz *f*; **to slog** *or* **work one's ~s out** (*inf*) wie blöd schuften (*inf*); **to hate sb's ~s** (*inf*) jdn auf den Tod nicht ausstehen können (*inf*); **~ reaction** rein gefühlsmäßige Reaktion; **my ~ feeling is that ...** rein gefühlsmäßig würde ich sagen, dass ...
(c) **guts** PL (*inf*: = *courage*) Mumm *m* (*inf*)
2 VT (a) *animal* ausnehmen
(b) (*fire*) ausbrennen; (= *remove contents*) ausräumen; **it was completely ~ted by the fire** es war völlig ausgebrannt; *see also* **gutted**

gutless [ˈgʌtlɪs] ADJ (*fig inf*) feige

gutsy [ˈgʌtsɪ] ADJ (*inf*) *person, action, effort* mutig; *performance, approach* kämpferisch

gutted [ˈgʌtɪd] ADJ (*esp Brit inf*) **I was ~** ich war total am Boden (*inf*); **he was ~ by the news** die Nachricht machte ihn völlig fertig (*inf*)

gutter [ˈgʌtə^r] **1** N (*on roof*) Dachrinne *f*; (*in street*) Gosse *f* (*also fig*); **the language of the ~** die Gassensprache **2** VI (*candle, flame*) flackern

guttering [ˈgʌtərɪŋ] **1** N Regenrinnen *pl* **2** ADJ flackernd

gutter press N (*Brit pej*) Boulevardpresse *f*

guttural [ˈgʌtərəl] **1** N Guttural(laut) *m*, Kehllaut *m* **2** ADJ *voice, accent* guttural, kehlig; (*Phon*) *sound* guttural

guy¹ [gaɪ] N (a) (*inf*) Typ *m* (*inf*), Kerl *m* (*inf*); **hey, you ~s** he Leute (*inf*); **great ~s** dufte Typen *pl* (*inf*); **I'll ask the ~ next door** ich werde (den Typ von) nebenan fragen (*inf*); **are you ~s ready?** seid ihr fertig? (b) (*Brit*) (= *effigy*) (Guy-Fawkes-)Puppe *f*; (*inf*: = *sight*) Schießbudenfigur *f* (*inf*)

guy² N (*also* **~-rope**) Halteseil *nt*; (*for tent*) Zeltschnur *f*

Guyana [gaɪˈænə] N Guayana *nt*

Guyanese [ˌgaɪəˈniːz] N Guayaner(in) *m(f)*

guzzle [ˈgʌzl] (*inf*) **1** VI (= *eat*) futtern (*inf*); (= *drink*) schlürfen **2** VT (= *eat*) futtern (*inf*); (= *drink*) schlürfen; *fuel* saufen (*inf*)

gym [dʒɪm] N (= *gymnasium*) Turnhalle *f*; (*for working out*) Fitnesscenter *nt*; (= *gymnastics*) Turnen *nt*

gymnasium [dʒɪmˈneɪzɪəm] N, *pl* **-s** *or* (*form*) **gymnasia** [dʒɪmˈneɪzɪə] Turnhalle *f*

Be careful! **gymnasium** *is not translated by the German word* **Gymnasium**.

gymnast [ˈdʒɪmnæst] N Turner(in) *m(f)*

gymnastic [dʒɪmˈnæstɪk] ADJ turnerisch; **~ exercises** Turnübungen

gymnastics [dʒɪmˈnæstɪks] N (a) SING (= *discipline*) Gymnastik *f*, no *pl*; (*with apparatus*) Turnen *nt*, no *pl* (b) PL (= *exercises*) Übungen *pl*

gym: gym shoe N (*Brit*) Turnschuh *m*; **gym teacher** N Turnlehrer(in) *m(f)*

gynaecological, (*US*) **gynecological** [ˌgaɪnɪkəˈlɒdʒɪkəl] ADJ gynäkologisch

gynaecologist, (*US*) **gynecologist** [ˌgaɪnɪˈkɒlədʒɪst] N Gynäkologe *m*, Gynäkologin *f*, Frauenarzt *m*/-ärztin *f*

gynaecology, (*US*) **gynecology** [ˌgaɪnɪˈkɒlədʒɪ] N Gynäkologie *f*, Frauenheilkunde *f*

gypsy [ˈdʒɪpsɪ] **1** N Zigeuner(in) *m(f)* **2** ADJ Zigeuner-; **~ woman** Zigeunerin *f*; **~ camp** Zigeunerlager *nt*

gyrate [dʒaɪəˈreɪt] VI (= *whirl*) (herum)wirbeln; (= *rotate*) sich drehen; (*dancer*) sich drehen und winden

gyration [dʒaɪəˈreɪʃən] N (*of dancer*) Drehung und Windung *f* usu *pl*

gyroscope [ˈdʒaɪərəˌskəʊp] N Gyroskop *nt*

Hh

H, h [eɪtʃ] N H *nt*, h *nt*

h ABBR *of* **hour(s)** h

haberdashery [ˌhæbəˈdæʃərɪ] N (*Brit*) Kurzwaren *pl*; (*US*) (= *articles*) Herrenbekleidung *f*; (= *shop*) Herrenmodengeschäft *nt*

habit [ˈhæbɪt] N (a) Gewohnheit *f*; (*esp undesirable*) (An)gewohnheit *f*; **to be in the ~ of doing sth** die Angewohnheit haben, etw zu tun; **... as was his ~** ... wie es seine Gewohnheit war; **it became a ~** es wurde zur Gewohnheit; **from (force of) ~** aus Gewohnheit; **I don't make a ~ of inviting strangers in** (für) gewöhnlich bitte ich Fremde nicht herein; **to get into/to get sb into the ~ of doing sth** sich/jdm angewöhnen, etw zu tun; **to get** *or* **fall into bad ~s** in schlechte Gewohnheiten verfallen; **to get out of/to get sb out of the ~ of doing sth** sich/jdm abgewöhnen, etw zu tun; **to have a ~ of doing sth** die Angewohnheit haben, etw zu tun
(b) (= *addiction*) Sucht *f*; **to have a cocaine ~** kokainsüchtig sein
(c) (= *costume*) Gewand *nt*; (*esp monk's*) Habit *nt or m*

habitable [ˈhæbɪtəbl] ADJ bewohnbar

habitat [ˈhæbɪtæt] N Heimat *f*

habitation [ˌhæbɪˈteɪʃən] N **unfit for human ~** menschenunwürdig

habitual [həˈbɪtjʊəl] ADJ (a) (= *customary*) gewohnt
(b) (= *regular*) gewohnheitsmäßig; *liar* notorisch; **~ criminal** Gewohnheitsverbrecher(in) *m(f)*; **~ drinker** Gewohnheitstrinker(in) *m(f)*

habitually [həˈbɪtjʊəlɪ] ADV ständig; (= *regularly*) regelmäßig

hack¹ [hæk] **1** VT (a) (= *cut*) hacken; **to ~ sb/sth to pieces** (*lit*) jdn/etw zerstückeln; (*fig*) jdn/etw zerfetzen; **to ~ one's way through (sth)** sich (*dat*) einen Weg (durch etw) schlagen
(b) (*Sport*) **to ~ sb on the shin** jdn vors *or* gegen das Schienbein treten (c) (*inf*: = *cope*) **to ~ it** es bringen (*sl*) **2** VI hacken (*also Comput*); **he ~ed (away) at the branch** er schlug auf den Ast; **to ~ into the system** in das System eindringen
► **hack off** VT SEP abhacken; **to hack sth off sth** etw von etw abhacken

hack² N (a) (= *hired horse*) Mietpferd *nt* (b) (*pej*: = *literary ~*) Schreiberling *m*; **the newspaper ~s** die Zeitungsschreiber *pl* (c) (*pej inf*) (**party**) ~ (Partei)heini *m* (*inf*) (d) (*US*: = *taxi*) Taxi *nt*

hacker [ˈhækəʳ] N (*Comput*) Hacker(in) *m(f)*

hackie [ˈhækɪ] N (*US inf*) Taxifahrer(in) *m(f)*

hacking [ˈhækɪŋ] **1** ADJ **~ cough** trockener Husten **2** N (*Comput*) Hacken *nt*

hackles [ˈhæklz] PL **to get sb's ~ up, to raise sb's ~** jdn auf die Palme bringen (*inf*)

hackneyed [ˈhæknɪd] ADJ (*Brit*) abgenutzt, abgedroschen (*inf*); *image* stereotyp; **~ idea** Klischee *nt*

hacksaw [ˈhæksɔː] N Metallsäge *f*

had [hæd] PRET, PTP *of* **have**

haddock [ˈhædək] N Schellfisch *m*

hadn't [ˈhædnt] CONTR *of* **had not**

haemoglobin, (*US*) **hemoglobin** [ˌhiːməʊˈgləʊbɪn] N Hämoglobin *nt*

haemophilia, (*US*) **hemophilia** [ˌhiːməʊˈfɪlɪə] N Bluterkrankheit *f*

haemophiliac, (*US*) **hemophiliac** [ˌhiːməʊˈfɪlɪæk] N Bluter *m*

haemorrhage, (*US*) **hemorrhage** [ˈhemərɪdʒ] **1** N Blutung *f*; (*fig*) Abwanderung *f* **2** VI bluten

haemorrhoids, (*US*) **hemorrhoids** [ˈhemərɔɪdz] PL Hämorr(ho)iden *pl*

hag [hæg] N Hexe *f*

haggard [ˈhægəd] ADJ ausgezehrt; (*from tiredness*) abgespannt; (*from worry*) abgehärmt

haggis [ˈhægɪs] N schottisches Gericht aus gehackten Schafsinnereien und Hafer im Schafsmagen

haggle [ˈhægl] VI feilschen (*about or over* um); (= *argue also*) sich (herum)streiten (*over* um *or* wegen)

haggling [ˈhæglɪŋ] N Gefeilsche *nt*

Hague [heɪg] N **the ~** Den Haag *nt*; **in the ~** in Den Haag

hail¹ [heɪl] **1** N Hagel *m*; **a ~ of stones** ein Steinhagel *m*; **a ~ of blows** ein Hagel von Schlägen; **in a ~ of bullets** im Kugel- *or* Geschosshagel **2** VI hageln

hail² **1** VT (a) **to ~ sb/sth as sth** jdn/etw als etw feiern
(b) (= *call loudly*) zurufen (+*dat*); *ship* anrufen; *taxi* (*by calling*) rufen; (*by making sign*) anhalten; **within ~ing distance** in Rufweite **2** VI **they ~ from all parts of the world** sie kommen aus allen Teilen der Welt **3** INTERJ **the Hail Mary** das Ave Maria

hail: **hailstone** N Hagelkorn *nt*; **hailstorm** N Hagel(schauer) *m*

hair [heəʳ] **1** N (a) (*collective*) Haare *pl*, Haar *nt*; (= *total body ~*) Behaarung *f*; **body ~** Körperbehaarung *f*; **to do one's ~** sich frisieren; **to have one's ~ cut/done** sich (*dat*) die Haare schneiden/frisieren lassen; **to let one's ~ down** (*fig*) aus sich (*dat*) herausgehen; **keep your ~ on!** (*Brit inf*) ruhig Blut!
(b) (= *single ~, of animal, plant*) Haar *nt*; **not a ~ on his head was harmed** (*fig*) ihm wurde kein Haar gekrümmt; **not a ~ out of place** (*fig*) wie aus dem Ei gepellt; **I'm allergic to cat ~** ich bin gegen Katzenhaare allergisch
2 ATTR Haar-; (= *horsehair*) Rosshaar-

hair: **hairband** N Haarband *nt*; **hairbrush** N Haarbürste *f*; **hair clip** N Clip *m*; (*for ponytail etc*) Haarspange *f*; **haircut** N Haarschnitt *m*; **to have** *or* **get a ~** sich (*dat*) die Haare schneiden lassen; **hairdo** N (*inf*) Frisur *f*; **hairdresser** N Friseur *m*, Friseuse *f*; **the ~'s** der Friseur; **hairdressing salon** N Friseursalon *m*; **hairdrier** N Haartrockner *m*; (*hand-held also*) Föhn *m*

hair: **hair gel** N (Haar)gel *nt*; **hairgrip** N (*Brit*) Haarklemme *f*; **hairline** N Haaransatz *m*; **hairline crack** N Haarriss *m*; **hairline fracture** N Haarriss *m*; **hairnet** N Haarnetz *nt*; **hairpiece** N Haarteil *m*; (*for men*) Toupet *nt*; **hairpin** N Haarnadel *f*; **hairpin (bend)** N Haarnadelkurve *f*; **hair-raising** ADJ haarsträubend; **hair remover** N Haarentferner *m*; **hair restorer** N Haarwuchsmittel *nt*; **hair's breadth** N Haaresbreite *f*; **by a ~** um Haaresbreite; **he was within a ~ of winning** er hätte um ein Haar gewonnen; **hair slide** N (*Brit*) Haarspange *f*; **hairsplitting** **1** N Haarspalterei *f* **2** ADJ haarspalterisch; **hairspray** N Haarspray *m or nt*; **hairstyle** N Frisur *f*; **hair stylist** N Coiffeur *m*, Coiffeuse *f*

hairy [ˈheərɪ] ADJ (+ER) (a) *person, body, plant, spider* behaart; *leg, chest, armpits, coat* haarig (b) (*inf*: = *scary, risky*) haarig (*inf*); *situation* brenzlig (*inf*); *adventure* riskant; *driving* rasant (*inf*)

Haiti [ˈheɪtɪ] N Haiti *nt*

hake [heɪk] N See- *or* Meerhecht *m*

halcyon [ˈhælsɪən] ADJ **~ days** glückliche Tage *pl*

hale [heɪl] ADJ (+ER) **~ and hearty** gesund und munter

half [hɑːf] **1** N, *pl* **halves** (a) Hälfte *f*; **the first ~ of the year** die erste Jahreshälfte; **to cut sth in ~** etw halbieren; *salary etc* um *or* auf die Hälfte kürzen; **to break/tear sth in ~** etw durchbrechen/durchreißen; **~ of it/them** die Hälfte davon/ von ihnen; **~ the book/money** die Hälfte des Buches/Geldes; **~ a million dollars** eine halbe Million Dollar; **he gave me ~** er gab mir die Hälfte; **~ a cup/an hour** eine halbe Tasse/Stunde; **he's not ~ the man he used to be** er ist längst nicht mehr da, was er einmal war; **to go halves (with sb on sth)** (mit jdm mit etw) halbe-halbe machen (*inf*); **that's only ~ the story** das ist nur die halbe Geschichte; **bigger by ~** anderthalbmal so groß; **to increase sth by ~** etw um die Hälfte vergrößern; **he is too clever by ~** (*Brit inf*) das ist ein richtiger Schlaumeier; **one and a ~** eineinhalb, anderthalb; **an hour and a ~** eineinhalb *or* anderthalb Stunden; **he's two and a ~** er ist zweieinhalb; **he doesn't do things by halves** er macht keine halben Sachen; **~ and ~** halb und halb; **that's not the ~ of it** (*inf*), **I haven't told you the ~ of it yet** (*inf*) und das ist noch nicht einmal die Hälfte (*inf*); **my better ~** (*hum*) *or* **other ~** meine bessere Hälfte
(b) (*Sport*: *of match*) Halbzeit *f*
(c) (= *travel, admission fee*) halbe Karte (*inf*); **return ~** (*Brit*) Abschnitt *m* für die Rückfahrt; **two and a ~ (to London)**

zweieinhalb(mal London)
(d) (= *beer*) kleines Bier, Halbe(s) *nt*
2 ADJ halb; **a ~ cup** eine halbe Tasse; **at** *or* **for ~ price** zum halben Preis; **~ man ~ beast** halb Mensch, halb Tier
3 ADV **(a)** halb; **I ~ thought ...** ich hätte fast gedacht ...; **the work is only ~ done** die Arbeit ist erst halb *or* zur Hälfte erledigt; **to be ~ asleep** (= *almost asleep*) schon fast schlafen; **~ laughing, ~ crying** halb lachend, halb weinend; **he only ~ understands** er begreift *or* versteht nur die Hälfte; **she's ~ German and ~ Russian** sie ist zur Hälfte Deutsche und zur Hälfte Russin; **it's ~ past three** *or* **~ three** es ist halb vier; **he is ~ as big as his sister** er ist halb so groß wie seine Schwester; **~ as big again** anderthalbmal so groß; **he earns ~ as much as you** er verdient halb so viel wie Sie; **give me ~ as much again** gib mir noch die Hälfte dazu
(b) (*Brit inf*) **he's not ~ stupid/rich** *etc* er ist vielleicht *or* unheimlich dumm/reich *etc*; **it didn't ~ rain** es HAT vielleicht geregnet; **not ~!** und wie!

half: **half-a-dozen** N halbes Dutzend; **half-baked** ADJ (*fig*) unausgegoren; **half bottle** N kleine Flasche; **a ~ of wine** eine kleine Flasche Wein; **half-brother** N Halbbruder *m*; **half-caste** N (*dated, pej*) Mischling *m*; **half-circle** N Halbkreis *m*; **half-cooked** ADJ halb gar; **half-day** N (= *holiday*) halber freier Tag; **we've got a ~** wir haben einen halben Tag frei; **half-dead** ADJ (*lit, fig*) halb tot (*with* vor +*dat*); **half-dollar** N halber Dollar; **half-dozen** N halbes Dutzend; **half-dressed** ADJ halb bekleidet; **half-empty** ADJ halb leer; **half-fare** **1** N halber Fahrpreis **2** ADV zum halben Preis; **half-fill** VT halb füllen; **half-full** ADJ halb voll; **half-hearted** ADJ halbherzig; *manner* lustlos; **he was rather ~ about accepting** er nahm ohne rechte Lust an; **half-heartedly** ADV halben Herzens; **to do sth ~** etw ohne rechte Überzeugung *or* Lust tun; **half holiday** N (*Brit*) halber Urlaubstag; (= *public holiday*) halber Feiertag; **we've got a ~ tomorrow morning** wir haben morgen Vormittag frei; **half-hour** N halbe Stunde; **half-an-hour's** *or* **a ~ interval** eine halbe Stunde Pause; **half-hourly** **1** ADV jede *or* alle halbe Stunde, halbstündlich **2** ADJ halbstündlich; **half-length** ADJ **~ portrait** Brustbild *nt*; **half-light** N Halbdunkel *nt*; **half-mast** N **at ~** (auf) halbmast; **half measure** N halbe Maßnahme, Stehenbleiben *nt no pl* auf halbem Weg; **half-moon** N Halbmond *m*; **half-note** N (*US Mus*) halbe Note; **half-open** **1** ADJ halb offen **2** VT halb öffnen *or* aufmachen; **half-pay** N halber Lohn; (*of salaried employee*) halbes Gehalt; **to be on ~** den halben Lohn/das halbe Gehalt bekommen; **half-pint** N ≈ Viertelliter *m or nt*; (*of beer*) kleines Bier; **half-price** ADJ, ADV zum halben Preis; **to be ~** die Hälfte kosten; **half-sister** N Halbschwester *f*; **half term** N (*Brit*) Ferien *pl* in der Mitte des Trimesters; **we have three days at ~** wir haben drei Tage Ferien in der Mitte des Trimesters; **half-time** **1** N (*Sport*) Halbzeit *f*; **at ~** bei *or* zur Halbzeit **2** ATTR Halbzeit-, zur Halbzeit; **~ whistle/score** Halbzeitpfiff *m*/-stand *m*; **half-truth** N Halbwahrheit *f*; **half volley** N (*Tennis*) Halbvolley *m*

halfway [ˈhɑːfˌweɪ] **1** ADJ ATTR *measures* halb; **at the ~ stage of the Tour de France** in der Mitte der Tour de France; **when we reached the ~ stage** *or* **point on our journey** als wir die Hälfte der Reise hinter uns (*dat*) hatten; **we're past the ~ stage** wir haben die Hälfte geschafft
2 ADV **~ to** auf halbem Weg nach; **we drove ~ to London** wir fuhren die halbe Strecke *or* den halben Weg nach London; **~ between two points** (in der Mitte *or* genau) zwischen zwei Punkten; **I live ~ up the hill** ich wohne auf halber Höhe des Berges; **~ through a book** halb durch ein Buch (durch); **she dropped out ~ through the race** nach der Hälfte des Rennens gab sie auf; **to go ~** (*lit*) die halbe Strecke zurücklegen; **to meet sb ~** (*lit, fig*) jdm (auf halbem Weg) entgegenkommen; **~ decent** halbwegs anständig

halfway house N (*fig*) Zwischending *nt*

half: **halfwit** N (*fig*) Schwachkopf *m*; **halfwitted** ADJ schwachsinnig; **half-year** N Halbjahr *nt*; **half-yearly** **1** ADJ halbjährlich **2** ADV halbjährlich, jedes halbe Jahr

halibut [ˈhælɪbət] N Heilbutt *m*

hall [hɔːl] N **(a)** (= *entrance* ~ *of house*) Diele *f*
(b) (= *large building*) Halle *f*; (= *large room*) Saal *m*; (*Brit: of college*) Speisesaal *m*; (= *dance* ~) Tanzdiele *f*; (= *village* ~) Gemeindehaus *nt*; (= *school assembly* ~) Aula *f*
(c) (= *mansion*) Herrenhaus *nt*; (*Brit: = students' residence: also* **~ of residence**) Studenten(wohn)heim *nt*; **to live** *or* **be in ~**

(*Brit*) im Wohnheim wohnen
(d) (*US: = corridor*) Korridor *m*, Gang *m*

hallelujah [ˌhælɪˈluːjə] **1** INTERJ halleluja **2** N Halleluja *nt*

hallmark [ˈhɔːlmɑːk] N **(a)** (Feingehalts)stempel *m* **(b)** (*fig*) Kennzeichen *nt* (*of* +*gen*, für); **this is the ~ of a true genius** daran erkennt man das wahre Genie

hallo [həˈləʊ] INTERJ, N = **hello**

hallowed [ˈhæləʊd] ADJ geheiligt; **on ~ ground** auf heiligem Boden

Halloween, Hallowe'en [ˌhæləʊˈiːn] N Halloween *nt*

hallucinate [həˈluːsɪneɪt] VI halluzinieren

hallucination [həˌluːsɪˈneɪʃən] N Halluzination *f*

hallucinatory [həˈluːsɪnətərɪ] ADJ *drug* Halluzinationen hervorrufend *attr*, halluzinogen (*spec*); *state, effect* halluzinatorisch

hallway [ˈhɔːlweɪ] N Flur *m*, Korridor *m*

halo [ˈheɪləʊ] N, *pl* **-(e)s** (*of saint, fig iro*) Heiligenschein *m*

halogen lamp N Halogenlampe *f*; (*Aut*) Halogenscheinwerfer *m*

halt [hɔːlt] **1** N Pause *f*, (*Mil*) Halt *m*; (*in production*) Stopp *m*; **to come to a ~** zum Stillstand kommen; **to bring sth to a ~** etw zum Stillstand bringen; **to call a ~ to sth** einer Sache (*dat*) ein Ende machen *or* bereiten; **the government called for a ~ to the fighting** die Regierung verlangte die Einstellung der Kämpfe
2 VI zum Stillstand kommen; (*person*) stehen bleiben; (*Mil*) Halt machen; **we ~ed briefly before attempting the summit** wir hielten kurz an, bevor wir den Gipfel in Angriff nahmen
3 VT zum Stillstand bringen; *fighting* einstellen; *arms race, war* beenden; *troops* Halt machen lassen
4 INTERJ halt; (*traffic sign*) stop

halterneck [ˈhɒltənek] ADJ rückenfrei mit Nackenverschluss

halting [ˈhɔːltɪŋ] ADJ *voice, efforts, answer* zögernd; *speech, progress* stockend; *German, verse* holprig

haltingly [ˈhɔːltɪŋlɪ] ADV zögernd; *speak, progress* stockend

halt sign N (*Aut*) Stoppschild *nt*

halve [hɑːv] VT **(a)** (= *separate in two*) halbieren **(b)** (= *reduce by one half*) auf die Hälfte reduzieren

halves [hɑːvz] PL *of* **half**

ham [hæm] **1** N **(a)** (*Cook*) Schinken *m*; **~ sandwich** Schinkenbrot *nt* **(b)** (*Theat*) Schmierenkomödiant(in) *m(f)*
2 ADJ ATTR *acting* übertrieben; **~ actor** Schmierenkomödiant(in) *m(f)*
▸ **ham up** VT SEP (*inf*) **to ham it up** zu dick auftragen

hamburger [ˈhæmˌbɜːgəʳ] N Hamburger *m*

ham-fisted [ˈhæmˈfɪstɪd] ADJ ungeschickt

hammer [ˈhæməʳ] **1** N (*generally*) Hammer *m*; (*of gun*) Hahn *m*; **to go at it ~ and tongs** (*inf*) sich ins Zeug legen (*inf*); (= *quarrel*) sich in die Wolle kriegen (*inf*); (= *have sex*) es miteinander machen (*inf*); **to go/come under the ~** (*at auction*) unter den Hammer kommen; **in the ~** (*Sport*) im Hammerwurf
2 VT **(a)** *nail, metal* hämmern; **to ~ a nail into a wall** einen Nagel in die Wand schlagen; **to ~ sth into shape** *metal* etw zurechthämmern; (*fig*) *agreement* etw ausarbeiten; **to ~ sth into sb** *or* **into sb's head** (*inf*) jdm etw einbläuen (*inf*)
(b) (*inf*: = *defeat badly*) eine Schlappe beibringen +*dat* (*inf*)
(c) (*inf*: = *criticize*) kritisieren
(d) (*inf*: = *harm*) **small businesses have been ~ed by the recession** kleine Firmen sind von der Rezession schwer in Mitleidenschaft gezogen worden
3 VI hämmern; **to ~ on the door** an die Tür hämmern

➤ **hammer home** VT SEP Nachdruck verleihen (+*dat*); **he tried to hammer it home to the pupils that ...** er versuchte, den Schülern einzubläuen *or* einzuhämmern, dass...

➤ **hammer out** VT SEP (*fig*) *plan, agreement, solution* ausarbeiten; *difficulties* beseitigen; *tune* hämmern

hammering [ˈhæmərɪŋ] N (*esp Brit*) **(a)** (*inf.* = *defeat*) Schlappe *f* (*inf*); **our team took a ~** unsere Mannschaft musste eine Schlappe einstecken (*inf*) **(b)** (*inf.* = *criticism*) scharfe Kritik; **doctors took a terrible ~ in the report** die Ärzteschaft wurden in dem Bericht scharf unter Beschuss genommen (*inf*)

hammock [ˈhæmək] N Hängematte *f*

hamper¹ [ˈhæmpəʳ] N (*esp Brit*) (= *basket*) Korb *m*; (*as present*) Geschenkkorb *m*

hamper² VT behindern; **to be ~ed (by sth)** (durch etw) gehandikapt sein; **the police were ~ed in their search by the shortage of clues** der Mangel an Hinweisen erschwerte der Polizei die Suche

hamster [ˈhæmstəʳ] N Hamster *m*

hamstring [ˈhæmstrɪŋ], *vb: pret, ptp* **hamstrung** [ˈhæmstrʌŋ] **1** N (*Anat*) Kniesehne *f* **2** VT (*fig*) **to be hamstrung** aufgeschmissen sein (*inf*); (*project*) lahm gelegt sein

---

hand [hænd]

1 NOUN	**3** PHRASAL VERBS
2 TRANSITIVE VERB	

1 NOUN
(a) Hand *f*; (*of clock*) Zeiger *m*; **on (one's) hands and knees** auf allen vieren; **to take/lead sb by the hand** jdn an die *or* bei der Hand nehmen/an der Hand führen; **hand in hand** Hand in Hand; **to go hand in hand with sth** mit etw einhergehen *or* Hand in Hand gehen; **hands up!** Hände hoch!; **hands up who knows the answer** Hand hoch, wer es weiß; **hands off!** (*inf*) Hände weg!; **keep your hands off my wife** lass die Finger *or* Pfoten (*inf*) von meiner Frau!; **done** *or* **made by hand** handgearbeitet; **to deliver a letter by hand** einen Brief persönlich überbringen; **to live (from) hand to mouth** von der Hand in den Mund leben; **with a heavy/firm hand** (*fig*) mit harter/fester Hand; **to get one's hands dirty** (*fig*) sich (*dat*) die Hände schmutzig machen; **to give with one hand and take away with the other** mit einer Hand geben, mit der anderen nehmen; **it's a case of the right hand not knowing what the left hand's doing** das ist so ein Fall, wo die rechte Hand nicht weiß, was die linke tut; **we're forced to do it with one hand** *or* **both hands** *or* **our hands tied behind our back** (*fig*) wir sind gezwungen, es zu tun, während uns die Hände gebunden sind
(b) (= *side*) Seite *f*; **on the right hand** auf der rechten Seite; **on my right hand** rechts von mir; **on the one hand ... on the other hand ...** einerseits ..., andererseits ...
(c) (= *agency, possession*) **your future is in your own hands** Sie haben Ihre Zukunft (selbst) in der Hand; **he put the matter in the hands of his lawyer** er übergab die Sache seinem Anwalt; **to put oneself in(to) sb's hands** sich jdm anvertrauen; **to fall into the hands of sb** jdm in die Hände fallen; **to fall into the wrong hands** in die falschen Hände geraten; **to be in good hands** in guten Händen sein; **to change hands** den Besitzer wechseln; **he suffered terribly at the hands of the enemy** er machte in den Händen des Feindes Schreckliches durch; **he has too much time on his hands** er hat zu viel Zeit zur Verfügung; **he has a problem/five children on his hands** er hat ein Problem/fünf Kinder am Hals (*inf*); **she read everything she could get her hands on** sie las alles, was sie in die Finger bekommen konnte; **just wait till I get my hands on him!** warte nur, bis ich ihn zwischen die Finger kriege! (*inf*); **to take sb/sth off sb's hands** jdm jdn/etw abnehmen
(d) (= *applause*) **they gave him a big hand** sie gaben ihm großen Applaus; **let's give our guest a big hand** und nun großen Beifall für unseren Gast
(e) (= *worker*) Arbeiter(in) *m(f)*; **all hands on deck!** alle Mann an Deck!
(f) (= *expert*) **to be an old hand (at sth)** ein alter Hase (in etw *dat*) sein
(g) (= *handwriting*) Handschrift *f*

(h) (*of horse*) ≈ 10 cm
(i) (*Cards*) Blatt *nt*; (= *person*) Mann *m*; (= *game*) Runde *f*; **a hand of bridge** eine Runde Bridge; **to show one's hand** seine Karten aufdecken; (*fig*) sich (*dat*) in die Karten sehen lassen
(j) (*other phrases*) **to ask for a lady's hand (in marriage)** um die Hand einer Dame anhalten; **to have one's hands full with sb/sth** mit jdm/etw alle Hände voll zu tun haben; **to wait on sb hand and foot** jdn von vorne und hinten bedienen; **to have a hand in sth** *in decision* an etw (*dat*) beteiligt sein; *in crime* die Hand bei etw im Spiel haben; **I had no hand in it** ich hatte damit nichts zu tun; **to keep one's hand in** in Übung bleiben; **to lend** *or* **give sb a hand** jdm behilflich sein; **give me a hand!** hilf mir mal!; **to force sb's hand** jdn zwingen; **to be hand in glove with sb** mit jdm unter einer Decke stecken; **to win hands down** mühelos *or* spielend gewinnen; **to have the upper hand** die Oberhand behalten; **to get** *or* **gain the upper hand (of sb)** (über jdn) die Oberhand gewinnen

✦**at + hand to keep sth at hand** etw in Reichweite haben; **according to the information at hand** gemäß *or* laut der vorliegenden Informationen; **at first/second hand** aus erster/zweiter Hand

✦**in + hand he had the situation well in hand** er hatte die Situation im Griff; **to take sb in hand** (= *discipline*) jdn in die Hand nehmen; (= *look after*) jdn in Obhut nehmen; **stock in hand** (*Comm*) Warenlager *nt*; **he still had £600/a couple of hours in hand** er hatte £ 600 übrig/noch zwei Stunden Zeit; **the matter in hand** die vorliegende *or* (*in discussion*) die zur Debatte stehende Angelegenheit; **we still have a game in hand** wir haben noch ein Spiel ausstehen

✦**on + hand there were no experts on hand** es standen keine Experten zur Verfügung

✦**out + hand to eat out of sb's hand** (*lit, fig*) jdm aus der Hand fressen; **things got out of hand** die Dinge sind außer Kontrolle geraten; **I dismissed the idea out of hand** ich verwarf die Idee sofort

✦**to + hand I don't have the letter to hand** ich habe den Brief gerade nicht zur Hand; **we have little information to hand** wir haben kaum Informationen *pl* (zur Verfügung)

2 TRANSITIVE VERB reichen, geben (*sth to sb, sb sth* jdm etw); **you've got to hand it to him** (*fig inf*) das muss man ihm lassen (*inf*)

3 PHRASAL VERBS
➤ **hand (a)round** VT SEP herumreichen; (= *distribute*) *papers* austeilen
➤ **hand back** VT SEP zurückgeben
➤ **hand down** VT SEP **(a)** (*fig*) weitergeben; *tradition, belief* überliefern; *heirloom etc* vererben (*to* +*dat*); **the farm's been handed down from generation to generation** der Hof ist durch die Generationen weitervererbt worden **(b)** (*Jur*) *sentence* fällen
➤ **hand in** VT SEP abgeben; *forms, thesis also, resignation* einreichen
➤ **hand on** VT SEP weitergeben (*to an* +*acc*)
➤ **hand out** VT SEP austeilen, verteilen (*to sb* an jdn); *advice* erteilen (*to sb* jdm); *heavy sentence* verhängen
➤ **hand over** **1** VT SEP (= *pass over*) (herüber)reichen (*to dat*); (= *hand on*) weitergeben (*to an* +*acc*); (= *give up*) (her)geben (*to dat*); *criminal, prisoner* übergeben (*to dat*); (*from one state to another*) ausliefern; *leadership, authority, powers* abgeben (*to* an +*acc*); *the controls, property, business* übergeben (*to dat*, an +*acc*); **I now hand you over to our political correspondent** ich übergebe nun an unseren (politischen) Korrespondenten **2** VI **when the Conservatives handed over to Labour** als die Konservativen die Regierung an Labour abgaben

---

hand: **handbag** N Handtasche *f*; **hand baggage** N Handgepäck *nt*; **handball** N **(a)** (= *game*) Handball *m* **(b)** (*Ftbl*: = *foul*) Handspiel *nt* **2** INTERJ (*Ftbl*) Hand; **hand basin** N Handwaschbecken *nt*; **handbill** N Handzettel *m*; **handbook** N Handbuch *nt*; (*tourist's*) Reiseführer *m*; **handbrake** N (*esp Brit*) Handbremse *f*

h & c ABBR *of* **hot and cold (water)** k.u.w., kalt und warm

hand: **handclasp** N (*US*) Händedruck *m*; **handcuff** VT Handschellen anlegen (+*dat*); **the accused was ~ed to a police officer** der Angeklagte war (mit Handschellen) an einen Polizisten gefesselt; **handcuffs** PL Handschellen *pl*; **handdrier** N Händetrockner *m*

handful ['hændfʊl] N **(a)** Hand *f* voll; (*of hair, fur*) Büschel *nt*; **a ~ of soil** eine Hand voll Erde **(b)** (*fig*) **those children are a ~** die Kinder können einen ganz schön in Trab halten

hand: hand grenade N Handgranate *f*; **handgun** N Handfeuerwaffe *f*; **hand-held** ADJ im Taschenformat; *computer* Handheld-; **taken with a ~ camera** aus der (freien) Hand aufgenommen

handicap ['hændɪkæp] **1** N **(a)** (*Sport*) Handicap *nt*; (= *race*) Handikaprennen *nt* **(b)** (= *disadvantage*) Handikap *nt*; (*physical, mental*) Behinderung *f* **2** VT ein Handikap *nt* darstellen für; (*fig*) *person* benachteiligen; **to be (physically/ mentally) ~ped** (körperlich/geistig) behindert sein; **~ped children** behinderte Kinder *pl*

handicraft ['hændɪkrɑːft] N (= *work*) Kunsthandwerk *nt*; (= *needlework etc*) Handarbeit *f*; (= *woodwork, modelling etc*) Werken *nt*; **~s** (= *products*) Kunstgewerbe *nt*

handily ['hændɪlɪ] ADV **(a)** *situated* günstig **(b)** (*US*: = *easily*) mit Leichtigkeit

handiwork ['hændɪwɜːk] N, NO PL **(a)** (*lit*) Arbeit *f*; (= *needlework etc*) Handarbeit *f*; **examples of the children's ~** Werkarbeiten/ Handarbeiten *pl* der Kinder **(b)** (*fig*) Werk *nt*; (*pej*) Machwerk *nt*

handkerchief ['hæŋkətʃɪf] N Taschentuch *nt*

hand-knitted ['hænd,nɪtɪd] ADJ handgestrickt

handle ['hændl] **1** N Griff *m*; (*of door*) Klinke *f*; (*esp of broom, saucepan*) Stiel *m*; (*esp of basket, bucket, cup, jug etc*) Henkel *m*; **to fly off the ~** (*inf*) an die Decke gehen (*inf*); **to have/get a ~ on sth** (*inf*) etw im Griff haben/in den Griff bekommen **2** VT **(a)** (= *touch*) anfassen, berühren; (*Ftbl*) *ball* mit der Hand berühren; **be careful how you ~ that** gehen Sie vorsichtig damit um; **"~ with care"** „Vorsicht - zerbrechlich" **(b)** (= *deal with*) umgehen mit; *economy* handhaben; *legal or financial matters* erledigen; *legal case* bearbeiten; *applicant, matter, problem* sich befassen mit; (= *tackle*) *problem, interview etc* anpacken; (= *succeed in coping with*) *child, drunk, problem, emergency* fertig werden mit; (= *resolve*) *matter* erledigen; *vehicle, plane, ship* steuern; **how would you ~ the situation?** wie würden Sie sich in der Situation verhalten?; **I can't ~ pressure** ich komme unter Druck nicht zurecht; **you keep quiet, I'll ~ this** sei still, lass mich mal machen; **who's handling the publicity for this?** wer macht die Öffentlichkeitsarbeit dafür? **(c)** (*Comm*) *types of goods, items* handeln mit *or* in (+*dat*); *orders* bearbeiten; *shares, securities* handeln; *financial affairs* besorgen; **airport workers refused to ~ goods for Uganda** die Flughafenarbeiter weigerten sich, Waren nach Uganda abzufertigen **3** VI (*ship, plane*) sich steuern lassen; (*car, motorbike*) sich fahren *or* lenken lassen

handlebar(s) ['hændlbɑː', -bɑːz] N(PL) Lenkstange *f*

handler ['hændlə'] N (= *dog-~*) Hundeführer(in) *m(f)*; **baggage ~** Gepäckmann *m*

handling ['hændlɪŋ] N Umgang *m* (*of* mit); (*of matter, problem*) Behandlung *f* (*of* +*gen*); (*of legal or financial matters*) Erledigung *f*; (= *official ~ of matters, of legal case*) Bearbeitung *f*; **her adroit ~ of the economy** ihre geschickte Handhabung der Wirtschaft; **his ~ of the matter/situation** die Art, wie er die Angelegenheit/die Situation angefasst hat; **his successful ~ of the crisis** seine Bewältigung der Krise; **toxic waste requires very careful ~** mit Giftmüll muss sehr vorsichtig umgegangen werden

handling charge N Bearbeitungsgebühr *f*; (*in warehouse*) Umladekosten *pl*; (*in banking*) Kontoführungsgebühren *pl*

hand: hand lotion N Handlotion *f*; **hand luggage** N (*Brit*) Handgepäck *nt*; **handmade** ADJ handgearbeitet; **this is ~** das ist Handarbeit; **hand-me-down** (*inf*) **1** N abgelegtes Kleidungsstück **2** ADJ *clothes* abgelegt; **hand mirror** N Handspiegel *m*; **hand-out** N (= *money*) (Geld)zuwendung *f*; (= *food*) Essensspende *f*; (= *leaflet*) Flugblatt *nt*; (*with several pages*) Broschüre *f*; (*in school*) Arbeitsblatt *nt*; (= *publicity ~*) Reklamezettel *m*; **handover** N (*Pol*) Übergabe *f*; **~ of power** Machtübergabe *f*; **hand-picked** ADJ (*fig*) sorgfältig ausgewählt, handverlesen (*hum*); **hand puppet** N (*US*) Handpuppe *f*; **handrail** N (*of stairs etc*) Geländer *nt*; (*of ship*) Reling *f*; (*for bath etc*) Haltegriff *m*; **handset** N (*Telec*) Hörer *m*

hands-free ['hændz'friː] ADJ *telephone, microphone* Freisprech-; **~ kit** Freisprechset *nt or* -anlage *f*

handshake ['hændʃeɪk] N Händedruck *m*

hands-off ['hændz'ɒf] ADJ passiv; **a ~ manager** ein Geschäftsführer, der die Zügel gern locker lässt

handsome ['hænsəm] ADJ **(a)** (= *good-looking*) gut aussehend; (= *well-built*) stattlich; *face, features* attraktiv; *animal, building, place, furniture* schön; (= *elegant*) elegant; (= *imposing*) imposant; **he is ~/has a ~ face** er sieht gut aus **(b)** *profit, increase, salary* ansehnlich; *reward* großzügig; *sum* stattlich; *win, victory* deutlich

handsomely ['hænsəmlɪ] ADV **(a)** (= *attractively*) schön **(b)** *pay* großzügig; *reward, profit* reichlich; *win* überlegen

hands-on ['hændz'ɒn] ADJ aktiv, engagiert; **a ~ manager** ein Geschäftsführer, der die Zügel fest in die Hand nimmt

hand: handstand N Handstand *m*; **hand-to-hand** **1** ADV im Nahkampf **2** ADJ **~ fight/fighting** Nahkampf *m*; **hand-to-mouth** ADJ kümmerlich; **hand towel** N Händehandtuch *nt*; **handwriting** N Handschrift *f*; **handwritten** ADJ handgeschrieben

handy ['hændɪ] ADJ (+ER) **(a)** *tool, device* praktisch; *hint, tip* nützlich; *car, size* handlich; **to come in ~** sich als nützlich erweisen; **the salary increase comes in ~** die Gehaltserhöhung kommt sehr gelegen; **my experience as a teacher comes in ~** meine Lehrerfahrung kommt mir zugute **(b)** (= *skilful*) geschickt; **to be ~ with a tool** mit einem Werkzeug gut umgehen können **(c)** (= *conveniently close*) in der Nähe; **the house is (very) ~ for the shops** das Haus liegt (ganz) in der Nähe der Geschäfte; **to keep** *or* **have sth ~** etw griffbereit *or* zur Hand haben

handyman ['hændɪmæn] N, *pl* **-men** [-mən] Heimwerker *m*; (*as job*) Hilfskraft *f*

hang [hæŋ], *vb: pret, ptp* **hung** **1** VT **(a)** hängen; *painting, curtains, decorations, clothes* aufhängen; *door, gate* einhängen; **to ~ wallpaper** tapezieren; **to ~ sth from sth** etw an etw (*dat*) aufhängen; **the rooms of the castle were hung with priceless pictures** kostbare Gemälde hingen in den Räumen des Schlosses; **they hung the windows/streets with bunting** sie schmückten die Fenster/Straßen mit Fahnen; **to ~ one's head** den Kopf hängen lassen **(b)** *pret, ptp* **hanged** *criminal* hängen; **to ~ oneself** sich erhängen *or* aufhängen (*inf*) **(c)** (*inf*) **~ the cost!** ist doch piepegal, was es kostet (*inf*) **2** VI **(a)** (*curtains, painting*) hängen (*on an* +*dat*, *from* von); (*drapery, clothes, hair*) fallen; (*inelegantly*) (herunter)hängen **(b)** (*gloom, fog etc*) hängen (*over* über +*dat*); **the question was left ~ing in the air** die Frage blieb im Raum stehen; **time ~s heavy on my hands** die Zeit wird mir sehr lang **(c)** (*criminal*) gehängt werden; **to be sentenced to ~** zum Tod durch Erhängen verurteilt werden **3** N, NO PL (*inf*) **to get the ~ of sth** den (richtigen) Dreh bei etw herauskriegen (*inf*); **to get the ~ of doing sth** den Dreh herausbekommen, wie man etw macht (*inf*)

▶ **hang about** (*Brit*) *or* **around** **1** VI (*inf*) warten; (= *loiter*) sich herumtreiben (*inf*); **to keep sb hanging around** jdn warten lassen; **to hang around with sb** sich mit jdm herumtreiben (*inf*); **hang about, I'm just coming** wart mal, ich komm ja schon; (*inf*) **he doesn't hang around** (= *move quickly*) er ist einer von der schnellen Truppe (*inf*) **2** VI +PREP OBJ **to hang around a place** sich an einem Ort herumtreiben (*inf*)

▶ **hang back** VI (*lit*) sich zurückhalten; (*fig*: = *hesitate*) zögern

▶ **hang down** VI herunterhängen

▶ **hang in** VI (*inf*) **just hang in there!** bleib am Ball (*inf*)

▶ **hang on** **1** VI **(a)** (= *hold*) sich festhalten (*to sth* an etw *dat*) **(b)** (= *hold out*) durchhalten; (*Telec*) am Apparat bleiben; (*inf*: = *wait*) warten; **hang on (a minute)** einen Augenblick (mal) **2** VI +PREP OBJ **(a)** **he hangs on her every word** er hängt an ihren Lippen **(b)** (= *depend on*) **everything hangs on his decision/getting the cash** alles hängt von seiner Entscheidung ab/davon ab, ob man das Geld bekommt

▶ **hang on to** VI +PREP OBJ **(a)** (*lit*: = *hold on to*) festhalten; (*fig*) *hope* sich klammern an (+*acc*) **(b)** (= *keep*) behalten; **to hang on to power** sich an die Macht klammern

▶ **hang out** **1** VI **(a)** (*tongue, shirt tails etc*) heraushängen **(b)** (*inf*) sich aufhalten; (= *live*) hausen; (= *usually be found also*) sich herumtreiben (*inf*) **2** VT SEP hinaushängen

➤ **hang together** VI (*argument, ideas*) folgerichtig *or* zusammenhängend sein; (*alibi*) keinen Widerspruch enthalten; (*story, report etc*) zusammenhängen

➤ **hang up** ◧ VI (*Telec*) auflegen; **he hung up on me** er legte einfach auf ◨ VT SEP *hat, picture* aufhängen; *telephone receiver* auflegen

➤ **hang upon** VI +PREP OBJ = **hang on** 2

hangar ['hæŋə'] N Hangar *m*

hanger ['hæŋə'] N (*for clothes*) (Kleider)bügel *m*; (= *loop on garment*) Aufhänger *m*

hanger-on [hæŋər'ɒn] N, *pl* **hangers-on** Satellit *m*

hang: **hang-glide** VI Drachen fliegen; **hang-glider** N (= *device*) Drachen *m*; **hang-gliding** N Drachenfliegen *nt*

hanging ['hæŋɪŋ] N **(a)** (*of criminal*: = *event*) Hinrichtung *f* (durch den Strang); **to bring back ~** die Todesstrafe wieder einführen **(b) hangings** PL (= *curtains etc*) Vorhänge *pl*; (*on wall*) Tapete *f*; (= *tapestry*) Wandbehang *m* or -behänge *pl*

hanging basket N Blumen- *or* Hängeampel *f*

hang: **hangman** N Henker *m*; (= *game*) Galgen *m*; **hang-out** N (*inf*) (= *pub, café etc*) Stammlokal *nt*; (*of group*) Treff *m* (*inf*); **hangover** N **(a)** Kater *m* (*inf*) **(b)** (= *sth left over*) Überbleibsel *nt*; **hang-up** N (*inf*) Komplex *m* (*about* wegen); (= *obsession*) Fimmel *m* (*inf*); **he has a ~ about people smoking** er stellt sich furchtbar an, wenn Leute rauchen (*inf*)

hanker ['hæŋkə'] VI sich sehnen (*for or after sth* nach etw)

hankering ['hæŋkərɪŋ] N Sehnsucht *f*; **to have a ~ for sth** Sehnsucht nach etw haben

hankie, hanky ['hæŋkɪ] N (*inf*) Taschentuch *nt*

hanky-panky ['hæŋkɪ'pæŋkɪ] N (*inf*) **(a)** (*esp US* = *dishonest dealings*) Mauscheleien *pl* (*inf*); **there's some ~ going on** hier ist was faul (*inf*) **(b)** (*esp Brit*: = *intimate behaviour*) Gefummel *nt* (*inf*)

haphazard [hæp'hæzəd] ADJ willkürlich; **in a ~ way** *or* **fashion** planlos, wahllos

haphazardly [hæp'hæzədlɪ] ADV (ganz) willkürlich

happen ['hæpən] VI **(a)** (= *occur*) geschehen; (*special or important event*) sich ereignen; (*esp unexpected, unintentional or unpleasant event*) passieren; **it ~ed like this ...** es geschah *or* war so ...; **what's ~ing?** was ist los?; **it just ~ed** es ist (ganz) von allein passiert *or* gekommen; **as if nothing had ~ed** als ob nichts geschehen *or* gewesen wäre; **don't let it ~ again** dass das nicht noch mal passiert!; **what has ~ed to him?** was ist ihm passiert?; (= *what have they done to him*) was ist mit ihm passiert?; (= *what's wrong with him*) was ist mit ihm los?; (= *what has become of him*) was ist aus ihm geworden?; **if anything should ~ to me** wenn mir etwas zustoßen *or* passieren sollte; **it all ~ed so quickly** es ging alles so schnell **(b)** (= *chance*) **to ~ to do sth** zufällig(erweise) etw tun; **do you ~ to know whether ...?** wissen Sie vielleicht *or* zufällig, ob ...?; **I picked up the nearest paper, which ~ed to be the Daily Mail** ich nahm die erstbeste Zeitung zur Hand, es war zufällig die Daily Mail; **it so ~s** *or* **as it ~s I (don't) like that kind of thing** so etwas mag ich nun einmal (nicht); **as it ~s I've been there too** zufällig(erweise) bin ich auch dort gewesen

happening ['hæpnɪŋ] N Ereignis *nt*; (*not planned*) Vorfall *m*; **there have been some strange ~s in that house** in dem Haus sind sonderbare Dinge vorgegangen

happily ['hæpɪlɪ] ADV **(a)** glücklich; *say, play* vergnügt; **it all ended ~** es ging alles gut aus; **they lived ~ ever after** (*in fairy tales*) und wenn sie nicht gestorben sind, dann leben sie noch heute **(b)** (= *harmoniously*) *live together, combine* harmonisch **(c)** (= *gladly*) gern; **I would ~ have lent her the money** ich hätte ihr das Geld ohne weiteres geliehen **(d)** (= *fortunately*) glücklicherweise, zum Glück; **~ for him, he can afford it** zu seinem Glück kann er es sich leisten

happiness ['hæpɪnɪs] N Glück *nt*; (= *feeling of contentment*) Zufriedenheit *f*; (= *cheerfulness*) Fröhlichkeit *f*

happy ['hæpɪ] ADJ (+ER) **(a)** glücklich; *atmosphere* harmonisch; **the ~ couple** (= *newlyweds*) das Brautpaar; **a ~ ending** ein Happy End *nt*; **~ birthday (to you)** herzlichen Glückwunsch zum Geburtstag; **Happy Easter/Christmas** frohe Ostern/Weihnachten **(b)** (= *content, satisfied*) **(not) to be ~ about** *or* **with sth** mit etw (nicht) zufrieden sein; **to be ~ to do sth** (= *willing*) etw gern tun; (= *pleased*) sich freuen, etw zu tun; (= *relieved*) froh sein,

etw zu tun; **I was ~ to hear that you passed your exam** es hat mich gefreut zu hören, dass du die Prüfung bestanden hast

happy: **happy event** N (*inf*) frohes *or* freudiges Ereignis; **happy-go-lucky** ADJ unbekümmert, sorglos; **happy hour** N (*in pubs etc*) Zeit, in der Getränke zu ermäßigten Preisen angeboten werden

harangue [hə'ræŋ] ◧ N (Straf)predigt *f* ◨ VT eine (Straf)predigt halten (+*dat*)

harass ['hærəs] VT belästigen; (= *mess around*) schikanieren; **don't ~ me** dräng *or* hetz (*inf*) mich doch nicht so!; **he sexually ~ed her** er belästigte sie (sexuell); **they eventually ~ed him into resigning** sie setzten ihm so lange zu, bis er schließlich zurücktrat

harassed ['hærəst] ADJ abgespannt, mitgenommen; (= *worried*) von Sorgen gequält; **a ~ father** ein (viel) geplagter Vater

harassment ['hærəsmənt] N (= *act*) Belästigung *f*; (= *messing around*) Schikanierung *f*; (= *state*) Bedrängnis *f*; **police ~** Schikane *f* von Seiten der Polizei; **racial ~** rassistisch motivierte Schikanierung; **sexual ~** sexuelle Belästigung

harbour, (*US*) **harbor** ['hɑ:bə'] ◧ N Hafen *m* ◨ VT **(a)** *criminal etc* Unterschlupf gewähren (+*dat*) **(b)** *suspicions, doubts, resentment* hegen; *ambitions, feelings* haben; *regrets* empfinden

harbour master N Hafenmeister(in) *m(f)*

hard [hɑ:d] ◧ ADJ (+ER) **(a)** hart; *work, day* hart, anstrengend; *winter, frost* streng; **as ~ as rocks** *or* **iron** steinhart; **he leaves all the ~ work to me** die ganze Schwerarbeit überlässt er mir; **to be a ~ worker** sehr fleißig sein; **it was ~ going** man kam nur mühsam voran; **this novel is ~ going** durch diesen Roman muss man sich mühsam durchbeißen; **to be ~ on sb** (= *cause strain or wear*) jdn strapazieren; (*person*) hart zu *or* streng mit jdm sein; **to be ~ on sth** (= *cause strain or wear*) etw strapazieren; (*person*) etw kritisieren; **to have a ~ time** es schwer *or* nicht leicht haben; **I had a ~ time finding a job** ich hatte Schwierigkeiten, eine Stelle zu finden; **to give sb a ~ time** jdm das Leben schwer machen; **there are no ~ feelings between them** sie sind einander nicht böse; **no ~ feelings?** nimm es mir nicht übel; **to be as ~ as nails** knallhart sein (*inf*)
(b) (= *difficult*) schwer, schwierig; **this is ~ to do, it is ~ to do** es ist schwer, das zu tun; **stories that are ~ to understand** Geschichten, die schwer verständlich sind; **that is a very ~ question to answer** diese Frage lässt sich nur schwer beantworten; **she is ~ to please** man kann ihr kaum etwas recht machen; **it's ~ to tell** es ist schwer zu sagen; **I find it ~ to believe** ich kann es kaum glauben; **she found it ~ to make friends** sie fiel ihr schwer, Freunde zu finden; **to play ~ to get** so tun, als sei man nicht interessiert
(c) *tug, kick* kräftig; *blow, punch* heftig; **to give sb/sth a ~ push** jdm/etw einen harten Stoß versetzen; **to give sth a ~ pull** *or* **tug** kräftig an etw (*dat*) ziehen; **it was a ~ blow** *or* **knock (for** *or* **to them)** (*fig*) es war ein schwerer Schlag (für sie)
(d) *facts, information* gesichert; **~ evidence** sichere Beweise *pl* ◨ ADV *work* hart, schwer; *run, drive* sehr schnell; *breathe* schwer; *study, play* eifrig; *listen, look* genau; *think* scharf; *push, pull, blow* kräftig; *rain, snow* stark; **I've been ~ at work** *or* **(going)** = at it (*inf*) **since 7 this morning** ich bin seit heute Morgen um 7 schwer am Werk *or* schwer dabei (*inf*); **she works ~ at keeping herself fit** sie gibt sich viel Mühe, sich fit zu halten; **to try ~** sich wirklich Mühe geben; **no matter how ~ I try ...** wie sehr ich mich auch anstrenge, ...; **it was freezing ~** es herrschte strenger Frost; **to be ~ pushed** *or* **put to do sth** es sehr schwer finden, etw zu tun; **to be ~ done by** übel dran sein; (= *unfairly treated*) ungerecht behandelt sein; **they are ~ hit by the cuts** sie sind von den Kürzungen schwer getroffen; **~ right/left** scharf rechts/links; **bear ~ round to your left** halten Sie sich scharf links; **to follow ~ upon sth** unmittelbar auf etw (*acc*) folgen; **my sister was ~ behind me** meine Schwester war direkt hinter mir

hard: **hard and fast** ADJ fest; **hardback** ◧ ADJ (*also* ~ed) *book* gebunden ◨ N gebundene Ausgabe; **hardball** N (*US*) **(a)** (*Baseball*) Hardball *m* **(b)** (*fig*) **to play ~** rücksichtslos sein *or* vorgehen; **hardboard** N Hartfaser- *or* Pressspanplatte *f*; **hard-boiled** ADJ **(a)** *egg* hart gekocht **(b)** (*fig*: = *unsentimental*) kaltschnäuzig (*inf*); **hard cash** N Bargeld *nt*; **hard copy** N Ausdruck *m*, Hardcopy *f*; **hard core** N (*fig*) harter Kern; **hard-core** ADJ **(a)** *pornography* hart; **~ film** harter Pornofilm **(b)** (= *committed*) *members* zum harten Kern gehörend; **hard court** N Hartplatz *m*; **hardcover** ADJ, N (*US*) = hardback; **hard currency** N harte Währung; **hard disk** N (*Comput*) Festplatte *f*; **hard disk drive** N Festplattenlaufwerk *nt*; **hard drug** N harte Droge; **hard-earned** ADJ *wages, cash* sauer verdient; *savings* mühsam erspart; *reward* redlich verdient; *victory* hart erkämpft; **hard-edged** ADJ (*fig*) hart, kompromisslos; *reality* hart

harden ['hɑːdn] **1** VT *steel* härten; *person* (*physically*) abhärten; (*emotionally*) abstumpfen (*pej*); **this ~ed his attitude** dadurch hat sich seine Haltung verhärtet; **to ~ oneself to sth** (*physically*) sich gegen etw abhärten; (*emotionally*) gegen etw unempfindlich werden **2** VI (*substance*) hart werden; (*fig*) (*attitude*) sich verhärten; (*St Ex*) (= *cease to fluctuate*) sich stabilisieren; (= *rise*) anziehen; **his face ~ed** sein Gesicht bekam einen harten Ausdruck

hardened ['hɑːdnd] ADJ *steel* gehärtet; *troops* abgehärtet; *arteries* verkalkt; **~ criminal** Gewohnheitsverbrecher(in) *m(f)*; **you become ~ to it after a while** daran gewöhnt man sich mit der Zeit

hardening ['hɑːdnɪŋ] N **~ of the arteries** Arterienverkalkung *f*

hard: **hard-fought** ADJ *battle, campaign* erbittert; *victory* hart erkämpft; *boxing match, competition, game* hart; **a ~ election** eine (erbitterte) Wahlschlacht; **hard hat** N Schutzhelm *m*; **hard-headed** ADJ nüchtern; **hardhearted** ADJ hartherzig (*towards sb* jdm gegenüber); **hard-hitting** ADJ *speech, report* äußerst kritisch; **hard labour,** (*US*) **hard labor** N Zwangsarbeit *f*; **hard left** N (*Pol*) **the ~** die extreme Linke; **hard lens** N (*Opt*) harte Kontaktlinse; **hard line** N harte Haltung, harte Linie; **to take a ~** eine harte Linie verfolgen; **hardline** ADJ kompromisslos; **hardliner** N Vertreter(in) *m(f)* der harten Linie, Hardliner(in) *m(f)* (*esp Pol*); **hard luck** N (*inf*) Pech *nt* (*on* für); **~!** Pech gehabt!; **it was very ~ on him** da hat er aber wirklich Pech gehabt

hardly ['hɑːdlɪ] ADV **(a)** (= *barely*) kaum; **I ~ knew him** ich kannte ihn kaum; **the boy was ~ seventeen** der Junge war kaum *or* keine siebzehn; **~ ever** fast nie; **~ any money** fast kein Geld; **it's worth ~ anything** es ist fast nichts wert; **you've ~ eaten anything** du hast (ja) kaum etwas gegessen; **there was ~ anywhere to go** man konnte fast nirgends hingehen **(b)** (= *certainly not*) wohl kaum; **will she remember? – ~!** wird sie daran denken? – bestimmt nicht!

hardness ['hɑːdnɪs] N **(a)** Härte *f* **(b)** (= *difficulty*) Schwierigkeit *f*

hard: **hard-nosed** ADJ (*inf*) *person, government* abgebrüht (*inf*); *approach, attitude, leadership* rücksichtslos; **hard on** N (*sl*) Ständer *m* (*inf*); **to have a ~** einen stehen *or* einen Ständer haben (*inf*); **hard-pressed** ADJ hart bedrängt; **to be ~ to do sth** es sehr schwer finden, etw zu tun; **hard right** N (*Pol*) **the ~** die extreme Rechte; **hard sell** N aggressive Verkaufstaktik

hardship ['hɑːdʃɪp] N (= *condition*) Not *f*; (= *instance*) Härte *f*; (= *deprivation*) Entbehrung *f*; **economic/financial ~** wirtschaftliche/finanzielle Not; **to suffer great ~s** große Not leiden; **is that such a great ~?** ist das wirklich ein solches Unglück?

hard shoulder N (*Brit*) Seitenstreifen *m*

hardware ['hɑːdwɛəʳ] **1** N **(a)** Eisenwaren *pl*; (= *household goods*) Haushaltswaren *pl* **(b)** (*Comput*) Hardware *f* **(c)** (*Mil*) (Wehr)material *nt* **(d)** (*US inf*: = *gun*) Schießeisen *nt* (*hum inf*) **2** ATTR **(a)** **~ shop** *or* **store** Eisenwarenhandlung *f*; (*including household goods*) Haushalts- und Eisenwarengeschäft *nt* **(b)** (*Comput*) Hardware-; **~ manufacturer** Hardwarehersteller *m*

hard: **hard-wearing** ADJ widerstandsfähig; *cloth, clothes* strapazierfähig; **hard-won** ADJ hart *or* schwer erkämpft; **hardwood** N Hartholz *nt*; **hard-working** ADJ fleißig

hardy ['hɑːdɪ] ADJ (+ER) *person, animal* robust, zäh; (= *hardened*) abgehärtet; (*Bot*) *plant* winterhart

hardy perennial N mehrjährige winterharte Pflanze

hare [hɛəʳ] **1** N (Feld)hase *m* **2** VI (*Brit inf*) sausen, flitzen (*inf*); **to ~ off** lossausen *or* -flitzen (*inf*)

harebrained ['hɛəbreɪnd] ADJ verrückt

harem [hɑːˈriːm] N Harem *m*

haricot ['hærɪkəʊ] N **~ (bean)** Gartenbohne *f*

hark [hɑːk] VI **~ at him!** (*inf*) hör sich einer den an! (*inf*)

➤ **hark back to** VI +PREP OBJ zurückkommen; **this custom harks back to the days when ...** dieser Brauch geht auf die

Zeit zurück, als ...; **he's always harking back to the good old days** er fängt immer wieder von der guten alten Zeit an

harm [hɑːm] **1** N (*bodily*) Verletzung *f*; (= *material damage, to relations, psychological*) Schaden *m*; **to do ~ to sb** jdm eine Verletzung/jdm Schaden zufügen; **to do ~ to sth** einer Sache (*dat*) schaden; **you could do somebody/yourself ~ with that knife** mit dem Messer können Sie jemanden/sich verletzen; **he never did anyone any ~** er hat keiner Fliege jemals etwas zuleide getan; **you will come to no ~** es wird Ihnen nichts geschehen; **it will do more ~ than good** es wird mehr schaden als nützen; **it won't do you any ~** es wird dir nicht schaden; **to mean no ~** es nicht böse meinen; **no ~ done** es ist nichts Schlimmes passiert; **there's no ~ in asking/trying** es kann nicht schaden, zu fragen/es zu versuchen; **where's** *or* **what's the ~ in that?** was kann denn das schaden?; **to keep** *or* **stay out of ~'s way** der Gefahr (*dat*) aus dem Weg gehen; **I've put those tablets in the cupboard out of ~'s way** ich habe die Tabletten im Schrank in Sicherheit gebracht **2** VT *person* verletzen; *thing, environment, relations etc* schaden (+*dat*); **don't ~ the children** tu den Kindern nichts (an); **it wouldn't ~ you to be a little more polite** es würde nicht(s) schaden, wenn du ein bisschen höflicher wärst

harmful ['hɑːmfʊl] ADJ schädlich (*to* für); *remarks* verletzend; **~ to one's health** gesundheitsschädlich

harmless ['hɑːmlɪs] ADJ (*lit, fig*) harmlos; **the bomb was rendered ~** die Bombe wurde entschärft

harmlessly ['hɑːmlɪslɪ] ADV harmlos; **the missile exploded ~ outside the town** die Rakete explodierte außerhalb der Stadt, ohne Schaden anzurichten

harmonic [hɑːˈmɒnɪk] ADJ (*Mus, Phys*) harmonisch

harmonica [hɑːˈmɒnɪkə] N Harmonika *f*

harmonious ADJ, **harmoniously** ADV [hɑːˈməʊnɪəs, -lɪ] (*Mus, fig*) harmonisch

harmonization [ˌhɑːmənaɪˈzeɪʃən] N (*Mus, fig*) Harmonisierung *f*

harmonize ['hɑːmənaɪz] **1** VT (*Mus, fig*) harmonisieren; *ideas etc* miteinander in Einklang bringen; *plans, colours* aufeinander abstimmen (*sth with sth* etw auf etw *acc*) **2** VI **(a)** (*notes, colours, people etc*) harmonieren **(b)** (= *sing in harmony*) mehrstimmig singen

harmony ['hɑːmənɪ] N Harmonie *f*; (*fig*: = *harmonious relations*) Eintracht *f*; **to live/work in perfect ~ with sb** in Harmonie *or* Eintracht mit jdm leben/zusammenarbeiten; **to be in/out of ~ with** (*lit*) harmonieren/nicht harmonieren mit; **to sing in ~** mehrstimmig singen; (= *in tune*) rein singen

harness ['hɑːnɪs] **1** N **(a)** Geschirr *nt*; **to be back in ~** (*fig*) wieder im gewohnten Trott sein; **to work in ~** (*fig*) zusammenarbeiten **(b)** (*of parachute*) Gurtwerk *nt*; (*for baby*) Laufgurt *m* **2** VT **(a)** *horse* anschirren; **to ~ a horse to a carriage** ein Pferd vor einen Wagen spannen **(b)** (= *utilize*) nutzen; *river etc also* nutzbar machen

harp [hɑːp] N Harfe *f*

➤ **harp on** VI (*inf*) **to harp on sth** auf etw (*dat*) herumreiten; **he's always harping on about the need for ...** er spricht ständig von der Notwendigkeit +*gen* ...

harpoon [hɑːˈpuːn] **1** N Harpune *f*; **~ gun** Harpunenkanone *f* **2** VT harpunieren

harpsichord ['hɑːpsɪkɔːd] N Cembalo *nt*

harrow ['hærəʊ] N (*Agr*) Egge *f*

harrowing ['hærəʊɪŋ] ADJ *story, picture etc* erschütternd; *experience* grauenhaft; *time* entsetzlich

harry ['hærɪ] VT (= *hassle*) bedrängen

harsh [hɑːʃ] ADJ (+ER) *winter* streng; *weather, climate, environment* rau; *sound, voice also* kratzig; *conditions, verdict, punishment, treatment* hart; *words, remarks, criticism* scharf; *taste, wine, whisky* herb; *light, glare, colours* grell; *reality, facts, truth* bitter; **to be ~ with** *or* **on sb** jdn hart anfassen; **don't be too ~ with him** sei nicht zu streng mit *or* hart zu ihm

harshly ['hɑːʃlɪ] ADV **(a)** *judge, treat* streng; *criticize* scharf **(b)** *say* schroff; **he never once spoke ~ to her** (= *unkindly*) er sprach sie nie in einem scharfen Ton an

harshness ['hɑːʃnɪs] N Härte *f*; (*of weather, climate, environment*) Rauheit *f*; (*of words, criticism*) Schärfe *f*

harvest ['hɑːvɪst] **1** N Ernte *f*; (*of wines, berries also*) Lese *f*; **a bumper potato ~** eine Rekordkartoffelernte **2** VT (= *reap*) ernten; *vines also* lesen; (= *bring in*) einbringen

harvester ['hɑːvɪstəʳ] N Mähmaschine f; (which cuts and binds) Mähbinder m; (= combine ~) Mähdrescher m

harvest festival N Erntedankfest nt

has [hæz] 3RD PERS SING PRESENT of **have**

has-been ['hæzbiːn] N (pej) vergangene Größe

hash [hæʃ] N **(a)** (fig) (= mess) Durcheinander nt; (= bad work) Pfusch m (inf); **to make a ~ of sth** etw verpfuschen or vermasseln (inf) **(b)** (Telec) Doppelkreuz nt **(c)** (inf: = hashish) Hasch nt (inf)

hash browns [hæʃ'braʊnz] PL ≈ Kartoffelpuffer pl

hashish ['hæʃɪʃ] N Haschisch nt

hasn't ['hæznt] CONTR of **has not**

hasp [hɑːsp] N (for chest, door etc) Überfall m

hassle ['hæsl] (inf) **1** N Auseinandersetzung f; (= bother, trouble) Mühe f; **we had a real ~ getting these tickets for tonight** es hat uns (dat) viel Mühe gemacht, diese Karten für heute Abend zu bekommen; **getting there is such a ~** es ist so umständlich, dorthin zu kommen; **don't give me any ~** mach kein Theater (inf) **2** VT bedrängen; **stop hassling me** lass mich in Ruhe!; **I'm feeling a bit ~d** ich fühle mich etwas im Stress (inf) or unter Druck

haste [heɪst] N Eile f; (nervous) Hast f; **to do sth in ~** etw in Eile tun; **to make ~** sich beeilen, etw zu tun

hasten ['heɪsn] **1** VI sich beeilen; **I ~ to add that ...** ich muss allerdings hinzufügen, dass ... **2** VT beschleunigen; **to ~ sb's departure** jdn zum Aufbruch drängen

hastily ['heɪstɪlɪ] ADV **(a)** arranged eilig; examine, glance flüchtig; dress, dash, eat hastig; say, add schnell **(b)** (= too quickly) übereilt; judge, speak vorschnell

hasty ['heɪstɪ] ADJ (+ER) **(a)** hastig; kiss, glance, examination flüchtig; departure plötzlich; **to beat a ~ retreat, to make a ~ escape** sich schnellstens aus dem Staub machen (inf) **(b)** (= rash, too quick) übereilt; action voreilig; judgement vorschnell; **don't be ~!** nicht so schnell or hastig!; **I had been too ~** ich hatte voreilig gehandelt

hat [hæt] N **(a)** Hut m; (of cook) Mütze f; **to put on one's ~** den or seinen Hut aufsetzen; **to take one's ~ off** den Hut abnehmen

(b) (fig) **I'll eat my ~ if ...** ich fresse einen Besen, wenn ... (inf); **I take my ~ off to him** Hut ab vor ihm!; **~s off to them for supporting us** Hut ab vor ihnen, dass sie uns unterstützt haben; **to talk through one's ~** (inf) dummes Zeug reden; **to keep sth under one's ~** (inf) etw für sich behalten; **at the drop of a ~** auf der Stelle; **that's old ~** (inf) das ist ein alter Hut (inf); **to pass round the ~ for sb** für jdn sammeln or den Hut rumgehen lassen (inf); **with my accountant's ~ on I would say ...** (inf) als Buchhalter würde ich sagen ...

hat: **hatband** N Hutband nt; **hatbox** N Hutschachtel f

hatch¹ [hætʃ] **1** VT, (also ~ out) ausbrüten; (fig) plot, scheme also aushecken **2** VI (also ~ out: bird) ausschlüpfen; **when will the eggs ~?** wann schlüpfen die Jungen aus?

hatch² N **(a)** (Naut) Luke f; (in floor, ceiling) Bodenluke f; (= half-door) Halbtür f **(b)** (service) ~ Durchreiche f **(c)** **down the ~!** (inf) hoch die Tassen! (inf)

hatchback ['hætʃbæk] N Hecktürmodell nt

hatchet ['hætʃɪt] N Beil nt; (= tomahawk) Kriegsbeil nt; **to bury the ~** (fig) das Kriegsbeil begraben

hatchet job N (inf) **to do a ~ on sb** jdn fertig machen (inf)

hatchway ['hætʃweɪ] N = **hatch²** (a)

hate [heɪt] **1** VT hassen; **to ~ to do sth** or **doing sth** es hassen, etw zu tun; (weaker) etw äußerst ungern tun; **I ~ seeing** or **to see her in pain** ich kann es nicht ertragen, sie leiden zu sehen; **I ~ it when people accuse me of lying** ich kann es nicht ausstehen, wenn man mich als Lügner bezeichnet; **I ~ to bother you** es ist mir sehr unangenehm, dass ich Sie belästigen muss; **I ~ to admit it but ...** es fällt mir sehr schwer, das zuzugeben zu müssen, aber ...; **she ~s me having any fun** sie kann es nicht haben, wenn ich Spaß habe; **I'd ~ to think I'd never see him again** ich könnte den Gedanken, ihn nie wiederzusehen, nicht ertragen **2** N Hass m (for, of auf +acc); **one of his pet ~s is plastic cutlery/having to wait** Plastikbesteck/Warten ist ihm ein Gräuel

hate campaign N Hasskampagne f

hated ['heɪtɪd] ADJ verhasst

hateful ['heɪtfʊl] ADJ **(a)** abscheulich; remarks also hässlich; person unausstehlich **(b)** (= full of hate) hasserfüllt

hate mail N beleidigende Briefe pl

hatpin ['hætpɪn] N Hutnadel f

hatred ['heɪtrɪd] N Hass m (for, of auf +acc); (of spinach, spiders etc) Abscheu m (of vor +dat); **racial ~** Rassenhass m

hat: **hat stand**, (US) **hat tree** N Garderobenständer m; **hat trick** N Hattrick m; **to score a ~** einen Hattrick erzielen

haughtily ['hɔːtɪlɪ] ADV say überheblich; dismiss, ignore arrogant; look geringschätzig

haughty ['hɔːtɪ] ADJ (+ER) überheblich; disdain, person also arrogant; look geringschätzig

haul [hɔːl] N **(a)** (= journey) Strecke f; **it's a long ~ to recovery** es ist ein weiter Weg bis zum Aufschwung; **short/long/ medium ~ aircraft** Kurz-/Lang-/Mittelstreckenflugzeug nt; **over the long ~** (esp US) langfristig

(b) (Fishing) (Fisch)fang m; (fig) (= booty) Beute f; (of cocaine etc) Fund m; **drugs ~** Drogenfund m

2 VT **(a)** (= pull) ziehen; **he ~ed himself/Paul to his feet** er wuchtete sich/Paul wieder auf die Beine

(b) (= transport) befördern, transportieren

▶ **haul in** VT SEP einholen; rope einziehen; (police) festnehmen

▶ **haul up** VT SEP (fig inf) **to haul sb up before the magistrate** jdn vor den Kadi schleppen (inf); **he's been hauled up on a drugs charge** er wurde wegen einer Rauschgiftsache vor den Kadi gebracht (inf)

haulage ['hɔːlɪdʒ] N (Brit) Transport m

haulage business N (esp Brit) (= firm) Transportunternehmen nt, Spedition(sfirma) f; (= trade) Speditionsbranche f

haulier ['hɔːlɪəʳ], (US) **hauler** ['hɔːləʳ] N (= company) Spedition f

haunch [hɔːntʃ] N (of person) Hüfte f; (= hip area) Hüftpartie f; (of animal) = hindquarters) Hinterbacke f; (= top of leg) Keule f; (Cook) Lendenstück nt; **~es** Gesäß nt; (of animal) Hinterbacken pl; **to squat on one's ~es** in der Hocke sitzen; **~ of venison** (Cook) Rehkeule f

haunt [hɔːnt] **1** VT **(a)** (ghost) spuken in (+dat) **(b)** person verfolgen; (memory) nicht loslassen; (fear, decision) quälen **(c)** (= frequent) verkehren in (+dat), frequentieren; (animal) vorkommen **2** N (of person) Stammlokal nt; (= pub etc) Stammlokal nt; (= favourite resort) Lieblingsort m; (of criminals) Treff(punkt) m; (of animal) Heimat f; **her usual childhood ~s** Stätten, die sie in ihrer Kindheit oft aufsuchte

haunted ['hɔːntɪd] ADJ **(a)** Spuk-; **~ castle** Spukschloss nt; **this place is ~** hier spukt es; **is it ~?** spukt es da? **(b)** look gequält

haunting ['hɔːntɪŋ] ADJ eindringlich; memory lastend; music schwermütig

haute couture [əʊtkuːˈtʊəʳ] **1** N Haute Couture f **2** ADJ ATTR der Haute Couture

---

have [hæv]

1 AUXILIARY VERB	**3** TRANSITIVE VERB
2 MODAL AUXILIARY VERB	**4** PHRASAL VERBS

pret, ptp **had**, *3rd person singular present* **has**

*When **have** is part of a set combination, eg **have a look**, **have a dream**, **have a good time**, look up the noun.*

1 AUXILIARY VERB
(a) haben

*The verb **haben** is the auxiliary used with most verbs to form past tenses in German. For important exceptions see **2**.*

to have seen/heard/eaten gesehen/gehört/gegessen haben; **I have/had seen** ich habe/hatte gesehen; **I have not/had not** or **I haven't/I hadn't seen him** ich habe/hatte ihn nicht gesehen; **had I seen him, if I had seen him** hätte ich ihn gesehen, wenn ich ihn gesehen hätte; **having seen him** (= after I had) als ich ihn gesehen hatte; **having realized this** (= since I had) nachdem ich das erkannt hatte

Note the tenses used in the following.

I have lived or **have been living here for 10 years/since January** ich wohne or lebe schon 10 Jahre/seit Januar hier **(b)** sein

The verb **sein** *is used with verbs of motion, eg.* **gehen, fahren,** *or verbs implying development, eg.* **wachsen,** *and to form past tenses.*

to have gone/run gegangen/gelaufen sein; **you HAVE grown!** du bist aber gewachsen!; **to have been** gewesen sein; **I have been against this for years** ich bin schon seit Jahren dagegen **(c)** *(in tag questions etc)* **you've seen her, haven't you?** du hast sie gesehen, oder nicht?; **you haven't seen her, have you?** du hast sie nicht gesehen, oder?; **you haven't seen her – yes, I have** du hast sie nicht gesehen – doch or wohl *(inf)*; **you've made a mistake – no, I haven't** du hast einen Fehler gemacht – nein(, hab ich nicht); **I have seen a ghost – have you?** ich habe ein Gespenst gesehen – tatsächlich?

2 MODAL AUXILIARY VERB

✦**to have to do sth** (= *to be obliged*) etw tun müssen; **I have (got** *esp Brit*) **to do it** ich muss es tun or machen; **she was having to get up at 6 o'clock each morning** sie musste jeden Morgen um 6 Uhr aufstehen; **we've had to go and see her twice this week** wir mussten diese Woche schon zweimal zu ihr (hin); **the letter will have to be written tomorrow** der Brief muss morgen unbedingt geschrieben werden

✦**don't/doesn't have to** or *(esp Brit)* **haven't/hasn't got to I haven't got to do it** *(esp Brit)*, **I don't have to do it** ich muss es nicht tun, ich brauche es nicht zu tun; **you didn't have to tell her** das hätten Sie ihr nicht unbedingt sagen müssen or brauchen

3 TRANSITIVE VERB

(a) haben; **have you (got** *esp Brit*) or **do you have a car?** hast du ein Auto?; **I haven't (got** *esp Brit*) or **I don't have a pen** ich habe keinen Kugelschreiber; **I have (got** *esp Brit*) **work/a translation to do** ich habe zu arbeiten/eine Übersetzung zu erledigen; **I must have more time** ich brauche mehr Zeit; **I have it!** ich habs!; **what time do you have?** *(US)* wie spät hast du es?; **I must have something to eat** ich muss dringend etwas zu essen haben; **there are some great bargains to be had in the shops** in den Geschäften gibt es tolle Angebote; **I'll have the bed in this room** das Bett möchte or werde ich in dieses Zimmer stellen; **thanks for having me** vielen Dank für Ihre Gastfreundschaft; **he has diabetes** er ist zuckerkrank, er hat Zucker *(inf)*; **to have a heart attack** einen Herzinfarkt bekommen; **I've (got** *esp Brit*) **a headache** ich habe Kopfschmerzen; **to have a pleasant evening** einen netten Abend verbringen; **to have a good time** Spaß haben; **have a good time!** viel Spaß!; **to have a walk** einen Spaziergang machen; **to have a swim** schwimmen gehen; **to have a child** or **baby** ein Kind or Baby bekommen; **our cat has had kittens** unsere Katze hat Junge bekommen; **he had the audience in hysterics** das Publikum kugelte sich vor Lachen; **he had the police baffled** die Polizei stand vor einem Rätsel; **as rumour** *(Brit)* or **rumor** *(US)* **has it** Gerüchten zufolge; **I won't have this sort of rudeness!** diese Unhöflichkeit lasse ich mir ganz einfach nicht bieten; **I won't have him insulted** ich lasse es nicht zu or dulde es nicht, dass man ihn beleidigt; **I'm not having any of that!** *(inf)* mit mir nicht! *(inf)*

✦**to let sb have sth** jdm etw geben

(b) to have breakfast frühstücken; **to have lunch/dinner** zu Mittag/Abend essen; **to have tea with sb** mit jdm (zusammen) Tee trinken; **will you have tea or coffee?** möchten Sie lieber Tee oder Kaffee?; **will you have a drink/ cigarette?** möchten Sie etwas zu trinken/eine Zigarette?; **what will you have? – I'll have the steak** was möchten or hätten Sie gern(e)? – ich hätte or möchte gern das Steak; **he had a cigarette/drink/steak** er rauchte eine Zigarette/trank etwas/aß ein Steak

(c) (= *catch, hold*) (gepackt) haben; **he had (got** *esp Brit*) **me by the throat/the hair** er hatte or hielt mich am Hals/bei den Haaren gepackt; **I'll have you** *(inf)* dich krieg ich (beim Kragen); **you have me there** da bin ich überfragt

(d) (= *hold, organize*) party geben, machen; *meeting* abhalten; **are you having a reception?** gibt es einen Empfang?
(e) (*wish*) mögen; **which one will you have?** welche(n, s) möchten Sie haben or hätten Sie gern?
(f) (*set structures*)

✦**to have sth done** etw tun lassen; **to have one's hair cut** sich *(dat)* die Haare schneiden lassen; **I had my cases brought up** ich habe (mir) meine Koffer nach oben bringen lassen; **they had him shot** sie ließen ihn erschießen; **he had his car stolen** man hat ihm sein Auto gestohlen; **I've had three windows broken** (bei) mir sind drei Fenster eingeworfen worden

✦**to have sb do sth** jdn etw tun lassen; **I'll have you know ...** Sie müssen nämlich wissen ...; **I had my friends turn against me** ich musste es erleben, wie or dass sich meine Freunde gegen mich wandten

✦**to have had it** *(inf)* **that coat has had it** der Mantel ist im Eimer *(inf)*; **if I miss the last bus, I've had it** wenn ich den letzten Bus verpasse, bin ich geliefert *(inf)*

✦**let him have it!** *(inf)* gibs ihm! *(inf)*

✦**have it your own way** halten Sie es, wie Sie wollen

✦**to be had** *(inf)* **you've been had!** da hat man dich übers Ohr gehauen *(inf)*

4 PHRASAL VERBS

➤ **have around** VT ALWAYS SEPARATE **(a)** (bei sich) zu Besuch haben; (= *invite*) einladen **(b) he's a useful man to have around** es ist ganz praktisch, ihn zur Hand zu haben

➤ **have back** VT SEP zurückhaben

➤ **have in** VT *always separate* **(a)** (*in the house*) im Haus haben **(b) to have it in for sb** *(inf)* jdn auf dem Kieker haben *(inf)* **(c) I didn't know he had it in him** ich hätte ihm das nicht zugetraut

➤ **have off** VT ALWAYS SEPARATE **(a) to have it off with sb** *(Brit inf)* es mit jdm treiben *(inf)* **(b) he had to have his leg off** ihm musste das Bein abgenommen werden

➤ **have on 1** VT SEP (= *wear*) anhaben (*also radio, TV*) **2** VT *always separate* **(a)** (= *have arranged*) vorhaben; (= *be busy with*) zu tun haben; **we've (got** *esp Brit*) **a big job on** wir haben ein großes Projekt in Arbeit **(b)** *(inf)* (= *trick*) übers Ohr hauen *(inf)*; (= *tease*) auf den Arm nehmen *(inf)* **(c) to have nothing on sb** nichts gegen jdn in der Hand haben; **they've got nothing on me!** mir kann keiner! *(inf)*

➤ **have out** VT *always separate* **(a)** (= *have taken out*) herausnehmen bekommen; **he had his tonsils out** ihm wurden die Mandeln herausgenommen **(b)** (= *discuss*) ausdiskutieren; **I'll have it out with him** ich werde mit ihm reden

➤ **have over** or *(esp Brit)* **round** VT ALWAYS SEPARATE (bei sich) zu Besuch haben; (= *invite*) (zu sich) einladen

➤ **have up** VT ALWAYS SEPARATE (*inf:* = *cause to appear in court*) drankriegen *(inf)*; **he's been had up again** er war schon wieder vor dem Kadi *(inf)*

have-a-go [ˌhævəˈgəʊ] ADJ ATTR (*Brit inf*) **~-hero** heldenmütiger Kämpfer

haven [ˈheɪvən] N (*fig*) Zufluchtsstätte *f*

haven't [ˈhævnt] CONTR of **have not**

haves [hævz] PL (*inf*) **the ~** die Betuchten *pl* (*inf*); **the ~ and the have-nots** die Betuchten und die Habenichtse

havoc [ˈhævək] N verheerender Schaden; (= *chaos*) Chaos *nt*; **to cause** or **create ~** ein Chaos verursachen; **to wreak ~ in/on/ with sth, to play ~ with sth** bei etw verheerenden Schaden anrichten; *with health, part of the body* für etw üble or schlimme Folgen haben; *with life, career* etw ruinieren; **the tornado wreaked ~ all along the coast** der Tornado richtete entlang der ganzen Küste große Verwüstungen an; **this wreaked ~ with their plans** das brachte ihre Pläne völlig durcheinander

Hawaii [həˈwaɪiː] N Hawaii *nt*

Hawaiian [həˈwaɪjən] **1** ADJ hawaii(ani)sch, Hawaii-; **~ island** Hawaii-Insel *f*; **~ Standard Time** (*US*) hawaiische Zeit **2** N Hawaiianer(in) *m(f)*

Hawaiian shirt N grellbuntes Hemd

hawk1 [hɔːk] N **(a)** (*Orn*) Habicht *m*; **to watch sb like a ~** jdn ganz genau beobachten **(b)** (*fig:* = *politician*) Falke *m*

hawk² VT hausieren (gehen) mit; (*in street*) verkaufen, feilbieten

➤ **hawk around** VT SEP (*lit, fig*) hausieren (gehen) mit

hawker ['hɔːkəʳ] N (*door-to-door*) Hausierer(in) *m(f)*; (*in street*) Straßenhändler(in) *m(f)*

hawk-eyed ['hɔːkaɪd] ADJ scharfsichtig, adleräugig

hawthorn ['hɔːθɔːn] N (*also* ~ **bush/tree**) Weiß- *or* Rot- *or* Hagedorn *m*

hay [heɪ] N Heu *nt*; **to make** ~ **while the sun shines** (*Prov*) das Eisen schmieden, solange es heiß ist (*Prov*)

hay: hay fever N Heuschnupfen *m*; **hayrick, haystack** N Heuhaufen *m*

haywire ['heɪwaɪəʳ] ADJ PRED (*inf*) **to go** ~ (= *go crazy*) durchdrehen (*inf*); (*plans, arrangements*) über den Haufen geworfen werden (*inf*); (*machinery*) verrückt spielen (*inf*)

hazard ['hæzəd] **1** N (a) Gefahr *f*; (= *risk*) Risiko *nt*; **it's a fire** ~ es stellt eine Feuergefahr dar; **to pose a** ~ **(to sb/sth)** eine Gefahr (für jdn/etw) darstellen (b) **hazards** PL (*Aut: also* ~ **(warning) lights**) Warnblinklicht *nt* **2** VT riskieren; *guess also* wagen; **if I might** ~ **a suggestion** wenn ich mir einen Vorschlag erlauben darf; **to** ~ **a guess** (es) wagen, eine Vermutung anzustellen

hazardous ['hæzədəs] ADJ gefährlich; (= *risky*) riskant; **such jobs are** ~ **to one's health** solche Arbeiten gefährden die Gesundheit

hazardous waste N Sondermüll *m*

haze [heɪz] N (a) Dunst *m* (b) (*fig*) **he/his mind was in a** ~ er war vollkommen verwirrt

hazel ['heɪzl] ADJ (*colour*) haselnussbraun

hazelnut ['heɪzlnʌt] N Haselnuss *f*

hazy ['heɪzɪ] ADJ (+ER) *day, weather* diesig; *sunshine, sky* trübe; *view, outline, vision* verschwommen; *notion, details, memory* unklar, vage; **I'm a bit** ~ **about that** ich bin mir nicht ganz im Klaren darüber

H-bomb ['eɪtʃbɒm] N H-Bombe *f*

he [hiː] **1** PERS PRON er; **he didn't do it, I did it** nicht er hat das getan, sondern ich; **Harry Rigg? who's he?** Harry Rigg? wer ist das denn? **2** N (*of animal*) Männchen *nt*; **it's a he** (*inf: of newborn baby*) es ist ein Er **3** PREF männlich

---

head [hed]

1 NOUN	**3** INTRANSITIVE VERB
2 TRANSITIVE VERB	**4** PHRASAL VERBS

1 NOUN

(a) Kopf *m* (*also Comput*); (= *intellect also*) Verstand *m*; (*of arrow, spear*) Spitze *f*; (*of bed*) Kopf(ende *nt*) *m*; (*on beer*) Blume *f*; (*Archit: of column*) Kapitell *nt*; (*of stream*) (= *upper area*) Oberlauf *m*; (= *source*) Ursprung *m*; **from head to foot** von Kopf bis Fuß; **he can hold his head high in any company** er kann sich in jeder Gesellschaft sehen lassen; **to keep one's head above water** (*fig*) sich über Wasser halten; **to go to one's head** (*whisky, power*) einem in den *or* zu Kopf steigen; **I can't make head nor tail of it** daraus werde ich nicht schlau; **by a short head** (*Horse Racing, fig*) um Nasenlänge; **use your head** streng deinen Kopf an; **it never entered his head that ...** es kam ihm nie in den Sinn, dass ...; **we put our heads together** wir haben unsere Köpfe zusammengesteckt; **the joke went** *or* **was over his head** er verstand *or* kapierte (*inf*) den Witz nicht; **to keep one's head** den Kopf nicht verlieren; **to lose one's head** den Kopf verlieren; **head of steam/water** (= *pressure*) Dampf-/Wasserdruck *m*; **at the head of the page/stairs** oben auf der Seite/an der Treppe; **at the head of the table** am Kopf(ende) des Tisches; **at the head of the queue** (*Brit*)**/army** an der Spitze der Schlange/des Heeres

✦**a** *or* **per head** pro Kopf

✦**head and shoulders** to **stand** *or* **be head and shoulders above sb** (*fig*) jdm haushoch überlegen sein

✦**head over heels** to **fall head over heels in love with sb** sich bis über beide Ohren in jdn verlieben; **to fall head over heels down the stairs** kopfüber die Treppe herunterfallen

✦**on one's/its head** to **stand on one's head** auf dem Kopf stehen; **to stand** *or* **turn sth on its head** etw auf den Kopf stellen; (*fig*) etw umkehren

✦**one's head off** to **laugh one's head off** (*inf*) sich fast totlachen (*inf*); **to shout one's head off** (*inf*) sich (*dat*) die Lunge aus dem Leib schreien (*inf*); **to scream one's head off** (*inf*) aus vollem Halse schreien

✦**into one's/sb's head** he **can't get it into his head that ...** es will ihm nicht in den Kopf, dass ...; **I can't get it into his head that ...** ich kann es ihm nicht begreiflich machen, dass ...; **to take it into one's head to do sth** sich (*dat*) in den Kopf setzen, etw zu tun; **don't put ideas into his head** bring ihn bloß nicht auf dumme Gedanken!; (= *unrealistic wish*) setz ihm bloß keinen Floh ins Ohr! (*inf*)

✦**out of one's head** to **put** *or* **get sb/sth out of one's head** sich (*dat*) jdn/etw aus dem Kopf schlagen

✦**off one's head** he **is off his head** (*Brit inf*) er ist (ja) nicht (ganz) bei Trost (*inf*); (*with drugs*) er ist auf dem Trip (*inf*)

✦**a (good) head (for)** he **has a good head for figures** er ist ein guter Rechner; **you need a good head for heights** Sie müssen schwindelfrei sein

✦**to a head** to **come to a head** sich zuspitzen; **to bring matters to a head** die Sache auf die Spitze treiben

(b) twenty head of cattle zwanzig Stück Vieh

(c) (= *leader*) (*of family*) Oberhaupt *nt*; (*of business, organization*) Chef(in) *m(f)*; (*of department*) Leiter(in) *m(f)*; (*of office, sub-department*) Vorsteher(in) *m(f)*; (*Sch*) Schulleiter(in) *m(f)*; **head of department** (*in business*) Abteilungsleiter(in) *m(f)*; (*Sch, Univ*) Fachbereichsleiter(in) *m(f)*; **head of state** Staatsoberhaupt *nt*

(d) (*of coin*) Kopfseite *f*; **heads or tails?** Kopf oder Zahl?; **heads you win** bei Kopf gewinnst du

(e) (*Tech*) (*on tape recorder*) Tonkopf *m*; (*Comput:* = *read/write head*) Kopf *m*

2 TRANSITIVE VERB

(a) (= *be at the head of*) anführen; (= *be in charge of*) führen; *team* leiten; **a coalition government headed by Mr Schröder** eine Koalitionsregierung unter der Führung von Herrn Schröder

(b) in the chapter headed ... in dem Kapitel mit der Überschrift ...

(c) (*Ftbl*) köpfen

3 INTRANSITIVE VERB gehen; (*vehicle*) fahren; **and the tornado was heading our way** und der Tornado kam auf uns zu

4 PHRASAL VERBS

➤ **head back** VI zurückgehen/-fahren; **it's time we were heading back now** es ist Zeit, sich auf den Rückweg zu machen

➤ **head for** VI +PREP OBJ (a) *place, person* zugehen/zufahren auf (+*acc*); *town, country, direction* gehen/fahren in Richtung (+*gen*); *door, pub, bargain counter, prettiest girl* zusteuern auf (+*acc*) (*inf*); (*ship*) zufahren *or* Kurs halten auf (+*acc*); **where are you heading** *or* **headed for?** wo gehen/fahren Sie hin? (b) (*fig*) zusteuern auf (+*acc*); **you're heading for trouble** du bist auf dem besten Weg, Ärger zu bekommen; **to head for victory/defeat** auf einen Sieg/eine Niederlage zusteuern

➤ **head off** **1** VT SEP (a) (= *divert*) umdirigieren (b) *quarrel, war, strike* abwenden; *questions* abbiegen **2** VI (= *set off*) sich aufmachen

---

head IN CPDS (= *top, senior*) Ober-; **headache** N Kopfschmerzen *pl*; (*inf:* = *problem*) Problem *nt*; **to have a** ~ Kopfschmerzen haben; **this is a bit of a** ~ **(for us)** das macht *or* bereitet uns ziemliches Kopfzerbrechen; **headband** N Stirnband *nt*; **headboard** N Kopfteil *nt*; **head boy** N *vom Schulleiter bestimmter Schulsprecher*; **headbutt** VT mit dem Kopf stoßen; **head cold** N Kopfgrippe *f*; **headcount** N (a) (*Ind:* = *workforce*) Beschäftigtenzahl *f* (b) **to have** *or* **take a** ~ abzählen; **headdress** N Kopfschmuck *m*

headed notepaper N Schreibpapier *nt* mit Briefkopf

header ['hedəʳ] N (*Ftbl*) Kopfball *m*

head: headfirst ADV (*lit, fig*) kopfüber; **headgear** N Kopfbedeckung *f*; **head girl** N *vom Schulleiter bestimmte Schulsprecherin*; **head-hunt** VT abwerben; **I've been** ~**ed** ich bin abgeworben worden; (= *have been approached*) man hat versucht, mich abzuwerben; **head-hunter** N (*fig*) Kopfjäger(in) *m(f)*, Headhunter(in) *m(f)*

heading ['hedɪŋ] N Überschrift f; (on letter, document) Kopf m; (in encyclopedia) Stichwort nt

head: **headlamp, headlight** N Scheinwerfer m; **headland** N Landspitze f; **headlight** N = headlamp; **headline** ◨ N (Press) Schlagzeile f; **he is always in the ~s** er macht immer Schlagzeilen; **to grab** or **hit** or **make the ~s** Schlagzeilen machen; **the news ~s** Kurznachrichten pl ◨ VT **(a) an article ~ ...** ein Artikel mit der Überschrift ... **(b)** festival, event die Hauptattraktion sein bei; **headline news** N, NO PL **to be ~ in** den Schlagzeilen sein; **headlong** ◨ ADV (lit, fig) überstürzt, Hals über Kopf (inf); fall vornüber; **he ran ~ down the stairs** er rannte in Windeseile die Treppe hinunter ◨ ADJ überstürzt; **headmaster** N (esp Brit) Schulleiter m; (of secondary school also) Direktor m; (of primary school also) Rektor m; **headmistress** N (esp Brit) Schulleiterin f; (of secondary school also) Direktorin f; (of primary school also) Rektorin f; **head office** N Zentrale f; **head-on** ◨ ADV (a) collide, crash frontal **(b)** (fig) meet, tackle direkt; **to confront sb/sth ~** jdm/einer Sache ohne Umschweife entgegentreten ◨ ADJ (a) ~ **collision** or **smash** Frontalzusammenstoß m **(b)** (fig) conflict, confrontation offen; **headphones** PL Kopfhörer pl; **headquarters** N SING or PL (Mil) Hauptquartier nt; (of business) Zentrale f; (of political party) Parteizentrale f; **headrest** N Kopfstütze f; **headroom** N lichte Höhe; (in car) Kopfraum m; **headscarf** N Kopftuch nt; **headset** N Kopfhörer pl; **head start** N Vorsprung m (on sb jdm gegenüber); **headstone** N (on grave) Grabstein m; **headstrong** ADJ dickköpfig; **head teacher** N (Brit) = headmaster, headmistress; **head waiter** N Oberkellner m; **headway** N **to make ~** (lit, fig) vorankommen; **did you make any ~ with the unions?** haben Sie bei den Gewerkschaften etwas erreicht?; **headwind** N Gegenwind m

heady ['hedɪ] ADJ (+ER) berauschend; experience aufregend; **the air is ~ with spices** der berauschende Duft von Gewürzen hängt in der Luft; **to be ~ with success** im Erfolgsrausch sein

heal [hiːl] VI (Med, fig) heilen ◨ VT (a) (Med) heilen **(b)** (fig) differences etc beilegen; (third party) schlichten; **they succeeded in ~ing the rift between them** es gelang ihnen, die Kluft zwischen ihnen zu überbrücken

▶ **heal up** VI zuheilen

healer ['hiːləʳ] N Heiler(in) m(f) (geh); **time is a great ~** (prov) die Zeit heilt alle Wunden (Prov)

healing ['hiːlɪŋ] ◨ N Heilung f; (of wound) (Zu)heilen nt ◨ ADJ (Med) Heil-, heilend; (fig) besänftigend; ~ **process** Heilprozess m; ~ **powers** Heilkräfte pl

health [helθ] N (lit, fig) Gesundheit f; (= state of ~) Gesundheitszustand m; **in good ~** bei guter Gesundheit; **in poor ~** bei schlechter Gesundheit; **how is his ~?** wie geht es ihm gesundheitlich?; **to suffer from poor** or **bad ~** kränklich sein; **to be good/bad for one's ~** gesund/ungesund or gesundheitsschädlich sein; ~ **and safety regulations** Arbeitsschutzvorschriften pl; **Ministry of Health** Gesundheitsministerium nt; **to drink (to) sb's ~** auf jds Wohl (acc) or Gesundheit (acc) trinken; **your ~!, good ~!** zum Wohl!

health: **Health and Social Services** PL (US) das amerikanische Gesundheits- und Sozialministerium; **health authority** N Gesundheitsbehörde f; **health care** N Gesundheitsfürsorge f; **health centre** N (Brit Med) Ärztezentrum nt; **health certificate** N Gesundheitszeugnis nt; **health club** N Fitnesscenter nt; **health farm** N Gesundheitsfarm f; **health food** N Reformkost f; **health food shop** (Brit), **health food store** (esp US) N Reformhaus nt, Bioladen m

healthily ['helθɪlɪ] ADV (a) eat, live gesund; grow kräftig **(b)** (fig) ~ **cynical/irreverent** erfrischend zynisch/respektlos

health: **health insurance** N Krankenversicherung f; **permanent ~** freiwillige Krankenversicherung mit Krankengeldanspruch; **health problem** N **to have ~s** gesundheitliche Probleme haben; **health resort** N Kurort m; **Health Service** N (Brit) **the ~** das Gesundheitswesen; ~ **doctor** Kassenarzt m/-ärztin f; **health warning** N (on cigarette packet) (gesundheitlicher) Warnhinweis

healthy ['helθɪ] ADJ (+ER) (lit, fig) gesund; **to earn a ~ profit** einen ansehnlichen Gewinn machen; **he has a ~ bank balance** sein Kontostand ist gesund

heap [hiːp] ◨ N Haufen m; **he fell in a ~ on the floor** er sackte zu Boden; **at the bottom/top of the ~** (fig) ganz unten/oben; **~s of** (inf) ein(en) Haufen (inf); **it's happened ~s of times** es

ist schon zigmal vorgekommen (inf); **she has ~s of enthusiasm/time** sie hat jede Menge Enthusiasmus/Zeit (inf) ◨ ADV ~**s** (inf) (unheimlich) viel ◨ VT häufen; **to ~ praise on sb/sth** über jdn/etw voll des Lobes sein (geh); (in addressing) jdn mit Lob überschütten; **to ~ scorn on sb/sth** jdn/etw mit Spott übergießen; **a ~ed spoonful** ein gehäufter Löffel

▶ **heap up** VT SEP aufhäufen

hear [hɪəʳ], pret, ptp **heard** ◨ VT (= also learn) hören; **I ~d him say that ...** ich habe ihn sagen hören, dass ...; **I ~d somebody come in** ich habe jemanden (herein)kommen hören; **there wasn't a sound to be ~d** es war kein Laut zu hören; **to make oneself ~d** sich (dat) Gehör verschaffen; **you're not going, do you ~ me!** du gehst nicht, hörst du (mich)!; **I've often ~d it said that ...** ich habe oft gehört or sagen hören, dass ...; **I ~ you play chess** ich höre, Sie spielen Schach; **I've ~d it all before** ich habe das schon hundertmal gehört; **I must be ~ing things** ich glaube, ich höre nicht richtig; **to ~ a case** (Jur) einen Fall verhandeln; **to ~ evidence** (Jur) Zeugen vernehmen

◨ VI hören; **he does not** or **cannot ~ very well** er hört nicht sehr gut; ~**, ~!** (sehr) richtig!; (Parl) hört!, hört!; **he's left his wife – yes, so I ~** er hat seine Frau verlassen – ja, ich habe es gehört; **to ~ about sth** von etw hören or erfahren; **never ~d of him/it** nie (von ihm/davon) gehört; **he was never ~d of again** man hat nie wieder etwas von ihm gehört; **I've never ~d of such a thing!** das ist ja unerhört!

▶ **hear of** VI +PREP OBJ (fig: = allow) hören wollen von; **I won't hear of it** ich will davon (gar) nichts hören

▶ **hear out** VT SEP person ausreden lassen; story zu Ende hören

heard [hɜːd] PRET, PTP of **hear**

hearing ['hɪərɪŋ] N (a) Gehör nt; **to have a keen sense of ~** ein gutes Gehör haben **(b)** within/out of ~ **(distance)** in/außer Hörweite; **he said that in/out of my ~** ich war in Hörweite/ nicht in Hörweite, er las das sagte **(c)** (Pol) Anhörung f; (Jur) Verhandlung f; **disciplinary ~** Disziplinarverfahren nt; **he didn't get a fair ~** man hörte ihn nicht richtig an; (Jur) er bekam keinen fairen Prozess

hearing: **hearing aid** N Hörgerät nt; **hearing-impaired** ['hɪərɪŋɪmˌpeəd] ◨ ADJ (= deaf) gehörlos; (= partially deaf) hörgeschädigt ◨ **the ~** (= deaf) Gehörlose pl; (= partially deaf) Hörgeschädigte pl

hearsay ['hɪəseɪ] N Gerüchte pl; **to know sth from** or **by ~** etw vom Hörensagen wissen or haben

hearse [hɜːs] N Leichenwagen m

heart [hɑːt] N (a) (lit, fig) Herz nt; **to break sb's ~** jdm das Herz brechen; **it breaks my ~ to think that ...** mir bricht das Herz, wenn ich daran denke, dass ...; **to have a change of ~** sich anders besinnen; **to be close** or **dear to one's ~** (cause, subject) jdm am Herzen liegen; **to learn/know/recite sth (off) by ~** etw auswendig lernen/können/aufsagen; **he knew in his ~ she was right** er wusste im Grunde seines Herzens, dass sie Recht hatte; **with all my ~** von ganzem Herzen; **from the bottom of one's ~** aus tiefstem Herzen; **to be the ~ and soul of sth** das Herz und die Seele einer Sache (gen) sein; **to put (one's) ~ and soul into sth** sich mit Leib und Seele einer Sache (dat) widmen; **to take sth to ~** sich (dat) etw zu Herzen nehmen; **we (only) have your interests at ~** uns liegen doch nur Ihre Interessen am Herzen; **to set one's ~ on sth** sein Herz an etw (acc) hängen (geh); **to one's ~'s content** nach Herzenslust; **most men are boys at ~** die meisten Männer sind im Grunde (ihres Herzens) noch richtige Kinder; **his ~ isn't in his work/in it** er ist nicht mit dem Herzen bei der Sache/dabei; **to give sb ~** jdm Mut machen; **to lose ~** den Mut verlieren; **to take ~** Mut fassen; **her ~ is in the right place** (inf) sie hat das Herz auf dem rechten Fleck (inf); **to have a ~ of stone** ein Herz aus Stein haben; **my ~ was in my mouth** (inf) mir schlug das Herz bis zum Hals; **I didn't have the ~ to say no** ich brachte es nicht übers Herz, nein zu sagen; **she has a ~ of gold** sie hat ein goldenes Herz; **my ~ sank** (= I was discouraged) mein Mut sank; **in the ~ of the forest** im tiefsten or mitten im Wald; **the ~ of the matter** der Kern der Sache **(b)** hearts PL (Cards) Herz nt; (Bridge) Coeur nt; **queen of ~s** Herz-/Coeurdame f

heart: **heartache** N Kummer m, Herzweh nt (geh); **heart attack** N Herzanfall m; (= thrombosis) Herzinfarkt m; **I nearly had a ~** (fig inf) ich habe fast einen Herzschlag gekriegt (inf); **heartbeat** N Herzschlag m; **heartbreak** N großer Kummer,

Leid *nt*; **heartbreaking** ADJ herzzerreißend; **it was ~ to see him with crutches** es brach einem das Herz, ihn an Krücken zu sehen; **heartbroken** ADJ untröstlich, todunglücklich; **she was ~ about it** sie war darüber todunglücklich; **heartburn** N Sodbrennen *nt*; **heart condition** N Herzleiden *nt*; **he has a ~** er ist herzleidend; **heart disease** N Herzkrankheit *f*

hearten ['hɑːtn] VT ermutigen

heartening ['hɑːtnɪŋ] ADJ *news* ermutigend

heart: **heart failure** N Herzversagen *nt*; **he suffered ~** sein Herz hat versagt; **heartfelt** ADJ *thanks, apology* aufrichtig; *sympathy, tribute, appeal* tief empfunden

hearth [hɑːθ] N Feuerstelle *f*; (= *whole fireplace*) Kamin *m*; (*fig*: = *home*) (häuslicher) Herd

hearthrug ['hɑːθrʌg] N Kaminvorleger *m*

heartily ['hɑːtɪlɪ] ADV **(a)** *laugh, say* herzlich; *sing* aus voller Kehle; *eat* tüchtig **(b)** *recommend* uneingeschränkt; *agree* voll und ganz; *endorse, welcome* von Herzen; **to ~ dislike doing sth** etw äußerst ungern tun; **to be ~ sick of sth** etw herzlich leid sein

heart: **heartland** N **in the Tory ~s** in den Hochburgen der Konservativen; **heartless** ADJ herzlos; (= *cruel also*) grausam; **heartlessly** ADV grausam; **heart-rending** ADJ herzzerreißend; **heartstrings** PL **to pull** *or* **tug at sb's ~** jdn zu Tränen rühren; **heart-throb** N (*inf*) Schwarm *m* (*inf*); **heart-to-heart** 🔢 ADJ ganz offen; **to have a ~ talk with sb** sich mit jdm ganz offen aussprechen 🔢 N offene Aussprache; **it's time we had a ~** es ist Zeit, dass wir uns einmal offen aussprechen; **heart transplant** N Herztransplantation *f*; **heart trouble** N Herzbeschwerden *pl*; **heart-warming** ADJ herzerfreuend

hearty ['hɑːtɪ] ADJ (+ER) **(a)** *laugh, voice, greeting* herzlich; *person, manner* (= *boisterous*) raubeinig; (= *over-familiar*) plumpvertraulich **(b)** *endorsement, condemnation* uneingeschränkt; *hatred, dislike* tief; **~ welcome** herzlicher Empfang **(c)** *food, meal* herzhaft; *appetite* gesund; **to be a ~ eater** einen gesunden Appetit haben

heat [hiːt] 🔢 N **(a)** (*lit, fig*) Hitze *f*; (*pleasant, Phys*) Wärme *f*; (= *heating*) Heizung *f*; **on** *or* **over** (a) **low ~** bei schwacher Hitze; **in the ~ of the moment** in der Hitze des Gefechts; (*when upset*) in der Erregung; **to take the ~ out of the situation/an argument** die Situation/Diskussion entschärfen; **in the ~ of the election campaign** in der Aufregung des Wahlkampfs
(b) (*inf*: = *pressure*) Druck *m*; **to put the ~ on** Druck machen (*inf*)
(c) (*Sport*) Vorlauf *m*; (*Boxing etc*) Vorkampf *m*
(d) on (*Brit*) *or* **in** (*esp US*) **~** brünstig; (*Hunt*) brunftig; (*dog, cat*) läufig
🔢 VT erhitzen; *room* heizen; *house, town, pool* beheizen
🔢 VI warm werden; **your dinner is ~ing in the oven** dein Essen steht (im Backofen) warm

➤ **heat up** 🔢 VI sich erwärmen, warm werden; (= *get very hot*) sich erhitzen; (*engine*) heißlaufen; (*fig: situation*) sich zuspitzen 🔢 VT SEP erwärmen; *food* aufwärmen

heated ['hiːtɪd] ADJ **(a)** (*lit*) *swimming pool, greenhouse etc* beheizt; *room* geheizt; *rear window, towel rail* heizbar **(b)** (*fig*) *debate, meeting* hitzig; *argument, exchange* heftig; *words* erregt; **to grow** *or* **become ~** (*person*) sich aufregen; (*debate*) hitzig werden

heatedly ['hiːtɪdlɪ] ADV hitzig; *argue* heftig

heater ['hiːtə'] N Ofen *m*; (*electrical also*) Heizgerät *nt*; (*in car*) Heizung *f*; **turn the ~ on** stell die Heizung an

heath [hiːθ] N Heide *f*

heathen ['hiːðən] 🔢 ADJ heidnisch 🔢 N Heide *m*, Heidin *f*; **the ~** (*collectively*) die Heiden

heather ['heðə'] N Heidekraut *nt*, Erika *f*

heating ['hiːtɪŋ] N Heizung *f*; (= *act*) (*of room, house*) (Be)heizen *nt*; (*of substances*) Erhitzen *nt*

heating: **heating engineer** N Heizungsinstallateur(in) *m(f)*; **heating system** N Heizungssystem *nt*; (= *apparatus*) Heizungsanlage *f*

heat: **heatproof** ADJ hitzebeständig; **heat rash** N Hitzeausschlag *m*; **heat-resistant** ADJ hitzebeständig; **heatstroke** N Hitzschlag *m*; **heat wave** N Hitzewelle *f*

heave [hiːv] 🔢 VT **(a)** (= *lift*) (hoch)hieven (*onto* auf +*acc*); (= *drag*) schleppen; **he ~d himself out of bed** er hievte sich aus dem Bett (*inf*) **(b)** (= *throw*) werfen, schmeißen (*inf*)

(c) *sigh* ausstoßen 🔢 VI **(a)** (= *pull*) ziehen, hieven **(b)** (*sea, waves, bosom*) wogen (*geh*); (*stomach*) sich umdrehen

heaven ['hevn] N (*lit, fig inf*) Himmel *m*; **the ~s** (*liter*) der Himmel; **in ~** im Himmel; **to go to ~** in den Himmel kommen; **he is in (seventh) ~** er ist im siebten Himmel; **to move ~ and earth** Himmel und Hölle in Bewegung setzen; **it was ~** es war einfach himmlisch; **(good) ~s!** (du) lieber Himmel! (*inf*); **would you like to? – (good) ~s no!** möchten Sie? – um Himmels willen, bloß nicht!; **~ knows what ...** weiß der Himmel, was ... (*inf*); **~ forbid!** bloß nicht, um Himmels willen! (*inf*); **for ~'s sake!** um Himmels willen!; **what in ~'s name ...?** was um Himmels willen ...?

heavenly ['hevnlɪ] ADJ **(a)** himmlisch, Himmels-; **~ body** Himmelskörper *m* **(b)** (*inf*: = *delightful*) himmlisch

heavily ['hevɪlɪ] ADV stark; *populated, wooded* dicht; *armed, fortified, breathe, land, lean, fall* schwer; *guarded* streng; *move, walk* schwerfällig; **to borrow ~** hohe Kredite aufnehmen; (*fig*) viele Anleihen machen (*from* bei); **~ disguised** (*lit, fig*) völlig unkenntlich gemacht; **to lose ~** hoch verlieren; **to draw ~ on sth** sich zum großen Teil auf etw (*acc*) stützen; **to be ~ involved in** *or* **with sth** sehr viel mit etw zu tun haben; **to be ~ into sth** (*inf*) voll auf etw (*acc*) abfahren (*inf*); **to be ~ fined** zu einer hohen Geldstrafe verurteilt werden; **to be ~ outnumbered** zahlenmäßig stark unterlegen sein; **to be ~ defeated** eine schwere Niederlage erleiden; **~ laden** schwer beladen; **~ built** kräftig gebaut; **she sat down ~ on the bed** sie setzte sich schwerfällig aufs Bett

heavy ['hevɪ] 🔢 ADJ (+ER) **(a)** schwer; *features* grob; *rain, traffic, drinker, smoker, period* stark; *expenses, taxes* hoch; *landing, fall* hart; **with a ~ heart** schweren Herzens; **the air was ~ with smoke/the smell of cooking** der Rauch/Essensgeruch hing schwer in der Luft; **~ breathing** schweres Atmen; **to be ~ on petrol** (*Brit*) *or* **gas** (*US*) viel Benzin brauchen; **to be ~ on the stomach** schwer im Magen liegen; **the conversation was ~ going** die Unterhaltung war mühsam; **this book is very ~ going** das Buch liest sich schwer
(b) *manner, style, sense of humour* schwerfällig
(c) *silence* bedrückend; *weather, air* schwül; *sky* bedeckt
(d) (*inf*: = *threatening*) bedrohlich; **he got really ~ with me** er hat mich echt bedroht (*inf*)
🔢 ADV schwer
🔢 N (*Brit inf*: = *thug*) Schlägertyp *m*

heavy: **heavy-duty** ADJ *clothes, tyres etc* strapazierfähig; *plastic, flex* dick; **heavy goods vehicle** N Lastkraftwagen *m*; **heavy-handed** ADJ schwerfällig, ungeschickt; **heavy industry** N Schwerindustrie *f*; **heavy metal** N (*Mus*) Heavymetal *m*

heavyweight ['hevɪweɪt] 🔢 N **(a)** (*Sport*) Schwergewicht *nt*, Schwergewichtler(in) *m(f)* **(b)** (*fig inf*) großes Tier (*inf*); **the literary ~s** die literarischen Größen *pl* 🔢 ADJ **(a)** (*Sport*) **~ champion** Meister(in) *m(f)* im Schwergewicht; **~ boxer** (Boxer(in) *m(f)* im) Schwergewicht *nt* **(b)** (*fig inf*) *issue, subject* gewichtig; *writer, commentator, interviewer* ernst zu nehmend; *newspaper* seriös

Hebrew ['hiːbruː] 🔢 ADJ hebräisch 🔢 N **(a)** Hebräer(in) *m(f)* **(b)** (*Ling*) Hebräisch *nt*

Hebrides ['hebrɪdiːz] PL Hebriden *pl*

heck [hek] INTERJ (*inf*) **oh ~!** zum Kuckuck! (*inf*); **ah, what the ~!** ach, was solls! (*inf*); **what the ~ do you mean?** was zum Kuckuck soll das heißen? (*inf*); **I've a ~ of a lot to do** ich habe irrsinnig viel zu tun (*inf*)

heckle ['hekl] 🔢 VT (durch Zwischenrufe) stören 🔢 VI stören, Zwischenrufe machen

heckler ['heklə'] N Zwischenrufer(in) *m(f)*

heckling ['heklɪŋ] N Zwischenrufe *pl*

hectare ['hektɑː'] N Hektar *m or nt*

hectic ['hektɪk] ADJ hektisch

hectoring ['hektərɪŋ] ADJ tyrannisch

he'd [hiːd] CONTR *of* **he would, he had**

hedge [hedʒ] 🔢 N **(a)** Hecke *f*; (*fig*: = *protection*) Schutz *m*; **to be a ~ against sth** ein Schutz(wall) *m* gegen etw sein **(b)** (*St Ex*) Kurssicherungsgeschäft *nt*, Hedging *nt* 🔢 VI ausweichen; **to ~ on a question** einer Frage ausweichen; **to ~ against sth** sich vor etw (*dat*) schützen 🔢 VT **to ~ one's bets** (*lit, fig*) auf Nummer sicher gehen (*inf*)

➤ **hedge about** (*Brit*) *or* **around** VT SEP (*with restrictions etc*) *procedure* erschweren; *offer, reform* einschränken (*with* durch)

hedge: **hedgehog** N Igel *m*; **hedgerow** N Hecke *f*; **hedge trimmer** N Elektroheckenschere *f*

hedging ['hedʒɪŋ] N (*St Ex*) Kurssicherungsgeschäft *nt*, Hedging *nt*

hedonism ['hiːdənɪzəm] N Hedonismus *m*

heed [hiːd] **1** N **to take ~** Acht geben; **to pay ~ to sb/sth, to take ~ of sb/sth** jdm/einer Sache Beachtung schenken **2** VT beachten; **he never ~s my advice** er hört nie auf meinen Rat

heedless ['hiːdlɪs] ADJ rücksichtslos; *extravagance* leichtsinnig; **to be ~ of sth** etw nicht beachten

heel[1] [hiːl] **1** N Ferse *f*; (*of shoe*) Absatz *m*; **I like to wear ~s** ich trage gerne Schuhe mit hohen Absätzen; **with his dog at his ~s** gefolgt von seinem Hund; (*fig: = chase*) jdm auf den Fersen sein; **to be right on sb's ~s** jdm auf den Fersen folgen; (*fig: = chase*) jdm auf den Fersen sein; **panic buying came hard on the ~s of the government's announcement** Hamsterkäufe folgten der Erklärung der Regierung auf dem Fuße; **the police were hot on our ~s** die Polizei war uns dicht auf den Fersen; **to be down at ~** (*person, building*) heruntergekommen sein; **to take to one's ~s** sich aus dem Staub(e) machen; **~!** (*to dog*) (bei) Fuß!; **to bring sb to ~** jdn an die Kandare nehmen (*inf*); **to turn or spin on one's ~** auf dem Absatz kehrtmachen; **to cool or kick one's ~s** (*inf*) (= *wait*) warten; (= *do nothing*) Däumchen drehen **2** VT **these shoes need ~ing** diese Schuhe brauchen neue Absätze

heel[2] VI (*Naut: ship: also ~ over*) sich (auf die Seite) legen *or* neigen

heel bar N Absatzbar *f*

heft [heft] VT (*US inf*) (= *lift*) (hoch)heben; (= *assess weight*) abwägen

hefty ['heftɪ] ADJ (+ER) (*inf*) *person* kräftig (gebaut); *object* massiv; *fine, bill, increase, payment, kick, punch* saftig (*inf*); *profit* anständig (*inf*)

heifer ['hefə'] N Färse *f*

height [haɪt] N **(a)** (*lit, fig*) Höhe *f*; (*of person*) Größe *f*; (*of stupidity*) Gipfel *m*; **to be six feet in ~** sechs Fuß groß *or* (*wall etc*) hoch sein; **what ~ are you?** wie groß sind Sie?; **you can raise the ~ of the saddle** du kannst den Sattel höher stellen; **at shoulder/head ~** in Schulter-/Kopfhöhe; **at the ~ of his power** auf der Höhe seiner Macht; **the ~ of luxury** das Nonplusultra an Luxus; **it is the ~ of bad manners to ...** es verstößt gegen jede Etikette, zu ...; **at the ~ of the season** in der Hauptsaison; **at the ~ of summer** im Hochsommer; **at its ~ the company employed 12,000 people** in ihrer Glanzzeit hatte die Firma 12.000 Angestellte; **during the war emigration was at its ~** im Krieg erreichte die Auswanderungswelle ihren Höhepunkt; **to be the ~ of fashion** der letzte Schrei sein **(b) heights** PL (= *high place*) Höhen *pl*; **to be afraid of ~s** nicht schwindelfrei sein

heighten ['haɪtn] **1** VT (= *raise*) höher stellen *or* machen; (= *emphasize*) hervorheben; *intensity* steigern; *colour, feelings, fear, effect, tension* verstärken; **~ed awareness** erhöhte Aufmerksamkeit **2** VI (*fig: = increase*) wachsen

heinous ['heɪnəs] ADJ abscheulich

heir [ɛə'] N Erbe *m*, Erbin *f* (*to* +*gen*); **~ to the throne** Thronfolger(in) *m(f)*

heiress ['ɛəres] N Erbin *f*

heirloom ['ɛəluːm] N Erbstück *nt*

heist [haɪst] N (*esp US inf*) Raubüberfall *m*

held [held] PRET, PTP *of* **hold**

helicopter ['helɪkɒptə'] N Hubschrauber *m*

helicopter gunship N Kampfhubschrauber *m*

helipad ['helɪpæd] N Hubschrauberlandeplatz *m*

heliport ['helɪpɔːt] N Heliport *m*

helium ['hiːlɪəm] N Helium *nt*

hell [hel] N **(a)** (*lit, fig*) Hölle *f*; **to go to ~** (*lit*) in die Hölle kommen; **all ~ broke loose** die Hölle war los; **it's ~ working there** es ist die reine Hölle, dort zu arbeiten; **a living ~** die Hölle auf Erden; **to go through ~** Höllenqualen ausstehen; **she made his life ~** sie machte ihm das Leben zur Hölle; **to give sb ~** (*inf*) (= *tell off*) jdm die Hölle heiß machen; (= *make life unpleasant*) jdm das Leben zur Hölle machen; **there'll be ~ to pay when he finds out** wenn er das erfährt, ist der Teufel los (*inf*); **to play ~ with sth** etw total durcheinander bringen; **I did it (just) for the ~ of it** (*inf*) ich habe es nur zum Spaß

gemacht; **~ for leather** was das Zeug hält; **the mother-in-law from ~** die böse Schwiegermutter, wie sie im Buche steht; **the holiday from ~** der absolut katastrophale Urlaub **(b)** (*inf: intensifier*) **a ~ of a noise** ein Höllenlärm *m* (*inf*); **I was angry as ~** ich war stinksauer (*inf*); **to work like ~** arbeiten, was das Zeug hält (*inf*); **to run like ~** laufen, was die Beine hergeben; **it hurts like ~** es tut wahnsinnig weh (*inf*); **we had a or one ~ of a time** (= *bad, difficult*) es war grauenhaft; (= *good*) wir haben uns prima amüsiert (*inf*); **a ~ of a lot** verdammt viel (*inf*); **she's a or one ~ of a girl** die ist schwer in Ordnung (*inf*); **that's one or a ~ of a problem/climb** das ist ein wahnsinnig schwieriges Problem (*inf*)/eine wahnsinnige Kletterei (*inf*); **to ~ with you** hol dich der Teufel (*inf*); **to ~ with it!** verdammt noch mal! (*inf*); **go to ~!** scher dich zum Teufel! (*inf*); **what the ~ do you want?** was willst du denn, verdammt noch mal? (*inf*); **where the ~ is it?** wo ist es denn, verdammt noch mal? (*inf*); **you scared the ~ out of me** du hast mich zu Tode erschreckt; **like ~ he will!** den Teufel wird er tun (*inf*); **what the ~, I've nothing to lose** zum Teufel, ich habe nichts zu verlieren (*inf*)

he'll [hiːl] CONTR *of* **he shall**, **he will**

hellbent ['hel'bent] ADJ versessen (*on* auf +*acc*)

Hellenic [he'liːnɪk] ADJ hellenisch

hellish ['helɪʃ] ADJ (*fig inf*) höllisch (*inf*); *traffic, heat, cold* mörderisch (*inf*); **it's ~** es ist die reinste Hölle (*inf*)

hellishly ['helɪʃlɪ] ADV (*inf*) *hot, cold* höllisch (*inf*); *difficult, complicated* verteufelt (*inf*)

hello [hə'ləʊ] **1** INTERJ hallo; **say ~ to your aunt** sag deiner Tante mal schön „Guten Tag!"; **say ~ to your parents (from me)** grüß deine Eltern (von mir) **2** N Hallo *nt*

hell-raiser ['helreɪzə'] N (*inf*) ausschweifender Mensch

helluva ['heləvə] ADJ, ADV (*inf*) = **hell of a**; *see* **hell (b)**

helm [helm] N (*Naut*) Ruder *nt*, Steuer *nt*; **to be at the ~** (*lit, fig*) am Ruder sein

helmet ['helmɪt] N Helm *m*; (*Fencing*) Maske *f*

help [help] **1** N, NO PL Hilfe *f*; **with his brother's ~** mithilfe seines Bruders; **his ~ with the project** seine Mithilfe an dem Projekt; **to ask sb for ~** jdn um Hilfe bitten; **to be of ~ to sb** jdm helfen; **he isn't much ~ to me** er ist mir keine große Hilfe; **you're a great ~!** (*iro*) du bist mir eine schöne Hilfe! **2** VT **(a)** helfen (+*dat*); **to ~ sb (to) do sth** jdm (dabei) helfen, etw zu tun; **to ~ sb with the cooking/his bags** jdm beim Kochen/mit seinen Taschen helfen; **~! Hilfe!**; **can I ~ you?** kann ich (Ihnen) helfen *or* behilflich sein?; **that won't ~ you** das wird Ihnen nichts nützen; **this will ~ the pain** das wird gegen die Schmerzen helfen; **it will ~ the crops to grow** es wird das Wachstum des Getreides fördern; **to ~ sb down** jdm hinunterhelfen; **to ~ sb on/off with his/her etc coat** jdm in den/aus dem Mantel helfen; **to ~ sb through a difficult time** (*belief, hope, pills etc*) jdm in einer schwierigen Zeit durchhelfen; **to ~ sb up** (*from floor, chair etc*) jdm aufhelfen **(b)** **to ~ oneself to sth** (*dat*) etw nehmen; (*inf: = steal*) etw mitgehen lassen; **~ yourself!** nehmen Sie sich doch! **(c)** **he can't ~ it, he's only a baby** er kann nichts dafür, er ist doch noch ein Baby; **he can't ~** (*hum inf: he's stupid*) (d)er ist nun mal so (doof); **not if I can ~ it** nicht, wenn es nach mir geht; **I couldn't ~ laughing** ich konnte mir nicht helfen, ich musste (einfach) lachen; **I had to do it, I couldn't ~ it or myself** ich konnte mir nicht helfen, ich musste es einfach tun; **I couldn't ~ thinking** *or* **but think ...** ich konnte nicht umhin zu denken ...; **it can't be ~ed** das lässt sich nicht ändern; **I can't ~ it if he's always late** ich kann nichts dafür, dass er immer zu spät kommt

3 VI helfen; **and your attitude didn't ~ either** und Ihre Einstellung war auch nicht gerade hilfreich; **it ~s (to) fight pollution** es trägt zur Bekämpfung der Umweltverschmutzung bei

► **help out** **1** VI aushelfen (*with* bei) **2** VT SEP helfen (+*dat*) (*with* mit)

help desk N *telefonischer Informationsdienst*, Support *m*

helper ['helpə'] N Helfer(in) *m(f)*; (= *assistant*) Gehilfe *m*, Gehilfin *f*

helpful ['helpfʊl] ADJ **(a)** *person* (= *willing to help*) hilfsbereit; (= *giving help*) hilfreich; **to be ~ to sb** jdm behilflich *or* hilfreich sein; **they were very ~ with the move** sie haben beim Umzug viel geholfen **(b)** *advice, information, tool* nützlich; *remedy* hilfreich

helpfully [ˈhelpfəlɪ] ADV (= willing to help) hilfsbereit; (= giving help) hilfreich; (= thoughtfully) liebenswürdigerweise

helping [ˈhelpɪŋ] **1** N (at table, fig) Portion f; **to take a second ~ of sth** sich (dat) noch einmal von etw nehmen **2** ADJ ATTR **to give** or **lend a ~ hand to sb** jdm helfen, jdm behilflich sein

helpless [ˈhelplɪs] ADJ (= powerless) person machtlos (against gegen); (= vulnerable) child, victim hilflos; **he was ~ to prevent it** er konnte es nicht verhindern; **she was ~ with laughter** sie konnte sich vor Lachen kaum halten

helplessly [ˈhelplɪslɪ] ADV hilflos; (lit, fig: = impotently) watch machtlos

helplessness [ˈhelplɪsnɪs] N Hilflosigkeit f; (= powerlessness) Machtlosigkeit f

help: helpline N (for emergencies) Notruf m; (for information) Informationsdienst m; **help screen** N (Comput) Hilfsbildschirm m

helter-skelter [ˈheltəˈskeltəʳ] ADV Hals über Kopf (inf)

hem [hem] **1** N Saum m **2** VT säumen

➤ **hem in** VT SEP troops etc einschließen; (fig) einengen

he-man [ˈhiːmæn] N, pl **-men** [-men] (inf) sehr männlicher Typ

hemisphere [ˈhemɪsfɪəʳ] N Hemisphäre f; (of earth also) Halbkugel f; (of brain also) Gehirnhälfte f; **in the northern ~** auf der nördlichen Halbkugel

hemispheric [ˌhemɪˈsferɪk] ADJ (US Pol) relations, solidarity zwischen den Nord- und Südstaaten der USA; **a sense of ~ identity** ein Gefühl der Identität in den Nord- und Südstaaten der USA

hemline [ˈhemlaɪn] N Saum m; **~s are lower this year** der Rocksaum ist dieses Jahr etwas tiefer gerutscht

hemo- IN CPDS (US) = **haemo-**

hemp [hemp] N (Bot) Hanf m

hen [hen] N (a) Huhn nt, Henne f (b) (= female bird, lobster) Weibchen nt

hence [hens] ADV (a) (= for this reason) also; **~ the name** daher der Name (b) (= from now) **two years ~** in zwei Jahren

henceforth [hensˈfɔːθ], **henceforward** [ˌhensˈfɔːwəd] ADV (= from that time on) von da an; (= from this time on) von nun an

henchman [ˈhentʃmən] N, pl **-men** [-mən] (pej) Spießgeselle m, Kumpan m

henna [ˈhenə] **1** N Henna f **2** VT mit Henna färben

hen: hen night N für die Braut vor der Hochzeit arrangierte Damengesellschaft; **hen party** N (inf) Damenkränzchen nt; (before wedding) für die Braut vor der Hochzeit arrangierte Damengesellschaft; **henpeck** VT **he is ~ed** er steht unterm Pantoffel (inf)

hepatitis [ˌhepəˈtaɪtɪs] N Hepatitis f

her [hɜːʳ] **1** PERS PRON (dir obj, with prep +acc) sie; (indir obj, with prep +dat) ihr; (when she is previously mentioned in clause) sich; **it's ~** sie ists **2** POSS ADJ ihr; see also **my**

herald [ˈherəld] **1** N (fig) (Vor)bote m (geh); **~ of spring** Frühlingsbote m **2** VT ankündigen; **tonight's game is being ~ed as the match of the season** das Spiel heute Abend wird als die Begegnung der Saison groß herausgebracht

heraldry [ˈherəldrɪ] N Wappenkunde f, Heraldik f

herb [hɜːb] N Kraut nt

herbaceous [hɜːˈbeɪʃəs] ADJ krautig

herbaceous border N Staudenrabatte f

herbal [ˈhɜːbəl] ADJ Kräuter-; **~ tea** Kräutertee m

herb garden N Kräutergarten m

herbicide [ˈhɜːbɪsaɪd] N Herbizid nt

herculean [ˌhɜːkjʊˈliːən] ADJ herkulisch; effort übermenschlich; **a ~ task** eine Herkulesarbeit

herd [hɜːd] N (of cattle etc) Herde f; (of deer) Rudel nt; (fig pej: of people) Schar f; **to follow the ~** (fig) mit der Herde laufen **2** VT treiben

herdsman [ˈhɜːdzmən] N Hirte m

here [hɪəʳ] ADV hier; (with motion) hierher, hierhin; **~!** (at roll call) hier!; (to dog) hierher!; **come ~!** komm her!; **~ I am** da or hier bin ich; **~'s the taxi** das Taxi ist da; **~ he comes** da kommt or ist er ja; **spring is ~** der Frühling ist da; **this one ~** der/die/das hier or da; **John ~ reckons ...** John hier meint ...; **~ and now** auf der Stelle; **I won't be ~ for lunch** ich bin zum Mittagessen nicht da; **~ and there** hier und da; **around/about ~** ungefähr hier; **near ~** (hier) in der Nähe; **I've read down to**

~ ich habe bis hierher or hierhin gelesen; **it's in/over ~** es ist hier (drin)/hier drüben; **put it in/over ~** stellen Sie es hierherein/hierherüber; **from ~ on in** (esp US) von jetzt or nun an; **~ I would like to draw your attention to ...** an dieser Stelle möchte ich Sie auf ... aufmerksam machen; **~ you are** (giving sb sth) hier(, bitte); (on finding sb) da bist du ja!; (on finding sth) da or hier ist es ja; **~ we are, home again** so, da wären wir also wieder zu Hause; **~ we go again, another crisis** da hätten wir also wieder eine Krise; **~ goes!** dann mal los; **~, try this one** hier, versuchs mal damit; **~, let me do that** komm, lass mich das mal machen; **~'s to you!** (in toast) auf Ihr Wohl!; **it's neither ~ nor there** es spielt keine Rolle; **I've had it up to ~ (with him/it)** (inf) ich habe die Nase voll (von ihm/davon) (inf)

here: hereabouts [ˈhɪərəbaʊts] ADV hier (in der Gegend); **hereby** ADV (form) hiermit

hereditary [hɪˈredɪtərɪ] ADJ erblich; **~ disease** or **illness** Erbkrankheit f; **~ peer** Peer, der seine Peerswürde geerbt hat

heredity [hɪˈredɪtɪ] N Vererbung f

herein [hɪərˈɪn] ADV (form) hierin; **and ~ lies the problem** und das ist or hier liegt das Problem

heresy [ˈherəsɪ] N Ketzerei f; **heresies** ketzerische Lehren pl

heretic [ˈherətɪk] N Ketzer(in) m(f)

herewith [hɪəˈwɪð] ADV (form) hiermit

heritage [ˈherɪtɪdʒ] N (lit, fig) Erbe nt

heritage centre N (Brit) auf ein bestimmtes Gebiet spezialisiertes (Heimat)museum

hermaphrodite [hɜːˈmæfrədaɪt] N Zwitter m, Hermaphrodit m (geh)

hermetically [hɜːˈmetɪkəlɪ] ADV **~ sealed** hermetisch verschlossen; (fig) world, existence hermetisch abgeriegelt

hermit [ˈhɜːmɪt] N Einsiedler(in) m(f)

hernia [ˈhɜːnɪə] N (Eingeweide)bruch m

hero [ˈhɪərəʊ] N, pl **-es** Held m (also of novel); (fig: = object of ~-worship also) Idol nt

heroic [hɪˈrəʊɪk] **1** ADJ (a) person, struggle, resistance heldenhaft; (= brave) mutig; behaviour, action heroisch; **~ action** or **deed** Heldentat f; **~ attempt** tapferer Versuch (b) (Liter) Helden-; **~ character** or **figure** Heldengestalt f; (= hero/heroine) Held m, Heldin f **2** N **heroics** PL Heldentaten pl

heroically [hɪˈrəʊɪkəlɪ] ADV (a) heldenhaft; (= bravely) mutig (b) work, struggle, play mit heldenhaftem Einsatz

heroin [ˈherəʊɪn] N Heroin nt; **~ addict** Heroinsüchtige(r) mf

heroine [ˈherəʊɪn] N Heldin f

heroism [ˈherəʊɪzəm] N Heldentum nt; (= daring) Kühnheit f

heron [ˈherən] N Reiher m

hero worship N Verehrung f (of +gen); (of pop star etc) Schwärmerei f (of für)

herpes [ˈhɜːpiːz] N (Med) Herpes m

herring [ˈherɪŋ] N Hering m

herringbone [ˈherɪŋbəʊn] **1** N (= pattern) Fischgrät m **2** ADJ ATTR **~ pattern** Fischgrät(en)muster nt

hers [hɜːz] POSS PRON ihre(r, s); **~** (on towels etc) sie; see also **mine**[1]

herself [hɜːˈself] PERS PRON (a) (dir and indir obj, with prep) sich; see also **myself** (b) (emph) (sie) selbst

he's [hiːz] CONTR of **he is**, **he has**

hesitancy [ˈhezɪtənsɪ] N Zögern nt; (= indecision) Unschlüssigkeit f

hesitant [ˈhezɪtənt] ADJ zögernd; person (= undecided) unschlüssig; voice unsicher; **to be ~ to do sth** or **about doing sth** zögern, etw zu tun; (= reluctant) etw nicht tun wollen; (= doubtful) Bedenken haben, etw zu tun

hesitantly [ˈhezɪtəntlɪ] ADV zögernd

hesitate [ˈhezɪteɪt] VI zögern; (in speech) stocken; **I'd ~ to take** or **at taking on such a task** ich würde es mir gut überlegen, ob ich so eine Aufgabe übernehmen würde; **he didn't ~ at the idea of leaving home** er zögerte keinen Augenblick, von zu Hause wegzugehen; **I am still hesitating about what I should do** ich bin mir immer noch nicht schlüssig, was ich tun soll; **don't ~ to ask/contact me** fragen Sie mich ruhig/wenden Sie sich ruhig an mich; (more formally) zögern Sie nicht, mich zu fragen/sich an mich zu wenden

hesitation [ˌhezɪˈteɪʃən] N Zögern *nt*; **after some/a moment's ~** nach einigem/kurzem Zögern; **without the slightest ~** ohne auch nur einen Augenblick zu zögern; **I have no ~ in saying that ...** ich kann ohne weiteres sagen, dass ...

heterogeneous [ˌhetərəʊˈdʒiːnɪəs] ADJ heterogen

heterosexual [ˌhetərəʊˈseksjʊəl] **1** ADJ heterosexuell **2** N Heterosexuelle(r) *mf*

heterosexuality [ˌhetərəʊˌseksjʊˈælɪtɪ] N Heterosexualität *f*

het up [hetˈʌp] ADJ (*Brit inf*) aufgeregt; **to get ~ about/over sth** sich über etw (*acc*)/wegen einer Sache (*gen*) aufregen

hew [hjuː], *pret* **hewed**, *ptp* **hewn** *or* **hewed** VT hauen; (= *shape*) behauen

hex [heks] (*esp US inf*) **1** N Fluch *m*; **there must be a ~ on this project** dieses Projekt muss verhext sein (*inf*); **to put a ~ on sb/sth** jdn/etw verhexen **2** VT verhexen

hexagon [ˈheksəgən] N Sechseck *nt*

hexagonal [hekˈsægənəl] ADJ sechseckig

hey [heɪ] INTERJ (*to attract attention*) he (Sie/du); (*in surprise*) he, Mensch (*inf*)

heyday [ˈheɪdeɪ] N Glanzzeit *f*; **in the ~ of glam rock** als Glam-Rock groß in Mode war

HGV (*Brit*) ABBR *of* **heavy goods vehicle** LKW *m*

hi [haɪ] INTERJ hallo

hiatus [haɪˈeɪtəs] N Lücke *f*; **after a two-week ~** nach einer Unterbrechung von zwei Wochen

hibernate [ˈhaɪbəneɪt] VI Winterschlaf halten

hibernation [ˌhaɪbəˈneɪʃən] N (*lit, fig*) Winterschlaf *m*

hiccough, hiccup [ˈhɪkʌp] **1** N Schluckauf *m*; (*fig inf*: = *problem*) Problemchen *nt* (*inf*); **to have the ~s** den Schluckauf haben; **without any ~s** ohne Störungen **2** VI hicksen (*dial*); **he started ~ing** er bekam den Schluckauf

hick [hɪk] N (*US inf*) Hinterwäldler(in) *m(f)* (*inf*)

hickory [ˈhɪkərɪ] N (= *tree*) Hickory(nussbaum) *m*; (= *wood*) Hickory(holz) *nt*

hide¹ [haɪd], *vb*: *pret* **hid** [hɪd], *ptp* **hid** *or* **hidden** [ˈhɪdn] **1** VT verstecken (*from* vor +*dat*); *truth, tears, feelings, face* verbergen (*from* vor +*dat*); (= *obstruct from view*) *moon, rust* verdecken; **hidden from view** nicht zu sehen; **I have nothing to ~** ich habe nichts zu verbergen; **there is a hidden agenda** da steckt noch etwas anderes dahinter; **hidden defect** verborgener Mangel **2** VI sich verstecken, sich verbergen (*from sb* vor jdm); **he was hiding in the cupboard** er hielt sich im Schrank versteckt; **he's hiding behind a pseudonym** er verbirgt sich hinter einem Pseudonym **3** N Versteck *nt*

▶ **hide away** **1** VI sich verstecken, sich verbergen **2** VT SEP verstecken

▶ **hide out** VI sich verstecken; (= *to be hiding also*) sich versteckt halten

hide² N (*of animal*) Haut *f*; (*on furry animal*) Fell *nt*; (*processed*) Leder *nt*; **the bags are made out of rhino ~** die Taschen sind aus Nashornleder

hide: **hide-and-seek**, (*US*) **hide-and-go-seek** N Versteckspiel *nt*; **to play ~** Verstecken spielen; **hideaway** N Versteck *nt*; (= *refuge*) Zufluchtsort *m*; **hidebound** ADJ *person, views* engstirnig

hideous [ˈhɪdɪəs] ADJ grauenhaft, scheußlich; *colour* schrecklich; *embarrassment, price* fürchterlich

hideously [ˈhɪdɪəslɪ] ADV *painted, designed, deformed* grauenhaft; (*emph*) *expensive, slow, loud* schrecklich; **~ ugly** potthässlich (*inf*)

hideout [ˈhaɪdaʊt] N Versteck *nt*

hiding¹ [ˈhaɪdɪŋ] N **to be in ~** sich versteckt halten; **to go into ~** untertauchen

hiding² N **(a)** (= *beating*) Tracht *f* Prügel; **to give sb a good ~** jdm eine Tracht Prügel geben **(b)** (*inf*: = *defeat*) Schlappe *f* (*inf*); **the team took** *or* **got a real ~** die Mannschaft musste eine schwere Schlappe einstecken (*inf*)

hiding place N Versteck *nt*

hierarchic(al) [ˌhaɪəˈrɑːkɪk(əl)] ADJ hierarchisch

hierarchy [ˈhaɪərɑːkɪ] N Hierarchie *f*

hieroglyph [ˈhaɪərəglɪf] N Hieroglyphe *f*

hieroglyphics [ˌhaɪərəˈglɪfɪks] PL Hieroglyphen *pl*

hi-fi [ˈhaɪfaɪ] **1** N (= *system*) Hi-Fi-Anlage *f* **2** ADJ Hi-Fi-; **~ equipment** Hi-Fi-Geräte *pl*

higgledy-piggledy [ˈhɪgldɪˈpɪgldɪ] **1** ADV durcheinander **2** ADJ durcheinander; (= *confused*) wirr

high [haɪ] **1** ADJ (+ER) **(a)** hoch *pred*, hohe(r, s) *attr*; *reputation* hervorragend; *altitude* groß; *wind* stark; *complexion, colour* (hoch)rot; **a building 80 metres** (*Brit*) *or* **meters** (*US*) **~, an 80-metre** (*Brit*) *or* **80-meter** (*US*) **~ building** ein 80 Meter hohes Gebäude; **the building is 80 metres** (*Brit*) *or* **meters** (*US*) **~** das Gebäude ist 80 Meter hoch; **on one of the ~er floors** in einem der oberen Stockwerke; **at ~ tide** *or* **water** bei Flut *or* Hochwasser; **the river is quite ~** der Fluss führt ziemlich viel Wasser; **to be left ~ and dry** auf dem Trockenen sitzen (*inf*); **~ office** hohes Amt; **on the ~est authority** von höchster Stelle; **to be ~ and mighty** erhaben tun; **of the ~est calibre** (*Brit*) *or* **caliber** (*US*)/**quality** von bestem Format/bester Qualität; **casualties were ~** es gab viele Opfer; (*Mil*) es gab hohe Verluste; **the temperature was in the ~ twenties** die Temperatur lag bei fast 30 Grad; **to pay a ~ price for sth** (*lit, fig*) etw teuer bezahlen; **to the ~est degree** im höchsten Grad *or* Maß; **in (very) ~ spirits** in Hochstimmung; **~ in fat** fettreich; **it's ~ time you went home** es ist *or* wird höchste Zeit, dass du nach Hause gehst

(b) (*inf*: *on drugs*) high (*inf*); **to get ~ on cocaine** sich mit Kokain anturnen (*sl*)

2 ADV (+ER) hoch; **~ up** (*position*) hoch oben; (*motion*) hoch hinauf; **~er up the hill was a small farm** etwas weiter oben am Berg lag ein kleiner Bauernhof; **~ (up) on the agenda** ganz oben auf der Tagesordnung; **~ up in the organization** weit oben in der Organisationsstruktur; **one floor ~er** ein Stockwerk höher; **to throw sth ~ in(to) the air** etw hoch in die Luft werfen; **to go as ~ as £200** bis zu £ 200 (hoch) gehen; **feelings ran ~** die Gemüter erhitzten sich; **to search ~ and low** überall suchen

3 N **(a)** **unemployment/the pound has reached a new ~** die Arbeitslosenzahlen haben/das Pfund hat einen neuen Höchststand erreicht; **sales have reached an all-time ~** die Verkaufszahlen sind so hoch wie nie zuvor; **the ~s and lows of my career** die Höhen und Tiefen *pl* meiner Laufbahn **(b)** (*Met*) Hoch *nt* **(c)** **he's still on a ~** (*inf*: = *on drugs*) er ist immer noch high (*inf*) **(d)** (*US Aut*: = *top gear*) **in ~** im höchsten Gang **(e)** (*US inf*: = ~ *school*) Penne *f* (*inf*)

high: **high altar** N Hochaltar *m*; **high beam** N (*Aut*) Fernlicht *nt*; **highbrow** N Intellektuelle(r) *mf* **2** ADJ *interests* intellektuell; *tastes, music, author* anspruchsvoll; **highchair** N Hochstuhl *m*; **High Church** **1** N Hochkirche *f* **2** ADJ der Hochkirche; **to be very ~** streng hochkirchlich eingestellt sein; **high-class** ADJ erstklassig; **high court** N oberstes *or* höchstes Gericht; **high-density** ADJ (*Comput*) *disk* mit hoher Schreibdichte; **high-end** ADJ (*Brit Comm*) Spitzen-; **high-energy** ADJ energiereich

higher [ˈhaɪə^r] **1** ADJ **(a)** COMP *of* **high (b)** *animals, life-forms* höher (entwickelt) **2** N **Higher** (*Scot*) ≈ Abiturabschluss *m*; **to take one's Highers** ≈ das Abitur machen; **three Highers** ≈ das Abitur in drei Fächern

higher: **higher education** N Hochschulbildung *f*; **Higher National Certificate** N (*Brit*) ≈ Berufsschulabschluss *m*; **Higher National Diploma** N (*Brit*) *Qualifikationsnachweis in technischen Fächern*

high: **high explosive** N hochexplosiver Sprengstoff; **highfalutin** [ˌhaɪfəˈluːtɪn] ADJ (*inf*) *language, behaviour* hochtrabend; *scheme* großkotzig (*inf*); *idea* hochgestochen; **high-fibre**, (*US*) **high-fiber** ADJ ballaststoffreich; **high-five** N (*inf*) Highfive *nt*; **to give sb a ~** jdn mit Highfive begrüßen; **high-flier** N (*inf*) (= *successful person*) Senkrechtstarter(in) *m(f)*; (= *ambitious person*) Ehrgeizling *m* (*pej*); **he's a ~** er ist ein Erfolgstyp (*inf*); **high-flown** ADJ *style, speech* hochtrabend; **high-flyer** N = **high-flier**; **high-flying** ADJ (*fig*) *businessman etc* erfolgreich; *lifestyle* exklusiv; **high ground** N (*fig*) hoch liegendes Land; **snow on ~** Schnee in hoch liegenden Gebieten **(b)** (*fig*) **to take the political/intellectual ~** sich politisch/intellektuell aufs hohe Ross setzen; **to lose/claim the moral ~** die moralische Überlegenheit verlieren/für sich beanspruchen; **high-growth** ADJ (*Econ*) mit hohem Wachstum; **high-handed** ADJ selbstherrlich; *treatment* arrogant; **high hat** N (*US inf*) hochnäsiger Typ (*inf*); **high-hat**

(*US inf*) **1** ADJ hochnäsig (*inf*) **2** VT herablassend behandeln; **high-heeled** ADJ hochhackig; **high heels** PL hohe Absätze *pl*; **high-interest** ADJ (*Fin*) hoch verzinslich; **high jinks** PL (*inf*) ausgelassene Späße *pl*; **high jump** N (*Sport*) Hochsprung *m*; **highland** ADJ hochländisch; *area, town also* im Hochland; **Highlands** PL schottisches Hochland, (schottische) Highlands *pl*; **high-level** ADJ *talks* auf höchster Ebene; (*Comput*) *language* höher; **high life** N Highlife *nt*; **highlight** **1** N (a) ~s (*in hair*) Strähnchen *pl* (b) (*fig*) Höhepunkt *m* **2** VT (a) *problem, dangers* ein Schlaglicht werfen auf (+*acc*) (b) *text* (*with ~er*) hervorheben; (*on computer screen*) markieren; **highlighter** N (= *pen*) Leuchtstift *m*, Textmarker *m*

highly ['haɪlɪ] ADV (a) (*emph:* = *extremely*) äußerst; *inflammable* leicht; *spiced* stark; *individual, unusual, significant, efficient* höchst; ~ **charged** *atmosphere* aufgeladen; *debate* hitzig; **to be ~ critical of sb/sth** jdn/etw scharf kritisieren; ~ **trained** äußerst gut ausgebildet; *skilled worker* hoch qualifiziert; *sportsperson* durchtrainiert; ~ **skilled** äußerst geschickt; *worker, workforce* hoch qualifiziert; ~ **placed** (*in organization, society*) hoch gestellt; (*Sport: in league*) führend; ~ **respected/ educated/paid** hoch geachtet/gebildet/bezahlt; ~ **intelligent/ topical/toxic** hochintelligent/-aktuell/-giftig; ~ **unlikely** *or* **improbable** äußerst *or* höchst unwahrscheinlich (b) *regard, rate, prize* hoch; **they were** ~ **praised** sie wurden hoch gelobt; **I don't rate him very ~ at all** ich halte überhaupt nicht viel von ihm; **to speak ~ of sb/sth** sich sehr positiv über jdn/etw äußern; **to think ~ of sb/sth** eine hohe Meinung von jdm/etw haben; ~ **recommended** sehr empfehlenswert

highly strung ADJ (*Brit*) nervös

high: **High Mass** N Hochamt *nt*; **high-minded** ADJ *ideals* hoch; *intentions* hochgesinnt; *critics* anspruchsvoll

highness ['haɪnɪs] N **Her/Your Highness** Ihre/Eure Hoheit; **yes, Your Highness** ja, Hoheit

high: **high-octane** ADJ (*lit*) mit hoher Oktanzahl; (*fig:* = *powerful, exciting*) hochkarätig; **high-performance** ADJ Hochleistungs-; **high-pitched** ADJ *sound, voice* hoch; *scream, squeak* schrill; **high point** N Höhepunkt *m*; **high-powered** ADJ (a) *machine, engine, computer* leistungsfähig; *rifle, gun* leistungsstark; *car* stark(motorig); *laser* stark (b) *person* hoch gestellt; *academic etc* äußerst fähig; *job, career, course* anspruchsvoll; *delegation* hochkarätig (*inf*); **high-pressure** ADJ (*Met*) ~ **area** Hochdruckgebiet *nt*; **high priest** N (*lit, fig*) Hohepriester *m*; **a** ~ ein Hoher Priester *m*; **high priestess** N (*lit, fig*) Hohepriesterin *f*; **high-profile** ADJ profiliert; **high-ranking** ADJ hoch(rangig); **high-resolution** ADJ hoch auflösend; **high-rise** ADJ ~ **building** Hochhaus *nt*; ~ **office** (**block**) Bürohochhaus *nt*; ~ **flats** (*Brit*) (Wohn)hochhaus *nt*; **high-risk** ADJ risikoreich; ~ **group** Risikogruppe *f*; **high school** N (*Brit*) ≈ Oberschule *f* (für 11 bis 18-Jährige); (*US*) ≈ Oberschule *f* (für 15 bis 18-Jährige)

In den USA sind **high schools** *weiterführende Bildungseinrichtungen für alle Jugendlichen im Alter von 15 bis 18 Jahren (neunte bis zwölfte Klasse).* Junior high schools *beginnen bereits mit der siebten Klasse. Wenn die Schüler die zwölfte Klasse mindestens mit dem Prädikat „zufrieden stellend" abschließen, erhalten sie auf einer feierlichen Zeremonie ihr Highschool-Diplom. Zu diesem Anlass kaufen sie sich auch häufig eine ganz besonderen Jahrgangsring. Über jedes Schuljahr wird ein Jahrbuch angelegt, das die Schüler erwerben können.* ▶ PROM

high: **high-scoring** ADJ *game* (*Ftbl, Hockey, Handball*) torreich; (*Basketball*) punktreich; **high seas** PL **the** ~ die Meere *pl*; **on the** ~ auf hoher See; **high-security** ADJ ~ **prison** Hochsicherheitsgefängnis *nt*; ~ **wing** Hochsicherheitstrakt *m*; **high-sided** ADJ ~ **vehicle** hohes Fahrzeug; **high sign** N (*US inf*) vereinbartes Signal; **to give sb a** ~ jdm ein vereinbartes Signal geben; **high society** N Highsociety *f*; **high-speed** ADJ schnell; *drill* mit hoher Umdrehungszahl; ~ **car chase** wilde Verfolgungsjagd im Auto; ~ **train** Hochgeschwindigkeitszug *m*; ~ **film** hoch (licht)empfindlicher Film; **high-spirited** ADJ temperamentvoll; **high spirits** PL Hochstimmung *f*; *youthful* ~ jugendlicher Übermut; **high spot** N Höhepunkt *m*; **high street** N (*Brit*) Hauptstraße *f*; ~ **banks** Geschäftsbanken *pl*; ~ **shops** Geschäfte *pl* in der Innenstadt; **high-strung** ADJ (*US*) nervös

hightail ['haɪteɪl] VI (*US inf*) **to** ~ (**it**) **out of a place** (aus einem Ort) abhauen (*inf*)

high: **high tea** N (frühes) Abendessen; **hightech** N, ADJ = **hi-tech**; **high technology** N Hochtechnologie *f*; **high-tension** ADJ (*Elec*) Hochspannungs-; **high treason** N Hochverrat *m*; **high-up** **1** ADJ *person* hoch gestellt **2** N (*inf*) hohes Tier (*inf*); **highway** N (a) (*US*) Highway *m*, ≈ Autobahn *f* (b) (*Brit*) Landstraße *f*; **public** ~ öffentliche Straße; **Highway Code** N (*Brit*) Straßenverkehrsordnung *f*; **high wire** N Drahtseil *nt*; **high-yield** ADJ (*Agr*) ertragreich; (*Fin*) ertragsstark

hijack ['haɪdʒæk] **1** VT entführen; (*fig*) für sich beanspruchen **2** N Entführung *f*

hijacker ['haɪdʒækə^r] N Entführer(in) *m(f)*

hike [haɪk] **1** VI wandern **2** VT *prices, rates* erhöhen **3** N (a) (*lit*) Wanderung *f* (b) (*fig: in interest rates*) Erhöhung *f* ▶ **hike up** VT SEP (a) *trousers, skirt* hochziehen (b) *prices, rates* erhöhen

hiker ['haɪkə^r] N Wanderer *m*, Wanderin *f*

hiking ['haɪkɪŋ] N Wandern *nt*

hiking boots PL Wanderstiefel *pl*

hilarious [hɪ'lɛərɪəs] ADJ urkomisch (*inf*)

hilariously [hɪ'lɛərɪəslɪ] ADV sehr amüsant

hill [hɪl] N Hügel *m*; (*higher*) Berg *m*; (= *incline*) Hang *m*; **to park on a** ~ am Berg parken; **as old as the ~s** steinalt, uralt; **that joke's as old as the ~s** der Witz hat ja so einen langen Bart; **to be over the** ~ (*fig inf*) seine beste Zeit *or* die besten Jahre hinter sich (*dat*) haben

hillbilly ['hɪlbɪlɪ] (*US inf*) **1** N Hinterwäldler(in) *m(f)* (*pej*) **2** ADJ hinterwäldlerisch (*pej*); ~ **music** Hillbilly *no art*, Hillbillymusik *f*

hillock ['hɪlək] N Hügel *m*, Anhöhe *f*

hill: **hillside** N Hang *m*; **hilltop** N Gipfel *m*; **hill-walker** N Bergwanderer *m*, Bergwanderin *f*; **hill-walking** N Bergwandern *nt*

hilly ['hɪlɪ] ADJ (+ER) hüg(e)lig; (*higher*) bergig

hilt [hɪlt] N Heft *nt*; (*of dagger*) Griff *m*; (**up**) **to the** ~ (*fig*) voll und ganz; (*involved, in debt also*) bis über beide Ohren (*inf*); **I'll back you (up) to the** ~ ich stehe voll und ganz hinter Ihnen

him [hɪm] PERS PRON (a) (*dir obj, with prep* +*acc*) ihn; (*indir obj, with prep* +*dat*) ihm; (*when he is previously mentioned in clause*) sich (b) (*emph*) er; **it's** ~ er ist's

Himalayas [,hɪmə'leɪəz] PL Himalaya *m*

himself [hɪm'self] PERS PRON (a) (*dir and indir obj, with prep*) sich; *see also* **myself** (b) (*emph*) (er) selbst

hind[1] [haɪnd] N (*Zool*) Hirschkuh *f*

hind[2] ADJ Hinter-; ~ **legs** Hinterbeine *pl*; **he can** *or* **could talk the** ~ **leg(s) off a donkey** (*inf*) er kann einem ein Ohr *or* die Ohren abreden (*inf*)

hinder ['hɪndə^r] VT (a) (= *obstruct, impede*) behindern; (= *delay*) *person* aufhalten; *arrival* verzögern (b) (= *stop, prevent from happening*) verhindern; **to** ~ **sb from doing sth** jdn daran hindern, etw zu tun

Hindi ['hɪndiː] N Hindi *nt*

hindquarters ['haɪndkwɔːtəz] PL Hinterteil *nt*; (*of horse*) Hinterhand *f*

hindrance ['hɪndrəns] N Behinderung *f*; (= *obstacle*) Hindernis *nt* (*to für*); **the rules/children are a** ~ die Regeln/Kinder sind hinderlich; **it was a serious** ~ **to progress** es behinderte den Fortschritt sehr; **without** ~ unbehindert

hindsight ['haɪndsaɪt] N **with** ~ **it's easy to criticize** im Nachhinein ist es leicht zu kritisieren; **it was, in** ~**, a mistaken judgement** es war, rückblickend betrachtet, ein Fehlurteil

Hindu ['hɪnduː] **1** ADJ hinduistisch; ~ **people** Hindu(s) *pl* **2** N Hindu *m*

Hinduism ['hɪnduːɪzəm] N Hinduismus *m*

hinge [hɪndʒ] **1** N (*of door*) Angel *f*; (*of box etc*) Scharnier *nt* **2** VI (*fig*) abhängen (*on von*)

hinged [hɪndʒd] ADJ mit Scharnier/mit Scharnieren (versehen); *door* eingehängt; ~ **lid** Klappdeckel *m*

hint [hɪnt] **1** N (a) (= *suggestion*) Andeutung *f*, Hinweis *m*; **to give a/no** ~ **of sth** etw ahnen lassen/nicht ahnen lassen; **to give** *or* **drop sb a** ~ jdm einen Wink geben; **OK, I can take a** ~ schon recht, ich verstehe *or* ich habe den Wink mit dem Zaunpfahl verstanden (*inf*)

(b) (= *trace*) Spur *f*; **a ~ of garlic** eine Spur Knoblauch; **a ~ of irony** ein Hauch *m* von Spott; **with just a ~ of sadness in his smile** mit einem leichten Anflug von Traurigkeit in seinem Lächeln; **at the first ~ of trouble** beim ersten Zeichen von Ärger

(c) (= *tip, piece of advice*) Tipp *m*; **~s for travellers** (*Brit*) *or* **travelers** (*US*) Reisetipps *pl*

2 VT andeuten (*to* gegenüber); **what are you ~ing?** was wollen Sie damit sagen *or* andeuten?

➤ **hint at** VI +PREP OBJ **he hinted at changes in the cabinet** er deutete an, dass es Umbesetzungen im Kabinett geben würde; **he hinted at my involvement in the affair** er spielte auf meine Rolle in der Affäre an

hinterland [ˈhɪntəlænd] N Hinterland *nt*

hip¹ [hɪp] N Hüfte *f*; **with one's hands on one's ~s** die Arme in die Hüften gestemmt

hip² INTERJ **~! ~!, hurrah!** hipp hipp, hurra!

hip³ ADJ (*inf*) hip (*inf*)

hip IN CPDS Hüft-; **hipbone** N (*Anat*) Hüftbein *nt*; **hip flask** N Flachmann *m* (*inf*); **hip measurement** N Hüftumfang *m*

hippie N = **hippy**

hippo [ˈhɪpəʊ] N (*inf*) Nilpferd *nt*

hip pocket N Gesäßtasche *f*

hippopotamus [ˌhɪpəˈpɒtəməs] N, *pl* **-es** *or* **hippopotami** [ˌhɪpəˈpɒtəmaɪ] Flusspferd *nt*

hippy, hippie [ˈhɪpɪ] N Hippie *m*

hip replacement N Hüftoperation *f*; (= *device*) Hüftprothese *f*

hire [haɪəʳ] (*esp Brit*) **1** N (= *rental*) Mieten *nt*; (*of car also, of suit*) Leihen *nt*; (= *employment*) Einstellen *nt*; **the hall is available for ~** man kann den Saal mieten; **for ~** (*taxi*) frei; **it's on ~** (= *is a hired item*) es ist gemietet/geliehen; **to be (out) on ~** vermietet sein

2 VT **(a)** (= *rent*) mieten; *suit* leihen; **~d car** Mietwagen *m*, Leihwagen *m*

(b) (= *employ*) einstellen; **~d assassin** gedungener Mörder

(c) = **hire out**

➤ **hire out** VT SEP (*esp Brit*) vermieten, verleihen

hireling [ˈhaɪəlɪŋ] N (*pej*) Mietling *m* (*old pej*)

hire-purchase [ˌhaɪəˈpɜːtʃəs] N (*Brit*) Ratenkauf *m*, Teilzahlungskauf *m*; **on ~** auf Raten *or* Teilzahlung; **~ agreement** Teilzahlungs(kauf)vertrag *m*

his [hɪz] **1** POSS ADJ sein; *see also* **my 2** POSS PRON seine(r, s); **~** (*on towels etc*) er; *see also* **mine¹**

Hispanic [hɪsˈpænɪk] **1** ADJ hispanisch; *community* spanisch **2** N Hispanoamerikaner(in) *m(f)*

hiss [hɪs] **1** VI zischen; (*cat*) fauchen **2** VT zischen; **come here, he ~ed** komm her, zischte er **3** N Zischen *nt*; (*of cat*) Fauchen *nt*

histogram [ˈhɪstəgræm] N Säulendiagramm *nt*, Histogramm *nt*

historian [hɪsˈtɔːrɪən] N Historiker(in) *m(f)*

historic [hɪsˈtɒrɪk] ADJ (*also Gram*) historisch; **~ cost** (*Comm*) Anschaffungskosten *pl*

historical [hɪsˈtɒrɪkəl] ADJ historisch; **~ research** Geschichtsforschung *f*; **places of ~ interest** historisch *or* geschichtlich interessante Stätten *pl*

historically [hɪsˈtɒrɪkəlɪ] ADV **(a)** (= *traditionally*) traditionellerweise; **the country has ~ been very dependent on agriculture** das Land war immer schon stark von der Landwirtschaft abhängig **(b)** *important, accurate, consider* historisch; **~ unique** einmalig in der Geschichte

history [ˈhɪstərɪ] N Geschichte *f*; (= *study of ~*) Geschichtswissenschaft *f*; **that's all ~ now** (*fig*) das gehört jetzt alles der Vergangenheit an; **he's ~** er ist schon lange vergessen *or* passé (*inf*); **he has a ~ of violence** er hat eine Vorgeschichte als Gewalttäter; **he has a ~ of heart disease** er hat schon lange ein Herzleiden

histrionic [ˌhɪstrɪˈɒnɪk] ADJ theatralisch

histrionics [ˌhɪstrɪˈɒnɪks] PL theatralisches Getue

hit [hɪt], *vb*: *pret, ptp* **hit 1** N **(a)** (= *blow, also Baseball*) Schlag *m*; (*on target, Fencing*) Treffer *m*

(b) (= *success, also Theat*) Erfolg *m*; (= *song*) Hit *m*; **to be *or* make a (big) ~ with sb** bei jdm (ausgesprochen) gut ankommen

(c) (*Comput*) (= *response from Internet*) Treffer *m*; (= *visit to website*) Hit *m*

2 VT **(a)** (= *strike, score*) schlagen; (*Comput*) *key* drücken; **to ~ one's head against sth** sich (*dat*) den Kopf an etw (*dat*) stoßen; **he ~ his head on the table** er schlug mit dem Kopf auf den Tisch auf; **the car ~ a tree** das Auto fuhr gegen einen Baum; **he was ~ by a stone** er wurde von einem Stein getroffen; **the tree was ~ by lightning** der Baum wurde vom Blitz getroffen; **the hurricane ~ Miami last night** der Hurrikan erreichte gestern Abend Miami; **the smell ~ me as I entered the room** der Geruch schlug mir entgegen, als ich ins Zimmer kam; **you won't know what has ~ you** (*inf*) du wirst dein blaues Wunder erleben (*inf*); **to ~ a century** hundert Läufe machen

(b) *mark, target, top C* treffen; *speed, level, top form etc* erreichen; **that ~ home** (*fig*) das hat getroffen, das saß (*inf*); **you've ~ it (on the head)** (*fig*) du hast es (genau) getroffen; **he's been ~ in the leg** (= *wounded*) er ist am Bein getroffen worden

(c) (= *affect adversely*) betreffen; **the crops were ~ by the rain** der Regen hat der Ernte geschadet; **to be hard ~ by sth** von etw schwer getroffen werden

(d) (= *come to, arrive at*) *beaches etc* erreichen; **to ~ town** (*inf*) die Stadt erreichen; **we're going to ~ the rush hour** wir kommen direkt in den Stoßverkehr; **to ~ a problem** ein Problem stoßen

(e) (*US inf*) **to ~ sb for 50 dollars** jdn um 50 Dollar anhauen (*inf*)

(f) (*fig inf phrases*) **to ~ the bottle** zur Flasche greifen; **to ~ the roof** an die Decke *or* in die Luft gehen (*inf*); **to ~ the road** sich auf die Socken machen (*inf*); **to ~ the ground running** (*person*) sofort alles im Griff haben

3 VI (= *strike*) schlagen; **he ~s hard** er schlägt hart zu

➤ **hit back** VI, VT SEP (*lit, fig*) zurückschlagen; **he hit back at his critics** er gab seinen Kritikern Kontra

➤ **hit off** VT SEP **to hit it off with sb** (*inf*) sich gut mit jdm verstehen, prima mit jdm auskommen (*inf*); **they hit it off straight away** sie haben sich von Anfang an gut verstanden

➤ **hit on** VI +PREP OBJ **(a)** stoßen auf (+*acc*), finden **(b)** (*esp US inf*: = *chat up*) anmachen (*inf*)

➤ **hit out** VI **(a)** (*lit*) einschlagen (*at sb* auf jdn) **(b)** (*fig*) **to hit out at *or* against sb/sth** jdn/etw attackieren *or* scharf angreifen

➤ **hit up** VT SEP (*US inf*) **to hit sb up for 50 dollars** jdn um 50 Dollar anhauen (*inf*)

➤ **hit upon** VI +PREP OBJ = **hit on (a)**

hit: **hit-and-miss** ADJ = **hit-or-miss**; **hit-and-run** ADJ **~ accident** Unfall *m* mit Fahrerflucht; **~ driver** unfallflüchtiger Fahrer, unfallflüchtige Fahrerin

hitch [hɪtʃ] **1** N Haken *m*; (*in plan, proceedings, programme*) Problem *nt*; **a technical ~** eine technische Panne; **without a ~** reibungslos; **there's been a ~** da ist ein Problem aufgetaucht **2** VT **(a)** (= *fasten*) festmachen (*sth to sth* etw an etw *dat*)

(b) (*inf*) **to get ~ed** heiraten

(c) **to ~ a lift *or* ride** trampen; **she ~ed a lift *or* ride with a truck driver** ein Lastwagenfahrer nahm sie mit

3 VI (*esp Brit*) trampen

➤ **hitch up** VT SEP **(a)** *trailer etc* anhängen; **we hitched up the horses to the wagon** wir spannten die Pferde vor den Wagen **(b)** *trousers, skirt* hochziehen

hitcher [ˈhɪtʃəʳ] N (*esp Brit inf*) Anhalter(in) *m(f)*

hitch: **hitchhike** VI per Anhalter fahren, trampen; **hitchhiker** N Anhalter(in) *m(f)*; **hitchhiking** N Trampen *nt*

hi tech [ˈhaɪtek] N Spitzentechnologie *f*

hi-tech [ˈhaɪtek] ADJ Hitech-

hither [ˈhɪðəʳ] ADV **~ and thither** (*liter*) hierhin und dorthin

hitherto [ˌhɪðəˈtuː] ADV bisher, bis jetzt

hit: **hit list** N (*lit, fig*) Abschussliste *f*; **hitman** N (*inf*) Killer *m* (*inf*); **hit-or-miss** ADJ auf gut Glück *pred*; *methods, planning* schlampig; **it was a rather ~ affair** das ging alles aufs Geratewohl; **hit parade** N Hitparade *f*; **hit record** N Hit *m*; **hit show** N erfolgreiche Show; **hit single** N Hitsingle *f*; **hit song** N Hit *m*; **hit squad** N Killerkommando *nt*

HIV ABBR *of* **human immunodeficiency virus** HIV *nt*; **~ positive/negative** HIV-positiv/-negativ

hive [haɪv] N **(a)** (= *beehive*) Bienenstock *m*; (= *bees in a ~*) (Bienen)schwarm *m* **(b)** (*fig*) **the office was a ~ of activity** das Büro glich einem Bienenhaus

➤ **hive off** VT SEP *department, company* ausgliedern

hiya ['haɪjə] INTERJ hallo

HM ABBR *of* **His/Her Majesty** S. M./I. M.

HNC (*Brit*) ABBR *of* **Higher National Certificate**

HND (*Brit*) ABBR *of* **Higher National Diploma**

hoagie, hoagy ['həʊgɪ] N (*US*) großes, reichlich belegtes Sandwich, Jumbo-Sandwich *nt* (*inf*)

hoard [hɔːd] **1** N Vorrat *m*; (= *treasure*) Schatz *m*; **a ~ of weapons** ein Waffenlager *nt*; **~ of money** gehortetes Geld **2** VT (*also* **~ up**) *food etc* hamstern; *money, supplies, weapons* horten

hoarder ['hɔːdəʳ] N Hamsterer *m*, Hamsterin *f*

hoarding[1] ['hɔːdɪŋ] N (*of food etc*) Hamstern *nt*

hoarding[2] N (*Brit*: = *fence, board*) Bretterzaun *m*; (**advertising**) ~ Plakatwand *f*

hoarfrost ['hɔːfrɒst] N (Rau)reif *m*

hoarse [hɔːs] ADJ (+ER) heiser; **you sound rather ~** deine Stimme klingt heiser

hoary ['hɔːrɪ] ADJ (+ER) (*fig*: = *old*) uralt; **a ~ old joke** ein alter Hut

hoax [həʊks] N (= *practical joke*) Streich *m*; (= *trick etc*) Trick *m*; (= *false alarm*) blinder Alarm

hoax call N **a ~** ein blinder Alarm

hob [hɒb] N (*on modern cooker*) Kochfeld *nt*

hobble ['hɒbl] **1** VI humpeln **2** VT (*fig*) behindern; *economy* lahm legen

hobby ['hɒbɪ] N Hobby *nt*

hobbyhorse ['hɒbɪhɔːs] N (*lit, fig*) Steckenpferd *nt*

hobnailed ['hɒbneɪld] ADJ genagelt

hobnob ['hɒbnɒb] VI **she's been seen hobnobbing with the chairman and his wife** sie ist viel mit dem Vorsitzenden und seiner Frau zusammen gesehen worden

hobo ['həʊbəʊ] N (*US*) (a) (= *tramp*) Penner *m* (*inf*) (b) (= *worker*) Wanderarbeiter *m*

hock[1] [hɒk] N (= *wine*) weißer Rheinwein

hock[2] N (*inf*) **to be in ~ to sb** in jds Schuld stehen

hockey ['hɒkɪ] N Hockey *nt*; (*US*) Eishockey *nt*

hockey: **hockey pitch** N Hockeyfeld *nt*; **hockey player** N Hockeyspieler(in) *m(f)*; (*US*) Eishockeyspieler(in) *m(f)*; **hockey stick** N Hockeyschläger *m*

hocus-pocus ['həʊkəs'pəʊkəs] N (*inf*: = *trickery*) faule Tricks *pl* (*inf*), Hokuspokus *m*

hod [hɒd] N (*for bricks, mortar etc*) Tragmulde *f*

hodgepodge ['hɒdʒpɒdʒ] N (*US*) = **hotchpotch**

hoe [həʊ] **1** N Hacke *f* **2** VTI hacken

hoedown ['həʊdaʊn] N (*US*) Schwof *m* (*inf*)

hog [hɒg] **1** N (Mast)schwein *nt*; (*US*: = *pig*) Schwein *nt* **2** VT (*inf*) in Beschlag nehmen; **a lot of drivers ~ the middle of the road** viele Fahrer meinen, sie hätten das Straßenmitte gepachtet (*inf*); **to ~ the limelight** alle Aufmerksamkeit für sich beanspruchen

Hogmanay ['hɒgmə'neɪ] N (*Scot*) Silvester *nt*

hog: **hogtie** VT (*US*) an allen vieren fesseln; (*fig inf*) handlungsunfähig machen; **we're ~d** uns (*dat*) sind Hände und Füße gebunden; **hogwash** N (*inf*: = *nonsense*) Quatsch *m*

hoi polloi [ˌhɔɪpə'lɔɪ] N (*pej*) Pöbel *m*

hoist [hɔɪst] **1** VT hochheben; (= *pull up*) hochziehen; *flag* hissen; *sails* aufziehen **2** N Hebezeug *nt*, Hebevorrichtung *f*

---

hokey ['həʊkɪ] ADJ (*US inf*) (a) (= *phoney*) künstlich; *excuse* faul (*inf*); **it's ~** das ist Quatsch (b) (= *corny*) *excuse* abgedroschen; *story, song* kitschig

hold [həʊld]

| **1** NOUN | **3** INTRANSITIVE VERB |
| **2** TRANSITIVE VERB | **4** PHRASAL VERBS |

vb: pret, ptp **held**

1 NOUN

(a) (= *grip, clutch*) Griff *m*; (*Mountaineering, of hairspray*) Halt *m no pl*; **to release/loosen one's hold on sb/sth** jdn/etw loslassen

◆ **to have/get/keep** *etc* **(a) hold of** **to have/catch hold of sth** (*lit*) etw festhalten/fassen *or* packen; **to keep hold of sth** etw nicht loslassen; (= *keep*) etw behalten; **to seize** *or* **grab hold of sb/sth** jdn/etw fassen *or* packen; **grab hold of my hand** fass mich bei der Hand; **to get** *or* **take (a) hold of sth** sich an etw (*dat*) festhalten; **to get hold of sth** (*fig*: = *obtain*) etw finden *or* auftreiben (*inf*); *guns, drugs* etw in die Finger bekommen; *information, story, facts* etw in Erfahrung bringen; **where did you get hold of that idea?** wie kommst du denn auf die Idee?; **to get hold of sb** (*fig*) jdn finden *or* auftreiben (*inf*); (*on phone etc*) jdn erreichen

◆ **to lose one's hold** den Halt verlieren

◆ **to take hold** (*idea*) sich durchsetzen; (*fire, epidemic*) sich ausbreiten; (*disease*) sich verschlimmern; (*recession*) sich breit machen

◆ **on hold** **to be on hold** warten; (*fig*) auf Eis liegen; **to put sb on hold** (*Telec*) jdn zur Wartestellung schalten; (*in larger organizations*) jdn auf die Warteschlange legen; **to put sth on hold** (*fig*) etw auf Eis legen

◆ **no holds barred** **when those two have a row, there are no holds barred** (*fig*) wenn die beiden sich streiten, dann kennen sie nichts mehr (*inf*)

(b) (= *influence*) Einfluss *m* (*over* auf +*acc*)

◆ **hold on** *or* **over sb/sth** **to have a hold over** *or* **on sb** (großen) Einfluss auf jdn ausüben; *audience, followers* jdn in seiner Gewalt haben; **he hasn't got any hold on** *or* **over me** er kann mir nichts anhaben; **the president has consolidated his hold on power** der Präsident hat seine Macht gefestigt

(c) (*Naut, Aviat*) Laderaum *m*, Frachtraum *m*

2 TRANSITIVE VERB

(a) (= *grasp, carry*) halten; **to hold sb/sth tight** jdn/etw (ganz) festhalten; **the frightened children held each other tight** die verängstigten Kinder klammerten sich aneinander; **this car holds the road well** dieses Auto hat eine gute Straßenlage; **to hold sth in place** etw (fest)halten; **to hold oneself/sth ready** *or* **in readiness** sich/etw bereithalten

◆ **to hold hands** sich an der Hand halten; (*lovers, children etc*) Händchen halten

(b) (= *contain*) enthalten; (*bottle, tank etc*) fassen; (*bus, plane, hall etc*) Platz haben für; **this room holds twenty people** in diesem Raum haben zwanzig Personen Platz; **what does the future hold (for us)?** was bringt (uns) die Zukunft?

(c) (= *believe*) meinen; (= *maintain*) behaupten; **I have always held that …** ich habe schon immer behauptet, dass …; **to hold sth to be true/immoral** *etc* etw für wahr/unmoralisch *etc* halten; **to hold the view** *or* **opinion that …** die Meinung vertreten, dass …; **to hold sb responsible (for sth)** jdn (für etw) verantwortlich machen

(d) (= *restrain, retain, keep back*) *train* aufhalten; *suspect, hostages etc* festhalten; *parcel, confiscated goods etc* zurückhalten; **to hold sb (prisoner)** jdn gefangen halten; **to hold sb hostage** jdn als Geisel festhalten; **there's no holding him** er ist nicht zu bremsen (*inf*); **hold the line!** bleiben Sie am Apparat!; **she can/can't hold her drink** (*esp Brit*) sie verträgt was/nichts

◆ **to hold one's fire** (= *not shoot*) nicht schießen

◆ **to hold one's breath** (*lit*) den Atem anhalten; **don't hold your breath!** (*iro*) erwarte nicht zu viel!

◆ **hold it!** (*inf*) Moment mal (*inf*); **hold it there!** (*when taking photograph*) so ist gut

(e) (= *possess, occupy*) *post, position* innehaben; *passport,* permit, degree haben; power, shares besitzen; (= have) records führen; (on computer, disk) speichern; (Sport) record halten; (Mil) position halten; (against attack) behaupten; **she holds the key to the mystery** sie hat den Schlüssel zu dem Geheimnis; **to hold office** im Amt sein; **to hold its value** seinen Wert behalten; **to hold one's own** sich behaupten (können); **to hold one's serve** (Tennis) den Aufschlag behalten; **to hold sb's attention** jds Aufmerksamkeit fesseln; **to hold sb's interest** jds Interesse wach halten; **to hold a note** (Mus) einen Ton halten

✦**to hold sb to sth I'll hold you to your promise** or **to that!** ich werde Sie beim Wort nehmen

   (f) (meeting, debate, election) abhalten; talks führen; party geben; (Eccl) service (ab)halten; **to hold a conversation** eine Unterhaltung führen

🖪 INTRANSITIVE VERB

   (a) (rope, nail, roof etc) halten; **to hold firm** or **fast** halten; **to hold still** still halten; **to hold tight** festhalten; **will the weather hold?** wird sich das Wetter wohl halten?; **if his luck holds** wenn ihm das Glück treu bleibt

   (b) (Telec) **please hold!** bitte bleiben Sie am Apparat!; **I've been holding for five minutes** ich warte schon fünf Minuten

   (c) (= be valid, apply to) gelten; theory stimmen; **to hold good** (rule, promise etc) gelten

🖪 PHRASAL VERBS

➤ **hold against** VT ALWAYS SEPARATE **to hold sth against sb** jdm etw übel nehmen

➤ **hold back 🖪** VI sich zurückhalten; (= fail to act) zögern; **I held back from telling him just what I thought of him** ich unterließ es, ihm meine Meinung zu sagen **🖪** VT SEP **(a)** crowd zurückhalten; river, floods (auf)stauen; emotions unterdrücken; **to hold sb back from doing sth** jdn daran hindern, etw zu tun **(b)** (= prevent from making progress) daran hindern, voranzukommen; **nothing can hold him back now** jetzt ist er nicht mehr aufzuhalten **(c)** (= withhold) verheimlichen; information, report geheim halten; pay increase verzögern

➤ **hold down** VT SEP **(a)** (= keep on the ground) niederhalten; (= keep in its place) (fest)halten; (= keep in check) unter Kontrolle haben; prices, costs, numbers, pressure niedrig halten **(b)** job haben; **he can't hold any job down for long** er kann sich in keiner Stellung lange halten

➤ **hold forth** VI sich ergehen (geh), sich auslassen (on über +acc)

➤ **hold in** VT SEP stomach einziehen; **to hold in one's anger** seinen Ärger unterdrücken

➤ **hold off 🖪** VI **(a)** (= not act) warten; (enemy) nicht angreifen; **they held off eating until she arrived** sie warteten mit dem Essen, bis sie kam **(b)** (rain, storm) ausbleiben; **I hope the rain holds off** ich hoffe, dass es nicht regnet **🖪** VT SEP enemy, attack, challenge abwehren

➤ **hold on 🖪** VI (lit: = maintain grip) sich festhalten; (= endure, resist) aushalten; (= wait) warten; **hold on (a minute)!** Moment!; (Telec) einen Moment bitte!; **now hold on a minute!** Moment mal! **🖪** VT SEP (fest)halten; **to be held on by sth** mit etw befestigt sein

➤ **hold on to** VI +PREP OBJ **(a)** (lit) festhalten; **they held on to each other** sie hielten sich aneinander fest **(b)** (fig) hope nicht aufgeben; idea, belief festhalten an (+dat) **(c)** (= keep) behalten; position beibehalten; staff halten; **to hold on to the lead** in Führung bleiben; **to hold on to power** sich an der Macht halten

➤ **hold out 🖪** VI **(a)** (supplies etc) reichen **(b)** (= endure, resist) aushalten; (= refuse to yield) nicht nachgeben; **to hold out for sth** auf etw (dat) bestehen **🖪** VT SEP **(a)** (lit) ausstrecken; **to hold out sth to sb** jdm etw hinhalten; **hold your hand out** halt die Hand auf; **she held out her arms** sie breitete die Arme aus **(b)** (fig) prospects bieten; **I held out little hope of seeing him again** ich machte mir nur wenig Hoffnung, ihn wiederzusehen

➤ **hold over** VT SEP **(a)** question, matter vertagen; meeting also, decision verschieben (until auf +acc) **(b)** **to hold sth over sb** (= threaten) jdn etw nicht vergessen lassen

➤ **hold to** VI +PREP OBJ festhalten an (+dat), bleiben bei; **I hold to my belief that ...** ich bleibe dabei, dass ...

➤ **hold together** VI, VT SEP zusammenhalten

➤ **hold up 🖪** VI (theory) sich halten lassen **🖪** VT SEP **(a)** (= raise) hochheben, hochhalten; face nach oben wenden; **hold up your hand** heb die Hand; **to hold sth up to the light** etw gegen das Licht halten **(b)** (= support) (from above) halten; (from the side) stützen; (from beneath) tragen **(c)** **to hold sb/sth up to ridicule/scorn** jdn/etw lächerlich/verächtlich machen; **to hold sb up as an example** jdn als Beispiel hinstellen **(d)** (= stop) anhalten; (= delay) people aufhalten; traffic, production ins Stocken bringen; talks, delivery verzögern; **my application was held up by the postal strike** durch den Poststreik hat sich meine Bewerbung verspätet **(e)** (robbers) bank überfallen

➤ **hold with** VI +PREP OBJ (inf) **I don't hold with that** ich bin gegen so was (inf)

holdall [ˈhəʊldɔːl] N Reisetasche f

holder [ˈhəʊldəʳ] N **(a)** (= person) Besitzer(in) m(f); (of title, office, record, passport) Inhaber(in) m(f) **(b)** (= object) Halter m; (= cigarette-~) Spitze f

holding [ˈhəʊldɪŋ] N **(a)** (Fin: of shares) Anteil m (in an +dat) **(b)** (of land) Landgut nt

holding: holding company N Holding(gesellschaft) f; **holding operation** N provisorische Maßnahme

hold: holdout N (US) Verweigerer m; **hold-up** N **(a)** (= delay) Verzögerung f; (of traffic) Stockung f; **what's the ~?** warum dauert das so lange?; **the strike caused a two-week ~ in production** der Streik brachte die Produktion zwei Wochen lang ins Stocken **(b)** (= armed robbery) bewaffneter Raubüberfall

hole [həʊl] **🖪** N **(a)** Loch nt (also Golf); (fox's) Bau m; **to be full of ~s** (fig) (plot, story) viele Schwächen aufweisen; (argument, theory) unhaltbar sein; **an 18-~ course** ein 18-Loch-Platz m **(b)** (inf: = awkward situation) **to be in a ~** in der Patsche or Klemme sitzen (inf); **to get sb out of a ~** jdm aus der Patsche or Klemme helfen (inf) **(c)** (pej inf) Loch nt (inf); (= town) Kaff nt (inf) **(d)** (vulg: = vagina) Loch nt (vulg) **🖪** VT **(a)** **to be ~d** ein Loch bekommen **(b)** (Golf) ball einlochen

➤ **hole up** VI (inf) (= hide) sich verkriechen (inf) or verstecken; (= barricade themselves in) sich verschanzen

hole: hole in one N (Golf) Hole-in-One nt; **hole-in-the-wall 🖪** N (in die Wand eingebauter) Geldautomat m **🖪** ATTR machine in die Wand eingebaut; **hole puncher** N Locher m

holiday [ˈhɒlɪdeɪ] **🖪** N **(a)** (= day off) freier Tag; (= public ~) Feiertag m; **to take a ~** einen Tag frei nehmen **(b)** (esp Brit: = period) OFTEN PL Ferien pl (esp Sch), Urlaub m; **the school/Christmas ~s** die Schul-/Weihnachtsferien pl; **on ~** in den Ferien, auf or im Urlaub; **to go on ~** Ferien/Urlaub machen; **where are you going for your ~(s)?** wo fahren Sie in den Ferien/im Urlaub hin?; **to take a month's ~** einen Monat Urlaub nehmen; **~ with pay, paid ~s** bezahlter Urlaub **🖪** VI (esp Brit) Ferien or Urlaub machen

holiday IN CPDS (esp Brit) Ferien-, Urlaubs-; **holiday camp** N Feriendorf nt; **holiday entitlement** N Urlaubsanspruch m; **holiday home** N Ferienhaus nt/-wohnung f; **holiday-maker** N Urlauber(in) m(f); **holiday resort** N Ferienort m; **holiday season** N Urlaubszeit f

holier-than-thou [ˌhəʊlɪəðənˈðaʊ] ADJ selbstgefällig

holiness [ˈhəʊlɪnɪs] N Heiligkeit f; **His/Your Holiness** (Eccl) Seine/Eure Heiligkeit

holistic [həʊˈlɪstɪk] ADJ holistisch

Holland [ˈhɒlənd] N Holland nt

holler [ˈhɒləʳ] VTI (inf: also ~ **out**) brüllen

hollow [ˈhɒləʊ] **🖪** ADJ hohl; (= meaningless, empty) leer; victory geschenkt; (= insincere) person unaufrichtig; sound dumpf **🖪** N **(a)** (= cavity) Höhlung f; (in larger structure) Hohlraum m **(b)** (= depression) Vertiefung f; (= small valley) (Boden)senke f

➤ **hollow out** VT SEP aushöhlen

holly [ˈhɒlɪ] N **(a)** (= tree) Stechpalme f **(b)** (= foliage) Stechpalme(nzweige pl) f

holocaust [ˈhɒləkɔːst] N **(a)** Inferno nt; **nuclear ~** Atominferno nt **(b)** (in Third Reich) Holocaust m

hologram ['hɒləgræm] N Hologramm *nt*

hols [hɒlz] (*Brit inf*) ABBR *of* **holidays**

holster ['həʊlstə'] N (Pistolen)halfter *nt or f*

holy ['həʊlɪ] ADJ (*Rel*) heilig; *oil, bread, ground* geweiht

holy: **Holy Bible** N the ~ die Bibel, die Heilige Schrift; **Holy Communion** N die heilige Kommunion, das heilige Abendmahl; **Holy Father** N the ~ (= *the Pope*) der Heilige Vater; **Holy Ghost** N = **Holy Spirit**; **Holy Land** N the ~ das Heilige Land; **Holy Spirit** N the ~ der Heilige Geist; **holy water** N heiliges Wasser; (*in Catholic Church*) Weihwasser *nt*; **Holy Week** N Karwoche *f*

homage ['hɒmɪdʒ] N Huldigung *f*; **to pay** *or* **do ~ to sb** jdm huldigen; **in order to pay ~ to the dead king** um dem König die letzte Ehre zu erweisen

home [həʊm] **1** N (a) (= *where one lives*) Zuhause *nt*; (= *house*) Haus *nt*; (= *country, area etc*) Heimat *f* (*also Zool, Bot*); **a loving/ good ~** ein liebevolles/gutes Zuhause; **his ~ is in Brussels** er ist in Brüssel zu Hause; **Bournemouth is his second ~** Bournemouth ist seine zweite Heimat (geworden); **he invited us round to his ~** er hat uns zu sich (nach Hause) eingeladen; **away from ~** von zu Hause weg; **he worked away from ~** er hat auswärts gearbeitet; **let's concentrate on problems closer to ~** wir sollten uns auf unsere eigenen Probleme konzentrieren; **at ~** zu Hause; (*Comm*) im Inland; (*Sport*) auf eigenem Platz; **to be** *or* **feel at ~ with sb** sich in jds Gegenwart (*dat*) wohl fühlen; **he doesn't feel at ~ with English** er fühlt sich im Englischen nicht sicher *or* zu Hause; **to make oneself at ~** es sich (*dat*) gemütlich *or* bequem machen; **to make sb feel at ~** es jdm gemütlich machen; **to leave ~** von zu Hause weggehen; **Scotland is the ~ of the haggis** Schottland ist die Heimat des Haggis; **the city is ~ to some 1,500 students** in dieser Stadt wohnen etwa 1.500 Studenten

(b) (= *institution*) Heim *nt*; (*for orphans*) Waisenhaus *nt*; (*for blind also*) Anstalt *f*

2 ADV **(a)** zu Hause, zuhause (*Aus, Sw*); (*with verb of motion*) nach Hause, nachhause (*Aus, Sw*); **to go ~** (*to house*) nach Hause *or* (*Aus, Sw*) nachhause gehen/fahren; (*to country*) heimfahren; **to get ~** nach Hause *or* (*Aus, Sw*) nachhause kommen; **I have to get ~ before ten** ich muss vor zehn zu Hause *or* (*Aus, Sw*) zuhause sein; **to return ~ from abroad** aus dem Ausland zurückkommen

(b) to bring *or* **get sth ~ to sb** jdm etw klarmachen *or* beibringen; **to strike ~** (*fig: remark*) ins Schwarze treffen

➤ **home in** VI (*missiles*) sich ausrichten (*on sth* auf etw *acc*); **to home in on a target** ein Ziel finden *or* selbstständig ansteuern; **he immediately homed in on the essential point** er hat sofort den wichtigsten Punkt herausgegriffen

home: **home address** N (*as opposed to business address*) Privatanschrift *f*; **home-baked** ADJ selbst gebacken; **home banking** N Homebanking *nt*; **home base** N (*Baseball*) Homebase *nt*, Schlagmal *nt*; **homebody** N (*inf*) Heimchen *nt*; **home-brew** N selbst gebrautes Bier; **homecoming** N Heimkehr *f*; **home computer** N Heimcomputer *m*; **home cooking** N Hausmannskost *f*; **Home Counties** PL Grafschaften, die an London angrenzen; **home economics** N SING Hauswirtschaft(slehre) *f*; **home entertainment system** N Home-Entertainment-System *nt*; **home field** N (*US Sport*) eigener Platz; **home game** N (*Sport*) Heimspiel *nt*; **home ground** N (*Sport*) eigener Platz; **to be on ~** (*fig*) sich auf vertrautem Terrain bewegen; **home-grown** ADJ *vegetables* selbst gezogen; (= *not imported*) einheimisch; (*fig*) *talent, player* heimisch; **home help** N Haushaltshilfe *f*; **home key** N (*Comput*) Hometaste *f*; **homeland** N Heimat(land *nt*) *f*; **homeless 1** ADJ obdachlos **2** PL the ~ die Obdachlosen *pl*; **homelessness** N Obdachlosigkeit *f*; **home life** N Familienleben *nt*; **home loan** N Hypothek *f*

homely ['həʊmlɪ] ADJ (+ER) **(a)** *atmosphere, restaurant* heimelig, behaglich **(b)** *food* bürgerlich **(c)** (*US*: = *plain*) *person* unscheinbar; *face* reizlos

home: **home-made** ADJ selbst gemacht; **homemaker** N (*US*) Hausfrau *f*; **home movie** N Amateurfilm *m*; **home news** N Meldungen *pl* aus dem Inland; **Home Office** N (*Brit*) Innenministerium *nt*; (*with relation to aliens*) Einwanderungsbehörde *f*

homeopath etc (*US*) = **homoeopath** etc

home: **homeowner** N (*of house*) Hauseigentümer(in) *m(f)*; (*of flat*) Wohnungseigentümer(in) *m(f)*; **home page** N (*Comput*) Homepage *f*; **home rule** N Selbstverwaltung *f*; **home run** N (*Baseball*) Homerun *m*; **to hit a ~** um alle vier Male laufen; (*US fig*) das große Los ziehen; **Home Secretary** N (*Brit*) Innenminister(in) *m(f)*; **home shopping** N Homeshopping *nt*; **homesick** ADJ **to be ~** Heimweh haben (*for* nach); **homespun** ADJ (*fig*) einfach; (*pej*) hausbacken; **~ philosophy** Lebensweisheiten *pl*; **homestead** N **(a)** Heimstätte *f* **(b)** (*US*) Heimstätte *f* für Siedler; **homesteader** ['həʊmstedə'] N (*US*) Heimstättensiedler(in) *m(f)*; **home straight, home stretch** N (*Sport*) Zielgerade *f*; **we're in the ~ now** (*fig inf*) das Ende ist in Sicht; **home team** N (*Sport*) Gastgeber *pl*; **home town**, (*US*) **hometown** N Heimatstadt *f*; **home trade** N Binnenhandel *m*; **home truth** N (*Brit*) bittere Wahrheit; **to tell sb a few ~s** jdm die Augen öffnen; **home video** N Amateurvideo *nt*

homeward ['həʊmwəd] ADJ **~ journey/flight** Heimreise *f*/-flug *m*; **we are ~ bound** es geht Richtung Heimat

homeward(s) ['həʊmwəd(z)] ADV nach Hause *or* (*Aus, Sw*) nachhause; (= *to country also*) in Richtung Heimat

home: **homework** N (*Sch*) Hausaufgaben *pl*, Schulaufgaben *pl*; **to give sb sth as ~** jdm etw aufgeben; **the minister had not done his ~** (*inf*) der Minister hatte sich mit der Materie nicht vertraut gemacht; **homeworker** N Heimarbeiter(in) *m(f)*; **homeworking** N Heimarbeit *f*

homey ['həʊmɪ] ADJ (+ER) (*US inf*) gemütlich

homicidal [ˌhɒmɪ'saɪdl] ADJ gemeingefährlich; **that man is a ~ maniac** dieser Mann ist ein mordgieriger Verrückter

homicide ['hɒmɪsaɪd] N Totschlag *m*

homie ['həʊmi:] N (*US inf*) Homie *m*

homily ['hɒmɪlɪ] N Predigt *f*

homing pigeon N Brieftaube *f*

homoeopath, (*US*) **homeopath** ['həʊmɪəʊpæθ] N Homöopath(in) *m(f)*

homoeopathic, (*US*) **homeopathic** [ˌhəʊmɪəʊ'pæθɪk] ADJ homöopathisch

homoeopathy, (*US*) **homeopathy** [ˌhəʊmɪ'ɒpəθɪ] N Homöopathie *f*

homogeneous [ˌhɒmə'dʒi:nɪəs] ADJ homogen

homogenize [hə'mɒdʒənaɪz] VT homogenisieren; **~d milk** homogenisierte Milch

homogenous [hə'mɒdʒɪnəs] ADJ homogen

homophobia [ˌhəʊməʊ'fəʊbɪə] N Homophobie *f*

homophobic [ˌhəʊməʊ'fəʊbɪk] ADJ homophob

Homo sapiens [ˌhəʊməʊ'sæpɪəns] N Homo sapiens *m*

homosexual [ˌhɒmə'seksjʊəl] **1** ADJ homosexuell **2** N Homosexuelle(r) *mf*

homosexuality [ˌhɒməʊseksjʊ'ælɪtɪ] N Homosexualität *f*

homy ADJ (+ER) (*US inf*) = **homey**

Hon (a) ABBR *of* **honorary (b)** ABBR *of* **Honourable**

Honduras [hɒn'djʊərəs] N Honduras *nt*

hone [həʊn] VT *blade* schleifen; (*fig*) *skills* vervollkommnen

honest ['ɒnɪst] **1** ADJ **(a)** ehrlich; **to be ~ with sb** jdm die Wahrheit sagen; **to be ~ about sth** etw ehrlich darstellen; **to be perfectly ~ (with you), I don't really know** um (ganz) ehrlich zu sein, ich weiß es nicht genau; **the ~ truth** die reine Wahrheit

(b) (= *law-abiding, decent*) *person* redlich; *money, profit* ehrlich *or* redlich erworben; **to make an ~ living** *or* **penny** sein Geld ehrlich *or* redlich verdienen

(c) *mistake* echt; **good ~ cooking** gutbürgerliche Küche

2 ADV (*inf*) **I didn't know about it, ~** ich wusste nichts davon, ehrlich *or* Ehrenwort!; **it's true, ~ it is** es stimmt, ganz ehrlich

honestly ['ɒnɪstlɪ] ADV ehrlich; *think, expect* wirklich; **I don't mind, ~** es ist mir wirklich *or* ehrlich egal; **quite ~ I don't remember it** ehrlich gesagt *or* um ehrlich zu sein, ich kann mich daran nicht erinnern; **~!** (*showing exasperation*) also wirklich!

honesty ['ɒnɪstɪ] N Ehrlichkeit *f*; (= *being law-abiding, decent*) Redlichkeit *f*; **in all ~** ganz ehrlich

honey ['hʌnɪ] N **(a)** Honig *m* **(b)** (*inf*: = *dear*) Schätzchen *nt*

honey: **honeybee** N (Honig)biene *f*; **honeycomb** N (Bienen)wabe *f*; **honeydew melon** N Honigmelone *f*

honeymoon ['hʌnɪmu:n] **1** N Flitterwochen *pl*; (= *trip*) Hochzeitsreise *f*; **to be on one's ~** in den Flitterwochen/auf

Hochzeitsreise sein; **the ~ is over** *(fig inf)* jetzt werden andere Saiten aufgezogen *(inf)* **2** VI seine Hochzeitsreise machen; **they are ~ing in Spain** sie sind in Spanien auf Hochzeitsreise

honeymoon period N *(fig)* Schonzeit *f*

honeysuckle [ˈhʌnɪsʌkəl] N Geißblatt *nt*

Hong Kong [ˈhɒŋˈkɒŋ] N Hongkong *nt*

honk [hɒŋk] **1** VI **(a)** *(car)* hupen **(b)** *(geese)* schreien **2** VT horn drücken auf (+*acc*)

honor *etc (US)* = **honour** *etc*

honorarium [ˌɒnəˈrɛərɪəm] N, *pl* **honoraria** [ˌɒnəˈrɛərɪə] Honorar *nt*

honorary [ˈɒnərərɪ] ADJ Ehren-

honorary degree N ehrenhalber verliehener akademischer Grad

honor guard N *(US)* Ehrenwache *f*

honour, *(US)* **honor** [ˈɒnəʳ] **1** N **(a)** Ehre *f*; **sense of ~** Ehrgefühl *nt*; **he made it a point of ~** er betrachtete es als Ehrensache; **man of ~** Ehrenmann *m*; **in ~ of sb/sth** zu Ehren von jdm/etw; *of dead person/past thing* in ehrendem Andenken an jdn/etw; **if you would do me the ~ of accepting** *(form)* wenn Sie mir die Ehre erweisen würden anzunehmen *(geh)*; **to whom do I have the ~ of speaking?** *(form, hum)* mit wem habe ich die Ehre? *(geh, hum)*
(b) (= *title*) **Your Honour** Hohes Gericht; **His Honour** das Gericht
(c) (= *distinction, award*) **~s** Auszeichnung(en) *f(pl)*; **with full military ~s** mit militärischen Ehren
(d) to do the ~s *(inf)* die Honneurs machen; *(on private occasions)* den Gastgeber spielen
(e) *(Univ)* **~s** *(also* **~s degree***)* akademischer Grad mit Prüfung im Spezialfach; **to do** *or* **take ~s in English** Englisch belegen, um den „Honours Degree" zu erwerben; **to get first-class ~s** das Examen mit Auszeichnung *or* „sehr gut" bestehen
2 VT **(a)** *person* ehren; **I would be ~ed** es wäre mir eine Ehre; **I should be (deeply) ~ed if you ...** ich würde mich (zutiefst) geehrt fühlen, wenn Sie ...; **he ~ed us with his presence** *(also iro)* er beehrte uns mit seiner Gegenwart; **it's Angelika, we ARE ~ed** *(iro)* es ist Angelika, welche Ehre
(b) *cheque* annehmen; *debt* begleichen; *bill of exchange* respektieren; *obligation* nachkommen (+*dat*); *commitment* stehen zu; *pledge, promise* halten; *agreement, contract* erfüllen

honourable, *(US)* **honorable** [ˈɒnərəbl] ADJ **(a)** ehrenhaft; *peace, discharge* ehrenvoll; *exception* rühmlich; **to get an ~ mention** rühmend *or* lobend erwähnt werden **(b)** *(Brit Parl)* **the Honourable member for X** der (Herr)/die (Frau) Abgeordnete für X; **the Honourable member** *or* **gentleman is wrong** der geschätzte *or* ehrenwerte (Herr) Kollege täuscht sich

honourably, *(US)* **honorably** [ˈɒnərəblɪ] ADV in Ehren; *behave, act* ehrenhaft

honours, *(US)* **honors** [ˈɒnəz-]: **honours degree** N = honour 1(e); **honours list** N *(Brit)* Liste *f* der Titel- und Rangverleihungen *(die zweimal im Jahr veröffentlicht wird)*

hooch [huːtʃ] N *(inf)* Stoff *m (sl)*

hood [hʊd] N **(a)** Kapuze *f*; *(thief's)* Maske *f* **(b)** *(Aut)* (= *roof*) Verdeck *nt*; *(US:* = *bonnet)* (Motor)haube *f*; *(on cooker)* Abzugshaube *f* **(c)** *(esp US inf)* (= *gangster*) Gangster *m (inf)*; (= *young ruffian*) Rowdy *m*

hooded [ˈhʊdɪd] ADJ **the ~ robber** der maskierte Räuber

hoodlum [ˈhuːdləm] N Rowdy *m*; (= *member of gang*) Gangster *m (inf)*

hoodwink [ˈhʊdwɪŋk] VT *(inf)* (he)reinlegen *(inf)*; **to ~ sb into doing sth** jdn dazu verleiten, etw zu tun

hoof [huːf] N, *pl* **-s** *or* **hooves** Huf *m*; **to eat on the ~** *(inf)* unterwegs essen; **they tend to make policy on the ~** *(inf)* sie legen ihre Politik oft aus dem Stegreif fest

hook [hʊk] **1** N Haken *m (also Boxing)*; **he swallowed the story ~, line and sinker** er hat die Geschichte tatsächlich mit Stumpf und Stiel geschluckt *(inf)*; **he fell for it ~, line and sinker** er ging auf den Leim; **by ~ or by crook** mit Biegen und Brechen; **that lets me off the ~** *(inf)* damit bin ich aus dem Schneider *(inf)*; **to leave the phone off the ~** den Hörer neben das Telefon legen; *(unintentionally)* nicht auflegen; **the phone was ringing off the ~** *(US inf)* das Telefon klingelte pausenlos; **to do sth on one's own ~** *(US inf)* etw auf eigene Faust machen
2 VT **(a) to ~ a trailer to a car** einen Anhänger an ein Auto hängen; **to ~ one's arm/feet around sth** seinen Arm/seine

Füße um etw schlingen
(b) *fish* an die Angel bekommen
(c) to be/get ~ed on sth *(inf)* *on drugs* von etw abhängig sein/werden; *on film, food, place etc* auf etw *(acc)* stehen *(inf)*; **he's ~ed on the idea** er ist von der Idee besessen

➤ **hook on 1** VI (an)gehakt werden *(to an* +*acc)*; *(with towbar)* angekoppelt *or* angehängt werden *(to an* +*acc)* **2** VT SEP anhaken *(to an* +*acc)*; *(with towbar)* ankoppeln, anhängen

➤ **hook up 1** VI *(Rad, TV)* gemeinsam ausstrahlen; **to hook up with sb** sich jdm anschließen **2** VT SEP **(a)** *dress etc* zuhaken; **hook me** *or* **the dress up, please** mach mir bitte die Haken zu **(b)** *trailer, caravan* ankoppeln, anhängen **(c)** *computer etc* anschließen *(to an* +*acc)*; *(Rad, TV)* anschließen *(with an* +*acc)*

hook and eye N Haken und Öse *no art, pl vb*

hooked [hʊkt] ADJ **~ beak/nose** Hakenschnabel *m*/-nase *f*

hooker [ˈhʊkəʳ] N *(esp US inf)* Nutte *f (inf)*

hooky [ˈhʊkɪ] N *(US inf)* **to play ~** (die) Schule schwänzen *(inf)*

hooligan [ˈhuːlɪgən] N Rowdy *m*

hooliganism [ˈhuːlɪgənɪzəm] N Rowdytum *nt*

hoop [huːp] N Reifen *m*; *(in croquet)* Tor *nt*; *(in basketball)* Korb *m*; (= *earring*) Creole *f*; **they put him through** *or* **made him jump through ~s** *(fig)* sie haben ihn auf Herz und Nieren geprüft

hooray [huːˈreɪ] INTERJ = hurrah

hoot [huːt] **1** N **(a)** *(of owl)* Schrei *m*; **~s of laughter** johlendes Gelächter; **I don't care** *or* **give a ~ or two ~s** *(inf)* das ist mir piepegal *(inf)* *or* völlig schnuppe *(inf)*; **to be a ~** *(inf)* zum Schreien (komisch) sein
(b) *(Aut)* Hupen *nt no pl*
2 VI **(a)** *(owl)* schreien; *(person: derisively)* johlen; **to ~ with laughter** in johlendes Gelächter ausbrechen
(b) *(Aut)* hupen
3 VT *(esp Brit Aut)* **to ~ one's/the horn** hupen

hooter [ˈhuːtəʳ] N *(Brit)* **(a)** *(Aut)* Hupe *f*; *(at factory)* Sirene *f* **(b)** *(inf:* = *nose)* Zinken *m (inf)*

Hoover® [ˈhuːvəʳ] N *(Brit)* Staubsauger *m*

hoover [ˈhuːvəʳ] *(Brit)* VTI (staub)saugen

➤ **hoover up** VI +PREP OBJ (staub)saugen

hoovering [ˈhuːvərɪŋ] N **to do the ~** (staub)saugen

hooves [huːvz] PL *of* hoof

hop¹ [hɒp] **1** N **(a)** (kleiner) Sprung; *(of deer, rabbit)* Satz *m*; **to catch sb on the ~** *(fig inf)* jdn überraschen *or* überrumpeln **(b)** *(Aviat inf)* **a short ~** ein Katzensprung *m (inf)*
2 VI *(animal)* hüpfen; *(rabbit)* hoppeln; *(person)* (auf einem Bein) hüpfen; **to ~ on** aufsteigen; **to ~ on a train** in einen Zug einsteigen; *(while moving)* auf einen Zug aufspringen; **he ~ped on his bicycle** er schwang sich auf sein Fahrrad; **he ~ped over the wall** er sprang über die Mauer
3 VT *(Brit inf)* **~ it!** zieh Leine *(inf)*

hop² N *(Bot)* Hopfen *m*

hope [həʊp] **1** N *(also person)* Hoffnung *f*; **she is our best ~** sie ist unsere größte Hoffnung; **past** *or* **beyond ~** hoffnungslos; **my ~ is that ...** ich hoffe nur, dass ...; **in the ~ of doing sth** in der Hoffnung, etw zu tun; **to have (high** *or* **great) ~s of doing sth** hoffen, etw zu tun; **to live in ~ of sth** in der Hoffnung auf etw *(acc)* leben; **don't get** *or* **build your ~s up too much** mach dir keine allzu großen Hoffnungen; **there's no ~ of that** da braucht man sich gar keine Hoffnungen zu machen; **to give up/lose ~ of doing sth** die Hoffnung aufgeben, etw zu tun; **what a ~!** *(inf)*, **some ~(s)!** *(inf)* schön wärs! *(inf)*; **she hasn't got a ~ in hell of passing her exams** *(inf)* es besteht nicht die geringste Chance, dass sie ihre Prüfung besteht
2 VI hoffen *(for auf* +*acc)*; **to ~ for the best** das Beste hoffen; **a pay rise would be too much to ~ for** auf eine Gehaltserhöhung braucht man sich *(dat)* gar keine Hoffnungen zu machen; **I ~ so** hoffentlich; **I ~ not** hoffentlich nicht
3 VT hoffen; **I ~ to see you** hoffentlich sehe ich Sie; **the party cannot ~ to win** für die Partei besteht keine Hoffnung zu gewinnen; **to ~ against ~ that ...** trotz allem die Hoffnung nicht aufgeben, dass ...

hope chest N *(US)* Aussteuertruhe *f*

hoped-for [ˈhəʊptfɔːʳ] ADJ erhofft

hopeful [ˈhəʊpfʊl] **1** ADJ **(a)** hoffnungsvoll; **he was still ~ (that ...)** er machte sich *(dat)* immer noch Hoffnungen(, dass ...); **they weren't very ~** sie hatten keine große Hoffnung; **he was feeling more ~** er war optimistisch; **you're (being) ~!** (*iro*) du bist vielleicht ein Optimist! (*inf*) **(b)** *news* positiv; *forecast* optimistisch; **it is not a ~ sign for the future** es ist kein gutes Zeichen für die Zukunft **2** N (= *aspirant*) Anwärter(in) *m(f)*; (= *applicant*) Bewerber(in) *m(f)*; (= *candidate*) Kandidat(in) *m(f)*; **presidential ~s** Anwärter *pl* auf die Präsidentschaft

hopefully ['həʊpfəlɪ] ADV **(a)** hoffnungsvoll **(b)** (*inf*: = *with any luck*) hoffentlich

hopeless ['həʊplɪs] ADJ hoffnungslos; *love, attempt, task, cause* aussichtslos; (= *despairing*) *person, sigh, gesture* verzweifelt; *drunk, liar, romantic* unverbesserlich; **to feel ~** keine Hoffnung haben; **she's a ~ manager/organizer** als Managerin/ im Organisieren ist sie ein hoffnungsloser Fall; **I'm ~ at maths/sport** in Mathe/Sport bin ich hoffnungslos *or* ein hoffnungsloser Fall; **to be ~ at doing sth** etw absolut *or* überhaupt nicht können

hopelessly ['həʊplɪslɪ] ADV **(a)** (= *despairingly*) verzweifelt **(b)** (*emph*: = *utterly*) ~ **confused** völlig verwirrt; **I feel ~ inadequate** ich komme mir völlig minderwertig vor; **he got ~ lost in the fog** er hat sich im Nebel hoffnungslos verirrt

hopelessness ['həʊplɪsnɪs] N (*of situation*) Hoffnungslosigkeit *f*

hopper ['hɒpə'] N (*Tech*) Einfülltrichter *m*

hopping mad ['hɒpɪŋ'mæd] ADJ (*inf*) fuchsteufelswild (*inf*)

hop: hopscotch N Hopse *f* (*inf*); **hop, skip and jump** N, **hop, step and jump** N Dreisprung *m*; **it's a ~ from here** es ist nur ein Katzensprung von hier

horde ['hɔːd] N (*inf*) Masse *f*; (*of football fans, children etc*) Horde *f* (*pej*)

horizon [hə'raɪzn] N Horizont *m*; (*fig auch*) Gesichtskreis *m no pl*; **on the ~** am Horizont; (*fig*) in Sicht; **the sun was below the ~** die Sonne war hinter dem Horizont

horizontal [hɒrɪ'zɒntl] ADJ waag(e)recht, horizontal; ~ **line** Waag(e)rechte *f*

horizontal bar N Reck *nt*

horizontally [hɒrɪ'zɒntəlɪ] ADV horizontal

hormone ['hɔːməʊn] N Hormon *nt*

hormone replacement therapy N Hormonersatztherapie *f*

horn [hɔːn] N **(a)** (*of cattle, Mus*) Horn *nt*; ~**s** (*of deer*) Geweih *nt*; **to lock ~s** (*fig*) die Klingen kreuzen **(b)** (*Aut*) Hupe *f*; (*Naut*) (Signal)horn *nt*; **to sound** *or* **blow the ~** (*Aut*) hupen; (*Naut*) tuten

horned [hɔːnd] ADJ gehörnt

hornet ['hɔːnɪt] N Hornisse *f*; **to stir up a ~'s nest** (*fig*) in ein Wespennest stechen

horn-rimmed ['hɔːnrɪmd] ADJ ~ **glasses** *or* **spectacles** Hornbrille *f*

horny ['hɔːnɪ] ADJ (+ER) **(a)** (= *like horn*) hornartig; *hands etc* schwielig; *soles* hornig **(b)** (*inf*: = *sexually aroused*) scharf (*inf*), geil (*inf*)

horoscope ['hɒrəskəʊp] N Horoskop *nt*

horrendous [hɒ'rendəs] ADJ **(a)** *accident, injury, war, experience* grauenhaft; *crime, attack, violence* abscheulich **(b)** (*inf*) *conditions, traffic* fürchterlich (*inf*); *loss, cost, price, stupidity* horrend; **children's shoes are a ~ price** Kinderschuhe sind horrend teuer

horrendously [hɒ'rendəslɪ] ADV (*inf*: = *dreadfully*) fürchterlich (*inf*); *expensive* horrend

horrible ['hɒrɪbl] ADJ **(a)** (*inf*: = *awful*) schrecklich (*inf*); *food* grauenhaft (*inf*); *clothes, colour, sight, smell, taste* scheußlich; *person* gemein, fies (*inf*); **to be ~ to sb** fies (*inf*) *or* gemein zu jdm sein **(b)** (= *horrific*) *death, crime, accident, injury* grauenhaft

horribly ['hɒrɪblɪ] ADV **(a)** grauenhaft; **they died ~** sie starben einen grauenhaften Tod **(b)** (*inf*) *drunk, expensive, embarrassed* schrecklich (*inf*)

horrid ['hɒrɪd] ADJ fürchterlich, schrecklich; **don't be so ~** sei nicht so gemein (*inf*)

horrific [hɒ'rɪfɪk] ADJ entsetzlich, schrecklich; *documentary* erschreckend

horrifically [hɒ'rɪfɪkəlɪ] ADV grauenhaft; **he was ~ injured in the crash** bei dem Unfall trug er grauenhafte Verletzungen davon

horrify ['hɒrɪfaɪ] VT entsetzen; **it horrifies me to think what ...** ich denke (nur) mit Entsetzen daran, was ...

horrifying ['hɒrɪfaɪɪŋ] ADJ schrecklich, fürchterlich; *crash* entsetzlich

horror ['hɒrə'] **1** N **(a)** Entsetzen *nt*, Grauen *nt*; (= *strong dislike*) Horror *m* (*of* vor +*dat*); **to have a ~ of sth** einen Horror vor etw (*dat*) haben; **to have a ~ of doing sth** einen Horror davor haben, etw zu tun; **they watched in ~** sie sahen entsetzt zu **(b)** USU PL (= *horrifying thing, of war etc*) Schrecken *m* **(c)** (*inf*) **to be a real ~** furchtbar sein (*inf*); **you little ~!** du kleines Ungeheuer! (*inf*) **2** ATTR Horror-; ~ **film/story** Horrorfilm *m*/-geschichte *f*

horror-stricken ['hɒrə.strɪkən], **horror-struck** ['hɒrə.strʌk] ADJ von Entsetzen *or* Grauen gepackt

hors d'oeuvre [ɔː'dɜːv] N Vorspeise *f*

horse [hɔːs] N Pferd *nt* (*also Gymnastics*); **he lost a lot of money on the ~s** (*betting*) er hat beim Pferderennen *or* bei der Pferdewette viel Geld verloren; **to eat like a ~** wie ein Scheunendrescher *m* essen *or* fressen (*inf*); **I could eat a ~** ich könnte ein ganzes Pferd essen; **information straight from the ~'s mouth** Informationen *pl* aus erster Hand; **it's a case of ~s for courses** (*Brit*) man muss den Richtigen/die Richtige/das Richtige dafür finden

➤ **horse about** (*Brit*) *or* **around** VI (*inf*) herumalbern (*inf*)

horse: horse-and-buggy ADJ (*US*) *approach, system* vorsintflutlich (*inf*); **horseback** N **on ~** zu Pferd; **policemen on ~** berittene Polizisten; **horsebox** N (= *van*) Pferdetransporter *m*; (= *trailer*) Pferdetransportwagen *m*; **horse chestnut** N (= *tree, fruit*) Rosskastanie *f*; **horse-drawn** ADJ von Pferden gezogen; ~ **cart** Pferdewagen *m*; ~ **carriage** Kutsche *f*; **horsehair 1** N Rosshaar *nt* **2** ADJ ATTR Rosshaar-; ~ **mattress** Rosshaarmatratze *f*; **horseman** N Reiter *m*; **horsemanship** N Reitkunst *f*; **horseplay** N Alberei *f*; **horsepower** N Pferdestärke *f*; **a 200 ~ car/engine** ein Auto/ Motor mit 200 PS *or* Pferdestärken; **horse race** N Pferderennen *nt*; **horse racing** N Pferderennsport *m*; (= *races*) Pferderennen *pl*; **horseradish** N Meerrettich *m*; **horse-riding** N Reiten *nt*; **horseshoe** N Hufeisen *nt*; **horse trading** N (*fig*) Kuhhandel *m*; **horsewhip 1** N Reitpeitsche *f* **2** VT auspeitschen; **horsewoman** N Reiterin *f*

horsey, horsy ['hɔːsɪ] ADJ (+ER) **(a)** (= *keen on horses*) pferdenärrisch **(b)** (*pej*: = *horse-like*) pferdeähnlich

horticultural [hɔːtɪ'kʌltʃərəl] ADJ Garten(bau)-; ~ **show** Gartenbauausstellung *f*

horticulturalist [hɔːtɪ'kʌltʃərəlɪst] N Gärtner(in) *m(f)*

horticulture ['hɔːtɪkʌltʃə'] N Gartenbau(kunst *f*) *m*

hose [həʊz] **1** N Schlauch *m* **2** VT (*also* ~ **down**) abspritzen

Be careful! **hose** *is not translated by the German word* **Hose***.*

hosepipe ['həʊzpaɪp] N (*esp Brit*) Schlauch *m*

hosepipe ban N *durch Wasserknappheit bedingtes Verbot, den Rasen zu sprengen oder das Auto mit dem Gartenschlauch zu waschen*

hosiery ['həʊzərɪ] N Strumpfwaren *pl*

hospice ['hɒspɪs] N (*for terminally ill*) Pflegeheim *nt* (für unheilbar Kranke)

hospitable ['hɒspɪtəbl] ADJ *person* gastfreundlich; **to be ~ to sb** jdn gastfreundlich *or* gastlich aufnehmen **(b)** *place, climate* gastlich; *environment* freundlich

hospital ['hɒspɪtl] N Krankenhaus *nt*, Hospital *nt* (old, Sw); **in** *or* (*US*) **in the ~** im Krankenhaus

hospital IN CPDS Krankenhaus-; **hospital bed** N Krankenhausbett *nt*

hospitality [hɒspɪ'tælɪtɪ] N Gastfreundschaft *f*; (*Comm*) Bewirtung *f*

hospitalization [hɒspɪtəlaɪ'zeɪʃən] N **(a)** Einweisung *f* ins Krankenhaus; (= *stay in hospital*) Krankenhausaufenthalt *m* **(b)** (*US*: = ~ **insurance**) Versicherung *f* für Krankenhauspflege

hospitalize ['hɒspɪtəlaɪz] VT ins Krankenhaus einweisen; **he was ~d for three months** er lag drei Monate lang im Krankenhaus

Host [həʊst] N (*Eccl*) Hostie *f*

host[1] [həʊst] **1** N Gastgeber(in) *m(f)*; **to be** *or* **play ~ to sb** jds Gastgeber(in) *m(f)* sein; **to play ~ to an event** eine

Veranstaltung ausrichten **2** VT *banquet, ball, TV programme* Gastgeber(in) sein bei; (*country, city*) *event, conference, Olympics* ausrichten

host² N Menge *f*, Masse *f* (*inf*); **he has a ~ of friends** er hat eine Menge Freunde

hostage ['hɒstɪdʒ] N Geisel *f*; **to take/hold sb** jdn als Geisel nehmen/halten

hostage: hostage-taker N Geiselnehmer(in) *m(f)*; **hostage-taking** N Geiselnahme *f*

host country N Gastland *nt*

hostel ['hɒstəl] **1** N (Wohn)heim *nt* **2** VI **to go ~ling in** Jugendherbergen übernachten

hostess ['həʊstɪs] N **(a)** Gastgeberin *f*; **to be** *or* **play ~ to sb** jds Gastgeberin sein **(b)** (*in nightclub, at exhibition etc*) Hostess *f* **(c)** (= *air* ~) Stewardess *f*

hostess trolley N Servierwagen *m*

hostile ['hɒstaɪl] ADJ (= *antagonistic*) feindselig; (= *opposed in principle*) *society, press* feindlich (gesinnt); (*Mil, Econ, Fin*) *forces, takeover bid* feindlich; *conditions, environment, weather* unwirtlich; **to be ~ to sb** sich jdm gegenüber feindselig verhalten; **to be ~ to** *or* **toward(s) sth** einer Sache (*dat*) feindlich gegenüberstehen

hostility [hɒs'tɪlɪtɪ] N **(a)** Feindseligkeit *f*; (*between people*) Feindschaft *f*; **to show ~ to sth** einer Sache (*dat*) feindlich gegenüberstehen; **he feels no ~ toward(s) anybody** er ist niemandem feindlich gesinnt; **~ to foreigners** Ausländerfeindlichkeit *f* **(b) hostilities** PL Feindseligkeiten *pl*

hot [hɒt] **1** ADJ (+ER) **(a)** heiß; *meal, tap, drink* warm; **I am** *or* **feel ~** mir ist (es) heiß; **with ~ and cold water** mit warm und kalt Wasser; **the weather is ~** es ist heißes Wetter; **the room was ~** in dem Zimmer war es heiß; **Africa is a ~ country** in Afrika ist es heiß; **I'm getting ~** mir wird (es) warm **(b)** *curry, spices etc* scharf **(c)** (*inf*: = *in demand*) *product* zugkräftig **(d)** (*inf*: = *good, competent*) stark (*inf*); **he's pretty ~ at maths** in Mathe ist er ganz schön stark (*inf*); **I'm not feeling too ~** mir gehts nicht besonders (*inf*) **(e)** (*fig*) **to be (a) ~ favourite** (*Brit*) *or* **favorite** (*US*) der große Favorit sein; **~ tip** heißer Tipp; **a ~ issue** eine umstrittene Frage; **~ money** (*Fin*) vagabundierendes Kapital; **~ news** das Neuste vom Neuen; **~ off the press** gerade erschienen; **the latest designs ~ from Milan** die neuesten Entwürfe, gerade aus Mailand eingetroffen; **it's too ~ to handle** (*political issue etc*) das ist ein heißes Eisen; **that's a ~ button, that hits a ~ button** (*US*) das ist ein heißes Eisen; **to get into ~ water** in Schwulitäten kommen (*inf*); **to be/get (all) ~ and bothered** (*inf*) ganz aufgeregt sein/werden (*about* wegen); **to get ~ under the collar about sth** wegen etw in Rage geraten; **to make things too ~ for sb** (*inf*) jdm die Hölle heiß machen (*inf*) **2** ADV (+ER) **he keeps blowing ~ and cold** er sagt einmal hü und einmal hott **3** N **to have the ~s for sb** (*inf*) auf jdn scharf sein (*inf*)

➤ **hot up** VI (*inf*) **things are hotting up in the Middle East** die Lage im Nahen Osten spitzt sich zu *or* verschärft sich; **things are hotting up** es geht langsam los

hot: hot air N (*fig*) leeres Gerede; **hot-air balloon** N Heißluftballon *m*; **hotbed** N (*fig*) Brutstätte *f*, Nährboden *m* (*of* für); **hot-blooded** ADJ heißblütig

hotchpotch ['hɒtʃpɒtʃ] N (*Brit*) Durcheinander *nt*, Mischmasch *m*

hot dog N Hot dog *m or nt*

hotel [həʊ'tel] N Hotel *nt*

hotelier [həʊ'telɪə'] N Hotelier *m*

hotel: hotel manager N Hoteldirektor(in) *m(f)*; **hotel room** N Hotelzimmer *nt*

hot: hot flushes PL (*Med*) fliegende Hitze; **hotfoot** (*inf*) VT **he ~ed it back home/out of town** er ging schleunigst nach Hause/verließ schleunigst die Stadt; **hothead** N Hitzkopf *m*; **hot-headed** ADJ hitzköpfig; **hothouse 1** N (*lit, fig*) Treibhaus *nt* **2** ADJ ATTR (*lit*) Treibhaus-; (*fig*) *atmosphere* spannungsgeladen; **hot line** N (*Pol*) heißer Draht; (*TV etc*) Hotline *f*

hotly ['hɒtlɪ] ADV **(a)** *debate, deny, say, protest* heftig; *contest, dispute* heiß **(b) he was ~ pursued by two policemen** zwei Polizisten waren ihm dicht auf den Fersen (*inf*)

hot: hotplate N **(a)** (*of stove*) Kochplatte *f* **(b)** (= *plate warmer*) Warmhalteplatte *f*; **hot potato** N (*fig inf*) heißes Eisen; **hot seat** N **to be in the ~** auf dem Schleudersitz sein; **hotshot** (*inf*) **1** N Ass *nt* (*inf*) **2** ADJ ATTR Spitzen- (*inf*), erstklassig; **hot spot** N (*Pol*) Krisenherd *m*; (*inf*: = *club etc*) heißer Schuppen (*inf*); **hot spring** N heiße Quelle; **hot stuff** N (*inf*) **this is ~** (= *very good*) das ist große Klasse (*inf*); (= *provocative*) das ist Zündstoff; **she's/he's ~** (= *very good*) sie/er ist große Klasse (*inf*); (= *very sexy*) das ist eine scharfe Braut (*sl*)/ein scharfer Typ (*inf*); **hot-tempered** ADJ leicht aufbrausend; **hot-water bottle** N Wärmflasche *f*

hoummos, houm(o)us ['huːməs] N orientalische Creme aus Kichererbsen, Sesam und Knoblauch

hound [haʊnd] **1** N **(a)** (*Hunt*) (Jagd)hund *m*; **the ~s lost the scent** die Meute verlor die Spur **(b)** (*any dog*) Hund *m* **2** VT hetzen, jagen; **to be ~ed** gehetzt sein; **to be ~ed by the press** von der Presse verfolgt werden

➤ **hound out** VT SEP verjagen

hour ['aʊə'] N **(a)** (*lit, fig*) Stunde *f*; (= *time of day*) Zeit *f*; **half an ~, a half ~** eine halbe Stunde; **three-quarters of an ~** eine Dreiviertelstunde; **a quarter of an ~** eine Viertelstunde; **an ~ and a half** anderthalb *or* eineinhalb Stunden; **it's two ~s' walk from here** von hier sind es zu Fuß zwei Stunden; **at fifteen hundred/fifteen thirty ~s** (*spoken*) um fünfzehn Uhr/ fünfzehn Uhr dreißig; **~ by ~** mit jeder Stunde; **~ after ~** Stunde um Stunde; **on the ~** zur vollen Stunde; **every ~ on the ~** jede volle Stunde; **20 minutes past the ~** 20 Minuten nach; **at the ~ of his death** in seiner Todesstunde; **at all ~s (of the day and night)** zu jeder (Tages- und Nacht)zeit; **what! at this ~ of the night!** was! zu dieser nachtschlafenden Zeit!; **to drive at 50 kilometres an ~** 50 Kilometer in der Stunde *or* 50 Stundenkilometer fahren; **to be paid by the ~** stundenweise bezahlt werden; **for ~s** stundenlang; **he took ~s to do it** er brauchte stundenlang dazu; **his ~ has come** seine Stunde ist gekommen; **the man/hero of the ~** der Mann/Held der Stunde

(b) hours PL (*of banks, shops etc*) Geschäftszeit(en) *f(pl)*; (*of pubs, park etc*) Öffnungszeiten *pl*; (*of post office*) Schalterstunden *pl*; (= *office ~s*) Dienststunden *pl*; (= *working ~s etc*) Arbeitszeit *f*; (*of doctor etc*) Sprechstunde *f*; **out of/after ~s** (*in pubs*) außerhalb der gesetzlich erlaubten Zeit; (*in office etc*) außerhalb der Arbeitszeit/nach Dienstschluss; (*of doctor etc*) außerhalb/nach der Sprechstunde; **what are your ~s?** (*shops, pubs etc*) wann haben Sie geöffnet *or* offen?; (*employee*) wie ist Ihre Arbeitszeit?; **to work long ~s** einen langen Arbeitstag haben; (*doctors, policeman etc*) lange Dienststunden haben

hour: hourglass N Sanduhr *f*; **hour hand** N kleiner Zeiger

hourly ['aʊəlɪ] **1** ADJ **(a)** stündlich; **an ~ bus service** ein stündlich verkehrender Bus; **at ~ intervals** stündlich, jede Stunde; **at two-~ intervals** alle zwei Stunden **(b)** (= *per hour*) *earnings* pro Stunde; **~ wage** *or* **pay** Stundenlohn *m*; **~ rate** Stundensatz *m*; **on an ~ basis** stundenweise **2** ADV **(a)** (*lit*) stündlich, jede Stunde; (*fig*) (= *constantly*) ständig; *diminish, grow* mit jeder Stunde; *expect* stündlich, jeden Augenblick **(b)** *pay* stundenweise

house [haʊs] **1** N, *pl* **houses** ['haʊzɪz] **(a)** Haus *nt* (*also Comm, Theat*); (= *family, line also*) Geschlecht *nt*; (= *household*) Haushalt *m*; **at my ~** bei mir (zu Hause *or* zuhause (*Aus, Sw*)); **to my ~** zu mir (nach Hause *or* nachhause (*Aus, Sw*)); **to keep ~ (for sb)** (jdm) den Haushalt führen; **they set up ~ together** sie gründeten einen gemeinsamen Hausstand; **to put** *or* **set one's ~ in order** (*fig*) seine Angelegenheiten in Ordnung bringen; **they get on like a ~ on fire** (*inf*) sie kommen ausgezeichnet miteinander aus; **as safe as ~s** (*Brit*) bombensicher (*inf*); **the upper/lower ~** (*Pol*) das Ober-/ Unterhaus; **House of Commons/Lords** (*Brit*) (britisches) Unter-/Oberhaus; **House of Representatives** (*US*) Repräsentantenhaus *nt*; **the Houses of Parliament** das Parlament(sgebäude); **on the ~** auf Kosten des Hauses; (*on the company*) auf Kosten der Firma; **we ordered a bottle of ~ red** wir bestellten eine Flasche von dem roten Hauswein; **to bring the ~ down** (*inf*) ein Bombenerfolg (beim Publikum) sein (*inf*) **(b)** (*in boarding school*) Gruppenhaus *nt* **(c) full ~** (*Cards*) Full House *nt*; (= *bingo*) volle Karte

2 [hauz] VT unterbringen; **this building ~s three offices/ten families** in diesem Gebäude sind drei Büros/zehn Familien untergebracht

HOUSE

Britisches und amerikanisches Englisch haben für Häuser und Wohnungen häufig verschiedene Ausdrücke. Mit **flat** *(Brit) oder* **apartment** *(US) wird allgemein eine Wohnung innerhalb eines größeren Gebäudes bezeichnet. Bei einem* **condominium** *(US) handelt es sich um einen Wohnblock mit Eigentumswohnungen, dessen Gemeinschaftseinrichtungen allen Bewohnern gemeinsam gehören.* **Terraced** *(Brit) oder* **row** *(US) houses heißen die Reihenhäuser. Doppelhäuser heißen* **semi-detached** *(Brit) oder* **duplex** *(US) houses.* **Detached** *houses (Brit) sind frei stehende Eigenheime, die normalerweise von einem Garten umgeben sind. Für die USA typisch sind die* **ranch** *houses (US), lang gezogene, einstöckige Gebäude, und* **colonials** *(US), zweigeschossige Schindel- oder Backsteinhäuser im traditionellen Stil, denen eine überdachte Veranda vorgebaut ist.*

house IN CPDS Haus-; **house arrest** N Hausarrest *m*; **houseboat** N Hausboot *nt*; **housebound** ADJ ans Haus gefesselt; **housebreaking** N Einbruch(sdiebstahl) *m*; **house-broken** ADJ (*US*) stubenrein; **housecoat** N Morgenrock *or* -mantel *m*; **houseguest** N (Haus)gast *m*

household ['haʊshəʊld] **1** N Haushalt *m* **2** ATTR Haushalts-; **~ appliance** Haushaltsgerät *nt*; **~ chores** Hausarbeit *f*

householder ['haʊsˌhəʊldə'] N Haus-/Wohnungsinhaber(in) *m(f)*

household: household name N **to be a ~** ein Begriff sein; **to become a ~** zu einem Begriff werden; **household waste** N Hausmüll *m*; **household word** N Begriff *m*

house: house-hunt VI auf Haussuche sein; **they have started ~ing** sie haben angefangen, nach einem Haus zu suchen; **househusband** N Hausmann *m*; **housekeeper** N Haushälterin *f*, Wirtschafterin *f*; **housekeeping** N (**a**) Haushalten *nt* (**b**) (*Brit: also ~ money*) Haushalts- *or* Wirtschaftsgeld *nt*; **housemate** N **my ~s** meine Mitbewohner; **House music** N Hausmusik *f*; **house party** N mehrtägige Einladung; (*= group invited*) Gesellschaft *f*; **house plant** N Zimmerpflanze *f*; **house-proud** ADJ **she is ~** sie ist eine penible Hausfrau; **houseroom** N **I wouldn't give it ~** das wollte ich nicht geschenkt haben; **house-sit** VI **to ~ for sb** während jds Abwesenheit in dessen Haus/Wohnung einziehen, um darauf aufzupassen; **house-to-house** ADJ **a ~ search** eine Suche *or* Fahndung von Haus zu Haus; **to conduct ~ inquiries** von Haus zu Haus gehen und fragen; **~ collection** Haussammlung *f*; **house-trained** ADJ stubenrein; **house-warming (party)** N Einzugsparty *f*; **to have a ~** Einzug feiern; **housewife** N Hausfrau *f*; **house wine** N Hauswein *m*; **housework** N Hausarbeit *f*

housing ['haʊzɪŋ] N (**a**) (*act*) Unterbringung *f* (**b**) (*= houses*) Wohnungen *pl*; (*temporary*) Unterkunft *f* (**c**) (*= provision of houses*) Wohnungsbeschaffung *f*; (*= building of houses*) Wohnungsbau *m* (**d**) (*Tech*) Gehäuse *nt*

housing IN CPDS Wohnungs-; **housing association** N Wohnungsbaugesellschaft *f*; **housing benefit** N (*Brit*) Wohngeld *nt*; **housing development**, (*Brit also*) **housing estate** N Wohnsiedlung *f*; **housing scheme** N (*= estate*) Siedlung *f*; (*= project*) Siedlungsbauvorhaben *nt*

hovel ['hɒvəl] N armselige Hütte; (*fig pej*) Bruchbude *f*

hover ['hɒvə'] VI (**a**) (*helicopter, insect*) schweben (**b**) (*fig*) **he ~ed between two alternatives** er schwankte zwischen zwei Alternativen; **he was ~ing between life and death** er schwebte zwischen Leben und Tod; **the exchange rate is ~ing around 110 yen to the dollar** der Wechselkurs bewegt sich um die 110 Yen für den Dollar (**c**) (*fig: = stand around*) herumstehen; **don't ~ over me** geh endlich weg

➤ **hover about** (*Brit*) *or* **around** VI herumlungern; **he was hovering around, waiting to speak to us** er strich um uns herum und wartete auf eine Gelegenheit, mit uns zu sprechen

hover: hovercraft N Luftkissenboot *nt*; **hoverport** N Anlegestelle *f* für Luftkissenboote

how [haʊ] ADV (**a**) wie; **~ so?**, **~'s that?**, **~ come?** (*all inf*) wieso (denn das)?; **~ do you mean?** (*inf*) wie meinst du das?; **~ is it that we** *or* **~ come** (*inf*) **we earn less?** wieso *or* warum verdienen wir denn weniger?; **I see ~ it is** ich verstehe

(schon); **~ do you know that?** woher wissen Sie das?; **I'd like to learn ~ to swim/drive** *etc* ich würde gerne schwimmen/Auto fahren *etc* lernen; **~ nice!** wie nett!; **~ much** (+*vb*) wie sehr; (+*n, adj, adv, vbs of physical action*) wie viel; **~ many** wie viel, wie viele; **~ would you like to ...?** hätten Sie Lust, ... zu ...?; **~ do you do?** (*on introduction*) guten Tag/Abend!, angenehm! (*form*); **~ are you?** wie geht es Ihnen?; **~'s work/the new job?** *etc* was macht die Arbeit/die neue Stelle? *etc* (*inf*); **~ are things at school/in the office?** *etc* wie gehts in der Schule/im Büro? *etc*; **~ did the job interview go?** wie ist das Bewerbungsgespräch gelaufen?; **~ about ...?** wie wäre es mit ...?; **~ about it?** (*about suggestion*) wie wäre es damit?; **~ about going for a walk?** wie wärs mit einem Spaziergang?; **I've had enough, ~ about you?** mir reichts, wie siehts bei dir aus?; **and ~!** und ob *or* wie!; **~ he's grown!** er ist aber *or* vielleicht groß geworden; **look ~ he's grown!** sieh mal, wie groß er geworden ist

(**b**) (*= that*) dass

howdy ['haʊdɪ] INTERJ (*US inf*) Tag (*inf*)

however [haʊ'evə'] **1** CONJ jedoch, aber; **~, we finally succeeded** wir haben es schließlich doch noch geschafft **2** ADV (**a**) (*= no matter how*) wie ... auch, egal wie (*inf*); (*= in whatever way*) wie; **~ you do it** wie immer du es machst; **buy it ~ expensive it is** kaufen Sie es, egal, was es kostet; **~ much you cry** und wenn du noch so weinst; **wait 30 minutes or ~ long it takes** warte eine halbe Stunde oder so lange, wie es dauert; **~ that may be** wie dem auch sei (**b**) (*in question*) wie ... bloß *or* nur; **~ did you manage it?** wie hast du das bloß geschafft?

howl [haʊl] **1** N Schrei *m*; (*of animal, wind*) Heulen *nt no pl*; **the dog let out a ~** der Hund jaulte; **~s of laughter** brüllendes Gelächter; **~s (of protest)** Protestgeschrei *nt* **2** VI (*person*) brüllen; (*animal*) jaulen; (*wind, = weep noisily*) heulen; (*baby*) schreien; **to ~ with laughter** in brüllendes Gelächter ausbrechen **3** VT hinausbrüllen; **they ~ed their disapproval** sie äußerten lautstark ihr Missfallen

howler ['haʊlə'] N (*Brit inf*) Hammer *m* (*inf*), Schnitzer *m* (*inf*); **he made a real ~** da hat er sich (*dat*) einen Hammer geleistet (*inf*)

howling ['haʊlɪŋ] ADJ (*inf*) enorm; **a ~ success** ein Riesenerfolg *m*

HP, hp (**a**) ABBR *of* **hire purchase** (**b**) ABBR *of* **horse power** PS

HQ ABBR *of* **headquarters**

HRH ABBR *of* **His/Her Royal Highness** S. M./I. M.

HRT ABBR *of* **hormone replacement therapy**

HSS (*US*) ABBR *of* **Health and Social Services** *das amerikanische Gesundheits- und Sozialministerium*

HST (*US*) ABBR *of* **Hawaiian Standard Time** hawaiische Zeit

HTML (*Comput*) ABBR *of* **hypertext mark-up language** HTML

hub [hʌb] N (**a**) (*of wheel*) (Rad)nabe *f* (**b**) (*fig*) Zentrum *nt*, Mittelpunkt *m*; **a ~ of finance** ein finanzielles Zentrum

hub airport N (*US*) Großflughafen *m*

hubbub ['hʌbʌb] N Tumult *m*; **a ~ of voices** ein Stimmengewirr *nt*

hubby ['hʌbɪ] N (*inf*) Mann *m*

hubcap ['hʌbkæp] N Radkappe *f*

hubris ['hjuːbrɪs] N (*liter*) Anmaßung *f*

huckleberry ['hʌklbərɪ] N amerikanische Heidelbeere

huckster ['hʌkstə'] N (*US inf*) Reklamefritze *m* (*inf*)

huddle ['hʌdl] **1** N (*wirrer*) Haufen *m*; (*of people*) Gruppe *f*; **in a ~** dicht zusammengedrängt; **to go into a ~** (*inf*) die Köpfe zusammenstecken **2** VI (*also* **to be ~d**) (sich) kauern; **they ~d under the umbrella** sie drängten sich unter dem Schirm zusammen; **we ~d around the fire** wir saßen eng zusammengedrängt um das Feuer herum

➤ **huddle together** VI sich aneinander kauern; **to be huddled together** aneinander kauern

hue¹ [hjuː] N (*= colour*) Farbe *f*; (*= shade*) Schattierung *f*; (*fig: = political leaning*) Färbung *f*

hue² N **~ and cry** Zeter und Mordio (*against* gegen); **to set up** *or* **raise a ~ and cry** Zeter und Mordio schreien

huff [hʌf] N **to be/go off in a ~** beleidigt *or* eingeschnappt sein/abziehen (*inf*)

huffy ['hʌfɪ] ADJ (+ER) (*= in a huff*) beleidigt; (*= touchy*) empfindlich; **to get/be ~ about sth** wegen etw eingeschnappt (*inf*) *or* beleidigt sein

hug [hʌg] **1** N Umarmung f; **to give sb a ~** jdn umarmen **2** VT **(a)** (= hold close) umarmen; (bear etc) umklammern **(b)** (= keep close to) sich dicht halten an (+acc); (car, ship etc also) dicht entlangfahren an (+dat) **3** VI sich umarmen

huge [hjuːdʒ] ADJ (+ER) riesig; appetite, thirst, disappointment, deficit, selection, success Riesen- (inf); effort gewaltig; **a ~ job** eine Riesenarbeit (inf); **~ numbers of these children** ungeheuer viele von diesen Kindern

hugely [ˈhjuːdʒlɪ] ADV (emph) successful, expensive, important, entertaining, talented außerordentlich; enjoy oneself riesig; vary, increase ungemein; **the whole thing is ~ enjoyable** das Ganze macht ungeheuer viel Spaß

hugeness [ˈhjuːdʒnɪs] N gewaltiges or riesiges Ausmaß

hulk [hʌlk] N **(a)** (Naut) (Schiffs)rumpf m **(b)** (inf: = person) Hüne m (inf) **(c)** (= wrecked vehicle) Wrack nt; (= wrecked building etc) Ruine f

hulking [ˈhʌlkɪŋ] ADJ **~ great, great ~** massig; **a ~ great brute of a man** ein grobschlächtiger, brutaler Kerl

hull[1] [hʌl] N (Naut) Schiffskörper m; **~ insurance** Kaskoversicherung f

hull[2] **1** N Hülse f; (of strawberries etc) Blättchen nt **2** VT schälen; strawberries etc entstielen

hullabaloo [ˌhʌləbəˈluː] N (Brit inf) Spektakel m

hullo [hʌˈləʊ] INTERJ (Brit) = **hello**

hum [hʌm] **1** N (of insect, person) Summen nt; (of traffic) Brausen nt; (of engine, electric tool etc) Brummen nt; (of small machine, camera etc) Surren nt; (of voices) Gemurmel nt **2** VI **(a)** (insect, person) summen; (engine, electric tool etc) brummen; (small machine, camera etc) surren **(b)** (fig inf: party, concert etc) in Schwung kommen; **the headquarters was ~ming with activity** im Hauptquartier ging es zu wie in einem Bienenstock **(c)** **to ~ and haw** (inf) herumdrucksen (inf) (over, about um) **3** VT music, tune summen

human [ˈhjuːmən] **1** ADJ menschlich; health, brain, part of the body des Menschen; **~ dignity** die Menschenwürde; **~ error** menschliches Versagen; **~ chain** Menschenkette f; **~ shield** menschlicher Schutzschild; **I'm only ~** ich bin auch nur ein Mensch **2** N Mensch m

human being N Mensch m

humane [hjuːˈmeɪn] ADJ human; rearing of animals unter humanen Bedingungen; **a ~ method of killing animals** eine möglichst schmerzlose Methode, Tiere zu töten

humanely [hjuːˈmeɪnlɪ] ADV treat human; rear animals unter humanen Bedingungen; destroy, slaughter, kill (möglichst) schmerzlos

human interest N (in newspaper story etc) Emotionalität f; **a ~ story** eine ergreifende Story

humanism [ˈhjuːmənɪzəm] N Humanismus m

humanitarian [hjuːˌmænɪˈtɛərɪən] **1** N Vertreter(in) m(f) des Humanitätsgedankens **2** ADJ humanitär

humanitarianism [ˌhjuːmænɪˈtɛərɪənɪzəm] N Humanitarismus m; (of individual) humanitäre Gesinnung

humanity [hjuːˈmænɪtɪ] N **(a)** (= mankind) die Menschheit **(b)** (= humaneness) Humanität f, Menschlichkeit f; **to treat sb with ~** jdn human behandeln **(c)** **humanities** PL Geisteswissenschaften pl; (= Latin and Greek) Altphilologie f

humanize [ˈhjuːmənaɪz] VT humanisieren

humankind [ˌhjuːmənˈkaɪnd] N die Menschheit

humanly [ˈhjuːmənlɪ] ADV menschlich; **as far as ~ possible** soweit überhaupt möglich; **to do all that is or everything ~ possible** alles Menschenmögliche tun

human nature N die menschliche Natur; **it's ~ to do that** es liegt (nun einmal) in der Natur des Menschen, das zu tun

human: human race N **the ~** die Menschheit, das Menschengeschlecht (geh); **human resources** PL (Econ) Humankapital nt, Arbeitskräftepotenzial nt; (of company) Personal nt; **human-resources** ADJ ATTR Personal-; **~ manager** Personalleiter(in) m(f); **human resources department** N Personalabteilung f; **human rights** PL Menschenrechte pl; **~ organization** Menschenrechtsorganisation f; **~ activist** Menschenrechtler(in) m(f)

humble [ˈhʌmbl] **1** ADJ (+ER) bescheiden; (= modest, esp Rel also) demütig; curate, clerk, beginner einfach; origins niedrig; **my ~ apologies!** ich bitte inständig um Verzeihung!; **to eat ~ pie** klein beigeben; **in my ~ opinion** meiner bescheidenen

Meinung nach **2** VT demütigen; **to be/feel ~d** sich (dat) klein vorkommen

humbly [ˈhʌmblɪ] ADV bescheiden, demütig (esp Rel); **she ~ apologized** sie entschuldigte sich kleinlaut

humbug [ˈhʌmbʌg] N **(a)** (Brit: = sweet) Pfefferminzbonbon m or nt **(b)** (inf: = talk) Humbug m, Mumpitz m (inf) **(c)** (inf: = person) Gauner m (inf)

humdinger [ˈhʌmdɪŋəʳ] N (inf) **to be a ~** Spitze or große Klasse sein (inf); **a ~ of a job/girl** etc ein klasse Job/Mädchen etc (inf)

humdrum [ˈhʌmdrʌm] ADJ stumpfsinnig

humid [ˈhjuːmɪd] ADJ feucht; **it's (hot and) ~ today** es ist schwül heute

humidifier [hjuːˈmɪdɪfaɪəʳ] N Luftbefeuchter m

humidity [hjuːˈmɪdɪtɪ] N (Luft)feuchtigkeit f

humiliate [hjuːˈmɪlɪeɪt] VT demütigen, erniedrigen

humiliating [hjuːˈmɪlɪeɪtɪŋ] ADJ defeat, experience demütigend; blow, conditions beschämend

humiliation [hjuːˌmɪlɪˈeɪʃən] N Demütigung f, Erniedrigung f; (because of one's own actions) Beschämung f no pl; **the result is a ~ for the prime minister** das Ergebnis ist eine demütigende Niederlage für den Premierminister

humility [hjuːˈmɪlɪtɪ] N Demut f; (= unassumingness) Bescheidenheit f

humming [ˈhʌmɪŋ] N Summen nt

hummingbird [ˈhʌmɪŋbɜːd] N Kolibri m

hummus [ˈhʊməs] N = **hoummos**

humor etc (US) = **humour** etc

humorist [ˈhjuːmərɪst] N Humorist(in) m(f)

humorous [ˈhjuːmərəs] ADJ humorvoll; book, story etc also, situation komisch; idea, thought witzig

humorously [ˈhjuːmərəslɪ] ADV humorvoll; reflect, say heiter

humour, (US) **humor** [ˈhjuːməʳ] **1** N **(a)** Humor m; **a sense of ~** (Sinn m für) Humor m; **I don't see the ~ in that** ich finde das gar nicht komisch **(b)** (= mood) Stimmung f, Laune f; **to be in a good ~** gute Laune haben; **with good ~** gut gelaunt; **to be out of ~, to be in a bad ~** schlechte Laune haben **2** VT **to ~ sb** jdm seinen Willen lassen or tun; **do it just to ~ him** tus doch, damit er seinen Willen hat

humourless, (US) **humorless** [ˈhjuːməlɪs] ADJ humorlos; speech, book etc also trocken

hump [hʌmp] **1** N **(a)** (Anat) Buckel m; (of camel) Höcker m **(b)** (= hillock) Hügel m; **we're over the ~ now** (fig) wir sind jetzt über den Berg **(c)** (Brit inf) **he's got the ~** er ist sauer (inf); **he/that gives me the ~** er/das fällt mir auf den Wecker (inf) **2** VT (inf: = carry) schleppen; (on back, shoulders) auf dem Rücken/den Schultern tragen or schleppen

humpbacked [ˈhʌmpbækt] ADJ person buck(e)lig; bridge gewölbt

hunch [hʌntʃ] **1** N Gefühl nt, Ahnung f; **to act on a ~** einem inneren Gefühl zufolge handeln; **your ~ paid off** du hattest die richtige Ahnung, es hat sich gelohnt **2** VT (also ~ up) **to ~ one's shoulders** die Schultern hochziehen; **he was ~ed over his desk** er saß über seinen Schreibtisch gebeugt

hunch: **hunchback** N Buck(e)lige(r) mf; **hunchbacked** ADJ buck(e)lig

hundred [ˈhʌndrɪd] **1** ADJ hundert; **a or one ~ years** (ein)hundert Jahre; **two/several ~ years** zweihundert/ mehrere hundert Jahre; **a or one ~ and one** (lit) (ein)hundert(und)eins; (fig) tausend; **(one) ~ and first/ second** etc hundert(und)erste(r, s)/-zweite(r, s) etc; **a or one ~ thousand** (ein)hunderttausend; **a ~-mile walk** ein Hundertmeilenmarsch; **a or one ~ per cent** hundert Prozent; **a (one) ~ per cent increase** eine Erhöhung von or um hundert Prozent; **I'm not a or one ~ per cent fit/sure** ich bin nicht hundertprozentig fit/sicher; **I agree with you one ~ per cent** ich stimme hundertprozentig mit Ihnen überein **2** N hundert num; (written figure) Hundert f; **~s** (lit, fig) hunderte pl; (Math: figures in column) Hunderter pl; **one in a ~** einer unter hundert; **eighty out of a ~** achtzig von hundert; **~s of times** hundertmal; **~s and ~s** hunderte und aberhunderte; **~s of or thousands** hunderttausende pl; **~s and thousands** (Cook) Liebesperlen pl; **he earns nine ~ a month** er verdient neunhundert im Monat; **I'll lay (you) a ~ to one** ich wette hundert gegen eins; **it'll cost you a ~** das wird dich einen Hunderter kosten; **to live to be a ~** hundert

Jahre alt werden; **they came in (their) ~s** or **by the ~** sie kamen zu hunderten

hundredth ['hʌndrɪdθ] **1** ADJ (in series) hundertste(r, s); (of fraction) hundertstel **2** N Hundertste(r, s) decl as adj; (= fraction) Hundertstel nt; see also **sixth**

hundredweight ['hʌndrɪdweɪt] N Zentner m; (Brit) 50,8 kg; (US) 45,4 kg

hung [hʌŋ] PRET, PTP of **hang**

Hungarian [hʌŋ'gɛərɪən] **1** ADJ ungarisch **2** N (a) Ungar(in) m(f) (b) (Ling) Ungarisch nt

Hungary ['hʌŋgərɪ] N Ungarn nt

hunger ['hʌŋgə'] N (lit, fig) Hunger m (for nach); **to die of ~** verhungern

➤ **hunger after** or **for** VI +PREP OBJ (liter) hungern nach; news sehnsüchtig warten auf (+acc)

hunger strike N **to be on (a) ~** sich im Hungerstreik befinden; **to go on (a) ~** in (den) Hungerstreik treten

hung: **hung over** ADJ **to be ~** einen Kater haben (inf); **hung parliament** N Parlament nt ohne klare Mehrheitsverhältnisse; **the election resulted in a ~** die Wahl führte zu einem parlamentarischen Patt

hungrily ['hʌŋgrɪlɪ] ADV (lit, fig) hungrig

hungry ['hʌŋgrɪ] ADJ (+ER) (lit, fig) hungrig; **to be** or **feel/get ~** Hunger haben/bekommen; **to go ~** hungern; **~ for knowledge/love/power** bildungs-/liebes-/machthungrig; **to be ~ for news** sehnsüchtig auf Nachricht warten; **this is ~ work** das macht hungrig

hung up ADJ (inf) **to be/get ~ about sth** (= be neurotic) wegen etw einen Knacks weghaben (inf)/durchdrehen (inf); (= have complex) Komplexe wegen etw haben/kriegen; **he's ~ on her** (inf) er steht auf sie (sl)

hunk [hʌŋk] N (a) Stück nt (b) (fig inf: = man) **a gorgeous ~ (of a man)** ein Mann! (inf)

hunky-dory ['hʌŋkɪ'dɔːrɪ] ADJ (inf) **that's ~** das ist in Ordnung

hunt [hʌnt] **1** N Jagd f; (= huntsmen) Jagd(gesellschaft) f; (fig: = search) Suche f; **tiger ~** Tigerjagd f; **the ~ is on** die Suche hat begonnen; **to have a ~ for sth** nach etw fahnden (inf) **2** VT (Hunt) jagen; criminal fahnden nach; missing person, article etc suchen **3** VI (a) (Hunt) jagen; **to go ~ing** auf die Jagd gehen (b) (= search) suchen (for, after nach); **he is ~ing for a job** er sucht eine Stelle

➤ **hunt down** VT SEP (unerbittlich) Jagd machen auf (+acc); (= capture) zur Strecke bringen

➤ **hunt out** VT SEP heraussuchen; person, facts ausfindig machen

hunter ['hʌntə'] N Jäger(in) m(f)

hunting ['hʌntɪŋ] N die Jagd; **the ~ in these woods is excellent** diese Wälder sind ein gutes Jagdgebiet

hunt saboteur N (Brit) jd, der versucht, die Fuchsjagd durch Sabotageakte zu verhindern, Jagdsaboteur(in) m(f)

huntsman ['hʌntsmən] N, pl **-men** [-mən] Jagdreiter m

hurdle ['hɜːdl] N (Sport, fig) Hürde f; **~s** sing (= race) Hürdenlauf m; **the 100m ~s** (die) 100 m Hürden; **to fall at the first ~** (fig) (schon) über die erste or bei der ersten Hürde stolpern

hurdler ['hɜːdlə'] N (Sport) Hürdenläufer(in) m(f)

hurl [hɜːl] VT schleudern; **to ~ insults at sb** jdm Beleidigungen entgegenschleudern

hurly-burly ['hɜːlɪ'bɜːlɪ] N Rummel m (inf); **the ~ of politics** der Rummel der Politik

hurrah [hə'rɑː], **hurray** [hə'reɪ] INTERJ hurra; **~ for the king!** ein Hoch dem König!

hurricane ['hʌrɪkən] N Orkan m; (tropical) Hurrikan m

hurricane lamp N Sturmlaterne f

hurried ['hʌrɪd] ADJ eilig; letter, essay eilig or hastig geschrieben; ceremony, meeting hastig durchgeführt; work in Eile gemacht; departure, wedding etc überstürzt

hurriedly ['hʌrɪdlɪ] ADV eilig; say hastig; leave in großer Eile

hurry ['hʌrɪ] **1** N Eile f; **in my ~ to get it finished ...** vor lauter Eile, damit fertig zu werden ...; **to do sth in a ~** etw schnell or (too fast) hastig tun; **I need it in a ~** ich brauche es eilig; **to be in a ~** es eilig haben; **I won't do that again in a ~!** (inf) das mache ich so schnell nicht wieder!; **what's the ~?** was soll die Eile or Hast?; **there's no ~** es eilt nicht; **there's no need to**

2 VI sich beeilen; (= run/go quickly) laufen; **there's no need to**

~ **kein Grund zur Eile; don't ~!** lass dir Zeit!

3 VT person (= make act quickly) (zur Eile) antreiben; (= make move quickly) scheuchen (inf); work etc beschleunigen, schneller machen; (= do too quickly) überstürzen; **don't ~ me** hetz mich nicht so!; **don't ~ your meals** schling das Essen nicht so runter!; **I won't be hurried into a decision** ich lasse mich nicht zu einer schnellen Entscheidung drängen

➤ **hurry along 1** VI sich beeilen; **hurry along there, please!** schnell weitergehen, bitte! **2** VT SEP person weiterdrängen; (with work etc) zur Eile antreiben; things, work etc vorantreiben

➤ **hurry up 1** VI sich beeilen; **hurry up!** Beeilung!; **hurry up and put your coat on!** mach schon und zieh dir deinen Mantel an! **2** VT SEP person zur Eile antreiben; work, process etc vorantreiben

hurt [hɜːt] vb: pret, ptp **hurt** **1** VT (a) (lit, fig) (= cause pain) wehtun (+dat); (= injure) verletzen; **to ~ oneself** sich (dat) wehtun; **to ~ one's arm** sich (dat) am Arm wehtun; (= injure) sich (dat) den Arm verletzen; **my arm is ~ing me** mir tut der Arm weh; **if you go on like that someone is bound to get ~** wenn ihr so weitermacht, verletzt sich bestimmt noch jemand (b) (= harm) schaden (+dat); **it won't ~ him to wait** es schadet ihm gar nicht(s), wenn es etwas warten muss **2** VI (a) (= be painful, fig) wehtun; **that ~s!** (lit, fig) das tut weh! (b) (= do harm) schaden **3** N Schmerz m; (to feelings) Verletzung f (to +gen); (to reputation etc) Schädigung f (to +gen) **4** ADJ limb, feelings verletzt; tone, look gekränkt

hurtful ['hɜːtfʊl] ADJ verletzend; **it was very ~ to him** es verletzte ihn sehr

hurtle ['hɜːtl] VI rasen; **the car was hurtling along** das Auto sauste dahin; **he came hurtling round the corner** er kam um die Ecke gerast

husband ['hʌzbənd] **1** N Ehemann m; **my/her etc ~** mein/ihr etc Mann; **they are ~ and wife** sie sind Eheleute or verheiratet **2** VT strength, resources sparsam umgehen mit

hush [hʌʃ] **1** VT person zum Schweigen bringen **2** VI still sein **3** N Stille f; **a ~ fell over the crowd** die Menge verstummte plötzlich **4** INTERJ pst; **~, ~, it's all right** sch, sch, es ist ja gut

➤ **hush up** VT SEP vertuschen

hushed [hʌʃt] ADJ voices gedämpft; crowd schweigend; courtroom still; **in ~ tones** mit gedämpfter Stimme

hush-hush ['hʌʃ'hʌʃ] ADJ (inf) streng geheim

husk [hʌsk] N Schale f; (of wheat, rice) Spelze f; (of maize) Hüllblatt nt

husky¹ ['hʌskɪ] ADJ (+ER) (a) rau; (= hoarse) heiser (b) (= sturdy) stämmig

husky² N (= dog) Schlittenhund m

hussy ['hʌsɪ] N (= pert girl) Fratz m (inf); (= whorish woman) Flittchen nt (pej)

hustings ['hʌstɪŋz] PL (Brit) (= campaign) Wahlkampf m; (= meeting) Wahlveranstaltung f; **on the ~** im Wahlkampf; (= at election meeting) in or bei einer Wahlveranstaltung

hustle ['hʌsl] **1** N (= jostling) Gedränge nt; (= hurry) Eile f; **the ~ (and bustle) of the city centre** das geschäftige Treiben or das Gewühl (inf) in der Innenstadt **2** VT (a) **to ~ sb into a room/out of a building** jdn schnell in einen Raum/aus einem Gebäude bringen or befördern (inf) (b) (fig inf) drängen; **I won't be ~d into a decision** ich lasse mich nicht zu einer Entscheidung drängen; **I won't be ~d into selling my shares** ich lasse mich nicht dazu drängen, meine Aktien zu verkaufen **3** VI (a) (= solicit) auf den Strich gehen (inf); **to ~ for business** (entrepreneur etc) Aufträgen nachjagen (b) (US inf: = work quickly) sich ins Zeug legen (inf)

hut [hʌt] N Hütte f; (Mil) Baracke f

hutch [hʌtʃ] N Verschlag m

hyacinth ['haɪəsɪnθ] N Hyazinthe f

hyaena, hyena [haɪ'iːnə] N Hyäne f

hybrid ['haɪbrɪd] **1** N (Ling) hybride Bildung; (Bot, Zool) Kreuzung f; (fig) Mischform f **2** ADJ (Ling) hybrid (spec); (Bot, Zool) Misch-; **~ plant** Mischpflanze f

hydrant ['haɪdrənt] N Hydrant m

hydrate [haɪ'dreɪt] VT hydratisieren

hydraulic [haɪˈdrɒlɪk] ADJ hydraulisch
hydraulics [haɪˈdrɒlɪks] N SING Hydraulik f
hydro- [ˈhaɪdrəʊ-] PREF Hydro-, hydro-, Wasser-, wasser-; (Chem: +n) -wasserstoff m; **hydrocarbon** N Kohlenwasserstoff m; **hydrochloric acid** N Salzsäure f; **hydroelectric power** N durch Wasserkraft erzeugte Energie; **hydroelectric power station** N Wasserkraftwerk nt; **hydrofoil** N (= boat) Tragflächen- or Tragflügelboot nt; (= fin) Tragfläche f or -flügel m
hydrogen [ˈhaɪdrɪdʒən] N Wasserstoff m
hydrogen bomb N Wasserstoffbombe f
hydro-: **hydroplane** N (= boat) Gleitboot nt; **hydropower** N Wasserkraft f; **hydrotherapy** N Wasserbehandlung f
hyena [haɪˈiːnə] N = **hyaena**
hygiene [ˈhaɪdʒiːn] N Hygiene f; **personal ~** Körperpflege f
hygienic [haɪˈdʒiːnɪk] ADJ hygienisch
hymn [hɪm] N Kirchenlied nt
hymn book N Gesangbuch nt
hype [haɪp] (inf) **1** N Publicity f; **media ~** Medienrummel m (inf); **all this ~ about ...** dieser ganze Rummel um ... (inf) **2** VT (also ~ **up**) Publicity machen für; **the film was ~d up too much** um den Film wurde zu viel Rummel gemacht (inf)
hyped up [haɪptˈʌp] ADJ (inf) aufgeputscht; (= excited) aufgedreht (inf)
hyper- [ˈhaɪpəʳ] PREF Hyper-, hyper-, Über-, über-; **hyperactive** ADJ überaktiv; **a ~ thyroid** eine Überfunktion der Schilddrüse
hyperbola [haɪˈpɜːbələ] N (Math) Hyperbel f
hyperbole [haɪˈpɜːbəlɪ] N (Liter) Hyperbel f
hyperbolic(al) [ˌhaɪpəˈbɒlɪk(əl)] ADJ (Liter) hyperbolisch
hyper-: **hypercritical** [ˈhaɪpəˈkrɪtɪkəl] ADJ übertrieben kritisch; **hyperlink** (Comput) **1** N Hyperlink m **2** VT per Hyperlink verbinden; **hypermarket** N (Brit) Verbrauchermarkt m; **hypersensitive** ADJ überempfindlich; **hypertext** N (Comput) Hypertext m; **hyperventilate** [ˌhaɪpəˈvɛntɪleɪt] VI hyperventilieren
hyphen [ˈhaɪfən] N Bindestrich m; (at end of line) Trenn(ungs)strich m
hyphenate [ˈhaɪfəneɪt] VT mit Bindestrich schreiben; **~d word** Bindestrichwort nt

hyphenation [ˌhaɪfəˈneɪʃən] N Silbentrennung f
hypnosis [hɪpˈnəʊsɪs] N Hypnose f; **under ~** unter Hypnose
hypnotherapy [ˌhɪpnəʊˈθerəpɪ] N Hypnotherapie f
hypnotic [hɪpˈnɒtɪk] ADJ **(a)** regression, trance hypnotisch; **~ state** Hypnosezustand m **(b)** effect, music, eyes hypnotisierend
hypnotism [ˈhɪpnətɪzəm] N Hypnotismus m
hypnotist [ˈhɪpnətɪst] N Hypnotiseur(in) m(f)
hypnotize [ˈhɪpnətaɪz] VT hypnotisieren; **to be ~d by sb/sth** (= fascinated) von jdm/etw wie hypnotisiert sein
hypo- [haɪpəʊ-] PREF Hypo-, hypo-; **~allergenic** hypoallergen
hypochondria [ˌhaɪpəʊˈkɒndrɪə] N Hypochondrie f
hypochondriac [ˌhaɪpəʊˈkɒndrɪæk] N Hypochonder m
hypocrisy [hɪˈpɒkrɪsɪ] N (= hypocritical behaviour) Heuchelei f; (= sanctimony) Scheinheiligkeit f
hypocrite [ˈhɪpəkrɪt] N Heuchler(in) m(f), Scheinheilige(r) mf
hypocritical [ˌhɪpəˈkrɪtɪkəl] ADJ heuchlerisch, scheinheilig
hypodermic [ˌhaɪpəˈdɜːmɪk] N subkutane Spritze
hypodermic: **hypodermic needle** N (Injektions)nadel f; **hypodermic syringe** N (Injektions)spritze f
hypothermia [ˌhaɪpəʊˈθɜːmɪə] N Unterkühlung f
hypothesis [haɪˈpɒθɪsɪs] N, pl **hypotheses** [haɪˈpɒθɪsiːz] Hypothese f, Annahme f
hypothetical [ˌhaɪpəʊˈθetɪkəl] ADJ hypothetisch, angenommen
hypothetically [ˌhaɪpəʊˈθetɪkəlɪ] ADV (= in theory) theoretisch
hysterectomy [ˌhɪstəˈrektəmɪ] N Hysterektomie f (spec)
hysteria [hɪˈstɪərɪə] N Hysterie f
hysterical [hɪˈsterɪkəl] ADJ **(a)** (also Psych) hysterisch **(b)** (inf: = hilarious) wahnsinnig komisch (inf)
hysterically [hɪˈsterɪkəlɪ] ADV **(a)** scream, laugh hysterisch **(b)** (inf) **~ funny** wahnsinnig komisch (inf) **(c)** (= frantically) wie wahnsinnig (inf)
hysterics [hɪˈsterɪks] PL Hysterie f; **to go into** or **have ~** hysterisch werden; (fig inf: = laugh) sich totlachen; **to be in ~** hysterisch sein; (fig inf: = be laughing) sich (halb) totlachen (inf)
Hz ABBR of **hertz** Hz

Ii

I¹, i [aɪ] N I nt, i nt

I² PERS PRON ich; **it is I** (form) ich bin es

IATA [aɪˈɑːtə] ABBR of **International Air Transport Association** IATA f

Iberian Peninsula N Iberische Halbinsel

ibid ABBR of **ibidem** ib., ibd

ICC ABBR of **International Chamber of Commerce** IHK f, Internationale Handelskammer

ice [aɪs] ∎ N (a) Eis nt; (on roads) (Glatt)eis nt; **to be as cold as ~** eiskalt sein; **my hands are like ~** ich habe eiskalte Hände; **to keep** or **put sth on ~** (fig) etw auf Eis legen; **to break the ~** (fig) das Eis brechen; **to be skating on thin ~** (fig) sich aufs Glatteis begeben/begeben haben; **that cuts no ~ with me** (inf) das kommt bei mir nicht an
(b) (Brit: = ~ cream) (Speise)eis nt
∎ VT cake mit Zuckerguss überziehen
➤ **ice over** VI zufrieren; (windscreen) vereisen
➤ **ice up** VI (aircraft wings, windscreen etc) vereisen; (pipes etc) einfrieren

ice IN CPDS Eis-; **ice age** N Eiszeit f; **ice axe**, (US) **ice ax** N Eispickel m; **iceberg** N (lit, fig) Eisberg m; **icebound** ADJ port, lake zugefroren; ship, place vom Eis eingeschlossen; **icebox** N (Brit: in refrigerator) Eisfach nt; (US) Eisschrank m; (= insulated box) Kühltasche f; **icebreaker** N Eisbrecher m; **ice bucket** N Eiskühler m; **icecap** N Eisschicht f; (polar) Eiskappe f; **ice-cold** ADJ eiskalt; **ice-cool** ADJ (fig) person supercool (inf); **ice cream** N Eis nt, Eiskrem f; **ice-cream cone, ice-cream cornet** N Eistüte f; **ice-cream parlour**, (US) **ice-cream parlor** N Eisdiele f; **ice cube** N Eiswürfel m

iced [aɪst] ADJ (a) drink eisgekühlt; **~ tea** Eistee m; **~ coffee** Eiskaffee m (b) cake, bun mit Zuckerguss überzogen

ice: ice dancing N Eistanz m; **ice floe** N Eisscholle f; **ice hockey** N Eishockey nt

Iceland [ˈaɪslənd] N Island nt

Icelander [ˈaɪsləndəʳ] N Isländer(in) m(f)

Icelandic [aɪsˈlændɪk] ∎ ADJ isländisch ∎ N (Ling) Isländisch nt

ice: ice lolly N (Brit) Eis nt am Stiel; **ice pack** N (on head) Eisbeutel m; **ice pick** N Eispickel m; **ice rink** N (Kunst)eisbahn f, Schlittschuhbahn f; **ice-skate** VI Schlittschuh laufen or fahren; **ice skate** N Schlittschuh m; **ice-skater** N Schlittschuhläufer(in) m(f); (= figure-skater) Eiskunstläufer(in) m(f); **ice-skating** N Schlittschuhlaufen nt; (= figure-skating) Eiskunstlauf m; **ice storm** N (US) Eissturm m; **ice water** N Eiswasser nt

icicle [ˈaɪsɪkl] N Eiszapfen m

icily [ˈaɪsɪlɪ] ADV (fig) eisig; say, stare also frostig; smile kalt

icing [ˈaɪsɪŋ] N (Cook) Zuckerguss m; **this is the ~ on the cake** (fig) das ist die Krönung des Ganzen

icing sugar N (Brit) Puderzucker m

icon [ˈaɪkɒn] N (a) Ikone f (b) (Comput) Icon nt

iconic [aɪˈkɒnɪk] ADJ (culturally) **an ~ figure** eine Ikone; **to achieve ~ status** zur Ikone werden

iconoclastic [aɪˌkɒnəˈklæstɪk] ADJ (fig) bilderstürmerisch

ICT (Brit Sch) ABBR of **Information and Communications Technology** Informations- und Kommunikationstechnologie f, IKT f

icy [ˈaɪsɪ] ADJ (+ER) (a) road, pavement vereist; **the ~ conditions on the roads** das Glatteis auf den Straßen; **when it's ~** bei Glatteis (b) wind, river, hands, feet eiskalt; **~ cold** water, weather eiskalt (c) (fig) stare eisig; tone, reception, silence frostig

ID N ABBR of **identification, identity; I don't have any ID on me** ich habe keinen Ausweis dabei

I'd [aɪd] CONTR of **I would, I had**

id [ɪd] N (Psych) Es nt

ID card [aɪˈdiːkɑːd] N Ausweis m; (state-issued) Personalausweis m

idea [aɪˈdɪə] N (a) Idee f; (esp sudden) Einfall m; **good ~!** gute Idee!; **that's not a bad ~** das ist keine schlechte Idee; **whose bright ~ was that?** (iro) wer hat denn diese glänzende Idee gehabt?; **history of ~s** Geistesgeschichte f; **man of ~s** Denker m; **the very ~!** (nein,) so was!; **the very ~ of eating horse meat revolts me** der bloße Gedanke an Pferdefleisch ekelt mich; **he is full of (bright) ~s** ihm fehlt es nie an (guten) Ideen; **to hit upon the ~ of doing sth** den plötzlichen Gedanken haben, etw zu tun; **that gives me an ~, we could ...** da fällt mir ein, wir könnten ...; **he got the ~ for his novel while he was having a bath** die Idee zu seinem Roman kam ihm in der Badewanne; **somehow he's got the ~ into his head that ...** er bildet sich (dat) irgendwie ein, dass ...; **where did you get the ~ that I was ill?** wie kommst du auf den Gedanken, dass ich krank war?; **don't get ~s** or **don't you go getting ~s about promotion** machen Sie sich (dat) nur keine falschen Hoffnungen auf eine Beförderung; **to put ~s into sb's head** jdm einen Floh ins Ohr setzen; **the ~ was to meet at 6** wir wollten uns um 6 treffen; **what's the ~ of keeping him waiting?** was soll denn das, ihn warten zu lassen?; **what's the big ~?** (inf) was soll das denn?; **the ~ is to reduce expenditure** es geht darum, die Ausgaben zu senken; **that's the ~** genau (das ists)!; **you're getting the ~** Sie verstehen langsam, worum es geht
(b) (= opinion) Meinung f, Ansicht f; (= conception) Vorstellung f; **if that's your ~ of fun** wenn Sie das lustig finden; **this isn't my ~ of a holiday** so stelle ich mir den Urlaub nicht vor
(c) (= knowledge) Ahnung f; **you've no ~ how worried I've been** du kannst dir nicht vorstellen, welche Sorgen ich mir gemacht habe; **(I've) no ~** (ich habe) keine Ahnung; **I've got some ~ (of)** what this is all about ich weiß so ungefähr, worum es hier geht; **I have an ~ that ...** ich habe so das Gefühl, dass ...; **could you give me an ~ of how long ...?** könnten Sie mir ungefähr sagen, wie lange ...?; **to give you an ~ of how difficult it is** um Ihnen eine Vorstellung davon zu vermitteln, wie schwierig es ist

ideal [aɪˈdɪəl] ∎ N Ideal nt (of + gen) ∎ ADJ ideal; **~ solution** Ideallösung f; **~ weight** Idealgewicht nt; **he is ~ or the ~ person for the job** er ist für den Job ideal geeignet; **in an ~ world** im Idealfall

idealism [aɪˈdɪəlɪzəm] N Idealismus m

idealist [aɪˈdɪəlɪst] N Idealist(in) m(f)

idealistic [aɪˌdɪəˈlɪstɪk] ADJ idealistisch

idealize [aɪˈdɪəlaɪz] VT idealisieren

idealized [aɪˈdɪəlaɪzd] ADJ idealisiert; image, view idealisierend

ideally [aɪˈdɪəlɪ] ADV (a) (introducing sentence) idealerweise
(b) suited, situated ideal

identical [aɪˈdentɪkəl] ADJ (= exactly alike) identisch; (= same) der-/die-/dasselbe; **~ twins** eineiige Zwillinge pl; **we have ~ views** wir haben die gleichen Ansichten

identically [aɪˈdentɪkəlɪ] ADV identisch

identifiable [aɪˈdentɪˌfaɪəbl] ADJ erkennbar; (esp in scientific contexts) identifizierbar; **he is ~ by his red hair** er ist an seinem roten Haar zu erkennen

identification [aɪˌdentɪfɪˈkeɪʃən] N (a) (of criminal, dead person etc) Identifizierung f; (of goals) Setzen nt; (of problems) Erkennen nt (b) (= papers) Ausweispapiere pl
(c) (= sympathy, support) Identifikation f

identification parade N Gegenüberstellung f (zur Identifikation des Täters)

identifier [aɪˈdentɪfaɪəʳ] N (Comput) Kennzeichnung f

identify [aɪˈdentɪfaɪ] ∎ VT (a) identifizieren; plant, species etc bestimmen; (= mark identity of) kennzeichnen; (= recognize, pick out) erkennen; **to ~ one's goals** sich (dat) Ziele setzen; **to ~ sb/sth by sth** jdn/etw an etw (dat) erkennen
(b) (= consider as the same) gleichsetzen (with mit)
(c) (= associate with) assoziieren (with mit)
∎ VR (a) **to ~ oneself** sich ausweisen
(b) **to ~ oneself with sb/sth** sich mit jdm/etw identifizieren
∎ VI (with film hero etc) sich identifizieren

Identikit® [aɪˈdentɪkɪt] N **~ (picture)** Phantombild nt

identity [aɪˈdentɪtɪ] N Identität f; **to prove one's ~** sich ausweisen; **a driving licence will be accepted as proof of ~** ein Führerschein genügt, um sich auszuweisen; **proof of ~** (= permit) Legitimation f

identity: **identity card** N Ausweis *m*; (*state-issued*) Personalausweis *m*; **identity crisis** N Identitätskrise *f*; **identity papers** PL Ausweispapiere *pl*; **identity parade** N Gegenüberstellung *f*

ideological [ˌaɪdɪəˈlɒdʒɪkəl] ADJ ideologisch

ideologically [ˌaɪdɪəˈlɒdʒɪkəlɪ] ADV ideologisch; **to be ~ opposed to sth** etw vom ideologischen Standpunkt aus ablehnen

ideology [ˌaɪdɪˈɒlədʒɪ] N Weltanschauung *f*, Ideologie *f*

idiocy [ˈɪdɪəsɪ] N **(a)** NO PL Idiotie *f*, Schwachsinn *m* **(b)** (= *stupid act, words*) Dummheit *f*

idiom [ˈɪdɪəm] N **(a)** (= *special phrase*) Redewendung *f* **(b)** (= *language*) Sprache *f*, Idiom *nt*; (*of region*) Mundart *f*, Dialekt *m*; (*of author*) Ausdrucksweise *f*; **... to use the modern ~ ...** um es modern auszudrücken **(c)** (*in music, art*) Ausdrucksform *f*

idiomatic [ˌɪdɪəˈmætɪk] ADJ idiomatisch; **to speak ~ German** idiomatisch richtiges Deutsch sprechen; **an ~ expression** eine Redensart

idiomatically [ˌɪdɪəˈmætɪkəlɪ] ADV idiomatisch

idiosyncrasy [ˌɪdɪəˈsɪŋkrəsɪ] N Eigenheit *f*, Eigenart *f*

idiosyncratic [ˌɪdɪəsɪŋˈkrætɪk] ADJ eigenartig

idiot [ˈɪdɪət] N Idiot *m*, Schwachkopf *m*; **what an ~!** so ein Idiot *or* Dummkopf!; **this ~ brother of mine** dieser Schwachkopf *or* Idiot von meinem Bruder; **what an ~ I am/was!** ich Idiot!; **to feel like an ~** sich dumm vorkommen

idiotic [ˌɪdɪˈɒtɪk] ADJ blöd(sinnig), idiotisch

idiot-proof [ˈɪdɪətˌpruːf] ADJ (*inf*) idiotensicher (*inf*)

idle [ˈaɪdl] **1** ADJ **(a)** (= *not working*) *person* müßig; *moment* ruhig; **~ life** faules Leben; **his car was lying ~ most of the time** sein Auto stand meistens unbenutzt herum **(b)** (= *lazy*) faul **(c)** (*in industry*) *person* unbeschäftigt; *machine* stillstehend *attr*, außer Betrieb; **500 men have been made ~ by the strike** durch den Streik mussten 500 Leute ihre Arbeit einstellen; **the machine stood ~** die Maschine stand still **(d)** *promise, threat, words* leer; *speculation, talk* müßig; *remark* beiläufig; **~ boast** bloße Angeberei; **~ curiosity** pure *or* bloße Neugier **2** VI **(a)** (*person*) faulenzen; **a day spent idling on the river** ein Tag, den man untätig auf dem Wasser verbringt **(b)** (*engine*) leer laufen; **when the engine is idling** wenn der Motor im Leerlauf ist

➤ **idle away** VT SEP *one's time etc* vertrödeln

idleness [ˈaɪdlɪns] N **(a)** (= *state of not working*) Untätigkeit *f*; (*pleasurable*) Müßiggang (*liter*) *m* **(b)** (= *laziness*) Faulheit *f*

idler [ˈaɪdləʳ] N Faulenzer(in) *m(f)*

idly [ˈaɪdlɪ] ADV **(a)** (= *without working*) untätig; (= *pleasurably*) müßig; **to stand ~ by** untätig herumstehen **(b)** (= *lazily*) faul **(c)** *watch, toy with sth* gedankenverloren; *say, suggest* ohne sich/mir *etc* etwas dabei zu denken **(d)** *speculate* müßig

idol [ˈaɪdl] N (*lit*) Götze *m*; (*fig, Film, TV etc*) Idol *nt*

idolatry [aɪˈdɒlətrɪ] N (*lit*) Götzendienst *m*; (*fig*) Vergötterung *f*

idolize [ˈaɪdəlaɪz] VT abgöttisch lieben *or* verehren; **to ~ sth** etw anbeten

I'd've [ˈaɪdəv] CONTR *of* **I would have**

idyll [ˈɪdɪl] N **(a)** (*Liter*) Idylle *f* **(b)** (*fig*) Idyll *nt*

idyllic [ɪˈdɪlɪk] ADJ idyllisch

i.e. ABBR *of* **id est** i.e., d.h.

if [ɪf] **1** CONJ wenn; (= *in case also*) falls; (= *whether, in direct clause*) ob; **I would be really pleased if you could do it** wenn Sie das tun könnten, wäre ich sehr froh; **if I may say so** wenn ich das sagen darf; **I wonder if he'll come** ich bin gespannt, ob er kommt; **what if something happens to him?** was ist, wenn ihm etwas passiert?; **I'll let you know if and when I come to a decision** ich werde Ihnen mitteilen, ob und wenn ich mich entschieden habe; **(even) if** auch wenn; **even if they are poor, at least they are happy** sie sind zwar arm, aber wenigstens glücklich; **if only I had known!** wenn ich das nur gewusst hätte!; **I would like to see him, if only for a few hours** ich würde ihn gerne sehen, wenn auch nur für ein paar Stunden; **as if** als ob; **he acts as if he were *or* was** (*inf*) rich er tut so, als ob er reich wäre; **it's not as if I meant to hurt her** es ist nicht so, dass ich ihr hätte wehtun wollen; **he stood there as if he were dumb** er stand wie stumm da; **if necessary** falls nötig; **if so** wenn ja; **if not** falls nicht; **this is difficult, if**

not impossible, to do das ist schwer, wenn nicht sogar unmöglich; **if I were you/him** an Ihrer/seiner Stelle; **if anything this one is bigger** wenn überhaupt, dann ist dieses hier größer; **if I know Pete, he'll ...** so wie ich Pete kenne, wird er ...; **well, if it isn't old Jim!** (*inf*) ich werd verrückt, das ist doch der Jim (*inf*) **2** N Wenn *nt*; **it's a big if** das ist die große Frage; **ifs and buts** Wenn und Aber *nt*

iffy [ˈɪfɪ] ADJ (+ER) (*inf*) strittig, fraglich; *neighbourhood etc* zweifelhaft; **I was feeling a bit ~** ich fühlte mich nicht wohl

igloo [ˈɪgluː] N Iglu *m or nt*

ignite [ɪgˈnaɪt] **1** VT entzünden, anzünden; (*fig*) *passions, interest* erwecken **2** VI sich entzünden

ignition [ɪgˈnɪʃən] N (*Aut*) Zündung *f*

ignition (*Aut*) IN CPDS Zünd-; **ignition key** N Zündschlüssel *m*

ignoble [ɪgˈnəʊbl] ADJ schändlich, unwürdig

ignominious [ˌɪgnəˈmɪnɪəs] ADJ schmachvoll; (= *humiliating*) entwürdigend; *behaviour* schändlich

ignominy [ˈɪgnəmɪnɪ] N Schmach *f*, Schande *f*

ignoramus [ˌɪgnəˈreɪməs] N Nichtswisser(in) *m(f)*, Ignorant(in) *m(f)*

ignorance [ˈɪgnərəns] N Unwissenheit *f*, Ignoranz *f*; (*of particular subject etc*) Unkenntnis *f*; **to keep sb in ~ of sth** jdn in Unkenntnis über etw (*acc*) lassen

ignorant [ˈɪgnərənt] ADJ **(a)** unwissend, ignorant; (*of particular subject*) unwissend; (*of plan, requirements etc*) nicht informiert (*of* über +*acc*); **to be ~ of the facts** die Tatsachen nicht kennen **(b)** (= *ill-mannered*) ungehobelt

ignore [ɪgˈnɔːʳ] VT ignorieren; (= *pass over, pay no attention to*) nicht beachten; *remark* übergehen; *person* übersehen; **I'll ~ that** (*remark*) ich habe nichts gehört

iguana [ɪˈgwɑːnə] N Leguan *m*

ikon [ˈaɪkɒn] N = **icon**

ilk [ɪlk] N **people of that ~** solche Leute; **all things of that ~** dergleichen Dinge

ill [ɪl] **1** ADJ **(a)** PRED (= *sick*) krank; **to fall *or* take** (*inf*) ***or* be taken ~** krank werden; **I feel (terribly) ~** mir ist (ganz und gar) nicht gut; **he is ~ with fever/a cold** er hat Fieber/eine Erkältung; **to be ~ with chicken pox** an Windpocken erkrankt sein **(b)** *comp* **worse**, *superl* **worst** (= *adverse*) *effects* unerwünscht; **I don't bear them any ~ will** ich trage ihnen nichts nach; **to suffer ~ health** gesundheitlich angeschlagen sein; **due to ~ health** aus Gesundheitsgründen; **~ humour** *or* (*US*) **humor** schlechte Laune **2** N **(a)** (*liter*) **to bode *or* augur ~** Böses ahnen lassen; **to speak ~ of sb** schlecht über jdn reden **(b)** **ills** PL (= *misfortunes*) Missstände *pl*, Übel *pl* **3** ADV schlecht; **he can ~ afford to refuse** er kann es sich (*dat*) schlecht leisten abzulehnen

I'll [aɪl] CONTR *of* **I will, I shall**

ill: **ill-advised** ADJ unklug; **you would be ~ to trust her** Sie wären schlecht beraten, wenn Sie ihr trauten; **ill-at-ease** ADJ unbehaglich; **ill-bred** ADJ schlecht erzogen; **ill-conceived** ADJ *plan, policy* schlecht durchdacht; **ill-disposed** ADJ **to be ~ to(wards) sb** jdm übel gesinnt sein

illegal [ɪˈliːgəl] ADJ unrechtmäßig; (= *against a specific law*) gesetzwidrig; *trade, immigration, drugs, profits* illegal; *substance, organization* verboten

illegality [ˌɪliːˈgælɪtɪ] N Unrechtmäßigkeit *f*; (*against a specific law*) Gesetzwidrigkeit *f*; (*of trade, drug, organization, profits*) Illegalität *f*

illegally [ɪˈliːgəlɪ] ADV (= *against the law*) unrechtmäßig; (= *against a specific law*) gesetzwidrig; **~ imported** illegal eingeführt; **they were convicted of ~ possessing a handgun** sie wurden wegen unerlaubten Besitzes einer Handfeuerwaffe verurteilt

illegible ADJ, **illegibly** ADV [ɪˈledʒəbl, -ɪ] unleserlich

illegitimacy [ˌɪlɪˈdʒɪtɪməsɪ] N (*of child*) Unehelichkeit *f*

illegitimate [ˌɪlɪˈdʒɪtɪmɪt] ADJ **(a)** *child, birth* unehelich **(b)** *argument, inference, act* unzulässig; *government* unrechtmäßig

ill: **ill-fated** ADJ verhängnisvoll; **ill-fitting** ADJ *clothes, dentures* schlecht sitzend; *shoes* schlecht passend; **ill-gotten gains** PL unrechtmäßiger Gewinn

illiberal [ɪˈlɪbərəl] ADJ (= *narrow-minded*) engstirnig, intolerant; (= *reactionary*) reaktionär; (*Pol, Jur*) *law* restriktiv; *rule* antiliberal; *system, regime* autoritär

illicit [ɪˈlɪsɪt] ADJ illegal; *affair, relationship* verboten; ~ **trade** *or* **sale** Schwarzhandel *m*

ill-informed [ˈɪlɪnˌfɔːmd] ADJ *person* schlecht informiert (*about* über); *attack, criticism* wenig sachkundig

illiteracy [ɪˈlɪtərəsɪ] N Analphabetentum *nt*

illiterate [ɪˈlɪtərət] **1** ADJ des Schreibens und Lesens unkundig; *country, population* analphabetisch; (= *badly-educated, uncultured*) ungebildet; **he's** ~ er ist Analphabet; **economically/musically** ~ völlig unwissend, wenn es um Wirtschaft/Musik geht; **many people are computer-**~ viele Menschen kennen sich nicht mit Computern aus **2** N Analphabet(in) *m(f)*

ill: **ill-mannered** ADJ unhöflich; **ill-natured** ADJ bösartig

illness [ˈɪlnɪs] N Krankheit *f*

illogical [ɪˈlɒdʒɪkəl] ADJ unlogisch

illogically [ɪˈlɒdʒɪkəlɪ] ADV unlogisch; ~**, I felt guilty** entgegen jeder Logik hatte ich Schuldgefühle

ill: **ill-starred** ADJ *undertaking etc* unter einem ungünstigen Stern (stehend); **ill-tempered** ADJ (*habitually*) missmutig, übellaunig; (*on particular occasion*) schlecht gelaunt *pred*; **ill-timed** ADJ ungelegen, unpassend; *move, speech* zeitlich schlecht abgestimmt; **ill-treat** VT schlecht behandeln, misshandeln; **ill-treatment** N Misshandlung *f*, schlechte Behandlung

illuminate [ɪˈluːmɪneɪt] VT **(a)** *room, building* beleuchten; *sky* erleuchten; (*spotlight etc*) anstrahlen; (= *decorate with lights*) festlich beleuchten; ~**d sign** Leuchtzeichen *nt* **(b)** (*Art*) *manuscript* illuminieren; ~**d letters** (verzierte) Initialen *pl* **(c)** (*fig*) *subject* erläutern

illuminating [ɪˈluːmɪneɪtɪŋ] ADJ (= *instructive*) aufschlussreich

illumination [ɪˌluːmɪˈneɪʃən] N (*of street, room, building*) Beleuchtung *f*; **source of** ~ Lichtquelle *f* **illuminations** PL (= *decorative lights*) festliche Beleuchtung

ill-use [ˌɪlˈjuːz] VT schlecht behandeln; (*physically*) misshandeln

illusion [ɪˈluːʒən] N Illusion *f*; (= *misperception*) Täuschung *f*; **to be under the ~ that ...** sich (*dat*) einbilden, dass ...; **to be under** *or* **have no ~s** sich (*dat*) keine Illusionen machen; **it gives the ~ of space** es vermittelt die Illusion von räumlicher Weite

illusionist [ɪˈluːʒənɪst] N Illusionist(in) *m(f)*

illusory [ɪˈluːsərɪ] ADJ illusorisch, trügerisch

illustrate [ˈɪləstreɪt] VT (*lit, fig*) illustrieren; (*fig also*) veranschaulichen; **his lecture was** ~**d by coloured slides** er veranschaulichte seinen Vortrag mit Farbdias; ~**d (magazine)** Illustrierte *f*

illustration [ˌɪləˈstreɪʃən] N **(a)** (= *picture*) Abbildung *f*, Illustration *f* **(b)** (*fig*) (= *thing*) Beispiel *nt*; **by way of** ~ als Beispiel

illustrative [ˈɪləstrətɪv] ADJ veranschaulichend; ~ **of** bezeichnend *or* beispielhaft für; **for** ~ **purposes** zur Veranschaulichung

illustrator [ˈɪləstreɪtəʳ] N Illustrator(in) *m(f)*

illustrious [ɪˈlʌstrɪəs] ADJ glanzvoll; *person* berühmt; *deeds, past* glorreich

I'm [aɪm] CONTR *of* **I am**

image [ˈɪmɪdʒ] N **(a)** Bild *nt*; (= *mental picture also*) Vorstellung *f*; (= *carved, sculpted figure*) Figur *f* **(b)** (= *likeness*) Ebenbild *nt*, Abbild *nt*; **he is the (spitting** (*inf*) *or* **living)** ~ **of his father** er ist seinem Vater wie aus dem Gesicht geschnitten **(c)** (= *public face*) Image *nt*; **brand** ~ Markenimage *nt* **(d)** (*Liter*) **to think in** ~**s** in Bildern *or* Metaphern denken

imagery [ˈɪmɪdʒərɪ] N Metaphorik *f*; **visual** ~ Bildersymbolik *f*

imaginable [ɪˈmædʒɪnəbl] ADJ vorstellbar, denkbar; **the best excuse** ~ die beste Ausrede, die man sich vorstellen kann; **the easiest/fastest way** ~ der denkbar einfachste/schnellste Weg

imaginary [ɪˈmædʒɪnərɪ] ADJ *danger* eingebildet; *characters, friend* erfunden; ~ **world** Fantasiewelt *f*

imagination [ɪˌmædʒɪˈneɪʃən] N (*creative*) Fantasie *f*, Vorstellungskraft *f*; (*self-deceptive*) Einbildung *f*; **to have (a lively** *or* **vivid)** ~ (eine lebhafte *or* rege) Fantasie haben; **use your** ~ lassen Sie Ihrer Fantasie spielen; **to lack** ~ fantasielos

or einfallslos sein; **it's just your** ~! das bilden Sie sich (*dat*) nur ein!; **to capture sb's** ~ jdn in seinen Bann ziehen

imaginative ADJ, **imaginatively** ADV [ɪˈmædʒɪnətɪv, -lɪ] fantasievoll

imagine [ɪˈmædʒɪn] VT **(a)** sich (*dat*) vorstellen; ~ **you're rich/lying on a beach** stellen Sie sich mal vor, Sie wären reich/lägen am Strand; **you can** ~ **how I felt** Sie können sich vorstellen, wie mir zumute war; **I can't** ~ **living there** ich kann mir nicht vorstellen, dort zu leben; **you can't** ~ **it!** Sie machen sich keine Vorstellungen!
(b) (= *be under the illusion that*) sich (*dat*) einbilden; **don't** ~ **that ...** bilden Sie sich nur nicht ein, dass ...; **you're (just) imagining things** (*inf*) Sie bilden sich das alles nur ein **(c)** (= *suppose, conjecture*) annehmen, vermuten; **is that her father? – I would** ~ **so** ist das ihr Vater? – ich denke schon; **I would never have** ~**d he could have done that** ich hätte nie gedacht, dass er das tun würde

imbalance [ɪmˈbæləns] N Unausgeglichenheit *f*

imbecile [ˈɪmbəsiːl] N Idiot *m*, Schwachkopf *m*

imbibe [ɪmˈbaɪb] **1** VT (*form, hum*) trinken, bechern (*hum*) **2** VI (*hum*) viel trinken

imbue [ɪmˈbjuː] VT (*fig*) durchdringen

IMF ABBR *of* **International Monetary Fund** IWF *m*

imitate [ˈɪmɪteɪt] VT imitieren; *person, accent also* nachahmen; (= *counterfeit also*) nachmachen

imitation [ˌɪmɪˈteɪʃən] **1** N Imitation *f*, Nachahmung *f*; **to do an** ~ **of sb** jdn imitieren *or* nachahmen **2** ADJ unecht, künstlich; ~ **gold/pearl** Gold-/Perlenimitation *f*; ~ **leather** Lederimitation *f*, Kunstleder *nt*; ~ **jewellery** unechter Schmuck

imitative [ˈɪmɪtətɪv] ADJ nachahmend, imitierend

imitator [ˈɪmɪteɪtəʳ] N Nachahmer(in) *m(f)*, Imitator(in) *m(f)*

immaculate [ɪˈmækjʊlɪt] ADJ untadelig; *behaviour* tadellos; *manuscript etc* einwandfrei

immaculately [ɪˈmækjʊlɪtlɪ] ADV tadellos; *behave also* untadelig

immaterial [ˌɪməˈtɪərɪəl] ADJ *objection, question* nebensächlich, unwesentlich; **that's (quite)** ~ das spielt keine Rolle, das ist egal

immature [ˌɪməˈtjʊəʳ] ADJ (*lit, fig*) unreif; *plans, ideas etc also* unausgegoren; *wine* nicht ausreichend gelagert

immaturity [ˌɪməˈtjʊərɪtɪ] N Unreife *f*

immeasurable [ɪˈmeʒərəbl] ADJ unermesslich, grenzenlos

immeasurably [ɪˈmeʒərəblɪ] ADV unermesslich, grenzenlos; **it has helped** ~ **that ...** es hat ungeheuer geholfen, dass ...

immediacy [ɪˈmiːdɪəsɪ] N Unmittelbarkeit *f*, Direktheit *f*; (= *urgency*) Dringlichkeit *f*

immediate [ɪˈmiːdɪət] ADJ **(a)** unmittelbar; *cause, impact, successor* direkt; *reply, reaction* sofortig, umgehend; *access* direkt; **only the** ~ **family were invited** nur die engste Familie wurde eingeladen; **our** ~ **plan is to go to France** wir fahren zuerst einmal nach Frankreich; **to take** ~ **action** sofort handeln; **with** ~ **effect** mit sofortiger Wirkung; **the matter requires your** ~ **attention** die Sache bedarf sofort Ihrer Aufmerksamkeit
(b) *problem, concern* dringendste(r, s); **my** ~ **concern was for the children** mein erster Gedanke galt den Kindern

immediately [ɪˈmiːdɪətlɪ] **1** ADV **(a)** (= *at once*) sofort, gleich; *reply, return, depart* umgehend; ~ **after/before that** unmittelbar danach/davor **(b)** (= *directly*) direkt, unmittelbar **2** CONJ (*Brit*) sobald, sofort als ...

immemorial [ˌɪmɪˈmɔːrɪəl] ADJ uralt; **from time** ~ seit undenklichen Zeiten

immense [ɪˈmens] ADJ enorm, immens; *problem, difference also, ocean, heat* gewaltig; *self-confidence, success* enorm; *achievement* großartig

immensely [ɪˈmenslɪ] ADV unheimlich (*inf*), enorm

immerse [ɪˈmɜːs] VT **(a)** (*lit*) eintauchen (*in* in +*acc*); **to** ~ **sth in water** etw in Wasser tauchen; **to be** ~**d in water** unter Wasser sein **(b)** (*fig*) **to** ~ **oneself in one's work** sich in seine Arbeit vertiefen *or* stürzen (*inf*); **to** ~ **oneself in a language** sich vollkommen in eine Sprache vertiefen

immersion: **immersion course** N Intensivkurs *m*; **immersion heater** N (*Brit*) Boiler *m*

immigrant [ˈɪmɪɡrənt] **1** N Einwanderer *m*, Einwanderin *f*, Immigrant(in) *m(f)* **2** ATTR the ~ **population/community** die Einwanderer *pl*

immigrant labour N, **immigrant workers** PL ausländische Arbeitnehmer *pl*; (*esp in Germany*) Gastarbeiter *pl*; (*in Switzerland*) Fremdarbeiter *pl*

immigration [ˌɪmɪˈɡreɪʃən] N Einwanderung *f*, Immigration *f*; (*also* ~ **control**) Einwanderungsstelle *f*

immigration: **immigration authorities** PL, **immigration department** N Einwanderungsbehörde *f*; **immigration officer** N (*at customs*) Grenzbeamte(r) *m*/-beamtin *f*

imminent [ˈɪmɪnənt] ADJ nahe bevorstehend; **to be ~** nahe bevorstehen

immobile [ɪˈməʊbaɪl] ADJ unbeweglich; (= *not able to move*) *person* bewegungslos; (*through lack of transport*) immobil

immobilize [ɪˈməʊbɪlaɪz] VT *car, broken limb* stilllegen; *army* bewegungsunfähig machen; *enemy tanks* außer Gefecht setzen; **to be ~d by fear/pain** sich vor Angst/Schmerzen nicht bewegen können

immobilizer [ɪˈməʊbɪlaɪzəʳ] N (*Aut*) Wegfahrsperre *f*

immoderate [ɪˈmɒdərɪt] ADJ *desire* übermäßig; *views* übertrieben, extrem

immodest [ɪˈmɒdɪst] ADJ unbescheiden; (= *indecent*) unanständig

immoral [ɪˈmɒrəl] ADJ unmoralisch

immorality [ˌɪməˈrælɪtɪ] N Unmoral *f*

immorally [ɪˈmɒrəlɪ] ADV unmoralisch

immortal [ɪˈmɔːtl] **1** ADJ unsterblich; *fame also* unvergänglich; *life* ewig **2** N Unsterbliche(r) *mf*

immortality [ˌɪmɔːˈtælɪtɪ] N Unsterblichkeit *f*

immortalize [ɪˈmɔːtəlaɪz] VT verewigen; **the film which ~d her** der Film, der sie unsterblich machte

immovable [ɪˈmuːvəbl] ADJ (a) (*lit*) unbeweglich; (*fig*) *obstacle* unüberwindlich (b) (*fig: = steadfast*) fest; **John was ~ in his decision** John war von seiner Entscheidung nicht abzubringen

immune [ɪˈmjuːn] ADJ (a) (*Med*) immun (*from, to* gegen) (b) (*fig*) sicher (*from, to* vor +*dat*); (*from temptation etc*) gefeit (*from, to* gegen); (*to criticism etc*) unempfindlich, immun (*to* gegen); ~ **from prosecution** vor Strafverfolgung geschützt

immune system N Immunsystem *nt*

immunity [ɪˈmjuːnɪtɪ] N (*Med, diplomatic*) Immunität *f* (*to, against* gegen); ~ **from prosecution** Schutz *m* vor Strafverfolgung

immunization [ˌɪmjʊnaɪˈzeɪʃən] N Immunisierung *f*

immunize [ˈɪmjʊnaɪz] VT immunisieren

immutable [ɪˈmjuːtəbl] ADJ unveränderlich

imp [ɪmp] N Kobold *m*; (*inf: = child*) Racker *m* (*inf*)

impact [ˈɪmpækt] **1** N Aufprall *m* (*on, against* auf +*acc*); (*of two moving objects*) Zusammenprall *m*; (*of bomb*) (*on house, factory*) Einschlag *m* (*on* in +*acc*); (*on roof, ground*) Aufschlag *m* (*on* auf +*dat*); (= *force*) Wucht *f*; (*fig*) (*Aus*)wirkung *f* (*on* auf +*acc*); **on** ~ (**with**) beim Aufprall (auf +*acc*)/Zusammenprall (mit) *etc*; **his speech had a great ~ on his audience** seine Rede machte großen Eindruck auf seine Zuhörer **2** VI **to ~ on sb/sth** (*fig*) auf jdn/etw einwirken

impair [ɪmˈpeəʳ] VT beeinträchtigen; *relations also, health* schaden (+*dat*)

impairment [ɪmˈpeəmənt] N Schaden *m*; **hearing/visual ~** Hör-/Sehschaden *m*

impale [ɪmˈpeɪl] VT aufspießen (*on* auf +*dat*)

impart [ɪmˈpaːt] VT (a) *information, news* mitteilen, übermitteln; *knowledge* vermitteln; *secret* preisgeben (b) (= *bestow*) verleihen, geben (*to* +*dat*)

impartial [ɪmˈpaːʃəl] ADJ unparteiisch, unvoreingenommen

impartiality [ɪmˌpaːʃɪˈælɪtɪ] N Unparteilichkeit *f*, Unvoreingenommenheit *f*

impartially [ɪmˈpaːʃəlɪ] ADV *act* unparteiisch; *judge* unvoreingenommen

impassable [ɪmˈpaːsəbl] ADJ unpassierbar

impasse [ɪmˈpaːs] N (*fig*) Sackgasse *f*; **to have reached an ~** sich festgefahren haben

impassioned [ɪmˈpæʃnd] ADJ leidenschaftlich

impassive ADJ, **impassively** ADV [ɪmˈpæsɪv, -lɪ] gelassen

impatience [ɪmˈpeɪʃəns] N Ungeduld *f*; (= *intolerance*) Unduldsamkeit *f*

impatient [ɪmˈpeɪʃənt] ADJ ungeduldig; (= *intolerant*) unduldsam (*of* gegenüber); **to be ~ to do sth** unbedingt etw tun wollen

impatiently [ɪmˈpeɪʃəntlɪ] ADV ungeduldig

impeach [ɪmˈpiːtʃ] VT (*Jur*) *public official* (eines Amtsvergehens) anklagen; (*US*) *president* ein Amtsenthebungsverfahren *or* Impeachment einleiten gegen

impeachment [ɪmˈpiːtʃmənt] N (*Jur*) Anklage *f* (*wegen eines Amtsvergehens*); (*US: of president*) Amtsenthebungsverfahren *nt*, Impeachment *nt*

impeccable ADJ, **impeccably** ADV [ɪmˈpekəbl, -lɪ] tadellos

impecunious [ˌɪmpɪˈkjuːnɪəs] ADJ mittellos, unbemittelt

impede [ɪmˈpiːd] VT *person* hindern; *action, traffic, process* behindern

impediment [ɪmˈpedɪmənt] N (a) Hindernis *nt* (b) (*Med*) Behinderung *f*; **speech ~** Sprachfehler *m*

impel [ɪmˈpel] VT **to ~ sb to do sth** jdn (dazu) nötigen, etw zu tun

impending [ɪmˈpendɪŋ] ADJ bevorstehend; **a sense of ~ doom** eine Ahnung von unmittelbar drohendem Unheil

impenetrable [ɪmˈpenɪtrəbl] ADJ undurchdringlich; *fortress* uneinnehmbar; *enemy lines* undurchlässig; *mind, character, mystery* unergründlich; *theory* undurchschaubar; *accent* völlig unverständlich (*to sb* für jdn)

imperative [ɪmˈperətɪv] **1** ADJ *need, desire* dringend; *necessity* unbedingt; **immediate action is ~** sofortiges Handeln ist dringend geboten **2** N (a) **the political/economic ~** die politische/wirtschaftliche Notwendigkeit (b) (*Gram*) Imperativ *m*; **in the ~** im Imperativ, in der Befehlsform

imperceptible [ˌɪmpəˈseptəbl] ADJ (*to sb* für jdn) nicht wahrnehmbar; *difference, movement also* unmerklich

imperceptibly [ˌɪmpəˈseptəblɪ] ADV kaum wahrnehmbar; *move, differ also* unmerklich; (= *invisibly*) unsichtbar; (= *inaudibly*) unhörbar

imperfect [ɪmˈpɜːfɪkt] **1** ADJ unvollkommen; (= *faulty also*) mangelhaft; (= *incomplete also*) unvollständig; (*Comm*) *goods* fehlerhaft **2** N (*Gram*) Imperfekt *nt*, Vergangenheit *f*

imperfection [ˌɪmpəˈfekʃən] N Mangel *m*

imperfectly [ɪmˈpɜːfɪktlɪ] ADV unvollkommen; (= *incompletely*) unvollständig

imperial [ɪmˈpɪərɪəl] ADJ (a) (= *of empire*) Reichs-; (= *of emperor*) kaiserlich, Kaiser- (b) *weights, measures* englisch

In Großbritannien ist für Maß- und Gewichtsangaben zum Teil noch das imperial system in Gebrauch, auch wenn das metrische System offiziell bereits 1971 eingeführt wurde. Die Kinder rechnen in der Schule im metrischen Dezimalsystem, doch Lebensmittel werden oft immer noch in pounds verkauft, Bier wird nach pints abgezapft und viele Leute denken noch in stones und pounds, wenn es um das eigene Gewicht, bzw. in feet und inches, wenn es um die persönliche Größe geht. Entfernungen werden in miles angegeben. In den USA ist das imperial system sowieso noch für alle Gewichts- und Maßangaben gültig, wobei es bei den Flüssigkeiten einen kleinen Unterschied zu den britischen Maßen gibt: die amerikanischen Mengen von liquid ounce, pint und gallon sind etwas kleiner als die britischen Entsprechungen. Und über ihr persönliches Gewicht sprechen die Amerikaner nur in pounds.

imperialism [ɪmˈpɪərɪəlɪzəm] N Imperialismus *m* (*often pej*)

imperil [ɪmˈperɪl] VT gefährden, in Gefahr bringen

imperious ADJ, **imperiously** ADV [ɪmˈpɪərɪəs, -lɪ] herrisch, gebieterisch

impermanent [ɪmˈpɜːmənənt] ADJ unbeständig

impermeable [ɪmˈpɜːmɪəbl] ADJ undurchlässig

impersonal [ɪmˈpɜːsənl] ADJ unpersönlich (*also Gram*)

impersonally [ɪmˈpɜːsənəlɪ] ADV unpersönlich

impersonate [ɪmˈpɜːsəneɪt] VT (a) (= *pretend to be*) sich ausgeben als (b) (= *take off*) imitieren, nachahmen

impersonation [ɪmˌpɜːsəˈneɪʃən] N Imitation *f*, Nachahmung *f*; **he does ~s of politicians** er imitiert Politiker; **his Elvis ~** seine Elvis-Imitation

impersonator [ɪmˈpɜːsəneɪtəʳ] N (*Theat*) Imitator(in) *m(f)*

impertinence [ɪmˈpɜːtɪnəns] N Unverschämtheit *f*

impertinent [ɪm'pɜːtɪnənt] ADJ unverschämt (*to* zu, gegenüber)

imperturbable [ˌɪmpə'tɜːbəbl] ADJ unerschütterlich; **he is completely ~** er ist durch nichts zu erschüttern

impervious [ɪm'pɜːvɪəs] ADJ **(a)** *substance, rock* undurchlässig; **~ to rain/water** regen-/wasserundurchlässig **(b)** *(fig)* unzugänglich (*to* für); *(to criticism)* unberührt (*to* von)

impetuous [ɪm'petjʊəs] ADJ *act, person* ungestüm; *decision* impulsiv

impetuously [ɪm'petjʊəslɪ] ADV ungestüm

impetus ['ɪmpɪtəs] N *(lit, fig)* Impuls *m*; (= *force*) Kraft *f*; (= *momentum*) Schwung *m*; **to give (an) ~ to sth** *(fig)* einer Sache (*dat*) Impulse geben

impinge [ɪm'pɪndʒ] VI *(on sb's life, habits)* sich auswirken (*on* auf +*acc*), beeinflussen (*on* +*acc*); *(on sb's rights etc)* einschränken (*on* +*acc*)

impish ['ɪmpɪʃ] ADJ schelmisch

implacable [ɪm'plækəbl] ADJ unerbittlich; *fate* unausweichlich

implacably [ɪm'plækəblɪ] ADV unerbittlich

implant [ɪm'plɑːnt] **1** VT **(a)** *(fig)* einimpfen (*in sb* jdm) **(b)** *(Med)* implantieren **2** ['ɪmplɑːnt] N *(Med)* Implantat *nt*; **breast ~** Brustimplantat *nt*

implausible [ɪm'plɔːzəbl] ADJ nicht plausibel; *story, tale, excuse also* unglaubhaft; *combination* unwahrscheinlich

implement ['ɪmplɪmənt] **1** N Gerät *nt*; (= *tool*) Werkzeug *nt* **2** ['ɪmplɪment] VT *law* vollziehen; *plan, reform, measure etc* durchführen; *decisions, ceasefire* in die Tat umsetzen

implementation [ˌɪmplɪmen'teɪʃən] N (*of law*) Vollzug *m*; (*of plan etc*) Durchführung *f*; (*of decisions, ceasefire*) Durchführung *f*

implicate ['ɪmplɪkeɪt] VT **to ~ sb in sth** jdn in etw verwickeln

implication [ˌɪmplɪ'keɪʃən] N (*of statement, situation*) Implikation *f*; (*of law, agreement etc*) Auswirkung *f*; (*of events*) Bedeutung *f no pl*; **the ~ of your statement is that ...** Ihre Behauptung impliziert, dass ...; **by ~** implizit

implicit [ɪm'plɪsɪt] ADJ **(a)** implizit; *threat* indirekt; *agreement, recognition* stillschweigend; **to be ~ in sth** durch etw impliziert werden; *in contract etc* in etw (*dat*) impliziert sein **(b)** *belief, confidence* absolut, unbedingt

implicitly [ɪm'plɪsɪtlɪ] ADV **(a)** implizit; *accept, recognize* stillschweigend **(b)** **to trust/believe sb ~** jdm blind vertrauen/vorbehaltlos glauben

implied [ɪm'plaɪd] ADJ impliziert

implode [ɪm'pləʊd] VI implodieren

implore [ɪm'plɔː'] VT anflehen

imploring ADJ, **imploringly** ADV [ɪm'plɔːrɪŋ, -lɪ] flehentlich

imply [ɪm'plaɪ] VT **(a)** (= *suggest*) andeuten, implizieren; **are you ~ing** *or* **do you mean to ~ that ...?** wollen Sie damit vielleicht sagen *or* andeuten, dass ...? **(b)** (= *indicate, lead to conclusion*) schließen lassen auf (+*acc*) **(c)** (= *involve*) bedeuten

impolite [ˌɪmpə'laɪt] ADJ unhöflich (*to sb* jdm gegenüber)

imponderable [ɪm'pɒndərəbl] N unberechenbare *or* unwägbare Größe; **~s** Unwägbarkeiten *pl*

import ['ɪmpɔːt] **1** N **(a)** *(Comm)* Import *m*, Einfuhr *f* **(b)** (*of speech, document etc*) Bedeutung *f*; **to be of (great) ~ to sb** für jdn von (großer) Bedeutung sein **2** [ɪm'pɔːt] VT *(Comm, Comput)* importieren; *goods also* einführen

importance [ɪm'pɔːtəns] N Wichtigkeit *f*; (= *significance also*) Bedeutung *f*; **to be of great ~** äußerst wichtig sein; **to be of no (great) ~** nicht (besonders) wichtig sein; **to be without ~** unwichtig sein; **to attach the greatest ~ to sth** einer Sache (*dat*) größten Wert *or* größte Wichtigkeit beimessen

important [ɪm'pɔːtənt] ADJ wichtig; (= *significant also*) bedeutend; (= *influential*) einflussreich; **that's not ~** das ist unwichtig; **it's not ~** (= *doesn't matter*) das macht nichts; **the (most) ~ thing is to stay fit** das Wichtigste *or* die Hauptsache ist, fit zu bleiben; **he's trying to sound ~** er spielt sich auf; **to make sb feel ~** jdm das Gefühl geben, er/sie sei wichtig

importantly [ɪm'pɔːtəntlɪ] ADV **(a)** (*usu pej:* = *self-~*) wichtigtuerisch (*pej*) **(b)** (*qualifying sentence*) **I was hungry and, more/most ~, my children were hungry** ich hatte Hunger, und was noch wichtiger/am allerwichtigsten war, meine Kinder hatten Hunger

importation [ˌɪmpɔː'teɪʃən] N Einfuhr *f*, Import *m*

import duty N Einfuhrzoll *m*, Importzoll *m*

imported [ɪm'pɔːtɪd] ADJ importiert, Import-; **~ goods/cars** Importwaren/-autos *pl*

importer [ɪm'pɔːtə'] N Importeur(in) *m(f)* (*of* von)

import: **import-export trade** N Import-Export-Handel *m*, Ein- und Ausfuhr *f*; **import licence** N Einfuhrlizenz *f*, Importlizenz *f*

importune [ˌɪmpɔː'tjuːn] VT belästigen; (*creditor, with questions*) zusetzen (+*dat*)

impose [ɪm'pəʊz] **1** VT **(a)** *task, conditions* aufzwingen, auferlegen (*on sb* jdm); *sanctions, fine, sentence* verhängen (*on* gegen); *tax* erheben; *opinions, taste* aufzwingen (*on sb* jdm); **to ~ a tax on sth** etw mit einer Steuer belegen **(b)** **to ~ oneself on sb** sich jdm aufdrängen; **he ~d himself on them for three months** er ließ sich einfach drei Monate bei ihnen nieder **2** VI zur Last fallen (*on sb* jdm)

imposing [ɪm'pəʊzɪŋ] ADJ beeindruckend, imponierend

imposition [ˌɪmpə'zɪʃən] N Zumutung *f* (*on* für); **I'd love to stay if it's not too much of an ~ (on you)** ich würde liebend gern bleiben, wenn ich Ihnen nicht zur Last falle

impossibility [ɪmˌpɒsə'bɪlɪtɪ] N Unmöglichkeit *f*; **that's an ~** das ist unmöglich *or* ein Ding der Unmöglichkeit

impossible [ɪm'pɒsəbl] **1** ADJ **(a)** unmöglich; *dream* unerfüllbar; **~!** ausgeschlossen!; **it is ~ for him to leave/do that** er kann unmöglich gehen/das unmöglich tun; **this cooker is ~ to clean** es ist unmöglich, diesen Herd sauber zu kriegen; **to make it ~ for sb to do sth** es jdm unmöglich machen, etw zu tun **(b)** *situation, position* aussichtslos; **I am faced with an ~ choice** ich stehe vor einer unmöglichen Wahl; **you put me in an ~ position** du bringst mich in eine unmögliche Lage **(c)** (*inf*) *person* unmöglich (*inf*) **2** N Unmögliche(s) *nt*; **to do the ~** (*in general*) Unmögliches tun; (*in particular case*) das Unmögliche tun

impossibly [ɪm'pɒsəblɪ] ADV unmöglich; **an ~ high standard** ein unerreichbar hohes Niveau

impostor [ɪm'pɒstə'] N Betrüger(in) *m(f)*, Schwindler(in) *m(f)*

impotence ['ɪmpətəns] N **(a)** (*sexual*) Impotenz *f* **(b)** *(fig)* Schwäche *f*, Machtlosigkeit *f*

impotent ['ɪmpətənt] ADJ **(a)** (*sexually*) impotent **(b)** *(fig)* schwach, machtlos

impound [ɪm'paʊnd] VT **(a)** *goods, assets, contraband* beschlagnahmen **(b)** *car* abschleppen (lassen)

impoverish [ɪm'pɒvərɪʃ] VT in Armut bringen

impoverished [ɪm'pɒvərɪʃt] ADJ arm; (= *having become poor*) verarmt

impracticable [ɪm'præktɪkəbl] ADJ impraktikabel; *plan also* praktisch unmöglich; *design, size* unbrauchbar

impractical [ɪm'præktɪkəl] ADJ unpraktisch

impracticality [ɪmˌpræktɪ'kælɪtɪ] N Unbrauchbarkeit *f*

imprecise [ˌɪmprɪ'saɪs], **imprecisely** ADV [ɪmprɪ'saɪs, -lɪ] ungenau, unpräzis(e)

imprecision [ˌɪmprɪ'sɪʒən] N Ungenauigkeit *f*

impregnable [ɪm'pregnəbl] ADJ (*Mil*) *fortress, defences* uneinnehmbar; *(fig) position* unerschütterlich; *argument* unwiderlegbar

impregnate ['ɪmpregneɪt] VT (*Biol*) befruchten

impresario [ˌɪmpre'sɑːrɪəʊ] N Impresario *m*

impress [ɪm'pres] **1** VT **(a)** *person* beeindrucken; (= *arouse admiration in*) imponieren (+*dat*); **how did it/he ~ you?** wie fanden Sie das/ihn?; **he/it ~ed me favourably** er/das hat einen guten *or* günstigen Eindruck auf mich gemacht; **she is not easily ~ed** sie lässt sich nicht so leicht beeindrucken; **he doesn't ~ me as a politician** als Politiker macht er keinen Eindruck auf mich **(b)** (= *fix in mind*) einschärfen (*on sb* jdm); *idea, danger, possibility* (deutlich) klarmachen (*on sb* jdm) **2** VI Eindruck machen; (*person: deliberately*) Eindruck schinden (*inf*)

impression [ɪm'preʃən] N **(a)** Eindruck *m*; (= *feeling*) Gefühl *nt*; **the theatre made a lasting ~ on me** das Theater beeindruckte mich tief; **his words made an ~** seine Worte machten Eindruck; **he created an ~ of power** er erweckte den Eindruck von Macht; **to give sb the ~ that ...** jdm den Eindruck vermitteln, dass ...; **he gave the ~ of being unhappy/self-confident** er wirkte unglücklich/selbstsicher; **I was under the ~ that ...** ich hatte den Eindruck, dass ...

(b) (*on wax etc*) Abdruck *m*; (*of engraving*) Prägung *f*
(c) (= *take-off*) Nachahmung *f*, Imitation *f*; **to do an ~ of sb** jdn imitieren *or* nachahmen

impressionable [ɪmˈpreʃnəbl] ADJ für Eindrücke empfänglich, leicht zu beeindrucken *pred* (*pej*); **at an ~ age** in einem Alter, in dem man für Eindrücke besonders empfänglich ist

impressionism [ɪmˈpreʃənɪzəm] N Impressionismus *m*

impressionist [ɪmˈpreʃənɪst] N **(a)** Impressionist(in) *m(f)*
(b) (*Theat: = impersonator*) Imitator(in) *m(f)*

impressive [ɪmˈpresɪv] ADJ beeindruckend

impressively [ɪmˈpresɪvlɪ] ADV eindrucksvoll

imprest [ɪmˈprest] N (*Brit*) Kassenvorschuss *m*

imprint [ɪmˈprɪnt] VT (*fig*) einprägen (*on sb* jdm); **to be ~ed on sb's mind** sich jdm eingeprägt haben; **to be ~ed on sb's memory** sich in jds Gedächtnis (*acc*) eingeprägt haben

imprison [ɪmˈprɪzn] VT (*lit*) inhaftieren; (*fig*) gefangen halten; **to be ~ed** (*lit, fig*) gefangen sein

imprisonment [ɪmˈprɪznmənt] N (= *action*) Inhaftierung *f*; (= *state*) Gefangenschaft *f*; **to sentence sb to one month's/life ~** jdn zu einem Monat Gefängnis *or* Freiheitsstrafe/zu lebenslänglicher Freiheitsstrafe verurteilen

improbability [ɪmˌprɒbəˈbɪlɪtɪ] N Unwahrscheinlichkeit *f*

improbable [ɪmˈprɒbəbl] ADJ unwahrscheinlich

impromptu [ɪmˈprɒmptjuː] ADJ improvisiert; **an ~ speech** eine Stegreifrede

improper [ɪmˈprɒpəʳ] ADJ (= *unsuitable*) unpassend, unangebracht; (= *unseemly*) unschicklich; (= *indecent*) unanständig; *use* unsachgemäß; *practice* unlauter; *conduct* unehrenhaft; **it is ~ to do that** es gehört sich nicht, das zu tun; **~ use of drugs/one's position** Drogen-/Amtsmissbrauch *m*

improperly [ɪmˈprɒpəlɪ] ADV *act, dress* unpassend; *use, install* unsachgemäß; *behave* unangemessen; (= *indecently*) unanständig

impropriety [ˌɪmprəˈpraɪətɪ] N Unschicklichkeit *f*; **sexual/financial ~** sexuelles/finanzielles Fehlverhalten

improve [ɪmˈpruːv] **1** VT verbessern; *knowledge* erweitern; *salaries* aufbessern; *area, appearance* verschönern; *sauce, food etc* verfeinern; *production* steigern; **to ~ one's mind** sich weiterbilden **2** VI sich verbessern; (*area, appearance*) schöner werden; (*production*) steigen; **the invalid is improving** dem Kranken geht es besser; **things are improving** es sieht schon besser aus **3** VR **to ~ oneself** an sich (*dat*) arbeiten

➤ **improve (up)on** VI +PREP OBJ **(a)** übertreffen, besser machen; *nature, performance* verbessern **(b)** (*Comm, Fin*) offer überbieten

improved [ɪmˈpruːvd] ADJ besser, verbessert

improvement [ɪmˈpruːvmənt] N Verbesserung *f*; (*of area, appearance*) Verschönerung *f*; (*in production*) Steigerung *f*; (*in health*) Besserung *f*; **an ~ on the previous one** eine Verbesserung gegenüber dem Früheren; **to carry out ~s to a house** Ausbesserungs- *or* (*to appearance*) Verschönerungsarbeiten an einem Haus vornehmen

improvident [ɪmˈprɒvɪdənt] ADJ sorglos

improving [ɪmˈpruːvɪŋ] ADJ informativ, lehrreich; (= *morally ~*) erbaulich

improvisation [ˌɪmprəvaɪˈzeɪʃən] N Improvisation *f*

improvise [ˈɪmprəvaɪz] VTI improvisieren; **to ~ on a tune** (*Mus*) über eine Melodie improvisieren; **to ~ on a story** eine Geschichte abändern

imprudence [ɪmˈpruːdəns] N Unklugheit *f*

imprudent ADJ, **imprudently** ADV [ɪmˈpruːdənt, -lɪ] unklug

impudence [ˈɪmpjʊdəns] N Unverschämtheit *f*, Frechheit *f*; **he had the ~ to ask me** er hatte die Stirn *or* er besaß die Frechheit, mich zu fragen

impudent ADJ, **impudently** ADV [ˈɪmpjʊdənt, -lɪ] unverschämt, dreist

impugn [ɪmˈpjuːn] VT Zweifel hegen an (+*dat*)

impulse [ˈɪmpʌls] N Impuls *m*; (= *driving force*) (Stoß- *or* Trieb)kraft *f*; **she resisted an ~ to smile** sie widerstand dem Impuls zu lächeln; **to yield to a sudden ~** einem Impuls nachgeben *or* folgen; **on ~** aus einem Impuls heraus, impulsiv; **an ~ buy** *or* **purchase** ein Impulsivkauf *m*

impulse: impulse buyer N Spontankäufer(in) *m(f)*; **impulse buying** N impulsives *or* spontanes Kaufen

impulsive [ɪmˈpʌlsɪv] ADJ impulsiv; (= *spontaneous*) spontan

impulsively [ɪmˈpʌlsɪvlɪ] ADV impulsiv; (= *spontaneously*) spontan

impunity [ɪmˈpjuːnɪtɪ] N Straflosigkeit *f*; **with ~** ungestraft

impure [ɪmˈpjʊəʳ] ADJ unrein; *food* verunreinigt; *motives* unsauber

impurity [ɪmˈpjʊərɪtɪ] N Unreinheit *f*; (*of food*) Verunreinigung *f*

impute [ɪmˈpjuːt] VT zuschreiben (*to sb/sth* jdm/einer Sache); **to ~ a crime to sb** jdn eines Verbrechens bezichtigen

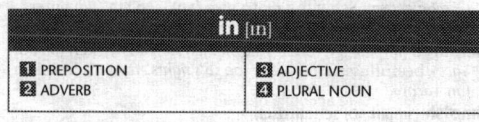

in [ɪn]

| **1** PREPOSITION | **3** ADJECTIVE |
| **2** ADVERB | **4** PLURAL NOUN |

1 PREPOSITION

> *When* **in** *is the second element of a phrasal verb, eg* **ask in**, **fill in**, **hand in**, *look up the verb. When it is part of a set combination, eg* **in danger**, **in the end**, **weak in**, **wrapped in**, *look up the other word.*

(a) in (+*dat*); (*with motion*) in (+*acc*); **it was in the lorry/bag/car** es war im Lastwagen/in der Tasche/im Auto; **he put it in the lorry/car/bag** er legte es auf den Lastwagen/ins Auto/ steckte es in die Tasche; **in here/there** hierin/darin, hier/da drin (*inf*); (*with motion*) hier/da hinein *or* rein (*inf*); **in the street** auf der/die Straße; **sitting in the window** am Fenster sitzend; **in (the) church** in der Kirche; **to stay in the house** im Haus *or* (*at home*) zu Hause *or* zuhause (*Aus, Sw*) bleiben; **in Germany/Switzerland/the United States** in Deutschland/der Schweiz/den Vereinigten Staaten

> *after the superlative,* **in** *is sometimes untranslated and the genitive case used instead.*

the highest mountain in Scotland der höchste Berg Schottlands *or* in Schottland; **the best in the class** der Klassenbeste
(b) (*people*) bei; **you can find examples of this in Dickens** man findet Beispiele dafür bei Dickens *or* in Dickens' Werken; **you have a great leader in him** in ihm habt ihr einen großen Führer; **he doesn't have it in him to ...** er bringt es nicht fertig, ... zu ...
(c) (*dates, seasons, time of day*) in (+*dat*); **in 1999** (im Jahre) 1999; **in May 1999** im Mai 1999; **in the sixties** in den sechziger Jahren; **in (the) spring** im Frühling; **in the morning(s)** morgens, am Vormittag; **in the afternoon** nachmittags, am Nachmittag; **in the daytime** tagsüber; **in those days** damals; **she is in her thirties** sie ist in den Dreißigern; **in old age** im Alter; **in my childhood** in meiner Kindheit; **she did it in three hours** sie machte es in drei Stunden *or* innerhalb von drei Stunden; **in a week('s time)** in einer Woche; **I haven't seen him in years** ich habe ihn jahrelang *or* seit Jahren nicht mehr gesehen; **in a moment** *or* **minute** sofort, gleich
(d) (*numbers, quantities*) zu; **packed in hundreds** zu Hunderten abgepackt; **to walk in twos** zu zweit gehen; **to count in fives** in Fünfern zählen; **in large/small quantities** in großen/kleinen Mengen
(e) (*ratios*) **he has a one in 500 chance of winning** er hat eine Gewinnchance von eins zu 500; **one (man) in ten** jeder Zehnte; **one book in ten** jedes zehnte Buch; **one in five children** ein Kind von fünf; **a tax of twenty pence in the pound** ein Steuersatz von zwanzig Prozent; **there are 12 inches in a foot** ein Fuß hat 12 Zoll
(f) (*manner, state, condition*) **to speak in a loud/soft voice** mit lauter/leiser Stimme sprechen; **to speak in German** Deutsch reden; **to pay in dollars** mit *or* in Dollar bezahlen; **to stand in a row/in groups** in einer Reihe/in Gruppen stehen; **in this way** so, auf diese Weise; **she squealed in delight** sie quietschte vor Vergnügen; **in anger** im Zorn; **in surprise** überrascht; **to live in luxury/poverty** im Luxus/in Armut leben
(g) (*clothes*) (+*dat*); **in one's best clothes** in Sonntagskleidung; **in his shirt** im Hemd; **dressed in white** weiß gekleidet
(h) (*substance, material*) **upholstered in silk** mit Seide

bezogen; **to paint in oils** in Öl malen; **to write in ink/pencil** mit Tinte/Bleistift schreiben; **in marble** in Marmor, marmorn
(i) (*in respect of*) **blind in the left eye** auf dem linken Auge blind; **a rise in prices** ein Preisanstieg *m*; **ten feet in height by thirty in length** zehn Fuß hoch auf dreißig Fuß lang; **the latest thing in hats** der letzte Schrei bei Hüten
(j) (*occupation, activity*) **he is in the army** er ist beim Militär; **he is in banking/the motor business** er ist im Bankwesen/in der Autobranche (tätig)
(k) (*set structures*)
✦**in + -ing** **in saying this, I ...** wenn ich das sage, ... ich; **in trying to save him she fell into the water herself** beim Versuch *or* als sie versuchte, ihn zu retten, fiel sie selbst ins Wasser
✦**in that** (= *seeing that*) insofern als; **the plan was unrealistic in that it didn't take account of the fact that ...** der Plan war unrealistisch, da *or* weil er nicht berücksichtigte, dass ...

2 ADVERB

When **in** *is the second element in a phrasal verb, eg* **come in**, **live in**, **sleep in**, *look up the verb.*

da; (*at home also*) zu Hause, zuhause (*Aus, Sw*); **there is nobody in** es ist niemand da/zu Hause

to be in *may require a more specific translation.*

the train is in der Zug ist da *or* angekommen; **the harvest is in** die Ernte ist eingebracht; **the tide is in** es ist Flut; **our team is in** (*Cricket*) unsere Mannschaft ist am Schlag; **the Socialists are in** (= *in power*) die Sozialisten sind an der Regierung; **my luck is in** ich habe einen Glückstag
✦**to be in for sth** **he's in for a surprise** er kann sich auf eine Überraschung gefasst machen; **we are in for rain/a cold spell** uns (*dat*) steht Regen/eine Kältewelle bevor
✦**to have it in for sb** (*inf*) es auf jdn abgesehen haben (*inf*)
✦**to be in on sth** an einer Sache beteiligt sein; **on secret etc** über etw (*acc*) Bescheid wissen
✦**to be (well) in with sb** sich gut mit jdm verstehen

3 ADJECTIVE (*inf*) in *inv* (*inf*); **long skirts are in** lange Röcke sind in (*inf*); **the in thing is to ...** es ist zur Zeit in (*inf*) *or* Mode, zu ...; **it's the in place to go** da gehen jetzt alle hin

4 PLURAL NOUN
(a) (= *details*)
✦**the ins and outs** die Einzelheiten *pl*; **to know the ins and outs of sth** bei einer Sache genau Bescheid wissen
(b) (*US*) (*Pol*) **the ins** die Regierungspartei

inability [ˌɪnəˈbɪlɪtɪ] N Unfähigkeit *f*, Unvermögen *nt*; **~ to pay** Zahlungsunfähigkeit *f*

inaccessible [ˌɪnækˈsesəbl] ADJ **(a)** unzugänglich (*to sb/sth* für jdn/etw); **to be ~ by land/sea** auf dem Landweg/Seeweg nicht erreichbar sein **(b)** (*fig*) *idea, music, novel* unverständlich

inaccuracy [ɪnˈækjʊrəsɪ] N Ungenauigkeit *f*; (= *incorrectness*) Unrichtigkeit *f*

inaccurate [ɪnˈækjʊrɪt] ADJ ungenau; (= *not correct*) unrichtig; **she was ~ in her judgement of the situation** ihre Beurteilung der Lage traf nicht zu; **it is ~ to say that ...** es ist nicht richtig zu sagen, dass ...

inaccurately [ɪnˈækjʊrɪtlɪ] ADV ungenau; (= *incorrectly*) unrichtig

inaction [ɪnˈækʃən] N Untätigkeit *f*

inactive [ɪnˈæktɪv] ADJ untätig; *mind* träge; (*Fin*) *account* umsatzlos

inactivity [ˌɪnækˈtɪvɪtɪ] N Untätigkeit *f*; (*Comm*) Flaute *f*

inadequacy [ɪnˈædɪkwəsɪ] N Unzulänglichkeit *f*; (*of measures*) Unangemessenheit *f*

inadequate [ɪnˈædɪkwɪt] ADJ unzulänglich, inadäquat (*geh*); *measures* unangemessen; **she makes him feel ~** sie gibt ihm das Gefühl der Unzulänglichkeit

inadequately [ɪnˈædɪkwɪtlɪ] ADV unzulänglich, inadäquat (*geh*)

inadmissible [ˌɪnədˈmɪsəbl] ADJ unzulässig

inadvertently [ˌɪnədˈvɜːtəntlɪ] ADV versehentlich

inadvisable [ˌɪnədˈvaɪzəbl] ADJ unratsam

inalienable [ɪnˈeɪlɪənəbl] ADJ *rights* unveräußerlich

inane [ɪˈneɪn] ADJ dumm

inanely [ɪˈneɪnlɪ] ADV dumm; **they chatted on ~** sie plauderten albern weiter

inanimate [ɪnˈænɪmɪt] ADJ leblos, tot; *nature, world* unbelebt

inapplicable [ɪnˈæplɪkəbl] ADJ *answer* unzutreffend; *laws, rules* nicht anwendbar (*to sb* auf jdn)

inappropriate [ˌɪnəˈprəʊprɪɪt] ADJ unpassend, unangebracht; *time* ungünstig; **you have come at a most ~ time** Sie kommen sehr ungelegen

inappropriately [ˌɪnəˈprəʊprɪɪtlɪ] ADV unpassend

inapt [ɪnˈæpt] ADJ ungeschickt; *comparison* unpassend

inarticulate [ˌɪnɑːˈtɪkjʊlɪt] ADJ schlecht *or* unklar ausgedrückt; *speech also* schwerfällig; **she's very ~** sie kann sich kaum *or* nur schlecht ausdrücken

inasmuch [ˌɪnəzˈmʌtʃ] ADV **~ as** da, weil; (= *to the extent that*) insofern als

inattention [ˌɪnəˈtenʃən] N Unaufmerksamkeit *f*; **~ to detail** Ungenauigkeit *f* im Detail

inattentive [ˌɪnəˈtentɪv] ADJ unaufmerksam

inaudible ADJ, **inaudibly** ADV [ɪnˈɔːdəbl, -ɪ] unhörbar (*to* für)

inaugural [ɪˈnɔːgjʊrəl] ADJ *lecture* Antritts-; *meeting, address, speech* Eröffnungs-

inaugurate [ɪˈnɔːgjʊreɪt] VT **(a)** *president, official etc* (feierlich) in sein/ihr Amt einführen, inaugurieren (*geh*) **(b)** *policy* einführen; *building* einweihen; *exhibition* eröffnen; *era* einleiten

inauguration [ɪˌnɔːgjʊˈreɪʃən] N **(a)** (*of president, official etc*) Amtseinführung *f*, Inauguration *f* (*geh*) **(b)** (*of building*) Einweihung *f*

inauspicious [ˌɪnɔːsˈpɪʃəs] ADJ Unheil verheißend; **to get off to an ~ start** (*career, campaign*) sich nicht gerade viel versprechend anlassen; (*person*) keinen viel versprechenden Anfang machen

in-between [ɪnbɪˈtwiːn] ADJ (*inf*) Mittel-, Zwischen-; **it is sort of ~** es ist so ein Mittelding; **~ stage** Zwischenstadium *nt*

inborn [ˈɪnˈbɔːn] ADJ angeboren

inbound [ˈɪnˌbaʊnd] ADJ *flight* ankommend

inbred [ˈɪnˈbred] ADJ angeboren (*in sb* jdm)

inbreeding [ˈɪnˈbriːdɪŋ] N Inzucht *f*

inbuilt [ˈɪnbɪlt] ADJ *safety features, error detection etc* integriert; *dislike, fear, awareness* instinktiv; *majority* automatisch; *predisposition, fondness, resistance* natürlich

Inc (*US*) ABBR *of* **Incorporated**

Inca [ˈɪŋkə] **1** N Inka *mf* **2** ADJ (*also* **~n**) Inka-, inkaisch; **~(n) empire** Inkareich *nt*

incalculable [ɪnˈkælkjʊləbl] ADJ unermesslich; *consequences* unabsehbar

incandescent [ˌɪnkænˈdesnt] ADJ (*lit*) (weiß) glühend; **~ light** Glühlampe *f*; **~ with rage** *or* **fury** bis zur Weißglut gereizt

incantation [ˌɪnkænˈteɪʃən] N Zauber(spruch) *m*, Zauberformel *f*

incapability [ɪnˌkeɪpəˈbɪlɪtɪ] N Unfähigkeit *f*, Unvermögen *nt* (*of doing sth* etw zu tun)

incapable [ɪnˈkeɪpəbl] ADJ unfähig; (*physically*) hilflos; **to be ~ of doing sth** unfähig *or* nicht imstande sein, etw zu tun; **she is physically ~ of lifting it** sie ist körperlich nicht in der Lage, es zu heben; **he was completely ~** (*because drunk*) er war volltrunken; **~ of working** arbeitsunfähig

incapacitate [ˌɪnkəˈpæsɪteɪt] VT unfähig machen (*from doing sth* etw zu tun); **to ~ sb for work** jdn arbeitsunfähig machen; **somewhat ~d by his broken ankle** durch seinen gebrochenen Knöchel ziemlich behindert

incapacity [ˌɪnkəˈpæsɪtɪ] N Unfähigkeit *f* (*for* für); **~ for work** Arbeitsunfähigkeit *f*

incapacity benefit N (*Brit*) Invalidenunterstützung *f*

in-car [ˈɪnkɑːʳ] ADJ ATTR Auto-; *entertainment, stereo* im Auto; **computer** Autocomputer *m*

incarcerate [ɪnˈkɑːsəreɪt] VT einkerkern

incarceration [ɪnˌkɑːsəˈreɪʃən] N (= *act*) Einkerkerung *f*; (= *period*) Kerkerhaft *f*

incarnate [ɪnˈkɑːnɪt] ADJ **he's the devil ~** er ist der leibhaftige Teufel *or* der Teufel in Person; **she is cynicism ~** sie ist der Zynismus in Person

incautious ADJ, **incautiously** ADV [ɪnˈkɔːʃəs, -lɪ] unvorsichtig

incendiary [ɪnˈsendɪərɪ] ADJ Brand-; **~ attack** Brandanschlag *m*

incendiary device N Brandsatz *m*

incense[1] [ɪnˈsens] VT wütend machen; **~d** wütend (*at, by* über *+acc*)

incense[2] [ˈɪnsens] N (*Eccl*) Weihrauch *m*; (*fig*) Duft *m*

incentive [ɪnˈsentɪv] N Anreiz *m*; **~ scheme** (*Ind*) Anreizsystem *nt*

inception [ɪnˈsepʃən] N Beginn *m*, Anfang *m*; **from its ~** von Anbeginn an; **at its ~** zu Anbeginn

incessant [ɪnˈsesnt] ADJ unaufhörlich, unablässig; *noise* ununterbrochen

incessantly [ɪnˈsesntlɪ] ADV unaufhörlich

incest [ˈɪnsest] N Inzest *m*, Blutschande *f*

incestuous [ɪnˈsestjʊəs] ADJ blutschänderisch

inch [ɪntʃ] **1** N Zoll *m*, Inch *m*; **3.5 ~ disk** 3,5-Zoll-Diskette *f*; **she's grown a few ~es** sie ist ein paar Zentimeter gewachsen; **he came within an ~ of being killed** er ist dem Tod um Haaresbreite entgangen; **they beat him (to) within an ~ of his life** sie haben ihn so geschlagen, dass er fast gestorben wäre; **the lorry missed me by ~es** der Lastwagen hat mich um Haaresbreite verfehlt; **he knows every ~ of the area** er kennt die Gegend wie seine Westentasche; **he is every ~ a soldier** er ist jeder Zoll ein Soldat; **they searched every ~ of the room** sie durchsuchten das Zimmer Zentimeter für Zentimeter **2** VI **to ~ forward/out/in** sich millimeterweise *or* stückchenweise vorwärts schieben/hinausschieben/ hineinschieben **3** VT langsam manövrieren; **he ~ed his way forward/through** er schob sich langsam vorwärts/durch

incidence [ˈɪnsɪdəns] N Häufigkeit *f*; **a high ~ of crime** eine hohe Verbrechensquote

incident [ˈɪnsɪdənt] N (a) Ereignis *nt*, Vorfall *m*; **a day full of ~** ein ereignisreicher Tag; **an ~ from his childhood** ein Kindheitserlebnis *nt* (b) (*diplomatic etc*) Zwischenfall *m*; (= *disturbance in bar etc*) Vorfall *m*; **without ~** ohne Zwischenfälle (c) (*in book, play*) Episode *f*

incidental [ˌɪnsɪˈdentl] ADJ nebensächlich; *remark* beiläufig

incidental expenses PL Nebenkosten *pl*

incidentally [ˌɪnsɪˈdentəlɪ] ADV übrigens

incidental music N Begleitmusik *f*

incident room N (*Police*) Einsatzzentrale *f*

incinerate [ɪnˈsɪnəreɪt] VT verbrennen

incineration [ɪnsɪnəˈreɪʃən] N Verbrennung *f*

incinerator [ɪnˈsɪnəreɪtər] N (Müll)verbrennungsanlage *f*; (= *garden ~*) Verbrennungsofen *m*

incipient [ɪnˈsɪpɪənt] ADJ anfangend, beginnend; *democracy* jung

incision [ɪnˈsɪʒən] N Schnitt *m*; (*Med*) Einschnitt *m*

incisive [ɪnˈsaɪsɪv] ADJ *style, tone, words* prägnant; *criticism, person* scharfsinnig; *mind* scharf

incisively [ɪnˈsaɪsɪvlɪ] ADV *speak, formulate* prägnant; *argue, criticize* scharfsinnig

incisor [ɪnˈsaɪzər] N Schneidezahn *m*

incite [ɪnˈsaɪt] VT aufhetzen; *racial hatred, violence* aufhetzen zu

incitement [ɪnˈsaɪtmənt] N, NO PL Aufhetzung *f*

incl ABBR **of inclusive(ly), including** incl., inkl.

inclement [ɪnˈklemənt] ADJ *weather* rau, unfreundlich

inclination [ˌɪnklɪˈneɪʃən] N Neigung *f*; **my (natural) ~ is to carry on** ich neige dazu, weiterzumachen; **I have no ~ to see him again** ich habe keinerlei Bedürfnis, ihn wiederzusehen; **he showed no ~ to leave** er schien nicht gehen zu wollen

incline 1 [ɪnˈklaɪn] VT (a) *head, body* neigen (b) (= *dispose*) veranlassen, bewegen; **this ~s me to think that he must be lying** das lässt mich vermuten, dass er lügt **2** VI (a) (= *slope*) sich neigen; (*ground*) abfallen (b) (= *be disposed, tend towards*) neigen; **to ~ to a point of view** zu einer Ansicht neigen *or* tendieren **3** [ˈɪnklaɪn] N Neigung *f*; (*of hill*) Abhang *m*; (= *gradient: Rail etc*) Gefälle *nt*

inclined [ɪnˈklaɪnd] ADJ **to be ~ to do sth** (= *feel that one wishes to*) Lust haben, etw zu tun; (= *have tendency to*) dazu neigen,

etw zu tun; **I am ~ to think that ...** ich neige zu der Ansicht, dass ...; **I'm ~ to disagree** ich möchte da doch widersprechen; **it's ~ to break** das bricht leicht; **if you feel ~** wenn Sie Lust haben *or* dazu aufgelegt sind; **if you're that way ~** wenn Ihnen so etwas liegt; **artistically ~** künstlerisch veranlagt

include [ɪnˈkluːd] VT einschließen, enthalten; (*on list, in group etc*) aufnehmen; **your name is not ~d on the list** Ihr Name ist nicht auf der Liste; **service not ~d** Bedienung nicht inbegriffen; **all ~d** alles inklusive *or* inbegriffen; **everyone, children ~d** alle einschließlich der Kinder; **the hostages ~d three Britons** unter den Geiseln befanden sich drei Briten; **does that ~ me?** gilt das auch für mich?; **I think we should ~ a chapter on ...** ich finde, wir sollten auch ein Kapitel über ... dazunehmen

including [ɪnˈkluːdɪŋ] PREP einschließlich, inklusive; **that makes seven ~ you** mit Ihnen sind das sieben; **that comes to 20 pounds ~ postage and packing** das kommt auf 20 Pfund inklusive *or* einschließlich Porto und Verpackung; **many people, ~ my father, had been invited** viele Leute, darunter mein Vater, waren eingeladen; **~ the service charge, ~ service** Bedienung (mit) inbegriffen; **up to and ~ March 4th** bis einschließlich 4. März

inclusion [ɪnˈkluːʒən] N Aufnahme *f*

inclusive [ɪnˈkluːsɪv] ADJ inklusive, einschließlich; **~ price** Inklusiv- *or* Pauschalpreis *m*; **~ sum** Pauschale *f*, Pauschalsumme *f*; **~ terms** Pauschalpreis *m*; **to be ~ of all charges** alle Gebühren einschließen; **from 1st to 6th May ~** vom 1. bis einschließlich *or* inklusive 6. Mai

incognito [ˌɪnkɒɡˈniːtəʊ] **1** ADV inkognito **2** ADJ **to remain ~** inkognito bleiben

incoherent [ˌɪnkəʊˈhɪərənt] ADJ *style, argument, speech* zusammenhanglos, unzusammenhängend; *person* sich unklar *or* undeutlich ausdrückend; *drunk etc* schwer verständlich; **he was ~ with rage** seine wütenden Worte waren kaum zu verstehen

incoherently [ˌɪnkəʊˈhɪərəntlɪ] ADV zusammenhanglos, unzusammenhängend

income [ˈɪnkʌm] N Einkommen *nt*; (= *receipts*) Einkünfte *pl*; **an annual ~ of £45,000** ein Jahreseinkommen von £ 45.000; **families on low ~s, low-~ families** einkommensschwache Familien *pl*

income: **income bracket** N Einkommensklasse *f*; **income group** N Einkommensgruppe *f*; **incomes policy** N Lohnpolitik *f*; **income statement** N (*US*) Gewinn- und Verlustrechnung *f*; **income support** N (*Brit*) ≈ Sozialhilfe *f*; **income tax** N Lohnsteuer *f*; (*on private income*) Einkommensteuer *f*

incoming [ˈɪnkʌmɪŋ] ADJ (a) ankommend; *missile* anfliegend; *mail, orders* eingehend; **~ tide** Flut *f*; **to receive ~ (phone) calls** (Telefon)anrufe entgegennehmen (b) *president etc* neu

incommunicado [ˌɪnkəmjuːnɪˈkɑːdəʊ] ADJ PRED ohne jede Verbindung zur Außenwelt, abgesondert; **he was held ~** er hatte keinerlei Verbindung zur Außenwelt; **to be ~** (*fig*) für niemanden zu sprechen sein

incomparable [ɪnˈkɒmpərəbl] ADJ nicht vergleichbar; *beauty, skill* unvergleichlich

incompatibility [ˈɪnkəmˌpætəˈbɪlɪtɪ] N (*of characters, ideas*) Unvereinbarkeit *f*; (*of drugs, blood groups, colours*) Unverträglichkeit *f*; (*of technical systems*) Inkompatibilität *f*; **divorce on grounds of ~** Scheidung aufgrund der Unvereinbarkeit der Charaktere der Ehepartner

incompatible [ˌɪnkəmˈpætəbl] ADJ *characters, ideas* unvereinbar; *technical systems* nicht kompatibel; *drugs, blood groups, colours* nicht miteinander verträglich; **we are ~, she said** wir passen überhaupt nicht zusammen *or* zueinander, sagte sie; **to be ~ with sb/sth** sich nicht mit jdm/etw vertragen; (= *not suit*) nicht zu jdm/etw passen

incompetence [ɪnˈkɒmpɪtəns] N Unfähigkeit *f*; (*for job*) Untauglichkeit *f*

incompetent [ɪnˈkɒmpɪtənt] **1** ADJ *person, institution* unfähig; (*for sth*) untauglich; *management* inkompetent; *piece of work* unzulänglich; **I was ~ at playing the piano** *or* **an ~ pianist** ich konnte nur sehr schlecht Klavier spielen **2** N Nichtskönner(in) *m(f)*

incompetently [ɪnˈkɒmpɪtəntlɪ] ADV schlecht, stümperhaft

incomplete [ˌɪnkəmˈpliːt] ADJ *collection, series* unvollständig; *knowledge, information* lückenhaft; *(referring to numbers)* nicht vollzählig

incomprehensible [ɪnˌkɒmprɪˈhensəbl] ADJ unverständlich *(to sb* jdm); *act also* unbegreiflich *(to sb* jdm)

inconceivable [ˌɪnkənˈsiːvəbl] ADJ unvorstellbar, undenkbar; **it was ~ to her that ...** sie konnte sich *(dat)* nicht vorstellen, dass ...

inconclusive [ˌɪnkənˈkluːsɪv] ADJ *result* unbestimmt; *election* ohne eindeutiges Ergebnis; *action, discussion, investigation* ergebnislos; *war* erfolglos; *evidence, argument* nicht überzeugend

inconclusively [ˌɪnkənˈkluːsɪvlɪ] ADV ergebnislos

incongruity [ˌɪnkɒnˈgruːɪtɪ] N, NO PL *(of remark, sb's presence)* Unpassende(s); *(of situation)* Absurdität *f*; *(of behaviour)* Unangebrachtheit *f*; **the ~ between what is said and what is left unsaid** das Missverhältnis zwischen dem, was gesagt wird, und dem, was ungesagt bleibt

incongruous [ɪnˈkɒŋgruəs] ADJ *couple, juxtaposition, mixture* wenig zusammenpassend *attr*; *thing to do, remark* unpassend; *behaviour* unangebracht; **it seems ~ that ...** es scheint abwegig *or* widersinnig, dass ...; **he was an ~ figure among the tourists** unter den Touristen wirkte er fehl am Platz

inconsequential [ɪnˌkɒnsɪˈkwenʃəl] ADJ unbedeutend, unwichtig

inconsiderable [ˌɪnkənˈsɪdərəbl] ADJ unbedeutend, unerheblich

inconsiderate [ˌɪnkənˈsɪdərɪt] ADJ rücksichtslos; *(in less critical sense)* unaufmerksam

inconsiderately [ˌɪnkənˈsɪdərɪtlɪ] ADV rücksichtslos

inconsistency [ˌɪnkənˈsɪstənsɪ] N **(a)** *(= contradictoriness)* Widersprüchlichkeit *f*; **the inconsistencies in his evidence** die Widersprüche in seiner Aussage **(b)** *(of work, in quality etc)* Unbeständigkeit *f*

inconsistent [ˌɪnkənˈsɪstənt] ADJ **(a)** *(= contradictory)* widersprüchlich; **to be ~ with sth** zu etw im Widerspruch stehen **(b)** *work* unbeständig; *person* inkonsequent

inconsistently [ˌɪnkənˈsɪstəntlɪ] ADV **(a)** *argue, behave* widersprüchlich **(b)** *work, perform* unbeständig, ungleichmäßig

inconsolable [ˌɪnkənˈsəʊləbl] ADJ untröstlich

inconspicuous [ˌɪnkənˈspɪkjuəs] ADJ unauffällig; **to make oneself ~** so wenig Aufsehen wie möglich erregen

inconspicuously [ˌɪnkənˈspɪkjuəslɪ] ADV unauffällig

incontestable [ˌɪnkənˈtestəbl] ADJ unbestreitbar

incontinence [ɪnˈkɒntɪnəns] N *(Med)* Inkontinenz *f*

incontinent [ɪnˈkɒntɪnənt] ADJ *(Med)* inkontinent

incontrovertible [ɪnˌkɒntrəˈvɜːtəbl] ADJ unbestreitbar; *evidence* unwiderlegbar; *argument* unanfechtbar

inconvenience [ˌɪnkənˈviːnɪəns] **1** N Unannehmlichkeit *f (to sb* für jdn); *(= trouble also)* Unannehmlichkeiten *pl*; **it's one of the ~s of getting old** es ist einer der Nachteile, wenn man älter wird; **it was something of an ~ not having a car** es war eine ziemliche Unannehmlichkeit, kein Auto zu haben; **the ~ of a delayed flight** die Unannehmlichkeiten, die durch einen verspäteten Flug verursacht werden; **I don't want to cause you any ~** ich möchte Ihnen keine Umstände bereiten *or* machen; **to put sb to great ~** jdm große Umstände bereiten
2 VT Unannehmlichkeiten *or* Umstände bereiten *(+dat)*; *(with reference to time)* ungelegen kommen *(+dat)*; **don't ~ yourself** machen Sie keine Umstände

inconvenient [ˌɪnkənˈviːnɪənt] ADJ **(a)** ungünstig; *shops* ungünstig gelegen; **if it's ~, I can come later** wenn es Ihnen ungelegen ist, kann ich später kommen; **it is ~ to have to wait** es ist lästig, warten zu müssen **(b)** *(= embarrassing) fact, information* unbequem

inconveniently [ˌɪnkənˈviːnɪəntlɪ] ADV ungünstig; **it was ~ timed** es fand zu einer ungünstigen Zeit statt; **he ~ decided to leave** er beschloss zu gehen *or* was sehr ungelegen kam

incorporate [ɪnˈkɔːpəreɪt] **1** VT **(a)** *(= integrate)* aufnehmen, einbauen *(into* in *+acc)*; **her proposals were ~d into the project** ihre Vorschläge gingen in das Projekt ein **(b)** *(= contain)* (in sich *dat*) vereinigen, enthalten; **the tax is ~d in the price** (die) Steuer ist im Preis enthalten **(c)** *(Jur, Comm)* **to ~ a company** eine Gesellschaft gründen; **~d**

company *(US)* Aktiengesellschaft *f* **2** VI *(Comm)* eine Gesellschaft gründen

incorporation [ɪnˌkɔːpəˈreɪʃən] N Aufnahme *f*, Integration *f (into, in* in *+acc)*; **certificate of ~** *(Comm)* Gründungsurkunde *f*

incorrect [ˌɪnkəˈrekt] ADJ **(a)** falsch; *text* fehlerhaft; **that is ~** das stimmt nicht; **you are ~** Sie haben Unrecht **(b)** *behaviour, dress* inkorrekt

incorrectly [ˌɪnkəˈrektlɪ] ADV *(= wrongly)* falsch; *(= improperly)* inkorrekt; **I had ~ assumed that ...** ich hatte fälschlich(erweise) angenommen, dass ...

incorrigible [ɪnˈkɒrɪdʒəbl] ADJ unverbesserlich

incorruptible [ˌɪnkəˈrʌptəbl] ADJ *person* charakterstark; *(= not bribable)* unbestechlich; **she's ~** man kann sie nicht verderben

Incoterms ABBR *of* **International Commercial Terms** Incoterms *pl, internationale Regeln für die Auslegung von Handelsklauseln*

increase [ɪnˈkriːs] **1** VI zunehmen; *(taxes)* erhöht werden; *(pride also, strength)* wachsen; *(price, sales, demand)* steigen; *(supply, joy, rage)* größer werden; *(rain, wind)* stärker werden; **to ~ in volume/weight** umfangreicher/schwerer werden; **to ~ in breadth/size/number** breiter/größer/mehr werden; **industrial output ~d by 2% last year** die Industrieproduktion wuchs im letzten Jahr um 2%
2 VT vergrößern; *darkness, noise, love, resentment also, effort* verstärken; *trade, sales* erweitern; *numbers, taxes, price, speed, demand, tension* erhöhen; *chances* verbessern; **he ~d his efforts** er strengte sich mehr an; **~d demand** erhöhte Nachfrage; **~d efficiency** Leistungssteigerung *f*; **they ~d her salary by £2,000 to £20,000 a year** sie erhöhten ihr Jahresgehalt um £ 2.000 auf £ 20.000
3 [ˈɪnkriːs] N Zunahme *f*; *(in size)* Vergrößerung *f*; *(in speed, spending)* Erhöhung *f (in +gen)*; *(in sales)* Zuwachs *m*; *(of demand)* Verstärkung *f*; *(of salary)* Gehaltserhöhung *f*; **to get an ~ of £5 per week** £ 5 pro Woche mehr bekommen; **to be on the ~** ständig zunehmen; **~ in value** Wertsteigerung *f*; **rent ~** Mieterhöhung *f*

increasing [ɪnˈkriːsɪŋ] ADJ zunehmend; **an ~ number of people are changing to ...** mehr und mehr Leute steigen auf *(+acc)* ... um; **there are ~ signs that ...** es gibt immer mehr Anzeichen dafür, dass ...

increasingly [ɪnˈkriːsɪŋlɪ] ADV zunehmend, immer mehr; **~, people are finding that ...** man findet in zunehmendem Maße, dass ...

incredible [ɪnˈkredəbl] ADJ unglaublich; *(inf: = amazing also)* unwahrscheinlich *(inf)*; *scenery, music* sagenhaft; **it seems ~ to me that ...** ich kann es nicht fassen, dass ...; **you're ~** *(inf)* du bist wirklich unschlagbar

incredibly [ɪnˈkredəblɪ] ADV unglaublich, unwahrscheinlich; **~, he wasn't there** unglaublicherweise war er nicht da

incredulity [ˌɪnkrɪˈdjuːlɪtɪ] N Ungläubigkeit *f*

incredulous [ɪnˈkredjʊləs] ADJ ungläubig; *look also* zweifelnd

incredulously [ɪnˈkredjʊləslɪ] ADV ungläubig

increment [ˈɪnkrɪmənt] N Zuwachs *m*, Steigerung *f*; *(in salary)* Gehaltserhöhung *f*

incremental [ˌɪnkrɪˈmentl] ADJ *(Brit)* ansteigend, zunehmend; *source* wachsend; *effect* steigernd; **~ costs** Grenzkosten *pl*

incriminate [ɪnˈkrɪmɪneɪt] VT belasten

incriminating [ɪnˈkrɪmɪneɪtɪŋ], **incriminatory** [ɪnˈkrɪmɪeɪtərɪ] ADJ belastend

in-crowd [ˈɪnkraʊd] N *(inf)* Schickeria *f (inf)*; **to be in with the ~** zur Schickeria gehören *(inf)*

incubate [ˈɪnkjʊbeɪt] **1** VT *egg* ausbrüten; *bacteria* züchten **2** VI ausgebrütet *or* bebrütet werden; **the virus can ~ for up to 10 days** das Virus hat eine Inkubationszeit von bis zu 10 Tagen

incubation [ˌɪnkjʊˈbeɪʃən] N *(of egg)* Ausbrüten *nt*; *(of bacteria)* Züchten *nt*

incubation period N *(Med)* Inkubationszeit *f*

incubator [ˈɪnkjʊbeɪtər] N *(for babies)* Brutkasten *m*; *(for chicks)* Brutapparat *m*

inculcate [ˈɪnkʌlkeɪt] VT einimpfen *(in sb* jdm)

incumbent [ɪnˈkʌmbənt] *(form)* **1** ADJ **to be ~ upon sb** jdm obliegen *(form)* **2** N Amtsinhaber(in) *m(f)*

incur [ɪnˈkɜːr] VT **(a)** *anger, injury* sich *(dat)* zuziehen; *penalty* belegt werden mit; **to ~ the wrath of sb** jds Zorn auf sich *(acc)* ziehen **(b)** (*Fin*) *loss* erleiden; *debts, expenses* machen; *costs* haben

incursion [ɪnˈkɜːʃən] N Einfall *m*, Eindringen *nt* (*into* in +*acc*); (*fig*) Ausflug *m* (*into* in +*acc*)

indebted [ɪnˈdetɪd] ADJ **(a)** (*fig*) verpflichtet; **to be ~ to sb for sth** jdm für etw (zu Dank) verpflichtet sein **(b)** (*Fin*) verschuldet (*to sb* bei jdm); **I was ~ to them for £3,000** ich schuldete ihnen £ 3000

indebtedness [ɪnˈdetɪdnɪs] N (*fig*) Verpflichtung *f* (*to* gegenüber); (*Fin*) Verschuldung *f*

indecency [ɪnˈdiːsnsɪ] N Unanständigkeit *f*, Anstößigkeit *f*

indecent [ɪnˈdiːsnt] ADJ unanständig, anstößig; *joke* schmutzig; *amount* unerhört; **with ~ haste** mit ungebührlicher Eile *or* Hast

indecent assault N Notzucht *f*

indecently [ɪnˈdiːsntlɪ] ADV unanständig; **to be ~ assaulted** sexuell missbraucht werden

indecipherable [ˌɪndɪˈsaɪfərəbl] ADJ nicht zu entziffern *pred*, nicht zu entziffernd *attr*; *handwriting* unleserlich

indecision [ˌɪndɪˈsɪʒən] N Unentschlossenheit *f*, Unschlüssigkeit *f*

indecisive [ˌɪndɪˈsaɪsɪv] ADJ **(a)** *person, manner* unschlüssig, unentschlossen (*in or about or over sth* in Bezug auf etw *acc*) **(b)** *discussion, vote* ergebnislos; *argument, battle* nicht(s) entscheidend *attr*; *result* nicht eindeutig

indecisively [ˌɪndɪˈsaɪsɪvlɪ] ADV unentschlossen; (= *inconclusively*) ergebnislos

indeed [ɪnˈdiːd] ADV **(a)** tatsächlich; (*showing interest, irony, surprise also*) wirklich; **I feel, ~ I know he is right** ich habe das Gefühl, ja ich weiß (sogar), dass er Recht hat; **who else? – ~, who else?** wer sonst? – in der Tat *or* ganz recht, wer sonst?; **isn't that strange? – ~ (it is)** ist das nicht seltsam? – allerdings; **are you coming? – ~ I am!** kommst du? – aber sicher *or* natürlich; **are you pleased? – yes, ~ or ~, yes!** bist du zufrieden? – oh ja, das kann man wohl sagen!; **did you/is it/has she** *etc* **~?** tatsächlich?; **~?** ach so?, ach wirklich?; **where ~?** ja, wo?; **what ~?** ja, was? **(b)** (*as intensifier*) wirklich; **very ... ~** wirklich sehr ...; **thank you very much ~** vielen herzlichen Dank **(c)** (*expressing possibility*) **if ~ ...** falls ... wirklich; **I may ~ come** es kann gut sein, dass ich komme

indefatigable ADJ, **indefatigably** ADV [ˌɪndɪˈfætɪgəbl, -ɪ] unermüdlich, rastlos

indefensible [ˌɪndɪˈfensəbl] ADJ *behaviour, remark etc* unentschuldbar; *cause, theory* unvertretbar; *policy* unhaltbar; **morally ~** moralisch nicht vertretbar

indefinable [ˌɪndɪˈfaɪnəbl] ADJ *colour, charm* undefinierbar; *feeling, impression* unbestimmt

indefinite [ɪnˈdefɪnɪt] ADJ unbestimmt; **at some ~ time** irgendwann einmal

indefinite article N (*Gram*) unbestimmter Artikel

indefinitely [ɪnˈdefɪnɪtlɪ] ADV *wait etc* unbegrenzt (lange), endlos; *postpone, continue, close* auf unbestimmte Zeit; **we can't go on like this ~** wir können nicht endlos so weitermachen

indelible [ɪnˈdeləbl] ADJ *stain* nicht zu entfernen; (*fig*) *impression* unauslöschlich; **~ pencil** Kopierstift *m*; **to leave an ~ mark on sb/sth** (*fig*) jdn/etw für immer zeichnen

indelibly [ɪnˈdeləblɪ] ADV (*fig*) unauslöschlich

indelicate [ɪnˈdelɪkət] ADJ *person* taktlos; *subject* peinlich; (= *crude*) geschmacklos

indemnify [ɪnˈdemnɪfaɪ] VT entschädigen (*for* für); (*for expenses*) erstatten (*sb for sth* jdm etw)

indemnity [ɪnˈdemnɪtɪ] N **(a)** (*for damage, loss etc*) Schadensersatz *m*; (*after war*) Wiedergutmachung *f* **(b)** (= *insurance*) Versicherungsschutz *m*; **professional ~** (*Brit*) Berufshaftpflicht *f*

indent [ɪnˈdent] VT (*Typ*) einrücken, einziehen

indentation [ˌɪndenˈteɪʃən] N (*in border, edge*) Kerbe *f*; (*Typ*) Einrückung *f*, Einzug *m*

independence [ˌɪndɪˈpendəns] N Unabhängigkeit *f* (*of* von); **to gain** *or* **achieve/declare ~** die Unabhängigkeit erlangen/erklären

Independence Day N (*US*) der Unabhängigkeitstag

independent [ˌɪndɪˈpendənt] **1** ADJ unabhängig (*of sb/sth* von jdm/etw) (*also Pol: country*); (*in attitude, spirit also*) selbstständig; **a man of ~ means** eine Person mit Privateinkommen; **to become ~** (*country*) die Unabhängigkeit erlangen; **~ retailer** (*US*) selbstständiger Einzelhändler, selbstständige Einzelhändlerin; **~ confirmation** Bestätigung *f* aus unabhängiger Quelle **2** N (*Pol*) Unabhängige(r) *mf*

independently [ˌɪndɪˈpendəntlɪ] ADV unabhängig (*of sb/sth* von jdm/etw); *live* ohne fremde Hilfe; *work* selbstständig; **they each came ~ to the same conclusion** sie kamen unabhängig voneinander zur gleichen Schlussfolgerung

independent school N freie *or* unabhängige Schule

in-depth [ˈɪndepθ] ADJ eingehend, gründlich; *interview* ausführlich

indescribable [ˌɪndɪˈskraɪbəbl] ADJ unbeschreiblich; (*inf*: = *terrible*) schrecklich

indestructible [ˌɪndɪˈstrʌktəbl] ADJ unzerstörbar

indeterminate [ˌɪndɪˈtɜːmɪnɪt] ADJ unbestimmt; **of ~ sex/age** von unbestimmbarem Geschlecht/Alter

index [ˈɪndeks] **1** N **(a)** *pl* **-es** (*in book*) Register *nt*, Index *m*; (*in library*) (*of topics*) (Schlagwort)katalog *m*; (*of authors*) (Verfasser)katalog *m*; (= *card ~*) Kartei *f* **(b)** *pl* **indices** (= *pointer*) **this is a good ~ of his character** das zeigt deutlich seinen Charakter **(c)** *pl* **-es** *or* **indices** (= *number showing ratio*) Index *m*; **cost-of-living ~** Lebenshaltungskostenindex *m* **2** VT **(a) the book is clearly ~ed** das Buch hat ein klares Register *or* einen klaren Index **(b) to ~ sth to inflation** etw an den Index binden; *pension* etw dynamisieren

index card N Karteikarte *f*

indexed [ˈɪndekst] ADJ (*Econ*) dynamisch

index: index finger N Zeigefinger *m*; **index-linked** ADJ *rate, salaries, trading* indexgebunden; *pensions, insurance* dynamisch

India [ˈɪndɪə] N Indien *nt*

India ink N (*US*) Tusche *f*

Indian [ˈɪndɪən] **1** ADJ **(a)** indisch **(b)** (= *American ~*) indianisch, Indianer- **2** N **(a)** Inder(in) *m(f)* **(b)** (= *American ~*) Indianer(in) *m(f)*

Indian: Indian ink N Tusche *f*; **Indian Ocean** N Indischer Ozean; **Indian sign** N (*US*) Zauber *m*; **to put an ~ on sb** jdn verzaubern *or* verhexen; **Indian summer** N Altweibersommer *m*; (*esp Brit fig*: = *success late in life*) späte Blüte

indicate [ˈɪndɪkeɪt] **1** VT **(a)** zeigen; (= *point out, mark also*) deuten auf (+*acc*); (= *gesture, express also*) andeuten; (= *point to*) zeigen *or* deuten auf (+*acc*); **large towns are ~d in red** Großstädte sind rot eingezeichnet *or* gekennzeichnet; **to ~ one's feelings** seine Gefühle zeigen *or* zum Ausdruck bringen; **to ~ one's intention to do sth** seine Absicht anzeigen, etw zu tun **(b)** (= *be a sign of, suggest*) erkennen lassen, (hin)deuten auf (+*acc*); **opinion polls ~ that ...** die Meinungsumfragen deuten darauf hin, dass ... **(c)** *temperature, speed* (an)zeigen **2** VI (*esp Brit Aut*) blinken

indication [ˌɪndɪˈkeɪʃən] N (An)zeichen *nt* (*also Med*) (*of* für), Hinweis *m* (*of* auf +*acc*); **he gave a clear ~ of his intentions** er ließ seine Absichten deutlich erkennen; **he gave no ~ that he was ready to compromise** nichts wies darauf hin, dass er zu einem Kompromiss bereit war; **that is some ~ of what we can expect** das gibt uns einen Vorgeschmack auf das, was wir zu erwarten haben

indicative [ɪnˈdɪkətɪv] **1** ADJ **(a)** bezeichnend (*of* für); **to be ~ of sth** auf etw (*acc*) schließen lassen, auf etw (*acc*) hindeuten; *of sb's character* für etw bezeichnend sein **(b)** (*Gram*) mood Indikativ *m*, Wirklichkeitsform *f* **2** N (*Gram*) Indikativ *m*, Wirklichkeitsform *f*; **in the ~** im Indikativ, in der Wirklichkeitsform

indicator [ˈɪndɪkeɪtər] N (= *instrument, gauge*) Anzeiger *m*; (= *needle*) Zeiger *m*; (*esp Brit Aut*) Blinker *m*; (*fig*: *of economic position etc*) Messlatte *f*; **altitude/pressure ~** Höhen-/Druckmesser *m*; **this is an ~ of economic recovery** dies ist ein Indikator für den Aufschwung

indices [ˈɪndɪsiːz] PL *of* **index**

indict [ɪnˈdaɪt] VT anklagen (*on a charge of sth* einer Sache *gen*); (*US Jur*) Anklage erheben gegen (*for* wegen +*gen*)

indictable [ɪnˈdaɪtəbl] ADJ strafbar

indictment [ɪnˈdaɪtmənt] N (*of person*) Beschuldigung *f*, Anschuldigung *f*; **to bring an ~ against sb** gegen jdn Anklage erheben; **to be an ~ of sth** (*fig*) ein Armutszeugnis *nt* für jдn sein; **the speech was a damning ~ of government policy** die Rede war eine vernichtende Anklage gegen die Regierungspolitik

indifference [ɪnˈdɪfrəns] N Gleichgültigkeit *f* (*to, towards* gegenüber); **it's a matter of complete ~ to me** das ist mir völlig egal *or* gleichgültig

indifferent [ɪnˈdɪfrənt] ADJ **(a)** gleichgültig (*to, towards* gegenüber); **he is quite ~ about it/to her** es/sie ist ihm ziemlich gleichgültig **(b)** (= *mediocre*) mittelmäßig, durchschnittlich

indigenous [ɪnˈdɪdʒɪnəs] ADJ einheimisch (*to* in +*dat*); *customs* landeseigen; **plants ~ to Canada** in Kanada heimische Pflanzen

indigestible [ˌɪndɪˈdʒestəbl] ADJ (*Med*) unverdaulich; (*fig*) schwer verdaulich

indigestion [ˌɪndɪˈdʒestʃən] N Verdauungsbeschwerden *pl*; **acid ~** Sodbrennen *nt*

indignant ADJ, **indignantly** ADV [ɪnˈdɪɡnənt, -lɪ] entrüstet, empört (*at, about, with* über +*acc*)

indignation [ˌɪndɪɡˈneɪʃən] N Entrüstung *f* (*at, about, with* über +*acc*)

indignity [ɪnˈdɪɡnɪtɪ] N Demütigung *f*

indigo [ˈɪndɪɡəʊ] ADJ indigofarben

indirect [ˌɪndɪˈrekt] ADJ indirekt; **by an ~ route/path/road** auf Umwegen *or* einem Umweg; **to make an ~ reference to sb/sth** auf jdn/etw anspielen *or* indirekt Bezug nehmen

indirect: **indirect costs** PL indirekte Kosten *pl*; **indirect discourse** (*US*) N (*Gram*) indirekte Rede

indirectly [ˌɪndɪˈrektlɪ] ADV indirekt

indirect: **indirect object** N (*Gram*) Dativobjekt *nt*; **indirect speech** N (*Gram*) indirekte Rede; **indirect taxation** N indirekte Besteuerung

indiscernible [ˌɪndɪˈsɜːnəbl] ADJ nicht erkennbar *or* sichtbar; *noise* nicht wahrnehmbar

indiscipline [ɪnˈdɪsɪplɪn] N Undiszipliniertheit *f*, Disziplinlosigkeit *f*

indiscreet [ˌɪndɪˈskriːt] ADJ indiskret; (= *tactless*) taktlos; **to be ~ about sth** in Bezug auf etw (*acc*) indiskret sein

indiscreetly [ˌɪndɪˈskriːtlɪ] ADV indiskret; (= *tactlessly*) taktlos

indiscretion [ˌɪndɪˈskreʃən] N Indiskretion *f*; (= *tactlessness*) Taktlosigkeit *f*; (= *affair*) Affäre *f*

indiscriminate [ˌɪndɪˈskrɪmɪnɪt] ADJ wahllos; *choice* willkürlich; *reader, shopper* unkritisch; *tastes* unausgeprägt

indiscriminately [ˌɪndɪˈskrɪmɪnɪtlɪ] ADV wahllos; *choose* willkürlich

indispensable [ˌɪndɪˈspensəbl] ADJ unentbehrlich

indisposed [ˌɪndɪˈspəʊzd] ADJ (= *unwell*) unwohl, indisponiert (*geh*)

indisposition [ˌɪndɪspəˈzɪʃən] N (= *illness*) Unwohlsein *nt*

indisputable [ˌɪndɪˈspjuːtəbl] ADJ unbestreitbar; *evidence* unanfechtbar

indistinct [ˌɪndɪˈstɪŋkt] ADJ verschwommen, unklar; *noise* schwach; *memory, voice* undeutlich; *line* unscharf

indistinctly [ˌɪndɪˈstɪŋktlɪ] ADV see nicht deutlich, verschwommen; *speak* undeutlich; *remember* dunkel

indistinguishable [ˌɪndɪˈstɪŋɡwɪʃəbl] ADJ nicht unterscheidbar; **the twins are ~ (from one another)** man kann die Zwillinge nicht (voneinander) unterscheiden

individual [ˌɪndɪˈvɪdjʊəl] **1** ADJ **(a)** (= *separate*) einzeln; **~ cases** Einzelfälle *pl* **(b)** (= *own*) eigen; (= *for one person*) einzeln; **~ portions cost 95p** eine Einzelportion kostet 95 Pence **(c)** (= *distinctive, characteristic*) eigen, individuell **2** N Individuum *nt*, Einzelne(r) *mf*; (*inf*) Individuum *nt*, Mensch *m*; **the freedom of the ~** die Freiheit des Einzelnen

individualistic [ˌɪndɪˈvɪdjʊəlɪstɪk] ADJ individualistisch

individuality [ˈɪndɪˌvɪdjʊˈælɪtɪ] N Individualität *f*, (eigene) Persönlichkeit

individualize [ˌɪndɪˈvɪdjʊəlaɪz] VT eine persönliche Note verleihen (+*dat*); **each patient has ~d treatment** jeder Patient bekommt eine individuelle Behandlung

individually [ˌɪndɪˈvɪdjʊəlɪ] ADV individuell; (= *separately*) einzeln

indivisible [ˌɪndɪˈvɪzəbl] ADJ unteilbar (*also Math*), untrennbar

Indo- [ˈɪndəʊ-] PREF Indo-; **Indo-China** N Indochina *nt*

indoctrinate [ɪnˈdɒktrɪneɪt] VT indoktrinieren

indoctrination [ɪnˌdɒktrɪˈneɪʃən] N Indoktrination *f*

Indo-European [ˌɪndəʊjʊərəˈpiːən] ADJ indoeuropäisch

indolence [ˈɪndələns] N Trägheit *f*

indolent [ˈɪndələnt] ADJ träge

indomitable [ɪnˈdɒmɪtəbl] ADJ *person, courage* unbezwingbar; *will* unbeugsam, eisern

Indonesia [ˌɪndəˈniːzɪə] N Indonesien *nt*

Indonesian [ˌɪndəˈniːzɪən] **1** ADJ indonesisch **2** N Indonesier(in) *m(f)*

indoor [ˈɪndɔːʳ] ADJ Innen-; *clothes* für zu Hause *or* zuhause (*Aus, Sw*); **~ aerial** Zimmerantenne *f*; **~ market** überdachter Markt; **~ plant** Zimmerpflanze *f*; **~ sport** Hallensport *m*; **~ swimming pool** (*public*) Hallenbad *nt*; (*private*) überdachter Swimmingpool *m*; **~ games** Spiele *pl* fürs Haus; (*Sport*) Hallenspiele *pl*

indoors [ɪnˈdɔːz] ADV drin(nen) (*inf*), innen; (= *at home*) zu Hause, zuhause (*Aus, Sw*); (= *into house*) ins Haus; **to stay ~** im Haus bleiben; **go and play ~** geh ins Haus *or* nach drinnen spielen

indorse *etc* = **endorse**

indubitably ADV [ɪnˈdjuːbɪtəblɪ] zweifellos, zweifelsohne

induce [ɪnˈdjuːs] VT **(a) to ~ sb to do sth** jdn dazu bewegen *or* bringen, etw zu tun **(b)** *reaction, change, sleep* herbeiführen; *relaxation* bewirken; *illness, vomiting* verursachen; *labour, birth* einleiten; **a stress-/drug-~d condition** ein durch Stress/ Drogen ausgelöstes Leiden

inducement [ɪnˈdjuːsmənt] N (= *motive, incentive*) Anreiz *m*, Ansporn *m* no *pl*; **to offer ~s** Anreize bieten; **cash/financial ~s** finanzielle Anreize *pl*

induct [ɪnˈdʌkt] VT **(a)** *bishop, president etc* in sein Amt einführen **(b)** (*US Mil*) einziehen, einberufen

inductee [ɪndʌkˈtiː] N (*US Mil*) (zum Wehrdienst) Eingezogene(r) *or* Einberufene(r) *mf*

induction [ɪnˈdʌkʃən] N **(a)** (*of bishop, president etc*) Amtseinführung *f*; (*of employee*) Einarbeitung *f*; (*US Mil*) Einberufung *f* **(b)** (*of labour, birth*) Einleitung *f*

induction course N Einführungskurs *m*

indulge [ɪnˈdʌldʒ] **1** VT nachgeben (+*dat*); (= *overindulge*) *children* verwöhnen; **he ~s her every whim** er erfüllt ihr jeden Wunsch; **she ~d herself with a glass of wine** sie gönnte sich (*dat*) ein Glas Wein **2** VI **to ~ in sth** sich (*dat*) etw gönnen; *in vice, drink, daydreams* sich einer Sache (*dat*) hingeben; **dessert came, but I didn't ~** (*inf*) der Nachtisch kam, aber ich konnte mich beherrschen

indulgence [ɪnˈdʌldʒəns] N **(a)** Nachsicht *f*; (= *overindulgence*) Verwöhnung *f*, Verhätschelung *f*; **~ in drink/food/sport** übermäßiges Trinken/Essen/Sporttreiben **(b)** (= *thing indulged in*) Luxus *m*; (= *food, drink, pleasure*) Genuss *m*

indulgent ADJ, **indulgently** ADV [ɪnˈdʌldʒənt, -lɪ] nachsichtig (*to* gegenüber)

industrial [ɪnˈdʌstrɪəl] ADJ industriell, Industrie-; **~ nation** Industriestaat *m*; **~ research** Arbeits- *or* Betriebsforschung *f*; **the Industrial Revolution** die industrielle Revolution

industrial: **industrial action** N Arbeitskampfmaßnahmen *pl*; **to take ~** in den Ausstand treten; **industrial design** N Konstruktionslehre *f*; **industrial dispute** N Auseinandersetzungen *pl* zwischen Arbeitgebern und Arbeitnehmern; (*about pay also*) Tarifkonflikt *m*; (= *strike*) Streik *m*; **industrial engineering** N Fertigungstechnik *f*; **industrial espionage** N Industriespionage *f*; **industrial estate** N (*Brit*) Industriegebiet *nt*

industrialist [ɪnˈdʌstrɪəlɪst] N Industrielle(r) *mf*

industrialization [ɪnˌdʌstrɪəlaɪˈzeɪʃən] N Industrialisierung *f*

industrialize [ɪnˈdʌstrɪəlaɪz] VTI industrialisieren; **~d nation** Industrienation *f*

industrial: **industrial park** N (*US*) Industriegelände *nt*; **industrial relations** PL Beziehungen *pl* zwischen

Arbeitgebern und Gewerkschaften; **industrial relations officer** N *leitender Angestellter für Arbeitgeber-Arbeitnehmerbeziehungen;* **industrial site** N Industriegelände *nt;* **industrial tribunal** N Arbeitsgericht *nt;* **industrial unrest** N Arbeitsunruhen *pl;* **industrial waste** N Industriemüll *m*

industrious ADJ, **industriously** ADV [ɪnˈdʌstrɪəs, -lɪ] arbeitsam, fleißig

industry [ˈɪndəstrɪ] N **(a)** Industrie *f;* **heavy/light** ~ Schwer-/Leichtindustrie *f;* **hotel** ~ Hotelgewerbe *nt;* **tourist** ~ Tourismusbranche *or* -industrie *f* **(b)** (= *industriousness*) Fleiß *m*

industry standard N Industrienorm *f*

inebriated [ɪˈniːbrɪeɪtɪd] ADJ (*form*) betrunken, unter Alkoholeinfluss (*form*)

inedible [ɪnˈedɪbl] ADJ nicht essbar; (= *unpleasant*) *meal etc* ungenießbar

ineffable [ɪnˈefəbl] ADJ (*form*) unsäglich (*geh*)

ineffective [ˌɪnɪˈfektɪv] ADJ unwirksam, ineffektiv; *person, government, management* unfähig; **to be** ~ **against sth** nicht wirksam gegen etw sein

ineffectively [ˌɪnɪˈfektɪvlɪ] ADV ineffektiv

ineffectiveness [ˌɪnɪˈfektɪvnɪs] N Unwirksamkeit *f,* Ineffektivität *f;* (*of person*) Unfähigkeit *f*

ineffectual [ˌɪnɪˈfektjʊəl] ADJ ineffektiv; (= *half-hearted*) halbherzig

inefficiency [ˌɪnɪˈfɪʃənsɪ] N (*of person*) Unfähigkeit *f,* Ineffizienz *f* (*geh*); (*of machine, engine*) geringe Leistung; (*of factory, company*) Unproduktivität *f;* **the** ~ **of this method** diese unrationelle Methode

inefficient [ˌɪnɪˈfɪʃənt] ADJ *person* unfähig, ineffizient (*geh*); *machine, engine* leistungsschwach; *method* unrationell; *use* unwirtschaftlich; *factory, company* unproduktiv; **to be** ~ **at doing sth** etw schlecht machen

inefficiently [ˌɪnɪˈfɪʃəntlɪ] ADV schlecht; **to work** ~ (*person*) unrationell arbeiten; (*machine*) unwirtschaftlich arbeiten

inelegant ADJ, **inelegantly** ADV [ɪnˈelɪgənt, -lɪ] unelegant

ineligible [ɪnˈelɪdʒəbl] ADJ (*for benefits, grant*) nicht berechtigt (*for zu* Leistungen +*gen*); (*for election*) nicht wählbar; (*for job, office, as husband*) ungeeignet; ~ **for military service** wehruntauglich; **to be** ~ **for a pension** nicht pensionsberechtigt sein

inept [ɪˈnept] ADJ ungeschickt; *behaviour, person also* unbeholfen; *performance also* stümperhaft (*pej*); *remark* unangebracht; *attempt* plump

ineptitude [ɪˈneptɪtjuːd], **ineptness** [ɪˈneptnɪs] N (*of person*) Ungeschick *nt,* Unbeholfenheit *f*

inequality [ˌɪnɪˈkwɒlɪtɪ] N Ungleichheit *f;* (= *instance of* ~) Unterschied *m;* ~ **of opportunity** Chancenungleichheit *f*

inequitable [ɪnˈekwɪtəbl] ADJ ungerecht

inequity [ɪnˈekwɪtɪ] N Ungerechtigkeit *f*

ineradicable [ˌɪnɪˈrædɪkəbl] ADJ *feeling of guilt, hatred* unauslöschlich; *disease, prejudice* unausrottbar

inert [ɪˈnɜːt] ADJ unbeweglich

inert gas N (*Chem*) Edelgas *nt*

inertia [ɪˈnɜːʃə] N (*lit, fig*) Trägheit *f;* ~**-reel seat belt** Automatikgurt *m*

inescapable [ˌɪnɪsˈkeɪpəbl] ADJ unvermeidlich; *fact, reality* unausweichlich; *consequence, logic, conclusion* zwangsläufig

inessential [ˌɪnɪˈsenʃəl] ADJ unwesentlich, unwichtig

inestimable [ɪnˈestɪməbl] ADJ unschätzbar

inevitability [ɪnˌevɪtəˈbɪlɪtɪ] N Unvermeidlichkeit *f*

inevitable [ɪnˈevɪtəbl] **1** ADJ unvermeidlich; **victory/defeat seemed** ~ der Sieg/die Niederlage schien unabwendbar **2** N **the** ~ das Unvermeidliche

inevitably [ɪnˈevɪtəblɪ] ADV zwangsläufig; **one question** ~ **leads to another** eine Frage zieht unweigerlich weitere nach sich; ~**, he got drunk** es konnte ja nicht ausbleiben, dass er sich betrank; **as** ~ **happens on these occasions** wie es bei solchen Anlässen immer ist

inexact [ˌɪnɪgˈzækt] ADJ ungenau

inexcusable [ˌɪnɪksˈkjuːzəbl] ADJ unverzeihlich

inexhaustible [ˌɪnɪgˈzɔːstəbl] ADJ unerschöpflich; *curiosity* unstillbar

inexorable [ɪnˈeksərəbl] ADJ erbarmungslos; (= *not to be stopped*) unaufhaltsam

inexorably [ɪnˈeksərəblɪ] ADV erbarmungslos; (= *unstoppably*) unaufhaltsam

inexpensive ADJ, **inexpensively** ADV [ˌɪnɪkˈspensɪv, -lɪ] billig

inexperience [ˌɪnɪkˈspɪərɪəns] N Unerfahrenheit *f*

inexperienced [ˌɪnɪkˈspɪərɪənst] ADJ unerfahren; *woodworker, skier etc* ungeübt; **to be** ~ **in doing sth** wenig Erfahrung darin haben, etw zu tun

inexpertly [ɪnˈekspɜːtlɪ] ADV unfachmännisch, laienhaft

inexplicable [ˌɪnɪkˈsplɪkəbl] ADJ unerklärlich

inexplicably [ˌɪnɪkˈsplɪkəblɪ] ADV (+*adj*) unerklärlich; (+*vb*) unerklärlicherweise

inexpressible [ˌɪnɪkˈspresəbl] ADJ unbeschreiblich

inexpressive [ˌɪnɪkˈspresɪv] ADJ *face* ausdruckslos; *style* blass

inextinguishable [ˌɪnɪkˈstɪŋgwɪʃəbl] ADJ *love, hope* unerschütterlich

in extremis [ˌɪnekˈstriːmɪs] ADV **to be** ~ sich in äußerster Not befinden

inextricable [ˌɪnɪkˈstrɪkəbl] ADJ *tangle* unentwirrbar; *confusion* unüberschaubar; *link, relationship* untrennbar

inextricably [ˌɪnɪkˈstrɪkəblɪ] ADV *entangled* unentwirrbar; *linked* untrennbar

infallibility [ɪnˌfæləˈbɪlɪtɪ] N Unfehlbarkeit *f* (*also Eccl*)

infallible [ɪnˈfæləbl] ADJ unfehlbar (*also Eccl*)

infallibly [ɪnˈfæləblɪ] ADV unfehlbar; *work* fehlerfrei

infamous [ˈɪnfəməs] ADJ berüchtigt (*for wegen*)

infamy [ˈɪnfəmɪ] N Verrufenheit *f*

infancy [ˈɪnfənsɪ] N frühe Kindheit; (*fig*) Anfangsstadium *nt;* **in early** ~ in früherer Kindheit; **when radio was still in its** ~ als das Radio noch in den Kinderschuhen steckte

infant [ˈɪnfənt] N (= *baby*) Säugling *m;* (= *young child*) Kleinkind *nt;* **she teaches** ~**s** sie unterrichtet Grundschulkinder; ~ **class** (*Brit*) erste und zweite Grundschulklasse

infantile [ˈɪnfəntaɪl] ADJ **(a)** (= *childish*) kindisch **(b)** (*Med*) Kinder-

infant mortality N Säuglingssterblichkeit *f*

infantry [ˈɪnfəntrɪ] N (*Mil*) Infanterie *f*

infantryman [ˈɪnfəntrɪmən] N, *pl* **-men** [-mən] Infanterist *m*

infant school N (*Brit*) Grundschule für die ersten beiden Jahrgänge

infatuated [ɪnˈfætjʊeɪtɪd] ADJ vernarrt, verknallt (*inf*) (*with* in +*acc*); **to become** ~ **with sb** sich in jdn vernarren

infatuation [ɪnˌfætjʊˈeɪʃən] N Vernarrtheit *f* (*with* in +*acc*)

infect [ɪnˈfekt] VT *wound, blood* infizieren; (*lit, fig*) *person* anstecken; *water* verseuchen; *meat* verderben; **to be** ~**ed with** *or* **by an illness** sich mit einer Krankheit angesteckt haben; **his wound became** ~**ed** seine Wunde entzündete sich

infected [ɪnˈfektɪd] ADJ infiziert; *water, place* verseucht; *meat* verdorben

infection [ɪnˈfekʃən] N Infektion *f,* Entzündung *f*

infectious [ɪnˈfekʃəs] ADJ (*Med, fig*) ansteckend

infer [ɪnˈfɜː] VT **(a)** (= *deduce*) schließen, folgern (*from* aus) **(b)** (= *imply*) andeuten

inference [ˈɪnfərəns] N Schluss(folgerung *f*) *m;* **it has a tiny head and, by** ~**, a tiny brain** es hat einen winzigen Kopf und demzufolge ein winziges Gehirn

inferior [ɪnˈfɪərɪə] **1** ADJ (*in quality*) minderwertig; *person* unterlegen; (*in rank*) untergeordnet; **an** ~ **workman** ein weniger guter Handwerker; **to be** ~ **to sth** (*in quality*) von minderer Qualität sein als etw; **to be** ~ **to sb** jdm unterlegen sein; (*in rank*) jdm untergeordnet sein; **he feels** ~ er kommt sich (*dat*) unterlegen *or* minderwertig vor **2** N **one's** ~**s** (*in social standing*) Leute *or* Personen *pl* aus einer niedrigeren Schicht; (*in rank*) seine Untergebenen *pl*

inferiority [ɪnˌfɪərɪˈɒrɪtɪ] N (*in quality*) Minderwertigkeit *f;* (*of person*) Unterlegenheit *f* (*to* gegenüber); (*in rank*) untergeordnete Stellung

inferiority complex N Minderwertigkeitskomplex *m*

infernal [ɪnˈfɜːnl] ADJ (*inf*) *impudence, nuisance* verteufelt; *noise* höllisch

inferno [ɪnˈfɜːnəʊ] N Flammenmeer *nt;* **a blazing** ~ ein flammendes Inferno

infertile [ɪnˈfɜːtaɪl] ADJ *soil, person* unfruchtbar; *animal* fortpflanzungsunfähig

infertility [ˌɪnfəˈtɪlɪtɪ] N (*of person*) Unfruchtbarkeit *f*

infertility treatment N Sterilitätsbehandlung *f*

infest [ɪnˈfest] VT (*rats, lice*) herfallen über (+*acc*); (*fig: unwanted people*) heimsuchen; (*crime, drugs etc*) verseuchen; **to be ~ed with rats** mit Ratten verseucht sein

infidel [ˈɪnfɪdəl] N (*Hist, Rel*) Ungläubige(r) *mf*

infidelity [ˌɪnfɪˈdelɪtɪ] N Untreue *f*

in-fighting [ˈɪnfaɪtɪŋ] N (*fig*) interner Machtkampf

infiltrate [ˈɪnfɪltreɪt] VT (*Pol*) *organization* unterwandern; *spies, informer* einschleusen

infiltration [ˌɪnfɪlˈtreɪʃən] N (*Pol*) Unterwanderung *f*

infiltrator [ˈɪnfɪlˌtreɪtəʳ] N (*Pol*) Unterwanderer *m*

infinite [ˈɪnfɪnɪt] **1** ADJ (*lit*) unendlich; *possibilities* unendlich viele; **the organizers, in their ~ wisdom, planned the two events for the same day** die Organisatoren, klug wie sie waren, legten die beiden Veranstaltungen auf den gleichen Tag **2** N **the ~** (= *space*) das Unendliche; (= *God*) der Unendliche

infinitely [ˈɪnfɪnɪtlɪ] ADV unendlich; *better, worse* unendlich viel

infinitesimal [ˌɪnfɪnɪˈtesɪməl] ADJ unendlich klein

infinitive [ɪnˈfɪnɪtɪv] N (*Gram*) Infinitiv *m*, Grundform *f*; **in the ~** im Infinitiv

infinity [ɪnˈfɪnɪtɪ] N (*lit*) Unendlichkeit *f*; (*Math*) das Unendliche; **to ~** (bis) ins Unendliche

infirm [ɪnˈfɜːm] ADJ gebrechlich, schwach

infirmary [ɪnˈfɜːmərɪ] N (= *hospital*) Krankenhaus *nt*; (*in school etc*) Krankenzimmer *nt or* -stube *f*; (*in prison, barracks*) Krankenstation *f*

infirmity [ɪnˈfɜːmɪtɪ] N Gebrechlichkeit *f*; **the infirmities of (old) age** die Altersgebrechen *pl*

inflame [ɪnˈfleɪm] VT (a) (*Med*) entzünden; **to become ~d** sich entzünden (b) *feelings* entfachen; *situation, public opinion* anheizen

inflammable [ɪnˈflæməbl] ADJ (*lit*) feuergefährlich; *fabric* leicht entflammbar; (*fig*) *situation* brisant, gereizt; **"highly ~"** „feuergefährlich"

inflammation [ˌɪnfləˈmeɪʃən] N (*Med*) Entzündung *f*

inflammatory [ɪnˈflæmətərɪ] ADJ *rhetoric, statement* aufrührerisch; **~ speech/pamphlet** Hetzrede/-schrift *f*

inflatable [ɪnˈfleɪtəbl] **1** ADJ aufblasbar; **~ dinghy** Schlauchboot *nt* **2** N (= *boat*) Gummiboot *nt*

inflate [ɪnˈfleɪt] **1** VT (a) (*lit*) aufpumpen; (*by mouth*) aufblasen (b) (*Econ*) *prices, bill* hoch treiben **2** VI (*lit*) sich mit Luft füllen

inflated [ɪnˈfleɪtɪd] ADJ *price, salary* überhöht; *ego* übersteigert

inflation [ɪnˈfleɪʃən] N (*Econ*) Inflation *f*; **~ rate** Inflationsrate *f*

inflationary [ɪnˈfleɪʃənərɪ] ADJ inflationär; **~ pressures/politics** Inflationsdruck *m*/-politik *f*

inflation-proof [ɪnˈfleɪʃənˌpruːf] ADJ inflationssicher

inflect [ɪnˈflekt] VI (*Gram*) flektierbar sein, gebeugt werden

inflected [ɪnˈflektɪd] ADJ (*Gram*) *form, ending* flektiert, gebeugt; *language* flektierend

inflection [ɪnˈflekʃən] N = **inflexion**

inflexibility [ɪnˌfleksɪˈbɪlɪtɪ] N (*fig*) Unbeugsamkeit *f*, Sturheit *f* (*pej*)

inflexible [ɪnˈfleksəbl] ADJ (*lit*) unbiegsam, starr; (*fig*) unbeugsam, stur (*pej*)

inflexion [ɪnˈflekʃən] N (a) (*Gram: of word, language*) Flexion *f*, Beugung *f* (b) (*of voice*) Tonfall *m*

inflict [ɪnˈflɪkt] VT *punishment, fine* verhängen (*on, upon* gegen); *suffering, damage, pain* zufügen (*on or upon sb* jdm); *wound, defeat* beibringen (*on or upon sb* jdm)

infliction [ɪnˈflɪkʃən] N (*of suffering, damage, pain*) Zufügen *nt*

in-flight [ˈɪnflaɪt] ADJ während des Fluges; *service* an Bord; **~ magazine** Bordmagazin *nt*

influence [ˈɪnfluəns] **1** N Einfluss *m* (*over* auf +*acc*); **to have an ~ on sb/sth** (*person*) Einfluss auf jdn/etw haben; **the book had** *or* **was a great ~ on him** das Buch hat ihn stark beeinflusst; **he was a great ~ in ...** er war ein bedeutender Faktor bei ...; **to use one's ~** seinen Einfluss einsetzen; **a man of ~** eine einflussreiche Person; **under the ~ of sb/sth** unter jds Einfluss/dem Einfluss einer Sache; **under the ~ of drink/drugs** unter Alkohol-/Drogeneinfluss; **under the ~** (*inf*) betrunken; **one of my early ~s was Beckett** einer der Schriftsteller, die mich schon früh beeinflusst haben, war Beckett

2 VT beeinflussen; **to be easily ~d** leicht beeinflussbar *or* zu beeinflussen sein

influential [ˌɪnfluˈenʃəl] ADJ einflussreich

influenza [ˌɪnfluˈenzə] N Grippe *f*

influx [ˈɪnflʌks] N (*of capital, shares, foreign goods*) Zufuhr *f*; (*of people*) Zustrom *m*; (*of ideas etc*) Zufluss *m*

info [ˈɪnfəʊ] N (*inf*) = **information**

inform [ɪnˈfɔːm] **1** VT informieren (*about* über +*acc*), unterrichten; **to ~ sb of sth** jdn über etw informieren; **I am pleased to ~ you that ...** ich freue mich, Ihnen mitteilen zu können, dass ...; **to ~ the police** die Polizei verständigen; **to keep sb/oneself ~ed** jdn/sich auf dem Laufenden halten (*of* über +*acc*) **2** VI **to ~ against** *or* **on sb** jdn anzeigen *or* denunzieren (*pej*)

informal [ɪnˈfɔːməl] ADJ (a) (*esp Pol*) *meeting, talks* nicht formell; *visit, arrangement* inoffiziell (b) *gathering, atmosphere, manner, tone* zwanglos; *language, speech* ungezwungen; *restaurant* gemütlich; **he is very ~** er ist sehr leger

informality [ˌɪnfɔːˈmælɪtɪ] N (a) (*esp Pol*) (*of meeting, talks*) nicht formeller Charakter; (*of visit, arrangement*) inoffizieller Charakter (b) (*of gathering, atmosphere, manner, tone*) Zwanglosigkeit *f*; (*of language, speech*) informeller Charakter *or* Ton

informally [ɪnˈfɔːməlɪ] ADV (= *unofficially*) inoffiziell; (= *casually*) zwanglos

informant [ɪnˈfɔːmənt] N (a) Informant(in) *m(f)*; **according to my ~ the book is out of print** wie man mir mitteilte, ist das Buch vergriffen (b) (*police*) ~ Polizeispitzel *m*

information [ˌɪnfəˈmeɪʃən] N (a) Auskunft *f*, Informationen *pl*; **a piece of ~** eine Auskunft *or* Information; **for your ~** zu Ihrer Information; (*indignantly*) damit Sie es wissen; **to give sb ~ about** *or* **on sb/sth** jdm Auskunft *or* Informationen über jdn/ etw geben; **to get ~ about** *or* **on sb/sth** sich über jdn/etw informieren; **"~"** „Auskunft"; **we have no ~ about that** wir wissen darüber nicht Bescheid; **for further ~ please contact this number ...** Näheres erfahren Sie unter Telefonnummer ...

(b) (*Comput*: = ~ *content*) Information *f*

information: information desk N Information *f*, Informationsschalter *m*; **information overload** N Informationsüberhang *m*; **information pack** N Informationsmaterial *nt*; **information superhighway** N Datenautobahn *f*; **information technology** N Informationstechnik *f*; **information transmission** N Informationsübermittlung *f*

informative [ɪnˈfɔːmətɪv] ADJ aufschlussreich, informativ (*geh*); **~ advertising** Social Spots *pl*

informed [ɪnˈfɔːmd] ADJ *observer, source* informiert; *guess, choice* fundiert

informer [ɪnˈfɔːməʳ] N Informant(in) *m(f)*, Denunziant(in) *m(f)* (*pej*); **police ~** Polizeispitzel *m*

infrared [ˈɪnfrəˈred] ADJ infrarot

infrastructure [ˈɪnfrəˌstrʌktʃəʳ] N Infrastruktur *f*

infrequency [ɪnˈfriːkwənsɪ] N Seltenheit *f*

infrequent [ɪnˈfriːkwənt] ADJ selten; **at ~ intervals** in großen Abständen

infrequently [ɪnˈfriːkwəntlɪ] ADV selten

infringe [ɪnˈfrɪndʒ] **1** VT verstoßen gegen; *rights* verletzen **2** VI **to ~ (up)on sb's rights** jds Rechte verletzen

infringement [ɪnˈfrɪndʒmənt] N **an ~ (of a rule)** ein Regelverstoß *m*; **~ of the law** Gesetzesverletzung *f*; **the ~ of sb's rights** die Verletzung von jds Rechten

infuriate [ɪnˈfjʊərɪeɪt] VT wütend *or* rasend machen, zur Raserei bringen

infuriating [ɪnˈfjʊərɪeɪtɪŋ] ADJ (äußerst) ärgerlich; **an ~ person** ein Mensch, der einen rasend *or* wütend machen kann

infuse [ɪnˈfjuːz] **1** VT (a) *courage, enthusiasm etc* einflößen, geben (*into sb* jdm) (b) (*Cook*) aufgießen **2** VI ziehen

infusion [ɪnˈfjuːʒən] N (*Cook*) Aufguss *m*; (*tea-like*) Tee *m*

ingenious ADJ, **ingeniously** ADV [ɪnˈdʒiːnɪəs, -lɪ] genial

ingenuity [ˌɪndʒɪˈnjuːɪtɪ] N Genialität f

ingenuous [ɪnˈdʒenjʊəs] ADJ offen, aufrichtig; (= naïve) naiv

ingenuously [ɪnˈdʒenjʊəslɪ] ADV offen, unbefangen; (= naïvely) naiv

ingot [ˈɪŋgət] N Barren m

ingrained [ˌɪnˈgreɪnd] ADJ (a) (fig) habit fest, eingefleischt; prejudice tief verwurzelt; belief fest verankert; **to be (deeply) ~ fest** verwurzelt sein **(b)** dirt tief eingedrungen

ingratiate [ɪnˈgreɪʃɪeɪt] VR **to ~ oneself with sb** sich bei jdm einschmeicheln

ingratiating [ɪnˈgreɪʃɪeɪtɪŋ] ADJ schmeichlerisch; smile süßlich

ingratitude [ɪnˈgrætɪtjuːd] N Undank m; **sb's ~** jds Undankbarkeit f

ingredient [ɪnˈgriːdɪənt] N Bestandteil m; (for recipe) Zutat f; **all the ~s for success** alles, was man zum Erfolg braucht

ingrowing [ˈɪngrəʊɪŋ] ADJ (Med) eingewachsen

inhabit [ɪnˈhæbɪt] VT bewohnen; (animals) leben in (+dat)

inhabitable [ɪnˈhæbɪtəbl] ADJ bewohnbar

inhabitant [ɪnˈhæbɪtənt] N Bewohner(in) m(f)

inhale [ɪnˈheɪl] **1** VT einatmen; (Med) inhalieren **2** VI (in smoking) inhalieren; **do you ~?** rauchen Sie auf Lunge?

inhaler [ɪnˈheɪləʳ] N Inhalationsapparat m

inherent [ɪnˈhɪərənt] ADJ innewohnend, eigen (to, in +dat)

inherently [ɪnˈhɪərəntlɪ] ADV von Natur aus

inherit [ɪnˈherɪt] VTI (lit, fig) erben; **the problems which we ~ed from the last government** die Probleme, die uns die letzte Regierung hinterlassen or vererbt hat

inheritance [ɪnˈherɪtəns] N Erbe nt (also fig), Erbschaft f; **~ tax** Erbschaftssteuer f

inherited [ɪnˈherɪtɪd] ADJ ererbt

inhibit [ɪnˈhɪbɪt] VT hemmen (also Psych, Sci); ability, performance beeinträchtigen; **to ~ sb from doing sth** jdn daran hindern, etw zu tun

inhibited [ɪnˈhɪbɪtɪd] ADJ gehemmt; **to be ~** Hemmungen haben, gehemmt sein

inhibition [ˌɪnhɪˈbɪʃən] N Hemmung f (also Psych, Sci); **he has no ~s about speaking French** er hat keine Hemmungen, Französisch zu sprechen

inhospitable [ˌɪnhɒˈspɪtəbl] ADJ ungastlich; climate, terrain, region unwirtlich

in-house [ˈɪnhaʊs] **1** ADJ hausintern; staff im Haus; jobs, work im Hause zu erledigend attr or zu erledigen pred **2** [ˈɪnˈhaʊs] ADV hausintern

inhuman [ɪnˈhjuːmən] ADJ unmenschlich

inhumane [ˌɪnhjuːˈmeɪn] ADJ inhuman; treatment menschenunwürdig

inhumanity [ˌɪnhjuːˈmænɪtɪ] N Unmenschlichkeit f

inimical [ɪˈnɪmɪkəl] ADJ (form) (= hostile) feindselig (to gegen); (= injurious) abträglich (to +dat)

inimitable [ɪˈnɪmɪtəbl] ADJ unnachahmlich

iniquitous [ɪˈnɪkwɪtəs] ADJ ungeheuerlich

iniquity [ɪˈnɪkwɪtɪ] N (no pl) Ungeheuerlichkeit f

initial [ɪˈnɪʃəl] **1** ADJ anfänglich, Anfangs-; **my ~ reaction** meine anfängliche Reaktion; **in the ~ stages** im Anfangsstadium; **~ cost** Startkosten pl **2** N Initiale f **3** VT document mit seinen Initialen unterzeichnen; (Comm) abzeichnen; (Pol) paraphieren

initially [ɪˈnɪʃəlɪ] ADV anfangs, zu or am Anfang

initiate [ɪˈnɪʃɪeɪt] VT (a) (= set in motion) den Anstoß geben zu, initiieren (geh); negotiations einleiten; discussion eröffnen; project in die Wege leiten; legislation einbringen **(b)** (into club etc) feierlich aufnehmen **(c)** (= instruct: in knowledge, skill) einweihen; **to ~ sb into sth** jdn in etw (acc) einführen

initiation [ɪˌnɪʃɪˈeɪʃən] N (into society) Aufnahme f

initiation ceremony N Aufnahmezeremonie f

initiative [ɪˈnɪʃɪətɪv] N Initiative f; **to take the ~** die Initiative ergreifen; **on one's own ~** aus eigener Initiative; **to have ~** Initiative haben; **to have the ~** überlegen sein; **to lose the ~** seine Überlegenheit verlieren

initiator [ɪˈnɪʃɪeɪtəʳ] N Initiator(in) m(f)

inject [ɪnˈdʒekt] VT (ein)spritzen; drugs, heroin spritzen; (fig) money into economy pumpen; **to ~ sb with sth** (Med) jdm etw spritzen; **I wanted to ~ some humour into my speech** ich

wollte etwas Humor in meine Rede bringen; **he ~ed new life into the team** er brachte neues Leben in das Team

injection [ɪnˈdʒekʃən] N (= substance injected) Injektion f, Spritze f; **to give sb an ~** jdm eine Injektion or Spritze geben; **a £250 million cash ~** eine Finanzspritze von 250 Millionen Pfund

injudicious ADJ, **injudiciously** ADV [ˌɪndʒʊˈdɪʃəs, -lɪ] unklug

injunction [ɪnˈdʒʌŋkʃən] N Anordnung f; (Jur) gerichtliche Verfügung; **to take out a court ~** eine gerichtliche Verfügung erwirken

injure [ˈɪndʒəʳ] VT (lit, fig) verletzen; reputation schaden (+dat); **to ~ one's leg** sich (dat) das Bein verletzen; **the horse was ~d** das Pferd verletzte sich; **how many were ~d?, how many ~d were there?** wie viele Verletzte gab es?; **the ~d** die Verletzten pl; **the ~d party** (Jur) der/die Geschädigte

injurious [ɪnˈdʒʊərɪəs] ADJ schädlich; **to be ~ to sb/sth** jdm/ einer Sache schaden or schädlich sein; **~ to health** gesundheitsschädigend or -schädlich

injury [ˈɪndʒərɪ] N Verletzung f (to +gen); (fig also) Kränkung f (to +gen); **to do sb/oneself an ~** sich/jdn verletzen; **to play ~ time** (Brit Sport) or **~ overtime** (US Sport) nachspielen

injustice [ɪnˈdʒʌstɪs] N (= unfairness, inequality) Ungerechtigkeit f; (= violation of sb's rights) Unrecht nt no pl; **to do sb an ~** jdm unrecht tun

ink [ɪŋk] N Tinte f; (Art) Tusche f; (Typ) Druckfarbe f; (for newsprint) Druckerschwärze f

ink IN CPDS Tinten-; (Art) Tusch-; **ink drawing** N Tuschzeichnung f; **ink-jet (printer)** N Tintenstrahldrucker m

inkling [ˈɪŋklɪŋ] N dunkle Ahnung; **he didn't have an ~** er hatte nicht die leiseste Ahnung or keinen blassen Schimmer (inf)

ink: ink pad N Stempelkissen nt; **inkstain** N Tintenfleck m; **inkwell** N Tintenfass nt (in eine Tischplatte eingelassen)

inky [ˈɪŋkɪ] ADJ (+ER) (a) (lit) tintenbeschmiert; **~ fingers** Tintenfinger pl **(b)** (fig) darkness, night tintenschwarz; blue, black tintig

inlaid [ɪnˈleɪd] **1** PTP of inlay **2** ADJ eingelegt; **~ table** Tisch m mit Einlegearbeit

inland [ˈɪnlænd] **1** ADJ binnenländisch; **~ town** Stadt f im Landesinneren; **~ waterway** Binnenwasserstraße f; **~ waterway transport** Binnenschifffahrt f **2** ADV landeinwärts

inland: inland lake N Binnensee m; **Inland Revenue** N (Brit) ≈ Finanzamt nt; **inland sea** N Binnenmeer nt

inlaw [ˈɪnlɔː] N angeheirateter Verwandter, angeheiratete Verwandte; **~s** (= parents-in-law) Schwiegereltern pl

inlay [ˈɪnleɪ] N Einlegearbeit f, Intarsien pl

inlet [ˈɪnlet] N **(a)** (of sea) Meeresarm m; (of river) Flussarm m **(b)** (Tech) Zuleitung f

in-line skates [ˈɪnlaɪnˌskeɪts] PL Inline-Skates pl

inmate [ˈɪnmeɪt] N Insasse m, Insassin f

inmost [ˈɪnməʊst] ADJ = innermost

inn [ɪn] N Gasthaus nt

innards [ˈɪnədz] PL Innereien pl (also fig), Eingeweide pl

innate [ɪˈneɪt] ADJ angeboren

innately [ɪˈneɪtlɪ] ADV von Natur aus

inner [ˈɪnəʳ] ADJ (lit, fig) innere(r, s); meaning verborgen; **~ side/ door** Innenseite/-tür f; **~ court/city** Innenhof m/-stadt f; **~ life** Seelenleben nt

inner: inner-city ADJ ATTR Innenstadt-; traffic innenstädtisch; housing in der Innenstadt; (= of cities generally) in den Innenstädten; decay, renewal, problem der Innenstadt/der Innenstädte; **~ area** Innenstadtbereich m; **innermost** ADJ innerste(r, s); his **~ being/heart** sein Innerstes; **inner tube** N Schlauch m

innings [ˈɪnɪŋz] N (Cricket) Innenrunde f; **he has had a good ~** (fig inf) er war lange an der Reihe; (= life) er hatte ein langes, ausgefülltes Leben

innocence [ˈɪnəsəns] N Unschuld f

innocent [ˈɪnəsənt] **1** ADJ **(a)** unschuldig; mistake unabsichtlich; **she is ~ of the crime** sie ist an dem Verbrechen unschuldig **(b)** question naiv; remark arglos; amusement harmlos **2** N Unschuld f

innocently [ˈɪnəsəntlɪ] ADV unschuldig; **the quarrel began ~ enough** der Streit begann ganz harmlos

innocuous ADJ, **innocuously** ADV [ɪˈnɒkjʊəs, -lɪ] harmlos

innovate [ˈɪnəʊveɪt] VI Neuerungen einführen

innovation [ˌɪnəʊˈveɪʃən] N Innovation f; (= *thing introduced also*) Neuerung f; **~ grant** Innovationszuschuss m

innovative [ˈɪnəˈveɪtɪv] ADJ innovativ; *idea* originell

innovator [ˈɪnəʊveɪtəʳ] N Neuerer m, Neuerin f

innuendo [ˌɪnjʊˈendəʊ] N, *pl* **-es** versteckte Andeutung; **sexual ~** sexuelle Anspielung

innumerable [ɪˈnjuːmərəbl] ADJ unzählig

inoculate [ɪˈnɒkjʊleɪt] VT impfen (*against* gegen)

inoculation [ɪˌnɒkjʊˈleɪʃən] N Impfung f

inoffensive [ˌɪnəˈfensɪv] ADJ harmlos

inoperable [ɪnˈɒpərəbl] ADJ inoperabel

inoperative [ɪnˈɒpərətɪv] ADJ **(a)** *law, rule* außer Kraft, ungültig **(b) to be ~** (*machine, radio*) nicht funktionieren

inopportune [ɪnˈɒpətjuːn] ADJ inopportun; *words* unpassend; **to be ~** ungelegen *or* zur Unzeit kommen

inordinate [ɪˈnɔːdɪnɪt] ADJ unmäßig; *number, size, sum of money* übermäßig; *demand, claim, fondness* übertrieben

inordinately [ɪˈnɔːdɪnɪtlɪ] ADV unmäßig; *large, high, long* übermäßig; **to be ~ fond of sth** etw allzu gern mögen

inorganic [ɪnɔːˈgænɪk] ADJ anorganisch

inpatient [ˈɪnpeɪʃənt] N stationär behandelter Patient/ behandelte Patientin

input [ˈɪnpʊt] **1** N **(a)** (*into computer*) Eingabe f; (*of capital*) Investition f; (*into project etc*) Beitrag m; **artistic/creative ~** künstlerische/kreative Beiträge pl; **~ port** (*Comput*) Eingabeport m; **~ tax** (*Brit*) Vorsteuer f **(b)** (= *point of ~, ~ terminal*) Eingang m **2** VT (*Comput*) eingeben

inquest [ˈɪnkwest] N (*Jur*) gerichtliche Untersuchung der Todesursache; (*fig*) Manöverkritik f

inquire, enquire [ɪnˈkwaɪəʳ] **1** VT sich erkundigen nach; **to ~ sth of sb** sich bei jdm nach etw erkundigen; **he ~d what/ whether/when** *etc* ... er erkundigte sich *or* fragte, was/ob/ wann *etc* ... **2** VI sich erkundigen (*about* nach); "**~ within**" „Näheres im Geschäft"
➤ **inquire about** *or* **after** VI +PREP OBJ sich erkundigen nach
➤ **inquire into** VI +PREP OBJ untersuchen

inquiring, enquiring [ɪnˈkwaɪərɪŋ] ADJ fragend; *mind* forschend

inquiry [ɪnˈkwaɪərɪ, (US) ˈɪnkwɪrɪ], **enquiry** [ɪnˈkwaɪərɪ] N, N **(a)** (= *question*) Anfrage f (*about* über +acc); (*for tourist information, direction etc*) Erkundigung f (*about* über +acc, nach); **to make inquiries** Erkundigungen einziehen; (*police etc*) Nachforschungen anstellen (*about sb* über jdn, *about sth* nach etw); **he is helping the police with their inquiries** (*euph*) er wird von der Polizei vernommen **(b)** (= *investigation*) Untersuchung f; **to hold an ~ into the cause of the accident** eine Untersuchung der Unfallursache durchführen

inquisitive [ɪnˈkwɪzɪtɪv] ADJ neugierig; (*for knowledge*) wissbegierig; **he's very ~ about my friends** er will alles über meine Freunde wissen

inquisitively [ɪnˈkwɪzɪtɪvlɪ] ADV neugierig

inroad [ˈɪnrəʊd] N (*fig*) **the Japanese are making ~s into the British market** die Japaner dringen in den britischen Markt ein; **these expenses are making great ~s into my bank account** diese Ausgaben greifen mein Bankkonto stark an

insane [ɪnˈseɪn] **1** ADJ **(a)** (*lit*) geisteskrank; (*fig inf*) wahnsinnig; **to drive sb ~** (*lit*) jdn um den Verstand bringen; (*fig inf*) jdn wahnsinnig machen; **that's ~!** (*inf*) das ist Wahnsinn! (*esp US*) **~ asylum/ward** Anstalt f/Abteilung f für Geisteskranke **2** PL **the ~** die Geisteskranken pl

insanely [ɪnˈseɪnlɪ] ADV irrsinnig

insanitary [ɪnˈsænɪtərɪ] ADJ unhygienisch

insanity [ɪnˈsænɪtɪ] N (*lit, fig*) Wahnsinn m

insatiable [ɪnˈseɪʃəbl] ADJ unersättlich; *curiosity, desire also* unstillbar

insatiably [ɪnˈseɪʃəblɪ] ADV **he is ~ hungry/curious** er hat einen unersättlichen Hunger/eine unstillbare Neugier

inscribe [ɪnˈskraɪb] VT **(a)** (*sth on sth* etw in etw *acc*) (*on ring, watch etc*) eingravieren; (*on rock, stone, wood*) einmeißeln; (*on tree*) einritzen **(b)** *book* eine Widmung schreiben in (+acc); **a watch, ~d ...** eine Uhr mit der Widmung ...

inscription [ɪnˈskrɪpʃən] N **(a)** Inschrift f; (*on coin*) Aufschrift f **(b)** (*in book*) Widmung f

inscrutable [ɪnˈskruːtəbl] ADJ unergründlich (*to* für); **~ face** undurchdringlicher Gesichtsausdruck

insect [ˈɪnsekt] N Insekt nt

insect bite N Insektenstich m

insecticide [ɪnˈsektɪsaɪd] N Insektengift nt, Insektizid nt (*form*)

insect repellent N Insektenbekämpfungsmittel nt

insecure [ˌɪnsɪˈkjʊəʳ] ADJ **(a)** unsicher; **~ future** ungesicherte Zukunft; **if they feel ~ in their jobs** wenn sie sich in ihrem Arbeitsplatz nicht sicher fühlen **(b)** *load, ladder* ungesichert

insecurity [ˌɪnsɪˈkjʊərɪtɪ] N Unsicherheit f

inseminate [ɪnˈsemɪneɪt] VT inseminieren (*spec*), befruchten; *cattle* besamen

insemination [ɪnˌsemɪˈneɪʃən] N Insemination f (*spec*), Befruchtung f; (*of cattle*) Besamung f

insensitive [ɪnˈsensɪtɪv] ADJ **(a)** (= *unfeeling, uncaring*) gefühllos; *remark* taktlos; *policy, action* rücksichtslos; **to be ~ to** *or* **about sb's problems/feelings** auf jds Probleme/Gefühle keine Rücksicht nehmen **(b)** (= *unappreciative*) unempfänglich; **to be ~ to the beauties of nature** *etc* für Schönheiten der Natur *etc* unempfänglich sein **(c)** (*physically*) unempfindlich (*to* gegen); **~ to pain/light** schmerz-/lichtunempfindlich

insensitivity [ɪnˌsensɪˈtɪvɪtɪ] N (= *unfeeling/uncaring attitude*) Gefühllosigkeit f (*towards* gegenüber); (*of remark*) Taktlosigkeit f; (*of policy, action*) Rücksichtslosigkeit f

inseparable [ɪnˈsepərəbl] ADJ untrennbar; *friends* unzertrennlich; **these two issues are ~** diese beiden Fragen sind untrennbar miteinander verbunden

inseparably [ɪnˈsepərəblɪ] ADV untrennbar

insert [ɪnˈsɜːt] **1** VT (= *stick into*) hineinstecken; (= *place in*) hineinlegen; (= *place between*) einfügen; *zip, pocket* einsetzen; *thermometer, suppository* einführen; *coin* einwerfen; (*Comput*) *disk* einlegen; **to ~ sth in(to) sth** (= *stick into*) etw in etw (*acc*) stecken; (= *place in*) etw in etw (*acc*) hineinlegen; (= *place between*) etw in etw (*acc*) einfügen; **to ~ an advert in a newspaper** eine Anzeige in die Zeitung setzen **2** [ˈɪnsɜːt] N (*in book*) Einlage f; (*in magazine*) Beilage f; (= *advertisement*) Inserat nt

insertion [ɪnˈsɜːʃən] N (= *sticking into*) Hineinstecken nt; (= *placing in*) Hineinlegen nt; (= *placing between*) Einfügen nt; (*of advert*) Aufgeben nt

in-service [ˈɪnˌsɜːvɪs] ADJ ATTR **~ training** (berufsbegleitende) Fortbildung

inset [ˈɪnset] N (*also* **~ map**) Nebenkarte f; (*on diagram*) Nebenbild nt

inshore [ˈɪnˈʃɔːʳ] **1** ADJ Küsten- **2** ADV in Küstennähe; **to go close ~** dicht an die Küste heranfahren

inside [ˈɪnˈsaɪd] **1** N **(a)** Innere(s) nt; (*of pavement*) Innenseite f; **the car overtook on the ~** das Auto überholte innen; **you'll have to ask someone on the ~** Sie müssen einen Insider *or* Eingeweihten fragen; **he's seen politics from the ~** er kennt die Politik von innen; **locked from** *or* **on the ~** von innen verschlossen; **the wind blew the umbrella ~ out** der Wind hat den Schirm umgestülpt; **your sweater's ~ out** du hast deinen Pullover links *or* verkehrt herum an; **to turn sth ~ out** etw umdrehen; (*fig*) *flat etc* etw auf den Kopf stellen; **to know sth ~ out** etw in- und auswendig kennen **(b)** (*inf*: = *stomach: also* **~s**) Eingeweide nt, Innere(s) nt **2** ADJ Innen-, innere(r, s); **it looks like an ~ job** (*crime*) es sieht nach dem Werk von Insidern aus (*inf*); **~ address** Empfängeranschrift f auf der Briefbogen; **~ leg measurement** innere Beinlänge; **~ pocket** Innentasche f **3** ADV innen; (= *indoors*) drin(nen); (*direction*) nach innen, herein; **look ~** sehen Sie innen; (= *search*) sehen Sie innen nach; **come ~!** kommen Sie herein!; **let's go ~** gehen wir hinein; **I heard music coming from ~** ich hörte von innen Musik; **to be ~** (*inf*: = *in prison*) sitzen (*inf*) **4** PREP (*esp US*: *also* **~ of**) **(a)** (*place*) innen in (+dat); (*direction*) in (+acc) ... (hinein); **don't let him come ~ the house** lassen Sie ihn nicht ins Haus (herein); **he was waiting ~ the house** er wartete im Haus; **something ~ me snapped** bei mir hakte etwas aus (*inf*) **(b)** (*time*) innerhalb; **he was 5 seconds ~ the record** er ist 5 Sekunden unter dem Rekord geblieben

inside: ~ **information** N Insiderinformationen pl; ~ **lane** N (*Sport*) Innenbahn f; (*Aut*) Innenspur f

insider [ɪnˈsaɪdəʳ] N Insider(in) m(f), Eingeweihte(r) mf

insider dealing, insider trading N (*Fin*) Insiderhandel m

insidious ADJ, **insidiously** ADV [ɪnˈsɪdɪəs, -lɪ] heimtückisch

insight ['ɪnsaɪt] N **(a)** NO PL Verständnis *nt*; **he lacks ~** ihm fehlt das Verständnis; **his ~ into my problems** sein Verständnis für meine Probleme **(b)** Einblick *m* (*into* in +*acc*); **to gain (an) ~ into sth** (einen) Einblick in etw gewinnen

insignia [ɪn'sɪgnɪə] PL Insignien *pl*

insignificance [ˌɪnsɪg'nɪfɪkəns] N Bedeutungslosigkeit *f*, Belanglosigkeit *f*

insignificant [ˌɪnsɪg'nɪfɪkənt] ADJ unbedeutend; *wound, alteration* geringfügig; *person, appearance* unscheinbar; *remark* belanglos

insincere [ˌɪnsɪn'sɪəʳ] ADJ unaufrichtig

insincerely [ˌɪnsɪn'sɪəlɪ] ADV unaufrichtig; *smile* falsch

insincerity [ˌɪnsɪn'serɪtɪ] N Unaufrichtigkeit *f*

insinuate [ɪn'sɪnjʊeɪt] VT **(a)** andeuten (*sth to sb* etw jdm gegenüber); **what are you insinuating?** was wollen Sie damit sagen?; **are you insinuating that I am lying?** willst du damit sagen, dass ich lüge? **(b) to ~ oneself into sb's favour** (*Brit*) *or* **favor** (*US*)/**the smart set** sich bei jdm/bei der Schickeria einschmeicheln

insinuating [ɪn'sɪnjʊeɪtɪŋ] ADJ anzüglich; *tone of voice* spitz

insinuation [ɪnˌsɪnjʊ'eɪʃən] N Anspielung *f* (*about* auf +*acc*); **he objected strongly to any ~ that ...** er wehrte sich heftig gegen jede Andeutung, dass ...

insipid [ɪn'sɪpɪd] ADJ fade; *colour* langweilig; *person, novel, lyrics* geistlos

insist [ɪn'sɪst] **1** VI **I ~!** ich bestehe darauf!; **if you ~** wenn Sie darauf bestehen; (= *if you like*) wenns unbedingt sein muss; **he ~s on his innocence** er behauptet beharrlich, unschuldig zu sein; **to ~ on a point** auf einem Punkt beharren; **to ~ on doing sth/on sb doing sth** darauf bestehen, etw zu tun/dass jd etw tut; **he will ~ on calling her by the wrong name** er redet sie beharrlich beim falschen Namen an **2** VT **to ~ that ...** darauf beharren *or* bestehen, dass ...; **he ~s that he is innocent** er behauptet beharrlich, unschuldig zu sein; **she ~s that she is right** sie besteht darauf, dass sie Recht hat

insistence [ɪn'sɪstəns] N Bestehen *nt* (*on* auf +*dat*); **I did it at his ~** ich tat es auf sein Drängen

insistent [ɪn'sɪstənt] ADJ **(a)** *person* hartnäckig; *salesman etc* aufdringlich; **he was most ~ about it** er beharrte *or* bestand hartnäckig darauf **(b)** *demand, tone* nachdrücklich, penetrant (*pej*); (= *constant*) unaufhörlich

insistently [ɪn'sɪstəntlɪ] ADV mit Nachdruck

in situ [ɪn'sɪtjuː] ADV in situ (*esp Med, Archeol*); **this part can be repaired ~** man braucht das Teil nicht auszubauen, um es zu reparieren

insofar [ˌɪnsəʊ'fɑːʳ] ADV **~ as** soweit

insole ['ɪnsəʊl] N Einlegesohle *f*; (= *part of shoe*) Brandsohle *f*

insolence ['ɪnsələns] N Unverschämtheit *f*, Frechheit *f*

insolent ADJ, **insolently** ADV ['ɪnsələnt, -lɪ] unverschämt, frech

insoluble [ɪn'sɒljʊbl] ADJ **(a)** *substance* unlöslich **(b)** *problem* unlösbar

insolvency [ɪn'sɒlvənsɪ] N Zahlungsunfähigkeit *f*, Insolvenz *f* (*geh*)

insolvent [ɪn'sɒlvənt] ADJ zahlungsunfähig, insolvent (*geh*)

insomnia [ɪn'sɒmnɪə] N Schlaflosigkeit *f*

insomniac [ɪn'sɒmnɪæk] N **to be an ~** an Schlaflosigkeit leiden

insomuch [ˌɪnsəʊ'mʌtʃ] ADV = **inasmuch**

inspect [ɪn'spekt] VT kontrollieren, prüfen; *school, hotel etc* inspizieren; **to ~ sth for sth** etw auf etw (*acc*) (hin) prüfen *or* kontrollieren

inspection [ɪn'spekʃən] N Kontrolle *f*, Prüfung *f*; (*of school, hotel etc*) Inspektion *f*; **to make an ~ of sth** etw kontrollieren *or* prüfen; *of school etc* etw inspizieren; **on ~** bei näherer Betrachtung

inspector [ɪn'spektəʳ] N (= *factory ~, on buses, trains*) Kontrolleur(in) *m(f)*; (*of schools*) Schulrat *m*, Schulrätin *f*; (*of police*) Polizeiinspektor(in) *m(f)*; (*higher*) Kommissar(in) *m(f)*

inspiration [ˌɪnspə'reɪʃən] N Inspiration *f* (*for* zu *or* für); **he gets his ~ from ...** er lässt sich von ... inspirieren; **his courage has been an ~ to us all** sein Mut hat uns alle inspiriert

inspirational [ˌɪnspə'reɪʃənl] ADJ inspirativ

inspire [ɪn'spaɪəʳ] VT **(a)** *respect, trust, awe* einflößen (*in sb* jdm); *hope, confidence etc* (er)wecken (*in* in +*dat*); *hate, fear* hervorrufen (*in* bei) **(b)** *person* inspirieren; **the book was ~d**

by a real person die Inspiration zu dem Buch kommt von einer wirklichen Person

inspired [ɪn'spaɪəd] ADJ genial; *author, performer, athlete etc* inspiriert; **it was an ~ guess/choice** das war genial geraten/gewählt; **the strike was politically ~** der Streik war politisch motiviert

inspiring [ɪn'spaɪərɪŋ] ADJ inspirierend; **she is an ~ teacher** als Lehrerin ist sie eine Inspiration

inst. ABBR *of* **instant** d. M.

instability [ˌɪnstə'bɪlɪtɪ] N Instabilität *f*

install [ɪn'stɔːl] VT installieren; *bathroom, fireplace* einbauen; *person* (in ein Amt) einführen; *government* einsetzen; **to have electricity ~ed** ans Elektrizitätsnetz angeschlossen werden

installation [ˌɪnstə'leɪʃən] N **(a)** (= *action*) Installation *f*; (*of telephone*) Anschluss *m*; (*of bath, kitchen, engine etc*) Einbau *m*; **~ program** (*Comput*) Installationsprogramm *nt* **(b)** (= *machine etc*) Anlage *f*, Einrichtung *f*

installment plan N (*US*) Ratenzahlung *f*; **to buy on the ~** auf Raten kaufen

instalment, (*US*) **installment** [ɪn'stɔːlmənt] N **(a)** (*of story, serial*) Fortsetzung *f*; (*Rad, TV*) (Sende)folge *f* **(b)** (*Fin, Comm*) Rate *f*; **monthly ~** Monatsrate *f*; **to pay in** *or* **by ~s** in Raten *or* ratenweise bezahlen

instance ['ɪnstəns] N (= *example*) Beispiel *nt*; (= *case*) Fall *m*; **for ~** zum Beispiel; **in the first ~** zuerst *or* zunächst (einmal)

instant ['ɪnstənt] **1** ADJ **(a)** unmittelbar **(b)** (*Cook*) Instant-; **~ mashed potatoes** fertiger Kartoffelbrei **2** N Augenblick *m*; **this (very) ~** auf der Stelle; **it was all over in an ~** in einem Augenblick war alles vorbei; **he left the ~ he heard the news** er ging sofort, als er die Nachricht hörte

instant access N (*Fin, Comput*) sofortiger Zugriff (*to* auf); **~ account** Sparkonto ohne Zugriffsbeschränkungen

instantaneous [ˌɪnstən'teɪnɪəs] ADJ unmittelbar; **death was ~** der Tod trat sofort ein

instantaneously [ˌɪnstən'teɪnɪəslɪ] ADV sofort, unverzüglich

instant: instant camera N Sofortbildkamera *f*; **instant coffee** N Pulver- *or* Instantkaffee *m*

instantly ['ɪnstəntlɪ] ADV sofort

instant replay N (*TV*) Wiederholung *f*

instead [ɪn'sted] **1** PREP **~ of** statt (+*gen or* (*inf*) +*dat*), anstelle von; **~ of going to school** (an)statt zur Schule zu gehen; **~ of that** statt dessen; **his brother came ~ of him** sein Bruder kam an seiner Stelle *or* statt ihm (*inf*) **2** ADV stattdessen, dafür; **if he doesn't want to go, I'll go ~** wenn er nicht gehen will, gehe ich (stattdessen)

instep ['ɪnstep] N **(a)** (*Anat*) Spann *m* **(b)** (*of shoe*) Blatt *nt*

instigate ['ɪnstɪgeɪt] VT anstiften; *violence* aufrufen zu; *new idea, reform etc* initiieren

instigation [ˌɪnstɪ'geɪʃən] N **at sb's ~** auf jds Betreiben *or* Veranlassung

instigator ['ɪnstɪgeɪtəʳ] N (*of crime etc*) Anstifter(in) *m(f)*; (*of new idea, reform etc*) Initiator(in) *m(f)*

instil, (*US*) **instill** [ɪn'stɪl] VT einflößen (*into sb* jdm); *knowledge, attitudes, discipline* beibringen (*into sb* jdm)

instinct ['ɪnstɪŋkt] N Instinkt *m*; **the sex/survival ~** der Geschlechts-/Überlebenstrieb; **by** *or* **from ~** instinktiv; **to have an ~ for business, to have a good business ~** einen ausgeprägten Geschäftssinn *or* -instinkt haben; **to follow one's ~s** sich auf seinen Instinkt verlassen

instinctive ADJ, **instinctively** ADV [ɪn'stɪŋktɪv, -lɪ] instinktiv

institute ['ɪnstɪtjuːt] **1** VT **(a)** *new laws, reforms etc* einführen; *organization etc* einrichten; *search* einleiten **(b)** (*Jur*) *inquiry* einleiten; *proceedings* anstrengen (*against* gegen) **2** N Institut *nt*; **Institute of Technology/Education** technische/pädagogische Hochschule; **women's ~** Frauenverein *m*

institution [ˌɪnstɪ'tjuːʃən] N Institution *f*, Einrichtung *f*; (= *organization also*) Einrichtung *f*; (= *building, home etc*) Anstalt *f*

institutional [ˌɪnstɪ'tjuːʃənl] ADJ institutionell; **~ care** Anstaltspflege *f*

institutionalized [ˌɪnstɪ'tjuːʃənəlaɪzd] ADJ institutionalisiert; **homelessness and destitution are becoming ~ here** Obdachlosigkeit und Elend werden hier zur Norm

in-store ['ɪnstɔːʳ] ADJ ATTR im Laden

instruct [ɪn'strʌkt] VT **(a)** (= *teach*) unterrichten **(b)** (= *tell, direct*) anweisen; (= *command*) die Anweisung erteilen (+*dat*);

(*Brit Jur*) *solicitor* unterrichten; (= *appoint*) *lawyer* beauftragen; **I've been ~ed to report to you** ich habe (An)weisung, Ihnen Meldung zu erstatten

instruction [ɪnˈstrʌkʃən] N **(a)** (= *teaching*) Unterricht *m*; **to give sb ~ in fencing** jdm Fechtunterricht erteilen **(b)** (= *order, command*) Anweisung *f*, Instruktion *f*; **what were your ~s?** welche Instruktionen *or* Anweisungen hatten Sie?; **~s for use** Gebrauchsanweisung *f*; **~ manual** (*Tech*) Bedienungsanleitung *f*

instructive [ɪnˈstrʌktɪv] ADJ instruktiv, aufschlussreich; (= *of educational value*) lehrreich

instructor [ɪnˈstrʌktəʳ] N (*also Sport*) Lehrer *m*; (*US*) Dozent *m*

instructress [ɪnˈstrʌktrɪs] N (*also Sport*) Lehrerin *f*; (*US*) Dozentin *f*

instrument [ˈɪnstrʊmənt] N **(a)** (*Mus, Med, Tech*) Instrument *nt* **(b)** (*fig*) Werkzeug *nt*

instrumental [ˌɪnstrʊˈmentl] ADJ **(a)** *role* entscheidend; **she was ~ in my release** sie hat bei meiner Freilassung eine entscheidende Rolle gespielt; **he was ~ in getting her the job** er hat ihr zu dieser Stelle verholfen **(b)** (*Mus*) Instrumental-; **~ music/version** Instrumentalmusik *f*/-version *f*

instrumentalist [ˌɪnstrʊˈmentəlɪst] N Instrumentalist(in) *m(f)*

instrumentation [ˌɪnstrʊmənˈteɪʃən] N Instrumentation *f*

instrument panel N (*Aviat*) Instrumententafel *f*; (*Aut*) Armaturenbrett *nt*

insubordinate [ˌɪnsəˈbɔːdɪnət] ADJ aufsässig

insubordination [ˈɪnsəˌbɔːdɪˈneɪʃən] N Aufsässigkeit *f*

insubstantial [ˌɪnsəbˈstænʃəl] ADJ wenig substanziell; *fear, hopes, accusation, rumour* gegenstandslos; *argument* haltlos; *amount* gering(fügig); *meal, plot, evidence* dürftig

insufferable ADJ, **insufferably** ADV [ɪnˈsʌfərəbl, -lɪ] unerträglich

insufficient [ˌɪnsəˈfɪʃənt] ADJ nicht genügend; **~ evidence** Mangel *m* an Beweisen; **~ funds** (*Fin*) mangelnde Deckung

insufficiently [ˌɪnsəˈfɪʃəntlɪ] ADV ungenügend, unzulänglich

insular [ˈɪnsjələʳ] ADJ (= *narrow-minded*) engstirnig

insularity [ˌɪnsjʊˈlærɪtɪ] N (= *narrow-mindedness*) Engstirnigkeit *f*

insulate [ˈɪnsjʊleɪt] VT **(a)** (*lit*) isolieren **(b)** (*fig: from unpleasantness etc*) abschirmen (*from gegen*)

insulating [ˈɪnsjʊleɪtɪŋ]: **insulating material** N Isoliermaterial *nt*; **insulating tape** N Isolierband *nt*

insulation [ˌɪnsjʊˈleɪʃən] N (*lit*) Isolierung *f*; (= *material*) Isoliermaterial *nt*

insulin [ˈɪnsjʊlɪn] N Insulin *nt*

insult [ɪnˈsʌlt] **▮** VT beleidigen **▮** [ˈɪnsʌlt] N Beleidigung *f*; **an ~ to my intelligence** eine Beleidigung meiner Intelligenz; **to add ~ to injury** das Ganze noch schlimmer machen

insulting [ɪnˈsʌltɪŋ] ADJ beleidigend; *question* unverschämt; **he was very ~ to her** er hat sich ihr gegenüber sehr beleidigend geäußert

insultingly [ɪnˈsʌltɪŋlɪ] ADV beleidigend; *behave* in beleidigender Weise

insuperable [ɪnˈsuːpərəbl] ADJ unüberwindlich

insurable [ɪnˈʃʊərəbl] ADJ versicherbar; **~ interest** versicherbares *or* versicherungsfähiges Interesse

insurance [ɪnˈʃʊərəns] N Versicherung *f*; (= *amount paid out*) Versicherungssumme *f*; **to take out ~** eine Versicherung abschließen (*against gegen*); **contract of ~** Versicherungsvertrag *m*

insurance: **insurance adjuster** N (*US*) Schadenssachverständige(r) *m(f)*; **insurance broker** N Versicherungsmakler(in) *m(f)*; **insurance certificate** N Versicherungspolice *f*, Versicherungsschein *m*; **insurance company** N Versicherungsgesellschaft *f*; **insurance policy** N Versicherungspolice *f*; **to take out an ~** eine Versicherung abschließen; **as an ~ against sth** (*fig*) als Sicherheitsvorkehrung gegen etw

insure [ɪnˈʃʊəʳ] VT versichern (lassen) (*against gegen*); **he ~d his house contents for £10,000** er schloss eine Hausratversicherung über £ 10.000 ab; **to ~ one's life** eine Lebensversicherung abschließen

insured [ɪnˈʃʊəd] **▮** ADJ versichert (*by, with* bei); **~ against fire** feuerversichert; **~ value** Versicherungswert *m* **▮** N **the ~** **(party)** der Versicherungsnehmer, die Versicherungsnehmerin

insurer [ɪnˈʃʊərəʳ] N Versicherer *m*, Versicherungsgeber *m*

insurmountable [ˌɪnsəˈmaʊntəbl] ADJ unüberwindlich

insurrection [ˌɪnsəˈrekʃən] N Aufstand *m*

intact [ɪnˈtækt] ADJ intakt; (= *not damaged also*) unversehrt; **not one window was left ~** kein einziges Fenster blieb ganz *or* heil; **his confidence remained ~** sein Vertrauen blieb ungebrochen *or* unerschüttert

intake [ˈɪnteɪk] N **(a)** **food ~** Nahrungsaufnahme *f*; **(sharp) ~ of breath** (plötzlicher) Atemzug **(b)** (*Sch, of immigrants*) Aufnahme *f*; (*Mil*) Rekrutierung *f*; **the latest ~ of graduates into our company** die Hochschulabsolventen, die kürzlich in unserer Firma eingestellt worden sind

intangible [ɪnˈtændʒəbl] ADJ unbestimmbar

intangible assets PL (*Jur, Comm*) immaterielle Werte *pl*

integer [ˈɪntɪdʒəʳ] N ganze Zahl

integral [ˈɪntɪgrəl] ADJ wesentlich, integral (*geh*); **to be ~ to sth** ein wesentlicher Bestandteil einer Sache (*gen*) sein

integrate [ˈɪntɪgreɪt] **▮** VT integrieren; **to ~ sb into** *or* **with sth** jdn in etw (*acc*) integrieren; **to ~ sth into sth** etw in etw (*acc*) integrieren; **to ~ sth with sth** etw auf etw (*acc*) abstimmen; **to ~ a school/college** (*US*) eine Schule/ein College auch für Schwarze *etc* zugänglich machen **▮** VI (*US: schools etc*) auch für Schwarze *etc* zugänglich werden

integrated [ˈɪntɪgreɪtɪd] ADJ integriert; *plan, piece of work* einheitlich; *school, town* ohne Rassentrennung

integration [ˌɪntɪˈgreɪʃən] N Integration *f* (*into* in +*acc*); **(racial) ~** Rassenintegration *f*

integrationist [ˌɪntɪˈgreɪʃənɪst] N (*US*) Vertreter(in) *m(f)* der Rassenintegration

integrity [ɪnˈtegrɪtɪ] N **(a)** (= *honesty*) Integrität *f* **(b)** (= *wholeness*) Einheit *f*

intellect [ˈɪntɪlekt] N **(a)** Intellekt *m*; **a man of keen ~** ein Mensch *m* mit einem scharfen Intellekt **(b)** (= *person*) großer Geist

intellectual [ˌɪntɪˈlektjʊəl] **▮** ADJ intellektuell; *freedom, climate, property, activity, interests* geistig **▮** N Intellektuelle(r) *mf*

intellectualize [ˌɪntɪˈlektjʊəlaɪz] VT intellektualisieren

intellectually [ˌɪntɪˈlektjʊəlɪ] ADV intellektuell

intelligence [ɪnˈtelɪdʒəns] N **(a)** Intelligenz *f*; **a man of little ~** ein Mensch von geringer Intelligenz; **if he hasn't got the ~ to wear a coat** wenn er nicht gescheit genug ist, einen Mantel anzuziehen **(b)** (= *news, information*) Informationen *pl* **(c)** (*Mil etc*) Geheim- *or* Nachrichtendienst *m*

intelligence: **intelligence service** N (*Pol*) Geheim- *or* Nachrichtendienst *m*; **intelligence test** N Intelligenztest *m*

intelligent ADJ, **intelligently** ADV [ɪnˈtelɪdʒənt, -lɪ] intelligent

intelligentsia [ɪnˌtelɪˈdʒentsɪə] N Intelligenz *f*

intelligible [ɪnˈtelɪdʒəbl] ADJ*pred* verständlich (*to sb* für jdn)

intemperate [ɪnˈtempərɪt] ADJ *person* maßlos; *language, comment* ausfallend, unbeherrscht

intend [ɪnˈtend] VT beabsichtigen; (+*n also*) wollen; (+*vb also*) fest vorhaben; **I ~ed no harm** es war (von mir) nicht böse gemeint; (*with action*) ich hatte nichts Böses beabsichtigt; **did you ~ that?** hatten Sie das beabsichtigt?; **it was ~ed as a compliment** das sollte ein Kompliment sein; **I wondered what he ~ed by that remark** ich fragte mich, was er mit dieser Bemerkung beabsichtigte; **this park is ~ed for the general public** dieser Park ist für die Öffentlichkeit gedacht *or* bestimmt; **I ~ to leave next year** ich beabsichtige *or* habe vor, nächstes Jahr zu gehen; **what do you ~ to do about it?** was beabsichtigen Sie, dagegen zu tun?; **this is ~ed to help me** das soll mir helfen; **did you ~ that to happen?** hatten Sie das beabsichtigt?

intended [ɪnˈtendɪd] **▮** ADJ *effect* beabsichtigt; *victim* ausgeguckt; *target* anvisiert **▮** N **my ~** (*inf*) mein Zukünftiger (*inf*), meine Zukünftige (*inf*)

intense [ɪnˈtens] ADJ intensiv; *disappointment* bitter; *pressure, interest, enthusiasm* enorm; *joy, effort* riesig; *heat, cold* ungeheuer; *desire* brennend; *competition, fighting, debate, speculation* heftig; *hatred, jealousy, anger* rasend; *person* ernsthaft

intensely [ɪnˈtenslɪ] ADV **(a)** (= *extremely*) äußerst; **I dislike it ~** ich kann es absolut nicht ausstehen **(b)** *feel, live, stare, study* intensiv

intensify [ɪnˈtensɪfaɪ] **▮** VT intensivieren; *meaning, fears* verstärken; *conflict, competition* verschärfen **▮** VI zunehmen

intensity [ɪnˈtensɪtɪ] N Intensität f

intensive [ɪnˈtensɪv] ADJ intensiv, Intensiv-; **to be in ~ care** (Med) auf der Intensivstation sein; **~ care unit** Intensivstation f; **~ farming** intensive Landwirtschaft

intensively [ɪnˈtensɪvlɪ] ADV intensiv

intent [ɪnˈtent] **1** N Absicht f; **to all ~s and purposes** im Grunde; **with ~ to** (esp Jur) in der Absicht or mit dem Vorsatz zu **2** ADJ **(a)** look durchdringend, forschend **(b) to be ~ on achieving sth** fest entschlossen sein, etw zu erreichen; **they were ~ on winning** sie wollten unbedingt gewinnen

intention [ɪnˈtenʃən] N **(a)** Absicht f, Intention f; **what was your ~ in publishing the article?** mit welcher Absicht haben Sie den Artikel veröffentlicht?; **it is my ~ to punish you severely** ich beabsichtige, Sie streng zu bestrafen; **I have every ~ of doing it** ich habe die feste Absicht, das zu tun; **to have no ~ of doing sth** nicht die Absicht haben, etw zu tun; **with the best of ~s** in der besten Absicht; **with the ~ of ...** in der Absicht zu ...
(b) ~s (inf) (Heirats)absichten pl; **his ~s are honourable** er hat ehrliche Absichten

intentional [ɪnˈtenʃənl] ADJ absichtlich, vorsätzlich (esp Jur); **it wasn't ~** das war keine Absicht

intentionally [ɪnˈtenʃənlɪ] ADV absichtlich

intently [ɪnˈtentlɪ] ADV konzentriert

inter [ɪnˈtɜːʳ] VT (form) bestatten

inter- [ˈɪntəʳ-] PREF zwischen-, Zwischen-; (esp with foreign words) inter-, Inter-; **~personal** zwischenmenschlich; **~disciplinary** interdisziplinär

interact [ˌɪntərˈækt] VI aufeinander wirken; (Phys) wechselwirken; (Psychol, Sociol) interagieren

interaction [ˌɪntərˈækʃən] N gegenseitige Einwirkung; (Phys) Wechselwirkung f; (Psychol, Sociol) Interaktion f

interactive [ˌɪntərˈæktɪv] ADJ interaktiv; **~ television** ineraktives Fernsehen

intercede [ˌɪntəˈsiːd] VI sich einsetzen, sich verwenden (with bei, for, on behalf of für); (in argument) vermitteln

intercept [ˌɪntəˈsept] VT abfangen; **they ~ed the enemy** sie schnitten dem Feind den Weg ab

interchange [ˈɪntəˌtʃeɪndʒ] N **(a)** (of roads) Kreuzung f; (of motorways) (Autobahn)kreuz nt **(b)** (= exchange) Austausch m

interchangeable [ˌɪntəˈtʃeɪndʒəbl] ADJ austauschbar; **the front wheels are ~ with the back ones** Vorder- und Hinterräder sind austauschbar

interchangeably [ˌɪntəˈtʃeɪndʒəblɪ] ADV **they are used ~** sie können ausgetauscht werden

intercity [ˌɪntəˈsɪtɪ] ADJ Intercity-; **~ train** Intercityzug m

intercollegiate [ˈɪntəkəˈliːdʒət] ADJ zwischen Colleges

intercom [ˈɪntəkɒm] N (Gegen)sprechanlage f; (in ship, plane) Bordverständigungsanlage f; (in schools etc) Lautsprecheranlage f

interconnect [ˌɪntəkəˈnekt] **1** VT **~ed problems/events** etc zusammenhängende Probleme/Ereignisse etc; **are these events ~ed in any way?** besteht irgendein Zusammenhang zwischen diesen Vorfällen? **2** VI in Zusammenhang stehen

intercontinental [ˈɪntəˌkɒntɪˈnentl] ADJ interkontinental, Interkontinental-; **~ ballistic missile** ballistische Interkontinentalrakete f

intercourse [ˈɪntəkɔːs] N Verkehr m; **human ~** Verkehr m mit Menschen; **social ~** gesellschaftlicher Verkehr; **(sexual) ~** (Geschlechts)verkehr m

interdepartmental [ˈɪntəˌdiːpɑːtˈmentl] ADJ relations, quarrel zwischen den Abteilungen; conference, projects mehrere Abteilungen betreffend; committee abteilungsübergreifend

interdependent [ˌɪntədɪˈpendənt] ADJ wechselseitig voneinander abhängig

interest [ˈɪntrɪst] **1** N **(a)** Interesse nt (in für); **do you have any ~ in chess?** interessieren Sie sich für Schach?; **to take an ~ in sb/sth** sich für jdn/etw interessieren; **to show (an) ~ in sb/sth** Interesse für jdn/etw zeigen; **is it of any ~ to you?** (= do you want it?) sind Sie daran interessiert?; **he has lost ~** er hat das Interesse verloren; **his ~s are ...** er interessiert sich für ...; **to act in sb's/one's own (best) ~(s)** in jds/im eigenen Interesse handeln; **in the ~(s) of sth** im Interesse einer Sache (gen); **in the public ~** im öffentlichen Interesse
(b) (Fin) Zinsen pl; **~ on an investment** Zinsen aus einer Kapitalanlage; **to bear ~ at 4%** mit 4% verzinst sein; **to repay a loan with ~** ein Darlehen mit Zins und Zinseszins zurückzahlen; **~ cover** Verhältnis zwischen Gewinn vor Steuern und dem Zinsaufwand für Bankkredite, Anleihen usw.
(c) (Comm) (= share, stake) Anteil m; (= group) Kreise pl, Interessentengruppe f; **shipping/oil ~s** (= shares) Reederei-/ Ölanteile pl; (= people) Reedereikreise pl/Vertreter pl von Ölinteressen; **he has a financial ~ in the company** er ist finanziell an der Firma beteiligt; **German ~s in Africa** deutsche Interessen pl in Afrika
2 VT interessieren (in für, an +dat); **to ~ sb in doing sth** jdn dafür interessieren, etw zu tun; **can I ~ you in a drink?** kann ich Sie zu etwas Alkoholischem überreden?

interest-bearing [ˈɪntrɪstˌbeərɪŋ] ADJ zinsbringend

interested [ˈɪntrɪstɪd] ADJ **(a)** interessiert (in an +dat); **I'm not ~** das interessiert mich nicht; **to be ~ in sb/sth** sich für jdn/etw interessieren, an jdm/etw interessiert sein; **I'm going to the cinema, are you ~ (in coming)?** ich gehe ins Kino, haben Sie Lust mitzukommen?; **I'm selling my car, are you ~?** ich verkaufe meinen Wagen, sind Sie interessiert?; **the company is ~ in expanding its sales** die Firma hat Interesse daran or ist daran interessiert, ihren Absatz zu vergrößern; **I'd be ~ to know how ...** es würde mich ja schon interessieren, wie ...; **to get sb ~ (in sth)** jdn (für etw) interessieren
(b) (= having personal or financial interest) befangen; (= involved) beteiligt; **he is an ~ party** er ist befangen, er ist daran beteiligt

interest: interest-free ADJ, ADV zinslos; **interest group** N Interessengruppe f

interesting [ˈɪntrɪstɪŋ] ADJ interessant; **the ~ thing about it is that ...** das Interessante daran ist, dass ...

interestingly [ˈɪntrɪstɪŋlɪ] ADV **~ enough, I saw him yesterday** interessanterweise habe ich ihn gestern gesehen

interest rate N (Fin) Zinssatz m

interface [ˈɪntəfeɪs] N **(a)** Grenzfläche f; **there's a bigger ~ between these two fields than I thought** diese beiden Gebiete haben mehr Berührungspunkte, als ich gedacht hätte
(b) (Comput) Schnittstelle f, Interface nt

interfere [ˌɪntəˈfɪəʳ] VI (in argument, sb's affairs) sich einmischen (in in +acc); (with machinery, sb's property) sich zu schaffen machen (with an +dat); (euph: sexually) sich vergehen (with an +dat); **don't ~ with the machine** lass die Finger von der Maschine; **to ~ with sth** (= disrupt) etw stören (also Rad); **with work, ability to do sth** etw beeinträchtigen; **to ~ with sb's plans** jds Pläne durchkreuzen

interference [ˌɪntəˈfɪərəns] N **(a)** (= meddling) Einmischung f **(b)** (= disruption, Rad, TV) Störung f (with +gen)

interfering [ˌɪntəˈfɪərɪŋ] ADJ person sich ständig einmischend

intergovernmental [ˌɪntəgʌvənˈmentl] ADJ zwischenstaatlich

interim [ˈɪntərɪm] **1** N Zwischenzeit f; **in the ~** in der Zwischenzeit **2** ADJ vorläufig; **~ agreement/solution** Übergangsabkommen nt/-lösung f; **~ report** Zwischenbericht m; **~ government/president** Interims- or Übergangsregierung f/-präsident(in) m(f); **~ period** Zwischenzeit f; (= transitional) Übergangszeit f; **~ payment** Interimszahlung f

interior [ɪnˈtɪərɪəʳ] **1** ADJ Innen-; **~ wall** Innenwand f; **~ minister** Innenminister(in) m(f); **~ ministry** Innenministerium nt **2** N (of country) Innere(s) nt; (of house) Innenausstattung f, Interieur nt (geh); **Department of the Interior** (US) Innenministerium nt; **the ~ of the house has been newly decorated** das Haus ist innen neu gemacht

interior: interior angle N Innenwinkel m; **interior decoration** N Innenausstattung f; **interior decorator** N Innenausstatter(in) m(f); **interior design** N Innenarchitektur f; **interior designer** N Innenarchitekt(in) m(f)

interject [ˌɪntəˈdʒekt] VT einwerfen; **..., he ~ed ...**, rief er dazwischen

interjection [ˌɪntəˈdʒekʃən] N (= exclamation) Ausruf m; (= remark) Einwurf m

interlibrary loan [ˈɪntəˌlaɪbrənˈləʊn] N Fernleihe f; **to have a book on ~** ein Buch über die Fernleihe (ausgeliehen) haben

interlink [ˌɪntəˈlɪŋk] VI ineinander hängen; (fig: theories etc) zusammenhängen; **a transport network with bus and rail services ~ing** ein Verkehrsnetz nt, in dem Bus und Bahn im Verbund fahren

interlock [ˌɪntəˈlɒk] VI ineinander greifen; (fig) verkettet sein

interlocutor [ˌɪntəˈlɒkjʊtəʳ] N Gesprächspartner(in) m(f); (asking questions) Fragesteller(in) m(f)

interloper [ˈɪntələʊpəʳ] N Eindringling m

interlude [ˈɪntəluːd] N Periode f; (Theat) (= interval) Pause f; (= performance) Zwischenspiel nt; (Mus) Interludium nt; (= episode) Intermezzo nt; **a peaceful ~ in his busy life** eine friedliche Unterbrechung seines geschäftigen Lebens

intermediary [ˌɪntəˈmiːdɪərɪ] **1** N (Ver)mittler(in) m(f) **2** ADJ (= intermediate) mittlere(r, s); (= mediating) vermittelnd; ~ **role** Vermittlerrolle f

intermediate [ˌɪntəˈmiːdɪət] **1** ADJ Zwischen-; French, maths etc für fortgeschrittene Anfänger; ~ **stage** Zwischenstadium nt; **the ~ stations** die dazwischenliegenden Bahnhöfe; **an ~ student** ein fortgeschrittener Anfänger, eine fortgeschrittene Anfängerin **2** N fortgeschrittener Anfänger, fortgeschrittene Anfängerin

interminable [ɪnˈtɜːmɪnəbl] ADJ endlos; **after what seemed an ~ journey** nach einer Reise, die nicht enden zu wollen schien

interminably [ɪnˈtɜːmɪnəblɪ] ADV endlos, ewig

intermingle [ˌɪntəˈmɪŋɡl] VI sich mischen (with unter +acc)

intermission [ˌɪntəˈmɪʃən] N (Theat, Film) Pause f

intermittent [ˌɪntəˈmɪtənt] ADJ periodisch auftretend

intermittently [ˌɪntəˈmɪtəntlɪ] ADV periodisch

intern¹ [ɪnˈtɜːn] VT person internieren

intern² [ˈɪntɜːn] N (US) (a) (= junior doctor) Assistenzarzt m/ -ärztin f (b) (= trainee) Praktikant(in) m(f)

internal [ɪnˈtɜːnl] ADJ innere(r, s); (Math) angle, diameter Innen-; (= within country) Binnen-; (= within organization) intern; ~ **call** internes or innerbetriebliches Gespräch; ~ **flight** Inlandsflug m; **Internal Revenue Service** (US) Finanzamt nt; ~ **structure** (of company) interne (Unternehmens)struktur; ~ **trade** Binnenhandel m; ~ **wall** Innenwand f

internal: **internal affairs** PL innere Angelegenheiten pl, Inneres nt; **internal bleeding** N innere Blutungen pl; **internal combustion engine** N Verbrennungsmotor m

internally [ɪnˈtɜːnəlɪ] ADV innen, im Inneren; (= in body) innerlich; (= in country) landesintern; (= in organization) intern; **"not to be taken ~"** „nicht zum Einnehmen"

internal market N (Econ) Binnenmarkt m; (in health service etc, within organization) marktwirtschaftliche Struktur

international [ˌɪntəˈnæʃnəl] **1** ADJ international; ~ **access code** (Telec) internationale Vorwahl; ~ **economic order** Weltwirtschaftsordnung f; ~ **money order** Auslandsanweisung f; ~ **reply coupon** internationaler Rückantwortschein; ~ **trade relations** Weltwirtschaftsbeziehungen pl **2** N (Sport) (= match) Länderspiel nt; (= player) Nationalspieler(in) m(f)

International: **International Bank for Reconstruction and Development** N Internationale Bank für Wiederaufbau und Entwicklung; **International Chamber of Commerce** N Internationale Handelskammer; **International Court of Justice** N Internationaler Gerichtshof; **International Date Line** N Datumsgrenze f; **international law** N internationales Recht

internationally [ˌɪntəˈnæʃnəlɪ] ADV international; compete auf internationaler Ebene

International: **International Monetary Fund** N (Econ) Internationaler Währungsfonds; **International Phonetic Alphabet** N internationale Lautschrift

internecine [ˌɪntəˈniːsaɪn] ADJ (a) ~ **war** gegenseitiger Vernichtungskrieg (b) quarrel, conflict intern; ~ **strife** innere Zerrissenheit

internee [ˌɪntɜːˈniː] N Internierte(r) mf

Internet [ˈɪntənet] N **the ~** das Internet; **to surf the ~** im Internet surfen

Internet: **Internet banking** N Internetbanking nt; **Internet café** N Internet-Café nt; **Internet service provider** N Internet-Anbieter m

internment [ɪnˈtɜːnmənt] N Internierung f; ~ **camp** Internierungslager nt

internship [ˈɪntɜːnʃɪp] N (US) (a) (Med) Medizinalpraktikum nt (b) (as trainee) Praktikum nt

interplay [ˈɪntəpleɪ] N Zusammenspiel nt

Interpol [ˈɪntəpɒl] N Interpol f

interpolate [ɪnˈtɜːpəleɪt] VT remark einwerfen; matter into book etc einfügen

interpose [ˌɪntəˈpəʊz] VT (a) object zwischenstellen/-legen; **to ~ sth between two things** etw zwischen zwei Dinge stellen/legen; **to ~ oneself between two people** sich zwischen zwei Leute stellen (b) remark, question einwerfen

interpret [ɪnˈtɜːprɪt] **1** VT (a) (= translate orally) dolmetschen (b) (= explain, understand) auslegen, interpretieren (also Theat, Mus); omen, dream deuten; world verstehen; **how would you ~ what he said?** wie würden Sie seine Worte verstehen or auffassen? **2** VI dolmetschen

interpretation [ɪnˌtɜːprɪˈteɪʃən] N (= explanation) Auslegung f, Interpretation f (also Theat, Mus); (of omen, dream) Deutung f; (of world) Verständnis nt; **she put quite a different ~ on the figures** sie interpretierte die Zahlen ganz anders

interpreter [ɪnˈtɜːprɪtəʳ] N (a) Dolmetscher(in) m(f) (b) (Comput) Interpreter m

interpreting [ɪnˈtɜːprɪtɪŋ] N (= profession) Dolmetschen nt

interquartile [ˌɪntəˈkwɔːtaɪl] ADJ (Comm) Quartils-; ~ **range** Quartilsabstand m

interrelate [ˌɪntərɪˈleɪt] **1** VT **to be ~d** zueinander in Beziehung stehen **2** VI zueinander in Beziehung stehen; **this influences the way in which we ~ with others** das beeinflusst unsere Beziehungen zu anderen

interrogate [ɪnˈterəgeɪt] VT verhören; (father, headmaster etc) regelrecht verhören

interrogation [ɪnˌterəˈgeɪʃən] N Verhör nt

interrogative [ˌɪntəˈrɒgətɪv] **1** ADJ look, tone fragend; (Gram) Interrogativ-; ~ **pronoun/clause** Interrogativpronomen nt/ -satz m **2** N (Gram) (= pronoun) Interrogativpronomen nt, Fragefürwort nt; (= mood) Interrogativ m, Frageform f; **in the ~** in der Frageform

interrogator [ɪnˈterəgeɪtəʳ] N Vernehmungsbeamte(r) mf (form); **my ~s** die, die mich verhören

interrupt [ˌɪntəˈrʌpt] **1** VT unterbrechen (also Elec); (in conversation: rudely also) ins Wort fallen (+dat); activity, work, traffic flow also stören; view versperren **2** VI (in conversation) unterbrechen; (= ~ sb's work etc) stören; **stop ~ing!** fall mir/ ihm etc nicht dauernd ins Wort!

interruption [ˌɪntəˈrʌpʃən] N Unterbrechung f; (of work, activity, traffic flow also) Störung f

intersect [ˌɪntəˈsekt] VI sich kreuzen; (Geometry, in set theory) sich schneiden

intersection [ˌɪntəˈsekʃən] N (= crossroads) Kreuzung f; (Geometry) Schnittpunkt m; **point of ~** Schnittpunkt m

intersperse [ˌɪntəˈspɜːs] VT verteilen; ~**d with sth** mit etw dazwischen; **a speech ~d with quotations** eine mit Zitaten gespickte Rede; **periods of sunshine ~d with showers** von Schauern unterbrochener Sonnenschein

interstate [ˌɪntəˈsteɪt] **1** ADJ (US) zwischen den (US-Bundes)staaten, zwischenstaatlich; ~ **highway** Interstate Highway m **2** N (US) Interstate (Highway) m

intertwine [ˌɪntəˈtwaɪn] VI sich ineinander verschlingen; (threads) verschlungen sein; (fig: destinies) sich verbinden

interurban [ˌɪntəˈɜːbən] ADJ (US) railroad städteverbindend

interval [ˈɪntəvəl] N (a) (in space, time) Abstand m, Intervall nt (form); **at ~s** in Abständen; **at two-weekly ~s** in Abständen von zwei Wochen; **at ~s of two metres** (Brit) or **meters** (US) in Abständen von zwei Metern; **sunny ~s** (Met) Aufheiterungen pl (b) (Sch, Theat etc) Pause f (c) (Mus) Intervall nt

intervene [ˌIntəˈviːn] VI (person) einschreiten (in bei), intervenieren; (= interrupt) unterbrechen; (event, fate) dazwischenkommen

intervening [ˌɪntəˈviːnɪŋ] ADJ dazwischenliegend; **in the ~ period** in der Zwischenzeit

intervention [ˌɪntəˈvenʃən] N Eingreifen nt, Intervention f

interventionist [ˌɪntəˈvenʃənɪst] ADJ interventionistisch

interview [ˈɪntəvjuː] **1** N (a) (for job) Vorstellungsgespräch nt; (with authorities, employer etc) Gespräch nt; (for grant) Auswahlgespräch nt (b) (Press, TV etc) Interview nt **2** VT (a) job applicant ein/das Vorstellungsgespräch führen mit; applicant for grant etc Fragen stellen (+dat) (b) (Press, TV etc) interviewen **3** VI (for job) das Vorstellungsgespräch/die Vorstellungsgespräche führen (b) (Press, TV etc) interviewen

interviewee [ˌɪntəvjuːˈiː] N (for job) Kandidat(in) m(f) (für die Stelle); (Press, TV etc) Interviewte(r) mf

interviewer [ˈɪntəvjuːəʳ] N (*for job*) Leiter(in) *m(f)* des Vorstellungsgesprächs; (*Press, TV etc*) Interviewer(in) *m(f)*

interwar [ˈɪntəˈwɔːʳ] ADJ zwischen den Weltkriegen

interweave [ˌɪntəˈwiːv] ⬛ VT (*lit, fig*) verweben ⬛ VI sich verweben

intestate [ɪnˈtestɪt] ADJ (*Jur*) **to die** ~ ohne Testament sterben

intestinal [ɪnˈtestɪnl] ADJ Darm-; ~ **cancer** Darmkrebs *m*

intestine [ɪnˈtestɪn] N Darm *m*; **small/large** ~ Dünn-/Dickdarm *m*

intimacy [ˈɪntɪməsɪ] N Vertrautheit *f*; (*euph.* = *sexual* ~) Intimität *f*

intimate¹ [ˈɪntɪmɪt] ⬛ ADJ eng; *friend also* vertraut; (*sexually, fig*) intim; *feelings, thoughts also* geheim; **to be on** ~ **terms with sb** mit jdm auf vertraulichem Fuß stehen; **to be/become** ~ **with sb** mit jdm vertraut sein/werden; (*sexually*) mit jdm intim sein/werden; **to have an** ~ **knowledge of sth** über etw (*acc*) in allen Einzelheiten Bescheid wissen ⬛ N Vertraute(r) *mf*

intimate² [ˈɪntɪmeɪt] VT andeuten; **he** ~**d to them that they should stop** er gab ihnen zu verstehen, dass sie aufhören sollten

intimately [ˈɪntɪmɪtlɪ] ADV *acquainted* bestens; *related, connected* eng; *know* genau

intimidate [ɪnˈtɪmɪdeɪt] VT einschüchtern; **they** ~**d him into not telling the police** sie schüchterten ihn so ein, dass er der Polizei nichts erzählte

intimidation [ɪnˌtɪmɪˈdeɪʃən] N Einschüchterung *f*

into [ˈɪntʊ] PREP **(a)** in (+*acc*); *crash, drive* gegen; **to translate sth** ~ **French** etw ins Französische übersetzen; **to change euros** ~ **pounds** Euro in Pfund umtauschen; **to divide 3** ~ **9** 9 durch 3 teilen *or* dividieren; **3** ~ **9 goes 3** 3 geht dreimal in 9; **he's well** ~ **his sixties** er ist in den späten Sechzigern; **research** ~ **AIDS/cancer** Aids-/Krebsforschung *f*
(b) (*inf*) **to be** ~ **sb/sth** (= *like*) auf jdn/etw (*acc*) stehen (*inf*); (= *be interested in*) sich für jdn/etw interessieren; **to be** ~ **sth** (= *use*) drugs etc etw nehmen; **he's** ~ **wine** (= *likes*) er ist Weinliebhaber; (= *is expert*) er ist Weinkenner; **he's** ~ **computers** er ist Computerfan (*inf*)

intolerable ADJ, **intolerably** ADV [ɪnˈtɒlərəbl, -ɪ] unerträglich

intolerance [ɪnˈtɒlərəns] N Intoleranz *f* (*of* gegenüber)

intolerant [ɪnˈtɒlərənt] ADJ intolerant (*of* gegenüber)

intonation [ˌɪntəˈneɪʃən] N Intonation *f*

intoxicated [ɪnˈtɒksɪkeɪtɪd] ADJ betrunken, berauscht (*also fig*); **to become** ~ sich berauschen (*also fig*) (*by, with* an +*dat*, von); ~ **by** *or* **with success** vom Erfolg berauscht

intoxication [ɪnˌtɒksɪˈkeɪʃən] N Rausch *m* (*also fig*); **in a state of** ~ (*form*) im Rausch

intractable [ɪnˈtræktəbl] ADJ *metal* unnachgiebig; *nature, problem, illness* hartnäckig; *conflict* unlösbar; *issue* äußerst schwierig

intramural [ˌɪntrəˈmjʊərəl] ADJ (*esp Univ*) *course* innerhalb der Universität; *activities* studienspezifisch

intranet [ˈɪntrənet] N (*Comput*) Intranet *nt*

intransigence [ɪnˈtrænsɪdʒəns] N Unnachgiebigkeit *f*

intransigent [ɪnˈtrænsɪdʒənt] ADJ unnachgiebig

intransitive [ɪnˈtrænsɪtɪv] ADJ intransitiv

intrastate [ˌɪntrəˈsteɪt] ADJ (*US*) innerhalb des (Bundes)staates

intrauterine device [ˌɪntrəˈjuːtərəndɪˌvaɪs] N Intrauterinpessar *nt*

intravenous [ˌɪntrəˈviːnəs] ADJ intravenös; ~ **drip** (*Med*) intravenöse Infusion; ~ **drug user** Drogenabhängige(r) *mf*, der/die intravenös spritzt

intravenously [ˌɪntrəˈviːnəslɪ] ADV intravenös

in-tray [ˈɪntreɪ] N Ablage *f* für Eingänge

intrepid [ɪnˈtrepɪd] ADJ unerschrocken, kühn

intricacy [ˈɪntrɪkəsɪ] N Kompliziertheit *f*; (= *intricate part: of law, chess etc*) Feinheit *f*; **the intricacies of the job** die Feinheiten der Arbeit

intricate ADJ, **intricately** ADV [ˈɪntrɪkɪt, -ɪ] kompliziert

intrigue [ɪnˈtriːɡ] ⬛ VI intrigieren ⬛ VT (= *arouse interest of*) faszinieren; (= *arouse curiosity of*) neugierig machen; **to be** ~**d with** *or* **by sth** von etw fasziniert sein; **I would be** ~**d to know why ...** es würde mich schon interessieren, warum ...
⬛ [ˈɪntriːɡ] N (= *plot*) Intrige *f*; (*no pl*: = *plotting*) Intrigen(spiel *nt*) *pl*

intriguing [ɪnˈtriːɡɪŋ] ADJ faszinierend

intrinsic [ɪnˈtrɪnsɪk] ADJ *merit, value* immanent; (= *essential*) wesentlich; **financial insecurity is** ~ **to capitalism** finanzielle Unsicherheit gehört zum Wesen des Kapitalismus

intrinsically [ɪnˈtrɪnsɪkəlɪ] ADV an sich

intro [ˈɪntrəʊ] N (*inf*) ABBR *of* **introduction** Intro *nt* (*inf*)

introduce [ˌɪntrəˈdjuːs] VT **(a)** (*to person*) vorstellen (*to sb* jdm); (*butler*) ankündigen; (*to subject*) einführen (*to* in +*acc*); **I don't think we've been** ~**d** ich glaube nicht, dass wir uns kennen; **allow me to** *or* **let me** ~ **myself** darf ich mich vorstellen?; **who** ~**d him to heroin?** durch wen ist er ans Heroin geraten?
(b) *fashion, practice, reform, invention* einführen; (*Parl*) *bill* einbringen; *mood, competition* bringen (*into* in +*acc*); *book, subject, era* einleiten; *speaker, programme* ankündigen; **to** ~ **sth onto the market** etw auf dem Markt einführen
(c) (= *insert*) einführen (*into* in +*acc*)

introduction [ˌɪntrəˈdʌkʃən] N **(a)** (*to person*) Vorstellung *f*; **to make** *or* **perform the** ~**s** die Vorstellung übernehmen; **letter of** ~ Einführungsbrief *m or* -schreiben *nt*
(b) (= *introductory part: to book, music*) Einleitung *f* (*to* zu)
(c) (*of fashion, practice, reform etc*) Einführung *f*; (*of bill, competition*) Einbringen *nt*; **our next guest needs no** ~ unser nächster Gast braucht nicht vorgestellt zu werden; **an** ~ **to French** (= *elementary course*) eine Einführung ins Französische

introductory [ˌɪntrəˈdʌktərɪ] ADJ *page, paragraph, chapter* einleitend; *words, remarks* einführend; *course, fee, offer* Einführungs-; ~ **speech** Einführungsrede *f*

introspective [ˌɪntrəʊˈspektɪv] ADJ selbstbeobachtend, introspektiv (*geh*)

introvert [ˈɪntrəʊvɜːt] N (*Psych*) Introvertierte(r) *mf*; **to be an** ~ introvertiert sein

introverted [ˈɪntrəʊvɜːtɪd] ADJ introvertiert

intrude [ɪnˈtruːd] VI stören; **to** ~ **on sb** jdn stören; **to** ~ **on sb's privacy** jds Privatsphäre verletzen; **to** ~ **on a meeting** eine Besprechung stören; **personal feelings cannot be allowed to** ~ für persönliche Gefühle ist kein Platz

intruder [ɪnˈtruːdəʳ] N Eindringling *m*

intrusion [ɪnˈtruːʒən] N Störung *f*; **forgive the** ~**, I just wanted to ask ...** entschuldigen Sie, wenn ich hier so eindringe, ich wollte nur fragen ...

intrusive [ɪnˈtruːsɪv] ADJ *person* aufdringlich; *presence* störend; *government, legislation* einmischend

intuition [ˌɪntjuːˈɪʃən] N Intuition *f*

intuitive [ɪnˈtjuːɪtɪv] ADJ intuitiv; *guess, feeling, assessment* instinktiv

intuitively [ɪnˈtjuːɪtɪvlɪ] ADV intuitiv; ~ **I'd say 50** ich hätte instinktiv 50 gesagt

inundate [ˈɪnʌndeɪt] VT (*lit, fig*) überschwemmen; (*with work*) überhäufen; **have you a lot of work on? – I'm** ~**d** haben Sie viel Arbeit? – ich ersticke darin

inure [ɪnˈjʊəʳ] VT **to become** ~**d to sth** sich an etw (*acc*) gewöhnen; (*physically*) sich gegen etw abhärten; **to** *danger* sich gegen ein stählen

invade [ɪnˈveɪd] VT (*Mil*) einmarschieren in (+*acc*); (*fig*) überfallen, heimsuchen; *privacy* eindringen in (+*acc*), stören

invader [ɪnˈveɪdəʳ] N (*Mil*) Invasor *m*

invading [ɪnˈveɪdɪŋ] ADJ einmarschierend; *Vikings etc* einfallend; ~ **army/troops** Invasionsarmee *f*/-truppen *pl*

invalid¹ [ˈɪnvəlɪd] ⬛ ADJ **(a)** krank; (= *disabled*) körperbehindert **(b)** (= *for* ~s) Kranken-, Invaliden- ⬛ N Kranke(r) *mf*; (= *disabled person*) Invalide *m*, Invalidin *f*, Körperbehinderte(r) *mf*

➤ **invalid out** VT SEP **to be invalided out of the army** wegen Dienstunfähigkeit aus der Armee entlassen werden

invalid² [ɪnˈvælɪd] ADJ (*esp Jur*) ungültig; *deduction, argument* nicht stichhaltig; *assumption* nicht zulässig; **to declare sth** ~ etw für ungültig erklären

invalidate [ɪnˈvælɪdeɪt] VT ungültig machen; *theory* entkräften

invaluable [ɪnˈvæljʊəbl] ADJ unbezahlbar; *service, role, help, contribution* unschätzbar; *advice, experience* von unschätzbarem Wert; **to be** ~ **(to sb)** (für jdn) von unschätzbarem Wert sein

invariable [ɪnˈvɛərɪəbl] ADJ (*also Math*) unveränderlich; *reply, characteristic* gleich bleibend; *bad luck* konstant, ständig

invariably [ɪnˈvɛərɪəblɪ] ADV ständig, unweigerlich; **do you trust his judgement? – ~!** trauen Sie seinem Urteil? – ausnahmslos!

invasion [ɪnˈveɪʒən] N (*lit, fig*) Invasion *f*; (*of privacy etc*) Eingriff *m* (*of* in *+acc*); **the German ~ of Poland** der Einmarsch *or* Einfall der Deutschen in Polen

invasive [ɪnˈveɪsɪv] ADJ (*Med*) invasiv

invective [ɪnˈvɛktɪv] N Beschimpfungen *pl* (*against +gen*)

inveigh [ɪnˈveɪ] VI **to ~ against sb/sth** (*liter*) sich in Schimpfreden gegen jdn/etw ergehen (*geh*)

invent [ɪnˈvɛnt] VT erfinden

invention [ɪnˈvɛnʃən] N **(a)** Erfindung *f*; **of one's own ~** selbsterfunden **(b)** (= *inventiveness*) Fantasie *f*

inventive [ɪnˈvɛntɪv] ADJ *powers, skills, mind* schöpferisch; *novel, design, menu* einfallsreich; (= *resourceful*) erfinderisch

inventiveness [ɪnˈvɛntɪvnɪs] N Einfallsreichtum *m*

inventor [ɪnˈvɛntəʳ] N Erfinder(in) *m(f)*

inventory [ˈɪnvəntrɪ] N Bestandsaufnahme *f*; **to make** *or* **take an ~ of sth** Inventar von etw *or* den Bestand einer Sache (*gen*) aufnehmen; **~ turnover** (*US*) Lagerumschlag *m*

inverse [ˈɪnˈvɜːs] **1** ADJ umgekehrt, entgegengesetzt; **in ~ order** in umgekehrter Reihenfolge **2** N Gegenteil *nt*

inversion [ɪnˈvɜːʃən] N (*fig: of roles, values*) Umkehrung *f*

invertebrate [ɪnˈvɜːtɪbrɪt] N Wirbellose(r) *m*

inverted commas PL (*Brit*) Anführungszeichen *pl*; **his new job, in ~** sein so genannter neuer Job

invest [ɪnˈvɛst] **1** VT **(a)** (*Fin*) investieren (*in* in *+acc or dat*), anlegen (*in* in *+dat*); (*fig*) investieren (*in* in *+acc*) **(b)** (*form*) **to ~ sb/sth with sth** jdm/einer Sache etw verleihen **2** VI investieren, Geld anlegen (*in* in *+acc or dat, with* bei); **to ~ in a new car** sich (*dat*) ein neues Auto anschaffen

investigate [ɪnˈvɛstɪgeɪt] **1** VT untersuchen; *sb's political beliefs, insurance claim, business affairs* überprüfen; *complaint* nachgehen (*+dat*); *motive, reason, cause* erforschen; **to ~ a case** in einem Fall ermitteln *or* Ermittlungen anstellen **2** VI nachforschen; (*police*) ermitteln

investigation [ɪnˌvɛstɪˈgeɪʃən] N **(a)** Untersuchung *f* (*into +gen*); **to order an ~ into** *or* **of sth** anordnen, dass in einer Sache (*dat*) ermittelt wird; **on ~ it turned out that ...** bei näherer Untersuchung stellte (es) sich heraus, dass ...; **to be under ~** überprüft werden; **he is under ~** (*by police*) gegen ihn wird ermittelt
(b) (= *scientific research*) (*in field*) Forschung *f*; (*of bacteria, object etc*) Erforschung *f* (*into +gen*)

investigative [ɪnˈvɛstɪgətɪv] ADJ investigativ; **~ journalism** Enthüllungsjournalismus *m*

investigator [ɪnˈvɛstɪgeɪtəʳ] N Ermittler(in) *m(f)*; (= *private ~*) (Privat)detektiv(in) *m(f)*

investiture [ɪnˈvɛstɪtʃəʳ] N (*of president etc*) Amtseinführung *f*; (*of royalty*) Investitur *f*

investment [ɪnˈvɛstmənt] N (*Fin*) Investition *f*; **we need more ~ in industry** in die Industrie muss mehr investiert werden; **foreign ~** Auslandsinvestition(en *pl*) *f*; **oil/this company is a good ~** Öl/diese Firma ist eine gute (Kapital)anlage; **a portable TV is a good ~** ein tragbarer Fernseher macht sich bezahlt

investment: **investment analyst** N (*Fin*) Fundamentalanalytiker(in) *m(f)*; **investment company** N Investmentgesellschaft *f*; **investment fund** N Investmentfonds *m*; **investment grant** N (*Econ*) Investitionszulage *f*; **investment income** N Kapitalerträge *pl*; **investment manager** N Investmentmanager(in) *m(f)*; **investment ratio** N (*Comm, Fin*) Investitionskennziffer *f*; **investment trust** N Investmenttrust *m*

investor [ɪnˈvɛstəʳ] N Kapitalanleger(in) *m(f)*, Investor(in) *m(f)*; **the small ~** die Kleinanleger *pl*

inveterate [ɪnˈvɛtərɪt] ADJ *dislike, hatred* tief verwurzelt; *laziness* chronisch; *opposition, prejudice, habit* hartnäckig; *liar, gambler* unverbesserlich; *collector, traveller* passioniert; **~ smoker/criminal** Gewohnheitsraucher(in) *m(f)*/-verbrecher(in) *m(f)*

invidious [ɪnˈvɪdɪəs] ADJ *remark* gehässig; *task, position* unangenehm; *behaviour, conduct* gemein; *distinctions, comparison, discrimination* ungerecht; **it would be ~ to ...** es wäre ungerecht, zu ...

invigilate [ɪnˈvɪdʒɪleɪt] (*Brit*) **1** VT Aufsicht führen bei **2** VI Aufsicht führen

invigilator [ɪnˈvɪdʒɪleɪtəʳ] N (*Brit*) Aufsicht *f*, Aufsichtsperson *f*

invigorate [ɪnˈvɪgəreɪt] VT beleben; (*tonic, cure*) kräftigen

invigorating [ɪnˈvɪgəreɪtɪŋ] ADJ *climate* gesund; *sea air, shower* erfrischend; *tonic, cure* kräftigend; (*fig*) *attitude, frankness* (herz)erfrischend

invincible [ɪnˈvɪnsəbl] ADJ unbesiegbar, unschlagbar; *courage, determination* unerschütterlich

inviolable [ɪnˈvaɪələbl] ADJ unantastbar; *law, oath* heilig

invisible [ɪnˈvɪzəbl] **1** ADJ unsichtbar; **~ to the naked eye** mit dem bloßen Auge nicht erkennbar **2** N **~s** (*Comm*) Dienstleistungsverkehr *m*

invisible: **invisible earnings** PL (*Econ*) geldwerte Leistungen *pl*; **invisible exports** PL (*Econ*) Ausfuhr *f* von Dienstleistungen; **invisible ink** N Geheimtinte *f*

invitation [ˌɪnvɪˈteɪʃən] N Einladung *f*; **by ~ (only)** nur auf Einladung; **at sb's ~** auf jds Aufforderung (*acc*) (hin); **an ~ to burglars** eine Aufforderung zum Diebstahl; **~ to tender** Ausschreibung *f*

invite [ɪnˈvaɪt] **1** VT **(a)** *person* einladen; **to ~ sb to do sth** jdn auffordern *or* bitten, etw zu tun **(b)** *suggestions, questions* bitten um; (*behaviour*) *ridicule, contempt, trouble* auslösen; **it ~s comparison with another theory** der Vergleich mit einer anderen Theorie drängt sich auf; **you're inviting ridicule/criticism** du machst dich lächerlich/setzt dich der Kritik aus; **to ~ a tender** (öffentlich) ausschreiben **2** [ˈɪnvaɪt] N (*inf*) Einladung *f*

➤ **invite (a)round** VT SEP (zu sich) einladen

➤ **invite in** VT SEP hereinbitten; **could I invite you in for (a) coffee?** möchten Sie auf eine Tasse Kaffee hereinkommen?

➤ **invite out** VT SEP einladen; **I invited her out** ich habe sie gefragt, ob sie mit mir ausgehen möchte; **to invite sb out for a meal** jdn in ein Restaurant einladen

inviting [ɪnˈvaɪtɪŋ] ADJ einladend; *prospect, idea, meal, water* verlockend

in vitro [ɪnˈviːtrəʊ] ADJ (*Biol*) **~ fertilization** künstliche Befruchtung

invoice [ˈɪnvɔɪs] **1** N (= *bill*) (Waren)rechnung *f*; (= *list*) Lieferschein *m*; **~ amount** Rechnungsbetrag *m*; **to ~ goods** in Rechnung stellen, berechnen; **to ~ sb for sth** jdm für etw eine Rechnung ausstellen; **we'll ~ you** wir senden Ihnen die Rechnung

invoicing [ˈɪnvɔɪsɪŋ] N Fakturierung *f*

invoke [ɪnˈvəʊk] VT **(a)** *God, the law* anrufen; **to ~ the name of Marx** Marx ins Feld führen **(b)** *treaty etc* sich berufen auf (*+acc*)

involuntarily [ɪnˈvɒləntərɪlɪ] ADV unbeabsichtigt, unabsichtlich; (= *automatically*) unwillkürlich

involuntary [ɪnˈvɒləntərɪ] ADJ unbeabsichtigt, ungewollt; *repatriation* unfreiwillig; *shudder, twitch etc* unwillkürlich

involve [ɪnˈvɒlv] VT **(a)** (= *entangle*) verwickeln (*sb in sth* jdn in etw *acc*); (= *include*) beteiligen (*sb in sth* jdn an etw *dat*); (= *concern*) betreffen; **the book doesn't ~ the reader** das Buch fesselt *or* packt den Leser nicht; **it wouldn't ~ you at all** du hättest damit gar nichts zu tun; **to be ~d in sth** etwas mit etw zu tun haben; **to get ~d in sth** in etw (*acc*) verwickelt werden; **to ~ oneself in sth** sich in etw (*dat*) engagieren; **I didn't want to get ~d** ich wollte damit/mit ihm *etc* nichts zu tun haben; **a matter of principle is ~d** es geht ums Prinzip; **the person ~d** die betreffende Person; **to be/get ~d with sth** etwas mit etw zu tun haben; (= *have part in*) an etw (*dat*) beteiligt sein; *with work etc* mit etw beschäftigt sein; **to be ~d with sb** mit jdm zu tun haben; (*sexually*) mit jdm ein Verhältnis haben; **to get ~d with sb** mit jdm Kontakt bekommen, sich mit jdm einlassen (*pej*); **he got ~d with a girl** er hat eine Beziehung mit einem Mädchen angefangen
(b) (= *entail*) mit sich bringen; (= *encompass*) umfassen; (= *mean*) bedeuten; **what does the job ~?** worin besteht die Arbeit?; **will the post ~ much foreign travel?** ist der Posten mit vielen Auslandsreisen verbunden?; **he doesn't understand what's ~d in this sort of work** er weiß nicht, worum es bei dieser Arbeit geht; **about £1,000 was ~d** es ging dabei um etwa £ 1.000; **it would ~ moving to Germany** das würde bedeuten, nach Deutschland umzuziehen

involved [ɪnˈvɒlvd] ADJ kompliziert

involvement [ɪnˈvɒlvmənt] N Beteiligung *f* (*in* an *+dat*); (*in quarrel, crime etc*) Verwicklung *f* (*in* in *+acc*); **she denied any**

~ **in** or **with drugs** sie leugnete, dass sie etwas mit Drogen zu tun hatte

invulnerable [ɪnˈvʌlnərəbl] ADJ unverwundbar, unverletzbar; *fortress* uneinnehmbar; (*lit, fig*) *position* unangreifbar

inward [ˈɪnwəd] **1** ADJ (**a**) (= *inner*) innere(r, s) (**b**) (= *incoming*) nach innen (**c**) (*Fin*) ~ **investment** Investitionen *pl* aus dem Ausland; ~ **trade mission** (*Brit*) fremde Handelsdelegation **2** ADV = **inwards**

inward-looking [ˈɪnwədˈlʊkɪŋ] ADJ in sich gekehrt, beschaulich

inwardly [ˈɪnwədlɪ] ADV innerlich, im Inneren; **to** ~ **digest sth** etw geistig verarbeiten

inwards [ˈɪnwədz] ADV nach innen

in-your-face, in-yer-face [ˌɪnjəˈfeɪs] ADJ (*inf*) *attitude etc* provokativ

iodine [ˈaɪədiːn] N Jod *nt*

Ionian [aɪˈəʊnɪən] ADJ ~ **Sea** Ionisches Meer

iota [aɪˈəʊtə] N **not an** or **one** ~ nicht ein Jota; **not an** ~ **of truth** kein Funke *m* or Körnchen *nt* Wahrheit; **it won't make an** ~ **of difference** es wird nicht den geringsten Unterschied machen

IOU ABBR *of* **I owe you** Schuldschein *m*; **to give sb an** ~ jdm einen Schuldschein ausschreiben

IPA ABBR *of* **International Phonetic Alphabet**

IQ ABBR *of* **intelligence quotient** IQ *m*, Intelligenzquotient *m*; **IQ test** Intelligenztest *m*

IRA ABBR *of* **Irish Republican Army** IRA *f*

Iran [ɪˈrɑːn] N (der) Iran

Iranian [ɪˈreɪnɪən] **1** ADJ iranisch **2** N Iraner(in) *m(f)*

Iraq [ɪˈrɑːk] N (der) Irak

Iraqi [ɪˈrɑːkɪ] **1** ADJ irakisch **2** N Iraker(in) *m(f)*

irascible [ɪˈræsɪbl] ADJ reizbar, jähzornig

irate [aɪˈreɪt] ADJ zornig; *crowd* wütend

ire [aɪəʳ] N (*liter*) Zorn *m*

Ireland [ˈaɪələnd] N Irland *nt*; **Northern** ~ Nordirland *nt*; **Republic of** ~ Republik *f* Irland

iris [ˈaɪərɪs] N Iris *f*; (*of eye also*) Regenbogenhaut *f*; (*Bot also*) Schwertlilie *f*

Irish [ˈaɪərɪʃ] **1** ADJ irisch; ~**man** Ire *m*, Irländer *m*; ~**woman** Irin *f*, Irländerin *f* **2** N (**a**) PL **the** ~ die Iren *pl*, die Irländer *pl* (**b**) (*Ling*) Irisch *nt*

Irish: Irish coffee N Irishcoffee *m*; **Irish Sea** N Irische See; **Irish stew** N Irishstew *nt*

irk [ɜːk] VT verdrießen (*geh*), ärgern

irksome [ˈɜːksəm] ADJ lästig

iron [ˈaɪən] **1** N (**a**) Eisen *nt* (*also Golf*); ~ **tablets** *pl* Eisentabletten *pl*; **a will of** ~ ein eiserner Wille; **to rule with a rod of** ~ (*Brit*) mit eiserner Rute or Hand herrschen; **to pump** ~ (*inf*) Krafttraining machen (**b**) (= *electric* ~) Bügeleisen *nt*; **he has too many ~s in the fire** er macht zu viel auf einmal; **to strike while the** ~ **is hot** (*Prov*) das Eisen schmieden, solange es heiß ist (*Prov*) **2** ADJ (**a**) (*Chem*) Eisen-; (= *made of* ~) Eisen-, eisern; ~ **bar** Eisenstange *f*; ~ **deficiency** Eisenmangel *m* (**b**) (*fig*) *constitution, hand, will* eisern; *rule* streng; **to rule with an** ~ **hand** mit eiserner Faust regieren **3** VTI bügeln

➤ **iron out** VT SEP (*lit, fig*) ausbügeln

iron: Iron Age N Eisenzeit *f*; **Iron Curtain** N Eiserne(r) Vorhang

ironic(al) [aɪˈrɒnɪk(əl)] ADJ ironisch; *position* paradox; **it's really** ~ **das ist** wirklich witzig (*inf*)

ironically [aɪˈrɒnɪkəlɪ] ADV ironisch; **and then,** ~**, it was he himself who had to do it** und dann hat ausgerechnet er es tun müssen

ironing [ˈaɪənɪŋ] N (= *process*) Bügeln *nt*; (= *clothes*) Bügelwäsche *f*; **to do the** ~ (die Wäsche) bügeln

ironing board N Bügelbrett *nt*

iron: ironmonger's (shop) N (*Brit*) Eisen- und Haushaltswarenhandlung *f*; **iron ore** N Eisenerz *nt*

irony [ˈaɪərnɪ] N Ironie *f* no *pl*; **the** ~ **of it is that ...** das Ironische daran ist, dass ...; **one of the great ironies of history** eine der ironischsten Fügungen der Geschichte

irradiate [ɪˈreɪdɪeɪt] VT bestrahlen; ~**d food** strahlungsbehandelte Lebensmittel *pl*

irrational [ɪˈræʃənl] ADJ (*also Math, Psych*) irrational; (= *not sensible*) unvernünftig; **if you maintain X, then it is** ~ **to deny Y** wenn Sie X behaupten, ist es widersinnig or unlogisch, Y zu leugnen

irrationally [ɪˈræʃnəlɪ] ADV irrational; (= *not sensibly*) unvernünftig; **quite** ~**, he believed ...** er glaubte gegen jede Vernunft or völlig unsinnigerweise ...

irreconcilable [ɪˌrekənˈsaɪləbl] ADJ unvereinbar

irrecoverable [ˌɪrɪˈkʌvərəbl] ADJ *debt* uneinbringlich; **the company's losses are** ~ die Verluste der Firma können nicht mehr wettgemacht werden

irredeemable [ˌɪrɪˈdiːməbl] ADJ *currency, pawned object* nicht einlösbar; *bonds* unkündbar, untilgbar; *annuity, debt* nicht ablösbar; ~ **securities** (*Fin*) Wertpapiere *pl* ohne Rückkaufmöglichkeit; (*fig*) *sinner* (rettungslos) verloren; *loss* unwiederbringlich; *transgression* unverzeihlich

irredeemably [ˌɪrɪˈdiːməblɪ] ADV *lost* rettungslos; **democracy was** ~ **damaged** die Demokratie hatte irreparablen Schaden genommen

irrefutable [ˌɪrɪˈfjuːtəbl] ADJ unwiderlegbar, unbestreitbar

irregular [ɪˈregjʊləʳ] **1** ADJ (**a**) (= *uneven, Gram*) unregelmäßig; *teeth, shape, coastline* ungleichmäßig; *surface* uneben; **he's been a bit** ~ **recently** (*inf*) er hat in letzter Zeit ziemlich unregelmäßigen Stuhlgang (**b**) (= *contrary to rules*) unvorschriftsmäßig; (= *contrary to law*) ungesetzlich; *behaviour* ungebührlich; **well, it's a bit** ~**, but I'll ...** eigentlich dürfte ich das nicht tun, aber ich ... **2** N (*Mil*) Irreguläre(r) *mf*; **the** ~**s** die irreguläre Truppe

irregularity [ɪˌregjʊˈlærɪtɪ] N (**a**) (= *unevenness*) Unregelmäßigkeit *f*; (*of teeth, shape, coastline*) Ungleichmäßigkeit *f*; (*of surface*) Unebenheit *f* (**b**) (= *non-observation of rules*) Unvorschriftsmäßigkeit *f*; (= *unlawfulness*) Ungesetzlichkeit *f*

irregularly [ɪˈregjʊləlɪ] ADV (= *unevenly*) unregelmäßig; *shaped* ungleichmäßig; *eat, occur, go etc* in unregelmäßigen Abständen

irrelevance [ɪˈreləvəns] N Irrelevanz *f* no *pl*; (*of titles, individuals*) Bedeutungslosigkeit *f*; **it's become something of an** ~ es ist ziemlich irrelevant geworden

irrelevant [ɪˈreləvənt] ADJ irrelevant; *details also, information* unwesentlich, nebensächlich; *titles etc* bedeutungslos; **these issues are** ~ **to the younger generation** diese Fragen sind für die jüngere Generation irrelevant

irreligious [ˌɪrɪˈlɪdʒəs] ADJ unreligiös; *youth* gottlos; (= *lacking respect*) pietätlos

irremediable [ˌɪrɪˈmiːdɪəbl] ADJ nicht wieder gutzumachen *pred*, nicht wieder gutzumachend *attr*

irreparable [ɪˈrepərəbl] ADJ irreparabel; *harm also* bleibend; *loss* unersetzlich

irreparably [ɪˈrepərəblɪ] ADV irreparabel; **his reputation was** ~ **damaged** sein Ruf war unwiderruflich geschädigt

irreplaceable [ˌɪrɪˈpleɪsəbl] ADJ unersetzlich

irrepressible [ˌɪrɪˈpresəbl] ADJ *urge, curiosity, energy, spirit* unbezähmbar; *optimism, sense of humour* unverwüstlich; *person* nicht kleinzukriegen

irreproachable [ˌɪrɪˈprəʊtʃəbl] ADJ tadellos, einwandfrei

irresistible [ˌɪrɪˈzɪstəbl] ADJ unwiderstehlich (*to* für)

irresolute [ɪˈrezəluːt] ADJ unentschlossen

irrespective [ˌɪrɪˈspektɪv] ADJ ~ **of** ungeachtet (+*gen*), unabhängig von; **candidates should be chosen** ~ **of sex/race** bei der Auswahl der Kandidaten sollte das Geschlecht/die Rasse keine Rolle spielen; ~ **of whether they want to or not** egal, ob sie wollen oder nicht

irresponsibility [ˌɪrɪˌspɒnsəˈbɪlɪtɪ] N (*of action, behaviour*) Unverantwortlichkeit *f*; (*of person*) Verantwortungslosigkeit *f*

irresponsible [ˌɪrɪˈspɒnsəbl] ADJ *action, behaviour* unverantwortlich; *person* verantwortungslos

irresponsibly [ˌɪrɪˈspɒnsəblɪ] ADV unverantwortlich

irretrievable [ˌɪrɪˈtriːvəbl] ADJ (**a**) nicht mehr wiederzubekommen; *past, happiness etc* unwiederbringlich; *loss* unersetzlich; **the erased information is** ~ die gelöschte Information kann nicht mehr abgerufen werden (**b**) *damage, harm* irreparabel

irretrievably [ˌɪrɪˈtriːvəblɪ] ADV ~ **lost** für immer verloren; ~ **damaged** irreparabel; **her marriage broke down** ~ ihre Ehe war (unheilbar) zerrüttet

irreverent [ɪˈrevərənt] ADJ *behaviour* unehrerbietig; *remark, attitude, book, author* respektlos; *(towards religion, the dead)* pietätlos

irreversible [ˌɪrɪˈvɜːsəblɪ] ADJ nicht rückgängig zu machen; *decision, judgement* unwiderruflich; *(Med, Phys, Chem)* irreversibel; *damage* bleibend

irreversibly [ˌɪrɪˈvɜːsəblɪ] ADV für immer; **the peace process has been ~ damaged** der Friedensprozess hat einen nicht wiedergutzumachenden Schaden davongetragen

irrevocable ADJ, **irrevocably** ADV [ɪˈrevəkəbl, -ɪ] unwiderruflich

irrigate [ˈɪrɪɡeɪt] VT bewässern

irrigation [ˌɪrɪˈɡeɪʃən] N *(Agr)* Bewässerung *f*

irritable [ˈɪrɪtəbl] ADJ *(as characteristic)* reizbar; *(on occasion)* gereizt; **don't be so ~** sei doch nicht so gereizt

irritably [ˈɪrɪtəblɪ] ADV gereizt

irritant [ˈɪrɪtənt] N *(Med)* Reizerreger *m*; *(= noise etc)* Ärgernis *nt*

irritate [ˈɪrɪteɪt] VT *(= annoy)* ärgern; *(deliberately, Med)* reizen; *(= get on nerves of)* irritieren; **to get ~d** ärgerlich werden; **I get ~d at** *or* **with him** er reizt *or* ärgert mich

irritating [ˈɪrɪteɪtɪŋ] ADJ ärgerlich; *cough* lästig; **I find his jokes most ~** seine Witze regen mich wirklich auf; **the ~ thing is that …** das Ärgerliche ist, dass …

irritation [ˌɪrɪˈteɪʃən] N (a) *(= state)* Ärger *m*; *(= thing that irritates)* Ärgernis *nt*; **to avoid the ~ of a long delay** um eine ärgerliche *or* lästige Verzögerung zu vermeiden (b) *(Med)* Reizung *f*

IRS ABBR *of* **Internal Revenue Service**

is [ɪz] 3RD PERSON SING PRESENT *of* **be**

ISA [ˈaɪsə] N ABBR *of* **Individual Savings Account** *(Brit Fin)* von Zinsabschlagsteuer befreites Sparkonto

Islam [ˈɪzlɑːm] N *(= religion)* der Islam; *(= Moslems collectively)* die Moslems *pl*

Islamic [ɪzˈlæmɪk] ADJ islamisch

island [ˈaɪlənd] N *(lit, fig)* Insel *f*

islander [ˈaɪləndəʳ] N Insulaner(in) *m(f)*, Inselbewohner(in) *m(f)*

island-hopping [ˈaɪləndˌhɒpɪŋ] *(inf)* N Inselhüpfen *nt* *(inf)*; **to go ~** von Insel zu Insel reisen

isle [aɪl] N **the Isle of Man** die Insel Man

isn't [ˈɪznt] CONTR *of* **is not**

isobar [ˈaɪsəʊbɑːʳ] N Isobare *f*

isolate [ˈaɪsəʊleɪt] VT (a) isolieren *(also Med, Chem)*; *(= cut off also)* abschneiden; *(= separate)* absondern; **to ~ oneself from other people** sich (von anderen) abkapseln (b) *(= pinpoint)* herausfinden; *essential factor* herauskristallisieren

isolated [ˈaɪsəʊleɪtɪd] ADJ (a) abgeschnitten, isoliert; *(= remote)* abgelegen; *existence* zurückgezogen; **the islanders feel ~** die Inselbewohner fühlen sich von der Außenwelt abgeschnitten (b) *(= single)* einzeln; **~ instances** Einzelfälle *pl*

isolation [ˌaɪsəʊˈleɪʃən] N *(= state)* Isoliertheit *f*, Abgeschnittenheit *f*; *(= remoteness)* Abgelegenheit *f*; **he felt a sense of ~** er fühlte sich isoliert; **he was in ~ for three months** er war drei Monate lang isoliert; *(in hospital)* er war drei Monate auf der Isolierstation; **to live in ~** zurückgezogen leben; **to consider sth in ~** etw gesondert *or* isoliert betrachten; **it doesn't make much sense (when taken) in ~** ohne Zusammenhang ist es ziemlich unverständlich

isolationism [ˌaɪsəʊˈleɪʃənɪzəm] N Isolationismus *m*

isolation ward N Isolierstation *f*

isosceles [aɪˈsɒsɪliːz] ADJ ~ **triangle** gleichschenkliges Dreieck

ISP *(Comput)* ABBR *of* **Internet service provider** Provider *m*

Israel [ˈɪzreɪl] N Israel *nt*

Israeli [ɪzˈreɪlɪ] **1** ADJ israelisch **2** N Israeli *mf*

issue [ˈɪʃuː] **1** VT (a) *passport, documents etc* ausstellen; *tickets, library books, shares, banknotes, rations, ammunition* ausgeben; *stamps* herausgeben; *order* erteilen *(to +dat)*; *warning, declaration, statement* abgeben; *details* bekanntgeben; *ultimatum* stellen; **~d share capital** ausgegebenes Aktienkapital; **issuing bank** Emissionsbank *f*; **issuing price** *(St Ex)* Ausgabepreis *m*; **to ~ sth to sb/sb with sth** etw an jdn ausgeben; **all troops are ~d with …** alle Truppen sind

mit … ausgerüstet (b) *book, newspaper* herausgeben **2** VI *(from aus)* *(liquid, gas)* austreten; *(sound)* (hervor- *or* heraus)dringen **3** N (a) *(= question)* Frage *f*; *(= matter)* Angelegenheit *f*; *(problematic)* Problem *nt*; **she raised the ~ of human rights** sie brachte die Frage der Menschenrechte zur Sprache; **the whole future of the country is at ~** es geht um die Zukunft des Landes; **this matter/question is not at ~** diese Angelegenheit/Frage steht nicht zur Debatte; **to take ~ with sb over sth** jdm in etw *(dat)* widersprechen; **to make an ~ of sth** etw aufbauschen; **to avoid the ~** ausweichen; **to have ~s with** *or* **about sth** Probleme *pl* mit etw haben (b) *(= outcome, result)* Ergebnis *nt*; **to force the ~** eine Entscheidung erzwingen (c) *(of banknotes, shares etc)* Ausgabe *f*; **date of ~** *(of tickets)* Ausstellungsdatum *nt*; **~ by prospectus** *(St Ex)* Aktienausgabe *f* durch Emissionsprospekt; **~ by tender** *(St Ex)* Emission *f* auf dem Submissionsweg; **~ prospectus** *(St Ex)* Emissionsbedingung *f* (d) *(= magazine etc)* Ausgabe *f*

issuer [ˈɪʃuːəʳ] N *(Fin)* Emittent(in) *m(f)*

IT ABBR *of* **information technology**

it [ɪt] PRON (a) *(when replacing German noun)* *(subj)* er/sie/es; *(dir obj)* ihn/sie/es; *(indir obj)* ihm/ihr/ihm; **of it** davon; **behind/over/under** *etc* **it** dahinter/darüber/darunter *etc*; **who is it? – it's me** *or* *(form)* **I** wer ist da? – ich (bins); **what is it?** was ist das?; *(= what's the matter?)* was ist los?; **that's not it** *(= not the trouble)* das ist es (gar) nicht; *(= not the point)* darum gehts gar nicht; **the cheek of it!** so eine Frechheit!; **I like it here** mir gefällt es hier (b) *(indef subject)* es; **it's raining** es regnet; **yes, it is a problem** ja, das ist ein Problem; **it seems simple to me** mir scheint das ganz einfach; **if it hadn't been for her, we would have come** wenn sie nicht gewesen wäre, wären wir gekommen; **why is it always me who has to …?** warum muss (ausgerechnet) immer ich …?; **it wasn't me** ICH wars nicht; **I don't think it (is) wise of you …** ich halte es für unklug, wenn du …; **it is said that …** man sagt, dass … (c) *(emph)* **it was him** *or* **he** *(form)* **who asked her** ER hat sie gefragt; **it was a cup that he dropped and not …** er hat eine TASSE fallen lassen und nicht …; **it's his appearance I object to** ich habe nur etwas gegen sein Äußeres (d) *(inf phrases)* **that's it!** *(agreement)* ja, genau!; *(annoyed)* jetzt reichts mir!; **this is it!** *(before action)* jetzt gehts los! **2** N *(inf)* (a) *(in children's games)* **you're it!** du bist! (b) **this is really it!** das ist genau das richtige; **he really thinks he's it** er bildet sich *(dat)* ein, er sei sonst wer

Italian [ɪˈtæljən] **1** ADJ italienisch **2** N (a) Italiener(in) *m(f)* (b) *(Ling)* Italienisch *nt*

italic [ɪˈtælɪk] **1** ADJ kursiv **2** N **italics** PL Kursivschrift *f*, Kursive *f*; **in ~s** kursiv (gedruckt)

Italy [ˈɪtəlɪ] N Italien *nt*

itch [ɪtʃ] **1** N (a) *(lit)* Jucken *nt*, Juckreiz *m*; **I have an ~** mich juckt es (b) *(fig inf)* Lust *f*; **I have the ~ to do sth** es reizt *or* juckt *(inf)* mich, etw zu tun **2** VI (a) *(lit)* jucken; **my back is ~ing** mir *or* mich juckt der Rücken (b) *(fig inf)* **he is ~ing to …** es reizt *or* juckt *(inf)* ihn, zu …

itchy [ˈɪtʃɪ] ADJ (+ER) (a) *(= itching)* juckend; **my back is ~** mein Rücken juckt; **I've got an ~ leg** mir juckt das Bein; **I've got ~ feet** *(inf)* ich will hier weg *(inf)* (b) *cloth* kratzig

it'd [ˈɪtəd] CONTR *of* **it would**, **it had**

item [ˈaɪtəm] N (a) *(in programme, on agenda etc)* Punkt *m*; *(Comm: in account book)* *(Rechnungs)*posten *m*; *(= article)* Stück *nt*, Gegenstand *m*; *(in catalogue etc)* Artikel *m*; *(Brit: in variety show)* Nummer *f*; **~s of furniture/clothing** Möbel-/Kleidungsstücke *pl* (b) *(of news)* Bericht *m*; *(short: Rad, TV)* Meldung *f*; **the main news ~** die wichtigste Nachricht (c) *(inf)* **Lynn and Craig are an ~** zwischen Lynn und Craig spielt sich was ab *(inf)*

itemize [ˈaɪtəmaɪz] VT einzeln aufführen; **to ~ a bill** die Rechnungsposten einzeln aufführen

itinerant [ɪˈtɪnərənt] ADJ umherziehend, wandernd; **an ~ lifestyle** ein Wanderleben *nt*; **~ worker** Wanderarbeiter(in) *m(f)*

itinerary [aɪˈtɪnərərɪ] N (= route) (Reise)route f; (= map) Straßenkarte f

it'll [ˈɪtl] CONTR of **it will, it shall**

its [ɪts] POSS ADJ sein(e)/ihr(e)/sein(e)

it's [ɪts] CONTR of **it is, it has** as aux

itself [ɪtˈsɛlf] PRON **(a)** (reflexive) sich
(b) (emph) selbst; **and now we come to the text ~** und jetzt kommen wir zum Text selbst; **the frame ~ is worth £1,000** der Rahmen allein ist £ 1.000 wert; **she has been kindness ~** sie war die Freundlichkeit in Person; **in ~, the actual amount is not important** der Betrag an sich ist unwichtig
(c) by ~ (= alone) allein; (= automatically) von selbst, selbsttätig; **seen by ~** einzeln betrachtet; **the bomb went off by ~** die Bombe ging von selbst los

ITV (Brit) ABBR of **Independent Television** britische Fernsehanstalt

IUD ABBR of **intrauterine device**

I've [aɪv] CONTR of **I have**

ivory [ˈaɪvərɪ] **1** N **(a)** (also colour) Elfenbein nt; **the ~ trade** der Elfenbeinhandel **(b)** (inf) **ivories** (= piano keys) Tasten pl **2** ADJ **(a)** elfenbeinern **(b)** (colour) elfenbeinfarben

ivory tower N (fig) Elfenbeinturm m

ivy [ˈaɪvɪ] N Efeu m

Ivy League N (US) Eliteuniversitäten pl der USA

Jj

J, j [dʒeɪ] N J *nt*, j *nt*

jab [dʒæb] ◨ VT *(with stick, elbow etc)* stoßen; *(with knife)* stechen; **she ~bed the jellyfish with a stick** sie pik(s)te mit einem Stock in die Qualle (hinein) *(inf)*; **he ~bed his finger at the map** er tippte mit dem Finger auf die Karte ◩ VI stoßen *(at sb* nach jdm) ◪ N **(a)** *(with stick, elbow)* Stoß *m*; *(with needle, knife)* Stich *m* **(b)** *(Brit inf: = injection)* Spritze *f*

jabber ['dʒæbəʳ] VI *(also* ~ **away)** plappern, quasseln *(inf)*; **they sat there ~ing away in Spanish** sie saßen da und quasselten spanisch *(inf)*

jack [dʒæk] N **(a)** Hebevorrichtung *f*; *(Aut)* Wagenheber *m* **(b)** *(Cards)* Bube *m* **(c)** *(Bowling)* Zielkugel *f*

➤ **jack in** VT SEP *(Brit inf)* job etc stecken *(sl)*, aufgeben; **jack it in!** *(= stop it)* hör auf damit!

➤ **jack up** VT SEP **(a)** car aufbocken **(b)** *(inf)* prices, wages etc (in die Höhe) treiben

jackal ['dʒækɔːl] N Schakal *m*

jackdaw ['dʒækdɔː] N Dohle *f*

jacket ['dʒækɪt] N **(a)** Jacke *f*; *(= man's tailored ~)* Jackett *nt* **(b)** *(of book)* Schutzumschlag *m*; *(US: of record)* Plattenhülle *f* **(c)** *(esp US: for papers etc)* Umschlag *m* **(d)** ~ **potatoes, potatoes (baked) in their ~s** (in der Schale) gebackene Kartoffeln *pl*

jackknife ['dʒæknaɪf] VI **the lorry ~d** der Lastwagenanhänger hat sich quer gestellt

jack of all trades [dʒækəvˈɔːltreɪdz] N **to be (a) ~ (and master of none)** *(prov)* ein Hansdampf *m* in allen Gassen sein

jackpot ['dʒækpɒt] N Pott *m* *(inf)*, Jackpot *m*; *(in lottery etc)* Hauptgewinn *m*; **to hit the ~** *(in lottery)* den Hauptgewinn bekommen; *(fig)* das große Los ziehen

Jacobean [ˌdʒækəˈbiːən] ADJ aus der Zeit Jakobs I.

Jacuzzi® [dʒəˈkuːzɪ] N Whirlpool *m*

jade [dʒeɪd] ◨ N *(= stone)* Jade *m or f*; *(= colour)* Jadegrün *nt* ◩ ADJ Jade-; *(colour)* jadegrün

jaded ['dʒeɪdɪd] ADJ *(physically)* matt; *(permanently)* verbraucht; *(= mentally dulled)* stumpfsinnig; *(from overindulgence etc)* übersättigt; appearance verbraucht

jagged ['dʒægɪd] ADJ zackig; teeth gezackt; wound, tear ausgefranst; coastline, rocks zerklüftet; mountains, peaks spitz

jaguar ['dʒægjuəʳ] N Jaguar *m*

jail [dʒeɪl] ◨ N Gefängnis *nt*; **in ~** im Gefängnis; **to go to ~** ins Gefängnis kommen ◩ VT ins Gefängnis sperren

jail: jailbird N *(inf)* Knastbruder *m*/-schwester *f* *(inf)*; **jailbreak** N Ausbruch *m* *(aus dem Gefängnis)*; **jailhouse** N *(US)* Gefängnis *nt*; **jail sentence** N Gefängnisstrafe *f*

jam¹ [dʒæm] N *(Brit)* Marmelade *f*, Konfitüre *f*

jam² ◨ N **(a)** *(= traffic ~)* (Verkehrs)stau *m* **(b)** *(= blockage)* Stauung *f* **(c)** *(inf: = tight spot)* **to be in a ~** in der Klemme *or* Patsche sitzen *(inf)*; **to get oneself into a ~** ins Gedränge kommen *(inf)*; **to get sb/oneself out of a ~** jdn/sich aus der Patsche ziehen *(inf)* ◩ VT **(a)** *(= wedge)* festklemmen; *(between two things)* einklemmen; **to ~ a door open/shut** eine Tür festklemmen(, so dass sie auf/zu bleibt); **they had him ~med up against the wall** sie hatten ihn gegen die Wand gedrängt; **it's ~med** es klemmt; **he got his finger ~med** *or* **he ~med his finger in the door** er hat sich *(dat)* den Finger in der Tür eingeklemmt **(b)** *(= cram, squeeze)* *(into* in +acc) stopfen; people quetschen, pferchen; **to be ~med together** *(things)* zusammengezwängt sein; *(people)* zusammengedrängt sein **(c)** street, town etc verstopfen, blockieren; phone lines blockieren; **the switchboard has been ~med all day** sämtliche Leitungen der Telefonzentrale waren den ganzen Tag blockiert **(d)** **to ~ one's foot on the brake** eine Vollbremsung machen ◪ VI **(a)** *(brake)* sich verklemmen; *(gun)* Ladehemmung haben; *(door, window etc)* klemmen; **the key ~med in the lock** der Schlüssel blieb im Schloss stecken **(b)** *(Mus)* eine Jamsession machen

➤ **jam in** VT SEP einkeilen; **he was jammed in by the crowd** er war in der Menge eingekeilt

➤ **jam on** VT SEP **(a)** **to jam on the brakes** eine Vollbremsung machen **(b)** **to jam on one's hat** sich *(dat)* den Hut aufstülpen

Jamaica [dʒəˈmeɪkə] N Jamaika *nt*

Jamaican [dʒəˈmeɪkən] ◨ ADJ jamaikanisch ◩ N Jamaikaner(in) *m(f)*

jamb [dʒæm] N *(of door/window)* (Tür-/Fenster)pfosten *m*

jam jar N *(Brit)* Marmeladenglas *nt*

jammy ['dʒæmɪ] ADJ (+ER) *(Brit inf)* Glücks-; **a ~ shot** ein Glückstreffer *m*; **the ~ bugger won three in a row** der verdammte Glückspilz hat dreimal nacheinander gewonnen *(inf)*

jam: jam-packed ADJ überfüllt; **~ with tourists** voller Touristen; **jam session** N Jamsession *f*; **jam tart** N Marmeladenkuchen *m*, Marmeladentörtchen *nt*

Jan ABBR *of* **January** Jan.

jangle ['dʒæŋgl] ◨ VI *(bells)* bimmeln *(inf)*; **my nerves are jangling** ich bin genervt *(inf)* ◩ VT money klimpern mit; keys, chains rasseln mit

janitor ['dʒænɪtəʳ] N Hausmeister(in) *m(f)*

January ['dʒænjuərɪ] N Januar *m*; *see also* **September**

Japan [dʒəˈpæn] N Japan *nt*

Japanese [ˌdʒæpəˈniːz] ◨ ADJ japanisch ◩ N **(a)** Japaner(in) *m(f)* **(b)** *(Ling)* Japanisch *nt*

jar¹ [dʒɑːʳ] N **(a)** *(for jam etc)* Glas *nt*; *(without handle)* Topf *m*, Gefäß *nt* **(b)** *(Brit inf)* Bierchen *nt* *(inf)*; **fancy a ~?** kommst du (mit) auf ein Bierchen? *(inf)*

jar² ◨ N *(= jolt)* Ruck *m* ◩ VI *(note)* schauerlich klingen; *(colours, patterns)* sich beißen *(inf)*; *(ideas, opinions)* sich nicht vertragen ◪ VT building etc, brain erschüttern; back, knee sich *(dat)* stauchen; *(= jolt continuously)* durchrütteln; **he must have ~red the camera** er muss mit dem Fotoapparat gewackelt haben

➤ **jar on** VI +PREP OBJ Schauer über den Rücken jagen *(+dat)*; **this noise jars on my nerves** dieser Lärm geht mir auf die Nerven

jargon ['dʒɑːgən] N Jargon *m* *(pej)*, Fachsprache *f*

jarring ['dʒɑːrɪŋ] ADJ **to strike a ~ note** einen Misston anschlagen

jaundice ['dʒɔːndɪs] N Gelbsucht *f*

jaundiced ['dʒɔːndɪst] ADJ attitude verbittert; **to take a ~ view of sth** in Bezug auf etw *(acc)* zynisch sein

jaunt [dʒɔːnt] N Trip *m*, Spritztour *f*; **to go for a ~** eine Spritztour machen

jauntily ['dʒɔːntɪlɪ] ADV munter, fröhlich; **with his hat perched ~ over one ear** den Hut keck auf einem Ohr

jaunty ['dʒɔːntɪ] ADJ (+ER) munter, fröhlich; tune also, hat flott; **with a ~ air** unbeschwert

javelin ['dʒævlɪn] N Speer *m*; **in the ~** *(Sport)* im Speerwurf

jaw [dʒɔː] N **(a)** Kiefer *m*, Kinnlade *f*; **the lion opened its ~s** der Löwe riss seinen Rachen auf; **his ~ dropped** sein Unterkiefer klappte herunter **(b)** *(of pincer, vice)* (Klemm)backe *f*

jawbone ['dʒɔːbəʊn] N Kieferknochen *m*

jay [dʒeɪ] N Eichelhäher *m*

jay: jaywalker N unachtsamer Fußgänger, unachtsame Fußgängerin; **jaywalking** N Unachtsamkeit *f* (eines Fußgängers) im Straßenverkehr

jazz [dʒæz] ◨ N **(a)** *(Mus)* Jazz *m* **(b)** *(inf: = talk)* Getön *nt* *(inf)*; **... and all that ~** ... und all so 'n Zeug *(inf)* ◩ ATTR Jazz-; **~ band** Jazzband *f*

➤ **jazz up** VT SEP aufmöbeln *(inf)*

jazzy ['dʒæzɪ] ADJ (+ER) **(a)** colour, dress, tie knallig *(inf)*; pattern auffallend **(b)** music verjazzt

JCB® N Erdräummaschine *f*

jealous ['dʒeləs] ADJ **(a)** husband etc eifersüchtig; *(= envious: of sb's success etc)* neidisch; **to be ~ of sb** auf jdn eifersüchtig sein; *(= envious)* jdn beneiden; **I'm not at all ~ of his success** ich beneide ihn nicht um seinen Erfolg **(b)** *(= watchful, careful)* sehr besorgt *(of* um), bedacht *(of* auf +acc)

jealously ['dʒeləslɪ] ADV **(a)** eifersüchtig; (= *enviously*) neidisch **(b)** *guard* eifersüchtig

jealousy ['dʒeləsɪ] N Eifersucht *f* (*of* auf +*acc*); (= *envy*) Neid *m*

jeans [dʒiːnz] PL Jeans *pl*; **a pair of ~** (ein Paar) Jeans *pl*

Jeep® [dʒiːp] N Jeep *m*

jeepers (creepers) ['dʒiːpəz('kriːpəz)] INTERJ (*US inf*) Mensch (*inf*)

jeer [dʒɪəʳ] **1** N **~s** Johlen *nt no pl*; (= *laughter*) Hohngelächter *nt* **2** VI höhnische Bemerkungen machen; (= *shout, boo*) buhen; (= *laugh*) höhnisch lachen; **to ~ at sb** jdn (laut) verhöhnen **3** VT verhöhnen

jeering ['dʒɪərɪŋ] N höhnische Bemerkungen *pl*; (= *shouting, booing*) Gejohle *nt*; (= *laughing*) Hohngelächter *nt*

Jehovah's Witness N Zeuge *m*/Zeugin *f* Jehovas

Jell-O® ['dʒeləʊ] N (*US*) Wackelpeter *m* (*inf*)

jelly ['dʒelɪ] N Gelee *nt*; (*esp Brit*: = *dessert*) Wackelpeter *m* (*inf*); (*esp US*: = *jam*) Marmelade *f*; (*round meat etc*) Aspik *m or nt*; **my legs were like ~** ich hatte Pudding in den Beinen (*inf*)

jelly: jellyfish N Qualle *f*; **jelly jar** N (*US*) = **jam jar**

jeopardize ['dʒepədaɪz] VT gefährden

jeopardy ['dʒepədɪ] N Gefahr *f*; **in ~** in Gefahr, gefährdet; **to put sb/sth in ~** jdn/etw gefährden

jerk [dʒɜːk] **1** N **(a)** Ruck *m*; (= *spasm, twitch*) Zucken *nt no pl*; **to give sth a ~** einer Sache (*dat*) einen Ruck geben; *rope, fishing line* an etw (*dat*) ruckartig ziehen; **to give a ~** (*car*) rucken; **the train stopped with a ~** der Zug hielt mit einem Ruck an **(b)** (*inf*: = *person*) Trottel *m* (*inf*) **2** VT rucken *or* ruckeln (*inf*) an (+*dat*); **the impact ~ed his head forward/back** beim Aufprall wurde sein Kopf nach vorn/hinten geschleudert; **he ~ed his head back to avoid the punch** er riss den Kopf zurück, um dem Schlag auszuweichen **3** VI **the car ~ed forward** der Wagen machte einen Ruck nach vorn; **the car ~ed to a stop** das Auto hielt ruckweise an

➤ **jerk off** VI (*sl*) sich (*dat*) einen runterholen (*inf*)

jerky ['dʒɜːkɪ] ADJ (+ER) ruckartig

Jersey ['dʒɜːzɪ] N **(a)** Jersey *nt* **(b)** (= *cow*) Jersey(rind) *nt*

jersey ['dʒɜːzɪ] N Pullover *m*; (*Cycling, Ftbl etc*) Trikot *nt*

Jerusalem [dʒəˈruːsələm] N Jerusalem *nt*

Jerusalem artichoke N Jerusalem- *or* Erdartischocke *f*

jest [dʒest] **1** N Scherz *m*, Witz *m*; **in ~** im Spaß **2** VI scherzen, spaßen; **to ~ with sb** mit jdm spaßen; **to ~ about sth** über etw (*acc*) Scherze *or* Witze machen

jester ['dʒestəʳ] N (*Hist*) Narr *m*

Jesuit ['dʒezjʊɪt] N Jesuit *m*

Jesus ['dʒiːzəs] **1** N Jesus *m*; **~ Christ** Jesus Christus **2** INTERJ (*sl*) Mensch (*inf*); **~ Christ!** Herr Gott, (noch mal)! (*inf*); (*surprised*) Menschenskind! (*inf*)

jet [dʒet] **1** N **(a)** (*of water, vapour*) Strahl *m*; **a thin ~ of water** ein dünner Wasserstrahl **(b)** (= *nozzle*) Düse *f* **(c)** (*also ~ plane*) Düsenflugzeug *nt*, Jet *m* **2** ATTR (*Aviat*) Düsen-, Jet-; **~ pilot** Jetpilot(in) *m(f)*

➤ **jet off** VI düsen (*inf*) (*to* nach)

jet-black [ˌdʒetˈblæk] ADJ kohl(pech)rabenschwarz

jet: jet engine N Düsentriebwerk *nt*; **jet foil** N Tragflügelboot *nt*; **jet lag** N Jetlag *nt*; **he's suffering from ~** er hat Jetlag; **jetlagged** ADJ **to be ~** an Jetlag leiden; **jetliner** N Jet *m*; **jet plane** N Düsenflugzeug *nt*

jetsam ['dʒetsəm] N über Bord geworfenes Gut; (*on beach*) Strandgut *nt*

jet: jet set N Jetset *m*; **jet-setter** N Jetsetter(in) *m(f)*; **jet ski** N Wassermotorrad *nt*; **jet-ski** VI Wassermotorrad fahren

jettison ['dʒetɪsn] VT **(a)** (*Naut, Aviat*) (als Ballast) abwerfen **(b)** (*fig*) *plan, policy* über Bord werfen; *unwanted articles* wegwerfen

jetty ['dʒetɪ] N (= *breakwater*) Mole *f*, Hafendamm *m*; (= *landing pier*) Pier *m*, Landungsbrücke *f*

Jew [dʒuː] N Jude *m*, Jüdin *f*

jewel ['dʒuːəl] N **(a)** Edelstein *m*, Juwel *nt* (*geh*); (= *piece of jewellery*) Schmuckstück *nt* **(b)** (*fig*: = *person*) Juwel *nt*, Goldstück *nt* (*inf*)

jewel box, jewel case N Schmuckkästchen *nt*

jeweller, (*US*) **jeweler** ['dʒuːələʳ] N Juwelier(in) *m(f)*; (*making jewellery*) Goldschmied(in) *m(f)*; **at the ~'s (shop)** beim Juwelier

jewellery, (*US*) **jewelry** ['dʒuːəlrɪ] N Schmuck *m no pl*; **a piece of ~** ein Schmuckstück *nt*

Jewish ['dʒuːɪʃ] ADJ jüdisch

jib [dʒɪb] **1** N (*Naut*) Klüver *m* **2** VI **to ~ at sth** (*person*) sich gegen etw sträuben

jibe [dʒaɪb] N, VI = **gibe**

jiffy ['dʒɪfɪ], **jiff** [dʒɪf] N (*inf*) Minütchen *nt* (*inf*); **I won't be a ~** ich komme sofort *or* gleich; (= *back soon*) ich bin sofort *or* gleich wieder da; **in a ~** sofort, gleich

Jiffy bag® N (*Brit*) (gepolsterte) Versandtasche; (*smaller*) gefütterter Briefumschlag

jig [dʒɪg] **1** N *lebhafter Volkstanz* **2** VI (*fig: also ~ about*) herumhüpfen; **to ~ up and down** herumspringen

jiggery-pokery ['dʒɪgərɪ'pəʊkərɪ] N (*inf*) Schmu *m* (*inf*); **I think there's been some ~ going on here** ich glaube, hier ist was faul (*inf*)

jiggle ['dʒɪgl] **1** VT wackeln mit; *door handle* rütteln an (+*dat*) **2** VI (*also ~ about*) herumzappeln

jigsaw ['dʒɪgsɔː] N **(a)** (*Tech*) Tischlerbandsäge *f* **(b)** (*also ~ puzzle*) Puzzle(spiel) *nt*

jilt [dʒɪlt] VT *lover* den Laufpass geben (+*dat*); *girl* sitzen lassen; **~ed** verschmäht

Jim Crow [dʒɪmˈkrəʊ] **1** N (*pej*: = *negro*) Nigger (*pej*), Schwarze(r) *m*; (= *discrimination*) Rassendiskriminierung *f* **2** ATTR *law, policy* (gegen Schwarze) diskriminierend; *saloon etc* für Schwarze

jingle ['dʒɪŋgl] **1** N (*advertising*) ~ Jingle *m* **2** VI (*keys, coins etc*) klimpern; (*bells*) bimmeln **3** VT *keys, coins* klimpern mit; *bells* bimmeln lassen

jingoism ['dʒɪŋgəʊɪzəm] N Hurrapatriotismus *m*

jingoistic [ˌdʒɪŋgəʊˈɪstɪk] ADJ hurrapatriotisch

jinks [dʒɪŋks] PL (*inf*) *see* **high jinks**

jinx [dʒɪŋks] N **there must be** *or* **there's a ~ on it** das ist verhext; **there must be** *or* **there's a ~ on us** wir sind vom Unglück verfolgt; **to put a ~ on sth** etw verhexen

jinxed [dʒɪŋkst] ADJ verhext

jitney ['dʒɪtnɪ] N (*US inf*) Fünfcentmünze *f*; (= *bus*) billiger Bus

jitters ['dʒɪtəz] PL (*inf*) **he had (a bad case of) the ~ about the exam** er hatte wegen der Prüfung das große Zittern (*inf*); **to give sb the ~** jdn ganz rappelig machen (*inf*)

jittery ['dʒɪtərɪ] ADJ (*inf*) nervös, rappelig (*inf*)

jiujitsu [dʒuːˈdʒɪtsuː] N Jiu-Jitsu *nt*

jive [dʒaɪv] **1** N **(a)** (= *dance*) Swing *m* **(b)** (*US inf*) **don't give me that ~** hör bloß mit dem Quatsch auf (*inf*) **2** VI swingen, Swing tanzen

job [dʒɒb] **1** N **(a)** (= *piece of work*) Arbeit *f*; (*Comput*) Job *m*; **I have a ~ to do** ich habe zu tun; **I have a little ~ for you** ich habe da eine kleine Arbeit *or* Aufgabe für Sie; **the plumbers have a lot of ~s on just now** die Klempner haben zurzeit viele Aufträge; **he's on the ~** (*inf*: = *at work*) er ist bei *or* an der Arbeit; **to make a good/bad ~ of sth** bei etw gute/schlechte Arbeit leisten; **we could do a far better ~ of running the company** wir könnten die Firma viel besser leiten; **he knows his ~** er versteht sein Handwerk **(b)** (= *employment*) Stelle *f*, Job *m* (*inf*); **to look for/get/have a ~** eine Stelle suchen/bekommen/haben; **to lose one's ~** seine Stelle verlieren; **I've got a Saturday ~** ich habe einen Samstagsjob (*inf*); **500 ~s lost** 500 Arbeitsplätze verloren gegangen **(c)** (= *duty*) Aufgabe *f*; **that's not my ~** dafür bin ich nicht zuständig; **it's not my ~ to tell him** es ist nicht meine Aufgabe, ihm das zu sagen; **I had the ~ of breaking the news to her** es fiel mir zu, ihr die Nachricht beizubringen; **he's not doing his ~** er erfüllt seine Aufgabe(n) nicht; **I'm only doing my ~** ich tue nur meine Pflicht **(d)** **that's a good ~!** so ein Glück; **what a good ~** *or* **it's a good ~ I brought my cheque book** nur gut, dass ich mein Scheckbuch mitgenommen habe; **to give sb/sth up as a bad ~** jdn/etw aufgeben; **to make the best of a bad ~** das Beste daraus machen; **that should do the ~** das müsste hinhauen (*inf*); **this is just the ~** das ist genau das Richtige **(e)** (= *difficulty*) **I had a ~ convincing him** *or* **to convince him** es war gar nicht so einfach, ihn zu überzeugen; **you'll have a ~**

das wird gar nicht so einfach sein
(f) (*inf*: = *crime*) Ding *nt* (*sl*); **remember that bank ~?** erinnerst du dich an das große Ding in der Bank? (*sl*)
(g) (*inf*: = *operation*) Korrektur *f*; **to have a nose/chin ~ (done)** eine Nasen-/Kinnkorrektur machen lassen
2 VI Gelegenheitsarbeiten tun, jobben (*inf*); **a graphic designer who ~s for various advertising firms** ein Grafiker, der für verschiedene Werbeagenturen Aufträge *or* Arbeiten ausführt

job advertisement N Stellenanzeige *f*

jobbing [ˈdʒɒbɪŋ] ADJ Gelegenheits-; **~ worker/actor** Gelegenheitsarbeiter(in) *m(f)*/-schauspieler *m*

job: Jobcentre N (*Brit*) Arbeitsamt *nt*; **job creation** N Arbeitsbeschaffung *f*; **~ scheme** Arbeitsbeschaffungsmaßnahme *f*; **job cuts** PL Arbeitsplatzabbau *m*; **job description** N Tätigkeitsbeschreibung *f*; **job-hunting** **1** N Arbeitssuche *f*; **to be ~** auf Arbeitssuche sein; **jobless 1** ADJ arbeitslos **2** N **the ~** *pl* die Arbeitslosen *pl*; **job loss** N **there were 1,000 ~es** 1 000 Arbeitsplätze gingen verloren; **job lot** N (*Comm*) (Waren)posten *m*; **job satisfaction** N Zufriedenheit *f* am Arbeitsplatz; **job security** N Arbeitsplatzsicherheit *f*; **jobseeker** N Arbeitssuchende(r) *mf*; **~'s allowance** (*Brit*) Arbeitslosengeld *nt*; **job sharing 1** N Arbeitsplatzteilung *f*, Jobsharing *nt* **2** ATTR *scheme* zur Arbeitsplatzteilung

jockey [ˈdʒɒkɪ] **1** N Jockey *m* **2** VI **to ~ for position** (*fig*) rangeln

jockey shorts PL Jockeyshorts *pl*

jockstrap [ˈdʒɒkstræp] N Suspensorium *nt*

jocular [ˈdʒɒkjʊləʳ] ADJ lustig, spaßig; **to be in a ~ mood** zu Scherzen *or* Späßen aufgelegt sein

jodhpurs [ˈdʒɒdpəz] PL Reithose(n) *f(pl)*

jog [dʒɒg] **1** VT stoßen an (+*acc*) *or* gegen; *person* anstoßen; **to ~ sb's memory** jds Gedächtnis (*dat*) nachhelfen **2** VI trotten, zuckeln (*inf*); (*Sport*) joggen **3** N **(a)** (= *push, nudge*) Stoß *m*, Schubs *m*; **to give sb's memory a ~** jds Gedächtnis (*dat*) nachhelfen **(b)** (= *run*) Trott *m*; (*Sport*) Dauerlauf *m*; **he broke into a ~** er fing an zu traben; **to go for a ~** (*Sport*) joggen (gehen)
▶ **jog along** VI **(a)** (= *go along*: *person, vehicle*) entlangzuckeln **(b)** (*fig*) vor sich (*acc*) hin wursteln (*inf*)

jogger [ˈdʒɒgəʳ] N Jogger(in) *m(f)*

jogging [ˈdʒɒgɪŋ] N Jogging *nt*, Joggen *nt*

jogging: jogging pants PL Jogginghose *f*; **jogging shoes** PL Joggingschuhe *pl*; **jogging suit** N Jogginganzug *m*

john [dʒɒn] N (*esp US inf*) (= *toilet*) Klo *nt* (*inf*)

John: John Bull N (= *the English*) die Engländer *pl*; **John Doe** N (*US*) (= *average man*) Otto Normalverbraucher *m* (*inf*)

johnny [ˈdʒɒnɪ] N (*Brit inf*) Pariser *m* (*inf*)

joie de vivre [ˌʒwædəˈviːvr] N Lebensfreude *f*

join [dʒɔɪn] **1** VT **(a)** (*lit, fig*: = *connect, unite*) verbinden (**to** mit); **to ~ two things together** zwei Dinge (miteinander) verbinden; **to ~ hands** (*lit, fig*) sich (*dat*) einander die Hände reichen
(b) *army* gehen zu; *NATO, the EU* beitreten (+*dat*); *political party, club, religious order* eintreten in (+*acc*); *firm* anfangen bei; *group of people, one's regiment, procession* sich anschließen (+*dat*); **to ~ the queue** sich in die Schlange stellen; **he ~ed us in France** er stieß in Frankreich zu uns; **I'll ~ you in five minutes** ich bin in fünf Minuten bei Ihnen; (= *follow you*) ich komme in fünf Minuten nach; **may I ~ you?** kann ich mich Ihnen anschließen?; (= *sit with you*) darf ich mich zu Ihnen setzen?; (*in game, plan etc*) kann ich mitmachen?; **will you ~ us?** machen Sie mit?; (= *sit with us*) wollen Sie sich (nicht) zu uns setzen?; (= *come with us*) kommen Sie mit?; **will you ~ me in a drink?** trinken Sie ein Glas mit mir?; **Paul ~s me in wishing you ...** Paul schließt sich meinen Wünschen für ... an
(c) (*river*) einmünden *or* fließen in (+*acc*); (*road*) (ein)münden in (+*acc*)
2 VI **(a)** (*also* **~ together**) (= *be attached*) (miteinander) verbunden sein; (= *be attachable*) sich (miteinander) verbinden lassen; (= *grow together*) zusammenwachsen; (= *meet, be adjacent*) zusammentreffen; (*rivers*) zusammenfließen; (*roads*) sich treffen; **to ~ together in doing sth** etw gemeinsam tun

(b) (*club member*) beitreten
3 N Naht(stelle) *f*; (*in pipe, knitting*) Verbindungsstelle *f*
▶ **join in** VI (*in activity*) mitmachen (**prep obj** bei); (*in demonstration also, in protest*) sich anschließen (**prep obj** +*dat*); (*in conversation*) sich beteiligen (**prep obj** an +*dat*); **everybody joined in the chorus** sie sangen alle zusammen den Refrain; **he didn't want to join in the fun** er wollte nicht mitmachen
▶ **join on 1** VI (= *be attachable*) sich verbinden lassen (**prep obj**, -**to** mit); (= *be attached*) verbunden sein (**prep obj**, -**to** mit); (*people: in procession etc*) sich anschließen (**prep obj**, -**to** +*dat*, **an** +*acc*) **2** VT SEP verbinden (**prep obj**, -**to** mit); (= *extend with*) ansetzen (**prep obj**, -**to an** +*acc*)
▶ **join up 1** VI **(a)** (*Brit Mil*) Soldat werden **(b)** (= *meet*: *roads etc*) sich treffen; (= *join forces*) sich zusammenschließen **2** VT SEP (miteinander) verbinden

joiner [ˈdʒɔɪnəʳ] N Tischler(in) *m(f)*, Schreiner(in) *m(f)*

joint [dʒɔɪnt] **1** N **(a)** (*Anat, tool, in armour etc*) Gelenk *nt*; **ankle ~** Knöchel *m*; **knee ~** Kniegelenk *nt*
(b) (*in woodwork*) Fuge *f*; (*in pipe etc*) Verbindung(sstelle) *f*; (*welded etc*) Naht(stelle) *f*
(c) (*Brit Cook*) Braten *m*; **a ~ of beef** ein Rinderbraten *m*
(d) (*inf*: = *place*) Laden *m* (*inf*); (*for gambling*) Spielhölle *f*
(e) (*inf*: *of marijuana*) Joint *m* (*inf*)
2 ADJ ATTR gemeinsam; *influence, strength* vereint; **he finished ~ second** *or* **in ~ second place** (*Brit*) er belegte gemeinsam mit einem anderen den zweiten Platz; **~ action** Gemeinschaftsaktion *f*; **it was a ~ effort** das ist in Gemeinschaftsarbeit entstanden

joint account N gemeinsames Konto

jointed [ˈdʒɔɪntɪd] ADJ mit Gelenken versehen; **a ~ doll** eine Gliederpuppe

jointly [ˈdʒɔɪntlɪ] ADV gemeinsam; **to be ~ owned by ...** im gemeinsamen Besitz von ... sein

joint: joint owner N Mitbesitzer(in) *m(f)*; **joint ownership** N Miteigentum *nt*, Mitbesitz *m*; **joint stock** N Aktienkapital *nt*; **joint stock company** N ≈ Kapitalgesellschaft *f*; **joint venture** N Joint-venture *nt* (*Comm*)

joist [dʒɔɪst] N Balken *m*; (*of metal, concrete*) Träger *m*

joke [dʒəʊk] **1** N Witz *m*; (= *hoax*) Scherz *m*; (= *prank*) Streich *m*; (= *laughing stock*) Gespött *nt*; **for a ~** zum Spaß; **I don't see the ~** ich möchte wissen, was daran so lustig ist *or* sein soll; **he can/can't take a ~** er versteht Spaß/keinen Spaß; **what a ~!** zum Totlachen! (*inf*); **it's no ~** das ist nicht witzig; **this is getting beyond a ~** (*Brit*) das geht (langsam) zu weit; **the ~ was on me** der Spaß ging auf meine Kosten; **I'm not in the mood for ~s** ich bin nicht zu(m) Scherzen aufgelegt; **to play a ~ on sb** jdm einen Streich spielen; **to make a ~ of sth** Witze über etw (*acc*) machen; **to make ~s about sb/sth** sich über jdn/etw lustig machen
2 VI Witze machen (**about** über +*acc*); (= *pull sb's leg*) Spaß machen; **I'm not joking** ich meine das ernst; **you must be joking!** das soll wohl ein Witz sein; **you're joking!** mach keine Witze!

joker [ˈdʒəʊkəʳ] N **(a)** (= *person*) Witzbold *m* **(b)** (*Cards*) Joker *m*

jokey [ˈdʒəʊkɪ] ADJ lustig

jokily [ˈdʒəʊkɪlɪ] ADV lustig; *say* scherzhaft

joking [ˈdʒəʊkɪŋ] **1** ADJ *tone* scherzhaft; **it's no ~ matter** darüber macht man keine Witze **2** N Witze *pl*; **~ apart** *or* **aside** Spaß beiseite

jokingly [ˈdʒəʊkɪŋlɪ] ADV im Spaß

joky [ˈdʒəʊkɪ] ADJ lustig

jolly [ˈdʒɒlɪ] **1** ADJ (+*ER*) (*esp Brit*) fröhlich, vergnügt **2** ADV (*dated Brit inf*) ganz schön (*inf*), vielleicht (*inf*); *nice, warm, pleased* mächtig (*inf*); **~ good** prima (*inf*); **a ~ good idea** eine tolle Idee; **I should ~ well hope/think so!** das will ich auch hoffen/gemeint haben!

jolt [dʒəʊlt] **1** VI (*vehicle*) holpern; (= *give one ~*) einen Ruck machen; **to ~ to a halt** ruckweise anhalten
2 VT (*lit*) = *shake*) durchschütteln; (*once*) einen Ruck geben *or* versetzen (+*dat*); (*fig*) aufrütteln; **she was ~ed awake** sie wurde wachgerüttelt; **to ~ sb out of his complacency** jdn aus seiner Zufriedenheit aufrütteln
3 N **(a)** (= *jerk*) Ruck *m*
(b) (*fig inf*) Schock *m*; **he realized with a ~ ...** mit einem Schlag wurde ihm klar, ...

Jordan [ˈdʒɔːdn] N Jordanien *nt*

josh [dʒɒʃ] (*esp US inf*) **1** VT aufziehen (*inf*), veräppeln (*inf*) **2** VI Spaß machen (*inf*)

joss stick [ˈdʒɒsstɪk] N Räucherstäbchen *nt*

jostle [ˈdʒɒsl] **1** VI drängeln; **they are jostling for the top job** sie streiten sich *or* rangeln um den Spitzenjob **2** VT anrempeln, schubsen

jot [dʒɒt] N (*inf*) Funken *m*, Körnchen *nt*; **it won't do a ~ of good** das nützt gar nichts *or* kein bisschen; **this won't affect my decision one ~** das wird meine Entscheidung nicht im Geringsten beeinflussen
➤ **jot down** VT SEP sich (*dat*) notieren, sich (*dat*) eine Notiz machen von; **to jot down notes** Notizen machen

jotter [ˈdʒɒtəʳ] N (*Brit*) (= *note pad*) Notizblock *m*; (= *notebook*) Notizheft(chen) *nt*

jottings [ˈdʒɒtɪŋz] PL Notizen *pl*

journal [ˈdʒɜːnl] N (**a**) (= *magazine*) Zeitschrift *f*; (= *newspaper*) Zeitung *f* (**b**) (= *diary*) Tagebuch *nt*; **to keep a ~** Tagebuch führen

journalese [ˌdʒɜːnəˈliːz] N Zeitungs- *or* Pressejargon *m*

journalism [ˈdʒɜːnəlɪzəm] N Journalismus *m*

journalist [ˈdʒɜːnəlɪst] N Journalist(in) *m(f)*

journey [ˈdʒɜːnɪ] **1** N Reise *f*; (*by car, train etc also*) Fahrt *f*; **to go on a ~** verreisen; **it's a ~ of 50 miles** *or* **a 50-mile ~** es liegt 50 Meilen entfernt; **it's a two-day ~ to get to ... from here** man braucht zwei Tage, um von hier nach ... zu kommen; **a bus/train ~** eine Bus-/Zugfahrt; **the ~ home** die Heimreise; **he has quite a ~ to get to work** er muss ziemlich weit fahren, um zur Arbeit zu kommen; **a ~ of discovery** eine Entdeckungsreise **2** VI reisen

joust [dʒaʊst] VI im Turnier kämpfen; (*fig*) sich rangeln

jousting [ˈdʒaʊstɪŋ] N Turnier(kämpfe *pl*) *nt*; (*fig*) Rangeleien *pl*

jovial [ˈdʒəʊvɪəl] ADJ fröhlich, jovial (*esp pej*); **in a ~ mood** gut gelaunt

jowl [dʒaʊl] N (*often pl*) (= *cheek*) Backe *f*; (= *fold of flesh*) Hängebacke *f*

joy [dʒɔɪ] N (**a**) Freude *f*; **to my great ~** zu meiner großen Freude; **this car is a ~ to drive** es ist eine Freude, dieses Auto zu fahren; **one of the ~s of this job is ...** eine der erfreulichen Seiten dieses Berufs ist ...; **that's the ~ of this system** das ist das Schöne an diesem System (**b**) NO PL (*Brit inf*: = *success*) Erfolg *m*; **any ~?** hat es geklappt? (*inf*); **you won't get any ~ out of him** bei ihm werden Sie keinen Erfolg haben

joyful [ˈdʒɔɪfʊl] ADJ freudig, froh

joyfully [ˈdʒɔɪfəlɪ] ADV freudig

joyless [ˈdʒɔɪlɪs] ADJ freudlos

joyous [ˈdʒɔɪəs] ADJ (*liter*) freudig, froh

joy: **joyride** N Spritztour *f* (*in einem gestohlenen Auto*); **joyrider** N Joyrider(in) *m(f)*; **joyriding** N Joyriding *nt*; **joystick** N (*Aviat*) Steuerknüppel *m*; (*Comput*) Joystick *m*

Jr ABBR *of* **junior** jr., jun.

jubilant [ˈdʒuːbɪlənt] ADJ überglücklich; (= *expressing joy*) jubelnd *attr*; **to be ~** überglücklich sein, jubeln

jubilation [ˌdʒuːbɪˈleɪʃən] N Jubel *m*

jubilee [ˈdʒuːbɪliː] N Jubiläum *nt*

Judaism [ˈdʒuːdeɪɪzəm] N Judaismus *m*

judder [ˈdʒʌdəʳ] VI (*Brit*) erzittern; (*car etc*) ruckeln; **the train ~ed to a halt** der Zug kam ruckartig zum Stehen

judge [dʒʌdʒ] **1** N (*a*) (*Jur*) Richter(in) *m(f)*; (*of competition*) Preisrichter(in) *m(f)*; (*Sport*) Kampfrichter(in) *m(f)*
(**b**) (*fig*) Kenner(in) *m(f)*; **he's a good/bad ~ of character** er ist ein guter/schlechter Menschenkenner; **I'll be the ~ of that** das müssen Sie mich schon selbst beurteilen lassen
2 VT (**a**) (*Jur*) *case* verhandeln
(**b**) *competition* beurteilen, bewerten; (*Sport*) Kampfrichter sein bei
(**c**) (*fig*: = *pass judgement on*) ein Urteil fällen über (+*acc*); **you shouldn't ~ people by appearances** Sie sollten Menschen nicht nach ihrem Äußeren beurteilen
(**d**) (= *consider*) halten für; **you can ~ for yourself which is better** Sie können selbst beurteilen, was besser ist; **how would you ~ him?** wie würden Sie ihn beurteilen *or* einschätzen?
(**e**) *speed, distance etc* einschätzen
3 VI (**a**) (*at competition*) Preisrichter sein
(**b**) (*fig*: = *pass judgement*) ein Urteil fällen; (= *form an*

opinion*) (be)urteilen; **as** *or* **so far as one can ~** soweit man (es) beurteilen kann; **judging by** *or* **from sth** nach etw zu urteilen; **to ~ by appearances** nach dem Äußeren urteilen; **he let me ~ for myself** er überließ es meinem Urteil

judg(e)ment [ˈdʒʌdʒmənt] N (**a**) (*Jur*) (Gerichts)urteil *nt*; **to await ~** (*Jur*) auf sein *or* das Urteil warten; **to pass** *or* **give ~** (*also fig*) das Urteil sprechen (*on* über +*acc*); **I don't want to sit in ~ on you** ich möchte nicht zu Ihrem Richter aufspielen
(**b**) (= *opinion*) Meinung *f*, Ansicht *f*; (= *moral judg(e)ment, value judg(e)ment*) Werturteil *nt*; (*of distance, speed etc*) Einschätzung *f*; **to give one's ~ on sth** sein Urteil über etw (*acc*) abgeben, seine Meinung zu etw äußern; **in my ~** meiner Meinung nach; **against one's better ~** wider besseres Wissen
(**c**) (= *discernment*) Urteilsvermögen *nt*; **to show ~** ein gutes Urteilsvermögen beweisen

judg(e)mental [dʒʌdʒˈmentl] ADJ wertend; **don't be so ~** nimm nicht immer gleich Wertungen vor

judg(e)ment: **judg(e)ment call** N (*esp US*) Gewissensentscheidung *f*; **to make a ~** eine Gewissensentscheidung treffen; **Judg(e)ment Day** N Tag *m* des Jüngsten Gerichts

judicial [dʒuːˈdɪʃəl] ADJ (*Jur*) gerichtlich; **~ system** Justizsystem *nt*

judiciary [dʒuːˈdɪʃərɪ] N (= *branch of administration*) Gerichtsbehörden *pl*; (= *judges*) Richterstand *m*

judicious ADJ, **judiciously** ADV [dʒuːˈdɪʃəs, -lɪ] klug, umsichtig

judo [ˈdʒuːdəʊ] N Judo *nt*

jug [dʒʌg] N (*with lid*) Kanne *f*; (*without lid*) Krug *m*; (*small*) Kännchen *nt*

juggernaut [ˈdʒʌgənɔːt] N (*Brit*) Schwerlaster *m*

juggle [ˈdʒʌgl] **1** VI jonglieren **2** VT *balls* jonglieren (mit); *figures* so hindrehen, dass sie passen; *debts* umverteilen; **many women have to ~ (the demands of) family and career** viele Frauen müssen (die Anforderungen von) Familie und Beruf miteinander vereinbaren

juggler [ˈdʒʌgləʳ] N (*lit*) Jongleur(in) *m(f)*

juggling [ˈdʒʌglɪŋ] N (**a**) (*lit*) Jonglieren *nt* (**b**) (*fig*) **~ with words/figures** Wort-/Zahlenakrobatik *f*

juggling act N (*fig*) Balanceakt *m*

jugular [ˈdʒʌgjʊləʳ] N (= **vein**) Drosselvene *f*; **to go for the ~** (*fig*) zum entscheidenden Schlag ausholen (*fig*)

juice [dʒuːs] N (*lit, fig inf*) Saft *m*

juice up VT SEP (*US inf*) (**a**) *car* frisieren (*inf*) (**b**) *party* aufpeppen (*inf*); *image, brand* aufmöbeln (*inf*)

juicy [ˈdʒuːsɪ] ADJ (+ER) (*lit, fig inf*) saftig

jujitsu [dʒuːˈdʒɪtsuː] N Jiu-Jitsu *nt*

jukebox [ˈdʒuːkbɒks] N Jukebox *f*

Jul ABBR *of* **July**

July [dʒuːˈlaɪ] N Juli *m*; *see also* **September**

jumble [ˈdʒʌmbl] **1** VT (*also ~ up*) (**a**) (*lit*) durcheinander werfen; **~d up** durcheinander; **a ~d mass of wires** ein Wirrwarr *m* von Kabeln; **his clothes are ~d together on the bed** seine Kleider liegen in einem unordentlichen Haufen auf dem Bett (**b**) (*fig*) *facts* durcheinander bringen **2** N (**a**) (*of objects*) Durcheinander *nt*; (*of ideas, words*) Wirrwarr *m* (**b**) NO PL (*for ~ sale*) gebrauchte Sachen *pl*

jumble sale N (*Brit*) ≈ Flohmarkt *m* (*von Vereinen veranstalteter Verkauf von gebrauchten Sachen*); (*for charity*) Wohltätigkeitsbasar *m*

jumbo [ˈdʒʌmbəʊ] N (= **~ jet**) Jumbo(jet) *m*

jump [dʒʌmp] **1** N (**a**) (*lit, fig*) Sprung *m*; (*with parachute*) Absprung *m*; (*on race-course*) Hindernis *nt*; (*of prices*) (plötzlicher *or* sprunghafter) Anstieg; **it's a big ~ from medical student to doctor** es ist ein großer Sprung vom Medizinstudenten zum Arzt; **he's always one ~ ahead** er ist immer einen Schritt voraus
(**b**) (= *start*) **to give a ~** zusammenfahren
(**c**) (*esp US inf*) **to get a** *or* **the ~ on sb/sth** jdm/etw gegenüber im Vorteil sein
2 VI (**a**) (*lit, fig*) springen (*also Sport*); (*lit also*) einen Satz machen; (*parachutist*) ab)springen; (*prices, shares*) sprunghaft ansteigen; **to ~ for joy** einen Freudensprung machen; **to ~ to one's feet** aufspringen; **they're ~ing up and down about it** (*fig*) sie regen sich furchtbar darüber auf; **to ~ to conclusions** vorschnelle Schlüsse ziehen; **~ to it!** mach

schon!; **the film suddenly ~s from the 18th into the 20th century** der Film macht plötzlich einen Sprung vom 18. ins 20. Jahrhundert; **her salary ~ed from £15,000 to £22,000** ihr Gehalt schnellte von £ 15.000 auf £ 22.000; **if you keep ~ing from one thing to another** wenn Sie nie an einer Sache bleiben
(b) (= *start*) zusammenfahren, zusammenzucken; **you made me ~** du hast mich (aber) erschreckt
3 VT **(a)** *ditch, fence etc* überspringen, hinüberspringen über (+*acc*); **he ~ed two metres** er hat zwei Meter übersprungen
(b) (*inf usages*) **to ~ bail** (*Jur*) abhauen (*inf*) (*während man auf Kaution freigelassen ist*); **to ~ the lights** *or* **a red light** bei Rot über die Kreuzung fahren; **to ~ the queue** (*Brit*) sich vordrängeln; **to ~ ship** (*Naut*) heimlich abheuern; (*fig*) das sinkende Schiff verlassen

➤ **jump at** VI +PREP OBJ *offer* sofort zugreifen bei; *suggestion* sofort aufgreifen; *chance* sofort beim Schopf ergreifen

➤ **jump down** VI herunterhüpfen *or* -springen (*from* von); **to jump down sb's throat** jdn anfahren

➤ **jump in** VI hineinspringen; **jump in!** (*to car*) steig ein!; (*at swimming pool etc*) spring rein!

➤ **jump off** VI herunterspringen (*prep obj* von); (*from train, bus*) aussteigen (*prep obj* aus); (*when moving*) abspringen (*prep obj* von); (*from bicycle, horse*) absteigen (*prep obj* von)

➤ **jump on 1** VI (*lit*) *onto vehicle* einsteigen (*prep obj*, *-to* in +*acc*); (*onto moving train, bus*) aufspringen (*prep obj*, *-to* auf +*acc*); (*onto bicycle, horse*) aufsteigen (*prep obj*, *-to* auf +*acc*); **to jump on(to) sb/sth** auf jdn/etw springen **2** VI +PREP OBJ (*inf*) *person* (= *criticize*) anfahren (*inf*); (= *attack*) überfallen; *suggestion* heruntermachen (*inf*)

➤ **jump out** VI hinausspringen; (*from vehicle*) aussteigen (*of* aus); (*when moving*) abspringen (*of* von); **to jump out of bed/the window** aus dem Bett/Fenster springen; **the caption jumps out at you** die Überschrift springt einem ins Auge

➤ **jump up** VI hochspringen; (*onto sth*) hinaufspringen (*onto* auf +*acc*)

jumped-up [ˈdʒʌmptˈʌp] ADJ (*inf*), **this new ~ manageress** dieser kleine Emporkömmling von einer Abteilungsleiterin

jumper [ˈdʒʌmpəʳ] N (*Brit*) Pullover *m*; (*US*: = *dress*) Trägerkleid *nt*

jumper cables N (*US Aut*) = **jump leads**

jump: **jump leads** N (*Brit Aut*) Starthilfekabel *nt*; **jump rope** N (*US*) Hüpf- *or* Sprungseil *nt*; **jump suit** N Overall *m*

jumpy [ˈdʒʌmpɪ] ADJ (+ER) (*inf*) *person* nervös; (= *easily startled*) schreckhaft; *market* unsicher

Jun ABBR *of* **June**

junction [ˈdʒʌŋkʃən] N (*Rail*) Gleisanschluss *m*; (*of roads*) Kreuzung *f*; (*of rivers*) Zusammenfluss *m*

junction box N (*Elec*) Verteilerkasten *m*

juncture [ˈdʒʌŋktʃəʳ] N **at this ~** zu diesem Zeitpunkt

June [dʒuːn] N Juni *m*; *see also* **September**

jungle [ˈdʒʌŋgl] N Dschungel *m* (*also fig*); **concrete ~** Betonwüste *f*

junior [ˈdʒuːnɪəʳ] **1** ADJ **(a)** (= *younger*) jünger; **Hiram Schwarz, ~** Hiram Schwarz junior
(b) (= *subordinate*) *employee* untergeordnet; *officer* rangniedriger; **to be ~ to sb** unter jdm stehen
(c) (*Sport*) Junioren-; **~ team** Juniorenmannschaft *f*
2 N **(a)** **he is my ~ by two years, he is two years my ~** er ist zwei Jahre jünger als ich
(b) (*Brit Sch*) (*at primary school*) Grundschüler(in) *m(f)*; (*at secondary school*) Unterstufenschüler(in) *m(f)*
(c) (*US Univ*) Student(in) im vorletzten Studienjahr
(d) (*Sport*) Junior(in) *m(f)*

junior: **junior college** N (*US Univ*) College, an dem man die ersten zwei Jahre eines 4-jährigen Studiums absolviert; **junior high (school)** N (*US*) ≈ Mittelschule *f*; **Junior League** N (*Brit Sport*) Amateurliga *f*; **junior minister** N Staatssekretär(in) *m(f)*; **junior partner** N jüngerer Teilhaber, (*in coalition*) kleinerer (Koalitions)partner *m*; **junior school** N (*Brit*) Grundschule *f*

junk¹ [dʒʌŋk] **1** N **(a)** (= *discarded objects*) Trödel *m* **(b)** (*inf*: = *trash*) Ramsch *m* **2** VT (*inf*) *object* wegschmeißen (*inf*); *idea, attempt* aufgeben

junk² N (*boat*) Dschunke *f*

junk: **junk bond** N (*Fin*) Junk Bond *m, niedrig eingestuftes Wertpapier mit hohen Ertragschancen bei erhöhtem Risiko*; **junk food** N Junk food *nt* (*inf*), ungesundes Essen

junkie [ˈdʒʌŋkɪ] N (*inf*) Fixer(in) *m(f)* (*inf*), Junkie *m* (*inf*); **fast food ~** Fan *m* von Fastfood; **computer ~** Computerfreak *m* (*sl*)

junk: **junk mail** N (Post)wurfsendungen *pl*; **junk room** N Rumpelkammer *f*; **junk shop** N Trödelladen *m*

junta [ˈdʒʌntə] N Junta *f*

Jupiter [ˈdʒuːpɪtəʳ] N Jupiter *m*

jurisdiction [ˌdʒʊərɪsˈdɪkʃən] N Gerichtsbarkeit *f*; (= *range of authority*) Zuständigkeit(sbereich *m*) *f*; **this court has no ~ over him** er untersteht diesem Gericht nicht; **that's not within my ~** dafür bin ich nicht zuständig

juror [ˈdʒʊərəʳ] N Schöffe *m*, Schöffin *f*; (*for capital crimes*) Geschworene(r) *mf*

jury [ˈdʒʊərɪ] N **(a)** (*Jur*) **the ~** die Schöffen *pl*; (*for capital crimes*) die Geschworenen *pl*; **to sit** *or* **be on the ~** Schöffe/Geschworener sein; **the ~ is (still) out** (*lit*) die Schöffen/Geschworenen beraten noch; (*fig*) es ist noch nichts enschieden **(b)** (*for exhibition, competition*) Jury *f*

jury: **jury box** N Schöffenbank *f*; (*for capital crimes*) Geschworenenbank *f*; **jury service** N Schöffenamt *nt*; (*for capital crimes*) Amt *nt* des Geschworenen; **to do ~** Schöffe/Geschworener sein

just¹ [dʒʌst] ADV **(a)** (*with time*) gerade; **they have ~ left** sie sind gerade *or* (so)eben gegangen; **she left ~ before I came** sie war, kurz bevor ich kam, weggegangen; **I met him ~ after lunch** ich habe ihn direkt *or* gleich nach dem Mittagessen getroffen; **he's ~ coming** er kommt gerade; **I'm ~ coming** ich komme ja schon; **I was ~ going to ...** ich wollte gerade ...; **~ as I was going** gerade, als ich gehen wollte; **~ now** (*in past*) gerade erst; **not ~ now** im Moment nicht; **~ now?** jetzt gleich?
(b) (= *barely, almost not*) gerade noch, knapp Not; **it ~ missed** es hat fast *or* beinahe getroffen; **I've got only ~ enough to live on** mir reicht es gerade so noch zum Leben; **I arrived ~ in time** ich bin gerade (noch) rechtzeitig gekommen
(c) (= *exactly*) genau, gerade; **that's ~ like you** das sieht dir ähnlich; **that's ~ it!** das ists ja gerade *or* eben!; **that's ~ what I was going to say** genau das wollte ich (auch) sagen; **~ what do you mean by that?** was wollen Sie damit sagen?
(d) (= *only, simply*) nur, bloß; **~ you and me** nur wir beide; **he's ~ a boy** er ist doch noch ein Junge; **why don't you want to/like it? – I ~ don't** warum willst du nicht/magst du es nicht? – ich will/mags eben nicht; **~ like that** (ganz) einfach so; **you can't ~ assume ...** Sie können doch nicht ohne weiteres annehmen ...; **it's ~ not good enough** es ist einfach nicht gut genug
(e) (= *a small distance: with position*) gleich; **~ round the corner** gleich um die Ecke; **~ above the trees** direkt über den Bäumen; **put it ~ over there** stells mal da drüben hin; **~ here** (genau) hier
(f) (= *absolutely*) einfach, wirklich; **it's ~ terrible** das ist ja schrecklich!
(g) **~ as** genauso, ebenso; **the blue hat is ~ as nice as the red one** der blaue Hut ist genauso hübsch wie der rote; **she didn't understand you – it's ~ as well!** sie hat Sie nicht verstanden – das vielleicht auch besser so; **it's ~ as well you didn't go out** nur gut, dass Sie nicht weggegangen sind; **come ~ as you are** kommen Sie so, wie Sie sind; **~ as I thought!** ich habe es mir doch gedacht!
(h) **~ about** in etwa, so etwa; **I am ~ about ready** ich bin so gut wie fertig; **did he make it in time? – ~ about** hat ers (rechtzeitig) geschafft? – so gerade; **will this do? – ~ about** ist das recht so? – so in etwa; **I am ~ about fed up with it!** (*inf*) langsam aber sicher hängt es mir zum Hals raus (*inf*)
(i) (*other uses*) **~ think** denk bloß; **~ listen** hör mal; **~ try** versuchs doch mal; **~ shut up!** sei bloß still!; **~ wait here a moment** warten Sie hier mal (für) einen Augenblick; **~ a moment** *or* **minute!** Moment mal!; **I can ~ see him as a soldier** ich kann ihn mir gut als Soldat vorstellen; **can I ~ finish this?** kann ich das eben noch fertig machen?; **don't I ~!** und ob (ich ...); **~ watch it** nimm dich bloß in Acht; **~ you dare** wehe, wenn dus wagst

just² ADJ (+ER) gerecht (*to* gegenüber); **a ~ cause** eine gerechte Sache; **I had ~ cause to be alarmed** ich hatte guten Grund, beunruhigt zu sein

justice [ˈdʒʌstɪs] N **(a)** Gerechtigkeit *f* (*also Jur*); (*system*) Justiz *f*; (*of claims*) Rechtmäßigkeit *f*; **British** ~ britisches Recht; **to bring sb to** ~ jdn vor Gericht bringen; **to do him** ~ um ihm gegenüber gerecht zu sein; **this photograph doesn't do her** ~ auf diesem Foto ist sie nicht gut getroffen; **that's not true, you're not doing yourself** ~ das stimmt nicht, Sie unterschätzen sich; **you didn't do yourself** ~ **in the exams** Sie haben im Examen nicht gezeigt, was Sie können; **ministry of** ~ (*Brit*), **Department of Justice** (*US*) Justizministerium *nt* **(b)** (= *judge*) Richter(in) *m(f)*; **Justice of the Peace** Friedensrichter(in) *m(f)*; **Mr Justice Buchanan** Richter Buchanan

justifiable [dʒʌstɪˈfaɪəbl] ADJ gerechtfertigt, berechtigt

justifiably [dʒʌstɪˈfaɪəblɪ] ADV mit *or* zu Recht; **and ~ so** und das mit *or* zu Recht

justification [dʒʌstɪfɪˈkeɪʃən] N Rechtfertigung *f* (*of* +*gen, for* für); **as (a)** ~ **for his action** zur Rechtfertigung seiner Handlungsweise

justify [ˈdʒʌstɪfaɪ] VT **(a)** rechtfertigen (*sth to sb* etw vor jdm *or* jdm gegenüber); **am I justified in believing that ...?** glaube ich zu Recht, dass ...?; **this does not ~ his being late** das ist kein Grund für sein Zuspätkommen; **he was justified in doing that** es war gerechtfertigt, dass er das tat **(b)** (*Typ*) justieren; (*Comput*) ausrichten; **right/left justified** rechts-/linksbündig

just-in-time [dʒʌstɪnˈtaɪm] ADJ (*Ind*) Just-in-time-

justly [ˈdʒʌstlɪ] ADV zu Recht, mit Recht; *treat, try* gerecht; *condemn* gerechterweise

jut [dʒʌt] VI (*also* ~ **out**) hervorstehen; (*chin, jaw*) vorspringen; **the peninsula ~s out into the sea** die Halbinsel ragt ins Meer hinaus; **to ~ out over the street** über die Straße hinausragen

juvenile [ˈdʒuːvənaɪl] **1** N (*Admin*) Jugendliche(r) *mf* **2** ADJ (= *for young people*) für Jugendliche; (*pej*) kindisch; **~ crime** Jugendkriminalität *f*

juvenile: **juvenile center** N (*US*) Heim *nt* für jugendliche Straftäter; **juvenile court** N Jugendgericht *nt*; **juvenile delinquency** N Jugendkriminalität *f*; **juvenile delinquent** N jugendlicher Straftäter, jugendliche Straftäterin; **juvenile home** N (*US*) Heim *nt* für jugendliche Straftäter

juxtapose [ˈdʒʌkstəˌpəʊz] VT nebeneinander stellen; *colours* nebeneinander setzen

juxtaposition [dʒʌkstəpəˈzɪʃən] N (= *act*) Nebeneinanderstellung *f*; **in ~ (with each other)** (direkt) nebeneinander

Kk

K, k [keɪ] N K *nt*, k *nt*

k N (*Comput*) ABBR *of* **kilobyte** KB

K ABBR (*in salaries etc*) -tausend; **15 K** 15.000

kaleidoscope [kə'laɪdəskəʊp] N Kaleidoskop *nt*; **a ~ of emotion** ein Wechselspiel *nt* der Gefühle

kamikaze [kæmɪ'kɑːzɪ] N ~ **pilot** Kamikazeflieger *m*; ~ **mission** Kamikaze-Mission *f*

kangaroo [ˌkæŋgə'ruː] N Känguru *nt*

kaput [kə'pʊt] ADJ (*inf*) kaputt (*inf*)

karaoke [ˌkærə'əʊkɪ] N Karaoke *nt*

karaoke machine N Karaoke-Gerät *nt*

karate [kə'rɑːtɪ] N Karate *nt*

karate chop N Karateschlag *or* -hieb *m*

karma [ˈkɑːmə] N Karma *nt*

kayak [ˈkaɪæk] N Kajak *m or nt*

kcal [ˈkɛtkæl] ABBR *of* **kilocalorie** kcal

kebab [kə'bæb] N Kebab *m*

keel [kiːl] N (*Naut*) Kiel *m*; **he put the business back on an even ~** er brachte das Geschäft wieder auf die Beine (*inf*)
➤ **keel over** VI (*ship*) kentern; (*fig inf*) umkippen

keen [kiːn] ADJ (+ER) **(a)** *appetite* kräftig; *interest, desire* stark; *pleasure* groß; *anticipation* gespannt; *mind, intelligence, sense of humour, wit, competition* scharf; *sight, eye, hearing, ear* gut; **to have a ~ nose for sth** eine gute *or* feine Nase für etw haben; **they have a ~ awareness** *or* **appreciation of the dangers** sie sind sich der Gefahren deutlich bewusst
(b) (= *enthusiastic*) begeistert; (= *eager, interested*) stark interessiert; (= *hardworking*) eifrig; ~ **to learn** lernbegierig; **to be ~ on sb** von jdm sehr angetan sein; (= *sexually attracted*) scharf auf jdn sein (*inf*); *on pop group, actor, author* von jdm begeistert sein; **to be ~ on sth** etw sehr gern mögen; *on classical music, football* sehr viel für etw übrig haben; **to be ~ on doing sth** (= *like to do*) etw gern *or* mit Begeisterung tun; **to be ~ to do sth** (= *want to do*) sehr darauf erpicht sein *or* scharf darauf sein (*inf*), etw zu tun; **to be ~ on mountaineering/dancing** begeisterter *or* leidenschaftlicher Bergsteiger/Tänzer sein; **he is very ~ on golf/tennis** *etc* er ist ein Golf-/Tennisfan *m etc*; **I'm not very ~ on him/that idea** ich bin von ihm/dieser Idee nicht gerade begeistert; **he's not ~ on her coming** er legt keinen (gesteigerten) Wert darauf, dass sie kommt; **he's very ~ that we should go/for us to go** er legt sehr großen Wert darauf, dass wir gehen
(c) *blade, wind* scharf; *frost* klirrend
(d) (*esp Brit*) *prices* günstig

keenly [ˈkiːnlɪ] ADV **(a)** *feel* leidenschaftlich; *interested, observe* stark; *listen* aufmerksam; **the match was ~ contested** in dem Spiel wurde hart gekämpft **(b)** (= *enthusiastically*) mit Begeisterung; ~ **awaited** mit Ungeduld erwartet **(c)** (*esp Brit*) ~ **priced goods** Waren *pl* zu scharf kalkulierten Preisen

keenness [ˈkiːnnɪs] N (= *enthusiasm*) Begeisterung *f*; (*of fan, golfer*) Leidenschaftlichkeit *f*; (*of applicant, learner*) starkes Interesse; (= *hardworking nature*) Eifer *m*

---

keep [kiːp]

1 TRANSITIVE VERB	**3** NOUN
2 INTRANSITIVE VERB	**4** PHRASAL VERBS

vb: pret, ptp **kept**

When **keep** *is part of a set combination, e.g.* **keep in mind**, **keep house**, **keep goal** *etc, look up the noun. For combinations of* **keep** *with adverbs and prepositions, e.g.* **keep in**, **keep on**, **keep up** *etc, see also the phrasal verbs section.*

1 TRANSITIVE VERB

(a) (= *retain*) behalten; **you can keep this book** du kannst dieses Buch behalten; **to keep a place for sb** einen Platz für jdn freihalten; **to keep one's place in a book** sich (*dat*) die Stelle im Buch markieren; **to keep a note of sth** sich (*dat*) etw notieren

(b) (= *maintain in a certain state, place etc*) halten; **he kept his hands in his pockets** er hat die Hände in der Tasche gelassen; **the garden was well kept** der Garten war (gut) gepflegt

✦**to keep sb/sth doing sth to keep sb waiting** jdn warten lassen; **can't you keep him talking?** können Sie ihn nicht in ein Gespräch verwickeln?; **to keep the traffic moving** den Verkehr am Fließen halten; **to keep the conversation going** das Gespräch in Gang halten

✦**to keep sb/sth + ADJ to keep one's dress clean** sein Kleid nicht schmutzig machen; **to keep sb quiet** zusehen *or* dafür sorgen, dass jd still ist; **just to keep her happy** damit sie zufrieden ist; **to keep sb alive** jdn am Leben halten; **to keep oneself busy** sich selbst beschäftigen; **to keep oneself warm** sich warm halten

(c) (= *have in a certain place, look after*) aufbewahren; **where does he keep his money?** wo bewahrt er sein Geld auf?; **where do you keep your spoons?** wo sind die Löffel?

(d) (= *put aside*) aufheben; **I've been keeping it for you** ich habe es für Sie aufgehoben

(e) (= *detain*) aufhalten, zurückhalten; **I mustn't keep you** ich will Sie nicht aufhalten; **what kept you?** wo waren Sie denn so lang?; **what's keeping him?** wo bleibt er denn?; **to keep sb prisoner** jdn gefangen halten; **to keep sb in prison** jdn in Haft halten; **they kept him in hospital over night** sie haben ihn über Nacht im Krankenhaus behalten

(f) (*shop, hotel, restaurant*) führen; *stock also* (zu verkaufen) haben; *bees, pigs etc* halten

(g) (= *support*) versorgen, unterhalten; **I earn enough to keep myself** ich verdiene genug für mich (selbst) zum Leben; **I have six children to keep** ich habe sechs Kinder zu unterhalten

(h) (*promise*) halten; *law, rule* befolgen; *appointment* einhalten; **to keep a vow** einen Schwur halten; **to keep late hours** lange aufbleiben

(i) (= *guard, protect*) (be)hüten; *sheep etc* hüten

(j) (*accounts, diary etc*) führen (*of* über +*acc*)

(k) (*US*) *road, path* weitergehen/-fahren; *direction* einhalten; **to keep one's course** (den) Kurs (ein)halten; **to keep one's room** auf seinem Zimmer bleiben; **to keep one's seat** sitzen bleiben

2 INTRANSITIVE VERB

(a) **to keep (to the) left/right** sich links/rechts halten; **to keep to the left** (*Aut*) links fahren; **keep north** gehen/fahren Sie immer Richtung Norden

(b) (= *remain in a certain state, position*) bleiben; **how are you keeping?** wie geht es Ihnen so?

✦**to keep + ADJ to keep fit** fit bleiben; **to keep quiet** still sein; **to keep silent** schweigen; **to keep calm** ruhig bleiben

✦**to keep doing sth** (= *not stop*) etw weiter tun; (*repeatedly*) etw immer wieder tun; (*constantly*) etw dauernd tun; **to keep walking** weitergehen; **keep going** machen Sie weiter; **I keep hoping she's still alive** ich hoffe immer noch, dass sie noch lebt; **I keep thinking ...** ich denke immer ...

(c) (*food etc*) sich halten

3 NOUN

(a) (= *livelihood, food*) Unterhalt *m*; **I got £300 a week and my keep** ich bekam £ 300 pro Woche und freie Kost und Logis; **to earn one's keep** seinen Lebensunterhalt verdienen

(b)

✦**for keeps** (*inf*) für immer; **it's yours for keeps** das darfst du behalten

4 PHRASAL VERBS

➤ **keep ahead** VI vorne bleiben; **to keep ahead of one's rivals** seinen Konkurrenten vorausbleiben

➤ **keep at** **1** VI +PREP OBJ weitermachen mit; **keep at it** machen Sie weiter so **2** VT +PREP OBJ **to keep sb (hard) at it** jdn hart rannehmen (*inf*)

➤ **keep away** ◼ VI (*lit*) wegbleiben; (= *not approach*) nicht näher herankommen (*from* an +*acc*); **keep away!** nicht näher kommen!; **keep away from that place** gehen Sie da nicht hin; **I just can't keep away** es zieht mich immer wieder hin; **keep away from him** lassen Sie die Finger von ihm
◼ VT (*always separate*) person, pet etc fern halten (*from* von); **to keep sth away from sth** etw nicht an etw (*acc*) kommen lassen; **keep them away from each other** halten Sie sie auseinander; **to keep sb away from school** jdn nicht in die Schule (gehen) lassen

➤ **keep back** ◼ VI zurückbleiben, nicht näher kommen; **keep back!** bleiben Sie, wo Sie sind!; **please keep back from the edge** bitte gehen Sie nicht zu nahe an den Rand
◼ VT SEP **(a)** person, hair, crowds, enemy zurückhalten; tears unterdrücken; **to keep sb/sth back from sb** jdn/etw von jdm abhalten
(b) money, taxes einbehalten; information, facts etc verschweigen (*from sb* jdm); **they are keeping back the names of the victims** die Namen der Opfer werden nicht bekannt gegeben

➤ **keep down** ◼ VI unten bleiben
◼ VT SEP **(a)** (*lit*) unten lassen; (= *hold down*) unten halten; head ducken; **keep your voices down** reden Sie leise *or* nicht so laut
(b) people, revolt unterdrücken; dog bändigen; rebellious person im Zaum halten; rabbits, weeds etc unter Kontrolle halten
(c) taxes, rates, prices niedrig halten; spending einschränken; costs, wages drücken; **to keep numbers down** die Zahlen gering halten; **to keep one's weight down** nicht zunehmen
(d) food, drink bei sich behalten

➤ **keep from** ◼ VT +PREP OBJ **(a)** sb hindern an (+*dat*); (*from going, doing sth also*) abhalten von; **I couldn't keep him from doing it** ich konnte ihn nicht daran hindern *or* davon abhalten, das zu tun; **the bells keep me from sleeping** die Glocken lassen mich nicht schlafen; **keep them from getting wet** verhindern Sie es, dass sie nass werden
(b) (= *protect*) **to keep sb from sth** jdn vor etw (*dat*) bewahren; **to keep sb from harm** jdn vor Schaden (*dat*) bewahren
(c) (= *withhold*) **to keep sth from sb** jdm etw verschweigen; **can you keep this from your mother?** können Sie das vor Ihrer Mutter geheim halten *or* verbergen?
◼ VI +PREP OBJ **to keep from doing sth** etw nicht tun; **she couldn't keep from laughing** sie musste einfach lachen

➤ **keep in** VT SEP **(a)** schoolboy nachsitzen lassen; **I've been kept in!** ich musste nachsitzen!; **his parents have kept him in** seine Eltern haben ihn nicht weggelassen *or* gehen lassen
(b) feelings zügeln

➤ **keep in with** VI +PREP OBJ sich gut stellen mit; **he's just trying to keep in with her** er will sich nur bei ihr lieb Kind machen

➤ **keep off** ◼ VI (*person*) wegbleiben; **if the rain keeps off** wenn es nicht regnet; **"keep off!"** „Betreten verboten!"
◼ VT SEP **(a)** dog, person fern halten (*prep obj* von); one's hands abhalten (*prep obj* von); **to keep one's mind off sth** nicht an etw (*acc*) denken; **keep him off me** halten Sie ihn mir vom Leib; **keep your hands off** Hände weg!
(b) jacket etc ausbehalten; hat abbehalten
◼ VI +PREP OBJ vermeiden; **"keep off the grass"** „Betreten des Rasens verboten"; **keep off the whisky** lassen Sie das Whiskytrinken

➤ **keep on** ◼ VI **(a)** (= *continue*) weitermachen, nicht aufhören; **to keep on doing sth** etw weiter tun; (*repeatedly*) etw immer wieder tun; (*incessantly*) etw dauernd tun; **if you keep on like this** wenn du so weitermachst; **I keep on telling you** ich sage dir ja immer; **to keep on at sb** (*inf*) dauernd an jdm herummeckern (*inf*); **they kept on at him until he agreed** sie haben ihm so lange keine Ruhe gelassen, bis er zustimmte; **there's no need to keep on about sth** (*inf*) unaufhörlich von etw reden; **there's no need to keep on about it** (*inf*) es ist wirklich nicht nötig, ewig darauf herumzuhacken (*inf*)
(b) (= *keep going*) weitergehen/-fahren; **keep straight on** immer geradeaus
◼ VT SEP **(a)** servant, employee weiterbeschäftigen
(b) coat etc anbehalten; hat aufbehalten

➤ **keep out** ◼ VI (*of room, building*) draußen bleiben; (*of property, area*) etw nicht betreten; **keep out of my room!** geh/komm nicht in mein Zimmer; **"keep out"** „Zutritt verboten"; **to keep out of the rain/sun** nicht in den Regen/die Sonne gehen; **to keep out of sight** sich nicht zeigen; (*hiding*) in Deckung bleiben; **to keep out of danger** Gefahr meiden; **to keep out of debt** keine Schulden machen; **you keep out of this!** halten Sie sich da raus!
◼ VT SEP person nicht hereinlassen (*of* in +*acc*); light, cold, rain, enemy etc abhalten; **this screen keeps the sun out of your eyes** diese Blende schützt Ihre Augen vor Sonne; **I wanted to keep him out of this** ich wollte nicht, dass er da mit hereingezogen wurde; **to keep sb's name out of the papers** jds Namen nicht in der Zeitung erwähnen

➤ **keep to** ◼ VI +PREP OBJ **(a)** **to keep to one's promise** sein Versprechen halten; **keep to the main road** bleiben Sie auf der Hauptstraße; **to keep to the schedule/plan** den Zeitplan einhalten; **to keep to the speed limit** sich an die Geschwindigkeitsbegrenzung halten; **to keep to the subject/point** bei der Sache *or* beim Thema bleiben
(b) (= *keep oneself to oneself*) nicht sehr gesellig sein; **they keep (themselves) to themselves** (*as a group*) sie bleiben unter sich
◼ VT +PREP OBJ **to keep sb to his word/promise** jdn beim Wort nehmen; **to keep sth to a minimum** etw auf ein Minimum beschränken; **to keep sth to oneself** etw für sich behalten; **keep your hands to yourself!** nehmen Sie Ihre Hände weg!

➤ **keep together** ◼ VI zusammenbleiben; (*as friends, community etc*) zusammenhalten; (*singers, oarsmen etc*) im Einklang *or* Takt sein ◼ VT SEP zusammen aufbewahren; (= *fix together, unite*) things, people zusammenhalten

➤ **keep up** ◼ VI **(a)** (*tent, pole*) stehen bleiben
(b) (*rain*) (an)dauern; (*weather, hurricane etc*) anhalten; (*morale, strength, determination*) nicht nachlassen
(c) (= *keep up with sb/sth*) (*in race, work, with prices*) (mit jdm/etw) Schritt halten, (mit jdm/etw) mithalten können (*inf*); (*in comprehension*) (jdm/einer Sache) folgen können; **they bought it just to keep up with the Joneses** sie kauften es nur, um den Nachbarn nicht nachzustehen; **to keep up with the times** mit der Zeit gehen; **to keep up with the news** sich auf dem Laufenden halten
◼ VT SEP **(a)** pole, tent aufrecht halten; **to keep his trousers up** damit die Hose nicht herunterrutscht
(b) (= *not stop*) nicht aufhören mit; study etc fortsetzen; quality, prices, output, friendship, tradition aufrechterhalten; subscription beibehalten; payments etc weiterbezahlen; workrate, speed (= *maintain*) halten; (= *endure*) durchhalten; **I try to keep up my Spanish** ich versuche, mit meinem Spanisch nicht aus der Übung zu kommen; **to keep one's morale up** den Mut nicht verlieren; **keep it up!** (machen Sie) weiter so!; **he couldn't keep it up** er hat schlappgemacht (*inf*)
(c) house unterhalten; road instand halten
(d) (= *prevent from going to bed*) am Schlafengehen hindern; **that child kept me up all night** das Kind hat mich die ganze Nacht nicht schlafen lassen

keeper ['ki:pə'] N (*in asylum, zoo*) Wärter(in) *m(f)*; (*of museum*) Kustode *m*, Kustodin *f*; (*Brit inf*: = *goalkeeper*) Torhüter(in) *m(f)*

keep fit N Fitnessübungen *pl*

keeping ['ki:pɪŋ] N **in ~ with** in Übereinstimmung *or* Einklang mit; **her behaviour was out of ~ with the dignity of the occasion** ihr Benehmen entsprach nicht der Feierlichkeit des Anlasses

keepsake ['ki:pseɪk] N Andenken *nt*

keg [keg] N **(a)** kleines Fass **(b)** (*also ~ beer*) Bier *nt* vom Fass

ken [ken] ◼ N **that is beyond my ~** das entzieht sich meiner Kenntnis ◼ VTI (*Scot*) = **know**

kennel ['kenl] N **(a)** Hundehütte *f* **(b)** **~s** (= *cage*) Hundezwinger *m*; (*for breeding*) Hundezucht *f*; (*boarding*) (Hunde)heim *nt*; **to put a dog in ~s** einen Hund in Pflege geben

Kenya ['kenjə] N Kenia *nt*

Kenyan ['kenjən] ◼ N Kenianer(in) *m(f)* ◼ ADJ kenianisch

kept [kept] PRET, PTP *of* **keep**

kerb [kɜ:b] N (*Brit*) Bordkante *f*, Randstein *m*

kerb: **kerb crawler** N Freier *m* im Autostrich (*inf*); **kerb crawling** N Autostrich *m*

kernel ['kɜ:nl] N (*lit, fig*) Kern *m*

kerosene [ˈkerəsiːn] N Kerosin nt

kestrel [ˈkestrəl] N Turmfalke m

ketchup [ˈketʃəp] N Ket(s)chup nt or m

kettle [ˈketl] N Kessel m; **I'll put the ~ on** ich stelle mal eben (Kaffee-/Tee)wasser auf; **the ~'s boiling** das Wasser kocht; **this is a different ~ of fish** (Brit inf) das ist doch was ganz anderes

kettledrum [ˈketldrʌm] N (Kessel)pauke f

key [kiː] **1** N **(a)** (lit, fig) Schlüssel m; **education is the ~ to success** Bildung ist der Schlüssel zum Erfolg; **this was the ~ to the murderer's identity** das gab Aufschluss darüber, wer der Mörder war
(b) (= answers) Lösungen pl; (Sch) Schlüssel m; (Math etc) Lösungsheft nt; (for maps etc) Zeichenerklärung f
(c) (of piano, typewriter, Comput) Taste f
(d) (Mus) Tonart f; **to sing off ~** falsch singen; **change of ~** Tonartwechsel m
2 ADJ ATTR Schlüssel-; witness wichtigste(r, s); **~ factor** Schlüsselfaktor m (in sth bei etw); **education is a ~ issue** Bildung ist eines der entscheidenden Themen; **~ position** Schlüsselposition or -stellung f; **~ role** Schlüsselrolle f
3 VT (Comput) text, data eingeben; (= hit) character, F7 etc drücken

➤ **key in** VT SEP (Comput) eingeben

➤ **key up** VT SEP **she was (all) keyed up about the interview** sie war wegen des Interviews ganz aufgedreht (inf); **he was all keyed up for the big race** er hatte sich schon ganz auf das große Rennen eingestellt

keyboard [ˈkiːbɔːd] N (of piano) Klaviatur f; (of organ) Manual nt; (of typewriter, Comput) Tastatur f; **~ skills** (Comput) Fertigkeiten pl in der Texterfassung

keyboarder [ˈkiːbɔːdə] N (Typ, Comput) Texterfasser(in) m(f)

keyboarding [ˈkiːbɔːdɪŋ] N (Comput) Texteingabe f; **~ skills** Fertigkeiten pl in der Texterfassung

keyboard: **keyboard instrument** N (Mus) Tasteninstrument nt; **keyboard operator** N Texterfasser(in) m(f)

key: **key card** N (at hotel etc) Schlüsselkarte f; **key currency** N (Fin) Leitwährung f; **keyhole** N Schlüsselloch nt; **keyhole surgery** N minimal invasive Chirurgie

keying [ˈkiːɪŋ] N (Comput) Texteingabe f

keynesian [ˈkeɪnzɪən] ADJ (Econ) keynessch attr, auf Keynes zurückgehend

key: **keynote** **1** N (of a speech) Leitgedanke m **2** ADJ ATTR **~ speech** (Pol etc) programmatische Rede; **keypad** N (Comput) Tastenfeld nt; **keyring** N Schlüsselring m; **keyworker** [ˈkiːwɜːkəʳ] N (Med, Social Work) Koordinator(in) m(f)

kg ABBR of **kilogramme(s)**, **kilogram(s)** kg

khaki [ˈkɑːkɪ] **1** N Khaki nt **2** ADJ khaki(braun or -farben)

kibbutz [kɪˈbʊts] N, pl **-im** [kɪbʊtˈsiːm] Kibbuz m

kick [kɪk] **1** N **(a)** Tritt m, Stoß m; **to give sth a ~** einer Sache (dat) einen Tritt versetzen; **what he needs is a good ~ up the backside** or **in the pants** (inf) er braucht mal einen kräftigen Tritt in den Hintern (inf)
(b) (inf: = thrill) **she gets a ~ out of it** es macht ihr einen Riesenspaß (inf); (physically) sie verspürt einen Kitzel dabei; **to do sth for ~s** etw zum Spaß tun; **how do you get your ~s?** was machen Sie zu ihrem Vergnügen?
2 VI (person) treten; (= struggle) um sich treten; (baby, while sleeping) strampeln; (animal) ausschlagen; **~ing and screaming** (fig) unter großem Protest
3 VT **(a)** (person, horse) sb, object einen Tritt versetzen (+dat); door treten gegen; football kicken (inf); **to ~ sb in the head/stomach** jdm gegen den Kopf/in den Bauch treten; **to ~ the bucket** (inf) ins Gras beißen (inf); **I could have ~ed myself** (inf) ich hätte mir in den Hintern beißen können (inf)
(b) (inf) **to ~ heroin** vom Heroin runterkommen (inf); **to ~ the habit** es sich (dat) abgewöhnen

➤ **kick about** (Brit) or **around 1** VI (inf) (person) rumhängen (inf) (prep obj in +dat); (thing) rumliegen (inf) (prep obj in +dat) **2** VT SEP **to kick a ball about** or **around** (herum)bolzen (inf); **you shouldn't let them kick you about** or **around** Sie sollten sich nicht so herumschubsen lassen; **to kick an idea about** or **around** (inf) eine Idee durchdiskutieren

➤ **kick away** VT SEP wegstoßen; (= knock down) niedertreten

➤ **kick back** VT SEP ball zurückspielen or -schießen

➤ **kick down** VT SEP door eintreten

➤ **kick in 1** VT SEP door eintreten; **to kick sb's teeth in** jdm die Zähne einschlagen **2** VI (system, fear) ausgelöst werden; (drug etc) wirken

➤ **kick off 1** VI (Ftbl) anstoßen; (fig inf) losgehen (inf); **who's going to kick off?** (fig inf) wer fängt an? **2** VT SEP wegtreten; shoes von sich schleudern; **they kicked him off the committee** (inf) sie warfen ihn aus dem Ausschuss

➤ **kick out 1** VI (horse) ausschlagen; (person) um sich treten; **to kick out at sb** nach jdm treten **2** VT SEP hinauswerfen (of aus)

➤ **kick up** VT SEP (fig inf) **to kick up a fuss** or **a stink** Krach schlagen (inf)

kick: **kickback** N (inf: as bribe) Provision f; **kickoff** N **(a)** (Sport) Anpfiff m, Anstoß m **(b)** **for a ~** (= to begin with) erst mal, zunächst; **kick-start(er)** N Kickstarter m

kid [kɪd] **1** N **(a)** (= young goat) Kitz nt
(b) (inf: = child) Kind nt; **when I was a ~** als ich klein war; **to get the ~s to bed** die Kleinen ins Bett bringen; **it's ~'s stuff** (= for children) das ist was für kleine Kinder (inf); (= easy) das ist doch ein Kinderspiel; **to be like a ~ in a candy store** (US) sich wie ein verwöhntes Kind aufführen
(c) (inf) (= man) Junge m; (= woman) Kleine f (inf); **listen ~, you keep out of this** hör mal Kleiner, du hältst dich hier raus
2 ADJ ATTR (inf) **~ sister** kleine Schwester
3 VT (inf) **to ~ sb** (= tease) jdn aufziehen (inf); (= deceive) jdn an der Nase rumführen (inf); **don't ~ yourself!** machen Sie sich doch nichts vor!; **who is she trying to ~?, who is she ~ding?** wem will sie was weismachen?
4 VI (inf) Jux machen (inf); **no ~ding** im Ernst; **you've got to or you must be ~ding!** das ist doch wohl nicht dein Ernst!

kid gloves [kɪdˈglʌvz] PL Glacéhandschuhe pl; **to handle** or **treat sb with ~** (fig) jdn mit Samthandschuhen anfassen

kidnap [ˈkɪdnæp] **1** VT entführen, kidnappen **2** N Entführung f, Kidnapping nt

kidnapper [ˈkɪdnæpəʳ] N Entführer(in) m(f), Kidnapper(in) m(f)

kidnapping [ˈkɪdnæpɪŋ] N Entführung f, Kidnapping nt

kidney [ˈkɪdnɪ] N (Anat, Cook) Niere f

kidney: **kidney bean** N Kidneybohne f; **kidney machine** N künstliche Niere

kill [kɪl] **1** VT **(a)** (lit, fig) töten; (lit, shock also) umbringen; feelings, love etc also zerstören; (Hunt) erlegen; pain beseitigen; weeds, hopes vernichten; taste, performance verderben; **to be ~ed in action** fallen; **to be ~ed in battle/in the war** im Kampf/Krieg fallen; **her brother was ~ed in a car accident** ihr Bruder ist bei einem Autounfall ums Leben gekommen; **how many were ~ed?** wie viel Todesopfer gab es?; **she ~ed herself** sie brachte sich um; **many people were ~ed by the plague** viele Menschen sind der Pest zum Opfer gefallen; **she was ~ed with a knife** sie wurde (mit einem Messer) erstochen; **I'll ~ him!** (also fig) den bring ich um (inf); **to ~ time** die Zeit totschlagen; **we have two hours to ~** wir haben noch zwei Stunden übrig; **to ~ two birds with one stone** (Prov) zwei Fliegen mit einer Klappe schlagen (Prov); **she was ~ing herself (laughing)** (inf) sie hat sich totgelacht or kaputtgelacht (inf); **a few more weeks won't ~ you** (inf) noch ein paar Wochen bringen dich nicht um (inf); **my feet are ~ing me** (inf) mir brennen die Füße; **I'll do it (even) if it ~s me** (inf) ich mache es, und wenn es mich umbringt (inf)
(b) parliamentary bill, proposal zu Fall bringen; project zum Scheitern bringen
(c) sound schlucken
(d) (Tech) engine etc abschalten, ausschalten
2 VI töten; **cigarettes can ~** Zigaretten können tödlich sein
3 N **(a)** (of the wolves gathered round for the ~ die Wölfe kreisten die Beute ein, um sie zu erlegen; **to be in at the ~** (fig) den Schlussakt miterleben; **to move** or **close in for the ~** (fig) zum entscheidenden Schlag ausholen
(b) (Hunt etc: = animals killed) Beute f no pl

➤ **kill off** VT SEP **(a)** vernichten, töten; whole race ausrotten; cows, pigs, elephants abschlachten; weeds vertilgen; character in TV series sterben lassen **(b)** (fig) hopes zerstören; speculation ein Ende machen (+dat)

killer [ˈkɪləʳ] N (person) Mörder(in) m(f), Killer(in) m(f) (inf); **this disease is a ~** diese Krankheit ist tödlich; **it's a ~** (inf: race, job etc) das ist der glatte Mord (inf)

killer whale N Schwertwal *m*

killing ['kɪlɪŋ] N **(a)** Töten *nt*, Tötung *f*; **three more ~s in Belfast** drei weitere Morde in Belfast **(b)** (*fig*) **to make a ~** einen Riesengewinn machen

killjoy ['kɪldʒɔɪ] N Spielverderber(in) *m(f)*

kiln [kɪln] N (*for baking, burning*) (Brenn)ofen *m*; (*for drying bricks etc*) Trockenofen *m*

kilo ['kiːləʊ] N Kilo *nt*

kilobyte ['kiːləʊbaɪt] N Kilobyte *nt*

kilogramme, (*US*) **kilogram** ['kɪləʊɡræm] N Kilogramm *nt*

kilohertz ['kɪləhɜːts] N Kilohertz *nt*

kilometre, (*US*) **kilometer** [kɪ'lɒmɪtə'] N Kilometer *m*

kilowatt ['kɪləʊwɒt] N Kilowatt *nt*; **~-hour** Kilowattstunde *f*

kilt [kɪlt] N Kilt *m*, Schottenrock *m*

kimono [kɪ'məʊnəʊ] N Kimono *m*

kin [kɪn] N Familie *f*, Verwandtschaft *f*; **has he any ~?** hat er Verwandte *or* Familie?

kind¹ [kaɪnd] N **(a)** (= *class, variety, nature*) Art *f*; (*of coffee, sugar, paint etc*) Sorte *f*; **several ~s of flour** mehrere Mehlsorten; **this ~ of book** diese Art Buch; **all ~s of ...** alle möglichen ...; **what ~ of ...?** was für ein(e) ...?; **the only one of its ~** das Einzige seiner Art; **a funny ~ of name** ein komischer Name; **he's not that ~ of person** so ist er nicht; **they're two of a ~** die beiden sind vom gleichen Typ; (*people*) sie sind vom gleichen Schlag; **she's one of a ~** sie ist wirklich einzigartig; **this ~ of thing** so etwas; **you know the ~ of thing I mean** Sie wissen, was ich meine; **... of all ~s** alle möglichen ...; **something of the ~** so etwas Ähnliches; **you'll do nothing of the ~** du wirst das schön bleiben lassen!; **it's not my ~ of holiday** solche Ferien sind nicht mein Fall (*inf*); **a ~ of ...** eine Art ...; (*so etwas*) ...; **a ~ of box** eine Art Schachtel; **he was so ~ of worried-looking** (*inf*) er sah irgendwie bedrückt aus; **I ~ of thought that he ...** (*inf*) (*and he didn't*) ich habe eigentlich gedacht, dass er ...; (*and he did*) ich habe es mir beinahe gedacht, dass er ...; **are you nervous? – ~ of** (*inf*) bist du nervös? – ja, schon (*inf*)
(b) payment in ~ Bezahlung *f* in Naturalien; **I shall pay you back in ~** (*fig*) ich werde es Ihnen in gleicher Münze heimzahlen

kind² ADJ (+ER) *person* liebenswürdig, nett (*to* zu); *voice, smile, face, description, words* freundlich; **he's ~ to animals** er ist gut zu Tieren; **would you be ~ enough to open the door** wären Sie (vielleicht) so nett *or* freundlich, die Tür zu öffnen; **he was so ~ as to show me the way** er war so nett *or* freundlich *or* lieb und zeigte mir den Weg; **it was very ~ of you to help me** es war wirklich nett von Ihnen, mir zu helfen

kindergarten ['kɪndəɡɑːtn] N Kindergarten *m*

kind-hearted ['kaɪnd'hɑːtɪd] ADJ gütig

kindle ['kɪndl] VT entfachen; *fire also* entzünden; *imagination* anregen; *interest* wecken

kindliness ['kaɪndlɪnɪs] N Freundlichkeit *f*, Güte *f*

kindly ['kaɪndlɪ] **1** ADV **(a)** *speak, act, treat* freundlich; *give, donate, offer* großzügig; *invite* freundlicherweise; **to look ~ (up)on sb** jdm gewogen sein; **to look ~ (up)on sth** etw positiv betrachten
(b) (*with request*) bitte; **~ shut the door** machen Sie doch bitte die Tür zu; **will you ~ do it now** tun Sie das sofort, wenn ich bitten darf
(c) he won't take at all ~ to that das wird ihm gar nicht gefallen; **I don't take ~ to not being asked** es ärgert mich, wenn ich nicht gefragt werde
2 ADJ (+ER) freundlich; *person also* nett; *advice* gut gemeint; *voice* sanft

kindness ['kaɪndnɪs] N **(a)** NO PL Freundlichkeit *f* (*towards* gegenüber), Liebenswürdigkeit *f* (*towards* gegenüber); (= *goodness of heart*) Güte *f* (*towards* gegenüber); **thank you very much for all your ~** vielen Dank, dass Sie so freundlich *or* liebenswürdig waren; **out of the ~ of one's heart** aus reiner Nächstenliebe
(b) (= *act of ~*) Gefälligkeit *f*, Aufmerksamkeit *f*; **to do sb a ~** jdm eine Gefälligkeit erweisen; **it would be a ~ to tell him** man würde ihm einen Gefallen tun, wenn man es ihm sagen würde

kindred ['kɪndrɪd] **1** N, NO PL Verwandtschaft *f* **2** ADJ verwandt; **~ spirit** Gleichgesinnte(r) *mf*

kinematics [ˌkɪnɪ'mætɪks] N SING Kinematik *f*, Bewegungslehre *f*

kinetic [kɪ'netɪk] ADJ kinetisch

king [kɪŋ] N (*lit, fig*) König *m* (*also Chess, Cards*); (*Draughts*) Dame *f*; **to live like a ~** leben wie ein Fürst; **an oil ~** ein Ölmagnat *m*

kingdom ['kɪŋdəm] N **(a)** (*lit*) Königreich *nt* **(b)** (*Rel*) **~ of heaven** Himmelreich *nt*; **to blow sth to ~ come** (*inf*) etw in die Luft jagen (*inf*); **you can go on doing that till ~ come** (*inf*) Sie können (so) bis in alle Ewigkeit weitermachen **(c)** (*Zool, Bot*) Reich *nt*; **the animal/plant ~** das Tier-/Pflanzenreich

king: **kingfisher** N Eisvogel *m*; **kingpin** N (*fig*: = *person*) Stütze *f*; **he's the ~ of the whole organization** mit ihm steht und fällt die ganze Organisation; **king prawn** N Königskrabbe *f*; **king-size(d)** ADJ (*inf*) großformatig; *cigarettes* King-size; *bed* extra groß

kink [kɪŋk] N (*in rope etc*) Knick *m*; (*in hair*) Welle *f*; **to work out** *or* **iron out the ~s** (*fig*) die Sache geradebiegen (*inf*)

kinky ['kɪŋkɪ] ADJ (+ER) (*inf*) abartig; *underwear, leather gear* sexy *inv*

kiosk ['kiːɒsk] N **(a)** Kiosk *m* **(b)** (*Brit Telec*) (Telefon)zelle *f*

kip [kɪp] (*Brit*) **1** N Schläfchen *nt*; **I've got to get some ~** ich muss mal 'ne Runde pennen (*inf*) **2** VI (*also ~ down*) pennen (*inf*)

kipper ['kɪpə'] N Räucherhering *m*

kirk [kɜːk] N (*Scot*) Kirche *f*; **the Kirk** die Presbyterianische Kirche Schottlands

kiss [kɪs] **1** N Kuss *m*; **~ of life** Mund-zu-Mund-Beatmung *f*; **that will be the ~ of death for them** das wird ihnen den Todesstoß versetzen
2 VT küssen; (*fig*: = *touch gently*) sanft berühren; **to ~ sb's cheek** jdn auf die Wange küssen; **to ~ sb's hand** jdm die Hand küssen; *woman's hand* (*in greeting*) jdm einen Handkuss geben; **they ~ed each other** sie küssten sich; **to ~ sb good night/goodbye** jdm einen Gutenachtkuss/ Abschiedskuss geben; **to ~ sth goodbye** (*fig inf*) sich (*dat*) etw abschminken (*inf*)
3 VI küssen; (= *each other*) sich küssen; **to ~ and make up** sich mit einem Kuss versöhnen; **to ~ and tell** Informationen über eine Affäre an die Medien verkaufen

kiss: **kiss-and-tell** ADJ **~ story** Enthüllungsstory *f* (*mit Details einer Affäre mit einer prominenten Person*); **kiss-off** N (*US inf*) **to give sb the ~** jdn in die Wüste schicken (*inf*); *boyfriend etc* jdm den Laufpass geben (*inf*)

kit [kɪt] N **(a)** (= *equipment, clothes*) Ausrüstung *f*; **gym ~** Sportzeug *nt*; **get your ~ off!** (*inf*) zieh dich aus! **(b)** (= *belongings, luggage etc*) Sachen *pl* **(c)** (*for self-assembly*) Bastelsatz *m* **(d)** (*Brit sl*: = *heroin*) H *nt* (*sl*), Sugar *m* (*sl*)
▶ **kit out** *or* **up** VT SEP (*Brit*) ausrüsten (*esp Mil*), ausstatten; (= *clothe*) einkleiden; **he arrived kitted out in oilskins** er erschien in Ölzeug

kitbag ['kɪtbæg] N Seesack *m*

kitchen ['kɪtʃɪn] N Küche *f*

kitchenette [ˌkɪtʃɪ'net] N (= *separate room*) kleine Küche; (= *part of one room*) Kochnische *f*

kitchen: **kitchen foil** N Alufolie *f*; **kitchen garden** N Gemüsegarten *m*; **kitchen knife** N Küchenmesser *nt*; **kitchen roll** N Küchenrolle *f*; **kitchen scales** PL Küchenwaage *f*; **kitchen sink** N **I've packed everything but the ~** (*inf*) ich habe den ganzen Hausrat eingepackt; **kitchen-sink drama** N Alltagsdrama *nt*; **kitchen unit** N Küchenschrank *m*

kite [kaɪt] N Drachen *m*; **to fly a ~** (*lit*) einen Drachen steigen lassen; (*fig*) einen Versuchsballon steigen lassen

Kite mark N (*Brit*) *dreieckiges Gütezeichen*

kith [kɪθ] N **~ and kin** Blutsverwandte *pl*

kitsch [kɪtʃ] N Kitsch *m*

kitschy ['kɪtʃɪ] ADJ (+ER) kitschig

kitten ['kɪtn] N Kätzchen *nt*; **to have ~s** (*fig inf*) Zustände kriegen (*inf*)

kitty ['kɪtɪ] N (gemeinsame) Kasse; (*Cards etc*) (Spiel)kasse *f*; **there's nothing left in the ~** die Kasse ist leer

kiwi ['kiːwiː] N **(a)** Kiwi *m* **(b)** (*also ~ fruit*) Kiwi(frucht) *f* **(c)** (*inf*: = *New Zealander*) Neuseeländer(in) *m(f)*, Kiwi *m* (*inf*)

Kleenex® ['kliːneks] N Tempo(taschentuch)® *nt*

kleptomaniac [ˌkleptəʊ'meɪnɪæk] N Kleptomane *m*, Kleptomanin *f*

km ABBR *of* **kilometre(s)** km

km/h, kmph ABBR *of* **kilometres per hour** km/h

knack [næk] N Trick *m*, Kniff *m*; (= *talent*) Talent *nt*; **there's a (special) ~ to opening it** da ist ein Trick dabei, wie man das aufbekommt; **you'll soon get the ~ of it** Sie werden den Dreh bald rausbekommen *or* raushaben; **she's got a ~ of saying the wrong thing** sie hat ein Talent, immer das Falsche zu sagen

knackered ['nækəd] ADJ (*Brit inf*) (= *exhausted*) geschafft (*inf*); (= *broken*) kaputt (*inf*)

knapsack ['næpsæk] N Proviantbeutel *m*, Tornister *m* (*esp Mil*)

knead [niːd] VT *dough* kneten; *muscles* massieren

knee [niː] **■** N Knie *nt*; **to be on one's ~s** (*lit, fig*) auf den Knien liegen; **on one's ~s, on bended ~(s)** (*liter, hum*) kniefällig; **to go (down) on one's ~s** (*lit*) niederknien; (*fig*) sich auf die Knie werfen; **to bring a country to its ~s** ein Land in die Knie zwingen **■** VT mit dem Knie stoßen; **to ~ sb in the groin** jdm das Knie zwischen die Beine stoßen

knee: **kneecap** N Kniescheibe *f*; **knee-deep** ADJ knietief; **he was ~ in mud** er steckte knietief im Schlamm; **knee-high** ADJ kniehoch; **kneejerk reaction** N Kurzschlussreaktion *f*

kneel [niːl], *pret, ptp* **knelt** *or* **kneeled** VI (*before* vor +*dat*) knien; (*also ~ down*) niederknien

knee-length ['niːlɛŋθ] ADJ *skirt* knielang; *boots* kniehoch; **~ socks** Kniestrümpfe *pl*

knelt [nɛlt] PRET, PTP *of* **kneel**

knew [njuː] PRET *of* **know**

knickers ['nɪkəz] PL (*Brit*) Schlüpfer *m*; **to get one's ~ in a twist (over sth)** (*inf*) sich (*dat*) (wegen etw) ins Hemd machen (*sl*); **don't get your ~ in a twist!** (*inf*) dreh nicht gleich durch! (*inf*)

knick-knack ['nɪknæk] N nette Kleinigkeit; **~s** Krimskrams *m*; (= *figurines*) Nippes *pl*

knife [naɪf] **■** N, *pl* **knives** Messer *nt*; **~, fork and spoon** Besteck *nt*; **to turn** *or* **twist the ~ (in the wound)** (*fig*) Salz in die Wunde streuen; **to put** *or* **stick the ~ in** (*inf*) böse zuschlagen (*inf*); **the knives are out for him** (*esp Brit inf*) für ihn wird schon das Messer gewetzt; **you could have cut the atmosphere with a ~** die Stimmung war zum Zerreißen gespannt **■** VT einstechen auf (+*acc*) (*fatally*) erstechen

knife: **knife edge** N **to be balanced on a ~** (*fig*) auf Messers Schneide stehen; **knife-point** N **to hold sb at ~** jdn mit einem Messer bedrohen; **knife sharpener** N Messerschärfer *m*

knight [naɪt] **■** N (= *title, Hist*) Ritter *m*; (*Chess*) Springer *m*; **a ~ in shining armour** (*fig*) ein Märchenprinz *m*; **white ~** (*Fin*) weißer Ritter, Retter *m* in der Not; **black ~** (*Fin*) schwarzer Ritter, Firmenjäger *m*; **grey ~** (*Fin*) grauer Ritter, *Anleger, dessen Absichten unklar sind* **■** VT adeln, zum Ritter schlagen

knighthood ['naɪthʊd] N Ritterstand *m*; **to receive a ~** in den Adelsstand erhoben werden

knit [nɪt], *pret, ptp* **knitted** *or* **knit** **■** VT stricken; **to ~ sth for sb, to ~ sb sth** jdm etw stricken; **~ three, purl two** drei rechts, zwei links; **to ~ one's brows** die Stirn runzeln **■** VI (a) stricken (b) (*bones: also ~ together, ~ up*) verwachsen

knitted ['nɪtɪd] ADJ gestrickt; *cardigan, dress etc* Strick-

knitting ['nɪtɪŋ] N Stricken *nt*; (= *material being knitted*) Strickzeug *nt*; **she was doing her ~** sie strickte

knitting: **knitting machine** N Strickmaschine *f*; **knitting needle** N Stricknadel *f*

knitwear ['nɪtwɛəʳ] N Strickwaren *pl*

knives [naɪvz] PL *of* **knife**

knob [nɒb] N (a) (*on walking stick, door*) Knauf *m*; (*on instrument etc*) Knopf *m*; **and the same to you with (brass) ~s on** (*Brit inf*) das beruht auf Gegenseitigkeit (b) **a ~ of butter** ein Stich *m* Butter (c) (*sl: = penis*) Prügel *m* (*sl*), Lanze *f* (*sl*)

knobbly ['nɒblɪ] ADJ (+ER) *wood* knorrig; *surface* uneben; **~ knees** Knubbelknie *pl* (*inf*)

knock [nɒk] **■** N (a) (*esp Brit*) (= *blow*) Stoß *m*; (*esp with hand, tool etc*) Schlag *m*; **to get a ~** einen Stoß/Schlag abbekommen; **I got a ~ on the head** ich habe einen Schlag auf den Kopf bekommen; **the car took a few ~s** mit dem Auto hat es ein paar Mal gebumst (*inf*); **he gave himself a nasty ~** er hat sich böse angestoßen

(b) (= *noise*) **there was a ~ at the door** es hat (an der Tür) geklopft; **I heard a ~** ich habe es klopfen hören

(c) (*esp Brit*) (*fig*: = *setback*) (Tief)schlag *m*; **to (have to) take a lot of ~s** viele Tiefschläge einstecken (müssen); (= *be criticized*) unter starken Beschuss kommen; **to take a ~** (*self-*

confidence, pride etc) erschüttert werden; (*reputation*) geschädigt werden

■ VT (a) stoßen; (*with hand, tool etc*) schlagen; *one's knee, head etc* anstoßen (*on* an +*dat*); (= *nudge, jolt*) stoßen gegen; **to ~ one's head/elbow** *etc* sich (*dat*) den Kopf/Ellbogen *etc* anstoßen; **he ~ed his foot against the table** er stieß mit dem Fuß gegen den Tisch; **to ~ sb on the head** jdn an *or* auf den Kopf schlagen; **I decided to ~ it on the head** (*Brit inf*) ich beschloss, der Sache (*dat*) ein Ende zu machen; **to ~ sb to the ground** jdn zu Boden werfen; **to ~ sb unconscious** jdn bewusstlos werden lassen; (*person*) jdn bewusstlos schlagen; **he ~ed some holes in the side of the box** er machte ein paar Löcher in die Seite der Kiste; **she ~ed the glass to the ground** sie stieß gegen das Glas und es fiel zu Boden; **watch you don't ~ your glass off the table** pass auf, dass du dein Glas nicht vom Tisch stößt; **to ~ some sense into sb** jdn zur Vernunft bringen; **he was ~ed sideways by it** (*fig inf*) es haute ihn um (*inf*)

(b) (*inf*: = *criticize*) (he)runtermachen (*inf*)

■ VI (a) klopfen (*also engine etc*); **to ~ at** *or* **on the door** anklopfen; **to ~ at** *or* **on the window** gegen das Fenster klopfen; **~ before entering** bitte anklopfen

(b) (= *bump*) stoßen (*into, against* gegen); **he ~ed into** *or* **against the gatepost** er rammte den Türpfosten; **his knees were ~ing (together)** ihm zitterten die Knie

▶ **knock about** (*Brit*) *or* **around** **■** VI (*inf*) (a) (*person*) herumziehen (*prep obj* in +*dat*); **he has knocked about** *or* **around a bit** er ist schon (ganz schön) (he)rumgekommen (*inf*); **who's he knocking about** *or* **around with these days?** mit wem hängt er denn jetzt so herum? (*inf*)

(b) (*object*) herumliegen (*prep obj* in +*dat*)

■ VT SEP (a) (= *ill-treat*) verprügeln, schlagen; **he was badly knocked about in the accident** er ist bei dem Unfall ziemlich zugerichtet worden

(b) (= *damage*) beschädigen

(c) **to knock a ball about** *or* **around** ein paar Bälle schlagen

▶ **knock back** VT SEP (*inf*) **he knocked back his whisky** er kippte sich (*dat*) den Whisky hinter die Binde (*inf*); **come on, knock it back** nun trink schon (aus) (*inf*)

▶ **knock down** VT SEP (a) *person, thing* umwerfen; *opponent* (*by hitting*) niederschlagen; (*car, driver*) anfahren; *building* abreißen; *obstacle, fence* niederreißen; **she was knocked down and killed** sie wurde überfahren (b) *price* (*buyer*) herunterhandeln (*to* auf +*acc*); (*seller*) heruntergehen mit; **I knocked him down to £15** ich habe es auf £ 15 heruntergehandelt

▶ **knock off** **■** VI (*inf*) aufhören, Feierabend *or* Schluss machen (*inf*); **to knock off for lunch** Mittag machen (*inf*) **■** VT SEP (a) (*lit*) *vase, cup, person etc* hinunterstoßen; *nose off statue etc* abschlagen; *high jump bar* reißen; **the branch knocked the rider off (his horse)** der Ast riss den Reiter vom Pferd

(b) (*inf*: = *reduce price by*) nachlassen (*for sb* jdm), runtergehen (*inf*); **I got something knocked off** ich habe es billiger bekommen

(c) (*inf*) *essay, painting* hinhauen (*inf*); (*with good result*) aus dem Ärmel schütteln (*inf*)

(d) (*Brit inf*: = *steal*) klauen (*inf*)

(e) (*inf*) **to knock off work** Feierabend machen; **knock it off!** nun hör schon auf!

▶ **knock on** VI (*Brit inf*) **he's knocking on for fifty** er geht auf die fünfzig zu

▶ **knock out** VT SEP (a) *tooth* ausschlagen; *nail* herausschlagen (*of* aus); *pipe* ausklopfen (b) (= *stun*) bewusstlos werden lassen; (*by hitting*) bewusstlos schlagen; (*Boxing*) k. o. schlagen (c) (*from competition*) besiegen (*of* in +*acc*); **to be knocked out** ausscheiden (*of* aus)

▶ **knock over** VT SEP umwerfen; (*car*) anfahren

▶ **knock together** VT SEP (a) *shelter, object* zusammenzimmern; *meal, snack* auf die Beine stellen (*inf*) (b) **I'd like to knock their heads together** man sollte die beiden zur Räson bringen

▶ **knock up** **■** VI (*Brit Sport*) sich einspielen **■** VT SEP *meal* auf die Beine stellen (*inf*); *building* hochziehen; *shelter* zusammenzimmern

knockback ['nɒkbæk] N (*inf*: = *setback*) Rückschlag *m*

knockdown ['nɒkdaʊn] ADJ ATTR **~ price** Schleuderpreis *m*

knocker ['nɒkə^r] N **(a)** (= *door ~*) (Tür)klopfer *m* **(b)** (*inf*) **(pair of)** ~**s** Titten *pl* (*sl*)
knocking ['nɒkɪŋ] N (*in engine*) Klopfen *nt*
knocking-off time [ˌnɒkɪŋ'ɒftaɪm] N (*inf*) Feierabend *m*
knock: **knock-kneed** ADJ x-beinig; **to be** ~ X-Beine haben;
  knock-on effect N (*Brit*) Folgewirkungen *pl* (*on* auf +*acc*)
knockout ['nɒkaʊt] **1** N **(a)** (*Boxing*) K. o. *m*; **he won by a** ~ er gewann durch K. o. **(b)** (*inf*: = *person, thing*) Wucht *f* (*inf*) **2** ATTR **(a)** (*Boxing, fig*) **to deliver a** ~ **blow** einen K.-o.-Schlag landen *or* versetzen (*fig*) **(b)** ~ **competition** Ausscheidungskampf *m*
knot [nɒt] **1** N **(a)** (*lit, fig*) Knoten *m* (*also Naut*); **to tie/undo** *or* **untie a** ~ einen Knoten machen/aufmachen; **to tie the** ~ (*fig*) den Bund fürs Leben schließen; **to tie oneself (up) in** ~**s** (*fig*) sich immer mehr verwickeln; **there was a** ~ **in his stomach** sein Magen krampfte sich zusammen **(b)** (*in wood*) Ast *m*, Verwachsung *f* **2** VT einen Knoten machen in (+*acc*); (= ~ *together*) verknoten; **get** ~**ted!** (*Brit inf*) du kannst mich mal! (*inf*)
➤ **knot together** VT SEP verknoten
knotty ['nɒtɪ] ADJ (+ER) *wood* knorrig; *problem* verwickelt

know [nəʊ]

1 TRANSITIVE VERB	**4** NOUN
2 INTRANSITIVE VERB	**5** PHRASAL VERBS
3 SET STRUCTURES	

vb: pret **knew**, ptp **known**

1 TRANSITIVE VERB

(a) (= *have knowledge about*) *answer, facts, details, results etc* wissen; *French, English etc* können; **he knew her to be guilty** er wusste, dass sie schuldig war; **to know what one is talking about** wissen, wovon man redet; **to know one's own mind** wissen, was man will; **he might even be dead for all I know** vielleicht ist er sogar tot, was weiß ich; **that's worth knowing** das ist ja interessant; **before you know where you are** ehe man sichs versieht; **she's angry!** – **don't I know it!** (*inf*) sie ist wütend! – wem sagst du das! (*inf*)
(b) (= *be acquainted with*) *people, places, book, author* kennen; **if I know John, he'll already be there** wie ich John kenne, ist er schon da; **he didn't want to know me** er wollte nichts mit mir zu tun haben
(c) (= *recognize*) erkennen; **to know sb by his voice/walk** *etc* jdn an der Stimme/am Gang *etc* erkennen; **he knows a bargain when he sees one** er weiß, was ein guter Kauf ist; **this is the end of the welfare system as we know it** das ist das Ende des uns bekannten Wohlfahrtssystems
(d) (= *be able to distinguish*) unterscheiden können; **don't you know your right from your left?** können Sie rechts und links nicht unterscheiden?; **do you know the difference between…?** wissen Sie, was der Unterschied zwischen … ist?
(e) (= *experience*) erleben; **I've never known it to rain so heavily** so einen starken Regen habe ich noch nie erlebt; **I've never known him (to) smile** ich habe ihn noch nie lächeln sehen; **have you ever known me (to) tell a lie?** haben Sie mich jemals lügen hören?

2 INTRANSITIVE VERB wissen; **who knows?** wer weiß?; **I know!** ich weiß!; (*having a good idea*) ich weiß was!; **I don't know** (das) weiß ich nicht; **as far as I know** soviel ich weiß; **he just didn't want to know** er wollte einfach nicht hören; **I wouldn't know** (*inf*) weiß ich (doch) nicht (*inf*); **how should I know?** wie soll ich das wissen?; **how was I to know?** wie sollte ich das wissen?

3 SET STRUCTURES

✦**to know that …** wissen, dass …

Note that while in English **that** *can be omitted, in German* **dass** *must be used to introduce the next sentence.*

when I saw the ambulance, I knew (that) something was wrong als ich den Krankenwagen sah, wusste ich, dass etwas nicht stimmte
✦**to know why…** wissen, warum …; **he didn't know why** er wusste nicht, warum

✦**to know how** to know how to do sth (*in theory*) wissen, wie man etw macht; (*in practice*) etw tun können; **I don't know how you can say that!** wie kannst du das nur sagen!
✦**to know better** **I know better than that** ich bin ja nicht ganz dumm; **I know better than to say something like that** ich werde mich hüten, so etwas zu sagen; **he/you ought to have known better** das war dumm (von ihm/dir); **they don't know any better** sie kennens nicht anders
✦**to know best** OK, **you know best** o.k., Sie müssens wissen
✦**to get to know** to get to know sb jdn kennen lernen; **to get to know sth** *methods, style, pronunciation etc* etw lernen; *habits, faults, shortcuts etc* etw herausfinden; **to get to know a place** einen Ort kennen lernen
✦**to let sb know** to let sb know sth (= *not keep back*) jdn etw wissen lassen; (= *tell, inform*) jdm von etw Bescheid geben
✦**you know…** you know, we could/there is … weißt du, wir könnten/da ist …; **it's raining, you know** es regnet; **wear the black dress, you know, the one with the red belt** zieh das schwarze Kleid an, du weißt schon, das mit dem roten Gürtel; **(if you) know what I mean** du weißt schon
✦**you never know** man kann nie wissen
✦**I'll have you know** it was nothing to do with me, **I'll have you know!** es hatte nichts mit mir zu tun, damit du es weißt!
✦**there's no knowing** (*inf*) there's no knowing what he'll do man weiß nie, was er noch tut
✦**what do you know!** (*inf*) sieh mal einer an!
✦**to be known** to be known (to sb) (jdm) bekannt sein; **it is (well) known that …** es ist (allgemein) bekannt, dass …; **to be known for sth** für etw bekannt sein; **he is known to have been here** man weiß, dass er hier war; **he is known as Mr Smith** man kennt ihn als Herrn Smith; **she wishes to be known as Mrs White** sie möchte Frau White genannt werden
✦**to make sb/sth known** jdn/etw bekannt machen; **to make it known that …** bekannt geben, dass …; **to make oneself known** sich melden (*to sb* bei jdm); (= *introduce oneself*) sich vorstellen (*to sb* jdm)
✦**to become known** bekannt werden
✦**to let it be known that …** bekannt geben, dass …

4 NOUN

✦**to be in the know** (*inf*) im Bild sein (*inf*), Bescheid wissen (*inf*)

5 PHRASAL VERBS

➤ **know about** **1** VI +PREP OBJ *history, maths, politics* sich auskennen in (+*dat*); *Africa* Bescheid wissen über (+*acc*); *women, men, cars, horses* sich auskennen mit; (= *be aware of, have been told about*) wissen von; **I know about that** das weiß ich; **I'd rather not know about it** das möchte ich lieber nicht wissen; **did you know about Maggie?** weißt du über Maggie Bescheid?; **to get to know about sb/sth** von jdm/etw hören; **I don't know about that** davon weiß ich nichts; (= *don't agree*) da bin ich aber nicht so sicher; **I don't know about you, but I'm hungry** ich weiß nicht, wie es Ihnen geht, aber ich habe Hunger
2 VT SEP +PREP OBJ **to know a lot/nothing/something about sth** viel/nichts/einiges über etw (*acc*) wissen; (*in history, maths etc*) in etw (*dat*) gut/nicht/ein bisschen Bescheid wissen; (*about cars, horses etc*) viel/nichts/einiges von etw verstehen; (= *be aware of, have been told about*) viel/nichts/einiges von etw wissen; **that was the first I knew about it** davon hatte ich nichts gewusst; **I know all about that** da kenne ich mich aus; (= *I'm aware of that*) das weiß ich; (= *I've been told about it*) ich weiß Bescheid; **I know all about you** ich weiß über Sie Bescheid

➤ **know of** VI +PREP OBJ *café, better method* kennen; *sb, sb's death* gehört haben von; **I soon got to know of all the facts** ich war bald über alle Fakten informiert; **not that I know of** nicht, dass ich wüsste

know: **know-all** N (*Brit inf*) Alleswisser(in) *m(f)*; **know-how** N Know-how *nt*; **he hasn't got the** ~ **for** *or* **to do the job** er hat nicht die nötige Sachkenntnis für diese Arbeit
knowing ['nəʊɪŋ] ADJ *look, smile* wissend; *person* verständnisvoll
knowingly ['nəʊɪŋlɪ] ADV **(a)** (= *consciously*) absichtlich **(b)** *look, smile* wissend

know-it-all [ˈnəʊɪtɔːl] N (*US inf*) = **know-all**

knowledge [ˈnɒlɪdʒ] N **(a)** (= *understanding, awareness*) Wissen *nt*, Kenntnis *f*; **to have ~ of** wissen von; **to have no ~ of** nichts wissen von; **to (the best of) my ~** soviel ich weiß; **not to my ~** nicht, dass ich wüsste **(b)** (= *learning, facts learned*) Kenntnisse *pl*, Wissen *nt*; **my ~ of English** meine Englischkenntnisse *pl*; **my ~ of D.H. Lawrence** was ich von D. H. Lawrence kenne; **the police have no ~ of him** die Polizei weiß nichts über ihn

knowledgeable [ˈnɒlɪdʒəbl] ADJ kenntnisreich, bewandert; **to be ~** viel wissen (*about* über +*acc*)

known [nəʊn] **1** PTP *of* **know 2** ADJ bekannt; *expert also* anerkannt; **it is a ~ fact that ...** es ist (allgemein) bekannt, dass ...; **~ quantity** bekannte Größe

knuckle [ˈnʌkl] N (Finger)knöchel *m*; (*of meat*) Hachse *f*
➤ **knuckle down** VI (*inf*) sich dahinter klemmen (*inf*)
➤ **knuckle under** VI (*inf*) spuren (*inf*); (*to demands*) sich beugen (*to* +*dat*)

KO 1 N K.-o.-Schlag *m* **2** VT (*Boxing*) k. o. schlagen

koala [kəʊˈɑːlə] N (*also* ~ **bear**) Koala(bär) *m*

kooky [ˈkuːkɪ] ADJ (+ER) (*US inf*) komisch (*inf*), verrückt (*inf*)

Koran [kɒˈrɑːn] N Koran *m*

Korea [kəˈrɪə] N Korea *nt*

Korean [kəˈrɪən] **1** ADJ koreanisch; **~ war** Koreakrieg *m* **2** N Koreaner(in) *m(f)*

kosher [ˈkəʊʃəʳ] ADJ **(a)** koscher **(b)** (*inf*) in Ordnung

Kosovo [ˈkɒsɒvəʊ] N Kosovo *nt*

kowtow [ˈkaʊtaʊ] VI **to ~ to sb** vor jdm dienern *or* katzbuckeln (*inf*)

kph ABBR *of* **kilometres per hour** kph

Kremlin [ˈkremlɪn] N **the ~** der Kreml

kudos [ˈkjuːdɒs] N Ansehen *nt*, Ehre *f*

kung fu [ˈkʌŋˈfuː] N Kung-Fu *nt*

Kurd [kɜːd] N Kurde *m*, Kurdin *f*

Kurdish [ˈkɜːdɪʃ] ADJ kurdisch

Kuwait [kʊˈweɪt] N Kuwait *nt*

Kuwaiti [kʊˈweɪtɪ] **1** ADJ kuwaitisch **2** N Kuwaiter(in) *m(f)*

kw ABBR *of* **kilowatt(s)** kW

Ll

L, l [el] N L *nt*, l *nt*
L (a) (*Brit Mot*) ABBR *of* **Learner (b)** ABBR *of* **large**
l (a) ABBR *of* **litre(s)** l. **(b)** ABBR *of* **left** l
lab [læb] ABBR *of* **laboratory**
label ['leɪbl] **1** N (*lit*) Etikett *nt* (*also fig*), *usu pej* Label *nt*; (*showing contents, instructions etc*) Aufschrift *f*; (*on specimen, cage*) Schild *nt*; (*tied on*) Anhänger *m*; (*adhesive*) Aufkleber *m*; (*of record company*) Label *nt*; **on the Pye ~** unter dem Pye-Label; **green ~** (*Comm*) Umweltetikett *nt*, ≈ blauer Engel **2** VT **(a)** (*lit*) etikettieren; (= *write on*) beschriften; **the bottle was labelled** (*Brit*) *or* **labeled** (= *US*) **"poison"** die Flasche trug die Aufschrift „Gift"
(b) (*fig*) *ideas* bezeichnen; (*pej*) abstempeln; **to ~ sb (as) sth** jdn als etw abstempeln
labor *etc* (*US*) = **labour** *etc*; **labor union** (*US*) Gewerkschaft *f*

laboratory [lə'bɒrətərɪ, (*US*) 'læbrə,tɔːrɪ] N Labor(atorium) *nt*; **~ assistant** Laborant(in) *m(f)*
laborious [lə'bɔːrɪəs] ADJ *task* mühsam; *style* umständlich
laboriously [lə'bɔːrɪəslɪ] ADV mühsam; *speak* umständlich
labour, (*US*) **labor** ['leɪbəʳ] **1** N **(a)** (= *work in general*) Arbeit *f*; (= *toil*) Anstrengung *f*, Mühe *f*
(b) (= *task*) Aufgabe *f*; **it was a ~ of love** ich/er *etc* tat es aus Liebe zur Sache
(c) (= *persons*) Arbeitskräfte *pl*; **to withdraw one's ~** die Arbeit verweigern; **~ legislation** Arbeitsgesetzgebung *f*
(d) (*Brit Pol*) **Labour** die Labour Party
(e) (*Med*) Wehen *pl*; **to be in ~** in den Wehen liegen; **to go into ~** die Wehen bekommen
2 VT *point, subject* auswalzen; **I won't ~ the point** ich will nicht darauf herumreiten
3 VI **(a)** (*in fields etc*) arbeiten; (= *work hard*) sich abmühen (*at, with* mit); **to ~ under a misapprehension** sich einer Illusion (*dat*) hingeben
(b) (= *move etc with effort or difficulty*) sich quälen; **to ~ up a hill** sich einen Hügel hinaufquälen
labour camp, (*US*) **labor camp** N Arbeitslager *nt*
Labour Day N der Tag der Arbeit
laboured, (*US*) **labored** ['leɪbəd] ADJ schwerfällig; *breathing* schwer
labourer, (*US*) **laborer** ['leɪbərəʳ] N (Hilfs)arbeiter(in) *m(f)*; (= *farm ~*) Landarbeiter(in) *m(f)*
labour, (*US*) **labor**: **labour force** N Arbeiterschaft *f*; (*of company*) Belegschaft *f*; **labour-intensive** ADJ arbeitsintensiv; **labour market** N Arbeitsmarkt *m*; **labour pains** PL Wehen *pl*
Labour Party N (*Brit*) Labour Party *f*
labour-saving, (*US*) **labor-saving** ['leɪbəseɪvɪŋ] ADJ arbeitssparend
Labrador ['læbrədɔːʳ] N (= *dog*) Labradorhund *m*
labyrinth ['læbɪrɪnθ] N (*lit, fig*) Labyrinth *nt*
lace [leɪs] **1** N **(a)** (= *fabric*) Spitze *f* **(b)** (*of shoe*) Schnürsenkel *m* **2** VT **(a)** *shoe* zubinden **(b) to ~ a drink with drugs/poison** Drogen/Gift in ein Getränk mischen; **~d with brandy** mit einem Schuss Weinbrand **(c)** (*fig*) **her comments were ~d with sarcasm** ihre Bemerkungen waren mit Sarkasmus gewürzt
▶ **lace up** VT SEP (zu)schnüren
lacerate ['læsəreɪt] VT (*lit*) *hand, skin* verletzen; *clothes* aufreißen; (*by glass etc*) zerschneiden; (*by claws, whip*) zerfetzen; **he ~d his arm** er zog sich (*dat*) tiefe Wunden am Arm zu
laceration [,læsə'reɪʃən] N Fleischwunde *f*; (= *tear*) Risswunde *f*

lace-up (shoe) ['leɪsʌp(ʃuː)] N Schnürschuh *m*
lack [læk] **1** N Mangel *m*; **for** *or* **through ~ of sth** aus Mangel an etw (*dat*); **though it wasn't for ~ of trying** nicht, dass er sich/ich mich *etc* nicht bemüht hätte; **there was a complete ~ of interest** es bestand überhaupt kein Interesse; **~ of water/time** Wasser-/Zeitmangel *m*; **there was no ~ of applicants** es fehlte nicht an Bewerbern
2 VT **they ~ the necessary equipment/talent** es fehlt ihnen an der notwendigen Ausrüstung/am richtigen Talent
3 VI **to be ~ing** fehlen; **innovation has been sadly ~ing throughout the project** es fehlte leider während des ganzen Projektes an Innovationen; **he is ~ing in confidence** ihm fehlt es an Selbstvertrauen; **he is completely ~ing in any sort of decency** er besitzt überhaupt keinen Anstand; **he ~ed for nothing** es fehlte ihm an nichts
lackadaisical [,lækə'deɪzɪkəl] ADJ (= *lacking energy*) lustlos; (= *careless*) nachlässig
lackey ['lækɪ] N (*lit, fig*) Lakai *m*
lacking ['lækɪŋ] ADJ **to be found ~** sich nicht bewähren
lacklustre, (*US*) **lackluster** ['læk,lʌstəʳ] ADJ *surface* stumpf, glanzlos; *style* langweilig
laconic [lə'kɒnɪk] ADJ lakonisch; *prose, style* knapp
lacquer ['lækəʳ] **1** N Lack *m*; (= *hair ~*) Haarspray *nt* **2** VT lackieren; *hair* sprayen
lacquered ['lækəd] ADJ lackiert; *hair* gesprayt; **~ table** Lacktisch *m*
lacrosse [lə'krɒs] N Lacrosse *nt*
lactose ['læktəʊs] N Laktose *f*
lacy ['leɪsɪ] ADJ (+ER) Spitzen-; (= *like lace*) spitzenartig; **~ underwear** Spitzenunterwäsche
lad [læd] N Junge *m*; (*in stable etc*) Bursche *m*; **young ~** junger Mann; **listen, ~** hör mir mal zu, mein Junge!; **when I was a ~** als ich ein junger Bursche war; **all together, ~s, push!** alle Mann anschieben!; **he's a bit of a ~** (*inf*) er ist ein ziemlicher Draufgänger; **he's one of the ~s** (*Brit inf*) er gehört dazu; **he likes a night out with the ~s** (*Brit inf*) er geht gern mal mit seinen Kumpels weg (*inf*)
ladder ['lædəʳ] **1** N **(a)** (*lit, fig*) Leiter *f*; **to be at the top/bottom of the ~** ganz oben/unten auf der Leiter stehen; **to move up the social/career ~** gesellschaftlich/beruflich aufsteigen
(b) (*Brit: in stocking*) Laufmasche *f*; (*US*) *stocking* zerreißen; **I've ~ed my tights** ich habe mir eine Laufmasche (in meiner Strumpfhose) geholt **3** VI (*Brit: stocking*) Laufmaschen bekommen
laddish ['lædɪʃ] ADJ (*Brit inf*) machohaft *inf*
laden ['leɪdn] ADJ (*lit, fig*) beladen (*with* mit)
la-di-da ['lɑːdɪ'dɑː] ADJ, ADV (*inf*) affektiert, affig (*inf*)
ladle ['leɪdl] **1** N (Schöpf- *or* Suppen)kelle *f* **2** VT schöpfen
▶ **ladle out** VT SEP *soup etc, money* austeilen
lady ['leɪdɪ] N **(a)** Dame *f*; **"Ladies"** (= *lavatory*) „Damen"; **where is the ladies** *or* **the ladies' room?** wo ist die Damentoilette?; **ladies and gentlemen!** sehr geehrte Damen und Herren!; **the old ~** (*inf*) (= *mother*) die alte Dame (*inf*); (= *wife*) meine/deine/seine Alte (*inf*); **young ~** junge Dame; (*scoldingly*) mein Fräulein; **his young ~** seine Freundin; **ladies' bicycle** Damen(fahr)rad *nt*
(b) (= *noble*) Adlige *f*; **Lady** (*as a title*) Lady *f*; **dinner is served, my ~** es ist angerichtet, Mylady *or* gnädige Frau
lady: ladybird, (*US*) **ladybug** N Marienkäfer *m*; **lady doctor** N Ärztin *f*; **lady friend** N Dame *f*; **ladylike** ADJ damenhaft, vornehm; **it's not ~** es gehört sich nicht für eine Dame
lag¹ [læg] **1** N (= *time-~*) Zeitabstand *m*; (= *delay*) Verzögerung *f*; **after a ~ of six months** nach sechs Monaten **2** VI (*in pace*) zurückbleiben
▶ **lag behind** VI zurückbleiben; **we lag behind in space exploration** in der Raumforschung liegen wir (weit) zurück; **the government is lagging behind in the polls** die Regierung liegt in den Meinungsumfragen zurück
lag² VT *boiler, pipe* isolieren
lager ['lɑːgəʳ] N helles Bier; **a glass of ~** ein (Glas) Helles
lager lout N (*Brit inf*) betrunkener Rowdy

lagging ['lægɪŋ] N Isolierschicht f; (= material) Isoliermaterial nt

lagoon [lə'guːn] N Lagune f

lah-di-dah ['lɑːdɪ'dɑː] ADJ, ADV (inf) = **la-di-da**

laid [leɪd] PRET, PTP of **lay**³

laid-back [ˌleɪd'bæk] ADJ (inf) cool (inf)

lain [leɪn] PTP see **lie**²

lair [lɛəʳ] N Lager nt; (= cave) Höhle f; (= den) Bau m

laissez-faire ['leɪseɪ'fɛəʳ] ADJ (Econ) Laisser-faire-; ~ **economics** Laisser-faire-Wirtschaftspolitik f

laity ['leɪtɪ] N Laien pl

lake [leɪk] N See m

Lake District N Lake District m (Seengebiet im NW Englands)

la-la land ['lɑːlɑːˌlænd] N (esp US inf) Bezeichnung für Los Angeles, insbesondere Hollywood; **to be in ~** (fig) ganz weit weg sein

lamb [læm] **1** N (a) (= young sheep) Lamm nt (b) (= meat) Lamm(fleisch) nt (c) (= person) **you poor ~!** du armes Lämmchen!; **like a ~ to the slaughter** wie das Lamm zur Schlachtbank **2** VI lammen; **the ~ing season** die Lammungszeit

lambast [læm'bæst], **lambaste** [læm'beɪst] VT fertig machen (inf); **to ~ sb for sth** es jdm wegen etw tüchtig geben (inf)

lamb: lamb chop N Lammkotelett nt; **lamb's lettuce** N Feldsalat m; **lambswool** N Lammwolle f

lame [leɪm] ADJ (+ER) (a) lahm; (as result of stroke etc) gelähmt; **to be ~ in one leg** auf einem Bein lahm sein; **the animal was ~** das Tier lahmte (b) (fig) excuse faul; argument schwach

lamé [lɑː'meɪ] N Lamé nt

lame duck N Niete f (inf); ~ **company** unwirtschaftliche Firma

lamely ['leɪmlɪ] ADV argue, say etc lahm

lament [lə'ment] **1** N (a) Klagen pl, (Weh)klage f (b) (Liter, Mus) Klagelied nt **2** VT **to ~ the fact that ...** die Tatsache bedauern, dass ...

lamentable ['læməntəbl] ADJ beklagenswert; piece of work erbärmlich

lamentably ['læməntəblɪ] ADV erbärmlich, beklagenswert; **he failed ~** er scheiterte kläglich

laminated ['læmɪneɪtɪd] ADJ geschichtet; card, book cover laminiert; ~ **glass** Verbundglas nt; ~ **wood** Sperrholz nt; ~ **plastic** Resopal® nt; ~ **working surfaces** Arbeitsflächen aus Resopal®

lamp [læmp] N Lampe f; (in street) Laterne f; (Aut, Rail) Scheinwerfer m; (= rear ~) Rücklicht nt; (= sun ~) Höhensonne f

lamplight ['læmplaɪt] N **by ~** bei Lampenlicht; **in the ~** im Schein der Lampe(n)

lampoon [læm'puːn] **1** N Spott- or Schmähschrift f **2** VT verspotten

lamp: lamppost N Laternenpfahl m; **lampshade** N Lampenschirm m

lance [lɑːns] **1** N Lanze f **2** VT (Med) öffnen

lance corporal N Obergefreite(r) mf

land [lænd] **1** N (a) (lit, fig) Land nt; (= soil) Boden m; **by ~** auf dem Landweg; **to see how the ~ lies** (fig) die Lage peilen; **to be in the ~ of the living** unter den Lebenden sein; **to work on the ~** das Land bebauen; **to live off the ~** (= grow own food) sich vom Lande ernähren
(b) (as property) Grund und Boden m; (= estates) Ländereien pl; **to own ~** Land besitzen; **she's bought a piece of ~** sie hat ein Stück Land or (for building) ein Grundstück gekauft; **get off my ~!** verschwinden Sie von meinem Grund und Boden!; ~ **utilization** Bodennutzung f
2 VT (a) passengers absetzen; troops landen; goods (from boat) an Land bringen; (from plane) abladen; fish at port anlanden; boat, fish on hook an Land ziehen; **to ~ a plane** (mit einem Flugzeug) landen
(b) (inf: = obtain) kriegen (inf); contract sich (dat) verschaffen; prize (sich dat) holen (inf); job an Land ziehen (inf)
(c) (Brit inf) blow landen (inf); **he ~ed him one, he ~ed him a punch on the jaw** er versetzte ihm einen Kinnhaken
(d) (inf: = place) bringen; **behaviour** (Brit) or **behavior** (US) **like that will ~ you in trouble/jail** bei einem solchen Betragen wirst du noch mal Ärger bekommen/im Gefängnis landen; **it ~ed me in a mess** dadurch bin ich in einen ganz schönen Schlamassel gekommen (inf); **I've ~ed myself in a real mess**

ich bin (ganz schön) in die Klemme geraten (inf)
(e) (inf: = lumber) **to ~ sb with sth** jdm etw andrehen (inf); **I got ~ed with him for two hours** ich hatte ihn zwei Stunden lang auf dem Hals
3 VI (from ship) an Land gehen; **we're coming in to ~** wir setzen zur Landung an; **the bomb ~ed on the building** die Bombe fiel auf das Gebäude; **to ~ on one's feet** (lit) auf den Füßen landen; (fig) auf die Füße fallen; **to ~ on one's head** auf den Kopf fallen

▶ **land up** VI (inf) landen (inf); **you'll land up in trouble** du wirst noch mal Ärger bekommen; **I landed up with nothing** ich hatte schließlich nichts mehr

landed ['lændɪd] ADJ ~ **gentry** Landadel m

landing ['lændɪŋ] N (a) (Aviat) Landung f (b) (on stairs) (inside house, outside flat door) Treppenabsatz m; (corridor outside flat doors) Gang m, Etagenabsatz m

landing: landing card N Einreisekarte f; **landing charges** (Brit), **landing fees** (US) N Landegebühren pl; **landing gear** N Fahrgestell nt; **landing stage** N (Naut) Landesteg m; **landing strip** N Landebahn f

land: landlady N (of flat etc) Vermieterin f; (of pub) Wirtin f; **land line** N (Telec) Landkabel nt; **landlocked** ADJ von Land eingeschlossen; **landlord** N m (of flat etc) Vermieter m; (of pub) Wirt m; **landmark** **1** N (Naut) Landmarke f; (= well-known thing) Wahrzeichen nt; (fig) Meilenstein m **2** ADJ ruling, victory historisch; decision, event von historischer Bedeutung; **land mine** N Landmine f; **landowner** N Grundbesitzer(in) m(f); **landowning** ADJ ATTR mit Grundbesitz; **the ~ class** die Grundbesitzer pl; **land register** N (Brit) Grundbuch nt; **landscape** ['lændskeɪp] **1** N Landschaft f **2** VT big area, natural park landschaftlich gestalten; garden, grounds gärtnerisch gestalten; **landscape gardener** N (for big areas etc) Landschaftsgärtner(in) m(f); (for gardens etc) Gartengestalter(in) m(f); **landscape gardening** N Landschaftsgärtnerei or -gestaltung f; **landslide** N (lit, fig) Erdrutsch m

lane [leɪn] N (in country) (for walking) (Feld)weg m; (for driving) Sträßchen nt; (in town) Gasse f; (Sport) Bahn f; (on road) Spur f; (= shipping ~) Schifffahrtsweg m; (= air ~) (Flug)route f; **in the left-hand ~** (Aut) in or auf der linken Spur; ~ **markings** (in road) Spurmarkierungen pl; **"get in ~"** „einordnen"

language ['læŋgwɪdʒ] N Sprache f; **your ~ is appalling** deine Ausdrucksweise ist entsetzlich; **it's a bloody nuisance! – ~!** verfluchter Mist! – na, so was sagt man doch nicht!; **bad ~** Kraftausdrücke pl; **strong ~** Schimpfwörter pl; (= forceful ~) starke Worte pl; **putting it in plain ~ ...** (= simply) einfach ausgedrückt ...; (= bluntly) um es ganz direkt or ohne Umschweife zu sagen, ...; **to talk sb's ~** jds Sprache sprechen

language: language barrier N Sprachbarriere f; **language course** N Sprachkurs(us) m; **language lab(oratory)** N Sprachlabor nt; **language learning** N Sprachenlernen nt; **language-learning** ADJ facilities, skills zum Sprachenlernen; **language school** N Sprachschule f

languid ['læŋgwɪd] ADJ träge; gesture matt; manner lässig; voice müde

languish ['læŋgwɪʃ] VI schmachten; **the products ~ on the shelves** die Waren bleiben in den Regalen liegen

languorous ['læŋgərəs] ADJ träge; tone, voice schläfrig

lank [læŋk] ADJ hair strähnig

lanky ['læŋkɪ] ADJ (+ER) schlaksig

lantern ['læntən] N Laterne f

lap¹ [læp] N Schoß m; **in or on her ~** auf dem/ihrem Schoß; **it's in the ~ of the gods** es liegt im Schoß der Götter; **to live in the ~ of luxury** ein Luxusleben führen

lap² (Sport) **1** N (= round) Runde f; (fig: = stage) Etappe f; ~ **of honour** (esp Brit) Ehrenrunde f; **we're on the last ~ now** (fig) wir haben es bald geschafft **2** VT überrunden

lap³ VI (waves, water) plätschern (against an +acc)

▶ **lap up** VT SEP (a) liquid auflecken; **the children hungrily lapped up their soup** die Kinder löffelten hungrig ihre Suppe
(b) praise, sunshine genießen

lapel [lə'pel] N Aufschlag m, Revers nt or m

lapse [læps] **1** N (a) (= error) Fehler m; (moral) Fehltritt m; ~ **of judgement** Fehlurteil nt; **he had a momentary ~ of concentration** seine Konzentration ließ einen Augenblick nach; **to suffer from ~s of memory** or **memory ~s** an

Gedächtnisschwäche leiden; **a serious security** ~ ein schwerer Verstoß gegen die Sicherheitsvorkehrungen **(b)** (*of time*) Zeitraum *m*; **time** ~ Zeitraum *m*; **after a** ~ **of 4 months** nach (einem Zeitraum von) 4 Monaten; **there was a** ~ **in the conversation** es gab eine Gesprächspause **②** VI **(a)** (= *decline*) verfallen (*into* in +*acc*); **to** ~ **into one's old ways** wieder in seine alten Gewohnheiten verfallen; **he ~d into silence** er versank in Schweigen; **he ~d into a coma** er sank in ein Koma
(b) (= *expire*) ablaufen; (*claims*) verfallen; **after two months have ~d** nach (Ablauf von) zwei Monaten

lapsed [læpst] ADJ *Catholic* abtrünnig; *insurance policy* verfallen

laptop [ˈlæptɒp] (*Comput*) **①** N Laptop *m* **②** ATTR Laptop-; ~ **PC/computer** Laptop-PC/Computer) *m*

larch [lɑːtʃ] N (*also* ~ **tree**) Lärche *f*

lard [lɑːd] N Schweineschmalz *nt*

larder [ˈlɑːdəʳ] N (*esp Brit*) (= *room*) Speisekammer *f*; (= *cupboard*) Speiseschrank *m*

large [lɑːdʒ] **①** ADJ (+ER) groß; *person* stark, korpulent; *meal* reichlich; ~ **print** Großdruck *m*; "~" (*on clothing label*) „Large"; **I need a ~r size** ich brauche eine größere Größe; **there he/it was as ~ as life** da war er/es in voller Lebensgröße **②** N **(a) at** ~ (= *in general*) im Großen und Ganzen, im Allgemeinen; **people** *or* **the world at** ~ die Allgemeinheit **(b) to be at** ~ (= *free*) frei herumlaufen

largely [ˈlɑːdʒlɪ] ADV zum größten Teil

large: large-print ADJ *book* in Großdruck; **large-scale** ADJ groß angelegt; *reception, party, changes* in großem Rahmen; ~ **production** (*Ind*) Massenproduktion *f*; **a** ~ **map** eine (Land)karte in großem Maßstab

largesse [lɑːˈʒes] N Großzügigkeit *f*

lark¹ [lɑːk] N (*Orn*) Lerche *f*

lark² N (*inf*) **(a)** (*esp Brit*: = *joke, fun*) Jux *m* (*inf*), Spaß *m*; **let's go to the party, it'll be a bit of a** ~ gehen wir zu der Party, das wird bestimmt lustig; **to do sth for a** ~ etw (nur) zum Spaß *or* aus Jux machen **(b)** (*Brit inf*: = *business, affair*) **this whole agency** ~ **is …** die ganze Geschichte mit der Agentur ist … (*inf*); **I don't believe in all this horoscopes** ~ ich glaube nicht an diesen Blödsinn mit den Horoskopen (*inf*)
➤ **lark about** *or* **around** VI (*Brit inf*) herumblödeln; **to lark about with sth** mit etw herumspielen

larva [ˈlɑːvə] N, *pl* **-e** [ˈlɑːvɪ] Larve *f*

laryngitis [ˌlærɪnˈdʒaɪtɪs] N Kehlkopfentzündung *f*

larynx [ˈlærɪŋks] N Kehlkopf *m*

lasagne, lasagna [ləˈzænjə] N Lasagne *pl*

lascivious [ləˈsɪvɪəs] ADJ lasziv (*geh*)

laser [ˈleɪzəʳ] N Laser *m*

laser IN CPDS Laser-; **laser beam** N Laserstrahl *m*; **laser disc** N Laserdisc *f*; **laser gun** N Laserkanone *f*; **laser printer** N Laserdrucker *m*; **laser surgery** N Laserchirurgie *f*

lash¹ [læʃ] N (= *eyelash*) Wimper *f*

lash² **①** N (*as punishment*) (Peitschen)schlag *m* **②** VT **(a)** (= *beat*) peitschen; (*as punishment*) auspeitschen; (*hail, rain, waves*) peitschen gegen **(b)** (= *tie*) festbinden (*to* an +*dat*); **to** ~ **sth together** etw zusammenbinden **③** VI **to** ~ **against** peitschen gegen
➤ **lash out** VI **(a)** (*physically*) (*wild*) um sich schlagen; (*horse*) ausschlagen; **to lash out at sb** auf jdn losgehen **(b)** (*in words*) vom Leder ziehen (*inf*); **to lash out against** *or* **at sb/sth** gegen jdn/etw wettern **(c)** (*inf: with money*) sich in Unkosten stürzen; **to lash out on sth** sich (*dat*) etw was kosten lassen (*inf*); **I'm going to lash out on a new car** ich werde mir ein neues Auto leisten

lashing [ˈlæʃɪŋ] N **(a)** (= *punishment*) Auspeitschung *f* **(b) lashings** PL (*inf*) eine Unmenge (*inf*); ~**s of money/cream** eine Unmenge Geld/Schlagsahne (*inf*)

lass [læs] N (junges) Mädchen

lasso [læˈsuː] **①** N, *pl* **-(e)s** Lasso *m* *or nt* **②** VT mit dem Lasso einfangen

last¹ [lɑːst] **①** ADJ letzte(r, s); **he was** ~ **to arrive** er kam als Letzter an; **the** ~ **person** der Letzte; **the** ~ **but one, the second** ~ **(one)** der/die/das Vorletzte; ~ **Monday, on Monday** ~ letzten Montag; ~ **year** letztes Jahr; **during the** ~ **20 years, these** ~ **20 years** in den letzten 20 Jahren; ~ **but not least** nicht zuletzt, last not least; **that's the** ~ **thing I worry about** das ist das Letzte, worüber ich mir Sorgen machen würde;

that was the ~ **thing I expected** damit hatte ich am wenigsten gerechnet
② N der/die/das Letzte; **he was the** ~ **of the visitors to leave** er ging als Letzter der Besucher; **I'm always the** ~ **to know** ich erfahre immer alles als Letzter; **he withdrew the** ~ **of his money from the bank** er hob sein letztes Geld von der Bank ab; **this is the** ~ **of the cake** das ist der Rest des Kuchens; **that was the** ~ **we saw of him** danach haben wir ihn nicht mehr gesehen; **I hope this is the** ~ **we'll hear of it** ich hoffe, damit ist die Sache erledigt; **the** ~ **I heard, they were getting married** das Letzte, was ich gehört habe, war, dass sie heiraten; **we shall never hear the** ~ **of it** das werden wir noch lange zu hören kriegen; **at** ~ endlich; **at long** ~ schließlich und endlich; **so you're ready at long** ~**!** du bist also endlich fertig geworden!; **to the** ~ bis zum Schluss
③ ADV **when did you** ~ **have a bath** *or* **have a bath** ~**?** wann hast du das letzte Mal gebadet?; **I** ~ **heard from him a month ago** vor einem Monat habe ich das letzte Mal von ihm gehört; **he spoke** ~ er sprach als Letzter; **the horse came in** ~ das Pferd ging als letztes durchs Ziel

last² **①** VT **the car has** ~**ed me eight years** das Auto hat acht Jahre (lang) gehalten; **these cigarettes will** ~ **me a week** diese Zigaretten reichen mir eine Woche; **I didn't think he'd** ~ **the week** ich hätte nicht gedacht, dass er die Woche durchhält **②** VI (= *continue*) dauern; (= *remain intact: cloth, flowers, marriage*) halten; **it can't** ~ es hält nicht an; **it won't** ~ es wird nicht lange so bleiben; **it's too good to** ~ das ist zu schön, um wahr zu sein; **he won't** ~ **long in this job** er wird in dieser Stelle nicht alt werden (*inf*); **the previous boss only** ~**ed a week** der vorige Chef blieb nur eine Woche
➤ **last out** **①** VT SEP ausreichen für; (*people*) durchhalten **②** VI (*money, resources*) ausreichen; (*person*) durchhalten

last-ditch [ˈlɑːstdɪtʃ] ADJ allerletzte(r, s); *attempt, proposals, talks etc* in letzter Minute

lasting [ˈlɑːstɪŋ] ADJ *relationship* dauerhaft; *shame etc* anhaltend

lastly [ˈlɑːstlɪ] ADV schließlich, zum Schluss

last: last-minute ADJ in letzter Minute; **last rites** PL Letzte Ölung; **last word** N **the** ~ (*in fashion*) der letzte Schrei; **to have the** ~ **(on sth)** das letzte Wort (zu etw) haben

latch [lætʃ] N Riegel *m*; **to be on the** ~ nicht verschlossen sein; **to leave the door on the** ~ die Tür nur einklinken
➤ **latch on** VI (*inf*) **(a)** (= *attach o.s.*) sich anschließen (*to* +*dat*); **she latched on to me at the party** sie hängte sich auf der Party an mich (*inf*) **(b)** (= *understand*) kapieren (*inf*)

late [leɪt] **①** ADJ (+ER) **(a)** spät; *opening hours* lang; **to be** ~ **(for sth)** (zu etw) zu spät kommen; **the train/bus is (five minutes)** ~ der Zug/Bus hat (fünf Minuten) Verspätung; **he is** ~ **with his rent** er hat seine Miete noch nicht bezahlt; **my period is** ~**, I am** ~ meine Periode ist noch nicht da; **that made me** ~ **for work** dadurch bin ich zu spät zur Arbeit gekommen; **that made the coach** ~ dadurch hatte der Bus Verspätung; **due to the** ~ **arrival of …** wegen der verspäteten Ankunft … (+*gen*); **it's too** ~ **in the day (for you) to do that** es ist zu spät (für dich), das noch zu tun; **it's** ~ es ist spät; **it's getting** ~ es ist schon spät; ~ **train/bus** Spätzug/-bus *m*; **at this** ~ **hour** zu so später Stunde; **they work** ~ **hours** sie arbeiten bis spät (am Abend); **they had a** ~ **dinner yesterday** sie haben gestern spät zu Abend gegessen; "~ **opening until 7pm on Fridays**" „freitags verlängerte Öffnungszeiten bis 19 Uhr"; **he's a** ~ **developer** er ist ein Spätentwickler; **they scored two** ~ **goals** sie erzielten zwei Tore in den letzten Spielminuten; **it happened in the** ~ **eighties** es geschah Ende der achtziger Jahre; **a man in his** ~ **eighties** ein Mann hoch in den Achtzigern; **in the** ~ **morning** am späten Vormittag; **a** ~ **18th-century building** ein Gebäude aus dem späten 18. Jahrhundert; **he came in** ~ **June** er kam Ende Juni
(b) (= *deceased*) verstorben; **the** ~ **John F. Kennedy** John F. Kennedy
② ADV spät; **to come** *or* **arrive** ~ (*person*) zu spät kommen; (*bus, train*) Verspätung haben; **I'll be home** ~ **today** ich komme heute spät nach Hause; **the train arrived/was running eight minutes** ~ der Zug hatte acht Minuten Verspätung; **the baby was born two weeks** ~ das Baby kam zwei Wochen nach dem Termin; **we're running** ~ **today** wir sind heute spät dran; **better** ~ **than never** besser spät als gar nicht; **to sit** *or* **stay up** ~ lange aufbleiben; **the chemist is open** ~ **on Thursdays** die Apotheke hat donnerstags länger geöffnet; **to work** ~ **at the office** länger im Büro arbeiten; ~ **at night** spät

abends; **~ last night** spät gestern Abend; **~ into the night** bis spät in die Nacht; **~ in the afternoon** am späten Nachmittag; **~ last century/in the year** (gegen) Ende des letzten Jahrhunderts/Jahres; **they scored ~ in the second half** gegen Ende der zweiten Halbzeit gelang ihnen ein Treffer; **we decided rather ~ in the day to come too** wir haben uns ziemlich spät entschlossen, auch zu kommen; **of ~** in letzter Zeit; **it was as ~ as 1900 before child labour** (Brit) or **labor** (US) **was abolished** erst 1900 wurde die Kinderarbeit abgeschafft

latecomer [ˈleɪtkʌməʳ] N Nachzügler(in) m(f) (inf)

lately [ˈleɪtlɪ] ADV in letzter Zeit; **till ~** bis vor kurzem

late-night [ˈleɪtˌnaɪt] ADJ **~ movie** Spätfilm m; **~ shopping** Einkauf m am (späten) Abend

latent [ˈleɪtənt] ADJ latent; *energy* ungenutzt

late payment notice N (US) Mahnschreiben nt

later [ˈleɪtəʳ] ADJ, ADV später; **at a ~ hour, at a ~ time** später; **in (his) ~ years** or **life** in späteren Jahren; **the weather cleared up ~ (on) in the day** das Wetter klärte sich im Laufe des Tages auf; **~ (on) in life** später im Leben; **~ (on) in the play** im weiteren Verlauf des Stückes; **I'll tell you ~ (on)** ich erzähle es dir später; **see you ~!** bis später; **they must be handed in no ~ than Monday** sie müssen bis spätestens Montag abgegeben werden

lateral ADJ, **laterally** ADV [ˈlætərəl, -ɪ] seitlich

lateral thinking N unkonventionelles Denken, Querdenken nt

latest [ˈleɪtɪst] **1** ADJ **(a)** *fashion, version* neu(e)ste(r, s); *technology* modernste(r, s); **the ~ news** das Neu(e)ste; **the ~ attempt to rescue them** der jüngste Versuch, sie zu retten **(b)** späteste(r, s); **what is the ~ date you can come?** wann kannst du spätestens kommen? **2** N **the ~ in a series of attacks** der jüngste in einer Reihe von Anschlägen; **what's the ~ (about John)?** was gibts Neues (über John)?; **wait till you hear the ~!** warte, bis du das Neueste gehört hast!; **it's the ~ in computer games/in technology** es ist das neueste Computerspiel/die neueste Technik; **at the (very) ~** spätestens

latex [ˈleɪteks] N Latex m

lathe [leɪð] N Drehbank f

lather [ˈlɑːðəʳ] N (Seifen)schaum m; **to get** or **work oneself up into a ~ (about sth)** (inf) sich (über etw acc) aufregen

Latin [ˈlætɪn] **1** ADJ **(a)** (= *Roman*) römisch **(b)** romanisch; *temperament, charm* südländisch **2** N **(a)** (= *person*) Südländer(in) m(f) **(b)** (*Ling*) Latein(isch) nt

Latin: Latin America N Lateinamerika nt; **Latin American 1** ADJ lateinamerikanisch **2** N Lateinamerikaner(in) m(f)

latitude [ˈlætɪtjuːd] N Breite f; (*fig*) Spielraum m

latte [ˈlɑːteɪ] N Caffè latte m

latter [ˈlætəʳ] **1** ADJ **(a)** (= *second of two*) letztere(r, s) **(b)** (= *at the end*) **the ~ part of the book/story is better** gegen Ende wird das Buch/die Geschichte besser; **the ~ half of the week/year** die zweite Hälfte der Woche/des Jahres **2** N **the ~** der/die/das/Letztere; (*more than one*) die Letzteren pl

latter-day [ˈlætəˈdeɪ] ADJ modern

latterly [ˈlætəlɪ] ADV (= *recently*) in letzter Zeit; (= *towards end of period*) zuletzt; (= *towards end of life*) in späteren Jahren

lattice [ˈlætɪs] N Gitter nt

latticework [ˈlætɪswɜːk] N Gitterwerk nt

Latvia [ˈlætvɪə] N Lettland nt

Latvian [ˈlætvɪən] **1** ADJ lettisch **2** N Lette m, Lettin f

laud [lɔːd] VT (*old*) preisen (*geh*)

laudable [ˈlɔːdəbl] ADJ lobenswert

laugh [lɑːf] **1** N **(a)** Lachen nt; **no, she said, with a ~** nein, sagte sie lachend; **she let out** or **gave a loud ~** sie lachte laut auf; **to have a good ~ over** or **about sth** sich köstlich über etw (*acc*) amüsieren; **it'll give us a ~** (*inf*) das wird lustig; **to have the last ~ (over** or **on sb)** es jdm zeigen (*inf*); **to get a ~** einen Lacherfolg verbuchen; **to play for ~s** Lacherfolge haben wollen

(b) (*inf*: = *fun*) **what a ~** (das ist ja) zum Totlachen or zum Schreien (*inf*!); **just for a ~** or **for ~s** nur (so) aus Spaß; **it'll be a good ~** es wird bestimmt lustig; **he's a (good) ~** er ist urkomisch or zum Schreien (*inf*)

2 VI lachen (*about, at, over* über +*acc*); **to ~ at sb** sich über jdn lustig machen; **it's nothing to ~ about** das ist nicht zum Lachen; **you'll be ~ing on the other side of your face** (*Brit*) or

mouth (*US*) **soon** dir wird das Lachen noch vergehen; **to ~ out loud** laut auflachen; **to ~ in sb's face** jdm ins Gesicht lachen; **you've got to ~** es ist eigentlich zum Lachen; **don't make me ~!** (*iro inf*) dass ich nicht lache! (*inf*); **if you've got your own house, you're ~ing** (*inf*) wenn man ein eigenes Haus hat, hat man es gut

3 VT **to ~ oneself silly** sich tot- or kaputtlachen (*inf*); **the idea was ~ed out of court** die Idee wurde verlacht; **don't be silly, he ~ed** red keinen Unsinn, sagte er lachend

► **laugh off** VT **(a)** ALWAYS SEPARATE **to laugh one's head off** sich tot- or kaputtlachen (*inf*) **(b)** SEP (= *dismiss*) mit einem Lachen abtun

laughable [ˈlɑːfəbl] ADJ lachhaft, lächerlich

laughing [ˈlɑːfɪŋ] **1** ADJ lachend; **it's no ~ matter** das ist nicht zum Lachen **2** N Lachen nt; **hysterical ~** hysterisches Gelächter

laughing gas N Lachgas nt

laughingly [ˈlɑːfɪŋlɪ] ADV lächerlicherweise; **what the government ~ calls its economic policy** das, was die Regierung als Wirtschaftspolitik bezeichnet, obwohl das eigentlich ein Witz ist

laughing stock N Witzfigur f

laughter [ˈlɑːftəʳ] N Gelächter nt; **~ broke out among the audience** das Publikum brach in Gelächter aus

launch [lɔːntʃ] **1** N **(a)** (= *vessel*) Barkasse f **(b)** (= *launching*) (*of ship*) Stapellauf m; (*of lifeboat*) Aussetzen nt; (*of rocket*) Abschuss m **(c)** (= *launching*) (*of company*) Gründung f; (*of new product*) Einführung f; (*with party, publicity: of film, play, book*) Lancierung f; (*bringing out*) (*of film, play*) Premiere f; (*of book*) Herausgabe f; (*of shares*) Emission f **2** VT **(a)** *new vessel* vom Stapel lassen; *lifeboat* aussetzen; *rocket* abschießen

(b) *company, newspaper, initiative* gründen; *new product, programme, trend* einführen; (*with party, publicity*) *film, play, book* lancieren; (= *bring out*) *film* anlaufen lassen; *play* auf die Bühne bringen; *book, series* herausbringen; *plan, investigation* in die Wege leiten; *career* starten; *policy* in Angriff nehmen; *shares* emittieren; **the attack was ~ed at 15.00 hours** der Angriff fand um 15.00 Uhr statt; **to ~ sb on his way** jdm einen guten Start geben; **to ~ a takeover bid** (*Comm*) ein Übernahmeangebot machen

► **launch into** VI +PREP OBJ angreifen; **the author launches straight into his main theme** der Autor kommt gleich zum Hauptthema; **he launched into a description of his new house** er legte mit einer Beschreibung seines neuen Hauses los (*inf*)

launching: launching pad N Start- or Abschussrampe f; (*fig*) Sprungbrett nt; **launching site** N Abschussbasis f

launch pad N = **launching pad**

launder [ˈlɔːndəʳ] VT waschen und bügeln; (*fig*) *money* waschen

Launderette® [lɔːndəˈret], **laundrette** [lɔːnˈdret] N (*Brit*) Waschsalon m

Laundromat® [ˈlɔːndrəʊmæt] N (*US*) Waschsalon m

laundry [ˈlɔːndrɪ] N (= *establishment*) Wäscherei f; (= *clothes*) (*dirty*) schmutzige Wäsche; (*washed*) Wäsche f; **to do the ~** (Wäsche) waschen

laundry basket N Wäschekorb m

laurel [ˈlɔrəl] N Lorbeer m; **to rest on one's ~s** sich auf seinen Lorbeeren ausruhen

lava [ˈlɑːvə] N Lava f

lavatory [ˈlævətrɪ] N Toilette f

lavatory: lavatory attendant N Toilettenfrau f/-mann m; **lavatory paper** N Toilettenpapier nt; **lavatory seat** N Toilettensitz m

lavender [ˈlævɪndəʳ] N (= *flower*) Lavendel m

lavish [ˈlævɪʃ] **1** ADJ *gifts* großzügig; *praise, affection* überschwänglich; *banquet* üppig; *party* feudal; *expenditure* verschwenderisch (*also pej*); **to be ~ in** or **with sth** mit etw verschwenderisch umgehen; **to be ~ with one's money** das Geld mit vollen Händen ausgeben **2** VT **to ~ sth on sb** jdn mit etw überhäufen; *praise, attention* jdn mit etw überschütten

lavishly [ˈlævɪʃlɪ] ADV *give, equipped* großzügig; *praise* überschwänglich; *entertain* reichlich; *illustrated* reich; **~**

furnished luxuriös einngerichtet; **to spend (money)** ~ das Geld mit vollen Händen ausgeben (*on für*)

law [lɔː] N **(a)** Gesetz *nt*; (= *system*) Recht *nt*; **it's the** ~ das ist Gesetz; **to become** ~ rechtskräftig werden; **is there a** ~ **against it?** ist das verboten?; **he is a** ~ **unto himself** er macht, was er will; **according to** *or* **in** *or* **by** *or* **under French** ~ nach französischem Recht; **by** ~ **all restaurants must display their prices outside** alle Restaurants sind gesetzlich dazu verpflichtet, ihre Preise draußen auszuhängen; **he is above the** ~ er steht über dem Gesetz; **to keep within the** ~ sich im Rahmen des Gesetzes bewegen; **in** ~ vor dem Gesetz; **civil/criminal** ~ Zivil-/Strafrecht *nt*; ~ **of contract** Vertragsrecht *nt*; **to practise** (*Brit*) *or* **practice** (*US*) ~ eine Anwaltspraxis haben; **to go to** ~ vor Gericht gehen; **to take the** ~ **into one's own hands** das Recht selbst in die Hand nehmen; ~ **and order** Recht und Ordnung

(b) (*as study*) Jura *no art*, Recht(swissenschaft *f*) *nt*

(c) the ~ (*inf*) die Bullen (*sl*); **I'll get the** ~ **on you** (*Brit inf*) ich hole die Polizei

law: law-abiding ADJ gesetzestreu; **law court** N Gerichtshof *m*

lawful [ˈlɔːfʊl] ADJ rechtmäßig

lawfully [ˈlɔːfəlɪ] ADV rechtmäßig; **he is** ~ **entitled to compensation** er hat einen Rechtsanspruch auf Entschädigung

lawless [ˈlɔːlɪs] ADJ *act* gesetzwidrig; *society* gesetzlos; *country* ohne Gesetzgebung

lawlessness [ˈlɔːlɪsnɪs] N (*of society, country*) Gesetzlosigkeit *f*

lawn [lɔːn] N Rasen *m no pl*

lawn: lawn mower N Rasenmäher *m*; **lawn tennis** N Rasentennis *nt*

law: law school N (*US*) juristische Fakultät; **law student** N Jurastudent(in) *m(f)*; **lawsuit** N Prozess *m*, Klage *f*; **to bring a** ~ **against sb** gegen jdn einen Prozess anstrengen

lawyer [ˈlɔːjəʳ] N (Rechts)anwalt *m*, (Rechts)anwältin *f*

LAWYER

*In Großbritannien gibt es zwei verschiedene Arten von **lawyers**, Rechtsanwälten: **solicitors** und **barristers** (die in Schottland **advocates** genannt werden). **Solicitors** beschäftigen sich normalerweise mit den allgemeinen Rechtsgeschäften wie An- und Verkauf von Eigentum, Testamenten, Schuldeneintreibung oder Scheidung, und werden von den Klienten direkt angesprochen. **Barristers** beraten in Rechtsfällen, die ihnen meist von den **solicitors**, nicht von den Klienten direkt, vorgelegt werden. Sie haben sich darauf spezialisiert, an den höheren Gerichten zu arbeiten, während die **solicitors** ihre Klienten in den unteren Instanzen vertreten.*

*In den USA werden die Rechtsanwälte allgemein **attorneys** genannt. Sie können jede Art von Rechtsfall übernehmen und ihre Klienten in allen Instanzen vor Bundes- und Staatsgerichten vertreten.*

lax [læks] ADJ (+ER) lax; *morals* locker; **to be** ~ **about sth** etw vernachlässigen; **he's** ~ **about washing** er nimmts mit dem Waschen nicht so genau

laxative [ˈlæksətɪv] **1** ADJ abführend **2** N Abführmittel *nt*

laxity [ˈlæksɪtɪ] N Laxheit *f*

lay¹ [leɪ] ADJ Laien-

lay² PRET *of* **lie²**

lay³ *vb: pret, ptp* **1** VT **laid (a)** legen (*sth on sth* etw auf etw *acc*); *wreath* niederlegen; *cable, mains, pipes* verlegen; *carpet, lino* (ver)legen; **to** ~ **(one's) hands on** (= *get hold of*) erwischen; (= *find*) finden; **he took all the money he could** ~ **his hands on** er nahm alles Geld, das ihm in die Finger kam (*inf*) **(b)** *plans* schmieden; (*esp Brit*) *table* decken; **to** ~ **a trap for sb** jdm eine Falle stellen

(c) (*non-material things*) *burden* auferlegen (*on sb* jdm); **to** ~ **the blame for sth on sb/sth** jdm/einer Sache die Schuld an etw (*dat*) geben; **to** ~ **responsibility for sth on sb** jdn für etw verantwortlich machen; **to** ~ **waste** verwüsten

(d) *eggs* (*hen*) legen; (*fish, insects*) ablegen; **to** ~ **bets on sth** auf etw (*acc*) wetten; **to** ~ **a fiver on it!** ich wette mit dir um 5 Pfund!; **I'll** ~ **you anything** ich gehe mit dir jede Wette ein ...

2 VI (*hen*) legen

➤ **lay aside** *or* **away** VT SEP *work etc* weglegen; (= *keep in reserve, save*) auf die Seite legen

➤ **lay down** VT SEP **(a)** *book, pen etc* hinlegen; **he laid his bag down on the table** er legte seine Tasche auf den Tisch **(b)** to **lay down one's arms** die Waffen niederlegen; **to lay down one's life** sein Leben lassen **(c)** *condition* festlegen; *policy* bestimmen; *rules* aufstellen; **to lay down the law** (*inf*) Vorschriften machen (*to sb* jdm)

➤ **lay into** VI +PREP OBJ (*inf*) **to lay into sb** auf jdn losgehen; (*verbally*) jdn fertig machen (*inf*) *or* runterputzen (*inf*)

➤ **lay off** **1** VI (*inf*) aufhören (*prep obj* mit); **you'll have to lay off smoking** du wirst das Rauchen aufgeben müssen (*inf*); **lay off my little brother, will you!** lass bloß meinen kleinen Bruder in Ruhe! **2** VT SEP *workers* Feierschichten machen lassen; (*permanently*) entlassen; **to be laid off** Feierschichten einlegen müssen; (*permanently*) entlassen werden

➤ **lay on** VT SEP *hospitality* bieten (*for sb* jdm); *entertainment* sorgen für; *excursion* veranstalten; *extra buses* einsetzen; *water, electricity* anschließen; **if you lay on the drinks I'll get the food** wenn du die Getränke stellst, besorge ich das Essen

➤ **lay out** VT SEP **(a)** (= *spread out*) ausbreiten **(b)** (= *present*) darlegen; **he laid out his plans for the country** er legte seine Pläne für das Land dar **(c)** *clothes* zurechtlegen; *corpse* (waschen und) aufbahren **(d)** (= *design, arrange*) anlegen; *rooms in house* anordnen; *office* aufteilen; *book* gestalten; *page* umbrechen; (*in magazines*) das Lay-out (+*gen*) machen **(e)** *money* (= *spend*) ausgeben; (= *invest*) investieren **(f)** (= *knock out*) **to lay sb out** jdn k. o. schlagen

➤ **lay over** VI (*US*) Aufenthalt haben

➤ **lay up** VT SEP **to be laid up (in bed)** auf der Nase (*inf*) *or* im Bett liegen

lay: layabout N (*Brit*) Nichtstuer(in) *m(f)*, Arbeitsscheue(r) *mf*; **lay-by** N (*Brit*) (*in town*) Parkbucht *f*; (*in country*) Parkplatz *m*; (*big*) Rastplatz *m*; **lay day** N (*Naut*) Liegetag *m*

layer [ˈleɪəʳ] **1** N Schicht *f* (*also Geol*), Lage *f*; **to arrange the vegetables in** ~**s** das Gemüse schichten; **several** ~**s of clothing** mehrere Kleidungsstücke übereinander **2** VT **(a)** *hair* abstufen **(b)** *vegetables etc* schichten

lay: layman N Laie *m*; **lay-off** N further ~**s were unavoidable** weitere Arbeiter mussten Feierschichten einlegen *or* (*permanent*) mussten entlassen werden; **layout** N Anordnung *f*; (*Typ*) Lay-out *nt*; **we have changed the** ~ **of this office** wir haben dieses Büro anders aufgeteilt; **layover** N (*US*) Aufenthalt *m*; **layperson** N Laie *m*

laze [leɪz] VI (*also* ~ **about,** ~ **around**) faulenzen

lazily [ˈleɪzɪlɪ] ADV faul; (= *languidly, unhurriedly*) träge; *drift, float* gemächlich

laziness [ˈleɪzɪnɪs] N Faulheit *f*

lazy [ˈleɪzɪ] ADJ (+ER) **(a)** faul; **to be** ~ **about doing sth** zu faul sein, etw zu tun **(b)** (= *slow-moving, lacking activity*) träge; *dinner, evening* gemütlich; **the long,** ~ **days of summer** die langen, trägen Sommertage; **I enjoy a** ~ **day at home** ich mache mir gerne einen faulen *or* gemütlichen Tag zu Hause **(c)** (*pej: = sloppy*) schluderig (*inf*)

lazybones [ˈleɪzɪˌbəʊnz] N SING (*inf*) Faulpelz *m*

lb N (*weight*) ≈ Pfd.

L/C ABBR *of* **letter of credit**

LCD ABBR *of* **liquid crystal display** LCD *nt*; ~ **screen** LCD-Bildschirm *m*

L-driver [ˈelˌdraɪvəʳ] N (*Brit inf*) Fahrschüler(in) *m(f)*

lead¹ [led] N **(a)** (= *metal*) Blei *nt* **(b)** (*in pencil*) Graphit *nt*; (= *single* ~) Mine *f*

lead² [liːd] *vb: pret, ptp* **led** **1** N **(a)** (= *leading position, Sport*) Führung *f*; **to be in the** ~ in Führung liegen; (*Sport*) in Führung *or* vorn liegen; **to take the** ~, **to move into the** ~ in Führung gehen; (*in league*) Tabellenführer werden **(b)** (= *distance, time ahead*) Vorsprung *m*; **to have two minutes'** ~ **over sb** zwei Minuten Vorsprung vor jdm haben **(c)** (= *example*) **to give sb a** ~ jdm etw vormachen; **to take the** ~, **to show a** ~ mit gutem Beispiel vorangehen **(d)** (= *clue*) Indiz *nt*, Anhaltspunkt *m*; (*in guessing etc*) Hinweis *m*; **the police have a** ~ die Polizei hat eine Spur **(e)** (*Theat*) (= *part*) Hauptrolle *f*; (= *person*) Hauptdarsteller(in) *m(f)*; **to sing the** ~ die Titelpartie singen **(f)** (= *leash*) Leine *f*; **on a** ~ an der Leine **(g)** (*Elec*) Leitung(skabel *nt*) *f*, Kabel *nt*

2 VT **(a)** führen; **to** ~ **sb in/out** *etc* jdn hinein-/hinaus- *etc* führen; **that road will** ~ **you back to the station** auf dieser Straße kommen Sie zum Bahnhof zurück; **to** ~ **the way** (*lit, fig*) vorangehen; (*fig: = be superior*) führend sein; **all this talk**

is ~**ing us nowhere** dieses ganze Gerede bringt uns nicht weiter; **to** ~ **sb to do sth** jdn dazu bringen, etw zu tun; **what led him to change his mind?** wie kam er dazu, seine Meinung zu ändern?; **I am led to believe that ...** ich habe Grund zu der Annahme, dass ...; **to** ~ **sb into trouble** jdn in Schwierigkeiten bringen; **I am led to the conclusion that ...** ich komme zu dem Schluss, dass ...
 (b) (= *be the leader of, direct*) (an)führen; *expedition, team* leiten; *movement, revolution* anführen; *orchestra* (*conductor*) leiten; (*first violin*) führen; **to** ~ **a party** den Parteivorsitz führen
 (c) (= *be first in*) anführen; **they led us by 30 seconds** sie lagen mit 30 Sekunden vor uns (*dat*); **Britain** ~**s the world in textiles** Großbritannien ist auf dem Gebiet der Textilproduktion führend in der Welt
 3 VI **(a)** führen; (*street etc also*) gehen; **it** ~**s into that room** es führt zu diesem Raum; **all this talk is** ~**ing nowhere** dieses ganze Gerede führt zu nichts; **remarks like that could** ~ **to trouble** solche Bemerkungen können unangenehme Folgen haben
 (b) (= *go in front*) vorangehen; (*in race*) in Führung liegen; **the "Times" led with a story about the financial crisis** die „Times" berichtete auf der ersten Seite ausführlich über die Finanzkrise
 (c) (*Cards*) ausspielen (*with sth* etw)
➤ **lead away** VT SEP wegführen *or* -bringen; *criminal, prisoner* abführen
➤ **lead off** VI (= *go off from*) abgehen; **several streets led off the square** mehrere Straßen gingen von dem Platz ab
➤ **lead on** VT SEP (= *deceive*) anführen (*inf*); (= *tease*) auf den Arm nehmen (*inf*)
➤ **lead on to** VI +PREP OBJ führen zu
➤ **lead up 1** VT SEP (= *lead across*) führen (*to* zu); **to lead sb up the garden path** (*fig*) jdn an der Nase herumführen **2** VI **the events/years that led up to the war** die Ereignisse/Jahre, die dem Krieg voran- *or* vorausgingen; **he was obviously leading up to an important announcement** er schickte sich offensichtlich an, etwas Wichtiges anzukündigen; **what are you leading up to?** worauf willst du hinaus?; **what's all this leading up to?** was soll das Ganze?

leaded [ˈlɛdɪd] ADJ *petrol* verbleit; ~ **window** Bleiglasfenster *nt*
leaden [ˈlɛdn] ADJ **(a)** *sky, colour, clouds* bleiern (*geh*); *heart, limbs, steps* bleischwer **(b)** (*pej*) *translation, dialogue* schwerfällig
leader [ˈliːdə̯] N **(a)** Führer(in) *m(f)*; (*of union, party*) Vorsitzende(r) *mf*; (*military*) Befehlshaber(in) *m(f)*; (*of gang, rebels*) Anführer(in) *m(f)*; (*of expedition, project, choir*) Leiter(in) *m(f)*; (*Sport*) (*in league*) Tabellenführer(in); (*in race*) der/die Erste; (*Mus: of orchestra*) Konzertmeister(in) *m(f)*; **to be the** ~ (*in race, competition*) in Führung liegen; **the** ~**s** (*in race, competition*) die Spitzengruppe; ~ **of the opposition** Oppositionsführer(in) *m(f)*; **the product is a** ~**/the world** ~ **in its field** dieses Produkt ist auf diesem Gebiet führend/ weltweit führend; **we are still the** ~**s in biochemical research** wir sind auf dem Gebiet der biochemischen Forschung immer noch führend
 (b) (*Brit Press*) Leitartikel *m*; ~ **writer** Leitartikler(in) *m(f)*
leadership [ˈliːdə̯ʃɪp] N **(a)** Führung *f*, Leitung *f*; (= *office*) Vorsitz *m*; **under the** ~ **of** unter (der) Führung von
 (b) (= *quality*) Führungsqualitäten *pl*; **he has** ~ **potential** er besitzt Führungsqualitäten
lead-free [ˈlɛdfriː] **1** ADJ bleifrei **2** N (= *petrol*) bleifreies Benzin
leading [ˈliːdɪŋ] ADJ **(a)** (= *first*) vorderste(r, s) **(b)** (= *most important*) *person, writer, politician, company* führend; ~ **product/sportsman** Spitzenprodukt *nt*/-sportler *m*; ~ **part** *or* **role** (*Theat*) Hauptrolle *f*; (*fig*) führende Rolle (*in* bei)
leading [ˈliːdɪŋ]: **leading article** N Leitartikel *m*; **leading edge** N **to be at** *or* **on the** ~ **of technology** (*machine etc*) zur Spitzentechnologie gehören; (*country etc*) in der Technologie führend sein; **leading-edge** ADJ führend; ~ **technology** Spitzentechnologie *f*; **leading light** N Nummer eins *f*; (= *person also*) großes Licht; **leading question** N Suggestivfrage *f*
lead [liːd]: **lead singer** N Leadsänger(in) *m(f)*; **lead story** N Hauptartikel *m*

leaf [liːf] **1** N, *pl* **leaves (a)** Blatt *nt*; **he swept the leaves into a pile** er fegte das Laub auf einen Haufen **(b)** (*of paper*) Blatt *nt*; **to take a** ~ **out of** *or* **from sb's book** sich (*dat*) von jdm eine Scheibe abschneiden; **to turn over a new** ~ einen neuen Anfang machen **2** VI **to** ~ **through a book** ein Buch durchblättern
leaflet [ˈliːflət] **1** N Prospekt *m*; (= *single page*) Handzettel *m*; (= *handout*) Flugblatt *nt*; (= *brochure for information*) Broschüre *f* **2** VT *area* Flugblätter verteilen in (+*dat*); (*Comm*) Werbematerial verteilen in (+*dat*)
leafy [ˈliːfɪ] ADJ *branch, tree* belaubt; *lane* grün
league [liːg] N **(a)** Verband *m*, Liga *f*; **League of Nations** Völkerbund *m*; **to be in** ~ **with sb** jdm gemeinsame Sache machen; **these two boys must be in** ~ **with each other** diese beiden Jungen stecken sicher unter einer Decke (*inf*)
 (b) (*Sport*) Liga *f*; **the club is top of the** ~ der Klub ist Tabellen- *or* Ligaführer; **he was not in the same** ~ (*fig*) er hatte nicht das gleiche Format; **this is way out of your** ~**!** das ist einige Nummern zu groß für dich!
league: **league game** N Ligaspiel *nt*; **league match** N (*Brit*) Ligaspiel *nt*; **league table** N (*esp Brit: of schools, companies etc*) Leistungstabelle *f*
leak [liːk] **1** N **(a)** (*lit, fig*) undichte Stelle; (*in container*) Loch *nt*; (= *escape of liquid*) Leck *nt* (*also Naut*); **to have a** ~ undicht sein; (*bucket etc*) lecken; **my pen has a** ~ mein Kugelschreiber läuft aus; **a gas** ~ eine undichte Stelle in der Gasleitung; **a security/news** ~ eine undichte Stelle; **a** ~ **to the press** eine Indiskretion der Presse gegenüber
 2 VT **(a)** (*lit*) durchlassen; *fuel* verlieren; **that tank is** ~**ing acid** aus diesem Tank läuft Säure aus
 (b) (*fig*) *information etc* zuspielen (*to sb* jdm)
 3 VI (*ship, receptacle, pipe*) lecken; (*roof*) undicht sein; (*pen, liquid*) auslaufen; (*gas*) ausströmen; (= *ooze out*) tropfen (*from* aus); **water is** ~**ing (in) through the roof** es regnet durch (das Dach durch)
➤ **leak out** VI **(a)** (*liquid*) auslaufen **(b)** (*news*) durchsickern
leakage [ˈliːkɪdʒ] N (= *act*) Auslaufen *nt*; **there's still a slight** ~ es ist immer noch etwas undicht
leaky [ˈliːkɪ] ADJ (+ER) undicht; *boat also* leck
lean¹ [liːn] ADJ (+ER) mager; *face, person* schmal; (*through lack of food*) hager; (*Comm*) schlank; ~ **er companies** verschlankte Firmen *pl*; **to go through a** ~ **patch** eine Durststrecke durchlaufen
lean² *pret, ptp* **leant** (*esp Brit*) *or* **leaned 1** VT **(a)** (= *put in sloping position*) lehnen (*against* gegen, an +*acc*); **to** ~ **one's head on sb's shoulder** seinen Kopf an jds Schulter (*acc*) lehnen
 (b) (= *rest*) aufstützen (*on* auf +*dat or acc*); **to** ~ **one's elbow on sth** sich mit dem Ellbogen auf etw (*acc*) stützen
 2 VI **(a)** (= *be off vertical*) sich neigen (*to* nach); **he** ~**ed across the counter** er beugte sich über den Ladentisch
 (b) (= *rest*) sich lehnen; **to** ~ **against sth** sich gegen etw lehnen; **she** ~**ed on my arm** sie stützte sich auf meinen Arm; **to** ~ **on one's elbow** sich mit dem Ellbogen aufstützen
 (c) (= *tend in opinion etc*) **to** ~ **toward(s) the left/socialism** nach links/zum Sozialismus tendieren
➤ **lean back** VI sich zurücklehnen
➤ **lean forward** VI sich vorbeugen
➤ **lean on** VI **(a)** (= *depend on*) **to lean on sb** sich auf jdn verlassen; (*inf*: = *put pressure on*) **to lean on sb** jdn bearbeiten (*inf*)
➤ **lean out** VI sich hinauslehnen (*of* aus)
➤ **lean over** VI (= *be off vertical*) sich (vor)neigen
leaning [ˈliːnɪŋ] **1** ADJ schräg, schief; **the Leaning Tower of Pisa** der Schiefe Turm von Pisa **2** N Hang *m*, Neigung *f*; **he had a** ~ **toward(s) the left** er hatte einen Hang nach links
leant [lɛnt] (*esp Brit*) PRET, PTP *of* **lean²**
leap [liːp], *vb: pret, ptp* **leapt** (*esp Brit*) *or* **leaped 1** N Sprung *m*; (*fig: in profits, unemployment etc*) sprunghafter Anstieg; **to take a** ~ einen Satz machen; **a great** ~ **forward** (*fig*) ein großer Sprung nach vorn; **a** ~ **into the unknown, a** ~ **in the dark** (*fig*) ein Sprung ins Ungewisse; **by** *or* **in** ~**s and bounds** (*fig*) sprunghaft
 2 VI springen; **to** ~ **about** herumspringen; **to** ~ **to one's feet** aufspringen; **the shares** ~**t by 21p** die Aktien stiegen mit einem Sprung um 21 Pence

➤ **leap at** VI +PREP OBJ **to leap at a chance** eine Gelegenheit beim Schopf packen; **to leap at an offer** sich (förmlich) auf ein Angebot stürzen

➤ **leap out** VI hinausspringen (*of* aus +*dat*); **he leapt out of the car** er sprang aus dem Auto

➤ **leap up** VI (*prices*) sprunghaft ansteigen

leapfrog ['liːpfrɒg] ▊ N Bockspringen *nt*; **to play ~** Bockspringen spielen *or* machen (*inf*) ▊ VT **he ~ged his way to the top of the company** er machte in der Firma eine Blitzkarriere

leapt [lept] (*esp Brit*) PRET, PTP *of* **leap**

leap year N Schaltjahr *nt*

learn [lɜːn], *pret, ptp* **learnt** (*Brit*) *or* **learned** ▊ VT (a) lernen; (= *memorize*) *poem etc* auswendig lernen; **I ~ed (how) to swim** ich habe schwimmen gelernt (b) (= *be informed*) erfahren ▊ VI (a) lernen; **to ~ from experience** aus der Erfahrung *or* durch Erfahrung lernen (b) (= *find out*) hören, erfahren (*about, of* von)

learned ['lɜːnɪd] ADJ gelehrt; *book also, journal* wissenschaftlich; *society also, profession* akademisch; **a ~ man** ein Gelehrter *m*

learner ['lɜːnə'] N Anfänger(in) *m(f)*, Lerner(in) *m(f)* (*esp Ling*); (= *student*) Lernende(r) *mf*; (= ~ *driver*) Fahrschüler(in) *m(f)*

learning ['lɜːnɪŋ] N (a) (= *act*) Lernen *nt* (b) (= *erudition*) Gelehrtheit *f*; **a man of ~** ein Gelehrter *m*

learning: learning by doing N Lernen *nt* durch praktische Anwendung; **learning curve** N **to be on a steep ~** viel dazulernen

learnt [lɜːnt] (*Brit*) PRET, PTP *of* **learn**

lease [liːs] ▊ N (*of land, farm, business premises etc*) Pacht *f*; (= *contract*) Pachtvertrag *m*; (*of house, flat, office*) Miete *f*; (= *contract*) Mietvertrag *m*; (*of equipment*) Leasing *nt*; (= *contract*) Leasingvertrag *m*; **to take a ~ on a house** ein Haus mieten; **to take a ~ on business premises** ein Geschäft(sgrundstück) *nt* pachten; **to give sb a new ~ of life** jdm (neuen) Aufschwung geben ▊ VT (= *take*) pachten (*from* von), in Pacht nehmen (*from* bei); *house, flat, office* mieten (*from* von); *equipment* leasen (*from* von); (= *give: also ~ out*) verpachten (*to* an +*acc*), in Pacht geben (*to sb* jdm); *house, flat, office* vermieten (*to* an +*acc*); *equipment* leasen (*to* an +*acc*)

lease: leasehold ▊ N (= *property*) Pachtbesitz *m*; (= *contract, tenure*) Pachtvertrag *m*; **who has the ~ on the property?** wer hat das Land/Gebäude gepachtet? ▊ ADJ gepachtet; *property* (*generally*) Pachtbesitz *m*; (= *land*) Pachtland *nt*; (= *building*) Pachtobjekt *nt*; **leaseholder** N Pächter(in) *m(f)*

leash [liːʃ] N Leine *f*; **on a ~** an der Leine; **to give sb a longer ~** (*esp US fig*) jdm mehr Freiheit geben

leasing ['liːsɪŋ] N Leasing *nt*

least [liːst] ▊ ADJ (a) (= *slightest, smallest*) geringste(r, s) (b) (*with uncountable nouns*) wenigste(r, s); **he has the ~ money** er hat am wenigsten Geld ▊ ADV (a) (+*vb*) am wenigsten; **~ of all would I wish to offend him** auf gar keinen Fall möchte ich ihn beleidigen (b) (+*adj*) **the ~ expensive car** das billigste Auto; **of all my worries that's the ~ important** das ist meine geringste Sorge; **the ~ talented player** der am wenigsten talentierte Spieler; **the ~ known** der/die/das Unbekannteste; **the ~ interesting** der/die/das Uninteressanteste; **not the ~ bit drunk** kein bisschen *or* nicht im Geringsten betrunken ▊ N **the ~** der/die/das Geringste *or* wenigste; **that's the ~ of my worries** darüber mache ich mir die wenigsten Sorgen; **it's the ~ I can do** das ist das wenigste, was ich tun kann; **at ~, I think so** ich glaube wenigstens; **at ~ it's not raining** wenigstens regnet es nicht; **we can at ~ try** wir können es wenigstens versuchen; **there were at ~ eight** es waren mindestens acht da; **we need three at the very ~** allermindestens brauchen wir drei; **all nations love football, not ~ the British** alle Völker lieben Fußball, nicht zuletzt die Briten; **he was not in the ~ upset** er war kein bisschen verärgert; **to say the ~** um es milde zu sagen; **the ~ said, the better** je weniger man darüber spricht, desto besser

leather ['leðə'] ▊ N Leder *nt* ▊ ADJ Leder-, ledern; **~ goods** Lederwaren *pl*; **~ shoes** Lederschuhe *pl*

leathery ['leðərɪ] ADJ *skin* ledern

leave [liːv], *vb: pret, ptp* **left** ▊ N (a) (= *permission*) Erlaubnis *f*; **to ask sb's ~ to do sth** jdn um Erlaubnis bitten, etw zu tun;

---

he borrowed my car without so much as a by your ~ er hat sich (*dat*) einfach so mein Auto geliehen

(b) (= *permission to be absent, Mil*) Urlaub *m*; **to be on ~** auf Urlaub sein; **I've got ~ to attend the conference** ich habe freibekommen, um an der Konferenz teilzunehmen; **~ of absence** Beurlaubung *f*

(c) **to take one's ~** sich verabschieden; **to take ~ of sb** sich von jdm verabschieden; **to take ~ of one's senses** den Verstand verlieren

▊ VT (a) *place, person* verlassen; **the train left the station** der Zug fuhr aus dem Bahnhof; **when the plane left Rome** als das Flugzeug von Rom abflog; **when he left Rome** als er von Rom wegging/wegfuhr/abflog *etc*; **to ~ the country** das Land verlassen; (*permanently*) auswandern; **to ~ home** von zu Hause weggehen/wegfahren; (*permanently*) von zu Hause weggehen; **to ~ school** die Schule verlassen; **to ~ the table** vom Tisch aufstehen; **to ~ one's job** seine Stelle aufgeben; **to ~ the road** (= *crash*) von der Straße abkommen; (= *turn off*) von der Straße abbiegen; **to ~ the rails** entgleisen; **I'll ~ you at the station** am Bahnhof trennen wir uns dann; (*in car*) ich setze dich am Bahnhof ab

(b) (= *allow or cause to remain*) lassen; *bad taste, dirty mark, message, scar, impression* hinterlassen; **I'll ~ my address with you** ich lasse Ihnen meine Adresse da; **I'll ~ the key with the neighbours** (*Brit*) *or* **neighbors** (*US*) ich hinterlege *or* lasse den Schlüssel bei den Nachbarn; **to ~ one's supper** sein Abendessen stehen lassen; **to ~ two pages blank** zwei Seiten frei lassen; **this ~s me free for the afternoon/free to go shopping** dadurch habe ich den Nachmittag frei/Zeit zum Einkaufen; **~ the dog alone** lass den Hund in Ruhe; **to ~ well alone** die Finger davonlassen (*inf*); **to ~ sb to do sth** es jdm überlassen, etw zu tun; **I'll ~ you to it** lasse Sie jetzt allein weitermachen; **to ~ go of sb/sth** jdn/etw loslassen; **let's ~ it at that** lassen wir es dabei (bewenden); **to ~ sth to the last minute** mit etw bis zur letzten Minute warten; **let's ~ this now** (= *stop*) lassen wir das jetzt mal

(c) (= *forget*) liegen lassen, stehen lassen

(d) (*after death*) *person, money* hinterlassen; **he left his wife very badly off** er ließ seine Frau mittellos zurück

(e) **to be left** (= *remain, be over*) übrig bleiben; **all I have left** alles, was ich noch habe; **I've (got) £6 left** ich habe noch 6 Pfund (übrig); **how many are there left?** wie viele sind noch übrig?; **3 from 10 ~s 7** 10 minus 3 ist *or* (ist) gleich 7; **there was nothing left for me to do but to sell it** mir blieb nichts anderes übrig, als es zu verkaufen

(f) (= *entrust*) überlassen (*up to sb* jdm); **~ it to me** lass mich nur machen; **to ~ sth to chance** etw dem Zufall überlassen

▊ VI (*person*) (weg)gehen; (*in vehicle*) abfahren; (*in plane*) abfliegen; **we ~ for Sweden tomorrow** wir fahren morgen nach Schweden

➤ **leave aside** VT SEP **leaving aside the fact that ...** wenn man die Tatsache außer Acht lässt, dass ...

➤ **leave behind** VT SEP (a) *the car, the children* zurücklassen; *fingerprints, chaos* hinterlassen; *the past* hinter sich (*dat*) lassen; **we've left all that behind us** das alles liegt hinter uns; **he left all his fellow students behind** er stellte alle seine Kommilitonen in den Schatten (b) (= *forget*) liegen lassen, stehen lassen

➤ **leave in** VT SEP nicht herausnehmen; **don't leave the dog in all day** lassen Sie den Hund nicht den ganzen Tag im Haus

➤ **leave off** ▊ VT SEP *clothes* nicht anziehen; *lid* nicht darauftun; *radio, lights* auslassen; **you left her name off the list** Sie haben ihren Namen nicht in die Liste aufgenommen ▊ VI, VI +PREP OBJ (*inf*) aufhören; **leave off doing that, will you!** hör auf damit, ja?; **leave off!** lass das!; **he picked up where he left off last year** er machte weiter, wo er letztes Jahr aufgehört hatte

➤ **leave on** VT SEP *clothes* anbehalten; *lights, fire etc* anlassen

➤ **leave out** VT SEP (a) (= *not bring in*) draußen lassen (b) (= *omit*) auslassen; (= *exclude*) *people* ausschließen (*of* von); **he was instructed to leave out all references to politics** er bekam Anweisung, alle Hinweise auf Politik wegzulassen; **you leave my wife/politics out of this** lassen Sie meine Frau/die Politik aus dem Spiel; **he got left out of things at school** er wurde in der Schule nie mit einbezogen (c) (= *not put away*) nicht wegräumen, liegen lassen

➤ **leave over** VT SEP **to be left over** übrig (geblieben) sein

leaves [liːvz] PL *of* **leaf**

leaving [ˈliːvɪŋ]: **leaving certificate** N (Brit) Abgangszeugnis nt; **leaving party** N Abschiedsfeier or -party f

Lebanese [lebəˈniːz] 🔟 ADJ libanesisch 🔟 N Libanese m, Libanesin f

Lebanon [ˈlebənən] N the ~ der Libanon

lecher [ˈletʃəʳ] N Lüstling m; (hum) Lustmolch m

lecherous [ˈletʃərəs] ADJ lüstern

lechery [ˈletʃərɪ] N Lüsternheit f

lectern [ˈlektɜːn] N Pult nt

lecture [ˈlektʃəʳ] 🔟 N **(a)** Vortrag m; (Univ) Vorlesung f; **to give a ~** einen Vortrag/eine Vorlesung halten (to für, on sth über etw acc)
(b) (= scolding) (Straf)predigt f; **to give sb a ~** jdm eine Strafpredigt halten (about wegen) inf
🔟 VT **(a)** (= give a ~) **to ~ sb on sth** jdm einen Vortrag/eine Vorlesung über etw (acc) halten; **he ~s us in French** wir hören bei ihm (Vorlesungen in) Französisch
(b) (= scold) **to ~ sb** jdm eine Strafpredigt halten (on wegen) 🔟 VI einen Vortrag halten; (Univ) (= give ~) eine Vorlesung halten; (= give ~ course) lesen, Vorlesungen halten (on über +acc); **he ~s in English** er ist Dozent für Anglistik; **he ~s at Princeton** er lehrt in Princeton

Be careful! **lecture** is not translated by the German word **Lektüre**.

lecture: lecture hall N Hörsaal m; **lecture notes** PL (professor's) Manuskript nt; (student's) Aufzeichnungen pl; (= handout) Vorlesungsskript nt

lecturer [ˈlektʃərəʳ] N Dozent(in) m(f); (= speaker) Redner(in) m(f); **assistant ~** ≈ Assistent(in) m(f); **senior ~** Dozent(in) in höherer Position

lectureship [ˈlektʃəʃɪp] N Dozentenstelle f

lecture theatre, (US) **lecture theater** N Hörsaal m

led [led] PRET, PTP of lead²

ledge [ledʒ] N Leiste f, Kante f; (along wall) Leiste f; (of window) (inside) Fensterbrett nt; (outside) (Fenster)sims nt or m; (= shelf) Bord nt; (= mountain ~) (Fels)vorsprung m

ledger [ˈledʒəʳ] N Hauptbuch nt

leech [liːtʃ] N Blutegel m; (fig) Blutsauger(in) m(f)

leek [liːk] N Porree m

leer [lɪəʳ] 🔟 N (knowing, sexual) anzügliches Grinsen; (evil) heimtückischer Blick 🔟 VI anzüglich grinsen; einen heimtückischen Blick haben; **he ~ed at the girl** er warf dem Mädchen lüsterne Blicke zu

leeway [ˈliːweɪ] N (fig) Spielraum m; (in a decision) Freiheit f; **he has given them too much ~** er hat ihnen zu viel Freiheit or Spielraum gelassen; **there's a lot of ~ to make up** es gibt viel nachzuarbeiten

left¹ [left] PRET, PTP of leave

left² 🔟 ADJ (also Pol) linke(r, s); **no ~ turn** Linksabbiegen verboten; **he's got two ~ feet** (inf) er ist sehr ungelenk; **to come out of ~ field** (esp US) überraschend kommen
🔟 ADV links (of von); **turn ~** (Aut) links abbiegen; **keep ~** links fahren
🔟 N **(a)** Linke(r, s); **on the ~** links (of von); **on or to sb's ~** links von jdm; **take the first (on the) ~ after the church** biegen Sie hinter der Kirche die erste (Straße) links ab; **the third/fourth etc ... from the ~** der/die/das dritte/vierte etc ... von links; **to keep to the ~** sich links halten; **to drive on the ~** links fahren
(b) (Pol) Linke f; **to be on the ~** links stehen; **to move to the ~** nach links rücken

left: left back N linker Verteidiger; **left-click** (Comput) 🔟 VI links klicken 🔟 VT links klicken auf (+acc); **left-footed** (Ftbl) ADJ shot mit dem linken Fuß; **~ player** Linksfüßer(in) m(f); **left-hand** ADJ **~ drive** Linkssteuerung f; **~ side** linke Seite; **he stood on the ~ side of the king** er stand zur Linken des Königs; **take the ~ turn** bieg links ab; **left-handed** 🔟 ADJ linkshändig; tool für Linkshänder; **both the children are ~** beide Kinder sind Linkshänder 🔟 ADV mit links; **left-hander** N (= punch) Linke f; (= person) Linkshänder(in) m(f)

leftist [ˈleftɪst] 🔟 ADJ linke(r, s), linksgerichtet 🔟 N Linke(r) mf

left: left-luggage locker N (Brit) Gepäckschließfach nt; **left-luggage (office)** N (Brit) Gepäckaufbewahrung f; **left-of-centre**, (US) **left-of-center** ADJ politician links von der Mitte

stehend; **~ party** Mitte-Links-Partei f; **leftover** 🔟 ADJ übrig geblieben 🔟 N **(a)** **~s** (Über)reste pl **(b)** (fig) **to be a ~ from the past** ein Überbleibsel nt aus der Vergangenheit sein

leftward(s) [ˈleftwəd(z)] 🔟 ADJ nach links; **a leftward shift** (Pol) ein Linksruck m 🔟 ADV (Pol) nach links

left: left wing N linker Flügel (also Sport); **on the ~** (Pol, Sport) auf dem linken Flügel; **left-wing** ADJ (Pol) linke(r, s); **left-winger** N (Pol) Linke(r) mf; (Sport) Linksaußen m

leg [leg] 🔟 N **(a)** (also of trousers, furniture) Bein nt; (of bed) Fuß m; **to be on one's last ~s** (= dying) in den letzten Zügen liegen (inf); (= exhausted) auf dem letzten Loch pfeifen (inf); **he hasn't (got) a ~ to stand on** (fig) (= no excuse) er kann sich nicht herausreden; (= no proof) das kann er ihm nicht belegen; **to have ~s** (esp US inf) (idea, plan) klappen; (story) laufen (inf) **(b)** (as food) Keule f; **~ of lamb** Lammkeule f **(c)** (= stage) Etappe f
🔟 VT **to ~ it** (inf: = run) laufen; (= run away) abhauen (inf)

legacy [ˈlegəsɪ] N (lit, fig) Erbschaft f, Vermächtnis nt; (fig pej) Hinterlassenschaft f; **to leave sb a ~ of sth** (fig) jdm etw hinterlassen

legal [ˈliːgl] ADJ **(a)** (= lawful) legal; restrictions, obligation, limit gesetzlich; fare, speed zulässig; will, purchase rechtsgültig; **to make sth ~** etw legalisieren; **it is not ~ to sell drink to children** es ist gesetzlich verboten, Alkohol an Kinder zu verkaufen; **~ limit** (of blood alcohol when driving) Promillegrenze f; **they don't know what their ~ rights are** sie kennen ihre eigenen Rechte nicht; **women had no ~ status** Frauen waren nicht rechtsfähig
(b) (= relating to the law) Rechts-; matters, advice, services, journal, mind juristisch; decision richterlich; inquiry, investigation gerichtlich; **for ~ reasons** aus rechtlichen Gründen; **~ charges** or **fees** or **costs** (solicitor's) Anwaltskosten pl; (court's) Gerichtskosten pl; **to take ~ advice** on or over or about sth in Bezug auf etw (acc) juristischen Rat einholen; **to start ~ proceedings against sb** gegen jdn Klage erheben; **the British ~ system** das britische Rechtssystem; **the ~ profession** die Anwaltschaft; (including judges) die Juristenschaft; **~ entity** juristische Person; **~ personality** Rechtspersönlichkeit f

legal: legal action N Klage f; **to take ~ against sb** gegen jdn Klage erheben; **legal adviser** N Rechtsberater(in) m(f); **legal aid** N Rechtshilfe f; **legal department** N Rechtsabteilung f

legality [liːˈgælɪtɪ] N Legalität f; (of claim) Rechtmäßigkeit f; (of contract, will, marriage, purchase, decision, limit) Rechtsgültigkeit f

legalize [ˈliːgəlaɪz] VT legalisieren

legally [ˈliːgəlɪ] ADV transacted, acquire, trade legal; married rechtmäßig; guaranteed, obliged gesetzlich; (= relating to the law) advise juristisch; indefensible rechtlich; **what's the position ~?** wie ist die Lage rechtlich gesehen?; **~ responsible** vor dem Gesetz verantwortlich; **to be ~ entitled to sth** einen Rechtsanspruch auf etw (acc) haben; **~ binding** rechtsverbindlich; **~ valid** rechtsgültig

legal tender N gesetzliches Zahlungsmittel

legation [lɪˈgeɪʃən] N (= diplomats) Vertretung f; (= building) Gesandtschaftsgebäude nt

legend [ˈledʒənd] N Legende f; (fictitious) Sage f; **heroes of Greek ~** griechische Sagenhelden pl; **to become a ~ in one's lifetime** schon zu Lebzeiten zur Legende werden

legendary [ˈledʒəndərɪ] ADJ **(a)** legendär **(b)** (= famous) berühmt

-legged [-legd, -legɪd] ADJ SUF -beinig; **two-/four-legged** zwei-/vierbeinig; **bare-legged** ohne Strümpfe

leggings [ˈlegɪŋz] PL (hohe or lange) Gamaschen pl; (= trousers) Leggings pl

leggy [ˈlegɪ] ADJ (+ER) langbeinig

legible [ˈledʒɪbl] ADJ lesbar

legibly [ˈledʒɪblɪ] ADV lesbar; write leserlich

legion [ˈliːdʒən] N Legion f; (= army) Armee f; **American/British Legion** American/British Legion f (Verband der Kriegsveteranen)

legislate [ˈledʒɪsleɪt] VI **(a)** Gesetze/ein Gesetz erlassen **(b)** (fig) **to ~ for sth** etw berücksichtigen; (= give ruling on) für etw Regeln aufstellen

legislation [ledʒɪsˈleɪʃən] N (= making laws) Gesetzgebung f; (= laws) Gesetze pl

legislative ['ledʒɪslətɪv] ADJ gesetzgebend; **~ reforms** Gesetzesreformen pl; **~ programme** (Brit) or **program** (US) (of government) Gesetzgebungsprogramm nt

legislator ['ledʒɪsleɪtə'] N Gesetzgeber m

legislature ['ledʒɪsleɪtʃə'] N Legislative f

legitimacy [lɪ'dʒɪtɪməsɪ] N Rechtmäßigkeit f, Legitimität f

legitimate [lɪ'dʒɪtɪmət] ADJ **(a)** legitim; (= reasonable) berechtigt; excuse begründet; reason zulässig; **it's perfectly ~ to ask questions** es ist vollkommen in Ordnung, Fragen zu stellen **(b)** (= born in wedlock) ehelich

legitimately [lɪ'dʒɪtɪmətlɪ] ADV legitim; (= with reason) berechtigterweise

legitimize [lɪ'dʒɪtɪmaɪz] VT legitimieren

leg: legless ADJ (inf) sternhagelvoll (inf); **legroom** N Beinfreiheit f; **leg-up** N **to give sb a ~** jdm hochhelfen; **legwarmer** N Legwarmer m

leisure ['leʒə'] N Freizeit f; **a gentleman of ~** ein Privatier m (dated); **to lead a life of ~** ein Leben in or der Muße führen (geh); **do it at your ~** (= in own time) tun Sie es, wenn Sie Zeit dazu haben; (= at own speed) lassen Sie sich (dat) Zeit damit

leisure: leisure activities PL Hobbys pl, Freizeitbeschäftigungen pl; **leisure centre** N (Brit) Freizeitzentrum nt; **leisure hours** PL Freizeit f

leisurely ['leʒəlɪ] **1** ADJ geruhsam; **to go at a ~ pace** (person) gemächlich gehen; (vehicle) in gemächlichem Tempo fahren; **to have a ~ bath/breakfast** in aller Ruhe baden/frühstücken **2** ADV walk, stroll gemächlich

leisure: leisure time N Freizeit f; **leisurewear** N Freizeitbekleidung f

lemon ['lemən] **1** N Zitrone f; (= colour) Zitronengelb nt; (= tree) Zitrone(nbaum m) f **2** ADJ Zitronen-

lemonade [lemə'neɪd] N Limonade f; (with lemon flavour) Zitronenlimonade f

lemon: lemon cheese, lemon curd N zähflüssiger Brotaufstrich mit Zitronengeschmack; **lemon juice** N Zitronensaft m; **lemon sole** N Rotzunge f; **lemon squash** N Zitronensaft m; (in bottle) Zitronensirup m; **lemon squeezer** N Zitronenpresse f; **lemon tea** N Zitronentee m

lend [lend], pret, ptp **lent** **1** VT **(a)** leihen (to sb jdm); (banks) money verleihen (to an +acc) **(b)** (fig: = give) verleihen (to +dat); **to ~ (one's) support to sb/sth** jdn/etw unterstützen; **to ~ a hand** helfen **2** VR **to ~ oneself to sth** (= be suitable) sich für etw eignen; **the programme** (Brit) or **program** (US) **doesn't really ~ itself to radio** die Sendung ist eigentlich für den Hörfunk ungeeignet

➤ **lend out** VT SEP verleihen; books also ausleihen

lender ['lendə'] N (professional) Geldverleiher(in) m(f)

lending ['lendɪŋ] **1** ADJ **~ bank** kreditierende Bank **2** N Darlehen nt

lending: lending library N Leihbücherei f; **lending rate** N (Darlehens)zinssatz m

length [leŋθ] N **(a)** Länge f (also Sport); **to be 4 feet in ~** 4 Fuß lang sein; **what ~ is it?** wie lang ist es?; **along the whole ~ of the river/lane** den ganzen Fluss/Weg entlang; **(through) the ~ and breadth of England** in ganz England; travel kreuz und quer durch ganz England; **to win by half a ~** mit einer halben Länge siegen

(b) (of cloth, rope, pipe) Stück nt; (of wallpaper, pool) Bahn f **(c)** (of time) Dauer f; (= great ~) lange Dauer; **at such ~** so lange; **for any ~ of time** für längere Zeit; **~ of life** (of people) Lebenserwartung f; (of animals) Lebensalter nt; (of machine) Lebensdauer f; **at ~** (= finally) schließlich; (for a long time) lange, ausführlich

(d) to go to any ~s to do sth vor nichts zurückschrecken, um etw zu tun; **to go to great ~s to do sth** sich (dat) sehr viel Mühe geben, um etw zu tun

lengthen ['leŋθən] **1** VT verlängern; clothes länger machen; **to ~ one's stride** größere Schritte machen **2** VI länger werden

lengthways ['leŋθweɪz], **lengthwise** ['leŋθwaɪz] **1** ADJ Längen-, Längs-; **~ cut** Längsschnitt m **2** ADV der Länge nach

lengthy ['leŋθɪ] ADJ (+ER) sehr lang; (= dragging on) langwierig; speech ausführlich, langatmig (pej); meeting, war lang andauernd; article, report, statement sehr umfangreich; interview, explanation sehr ausführlich; **a ~ prison sentence** eine lange or hohe Gefängnisstrafe

leniency ['liːnɪənsɪ] N Nachsicht f (towards gegenüber); (of judge, attitude, treatment, sentence) Milde f

lenient ['liːnɪənt] ADJ nachsichtig (towards gegenüber); judge, attitude, treatment, sentence milde; **to be ~ with sb** mit jdm milde umgehen

leniently ['liːnɪəntlɪ] ADV nachsichtig; judge milde

lens [lenz] N (Anat, Opt, Phot) Linse f; (in spectacles) Glas nt; (= camera part containing ~) Objektiv nt; (= eyeglass) Klemmlupe f; (for stamps etc) Lupe f

lens cap N Schutzkappe f

Lent [lent] N Fastenzeit f

lent [lent] PRET, PTP of **lend**

lentil ['lentl] N Linse f; **~ soup** Linsensuppe f

Leo ['liːəʊ] N (Astrol) Löwe m; **he's (a) ~** er ist Löwe

leopard ['lepəd] N Leopard m

leotard ['liːətɑːd] N Trikot nt; (Gymnastics) Gymnastikanzug m

leper ['lepə'] N Leprakranke(r) mf, Aussätzige(r) mf (old, fig)

leprosy ['leprəsɪ] N Lepra f, Aussatz m (old)

lesbian ['lezbɪən] **1** ADJ lesbisch; **~ and gay rights/issues** Rechte pl/Probleme pl der Lesben und Schwulen; **the ~ and gay community** die Lesben und Schwulen **2** N Lesbe f (inf)

lesbianism ['lezbɪənɪzəm] N (in general) lesbische Liebe; (of one person) Lesbiertum nt

lesion ['liːʒən] N Verletzung f; **~s in the brain** Gehirnverletzungen pl

less [les] **1** ADJ, ADV, N weniger; **~ noise, please!** nicht so laut, bitte!; **no ~ a person than the bishop** kein Geringerer als der Bischof; **to grow ~** weniger werden; (= grow at slow rate) langsamer wachsen; (= decrease) abnehmen; **~ and ~** immer weniger; **she saw him ~ and ~ (often)** sie sah ihn immer seltener; **a sum ~ than £1** eine Summe unter £ 1; **it's nothing ~ than disgraceful/than a disaster** es ist wirklich eine Schande/ein Unglück nt; **he was ~ frightened than angry** er war nicht so sehr ängstlich, sondern eher ärgerlich; **~ beautiful** nicht so schön; **~ quickly** nicht so schnell; **none the ~** nichtsdestoweniger; **I don't love her any the ~** ich liebe sie nicht weniger; **can't you let me have it for ~?** können Sie es mir nicht etwas billiger lassen?; **I hope you won't think (any the) ~ of me** ich hoffe, du denkst nicht schlecht von mir; **~ of that!** komm mir nicht so! **2** PREP weniger; (Comm) abzüglich; **6 ~ 4 is 2** 6 weniger or minus 4 ist 2

lessen ['lesn] **1** VT verringern; cost senken; effect, impact abschwächen; pain lindern **2** VI nachlassen; (value of money) abnehmen

lesser ['lesə'] ADJ geringer; (in names) klein; **to a ~ extent** in geringerem Maße; **a ~ amount** ein kleinerer Betrag; **which is the ~ crime?** welches Verbrechen ist weniger schlimm?

lesson ['lesn] N **(a)** (Sch etc) Stunde f; (= unit of study) Lektion f; **~s** Unterricht m; **~s begin at 9** der Unterricht or die Schule beginnt um 9; **a French ~** eine Französischstunde; **a driving ~** eine Fahrstunde; **to give** or **teach a ~** eine Stunde geben **(b)** (fig) Lehre f; **he has learned his ~** er hat seine Lektion gelernt; **to teach sb a ~** jdm eine Lektion erteilen; **what ~ can we learn from this story?** was können wir von dieser Geschichte lernen?

lest [lest] CONJ (form) (= for fear that) aus Furcht, dass; (in order that ... not) damit ... nicht; (= in case) für den Fall, dass; **I didn't do it ~ somebody should object** ich habe es aus Furcht, dass jemand dagegen sein könnte, nicht getan; **~ we forget** damit wir nicht vergessen

let pret, ptp **let** VT **(a)** lassen; **to ~ sb do sth** jdn etw tun lassen; **she ~ me borrow the car** sie lieh mir das Auto; **we can't ~ that happen** wir dürfen das nicht zulassen; **he wants to but I won't ~ him** er möchte gern, aber ich lasse ihn nicht or erlaube es ihm nicht; **~ me know what you think** sagen Sie mir (Bescheid), was Sie davon halten; **to ~ sb be** jdn (in Ruhe) lassen; **to ~ sb/sth go**, **to ~ go of sb/sth** jdn/etw loslassen; **to ~ oneself go** (= neglect oneself) sich gehen lassen; (= relax) aus sich herausgehen; **to ~ it go at that** es dabei bewenden lassen; **we'll ~ it pass** or **go this once** (= disregard) error wir wollen es mal durchgehen lassen; **~ it be known that ...** alle sollen wissen, dass ...; **to ~ sb/sth alone** jdn/etw in Ruhe lassen; **we can't improve it any more, we'd better ~ it alone** wir können es nicht mehr verbessern, also lassen wir es lieber so

(b) ~ **alone** (= *much less*) geschweige denn

(c) ~**'s go home** komm, wir gehen nach Hause; ~**'s go!** gehen wir!; **yes,** ~**'s** oh ja!; ~**'s not** lieber nicht; **don't** ~**'s** *or* ~**'s not fight** wir wollen uns doch nicht streiten; ~**'s be friends** wir wollen Freunde sein; ~**'s look at this in more detail** wir wollen das einmal genauer betrachten; ~ **him try (it)!** das soll er nur *or* mal versuchen!; ~ **me think** *or* **see, where did I put it?** warte mal, wo habe ich das nur hingetan?; ~ **us pray** lasst uns beten; ~ **us suppose ...** nehmen wir (mal) an, dass ...

(d) (*esp Brit*: = *hire out*) vermieten; **"to** ~**"** „zu vermieten"; **we can't find a house to** ~ wir können kein Haus finden, das zu mieten ist

➤ **let down** VT SEP **(a)** (= *lower*) herunterlassen; *seat* herunterklappen; **I tried to let him down gently** (*fig*) ich versuchte, ihm das schonend beizubringen

(b) (= *lengthen*) *dress* länger machen; *hem* auslassen

(c) (= *deflate*) **to let a tyre** (*Brit*) *or* **tire** (*US*) **down** die Luft aus einem Reifen lassen

(d) (= *fail to help*) **to let sb down** jdn im Stich lassen (*over* mit); **the weather let us down** das Wetter machte uns einen Strich durch die Rechnung

(e) (= *disappoint*) enttäuschen; **to feel let down** enttäuscht sein; **to let the school/oneself down** die Schule/sich blamieren

➤ **let in** VT SEP **(a)** *water* durchlassen

(b) *air, cat, visitor* hereinlassen; (*to club etc*) zulassen (*to* zu); **he let himself in (with his key)** er schloss die Tür auf und ging hinein; **he let her into the apartment** er ließ sie in die Wohnung hinein

(c) (= *involve in*) **see what you've let me in for now** da hast du mir aber was eingebrockt! (*inf*); **to let oneself in for sth** sich auf etw (*acc*) einlassen

(d) (= *allow to know*) **to let sb in on sth, to let sb into sth** jdn in etw (*acc*) einweihen; **she let me in on the secret** sie hat es mir verraten

➤ **let off** ❶ VT SEP **(a)** *gun, shot* abfeuern

(b) *firework, bomb* hochgehen lassen

(c) *gases* absondern; *smell* verbreiten; **to let off steam** (*lit*) Dampf ablassen; (*fig also*) sich abreagieren

❷ VT ALWAYS SEPARATE **(a)** **to let sb off** jdm etw durchgehen lassen; **I'll let you off this time** diesmal drücke ich noch ein Auge zu; **to let sb off with a warning/fine** jdn mit einer Verwarnung/Geldstrafe davonkommen lassen; **he's been let off** man hat ihn laufen lassen

(b) (= *allow to go*) gehen lassen; **we were let off early** wir durften früher gehen; **I let the dog off (the leash)** ich machte den Hund (von der Leine) los

➤ **let on** VI **(a)** (*inf*) verraten; **don't let on you know** lass dir bloß nicht anmerken, dass du das weißt **(b)** (= *pretend*) **to let on that ...** vorgeben, dass ...

➤ **let out** VT SEP **(a)** *cat, smell, air* herauslassen; (*from car*) absetzen; **I'll let myself out** ich finde alleine hinaus; **to let out a long sigh** tief seufzen; **to let out a scream** einen Schrei ausstoßen; **to let out a groan** (auf)stöhnen **(b)** *prisoner* entlassen; *secret* verraten **(c)** *dress* auslassen **(d)** (*esp Brit*: = *rent*) vermieten

➤ **let up** VI **(a)** (= *cease*) aufhören **(b)** (= *ease up*) nachlassen **(c)** **to let up on sb** jdn in Ruhe lassen

letdown ['letdaʊn] N (*inf*) Enttäuschung *f*

lethal ['liːθəl] ADJ **(a)** tödlich; **to be executed by** ~ **injection** durch die Todesspritze hingerichtet werden **(b)** (*fig*) *opponent* äußerst gefährlich; (*inf*: = *strong*) *drink* tödlich stark (*inf*); *curry* höllisch scharf (*inf*)

lethargic [lɪˈθɑːdʒɪk] ADJ **(a)** träge, lethargisch; (= *uninterested*) lustlos; **to feel** ~ sich träge fühlen **(b)** (*Comm, St Ex*) *sales, trading* stagnierend; *market* lustlos

lethargy ['leθədʒɪ] N Lethargie *f*, Trägheit *f*

let's [lets] CONTR *of* **let us**

letter ['letəʳ] N **(a)** (*of alphabet*) Buchstabe *m*; **to the** ~ buchstabengetreu **(b)** (= *written message*) Brief *m*; (*Comm etc*) Schreiben *nt* (*form*) (*to an* +*acc*); **by** ~ schriftlich; **to write a** ~ **of complaint/apology** sich schriftlich beschweren/ entschuldigen; ~ **of recommendation** (*US*) Arbeitszeugnis *nt* **(c)** (*Liter*) ~**s** Literatur *f*; **man of** ~**s** Belletrist *m*; (= *writer*) Literat *m*

letter: **letter bomb** N Briefbombe *f*; **letter box** N (*Brit*) Briefkasten *m*; **letterhead** N Briefkopf *m*

lettering ['letərɪŋ] N Beschriftung *f*

letter: **letter quality** N Schönschrift *f*; **letter-quality** ADJ ~ **printer** Schönschriftdrucker *m*

letters page ['letəzˌpeɪdʒ] N (*Press*) Leserbriefseite *f*

lettuce ['letɪs] N Kopfsalat *m*

let-up ['letʌp] N (*inf*) Pause *f*; (= *easing up*) Nachlassen *nt*; **if there is a** ~ **in the rain** wenn der Regen aufhört/nachlässt

leukaemia, (*US*) **leukemia** [luːˈkiːmɪə] N Leukämie *f*

level ['levl] ❶ ADJ **(a)** *ground, surface, floor* eben; *spoonful* gestrichen

(b) (= *at the same height*) auf gleicher Höhe (*with* mit); (= *parallel*) parallel (*with* zu); **the bedroom is** ~ **with the ground** das Schlafzimmer liegt ebenerdig

(c) (= *equal*) gleichauf; (*fig*) gleich gut; **Jones was almost** ~ **with the winner** Jones kam fast auf gleiche Höhe mit dem Sieger; **the two teams are** ~ **in the league** die beiden Mannschaften haben den gleichen Tabellenstand

(d) (= *steady*) *tone of voice* ruhig; (= *well-balanced*) ausgeglichen; *judgement* abgewogen, ausgewogen; **to have/ keep a** ~ **head** einen kühlen Kopf haben/bewahren

❷ ADV ~ **with** in Höhe (+*gen*); **it should lie** ~ **with ...** es sollte gleich hoch sein wie ...; **to draw** ~ **with sb** mit jdm gleichziehen; (*in league etc*) punktegleich mit jdm sein

❸ N **(a)** (= *altitude*) Höhe *f*; **on a** ~ **(with)** auf gleicher Höhe (mit); **at eye** ~ in Augenhöhe; **the trees were very tall, almost at roof** ~ die Bäume waren sehr hoch, sie reichten fast bis zum Dach

(b) (= *storey*) Etage *f*, Stockwerk *nt*; **the house is on four** ~**s** das Haus hat vier Etagen

(c) (= *position on scale*) Ebene *f*; (*social, intellectual etc*) Niveau *nt*; **they're on a different** ~ sie haben ein unterschiedliches Niveau; **to descend** *or* **come down to that** ~ auf ein so tiefes Niveau absinken; **he tried to raise the** ~ **of the conversation** er versuchte, der Unterhaltung etwas mehr Niveau zu geben; **if profit stays at the same** ~ wenn sich der Gewinn auf dem gleichen Stand hält; **the pound has been left to find its own** ~ der Pfundkurs wurde freigegeben, um seinen natürlichen Stand zu erreichen; **the rising** ~ **of inflation** die steigende Inflationsrate; **a high** ~ **of interest** sehr großes Interesse; **a high** ~ **of support** sehr viel Unterstützung; **the talks were held at a very high** ~ die Gespräche fanden auf hoher Ebene statt; **a low** ~ **of sales** ein sehr geringer Absatz; **on a purely personal** ~ rein persönlich

(d) (= *amount, degree*) **a high** ~ **of hydrogen** ein hoher Wasserstoffanteil; **the** ~ **of alcohol in the blood** der Alkoholspiegel im Blut; **cholesterol** ~ Cholesterinspiegel *m*; **the** ~ **of violence** das Ausmaß der Gewalttätigkeit

(e) **it's on the** ~ (*inf*) (*business*) es ist reell; (*proposition*) es ist ehrlich gemeint; **is he on the** ~**?** meint er es ehrlich?

❹ VT *ground, site etc* einebnen, planieren; *building* abreißen; *town* dem Erdboden gleichmachen

(b) *weapon* richten (*at* auf +*acc*); *accusation* erheben (*at* gegen); *criticism* üben (*at an* +*dat*)

(c) (*Sport*) **to** ~ **the match** den Ausgleich erzielen; **to** ~ **the score** gleichziehen

❺ VI (*inf*) **I'll** ~ **with you** ich werd ehrlich mit dir sein

➤ **level out** VI (*also* **level off**) (*ground*) eben *or* flach werden; (*fig*) sich einpendeln; (*output, growth*) sich stabilisieren

level: **level crossing** N (*Brit*) (beschrankter) Bahnübergang; **level-headed** ADJ *person* ausgeglichen; *attitude* ausgewogen; **level pegging** ADJ (*Brit*) punktgleich; **it's** ~ **as they go round the final bend** sie liegen in der letzten Kurve auf gleicher Höhe

lever ['liːvəʳ, (*US*) 'levəʳ] ❶ N Hebel *m*; (= *crowbar*) Brechstange *f*; (*fig*) Druckmittel *nt* ❷ VT (hoch)stemmen; **he** ~**ed the machine-part into place** er hob das Maschinenteil durch Hebelwirkung an seinen Platz; **he** ~**ed the box open** er stemmte die Kiste auf; **he** ~**ed himself onto the ledge** er hievte sich auf den Felsvorsprung (hoch)

leverage ['liːvərɪdʒ, (*US*) 'levərɪdʒ] N Hebelkraft *f*; (*fig*) Einfluss *m*; **to use sth as** ~ (*fig*) etw als Druckmittel benutzen; (= *to one's own advantage*) etw zu seinem Vorteil ausnützen; **this gave us a bit of** ~ **with the authorities** dadurch konnten wir etwas Druck auf die Behörden ausüben

Levis, levis® ['liːvaɪz] PL Levis® *f*, Jeans *pl*

levy ['levɪ] ❶ N (= *act*) (Steuer)einziehung *f or* -eintreibung *f*; (= *tax*) Steuer *f* ❷ VT *tax, charge* erheben; **to** ~ **a tax on beer** Steuern *pl* auf Bier erheben; **to** ~ **execution against sb** jdn pfänden lassen

lewd [luːd] ADJ (+ER) unanständig; (= *lustful*) lüstern; *remark* anzüglich

lexicographer [ˌleksɪˈkɒɡrəfəʳ] N Lexikograf(in) *m(f)*

lexicography [ˌleksɪˈkɒɡrəfɪ] N Lexikografie *f*

lexicon [ˈleksɪkən] N Wörterbuch *nt*; (*in linguistics*) Lexikon *nt*

liability [ˌlaɪəˈbɪlɪtɪ] N **(a)** (= *burden*) Belastung *f* **(b)** one's ~ for tax jds Steuerpflicht *f*; **he has a tax ~ of £1,000** er muss £ 1000 Steuern bezahlen **(c)** (= *responsibility*) Haftung *f*; **we accept no ~ for ...** wir übernehmen keine Haftung für ...; **~ company** Gesellschaft *f* mit beschränkter Haftung **(d)** (*Fin*) **liabilities** Verbindlichkeiten *pl*; (*on balance sheet*) Aktiva *pl*

liable [ˈlaɪəbl] ADJ **(a)** to be ~ for *or* to sth einer Sache (*dat*) unterliegen; **to be ~ for tax** (*things*) besteuert werden; (*income, person*) steuerpflichtig sein; **~ to VAT** umsatzsteuerpflichtig; **to be ~ to prosecution** der Strafverfolgung unterliegen
(b) (= *prone to*) anfällig; **~ to inflation** inflationsanfällig **(c)** (= *responsible*) **to be ~** haften, haftbar sein; **to be ~ for sth** für etw haftbar sein *or* haften; **he is not legally ~ to pay** er ist nicht gesetzlich verpflichtet zu zahlen
(d) (= *likely to*) **to be ~ to do sth** (*in future*) wahrscheinlich etw tun (werden); (*habitually*) dazu neigen, etw zu tun; **we are ~ to get shot here** wir können hier leicht beschossen werden; **if you don't write it down I'm ~ to forget it** wenn Sie das nicht aufschreiben, kann es durchaus sein, dass ich es vergesse; **the car is ~ to run out of petrol** (*Brit*) *or* **gas** (*US*) **any minute** dem Auto kann jede Minute das Benzin ausgehen

liaise [liːˈeɪz] VI (= *be the contact person*) als Verbindungsperson fungieren; (= *get in contact*) sich in Verbindung setzen; (= *be in contact*) in Verbindung stehen; **social services and health workers ~ closely** das Sozialamt und der Gesundheitsdienst arbeiten eng zusammen

liaison [liːˈeɪzɒn] N **(a)** (= *coordination*) Verbindung *f*, Zusammenarbeit *f*; (= *person*) Verbindungsmann *m*/-frau *f*
(b) (= *affair*) Liaison *f*

liaison officer N Verbindungsmann *m*/-frau *f*; **the firm's ~** der/die Firmensprecher(in)

liar [ˈlaɪəʳ] N Lügner(in) *m(f)*

lib [lɪb] N ABBR *of* **liberation**

Lib Dem [ˌlɪbˈdem] (*Brit Pol*) ABBR *of* **Liberal Democrat**

libel [ˈlaɪbl] **1** N (schriftlich geäußerte) Verleumdung (*on +gen*); **to begin a ~ action against sb** jdn wegen Verleumdung verklagen **2** VT verleumden

libellous, (*US*) **libelous** [ˈlaɪbələs] ADJ verleumderisch

liberal [ˈlɪbərəl] **1** ADJ *offer, supply* großzügig; *helping of food* reichlich; **to be ~ with one's praise/comments** mit Lob/ seinen Kommentaren freigebig sein; **to be ~ with one's money** mit seinem Geld großzügig umgehen **(b)** (= *broad-minded, Pol*) liberal; **the Liberal Party** (*Brit Hist, in Canada*) die Liberale Partei **2** N **(a)** (*Pol*) Liberale(r) *mf* **(b)** (= *~-minded person*) Liberalbesinnte(r) *mf*

liberal: **liberal arts** PL **the ~** (*esp US*) die geisteswissenschaftlichen Fächer; **Liberal Democrat** (*Brit Pol*) **1** N Liberaldemokrat(in) *m(f)* **2** ADJ liberaldemokratisch; *gain, loss, policy* der Liberaldemokraten; **the ~ Party** die liberaldemokratische Partei; **liberal education** N Allgemeinbildung *f*

liberalization [ˌlɪbərəlaɪˈzeɪʃən] N Liberalisierung *f*

liberalize [ˈlɪbərəlaɪz] VT liberalisieren

liberally [ˈlɪbərəlɪ] ADV (= *broad-mindedly*) liberal; (= *generously*) großzügig; (= *in large quantities*) reichlich

liberal-minded [ˌlɪbərəlˈmaɪndɪd] ADJ liberal

liberate [ˈlɪbəreɪt] VT befreien; **to ~ sb from sth** jdn von etw befreien

liberated [ˈlɪbəreɪtɪd] ADJ *women, times* emanzipiert

liberation [ˌlɪbəˈreɪʃən] N Befreiung *f*

libertarian [ˌlɪbəˈtɛərɪən] **1** ADJ (= *freedom-loving*) freiheitsliebend; (= *opposed to authority*) libertär; *policy, politics* liberalistisch **2** N Verfechter(in) *m(f)* des freien Willens, Liberalist(in) *m(f)* (*esp Pol*)

liberty [ˈlɪbətɪ] N **(a)** Freiheit *f*; **to be at ~ to do sth** (= *be permitted*) etw tun dürfen; **I am not at ~ to comment** es ist mir nicht gestattet, darüber zu sprechen; **you are at ~ to go** es steht Ihnen frei zu gehen **(b)** **I have taken the ~ of giving your name** ich habe mir erlaubt, Ihren Namen anzugeben; **to take liberties with the truth** es mit der Wahrheit nicht so genau nehmen; **to take liberties with sb** sich jdm gegenüber Freiheiten herausnehmen

libido [lɪˈbiːdəʊ] N Libido *f*

Libra [ˈliːbrə] N Waage *f*; **she's (a) ~** sie ist Waage

librarian [laɪˈbrɛərɪən] N Bibliothekar(in) *m(f)*

library [ˈlaɪbrərɪ] N Bibliothek *f*; (*public also*) Bücherei *f*; (= *collection of books/records*) (Bücher-/ Schallplatten)sammlung *f*

library: **library book** N Leihbuch *nt*; **library ticket** N Leserausweis *m*

libretto [lɪˈbretəʊ] N Libretto *nt*

Libya [ˈlɪbɪə] N Libyen *nt*

Libyan [ˈlɪbɪən] **1** ADJ libysch **2** N Libyer(in) *m(f)*

lice [laɪs] PL *of* **louse**

licence, (*US*) **license** [ˈlaɪsəns] N **(a)** Genehmigung *f*; (*by authority*) behördliche Genehmigung; (*Comm*) Lizenz *f*; (= *driving ~*) Führerschein *m*; (= *gun ~*) Waffenschein *m*; (= *hunting ~*) Jagdschein *m*; (= *radio/television ~*) (Rundfunk-/ Fernseh)genehmigung *f*; **you have to have a (television) ~** man muss Fernsehgebühren bezahlen; **a ~ to practise medicine** (*Brit*), **a license to practice medicine** (*US*) die Approbation; **the restaurant has lost its ~ (to sell drinks)** das Restaurant hat seine Schankerlaubnis verloren; **it is just a ~ to print money** (*fig*) es ist ein sehr lukratives Geschäft; **to manufacture sth under ~** etw in Lizenz herstellen; **to give sb ~ to do sth** jdm erlauben, etw zu tun
(b) (= *freedom*) Freiheit *f*

licence: **licence fee** N (*Brit TV*) ≈ Fernsehgebühr *f*; **licence number**, (*US*) **license number** N (*Aut*) Kraftfahrzeug- *or* Kfz-Kennzeichen *nt*; **licence plate**, (*US*) **license plate** N (*Aut*) Nummernschild *nt*

license [ˈlaɪsəns] **1** N (*US*) = **licence 2** VT eine Lizenz/ Konzession vergeben an (*+acc*); **to be ~d to do sth** die Genehmigung haben, etw zu tun; **he is ~d to practise** (*Brit*) *or* **practice** (*US*) **medicine** er ist approbierter Arzt; **we are not ~d to sell alcohol** wir haben keine Schankerlaubnis

licensed [ˈlaɪsənst] ADJ **(a)** *pilot* mit Pilotenschein; *taxi driver* mit Taxischein; *physician* approbiert **(b)** **~ bar/premises** Lokal *nt* mit Schankerlaubnis; **fully ~** mit voller Schankerlaubnis; **he won't stay at a hotel unless it's ~** er übernachtet nur in Hotels mit Alkoholausschank

licensee [ˌlaɪsənˈsiː] N (*of bar*) Inhaber(in) *m(f)* einer Schankerlaubnis; **the ~ of our local pub** (*Brit*) *or* **bar** der Wirt unserer Stammkneipe

licensing [ˈlaɪsənsɪŋ] **1** ADJ **~ hours** Ausschankzeiten *pl*; **~ laws** Gesetz *nt* über den Ausschank und Verkauf alkoholischer Getränke **2** N Zulassung *f*, Genehmigung *f*

LICENSING LAWS

*In Großbritannien werden alle Gesetze und Verordnungen bezüglich des Verkaufs und Konsums von alkoholischen Getränken unter dem Begriff der **licensing laws** zusammengefasst. Das Mindestalter, ab dem der Konsum von Alkohol in Pubs oder Clubs gestattet ist, liegt bei 18 Jahren. Pubs, Clubs und Restaurants dürfen nur dann Alkohol ausschenken, wenn sie eine Schankerlaubnis, **licence**, besitzen, und auch dann nur zu bestimmten Uhrzeiten. Ein gutes Sortiment verschiedenster Biere und Weine findet sich an fast jeder Ecke in Fachgeschäften, den so genannten **off-licences**, die so heißen, da der dort verkaufte Alkohol nur privat, außerhalb „off" der lizenzierten Räumlichkeiten konsumiert werden darf.*

*In den USA bestehen in den einzelnen Bundesstaaten verschiedene Regelungen. Das Mindestalter für den Alkoholkonsum schwankt zwischen 18 und 21 Jahren, einige Staaten haben regelrechte „trockene" Counties, in denen der Konsum und der Verkauf von Alkohol komplett untersagt ist. In einigen Bundesstaaten können alkoholische Getränke nur in den so genannten **liquor stores** oder auch **package stores** erworben werden. Dafür sind die meisten Restaurants und Clubs im Besitz einer **liquor permit** für den Alkoholausschank.*

---

licentious [laɪˈsenʃəs] ADJ ausschweifend; *behaviour* unzüchtig; *book* sehr freizügig

lichen [ˈlaɪkən] N Flechte *f*

lick [lɪk] **1** N **(a) to give sth a ~** an etw (*dat*) lecken **(b)** (*inf*: = *small quantity*) **it's time we gave the kitchen a ~ of paint** die Küche könnte auch mal wieder etwas Farbe vertragen (*inf*)

(c) (*Brit inf*) **to go/drive at a fair old ~** einen ganz schönen Zahn draufhaben (*inf*)

2 VT **(a)** lecken; **he ~ed the stamp** er leckte an der Briefmarke; **he ~ed the ice cream** er leckte am Eis; **to ~ one's lips** sich (*dat*) die Lippen lecken; (*fig*) sich (*dat*) die Finger lecken; **to ~ one's wounds** (*fig*) seine Wunden lecken; **to ~ sb's boots** (*fig*) vor jdm kriechen (*inf*)
(b) (*flames*) züngeln an (+*dat*)
(c) (*inf*: = *beat, defeat*) in die Pfanne hauen (*inf*); **I think we've got it ~ed** ich glaube, wir haben die Sache jetzt im Griff

licking [ˈlɪkɪŋ] N (*inf*) **to give sb a ~** (= *beating*) jdm eine Abreibung geben (*inf*); (= *defeat*) jdn in die Pfanne hauen (*inf*)

licorice [ˈlɪkərɪs] N = **liquorice**

lid [lɪd] N Deckel *m*; **that puts the (tin) ~ on it** (*inf*) das ist doch die Höhe, das schlägt dem Fass den Boden aus; **a documentary that really takes the ~ off Hollywood** ein Dokumentarfilm, der das wahre Gesicht Hollywoods zeigt; **to keep a ~ on sth** etw unter Kontrolle halten; *on information* etw geheim halten

lie¹ [laɪ] **1** N Lüge *f*; **to tell a ~** lügen; **I tell a ~, it's actually tomorrow** ich hab mich vertan, es ist morgen; **to give the ~ to a claim** die Unwahrheit einer Behauptung (*gen*) zeigen *or* beweisen **2** VI lügen; **to ~ to sb** jdn belügen *or* anlügen

lie² *vb*: *pret* **lay**, *ptp* **lain** **1** N (= *position*) Lage *f*, Position *f* **2** VI **(a)** liegen; (= ~ *down*) sich legen; **~ on your back** leg dich auf den Rücken; **the runner who is lying third** (*esp Brit*) der Läufer, der auf dem dritten Platz liegt; **our road lay along the river** unsere Straße führte am Fluss entlang; **our futures ~ in quite different directions** unsere zukünftigen Wege führen in verschiedene Richtungen; **to ~ asleep** (daliegen und) schlafen; **to ~ dying** im Sterben liegen; **the book lay unopened** das Buch lag ungeöffnet da; **to ~ low** untertauchen; **it ~s with you to solve the problem** es liegt bei dir, das Problem zu lösen; **he did everything that lay in his power to help us** er tat alles in seiner Macht Stehende, um uns zu helfen; **that responsibility ~s with your department** dafür ist Ihre Abteilung verantwortlich
(b) (= *be buried*) ruhen

➤ **lie about** (*Brit*) *or* **around** VI herumliegen

➤ **lie back** VI **(a)** (= *recline*) sich zurücklehnen **(b)** (*fig*: = *take no action*) sich ausruhen

➤ **lie behind** VI +PREP OBJ *decision, remarks* stehen hinter (+*dat*)

➤ **lie down** VI **(a)** (*lit*) sich hinlegen; **he lay down on the bed** er legte sich aufs Bett **(b)** (*fig*) **he won't take that lying down!** das lässt er sich nicht gefallen *or* bieten!

➤ **lie in** VI (= *stay in bed*) im Bett bleiben

lie detector N Lügendetektor *m*

lie-down [ˌlaɪˈdaʊn] N (*inf*) **to have a ~** ein Schläfchen *or* Nickerchen machen (*inf*)

lie-in [ˈlaɪɪn] N (*Brit inf*) **to have a ~** (sich) ausschlafen

lieu [luː] N (*form*) **money in ~** stattdessen Geld; **in ~ of X** an Stelle von X; **I work weekends and get time off in ~** (*esp Brit*) ich arbeite an Wochenenden und kann mir dafür (an anderen Tagen) frei nehmen

lieutenant [lefˈtenənt, (*US*) luːˈtenənt] N Leutnant *m*; (*Brit*) Oberleutnant *m*

life [laɪf] N, *pl* **lives (a)** Leben *nt*; **bird/plant** ~ die Vogel-/Pflanzenwelt; **the battle resulted in great loss of ~** bei der Schlacht kamen viele ums Leben; **this is a matter of ~ and death** hier geht es um Leben und Tod; **to bring sb back to ~** jdn wieder beleben; **his book brings history to ~** sein Buch lässt die Geschichte lebendig werden; **to come to ~** (*fig*) lebendig werden; **after half an hour the discussion came to ~** nach einer halben Stunde kam Leben in die Diskussion; **to put new ~ into sb** jdm wieder Auftrieb geben; **at my time of ~** in meinem Alter; **he's got a job for ~** er hat eine Stelle auf Lebenszeit; **he's doing ~ (for murder)** (*inf*) er sitzt lebenslänglich (wegen Mord) (*inf*); **he got ~** (*inf*) er hat lebenslänglich gekriegt (*inf*); **how many lives were lost?** wie viele (Menschen) sind ums Leben gekommen?; **the lives of the prisoners** das Leben der Gefangenen; **to take one's own ~** sich (*dat*) das Leben nehmen; **to save sb's ~** (*lit*) jdm das Leben retten; (*fig*) jdn retten; **I couldn't do it to save my ~** ich kann es beim besten Willen nicht; **the church is my ~** die Kirche ist mein ganzes Leben; **early in ~**, **in early ~** in frühen Jahren; **later in ~**, **in later ~** in späteren Jahren; **she leads a busy ~** bei ihr ist immer etwas los; **she began (her working) ~ as a teacher** sie begann ihr Berufsleben als Lehrerin; **all his ~** sein ganzes Leben lang; **I've never been to London in my ~** ich war in meinem ganzen Leben noch nicht in London; **to fight for one's ~** um sein Leben kämpfen; **run for your lives!** rennt um euer Leben!; **I can't for the ~ of me ...** (*inf*) ich kann beim besten Willen nicht ...; **never in my ~ have I heard such nonsense** ich habe noch nie im Leben so einen Unsinn gehört; **not on your ~!** (*inf*) ich bin doch nicht verrückt! (*inf*); **get a ~!** (*inf*) sonst hast du keine Probleme? (*inf*); **to have a ~ of one's own** sein eigenes Leben führen; **it seemed to have a ~ of its own** es scheint seinen eigenen Willen zu haben; **those children are full of ~!** diese Kinder sind sehr lebhaft!; **the city centre** (*Brit*) *or* **center** (*US*) **was full of ~** im Stadtzentrum ging es sehr lebhaft zu; **he is the ~ and soul** (*Brit*) *or* ~ (*US*) **of every party** er bringt Leben in jede Party; **village ~** das Leben auf dem Dorf; **this is the ~!** ja, ist das ein Leben!; **what a ~!** was für ein Leben!; **such is ~, that's ~** so ist das Leben; **the good ~** das süße Leben
(b) (= *the world, social activity*) **to see ~** die Welt sehen
(c) (= *useful or active ~*) Lebensdauer *f*; **during the ~ of the present Parliament** während der Legislaturperiode des gegenwärtigen Parlaments
(d) (= *biography*) Biografie *f*; (*of saint, king etc*) Lebensbeschreibung *f*

life: **life assurance** N (*Brit*) Lebensversicherung *f*; **whole** (*Brit*) *or* **straight** (*US*) ~ Todesfallversicherung *f*; **term** ~ Risikolebensversicherung *f*; **lifebelt** N Rettungsgürtel *m*; **lifeboat** N Rettungsboot *nt*; **lifebuoy** N Rettungsring *m*; **life class** N (*Art*) Kurs *m* im Modellzeichnen; **life cycle** N Lebenszyklus *m*; **life expectancy** N Lebenserwartung *f*; **lifeguard** N (*on beach*) Rettungsschwimmer(in) *m(f)*; (*in baths*) Bademeister(in) *m(f)*; **life imprisonment** N lebenslängliche Freiheitsstrafe; **life insurance** N = **life assurance**; **life jacket** N Schwimmweste *f*

lifeless [ˈlaɪflɪs] ADJ leblos; (= *inanimate also*) tot

life: **lifelike** ADJ lebensecht; **lifeline** N (*fig*) Rettungsanker *m*; **the telephone is a ~ for many old people** das Telefon ist für viele alte Leute lebenswichtig; **lifelong** ADJ lebenslang; **they are ~ friends** sie sind schon ihr Leben lang Freunde; **his ~ devotion to the cause** die Sache, in deren Dienst er sein Leben gestellt hat; **life membership** N Mitgliedschaft *f* auf Lebenszeit; **life-or-death** ADJ *struggle* Kampf *m* auf Leben und Tod; **life peer** N Peer *m* auf Lebenszeit; **life preserver** N (*US*) Schwimmweste *f*; **life raft** N Rettungsfloß *nt*; **life-saver** N (*fig*) Retter *m* in der Not; **it was a real ~!** das hat mich gerettet; **life-saving** **1** N Rettungsschwimmen *nt* **2** ADJ *techniques, apparatus* zur Lebensrettung; *phone call, drug, operation, treatment* lebensrettend; **life sentence** N lebenslängliche Freiheitsstrafe; **life-size(d)** ADJ in Lebensgröße, lebensgroß; **lifespan** N (*of people*) Lebenserwartung *f*; (*of animals, plants*) Leben(sdauer *f*) *nt*; **life story** N Lebensgeschichte *f*; **lifestyle** N Lebensstil *m*; **life support machine** N Herz-Lungen-Maschine *f*; **life support system** N Lebenserhaltungssystem *nt*; **life-threatening** ADJ lebensbedrohend; **lifetime** N **(a)** Lebenszeit *f*; (*of battery, machine, animal*) Lebensdauer *f*; **once in a ~** einmal im Leben; **during** *or* **in my ~** während meines Lebens; **the chance of a ~** eine einmalige Chance **(b)** (*fig*) Ewigkeit *f*

LIFO (*Comm*) ABBR *of* **last-in-first-out** Lifo; **~ costing** Lifo-Kostenerfassung *f*

lift [lɪft] **1** N **(a)** (= *lifting*) **give me a ~ up** heb mich mal hoch **(b)** (= *emotional uplift*) **to give sb a ~** jdn aufmuntern; (*drug*) jdn aufputschen; (*prospect*) jdm Auftrieb geben **(c)** (*in car etc*) Mitfahrgelegenheit *f*; **to give sb a ~** jdn mitnehmen; (*as special journey*) jdn fahren; **want a ~?** möchten Sie mitkommen?, soll ich dich fahren? **(d)** (*Brit*: = *elevator*) Fahrstuhl *m*; (*for goods*) Aufzug *m*; **he took the ~** er fuhr mit dem Fahrstuhl **2** VT **(a)** (*also* ~ **up**) hochheben; *window* hochschieben; *feet, head* heben; *hat* ziehen; *potatoes etc* ernten; **to ~ the baby out of his playpen** das Baby aus dem Laufgitter heben; **to ~ the phone** den Hörer abnehmen; **to have one's face ~ed** sich (*dat*) das Gesicht liften lassen **(b)** (*fig*: *also* ~ **up**) **to ~ the spirits/mood** die Stimmung heben; **the news ~ed him out of his depression** durch die Nachricht verflog seine Niedergeschlagenheit **(c)** *restrictions etc* aufheben

(d) (*inf*: = *steal*) klauen (*inf*); (= *plagiarize*) abkupfern (*inf*) 🔟 VI (*mist*) sich lichten; (*mood, spirits*) sich heben

liftoff [ˈlɪftɒf] N (*Space*) Abheben *nt*, Start *m*; **we have ~** der Start ist erfolgt

ligament [ˈlɪgəmənt] N Band *nt*; **he's torn a ~ in his shoulder** er hat einen Bänderriss in der Schulter

light¹ [laɪt], *vb*: pret, ptp **lit** or **lighted** 🔟 N **(a)** (*in general*) Licht *nt*; (= *lamp*) Lampe *f*; **by the ~ of a candle/the fire** im Schein einer Kerze/des Feuers; **at first ~** bei Tagesanbruch; **to cast** or **throw** or **shed ~ on sth** (*fig*) Licht in etw (*acc*) bringen; **to cast a new** or **fresh ~ on sth** neues Licht auf etw (*acc*) werfen; **in the cold ~ of day** (*fig*) bei Licht besehen; **to see sb/sth in a different ~** jdn/etw in einem anderen Licht sehen; **it showed him in a different ~** es zeigte ihn in einem anderen Licht; **to see sth in a new ~** etw mit anderen Augen betrachten; **in the ~ of** angesichts (+*gen*); **in the ~ of what you say** in Anbetracht dessen, was Sie sagen; **to bring sth to ~** etw ans Tageslicht bringen; **to come to ~** ans Tageslicht kommen; **finally I saw the ~** (*inf*) endlich ging mir ein Licht auf (*inf*); (*morally*) endlich wurden mir die Augen geöffnet; **to see the ~ of day** (*report*) veröffentlicht werden; (*project*) verwirklicht werden; **to go out like a ~** sofort weg sein (*inf*); **put out the ~s before you go to bed** mach das Licht aus, bevor du ins Bett gehst; **(traffic)** ~s Ampel *f*; **the ~s** (*of a car*) die Beleuchtung; **~s out for the boys was at 8 pm** um 20 Uhr mussten die Jungen das Licht ausmachen; **~s out!** Licht aus(machen)!
(b) (= *flame*) **have you (got) a ~?** haben Sie Feuer?; **to put a ~ to sth, to set ~ to sth** etw anzünden
🔟 ADJ (+ER) hell; **a ~ green dress** ein hellgrünes Kleid; **it's getting** or **growing ~** es wird hell
🔟 VT **(a)** (= *illuminate*) beleuchten; *lamp, light* anmachen; **to ~ the way for sb** jdm leuchten
(b) (= *ignite*) anzünden; **to ~ a fire under sb** (*esp US fig*) jdm Feuer unter dem Hintern machen (*inf*)
🔟 VI **this fire won't ~** das Feuer geht nicht an

▶ **light up** 🔟 VI **(a)** (= *be lit, eyes*) aufleuchten; (*face*) sich erhellen **(b)** **the men took out their pipes and lit up** die Männer holten ihre Pfeifen hervor und zündeten sie an
🔟 VT SEP **(a)** beleuchten; **a smile lit up his face** ein Lächeln erhellte sein Gesicht; **Piccadilly Circus was all lit up** der Piccadilly Circus war hell erleuchtet; **flames lit up the night sky** Flammen erleuchteten den Nachthimmel **(b)** *cigarette etc* anzünden

light² 🔟 ADJ (+ER) leicht; *punishment* milde; **to be a ~ eater** kein großer Esser sein; **~ comedy** Lustspiel *nt*; **~ industry** Leichtindustrie *f*; **~ opera** Operette *f*; **~ reading** Unterhaltungslektüre *f*; **with a ~ heart** leichten Herzens; **as ~ as a feather** federleicht; **to make ~ of one's difficulties** seine Schwierigkeiten auf die leichte Schulter nehmen; **you shouldn't make ~ of her problems** du solltest dich über ihre Probleme nicht lustig machen; **to make ~ work of sth** spielend fertig werden mit
🔟 ADV **to travel ~** mit wenig or leichtem Gepäck reisen

▶ **light (up)on** VI +PREP OBJ (*inf*) entdecken, stoßen auf (+*acc*)

light: light bulb N Glühlampe or -birne *f*; **light-coloured**, (*US*) **light-colored** ADJ, *comp* **lighter-colo(u)red**, *superl* **lightest-colo(u)red** hell; **light cream** N (*US*) Sahne *f* (*mit geringem Fettgehalt*)

lighten¹ [ˈlaɪtn] 🔟 VT erhellen; *colour, hair* aufhellen; *gloom* aufheitern 🔟 VI hell werden; (*mood*) sich heben; (*atmosphere*) sich entspannen

lighten² VT *load* leichter machen; **to ~ sb's burden** or **load** (*fig*) jds Lage erleichtern; **to ~ sb's workload** jdm etwas Arbeit abnehmen

▶ **lighten up** VI (*inf*) die Dinge leichter nehmen; **lighten up!** nimms leicht!

lighter [ˈlaɪtər] N Feuerzeug *nt*

lighter fuel N Feuerzeugbenzin *nt*

light: light-fingered [laɪtˈfɪŋgəd] ADJ, *comp* **lighter-fingered**, *superl* **lightest-fingered** langfingerig; **light fitting, light fixture** N (= *lightbulb holder*) Fassung *f*; (= *bracket*) (Lampen)halterung *f*; **light-headed** ADJ, *comp* **lighter-headed**, *superl* **lightest-headed** benebelt (*inf*); (= *frivolous*) oberflächlich, leichtfertig; **I felt quite ~ when I heard I'd passed the exam** ich wurde ganz ausgelassen or übermütig, als ich hörte, dass ich die Prüfung bestanden hatte; **light-hearted** ADJ unbeschwert; *chat* zwanglos; *reply* scherzhaft

book, film vergnüglich; *comedy* leicht; **light-heartedly** ADV unbekümmert, leichten Herzens; (= *jokingly*) *reply* scherzhaft; **lighthouse** N Leuchtturm *m*

lighting [ˈlaɪtɪŋ] N Beleuchtung *f*

lightish [ˈlaɪtɪʃ] ADJ *colour* hell; **a ~ brown** ein helleres Braun

lightly [ˈlaɪtlɪ] ADV **(a)** leicht; *walk, tread* leise; **to sleep ~** einen leichten Schlaf haben; **~ clad (in sth)** leicht (mit etw) bekleidet; **to get off ~** glimpflich davonkommen; **to touch ~ on a subject** ein Thema nur berühren or streifen
(b) (= *casually*) **to speak ~ of sb/sth** sich abfällig or geringschätzig über jdn/etw äußern; **he spoke ~ of his illness** er nahm seine Krankheit auf die leichte Schulter; **to treat sth too ~** etw nicht ernst genug nehmen; **a responsibility not to be ~ undertaken** eine Verantwortung, die man nicht unüberlegt auf sich nehmen sollte

light meter N Belichtungsmesser *m*

lightning [ˈlaɪtnɪŋ] 🔟 N Blitz *m*; **a flash of ~** ein Blitz *m*; (*doing damage*) ein Blitzschlag *m*; **struck by ~** vom Blitz getroffen; **we had some ~ an hour ago** vor einer Stunde hat es geblitzt; **as quick as ~, like (greased) ~** wie der Blitz 🔟 ATTR blitzschnell, Blitz-; **~ strike** spontaner Streik; **with ~ speed** blitzschnell; **~ visit** Blitzbesuch *m*

lightning conductor, (*US*) **lightning rod** N Blitzableiter *m*

light: light pen N (*Comput*) Lichtgriffel *m*; **light show** N Lightshow *f*; **light switch** N Lichtschalter *m*; **lightweight** 🔟 ADJ leicht; (*fig*) schwach; **~ boxer** Leichtgewichtsboxer(in) *m(f)* 🔟 N Leichtgewicht *nt also fig* (*Boxing*) Leichtgewichtler(in) *m(f)*; **he is regarded as a ~ in academic circles** er wird in akademischen Kreisen nicht für voll genommen; **light year** N Lichtjahr *nt*; **to be ~s ahead of sb** jdm um Lichtjahre voraus sein

likable ADJ = **likeable**

like¹ [laɪk] 🔟 ADJ (= *similar*) ähnlich
🔟 PREP wie; **to be ~ sb/sth** jdm ähnlich sein; **they are very ~ each other** sie sind sich (*dat*) sehr ähnlich; **to look ~ sb** jdm ähnlich sehen; **what's he ~?** wie ist er?; **he's just bought a new car – what is it ~?** er hat sich gerade ein neues Auto gekauft – wie sieht es aus?; **she was ~ a sister to me** sie war wie eine Schwester zu mir; **that's just ~ him!** das sieht ihm ähnlich!; **it's not ~ him** es ist nicht seine Art; **I never saw anything ~ it** so (et)was habe ich noch nie gesehen; **that's more ~ it!** so ist es schon besser!; **it's on company advice – orders, more ~** (*inf*) es ist auf Anraten der Firma – besser gesagt auf Anordnung; **that hat's nothing ~ as nice as this one** der Hut ist bei weitem nicht so hübsch wie dieser; **there's nothing ~ a nice cup of tea!** es geht nichts über eine schöne Tasse Tee!; **is this what you had in mind? – it's something/nothing ~ it** hattest du dir so etwas vorgestellt? – ja, so ähnlich/nein, überhaupt nicht; **the Americans are ~ that** so sind die Amerikaner; **people ~ that** solche Leute; **a car ~ that** so ein Auto; **I found one ~ it** ich habe ein Ähnliches gefunden; **it will cost something ~ £10** es wird etwa or so ungefähr £ 10 kosten; **that sounds ~ a good idea** das hört sich gut an; **~ mad** (*Brit inf*), **~ anything** (*inf*) wie verrückt (*inf*); **~ that** so; **it wasn't ~ that at all** so wars doch gar nicht
🔟 ADV (*inf*) **(as) ~ as not** höchstwahrscheinlich
🔟 CONJ (*strictly incorrect*) **I said ~** wie gesagt; **it's just ~ I say** das sage ich ja immer; **do it ~ I do** mach es so wie ich
🔟 N (= *equal etc*) **we shall not see his ~ again** so etwas wie ihn bekommen wir nicht wieder (*inf*); **did you ever see the ~?** (*inf*) hast du so was schon gesehen?; **and the ~, and such ~** und dergleichen; **I've no time for the ~s of him** (*inf*) mit solchen Leuten gebe ich mich nicht ab (*inf*)

like² 🔟 N USU PL **she tried to find out his ~s and dislikes** sie wollte herausbekommen, was er mochte und was nicht
🔟 VT **(a)** *person* mögen, gern haben; **how do you ~ him?** wie gefällt er dir?; **I don't ~ him** ich kann ihn nicht leiden; **he is well ~d here** er ist hier sehr beliebt
(b) **I ~ black shoes** ich mag schwarze Schuhe, mir gefallen schwarze Schuhe; **I ~ it** das gefällt mir; **I ~ chocolate** ich esse gern Schokolade; **I ~ football** (= *playing*) ich spiele gerne Fußball; (= *watching*) ich finde Fußball gut; **I ~ dancing** ich tanze gern; **we ~ it here** es gefällt uns hier; **that's one of the things I ~ about you** das ist eines der Dinge, die ich an dir mag; **how do you ~ your coffee?** wie trinken Sie Ihren Kaffee?; **how do you ~ Cádiz?** wie gefällt Ihnen Cádiz?; **how would you ~ to go for a walk?** was hältst du von einem Spaziergang?; **well, I ~ that!** (*inf*) das ist ein starkes Stück! (*inf*)

(c) (= *wish, wish for*) **I'd ~ an explanation** ich hätte gerne eine Erklärung; **I should ~ more time** ich würde mir gerne noch etwas Zeit lassen; **they would have ~d to come** sie wären gern gekommen; **I should ~ to know why** ich wüsste (gerne), warum; **I should ~ you to do it** ich möchte, dass du es tust; **whether he ~s it or not** ob es ihm passt oder nicht; **I didn't ~ to disturb him** ich wollte ihn nicht stören; **what would you ~?** was hätten *or* möchten Sie gern?; **would you ~ a drink?** möchten Sie etwas trinken?; **I would ~ to take this opportunity to welcome Dr Allan** ich möchte diese Gelegenheit ergreifen, um Dr. Allan willkommen zu heißen ⬛ VI **he is free to act as he ~s** es steht ihm frei, zu tun, was er will; **as you ~** wie Sie wollen; **if you ~** wenn Sie wollen

-like ADJ SUF -ähnlich, -artig; **cement-like** zementartig *or* -ähnlich

likeable (*Brit*), **likable** ['laɪkəbl] ADJ sympathisch, liebenswert

likelihood ['laɪklɪhʊd] N Wahrscheinlichkeit *f*; **in all ~** aller Wahrscheinlichkeit nach; **the ~ is that …** es ist wahrscheinlich, dass …; **there is little/every ~ that …** es ist kaum/durchaus wahrscheinlich, dass …; **is there any ~ of him coming?** besteht die Möglichkeit, dass er kommt?

likely ['laɪklɪ] ⬛ ADJ (+ER) **(a)** wahrscheinlich; **he is not ~ to come** es ist unwahrscheinlich, dass er kommt; **they are ~ to accept/refuse** sie werden wahrscheinlich zusagen/ablehnen; **the plan most ~ to succeed** der erfolgversprechendste Plan; **a ~ explanation** eine wahrscheinliche Erklärung; **a ~ story** *or* **tale!** (*iro*) das soll mal einer glauben! **(b)** (*inf*: = *suitable*) geeignet; **he is a ~ person for the job** er kommt für die Stelle infrage; **~ candidates** aussichtsreiche Kandidaten ⬛ ADV wahrscheinlich; **as ~ as not** höchstwahrscheinlich; **it's more ~ to be early than late** es wird eher früh als spät werden; **not ~!** (*inf iro*) wohl kaum (*inf*)

like-minded ['laɪk'maɪndɪd] ADJ gleich gesinnt; **~ people** Gleichgesinnte *pl*

liken ['laɪkən] VT vergleichen (*to* mit)

likeness ['laɪknɪs] N (= *resemblance*) Ähnlichkeit *f*; (= *portrait*) Bild(nis) *nt*; **to have a ~ to sb/one another** jdm/einander ähnlich sehen; **the painting is a good ~ of him** er ist auf dem Gemälde gut getroffen

likewise ['laɪkwaɪz] ADV ebenso, gleichermaßen; **he did ~** er tat das Gleiche; **have a nice weekend – ~** schönes Wochenende! – danke gleichfalls!

liking ['laɪkɪŋ] N **(a) to have a ~ for sb** jdn gern haben; **she took a ~ to him** er war ihr sympathisch **(b) to have a ~ for sth** eine Vorliebe für etw haben; **to take a ~ to sth** eine Vorliebe für etw bekommen; **to be to sb's ~** nach jds Geschmack sein; **she asks too many questions for my ~** für meinen Geschmack stellt sie zu viele Fragen

lilac ['laɪlək] ⬛ N **(a)** (= *plant*) Flieder *m* **(b)** (= *colour*) (Zart)lila *nt* ⬛ ADJ (zart)lila

Lilo® ['laɪ,ləʊ] N (*Brit*) Luftmatratze *f*

lilt [lɪlt] N singender Tonfall; **she spoke with a Welsh ~** sie sprach mit dem singenden Tonfall der Waliser

lilting ['lɪltɪŋ] ADJ *accent* singend; *ballad, tune, melody* beschwingt

lily ['lɪlɪ] N Lilie *f*; (= *water ~*) Seerose *f*; **~ of the valley** Maiglöckchen *nt*

limb [lɪm] N **(a)** (*Anat*) Glied *nt*; **~s** *pl* Gliedmaßen *pl*; **the lower ~s** die unteren Gliedmaßen; **to tear sb ~ from ~** jdn in Stücke reißen; **to risk life and ~** Leib und Leben riskieren **(b) to be out on a ~** (*fig*) exponiert sein; **to go out on a ~** (*fig*) sich exponieren

➤ **limber up** VI Lockerungsübungen machen; (*fig*) sich vorbereiten

limbo ['lɪmbəʊ] N (*fig*) Übergangs- *or* Zwischenstadium *nt*; **our expansion plans are in ~ because of lack of money** unsere Erweiterungspläne sind wegen Geldmangels in der Schwebe; **I'm in a sort of ~** ich hänge in der Luft (*inf*)

lime¹ [laɪm] N (*Geol*) Kalk *m*

lime² N (*Bot*: = *linden, also* **~ tree**) Linde(nbaum *m*) *f*

lime³ N (*Bot*: = *citrus fruit*) Limone(lle) *f*

lime juice N Limonensaft *m*

limelight ['laɪmlaɪt] N Rampenlicht *nt*; **to be in the ~** im Licht der Öffentlichkeit stehen

limerick ['lɪmərɪk] N Limerick *m*

limestone ['laɪmstəʊn] N Kalkstein *m*

limit ['lɪmɪt] ⬛ N **(a)** Grenze *f*; (= *limitation*) Begrenzung *f*; (= *speed ~*) Geschwindigkeitsbegrenzung *f*; (*Comm*) Limit *nt*; **the city ~s** die Stadtgrenzen *pl*; **a 40-mile ~** eine Vierzigmeilengrenze; **the 50 km/h ~** die Geschwindigkeitsbegrenzung von 50 Stundenkilometern; **is there any ~ on the size?** ist die Größe begrenzt *or* beschränkt?; **to put a ~ on sth, to set a ~ to** *or* **on sth** etw begrenzen; **there is a ~ to what one person can do** ein Mensch kann nur so viel tun und nicht mehr; **there's a ~ to the amount of money we can spend** wir können nicht unbegrenzt Geld ausgeben; **without ~** unbegrenzt; **off ~s to military personnel** Zutritt für Militär verboten; **over the ~** zu viel; (*in time*) zu lange; **you are** *or* **your baggage is over the ~** Ihr Gepäck hat Übergewicht; **you shouldn't drive, you're over the ~** du solltest dich nicht ans Steuer setzen, du hast zu viel getrunken; **he was three times over the ~** er hatte dreimal so viel Promille wie gesetzlich erlaubt; **50 pages per week is my ~** 50 Seiten pro Woche sind mein Limit; (*St Ex*) **at ~** Limit-; **to buy at ~** einen Limitauftrag erteilen

(b) (*inf*) **that's (just) the ~!** das ist die Höhe (*inf*); **that child is the ~!** dieses Kind ist eine Zumutung! (*inf*); **he's the ~!, isn't he the ~?** das ist 'ne Type! (*inf*) ⬛ VT begrenzen, beschränken; *freedom, spending, possibilities* einschränken; *imagination* hemmen; **to ~ sb/sth to sth** jdn/ etw auf etw (*acc*) beschränken; **to ~ oneself to a few remarks** sich auf einige (wenige) Bemerkungen beschränken

limitation [lɪmɪ'teɪʃən] N Beschränkung *f*; (*of freedom, spending*) Einschränkung *f*; **damage ~** Schadensbegrenzung *f*; **there is no ~ on exports of coal** es gibt keine Beschränkungen für den Kohleexport; **to have one's/its ~s** seine Grenzen haben

limited ['lɪmɪtɪd] ADJ **(a)** begrenzt, beschränkt; **this offer is for a ~ period only** dieses Angebot ist (zeitlich) befristet; **this is only true in a ~ sense** *or* **to a ~ extent** dies ist nur in gewissem Maße wahr; **he can only get about/look after himself to a ~ extent** er kann sich nur eingeschränkt bewegen/sich nur teilweise selber versorgen **(b)** (*esp Brit Comm*) *liability, right, authority* beschränkt; **ABC Travel Limited** ≈ ABC-Reisen GmbH

limited: limited company N (*esp Brit Comm*) ≈ Gesellschaft *f* mit beschränkter Haftung; **limited edition** N limitierte Auflage; (*of car*) limitierte Serie; **limited liability company** N (*esp Brit Comm*) = **limited company**

limitless ['lɪmɪtlɪs] ADJ grenzenlos

limo ['lɪməʊ] N (*inf*) Limousine *f*

limousine ['lɪməzi:n] N Limousine *f*

limp¹ [lɪmp] ⬛ N Hinken *nt*, Humpeln *nt*; **to walk with a ~** hinken, humpeln ⬛ VI hinken, humpeln

limp² ADJ (+ER) schlapp; *handshake* schlaff; *flowers* welk; *material, cloth* weich; **to hang ~** schlaff herunterhängen; **let your body go ~** alle Muskeln entspannen

limpid ['lɪmpɪd] ADJ klar

limply ['lɪmplɪ] ADV schlapp

linchpin ['lɪntʃpɪn] N (*fig*) Stütze *f*

linden ['lɪndən] N (*also* **~ tree**) Linde *f*

---

line¹ [laɪn]

⬛ NOUN	⬛ PHRASAL VERB
⬛ TRANSITIVE VERB	

⬛ NOUN

(a) (*for washing, fishing*) Leine *f*

(b) (= *mark*) (*on paper, on tennis court etc, on palm*) Linie *f*

(c) (= *wrinkle*) Falte *f*

(d) (= *boundary*) Grenze *f*; **the (fine** *or* **thin) line between right and wrong** der (feine) Unterschied zwischen Recht und Unrecht; **to draw a line between** (*fig*) einen Unterschied machen zwischen

(e) (= *row*) (*of people, cars*) (*side by side*) Reihe *f*; (*one behind the other, US*: = *queue*) Schlange *f*; (*Sport*) Linie *f*; **in (a) line** in einer Reihe; **in a straight line** geradlinig; **a line of traffic** eine Autoschlange; **to stand in line** Schlange stehen

✦**to be in line** (*buildings etc*) geradlinig sein; **to be in line (with)** (*fig*) in Einklang stehen (mit)

✦**to keep sb in line** (fig) dafür sorgen, dass jd nicht aus der Reihe tanzt

✦**into line** to bring sb/sth into line (with sth) (fig) jdn/etw auf die gleiche Linie (wie etw) bringen; **it's time these rebels were brought into line** es wird Zeit, dass die Rebellen zurückgepfiffen werden; **to fall** or **get into line** (= abreast) sich in Reih und Glied aufstellen; (= behind one another) sich in einer Reihe aufstellen; **he refused to fall into line with the new proposals** er weigerte sich, mit den neuen Vorschlägen konform zu gehen

✦**out of line** to be out of line nicht geradlinig sein; **to step out of line** (fig) aus der Reihe tanzen
(f) (Fin) **line of credit, credit line** Kreditrahmen m, Kreditlinie f
(g) (= company) (of aircraft, liners, buses) Gesellschaft f, Linie f; (= shipping company) Reederei f
(h) (indicating succession) **he was descended from a long line of farmers** er stammte aus einem alten Bauerngeschlecht; **it's the latest in a long line of tragedies** es ist die neueste Tragödie in einer ganzen Serie; **to be next in line** als Nächste(r) an der Reihe sein
(i) (Rail) (in general) Strecke f, Bahnlinie f; (= section of track) Strecke f; **lines** pl Gleise pl; **to reach the end of the line** (fig) am Ende sein
(j) (Telec) Leitung f; **this is a very bad line** die Verbindung ist sehr schlecht; **to be on the line to sb** mit jdm telefonieren; **hold the line** bleiben Sie am Apparat!
(k) (written) Zeile f; **the teacher gave me 200 lines** der Lehrer ließ mich 200 mal ... schreiben; **lines** (Theat) Text m; **to learn one's lines** seinen Text auswendig lernen; **he gets all the funny lines** er bekommt immer die lustigen Stellen; **to drop sb a line** jdm ein paar Zeilen schreiben
(l) (= direction) **line of argument** Argumentation f; **line of attack** (fig) Taktik f; **the police refused to reveal their lines of inquiry** die Polizei weigerte sich zu sagen, in welcher Richtung sie ermittelte; **line of thought** Denkrichtung f; **to be on the right lines** (fig) auf dem richtigen Weg sein

✦**to take + line** we must take a firm or strong line with these people wir müssen diesen Leuten gegenüber sehr bestimmt auftreten; **what sort of line do you think I should take when I see him?** wie meinen Sie, soll ich mich verhalten, wenn ich ihn sehe?; **he took the line that ...** er vertrat den Standpunkt, dass ...
(m) (Mil) **line of battle** Kampflinie f; **to draw up the battle lines** or **the lines of battle** (fig) (Kampf)stellung beziehen; **enemy lines** feindliche Stellungen or Linien pl; **lines of communication** Verbindungswege pl
(n) (= field) Branche f; **what line (of work) is he in?, what's his line (of work)?** was macht er beruflich?; **that's not in my line of business** damit habe ich nichts zu tun; **we're in the same line of business** wir sind in der gleichen Branche tätig; **that's not in my line** das liegt mir nicht; **it's all in the line of duty** das gehört zu meinen/seinen etc Pflichten
(o) (in shop) (= item) Modell nt; (= range) Kollektion f
(p) (set structures)

✦**along the line** somewhere along the line (= at some time) irgendwann; **all along the line** (fig) auf der ganzen Linie

✦**along the lines of** to be along the lines of ... ungefähr so etwas wie ... sein

✦**along these/the same lines** along these lines ungefähr so; **something along these lines** etwas in dieser Richtung or Art; **I was thinking along the same lines** ich hatte etwas Ähnliches gedacht

✦**to lay it on the line** (inf) die Karten auf den Tisch legen (inf); **they laid it on the line to the government, that ...** sie erklärten der Regierung klipp und klar, dass ... (inf)

✦**to put one's life/job** etc **on the line** (inf) sein Leben/seine Stelle etc riskieren

2 TRANSITIVE VERB (= border) säumen; **the streets were lined with cheering crowds** eine jubelnde Menge säumte die Straßen; **portraits lined the walls** an den Wänden hing ein Porträt neben dem andern

3 PHRASAL VERB

➤ **line up 1** VI (= stand in line) sich aufstellen; (= queue) sich anstellen; **the party lined up behind/against their leader** (fig) die Partei stellte sich hinter/gegen ihren Vorsitzenden

2 VT SEP **(a)** troops, pupils, prisoners antreten lassen; boxes, books etc in einer Reihe aufstellen; **they lined the prisoners up along the wall** die Gefangenen mussten sich an der Wand entlang aufstellen
(b) (= prepare, arrange) entertainment sorgen für; speakers verpflichten; support mobilisieren; **what have you got lined up for me today?** was haben Sie heute für mich geplant?; **I've lined up a meeting with the directors** ich habe ein Treffen mit den Direktoren arrangiert

line² VT clothes füttern; pipe auskleiden; ~ **the box with paper** den Karton mit Papier auskleiden; **the membranes which ~ the stomach** die Schleimhäute, die den Magen auskleiden; **to ~ one's own pockets** (fig) in die eigene Tasche arbeiten or wirtschaften (inf)

lineage ['lɪnɪdʒ] N (= descent) Abstammung f; (= descendants) Geschlecht nt

linear ['lɪnɪə'] ADJ linear; (also Math, Phys) time linear fortlaufend

lined [laɪnd] ADJ face etc (of old people) faltig; (through worry, tiredness etc) gezeichnet; paper liniert

line: **line dancing** N Line-Country-Dance m; **line drawing** N Zeichnung f; **line manager** N Vorgesetzte(r) mf

linen ['lɪnɪn] **1** N Leinen nt; (= table ~) Tischwäsche f; (= sheets, garments etc) Wäsche f **2** ADJ Leinen-; ~ **blouse** Leinenbluse f

linen closet, linen cupboard N Wäscheschrank m

line printer N (Comput) Zeilendrucker m

liner ['laɪnə'] N (= ship) Liniendampfer m

liner note N USU PL (US) Covertext m

linesman ['laɪnzmən] N, pl **-men** [-mən] (Sport) Linienrichter m

line: **line spacing** N Zeilenabstand m; **line-up** N (Sport) Aufstellung f; (= cast) Besetzung f; **she picked the thief out of the ~** sie erkannte den Dieb bei der Gegenüberstellung

linger ['lɪŋə'] VI **(a)** (also ~ **on**) (zurück)bleiben, verweilen (liter); (in dying) zwischen Leben und Tod schweben; (doubts, suspicions) zurückbleiben; (feeling, emotion, pain) anhalten; (memory) bleiben; (scent) sich halten; **the party was over, but many of the guests ~ed in the hall** die Party war vorbei, aber viele Gäste standen noch im Flur herum; **to ~ on a subject** bei einem Thema verweilen (geh); **to ~ over a meal** sich (dat) bei einer Mahlzeit Zeit lassen
(b) (= delay) sich aufhalten, verweilen (liter)

lingerie ['læ̃ʒəriː] N (Damen)unterwäsche f

lingering ['lɪŋgərɪŋ] ADJ lang, ausgedehnt; death langsam; illness langwierig; doubt zurückbleibend; look sehnsüchtig; kiss innig

lingo ['lɪŋgəʊ] N (inf) Sprache f; (= specialist jargon) Jargon m

linguist ['lɪŋgwɪst] N **(a)** (= speaker of languages) Sprachkundige(r) mf; **he's a good ~** er ist sehr sprachbegabt
(b) (= specialist in linguistics) Linguist(in) m(f)

linguistic [lɪŋ'gwɪstɪk] ADJ **(a)** (= concerning language) sprachlich; ~ **competence** or **ability** Sprachfähigkeit f
(b) (= concerning language science) linguistisch, sprachwissenschaftlich

linguistics [lɪŋ'gwɪstɪks] N SING Linguistik f, Sprachwissenschaft f

lining ['laɪnɪŋ] N (of clothes etc) Futter nt; (= ~ material) Futterstoff m; (of brake) (Brems)belag m; (of pipe) Auskleidung f; **the ~ of the stomach** die Magenschleimhaut

link [lɪŋk] **1** N **(a)** (of chain, fig) Glied nt; (person) Verbindungsmann m/-frau f
(b) (= connection) Verbindung f; **a new rail ~ for the village** eine neue Bahnverbindung zum Dorf; **cultural ~s** kulturelle Beziehungen pl; **the strong ~s between Britain and Australia** die engen Beziehungen zwischen Großbritannien und Australien
(c) (Comput) Link m
2 VT **(a)** verbinden; **to ~ arms** sich unterhaken (with bei); **we are ~ed by telephone to ...** wir sind telefonisch verbunden mit ...; **do you think these two murders are ~ed?** glauben Sie, dass zwischen den beiden Morden eine Verbindung besteht?; **his name has been ~ed with several famous women** sein Name ist mit mehreren berühmten Frauen in Verbindung gebracht worden
(b) (Comput) per Link verbinden

3 VI **(a) to ~ (together)** (*parts of story*) sich zusammenfügen lassen; (*parts of machine*) verbunden werden
(b) (*Comput*) **to ~ to a site** einen Link zu einer Website haben

➤ **link up 1** VI zusammenkommen; (*people*) sich zusammentun; (*facts*) zusammenpassen; (*companies*) sich zusammenschließen; **how does that link up with what Freud says?** wie hängt das mit dem zusammen, was Freud sagt? **2** VT SEP miteinander verbinden; *bits of evidence* miteinander in Verbindung bringen

link: link road N (*Brit*) Verbindungsstraße *f*; **linkup** N (*Telec, general*) Verbindung *f*

lino [ˈlaɪnəʊ] (*esp Brit*), **linoleum** [lɪˈnəʊlɪəm] N Linoleum *nt*

linseed [ˈlɪnsiːd] N Leinsamen *m*

linseed oil N Leinöl *nt*

lintel [ˈlɪntl] N (*Archit*) Sturz *m*

lion [ˈlaɪən] N Löwe *m*; **to throw sb to the ~s** (*fig*) jdn den Löwen zum Fraß vorwerfen; **the ~'s share** der Löwenanteil

lioness [ˈlaɪənɪs] N Löwin *f*

lip [lɪp] N **(a)** (*Anat*) Lippe *f*; **to keep a stiff upper ~** Haltung bewahren; **to lick** *or* **smack one's ~s** sich (*dat*) die Lippen lecken; **the question on everyone's ~s** die Frage, die sich (*dat*) jeder stellt **(b)** (*of jug*) Schnabel *m*; (*of cup, crater*) Rand *m* **(c)** (*inf: = cheek*) **to give sb a lot of ~** jdm gegenüber eine (dicke *or* freche) Lippe riskieren (*inf*); **none of your ~!** sei nicht so frech

lip gloss N Lipgloss *m*

liposuction [ˈlɪpəʊˌsʌkʃən] N Fettabsaugung *f*

lip: lip-read VI von den Lippen *or* vom Mund ablesen; **lip salve** N Lippenpflegestift *m*; **lip service** N **to pay ~ to an idea** ein Lippenbekenntnis zu einer Idee ablegen; **lipstick** N Lippenstift *m*

liquefy [ˈlɪkwɪfaɪ] **1** VT verflüssigen **2** VI sich verflüssigen

liqueur [lɪˈkjʊəʳ] N Likör *m*

liquid [ˈlɪkwɪd] **1** ADJ flüssig; (*also Comm*) **2** N Flüssigkeit *f*; **she can only take ~s** sie kann nur Flüssiges zu sich nehmen

liquidate [ˈlɪkwɪdeɪt] VT liquidieren (*also Comm*) **~d damages** Konventional- *or* Vertragsstrafe *f*

liquidation [ˌlɪkwɪˈdeɪʃən] N (*Comm*) Liquidation *f*; **to go into ~** in Liquidation gehen

liquidator [ˈlɪkwɪdeɪtəʳ] N Liquidator *m*

liquid-crystal [ˈlɪkwɪdˈkrɪstl] ADJ Flüssigkristall-; **~ display** Flüssigkristallanzeige *f*

liquidity [lɪˈkwɪdɪtɪ] N Liquidität *f*

liquidize [ˈlɪkwɪdaɪz] VT (im Mixer) pürieren

liquidizer [ˈlɪkwɪdaɪzəʳ] N Mixgerät *nt*

liquor [ˈlɪkəʳ] N (= *whisky, brandy etc*) Spirituosen *pl*; (= *alcohol*) Alkohol *m*; **he can't take his ~** er verträgt nichts

liquorice, licorice [ˈlɪkərɪs] N Lakritze *f*

liquor store N (*US*) ≈ Wein- und Spirituosengeschäft *nt*

lira [ˈlɪərə] N Lira *f*; **500 ~(s)** 500 Lire

Lisbon [ˈlɪzbən] N Lissabon *nt*

lisp [lɪsp] **1** N Lispeln *nt*; **to speak with a ~**, **to have a ~** lispeln **2** VTI lispeln

list¹ [lɪst] **1** N Liste *f*; (= *shopping ~*) Einkaufszettel *m*; **it's not on the ~** es steht nicht auf der Liste; **~ of names** Namensliste *f*; (*esp in book*) Namensverzeichnis *nt*; **~ of prices** Preisliste *f* **2** VT notieren; *single item* in die Liste aufnehmen; (*verbally*) aufzählen; **it is not ~ed** es ist nicht aufgeführt

list² (*Naut*) **1** N Schlagseite *f* **2** VI Schlagseite haben; **to ~ badly** schwere Schlagseite haben

listed [ˈlɪstɪd] ADJ (*Brit*) *building* unter Denkmalschutz (stehend *attr*); **it's a ~ building** es steht unter Denkmalschutz

listen [ˈlɪsn] **(a)** (= *hear*) hören (*to sth* etw *acc*); **to ~ to the radio** Radio hören; **if you ~ hard, you can hear the sea** wenn du genau hinhörst, kannst du das Meer hören; **she ~ed carefully to everything he said** sie hörte ihm genau zu; **to ~ for sth** auf etw (*acc*) horchen; **to ~ for sb** horchen *or* hören, ob jd kommt
(b) (= *heed*) zuhören; **~ to me!** hör mir zu!; **~, I know what we'll do** pass auf, ich weiß, was wir machen; **don't ~ to him** hör nicht auf ihn

➤ **listen in** VI mithören (*on sth* etw *acc*); **I'd like to listen in on** *or* **to your discussion** ich möchte mir Ihre Diskussion mit anhören

listener [ˈlɪsnəʳ] N Zuhörer(in) *m(f)*; (*Rad*) Hörer(in) *m(f)*; **to be a good ~** gut zuhören können

listing [ˈlɪstɪŋ] N **(a)** Auflistung *f*, Verzeichnis *nt* **(b) listings** (*TV, Rad, Film*) Programm *nt*; **~s magazine** Programmzeitschrift *f*

listless [ˈlɪstlɪs] ADJ lustlos; *patient* teilnahmslos

listlessly [ˈlɪstlɪslɪ] ADV lustlos; **to watch ~** teilnahmslos *or* apathisch zusehen

list price N Listenpreis *m*

lit [lɪt] PRET, PTP *of* **light¹**

litany [ˈlɪtənɪ] N Litanei *f*

liter N (*US*) = **litre**

literacy [ˈlɪtərəsɪ] N Fähigkeit *f* lesen und schreiben zu können; **~ is high here** die Analphabetenquote hier ist niedrig; **~ test** Lese- und Schreibtest *m*

literal [ˈlɪtərəl] ADJ **(a)** *translation, meaning* wörtlich; **in the ~ sense (of the word)** im wörtlichen Sinne **(b)** (= *real*) **that is the ~ truth** das ist die reine Wahrheit **(c)** (= *prosaic*) nüchtern, prosaisch

literally [ˈlɪtərəlɪ] ADV **(a)** (= *word for word*) (wort)wörtlich; **to take sb/sth ~** jdn/etw wörtlich nehmen; **to be ~ true** wortwörtlich stimmen **(b)** (= *really*) buchstäblich, wirklich; **the best meal I've ever had, ~** wirklich das Beste, was ich je gegessen habe; **I was ~ shaking with fear** ich zitterte regelrecht vor Angst

literary [ˈlɪtərərɪ] ADJ literarisch; **a ~ man** ein Literaturkenner *m*; (= *author*) ein Literat *or* Autor *m*; **the ~ scene** die Literaturszene

literary: literary agent N Literaturagent(in) *m(f)*; **literary critic** N Literaturkritiker(in) *m(f)*; **literary criticism** N (*as subject*) Literaturwissenschaft *f*; (= *reviews*) Literaturkritik *f*; **literary theory** N Literaturtheorie *f*

literate [ˈlɪtərɪt] ADJ **(a) to be ~** lesen und schreiben können **(b)** (= *well-educated*) gebildet

literature [ˈlɪtərɪtʃəʳ] N Literatur *f*; (*inf: = brochures etc*) Informationsmaterial *nt*; (= *specialist ~*) (Fach)literatur *f*

lithe [laɪð] ADJ (+ER) geschmeidig

lithium [ˈlɪθɪəm] N Lithium *nt*

lithograph [ˈlɪθəʊɡrɑːf] N Lithografie *f*

Lithuania [ˌlɪθjʊˈeɪnɪə] N Litauen *nt*

Lithuanian [ˌlɪθjʊˈeɪnɪən] **1** ADJ litauisch **2** N Litauer(in) *m(f)*

litigate [ˈlɪtɪɡeɪt] VI einen Prozess führen *or* anstrengen

litigation [ˌlɪtɪˈɡeɪʃən] N Prozess *m*, Rechtsstreit *m*; **he threatened them with ~** er drohte ihnen mit einem Prozess

litmus [ˈlɪtməs]: **litmus paper** N Lackmuspapier *nt*; **litmus test** N (*fig*) entscheidender Test

litre, (*US*) **liter** [ˈliːtəʳ] N Liter *m or nt*

litter [ˈlɪtəʳ] **1** N **(a)** Abfälle *pl*; (= *papers, wrappings*) Papier *nt*; **the park was strewn with ~** der Park war mit Papier und Abfällen übersät; **don't leave** *or* **drop ~** (*on notice*) bitte keinen Abfall zurücklassen
(b) (*Zool*) Wurf *m*
(c) (= *bedding for animals*) Streu *f*; (*for plants*) Stroh *nt*; (= *cat ~*) Katzenstreu *f*
2 VT **to be ~ed with sth** (*lit, fig*) mit etw übersät sein; **glass from broken bottles ~ed the streets** Glasscherben lagen überall auf den Straßen herum
3 VI (*esp US*) Abfall wegwerfen

litter: litter basket N Abfallkorb *m*; **litter bin** N (*Brit*) Abfalleimer *m*; (*hooked on*) Abfallkorb *m*; (*bigger*) Abfalltonne *f*

little [ˈlɪtl] **1** ADJ klein; **a ~ house** ein Häuschen *nt*; **the ~ ones** die Kleinen *pl*; **a nice ~ profit** ein hübscher Gewinn; **he will have his ~ joke** er will auch einmal ein Witzchen machen; **to worry about ~ things** sich (*dat*) über Kleinigkeiten Gedanken machen; **a ~ while ago** vor kurzem; **in a ~ while** bald
2 ADV, N **(a)** wenig; **of ~ importance/interest** von geringer Bedeutung/geringem Interesse; **~ better than** kaum besser als; **~ more than a month ago** vor kaum einem Monat; **~ short of** fast schon; **~ did I think that ...** ich hätte kaum gedacht, dass ...; **~ does he know that ...** er hat keine Ahnung, dass ...; **I walk as ~ as possible** ich laufe so wenig wie möglich; **to spend ~ or nothing** so gut wie (gar) nichts ausgeben; **every ~ helps** Kleinvieh macht auch Mist (*Prov*); **he had ~ to say** er hatte nicht viel zu sagen; **I see very ~ of her nowadays** ich

sehe sie in letzter Zeit sehr selten; **there was ~ we could do** wir konnten nicht viel tun; **~ by ~** nach und nach; **I could make ~ of this book** ich konnte mit diesem Buch nicht viel anfangen

(b) a ~ ein wenig, ein bisschen; **a ~ (bit) hot** etwas *or* ein bisschen heiß; **with a ~ effort** mit etwas Anstrengung; **I'll give you a ~ advice** ich gebe dir einen kleinen Tipp; **a ~ after five** kurz nach fünf; **we walked on for a ~** wir liefen noch ein bisschen weiter; **after a ~** nach einer Weile; **for a ~** für ein Weilchen

liturgical [lɪˈtɜːdʒɪkəl] ADJ liturgisch

liturgy [ˈlɪtədʒɪ] N Liturgie *f*

live¹ [lɪv] **1** VT *life* führen; **he had been living a lie** sein Leben war eine Lüge; **to ~ one's own life** sein eigenes Leben leben; **he ~s and breathes golf** er lebt nur für Golf

2 VI **(a) there is no man living who can equal him** es gibt niemanden, der es ihm gleichtun könnte; **long ~ Queen Anne!** lang lebe Königin Anne!; **to ~ and let ~** leben und leben lassen; **to ~ like a king** *or* **lord** fürstlich *or* wie Gott in Frankreich leben; **not many people ~ to be a hundred** nicht viele Menschen werden hundert (Jahre alt); **to ~ to a ripe old age** ein hohes Alter erreichen; **his name will ~ for ever** sein Ruhm wird nie vergehen; **his music will ~ for ever** seine Musik ist unvergänglich; **to ~ by one's wits** sich (so) durchschlagen; **he ~d through two wars** er hat zwei Kriege miterlebt; **to ~ through an experience** eine Erfahrung durchmachen; **to ~ within one's income** nicht über seine Verhältnisse leben; **you'll ~ to regret it** das wirst du noch bereuen; **I want to ~** (= *experience real living*) ich will leben *or* was erleben (*inf*); **you've never skied? you haven't ~d!** du bist noch nie Ski gefahren? du weißt gar nicht, was du versäumt hast!

(b) (= *reside*) wohnen; (*animals*) leben; **he ~s at 19 Marktstraße** er wohnt in der Marktstraße Nr. 19; **he ~s with his parents** er wohnt bei seinen Eltern; **a house not fit to ~ in** ein unbewohnbares Haus

➤ **live down** VT SEP *scandal, humiliation* hinwegkommen über (+*acc*); (*actively*) *scandal, mistake* Gras wachsen lassen über (+*acc*); **he'll never live it down** das wird man ihm nie vergessen

➤ **live in** VI im Haus/im Wohnheim *etc* wohnen, nicht außerhalb wohnen

➤ **live off** VI +PREP OBJ **(a) to live off one's relations** auf Kosten seiner Verwandten leben **(b)** = **live on 2**

➤ **live on** **1** VI (= *continue to live*) weiterleben **2** VI +PREP OBJ **to live on eggs** sich von Eiern ernähren; **he doesn't earn enough to live on** er verdient nicht genug, um davon zu leben

➤ **live out** VT SEP *life* verbringen

➤ **live together** VI (= *cohabit*) zusammenleben; (= *share a room, flat etc*) zusammen wohnen

➤ **live up** VI ALWAYS SEPARATE **to live it up** (*inf*) die Puppen tanzen lassen (*inf*); (*extravagantly*) in Saus und Braus leben (*inf*)

➤ **live up to** VI +PREP OBJ **the holiday** (*esp Brit*) *or* **vacation** (*US*) **lived up to (my) expectations/the advertiser's claims** der Urlaub hielt, was ich mir davon versprochen hatte/was die Werbung versprochen hatte; **sales have not lived up to expectations** die Verkaufszahlen entsprachen nicht den Erwartungen; **to live up to one's reputation** seinem Ruf gerecht werden; **he's got a lot to live up to** in ihn werden große Erwartungen gesetzt

live² [laɪv] **1** ADJ **(a)** (= *alive*) lebend; *issue, question* aktuell; **a real ~ duke** ein waschechter Herzog **(b)** *coal* glühend; *cartridge, shell* scharf; (*Elec*) geladen; **"danger, ~ wires!"** „Vorsicht Hochspannung!"; **she's a real ~ wire** (*fig*) sie ist ein richtiges Energiebündel **(c)** (*Rad, TV*) live; **a ~ programme** (*Brit*) *or* **program** (*US*) eine Livesendung **2** ADV (*Rad, TV*) live

live-in [ˈlɪvɪn] ADJ *cook, maid* in Haus wohnend

livelihood [ˈlaɪvlɪhʊd] N Lebensunterhalt *m*; **fishing is their ~** sie verdienen ihren Lebensunterhalt mit Fischfang; **to earn a ~** sich (*dat*) seinen Lebensunterhalt verdienen

liveliness [ˈlaɪvlɪnɪs] N Lebhaftigkeit *f*

lively [ˈlaɪvlɪ] ADJ (+ER) lebhaft; *scene, account, sense of humour, imagination* lebendig; *campaign* dynamisch; *pace* flott; *mind* aufgeweckt; *tune* schwungvoll; **things are getting ~** es geht hoch her (*inf*); **look ~!** mach schnell!

liven up [ˈlaɪvənˈʌp] **1** VT SEP beleben, Leben bringen in (+*acc*) (*inf*) **2** VI in Schwung kommen; (*person*) aufleben

liver [ˈlɪvəʳ] N (*Anat, Cook*) Leber *f*

liver: **liver pâté** N Leberpastete *f*; **liver sausage, liverwurst** [ˈlɪvəwɜːst] (*esp US*) N Leberwurst *f*

lives [laɪvz] PL *of* **life**

livestock [ˈlaɪvstɒk] N Vieh *nt*; (= *number of animals*) Viehbestand *m*

livid [ˈlɪvɪd] ADJ **(a)** (*inf*: = *furious*) wütend, fuchsteufelswild (*inf*) (*about, at* über +*acc*); **he was ~ about having to do it himself** er war höchst empört darüber, dass er es selbst machen musste **(b)** (= *dark purple*) dunkelviolett; (= *greyish*) purpurgrau; **~ red** purpurrot

living [ˈlɪvɪŋ] **1** ADJ lebend; *example* lebendig; **the greatest ~ playwright** der bedeutendste noch lebende Dramatiker; **I have no ~ relatives** ich habe keine Verwandten mehr; **a ~ creature** ein Lebewesen *nt*; **not a ~ soul** keine Menschenseele; **(with)in ~ memory** seit Menschengedenken **2** N **(a) the living** PL die Lebenden *pl*

(b) (= *way of*) **he is fond of good ~** er lebt gern gut; **healthy ~** gesundes Leben

(c) (= *livelihood*) Lebensunterhalt *m*; **to earn** *or* **make a ~** sich (*dat*) seinen Lebensunterhalt verdienen; **what does he do for a ~?** womit verdient er sich (*dat*) seinen Lebensunterhalt?; **it is possible to make a very good ~ from modelling** (*Brit*) *or* **modeling** (*US*) von der Arbeit als Model kann man sehr gut leben; **to work for one's ~** arbeiten, um sich (*dat*) seinen Lebensunterhalt zu verdienen

living: **living conditions** PL Wohnverhältnisse *pl*; **living expenses** PL Spesen *pl*; **living quarters** PL Wohnräume *pl*; (*for soldiers, sailors*) Quartier *nt*; **living room** N Wohnzimmer *nt*; **living wage** N ausreichender Lohn; **£65 a week is not a ~** von £ 65 pro Woche kann man nicht leben

lizard [ˈlɪzəd] N Eidechse *f*

llama [ˈlɑːmə] N Lama *nt*

load [ləʊd] **1** N Last *f*; (*on girder, axle etc, fig also*) Belastung *f*; (= *cargo*) Ladung *f*; **to put a ~ on sth** etw belasten; **the maximum ~ for that bridge is 10 tons** die maximale Tragfähigkeit dieser Brücke beträgt 10 Tonnen; (*work*) ~ (Arbeits)pensum *nt*; **he has a heavy teaching ~ this term** er hat in diesem Semester eine hohe Stundenzahl; **I put a ~ in the washing machine** ich habe die Maschine mit Wäsche gefüllt; **that's a ~ off my mind!** da fällt mir ein Stein vom Herzen!; **to take a ~ off sb's mind** jdm eine Last von der Seele nehmen

(b) (*Elec*) (*supplied*) Leistung *f*; (*carried*) Spannung *f*

(c) (*inf usages*) **~s of, a ~ of** jede Menge (*inf*); **~s, we have ~s** danke, wir haben jede Menge (*inf*); **it's a ~ of old rubbish** (*Brit*) das ist alles Blödsinn (*inf*) *or* Quatsch (*inf*); (*film, book, translation*) das ist alles Mist! (*inf*); **get a ~ of this!** (= *listen*) hör dir das mal an!; (= *look*) guck dir das mal an! (*inf*) **2** VT *goods, gun* laden *also Comput lorry etc* beladen; **the ship was ~ed with bananas** das Schiff hatte Bananen geladen; **to ~ a camera** einen Film in (einen Fotoapparat) einlegen; **is this camera ~ed?** ist ein Film im Apparat? **3** VI laden *also Comput* "~ing and unloading" „Be- und Entladen"; **how does this gun ~?** wie lädt man dieses Gewehr?

➤ **load down** VT SEP (*schwer*) beladen; (*fig*) überladen

➤ **load up** **1** VI aufladen **2** VT SEP **(a)** *lorry* beladen; *goods* aufladen **(b)** (*Comput*) laden

loaded [ˈləʊdɪd] ADJ beladen; *dice* präpariert; *camera* mit eingelegtem Film; *gun, software* geladen; **the dice are ~ in their favour** (*Brit*) *or* **favor** (*US*)/**against them** (*fig*) alles spricht für/gegen sie; **a ~ question** eine Fangfrage; **that's a ~ term** das ist kein neutraler Ausdruck; **he's ~** (*inf*) (= *rich*) er ist stinkreich (*inf*)

loading bay [ˈləʊdɪŋbeɪ] N Ladeplatz *m*

loaf [ləʊf] N, pl **loaves** Brot *nt*; (*unsliced*) (Brot)laib *m*; **a ~ of bread** ein (Laib) Brot; **a small white ~** ein kleines Weißbrot; **half a ~ is better than none** (*Prov*) (wenig ist) besser als gar nichts; **use your ~!** (*inf*) streng deinen Grips an (*inf*)

➤ **loaf about** (*Brit*) *or* **around** VI (*inf*) faulenzen

loafer [ˈləʊfəʳ] N (*esp US*: = *casual shoe*) Halbschuh *m*

loan [ləʊn] **1** N **(a)** (= *thing lent*) Leihgabe *f*; (*from bank etc*) Darlehen *nt*; (= *public ~*) Anleihe *f*; **my friend let me have the money as a ~** mein Freund hat mir das Geld geliehen **(b) he gave me the ~ of his bicycle** er hat mir sein Fahrrad

geliehen; **it's on** ~ es ist geliehen; (= *out on* ~) es ist verliehen *or* ausgeliehen; **the machinery is on** ~ **from the American government** die Maschinen sind eine Leihgabe der amerikanischen Regierung; **she's on** ~ **to us from the CIA** sie ist vom CIA an uns abgestellt worden; **to have sth on** ~ etw geliehen haben (*from* von)
2 VT leihen (*to sb* jdm)

loan: **loan agreement** N Darlehensvertrag *m*; **loan capital** N Anleihekapital *nt*; **loan shark** N (*inf*) Kredithai *m* (*inf*)

loath, loth [ləʊθ] ADJ **to be** ~ **to do sth** etw ungern tun; **he is** ~ **for us to go** er ließ uns ungern gehen

loathe [ləʊð] VT *thing, person* verabscheuen; *modern art, spinach, jazz etc* nicht ausstehen können; **I** ~ **doing it** (*in general*) ich hasse es, das zu tun; (*on particular occasion*) es ist mir zuwider, das zu tun

loathing ['ləʊðɪŋ] N Abscheu *m*

loathsome ['ləʊðsəm] ADJ *thing, person* widerlich; *task* verhasst

loaves [ləʊvz] PL *of* loaf

lob [lɒb] **1** N (*Tennis*) Lob *m* **2** VT *ball* lobben; **he** ~**bed the grenade over the wall** er warf die Granate im hohen Bogen über die Mauer

lobby ['lɒbɪ] **1** N Vor- *or* Eingangshalle *f*; (*of hotel, theatre*) Foyer *nt*; (*Pol, = place in Parliament*) Lobby *f*; **the gun** ~ die Waffenlobby **2** VT **to** ~ **one's Member of Parliament** auf seinen Abgeordneten Einfluss nehmen **3** VI **the farmers are** ~**ing for higher subsidies** die Bauernlobby will höhere Subventionen durchsetzen

lobe [ləʊb] N (*Anat*) (*of ear*) Ohrläppchen *nt*

lobotomy [ləʊ'bɒtəmɪ] N (*Med*) Lobotomie *f*

lobster ['lɒbstər] N Hummer *m*

local ['ləʊkəl] **1** ADJ örtlich; (= *in this area*) hiesig; (= *in that area*) dortig; ~ **radio** Lokalradio *nt*; ~ **radio station** Regionalsender *m*; ~ **news** Lokalnachrichten *pl*; ~ **newspaper** Lokalzeitung *f*; **all the** ~ **residents** alle Ortsansässigen *pl*; **he's a** ~ **man** er ist ein Ortsansässiger; ~ **community** Kommune *f*; ~ **currency** Landeswährung *f*; **at** ~ **level** auf lokaler Ebene; **it's only of** ~ **interest** es ist nur für die Einheimischen interessant; ~ **train** Nahverkehrszug *m*; ~ **traffic** Ortsverkehr *m*; ~ **time** Ortszeit *f*; **go into your** ~ **branch** gehen Sie zu Ihrer Zweigstelle; **vote for your** ~ **candidate** wählen Sie den Kandidaten Ihres Wahlkreises; **the best** ~ **wine** der beste Wein der Gegend; ~ **anaesthetic** *or* **anesthetic** (*US*) örtliche Betäubung
2 N (**a**) (*Brit inf: = pub*) **the** ~ (*in village*) die Dorfkneipe (*inf*); (*in community*) das Stammlokal; **our** ~ unsere Stammkneipe (*inf*)
(**b**) (*born in*) Einheimische(r) *mf*; (*living in*) Einwohner(in) *m(f)*
(**c**) (*US*) (= *branch*) Zweigstelle *f*; (= *train*) Nahverkehrszug *m*

local: **local area network** N (*Comput*) lokales Rechnernetz, LAN *nt*; **local authority** N Kommunalbehörde *f*; **local call** N (*Telec*) Ortsgespräch *nt*

locale [ləʊ'kɑːl] N Schauplatz *m*

local: **local education authority** N örtliche Schulbehörde; **local government** N Kommunalverwaltung *f*; ~ **elections** Kommunalwahlen *pl*

locality [ləʊ'kælɪtɪ] N Gegend *f*

localize ['ləʊkəlaɪz] VT **this custom, once widespread, has now become very** ~**d** die einst weit verbreitete Sitte ist jetzt auf wenige Orte begrenzt

locally ['ləʊkəlɪ] ADV am Ort; **I prefer to shop** ~ ich kaufe lieber im Ort ein; **do you live** ~? wohnen Sie am Ort?; **was she well-known** ~? war sie in dieser Gegend sehr bekannt?; **it was organized both nationally and** ~ es wurde sowohl auf nationaler als auch auf lokaler Ebene organisiert; ~ **grown** *or* **produced** in der Region angebaut

locate [ləʊ'keɪt] VT (**a**) (= *position*) legen; *headquarters* einrichten; (*including act of building*) errichten; *sportsground, playground* anlegen; **to be** ~**d at** *or* **in** sich befinden in (+*dat*); **the hotel is centrally** ~**d** das Hotel liegt zentral (**b**) (= *find*) ausfindig machen; *submarine, plane* orten

location [ləʊ'keɪʃən] N (**a**) (= *position, site*) Lage *f*; (*of building*) Standort *m*; (*of ship*) Position *f*; **this would be an ideal** ~ **for the airport** das wäre ein ideales Gelände für den Flughafen (**b**) (= *positioning, siting*) **they discussed the** ~ **of the proposed airport** sie diskutierten, wo der geplante Flughafen gebaut werden sollte
(**c**) (*Film*) Drehort *m*; **to be on** ~ **in Mexico** (*person*) bei Außenaufnahmen in Mexiko sein; **part of the film was shot on** ~ **in Mexico** ein Teil der Außenaufnahmen für den Film wurde in Mexiko gedreht

loch [lɒx] N (*Scot*) See *m*; (= *sea* ~) Meeresarm *m*

lock¹ [lɒk] N (*of hair*) Locke *f*; **her wavy** ~**s** ihr gewelltes Haar

lock² **1** N (**a**) (*on door, box, gun*) Schloss *nt*; **to put/keep sb under** ~ **and key** jdn hinter Schloss und Riegel bringen/ verwahren; **to put sth under** ~ **and key** etw wegschließen; **he offered me the house** ~**, stock and barrel** er bot mir das Haus mit allem Drum und Dran an (*inf*)
(**b**) (= *canal* ~) Schleuse *f*
2 VT *door etc* ab- *or* zuschließen; *steering wheel* sperren; *wheel* blockieren; (*Comput*) *keyboard* verriegeln; **to** ~ **sb in a room** jdn in einem Zimmer einschließen; **the armies were** ~**ed in combat** die Armeen waren in Kämpfe verwickelt; **they were** ~**ed in each other's arms** sie hielten sich fest umschlungen; **this bar** ~**s the wheel in position** diese Stange hält das Rad fest
3 VI schließen; (*wheel*) blockieren; **a suitcase that** ~**s** ein verschließbarer Koffer

▶ **lock away** VT SEP wegschließen; *person* einsperren; **he locked the money away in his safe** er schloss das Geld in seinem Safe ein

▶ **lock in** VT SEP *person, animal* einschließen; **to be locked in** eingesperrt sein

▶ **lock on** VI (*spaceship etc*) gekoppelt werden (*to* mit); **the missile locks onto its target** das Geschoss richtet sich auf das Ziel

▶ **lock out** VT SEP *workers* aussperren; **I've locked myself out** ich habe mich ausgesperrt

▶ **lock up** **1** VT SEP (**a**) *thing, house* abschließen; *person* einsperren; **to lock sth up in sth** etw in etw (*dat*) einschließen (**b**) (*Comm*) *capital* fest anlegen **2** VI abschließen

locker ['lɒkər] N Schließfach *nt*; (*Naut, Mil*) Spind *m*

locker room N Umkleideraum *m*

locket ['lɒkɪt] N Medaillon *nt*

lock: **lock gate** N Schleusentor *nt*; **lockout** N Aussperrung *f*; **locksmith** N Schlosser(in) *m(f)*; **lock-up** N (= *shop*) Laden *m*, Geschäft *nt*; (= *garage*) Garage *f*

locomotive [ˌləʊkə'məʊtɪv] N Lokomotive *f*

locum (tenens) ['ləʊkəm('tenenz)] N (*Brit*) Vertreter(in) *m(f)*

locust ['ləʊkəst] N Heuschrecke *f*

lodge [lɒdʒ] **1** N (*in grounds*) Pförtnerhaus *nt*; (= *shooting* ~, *skiing* ~ *or* *porter's* ~) Hütte *f*; (= *porter's* ~) Pförtnerloge *f*
2 VT (**a**) (*Brit*) *person* unterbringen
(**b**) (*with* bei) *complaint* einlegen; *protest* erheben; *claim* geltend machen; *charge, petition, application* einreichen; **to** ~ **an appeal** Einspruch erheben; (*Jur*) Berufung einlegen
(**c**) (= *insert*) **to be** ~**d** (fest)stecken
3 VI (**a**) (*Brit: = live*) (zur *or* in Untermiete) wohnen (*with sb, at sb's* bei); (*at boarding house*) wohnen (*in* in +*dat*)
(**b**) (*object, bullet*) stecken bleiben; **to** ~ **in sb's mind** jdm in Erinnerung bleiben

lodger ['lɒdʒər] N Untermieter(in) *m(f)*

lodging ['lɒdʒɪŋ] N (**a**) Unterkunft *f* (**b**) **lodgings** PL ein möbliertes Zimmer, möblierte Zimmer *pl*; **we took** ~**s with Mrs B** wir mieteten uns bei Frau B ein

lodging house N Pension *f*

loft [lɒft] N (**a**) Boden *m*; **in the** ~ auf dem Boden *or* Speicher (**b**) (= *apartment*) Loftwohnung *f*

loft conversion N Dachausbau *m*

loftily ['lɒftɪlɪ] ADV stolz, hochmütig

lofty ['lɒftɪ] ADJ (+ER) (**a**) *ideals, ambitions* hochfliegend; *sentiments* erhaben (**b**) (= *haughty*) stolz, hochmütig

log¹ [lɒg] N Baumstamm *m*; (= *short length of tree trunk*) Block *m*; (*for a fire*) Scheit *nt*; **to sleep like a** ~ wie ein Stein schlafen

log² **1** N (= *record*) Aufzeichnungen *pl*; (*Naut*) Logbuch *nt*; **to keep a** ~ **of sth** über etw (*acc*) Buch führen **2** VT Buch führen über (+*acc*); (*Naut*) (ins Logbuch) eintragen; **details are** ~**ged in the computer** Einzelheiten sind im Computer gespeichert

▶ **log in** VI (*Comput*) einloggen

▶ **log off** (*Comput*) VI ausloggen

▶ **log on** (*Comput*) VI einloggen

➤ **log out** VI (*Comput*) ausloggen

➤ **log up** VT SEP (= *clock up*) *distance* zurücklegen; (*fig*) *successes* einheimsen (*inf*)

log³ ABBR *of* **logarithm** log; ~ **tables** Logarithmentafel *f*

logarithm ['lɒgərɪθəm] N Logarithmus *m*

log: **logbook** N (*Naut*) Logbuch *nt*; (*Aviat*) Bordbuch *nt*; (*of lorries*) Fahrtenbuch *nt*; (*Aut*: = *registration book*) Kraftfahrzeug- *or* Kfz-Brief *m*; (*in hospitals, police stations etc*) Dienstbuch *nt*; **log cabin** N Blockhaus *nt*

loggerheads ['lɒgəhedz] PL **to be at ~ (with sb)** (*esp Brit*) sich (*dat*) (mit jdm) in den Haaren liegen (*inf*)

logic ['lɒdʒɪk] N Logik *f*; **there's no ~ in that** das ist völlig unlogisch

logical ['lɒdʒɪkəl] ADJ logisch; **he has a ~ mind** er denkt logisch

logically ['lɒdʒɪkəlɪ] ADV logisch; **~, he may be right** logisch gesehen könnte er Recht haben

logistic [lɒ'dʒɪstɪk] ADJ logistisch

logistics [lɒ'dʒɪstɪks] N SING Logistik *f*

logo ['ləugəu, 'lɒgəu] N Logo *nt*, Emblem *nt*

loiter ['lɔɪtəʳ] VI herumlungern; **"no ~ing"** „unberechtigter Aufenthalt verboten"

loll [lɒl] VI (**a**) sich lümmeln; **he was ~ing in an easy chair** er hing (*inf*) *or* räkelte sich im Sessel; **to ~ against sth** sich (lässig) gegen *or* an etw (*acc*) lehnen (**b**) (*head*) hängen; (*tongue*) heraushängen

➤ **loll about** (*Brit*) *or* **around** VI herumlümmeln

lollipop ['lɒlɪpɒp] N Lutscher *m*; (= *iced ~*) Eis *nt* am Stiel

lollipop (*Brit inf*): **lollipop lady** N ≈ Schülerlotsin *f*; **lollipop man** N ≈ Schülerlotse *m*

lolly ['lɒlɪ] N (*esp Brit*) (**a**) (*inf*: = *lollipop*) Lutscher *m*; **an ice ~** ein Eis *nt* am Stiel (**b**) (*inf*: = *money*) Kohle *f* (*inf*)

London ['lʌndən] **1** N London *nt* **2** ADJ Londoner

lone [ləun] ADJ (= *single*) einzeln; (= *isolated*) einsam; *survivor, success* einzig; **to fight a ~ battle** einen einsamen Kampf führen; **~ parent** Alleinerziehende(r) *mf*; **~ parent family** Einelternfamilie *f*

loneliness ['ləunlɪnɪs] N Einsamkeit *f*

lonely ['ləunlɪ] ADJ (+ER) einsam; **~ hearts ad** Kontaktanzeige *f*; **~ hearts column** Kontaktanzeigen *pl*; **~ hearts club** Singletreff *m*

loner ['ləunəʳ] N Einzelgänger(in) *m(f)*

lonesome ['ləunsəm] ADJ (*esp US*) einsam

long¹ [lɒŋ] **1** ADJ (+ER) lang; *glass* hoch; *journey* weit; *job* langwierig; **it is 6 feet ~** es ist 6 Fuß lang; **to pull a ~ face** ein langes Gesicht machen; **it's a ~ way** das ist weit; **to have a ~ memory** ein gutes Gedächtnis haben; **to be ~ in the tooth** (*inf*) nicht mehr der/die Jüngste sein; **it's a ~ time since I saw her** ich habe sie schon lange nicht mehr gesehen; **he's been here (for) a ~ time** er ist schon lange hier; **she was abroad for a ~ time** sie war (eine) lange Zeit im Ausland; **to take a ~ look at sth** etw lange *or* ausgiebig betrachten; **how ~ is the film?** wie lange dauert der Film?; **a ~ drink** (*mixed*) ein Longdrink *m*

2 ADV lang(e); **to be ~ in** *or* **about doing sth** lange zu etw brauchen; **don't be ~!** beeil dich!; **don't be too ~ about it** lass dir nicht zu viel Zeit; **I shan't be ~** (*in finishing*) ich bin gleich fertig; (*in returning*) ich bin gleich wieder da; **all night ~** die ganze Nacht; **~ ago** vor langer Zeit; **not ~ ago** vor kurzem; **not ~ before I met you** kurz bevor ich dich kennen lernte; **those days are ~ (since) past** diese Tage sind schon lange vorbei; **we waited as ~ as we could** wir haben gewartet, solange wir konnten; **as ~ as, so ~ as** (= *provided that*) solange; **how much ~er can you stay?** wie lange können Sie noch bleiben?; **I can't wait any ~er** ich kann nicht mehr länger warten; **if that noise goes on any ~er** wenn der Lärm weitergeht; **no ~er** (= *not any more*) nicht mehr; **so ~!** (*inf*) tschüs(s)! (*inf*)

3 N **before ~** bald; **are you going for ~?** werden Sie länger weg sein?; **it won't take ~** das dauert nicht lange; **it didn't take ~ before ...** es dauerte nicht lange, bis ...; **I won't take ~** ich brauche nicht lange (dazu)

long² VI sich sehnen (*for* nach); (*less passionately*) herbeisehnen (*for sth* etw *acc*); **he ~ed for his wife to return** er wartete sehnsüchtig auf die Rückkehr seiner Frau; **he is ~ing for me to make a mistake** er möchte zu gern, dass ich einen Fehler mache; **I am ~ing to go abroad** ich brenne

---

darauf, ins Ausland zu gehen; **I'm ~ing to see that film** ich will den Film unbedingt sehen

long: **long-dated** ADJ (*Fin*) langfristig; **~ bonds** langfristige Anleihen *pl*, Langläufer *pl*; **long-distance 1** ADJ **~ call** Ferngespräch *nt*; **~ lorry driver** (*Brit*) Fernfahrer(in) *m(f)*; **~ flight/race** Langstreckenflug *m*/-rennen *nt*; **~ runner** Langstreckenläufer(in) *m(f)*; **~ journey/travel** Fernreise *f*/-reisen *pl* **2** ADV **to call ~** ein Ferngespräch führen; **long division** N schriftliche Division; **long-drawn-out** ADJ *speech, argument* langatmig; *meeting* ausgedehnt; *affair, war* sich lange hinziehend; *process* langwierig

longed-for ['lɒŋdfɔːʳ] ADJ ersehnt

long: **long-grain** ADJ **~ rice** Langkornreis *m*; **longhand** ADV in Langschrift; **long-haul** ADJ **~ truck driver** Fernfahrer(in) *m(f)*

longing ['lɒŋɪŋ] **1** ADJ *look* sehnsüchtig **2** N Sehnsucht *f* (*for* nach); **to have a (great) ~ to do sth** sich (sehr) danach sehnen, etw zu tun

longingly ['lɒŋɪŋlɪ] ADV sehnsüchtig

longish ['lɒŋɪʃ] ADJ ziemlich lang

longitude ['lɒŋgɪtjuːd] N Länge *f*

long: **long johns** PL (*inf*) lange Unterhosen *pl*; **long jump** N Weitsprung *m*; **long-life** ADJ *battery etc* mit langer Lebensdauer; **long-life milk** N H-Milch *f*; **long-lost** ADJ *person* verloren geglaubt; *ideals, enthusiasm etc* verloren gegangen; **long-playing** ADJ **~ record** Langspielplatte *f*; **long position** N (*St Ex*) Hausseposition *f*; **long-range** ADJ *gun* mit hoher Reichweite; *forecast, plan* langfristig; **~ aircraft** Langstreckenflugzeug *nt*; **~ missile** Langstreckenrakete *f*; **long-running** ADJ *series* lange laufend; *feud* lange andauernd; **longshoreman** N (*US*) Hafenarbeiter *m*; **long shot** N (*inf*) **it's a ~, but it may pay off** es ist gewagt, aber es könnte sich auszahlen; **not by a ~** bei weitem nicht; **long-sighted** ADJ (*Brit lit, fig*) weitsichtig; **long-standing** ADJ alt; *friendship* langjährig; *interest, invitation* schon lange bestehend; **long-stay** ADJ (*Brit*) *hospital, patient* Langzeit-; *car park* Dauer-; **long-suffering** ADJ schwer geprüft; **long term** N **in the ~** langfristig gesehen; **long-term** ADJ langfristig; *relationship* dauerhaft; **~ memory** Langzeitgedächtnis *nt*; **the ~ unemployed** die Langzeitarbeitslosen *pl*; **~ securities** (*Fin*) langlaufende Staatstitel; **long vacation** N (*Univ*) (Sommer)semesterferien *pl*; (*Sch*) große Ferien *pl*; **long wave** N Langwelle *f*; **long-wearing** ADJ (*US*) strapazierfähig; **long-winded** ADJ umständlich; *story, speech* langatmig

loo [luː] N (*Brit inf*) Klo *nt* (*inf*); **to go to the ~** aufs Klo gehen (*inf*); **in the ~** auf dem Klo (*inf*)

look [luk] **1** N (**a**) (= *glance*) Blick *m*; **she gave me a dirty ~, I got a dirty ~ from her** sie warf mir einen vernichtenden Blick zu; **she gave me a ~ of disbelief** sie sah mich ungläubig an; **to have** *or* **take a ~ at sth** sich (*dat*) etw ansehen; **can I have a ~?** darf ich mal sehen?; **let's have a ~ at it** lass mal sehen; **let's have a ~ at you** lass dich mal ansehen; **to take a good ~ at sth** sich (*dat*) etw genau ansehen; **to have a ~ for sth** sich nach etw umsehen; **to have a ~ (a)round** sich umsehen; **shall we have a ~ (a)round the town?** sollen wir uns (*dat*) die Stadt ansehen?

(**b**) (= *air, appearance*) Aussehen *nt*; **there was a ~ of despair in his eyes** ein verzweifelter Blick war in seinen Augen; **I don't like the ~ of him/this wound** er/die Wunde gefällt mir gar nicht; **by the ~ of him** so, wie er aussieht; **to give sth a new ~** einer Sache (*dat*) ein neues Aussehen verleihen; **the town has now taken on a new ~** die Stadt hat ein neues Gesicht bekommen

(**c**) **looks** PL Aussehen *nt*; **good ~s** gutes Aussehen; **~s aren't everything** auf das Aussehen allein kommt es nicht an

2 VT **he ~s his age** man sieht ihm sein Alter an; **he's not ~ing himself these days** er sieht in letzter Zeit ganz verändert aus; **he's ~ing his old self again** er ist wieder ganz der Alte; **I want to ~ my best tonight** ich möchte heute Abend besonders gut aussehen; **~ what you've done!** sieh dir mal an, was du da angestellt hast!; **~ where you're going!** pass auf, wo du hintrittst!; **who's here!** guck mal, wer da ist! (*inf*)

3 VI (**a**) (= *see, glance*) gucken (*inf*); **to ~ (a)round** sich umsehen; **to ~ carefully** genau hinsehen; **to ~ and see** nachsehen; **~ here!** hör (mal) zu!; **now ~ here, it wasn't my fault** Moment mal, das war aber nicht meine Schuld; **~, I know you're tired, but ...** ich weiß ja, dass du müde bist, aber ...; **~, there's a much better solution** da gibt es doch eine wesentlich bessere Lösung; **to ~ the other way** (*fig*) die Augen

verschließen; **to ~ over sb's shoulder** jdm über die Schulter sehen; **~ before you leap** (*Prov*) erst wägen, dann wagen (*Prov*)
(b) (= *search*) suchen, nachsehen
(c) (= *seem*) aussehen; **it ~s all right to me** es scheint mir in Ordnung zu sein; **how does it ~ to you?** was meinst du dazu?; **the car ~s about 10 years old** das Auto sieht so aus, als ob es 10 Jahre alt wäre; **to ~ like** aussehen wie; **the picture doesn't ~ like him** das Bild sieht ihm nicht ähnlich; **it ~s like rain, it ~s as if it will rain** es sieht nach Regen aus; **it ~s as if we'll be late** es sieht (so) aus, als würden wir zu spät kommen; **the festival ~s like being busy** auf dem Festival wird es wahrscheinlich sehr voll (werden)

▶ **look after** VI +PREP OBJ **(a)** sich kümmern um; **to look after oneself** (= *cook etc*) für sich selbst sorgen; (= *be capable, strong etc*) auf sich (*acc*) aufpassen; **he's only looking after his own interests** er handelt nur im eigenen Interesse
(b) (*temporarily*) sehen nach; **children** aufpassen auf (+*acc*)

▶ **look ahead** VI **(a)** (*lit*) nach vorne sehen *or* gucken (*inf*)
(b) (*fig*) vorausschauen; **when we look ahead to the next 30 years** wenn wir die nächsten 30 Jahre betrachten

▶ **look around** VI **(a)** (*generally*) sich umsehen (**for sth** nach etw) **(b)** (*in shop etc*) sich umsehen; (+*prep obj*) sich (*dat*) ansehen *or* angucken (*inf*)

▶ **look at** VI +PREP OBJ **(a)** (= *observe*) ansehen, angucken (*inf*); **just look at him!** sieh *etc* dir den mal an!; **look at the time, I'd better go!** so spät ist es schon, ich muss los!; **he looked at his watch** er sah *etc* auf die Uhr; **he/it isn't much to look at** (= *not attractive*) er/es sieht nicht besonders (gut) aus; (= *nothing special*) er/es sieht nach nichts aus; **to look at him ...** wenn man ihn sieht ...
(b) (= *examine*) sich (*dat*) ansehen *or* -gucken (*inf*); *offer* prüfen; **has the manuscript been looked at yet?** ist das Manuskript schon durchgesehen worden?
(c) (= *view*) betrachten, sehen; **they look at life in a different way** sie haben eine andere Einstellung zum Leben
(d) (= *consider*) *possibilities* sich (*dat*) überlegen; *suggestions, offer* in Betracht ziehen

▶ **look away** VI (*person*) wegsehen

▶ **look back** VI sich umsehen; (*fig*) zurückblicken (**on sth, to sth** auf etw *acc*); **he's never looked back** (*fig inf*) es ist ständig mit ihm bergauf gegangen

▶ **look down** VI hinunter-/heruntersehen *or* -gucken (*inf*)

▶ **look down on** VI +PREP OBJ herabsehen auf (+*acc*)

▶ **look for** VI +PREP OBJ **(a)** suchen; **he's looking for trouble** er wird sich (*dat*) Ärger einhandeln; (*actively*) er sucht Streit
(b) (= *expect*) erwarten

▶ **look forward to** VI +PREP OBJ sich freuen auf (+*acc*); **I'm so looking forward to seeing you again** ich freue mich so darauf, dich wiederzusehen; **I look forward to hearing from you** ich hoffe, bald von Ihnen zu hören

▶ **look in** VI (= *visit*) vorbeikommen (**on sb** bei jdm)

▶ **look into** VI +PREP OBJ **(a)** **to look into sb's face** jdm ins Gesicht sehen; **to look into the future** in die Zukunft sehen *or* blicken **(b)** (= *investigate*) untersuchen; *matter, complaint etc* prüfen

▶ **look on** VI **(a)** zusehen, zugucken (*inf*) **(b)** **to look onto** (*window*) (hinaus)gehen auf (+*acc*); (*building*) liegen an (+*dat*)
(c) +PREP OBJ (*also* **look upon**) betrachten; **I look on him as a good doctor** ich halte ihn für einen guten Arzt

▶ **look out** VI **(a)** (*of window etc*) hinaus-/heraussehen *or* -gucken (*inf*); **to look out (of) the window** zum Fenster hinaussehen *etc* **(b)** (= *take care*) aufpassen; **look out!** pass auf!, Vorsicht!

▶ **look out for** VI +PREP OBJ **(a)** **we'll look out for you at the station/after the meeting** wir werden am Bahnhof/nach der Versammlung nach dir Ausschau halten; **look out for pickpockets/his left hook** nimm dich vor Taschendieben/ seinem linken Haken in Acht **(b)** (= *take care of*) sich kümmern um

▶ **look over** VT SEP *papers, notes etc* durchsehen; *house* sich (*dat*) ansehen

▶ **look round** VI (*esp Brit*) = **look around**

▶ **look through** ■ VI +PREP OBJ **he looked through the window** er sah zum Fenster hinein/herein/hinaus/heraus ② VT SEP (= *examine*) durchsehen; (= *read*) durchlesen

▶ **look to** VI +PREP OBJ **(a)** (= *rely on*) sich verlassen auf (+*acc*); **they looked to him to solve the problem** sie verließen sich

darauf, dass er das Problem lösen würde; **we look to you for support** wir rechnen auf Ihre *or* mit Ihrer Hilfe **(b) to look to the future** in die Zukunft blicken

▶ **look up** ■ VI **(a)** (*lit*) aufsehen *or* -blicken; **don't look up** guck nicht hoch (*inf*) **(b)** (= *improve*) besser werden; (*shares*) steigen; **things are looking up** es geht bergauf ② VT SEP **(a) to look sb up and down** jdn von oben bis unten ansehen *or* mustern **(b)** (= *visit*) **to look sb up** bei jdm vorbeischauen **(c)** *word* nachschlagen; *phone number, address* heraussuchen

▶ **look upon** VI +PREP OBJ = **look on**

▶ **look up to** VI +PREP OBJ **to look up to sb** zu jdm aufsehen

look: lookalike N Doppelgänger(in) *m(f)*; **a Rupert Murdoch ~** ein Doppelgänger von Rupert Murdoch; **look-in** [ˈlʊkɪn] N (*inf*) Chance *f*; **he didn't get a ~** er hatte keine Chance; **lookout** N **(a)** **~ post/station/tower** Beobachtungsposten *m*/-station *f*/-turm *m* **(b)** (*Mil*: = *person*) Wachtposten *m* **(c)** **to keep a ~** Ausschau halten; **to be on the ~ for, to keep a ~ for** = **look out for (d)** (*inf*) **that's his ~!** das ist sein Problem!

loom¹ [luːm] N Webstuhl *m*

loom² VI (*also* **~ ahead** *or* **up**) (*lit, fig*) sich abzeichnen; (*storm*) heraufziehen; (*disaster*) zusammenbrauen; (*danger*) drohen; (*difficulties*) sich auftürmen; (*exams*) bedrohlich näherrücken; **the ship ~ed (up) out of the mist** das Schiff tauchte bedrohlich aus dem Nebel (auf); **to ~ large** eine große Rolle spielen

loony [ˈluːnɪ] (*inf*) ■ ADJ (+ER) bekloppt (*inf*) ② N Verrückte(r) *mf* (*inf*)

loop [luːp] ■ N **(a)** (= *curved shape*) Schlaufe *f*; (*of wire*) Schlinge *f*; **to knock** *or* **throw sb for a ~** (*esp US inf*) jdn völlig umhauen (*inf*) **(b)** (*Aviat*) **to ~ the ~** einen Looping machen **(c)** (*Comput*) Schleife *f* ② VT *rope etc* schlingen

loophole [ˈluːphəʊl] N (*fig*) Hintertürchen *nt*; **a ~ in the law** eine Lücke im Gesetz

loose [luːs] ■ ADJ (+ER) **(a)** lose; *weave, morals, arrangement* locker; *dress, collar* weit; *tooth, bandage, knot, screw, soil, translation* frei; **a ~ connection** (*Elec*) ein Wackelkontakt *m*; **to come** *or* **work ~** (*screw, handle etc*) sich (los)lösen; (*sole, cover etc*) sich (los)lösen; (*button*) abgehen; **to hang ~** lose herunterhängen; **to sell sth ~** (= *not pre-packed*) etw lose verkaufen; **in a ~ sense** (= *approximately*) im weiteren Sinne; (= *approximately*) grob gesagt; **to have a ~ tongue** nichts für sich behalten können; **~ talk** leichtfertiges Gerede
(b) to break *or* **get ~** (*person, animal*) sich losreißen (**from** von); (*ship*) sich (von der Vertäuung) losreißen; (**from** *group of players etc*) sich trennen; (= *break out*) ausbrechen; (**from** *commitment, parental home etc*) sich freimachen (**from** von); **to turn** *or* **let** *or* **set ~** *animal* frei herumlaufen lassen; *prisoner* freilassen; **to let ~ political forces that will be difficult to control** politische Kräfte entfesseln, die nur schwer unter Kontrolle zu bringen sind; **to be at a ~ end** (*fig*) nichts mit sich anzufangen wissen; **to tie up the ~ ends** (*fig*) ein paar offene Probleme lösen
② N (*inf*) **to be on the ~** frei herumlaufen
③ VT **(a)** (= *untie*) losmachen
(b) (= *slacken*) lockern

loose: loose change N Kleingeld *nt*; **loose-fitting** ADJ weit; **loose-leaf** N **~ binder** Ringbuch *nt*; **~ pad** Ringbucheinlage *f*

loosely [ˈluːslɪ] ADV **(a)** lose, locker; *knit, weave* locker; *organized* lose; **a ~ knit group** eine lose Gruppe
(b) (= *imprecisely*) **~ translated** frei übersetzt; **~ based on Shakespeare** frei nach Shakespeare; **what is ~ termed socialist realism** was man ganz allgemein als sozialistischen Realismus bezeichnet; **I was using the word rather ~** ich habe das Wort ziemlich frei gebraucht; **they are ~ connected** sie hängen lose zusammen

loosen [ˈluːsn] ■ VT **(a)** lösen; (= *untie also*) losmachen **(b)** (= *slacken*) lockern; *belt* weiter machen; *soil* auflockern; *collar* aufmachen; *reins* locker lassen; **to ~ one's grip on sth** (*lit*) seinen Griff um etw lockern; (*fig*) **on the party, on power** etw nicht mehr so fest im Griff haben ② VI sich lockern

▶ **loosen up** ■ VT SEP *muscles* lockern; *soil* auflockern ② VI (*muscles*) locker werden; (*athlete*) sich (auf)lockern; (= *relax*) auftauen

loot [luːt] ■ N Beute *f* ② VTI plündern

looter [ˈluːtəʳ] N Plünderer *m*

lop [lɒp] VT (*also* **~ off**) abhacken

lope [ləʊp] VI in großen Sätzen springen; **he ~d along beside her** er lief mit großen Schritten neben ihr her

lopsided ['lɒp'saɪdɪd] ADJ schief; (fig) einseitig

loquacious [lə'kweɪʃəs] ADJ redselig

lord [lɔːd] **1** N **(a)** (= master, ruler) Herr m; **~ and master** Herr und Meister m; (hum: = husband) Herr und Gebieter m **(b)** (Brit: = nobleman) Lord m; **the (House of) Lords** das Oberhaus **(c)** (Rel) **Lord** Herr m; **the Lord (our) God** Gott, der Herr; **(good) Lord!** (inf) ach, du lieber Himmel! (inf); (annoyed) mein Gott! (inf); **Lord knows** (inf) wer weiß **2** VT **to ~ it over sb** jdn herumkommandieren

Lord Mayor N (Brit) ≈ Oberbürgermeister m

Lordship ['lɔːdʃɪp] N **His/Your** ~ Seine/Eure Lordschaft; (to bishop) Seine/Eure Exzellenz; (to judge) Seine/Euer Ehren or Gnaden

Lord's Prayer ['lɔːdz'preəʳ] N (Rel) **the** ~ das Vaterunser

lore [lɔːʳ] N Überlieferungen pl

lorry ['lɒrɪ] N (Brit) Last(kraft)wagen m, Lkw m; **it fell off the back of a** ~ (hum inf) ich hab/er hat etc das „gefunden" (hum inf)

lorry driver N (Brit) Last(kraft)wagenfahrer(in) m(f), Lkw-Fahrer(in) m(f)

lose [luːz], pret, ptp **lost** **1** VT **(a)** (generally) verlieren; pursuer abschütteln; **to ~ one's job/(driving) licence** (Brit) **or (driver's) license** (US) die Stelle/den Führerschein verlieren; **many men ~ their hair** vielen Männern gehen die Haare aus; **the cat has lost a lot of hair** die Katze hat viel Haar verloren; **the shares have lost 15% in a month** die Aktien sind in einem Monat um 15% gefallen; **to ~ one's way** (lit) sich verirren; (fig) die Richtung verlieren; **you will ~ nothing by helping them** es kann dir nicht schaden, wenn du ihnen hilfst; **that mistake lost him his job/the game** dieser Fehler kostete ihn die Stellung/den Sieg; **she lost her brother in the war** sie hat ihren Bruder im Krieg verloren; **he lost the use of his legs in the accident** seit dem Unfall kann er seine Beine nicht mehr bewegen; **to ~ no time in doing sth** etw sofort tun; **my watch lost three hours** meine Uhr ist drei Stunden nachgegangen; **you've lost me now with all this abstract argument** bei dieser abstrakten Argumentation komme ich nicht mehr mit **(b)** (= not catch) opportunity verpassen **(c)** (inf) **he's lost it** (inf) (= doesn't know what he's doing) er ist total daneben (inf); (= has lost his touch) er ist nicht mehr ganz auf der Höhe (inf); **she's finally lost it** jetzt ist sie völlig durchgedreht (inf) **(d)** (passive usages) **to be lost** (things) verschwunden sein; (people) sich verlaufen haben; (fig) verloren sein; (words) untergehen; **I can't follow the reasoning, I'm lost** ich kann der Argumentation nicht folgen, ich verstehe nichts mehr; **he was soon lost in the crowd** er hatte sich bald in der Menge verloren; **to be lost at sea** auf See geblieben sein; (ship) auf See vermisst sein; **all is (not) lost!** (noch ist nicht) alles verloren!; **to get lost** sich verlaufen or verirren; (boxes etc) verloren gehen; **get lost!** (inf) verschwinde! (inf); **to give sb up for lost** jdn verloren geben; **to give sth up for lost** etw abschreiben; **I'm lost without my watch** ohne meine Uhr bin ich verloren or aufgeschmissen (inf); **classical music is lost on him** er hat keinen Sinn für klassische Musik; **the joke was lost on her** der Witz kam bei ihr nicht an; **the irony was not lost on me** ich verstand die Ironie durchaus; **to be lost for words** sprachlos sein; **to be lost in thought** in Gedanken versunken sein **2** VI verlieren; (watch) nachgehen; **you can't ~** du kannst nichts verlieren; **you will not ~ by helping him** es kann dir nicht schaden, wenn du ihm hilfst

▶ **lose out** VI (inf) schlecht wegkommen (inf); **to lose out to sb/sth** von jdm/etw verdrängt werden

loser ['luːzəʳ] N Verlierer(in) m(f); **what a ~!** (inf) was für eine Null! (inf)

losing ['luːzɪŋ] ADJ **the ~ team** die unterlegene Mannschaft; **to fight a ~ battle** einen aussichtslosen Kampf führen; **to be on the ~ side** verlieren

loss [lɒs] N **(a)** Verlust m; **hair ~** Haarausfall m; **weight ~** Gewichtsverlust m; **~ of memory, memory ~** Gedächtnisverlust m; **the factory closed with the ~ of 300 jobs** bei der Schließung der Fabrik gingen 300 Stellen verloren; **he felt her ~ very deeply** ihr Tod war ein schwerer Verlust für ihn; **there was a heavy ~ of life** viele kamen ums Leben; **job ~es** Stellenkürzungen pl; **his business is running at a ~** er arbeitet mit Verlust; **to sell sth at a ~** etw mit Verlust verkaufen; **it's your ~** es ist deine Sache; **a dead ~** (Brit inf) ein böser Reinfall (inf); (= person) ein hoffnungsloser Fall (inf); **to cut one's ~es** (fig) Schluss machen, ehe der Schaden (noch) größer wird **(b) to be at a ~** nicht mehr weiterwissen; **we are at a ~ for what to do** wir wissen nicht mehr aus noch ein; **to be at a ~ to explain sth** etw nicht erklären können; **to be at a ~ for words** nicht wissen, was man sagen soll

loss: **loss adjuster** N (Brit Insur) Schadenssachverständige(r) mf; **lossmaking** ADJ **a ~ company** ein Unternehmen, das mit Verlust arbeitet

lost [lɒst] **1** PRET, PTP of **lose** **2** ADJ ATTR verloren; civilization untergegangen; cause aussichtslos; person vermisst; dog, cat entlaufen; book, glasses etc verlegt; opportunity versäumt

lost: **lost-and-found (department)** N (US) Fundbüro nt; **lost property** N (Brit) **(a)** (= items) Fundstücke pl **(b)** = **lost property office**; **lost property office** N (Brit) Fundbüro nt

lot¹ [lɒt] N **(a) to draw ~s** losen, Lose ziehen; **they drew ~s to see who would begin** sie losten aus, wer anfangen sollte **(b)** (= destiny, at auction) Los nt; **failure was his ~ in life** es war sein Los, immer zu versagen; **to throw in one's ~ with sb** sich mit jdm zusammentun; **to improve one's ~** seine Lage verbessern **(c)** (= plot) Parzelle f; (Film) Filmgelände nt; **building ~** Bauplatz m; **parking ~** (US) Parkplatz m; **all over the ~** (US inf) (= everywhere) überall; (= in confusion) völlig durcheinander **(d)** (esp Brit) **where shall I put this ~?** wo soll ich das hier or das Zeug (inf) hintun?; **can you carry that ~ by yourself?** kannst du das (alles) alleine tragen?; **divide the books up into three ~s** teile die Bücher in drei Teile or Stapel ein; **we moved the furniture in two ~s** wir haben die Möbel in zwei Fuhren befördert; **he/she is a bad ~** (inf) er/sie taugt nichts; **they are a bad ~** (inf) das ist ein übles Pack **(e)** (esp Brit inf: = group) Haufen m; **that ~ in the next office** die Typen vom Büro nebenan (inf); **are you ~ coming to the pub?** kommt ihr (alle) in die Kneipe? **(f) the ~** (inf) alle; alles; **that's the ~** das ist alles; **the whole ~ of them** sie alle; **he's eaten the ~** er hat alles aufgegessen

lot² N, ADV **a ~, ~s** viel; **a ~ of money** viel or eine Menge Geld; **a ~ of books, ~s of books** viele or eine Menge Bücher; **such a ~** so viel; **what a ~!** was für eine Menge!; **how much has he got? — ~s** or **a ~** wie viel hat er? — jede Menge (inf) or viel; **such a ~ of books** so viele Bücher; **he made ~s and ~s of mistakes** er hat eine Unmenge Fehler gemacht; **we see a ~ of John these days** wir sehen John in letzter Zeit sehr oft; **things have changed a ~** es hat sich vieles geändert; **I like him a ~** ich mag ihn sehr; **I feel ~s** or **a ~ better** es geht mir sehr viel besser

lotion ['ləʊʃən] N Lotion f

lottery ['lɒtərɪ] N Lotterie f; **life is a ~** das Leben ist ein Glücksspiel

lotus position ['ləʊtəspəzɪʃən] N Lotossitz m

loud [laʊd] **1** ADJ (+ER) **(a)** laut; protest, complaint lautstark **(b)** behaviour aufdringlich; colour grell; tie, clothes knallbunt **2** ADV laut; **~ and clear** laut und deutlich; **to say/read sth out ~** etw laut sagen/lesen; **to laugh/think out ~** ~ laut lachen/denken

loud-hailer [laʊd'heɪləʳ] N Megafon nt

loudly ['laʊdlɪ] ADV laut; complain, oppose, criticize lautstark

loud: **loudmouth** N (inf) Großmaul nt (inf); **loudmouthed** ['laʊd,maʊθd] ADJ (inf) großmäulig (inf)

loudness ['laʊdnɪs] N Lautstärke f; **the ~ of his voice** seine laute Stimme

loudspeaker [laʊd'spiːkəʳ] N Lautsprecher m

lounge [laʊndʒ] **1** N (in house) Wohnzimmer nt; (in hotel) Gesellschaftsraum m; (at airport) Warteraum m **2** VI faulenzen; **to ~ about** (Brit) or **around** herumliegen/-sitzen; **to ~ against a wall** sich lässig gegen eine Mauer lehnen

lounge bar N Salon m (vornehmerer Teil einer Gaststätte)

lounger ['laʊndʒəʳ] N (Brit: = reclining chair) Ruhesessel m

louse [laʊs] N, pl **lice (a)** (Zool) Laus f **(b)** (inf) fieser Kerl (inf)

lousy ['laʊzɪ] ADJ (inf) mies (inf); (= meagre also) lausig; trick etc fies (inf); **I'm ~ at arithmetic** in Mathe bin ich mies or miserabel (inf); **he is ~ at (playing) golf** or **a ~ golfer** er spielt miserabel Golf (inf); **you've done a ~ job** du hast saumäßig

gearbeitet (sl); **to feel ~** sich mies fühlen (inf); **a ~ £3** popelige or lausige drei Pfund (inf)

lout [laʊt] N Rüpel m, Flegel m

loutish ['laʊtɪʃ] ADJ rüpelhaft, flegelhaft

louvre, (US) **louver** ['luːvəʳ] N Jalousie f; **~ door** Lamellentür f

lovable ['lʌvəbl] ADJ liebenswert

love [lʌv] **1** N **(a)** Liebe f; **to have a ~ for** or **of sb/sth** jdn/etw sehr lieben; **~ of learning** Freude f am Lernen; **~ of adventure** Abenteuerlust f; **~ of books** Liebe f zu Büchern; **~ of (one's) country** Vaterlandsliebe f; **for ~** aus Liebe; **for the ~ of** aus Liebe zu; **to be in ~ (with sb)** (in jdn) verliebt sein; **to fall in ~ (with sb)** sich (in jdn) verlieben; **there is no ~ lost between them** sie können sich nicht ausstehen; **to make ~** (sexually) miteinander schlafen; **to make ~ to sb** (sexually) mit jdm schlafen; **yes, (my) ~** ja, Liebling or Schatz; **she's the ~ of my life** sie ist die große Liebe meines Lebens
(b) (= greetings: in letters etc) **with all my ~** mit herzlichen Grüßen; **~ from Anna** herzliche Grüße von Anna; **give him my ~** grüß ihn von mir; **he sends his ~** er lässt grüßen
(c) (inf: form of address) mein Lieber/meine Liebe; **I'm afraid the bus is full, ~** der Bus ist leider voll
(d) (Tennis) null; **fifteen ~** fünfzehn null
2 VT lieben; (= like) thing gern mögen; **they ~ each other** sie lieben sich; **I ~ tennis** ich mag Tennis sehr gern; (to play) ich spiele sehr gern Tennis; **I'd ~ a cup of tea** ich hätte (liebend) gern(e) eine Tasse Tee; **I'd ~ to come** ich würde sehr or liebend gern(e) kommen; **we'd all ~ you to come with us** wir würden uns alle sehr freuen, wenn du mitkommen würdest; **I ~ the way she smiles** ich mag es, wie sie lächelt; **I ~ the way he leaves us to do all the work** (iro) ist es nicht toll, wie er uns die ganze Arbeit überlässt (iro)
3 VI lieben

love: love affair N Verhältnis nt; **the Americans' ~ with firearms** das innige Verhältnis der Amerikaner zu Schusswaffen; **lovebite** N Knutschfleck m (inf); **love-hate relationship** N Hassliebe f; **they have a ~** zwischen ihnen besteht eine Hassliebe; **loveless** ADJ life, marriage ohne Liebe; home, family, environment lieblos; **love letter** N Liebesbrief m; **love life** N Liebesleben nt

lovely ['lʌvlɪ] ADJ (+ER) (= beautiful) wunderschön; (= delightful also) herrlich; baby niedlich; (= charming, likeable) liebenswürdig, nett; personality einnehmend; smile gewinnend; **that dress looks ~ on you** dieses Kleid steht dir sehr gut; **we had a ~ time** es war sehr schön; **it's ~ and warm in this room** es ist schön warm in diesem Zimmer; **he made a ~ job of it** er hat das wunderbar gemacht; **have a ~ holiday** (esp Brit) or **vacation** (US)! schöne Ferien!; **it's been ~ to see you** es war schön, dich zu sehen

lovemaking ['lʌvmeɪkɪŋ] N (sexual) Liebe f

lover ['lʌvəʳ] N **(a)** Liebhaber m, Geliebte f; **the ~s** das Liebespaar; **we were ~s for two years** wir waren zwei Jahre lang verliebt **(b)** **a ~ of books** ein(e) Bücherfreund(in) m(f); **a ~ of good food** ein(e) Freund(in) or Liebhaber(in) m(f) von gutem Essen; **music-~** Musikliebhaber(in) m(f) or -freund(in) m(f); **soccer ~s** Fußballanhänger or -begeisterte pl

love: lovesick ADJ liebeskrank; **to be ~** Liebeskummer m haben; **love song** N Liebeslied nt; **love story** N Liebesgeschichte f; **lovestruck** ADJ bis über beide Ohren verliebt

loving ['lʌvɪŋ] ADJ liebend; look, disposition, relationship, marriage liebevoll; **your ~ son ...** in Liebe euer Sohn ...; **they are such a ~ couple/family** sie gehen so liebevoll miteinander um

lovingly ['lʌvɪŋlɪ] ADV liebevoll

low [ləʊ] **1** ADJ (+ER) niedrig; form of life, musical key nieder; bow, note tief; density, intelligence, quality, resistance gering; food supplies knapp; trick gemein; morale schlecht; light gedämpft; (pej) minderwertig (pej); **the sun was ~ in the sky** die Sonne stand tief am Himmel; **her dress was ~ at the neck** ihr Kleid hatte einen tiefen Ausschnitt; **the river is ~** der Fluss führt wenig Wasser; **a ridge of ~ pressure** ein Tiefdruckkeil m; **activity on the stock exchange is at its ~est** die Börsentätigkeit hat ihren Tiefstand erreicht; **to speak in a ~ voice** leise sprechen; **how ~ can you get!** wie kann man nur so tief sinken!; **to feel ~** (physically) sich nicht wohl or gut fühlen; (emotionally) niedergeschlagen sein
2 ADV aim nach unten; speak, sing leise; fly, bow tief; **they**

turned the lamps down ~ sie drehten die Lampen herunter; **a dress cut ~ in the back** ein Kleid mit tiefem Rückenausschnitt; **I would never sink so ~ as to ...** so tief würde ich nie sinken, dass ich ...; **he's been laid ~ with the flu** (Brit) er liegt mit Grippe im Bett; **to run** or **get ~** knapp werden; **we are getting ~ on petrol** (Brit) or **gas** (US) uns (dat) geht das Benzin aus
3 N (Met, fig) Tief nt; **to reach a new ~** einen neuen Tiefstand erreichen

low: low-alcohol ADJ alkoholarm; **lowbrow** ADJ (geistig) anspruchslos; **low-cal** ADJ (inf), **low-calorie** ADJ kalorienarm; **a low-calorie diet** eine kalorienarme Diät; **low-cost** ADJ preiswert; **Low Countries** PL **the ~** die Niederlande pl; **low-cut** ADJ dress tief ausgeschnitten; **low-down** ADJ (esp US inf) gemein, fies (inf); **lowdown** N (inf) Informationen pl; **what's the ~ on Kowalski?** was wissen or haben (inf) wir über Kowalski?; **he gave me the ~ on it** er hat mich darüber aufgeklärt

lower ['ləʊəʳ] **1** ADJ **(a)** (in height) niedriger; part, limb, storey, latitude untere(r, s); note tiefer; (Geog) Nieder-; **the Lower Rhine** der Niederrhein; **~ leg/arm** Unterschenkel m/-arm m; **the ~ of the two holes** das untere der beiden Löcher; **hemlines are ~ this year** die Röcke sind dieses Jahr länger; **the ~ deck** (of bus) das untere Deck; (of ship) das Unterdeck
(b) rank, level, animals niedere(r, s); **the ~ classes** (Sociol) die unteren Schichten; **a ~ middle-class family** eine Familie aus der unteren Mittelschicht; **the ~ school** die unteren Klassen
2 ADV tiefer, leiser; **~ down the mountain** weiter unten am Berg; **~ down the list** weiter unten auf der Liste
3 VT **(a)** boat, injured man, load herunterlassen; eyes, gun senken; mast umlegen; sail, flag einholen; bicycle saddle niedriger machen; **he ~ed himself into an armchair** er ließ sich in einen Sessel nieder
(b) pressure, risk verringern; price, interest rates, tone, temperature senken; morale, resistance schwächen; standard herabsetzen; **~ your voice** sprich leiser; **to ~ oneself** sich hinunterlassen; (socially) sich unter sein Niveau begeben

lower: lower case **1** N Kleinbuchstaben pl **2** ADJ klein; **Lower Chamber** N Unterhaus nt, zweite Kammer; **lower-class** ADJ der Unterschicht; habit, vocabulary der unteren or niederen Schichten; **a ~ neighbourhood** (Brit) or **neighborhood** (US) eine sozial schwache Gegend; **lower-income** ADJ household mit niedrigen Einkommen; **in the ~ bracket** in der Steuerklasse für Niedrigeinkommen; **lower sixth (form)** N (Brit Sch) vorletztes Schuljahr

low: low-flying ADJ **~ plane** Tiefflieger m; **low-heeled** ADJ shoes mit flachem Absatz; **low-key** ADJ approach gelassen; handling besonnen; reception reserviert; **lowland** **1** N **the Lowlands of Scotland** das schottische Tiefland; **the ~s of Central Europe** die Tiefebenen pl Mitteleuropas **2** ADJ des Flachlands; (of Scotland) des Tieflands; **low-level** ADJ radiation niedrig; (Comput) language nieder; **lowlife** N niederes Milieu

lowly ['ləʊlɪ] ADJ (+ER) bescheiden

low: low-lying ADJ tief gelegen; **low-necked** ADJ tief ausgeschnitten; **low-pitched** ADJ tief; **low-priced** ADJ günstig; **low-profile** ADJ wenig profiliert; **low-rent** ADJ mit niedriger Miete; **low-rise** ATTR niedrig (gebaut); **low season** N Nebensaison f; **low-tar** ADJ cigarette teerarm; **low-tech** ADJ nicht mit Hi-Tech ausgestattet; **it's pretty ~** es ist nicht gerade hi-tech; **low tide, low water** N Niedrigwasser nt; **at ~** bei Niedrigwasser; **low-wage** ADJ ATTR Niedriglohn-; **~ country** Niedriglohnland nt

loyal ['lɔɪəl] ADJ (+ER) **(a)** treu; **he was very ~ to his friends/country** er hielt (treu) zu seinen Freunden/seinem Land; **he remained ~ to his wife/the king** er blieb seiner Frau/dem König treu **(b)** (= without emotional involvement) loyal (to a party einer Partei gegenüber)

loyalist ['lɔɪəlɪst] **1** N Loyalist(in) m(f) **2** ADJ loyal; army, troops regierungstreu

loyally ['lɔɪəlɪ] ADV **(a)** treu **(b)** (= without emotional involvement) loyal

loyalty ['lɔɪəltɪ] N **(a)** Treue f **(b)** (non-emotional) Loyalität f

loyalty card N (Brit Comm) Kundenkarte f

lozenge ['lɒzɪndʒ] N **(a)** (Med) Pastille f **(b)** (= shape) Raute f, Rhombus m

LP ABBR of **long player, long-playing record** LP f

LPG ABBR *of* **liquefied petroleum gas** Flüssiggas *nt*, Autogas *nt*

L-plate ['elpleɪt] N *Schild mit der Aufschrift „L" (für Fahrschüler)*

LRP (*Brit*) N ABBR *of* **lead replacement petrol** Benzin mit integriertem Bleiersatz-Additiv

LSD ABBR *of* **lysergic acid diethylamide** LSD *nt*

Ltd ABBR *of* **Limited** GmbH

lube [lu:b] (*US inf*) **1** N Schmieröl *nt*; (*Med*) Gleitmittel *nt* **2** VT schmieren

lubricant ['lu:brɪkənt] N Schmiermittel *nt*

lubricate ['lu:brɪkeɪt] VT (*lit, fig*) schmieren

Lucerne [lu:'sɜːn] N Luzern *nt*; **Lake ~** Vierwaldstätter See *m*

lucid ['lu:sɪd] ADJ (+ER) **(a)** klar; *account* präzise; *explanation* einleuchtend **(b)** (= *sane*) **~ intervals** lichte Augenblicke; **he was ~ for a few minutes** ein paar Minuten lang war er bei klarem Verstand

lucidly ['lu:sɪdlɪ] ADV klar; *explain* einleuchtend; *write* verständlich

luck [lʌk] N Glück *nt*; **by ~** durch einen glücklichen Zufall; **bad ~** Unglück *nt*, Pech *nt*; **bad** *or* **hard** *or* **tough ~!** so ein Pech!; **good ~, good ~!** viel Glück!; **good ~ to them!** (*iro*), **and the best of (British) ~!** (*iro*) na dann viel Glück!; **no such ~!** schön wärs! (*inf*); **just my ~!** Pech (gehabt), wie immer!; **with any ~** mit etwas Glück; **any ~?** (= *did it work?*) hats geklappt?; (= *did you find it?*) hast du es gefunden?; **worse ~!** wie schade!; **to be in ~** Glück haben; **to be out of ~** kein Glück haben; **he was a bit down on his ~** er hatte eine Pechsträhne; **to bring sb good/bad ~** jdm Glück/Unglück bringen; **as ~ would have it** wie es der Zufall wollte; **Bernstein kisses his cuff links for ~** Bernstein küsst seine Manschettenknöpfe, damit sie ihm Glück bringen; **to try one's ~** sein Glück versuchen

▶ **luck out** VI (*US inf*) Schwein haben (*inf*)

luckily ['lʌkɪlɪ] ADV glücklicherweise; **~ for me** zu meinem Glück

lucky ['lʌkɪ] ADJ (+ER) (= *having, bringing luck*) Glücks-; *coincidence* glücklich; **a ~ shot** ein Glückstreffer *m*; **you ~ thing!, ~ you!** du Glückliche(r) *mf*; **the ~ winner** der glückliche Gewinner, die glückliche Gewinnerin; **to be ~** Glück haben; **I was ~ enough to meet him** ich hatte das (große) Glück, ihn kennen zu lernen; **you are ~ to be alive** du kannst von Glück sagen, dass du noch lebst; **you were ~ to catch him** du hast Glück gehabt, dass du ihn erwischt hast; **you'll be ~ to make it in time** wenn du das noch schaffst, hast du (aber) Glück; **I want another £500 – you'll be ~!** ich will nochmal £ 500 haben – viel Glück!; **to be ~ (in)** that **...** Glück haben, dass ...; **~ number** Glückszahl *f*; **~ charm** Glücksbringer *m*; **it must be my ~ day** ich habe wohl heute meinen Glückstag; **to be ~** (*charm, number etc*) Glück bringen; **it was ~ I stopped him in time** ein Glück, dass ich ihn rechtzeitig aufgehalten habe; **that was a ~ escape** da habe ich/hast du *etc* noch mal Glück gehabt

lucky dip N ≈ Glückstopf *m*

lucrative ['lu:krətɪv] ADJ lukrativ

ludicrous ['lu:dɪkrəs] ADJ lächerlich; *idea, prices, wages, speed* haarsträubend

ludicrously ['lu:dɪkrəslɪ] ADV grotesk; *small, little, low* lächerlich; *high, fast* haarsträubend; **~ expensive** absurd teuer; **the description is ~ inadequate** die Beschreibung ist hoffnungslos unzulänglich

lug [lʌg] VT schleppen; **to ~ sth around with one** etw mit sich herumschleppen

luggage ['lʌgɪdʒ] N Gepäck *nt*

luggage: luggage locker N Gepäckschließfach *nt*; **luggage rack** N (*Rail etc*) Gepäckablage *ntf* (*Aut*) Gepäckträger *m*; **luggage trolley** N Kofferkuli *m*; **luggage van** N (*Brit Rail*) Gepäckwagen *m*

lugubrious [lu:'gu:brɪəs] ADJ *person, song* schwermütig; *smile, tune* wehmütig; *face, expression* kummervoll

lukewarm ['lu:kwɔːm] ADJ (*lit, fig*) lauwarm; *friendship* lau, oberflächlich; **he's ~ about** *or* **on the idea/about her** er ist von der Idee/von ihr nur mäßig begeistert

lull [lʌl] **1** N Pause *f*; (*Comm*) Flaute *f*; **a ~ in the conversation/fighting** eine Gesprächs-/Gefechtspause; **the ~ before the storm** (*fig*) die Ruhe vor dem Sturm **2** VT *baby* beruhigen; (*fig*) einlullen; *fears etc* zerstreuen; **to ~ a baby to sleep** ein Baby in den Schlaf wiegen; **he ~ed them into a false sense of security** er wiegte sie in trügerische Sicherheit

lullaby ['lʌləbaɪ] N Schlaflied *nt*

lumbago [lʌm'beɪgəʊ] N Hexenschuss *m*

lumber¹ ['lʌmbə'] **1** N (*esp US*) (Bau)holz *nt* **2** VT (*Brit inf*) **to ~ sb with sth** jdm etw aufhalsen (*inf*); **I got ~ed with her for the evening** ich hatte sie den ganzen Abend auf dem Hals (*inf*)

lumber² VI (*cart*) rumpeln; (*tank*) walzen; (*elephant, person*) trampeln; (*bear*) tapsen

lumber: lumberjack N Holzfäller *m*; **lumber room** N Rumpelkammer *f*; **lumberyard** N (*US*) Holzlager *nt*

luminary ['lu:mɪnərɪ] N (*fig*) Koryphäe *f*

luminous ['lu:mɪnəs] ADJ leuchtend; **~ paint/colour** (*Brit*) *or* **color** (*US*) Leuchtfarbe *f*; **~ dial** Leuchtzifferblatt *nt*; **my watch is ~** meine Uhr leuchtet im Dunkeln

lump [lʌmp] **1** N **(a)** Klumpen *m*; (*of sugar*) Stück *nt* **(b)** (= *swelling*) Beule *f*; (*inside the body*) Geschwulst *f*; (*in breast*) Knoten *m*; (*on surface*) Huppel *m* (*inf*), kleine Erhebung *f*; **with a ~ in one's throat** (*fig*) mit einem Kloß im Hals; **it brings a ~ to my throat** dabei schnürt sich mir die Kehle zu **(c)** **to pay money in a ~** (= *at once*) auf einmal bezahlen; (= *covering different items*) pauschal bezahlen **2** VT (*esp Brit inf*) **to ~ it** sich damit abfinden; **like it or ~ it** you'll have to go to work (*inf*) du musst zur Arbeit, ob es dir passt oder nicht; **if he doesn't like it he can ~ it** wenns ihm nicht passt, hat er eben Pech gehabt (*inf*)

▶ **lump together** VT SEP **(a)** (= *put together*) zusammentun; *expenses, money* zusammenlegen **(b)** (= *judge together*) *persons, topics* in einen Topf werfen

lump: lump payment N (*at once*) einmalige Bezahlung; (*covering different items*) Pauschalbezahlung *f*; **lump sugar** N Würfelzucker *m*; **lump sum** N Pauschalbetrag *m*; **to pay sth in a ~** etw pauschal bezahlen

lumpy ['lʌmpɪ] ADJ (+ER) *liquid etc, mattress, cushion* klumpig; *figure* pummelig, plump; **to go ~** (*sauce, rice*) klumpen

lunacy ['lu:nəsɪ] N Wahnsinn *m*

lunar ['lu:nə'] ADJ Mond-; **~ landscape** Mondlandschaft *f*

lunar: lunar eclipse N Mondfinsternis *f*; **lunar module** N Mondlandefähre *f*

lunatic ['lu:nətɪk] **1** ADJ wahnsinnig **2** N Wahnsinnige(r) *mf*

lunatic asylum N Irrenanstalt *f*

lunch [lʌntʃ] **1** N Mittagessen *nt*; **to have** *or* **take ~** (zu) Mittag essen; **let's do ~** (*inf*) wir sollten uns zum Mittagessen treffen; **how long do you get for ~?** wie lange haben Sie Mittagspause?; **he's at ~** er ist beim Mittagessen **2** VI (zu) Mittag essen; **we ~ed on a salad** zum (Mittag)essen gab es einen Salat

lunch: lunchbox N Lunchbox *f*; **lunch break** N Mittagspause *f*; **lunch counter** N (*US*) (= *café*) Imbiss *m*; (= *counter*) Imbisstheke *f*

luncheon ['lʌntʃən] N (*form*) Mittagessen *nt*

luncheon: luncheon meat N Frühstücksfleisch *nt*; **luncheon voucher** N Essen(s)bon *m*

lunch: lunch hour N Mittagsstunde *f*; (= *lunch break*) Mittagspause *f*; **lunch money** N (*US Sch*) Essensgeld *nt*; **lunchpail** N (*US*) Lunchbox *f*; **lunchroom** N (*US*) Imbissstube *f*; (= *canteen*) Kantine *f*; **lunchtime** N Mittagspause *f*; **they arrived at ~** sie kamen gegen Mittag an

lung [lʌŋ] N Lunge *f*; **he has weak ~s** er hat keine gute Lunge

lung cancer N Lungenkrebs *m*

lunge [lʌndʒ] **1** N Satz *m* nach vorn; **he made a ~ at his opponent** er stürzte sich auf seinen Gegner **2** VI (sich) stürzen; **to ~ at sb** sich auf jdn stürzen

lurch¹ [lɜːtʃ] N **to leave sb in the ~** (*inf*) jdn hängen lassen (*inf*)

lurch² **1** N **to give a ~** einen Ruck machen; (*boat*) schlingern; **the party's ~ to the right** der Rechtsruck der Partei **2** VI **(a)** einen Ruck machen **(b)** (= *move with lurches*) sich ruckartig bewegen; (*boat*) schlingern; (*person*) taumeln; **the train ~ed to a standstill** der Zug kam mit einem Ruck zum Stehen; **the bus ~ed off down the bumpy track** der Bus ruckelte den holprigen Weg hinunter; **the government ~es from one crisis to the next** die Regierung schlittert von einer Krise in die andere

lure [ljʊəʳ] **1** N (= *bait*) Köder *m*; (= *person, for hawk*) Lockvogel *m*; (*general*) Lockmittel *nt*; (*fig: of city, sea etc*) Verlockungen *pl*; **the ~ of the wild** der lockende Ruf der Wildnis **2** VT anlocken; **to ~ sb away from sth** jdn von etw weglocken; **to ~ sb/an animal into a trap** jdn/ein Tier in eine Falle locken

lurid [ˈljʊərɪd] ADJ **(a)** *colour, sky* grell; *dress* grellfarben; *poster* schreiend; **she was painting her toenails a ~ red** sie lackierte sich die Fußnägel grellrot **(b)** (*fig*) *language, headline, imagination, description* reißerisch; (= *sordid*) *detail, crime* widerlich; *photo, image* schaurig; (= *prurient*) anzüglich; **~ tale** Schauergeschichte *f*

luridly [ˈljʊərɪdlɪ] ADV *coloured* grell

lurk [lɜːk] VI lauern; **a nasty suspicion ~ed at the back of his mind** er hegte einen fürchterlichen Verdacht

➤ **lurk about** (*Brit*) *or* **around** VI herumschleichen

lurking [ˈlɜːkɪŋ] ADJ heimlich; *doubt* nagend

luscious [ˈlʌʃəs] ADJ **(a)** (= *delicious*) köstlich **(b)** *colour* satt; *girl, boy* zum Anbeißen (*inf*); *figure, lips* üppig

lush [lʌʃ] ADJ **(a)** *grass, meadows* saftig; *vegetation* üppig **(b)** (*inf*) *hotel, house* feudal; *lifestyle* üppig

lust [lʌst] **1** N Wollust *f*; (= *wanting to acquire*) Begierde *f* (*for* nach); (= *greed*) Gier *f* (*for* nach); **~ for power** Machtgier *f* **2** VI **to ~ after** (*sexually*) begehren (+*acc*); (*greedily*) gieren nach

luster N (*US*) = **lustre**

lustful [ˈlʌstfʊl] ADJ lüstern

lustily [ˈlʌstɪlɪ] ADV *eat* herzhaft; *sing* aus voller Kehle; *cry, cheer* aus vollem Hals(e)

lustre, (*US*) **luster** [ˈlʌstəʳ] N **(a)** Schimmer *m* **(b)** (*fig*) Glanz *m*

lusty [ˈlʌstɪ] ADJ (+ER) *appetite* herzhaft; *cheer, cry* laut

lute [luːt] N Laute *f*

Luxembourg [ˈlʌksəmbɜːg] N Luxemburg *nt*

luxuriant [lʌgˈzjʊərɪənt] ADJ üppig; *forest* dicht

luxuriate [lʌgˈzjʊərɪeɪt] VI **to ~ in sth** (*people*) sich in etw (*dat*) aalen

luxurious [lʌgˈzjʊərɪəs] ADJ luxuriös; *food* üppig; **a ~ hotel** ein Luxushotel *nt*; **he is a man of ~ tastes** er hat einen Hang zum Luxus

luxury [ˈlʌkʃərɪ] **1** N (*in general*) Luxus *m*; (*of car, house etc*) Komfort *m*; **to live a life of ~** ein Luxusleben führen; **we can't allow ourselves many luxuries** wir können uns (*dat*) nicht viel Luxus leisten **2** ADJ ATTR Luxus-; **~ car** Luxusauto *nt*

LW ABBR *of* **long wave** LW

lychee [ˈlaɪtʃiː] N Litschi *f*

Lycra® [ˈlaɪkrə] N Lycra® *nt*

lying [ˈlaɪɪŋ] **1** ADJ verlogen **2** N Lügen *nt*; **that would be ~** das wäre gelogen

lynch [lɪntʃ] VT lynchen

lynx [lɪŋks] N Luchs *m*

lyric [ˈlɪrɪk] **1** ADJ lyrisch **2** N (= *poem*) lyrisches Gedicht; (= *often pl: words of pop song*) Text *m*

lyrical [ˈlɪrɪkəl] ADJ lyrisch; (*fig: = enthusiastic*) schwärmerisch; **to wax ~ about sth** über etw (*acc*) ins Schwärmen geraten

lyricism [ˈlɪrɪsɪzəm] N Lyrik *f*

lyricist [ˈlɪrɪsɪst] N (*Mus*) Texter(in) *m(f)*

Mm

M, m [ɛm] N M *nt*, m *nt*
M ABBR *of* **medium**
m (a) ABBR *of* **million(s)** Mio. **(b)** ABBR *of* **metre(s)** m **(c)** ABBR *of* **mile(s) (d)** ABBR *of* **married** verh. **(e)** ABBR *of* **masculine** m.
MA ABBR *of* **Master of Arts** M. A.
ma [mɑː] N (*inf*) Mama *f* (*inf*)
ma'am [mæm] N gnä' Frau *f* (*form*); *see also* **madam**
mac [mæk] N (*Brit inf*) Regenmantel *m*
macabre [məˈkɑːbrə] ADJ makaber
macaroni [ˌmækəˈrəʊnɪ] N Makkaroni *pl*
macaroni cheese N Käsemakkaroni *pl*
macaroon [ˌmækəˈruːn] N Makrone *f*
macaw [məˈkɔː] N Ara *m*
mace [meɪs] N (*mayor's*) Amtsstab *m*
Macedonia [ˌmæsɪˈdəʊnɪə] N Mazedonien *nt*
machete [məˈtʃeɪtɪ] N Buschmesser *nt*
machination [ˌmækɪˈneɪʃən] N USU PL Machenschaften *pl*
machine [məˈʃiːn] ■ N Maschine *f*; (= *vending ~*) Automat *m*; **the party ~** (*Pol*) der Parteiapparat; **the publicity/propaganda ~** die Publicity-/Propagandamaschine ■ VT (*Tech*) maschinell herstellen; (= *treat with ~*) maschinell bearbeiten; (*Sew*) mit der Maschine nähen
machine: machine code N Maschinenkode *m*; **machine gun** N Maschinengewehr *nt*; **machine language** N (*Comput*) Maschinensprache *f*; **machine operator** N Maschinenarbeiter(in) *m(f)*; (*skilled*) Maschinist(in) *m(f)*; **machine-readable** ADJ (*Comput*) maschinenlesbar
machinery [məˈʃiːnərɪ] N (*lit, fig*) Maschinerie *f*; (= *mechanism*) Mechanismus *m*; **the ~ of government** der Regierungsapparat
machine: machine shop N Maschinensaal *m*; **machine tool** N Werkzeugmaschine *f*; **machine translation** N maschinelle Übersetzung; **machine-washable** ADJ waschmaschinenfest
machinist [məˈʃiːnɪst] N (*Tech*) Maschinist(in) *m(f)*; (*Sew*) Näherin *f*
macho [ˈmætʃəʊ] ADJ macho *pred*, Macho-; **~ image** Macho-Image *nt*; **a ~ type** ein Macho-Typ *m*
mackerel [ˈmækrəl] N Makrele *f*
mackintosh [ˈmækɪntɒʃ] N Regenmantel *m*
macro [ˈmækrəʊ] N (*Comput*) Makro *nt*
macro- PREF makro-, Makro-; **~language** Makrosprache *f*
macrobiotic [ˈmækrəʊbaɪɒtɪk] ADJ makrobiotisch
macrocosm [ˈmækrəʊkɒzəm] N Makrokosmos *m*; **the ~ of Italian society** die italienische Gesellschaft in ihrer Gesamtheit
macroeconomics [ˌmækrəʊˌiːkəˈnɒmɪks] N SING or PL Makroökonomie *f*
mad [mæd] ■ ADJ (+ER) **(a)** wahnsinnig (*with* vor +*dat*); (= *genuinely insane*) geisteskrank; (*inf*: = *crazy*) verrückt; (= *with rabies*) animal tollwütig; **to go ~** wahnsinnig werden; (*lit*: = *go insane*) den Verstand verlieren; **to drive sb ~** jdn wahnsinnig machen; (*lit*: = *drive sb insane*) jdn um den Verstand bringen; **it's enough to drive you ~** es ist zum Verrücktwerden; **you must be ~!** du bist wohl wahnsinnig!; **I must have been ~ to believe him** ich war wohl von Sinnen, ihm zu glauben; **they made a ~ rush** *or* **dash for the door** sie stürzten wie wild zur Tür; **why the ~ rush?** warum diese Hektik?; **this is bureaucracy gone ~** das ist Bürokratie hoch drei; **she's ~ doing something like that** sie ist verrückt, so etwas zu tun
(b) (*inf*: = *angry*) sauer (*inf*); **to be ~ at sb** auf jdn sauer sein (*inf*); **to be ~ about** *or* **at sth** über etw (*acc*) sauer sein (*inf*); **this makes** *or* **drives me ~** das bringt mich auf die Palme (*inf*)
(c) (*esp Brit inf*: = *very keen*) **to be ~ about** *or* **on sth** auf etw (*acc*) verrückt sein; **I'm not exactly ~ about this job** ich bin nicht gerade versessen auf diesen Job; **I'm (just) ~ about you** ich bin (ganz) verrückt nach dir!; **don't go ~!** (= *don't overdo it*) übertreib es nicht
■ ADV (*inf*) **to be ~ keen on sb/sth** ganz scharf auf jdn/etw sein (*inf*); **like ~** wie verrückt; **he ran like ~** er rannte wie wild

Madagascar [ˌmædəˈɡæskəʳ] N Madagaskar *nt*
madam [ˈmædəm] N gnädige Frau (*old, form*); **yes, ~** ja(wohl); **can I help you, ~?** kann ich Ihnen behilflich sein?; **Dear Madam** (*esp Brit*) sehr geehrte gnädige Frau; **Dear Sir or Madam** (*esp Brit*) Sehr geehrte Damen und Herren
madcap [ˈmædkæp] ADJ *idea* versponnen; *scheme* hirnverbrannt
mad cow disease N Rinderwahn(sinn) *m*
madden [ˈmædn] VT ärgern, fuchsen (*inf*)
maddening [ˈmædnɪŋ] ADJ unerträglich; *habit* aufreizend
maddeningly [ˈmædnɪŋlɪ] ADV unerträglich; **the train ride was ~ slow** es war zum Verrücktwerden, wie langsam der Zug fuhr
made [meɪd] PRET, PTP *of* **make**
made-to-measure [ˈmeɪdtəˈmeʒəʳ] ADJ (*Brit*) maßgeschneidert; *curtains* nach Maß; *furniture etc* spezialangefertigt; **~ suit** Maßanzug *m*; **~ clothes** Maßkonfektion *f*
made-up [ˈmeɪdʌp] ADJ **(a)** (= *invented*) erfunden **(b)** (= *wearing make-up*) geschminkt **(c)** (= *ready-made*) vorgefertigt; *curtains* fertig genäht
madhouse [ˈmædhaʊs] N (*lit, fig*) Irrenhaus *nt*
madly [ˈmædlɪ] ADV **(a)** wie verrückt **(b)** (*inf*: = *extremely*) wahnsinnig; **to be ~ in love (with sb)** bis über beide Ohren (in jdn) verliebt sein
madman [ˈmædmən] N, *pl* **-men** [-mən] Verrückte(r) *m*
madness [ˈmædnɪs] N Wahnsinn *m*
Madonna [məˈdɒnə] N Madonna *f*
Madrid [məˈdrɪd] N Madrid *nt*
madwoman [ˈmædwʊmən] N Verrückte *f*
maelstrom [ˈmeɪlstrəʊm] N (*fig*) Malstrom *m* (*liter*), Sog *m*; **he returned to the ~ of public life** er kehrte in den Trubel des öffentlichen Lebens zurück
maestro [ˈmaɪstrəʊ] N Maestro *m*
Mafia [ˈmæfɪə] N Mafia *f*
mag [mæɡ] N (*inf*) Magazin *nt*; **porn ~** Pornoheft *nt*
magazine [ˌmæɡəˈziːn] N **(a)** Magazin *nt* **(b)** (*Mil*: = *store*) Depot *nt*
maggot [ˈmæɡət] N Made *f*
magic [ˈmædʒɪk] ■ N **(a)** Magie *f*; **he entertained them with a display of ~** er unterhielt sie mit ein paar Zauberkunststücken; **he made the spoon disappear by ~** er zauberte den Löffel weg; **as if by ~** wie durch Zauberei; **it worked like ~** (*inf*) es klappte wie am Schnürchen (*inf*) **(b)** (= *mysterious charm*) Zauber *m*
■ ADJ **(a)** Zauber-; *powers, square* magisch; **~ formula** Zauberformel *f*; **the ~ word** (*having special effect*) das Stichwort; (*making sth possible*) das Zauberwort; **he hasn't lost his ~ touch** er hat nichts von seiner Genialität verloren **(b)** (*inf*: = *fantastic*) toll (*inf*), super (*inf*)
magical [ˈmædʒɪkəl] ADJ *powers, attraction* magisch; *atmosphere* unwirklich; **the effect was ~** das wirkte (wahre) Wunder; (*visually*) die Wirkung war zauberhaft
magically [ˈmædʒɪklɪ] ADV wunderbar; **~ transformed** auf wunderbare Weise verwandelt
magic carpet N fliegender Teppich
magician [məˈdʒɪʃən] N Magier *m*; (= *conjuror*) Zauberkünstler(in) *m(f)*; **I'm not a ~!** ich kann doch nicht hexen!
magic: magic mushroom N (*inf*) Magic Mushroom *m*, Zauberpilz *m*; **magic spell** N Zauber *m*; (= *words*) Zauberspruch *m*; **the witch cast a ~ on her** die Hexe verzauberte sie; **magic wand** N Zauberstab *m*; **to wave a ~** (*lit, fig*) den Zauberstab schwingen
magisterial [ˌmædʒɪˈstɪərɪəl] ADJ gebieterisch
magistrate [ˈmædʒɪstreɪt] N Schiedsmann *m*/-frau *f*
magistrates' court [ˈmædʒɪstreɪtsˈkɔːt] N (*Brit*) Schiedsgericht *nt*
magna cum laude [ˈmæɡnəkʊmˈlaʊdeɪ] ADV (*US*) magna cum laude, sehr gut
magnanimity [ˌmæɡnəˈnɪmɪtɪ] N Großmut *f*

magnanimous [mæg'nænɪməs] ADJ großmütig; (= *generous*) großzügig; **he was ~ in victory/defeat** er zeigte Großmut im Sieg/in der Niederlage

magnanimously [mæg'nænɪməslɪ] ADV großmütig; (= *generously*) großzügig

magnate ['mægneɪt] N Magnat *m*

magnesium [mæg'niːzɪəm] N Magnesium *nt*

magnet ['mægnɪt] N (*lit, fig*) Magnet *m*

magnetic [mæg'netɪk] ADJ (*lit*) magnetisch; **he has a ~ personality** er hat ein sehr anziehendes Wesen

magnetic: magnetic disk N (*Comput*) Magnetplatte *f*; **magnetic field** N Magnetfeld *nt*; **magnetic north** N nördlicher Magnetpol; **magnetic strip, magnetic stripe** N Magnetstreifen *m*; **magnetic tape** N Magnetband *nt*

magnetism ['mægnɪtɪzəm] N Magnetismus *m*; (*fig*) Anziehungskraft *f*

magnification [ˌmægnɪfɪ'keɪʃən] N Vergrößerung *f*; **high/low ~** starke/geringe Vergrößerung

magnificence [mæg'nɪfɪsəns] N (a) Großartigkeit *f* (b) (= *splendid appearance*) Pracht *f*

magnificent [mæg'nɪfɪsənt] ADJ (a) großartig; *food, meal* hervorragend; **he has done a ~ job** er hat das ganz hervorragend gemacht (b) (= *of splendid appearance*) prächtig

magnificently [mæg'nɪfɪsəntlɪ] ADV großartig

magnify ['mægnɪfaɪ] VT (a) vergrößern (b) (= *exaggerate*) aufbauschen

magnifying glass ['mægnɪfaɪɪŋ'glɑːs] N Vergrößerungsglas *nt*

magnitude ['mægnɪtjuːd] N Ausmaß *nt*; (= *importance*) Bedeutung *f*; **I didn't appreciate the ~ of the task** ich war mir über den Umfang der Aufgabe nicht im Klaren; **in operations of this ~** bei Vorhaben dieser Größenordnung; **a matter of the first ~** eine Angelegenheit von äußerster Wichtigkeit

magnolia [mæg'nəʊlɪə] N Magnolie *f*; (*also ~* **tree**) Magnolienbaum *m*

magnum opus [ˌmægnəm'əʊpəs] N Hauptwerk *nt*

magpie ['mægpaɪ] N Elster *f*

maharajah [ˌmɑːhə'rɑːdʒə] N Maharadscha *m*

mahogany [mə'hɒgənɪ] N Mahagoni *nt* ADJ Mahagoni-; (*colour*) mahagoni(farben); **~ furniture** Mahagonimöbel *pl*

maid [meɪd] N (= *servant*) Dienstmädchen *nt*; (*in hotel*) Zimmermädchen *nt*; (= *lady's ~*) Zofe *f*

maiden ['meɪdn] N (*liter*) Mädchen *nt* ADJ ATTR Jungfern-; **~ flight** Jungfernflug *m*; **~ voyage** Jungfernfahrt *f*

maiden: maiden name N Mädchenname *m*; **maiden speech** N Jungfernrede *f*

maid: maid of honour, (*US*) **maid of honor** N Brautjungfer *f*; **maidservant** N Hausmädchen *nt*

mail [meɪl] N Post *f*; **to send sth by ~** etw mit der Post schicken; **is there any ~ for me?** ist Post für mich da? VT (a) aufgeben; (= *put in letter box*) einwerfen; (= *send by ~*) mit der Post schicken (b) (= *send by e-~*) per E-Mail senden, mailen (*inf*); **to ~ sb** jdm eine E-Mail senden

mail: mailbag N Postsack *m*; **mail bomb** N (*US*) Briefbombe *f*; **mailbox** N (a) (*US*) Briefkasten *m* (b) (*Comput*) Mailbox *f*; **mail drop** N (*US*) Briefschlitz *m*

mailing ['meɪlɪŋ] N Rundschreiben *nt*

mailing: mailing address N (*US*) Postanschrift *f*; **mailing list** N Adressenliste *f*; (*e-mail*) Mailingliste *f*

mail: mailman N (*US*) Briefträger *m*; **mail merge** N (*Comput*) Mailmerge *nt*; **mail order** N Postversand *m*; **mail-order** ADJ Versand-; **~ catalogue** (*Brit*) *or* **catalog** (*US*) Versandhauskatalog *m*; **~ firm** *or* **house** Versandhaus *nt*; **mailroom** N (*esp US*) Poststelle *f*; **mailshot** N (*Brit*) Mailshot *m*; **mail train** N Postzug *m*; **mail van** N (*on roads*) Postauto *nt*; (*Brit Rail*) Postwagen *m*; **mailwoman** N (*US*) Briefträgerin *f*

maim [meɪm] VT (= *mutilate*) verstümmeln; (= *cripple*) zum Krüppel machen; **he will be ~ed for life** er wird sein Leben lang ein Krüppel bleiben

main [meɪn] ADJ ATTR Haupt-; **the ~ reason** der Hauptgrund; **the ~ thing is to ...** die Hauptsache ist, dass ...; **the ~ thing is you're still alive** Hauptsache, du lebst noch; **~ market** (*St Ex*) Hauptbörsenplatz *m*, bedeutendster Börsenplatz N (a) (= *pipe*) Hauptleitung *f*; **the ~s** (*of town*) das

---

öffentliche Versorgungsnetz; (*for electricity*) das Stromnetz; (*of house*) der Haupthahn; (*for electricity*) der Hauptschalter; **the machine is run directly off the ~s** das Gerät wird direkt ans Stromnetz angeschlossen; **the water/gas/electricity was switched off at the ~s** der Haupthahn/Hauptschalter für Wasser/Gas/Elektrizität wurde abgeschaltet (b) **in the ~** im Großen und Ganzen

main: main clause N (*Gram*) Hauptsatz *m*; **main course** N Hauptgericht *nt*; **main deck** N Hauptdeck *nt*; **main drag** N (*US inf*) Hauptstraße *f*; **mainframe (computer)** N Mainframe *m*; **mainframe network** N (*Comput*) vernetzte Großanlage; **mainland** N Festland *nt*; **on the ~ of Europe** auf dem europäischen Festland; **main line** N (*Rail*) Hauptstrecke *f*; **main-line** ADJ **~ train** Schnellzug *m*

mainly ['meɪnlɪ] ADV hauptsächlich; **the meetings are held ~ on Tuesdays** die Besprechungen finden meistens dienstags statt; **the climate is ~ wet** das Klima ist vorwiegend feucht

main: main office N Zentrale *f*; **main road** N Hauptstraße *f*; **mains-operated** ['meɪnzˌɒpəreɪtɪd], **mains-powered** ['meɪnzˌpaʊəd] ADJ für Netzbetrieb;

main: mainspring N (*fig*) Triebfeder *f*; **mainstay** N (*fig*) Stütze *f*

mainstream ['meɪnstriːm] N Hauptrichtung *f*; **to be in the ~ of sth** der Hauptrichtung einer Sache (*gen*) angehören ADJ (a) *politician, party, politics* der Mitte; *philosophy, opinion etc* vorherrschend; *schools, education* regulär; **~ society** die Mitte der Gesellschaft (b) **~ cinema** Mainstreamkino *nt*; **~ jazz** Mainstreamjazz *m* VT (*US Sch*) in die reguläre Schule schicken

main street N Hauptstraße *f*

maintain [meɪn'teɪn] VT (a) (= *keep up*) aufrechterhalten; *law and order, peace etc* wahren; *speed, attitude* beibehalten; *prices* halten; *life* erhalten; **to ~ sth at a constant temperature** etw bei gleich bleibender Temperatur halten (b) (= *support*) *family* unterhalten (c) *machine* warten; *roads, building* instand halten; *car* pflegen; **products which help to ~ healthy skin** Produkte, die die Haut gesund erhalten (d) (= *claim*) behaupten; **he still ~ed he was innocent, he still ~ed his innocence** er beteuerte immer noch seine Unschuld

maintained school [meɪn'teɪndskuːl] N (*Brit*) staatliche Schule

maintenance ['meɪntnəns] N (a) (= *keeping up*) Aufrechterhaltung *f*; (*of law and order, peace etc*) Wahrung *f*; (*of life*) Erhaltung *f* (b) (*Brit*) (*of family*) Unterhalt *m*; (= *social security*) Unterstützung *f*; **he has to pay ~** er ist unterhaltspflichtig (c) (*of machine, car*) Wartung *f*; (*of road, building etc*) Instandhaltung *f*; (*of gardens*) Pflege *f*; (= *cost*) Unterhalt *m*

maintenance: maintenance costs PL Unterhaltskosten *pl*; **maintenance payments** PL Unterhaltszahlungen *pl*

maisonette [ˌmeɪzə'net] N Appartement *nt*

maître d' [ˌmetrə'diː] N (*US*) Oberkellner *m*

maize [meɪz] N Mais *m*

majestic [mə'dʒestɪk] ADJ majestätisch; *proportions* stattlich; *music* getragen; (= *not slow*) erhaben

majestically [mə'dʒestɪkəlɪ] ADV majestätisch

majesty ['mædʒɪstɪ] N Majestät *f*; **His/Her Majesty** Seine/Ihre Majestät; **Your Majesty** Eure Majestät

major ['meɪdʒəʳ] ADJ (a) Haupt-; (= *of great importance*) bedeutend; (= *of great extent*) groß *also Pol cause, factor* wesentlich; *incident* schwerwiegend; *part, role* führend; **~ customer** Großkunde *m*, Großkundin *f*; **a ~ road** eine Hauptverkehrsstraße; **a ~ poet** ein bedeutender Dichter; **of ~ importance** von großer Bedeutung; **a ~ operation** eine größere Operation; **a ~ work of art** ein bedeutendes Kunstwerk (b) (*Mus*) Dur-; **~ key** Durtonart *f*; **A ~** A-Dur *f* N (a) (*Mil*) Major(in) *m(f)* (b) (*US*: = *subject*) Hauptfach *nt*; **he's a psychology ~** Psychologie ist/war sein Hauptfach VI (*US*) **to ~ in French** Französisch als Hauptfach studieren

Majorca [mə'jɔːkə] N Mallorca *nt*

majorette [ˌmeɪdʒə'ret] N Majorette *f*

majority [mə'dʒɒrɪtɪ] N (a) Mehrheit *f*; **to be in a** *or* **the ~** in der Mehrzahl sein; **to be in a ~ of 3** eine Mehrheit von 3 Stimmen haben; **to have/get a ~** die Mehrheit haben/

bekommen **(b)** (*Jur*) Volljährigkeit *f*; **to reach the age of ~** volljährig werden

majority: **majority decision** N Mehrheitsbeschluss *m*; **majority rule** N Mehrheitsregierung *f*; **majority vote** N Mehrheitsbeschluss *m*

---

make [meɪk]

1	TRANSITIVE VERB	**4**	NOUN
2	INTRANSITIVE VERB	**5**	PHRASAL VERBS
3	REFLEXIVE VERB		

---

vb: pret, ptp **made**

1 TRANSITIVE VERB

(a) machen; *bread* backen; *cars* herstellen; *dress* nähen; *coffee* kochen; *peace* stiften; *speech* halten; *choice, arrangements, decision* treffen; **she made it into a suit** sie machte einen Anzug daraus; **God made the world** Gott erschuf die Welt; **to make an application** sich bewerben; **to make a guess** raten

◆**made in/of/for/to** made in Deutschland hergestellt, made in Germany; **it's made of gold** es ist aus Gold; **to show what one is made of** zeigen, was in einem steckt; **the job is made for him** die Arbeit ist wie für ihn geschaffen; **they're made for each other** sie sind wie geschaffen füreinander

◆**to make sb/sth +** *ADJ* **to make sb happy/angry** *etc* jdn glücklich/wütend *etc* machen; **to make one's voice heard** mit seiner Stimme durchdringen

◆**to make sb/sth +** *NOUN* **he was made a judge** man ernannte ihn zum Richter; **Shearer made it 1-0** Shearer erzielte das 1:0; **they'll never make a soldier of him** *or* **out of him** aus ihm wird nie ein Soldat

◆**to make a day/night of it** **we decided to make a day/night of it** wir beschlossen, den ganzen Tag dafür zu nehmen/(die Nacht) durchzumachen

◆**to make something of oneself/one's life** etwas aus sich/ seinem Leben machen

(b) (= *cause to do or happen*) (dazu) bringen; (= *compel to do*) zwingen

◆**to make sb do sth** (= *cause to do*) jdn dazu bringen, etw zu tun; (= *compel to do*) jdn zwingen, etw zu tun; **what made you come to this town?** was hat Sie dazu veranlasst, in diese Stadt zu kommen?; **what makes you say that?** warum sagst du das?; **what makes you think you can do it?** was macht Sie glauben, dass Sie es schaffen können?; **he makes his heroine die** er lässt seine Heldin sterben; **you can't make me!** mich kann keiner zwingen!

◆**to make sth do sth** **what made it explode?** was hat die Explosion bewirkt?; **it makes the room look smaller** es lässt den Raum kleiner wirken; **the chemical makes the plant grow faster** die Chemikalie bewirkt, dass die Pflanze schneller wächst; **that made the cloth shrink** dadurch ging der Stoff ein; **you can't make things happen** man kann den Lauf der Dinge nicht erzwingen

◆**to make do to** make do with sth sich mit etw begnügen; **to make do with less money** mit weniger Geld auskommen

(c) (*money*) verdienen; *profit, loss, fortune* machen (*on* bei); *reputation* sich (*dat*) verschaffen

(d) (= *reach, achieve*) schaffen; *train, plane etc* erwischen (*inf*); *summit, top, shore etc* es schaffen zu; **we made good time** wir kamen schnell voran; **sorry I couldn't make your party last night** tut mir Leid, ich habe es gestern Abend einfach nicht zu deiner Party geschafft; **we'll never make the airport in time** wir kommen garantiert nicht rechtzeitig zum Flughafen; **the story made the front page** die Geschichte kam auf die Titelseite

◆**to make it** (= *succeed*) es schaffen; **he just made it** er hat es gerade noch geschafft; **he'll never make it through the winter** (= *survive*) er wird den Winter nie überstehen

◆**to make good** **to make good as a writer** es als Schriftsteller(in) schaffen; **he is a poor boy made good** er ist ein armer Junge, der es zu etwas gebracht hat

(e) (= *cause to succeed*) berühmt machen; **this film made her** mit diesem Film schaffte sie den Durchbruch; **his performance makes the play** das Stück lebt von seiner schauspielerischen Leistung; **he's got it made** (*inf*) er hat ausgesorgt

◆**to make sb's day** **that makes my day!** das freut mich unheimlich!; (*iro*) **das hat mir gerade noch gefehlt!; you've made my day** ich könnte dir um den Hals fallen! (*inf*)

◆**to make or break sth/sb** **he can make or break you** er hat dein Schicksal in der Hand

(f) (= *be, constitute*) machen, abgeben; **he made a good father** er gab einen guten Vater ab; **he'll never make a soldier** aus dem wird nie ein Soldat; **he'd make a fantastic Hamlet/a good teacher** er wäre ein fantastischer Hamlet/ein guter Lehrer; **they make a good couple** sie sind ein gutes Paar

(g) (= *equal*) sein, (er)geben; **2 plus 2 makes 4** 2 und 2 ist 4; **that makes £55 you owe me** Sie schulden mir damit (nun) £ 55; **how much does that make altogether?** was macht das insgesamt?

(h) (= *reckon*) *distance, total* schätzen auf (*+acc*); **I make the total 107** ich komme auf 107

◆**to make it +** *time, date, figure* **what time do you make it?** wie spät hast du es?; **I make it 3.15** ich habe 3.15 Uhr; **I make it 3 miles** ich schätze 3 Meilen; **shall we make it 7 o'clock?** (= *agree*) sagen wir 7 Uhr?

(l) (*Elec*) *circuit* schließen; *contact* herstellen

2 INTRANSITIVE VERB

(a) **to make on a deal** bei einem Geschäft verdienen

(b) (= *act*)

◆**to make as if to do sth** Anstalten machen, etw zu tun; (*as deception*) so tun, als wolle man etw tun

◆**to make to...** (= *try*) **I made to speak** ich setzte zur Rede an

◆**to make like...** (*inf*) so tun, als ob...; **he made like he was dying** er tat so, als ob er am Sterben wäre

3 REFLEXIVE VERB

◆**to make oneself +** *ADJ or NOUN* **to make oneself comfortable** es sich (*dat*) bequem machen; **you'll make yourself ill!** du machst dich damit krank!; **to make oneself heard** sich (*dat*) Gehör verschaffen; **to make oneself understood** sich verständlich machen

◆**to make oneself sth** sich (*dat*) etw machen; **she made herself a lot of money on the deal** sie hat bei dem Geschäft eine Menge Geld verdient

◆**to make oneself do sth** sich dazu zwingen, etw zu tun; **he's just made himself look ridiculous** er hat sich nur lächerlich gemacht

4 NOUN

(a) (= *brand*) Marke *f*; **what make of car do you have?** welche (Auto)marke fahren Sie?

(b)

◆**on the make** (*pej inf*) (*for profit*) profitgierig (*inf*); (= *ambitious*) karrieresüchtig (*inf*)

5 PHRASAL VERBS

➤ **make for** VI +PREP OBJ **(a)** (= *head for*) zuhalten auf (*+acc*); (*crowd*) zuströmen (*+dat*, auf *+acc*); (*vehicle*) losfahren auf (*+acc*); **we are making for London** wir wollen nach London; (*by vehicle*) wir fahren Richtung London; (*by ship*) wir halten Kurs auf London **(b)** (= *promote*) führen zu; *happy marriage, successful parties* den Grund legen für; **such tactics don't make for good industrial relations** solche Praktiken wirken sich nicht gerade günstig auf das Arbeitsklima aus

➤ **make of** VI +PREP OBJ halten von; **don't make too much of it** überbewerten Sie es nicht

➤ **make off** VI sich davonmachen

➤ **make out** **1** VT SEP **(a)** *cheque, receipt* ausstellen (*to* auf *+acc*); *list, bill* aufstellen; **to make out a case for sth** für etw argumentieren

(b) (= *see, discern*) ausmachen; (= *decipher*) entziffern; (= *understand*) verstehen; *person, actions* schlau werden aus; **I can't make out what he wants** ich komme nicht dahinter, was er will; **how do you make that out?** wie kommst du darauf?

(c) (= *claim*) behaupten

(d) (= *imply*) **to make out that ...** es so hinstellen, als ob ...; **he made out that he was hurt** er tat, als sei er verletzt; **to make sb out to be clever/a genius** jdn als klug/Genie hinstellen **2** VI (*inf*) (= *get on*) zurechtkommen; (*with people*) auskommen; (= *succeed*) es schaffen

➤ **make over** VT SEP **(a)** (= *assign*) überschreiben (*to sb* jdm); (= *bequeath*) vermachen (*to sb* jdm) **(b)** (= *convert*) umändern; *house* umbauen; **the gardens have been made over into a parking lot** man hat die Anlagen in einen Parkplatz umgewandelt

➤ **make up** 🚺 VT SEP **(a)** (= *constitute*) bilden; **to be made up of** bestehen aus

(b) *food, medicine, bed* zurechtmachen; *parcel* packen; *list, accounts, team* zusammenstellen; (*Typ*) *page* umbrechen; **to make material up into sth** Material zu etw verarbeiten

(c) *quarrel* beilegen; **to make it up (with sb)** sich (mit jdm) aussöhnen

(d) *face, eyes* schminken; **to make sb/oneself up** jdn/sich schminken

(e) to make up one's mind (to do sth) sich (dazu) entschließen(, etw zu tun); **my mind is quite made up** mein Entschluss steht fest; **to make up one's mind about sb/sth** sich (*dat*) eine Meinung über jdn/etw bilden; **I can't make up my mind about him** ich weiß nicht, was ich von ihm halten soll

(f) (= *invent*) erfinden; **you're making that up!** jetzt schwindelst du aber! (*inf*)

(g) (= *complete*) crew vollständig machen; **I'll make up the other £20** ich komme für die restlichen £ 20 auf; **he made the gift up to £50** er rundete das Geschenk auf £ 50 auf

(h) *loss* ausgleichen; *time* einholen, aufholen; *sleep* nachholen; **to make it up to sb (for sth)** (= *compensate*) jdn (für etw) entschädigen; (*emotionally, return favour etc*) jdm etw wieder gutmachen

🚺 VI (*after quarrelling*) sich wieder vertragen

➤ **make up for** VI +PREP OBJ **to make up for sth** etw ausgleichen; **to make up for lost time** verlorene Zeit aufholen; **to make up for the lack of sth** etw ersetzen; **that still doesn't make up for the fact that you were very rude** das macht noch lange nicht ungeschehen, dass du sehr unhöflich warst

➤ **make with** VI +PREP OBJ (*US inf*) **he started making with his trumpet** er legte mit seiner Trompete los (*inf*); **OK, let's make with the paint brushes** na dann, schnappen wir uns die Pinsel (*inf*)

---

make: makebelieve VT sich (*dat*) vorstellen; **make-believe** 🚺 ADJ ATTR Fantasie-, imaginär; **a ~ world** eine Fantasie- *or* Scheinwelt 🚺 N Fantasie *f*; **don't be afraid, it's only ~** hab keine Angst, das ist doch nur eine Geschichte; **make-or-break** ADJ ATTR (*inf*); **makeover** N (= *beauty treatment*) Schönheitskur *f*; (*of car, building*) Verschönerung *f*; **to give sb a complete ~** jdm einen neuen Look verpassen (*inf*)

maker ['meɪkə'] N (= *manufacturer*) Hersteller(in) *m(f)*; (*of bill of exchange*) Aussteller(in) *m(f)*

makeshift ['meɪkʃɪft] ADJ improvisiert; *office* provisorisch; *weapon, tool, repairs* behelfsmäßig; **~ accommodation** Notunterkunft *f*

make-up ['meɪkʌp] N **(a)** Make-up *nt*; (*Theat*) Maske *f*; **she spends hours on her ~** sie braucht Stunden zum Schminken **(b)** (*of team, party etc*) Zusammenstellung *f*; (= *character*) Veranlagung *f*; **psychological ~** Psyche *f*; **it's part of their national ~** das gehört zu ihrem Nationalcharakter

make-up bag N Kosmetiktasche *f*

makeweight ['meɪkweɪt] N (*fig*) Lückenbüßer *m*; (= *person*) Lückenbüßer(in) *m(f)*

making ['meɪkɪŋ] N **(a)** (= *production*) Herstellung *f*; (*of food*) Zubereitung *f*; **the film was three months in the ~** der Film wurde in drei Monaten gedreht; **a star/dictator in the ~** ein werdender Star/Diktator; **it's a disaster in the ~** es bahnt sich eine Katastrophe an; **many of her problems are of her own ~** an vielen ihrer Probleme ist sie selbst schuld; **it was the ~ of him** das hat ihn zu dem gemacht, was er (heute) ist **(b) makings** PL Voraussetzungen *pl* (*of* zu); **he has the ~s of an actor/a general** *etc* er hat das Zeug zu einem Schauspieler/ General *etc*; **the situation has all the ~s of a strike** die Situation bietet alle Voraussetzungen für einen Streik

maladjusted [ˌmælə'dʒʌstɪd] ADJ (*Psych, Sociol*) verhaltensgestört

maladministration ['mælədˌmɪnɪs'treɪʃən] N schlechte Verwaltung

---

malady ['mælədɪ] N Leiden *nt*; **social ~** gesellschaftliches Übel

malaise [mæ'leɪz] N Unwohlsein *nt*; (*fig*) Unbehagen *nt*

malaria [mə'lɛərɪə] N Malaria *f*

Malawi [mə'lɑːwɪ] N Malawi *nt*

Malaya [mə'leɪə] N Malaya *nt*

Malayan [mə'leɪən] 🚺 ADJ malaiisch 🚺 N Malaie *m*, Malaiin *f*

Malaysia [mə'leɪzɪə] N Malaysia *nt*

Malaysian [mə'leɪzɪən] 🚺 ADJ malaysisch 🚺 N Malaysier(in) *m(f)*

malcontent ['mælkən,tent] N Unzufriedene(r) *mf*

maldistribution [ˌmældɪstrɪ'bjuːʃən] N (*of goods*) Fehlverteilung *f*

male [meɪl] 🚺 ADJ männlich; *choir, voice* Männer-; **~ child** Junge *m*; **a ~ doctor** ein Arzt *m*; **~ nurse** Krankenpfleger *m*; **~ sparrow/crocodile** Spatzen-/Krokodilmännchen *nt*; **that's a typical ~ attitude** das ist typisch männlich; **~ bonding** Verbundenheit *f* unter Männern 🚺 N (= *animal*) Männchen *nt*; (*inf*: = *man*) Mann *m*

male: male chauvinism N Chauvinismus *m*; **male chauvinist** N Chauvi *m* (*inf*); **~ attitude** chauvinhafte Haltung (*inf*)

malevolence [mə'levələns] N Boshaftigkeit *f*

malevolent [mə'levələnt] ADJ boshaft; *action* böswillig; *power, force* böse; *fate* grausam

malformed [mæl'fɔːmd] ADJ missgebildet

malfunction [mæl'fʌŋkʃən] 🚺 N (*of liver etc*) Funktionsstörung *f*; (*of machine*) Defekt *m* 🚺 VI (*liver etc*) nicht richtig arbeiten; (*machine, system*) nicht richtig funktionieren; **the ~ing part** das defekte Teil

malice ['mælɪs] N Bosheit *f*; **I bear him no ~** ich bin ihm nicht böse

malicious [mə'lɪʃəs] ADJ **(a)** *person, words* boshaft; *behaviour, action* böswillig; *letter, phone call* bedrohend **(b)** (*Jur*) *damage* mutwillig; **with ~ intent** in böswilliger Absicht

maliciously [mə'lɪʃəslɪ] ADV *act* böswillig; *say, smile* boshaft

malign [mə'laɪn] 🚺 ADJ (*liter*) *influence, effect* unheilvoll 🚺 VT verleumden; (= *run down*) schlecht machen

malignant [mə'lɪgnənt] ADJ bösartig; *effect* negativ; **a ~ growth** (*Med, fig*) ein bösartiges Geschwür

malingerer [mə'lɪŋgərə'] N Simulant(in) *m(f)*

mall [mɔːl, mæl] N (*US: also* **shopping ~**) Einkaufszentrum *nt*

malleable ['mælɪəbl] ADJ formbar (*also fig*), weich; (*of clay, wax*) geschmeidig

mallet ['mælɪt] N Holzhammer *m*; (*Croquet*) (Krocket)hammer *m*; (*Polo*) (Polo)schläger *m*

malnourished [mæl'nʌrɪʃt] ADJ (*form*) unterernährt

malnutrition [ˌmælnjʊ'trɪʃən] N Unterernährung *f*

malpractice [ˌmæl'præktɪs] N Berufsvergehen *nt*; **~ insurance** (*US*) Berufshaftpflicht *f*

malt [mɔːlt] N Malz *nt*

Malta ['mɔːltə] N Malta *nt*

Maltese [ˌmɔːl'tiːz] 🚺 ADJ maltesisch 🚺 N Malteser(in) *m(f)*

malt: malt liquor N *aus Malz gebrautes alkoholisches Getränk*; (*US: = beer*) Starkbier *nt*; **malt loaf** N ≈ Rosinenbrot *nt*

maltreat [ˌmæl'triːt] VT schlecht behandeln; (*using violence*) misshandeln

maltreatment [ˌmæl'triːtmənt] N schlechte Behandlung; (*violent*) Misshandlung *f*

malt whisky N Malt Whisky *m*

mam(m)a [mə'mɑː] N (*inf*) Mama *f* (*inf*)

mammal ['mæməl] N Säugetier *nt*

mammary ['mæmərɪ] ADJ Brust-; **~ gland** Brustdrüse *f*

mammoth ['mæməθ] 🚺 N Mammut *nt* 🚺 ADJ Mammut-; *enterprise* kolossal; *proportions* riesig

mammy ['mæmɪ] N (*inf*) Mami *f* (*inf*)

man [mæn] 🚺 N, pl **men** [men] Mann *m*; (= *servant*) Bedienstete(r) *m*; **this incident made a ~ out of him** dieses Ereignis hat zum Mann gemacht; **he took it like a ~** er hat es wie ein Mann ertragen; **her ~** (*inf*) ihr Mann; **they are ~ and wife** sie sind Mann und Frau; **the ~ in the street** der Mann auf der Straße; **~ of God** Mann *m* Gottes; **~ of letters** (= *writer*) Literat *m*; (= *scholar*) Gelehrter *m*; **~ of property** vermögender Mann; **he used to be something of a ~ about town** (*Brit*) er hatte früher ein reges gesellschaftliches Leben; **a ~ of the world** ein Mann *m* von Welt; **to be ~ enough** Manns genug sein; **~'s bicycle/jacket** Herrenfahrrad *nt*/-jacke *f*; **the right/ wrong ~** der Richtige/Falsche; **you've come to the right ~** da sind Sie bei mir richtig; **he's not the ~ for the job** er ist nicht der Richtige für diese Aufgabe; **he's not a ~ to ...** er ist nicht der Typ, der ...; **he's not a ~ to meddle with** mit ihm ist nicht gut Kirschen essen; **he is a Cambridge ~** er hat in Cambridge studiert; **he's a family ~** er ist sehr häuslich; **it's got to be a local ~** es muss jemand aus dieser Gegend sein; **I'm not a drinking ~** ich bin kein großer Trinker; **you can't do that, ~** (*inf*) Mann, das kannst du doch nicht machen! (*inf*); **she has a ~ to do the garden** sie hat jemanden, der den Garten macht; **follow me, men!** mir nach, Leute!

(b) (= *human race: also* **Man**) der Mensch, die Menschen **(c)** (= *person*) man; **no ~** niemand; **any ~** jeder; **any ~ who believes that ...** wer das glaubt, ...; **that ~!** dieser Mensch!; **the strong ~ of the government** der starke Mann (in) der Regierung; **they are communists to a ~** sie sind allesamt Kommunisten

(d) (*Chess*) Figur *f*; (*in draughts*) Stein *m*

2 VT *ship* bemannen; *fortress, barricades, checkpoint* besetzen; *power station, pump, gun, telephone etc* bedienen; **the ship is ~ned by a crew of 30** das Schiff hat 30 Mann Besatzung

manacle ['mænəkl] **1** N USU PL Ketten *pl* **2** VT *person* in Ketten legen; *hands* fesseln; **he was ~d to the wall** er war an die Wand gekettet

manage ['mænɪdʒ] **1** VT **(a)** *company, organization, economy* leiten; *property* verwalten; *affairs* regeln; *time, money, resources* einteilen; *football team, pop group* managen **(b)** (= *handle, control*) *person, animal* zurechtkommen mit; **I can ~ him** mit dem werde ich schon fertig **(c)** *task* bewältigen; **£50/two hours is the most I can ~** ich kann mir höchstens £ 50 leisten/zwei Stunden erlauben; **I'll ~ it** das werde ich schon schaffen; **he ~d it very well** er hat das sehr gut gemacht; **can you ~ the cases?** kannst du die Koffer (allein) tragen?; **thanks, I can ~ them** danke, das geht schon; **she can't ~ the stairs** sie schafft die Treppe nicht; **can you ~ two more in the car?** kriegst du noch zwei Leute in dein Auto? (*inf*); **can you ~ 8 o'clock?** 8 Uhr, ginge *or* geht das?; **can you ~ another cup?** darfs noch eine Tasse sein?; **I think I could ~ another piece of cake** ich glaube, ich könnte noch ein Stück Kuchen vertragen; **she ~d a weak smile** sie brachte ein schwaches Lächeln über sich (*acc*); **to ~ to do sth** es schaffen, etw zu tun; **we have ~d to reduce our costs** es ist uns gelungen, die Kosten zu senken; **do you think you'll ~ to do it?** meinen Sie, Sie schaffen das?; **he ~d to control himself** es gelang ihm, sich zu beherrschen; **how could you possibly ~ to do that?** wie hast du denn das fertig gebracht?

2 VI zurechtkommen; **can you ~?** geht es?; **thanks, I can ~** danke, es geht schon; **how do you ~?** wie schaffen Sie das bloß?; **to ~ without sth** ohne etw auskommen; **we'll just have to ~ without** wir müssen wir eben so auskommen; **I can ~ by myself** ich komme (schon) allein zurecht; **how do you ~ on £100 a week?** wie kommen Sie mit £100 pro Woche aus?

manageable ['mænɪdʒəbl] ADJ *amount, task* zu bewältigen; *hair* leicht frisierbar; *number, proportions* überschaubar; **the situation is ~** die Situation lässt sich in den Griff bekommen; **to keep sth to a ~ level** etw im überschaubaren Rahmen halten; **pieces of a more ~ size** Stücke, die leichter zu handhaben sind

managed fund ['mænɪdʒd'fʌnd] N Investmentfonds *m* (*mit gelegentlicher Umschichtung des Aktienbestandes*)

management ['mænɪdʒmənt] N **(a)** (= *act*) Leitung *f*; (*of estate, assets, money*) Verwaltung *f*; (*of affairs*) Regelung *f*; **crisis/ time/people ~** Krisen-/Zeit-/Personalmanagement *nt*; **~ by objectives** zielgesteuerte Unternehmensführung **(b)** (= *persons*) Unternehmensleitung *f*; (*of single unit or smaller factory*) Betriebsleitung *f*; (*non-commercial*) Leitung *f*; (*Theat*) Intendanz *f*; **"under new ~"** „neuer Inhaber"; (*shop*) „neu eröffnet"

management: management buyout N *Aufkauf eines Unternehmens durch Mitglieder der Geschäftsleitung,* Management-Buy-out *nt*; **management consultancy** N Unternehmensberatung *f*; **management consultant** N Unternehmensberater(in) *m(f)*; **management course** N Managerkurs *m*; **management fee** N Verwaltungsgebühr *f*; **management skills** PL Führungsqualitäten *pl*; **management studies** N Betriebswirtschaft *f*

manager ['mænɪdʒər] N (*Comm etc*) Geschäftsführer(in) *m(f)*; (*of smaller firm or factory*) Betriebsleiter(in) *m(f)*; (*of bank, chain store*) Filialleiter(in) *m(f)*; (*of department*) Abteilungsleiter(in) *m(f)*; (*of estate etc*) Verwalter(in) *m(f)*; (*Theat*) Intendant(in) *m(f)*; (*of hotel*) Direktor(in) *m(f)*; (*of pop group, boxer etc*) Manager(in) *m(f)*; (*of team*) Trainer(in) *m(f)*; **sales ~** Verkaufsleiter(in) *m(f)*; **business ~** (*for theatre*) Verwaltungsdirektor(in) *m(f)*; (*of pop star etc*) Manager(in) *m(f)*

manageress [,mænɪdʒə'res] N (*Comm etc*) Geschäftsführerin *f*; (*of restaurant*) Geschäftsführerin *f*; (*of chain store*) Filialleiterin *f*; (*of hotel*) Direktorin *f*

managerial [,mænə'dʒɪərɪəl] ADJ geschäftlich; (= *executive*) Management-; *post, staff* leitend; **at ~ level** auf der Führungsebene; **proven ~ skills** nachgewiesene Leitungsfähigkeit *f*; **~ responsibilities** Führungsaufgaben *pl*; **~ style** Führungsstil *m*

managing director ['mænɪdʒɪŋdɪ'rektər] N Geschäftsführer(in) *m(f)*

mandarin ['mændərɪn] N **(a)** (= *official*) hoher Funktionär **(b)** (*Ling*) **Mandarin** Hochchinesisch *nt* **(c)** (= *fruit*) Mandarine *f*

mandate ['mændeɪt] N Auftrag *m*; (*Pol*) Mandat *nt*; **to give sb a ~ to do sth** jdn damit beauftragen, etw zu tun; **we have a clear ~ from the country to ...** wir haben den eindeutigen Wählerauftrag, zu ...

mandatory ['mændətərɪ] ADJ **(a)** obligatorisch; **~ retirement age** vorgeschriebenes Rentenalter; **union membership is ~** Mitgliedschaft in der Gewerkschaft ist Pflicht **(b)** (*Jur*) *sentence etc* vorgeschrieben; **murder carries a ~ death sentence** bei Mord ist die Todesstrafe vorgeschrieben

mandolin(e) ['mændəlɪn] N Mandoline *f*

mane [meɪn] N (*lit, fig*) Mähne *f*

man-eating ['mænˌiːtɪŋ] ADJ Menschen fressend; **~ shark** Menschenhai *m*

maneuver N, VTI (*US*) = **manoeuvre**

manfully ['mænfəlɪ] ADV mutig

manger ['meɪndʒər] N Krippe *f*

mangetout ['mɑ̃ːʒ'tuː] N (*Brit: also* **~ pea**) Zuckererbse *f*

mangle[1] ['mæŋgl] N Mangel *f*

mangle[2] VT (*also* **~ up**) (übel) zurichten

mango ['mæŋgəʊ] N (= *fruit*) Mango *f*; (= *tree*) Mangobaum *m*

mangy ['meɪndʒɪ] ADJ (+ER) *dog* räudig

manhandle ['mænhændl] VT **(a)** *person* grob behandeln; **he was ~d into the back of the van** er wurde recht unsanft in den Laderaum des Wagens verfrachtet **(b)** *piano etc* hieven

manhole ['mænhəʊl] N Kanalschacht *m*

manhood ['mænhʊd] N **(a)** (= *state*) Mannesalter *nt* **(b)** (= *manliness*) Männlichkeit *f* **(c)** (= *men*) Männer *pl*; **a fine example of American ~** ein gutes Beispiel für den amerikanischen Mann

man: man-hour N Arbeitsstunde *f*; **manhunt** N Fahndung *f*

mania ['meɪnɪə] N Manie *f also inf persecution ~** Verfolgungswahn *m*; **this ~ for nationalization** diese Verstaatlichungsmanie; **he has a ~ for collecting things** er hat einen Sammeltick (*inf*)

maniac ['meɪnɪæk] **1** ADJ wahnsinnig **2** N **(a)** Wahnsinnige(r) *mf* **(b)** (*fig*) **these sports ~s** diese Sportfanatiker *pl*; **you ~** du bist ja wahnsinnig!

maniacal [mə'naɪəkəl] ADJ wahnsinnig

manic ['mænɪk] ADJ **(a)** *activity, excitement* fieberhaft; *energy, person, jealousy* rasend; *grin, laughter, sense of humour* irre **(b)** (*Psych*) manisch

manic-depressive ['mænɪkdɪ'presɪv] **1** ADJ manisch-depressiv **2** N Manisch-Depressive(r) *mf*; **he is a ~** er ist manisch-depressiv

manicure ['mænɪˌkjʊər] **1** N Maniküre *f*; **to have a ~** sich (*dat*) (die Hände) maniküren lassen **2** VT maniküren

manicured ['mænɪkjʊəd] ADJ *nails, hands* manikürt; *lawn, garden* gepflegt

manicure set N Nagelnecessaire *nt*

manicurist ['mænɪˌkjʊərɪst] N Handpflegerin *f*

manifest ['mænɪfest] **1** ADJ offenbar; (= *definite*) eindeutig; **to make sth ~** etw deutlich machen **2** VT bekunden **3** VR sich zeigen; (Sci, Psych etc) sich manifestieren; (guilt etc) sich offenbaren

manifestation [ˌmænɪfeˈsteɪʃən] N Anzeichen nt

manifestly [ˈmænɪfestlɪ] ADV offensichtlich; **the policy ~ failed to work** die Politik funktionierte offenkundig nicht

manifesto [ˌmænɪˈfestəʊ] N, pl **-(e)s** Manifest nt

manifold [ˈmænɪfəʊld] ADJ vielfältig; **there are ~ problems** es gibt vielfache Probleme

manila, manilla [məˈnɪlə] N (= ~ paper) Hartpapier nt; **~ envelopes** braune Umschläge

manipulate [məˈnɪpjʊleɪt] VT **(a)** manipulieren; **to ~ sb into doing sth** jdn so manipulieren, dass er/sie etw tut **(b)** machine etc handhaben; bones einrenken; (after fracture) zurechtrücken

manipulation [məˌnɪpjʊˈleɪʃən] N Manipulation f

manipulative [məˈnɪpjʊlətɪv] ADJ (pej) behaviour, skill manipulativ; film, article, speech manipulierend; **he was very ~** er konnte andere sehr gut manipulieren

manipulator [məˈnɪpjʊleɪtəʳ] N Manipulator(in) m(f)

mankind [mænˈkaɪnd] N die Menschheit

manly [ˈmænlɪ] ADJ (+ER) männlich

man-made [ˈmænˈmeɪd] ADJ **(a)** (= artificial) künstlich; **~ fibres** (Brit) or **fibers** (US) Kunstfasern pl **(b)** disaster, pollution vom Menschen verursacht; world, environment, laws vom Menschen geschaffen

manned [mænd] ADJ satellite etc bemannt

manner [ˈmænəʳ] N **(a)** Art f; **in** or **after this ~** auf diese Art und Weise; **in the Spanish ~** im spanischen Stil; **in such a ~ that ...** so ..., dass ...; **in a ~ of speaking** sozusagen; **he has a very kind ~** er hat ein sehr freundliches Wesen; **all ~ of birds** die verschiedensten Arten von Vögeln; **we saw all ~ of interesting things** wir sahen so manches Interessante **(b) manners** PL (good, bad etc) Benehmen nt; (of society) Sitten (und Gebräuche) pl; **a comedy of ~s** eine Sittenkomödie; **~s!** benimm dich!; **it's bad ~s to ...** es gehört sich nicht, zu ...; **he has no ~s** er kann sich nicht benehmen

mannered [ˈmænəd] ADJ style, work of art, gestures manieriert; friendliness, subservience etc betont

mannerism [ˈmænərɪzəm] N **(a)** (in behaviour, speech) Eigenheit f **(b)** (of style) Manieriertheit f; **his ~s** seine Manierismen

mannish [ˈmænɪʃ] ADJ männlich wirkend

manoeuvrable, (US) **maneuverable** [məˈnuːvrəbl] ADJ manövrierfähig; **easily ~** leicht zu manövrieren

manoeuvre, (US) **maneuver** [məˈnuːvəʳ] ■ N **(a)** (Mil) Feldzug m
(b) manoeuvres PL (Mil) Manöver nt or pl, Truppenübung f; **the troops were out on ~s** die Truppen befanden sich im Manöver
(c) (= clever plan) Manöver nt
■ VTI manövrieren; **to ~ a gun into position** ein Geschütz in Stellung bringen; **to ~ sb into doing sth** jdn dazu bringen, etw zu tun; **to ~ for position** (lit, fig) sich in eine günstige Position manövrieren; **room to ~** Spielraum m

manor [ˈmænəʳ] N (Land)gut nt; **lord/lady of the ~** Gutsherr m/-herrin f

manor house N Herrenhaus nt

manpower [ˈmænˌpaʊəʳ] N Leistungspotential nt; (Mil) Stärke f; **we haven't got the ~** wir haben dazu nicht genügend Personal

manservant [ˈmænsɜːvənt] N, pl **menservants** [ˈmensɜːvənts] Diener m

mansion [ˈmænʃən] N Villa f; (of ancient family) Herrenhaus nt

manslaughter [ˈmænslɔːtəʳ] N Totschlag m

mantelpiece [ˈmæntlpiːs] N (above fireplace) Kaminsims nt or m; (around fireplace) Kaminverkleidung f

man-to-man [ˌmæntəˈmæn] ADJ, ADV von Mann zu Mann; **a ~ talk** ein Gespräch nt von Mann zu Mann

manual [ˈmænjʊəl] ■ ADJ manuell; labour körperlich; **~ work** manuelle Arbeit; **~ labourer** (Brit) or **laborer** (US) Schwerarbeiter(in) m(f); **~ worker** Handarbeiter(in) m(f); **~ gear change** or **shift** (US) Schaltung f von Hand; **~ operation** Handbetrieb m ■ N (= book) Handbuch nt

manual gearbox [ˈmænjʊəlˈɡɪəbɒks] N (Brit) Schaltgetriebe nt

manually [ˈmænjʊəlɪ] ADV manuell; **~ operated** handbetrieben

manual transmission N Schaltgetriebe nt

manufacture [ˌmænjʊˈfæktʃəʳ] ■ N Herstellung f ■ VT **(a)** (lit) herstellen; **~d goods** Industriewaren pl, Industriegüter pl **(b)** (fig) excuse erfinden

manufacturer [ˌmænjʊˈfæktʃərəʳ] N (= person) Hersteller(in) m(f); (= company) Hersteller m

manufacturing [ˌmænjʊˈfæktʃərɪŋ] ■ ADJ Herstellungs-; industry verarbeitend; **~ company** Herstellerfirma f; **~ town/city** Industriestadt f; **~ output** Produktionsmenge f; **the ~ sector** das verarbeitende Gewerbe ■ N Herstellung f

manure [məˈnjʊəʳ] N Dung m, Mist m; (esp artificial) Dünger m; **liquid ~** Jauche f

manuscript [ˈmænjʊskrɪpt] N Manuskript nt; **the novel is still in ~** der Roman ist noch in Manuskriptform

Manx [mæŋks] ADJ der Insel Man

many [ˈmenɪ] ■ ADJ, PRON viele; **~ people** viele (Menschen); **she has ~** sie hat viele (davon); **there were as ~ as 20** es waren sogar 20 da; **fifty went to France and as ~ to Germany** fünfzig gingen nach Frankreich und ebenso viele nach Deutschland; **as ~ again** noch einmal so viele; **there's one too ~** einer ist zu viel; **he's had one too ~** (inf) er hat einen zu viel getrunken (inf); **a good/great ~ houses** eine (ganze) Anzahl Häuser; **~ a good soldier** so mancher gute Soldat; **~ a time** so manches Mal; **~'s the time I've heard that old story** ich habe diese alte Geschichte so manches Mal gehört ■ N **the ~** die (große) Masse

many: many-coloured, (US) **many-colored** ADJ vielfarbig; **many-sided** ADJ vielseitig; **it's a ~ problem** das Problem hat sehr viele verschiedene Aspekte

Maori [ˈmaʊrɪ] ■ ADJ Maori-; **~ chief** Maorihäuptling m ■ N Maori mf

map [mæp] ■ N (Land)karte f; (of streets, town) Stadtplan m; (showing specific item) Karte f; **this will put Cheam on the ~** (fig) das wird Cheam zu einem Namen verhelfen; **entire cities were wiped off the ~** ganze Städte wurden ausradiert ■ VT eine Karte anfertigen von

> Be careful! **map** is not translated by the German word **Mappe**.

➤ **map out** VT SEP **(a)** (lit) = **map 2 (b)** (fig: = plan) entwerfen; **the conference schedule was all mapped out in advance** der Zeitplan für die Konferenz war schon im Voraus genau festgelegt

maple [ˈmeɪpl] N (= wood, tree) Ahorn m

maple: maple leaf N Ahornblatt nt; **maple syrup** N Ahornsirup m

Mar ABBR of **March** Mrz.

mar [maːʳ] VT verderben; happiness trüben; beauty mindern; **his essay was ~red by careless mistakes** durch seine Flüchtigkeitsfehler verdarb er (sich) den ganzen Aufsatz

marathon [ˈmærəθən] ■ N (lit) Marathon(lauf) m; **~ runner** Marathonläufer(in) m(f) ■ ADJ Marathon-; negotiations endlos (lang)

marauder [məˈrɔːdəʳ] N Plünderer m, Plünderin f

marauding [məˈrɔːdɪŋ] ADJ plündernd

marble [ˈmaːbl] ■ N **(a)** Marmor m **(b)** (= work in ~) Marmorplastik f **(c)** (= glass ball) Murmel f; **he's lost his ~s** (inf) er hat nicht mehr alle Tassen im Schrank (inf) ■ ADJ Marmor-; **~ pillar** Marmorsäule f

marbled [ˈmaːbld] ADJ marmoriert; **~ effect/finish** Marmoreffekt m

March [maːtʃ] N März m; see also **September**

march [maːtʃ] ■ N **(a)** (Mil, Mus) Marsch m; (= demonstration) Demonstration f; (fig: = long walk) Weg m; **it's two days' ~** es ist ein Zwei-Tage-Marsch **(b)** (of time, history, events) Lauf m **(c) to steal a ~ on sb** jdm zuvorkommen ■ VTI marschieren; **to ~ sb off** jdn abführen; **forward ~!** vorwärts(, marsch)!; **quick ~!** im Laufschritt, marsch!; **she ~ed straight up to him** sie marschierte schnurstracks auf ihn zu

marcher [ˈmaːtʃəʳ] N (in demo) Demonstrant(in) m(f)

marching orders [ˈmaːtʃɪŋɔːdəz] PL (Brit) **the new manager got his ~** der neue Manager ist gegangen worden (inf); **she gave him his ~** sie hat ihm den Laufpass gegeben

marchioness [ˈmaːʃənɪs] N Marquise f

Mardi Gras [ˈmaːdɪˈɡraː] N Karneval m

mare [mɛəʳ] N Stute f

margarine [ˌmɑːdʒəˈriːn], **marge** [mɑːdʒ] *(inf)* N Margarine *f*

margin [ˈmɑːdʒɪn] N **(a)** *(on page)* Rand *m*; **a note (written) in the ~** eine Randbemerkung **(b)** *(= extra amount)* Spielraum *m*; **to allow for a ~ of error** etwaige Fehler mit einkalkulieren; **by a narrow ~** knapp; **it's within the safety ~** das ist noch sicher **(c)** *(Comm: also* **profit ~)** Gewinnspanne *f*

marginal [ˈmɑːdʒɪnl] ADJ **(a)** *improvement, difference* geringfügig, unwesentlich; *issue* nebensächlich; **~ figure** Randfigur *f*
(b) *(Sociol) people, groups* randständig
(c) *(Brit Parl) constituency, seat* mit knapper Mehrheit; **~ case** Grenzfall *m*
(d) *business* kaum rentabel; *land* ertragsarm; **~ cost** Grenzkosten *pl*; **~ costing** Teilkostenrechnung *f*; **~ utility** *(Econ)* Grenznutzen *m*
(e) **~ note** Randbemerkung *f*

marginalize [ˈmɑːdʒɪnəlaɪz] VT marginalisieren *(geh)*

marginally [ˈmɑːdʒɪnəlɪ] ADV geringfügig; *higher, faster etc* etwas; **is that better? – ~** ist das besser? – etwas *or* ein wenig

marigold [ˈmærɪɡəʊld] N Tagetes *f*

marihuana, marijuana [ˌmærɪˈhwɑːnə] N Marihuana *nt*

marina [məˈriːnə] N Jachthafen *m*

marinade [ˌmærɪˈneɪd] N Marinade *f*

marinate [ˈmærɪneɪt] VT marinieren

marine [məˈriːn] **1** ADJ Meeres-; **~ life** Meeresfauna und -flora *f* **2** N Marineinfanterist(in) *m(f)*; **the ~s** die Marinetruppen *pl*

marine biologist N Meeresbiologe *m*, Meeresbiologin *f*

mariner [ˈmærɪnəʳ] N Seemann *m*

marital [ˈmærɪtl] ADJ ehelich

marital: **marital status** N Familienstand *m*; **marital vows** PL Ehegelübde *nt*

maritime [ˈmærɪtaɪm] ADJ See-; **~ warfare** Seekrieg *m*; **~ regions** Küstenregionen *pl*; **~ museum** Schifffahrtsmuseum *nt*

maritime: **maritime law** N Seerecht *nt*; **maritime power** N Seemacht *f*

marjoram [ˈmɑːdʒərəm] N Majoran *m*

mark¹ [mɑːk] N *(Hist: = currency)* Mark *f*

mark² **1** N **(a)** *(= stain, spot etc)* Fleck *m*; *(= scratch)* Kratzer *m*; *(= marking: on person)* Mal *nt*; *(on plane, football pitch etc)* Markierung *f*; *(= sign: on monument etc)* Zeichen *nt*; **to make a ~ on sth** einen Fleck/Kratzer auf etw *(acc)* machen; **dirty ~s** Schmutzflecken *pl*; **with not a ~ on it** in makellosem Zustand; **the corpse didn't have a ~ on it** die Leiche wies keine Verletzungen auf
(b) *(in exam)* Note *f*; **high** *or* **good ~s** gute Noten *pl*; **there are no ~s for guessing** *(fig)* das ist ja wohl nicht schwer zu erraten; **he gets full ~s for punctuality** *(fig)* in Pünktlichkeit verdient er eine Eins
(c) *(= sign, indication)* Zeichen *nt*; **it bears the ~s of genius** das trägt geniale Züge; **to make one's ~** *(instead of signature)* drei Kreuze (als Unterschrift) machen
(d) *(= level)* **expenses have reached the £100 ~** die Ausgaben haben die 100-Pfund-Grenze erreicht; **the temperature reached the ~ of 35°** die Temperatur stieg bis auf 35° an
(e) **Cooper Mark II** Cooper, II
(f) **to be quick off the ~** *(Sport)* einen guten Start haben; *(fig)* blitzschnell handeln; **to be slow off the ~** *(Sport)* einen schlechten Start haben; *(fig)* nicht schnell genug reagieren; *(as characteristic)* eine lange Leitung haben *(inf)*; **to be up to the ~** den Anforderungen entsprechen; **to leave one's ~ (on sth)** seine Spuren (an etw *dat*) hinterlassen; **to make one's ~** sich *(dat)* einen Namen machen; **on your ~s!** auf die Plätze!; **to be wide of the ~** *(shooting)* danebentreffen; *(fig: in guessing, calculating)* danebentippen; **to hit the ~** *(lit, fig)* ins Schwarze treffen
2 VT **(a)** *(adversely)* beschädigen; *(= stain)* schmutzig machen; *(= scratch)* zerkratzen; **the experience ~ed him for life** das Erlebnis hat ihn für sein Leben gezeichnet
(b) *(for recognition, identity)* markieren; *(= label)* beschriften; **the bottle was ~ed "poison"** die Flasche trug die Aufschrift „Gift"; **the chair is ~ed at £30** der Stuhl ist mit £30 ausgezeichnet; **~ where you have stopped in your reading** mach dir ein Zeichen, bis wohin du gelesen hast; **to ~ sth with an asterisk** etw mit einem Sternchen versehen; **the teacher ~ed him absent** der Lehrer trug ihn als fehlend ein;

it's not ~ed on the map es ist nicht auf der Karte eingezeichnet; **it's ~ed with a blue dot** es ist mit einem blauen Punkt gekennzeichnet
(c) *(= characterize)* kennzeichnen; **a decade ~ed by violence** ein Jahrzehnt, das im Zeichen der Gewalt stand; **the new bill ~s a change of policy** das neue Gesetz deutet auf einen politischen Kurswechsel hin; **it ~ed the end of an era** damit ging eine Ära zu Ende
(d) *exam, paper* korrigieren (und benoten); **to ~ a candidate** einem Kandidaten eine Note geben; **to ~ sth wrong** etw anstreichen
(e) *(= heed)* hören auf *(+acc)*; **~ my words** das kann ich dir sagen; **~ you, he may have been right** er könnte gar nicht so Unrecht gehabt haben
(f) *(Sport) player, opponent* decken
(g) **to ~ time** *(Mil, fig)* auf der Stelle treten

➤ **mark down** VT SEP *prices* heruntersetzen

➤ **mark off** VT SEP kennzeichnen; *boundary* markieren; *football pitch etc* abgrenzen; *danger area etc* absperren; **these characteristics mark him off from the others** durch diese Eigenschaften unterscheidet er sich von den anderen

➤ **mark out** VT SEP **(a)** *tennis court etc* abstecken **(b)** *(= note)* bestimmen *(for* für); **he's been marked out for promotion** er ist zur Beförderung vorgesehen *(für)*; **his speeches have marked him out as a communist** aus seinen Reden kann man schließen, dass er Kommunist ist

➤ **mark up** VT SEP *price* erhöhen

marked [mɑːkt] ADJ **(a)** *contrast, accent* deutlich; *improvement* spürbar; **in ~ contrast (to sb/sth)** in scharfem Gegensatz (zu jdm/etw) **(b)** **he's a ~ man** er steht auf der schwarzen Liste **(c)** *path, trail* ausgezeichnet

markedly [ˈmɑːkɪdlɪ] ADV *improve, increase, differ, change* merklich; *quicker, slower, more, less* wesentlich

marker [ˈmɑːkəʳ] N **(a)** Marke *f*; *(to turn at)* Wendemarke *f*; *(on road)* Wegweiser *m*; *(in book)* Lesezeichen *nt* **(b)** *(= indication)* **a ~ for sth** eine Kennzeichnung für etw **(c)** *(for exams)* Korrektor(in) *m(f)* **(d)** *(Ftbl)* Beschatter(in) *m(f)* **(e)** *(= pen)* Markierstift *m*

market [ˈmɑːkɪt] **1** N **(a)** Markt *m*; *(= area of demand)* Absatzmarkt *m*; **when is the next ~?** wann ist wieder Markt(tag)?; **at the ~** auf dem Markt; **to go to ~** auf den Markt gehen; **world ~** Weltmarkt *m*; **to be in the ~ for sth** an etw *(dat)* interessiert sein; **to be on the ~** auf dem Markt sein; **to come on(to) the ~** auf den Markt kommen; **to put on the ~** auf den Markt bringen; *house* zum Verkauf anbieten; **to create a ~** Nachfrage erzeugen
(b) *(= stock ~)* Börse *f*; **to play the ~** (an der Börse) spekulieren; **at ~** bestens, billigst
2 VT vertreiben; **to ~ a (new) product** ein (neues) Produkt auf den Markt bringen; **it's a nice idea, but we can't ~ it** das ist eine gute Idee, sie lässt sich nur nicht vermarkten

marketability [ˌmɑːkɪtəˈbɪlɪtɪ] N Marktfähigkeit *f*

marketable [ˈmɑːkɪtəbl] ADJ marktfähig; *(fig) actor, sportsperson* vermarktbar

market: **market conditions** PL Marktbedingungen *pl*; **market-driven, market-led** ADJ marktbestimmt; **market forces** PL Marktkräfte *pl*; **market garden** N Gemüseanbaubetrieb *m*; **market gardener** N Gärtner(in) *m(f)*; **market gardening** N Anbau *m* von Gemüse

marketing [ˈmɑːkɪtɪŋ] N Marketing *nt*; **~ co-operative** Vermarktungsgenossenschaft *f*; **~ department** Marketingabteilung *f*; **~ manager** Marketingmanager(in) *m(f)*

market: **market leader** N Marktführer *m*; **market maker** N *(St Ex)* marktbestimmender Börsenteilnehmer; **market-oriented** ADJ marktorientiert; **marketplace** N **(a)** Marktplatz *m* **(b)** *(= world of trade)* Markt *m*; **in the ~** auf dem Markt; **market price** N Marktpreis *m*; **at ~** zu Marktpreisen; **market research** N Marktforschung *f*; **market share** N Marktanteil *m*; **market town** N Marktstädtchen *nt*; **market trader** N *(Brit)* Markthändler(in) *m(f)*; **market value** N Marktwert *m*

marking [ˈmɑːkɪŋ] N **(a)** Markierung *f*; *(on animal)* Zeichnung *f* **(b)** *(of exams)* *(= correcting)* Korrektur *f*; *(= grading)* Benotung *f* **(c)** *(Sport)* Deckung *f*

marksman [ˈmɑːksmən] N, *pl* **-men** [-mən] Schütze *m*; *(police etc)* Scharfschütze *m*

mark-up ['mɑːkʌp] N Handelsspanne f; (= amount added) Preisaufschlag m; ~ **price** Verkaufspreis m

marmalade ['mɑːməleɪd] N Marmelade f aus Zitrusfrüchten; **(orange)** ~ Orangenmarmelade f

maroon[1] [mə'ruːn] **1** ADJ kastanienbraun **2** N Kastanienbraun nt

maroon[2] VT ~**ed** von der Außenwelt abgeschnitten; ~**ed by floods** vom Hochwasser eingeschlossen

marque [mɑːk] N (= brand) Marke f

marquee [mɑːˈkiː] N **(a)** Festzelt nt **(b)** (US: of theatre etc) Vordach nt, Canopy m

marquess, marquis ['mɑːkwɪs] N Marquis m

marriage ['mærɪdʒ] N **(a)** (state) die Ehe; (= wedding) Hochzeit f; (= ~ ceremony) Trauung f; ~ **of convenience** Vernunftehe f; **to be related by** ~ (in-laws) miteinander verschwägert sein; (others) miteinander verwandt sein; **an offer of** ~ ein Heiratsantrag m **(b)** (fig) Verbindung f; **a** ~ **of two minds** eine geistige Ehe

marriage: **marriage ceremony** N Trauzeremonie f; **marriage certificate** N Heiratsurkunde f; **marriage guidance** N Eheberatung f; **marriage guidance counsellor**, (US) **marriage guidance counselor** N Eheberater(in) m(f); **marriage licence**, (US) **marriage license** N Eheerlaubnis f; **marriage vow** N Ehegelübde nt

married ['mærɪd] ADJ verheiratet (to sb mit jdm); **just** or **newly** ~ **couple** Ehepaar nt; ~ **couple's allowance** Steuerfreibetrag m für Verheiratete; ~ **life** das Eheleben; **he/ she is a** ~ **man/woman** er/sie ist verheiratet

married name N Ehename m

marrow ['mærəʊ] N **(a)** (Anat) (Knochen)mark nt; **to be frozen to the** ~ völlig durchgefroren sein **(b)** (Brit Bot: also **vegetable** ~) Gartenkürbis m

marrowbone ['mærəʊbəʊn] N Markknochen m

marry ['mærɪ] **1** VT **(a)** (= get married to) heiraten; **will you** ~ **me?** willst du mich heiraten? **(b)** (priest) trauen **(c)** (father) verheiraten; **he married all his daughters into very rich families** er hat zugesehen, dass alle seine Töchter in reiche Familien einheirateten **2** VI (also **get married**) heiraten; **to** ~ **into a rich family** in eine reiche Familie einheiraten

➤ **marry off** VT SEP an den Mann/die Frau bringen (inf); **he has married off his daughter to a rich young lawyer** er hat dafür gesorgt, dass seine Tochter einen reichen jungen Anwalt heiratet

Mars [mɑːz] N Mars m

marsh [mɑːʃ] N Sumpf m

marshal ['mɑːʃəl] **1** N (at sports meeting etc) Platzwärter(in) m(f); (at demo etc) Ordner(in) m(f); (US) Bezirkspolizeichef(in) m(f) **2** VT facts, arguments ordnen; (= lead) geleiten, führen

marsh: **marshland** N Marschland nt; **marshmallow** N (= sweet) Marshmallow nt

marshy ['mɑːʃɪ] ADJ (+ER) sumpfig

marsupial [mɑːˈsuːpɪəl] N Beuteltier nt

martial ['mɑːʃəl] ADJ music kriegerisch; bearing soldatisch

martial: **martial art** N the ~**s** die Kampfkunst; **martial law** N Kriegsrecht nt

Martian ['mɑːʃən] N Marsmensch m

martini [mɑːˈtiːnɪ] N Martini m

martyr ['mɑːtə'] **1** N Märtyrer(in) m(f); **he was a** ~ **to the cause of civil rights** er wurde zum Märtyrer für die Sache der Bürgerrechtsbewegung; **to be a** ~ **to arthritis** entsetzlich unter Arthritis zu leiden haben **2** VT **thousands of Christians were** ~**ed** tausende von Christen starben den Märtyrertod

martyrdom ['mɑːtədəm] N (= suffering) Martyrium nt; (= death) Märtyrertod m

marvel ['mɑːvəl] **1** N Wunder nt; **the** ~**s of modern science** die Wunder der modernen Wissenschaft; **it's a** ~ **to me how he does it** (inf) es ist mir einfach unerklärlich, wie er das macht **2** VI staunen (at über +acc)

marvellous, (US) **marvelous** ['mɑːvələs] ADJ wunderbar; **isn't it** ~? ist das nicht herrlich?; (iro) gut, nicht! (iro); **they've done a** ~ **job** das haben sie hervorragend gemacht

marvellously, (US) **marvelously** ['mɑːvələslɪ] ADV (with adj) herrlich; (with vb) großartig

Marxism ['mɑːksɪzəm] N der Marxismus

Marxist ['mɑːksɪst] **1** ADJ marxistisch **2** N Marxist(in) m(f)

marzipan [ˌmɑːzɪˈpæn] N Marzipan nt or m

mascara [mæˈskɑːrə] N Wimperntusche f

mascot ['mæskət] N Maskottchen nt

masculine ['mæskjʊlɪn] **1** ADJ männlich; woman, decor maskulin; (Gram) maskulin, männlich **2** N (Gram) Maskulinum nt

masculinity [ˌmæskjʊˈlɪnɪtɪ] N Männlichkeit f

mash [mæʃ] **1** N Brei m; (for animals) Futterbrei m; (= potatoes) Püree nt **2** VT zerstampfen

mashed [mæʃt] ADJ ~ **potatoes** Kartoffelbrei m

masher ['mæʃə'] N (for potatoes) Kartoffelstampfer m

mask [mɑːsk] **1** N (lit, fig, Comput) Maske f; **surgeon's** ~ Mundschutz m **2** VT maskieren; (clouds, trees etc) verdecken; feelings verbergen

masked [mɑːskt] ADJ maskiert

masked ball N Maskenball m

masochism ['mæsəʊkɪzəm] N Masochismus m

masochist ['mæsəʊkɪst] N Masochist(in) m(f)

masochistic [ˌmæsəʊˈkɪstɪk] ADJ masochistisch

mason ['meɪsn] N **(a)** Steinmetz(in) m(f) **(b)** (= freemason) Freimaurer m

masonic [məˈsɒnɪk] ADJ Freimaurer-; ~ **lodge/order** Freimaurerloge f/-orden m

masonry ['meɪsnrɪ] N Mauerwerk nt

masquerade [ˌmæskəˈreɪd] **1** N Maskerade f; **that's just a** ~ (fig) das ist alles nur Theater **2** VI **to** ~ **as ...** (fig) sich ausgeben als ...; **this cheap trash masquerading as literature** dieser Schund, der als Literatur ausgegeben wird

mass[1] [mæs] N (Eccl) Messe f; **to go to** ~ zur Messe gehen

mass[2] **1** N **(a)** (general, Phys) Masse f; (of people) Menge f; **a** ~ **of snow** eine Schneemasse; **a** ~ **of rubble** ein Schutthaufen m; **a** ~ **of red hair** ein Wust m roter Haare; **the** ~**es** die Masse(n pl); **the great** ~ **of the population** die (breite) Masse der Bevölkerung; **the great** ~ **of the mountains** das riesige Bergmassiv

(b) masses PL (inf) massenhaft, eine Masse (inf); **he has** ~**es of money/time** er hat massenhaft Geld/Zeit; **the factory is producing** ~**es of cars** die Fabrik produziert Unmengen von Autos; **I've got** ~**es (of things) to do** ich habe noch massig zu tun (inf) **2** VI (Mil) sich massieren; (demonstrators etc) sich versammeln; **they're** ~**ing for an attack** sie sammeln sich zum Angriff

massacre ['mæsəkə'] **1** N Massaker nt **2** VT massakrieren; **last Saturday they** ~**d us 6-0** (inf) letzten Samstag haben sie uns mit 6:0 fertig gemacht (inf)

massage ['mæsɑːʒ] **1** N Massage f **2** VT massieren

massage parlour, (US) **massage parlor** N Massagesalon m

mass destruction N **weapons of** ~ Massenvernichtungswaffen pl

massed [mæst] ADJ troops, tanks zusammengezogen; people dicht gedrängt; ~ **ranks** dicht gedrängte Reihen

masseur [mæˈsɜː'] N Masseur m

masseuse [mæˈsɜːz] N Masseuse f

mass: **mass grave** N Massengrab nt; **mass hysteria** N Massenhysterie f

massive ['mæsɪv] ADJ riesig; task gewaltig; attack, pressure, support, heart attack, structure massiv; boxer massig; **on a** ~ **scale** in riesigem Umfang

massively ['mæsɪvlɪ] ADV enorm

mass: **mass killing** N Massenmord m; **mass market** N Massenmarkt m; **mass media** PL Massenmedien pl; **mass meeting** N Massenveranstaltung f; (in company) Betriebsversammlung f; (of trade union) Vollversammlung f; (Pol) Massenkundgebung f; **mass murderer** N Massenmörder(in) m(f); **mass-produce** VT in Massenproduktion herstellen; cars, engines etc serienweise herstellen; **mass-produced** ADJ ~ **items** Massenartikel pl; **mass production** N Massenproduktion f; **mass protests** PL Massenproteste pl; **mass tourism** N Massentourismus m; **mass unemployment** N Massenarbeitslosigkeit f

mast [mɑːst] N (Naut) Mast(baum) m; (Rad etc) Sendeturm m

mastectomy [mæˈstektəmɪ] N Brustamputation f

master ['mɑːstə'] **1** N **(a)** (of the house, dog, servants) Herr m; **to be ~ in one's own house** (also fig) Herr im Hause sein; **to be one's own ~** sein eigener Herr sein; **to be ~ of sth** etw beherrschen; **to be ~ of the situation** Herr m der Lage sein **(b)** (Naut) Kapitän m; **~'s certificate** Kapitänspatent nt; **~'s copy** (of bill of lading) Kapitänskopie f **(c)** (= musician, painter etc) Meister(in) m(f) **(d)** (= teacher) Lehrer m; (of apprentice) Meister m **(e)** (= boy's title) Master m **(f)** (= ~ copy) Original nt **2** VT meistern; one's emotions unter Kontrolle bringen; technique, method beherrschen; **to ~ the violin** das Geigenspiel beherrschen

master IN CPDS (with trades) -meister(in) m(f); **master baker** N Bäckermeister(in) m(f); **master bedroom** N großes Schlafzimmer; **master copy** N Original nt; **master craftsman** N Handwerksmeister m; **master disk** N Hauptplatte f; **master file** N (Comput) Stammdatei f

masterful ['mɑːstəfʊl] ADJ meisterhaft; personality gebieterisch

master key N Generalschlüssel m

masterly ['mɑːstəlɪ] ADJ meisterhaft

master: mastermind 1 N (führender) Kopf **2** VT who ~ed the robbery? wer steckt hinter dem Raubüberfall?; **Master of Arts/Science** N ≈ Magister m (der philosophischen/ naturwissenschaftlichen Fakultät); **master of ceremonies** N (at function) Zeremonienmeister(in) m(f); (on stage) Conférencier m; (on TV) Showmaster(in) m(f); **masterpiece** N Meisterwerk nt; **master plan** N (overall) Gesamtplan m; (masterly) Meisterplan m; **masterstroke** N Meisterstück nt; **master tape** N Originalband nt; (Comput) Stammband nt; **masterwork** N Meisterwerk nt

mastery ['mɑːstərɪ] N (of language, technique, instrument etc) Beherrschung f; (= control) Können nt; (over competitors etc) Oberhand f; **the painter's ~ of form** des Malers meisterhafter Gebrauch von Form

masthead ['mɑːsthed] N (Press) Impressum nt

masturbate ['mæstəbeɪt] VI masturbieren

masturbation [ˌmæstə'beɪʃən] N Masturbation f

mat [mæt] N Matte f; (= door ~) Fußmatte f; (on table) Untersetzer m; (of cloth) Deckchen nt; **to go to the ~ for sb** (US) sich für jdn auf einen Streit einlassen; **to go to the ~ to do sth** (US) einen Streit riskieren, um etw zu tun

matador ['mætədɔː'] N Matador m

match¹ [mætʃ] N Streichholz nt

match² **1** N **(a) to be** or **make a good ~** gut zusammenpassen; **I want a ~ for this yellow paint** ich möchte Farbe in diesem Gelbton; **to be a/no ~ for sb** (= be able to compete with) sich mit jdm messen/nicht messen können; (= be able to handle) jdm gewachsen/nicht gewachsen sein; **to meet one's ~** seinen Meister finden **(b)** (= marriage) Heirat f; **she made a good ~** sie hat eine gute Partie gemacht **(c)** (Sport) (general) Wettkampf m; (= team game) Spiel nt; (Tennis) Match nt; (Boxing, Fencing) Kampf m; **athletics ~** Leichtathletikkampf m; **we must have another ~ some time** wir müssen wieder einmal gegeneinander spielen **2** VT **(a)** (= pair off) (einander) anpassen **(b)** (= equal) gleichkommen (+dat) (in an +dat); **nobody can ~ him in argument** niemand kann so gut argumentieren wie er; **a quality that has never been ~ed since** eine Qualität, die bislang unerreicht ist or noch ihresgleichen sucht (geh); **~ that if you can!** das soll erst mal einer nachmachen, das macht so leicht keiner nach! **(c)** (= correspond to) entsprechen (+dat) **(d)** (clothes, colours) passen zu; **to ~ textures and fabrics so that ...** Strukturen und Stoffe so aufeinander abstimmen, dass ... **(e)** (= pit) **to be ~ed against sb** gegen jdn antreten; **to ~ one's wits against sb** sich geistig mit jdm messen; **to ~ one's strength against sb** seine Kräfte mit jdm messen **3** VI zusammenpassen; **it doesn't ~** das passt nicht (zusammen); **with a skirt to ~** (dazu) passenden Rock

➤ **match up 1** VI zusammenpassen **2** VT SEP colours aufeinander abstimmen; **I matched the lampshade up with the wallpaper** ich fand den passenden Lampenschirm zu der Tapete

match: matchbook N (esp US) Streichholzheftchen nt; **matchbox** N Streichholzschachtel f

matched [mætʃt] ADJ pair, set zusammenpassend; **they're well ~** (couple) die beiden passen gut zusammen; **the two boxers were well ~** die beiden Boxer waren einander ebenbürtig

matching ['mætʃɪŋ] ADJ (dazu) passend; **they form a ~ pair** sie passen zusammen; **a ~ set of wine glasses** ein Satz m Weingläser

matchless ['mætʃlɪs] ADJ einzigartig, unvergleichlich

match: matchmaker N Ehestifter(in) m(f), Kuppler(in) m(f) (pej); **match point** N (Tennis) Matchball m; **matchstick** N Streichholz nt

mate¹ [meɪt] (Chess) **1** N Matt nt **2** VT matt setzen

mate² **1** N **(a)** (= fellow worker) Arbeitskollege m/-kollegin f; (= helper) Gehilfe m, Gehilfin f **(b)** (Naut) Maat m; **~'s receipt** (of bill of lading) Bordempfangsbescheinigung f **(c)** (of animal) (male) Männchen nt; (female) Weibchen nt; **his ~** das Weibchen **(d)** (inf: = friend) Freund(in) m(f); **listen, ~** hör mal, Freundchen! (inf) **2** VI (Zool) sich paaren

material [mə'tɪərɪəl] **1** ADJ **(a)** materiell; **~ damage** Sachschaden m **(b)** (esp Jur) evidence, witness wesentlich **2** N (also **~s**) Material nt; (for report, novel etc, = cloth) Stoff m; **raw ~s** Rohstoffe pl; **writing ~s** Schreibzeug nt; **~s handling** Materialtransport m; **~s planning** Marktplanung f

materialism [mə'tɪərɪəlɪzəm] N Materialismus m

materialistic [mə,tɪərɪə'lɪstɪk] ADJ materialistisch

materialize [mə'tɪərɪəlaɪz] VI (idea, plan) sich verwirklichen; (promises, hopes etc) wahr werden; **the meeting never ~d** das Treffen kam nie zustande; **the money he'd promised me never ~d** von dem Geld, das er mir versprochen hatte, habe ich nie etwas gesehen

materially [mə'tɪərɪəlɪ] ADV wesentlich

maternal [mə'tɜːnl] ADJ mütterlich; **~ grandfather** Großvater mütterlicherseits; **~ affection** or **love** Mutterliebe f

maternity [mə'tɜːnɪtɪ]: **maternity allowance, maternity benefit** N (Brit) Mutterschaftshilfe f; **maternity dress** N Umstandskleid nt; **maternity leave** N Mutterschaftsurlaub m; **maternity pay** N (Brit) Mutterschaftsgeld nt (als Lohnfortzahlung); **maternity rights** PL Anspruchsberechtigung f von Müttern; **maternity ward** N Entbindungsstation f

matey ['meɪtɪ] (Brit inf) ADJ (+ER) kollegial; (pej) vertraulich; **careful what you say, he's ~ with the director** sei vorsichtig mit dem, was du sagst, er steht mit dem Direktor auf Du und Du

math [mæθ] N (US inf) Mathe f (inf)

mathematical [ˌmæθə'mætɪkəl] ADJ mathematisch

mathematician [ˌmæθəmə'tɪʃən] N Mathematiker(in) m(f)

mathematics [ˌmæθə'mætɪks] N **(a)** SING Mathematik f **(b)** PL **the ~ of this are complicated** das ist mathematisch kompliziert

maths [mæθs] N SING (Brit inf) Mathe f (inf)

matinée ['mætɪneɪ] N Matinee f; (in the afternoon) Frühvorstellung f

mating ['meɪtɪŋ] N Paarung f

mating: mating call N Lockruf m; **mating season** N Paarungszeit f

matriarch ['meɪtrɪɑːk] N Matriarchin f

matriarchal [ˌmeɪtrɪ'ɑːkl] ADJ matriarchalisch

matriarchy ['meɪtrɪɑːkɪ] N Matriarchat nt

matriculate [mə'trɪkjʊleɪt] VI sich immatrikulieren

matriculation [mə,trɪkjʊ'leɪʃən] N Immatrikulation f

matrimonial [ˌmætrɪ'məʊnɪəl] ADJ ehelich

matrimonial law N Eherecht nt

matrimony ['mætrɪmənɪ] N (form) Ehe f

matron ['meɪtrən] N **(a)** (in hospital) Oberin f; (in school) Schwester f **(b)** (= married woman) Matrone f

matronly ['meɪtrənlɪ] ADJ matronenhaft

matt [mæt] ADJ matt; **a paint with a ~ finish** ein Mattlack m

matted ['mætɪd] ADJ verfilzt; **hair ~ with blood/mud** mit Blut/ Schlamm verkrustetes Haar

matter ['mætə'] **1** N **(a)** (= substance, not mind) die Materie **(b)** (particular kind) Stoff m; **vegetable ~** pflanzliche Stoffe pl **(c)** (= question, affair) Sache f; (= topic) Thema nt; **can I talk to you on a ~ of great urgency?** kann ich Sie in einer äußerst dringenden Angelegenheit sprechen?; **in the ~ of ...** was ... (+*acc*) anbelangt; **there's the ~ of my expenses** da ist (noch) die Sache mit meinen Ausgaben; **that's quite another ~** das ist etwas (ganz) anderes; **it will be no easy ~ (to) ...** es wird nicht einfach sein, zu ...; **the ~ is closed** die Sache *or* der Fall ist erledigt; **for that ~** eigentlich; **a ~ of** eine Frage (+*gen*); **it's a ~ of time** das ist eine Frage der Zeit; **it's a ~ of taste/opinion** das ist Geschmacks-/Ansichtssache; **it's a ~ of adjusting this part exactly** es geht darum, dieses Teil genau einzustellen; **it will be a ~ of a few weeks** es wird ein paar Wochen dauern; **in a ~ of minutes** innerhalb von Minuten; **it's a ~ of great concern to us** die Sache ist für uns von großer Bedeutung; **it's not just a ~ of increasing the money supply** es ist nicht damit getan, die Geldzufuhr zu erhöhen; **as a ~ of course** selbstverständlich; **you should always take your passport with you as a ~ of course** es sollte für Sie eine Selbstverständlichkeit sein, stets Ihren Pass bei sich zu haben; **no ~!** macht nichts; **no ~ how/what/when/where** *etc* ... egal, wie/was/wann/wo *etc* ...; **no ~ how you do it** wie du es auch machst; **no ~ how hard he tried** so sehr er sich auch anstrengte; **sth is the ~ with sb/sth** etw ist mit jdm/etw los; (*ill*) etw fehlt jdm; **what's the ~?** was ist (denn) los?; **what's the ~ with you this morning?** – **nothing's the ~** was hast du denn heute Morgen? – gar nichts; **something's the ~ with the lights** mit dem Licht ist irgendetwas nicht in Ordnung **(d) matters** PL Angelegenheiten *pl*; **as ~s stand** wie die Dinge liegen; **to make ~s worse** zu allem Unglück (noch) 🄑 VI **it doesn't ~** macht nichts; **I forgot it, does it ~?** – **yes, it does** – ich habs vergessen, ist das schlimm? – ja, das ist schlimm; **why should it ~ to me?** warum sollte mir das etwas ausmachen?; **it doesn't ~ to me what you do** es ist mir (ganz) egal, was du machst; **the things which ~ in life** was im Leben wichtig ist; **poverty ~s** Armut geht jeden etwas an

matter-of-fact [ˌmætərəv'fækt] ADJ sachlich; **he was very ~ about it** er blieb sehr sachlich

matting ['mætɪŋ] N Matten *pl*; (= *material*) Mattenmaterial *nt*

mattress ['mætrɪs] N Matratze *f*

mature [mə'tjʊə*r*] 🄑 ADJ (+ER) *child* reif; *wine* ausgereift; *plant* ausgewachsen; *child* verständig, vernünftig; (*euph.* = *middle-aged*) gereift; **of ~ years** im reiferen Alter; **after ~ deliberation** nach reiflicher Überlegung 🄑 VI **(a)** (*person*) reifer werden; (*animal*) auswachsen **(b)** (*wine, cheese*) reifen **(c)** (*Comm*) fällig werden

maturely [mə'tjʊəlɪ] ADV *behave* vernünftig

mature student N Spätstudierende(r) *mf*

maturity [mə'tjʊərɪtɪ] N **(a)** Reife *f*; **to reach ~** (*person*) erwachsen werden; (*legally*) volljährig werden **(b)** (*Comm*) Fälligkeit *f*; (= *date*) Fälligkeitsdatum *nt*

maudlin ['mɔːdlɪn] ADJ rührselig; *person* sentimental

maul [mɔːl] VT übel zurichten; (*fig*) *writer, play etc* verreißen

mauling ['mɔːlɪŋ] N **to get a ~** (*player, team*) vernichtend geschlagen werden; (*author, book*) von der Kritik verrissen werden

Mauritius [mə'rɪʃəs] N Mauritius *nt*

mausoleum [ˌmɔːsə'lɪəm] N Mausoleum *nt*

mauve [məʊv] 🄑 ADJ mauve 🄑 N Mauvein *nt*

maverick ['mævərɪk] N **(a)** (= *dissenter*) Abtrünnige(r) *mf* **(b)** (= *independent person*) Einzelgänger(in) *m(f)*

mawkish ['mɔːkɪʃ] ADJ sentimental

max N ABBR *of* **maximum** max.

maxim ['mæksɪm] N Maxime *f*

maximize ['mæksɪmaɪz] VT maximieren

maximum ['mæksɪməm] 🄑 ADJ ATTR Höchst-; *size, height, costs, length* maximal; **~ penalty/sentence** Höchststrafe *f*; **~ fine** maximale Geldstrafe; **for ~ effect** um die größte Wirkung zu erzielen; **he scored ~ points** er hat die höchste Punktzahl erreicht; **~ security wing/prison** Hochsicherheitstrakt *m*/-gefängnis *nt* 🄑 N, *pl* **-s** *or* **maxima** ['mæksɪmə] Maximum *nt*; **up to a ~ of £8** bis zu maximal £ 8; **temperatures reached a ~ of 34°** die Höchsttemperatur betrug 34°; **is that the ~ you can offer?** ist das Ihr höchstes Angebot? 🄰 ADV (= *at the most*) maximal; **drink two cups of coffee a day ~** trinken Sie maximal zwei Tassen Kaffee pro Tag

May [meɪ] N Mai *m*

may [meɪ] VI, *pret* **might** *see also* **might**[1] **(a)** (*possibility: also* **might**) können; **it ~ rain** es könnte regnen; **it ~ be that ...** vielleicht..., es könnte sein, dass ...; **although it ~ have been useful** obwohl es hätte nützlich sein können; **he ~ not be hungry** vielleicht hat er keinen Hunger; **I ~ have said so** es könnte sein, dass ich das gesagt habe; **they ~ be brothers for all I know** es könnte sein, dass sie Brüder sind; **yes, I ~** ja, das kann sein; **that's as ~ be** (*not might*) das mag ja sein(, aber ...); **you ~ well ask** das kann man wohl fragen **(b)** (*permission*) dürfen; **~ I go now?** darf ich jetzt gehen? **(c)** **I had hoped he might succeed this time** ich hatte gehofft, es würde ihm diesmal gelingen; **we ~ or might as well go** ich glaube, wir können (ruhig) gehen; **if they don't have it we ~ or might as well go to another firm** wenn sie es nicht haben, gehen wir am besten zu einer anderen Firma **(d)** (*in wishes*) **~ you be very happy together** ich wünsche euch, dass ihr sehr glücklich miteinander werdet; **~ the Lord have mercy on your soul** der Herr sei deiner Seele gnädig **(e)** (*in questions*) **who ~ or might you be?** und wer sind Sie?

maybe ['meɪbiː] ADV vielleicht; **that's as ~** kann schon sein; **~, ~ not** vielleicht, vielleicht auch nicht

May: **May Day** N der 1. Mai, der Maifeiertag; **Mayday** N Maydaysignal *nt*; (*said*) Mayday

mayhem ['meɪhem] N Chaos *nt*

mayo ['meɪəʊ] N (*US inf*) Majo *f* (*inf*)

mayonnaise [ˌmeɪə'neɪz] N Majonäse *f*

mayor [mɛə*r*] N Bürgermeister(in) *m(f)*

mayoress ['mɛərɛs] N Frau *f* Bürgermeister; (= *lady mayor*) Bürgermeisterin *f*

maze [meɪz] N Irrgarten *m*; (= *puzzle*) Labyrinth *nt*; (*fig*) Gewirr *nt*

MBA ABBR *of* **Master of Business Administration**; **he's doing an ~** er studiert Betriebswirtschaft; **he has** *or* **is an ~** er ist Betriebswirt

MBE ABBR *of* **Member of the Order of the British Empire** *britischer Verdienstorden*

MC ABBR *of* **Master of Ceremonies**

McCoy [mə'kɔɪ] N *see* **real**

MD (a) ABBR *of* **Doctor of Medicine** Dr. med. **(b)** ABBR *of* **managing director**

me [miː] PRON **(a)** (*dir obj, with prep +acc*) mich; (*indir obj, with prep +dat*) mir; **with my books about me** mit meinen Büchern um mich herum; **he's older than me** er ist älter als ich **(b)** (*emph*) ich; **it's me** ich bins

meadow ['medəʊ] N Wiese *f*; **in the ~** auf der Wiese

meagre, (*US*) **meager** ['miːgə*r*] ADJ spärlich; *amount, crowd* kläglich; *meal* kärglich; **he earns a ~ £500 a month** er verdient magere £500 im Monat

meal[1] [miːl] N Schrot(mehl *nt*) *m*

meal[2] N Mahlzeit *f*; (= *food*) Essen *nt*; **come round for a ~** komm zum Essen (zu uns); **to go for a ~** essen gehen; **to have a (good) ~** (gut) essen; **hot ~s** warmes Essen; **to make a ~ of sth** (*inf*) etw auf sehr umständliche Art machen; **don't make a ~ of it** (*inf*) nun übertreibs mal nicht (*inf*)

meal: **meals on wheels** N Essen *nt* auf Rädern; **meal ticket** N **(a)** (*US: lit*) Essensmarke *f* **(b)** (*fig*) **that letter of introduction was his ~ for the next few months** dank des Empfehlungsschreibens konnte er sich die nächsten paar Monate über Wasser halten; **a boyfriend is just a ~ to a lot of girls** viele Mädchen haben nur einen Freund, um sich von ihm aushalten zu lassen; **mealtime** N Essenszeit *f*; **you shouldn't smoke at ~s** Sie sollten während des Essens nicht rauchen

mealy-mouthed ['miːlɪ'maʊðd] ADJ unaufrichtig; *politician* schönfärberisch

mean[1] [miːn] ADJ (+ER) **(a)** (*esp Brit*: = *miserly*) geizig; **you ~ thing!** du Geizhals! **(b)** (= *unkind, spiteful*) gemein; **don't be ~!** sei nicht so gemein!; **you ~ thing!** du Miststück! (*inf*) **(c)** *birth, motives* niedrig **(d)** (= *vicious*) bösartig; *look* gehässig, hinterhältig **(e)** **he is no ~ player** er ist ein beachtlicher Spieler; **he plays a ~ game of poker** er ist ein ausgefuchster Pokerspieler (*inf*); **that's no ~ feat** diese Aufgabe ist nicht zu unterschätzen

mean[2] N (*Math*) Mittelwert *m*; **the golden** *or* **happy ~** die goldene Mitte

mean³ *pret, ptp* **meant** VT **(a)** bedeuten; (*person*: = *refer to, have in mind*) meinen; **what do you ~ by that?** was willst du damit sagen?; **the name ~s nothing to me** der Name sagt mir nichts; **it ~s starting all over again** das bedeutet, dass wir wieder ganz von vorne anfangen müssen; **this will ~ great changes** dies wird bedeutende Veränderungen zur Folge haben; **your friendship/he ~s a lot to me** deine Freundschaft/er bedeutet mir viel
(b) (= *intend*) beabsichtigen; **to ~ to do sth** etw tun wollen; (= *do on purpose*) etw absichtlich tun; **to be ~t for sb/sth** für jdn/etw bestimmt sein; **to ~ sb to do sth** wollen, dass jd etw tut; **sth is ~t to be sth** etw soll etw sein; **of course it hurt, I ~t it** to *or* it was ~t to natürlich tat das weh, das war Absicht; **I ~t it as a joke** das sollte ein Witz sein; **I ~t you to have it** das solltest du haben; **I was ~t to do that** ich hätte das tun sollen; **you are ~t to be on time** du solltest pünktlich sein; **I thought it was ~t to be hot in the south** ich dachte immer, dass es im Süden so heiß sei; **I ~ to have it** ich bin fest entschlossen, es zu bekommen; **this pad is ~t for drawing** dieser Block ist zum Zeichnen gedacht; **he ~s well/no harm** er meint es gut/nicht böse; **to ~ sb no harm** es gut mit jdm meinen; (*physically*) jdm nichts tun wollen; **I ~t no harm by what I said** was ich da gesagt habe, war nicht böse gemeint
(c) (= *be serious about*) ernst meinen; **I ~ it!** das ist mein Ernst!; **do you ~ to say you're not coming?** willst du damit sagen, dass du nicht kommst?; **I ~ what I say** ich sage das im Ernst

meander [mi'ændə'] VI (*river*) sich (dahin)schlängeln; (*person*) (= *go off subject*) (vom Thema) abschweifen; (*walking*) schlendern

meaning ['mi:nɪŋ] N Bedeutung *f*; **what's the ~ of (the word) "hick"?** was soll das Wort „hick" bedeuten?; **do you get my ~?** haben Sie mich (richtig) verstanden?; **you don't know the ~ of love** du weißt ja gar nicht, was Liebe ist; **what's the ~ of this?** was hat denn das zu bedeuten?

Be careful! **meaning** *is not translated by the German word* **Meinung.**

meaningful ['mi:nɪŋfʊl] ADJ **(a)** *word, statement, symbol* mit Bedeutung; *poem, film, look, glance* bedeutungsvoll; **to be ~** eine Bedeutung haben **(b)** (= *comprehensible, purposeful*) sinnvoll; *relationship* tiefer gehend

meaningfully ['mi:nɪŋfʊlɪ] ADV **(a)** *look* bedeutungsvoll; *say, add* vielsagend **(b)** *spend one's time, participate, negotiate* sinnvoll

meaningless ['mi:nɪŋlɪs] ADJ bedeutungslos; **my life is ~** mein Leben hat keinen Sinn

meanly ['mi:nlɪ] ADV *behave, treat* gemein

meanness ['mi:nnɪs] N **(a)** (*esp Brit*: = *miserliness*) Geiz *m* **(b)** (= *unkindness, spite*) Gemeinheit *f* **(c)** (= *viciousness*) Bösartigkeit *f*

means [mi:nz] N **(a)** SING (= *method*) Möglichkeit *f*; (= *instrument*) Mittel *nt*; (= *production* Produktionsmittel *pl*; **a ~ of transport** ein Beförderungsmittel *nt*; **a ~ of escape** eine Fluchtmöglichkeit; **a ~ to an end** ein Mittel *nt* zum Zweck; **I have/there is no ~ of doing it** es ist mir/es ist unmöglich, das zu tun; **is there any ~ of doing it?** ist es irgendwie möglich, das zu tun?; **we've no ~ of knowing** wir können nicht wissen; **by ~ of sth** durch etw; **by ~ of doing sth** dadurch, dass man etw tut; **by this ~** dadurch **(b)** SING **by all ~!** (aber) selbstverständlich!; **by no ~, not by any ~** keineswegs; (= *under no circumstances*) auf keinen Fall **(c)** PL (= *wherewithal*) Mittel *pl*; **a man of ~** ein vermögender Mann; **private ~** private Mittel *pl*; **that is within/beyond my ~** das kann ich mir leisten/nicht leisten; **to live beyond one's ~** über seine Verhältnisse leben; **to live within one's ~** seinen Verhältnissen entsprechend leben

means test N Vermögensveranlagung *f*

meant [ment] PRET, PTP *of* **mean³**

meantime ['mi:ntaɪm] ▨ ADV inzwischen ▨ N **for the ~** vorerst; **in the ~** in der Zwischenzeit

meanwhile ['mi:nwaɪl] ADV inzwischen

measles ['mi:zlz] N SING Masern *pl*

measly ['mi:zlɪ] ADJ (+ER) (*inf*) mick(e)rig (*inf*)

measurably ['meʒərəblɪ] ADV deutlich

measure ['meʒə'] ▨ N **(a)** Maß *nt*; (*fig*: = *yardstick*) Maßstab *m* (*of* für); **a ~ of length** ein Längenmaß *nt*; **to have sth made to ~** etw nach Maß anfertigen lassen; **the furniture has been made to ~** die Möbel sind Maßarbeit; **beyond ~** grenzenlos; **can we regard this exam as a ~ of intelligence?** kann diese Prüfung als Intelligenzmaßstab gelten?; **it gave us some ~ of the difficulty** es gab uns einen Begriff von der Schwierigkeit; **it's a ~ of his skill as a writer that ...** seine schriftstellerischen Fähigkeiten lassen sich daran beurteilen, dass ...
(b) (= *amount measured*) Menge *f*; **a small ~ of flour** ein wenig Mehl; **wine is sold in ~s of 1/4 litre** (*Brit*) *or* **liter** (*US*) Wein wird in Vierteln ausgeschenkt; **for good ~** sicherheitshalber
(c) (= *extent*) **in some ~** in gewisser Hinsicht; **some ~ of** ein gewisses Maß an; **to a large ~, in large ~** in hohem Maße; **to get the ~ of sb/sth** jdn/etw (richtig) einschätzen
(d) (= *step*) Maßnahme *f*; **to take ~s to do sth** Maßnahmen ergreifen, um etw zu tun
▨ VT messen; (= *take sb's measurements*) Maß nehmen bei; (*fig*) beurteilen; *words* abwägen
▨ VI messen; **what does it ~?** wie groß ist es?

➤ **measure out** VT SEP abmessen; *weights* abwiegen

➤ **measure up** ▨ VT SEP *wood, room etc* abmessen; *person for suit etc* Maß nehmen bei ▨ VI messen; **to measure up** enttäuscht; **to measure up to sth** an etw (*acc*) herankommen **(b)** (= *take measurements*) Maß nehmen

measured ['meʒəd] ADJ *tread* gemessen (*liter*); *tone* bedächtig; *words* wohl überlegt; *approach, response* maßvoll; **at a ~ pace** in gemäßigtem Tempo

measurement ['meʒəmənt] N **(a)** (= *act*) Messung *f* **(b)** (= *measure*) Maß *nt*; (= *figure*) Messwert *m*; (*fig*) Maßstab *m*; **to take sb's ~s** an jdm *or* bei jdm Maß nehmen

measuring ['meʒərɪŋ] IN CPDS Mess-; **measuring device** N Messgerät *nt*; **measuring jug** N Messbecher *m*

meat [mi:t] N **(a)** Fleisch *nt*; **assorted cold ~s** Aufschnitt *m* **(b)** (*fig*: *of argument, book*) Substanz *f*; **a book with some ~ in it** ein aussagestarkes Buch

meat IN CPDS Fleisch-; **meatball** N Fleischkloß *m*; **meat loaf** N ≈ Fleischkäse *m*

meaty ['mi:tɪ] ADJ (+ER) **(a)** mit viel Fleisch; **~ chunks** Fleischbrocken *pl* **(b)** (= *fleshy*) *arms, hands* fleischig **(c)** (*fig*) *book* gehaltvoll; *role, part* anspruchsvoll

Mecca ['mekə] N (*lit, fig*) Mekka *nt*

mechanic [mɪ'kænɪk] N Mechaniker(in) *m(f)*

mechanical [mɪ'kænɪkl] ADJ (*lit, fig*) mechanisch; *toy* technisch; **a ~ device** ein Mechanismus *m*

mechanical: mechanical engineer N Maschinenbauer(in) *m(f)*; **mechanical engineering** N Maschinenbau *m*

mechanically [mɪ'kænɪkəlɪ] ADV (*lit, fig*) mechanisch

mechanics [mɪ'kænɪks] N **(a)** SING (= *subject*) (= *engineering*) Maschinenbau *m*; (*Phys*) Mechanik *f* **(b)** PL (= *technical aspects*) Mechanik *f*; (*fig: of writing etc*) Technik *f*; **I don't understand the ~ of parliamentary procedure** ich verstehe den Mechanismus parlamentarischer Abläufe nicht

mechanism ['mekənɪzəm] N Mechanismus *m*

mechanization [,mekənaɪ'zeɪʃən] N Mechanisierung *f*

mechanize ['mekənaɪz] VT mechanisieren

mechanized ['mekənaɪzd] ADJ mechanisiert

medal ['medl] N Medaille *f*; (= *decoration*) Orden *m*

medalist N (*US*) = **medallist**

medallion [mɪ'dæljən] N Medaillon *nt*; (= *medal*) Medaille *f*

medallist, (*US*) **medalist** ['medəlɪst] N Medaillengewinner(in) *m(f)*

meddle ['medl] VI (= *interfere*) sich einmischen (*in in* +*acc*); (= *tamper*) sich zu schaffen machen (*with an* +*dat*); **to ~ with sb** sich mit jdm einlassen; **he's not a man to ~ with** mit ihm ist nicht gut Kirschen essen

meddlesome ['medlsəm] ADJ, **meddling** ['medlɪŋ] ADJ ATTR **she's a ~ old busybody** sie mischt sich dauernd in alles ein

media ['mi:dɪə] N PL *of* **medium** Medien *pl*; **he works in the ~** er ist im Mediensektor tätig; **to get too much ~ coverage** zu viel Publicity bekommen

mediaeval ADJ = **medieval**

media event N Medienereignis *nt*

median ['mi:dɪən] ADJ mittlere(r, s)

median strip N (*US*) Mittelstreifen *m*

media studies PL Medienwissenschaft *f*

mediate [ˈmiːdɪeɪt] **1** VI vermitteln **2** VT *settlement* aushandeln

mediation [ˌmiːdrˈeɪʃən] N Vermittlung *f*

mediator [ˈmiːdɪeɪtər] N Vermittler(in) *m(f)*

medic [ˈmedɪk] N *(inf)* Mediziner(in) *m(f) (inf)*

Medicaid [ˈmedɪkeɪd] N *(US) staatliche Krankenversicherung und Gesundheitsfürsorge für Einkommensschwache unter 65 in den USA; see also* **Medicare**

medical [ˈmedɪkəl] **1** ADJ medizinisch; *(in military contexts)* Sanitäts-; *examination, treatment, advice, expertise, staff* ärztlich; **the ~ profession** die Ärzteschaft; **~ condition** *or* **disorder** Erkrankung *f* **2** N (ärztliche) Untersuchung; **have you had your ~?** bist du zur Untersuchung gewesen?

medical: **medical certificate** N ärztliches Attest; **medical examiner** N *(US Jur)* Gerichtsmediziner(in) *m(f)*; **medical history** N her – ihre Krankengeschichte; **medical insurance** N Krankenversicherung *f*

medically [ˈmedɪkəlɪ] ADV medizinisch; **to be ~ qualified/trained** eine medizinische Ausbildung absolviert/gemacht haben

medical: **medical officer** N *(Mil)* Stabsarzt *m*; *(= official)* Amtsarzt *m*; **medical practice** N *(= business)* Arztpraxis *f*; **medical practitioner** N Arzt *m*, Ärztin *f*; **medical record** N *(= medical background)* Krankengeschichte *f*; **~s** Krankenblatt *nt*; **medical school** N ≈ medizinische Fakultät; **medical science** N die ärztliche Wissenschaft; **medical student** N Medizinstudent(in) *m(f)*

Medicare [ˈmedɪkeər] N *(US) staatliche Krankenversicherung und Gesundheitsfürsorge für ältere Bürger in den USA; see also* **Medicaid**

medicated [ˈmedɪkeɪtɪd] ADJ medizinisch

medication [ˌmedrˈkeɪʃən] N Medikamente *pl*

medicinal [meˈdɪsɪnl] ADJ Heil-, heilend; **for ~ purposes** zu medizinischen Zwecken; **the ~ properties of various herbs** die Heilkraft verschiedener Kräuter

medicine [ˈmedsm, ˈmedɪsm] N **(a)** Medizin *f (inf)*; *(= one particular preparation)* Medikament *nt*; **to take one's ~** seine Arznei einnehmen; **to give sb a taste of his own ~** *(fig)* es jdm mit gleicher Münze heimzahlen **(b)** *(= science)* Medizin *f*; **to practise** *(Brit) or* **practice** *(US)* **~** den Arztberuf ausüben

medicine chest N Arzneischränkchen *nt*

medieval [ˌmedrˈiːvəl] ADJ *(lit, fig)* mittelalterlich; **in ~ times** im Mittelalter

medieval history N die Geschichte des Mittelalters

mediocre [ˌmiːdrˈəʊkər] ADJ mittelmäßig

mediocrity [ˌmiːdrˈɒkrɪtɪ] N **(a)** Mittelmäßigkeit *f* **(b)** *(= person)* kleines Licht

meditate [ˈmedɪteɪt] VI nachdenken *(upon, on über +acc)*; *(Rel, Philos)* meditieren

meditation [ˌmedrˈteɪʃən] N Nachdenken *nt*; *(Rel, Philos)* Meditation *f*

meditative [ˈmedɪtətɪv] ADJ nachdenklich; *(Rel, Philos)* Meditations-; **~ techniques** Meditationstechniken *pl*

meditatively [ˈmedɪtətɪvlɪ] ADV nachdenklich; *sit, look* meditierend

Mediterranean [ˌmedɪtəˈreɪmən] **1** N Mittelmeer *nt*; **in the ~** *(= in sea)* im Mittelmeer; *(= in region)* am Mittelmeer **2** ADJ Mittelmeer-; *scenery, character, person* südländisch; **~ island** Mittelmeerinsel *f*; **~ types** Südländer *pl*; **~ cruise** Kreuzfahrt *f* im Mittelmeer; **~ holiday** *(Brit) or* **vacation** *(US)* Urlaub *m* im Mittelmeerraum

Mediterranean Sea N **the ~** das Mittelmeer

medium [ˈmiːdɪəm] **1** ADJ mittlere(r, s); *steak* medium; *(= ~-sized)* mittelgroß; **~ brown** mittelbraun; **of ~ height/build/size** mittelgroß; **cook over a ~ heat** bei mittlerer Hitze kochen; **in/over the ~ term** mittelfristig **2** N, pl **media** *or* **-s (a)** *(= means)* Mittel *nt*; *(TV, Rad, Press)* Medium *nt*; *(Art, Liter)* Ausdrucksmittel *nt*; **through the ~ of the press** durch die Presse; **advertising ~** Werbeträger *m* **(b)** *(= midpoint)* **to strike a happy ~** den goldenen Mittelweg finden **(c)** *(= spiritualist)* Medium *nt*

medium IN CPDS mittel-; **medium-dry** ADJ halbtrocken; **medium-priced** ADJ **a ~ hotel/whisky** ein Hotel *nt*/ein Whisky *m* mittlerer Preislage; **medium-range** ADJ **~ aircraft/missile**

Mittelstreckenflugzeug *nt*/-rakete *f*; **medium-rare** ADJ rosa; **medium-sized** ADJ mittelgroß; **medium-sweet** ADJ *wine* fruchtig; *sherry, cider* halbsüß; **medium-term** ADJ mittelfristig; **medium wave** N Mittelwelle *f*; **medium-wave** ADJ **~ transmitter** Mittelwellensender *m*

medley [ˈmedlɪ] N Gemisch *nt*; *(Mus)* Medley *nt*

meek [miːk] ADJ (+ER) sanft(mütig); *(pej)* duckmäuserisch; *(= uncomplaining)* duldsam, geduldig; *voice* schüchtern; *acceptance* widerstandslos

meekly [ˈmiːklɪ] ADV sanft; *(pej)* duckmäuserisch; *agree* widerspruchslos; *submit, accept* widerstandslos

meet [miːt], vb: pret, ptp **met** **1** VT **(a)** treffen; *difficulty* stoßen auf *(+acc)*; *(= converge with)* sich vereinigen mit; *(river)* münden in *(+acc)*; *(= intersect)* schneiden; *(= touch)* berühren; **he met his death in 1800** im Jahre 1800 fand er den Tod; **to arrange to ~ sb** sich mit jdm verabreden; **to ~ a challenge** sich einer Herausforderung *(dat)* stellen; **his eyes** *or* **gaze met mine** unsere Blicke trafen sich; **there's more to it than ~s the eye** da steckt mehr dahinter, als man auf den ersten Blick meint

(b) *(= get to know)* kennen lernen; *(= be introduced to)* bekannt gemacht werden mit; **pleased to ~ you!** guten Tag/Abend

(c) *(= await arrival, collect)* abholen *(at an +dat, von)*; *(= connect with)* train, boat *etc* Anschluss haben an *(+acc)*

(d) *expectations, target, deadline* erfüllen; *requirement, demand, wish* entsprechen *(+dat)*, gerecht werden *(+dat)*; *expenses, needs* decken; *debt* begleichen; *charge, objection, criticism* begegnen *(+dat)*

2 VI **(a)** *(= encounter) (people)* sich begegnen; *(by arrangement)* sich treffen; *(society, committee etc)* zusammenkommen, tagen; *(Sport)* aufeinander treffen; **keep it until we ~ again** behalten Sie es, bis wir uns mal wiedersehen; **to ~ halfway** einen Kompromiss schließen

(b) *(= become acquainted)* sich kennen lernen; *(= be introduced)* bekannt gemacht werden; **we've met before** wir kennen uns bereits; **haven't we met before somewhere?** sind wir uns nicht schon mal begegnet?

(c) *(= join)* sich treffen, aufeinander stoßen; *(= converge)* sich vereinigen; *(rivers)* ineinander fließen; *(= intersect)* sich schneiden; *(= touch)* sich berühren; **our eyes met** unsere Blicke trafen sich

3 N *(Brit Hunt)* Jagd *f*; *(US) (Athletics)* Sportfest *nt*; *(Swimming)* Schwimmfest *nt*

➤ **meet up** VI sich treffen

➤ **meet with** VI +PREP OBJ **(a)** *hostility, opposition, problems* stoßen auf *(+acc)*; *success, accident* haben; *disaster, loss, shock* erleiden; *setback* erleben; *approval, encouragement, an untimely death* finden; **to meet with kindness/a warm welcome** freundlich behandelt/herzlich empfangen werden; **I was met with a blank stare** sie/er *etc* starrte mich unwissend an **(b)** *person* treffen; *(esp US: = have a meeting with)* zusammenkommen mit

meeting [ˈmiːtɪŋ] N **(a)** Begegnung *f*; *(arranged)* Treffen *nt*; *(= business ~)* Besprechung *f*; **the minister had a ~ with the ambassador** der Minister traf zu Gesprächen mit dem Botschafter zusammen **(b)** *(of committee, council)* Sitzung *f*; *(of members, employees, citizens)* Versammlung *f*; **the committee has three ~s a year** der Ausschuss tagt dreimal im Jahr **(c)** *(Sport)* Veranstaltung *f*; *(between teams, opponents)* Begegnung *f*

meeting: **meeting place** N Treffpunkt *m*; **meeting point** N Treffpunkt *m*; *(of rivers)* Zusammenfluss *m*; *(of lines)* Berührungspunkt *m*

mega- [ˈmegə-] PREF Mega-

megabyte [ˈmegəbaɪt] N *(Comput)* Megabyte *nt*; **a 40-~ memory** ein 40-Megabyte-Speicher *m*

megalomania [ˌmegələʊˈmeɪnɪə] N Größenwahn *m*, Megalomanie *f (spec)*

megalomaniac [ˌmegələʊˈmeɪnɪæk] N Größenwahnsinnige(r) *mf*; **he's a ~** er ist größenwahnsinnig

mega: **megaphone** N Megaphon *nt*; **megastar** N Megastar *m*; **megastore** N Großmarkt *m*

melancholic [ˌmelənˈkɒlɪk] ADJ melancholisch

melancholy [ˈmelənkəlɪ] **1** ADJ melancholisch; *sight, truth etc* traurig; *place* trist **2** N Melancholie *f*

mêlée ['melei] N (= *confused struggle*) Gedränge *nt*; (= *fighting*) Handgemenge *nt*

mellow ['melǝʊ] **1** ADJ (+ER) **(a)** *wine* ausgereift; *brandy, whisky, flavour* mild; *colour, light, stone* warm; *sound* voll; (= *soft*) weich; *voice* sanft **(b)** *person* (= *relaxed*) abgeklärt; (= *affable*) umgänglich; (= *in a good mood*) gut gelaunt; (*fig*: = *slightly drunk*) angeheitert; **in a ~ mood** guter Laune **2** VT heiter stimmen; **the rum began to ~ her** der Rum versetzte sie allmählich in freundlichere Stimmung **3** VI (*person*) (= *become more relaxed*) abgeklärter werden; (= *become more affable*) umgänglicher werden

melodic ADJ, **melodically** ADV [mɪ'lɒdɪk, -əlɪ] melodisch

melodrama ['melǝʊdrɑːmǝ] N Melodrama *nt*

melodramatic ADJ, **melodramatically** ADV [ˌmelǝʊdrǝ'mætɪk, -əlɪ] melodramatisch

melody ['melǝdɪ] N Melodie *f*; (*fig*: *of poetry etc*) Melodik *f*

melon ['melǝn] N Melone *f*

melt [melt] **1** VT **(a)** (*lit*) schmelzen; *butter* zerlassen; *sugar, grease* auflösen **(b)** (*fig*) *heart etc* erweichen **2** VI **(a)** schmelzen; (*sugar, grease*) sich (auf)lösen **(b)** (*fig*: *person*) dahinschmelzen; **... and then his heart ~ed** ... und dann ließ er sich erweichen

➤ **melt away** VI **(a)** (*lit*) (weg)schmelzen **(b)** (*fig*) sich auflösen; (*crowd*) dahinschmelzen; (*anger, anxiety*) verfliegen

➤ **melt down** VT SEP einschmelzen

meltdown ['meltdaʊn] N Kernschmelze *f*; (*fig*) (*of market, industry*) Crash *m*; (*of company*) Zusammenbruch *m*; (= *disaster*) Katastrophe *f*

melting pot ['meltɪŋpɒt] N (*fig*) Schmelztiegel *m*

member ['membǝʳ] N **(a)** Mitglied *nt*; (*of tribe, species*) Angehörige(r) *mf*; **"~s only"** „nur für Mitglieder"; **~ of the family** Familienmitglied *nt*; **if any ~ of the audience ...** falls einer der Zuschauer/Zuhörer ...; **the ~ countries/states** die Mitgliedsstaaten *pl* **(b)** (*Parl*) Abgeordnete(r) *mf*; **~ of parliament** Parlamentsmitglied *nt*

membership ['membǝʃɪp] N Mitgliedschaft *f* (*of* in +*dat*); (= *number of members*) Mitgliederzahl *f*

membership: **membership card** N Mitgliedsausweis *m*; **membership fee** N Mitgliedsbeitrag *m*

membrane ['membreɪn] N Membran(e) *f*

memento [mǝ'mentǝʊ] N, *pl* -(**e**)**s** Andenken *nt* (*of* an +*acc*)

memo ['memǝʊ] N ABBR *of* **memorandum** Memo *nt*

memoir ['memwɑː^r] N **(a)** Kurzbiografie *f* **(b)** **memoirs** PL Memoiren *pl*

memo pad N Notizblock *m*

memorable ['memǝrǝbl] ADJ unvergesslich; (= *important*) denkwürdig

memorandum [ˌmemǝ'rændǝm] N, *pl* **memoranda** [ˌmemǝ'rændǝ] (*in business*) Mitteilung *f*; (= *personal reminder*) Notiz *f*; **~ of association** (*Brit*) Gesellschaftsvertrag *m*, Gründungsurkunde *f* und Satzung

memorial [mɪ'mɔːrɪǝl] **1** ADJ Gedenk-; **~ plaque** Gedenktafel *f* **2** N Denkmal *nt* (*to* für)

memorial: **Memorial Day** N (*US*) ≈ Volkstrauertag *m*; **memorial service** N Gedenkgottesdienst *m*

memorize ['memǝraɪz] VT sich (*dat*) einprägen

memory ['memǝrɪ] N **(a)** Gedächtnis *nt*; (= *faculty*) Erinnerungsvermögen *nt*; **from ~** aus dem Kopf; **to lose one's ~** sein Gedächtnis verlieren; **to commit sth to ~** sich (*dat*) etw einprägen; *poem* etw auswendig lernen; **I have a bad ~ for faces/names** ich habe ein schlechtes Personengedächtnis/Namensgedächtnis; **if my ~ serves me right** wenn ich mich recht entsinne **(b)** (= *thing remembered*) Erinnerung *f* (*of* an +*acc*); **I have no ~ of it** ich kann mich nicht daran erinnern; **he had happy memories of his father** er verband angenehme Erinnerungen mit seinem Vater; **to honour** (*Brit*) *or* **honor** (*US*) **sb's ~** jds Andenken *nt* ehren; **in ~ of** zur Erinnerung an (+*acc*) **(c)** (*Comput*) Speicher *m*

memory: **memory bank** N (*Comput*) Datenbank *f*; **memory expansion card** N (*Comput*) Speichererweiterungskarte *f*

men [men] PL *of* **man**

menace ['menɪs] **1** N **(a)** Bedrohung *f* (*to* +*gen*); (*issued by a person*) Drohung *f*; (= *imminent danger*) drohende Gefahr **(b)** (*inf*: = *nuisance*) (Land)plage *f*; **she's a ~ on the roads** sie gefährdet den ganzen Verkehr **2** VT bedrohen

menacing ['menɪsɪŋ] ADJ drohend; *threat* gefährlich; **to look ~** bedrohlich aussehen

menacingly ['menɪsɪŋlɪ] ADV drohend; **..., he said ~ ...**, sagte er mit drohender Stimme

menagerie [mɪ'nædʒǝrɪ] N Menagerie *f*

mend [mend] **1** N (*in shoe*) reparierte Stelle; **to be on the ~** (*fig, lit*: *person*) sich (langsam) erholen **2** VT **(a)** reparieren; *roof, fence also* ausbessern; *hole, clothes* flicken **(b)** **to ~ one's ways** sich bessern; **you'd better ~ your ways** das muss aber anders werden mit dir!; **to ~ fences** (*fig*) Unstimmigkeiten ausbügeln **3** VI (*bone*) (ver)heilen

mending ['mendɪŋ] N (= *articles to be mended*) Flickarbeit *f*

menial ['miːnɪǝl] ADJ niedrig; **she regards no task as too ~ for her** sie betrachtet keine Arbeit für unter ihrer Würde

meningitis [ˌmenɪn'dʒaɪtɪs] N Hirnhautentzündung *f*

menopause ['menǝʊpɔːz] N Wechseljahre *pl*

men's room ['menzruːm] N (*esp US*) Herrentoilette *f*

menstrual ['menstrʊǝl] ADJ Menstruations-

menstrual cycle N Menstruationszyklus *m*

menstruate ['menstrʊeɪt] VI menstruieren

menstruation [ˌmenstrʊ'eɪʃǝn] N Menstruation *f*

mental ['mentl] ADJ **(a)** geistig; *strain* psychisch; *cruelty* seelisch; **to make a ~ note of sth** sich (*dat*) etw merken; **~ process** Denkvorgang *m*; **the causes are ~ not physical** die Ursachen sind eher psychischen als physischer Natur **(b)** (*inf*: = *mad*) übergeschnappt (*inf*)

mental: **mental arithmetic** N Kopfrechnen *nt*; **mental block** N **to have a ~** (*in exam*) ein Brett vor dem Kopf haben (*inf*); **mental breakdown** N Nervenzusammenbruch *m*; **mental health** N Geisteszustand *m*; **mental hospital** N psychiatrische Klinik, Nervenklinik *f*; **mental illness** N Geisteskrankheit *f*

mentality [men'tælɪtɪ] N Mentalität *f*

mentally ['mentǝlɪ] ADV **(a)** geistig; **~ handicapped** geistig behindert; **he is ~ ill** er ist geisteskrank **(b)** (= *in one's head*) im Kopf

menthol ['menθɒl] N Menthol *nt*; **~ cigarettes** Mentholzigaretten *pl*

mention ['menʃǝn] **1** N Erwähnung *f*; **to get** *or* **receive a ~** erwähnt werden; **to give sb/sth a ~** jdn/etw erwähnen; **there is a/no ~ of it** es wird erwähnt/nicht erwähnt; **his contribution deserves special ~** sein Beitrag verdient es, besonders hervorgehoben zu werden; **at the ~ of his name/ the police ...** als sein Name/das Wort Polizei fiel *or* erwähnt wurde ... **2** VT erwähnen (*to sb* jdm gegenüber); **not to ~ ...** nicht zu vergessen ...; **France and Spain, not to ~ Holland** Frankreich und Spanien, von Holland ganz zu schweigen; **don't ~ it!** (bitte,) gern geschehen!; **to ~ sb in one's will** jdn in seinem Testament berücksichtigen

mentor ['mentɔː^r] N Mentor(in) *m(f)*

menu ['menjuː] N (= *bill of fare*) Speisekarte *f*; (= *dishes served*) Menü *nt also Comput*; **may we see the ~?** können Sie uns bitte die Karte bringen?; **what's on the ~?** was gibt es heute (zu essen)?

menu (*Comput*): **menu bar** N Menüzeile *f*; **menu-driven** ADJ menügesteuert

MEP ABBR *of* **Member of the European Parliament** Mitglied *nt* des Europäischen Parlaments

mercenary ['mɜːsɪnǝrɪ] **1** ADJ **(a)** *person* geldgierig; **don't be so ~** sei doch nicht so hinter dem Geld her (*inf*) **(b)** (*Mil*) **~ army** Söldnerarmee *f* **2** N Söldner(in) *m(f)*

merchandise ['mɜːtʃǝndaɪz] N (Handels)ware *f*

merchandising ['mɜːtʃǝndaɪzɪŋ] N Verkaufsförderung *f*

merchant ['mɜːtʃǝnt] N Kaufmann *m*/-frau *f*; **corn/diamond ~** Getreide-/Diamantenhändler(in) *m(f)*

merchantable ['mɜːtʃǝntǝbl] ADJ marktgängig, zum Verkauf geeignet

merchant: **merchant bank** N (*Brit*) Handelsbank *f*; **merchant banker** N (*Brit*) Handelsbankier *m*; **merchant marine** N (*US*) Handelsmarine *f*; **merchant navy** N (*Brit*) Handelsmarine *f*

merciful ['mɜːsɪfʊl] ADJ gnädig (*to sb* jdm gegenüber); **his death was a ~ release from pain** sein Tod war für ihn eine Erlösung

mercifully ['mɜːsɪfəlɪ] ADV *act* barmherzig; *treat sb* gnädig; (= *fortunately*) glücklicherweise; **his suffering was ~ short** es war ein Glück, dass er nicht lange leiden musste

merciless ['mɜːsɪlɪs] ADJ unbarmherzig; *destruction* schonungslos; (= *unrelenting*) gnadenlos

mercilessly ['mɜːsɪlɪslɪ] ADV erbarmungslos; *glare* gnadenlos

Mercury ['mɜːkjʊrɪ] N Merkur *m*

mercury ['mɜːkjʊrɪ] N Quecksilber *nt*

mercy ['mɜːsɪ] N **(a)** NO PL (= *feeling of compassion*) Erbarmen *nt*; (= *action, forbearance from punishment*) Gnade *f*; (= *God's ~*) Barmherzigkeit *f*; **to beg for ~** um Gnade bitten; **to have ~/ no ~ on sb** mit jdm Erbarmen/kein Erbarmen haben; **to show sb ~/no ~** Erbarmen/kein Erbarmen mit jdm haben; **to be at the ~ of sb** jdm (auf Gedeih und Verderb) ausgeliefert sein; **to be at the ~ of sth** einer Sache (*dat*) ausgeliefert sein; **we're at your ~** wir sind in Ihrer Hand **(b)** (*inf*: = *blessing*) Segen *m*; **we must be thankful for small mercies** man muss schon mit wenigem zufrieden sein

mere [mɪəʳ] ADJ bloß; *formality also, nonsense* rein; **a ~ mortal** ein gewöhnlicher Sterblicher, eine gewöhnliche Sterbliche; **he's a ~ clerk** er ist bloß ein kleiner Angestellter; **a ~ 3%/two hours** bloß 3%/zwei Stunden; **the ~ thought of food made me hungry** schon beim Gedanken an Essen bekam ich Hunger **(b)** **the ~st ...** (= *slightest*) der/die/das kleinste ...; *suspicion, sign* der/die/das geringste ...

merely ['mɪəlɪ] ADV lediglich, bloß

merge [mɜːdʒ] **1** VI **(a)** (= *zusammenkommen*; (*colours*) ineinander übergehen; (*roads*) zusammenführen; (*US Aut*) sich einordnen; **to ~ with sth** sich mit etw vereinen; (*colour*) in etw (*acc*) übergehen; (*road*) in etw (*acc*) einmünden; **to ~ (in) with/into the crowd** in der Menge untergehen/ untertauchen; **to ~ into sth** in etw (*acc*) übergehen **(b)** (*Comm*) fusionieren **2** VT **(a)** miteinander vereinen; (*Comput*) *files* mischen **(b)** (*Comm*) fusionieren; **they were ~d into one company** sie wurden zu einer Firma zusammengeschlossen; **they were ~d with ...** sie haben mit ... fusioniert

merger ['mɜːdʒəʳ] N (*Comm*) Fusion *f*

merging lane ['mɜːdʒɪŋˌleɪn] N (*US*) Abbiegespur *f*

meringue [məˈræŋ] N Baiser *nt*

merit ['merɪt] **1** N (= *achievement*) Verdienst *nt*; (= *advantage*) Vorzug *m*; **to look** *or* **inquire into the ~s of sth** etw auf seine Vorteile untersuchen; **a work of great literary ~** ein Werk von großem literarischem Wert; **she was elected on ~ alone** sie gewann die Wahl aufgrund persönlicher Fähigkeiten; **to judge a case on its ~s** einen Fall gesondert behandeln; **I don't see any ~ in being rich** ich betrachte Reichtum als kein besonderes Verdienst; **to pass an exam with ~** ein Examen mit Auszeichnung bestehen **2** VT verdienen; **it ~s your consideration** das ist es wert, dass Sie sich damit beschäftigen

merit: **merit goods** PL (*Econ*) meritorische Güter *pl*; **merit pay** N leistungsbezogener Lohn

mermaid ['mɜːmeɪd] N Meerjungfrau *f*

merrily ['merɪlɪ] ADV **(a)** vergnügt; **to burn ~** munter vor sich hin brennen **(b)** (= *blithely*) *continue, say* munter

merry ['merɪ] ADJ (+ER) **(a)** fröhlich; **Merry Christmas!** frohe Weihnachten! **(b)** (*fig*) **to lead sb a ~ dance** jdn ganz schön an der Nase herumführen; **to play ~ hell with sth** (*inf*) etw total durcheinander bringen **(c)** (*Brit inf*: = *tipsy*) beschwipst (*inf*)

merry-go-round ['merɪɡəʊˌraʊnd] N Karussell *nt*

mesh [meʃ] **1** N **(a)** (= *hole*) Masche *f*; (= *size of hole*) Maschenweite *f*; **fine ~ stockings** feinmaschige Strümpfe *pl*; **a 5mm ~ screen** ein 5-mm-Maschendraht **(b)** (*material*) (= *wire ~*) Maschendraht *m*; (= *network of wires*) Drahtgeflecht *nt*; (*Tex*) Gittergewebe *nt* **2** VI **(a)** (*Mech*) eingreifen (*with* in +*acc*); **the gears ~ (together)** die Zahnräder greifen ineinander **(b)** (*fig*: *views, approach*) sich vereinen lassen

mesmerize ['mezməraɪz] VT hypnotisieren; (*fig*) fesseln; **the audience sat ~d** die Zuschauer saßen wie gebannt

mesmerizing ['mezməraɪzɪŋ] ADJ *effect* hypnotisch; *smile, voice* faszinierend

mess¹ [mes] **1** N **(a)** Durcheinander *nt*; (*dirty*) Schweinerei *f*; **to be (in) a ~** in einem fürchterlichen Zustand sein; (= *disorganized*) ein einziges Durcheinander sein; (*fig*: *one's life, career etc*) verkorkst sein (*inf*); **to be a ~** (*piece of work*) eine Schweinerei sein (*inf*); (*person*) (*in appearance*) unordentlich aussehen; (*psychologically*) verkorkst sein (*inf*); **to make a ~** (= *be untidy*) Unordnung machen; (= *be dirty*) eine Schweinerei machen (*inf*); **to make a ~ of sth** (= *make untidy*) etw durcheinander bringen; (= *make dirty*) etw verdrecken; (= *bungle, botch*) etw verpfuschen; **of one's life** etw verkorksen (*inf*); **you've really made a ~ of things** du hast alles total vermasselt (*inf*); **what a ~!** das sieht ja vielleicht aus!; (*fig*) ein schöner Schlamassel! (*inf*); **I'm not tidying up your ~** ich räume nicht für dich auf **(b)** (= *awkward predicament*) Schwierigkeiten *pl*; **cheating got him into a ~** durch seine Mogelei ist er in ziemliche Schwierigkeiten geraten **(c)** (*euph*: = *excreta*) Dreck *m*; **the cat has made a ~ on the carpet** die Katze hat auf den Teppich gemacht **2** VI = **mess about 2**

➤ **mess about** (*Brit*) *or* **around** (*inf*) **1** VT SEP *person* an der Nase herumführen (*inf*); (*boss, person in authority*) herumschikanieren; (*by delaying decision*) hinhalten **2** VI **(a)** (= *play the fool*) herumalbern **(b)** (= *do nothing in particular*) herumgammeln (*inf*); **he enjoys messing about** *or* **around on the river** (*in boat*) er gondelt gern (im Boot) auf dem Fluss herum **(c)** (= *tinker, fiddle*) herumfummeln (*inf*) (*with* an +*dat*); (*as hobby etc*) herumbasteln (*with* an +*dat*) (*inf*); **I don't like film directors messing about** *or* **around with my scripts** ich kann es nicht haben, wenn Regisseure an meinen Drehbüchern herumändern **(d)** **to mess around with sb** (= *associate with*) sich mit jdm einlassen; (= *not take seriously*) jdn zum Narren haben; **he was messing about** *or* **around with my wife** er trieb es mit meiner Frau

➤ **mess up** VT SEP durcheinander bringen; (= *make dirty*) verdrecken; (= *botch, bungle*) verpfuschen; *marriage* ruinieren; *life, person* verkorksen (*inf*); **that's really messed things up** das hat wirklich alles verdorben

mess² N (*Mil*) Kasino *nt*; (*on ships*) Messe *f*

message ['mesɪdʒ] N **(a)** Nachricht *f*; (= *report, police ~*) Meldung *f*; **to give sb a ~** (*verbal*) jdm etwas ausrichten; (*written*) jdm eine Nachricht geben; **would you give John a ~ (for me)?** könnten Sie John etwas (von mir) ausrichten?; **to send a ~ to sb, to send sb a ~** jdn benachrichtigen; **to leave a ~ for sb** (*written*) jdm eine Nachricht hinterlassen; (*verbal*) jdm etwas ausrichten lassen; **can I take a ~ (for him)?** (*on telephone*) kann ich (ihm) etwas ausrichten? **(b)** (= *moral*) Botschaft *f*; **the ~ of the play is ...** die Aussage des Stückes ist ...; **to get the** *or* **one's ~ across to sb** es jdm verständlich machen **(c)** (*fig inf*) **to get the ~** kapieren (*inf*)

messenger ['mesɪndʒəʳ] N Bote *m*, Botin *f*

Messiah [mɪˈsaɪə] N Messias *m*

messily ['mesɪlɪ] ADV unordentlich

mess kit N (*US*) Essgeschirr *nt*

Messrs ['mesəz] PL *of* **Mr** ABBR *of* **Messieurs**; **to ~ ...** an die Herren ...

messy ['mesɪ] ADJ (+ER) **(a)** (= *dirty*) schmutzig; (= *untidy*) unordentlich; **he's a ~ eater** er kann nicht ordentlich essen **(b)** (*fig*) *situation* verfahren; *process, relationship* schwierig; *dispute* unschön; **their divorce was a ~ business, they had a ~ divorce** ihre Scheidung war eine unerfreuliche Angelegenheit

met [met] PRET, PTP *of* **meet**

meta- ['metə-] PREF meta-, Meta-

metabolism [meˈtæbəlɪzəm] N Stoffwechsel *m*

metal ['metl] **1** N Metall *nt* **2** VT (*Brit*) **~led road** Asphaltstraße *f*

metal: **metal detector** N Metallsuchgerät *nt*; **metal exchange** N (*St Ex*) Metallbörse *f*

metallic [mɪˈtælɪk] ADJ metallisch; **~ finish/paint** Metalliclackierung *f*/-lack *m*; **~ blue/green** blau-/ grünmetallic; **a ~ blue car** ein Auto *nt* in Blaumetallic

metallurgy [me'tælədʒɪ] N Metallurgie f

metal IN CPDS Metall-; **metal polish** N Metallpolitur f; **metalwork** N Metall nt; **we did ~ at school** wir haben in der Schule Metallarbeiten gemacht

metamorphose [ˌmetə'mɔːfəʊz] **1** VT verwandeln; (Sci) umwandeln **2** VI sich verwandeln; (Sci) sich umwandeln

metamorphosis [ˌmetə'mɔːfəsɪs] N, pl **metamorphoses** [ˌmetə'mɔːfəsiːz] Metamorphose f; (fig) Verwandlung f

metaphor ['metəfə'] N Metapher f

metaphorical [ˌmetə'fɒrɪkəl] ADJ metaphorisch

metaphorically [ˌmetə'fɒrɪkəlɪ] ADV metaphorisch; **~ speaking** bildlich gesprochen

metaphysical [ˌmetə'fɪzɪkəl] ADJ metaphysisch

mete [miːt] VT **to ~ out punishment to sb** jdn bestrafen

meteor ['miːtɪə'] N Meteor m

meteoric [ˌmiːtɪ'ɒrɪk] ADJ (fig) kometenhaft

meteorite ['miːtɪəraɪt] N Meteorit m

meteorological [ˌmiːtɪərə'lɒdʒɪkəl] ADJ meteorologisch; **~ station** Wetterstation f

meteorologist [ˌmiːtɪə'rɒlədʒɪst] N Meteorologe m, Meteorologin f

meteorology [ˌmiːtɪə'rɒlədʒɪ] N Meteorologie f

meter[1] ['miːtə'] **1** N Zähler m; (= gas ~ also) Gasuhr f; (= water ~) Wasseruhr f; (= parking ~) Parkuhr f; (= exposure or light ~) Belichtungsmesser m; (= coin ~) Münzzähler m; **the ~ has run out** (parking ~) die Parkuhr ist abgelaufen; (coin ~) es ist kein Geld mehr im Zähler; **to turn the water/gas off at the ~** das Wasser/Gas am Hauptschalter abstellen; **to turn the electricity off at the ~** den Strom am Hauptschalter abschalten **2** VT messen

meter[2] N (US) = metre

methane ['miːθeɪn] N Methan nt

method ['meθəd] N Methode f; (= process) Verfahren nt; (Cook) Zubereitung f; (in experiment) Vorgehensweise f; **~ of payment/application** Zahlungs-/Anwendungsweise f; **~ analysis** or **study** (Comm) Arbeitsablaufstudie f

methodical ADJ, **methodically** ADV [mɪ'θɒdɪkəl, -ɪ] methodisch

Methodist ['meθədɪst] **1** ADJ methodistisch **2** N Methodist(in) m(f)

meths [meθs] N SING ABBR of **methylated spirits** Spiritus m; **~ drinker** ≈ Fuseltrinker(in) m(f)

methylated spirits ['meθɪleɪtɪd'spɪrɪts] N SING Äthylalkohol m

meticulous [mɪ'tɪkjʊləs] ADJ genau; **to be ~ about sth** es mit etw sehr genau nehmen

meticulously [mɪ'tɪkjʊləslɪ] ADV sorgfältig

met office ['met,ɒfɪs] N (Brit) Wetteramt nt

metre, (US) **meter** ['miːtə'] N **(a)** (Measure) Meter m or nt **(b)** (Poet) Metrum nt

metric ['metrɪk] ADJ metrisch; **the ~ system** das metrische Maßsystem; **to go ~** auf das metrische Maßsystem umstellen

metronome ['metrənəʊm] N Metronom nt

metropolis [mɪ'trɒpəlɪs] N Metropole f; (= capital) Hauptstadt f

metropolitan [ˌmetrə'pɒlɪtən] ADJ weltstädtisch; (of a capital) hauptstädtisch; **~ district/area** Stadtgebiet nt

mettle [metl] N Courage f; **to test sb's ~** (thing) zeigen, was in jdm steckt; **to be on one's ~** auf dem Posten sein

mews [mjuːz] N SING or PL (= houses) Siedlung ehemaliger zu modischen Wohnungen umgebauter Kutscherhäuschen; (= street) Gasse f; **a ~ cottage** ein ehemaliges Kutscherhäuschen

Mexican ['meksɪkən] **1** ADJ mexikanisch **2** N Mexikaner(in) m(f)

Mexico ['meksɪkəʊ] N Mexiko nt

Mexico City N Mexiko City nt

mezzanine ['mezəniːn] N Mezzanin nt

MFN ABBR of **Most Favoured Nation**

mg ABBR of **milligram(s), milligramme(s)** mg

MI5 (Brit) ABBR of **Military Intelligence, section 5** MI5 m, Spionageabwehrdienst der britischen Regierung

MI6 (Brit) ABBR of **Military Intelligence, section 6** MI6 m, britischer Auslandsgeheimdienst

miaow [miː'aʊ] (Brit) **1** N Miau(en) nt **2** VI miauen

mice [maɪs] PL of mouse

mickey ['mɪkɪ] N (Brit inf) **to take the ~ out of sb** jdn auf den Arm nehmen (inf); **are you taking the ~?** du willst mich/ihn etc wohl auf den Arm nehmen (inf)

Mickey Mouse ADJ ATTR (inf) company etc lachhaft; **~ money** Spielgeld nt

micro ['maɪkrəʊ] N (Comput) Mikro(computer) m

micro- PREF mikro-, Mikro-

microbe ['maɪkrəʊb] N Mikrobe f

micro: microbiology N Mikrobiologie f; **microchip** N Mikrochip nt; **microcomputer** N Mikrocomputer m; **microcosm** N Mikrokosmos m; **microfiche** N Mikrofiche m or nt; **microfilm** N Mikrofilm m; **microlight** N Ultraleichtflugzeug nt; **microorganism** N Mikroorganismus m; **microphone** N Mikrofon nt; **microprocessor** N Mikroprozessor m; **microscope** N Mikroskop nt

microscopic [ˌmaɪkrə'skɒpɪk] ADJ (in size) mikroskopisch (klein); **~ creature** mikroskopisch kleines Lebewesen; **in ~ detail** bis ins kleinste Detail

microsurgery N Mikrochirurgie f

microwavable ['maɪkrəʊweɪvəbl] ADJ mikrowellengeeignet

microwave N Mikrowelle f

microwave oven N Mikrowellenherd m

mid [mɪd] ADJ **in ~ January/June** Mitte Januar/Juni; **in the ~ 1950s** Mitte der fünfziger Jahre; **temperatures in the ~ eighties** Temperaturen um 85° Fahrenheit; **to be in one's ~ forties** Mitte vierzig sein; **in ~ morning/afternoon** am Vormittag/Nachmittag; **a ~-morning/-afternoon break** eine Frühstücks-/Nachmittagspause; **a ~-morning snack** ein zweites Frühstück; **in ~ air** in der Luft; **in ~ flight** während des Flugs

midday ['mɪd'deɪ] **1** N Mittag m; **at ~** mittags **2** ADJ ATTR mittäglich; **~ meal** Mittagessen nt; **~ sun/heat** Mittagssonne/-hitze f

middle ['mɪdl] **1** N Mitte f; (= central section: of book, film etc) Mittelteil m; (= inside: of fruit, nut etc) Innere(s) nt; (= stomach) Bauch m; (= waist) Taille f; **in the ~ of the table** mitten auf dem Tisch; (= in exact centre) in der Mitte des Tisches; **in the ~ of the night** mitten in der Nacht; **in the ~ of the day** mitten am Tag; (= around midday) gegen Mittag; **in the ~ of nowhere** am Ende der Welt; **in the ~ of summer** mitten im Sommer; (= height of summer season) im Hochsommer; **in or about the ~ of May** Mitte Mai; **we were in the ~ of lunch** wir waren mitten beim Essen; **to be in the ~ of doing sth** mitten dabei sein, etw zu tun; **down the ~** in der Mitte

2 ADJ mittlere(r, s); **to be in one's ~ twenties** Mitte zwanzig sein

middle IN CPDS Mittel-, mittel-; **middle age** N mittleres Lebensalter; **middle-aged** ADJ in den mittleren Jahren; **Middle Ages** PL Mittelalter nt; **Middle America** N (= class) die amerikanische Mittelschicht; **middlebrow** ADJ für den (geistigen) Normalverbraucher; **~ tastes** Durchschnittsgeschmack m; **middle-class** ADJ bürgerlich; **middle class(es)** N(PL) Mittelstand m; **middle-distance runner** N Mittelstreckenläufer(in) m(f); **Middle East** N Naher Osten; (from Iran and India) Mittlerer Osten; **Middle England** N (fig: = middle classes) die englische Mittelschicht; **middle finger** N Mittelfinger m; **middle-income** ADJ family mit mittlerem Einkommen; **middleman** N Mittelsmann m; (Comm) Zwischenhändler m; **middle management** N mittleres Management; **middle manager** N mittlere Führungskraft; **middle name** N zweiter (Vor)name; **modesty is my ~** (fig) mit der Bescheidenheit in Person; **middle-of-the-road** ADJ **(a)** (= moderate) gemäßigt; policy, politician der gemäßigten Mitte **(b)** (= conventional) style, person konventionell; music anspruchslos; **middle-ranking** ADJ mittlere(r, s); **~ army officers** Armeeoffiziere pl mittleren Ranges; **middle school** N (Brit) Schule für 9-12-jährige

middling ['mɪdlɪŋ] ADJ mittelmäßig; **how are you? - ~** wie geht es dir? - einigermaßen inf

Mideast [mɪd'iːst] (US) N **the ~** der Nahe Osten; (from Iran and Iraq to India) der Mittlere Osten

midfield [mɪd'fiːld] **1** N Mittelfeld nt **2** ADJ Mittelfeld-; **~ player/position** Mittelfeldspieler(in) m(f)/-position f

midge [mɪdʒ] N (Brit) Mücke f

midget ['mɪdʒɪt] **1** N Liliputaner(in) m(f) **2** ADJ winzig

mid: **Midlands** PL **the ~** die Midlands; **midlife crisis** N Midlife-Crisis f; **midnight** ◼ N Mitternacht f; **at ~** um Mitternacht ◼ ADJ ATTR mitternächtlich, Mitternachts-; **~ mass** Mitternachtsmesse f; **the ~ hour** die Mitternachtsstunde; **midpoint** N mittlerer Punkt; (Geometry) Mittelpunkt m; **mid-price** ◼ ADJ im mittleren Preisbereich ◼ N **at ~** im mittleren Preisbereich

midriff ['mɪdrɪf] N Taille f

midst [mɪdst] N Mitte f; **in the ~ of** mitten in; **in our ~** unter uns

mid: **midstream** N **in ~** (lit) in der Mitte des Flusses; (fig) auf halber Strecke, mittendrin; **midsummer** ◼ N Hochsommer m ◼ ADJ im Hochsommer; **Midsummer's Day** N Sommersonnenwende f; **midterm** ◼ N **in ~** (three-term year) mitten im Trimester; (two-term year) mitten im Schulhalbjahr or (Univ) Semester ◼ ADJ **~ elections** (Pol) Zwischenwahlen pl; **midtown** (US) ◼ N Stadtzentrum nt ◼ ADJ im Stadtzentrum; **a ~ Manhattan hotel** ein Hotel im Zentrum von Manhattan; **midway** ◼ ADV auf halbem Weg; **Düsseldorf is ~ between Krefeld and Cologne** Düsseldorf liegt auf halber Strecke zwischen Krefeld und Köln; **~ through sth** mitten in etw (dat) ◼ ADJ **we've now reached the ~ point** or **stage in the project** das Projekt ist jetzt zur Hälfte fertig; **midweek** ◼ ADV mitten in der Woche; **by ~** Mitte der Woche ◼ ADJ ATTR Mitte der Woche; **he booked a ~ flight** er buchte einen Flug für Mitte der Woche; **Midwest** N Mittelwesten m; **Midwestern** ADJ mittelwestlich

midwife ['mɪdwaɪf] N, pl **-wives** [-waɪvz] Hebamme f

midwinter [ˌmɪd'wɪntəʳ] ◼ N Wintermitte f ◼ ADJ mittwinterlich

miff [mɪf] VT (inf) **to be ~ed at** or **about sth** (= annoyed) über etw (acc) verärgert sein; (= offended) sich wegen etw auf den Schlips getreten fühlen (inf)

might[1] [maɪt] PRET of **may**; **they ~ be brothers, they look so alike** sie könnten Brüder sein, sie sehen sich so ähnlich; **as you ~ expect** wie zu erwarten war; **... I ~ add** ... möchte ich hinzufügen; **you ~ try Smith's** Sie könnten es ja mal bei Smiths versuchen; **he ~ at least have apologized** er hätte sich wenigstens entschuldigen können; **I ~ have known** das hätte ich mir denken können; **she was thinking of what ~ have been** sie dachte an das, was hätte sein können

might[2] N Macht f; **with all one's ~** mit aller Kraft

mightily ['maɪtɪlɪ] ADV (inf: = extremely) mächtig (inf); **~ impressive** höchst beeindruckend; **I was ~ impressed/relieved** ich war überaus beeindruckt/erleichtert

mightn't ['maɪtnt] CONTR of **might not**

mighty ['maɪtɪ] ◼ ADJ **(a)** person, force, army mächtig; **the ~** die Mächtigen pl **(b)** (= massive) gewaltig; cheer lautstark ◼ ADV (esp US inf) mächtig (inf)

migraine ['miːgreɪn] N Migräne f

migrant ['maɪgrənt] ◼ ADJ **~ bird** Zugvogel m; **~ worker** Wanderarbeiter(in) m(f); (esp in EU) Gastarbeiter(in) m(f) ◼ N **(a)** (= bird) Zugvogel m **(b)** (= worker) Wanderarbeiter(in) m(f); (esp in EU) Gastarbeiter(in) m(f)

migrate [maɪ'greɪt] VI (ab)wandern; (birds) nach Süden ziehen

migration [maɪ'greɪʃən] N Wanderung f; (of birds) (Vogel)zug m

migratory [maɪ'greɪtərɪ] ADJ **~ worker** Wanderarbeiter(in) m(f); **~ birds** Zugvögel pl

mike [maɪk] N (inf) Mikro nt (inf)

mil [mɪl] (inf) ABBR of **million(s)**; **half a ~** eine halbe Million

Milan [mɪ'læn] N Mailand nt

mild [maɪld] ◼ ADJ (+ER) mild; breeze, criticism, medicine, cigarettes, illness leicht; person, character sanft ◼ N (Brit: = beer) leichtes dunkles Bier

mildew ['mɪldjuː] N Schimmel m; (on plants) Mehltau m

mildly ['maɪldlɪ] ADV leicht; say, ask sanft; scold, rebuke, protest, curse, reply milde; **to put it ~** gelinde gesagt

mile [maɪl] N Meile f; **how many ~s per gallon does your car do?** wie viel verbraucht Ihr Auto?; **a fifty-~ journey** eine Fahrt von fünfzig Meilen; **it's 12 ~s to Manchester** bis Manchester sind es 12 Meilen; **~s (and ~s)** (inf) meilenweit; **to go the extra ~** (fig) besondere Anstrengungen unternehmen; **they live ~s away** sie wohnen meilenweit weg; **sorry, I was ~s away** (inf) tut mir Leid, ich war mit meinen Gedanken ganz woanders (inf); **you can tell it a ~ off, it stands** or **sticks out a ~** das sieht ja ein Blinder (mit Krückstock) (inf); **he's ~s better at tennis than she is** er spielt hundertmal besser

Tennis als sie (inf); **if she invited me for dinner, I'd run a ~** (fig inf) wenn sie mich zum Abendessen einladen würde, würde mich das kalte Grausen packen (inf); **to talk a ~ a minute** (US inf) das Blaue vom Himmel (herunter)reden (inf)

mileage ['maɪlɪdʒ] N Meilen pl; (on odometer) Meilenstand m; **you get a much better ~ (per gallon) from this car if ...** dieser Wagen ist viel sparsamer im Verbrauch, wenn ...; **~ allowance** ≈ Kilometerpauschale f; **we got a lot of ~ out of it** (fig inf) das war uns (dat) sehr dienlich

mileometer [maɪ'lɒmɪtəʳ] N (Brit) ≈ Kilometerzähler m

milestone ['maɪlstəʊn] N (lit, fig) Meilenstein m

milieu ['miːljɜː] N Milieu nt

militant ['mɪlɪtənt] ◼ ADJ militant ◼ N militantes Element; **the ~s among the students** die militanten Studenten

militarily ['mɪlɪtrɪlɪ] ADV militärisch

militarism ['mɪlɪtərɪzəm] N Militarismus m

militarist ['mɪlɪtərɪst] ◼ ADJ militaristisch ◼ N Militarist(in) m(f)

militaristic [ˌmɪlɪtə'rɪstɪk] ADJ militaristisch

military ['mɪlɪtərɪ] ◼ ADJ militärisch; **~ government** Militärregierung f; **~ personnel** Militärangehörige pl ◼ N **the ~** das Militär

military: **military base** N Militärstützpunkt m; **military police** N Militärpolizei f; **military policeman** N Militärpolizist m; **military service** N Militärdienst m; **to do one's ~** seinen Militärdienst ableisten; **he's doing his ~** er ist gerade beim Militär

militate ['mɪlɪteɪt] VI **to ~ against/in favour** (Brit) or **favor** (US) **of sth** für/gegen etw sprechen

militia [mɪ'lɪʃə] N Miliz f

militiaman [mɪ'lɪʃəmən] N, pl **-men** [-mən] Milizsoldat m

milk [mɪlk] ◼ N Milch f; **it's** or **there's no use crying over spilled ~** (prov) was passiert ist, ist passiert ◼ VT (lit, fig) melken; **the little old lady was ~ed dry by some heartless swindler** die alte Frau wurde von einem gewissenlosen Betrüger nach Strich und Faden ausgenommen (inf)

milk IN CPDS Milch-; **milk chocolate** N Vollmilchschokolade f; **milk float** N Milchauto nt

milking ['mɪlkɪŋ] N Melken nt

milk: **milkman** N Milchmann m; **milk of magnesia** N Magnesiamilch f; **milk product** N Milchprodukt nt; **milk pudding** N (Brit) Milchspeise f; **milk round** N (Brit) **(a)** (of milkman) Milchrunde f **(b)** (Univ) regelmäßige Besuche von Personalvertretern großer Firmen an Universitäten, um mögliche Mitarbeiter zu rekrutieren; **milkshake** N Milchshake m; **milk tooth** N Milchzahn m

milky ['mɪlkɪ] ADJ (+ER) milchig; **~ green/white** milchig grün/weiß; **~ coffee** Milchkaffee m

Milky Way [ˌmɪlkɪ'weɪ] N Milchstraße f

mill [mɪl] N **(a)** Mühle f; **in training you're really put through the ~** (inf) im Training wird man ganz schön hart rangenommen (inf) **(b)** (= paper, steel ~ etc) Fabrik f; (= cotton ~) (for thread) Spinnerei f; (for cloth) Weberei f

➤ **mill about** (Brit) or **around** VI umherlaufen; **people were milling about** or **around the office** es herrschte ein Kommen und Gehen im Büro

millennial [mɪ'lenɪəl] ADJ tausendjährig

millennium [mɪ'lenɪəm] N, pl **-s** or **millennia** [mɪ'lenɪə] (= 1,000 years) Jahrtausend nt

millennium bug N (Comput inf) Jahr-2000-Problem nt

miller ['mɪləʳ] N Müller(in) m(f)

milli- ['mɪlɪ-] PREF Milli-; **~second** Millisekunde f

milli: **milligram(me)** N Milligramm nt; **millilitre**, (US) **milliliter** N Milliliter m or nt; **millimetre**, (US) **millimeter** N Millimeter m or nt

milliner ['mɪlɪnəʳ] N Hutmacher m, Modistin f

millinery ['mɪlɪnərɪ] N (= articles) Hüte pl

million ['mɪljən] N Million f; **4 ~ people** 4 Millionen Menschen; **for ~s and ~s of years** für millionen und abermillionen von Jahren; **she's one in a ~** (inf) sie ist einsame Klasse (inf); **it will sell a ~** (inf) das wird ein Millionenerfolg; **I've done it ~s of times** (inf) das habe ich schon tausendmal gemacht; **to look (like) a ~ dollars** (inf) umwerfend aussehen (inf)

millionaire [ˌmɪljə'nɛəʳ] N Millionär m

millionairess [ˌmɪljəˈnɛəres] N Millionärin f
millionth [ˈmɪljənθ] **1** ADJ (= *fraction*) millionstel; (*in series*) millionste(r, s) **2** N Millionstel *nt*
millipede [ˈmɪlɪpiːd] N Tausendfüß(l)er *m*
millstone [ˈmɪlstəʊn] N Mahlstein *m*; **she's/it's a ~ around his neck** sie/das ist für ihn ein Klotz am Bein
mime [maɪm] **1** N Pantomime f **2** VT pantomimisch darstellen **3** VI Pantomimen spielen
mime artist N Pantomime *m*, Pantomimin f
mimic [ˈmɪmɪk] **1** N Imitator(in) *m(f)*; **he's a very good ~** er kann sehr gut Geräusche/andere Leute nachmachen **2** VT nachahmen; (= *ridicule*) nachäffen
mimicry [ˈmɪmɪkrɪ] N Nachahmung f
min (**a**) ABBR *of* **minute(s)** min (**b**) ABBR *of* **minimum** min.
minaret [ˌmɪnəˈret] N Minarett *nt*
mince [mɪns] **1** N (*esp Brit*) Hackfleisch *nt* **2** VT (*esp Brit*) *meat* durch den Fleischwolf drehen; **he doesn't ~ his words** er nimmt kein Blatt vor den Mund **3** VI (*Brit* = *walk*) tänzeln
mince: mincemeat N *süße Gebäckfüllung aus Dörrobst und Sirup*; **to make ~ of sb** (*inf*) (*physically*) Hackfleisch aus jdm machen (*inf*); (*verbally*) jdn zur Schnecke machen (*inf*); **mince pie** N *mit Mincemeat gefülltes Gebäck*
mincer [ˈmɪnsəʳ] N (*esp Brit*) Fleischwolf *m*

---

mind [maɪnd]

1 NOUN	**3** INTRANSITIVE VERB
2 TRANSITIVE VERB	**4** PHRASAL VERB

1 NOUN
(**a**) (= *intellect*) Geist *m* (*also Philos*), Verstand *m*; (= *way of thinking*) Denkweise f; (= *thoughts*) Gedanken *pl*; (= *memory*) Gedächtnis *nt*; **to have a good mind** ein heller Kopf sein; **it's all in the mind** das ist alles Einbildung; **to blow sb's mind** (*inf*) jdn umwerfen (*inf*); (*drugs*) jdn high machen (*inf*); **to have a literary/logical** *etc* **mind** literarisch/logisch *etc* veranlagt sein; **in the public mind prostitution is immoral** nach dem Empfinden der Öffentlichkeit ist Prostitution unmoralisch; **state** *or* **frame of mind** Geisteszustand *m*; **to be clear in one's mind about sth** sich (*dat*) über etw im Klaren sein; **to put** *or* **set one's mind to sth** sich anstrengen, etw zu tun; **he had something on his mind** ihn beschäftigte etwas; **I've a lot on my mind** ich muss mich um (so) viele Dinge kümmern; **you are always on my mind** ich denke ständig an dich; **keep your mind on the job** bleib mit den Gedanken bei der Arbeit; **she couldn't get** *or* **put the song/him out of her mind** das Lied/er ging ihr nicht aus dem Kopf; **to take sb's mind off sth** jdn etw vergessen lassen; **my mind isn't on my work** ich kann mich nicht auf meine Arbeit konzentrieren; **the idea never entered my mind** daran hatte ich überhaupt nicht gedacht; **nothing was further from my mind** nichts lag mir ferner; **in my mind's eye** vor meinem inneren Auge; **it went right out of my mind** daran habe ich überhaupt nicht mehr gedacht; **to bring** *or* **call sth to mind** an etw (*acc*) erinnern
✦**mind over matter** it's a question of mind over matter es ist eine Willensfrage
(**b**) (= *inclination*) Lust f; (= *intention*) Sinn *m*, Absicht f; **I've half a mind/a good mind to …** ich hätte Lust/große *or* gute Lust, zu …
(**c**) (= *opinion*) Meinung f, Ansicht f; **to change one's mind** seine Meinung ändern (*about* über +*acc*); **to be in two minds about sth** sich (*dat*) über etw (*acc*) nicht im Klaren sein; **to be of one** *or* **of the same mind** eines Sinnes (*geh*) *or* gleicher Meinung sein; **to have a mind of one's own** (*person*) (= *think for oneself*) eine eigene Meinung haben; (= *not conform*) seinen eigenen Kopf haben; (*hum: machine etc*) seine Mucken haben (*inf*)
(**d**) (= *sanity*) Verstand *m*, Sinne *pl*; **to lose one's mind** den Verstand verlieren; **nobody in his right mind** kein normaler Mensch
(**e**) (*set structures*)
✦**to bear** *or* **keep sth in mind** etw nicht vergessen; **to bear** *or* **keep sb in mind** an jdn denken; **with this in mind…** mit diesem Gedanken im Hinterkopf…; **to have sb/sth in mind** an jdn/etw denken; **it puts me in mind of sb/sth** es weckt in mir Erinnerungen an jdn/etw

✦**out of one's mind** to go out of one's mind den Verstand verlieren; **I'm bored out of my mind** ich langweile mich zu Tode

2 TRANSITIVE VERB
(**a**) (= *look after*) aufpassen auf (+*acc*); **sb's chair, seat** freihalten
(**b**) (= *be careful of*) aufpassen auf (+*acc*); (= *pay attention to*) achten auf (+*acc*); (= *act in accordance with*) beachten; **mind what you're doing!** pass (doch) auf!; **mind your language!** drück dich anständig aus!; **mind the step!** (*Brit*) Vorsicht Stufe!; **mind your head!** (*Brit*) Kopf einziehen (*inf*), Vorsicht, niedrige Tür/Decke *etc*; **mind your own business** kümmern Sie sich um Ihre eigenen Angelegenheiten
(**c**) (= *care about*) sich kümmern um; (= *object to*) etwas haben gegen; **I don't mind the cold** die Kälte macht mir nichts aus; **I don't mind what he does** es ist mir egal, was er macht; **do you mind coming with me?** würde es dir etwas ausmachen mitzukommen?; **would you mind opening the door?** wären Sie so freundlich, die Tür aufzumachen?; **do you mind my smoking?** macht es Ihnen etwas aus, wenn ich rauche?; **don't mind me** lass dich (durch mich) nicht stören; (*iro*) nimm auf mich keine Rücksicht; **I wouldn't mind a cup of tea** ich hätte nichts gegen eine Tasse Tee
✦**never mind** + *sb/sth* **never mind the expense** (es ist) egal, was es kostet; **never mind that now** das ist jetzt nicht wichtig; **never mind him** kümmere dich nicht um ihn

3 INTRANSITIVE VERB
(**a**) (= *care, worry*) sich (*dat*) etwas daraus machen; (= *object*) etwas dagegen haben; **nobody seemed to mind** niemand schien etwas dagegen zu haben; **I'd prefer to stand, if you don't mind** ich würde lieber stehen, wenn es Ihnen recht ist; **do you mind?** macht es Ihnen etwas aus?; **do you mind!** (*iro*) ich möchte doch sehr bitten!; **I don't mind if I do** ich hätte nichts dagegen
✦**never mind** macht nichts; (*in exasperation*) schon gut; **never mind, you'll find another** mach dir nichts draus, du findest bestimmt einen anderen; **oh, never mind, I'll do it myself** ach, schon gut, ich mache es selbst; **never mind about that now!** das ist doch jetzt nicht wichtig; **I'm not going to finish school, never mind go to university** ich werde die Schule nicht beenden und schon gar nicht zur Universität gehen
✦**never you mind!** kümmere du dich mal nicht darum; (= *none of your business*) das geht dich überhaupt nichts an!
(**b**) (= *be sure*) **mind you get that done** sieh zu, dass du das fertig bekommst; **I'm not saying I'll do it, mind** ich will damit aber nicht sagen, dass ich es tue; **he's not a bad lad, mind, just …** er ist eigentlich kein schlechter Junge, nur …
✦**mind you** allerdings; **it was raining at the time, mind you** allerdings hat es da geregnet; **mind you, he did try** er hat es immerhin versucht; **he's quite good, mind you** er ist eigentlich ganz gut

4 PHRASAL VERB
➤ **mind out** VI (*Brit*) aufpassen (*for* auf +*acc*)

---

mind: mind-bending ADJ (*inf*) Wahnsinns- (*inf*); **drug, substances** bewusstseinsverändernd; **mind-blowing** ADJ (*inf*) Wahnsinns- (*inf*); **mind-boggling** ADJ (*inf*) irrsinnig (*inf*), verrückt (*inf*)
-minded [ˈmaɪndɪd] ADJ SUF **she's very politically-minded** sie interessiert sich sehr für Politik
minder [ˈmaɪndəʳ] N (*inf*) Aufpasser(in) *m(f)*
mindful [ˈmaɪndfʊl] ADJ **to be ~ of sth** etw bedenken
mind: mindless ADJ **destruction, crime, violence** sinnlos; **work, entertainment, routine** stumpfsinnig; (= *stupid*) hirnlos; **mindlessly** ADV (= *tediously*) stumpfsinnig; (= *stupidly*) hirnlos; **mind-reader** N Gedankenleser(in) *m(f)*; **mindset** N Mentalität f
mine[1] [maɪn] POSS PRON meine(r, s); **this car is ~** dieses Auto gehört mir; **his friends and ~** seine und meine Freunde; **a friend of ~** ein Freund von mir; **a favourite** (*Brit*) *or* **favorite** (*US*) **expression of ~** einer meiner Lieblingsausdrücke
mine[2] **1** N (**a**) (*Min*) Bergwerk *nt*; **to work down the ~s** unter Tage arbeiten (**b**) (*Mil, Naut etc*) Mine f (**c**) (*fig*) **the book is a**

~ of information das Buch ist eine wahre Fundgrube; **he is a ~ of information** er ist ein wandelndes Lexikon (*inf*) **2** VT **(a)** *coal, metal* fördern **(b)** (*Mil, Naut*) *channel, road* verminen **3** VI **to ~ for sth** nach etw graben

minefield ['maɪnfiːld] N Minenfeld *nt*; **to enter a (political) ~** sich auf (politisch) gefährliches Terrain begeben

miner ['maɪnə^r] N Bergarbeiter(in) *m(f)*

mineral ['mɪnərəl] **1** N Mineral *nt* **2** ADJ mineralisch; **~ deposits** Mineralbestände *pl*

mineral water N Mineralwasser *nt*

minestrone [ˌmɪnɪ'strəʊnɪ] N Minestrone *f*

minesweeper ['maɪnswiːpə^r] N Minensucher *m*

mingle ['mɪŋgl] VI sich vermischen; (*people, groups*) sich untereinander vermischen; **he ~d with people of all classes** er hatte Umgang mit Menschen aller gesellschaftlichen Schichten; **to ~ with the crowd** sich unters Volk mischen; **she ~d for a while** (*at party*) sie mischte sich eine Zeit lang unter die Gäste

mini- ['mɪnɪ-] PREF Mini-

miniature ['mɪnɪtʃə^r] **1** N Miniaturausgabe *f*; (*Art*) Miniatur *f*; (= *bottle*) Miniflasche *f*; **in ~** im kleinen **2** ADJ ATTR Miniatur-

miniature golf N Minigolf *nt*

mini: minibar N Minibar *f*; **mini-break** N Kurzurlaub *m*; **minibus** N Kleinbus *m*; **minicab** N Kleintaxi *nt*; **minicam** N Minicam *f*; **Minidisc®** ['mɪnɪdɪsk] N (*Mus*) Minidisc *f*; **~ player** Minidisc-Spieler *m*

minim ['mɪnɪm] N (*Brit Mus*) halbe Note

minimal ['mɪnɪml] ADJ minimal; **at ~ cost** zu minimalen Kosten; **with ~ effort** mit minimalem Aufwand

minimalism ['mɪnɪməlɪzəm] N Minimalismus *m*

minimalist ['mɪnɪməlɪst] ADJ minimalistisch

minimize ['mɪnɪmaɪz] VT **(a)** *expenditure, time lost etc* minimieren (*form*) **(b)** (= *belittle, underestimate*) herabsetzen

minimum ['mɪnɪməm] **1** N Minimum *nt*; **with a ~ of inconvenience** mit einem Minimum an Unannehmlichkeiten; **what is the ~ you will accept?** was ist für Sie das Minimum *or* der Mindestbetrag?; **a ~ of 2 hours/ £50/10 people** mindestens 2 Stunden/£ 50/10 Leute; **to keep sth to a** *or* **the ~** etw auf ein Minimum beschränken; **at a** *or* **the ~** (= *at least*) mindestens **2** ADJ ATTR Mindest-; **~ age** Mindestalter *nt*; **~ charge** Mindestgebühr *f*; **~ temperature** Tiefsttemperatur *f*

minimum: minimum lending rate N (*Brit Fin*) Diskontsatz *m*; **minimum reserve (requirement)** N (*Fin*) Mindestreserve *f*; **minimum wage** N Mindestlohn *m*

mining ['maɪnɪŋ] N (*Min*) Bergbau *m*

mining: mining area N Bergbaugebiet *nt*; **mining industry** N Bergbau *m*; **mining town** N Bergarbeiterstadt *f*

minion ['mɪnɪən] N (*fig*) Trabant *m*; **she delegated the job to one of her ~s** sie beauftragte einen/eine ihrer Untergebenen, die Sache zu erledigen

miniskirt ['mɪnɪskɜːt] N Minirock *m*

minister ['mɪnɪstə^r] **1** N **(a)** (*Pol*) Minister(in) *m(f)* **(b)** (*Eccl*) Pfarrer(in) *m(f)* **2** VI **to ~ to sb** sich um jdn kümmern; **to ~ to sb's needs/wants** jds Bedürfnisse/Wünsche (*acc*) befriedigen

ministerial [ˌmɪnɪ'stɪərɪəl] ADJ (*Pol*) ministeriell; **~ post** Ministerposten *m*; **his ~ duties** seine Pflichten als Minister; **at ~ level** auf Ministerebene

ministry ['mɪnɪstrɪ] N **(a)** (*Pol*) Ministerium *nt*; **~ of education** Bildungsministerium *nt* **(b)** (*Eccl*) geistliches Amt; **to enter** *or* **go into the ~** Geistliche(r) werden

mink [mɪŋk] N Nerz *m*; **~ coat** Nerzmantel *m*

minor ['maɪnə^r] **1** ADJ **(a)** (= *of lesser extent*) kleiner; (= *of lesser importance*) unbedeutend; *offence, illness, operation, injuries* leicht; *surgery* klein; *interest, importance* geringer; **~ road** Nebenstraße *f*; **he only played a ~ role in the company** er spielte in der Firma nur eine untergeordnete Rolle **(b)** (*Mus*) Moll-; **~ key** Molltonart *f*; **G ~** g-Moll *nt* **2** N **(a)** (*Jur*) Minderjährige(r) *mf* **(b)** (*US Univ*) Nebenfach *nt* **3** VI (*US Univ*) im Nebenfach studieren (*in* +*acc*)

Minorca [mɪ'nɔːkə] N Menorca *nt*

minority [maɪ'nɒrɪtɪ] **1** N Minderheit *f*; **to be in a** *or* **the ~** in der Minderheit sein **2** ADJ ATTR **(a)** Minderheits-; **~ group** Minderheit *f*; **(ethnic) ~ students** Studenten *pl*, die einer (ethnischen) Minderheit angehören; **a ~ view** die Ansicht einer Minderheit; **~ rights** (*Pol*) Minderheitenrechte *pl* **(b)** (*US Pol*) **House/Senate Minority Leader** Oppositionsführer(in) *m(f)* (im Repräsentantenhaus/Senat)

minority: minority government N Minderheitsregierung *f*; **minority holding, minority interest** N (*Fin*) Minderheitsbeteiligung *f*; **minority shareholder** N (*Fin*) Kleinaktionär(in) *m(f)*

minor league ADJ **~ baseball** (*US*) Baseball *m or nt* in den unteren Ligen

minster ['mɪnstə^r] N Münster *nt*

minstrel ['mɪnstrəl] N (*medieval*) Spielmann *m*; (*wandering*) (fahrender) Sänger

mint¹ [mɪnt] **1** N Münzanstalt *f*; **(Royal) Mint** (König-lich-)Britische Münzanstalt; **to be worth a ~** (*inf*) unbezahlbar sein; **his father made a ~** (*inf*) sein Vater hat einen Haufen Geld gemacht (*inf*) **2** ADJ *stamp* ungestempelt; **in ~ condition** in tadellosem Zustand **3** VT *coin, phrase* prägen

mint² N (*Bot*) Minze *f*; (= *sweet*) Pfefferminz *nt*

mint: mint sauce N Minzsoße *f*; **mint tea** N Pfefferminztee *m*

minuet [ˌmɪnjʊ'et] N Menuett *nt*

minus ['maɪnəs] **1** PREP (a) minus, weniger; **£100 ~ taxes** £ 100 abzüglich (der) Steuern **(b)** (= *without*) ohne; **he returned from the war ~ an arm** er kam mit einem Arm weniger aus dem Krieg zurück **2** ADJ Minus-; *quantity, value* negativ; **~ point** Minuspunkt *m*; **~ three degrees centigrade** drei Grad minus; **an A ~** (*in grading*) eine Eins minus **3** N **(a)** (= *sign*) Minus(zeichen) *nt* **(b)** (= *disadvantage*) Minus *nt*

minuscule ['mɪnəskjuːl] ADJ winzig

minus sign N Minuszeichen *nt*

minute¹ ['mɪnɪt] **1** N **(a)** (*of time, degree*) Minute *f*; **it's 23 ~s past 3** es ist 3 Uhr und 23 Minuten; **in a ~** gleich, sofort; **this (very) ~!** auf der Stelle!; **at this very ~** gerade in diesem Augenblick; **I shan't be a ~** es dauert nicht lang; **just a ~!** einen Moment bitte!; **any ~ (now)** jeden Augenblick; **tell me the ~ he comes** sag mir sofort Bescheid, wenn er kommt; **have you got a ~?** hast du mal eine Minute Zeit?; **I don't believe for a** *or* **one ~ that ...** ich glaube nicht einen Augenblick, dass...; **at the last ~** in letzter Minute **(b)** (= *official note*) Notiz *f*; **~s** Protokoll *nt*; **to take the ~s** das Protokoll führen **2** VT *remark, fact* zu Protokoll nehmen

minute² [maɪ'njuːt] ADJ (= *small*) winzig; (= *detailed, exact*) minuziös; *detail* kleinste(r, s)

minute hand ['mɪnɪthænd] N Minutenzeiger *m*

minutely [maɪ'njuːtlɪ] ADV (= *by a small amount*) ganz geringfügig; (= *in detail*) genauestens; **anything ~ resembling a fish** alles, was auch nur annähernd nach Fisch aussieht; **a ~ detailed account** eine sehr detaillierte Schilderung

minutiae [mɪ'njuːʃiː] PL genaue Einzelheiten *pl*; **the ~ of daily life** die tägliche Kleinarbeit

miracle ['mɪrəkl] N Wunder *nt*; **to work** *or* **perform ~s** (*lit*) Wunder vollbringen; **I can't work ~s** ich kann nicht hexen; **by a ~** (*fig*), **by some ~** (*fig*) wie durch ein Wunder; **it'll take a ~ for us** *or* **we'll need a ~ to be finished on time** da müsste schon ein Wunder geschehen, wenn wir noch rechtzeitig fertig werden sollen

miracle drug N Wunderdroge *f*

miraculous [mɪ'rækjʊləs] ADJ **(a)** *escape, recovery* wundersam; **~ powers** Wunderkräfte *pl*; **that is nothing/little short of ~** das grenzt an ein Wunder **(b)** (= *unbelievable, wonderful*) wunderbar; *achievement, improvement, transformation* erstaunlich

miraculously [mɪ'rækjʊləslɪ] ADV **the baby was unhurt** es war wie ein Wunder, dass das Baby unverletzt blieb

mirage ['mɪrɑːʒ] N Fata Morgana *f*; (*fig*) Trugbild *nt*

mire [maɪə^r] N Morast *m* (*also fig*); **to drag sb/sth through the ~** (*fig*) jdn/etw in den Schmutz ziehen

mirror ['mɪrə^r] **1** N Spiegel *m* **2** VT (wider)spiegeln

mirror image N Spiegelbild *nt*

mirth [mɜːθ] N Freude *f*; (= *laughter*) Heiterkeit *f*

misadventure [ˌmɪsəd'ventʃə^r] N Missgeschick *nt*

misanthrope ['mɪzənθrəʊp] N Misanthrop(in) *m(f)*

misapply ['mɪsə'plaɪ] VT falsch anwenden

misapprehension ['mɪsˌæprɪ'henʃən] N Missverständnis *nt*; **he was under the ~ that ...** er hatte fälschlicherweise angenommen, dass ...

misappropriate ['mɪsə'prəuprɪeɪt] VT entwenden; *money* veruntreuen

misappropriation ['mɪsəˌprəuprɪ'eɪʃən] N Entwendung *f*; *(of money)* Veruntreuung *f*

misbehave ['mɪsbɪ'heɪv] VI sich schlecht benehmen

misbehaviour, *(US)* **misbehavior** ['mɪsbɪ'heɪvjəʳ] N schlechtes Benehmen

miscalculate ['mɪs'kælkjʊleɪt] **1** VT falsch berechnen; *(= misjudge)* falsch einschätzen **2** VI sich verrechnen; *(= estimate wrongly)* sich verkalkulieren; *(= misjudge)* sich verschätzen

miscalculation ['mɪsˌkælkjʊ'leɪʃən] N Rechenfehler *m*; *(= wrong estimation)* Fehlkalkulation *f*; *(= misjudgement)* Fehleinschätzung *f*

miscarriage ['mɪsˌkærɪdʒ] N **(a)** *(Med)* Fehlgeburt *f* **(b)** **~ of justice** Justizirrtum *m*

miscarry [ˌmɪs'kærɪ] VI *(Med)* eine Fehlgeburt haben

miscast ['mɪs'kɑːst], *pret, ptp* **miscast** VT **the actor was clearly ~ in this role** mit diesem Schauspieler war die Rolle eindeutig fehlbesetzt

miscellaneous [ˌmɪsɪ'leɪnɪəs] ADJ verschieden; *collection, crowd* bunt; **~ expenses/income** sonstige Aufwendungen/Erträge; **"~"** *(on agenda, list)* „Sonstiges"

mischief ['mɪstʃɪf] N **(a)** *(= roguery)* Schalk *m*; *(= naughty, foolish behaviour)* Unsinn *m*, Unfug *m*; **she's full of ~** sie hat nur Unfug im Kopf; **he's always getting into ~** er stellt dauernd etwas an; **to keep out of ~** keinen Unfug machen **(b)** *(= trouble)* **to cause** *or* **make ~** Unfrieden stiften; **to make ~ for sb** jdn in Schwierigkeiten bringen **(c)** *(= damage, physical injury)* Schaden *m*; **to do sb/oneself a ~** jdm/sich Schaden zufügen; *(physically)* jdm/sich etwas (an)tun

mischief-maker ['mɪstʃɪfˌmeɪkəʳ] N Unruhestifter(in) *m(f)*

mischievous ['mɪstʃɪvəs] ADJ **(a)** *(= roguish, playful)* verschmitzt; **a ~ person** ein Schlawiner *m*; **her son is really ~** ihr Sohn ist ein Schlingel **(b)** *(= malicious)* *rumour, suggestion* bösartig; *person* boshaft

mischievously ['mɪstʃɪvəslɪ] ADV **(a)** *(= roguishly)* *smile, say* verschmitzt; **to behave ~** Unfug anstellen **(b)** *(= maliciously)* bösartig

misconceived ['mɪskən'siːvd] ADJ *policy* verfehlt; *idea* irrig, falsch; *approach, action* falsch

misconception [ˌmɪskən'sepʃən] N fälschliche Annahme

misconduct [ˌmɪs'kɒndʌkt] N schlechtes Benehmen; *(professional)* Berufsvergehen *nt*; *(sexual)* Fehltritt *m*; **gross ~** grobes Fehlverhalten

misdemeanour, *(US)* **misdemeanor** [ˌmɪsdɪ'miːnəʳ] N schlechtes Benehmen; *(Jur)* Vergehen *nt*

misdiagnose ['mɪsdaɪəgnəʊz] VT **(a)** *(Med)* *illness* falsch diagnostizieren; *patient* eine falsche Diagnose stellen (+*dat*) **(b)** *problem, situation* falsch einschätzen

misdirect ['mɪsdɪ'rekt] VT *letter (= send to wrong address)* fehlleiten; *(= address wrongly)* falsch adressieren; *energies* vergeuden; *person (= send astray)* in die falsche Richtung schicken; *(= misinform)* falsch informieren

misdirected ['mɪsdɪ'rektɪd] ADJ *energy, effort* vergeudet

miser ['maɪzəʳ] N Geizhals *m*

miserable ['mɪzərəbl] ADJ **(a)** *(= unhappy)* *person* unglücklich; *colour* trist; *(= ill-tempered)* griesgrämig; **I feel ~ today** ich fühle mich heute elend *or (ill)* miserabel; **to make sb ~** jdn unglücklich machen; **to make life ~ for sb, to make sb's life ~** jdm das Leben zur Qual machen **(b)** *(= wretched)* *headache, cold, weather* grässlich; *existence, hovel, spectacle* erbärmlich; *place* trostlos **(c)** *(= contemptible)* jämmerlich; *person, treatment, behaviour* gemein; *sum* kläglich; **a ~ £3** mickrige 3 Pfund *(inf)*; **to be a ~ failure** kläglich versagen

miserably ['mɪzərəblɪ] ADV **(a)** *(= unhappily)* unglücklich **(b)** *(= wretchedly)* *live, die* jämmerlich, *poor* erbärmlich; **~ unhappy** todunglücklich *(inf)*; **it was ~ cold** es war erbärmlich kalt **(c)** *pay, feed, play* miserabel; *fail* kläglich; *treat, behave* gemein

miserly ['maɪzəlɪ] ADJ geizig; *offer* knauserig; **a ~ £8** mickrige £ 8 *(inf)*; **to be ~ with sth** mit etw geizen

misery ['mɪzərɪ] N **(a)** *(= sadness)* Trauer *f* **(b)** *(= suffering)* Qualen *pl*; *(= wretchedness)* Elend *nt*; **to make sb's life a ~** jdm das Leben zur Hölle machen; **to put an animal out of its ~** ein Tier von seinen Qualen erlösen; **to put sb out of his ~** *(fig)* jdn nicht länger auf die Folter spannen **(c)** *(Brit inf: = person)* Miesepeter *m (inf)*

misery-guts ['mɪzərɪgʌts] N *(Brit inf)* Miesmacher(in) *m(f) (inf)*

misfire ['mɪs'faɪəʳ] VI *(engine)* fehlzünden; *(plan)* fehlschlagen

misfit ['mɪsfɪt] N Außenseiter(in) *m(f)*; **he's a real ~** er ist ein sehr schwieriger Fall

misfortune [mɪs'fɔːtʃuːn] N *(= ill fortune, affliction)* (schweres) Schicksal *nt*; *(= bad luck)* Pech *nt no pl*; *(= unlucky incident)* Missgeschick *nt*; **it was my ~** *or* **I had the ~ to ...** ich hatte das Pech, zu ...

misgiving [mɪs'gɪvɪŋ] N Bedenken *pl*; **I had (certain) ~s about the scheme** bei dem Vorhaben war mir nicht ganz wohl; **I had (certain) ~s about lending him the money** bei dem Gedanken, ihm das Geld zu leihen, war mir nicht ganz wohl

misguided ['mɪs'gaɪdɪd] ADJ töricht; *opinions* irrig; *(= misplaced) kindness etc* unangebracht; **I think it was ~ of you** *or* **you were ~ to accept his proposal** meiner Ansicht nach waren Sie schlecht beraten, seinen Vorschlag anzunehmen

mishandle ['mɪs'hændl] VT *case* falsch handhaben

mishap ['mɪshæp] N Missgeschick *nt*; **he's had a slight ~** ihm ist ein kleines Missgeschick passiert

mishear ['mɪs'hɪəʳ], *pret, ptp* **misheard** ['mɪs'hɜːd] **1** VT falsch hören **2** VI sich verhören

misinform ['mɪsɪn'fɔːm] VT falsch informieren; **you've been ~ed** Sie sind falsch informiert

misinterpret ['mɪsɪn'tɜːprɪt] VT falsch auslegen; **he ~ed her silence as agreement** er deutete ihr Schweigen fälschlich als Zustimmung

misjudge ['mɪs'dʒʌdʒ] VT falsch einschätzen

misjudgement ['mɪs'dʒʌdʒmənt] N Fehleinschätzung *f*

mislay [mɪs'leɪ], *pret, ptp* **mislaid** [mɪs'leɪd] VT verlegen

mislead [mɪs'liːd], *pret, ptp* **misled** VT irreführen; **you have been misled** Sie irren *or* täuschen sich; **don't be misled by appearances** lassen Sie sich nicht durch Äußerlichkeiten täuschen

misleading [mɪs'liːdɪŋ] ADJ irreführend

misleadingly [mɪs'liːdɪŋlɪ] ADV *tell, say etc* irreführenderweise; *presented* irreführend

misled [ˌmɪs'led] PRET, PTP *of* **mislead**

mismanage ['mɪs'mænɪdʒ] VT *company, finances* schlecht verwalten; *affair, deal* schlecht handhaben

mismanagement ['mɪs'mænɪdʒmənt] N Misswirtschaft *f*

mismatch [mɪs'mætʃ] N **to be a ~** nicht zusammenpassen

misnomer ['mɪs'nəʊməʳ] N unzutreffende Bezeichnung

misogynist [mɪ'sɒdʒɪnɪst] N Frauenfeind *m*

misplace ['mɪs'pleɪs] VT **(a)** *document, file etc* falsch einordnen; *(= mislay)* verlegen **(b)** **to be ~d** *(confidence, trust)* unangebracht sein

misprint ['mɪsprɪnt] N Druckfehler *m*

mispronounce ['mɪsprə'naʊns] VT falsch aussprechen

misquote ['mɪs'kwəʊt] VT falsch zitieren; **he was ~d as having said ...** man unterstellte ihm, gesagt zu haben ...

misread ['mɪs'riːd], *pret, ptp* **misread** ['mɪs'red] VT falsch lesen; *(= misinterpret)* falsch verstehen

misremember [mɪsrɪ'membəʳ] VT *(esp US form)* falsch erinnern

misrepresent ['mɪsˌreprɪ'zent] VT falsch darstellen; *ideas* verfälschen; **he was ~ed in the papers** seine Worte *etc* wurden von der Presse verfälscht wiedergegeben

miss¹ [mɪs] **1** N **(a)** *(= shot)* Fehlschuss *m*; *(= failure)* Misserfolg *m*; **his first shot was a ~** sein erster Schuss ging daneben; **it was a near ~** *(fig)* das war eine knappe Sache; **we had a near ~ with that car** wir wären fast mit diesem Auto zusammengestoßen

(b) to give sth a ~ *(inf)* sich *(dat)* etw schenken **2** VT **(a)** *(= fail to hit, catch, experience, find, attend etc: by accident)* verpassen; *(= deliberately not attend)* nicht gehen zu *or* in (+*acc*); *(deliberately: = not experience)* sich *(dat)* entgehen lassen; *(= fail to hear or perceive)* nicht mitbekommen;

(*deliberately*) überhören/-sehen; (= *not hit, find*) *target, ball, step, vocation, place* verfehlen; **to ~ breakfast** nicht frühstücken; (= *be too late for*) das Frühstück verpassen; **they ~ed each other in the crowd** sie verpassten sich in der Menge; **to ~ the boat** *or* **bus** (*fig*) den Anschluss verpassen; **he ~ed school for a week** er hat eine Woche lang die Schule versäumt; **~ a turn** einmal aussetzen; **he doesn't ~ much** (*inf*) ihm entgeht so schnell nichts

(b) (= *fail to achieve*) *prize* nicht bekommen; **he narrowly ~ed being first/becoming president** er wäre beinahe auf den ersten Platz gekommen/Präsident geworden

(c) (= *avoid*) *obstacle* (noch) ausweichen können (+*dat*); (= *escape*) entgehen (+*dat*); **to ~ doing sth** etw um ein Haar tun; **the car just ~ed the tree** das Auto wäre um ein Haar gegen den Baum gefahren

(d) (= *overlook, fail to deal with*) übersehen

(e) (= *notice or regret absence of*) vermissen; **I ~ him/my old car** er/mein altes Auto fehlt mir; **he won't be ~ed** keiner wird ihn vermissen

3 VI (= *not hit*) nicht treffen; (*punching*) danebenschlagen; (*shooting*) danebenschießen; (= *not catch*) danebengreifen; (*ball, shot, punch*) danebengehen

➤ **miss out 1** VT SEP (= *accidentally not see*) übersehen; *last line or paragraph etc* weglassen **2** VI (*inf*) zu kurz kommen; **to miss out on sth** etw verpassen; (= *get less*) bei etw zu kurz kommen

miss² N **(a)** **Miss** Fräulein *nt*, Frl. *abbr* **(b)** (= *term of address*) (*to waitress etc*) Bedienung; (*to teacher*) Frau X

mis-sell [mɪsˈsel] VT *pension, insurance etc* mit Täuschungsabsicht verkaufen

mis-selling [mɪsˈselɪŋ] N (*of pensions etc*) Verkauf *m* mit Täuschungsabsicht

misshapen [mɪsˈʃeɪpən] ADJ missgebildet; *vegetables* unförmig, missraten

missile [ˈmɪsaɪl] N **(a)** (= *stone, javelin etc*) (Wurf)geschoss *nt* **(b)** (= *rocket*) Rakete *f*

missing [ˈmɪsɪŋ] ADJ (= *not able to be found*) *person, boat* vermisst; *object* verschwunden; (= *not there*) fehlend; **to be ~/have gone ~** fehlen; (*person, boat etc*) vermisst werden; **to go ~** (*person, boat etc*) vermisst werden; (*object*) verloren gehen; **the coat has two buttons ~, two buttons are ~ from the coat** an dem Mantel fehlen zwei Knöpfe; **my name is ~ from the list** mein Name fehlt auf der Liste; **~ in action** vermisst

missing person N Vermisste(r) *mf*; **~s bureau/file** Vermisstenbüro *nt*/-liste *f*

mission [ˈmɪʃən] N **(a)** (= *business, task*) Auftrag *m*; (= *calling*) Berufung *f*; (*Mil*) Befehl *m*; (= *operation*) Einsatz *m*; **our ~ is to ...** wir sind damit beauftragt, zu ...; **to send sb on a secret ~** jdn mit einer geheimen Mission beauftragen; **~ accomplished** (*Mil, fig*) Befehl ausgeführt; (*without military overtones*) Auftrag ausgeführt **(b)** (= *people on ~*) Delegation *f*; (*Pol*) Mission *f*; **trade ~** Handelsreise *f*

missionary [ˈmɪʃənrɪ] **1** N Missionar(in) *m(f)* **2** ADJ missionarisch

mission statement N (*of company*) (Kurzdarstellung der) Firmenphilosophie *f*

missis [ˈmɪsɪz] N (*Brit inf*: = *wife*) bessere Hälfte (*hum inf*); **yes, ~** ja(wohl)

Mississippi [mɪsɪˈsɪpɪ] N Mississippi *m*

misspell [ˈmɪsˈspel], *pret, ptp* **misspelled** *or* **misspelt** VT falsch schreiben

misspent [mɪsˈspent] ADJ **I regret my ~ youth** ich bedaure es, meine Jugend so vergeudet zu haben

missus [ˈmɪsɪz] N (*inf*) = **missis**

mist [mɪst] N Nebel *m*; (= *haze*) Dunst *m*; (*on glass etc*) Beschlag *m*

> [!NOTE]
> *Be careful!* **mist** *is not translated by the German word* **Mist**.

➤ **mist over** VI (*glass, mirror: also* **mist up**) (sich) beschlagen; **her eyes misted over with tears** Tränen verschleierten ihren Blick (*liter*)

mistake [mɪsˈteɪk] **1** N Fehler *m*; **to make a ~** (*in writing, calculating etc*) einen Fehler machen; (= *be mistaken*) sich irren; **to make the ~ of asking too much** den Fehler machen, zu viel zu verlangen; **by ~** aus Versehen; **there must be some**

~ da muss ein Fehler vorliegen; **let there be no ~ about it, make no ~ (about it)** ein(e)s steht fest: ...

2 VT, *pret* **mistook**, *ptp* **mistaken** *words, meaning etc* falsch verstehen; *seriousness, cause* nicht erkennen; *house, road, time of train* sich irren in (+*dat*); **to ~ sb's meaning** jdn falsch verstehen; **there's no mistaking her writing** ihre Schrift ist unverkennbar; **there's no mistaking what he meant** er hat sich unmissverständlich ausgedrückt; **there was no mistaking his anger** er war eindeutig wütend; **to ~ A for B** A mit B verwechseln; **to be ~n** sich irren; **to be ~n about sth/sb** sich in etw/jdm irren; **to be ~n in thinking that ...** fälschlicherweise annehmen, dass ...; **if I am not ~n ..., unless I am (very much) ~n ...** wenn mich nicht alles täuscht ...

mistaken [mɪsˈteɪkən] ADJ (= *wrong*) *idea* falsch; (= *misplaced*) *loyalty, kindness* unangebracht; *affection, trust* töricht; **in the ~ belief that ...** in der irrigen Annahme, dass ...; **a case of ~ identity** eine Verwechslung

mistakenly [mɪsˈteɪkənlɪ] ADV irrtümlicherweise; (= *by accident*) versehentlich

mister [ˈmɪstəʳ] N (*abbr* **Mr**) Herr *m*; (*on envelope*) Herrn; **please, ~, can you tell me ...?** können Sie mir bitte sagen ...?

mistime [ˈmɪsˈtaɪm] VT *act* einen ungünstigen Zeitpunkt wählen für; **he ~d his entrance** (*actor*) er trat zum falschen Zeitpunkt auf

mistletoe [ˈmɪsltəʊ] N Mistel *f*; (= *sprig*) Mistelzweig *m*

mistook [mɪsˈtʊk] PRET *of* **mistake**

mistranslate [ˈmɪstrænzˈleɪt] VT falsch übersetzen

mistreat [ˌmɪsˈtriːt] VT schlecht behandeln; (*violently*) misshandeln

mistreatment [mɪsˈtriːtmənt] N schlechte Behandlung; (*violent*) Misshandlung *f*

mistress [ˈmɪstrɪs] N **(a)** (*of house, dog*) Herrin *f* **(b)** (= *lover*) Geliebte *f* **(c)** (= *teacher*) Lehrerin *f*

mistrial [ˌmɪsˈtraɪəl] N **it was declared a ~** das Urteil wurde wegen Verfahrensmängeln aufgehoben

mistrust [ˈmɪsˈtrʌst] **1** N Misstrauen *nt* (*of* gegenüber) **2** VT misstrauen (+*dat*)

mistrustful [mɪsˈtrʌstfʊl] ADJ misstrauisch; **to be ~ of sb/sth** jdm/einer Sache misstrauen

misty [ˈmɪstɪ] ADJ (+ER) *day, morning* neblig; (= *hazy*) dunstig; **~ weather** Nebelwetter *nt*

misunderstand [ˈmɪsʌndəˈstænd], *pret, ptp* **misunderstood 1** VT missverstehen; **don't ~ me ...** verstehen Sie mich nicht falsch ... **2** VI **I think you've misunderstood** ich glaube, Sie haben das missverstanden

misunderstanding [ˈmɪsʌndəˈstændɪŋ] N **(a)** Missverständnis *nt*; **there must be some ~** da muss ein Missverständnis vorliegen **(b)** (= *disagreement*) Meinungsverschiedenheit *f*

misunderstood [ˈmɪsʌndəˈstʊd] **1** PTP *of* **misunderstand 2** ADJ *artist, playwright* verkannt

misuse 1 [ˈmɪsˈjuːs] N Missbrauch *m*; (*of words*) falscher Gebrauch; (*of funds*) Zweckentfremdung *f*; **~ of power/authority** Macht-/Amtsmissbrauch *m* **2** [ˈmɪsˈjuːz] VT missbrauchen; *words* falsch gebrauchen; *funds* zweckentfremden

mite¹ [maɪt] N (*Zool*) Milbe *f*

mite² ADV (*inf*) **a ~ surprised/disappointed** etwas *or* ein bisschen überrascht/enttäuscht

mitigate [ˈmɪtɪgeɪt] VT *pain* lindern; *punishment* mildern; **mitigating circumstances/factors** mildernde Umstände *pl*

mitigation [ˌmɪtɪˈgeɪʃən] N **to say something in ~** etwas zu jds/ seiner Verteidigung anführen

mitt [mɪt] N **(a)** = **mitten (b)** (= *baseball glove*) Baseballhandschuh *m* **(c)** (*inf*: = *hand*) Pfote *f* (*inf*)

mitten [ˈmɪtn] N Fausthandschuh *m*

mix [mɪks] **1** N Mischung *f*; **a real ~ of people** eine bunte Mischung von Menschen; **a broad racial ~** ein breites Spektrum verschiedener Rassen; **cement ~** Zementmischung *f*

2 VT (ver)mischen; *drinks* (= *prepare*) mixen; (*Cook*) *ingredients* verrühren; *dough* zubereiten; *salad* wenden; **you shouldn't ~ your drinks** man sollte nicht mehrere Sachen durcheinander trinken; **to ~ sth into sth** etw unter etw (*acc*) mengen; **I never ~ business with** *or* **and pleasure** ich vermische nie Geschäftliches und Privates

3 VI **(a)** (= *combine*) sich mischen lassen; (*chemical*

substances, races) sich vermischen
(b) (= *go together*) zusammenpassen; **business and pleasure don't** ~ Arbeit und Vergnügen lassen sich nicht verbinden
(c) (*people*) (= *get on*) miteinander auskommen; (= *mingle*) sich vermischen; (= *associate*) miteinander verkehren; **he finds it hard to** ~ er ist nicht sehr gesellig
➤ **mix in** VT SEP *egg, water* unterrühren
➤ **mix up** VT SEP **(a)** (= *get in a muddle*) durcheinander bringen; (= *confuse with sb/sth else*) verwechseln **(b) to be mixed up in sth** in etw (*acc*) verwickelt sein; **he's got himself mixed up with that gang** er hat sich mit dieser Bande eingelassen

mixed [mɪkst] ADJ gemischt; (= *both good and bad*) unterschiedlich; ~ **nuts/biscuits** Nuss-/Keksmischung *f*; **of** ~ **race** *or* **parentage** gemischtrassig; **a class of** ~ **ability** eine Klasse mit Schülern unterschiedlicher Leistungsstärke; **to have** ~ **feelings about sth** etw mit gemischten Gefühlen betrachten; **with** ~ **results** mit wechselndem Erfolg

mixed: mixed-ability ADJ *group, class* mit unterschiedlicher Leistungsstärke; **mixed bag** N bunte Mischung; **the students are a bit of a** ~ die Studenten sind eine ziemlich bunt gemischte Truppe (*inf*); **mixed blessing** N **it's a** ~ das ist ein zweischneidiges Schwert; **mixed doubles** PL (*Sport*) gemischtes Doppel; **mixed economy** N Mischwirtschaft *f*; **mixed grill** N Grillteller *m*; **mixed-media** ADJ *work* mittelmedial; **mixed metaphor** N gemischte Metapher; **mixed-race** ADJ *children* gemischtrassig; **mixed-up** ADJ ATTR, **mixed up** ADJ PRED durcheinander *pred*; (= *muddled*) *person also, ideas* konfus; **I'm all mixed up** ich bin völlig durcheinander; **he got all mixed up** er hat alles durcheinander gebracht

mixer [ˈmɪksəʳ] N **(a)** (= *food* ~) Mixer *m*; (= *cement* ~) Mischmaschine *f* **(b)** (*for drink*) Cola, Ginger Ale, Tonic etc zum Auffüllen von alkoholischen Mixgetränken **(c)** (= *sociable person*) **to be a good** ~ kontaktfreudig sein **(d)** (*US inf*) Party *f* zum Kennenlernen; (*for new students*) Erstsemesterfete *f*

mixture [ˈmɪkstʃəʳ] N Mischung *f*; (*Med*) Mixtur *f*; (*Cook*) Gemisch *nt*; (= *cake* ~, *dough*) Teig *m*; **fold the eggs into the cheese** ~ heben Sie die Eier in die Käsemischung unter

mix-up [ˈmɪksʌp] N Durcheinander *nt*; (= *mistake*) Verwechslung *f*; **there seemed to be some** ~ **about which train ...** es schien völlig unklar, welchen Zug ...; **there must have been a** ~ da muss irgendetwas schief gelaufen sein (*inf*)

MLA (*Brit Pol*) ABBR *of* **Member of the Legislative Assembly** Abgeordnete(r) *mf* der gesetzgebenden Versammlung

mm ABBR *of* **millimetre(s)** mm

mnemonic [nɪˈmɒnɪk] N Gedächtnishilfe *f*

mo [məʊ] N (*inf*) ABBR *of* **moment**

moan [məʊn] **1** N **(a)** (= *groan*) Stöhnen *nt* **(b)** (= *grumble*) Gejammer *nt no pl* (*inf*); **to have a** ~ **about sth** über etw (*acc*) jammern **2** VI **(a)** (= *groan*) stöhnen **(b)** (= *grumble*) jammern (*about* über +*acc*) **3** VT **..., he ~ed** ... stöhnte er

moaning [ˈməʊnɪŋ] N **(a)** Stöhnen *nt* **(b)** (= *grumbling*) Gestöhn(e) *nt*

mob [mɒb] **1** N **(a)** (= *crowd*) Horde *f*; (*riotous, violent*) Mob *m no pl*; **they went in a** ~ **to the town hall** sie stürmten zum Rathaus **(b)** (*inf*) (= *criminal gang*) Bande *f*; (*fig*: = *clique*) Haufen *m*; **the Mob** (= *the Mafia*) die Maf(f)ia **(c)** **the** ~ (*pej*: = *the masses*) die Masse(n *pl*) **2** VT herfallen über (+*acc*); *actor, pop star* belagern

mobile [ˈməʊbaɪl] **1** ADJ **(a)** *person* beweglich **(b)** *X-ray unit etc* fahrbar; *missile launcher, laboratory* mobil **2** N **(a)** (= ~ *phone*) Handy *nt* **(b)** (= *decoration*) Mobile *nt*

mobile: mobile home N Wohnwagen *m*; **mobile phone** N Mobiltelefon *nt*, Handy *nt*; **mobile walkway** N (*US*) Rollsteg *m*

mobility [məʊˈbɪlɪtɪ] N (*of person*) Beweglichkeit *f*; (*of work force*) Mobilität *f*; **a car gives you** ~ ein Auto macht Sie beweglich

mobilization [ˌməʊbɪlaɪˈzeɪʃən] N Mobilisierung *f*

mobilize [ˈməʊbɪlaɪz] **1** VT mobilisieren **2** VI mobil machen

mobster [ˈmɒbstəʳ] N (*esp US*) Gangster(in) *m(f)*

moccasin [ˈmɒkəsɪn] N Mokassin *m*

mocha [ˈmɒkə] N Mokka *m*

mock [mɒk] **1** N **mocks** (*Brit Sch inf*) Probeprüfungen *pl* **2** ADJ ATTR *emotions* gespielt; (*crash, examination* simuliert; *execution, trial* gestellt; ~ **leather/fur** Kunstleder *nt*/-pelz *m* **3** VT

(a) (= *ridicule*) sich lustig machen über (+*acc*), verspotten **(b)** (= *defy*) trotzen (+*dat*); *law* sich hinwegsetzen über (+*acc*) **4** VI **don't** ~ mokier dich nicht!, spotte nicht! (*geh*)

mockery [ˈmɒkərɪ] N **(a)** Spott *m* **(b)** (= *object of ridicule*) Gespött *nt*; **to make a** ~ **of sth** etw lächerlich machen; (= *prove its futility*) etw ad absurdum führen

mocking ADJ, **mockingly** ADV [ˈmɒkɪŋ, -lɪ] spöttisch

mock-up [ˈmɒkʌp] N Modell *nt* in Originalgröße

MOD (*Brit*) ABBR *of* **Ministry of Defence**

modal [ˈməʊdl] ADJ modal; ~ **verb** Modalverb *nt*

mod cons [ˈmɒdˈkɒnz] (*Brit inf*) PL ABBR *of* **modern conveniences** mod. Komf.

mode [məʊd] N **(a)** (= *way*) Art *f* (und Weise); (= *form*) Form *f*; ~ **of transport** Transportmittel *nt*; ~ **of life** Lebensweise *f* **(b)** (*Comput*) Modus *m*, Mode *m*

model [ˈmɒdl] **1** N **(a)** Modell *nt*; (= *fashion* ~) Mannequin *nt*; (= *male* ~) Dressman *m*; **to make sth on the** ~ **of sth** etw (*acc*) einer Sache (*dat*) nachbilden
(b) (= *perfect example*) Muster *nt* (*of* an +*dat*); **to hold sb up as a** ~ jdn als Vorbild hinstellen
2 ADJ **(a)** Modell-; ~ **railway** (*Brit*) *or* **railroad** (*US*) Modelleisenbahn *f*
(b) (= *perfect*) vorbildlich; ~ **pupil** Musterschüler(in) *m(f)*
3 VT **(a)** **to** ~ **X on Y** Y als Vorlage *or* Muster für X benutzen; **X is modelled** (*Brit*) *or* **modeled** (*US*) **on Y** Y dient als Vorlage *or* Muster für X; **the system was modelled** (*Brit*) *or* **modeled** (*US*) **on the American one** das System war nach amerikanischem Muster aufgebaut; **to** ~ **oneself on sb** sich (*dat*) jdn zum Vorbild nehmen
(b) (= *make a* ~) modellieren
(c) *dress etc* vorführen
4 VI (*Art, Phot*) als Modell arbeiten; (*Fashion*) als Mannequin/Dressman arbeiten

modelling, (*US*) **modeling** [ˈmɒdlɪŋ] N **to do some** ~ (*Phot, Art*) als Modell arbeiten; (*Fashion*) als Mannequin/Dressman arbeiten

modem [ˈməʊdem] N Modem *nt*

moderate [ˈmɒdərɪt] **1** ADJ gemäßigt (*also Pol*); *appetite, lifestyle, speed, increase* mäßig; *gain, improvement* leicht; *demands, price* vernünftig; *drinker, eater* maßvoll; *income, success* bescheiden; **a** ~ **amount** einigermaßen viel; **in a** ~ **oven** im Backofen bei mittlerer Hitze **2** N (*Pol*) Gemäßigte(r) *mf* **3** [ˈmɒdəreɪt] VT mäßigen

moderately [ˈmɒdərɪtlɪ] ADV **(a)** (*with adj/adv*) einigermaßen; *increase, decline* mäßig; **a** ~ **priced suit** ein nicht allzu teurer Anzug **(b)** *drink, eat, exercise* in Maßen

moderation [ˌmɒdəˈreɪʃən] N Mäßigung *f*; **in** ~ mit Maß(en)

modern [ˈmɒdən] ADJ modern; *history* neuere und neueste; **Modern Greek** etc Neugriechisch *nt* etc

modern-day [ˌmɒdənˈdeɪ] ADJ modern; ~ **America** das heutige Amerika

modernism [ˈmɒdənɪzəm] N Modernismus *m*

modernist [ˈmɒdənɪst] **1** ADJ modernistisch **2** N Modernist(in) *m(f)*

modernistic [ˌmɒdəˈnɪstɪk] ADJ modernistisch

modernization [ˌmɒdənaɪˈzeɪʃən] N Modernisierung *f*

modernize [ˈmɒdənaɪz] VT modernisieren

modern languages PL neuere Sprachen *pl*; (*Univ*) Neuphilologie *f*

modest [ˈmɒdɪst] ADJ **(a)** bescheiden; *price* mäßig; **to be** ~ **about one's successes** nicht mit seinen Erfolgen prahlen; **on a** ~ **scale** in bescheidenem Rahmen **(b)** (= *chaste, proper*) schamhaft; (*in one's behaviour*) anständig

modestly [ˈmɒdɪstlɪ] ADV **(a)** bescheiden; ~ **priced goods** Waren zu gemäßigten Preisen **(b)** (= *chastely, properly*) schamhaft; *behave, dress* anständig

modesty [ˈmɒdɪstɪ] N **(a)** (= *humbleness*) Bescheidenheit *f*; **in all** ~ bei aller Bescheidenheit **(b)** (= *chasteness*) Schamgefühl *nt*; (*in behaviour*) Anstand *m*; (*in dress*) Dezentheit *f*

modicum [ˈmɒdɪkəm] N **a** ~ (**of**) ein wenig; **a** ~ **of intelligence** ein Funke *m* (von) Intelligenz; **a** ~ **of truth** ein Körnchen *nt* Wahrheit

modification [ˌmɒdɪfɪˈkeɪʃən] N (Ver)änderung *f*; (*of design*) Abänderung *f*; (*of terms, contract, wording*) Modifizierung *f*; **to make** ~**s to sth** (Ver)änderungen an etw (*dat*) vornehmen; etw abändern; etw modifizieren

modifier ['mɒdɪfaɪəʳ] N (*Gram*) Bestimmungswort *nt*, nähere Bestimmung

modify ['mɒdɪfaɪ] VT **(a)** (ver)ändern; *design* abändern; *terms, contract, wording* modifizieren **(b)** (*Gram*) näher bestimmen

modish ['məʊdɪʃ] ADJ (= *fashionable*) modisch; (= *stylish*) schick

modular ['mɒdjʊləʳ] ADJ aus Elementen zusammengesetzt; (*Comput*) modular; (*esp Brit Sch, Univ*) *course, degree etc* modular aufgebaut

modulate ['mɒdjʊleɪt] VTI (*Mus, Rad*) modulieren

modulation [,mɒdjʊ'leɪʃən] N (*Mus, Rad*) Modulation *f*

module ['mɒdjuːl] N (Bau)element *nt*; (*in education*) Kurs *m*; (*Comput*) Modul *nt*; (*Space*) Raumkapsel *f*

mogul ['məʊgəl] N (*lit, fig*) Mogul *m*

mohair ['məʊhɛəʳ] N Mohair *m*

Mohammed [məʊ'hæmed] N Mohammed *m*

moist [mɔɪst] ADJ (+ER) feucht (*from, with* vor +*dat*)

moisten ['mɔɪsn] VT anfeuchten

moistener N Anfeuchter *m*

moisture ['mɔɪstʃəʳ] N Feuchtigkeit *f*

moisturizer ['mɔɪstʃəraɪzəʳ], **moisturizing cream** ['mɔɪstʃəraɪzɪŋ'kriːm] N Feuchtigkeitscreme *f*

molar (tooth) ['məʊləʳ(,tuː:θ)] N Backenzahn *m*

molasses [məʊ'læsɪz] N Melasse *f*

mold *etc* (*US*) = **mould** *etc*

mole¹ [məʊl] N (*Anat*) Pigmentmal *nt* (*form*), Leberfleck *m*

mole² N (*Zool*) Maulwurf *m*; (*inf*: = *secret agent*) Spion(in) *m(f)*

molecular [məʊ'lekjʊləʳ] ADJ Molekular-

molecular biology N Molekularbiologie *f*

molecule ['mɒlɪkjuːl] N Molekül *nt*

moleskin ['məʊlskɪn] N (= *coat/jacket etc*) Mantel/Jacke *etc* aus Maulwurfsfell; (= *fabric*) Moleskin *m or nt*

molest [məʊ'lest] VT belästigen

mollify ['mɒlɪfaɪ] VT beschwichtigen

mollusc ['mɒləsk] N Weichtier *nt*

mollycoddle ['mɒlɪ,kɒdl] VT verhätscheln

molt N, VTI (*US*) = **moult**

molten ['məʊltən] ADJ geschmolzen; *glass, lava* flüssig

mom [mɒm] N (*US inf*) = **mum²**

moment ['məʊmənt] N Augenblick *m*; **any ~ now**, (**at**) **any ~** jeden Augenblick; **at any ~** (= *any time*) jederzeit; **at the ~** im Augenblick; **at the ~ when ...** zu dem Zeitpunkt, als ...; **not at the** *or* **this ~** im Augenblick nicht; **at this (particular) ~ in time** augenblicklich; **for the ~** vorläufig; **not for a ~** *or* **one ~ ...** nie(mals) ...; **I didn't hesitate for a ~** ich habe keinen Augenblick gezögert; **in a ~** gleich; **it was all over in a ~** *or* **in a few ~s** das ganze dauerte nur wenige Augenblicke; **to leave things until the last ~** alles erst im letzten Moment erledigen; **just a ~!, wait a ~!** Moment mal!; **I shan't be a ~** ich bin gleich wieder da; (= *nearly ready*) ich bin gleich so weit; **I have just this ~ heard about it** ich habe es eben *or* gerade erst erfahren; **we haven't a ~ to lose** wir haben keine Minute zu verlieren; **not a ~'s peace** *or* **rest** keine ruhige Minute; **one ~ she was laughing, the next she was crying** zuerst lachte sie, einen Moment später weinte sie; **the ~ I saw him I knew ...** als ich ihn sah, wusste ich sofort ...; **tell me the ~ he comes** sagen Sie mir sofort Bescheid, wenn er kommt; **the ~ of truth** die Stunde der Wahrheit; **the film has its ~s** streckenweise hat der Film was (*inf*)

momentarily ['məʊməntərɪlɪ] ADV **(a)** (für) einen Augenblick **(b)** (*US*: = *very soon*) jeden Augenblick

momentary ['məʊməntərɪ] ADJ kurz; *lapse of memory/ concentration* momentan; **there was a ~ silence** einen Augenblick lang herrschte Stille

momentous [məʊ'mentəs] ADJ (= *memorable, important*) bedeutungsvoll; (= *of great consequence*) von großer Tragweite

momentum [məʊ'mentəm] N Schwung *m also fig* (*at moment of impact*) Wucht *f*; (*Phys*) Impuls *m*; **to gather** *or* **gain ~** (*lit*) sich beschleunigen; (*fig: idea, plan etc*) in Gang kommen; **to lose ~** (*lit, fig*) Schwung verlieren

Mon ABBR *of* **Monday** Mo

Monaco ['mɒnəkəʊ] N Monaco *nt*

monarch ['mɒnək] N Monarch(in) *m(f)*

monarchist ['mɒnəkɪst] N Monarchist(in) *m(f)*

monarchy ['mɒnəkɪ] N Monarchie *f*

monastery ['mɒnəstərɪ] N (Mönchs)kloster *nt*

monastic [mə'næstɪk] ADJ klösterlich; **~ life** Klosterleben *nt*; **~ order** Mönchsorden *m*

Monday ['mʌndɪ] N Montag *m*; *see also* **Tuesday**

monetarism ['mʌnɪtərɪzəm] N Monetarismus *m*

monetarist ['mʌnɪtərɪst] **1** N Monetarist(in) *m(f)* **2** ADJ monetaristisch

monetary ['mʌnɪtərɪ] ADJ währungspolitisch; **~ policy** Währungspolitik *f*; **~ system** Währungssystem *nt*; **~ union** Währungsunion *f*

monetary unit N Währungseinheit *f*

money ['mʌnɪ] N Geld *nt*; (= *medium of exchange*) Zahlungsmittel *nt*; **to make ~** (*person*) (viel) Geld verdienen; (*business*) etwas einbringen; **to lose ~** (*person*) Geld verlieren; (*business*) Verluste haben; **there's ~ in it** das ist sehr lukrativ; **what can you expect for the ~?** was kann man bei dem Preis schon verlangen?; **it's ~ for jam** *or* **old rope** (*Brit inf*) da wird einem das Geld ja nachgeworfen (*inf*); **to be in the ~** (*inf*) Geld wie Heu haben; **what's the ~ like in this job?** wie wird der Job bezahlt?; **to earn good ~** gut verdienen; **to get one's ~'s worth** etwas für sein Geld bekommen; **do you think I'm made of ~?** (*inf*) ich bin doch kein Krösus!; **to throw ~ at a problem** ein Problem dadurch zu lösen versuchen, dass man viel Geld dafür ausgibt; **to put one's ~ where one's mouth is** (*inf*) (nicht nur reden, sondern) Taten sprechen lassen; **his analysis was right on the ~** (*US*) seine Analyse stimmte haargenau

money: money belt N ≈ Gürteltasche *f* (*mit Geldfächern*); **moneybox** N Sparbüchse *f*; **moneylender** N Geldverleiher(in) *m(f)*; **moneylending** N Geldverleih *m*; **moneymaker** N (= *idea*) einträgliche Sache; (= *product*) Verkaufserfolg *m*; (= *company*) gewinnbringendes Unternehmen; **moneymaking 1** ADJ gewinnbringend **2** N Geldverdienen *nt*; **money market** N Geldmarkt *m*; **money order** N Zahlungsanweisung *f*; **money supply** N Geldvolumen *nt*

Mongolia [mɒŋ'gəʊlɪə] N Mongolei *f*

mongrel ['mʌŋgrəl] N Promenadenmischung *f*; (*pej*) Köter *m*

monitor ['mɒnɪtəʳ] **1** N **(a)** (*Sch*) Schüler(in) *m(f)* mit besonderen Pflichten; **book ~** Bücherwart(in) *m(f)* **(b)** (*TV, Tech*: = *screen*) Monitor *m* **(c)** (= *observer*) Überwacher(in) *m(f)* **2** VT **(a)** *foreign station, telephone conversation* abhören; *TV programme* mithören **(b)** (= *control, check*) überwachen; *personal expenditure etc* kontrollieren

monk [mʌŋk] N Mönch *m*

monkey ['mʌŋkɪ] **1** N Affe *m*; (*fig*: = *child*) Strolch *m*, Schlingel *m*; **I don't give a ~'s (about it)** (*Brit inf*) das ist mir scheißegal (*inf*) **2** VI **to ~ around** herumalbern; **to ~ around with sth** an etw (*dat*) herumfummeln (*inf*)

monkey: monkey business N (*inf*) **no ~!** mach(t) mir keine Sachen! (*inf*); **monkey puzzle (tree)** N Andentanne *f*; **monkey wrench** N Engländer *m*

mono ['mɒnəʊ] **1** N Mono *nt* **2** ADJ Mono-, mono-; **~ recording** Monoaufnahme *f*

mono- PREF Mono-, mono-

monochrome ['mɒnəkrəʊm] ADJ monochrom; **~ screen** Monochrombildschirm *m*

monocle ['mɒnəkəl] N Monokel *nt*

monogamous [mɒ'nɒgəməs] ADJ monogam

monogamy [mɒ'nɒgəmɪ] N Monogamie *f*

monogram ['mɒnəgræm] N Monogramm *nt*

monogrammed ['mɒnəgræmd] ADJ mit Monogramm

monolingual [,mɒnə'lɪŋgwəl] ADJ einsprachig

monolithic [,mɒnəʊ'lɪθɪk] ADJ (*lit*) monolithisch; (*fig*) gigantisch, riesig

monologue, (*US*) **monolog** ['mɒnəlɒg] N Monolog *m*

monopolistic [mə'nɒpəlɪstɪk] ADJ monopolistisch

monopolization [mə,nɒpəlaɪ'zeɪʃən] N (*lit*) Monopolisierung *f*

monopolize [mə'nɒpəlaɪz] VT (*lit*) *market* monopolisieren; (*fig*) *person, place, sb's time etc* mit Beschlag belegen; *conversation, discussion* beherrschen; **she wants to ~ his attention** sie möchte seine Aufmerksamkeit ganz für sich haben

monopoly [mə'nɒpəlɪ] N **(a)** (*lit*) Monopol *nt*; **coal is a government ~** der Staat hat das Kohlenmonopol; **Monopolies and Mergers Commission** (*Brit*) britisches

Kartellamt (b) (*fig*) **to have the** *or* a ~ **on** *or* **of sth** etw für sich gepachtet haben (*inf*)

monorail [ˈmɒnəreɪl] N Einschienenbahn *f*

monosyllabic [ˌmɒnəʊsɪˈlæbɪk] ADJ (*fig*) einsilbig

monotone [ˈmɒnətəʊn] N monotoner Klang; (= *voice*) monotone Stimme

monotonous [məˈnɒtənəs] ADJ (*lit, fig*) monoton; **with ~ regularity** regelmäßig; **it's getting ~** es wird allmählich langweilig

monotonously [məˈnɒtənəslɪ] ADV monoton

monotony [məˈnɒtənɪ] N (*lit, fig*) Monotonie *f*

monoxide [mɒˈnɒksaɪd] N Monoxid *nt*

monsoon [mɒnˈsuːn] N Monsun *m*; **the ~s, the ~ season** die Monsunzeit

monster [ˈmɒnstəʳ] **1** N (a) (= *big animal, thing*) Ungetüm *nt*; (= *animal*) Ungeheuer *nt* (b) (= *abnormal animal*) Monster *nt*; (= *legendary animal*) Fabelwesen *nt* (c) (= *cruel person*) Unmensch *m* **2** ATTR (= *enormous*) riesenhaft; **~ film** Monsterfilm *m*

monstrosity [mɒnˈstrɒsɪtɪ] N (= *thing*) Monstrosität *f*; (= *cruel deed*) Gräueltat *f*

monstrous [ˈmɒnstrəs] ADJ (a) (= *huge*) riesig (b) (= *shocking, horrible*) abscheulich; *crime, thought* grässlich; *suggestion* ungeheuerlich; **it's ~ that ...** es ist einfach ungeheuerlich, dass ...

montage [mɒnˈtɑːʒ] N Montage *f*

Montenegro [ˌmɒntɪˈniːgrəʊ] N Montenegro *nt*

month [mʌnθ] N Monat *m*; **in** *or* **for ~s** seit langem; **it went on for ~s** es hat sich monatelang hingezogen; **one ~'s salary** ein Monatsgehalt; **paid by the ~** monatlich bezahlt

monthly [ˈmʌnθlɪ] **1** ADJ, ADV monatlich; **~ magazine** Monats(zeit)schrift *f*; **~ salary** Monatsgehalt *nt*; **~ ticket/ payment** Monatskarte/-rate *f*; **they have ~ meetings** sie treffen sich einmal im Monat; **to pay on a ~ basis** monatlich zahlen; **twice ~** zweimal im *or* pro Monat **2** N Monats(zeit)schrift *f*

monty [ˈmɒntɪ] N (*inf*) **the full ~** absolut alles

monument [ˈmɒnjʊmənt] N Denkmal *nt*; (*small, on grave etc*) Gedenkstein *m*; (*fig*) Zeugnis *nt* (*to +gen*)

monumental [ˌmɒnjʊˈmentl] ADJ enorm; *proportions, achievement* gewaltig; *ignorance, stupidity, error* kolossal; **on a ~ scale, of ~ proportions** *disaster, crisis* von riesigem Ausmaß; *building, work of art* monumental

moo [muː] VI muhen

mooch [muːtʃ] (*inf*) VI tigern (*inf*); **I spent all day just ~ing about** (*Brit*) *or* **around the house** ich habe den ganzen Tag zu Hause herumgegammelt (*inf*)

mood[1] [muːd] N (*of party, town etc*) Stimmung *f*; (*of one person*) Laune *f*; (= *bad ~*) schlechte Laune; **he's in one of his ~s** er hat mal wieder eine seiner Launen; **he was in a good/bad/ foul ~** er hatte gute/schlechte/eine fürchterliche Laune; **to be in a cheerful ~** gut aufgelegt sein; **to be in a festive/ forgiving ~** feierlich/versöhnlich gestimmt sein; **I'm in no ~ for laughing** mir ist nicht nach *or* zum Lachen zumute; **to be in the ~ for sth** zu etw aufgelegt sein; **to be in the ~ to do sth** dazu aufgelegt sein, etw zu tun; **to be in no ~ to do sth** nicht in der Stimmung sein, etw zu tun; **I'm not in the ~ for work** *or* **to work** ich habe keine Lust zum Arbeiten; **I'm not in the ~** ich bin nicht dazu aufgelegt

mood[2] N (*Gram*) Modus *m*; **indicative ~** Indikativ *m*; **subjunctive ~** Konjunktiv *m*

moodiness [ˈmuːdɪnɪs] N Launenhaftigkeit *f*; (= *bad mood*) schlechte Laune; **his ~** sein launisches Wesen

moody [ˈmuːdɪ] ADJ (+ER) launisch; (= *bad-tempered*) schlecht gelaunt; *film, piece of music* stimmungsvoll

moon [muːn] N Mond *m*; **is there a ~ tonight?** scheint heute der Mond?; **when the ~ is full** bei Vollmond; **you're asking for the ~!** du verlangst Unmögliches!; **to promise sb the ~** jdm das Blaue vom Himmel versprechen; **to be over the ~** (*inf*) überglücklich sein

▶ **moon about** (*Brit*) *or* **around** VI (vor sich *acc* hin) träumen; **to moon about** *or* **around (in) the house** zu Hause hocken

moon IN CPDS Mond-; **moonbeam** N Mondstrahl *m*; **moon landing** N Mondlandung *f*; **moonless** ADJ *night* mondlos;

moonlight **1** N Mondlicht *nt*; **it was ~** der Mond schien; **a ~ walk** ein Mondscheinspaziergang *m* **2** VI (*inf*) schwarzarbeiten; **moonlighting** N (*inf*) Schwarzarbeit *f*; **moonlit** ADJ *object* mondbeschienen; *night, landscape, lawn* mondhell; **moonshine** N (a) (= *moonlight*) Mondschein *m* (b) (*inf: = nonsense*) Unsinn *m* (c) (*inf: = illegal whisky*) *illegal gebrannter Whisky*

moor[1] [mʊəʳ] N (Hoch)moor *nt*; **a walk on the ~s** ein Spaziergang *m* übers Moor

moor[2] **1** VT festmachen; (*at permanent moorings*) muren **2** VI festmachen

mooring [ˈmʊərɪŋ] N (= *place*) Anlegeplatz *m*; **~s** (= *ropes, fixtures*) Verankerung *f*

moose [muːs] N, *pl* - Elch *m*

moot [muːt] ADJ **a ~ point** *or* **question** eine fragliche Sache; **it's a ~ point** *or* **question whether ...** es ist noch fraglich, ob ...

mop [mɒp] **1** N (= *floor ~*) Mop *m*; (= *sponge ~*) Schwammmopp *m*; **her ~ of curls** ihr Wuschelkopf *m* **2** VT *floor, kitchen* wischen; **to ~ one's brow** sich (*dat*) den Schweiß von der Stirn wischen

▶ **mop up** VT SEP (a) *water etc* aufwischen; **she mopped up the sauce with a piece of bread** sie tunkte die Soße mit einem Stück Brot auf (b) (*Mil*) säubern (*inf*) **2** VI (auf)wischen

mope [məʊp] VI Trübsal blasen (*inf*)

▶ **mope about** (*Brit*) *or* **around** VI mit einer Jammermiene herumlaufen; **to mope about** *or* **around the house** zu Hause hocken und Trübsal blasen (*inf*)

moped [ˈməʊped] N Moped *nt*; (*very small*) Mofa *nt*

moral [ˈmɒrəl] **1** ADJ moralisch; (= *virtuous*) integer; (*sexually*) tugendhaft; **~ values** sittliche Werte *pl*, Moralvorstellungen *pl*; **~ code** (*of individual*) Auffassung *f* von Moral; (*of society*) Sitten- *or* Moralkodex *m*; **to give sb ~ support** jdn moralisch unterstützen; **to have a ~ right to sth** jedes Recht auf etw (*acc*) haben **2** N (a) (= *lesson*) Moral *f* (b) **morals** PL (= *principles*) Moral *f*; **his ~s are different from mine** er hat ganz andere Moralvorstellungen als ich; **to have loose ~s** eine recht lockere Moral haben

morale [mɒˈrɑːl] N Moral *f*; **to boost sb's ~** jdm (moralischen) Auftrieb geben

moralist [ˈmɒrəlɪst] N Moralist(in) *m(f)*

moralistic [ˌmɒrəˈlɪstɪk] ADJ moralisierend

morality [məˈrælɪtɪ] N Moralität *f*; (= *moral system*) Ethik *f*

moralize [ˈmɒrəlaɪz] VI moralisieren; **to ~ about sb/sth** sich über jdn/etw moralisch entrüsten

morally [ˈmɒrəlɪ] ADV (a) (= *ethically*) moralisch (b) (= *virtuously*) integer; (*sexually*) tugendhaft

Moral Majority N (*US Pol*) moralische Mehrheit

morass [məˈræs] N **a ~ of problems** ein Wust *m* von Problemen

moratorium [ˌmɒrəˈtɔːrɪəm] N Stopp *m*; (*on treaty etc*) Moratorium *nt*; **a ~ on nuclear armament** ein Atomwaffenstopp *m*

morbid [ˈmɔːbɪd] ADJ krankhaft; *sense of humour, talk etc* makaber; (= *gloomy*) *outlook, thoughts* düster; *person* trübsinnig; *poet, novel, music etc* morbid; **don't be so ~!** sieh doch nicht alles so schwarz!

more [mɔːʳ] **1** N, PRON mehr; (*of countable things*) noch welche; **~ and ~** immer mehr; **three ~** noch drei; **many/much ~** viel mehr; **not many/much ~** nicht mehr viele/viel; **no ~** nichts mehr; (*countable*) keine mehr; **some ~** noch etwas; (*countable*) noch welche; **there isn't/aren't any ~** mehr gibt es nicht; (*here, at the moment, left over*) es ist nichts/es sind keine mehr da; **is/are there any ~?** gibt es noch mehr?; (*left over*) ist noch etwas/sind noch welche da?; **even ~** noch mehr; **I shall have ~ to say about this** dazu habe ich noch etwas zu sagen; **let's say no ~ about it** reden wir nicht mehr darüber; **there's ~ to come** das ist noch nicht alles; **what ~ do you want?** was willst du denn noch?; **there's ~ to it** da steckt (noch) mehr dahinter; **there's ~ to bringing up children than just ...** zum Kindererziehen gehört mehr als nur ...; **and what's ~, he ...** und außerdem hat er ... (noch) ...; **(all) the ~** umso mehr; **the ~ you give him, the ~ he wants** je mehr du ihm gibst, desto mehr verlangt er; **the ~ the merrier** je mehr, desto besser

2 ADJ mehr; (*in addition*) noch mehr; **two/five ~ bottles** noch zwei/fünf Flaschen; **a lot/a little ~ money** viel/etwas mehr

Geld; (*in addition*) noch viel/noch etwas mehr Geld; **a few ~ weeks** noch ein paar Wochen; **no ~ friends** keine Freunde mehr; **no ~ squabbling!** Schluss mit dem Zanken!; **do you want some ~ tea/books?** möchten Sie noch etwas Tee/noch ein paar Bücher?; **there isn't any ~ wine** es ist kein Wein mehr da; **there aren't any ~ books** mehr Bücher gibt es nicht; (*here, at the moment*) es sind keine Bücher mehr da; **(the) ~ fool you!** du bist ja vielleicht ein Dummkopf!

3 ADV **(a)** mehr; **~ and ~** immer mehr; **it will weigh/grow a bit ~** es wird etwas mehr wiegen/noch etwas wachsen; **to like/ want sth ~** etw lieber mögen/wollen; **~ than** mehr als; **£5/2 hours ~ than I thought** £ 5 mehr/2 Stunden länger, als ich dachte; **it will ~ than meet the demand** das wird die Nachfrage mehr als genügend befriedigen; **he's ~ lazy than stupid** er ist eher faul als dumm; **no ~ than, not ~ than** nicht mehr als; **he's ~ like a brother to me** er ist eher wie ein Bruder (für mich); **no ~ do I** ich auch nicht; **he has resigned – that's no ~ than I expected** er hat gekündigt – das habe ich ja erwartet; **once ~** noch einmal; **no ~, not any ~** nicht mehr; **to be no ~** (*person*) nicht mehr leben; (*thing*) nicht mehr existieren; **if he comes here any ~ ...** wenn er noch länger hierher kommt ...; **~ or less** mehr oder weniger; **neither ~ nor less, no ~, no less** nicht mehr und nicht weniger

(b) (*to form comp of adj, adv*) -er (*than* als); **~ beautiful** schöner; **~ and ~ beautiful** immer schöner; **~ seriously** ernster; **no ~ stupid than I am** (auch) nicht dümmer als ich

moreish ['mɔːrɪʃ] ADJ (*Brit inf*) **these biscuits are very ~** diese Plätzchen schmecken nach mehr (*inf*)

moreover [mɔːˈrəʊvə^r] ADV zudem

morgue [mɔːɡ] N Leichenschauhaus *nt*

moribund ['mɒrɪbʌnd] ADJ (*fig*) *plan, policy* zum Scheitern verurteilt; *customs, way of life* zum Aussterben verurteilt

Mormon ['mɔːmən] **1** ADJ mormonisch; **~ church** Mormonenkirche *f* **2** N Mormone *m*, Mormonin *f*

morning ['mɔːnɪŋ] **1** N Morgen *m*; **in the ~** morgens; (= *tomorrow*) morgen früh; **early in the ~** am frühen Morgen; (= *tomorrow*) morgen früh; **(at) 7 in the ~** (um) 7 Uhr morgens *or* früh; (= *tomorrow*) morgen (früh) um 7; **I didn't get back until 2 in the ~** ich bin erst um 2 Uhr früh nach Hause gekommen; **this/yesterday ~** heute/gestern Morgen; **tomorrow ~** morgen früh; **it was the ~ after** es war am nächsten Morgen

2 ATTR am Morgen; (= *regularly in the ~*) morgendlich; **~ flight** Vormittagsflug *m*; **~ train** Frühzug *m*

morning: **morning dress** N, NO PL Cut(away) *m*; (*dark*) Stresemann *m*; **morning sickness** N (Schwangerschafts)übelkeit *f*; **morning suit** N Cut(away) *m*; (*dark*) Stresemann *m*

Moroccan [məˈrɒkən] **1** ADJ marokkanisch **2** N Marokkaner(in) *m(f)*

Morocco [məˈrɒkəʊ] N Marokko *nt*

moron ['mɔːrɒn] N (*inf*) Trottel *m* (*inf*)

moronic [məˈrɒnɪk] ADJ (*inf*) idiotisch (*inf*)

morose ADJ, **morosely** ADV [məˈrəʊs, -lɪ] missmutig

morphine ['mɔːfiːn] N Morphium *nt*

morphology [mɔːˈfɒlədʒɪ] N Morphologie *f*

morse [mɔːs] N (*also* Morse code) Morseschrift *f*

morsel ['mɔːsl] N (*of food*) Bissen *m*; (*fig*) bisschen *nt*; (*of information*) Brocken *m*

mortal ['mɔːtl] **1** ADJ sterblich; (= *causing death, extreme*) tödlich; **to deal (sb/sth) a ~ blow** (jdm/einer Sache) einen tödlichen Schlag versetzen; **to live in ~ fear** *or* **dread that ...** eine Todesangst haben, dass ...; **~ enemy** Todfeind(in) *m(f)* **2** N Sterbliche(r) *mf*; **ordinary ~** (*inf*) Normalsterbliche(r) *mf* (*inf*); **a mere ~** ein bloßer Sterblicher

mortality [mɔːˈtælɪtɪ] N (= *number of deaths*) Todesfälle *pl*; (= *rate*) Sterblichkeit(sziffer) *f*; **~ rate, rate of ~** Sterblichkeitsziffer *f*

mortally ['mɔːtəlɪ] ADV (*lit, fig*) tödlich; **~ ill** todkrank; *wounded* (*fig*) zutiefst

mortal sin N Todsünde *f*

mortar ['mɔːtə^r] N Mörtel *m*

mortarboard ['mɔːtəbɔːd] N (*Univ*) Doktorhut *m*

mortgage ['mɔːɡɪdʒ] **1** N Hypothek *f* (*on* auf +*acc/dat*); **a ~ for £50,000** eine Hypothek über £ 50.000 **2** VT hypothekarisch belasten

mortgage rate N Hypothekenzinssatz *m*

mortician [mɔːˈtɪʃən] N (*US*) Bestattungsunternehmer(in) *m(f)*

mortification [mɔːtɪfɪˈkeɪʃən] N **I discovered to my ~ that I had made a mistake** ich stellte zu meiner größten Verlegenheit fest, dass ich einen Fehler gemacht hatte

mortify ['mɔːtɪfaɪ] VT **he was mortified** er empfand das als beschämend; (= *embarrassed*) es war ihm äußerst peinlich

mortuary ['mɔːtjʊərɪ] N Leichenhalle *f*

mosaic [məʊˈzeɪɪk] N Mosaik *nt*

Moscow ['mɒskəʊ] N Moskau *nt*

Moslem ['mɒzlem] **1** ADJ mohammedanisch **2** N Muslim(in) *m(f)*

mosque [mɒsk] N Moschee *f*

mosquito [mɒsˈkiːtəʊ] N, *pl* **-es** Stechmücke *f*; (*in tropics*) Moskito *m*

mosquito net N Moskitonetz *nt*

moss [mɒs] N Moos *nt*

mossy ['mɒsɪ] ADJ (+ER) moosbedeckt

most [məʊst] **1** ADJ SUPERL **(a)** meiste(r, s); *satisfaction, pleasure etc* größte(r, s); *speed etc* höchste(r, s); **who has (the) ~ money?** wer hat am meisten Geld?; **for the ~ part** größtenteils; (= *by and large*) im Großen und Ganzen

(b) (= *the majority of*) die meisten; **~ men/people** die meisten (Menschen/Leute)

2 N, PRON (*uncountable*) das meiste; (*countable*) die meisten; **~ of it** das meiste; **~ of them** die meisten (von ihnen); **~ of the money** das meiste Geld; **~ of his friends** die meisten seiner Freunde; **~ of the day** fast den ganzen Tag über; **~ of the time** die meiste Zeit; (= *usually*) meist(ens); **at (the) ~** höchstens; **to make the ~ of sth** (= *make good use of*) etw voll ausnützen; (= *enjoy*) etw in vollen Zügen genießen

3 ADV **(a)** SUPERL (+*vbs*) am meisten; (+*adj*) -ste(r, s); (+*adv*) am -sten; **the ~ beautiful/difficult** *etc* ... der/die/das schönste/ schwierigste *etc* ...; **what ~ displeased him ...**, **what ~ displeased him ~ ...** was ihm am meisten missfiel ...; **~ of all** allermeisten

(b) (= *very*) äußerst; **~ likely** höchstwahrscheinlich

Most Favoured Nation N Staat *m* mit Meistbegünstigung

mostly ['məʊstlɪ] ADV (= *principally*) hauptsächlich; (= *most of the time*) meistens; (= *by and large*) zum größten Teil; **they are ~ women** die meisten sind Frauen

MOT [ˌeməʊˈtiː] (*Brit*) **1** N ~ (**test**) ≈ TÜV *m*; **it failed its ~** ≈ es ist nicht durch den TÜV gekommen; **~ certificate** ≈ TÜV-Plakette *f* **2** VT **to get one's car ~'d** ≈ sein Auto zum TÜV bringen; **I got my car ~'d** (*successfully*) ≈ mein Auto hat den TÜV bestanden; **the car is ~'d till June** ≈ das Auto hat noch TÜV bis Juni

motel [məʊˈtel] N Motel *nt*

moth [mɒθ] N Nachtfalter *m*; (*wool-eating*) Motte *f*

moth: **mothball** **1** N Mottenkugel *f* **2** VT *plan, equipment etc* einmotten; *factory* stilllegen; **moth-eaten** ADJ (*lit*) mottenzerfressen; (*fig*) vermottet (*inf*)

mother ['mʌðə^r] **1** N Mutter *f*; (= *animal also*) Muttertier *nt*; **she's a ~ of three** sie hat drei Kinder; **the ~ of all battles** die Mutter aller Kriege **2** ATTR Mutter-; **~ bird** Vogelmutter *f*; **~ hen** Glucke *f* **3** VT (= *care for*) großziehen; (= *cosset*) bemuttern

mother: **motherboard** N (*Comput*) Mutterplatine *f*; **mother country** N (= *native country*) Heimat *f*; (= *head of empire*) Mutterland *nt*; **mother figure** N Mutterfigur *f*; **motherhood** N Mutterschaft *f*; **mother-in-law** N, *pl* **mothers-in-law** Schwiegermutter *f*; **motherland** N (= *native country*) Heimat *f*; (= *ancestral country*) Land *nt* der Vorfahren; **motherless** ADJ mutterlos; **he was left ~ at the age of 2** er verlor mit 2 Jahren seine Mutter

motherly ['mʌðəlɪ] ADJ mütterlich

mother-of-pearl [ˌmʌðərəvˈpɜːl] **1** N Perlmutt *nt* **2** ADJ Perlmutt-; **~ button** Perlmuttknopf *m*

Mother's Day N Muttertag *m*

mother: **mother-to-be** N, *pl* **mothers-to-be** werdende Mutter; **mother tongue** N Muttersprache *f*

motif [məʊˈtiːf] N (*Art, Mus*) Motiv *nt*; (*Sew*) Muster *nt*

motion ['məʊʃən] **1** N **(a)** Bewegung *f*; **to be in ~** sich bewegen; (*train, bus etc*) fahren; **to set** *or* **put sth in ~** etw in Gang setzen; **to go through the ~s of doing sth** (*because*

protocol etc demands it) etw der Form halber tun; (= *pretend*) den Anschein erwecken, etw zu tun; (= *do mechanically*) etw völlig mechanisch tun
(b) (= *proposal*) Antrag *m*; **to propose** *or* **make** (*US*) **a ~** einen Antrag stellen
(c) (*in debate*) Thema *nt*
2 VT **to ~ sb to do sth** jdm ein Zeichen geben, dass er etw tun solle; **he ~ed me to a chair** er wies mir einen Stuhl an
3 VI **to ~ to sb to do sth** jdm ein Zeichen geben, dass er etw tun solle

motion: motionless ADJ reg(ungs)los; **to stand ~** bewegungslos dastehen; **motion picture** N (*esp US*) Film *m*

motivate ['məʊtɪveɪt] VT motivieren

motivated ['məʊtɪveɪtɪd] ADJ motiviert; **to keep sb ~** jds Motivation erhalten; **he's just not ~ enough** es fehlt ihm einfach die nötige Motivation

motivation [,məʊtɪ'veɪʃən] N Motivation *f*

motive ['məʊtɪv] N Motiv *nt*, Beweggrund *m*; (*for crime*) (Tat)motiv *nt*

motiveless ['məʊtɪvlɪs] ADJ unmotiviert

motley ['mɒtlɪ] ADJ kunterbunt

motor ['məʊtə'] **1** N **(a)** Motor *m* **(b)** (*Brit inf*: = *car*) Auto *nt* **2** ATTR **(a)** (*Physiol*) motorisch **(b)** (= *~-driven*) Motor-; **~ yacht** Motorjacht *f* **(c)** (= *relating to ~ vehicles*) Kraftfahrzeug-; **the ~ trade** die Kraftfahrzeugbranche

motor: motorbike N Motorrad *nt*; **motorboat** N Motorboot *nt*

motorcade ['məʊtəkeɪd] N Fahrzeugkolonne *f*

motor: motorcycle N Motorrad *nt*; **motorcycling** N Motorradfahren *nt*; (*Sport*) Motorradsport *m*; **motorcyclist** N Motorradfahrer(in) *m(f)*

motoring ['məʊtərɪŋ] (*esp Brit*) **1** ADJ ATTR Auto-; **~ offence** Verkehrsdelikt *nt* **2** N Autofahren *nt*; **school of ~** Fahrschule *f*

motor inn N (*US*) Motel *nt*

motor insurance N Kraftfahrzeugversicherung *f*

motorist ['məʊtərɪst] N Autofahrer(in) *m(f)*

motorize ['məʊtəraɪz] VT **to be ~d** motorisiert sein

motor: motor lodge N (*US*) Motel *nt*; **motor mechanic** N Kraftfahrzeugmechaniker(in) *m(f)*; **motor racing** N Rennsport *m*; **motor show** N Automobilausstellung *f*; **motor sport** N Motorsport *m*; **motor vehicle** N (*form*) Kraftfahrzeug *nt*; **motorway** N (*Brit*) Autobahn *f*; **~ driving** das Fahren auf der Autobahn

mottled ['mɒtld] ADJ gesprenkelt; *complexion* fleckig; **~ brown and white** braun und weiß gesprenkelt

motto ['mɒtəʊ] N, *pl* **-es** Motto *nt*; (*in cracker, on calendar*) Spruch *m*; **the school ~** das Motto der Schule

mould¹ (*US*) **mold** [məʊld] **1** N **(a)** (= *hollow form*) (Guss)form *f*; (= *shape, Cook*) Form *f* **(b)** (*fig*) **to be cast in** *or* **from the same/a different ~** (*people*) vom gleichen/von einem anderen Schlag sein; **to break the ~** (*fig*) mit der Tradition brechen **2** VT (*lit, fig*) formen (*into* zu); **to ~ sb into sth** etw aus jdm machen

mould² (*US*) **mold** N (= *fungus*) Schimmel *m*

moulder, (*US*) **molder** ['məʊldə'] VI (*lit*) vermodern; (*food*) verderben; (*carcass*) verwesen; (*fig*) (*building*) zerfallen; (*equipment*) vergammeln (*inf*)

mouldy, (*US*) **moldy** ['məʊldɪ] ADJ (+ER) verschimmelt; (= *musty*) mod(e)rig; **to go ~** (*food*) verschimmeln

moult, (*US*) **molt** [məʊlt] VI (*bird*) sich mausern; (*mammals*) sich haaren; (*snake*) sich häuten

mound [maʊnd] N **(a)** (= *hill, burial ~*) Hügel *m*; (= *earthwork*) Wall *m*; (*Baseball*) Wurfmal *nt* **(b)** (= *pile*) Haufen *m*; (*of books, letters*) Stapel *m*

mount¹ [maʊnt] N (*in names*) **Mount Etna/Kilimanjaro** *etc* der Ätna/Kilimandscharo *etc*; **Mount Everest** Mount Everest *m*; **on Mount Sinai** auf dem Berg(e) Sinai

mount² **1** N **(a)** (= *horse etc*) Reittier *nt* **(b)** (= *support, base*) (*of machine*) Sockel *m*; (*of jewel*) Fassung *f*; (*of photo, picture*) Passepartout *nt*; (= *backing*) Unterlage *f* **2** VT **(a)** (= *climb onto*) besteigen
(b) (= *place in/on ~*) montieren; *picture, photo* aufziehen; *colour slide* rahmen; *microscope slide, specimen, animal* präparieren; *jewel* (ein)fassen; *stamp* aufkleben
(c) *play* inszenieren; *attack, expedition, exhibition*

organisieren; **to ~ a guard** eine Wache aufstellen
(d) (= *mate with*) bespringen
3 VI **(a)** (= *get on*) aufsteigen; (*on horse*) aufsitzen
(b) (*also ~ up*) zunehmen; (*evidence*) sich häufen; **the death toll has ~ed to 800** die Todesziffer ist auf 800 gestiegen; **pressure is ~ing on him to resign** er sieht sich wachsendem Druck ausgesetzt, zurückzutreten

mountain ['maʊntɪn] N (*lit, fig*) Berg *m*; **in the ~s** in den Bergen; **to make a ~ out of a molehill** aus einer Mücke einen Elefanten machen (*inf*)

mountain IN CPDS Berg-; (*alpine, Himalayan etc*) Gebirgs-; **~ road** Bergstraße *f*; **mountain bike** N Mountainbike *nt*

mountaineer [,maʊntɪ'nɪə'] N Bergsteiger(in) *m(f)*

mountaineering [,maʊntɪ'nɪərɪŋ] N Bergsteigen *nt*

mountainous ['maʊntɪnəs] ADJ gebirgig; (*fig*: = *huge*) riesig; *waves* meterhoch

mountain: mountain range N Gebirgszug *m*; **mountainside** N (Berg)hang *m*

mounted ['maʊntɪd] ADJ (= *on horseback*) beritten

Mountie ['maʊntɪ] N (*inf*) *berittener kanadischer Polizist*

mounting ['maʊntɪŋ] ADJ wachsend; **there is ~ evidence that ...** es häufen sich die Beweise dafür, dass ...

mourn [mɔːn] **1** VT betrauern; (*fig*) nachtrauern (+*dat*); **he is still ~ing the break-up of his relationship** er trauert noch immer über das Ende seiner Beziehung **2** VI trauern; (= *wear mourning*) Trauer tragen; **to ~ for** *or* **over sb** um jdn trauern; **to ~ for** *or* **over sth** einer Sache (*dat*) nachtrauern

mourner ['mɔːnə'] N Trauernde(r) *mf*; (= *non-relative at funeral*) Trauergast *m*

mournful ['mɔːnfʊl] ADJ *person, occasion, look* traurig; *person (as character trait), voice* weinerlich; *sound, cry* klagend

mourning ['mɔːnɪŋ] N (= *period etc*) Trauerzeit *f*; (= *dress*) Trauer(kleidung) *f*; **to be in ~ for sb** um jdn trauern; (= *wear ~*) Trauer tragen; **next Tuesday has been declared a day of national ~** für den kommenden Dienstag wurde Staatstrauer angeordnet

mouse [maʊs] N, *pl* **mice** Maus *f* (*also Comput*)

mouse: mouse mat, mouse pad N (*Comput*) Mausmatte *f*; **mousetrap** N Mausefalle *f*

mousey ADJ = **mousy**

mousse [muːs] N **(a)** Creme(speise) *f* **(b)** (*also styling ~*) Schaumfestiger *m*

moustache, (*US*) **mustache** [mə'stɑːʃ] N Schnurrbart *m*

mousy, mousey ['maʊsɪ] ADJ (+ER) *colour, hair* mausgrau

mouth [maʊθ] **1** N (*of person*) Mund *m*; (*of animal*) Maul *nt*; (*of bird*) Rachen *m*; (*of bottle, cave, vice etc*) Öffnung *f*; (*of river*) Mündung *f*; (*of harbour*) Einfahrt *f*; **to keep one's (big) ~ shut (about sth)** (*inf*) (über etw *acc*) die Klappe halten (*inf*); **me and my big ~!** (*inf*) ich konnte wieder nicht die Klappe halten (*inf*); **to speak** *or* **talk out of both sides of one's ~** (*US*) mit gespaltener Zunge sprechen; **he has three ~s to feed** er hat drei Mäuler zu stopfen (*inf*)
2 [maʊð] VT (= *say affectedly*) (über)deutlich artikulieren; (= *articulate soundlessly*) mit Lippensprache sagen

mouthful ['maʊθfʊl] N (*of drink*) Schluck *m*; (*of food*) Bissen *m*; (*fig*: = *difficult word*) Zungenbrecher *m*; (= *long word*) Bandwurm *m*

mouth IN CPDS Mund-; **mouth organ** N Mundharmonika *f*; **mouthpiece** N Mundstück *nt*; (*of telephone*) Sprechmuschel *f*; (*fig*) Sprachrohr *nt*; **mouth-to-mouth** ADJ **~ resuscitation** Mund-zu-Mund-Beatmung *f*; **mouthwash** N Mundwasser *nt*; **mouthwatering** ADJ lecker; (*fig*) verlockend

movable ['muːvəbl] ADJ beweglich (*auch Jur*); (= *transportable*) transportierbar

move [muːv]	
1 TRANSITIVE VERB	**3** NOUN
2 INTRANSITIVE VERB	**4** PHRASAL VERBS

1 TRANSITIVE VERB
(a) bewegen; *wheel, windmill etc* (an)treiben; (= *shift*) *objects, furniture* woanders hinstellen; (= *move away*) wegstellen; (= *shift about*) umräumen; *chest, chair* rücken; *vehicle (driver)*

wegfahren; (= *transport*) befördern; (= *remove*) *soil, rubble* wegschaffen; *obstacle* aus dem Weg räumen; *rock* von der Stelle bewegen; *chess piece etc* ziehen mit; (= *take away*) *arm* wegnehmen; *one's foot, hand* wegziehen; *enemy, demonstrators* vertreiben; *patient* (= *transport*) transportieren; (= *transfer*) verlegen; *refugees* transportieren; (*out of area*) evakuieren; *employee* (*to different department,*) *pupil* (*by authorities*) versetzen; **he moved his face a little closer** er ging mit dem Gesicht etwas näher heran; **move your feet off the table!** nimm deine Füße vom Tisch!; **to move sth to a different place** etw an einen anderen Platz stellen; **I can't move this lid/handle** der Deckel/Griff lässt sich nicht bewegen; **you'll have to move these books/your car (out of the way)** Sie müssen diese Bücher wegräumen/Ihr Auto wegfahren; **move those people** schicken Sie die Leute da weg; **his parents moved him to another school** seine Eltern haben ihn in eine andere Schule getan

(b) (= *change location/timing of*) verlegen; (*Comput*) *text block* (= *postpone*) verschieben; **we've been moved to a new office** wir mussten in ein anderes Büro umziehen

✦**to move house** (*Brit*) umziehen

✦**to move office** (in ein anderes Büro) umziehen

(c) (= *cause emotion*) rühren; (= *upset*) erschüttern; **to be moved** gerührt/erschüttert sein; **his speech really moved them** sie waren von seiner Rede tief bewegt

✦**to move sb to...** to move sb to tears jdn zu Tränen rühren

✦**to move sb to do sth** jdn dazu bringen, etw zu tun

(d) (= *propose*) (*form*) beantragen; **I move that we adjourn** ich beantrage eine Vertagung

(e) (*Comm*) (= *sell*) absetzen

2 INTRANSITIVE VERB

(a) sich bewegen; (*vehicle, ship*) fahren; (*traffic*) vorankommen; **the wheel began to move** das Rad setzte sich in Bewegung; **nothing/nobody moved** nichts/niemand rührte sich; **don't move!** stillhalten!; **to keep moving** nicht stehen bleiben; **to keep sb/sth moving** jdn/etw in Gang halten; **to move (away) from sth** sich von etw entfernen; **to move (closer) to(wards) sth** sich einer Sache (*dat*) nähern; **things are moving at last** endlich kommen die Dinge in Gang; **to move with the times** mit der Zeit gehen; **to move in high society/in royal circles** *etc* in der feinen Gesellschaft/in königlichen Kreisen *etc* verkehren

(b) (= *move house*) umziehen; **we moved to London/to a bigger house** wir sind nach London/in ein größeres Haus umgezogen; **they moved to Germany** sie sind nach Deutschland gezogen

(c) (= *change place*) gehen; (*in vehicle*) fahren; **he has moved to room 52** er ist jetzt in Zimmer 52; **she has moved to another department/a different company** sie hat die Abteilung/Firma gewechselt; **move!** weitergehen!; (= *go away*) verschwinden Sie!; **don't move** gehen Sie nicht weg

(d) (= *go fast*) (*inf*) ein Tempo draufhaben (*inf*); (= *hurry up*) zumachen (*inf*); **he can really move** der ist unheimlich schnell (*inf*)

(e) (*in games*) (= *make a move*) ziehen

(f) (= *act*) (*fig*) etwas unternehmen; **we'll have to move quickly (in order to avoid this)** wir müssen schnell handeln(, um dies zu vermeiden)

(g) (*Comm*) (= *sell*) sich absetzen lassen

3 NOUN

(a) (*in game*) Zug *m*; (*fig*) (= *step, action*) Schritt *m*; (= *measure taken*) Maßnahme *f*; **it's my move** (*lit, fig*) ich bin am Zug

✦**to make a move** (*lit, fig*) einen Zug machen

✦**to make the first move** (*fig*) den ersten Zug machen

(b) (= *movement*) Bewegung *f*; **to watch sb's every move** jdn nicht aus den Augen lassen

✦**to make a move** (= *go, leave*) **it's time we made a move** es wird Zeit, dass wir gehen

✦**to make a move to do sth** (*fig*) Anstalten machen, etw zu tun

✦**to be on the move** (*things, people*) in Bewegung sein; (*person: in different places*) unterwegs sein; (*vehicle*) fahren

✦**to get a move on** (*inf*: = *hurry up*) sich beeilen; (= *make quick progress*) (mit etw) vorankommen; **get a move on!** nun mach schon! (*inf*)

(c) (= *change*) (*of house etc*) Umzug *m*; (*to different job*) Stellenwechsel *m*; (*to different department*) Wechsel *m*

4 PHRASAL VERBS

➤ **move about** (*Brit*) **1** VT SEP umarrangieren; *furniture, ornaments etc* umräumen; *parts of body* (hin und her) bewegen **2** VI sich (hin und her) bewegen; (= *fidget*) herumzappeln; (= *travel*) unterwegs sein; (= *move house*) umziehen; **I can hear him moving about** ich höre ihn herumlaufen

➤ **move along 1** VT SEP weiterrücken; *car* vorfahren; *bystanders etc* zum Weitergehen veranlassen; **they are trying to move things along** sie versuchen, die Dinge voranzutreiben **2** VI (*along seat etc*) aufrücken; (*along pavement, bus etc*) weitergehen; (*cars*) weiterfahren

➤ **move around** VTI SEP = **move about**

➤ **move aside 1** VT SEP zur Seite schieben; *person* beiseite drängen **2** VI zur Seite gehen

➤ **move away 1** VT SEP wegräumen; *car* wegfahren; *person* wegschicken; (*to different town, job etc*) versetzen; (*pupil*) wegsetzen; **to move sb away from sth/sth** jdn von jdm/etw entfernen **2** VI **(a)** (= *move aside*) aus dem Weg gehen; (= *leave*) (*people*) weggehen; (*vehicle*) losfahren; (= *move house*) wegziehen (*from* aus, von) **(b)** (*fig*) sich entfernen (*from* von)

➤ **move back 1** VT SEP **(a)** (*to former place*) zurückstellen; *people* zurückbringen; (*into old house, town*) wieder unterbringen (*into* in +*dat*); (*to job*) zurückversetzen **(b)** (*to the rear*) things zurückschieben; *car* zurückfahren; *people* zurückdrängen; *troops* zurückziehen **2** VI **(a)** (*to former place*) zurückkommen; (*into one's house*) wieder einziehen (*into* in +*acc*); (*into old job*) zurückgehen (*to* zu) **(b)** (*to the rear*) zurückweichen; (*troops*) sich zurückziehen; (*car*) zurückfahren; **move back, please!** bitte zurücktreten!

➤ **move down 1** VT SEP (*downwards*) (weiter) nach unten stellen; (*along*) (weiter) nach hinten stellen; *pupil* zurückstufen; (*Sport*) absteigen lassen **2** VI (*downwards*) nach unten rücken; (*along*) weiterrücken; (*in bus etc*) nach hinten aufrücken; (*team etc*) absteigen; **he had to move down a year** (*pupil*) er musste eine Klasse zurück

➤ **move forward 1** VT SEP **(a)** *person* vorgehen lassen; *chair, table etc* vorziehen; *car* vorfahren; *troops* vorrücken lassen **(b)** (*fig*) *event, date* vorverlegen **2** VI (*person, troops*) vorrücken; (*crowd*) sich vorwärts bewegen; (*car*) vorwärts fahren

➤ **move in 1** VT SEP *troops, extra staff* einsetzen (*-to* in +*dat*) **2** VI **(a)** (*into accommodation*) einziehen (*-to* in +*acc*) **(b)** (= *come closer*) sich nähern (*on dat*); (*camera*) näher herangehen (*on an* +*acc*); (*police, troops*) anrücken; (= *start operations*) (*workers*) (an)kommen; (*hooligans, firms*) auf den Plan treten; **to move in on sb** (*police, troops*) gegen jdn vorrücken

➤ **move off 1** VT SEP *people* wegschicken **2** VI **(a)** (= *go away*) (*people*) weggehen; (*troops*) abziehen **(b)** (= *start moving*) sich in Bewegung setzen

➤ **move on 1** VT SEP **the policeman moved them on** der Polizist forderte sie auf weiterzugehen/weiterzufahren **2** VI (*people*) weitergehen; (*vehicles*) weiterfahren; **it's about time I was moving on** (*fig*: to new job etc) es wird Zeit, dass ich (mal) etwas anderes mache; **time is moving on** die Zeit vergeht

➤ **move out 1** VT SEP **(a)** *car* herausfahren (*of* aus); **we had to move the furniture out** wir mussten die Möbel hinausräumen; **move the table out of the corner** stellen *or* rücken Sie den Tisch von der Ecke weg **(b)** *troops* abziehen; **they moved everybody out of the danger zone** alle mussten die Gefahrenzone räumen **2** VI **(a)** (= *leave accommodation*) ausziehen; (= *withdraw: troops*) abziehen **(b)** (= *leave: train etc*) abfahren

➤ **move over 1** VT SEP herüberschieben; **he moved the car over to the side** er fuhr an die Seite heran **2** VI zur Seite rücken; **move over, we all want to sit down** rück mal ein Stück, wir wollen uns auch hinsetzen (*inf*); **to move over to a new system** ein neues System einführen

➤ **move up 1** VT SEP **(a)** (weiter) nach oben stellen; (= *promote*) befördern; *pupil* versetzen; (*Sport*) aufsteigen lassen; **they moved him up two places** sie haben ihn zwei Plätze vorgerückt **(b)** *troops etc* (*into battle area*) aufmarschieren lassen; (*to front line*) vorrücken lassen; *guns, artillery* auffahren **2** VI (*fig*) aufsteigen; (*shares, rates etc*) steigen; (= *be promoted*) befördert werden; (*Sch*) versetzt werden

moveable ADJ = **movable**

movement ['muːvmənt] N **(a)** (= *also political etc* ~) Bewegung *f*; (*fig*: = *trend*) Trend *m* (*towards* zu); **the ~ of traffic** der Verkehrsfluss; **the ~ of capital and goods** der freie Kapital- und Warenverkehr **(b)** (= *transport: of goods etc*) Beförderung *f*; **~ certificate** (*Comm*) Waren(verkehrs)-bescheinigung *f* **(c)** (*Mus*) Satz *m* **(d)** (= *mechanism*) Antrieb *m*; (*of clock*) Uhrwerk *nt*

mover ['muːvəʳ] N **(a)** (= *walker, dancer etc*) **he is a good/poor** *etc* ~ seine Bewegungen sind schön/plump *etc* **(b) to be a fast ~** (*inf*) von der schnellen Truppe sein (*inf*)

movie ['muːvɪ] N (*esp US*) Film *m*; **(the) ~s** der Film; **to go to the ~s** ins Kino gehen

MOVIE RATING, FILM RATING

Es ist Aufgabe des „British Board of Film Classification", die in Großbritannien erscheinenden Filme und Videos einzustufen. Jeder Film erhält danach eine Klassifizierung: U (Universal) - für jedes Alter geeignet; PG (Parental Guidance) - einige Szenen könnten für jüngere Kinder ungeeignet sein; „12", „15" oder „18" - das ist das jeweilige Mindestalter der Zuschauer; „Restricted 18" - darf nur in bestimmten Lokalitäten, z. B. Kinoklubs, gezeigt werden.

In den USA erfüllt die „Motion Picture Association of America" eine ähnliche Aufgabe. Hier werden folgende Klassifizierungen vergeben: G (General) - für jedes Alter geeignet; PG (Parental Guidance) - einige Szenen könnten für jüngere Kinder ungeeignet sein; „PG13" - einige Szenen könnten für Kinder unter 13 nicht geeignet sein; „R" (Restricted) - jeder unter 17 muss von einem Elternteil oder einer erwachsenen Aufsichtsperson begleitet werden; „NC-17" oder „X" - keine Jugendlichen unter 17.

movie (*esp US*) IN CPDS Film-; **movie camera** N Filmkamera *f*; **moviegoer** N Kinogänger(in) *m(f)*; **movie star** N Filmstar *m*; **movie theater** N Kino *nt*

moving ['muːvɪŋ] ADJ **(a)** beweglich **(b)** (= *causing emotion*) ergreifend; *tribute* rührend

moving (*US*): **moving company** N Umzugsunternehmen *nt*; **moving van** N Möbelwagen *m*

mow [məʊ], *pret* **mowed**, *ptp* **mown** *or* **mowed** VTI mähen

➤ **mow down** VT SEP (*fig*) niedermähen

mower ['məʊəʳ] N (= *lawnmower*) Rasenmäher *m*

mown [məʊn] PTP *of* **mow**

MP ABBR *of* **Member of Parliament**

mpg ABBR *of* **miles per gallon**

mph ABBR *of* **miles per hour**

MPhil ABBR *of* **Master of Philosophy**

Mr ['mɪstəʳ] ABBR *of* **Mister** Herr *m*

Mrs ['mɪsɪz] ABBR *of* **Mistress** Frau *f*

MS N ABBR *of* **multiple sclerosis**

Ms [mɪz] N Frau *f* (*auch für Unverheiratete*)

Ms

Ms ist die schriftliche Anredeform für Frauen, mit der man die traditionelle Unterscheidung nach verheiratetem (Mrs) und unverheiratetem (Miss) Familienstand vermeidet.

MSc ABBR *of* **Master of Science**

MSP (*Brit Pol*) ABBR *of* **Member of the Scottish Parliament** Abgeordnete(r) *mf* des schottischen Parlaments

Mt ABBR *of* **Mount**

much [mʌtʃ] **1** ADJ, N viel *inv*; **how ~** wie viel *inv*; **not ~** nicht viel; **that ~** so viel; **but that ~ I do know** aber DAS weiß ich; **we don't see ~ of each other** wir sehen uns nicht oft *or* nur selten; **he's/it's not up to ~** (*inf*) er/es ist nicht gerade berühmt (*inf*); **I'm not ~ of a musician/cook/player** ich bin nicht sehr musikalisch/keine große Köchin/kein (besonders) guter Spieler; **that wasn't ~ of a party** die Party

war nicht gerade besonders; **I find that a bit (too) ~ after all** I've done for him nach allem was ich für ihn getan habe, finde ich das ein ziemlich starkes Stück (*inf*); **too ~** (*in quantity etc, inf*: = *more than one can bear*) zu viel *inv*; (*inf*) (= *marvellous, hilarious*) Spitze (*sl*); (= *ridiculous*) das Letzte (*inf*); **that insult was too ~ for me** die Beleidigung ging mir zu weit; **this job is too ~ for me** ich bin der Arbeit nicht gewachsen; **far too ~** viel zu viel; **(just) as ~** ebenso viel *inv*, genauso viel *inv*; **about/not as ~** ungefähr/nicht so viel; **as ~ as you want/can** *etc* so viel du willst/kannst *etc*; **they hope to raise as ~ as £2m** sie hoffen, nicht weniger als zwei Millionen Pfund aufzubringen; **as ~ again** noch einmal so viel; **I feared/thought** *etc* **as ~** (= *genau*) das habe ich befürchtet/mir gedacht *etc*; **it's as ~ as I can do to stand up** es fällt mir schwer genug aufzustehen; **so ~** so viel *inv*; **it's not so ~ a problem of modernization as ...** es ist nicht so sehr ein Problem der Modernisierung, als ...; **to make ~ of sb/sth** viel Wind um jdn/etw machen; **Glasgow makes ~ of its large number of parks** Glasgow rühmt sich seiner vielen Parks; **I couldn't make ~ of that chapter** mit dem Kapitel konnte ich nicht viel anfangen (*inf*)

2 ADV **(a)** viel; **a ~-admired woman** eine viel bewunderte Frau; **so ~** so viel; so sehr; **too ~** zu viel, zu sehr; **I like it very ~** es gefällt mir sehr gut; **I don't like him/it too ~** ich kann ihn/es nicht besonders leiden; **thank you very ~** vielen Dank; **I don't ~ care** *or* **care ~** es ist mir ziemlich egal; **however ~ he tries** sosehr *or* wie sehr er sich auch bemüht; **~ as I like him** sosehr ich ihn mag

(b) (= *by far*) weitaus, bei weitem; **I would ~ prefer to** *or* **~ rather stay** ich würde viel lieber bleiben

(c) (= *almost*) beinahe; **they are produced in ~ the same way** sie werden auf sehr ähnliche Art hergestellt

muchness ['mʌtʃnɪs] N (*Brit inf*) **they're much of a ~** (*things*) das ist eins wie das andere; (*people*) sie sind einer wie der andere

muck [mʌk] N **(a)** (= *dirt*) Dreck *m*; (= *manure*) Dung *m*, Mist *m* **(b)** (*fig*) (= *rubbish*) Mist *m*; (= *obscenities*) Schund *m*; (= *food etc*) Zeug *nt*

➤ **muck about** *or* **around** (*Brit inf*) **1** VT SEP **to muck sb about** jdn verarschen (*inf*); (*by not committing oneself*) jdn hinhalten; **stop mucking me about!** sag mir endlich, was los ist! **2** VI **(a)** (= *lark about*) herumalbern (*inf*); (= *do nothing in particular*) herumgammeln (*inf*) **(b)** (= *tinker with*) herumfummeln (*with* an +*dat*)

➤ **muck in** VI (*Brit inf*) mit anpacken (*inf*)

➤ **muck out** (*Brit*) **1** VT SEP (aus)misten **2** VI ausmisten

➤ **muck up** VT SEP (*Brit inf*) **(a)** (= *dirty*) dreckig machen (*inf*) **(b)** (= *spoil*) vermasseln (*inf*); **that's really mucked me/my plans up** das hat mir alles/meine Pläne vermasselt (*inf*)

muckraking ['mʌkreɪkɪŋ] N (*fig inf*) Sensationsmache(rei) *f* (*inf*)

mucky ['mʌkɪ] ADJ (+ER) dreckig (*inf*), schmutzig; **you ~ thing** *or* **pup!** (*Brit inf*) du Ferkel! (*inf*)

mud [mʌd] N **(a)** Schlamm *m*; (*on roads etc*) Matsch *m* **(b)** (*fig*) **his name is ~** (*inf*) er ist unten durch (*inf*); **to drag sb/sb's name** *or* **reputation through the ~** jdn/jds guten Namen in den Schmutz ziehen

mud bath N Schlammbad *nt*

muddle ['mʌdl] **1** N Durcheinander *nt*; **to get in(to) a ~** (*things*) durcheinander geraten; (*person*) konfus werden; **to get oneself in(to) a ~ over sth** mit etw nicht klarkommen (*inf*); **to be in a ~** völlig durcheinander sein **2** VT durcheinander bringen; **two things** *or* **people** verwechseln; (= *make confused*) *person* verwirren

➤ **muddle along** VI vor sich (*acc*) hinwursteln (*inf*)

➤ **muddle through** VI sich (irgendwie) durchschlagen

➤ **muddle up** VT SEP = **muddle 2**

muddled ['mʌdld] ADJ *koriers; thoughts, ideas* wirr; **to get ~ (up)** (*things*) durcheinander geraten; (*person*) konfus werden

muddy ['mʌdɪ] **1** ADJ (+ER) *floor, shoes, hands etc* schmutzig; *road, ground etc* matschig; *liquid* schlammig; **I'm all ~** ich bin ganz voll Schlamm **2** VT schmutzig machen; (*fig*) *situation, issue* in Verwirrung bringen

mud: **mudflap** N Schmutzfänger *m*; **mudguard** N (*Brit*) (*on cycles*) Schutzblech *nt*; (*on cars*) Kotflügel *m*; **mudpack** N Schlammpackung *f*

muesli ['mjuːzlɪ] N Müsli *nt*

muff¹ [mʌf] N Muff *m*

muff² VT (*inf*) vermasseln (*inf*); *kick, shot, ball* danebensetzen (*inf*); *lines, text* verpatzen (*inf*)

muffin ['mʌfɪn] N **(a)** Muffin *m, kleiner, in Förmchen gebackener Kuchen* **(b)** (*Brit*) weiches, flaches Milchbrötchen, *meist warm gegessen*

muffle ['mʌfl] VT *sound, shot etc* dämpfen; *noise* abschwächen

muffled ['mʌfld] ADJ *sound, voice etc* gedämpft; *shouts* erstickt

muffler ['mʌflə'] N (*US Aut*) Auspuff(topf) *m*

mug [mʌg] **1** N **(a)** (= *cup*) Becher *m*; (*for beer*) Krug *m* **(b)** (*esp Brit inf*: = *dupe*) Trottel *m* (*inf*); **have you found some ~ to do it?** hast du einen Dummen dafür gefunden? (*inf*); **that's a ~'s game** das ist doch schwachsinnig **(c)** (*inf*: = *face*) Visage *f* (*inf*) **2** VT überfallen

➤ **mug up** VT SEP (*Brit inf*: *also* **mug up on**) **to mug up sth/one's French up, to mug up on sth/one's French** etw/Französisch pauken (*inf*)

mugger ['mʌgə'] N Straßenräuber(in) *m(f)*

mugging ['mʌgɪŋ] N Straßenraub *m no pl*

muggy ['mʌgɪ] ADJ (+ER) schwül; *heat* drückend

mug shot N (*inf*) Verbrecherfoto *nt* (*inf*)

mulberry ['mʌlbərɪ] N (= *fruit*) Maulbeere *f*; (= *tree*) Maulbeerbaum *m*

mulch [mʌltʃ] (*Hort*) **1** N Krümelschicht *f* **2** VT abdecken

mule¹ [mju:l] N (*of donkey and mare*) Maultier *nt*; (*of stallion and donkey*) Maulesel *m*; **(as) stubborn as a ~** (so) störrisch wie ein Maulesel

mule² N (= *slipper*) Pantoffel *m*

➤ **mull over** VT SEP sich (*dat*) durch den Kopf gehen lassen

mulled wine [,mʌld'waɪn] N Glühwein *m*

multi- PREF mehr-, Mehr-; (*with Latin stem in German*) Multi-, multi-; **~syllabic** mehrsilbig; **~disciplinary** multidisziplinär

multi: multichannel ADJ (*TV*) mehrkanalig, Mehrkanal-; **multicoloured**, (*US*) **multicolored** ADJ mehrfarbig; *material, lights, decorations* bunt; **multicultural** ADJ multikulturell; **multifunctional** ADJ multifunktional; **multigrade** ADJ ~ **oil** Mehrbereichsöl *nt*; **multilateral** ADJ (*Pol*) multilateral; **multilingual** ADJ mehrsprachig; **multimedia** ADJ multimedial; (*Comput*) Multimedia-; **multimillionaire** N Multimillionär(in) *m(f)*; **multinational** **1** N Multi *m* (*inf*) **2** ADJ multinational; *aid, effort* international; **multiparty** ADJ (*Pol*) Mehrparteien-

multiple ['mʌltɪpl] **1** ADJ **(a)** (*with sing n*: = *of several parts*) mehrfach; **~ collision** *or* **crash** Massenkarambolage *f* **(b)** (*with pl n*: = *many*) mehrere; **he died of ~ injuries** er erlag seinen zahlreichen Verletzungen **2** N (*Math*) Vielfache(s) *nt*; **eggs are usually sold in ~s of six** Eier werden gewöhnlich in Einheiten zu je sechs verkauft

multiple: multiple choice N Multiplechoice *nt*; **multiple sclerosis** N multiple Sklerose

multiplication [,mʌltɪplɪ'keɪʃən] N **(a)** (*Math*) Multiplikation *f* **(b)** (*fig*) Vervielfachung *f*

multiplication: multiplication sign N (*Math*) Multiplikationszeichen *nt*; **multiplication table** N (*Math*) Multiplikationstabelle *f*; **he knows all his ~s** er kann das Einmaleins

multiplicity [,mʌltɪ'plɪsɪtɪ] N Vielzahl *f*; **for a ~ of reasons** aus vielerlei Gründen

multiply ['mʌltɪplaɪ] **1** VT **(a)** (*Math*) multiplizieren; **4 multiplied by 6 is 24** 4 mal 6 ist 24 **(b)** (*fig*) vervielfachen **2** VI **(a)** (*fig*) sich vervielfachen **(b)** (= *breed*) sich vermehren

multi: multipurpose ADJ Mehrzweck-; **~ cleaner** Allzweckreiniger *m*; **multiracial** ADJ gemischtrassig; **multiskilled** ADJ mehrfach qualifiziert; **multistorey**, (*US*) **multistory** ADJ mehrstöckig; **~ flats** (*Brit*), **multistorey apartments** (*US*) (Wohn)hochhäuser *pl*; **~ car park** (*Brit*) Park(hoch)haus *nt*; **multitasking** N (*Comput*) Multitasking *nt*

multitude ['mʌltɪtju:d] N Menge *f*; **a ~ of** eine Vielzahl von, eine Menge

mum¹ [mʌm] ADJ (*inf*) **to keep** *or* **stay ~** den Mund halten (*about* über +*acc*) (*inf*)

mum² N (*Brit inf*) Mutter *f*; (*as address*) Mutti *f* (*inf*)

mumble ['mʌmbl] **1** VT murmeln **2** VI vor sich hin murmeln; (= *speak indistinctly*) nuscheln

mumbo jumbo ['mʌmbəʊ'dʒʌmbəʊ] N (= *empty ritual, superstition*) Hokuspokus *m*; (= *gibberish*) Kauderwelsch *nt*

mummy¹ ['mʌmɪ] N (= *corpse*) Mumie *f*

mummy² N (*Brit inf*: = *mother*) Mama *f* (*inf*)

mumps [mʌmps] N SING Mumps *m or f* (*inf*) *no art*

munch [mʌntʃ] VTI mampfen (*inf*)

munchies ['mʌntʃɪz] PL (*US inf*) Knabberei *f* (*inf*)

mundane [,mʌn'deɪn] ADJ (*fig*: = *everyday*) alltäglich; (*pej*) (= *humdrum*) banal; (= *boring*) langweilig

Munich [mjuː'nɪk] N München *nt*

municipal [mjuː'nɪsɪpəl] ADJ städtisch; **~ elections** Gemeinderatswahl *f*

municipality [mjuː,nɪsɪ'pælɪtɪ] N Gemeinde *f*

munition [mjuː'nɪʃən] N USU PL Waffen *pl* und Munition *f*

mural ['mjʊərəl] N Wandgemälde *nt*

murder ['mɜ:də'] **1** N **(a)** (*lit*) Mord *m*; **the ~ of John F. Kennedy** der Mord an John F. Kennedy **(b)** (*fig inf*) **it was ~** es war mörderisch; **it'll be ~** es wird schrecklich werden; (= *exhausting*) das ist glatter Mord (*inf*); **to get away with ~** sich (*dat*) alles erlauben können **2** VT (*lit*) ermorden; (= *slaughter*) morden

> *Be careful!* **murder** *is not translated by the German word* **Mörder**.

murderer ['mɜ:dərə'] N Mörder(in) *m(f)*

murderess ['mɜ:dərɪs] N Mörderin *f*

murderous ['mɜ:dərəs] ADJ *villain, soldiers etc* blutrünstig; **~ attack** Mordanschlag *m*

murk [mɜ:k] N Düsternis *f*; (*in water*) trübes Wasser

murky ['mɜ:kɪ] ADJ (+ER) (*lit, fig*) trüb; *water also* schmutzig; *room, street* düster, dunkel; *night, character, deed* finster; *past* dunkel; **it's really ~ outside** draußen ist es so düster

murmur ['mɜ:mə'] **1** N Murmeln *nt*; (*of water, wind, leaves, traffic*) Rauschen *nt*; **there was a ~ of approval/discontent** ein beifälliges/unzufriedenes Murmeln erhob sich; **without a ~** ohne zu murren **2** VT murmeln; (*with discontent*) murren **3** VI murmeln; (*with discontent*) murren (*about, against* über +*acc*); (*fig*) rauschen

murmuring ['mɜ:mərɪŋ] N **~s (of discontent)** Unmutsäußerungen *pl* (*from* +*gen*)

muscle ['mʌsl] N Muskel *m*; (*fig*: = *power*) Macht *f*; **to have financial ~** finanzstark sein; **he never moved a ~** er rührte sich nicht

➤ **muscle in** VI (*inf*) mitmischen (*inf*) (*on* bei)

muscle-bound ['mʌslbaʊnd] ADJ (*inf*) muskelbepackt (*inf*); **to be ~** ein Muskelpaket *m* sein (*inf*)

muscl(e)y ['mʌsəlɪ] ADJ (*inf*) muskelbepackt (*inf*)

muscular ['mʌskjʊlə'] ADJ **(a)** (= *relating to muscles*) Muskel-; **~ cramp** *or* **spasm** Muskelkrampf *m* **(b)** (= *having strong muscles*) muskulös

muscular dystrophy N Muskelschwund *m*

muse [mju:z] **1** VI nachgrübeln (*about, on* über +*acc*) **2** VT grüblerisch sagen **3** N Muse *f*

museum [mjuː'zɪəm] N Museum *nt*

mush [mʌʃ] N **(a)** Brei *m* **(b)** (*inf*) Schmalz *m*; **he always sings such ~** er singt immer solche Schnulzen

mushroom ['mʌʃrʊm] **1** N (*essbarer*) Pilz; (= *button ~*) Champignon *m* **2** ATTR Pilz-; **~ soup** Pilz- *or* Champignonsuppe *f* **3** VI **(a) to go ~ing** Pilze sammeln (gehen) **(b)** (= *grow rapidly*) wie die Pilze aus dem Boden schießen; **unemployment has ~ed** die Arbeitslosigkeit ist explosionsartig angestiegen

mushy ['mʌʃɪ] ADJ (+ER) **(a)** matschig; *liquid, consistency* breiig; (= *puréed*) püriert; **~ snow** Schneematsch *m*; **to go ~** zu Brei werden; (= *go off*: *fruit*) matschig werden **(b)** (*inf*: = *maudlin*) schmalzig

mushy peas PL Erbsenmus *nt*

music ['mju:zɪk] N Musik *f*; (= *written score*) Noten *pl*; **to set** *or* **put sth to ~** etw vertonen; **it was (like) ~ to my ears** das war Musik in meinen Ohren; **to face the ~** (*fig*) dafür gradestehen

musical ['mju:zɪkəl] **1** ADJ **(a)** musikalisch; **~ note** Note *f*; **~ evening** Musikabend *m* **(b)** (= *tuneful*) melodisch **2** N Musical *nt*

musical: musical box N Spieluhr *f*; **musical chairs** N SING Reise *f* nach Jerusalem; **musical director** N (*esp US*) (*of orchestra*) Chefdirigent(in) *m(f)*; (*of show*) musikalischer Leiter, musikalische Leiterin; **musical instrument** N Musik-instrument *nt*

musically ['mjuːzɪkəlɪ] ADV musikalisch; **I'm ~ trained** ich habe eine musikalische Ausbildung

musical score N (*written*) Partitur *f*; (*for film etc*) Musik *f*

music IN CPDS Musik-; **music box** N Spieldose *f*; **music hall** N Varietee *nt*

musician [mjuːˈzɪʃən] N Musiker(in) *m(f)*

music: **music paper** N Notenpapier *nt*; **music stand** N Notenständer *m*; **music video** N Musikvideo *nt*

musk [mʌsk] N Moschus *m*

musky ['mʌskɪ] ADJ (+ER) **~ smell** *or* **scent** Moschusduft *m*

Muslim ['mʊzlɪm] ADJ, N = **Moslem**

muslin [mʌzlɪn] **1** N Musselin *m* **2** ADJ aus Musselin

muss [mʌs] VT (*also ~ up*) in Unordnung bringen

mussel ['mʌsl] N (Mies)muschel *f*

must [mʌst] **1** VB AUX PRESENT TENSE ONLY **(a)** müssen; **you ~ (go and) see this church** Sie müssen sich (*dat*) diese Kirche unbedingt ansehen; **if you ~ know** wenn du es unbedingt wissen willst; **~ you/I** *etc*? (= *really?*) ja (wirklich)?; (= *do you/ I have to?*) muss das sein?
(b) (*in neg sentences*) dürfen; **I ~n't forget that** ich darf das nicht vergessen
(c) (= *be certain to*) **he ~ be there by now** er ist wohl inzwischen da; (= *is bound to*) er muss (wohl) inzwischen da sein; **I ~ have lost it** ich muss es wohl verloren haben; **he ~ be older than that** er muss älter sein; **it ~ be about 3 o'clock** es muss so gegen 3 Uhr sein; **I ~ have been dreaming** da habe ich wohl geträumt; **you ~ be crazy!** du bist ja *or* wohl wahnsinnig!
2 N (*inf*) Muss *nt*; **a sense of humour** (*Brit*) *or* **humor** (*US*) **is a ~** man braucht unbedingt Humor

mustache N (*US*) = **moustache**

mustard ['mʌstəd] **1** N Senf *m* **2** ATTR Senf-; (= *yellow*) senffarben; **~ sauce** Senfsoße *f*

mustard powder N Senfmehl *nt*

muster ['mʌstəʳ] **1** N **to pass ~** (*fig*) den Anforderungen genügen **2** VT (*fig: also ~ up*) *intelligence* aufbieten; *strength, courage* aufbringen; *all one's strength, courage* zusammennehmen

mustn't ['mʌsnt] CONTR *of* **must not**

musty ['mʌstɪ] ADJ (+ER) *air* moderig; *air* muffig

mutant ['mjuːtənt] N Mutation *f*

mutation [mjuːˈteɪʃən] N (= *result*) Variante *f*; (*Biol*) Mutation *f*

mute [mjuːt] **1** ADJ stumm (*also Ling*); **to sit ~** schweigend dasitzen **2** N Stumme(r) *mf*

muted ['mjuːtɪd] ADJ gedämpft; (*fig*) *criticism etc* leise

mutilate ['mjuːtɪleɪt] VT verstümmeln; *painting, building etc* verschandeln (*inf*)

mutilation [mjuːtɪˈleɪʃən] N Verstümmelung *f*

mutinous ['mjuːtɪnəs] ADJ (*Naut*) meuterisch; (*fig*) rebellisch

mutiny ['mjuːtɪnɪ] (*Naut, fig*) **1** N Meuterei *f* **2** VI meutern

mutter ['mʌtəʳ] **1** N Murmeln *nt*; **a ~ of discontent** ein unzufriedenes Murren **2** VT murmeln; **they ~ed their discontent** sie murrten unzufrieden **3** VI murmeln; (*with discontent*) murren

muttering ['mʌtərɪŋ] N Gemurmel *nt no pl*, Meckerei *f* (*inf*)

mutton ['mʌtn] N Hammel(fleisch *nt*) *m*

mutual ['mjuːtjʊəl] ADJ *trust, respect, affection etc* gegenseitig; *efforts, détente, satisfaction* beiderseitig; *interest, friends, dislikes*

etc gemeinsam; **the divorce was by ~ consent** sie haben sich im gegenseitigen Einvernehmen scheiden lassen; **it would be for our ~ benefit** es wäre für uns beide von Vorteil; **the feeling is ~** das beruht (ganz) auf Gegenseitigkeit

mutual fund N (*US Fin*) offener Investmentfonds

mutually ['mjuːtjʊəlɪ] ADV beide; *satisfactory, beneficial* für beide Seiten; *agreed, rejected* von beiden Seiten; **at a ~ convenient time** zu einem für beide Seiten annehmbaren Zeitpunkt

Muzak® ['mjuːzæk] N Berieselungsmusik *f* (*inf*)

muzzle ['mʌzl] **1** N **(a)** (= *snout, mouth*) Maul *nt* **(b)** (*for dog etc*) Maulkorb *m* **(c)** (*of gun*) Mündung *f* **2** VT *animal* einen Maulkorb umlegen (+*dat*); (*fig*) *the press etc* mundtot machen

MVP N (*US Sport*) ABBR *of* **most valuable player** bester Spieler, beste Spielerin

MW ABBR *of* **medium wave** MW

my [maɪ] **1** POSS ADJ mein; **I've hurt my leg/arm** ich habe mir das Bein/den Arm verletzt; **in my country** bei uns **2** INTERJ (*surprise*) (du) meine Güte; (*delight*) ach, oh

myopia [maɪˈəʊpɪə] N Kurzsichtigkeit *f*

myopic [maɪˈɒpɪk] ADJ kurzsichtig

myriad ['mɪrɪəd] **1** N **a ~ of** Myriaden von **2** ADJ unzählige

myself [maɪˈself] PERS PRON **(a)** (*dir obj, with prep +acc*) mich; (*indir obj, with prep +dat*) mir; **I said to ~** ich sagte mir; **singing to ~** vor mich hin singend; **I wanted to see (it) for ~** ich wollte es selbst *or* selber sehen; **I addressed the letter to ~** ich habe den Brief an mich selbst adressiert
(b) (*emph*) (ich) selbst; **my wife and ~** meine Frau und ich; **I thought so ~** das habe ich auch gedacht; **... if I say so** *or* **it ~ ...** auch wenn ich es selbst sage; **(all) by ~** (= *ganz*) allein(e)
(c) (= *one's normal self*) **I'm not (feeling) ~ today** mit mir ist heute etwas nicht in Ordnung; **I just tried to be ~** ich versuchte, mich ganz natürlich zu benehmen

mysterious [mɪˈstɪərɪəs] ADJ (= *puzzling*) rätselhaft, mysteriös; *atmosphere, stranger* (= *secretive also*) geheimnisvoll; **she is being quite ~ about it/him** sie macht ein großes Geheimnis daraus/um ihn; **for some ~ reason** aus unerfindlichen Gründen

mystery ['mɪstərɪ] N (= *puzzle*) Rätsel *nt*; (= *secret*) Geheimnis *nt*; **to be shrouded** *or* **surrounded in ~** von einem Geheimnis umgeben sein; **there's no ~ about it** da ist überhaupt nichts Geheimnisvolles dabei

mystery: **mystery novel, mystery story** N Kriminalgeschichte *f*; **mystery tour** N Fahrt *f* ins Blaue

mystic ['mɪstɪk] **1** ADJ mystisch **2** N Mystiker(in) *m(f)*

mystical ['mɪstɪkəl] ADJ mystisch

mysticism ['mɪstɪsɪzəm] N Mystizismus *m*

mystified ['mɪstɪfaɪd] ADJ verblüfft; **I am ~ as to how this could happen** es ist mir ein Rätsel, wie das passieren konnte

mystify ['mɪstɪfaɪ] VT vor ein Rätsel stellen

mystifying ['mɪstɪfaɪɪŋ] ADJ rätselhaft

mystique [mɪˈstiːk] N geheimnisvoller Nimbus

myth [mɪθ] N Mythos *m*; (*fig*) Märchen *nt*

mythic ['mɪθɪk] ADJ = **mythical**

mythical ['mɪθɪkəl] ADJ **(a)** (*of myth*) mythisch; **the ~ figure/ character of Arthur** die Sagengestalt des Artus **(b)** *proportions, status, figure* legendär **(c)** (= *unreal*) *figure, world* fantastisch; (= *invented*) erfunden

mythological [mɪθəˈlɒdʒɪkəl] ADJ mythologisch

mythology [mɪˈθɒlədʒɪ] N Mythologie *f*

Nn

N, n [en] N N *nt*, n *nt*

N ABBR *of* **north** N

n ABBR *of* **noun** Subst.

'n (*inf*) = **and**

n/a ABBR *of* **not applicable** entf.

NAACP (*US*) ABBR *of* **National Association for the Advancement of Colored People** *Vereinigung zur Förderung Farbiger*

nab [næb] VT (*inf*) **(a)** (= *catch*) erwischen; (*police*) schnappen (*inf*) **(b)** (= *take for oneself*) sich (*dat*) grapschen (*inf*); **somebody had ~bed my seat** mir hatte jemand den Platz geklaut (*inf*)

naff [næf] ADJ (*Brit inf*) **(a)** (= *stupid*) blöd (*inf*) **(b)** colour, design, car ordinär

➤ **naff off** VI (*Brit inf*) verschwinden (*inf*); **naff off!** (= *go away*) hau ab! (*inf*); (*expressing refusal*) du spinnst wohl!

NAFTA [ˈnæftə] N ABBR *of* **North American Free Trade Agreement** NAFTA *f*

nag¹ [næg] **1** VT (= *find fault with*) herumnörgeln an (+*dat*); (= *pester*) keine Ruhe lassen (+*dat*) (*for* wegen); **don't ~ me** nun lass mich doch in Ruhe!; **to ~ sb about sth** jdm wegen etw keine Ruhe lassen; **to ~ sb to do sth** jdm schwer zusetzen, damit er etw tut **2** VI (= *find fault*) herumnörgeln; (= *be insistent*) keine Ruhe geben; **stop ~ging** hör auf zu meckern (*inf*) **3** N Nörgler(in) *m(f)*; (*pestering*) Quälgeist *m*

nag² N (= *old horse*) Mähre *f*; (*inf: = horse*) Gaul *m*

nagging [ˈnægɪŋ] ADJ *pain* dumpf; *worry, doubt* quälend; *question* brennend; *fear* drückend

nail [neɪl] **1** N (*Anat, Tech*) Nagel *m*; **as hard as ~s** knallhart (*inf*), (unheimlich) hart; (*physically*) zäh wie Leder; **to hit the ~ (right) on the head** (*fig*) den Nagel auf den Kopf treffen; **to be a ~ in sb's coffin** (*fig*) ein Nagel zu jds Sarg sein **2** VT **(a)** nageln; **to ~ sth to the floor/wall** etw an den Boden/an die Wand nageln **(b)** (*inf*) **to ~ sb** sich (*dat*) jdn schnappen (*inf*); (= *charge*) jdn drankriegen (*inf*)

➤ **nail down** VT SEP festnageln

➤ **nail up** VT SEP *picture etc* annageln; *door, window* vernageln; *box* zunageln

nail IN CPDS Nagel-; **nail-biting** ADJ (*inf*) *suspense* atemlos; *match* spannungsgeladen; **nailbrush** N Nagelbürste *f*; **nail clippers** PL Nagelzwicker *m*; **nailfile** N Nagelfeile *f*; **nail polish** N Nagellack *m*; **nail polish remover** N Nagellackentferner *m*; **nail scissors** PL Nagelschere *f*; **nail varnish** N (*Brit*) Nagellack *m*

naïve [naɪˈiːv] ADJ (+ER) naiv (*also Art*)

naïvely [naɪˈiːvlɪ] ADV naiv; **I ~ thought that ...** naiverweise dachte ich, dass ...

naked [ˈneɪkɪd] ADJ **(a)** *person, truth, hatred* nackt; *flame, light* ungeschützt; *wire* blank; **to go ~** nackt gehen; **~ to the waist** mit nacktem Oberkörper; **visible/invisible to the ~ eye** mit bloßem Auge erkennbar/nicht erkennbar **(b)** (= *defenceless*) schutzlos; **the army was left ~** das Heer stand schutzlos da **(c)** (*Fin*) *debenture* ungesichert

Nam [næm] N (*US*) ABBR *of* **Vietnam**

name [neɪm] **1** N **(a)** Name *m*; **what's your ~?** wie heißen Sie?; **my ~ is ...** ich heiße ...; **what's the ~ of this street?** wie heißt diese Straße?; **a man (going) by the ~ of Gunn** ein Mann namens Gunn; **he knows all his customers by ~** er kennt alle seine Kunden mit Namen; **to refer to sb/sth by ~** jdn/etw namentlich *or* mit Namen nennen; **what ~ shall I say?** wie ist Ihr Name, bitte?; (*on telephone*) wer ist am Apparat?; (*before showing sb in*) wen darf ich melden?; **to have one's ~ taken** (*Ftbl, Police etc*) aufgeschrieben werden; **in the ~ of** im Namen (+*gen*); **I'll put my/your ~ down** (*on list, in register etc*) ich trage mich/dich ein; (*for school, class, excursion, competition etc*) ich melde mich/dich an (*for* zu, *for a school* in einer Schule); (*for tickets, goods etc*) ich lasse mich/dich vormerken; (*on waiting list*) ich lasse mich/dich auf die Warteliste setzen; **to call sb ~s** jdn beschimpfen; **not to have a penny/cent to one's ~** völlig pleite sein (*inf*); **in all but ~** praktisch; **for these people survival is the ~ of the game** diesen Leuten geht es ums Überleben

(b) (= *reputation*) Ruf *m*; **to have a good/bad ~** einen guten/ schlechten Ruf haben; **to get a bad ~ in** Verruf kommen; **to give sb a bad ~** jdn in Verruf bringen; **to make one's ~ as, to make a ~ for oneself as** sich (*dat*) einen Namen machen als; **this book made his ~** mit diesem Buch machte er sich einen Namen

(c) (= *important person*) Persönlichkeit *f*

2 VT **(a)** (= *call by a ~, give a ~ to, specify*) person nennen; *ship, plant, new star etc* einen Namen geben (+*dat*); **I ~ this child/ ship X** ich taufe dieses Kind/Schiff auf den Namen X; **the child is ~d Peter** das Kind hat den Namen Peter; **they refused to ~ the victim** sie hielten den Namen des Opfers geheim; **to ~ ~s** Namen nennen; **the main plays by Shakespeare** nenne mir die wichtigsten Dramen Shakespeares; **to ~ the day** (*inf*) den Hochzeitstag festsetzen; **you ~ it, they have it/he's done it** es gibt nichts, was sie nicht haben/was er noch nicht gemacht hat

(b) (= *appoint, nominate*) ernennen; **to ~ sb mayor/as leader** jdn zum Bürgermeister/Führer ernennen; **they ~d her as the winner of the award** sie haben ihr den Preis verliehen; **to ~ sb as one's heir** jdn zu seinem Erben bestimmen

-named [-neɪmd] ADJ SUF genannt; **the first-/last-named** der Erst-/Letztgenannte

name: **name-dropping** N (*inf*) Angeberei *f* mit berühmten Bekannten; **nameless** ADJ **a person who shall be/remain ~** jemand, der nicht genannt werden soll/der ungenannt bleiben soll

namely [ˈneɪmlɪ] ADV nämlich

name: **nameplate** N Namensschild *nt*; (*on business premises*) Firmenschild *nt*; **namesake** N Namensvetter(in) *m(f)*

nan(a) [ˈnæn(ə)] N Oma *f* (*inf*)

nan bread [ˈnɑːnbred] N *warm serviertes, fladenförmiges Weißbrot als Beilage zu indischen Fleisch- und Gemüsegerichten*

nanny [ˈnænɪ] N **(a)** Kindermädchen *nt* **(b)** (*inf: also nana*) Oma *f* (*inf*)

nap [næp] **1** N Nickerchen *nt*; **afternoon ~** Nachmittagsschläfchen *nt*; **to have** *or* **take a ~** ein Nickerchen machen **2** VI **to catch sb ~ping** (*fig*) jdn überrumpeln

napalm [ˈneɪpɑːm] N Napalm *nt*

nape [neɪp] N **~ of the/one's neck** Genick *nt*

napkin [ˈnæpkɪn] N Serviette *f*

napkin ring N Serviettenring *m*

Naples [ˈneɪplz] N Neapel *nt*

nappy [ˈnæpɪ] N (*Brit*) Windel *f*

nappy rash N **little Jonathan's got ~** der kleine Jonathan ist wund

narcissism [nɑːˈsɪsɪzəm] N Narzissmus *m*

narcissistic [nɑːsɪˈsɪstɪk] ADJ narzisstisch

narco- [nɑːkəʊ] PREF Drogen-

narcotic [nɑːˈkɒtɪk] **1** ADJ **(a)** **~ substance/drug** Rauschgift *nt* **(b)** (*Med*) narkotisch **2** N **(a)** Rauschgift *nt*; **~s** Rauschgift *nt* **(b)** (*Med*) Narkotikum *nt*

narrate [nəˈreɪt] VT erzählen; *events, journey etc* schildern

narration [nəˈreɪʃən] N Erzählung *f*; (*of events, journey*) Schilderung *f*

narrative [ˈnærətɪv] **1** N **(a)** (= *story*) Erzählung *f*; (= *account*) Schilderung *f* **(b)** (= *act of narrating*) **he has a gift for ~** er ist ein talentierter Erzähler **2** ADJ erzählend; *ability etc* erzählerisch; **~ structure** Erzählstruktur *f*

narrator [nəˈreɪtəʳ] N Erzähler(in) *m(f)*; **first-person ~** Icherzähler(in) *m(f)*

narrow [ˈnærəʊ] **1** ADJ (+ER) (*lit, fig*) eng; *shoulders, hips* schmal; *attitudes, ideas, views* engstirnig; *majority, victory, defeat, lead* knapp; **to become ~** eng werden; (*road etc*) sich verengen; **to have a ~ mind** engstirnig sein; **to have a ~ escape** mit knapper Not davonkommen

2 VT *road etc* verengen; *gap* verkleinern; **to ~ the field** (*fig*) die Auswahl reduzieren (*to* auf +*acc*); **they decided to ~ the focus of their investigation** sie beschlossen, ihre Untersuchung einzuengen

3 VI sich verengen; **the field ~ed to two candidates** die Auswahl war auf zwei Kandidaten zusammengeschrumpft
➤ **narrow down** VT SEP (*to auf +acc*) (= *limit*) beschränken; **that narrows it down a bit** dadurch wird die Auswahl kleiner
narrow boat N (*esp Brit*) (schmales) Kanalboot
narrowly ['nærəʊlɪ] ADV (**a**) *defeat, fail, avoid* knapp; *escape* mit knapper Not; **he ~ escaped being knocked down** er wäre beinahe überfahren worden (**b**) *interpret, define, focus* eng; **to focus too ~ on sth** sich zu sehr auf etw (*acc*) beschränken
narrow: narrow-minded ADJ, **narrow-mindedly** ADV engstirnig; **narrow-mindedness** N Engstirnigkeit *f*
NASA ['næsə] ABBR *of* **National Aeronautics and Space Administration** NASA *f*
nasal ['neɪzl] ADJ (**a**) (*Anat, Med*) Nasen- (**b**) (*Ling*) nasal; *accent, voice, intonation* näselnd; **to speak in a ~ voice** durch die Nase sprechen; **~ sound** Nasallaut *m*
nasal spray N Nasenspray *nt*
nastily ['nɑːstɪlɪ] ADV *behave* gemein; **to speak ~ to sb** zu jdm gehässig sein
nasty ['nɑːstɪ] ADJ (+ER) (**a**) (= *unpleasant*) scheußlich; *medicine* ekelhaft; *weather, habit, behaviour, word, names* abscheulich; *surprise, moment, break, cough, fall* böse; *situation, problem, accident* schlimm; (= *dirty*) schmutzig; (= *dangerous*) *virus, bend, fog* gefährlich; **that's a ~-looking cut** der Schnitt sieht böse aus; **to turn ~** (*situation, person*) unangenehm werden; (*animal*) wild werden; (*weather*) schlecht umschlagen (**b**) (= *malicious*) gemein; *rumour* gehässig; **he has a ~ temper** mit ihm ist nicht gut Kirschen essen; **to be ~ about sb** gemein über jdn reden; **that was a ~ thing to say/do** das war gemein *or* fies (*inf*); **what a ~ man** was für ein ekelhafter Mensch (**c**) (= *offensive*) anstößig
nation ['neɪʃən] N Volk *nt*; (= *people of one country*) Nation *f*; **to address the ~** zum Volk sprechen; **the whole ~ watched him do it** das ganze Land sah ihm dabei zu
national ['næʃənəl] **1** ADJ national; *election, strike, scandal* landesweit; *agreement, radio station, press etc* überregional; **the ~ average** der Landesdurchschnitt; **~ character** Nationalcharakter *m*; **~ language** Landessprache *f* **2** N Staatsbürger(in) *m(f)*; **foreign ~** Ausländer(in) *m(f)*; **Commonwealth ~s** Angehörige *pl* des Commonwealth
national: national anthem N Nationalhymne *f*; **national costume, national dress** N Nationaltracht *f*
national debt N Staatsverschuldung *f*
national flag N Nationalflagge *f*
National Front N (*Brit*) *rechtsradikale Partei*
National Guard N (*esp US*) Nationalgarde *f*
National Health ADJ ATTR ≈ Kassen-; **~ patient** ≈ Kassenpatient(in) *m(f)*
National Health (Service) N (*Brit*) staatlicher Gesundheitsdienst; **I got it on the ~** ≈ das hat die Krankenkasse bezahlt
national holiday N gesetzlicher Feiertag
national insurance N (*Brit*) Sozialversicherung *f*; **~ contributions** Sozialversicherungsbeiträge *pl*

nationalism ['næʃnəlɪzəm] N Nationalismus *m*
nationalist ['næʃnəlɪst] **1** ADJ nationalistisch **2** N Nationalist(in) *m(f)*
nationalistic [ˌnæʃnə'lɪstɪk] ADJ nationalistisch
nationality [ˌnæʃə'nælɪtɪ] N Staatsangehörigkeit *f*; **what ~ is he?** welche Staatsangehörigkeit hat er?; **she is of German ~** sie hat die deutsche Staatsangehörigkeit
nationalization [ˌnæʃnəlaɪ'zeɪʃən] N Verstaatlichung *f*
nationalize ['næʃnəlaɪz] VT verstaatlichen

National Lottery N (*Brit*) ≈ Lotto *nt*
nationally ['næʃnəlɪ] ADV (= *as a nation*) als Nation; (= *nationwide*) landesweit
national: national park N Nationalpark *m*; **National Savings** PL (*Brit*) ≈ Postsparkasse *f*; **national security** N Staatssicherheit *f*; **National Security Council** N (*US*) Nationaler Sicherheitsrat; **national service** N Wehrdienst *m*; **National Trust** N (*Brit*) National Trust *m, Natur- und Denkmalschutzverein in Großbritannien*
nationwide ['neɪʃənˌwaɪd] ADJ, ADV landesweit; **we have 300 branches ~** wir haben 300 Niederlassungen im ganzen Land
native ['neɪtɪv] **1** ADJ einheimisch; (= *associated with ~s*) der Eingeborenen; *population* eingeboren; **~ town/city** Heimatstadt *f*; **~ language** *or* **tongue** Muttersprache *f*; **a ~ German** ein gebürtiger Deutscher, eine gebürtige Deutsche; **an animal ~ to India** ein in Indien beheimatetes Tier; **to go ~** wie die Eingeborenen leben **2** N (**a**) (= *person*) Einheimische(r) *mf*; (*in colonial contexts*) Eingeborene(r) *mf*; (= *original inhabitant*) Ureinwohner(in) *m(f)*; **a ~ of Britain/Germany** ein gebürtiger Brite/Deutscher, eine gebürtige Britin/Deutsche (**b**) **to be a ~ of ...** (*plant, animal*) in ... beheimatet sein
Native American **1** ADJ indianisch **2** N Indianer(in) *m(f)*

native: native-born ADJ ATTR gebürtig; **native country** N Heimatland *nt*; **native speaker** N Muttersprachler(in) *m(f)*; **I'm not a ~ of English** Englisch ist nicht meine Muttersprache
nativity [nə'tɪvɪtɪ] N **the Nativity** Christi Geburt *f*; (= *picture*) die Geburt Christi; **~ play** Krippenspiel *nt*
NATO ['neɪtəʊ] ABBR *of* **North Atlantic Treaty Organization** NATO *f*
natter ['nætə'] (*Brit inf*) **1** VI schwatzen (*inf*) **2** N **to have a ~** einen Schwatz halten (*inf*)
natty ['nætɪ] ADJ (+ER) (*inf*) *dress, person* schick; **he's a ~ dresser** er zieht sich immer elegant an
natural ['nætʃrəl] **1** ADJ (**a**) natürlich; *laws, phenomena, silk* Natur-; (= *understandable*) *mistake* verständlich; **~ resources** Rohstoffquellen *pl*; **it is (only) ~ for him to think ...** es ist nur natürlich, dass er denkt ...; **the ~ world** die Natur; **in its ~ state** im Naturzustand; **to die a ~ death** *or* **of ~ causes** eines natürlichen Todes sterben; **~ remedy** Naturheilmittel *nt*; **she is a ~ blonde** sie ist von Natur aus blond (**b**) *gift, ability, quality* angeboren; **to have a ~ talent for sth** eine natürliche Begabung für etw haben; **he is a ~ artist/comedian** er ist der geborene Künstler/Komiker (**c**) *parents* leiblich **2** N (**a**) (*Mus*) (= *symbol*) Auflösungszeichen *nt*; (= *note*) Note *f* ohne Vorzeichen; **B ~** H, h; **D ~** D, d (**b**) (*inf*: = *person*) Naturtalent *nt*; **he's a ~ for this part** diese Rolle ist ihm wie auf den Leib geschrieben
natural: natural childbirth N natürliche Geburt; (= *method*) die schmerzlose Geburt; **natural disaster** N Naturkatastrophe *f*; **natural gas** N Erdgas *nt*; **natural history** N Naturkunde *f*; (*concerning evolution*) Naturgeschichte *f*
naturalist ['nætʃrəlɪst] N Naturforscher(in) *m(f)*
naturalistic [ˌnætʃrə'lɪstɪk] ADJ (*Art, Liter*) naturalistisch
naturalization [ˌnætʃrəlaɪ'zeɪʃən] N Einbürgerung *f*; **~ papers** Einbürgerungsurkunde *f*
naturalize ['nætʃrəlaɪz] VT *person* einbürgern; **to become ~d** eingebürgert werden
naturally ['nætʃrəlɪ] ADV natürlich; (= *understandably*) verständlicherweise; (= *by nature*) von Natur aus; **he is ~ artistic/lazy** er ist künstlerisch veranlagt/von Natur aus faul; **to do what comes ~** seiner Natur folgen; **it comes ~ to him** das fällt ihm leicht
natural: natural science N Naturwissenschaft *f*; **the ~s** die Naturwissenschaften *pl*; **natural wastage** N natürliche Personalreduzierung; **to make job cuts through ~** Personal durch natürliche Fluktuation abbauen

nature [ˈneɪtʃəʳ] N **(a)** Natur f; **Nature** die Natur; **laws of ~** Naturgesetze pl; **against ~** gegen die Natur; **to paint from ~** nach der Natur malen; **it is not in my ~ to say things like that** es entspricht nicht meiner Art, so etwas zu sagen; **it is in the ~ of young people to want to travel** es liegt im Wesen junger Menschen, reisen zu wollen **(b)** (of object, material) Beschaffenheit f; **it's in the ~ of things** das liegt in der Natur der Sache; **the ~ of the case is such ...** der Fall liegt so ...; **cash is, by its (very) ~, easy to steal** Geld ist aufgrund seiner Beschaffenheit leicht zu stehlen **(c)** (= type, sort) Art f; **things of this ~** derartiges; **... or something of that ~** ... oder etwas in der Art

nature: nature reserve N Naturschutzgebiet nt; **nature study** N Naturkunde f; **nature trail** N Naturlehrpfad m

naturism [ˈneɪtʃərɪzəm] N Freikörperkultur f, FKK no art

naturist [ˈneɪtʃərɪst] **1** N FKK-Anhänger(in) m(f) **2** ADJ FKK-; **~ beach** FKK-Strand m

naughtily [ˈnɔːtɪlɪ] ADV frech; behave unartig

naughty [ˈnɔːtɪ] ADJ (+ER) **(a)** frech; child, dog unartig; (= disobedient) ungehorsam; **it was ~ of him to break it** das war aber gar nicht lieb von ihm, dass er das kaputtgemacht hat **(b)** joke, word, story unanständig

nausea [ˈnɔːsɪə] N (Med) Übelkeit f; (fig) Ekel m; **a feeling of ~** Übelkeit f; (fig) ein Gefühl nt des Ekels

nauseate [ˈnɔːsɪeɪt] VT **to ~ sb** (Med) in jdm Übelkeit erregen; (fig) jdn anwidern

nauseating [ˈnɔːsɪeɪtɪŋ] ADJ Ekel erregend; hypocrisy widerlich; person ekelhaft

nauseous [ˈnɔːsɪəs] ADJ (Med) **that made me (feel) ~** dabei wurde mir übel

nautical [ˈnɔːtɪkəl] ADJ nautisch; stories von der Seefahrt; language, tradition, appearance seemännisch; **~ chart** Seekarte f

nautical mile N Seemeile f

naval [ˈneɪvəl] ADJ der Marine

naval: naval academy N Marineakademie f; **naval base** N Flottenbasis f; **naval battle** N Seeschlacht f; **naval officer** N Marineoffizier(in) m(f)

nave [neɪv] N (of church) Hauptschiff nt

navel [ˈneɪvl] N (Anat) Nabel m

navel-gazing [ˈneɪvlˌgeɪzɪŋ] N (pej) Nabelschau f

navigable [ˈnævɪgəbl] ADJ schiffbar; **in a ~ condition** ship seetüchtig

navigate [ˈnævɪgeɪt] **1** VI (in plane, ship) navigieren; (in car) den Fahrer dirigieren; (in rally) der Beifahrer sein; **I don't know the route, you'll have to ~** ich kenne die Strecke nicht, du musst mich dirigieren **2** VT **(a)** aircraft, ship navigieren; **to ~ sth through sth** etw durch etw navigieren; (fig) etw durch etw hindurchschleusen **(b)** (= journey through) durchfahren; (plane, pilot) durchfliegen; ocean durchqueren; river befahren

navigation [ˌnævɪˈgeɪʃən] N **(a)** Navigation f **(b)** (= shipping) Schiffsverkehr m

navigator [ˈnævɪgeɪtəʳ] N (Naut) Navigationsoffizier(in) m(f); (Aviat) Navigator(in) m(f); (Mot) Beifahrer(in) m(f)

navvy [ˈnævɪ] N (Brit) Bauarbeiter(in) m(f)

navy [ˈneɪvɪ] **1** N **(a)** (Kriegs)marine f; **to serve in the ~** in der Marine dienen **(b)** (also **~ blue**) Marineblau nt **2** ADJ **(a)** ATTR Marine- **(b)** (also **~-blue**) marineblau

nay [neɪ] ADV (liter) **surprised, ~ astonished** überrascht, nein vielmehr verblüfft

Nazi [ˈnɑːtsɪ] **1** N Nazi m **2** ADJ Nazi-

NB ABBR of **nota bene** NB

NC ABBR of **numerical control** numerische Steuerung

NE ABBR of **north-east** NO

near [nɪəʳ]	
1 ADVERB	**4** TRANSITIVE VERB
2 PREPOSITION	**5** INTRANSITIVE VERB
3 ADJECTIVE	

1 ADVERB

(a) (= close in space or time) nahe; **he lives quite near** er wohnt ganz in der Nähe; **you live nearer/nearest** du wohnst näher/am nächsten; **could you move nearer together?** könnten Sie enger zusammenrücken?; **that was the nearest I ever got to seeing him** da hätte ich ihn fast gesehen; **this is the nearest I can get to solving the problem** besser kann ich das Problem nicht lösen; **the nearer it gets to the election, the more they look like losing** je näher die Wahl kommt or rückt, desto mehr sieht es danach aus, dass sie verlieren werden

✦**to be near at hand** zur Hand sein; (shops) in der Nähe sein; (help) ganz nahe sein; (event) unmittelbar bevorstehen **(b)** (= closely, accurately) genau; **as near as I can tell** soweit ich es beurteilen kann

✦**near enough** (that's) **near enough** das haut so ungefähr hin (inf) **(c)** (= almost) fast; **dead** nahezu; **he very near succeeded** fast wäre es ihm gelungen **(d)** (in negative statements) **it's nowhere near enough** das ist bei weitem nicht genug; **we're not any nearer (to) solving the problem** wir sind der Lösung des Problems kein bisschen näher gekommen; **you are nowhere or not anywhere near the truth** das ist weit gefehlt; **he is nowhere or not anywhere near as clever as you** er ist bei weitem nicht so klug wie du

2 PREPOSITION (also ADV: **near to**)

(a) (= close to) (position) nahe an (+dat); (with motion) nahe an (+acc); (= in the vicinity of) in der Nähe von or +gen; (with motion) in die Nähe von or +gen; **he lives near (to) the border** er wohnt in der Nähe der Grenze; **the hotel is very near (to) the station** das Hotel liegt ganz in der Nähe des Bahnhofs; **move the chair near/nearer (to) the table** rücken Sie den Stuhl an den/näher an den Tisch; **to get near/nearer (to) sb/sth** nahe/näher an jdn/etw herankommen; **keep near me** bleib in meiner Nähe; **near here/there** nahe hier/dort in der Nähe; **don't come near me** komm mir nicht zu nahe; **near (to) where I had seen him** nahe der Stelle, wo ich ihn gesehen hatte; **to be nearest to sth** einer Sache (dat) am nächsten sein; **take the chair nearest (to) you** nehmen Sie den Stuhl direkt neben Ihnen; **that's nearer it** das trifft schon eher zu **(b)** (= close in time) (with time stipulated) gegen; **near (to) death** dem Tode nahe; **phone again nearer (to) Christmas** rufen Sie vor Weihnachten noch einmal an; **come back nearer (to) 3 o'clock** kommen Sie gegen 3 Uhr wieder; **near (to) the end of my stay/the play** gegen Ende meines Aufenthalts/des Stücks; **I'm near (to) the end of the book** ich habe das Buch fast zu Ende gelesen; **she's near (to) the end of her stay** ihr Aufenthalt ist fast zu Ende; **her birthday is near (to) mine** ihr und mein Geburtstag liegen nahe beieinander **(c)** (= on the point of) **to be near (to) doing sth** nahe daran sein, etw zu tun; **to be near (to) tears/despair** etc den Tränen/ der Verzweiflung etc nahe sein; **the project is near (to) completion** das Projekt steht vor seinem Abschluss **(d)** (= similar to) ähnlich (+dat); **German is nearer (to) Dutch than English is** Deutsch ist dem Holländischen ähnlicher als Englisch; **it's the same thing or near it** es ist so ziemlich das Gleiche

3 ADJECTIVE

(a) (= close in space or time) nahe; **to be near** (person, object) in der Nähe sein; (danger, end, help) nahe sein; (event, departure) bevorstehen; **to be nearer/nearest** näher/am nächsten sein; **it looks very near** es sieht so aus, als ob es ganz nah wäre; **his answer was nearer than mine/nearest** seine Antwort traf eher zu als meine/traf die Sachlage am ehesten **(b)** (fig) escape knapp; **a near disaster/accident** fast ein Unglück nt/ein Unfall m; **his nearest rival** sein schärfster Rivale, seine schärfste Rivalin; **to be in a state of near collapse/ hysteria** am Rande eines Zusammenbruchs/der Hysterie sein; **round up the figure to the nearest pound** runden Sie die Zahl auf das nächste Pfund auf; **£50 or nearest offer** (Comm) Verhandlungsbasis £ 50; **this is the nearest equivalent** das kommt dem am Nächsten; **that's the nearest thing you'll get to an answer** eine bessere Antwort kannst du kaum erwarten **(c)** (= closely related) **my nearest and dearest** meine Lieben pl

4 TRANSITIVE VERB sich nähern (+dat); **to be nearing sth** (fig) auf etw (acc) zugehen; **she was nearing fifty** sie ging auf die Fünfzig zu; **to near completion** kurz vor dem Abschluss stehen

5 INTRANSITIVE VERB (time, event) näher rücken

nearby [nɪəˈbaɪ] **1** ADV (*also* **near by**) in der Nähe **2** ADJ nahe gelegen

Near East N Naher Osten; **in the ~** im Nahen Osten

nearly [ˈnɪəlɪ] ADV fast; **I ~ laughed** ich hätte fast gelacht; **we are ~ there** (*at a place*) wir sind fast da; (*with a job*) wir sind fast so weit; **he very ~ drowned** er wäre um ein Haar ertrunken; **not ~** bei weitem nicht

nearly-new [ˌnɪəlɪˈnjuː] ADJ *clothes* fast neu; **~ shop** Second-Hand-Laden *m* (*der besonders gute Qualität anbietet*)

near: near miss N (*Aviat*) Beinahezusammenstoß *m*; **nearside 1** ADJ auf der Beifahrerseite **2** N Beifahrerseite *f*; **near-sighted** ADJ kurzsichtig; **near thing** N **that was a ~** das war knapp

neat [niːt] ADJ (+ER) **(a)** (= *tidy*) ordentlich; *hair, appearance* gepflegt; **he likes everything ~ and tidy** er will alles hübsch ordentlich haben
(b) (= *precise*) fit genau; *division* sauber; *summary* prägnant; *explanation* prägnant formuliert
(c) (= *pleasing*) *clothes, figure* nett
(d) (= *skilful*) *style* gewandt; *solution, plan* elegant; *trick* schlau
(e) (*esp Brit*) *spirits* pur; **to drink one's whisky ~** Whisky pur trinken
(f) (*US inf*: = *excellent*) prima (*inf*)

neatly [ˈniːtlɪ] ADV **(a)** (= *tidily*) ordentlich **(b)** (= *pleasingly*) nett **(c)** (= *skilfully*) gewandt; *solve* elegant; **~ put** prägnant formuliert

neatness [ˈniːtnɪs] N Ordentlichkeit *f*

nebulous [ˈnebjʊləs] ADJ (*fig*) unklar

necessarily [ˈnesɪsərɪlɪ] ADV notwendigerweise, unbedingt; **not ~** nicht unbedingt

necessary [ˈnesɪsərɪ] **1** ADJ **(a)** notwendig; **it is ~ to ...** man muss ...; **is it really ~ for me to come too?** muss ich denn wirklich auch kommen?; **it's not ~ for you to come** Sie brauchen nicht zu kommen; **all the ~ qualifications** alle erforderlichen Qualifikationen; **to be/become ~ to sb** jdm unentbehrlich sein/werden; **if/when ~** wenn nötig; **that won't be ~** das wird nicht nötig sein; **to make the ~ arrangements** die notwendigen Maßnahmen treffen; **to do everything ~, to do whatever is ~** alles Nötige tun
(b) *conclusion, change, result* unausweichlich; **a ~ evil** ein notwendiges Übel
2 N USU PL **the ~** *or* **necessaries** das Notwendige

necessitate [nɪˈsesɪteɪt] VT notwendig machen; **the heat ~d our staying indoors** die Hitze zwang uns, im Haus zu bleiben

necessity [nɪˈsesɪtɪ] N Notwendigkeit *f*; **from** *or* **out of ~** aus Not; **of ~** notgedrungen; **the bare necessities (of life)** das Notwendigste (zum Leben)

neck [nek] N **(a)** Hals *m*; **to break one's ~** sich (*dat*) den Hals brechen; **to risk one's ~** Kopf und Kragen riskieren; **to save one's ~** seinen Hals aus der Schlinge ziehen; **to be up to one's ~ in work** bis über den Hals in der Arbeit stecken; **to stick one's ~ out** seinen Kopf riskieren; **in this ~ of the woods** (*inf*) in diesen Breiten **(b)** (*of dress etc*) Ausschnitt *m*; **it has a high ~** es ist hochgeschlossen **(c)** (*also* **~ measurement**) Halsweite *f*

neck: neck and neck ADV (*lit, fig*) Kopf an Kopf; **necklace** [ˈneklɪs] N (Hals)kette *f*; **neckline** N Ausschnitt *m*; **necktie** N (*esp US*) Krawatte *f*

nectar [ˈnektəʳ] N (*lit, fig*) Nektar *m*

nectarine [ˈnektərɪn] N Nektarine *f*

née [neɪ] ADJ **Mrs Smith, ~ Jones** Frau Smith, geborene Jones

need [niːd] **1** N **(a)** NO PL (= *necessity*) Notwendigkeit *f* (*for* +*gen*); **if ~ be** nötigenfalls; **in case of ~** notfalls; **(there is) no ~ for sth** etw ist nicht nötig; **(there is) no ~ to do sth** etw braucht nicht getan zu werden; **there is no ~ for sb to do sth** jd braucht etw nicht zu tun; **there was no ~ to send it immediately** es war nicht nötig, es sofort zu schicken; **to be (badly) in ~ of sth** (*person*) etw (dringend) brauchen; **to be in ~ of repair** reparaturbedürftig sein; **to have no ~ of sth** etw nicht brauchen; **to have no ~ to do sth** etw nicht zu tun brauchen
(b) NO PL (= *misfortune, poverty*) Not *f*; **in time(s) of ~** in schwierigen Zeiten; **to be in great ~** große Not leiden; **those in ~** die Notleidenden *pl*
(c) (= *requirement*) Bedürfnis *nt*; **my ~s are few** ich stelle nur geringe Ansprüche; **your ~ is greater than mine** Sie haben es nötiger als ich; **there is a great ~ for ...** es besteht ein großer

Bedarf an (+*dat*) ...
2 VT brauchen; **much ~ed** dringend notwendig; **just what I ~ed** genau das Richtige; **that's/you're all I ~ed** (*iro*) das hat/du hast mir gerade noch gefehlt; **this incident ~s some explanation** dieser Vorfall bedarf einer Erklärung (*gen*); **it ~s a coat of paint/careful consideration** es muss gestrichen/gründlich überlegt werden; **is a visa ~ed to enter the USA?** braucht man für die Einreise in die USA ein Visum?; **sth ~s doing** *or* **to be done** etw muss gemacht werden; **to ~ to do sth** (= *have to*) etw tun müssen; **not to ~ to do sth** etw nicht zu tun brauchen; **you shouldn't ~ to be told** das müsste man dir nicht erst sagen müssen; **she ~s to have everything explained to her** man muss ihr alles erklären
3 VB AUX **(a)** (*in positive contexts*) müssen; **~ he go?** muss er gehen?; **I ~ hardly say that ...** ich brauche wohl kaum zu erwähnen, dass ...; **no-one ~ go** *or* **~s to go home yet** es braucht noch keiner nach Hause zu gehen; **you only ~ed (to) ask** du hättest nur (zu) fragen brauchen
(b) (*in negative contexts*) brauchen; **we ~n't have come/gone** wir hätten gar nicht kommen/gehen brauchen; **I/you ~n't have bothered** das war nicht nötig
(c) (*indicating logical necessity*) **that ~n't be the case** das muss nicht unbedingt der Fall sein; **it ~ not follow that ...** daraus folgt nicht unbedingt, dass ...

needle [ˈniːdl] **1** N Nadel *f*; **it's like looking for a ~ in a haystack** es ist, als ob man eine Stecknadel im Heuhaufen suchte **2** VT (*inf*) ärgern; **what's needling him?** was ist ihm über die Leber gelaufen? (*inf*)

needless [ˈniːdlɪs] ADJ unnötig; *death, killing, pain, destruction* sinnlos; **~ to say, he didn't come** er kam natürlich nicht

needlessly [ˈniːdlɪslɪ] ADV unnötig(erweise); *destroy, kill* sinnlos; **you are worrying quite ~** Ihre Sorgen sind vollkommen unbegründet

needlework [ˈniːdlwɜːk] N Handarbeit *f*; **a piece of ~** eine Handarbeit

needy [ˈniːdɪ] **1** ADJ (+ER) bedürftig **2** N **the ~** die Bedürftigen *pl*

negate [nɪˈgeɪt] VT (= *nullify*) zunichte machen

negative [ˈnegətɪv] **1** ADJ negativ; *answer* verneinend; (*Gram*) *form* verneint; **I got a ~ reply to my request** ich habe auf meinen Antrag einen abschlägigen Bescheid bekommen
2 N **(a)** (*also Gram*) Verneinung *f*; **to answer in the ~** eine verneinende Antwort geben; (= *say no*) mit Nein antworten; (= *refuse*) einen abschlägigen Bescheid geben; **put this sentence into the ~** verneinen Sie diesen Satz
(b) (*Gram*: = *word*) Negation *f*; (*Math*) negative Zahl; **two ~s make a positive** (*Math*) zweimal minus gibt plus
(c) (*Phot*) Negativ *nt*
(d) (*Elec*) negativer Pol
3 INTERJ nein

negative feedback N (= *criticism*) negative Reaktion; **to get ~ (about sb/sth)** eine negative Rückmeldung (zu jdm/etw) erhalten

negatively [ˈnegətɪvlɪ] ADV negativ; (= *in the negative*) verneinend

neglect [nɪˈglekt] **1** VT vernachlässigen; *promise* nicht einhalten; *advice* nicht befolgen; *opportunity* versäumen; **to ~ to do sth** es versäumen, etw zu tun **2** N Nachlässigkeit *f*; **to be in a state of ~** verwahrlost sein

neglected [nɪˈglektɪd] ADJ vernachlässigt; *area, garden etc* verwahrlost; **to feel ~** sich vernachlässigt fühlen

neglectful [nɪˈglektfʊl] ADJ nachlässig; *father, government etc* pflichtvergessen; **to be ~ of sb/sth** jdn/etw vernachlässigen

négligé(e) [ˈneglɪʒeɪ] N Negligee *nt*

negligence [ˈneglɪdʒəns] N Nachlässigkeit *f*; (*causing danger, Jur*) Fahrlässigkeit *f*

negligent [ˈneglɪdʒənt] ADJ nachlässig; (*causing danger, damage*) fahrlässig; **both drivers were ~** beide Fahrer haben sich fahrlässig verhalten

negligently [ˈneglɪdʒəntlɪ] ADV nachlässig; (= *causing danger, damage*) fahrlässig

negligible [ˈneglɪdʒəbl] ADJ unwesentlich; **the opposition in this race is ~** in diesem Rennen gibt es keinen ernst zu nehmenden Gegner

negotiable [nɪˈgəʊʃɪəbl] ADJ **(a)** (*Comm*) (= *can be sold*) veräußerlich; (= *can be transferred*) übertragbar; *bill of exchange, promissory note* begebbar, umlauffähig **(b)** these

terms are ~ über diese Bedingungen kann verhandelt werden

negotiate [nɪˈɡəʊʃɪeɪt] **1** VT **(a)** (= *discuss*) verhandeln über (+*acc*); (= *bring about*) aushandeln **(b)** *bend in road, fence* nehmen; *river, mountain, rapids* passieren; *obstacle, difficulty* überwinden **(c)** (*Comm*) *shares* handeln mit; *sale* tätigen (*form*) **2** VI verhandeln (*for* über +*acc*)

negotiating table [nɪˈɡəʊʃɪeɪtɪŋˌteɪbl] N Verhandlungstisch *m*

negotiation [nɪˌɡəʊʃɪˈeɪʃən] N Verhandlung *f*; **the matter is still under** ~ über diese Sache wird noch verhandelt; **the price is a matter for** ~ über den Preis kann verhandelt werden; **to be in** ~**(s) with sb** mit jdm in Verhandlungen stehen

negotiator [nɪˈɡəʊʃɪeɪtəʳ] N Unterhändler(in) *m(f)*

neigh [neɪ] VI wiehern

neighbour, (*US*) **neighbor** [ˈneɪbəʳ] N Nachbar(in) *m(f)*; (*at table*) Tischnachbar(in) *m(f)*

neighbourhood, (*US*) **neighborhood** [ˈneɪbəhʊd] N (= *district*) Gegend *f*; (= *people*) Nachbarschaft *f*; **your friendly** ~ **policeman** der freundliche Polizist in Ihrer Nachbarschaft; **in the** ~ **of sth** in der Nähe von etw; (*fig*: = *approximately*) um etw herum

neighbourhood watch N (*Brit*) *Vereinigung von Bürgern, die durch Straßenwachen etc in ihrem Bezirk die Polizei bei der Verbrechensbekämpfung unterstützen*

neighbouring, (*US*) **neighboring** [ˈneɪbərɪŋ] ADJ benachbart; ~ **village/house** Nachbardorf/-haus *nt*; ~ **country** Nachbarland *nt*

neighbourly, (*US*) **neighborly** [ˈneɪbəlɪ] ADJ *person* nachbarlich; *action, relations* gutnachbarlich

neither [ˈnaɪðəʳ] **1** ADV ~ ... **nor** weder ... noch; **he** ~ **knows nor cares** er weiß es nicht und will es auch nicht wissen **2** CONJ auch nicht; **if you don't go,** ~ **shall I** wenn du nicht gehst, gehe ich auch nicht; **he didn't do it (and)** ~ **did his sister** weder er noch seine Schwester haben es getan; **I can't go,** ~ **do I want to** ich kann und will auch nicht gehen **3** ADJ keine(r, s) (der beiden); ~ **one of them** keiner von beiden **4** PRON keine(r, s); ~ **of them** keiner von beiden

neo- [ˈniːəʊ-] PREF neo-, Neo-; **neoclassical** ADJ klassizistisch

neologism [nɪˈɒlədʒɪzəm] N (*Ling*) Neologismus *m*

neon [ˈniːɒn] ADJ ATTR Neon-; ~ **tube** Neonröhre *f*

neo-Nazi [ˌniːəʊˈnɑːtsɪ] **1** N Neonazi *m* **2** ADJ neonazistisch

neon: neon light N Neonlicht *nt*; **neon sign** N (= *name*) Neonschild *nt*; (= *advertisement*) Neonreklame *f*

Nepal [nɪˈpɔːl] N Nepal *nt*

nephew [ˈnevjuː, ˈnefjuː] N Neffe *m*

nepotism [ˈnepətɪzəm] N Vetternwirtschaft *f*

Neptune [ˈneptjuːn] N (*Astron, Myth*) Neptun *m*

nerd [nɜːd] N (*inf*) Dumpfbacke *f* (*sl*); **computer** ~ Computerfreak *m* (*inf*)

nerve [nɜːv] **1** N **(a)** (*Anat*) Nerv *m*; **to suffer from** ~**s** nervös sein; **to have an attack of** ~**s** in Panik geraten; **it's only** ~**s** du bist/er ist *etc* nur nervös; **his** ~**s are bad** er hat schlechte Nerven; **to get on sb's** ~**s** (*inf*) jdm auf die Nerven gehen; **his speech touched** *or* **struck a (raw)** ~ seine Rede berührte einen wunden Punkt

(b) NO PL (= *courage*) Mut *m*; **to lose/hold** *or* **keep one's** ~ die Nerven verlieren/nicht verlieren; **his** ~ **failed him** ihn verließ der Mut; **to have the** ~ **to do sth** sich trauen, etw zu tun **(c)** NO PL (*inf*: = *impudence*) Frechheit *f*; **to have the** ~ **to do sth** die Frechheit besitzen, etw zu tun; **he's got a** ~! der hat Nerven! (*inf*)

2 VR **to** ~ **oneself for sth/to do sth** sich seelisch und moralisch auf etw (*acc*) vorbereiten/darauf vorbereiten, etw zu tun

nerve IN CPDS Nerven-; **nerve centre**, (*US*) **nerve center** N (*fig*) Schaltzentrale *f*; **nerve gas** N Nervengas *nt*; **nerve-racking, nerve-wracking** ADJ nervenaufreibend

nervous [ˈnɜːvəs] ADJ **(a)** *disorder, exhaustion* nervös; ~ **strain** Nervenbelastung *f*; ~ **tension** Nervenanspannung *f* **(b)** (= *apprehensive, timid*) ängstlich; (= *on edge*) nervös; **to be** *or* **feel** ~ (= *be afraid*) Angst haben; (= *be worried*) sich (*dat*) Sorgen machen; (= *be on edge*) nervös sein; **I am** ~ **about the exam/him** mir ist bange vor dem Examen/um ihn; **I was rather** ~ **about giving him the job** mir war nicht wohl bei dem

Gedanken, ihm die Stelle zu geben; **I am rather** ~ **about diving** ich habe eine ziemliche Angst vor dem Tauchen

nervous IN CPDS Nerven-; **nervous breakdown** N Nervenzusammenbruch *m*; **nervous energy** N Vitalität *f*

nervously [ˈnɜːvəslɪ] ADV (= *apprehensively*) ängstlich; (= *on edge*) nervös

nervous: nervous system N Nervensystem *nt*; **nervous wreck** N (*inf*) **to be a** ~ mit den Nerven völlig am Ende sein

nervy [ˈnɜːvɪ] ADJ (+ER) (*Brit*) nervös

nest [nest] **1** N **(a)** Nest *nt* **(b)** (*of boxes etc*) Satz *m*; **a** ~ **of tables** ein Satz *m* Tische *or* von Tischen **(c)** (*fig*: = *den*) Schlupfwinkel *m* **2** VI nisten

nest egg N (*fig*) Notgroschen *m*

nestle [ˈnesl] VI **to** ~ **up to sb** sich an jdn schmiegen; **to** ~ **against sb** sich an jdn anschmiegen; **the village nestling in the hills** das Dorf, das zwischen den Bergen eingebettet liegt

Net [net] N (*inf*) **the** ~ (*Comput*) das Internet

net¹ [net] **1** N **(a)** (*lit, fig*) Netz *nt* also *Sport* **he felt the** ~ **closing round him** (*fig*) er fühlte, wie sich die Schlinge immer enger zog; **to cast one's** ~ **wider** die Auswahl erweitern; **to slip through the** ~ (*criminal*) durch die Maschen schlüpfen; **to come up to the** ~ ans Netz gehen **(b)** (*Tex*) Netzgewebe *nt*; (*for curtains, clothes etc*) Tüll *m* **2** VT *fish, butterfly* mit dem Netz fangen; (*fig*) *criminal* fangen

net² **1** ADJ **(a)** *price, income, weight* Netto-; ~ **disposable income** verfügbares Nettoeinkommen **(b)** (*fig*) End-, letztendlich; ~ **result** Endergebnis *nt*; ~ **effect** Endeffekt *m* **2** VT netto einnehmen; (*in wages, salary*) netto verdienen; (*show, deal etc*) einbringen; **I** ~**ted a salary of £850 a month** ich hatte ein monatliches Nettogehalt von £ 850

net: netball N (*Brit*) Korbball *m*; **net curtain** N (*Brit*) Tüllgardine *f*

Netherlands [ˈneðələndz] PL **the** ~ die Niederlande *pl*

net: net loss N Reinverlust *m*; **net national product** N Nettosozialprodukt *nt*; **net payment** N Nettozahlung *f*; **net profit** N Reingewinn *m*, Nettoertrag *m*

netsurfing [ˈnetsɜːfɪŋ] N (*Comput*) Internetsurfen *nt*

netting [ˈnetɪŋ] N Netz *nt*; (= *wire* ~) Maschendraht *m*; (= *fabric*) Netzgewebe *nt*; (*for curtains etc*) Tüll *m*

nettle [ˈnetl] **1** N (*Bot*) Nessel *f*; **to grasp the** ~ (*fig*) in den sauren Apfel beißen **2** VT (*fig inf*) *person* wurmen (*inf*)

net weight N Nettogewicht *nt*

network [ˈnetwɜːk] **1** N **(a)** (*lit, fig*) Netz *nt* **(b)** (*Rad, TV*) Sendenetz *nt*; (*Elec, Comput*) Netzwerk *nt*; ~ **driver/server** (*Comput*) Netzwerktreiber *m*/-server *m* **2** VT *programme* im ganzen Netzbereich ausstrahlen; (*Comput*) vernetzen **3** VI (*people*) im Netzwerk arbeiten

networking [ˈnetwɜːkɪŋ] N **(a)** (*Comput*) Networking *nt* **(b)** (= *making contacts*) Knüpfen *nt* von Kontakten

neuro- [ˈnjʊərəʊ-] IN CPDS Neuro-, neuro-; **neurobiology** N Neurobiologie *f*

neurological [ˌnjʊərəˈlɒdʒɪkəl] ADJ neurologisch

neurologist [njʊəˈrɒlədʒɪst] N Neurologe *m*, Neurologin *f*

neurology [njʊəˈrɒlədʒɪ] N Neurologie *f*

neurosis [njʊəˈrəʊsɪs] N, *pl* **neuroses** [njʊəˈrəʊsiːz] Neurose *f*

neurosurgery [ˈnjʊərəʊsɜːdʒərɪ] N Neurochirurgie *f*

neurotic [njʊəˈrɒtɪk] **1** ADJ neurotisch; **to be** ~ **about sth** in Bezug auf etw (*acc*) neurotisch sein **2** N Neurotiker(in) *m(f)*

neuter [ˈnjuːtəʳ] **1** ADJ (*Gram*) sächlich **2** VT *cat, dog* kastrieren

neutral [ˈnjuːtrəl] **1** ADJ neutral; (= *colourless*) farblos **2** N **(a)** (= *person*) Neutrale(r) *mf*; (= *country*) neutrales Land **(b)** (*Aut*) Leerlauf *m*; **to be in** ~ im Leerlauf sein; **to put the car/gear in** ~ den Gang herausnehmen

neutrality [njuːˈtrælɪtɪ] N Neutralität *f*

neutralize [ˈnjuːtrəlaɪz] VT neutralisieren (*also Chem*); (*fig*) aufheben; *the force of an argument* die Spitze nehmen (+*dat*)

neutron [ˈnjuːtrɒn] N Neutron *nt*

never [ˈnevəʳ] ADV **(a)** nie, niemals (*geh*); **I** ~ **eat it** das esse ich nie; **I have** ~ **seen him** ich habe ihn (noch) nie gesehen; ~ **again** nie wieder; ~ **before** noch nie; ~ **before had there been such a disaster** eine solche Katastrophe hatte es noch nie (zuvor) gegeben; ~ **even** nicht einmal; **I have** ~ **ever been so insulted** ich bin noch nie so beleidigt worden **(b)** (*emph*: = *not*) **I** ~ **slept a wink** (*inf*) ich habe kein Auge zugetan; **he** ~ **so much as smiled** er hat nicht einmal gelächelt; **you've ~ left it behind!** (*inf*) du hast es doch wohl nicht etwa liegen lassen! (*inf*); **would you do it again? ~ ~!** würdest du das noch einmal machen? – bestimmt nicht; **Spurs were beaten – ~!** (*inf*) Spurs ist geschlagen worden – nein!; **well I ~ (did)!** (*inf*) nein, so was!; **~ fear** keine Angst

never-ending ['nevər'endıŋ] ADJ endlos

nevertheless [nevəðə'les] ADV dennoch

new [njuː] ADJ (+ER) neu; *wine* jung; *bread* frisch; (= *modern, novel*) modern; **the ~ people at number five** die Neuen in Nummer fünf; **that's nothing ~** das ist nichts Neues; **what's ~?** (*inf*) was gibts Neues? (*inf*); **as ~** wie neu; **he is a ~ man** (*fig*) er ist ein neuer Mensch; **that's a ~ one on me** (*inf*) das ist mir ja ganz neu; **the ~ woman** die moderne Frau; **I'm quite ~ to this job/to the company** ich bin neu in dieser Stelle/Firma; **to be ~ to business** ein Neuling *m* im Geschäftsleben sein; **she's ~ to the game** (*Sport*) sie ist erst seit kurzem bei diesem Sport dabei; (*fig*) sie ist neu auf diesem Gebiet

new: New Age Traveller N (*Brit*) Aussteiger(in) *m(f)*; **new blood** N (*fig*) frisches Blut; **newborn** ADJ neugeboren; **the ~ babies** die Neugeborenen; **newcomer** N (*who has just arrived*) Neuankömmling *m*; (*in job, subject etc*) Neuling *m* (*to* in +*dat*); **they are ~s to this town** sie sind neu in dieser Stadt; **New England** N Neuengland *nt*; **new face** N neues Gesicht; **newfangled** ADJ neumodisch; **new-found** ADJ *happiness* neu(gefunden); *confidence* neugeschöpft

Newfoundland ['njuːfəndlənd] N Neufundland *nt*

newish ['njuːıʃ] ADJ ziemlich neu

newly ['njuːlı] ADV frisch; **~ made** ganz neu; *bread, cake etc* frisch gebacken; **~ arrived** neu angekommen; **~ married** frisch vermählt

newlyweds ['njuːlıwedz] PL (*inf*) Frischvermählte *pl*

new: New Mexico N New Mexico *nt*; **new moon** N Neumond *m*; **there's a ~ tonight** heute Nacht ist Neumond

news [njuːz] N, NO PL **(a)** (= *report, information*) Nachricht *f*; (= *recent development*) Neuigkeit(en) *f(pl)*; **a piece of ~** eine Neuigkeit; **I have ~/no ~ of him** ich habe von ihm gehört/ nicht von ihm gehört; **there is no ~** es gibt nichts Neues zu berichten; **have you heard the ~?** haben Sie schon (das Neueste) gehört?; **tell us your ~** erzähl uns das Neueste; **I have ~ for you** (*iro*) ich habe eine Überraschung für dich; **bad/sad/good ~** schlechte/traurige/gute Nachricht(en); **that's bad ~ for English football** das ist ein schwerer Schlag für den englischen Fußball; **as far as I'm concerned, he's bad ~** (*inf*) für mich bedeutet er nichts als) Ärger; **no ~ is good ~** keine Nachricht ist gute Nachricht; **who will break the ~ to him?** wer wird es ihm sagen *or* beibringen?; **that is ~ (to me)!** das ist (mir) ganz neu!

(b) (*Press, Film, Rad, TV*) Nachrichten *pl*; **~ in brief** Kurznachrichten *pl*; **financial ~** Wirtschaftsbericht *m*; **sports ~** Sportnachrichten *pl*; **it was on the ~** das kam in den Nachrichten; **to be in the ~** von sich reden machen

news: news agency N Nachrichtenagentur *f*; **newsagent** N (*Brit*) Zeitungshändler(in) *m(f)*; **newsboy** N (*US*) Zeitungsjunge *m*; **news bulletin** N Bulletin *nt*; **newscaster** N Nachrichtensprecher(in) *m(f)*; **newsdealer** N (*US*) Zeitungshändler(in) *m(f)*; **newsflash** N Kurzmeldung *f*; **newsgirl** N (*US*) Reporterin *f*; **news headlines** PL Kurznachrichten *pl*; (= *recap*) Nachrichten *pl* in Kürze; **news item** N Nachricht *f*; **newsletter** N Rundschreiben *nt*

newspaper ['njuːzˌpeɪpər] N Zeitung *f*; **daily/weekly ~** Tages-/ Wochenzeitung *f*

newspaper: newspaper article N Zeitungsartikel *m*; **newspaperman** N Zeitungsmann *m* (*inf*); (= *journalist*) Journalist *m*; **newspaperwoman** N Zeitungsfrau *f* (*inf*); (= *journalist*) Journalistin *f*

news: newsreader N Nachrichtensprecher(in) *m(f)*; **news release** N (*esp US*) Pressemitteilung *f*; **newsroom** N (*of newspaper*) Nachrichtenredaktion *f*; **news sheet** N Informationsblatt *nt*; **newsstand** N Zeitungsstand *m*

new-style ['njuːstaɪl] ADJ im neuen Stil

news vendor N Zeitungsverkäufer(in) *m(f)*

newsworthy ['njuːzwɜːðɪ] ADJ **to be ~** Neuigkeitswert haben

newt [njuːt] N Wassermolch *m*

new: New Testament N **the ~** das Neue Testament; **new town** N neue Stadt, ≈ Retortenstadt *f* (*pej*); **new wave** N (*in films*)

neue Welle ☑ ADJ ATTR der neuen Welle; **New World** N **the ~** die Neue Welt

New Year N neues Jahr; (= ~'**s Day**) Neujahr *nt*; **to bring in** *or* **see in the ~** das neue Jahr begrüßen; **Happy ~!** (ein) gutes neues Jahr!; **over/at ~** über/an Neujahr; **she's expecting a baby in the ~** sie erwartet im neuen Jahr ihr Baby; **~ resolution** (guter) Vorsatz für das neue Jahr

New Year's ['njuːjɪəz] N (*US inf*) = **New Year's Day, New Year's Eve**

New Year's: New Year's Day N Neujahr *nt*; **New Year's Eve** N Sylvester *nt*

New: New York ☑ N New York *nt* ☑ ADJ ATTR New Yorker; **~ Stock Exchange** wichtigste New Yorker Börse; **New Zealand** ☑ N Neuseeland *nt* ☑ ADJ ATTR Neuseeländer *attr*, neuseeländisch; **New Zealander** N Neuseeländer(in) *m(f)*

next [nekst] ☑ ADJ nächste(r, s); **come back ~ week/Tuesday** kommen Sie nächste Woche/nächsten Dienstag wieder; **he came back the ~ day/week** er kam am nächsten Tag/in der nächsten Woche wieder; **(the) ~ time I see him** wenn ich ihn das nächste Mal sehe; **(the) ~ moment he was gone** im nächsten Moment war er weg; **from one moment to the ~** von einem Moment zum anderen; **this time ~ week** nächste Woche um diese Zeit; **the year after ~** übernächstes Jahr; **the ~ day but one** der übernächste Tag; **who's ~?** wer ist der Nächste?; **you're ~** Sie sind dran (*inf*) *or* an der Reihe; **my name is ~ on the list** mein Name kommt als nächster auf der Liste; **the ~ but one** der/die/das Übernächste; **the ~ thing I knew I ...** bevor ich wusste, wie mir geschah, ... ich ...; (*after fainting etc*) das Nächste, woran ich mich erinnern kann, war, dass ich ...; **the ~ size up/down** die nächstkleinere/ nächstgrößere Größe

☑ ADV **(a)** (= *the ~ time*) das nächste Mal; (= *afterwards*) danach; **what shall we do ~?** und was sollen wir als Nächstes machen?; **whatever ~?** (*in surprise*) Sachen gibts! (*inf*); (*despairingly*) wo soll das nur hinführen?

(b) **~ to sb/sth** neben jdm/etw; (*with motion*) neben jdn/etw; **the ~ to last row** die vorletzte Reihe; **~ to the skin** (direkt) auf der Haut; **~ to nothing/nobody** so gut wie nichts/niemand; **~ to impossible** nahezu unmöglich

(c) **the ~ best** der/die/das Nächstbeste; **this is the ~ best thing** das ist das Nächstbeste; **the ~ tallest/oldest boy** (= *second in order*) der zweitgrößte/zweitälteste Junge

☑ N Nächste(r) *mf*; (= *child*) Nächste(s) *nt*

next door ['neks'dɔːr'] ADV nebenan; **let's go ~** gehen wir nach nebenan; **they live ~ to us** sie wohnen (direkt) neben uns; **he has the room ~ to me** er hat das Zimmer neben mir; **we live ~ to each other** wir wohnen Tür an Tür; **the boy ~** der Junge von nebenan

next-door ['neks'dɔːr'] ADJ **the ~ neighbour** (*Brit*) *or* **neighbor** (*US*) der direkte Nachbar; **we are ~ neighbours** (*Brit*) *or* **neighbors** (*US*) wir wohnen Tür an Tür; **the ~ house** das Nebenhaus

next of kin N, *pl* - nächster Verwandter, nächste Verwandte

NF (*Brit*) ABBR *of* **National Front**

NFL (*US*) ABBR *of* **National Football League** amerikanische Fußball-Nationalliga

NHS (*Brit*) ABBR *of* **National Health Service**

Niagara [naɪ'ægrə] N **~ Falls** die Niagarafälle *pl*

nib [nɪb] N Feder *f*

nibble ['nɪbl] ☑ VT knabbern; (= *pick at*) herumnagen an (+*dat*) (*inf*) ☑ VI (*at an* +*dat*) knabbern; (= *pick at*) herumnagen ☑ N **~s** (*Brit*) Knabbereien *pl*

Nicaragua [nɪkə'rægjʊə] N Nicaragua *nt*

nice [naɪs] ADJ (+ER) **(a)** nett; *weather, taste, smell, meal, whisky, work, manners* gut; *warmth, feeling, car, words* schön; *district* fein; **be ~ to him** sei nett zu ihm; **to have a ~ time** sich gut amüsieren; **have a ~ day!** (*esp US*) schönen Tag noch!; **that**

was the ~ **thing about Venice** das war das Schöne an Venedig; **it's (so) ~ to see you again** es freut mich (sehr), Sie wieder zu treffen; **it's been ~ meeting you** ich habe mich gefreut, Sie kennen zu lernen; **I had a ~ rest** ich habe mich schön ausgeruht; **~ one!** toll! (inf); **not a ~ word/district/book** gar kein schönes Wort/Viertel/Buch
(b) (intensifier) schön; **a ~ long bath** ein schönes, langes Bad; **~ and warm/near/quickly** schön warm/nahe/schnell; **take it ~ and easy** überanstrengen Sie sich nicht
(c) (iro) **you're in a ~ mess** du sitzt schön im Schlamassel (inf); **that's a ~ way to talk to your mother** das ist ja eine schöne Art, mit deiner Mutter zu sprechen
(d) (= subtle) **that was a ~ point** das war eine gute Bemerkung

nice-looking ['naɪs'lʊkɪŋ] ADJ schön; woman, man gut aussehend; face, dress etc nett; hotel, village hübsch; **to be ~** gut aussehen

nicely ['naɪslɪ] ADV (= pleasantly) nett; (= well) go, speak, behave, placed gut; **to be coming along ~** sich gut machen; **to ask ~** höflich fragen; **say thank you ~!** sag mal schön danke!; **that will do ~** das reicht vollauf; **he's doing very ~ for himself** er ist sehr gut gestellt, er scheffelt Geld (inf); **to be ~ spoken** sich gepflegt ausdrücken; **~ done** gut gemacht

niceties ['naɪsɪtɪz] PL Feinheiten pl

niche [niːʃ] N (Archit) Nische f; (fig) Plätzchen nt; **to carve a ~ for oneself** eine Nische für sich finden; **~ market** (Comm) Nischenmarkt m

nick¹ [nɪk] N **(a)** Kerbe f **(b) in the ~ of time** gerade noch (rechtzeitig) **(c)** (Brit inf) **in good/bad ~** gut/nicht gut in Schuss (inf) 🔁 VT **(a) to ~ oneself** (inf) sich schneiden **(b)** (bullet) streifen

nick² (Brit) 🔁 VT **(a)** (= arrest) einsperren (inf) **(b)** (= steal) klauen (inf) 🔁 N (inf: = prison) Knast m (inf)

nickel ['nɪkl] N **(a)** (= metal) Nickel nt **(b)** (US) Fünfcentstück nt

nickel-and-dime ['nɪklən'daɪm] ADJ (US inf) billig; criminal etc klein

nickel-plated ['nɪkl'pleɪtɪd] ADJ vernickelt

nickname ['nɪkneɪm] 🔁 N Spitzname m 🔁 VT **they ~d him Baldy** sie gaben ihm den Spitznamen Baldy; **Chicago is ~d the Windy City** Chicago hat den Spitznamen Windy City

nicotine ['nɪkətiːn] N Nikotin nt

nicotine: **nicotine patch** N Nikotinpflaster nt; **nicotine poisoning** N Nikotinvergiftung f

niece [niːs] N Nichte f

nifty ['nɪftɪ] ADJ (+ER) (inf) flott (inf); gadget, tool schlau (inf); **a ~ piece of work** gute Arbeit; **a ~ little car** ein netter kleiner Flitzer (inf)

Nigeria [naɪ'dʒɪərɪə] N Nigeria nt

Nigerian [naɪ'dʒɪərɪən] 🔁 ADJ nigerianisch 🔁 N Nigerianer(in) m(f)

niggardly ['nɪɡədlɪ] ADJ person knaus(e)rig; amount, portion armselig

niggle ['nɪɡl] 🔁 VI (= complain) herumkritteln (inf) (about an +dat) 🔁 VT (= worry) quälen

niggling ['nɪɡlɪŋ] ADJ question, doubt, pain quälend; feeling ungut

nigh [naɪ] 🔁 ADJ (old, liter) nahe; **the end (of the world) is ~** das Ende der Welt ist nah 🔁 ADV **~ on** nahezu (geh); **well ~ impossible** nahezu unmöglich

night [naɪt] 🔁 N Nacht f; (= evening, Theat) Abend m; **I saw him last ~** ich habe ihn gestern Abend gesehen; **I'll see him tomorrow ~** ich treffe ihn morgen Abend; **I stayed with them last ~** ich habe letzte Nacht bei ihnen übernachtet; **to stay four ~s with sb** vier Nächte lang bei jdm bleiben; **I'll stay with them tomorrow ~** ich übernachte morgen Nacht bei ihnen; **on Friday ~** Freitag Abend/Nacht; **11 o'clock at ~** 11 Uhr nachts; **6 o'clock at ~** 6 Uhr abends; **she works at ~** sie arbeitet nachts; **in/during the ~** in/während der Nacht; **the ~ before they were ...** am Abend/die Nacht zuvor waren sie ...; **the ~ before last they were ...** vorgestern Abend/vorletzte Nacht waren sie ...; **to spend the ~ at a hotel** in einem Hotel übernachten; **to have a good/bad ~** or **~'s sleep** gut/schlecht schlafen; **~~!** (inf) gut Nacht! (inf); **all ~ (long)** die ganze Nacht; **to have a ~ out** (abends) ausgehen; **to make a ~ of it** durchmachen (inf); **to have a late/an early ~** spät/früh schlafen gehen; **to be on ~s** Nachtdienst haben; (shift worker)

Nachtschicht haben; **a Mozart ~** ein Mozartabend m 🔁 ADV **~s** (esp US) nachts

night IN CPDS Nacht-; **nightcap** N (= drink) Schlaftrunk m (inf); **nightclub** N Nachtklub m; **night depository** N (US) Nachttresor m; **nightdress** N Nachthemd nt; **nightfall** N Einbruch m der Dunkelheit; **at ~** bei Einbruch der Dunkelheit; **night flight** N Nachtflug m; **nightgown** N Nachthemd nt

nightie ['naɪtɪ] N (inf) Nachthemd nt

nightingale ['naɪtɪŋɡeɪl] N Nachtigall f

night: **nightlife** N Nachtleben nt; **night-light** N (for child etc) Nachtlicht nt

nightly ['naɪtlɪ] 🔁 ADJ (= every night) (all)nächtlich; (= every evening) (all)abendlich; **~ performances** (Theat) allabendliche Vorstellung; **the ~ television news** die Abendnachrichten im Fernsehen 🔁 ADV (= every night) jede Nacht; (= every evening) jeden Abend; **three performances ~** jeden Abend drei Vorstellungen; **twice ~** zweimal pro Abend

nightmare ['naɪtmeə^r] N (lit, fig) Albtraum m; **that was a ~ of a journey** die Reise war ein Albtraum

night: **night owl** N (inf) Nachteule f (inf); **night porter** N Nachtportier m; **night safe** N Nachttresor m; **night school** N Abendschule f; **night shift** N Nachtschicht f; **to be** or **work on ~** Nachtschicht haben; **nightshirt** N (Herren)nachthemd nt; **nightspot** N Nachtlokal nt; **night stick** N (US) Schlagstock m; **night-time** 🔁 N Nacht f; **at ~** nachts 🔁 ADJ ATTR nächtlich; **~ temperature** Nachttemperatur f; **night watchman** N Nachtwächter(in) m(f)

nihilistic [naɪ'lɪstɪk] ADJ nihilistisch

Nikkei average [nɪ,keɪ'ævərɪdʒ], **Nikkei index** [nɪ,keɪ'ɪndeks] N Nikkei-Index m

nil [nɪl] N (= zero) null; (= nothing) nichts; **the score was one-~** es stand eins zu null; see also **zero**

Nile [naɪl] N Nil m

nimble ['nɪmbl] ADJ (+ER) (= quick) flink; (= agile) gelenkig; mind beweglich

nimbly ['nɪmblɪ] ADV dance leicht(füßig); jump, climb, step gelenkig

nine [naɪn] 🔁 ADJ neun; **~ times out of ten** in neun Zehntel der Fälle 🔁 N Neun f; **dressed (up) to the ~s** in Schale (inf); **999 call** (Brit), **911 call** (US) Notruf m; **to call 999** (Brit) or **911** (US) den Notruf wählen; see also **six**

nineteen ['naɪn'tiːn] 🔁 ADJ neunzehn 🔁 N Neunzehn f; **she talks ~ to the dozen** (Brit inf) sie redet wie ein Wasserfall (inf)

nineteenth ['naɪn'tiːnθ] 🔁 ADJ (in series) neunzehnte(r, s); (as fraction) neunzehntel 🔁 N Neunzehnte(r, s); (= fraction) Neunzehntel nt; see also **sixteenth**

ninetieth ['naɪntɪɪθ] 🔁 ADJ (in series) neunzigste(r, s); (as fraction) neunzigstel 🔁 N Neunzigste(r, s); (= fraction) Neunzigstel nt

nine-to-five [,naɪntə'faɪv] ADJ Büro-; **~ job/worker** Bürojob m/-angestellte(r) mf

ninety ['naɪntɪ] 🔁 ADJ neunzig 🔁 N Neunzig f; see also **sixty**

ninth [naɪnθ] 🔁 ADJ (in series) neunte(r, s); (as fraction) neuntel 🔁 N Neunte(r, s); (= fraction) Neuntel nt; see also **sixth**

nip¹ [nɪp] 🔁 N **(a)** (= pinch) Kniff m; (= bite: from animal etc) Biss m; **to give sb a ~ on the leg** jdn ins Bein kneifen; (dog) jdn leicht ins Bein beißen
(b) there's a ~ in the air today es ist ganz schön frisch heute 🔁 VT **(a)** (= bite) zwicken; (= pinch) kneifen; **the dog ~ped his ankle** der Hund hat ihn am Knöchel gezwickt
(b) (Hort) bud, shoot abknipsen; **to ~ sth in the bud** (fig) etw im Keim ersticken
🔁 VI (Brit inf) sausen (inf); **to ~ up(stairs)/down(stairs)** hoch-/runterflitzen (inf); **I'll just ~ down to the shops** ich gehe mal kurz einkaufen (inf); **I'll just ~ round to his place** ich gehe mal kurz bei ihm vorbei (inf)

► **nip out** VI (Brit inf) kurz weggehen (inf)

nip² N (inf: = drink) Schlückchen nt

nipper ['nɪpə^r] N (Brit inf) Steppke m (inf)

nipple ['nɪpl] N (Anat) Brustwarze f, Nippel m (inf); (US: on baby's bottle) Sauger m

nippy ['nɪpɪ] ADJ (+ER) **(a)** (Brit inf) flott; car, motor spritzig **(b)** weather, wind frisch

nit [nɪt] N **(a)** (Zool) Nisse f **(b)** (Brit inf) Schwachkopf m (inf)

nit-pick ['nɪtpɪk] VI (inf) pingelig sein (inf)

nit-picking ['nɪtpɪkɪŋ] ADJ (inf) pingelig (inf)

nitrate ['naɪtreɪt] N Nitrat nt

nitric acid [,naɪtrɪk'æsɪd] N Salpetersäure f

nitrogen ['naɪtrədʒən] N Stickstoff m

nitty-gritty ['nɪtɪ'grɪtɪ] N (inf) **to get down to the ~** zur Sache kommen; **the ~ of everyday life** die wahre Realität des alltäglichen Lebens

nitwit ['nɪtwɪt] N (inf) Schwachkopf m (inf)

NNP ABBR of **net national product**

No, no ABBR of **number** Nr.

no [nəʊ] **1** ADV (a) (negative) nein; **to answer no** (to question) mit Nein antworten; (to request) Nein sagen
(b) (with comp) nicht; **I can bear it no longer** ich kann es nicht länger ertragen; **I have no more money** ich habe kein Geld mehr; **he returned to England in an aircraft carrier no less** er kehrte auf nichts Geringerem als einem Flugzeugträger nach England zurück
2 ADJ kein; **no one person could do it** keiner könnte das allein tun; **no other man** kein anderer; **it's of no interest/importance** das ist belanglos/unwichtig; **it's no use** or **no good** das hat keinen Zweck; **no parking/smoking** Parken/Rauchen verboten; **there's no saying** or **telling what he'll do next** man kann nie wissen, was er als Nächstes tun wird; **there's no denying it** es lässt sich nicht leugnen; **there's no pleasing him** ihm kann man es auch nie recht machen; **he's no genius** er ist nicht gerade ein Genie; **this is no place for children** das ist hier nichts für Kinder; **in no time** im Nu; **it's no small matter** das ist keine Kleinigkeit; **at no little expense** zu großen Kosten; **there is no such thing** so etwas gibt es nicht; **I'll do no such thing** ich werde mich hüten
3 N, pl **-es** Nein nt; (= no vote) Neinstimme f; **I won't take no for an answer** ich bestehe darauf; **the noes have it** die Mehrheit ist dagegen

nobble ['nɒbl] VT (Brit inf) (a) horse, dog lahm legen (inf)
(b) jury, witness bestechen

Nobel ['nəʊbel] N **~ prize** Nobelpreis m; **~ peace prize** Friedensnobelpreis m

nobility [nəʊ'bɪlɪtɪ] N, NO PL (a) (= people) (Hoch)adel m
(b) (= quality) Edle(s) nt

noble ['nəʊbl] **1** ADJ (+ER) (a) (= aristocratic) adlig; **to be of ~ birth** adlig sein (b) (= fine, distinguished) person, deed, thought etc nobel; appearance vornehm; monument prächtig; resistance heldenhaft; **a ~ attempt** das war ein heldenhafter Versuch (c) (inf: = selfless) edelmütig; **how ~ of you!** (iro) zu gütig **2** N Adlige(r) mf

noble: **nobleman** N Adlige(r) m; **noblewoman** N Adlige f

nobly ['nəʊblɪ] ADV (a) (= finely) vornehm; (= bravely) heldenhaft (b) (inf: = selflessly) großmütig; **he ~ gave up his weekend** großmütigerweise opferte er sein Wochenende

nobody ['nəʊbədɪ] **1** PRON niemand; **there was ~ else** da war sonst niemand; **~ else but you can do it** außer dir kann das niemand; **~ else offered to give them money** sonst hat sich niemand angeboten, ihnen Geld zu geben; **like ~'s business** wie nichts **2** N Niemand m no pl, Nichts nt no pl; **they are nobodies** sie sind doch niemand

no-claim(s) bonus ['nəʊ,kleɪm(z)'bəʊnəs] N Schadenfreiheitsrabatt m

nocturnal [nɒk'tɜːnl] ADJ nächtlich; **~ animal/bird** Nachttier nt/-vogel m

nod [nɒd] **1** N Nicken nt; **he gave a quick ~** er nickte kurz; **to give sb a ~** jdm zunicken; **to give sb the ~** (fig) jdm grünes Licht geben; **to go through on the ~** (inf) ohne Einwände angenommen werden
2 VI nicken; **to ~ to sb** jdm zunicken; **to ~ toward(s) sth** mit dem Kopf auf etw zeigen; **he ~ded to me to leave** er gab mir durch ein Nicken zu verstehen, dass ich gehen sollte
3 VT (a) **to ~ one's head** mit dem Kopf nicken; **to ~ one's agreement/approval** zustimmend nicken
(b) (Sport) ball köpfen

➤ **nod in** VT SEP goal, ball einköpfen

➤ **nod off** VI einnicken (inf)

node [nəʊd] N Knoten m

nodule ['nɒdjuːl] N (Med, Bot) Knötchen nt

no: **no-fault** ADJ (US) (a) divorce in gegenseitigem Einvernehmen (b) (Insur) coverage mit garantierter

Entschädigungssumme; **no-frills** ADJ ATTR package, deal etc ohne (alle) Extras; style, decor etc einfach; **no-go area** N Sperrgebiet nt; **this street is a ~** diese Straße sollte man meiden; **no-good** ADJ person nichtsnutzig; **no-holds-barred** ADJ contest, attack kompromisslos

noise [nɔɪz] N Geräusch nt; (= loud, irritating sound) Lärm m; (Elec: = interference) Rauschen nt; **what was that ~?** was war das für ein Geräusch?; **the ~ of the traffic** der Straßenlärm; **it made a lot of ~** es war sehr laut; **don't make a ~!** sei leise!; **stop making such a (lot of) ~** hör auf, solchen Lärm zu machen; **he's always making ~s about resigning** er redet dauernd davon, dass er zurücktreten will; **to make reassuring ~s** beruhigende Geräusche machen; **she made (all) the right ~s** sie reagierte richtig; **~ abatement/prevention** Lärmbekämpfung f

noiselessly ['nɔɪzlɪslɪ] ADV geräuschlos

noise level N Geräuschpegel m

noisily ['nɔɪzɪlɪ] ADV laut; protest, welcome, debate lautstark

noisy ['nɔɪzɪ] ADJ (+ER) laut; protest, welcome, debate lautstark; **this is a ~ house** in dem Haus ist es laut

nomad ['nəʊmæd] N Nomade m, Nomadin f

nomadic [nəʊ'mædɪk] ADJ nomadisch; **~ tribe** Nomadenstamm m; **~ lifestyle** Nomadenleben nt

no-man's-land ['nəʊmænzlænd] N (lit, fig) Niemandsland nt

nominal ['nɒmɪnl] ADJ nominell; share capital Nominal-; **~ shares** Stammaktien pl

nominally ['nɒmɪnəlɪ] ADV nominell; **it's ~ worth £500** auf dem Papier ist es £ 500 wert

nominal value N Nennwert m

nominate ['nɒmɪneɪt] VT (a) (= appoint) ernennen; **he was ~d chairman** er wurde zum Vorsitzenden ernannt
(b) (= propose) nominieren; **he was ~d for the presidency** er wurde als Präsidentschaftskandidat aufgestellt; **to ~ sb/sth for an award** jdn/etw für eine Auszeichnung nominieren

nomination [,nɒmɪ'neɪʃən] N (a) (= appointment) Ernennung f
(b) (= proposal) Nominierung f

nominative ['nɒmɪnətɪv] (Gram) **1** N Nominativ m **2** ADJ **(the) ~ case** der Nominativ

nominee [,nɒmɪ'niː] N Kandidat(in) m(f)

non- [nɒn-] PREF nicht-; **nonaggression** N **~ treaty** or **pact** Nichtangriffspakt m; **nonalcoholic** ADJ alkoholfrei; **nonaligned** (Pol) blockfrei; **non-binding** ADJ (Comm) unverbindlich; **non-callable** ADJ (St Ex) nicht kündbar; **non-cash** ADJ (Fin) payment bargeldlos; **~ assets** Sachwerte pl; **~ benefits** geldwerte Vorteile pl

nonchalance ['nɒnʃələns] N Lässigkeit f

nonchalant ADJ, **nonchalantly** ADV ['nɒnʃələnt, -lɪ] lässig

non: **noncombatant** **1** N Nichtkämpfer(in) m(f) **2** ADJ nicht am Kampf beteiligt; **noncommissioned** ADJ (Mil) **~ officer** Unteroffizier(in) m(f); **noncommittal** ADJ zurückhaltend; **to be ~ about whether …** sich nicht festlegen, ob …; **noncommittally** ADV unverbindlich; **nonconformist** **1** N Nonkonformist(in) m(f) **2** ADJ nonkonformistisch; **noncontributory** ADJ benefits, insurance etc ohne Eigenbeteiligung; member beitragsfrei; **nonconvertible** ADJ (Fin) nicht konvertierbar; **non-degradable** ADJ nicht abbaubar

nondescript ['nɒndɪskrɪpt] ADJ taste, colour unbestimmbar; person, appearance unauffällig

non: **nondrinker** N Nichttrinker(in) m(f); **she is a ~** sie trinkt keinen Alkohol; **nondriver** N Nichtfahrer(in) m(f); **non-durable** ADJ goods kurzlebig

none [nʌn] **1** PRON keine(r, s); (on form) keine; **~ of the boys/the chairs/them** keiner der Jungen/Stühle/von ihnen; **~ of the girls** keines der Mädchen; **~ of this/the cake** nichts davon/von dem Kuchen; **~ of this is any good** das ist alles nicht gut; **~ of this money is mine** von dem Geld gehört mir nichts; **do you have any bread/apples? – ~ (at all)** haben Sie Brot/Äpfel? – nein, gar keines/keine; **there is ~ left** es ist nichts übrig; **their guest was ~ other than …** ihr Gast war kein anderer als …; **I want ~ of this/this nonsense** ich will davon/von diesem Unsinn nichts hören; **he would have ~ of it** er wollte davon nichts wissen
2 ADV **to be ~ the wiser** um nichts schlauer sein; **she looks ~ the worse for her ordeal** trotz allem, was sie durchzustehen hatte, sieht sie gut aus; **it's ~ too warm** es ist keineswegs zu

warm; **he was ~ too happy about it** er war darüber gar nicht erfreut; **~ too sure/easy** durchaus nicht sicher/einfach

nonentity [nɒ'nentɪtɪ] N unbedeutende Figur

nonessential [nɒnɪ'senʃəl] **1** ADJ unnötig; *workers* nicht unbedingt nötig; *services* nicht lebenswichtig **2** N **nonessentials** PL nicht (lebens)notwendige Dinge *pl*

nonetheless [ˌnʌnðə'les] ADV trotzdem

non: **nonevent** N (*inf*) Reinfall *m* (*inf*); **nonexecutive** ADJ **in a ~ capacity** ohne Entscheidungsbefugnis; **~ director** ≈ Aufsichtsratsmitglied *nt* (*ohne Entscheidungsbefugnis*); **nonexistent** ADJ nicht vorhanden; **discipline is practically ~ here** hier herrscht praktisch keine Disziplin; **non-fading** ADJ lichtecht; **non-fat** ADJ *diet* fettlos; **non-fat milk** N Milchersatz *m* (*auf pflanzlicher Basis*); **nonfattening** ADJ nicht dick machend *attr*; **fruit is ~** Obst macht nicht dick; **nonfiction 1** N Sachbücher *pl* **2** ADJ **~ book/publication** Sachbuch *nt*; **nonflammable** ADJ nicht entzündbar; **non-food** ADJ Non-food-; **nonhereditary** ADJ nicht vererbbar; **nonintervention** N (*Pol etc*) Nichteinmischung *f* (*in* in +*acc*); **non-manual** ADJ nicht manuell; **nonmember** N open to **~s** Gäste willkommen; **non-moving** ADJ (*Comm*) schwer verkäuflich; **non-negotiable** ADJ *ticket* nicht übertragbar; **the price is ~** über den Preis lässt sich nicht verhandeln

no-no ['nəʊnəʊ] N (*inf*) **that's/she's a ~!** das/sie kommt nicht infrage (*inf*); **that's a ~!** (= *you mustn't do it*) das gibts nicht!

no-nonsense ['nəʊˌnɒnsəns] ADJ (kühl und) sachlich

non: **non-operating** ADJ (*Comm*) betriebsfremd; **nonpayment** N Nichtzahlung *f*

nonplus ['nɒn'plʌs] VT **completely ~sed** völlig verdutzt

non: **nonpolitical** ADJ nicht politisch; **nonproductive** ADJ **~ industries** Dienstleistungssektor *m*; **~ worker** Angestellte(r) *mf* im Dienstleistungssektor; **non-profit-making**, (*US*) **nonprofit** ADJ keinen Gewinn anstrebend *attr*; *charity etc* gemeinnützig; **on a ~ basis** auf gemeinnütziger Basis; **nonproliferation** N **~ treaty** Atomsperrvertrag *m*; **non-redeemable** ADJ (*Fin*) nicht einlösbar, unkündbar; *securities* ohne Rückkaufmöglichkeit; **non-registered** ADJ (*Comm*) nicht eingetragen; **non-renewable** ADJ nicht erneuerbar; **nonresident 1** ADJ nicht ansässig; (*in hotel*) nicht im Hause wohnend **2** N Nicht(orts)ansässige(r) *mf*; (*in hotel*) nicht im Haus wohnender Gast; **open to ~s** auch für Nichthotelgäste; **nonreturnable** ADJ **~ bottle** Einwegflasche *f*; **~ deposit** Anzahlung *f*; **nonscheduled** ADJ außerplanmäßig

nonsense ['nɒnsəns] N, NO PL (*also as interjection*) Unsinn *m*; (= *silly behaviour*) Dummheiten *pl*; **that's a lot of ~!** das ist (ja) alles dummes Zeug!; **I've had enough of this ~** jetzt reichts mir aber; **what's all this ~ about a cut in salary/about them not wanting to go?** was soll all das Gerede von einer Gehaltskürzung/all das Gerede, dass sie nicht mitgehen wollen?; **and no ~** und keine Dummheiten; **he will stand no ~ from anybody** er lässt nicht mit sich spaßen

nonsensical [nɒn'sensɪkəl] ADJ unsinnig

non sequitur [ˌnɒn'sekwɪtəʳ] N unlogische (Schluss)folgerung

non: **nonshrink** ADJ nicht einlaufend; **to be ~** nicht einlaufen; **nonslip** ADJ rutschfest; **nonsmoker** N (**a**) Nichtraucher(in) *m(f)* (**b**) (*Rail*) Nichtraucherabteil *nt*; **nonsmoking** ADJ Nichtraucher-; **~ area** *or* **section** Nichtraucherbereich *m*; **we have a ~ policy** bei uns herrscht Rauchverbot; **nonstandard** ADJ nicht der Norm entsprechend; (= *not usually supplied*) *fittings* nicht üblich; **~ size** Sondergröße *f*; **nonstarter** N (**a**) (*in race*) **there were two ~s** zwei traten nicht an (**b**) (*fig*: = *idea*) Blindgänger *m*; **nonstick** ADJ kunststoffbeschichtet; **nonstop 1** ADJ *train* durchgehend; *journey, performances* ohne Unterbrechung; *music* dauernd; **~ flight** Nonstopflug *m* **2** ADV *talk, work* ununterbrochen; *fly, travel* nonstop; **nonswimmer** N Nichtschwimmer(in) *m(f)*; **nontaxable** ADJ nicht steuerpflichtig; **nontoxic** ADJ ungiftig; **nonunion** ADJ *worker, labour* nicht organisiert; **nonverbal** ADJ nichtverbal; **nonviolence** N Gewaltlosigkeit *f*; **nonviolent** ADJ gewaltlos; *crime, offender* nicht gewalttätig; **nonvocational** ADJ *subject, course* nicht berufsorientiert; **nonvoter** N Nichtwähler(in) *m(f)*; **nonvoting** ADJ **~ shares** stimmrechtslose Aktien *pl*; **non-White 1** ADJ **(a)** Nicht-Weiße(r) *mf* **2** ADJ farbig

noodle ['nuːdl] N (**a**) (*Cook*) Nudel *f* (**b**) (*US inf*: = *head*) Birne *f* (*inf*); **use your ~** streng deinen Grips an (*inf*)

nook [nʊk] N Winkel *m*; **in every ~ and cranny** in jedem Winkel

noon [nuːn] **1** N Mittag *m*; **at ~** um 12 Uhr mittags **2** ADJ 12-Uhr-; *deadline* bis 12 Uhr

no-one, no one ['nəʊwʌn] PRON = **nobody**

noontime (*esp US*) **1** N Mittagszeit *f*; **at ~** um die Mittagsstunde (*geh*) **2** ADJ zur Mittagszeit

noose [nuːs] N Schlinge *f*

nope [nəʊp] ADV (*inf*) ne(e) (*dial*), nein

no place ADV (*esp US inf*) = **nowhere**

nor [nɔːʳ] CONJ **(a)** noch; **neither ... ~** weder ... noch **(b)** (= *and not*) und ... auch nicht; **I shan't go, ~ will you** ich gehe nicht, und du auch nicht; **~ do/have/am I** ich auch nicht

Nordic ['nɔːdɪk] ADJ nordisch

norm [nɔːm] N Norm *f*

normal ['nɔːməl] **1** ADJ normal; (= *customary*) üblich; **it's ~ practice** das ist so üblich; **he is not his ~ self today** er ist heute so anders; **a higher than ~ risk of infection** ein Infektionsrisiko, das über dem Normalen liegt **2** N, NO PL **temperatures below ~** Temperaturen unter dem Durchschnitt; **her temperature is below/above ~** sie hat Untertemperatur/erhöhte Temperatur; **when things/we are back to** *or* **return to ~** wenn sich alles wieder normalisiert hat; **just carry on as ~** machen Sie einfach normal weiter

normality [nɔː'mælɪtɪ] N Normalität *f*; **to return to ~** sich wieder normalisieren

normally ['nɔːməlɪ] ADV (= *usually*) normalerweise; (= *in normal way*) normal

Norman ['nɔːmən] **1** ADJ normannisch; **the ~ Conquest** der normannische Eroberungszug **2** N Normanne *m*, Normannin *f*

Normandy ['nɔːməndɪ] N Normandie *f*

Norse [nɔːs] ADJ altnordisch

north [nɔːθ] **1** N Norden *m*; **in/from the ~** im/aus dem Norden; **to the ~ of** nördlich von; **the wind is in the ~** es ist Nordwind; **to face (the) ~** nach Norden liegen; **the North (of Scotland/England)** Nordschottland/-england *nt* **2** ADJ ATTR Nord-; **North German** norddeutsch **3** ADV (= *towards North*) nach Norden; **~ of** nördlich von

north IN CPDS Nord-; **North Africa** N Nordafrika *nt*; **North America** N Nordamerika *nt*; **North American 1** ADJ nordamerikanisch; **~ Free Trade Area** Nordamerikanische Freihandelszone **2** N Nordamerikaner(in) *m(f)*; **North Atlantic** N Nordatlantik *m*; **northbound** ADJ *carriageway* nach Norden (führend); *traffic* in Richtung Norden; **North Dakota** [ˌnɔːθdə'kəʊtə] N Norddakota *nt*; **northeast 1** N Nordosten *m*; **in the ~** im Nordosten; **from the ~** von Nordost **2** ADJ Nordost-, nordöstlich; **~ England** Nordostengland *nt* **3** ADV nach Nordosten; **~ of** nordöstlich von; **northeasterly** ADJ nordöstlich; **northeastern** ADJ nordöstlich, im Nordosten; **northeastwards** ADV nordostwärts

northerly ['nɔːðəlɪ] ADJ nördlich

northern ['nɔːðən] ADJ nördlich; **~ Germany/Italy** Norddeutschland/-italien *nt*; **Northern Irish** nordirisch

northerner ['nɔːðənəʳ] N (**a**) Nordländer(in) *m(f)*/-deutsche(r) *mf etc*; **he is a ~** er kommt aus dem Norden (des Landes) (**b**) (*US*) Nordstaatler(in) *m(f)*

Northern Ireland N Nordirland *nt*

northernmost ['nɔːðənməʊst] ADJ nördlichste(r, s)

north: **North Korea** N Nordkorea *nt*; **North Korean 1** ADJ nordkoreanisch **2** N Nordkoreaner(in) *m(f)*; **North Pole** N Nordpol *m*; **North Sea 1** N Nordsee *f* **2** ADJ Nordsee-; **~ gas/ oil** Nordseegas *nt*/-öl *nt*; **North-South divide** N Nord-Süd-Gefälle *nt*; **North Vietnam** N Nordvietnam *nt*; **North Vietnamese 1** ADJ nordvietnamesisch **2** N Nordvietnamese *m*/-vietnamesin *f*; **northward 1** ADJ nördlich **2** ADV (*also* **~s**) nordwärts; **northwest 1** N Nordwesten *m* **2** ADJ Nordwest-, nordwestlich; **~ England** Nordwestengland *nt* **3** ADV nach Nordwest(en); **~ of** nordwestlich von; **northwesterly** ADJ nordwestlich

Norway ['nɔːweɪ] N Norwegen *nt*

Norwegian [nɔː'wiːdʒən] **1** ADJ norwegisch **2** N (**a**) Norweger(in) *m(f)* (**b**) (*Ling*) Norwegisch *nt*

Nos., nos. ABBR *of* **numbers** Nrn.

nose [nəʊz] **1** N Nase *f*; (*of car*) Schnauze *f*; (*of boat*) Bug *m*; (*of torpedo*) Kopf *m*; **to hold one's ~** sich (*dat*) die Nase zuhalten; **my ~ is bleeding** ich habe Nasenbluten; **follow your ~** immer der Nase nach; **she always has her ~ in a book** sie hat dauernd den Kopf in einem Buch (vergraben); **to do sth under sb's (very)** ~ etw vor jds Augen tun; **it was right under his ~ all the time** er hatte es die ganze Zeit direkt vor der Nase; **he can't see beyond** or **further than the end of his ~** er kann nicht weiter sehen, als sein eigener Schatten reicht; **to get up sb's ~** (fig inf) jdm auf den Geist gehen (inf); **to poke** or **stick one's ~ into sth** (fig) seine Nase in etw (acc) stecken; **you keep your ~ out of this** (inf) halt du dich da raus (inf); **to cut off one's ~ to spite one's face** (prov) sich ins eigene Fleisch schneiden; **to look down one's ~ at sb/sth** auf jdn/etw herabblicken; **to pay through the ~** (inf) sich dumm und dämlich zahlen (inf); **to put sb's ~ out of joint** jdn vor den Kopf stoßen; **to keep one's ~ clean** (inf) sauber bleiben (inf); **to have a ~ for sth** (fig) eine Nase für etw haben; **~ to tail** cars Stoßstange an Stoßstange

☑ VT the car/ship ~d its way through the fog das Auto/Schiff tastete sich durch den Nebel; **the car ~d its way into the stream of traffic** das Auto schob sich in den fließenden Verkehr vor

➤ **nose about** (Brit) or **around** VI herumschnüffeln (inf)

➤ **nose out** VT SEP (Brit inf) aufspüren; secret, scandal ausschnüffeln (inf)

nose: nosebleed N Nasenbluten nt; **to have a ~** Nasenbluten haben; **nosedive ☑** N (Aviat) Sturzflug m; **to go into a ~** zum Sturzflug ansetzen; **the company's profits took a ~** mit der Firma ging es rapide bergab; **his career took a ~** seine Karriere nahm einen scharfen Knick nach unten **☑** VI (plane) im Sturzflug herabgehen; (fig) den Bach runtergehen (inf); **nosedrops** PL Nasentropfen pl

nosey ADJ = **nosy**

nosey parker [ˌnəʊzɪˈpɑːkə'] N (Brit inf) Schnüffler(in) m(f) (inf)

nosh [nɒʃ] (Brit sl) N (= food) Futter nt (inf); (= meal) Schmaus m; **to have some ~** was futtern (inf)

nosh-up [ˈnɒʃʌp] N (Brit inf) Fressgelage nt (inf)

nostalgia [nɒˈstældʒɪə] N Nostalgie f (for nach); **to feel ~ for sth** sich nach etw zurücksehnen

nostalgic [nɒˈstældʒɪk] ADJ nostalgisch; (= wistful) wehmütig; **to feel/be ~ for** or **about sth** sich nach etw zurücksehnen

nostalgically [nɒˈstældʒɪklɪ] ADV nostalgisch; (= wistfully) wehmütig; **they look back ~ to the war** sie blicken mit Nostalgie auf den Krieg zurück

no-strike [ˈnəʊstraɪk] ADJ ATTR ~ **deal/agreement** Streikverzichtabkommen nt

nostril [ˈnɒstrəl] N Nasenloch nt; (of horse, zebra etc) Nüster f

nosy [ˈnəʊzɪ] ADJ (+ER) (inf) neugierig

not [nɒt] ADV (a) nicht; **he told me ~ to do that** er sagte, ich solle das nicht tun; **that's how ~ to do it** so sollte man es nicht machen; ~ **wanting to be heard, he ...** da er nicht gehört werden wollte, ... er ...; ~ **a sound/word** etc kein Ton/ Wort etc; ~ **a bit** kein bisschen; ~ **one of them** kein Einziger; ~ **a thing** überhaupt nichts; ~ **any more** nicht mehr; ~ **yet** noch nicht; ~ **even** nicht einmal; ~ **so** (as reply) nein; **it would seem** or **appear** ~ anscheinend nicht; **he's decided ~ to do it – I should think/hope** ~ er hat sich entschlossen, es nicht zu tun – das möchte ich auch meinen/hoffen; **are you cold? – ~ at all** ist dir kalt? – überhaupt nicht; **thank you very much – ~ at all** vielen Dank – gern geschehen; ~ **that I care** nicht, dass es mir etwas ausmacht(e); ~ **that I know of** nicht, dass ich wüsste; **it's ~ that I don't believe him** ich glaube ihm ja

(b) (in tag or rhetorical questions) **it's hot, isn't it?** es ist heiß, nicht wahr or nicht? (inf); **isn't it hot?** (es ist) heiß, nicht wahr?; **isn't he naughty!** ist er nicht frech?; **you are coming, aren't you?** Sie kommen doch, oder?; **you have got it, haven't you?** Sie haben es doch, oder?; **you like it, don't you?** das gefällt dir, nicht (wahr)?; **you are ~ angry, are you?** Sie sind nicht böse, oder?

notable [ˈnəʊtəbl] ADJ (= eminent) bedeutend; (= big) beträchtlich; (= conspicuous) auffallend; **with a few ~ exceptions** bis auf einige rühmliche Ausnahmen

notably [ˈnəʊtəblɪ] ADV (a) (= strikingly) auffallend; improved, different beträchtlich (b) (= in particular) insbesondere; **most ~** vor allem

notary (public) [ˈnəʊtərɪˈpʌblɪk)] N Notar(in) m(f)

notation [nəʊˈteɪʃən] N (= system) Zeichensystem nt; (= symbols) Zeichen pl; (Mus) Notenschrift f

notch [nɒtʃ] N Kerbe f; (of handbrake, for adjustment etc) Raste f; (in belt) Loch nt; **our team is a ~ above theirs** unsere Mannschaft ist eine Klasse besser als ihre

➤ **notch up** VT SEP score, points erzielen; success verzeichnen können

note [nəʊt] **☑** N (a) Notiz f; (= footnote) Anmerkung f; (official: in file etc) Vermerk m; (= informal letter) Briefchen nt; **~s** (= summary) Aufzeichnungen pl; (= plan, draft) Konzept nt; **to speak without ~s** frei sprechen; **to send/leave sb a ~** jdm ein paar Zeilen schicken/hinterlassen; **to take** or **make ~s** Notizen machen; (in lecture also, in interrogation) mitschreiben; **to take** or **make a ~ of sth** sich (dat) etw notieren

(b) NO PL (= notice) **to take ~ of sth** von etw Notiz nehmen; (= heed) einer Sache (dat) Beachtung schenken

(c) NO PL (= importance) **a man of ~** ein bedeutender Mann; **nothing of ~** nichts Erwähnenswertes

(d) (Mus: = sign) Note f; (= quality, tone, Mus: = sound) Ton m; **to play/sing the right/wrong ~** richtig/falsch spielen/singen; **to strike the right ~** (fig) den richtigen Ton treffen; **it struck a wrong** or **false ~** (fig) da hat er etc sich im Ton vergriffen; (= wasn't genuine) es klang nicht echt; **on a personal ~** persönlich gesprochen; **on a more optimistic/positive ~** aus optimistischer/positiver Sicht; **to sound a ~ of caution** zur Vorsicht mahnen; **there was a ~ of warning in his voice** seine Stimme hatte einen warnenden Unterton

(e) (Brit Fin) Schein m; **a £5 ~, a five-pound ~** ein Fünfpfundschein m

(f) (Fin) **~s payable** Schuldwechsel pl

☑ VT (a) (= notice) bemerken; (= take ~ of) zur Kenntnis nehmen; (= pay attention to) beachten

(b) = **note down**

➤ **note down** VT SEP notieren; (as reminder) sich (dat) notieren

notebook [ˈnəʊtbʊk] N Notizbuch nt; ~ **(computer)** Notebook m

noted [ˈnəʊtɪd] ADJ berühmt (for für, wegen)

notelet [ˈnəʊtlɪt] N Briefkarte f

note: notepad N Notizblock m; **notepaper** N Briefpapier nt; **noteworthy** ADJ beachtenswert

nothing [ˈnʌθɪŋ] **☑** N, PRON, ADV nichts; **it was reduced to ~** es blieb nichts davon übrig; **it was all or ~** es ging um alles oder nichts; **£500 is ~ to her** £ 500 sind für sie gar nichts; **it came to ~** da ist nichts draus geworden; **I can make ~ of it** das sagt mir nichts; **he thinks ~ of doing that** er findet nichts dabei(, das zu tun); **think ~ of it** keine Ursache!; **there was ~ doing at the club** (inf) im Klub war nichts los; **for ~** (= free, in vain) umsonst; **there's ~ (else) for it but to leave** da bleibt einem nichts übrig als zu gehen; **there was ~ in it for me** das hat sich für mich nicht gelohnt; **there's ~ in the rumour** (Brit) or **rumor** (US) an dem Gerücht ist nichts (Wahres); **there's ~ to it** (inf) das ist kinderleicht (inf); ~ **but** nur; ~ **else** sonst nichts; ~ **more** nicht mehr than that ich möchte nichts lieber als das; ~ **much** nicht viel; ~ **if not polite** äußerst höflich; ~ **new** nichts Neues; **it was ~ like as big as we thought** es war lange nicht so groß, wie wir dachten; **in ~ flat** (US inf) in null Komma nichts (inf) **☑** N (a) (Math) Null f

(b) (= thing, person of no value) Nichts nt; **thank you – it was ~** danke – das war doch selbstverständlich; **please don't apologize, it's ~** entschuldige dich nicht, es ist nicht der Rede wert; **what's wrong with you? – (it's) ~** was ist mit dir los? – nichts

nothingness [ˈnʌθɪŋnɪs] N Nichts nt

no through road N **it's a ~** es ist keine Durchfahrt

notice [ˈnəʊtɪs] **☑** N (a) (= warning, communication) Bescheid m; (= written notification) Mitteilung f; (of forthcoming event, film etc) Ankündigung f; ~ **to pay** (Comm) Zahlungsaufforderung f; **final** ~ letzte Aufforderung; **we need three weeks'** ~ wir müssen drei Wochen vorher Bescheid wissen; **to give** ~ **of sth** von etw Bescheid geben; of film, change etc etw ankündigen; of arrival etc melden; **to give sb** ~ **of sth** jdm etw mitteilen; **he didn't give us much** ~, **he gave us rather short** ~ er hat uns nicht viel Zeit gegeben; **at short** ~ kurzfristig; **at a moment's** ~ jederzeit; **at three days'** ~ innerhalb von drei Tagen; **until further** ~ bis auf weiteres

(b) (= public announcement) (on ~ board etc) Anschlag m; (= poster) Plakat nt; (= sign) Schild nt; (in newspaper) Bekanntmachung f; (short) Notiz f; (of birth, wedding, vacancy

etc) Anzeige *f*; **birth/marriage/death** ~ Geburts-/Heirats-/Todesanzeige *f*; **I saw a ~ in the paper about the concert** ich habe das Konzert in der Zeitung angekündigt gesehen
(c) (*prior to end of employment, residence etc*) Kündigung *f*; ~ **to quit** (*Brit*) *or* **to vacate** (*US*) Kündigung *f*; **to give sb ~** *employer, landlord* jdm kündigen; (*lodger, employee also*) bei jdm kündigen; **to give** *or* **hand** *or* **turn** (*US*) **in one's ~** kündigen; **I got my ~** mir ist gekündigt worden; **a month's ~** eine einmonatige Kündigungsfrist; **she gave me** *or* **I was given a month's ~** mir wurde zum nächsten Monat gekündigt
(d) (= *review*) Rezension *f*
(e) (= *attention*) **to take ~ of sth** von etw Notiz nehmen; (= *heed*) etw beachten; **to take no ~ of sb/sth** von jdm/etw keine Notiz nehmen; **take no ~!** kümmern Sie sich nicht darum!; **to bring sth to sb's ~** jdn auf etw (*acc*) aufmerksam machen; (*in letter etc*) jdn von etw in Kenntnis setzen
2 VT bemerken; (= *recognize, acknowledge existence of*) zur Kenntnis nehmen; *difference* feststellen; **without my noticing it** ohne dass ich etwas bemerkt habe; **I ~d her hesitating** ich merkte, dass sie zögerte; **to get oneself ~d** auf sich (*acc*) aufmerksam machen; (*negatively*) auffallen

noticeable ['nəʊtɪsəbl] ADJ erkennbar; (= *visible*) sichtbar; (= *obvious, considerable*) deutlich; *relief, pleasure, disgust etc* merklich; **the stain is very ~** der Fleck fällt ziemlich auf; **the change was ~** man konnte eine Veränderung feststellen; **it is ~ that ...** man merkt, dass ...

noticeably ['nəʊtɪsəbli] ADV deutlich; *relieved, annoyed etc* sichtlich

notice board ['nəʊtɪsbɔːd] N (*esp Brit*) Anschlagbrett *nt*

notifiable ['nəʊtɪfaɪəbl] ADJ meldepflichtig

notification [ˌnəʊtɪfɪ'keɪʃən] N Benachrichtigung *f*; (*of disease, crime, damage etc*) Meldung *f*; (= *written ~: of birth etc*) Anzeige *f*; **to send ~ of sth to sb** jdm etw schriftlich mitteilen

notify ['nəʊtɪfaɪ] VT benachrichtigen; **to ~ sb of sth** jdn von etw benachrichtigen; *authorities, insurance company* jdm etw melden

notion ['nəʊʃən] N **(a)** (= *idea, thought*) Idee *f*; (= *conception*) Vorstellung *f*; (= *vague knowledge*) Ahnung *f*; (= *opinion*) Meinung *f*; **I have no ~ of time** ich habe überhaupt kein Zeitgefühl; **where did you get the ~** *or* **what gave you the ~ that I ...?** wie kommst du denn auf die Idee, dass ich ...?; **he got the ~ (into his head) that she wouldn't help him** irgendwie hat er sich (*dat*) eingebildet, sie würde ihm nicht helfen
(b) notions PL (*esp US inf*) Kurzwaren *pl*

notional ['nəʊʃənl] ADJ **(a)** (= *hypothetical*) angenommen; (= *nominal*) nominell **(b)** (*esp US*) versponnen

notoriety [ˌnəʊtə'raɪətɪ] N traurige Berühmtheit

notorious [nəʊ'tɔːrɪəs] ADJ berüchtigt; *gambler, criminal, liar* notorisch; **a ~ woman** eine Frau von schlechtem Ruf

notoriously [nəʊ'tɔːrɪəslɪ] ADV bekanntlich; **it is ~ difficult to treat** es lässt sich bekanntlich nur sehr schwer behandeln; **to be ~ unreliable/inefficient** *etc* für seine Unzuverlässigkeit/Untüchtigkeit *etc* berüchtigt sein

notwithstanding [ˌnɒtwɪθ'stændɪŋ] (*form*) **1** PREP ungeachtet (+*gen*) (*form*) **2** ADV nichtsdestotrotz (*form*)

nougat ['nuːgɑː] N Nougat *m*

nought [nɔːt] N **(a)** (= *number*) Null *f* **(b)** (*liter*) Nichts *nt*; **to come to ~** sich zerschlagen

noun [naʊn] N Substantiv *nt*

nourish ['nʌrɪʃ] VT **(a)** (*lit*) nähren; *person* ernähren **(b)** (*fig*) *hopes etc* hegen

nourishing ['nʌrɪʃɪŋ] ADJ nahrhaft

nourishment ['nʌrɪʃmənt] N Nahrung *f*; **to take ~** Nahrung *f* zu sich (*dat*) nehmen

nous [naʊs] N (*Brit inf*) Grips *m* (*inf*)

nouveau riche [ˌnuːvəʊ'riːʃ] N, *pl* **-x -s** [ˌnuːvəʊ'riːʃ] Neureiche(r) *mf*

Nov ABBR *of* **November** Nov

Nova Scotia ['nəʊvə'skəʊʃə] N Neuschottland *nt*

novel[1] ['nɒvəl] N Roman *m*

novel[2] ADJ neu(artig)

novelist ['nɒvəlɪst] N Romanschriftsteller(in) *m(f)*

novella [nə'velə] N Novelle *f*

novelty ['nɒvəltɪ] N **(a)** Neuheit *f*; **once the ~ has worn off** wenn der Reiz des Neuen vorbei ist; **it was quite a ~** das war etwas ganz Neues **(b)** (*Comm*: = *trinket*) Krimskrams *m*

November [nəʊ'vembə[r]] N November *m*; *see also* **September**

novice ['nɒvɪs] N (*fig*) Neuling *m*, Anfänger(in) *m(f)* (*at* bei)

now [naʊ] **1** ADV **(a)** (= *immediately*) jetzt; (= *at this very moment*) gerade; (= *nowadays*) heute; **she ~ realized why ...** jetzt erkannte sie, warum ...; **just ~** gerade; (= *immediately*) gleich, sofort; **I'll do it just** *or* **right ~** ich mache es jetzt gleich; **it's ~ or never** jetzt oder nie; **what is it ~?** was ist denn jetzt *or* nun schon wieder?; **by ~** (*present, past*) inzwischen; **they have never met before ~** sie haben sich bis jetzt noch nie getroffen; **we'd have heard before ~** das hätten wir (inzwischen) schon gehört; **for ~** vorläufig; **even ~** selbst jetzt noch; **any day/moment ~** jetzt jeden Tag/Moment; **from ~ on(wards)** von nun an; **between ~ and the end of the week** bis zum Ende der Woche; **in three days from ~** (heute) in drei Tagen
(b) (*alternation*) ~ ... ~ ... bald ... bald; (*every*) ~ **and then**, ~ **and again** ab und zu
2 CONJ **(a)** ~ (**that**) **you've seen him** jetzt, wo Sie ihn gesehen haben
(b) (*in explanation etc*) nun
3 INTERJ **now** ~, ~! na, na!; **well** ~ also; ~ **then** also (jetzt); **stop that ~!** Schluss jetzt!; ~, **why didn't I think of that?** warum habe ich bloß nicht daran gedacht?

nowadays ['naʊədeɪz] ADV heute

no way ADV *see* **way**

nowhere ['nəʊweə[r]] ADV nirgendwo; (*with verbs of motion*) nirgendwohin; ~ **is** *or* **there is ~ more romantic than Paris** nirgends ist es romantischer als in Paris; **they have ~ (else) to go** sie können (sonst) nirgends unterkommen; **there was ~ to hide** man konnte sich nirgends verstecken; **to appear from** *or* **out of ~** aus heiterem Himmel auftauchen; **to come ~** (*Sport*) unter „ferner liefen" kommen; **to come from ~ and win** (*Sport*) überraschend siegen; **we're getting ~ (fast)** wir kommen nicht weiter; **rudeness will get you ~** Grobheit bringt dir gar nichts ein; **a pound goes ~ these days** mit einem Pfund kommt man heute nicht mehr weit

no-win situation [nəʊwɪnsɪtjʊ'eɪʃən] N **it's a ~** wie mans macht ists falsch

noxious ['nɒkʃəs] ADJ (= *harmful*) schädlich; (= *toxic*) giftig

nozzle ['nɒzl] N Düse *f*

nr ABBR *of* **near** b., bei

NT ABBR *of* **New Testament** N. T. *nt*

nth [enθ] ADJ **the ~ power** *or* **degree** die n-te Potenz; **for the ~ time** zum x-ten Mal (*inf*)

nuance ['njuːɑːns] N Nuance *f*

nub [nʌb] N (*fig*) **the ~ of the matter** der springende Punkt

nubile ['njuːbaɪl] ADJ *girl* gut entwickelt

nuclear ['njuːklɪə[r]] ADJ Atom-; *fuel* nuklear

nuclear: nuclear deterrent N nukleares Abschreckungsmittel; **nuclear disarmament** N nukleare Abrüstung; **nuclear energy** N = **nuclear power**; **nuclear family** N Kleinfamilie *f*; **nuclear-free** ADJ atomwaffenfrei; **nuclear missile** N Atomrakete *f*; **nuclear physicist** N Kernphysiker(in) *m(f)*; **nuclear physics** N Kernphysik *f*; **nuclear power** N Atomkraft *f*; **nuclear-powered** ADJ atomgetrieben; **nuclear power station** N Atomkraftwerk *nt*; **nuclear reactor** N Atomreaktor *m*; **nuclear reprocessing plant** N nukleare Wiederaufbereitungsanlage; **nuclear submarine** N Atom-U-Boot *nt*; **nuclear test** N Atom(waffen)test *m*; **nuclear war** N Atomkrieg *m*; **nuclear waste** N Atommüll *m*; **nuclear weapon** N Atomwaffe *f*

nucleus ['njuːklɪəs] N, *pl* **nuclei** [-lɪaɪ] (*Phys, fig*) Kern *m*; (*Biol: of cell also*) Nukleus *m*

nude [njuːd] **1** ADJ nackt; (*Art*) Akt-; ~ **figure/portrait** Akt *m*; ~ **scene** (*Film*) Nacktszene *f* **2** N (*Art*) Akt *m*; **in the ~** nackt

nudge [nʌdʒ] **1** VT anstoßen; **she ~d him forward** sie schubste ihn vorwärts; **to ~ sb into doing sth** jdm den Anstoß dazu geben, etw zu tun; **the temperature was nudging 35°C** die Temperatur erreichte fast 35°C; **she's nudging 40** sie geht stramm auf die 40 zu **2** N Stups *m*

nudist ['njuːdɪst] N Nudist(in) *m(f)*

nudist beach N Nacktbadestrand *m*

nudity ['njuːdɪtɪ] N Nacktheit *f*

nugget [ˈnʌgɪt] N (*of gold etc*) Klumpen *m*; (*fig: of information*) Brocken *m*

nuisance [ˈnjuːsns] N **(a)** (= *person*) Plage *f*; (*esp pestering*) Nervensäge *f*; (*esp child*) Quälgeist *m*; **sorry to be a ~** entschuldigen Sie, wenn ich störe; **to make a ~ of oneself** lästig werden **(b)** (= *thing, event*) **to be a ~** lästig sein; (*annoying*) ärgerlich sein; **what a ~, having to do it again** wie ärgerlich, das noch einmal machen zu müssen

nuke [njuːk] VT (*sl*) mit Atomwaffen angreifen

null [nʌl] ADJ (*Jur*) (null und) nichtig; **to render sth ~ and void** etw null und nichtig machen

nullify [ˈnʌlɪfaɪ] VT annullieren

numb [nʌm] **1** ADJ (+ER) taub; (*emotionally*) benommen; **hands ~ with cold** Hände, die vor Kälte taub sind; **~ with grief** wie betäubt vor Schmerz **2** VT (*cold*) taub machen; (*injection, fig*) betäuben

number [ˈnʌmbə^r] **1** N **(a)** (*Math*) Zahl *f*; (= *numeral*) Ziffer *f* **(b)** (= *quantity, amount*) Anzahl *f*; **a ~ of problems/applicants** eine (ganze) Anzahl von Problemen/Bewerbern; **large ~s of people/books** (sehr) viele Leute/Bücher; **on a ~ of occasions** des Öfteren; **boys and girls in equal ~s** ebenso viele Jungen wie Mädchen; **in a small ~ of cases** in wenigen Fällen; **ten in ~** zehn an der Zahl; **to be found in large ~s** zahlreich vorhanden sein; **in small/large ~s** in kleinen/großen Mengen; **any ~ can play** beliebig viele Spieler können teilnehmen; **any ~ of cards** *etc* (*when choosing*) beliebig viele Karten *etc*; (= *many*) sehr viele Karten *etc* **(c)** (*of house, room, phone*) (= *song, act, issue*) Nummer *f*; (*of page*) Seitenzahl *f*; (*of car*) (Auto)nummer *f*; **at ~ 4** (in) Nummer 4; **Number Ten (Downing Street)** Nummer zehn (Downing Street); **the ~ 47 bus** die Buslinie 47; **I've got the wrong ~** ich habe mich verwählt; **it was a wrong ~** ich/er *etc* war falsch verbunden; **the ~ one tennis player** (*inf*) der Tennisspieler Nummer eins (*inf*); **the single went straight to** *or* **straight in at ~ one** die Single stieg gleich auf Nummer eins ein; **to take care of** *or* **look after ~ one** (*inf*) (vor allem) an sich (*acc*) selbst denken; **his ~'s up** (*inf*) er ist dran (*inf*); **to get sb's ~** (*inf*) jdn durchschauen **(d)** (= *song, act, issue of magazine*) Nummer *f*; (= *dress*) Kreation *f* **(e)** (= *company*) **one of their/our ~** eine(r) aus ihren/unseren Reihen **(f) numbers** PL (= *arithmetic*) Rechnen *nt* **2** VT **(a)** (= *give a ~ to*) nummerieren **(b)** (= *include, amount to*) zählen (*among* zu); **the group ~ed 50** es waren 50 (Leute in der Gruppe); **his days are ~ed** seine Tage sind gezählt

number (*Comput*): **number cruncher** N Supercomputer *m*; (= *person*) Zahlenzauberer *m*, Zahlenzauberin *f*; **number crunching** N Numbercrunching *nt*

numbering [ˈnʌmbərɪŋ] N (*of houses etc*) Nummerierung *f*

number: **numberplate** N (*Brit*) Nummernschild *nt*; **numbers lock** N (*Comput*) Zahlenverriegelung *f*

numbly [ˈnʌmlɪ] ADV benommen

numbness [ˈnʌmnɪs] N (*of limbs etc*) Taubheit *f*

numeracy [ˈnjuːmərəsɪ] N Rechnen *nt*

numeral [ˈnjuːmərəl] N Ziffer *f*

numerate [ˈnjuːmərɪt] ADJ rechenkundig; **to be (very) ~** (gut) rechnen können

numeric [njuːˈmerɪk] ADJ **~ keypad** numerisches Tastenfeld

numerical [njuːˈmerɪkəl] ADJ *order, data* numerisch; *superiority* zahlenmäßig; **~ control** numerische Steuerung

numerically [njuːˈmerɪkəlɪ] ADV zahlenmäßig; **~ controlled** numerisch gesteuert

numerous [ˈnjuːmərəs] ADJ zahlreich; **on ~ occasions** bei vielen Gelegenheiten

nun [nʌn] N Nonne *f*

nuptials [ˈnʌpʃəlz] PL (*hum, liter*) **the ~** die Hochzeit *f*

nurd N (*US sl*) = **nerd**

Nuremberg [ˈnjʊərəmbɜːg] N Nürnberg *nt*

nurse [nɜːs] **1** N Schwester *f*; (*as professional title*) Krankenschwester *f*; (= *nanny*) Kindermädchen *nt*; **male ~** Krankenpfleger *m* **2** VT **(a)** pflegen; (*fig*) *plan, hope, wrath etc* hegen; (= *treat carefully*) schonen; *business* sorgsam verwalten; **to ~ sb back to health** jdn gesund pflegen; **to ~ sb through an illness** jdn während einer Krankheit pflegen; **to ~ a cold** an einer Erkältung herumlaborieren (*inf*); **he stood there nursing his bruised arm** er stand da und hielt seinen verletzten Arm **(b)** (= *suckle*) *child* stillen; (= *cradle*) (in den Armen) wiegen

nursery [ˈnɜːsərɪ] N **(a)** (= *room*) Kinderzimmer *nt*; (*in hospital*) Säuglingssaal *m*; (= *institution*) Kindergarten *m*; (*all-day*) Kindertagesstätte *f* **(c)** (*Agr, Hort*) Gärtnerei *f*; (*for trees*) Baumschule *f*

nursery: **nursery nurse** N Kindermädchen *nt*; **nursery rhyme** N Kinderreim *m*; **nursery school** N Kindergarten *m*; **nursery school teacher** N Kindergärtner(in) *m(f)*; **nursery slope** N (*Ski*) Idiotenhügel *m* (*hum*)

nursing [ˈnɜːsɪŋ] **1** N **(a)** (= *care of invalids*) Pflege *f* **(b)** (= *profession*) Krankenpflege *f*; **she's going in for ~** sie will in die Krankenpflege arbeiten **2** ADJ ATTR Pflege-; **~ staff** Pflegepersonal *nt*; **the ~ profession** die Krankenpflege; (= *nurses collectively*) die Pflegeberufe *pl*

nursing home N Privatklinik *f*; (= *convalescent home*) Pflegeheim *nt*

nurture [ˈnɜːtʃə^r] VT *sb's talent* entwickeln; *idea, ambitions* hegen

NUS (*Brit*) ABBR *of* **National Union of Students** Studentengewerkschaft

nut [nʌt] N **(a)** (*Bot*) Nuss *f*; **a hard** *or* **tough ~ to crack** (*fig*) eine harte Nuss **(b)** (*inf*: = *head*) Nuss *f* (*inf*) **(c)** (*inf*: = *person*) Spinner(in) *m(f)* (*inf*) **(d)** (*Mech*) (Schrauben)mutter *f*; **the ~s and bolts of a theory** die Grundbestandteile einer Theorie

nut: **nutcase** N (*inf*) Spinner(in) *m(f)* (*inf*); **nutcracker** N, **nutcrackers** PL Nussknacker *m*; **nutmeg** N Muskatnuss *f*

nutrient [ˈnjuːtrɪənt] N Nährstoff *m*

nutrition [njuːˈtrɪʃən] N Ernährung *f*

nutritional [njuːˈtrɪʃənl] ADJ Nähr-; **~ value** Nährwert *m*; **~ information** Nährwertangaben *pl*

nutritious [njuːˈtrɪʃəs] ADJ nahrhaft

nuts [nʌts] ADJ PRED (*inf*) **to be ~** spinnen (*inf*); **to be ~ about sb/sth** ganz verrückt nach jdm/auf etw (*acc*) sein (*inf*)

nutshell [ˈnʌtʃel] N **in a ~** (*fig*) mit einem Wort

nutter [ˈnʌtə^r] N (*Brit inf*) Spinner(in) *m(f)* (*inf*); (*dangerous*) Verrückte(r) *mf*; **he's a ~** er hat einen Stich (*inf*)

nutty [ˈnʌtɪ] ADJ (+ER) **(a)** (= *like nuts*) nussartig; (= *with nuts*) mit Nüssen **(b)** (*inf*: = *crazy*) bekloppt (*inf*)

nuzzle [ˈnʌzl] **1** VT beschnüffeln **2** VI **to ~ (up) against sb, to ~ up to sb** (*person, animal*) sich an jdn schmiegen

NW ABBR *of* **north-west** NW

NY ABBR *of* **New York**

nylon [ˈnaɪlɒn] **1** N **(a)** (*Tex*) Nylon *nt* **(b) nylons** PL Nylonstrümpfe *pl* **2** ADJ Nylon-; **~ shirt** Nylonhemd *nt*

nymph [nɪmf] N (*Myth*) Nymphe *f*

nymphomaniac [ˌnɪmfəʊˈmeɪnɪæk] N Nymphomanin *f*

NYSE ABBR *of* **New York Stock Exchange**

NZ ABBR *of* **New Zealand**

O, o [əʊ] N **(a)** O nt, o nt **(b)** (Brit) əʊ, (US) 'zɪərəʊ) (Telec) Null f

O INTERJ oh; **O to be in France** (ach,) wäre ich nur in Frankreich!

o' [ə] PREP ABBR of of

oaf [əʊf] N Flegel m; **you clumsy ~!** du altes Trampel! (inf)

oak [əʊk] N Eiche f; (= wood also) Eichenholz nt

OAP (Brit) ABBR of old-age pensioner

oar [ɔː'] N Ruder nt; **he always has to put** or **stick his ~ in** (fig inf) er muss (aber auch) immer mitmischen (inf)

OAS ABBR of Organization of American States OAS f

oasis [əʊ'eɪsɪs] N, pl oases [əʊ'eɪsiːz] (lit, fig) Oase f

oat [əʊt] N USU PL Hafer m; **~s** pl (Cook) Haferflocken pl

oatcake ['əʊtkeɪk] N Haferkeks m

oath [əʊθ] N **(a)** Schwur m; (Jur) Eid m; **to take** or **swear an ~** schwören; (Jur) einen Eid ablegen or leisten; **he took an ~ of loyalty to the government** er schwor der Regierung Loyalität; **to declare under ~** or **on ~** (Jur) unter Eid aussagen; **to be under ~** (Jur) unter Eid stehen; **to take the ~** (Jur) vereidigt werden **(b)** (= curse, profanity) Fluch m

oatmeal ['əʊtmiːl] **1** N, NO PL Haferschrot m **2** ADJ **(a)** biscuits, bread aus Haferschrot **(b)** colour, dress hellbeige

OAU ABBR of Organization of African Unity OAU f

obdurate ['ɒbdjʊrɪt] ADJ hartnäckig

OBE ABBR of Officer of the Order of the British Empire britischer Verdienstorden

obedience [ə'biːdɪəns] N, NO PL Gehorsam m

obedient [ə'biːdɪənt] ADJ gehorsam; **to be ~** gehorchen (to dat)

obediently [ə'biːdɪəntlɪ] ADV gehorsam

obese [əʊ'biːs] ADJ fettleibig

obesity [əʊ'biːsɪtɪ] N Fettleibigkeit f

obey [ə'beɪ] **1** VT gehorchen (+dat); law, rules, order befolgen; (Jur) summons nachkommen (+dat); **I expect to be ~ed** ich erwarte, dass man meine Anordnungen befolgt **2** VI gehorchen

obituary [ə'bɪtjʊərɪ] N Nachruf m; **~ notice** Todesanzeige f; **~ column** Sterberegister nt

object¹ ['ɒbdʒɪkt] N **(a)** (= thing) Gegenstand m; **she became an ~ of pity** mit ihr musste man Mitleid haben; **he was an ~ of scorn** er war die Zielscheibe der Verachtung **(b)** (= aim) Ziel nt; **with this ~ in view** or **in mind** mit diesem Ziel vor Augen; **what's the ~ (of staying here)?** zu welchem Zweck (bleiben wir hier)?; **the ~ of the exercise** der Zweck der Übung; **that defeats the ~** das verfehlt seinen Zweck **(c)** (= obstacle) money/distance **is no ~** Geld/Entfernung spielt keine Rolle **(d)** (Gram) Objekt nt

object² [əb'dʒekt] **1** VI dagegen sein; (= make objection, protest) protestieren; (= be against: in discussion etc) Einwände haben (to gegen); (= raise objection) Einwände erheben; **to ~ to sth** (= disapprove) etw missbilligen; **I don't ~ to that** ich habe nichts dagegen (einzuwenden); **he ~s to my drinking** er nimmt daran Anstoß, dass ich trinke; **I ~ to your tone** ich verbitte mir diesen Ton; **I ~ to people smoking in my living room** ich verbitte mir, dass in meinem Wohnzimmer geraucht wird; **I ~ to him bossing me around** ich wehre mich dagegen, dass er mich (so) herumkommandiert; **I ~!** ich protestiere! **2** VT einwenden

objection [əb'dʒekʃən] N **(a)** Einwand m (to gegen); **to make** or **raise an ~ (to sth)** einen Einwand (gegen etw) machen; **I have no ~ to his going away** ich habe nichts dagegen (einzuwenden), dass er weggeht; **are there any ~s?** irgendwelche Einwände?; **~!** (Jur) Einspruch! **(b)** (= dislike) **I have no ~ to him** ich habe nichts gegen ihn

objectionable [əb'dʒekʃənəbl] ADJ störend; conduct, remark, language anstößig; **he's a most ~ person** er ist unausstehlich; **I find this (really) ~** ich habe starke Einwände dagegen; (= offensive) ich finde das anstößig

objective [əb'dʒektɪv] **1** ADJ objektiv; **~ fact** Tatsache f **2** N (= aim) Ziel nt; (esp Comm) Zielvorstellung f; (Mil) Angriffsziel nt

objectively [əb'dʒektɪvlɪ] ADV objektiv

objectivity [,ɒbdʒek'tɪvɪtɪ] N Objektivität f

object lesson ['ɒbdʒɪkt,lesn] N (fig) Musterbeispiel nt (in, on für)

objector [əb'dʒektə'] N Gegner(in) m(f) (to +gen)

objet d'art ['ɒbʒeɪ'dɑː] N Kunstgegenstand m

obligation [ɒblɪ'geɪʃən] N Verpflichtung f; **to be under an ~ to do sth** verpflichtet sein, etw zu tun; **to be under** or **have an ~ to sb** jdm verpflichtet sein; **without ~** (Comm) unverbindlich

obligatory [ɒ'blɪgətərɪ] ADJ obligatorisch; **~ subject** Pflichtfach nt; **biology is ~** Biologie ist Pflicht; **attendance is ~** Anwesenheit ist vorgeschrieben; **identity cards were made ~** Personalausweise wurden Vorschrift; **with the ~ piper** mit dem obligaten Dudelsackpfeifer

oblige [ə'blaɪdʒ] **1** VT **(a)** (= compel) zwingen; (because of duty) verpflichten; **sb to do sth** jdn, etw zu tun; (Jur) vorschreiben; **(sb to do sth** jdm, etw zu tun); **to feel ~d to do sth** sich verpflichtet fühlen, etw zu tun; **you are not ~d to answer this question** Sie brauchen diese Frage nicht zu beantworten **(b)** (= do a favour to) einen Gefallen tun (+dat); **he ~d us with a song** er gab uns ein Lied zum Besten; **would you ~ me by not interrupting, I would be ~d if you wouldn't interrupt** hätten Sie die Güte, mich nicht zu unterbrechen; **much ~d!** herzlichen Dank!; **I am much ~d to you for this!** ich bin Ihnen dafür sehr dankbar **2** VI **she is always ready to ~** sie ist immer sehr gefällig; **anything to ~** stets zu Diensten!

obliging [ə'blaɪdʒɪŋ] ADJ entgegenkommend

obligingly [ə'blaɪdʒɪŋlɪ] ADV entgegenkommenderweise

oblique [ə'bliːk] **1** ADJ **(a)** line schräg; angle schief **(b)** (fig) indirekt; warning versteckt; criticism verdeckt **2** N Schrägstrich m; **and ~** or und Strich oder

obliquely [ə'bliːklɪ] ADV (fig) indirekt

obliterate [ə'blɪtəreɪt] VT auslöschen; city vernichten; **by the 19th century this disease had been completely ~d** im 19. Jahrhundert war dann diese Krankheit völlig ausgerottet

oblivion [ə'blɪvɪən] N Vergessenheit f; **to sink** or **fall into ~** in Vergessenheit geraten; **to rescue sb/sth from ~** jdn/etw wieder ins Bewusstsein bringen

oblivious [ə'blɪvɪəs] ADJ **to be ~ of** or **to sth** sich (dat) einer Sache (gen) nicht bewusst sein; **he was quite ~ of his surroundings** er nahm seine Umgebung gar nicht wahr; **he was totally ~ of what was going on in his marriage** er (be)merkte gar nicht, was in seiner Ehe vor sich ging

obliviously [ə'blɪvɪəslɪ] ADV **to carry on ~** einfach (unbeirrt) weitermachen

oblong ['ɒblɒŋ] **1** ADJ rechteckig **2** N Rechteck nt

obnoxious [əb'nɒkʃəs] ADJ widerwärtig; person, behaviour unausstehlich; **an ~ person** ein Ekel nt (inf); **don't be so ~ to her** sei nicht so gemein zu ihr

obnoxiously [əb'nɒkʃəslɪ] ADV widerlich; behave unausstehlich

oboe ['əʊbəʊ] N Oboe f

obscene [əb'siːn] ADJ obszön; (= repulsive) Ekel erregend; prices, demands unverschämt; **~ publication** Veröffentlichung f mit pornografischem Inhalt

obscenely [əb'siːnlɪ] ADV obszön; (= repulsively) Ekel erregend; **she earns ~ large amounts of money** sie verdient unverschämt viel Geld

obscenity [əb'senɪtɪ] N Obszönität f; **he used an ~** er gebrauchte einen ordinären Ausdruck

obscure [əb'skjʊə'] **1** ADJ (+ER) **(a)** (= hard to understand) dunkel; style undurchsichtig; argument verworren; language, word, book, poet schwer verständlich **(b)** (= indistinct) **for some ~ reason** aus einem unerfindlichen Grund **(c)** (= unknown, little known) obskur; poet, village unbekannt; (= humble) beginnings unbedeutend **2** VT **(a)** sun, view verdecken **(b)** truth, facts, issues verschleiern

obscurely [əb'skjʊəlɪ] ADV undeutlich

obscurity [əb'skjʊərɪtɪ] N **(a)** (of style, ideas, argument) Unklarheit f; **he threw some light on the obscurities of the**

text er erhellte einige der unklaren Textstellen **(b)** NO PL *(of birth, origins)* Dunkel *nt;* **to live in** ~ zurückgezogen leben; **to sink into** ~ in Vergessenheit geraten

obsequious [əb'siːkwɪəs] ADJ unterwürfig *(to(wards)* gegenüber)

observable [əb'zɜːvəbl] ADJ erkennbar; **there has been no ~ change in his condition today** es wurde heute keine Veränderung seines Befindens beobachtet

observance [əb'zɜːvəns] N *(of law)* Befolgung *f*

observant [əb'zɜːvənt] ADJ *person* aufmerksam; **that's very ~ of you** das hast du aber gut bemerkt

observation [ˌɒbzə'veɪʃən] N **(a)** Beobachtung *f;* **to keep sb/sth under** ~ jdn/etw unter Beobachtung halten; *(by police)* jdn/etw observieren *(form);* **powers of** ~ Beobachtungsgabe *f;* **he's in hospital for** ~ er ist zur Beobachtung im Krankenhaus **(b)** *(= remark)* Bemerkung *f;* **~s on Kant** Betrachtungen zu Kant

observation post N Beobachtungsposten *m*

observatory [əb'zɜːvətrɪ] N Observatorium *nt*

observe [əb'zɜːv] VT **(a)** beobachten; *(by police)* überwachen **(b)** *(= remark)* bemerken **(c)** *(= obey)* achten auf *(+acc); rule, custom, ceasefire, Sabbath* einhalten; *anniversary etc* begehen; **to ~ a minute's silence** eine Schweigeminute einlegen

observer [əb'zɜːvəʳ] N Zuschauer(in) *m(f);* *(Mil, Pol)* Beobachter(in) *m(f)*

obsess [əb'ses] VT **to be ~ed by** *or* **with sb/sth** von jdm/etw besessen sein; **to be ~ed about sth** von etw besessen sein

obsession [əb'seʃən] N **(a)** *(= fixed idea)* fixe Idee; *(= fear etc)* Zwangsvorstellung *f;* **it's an ~ with him** das ist eine fixe Idee von ihm; *(hobby etc)* er ist davon besessen **(b)** *(= state)* Besessenheit *f (with von);* **this ~ with order/quality** dieser Ordnungs-/Qualitätswahn *m*

obsessional [əb'seʃənl] ADJ *(Psych) behaviour, personality* zwanghaft; *love, hatred, jealousy* obsessiv

obsessive [əb'sesɪv] **1** ADJ zwanghaft; **to be ~ about sth** von etw besessen sein; **to be ~ about cleanliness** einen Sauberkeitsfimmel haben *(inf);* **to become ~** zum Zwang werden **2** N Zwangsneurotiker(in) *m(f)*

obsessively [əb'sesɪvlɪ] ADV wie besessen

obsolescent [ˌɒbsə'lesnt] ADJ **to be ~** anfangen zu veralten; *(machine, process etc)* technisch (fast) überholt sein

obsolete ['ɒbsəliːt] ADJ überholt; **to become ~** veralten

obstacle ['ɒbstəkl] N *(lit, fig)* Hindernis *nt;* **to be an ~ to sb/sth** jdm/einer Sache im Weg(e) stehen; **if they put any ~ in the way of our plans** wenn man uns Steine in den Weg legt; **all the ~s to progress/peace** *etc* alles, was den Fortschritt/Frieden *etc* behindert

obstetric(al) [ɒb'stetrɪk(əl)] ADJ *(Med) techniques etc* bei der Geburtshilfe; **obstetric care** Geburtshilfe *f*

obstetrician [ˌɒbstə'trɪʃən] N Geburtshelfer(in) *m(f)*

obstetrics [ɒb'stetrɪks] N SING Geburtshilfe *f*

obstinacy ['ɒbstɪnəsɪ] N Hartnäckigkeit *f;* **his ~ in doing sth** die Hartnäckigkeit, mit der er etw tut

obstinate ['ɒbstɪnɪt] ADJ hartnäckig; *nail etc* widerspenstig; **to remain ~** stur bleiben

obstinately ['ɒbstɪnɪtlɪ] ADV hartnäckig; **unemployment figures remain ~ high** die Arbeitslosenzahlen verharren auf unverändert hohem Niveau

obstreperous [əb'strepərəs] ADJ aufmüpfig *(inf); child* aufsässig

obstruct [əb'strʌkt] VT **(a)** *(= block)* blockieren; *view* versperren; **you're ~ing my view** Sie versperren mir die Sicht **(b)** *(= hinder)* behindern; *(Sport)* sperren; **to ~ (the course of) justice** die Rechtsfindung behindern; **to ~ the police** die Arbeit der Polizei behindern

obstruction [əb'strʌkʃən] N **(a)** *(= hindering)* Behinderung *f;* *(Sport)* Sperren *nt;* **to cause an ~** den Verkehr behindern **(b)** *(= obstacle)* Hindernis *nt;* **there is an ~ in the pipe** das Rohr ist verstopft

obstructive [əb'strʌktɪv] ADJ obstruktiv *(esp Pol),* behindernd; **to be ~** (person) Schwierigkeiten machen

obtain [əb'teɪn] **1** VT erhalten; *knowledge* erwerben; **to ~ sth through hard work** etw durch harte Arbeit erreichen; *possession* sich *(dat)* etw mühsam erarbeiten; **to ~ sth for sb** jdm etw beschaffen; **they ~ed the release of the hostages** sie

erreichten die Freilassung der Geiseln **2** VI *(form)* gelten; *(customs)* herrschen

obtainable [əb'teɪnəbl] ADJ erhältlich

obtrude [əb'truːd] VI sich aufdrängen

obtrusive [əb'truːsɪv] ADJ *person, music, smell* aufdringlich; *building, furniture* zu auffällig

obtuse [əb'tjuːs] ADJ **(a)** *(Geometry)* stumpf **(b)** *person* begriffsstutzig; **are you just being ~?** tust du nur so beschränkt?

obverse ['ɒbvɜːs] N Kehrseite *f*

obviate ['ɒbvɪeɪt] VT vermeiden; *need* vorbeugen *(+dat)*

obvious ['ɒbvɪəs] ADJ offensichtlich; *(= not subtle)* plump; *proof, difference, fact* eindeutig; *statement* nahe liegend; *reason* (leicht) ersichtlich; *dislike, reluctance, surprise* sichtlich; **that's the ~ solution** das ist die nächstliegende Lösung; **for ~ reasons** aus nahe liegenden Gründen; **it was ~ he didn't want to come** er wollte offensichtlich nicht kommen; **it's quite ~ he doesn't understand** es ist doch klar, dass er nicht versteht; **I would have thought that was perfectly ~** das liegt doch auf der Hand; *(= noticeable)* das springt doch ins Auge; **with the ~ exception of ...** natürlich mit Ausnahme von ...; **even if I am stating the ~** selbst wenn ich hier etwas längst Bekanntes sage; **what's the ~ thing to do?** was ist das Naheliegendste?

obviously ['ɒbvɪəslɪ] ADV offensichtlich; **he's ~ French** er ist eindeutig ein Franzose; **~!** natürlich!; **he's not going to like it** das wird ihm natürlich nicht gefallen; **he's ~ not going to get the job** er bekommt die Stelle nicht, das ist ja klar *(inf)*

occasion [ə'keɪʒən] N **(a)** *(= point in time)* Gelegenheit *f;* **on that ~** zu jener Gelegenheit; **on another ~** ein anderes Mal; **on several ~s** mehrmals; **(on) the first ~** beim ersten Mal; **to rise to the ~** sich der Lage gewachsen zeigen **(b)** *(= special time)* Ereignis *nt;* **on the ~ of his birthday** anlässlich seines Geburtstages *(geh)* **(c)** *(= reason)* Anlass *m;* **should the ~ arise** sollte es nötig werden; **if you have ~ to ...** sollten Sie Veranlassung haben, zu ...; **not an ~ for merriment** kein Grund zur Freude

occasional [ə'keɪʒənl] ADJ gelegentlich; **he likes an** *or* **the ~ cigar** er raucht gelegentlich ganz gern eine Zigarre; **she made ~ visits to England** sie fuhr ab und zu nach England

occasionally [ə'keɪʒənəlɪ] ADV gelegentlich; **very ~** sehr selten

occult [ɒ'kʌlt] **1** ADJ okkult; *(= of occultism)* okkultistisch; *(= secret)* geheimnisvoll **2** N Okkulte(s) *nt*

occultism ['ɒkəltɪzəm] N Okkultismus *m*

occupancy ['ɒkjʊpənsɪ] N Bewohnen *nt;* *(= period)* Wohndauer *f;* **a change of** ~ ein Besitzerwechsel *m;* *(of rented property)* ein Mieterwechsel *m;* **levels of hotel** ~ Übernachtungsziffern *pl*

occupant ['ɒkjʊpənt] N *(of house)* Bewohner(in) *m(f);* *(of post)* Inhaber(in) *m(f);* *(of car)* Insasse *m,* Insassin *f*

occupation [ˌɒkjʊ'peɪʃən] N **(a)** *(= employment)* Beruf *m;* **what is his ~?** was ist er von Beruf?; **he is a teacher by ~** er ist Lehrer von Beruf **(b)** *(= pastime)* Beschäftigung *f* **(c)** *(Mil)* Okkupation *f;* **army of ~** Besatzungsarmee *f*

occupational [ˌɒkjʊ'peɪʃənl] ADJ Berufs-, beruflich; **~ hazard** *or* **risk** Berufsrisiko *nt*

occupational: occupational pension (scheme) N betriebliche Altersversorgung; **occupational therapist** N Beschäftigungstherapeut(in) *m(f);* **occupational therapy** N Beschäftigungstherapie *f*

occupied ['ɒkjʊpaɪd] ADJ **(a)** *house, room* belegt; **a room ~ by four people** ein von vier Personen bewohntes Zimmer; **is this seat ~?** ist dieser Platz belegt? **(b)** *(Mil etc) country, territory* besetzt **(c)** *(= busy)* beschäftigt; **to be ~ with sth** mit etw beschäftigt sein; **to keep sb ~** jdn beschäftigen; **he kept his mind ~** er ist beschäftigte sich geistig

occupier ['ɒkjʊpaɪəʳ] N *(of house, land)* Bewohner(in) *m(f)*

occupy ['ɒkjʊpaɪ] VT **(a)** *house* bewohnen; *seat, room* belegen **(b)** *(Mil etc)* besetzen **(c)** *post, position* innehaben **(d)** *(= take up)* beanspruchen; *space* einnehmen; *time* in Anspruch nehmen; *(= help pass)* ausfüllen **(e)** *(= busy)* beschäftigen

occur [ə'kɜːʳ] VI **(a)** *(event)* geschehen; *(difficulty)* sich ergeben; *(change)* stattfinden; **that doesn't ~ very often** das gibt es nicht oft; **should a fault ~** sollte ein Fehler auftreten **(b)** *(= be found: disease)* vorkommen **(c)** *(= come to mind)* einfallen *(to sb* jdm); **it ~s to me that ...** ich habe den Eindruck, dass ...; **the idea just ~red to me** es ist mir gerade eingefallen; **it never ~red to me** darauf bin ich noch nie gekommen; **it didn't even ~ to him to ask** er kam erst gar nicht auf den Gedanken, zu fragen

occurrence [ə'kʌrəns] N **(a)** (= *event*) Ereignis *nt* **(b)** (= *presence, taking place*) Auftreten *nt*; **further ~s of this nature must be avoided** weitere Vorkommnisse dieser Art müssen vermieden werden

ocean ['əʊʃən] N Ozean *m*

ocean-going ['əʊʃəngəʊɪŋ] ADJ hochseetauglich

Oceania [əʊʃɪ'eɪnɪə] N Ozeanien *nt*

oceanic [əʊʃɪ'ænɪk] ADJ Meeres-; **~ plant** Meerespflanze *f*

ocean liner N Ozeandampfer *m*

oceanography [əʊʃə'nɒgrəfɪ] N Meereskunde *f*

ochre, (*US*) **ocher** ['əʊkə'] 1 N Ocker *m* or *nt* 2 ADJ ockerfarben

o'clock [ə'klɒk] ADV **at 5** ~ um 5 Uhr; **it is 5 ~ in the morning/ evening** es ist 5 Uhr morgens/abends; **the 9 ~ news** die 9-Uhr-Nachrichten; **the 9 ~ train** der 9-Uhr-Zug

Oct ABBR *of* **October** Okt.

octagon ['ɒktəgən] N Achteck *nt*

octagonal [ɒk'tægənl] ADJ achteckig

octane ['ɒkteɪn] N Oktan *nt*; **high-~ fuel** Benzin *nt* mit hoher Oktanzahl

octave ['ɒktɪv] N (*Mus*) Oktave *f*

October [ɒk'təʊbə'] N Oktober *m*; *see also* **September**

octogenarian [ɒktəʊdʒɪ'neərɪən] N Achtzigjährige(r) *mf*

octopus ['ɒktəpəs] N Tintenfisch *m*

OD (*inf*) 1 N Überdosis *f* 2 VI eine Überdosis nehmen; **to OD on heroin** sich (*dat*) den goldenen Schuss setzen (*inf*)

odd [ɒd] 1 ADJ (+ER) **(a)** (= *peculiar*) seltsam; **how ~ that we should meet him** wie seltsam, dass wir ihn trafen; **the ~ thing about it is that ...** das Merkwürdige *etc* daran ist, dass ...; **it seemed ~ to me** es kam mir komisch vor **(b)** *number* ungerade **(c)** (= *one of a pair or a set*) shoe, glove einzeln; **he/she is (the) ~ man** or **one out** er/sie ist überzählig; (*in character*) er/sie steht (immer) abseits; **in each group underline the word/ picture which is the ~ man** or **one out** unterstreichen Sie in jeder Gruppe das nicht dazugehörige Wort/Bild **(d)** (= *slightly over*) **600-~ pounds** gut 600 Pfund **(e)** (= *surplus, extra*) übrig; **the ~ one left over** der/die/das Überzählige **(f)** *moments, times* zeitweilig; (*Comm*) size ausgefallen; **at ~ moments** or **times** ab und zu; **he likes the ~ drink** er trinkt gerne mal einen; **he does all the ~ jobs** er macht alles, was an Arbeit anfällt 2 ADV (*inf*) **he was acting a bit ~** er benahm sich etwas komisch

oddball ['ɒdbɔːl] (*inf*) N Spinner(in) *m(f)*

oddity ['ɒdɪtɪ] N (= *odd person*) komischer Kauz; (*who doesn't fit,* = *odd thing*) Kuriosität *f*

odd-jobman [ˌɒd'dʒɒbmæn] Mädchen *nt* für alles

oddly ['ɒdlɪ] ADV merkwürdig; **an ~ shaped room** ein Raum, der eine seltsame Form hat; **the street was ~ familiar** die Straße kam mir merkwürdig bekannt vor; **~ enough she was at home** merkwürdigerweise war sie zu Hause

oddment ['ɒdmənt] N USU PL Restposten *m*

odds [ɒdz] PL **(a)** (*Betting*) Odds *pl*; (*of bookmaker*) Kurse *pl*; **the ~ are 6 to 1** die Chancen stehen 6 zu 1 (*written: 6:1*); **I'll lay ~ (of 3 to 1) that ...** (*fig*) ich wette (3 gegen 1), dass ...; **to pay over the ~** (*inf*) zu viel bezahlen **(b)** (= *chances for or against*) Chance(n) *f(pl)*; **the ~ were against us** alles sprach gegen uns; **the ~ were in our favour** (*Brit*) or **favor** (*US*) alles sprach für uns; **against all the ~ he won** entgegen allen Erwartungen gewann er; **what are the ~ on/against ...?** wie sind or stehen die Chancen, dass .../ dass ... nicht?; **the ~ are that he will come** es sieht ganz so aus, als ob er käme **(c)** (= *difference*) **it makes no ~** es spielt keine Rolle; **it makes no ~ to me** es ist mir (völlig) einerlei **(d)** (= *variance*) **to be at ~ with sb over sth** mit jdm in etw (*dat*) nicht übereinstimmen; **we are at ~ as to the best solution** wir gehen nicht darin einig, wie das am besten gelöst werden soll

odds and ends PL Krimskrams *m*; (*of food, cloth*) Reste *pl*; **bring all your ~** bringen Sie Ihren ganzen Kram

odds-on ['ɒdzɒn] 1 ADJ **the ~ favourite** (*Brit*) or **favorite** (*US*) der klare Favorit; **she's ~ favourite** (*Brit*) or **favorite** (*US*) **for the job** sie hat die größten Aussichten, die Stelle zu bekommen; **he has an ~ chance (of winning)** er hat die besten (Gewinn)chancen 2 ADV **it's ~ that he'll come** es ist so gut wie sicher, dass er kommt

ode [əʊd] N Ode *f* (*to, on* an +*acc*)

odious ['əʊdɪəs] ADJ *person* abstoßend; *action* abscheulich; **an ~ person** ein Ekel *nt*

odometer [ɒ'dɒmɪtə'] N Kilometerzähler *m*

odour, (*US*) **odor** ['əʊdə'] N (*lit, fig*) Geruch *m*; (= *sweet smell*) Duft *m*; (= *bad smell*) Gestank *m*

odourless, (*US*) **odorless** ['əʊdəlɪs] ADJ geruchlos

Odyssey ['ɒdɪsɪ] N (*Myth, fig*) Odyssee *f*

Oedipus complex ['iːdɪpəs'kɒmpleks] N Ödipuskomplex *m*

oesophagus, (*US*) **esophagus** [iː'sɒfəgəs] N Speiseröhre *f*

of [ɒv, əv] PREP **(a)** von (+*dat*), *use of gen*; **the wife of the doctor** die Frau des Arztes, die Frau vom Arzt; **a friend of ours** ein Freund/eine Freundin von uns; **a painting of the Queen** ein Gemälde *nt* von der Königin; **a painting of the Queen's** (= *belonging to her*) ein Gemälde (im Besitz) der Königin; **of it** davon; **the first of May** der Erste Mai; **that damn dog of theirs** (*inf*) ihr verdammter Hund (*inf*); **it is very kind of you** es ist sehr freundlich von Ihnen; **south of Paris** südlich von Paris; **within a month of his death** einen Monat nach seinem Tod; **a quarter of six** (*US*) Viertel vor sechs; **fear of God** Gottesfurcht *f*; **his love of his father** die Liebe zu seinem Vater; **he is a leader of men** er hat die Fähigkeit, Menschen zu führen; **writer of legal articles** Verfasser von juristischen Artikeln; **love of God for man** Liebe Gottes zu den Menschen; **affection of a mother** Mutterliebe *f*; **the whole of the house** das ganze Haus; **half of the house** das halbe Haus; **how many of them do you want?** wie viele möchten Sie (davon)?; **there were six of us** wir waren zu sechst; **he is not one of us** er gehört nicht zu uns; **one of the best** einer der Besten; **he asked the six of us to lunch** er lud uns sechs zum Mittagessen ein; **of the ten only one was absent** von den zehn fehlte nur einer; **today of all days** ausgerechnet heute; **you of all people ought to know** gerade Sie sollten das wissen; **he warned us of the danger** er warnte uns vor der Gefahr; **doctor of medicine** Doktor der Medizin; **what of it?** ja und? **(b)** (*indicating cause*) **he died of poison/cancer** er starb an Gift/Krebs; **he died of hunger** er verhungerte; **it tastes of garlic** es schmeckt nach Knoblauch **(c)** (*indicating material*) aus; **a dress made of wool** ein Wollkleid *nt* **(d)** (*indicating quality, identity etc*) **a man of courage** ein mutiger Mensch; **a girl of ten** ein zehnjähriges Mädchen; **a matter of no importance** eine Sache ohne Bedeutung; **the city of Paris** die Stadt Paris; **where is that rascal of a boy?** wo ist dieser verflixte Bengel?; **that idiot of a waiter** dieser Idiot von Kellner **(e)** (*in temporal phrases*) **he's become very quiet of late** er ist letztlich so ruhig geworden; **they go out of an evening** (*inf*) sie gehen abends (schon mal) aus (*inf*)

Ofcom ['ɒfkɒm] N (*Brit*) ABBR *of* **Office of Communications Regulation** *Regulierungsbehörde für die Kommunikations-industrie*

off [ɒf] 1 ADV **(a)** (*distance*) **the house is 5 km ~** das Haus ist 5 km entfernt; **it's a long way ~** das ist weit weg; (*time*) das liegt in weiter Ferne; **August isn't/the exams aren't very far ~** es ist nicht mehr lang bis August/bis zu den Prüfungen **(b)** (*departure*) **to be/go ~** gehen; **he's ~ to school** er ist zur Schule gegangen; **I must be ~** ich muss (jetzt) weg (*inf*); **where are you ~ to?** wohin gehen Sie denn?; **~ we go!** los!; **they're ~** (*Sport*) sie sind vom Start; **she's ~ again** (*inf*: = *complaining etc*) sie legt schon wieder los (*inf*) **(c)** (*removal*) **he helped me ~ with my coat** er half mir aus dem Mantel; **with his shirt ~** ohne Hemd; **~ with those wet clothes!** raus aus den nassen Kleidern!; **the handle has come ~** der Griff ist abgegangen **(d)** (= *discount*) **3% ~** (*Comm*) 3% Nachlass; **to give sb £5/ something** ~ jdm £ 5 Ermäßigung/eine Ermäßigung geben; **he let me have £5 ~** er gab es mir (um) £ 5 billiger **(e)** (= *not at work*) **to have time ~ to do sth** (Zeit) freibekommen haben, um etw zu tun; **I've got a day ~** ich habe einen Tag frei(bekommen); **to be ~ sick** wegen

Krankheit fehlen
(f) (*in phrases*) ~ **and on, on and** ~ ab und zu; **right** *or* **straight**
~ **gleich**

2 ADJ **(a)** ATTR *year, day etc* schlecht; **I'm having an** ~ **day today**
ich bin heute nicht in Form
(b) PRED (*Brit*: = *not fresh*) verdorben; *milk* schlecht; *butter*
ranzig; **to go** ~ schlecht werden
(c) PRED *match, party, talks* abgesagt; **I'm afraid veal is** ~ **today**
Kalbfleisch gibt es heute leider nicht; **the bet/agreement is** ~
die Wette/Abmachung gilt nicht (mehr); **their engagement
is** ~ ihre Verlobung ist gelöst
(d) *TV, light, machine* aus(geschaltet); *tap* zu(gedreht); **the
gas/electricity was** ~ das Gas/der Strom war abgeschaltet; **the
brake was** ~ die Bremse war gelöst
(e) **they are badly/well** *or* **comfortably** ~ sie sind nicht gut/
(ganz) gut gestellt; **he is better/worse** ~ **staying in England** er
steht sich in England besser/schlechter; **he was quite a bit** ~
in his calculations er hatte sich in seinen Berechnungen
ziemlich vertan
(f) PRED (*inf*) **that's a bit** ~**!** das ist ein dicker Hund! (*inf*); **it's a
bit** ~ **not letting me know** das ist ja nicht die feine Art, mir
nicht Bescheid zu sagen

3 PREP **(a)** von (+*dat*); **he jumped** ~ **the roof** er sprang vom
Dach; **I got it** ~ **my friend** (*inf*) ich habs von meinem Freund
(gekriegt) (*inf*); **we live** ~ **cheese on toast** wir leben von Käse
und Toastbrot; **he got £2** ~ **the shirt** er bekam das Hemd £ 2
billiger; **the lid had been left** ~ **the tin** jemand hatte den
Deckel nicht wieder auf die Büchse getan
(b) (= *distant from*) ab(gelegen) von (+*dat*); (= *in a side street
from*) in einer Nebenstraße von (+*dat*); **the house was just** ~
the main road das Haus lag in unmittelbarer Nähe der
Hauptstraße; **a road** ~ **Bank Street** eine Querstraße zur Bank
Street
(c) ~ **the map** nicht auf der Karte; **I just want it** ~ **my hands**
ich möchte das nur loswerden; **I'm** ~ **sausages/beer/him**
Wurst/Bier/er kann mich zur Zeit nicht reizen

off air ADV (*TV, Rad*) nicht auf Sendung; **to go** ~ (*broadcast*)
enden; (*for good: station*) den Sendebetrieb einstellen

offal [ˈɒfəl] N, NO PL Innereien *pl*

off: **offbeat** ADJ unkonventionell; **off-Broadway** ADJ *in New
York außerhalb des Broadway aufgeführt/gelegen*, Off-
Broadway-; ~ **musical** Off-Broadway-Musical *nt*

*Off-Broadway heißen in New York diejenigen Theaterproduktionen, die
nicht in den berühmten Broadway-Häusern gespielt werden. Off-
Broadway-Theater sind normalerweise kleiner und die Eintrittskarten
kosten weniger als bei den berühmteren Häusern, wobei neben
professionellen Truppen auch Laiengruppen Aufführungen anbieten.*

off: **off-campus** **1** ADJ (*Univ*) *activities* außerhalb der
Universität; **several colleges hold classes at** ~ **sites** mehrere
Institute halten Lehrveranstaltungen ab außerhalb des
Universitätsgeländes; **off-centre**, (*US*) **off-center** **1** ADJ (*lit*)
nicht in der Mitte; *construction* asymmetrisch **2** ADV schief;
off chance N **I just did it on the** ~ ich habe es auf gut Glück
getan; **I came on the** ~ **of seeing her** ich kam in der
Hoffnung, sie vielleicht zu sehen; **off-colour**, (*US*) **off-color**
ADJ (*esp Brit*) **(a)** (= *unwell*) unwohl; **to feel/be** ~ sich nicht
wohl fühlen **(b)** (= *indecent*) gewagt; **off-duty** ADJ ATTR außer
Dienst

offence, (*US*) **offense** [əˈfens] N **(a)** (*Jur*) Straftat *f*; (*minor*)
Vergehen *nt*; **to commit an** ~ sich strafbar machen; **it is an** ~
to … … ist bei Strafe verboten
(b) NO PL (*to sb's feelings*) Kränkung *f*; (*to sense of decency,
morality etc*) Anstoß *m*; **to cause** *or* **give** ~ **to sb** jdn kränken;
to take ~ **at sth** wegen etw gekränkt sein; **no** ~ **to the
Germans, of course!** damit will ich natürlich nichts gegen
die Deutschen gesagt haben; **no** ~ **(meant)** nichts für ungut;
no ~ **(taken)** ich nehme dir das nicht übel
(c) [ˈɒfens] (*US*: = *attacking part of team*) Angriff *m*

offend [əˈfend] **1** VT (= *hurt feelings of*) kränken; (= *be
disagreeable to*) Anstoß erregen bei **2** VI (*ein*) Unrecht tun

➤ **offend against** VI +PREP OBJ verstoßen gegen

offended [əˈfendɪd] ADJ beleidigt; **don't be** ~ seien Sie (doch)
nicht beleidigt; **to be** ~ **by sth** sich von etw verletzt fühlen

offender [əˈfendəʳ] N (= *law-breaker*) (Straf)täter(in) *m(f)*;
(*against traffic laws*) Verkehrssünder(in) *m(f)*; **sex** ~
Sexualstraftäter(in) *m(f)*

offending [əˈfendɪŋ] ADJ **(a)** *person* zuwiderhandelnd; **the** ~
party (*Jur*) die schuldige Partei; (*fig*) der/die Schuldige
(b) (= *causing problem*) störend; *wire, part* defekt

offense N (*US*) = **offence**

offensive [əˈfensɪv] **1** ADJ **(a)** (*Mil*) Offensiv-; *action* offensiv; ~
player Offensivspieler(in) *m(f)*
(b) *smell, sight* abstoßend; *language, film, book* anstößig;
remark, gesture, behaviour beleidigend; **to find sb/sth** ~ jdn/
etw abstoßend finden; *behaviour, language* Anstoß an etw
(*dat*) nehmen; **he was** ~ **to her** er beleidigte sie; **I don't mean
to be** ~ ich möchte nicht beleidigend wirken
2 N (*Mil, Sport*) Offensive *f*; **to take the** ~ in die Offensive
gehen; **to go over** *or* **on to the** ~ zum Angriff übergehen; **on
the** ~ in der Offensive

offensively [əˈfensɪvlɪ] ADV (= *unpleasantly*) widerlich; (*in moral
sense*) anstößig; (= *abusively*) beleidigend; (= *obscenely*)
unflätig

offer [ˈɒfəʳ] **1** N Angebot *nt*; **the** ~**'s there** das Angebot gilt; **did
you have many** ~**s of help?** haben Ihnen viele Leute ihre Hilfe
angeboten?; **any** ~**s?** ist jemand interessiert?; **he made me an**
~ (**of £50**) er machte mir ein Angebot (von £ 50); ~**s over
£75,000** Angebote nicht unter £ 75.000; **on** ~ (= *Comm*) (= *on
special* ~) im Angebot; (= *for sale*) verkäuflich
2 VT **(a)** anbieten; *reward, prize* aussetzen; *suggestion*
unterbreiten; *excuse* vorbringen; *condolences* aussprechen; **to**
~ **to do sth** anbieten, etw zu tun; (= ~ *one's services*) sich
bereit erklären, etw zu tun; **he** ~**ed to help** er bot seine Hilfe
an; **to** ~ **one's services** sich anbieten; **did he** ~ **to?** hat er sich
angeboten?; **to** ~ **an opinion** sich (dazu) äußern; **to** ~ **one's
resignation** seinen Rücktritt anbieten
(b) *prayers, homage, sacrifice* darbringen; *one's life* opfern
(c) *resistance* bieten
3 VI **did he** ~**?** hat er es angeboten?

➤ **offer up** VT SEP *prayers, sacrifice* darbringen (*to sb* jdm)

offering [ˈɒfərɪŋ] N Gabe *f*; (*Rel*) (= *collection*) Opfergabe *f*;
(= *sacrifice*) Opfer *nt*; (*iro*: = *essay, play etc*) Vorstellung *f*

offer price N Angebotspreis *m*

offertory [ˈɒfətərɪ] N (*Eccl*) (= *part of service*) Opferung *f*;
(= *collection*) Kollekte *f*

offhand [ˌɒfˈhænd] **1** ADJ lässig; **to be** ~ **with sb** sich jdm
gegenüber lässig benehmen; **to be** ~ **about sth** etw leichthin
abtun **2** ADV so ohne weiteres; **I couldn't tell you** ~ das
könnte ich Ihnen auf Anhieb nicht sagen

office [ˈɒfɪs] N **(a)** Büro *nt*; (*of lawyer*) Kanzlei *f*; (= *part of
organization*) Abteilung *f*; (= *branch*) Geschäftsstelle *f*; **at the**
~ im Büro **(b)** (= *public position*) Amt *nt*; **to take** ~ das Amt
antreten; (*political party*) die Regierung übernehmen; **to be in**
or **hold** ~ im Amt sein; (*party*) an der Regierung sein **(c)** USU
PL **through his good** ~**s** durch seine guten Dienste; **through
the** ~ **of …** durch Vermittlung von …

office: **office block** N Bürogebäude *nt*; **office chair** N
Bürostuhl *m*; **office holder** N Amtsinhaber(in) *m(f)*; **office
hours** PL Dienstzeit *f*; (*on sign*) Geschäftszeiten *pl*; **to work** ~
normale Arbeitszeiten haben; **office job** N Stelle *f* im Büro;
office junior N Bürogehilfe *m*/-gehilfin *f*; **office
manager(ess)** N Büroleiter(in) *m(f)*; **Office of Fair Trading** N
(*Brit*) Behörde *f* gegen unlauteren Wettbewerb; **office party**
N Büroparty *f*

officer [ˈɒfɪsəʳ] N **(a)** (*Mil, Naut, Aviat*) Offizier(in) *m(f)*
(b) (= *official*) Beamte(r) *m*, Beamtin *f*; (= *police* ~) Polizist(in)
m(f); (*of club, society*) Funktionär(in) *m(f)*

officers' mess [ˈɒfɪsəzˈmes] N Offizierskasino *nt*

office: **office supplies** PL Bürobedarf *m*; **office worker** N
Büroangestellte(r) *mf*

official [əˈfɪʃəl] **1** ADJ offiziell; (= *formal*) formell; *biography*
autorisiert; ~ **language** Amtssprache *f*; **is that** ~? ist das
amtlich?; (= *publicly announced*) ist das offiziell?; **acting in
one's** ~ **capacity** in Ausübung seiner Amtsgewalt
2 N (= *railway* ~, *post office* ~ *etc*) Beamte(r) *m*, Beamtin *f*; (*of
club, at race-meeting*) Funktionär(in) *m(f)*; **government** ~
Regierungsbeamte(r) *m*/-beamtin *f*; **trade union** ~ (*Brit*)
Gewerkschaftsfunktionär(in) *m(f)*

officialdom [əˈfɪʃəldəm] N (*pej*) Beamtentum *nt*

officially [əˈfɪʃəlɪ] ADV offiziell

officiate [əˈfɪʃɪeɪt] VT amtieren (*at* bei); **to ~ at a wedding** eine Trauung vornehmen

officious [əˈfɪʃəs] ADJ (dienst)beflissen; **to be ~** sich vor (Dienst)eifer überschlagen

offing [ˈɒfɪŋ] N **in the ~** in Sicht; **there's a pay rise** (*Brit*) *or* **raise** (*US*) **in the ~ for us** uns steht eine Gehaltserhöhung bevor

off: **off key** ADJ PRED (*Mus*) falsch; **off-licence** N (*Brit*) Wein- und Spirituosenhandlung *f*; **off limits** ADJ PRED **(a) this area is ~** das Betreten dieses Gebiets ist verboten; **this room is ~ to** *or* **for the kids** die Kinder dürfen diesen Raum nicht betreten; *see also* **limit (b)** (*fig*: = *forbidden*) *activity* verboten; **chocolates are ~** Pralinen sind nicht erlaubt; **off line** (*Comput*) **1** ADJ PRED offline **2** ADV off line; **to go ~** auf Offlinebetrieb schalten; **off-line** ADJ ATTR (*Comput*) Offline-; **off-load** VT *goods* ausladen, entladen; *passengers* aussteigen lassen; **off-message** ADJ (*esp Pol*) nicht auf Linie; **off-peak** ADJ **~ central heating** Nacht(strom)speicherheizung *f*; **~ electricity** Nachtstrom *m*; **~ charges** verbilligter Tarif; (*Elec*) ≈ Nachttarif *m*; **at ~ times, during ~ hours** außerhalb der Stoßzeiten; (*Telec*) außerhalb der Spitzenzeiten; **~ service** (*Rail*) Zugverkehr *m* außerhalb der Hauptverkehrszeit; **off-piste** ADJ, ADV abseits der Piste; **off-putting** ADJ (*esp Brit*) *smell, behaviour, sight* abstoßend; *meal* wenig einladend; *thought, idea, story* wenig ermutigend; (= *daunting*) entmutigend; *interviewer* wenig entgegenkommend; **off-road** ADJ *driving, racing* im Gelände; **~ vehicle** Geländefahrzeug *nt*; **off-roader** N Geländefahrzeug *nt*; **off-screen** ADJ, ADV (*Film, TV*) im wirklichen Leben; **off season** N (*in tourism*) Nebensaison *f*; **in the ~** außerhalb der Saison; **off-season** ADJ *travel, prices* außerhalb der Saison

offset [ˈɒfset], *pret, ptp* **offset** VT (*financially, statistically etc*) ausgleichen; (= *make up for*) wettmachen

offshoot [ˈɒfʃuːt] N (*fig*) (*of organization*) Nebenzweig *m*; (*of discussion, argument etc*) Randergebnis *nt*

offshore [ˈɒfʃɔːʳ] **1** ADJ **(a)** *island* küstennah; *wind* ablandig; *oilfield, installations etc* im Meer **(b)** (*Fin*) *investment, funds* im Ausland **2** [ˌɒfˈʃɔːʳ] ADV **(a) 20 miles ~** 20 Meilen vor der Küste; **the ship anchored ~** das Schiff ankerte vor der Küste **(b)** (*Fin*) im Ausland; **to move one's operation ~** sein Unternehmen ins Ausland verlegen

offshore: **offshore banking** N (*Fin*) Offshorebankgeschäfte *pl*; **offshore company** N (*Fin*) Offshorefirma *f*

offside [ˈɒfsaɪd] **1** ADJ **(a)** (*Sport*) im Abseits; **to be ~** (*player*) im Abseits sein *or* stehen; (*goal*) ein Abseitstreffer *m* sein; **~ rule** Abseitsregel *f*; **~ trap** Abseitsfalle *f* **(b)** (*Aut*) auf der Fahrerseite **2** N (*Aut*) Fahrerseite *f* **3** ADV (*Sport*) abseits

offspring [ˈɒfsprɪŋ] N **(a)** SING Sprössling *m*; (*of animal*) Junge(s) *nt* **(b)** PL (*form, hum*) (*of people*) Nachkommen *pl*; (*of animals*) Junge *pl*

offstage [ˈɒfˈsteɪdʒ] **1** ADJ hinter den Kulissen; *voice, music etc* aus den Kulissen **2** ADV *go, walk* von der Bühne; *stand* hinter den Kulissen

off: **off-street parking** N (= *single place*) Stellplatz *m*; (= *spaces*) Stellplätze *pl*; **off-the-cuff** ADJ *remark, speech* aus dem Stegreif; **off-the-peg** ADJ ATTR, **off the peg** ADJ PRED (*Brit*), **off-the-rack** ADJ ATTR, **off the rack** ADJ PRED (*US*) *dress, suit* von der Stange; **off-the-record** ADJ ATTR, **off the record** ADJ PRED inoffiziell; (= *confidential*) vertraulich; **off-the-shelf** ADJ, **off the shelf** ADV (*Comm*) ab Lager; **off-the-shoulder** ADJ *dress* schulterfrei; **off-the-wall** ADJ ATTR, **off the wall** ADJ PRED (*inf*) irre (*inf*), verrückt; **off-white** **1** ADJ gebrochen weiß **2** N gebrochenes Weiß

oft [ɒft] ADV (*liter*) oft; **an ~-told story** eine gar oft erzählte Geschichte (*liter*)

often [ˈɒfən] ADV oft; **he went there ~, he ~ went there** er ging oft da hin; **not as ~ as** twice a week weniger als zweimal in der Woche; **more ~ than not, as ~ as not** meistens; **every so ~** öfters; **how ~?** wie oft?; **it is not ~ that ...** es kommt selten vor, dass ...

ogle [ˈəʊgl] VT kein Auge lassen von; (*flirtatiously*) liebäugeln mit; *legs, girls* schielen nach

ogre [ˈəʊgəʳ] N Ungeheuer *nt*

oh [əʊ] INTERJ ach; (*admiring, surprised, disappointed*) oh; (*questioning, disinterested, in confirmation*) tatsächlich; **oh good!** prima! (*inf*); **oh well** na ja!; **oh dear!** o je!; **oh yes?** (*interested*) ach ja?; (*disbelieving*) so, so; **oh yes, that's right** ach ja, das stimmt

ohm [əʊm] N Ohm *nt*

oi [ɔɪ] INTERJ (*Brit inf*) he!

oil [ɔɪl] **1** N **(a)** Öl *nt*; **to pour ~ on troubled waters** die Wogen glätten **(b)** (= *petroleum*) (Erd)öl *nt*; **to strike ~** auf Öl stoßen **(c)** (*Art*: = *painting*) Ölgemälde *nt*; **to paint in ~s** in Öl malen **2** VT ölen; *table, furniture* einölen; **to ~ the wheels** (*fig*) die Dinge erleichtern

oil IN CPDS Öl-; **oil baron** N Ölmagnat *m*; **oil-based** ADJ **~ paint** Ölfarbe *f*; **oilcan** N Ölkanne *f*; **oil change** N Ölwechsel *m*; **I took the car in for an ~** ich habe den Wagen zum Ölwechsel gebracht; **oil company** N Ölkonzern *m*; **oil driller** N Ölbohrarbeiter(in) *m(f)*; **oil-exporting** ADJ Öl exportierend; **oilfield** N Ölfeld *nt*; **oil-fired** ADJ Öl-, mit Öl befeuert; **~ power station** Ölkraftwerk *nt*; **oil gauge** N Ölstandsmesser *m*; **oil industry** N Ölindustrie *f*; **oil lamp** N Öllampe *f*; **oil level** N Ölstand *m*; **oil painting** N (= *picture*) Ölgemälde *nt*; (= *art*) Ölmalerei *f*; **oil platform** N Bohrinsel *f*; **oil-producing** ADJ ölproduzierend; **oil rig** N (Öl)bohrinsel *f*; **oilskins** PL Ölzeug *nt*; **oil slick** N Ölteppich *m*; **oil spill** N Ölkatastrophe *f*; **oil stove** N Ölofen *m*; **oil tanker** N (= *ship*) (Öl)tanker *m*; (= *lorry*) Tankwagen *m*; **oil well** N Ölquelle *f*

oily [ˈɔɪlɪ] ADJ (+ER) (*lit, fig*) ölig; *hair, skin, food* fettig; *clothes, fingers* voller Öl; **~ fish** Fisch *m* mit hohem Ölgehalt

ointment [ˈɔɪntmənt] N Salbe *f*

OJ N (*US inf*) ABBR *of* **orange juice** O-Saft *m*

OK, okay [ˈəʊˈkeɪ] (*inf*) **1** INTERJ okay (*inf*); (= *agreed also*) in Ordnung; **OK, OK!** ist ja gut! (*inf*); **OK, let's go!** also, gehen wir!

2 ADJ in Ordnung, okay (*inf*); **that's OK with** *or* **by me** (= *that's convenient*) das ist mir recht; (= *I don't mind that*) von mir aus; **is it OK (with you) if ...?** macht es (dir) etwas aus, wenn ...?; **how's your mother? – she's OK** wie gehts deiner Mutter? – gut *or* (*not too well*) so einigermaßen (*inf*); **I feel OK** es geht mir einigermaßen (*inf*); **to be OK (for time/money)** (noch) genug (Zeit/Geld) haben; **is that OK?** geht das?; **what do you think of him? – he's OK** was halten Sie von ihm? – der ist in Ordnung (*inf*); **he's an OK guy** (*esp US*) er ist ein prima Kerl (*inf*) **3** ADV **(a)** (= *well*) gut; (= *not too badly*) einigermaßen (gut); (= *for sure*) schon; **to do OK** ganz gut zurechtkommen; (*Sch*: *in subject*) nicht schlecht sein; **they must be doing OK** (= *be affluent*) es muss ihnen ganz gut gehen; **can you manage it OK?** kommst du damit klar? **(b)** (*inf*: = *admittedly*) **OK it's difficult but ...** zugegeben, es ist schwer, aber ...; **OK, so he's not a real count** na gut, er ist also kein richtiger Graf **4** VT *order, plan, suggestion* gutheißen; *document, proposed expenses* genehmigen; **you have to get the boss to OK it, you have to OK it with the boss** das muss der Chef bewilligen **5** N **to give (sb/sth) the OK** (jdm/zu etw) seine Zustimmung geben; **I can start work as soon as I get the OK** ich kann mit der Arbeit anfangen, sobald ich grünes Licht bekomme

ol' [əʊl] ADJ (*esp US inf*) = **old**

old [əʊld] **1** ADJ (+ER) **(a)** alt; **~ people** *or* **folk(s)** alte Leute; **Mr Smith, ~ man Smith** (*esp US*) der alte (Herr) Smith; **he/the building is 40 years ~** er/das Gebäude ist 40 Jahre alt; **at ten months ~** im Alter von zehn Monaten; **two-year-~** Zweijährige(r) *mf*; **the ~ (part of) town** die Altstadt; **in the ~ days** früher; **the good/bad ~ days** die gute/schlechte alte Zeit; **my ~ school** meine alte Schule **(b)** (*inf*: *as intensifier*) **she dresses any ~ how** die ist vielleicht immer angezogen (*inf*); **any ~ thing** irgendwas; **any ~ bottle/blouse etc** irgendeine Flasche/Bluse *etc* (*inf*); **good ~ Tim** (*inf*) der gute alte Tim; **always the same ~ excuse** immer wieder dieselbe Ausrede; **funny ~ guy** komischer Typ (*inf*) **2** N PL (= ~ *people*) **the ~** die Alten; **it caters for young and ~** es hat Angebote für Jung und Alt

old: **old age** N das Alter; **in one's ~** im Alter; **old-age pension** N (Alters)rente *f*; **old-age pensioner** N Rentner(in) *m(f)*; **old boy** N **(a)** (*Brit Sch*) Ehemalige(r) *m*; **the old-boy network** Beziehungen *pl* (von der Schule her) **(b)** (*inf*: = *old man*) **the ~ next door** der Alte von nebenan

olden [ˈəʊldən] ADJ (*liter*) **in ~ times** *or* **days** in alten Zeiten

old: **old-fashioned** [ˈəʊldˈfæʃnd] ADJ altmodisch; **old flame** N alte Liebe; **old girl** N **(a)** (*inf*: = *old woman*) Alte *f* **(b)** (*Brit Sch*) Ehemalige *f*; **Old Glory** N (*US*: = *flag*) das Sternenbanner; **old guard** N (*fig*) alte Garde; **old hand** N alter Hase

oldie [ˈəʊldɪ] N (inf) (= song) Oldie m; **the ~s** (= people) die Alten pl

old: old lady N (inf) my ~ (= wife, mother) meine Alte (inf); **old maid** N alte Jungfer; **old man** N (inf) my ~ (= husband, father) mein Alter (inf); **old master** N alter Meister; **old people's home** N Altenheim nt; **old school** N (fig) alte Schule

oldster [ˈəʊldstəˈ] N (US inf) älterer Mann; **some of us ~s** einige von uns Alten

old: old-style ADJ im alten Stil; furniture, car etc altertümlich; **Old Testament** N (Bibl) Altes Testament; **old-timer** N Veteran(in) m(f); **old wives' tale** N Ammenmärchen nt; **old woman** N he's an ~ er ist wie ein altes Weib; **Old World** N the ~ die Alte Welt; **old-world** ADJ politeness, manners altväterlich; cottage, atmosphere heimelig

O level [ˈəʊlevl] N (Brit formerly) ≈ mittlere Reife; **to do one's ~s** ≈ die mittlere Reife machen; **to have an ~ in English** ≈ bis zur mittleren Reife Englisch gelernt haben; **3 ~s** ≈ die mittlere Reife in 3 Fächern

oligarchy [ˈɒlɪgɑːkɪ] N Oligarchie f

oligopoly [ɒlɪˈgɒpəlɪ] N Oligopol nt

olive [ˈɒlɪv] **1** N (a) Olive f; (also ~ tree) Olivenbaum m (b) (= colour) Olive nt **2** ADJ (also ~-coloured) olivgrün

olive: olive branch N to hold out or offer the ~ to sb (fig) jdm seinen Willen zum Frieden bekunden; **olive green** N Olivgrün nt; **olive-green** ADJ olivgrün; **olive grove** N Olivenhain m; **olive oil** N Olivenöl nt

Olympiad [əˈlɪmpɪæd] N Olympiade f

Olympian [əˈlɪmpɪən] **1** ADJ olympisch **2** N the ~s die Olympier pl

Olympic [əˈlɪmpɪk] **1** ADJ olympisch; ~ **medallist** (Brit) or **medalist** (US) Olympiamedaillengewinner(in) m(f) **2** N **Olympics** PL the ~s die Olympiade, die Olympischen Spiele

Olympic: Olympic champion N Olympiasieger(in) m(f); **Olympic Games** PL the ~ die Olympischen Spiele

Oman [əʊˈmɑːn] N Oman nt

ombudsman [ˈɒmbʊdzmən] N, pl **-men** [-mən] Ombudsmann m

omega [ˈəʊmɪgə] N Omega nt

omelette, (US) **omelet** [ˈɒmlɪt] N Omelett(e) nt

omen [ˈəʊmen] N Omen nt

ominous [ˈɒmɪnəs] ADJ bedrohlich; **that's ~** das lässt nichts Gutes ahnen

ominously [ˈɒmɪnəslɪ] ADV bedrohlich; say in einem Unheil verkündenden Ton; **more ~, the government is talking of reprisals** schlimmer noch, die Regierung spricht von Vergeltungsmaßnahmen

omission [əˈmɪʃən] N (= omitting) Auslassen nt; (= word, thing etc left out) Auslassung f; (= failure to do sth) Unterlassung f

omit [əˈmɪt] VT (a) (= leave out) auslassen (b) (= fail) (to do sth etw zu tun) unterlassen; (accidentally) versäumen

omnibus [ˈɒmnɪbəs] N (also ~ edition) (= book) Sammelband m; (TV, Rad) Fernseh- oder Radioprogramm, das zwei oder mehrere Folgen wiederholt

omnipotence [ɒmˈnɪpətəns] N, NO PL Omnipotenz f

omnipotent [ɒmˈnɪpətənt] ADJ omnipotent

omnipresent [ˈɒmnɪˈprezənt] ADJ allgegenwärtig

omniscient [ɒmˈnɪsɪənt] ADJ allwissend

omnivore [ˈɒmnɪˌvɔːˈ] N Allesfresser m

omnivorous [ɒmˈnɪvərəs] ADJ (lit) alles fressend; **an ~ reader** ein Vielfraß m, was Bücher angeht

on [ɒn]

| **1** PREPOSITION | **3** ADJECTIVE |
| **2** ADVERB | |

1 PREPOSITION

When **on** is the second element in a phrasal verb, eg **live on**, **lecture on**, look up the verb. When it is part of a set combination, eg **on the right**, **on request**, **on occasion**, look up the other word.

(a) (indicating place, position) auf (+dat); (with vb of motion) auf (+acc); (on vertical surface, part of body) an (+dat); (with vb of motion) an (+acc); **the book is on the table** das Buch ist auf dem Tisch; **he put the book on the table** er legte das Buch auf den Tisch; **he hung it on the wall/nail** er hängte es an die Wand/den Nagel; **a house on the coast/main road** ein Haus am Meer/an der Hauptstraße; **with a smile on her face** mit einem Lächeln auf den Lippen; **a ring on his finger** ein Ring am Finger; **on TV/the radio** im Fernsehen/Radio; **on video** auf Video; **held on computer** auf Computer (dat) gespeichert; **who's on his show tonight?** wer ist heute in seiner Show?; **I have no money on me** ich habe kein Geld bei mir; **we had something to eat on the train** wir haben im Zug etwas gegessen; see also **onto**

(b) (= by means of, using) **we went on the train/bus** wir fuhren mit dem Zug/Bus; **on a bicycle** mit dem (Fahr)rad; **the heating runs on oil** die Heizung wird mit Öl betrieben; **to count sth on one's fingers** etw an den Fingern abzählen; **he played (it) on the violin/trumpet** er spielte (es) auf der Geige/Trompete; **on drums/piano** am Schlagzeug/Klavier

(c) (= about, concerning) über (+acc); **have you heard him on the subject?** haben Sie ihn zu diesem Thema gehört?; **he has nothing on me** (= no damaging information etc) er hat nichts gegen mich in der Hand

(d) (in expressions of time) an (+dat); **on Sunday** (am) Sonntag; **on Sundays** sonntags; **on December the first** am ersten Dezember; **on or about the twentieth** um den Zwanzigsten herum

(e) (= at the time of) bei (+dat); **on examination** bei der Untersuchung; **on hearing this he left** als er das hörte, ging er

(f) (= as a result of) auf ... (acc) hin; **on receiving my letter** auf meinen Brief hin

(g) (indicating membership) in (+dat); **he is on the committee/the board** er sitzt im Ausschuss/Vorstand; **he is on the teaching staff** er gehört zum Lehrpersonal

(h) (= compared with) im Vergleich zu; **prices are up on last year('s)** im Vergleich zum letzten Jahr sind die Preise gestiegen; **month on month** monatlich; **year on year** jährlich; **he has nothing on me** (= not as good as) er kann mir nicht das Wasser reichen

(i) **to be on drugs/the pill** Drogen/die Pille nehmen; **what is he on?** (inf) er tickt wohl nicht ganz richtig! (inf); **I'm on £28,000 a year** ich bekomme £ 28.000 im Jahr; **he retired on a good pension** er trat mit einer guten Rente in den Ruhestand; **this round is on me** diese Runde geht auf meine Kosten; **have it on me** ich gebe (dir) das aus

2 ADVERB

(a) (= in place, covering) **he screwed the lid on** er schraubte den Deckel drauf; **she had nothing on** sie hatte nichts an; **he had his hat on crooked** er hatte den Hut schief auf

(b) (indicating position) **put it this way on** stellen/legen Sie es so herum (darauf); **sideways on** längs

(c) (indicating time) **from that day on** von diesem Tag an; **it was well on into September** es war spät im September

(d) (set structures)

✦**on and on** **they talked on and on** sie redeten und redeten; **the noise went on and on** der Lärm hörte überhaupt nicht auf; **she went on and on** sie hörte gar nicht mehr auf

✦**to be on at sb** (inf) **he's always on at me** er hackt dauernd auf mir herum; **he's always on at me to get my hair cut** er liegt mir dauernd in den Ohren, dass ich mir die Haare schneiden lassen soll

✦**to be on about sth** (inf) **she's always on about her experiences in Italy** sie kommt dauernd mit ihren Italienerfahrungen (inf); **what's he on about?** wovon redet er nun schon wieder?

3 ADJECTIVE

(a) (lights, TV, radio) an; brake angezogen; electricity, gas an(gestellt); **to leave the engine on** den Motor laufen lassen; **the "on" switch** der Einschalter; **in the "on" position** auf „ein" gestellt

(b) (lid, cover) drauf

(c) (= taking place, performing) **there's a tennis match on at the moment** ein Tennismatch ist gerade im Gang; **there's a tennis match on tomorrow** morgen findet ein Tennismatch statt; **I have nothing on tonight** ich habe heute Abend nichts vor; **what's on in London?** was ist los in London?; **the search is on for a new managing director** jetzt wird nach einem neuen Geschäftsführer gesucht; **to be on** (in theatre, cinema) gegeben werden; (on TV, radio) gesendet werden; **the play is still on** (= still running) das Stück wird immer noch gegeben; **what's on tonight?** was steht heute Abend auf dem Programm?; **you're on now** (Theat, Rad, TV) Sie sind (jetzt) dran (inf); **tell me when the English team is on** sagen Sie mir, wenn die englische Mannschaft dran ist or drankommt **(d) to be on** (bet, agreement) gelten; **you're on!** abgemacht!; **are you on for dinner tonight?** sehen wir uns zum Abendessen?; **it's just not on** (Brit inf) das ist einfach nicht drin (inf)

once [wʌns] **1** ADV **(a)** einmal; **~ a week/month/year** einmal in der Woche/im Monat/im Jahr; **~ again** or **more** noch einmal; **~ again we find that ...** wir stellen erneut fest, dass ...; **~ or twice** (fig) nur ein paar Mal; **~ and for all** ein für alle Mal; **(every) ~ in a while** ab und zu mal; **you can come (just) this ~** dieses eine Mal können Sie kommen; **for ~** ausnahmsweise einmal; **he was ~ famous** er war früher einmal berühmt; **~ upon a time there was ...** es war einmal ... **(b) at ~** (= immediately) sofort; (= at the same time) auf einmal; **all at ~** auf einmal; (= suddenly) ganz plötzlich; **they came all at ~** sie kamen alle zur gleichen Zeit; **don't spend it all at ~** gib es nicht alles auf einmal aus **2** CONJ wenn; (with past tense) als; **~ you understand, it's easy** wenn Sie es einmal verstehen, ist es einfach; **~ the sun had set, it turned cold** als die Sonne erst untergegangen war, wurde es kalt

once-over [ˈwʌnsəʊvəʳ] N (inf) **to give sb/sth the** or **a ~** (= appraisal) jdn/etw mal kurz überprüfen

oncoming [ˈɒnkʌmɪŋ] ADJ car entgegenkommend; **the ~ traffic** der Gegenverkehr

one [wʌn] **1** ADJ **(a)** (= number) ein/eine/ein; (counting) eins; **there was ~ person too many** da war einer zu viel; **~ girl was pretty, the other was ugly** das eine Mädchen war hübsch, das andere hässlich; **the baby is ~ (year old)** das Kind ist ein Jahr (alt); **it is ~ (o'clock)** es ist ein Uhr; **~ hundred pounds** (ein)hundert Pfund **(b)** (indefinite) **~ morning/day** etc **he realized ...** eines Morgens/Tages etc bemerkte er ...; **~ day next week** nächste Woche einmal; **~ day soon** bald einmal **(c)** (= a certain) **~ Mr Smith** ein gewisser Herr Smith **(d) my ~ (and only) hope** meine einzige Hoffnung; **the ~ and only Brigitte Bardot** die unvergleichliche Brigitte Bardot; **they all came in the ~ car** sie kamen alle in dem einen Auto; **it is ~ and the same thing** das ist ein und dasselbe; **the crowd rose as ~** die Menge erhob sich geschlossen **2** PRON **(a)** eine(r, s); **the ~ who ...** der(jenige), der .../ die(jenige), die .../das(jenige), das ...; **he/that was the ~** er/das war's; **do you have ~?** haben Sie einen/eine/ein(e)s?; **the red/big** etc **~** der/die/das Rote/Große etc; **he has some very fine ~s** er hat sehr Schöne; **my ~** (inf) meiner/meine/ mein(e)s; **not (a single) ~ of them** nicht eine(r, s) von ihnen; **any ~** irgendeine(r, s); **every ~** jede(r, s); **this ~** diese(r, s); **that ~** der/die/das, jene(r, s) (geh); **which ~?** welche(r, s)?; **let's have a quick ~ after work** (inf) lasst uns nach der Arbeit noch kurz einen trinken gehen; **I am not much of a ~ for cakes** (inf) ich bin kein großer Freund von Kuchen (inf); **he's never ~ to say no** er sagt nie Nein; **he's a great ~ for discipline/turning up late** der ist ganz groß, wenns um Disziplin/ums Zuspätkommen geht; **I, for ~, think otherwise** ich, zum Beispiel, denke anders; **~ by ~** einzeln; **~ after the other** eine(r, s) nach dem/der anderen; **take ~ or the other** nehmen Sie das eine oder das andere; **he is ~ of us** er ist einer von uns; **~ who knows the country** jemand, der das Land kennt; **like ~ possessed** wie besessen **(b)** (impers) (nom) man; (acc) einen; (dat) einem; **~ must learn to keep quiet** man muss lernen, still zu sein; **to hurt ~'s foot** sich (dat) den Fuß verletzen **3** N (= written figure) Eins f; **in ~s and twos** in kleinen Gruppen; **to be at ~ (with sb)** sich (dat) (mit jdm) einig sein; **it was a bedroom and sitting room (all) in ~** es war Schlaf- und Wohnzimmer in einem; **to be ~ up on sb** (inf) (= know more) jdm eins voraus sein; (= have more) jdm etwas vor+bhaben; **Rangers were ~ up after the first half** Rangers hatten nach der ersten Halbzeit ein Tor Vorsprung

one: **one-act play** N Einakter m; **one another** = **each other;** see **each;** **one-armed bandit** N (inf) einarmiger Bandit; **one-day** ADJ seminar, course eintägig; **one-dimensional** ADJ

eindimensional; **one-horse** ADJ **(a) to be a ~ race** (fig) einen sicheren Sieger haben **(b)** (inf) **~ town** Kuhdorf nt (inf); **one-liner** N (inf) witzige Bemerkung; **one-man band** N Einmannkapelle f; (fig inf) Einmannbetrieb m; **one-man show** N (Theat etc) Einmannshow f; **one-night stand** N (fig) One-Night Stand m; **one-off** (Brit inf) **1** ADJ einmalig **2** N a ~ etwas Einmaliges; **that mistake** etc **was just a ~** dieser Fehler etc war eine Ausnahme; **one-on-one, one-to-one** ADJ, ADV, N (US) = **one-to-one;** **one-parent family** N Einelternteilfamilie f; **one-party** ADJ (Pol) **~ state/system** Einparteienstaat m/- system nt; **one-piece** **1** ADJ einteilig **2** N (= bathing costume) Einteiler m; **one-room** ATTR, **one-roomed** ADJ **~ flat** (Brit) or **apartment** Einzimmerwohnung f

onerous [ˈɒnərəs] ADJ responsibility schwer(wiegend); task, duty schwer

oneself [wʌnˈself] PRON **(a)** (dir and indir, with prep) sich; (= ~ personally) sich selbst **(b)** (emph) (sich) selbst; see also **myself**

one: **one-sided** ADJ einseitig; **one-time** ADJ ehemalig; **one-to-one** **1** ADJ **(a)** (= between two people) conversation, meeting unter vier Augen; **~ teaching** or **tuition** Einzelunterricht m **(b)** (= corresponding exactly) sich Punkt für Punkt entsprechend; **a ~ exchange rate** ein Wechselkurs m im Verhältnis eins zu eins **2** ADV talk, discuss unter vier Augen **3** N **to have a ~ with sb** unter vier Augen mit jdm führen; **one-touch** ADJ Berührungs-, Sensor-; **one-track** ADJ **he's got a ~ mind** der hat immer nur das eine im Sinn or Kopf; **one-upmanship** [wʌnˈʌpmənʃɪp] N **that's just a form of ~** damit will er/sie den anderen nur um eine Nasenlänge voraus sein; **one-way** ADJ **(a)** traffic etc in einer Richtung; **~ street** Einbahnstraße f; **~ system** System nt von Einbahnstraßen; **~ ticket** (US Rail) einfache Fahrkarte; **~ trip** einfache Fahrt **(b)** mirror, glass von einer Seite durchsichtig; **one-woman** ADJ Einfrau-; **~ show** Einfraushow f

ongoing [ˈɒŋgəʊɪŋ] ADJ research, project laufend; (= long-term, continuing) development, relationship andauernd; **~ crisis** Dauerkrise f; **this is an ~ situation** diese Situation ist von Dauer

onion [ˈʌnjən] N Zwiebel f

onion: **onion ring** N (Cook) Zwiebelring m; **onion soup** N Zwiebelsuppe f

on line [ɒnˈlaɪn] (Comput) **1** ADJ PRED online **2** ADV on line; **to go ~** auf Onlinebetrieb schalten

on-line [ˈɒnlaɪn] ADJ ATTR (Comput) Online-

onlooker [ˈɒnlʊkəʳ] N Zuschauer(in) m(f)

only [ˈəʊnlɪ] **1** ADJ ATTR einzige(r, s); **he's an/my ~ child** er ist ein Einzelkind nt/mein einziges Kind; **the ~ one** or **person** der/ die Einzige; **the ~ ones** or **people** die Einzigen; **he was the ~ one to leave** or **who left** er ist als Einziger gegangen; **the ~ thing** die Einzige; **the ~ thing I have against it is that ...** ich habe nur eins dagegen einzuwenden, nämlich, dass ...; **the ~ thing** or **problem is ...** nur ...; **my ~ wish/regret** das einzige, was ich mir wünsche/was ich bedaure **2** ADV nur; **it's ~ five o'clock** es ist erst fünf Uhr; **~ yesterday/ last week** erst gestern/letzte Woche; **I ~ hope he gets here in time** ich hoffe nur, dass er es noch rechtzeitig hier eintrifft; **you ~ have to ask** Sie brauchen nur zu fragen; **"members ~"** „(Zutritt) nur für Mitglieder"; **I'd be ~ too pleased to help** ich würde nur zu gerne helfen; **if ~ that hadn't happened** wenn das nur nicht passiert wäre; **we ~ just caught the train** wir haben den Zug gerade noch gekriegt; **he has ~ just arrived** er ist gerade erst angekommen; **not ~ ... but also ...** nicht nur ..., sondern auch ... **3** CONJ bloß, nur; **I would do it myself, ~ I haven't time** ich würde es selbst machen, ich habe nur keine Zeit

on-message ADJ (esp Pol) auf Linie

ono ABBR **of or near(est) offer**

on-off switch [ˈɒnˈɒfswɪtʃ] N Ein- und Ausschalter m

onomatopoeia [ˌɒnəʊmætəʊˈpiːə] N Lautmalerei f

onrush [ˈɒnrʌʃ] N (of people) Ansturm m; (of water) Schwall m

on-screen [ˈɒnskriːn] **1** ADJ **(a)** (Comput) auf dem Bildschirm; **~ display** Bildschirmanzeige f **(b)** romance, kiss etc (TV) Bildschirm-; (Film) Film- **2** ADV [ɒnˈskriːn] (Film) auf der Leinwand; (TV, Comput) auf dem Bildschirm

onset [ˈɒnset] N Beginn m; (of illness) Ausbruch m; **with the ~ of old age he ...** als er alt zu werden begann ...

onshore ['ɒnʃɔːʳ] **1** ADJ an Land; *oilfield, job* auf dem Festland; **~ wind** Seewind *m* **2** [ɒnʃɔːʳ] ADV (*also* **on shore**) an Land; (*= on the mainland*) auf dem Festland

onside [ɒnsaɪd] ADV (*Ftbl*) nicht im Abseits; **to keep sb ~** (*fig*) jdn auf seiner Seite behalten

on-site [ɒnsaɪt] ADJ vor Ort

onslaught ['ɒnslɔːt] N (*Mil, fig*) Angriff (*on auf +acc*); **to make an ~ on sb/sth** (*fig*) (*verbally*) jdn/etw angreifen

on-the-job training ['ɒnðəˌdʒɒb'treɪnɪŋ] N Ausbildung *f* am Arbeitsplatz

on-the-spot [ˌɒnðə'spɒt] ADJ *fine* an Ort und Stelle verhängt; *decision, diagnosis, investigation* an Ort und Stelle; *reporting, coverage* vom Ort des Geschehens

onto ['ɒntu] PREP **(a)** (*= upon, on top of*) auf (*+acc*); (*on sth vertical*) an (*+acc*); **to clip sth ~ sth** etw an etw (*acc*) anklemmen; **to get ~ the committee** in den Ausschuss kommen **(b)** (*in verbal expressions, see also vb +on*) **to come ~ the market** auf den Markt kommen; **when will you get ~ the next chapter?** wann kommen Sie zum nächsten Kapitel?; **to be ~ or on to sb** (*= find sb out*) jdm auf die Schliche gekommen sein (*inf*); (*police*) jdm auf der Spur sein; **I think we're ~ something** ich glaube, hier sind wir auf etwas gestoßen

onus ['əʊnəs] N, NO PL Pflicht *f*; (*= burden*) Last *f*; **to shift the ~ for sth onto sb** jdm die Verantwortung für etw zuschieben; **the ~ to do it is on him** *or* **lies with him** es liegt an ihm, das zu tun

onward ['ɒnwəd] **1** ADJ *of* **flight** Anschlussflug *m*; **~ journey** Weiterreise *f* **2** ADV (*also* **~s**) vorwärts; *march* weiter; **from today/this time ~** von heute/der Zeit an

onyx ['ɒnɪks] **1** N Onyx *m* **2** ADJ Onyx-

oodles ['uːdlz] PL (*inf*) **~ (of)** jede Menge (*inf*); **~ (and ~) of money** Geld wie Heu (*inf*); **~ (and ~) of time** massenhaft Zeit (*inf*)

oomph [ʊmf] N (*inf: = energy*) Pep *m* (*inf*)

ooze [uːz] **1** N Schlamm *m* **2** VI (*lit*) triefen; (*wound*) nässen; (*resin, mud, glue*) (heraus)quellen **3** VT **(a)** *blood* triefen von; **my shoes were oozing water** das Wasser quoll mir aus den Schuhen **(b)** (*fig*) *charm* triefen von (*pej*), verströmen; *confidence, sex appeal* strotzen von

➤ **ooze out** VI herausquellen; (*water, blood etc*) heraussickern

op [ɒp] N (*inf*) = **operation**

opal ['əʊpəl] **1** N Opal *m* **2** ADJ Opal-

opaque [əʊ'peɪk] ADJ **(a)** opak; *liquid* trüb; *paper, glass* undurchsichtig; *tights, stockings* blickdicht **(b)** (*fig*) *prose, text* undurchsichtig

op cit [ɒp'sɪt] ABBR *of* **opere citato** op. cit.

OPEC ['əʊpek] ABBR *of* **Organization of Petroleum Exporting Countries** OPEC *f*

open ['əʊpən] **1** ADJ **(a)** offen; (*= ~ for business*) geöffnet; *lines of communication, view, river* frei (*to* für); (*Mus*) *string* leer; (*= public*) *meeting, trial* öffentlich; **to keep/hold the door ~** die Tür offen lassen/halten; **a shirt ~ at the neck** ein am Hals offenes Hemd; **the baker/baker's shop is ~** der Bäcker/Bäckerladen hat geöffnet; **in the ~ air** im Freien; **on ~ ground** auf offenem *or* freiem Gelände; **~ to traffic/shipping** für den Verkehr/die Schifffahrt freigegeben; **"road ~ to traffic"** „Durchfahrt frei"; **to be ~ to sb** (*competition, membership, possibility*) jdm offen stehen; (*place*) für jdn geöffnet sein; (*park*) jdm zur Verfügung stehen; **in ~ court** (*Jur*) in öffentlicher Verhandlung; **~ to the public** der Öffentlichkeit zugänglich; **she gave us an ~ invitation to visit** sie lud uns ein, jederzeit bei ihr vorbeizukommen; **to be ~ to suggestions/ideas** Vorschlägen/Ideen gegenüber offen sein; **I'm ~ to persuasion** ich lasse mich gern überreden; **I'm ~ to offers** ich lasse gern mit mir reden; **to keep one's options ~** es offen lassen; **to keep an ~ mind** alles offen lassen; **to have an ~ mind on sth** einer Sache (*dat*) aufgeschlossen gegenüberstehen; **to be ~ to debate** zur Debatte stehen **(b)** (*= officially in use*) *building* eingeweiht; *road, bridge* (offiziell) freigegeben; *exhibition* eröffnet **(c)** (*= exposed, not protected*) **to be ~ to criticism/attack** der Kritik/Angriffen ausgesetzt sein; **to lay oneself ~ to criticism/attack** sich der Kritik/Angriffen aussetzen; **to be ~ to abuse** sich leicht missbrauchen lassen; **to be ~ to doubt** anzweifelbar sein

2 N **in the ~** (*= outside*) im Freien; (*= on ~ ground*) auf freiem Feld; **to bring sth out into the ~** mit etw nicht länger hinterm Berg halten; **to come out into the ~** (*fig*) (*person*) Farbe bekennen; (*affair*) herauskommen

3 VT **(a)** öffnen; *also Med* **to ~ one's heart to sb** sich jdm eröffnen (*geh*); **~ your mind to new possibilities** öffnen Sie sich (*dat*) den Blick für neue Möglichkeiten; **to ~ the bowels** (*medicine*) abführen **(b)** (*officially*) *exhibition* eröffnen; *building* einweihen; *motorway* (für den Verkehr) freigeben **(c)** *case, trial, account, shop* eröffnen; *debate, conversation etc* beginnen; *school* einrichten; **to ~ fire** (*Mil*) das Feuer eröffnen (*on auf +acc*)

4 VI **(a)** aufgehen; (*eyes, door, flower, book, wound, window*) sich öffnen; **I can't get the box/bottle to ~** ich habe die Schachtel/Flasche nicht aufbekommen **(b)** (*shop, museum*) öffnen **(c)** (*= afford access: door*) führen (*into* in +acc) **(d)** (*= start*) beginnen; (*Cards, Chess*) eröffnen; **the play ~s next week** das Stück wird ab nächster Woche gegeben

➤ **open on to** VI +PREP OBJ (*window, door*) gehen auf (*+acc*)

➤ **open out 1** VI **(a)** (*= become wider*) (*river, street*) sich verbreitern (*into* zu); (*view*) sich weiten **(b)** (*map*) sich ausfalten lassen **2** VT SEP *map, newspaper etc* auseinander falten

➤ **open up 1** VI **(a)** (*fig*) (*prospects*) sich eröffnen; (*field, new horizons*) sich erschließen **(b)** (*= become expansive*) gesprächiger werden; **to get sb to open up** jdn zum Reden bringen **(c)** (*= unlock doors: of house, shop etc*) aufschließen; **open up!** aufmachen! **2** VT SEP **(a)** (*= make accessible*) *territory, mine, prospects, new horizons etc* erschließen; **to open up a country to trade** ein Land für den Handel erschließen **(b)** (*= unlock*) *house, shop, car etc* aufschließen **(c)** (*= start*) *business, shop* eröffnen

open: **open-air** ADJ im Freien; **open-air concert** N Freilichtkonzert *nt*; **open-air swimming pool** N Freibad *nt*; **open-air theatre**, (*US*) **open-air theater** N Freilichtbühne *f*; **open-and-shut** ADJ **it's an ~ case** es ist ein glasklarer Fall; **open cheque** N (*Brit*) Barscheck *m*; **open day** N (*Brit*) Tag *m* der offenen Tür; **open-door** ADJ **~ policy** Politik *f* der offenen Tür; **open-ended** ADJ (*fig*) *contract* zeitlich nicht begrenzt; *offer, commitment* unbegrenzt; *discussion* alles offen lassend *attr*; **open enrollment** N (*US Univ*) Einschreibung ohne Zulassungsvoraussetzungen

opener ['əʊpnəʳ] N Öffner *m*

open: **open-face sandwich** N (*US*) belegtes Brot; **open-heart surgery** N Eingriff *m* am offenen Herzen; **open house** N **to keep ~** ein offenes Haus führen

opening ['əʊpnɪŋ] **1** N **(a)** Öffnung *f*; (*in traffic stream*) Lücke *f*; (*= forest clearing*) Lichtung *f*; (*fig: in conversation*) Anknüpfungspunkt *m* **(b)** (*= beginning, initial stages*) Anfang *m*; (*Chess, Cards*) Eröffnung *f* **(c)** (*= official ~*) Eröffnung *f*; (*of motorway*) Freigabe *f* (für den Verkehr); **Opening of Parliament** Parlamentseröffnung *f* **(d)** (*= opportunity*) Möglichkeit *f*; (*= job vacancy*) (freie) Stelle **2** ATTR (*= initial, first*) erste(r, s); *remarks* einführend; **~ speech** Eröffnungsrede *f*

opening: **opening ceremony** N Eröffnungsfeierlichkeiten *pl*; **opening hours** PL Öffnungszeiten *pl*; **opening night** N Eröffnungsvorstellung *f* (am Abend); **opening price** N (*St Ex*) Eröffnungskurs *m*; **opening time** N Öffnungszeit *f*; **what are the bank's ~s?** wann hat die Bank geöffnet?

openly ['əʊpənli] ADV offen; (*= publicly*) öffentlich; **he was ~ gay** er machte keinen Hehl aus seiner Homosexualität

open: **open-minded** ADJ aufgeschlossen; **open-mouthed** [ˌəʊpn'maʊðd] ADJ (*in surprise or stupidity*) mit offenem Mund; **open-necked** ADJ *shirt* mit offenem Kragen

openness ['əʊpnnɪs] N Offenheit *f*, Aufrichtigkeit *f*

open: **open-plan** ADJ ~ **office** Großraumbüro *nt*; **open sandwich** N (*Brit*) belegtes Brot; **Open University** N (*Brit*) Fernuniversität *f*; **to do an ~ course** ein Fernstudium machen *or* absolvieren

opera ['ɒpərə] N Oper *f*; **to go to the ~** in die Oper gehen

operable ['ɒpərəbl] ADJ (*Med*) operabel

opera IN CPDS Opern-; **opera company** N Opernensemble *nt*; **opera glasses** PL Opernglas *nt*; **opera house** N Opernhaus *nt*; **opera singer** N Opernsänger(in) *m(f)*

operate ['ɒpəreɪt] **1** VI (a) (*machine, mechanism*) funktionieren; (= *be powered*) betrieben werden (*by, on* mit); (= *be in operation*) laufen; **to ~ at maximum capacity** (*lit, fig*) Höchstleistung bringen
(b) (*theory, plan, law*) sich auswirken; (*organization, system*) arbeiten; **I don't understand how his mind ~s** ich verstehe seine Gedankengänge nicht
(c) (= *carry on one's business*) operieren; (*airport, station*) in Betrieb sein; **I don't like the way he ~s** ich mag seine Methoden nicht
(d) (*Med*) operieren (*on sb/sth* jdn/etw); **to be ~d on** operiert werden; **he ~d on him for appendicitis/a cataract** er operierte ihn am Blinddarm/auf grauen Star
2 VT (a) (*person*) *machine, switchboard etc* bedienen; (= *set in operation*) in Betrieb setzen; *brakes etc* betätigen; (*lever, button etc*) betätigen; (*electricity, batteries etc*) betreiben
(b) (= *manage*) *business* führen
(c) *system, law, policy* anwenden

operatic [ɒpə'rætɪk] ADJ Opern-

operatics [ɒpə'rætɪks] N SING (*amateur*) ~ Amateuropern *pl*

operating ['ɒpəreɪtɪŋ] ADJ ATTR (a) (*Tech, Comm*) Betriebs-; ~ **costs** *or* **expenses** Betriebsausgaben *pl*, betriebliche Aufwendungen *pl*; ~ **profit** Betriebsgewinn *m*; ~ **statement** (*US*) Gewinn- und Verlustrechnung *f* (b) (*Med*) Operations-

operating: **operating room** N (*US Med*) Operationssaal *m*; **operating system** N (*Comput*) Betriebssystem *nt*; **operating theatre** N (*Brit Med*) Operationssaal *m*

operation [ɒpə'reɪʃən] N (a) **to be in ~** (*machine*) in Betrieb sein; (*law*) in Kraft sein; (*plan*) durchgeführt werden; **to come into ~** (*law*) in Kraft treten; (*plan*) zur Anwendung gelangen; **to put a law into ~** ein Gesetz in Kraft setzen
(b) (*Med*) Operation *f* (*on an +dat*); **to have an ~** operiert werden; **to have a heart ~** sich einer Herzoperation unterziehen; **to have an ~ for a hernia** wegen eines Bruchs operiert werden
(c) (= *enterprise, Math, Mil*) Operation *f*; (= *task, stage in undertaking*) Arbeitsgang *m*; (= *campaign: in police force etc*) Einsatz *m*; **Operation Cynthia** Operation Cynthia; **(business)** ~**s** Geschäfte *pl*; **to cease/resume** ~**s** den Geschäftsverkehr einstellen/wieder aufnehmen

operational [ɒpə'reɪʃənl] ADJ (a) (= *ready for use or action*) *machine, vehicle* betriebsbereit; *army unit, aeroplane, tank etc* einsatzbereit; (= *in use or action*) *machine, vehicle, airport* in Betrieb; *army unit etc* im Einsatz (b) (= *relating to operation*) (*Tech, Comm*) Betriebs-; (*Mil*) Einsatz-; *problems, duties* operativ; ~ **costs** Betriebskosten *pl*

operations room [ɒpə'reɪʃənz'ruːm] N (*Mil, Police*) Hauptquartier *nt*

operative ['ɒpərətɪv] **1** ADJ *measure, laws* wirksam; *law* geltend; *plan, system, service* operativ; **"if" being the ~ word** wobei „wenn" das entscheidende Wort ist **2** N (*of machinery*) Maschinenarbeiter(in) *m(f)*; (= *spy*) Agent(in) *m(f)*; (*US Pol*: = *campaign worker*) Parteiarbeiter(in) *m(f)*

operator ['ɒpəreɪtə'] N (a) (*Telec*) Vermittlung *f*; **a call through the ~** ein handvermitteltes Gespräch
(b) (*of machinery*) (Maschinen)arbeiter(in) *m(f)*; (*of electrical equipment*) Bediener(in) *m(f)*; (*of computer etc*) Operator(in) *m(f)*; **lathe** *etc* ~ Arbeiter(in) *m(f)* an der Drehbank *etc*

(c) (= *private company*) Unternehmen *nt*; (= *company owner*) Unternehmer(in) *m(f)*; (*Fin*) (Börsen)makler(in) *m(f)*; (= *tour* ~) Veranstalter(in) *m(f)*
(d) (*inf*) **to be a smooth/clever ~** raffiniert vorgehen

operetta [ɒpə'retə] N Operette *f*

ophthalmic [ɒf'θælmɪk] ADJ Augen-

ophthalmic surgeon N Augenchirurg(in) *m(f)*

ophthalmologist [ɒfθæl'mɒlədʒɪst] N Ophthalmologe *m*, Ophthalmologin *f*

opinion [ə'pɪnjən] N Meinung *f* (*about, on* zu); (*political, religious*) Anschauung *f*; (= *professional advice*) Gutachten *nt*; (*esp Med*) Befund *m*; **in my ~** meiner Meinung nach; **in the ~ of the experts** nach Ansicht der Experten; **to be of the ~ that ...** der Meinung *or* Ansicht sein, dass ...; **to ask sb's ~** jdn nach seiner Meinung fragen; **it is a matter of ~** das ist Ansichtssache; **to have a good** *or* **high/low** *or* **poor ~ of sb/sth** eine gute/schlechte Meinung von jdm/etw haben; **it is the ~ of the court that ...** das Gericht ist zu der Auffassung gekommen, dass ...; **to seek** *or* **get a second ~** (*esp Med*) ein zweites Gutachten einholen

opinionated [ə'pɪnjəneɪtɪd] ADJ rechthaberisch

opinion: **opinion former, opinion maker** N Meinungsmacher(in) *m(f)*; **opinion poll** N Meinungsumfrage *f*

opium ['əʊpɪəm] N Opium *nt*

opossum [ə'pɒsəm] N Opossum *nt*

opponent [ə'pəʊnənt] N Gegner(in) *m(f)*

opportune ['ɒpətjuːn] ADJ *time* günstig; *remark* an passender Stelle; *action, event* rechtzeitig; **at an ~ moment** zu einem günstigen Zeitpunkt

opportunism [ɒpə'tjuːnɪzəm] N Opportunismus *m*

opportunist [ɒpə'tjuːnɪst] **1** N Opportunist(in) *m(f)* **2** ADJ opportunistisch; ~ **thief** Gelegenheitsdieb(in) *m(f)*

opportunity [ɒpə'tjuːnɪtɪ] N (a) Gelegenheit *f*; **at the first** *or* **earliest ~** bei der erstbesten Gelegenheit; **to take/seize the ~ to do sth** *or* **of doing sth** die Gelegenheit nutzen/ergreifen, etw zu tun; **as soon as I get the ~** sobald sich die Gelegenheit ergibt (b) (= *chance to better oneself*) Chance *f*; **opportunities for promotion** Aufstiegschancen *pl*; **equality of ~** Chancengleichheit *f*

opportunity cost N (*Econ*) Opportunitätskosten *pl*

oppose [ə'pəʊz] VT (a) (= *be against*) ablehnen; (= *fight against*) sich entgegensetzen (+*dat*); *leadership, orders, plans, sb's wishes* sich widersetzen (+*dat*); *government* sich stellen gegen; **he ~s our coming** er ist absolut dagegen, dass wir kommen (b) (= *stand in opposition*: *candidate*) kandidieren gegen

opposed [ə'pəʊzd] ADJ (a) PRED (= *hostile*) dagegen; **to be ~ to sb/sth** gegen jdn/etw sein; **I am ~ to your going away** ich bin dagegen, dass Sie gehen (b) **as ~ to** im Gegensatz zu

opposing [ə'pəʊzɪŋ] ADJ *team* gegnerisch; *army* feindlich; *views* gegensätzlich; **to be on ~ sides** auf entgegengesetzten Seiten stehen

opposite ['ɒpəzɪt] **1** ADJ entgegengesetzt (*to, from* +*dat*, zu); (= *facing*) gegenüberliegend *attr*; **to be ~** gegenüberliegen/-stehen/-sitzen *etc*; **on the ~ page** auf der gegenüberliegenden Seite; **in the ~ direction** in entgegengesetzter Richtung; **the ~ sex** das andere Geschlecht; **it had the ~ effect** es bewirkte das genaue Gegenteil
2 N Gegenteil *nt*; (= *contrast: of pair*) Gegensatz *m*; **quite the ~!** ganz im Gegenteil!
3 ADV gegenüber; **they sat ~** sie saßen uns/ihnen/sich *etc* gegenüber
4 PREP gegenüber (+*dat*); ~ **one another** sich gegenüber; **they live ~ us** sie wohnen uns gegenüber

opposite number N Pendant *nt*

opposition [ɒpə'zɪʃən] N (a) Opposition *f*; **to act in ~ to sth** einer Sache (*dat*) zuwiderhandeln; **without ~** widerstandslos; **the Opposition, Her Majesty's Opposition** (*esp Brit Parl*) die Opposition; **leader of the Opposition** Oppositionsführer(in) *m(f)* (b) (*Sport*) Gegner *pl*

oppress [ə'pres] VT (a) (= *tyrannize*) unterdrücken (b) (= *weigh down*) bedrücken; (*heat*) lasten auf (+*dat*); **the climate ~es me** das Klima macht mir schwer zu schaffen

oppression [ə'preʃən] N Unterdrückung *f*

oppressive [əˈpresɪv] ADJ **(a)** *regime, laws* repressiv; *taxes* (er)drückend **(b)** *(fig)* drückend; *thought, mood* bedrückend

oppressor [əˈpresəʳ] N Unterdrücker(in) *m(f)*

opprobrium [əˈprəʊbrɪəm] N (= *disgrace*) Schmach *f*; (= *scorn, reproach*) Schmähung *f*

opt [ɒpt] VI **to ~ for sth** sich für etw entscheiden; **to ~ to do sth** sich entscheiden, etw zu tun

➤ **opt in** VI beitreten (+*dat*)

➤ **opt out** VI sich anders entscheiden; (*of insurance scheme*) kündigen (*of* +*acc*); (*Brit: school, hospital*) aus der Kontrolle der Kommunalverwaltung austreten

optic [ˈɒptɪk], **optical** [ˈɒptɪkəl] ADJ optisch

optical: optical character reader N (*Comput*) optischer Klarschriftleser; **optical disk** N optische Platte; **optical fibre**, (*US*) **optical fiber** N (= *material*) Glasfaser *f*; (= *cable*) Glasfaserkabel *nt*; **optical illusion** N optische Täuschung

optician [ɒpˈtɪʃən] N Optiker(in) *m(f)*

optic nerve N Sehnerv *m*

optics [ˈɒptɪks] N SING Optik *f*

optimal [ˈɒptɪml] ADJ optimal

optimism [ˈɒptɪmɪzəm] N Optimismus *m*

optimist [ˈɒptɪmɪst] N Optimist(in) *m(f)*

optimistic [ˌɒptɪˈmɪstɪk] ADJ optimistisch; **to be ~ about sth** in Bezug auf etw (*acc*) optimistisch sein; **I'm not very ~ about it** da bin ich nicht sehr optimistisch

optimistically [ˌɒptɪˈmɪstɪkəlɪ] ADV optimistisch

optimize [ˈɒptɪmaɪz] VT optimieren

optimum [ˈɒptɪməm] ADJ optimal

option [ˈɒpʃən] N **(a)** (= *choice*) Wahl *f no pl*; (= *possible course of action*) Möglichkeit *f*; **you have the ~ of leaving or staying** Sie haben die Wahl, ob Sie gehen oder bleiben wollen; **to give sb the ~ of doing sth** jdm die Wahl lassen, etw zu tun; **I have little/no ~** mir bleibt kaum eine/keine andere Wahl; **he had no ~ but to come** ihm blieb nichts anderes übrig, als zu kommen; **to keep** *or* **leave one's ~s open** sich (*dat*) alle Möglichkeiten offen lassen

(b) (*Comm*) Option *f* (*on* auf +*acc*); (*on house, goods etc*) Vorkaufsrecht *nt* (*on* an +*dat*); (*on shares*) Bezugsrecht *nt* (*on* für); **with an ~ to buy** mit einer Kaufoption *or* (*on shares*) Bezugsoption; (= *on approval*) zur Ansicht

(c) (*Univ, Sch*) Wahlfach *nt*

optional [ˈɒpʃənl] ADJ (= *not compulsory*) freiwillig; (= *not basic*) *trim, mirror etc* auf Wunsch erhältlich; **"evening dress ~"** „Abendkleidung nicht Vorschrift"; **~ extras** Extras *pl*; **~ subject** (*Sch, Univ*) Wahlfach *nt*

optometrist [ɒpˈtɒmətrɪst] N (*US:* = *optician*) Optiker(in) *m(f)*

opt-out [ˈɒptaʊt] **1** ADJ ATTR **~ clause** Rücktrittsklausel *f* **2** N **(a)** (*Brit: by school, hospital*) Austritt *m* aus der Kontrolle der Kommunalverwaltung **(b)** (*from agreement, treaty*) Rücktritt *m*

opulence [ˈɒpjʊləns] N, NO PL Reichtum *m*; (*of clothes, building, room*) Prunk *m*; (*of décor, lifestyle*) Üppigkeit *f*

opulent [ˈɒpjʊlənt] ADJ reich; *clothes, building, room* prunkvoll; *décor, lifestyle* üppig

or [ɔːʳ] CONJ **(a)** oder; **he could not read or write** er konnte weder lesen noch schreiben; **in a day/month or two** in ein bis or oder zwei Tagen/Monaten **(b)** (= *that is*) (oder) auch; **Rhodesia, or rather, Zimbabwe** Rhodesien, beziehungsweise Simbabwe **(c)** (= *otherwise*) sonst; **you'd better go or (else) you'll be late** gehen Sie jetzt besser, sonst kommen Sie zu spät

oracle [ˈɒrəkl] N Orakel *nt*; (= *person*) Seher(in) *m(f)*; (*fig*) Alleswisser(in) *m(f)*

oracy [ˈɒrəsɪ] N mündliche Kommunikationsfähigkeit

oral [ˈɔːrəl] **1** ADJ **(a)** oral; *vaccine* oral verabreicht; *medicine* zum Einnehmen **(b)** (= *verbal*) mündlich; **to give ~ evidence to a committee** vor einer Kommission aussagen; **to improve one's ~ skills in a language** eine Sprache besser sprechen lernen **2** N Mündliche(s) *nt*

oral: oral history N mündliche Geschichtsdokumentation; **oral hygiene** N Mundhygiene *f*

orally [ˈɔːrəlɪ] ADV **(a)** oral **(b)** (= *verbally*) mündlich

oral sex N Oralverkehr *m*

orange [ˈɒrɪndʒ] **1** N **(a)** (= *fruit*) Orange *f*; (= *drink*) Orangensaft *m* **(b)** (= *colour*) Orange *nt* **2** ADJ **(a)** Orangen-;

~ flavour (*Brit*) *or* **flavor** (*US*) Orangengeschmack *m* **(b)** (*colour*) orange *inv*, orange(n)farben *or* -farbig

orange: orange juice N Orangensaft *m*; **Orange Order** N Oranierorden *m* (*protestantische Vereinigung, die den Namen Wilhelms von Oranien trägt*); **orange squash** N (*Brit*) Orangenkonzentrat *nt*; (*diluted*) Orangengetränk *nt*

orang-outang, orang-utan [ɔːˌræŋuːˈtæn, -n] N Orang-Utan *m*

oration [ɒˈreɪʃən] N Ansprache *f*; **funeral ~** Grabrede *f*

orator [ˈɒrətəʳ] N Redner(in) *m(f)*

oratory [ˈɒrətərɪ] N Redekunst *f*

orbit [ˈɔːbɪt] **1** N **(a)** (*Astron, Space*) (= *path*) Umlaufbahn *f*; (= *single circuit*) Umkreisung *f*; **to be in ~** ((a)round the earth) in der (Erd)umlaufbahn sein; **to go into ~** ((a)round the sun) in die (Sonnen)umlaufbahn eintreten **(b)** (*fig*) Kreis *m*; (= *sphere of influence*) Einflusssphäre *f* **2** VT umkreisen

orbital [ˈɔːbɪtl] N (*also* **~ motorway**) Ringautobahn *f*

orchard [ˈɔːtʃəd] N Obstgarten *m*; (*commercial*) Obstplantage *f*; **apple/cherry ~** Obstgarten *m* mit Apfel-/Kirschbäumen; (*commercial*) Apfel-/Kirschplantage *f*

orchestra [ˈɔːkɪstrə] N Orchester *nt*

orchestral [ɔːˈkestrəl] ADJ Orchester-; **~ music** Orchestermusik *f*

orchestra pit N Orchestergraben *m*

orchestrate [ˈɔːkɪstreɪt] VT orchestrieren

orchestrated [ˈɔːkɪstreɪtɪd] ADJ (*fig*) *attempt, campaign* gezielt; **a carefully ~ protest** eine sorgfältig organisierte Protestaktion

orchestration [ˌɔːkɪsˈtreɪʃən] N Orchestrierung *f*

orchid [ˈɔːkɪd] N Orchidee *f*

ordain [ɔːˈdeɪn] VT **(a)** *sb* ordinieren; (*Eccl*) *a priest* weihen **(b)** (= *destine, decree*) bestimmen; (*ruler*) verfügen

ordeal [ɔːˈdiːl] N Tortur *f*; (= *torment, emotional ~*) Qual *f*

order [ˈɔːdəʳ] **1** N **(a)** (= *sequence*) (Reihen)folge *f*; **are they in ~/in the right ~?** sind sie geordnet/in der richtigen Reihenfolge?; **in ~ of preference/merit** in der bevorzugten/in der ihren Auszeichnungen entsprechenden Reihenfolge; **to put sth in (the right) ~** etw ordnen; **to be in the wrong ~** *or* **out of ~** durcheinander sein; (*one item*) an eine falsche Stelle kommen

(b) (= *system, discipline*) Ordnung *f also Mil* **there's no ~ in his work** seiner Arbeit fehlt die Systematik; **it is in the ~ of things** es liegt in der Natur der Dinge; **his passport was in ~** sein Pass war in Ordnung; **to put one's affairs in ~** Ordnung in seine Angelegenheiten bringen; **to keep ~** die Ordnung wahren; **to keep the children in ~** die Kinder unter Kontrolle halten; **~, ~!** Ruhe!; **to be out of ~** (*at meeting etc*) gegen die Verfahrensordnung verstoßen; (*fig*) aus dem Rahmen fallen; **to call sb to ~** jdn ermahnen, sich an die Verfahrensordnung zu halten; **to call the meeting to ~** die Versammlung zur Ordnung rufen; **congratulations are in ~** Glückwünsche sind angebracht; **is it in ~ for me to go to Paris?** ist es in Ordnung, wenn ich nach Paris fahre?

(c) (= *working condition*) Zustand *m*; **to be out of/in ~** nicht funktionieren/funktionieren; **"out of ~"** „außer Betrieb"

(d) (= *command*) Befehl *m*; **I don't take ~s from anyone** ich lasse mir von niemandem befehlen; **to be under ~s to do sth** Instruktionen haben, etw zu tun; **until further ~s** bis auf weiteren Befehl

(e) (*in restaurant etc, Comm*) Bestellung *f*; (= *contract to manufacture or supply*) Auftrag *m*; **to place an ~ with sb** eine Bestellung bei jdm aufgeben/jdm einen Auftrag geben; **to be on ~** bestellt sein; **two ~s of French fries** (*esp US*) zwei Portionen Pommes frites; **made to ~** auf Bestellung (gemacht *or* hergestellt)

(f) (*Fin*) **pay to the ~ of** zahlbar an (+*acc*)

(g) **in ~ to do sth** um etw zu tun; **in ~ that** damit

(h) (*fig*: = *class, degree*) Art *f*; **something in the ~ of ten per cent** in der Größenordnung von zehn Prozent; **something in the ~ of one in ten applicants** etwa einer von zehn Bewerbern

(i) (*Eccl*: *of monks etc*) Orden *m*; **Benedictine ~** Benediktinerorden *m*

(j) orders PL (holy) **~s** (*Eccl*) Weihe *f*; (*of priesthood*) Priesterweihe *f*; **to take (holy) ~s** die Weihe empfangen **2** VT **(a)** (= *command, decree*) *sth* befehlen; (= *prescribe: doctor*) verordnen (*for sb* jdm); **to ~ sb to do sth** jdm befehlen *or* (*doctor*) verordnen, etw zu tun; (*esp Mil*) jdn dazu beordern, etw zu tun; **to ~ sb's arrest** jds Verhaftung anordnen; **he ~ed his gun to be brought (to him)** er ließ sich (*dat*) sein Gewehr bringen **(b)** (= *direct, arrange*) *one's affairs* ordnen **(c)** (*Comm etc*) *goods, dinner, taxi* bestellen; (*to be manufactured*) *ship, suit etc* in Auftrag geben (*from sb* bei jdm) **3** VI bestellen

➤ **order about** (*Brit*) *or* **around** VT SEP herumkommandieren **order**: **order book** N (*Comm*) Auftragsbuch *nt*; **the ~s are full** die Auftragsbücher sind voll; **order confirmation** Auftragsbestätigung *f*; **order form** N Bestellformular *nt*

orderly [ˈɔːdəlɪ] **1** ADJ **(a)** (= *tidy, methodical*) ordentlich; *person, mind* methodisch; **in an ~ fashion** *or* **manner** geordnet **(b)** *group, demonstration* friedlich **2** N **(medical)** ~ Pfleger(in) *m(f)*; (*Mil*) Sanitäter(in) *m(f)*

ordinal [ˈɔːdɪnl] N (*Math*) Ordinalzahl *f*

ordinal number N (*Math*) Ordnungszahl *f*, Ordinalzahl *f*

ordinarily [ˈɔːdnrɪlɪ] ADV gewöhnlich

ordinary [ˈɔːdnrɪ] **1** ADJ gewöhnlich; (= *average*) durchschnittlich; **the ~ Englishman** der normale Engländer; **this is no ~ car** dies ist kein gewöhnliches Auto **2** N **out of the ~** außergewöhnlich; **nothing/something out of the ~** nichts/etwas Außergewöhnliches

---

Be careful! **ordinary** *is not translated by the German word* **ordinär**.

---

ordinary share, ordinary stock N (*Fin*) Stammaktie *f*

ordination [ˌɔːdɪˈneɪʃən] N Ordination *f*

ordnance [ˈɔːdnəns] (*Mil*) N **(a)** (= *artillery*) (Wehr)material *nt* **(b)** (= *supply*) Versorgung *f*

Ordnance Survey map N (*Brit*) amtliche topografische Karte

ore [ɔːʳ] N Erz *nt*

oregano [ɒrɪˈɡɑːnəʊ] N Oregano *m*

organ [ˈɔːɡən] N **(a)** (*Anat*) (= *newspaper*) Organ *nt*; (= *mouthpiece of opinion*) Sprachrohr *nt* **(b)** (*Mus*) Orgel *f*; **to be at the ~** die Orgel spielen

organ donor N Organspender(in) *m(f)*

organic [ɔːˈɡænɪk] ADJ **(a)** (*Sci, Med, fig*) organisch **(b)** *vegetables, farming* biodynamisch; **~ wine/flour** Wein *m*/ Mehl *nt* aus biologisch kontrolliertem Anbau; **~ meat** Fleisch *nt* aus biologisch kontrollierter Zucht

organically [ɔːˈɡænɪkəlɪ] ADV *farm, grow* biodynamisch

organic: **organic chemistry** N organische Chemie; **organic farm** N Bio-Landwirtschaftsbetrieb *m*

organism [ˈɔːɡənɪzəm] N (*Biol, fig*) Organismus *m*

organist [ˈɔːɡənɪst] N Organist(in) *m(f)*

organization [ˌɔːɡənaɪˈzeɪʃən] N Organisation *f* (*also Pol*); (= *arrangement*) Ordnung *f*; (*of time*) Einteilung *f*; (*of essay*) Aufbau *m*; (*Comm*) Unternehmen *nt*

organizational [ˌɔːɡənaɪˈzeɪʃənəl] ADJ organisatorisch; **at an ~ level** im strukturellem Bereich

organize [ˈɔːɡənaɪz] VT (= *systematize*) ordnen; (= *arrange*) organisieren; *time* (*into teams, groups*) einteilen; *essay* aufbauen; *one's/sb's life* planen; *food, music for party etc* sorgen für; **to get (oneself) ~d** (= *get ready*) alles vorbereiten; (*to go out*) sich fertig machen; (*for term, holiday etc*) sich vorbereiten; (= *sort things out*) seine Sachen in Ordnung bringen; **to ~ things so that …** es so einrichten, dass …; **they ~d (it) for me to go to London** sie haben meine Londonreise arrangiert

organized [ˈɔːɡənaɪzd] ADJ organisiert; **he isn't very ~** bei ihm geht alles drunter und drüber (*inf*); **you have to be ~** du musst mit System vorgehen

organized labour, (*US*) **organized labor** N organisierte Arbeitnehmerschaft

organizer [ˈɔːɡənaɪzəʳ] N **(a)** Organisator(in) *m(f)*; (*of sports event*) Ausrichter(in) *m(f)* **(b)** = **personal organizer**

orgasm [ˈɔːɡæzəm] N Orgasmus *m*

orgy [ˈɔːdʒɪ] N (*lit, fig*) Orgie *f*; **drunken ~** Sauforgie *f*; **an ~ of killing** eine Blutorgie

orient [ˈɔːrɪənt] **1** N (*also* **Orient**) Orient *m* **2** VT = **orientate**

oriental [ˌɔːrɪˈentl] ADJ orientalisch; **~ rug** Orientteppich *m*

orientate [ˈɔːrɪənteɪt] **1** VR (*lit*) sich orientieren (*by an* +*dat, by the map* nach der Karte); (*fig also*) sich zurechtfinden **2** VT ausrichten (*towards* auf +*acc*); *thinking* orientieren (*towards*

an +*dat*); **money-~d** materiell ausgerichtet; **family-~d** familienorientiert

orientation [ˌɔːrɪənˈteɪʃən] N (*fig*) Orientierung *f*; (= *attitude*) Einstellung *f* (*towards* zu); (= *leaning*) Ausrichtung *f* (*towards* auf +*acc*); **sexual ~** sexuelle Orientierung

-oriented [ˈɔːrɪəntɪd] ADJ SUF -orientiert; **market-oriented** marktorientiert

orienteering [ˌɔːrɪənˈtɪərɪŋ] N Orientierungslauf *m*

orifice [ˈɒrɪfɪs] N Öffnung *f*

origami [ˌɒrɪˈɡɑːmɪ] N Origami *nt*

origin [ˈɒrɪdʒɪn] N Ursprung *m*; (*of person, family*) Herkunft *f*; **to have its ~ in sth** auf etw (*acc*) zurückgehen; **country of ~** Herkunftsland *nt*; **nobody knew the ~ of that story** niemand wusste, wie die Geschichte entstanden war

original [əˈrɪdʒɪnl] **1** ADJ **(a)** (= *first, earliest*) ursprünglich; **~ inhabitants of a country** Ureinwohner *pl* eines Landes; **~ version** (*of book, play*) Urfassung *f*; (*of film, song*) Originalversion *f*; **in the ~ German** im deutschen Originaltext **(b)** (= *not imitative*) *painting* original; *idea, writer, play* originell; **~ research** eigene Forschung **2** N Original *nt*; (*of model*) Vorlage *f*

originality [əˌrɪdʒɪˈnælɪtɪ] N Originalität *f*

originally [əˈrɪdʒənəlɪ] ADV ursprünglich

original sin N die Erbsünde

originate [əˈrɪdʒɪneɪt] **1** VT hervorbringen; *policy* ins Leben rufen; *product* erfinden; **who ~d the idea?** von wem stammt die Idee? **2** VI **(a)** entstehen; **to ~ from a country** aus einem Land stammen; **to ~ from** *or* **with sb** von jdm stammen **(b)** (*US: bus, train etc*) ausgehen (*in* von)

originator [əˈrɪdʒɪneɪtəʳ] N (*of plan, idea*) Urheber(in) *m(f)*; (*of product*) Erfinder(in) *m(f)*

Orkney Islands [ˈɔːknɪˈaɪləndz], **Orkneys** [ˈɔːknɪz] PL Orkneyinseln *pl*

ornament [ˈɔːnəmənt] N **(a)** (= *decorative object*) Verzierung *f*; (*on mantelpiece etc*) Ziergegenstand *m*; (*fig*) Zierde *f* (*to* +*gen*) **(b)** NO PL (= *ornamentation*) Ornamente *pl*; (= *decorative articles, on clothes etc*) Verzierungen *pl*; **by way of ~**, **for ~** zur Verzierung

ornamental [ˌɔːnəˈmentl] ADJ dekorativ; *detail* schmückend; **to be purely ~** zur Verzierung (da) sein; **~ garden/pond** Ziergarten *m*/-teich *m*

ornamentation [ˌɔːnəmenˈteɪʃən] N Verzierungen *pl*; (*Art, Archit*) Ornamentik *f*

ornate [ɔːˈneɪt] ADJ kunstvoll; (*of larger objects*) prunkvoll; *decoration* aufwändig; *language, style* umständlich (*pej*), reich

ornately [ɔːˈneɪtlɪ] ADV kunstvoll; *written* in reicher Sprache

ornithologist [ˌɔːnɪˈθɒlədʒɪst] N Ornithologe *m*, Ornithologin *f*

ornithology [ˌɔːnɪˈθɒlədʒɪ] N Ornithologie *f*

orphan [ˈɔːfən] **1** N Waisenkind *nt*; **the accident left him an ~** der Unfall machte ihn zum Waisenkind **2** VT zur Waise machen; **to be ~ed** zur Waise werden

orphanage [ˈɔːfənɪdʒ] N Waisenhaus *nt*

orthodontic [ˌɔːθəˈdɒntɪk] ADJ kieferorthopädisch

orthodox [ˈɔːθədɒks] ADJ (*Rel*) orthodox; **the Orthodox (Eastern) Church** die orthodoxe (Ost)kirche **(b)** (*fig*) konventionell; *view, method, approach etc* orthodox

orthodoxy [ˈɔːθədɒksɪ] N **(a)** (*fig*) Konventionalität *f*; (*of view, method, approach etc*) Orthodoxie *f* **(b)** (= *orthodox belief, practice etc*) orthodoxe Konvention

orthopaedic, (*US*) **orthopedic** [ˌɔːθəˈpiːdɪk] ADJ orthopädisch; **~ bed** orthopädisches Bett; **~ surgeon** orthopädischer Chirurg, orthopädische Chirurgin

OS ABBR *of* **outsize**

Oscar [ˈɒskəʳ] N (*Film*) Oscar *m*

oscillate [ˈɒsɪleɪt] VI (*Phys*) schwingen; (*compass needle etc, fig*) schwanken

osmosis [ɒzˈməʊsɪs] N Osmose *f*

ossify [ˈɒsɪfaɪ] **1** VT (*fig*) erstarren lassen; **to be ossified** erstarrt sein; **to become ossified** (*fig*) erstarren **2** VI (*fig*) erstarren

Ostend [ɒˈstend] N Ostende *nt*

ostensible ADJ, **ostensibly** ADV [ɒˈstensəbl, -ɪ] angeblich

ostentation [ˌɒstenˈteɪʃən] N (*of wealth etc*) Pomp *m*; (*of skills etc*) Großtuerei *f*

ostentatious [ˌɒstenˈteɪʃəs] ADJ **(a)** (= *pretentious*) pompös **(b)** (= *conspicuous*) ostentativ

ostentatiously [ˌɒstenˈteɪʃəslɪ] ADV **(a)** (= *pretentiously*) pompös; *live* auf großem Fuße **(b)** (= *conspicuously*) ostentativ

osteopath [ˈɒstɪəpæθ] N Osteopath(in) *m(f)*

ostracism [ˈɒstrəsɪzəm] N Ächtung *f*

ostracize [ˈɒstrəsaɪz] VT ächten

ostrich [ˈɒstrɪtʃ] N Strauß *m*

OT ABBR *of* **Old Testament** A. T. *nt*

other [ˈʌðəʳ] **1** ADJ, PRON andere(r, s); ~ **people** andere (Leute); **do you have any** ~ **questions?** haben Sie sonst noch Fragen?; **he had no** ~ **questions** er hatte sonst keine Fragen; **the man was none** ~ **than my father** der Mann war niemand anders als mein Vater; **the** ~ **day** neulich; **the** ~ **world** das Jenseits, jene andere Welt (*liter*); **some** ~ **time** (*in future*) ein andermal; (*in past*) ein anderes Mal; ~ **people's property** fremdes Eigentum; **every** ~ ... (= *alternate*) jede(r, s) zweite ...; ~ **than** (= *except*) außer (+*dat*); (= *different to*) anders als; **some time or** ~ irgendwann (einmal); **some writer/house** *etc* **or** ~ irgendein Schriftsteller/Haus *etc*; **he doesn't like hurting** ~**s** er mag niemandem wehtun; **there are 6** ~**s** da sind noch 6 (andere); **there were no** ~**s there** es waren sonst keine da; **something/someone or** ~ irgendetwas/-jemand; **can you tell one from the** ~? kannst du sie auseinander halten? **2** ADV **he could do no** ~ (**than come**) er konnte nicht anders (als kommen); **I've never seen her** ~ **than with her husband** ich habe sie immer nur mit ihrem Mann gesehen; **somehow or** ~ irgendwie; **somewhere or** ~ irgendwo

otherwise [ˈʌðəwaɪz] **1** ADV **(a)** (= *in a different way*) anders; **I am** ~ **engaged** (*form*) ich bin anderweitig beschäftigt; **except where** ~ **stated** (*form*) sofern nicht anders angegeben; **Richard I,** ~ (**known as**) **the Lionheart** Richard I., auch bekannt als Löwenherz; **you seem to think** ~ Sie scheinen anderer Meinung zu sein **(b)** (= *in other respects*) ansonsten **2** CONJ (= *or else*) sonst

otherworldly [ˌʌðəˈwɜːldlɪ] ADJ weltfern

OTT (*inf*) ABBR *of* **over the top**

otter [ˈɒtəʳ] N Otter *m*

ouch [aʊtʃ] INTERJ autsch

ought [ɔːt] V AUX **I** ~ **to do it** ich sollte *or* müsste es tun; **he** ~ **to have come** er hätte kommen sollen; ~ **I to go too?** – **yes, you** ~ **(to)/no, you** ~**n't (to)** sollte ich auch (hin)gehen? – ja doch/nein, das sollen Sie nicht; ~**n't you to have left by now?** hätten Sie nicht schon gehen müssen?; **you** ~ **to see that film** den Film sollten Sie sehen; **you** ~ **to have seen his face** sein Gesicht hätten Sie sehen müssen; **she** ~ **to have been a teacher** sie hätte Lehrerin werden sollen; **he** ~ **to win the race** er müsste (eigentlich) das Rennen gewinnen; **he** ~ **to have left by now** er müsste inzwischen gegangen sein; **... and I** ~ **to know!** ... und ich muss es doch wissen!

ounce [aʊns] N Unze *f*; **there's not an** ~ **of truth in it** daran ist kein Fünkchen Wahrheit; **if he had an** ~ **of sense** wenn er nur einen Funken Verstand hätte

our [aʊəʳ] POSS ADJ unser; **Our Father** (*in prayer*) Vater unser; *see also* **my**

ours [aʊəz] POSS PRON unsere(r, s); *see also* **mine**

ourselves [aʊəˈselvz] PERS PRON (*dir, indir obj* +*prep*) uns; (*emph*) selbst; *see also* **myself**

oust [aʊst] VT herausbekommen; *government* absetzen; *politician, colleague etc* ausbooten (*inf*); (= *take place of*) verdrängen; **to** ~ **sb from office/his position** jdn aus seinem Amt/seiner Stellung entfernen *or* (*by intrigue*) hinausmanövrieren; **to** ~ **sb from power** jdn von der Macht verdrängen

out [aʊt] **1** ADV **(a)** (= *not in container, car etc*) außen; (= *not in building, room, prison*) draußen; (*indicating motion*) (*seen from inside*) hinaus; (*seen from outside*) heraus; **to be** ~ weg sein; (*when visitors come*) nicht da sein; **they are** ~ **fishing/shopping** sie sind zum Fischen/Einkaufen (gegangen); **she was** ~ **all night** sie war die ganze Nacht weg; **it's cold** ~ **here/there** es ist kalt hier/dort draußen; **you go!** hinaus mit dir! *inf* **at weekends I like to be** ~ **and about** an den Wochenenden will ich (immer) raus; **we had a day** ~ **at the beach/in London** wir haben einen Tag am Meer/in London verbracht; **the journey** ~ die Hinreise; (*seen from destination*) die Herfahrt; **the book is** ~ (*from library*) das Buch ist ausgeliehen; **the workers are** ~ (= *on strike*) die Arbeiter streiken; **school is** ~ die Schule ist aus; **the tide is** ~ es ist Ebbe; **their secret was** ~ ihr Geheimnis war herausgekommen; **the truth will** ~ die Wahrheit will heraus; ~ **with it!** heraus damit!; **before the day/month is/was** ~ vor Ende des Tages/Monats **(b)** (*indicating distance*) **when he was** ~ **in Persia** als er in Persien war; **to go** ~ **to China** nach China fahren; **Wilton Street? isn't that** ~ **your way?** Wilton Street? ist das nicht da (hinten) bei euch in der Gegend?; **the boat was ten miles** ~ das Schiff war zehn Meilen weit draußen **(c) to be** ~ (*sun*) (he)raus sein; (*stars, moon*) am Himmel sein; (*flowers*) blühen; (= *be published*) herausgekommen sein; **when will it be** ~? (= *be published*) wann kommt es heraus?; **there's a warrant** ~ **for him** *or* **for his arrest** es besteht Haftbefehl gegen ihn **(d)** (*light, fire*) (*Sport*) aus; (*dirt, stain etc*) (he)raus; (= *not in fashion*) aus der Mode, passé, out (*inf*); (= ~ *of the question*) ausgeschlossen; **to be** ~ (= *unconscious*) bewusstlos sein **(e) he was** ~ **in his calculations, his calculations were** ~ er hatte sich in seinen Berechnungen geirrt; **you're not far** ~ Sie haben es fast (getroffen); **we were £5/20%** ~ wir hatten uns um £ 5/20% verrechnet *or* vertan (*inf*) **(f) to be** ~ **for sth** auf etw (*acc*) aus sein; **to be** ~ **for a good time** sich amüsieren wollen; **he's** ~ **for all he can get** er will haben, was er nur bekommen kann; **he's** ~ **to get her** er ist hinter ihr her; **he's just** ~ **to make money** ihm geht es nur um Geld **2** N **(a)** *see* **in (b)** (*esp US inf*: = *way* ~) Hintertürchen *nt* **3** PREP aus (+*dat*); **to go** ~ **the door/window** zur Tür/zum Fenster hinausgehen; *see also* **out of 4** VT homosexual outen

out- PREF WITH VBS **to** ~**-dance** *etc* **sb** jdn im Tanzen *etc* übertreffen

out-and-out [ˈaʊtənˈaʊt] ADJ *liar, lie, fool* ausgemacht; *racist, fascist* eingefleischt; *winner, success* überragend; *defeat* total; **he is an** ~ **revolutionary/conservative** er ist ein Revolutionär durch und durch/ein Erzkonservativer

outback [ˈaʊtbæk] N (*in Australia*) **the** ~ das Hinterland

out: outbid *pret, ptp* **outbid** VT überbieten; **outboard** ADJ ~ **motor** Außenbordmotor *m*; **outbound** ADJ *ship* auslaufend; ~ **flight/journey** Hinflug *m*/-reise *f*

outbreak [ˈaʊtbreɪk] N Ausbruch *m*; **if there should be an** ~ **of fire** wenn ein Feuer ausbricht

outbuilding [ˈaʊtbɪldɪŋ] N Nebengebäude *nt*

outburst [ˈaʊtbɜːst] N Ausbruch *m*; ~ **of temper** *or* **anger** Wutanfall *m*

outcast [ˈaʊtkɑːst] N Ausgestoßene(r) *mf*; **social** ~ gesellschaftlicher Außenseiter, gesellschaftliche Außenseiterin

outclass [aʊtˈklɑːs] VT in den Schatten stellen

outcome [ˈaʊtkʌm] N Ergebnis *nt*; **what was the** ~? was ist dabei herausgekommen?

outcrop [ˈaʊtkrɒp] N (*Geol*) **an** ~ (**of rock**) eine Felsnase

outcry [ˈaʊtkraɪ] N Aufschrei *m* der Empörung (*against* über +*acc*); (= *public protest*) Protestwelle *f* (*against* gegen); **to cause an** ~ **against sb/sth** zu lautstarkem Protest gegen jdn/ etw führen

out: outdated ADJ *idea, theory* überholt; *technology, equipment, method, word, style, custom* veraltet; *image, concept, practice* überkommen; **outdid** PRET *of* **outdo**; **outdistance** VT hinter sich (*dat*) lassen

outdo [aʊtˈduː], *pret* **outdid** [aʊtˈdɪd], *ptp* **outdone** [aʊtˈdʌn] VT übertreffen (*sb in sth* jdn an etw *dat*); **but Jimmy was not to be** ~**ne** aber Jimmy wollte da nicht zurückstehen

outdoor [ˈaʊtdɔːʳ] ADJ ~ **café** Café *nt* im Freien; (*in street*) Straßencafé *nt*; ~ **clothes** Kleidung *f* für draußen; ~ **shoes** Straßenschuhe *pl*; ~ **market** Markt *m* im Freien; (*in street*) Straßenmarkt *m*; ~ **swimming pool** Freibad *nt*

outdoors [ˈaʊtˈdɔːz] **1** ADV im Freien; **to go** ~ nach draußen gehen **2** N **the great** ~ (*hum*) die freie Natur

outer [ˈaʊtəʳ] ADJ ATTR äußere(r, s); ~ **office** (= *reception area*) Vorzimmer *nt*

Outer London N die Peripherie Londons

outermost [ˈaʊtəməʊst] ADJ äußerste(r, s)

outer space N der Weltraum

outfit ['aʊtfɪt] N **(a)** (= *clothes*) Kleidung f; (*Fashion*) Ensemble nt; (= *fancy dress*) Kostüm nt **(b)** (*inf*) (= *organization*) Verein m (*inf*); (*Mil*) Einheit f

out: outflank VT **(a)** (*Mil*) umfassen, von der Flanke/den Flanken angreifen **(b)** (*fig*: = *outwit*) überlisten; **outflow** N (= *act*) (*of water etc*) Ausfluss m; (*of money, capital*) Abfluss m; (*of refugees*) Strom m; **outfox** VT überlisten; **outgo** N (*US*) Ausgabe(n) f(pl)

outgoing ['aʊt'gəʊɪŋ] **1** ADJ **(a)** *office holder* scheidend; *flight* hinausgehend; *call, shipment* abgehend **(b)** *personality* kontaktfreudig **2** PL ~s Ausgaben pl

outgrow [aʊt'grəʊ], *pret* **outgrew** [aʊt'gruː], *ptp* **outgrown** [aʊt'grəʊn] VT **(a)** *clothes* herauswachsen aus **(b)** *habit* entwachsen (+*dat*); **he has ~n such childish pastimes** über solche Kindereien ist er hinaus

outhouse ['aʊthaʊs] N Seitengebäude nt

outing ['aʊtɪŋ] N **(a)** Ausflug m; **school's/firm's ~** Schul-/Betriebsausflug m; **to go on an ~** einen Ausflug machen **(b)** (*of homosexual*) Outen nt

outlandish [aʊt'lændɪʃ] ADJ absonderlich; *prose, style, description etc* eigenwillig; *name, clothes, appearance etc* ausgefallen; *theory* obskur

outlast [aʊt'lɑːst] VT (*thing*) länger halten als; (*idea etc*) überdauern

outlaw ['aʊtlɔː] **1** N Geächtete(r) mf; (*in Western etc*) Bandit m **2** VT ächten; *newspaper, action etc* verbieten

outlay ['aʊtleɪ] N (Kosten)aufwand m; (*recurring, continuous*) Kosten pl; **the initial ~** die anfänglichen Aufwendungen; **capital ~** Kapitalaufwand m

outlet ['aʊtlet] N **(a)** (*for water etc*) Abfluss m; (*for steam etc*) Abzug m; (*of river*) Ausfluss m **(b)** (*Comm*) Absatzmarkt m; (= *merchant*) Abnehmer(in) m(f); (= *shop*) Verkaufsstelle f **(c)** (*fig*) (*for talents etc*) Betätigungsmöglichkeit f; (*for emotion*) Ventil nt

outline ['aʊtlaɪn] **1** N **(a)** (*of objects*) Umriss m; (= *line itself*) Umrisslinie f; (= *silhouette*) Silhouette f; (*of face*) Züge pl; **he drew the ~ of a head** er zeichnete einen Kopf im Umriss **(b)** (*fig*: = *summary*) Abriss m; **just give (me) the broad ~s** umreißen Sie es (mir) grob **2** VT **(a)** **the mountain was ~d against the sky** die Umrisse des Berges zeichneten sich gegen den Himmel ab **(b)** (= *give summary of*) umreißen

outlive [aʊt'lɪv] VT *person* überleben; **to have ~d one's/its usefulness** ausgedient haben; (*method, system*) sich überlebt haben

outlook ['aʊtlʊk] N **(a)** (= *view*) Aussicht f (*over* über +*acc, on to* auf +*acc*) **(b)** (= *prospects, Met*) Aussichten pl **(c)** (= *mental attitude*) Einstellung f; **his ~ (up)on life** seine Lebensauffassung; **narrow ~** beschränkter Horizont

out: outlying ADJ (= *distant*) entlegen; (= *outside the town boundary*) umliegend; **~ district** (*of town*) Außenbezirk m; **outmanoeuvre,** (*US*) **outmaneuver** VT (*fig*) ausmanövrieren; **outmoded** ADJ altmodisch; *technology* veraltet

outnumber [aʊt'nʌmbə'] VT zahlenmäßig überlegen sein (+*dat*); **we were ~ed (by them)** wir waren (ihnen) zahlenmäßig unterlegen

out of PREP **(a)** (= *outside, away from*) (*position*) nicht in (+*dat*); (*motion*) aus (+*dat*); (*fig*) außer (+*dat*); **I'll be ~ town all week** ich werde die ganze Woche (über) nicht in der Stadt sein; **to go/be ~ the country** außer Landes gehen/sein; **he went ~ the door** er ging zur Tür hinaus; **to look ~ the window** aus dem Fenster sehen; **I saw him ~ the window** ich sah ihn durchs Fenster; **to keep ~ the sun** nicht in die Sonne gehen; **danger/sight** außer Gefahr/Sicht; **he's ~ the tournament** er ist aus dem Turnier ausgeschieden; **he feels ~ it** (*inf*) er fühlt sich ausgeschlossen; **he lives 10 miles ~ London** er wohnt 10 Meilen außerhalb Londons; **you're well ~ it** (*inf*) so ist es besser für dich

(b) (*cause, motive, origins*) aus (+*dat*); **~ curiosity** aus Neugier; **to drink ~ a glass** aus einem Glas trinken; **made ~ silver** aus Silber (gemacht)

(c) (= *from among*) von (+*dat*); **in seven cases ~ ten** in sieben von zehn Fällen; **he picked one ~ the pile** er nahm einen aus dem Stapel (heraus)

(d) (= *without*) **we are ~ money/bread** wir haben kein Geld/Brot mehr

out: out-of-court ADJ *settlement* außergerichtlich; **out-of-date** ADJ ATTR, **out of date** ADJ PRED **(a)** *methods, technology, ideas, customs* veraltet; *clothes, records* altmodisch **(b)** (= *expired*) *ticket* abgelaufen; *food, medicine* mit abgelaufenem Verfallsdatum; **out-of-doors** ADV = **outdoors; out-of-pocket** ADJ ATTR, **out of pocket** ADJ PRED (*Brit*) **~ expenses** Barauslagen pl; **to be out of pocket** draufzahlen; **I was £5 out of pocket** ich habe £ 5 aus eigener Tasche bezahlt; **out-of-the-way** ADJ ATTR, **out of the way** ADJ PRED (= *remote*) *spot* abgelegen; (= *unusual*) *theory* ungewöhnlich; **out-of-town** ADJ *shopping centre, cinema* außerstädtisch; **out-of-towner** N (*esp US*) Auswärtige(r) mf; **outpace** VT schneller sein als; **outpatient** N ambulanter Patient, ambulante Patientin; **~s' (department)** Ambulanz f; **outperform** VT ausstechen (*inf*); **outplay** VT (*Sport*) besser spielen als; **outpost** N (*Mil, fig*) Vorposten m; **outpouring** N OFTEN PL Erguss m (*fig*)

output ['aʊtpʊt] N Produktion f; (= *of computer*) Output m or nt; **this factory has an ~ of 600 radios a day** diese Fabrik produziert täglich 600 Radios

output tax N (*Brit*) Bruttomehrwertsteuer f

outrage ['aʊtreɪdʒ] **1** N **(a)** (= *wicked, violent deed*) Untat f; (*cruel*) Gräueltat f; (*by police, demonstrators etc*) Ausschreitung f

(b) (= *indecency, injustice*) Skandal m; **an ~ against humanity** ein Verbrechen nt gegen die Menschlichkeit

(c) (= *sense of ~*) Empörung f (*at* über +*acc*), Entrüstung f (*at* über +*acc*)

2 [aʊt'reɪdʒ] VT *morals, conventions* Hohn sprechen (+*dat*); *sense of decency* beleidigen; *person* empören; **public opinion was ~d by this injustice** die öffentliche Meinung war über diese Ungerechtigkeit empört

outraged [aʊt'reɪdʒd] ADJ empört (*at, about* über +*acc*)

outrageous [aʊt'reɪdʒəs] ADJ **(a)** (= *cruel, violent*) verabscheuenswürdig **(b)** *remark, story, price, claim, behaviour* unerhört; *demand, insolence, lie, arrogance etc* unverschämt; *nonsense* haarsträubend; *language* unflätig; *charge, defamation etc* ungeheuerlich; *clothes, make-up etc* unmöglich (*inf*); **it's absolutely ~ that ...** es ist einfach unerhört, dass ...

outrageously [aʊt'reɪdʒəslɪ] ADV *expensive* unerhört; *behave also* unmöglich

outran PRET *of* **outrun**

outrider ['aʊtraɪdə'] N (*on motorcycle*) Kradbegleiter(in) m(f)

outright **1** ['aʊt'raɪt] ADV **(a)** (= *entirely*) *reject* rundweg; *own* vollständig; **to buy sth ~** etw komplett kaufen; (= *not on HP*) den ganzen Preis für etw sofort bezahlen; **to win ~** einen klaren Sieg davontragen

(b) (= *at once*) sofort; **he was killed ~** er war sofort tot

(c) (= *openly*) geradeheraus

2 ['aʊtraɪt] ADJ **(a)** total; *deception, lie* glatt (*inf*); *majority* absolut; *hostility, condemnation* offen; *winner* klar; *defeat* gründlich; **that's ~ arrogance** das ist die reine Arroganz

(b) (*Comm*) **~ sale/purchase** Verkauf m/Kauf m gegen sofortige Zahlung der Gesamtsumme; **~ owner** Volleigentümer(in) m(f)

out: outrun *pret* **outran,** *ptp* **outrun** VT schneller laufen als; (= *outdistance*) davonlaufen (+*dat*); **outset** N Anfang m; **at the ~** zu or am Anfang; **from the ~** von Anfang an; **outshine** *pret, ptp* **outshone** VT (*fig*) in den Schatten stellen

outside ['aʊt'saɪd] **1** N (*of house, car, object*) Außenseite f; **the ~ of the car is green** das Auto ist (von) außen grün; **to open the door from the ~** die Tür von außen öffnen; **people on the ~ (of society)** Menschen außerhalb der Gesellschaft; **to overtake on the ~** (*Brit*) außen überholen; **at the (very) ~** äußerstenfalls

2 ADJ **(a)** (= *external*) äußere(r, s); *consultant, investor, examiner, opinion* extern; **an ~ broadcast from Wimbledon** eine Sendung aus Wimbledon; **to get some ~ help** Hilfe von außen holen; **~ line** (*Telec*) Amtsleitung f; **~ work** freie Mitarbeit

(b) *price* äußerste(r, s)

(c) (= *very unlikely*) **an ~ chance** eine kleine Chance

3 ADV außen; (*of house, room, vehicle*) draußen; **to be ~** draußen sein; **to go ~** nach draußen gehen

4 PREP (*also* **~ of**) **(a)** außerhalb (+*gen*); **~ California** außerhalb Kaliforniens; **~ London** außerhalb von London; **to go ~ sth** aus etw gehen; **he went ~ the house** er ging nach draußen; **he is waiting ~ the door** er wartet vor der Tür; **the**

car ~ **the house** das Auto vorm Haus; **it is ~ our agreement** es geht über unsere Vereinbarung hinaus; **this falls ~ the scope of ...** das geht über den Rahmen (+gen) ... hinaus; **you'll have to do it ~ office hours** Sie müssen das nach Büroschluss erledigen

(b) (= apart from) außer (+dat), abgesehen von (+dat)

outside: outside lane N Überholspur f; **outside line** N (Tel) Amtsanschluss m

outsider [ˈaʊtˈsaɪdəʳ] N Außenseiter(in) m(f)

outside: outside temperature N Außentemperatur f; **outside toilet** N Außentoilette f; **outside wall** N Außenwand f; **outside world** N Außenwelt f

out: outsize ADJ **(a)** übergroß; ~ **clothes** Übergrößen pl **(b)** (inf: = enormous) riesig; **outskirts** PL (of town) Stadtrand m; **outsmart** VT (inf) überlisten

outspoken [ˈaʊtˈspəʊkən] ADJ person, criticism, speech, book freimütig; attack, remark direkt; **he is ~** er nimmt kein Blatt vor den Mund

outstanding [ˈaʊtˈstændɪŋ] ADJ **(a)** (= exceptional) hervorragend; talent, beauty außerordentlich; **of ~ ability** außerordentlich begabt **(b)** (= prominent, conspicuous) event bemerkenswert; detail auffallend; feature hervorstehend **(c)** (Comm, Fin) business unerledigt; amount, account, bill, interest ausstehend; **are there any problems still ~?** gibt es noch irgendwelche ungeklärten Probleme?; ~ **debts** Außenstände pl

outstandingly [ˈaʊtˈstændɪŋlɪ] ADV hervorragend; good, beautiful, successful außergewöhnlich; **the party did ~ well in the elections** die Partei hat in den Wahlen außergewöhnlich gut abgeschnitten

out: outstay VT **I don't want to ~ my welcome** ich will eure Gastfreundschaft nicht überbeanspruchen; **outstretched** ADJ body ausgestreckt; arms also ausgebreitet; **outstrip** VT (fig) übertreffen (in an +dat); **outtake** N für die endgültige Fassung nicht verwendete, herausgeschnittene Filmsequenz, Outtake m; **out tray** N Ablage f für Ausgänge; **outvote** VT überstimmen

outward [ˈaʊtwəd] **I** ADJ **(a)** appearance, form äußere(r, s); **he put on an ~ show of confidence** er gab sich den Anstrich von Selbstsicherheit **(b)** (= going out) ~ **journey/voyage** Hinreise f; ~ **flight** Hinflug m; ~ **investment** Auslandsinvestitionen pl; ~ **trade mission** (Brit) Handelsdelegation f **II** ADV nach außen; ~ **bound** ship auslaufend

outward-looking [ˈaʊtwədˌlʊkɪŋ] ADJ person, organization, country aufgeschlossen

outwardly [ˈaʊtwədlɪ] ADV nach außen hin

outwards [ˈaʊtwədz] ADV nach außen; **the journey ~** die Hinreise

out: outweigh VT mehr Gewicht haben als; **outwit** VT überlisten

oval [ˈəʊvəl] ADJ oval

ovarian [əʊˈvɛərɪən] ADJ (Anat) des Eierstocks/der Eierstöcke; ~ **cyst** Zyste f im Eierstock

ovary [ˈəʊvərɪ] N (Anat) Eierstock m

ovation [əʊˈveɪʃən] N Ovation f; **to give sb an ~** jdm eine Ovation darbringen

oven [ˈʌvn] N (Cook) (Back)ofen m; (for baking pottery etc) (Brenn)ofen m; **to put sth in the ~** etw in den Ofen tun or stecken; **to cook in a hot** or **quick/moderate/slow ~** bei starker/mittlerer/schwacher Hitze backen; **it's like an ~ in here** hier ist ja der reinste Backofen

oven: oven cleaner N Ofenreiniger m; **oven glove** N (Brit) Topfhandschuh m; **ovenproof** ADJ feuerfest; **oven-ready** ADJ bratfertig

over [ˈəʊvəʳ] **I** PREP **(a)** (indicating motion) über (+acc); (indicating position: = above, on top of) über (+dat); **he spilled coffee ~ it** er goss Kaffee darüber; **to hit sb ~ the head** jdm auf den Kopf schlagen; **bent ~ one's books** über die Bücher gebeugt; **to look ~ the wall** über die Mauer schauen; **it's ~ the page** es ist auf der nächsten Seite; **he looked ~ my shoulder** er sah mir über die Schulter; **she has to keep looking ~ her shoulder** (fig) sie ist verängstigt; **the house ~ the road** das Haus gegenüber; **it's just ~ the road from us** das ist von uns (aus) nur über die Straße; **the bridge ~ the river** die Brücke über den Fluss; **we're ~ the main obstacles now** wir haben jetzt die größten Hindernisse hinter uns (dat)

(b) (= in or across every part of) in (+dat); **they came from all ~** England sie kamen aus ganz England; **you've got ink all ~ you/your hands** Sie/Ihre Hände sind ganz voller Tinte; **to be all ~ sb** (inf) ein Mordstheater um jdn machen (inf)

(c) (= superior to) über (+dat); **he has no control ~ his urges/his staff** er hat seine Triebe/seine Angestellten nicht unter Kontrolle; **we were all ~ them** (inf) wir waren ihnen haushoch überlegen

(d) (= more than, longer than) (in expressions of time) über (+acc); (= during) während (+gen), in (+dat); ~ **and above that** darüber hinaus; **that was well ~ a year ago** das war vor gut einem Jahr; ~ **Christmas** über Weihnachten; ~ **the summer** den Sommer über; ~ **the (past) years** den Sommer über; ~ **the (past) years I've come to realize ...** im Laufe der (letzten) Jahre ist mir klar geworden ...; **the visits were spread ~ several months** die Besuche verteilten sich über mehrere Monate

(e) let's discuss that ~ **dinner/a beer** besprechen wir das beim Essen/bei einem Bier; **they'll be a long time ~ it** sie werden dazu lange brauchen; **he told me ~ the phone** er hat es mir am Telefon gesagt; **a voice came ~ the intercom** eine Stimme kam über die Sprechanlage; **what is 7 ~ 3?** wie viel ist 7 durch 3?

(f) (= about) über (+acc); **it's not worth arguing ~** es lohnt (sich) nicht, darüber zu streiten

II ADV **(a)** (= across) (away from speaker) hinüber; (towards speaker) herüber; (= on the other side) drüben; **come ~ tonight** kommen Sie heute Abend vorbei; **he is ~ here/there** er ist hier/dort drüben; ~ **to you!** Sie sind daran; **and now ~ to Paris where ...** und nun (schalten wir um) nach Paris, wo ...; **he has gone ~ to America** er ist nach Amerika gefahren; **famous the world ~** in der ganzen Welt berühmt; **I've been looking for it all ~** ich habe überall danach gesucht; **I am aching all ~** mir tut alles weh; **he was shaking all ~** er zitterte am ganzen Leib; **I'm wet all ~** ich bin völlig nass; **that's Fred all ~** das ist typisch (für) Fred

(b) (= ended) zu Ende; **the danger was ~** es bestand keine Gefahr mehr; **when all this is ~** wenn das alles vorbei ist; **it's all ~ between us** es ist aus zwischen uns

(c) (indicating repetition) **to start (all) ~ again** (Brit) or ~ (US) noch einmal (ganz) von vorn anfangen; ~ **and ~ (again)** immer (und immer) wieder; **he did it five times ~** er hat es fünfmal wiederholt

(d) (= remaining) übrig; **there was no/a lot of meat (left) ~** es war kein Fleisch mehr übrig/viel Fleisch übrig; **7 into 22 goes 3 and ~** 22 durch 7 ist 3, Rest 1; **6 feet and a little ~** 6 Fuß und ein bisschen

(e) (= more) **children of 8 and ~** Kinder ab 8; **if it takes three hours or ~** wenn es drei oder mehr Stunden dauert

(f) (Telec) **come in, please,** ~ bitte kommen, over; ~ **and out** Ende der Durchsage; (Aviat) over and out

III N (Cricket) 6 aufeinanderfolgende Würfe

over- PREF über-, Über-; **overact** (Theat) VI übertreiben (also fig), chargieren; **overactive** ADJ überaktiv

overage [ˈəʊvərˈeɪdʒ] ADJ zu alt

overall¹ [ˈəʊvərˈɔːl] **I** ADJ **(a)** gesamt, Gesamt-; ~ **width/length** Gesamtbreite f/-länge f; ~ **majority** absolute Mehrheit; ~ **winner** Gesamtsieger(in) m(f); **Labour gained ~ control** Labour erlangte die vollständige Kontrolle

(b) (= general) allgemein; **the ~ effect of this was to ...** dies hatte das Endergebnis, dass ...

II ADV **(a)** insgesamt; **he came second ~** (Sport) er belegte in der Gesamtwertung den zweiten Platz

(b) (= in general, on the whole) im Großen und Ganzen

overall² [ˈəʊvərɔːl] N (Brit) Kittel m

overalls [ˈəʊvərɔːlz] PL Overall m; (US: = dungarees) Latzhose f

over: overambitious ADJ zu ehrgeizig; **overanxious** ADJ übertrieben besorgt; (on particular occasion) übermäßig nervös; **overarm** ADJ, ADV (Sport) throw mit gestrecktem (erhobenem) Arm; serve über Kopf; **overate** PRET of overeat; **overawe** VT (= intimidate) einschüchtern; (= impress) überwältigen; **overbalance** VI aus dem Gleichgewicht kommen

overbearing [ˈəʊvəˈbɛərɪŋ] ADJ herrisch

overblown ADJ prose, rhetoric geschwollen

overboard [ˈəʊvəbɔːd] ADV **(a)** (Naut) über Bord; **to fall ~** über Bord gehen or fallen; **man ~!** Mann über Bord! **(b)** (fig inf) **to go ~, there's no need to go ~ (about it)** übertreib es nicht

over: overbook VI zu viele Buchungen vornehmen; **overburden** VT (fig) überlasten; **overcame** PRET of overcome;

overcapacity N Überkapazität f; **overcast** ADJ *weather, sky* bedeckt; **overcautious** ADJ übervorsichtig

overcharge [əʊvəˈtʃɑːdʒ] **1** VT *person* zu viel berechnen (+*dat*) (*for* für); **they ~d me by £2** sie haben mir £ 2 zu viel berechnet **2** VI zu viel verlangen (*for* für)

overcoat [ˈəʊvəkəʊt] N Mantel *m*

overcome [əʊvəˈkʌm], *pret* **overcame** [əʊvəˈkeɪm], *ptp* **overcome** VT *enemy* überwältigen; *shyness, nerves, difficulty, anger, obstacle etc* überwinden; *temptation* widerstehen (+*dat*); *disappointment* hinwegkommen über (+*acc*); **he was ~ by the fumes** die giftigen Gase machten ihn bewusstlos; **he was ~ by emotion** Rührung übermannte ihn; **he was ~ by remorse/ (a feeling of) despair** Reue f/(ein Gefühl *nt* der) Verzweiflung f überkam ihn; **~ (with emotion)** ergriffen, gerührt

over: overcompensate VI **to ~ for sth** etw überkompensieren; **overconfident** ADJ übertrieben selbstsicher; **overconsumption** N zu starker Verbrauch (*of an* +*dat*); **overcook** VT verbraten; (= *boil too long*) verkochen; **overcrowded** ADJ (*with things*) überfüllt; *town also* übervölkert; (= *overpopulated*) überbevölkert; **overcrowding** N Überfüllung f; (*of town*) Überbevölkerung f; **overdeveloped** ADJ überentwickelt

overdo [əʊvəˈduː], *pret* **overdid** [əʊvəˈdɪd], *ptp* **overdone** [əʊvəˈdʌn] VT **(a)** (= *exaggerate*) übertreiben; **you are ~ing it or things** (= *going too far*) Sie gehen zu weit; (= *tiring yourself*) Sie übernehmen sich; **I'm afraid you've rather overdone it with the garlic** ich fürchte, du hast es mit dem Knoblauch etwas zu gut gemeint **(b)** (= *cook too long*) verbraten; (= *boil too long*) verkochen

over: overdone ADJ **(a)** (= *exaggerated*) übertrieben **(b)** (= *cooked too long*) verbraten; (= *boiled too long*) verkocht; **overdose** **1** N (*lit*) Überdosis f; (*fig*) Zuviel *nt* (*of an* +*dat*) **2** VI eine Überdosis nehmen; **to ~ on heroin** eine Überdosis Heroin nehmen; **overdraft** N Kontoüberziehung f; **to have an ~ of £100** (= *be in debt*) sein Konto um £ 100 überzogen haben; **overdraft facility** N Überziehungskredit *m*; **overdrawn** [əʊvəˈdrɔːn] ADJ (*Fin*) *account* überzogen; **to be £100 ~, to be ~ by £100** sein Konto um £ 100 überzogen haben; **overdress** [əʊvəˈdres] VT **to be ~ed** zu vornehm angezogen sein; **overdue** ADJ *book, change, visit* überfällig; *sum of money, salary* fällig; **long** ~ schon seit langem fällig; **overeager** ADJ übereifrig; **overeat** *pret* **overate**, *ptp* **overeaten** VI sich überessen; **overeating** N Überessen *nt*; **overemphasis** N Überbetonung f; **an ~ on money** eine Überbewertung des Geldes; **overemphasize** VT überbetonen; **one cannot ~ the importance of this** man kann nicht genug betonen, wie wichtig das ist; **overenthusiastic** ADJ übertrieben begeistert; **not exactly ~** nicht gerade hingerissen; **overestimate** **1** [əʊvərˈestɪmeɪt] VT überschätzen **2** [əʊvərˈestɪmɪt] N (*of price*) zu hohe Schätzung; **overexcited** ADJ *person* überreizt; *children* aufgedreht; **overexpose** VT (*Phot*) überbelichten; **overexposure** N **the President's image is suffering from ~ (in the media)** das Image des Präsidenten leidet darunter, dass er zu oft in den Medien erscheint; **overfamiliar** ADJ **to be ~ with sb** etwas zu vertraulich or intim mit jdm sein; **I'm not ~ with their methods** ich bin nicht allzu vertraut mit ihren Methoden; **overfeed** *pret, ptp* **overfed** VT überfüttern; **overfill** VT überfüllen

overflow [ˈəʊvəfləʊ] **1** N **(a)** (= *amount*) Übergelaufene(s) *nt* **(b)** (= *outlet*) Überlauf *m* **(c)** (= *excess: of people*) Überschuss *m* (*of an* +*dat*) **2** [əʊvəˈfləʊ] VT **the river has ~ed its banks** der Fluss ist über die Ufer getreten **3** [əʊvəˈfləʊ] VI **(a)** (*liquid, river, container*) überlaufen; (*room, vehicle*) überfüllt sein; **full to ~ing** *bowl, cup* zum Überlaufen voll; *room* überfüllt; **the crowd at the meeting ~ed into the street** die Leute bei der Versammlung standen bis auf die Straße **(b)** (*fig*) überfließen (*with von*); **his heart was ~ing with love** sein Herz floss über vor Liebe

over: overflow pipe N Überlaufrohr *nt*; **overground** (*Transport*) ADJ oberirdisch; **overgrown** ADJ überwachsen (*with von*); **overhang** [əʊvəˈhæŋ], *vb: pret, ptp* **overhung** **1** VT hängen über (+*acc*); (*rocks, balcony*) hinausragen über (+*acc*) **2** N [ˈəʊvəhæŋ] (*of rock, building*) Überhang *m*; (*Archit*) Überkragung f; **overhaul** [ˈəʊvəhɔːl] **1** N Überholung f; **the machine needs an ~** die Maschine muss überholt werden **2** VT [əʊvəˈhɔːl] *engine* überholen; *plans* überprüfen;

overhead¹ [ˈəʊvəhed] **1** ADV oben; (= *in the sky: position*) am Himmel; **a plane flew ~** ein Flugzeug flog über uns *etc* (*acc*) (hinweg) **2** [ˈəʊvəhed] ADJ ~ **railway** (*Brit*) Hochbahn f; ~ **lighting** Deckenbeleuchtung f; **overhead²** [ˈəʊvəhed] N (*US*) = **overheads**; **overhead cable** N (*high voltage*) Hochspannungsleitung f; **overhead projector** N Overheadprojektor *m*; **overheads** [ˈəʊvəhedz] PL (*Brit*) allgemeine Unkosten *pl*; **overhear** [əʊvəˈhɪəʳ], *pret, ptp* **overheard** [əʊvəˈhɜːd] VT zufällig mit anhören; **we don't want him to ~ us** wir wollen nicht, dass er uns zuhören kann; **I ~d them plotting** ich hörte zufällig, wie sie etwas ausheckten; **overheat** **1** VT *engine* überhitzen; *room* überheizen **2** VI (*engine*) heißlaufen; (*fig: economy*) sich überhitzen; **overheated** ADJ **(a)** heißgelaufen; *room* überheizt **(b)** *economy, market* überhitzt; **overhung** PRET, PTP *of* **overhang**; **overimpressed** ADJ **I'm not ~ with him** er imponiert mir nicht besonders; **I'm not ~ with his work** ich bin nicht gerade von seiner Arbeit begeistert; **overindebted** ADJ überschuldet; **overindebtedness** N Überschuldung f; **overindulge** **1** VT *person* zu nachsichtig sein mit **2** VI zu viel genießen; **I ~d at the party** ich habe auf der Party ein bisschen zu viel des Guten gehabt; **overindulgent** ADJ zu nachsichtig (*to(wards) sb* mit jdm); **overinsurance** N Überversicherung f; **overinsure** VT überversichern

overjoyed [əʊvəˈdʒɔɪd] ADJ überglücklich (*at, by, with über* +*acc*); **to be ~ to see sb** überglücklich sein, jdn zu sehen

over: overkill N **repainting the whole room would definitely be ~** das ganze Zimmer neu zu streichen wäre des Guten zu viel *or* wäre übertrieben; **overladen** ADJ (*lit, fig*) überladen; **overlaid** PRET, PTP *of* **overlay**; **overland** **1** ADJ *journey* auf dem Landweg; ~ **route** Route f auf dem Landweg **2** ADV *travel etc* über Land

overlap [ˈəʊvəlæp] **1** N Überschneidung f; (*spatial*) Überlappung f; (*of concepts*) teilweise Entsprechung; **3 inches' ~** 3 Zoll Überlapp(ung) **2** [əʊvəˈlæp] VI **(a)** (*tiles, boards*) überlappen **(b)** (*visits, dates, responsibilities*) sich überschneiden; (*ideas, plans, work areas*) sich teilweise decken **3** [əʊvəˈlæp] VT *part* liegen über (+*dat*)

over: overlay *vb: pret, ptp* **overlaid** [əʊvəˈleɪ] VT überziehen; (*with metal*) belegen; **overleaf** ADV umseitig; **the illustration ~** die umseitige Abbildung; **see ~** siehe umseitig; **overload** VT überladen; (*Elec, Mech*) überlasten

overlook [əʊvəˈlʊk] VT **(a)** (= *have view onto*) überblicken; **we had a room ~ing the park** wir hatten ein Zimmer mit Blick auf den Park; **the castle ~s the whole town** vom Schloss aus hat man Aussicht auf die ganze Stadt **(b)** (= *fail to notice*) übersehen **(c)** (= *ignore*) hinwegsehen über (+*acc*); **I am prepared to ~ it this time** diesmal will ich noch ein Auge zudrücken

overly [ˈəʊvəlɪ] ADV übermäßig, allzu

over: overmanned ADJ **to be ~** eine zu große Belegschaft haben; **overmanning** N zu große Belegschaft(en *pl*); **overmuch** ADV übermäßig

overnight [ˈəʊvənaɪt] **1** ADV (*lit, fig*) über Nacht; **we drove ~** wir sind die Nacht durchgefahren; **to stay ~ (with sb)** (bei jdm) übernachten **2** ADJ **(a)** Nacht-; ~ **accommodation** Übernachtungsmöglichkeit f; ~ **train** Nachtzug *m* **(b)** (*fig: = sudden*) ganz plötzlich; **an ~ success** ein Blitzerfolg *m*; **she became an ~ star** sie wurde über Nacht zum Star

overnight: overnight bag N Reisetasche f; **overnight stay** N Übernachtung f

over: overpaid PRET, PTP *of* **overpay**; **overpass** N Überführung f; **overpay** *pret, ptp* **overpaid** VT überbezahlen; **overplay** VT (= *overact*) übertrieben spielen; **to ~ one's hand** (*fig*) es übertreiben; **overpopulated** ADJ überbevölkert; **overpopulation** N Überbevölkerung f

overpower [əʊvəˈpaʊəʳ] VT überwältigen

overpowering [əʊvəˈpaʊərɪŋ] ADJ überwältigend; *smell* penetrant; *colour, decoration, perfume, person* aufdringlich; *heat* glühend; **I felt an ~ desire ...** ich fühlte den unwiderstehlichen Drang, ...

over: overprice VT einen zu hohen Preis verlangen für; **at £50 it's ~d** £ 50 ist zu viel dafür; **overproduction** N Überproduktion f; **overprotective** ADJ überängstlich; **overran** PRET *of* **overrun**; **overrate** VT überschätzen; *book, play* überbewerten; **to be ~d** überschätzt werden; **overreach** VI sich übernehmen; **overreact** VI übertrieben reagieren (*to* auf +*acc*); **overreaction** N übertriebene Reaktion (*to* auf +*acc*)

override [əʊvə'raɪd], *pret* **overrode** [əʊvə'rəʊd], *ptp* **overridden** [əʊvə'rɪdn] VT **(a)** (= *disregard*) sich hinwegsetzen über (+*acc*) **(b)** *order, decision, ruling* aufheben; *objection* ablehnen

overriding [əʊvə'raɪdɪŋ] ADJ *principle* vorrangig; *priority* vordringlich; *desire* dringendste(r, s); **matters of ~ importance** äußerst bedeutende Angelegenheiten

over: overripe ADJ überreif; **overrode** PRET *of* **override**

overrule [əʊvə'ruːl] VT ablehnen; *verdict, decision* aufheben; **his objection was ~d** sein Einspruch wurde abgewiesen; **we were ~d** unser Vorschlag/unsere Entscheidung *etc* wurde abgelehnt

overrun [əʊvə'rʌn], *pret* **overran** [əʊvə'ræn], *ptp* **overrun** ▮ VT **(a)** (*weeds*) überwuchern, überwachsen; **the town was ~ by tourists** die Stadt war von Touristen überlaufen; **the house was ~ by mice** das Haus war voller Mäuse **(b)** (*troops etc*: = *invade*) einfallen in (+*dat*), herfallen über (+*acc*) **(c)** (= *go past*) *mark* hinauslaufen über (+*acc*); (*train*) *platform* hinausfahren über (+*acc*); (*plane*) *runway* hinausrollen über (+*acc*) ▮ VI (*in time*) überziehen; **his speech overran by ten minutes** seine Rede dauerte zehn Minuten zu lang

oversaw [əʊvə'sɔː] PRET *of* **oversee**

overseas [əʊvə'siːz] ▮ ADJ **(a)** (= *beyond the sea*) in Übersee *pred*; *country, market* überseeisch; **an ~ visitor** ein Besucher *m* aus Übersee **(b)** (= *abroad*) ausländisch; **an ~ visitor** ein Besucher *m* aus dem Ausland; **~ trip** Auslandsreise *f* ▮ ADV **to be/work ~** in Übersee/im Ausland sein/arbeiten; **to go ~** nach Übersee/ins Ausland gehen; **from ~** aus Übersee/dem Ausland

over: oversee *pret* **oversaw**, *ptp* **overseen** VT *person, work* beaufsichtigen; **overseer** N Aufseher(in) *m(f)*; (= *foreman*) Vorarbeiter(in) *m(f)*; **oversell** *pret, ptp* **oversold** VT (= *promote too much*) zu viel Reklame machen für; **to ~ oneself** sich zu gut verkaufen; **oversensitive** ADJ überempfindlich; **oversexed** ADJ **to be ~** einen übermäßig starken Sexualtrieb haben; **overshadow** VT (*lit, fig*) überschatten

overshoot [əʊvə'ʃuːt], *pret, ptp* **overshot** [əʊvə'ʃɒt] VT *target, runway* hinausschießen über (+*acc*); *production target etc* übertreffen

oversight [əʊvəsaɪt] N Versehen *nt*; **by** *or* **through an ~** aus Versehen

over: oversimplification N (zu) grobe Vereinfachung; **oversimplify** VT zu sehr vereinfachen; **oversize(d)** ADJ übergroß; **oversleep** *pret, ptp* **overslept** VI verschlafen; **oversold** PRET, PTP *of* **oversell**; **overspend** [əʊvə'spend], *vb: pret, ptp* **overspent** VI zu viel ausgeben; **we've overspent by £10** wir haben £ 10 zu viel ausgegeben; **overspending** N zu hohe Ausgaben *pl*; **overspill** [ə'spɪl] N (*Brit*) Bevölkerungsüberschuss *m*; **~ town** Trabantenstadt *f*; **overstaffed** ADJ überbesetzt; **this office is ~** dieses Büro hat zu viel Personal; **overstaffing** N Personalüberschuss *m*; **overstate** VT *facts, case* übertreiben; **overstatement** N Übertreibung *f*, übertriebene Darstellung; **overstay** VT = **outstay**; **overstep** VT überschreiten; **to ~ the mark** zu weit gehen

overstretch [əʊvə'stretʃ] VT (*fig*) *resources, finances* zu sehr belasten; **to ~ oneself** sich übernehmen

over: oversubscribe VT (*Fin*) überzeichnen; **the zoo outing was ~d** zu viele (Leute) hatten sich für den Ausflug in den Zoo angemeldet; **oversupply** N Überangebot *nt* (*of* an +*dat*)

overt [əʊ'vɜːt] ADJ offen; *hostility* unverhohlen

overtake [əʊvə'teɪk], *pret* **overtook** [əʊvə'tʊk], *ptp* **overtaken** [əʊvə'teɪkən] ▮ VT **(a)** *competitor, rival* einholen; (*esp Brit*: = *pass*) *runner, car etc* überholen **(b)** (= *take by surprise, fate*) ereilen (*geh*); **we were ~n by events, events have ~n us** wir waren auf die Entwicklung der Dinge nicht gefasst ▮ VI (*esp Brit*) überholen

overtaking [əʊvə'teɪkɪŋ] N (*esp Brit*) Überholen *nt*

over: overtax VT (*fig*) *person, heart* überlasten; **over-the-counter** ADJ *drugs* nicht rezeptpflichtig; (*St Ex*) *securities, transactions* außerbörslich; **overthrow** *vb: pret* **overthrew**, *ptp* **overthrown** ▮ ['əʊvəθrəʊ] N (*of dictator etc*) Sturz *m* ▮ [əʊvə'θrəʊ] VT *dictator etc* stürzen

overtime ['əʊvətaɪm] ▮ N **(a)** Überstunden *pl*; **I am on ~** *or* **doing ~** ich mache Überstunden **(b)** (*US Sport*) Verlängerung *f*; **we had to play ~** es gab eine Verlängerung ▮ ADV **to work ~** Überstunden machen; **my imagination was working ~** (*inf*) meine Fantasie lief auf Hochtouren (*inf*)

overtime pay N Überstundenlohn *m*

overtly [əʊ'vɜːtlɪ] ADV offen

overtone ['əʊvətəʊn] N (*fig*) Unterton *m*; **political ~s** politische Untertöne *pl*

overtook PRET *of* **overtake**

overture ['əʊvətjʊə'] N **(a)** (*Mus*) Ouvertüre *f* **(b)** USU PL (= *approach*) Annäherungsversuch *m*; **to make ~s to sb** Annäherungsversuche bei jdm machen

overturn [əʊvə'tɜːn] ▮ VT **(a)** (*lit*) umkippen; (= *capsize*) *boat* zum Kentern bringen **(b)** (*fig*) *regime* stürzen; *philosophy, world view* umstürzen; *law, ban, conviction* aufheben ▮ VI (*chair*) umkippen; (*boat*) kentern

over: overuse ▮ [əʊvə'juːs] N übermäßiger Gebrauch ▮ [əʊvə'juːz] VT übermäßig oft gebrauchen; **overvalue** VT *goods* zu hoch schätzen; **overview** N Überblick *m* (*of* über +*acc*)

overweening [əʊvə'wiːnɪŋ] ADJ maßlos

overweight ['əʊvə'weɪt] ADJ *thing* zu schwer; *person* übergewichtig; **to be five kilos ~** (*person, box etc*) fünf Kilo Übergewicht haben; **you're ~** Sie haben Übergewicht

overwhelm [əʊvə'welm] VT **(a)** überwältigen; *country* besiegen; (*Sport*) *defence* überrennen; **he was ~ed when they gave him the present** er war zutiefst gerührt, als sie ihm das Geschenk gaben **(b)** (*fig*) (*with praise, work*) überhäufen; (*with questions*) bestürmen

overwhelming [əʊvə'welmɪŋ] ADJ überwältigend; *desire* unwiderstehlich; **they won despite ~ odds** sie gewannen obwohl ihre Chancen sehr schlecht standen

overwhelmingly [əʊvə'welmɪŋlɪ] ADV *reject, support* mit überwältigender Mehrheit; *white, positive* größtenteils

over: overwork ▮ N Überarbeitung *f* ▮ VT *horse etc* schinden; *person* überanstrengen; *image, idea, theme etc* überstrapazieren; **to ~ oneself** sich überarbeiten ▮ VI sich überarbeiten; **overwrite** *pret* **overwrote**, *ptp* **overwritten** VTI (*Comput*) überschreiben; **overwrought** [əʊvə'rɔːt] ADJ überreizt; **overzealous** [əʊvə'zeləs] ADJ übereifrig

ovulate ['ɒvjʊleɪt] VI ovulieren

ovulation [ɒvjʊ'leɪʃən] N Eisprung *m*

owe [əʊ] ▮ VT **(a)** *money* schulden (*sb sth, sth to sb* jdm etw); **how much do I ~ you?** (*in shop etc*) was bin ich schuldig? **(b)** *obedience, loyalty, allegiance* schulden (*to sb* jdm) **(c)** (= *be under an obligation for*) verdanken (*sth to sb* jdm etw); **I ~ my life to him** ich verdanke ihm mein Leben; **to what do I ~ the honour** (*Brit*) *or* **honor** (*US*) **of your visit?** (*iro*) und was verschafft mir die Ehre Ihres Besuches?; **you ~ it to yourself to keep fit** du bist es dir schuldig, fit zu bleiben; **I think you ~ me an explanation** ich glaube, du bist mir eine Erklärung schuldig ▮ VI **to ~ sb for sth** jdm Geld für etw schulden; **I still ~ him for the meal** ich muss ihm das Essen noch bezahlen

owing ['əʊɪŋ] ▮ ADJ unbezahlt; **the amount ~ on the house** die Schulden, die auf dem Haus liegen; **how much is still ~?** wie viel steht noch aus? ▮ PREP **~ to** wegen (+*gen or* (*inf*) +*dat*), infolge (+*gen*); **~ to the circumstances** umständehalber; **~ to his being foreign** weil er Ausländer ist

owl [aʊl] N Eule *f*

own[1] [əʊn] ▮ VT **(a)** (= *possess*) besitzen; **who ~s that?** wem gehört das?; **he looks as if he ~s the place** er sieht so aus, als wäre er hier zu Hause **(b)** (= *admit*) zugeben; (= *recognize*) anerkennen ▮ VI **to ~ to sth** etw eingestehen; **he ~ed to having done it** er gestand, es getan zu haben

➤ **own up** VI es zugeben; **to own up to sth** etw zugeben; **he owned up to stealing the money** er gab zu, das Geld gestohlen zu haben

own[2] ▮ ADJ ATTR eigen; **his ~ car** sein eigenes Auto; **one's ~ car** ein eigenes Auto; **he's his ~ man** er geht seinen eigenen Weg; **he likes beauty for its ~ sake** er liebt die Schönheit um ihrer selbst willen; **he does (all) his ~ cooking** er kocht für sich selbst; **thank you, I'm quite capable of finding my ~ way out** danke, ich finde sehr gut alleine hinaus ▮ PRON **(a)** **to make sth one's ~** sich (*dat*) etw zu eigen

machen; **my time is my** ~ ich kann mit meiner Zeit machen, was ich will; **a house of one's** ~ ein eigenes Haus; **I have money of my** ~ ich habe selbst Geld; **it has a beauty all its** ~ *or of its* ~ es hat eine ganz eigene Schönheit; **for reasons of his** ~ aus irgendwelchen Gründen
  (b) (*in phrases*) **to get one's** ~ **back on sb** (*esp Brit*) es jdm heimzahlen; **(all) on one's** ~ (ganz) allein; **on its** ~ von selbst; **the goalkeeper came into his** ~ **with a series of brilliant saves** der Torwart zeigte sich von seiner besten Seite, als er eine Reihe von Bällen geradezu fantastisch abwehrte

own brand N Hausmarke *f*

owner [ˈəʊnəʳ] N Besitzer(in) *m(f)*; (*of shop, factory, firm etc*) Inhaber(in) *m(f)*; (*of dogs, car, slaves*) Halter(in) *m(f)*; **at** ~**'s risk** auf eigene Gefahr; ~**'s equity** (*Fin*) Eigenkapital *nt*

owner-occupier N Bewohner(in) *m(f)* im eigenen Haus, Eigennutzer(in) *m(f)* (*form*)

ownership [ˈəʊnəʃɪp] N Besitz *m*; **to establish the** ~ **of sth** den Besitzer einer Sache (*gen*) feststellen; **under new** ~ unter neuer Leitung

own goal N (*lit, fig*) Eigentor *nt*; **to score an** ~ (*lit, fig*) ein Eigentor schießen

ox [ɒks] N, *pl* **-en** Ochse *m*

Oxfam [ˈɒksfæm] N ABBR *of* **Oxford Committee for Famine Relief** *britische karitative Vereinigung zur Hungerhilfe*

oxide [ˈɒksaɪd] N (*Chem*) Oxid *nt*

oxidize [ˈɒksɪdaɪz] VTI oxidieren

oxtail soup [ˈɒksteɪlˈsuːp] N Ochsenschwanzsuppe *f*

oxyacetylene [ˈɒksɪəˈsetɪliːn] ADJ ~ **burner** *or* **lamp** *or* **torch** Schweißbrenner *m*; ~ **welding** Autogenschweißen *nt*

oxygen [ˈɒksɪdʒən] N Sauerstoff *m*

oxygen: oxygen mask N Sauerstoffmaske *f*; **oxygen tent** N Sauerstoffzelt *nt*

oxymoron [ˌɒksɪˈmɔːrɒn] N Oxymoron *nt*

oyster [ˈɔɪstəʳ] N Auster *f*; **the world's his** ~ die Welt steht ihm offen

oz ABBR *of* **ounce(s)**

ozone [ˈəʊzəʊn] N Ozon *nt*; ~ **depletion** Verringerung *f* der Ozonschicht

ozone: ozone-friendly ADJ *spray etc* FCKW-frei; **ozone layer** N Ozonschicht *f*; **a hole in the** ~ ein Ozonloch *nt*

Pp

P, p [pi:] N P *nt*, p *nt*

p (a) ABBR *of* **page** S. **(b)** ABBR *of* **penny, pence**

PA (a) ABBR *of* **personal assistant (b)** ABBR *of* **public address (system)**

pa [pɑ:] N (*inf*) Papa *m inf*

p.a. ABBR *of* **per annum**

pace [peɪs] **1** N **(a)** (= *step*) Schritt *m*; **at 20 ~s** auf 20 Schritte Entfernung; **to put sb/a new car through his/its ~s** (*fig*) jdn/ein neues Auto auf Herz und Nieren prüfen **(b)** (= *speed*) Tempo *nt*; **the more leisurely ~ of life in those days** die geruhsamere Leben damals; **at a good** *or* **smart ~** recht schnell; **at a slow ~** langsam; **to learn at one's own ~** in seinem eigenen Tempo lernen; **I can't keep ~ with events** ich komme mit den Ereignissen nicht mit; **to make** *or* **set the ~** das Tempo angeben; **to quicken one's ~** seinen Schritt beschleunigen; (*working*) sein Tempo beschleunigen; **I'm getting old, I can't stand the ~ any more** (*inf*) ich werde alt, ich kann nicht mehr mithalten **2** VT (*in anxiety etc*) auf und ab gehen in (+*dat*) **3** VI **to ~ up and down** auf und ab gehen

pacemaker ['peɪsmeɪkə'] N **1** (*Med*) Schrittmacher *m* **2** (*Sport*) Tempomacher(in) *m(f)*

pacesetter ['peɪssetə'] N (*Sport*) Tempomacher(in) *m(f)*

Pacific [pə'sɪfɪk] N **the ~ (Ocean)** der Pazifische *or* Stille Ozean, der Pazifik; **a ~ island** eine Insel im Pazifik; **the ~ Rim** die Pazifikanrainerstaaten *pl*

Pacific Standard Time N pazifische Zeit

pacifier ['pæsɪfaɪə'] N (*US: for baby*) Schnuller *m*

pacifism ['pæsɪfɪzəm] N Pazifismus *m*

pacifist ['pæsɪfɪst] N Pazifist(in) *m(f)*

pacify ['pæsɪfaɪ] VT baby beruhigen; *warring countries* miteinander aussöhnen; *critics* besänftigen

pack [pæk] **1** N **(a)** (*on animal*) Last *f*; (= *rucksack*) Rucksack *m*; (*Mil*) Gepäck *nt no pl* **(b)** (= *packet: of cereal etc*) Paket *nt*; (*esp US: of cigarettes*) Packung *f*; **a ~ of six** ein Sechserpack *m* **(c)** (*Hunt*) Meute *f* **(d)** (*of wolves, cubs*) Rudel *nt* **(e)** (*pej: = group*) Horde *f*; **a ~ of thieves** eine Diebesbande; **it's all a ~ of lies** es ist alles erlogen **(f)** (*of cards*) (Karten)spiel *nt* **2** VT **(a)** *crate, container etc* voll packen; *fish, meat in tin etc* abpacken **(b)** *case, trunk* (= *crowd, cram*) packen; *things in case, clothes etc* (= *wrap, put into parcel*) einpacken; **the box was ~ed full of explosives** die Kiste war voll mit Sprengstoff; **the crowds that ~ed the stadium** die Menschenmassen, die sich im Stadium drängten; **to be ~ed** (= *full*) gerammelt voll sein (*inf*); **a weekend ~ed with excitement** ein Wochenende voller aufregender Erlebnisse **(c)** (= *make firm*) *soil etc* festdrücken; **the snow on the path was ~ed hard** der Schnee auf dem Weg war festgetrampelt **(d)** (*US inf*) *gun* tragen **(e)** (*inf*) **to ~ a (heavy) punch** (*person*) kräftig zuschlagen; **the film ~s a real punch** (*fig*) der Film ist total spannend **3** VI **(a)** (*person*) packen **(b)** (= *crowd*) **the crowds ~ed into the stadium** die Menge drängte sich in das Stadion; **we can't all ~ into one car** wir können uns nicht alle in ein Auto zwängen **(c)** (*inf*) **to send sb ~ing** jdn kurz abfertigen

▶ **pack away** VT SEP wegpacken; **I've packed all your books away in the attic** ich habe alle deine Bücher auf den Boden geräumt

▶ **pack in 1** VT SEP **(a)** *people* hineinpferchen in (+*acc*) **(b)** (*Brit inf*) *job* hinschmeißen (*inf*); *girlfriend* sausen lassen (*inf*); *work, activity* Schluss machen mit; **to pack it all in** Schluss machen; **pack it in!** lass es gut sein! **2** VI (*Brit inf*) (*engine*) seinen Geist aufgeben (*hum*); (*person*) Feierabend machen (*inf*)

▶ **pack off** VT SEP **she packed them off to bed** sie schickte sie ins Bett

▶ **pack out** VT SEP USU PASS **to be packed out** (*theatre etc*) überfüllt sein

▶ **pack up 1** VT SEP zusammenpacken **2** VI **(a)** packen; **he just packed up and left** er packte seine Sachen und ging **(b)** (*Brit inf*) (*engine*) seinen Geist aufgeben (*hum*); (*person*) Feierabend machen (*inf*)

package ['pækɪdʒ] **1** N Paket *nt*; (*of cardboard*) Schachtel *f*; **software ~** Softwarepaket *nt* **2** VT **(a)** *goods* verpacken **(b)** (*in order to enhance sales*) präsentieren

package: package deal N Pauschalangebot *nt*; **package holiday** N Pauschalreise *f*; **package store** N (*US*) Spirituosenhandlung *f*; **package tour** N Pauschalreise *f*

packaging ['pækɪdʒɪŋ] N **(a)** (= *material*) Verpackung *f*; **~ tax** Verpackungssteuer *f* **(b)** (= *presentation of product*) Präsentation *f*

packaging date N (*US*) Datumskennzeichnung *f*

packed lunch [pækt'lʌntʃ] N (*Brit*) Lunchpaket *nt*

packer ['pækə'] N Packer(in) *m(f)*

packet ['pækɪt] N (*esp Brit*) **(a)** Paket *nt*; (*of cigarettes*) Schachtel *f*; (= *small box*) Schachtel *f* **(b)** (*Brit inf*) **to make a ~** ein Schweinegeld verdienen (*inf*); **that must have cost a ~** das muss ein Heidengeld gekostet haben (*inf*)

packet soup N (*esp Brit*) Tütensuppe *f*

pack ice N Packeis *nt*

packing ['pækɪŋ] N (= *act*) Packen *nt*; (= *material*) Verpackung *f*; **to do one's ~** packen

packing case N Kiste *f*

packsack ['pæksæk] N (*US*) Rucksack *m*

pact [pækt] N Pakt *m*; **to make a ~ with sb** mit jdm einen Pakt schließen

pad¹ [pæd] VI **to ~ about** (*Brit*) *or* **around** umhertapsen

pad² **1** N **(a)** (*for comfort etc*) Polster *nt*; (*for protection*) Schützer *m*; (*in bra*) Einlage *f*; (= *brake ~ etc*) Belag *m* **(b)** (*of paper*) Block *m* **(c)** (*inf: = room, home*) Bude *f* (*inf*); **at your ~** bei dir **2** VT *shoulders etc* polstern

▶ **pad out** VT SEP (*fig*) *article, essay etc* auffüllen; *speech* ausdehnen

padded ['pædɪd] ADJ *shoulders, bra* wattiert; *dashboard, seat* gepolstert; **~ envelope** gefütterter (Brief)umschlag

padding ['pædɪŋ] N **(a)** (= *material*) Polsterung *f* **(b)** (*fig: in essay etc*) Füllwerk *nt*

paddle ['pædl] **1** N **(a)** (= *oar*) Paddel *nt* **(b) to go for a ~, to have a ~** durchs Wasser waten **2** VT **(a)** *boat* paddeln **(b)** (*US: = spank*) verhauen **3** VI **(a)** (*in boat*) paddeln **(b)** (= *walk in shallow water*) waten

paddle: paddle boat N Raddampfer *m*; (*small, on pond*) Paddelboot *nt*; **paddle steamer** N Raddampfer *m*

paddling pool ['pædlɪŋ,pu:l] N (*Brit*) Plan(t)schbecken *nt*

paddock ['pædək] N Koppel *f*; (*of racecourse*) Sattelplatz *m*

paddy ['pædɪ] N (*also* **~ field**) Reisfeld *nt*

paddy wagon N (*US inf*) grüne Minna (*inf*)

padlock ['pædlɒk] **1** N Vorhängeschloss *nt* **2** VT (mit einem Vorhängeschloss) verschließen

padre ['pɑ:drɪ] N (*Mil*) Feldgeistliche(r) *m*

paean ['pi:ən] N Lobrede *f*

paediatric, (*US*) **pediatric** [,pi:dɪˈætrɪk] ADJ Kinder-

paediatrician, (*US*) **pediatrician** [,pi:dɪəˈtrɪʃən] N Kinderarzt *m*/-ärztin *f*

paediatrics, (US) **pediatrics** [ˌpiːdɪˈætrɪks] N Kinderheilkunde f

paedophile, (US) **pedophile** [ˈpiːdəfaɪl] N Pädophile(r) mf

paedophilia, (US) **pedophilia** [ˌpiːdəʊˈfɪlɪə] N Pädophilie f

pagan [ˈpeɪɡən] **1** ADJ heidnisch **2** N Heide m, Heidin f

paganism [ˈpeɪɡənɪzəm] N Heidentum nt

page¹ [peɪdʒ] **1** N (also ~**boy**) Page m **2** VT **to ~ sb** jdn ausrufen lassen; **paging Mr Cousin** Herr Cousin, bitte!

page² N Seite f; **on ~ 14** auf Seite 14; **write on both sides of the ~** beschreiben Sie beide Seiten; **to be on the same ~** (US: = in agreement) auf der gleichen Wellenlänge liegen; **the sports ~s** die Sportseiten pl

pageant [ˈpædʒənt] N (= show) historische Aufführung, Historienspiel nt; (= procession) Festzug m; **Christmas ~** Weihnachtsspiel nt

pageantry [ˈpædʒəntrɪ] N Prunk m, Gepränge nt

page: **pageboy** N Page m; (Brit: = attendant at wedding) Junge, der bei der Hochzeitszeremonie assistiert; **page break** N (Comput) Seitenwechsel m; **page number** N Seitenzahl f; **page preview** N (Comput) Preview m; **page printer** N (Comput) Seitendrucker m

pager [ˈpeɪdʒəʳ] N (Telec) Funkempfänger m, Pieper m (inf)

paginate [ˈpædʒɪneɪt] VT paginieren

pagination [ˌpædʒɪˈneɪʃən] N Paginierung f

pagoda [pəˈɡəʊdə] N Pagode f

paid [peɪd] **1** PRET, PTP of **pay 2** ADJ **(a)** official, work bezahlt; **a highly ~ job** ein hoch bezahlter Posten **(b)** (esp Brit) **to put ~ to sth** etw zunichte machen; **that's put ~ to my weekend** damit ist mein Wochenende geplatzt **3** N **the low/well ~** die Gering-/Gutverdienenden pl

paid-up [ˈpeɪdˈʌp] ADJ share eingezahlt; **500 ~ members** 500 zahlende Mitglieder; **fully ~ member** Mitglied nt ohne Beitragsrückstände

pail [peɪl] N Eimer m

pain [peɪn] **1** N **(a)** Schmerz m; (mental) Qualen pl; **where is the ~ exactly?** wo tut es denn genau weh?; **to be in ~** Schmerzen haben; **he screamed in ~** er schrie vor Schmerzen; **stomach/chest ~s** Magen-/Brustschmerzen pl; **my ankle has been giving** or **causing me a lot of ~** mein Knöchel tut mir sehr weh; **I felt a ~ in my leg** ich hatte Schmerzen im Bein; **he suffered great mental ~** er litt Seelenqualen; **the decision caused me a lot of ~** die Entscheidung war sehr schmerzlich für mich
(b) **pains** PL (= efforts) Mühe f; **to be at (great) ~s to do sth** sich (dat) (große) Mühe geben, etw zu tun; **to take ~s to do sth** sich (dat) Mühe geben, etw zu tun; **she takes great ~s with her appearance** sie verwendet sehr viel Sorgfalt auf ihr Äußeres; **see what you get for your ~s!** das hast du nun für deine Mühe!
(c) (= penalty) **on** or **under ~ of death** bei Todesstrafe
(d) (inf: also ~ **in the neck** or **arse** Brit sl) **to be a (real) ~** einem auf den Wecker gehen (inf) sl
2 VT (mentally) schmerzen; **it ~s me to see their ignorance** ihre Unwissenheit tut schon weh

pained [peɪnd] ADJ expression, voice schmerzerfüllt

painful [ˈpeɪnfʊl] ADJ injury schmerzhaft; (= unpleasant, distressing) schmerzlich; **is it ~?** tut es weh?; **it is my ~ duty to tell you that ...** ich habe die traurige Pflicht, Ihnen mitteilen zu müssen, dass ...

painfully [ˈpeɪnfəlɪ] ADV **(a)** (physically) schmerzhaft; move, walk unter Schmerzen **(b)** (fig) learn, understand schmerzlich **(c)** (= very) schrecklich; thin furchtbar; slow schmerzlich; **it was ~ obvious** es war nicht zu übersehen

painkiller [ˈpeɪnkɪləʳ] N schmerzstillendes Mittel

painless [ˈpeɪnlɪs] ADJ schmerzlos; **a procedure which makes paying completely ~** (inf) ein Verfahren, bei dem Sie von der Bezahlung überhaupt nichts merken; **don't worry, it's quite ~** (inf) keine Angst, es tut gar nicht weh

painlessly [ˈpeɪnlɪslɪ] ADV schmerzlos

painstaking ADJ, **painstakingly** ADV [ˈpeɪnzˌteɪkɪŋ, -lɪ] sorgfältig

paint [peɪnt] **1** N **(a)** Farbe f; (on car, furniture) Lack m **(b)** **paints** PL Farben pl; **box of ~s** Farbkasten m
2 VT **(a)** wall, fence, door streichen; car lackieren; **to ~ one's face** (with make-up) sich anmalen (inf); **to ~ the town red** (inf) die Stadt unsicher machen (inf); **to ~ oneself/sb into a corner**

(fig) sich selbst/jdn in die Enge treiben
(b) picture, person malen; **he ~ed a very convincing picture of life on the moon** er zeichnete ein sehr überzeugendes Bild vom Leben auf dem Mond
3 VI malen; (= decorate) (an)streichen

paint: **paintbox** N Farbkasten m; **paintbrush** N Pinsel m

painter [ˈpeɪntəʳ] N (Art) Maler(in) m(f); (= decorator) Anstreicher(in) m(f)

painting [ˈpeɪntɪŋ] N **(a)** (= picture) Gemälde nt **(b)** NO PL (Art) Malerei f

paint: **paint pot** N Farbtopf m; **paint spray(er)** N Spritzpistole f; **paint stripper** N Abbeizmittel nt; **paintwork** N (on car etc) Lack m; (on wall, furniture) Anstrich m

pair [pɛəʳ] **1** N **(a)** (of gloves, people) Paar nt; (of animals, cards) Pärchen nt; **these socks are not a ~** diese beiden Socken gehören nicht zusammen; **a ~ of scissors** eine Schere; **six ~s of scissors** sechs Scheren; **a new ~** (of trousers) eine neue (Hose); (of shoes) ein Paar neue; **I've only got one ~ of hands** ich habe auch nur zwei Hände; **to be** or **have a safe ~ of hands** zuverlässig sein; **in ~s** paarweise; hunt, arrive, go out zu zweit; be seated in Zweiergruppen; **you're a fine ~ you are!** (iro) ihr seid mir (vielleicht) ein sauberes Pärchen (iro)
(b) **pairs** SING or PL **the ~** (Skating) Paarlauf m; (Rowing) Zweier m; **in the ~s** im Paarlauf/Zweier
2 VT **I was ~ed with Bob for the next round** in der nächsten Runde musste ich mit Bob ein Paar bilden

➤ **pair off** **1** VT SEP in Zweiergruppen einteilen; **to pair sb off with sb** (= find boyfriend etc for) jdn mit jdm zusammenbringen or verkuppeln (inf) **2** VI Paare bilden (with mit); **all the people at the party had paired off** bei der Party hatten alle Pärchen gebildet

paisley [ˈpeɪzlɪ] ADJ pattern türkisch; shirt türkisch gemustert

pajamas [pəˈdʒɑːməz] PL (US) = **pyjamas**

Paki [ˈpækɪ] (pej inf) **1** N (= person) Pakistani mf **2** ADJ shop etc pakistanisch

Pakistan [ˌpɑːkɪsˈtɑːn] N Pakistan nt

Pakistani [ˌpɑːkɪsˈtɑːnɪ] **1** ADJ pakistanisch **2** N Pakistani mf

pal [pæl] N (inf) Kumpel m (inf); **be a ~!** sei so nett!

palace [ˈpælɪs] N (lit, fig) Palast m; **bishop's ~** bischöfliche Residenz; **royal ~** (Königs)schloss nt

palaeo- [ˈpælɪəʊ-] PREF = **paleo-**

palatable [ˈpælətəbl] ADJ **(a)** genießbar **(b)** (fig) experience attraktiv; **to make sth ~ to sb** jdm etw schmackhaft machen

palate [ˈpælɪt] N (lit) Gaumen m

palatial [pəˈleɪʃəl] ADJ (= spacious) palastartig; (= luxurious) prunkvoll

palaver [pəˈlɑːvəʳ] N (inf) Theater nt (inf)

pale¹ [peɪl] **1** ADJ (+ER) blass; (implying unhealthy etc) bleich; light, moon, sun fahl; **~ green/orange** etc zartgrün-/orange etc; **but a ~ imitation of the real thing** nur ein Abklatsch m des Originals **2** VI (person) erbleichen; **to ~ (into insignificance) beside** or **alongside sth** neben etw (dat) bedeutungslos sein

pale² N **those last few remarks were quite beyond the ~** diese letzten Bemerkungen haben eindeutig die Grenzen überschritten

pale ale N (Brit) helleres Dunkelbier

paleness [ˈpeɪlnɪs] N Blässe f

paleo- [ˈpælɪəʊ-] PREF paläo-, Paläo-

paleontology [ˌpælɪɒnˈtɒlədʒɪ] N Paläontologie f

Palestine [ˈpælɪstaɪn] N Palästina nt

Palestinian [ˌpælɪˈstɪnɪən] **1** ADJ palästinensisch **2** N Palästinenser(in) m(f)

palette [ˈpælɪt] N Palette f

palette knife N Palettenmesser nt

palimony [ˈpælɪmənɪ] N (esp US inf) Unterhaltszahlung f (bei der Auflösung einer Ehe ohne Trauschein)

palindrome [ˈpælɪndrəʊm] N Palindrom nt

paling [ˈpeɪlɪŋ] N (= stake) Zaunpfahl m; (= fence) Lattenzaun m; (bigger) Palisadenzaun m

palisade [ˌpælɪˈseɪd] N Palisade f

pall¹ [pɔːl] N (over coffin) Sargtuch nt; **a ~ of smoke** (fig) eine Dunstglocke

pall² VI an Reiz verlieren (on sb für jdn)

pallbearer [ˈpɔːlˌbɛərəʳ] N Sargträger(in) m(f)

pallet ['pælɪt] N Palette f
palliative ['pælɪətɪv] (form) ▊ ADJ lindernd ▊ N
Linderungsmittel nt
pallid ['pælɪd] ADJ blass; (= unhealthy looking) bleich
pallor ['pælə'] N Blässe f
pally ['pælɪ] ADJ (+ER) (Brit inf) they're very ~ sie sind dicke
Freunde (inf); to be ~ with sb mit jdm gut Freund sein; to get
~ with sb sich mit jdm anfreunden
palm[1] [pɑːm] N (Bot) Palme f
palm[2] N (Anat) Handteller m; he had the audience in the ~ of
his hand er hielt das Publikum ganz in seinem Bann; to
grease sb's ~ (fig) jdn schmieren (inf); to read sb's ~ jdm aus
der Hand lesen
➤ **palm off** VT SEP (inf) rubbish, goods andrehen (on(to) sb jdm)
(inf); person (with explanation) abspeisen (inf); they palmed
him off on me sie haben ihn mir aufgehalst (inf)
palmcorder ['pɑːmkɔːdə'] N Palmcorder m
palmistry ['pɑːmɪstrɪ] N Handlesekunst f
palm: palm leaf N Palmwedel m; **palm oil** N Palmöl nt; **Palm
Sunday** N Palmsonntag m; **palmtop** N (Comput) Palmtop m;
palm tree N Palme f
palpable ['pælpəbl] ADJ nonsense vollkommen
palpably ['pælpəblɪ] ADV (= clearly) eindeutig
palpitate ['pælpɪteɪt] VI (heart) heftig klopfen
palpitation [ˌpælpɪ'teɪʃən] N (of heart) Herzklopfen nt; to have
~s Herzklopfen haben
palsy ['pɔːlzɪ] N Lähmung f
paltry ['pɔːltrɪ] ADJ armselig; he gave some ~ excuse er brachte
irgendeine armselige Entschuldigung hervor
pamper ['pæmpə'] VT verwöhnen
pamphlet ['pæmflɪt] N (informative) Broschüre f; (political,
handed out in street) Flugblatt nt
pan [pæn] N (Cook) Pfanne f; (= saucepan) Topf m
➤ **pan out** VI (inf) sich entwickeln; it didn't pan out es hat
nicht geklappt (inf)
pan- PREF pan-, Pan-
panache [pə'næʃ] N Schwung m, Elan m
Panama [ˌpænə'mɑː] N Panama nt; ~ Canal Panamakanal m
Panamanian [ˌpænə'meɪnɪən] ▊ ADJ panamaisch ▊ N Panamese
m, Panamesin f
pancake ['pænkeɪk] N Pfannkuchen m
pancreas ['pæŋkrɪəs] N Bauchspeicheldrüse f
panda ['pændə] N Panda m
panda car N (Brit) (Funk)streifenwagen m
pandemonium [ˌpændɪ'məʊnɪəm] N Chaos nt; scenes of ~
chaotische Szenen pl
pander ['pændə'] VI nachgeben (to +dat); to ~ to sb's whims jds
Launen (acc) befriedigen wollen; to ~ to sb's ego jdm um
den Bart gehen
p and p ABBR of post(age) and packing
pane [peɪn] N Glasscheibe f
panel ['pænl] N (a) (= piece of wood) Tafel f; (in ceiling, door)
Feld nt; (in car) Türblech nt (b) (of instruments etc)
Schalttafel f; instrument ~ Armaturenbrett nt; (on machine)
Kontrolltafel f (c) (of interviewers etc) Gremium nt; (in
discussion) Diskussionsrunde f; (in quiz) Rateteam nt; a ~ of
experts ein Sachverständigengremium nt; a ~ of judges eine
Jury
panel: panel discussion N Podiumsdiskussion f; **panel game**
N Ratespiel nt
panelled, (US) **paneled** ['pænld] ADJ paneeliert
panelling, (US) **paneling** ['pænəlɪŋ] N Täfelung f
panellist, (US) **panelist** ['pænəlɪst] N
Diskussionsteilnehmer(in) m(f)
panel truck N (US) Lieferwagen m
pang [pæŋ] N I felt a ~ of conscience ich hatte Gewissensbisse;
a ~ of jealousy ein Eifersuchtsanfall m; a ~ of regret ein
Anfall m von Bedauern; ~s of hunger quälender Hunger
pan: panhandle VI (US inf) die Leute anhauen (inf); **panhandler**
N (US inf) Bettler(in) m(f)
panic ['pænɪk], vb: pret, ptp panicked ▊ N Panik f; ~ on the
stock exchange Börsenpanik f; in a (blind) ~ in (heller) Panik;
to flee in ~ panikartig die Flucht ergreifen; a ~ reaction eine
Kurzschlussreaktion; the country was thrown into a (state of)

~ das Land wurde von Panik erfasst; ~ buying/selling (esp St
Ex) Panikkäufe pl/-verkäufe pl; (of goods also) Hamsterkäufe
pl/Angstverkäufe pl
▊ VI in Panik geraten; don't ~ nur keine Panik!
▊ VT Panik auslösen unter (+dat)
panic attack N (Psych) Panikanfall m; to have a ~ einen
Panikanfall bekommen
panicky ['pænɪkɪ] ADJ person überängstlich; voice panisch;
measure, behaviour panikartig; to feel ~ panische Angst
haben; to get ~ in Panik geraten
panic-stricken ['pænɪkˌstrɪkən] ADJ von panischem Schrecken
ergriffen; look panisch
pannier ['pænɪə'] N Korb m; (on motor-cycle etc) Satteltasche f
panorama [ˌpænə'rɑːmə] N (lit, fig) Panorama nt (of +gen)
panoramic [ˌpænə'ræmɪk] ADJ Panorama-
panoramic view N Panoramablick m; a ~ of the hills ein Blick
m auf das Bergpanorama
pansy ['pænzɪ] N (a) (Bot) Stiefmütterchen nt (b) (Brit pej:
= homosexual) Schwuchtel f (pej inf)
pant [pænt] VI keuchen; (dog) hecheln; he was ~ing for breath
er schnappte nach Luft (inf)
pantheon ['pænθɪən] N Pantheon nt
panther ['pænθə'] N Pant(h)er m
panties ['pæntɪz] PL Höschen nt; a pair of ~ ein Höschen nt
panto ['pæntəʊ] N (Brit inf) = pantomime (a)
pantomime ['pæntəmaɪm] N (a) (in GB) ≈ Weihnachtsmärchen
nt; what a ~! (inf) was für ein Theater! (inf) (b) (= mime)
Pantomime f

PANTOMIME

Eine **pantomime**, oder kurz panto, hat mit der deutschen Form von
Pantomime wenig gemein. Es handelt sich dabei vielmehr um ein
normalerweise zur Weihnachtszeit aufgeführtes Märchenspiel für die
ganze Familie. Die Handlung basiert auf einer bekannten Geschichte,
wie z. B. Aschenputtel oder Aladin. Häufig ist die Mithilfe des Publikums,
vor allem der Kinder, gefordert. Die männlichen und weiblichen
Hauptrollen werden gern Vertretern des jeweils anderen Geschlechts
übertragen, wobei bei den bekannteren Aufführungen Prominente die
Rollen übernehmen.

pantry ['pæntrɪ] N Speisekammer f
pants [pænts] PL (esp US: = trousers) Hose f; (Brit: = underpants)
Unterhose f; a pair of ~ eine Hose/Unterhose; to charm the ~
off sb (inf) jdm um den Bart gehen; to wear the ~ (US fig) die
Hosen anhaben (inf); to be ~ (Brit sl: = awful) beknackt or
beschissen sein (sl)
pantsuit ['pæntsuːt] N (US) Hosenanzug m
panty ['pæntɪ]: **pantyhose** N (US) Strumpfhose f; **panty-liner** N
Slipeinlage f
paparazzo [ˌpæpə'rætsəʊ], pl **paparazzi** [ˌpæpə'rætsɪ] N Paparazzo
m
papaya [pə'paɪə] N Papayabaum f; (= fruit) Papaya f
paper ['peɪpə'] ▊ N (a) Papier nt; to get or put sth down on ~
etw schriftlich festhalten; can we get your acceptance down
on ~? können wir Ihre Einwilligung schriftlich haben?; on ~
they're the best firm auf dem Papier ist das die beste Firma;
it's not worth the ~ it's written on das ist schade ums Papier,
auf dem es steht
(b) (= newspaper) Zeitung f; to write to the ~s about sth
Leserbriefe/einen Leserbrief über etw (acc) schreiben; he's
always in the ~s er steht ständig in der Zeitung
(c) papers PL (= identity ~s) Papiere pl
(d) (= set of questions in exam) Testbogen m; (= exam) (Univ)
Klausur f; (Sch) Arbeit f; to do a good ~ in maths eine gute
Mathematikklausur/-arbeit schreiben
(e) (academic) Referat nt
(f) (= wallpaper) Tapete f
(g) (Parl) a white ~ ein Weißbuch nt
▊ VT wall, room tapezieren
➤ **paper over** VT SEP überkleben; to paper over the cracks (fig)
die Risse übertünchen; (= cover up mistakes) die Fehler
übertünchen
paper IN CPDS Papier-; **paperback** N Taschenbuch nt; ~
edition Taschenbuchausgabe f; **paper bag** N Papiertüte f;
paperboy N Zeitungsjunge m; **paper chain** N Girlande f;
paperclip N Büroklammer f; **paper cup** N Pappbecher m;

paper cutter N (US) Schneidemaschine f; **paper feed** N (Comput) Papiervorschub m; **paper girl** N Zeitungsmädchen nt; **paper handling** N (Comput) Papierführung f; **paperless** ADJ papierlos; **paper money** N Papiergeld nt; **paper plate** N Pappteller m; **paper profit** N rechnerischer Gewinn; **paper round** N (Brit) **to have** or **do a** ~ Zeitungen austragen; **paper route** N (US) = paper round; **paper shop** N (Brit) Zeitungsladen m; **paper-thin** ADJ hauchdünn; **paper trail** N (US) belastende Unterlagen pl; **paper tray** N (Comput) Papierschacht m; **paperweight** N Briefbeschwerer m; **paperwork** N Schreibarbeit f

papier mâché [ˈpæpɪeɪˈmæʃeɪ] **1** N Pappmaché nt **2** ADJ aus Pappmaché

paprika [ˈpæprɪkə] N Paprika m

Papua [ˈpæpjʊə] N Papua nt

Papuan [ˈpæpjʊən] **1** ADJ papuanisch **2** N Papua mf

Papua New Guinea N Papua-Neuguinea nt

par [pɑːʳ] N **(a)** (Fin) Nennwert m; **to be above/below** ~ über/unter dem Nennwert stehen; **at** ~ zum Nennwert, al pari **(b) to be on a** ~ **with sb/sth** sich mit jdm/etw messen können; **this objection is on a** ~ **with Harry's** dieser Einwand liegt auf der gleichen Ebene wie Harrys; **he's nowhere near on a** ~ **with her** er kann ihr nicht das Wasser reichen; **this puts him on a** ~ **with the champion** dadurch hat er mit dem Meister gleichgezogen **(c) below** ~ (fig) unter Niveau; **I'm feeling physically below** or **under** ~ ich fühle mich körperlich nicht auf der Höhe **(d)** (Golf) Par nt; ~ **three** Par 3; **that's** ~ **for the course for him** (fig inf) das kann man von ihm erwarten

parable [ˈpærəbl] N Parabel f, Gleichnis nt

paracetamol [ˌpærəˈsiːtəmɒl] N Schmerztablette f

parachute [ˈpærəʃuːt] **1** N Fallschirm m; **by** ~ mit dem Fallschirm **2** VI (also ~ **down**) (mit dem Fallschirm) abspringen; **to** ~ **to safety** sich mit dem Fallschirm retten ➤ **parachute in 1** VT SEP troops mit dem Fallschirm absetzen; supplies abwerfen **2** VI (mit dem Fallschirm) abspringen

parachute: parachute drop N (of supplies) (Fallschirm)abwurf m; **parachute jump** N Absprung m (mit dem Fallschirm)

parachutist [ˈpærəʃuːtɪst] N Fallschirmspringer(in) m(f)

parade [pəˈreɪd] **1** N **(a)** (= procession) Umzug m; (Mil, of circus, = display) Parade f; (political) Demonstration f; (of wealth etc) Zurschaustellung f; **to be on** ~ (Mil) eine Parade abhalten **(b)** (= fashion ~) Modenschau f **2** VT **(a)** troops aufmarschieren lassen; military might demonstrieren; placards vor sich her tragen **(b)** (= show off) zur Schau stellen **3** VI (Mil) aufmarschieren; **the strikers** ~**d through the town** die Streikenden zogen durch die Stadt; **she** ~**d up and down with the hat on** sie stolzierte mit ihrem Hut auf und ab

paradise [ˈpærədaɪs] N (lit, fig) Paradies nt; **a shopper's** ~ ein Einkaufsparadies nt; **an architect's** ~ ein Paradies nt für Architekten; **living there must be** ~ **compared with this place** dort zu leben muss geradezu paradiesisch sein verglichen mit hier

paradox [ˈpærədɒks] N Paradox nt

paradoxical [ˌpærəˈdɒksɪkəl] ADJ paradox

paradoxically [ˌpærəˈdɒksɪkəli] ADV paradoxerweise

paraffin [ˈpærəfɪn] N Paraffin nt

paragliding [ˈpærəɡlaɪdɪŋ] N Gleitschirmfliegen nt

paragraph [ˈpærəɡrɑːf] N Abschnitt m

Paraguay [ˈpærəɡwaɪ] N Paraguay nt

Paraguayan [ˌpærəˈɡwaɪən] **1** ADJ paraguayisch **2** N Paraguayer(in) m(f)

paralegal [ˌpærəˈliːɡəl] (esp US) **1** N Rechtsassistent(in) m(f) **2** ADJ ~ **assistant** Rechtsassistent(in) m(f)

parallel [ˈpærəlel] **1** ADJ (lit, fig) parallel; career, development parallel verlaufend; ~ **to** or **with** parallel zu or mit; ~ **interface** (Comput) Parallelschnittstelle f; ~ **market** (Econ) Parallelmarkt m; ~ **printer** Paralleldrucker m; **the two systems developed along** ~ **lines** die Entwicklung der beiden Systeme verlief vergleichbar **2** ADV **to run** ~ (roads, careers) parallel verlaufen (**to sth** zu etw) **3** N (fig) Parallele f; **without** ~ ohne Parallele; **to draw a** ~ **between X and Y** eine Parallele zwischen X und Y ziehen; **in** ~ **with** parallel mit

4 VT (fig) gleichen (+dat); **a case** ~**led only by ...** ein Fall, zu dem es nur eine einzige Parallele gibt, nämlich ...

parallel: parallel import N (Econ) Parallelimport m; **parallel processing** N (Comput) Parallelverarbeitung f

paralysis [pəˈræləsɪs] N, pl **paralyses** [pəˈrælɪsiːz] Lähmung f

paralytic [ˌpærəˈlɪtɪk] (Brit inf: = very drunk) voll dicht (sl)

paralyze [ˈpærəlaɪz] VT **(a)** (lit) lähmen **(b)** (fig) industry, economy lahm legen

paralyzed [ˈpærəlaɪzd] ADJ **(a)** (lit) gelähmt; **he was left partially** ~ er behielt teilweise Lähmungen zurück; ~ **from the waist down** von der Hüfte abwärts gelähmt **(b)** (fig) **to be** ~ **with fear** vor Angst (wie) gelähmt sein

paralyzing [ˈpærəlaɪzɪŋ] ADJ (fig) fear etc lähmend

paramedic [ˌpærəˈmedɪk] N Sanitäter(in) m(f); (in hospital) medizinisch-technischer Assistent, medizinisch-technische Assistentin

parameters [pəˈræmətəz] PL (= framework, limits) Rahmen m; **to define** or **establish** or **set the** ~ **of** or **for sth** die Parameter für etw festsetzen

paramilitary [ˌpærəˈmɪlɪtəri] ADJ paramilitärisch

paramount [ˈpærəmaʊnt] ADJ Haupt-; **to be** ~ Priorität haben; **of** ~ **importance** von höchster Wichtigkeit

paranoia [ˌpærəˈnɔɪə] N Paranoia f; (inf) Verfolgungswahn m

paranoid [ˈpærənɔɪd] ADJ paranoid; **or am I just being** ~? oder bilde ich mir das nur ein?; **aren't you being rather** ~? du scheinst unter Wahnvorstellungen zu leiden; **to be** ~ **about sth** von etw Wahnvorstellungen haben; **she's getting** ~ **about what other people think of her** die Angst vor dem, was andere von ihr denken, wird bei ihr langsam zur Manie

paranormal [ˌpærəˈnɔːməl] **1** ADJ paranormal **2** N **the** ~ das Paranormale

paraphernalia [ˈpærəfəˈneɪlɪə] PL Drum und Dran nt

paraphrase [ˈpærəfreɪz] VT umschreiben

paraplegic [ˌpærəˈpliːdʒɪk] N Paraplegiker(in) m(f) (spec)

parasite [ˈpærəsaɪt] N (lit) Parasit m; (fig) Schmarotzer(in) m(f)

parasitic(al) [ˌpærəˈsɪtɪk(əl)] ADJ parasitär (also fig)

paratrooper [ˈpærətruːpəʳ] N Fallschirmjäger(in) m(f)

paratroops [ˈpærətruːps] PL Fallschirmjäger pl

parcel [ˈpɑːsl] N (esp Brit) Paket nt; ~ **post** Paketpost f ➤ **parcel up** VT SEP als Paket verpacken

parcel bomb N (Brit) Paketbombe f

parcel(s) office N (Brit Rail) Paketstelle f

parched [pɑːtʃt] ADJ ausgetrocknet; **I'm** ~ ich habe furchtbaren Durst

parchment [ˈpɑːtʃmənt] N Pergament nt

pardon [ˈpɑːdn] **1** N **(a)** (Jur) Begnadigung f; **to grant sb a** ~ jdn begnadigen **(b) to beg sb's** ~ jdn um Verzeihung bitten; **I beg your** ~! erlauben Sie mal!; ~? (Brit), **I beg your** ~? (Brit) (wie) bitte?; **I beg your** ~ (apology) Entschuldigung **2** VT **(a)** (Jur) begnadigen **(b)** (= forgive) verzeihen; **to** ~ **sb sth** jdm etw verzeihen; ~ **me, but could you ...?** entschuldigen Sie bitte, könnten Sie ...?; ~ **me!** Entschuldigung!; ~ **me?** (US) (wie) bitte?

pare [peəʳ] VT (fig) budget etc zurückschneiden ➤ **pare back** VT SEP budget etc zurückschneiden ➤ **pare down** VT SEP (fig) expenses einschränken; personnel einsparen; **to pare sth down to the minimum** etw auf ein Minimum beschränken

parent [ˈpeərənt] N Elternteil m; ~**s** Eltern pl

parentage [ˈpeərəntɪdʒ] N Herkunft f; **children of racially mixed** ~ gemischtrassige Kinder pl

parental [pəˈrentl] ADJ care etc elterlich attr; ~ **leave** Elternschaftsurlaub m

parental leave N Elternurlaub m

parent company N Muttergesellschaft f

parenthesis [pəˈrenθɪsɪs] N, pl **parentheses** [pəˈrenθɪsiːz] Klammer f; **in** ~ in Klammern

parenthood [ˈpeərənthʊd] N Elternschaft f

parent teacher association N (Sch) Lehrer- und Elternverband m

par excellence [ˌpɑːˈreksəlɑ̃ːns] ADV par excellence

Paris [ˈpærɪs] N Paris nt

parish [ˈpærɪʃ] N Gemeinde f; (= district also) Pfarrbezirk m

parish: **parish church** N Pfarrkirche f; **parish council** N Gemeinderat m

parishioner [pəˈrɪʃənəʳ] N Gemeinde(mit)glied nt

parish priest N Pfarrer m

parity [ˈpærɪtɪ] N **(a)** (= equality) Gleichstellung f; (of opportunities) Gleichheit f; **~ of pay** Lohngleichheit f **(b)** (Fin, Sci, Comput) Parität f; **the ~ of the dollar** die Dollarparität; **odd/even ~** ungerade/gerade Parität **(c)** (US Agr) Preisparität f

park [pɑːk] **1** N Park m; **national ~** Nationalpark m **2** VT **(a)** car parken; bicycle abstellen; **a ~ed car** ein parkendes Auto; **there's been a car ~ed outside for days** draußen parkt schon seit Tagen ein Auto **(b)** (inf: = put) abstellen; **he ~ed himself right in front of the fire** er pflanzte sich direkt vor den Kamin (inf) **3** VI parken; **there was nowhere to ~** es gab nirgendwo einen Parkplatz; **to find a place to ~** einen Parkplatz finden; (in line of cars) eine Parklücke finden

park: **park-and-ride** N Park-and-Ride-System nt; **park bench** N Parkbank f

parking [ˈpɑːkɪŋ] N Parken nt; **there's no ~ on this street** in dieser Straße ist Parken verboten or ist Parkverbot; **"no ~"** „Parken verboten"; **"~ for 50 cars"** "50 (Park)plätze"

parking: **parking attendant** N Parkplatzwächter(in) m(f); **parking bay** N Parkbucht f; **parking fine** N Geldbuße f (für Parkvergehen); **parking garage** N (US) Parkhaus nt; **parking lot** N (US) Parkplatz m; **parking meter** N Parkuhr f; **parking place** N Parkplatz m; **parking ticket** N Strafzettel m

Parkinson's (disease) [ˈpɑːkɪnsənz(drˈziːz)] N parkinsonsche Krankheit

park: **park keeper** N Parkwächter(in) m(f); **parkland** N Grünland nt; **park ranger**, **park warden** N (in national park) Aufseher(in) m(f) in einem Nationalpark; **parkway** N (US) Allee f

parliament [ˈpɑːləmənt] N Parlament nt; **the German ~** der Bundestag; **the Swiss ~** die Bundesversammlung; **the Austrian ~** der Nationalrat

parliamentary [pɑːləˈmentərɪ] ADJ parlamentarisch; **~ seat** Parlamentssitz m

parliamentary: **parliamentary candidate** N Parlamentskandidat(in) m(f); **parliamentary election** N Parlamentswahlen pl

parlor car N (US) Salonwagen m

parlour, (US) **parlor** [ˈpɑːləʳ] N (= beauty ~ etc) Salon m; **ice-cream ~** Eisdiele f

Parmesan [ˌpɑːmɪˈzæn] N Parmesan m

parody [ˈpærədɪ] **1** N **(a)** Parodie f (of auf +acc) **(b)** (= travesty) Abklatsch m; **a ~ of justice** eine Parodie auf die Gerechtigkeit **2** VT parodieren

parole [pəˈrəʊl] **1** N (Jur) Bewährung f; (= temporary release) Strafunterbrechung f; **to let sb out on ~** jdn auf Bewährung entlassen; (temporarily) jdm Strafunterbrechung gewähren; **to be on ~** unter Bewährung stehen; (temporarily) auf Kurzurlaub sein; **he's on six months' ~** er hat sechs Monate Bewährung(sfrist) **2** VT auf Bewährung entlassen; (temporarily) Strafunterbrechung gewähren (+dat)

parrot [ˈpærət] N Papagei m; **he felt as sick as a ~** (Brit inf) ihm war kotzübel (inf)

parrot-fashion [ˈpærətfæʃən] ADV **to repeat sth ~** etw wie ein Papagei nachplappern; **he learned the poem ~** er lernte das Gedicht stur auswendig

parry [ˈpærɪ] VTI (Fencing, fig) parieren; (Boxing, Ftbl) abwehren

parser [ˈpɑːsəʳ] N (Comput) Parser m

parsing [ˈpɑːsɪŋ] N (Comput) Parsing nt

parsley [ˈpɑːslɪ] N Petersilie f

parsnip [ˈpɑːsnɪp] N Pastinake f

parson [ˈpɑːsn] N Pfarrer m

part [pɑːt] **1** N **(a)** Teil m; **you haven't heard the best ~ yet** ihr habt ja das Beste noch gar nicht gehört; **in ~** teilweise; **a ~ of the country/city I don't know** eine Gegend, die ich nicht kenne; **during the darkest ~ of the night** in tiefster Nacht; **I lost ~ of the manuscript** ich habe einen Teil des Manuskripts verloren; **for the most ~** zum größten Teil; **her performance was for the most ~ well executed** ihre Leistung war im Großen und Ganzen gelungen; **in the latter ~ of the year** gegen Ende des Jahres; **the remaining ~ of our holidays** der

Rest unseres Urlaubs; **she's become (a) ~ of me** sie ist ein Teil von mir geworden; **it's all ~ of growing up** das gehört alles zum Erwachsenwerden dazu; **to be ~ and parcel of sth** fester Bestandteil einer Sache (gen) sein; **it is ~ and parcel of the job** das gehört zu der Arbeit dazu; **spare ~** Ersatzteil nt; **moving ~s** bewegliche Teile pl

(b) (Gram) **~ of speech** Wortart f

(c) (of series) Folge f; (of serial) Fortsetzung f; (of encyclopaedia etc) Lieferung f; **end of ~ one** (TV) Ende des ersten Teils

(d) (= share, role) (An)teil m; (Theat) Rolle f; **to play one's ~** (fig) seinen Beitrag leisten; **to take ~ in** an etw (dat) teilnehmen; **who is taking ~?** wer macht mit?; **he's taking ~ in the play** er spielt in dem Stück mit; **he looks the ~** (fig) so sieht (d)er auch aus; **to play a ~** (Theat, fig) eine Rolle spielen; **to play no ~ in sth** (person) nicht an etw (dat) beteiligt sein; **we want no ~ of it** wir wollen damit nichts zu tun haben

(e) parts PL (= region) Gegend f; **from all ~s** von überall her; **in** or **around these ~s** in dieser Gegend; **in foreign ~s** in fremden Ländern; **he's not from these ~s** er ist nicht aus dieser Gegend

(f) (= side) Seite f; **to take sb's ~** für jdn Partei ergreifen; **for my ~** was mich betrifft; **a miscalculation on my ~** eine Fehlkalkulation meinerseits; **on the ~ of** seitens (+gen)

(g) (US: in hair) Scheitel m

2 ADV teils, teilweise; **is it X or Y? - ~ one and ~ the other** ist es X oder Y? - teils (das eine), teils (das andere); **it is ~ iron and ~ copper** es ist teils aus Eisen, teils aus Kupfer

3 VT **(a)** (= divide) teilen; hair scheiteln; legs aufmachen; lips öffnen

(b) (= separate) trennen; **to ~ sb from sb/sth** jdn von jdm/etw trennen; **till death us do ~** bis dass der Tod uns scheidet; **to ~ company with sb/sth** sich von jdm/etw trennen

4 VI **(a)** (= divide) sich teilen; (curtains) sich öffnen; **her lips ~ed in a smile** ihre Lippen öffneten sich zu einem Lächeln

(b) (= separate) (people) sich trennen; (things) sich lösen; **to ~ from** or **with sb** sich von jdm trennen; **we ~ed friends** wir gingen als Freunde auseinander; **to ~ with sth** sich von etw trennen; **to ~ with money** Geld ausgeben

part consignment N (Brit) Teillieferung f, Teilsendung f

parterre [pɑːˈtɛəʳ] N (US) Parterre nt

part exchange N **to offer/take sth in ~** etw in Zahlung geben/nehmen

partial [ˈpɑːʃəl] ADJ teilweise; **a ~ success** ein Teilerfolg m; **to make a ~ recovery** eine teilweise Erholung durchmachen; **to reach a ~ agreement** teilweise Übereinstimmung erzielen; **~ consignment** (US) Teillieferung f, Teilsendung f; **~ loss** Teilverlust m; (damage) Teilschaden m; **~ payment** (US) Abschlags- or Teilzahlung f

partially [ˈpɑːʃəlɪ] ADV teilweise; **~ deaf** eingeschränkt hörfähig

partially sighted ADJ eingeschränkt sehfähig

participant [pɑːˈtɪsɪpənt] N Teilnehmer(in) m(f) (in an +dat)

participate [pɑːˈtɪsɪpeɪt] VI sich beteiligen (in an +dat); **to ~ in sport** (Sch) am Schulsport teilnehmen; **participating preferred stock** (St Ex) Beteiligungsvorzugsaktie f

participation [pɑːˌtɪsɪˈpeɪʃən] N Beteiligung f; (in competition etc) Teilnahme f; (= worker ~) Mitbestimmung f; **~ in the profits** Gewinnbeteiligung f

particle [ˈpɑːtɪkl] N (of sand etc) Körnchen nt; (Phys) Teilchen nt; **~ of dust**, **dust ~** Staubkörnchen nt

particular [pəˈtɪkjʊləʳ] **1** ADJ **(a)** (= as against others) **this ~ house is very nice** dies (eine) Haus ist sehr hübsch; **in this ~ instance** in diesem besonderen Fall; **there's a ~ town in France where ...** in Frankreich gibt es eine Stadt, wo ...; **is there any one ~ city you prefer?** bevorzugen Sie eine bestimmte Stadt?

(b) (= special) besondere(r, s); **in ~** insbesondere; **the wine in ~ was excellent** vor allem der Wein war hervorragend; **nothing in ~** nichts Besonderes; **is there anything in ~ you'd like?** haben Sie einen besonderen Wunsch?; **did you want to speak to anyone in ~?** wollten Sie mit jemand(em) Bestimmtem sprechen?; **for no ~ reason** aus keinem besonderen Grund; **at a ~ time** zu einer bestimmten Zeit; **at that ~ time** zu (genau) diesem Zeitpunkt; **in a ~ way** auf bestimmte Art und Weise; **to be of ~ concern to sb** jdm ein besonderes Anliegen sein

(c) (= fussy) eigen; (= choosy) wählerisch; **he is very ~ about cleanliness** er nimmt es mit der Sauberkeit; **he's ~ about his car** er ist sehr eigen mit seinem Auto (inf)

2 N particulars PL Einzelheiten *pl*; *(about person)* Personalien *pl*; **for further ~s apply to the personnel manager** weitere Auskünfte erteilt der Personalchef

particularly [pə'tɪkjʊlɪ] ADV besonders; **do you want it ~ for tomorrow?** brauchen Sie es unbedingt morgen?; **we are ~ pleased to have with us today …** wir freuen uns besonders, heute … bei uns zu haben; **not ~** nicht besonders; **it's important, ~** since time is getting short es ist wichtig, zumal die Zeit knapp wird

parting ['pɑːtɪŋ] **1 N (a)** Abschied *m* **(b)** *(Brit: in hair)* Scheitel *m* **2 ADJ** abschließend; **Charles knows all about it already, was her ~ shot** Charles weiß schon alles, schleuderte sie ihm nach; **his ~ words** seine Abschiedsworte *pl*

partisan [ˌpɑːtɪ'zæn] N *(Mil)* Partisan(in) *m(f)*

partition [pɑː'tɪʃən] **1 N (a)** Teilung *f* **(b)** *(= wall)* Trennwand *f* **(c)** *(= section)* Abteilung *f* **2 VT** *country* teilen; *room* aufteilen

part load N *(Comm)* Teilladung *f*

partly ['pɑːtlɪ] ADV teilweise

partner ['pɑːtnə'] N Partner(in) *m(f)*; **junior/senior ~** Junior-/Seniorpartner(in) *m(f)*

partnership ['pɑːtnəʃɪp] N **(a)** Partnerschaft *f*; **to do sth in ~ with sb** etw mit jdm gemeinsam machen **(b)** *(Comm)* Personengesellschaft *f*; **to enter into a ~** in eine Gesellschaft eintreten; **to go into ~ with sb** mit jdm eine Personengesellschaft gründen; **general ~** offene Handelsgesellschaft; **~ articles** *(Brit)*, **articles of ~** *(US)* Gesellschaftsvertrag *m* einer Handelsgesellschaft

part: part owner N Mitbesitzer(in) *m(f)*; **part payment** N Teilzahlung *f*

partridge ['pɑːtrɪdʒ] N Rebhuhn *nt*

part: part-time 1 ADJ ~ job/worker Teilzeitarbeit *f*/-arbeiter(in) *m(f)*; **I'm just ~** ich arbeite nur Teilzeit; **on a ~ basis** auf Teilzeitbasis **2 ADV can I do the job ~?** kann ich (auf) Teilzeit arbeiten?; **she only teaches ~** sie unterrichtet nur stundenweise; **she is studying ~** sie ist Teilzeitstudentin; **part-timer** N Teilzeitbeschäftigte(r) *m(f)*

party ['pɑːtɪ] **1 N (a)** *(Pol, Jur, fig)* Partei *f*; **to be a member of the ~** Parteimitglied sein; **a third ~** ein Dritter *m*; **the third ~** der Dritte **(b)** *(= group)* Gruppe *f*; **a ~ of tourists** eine Reisegesellschaft **(c)** *(= celebration)* Party *f*; *(more formal)* Gesellschaft *f*; **to have or give or throw** *(inf)* **a ~** eine Party geben; **at the ~** auf der Party; *(more formal)* bei der Gesellschaft **2 VI** *(inf)* feiern

party: party dress N Partykleid *nt*; **partygoer** N Partygänger(in) *m(f)*; **party hat** N Partyhut *m*; **party political broadcast** N parteipolitische Sendung; **party pooper** N *(inf)* Partymuffel *m* *(inf)*; **party popper** N Partyknaller *m*; **party spirit** N Partylaune *f*

pass [pɑːs] **1 N (a)** *(= permit)* Ausweis *m*; *(Mil etc)* Passierschein *m* **(b)** *(Geog, Sport)* Pass *m*; *(Ftbl: for shot at goal)* Vorlage *f* **(c) things had come to such a ~ that …** die Lage hatte sich so zugespitzt, dass …; **things have come to a pretty ~ when …** so weit ist es schon gekommen, dass …; **this is a pretty ~!** das ist ja eine schöne Bescherung! **(d) to make a ~ at sb** bei jdm Annäherungsversuche machen **(e)** *(Aviat)* **the jet made three ~es over the ship** der Düsenjäger flog dreimal über das Schiff **2 VT (a)** *(= move past)* vorbeigehen/-fahren/-fliegen an *(+dat)*; **he ~ed me without even saying hello** er ging ohne zu grüßen an mir vorbei **(b)** *(= overtake)* überholen **(c)** *frontier etc* passieren; *deadline* überschreiten; **not a word ~ed her lips** kein Wort kam über ihre Lippen **(d)** *(= reach, hand)* reichen; **they ~ed the photograph around** sie reichten das Foto herum; **~ (me) the salt, please** reich mir doch bitte das Salz!; **the characteristics which he ~ed to his son** die Eigenschaften, die er an seinen Sohn weitergab **(e)** *exam* bestehen; *candidate* bestehen lassen **(f)** *(= approve)* *motion* annehmen; *plan* gutheißen; *(Parl)* verabschieden **(g)** *(Sport)* **to ~ the ball to sb** jdm den Ball zuspielen **(h) ~ the thread through the hole** führen Sie den Faden durch die Öffnung; **he ~ed a chain around the front axle** er legte eine Kette um die Vorderachse

(i) *time* verbringen; **he did it just to ~ the time** er tat das nur, um sich *(dat)* die Zeit zu vertreiben **(j)** *(Jur)* *sentence* verhängen; *judgement* fällen; **to ~ comment (on sth)** einen Kommentar (zu etw) abgeben **(k)** *excrement, blood* ausscheiden; **to ~ water** Wasser lassen **3 VI (a)** *(= move past)* vorbeigehen/-fahren; **the street was too narrow for the cars to ~** die Straße war so eng, dass die Wagen nicht aneinander vorbeikamen; **we ~ed in the corridor** wir gingen im Korridor aneinander vorbei **(b)** *(= overtake)* überholen **(c)** *(= move, go)* **what has ~ed between us** was sich zwischen uns zugetragen hat; **if you ~ by the grocer's …** wenn du beim Kaufmann vorbeikommst …; **the procession ~ed down the street** die Prozession zog die Straße entlang; **the virus ~es easily from one person to another** der Virus ist leicht von einer Person auf die andere übertragbar; **the land has now ~ed into private hands** das Land ist jetzt in Privatbesitz übergegangen; **to ~ into history** in die Geschichte eingehen; **to ~ out of sight** außer Sichtweite geraten; **the manuscript has ~ed through a lot of hands** das Manuskript ist durch viele Hände gegangen; **the thread ~es through this hole** der Faden geht durch diese Öffnung; **he ~ed under the archway** er ging/fuhr durch das Tor **(d)** *(time: also ~ by)* vergehen; *(deadline)* verfallen **(e)** *(= disappear, end: anger, era etc)* vorübergehen; *(storm)* *(= go over)* vorüberziehen; *(= abate)* sich legen; *(rain)* vorbeigehen; **to let an opportunity ~** eine Gelegenheit verstreichen lassen; **it'll ~** das geht vorüber! **(f)** *(= be acceptable)* gehen; **to let sth ~** etw durchgehen lassen; **let it ~!** vergiss es! **(g)** *(= be considered, be accepted)* angesehen werden *(for or as sth* als etw); **this little room has to ~ for an office** dieses kleine Zimmer dient als Büro; **she could easily ~ for 25** sie könnte leicht für 25 durchgehen; **or what ~es nowadays for a hat** oder was heute so als Hut betrachtet wird **(h)** *(in exam)* bestehen; **I ~ed!** ich habe bestanden! **(i)** *(Sport)* abspielen; **to ~ to sb** jdm zuspielen **(j)** *(Cards)* passen; **(I) ~!** passe!; **I'll ~ on that** da passe ich

➤ **pass away** VI *(euph.* = *die)* entschlafen

➤ **pass by** VI vorbeigehen; *(car etc)* vorbeifahren; *(time)* vergehen **2 VT SEP** *(= ignore)* *problems* übergehen; **life has passed her by** das Leben ist an ihr vorübergegangen

➤ **pass down** VT SEP *traditions* weitergeben *(to +dat)*; *characteristics* weitergeben *(to an +acc)*; **passed down by word of mouth** mündlich überliefert

➤ **pass off 1 VI (a)** *(= take place)* ablaufen **(b)** *(= be taken as)* durchgehen *(as als)*; **she could pass off as an Italian** sie würde als Italienerin durchgehen **2 VT SEP to pass oneself/sb/sth off as sth** sich/jdn/etw als *or* für etw ausgeben

➤ **pass on 1 VI (a)** *(euph.* = *die)* entschlafen **(b)** *(= proceed)* übergehen *(to zu)* **2 VT SEP** *news, cost etc* weitergeben; *disease* übertragen; **pass it on!** weitersagen!; **take a leaflet and pass them on** nehmen Sie ein Blatt und geben Sie die anderen weiter

➤ **pass out** VI *(= become unconscious)* in Ohnmacht fallen; **he drank till he passed out** er trank bis zum Umfallen

➤ **pass over** VT SEP übergehen

➤ **pass through** VI **I'm only passing through** ich bin nur auf der Durchreise

➤ **pass up** VT SEP *chance* vorübergehen lassen

passable ['pɑːsəbl] ADJ **(a)** passierbar **(b)** *(= tolerable)* passabel

passage ['pæsɪdʒ] N **(a)** *(= transition)* Übergang *m*; **in or with the ~ of time** mit der Zeit **(b)** *(= right of ~)* Durchreisegenehmigung *f* **(c)** *(= corridor)* Gang *m*; **secret ~** Geheimgang *m* **(d)** *(in book, Mus)* Passage *f*; **a ~ from Shakespeare** eine Shakespearestelle

passageway ['pæsɪdʒweɪ] N Durchgang *m*

passbook ['pɑːsbʊk] N Sparbuch *nt*

passenger ['pæsɪndʒə'] N *(on bus, in taxi)* Fahrgast *m*; *(on train)* Reisende(r) *mf*; *(on ship, plane)* Passagier(in) *m(f)*; *(in car, on motorcycle)* Beifahrer(in) *m(f)*

passenger: passenger aircraft N Passagierflugzeug *nt*; **passenger door** N Beifahrertür *f*; **passenger ferry** N Personenfähre *f*; **passenger seat** N Beifahrersitz *m*; **passenger ship** N Passagierschiff *nt*; **passenger train** N Zug *m* im Personenverkehr

passer-by ['pɑːsə'baɪ] N, *pl* **passers-by** Passant(in) *m(f)*

passing ['pɑːsɪŋ] **1** N **(a)** Vorübergehen *nt*; *(of procession)* Passieren *nt*, Vorüberziehen *nt*; **I would like to mention in ~ that ...** ich möchte beiläufig noch erwähnen, dass ...
(b) (= *overtaking*) Überholen *nt*
(c) (*euph*: = *death*) Heimgang *m*
(d) (*Ftbl*) Ballabgabe *f*
2 ADJ **(a)** *car* vorbeifahrend; *clouds* vorüberziehend; *years* vergehend; **with every** *or* **each ~ day** mit jedem Tag, der vergeht
(b) *glance, thought, interest* flüchtig; *comments* beiläufig; *fancy, fashion* vorübergehend; **to make (a) ~ reference to sth** auf etw (*acc*) beiläufig hinweisen; **to bear a ~ resemblance to sb/sth** mit jdm/etw eine flüchtige Ähnlichkeit haben

passion ['pæʃən] N Leidenschaft *f*; (= *fervour*) Leidenschaftlichkeit *f*; **to have a ~ for sth** eine Leidenschaft für etw haben; **~s were running high** die Erregung schlug hohe Wellen; **his ~ is Mozart** Mozart ist seine Passion

passionate ['pæʃənɪt] ADJ leidenschaftlich; **to be ~ about sth** für etw eine Leidenschaft haben

passionately ['pæʃənɪtlɪ] ADV leidenschaftlich; **oh yes, she said ~** o ja, sagte sie voller Leidenschaft; **to be ~ fond of sth** etw unwahrscheinlich gern haben; **a ~ held belief** eine felsenfeste Überzeugung

passion: passion fruit N Passionsfrucht *f*; **Passion play** N Passionsspiel *nt*; **Passion Week** N Karwoche *f*

passive ['pæsɪv] **1** ADJ **(a)** passiv; *acceptance* widerspruchslos **(b)** (*Gram*) Passiv-; **~ form** Passivform *f* **2** N (*Gram*) Passiv *nt*; **in the ~** im Passiv

passively ['pæsɪvlɪ] ADV passiv; *accept* widerspruchslos; *watch etc* tatenlos

passive smoking N Passivrauchen *nt*

Passover ['pɑːsəʊvəʳ] N Passah *nt*

passport ['pɑːspɔːt] N (Reise)pass *m*; (*fig*) Schlüssel *m* (*to* zu)

passport: passport control N Passkontrolle *f*; **passport holder** N Passinhaber(in) *m(f)*; **are you a British ~?** haben Sie einen britischen Pass?; **passport office** N Passamt *nt*

password ['pɑːswɜːd] N Kennwort *nt*; (*Comput*) Passwort *nt*

past [pɑːst] **1** ADJ **(a)** frühe(r, s) *attr*; **for some time ~** seit einiger Zeit; **in times ~** in früheren Zeiten; **it's ~ history now** das gehört jetzt der Vergangenheit an; **all that is now ~** das ist jetzt alles vorüber; **what's ~ is ~** was vorbei ist, ist vorbei; **in the ~ week** vergangene Woche
(b) (*Gram*) **~ tense** Vergangenheit *f*
2 N Vergangenheit *f* (*also Gram*); **in the ~** in der Vergangenheit; **to be a thing of the ~** der Vergangenheit (*dat*) angehören; **that's all in the ~ now** das ist jetzt alles Vergangenheit; **the verb is in the ~** das Verb steht in der Vergangenheit
3 PREP **(a)** (*motion*) an (+*dat*) ... vorbei; (*position*: = *beyond*) hinter (+*dat*); **to run ~ sb** an jdm vorbeilaufen
(b) (*time*) nach (+*dat*); **ten (minutes) ~ three** zehn (Minuten) nach drei; **half ~ four** halb fünf; **a quarter ~ nine** Viertel nach neun; **it's ~ 12** es ist schon nach 12; **the trains run at a quarter ~ the hour** die Züge gehen jeweils um Viertel nach; **it's (well) ~ your bedtime** du solltest schon längst im Bett liegen; **~ due** (*Comm*) überfällig, im Rückstand
(c) (= *beyond*) über (+*acc*); **~ forty** über vierzig; **the patient is ~ saving** der Patient ist nicht mehr zu retten; **we're ~ caring** es kümmert uns nicht mehr; **to be ~ it** für etw zu alt sein; **he's ~ it** (*inf*) er brings nicht mehr (*sl*); **I wouldn't put it ~ him** (*inf*) ich würde es ihm schon zutrauen
4 ADV vorüber; **to walk ~** vorübergehen; **to run ~** vorbeirennen

pasta ['pæstə] N Nudeln *pl*

paste [peɪst] **1** N **(a)** (*for sticking*) Kleister *m* **(b)** **mix to a smooth/firm ~** (*glue etc*) zu einem lockeren/festen Brei anrühren; (*cake mixture etc*) zu einem glatten/festen Teig anrühren **(c)** (= *spread*) Brotaufstrich *m*; (= *tomato ~*) Mark *nt* **2** VT *wallpaper etc* einkleistern; (= *affix*) kleben; (*Comput*) einfügen; **to ~ sth to sth** etw an etw (*acc*) kleben

pastel ['pæstl] **1** N (= *crayon*) Pastellstift *m*; (= *colour*) Pastellton *m* **2** ADJ ATTR **~ colour** (*Brit*) *or* **color** (*US*) Pastellfarbe *f*; **~ drawing** Pastellzeichnung *f*

pasteurize ['pæstəraɪz] VT pasteurisieren

pastille ['pæstɪl] N Pastille *f*

pastime ['pɑːstaɪm] N Zeitvertreib *m*

pastor ['pɑːstəʳ] N Pfarrer(in) *m(f)*

pastoral ['pɑːstərəl] ADJ *land, farming, life* ländlich; (*Art, Liter, Mus, Eccl*) pastoral; *duties, responsibility* seelsorgerisch

past: past participle N Partizip Perfekt *nt*; **past perfect** N Plusquamperfekt *nt*

pastry ['peɪstrɪ] N Teig *m*; (= *cake etc*) Stückchen *nt*; **pastries** *pl* Gebäck *nt*

pastry chef, pastry cook N Konditor(in) *m(f)*; (*with higher qualification*) Konditormeister(in) *m(f)*

pasture ['pɑːstʃəʳ] N **(a)** (= *field*) Weide *f*; **to move on to ~s new** (*fig*) sich (*dat*) etwas Neues suchen **(b)** NO PL (*also* **~ land**) Weideland *nt*

pasty¹ ['peɪstɪ] ADJ *colour* blässlich; *look* kränklich

pasty² ['pæstɪ] N (*esp Brit*) Pastete *f*

pasty-faced ['peɪstɪ'feɪst] ADJ bleichgesichtig

pat¹ [pæt] N (*of butter*) Portion *f*; **cow ~** Kuhfladen *m*

pat² ADV **to know** *or* **have sth off ~** etw wie aus dem Effeff können (*inf*); **to learn sth off ~** etw in- und auswendig lernen

pat³ **1** N Klaps *m*; **he gave his nephew a ~ on the head** er tätschelte seinem Neffen den Kopf; **to give one's horse a ~** sein Pferd tätscheln; (*once*) seinem Pferd einen Klaps geben; **to give sb/oneself a ~ on the back** (*fig*) jdm/sich selbst auf die Schulter klopfen; **that's a ~ on the back for you** das ist ein Kompliment für dich
2 VT tätscheln; *ball* leicht schlagen; *face* abtupfen; **to ~ sb on the head** jdm den Kopf tätscheln; **to ~ sth/one's face dry** etw/ sein Gesicht trockentupfen; **to ~ sb on the back** (*lit*) jdm auf den Rücken klopfen; **to ~ sb/oneself on the back** (*fig*) jdm/ sich selbst auf die Schulter klopfen
➤ **pat down** VT SEP festklopfen; *hair* festdrücken

Patagonia [,pætə'gəʊnɪə] N Patagonien *nt*

Patagonian [,pætə'gəʊnɪən] **1** ADJ patagonisch **2** N Patagonier(in) *m(f)*

patch [pætʃ] **1** N **(a)** (*for mending*) Flicken *m*; (*on new garments*) Flecken *m*; (= *eye ~*) Augenklappe *f*
(b) (= *small area, stain*) Fleck *m*; (= *piece of land*) Stück *nt*; (*of garden*) Beet *nt*; (= *part, section*) Stelle *f*; (*of time*) Phase *f*; (*inf*: *of policeman etc*) Revier *nt*; **a ~ of blue sky** ein Stückchen *nt* blauer Himmel; **a ~ of oil** ein Ölfleck *m*; **he's going through a bad** *or* **rough ~ at the moment** ihm gehts im Augenblick nicht sonderlich gut; **it's/he's not a ~ on ...** (*Brit inf*) das/er ist gar nichts gegen ...
(c) (*Comput*) Korrekturroutine *f*
2 VT flicken
➤ **patch up** VT SEP zusammenflicken; *quarrel* beilegen; **I want to patch things up between us** ich möchte unsere Beziehung wieder ins Lot bringen

patchwork ['pætʃwɜːk] N Patchwork *nt*; **~ quilt** Flickendecke *f*

patchy ['pætʃɪ] ADJ (+*ER*) **(a)** *work* ungleichmäßig; *knowledge, evidence* lückenhaft **(b)** (*lit*) *beard, grass* licht; **~ fog on the coast** an der Küste stellenweise Nebel

pâté ['pæteɪ] N Pastete *f*

patent ['peɪtənt] **1** N Patent *nt*; **~ applied for** *or* **pending** Patent angemeldet; **to take out a ~ on sth** etw (*acc*) patentieren lassen **2** VT patentieren lassen; **is it ~-ed?** ist das patentrechtlich geschützt?

patentable ['peɪtəntəbl] ADJ patentierbar

patent: patent application N Patentanmeldung *f*; **patent attorney** N Patentanwalt *m*/-anwältin *f*; **patent holder** N Patentinhaber(in) *m(f)*; **patent leather** N Lackleder *nt*; **~ shoes** Lackschuhe *pl*

patently ['peɪtəntlɪ] ADV offensichtlich; **~ obvious** ganz offensichtlich

Patent Office N Patentamt *nt*

paternal [pə'tɜːnl] ADJ väterlich; **my ~ grandmother** *etc* meine Großmutter *etc* väterlicherseits

paternity [pə'tɜːnɪtɪ] N Vaterschaft *f*

paternity leave N Vaterschaftsurlaub *m*

path [pɑːθ] N (*lit, fig*) Weg *m*; (*in field*) Feldweg *m*; (= *trajectory, route*) Bahn *f*; (*Comput*) Pfad *m*

path-breaking ['pɑːθ,breɪkɪŋ] ADJ (*esp US*) bahnbrechend

pathetic [pə'θetɪk] ADJ **(a)** (= *piteous*) Mitleid erregend; **the exhausted refugees made a ~ sight** die erschöpften Flüchtlinge boten ein Bild des Jammers **(b)** (= *poor*) erbärmlich; **it's ~** es ist zum Heulen (*inf*); **honestly you're ~,**

can't you even boil an egg? ehrlich, dich kann man zu nichts brauchen, kannst du nicht einmal ein Ei kochen?

pathetically [pəˈθetɪkəlɪ] ADV **(a)** (= *piteously*) Mitleid erregend; **~ thin** erschreckend dünn **(b)** *slow, inefficient* erbärmlich; **a ~ weak attempt** ein kläglicher Versuch; **it had become ~ obvious that she was ignoring him** es war schon peinlich zu sehen, wie sie ihn ignorierte

path name N (*Comput*) Pfad(name) *m*

pathological [ˌpæθəˈlɒdʒɪkəl] ADJ (*lit, fig*) pathologisch

pathologically [ˌpæθəˈlɒdʒɪkəlɪ] ADV krankhaft

pathologist [pəˈθɒlədʒɪst] N Pathologe *m*, Pathologin *f*

pathology [pəˈθɒlədʒɪ] N (*science*) Pathologie *f*

pathway [ˈpɑːθweɪ] N Weg *m*

patience [ˈpeɪʃəns] N **(a)** Geduld *f*; **to have ~/no ~ (with sb/sth)** Geduld/keine Geduld (mit jdm/etw) haben; **to have no ~ with sb/sth** (*fig inf*: = *dislike*) für jdn/etw nichts übrig haben; **to lose (one's) ~ (with sb/sth)** (mit jdm/etw) die Geduld verlieren; **to try** *or* **test sb's ~** jds Geduld auf die Probe stellen **(b)** (*Brit Cards*) Patience *f*; **to play ~** eine Patience legen

patient [ˈpeɪʃənt] **1** ADJ geduldig; **to be ~ with sb/sth** mit jdm/ etw geduldig sein; **we have been ~ long enough!** unsere Geduld ist erschöpft! **2** N Patient(in) *m(f)*; **cancer/heart ~** Krebs-/Herzpatient(in) *m(f)*

patiently [ˈpeɪʃəntlɪ] ADV geduldig

patio [ˈpætɪəʊ] N Terrasse *f*; (= *inner court*) Innenhof *m*; **~ door(s)** Terrassentür *f*

patriarchal [ˌpeɪtrɪˈɑːkəl] ADJ patriarchalisch

patriarchy [ˌpeɪtrɪˈɑːkɪ] N Patriarchat *nt*

patriot [ˈpeɪtrɪət] N Patriot(in) *m(f)*

patriotic ADJ, **patriotically** ADV [ˌpætrɪˈɒtɪk, -əlɪ] patriotisch

patriotism [ˈpætrɪətɪzəm] N Patriotismus *m*

patrol [pəˈtrəʊl] **1** N (*police*) Streife *f*; (*Mil*) Patrouille *f*; (*by watchman etc*) Runde *f*; **the navy carry out** *or* **make weekly ~s of the area** die Marine patrouilliert das Gebiet wöchentlich; **on ~** (*Mil*) auf Patrouille; (*police*) auf Streife; (*guard dogs, detectives etc*) im Einsatz **2** VT (*Mil*) patrouillieren; (*policeman, watchman*) seine Runden machen in (+*dat*); (*police car*) Streife fahren in (+*dat*); (*guard dogs, gamewarden*) einen Rundgang machen in (+*dat*) **3** VI (*Mil*) patrouillieren; (*policeman*) seine Streife machen; (*watchman, store detective etc*) seine Runden machen; **to ~ up and down** auf und ab gehen

patrol: patrol boat N Patrouillenboot *nt*; **patrol car** N Streifenwagen *m*; **patrolman** N *m*; (*US:* = *policeman*) Polizist *m*; **patrol wagon** N (*US*) Gefangenenwagen *m*; **patrolwoman** N Wächterin *f*; (*US:* = *policewoman*) Polizistin *f*

patron [ˈpeɪtrən] N (*of shop*) Kunde *m*, Kundin *f*; (*of restaurant, hotel*) Gast *m*; (*of society*) Schirmherr(in) *m(f)*; (*of artist*) Förderer *m*, Förderin *f*; (= *saint*) Schutzpatron(in) *m(f)*; **~ of the arts** Kunstmäzen(in) *m(f)*

patronage [ˈpætrənɪdʒ] N Schirmherrschaft *f*; **his lifelong ~ of the arts** seine lebenslange Förderung der Künste

patroness [ˈpeɪtrənes] N Gönnerin *f*; **~ of the arts** Kunstmäzenin *f*

patronize [ˈpætrənaɪz] VT (= *treat condescendingly*) herablassend behandeln; (= *support*) fördern

patronizing [ˈpætrənaɪzɪŋ] ADJ herablassend; **to be ~ to** *or* **toward(s) sb** jdn herablassend behandeln

patronizingly [ˈpætrənaɪzɪŋlɪ] ADV herablassend

patter [ˈpætə^r] **1** N **(a)** (*of feet*) Getrippel *nt*; (*of rain*) Platschen *nt*; **the ~ of tiny feet** (*fig*) Kindergetrappel *nt* **(b)** (*of salesman etc*) Sprüche *pl* (*inf*); **sales ~** Vertretersprüche *pl* **2** VI (*person, feet*) trippeln; (*rain: also* **~ down**) platschen

pattern [ˈpætən] **1** N **(a)** (*lit, fig: in events etc*) Muster *nt*; (*fig: set*) Schema *nt*; (*fig: recurrent*) Regelmäßigkeit *f*; **to make a ~** ein Muster bilden; **there's a distinct ~/no ~ to these crimes** in diesen Verbrechen steckt ein bestimmtes Schema/kein Schema; **the ~ of events leading up to the war** der Ablauf der Ereignisse, die zum Krieg geführt haben; **behaviour ~s** Verhaltensmuster *pl*; **eating/sleeping ~** Ess-/ Schlafverhalten *nt*; **the daily ~ of his existence** die tägliche Routine seines Lebens; **to follow the usual/same ~** nach dem üblichen/gleichen Schema verlaufen
(b) (*Sew*) Schnittmuster *nt*; (*Knitting*) Strickanleitung *f*
(c) (*fig:* = *model*) Vorbild *nt*; **according to a ~** nach einem

(festen) Schema; **to set a** *or* **the ~ for sth** ein Vorbild für etw sein
2 VT **(a)** (*esp US:* = *model*) machen (*on* nach); **to be ~ed on sth** einer Sache (*dat*) nachgebildet sein; **to ~ oneself on sb** sich (*dat*) jdn zum Vorbild nehmen
(b) (= *put ~s on*) mit einem Muster versehen

pattern card N Musterkarte *f*

patterned [ˈpætənd] ADJ gemustert

paunch [pɔːntʃ] N Bauch *m*

pauper [ˈpɔːpə^r] N Arme(r) *mf*

pause [pɔːz] **1** N Pause *f*; **an anxious/a pregnant ~** ein ängstliches/vielsagendes Schweigen; **there was a ~ while ...** es entstand eine Pause, während ...
2 VI stehen bleiben; (*speaker*) innehalten; **he ~d dramatically** er legte eine Kunstpause ein; **he ~d for breath** er machte eine Pause, um Luft zu holen; **to ~ for thought** (zum Nachdenken) innehalten; **he spoke for thirty minutes without once pausing** er sprach eine halbe Stunde ohne eine einzige Pause; **it made him ~** das machte ihn nachdenklich

pave [peɪv] VT befestigen (*in, with* mit); *road, path* (*with stones also*) pflastern; **to ~ the way for sb/sth** (*fig*) jdm/einer Sache (*dat*) den Weg ebnen

pavement [ˈpeɪvmənt] N (*Brit*) Gehsteig *m*; (*US:* = *paved road*) Straße *f*

pavilion [pəˈvɪlɪən] N Pavillon *m*; (*Brit Sport*) (= *changing ~*) Umkleideräume *pl*; (= *clubhouse*) Klubhaus *nt*

paving stone [ˈpeɪvɪŋstəʊn] (*n*) Platte *f*

paw [pɔː] **1** N (*of animal*) Pfote *f*; (*of lion, bear*) Tatze *f*; (*pej inf:* = *hand*) Pfote *f* (*inf*) **2** VT **(a)** (= *touch*) tätscheln; (*lion etc*) mit der Tatze berühren **(b)** (*pej inf:* = *handle*) betatschen (*inf*) **3** VI **to ~ at sb/sth** jdn/etw betätscheln

pawn¹ [pɔːn] N (*Chess*) Bauer *m*; (*fig*) Schachfigur *f*

pawn² VT verpfänden

pawn: pawnbroker N Pfandleiher(in) *m(f)*; **pawnbroker's (shop), pawnshop** N Pfandhaus *nt*

pay [peɪ] *vb: pret, ptp* **paid** **1** N Lohn *m*; (*of salaried employee*) Gehalt *nt*; (*Mil*) Sold *m*; **three months' ~** drei Monatslöhne; (*of salaried employees*) drei Monatsgehälter; **what's the ~ like?** wie ist die Bezahlung?; **it comes out of my ~** es wird mir vom Gehalt/Lohn abgezogen; **a low-~ country** ein Niedriglohnland *nt*
2 VT **(a)** zahlen; *person, bill, debt* bezahlen; **to ~ sb £10** jdm £ 10 zahlen; **to ~ shareholders** Dividenden ausschütten; **how much is there still to ~?** wie viel steht noch aus?; **to be** *or* **get paid** (*in regular job*) seinen Lohn/sein Gehalt bekommen; **savings accounts that ~ 5%** Sparkonten, die 5% Zinsen bringen; **to ~ the price for sth** den Preis für etw zahlen
(b) **to ~ (sb/a place) a visit** *or* **call, to ~ a visit to** *or* **a call on sb/a place** jdn/einen Ort besuchen; **to ~ a visit to the doctor** den Arzt aufsuchen
3 VI **(a)** zahlen; **to ~ on account** auf Rechnung zahlen; **they ~ well for this sort of work** diese Arbeit wird gut bezahlt; **to ~ for sth** etw bezahlen; **it's already paid for** es ist schon bezahlt; **to ~ for sb** für jdn zahlen; **I'll ~ for this time** dieses Mal zahle ich; **they paid for her to go to America** sie zahlten ihr die Reise nach Amerika
(b) (= *be profitable*) sich lohnen; **it's a business that ~s** es ist ein rentables Geschäft; **it will ~ for itself within two years** innerhalb von zwei Jahren wird sich das rentiert haben; **crime doesn't ~** (*prov*) Verbrechen lohnt sich nicht
(c) (*fig:* = *suffer*) **to ~ for sth** für etw bezahlen; **you'll ~ for that!** dafür wirst du (mir) büßen; **to make sb ~ (for sth)** jdn (für etw) büßen lassen

➤ **pay back** VT SEP **(a)** *money* zurückzahlen; **when do you want me to pay you back?** wann willst du das Geld wiederhaben?; **pay me back when you like** gibs mir zurück, wenn du willst **(b)** *insult, trick* sich revanchieren für; **to pay sb back** es jdm heimzahlen

➤ **pay in** VI, VT SEP einzahlen; **to pay money into an account** Geld auf ein Konto einzahlen

➤ **pay off** **1** VT SEP *workmen* auszahlen; *debt* abbezahlen; *HP* abzahlen; *mortgage* abtragen; *creditor* befriedigen **2** VI sich auszahlen

➤ **pay out** **1** VT SEP *money* (= *spend*) ausgeben **2** VI bezahlen

➤ **pay up** **1** VT SEP *what one owes* zurückzahlen; *subscription* bezahlen; **his account is paid up** er hat alles bezahlt **2** VI zahlen

payable [ˈpeɪəbl] ADJ zahlbar; (= *due*) fällig; ~ **to order** zahlbar an Order; **to make a cheque** (*Brit*) *or* **check** (*US*) ~ **to sb** einen Scheck auf jdn ausstellen

pay: **pay-and-display** ADJ (*Brit*) ~ **parking space** Parkplatz, auf dem der Parkschein sichtbar im Wagen ausgelegt werden muss; **pay-as-you-earn** ATTR ~ **tax system** Lohnsteuerabzugsverfahren *nt*; **pay-as-you-go** (**mobile phone**) N Handy *nt* mit Guthabenkarte; **pay award** N Lohn-/Gehaltserhöhung *f*; **payback** N (*fig*) (a) (= *return*) Ertrag *m*; **to have a big** ~ sich rentieren (b) (= *revenge*) Rache *f*; **it's** ~ **time** die Zeit der Rache ist gekommen; **pay bargaining** N Tarifverhandlungen *pl*; **pay cheque**, (*US*) **paycheck** N Lohn-/Gehaltsscheck *m*; **pay claim** Lohn-/Gehaltsforderung *f*; **payday** N Zahltag *m*

PAYE (*Brit*) ABBR *of* **pay-as-you-earn**

payee [peɪˈiː] N Zahlungsempfänger(in) *m(f)*

pay envelope N (*US*) Lohntüte *f*

payer [ˈpeɪəʳ] N Zahler(in) *m(f)*; **late/slow** ~ säumiger Zahler, säumige Zahlerin

pay: **pay freeze** N Lohnstopp *m*; **pay increase** N Lohn-/Gehaltserhöhung *f*

paying [ˈpeɪɪŋ] ADJ (a) (= *profitable*) rentabel (b) ~ **guest** zahlender Gast

paying-in slip [peɪɪŋˈɪnslɪp] N (*Brit*) Einzahlungsschein *m*

payment [ˈpeɪmənt] N (= *paying*) Bezahlung *f*; (*of debt, mortgage*) Rückzahlung *f*; (*of interest etc, = sum paid*) Zahlung *f*; **three monthly ~s** drei Monatsraten; **in** ~ **of a debt** in Begleichung einer Schuld; **to accept sth as** *or* **in** ~ (**for …**) etw als Bezahlung (für …) annehmen; **on** ~ **of** bei Begleichung/Bezahlung von; **to make a** ~ eine Zahlung leisten; **to stop ~s** die Zahlungen *pl* einstellen; **to stop** ~ **of a cheque** (*Brit*) *or* **check** (*US*) einen Scheck sperren

pay: **pay negotiations** PL = **pay talks**; **payoff** N (= *final payment*) Abschlusszahlung *f*; (*inf*: = *bribe*) Bestechungsgeld *nt*; **payout** N (*in competition*) Preis *m*; (*from insurance*) (Aus)zahlung *f*; **pay packet** N Lohntüte *f*; **pay-per-view** ATTR Pay-per-View-; **payphone** N Münzfernsprecher *m*; **pay rise** N Lohn-/Gehaltserhöhung *f*; **payroll** N **they have 500 people on the** ~ sie haben 500 Beschäftigte; **a monthly** ~ **of £75,000** eine monatliche Lohn- und Gehaltssumme von £ 75.000; ~ **office** Lohnbüro *nt*, Lohnbuchhaltung *f*; ~ **tax** Lohnsteuer *f*; **payslip** N Lohn-/Gehaltsstreifen *m*; **pay talks** PL Lohnverhandlungen *pl*; (*for profession, area of industry*) Tarifverhandlungen *pl*; **pay television**, **pay TV** N Pay-TV *nt*

PC (*Brit*) (a) ABBR *of* **Police Constable**; **PC Plod** (*inf*) Streifenpolizist(in) *m(f)* (b) ABBR *of* **personal computer** PC *m* (c) ABBR *of* **politically correct**

PCI (*Comput*) ABBR *of* **Peripheral Component Interconnect** PCI

pcm ABBR *of* **per calendar month** monatl.; "**rent £230 ~**" „Miete £ 230 monatl."

PDQ (*inf*) ABBR *of* **pretty damned quick** verdammt schnell (*inf*)

PDSA (*Brit*) ABBR *of* **People's Dispensary for Sick Animals** *kostenloses Behandlungszentrum für Haustiere*

PDT (*US*) ABBR *of* **Pacific Daylight Time** pazifische Sommerzeit

PE ABBR *of* **physical education**

pea [piː] N Erbse *f*

peace [piːs] N (a) Frieden *m*; **a man of** ~ ein friedfertiger *or* friedliebender Mensch; **to be at** ~ **with sb/sth** mit jdm/etw in Frieden leben; **the two countries are now at** ~ zwischen den beiden Ländern herrscht jetzt Frieden; **he is at** ~ (*euph*: = *dead*) er ruht in Frieden; **to make (one's)** ~ (**with sb**) sich (mit jdm) versöhnen; **to make** ~ **between …** Frieden stiften zwischen (+*dat*) …; **to keep the** ~ (*Jur*) (*demonstrator, citizen*) die öffentliche Ordnung wahren; (*policeman*) die öffentliche Ordnung aufrechterhalten; (*fig*) Frieden bewahren (b) (= *tranquillity*) Ruhe *f*; ~ **of mind** innere Ruhe; ~ **and quiet** Ruhe und Frieden; **to give sb some** ~ jdn in Ruhe *or* Frieden lassen; **to give sb no** ~ jdm keine Ruhe lassen; **to get some/no** ~ zur Ruhe/nicht zur Ruhe kommen

peace: **peace campaigner** N Friedenskämpfer(in) *m(f)*; **peace conference** N Friedenskonferenz *f*

peaceful [ˈpiːsfʊl] ADJ friedlich; (= *peaceable*) friedfertig; *holiday, sleep etc* ruhig; *death* sanft; **a ~ transition to independence** die Erlangung der Unabhängigkeit auf friedlichem Wege

peacefully [ˈpiːsfʊlɪ] ADV friedlich; **to die** ~ (**in one's sleep**) sanft sterben

peacefulness [ˈpiːsfʊlnɪs] N Friedlichkeit *f*; (*of place, holiday, sleep*) Ruhe *f*; (*of death*) Sanftheit *f*; **the** ~ **of the demonstration** der friedliche Charakter der Demonstration

peace: **peacekeeper** N Friedenswächter(in) *m(f)*; **peacekeeping 1** N Friedenssicherung *f* **2** ADJ zur Friedenssicherung; ~ **troops** Friedenstruppen *pl*; **UN troops have a purely ~ role** die UN-Truppen sind eine reine Friedenstruppe; **a ~ operation** Maßnahmen *pl* zur Sicherung des Friedens; **peace-loving** ADJ friedliebend; **peacemaker** N Friedensstifter(in) *m(f)*; **peacemaking 1** N Friedensbemühungen *pl* **2** ADJ friedensstiftend; **peace process** N Friedensprozess *m*; **peace talks** PL Friedensverhandlungen *pl*; **peacetime 1** N Friedenszeiten *pl* **2** ADJ in Friedenszeiten

peach [piːtʃ] **1** N (= *fruit*) Pfirsich *m* **2** ADJ pfirsichfarben

pea: **peacock** N Pfau *m*; (*fig*: = *man*) Geck *m*; **pea-green** ADJ erbsengrün

peak [piːk] **1** N (a) (*of mountain*) Gipfel *m*; (*of roof*) First *m*; (= *sharp point*) Spitze *f* (b) (*of cap*) Schirm *m* (c) (= *maximum*) Höhepunkt *m*; (*on graph*) Scheitelpunkt *m*; (*St Ex*) Höchststand *m*, Höchstwert *m*; **when his career was at its** ~ als er auf dem Höhepunkt seiner Karriere war; **when demand is at its** ~ wenn die Nachfrage ihren Höhepunkt erreicht hat **2** ADJ ATTR höchste(r, s); **in ~ condition** (*athlete*) in Höchstform; ~ **level** Höchstniveau *nt*; **at ~ time** (*TV, Radio*) zur Hauptsendezeit; ~ **viewing period** (*TV*) Hauptsendezeit *f* **3** VI den Höchststand erreichen; (*athlete*) seine Spitzenform erreichen; **inflation ~ed at 9%** die Inflationsrate erreichte ihren Höchstwert bei 9%; **to have ~ed** auf dem absteigenden Ast sein (*inf*)

peaked [piːkt] ADJ *cap etc* spitz

peak: **peak-hour** ADJ ~ **travel costs more** in der Hauptverkehrszeit sind die öffentlichen Verkehrsmittel teurer; **peak hours** PL (*of traffic*) Hauptverkehrszeit *f*; (*Telec, Elec*) Hauptbelastungszeit *f*; **peak rate** N (*Telec*) Höchsttarif *m*; **peak season** N Hochsaison *f*; **peak-time** ADJ (*Brit*) zu Spitzenzeiten; ~ **traffic** Stoßverkehr *m*; ~ **train services** Zugverbindungen *pl* während der Hauptbelastungszeit; **peak times** PL Hauptbelastungszeit *f*

peal [piːl] **1** N ~ **of bells** Glockenläuten *nt*; ~**s of laughter** schallendes Gelächter; ~ **of thunder** Donnerrollen *nt* **2** VI (*bell*) läuten

➤ **peal out** VI verhallen

peanut [ˈpiːnʌt] N Erdnuss *f*; ~**s** (*inf*: = *not much money*) Peanuts *pl* (*inf*); **the pay is ~s** die Bezahlung ist lächerlich (*inf*)

peanut butter N Erdnussbutter *f*

peapod [ˈpiːpɒd] N Erbsenschote *f*

pear [peəʳ] N Birne *f*; (= *tree*) Birnbaum *m*

pearl [pɜːl] **1** N (*lit, fig*) Perle *f*; (= *colour*) Grauweiß *nt*; ~ **of wisdom** weiser Spruch **2** ADJ ~ **necklace** Perlenkette *f*

pearly-white [ˈpɜːlɪˈwaɪt] ADJ strahlend weiß; *teeth* perlweiß

pear-shaped [ˈpeəʃeɪpt] ADJ birnenförmig; **to be** ~ (*woman*) eine birnenförmige Körperform haben; **to go** ~ (*Brit fig inf*) völlig danebengehen (*inf*)

peasant [ˈpezənt] **1** N (*lit*) (armer) Bauer, (arme) Bäuerin **2** ADJ ATTR bäuerlich; ~ **boy/girl** Bauernjunge *m*/-mädchen *nt*; ~ **farmer** (armer) Bauer; ~ **woman** (arme) Bäuerin

peasantry [ˈpezəntrɪ] N Bauernschaft *f*; (= *class, status*) Bauerntum *nt*

peat [piːt] N Torf *m*; (= *piece*) Stück *nt* Torf

pebble [ˈpebl] N Kieselstein *m*

pebbly [ˈpeblɪ] ADJ steinig

pecan [ˈpiːkæn] N Pecannuss *f*

peck [pek] **1** N (*inf*: = *kiss*)*m* Küsschen *nt* **2** VT (*bird*) picken **3** VI picken (*at* nach)

pecking order [ˈpekɪŋˌɔːdəʳ] N (*lit, fig*) Hackordnung *f*

peckish [ˈpekɪʃ] ADJ (*Brit inf*) **I'm (feeling) a bit** ~ ich könnte etwas zwischen die Zähne gebrauchen (*inf*)

peculiar [pɪˈkjuːlɪəʳ] ADJ (a) (= *strange*) seltsam; **to feel** ~ sich seltsam fühlen (b) (= *exclusive, special*) eigentümlich; **to be** ~ **to sth** *to period, group etc* für etw eigentümlich sein; **his own** ~ **style** der ihm eigene Stil

peculiarity [pɪˌkjuːlɪˈærɪtɪ] N **(a)** (= *strangeness*) Seltsamkeit *f* **(b)** (= *unusual feature*) Eigentümlichkeit *f*

peculiarly [pɪˈkjuːlɪəlɪ] ADV (= *strangely*) seltsam

pedal [ˈpedl] **1** N Pedal *nt*; (*on waste bin etc*) Trethebel *m* **2** VI treten; **he ~led for all he was worth** er trat in die Pedale, er strampelte (*inf*) so sehr er konnte

pedal: **pedal bin** N (*Brit*) Treteimer *m*; **pedal boat** N Tretboot *nt*; **pedal car** N Tretauto *nt*

pedantic [pɪˈdæntɪk] ADJ pedantisch; **to be ~ about sth** in Bezug auf etw (*acc*) pedantisch sein

pedantically [pɪˈdæntɪkəlɪ] ADV pedantisch

peddle [ˈpedl] VT verkaufen; **to ~ drugs** mit Drogen handeln

pedestal [ˈpedɪstl] N Sockel *m*; **to put** *or* **set sb (up) on a ~** (*fig*) jdn in den Himmel heben

pedestrian [pɪˈdestrɪən] **1** N Fußgänger(in) *m(f)* **2** ADJ ATTR **~ lights** Fußgängerampel *f*; **~ precinct** *or* (*US*) **zone** Fußgängerzone *f*

pedestrian crossing N Fußgängerüberweg *m*

pedestrianize [pɪˈdestrɪənaɪz] VT in eine Fußgängerzone umwandeln

pedestrian mall N (*US*) Fußgängerzone *f*

pediatric *etc* [ˌpiːdɪˈætrɪk] (*US*) = **paediatric** *etc*

pedigree [ˈpedɪgriː] **1** N (*lit, fig*) Stammbaum *m* **2** ATTR reinrassig

pedology *etc* (*US*) = **paedology** *etc*

pedophile *etc* (*US*) = **paedophile** *etc*

pee [piː] (*inf*) **1** N Urin *m*, Pipi *nt* (*baby-talk*); **to need a ~** pinkeln müssen (*inf*); **I'm just going for a ~** ich geh mal eben pinkeln (*inf*) **2** VI pinkeln (*inf*)

peek [piːk] **1** N kurzer Blick; (*furtive*) verstohlener Blick; **to take** *or* **have a ~** kurz/verstohlen gucken (*at* nach); **to get a ~ at sb/sth** jdn/etw kurz zu sehen bekommen **2** VI gucken (*at* nach)

peel [piːl] **1** N Schale *f* **2** VT schälen **3** VI (*wallpaper*) sich lösen; (*paint*) abblättern; (*skin, person*) sich schälen

➤ **peel away** VI (*lit, fig*) sich lösen (*from* von)

➤ **peel back** VT SEP abziehen

➤ **peel off 1** VT SEP (+*prep obj* von) sticky tape, wallpaper, paint abziehen; *wrapper, dress, glove etc* abstreifen **2** VI = **peel away**

peep¹ [piːp] **1** N (*of bird etc*) Piep *m*; (*of horn, whistle, inf: of person*) Ton *m*; **we haven't heard a ~ out of him** wir haben keinen Pieps von ihm gehört (*inf*); **one ~ out of you and ...** (*inf*) noch einen Pieps und ... (*inf*); **~! ~!** (*of horn*) tut! tut!; (*of whistle*) tüt! tüt! **2** VI (*bird etc*) piepen; (*horn, car*) tuten; (*whistle*) pfeifen **3** VT **I ~ed my horn at him, I ~ed him** (*inf*) ich habe ihn angehupt (*inf*)

peep² 1 N (= *look*) kurzer Blick; (*furtive*) verstohlener Blick; **to get a ~ at sth** etw kurz zu sehen bekommen; **to take** *or* **have a ~ (at sth)** kurz/verstohlen (nach etw) gucken **2** VI gucken (*at* nach); **to ~ from behind sth** hinter etw (*dat*) hervorschauen; **no ~ing!, don't ~!** (aber) nicht gucken!

➤ **peep out** VI herausgucken; **the sun peeped out from behind the clouds** die Sonne kam hinter den Wolken hervor

peep: **peephole** N Guckloch *nt*; (*in door*) Spion *m*; **peepshow** N Peepshow *f*

peer¹ [pɪəʳ] N **(a)** (= *noble*) Peer *m* **(b)** (= *equal*) Gleichrangige(r) *mf*; **he was well-liked by his ~s** er war bei seinesgleichen beliebt

peer² VI starren; (*short-sightedly, inquiringly*) schielen; **to ~ (hard) at sb** jdn anstarren/anschielen; **to ~ (hard) at sth** etw anstarren; **the driver ~ed through the fog** der Fahrer versuchte angestrengt, im Nebel etwas zu erkennen

peerage [ˈpɪərɪdʒ] N **(a)** (= *peers*) Adelsstand *m*; (*in GB*) Peers *pl* **(b)** (= *rank*)*m* Adelswürde *f*; (*in GB*) Peerswürde *f*; **to give sb a ~** jdm einen Adelstitel verleihen; **to get a ~** geadelt werden

peer: **peer group** N Peergroup *f*; (*employees*) gleichrangige Mitarbeiter *pl*; **peer pressure** N Gruppendruck *m* (*vonseiten Gleichaltriger*)

peeved [piːvd] ADJ (*inf*) eingeschnappt; *look* verärgert

peevish [ˈpiːvɪʃ] ADJ (= *irritated*) gereizt; (= *irritable*) reizbar

peevishly [ˈpiːvɪʃlɪ] ADV gereizt

peg [peg] **1** N (= *stake*) Pflock *m*; (= *tent ~*) Hering *m*; (*Brit*: = *clothes ~*) (Wäsche)klammer *f*; **off the ~** von der Stange; **to take** *or* **bring sb down a ~ or two** (*inf*) jdm einen Dämpfer geben **2** VT **(a)** (*with stake*) anpflocken; (*with clothes ~*)

anklammern; (*with tent ~*) festpflocken **(b)** (*fig*) *prices, wages* festsetzen

➤ **peg out 1** VT SEP **(a)** *washing* aufhängen **(b)** (= *mark out*) *area* abstecken **2** VI (*Brit sl*) (= *die*) den Löffel abgeben (*inf*); (*with exhaustion*) umkippen (*inf*)

pejorative ADJ, **pejoratively** ADV [prɪˈdʒɒrɪtɪv, -lɪ] abwertend

pekin(g)ese [ˌpiːkɪˈniːz] N, *pl* **-** (= *dog*) Pekinese *m*

pelican [ˈpelɪkən] N Pelikan *m*

pelican crossing N (*Brit*) Fußgängerüberweg *m* (*mit Ampel*)

pellet [ˈpelɪt] N Kügelchen *nt*; (*for gun*) Schrotkugel *m*

Peloponnese [ˌpeləpəˈniːz] N Peloponnes *m*

Peloponnesian [ˌpeləpəˈniːzɪən] ADJ peloponnesisch

pelt [pelt] **1** VT schleudern (*at* nach); **to ~ sb/sth (with sth)** jdn/etw mit etw) bewerfen **2** VI (*inf*) **(a)** (= *go fast*) pesen (*inf*) **(b)** **it ~ed (with rain)** es hat nur so geschüttet (*inf*) **3** N (*inf*) **at full ~** volle Pulle (*inf*)

➤ **pelt down** VI it *or* **the rain really pelted down** der Regen prasselte nur so herunter; **it's pelting down** es regnet in Strömen

pelvic bone [ˈpelvɪkˌbəʊn] N Beckenknochen *m*

pelvis [ˈpelvɪs] N Becken *nt*

pen¹ [pen] N (= *dip ~*) Feder *f*; (= *fountain ~*) Füller *m*; (= *ballpoint ~*) Kugelschreiber *m*; **to put ~ to paper** zur Feder greifen

pen² N **(a)** (*for cattle etc*) Pferch *m*; (*for sheep*) Hürde *f*; (*for pigs*) Koben *m* **(b)** (*US inf*: = *prison*) Bau *m* (*inf*), Knast *m* (*inf*)

➤ **pen in** VT SEP einsperren; (*fig*) *car etc* einkeilen

penal [ˈpiːnl] ADJ **~ institution** Strafanstalt *f*; **~ reform** Strafrechtsreform *f*

penal: **penal code** N Strafgesetzbuch *nt*; **penal colony** N Strafkolonie *f*

penalize [ˈpiːnəlaɪz] VT **(a)** (*also Sport*) bestrafen **(b)** (*fig*) benachteiligen

penal system N Strafrecht *nt*

penalty [ˈpenltɪ] N **(a)** (= *punishment*) Strafe *f*; (*for late payment*) Säumniszuschlag *m*; (*for breach of contract*) Konventionalstrafe *f*; **the ~ (for this) is death** darauf steht die Todesstrafe; **you know the ~** Sie wissen, welche Strafe darauf steht; **"~ £50"** „bei Zuwiderhandlung wird eine Geldstrafe von £ 50 erhoben"; **to carry the death ~** mit dem Tod bestraft werden; **on ~ of £200** bei einer Geldstrafe von £ 200; **to pay the ~** dafür büßen **(b)** (*Sport*) Strafstoß *m*; (*Ftbl*) Elfmeter *m*

penalty: **penalty area** N Strafraum *m*; **penalty box** N (*Ftbl*) Strafraum *m*; (*Ice Hockey*) Strafbank *f*; **penalty clause** N Konventionalstrafklausel *f*; **penalty goal** N (*Rugby*) Straftor *nt*; **penalty kick** N Strafstoß *m*; **penalty point** N (*Aut, Jur, Sport*) Strafpunkt *m*; **penalty shoot-out** N (*Ftbl*) Elfmeterschießen *nt*; **penalty spot** N (*Ftbl*) Elfmeterpunkt *m*

penance [ˈpenəns] N (*Rel*) Buße *f*; (*fig*) Strafe *f*; **to do ~** Buße tun; (*fig*) büßen

pence [pens] N PL *of* **penny** Pence *pl*

pencil [ˈpensl] **1** N Bleistift *m* **2** ATTR Bleistift-; *line* mit Bleistift gezogen; **~ sketch** Bleistiftskizze *f*

➤ **pencil in** VT SEP (= *arrange provisionally*) vorläufig vormerken; **can I pencil you in for Tuesday?** kann ich Sie erst mal für Dienstag vormerken?

pencil: **pencil case** N Federmäppchen *nt*; **pencil sharpener** N (Bleistift)spitzer *m*

pendant [ˈpendənt] N Anhänger *m*

pending [ˈpendɪŋ] **1** ADJ anstehend; *lawsuit* anhängig; **to be ~** (*decision etc*) noch anstehen; (*trial*) noch anhängig sein **2** PREP **~ his arrival** bis zu seiner Ankunft; **~ a decision** bis eine Entscheidung getroffen worden ist

pendulum [ˈpendjʊləm] N Pendel *nt*

penetrate [ˈpenɪtreɪt] **1** VT eindringen in (+*acc*); (= *go right through*) *walls etc* durchdringen; (*Mil*) *enemy lines* durchbrechen; (= *infiltrate*) *party* infiltrieren; *market* eindringen in **2** VI eindringen; (= *go right through*) durchdringen; **it just didn't ~** (*fig*) das ist mir/ihm *etc* nicht klar geworden

penetrating [ˈpenɪtreɪtɪŋ] ADJ *gaze* durchdringend; *insight* scharfsinnig; *question, analysis* treffend

penetration [ˌpenɪˈtreɪʃən] N (= *entering*) Eindringen *nt* (*into* in +*acc*); (= *going right through*) Durchdringen *nt* (*of* +*gen*); (*Mil*)

Durchbrechen *nt*; (= *infiltration: of party, group*) Infiltration *f*; (*during sex*) Penetration *f*

penetrative ['penɪtrətɪv] ADJ ~ **sex** penetrativer Sex

pen friend N Brieffreund(in) *m(f)*

penguin ['peŋgwɪn] N Pinguin *m*

penicillin [penɪ'sɪlɪn] N Penizillin *nt*

peninsula [pɪ'nɪnsjʊlə] N Halbinsel *f*

penis ['piːnɪs] N Penis *m*

penitence ['penɪtəns] N Reue *f* (*also Eccl*)

penitent ['penɪtənt] ADJ reuig (*also Eccl*)

penitentiary [penɪ'tenʃərɪ] N (*esp US*) Strafanstalt *f*

penknife ['pennaɪf] N Taschenmesser *nt*

penniless ['penɪlɪs] ADJ mittellos; **to be** ~ kein Geld haben

Pennines ['penaɪnz] PL Pennines *pl*, Gebirgszug in Nordengland

Pennsylvania [pensɪl'veɪnɪə] N Pennsylvania *nt*

Pennsylvania Dutch ☒ N **(a)** (*Ling*) Pennsylvania-Deutsch *nt* **(b)** PL (= *people*) Pennsylvania-Deutsche *pl* **☑** ADJ pennsylvania-deutsch

penny ['penɪ] N, *pl* (*coins*) **pennies** *or* (*sum*) **pence** Penny *m*; (*US*) Centstück *nt*; **it costs 50 pence** es kostet 50 Pence; **to count** *or* **watch the pennies** auf den Pfennig sehen; **magpies are two** *or* **ten a** ~ **in this area** Elstern gibt es in dieser Gegend jede Menge; **he keeps turning up like a bad** ~ (*inf*) der taucht immer wieder auf (*inf*); **to spend a** ~ (*Brit inf*) mal eben verschwinden (*inf*); **the** ~ **dropped** (*inf*) der Groschen ist gefallen (*inf*)

penny share N (*Brit St Ex*), **penny stock** N (*US St Ex*) Penny Stock *m*

pen pal N (*inf*) Brieffreund(in) *m(f)*

pension ['penʃən] N Rente *f*; (*for civil servants also*) Pension *f*; **company** ~ betriebliche Altersversorgung; **to be entitled to a** ~ Anspruch auf eine Rente *etc* haben, rentenberechtigt/pensionsberechtigt sein; **to get a** ~ eine Rente *etc* beziehen

pensionable ['penʃənəbl] ADJ *job* mit Pensionsberechtigung; **of** ~ **age** im Renten-/Pensionsalter; ~ **salary** Gehaltsanteil, *der zur Berechnung des Rentenversicherungsbeitrages herangezogen wird*

pensioner ['penʃənəʳ] N Rentner(in) *m(f)*; (= *former civil servant also*) Pensionär(in) *m(f)*

pension: pension fund N Rentenfonds *m*; **pension scheme** N Rentenversicherung *f*

pensive ADJ, **pensively** ADV ['pensɪv, -lɪ] nachdenklich; (= *sadly serious*) schwermütig

pentagon ['pentəgən] N **the Pentagon** das Pentagon

pentathlon [pen'tæθlən] N Fünfkampf *m*

Pentecost ['pentɪkɒst] N (*Jewish*) Erntefest *nt*; (*Christian*) Pfingsten *nt*

penthouse ['penthaʊs] N Penthouse *nt*

Pentium processor® [pentɪəm'prəʊsesəʳ] N Pentium-Prozessor® *m*

pent up ADJ PRED, **pent-up** ['pent'ʌp] ADJ ATTR *emotions etc* aufgestaut; (*Econ*) *demand* rege, lebhaft

penultimate [pe'nʌltɪmɪt] ADJ vorletzte(r, s)

people ['piːpl] PL **(a)** Menschen *pl*; (*not in formal context*) Leute *pl*; **French** ~ **are very fond of their food** die Franzosen lieben ihre gute Küche; **a job where you meet** ~ eine Arbeit, wo man mit Menschen zusammenkommt; **all** ~ **with red hair** alle Rothaarigen; **some** ~ **don't like it** manche Leute mögen es nicht; **aren't** ~ **funny?** was gibt es doch für seltsame Leute?; **why me of all** ~? warum ausgerechnet ich/mich?; **of all** ~ **who do you think I should meet?** stell dir mal vor, wen ich getroffen habe?; **what do you** ~ **think?** was haltet ihr denn davon?; **poor** ~ arme Leute *pl*; **disabled** ~ Behinderte *pl*; **middle-aged** ~ Menschen *pl* mittleren Alters; **old** ~ Senioren *pl*; **city** ~ Stadtmenschen *pl*; **country** ~ Menschen *pl* vom Land; **some** ~! Leute gibts!; **some** ~ **have all the luck** manche Leute haben einfach Glück
(b) (= *inhabitants*) Bevölkerung *f*; **Madrid has over 5 million** ~ Madrid hat über 5 Millionen Einwohner
(c) (= *one, they*) man; (= ~ *in general, the neighbours*) die Leute; ~ **say that ...** man sagt, dass ...; **what will** ~ **think!** was sollen die Leute denken!
(d) (= *nation, masses, subjects*) Volk *nt*; **the common** ~ das einfache Volk; **the Belgian** ~ das belgische Volk; **People's Republic** *etc* Volksrepublik *f etc*

people carrier N (*Aut*) Großraumlimousine *f*, Van *m*

pep [pep] N (*inf*) Pep *m* (*inf*)

➤ **pep up** VT SEP (*inf*) Schwung bringen in (+*acc*); *food, drink* pikanter machen; *person* munter machen

pepper ['pepəʳ] N Pfeffer *m*; (= *green, red* ~) Paprika *m*; **two ~s** zwei Paprikaschoten

pepper: pepper mill N Pfeffermühle *f*; **peppermint** N Pfefferminz *nt*; **pepper pot** N Pfefferstreuer *m*

peppery ['pepərɪ] ADJ gepfeffert

pep pill N Aufputschpille *f*

pep talk N (*inf*) aufmunternde Worte *pl*; **to give sb a** ~ jdm ein paar aufmunternde Worte sagen

per [pɜːʳ] PREP pro; **£500** ~ **annum** £ 500 im *or* pro Jahr; **60 km** ~ **hour** 60 km pro Stunde; **£2** ~ **dozen** das Dutzend für £ 2

per capita [pə'kæpɪtə] **☒** ADJ Pro-Kopf-; ~ **income** Pro-Kopf-Einkommen *nt* **☑** ADV pro Kopf

perceive [pə'siːv] VT wahrnehmen; (= *understand, realize, recognize*) erkennen; **to** ~ **oneself as ...** sich als ... empfinden

per cent, (*US*) **percent** [pə'sent] N Prozent *nt*; **what ~?** wie viel Prozent?; **20** ~ 20 Prozent; **a 10** ~ **discount** 10 Prozent Rabatt; **a ten** ~ **increase** eine zehnprozentige Steigerung; **to give 100** ~ 100 Prozent geben; **I'm 99** ~ **certain that ...** ich bin (zu) 99 Prozent sicher, dass ...

percentage [pə'sentɪdʒ] **☒** N Prozentsatz *m*; (= *commission, payment*) Anteil *m*; (= *proportion*) Teil *m*; **expressed as a** ~ prozentual ausgedrückt; **what ~?** wie viel Prozent?; **to get a** ~ **of all sales** prozentual am Umsatz beteiligt sein **☑** ATTR **on a** ~ **basis** auf Prozentbasis

perceptible [pə'septəbl] ADJ wahrnehmbar; *improvement, trend etc* spürbar

perceptibly [pə'septəblɪ] ADV merklich

perception [pə'sepʃən] N **(a)** NO PL Wahrnehmung *f*; (*of difficulties, meaning etc*) Erkennen *nt*; **his powers of** ~ sein Wahrnehmungsvermögen *nt* **(b)** (= *mental image, conception*) Auffassung *f* (*of* von); **one's** ~ **of the situation** die eigene Einschätzung der Lage **(c)** NO PL (= *perceptiveness*) Einsicht *f*

perceptive [pə'septɪv] ADJ *person* (= *quick to smell/see/hear*) aufmerksam; (= *quick to understand*) scharfsinnig; *analysis, speech* erkenntnisreich, scharfsinnig; *book, remark* aufschlussreich; ~ **ability** Wahrnehmungsvermögen *nt*

perceptively [pə'septɪvlɪ] ADV scharfsinnig

perceptiveness [pə'septɪvnɪs] N (= *quickness to see/hear/smell*) Aufmerksamkeit *f*; (= *quick realization: of analysis, speech, study*) Scharfsinnigkeit *f*

perch [pɜːtʃ] **☒** N (*of bird*) Stange *f*; (*in tree*) Ast *m* **☑** VT **to ~ sth on sth** etw auf etw (*acc*) setzen *or* (*upright*) stellen **☒** VI (*bird, fig: person*) hocken; (= *alight*) sich niederlassen

perched [pɜːtʃt] ADJ **(a)** (= *situated*) ~ **on sth** thronend auf +*dat*; **a village** ~ **on a hillside** ein Dorf, das auf dem Hang thront **(b)** (= *seated*) **to be** ~ **on sth** auf etw (*dat*) hocken **(c)** **with his glasses** ~ **on the end of his nose** mit der Brille auf der Nasenspitze

percolator ['pɜːkəleɪtəʳ] N Kaffeemaschine *f*

percussion [pə'kʌʃən] N (*Mus*) Schlagzeug *nt*

percussion instrument N (*Mus*) Schlaginstrument *nt*

percussionist [pə'kʌʃənɪst] N Schlagzeuger(in) *m(f)*

perennial [pə'renɪəl] ADJ *plant* mehrjährig; (= *perpetual, constant*) immer während; (= *regularly recurring*) immer wiederkehrend

perfect ['pɜːfɪkt] **☒** ADJ **(a)** perfekt; (*Comm:* = *not damaged*) einwandfrei; **to be** ~ **for doing sth** bestens geeignet sein, um etw zu tun; **it was the** ~ **moment** es war genau der richtige

Augenblick; **that's the ~ hairstyle for you** das ist genau die richtige Frisur für dich; **they make a ~ couple** sie sind das perfekte Paar; **in a ~ world** in einer idealen Welt
(b) (= *absolute, utter*) völlig; **a ~ stranger** ein wildfremder Mensch; **he's a ~ stranger to me** er ist mir völlig fremd
(c) (*Gram*) **~ tense** Perfekt *ntf*
2 N (*Gram*) Perfekt *nt*; **in the ~** im Perfekt
3 [pə'fekt] VT vervollkommnen; *technique, technology* perfektionieren

perfection [pə'fekʃən] N **(a)** Perfektion *f*; **to do sth to ~** etw perfekt tun **(b)** (= *perfecting*) Perfektionierung *f*

perfectionist [pə'fekʃənɪst] N Perfektionist(in) *m(f)*

perfectly ['pɜːfɪktlɪ] ADV **(a)** (= *flawlessly, completely*) perfekt; **the climate suited us ~** das Klima war ideal für uns; **I understand you ~** ich weiß genau, was Sie meinen
(b) (= *absolutely, utterly*) vollkommen; **we're ~ happy about it** wir sind damit völlig zufrieden; **you know ~ well that ...** du weißt ganz genau, dass ...; **to be ~ honest, ...** um ganz ehrlich zu sein, ...; **a Lada is a ~ good car** ein Lada ist durchaus ein gutes Auto

perform [pə'fɔːm] **1** VT *play, concerto* aufführen; *solo, duet* vortragen; *part* spielen; *trick* vorführen; *miracle* vollbringen; *task, duty* erfüllen; *operation* durchführen; *ritual, ceremony* vollziehen
2 VI **(a)** (= *appear: orchestra etc*) auftreten
(b) (*car, football team etc*) leisten; (*examination candidate etc*) abschneiden; **to ~ well** (*company etc*) gute Leistungen erbringen; **the choir ~ed very well** der Chor hat sehr gut gesungen; **how did the car ~?** wie ist der Wagen gelaufen?; **how does the metal ~ under pressure?** wie verhält sich das Metall unter Druck?; **the shares are ~ing strongly** die Aktien steigen stark

performance [pə'fɔːməns] N **(a)** (*esp Theat*) (*of play etc*) Aufführung *f*; (*cinema*) Vorstellung *f*; (*by actor*) Leistung *f*; (*of a part*) Darstellung *f*; **the late ~** die Spätvorstellung; **he gave a splendid ~** er hat eine ausgezeichnete Leistung geboten; **we are going to hear a ~ of Beethoven's 5th** wir werden Beethovens 5. Sinfonie hören
(b) (*of duty, task*) Erfüllung *f*; (*of operation*) Durchführung *f*; (*of ritual, ceremony*) Vollzug *m*; (*of trick*) Vorführung *f*; (*of miracle*) Vollbringung *f*; (*of play, concerto*) Aufführung *f*; (*of solo, duet*) Vortrag *m*; (*of part*) Darstellung *f*
(c) (*of machine, vehicle, sportsman etc*) Leistung *f*; (*of examination candidate etc*) Abschneiden *nt*; (*of shares*) Kursentwicklung *f*; **he put up a good ~** er hat sich gut geschlagen (*inf*)
(d) (*inf*: = *palaver*) Umstand *m*; (= *bad behaviour*) Benehmen *nt*

performer [pə'fɔːmə'] N Künstler(in) *m(f)*

performing [pə'fɔːmɪŋ] ADJ *animal* dressiert; *artist* darstellend; **the ~ arts** die darstellenden Künste

perfume ['pɜːfjuːm] N (= *substance*) Parfüm *nt*; (= *smell*) Duft *m*

perfumed ['pɜːfjuːmd] ADJ **(a)** (= *scented*) parfümiert
(b) (*naturally*) *flowers, air* duftend

perhaps [pə'hæps, præps] ADV vielleicht; **~ the greatest exponent of the art** der möglicherweise bedeutendste Vertreter dieser Kunst; **~ so** das mag sein; **~ not** vielleicht (auch) nicht; **~ I might keep it for a day or two?** könnte ich es vielleicht für ein oder zwei Tage behalten?

peril ['perɪl] N Gefahr *f*; **he is in great ~** er schwebt in großer Gefahr; **do it at your (own) ~** auf Ihre eigene Gefahr

perilous ['perɪləs] ADJ gefährlich

perilously ['perɪləslɪ] ADV gefährlich; **we came ~ close to bankruptcy** wir waren dem Bankrott gefährlich nahe; **she came ~ close to falling** sie wäre um ein Haar heruntergefallen

perimeter [pə'rɪmɪtə'] N (*Math*) Umfang *m*

period ['pɪərɪəd] N **(a)** (= *length of time*) Zeit *f*; (= *age, epoch*) Zeitalter *nt*; (*Geol*, = *menstruation*) Periode *f*; **for a ~ of eight weeks** für einen Zeitraum von acht Wochen; **within a three-month ~** innerhalb von drei Monaten; **for a three-month ~** drei Monate lang; **at that ~ (of my life)** zu diesem Zeitpunkt (in meinem Leben); **a ~ of cold weather** eine Kaltwetterperiode; **~ of notice** Kündigungsfrist *f*; **~ of payment** Zahlungsfrist *f*; **she missed a ~** sie bekam ihre Periode nicht
(b) (*Sch*) (Schul)stunde *f*; **double ~** Doppelstunde *f*

(c) (*form*: *of sentence*) Periode *f*; (*esp US*: = *full stop*) Punkt *m*; **I'm not going ~!** (*esp US*) ich gehe nicht, und damit basta (*inf*)!

periodic [ˌpɪərɪ'ɒdɪk] ADJ periodisch; (= *regular also*) regelmäßig

periodical [ˌpɪərɪ'ɒdɪkəl] **1** ADJ **= periodic 2** N Zeitschrift *f*; (*academic also*) Periodikum *nt*

periodically [ˌpɪərɪ'ɒdɪkəlɪ] ADV periodisch; (= *regularly also*) regelmäßig

period pains PL Menstruationsbeschwerden *pl*

peripheral [pə'rɪfərəl] **1** ADJ Rand-; (*fig*) peripher; (*Comput*) Peripherie-; **~ role** Nebenrolle *f*; **~ device** (*Comput*) Peripheriegerät *nt* **2** N (*Comput*) Peripheriegerät *nt*

periphery [pə'rɪfərɪ] N Peripherie *f*; **young people on the ~ of society** junge Menschen am Rande der Gesellschaft

periscope ['perɪskəʊp] N Periskop *nt*

perish ['perɪʃ] VI (*liter*) (= *die*) umkommen; (= *be destroyed*) untergehen; **~ the thought!** (*inf*) Gott behüte

perishable ['perɪʃəbl] **1** ADJ *food* verderblich; **"~"** „leicht verderblich" **2** PL **~s** leicht verderbliche Ware(n)

perished ['perɪʃt] ADJ (*inf*: *with cold*) durchgefroren

perishing ['perɪʃɪŋ] ADJ (*Brit inf*) *room, weather* eisig kalt; **I'm ~** ich geh fast ein vor Kälte (*inf*)

perjury ['pɜːdʒərɪ] N Meineid *m*; **to commit ~** einen Meineid leisten

perk [pɜːk] N Vergünstigung *f*
► **perk up 1** VT SEP **to perk sb up** (= *make lively*) jdn munter machen; (= *make cheerful*) jdn aufheitern **2** VI (= *liven up*) munter werden; (= *cheer up*) aufleben; (= *become interested*) hellhörig werden

perky ['pɜːkɪ] ADJ (+ER) munter

perm [pɜːm] ABBR *of* **permanent wave 1** N Dauerwelle *f* **2** VT **to ~ sb's hair** jdm eine Dauerwelle machen

permanence ['pɜːmənəns], **permanency** ['pɜːmənənsɪ] N Dauerhaftigkeit *f*; (*of relationship, arrangement also, of job*) Beständigkeit *f*

permanent ['pɜːmənənt] **1** ADJ permanent; *arrangement, position, building* fest; *job, relationship, dye, effect, solution* dauerhaft; *damage* bleibend; *agreement* unbefristet; *staff* fest angestellt; *member* ständig; **~ employees** Festangestellte *pl*; **to make sb ~** jdn fest anstellen; **on a ~ basis** dauerhaft; **I hope this is not going to become ~** ich hoffe, das wird kein Dauerzustand; **~ assets** Anlagevermögen *nt*; **~ capital** Anlagekapital *nt*; **~ feature** fester Bestandteil; **~ memory** (*Comput*) Festspeicher *m*; **~ residence/address** fester Wohnsitz
2 N (*US*) **= perm 1**

permanently ['pɜːmənəntlɪ] ADV permanent; *fixed* fest; *damage* bleibend; *change, tired, angry* ständig; *closed* dauernd; **~ employed** fest angestellt; **are you living ~ in Frankfurt?** ist Frankfurt Ihr fester Wohnsitz?

permanent wave N *see* **perm 1**

permeate ['pɜːmɪeɪt] **1** VT (*lit, fig*) durchdringen **2** VI dringen (*into* in +*acc, through* durch)

permissible [pə'mɪsɪbl] ADJ **(a)** erlaubt (*for sb* jdm); **the maximum ~ levels of radiation** die maximal zulässige Strahlenbelastung **(b)** (= *acceptable*) annehmbar

permission [pə'mɪʃən] N Erlaubnis *f*; **with your ~** mit Ihrer Erlaubnis; **without ~ from sb** ohne jds Erlaubnis; **to do sth with/by sb's ~** etw mit jds Erlaubnis tun; **to get ~** eine Erlaubnis erhalten; **to get sb's ~** jds Erlaubnis erhalten; **to give ~** die Erlaubnis erteilen; **to give sb ~ (to do sth)** jdm erlauben(, etw zu tun); **to ask sb's ~, to ask ~ of sb** jdn um Erlaubnis bitten; **"by (kind) ~ of ..."** „mit (freundlicher) Genehmigung (+*gen*) ..."

permissive [pə'mɪsɪv] ADJ nachgiebig; (*sexually*, = *tolerant*) freizügig; **the ~ society** die permissive Gesellschaft

permissiveness [pə'mɪsɪvnɪs] N Nachgiebigkeit *f*; (*sexually*, = *tolerance*) Freizügigkeit *f*

permit [pə'mɪt] **1** VT *sth* erlauben; **to ~ sb/oneself to do sth** jdm/sich (*dat*) erlauben, etw zu tun; **visitors are not ~ed after 10** nach 10 Uhr sind keine Besucher mehr erlaubt **2** VI **if the weather ~s, weather ~ting** wenn es das Wetter erlaubt **3** ['pɜːmɪt] N Genehmigung *f*; **~ holder** Inhaber(in) *m(f)* eines Berechtigungsscheins *or* (*for parking*) Parkausweises; **"~ holders only"** (*for parking*) „Parken nur mit Parkausweis"

pernickety [pəˈnɪkɪtɪ] ADJ (inf) pingelig (inf)

perpendicular [ˌpɜːpənˈdɪkjʊləʳ] **1** ADJ senkrecht (to zu); **a ~ cliff** eine senkrecht abfallende Klippe **2** N Senkrechte f

perpetrate [ˈpɜːpɪtreɪt] VT begehen

perpetration [ˌpɜːpɪˈtreɪʃən] N Begehen nt

perpetrator [ˈpɜːpɪtreɪtəʳ] N Täter(in) m(f); **the ~ of this crime** derjenige, der dieses Verbrechen begangen hat

perpetual [pəˈpetjʊəl] ADJ ständig, fortwährend; inventory laufend; **you're a ~ source of amazement to me** ich muss mich immer wieder über dich wundern

perpetually [pəˈpetjʊəlɪ] ADV ständig

perpetuate [pəˈpetjʊeɪt] VT aufrechterhalten; memory bewahren

perplex [pəˈpleks] VT verblüffen

perplexed ADJ, **perplexedly** ADV [pəˈplekst, -sɪdlɪ] verblüfft

perplexing [pəˈpleksɪŋ] ADJ verblüffend

perplexity [pəˈpleksɪtɪ] N Verblüffung f; **in some ~** verblüfft

persecute [ˈpɜːsɪkjuːt] VT verfolgen

persecution [ˌpɜːsɪˈkjuːʃən] N Verfolgung f (of von); **his ~ by the press** seine Verfolgung durch die Presse

persecutor [ˈpɜːsɪkjuːtəʳ] N Verfolger(in) m(f)

perseverance [ˌpɜːsɪˈvɪərəns] N Ausdauer f (with mit), Beharrlichkeit f (with bei)

persevere [ˌpɜːsɪˈvɪəʳ] VI durchhalten; **to ~ in one's studies** mit seinem Studium weitermachen; **to ~ in or with one's attempts/efforts to do sth** unermüdlich weiter versuchen, etw zu tun

persevering ADJ, **perseveringly** ADV [ˌpɜːsɪˈvɪərɪŋ, -lɪ] beharrlich

Persia [ˈpɜːʃə] N Persien nt

Persian [ˈpɜːʃən] **1** ADJ persisch; **the ~ Gulf** der Persische Golf **2** N **(a)** Perser(in) m(f) **(b)** (Ling) Persisch nt

Persian carpet N Perser(teppich) m

persist [pəˈsɪst] VI (= persevere) nicht lockerlassen; (= be tenacious) beharren (in auf +dat); (= last, continue) anhalten; **we shall ~ in or with our efforts** wir werden in unseren Bemühungen nicht nachlassen

persistence [pəˈsɪstəns], **persistency** [pəˈsɪstənsɪ] N (= tenacity) Beharrlichkeit f; (= perseverance) Ausdauer f

persistent [pəˈsɪstənt] ADJ demands, questions beharrlich; person, smell hartnäckig; attempts, efforts ausdauernd; drinking gewohnheitsmäßig; nagging, lateness, threats ständig; report wiederholt; rumour, problems, rain, pain, noise anhaltend; worry nicht nachlassend; **~ offender** Wiederholungstäter(in) m(f)

persistently [pəˈsɪstəntlɪ] ADV deny, ask beharrlich; claim, argue hartnäckig; fail, criticize ständig; **~ high inflation** anhaltend hohe Inflation

person [ˈpɜːsn] N **(a)** pl people or (form) -s Mensch m; (in official contexts) Person f; **I like him as a ~, but not as a teacher** ich mag ihn als Mensch, aber nicht als Lehrer; **no ~** kein Mensch; **I know no such ~** so jemanden kenne ich nicht; **any ~** jeder; **a certain ~** ein gewisser Jemand; **30 p per ~** 30 Pence pro Person; **I'm more of an outdoor/cat ~** ich bin mehr ein Typ m für draußen/ein Katzentyp m
(b) pl -s (Gram, Jur: = legal ~) Person f; **first ~ singular/plural** erste Person Singular/Plural
(c) pl -s (= body) Körper m; **in ~** persönlich

-person SUF in Berufsbezeichnungen etc als neutralere Form anstelle von „-man"; **chairperson** Vorsitzende(r) mf; **salesperson** Verkäufer(in) m(f)

personal [ˈpɜːsnl] **1** ADJ persönlich; **the ~ touch** der persönliche Touch; **~ hygiene** Körperpflege f; **it's nothing ~, I just don't think you're the right person** nicht, dass ich etwas gegen Sie persönlich hätte, Sie sind nur nicht der/die Richtige; **~ call** Privatgespräch nt; **~ friend** persönlicher Freund, persönliche Freundin; **~ liability** unbeschränkte Haftung; **~ services** (Econ) persönliche Dienstleistungen pl; **her ~ life** ihr Privatleben nt; **"~"** (on letter) „privat" **2** N (US Press: = advert) Privatanzeige f

personal: **personal ad** N (inf) private Kleinanzeige; **personal allowance** N (for tax purposes) persönlicher Freibetrag; **personal assistant** N persönlicher Assistent, persönliche Assistentin; (= secretary) Chefsekretär(in) m(f); **personal column** N Familienanzeigen pl; **personal computer** N

Personalcomputer m, PC m; **personal hygiene** N Körperpflege f; **personal insurance** N Privatversicherung f

personality [ˌpɜːsəˈnælɪtɪ] N Persönlichkeit f

personal loan N Personaldarlehen nt, Privatdarlehen nt

personally [ˈpɜːsnəlɪ] ADV persönlich; **~, I think that ...** ich persönlich bin der Meinung, dass ...; **I like him ~, but not as an employer** ich mag ihn als Mensch, aber nicht als Arbeitgeber; **to hold sb ~ responsible** jdn persönlich verantwortlich machen; **to be ~ involved** persönlich beteiligt sein

personal: **personal organizer** N Terminplaner m; (electronic) elektronisches Notizbuch; **personal stereo** N Walkman® m; **personal trainer** N privater Fitnesstrainer, private Fitnesstrainerin

personification [pɜːˌsɒnɪfɪˈkeɪʃən] N Personifizierung f; **he is the ~ of good taste** er ist der personifizierte gute Geschmack

personify [pɜːˈsɒnɪfaɪ] VT personifizieren; **he is evil personified** er ist das personifizierte Böse

personnel [ˌpɜːsəˈnel] **1** N SING or PL **(a)** Personal nt; (on plane, ship) Besatzung f; (Mil) Leute pl; **this firm employs 800 ~** diese Firma beschäftigt 800 Leute; **with a larger ~** mit mehr Personal **(b)** (= ~ department) die Personalabteilung; (= ~ work) Personalarbeit f **2** ATTR Personal-

personnel: **personnel department** N Personalabteilung f; **personnel manager** N Personalchef(in) m(f); **personnel officer** N Personalleiter(in) m(f)

person-to-person call [ˌpɜːsntəˈpɜːsnkɔːl] N (US) direktes Gespräch

perspective [pəˈspektɪv] N Perspektive f; **to get a different ~ on a problem** ein Problem aus einer anderen Perspektive or aus einem anderen Blickwinkel sehen; **try to keep/get things in ~** versuchen Sie, nüchtern und sachlich zu bleiben/das nüchtern und sachlich zu sehen; **to get sth out of ~** (fig) etw verzerrt sehen; **to see things from a different ~** die Dinge aus einem anderen Blickwinkel betrachten

perspiration [ˌpɜːspɪˈreɪʃən] N (= perspiring) Schwitzen nt; (= sweat) Schweiß m

perspire [pəˈspaɪəʳ] VI schwitzen

persuade [pəˈsweɪd] VT überreden; (= convince) überzeugen; **to ~ sb to do sth** jdn überreden, etw zu tun; **to ~ sb into doing sth** jdn dazu überreden, etw zu tun; **to ~ sb out of sth** jdm etw ausreden; **to ~ sb out of doing sth** jdn dazu überreden, etw nicht zu tun; **to ~ oneself/sb of sth** sich selbst/jdn von etw überzeugen; **to ~ sb that ...** jdn davon überzeugen, dass ...; **she is easily ~d** sie ist leicht zu überreden/ überzeugen; **he doesn't take much persuading** ihn braucht man nicht lange zu überreden

persuasion [pəˈsweɪʒən] N **(a)** (= persuading) Überredung f; **her powers of ~** ihre Überredungskünste; **she tried every possible means of ~ to get him to agree** sie setzte ihre ganze Überredungskunst ein, um seine Zustimmung zu erlangen; **I don't need much ~ to stop working** man braucht mich nicht lange zu überreden, damit ich aufhöre zu arbeiten **(b)** (= belief) Überzeugung f; **I am not of that ~** davon bin ich nicht überzeugt; **and others of that ~** und andere, die dieser Überzeugung anhängen

persuasive [pəˈsweɪsɪv] ADJ salesman, voice beredsam; arguments etc überzeugend; **he can be very ~** er kann einen gut überreden; (= convincing) er kann einen leicht überzeugen

persuasively [pəˈsweɪsɪvlɪ] ADV überzeugend; **..., he said ~ ...,** versuchte er sie/ihn etc zu überreden

persuasiveness [pəˈsweɪsɪvnɪs] N (of person, salesman etc) Überredungskunst f; (of argument etc) Überzeugungskraft f

pert [pɜːt] ADJ (+ER) keck

perturb [pəˈtɜːb] VT beunruhigen

perturbed [pəˈtɜːbd] ADJ beunruhigt

Peru [pəˈruː] N Peru nt

perusal [pəˈruːzəl] N Lektüre f; (careful) Prüfung f

Peruvian [pəˈruːvɪən] **1** ADJ peruanisch **2** N Peruaner(in) m(f)

perverse [pəˈvɜːs] ADJ (= contrary) abwegig; (= perverted) pervers

perversely [pəˈvɜːslɪ] ADV (= paradoxically) paradoxerweise; think, decide abwegigerweise

perversion [pəˈvɜːʃən] N **(a)** (esp sexual, Psych) Perversion f; (no pl: = act of perverting) Pervertierung f **(b)** (of truth etc) Verzerrung f

perversity [pə'vɜːsɪtɪ] N Perversität *f*
pervert 1 [pə'vɜːt] VT *person, mind* verderben; *truth, sb's words* verzerren; **to ~ the course of justice** (*Jur*) die Rechtsfindung behindern; (*by official*) das Recht beugen **2** ['pɜːvɜːt] N Perverse(r) *mf*
perverted [pə'vɜːtɪd] ADJ *mind, person* pervertiert; *phone call* pervers
pessimism ['pesɪmɪzəm] N Pessimismus *m*
pessimist ['pesɪmɪst] N Pessimist(in) *m(f)*
pessimistic [,pesɪ'mɪstɪk] ADJ pessimistisch; **I'm rather ~ about it** da bin ich ziemlich pessimistisch; **I'm ~ about our chances of success** ich bin pessimistisch, was unsere Erfolgschancen angeht
pessimistically [,pesɪ'mɪstɪkəlɪ] ADV pessimistisch
pest [pest] N **(a)** (*Zool*) Schädling *m*; **~ control** Schädlingsbekämpfung *f* **(b)** (*fig*) (= *person*) Nervensäge *f*; (= *thing*) Plage *f*
pester ['pestə'] VT belästigen; (*with requests etc*) plagen; **she ~ed me for the book** sie ließ mir keine Ruhe wegen des Buches; **to ~ sb to do sth** jdn bedrängen, etw zu tun
pesticide ['pestɪsaɪd] N Pestizid *nt*
pet [pet] **1** ADJ ATTR **(a) a ~ lion** ein zahmer Löwe; **her two ~ dogs** ihre beiden Hunde **(b)** (= *favourite*) Lieblings-; **~ theory** Lieblingstheorie *f*; **a ~ name** ein Kosename *m* **2** N **(a)** (= *animal*) Haustier *nt* **(b)** (= *favourite*) Liebling *m*; **teacher's ~** Lehrers Liebling *m*; (*as derogatory name*) Streber(in) *m(f)* **(c)** (*inf*: = *dear*) Schatz *m* **3** VT streicheln
petal ['petl] N Blütenblatt *nt*
Pete [piːt] N **for ~'s** *or* **pete's sake** (*inf*) um Himmels willen
peter out ['piːtər'aʊt] VI langsam zu Ende gehen; (*river*) versickern; (*song, noise*) verhallen; (*interest*) sich verlieren; (*excitement*) sich legen; (*plan*) im Sande verlaufen
pet food N Tierfutter *nt*
petit bourgeois ['petɪ'bʊəʒwɑː] **1** N Kleinbürger(in) *m(f)* **2** ADJ kleinbürgerlich
petite [pə'tiːt] ADJ zierlich
petite bourgeoisie [petɪ,bʊəʒwɑː'ziː] N Kleinbürgertum *nt*
petition [pə'tɪʃən] **1** N Unterschriftenliste *f*; **to get up a ~ (for/against sth)** Unterschriften (für/gegen etw) sammeln **2** VT (= *request, entreat*) ersuchen (*for* um); (= *hand ~ to*) eine Unterschriftenliste vorlegen (+*dat*) **3** VI (= *hand in ~*) eine Unterschriftenliste einreichen
pet passport N (*Brit*) Tierpass *m*
petrified ['petrɪfaɪd] ADJ (*fig*) **I was ~ (with fear)** ich war starr vor Schrecken; **she is ~ of spiders** sie hat panische Angst vor Spinnen; **to be ~ of doing sth** panische Angst davor haben, etw zu tun
petrify ['petrɪfaɪ] VT (= *frighten*) **he really petrifies me** er jagt mir schreckliche Angst ein; **a ~ing experience** ein schreckliches Erlebnis; **to be petrified by sth** sich panisch vor etw fürchten
petrochemical ['petrəʊ'kemɪkəl] **1** N petrochemisches Erzeugnis **2** ADJ petrochemisch
petrodollar ['petrəʊdɒlə'] N Petrodollar *m*
petrol ['petrəl] N (*Brit*) Benzin *nt*
petrol IN CPDS Benzin-; **petrol bomb** N Benzinbombe *f*, Molotowcocktail *m*; **petrol can** N Reservekanister *m*; **petrol cap** N Tankdeckel *m*
petroleum [pɪ'trəʊlɪəm] N Petroleum *nt*; **~ revenue tax** (*Brit*) Mineralölsteuer *f*
petrol: petrol gauge N Benzinuhr *f*; **petrol pump** N Zapfsäule *f*; **petrol station** N Tankstelle *f*; **petrol tank** N Benzintank *m*; **petrol tanker** N (Benzin)Tankwagen *m*
petticoat ['petɪkəʊt] N Unterrock *m*
pettiness ['petɪnɪs] N **(a)** (= *trivial nature*) Belanglosigkeit *f*, Unwichtigkeit *f* **(b)** (= *small-mindedness*) Kleinlichkeit *f*; (*of remark*) spitzer Charakter
petting ['petɪŋ] N Petting *nt*; **heavy ~** Heavy Petting *nt*
petty ['petɪ] ADJ (+ER) **(a)** (= *trivial*) belanglos; *excuse* billig; *crime* geringfügig **(b)** (= *small-minded*) kleinlich; *remark* spitz
petty: petty bourgeois N, ADJ = **petit bourgeois; petty bourgeoisie** N = **petite bourgeoisie; petty cash** N Portokasse *f*; **petty crime** N **(a)** NO PL (= *illegal activities*) Kleinkriminalität *f* **(b)** (= *illegal act*) Vergehen *nt*, Bagatelldelikt *nt*; **petty theft** N einfacher Diebstahl
petulant ['petjʊlənt] ADJ verdrießlich; *child* bockig (*inf*)

petulantly ['petjʊləntlɪ] ADV verdrießlich; (*used of child*) bockig (*inf*)
pew [pjuː] N (*Eccl*) (Kirchen)bank *f*; (*hum*: = *chair*) Platz *m*; **take a ~!** (*hum*) lass dich nieder! (*hum*)
PFI (*Brit Pol*) ABBR *of* **Private Finance Initiative**
phallic ['fælɪk] ADJ phallisch; **~ symbol** Phallussymbol *nt*
phallus ['fæləs] N, *pl* **-es** *or* **phalli** Phallus *m*
phantasy N = **fantasy**
phantom ['fæntəm] **1** N Phantom *nt*; (= *ghost*) Geist *m* **2** ADJ ATTR (= *imagined*) eingebildet; (= *mysterious*) Phantom-; **a ~ knight** *etc* der Geist eines Ritters *etc*; **~ company** Briefkastenfirma *f*; **~ withdrawal** (*from cash dispenser*) irrtümliche Abbuchung
Pharaoh ['feərəʊ] N Pharao *m*
pharmaceutical [,fɑːmə'sjuːtɪkəl] **1** ADJ pharmazeutisch **2** N USU PL Arzneimittel *nt*; **~(s) company** Pharmaunternehmen *nt*
pharmacist ['fɑːməsɪst] N Apotheker(in) *m(f)*
pharmacologist [,fɑːmə'kɒlədʒɪst] N Pharmakologe *m*, Pharmakologin *f*
pharmacology [,fɑːmə'kɒlədʒɪ] N Pharmakologie *f*
pharmacy ['fɑːməsɪ] N (*esp US*: = *shop*) Apotheke *f*
phase [feɪz] **1** N Phase *f*; (*of construction, project, history also*) Abschnitt *m*; **a passing ~** ein vorübergehender Zustand; **he's just going through a ~** das ist nur so eine Phase bei ihm **2** VT **(a)** (= *introduce gradually*) schrittweise durchführen **(b)** (= *coordinate, fit to one another*) aufeinander abstimmen; **a ~d withdrawal of troops** ein schrittweiser Truppenabzug
➤ **phase in** VT SEP allmählich einführen
➤ **phase out** VT SEP auslaufen lassen
PhD N Doktor *m*, Dr.; **~ thesis** Doktorarbeit *f*; **to do one's ~** promovieren; **to get one's ~** den Doktor bekommen; **he has a ~ in English** er hat in Anglistik promoviert
pheasant ['feznt] N Fasan *m*
phenix ['fiːnɪks] N (*US*) = **phoenix**
phenomena [fɪ'nɒmɪnə] PL *of* **phenomenon**
phenomenal [fɪ'nɒmɪnl] ADJ phänomenal; *person, beauty, figure* fabelhaft; *boredom, heat* unglaublich; **at a ~ rate** in phänomenalem Tempo
phenomenally [fɪ'nɒmɪnəlɪ] ADV außerordentlich; *bad, boring etc* unglaublich
phenomenon [fɪ'nɒmɪnən] N, *pl* **phenomena** Phänomen *nt*
phew [fjuː] INTERJ puh

philanderer [fɪ'lændərə'] N Schwerenöter *m*
philandering [fɪ'lændərɪŋ] ADJ **her ~ husband** ihr zu Seitensprüngen neigender Mann
philanthropic(al) [,fɪlən'θrɒpɪk(əl)] ADJ philanthropisch
philanthropist [fɪ'lænθrəpɪst] N Philanthrop(in) *m(f)*
philanthropy [fɪ'lænθrəpɪ] N Philanthropie *f*
-phile [-faɪl] SUF **1** N -phile(r) *mf*, -freund(in) *m(f)*; **Anglophile** Anglophile(r) *mf*, Englandfreund(in) *m(f)* **2** ADJ -phil, -freundlich; **Francophile** frankophil, frankreichfreundlich
philharmonic [,fɪlɑː'mɒnɪk] **1** ADJ philharmonisch **2** N **Philharmonic** Philharmonie *f*
Philippine ['fɪlɪpiːn] ADJ philippinisch
Philippines ['fɪlɪpiːnz] PL Philippinen *pl*
philistine ['fɪlɪstaɪn] **1** ADJ (*fig*) kulturlos **2** N (*fig*) Banause *m*, Banausin *f*
philology [fɪ'lɒlədʒɪ] N Philologie *f*
philosopher [fɪ'lɒsəfə'] N Philosoph(in) *m(f)*
philosophic(al) [,fɪlə'sɒfɪk(əl)] ADJ philosophisch; (*fig*) gelassen; **to be philosophical about sth** etw philosophisch betrachten

philosophically [fɪləˈsɒfɪkəlɪ] ADV philosophisch; *(fig)* gelassen

philosophize [fɪˈlɒsəfaɪz] VI philosophieren *(about, on* über *+acc)*

philosophy [fɪˈlɒsəfɪ] N Philosophie *f*

phlegm [flem] N *(= mucus)* Schleim *m*

phlegmatic [flegˈmætɪk] ADJ *(= cool)* seelenruhig; *(= stolid)* phlegmatisch

-phobe [-fəʊb] N SUF -phobe(r) *mf*, -feind(in) *m(f)*; **Anglophobe** Anglophobe(r) *mf*, Englandfeind(in) *m(f)*

phobia [ˈfəʊbɪə] N Phobie *f*; **she has a ~ about it** sie hat krankhafte Angst davor

-phobic [-ˈfəʊbɪk] ADJ SUF -phob, -feindlich

phoenix, *(US)* **phenix** [ˈfiːnɪks] N *(Myth)* Phönix *m*; **like a ~ from the ashes** wie ein Phönix aus der Asche

phone [fəʊn] **1** N Telefon *nt*; **to be on the ~** *(= be a subscriber)* Telefon haben; *(= be speaking)* am Telefon sein; **I'll give you a ~** *(inf)* ich ruf dich an **2** VT *person* anrufen; *message* telefonisch übermitteln **3** VI telefonieren

➤ **phone back** VTI SEP zurückrufen

➤ **phone in** **1** VI anrufen; **to phone in sick** sich telefonisch krankmelden **2** VT SEP *order* telefonisch aufgeben

➤ **phone up** **1** VI telefonieren **2** VT SEP anrufen

phone: **phone bill** N Telefonrechnung *f*; **phone booth (a)** Fernsprechhaube *f* **(b)** *(US: = call box)* Telefonzelle *f*; **phonecard** N Telefonkarte *f*; **phone-in** N Phone-in *nt*

phonetic ADJ, **phonetically** ADV [fəˈnetɪk, -əlɪ] phonetisch

phonetics [fəˈnetɪks] N SING *(= subject)* Phonetik *f*

phoney [ˈfəʊnɪ] *(inf)* **1** ADJ **(a)** *(= fake, pretentious)* unecht; *excuse, deal* faul *(inf)*; *name, accent* falsch; *passport, money* gefälscht; *story, report* erfunden; **a ~ doctor** ein Scharlatan *m*; **a ~ policeman** ein zwielichtiger Polizist; **a ~ company** eine Schwindelfirma; **a ~ war** kein echter Krieg **(b)** *(= insincere) person* falsch; *emotion* vorgetäuscht **2** N *(= thing)* Fälschung *f*; *(= bogus policeman etc)* Schwindler(in) *m(f)*; *(= doctor)* Scharlatan *m*; *(= pretentious person)* Angeber(in) *m(f)*

phony ADJ, N *(US inf)* = **phoney**

phosphate [ˈfɒsfeɪt] N *(Chem)* Phosphat *nt*; *(Agr: = fertilizer)* Phosphatdünger *m*

phosphorescent [fɒsfəˈresnt] ADJ phosphoreszierend

photo [ˈfəʊtəʊ] N Foto *nt*

photo: **photo booth** N Passfotoautomat *m*; **photocopier** N (Foto)kopierer *m*; **photocopy** **1** N Fotokopie *f* **2** VT fotokopieren **3** VI **this won't ~** das lässt sich nicht fotokopieren; **photo finish** N Fotofinish *nt*; **Photofit®** N *(also* **~ picture)** Phantombild *nt*

photogenic [fəʊtəʊˈdʒenɪk] ADJ fotogen

photograph [ˈfəʊtəɡræf] **1** N Fotografie *f*; **to take a ~ (of sb/ sth)** (jdn/etw) fotografieren; **~ album** Fotoalbum *nt* **2** VT fotografieren

Be careful! **photograph** *is not translated by the German word* **Fotograf***.*

photographer [fəˈtɒɡrəfə*ʳ*] N Fotograf(in) *m(f)*

photographic [fəʊtəˈɡræfɪk] ADJ fotografisch; *style of painting* naturgetreu; **~ agency** Fotoagentur *f*

photography [fəˈtɒɡrəfɪ] N Fotografie *f*; *(in film, book etc)* Bilder *pl*; **his ~ is marvellous** seine Fotografien sind hervorragend

photo: **photojournalism** N Fotojournalismus *m*; **photojournalist** N Fotojournalist(in) *m(f)*; **photomontage** [ˈfəʊtəʊmɒnˈtɑːʒ] N Fotomontage *f*

photon [ˈfəʊtɒn] N Photon *nt*

photo: **photo session** N Fotosession *f*; **photosynthesis** N Photosynthese *f*

phrasal verb [freɪzəlˈvɜːb] N Verb *nt* mit Präposition

phrase [freɪz] **1** N **(a)** *(Gram)* Satzteil *m*; *(in spoken language)* Phrase *f* **(b)** *(= mode of expression)* Ausdruck *m*; *(= set expression)* Redewendung *f* **2** VT formulieren

phrase book N Sprachführer *m*

pH-value [piːˈeɪtʃvæljuː] N pH-Wert *m*

physical [ˈfɪzɪkəl] **1** ADJ **(a)** physisch; *(= of the body, sexual)* körperlich; *world* fassbar; **you don't take/get enough ~ exercise** Sie bewegen sich nicht genug **(b)** *(= of physics)* physikalisch; **it's a ~ impossibility** es ist ein Ding der Unmöglichkeit **2** N ärztliche Untersuchung; *(Mil)* Musterung *f*

physical: **physical education** N *(abbr* **PE)** Sport *m*; **physical education teacher** N Sportlehrer(in) *m(f)*; **physical fitness** N körperliche Fitness *f*

physically [ˈfɪzɪkəlɪ] ADV physisch; *restrain, separate* körperlich; **to be ~ sick** sich übergeben; **~ impossible** praktisch unmöglich; **they removed him ~ from the meeting** sie haben ihn mit Gewalt aus der Versammlung entfernt; **as long as is ~ possible** so lange wie nur irgend möglich

physical: **physical science** N Naturwissenschaft *f*; **physical therapist** N *(US Med)* Physiotherapeut(in) *m(f)*; **physical therapy** N *(US Med)* Physiotherapie *f*

physician [fɪˈzɪʃən] N Arzt *m*, Ärztin *f*

physicist [ˈfɪzɪsɪst] N Physiker(in) *m(f)*

physics [ˈfɪzɪks] N *(sing: = subject)* Physik *f*

physio [ˈfɪzɪəʊ] N *(esp Brit inf)* Physiotherapeut(in) *m(f)*

physiological [fɪzɪəˈlɒdʒɪkəl] ADJ physiologisch

physiology [fɪzɪˈɒlədʒɪ] N Physiologie *f*

physiotherapist [fɪzɪəˈθerəpɪst] N Physiotherapeut(in) *m(f)*

physiotherapy [fɪzɪəˈθerəpɪ] N Physiotherapie *f*

physique [fɪˈziːk] N Körperbau *m*

pi [paɪ] N *(Math)* Pi *nt*

p/i ABBR *of* **pro forma invoice** Proforma-Rechnung *f*

pianist [ˈpɪənɪst] N Klavierspieler(in) *m(f)*; *(= concert ~)* Pianist(in) *m(f)*

piano [ˈpjænəʊ] N *(upright)* Klavier *nt*; *(= grand ~)* Flügel *m*

piano: **piano lesson** N Klavierstunde *f*; **piano music** N Klaviermusik *f*; **piano player** N Klavierspieler(in) *m(f)*; **piano stool** N Klavierhocker *m*; **piano teacher** N Klavierlehrer(in) *m(f)*

picayune [pɪkəˈjuːn] ADJ *(US)* *(= paltry)* minimal; *(= petty)* kleinlich

piccolo [ˈpɪkələʊ] N Pikkoloflöte *f*

pick [pɪk] **1** N **(a)** *(= pickaxe)* Spitzhacke *f* **(b)** *(= choice)* **she could have her ~ of any man in the room** sie könnte jeden Mann im Raum haben; **to have first ~** die erste Wahl haben; **take your ~!** such dir etwas/einen *etc* aus! **(c)** *(= best)* Beste(s) *nt* **2** VT **(a)** *(= choose)* (aus)wählen; **to ~ a team** eine Mannschaft aufstellen; **to ~ sb to do sth** jdn auswählen, etw zu tun; **to ~ sides** wählen; **to ~ a winner** *(lit)* den Sieger erraten; *(fig)* das große Los ziehen; **to ~ one's way through sth** seinen Weg durch etw finden **(b)** *(= pull bits off, make holes in)* jumper etc zupfen an *(+dat)*; *spot, scab* kratzen an *(+dat)*; *hole (with fingers, instrument)* bohren; **to ~ one's nose** sich *(dat)* in der Nase bohren; **to ~ one's teeth** sich *(dat)* in den Zähnen herumstochern; **to ~ a lock** ein Schloss knacken; **to ~ sth to pieces** *(fig)* etw verreißen; **to ~ holes in sth** *(fig)* etw bemäkeln; *in argument, theory* etw in ein paar Punkten widerlegen; **to ~ a fight or quarrel (with sb)** (mit jdm) einen Streit vom Zaun brechen; **to ~ sb's pocket** jdn bestehlen; **to ~ sb's brains (about sth)** jdn (nach etw) ausfragen **(c)** *flowers, fruit* pflücken **(d)** *(esp US)* strings, banjo zupfen **3** VI *(= choose)* wählen; **to ~ and choose** wählerisch sein

➤ **pick at** VI +PREP OBJ **to pick at one's food** im Essen herumstochern

➤ **pick off** VT SEP **(a)** *(= remove)* wegzupfen; *(= pluck)* fruit pflücken; *nail polish* abschälen **(b)** *(= shoot)* abschießen

➤ **pick on** VI +PREP OBJ *(esp Brit)* herumhacken auf *(+dat)*; **why pick on me?** *(inf)* warum gerade ich?; **pick on somebody your own size!** *(inf)* leg dich doch mit einem Gleichstarken an! *(inf)*

➤ **pick out** VT SEP **(a)** *(= choose)* auswählen **(b)** *(= remove)* heraussuchen **(c)** *(= see, distinguish)* ausmachen **(d)** *(= highlight)* hervorheben *(in,* with durch) **(e)** *(Mus)* **to pick out a tune (on the piano)** eine Melodie (auf dem Klavier) improvisieren

➤ **pick over** *or* **through** VI +PREP OBJ durchsehen

➤ **pick up** **1** VT SEP **(a)** *(= take up)* aufheben; *(= lift momentarily)* hochheben; **to pick up a child in one's arms** ein Kind auf den Arm nehmen; **to pick oneself up** aufstehen; **as soon as he picks up a book** sobald er ein Buch in die Hand nimmt; **to pick up the phone** (den Hörer) abnehmen; **you**

just have to pick up the phone du brauchst nur anzurufen; **to pick up the bill** (= *pay*) die Rechnung bezahlen; **to pick up a story** mit einer Geschichte fortfahren; **to pick up the pieces** (*lit, fig*) die Scherben aufsammeln

(b) (= *get*) holen; (= *buy*) bekommen; *habit* sich (*dat*) angewöhnen; *news, gossip* aufschnappen; *illness* sich (*dat*) holen; (= *earn*) verdienen; *medal* erhalten; **to pick sth up at a sale** etw im Ausverkauf erwischen; **to pick up speed** schneller werden; **he picked up a few extra points** er hat ein paar Extrapunkte gemacht

(c) (= *learn*) *skill etc* sich (*dat*) aneignen; *language* lernen; *accent, word* aufschnappen; *information, tips etc* herausbekommen; *idea* aufgreifen; **you'll soon pick it up** du wirst das schnell lernen; **where did you pick up that idea?** wo hast du denn die Idee her?

(d) (= *collect*) *person, goods* abholen; (*bus etc*) *passengers* aufnehmen; (*in car*) mitnehmen; (= *rescue: helicopter etc*) bergen; (= *arrest, catch*) schnappen (*inf*)

(e) (*inf*) *girl* aufgabeln (*inf*)

(f) (*Rad*) *station* hereinbekommen; *message* empfangen; (= *see*) *beacon etc* ausmachen

(g) (= *restore to health*) wieder auf die Beine stellen

(h) (= *spot, identify*) finden

(i) (*US inf* = *tidy*) auf Vordermann bringen (*inf*)

2 VI **(a)** (= *improve*) besser werden; (*appetite*) zunehmen; (*currency, business*) sich erholen; (*engine*) rund laufen; (= *accelerate*) schneller werden

(b) (= *continue*) weitermachen; **to pick up where one left off** da weitermachen, wo man aufgehört hat

pickaxe, (*US*) **pickax** [ˈpɪkæks] N Spitzhacke *f*

picket [ˈpɪkɪt] **1** N (*of strikers*) Streikposten *m* **2** VT *factory* Streikposten aufstellen vor (+*dat*); (*demonstrators etc*) demonstrieren vor (+*dat*) **3** VI Streikposten aufstellen

picketing [ˈpɪkɪtɪŋ] N Aufstellen *nt* von Streikposten

picket line N Streikpostenkette *f*; **to cross a ~** eine Streikpostenkette durchbrechen

picking [ˈpɪkɪŋ] N **pickings** PL Ausbeute *f*; (= *stolen goods*) Beute *f*; **there are rich ~s to be had** da gibt es reiche Beute

pickle [ˈpɪkl] **1** N **(a)** (= *food*) Pickles *pl* **(b)** (*inf*: = *predicament*) Klemme *f* (*inf*); **he was in a bit of a ~** er steckte in einer Klemme *f* (*inf*); **to get (oneself) into a ~** in ein Kuddelmuddel geraten (*inf*) **2** VT einlegen

> *Be careful!* **pickle** *is not translated by the German word* **Pickel**.

pickled [ˈpɪkld] ADJ eingelegt

pickpocket [ˈpɪkˌpɒkɪt] N Taschendieb(in) *m(f)*

pick-up [ˈpɪkʌp] N **(a)** (*also* **~ truck**) Kleintransporter *m* **(b)** (= *collection*) Abholen *nt*; **~ point** (*for excursion*) Treffpunkt *m*; (*on regular basis*) Haltestelle *f* **(c)** (= *improvement*) Verbesserung *f*; (= *increase*) Ansteigen *nt*

picky [ˈpɪkɪ] ADJ (+ER) (*inf*) pingelig (*inf*); *eater* wählerisch

picnic [ˈpɪknɪk], *vb: pret, ptp* **picnicked 1** N Picknick *nt*; **to have a ~** picknicken; **to go for** *or* **on a ~** ein Picknick machen; **a ~ lunch** ein Picknick *nt* **2** VI picknicken

picnic: picnic basket, picnic hamper N Picknickkorb *m*; **picnic site** N Rastplatz *m*; **picnic table** N Campingtisch *m*

picture [ˈpɪktʃəʳ] **1** N **(a)** Bild *nt*; (= *drawing*) Zeichnung *f*; (as) **pretty as a ~** bildschön; **have you got the general ~?** wissen Sie jetzt ungefähr Bescheid?; **to give you a ~ of what life is like here** damit Sie sich (*dat*) ein Bild vom Leben hier machen können; **to be in the ~** im Bilde sein; **to put sb in the ~** jdn ins Bild setzen; **to be left out of the ~** nicht informiert werden; **I get the ~** (*inf*) ich habs begriffen *or* kapiert (*inf*); **his face was a ~** sein Gesicht war ein Bild für die Götter (*inf*); **she looked** *or* **was the ~ of happiness/health** sie sah wie das Glück/die Gesundheit in Person aus

(b) (*Film*) Film *m*; **the ~s** (*Brit*) das Kino; **to go to the ~s** (*Brit*) ins Kino gehen

2 VT (= *imagine*) sich (*dat*) vorstellen; **to ~ sth to oneself** sich (*dat*) etw vorstellen

picture: picture book N Bildband *m*; (*for children*) Bilderbuch *nt*; **picture frame** N Bilderrahmen *m*; **picture gallery** N Gemäldegalerie *f*; **picture-in-picture** N (*TV, Comput*) Bild-in-Bild *nt*; **picture library** N Fotothek *f*; **picture postcard** N Ansichts(post)karte *f*

picturesque ADJ, **picturesquely** ADV [ˌpɪktʃəˈresk, -lɪ] malerisch

piddle [ˈpɪdl] (*inf*) **1** N Pipi *nt* (*inf*); **to do a ~** pinkeln (*inf*) **2** VI pinkeln (*inf*)

piddling [ˈpɪdlɪŋ] ADJ (*inf*) lächerlich

pidgin English [ˌpɪdʒɪnˈɪŋglɪʃ] N Pidgin-English *nt*

pie [paɪ] N Pastete *f*; (*sweet*) Obstkuchen *m*; (*individual*) Tortelett *nt*; **that's all ~ in the sky** (*inf*) das sind nur verrückte Ideen; **as easy as ~** (*inf*) kinderleicht; **she's got a finger in every ~** (*fig inf*) sie hat überall ihre Finger drin (*inf*)

piece [piːs] N **(a)** Stück *nt*; (= *part, member of a set*) Teil *nt*; (= *component part*) Einzelteil *nt*; (= *fragment: of glass etc*) Scherbe *f*; (*in draughts etc*) Stein *m*; (*in chess*) Figur *f*; (*Press:* = *article*) Artikel *m*; **a 50p ~** ein 50-Pence-Stück; **a ~ of cake/land/paper** ein Stück *nt* Kuchen/Land/Papier; **a ~ of furniture/luggage/clothing** ein Möbel-/Gepäck-/Kleidungsstück *nt*; **a ~ of news** eine Nachricht; **a ~ of information** eine Information; **a ~ of advice** ein Rat *m*; **a ~ of luck** ein Glücksfall *m*; **a ~ of work** eine Arbeit; **~ by ~** Stück für Stück; **to take sth to ~s** etw in seine Einzelteile zerlegen; **to come to ~s** (*collapsible furniture etc*) sich zerlegen lassen; **to come** *or* **fall to ~s** (*old book etc*) auseinanderfallen; (*glass, pottery*) zerbrechen; **to be in ~s** (= *taken apart*) (in Einzelteile) zerlegt sein; (= *broken*) zerbrochen sein; **to smash sth to ~s** etw kaputtschlagen; **he tore the letter (in)to ~s** er zerriss den Brief (in Stücke *or* Fetzen); **he tore me to ~s during the debate** er zerriss mich förmlich während der Debatte

(b) (*phrases*) **to go to ~s** (= *crack up*) durchdrehen (*inf*); (= *lose grip*) die Kontrolle verlieren; (*sportsman, team*) abbauen (*inf*); **his confidence is shot to ~s** (*inf*) sein Selbstvertrauen ist völlig zerstört; **all in one ~** heil; **are you still in one ~ after your trip?** hast du deine Reise heil überstanden?; **to give sb a ~ of one's mind** jdm ordentlich die Meinung sagen; **to say one's ~** seine Meinung sagen

> **piece together** VT SEP (*lit*) zusammenstückeln; (*fig*) sich (*dat*) zusammenreimen; *evidence* zusammenfügen

piece: piecemeal 1 ADV stückweise; (= *haphazardly*) kunterbunt durcheinander **2** ADJ stückweise; (= *haphazard*) wenig systematisch; **piece rate** N Akkordlohnsatz *m*; **piecework** N Akkordarbeit *f*; **to be on ~** im Akkord arbeiten; **pieceworker** N Akkordarbeiter(in) *m(f)*

pie chart N Kreisdiagramm *nt*

pier [pɪəʳ] N Pier *m or f*

pierce [pɪəs] VT durchstechen; (*knife, spear, bullet*) durchbohren; (*fig: sound, coldness etc*) durchdringen; **to ~ a hole in sth** etw durchstechen; **to have** *or* **get one's ears ~d** sich (*dat*) die Ohren durchstechen lassen

pierced [pɪəst] ADJ *object* durchstochen; *nose, nipple* gepierct

piercing [ˈpɪəsɪŋ] ADJ durchdringend; *wind, stare* stechend

piercingly [ˈpɪəsɪŋlɪ] ADV durchdringend

piety [ˈpaɪətɪ] N Pietät *f*, Frömmigkeit *f*

pig [pɪg] **1** N **(a)** (*lit, fig inf,* = *dirty/nasty person*) Schwein *nt*; (= *greedy person*) Vielfraß *m* (*inf*); **to make a ~ of oneself** (*dat*) den Bauch voll schlagen (*inf*); **~s might fly** (*Brit prov*) wers glaubt, wird selig; **they were living like ~s** sie haben wie die Schweine gehaust; **in a ~'s eye** (*US inf*) du spinnst wohl! (*inf*)

(b) (*sl*: = *policeman*) Bulle *m* (*sl*)

2 VR **to ~ oneself** (*inf*) sich voll stopfen (*inf*)

> **pig out** VI (*inf*) sich voll stopfen (*inf*)

pigeon [ˈpɪdʒən] N Taube *f*

pigeonhole [ˈpɪdʒənhəʊl] **1** N (*in desk etc*) Fach *nt*; **to put people in ~s** (*fig*) Menschen (in Kategorien) einordnen **2** VT (*fig*) einordnen

piggy [ˈpɪgɪ] ADJ (+ER) **(a)** ATTR **~ eyes** Schweinsaugen *pl* **(b)** (*inf*: = *greedy*) verfressen (*inf*)

piggyback [ˈpɪgɪbæk] **1** N **to give sb a ~** jdn huckepack nehmen **2** ADV (*US Rail, also Comput*) huckepack *inv*

piggy bank N Sparschwein *nt*

pig: pig-headed ADJ stur; **pig in the middle** N (*Brit*) **I'm just ~ on this project** (*inf*) ich stehe bei diesem Projekt nur hilflos dabei

piglet [ˈpɪglɪt] N Ferkel *nt*

pigment [ˈpɪgmənt] N Pigment *nt*

pigmy N = pygmy

pig: **pigpen** N (US) = pigsty; **pig's ear** N to make a ~ of sth (Brit inf) etw vermasseln (inf); **pigsty** N Schweinestall m; (fig also) Saustall m (inf); **pigswill** N Schweinefutter nt; **pigtail** N Zopf m

pike [paɪk] N (= fish) Hecht m

pilchard ['pɪltʃəd] N Sardine f

pile [paɪl] **1** N **(a)** (= heap) Stapel m; **to put things in a** ~ etw (auf)stapeln; **her things lay** or **were in a** ~ ihre Sachen lagen auf einem Haufen; **at the bottom/top of the** ~ (fig) untenan/obenauf
(b) (inf: = large amount) Menge f; **a great** ~ **of work** eine Menge Arbeit; **~s of money/food** eine or jede Menge Geld/Essen (inf); **a** ~ **of things to do** massenhaft zu tun (inf) **2** VT stapeln; **a table** ~**d high with books** ein Tisch mit Stapeln von Büchern; **the sideboard was** ~**d high with presents** auf der Anrichte stapelten sich die Geschenke
► **pile in 1** VI (inf) (-to in +acc) hineindrängen; (= get in) einsteigen **2** VT SEP einladen (-to in +acc)
► **pile on 1** VI (inf) hineindrängen (-to in +acc) **2** VT SEP (lit) aufhäufen (-to auf +acc); **she piled rice on(to) my plate** sie häufte Reis auf meinen Teller; **they are really piling on the pressure** sie setzen uns/euch etc ganz gehörig unter Druck
► **pile out** VI (inf) hinausdrängen (of aus)
► **pile up 1** VI (lit, fig) sich anhäufen; (traffic) sich stauen; (evidence) sich verdichten **2** VT SEP (auf)stapeln; (fig) debts anhäufen; evidence sammeln

piles [paɪlz] PL Hämorr(ho)iden pl

pile-up ['paɪlʌp] N (= car crash) (Massen)karambolage f

pilfer ['pɪlfər] VT stehlen

pilgrim ['pɪlgrɪm] N Pilger(in) m(f); **the Pilgrim Fathers** die Pilgerväter pl

---

PILGRIM FATHERS

*Die **Pilgrim Fathers**, die Pilgerväter, waren eine Gruppe von Puritanern, die 1620 England verließen, um der religiösen Verfolgung zu entgehen. Sie segelten in einem Schiff namens „Mayflower" über den Atlantik und gründeten New Plymouth in Neuengland. Die **Pilgrim Fathers** gelten als die Gründerväter der Vereinigten Staaten, und jedes Jahr wird am Thanksgiving Day wieder ihre erste Ernte gefeiert.*
► THANKSGIVING

---

pilgrimage ['pɪlgrɪmɪdʒ] N Pilgerfahrt f; **to go on** or **make a** ~ eine Pilgerfahrt machen

pill [pɪl] N Tablette f; **the** ~ die Pille; **to be/go on the** ~ die Pille nehmen

pillar ['pɪlər] N Säule f; **a** ~ **of society** eine Stütze der Gesellschaft

pillar box N (Brit) Briefkasten m

pillion ['pɪljən] **1** N Soziussitz m **2** ADV **to ride** ~ auf dem Soziussitz mitfahren; (on horse) hinter dem Sattel sitzen

pillow ['pɪləʊ] **1** N (Kopf)kissen nt **2** VT betten

pillow: **pillowcase** N (Kopf)kissenbezug m; **pillowslip** N = pillowcase

pilot ['paɪlət] **1** N **(a)** (Aviat) Pilot(in) m(f), Flugzeugführer(in) m(f); **~'s licence** Flugschein m **(b)** (TV) = (episode) Pilotfilm m **2** VT plane fliegen

pilot: **pilot light** N Zündflamme f; **pilot scheme** N Pilotprojekt nt; **pilot study** N Pilotstudie f; **pilot survey** N Pilot- or Vorlaufstudie f

pimp [pɪmp] **1** N Zuhälter m **2** VI Zuhälter sein

pimple ['pɪmpl] N Pickel m

PIN [pɪn] N ABBR of **personal identification number**; ~ **number** Geheimzahl f

pin [pɪn] **1** N **(a)** (Sew) Stecknadel f; (= tie ~, hair ~, on brooch) Nadel f; (Mech) Bolzen m; (= small nail) Stift m; (Comput) (on connector) Pin m; (on printhead) Nadel f; **a two-~ plug** ein zweipoliger Stecker; **I've got ~s and needles in my foot** mir ist der Fuß eingeschlafen; **to be on ~s and needles** wie auf (glühenden) Kohlen sitzen; **you could have heard a** ~ **drop** man hätte eine Stecknadel fallen hören können
(b) (esp US) (= brooch) Brosche f; (= badge: also lapel ~, fraternity ~) Abzeichen nt
2 VT **(a)** dress stecken; **to** ~ **sth to sth** etw an etw (acc) heften; **she** ~**ned her hair back** sie hatte ihr Haar hinten zusammengesteckt

(b) (fig) **to** ~ **sb to the ground/against a wall** jdn an den Boden/an eine Wand pressen; **to** ~ **sb's arm behind his back** jdm den Arm auf den Rücken drehen; **to** ~ **one's hopes on sb/sth** seine Hoffnungen auf jdn/etw setzen
(c) (inf: = accuse of) **to** ~ **sth on sb** jdm etw anhängen; **to** ~ **the blame (for sth) on sb** jdm die Schuld (an etw (dat)) anhängen (inf)
(d) (US inf) **to be** ~**ned** verlobt sein; **to get** ~**ned** sich verloben
► **pin down** VT SEP **(a)** (with pins) festheften; (= hold, weight down) niederhalten; **two of the gang pinned him down** zwei aus der Bande drückten ihn zu Boden **(b)** (fig) **to pin sb down** jdn festnageln; **he wouldn't be pinned down to any particular date** er ließ sich nicht auf ein bestimmtes Datum festnageln; **I've seen him somewhere before but I can't pin him down** ich habe ihn schon mal irgendwo gesehen, kann ihn aber nicht einordnen
► **pin up** VT SEP notice anheften; hair hochstecken; dress stecken

pinafore ['pɪnəfɔːr] N Schürze f

pincers ['pɪnsəz] PL **(a)** Kneifzange f; **a pair of** ~ eine Kneifzange **(b)** (Zool) Schere f

pinch [pɪntʃ] **1** N **(a)** (with fingers) Kneifen nt no pl **(b)** (= small quantity) Quäntchen nt; (Cook) Prise f **(c)** (= pressure) **to feel the** ~ die schlechte Lage zu spüren bekommen; **at** (Brit) or **in** (US) **a** ~ zur Not
2 VT **(a)** (with fingers) kneifen; **to** ~ **sb's bottom** jdn in den Hintern kneifen; **to** ~ **oneself** sich kneifen
(b) (Brit inf: = steal) klauen inf **don't let anyone** ~ **my seat** pass auf, dass mir niemand den Platz wegnimmt; **he** ~**ed Johnny's girlfriend** er hat Johnny (dat) die Freundin ausgespannt (inf)
3 VI (shoe, also fig) drücken

pinch-hit ['pɪntʃhɪt] VI (US fig) einspringen

pinch hitter ['pɪntʃˌhɪtər] N (US fig) Ersatz m

pine¹ [paɪn] N Kiefer f

pine² VI **(a)** **to** ~ **for sb/sth** sich nach jdm/etw sehnen **(b)** (= away, be sad) sich vor Kummer verzehren
► **pine away** VI sich (vor Kummer) verzehren

pineapple ['paɪnˌæpl] N Ananas f; ~ **juice** Ananassaft m

pine: **pine cone** N Kiefernzapfen m; **pine forest** N Kiefernwald m; **pine needle** N Kiefernnadel f; **pine tree** N Kiefer f; **pine wood** N Kiefernwald m; (= material) Kiefernholz nt

ping pong ['pɪŋpɒŋ] N Pingpong nt; ~ **ball** Pingpongball m

pink [pɪŋk] **1** N (= colour) Rosa nt **2** ADJ **(a)** rosa inv; cheeks, face rosig; **to go** or **turn** ~ erröten **(b)** (inf: = gay) economy, vote Schwulen- (inf)

pink slip N (US inf) Entlassungspapiere pl

PINK SLIP

*In den USA ist **pink slip** der umgangssprachliche Ausdruck für das Schreiben, mit dem ein Arbeitgeber seinem Angestellten die Kündigung mitteilt. Der Begriff stammt aus den zwanziger Jahren, als ein rosafarbener Durchschlag mit der Kündigung in die Lohntüte gesteckt wurde.*

---

pinnacle ['pɪnəkl] N (fig) Gipfel m

PIN number N Geheimzahl f

pin: **pinpoint 1** N Punkt m; **a** ~ **of light** ein Lichtpunkt m **2** VT (= locate) genau aufzeigen; (= define, identify) genau feststellen; **pinprick** N Nadelstich m; **pinstripe** N ~**d suit** Nadelstreifenanzug m

pint [paɪnt] N **(a)** (= measure) Pint nt **(b)** (esp Brit: = quantity) (of milk) Tüte f; (of beer) Glas nt (Bier); (= bottle) Flasche f; **to have a** ~ ein Bier trinken; **to go (out) for a** ~ auf ein Bier ausgehen; **he likes a** ~ er hebt ganz gern mal einen (inf); **she's had a few** ~**s** (inf) sie hat ein paar intus (inf)

pin: **pin-up** N (= picture) Pin-up-Foto nt; (= woman) Pin-up-Girl nt; (= man) Idol nt; **pin-up girl** N Pin-up-Girl nt

pioneer [paɪə'nɪər] **1** N (fig) Pionier(in) m(f) **2** ADJ ATTR see pioneering **3** VT way vorbereiten; (fig) Pionierarbeit f leisten für; **to** ~ **the use of sth** etw zum ersten Mal anwenden

pioneering [paɪə'nɪərɪŋ] ADJ ATTR method, research wegbereitend; ~ **spirit** Pioniergeist m; ~ **work** Pionierarbeit f

pious ['paɪəs] ADJ fromm; (pej also) frömmlerisch

piously ['paɪəslɪ] ADV fromm

pip[1] [pɪp] N **(a)** (*Bot*) Kern *m* **(b)** (*Rad, Telec*) **the ~s** das Zeitzeichen; (*in public telephone*) das Tut-Tut-Tut

pip[2] VT (*Brit inf*) knapp besiegen; **to ~ sb at** *or* **to the post** (*in race*) jdn um Haaresbreite schlagen; (*fig*) jdm um Haaresbreite zuvorkommen; (*in getting orders etc*) jdm etw vor der Nase wegschnappen

pipe [paɪp] **1** N **(a)** (*for water, gas etc*) Rohr *nt*; (= *fuel ~, for steam*) Leitung *f* **(b)** (*Mus*) Flöte *f*; **~s** (= *bagpipes*) Dudelsack *m* **(c)** (*for smoking*) Pfeife *f*; **to smoke a ~** Pfeife rauchen; **put that in your ~ and smoke it!** (*inf*) steck dir das hinter den Spiegel! (*inf*) **2** **(d)** VT *water, oil etc* in Rohren leiten; (*Cook*) spritzen
► **pipe down** VI (*inf*) die Luft anhalten (*inf*)
► **pipe up** VI (*inf*) (*person*) den Mund aufmachen; **suddenly a little voice piped up** plötzlich machte sich ein Stimmchen bemerkbar

pipe: **pipe dream** N Hirngespinst *nt*; **that's just a ~** das ist ja wohl nur ein frommer Wunsch; **pipeline** N (Rohr)leitung *f*; (*for oil, gas also*) Pipeline *f*; **to be in the ~** (*fig*) in Vorbereitung sein; **the pay rise hasn't come through yet but it's in the ~** die Lohnerhöhung ist noch nicht durch, steht aber kurz bevor

piper ['paɪpə'] N Flötenspieler(in) *m(f)*; (*on bagpipes*) Dudelsackpfeifer(in) *m(f)*

pipe: **pipe smoker** N Pfeifenraucher(in) *m(f)*; **pipe tobacco** N Pfeifentabak *m*

piping ['paɪpɪŋ] **1** N **(a)** (= *pipework*) Rohrleitungssystem *nt*; (= *pipe*) Rohrleitung *f* **(b)** (*Mus*) Flötenspiel *nt*; (*on bagpipes*) Dudelsackpfeifen *nt* **2** ADV **~ hot** kochend heiß

piquant ['pi:kənt] ADJ (*lit, fig*) pikant

pique [pi:k] **1** N Groll *m*; **he resigned in a fit of ~** er kündigte, weil er vergrämt war **2** VT kränken; **to be ~d at** *or* **by sth** über jdn/etw pikiert sein

piracy ['paɪərəsɪ] N Piraterie *f*; (*Econ also*) Produktpiraterie *f*; (*of book etc*) Raubdruck *m*; (*of record*) Raubpressung *f*

piranha (fish) [pɪ'rɑːnjə(fɪʃ)] N Piranha *m*

pirate ['paɪərɪt] **1** N Pirat(in) *m(f)* **2** VT *book* einen Raubdruck herstellen von; *invention, idea* stehlen; **a ~d copy of the record** eine Raubpressung; **~d edition** Raubdruck *m*

Pisces ['paɪsiːz] PL Fische *pl*; **I'm (a) ~** ich bin Fisch

piss [pɪs] (*sl*) **1** N Pisse *f* (*vulg*); **to have a ~** pissen (*vulg*); **to go for a ~** pissen gehen (*vulg*); **to take the ~ out of sb/sth** (*Brit sl*) jdn/etw verarschen (*inf*) **2** VI pissen (*inf*); **it's ~ing with rain** (*inf*) es pisst (*sl*) **3** VT pissen (*sl*) **4** VR sich bepissen (*vulg*); **we ~ed ourselves (laughing)** wir haben uns bepisst (*sl*)
► **piss about** *or* **around** VI (*Brit inf*) herummachen (*inf*)
► **piss down** VI (*Brit inf*) **it's pissing down** es pisst (*sl*)
► **piss off** **1** VI (*esp Brit sl*) sich verpissen (*sl*); **piss off!** (= *go away*) verpiss dich! (*sl*); (= *don't be stupid*) du kannst mich mal (*inf*) **2** VT (*esp Brit inf*) ankotzen (*sl*); **to be pissed off with sb/sth** von jdm/etw die Schnauze voll haben (*inf*)

piss artist N (*inf*) (= *drunk*) Säufer(in) *m(f)*; (= *boaster*) Großmaul *nt* (*inf*); (= *incompetent*) Niete *f* (*inf*)

pissed [pɪst] ADJ (*inf*) (*Brit*: = *drunk*) stockbesoffen (*inf*); (*US*: = *angry*) stocksauer (*inf*)

piss: **piss-take** N (*Brit sl*) Verarschung *f* (*inf*); **piss-up** N (*Brit sl*) Saufgelage *nt* (*inf*)

pistachio [pɪ'stɑːʃɪəʊ] N Pistazie *f*

piste [pi:st] N (*Ski*) Piste *f*

pistol ['pɪstl] N Pistole *f*; **~ shot** Pistolenschuss *m*

pit[1] [pɪt] **1** N **(a)** (= *hole, in garage*) Grube *f*; (*Brit*: = *coal mine*) Zeche *f*; (= *quarry*) Steinbruch *m*; **to have a sinking feeling in the ~ of one's stomach** ein ungutes Gefühl in der Magengegend haben; **to go down the ~** Bergmann werden; **he works down the ~(s)** er arbeitet unter Tage
(b) (*Sport*) **the ~s** (*Motor Racing*) die Box; **to make a ~ stop** einen Boxenstopp machen
(c) (*Theat*: = *orchestra ~*) Orchestergraben *m*
(d) (*US St Ex*) Börsensaal *m*
(e) **the ~s** (*inf*: = *very bad*) das Allerletzte
2 VT **(a) the surface of the moon is ~ted with small craters** die Mondoberfläche ist mit kleinen Kratern übersät; **where the meteorites have ~ted the surface** wo die Meteoriten Einschläge hinterlassen haben
(b) to ~ one's wits against sb/sth seinen Verstand an jdm/etw messen; **in the next round A is ~ted against B** in der nächsten Runde stehen sich A und B gegenüber

pit[2] (*US*) **1** N Stein *m* **2** VT entsteinen

pita (bread) ['pɪtə] N (*US*) = **pitta (bread)**

pitch **1** N **(a)** (= *throw*) Wurf *m*
(b) (*esp Brit Sport*) Platz *m*
(c) (*Brit*) (*in market, outside theatre etc*) Stand *m*; (*fig*: = *usual place*) Platz *m*
(d) (*inf*: = *sales ~*) (= *long talk*) Sermon *m* (*inf*); (= *technique*) Verkaufstaktik *f*
(e) (*Phon, also of note*) Tonhöhe *f*; (*of instrument*) Tonlage *f*; (*of voice*) Stimmlage *f*
(f) (= *angle, slope*) Schräge *f*
(g) (*fig*: = *degree*) **their frustration had reached such a ~ that ...** ihre Frustration hatte einen derartigen Grad erreicht, dass ...
(h) (*US inf*) **what's the ~?** was liegt an? (*inf*)
2 VT **(a)** *hay* gabeln; *ball* werfen
(b) (*Mus*) *note* (= *give*) angeben; (= *hit*) treffen; **she ~ed her voice higher** sie sprach mit einer höheren Stimme
(c) (*fig*) **the production must be ~ed at the right level for London audiences** das Stück muss auf das Niveau des Londoner Publikums abgestimmt werden; **to ~ sb a story** (*inf*) jdm eine Geschichte auftischen (*inf*); **to ~ sb into a crisis** jdn in die Krise stürzen
(d) *camp, tent* aufschlagen; *stand* aufstellen; (*advertise*) anpreisen (*to sb* jdm)
3 VI **(a)** (= *fall*) fallen, stürzen; **to ~ forward** vornüberfallen
(b) (*Naut*) stampfen; (*Aviat*) absacken
(c) (*Baseball*) werfen
► **pitch for** VI +PREP OBJ anpreisen
► **pitch in** VI (*inf*) einspringen; **so we all pitched in together** also packten wir alle mit an

pitch: **pitch-black** ADJ pechschwarz; **pitch-dark** **1** ADJ pechschwarz **2** N (tiefe) Finsternis

pitcher[1] ['pɪtʃə'] N (*esp US*) Krug *m*

pitcher[2] N (*Baseball*) Werfer(in) *m(f)*

pitchfork ['pɪtʃfɔːk] N Heugabel *f*; (*for manure*) Mistgabel *f*

piteous ['pɪtɪəs] ADJ Mitleid erregend; *sounds* kläglich

piteously ['pɪtɪəslɪ] ADV Mitleid erregend; *cry etc also* kläglich

pitfall ['pɪtfɔːl] N (*fig*) Falle *f*

pitiful ['pɪtɪfʊl] ADJ **(a)** (= *moving to pity*) *sight, story* Mitleid erregend; *person* bedauernswert; *cry* jämmerlich; **to be in a ~ state** in einem erbärmlichen Zustand sein **(b)** (= *poor, wretched*) erbärmlich

pitifully ['pɪtɪfəlɪ] ADV **(a)** jämmerlich; *look, say, complain* Mitleid erregend **(b)** *inadequate* erbärmlich

pitiless ['pɪtɪlɪs] ADJ mitleidlos; *sun, glare* unbarmherzig; *cruelty also* erbarmungslos

pitilessly ['pɪtɪlɪslɪ] ADV mitleidlos; *cruel* erbarmungslos

pits [pɪts] PL *see* **pit**[1]

pitta (bread) ['pɪtə] N ≈ Fladenbrot *nt*

pittance ['pɪtəns] N Hungerlohn *m*

pity ['pɪtɪ] **1** N **(a)** Mitleid *nt*; **for ~'s sake!** Erbarmen!; (*less seriously*) um Himmels willen!; **to have** *or* **take ~ on sb, to feel ~ for sb** mit jdm Mitleid haben; **to do sth out of ~ (for sb)** etw aus Mitleid (mit jdm) tun; **to feel no ~** kein Mitgefühl *etc* haben, kein Mitleid fühlen; **to move sb to ~** jds Mitleid (*acc*) erregen
(b) (= *cause of regret*) **(what a) ~!** (wie) schade!; **what a ~ he can't come** (wie) schade, dass er nicht kommen kann; **more's the ~!** leider; **it is a ~ that ...** es ist schade, dass ...; **it's a great ~** es ist sehr schade, es ist jammerschade; (*more formally*) es ist sehr bedauerlich; **it would be a ~ if he lost** *or* **were to lose this job** es wäre bedauerlich, wenn er seine Arbeit verlieren sollte
2 VT bedauern

pivot ['pɪvət], *vb*: *pret, ptp* **pivoted** **1** N Drehzapfen *m* **2** VI sich drehen; **to ~ on sth** (*fig*) sich um etw drehen

pivotal ['pɪvətl] ADJ (*fig*) zentral

pixel ['pɪksl] N (*Comput*) Pixel *nt*

pizza ['pi:tsə] N Pizza *f*

pizzeria [pi:tsə'ri:ə] N Pizzeria *f*

PJs ['pi:dʒeɪz] PL (*inf*) ABBR *of* **pyjamas** Pyjama *m*

placard ['plækɑːd] N Plakat *nt*

placate [plə'keɪt] VT beschwichtigen

place [pleɪs]

1 NOUN **2** TRANSITIVE VERB

1 NOUN

(a) (*general*) Platz *m*, Stelle *f* (*also in exam, competition*); **water is coming through in several places** an mehreren Stellen kommt Wasser durch; **from place to place** von einem Ort zum anderen; **in another place** woanders; **bed is the best place for him** im Bett ist er am besten aufgehoben; **we found a good place to watch the procession from** wir fanden einen Platz, von dem wir den Umzug gut sehen konnten; **in the right/wrong place** an der richtigen/falschen Stelle; **some/any place** irgendwo; **a poor man with no place to go** ein armer Mann, der nicht weiß, wohin; **this is no place for you** das ist kein Platz für dich; **it was the last place I expected to find him** da hätte ich ihn zuletzt vermutet; **this isn't the place to discuss politics** dies ist nicht der Ort, um über Politik zu sprechen; **I can't be in two places at once!** ich kann doch nicht an zwei Stellen gleichzeitig sein

(b) (= *geographical location*) (= *district*) Gegend *f*; (= *country*) Land *nt*; (= *building*) Gebäude *nt*; (= *town*) Ort *m*; (*in street names*) Platz *m*; **there's nothing to do in the evenings in this place** hier kann man abends nichts unternehmen; **a little place at the seaside** (= *village*) ein kleiner Ort am Meer

(c) (= *home*) Haus *nt*; **come round to my place some time** besuch mich mal, komm doch mal vorbei; **let's go back to my place** lass uns zu mir gehen; **I've never been to his place** ich bin noch nie bei ihm gewesen; **where's your place?** wo wohnst du?; **at Peter's place** bei Peter; **your place or mine?** (*hum inf*) gehen wir zu dir oder zu mir?

(d) (= *seat, position*) (*at table, in team*) Platz *m*; (*at university*) Studienplatz *m*; (= *job, in book etc*) Stelle *f*; (*Sport*) Platzierung *f*; **places for 500 students** 500 Studienplätze; **to give up one's place** (*in a queue*) jdm den Vortritt lassen; **to lose one's place** (*in a queue*) sich wieder hinten anstellen müssen; (*in book*) die Seite verblättern; (*on page*) die Zeile verlieren; **to take the place of sb/sth** den Platz von jdm/etw einnehmen; **to win first place** Erste(r, s) sein

(e) (*in hierarchy*) Rang *m*, Stellung *f*; **people in high places** Leute in hohen Positionen; **to know one's place** wissen, was sich (für einen) gehört; **it's not my place to comment** es steht mir nicht zu, einen Kommentar abzugeben; **to keep** *or* **put sb in his place** jdn in seine Schranken weisen

(f) (*Math*) Stelle *f*; **to work sth out to three decimal places** etw auf drei Stellen nach dem Komma berechnen

(g) (*set structures*)

✦**place of** + *noun* **place of birth** Geburtsort *m*; **place of residence** Wohnort *m*; **place of business** *or* **work** Arbeitsstelle *f*

✦**in places** stellenweise

✦**in place** **everything was in place** alles war an seiner Stelle; **make sure the wire is properly in place** achten Sie darauf, dass der Draht richtig sitzt; **the legislation is already in place** die gesetzlichen Regelungen gelten schon

✦**out of place** **to be out of place** (= *in the wrong place*) nicht an der richtigen Stelle sein; (= *untidy*) in Unordnung sein; (*fig: remark, person*) deplatziert sein; **to look out of place** fehl am Platz wirken

✦**all over the place** (= *everywhere*) überall; **she's all over the place** (*inf*: = *disorganized*) sie ist total chaotisch (*inf*)

✦**in place of** statt (+*gen*); **McCormack played in goal in place of Miller** McCormack stand anstelle von Miller im Tor

✦**to fall into place** Gestalt annehmen

✦**in the first place** (= *firstly*) erstens; **in the first place ..., in the second place ...** erstens ..., zweitens ...; **she shouldn't have been there in the first place** (= *anyway*) sie hätte überhaupt nicht dort sein sollen

✦**to take place** stattfinden

✦**to go places** (= *travel*) herumreisen

2 TRANSITIVE VERB

(a) (= *put*) setzen, stellen; (= *lay down*) legen; *guards* aufstellen; *announcement* (*in paper*) inserieren (*in* in +*dat*); *advertisement* setzen (*in* in +*acc*); **she slowly placed one foot in front of the other** sie setzte langsam einen Fuß vor den anderen; **she placed a finger on her lips** sie legte den Finger

auf die Lippen; **to place a strain on sth** etw belasten; **to place confidence/trust in sb/sth** Vertrauen in jdn/etw setzen; **to be placed** (*shop, town etc*) liegen; **how are you placed for time?** wie sieht es mit deiner Zeit aus?

✦**well/better placed** **we are well placed for the shops** was Einkaufsmöglichkeiten angeht, wohnen wir günstig; **Liverpool are well placed in the league** Liverpool liegt gut in der Tabelle

(b) (= *rank*) stellen; **that should be placed first** das sollte an erster Stelle stehen; **the German runner was placed third** der deutsche Läufer belegte den dritten Platz *or* wurde Dritter; **to be placed** (*Sport*) sich platzieren

(c) (*Comm*) *goods* absetzen; *order* erteilen (*with sb* jdm); *contract* abschließen (*with sb* mit jdm)

(d) (*money*) (= *deposit*) deponieren; (= *invest*) investieren; **to place money at sb's credit** jdm eine Geldsumme gutschreiben

(e) (= *find job for*) unterbringen (*with* bei)

place mat N Set *nt*

placement ['pleɪsmənt] N **(a)** (= *act: of teacher etc*) Platzierung *f*; (= *finding job for*) Vermittlung *f* **(b)** (*Brit*) (= *period: of trainee*) Praktikum *nt*; **I'm here on a six-month ~** (*for in-service training etc*) ich bin hier für sechs Monate zur Weiterbildung; (*on secondment*) ich bin für sechs Monate hierhin überwiesen worden

place: **place name** N Ortsname *m*; **place setting** N Gedeck *nt*

placid ['plæsɪd] ADJ ruhig; *person* gelassen; *disposition* friedfertig; *smile* still; *scene* beschaulich

placidly ['plæsɪdlɪ] ADV ruhig; *speak* bedächtig

plagiarize ['pleɪdʒjəraɪz] VT plagiieren

plague [pleɪɡ] **1** N (*Med*) Seuche *f*; (*Bibl, fig*) Plage *f*; **the ~** die Pest; **to avoid sb/sth like the ~** jdn/etw wie die Pest meiden **2** VT plagen; **to be ~d by doubts/injury** von Zweifeln/Verletzungen geplagt werden; **to ~ sb with questions** jdn ständig mit Fragen belästigen

plaice [pleɪs] N, NO PL Scholle *f*

plain [pleɪn] **1** ADJ (+ER) **(a)** (= *clear*) klar; *truth* schlicht; (= *obvious*) offensichtlich; **it is ~ to see that ...** es ist offensichtlich, dass ...; **to make sth ~ to sb** jdm etw klarmachen; **the reason is ~ to see** der Grund ist leicht einzusehen; **I'd like to make it quite ~ that ...** ich möchte gern klarstellen, dass ...; **it won't all be ~ sailing** es wird gar nicht so einfach sein; **from now on it'll be ~ sailing** von jetzt an geht es ganz einfach

(b) (= *simple*) einfach; *cooking, food* (gut)bürgerlich; *paper* unliniert; *colour* einheitlich; **in a ~ colour** (*Brit*) *or* **color** (*US*) einfarbig

(c) (= *sheer*) rein

(d) (= *not beautiful*) unattraktiv; **she really is so ~** sie ist recht unansehnlich

2 ADV **(a)** (*inf*: = *simply, completely*) (ganz) einfach

(b) **I can't put it ~er than that** deutlicher kann ich es nicht sagen

3 N (*Geog*) Ebene *f*; **the ~s** das Flachland; (*in North America*) die Prärie

plain: **plain chocolate** N (*Brit*) (Zart)bitterschokolade *f*; **plain-clothes** ADJ in Zivil; **plain flour** N Mehl *nt* (*ohne beigemischtes Backpulver*)

plainly ['pleɪnlɪ] ADV **(a)** (= *clearly*) eindeutig; *explain, remember, visible* klar; **~, these new techniques are impractical** es ist ganz klar, dass diese neuen Verfahren unpraktisch sind

(b) (= *frankly*) offen **(c)** (= *unsophisticatedly*) einfach

plaintiff ['pleɪntɪf] N Kläger(in) *m(f)*

plait [plæt] **1** N (*esp Brit*) Zopf *m* **2** VT flechten

plan [plæn] **1** N Plan *m*; (*for essay, speech*) Konzept *nt*; (= *town ~*) Stadtplan *m*; **~ of action** (*Mil, fig*) Aktionsprogramm *nt*; **the ~ is to meet at six** es ist geplant, sich um sechs zu treffen; **to make ~s (for sth)** Pläne (für etw) machen; **have you any ~s for tonight?** hast du (für) heute Abend (schon) etwas vor?; **according to ~** planmäßig

2 VT **(a)** planen; *programme etc* erstellen; *buildings etc* entwerfen

(b) (= *intend*) vorhaben; **we weren't ~ning to** wir hatten es nicht vor; **this development was not ~ned** diese Entwicklung war nicht eingeplant

3 VI planen; **to ~ months ahead** (auf) Monate vorausplanen

➤ **plan on** VI +PREP OBJ **(a) to plan on doing sth** vorhaben, etw zu tun **(b) to plan on sth** mit etw rechnen; **I hadn't planned on being paid for my help** ich hatte nicht damit gerechnet, für meine Hilfe bezahlt zu werden

➤ **plan out** VT SEP in Einzelheiten planen

plane N **(a)** (= *aeroplane*) Flugzeug *nt*; **to go by ~, to take a ~** fliegen **(b)** (*fig*) Ebene *f*; (*intellectual*) Niveau *nt*; (= *social ~*) Schicht *f*

planeload ['pleɪnləʊd] N Flugzeugladung *f*

planet ['plænɪt] N Planet *m*; **what ~ is he/she on?** (*inf*) lebt er/sie eigentlich auf dem Mond? (*inf*)

planetarium [plænɪ'teərɪəm] N Planetarium *nt*

plank [plæŋk] N Brett *nt*; (*Naut*) Planke *f*

planned [plænd] ADJ geplant

planned: planned economy N Planwirtschaft *f*; **planned obsolescence** N geplanter Verschleiß

planner ['plænəʳ] N Planer(in) *m(f)*

planning ['plænɪŋ] N Planung *f*

planning IN CPDS Planungs-; **~ commission** Planungsausschuss *m*; **~ manager** Planungsleiter(in) *m(f)*; **~ permission** Baugenehmigung *f*, baurechtliche Vorschriften *pl*

plant [plɑːnt] **1** N **(a)** (*Bot*) Pflanze *f*; **rare/tropical ~s** seltene/tropische Gewächse *pl* **(b)** NO PL (= *equipment*) Anlagen *pl*; (= *equipment and buildings*) Produktionsanlage *f*; (*US: of school, bank*) Einrichtungen *pl*; (= *factory*) Werk *nt*; **~ assets** Werksanlagevermögen *nt*, Betriebsvermögen *nt*; **~ manager** (*US*) Werks- *or* Betriebsleiter(in) *m(f)*; **~ utilization** Kapazitätsauslastung *f* **2** ATTR **~ life** Pflanzenwelt *f* **3** VT **(a)** *plants* pflanzen; *field* bepflanzen **(b)** (= *place in position*) setzen; *bomb* legen; *kiss* drücken; **to ~ sth in sb's mind** jdm etw in den Kopf setzen, jdn auf etw (*acc*) bringen **(c)** (*inf*) *incriminating evidence etc* manipulieren; (*in sb's car, home*) schmuggeln; **to ~ sth on sb** (*inf*) jdm etw unterjubeln (*inf*)

➤ **plant out** VT SEP auspflanzen

plantation [plæn'teɪʃən] N Plantage *f*; (*of trees*) Anpflanzung *f*

plant pot N (*esp Brit*) Blumentopf *m*

plaque [plæk] N **(a)** Plakette *f*; (*on building etc*) Tafel *f* **(b)** (*on teeth*) (Zahn)belag *m*

plasm ['plæzəm], **plasma** ['plæzmə] N Plasma *nt*

plaster ['plɑːstəʳ] **1** N **(a)** (*Build*) (Ver)putz *m* **(b)** (*Art, Med: also ~ of Paris*) Gips *m*; (*Brit Med:* = ~ *cast*) Gipsverband *m*; **to have one's leg in ~** das Bein in Gips haben **(c)** (*Brit: = sticking ~*) Pflaster *nt* **2** VT **(a)** (*Build*) *wall* verputzen **(b)** (*inf*) **to ~ one's face with make-up** sein Gesicht mit Make-up voll kleistern (*inf*); **~ed with mud** schlammbedeckt

plaster cast N (*Med*) Gipsverband *m*

plastered ['plɑːstəd] ADJ PRED (*inf*) voll (*inf*); **to get ~** sich voll laufen lassen (*inf*)

plastic ['plæstɪk] **1** N **(a)** Plastik *nt*; **~s** Kunststoffe *pl* **(b)** (*inf:* = *credit cards*) Kreditkarten *pl* **2** ADJ Plastik-; **~ bottle** Plastikflasche *f*

plastic: plastic bag N Plastiktüte *f*; **plastic explosive** N Plastiksprengstoff *m*

Plasticine® ['plæstɪsiːn] N (*Brit*) Plastilin *nt*

plastic: plastic surgeon N plastischer Chirurg; **plastic surgery** N plastische Chirurgie; **she decided to have ~ on her nose** sie entschloss sich zu einer Schönheitsoperation an ihrer Nase; **plastic wrap** N (*US*) Frischhaltefolie *f*

plate [pleɪt] N **(a)** Teller *m*; **~ supper** (*US*) Tellergericht *nt*; **a dinner at 45 dollars a ~** (*US*) ein Essen für *or* zu 45 Dollar pro Person; **to have sth handed to one on a ~** (*Brit fig inf*) etw auf einem Tablett serviert bekommen (*inf*); **to have enough/a lot on one's ~** (*fig inf*) genug/viel am Hals haben (*inf*) **(b)** (= *plated metal*) vergoldetes/versilbertes Metall **(c)** (*Tech, Phot, Typ*) Platte *f*; (= *name ~, number ~*) Schild *nt*

plateau ['plætəʊ] N, *pl* **-s** *or* **-x** (*Geog*) Hochebene *f*

plateful ['pleɪtfʊl] N Teller *m*

platform ['plætfɔːm] N Plattform *f*; (= *stage*) Bühne *f*; (*Rail*) Bahnsteig *m*

platform shoe N Plateauschuh *m*

platinum ['plætɪnəm] N Platin *nt*; **a ~ blonde** eine Platinblonde

platitude ['plætɪtjuːd] N Platitüde *f*

platonic [plə'tɒnɪk] ADJ platonisch

platoon [plə'tuːn] N (*Mil*) Zug *m*

platter ['plætəʳ] N Teller *m*; (= *serving dish*) Platte *f*; **to have sth handed to one on a (silver) ~** (*fig*) etw auf einem (silbernen) Tablett serviert bekommen

plausibility [plɔːzə'bɪlɪtɪ] N Plausibilität *f*

plausible ['plɔːzəbl] ADJ plausibel; *liar* geschickt; *manner, person* überzeugend

plausibly ['plɔːzəblɪ] ADV plausibel

play [pleɪ] **1** N **(a)** Spiel *nt*; **~ on words** Wortspiel *nt*; **to abandon ~** (*Sport*) das Spiel abbrechen; **in a clever piece of ~, in a clever ~** (*US*) in einem klugen Schachzug; **to be in ~/out of ~** (*ball*) im Spiel/im Aus sein **(b)** (*Theat*) (Theater)stück *nt*; (*Rad*) Hörspiel *nt*; (*TV*) Fernsehspiel *nt*; **the ~s of Shakespeare** Shakespeares Dramen **(c)** (*fig phrases*) **to come into ~** ins Spiel kommen; **to bring or call sth into ~** etw aufbieten; **the free ~ of market forces** das freie Spiel der Marktkräfte; **to make a ~ for sth** es auf etw (*acc*) abgesehen haben **2** VT spielen; *player* aufstellen; (= *perform in*) *town* spielen in (+*dat*); **to ~ sb (at a game)** gegen jdn (ein Spiel) spielen; **to ~ a joke on sb** jdm einen Streich spielen; **to ~ a mean/dirty trick on sb** jdn auf gemeine/schmutzige Art hereinlegen; **to ~ it safe** auf Nummer sicher gehen (*inf*); **to ~ the fool** den Clown spielen, herumblödeln (*inf*); **to ~ the piano** Klavier spielen **3** VI (*esp child*) spielen; (*fountain*) tanzen; (*Theat: = be performed*) gespielt werden; **to go out to ~** rausgehen und spielen; **can Johnny come out to ~?** darf Johnny zum Spielen rauskommen?; **to ~ at cowboys and Indians** Cowboy und Indianer spielen; **to ~ at being a fireman** Feuerwehrmann spielen; **to ~ in defence** (*Sport*) in der Abwehr spielen; **to ~ in goal** im Tor stehen; **what are you ~ing at?** (*inf*) was soll (denn) das? (*inf*); **to ~ for money** um Geld spielen; **to ~ for time** (*fig*) Zeit gewinnen wollen; **to ~ into sb's hands** (*fig*) jdm in die Hände spielen; **to ~ to sb** (*Mus*) jdm vorspielen

➤ **play about** (*Brit*) *or* **around** VI spielen; **to play around with sth** mit etw (herum)spielen; **he's been playing around (with another woman)** er hat mit einer anderen Frau herumgemacht (*inf*)

➤ **play along 1** VI mitspielen; **to play along with a suggestion** auf einen Vorschlag scheinbar eingehen; **to play along with sb** jdm zustimmen **2** VT ALWAYS SEPARATE ein falsches Spiel spielen mit

➤ **play back** VT SEP *tape recording* abspielen; *answering machine* abhören

➤ **play down** VT SEP herunterspielen

➤ **play off** VT SEP **to play X off against Y** X gegen Y ausspielen

➤ **play on 1** VI weiterspielen **2** VI +PREP OBJ (*also* **play upon**) *sb's fears, good nature* geschickt ausnutzen; **the hours of waiting played on my nerves** das stundenlange Warten zermürbte mich

➤ **play out** VT SEP (*Theat*) *scene* darstellen (*also fig*)

➤ **play through** VI +PREP OBJ *a few bars etc* durchspielen

➤ **play up 1** VI (*Brit inf:* = *cause trouble*) Schwierigkeiten machen **2** VT SEP (*inf:* = *cause trouble to*) **to play sb up** jdm Schwierigkeiten machen

➤ **play upon** VI +PREP OBJ = **play on 2**

➤ **play with** VI +PREP OBJ **we don't have much time/money to play with** wir haben zeitlich/finanziell nicht viel Spielraum; **we don't have that many alternatives to play with** so viele Alternativen haben wir nicht zur Verfügung; **to play with oneself** an sich (*dat*) herumfummeln

play: play-acting N (*dated Theat*) Schauspielerei *f*; (*fig*) Theater *nt*; **playbill** N (*US*) Theaterprogramm *nt*; **playboy** N Playboy *m*

Play-Doh® ['pleɪdəʊ] N (*esp US*) Play-Doh® *nt*, Knetmasse *f*

player ['pleɪəʳ] N (*Sport, Mus*) Spieler(in) *m(f)*

player-manager ['pleɪə'mænɪdʒəʳ] N Spieler-Manager *m*

playful ['pleɪfʊl] ADJ neckisch; *child, animal* verspielt; **the dog is just being ~** der Hund spielt nur; **she gave Philip's hand a ~ squeeze** sie drückte spielerisch Philips Hand

playfully ['pleɪfəlɪ] ADV neckisch; **he grasped her wrist ~** er ergriff spielerisch ihr Handgelenk

playfulness ['pleɪfʊlnɪs] N (of child, animal) Verspieltheit f; (of adult) Ausgelassenheit f

play: **playground** N Spielplatz m; (Sch) (Schul)hof m; **playgroup** N Spielgruppe f; **playhouse** N (a)nt (US: = doll's house) Puppenstube f **(b)** (Theat) Schauspielhaus nt

playing ['pleɪɪŋ]: **playing card** N Spielkarte f; **playing field** N Sportplatz m

play: **playmate** N Spielkamerad(in) m(f); **play-off** N Entscheidungsspiel nt; **play park** N Spielpark m; **playpen** N Laufstall m; **playschool** N (esp Brit) Kindergarten m; **playtime** N Zeit f zum Spielen; (Sch) große Pause

playwright ['pleɪraɪt] N Dramatiker(in) m(f)

plaza ['plɑːzə] N Piazza f; (US: = shopping complex) Einkaufszentrum nt

plc (Brit) ABBR of **public limited company** ≈ AG f

plea [pliː] N **(a)** Bitte f; (= general appeal) Appell m; **to make a ~ for sth** zu etw aufrufen **(b)** (Jur) Plädoyer nt

plead [pliːd], pret, ptp **pleaded** or (Scot, US) **pled** █ VT ignorance, insanity sich berufen auf (+acc) █ VI **(a)** bitten (for um); **to ~ with sb to do sth** jdn bitten, etw zu tun geh **to ~ with sb for sth** jdn um etw bitten **(b)** (Jur: counsel) das Plädoyer halten; **to ~ guilty/not guilty** sich schuldig/nicht schuldig bekennen

pleading ADJ, **pleadingly** ADV ['pliːdɪŋ, -lɪ] flehend

pleasant ['pl,eznt] ADJ angenehm; news erfreulich; person, face nett; manner, smile freundlich; building gefällig

pleasantly ['plezntlɪ] ADV angenehm; smile, greet, speak etc freundlich

pleasantness ['plezntnɪs] N Freundlichkeit f

pleasantry ['plezntrɪ] N (= joking remark) Scherz m; (= polite remark) Nettigkeit f

please [pliːz] █ INTERJ bitte; **(yes,)** (= acceptance) (ja,) bitte; (enthusiastic) oh ja, gerne; **~ pass the salt, pass the salt, ~** würden Sie mir bitte das Salz reichen?; **may I? - ~ do!** darf ich? - bitte sehr!
█ VI **(a)** (just) as you ~ ganz wie du willst; **bold as you ~, he entered the room** frech wie Oskar kam er ins Zimmer (inf); **to do as one ~s** machen or tun, was einem gefällt **(b)** (= cause satisfaction) gefallen; **eager to ~** darum bemüht, alles richtig zu machen; (servant) darum bemüht, jeden Wunsch zu erfüllen; **we aim to ~** wir wollen, dass Sie zufrieden sind
█ VT (= give pleasure to) eine Freude machen (+dat); (= satisfy) zufrieden stellen; (= do as sb wants) gefallen (+dat); **the idea ~d him** die Idee hat ihm gefallen; **just to ~ you** nur dir zuliebe; **it ~s me to see him so happy** es freut mich, dass er so glücklich ist; **you can't ~ everybody** man kann es nicht allen recht machen; **there's no pleasing him** er ist nie zufrieden; **he is easily ~d or easy to ~** er ist leicht zufrieden zu stellen
█ VR **to ~ oneself** tun, was einem gefällt; **~ yourself!** wie Sie wollen!; **you can ~ yourself about where you sit** es ist Ihnen überlassen, wo Sie sitzen

pleased [pliːzd] ADJ (= happy) freudig; (= satisfied) zufrieden; **to be ~ (about sth)** sich (über etw acc) freuen; **I'm ~ to hear that ...** es freut mich zu hören, dass ...; **~ to meet you** or **to make your acquaintance** freut mich; **we are ~ to inform you that ...** wir freuen uns, Ihnen mitteilen zu können, dass ...; **to be ~ at sth** über etw (acc) erfreut sein; **to be ~ with sb/sth** mit jdm/etw zufrieden sein; **~ with oneself** mit sich selbst zufrieden; **I was only too ~ to help** es war mir wirklich eine Freude zu helfen

pleasing ['pliːzɪŋ] ADJ angenehm; sight erfreulich

pleasurable ['pleʒərəbl] ADJ angenehm; anticipation freudig

pleasurably ['pleʒərəblɪ] ADV angenehm

pleasure ['pleʒəʳ] N **(a)** Freude f; **it's a ~, (my) ~** gern (geschehen)!; **with ~** sehr gerne; **the ~ is all mine** (form) das Vergnügen ist ganz meinerseits (form); **it's my very great ~ ...** es ist mir ein großes Vergnügen, ...; **it would give me great ~ to ...** es wäre mir ein Vergnügen, zu ...; **I have much ~ in informing you that ...** ich freue mich (sehr), Ihnen mitteilen zu können, dass ...; **to have the ~ of doing sth** das Vergnügen haben, etw zu tun; **to do sth for ~** etw zum Vergnügen tun; **to get ~ from** or **out of doing sth** Spaß daran haben, etw zu tun; **he seems to take ~ in annoying me** es scheint ihm Vergnügen zu bereiten, mich zu ärgern

(b) (= amusement, source of ~) Vergnügen nt; **is it business or ~?** (ist es) geschäftlich oder zum Vergnügen?; **it's a ~ to meet you** es freut mich, Sie kennenzulernen; **he's a ~ to teach** es ist ein Vergnügen, ihn zu unterrichten

pleasure IN CPDS Vergnügungs-; **pleasure boat** N Vergnügungsdampfer m

pleat [pliːt] █ N Falte f █ VT fälteln

pleated ['pliːtɪd] ADJ gefältelt; **~ skirt** Faltenrock m

pleb [pleb] N (Brit pej inf) Prolet(in) m(f) (pej inf); **the ~s** der Plebs (pej)

plectrum ['plektrəm] N Plektrum nt

pled [pled] (US, Scot) PRET, PTP of **plead**

pledge [pledʒ] █ N (in pawnshop, of love) Pfand nt; (= promise) Versprechen nt; **as a ~ of** als Zeichen (+gen); **election ~s** Wahlversprechen pl █ VT **(a)** (= give as security, pawn) verpfänden **(b)** (= promise) zusichern; **to ~ support for sb/sth** jdm/einer Sache seine Unterstützung zusichern; **to ~ (one's) allegiance to sb/sth** jdm/einer Sache Treue geloben

---

PLEDGE OF ALLEGIANCE

Die **Pledge of Allegiance**, ursprünglich 1892 geschrieben, wird jeden Tag von amerikanischen Schulkindern, besonders in der Grundschule, aufgesagt. Besonders die Traditionalisten halten an diesem Brauch fest, den sie als einen Kernpunkt des amerikanischen Patriotismus ansehen.

---

plentiful ['plentɪfʊl] ADJ reichlich; commodities, minerals etc reichlich vorhanden; **to be in ~ supply** reichlich vorhanden sein

plenty ['plentɪ] █ N **(a)** eine Menge; **in ~** im Überfluss; **three kilos will be ~** drei Kilo sind reichlich; **there's ~ here for six** es gibt mehr als genug für sechs; **that's ~, thanks!** danke, das ist reichlich; **you've already had ~** du hast schon reichlich gehabt; **to see ~ of sb** jdn oft sehen; **there's ~ to do** es gibt viel zu tun; **there's ~ more where that came from** davon gibt es genug; **there are still ~ left** es sind immer noch eine ganze Menge da
(b) **~ of** viel; **~ of time/milk** viel Zeit/Milch; **~ of eggs/reasons** viele Eier/Gründe; **there is no longer ~ of oil** Öl ist nicht mehr im Überfluss vorhanden; **a country with ~ of natural resources** ein Land mit umfangreichen Bodenschätzen; **has everyone got ~ of potatoes?** hat jeder reichlich Kartoffeln?; **there will be ~ of things to drink** es gibt dort ausreichend zu trinken; **he had been given ~ of warning** er ist genügend oft gewarnt worden; **we arrived in ~ of time to get a good seat** wir kamen so rechtzeitig, dass wir einen guten Platz kriegten; **don't worry, there's ~ of time** keine Angst, es ist noch viel Zeit; **take ~ of exercise** Sie müssen viel Sport treiben
█ ADJ (US inf) reichlich; **~ bananas** reichlich Bananen
█ ADV (esp US inf) **~ big (enough)** groß genug; **it rained ~** es hat viel geregnet; **sure, I like it ~** sicher, ich mag das sehr

pliable ['plaɪəbl], **pliant** ['plaɪənt] ADJ biegsam; leather geschmeidig; character, mind formbar; (= docile) fügsam

pliers ['plaɪəz] PL (also pair of ~) (Kombi)zange f

plight [plaɪt] N Elend nt; (of currency, economy etc) Verfall m; **the country's economic ~** die wirtschaftliche Misere des Landes

plod [plɒd] VI **(a)** (= trudge) trotten; **to ~ up a hill** einen Hügel hinaufstapfen; **to ~ along** or **on** weiterstapfen **(b)** (fig) sich abmühen; **to ~ away at sth** sich mit etw abmühen etc; **to ~ on** sich weiterkämpfen

plodder ['plɒdəʳ] N zäher Arbeiter, zähe Arbeiterin

plonk[1] [plɒŋk] VT (inf: also = down) hinschmeißen (inf); **to ~ oneself (down)** sich hinpflanzen (inf)

plonk[2] N (Brit inf: = wine) (billiger) Wein

plonker ['plɒŋkəʳ] N (Brit inf) **(a)** (= stupid person) Niete f **(b)** (= penis) Pimmel m (inf)

plop [plɒp] █ N Plumps m; (in water) Platsch m █ VI **(a)** (= make a plopping sound) platschen **(b)** (inf: = fall) plumpsen (inf)

plot [plɒt] █ N **(a)** (Agr) Stück nt Land; (= building ~) Grundstück nt; (= allotment) Parzelle f; **a ~ of land** ein Stück nt Land
(b) (US: = diagram) (of estate) Plan m; (of building) Grundriss m
(c) (= conspiracy) Verschwörung f

(d) (*Liter, Theat*) Handlung *f*; **to lose the ~** (*fig inf*) den Faden verlieren

2 VT **(a)** (= *plan*) planen; **they ~ted to kill him** sie planten gemeinsam, ihn zu töten

(b) *position, course* feststellen; (= *draw on map*) einzeichnen

3 VI sich verschwören; **to ~ against sb** sich gegen jdn verschwören

plotter ['plɒtə'] N (*Comput*) Plotter *m*

plough, (*US*) **plow** [plaʊ] **1** N Pflug *m*; **the Plough** (*Astron*) der Wagen **2** VT (*Agr*) pflügen; *furrow* ziehen **3** VI pflügen

➤ **plough back** VT SEP (*Comm*) reinvestieren (*into* in +*acc*)

➤ **plough into** **1** VI +PREP OBJ *car etc* hineinrasen in (+*acc*) **2** VT SEP *money* reinstecken in (+*acc*) (*inf*)

➤ **plough through** **1** VI +PREP OBJ **(a) we had to plough through the snow** wir mussten uns durch den Schnee kämpfen; **the car ploughed straight through our garden fence** der Wagen brach geradewegs durch unseren Gartenzaun **(b)** (*inf*) **to plough through a novel** *etc* sich durch einen Roman *etc* hindurchquälen

2 VT SEP **(a) the ship ploughed its way through the waves** das Schiff pflügte sich durch die Wellen; **we ploughed our way through the long grass** wir bahnten uns unseren Weg durch das hohe Gras **(b)** (*inf*) **to plough one's way through a novel** *etc* sich durch einen Roman *etc* durchackern (*inf*)

➤ **plough up** VT SEP *field* umpflügen

ploughing, (*US*) **plowing** ['plaʊɪŋ] N Pflügen *nt*; **the ~ back of profits into the company** die Reinvestierung von Gewinnen in die Firma

plough, (*US*) **plow**: **ploughman** N Pflüger *m*; **ploughman's lunch** N (*Brit*) Käse und Brot als Imbiss

plow *etc* (*US*) = **plough** *etc*

ploy [plɔɪ] N Trick *m*

pls ABBR *of* **please** b.

pluck [plʌk] **1** VT **(a)** *fruit, flower* pflücken; *chicken* rupfen; *guitar, eyebrows* zupfen; **to ~ (at) sb's sleeve** jdn am Ärmel zupfen; **she was ~ed from obscurity to become a film star** sie wurde von einer Unbekannten zum Filmstar gemacht; **he was ~ed to safety** er wurde in Sicherheit gebracht; **to ~ sth out of the air** etw aus der Luft greifen; **to ~ up (one's) courage** all seinen Mut zusammennehmen **(b)** (*also* ~ **out**) *hair, feather* auszupfen **2** VI **to ~ at sth** an etw (*dat*) (herum)zupfen

plug [plʌg] **1** N **(a)** (= *stopper*) Stöpsel *m*; (*for stopping a leak*) Propfen *m*; (*in barrel*) Spund *m*; **to pull the ~ on sb/sth** (*fig inf*) jdm/einer Sache den Boden unter den Füßen wegziehen **(b)** (*Elec*) Stecker *m*; (*Aut*: = *spark ~*) (Zünd)kerze *f* **(c)** (*inf*: *piece of publicity*) Schleichwerbung *f no pl*; **to give sb/ sth a ~** für jdn/etw Werbung machen **(d)** (*US*: = *fireplug*) Hydrant *m* **2** VT **(a)** *hole, leak* zustopfen **(b)** (*inf*: = *publicize*) Schleichwerbung machen für

➤ **plug away** VI (*inf*) ackern (*inf*); **to plug away at sth** sich mit etw herumschlagen (*inf*); **keep plugging away** (nur) nicht lockerlassen

➤ **plug in** **1** VT SEP einstöpseln; **to be plugged in** angeschlossen sein **2** VI sich anschließen lassen

➤ **plug up** VT SEP *hole, leak etc* verstopfen, zustopfen; *crack* zuspachteln

plug: **plug-and-play** ATTR (*Comput*) Plug-and-Play-; **plughole** N (*Brit*) Abfluss *m*; **to go down the ~** (*fig inf*) kaputtgehen (*inf*)

plum [plʌm] **1** N (= *fruit, tree*) Pflaume *f*; (= *Victoria ~, dark blue*) Zwetsch(g)e *f* **2** ADJ ATTR **(a)** (*inf*) *job, position* Bomben- (*inf*) **(b)** (*colour*) pflaumenblau

plumage ['pluːmɪdʒ] N Gefieder *nt*

plumb [plʌm] **1** ADV (*inf*) (= *completely*) total (*inf*); (= *exactly*) genau **2** VT (*fig*) *mystery etc* ergründen; **to ~ the depths of despair** die tiefste Verzweiflung erleben; **to ~ new depths** einen neuen Tiefstand erreichen

➤ **plumb in** VT SEP (*Brit*) anschließen

plumber ['plʌmə'] N Klempner(in) *m(f)*

plumbing ['plʌmɪŋ] N **(a)** (= *work*) Installieren *nt* **(b)** (= *fittings*) Leitungen *pl*

plume [pluːm] N Feder *f*; (*on helmet*) Federbusch *m*; **~ of smoke** Rauchfahne *f*

plummet ['plʌmɪt] VI (*bird, plane etc*) hinunterstürzen; (*Econ*) (*sales figures etc*) stark zurückgehen; (*currency, shares etc*) fallen; **the euro has ~ted to £0.60** der Euro ist auf £ 0,60 gefallen

plummeting ['plʌmɪtɪŋ] ADJ fallend; *popularity* schwindend

plump [plʌmp] **1** ADJ (+ER) mollig; *legs etc* stämmig; *face* rundlich; *chicken etc* gut genährt; *fruit* prall **2** VT (= *drop*) fallen lassen; (= *throw*) werfen; **to ~ sth down** etw hinfallen lassen/hinwerfen; **she ~ed herself down in the armchair** sie ließ sich in den Sessel fallen

> *Be careful!* **plump** *is not translated by the German word* **plump**.

➤ **plump for** VI +PREP OBJ sich entscheiden für

➤ **plump up** VT SEP *cushion* aufschütteln

plumpness ['plʌmpnɪs] N Molligkeit *f*; (*of legs etc*) Stämmigkeit *f*; (*of face*) Pausbäckigkeit *f*; (*of chicken*) Wohlgenährtheit *f*

plum tomato N italienische Tomate

plunder ['plʌndə'] **1** N Beute *f* **2** VT *place* plündern (*also hum*); (*completely*) ausplündern; *people* ausplündern; *thing* rauben **3** VI plündern

plundering ['plʌndərɪŋ] N (*of place*) Plünderung *f*; (*of things*) Raub *m*

plunge [plʌndʒ] **1** VT **(a)** (= *thrust*) stecken; (*into water etc*) tauchen; **he ~d the knife into his victim's back** er jagte seinem Opfer das Messer in den Rücken **(b)** (*fig*) **to ~ the country into war/debt** das Land in einen Krieg/in Schulden stürzen; **the room was ~d into darkness** das Zimmer war in Dunkelheit getaucht **2** VI **(a)** (= *dive*) tauchen **(b)** (= *rush*: *esp downward*) stürzen (*also Econ*); **to ~ to one's death** zu Tode stürzen; **he ~d into the crowd** er stürzte sich in die Massen; **sales have ~d by 24%** die Verkaufszahlen sind um 24% gefallen **3** VR (*into studies, job etc*) sich stürzen (*into* in +*acc*) **4** N **(a)** (*lit, fig*) Sturz *m*; **a downward ~** ein Absturz *m*; **shares took a ~ after the government's announcement** nach der Ankündigung der Regierung kam es zu einem Kurssturz; **a ~ in the value of the pound** ein Kurssturz *m* des Pfunds **(b)** (= *dive*) (Kopf)sprung *m*; **to take the ~** (*fig inf*) den Sprung wagen

➤ **plunge in** **1** VT SEP *knife* hineinjagen; *hand* hineinstecken; (*into water*) hineintauchen; **he was plunged straight in (at the deep end)** (*fig*) er musste gleich richtig ran (*inf*) **2** VI (= *dive*) hineinspringen

plunger ['plʌndʒə'] N Sauger *m*

plunging ['plʌndʒɪŋ] ADJ **(a)** *neckline* tief ausgeschnitten **(b)** *cost, currency, prices* stark fallend

pluperfect ['pluːˈpɜːfɪkt] **1** N Plusquamperfekt *nt* **2** ADJ **~ tense** Plusquamperfekt *nt*

plural ['plʊərəl] **1** ADJ (*Gram*) Plural-; **~ ending** Pluralendung *f* **2** N Plural *m*; **in the ~** im Plural

plus [plʌs] **1** PREP plus (+*dat*); (= *together with*) (außerdem); **~ or minus 10%** plus minus 10% **2** ADJ **(a)** (*Math, Elec, fig*) **a ~ figure** eine positive Zahl; **a ~ factor** ein Pluspunkt *m*; **on the ~ side** auf der Habenseite; **~ 10 degrees** 10 Grad über Null **(b)** (= *more than*) **he got B ~ in the exam** ≈ er hat in der Prüfung eine Zwei plus bekommen; **50 pages ~ a week** mehr als *or* über 50 Seiten pro Woche **3** N (= *sign*) Pluszeichen *nt*; (= *positive factor*) Pluspunkt *m*; (= *extra*) Plus *nt*

plush [plʌʃ] ADJ (+ER) (*inf*) feudal (*inf*); **a ~ hotel** ein Nobelhotel *nt* (*inf*)

plus sign N (*Math, Elec*) Pluszeichen *nt*

Pluto ['pluːtəʊ] N (*Astron*) Pluto *m*

plutonium [pluːˈtəʊnɪəm] N Plutonium *nt*

ply [plaɪ] VT **(a)** *trade* ausüben **(b)** **to ~ sb with questions** jdn mit Fragen überhäufen; **to ~ sb with drink(s)** jdn immer wieder zum Trinken auffordern

plywood ['plaɪwʊd] N Sperrholz *nt*

PM (*Brit inf*) ABBR *of* **Prime Minister**

pm ABBR *of* **post meridiem** p.m.

PMT [piːemˈtiː] N (*Brit*) ABBR *of* **pre-menstrual tension**

pneumatic drill [njuːˌmætɪkˈdrɪl] N Pressluftbohrer *m*

pneumonia [njuːˈməʊnɪə] N Lungenentzündung f
PO ABBR of **post office** PA
poach¹ [pəʊtʃ] VT egg pochieren; fish dünsten; **~ed egg** verlorenes Ei
poach² █ VT unerlaubt fangen; (fig) idea stehlen; members, customers abwerben █ VI (lit) wildern (for auf +acc)
poacher [ˈpəʊtʃə'] N Wilderer m, Wilderin f
poaching [ˈpəʊtʃɪŋ] N Wildern nt
P.O. box N Postfach nt
pocket [ˈpɒkɪt] █ N (a) Tasche f; (in suitcase, file etc) Fach nt; (Billiards) Loch nt; **to have sb/sth in one's ~** (fig) jdn/etw in der Tasche haben (inf); **to be in sb's ~** (fig) jdm hörig sein; **to live in each other's** or **one another's ~s** (fig) unzertrennlich sein **(b)** (= resources) Geldbeutel m; **to be a drain on one's ~** jds Geldbeutel strapazieren (inf); **I was £100 in ~ after the sale** nach dem Verkauf war ich um £ 100 reicher; **to pay for sth out of one's own ~** etw aus der eigenen Tasche bezahlen; **to have deep ~s** (fig) großzügig sein
(c) (= restricted area) Gebiet nt; **~ of resistance** Widerstandsnest nt
█ ADJ Taschen-; **~ diary** Taschenkalender m
█ VT **(a)** (= put in one's ~) einstecken
(b) (= gain) kassieren; (= misappropriate) einstecken (inf)
pocket: pocketbook N **(a)** (= notebook) Notizbuch nt
(b) (esp US: = wallet) Brieftasche f; **pocket calculator** N Taschenrechner m
pocketful [ˈpɒkɪtfʊl] N **a ~** eine Tasche voll
pocket: pocketknife N Taschenmesser nt; **pocket money** N (esp Brit) Taschengeld nt; **pocket-size(d)** ADJ book im Taschenformat; **~ camera/TV** Miniaturkamera f/-fernseher m
pockmarked [ˈpɒkmɑːkt] ADJ face pockennarbig; surface narbig
pod [pɒd] █ N (Bot) Hülse f █ VT peas enthülsen
podgy [ˈpɒdʒɪ] ADJ (+ER) (Brit inf) pummelig; face schwammig; **~ fingers** Wurstfinger pl
podiatrist [pɒˈdiːətrɪst] N (esp US) Fußspezialist(in) m(f)
podium [ˈpəʊdɪəm] N Podest nt
poem [ˈpəʊɪm] N Gedicht nt; **epic ~** Epos nt
poet [ˈpəʊɪt] N Dichter m
poetess [ˈpəʊɪtes] N Dichterin f
poetic [pəʊˈetɪk] ADJ poetisch; place, charm malerisch; **~ beauty** (visual) malerische Schönheit
poetical [pəʊˈetɪkəl] ADJ = **poetic**
poetically [pəʊˈetɪkəlɪ] ADV poetisch; **~ gifted** dichterisch begabt
poetic licence N dichterische Freiheit
poet laureate [ˈpəʊɪtˈlɔːrɪɪt] N Hofdichter(in) m(f)
poetry [ˈpəʊɪtrɪ] N **(a)** Dichtung f; **to write ~** Gedichte schreiben **(b)** (fig) Poesie f; **the dancing was ~ in motion** der Tanz war in Bewegung umgesetzte Poesie
po-faced [ˈpəʊfeɪst] ADJ (inf) mürrisch
pogrom [ˈpɒɡrəm] N Pogrom nt
poignancy [ˈpɔɪnjənsɪ] N Ergreifende(s) nt; (of look, memories) Wehmut f; (of distress, regret) Schmerzlichkeit f; **he writes with great ~** er schreibt sehr ergreifend
poignant [ˈpɔɪnjənt] ADJ ergreifend; memories, look wehmütig; distress, regret schmerzlich
poignantly [ˈpɔɪnjəntlɪ] ADV ergreifend

---

point [pɔɪnt]

█ NOUN	█ INTRANSITIVE VERB
█ PLURAL NOUN	█ PHRASAL VERB
█ TRANSITIVE VERB	

█ NOUN
(a) Punkt m; (on thermometer) Grad m; **from all points (of the compass)** aus allen (Himmels)richtungen; **points for/against** Plus-/Minuspunkte pl; **to win on points** nach Punkten gewinnen; **(nought) point seven (0.7)** null Komma sieben (0,7)
✦**up to a point** bis zu einem gewissen Grad
(b) (of chin, needle) Spitze f; (of a star) Zacke f
(c) (= place, time) Stelle f; **at this point** (= then) in diesem Augenblick; (= now) jetzt; **from that point on they were**

friends von da an waren sie Freunde; **at what point ...?** an welcher Stelle ...?; **at no point** nie; **at no point in the book** nirgends in dem Buch, an keiner Stelle des Buches
✦**point of** + NOUN **point of departure** (lit, fig) Ausgangspunkt m; **severe to the point of cruelty** streng bis an die Grenze der Grausamkeit; **to reach the point of no return** (fig) den Punkt erreichen, von dem an es kein Zurück gibt; **point of view** Standpunkt m; **from my point of view** von meinem Standpunkt aus; **from the point of view of productivity** von der Produktivität her gesehen; **point of reference** Orientierungspunkt m
✦**point of** + -ing **to be on the point of doing sth** im Begriff sein, etw zu tun; **he was on the point of telling me the story when ...** er wollte mir gerade die Geschichte erzählen, als ...
(d) (= matter, question) Punkt m; **a 12-point plan** ein Zwölfpunkteplan m; **a useful point** ein nützlicher Hinweis; **point by point** Punkt für Punkt; **my point was ...** was ich sagen wollte, war ...; **you have a point there** darin mögen Sie Recht haben; **would you put that point more succinctly?** können Sie das etwas knapper fassen?
✦**to make a/one's point** ein/sein Argument nt vorbringen; **he made the point that ...** er betonte, dass ...; **you've made your point!** das hast du ja schon gesagt!; **what point are you trying to make?** worauf wollen Sie hinaus?; **if I may make another point** wenn ich noch auf einen weiteren Punkt aufmerksam machen darf
✦**to take the/sb's point** I take your point, **point taken** ich akzeptiere, was Sie sagen; (in exasperation) ich habe schon begriffen; **do you take my point?** verstehst du mich?
✦**point of** + NOUN **a point of interest** ein interessanter Punkt; **a point of law** eine Rechtsfrage; **a point of principle** eine grundsätzliche Frage
(e) (= purpose) Sinn m; **there's no point in staying** es hat keinen Sinn zu bleiben; **I don't see the point of carrying on** ich sehe keinen Sinn darin, weiterzumachen; **what's the point?** was solls?; **the point of this is ...** Sinn und Zweck davon ist ...; **what's the point of trying?** wozu (es) versuchen?; **he doesn't understand the point of doing this** er versteht nicht, weswegen wir/sie etc das machen; **the point is that ...** die Sache ist die, dass ...; **that's the whole point** das ist es ja gerade; **that's the whole point of doing it this way** gerade darum machen wir das so; **the point of the joke/story** die Pointe; **that's not the point** darum geht es nicht; **his remarks are very much to the point** seine Bemerkungen sind sehr sachbezogen
✦**to get** or **see the point** verstehen, worum es geht; **do you see the point of what I'm saying?** weißt du, worauf ich hinauswill?
✦**to miss the point** nicht verstehen, worum es geht; **he missed the point of what I was saying** er hat nicht begriffen, worauf ich hinauswollte
✦**to come to the point** zur Sache kommen
✦**to keep** or **stick to the point** beim Thema bleiben
✦**beside the point** irrelevant; **I'm afraid that's beside the point** das ist nicht relevant
✦**a case in point** ein einschlägiger Fall
✦**to make a point of doing sth** Wert darauf legen, etw zu tun
(f) (= characteristic) **good/bad points** gute/schlechte Seiten pl

█ **points** PLURAL NOUN (Rail, Brit) Weichen pl

█ **TRANSITIVE VERB**
(a) (gun, telescope etc) richten (at auf +acc)
(b) (= mark, show) zeigen; **to point the way** (lit, fig) den Weg weisen
(c) (toes) strecken

█ **INTRANSITIVE VERB**
(a) (with finger etc) zeigen (at, to auf +acc); **it's rude to point (at strangers)** es ist unhöflich, mit dem Finger (auf Fremde) zu zeigen; **he pointed toward(s) the house** er zeigte zum Haus
(b) (= indicate) hindeuten (to auf +acc); **everything points that way** alles weist in diese Richtung; **all the signs point to success** alle Zeichen stehen auf Erfolg
(c) (gun, vehicle etc) gerichtet sein; (building, valley) liegen

⑤ PHRASAL VERB

➤ **point out** VT SEP **(a)** (= *show*) zeigen auf (+*acc*); **to point sth out to sb** jdn auf etw hinweisen; **could you point him out to me?** kannst du mir zeigen, wer er ist? **(b)** (= *mention*) **to point sth out (to sb)** (jdn) auf etw (*acc*) aufmerksam machen; **may I point out that …?** darf ich darauf aufmerksam machen, dass …?

point-blank ['pɔɪnt'blæŋk] **①** ADJ direkt; *refusal* glatt; **at** *or* **from ~ range** aus kürzester Entfernung **②** ADV *fire* aus kürzester Entfernung; *ask* rundheraus; **to ask sb ~** jdn geradeheraus fragen; **he refused ~ to help** er weigerte sich rundweg zu helfen

pointed ['pɔɪntɪd] ADJ **(a)** *stick, roof, chin etc* spitz; *window, arch* spitzbogig **(b)** *wit, criticism* scharf **(c)** *remark, comment, look* spitz; *reference* unverblümt; *question* gezielt; *absence, gesture* ostentativ; **that was rather ~** das war ziemlich deutlich

pointedly ['pɔɪntɪdlɪ] ADV *speak, look* spitz; *refer* unverblümt; *leave, stay away etc* ostentativ

pointer ['pɔɪntə˞] N **(a)** (= *indicator*) Zeiger *m* **(b)** (= *stick*) Zeigestock *m* **(c)** (*fig*) Hinweis *m*

pointless ['pɔɪntlɪs] ADJ sinnlos; **it is ~ her going** *or* **for her to go** es ist sinnlos, dass sie geht; **a ~ exercise** eine sinnlose Angelegenheit

pointlessly ['pɔɪntlɪslɪ] ADV sinnlos

pointlessness ['pɔɪntlɪsnɪs] N Sinnlosigkeit *f*

point of sale N (*Comm*) Verkaufsstelle *f*

pointy ['pɔɪntɪ] ADJ ATTR (+ER) spitz

poise [pɔɪz] **①** N **(a)** (*of body*) Haltung *f*; (= *grace*) Grazie *f* **(b)** (= *composure*) Gelassenheit *f*; (= *self-possession*) Selbstsicherheit *f*; **to recover** *or* **regain one's ~** seine Selbstbeherrschung wiedererlangen **②** VT **(a)** (= *balance*) balancieren; **she ~d her pen over her notebook** sie hielt den Kugelschreiber schreibbereit über ihrem Notizblock **(b)** (*in passive*) **to be/hang ~d** (*bird, rock, sword*) schweben; **the tiger was ~d ready to spring** der Tiger lauerte sprungbereit; **we sat ~d on the edge of our chairs** wir balancierten auf den Stuhlkanten

poised [pɔɪzd] ADJ **(a)** (= *suspended*) *hand* erhoben; *object* bereit **(b)** (= *ready*) bereit; **to be ~ to do sth** bereit sein, etw zu tun; **to be ~ for sth** für etw bereit sein; **the enemy are ~ to attack** der Feind steht angriffsbereit; **he was ~ to become champion** er war auf dem besten Weg, die Meisterschaft zu gewinnen; **to be ~ on the brink of sth** am Rande von etw stehen **(c)** (= *self-possessed*) selbstsicher

poison ['pɔɪzn] **①** N (*lit, fig*) Gift *nt*; **what's your ~?** (*inf*), **name your ~** (*inf*) was willst du trinken? **②** VT (*lit, fig*) vergiften; *atmosphere, rivers* verpesten; *marriage* zerrütten; **it won't ~ you** (*inf*) das wird dich nicht umbringen (*inf*); **to ~ sb's mind against sb** jdn gegen jdn aufstacheln

poisoned ['pɔɪznd] ADJ vergiftet

poisoning ['pɔɪznɪŋ] N (*lit, fig*) Vergiftung *f*; **the gradual ~ of the atmosphere by …** die zunehmende Luftverpestung durch …

poisonous ['pɔɪznəs] ADJ (*lit, fig*) giftig; *literature, doctrine* zersetzend; **~ mushroom** Giftpilz *m*; **~ snake** Giftschlange *f*

poison: poison-pen letter N anonymer Brief; **poison pill** N (*Fin*) zum Schutz gegen ein unerwünschtes Übernahmeangebot eingesetzte Maßnahmen, die im Falle der Übernahme zu einem Wertverlust der Firma führen

poke [pəʊk] **①** N Stoß *m*; **to give sb/sth a ~** (*with stick*) jdn/etw stoßen; (*with finger*) jdn/etw stupsen **②** VT **(a)** (= *jab*) (*with stick*) stoßen; (*with finger*) stupsen; **to ~ the fire** das Feuer schüren; **he accidentally ~d me in the eye** er hat mir aus Versehen ins Auge gestoßen **(b)** (= *thrust*) **to ~ one's finger/a stick** *etc* **into sth** seinen Finger/einen Stock *etc* in etw (*acc*) stecken; **he ~d his head round the door** er streckte seinen Kopf durch die Tür **(c)** (= *make by poking*) bohren; **to ~ holes in sb's story** jds Geschichte zerpflücken **③** VI **to ~ at sth** in etw (*dat*) stochern; **she ~d at her food with a fork** sie stocherte mit einer Gabel in ihrem Essen herum

➤ **poke about** (*Brit*) *or* **around** VI **(a)** (= *prod*) herumstochern **(b)** (*inf*: = *nose about*) schnüffeln (*inf*)

➤ **poke in** VT SEP hineinstecken; **I'll just poke my head in and say hello** (*inf*) ich will nur schnell vorbeischauen und Guten Tag sagen

➤ **poke out ①** VI vorstehen; **a handkerchief was poking out of his top pocket** ein Taschentuch guckte aus seiner Brusttasche hervor **②** VT SEP **(a)** (= *extend*) hinausstrecken **(b)** **he poked the dirt out with his fingers** er kratzte den Schmutz mit den Fingern heraus; **to poke sb's eye out** jdm ein Auge ausstechen

poker ['pəʊkə˞] N (*Cards*) Poker *nt*

poker-faced ['pəʊkə'feɪst] ADJ mit einem Pokergesicht

poky ['pəʊkɪ] ADJ (+ER) (*pej*) winzig; **it's so ~ in here** es ist so eng hier

Poland ['pəʊlənd] N Polen *nt*

polar ['pəʊlə˞] ADJ **(a)** Polar-, polar **(b)** (= *opposite*) polar

polar: polar bear N Eisbär *m*; **polar circle** N Polarkreis *m*

polarize ['pəʊləraɪz] **①** VT polarisieren **②** VI sich polarisieren

Polaroid® ['pəʊlərɔɪd] N (= *camera*) Polaroidkamera® *f*; (= *photograph*) Sofortbild *nt*

Pole [pəʊl] N Pole *m*, Polin *f*

pole¹ [pəʊl] N Stange *f*; (*for vaulting*) Stab *m*; **I wouldn't touch him with a ten-foot ~** (*US inf*) von so jemandem lasse ich die Finger (*inf*); (*because disgusting*) den würde ich noch nicht mal mit der Kneifzange anfassen (*inf*)

pole² N (*Geog, Astron, Elec*) Pol *m*; **they are ~s apart** sie (*acc*) trennen Welten

polecat ['pəʊlkæt] N Iltis *m*; (*US*) Skunk *m*

polemical [pə'lemɪkəl] ADJ polemisch

pole: pole position N (*Motor Racing*) Poleposition *f*; **to be** *or* **start in ~** aus der Poleposition starten; **pole star** N Polarstern *m*; **pole vault** N Stabhochsprung *m*; **pole-vaulter** N Stabhochspringer(in) *m(f)*

police [pə'liːs] **①** N Polizei *f*; **to join the ~** zur Polizei gehen; **he is in** *or* **a member of the ~** er ist bei der Polizei; **hundreds of ~** Hunderte von Polizisten; **extra ~ were called in** es wurden zusätzliche Polizeikräfte angefordert; **three ~ were injured** drei Polizisten wurden verletzt **②** VT kontrollieren

police: police car N Polizeiwagen *m*; **police constable** N (*Brit*) Polizist(in) *m(f)*; **police dog** N Polizeihund *m*; **police force** N Polizei *f*; **one of the best-equipped ~s in the world** eine der bestausgestatteten Polizeitruppen der Welt; **police headquarters** N SING *or* PL Polizeipräsidium *nt*; **policeman** N Polizist *m*; **police officer** N Polizeibeamte(r) *mf*; **police presence** N Polizeiaufgebot *nt*; **police station** N (Polizei)wache *f*; **policewoman** N Polizistin *f*

policing [pə'liːsɪŋ] N Kontrolle *f*; (*of agreement, pop concert also*) Überwachung *f*

policy¹ ['pɒlɪsɪ] N **(a)** Politik *f no pl*; (*of business*) Geschäftspolitik *f* (*on* bei); (= *principle*) Grundsatz *m*; **social and economic ~** Wirtschafts- und Sozialpolitik *f*; **our ~ on recruitment** unsere Einstellungspolitik; **a ~ of restricting immigration** eine Politik zur Einschränkung der Einwanderung; **a matter of ~** eine Grundsatzfrage; **~ decision** Grundsatzentscheidung *f*; **your ~ should always be to give people a second chance** du solltest es dir zum Grundsatz machen, Menschen eine zweite Chance zu geben; **my ~ is to wait and see** meine Devise heißt abwarten; **it's our ~ to cater for the mid-twenties** wir wenden uns mit unserer Firmenpolitik an die Mittzwanziger; **our ~ is one of expansion** wir verfolgen eine expansionsorientierte Geschäftspolitik **(b)** (= *prudence*) Taktik *f*; **it was good/bad ~** das war (taktisch) klug/unklug

policy² N (*also* **insurance ~**) (Versicherungs)police *f*; **to take out a ~** eine Versicherung abschließen

policy: policy document N Grundsatzpapier *nt*; **policyholder** N Versicherungsnehmer(in) *m(f)*; **policy-maker** N Parteiideologe *m*/-ideologin *f*; **policy-making** ADJ grundsatzpolitisch; **policy paper** N Grundsatzpapier *nt*

polio ['pəʊlɪəʊ] N Kinderlähmung *f*

Polish ['pəʊlɪʃ] **①** ADJ polnisch **②** N (*Ling*) Polnisch *nt*

polish ['pɒlɪʃ] **①** N **(a)** (= *shoe* ~) Creme *f*; (= *floor* ~) Bohnerwachs *nt*; (= *furniture* ~) Politur *f*; (= *metal* ~) Poliermittel *nt*; (= *nail* ~) Lack *m* **(b)** **to give sth a ~** etw polieren; *floor* etw bohnern; **my shoes need a ~** meine

Schuhe müssen geputzt werden **(c)** (= *shine*) Glanz *m* **2** VT (*lit*) polieren; *floor* bohnern

➤ **polish off** VT SEP (*inf*) *food* verputzen (*inf*); *drink* wegputzen (*inf*)

➤ **polish up** VT SEP **(a)** polieren **(b)** (*fig*) *style, one's French* aufpolieren; *work* überarbeiten

polished ['pɒlɪʃt] ADJ **(a)** *surface, furniture* poliert; *floor* gebohnert; *stone, glass, manners* geschliffen **(b)** *style etc* verfeinert; *performance, performer* brillant; *image* makellos

polite [pə'laɪt] ADJ (+ER) höflich; **it wouldn't be ~** es wäre unhöflich; **to be ~ to sb** höflich zu jdm sein

politely [pə'laɪtlɪ] ADV höflich

politeness [pə'laɪtnɪs] N Höflichkeit *f*

political [pə'lɪtɪkəl] ADJ politisch

political: political asylum N politisches Asyl; **he was granted/refused ~** ihm wurde politisches Asyl gewährt/nicht gewährt; **political correctness** N politische Korrektheit; **political economy** N Volkswirtschaft *f*

politically [pə'lɪtɪkəlɪ] ADV politisch

politically correct ADJ politisch korrekt

POLITICALLY CORRECT

*Die Woge der politischen Korrektheit entstand wie so vieles andere in den Vereinigten Staaten. Ursprünglich wollte man vermeiden, dass über ethnische Minderheiten, Frauen, Behinderte, Homosexuelle und benachteiligte Bevölkerungsgruppen in Worten gesprochen wird, die sie herabsetzen oder beleidigen. Heute wird der Ausdruck **politically correct** überwiegend als Schimpfwort von den Gegnern dieser „liberalen" Ansichten gebraucht.*

politically incorrect ADJ politisch inkorrekt

political: political party N politische Partei; **political prisoner** N politischer Gefangener, politische Gefangene

politician [pɒlɪ'tɪʃən] N Politiker(in) *m(f)*

politics ['pɒlɪtɪks] N Politik *f*; (= *views*) politische Ansichten *pl*; **to be in ~** in der Politik sein; **to go into ~** in die Politik gehen; **interested in ~** politisch interessiert; **office ~** Bürorangeleien *pl*

polka dot ['pɒlkədɒt] **1** N Tupfen *m* **2** ADJ getupft

poll [pəʊl] **1** N **(a)** (*Pol* = *voting*) Abstimmung *f*; (= *election*) Wahl *f*; **a ~ was taken among the villagers** unter den Dorfbewohnern wurde abgestimmt
(b) (= *total of votes cast*) Wahlbeteiligung *f*; (*for individual candidate*) Stimmenanteil *m*; **they got 34% of the ~** sie bekamen 34% der Stimmen
(c) **~s** (= *voting place*) Wahllokale *pl*; (= *election*) Wahl *f*; **to go to the ~s** zur Wahl gehen; **a crushing defeat at the ~s** eine vernichtende Wahlniederlage
(d) (= *opinion ~*) Umfrage *f*; **a telephone ~** eine telefonische Abstimmung
2 VT **(a)** *votes* erhalten
(b) (*in opinion ~*) befragen; **40% of those ~ed supported the Government** 40% der Befragten waren für die Regierung

pollen ['pɒlən] N Pollen *m*

pollen count N Pollenzahl *f*

pollinate ['pɒlɪneɪt] VT bestäuben

pollination [pɒlɪ'neɪʃən] N Bestäubung *f*

polling ['pəʊlɪŋ] N **(a)** Wahl *f*; **~ will be on Thursday** die Wahl ist am Donnerstag **(b)** (*Comput*) Sendeaufruf *m*

polling: polling booth N Wahlkabine *f*; **polling card** N Wahlausweis *m*; **polling day** N (*esp Brit*) Wahltag *m*; **polling station** N (*Brit*) Wahllokal *nt*

poll tax N Kopfsteuer *f*

pollutant [pə'luːtənt] N Schadstoff *m*

pollute [pə'luːt] VT verschmutzen; *atmosphere etc* verunreinigen

pollution [pə'luːʃən] N (*of environment*) Umweltverschmutzung *f*; (*of atmosphere*) Verunreinigung *f*

polo ['pəʊləʊ] N Polo *nt*

polo neck (*Brit*) **1** N (= *sweater*) Rollkragenpullover *m* **2** ADJ **~ sweater** Rollkragenpullover *m*

poltergeist ['pɒltəgaɪst] N Poltergeist *m*

polyester [pɒlɪ'estə'] N Polyester *m*

Polynesia [pɒlɪ'niːzɪə] N Polynesien *nt*

Polynesian [pɒlɪ'niːzɪən] **1** ADJ polynesisch **2** N Polynesier(in) *m(f)*

polystyrene [pɒlɪ'staɪriːn] **1** N Polystyrol *nt*; (*extended also*) Styropor® *nt* **2** ADJ Polystyrol-/Styropor-

polytechnic [pɒlɪ'teknɪk] N (*Brit*) ≈ Polytechnikum *nt*; (*degree-awarding*) technische Hochschule, TH *f*

polythene ['pɒlɪθiːn] N (*Brit*) Polyäthylen *nt*; (*in everyday language*) Plastik *nt*; **~ bag** Plastiktüte *f*

pomegranate ['pɒmə,grænɪt] N Granatapfel *m*

Pomerania [pɒmə'reɪnɪə] N Pommern *nt*

Pomeranian [pɒmə'reɪnɪən] **1** ADJ pommer(i)sch **2** N **(a)** Pommer(in) *m(f)* **(b)** (= *dog*) Spitz *m*

pomp [pɒmp] N Pomp *m*

Pompeii [pɒm'peiiː] N Pompe(j)i *nt*

pompom ['pɒmpɒm] N Troddel *f*

pomposity [pɒm'pɒsɪtɪ] N (*of person, behaviour*) Aufgeblasenheit *f*; (*of phrase*) Gespreiztheit *f*; (*of language, letter*) Schwülstigkeit *f*

pompous ['pɒmpəs] ADJ *person, behaviour* aufgeblasen; *phrase* gespreizt; *language, letter* schwülstig

pompously ['pɒmpəslɪ] ADV *write, speak* schwülstig; *behave* aufgeblasen

ponce about [pɒnsə'baʊt], **ponce around** [pɒnsə'raʊnd] VI (*Brit inf*) herumtänzeln

poncho ['pɒntʃəʊ] N Poncho *m*

poncy ['pɒnsɪ] ADJ (+ER) (*Brit inf*) *walk, actor* tuntig (*inf*)

pond [pɒnd] N Teich *m*; **the ~** (*inf*: = *Atlantic Ocean*) der Große Teich

ponder ['pɒndə'] **1** VT nachdenken über (+*acc*); *possibilities, consequences etc* erwägen **2** VI nachdenken (*on, over* über +*acc*)

ponderous ['pɒndərəs] ADJ (= *laboured, clumsy*) schwerfällig; (= *heavy*) massiv

ponderously ['pɒndərəslɪ] ADV schwerfällig

pone [pəʊn] N (*US*) Maisbrot *nt*

pong [pɒŋ] (*Brit inf*) **1** N Gestank *m*; **there's a bit of a ~ in here** hier stinkts **2** VI stinken

pontificate [pɒn'tɪfɪkeɪt] VI (*fig*) dozieren

pony ['pəʊnɪ] N Pony *nt*

pony: ponytail N Pferdeschwanz *m*; **she was wearing her hair in a ~** sie trug einen Pferdeschwanz; **pony trekking** N Ponyreiten *nt*

poo [puː] N, VI (*baby-talk*) = **pooh 2, 3**

pooch [puːtʃ] N (*inf*) Hündchen *nt*

poodle ['puːdl] N Pudel *m*

poof(ter) [pʊf(tə')] N (*dated Brit pej inf*) Schwule(r) *m* (*inf*)

pooh [puː] **1** INTERJ puh **2** N (*baby-talk*) Aa *nt* (*baby-talk*); **to do a ~** Aa machen (*baby-talk*) **3** VI (*baby-talk*) Aa machen (*baby-talk*)

pool¹ [puːl] N **(a)** Teich *m* **(b)** (*of rain*) Pfütze *f*; (*of spilled liquid*) Lache *f*; **a ~ of blood** eine Blutlache **(c)** (= *swimming ~*) (Schwimm)becken *nt*; (*in private garden, hotel*) Swimmingpool *m*; (= *swimming baths*) Schwimmbad *nt*; **to go to the (swimming) ~** ins Schwimmbad gehen

pool² **1** N **(a)** (= *common fund*) (gemeinsame) Kasse; **the ~ stood at £40** es waren £ 40 in der Kasse
(b) (= *typing ~*) Schreibzentrale *f*; (= *car ~*) Fahrbereitschaft *f*; (= *car-sharing*) Fahrgemeinschaft *f*
(c) pools PL (*Brit*) **the ~s** (= *football ~s*) Toto *m* or *nt*; **to do the ~s** Toto spielen; **he won £1000 on the ~s** er hat £ 1000 im Toto gewonnen
(d) (*form of snooker*) Poolbillard *nt*
(e) (*Comm*) Interessengemeinschaft *f*; (*US*: = *monopoly, trust*) Kartell *nt*
2 VT *resources, savings* zusammenlegen; *efforts* vereinen (*geh*)

pool: pool attendant N Bademeister(in) *m(f)*; **pool hall, pool room** N Billardzimmer *nt*; **pool table** N Billardtisch *m*

poop [puːp] VT (*inf*: = *exhaust*) schlauchen (*inf*)

poor [pʊə'] **1** ADJ (+ER) **(a)** arm; **to get** or **become ~er** verarmen; **he was now one thousand pounds (the) ~er** er war nun um eintausend Pfund ärmer; **~ relation** (*fig*) Sorgenkind *nt*; **you ~ (old) chap** (*inf*) du armer Kerl (*inf*); **~ you!** du Ärmste(r)!; **she's all alone, ~ woman** sie ist ganz allein, die arme Frau; **~ things, they look cold** die Ärmsten, ihnen scheint kalt zu sein

(b) (= *not good*) schlecht; (= *meagre*) mangelhaft; *leadership* schwach; **he is a ~ traveller** er verträgt Reisen nicht gut; **a ~ friend you are!** du bist mir ein schöner Freund!; **fruit wines are a ~ substitute for grape wine** Obstwein ist nur ein armseliger Ersatz für Wein aus Trauben; **a ~ chance of success** schlechte Erfolgsaussichten *pl*; **that's ~ consolation** das ist ein schwacher Trost; **this is a pretty ~ state of affairs** das sieht aber gar nicht gut aus; **he has a very ~ grasp of the subject** er beherrscht das Fach sehr schlecht; **he showed a ~ grasp of the facts** er zeigte wenig Verständnis für die Fakten **2** PL **the ~** die Armen *pl*

poorly ['pʊəlɪ] **1** ADV **(a)** arm; *dressed, furnished* ärmlich; **~ off** schlecht gestellt **(b)** (= *badly*) schlecht; **~-attended** schlecht besucht; **~-designed** schlecht konstruiert; **~-educated** ohne (ausreichende) Schulbildung; **~-equipped** schlecht ausgerüstet; **~-paid** schlecht bezahlt; **to do ~ (at sth)** (in etw *dat*) schlecht abschneiden **2** ADJ PRED (*Brit*: = *ill*) krank; **to be** *or* **feel ~** sich krank fühlen

poorness ['pʊənɪs] N Dürftigkeit *f*; (*of soil*) Magerkeit *f*

pop¹ [pɒp] N (*esp US inf*) (= *father*) Papa *m* (*inf*); (= *elderly man*) Opa *m* (*hum inf*)

pop² **1** N **(a)** (= *sound*) Knall *m* **(b)** (= *fizzy drink*) Limo *f* (*inf*) **2** ADV **to go ~** (*cork*) knallen; (*balloon*) platzen; **~!** peng! **3** VT **(a)** *balloon, corn* zum Platzen bringen **(b)** (*inf*: = *put*) stecken; **to ~ a letter into the postbox** (*Brit*) *or* **mailbox** (*US*) einen Brief einwerfen; **he ~ped his head round the door** er streckte den Kopf durch die Tür; **to ~ a jacket/hat on** sich (*dat*) ein Jackett überziehen/einen Hut aufsetzen; **to ~ one's clogs** (*Brit hum inf*) das Zeitliche segnen (*inf*); **to ~ the question** einen (Heirats)antrag machen **(c)** (*inf*) *pills* schlucken (*inf*) **4** VI (*inf*) **(a)** (*cork*) knallen; (*balloon*) platzen; (*seed pods, buttons, ~corn*) aufplatzen; (*ears*) knacken; **his eyes were ~ping out of his head** ihm fielen fast die Augen aus dem Kopf (*inf*) **(b)** **to ~ along/down to the baker's** schnell zum Bäcker laufen; **I'll just ~ upstairs** ich laufe mal eben nach oben; **~ across/over/round and see me sometime** komm doch mal auf einen Sprung bei mir vorbei (*inf*)

➤ **pop back** (*inf*) **1** VT SEP (schnell) zurücktun (*inf*); **pop it back in(to) the box** tu es wieder in die Schachtel **2** VI schnell zurücklaufen

➤ **pop in** (*inf*) **1** VT SEP hineintun; **to pop sth in(to) sth** etw in etw (*acc*) stecken **2** VI (= *visit*) auf einen Sprung vorbeikommen (*inf*); **to pop in for a short chat** auf einen kleinen Schwatz hereinschauen (*inf*); **we just popped into the pub for a quickie** wir gingen kurz in die Kneipe, um einen zu heben (*inf*); **just pop in any time you're passing** komm doch mal vorbei, wenn du in der Gegend bist

➤ **pop off** VI (*Brit inf*: = *go off*) verschwinden (*inf*) (*to* nach)

➤ **pop out** VI (*inf*) **(a)** (= *go out*) (schnell) rausgehen (*inf*); **he has just popped out for a beer** er ist schnell auf ein Bierchen gegangen (*inf*); **he has just popped out to buy a paper/to the shops** er ist schnell eine Zeitung kaufen gegangen/zum Einkaufen gegangen **(b)** (*eyes*) vorquellen

➤ **pop up** (*inf*) **1** VT SEP **(a)** *head* hochstrecken **(b)** (= *bring up*) schnell raufbringen (*inf*) **2** VI **(a)** (= *appear suddenly*) auftauchen; (*head, toast*) hochschießen (*inf*) **(b)** (= *come up*) (mal eben) raufkommen (*inf*); (= *go up*) (mal eben) raufgehen (*inf*)

pop: pop concert N Popkonzert *nt*; **popcorn** N Popcorn *nt*

Pope [pəʊp] N Papst *m*

pop: pop festival N Popfestival *nt*; **pop group** N Popgruppe *f*; **popgun** N Spielzeugpistole *f*

poplar ['pɒplə'] N Pappel *f*

pop music N Popmusik *f*

poppy ['pɒpɪ] N Mohn *m*

Poppy Day N (*Brit*) ≈ Volkstrauertag *m*

poppy seed N Mohn *m*; **poppy-seed cake** Mohnkuchen *m*

pops ['pɒps] N (*esp US inf*) Paps *m* (*inf*)

Popsicle® ['pɒpsɪkl] N (*US*) Eis *nt* am Stiel

pop: pop singer N Popsänger(in) *m(f)*; **pop song** N Popsong *m*; **pop star** N Popstar *m*

populace ['pɒpjʊlɪs] N Bevölkerung *f*; (= *masses*) breite Öffentlichkeit

popular ['pɒpjʊlə'] ADJ **(a)** (= *well-liked*) beliebt (*with* bei); **he was a very ~ choice** seine Wahl fand großen Anklang **(b)** (= *suitable for the general public*) populär; *music* leicht; *lectures, journal* populärwissenschaftlich; *newspaper* weit verbreitet; **~ appeal** Massenappeal *m*; **~ science** Populärwissenschaft *f* **(c)** *belief, fallacy, discontent* weit verbreitet; **contrary to ~ belief** *or* **opinion** entgegen der landläufigen Meinung; **fruit teas are becoming increasingly ~** Früchtetees erfreuen sich zunehmender Beliebtheit **(d)** (*Pol*) *government, approval, support* des Volkes; *vote, demand* allgemein; **~ uprising** Volksaufstand *m*; **by ~ request** auf allgemeinen Wunsch

popular culture N Populärkultur *f*

popularity [pɒpjʊ'lærɪtɪ] N Beliebtheit *f*; (*with the public also*) Popularität *f* (*with* bei); **he'd do anything to win ~** er würde alles tun, um sich beliebt zu machen; **the sport is growing/declining in ~** dieser Sport wird immer populärer/verliert immer mehr an Popularität

popularly ['pɒpjʊlälɪ] ADV **(a)** allgemein; **he is ~ believed** *or* **held** *or* **thought to be a rich man** nach allgemeiner Ansicht ist er ein reicher Mann; **to be ~ known as sb/sth** allgemeinhin als jd/etw bekannt sein **(b)** (= *democratically, publicly*) vom Volk

populate ['pɒpjʊleɪt] VT (= *inhabit*) bevölkern; (= *colonize*) besiedeln; **~d by** bevölkert von; **this area is ~d mainly by immigrants** in diesem Stadtteil leben hauptsächlich Einwanderer; **densely ~d areas** dicht besiedelte Gebiete *pl*; **densely ~d cities** dicht bevölkerte Städte *pl*

population [pɒpjʊ'leɪʃən] N (*of region, country*) Bevölkerung *f*; (*of village, town*) Bewohner *pl*; (= *colonization*) Besiedlung *f*; (= *number of inhabitants*) Bevölkerungszahl *f*; **the growing black ~ of London** die wachsende Zahl von Schwarzen in London

pop-up ['pɒpʌp] ADJ *toaster* automatisch; *book, picture* Hochklapp- (*inf*); **~ menu** (*Comput*) Pop-up-Menü *nt*

porcelain ['pɔːsəlɪn] **1** N Porzellan *nt* **2** ADJ Porzellan-

porch [pɔːtʃ] N (*of house*) Vorbau *m*; (*US*) Veranda *f*; (*of church*) Portal *nt*

porcupine ['pɔːkjʊpaɪn] N Stachelschwein *nt*

pore [pɔː'] N Pore *f*; **in/from every ~** (*fig*) aus allen Poren

➤ **pore over** VI +PREP OBJ (= *scrutinize*) genau studieren; (= *meditate*) nachgrübeln über (+*acc*); **to pore over one's books** über seinen Büchern hocken

pork [pɔːk] N Schweinefleisch *nt*

pork: pork chop N Schweinekotelett *nt*; **pork pie** N Schweinefleischpastete *f*; **pork sausage** N Schweinswurst *f*

porky ['pɔːkɪ] (*inf*) **1** ADJ (+*ER*) (= *fat*) fett **2** N Schwindelei *f*

porn [pɔːn] (*inf*) **1** N Pornografie *f*; **soft ~** weicher Porno; **hard ~** harter Porno **2** ADJ pornografisch; **~ actor** Pornodarsteller *m*; **~ shop** Pornoladen *m* (*inf*)

pornographic ADJ, **pornographically** ADV [pɔːnə'græfɪk, -əlɪ] pornografisch

pornography [pɔː'nɒgrəfɪ] N Pornografie *f*

porous ['pɔːrəs] ADJ *rock, substance* porös; *skin* porig

porpoise ['pɔːpəs] N Tümmler *m*

porridge ['pɒrɪdʒ] N (*esp Brit*) Haferbrei *m*

port¹ [pɔ:t] N (= *harbour, city*) Hafen *m*; **~ of destination** Ziel-
or Bestimmungshafen *m*; **~ of call** Halt *m*; **any ~ in a storm**
(*prov*) in der Not frisst der Teufel Fliegen (*Prov*)

port² N (*Comput*) Anschluss *m*, Port *m*

port³ 🟦 N (*Naut, Aviat*: = *left side*) Backbord *m*; **land to ~!** Land
an Backbord! 🟦 ADJ auf der Backbordseite

port⁴ N (*also* **~ wine**) Portwein *m*

portable ['pɔ:təbl] 🟦 ADJ (a) *computer, sound system* tragbar;
generator, toilets mobil; **easily ~** leicht zu tragen; **~ radio**
Kofferradio *nt*; **~ television** tragbarer Fernseher; **~
(tele)phone** Mobiltelefon *nt* (b) *pension, software, computer
language* übertragbar 🟦 N (*computer, TV*) Portable *nt*

portage ['pɔ:tɪdʒ] N (*Comm*) (= *act*) Transport *m*; (= *cost*)
Transportkosten *pl*

portal ['pɔ:tl] N (*Comput*) Portal *n*

porter ['pɔ:təʳ] N (*of office etc*) Pförtner(in) *m(f)*; (= *hospital ~*)
Assistent(in) *m(f)*; (*at hotel*) Portier *m*, Portiersfrau *f*; (*Rail, at
airport*) Gepäckträger(in) *m(f)*; (*US Rail*)
Schlafwagenschaffner(in) *m(f)*

portfolio [pɔ:t'fəʊlɪəʊ] N (a) (Akten)mappe *f* (b) (*Fin*)
Portefeuille *nt* (c) (*of artist, Comm*: = *range of products*)
Kollektion *f*; **~ income** Kapitaleinkünfte *pl*, Kapitalerträge *pl*

porthole ['pɔ:thəʊl] N Bullauge *nt*

portion ['pɔ:ʃən] N (a) (= *piece, part*) Teil *m*; (*of ticket*)
Abschnitt *m*; **my ~** mein Anteil *m* (b) (*of food*) Portion *f*

portrait ['pɔ:trɪt] N (*also in words*) Porträt *nt*; **to have one's ~
painted** sich malen lassen; **to paint a ~ of sb** jdn porträtieren

portrait: **portrait painter** N Porträtmaler(in) *m(f)*; **portrait
photographer** N Porträtfotograf(in) *m(f)*

portray [pɔ:'treɪ] VT darstellen; (= *paint*) malen

portrayal [pɔ:'treɪəl] N Darstellung *f*

Portugal ['pɔ:tjʊgəl] N Portugal *nt*

Portuguese [ˌpɔ:tjʊ'gi:z] 🟦 ADJ portugiesisch; **he is ~** er ist
Portugiese 🟦 N Portugiese *m*, Portugiesin *f*; (*Ling*)
Portugiesisch *nt*

pose [pəʊz] 🟦 N Haltung *f*; **to take up a ~** (*model*) eine
Haltung einnehmen
🟦 VT (a) (= *put forward*) *question* vortragen; **the question ~d
by his speech** die in seiner Rede aufgeworfene Frage
(b) (= *formulate*) *question* formulieren
(c) (= *constitute*) *difficulties* aufwerfen; *threat* darstellen
🟦 VI (a) (= *model*) posieren; **to ~ (in the) nude** für einen Akt
posieren; **to ~ for photographs** für Fotografien posieren
(b) **to ~ as** sich ausgeben als

poser ['pəʊzəʳ] N Angeber(in) *m(f)*

posh [pɒʃ] (*inf*) 🟦 ADJ (+ER) vornehm 🟦 ADV (+ER) **to talk ~** mit
vornehmem Akzent sprechen

position [pə'zɪʃən] 🟦 N (a) Platz *m*; (*of microphone, statue,
wardrobe etc*) Standort *m*; (*of spotlight, table, painting*)
Anordnung *f*; (*of town, house etc*) Lage *f*; (*of plane, ship, Sport*:
= *starting ~, Ftbl etc*) Position *f*; (*Mil*) Stellung *f*; **to be in/out
of ~** an der richtigen/falschen Stelle sein; **to jockey** *or* **jostle
for ~** (*lit*) um eine gute Ausgangsposition kämpfen; (*fig*) um
eine gute Position rangeln; **what ~ do you play?** auf welcher
Position spielst du?; **after the third lap he was in fourth ~**
nach der dritten Runde lag er auf dem vierten Platz
(b) (= *posture*) Haltung *f*; (*in love-making*) Stellung *f*; **in a
sitting ~** sitzend
(c) (= *social, professional standing*) Position *f*; (= *job*) Stelle *f*; **a
~ of trust** eine Vertrauensstellung; **to be in a ~ of power** eine
Machtposition innehaben
(d) (*fig*: = *situation*) Lage *f*; **to be in a ~ to do sth** in der Lage
sein, etw zu tun; **what is the ~ regarding ...?** wie sieht es
mit ... aus?; **I'm not in a ~ to say anything about that** ich kann
dazu nichts sagen
(e) (*fig*: = *point of view*) Standpunkt *m*; **what is the
government's ~ on ...?** welchen Standpunkt vertritt die
Regierung zu ...?
🟦 VT (a) *microphone, ladder, guards* aufstellen; *soldiers,
policemen* postieren; (*artist, photographer etc*) platzieren;
(*Comput*) *cursor* positionieren; **he ~ed himself where he could
see her** er stellte *or* (*seated*) setzte sich so, dass er sie sehen
konnte
(b) (*in marketing*) *product* positionieren; **to ~ on the market**
am Markt positionieren

positive ['pɒzɪtɪv] 🟦 ADJ (a) (= *affirmative, also Sci, Gram*)
positiv; *criticism, suggestion* konstruktiv; **~ pole** Pluspol *m*; **he
is a very ~ person** er hat eine sehr positive Einstellung zum
Leben; **to take ~ action** positive Schritte unternehmen
(b) (= *definite*) *instructions* streng; *evidence, answer* eindeutig;
to be ~ that ... sicher sein, dass ...; **to be ~ about** *or* **of sth** sich
(*dat*) einer Sache (*gen*) absolut sicher sein; **are you sure you
don't want her address? – ~** bist du sicher, dass du nicht ihre
Adresse willst? – ganz bestimmt; **this is a ~ disgrace** das ist
wirklich eine Schande; **he's a ~ genius** er ist ein wahres
Genie
🟦 ADV (a) (*Med*) **to test ~** einen positiven Befund haben
(b) **to think ~** positiv denken

positive feedback N positives Feedback; **to get ~ (about sb/
sth)** eine positive Rückmeldung (zu jdm/etw) erhalten

positively ['pɒzɪtɪvlɪ] ADV (a) (= *affirmatively, constructively, also
Sci*) positiv (b) (= *decisively*) bestimmt; (= *definitely*) definitiv;
to test ~ for drugs positiv auf Drogen getestet werden
(c) (= *absolutely*) wirklich; (*emph*: = *actively*) eindeutig; **Jane
doesn't mind being photographed, she ~ loves it** Jane hat
nichts dagegen, fotografiert zu werden, im Gegenteil, sie
hat es sehr gern

posse ['pɒsɪ] N (*US*) Aufgebot *nt*; (*fig*) Gruppe *f*; **~ of searchers**
Suchtrupp *m*

possess [pə'zes] VT besitzen; (*form*) *facts* verfügen über (+*acc*);
to be ~ed by demons von Dämonen besessen sein; **like a
man/woman ~ed** wie ein Besessener/eine Besessene; **whatever
~ed you to do that?** was ist bloß in Sie gefahren, so etwas zu
tun?

possession [pə'zeʃən] N (a) (= *ownership*) Besitz *m*; **to have sth
in one's ~** etw in seinem Besitz haben; **to have/take ~ of sth**
etw in Besitz haben/nehmen; **to come into/get ~ of sth** in
den Besitz von etw gelangen/kommen; **to be in ~ of sth** im
Besitz von etw sein; **I'm in full ~ of the facts** ich verfüge über
alle Tatsachen (b) (= *thing possessed*) Besitz *m no pl*;
(= *territory*) Besitzung *f*; **all his ~s** sein gesamter Besitz

possessive [pə'zesɪv] 🟦 ADJ (*towards belongings*) eigen;
boyfriend, manner etc besitzergreifend; **to be ~ about sth** seine
Besitzansprüche auf etw (*acc*) betonen; **to be ~ toward(s) sb**
an jdn Besitzansprüche stellen 🟦 N (*Gram*) Possessiv(um) *nt*

possessively [pə'zesɪvlɪ] ADV (*about things*) eigen; (*towards
people*) besitzergreifend

possessiveness [pə'zesɪvnɪs] N eigene Art (*about* mit); (*towards
people*) besitzergreifende Art (*towards* gegenüber)

possessive pronoun N (*Gram*) Possessivpronomen *nt*

possessor [pə'zesəʳ] N Besitzer(in) *m(f)*

possibility [ˌpɒsə'bɪlɪtɪ] N Möglichkeit *f*; **there's not much ~ of
success/of his** *or* **him being successful** die Aussichten auf
Erfolg/darauf, dass er Erfolg hat, sind nicht sehr groß; **it's
not beyond the realms** *or* **bounds of ~** es ist durchaus im
Bereich des Möglichen; **the ~ of doing sth** die Möglichkeit,
etw zu tun; **it's a distinct ~ that ...** es besteht eindeutig die
Möglichkeit, dass ...; **there is some** *or* **a ~ that ...** es besteht
die Möglichkeit, dass ...

possible ['pɒsəbl] 🟦 ADJ möglich; **anything is ~** möglich ist
alles; **as soon/often/far as ~** so bald/oft/weit wie möglich; **the
best/quickest ~ ...** der/die/das bestmögliche/
schnellstmögliche; **if (at all) ~** falls (irgend) möglich; **it's just
~ that I'll see you before then** eventuell sehe ich dich doch vorher
noch; **there is no ~ excuse for his behaviour** für sein
Verhalten gibt es absolut keine Entschuldigung; **the only ~
choice, the only choice ~** die einzig mögliche Wahl; **it will be
~ for you to return the same day** Sie haben die Möglichkeit,
am selben Tag zurückzukommen; **to make sth ~** etw
ermöglichen; **to make it ~ for sb to do sth** es jdm
ermöglichen, etw zu tun; **where ~** wo möglich; **wherever ~**
wo immer möglich
🟦 N Möglichkeit *f*; **a long list of ~s for the job** eine lange
Liste möglicher Kandidaten für die Stelle; **he is a ~ for the
English team** er kommt für die englische Mannschaft infrage

possibly ['pɒsəblɪ] ADV (a) **I can't ~ stay indoors all weekend**
ich kann unmöglich das ganze Wochenende in der
Wohnung sitzen; **nobody could ~ tell the difference** es war
unmöglich, einen Unterschied zu erkennen; **can that ~ be
true?** kann das (vielleicht doch) stimmen?; **very** *or* **quite ~**
durchaus möglich; **how could he ~ have known that?** wie
konnte er das nur wissen?; **he did all he ~ could** er tat, was

er nur konnte; **I have made myself as comfortable as I ~ can** ich habe es mir so bequem wie möglich gemacht; **if I ~ can** wenn ich irgend kann
(b) (= *perhaps*) vielleicht; **~ not** vielleicht nicht
post¹ [pəʊst] **1** N (= *pole, doorpost etc*) Pfosten *m*; (= *lamp ~*) Pfahl *m*; (= *telegraph ~*) Mast *m*; **a wooden ~** ein Holzpfahl *m*; **starting/winning** *or* **finishing ~** Start-/Zielpfosten *m* **2** VT **(a)** (= *display: also* **~ up**) anschlagen **(b)** (= *announce*) *gains, profits* veröffentlichen
post² **1** N **(a)** (*Brit*: = *job*) Stelle *f*; **to look for/take up a ~** eine Stelle suchen/antreten; **to hold a ~** eine Stelle innehaben **(b)** (*Mil*) Posten *m*; **a frontier** *or* **border ~** ein Grenzposten *m* **2** VT **(a)** (= *position*) postieren **(b)** (= *send, assign*) versetzen; (*Mil*) abkommandieren
post³ **1** N (*Brit*: = *mail*) Post *f*; **by ~** mit der Post; **it's in the ~** es ist in der Post; **to catch the ~** (*person*) rechtzeitig zur Leerung kommen; **to miss the ~** (*person*) die Leerung verpassen; **there is no ~ today** (= *no delivery*) heute kommt keine Post; (= *no letters*) heute ist keine Post (für uns) gekommen; **has the ~ been?** war die Post schon da? **2** VT **(a)** (*Brit*) (= *put in the ~*) aufgeben; (*in letterbox*) einwerfen; (= *send by ~*) mit der Post schicken; (*Comput*: = *send by e-mail*) mailen; **I ~ed it to you on Monday** ich habe es am Montag an Sie abgeschickt/gemailt
(b) to keep sb ~ed jdn auf dem Laufenden halten
(c) (= *enter in ledger: also* **~ up**) eintragen (*to* in +*acc*)
➤ **post off** VT SEP abschicken
post- [pəʊst-] PREF nach-; (*esp with words derived from Latin or Greek*) post-; **~communist** postkommunistisch; **~~traumatic** posttraumatisch
postage [ˈpəʊstɪdʒ] N Porto *nt*; **~ and packing** (*abbr* **p&p**) Porto und Verpackung; **~ paid** freigemacht, Entgelt bezahlt
postage stamp N Briefmarke *f*
postal [ˈpəʊstl] ADJ Post-; **~ charges** Postgebühren *pl*
postal: postal address N Postanschrift *f*; **postal card** N (*US*) (= *letter card*) Postkarte mit aufgedruckter Briefmarke für offizielle Zwecke; (= *postcard*) Postkarte *f*; (*with picture*) Ansichtskarte *f*; **postal code** N (*Brit*) Postleitzahl *f*; **postal order** N (*Brit*) ≈ Postanweisung *f*, Geldgutschein, der bei der Post gekauft und eingelöst wird; **postal receipt** N Posteinlieferungsschein *m*; **postal service** N Postdienst *m*; **postal vote** N to have a ~ per Briefwahl wählen; **postal worker** N Postbeamte(r) *m*, Postbeamtin *f*
post: postbag N (*Brit*) Postsack *m*; **postbox** N (*Brit*) Briefkasten *m*; **postcard** N Postkarte *f*; **(picture) ~** Ansichtskarte *f*; **post code** N (*Brit*) Postleitzahl *f*

post: postdate VT vordatieren; **postedit** VTI (*Comput*) redaktionell nachbearbeiten
poster [ˈpəʊstəʳ] N (*advertising*) Plakat *nt*; (*for decoration also*) Poster *nt*
posterior [pɒˈstɪərɪəʳ] N (*hum*) Allerwerteste(r) *m* (*hum*)
posterity [pɒˈsterɪtɪ] N die Nachwelt
post: post-free ADJ, ADV portofrei; **postgrad** [ˈpəʊstˌɡræd] N, ADJ (*Brit inf*) = **postgraduate**; **postgraduate** **1** N *jd, der seine Studien nach dem ersten akademischen Grad weiterführt*, Postgraduierte(r) *mf* **2** ADJ weiterführend; **~ course** Anschlusskurs *m*; **~ degree** zweiter akademischer Grad; **~ diploma** Postgraduiertendiplom *nt*; **~ student** Postgraduierte(r) *mf*
posthumous ADJ, **posthumously** ADV [ˈpɒstjʊməs, -lɪ] post(h)um
post: postman N (*Brit*) Briefträger *m*; **postmark** **1** N Poststempel *m*; **date as ~** Datum *nt* des Poststempels **2** VT (ab)stempeln; **the letter is ~ed "Birmingham"** der Brief ist in Birmingham abgestempelt; **postmaster** N (*Brit*) Postmeister *m*; **postmistress** N (*Brit*) Postmeisterin *f*; **postmodern** ADJ postmodern; **postmodernism** N Postmodernismus *m*;

postmortem [pəʊstˈmɔːtəm] N (*also* **~ examination**) Obduktion *f*; **postnatal** ADJ nach der Geburt; **post office** N Postamt *nt*; **the Post Office** (= *institution*) die Post; **~ box** (*abbr* **PO Box**) Postfach *nt*; **~ worker** Postarbeiter(in) *m(f)*; **post-paid** **1** ADJ portofrei; *envelope* frankiert **2** ADV portofrei
postpone [pəʊstˈpəʊn] VT aufschieben; (*for specified period*) verschieben; **it has been ~d till Tuesday** es ist auf Dienstag verschoben worden
postponement [pəʊstˈpəʊnmənt] N (= *act*) Verschiebung *f*; (= *result*) Aufschub *m*
postscript(um) [ˈpəʊstskrɪpt(əm)] N (*abbr* **PS**) (*to letter*) Postskriptum *nt*; (*to book etc*) Nachwort *nt*
posture [ˈpɒstʃəʳ] **1** N (*lit, fig*) Haltung *f*; (*pej*) Pose *f* **2** VI sich in Positur *or* Pose werfen
post: post-war ADJ Nachkriegs-; *event also* in der Nachkriegszeit; **~ era** Nachkriegszeit *f*; **postwoman** N (*esp Brit*) Briefträgerin *f*
pot [pɒt] **1** N **(a)** Topf *m*; (= *teapot, coffee ~*) Kanne *f*; **a pint ~** ≈ ein Humpen *m*; **to go to ~** (*inf*) (*person, business*) auf den Hund kommen (*inf*); (*plan, arrangement*) ins Wasser fallen (*inf*) **(b)** (*inf*) **to have ~s of money/time** jede Menge Geld/Zeit haben (*inf*) **(c)** (*inf*: = *marijuana*) Pot *nt* (*sl*) **(d)** (= *~shot*) Schuss *m* aufs Geratewohl **2** VT **(a)** *plant* eintopfen **(b)** (*Billiards*) *ball* einlochen
potassium [pəˈtæsɪəm] N Kalium *nt*
potato [pəˈteɪtəʊ] N, *pl* **-es** Kartoffel *f*
potato: potato chip N **(a)** (*esp US*) = **potato crisp (b)** (*Brit*: = *chip*) Pomme frite *m*; **potato crisp** N (*Brit*) Kartoffelchip *m*; **potato masher** N Kartoffelstampfer *m*; **potato peeler** N Kartoffelschäler *m*; **potato salad** N Kartoffelsalat *m*
pot: potbellied [ˈpɒtˈbelɪd] ADJ spitzbäuchig; (*through hunger*) blähbäuchig; **potbelly** N (*from overeating*) Spitzbauch *m*; (*from malnutrition*) Blähbauch *m*
potency [ˈpəʊtənsɪ] N (*of drink, drug, charm etc*) Stärke *f*; (*of argument, reason etc*) Durchschlagskraft *f*; (*of image*) Schlagkraft *f*
potent [ˈpəʊtənt] ADJ stark; *argument etc* durchschlagend; *reminder* beeindruckend
potential [pəʊˈtenʃəl] **1** ADJ (*also Phys*) potenziell **2** N Potenzial *nt* (*also Elec, Math, Phys*); **~ for growth** Wachstumspotenzial *nt*; **to have ~** ausbaufähig sein (*inf*); **he shows quite a bit of ~** es steckt einiges in ihm; **to achieve** *or* **fulfil** *or* **realize one's ~** die Grenze seiner Möglichkeiten verwirklichen; **to have great ~ (as/for)** große Möglichkeiten bergen (als/für); **to have the ~ to do sth** das Potenzial haben, um etw zu tun; **to have no/little ~** kein/kaum Potenzial haben; **she has management ~** sie hat das Zeug zur Managerin; **commercial ~** kommerzielle Möglichkeiten *pl*
potentially [pəʊˈtenʃəlɪ] ADV potenziell; **~, these problems are very serious** diese Probleme könnten sich als gravierend herausstellen
pothole [ˈpɒthəʊl] N **(a)** (*in road*) Schlagloch *nt* **(b)** (*Geol*) Höhle *f*
potion [ˈpəʊʃən] N Trank *m*
pot luck N **to take ~** nehmen, was es gerade gibt; **we took ~ and went to the nearest pub** wir gingen aufs Geratewohl in die nächste Kneipe
potpourri [pəʊˈpʊrɪ] N (*lit*) Duftsträußchen *nt*
pot: pot roast **1** N Schmorbraten *m* **2** VT schmoren; **pot shot** N Schuss *m* aufs Geratewohl; **to take a ~ at sb/sth** aufs Geratewohl auf jdn/etw schießen
potted [ˈpɒtɪd] ADJ **(a)** *meat* eingemacht; **~ plant** Topfpflanze *f* **(b)** (*shortened*) gekürzt
potter¹ [ˈpɒtəʳ] N Töpfer(in) *m(f)*; **~'s clay** Töpferton *m*; **~'s wheel** Töpferscheibe *f*
potter² (*US also*) **putter** [ˈpʌtəʳ] VI (= *do little jobs*) herumwerkeln; (= *wander aimlessly*) herumschlendern; **she ~s away in the kitchen for hours** sie hantiert stundenlang in der Küche herum; **to ~ round the house** im Haus herumwerkeln; **to ~ round the shops** einen Geschäftsbummel machen; **to ~ along the road** (*car, driver*) dahinzuckeln
pottery [ˈpɒtərɪ] N (= *workshop, craft*) Töpferei *f*; (= *pots*) Töpferwaren *pl*; (*glazed*) Keramik *f*
potting [ˈpɒtɪŋ]: **potting compost** N Pflanzerde *f*; **potting shed** N Schuppen *m*

potty¹ [ˈpɒtɪ] N Töpfchen *nt*; **~-trained** (*Brit*) sauber

potty² ADJ (+ER) (*Brit inf*: = *mad*) verrückt; **to go ~** verrückt werden; **to drive sb ~** jdn zum Wahnsinn treiben; **he's ~ about her** er ist verrückt nach ihr

pouch [paʊtʃ] N Beutel *m*; (*of pelican, hamster*) Tasche *f*

poultice [ˈpəʊltɪs] N Umschlag *m*

poultry [ˈpəʊltrɪ] N Geflügel *nt*

poultry: poultry farm N Geflügelfarm *f*; **poultry farmer** N Geflügelzüchter(in) *m(f)*

pounce [paʊns] **1** N Satz *m* **2** VI (*cat, lion etc*) einen Satz machen; (*bird*) niederstoßen; (*fig*) zuschlagen; **to ~ on sb/sth** (*lit, fig*) sich auf jdn/etw stürzen

pound¹ [paʊnd] N (a) (= *weight*) ≈ Pfund *nt*; **two ~s of apples** zwei Pfund Äpfel; **by the ~** pfundweise **(b)** (= *money*) Pfund *nt*; **one ~ sterling** ein Pfund *nt* Sterling; **five ~s** fünf Pfund; **a five-~ note** eine Fünfpfundnote

pound² **1** VT **(a)** (= *strike*) hämmern; *table* hämmern auf (+*acc*); *door, wall* hämmern gegen; (*waves, sea*) schlagen gegen; (*guns, shells*) ununterbrochen beschießen **(b)** (= *pulverize*) *corn etc* (zer)stampfen; *drugs, spices* zerstoßen **2** VI hämmern; (*heart*) (wild) pochen; (*waves, sea*) schlagen (*on, against* gegen); (*drums*) dröhnen; (*engine, hooves, runner*) stampfen; (= *walk heavily, stamp*) stapfen
➤ **pound away** VI hämmern; (*music, drums, guns*) dröhnen; **he was pounding away at the typewriter** er hämmerte auf der Schreibmaschine herum

pound³ N (*for stray dogs*) städtischer Hundezwinger; (*esp Brit: for cars*) Abstellplatz *m* (für amtlich abgeschleppte Fahrzeuge)

poundage [ˈpaʊndɪdʒ] N Gewicht *nt* (in Pfund)

-pounder [-ˈpaʊndə*ʳ*] N SUF -pfünder *m*; **quarter-pounder** Viertelpfünder *m*

pounding [ˈpaʊndɪŋ] **1** N Hämmern *nt*; (*of heart*) Pochen *nt*; (*of music, drums*) Dröhnen *nt*; (*of waves, sea*) Schlagen *nt*; (*of engine, hooves, feet etc*) Stampfen *nt*; (*of guns, shells*) Bombardement *nt*; **the ship took a ~ from the waves** das Schiff wurde von den Wellen stark mitgenommen **2** ADJ *heart* klopfend; *feet* trommelnd; *hooves, drums, waves* donnernd; *headache* pochend

pour [pɔː*ʳ*] **1** VT *liquid* gießen; *sugar, rice etc* schütten; *drink* eingießen; **to ~ sth for sb** jdm etw eingießen; **to ~ money into a project** Geld in ein Projekt pumpen (*inf*) **2** VI **(a)** (*lit, fig*) strömen; **the sweat ~ed off him** der Schweiß floss in Strömen an ihm herunter; **books are ~ing off the presses** Bücher werden in Massen ausgestoßen; **it's ~ing (with rain)** es gießt (in Strömen), es schüttet (*inf*); **the rain ~ed down** es goss in Strömen **(b)** (= ~ *out tea etc*) eingießen; (*US:* = *act as hostess*) als Gastgeberin fungieren; **this jug doesn't ~ well** dieser Krug gießt nicht gut
➤ **pour away** VT SEP weggießen
➤ **pour forth** VI, VT SEP = **pour out 1, 2(b, c)**
➤ **pour in** VI hereinströmen; (*donations, protests*) in Strömen eintreffen
➤ **pour out** **1** VI herausströmen (*of* aus); (*smoke also*) hervorquellen (*of* aus); (*words*) heraussprudeln (*of* aus) **2** VT SEP **(a)** *liquid* ausgießen; *sugar, rice etc* ausschütten; *drink* eingießen **(b)** (*factories, schools*) *cars, students* ausstoßen **(c)** (*fig*) *feelings, troubles* sich (*dat*) von der Seele reden; **to pour out one's heart (to sb)** (jdm) sein Herz ausschütten

pouring [ˈpɔːrɪŋ] ADJ **~ rain** strömender Regen

pout [paʊt] **1** VI Schmollmund *m* **2** VI **(a)** (*with lips*) einen Schmollmund machen **(b)** (= *sulk*) schmollen

poverty [ˈpɒvətɪ] N Armut *f*; **to be above/below/on the ~ line** oberhalb/unterhalb/an der Armutsgrenze leben

poverty-stricken [ˈpɒvətɪstrɪkən] ADJ Not leidend; **to be ~** Armut leiden

POW ABBR *of* **prisoner of war**

powder [ˈpaʊdə*ʳ*] **1** N Pulver *nt*; (= *face, talcum ~ etc*) Puder *m*; (= *dust*) Staub *m* **2** VT *face, body* pudern; **to ~ one's nose** (*euph*) kurz verschwinden (*euph*) **3** VI (= *crumble*) (zu Staub) zerfallen

powdered [ˈpaʊdəd] ADJ **(a)** (= *covered with powder*) gepudert **(b)** (= *in powder form*) löslich; **~ sugar** (*US*) Puderzucker *m*, Staubzucker *m* (*Aus*)

powdered milk N Milchpulver *nt*

powder: powder keg N (*lit, fig*) Pulverfass *nt*; **powder room** N Damentoilette *f*

powdery [ˈpaʊdərɪ] ADJ **(a)** (= *like powder*) pulvrig **(b)** (= *crumbly*) bröckelig

power [ˈpaʊə*ʳ*] **1** N (a) NO PL (= *physical strength*) Kraft *f*; (= *force: of blow, explosion etc*) Stärke *f*, Gewalt *f*, Wucht *f*; (*fig: of argument etc*) Überzeugungskraft *f*; **the ~ of love/logic** die Macht der Liebe/Logik; **earning ~** mögliche Verdiensthöhe; **purchasing** *or* **spending ~** Kaufkraft *f*
(b) (= *faculty, ability*) Vermögen *nt no pl*; **his ~s of hearing** sein Hörvermögen *nt*; **mental/hypnotic ~s** geistige/hypnotische Kräfte *pl*
(c) (= *capacity etc, nation*) Macht *f*; **he did all in his ~ to help them** er tat (alles), was in seiner Macht stand, um ihnen zu helfen; **a naval ~** eine Seemacht
(d) (*no pl:* = *authority*) Macht *f*; (*Jur, parental*) Gewalt *f*; (*usu pl:* = *thing one has authority to do*) Befugnis *f*; **he has the ~ to act** er ist handlungsberechtigt; **the ~ of the police** die Macht der Polizei; **to be in sb's ~** in jds Gewalt (*dat*) sein; **~ of attorney** (*Jur*) (Handlungs)vollmacht *f*; **the party now in ~** die Partei, die im Augenblick an der Macht ist; **to fall from ~** abgesetzt werden; **to come into ~** an die Macht kommen; **they have no ~ over economic matters** in Wirtschaftsfragen haben sie keine Befugnisse; **I have no ~ over her** ich habe keine Gewalt über sie
(e) (= *person or institution having authority*) Autorität *f*; **to be the ~ behind the scenes/throne** die graue Eminenz sein; **the ~s that be** (*inf*) die da oben (*inf*); **the ~s of evil** die Mächte des Bösen
(f) (*nuclear, electric ~ etc*) Energie *f*; **they cut off the ~** (= *electricity*) sie haben den Strom abgestellt
(g) (*of engine, machine, transmitter*) Leistung *f*; (*of lens, chemical*) Stärke *f*; **microwave on full ~ for one minute** eine Minute bei voller Leistung in der Mikrowelle erhitzen
(h) (*Math*) Potenz *f*; **to the ~ (of) 2** hoch 2
(i) (*inf*) **that did me a ~ of good** das hat mir ganz unheimlich gut getan (*inf*)
2 VT (*engine*) antreiben; (*fuel*) betreiben; **~ed by electricity** mit Elektroantrieb
3 VI rasen
➤ **power down** VT SEP *computer, engine* herunterfahren
➤ **power up** VI, VT SEP starten

power: power base N Machtbasis *f*; **power cable** N Stromkabel *nt*; **power cut** N (*accidental*) Stromausfall *m*; **power drill** N Bohrmaschine *f*; **power-driven** ADJ mit Motorantrieb; **power failure** N Stromausfall *m*

powerful [ˈpaʊəfʊl] ADJ **(a)** (= *influential*) mächtig **(b)** (= *strong*) stark; *build, arm, kick, light* kräftig; *swimmer, stroke, punch, detergent, voice* kraftvoll; *earthquake, storm, smell* massiv **(c)** (*fig*) *speaker, actor* mitreißend; *music, film, performance* ausdrucksvoll; *argument* durchschlagend

powerfully [ˈpaʊəfəlɪ] ADV **(a)** (*influence*) mächtig; *reinforce* massiv; *moving* stark; **~ built** kräftig gebaut **(b)** (*fig*) *speak, describe, act* kraftvoll; *argue* massiv (*inf*); **~ written** mitreißend geschrieben; **I was ~ affected by the book** das Buch hat mich stark beeindruckt

power: powerhouse N (*fig*) treibende Kraft (*behind* hinter +*dat*); **he's a real ~** er ist ein äußerst dynamischer Mensch; **powerless** ADJ machtlos; **to be ~ to resist** nicht die Kraft haben, zu widerstehen; **the government is ~ to deal with inflation** die Regierung steht der Inflation machtlos gegenüber; **power plant** N = **power station**; **power politics** PL Machtpolitik *f*; **power sharing** N (*Pol*) Machtteilung *f*; **power-sharing** ADJ (*Pol*) *executive* mit Machtteilung *pred*; **power station** N Kraftwerk *nt*; **power steering** N (*Aut*) Servolenkung *f*; **power structure** N Machtstruktur *f*; **power struggle** N Machtkampf *m*; **power supply** N (*Elec*) Stromversorgung *f*; **power tool** N Elektrowerkzeug *nt*

PPV ABBR *of* **pay-per-view**

PR [piːˈɑː*ʳ*] N ABBR *of* **public relations** PR *f*; **PR agency** PR-Agentur *f*; **PR man** PR-Mann *m*; **PR woman** PR-Frau *f*; **PR work** PR-Arbeit *f*

practicability [ˌpræktɪkəˈbɪlɪtɪ] N Durchführbarkeit *f*

practicable [ˈpræktɪkəbl] ADJ durchführbar

practical [ˈpræktɪkəl] ADJ praktisch; **for (all) ~ purposes** in der Praxis; **to be of no ~ use** ohne (jeden) praktischen Nutzen sein

practicality [ˌpræktɪˈkælɪtɪ] N **(a)** NO PL (of scheme etc) Durchführbarkeit f **(b)** (= practical detail) praktisches Detail

practical: **practical joke** N Streich m; **practical joker** N Witzbold m (inf)

practically [ˈpræktɪkəlɪ] ADV praktisch; ~ **speaking** konkret gesagt

practice [ˈpræktɪs] **1** N **(a)** (= habit, custom) (of individual) Gewohnheit f; (of group, in country) Brauch m; (= bad habit) Unsitte f; (in business) Praktik f; **he opposes the ~ of pubs being open on Sundays** er ist dagegen, dass Lokale am Sonntag geöffnet sind; **this is normal business ~** das ist im Geschäftsleben so üblich; **that's common ~** das ist allgemein üblich

(b) (= exercise, training) Übung f; (= rehearsal) Probe f; (Sport) Training nt; (= ~ game) Trainingsspiel nt; **~ makes perfect** (Prov) Übung macht den Meister (Prov); **this piece of music needs a lot of ~** für dieses (Musik)stück muss man viel üben; **you should do 10 minutes' ~ each day** du solltest täglich 10 Minuten (lang) üben; **to be out of ~** aus der Übung sein; **to have a ~ session** üben; (= rehearse) Probe haben; (Sport) trainieren

(c) (as opposed to theory, of doctor etc) Praxis f; **in ~** in der Praxis; **that won't work in ~** das lässt sich praktisch nicht durchführen; **to put one's ideas into ~** seine Ideen in die Praxis umsetzen; **to go into** or **set up in ~** eine Praxis aufmachen; **he's not in ~ any more** er praktiziert nicht mehr; **a large legal ~** eine große Rechtsanwaltspraxis

2 VTI (US) = **practise**

practice teacher N (US Sch) Referendar(in) m(f)

practise, (US) **practice** [ˈpræktɪs] **1** VT **(a)** üben; song, chorus proben; self-denial, torture praktizieren; **to ~ what one preaches** (prov) seine Lehren in die Tat umsetzen; **to ~ the violin** Geige üben; **to ~ doing sth** etw üben; **I'm practising my German on him** ich probiere mein Deutsch an ihm aus **(b)** profession, religion ausüben; **to ~ law/medicine** als Anwalt/Arzt praktizieren

2 VI **(a)** (in order to acquire skill) üben **(b)** (lawyer, doctor etc) praktizieren

practising, (US) **practicing** [ˈpræktɪsɪŋ] ADJ praktizierend

practitioner [prækˈtɪʃənəʳ] N (= medical ~) praktischer Arzt, praktische Ärztin; (= dental ~) Zahnarzt m/-ärztin f; (= legal ~) Rechtsanwalt m/-anwältin f

pragmatic ADJ, **pragmatically** ADV [prægˈmætɪk, -əlɪ] pragmatisch

pragmatism [ˈprægmətɪzəm] N Pragmatismus m

pragmatist [ˈprægmətɪst] N Pragmatiker(in) m(f)

Prague [prɑːg] N Prag nt

prairie [ˈprɛərɪ] N Grassteppe f; (in North America) Prärie f

praise [preɪz] **1** VT loben; **to ~ sb for having done sth** jdn dafür loben, etw getan zu haben; **~ God!** gelobt sei Gott! **2** N Lob nt no pl; **a hymn of ~** eine Lobeshymne; **he made a speech in ~ of their efforts** er hielt eine Lobrede auf ihre Bemühungen; **to win ~** (person) Lob ernten; (efforts) Lob einbringen; **I have nothing but ~ for him** ich kann ihn nur loben; **~ indeed!** (also iro) ein hohes Lob; **~(s) be!** Gott sei Dank!

praiseworthy [ˈpreɪzwɜːðɪ] ADJ lobenswert

praline [ˈprɑːliːn] N Praline f mit Nuss-Karamellfüllung

pram [præm] N (Brit) Kinderwagen m

prance [prɑːns] VI tänzeln; (= jump around) herumtanzen

prank [præŋk] N Streich m; (harmless also) Ulk m; **to play a ~ on sb** jdm einen Streich spielen

prankster [ˈpræŋkstəʳ] N Schelm(in) m(f)

prat [præt] N (Brit inf) Trottel m (inf)

prattle [ˈprætl] **1** N Geplapper nt **2** VI plappern

prawn [prɔːn] N Garnele f

pray [preɪ] VI beten; **let us ~** lasset uns beten; **to ~ for sb/sth** für jdn/um etw beten; **to ~ for sth** (= want it badly) stark auf etw (acc) hoffen

prayer [prɛəʳ] N Gebet nt; (= service, ~ meeting) Andacht f; **to say one's ~s** beten; **family ~s** Hausandacht f

prayer: **prayer book** N Gebetbuch nt; **prayer meeting** N Gebetsstunde f

pre- [priː-] PREF vor-; (esp with words derived from Latin or Greek) prä-; **~school** vorschulisch

preach [priːtʃ] **1** VT predigen; (fig) propagieren; **to ~ a sermon** (lit, fig) eine Predigt halten; **to ~ the gospel** das Evangelium verkünden **2** VI (lit, fig) predigen; **to ~ to the converted** (prov) offene Türen einrennen

preacher [ˈpriːtʃəʳ] N Prediger(in) m(f); (fig) Moralprediger(in) m(f)

preaching [ˈpriːtʃɪŋ] N (lit, fig) Predigen nt

prearrange [ˌpriːəˈreɪndʒ] VT im Voraus vereinbaren

prearranged [ˌpriːəˈreɪndʒd], **pre-arranged** ADJ meeting, sign im Voraus verabredet; route, location im Voraus bestimmt

precarious [prɪˈkɛərɪəs] ADJ unsicher; situation, relationship prekär; theory anfechtbar; peace instabil; **at a ~ angle** in einem gefährlich aussehenden Winkel

precariously [prɪˈkɛərɪəslɪ] ADV unsicher; **to be ~ balanced** (lit, fig) auf der Kippe stehen; **~ perched on the edge of the table** gefährlich nahe am Tischrand

precaution [prɪˈkɔːʃən] N Vorsichtsmaßnahme f; **security ~s** Sicherheitsmaßnahmen pl; **fire ~s** Brandschutzmaßnahmen pl; **to take ~s against sth** Vorsichtsmaßnahmen pl gegen etw treffen; **do you take ~s?** (euph: = use contraception) nimmst du (irgend)etwas?; **to take the ~ of doing sth** vorsichtshalber etw tun

precautionary [prɪˈkɔːʃənərɪ] ADJ Vorsichts-; **~ measure** Vorsichtsmaßnahme f

precede [prɪˈsiːd] VT (in order, time) vorangehen (+dat); **for the month preceding this** den (ganzen) Monat davor

precedence [ˈpresɪdəns] N (of person) vorrangige Stellung (over gegenüber); (of problem etc) Vorrang m (over vor +dat); **to take** or **have ~ over sb/sth** vor jdm/etw Vorrang haben; **to give ~ to sb/sth** jdm/einer Sache Vorrang geben

precedent [ˈpresɪdənt] N Präzedenzfall m; **without ~** noch nie da gewesen; **to establish** or **create** or **set a ~** einen Präzedenzfall schaffen; **there is no ~ for this decision** diese Entscheidung kann sich nicht an einem vergleichbaren Fall ausrichten

preceding [prɪˈsiːdɪŋ] ADJ vorhergehend

precinct [ˈpriːsɪŋkt] N **(a)** (Brit) (= pedestrian ~) Fußgängerzone f; (= shopping ~) Einkaufsviertel nt; (US) (= police ~) Revier nt; (= voting ~) Bezirk m **(b)** **precincts** PL (= grounds) Gelände nt; (= environs) Umgebung f

precious [ˈpreʃəs] **1** ADJ (= costly, rare) kostbar; (= treasured) wertvoll; **I have very ~ memories of that time** ich habe Erinnerungen an diese Zeit, die mir sehr wertvoll sind; **the loss of our ~ daughter** der Verlust unserer heiß geliebten Tochter **2** ADV (inf) **~ little/few** herzlich wenig/wenige (inf); **~ little else** herzlich wenig sonst; **I had ~ little choice** ich hatte keine große Wahl

precious: **precious metal** N Edelmetall nt; **precious stone** N Edelstein m

precipice [ˈpresɪpɪs] N (lit, fig) Abgrund m

precipitate [prəˈsɪpɪteɪt] VT (= hasten) beschleunigen

precise [prɪˈsaɪs] ADJ genau; (= meticulous) präzise; **at that ~ moment** genau in dem Augenblick; **please be more ~** drücken Sie sich bitte etwas genauer aus; **18, to be ~** 18, um genau zu sein; **or, to be more ~, ...** oder, um es genauer zu sagen, ...

precisely [prɪˈsaɪslɪ] ADV genau; use instrument exakt; **at ~ 7 o'clock, at 7 o'clock ~** Punkt 7 Uhr; **but it is ~ because the money supply is ...** aber gerade deshalb, weil das Kapital ... ist; **that is ~ why I don't want it** genau deshalb will ich es nicht; **or more ~ ...** oder genauer ...

precision [prɪˈsɪʒən] N Genauigkeit f; (of work, movement also) Präzision f

precision engineering N Präzisionsmechanik f, Feinmechanik f

preclude [prɪˈkluːd] VT ausschließen; **to ~ sb from doing sth** jdn daran hindern, etw zu tun

precocious [prɪˈkəʊʃəs] ADJ frühreif; way of speaking altklug

precociously [prɪˈkəʊʃəslɪ] ADV frühreif; talk altklug; **~ talented** früh begabt

preconceived [ˌpriːkənˈsiːvd] ADJ vorgefasst; **to have ~ ideas about sth** eine vorgefasste Meinung zu etw haben

preconception [ˌpriːkənˈsepʃən] N vorgefasste Meinung

precondition [ˌpriːkənˈdɪʃən] N (Vor)bedingung f

precursor [prɪ'kɜːsə^r] N Vorläufer(in) *m(f)*; (= *herald: of event etc*) Vorbote *m*, Vorbotin *f*

predate [ˌpriː'deɪt] VT (= *precede*) zeitlich vorangehen (+*dat*); *cheque, letter* zurückdatieren

predator ['predətə^r] N (= *animal*) Raubtier *nt*

predatory ['predətərɪ] ADJ *attack, behaviour* räuberisch; (*financially etc*) raubtierhaft; **~ instinct** Raubtierinstinkt *m*

predecessor ['priːdɪsesə^r] N (= *person*) Vorgänger(in) *m(f)*; (= *thing*) Vorläufer(in) *m(f)*; **our ~s** (= *ancestors*) unsere Ahnen *pl*

predestine [priː'destɪn] VT prädestinieren

predetermined [ˌpriːdɪ'tɜːmɪnd] ADJ *outcome* im Voraus festgelegt; *size* vorgegeben; *position* vorherbestimmt; **for a ~ period** für einen vorherbestimmten Zeitabschnitt

predicament [prɪ'dɪkəmənt] N Dilemma *nt*

predict [prɪ'dɪkt] VT vorhersagen

predictability [prəˌdɪktə'bɪlɪtɪ] N Vorhersagbarkeit *f*

predictable [prɪ'dɪktəbl] ADJ *event, reaction* vorhersagbar; *person* durchschaubar; **to be ~** vorhersagbar sein; **you're so ~** man weiß doch genau, wie Sie reagieren

predictably [prɪ'dɪktəblɪ] ADV *react* vorhersagbar; **~ (enough)**, **he was late** wie vorauszusehen, kam er zu spät

prediction [prɪ'dɪkʃən] N Prophezeiung *f*

predispose [ˌpriːdɪ'spəʊz] VT geneigt machen; (*Med*) anfällig machen (*to* für); **to ~ sb toward(s) sb/sth** jdn für jdn/etw einnehmen

predisposition [ˌpriːdɪspə'zɪʃən] N Neigung *f* (*to* zu); (*Med*) Anfälligkeit *f* (*to* für); **he has a natural ~ to violence** er hat eine natürliche Veranlagung zur Gewalttätigkeit

predominance [prɪ'dɒmɪnəns] N Überwiegen *nt*; **the ~ of women in the office** die weibliche Überzahl im Büro

predominant [prɪ'dɒmɪnənt] ADJ *idea, theory* vorherrschend; (= *dominating*) *person, animal* beherrschend; **those things which are ~ in your life** die Dinge, die in Ihrem Leben von größter Bedeutung sind

predominantly [prɪ'dɒmɪnəntlɪ] ADV überwiegend

predominate [prɪ'dɒmɪneɪt] VI (*in numbers*) vorherrschen; (*in influence etc*) überwiegen

predominately [prɪ'dɒmɪnɪtlɪ] ADV (= *mainly*) überwiegend

pre-election [ˌpriːɪ'lekʃən] ADJ vor der Wahl (durchgeführt); **~ promise** Wahlversprechen *nt*

pre-eminent [priː'emɪnənt] ADJ überragend

pre-empt [priː'empt] VT zuvorkommen (+*dat*)

pre-emptive [priː'emptɪv] ADJ präventiv, Präventiv-; **~ attack** Präventivschlag *m*; **~ right** (*US Fin*) Vorkaufsrecht *nt*

preen [priːn] **1** VT putzen **2** VI (*bird*) sich putzen **3** VR **to ~ oneself** (*bird*) sich putzen

pre-existent [ˌpriːɪg'zɪstənt] ADJ vorher vorhanden

prefabricated [ˌpriː'fæbrɪkeɪtɪd] ADJ vorgefertigt; **~ building** Fertighaus *nt*

preface ['prefɪs] N Vorwort *nt*; (*of speech*) Vorrede *f*

prefect ['priːfekt] N (*Brit Sch*) Aufsichtsschüler(in) *m(f)*

prefer [prɪ'fɜː^r] VT (= *like better*) vorziehen (*to dat*); (= *be more fond of*) lieber haben (*to* als); **he ~s coffee to tea** er trinkt lieber Kaffee als Tee; **I ~ it that way** es ist mir lieber so; **which (of them) do you ~?** (*of people*) wen mögen Sie lieber?; (*of things*) welche(n, s) finden Sie besser?; **I'd ~ something less ornate** ich hätte lieber etwas Schlichteres; **to ~ to do sth** etw lieber tun; **I ~ not to say** ich sage es lieber nicht; **would you ~ me to drive?** soll ich lieber fahren?; **I would ~ you to do it today** *or* **that you did it today** mir wäre es lieber, wenn Sie es heute täten

preferable ['prefərəbl] ADJ **X is ~ to Y** X ist Y (*dat*) vorzuziehen; **anything would be ~ to sharing a flat with Sophie** alles wäre besser, als mit Sophie zusammen wohnen zu müssen; **it would be ~ to do it that way** es wäre besser, es so zu machen; **infinitely ~** hundertmal besser

preferably ['prefərəblɪ] ADV am liebsten; **tea or coffee? – coffee, ~** Tee oder Kaffee? – lieber Kaffee; **but ~ not Tuesday** aber, wenn möglich, nicht Dienstag

preference ['prefərəns] N **(a)** (= *greater liking*) Vorliebe *f* **(b) just state your ~** nennen Sie einfach Ihre Wünsche; **I have no ~** mir ist das eigentlich gleich **(c)** (= *greater favour*) Vorzug *m*; **to give ~ to sb/sth** jdn/etw bevorzugen (*over* gegenüber)

preference shares ['prefərəns'ʃeəz] PL (*Brit Fin*) Vorzugsaktien *pl*

preferential [ˌprefə'renʃəl] ADJ bevorzugt; *creditor, rights* bevorrechtigt; **~ rate** Sonderpreis *m*; **to give sb ~ treatment** jdn bevorzugt behandeln; **to get** *or* **receive ~ treatment** eine Vorzugsbehandlung bekommen; **~ trade** (*Comm*) Präferenzhandel *m*; **~ trade area** präferenzielle Handelszone; **~ trading status** präferenzieller Handelsstatus; **~ tariff** (*Comm*) Präferenzzoll *m*

preferred [prɪ'fɜːd] ADJ *creditor* bevorrechtigt

preferred stock N (*US Fin*) Vorzugsaktien *pl*

prefix ['priːfɪks] N (*Gram*) Präfix *nt*; (*Telec*) Vorwahl *f*

pregnancy ['pregnənsɪ] N Schwangerschaft *f*; (*of animal*) Trächtigkeit *f*

pregnancy test N Schwangerschaftstest *m*

pregnant ['pregnənt] ADJ **(a)** *woman* schwanger; *animal* trächtig; **3 months ~** im vierten Monat schwanger; **she is ~ with her first child** sie ist zum ersten Mal schwanger; **Gill was ~ by her new boyfriend** Gill war von ihrem neuen Freund schwanger; **to become** *or* **get ~** (*woman*) schwanger werden **(b)** (*fig*) *silence, pause* bedeutungsschwer

preheat [priː'hiːt] VT vorheizen

prehistoric [ˌpriːhɪ'stɒrɪk] ADJ prähistorisch

prehistory [ˌpriː'hɪstərɪ] N Vorgeschichte *f*

prejudge [priː'dʒʌdʒ] VT im Voraus beurteilen; (*negatively*) im Voraus verurteilen

prejudice ['predʒʊdɪs] **1** N Vorurteil *nt*; **his ~ against …** seine Voreingenommenheit gegen …; **to have a ~ against sb/sth** gegen jdn/etw voreingenommen sein; **racial ~** Rassenvorurteile *pl* **2** VT beeinflussen

prejudiced ['predʒʊdɪst] ADJ *person* voreingenommen (*against* gegen); *opinion* vorgefasst; **to be ~ in favour of sb/sth** für jdn/etw voreingenommen sein; **to be racially ~** Rassenvorurteile haben

preliminary [prɪ'lɪmɪnərɪ] **1** ADJ *remarks, chapter* einleitend; *steps, measures* vorbereitend; *report, results, tests* vorläufig; *stage* früh; **~ negotiations** Vorverhandlungen *pl*; **~ investigation** Voruntersuchung *f*; **~ hearing** (*US Jur*) gerichtliche Voruntersuchung; **~ contacts** erste Kontakte; **~ round** Vorrunde *f*
2 N Einleitung *f* (*to* zu); (= *preparatory measure*) Vorbereitung *f*; (*Sport*) Vorspiel *nt*; **preliminaries** *pl* Präliminarien *pl* (*geh, Jur*); (*for speech*) einleitende Worte; (*Sport*) Vorrunde *f*; **let's dispense with the preliminaries** kommen wir gleich zur Sache

preliminary hearing N (*Jur*) Voruntersuchung *f*

prelude ['preljuːd] N (*fig*) Auftakt *m*

premarital [priː'mærɪtl] ADJ vorehelich

premature ['premətʃʊə^r] ADJ vorzeitig; *decision, action* verfrüht; **the baby was three weeks ~** das Baby wurde drei Wochen zu früh geboren; **~ baby** Frühgeburt *f*; **~ ejaculation** vorzeitiger Samenerguss

prematurely ['premətʃʊəlɪ] ADV vorzeitig; *decide* verfrüht; *act* voreilig; **he was born ~** er war eine Frühgeburt

premeditate [priː'medɪteɪt] VT vorsätzlich planen

premeditated [priː'medɪteɪtɪd] ADJ vorsätzlich

premenstrual [priː'menstrʊəl] ADJ prämenstruell

premenstrual syndrome, premenstrual tension N (*esp Brit*) prämenstruelles Syndrom

premier ['premɪə^r] **1** ADJ führend **2** N Premierminister(in) *m(f)*

première ['premɪeə^r] **1** N Premiere *f* **2** VT uraufführen

Premier League, Premiership ['premɪəʃɪp] N (*Ftbl*) erste Liga

premise ['premɪs] N **(a)** (*esp Logic*) Voraussetzung *f* **(b) premises** PL (*of school, factory*) Gelände *nt*; (= *building*) Gebäude *nt*; (= *shop*) Räumlichkeiten *pl*; **business ~s** Geschäftsräume *pl*; **drinking is not allowed in** *or* **on these ~s** es ist nicht erlaubt, hier Alkohol zu trinken; **will you escort him off the ~s?** würden Sie ihn bitte hinausbegleiten?

premiss N (*Logic*) Voraussetzung *f*

premium ['priːmɪəm] **1** N (= *bonus*) Bonus *m*; (= *surcharge*) Zuschlag *m*; (= *insurance* ~) Prämie *f*; (*St Ex*) Aufgeld *nt*; **~ bond** (*Brit*) Lotterieanleihe *f*; **to sell sth at a ~** etw über seinem Wert verkaufen; **to be at a ~** (*St Ex*) über pari stehen; (*fig*) hoch im Kurs stehen
2 ADJ **(a)** (= *top-quality*) erstklassig; **~ petrol** (*Brit*) *or* **gas** (*US*)

Superbenzin *nt*
(b) (= *inflated*) **~ price** Höchstpreis *m*; **callers are charged a ~ rate of 48p a minute** Anrufern wird ein Höchsttarif von 48 Pence pro Minute berechnet

premium-rate [ˈpriːmɪəmˌreɪt] ADJ (*Telec*) zum Höchsttarif

premonition [ˌpriːməˈnɪʃən] N (= *presentiment*) (böse) Vorahnung; (= *forewarning*) Vorwarnung *f*

prenatal [priːˈneɪtl] ADJ pränatal

preoccupation [priːˌɒkjʊˈpeɪʃən] N **her ~ with her appearance** ihre ständige Sorge um ihr Äußeres; **her ~ with making money was such that ...** sie war so sehr mit dem Geldverdienen beschäftigt, dass ...; **that was his main ~** das war sein Hauptanliegen

preoccupied [priːˈɒkjʊpaɪd] ADJ gedankenverloren; **to be ~ with sth** nur an etw (*acc*) denken; **he has been (looking) rather ~ recently** er sieht in letzter Zeit so aus, als beschäftige ihn etwas

preoccupy [priːˈɒkjʊpaɪ] VT (stark) beschäftigen

prepackaged [priːˈpækɪdʒd], **prepacked** [priːˈpækt] ADJ abgepackt

prepaid [priːˈpeɪd] **1** PTP *of* **prepay 2** ADJ *postage, goods* vorausbezahlt; *envelope* freigemacht; **~ envelope** (*Comm*) frankierter Rückumschlag; **~ mobile phone** Handy *nt* (*mit im Voraus entrichteter Grundgebühr*); **~ corporation tax** (*US*) Körperschaftssteuer-Vorauszahlung *f*

preparation [ˌprepəˈreɪʃən] N Vorbereitung *f*; (*of meal, medicine etc*) Zubereitung *f*; **in ~ for sth** als Vorbereitung für etw; **~s for war/a journey** Kriegs-/Reisevorbereitungen *pl*; **to make ~s** Vorbereitungen treffen

preparatory [prɪˈpærətərɪ] ADJ vorbereitend; **~ work** Vorbereitungsarbeit *f*; **the ~ arrangements** die Vorbereitungen *pl*

PREPARATORY SCHOOL

*In Großbritannien ist eine **preparatory school** oder auch **prep school** eine private Grundschule für Kinder im Alter von 7 bis 13 Jahren, in der die Schülerinnen und Schüler auf eine private weiterführende Schule vorbereitet werden sollen, und das sowohl in schulischer wie auch in gesellschaftlicher Hinsicht.*

*In den USA dagegen ist eine **preparatory school** eine private weiterführende Schule, die die Schülerinnen und Schüler auf das College oder die Universität vorbereiten soll. Wie in Großbritannien, so wird auch in den USA die **preparatory school** mit gesellschaftlicher Exklusivität, Privilegiertheit und Reichtum verbunden.*

---

prepare [prɪˈpɛəʳ] **1** VT vorbereiten (*sb for sth* jdn auf etw *acc*, *sth for sth* etw für etw); *meal, medicine* zubereiten; *guest room* zurechtmachen; (*Sci*) präparieren; *data* aufbereiten; **~ yourself for a shock!** mach dich auf einen Schock gefasst! **2** VI **to ~ for sth** sich auf etw (*acc*) vorbereiten; **the country is preparing for war** das Land trifft Kriegsvorbereitungen; **to ~ to do sth** Anstalten machen, etw zu tun

prepared [prɪˈpɛəd] ADJ **(a)** (*also* **ready ~**) vorbereitet (*for* auf +*acc*); **~ meal** Fertiggericht *nt*; **the country is ~ for war** das Land ist kriegsbereit *or* bereit zum Krieg **(b)** (= *willing*) **to be ~ to do sth** bereit sein, etw zu tun

prepay [priːˈpeɪ], *pret, ptp* **prepaid** VT im Voraus bezahlen

prepayment [priːˈpeɪmənt] N Vorauszahlung *f*

preponderance [prɪˈpɒndərəns] N Übergewicht *nt*; (*in number also*) Überwiegen *nt*

preposition [ˌprepəˈzɪʃən] N Präposition *f*

prepossessing [ˌpriːpəˈzesɪŋ] ADJ einnehmend

preposterous [prɪˈpɒstərəs] ADJ grotesk

preppie, preppy [ˈprepɪ] ADJ adrett

preprinted [ˈpriːˈprɪntɪd] ADJ vorgedruckt

preprogram [priːˈprəʊgræm] VT vorprogrammieren

prep school N = **preparatory school**

prerecord [ˌpriːrɪˈkɔːd] VT vorher aufzeichnen; **~ed cassette** bespielte Kassette

prerequisite [ˌpriːˈrekwɪzɪt] N Vorbedingung *f*

prerogative [prɪˈrɒgətɪv] N Vorrecht *nt*

Presbyterian [ˌprezbɪˈtɪərɪən] **1** ADJ presbyterianisch **2** N Presbyterianer(in) *m(f)*

---

preschool [ˈpriːˈskuːl] ADJ ATTR vorschulisch; **a child of ~ age** ein Kind *nt* im Vorschulalter; **~ education** Vorschulerziehung *f*

prescribe [prɪˈskraɪb] VT **(a)** (= *order, lay down*) vorschreiben **(b)** (*Med, fig*) verschreiben (*sth for sb* jdm etw); **the ~d dose** die verordnete Dosis

prescription [prɪˈskrɪpʃən] N (*Med*) Rezept *nt*; (*act of prescribing*) Verschreiben *nt*; **to make up** *or* **fill** (*US*) **a ~** eine Medizin zubereiten; **on ~** auf Rezept

prescription drugs PL verschreibungspflichtige Medikamente *pl*

presealed [ˈpriːˈsiːld] ADJ versiegelt

preseason [ˈpriːˈsiːzn] ADJ (*Sport*) vor der Saison; (*in tourism*) Vorsaison-

preselect [ˌpriːsɪˈlekt] VT vorher auswählen

presence [ˈprezns] N **(a)** Anwesenheit *f*; **in sb's ~, in the ~ of sb** in jds (*dat*) Anwesenheit; **your ~ is required** Ihre Anwesenheit ist erforderlich; **to make one's ~ felt** sich bemerkbar machen; **in the ~ of danger** im Angesicht der Gefahr; **a military/police ~** Militär-/Polizeipräsenz *f* **(b)** (= *bearing, dignity*) Auftreten *nt*; (*also* **stage ~**) Ausstrahlung *f*

presence of mind N Geistesgegenwart *f*

present¹ [ˈpreznt] **1** ADJ **(a)** (= *in attendance*) anwesend; **to be ~** anwesend sein; **~ company excepted** Anwesende ausgenommen; **all those ~** alle Anwesenden; **all ~ and correct** alle anwesend **(b)** (= *existing in sth*) vorhanden; **carbon is ~ in organic matter** Kohlenstoff ist in organischen Stoffen enthalten **(c)** **at the ~ time** gegenwärtig; *year, season etc* laufend; (= *at the ~ moment*) zum gegenwärtigen Zeitpunkt; **the ~ day** (= *nowadays*) heutzutage; **till** *or* **to** *or* **until the ~ day** bis zum heutigen Tag; **in the ~ circumstances** unter den gegenwärtigen Umständen **(d)** (*Gram*) **in the ~ tense** im Präsens; **~ participle** Partizip *nt* Präsens **2** N **(a)** Gegenwart *f*; **at ~** zur Zeit; **up to the ~** bis jetzt; **there's no time like the ~** (*prov*) was du heute kannst besorgen, das verschiebe nicht auf morgen (*Prov*); **that will be all for the ~** das ist vorläufig alles **(b)** (*Gram*) Präsens *nt*; **~ continuous** erweitertes Präsens

present² **1** N (= *gift*) Geschenk *nt*; **I got it** *or* **was given it as a ~** das habe ich geschenkt bekommen **2** [prɪˈzent] VT *medal, prize etc* übergeben; (= *give as a gift*) schenken; **to ~ sb with sth, to ~ sth to sb** jdm etw übergeben; (*as a gift*) jdm etw schenken **(b)** (= *put forward*) vorlegen; *cheque* (*for payment*) präsentieren **(c)** *target, view, opportunity* bieten; **his action ~ed us with a problem** seine Tat stellte uns vor ein Problem **(d)** (*Rad, TV*) präsentieren; (*Theat*) aufführen; (*commentator*) moderieren **(e)** (= *introduce*) vorstellen; **to ~ Mr X to Miss Y** Herrn X Fräulein Y (*dat*) vorstellen; **may I ~ Mr X?** (*form*) erlauben Sie mir, Herrn X vorzustellen (*form*) **3** [prɪˈzent] VR (*opportunity, problem etc*) sich ergeben; **he was asked to ~ himself for interview** er wurde gebeten, zu einem Vorstellungsgespräch zu erscheinen

presentable [prɪˈzentəbl] ADJ präsentabel; **to look ~** (*person*) präsentabel aussehen; **to make sth ~** etw so herrichten, dass man es zeigen kann; **to make oneself ~** sich zurechtmachen

presentation [ˌprezənˈteɪʃən] N **(a)** (*of gift etc*) Überreichung *f*; (*of prize, medal*) Verleihung *f*; (= *ceremony*) Verleihung(szeremonie) *f*; **to make the ~** die Preise/Auszeichnungen *etc* verleihen **(b)** (*of report, voucher, cheque etc*) Vorlage; (*Jur: of case, evidence*) Darlegung *f* **(c)** (= *manner of presenting*) Darbietung *f* **(d)** (*Theat*) Inszenierung *f*; (*TV, Rad*) Produktion *f*; (= *announcing*) Moderation *f*

present-day [ˈprezntˈdeɪ] ADJ ATTR heutig; **~ Britain** das heutige Großbritannien

presenter [prɪˈzentəʳ] N (*esp Brit*: *TV, Rad*) Moderator(in) *m(f)*

presently [ˈprezntlɪ] ADV **(a)** (= *soon*) bald; (= *shortly afterwards*) bald darauf **(b)** (= *at present*) derzeit

preservation [ˌprezəˈveɪʃən] N **(a)** (= *maintaining*) Erhaltung *f* **(b)** (*to prevent decay*) Konservierung *f*; (*of specimens*) Präservierung *f*; **to be in a good state of ~** gut erhalten sein

preservative [prɪˈzɜːvətɪv] N Konservierungsmittel *nt*

> *Be careful!* **preservative** *is not translated by the German word* **Präservativ**.

preserve [prɪˈzɜːv] **1** VT **(a)** erhalten; *dignity* wahren; *memory, reputation* aufrechterhalten; *sense of humour, silence* bewahren; **to ~ sb from sth** jdn vor etw (*dat*) bewahren **(b)** (= *keep from decay*) konservieren; *specimens etc* präservieren; *leather, wood* schützen **2** N **(a) preserves** PL (*Cook*) Eingemachtes *nt*; **peach ~(s)** (= *jam*) Pfirsichmarmelade *f* **(b)** (= *special domain*) Ressort *nt*; **this was once the ~ of the wealthy** dies war einst eine Domäne der Reichen; **game ~** (*Hunt*) Jagdrevier *nt*

preserved [prɪˈzɜːvd] ADJ **(a)** *food* konserviert; (*in jars*) eingemacht; (= *pickled*) eingelegt **(b)** (= *conserved*) erhalten; **well-~** gut erhalten

preset [priːˈset], pret, ptp **preset** VT vorher einstellen

preside [prɪˈzaɪd] VI (*at meeting etc*) den Vorsitz haben (*at* bei); **to ~ over an organization** *etc* eine Organisation *etc* leiten

presidency [ˈprezɪdənsɪ] N Präsidentschaft *f*; (*esp US: of company*) Aufsichtsratsvorsitz *m*; (*US Univ*) Rektorat *nt*

president [ˈprezɪdənt] N Präsident(in) *m(f)*; (*esp US: of company*) Aufsichtsratsvorsitzende(r) *mf*; (*US Univ*) Rektor(in) *m(f)*

presidential [prezɪˈdenʃəl] ADJ (*Pol*) des Präsidenten; **his ~ duties** seine Pflichten als Präsident

presidential (*Pol*): **presidential adviser** N Berater(in) *m(f)* des Präsidenten; **presidential campaign** N Präsidentschaftskampagne *f*; **presidential candidate** N Präsidentschaftskandidat(in) *m(f)*; **presidential election** N Präsidentenwahl *f*

press [pres] **1** N **(a)** (= *machine, newspapers etc*) Presse *f*; **the daily ~** die Tagespresse; **the weekly ~** die Wochenzeitungen *pl*; **to get a bad ~** eine schlechte Presse bekommen **(b)** (*Typ*) (Drucker)presse *f*; **to go to ~** in Druck gehen **(c)** (= *squeeze, push*) Druck *m* **2** VT **(a)** (= *push, squeeze*) drücken (*to* an +*acc*); *button, brake pedal* drücken auf (+*acc*); *clutch* treten; *grapes* (aus)pressen; *flowers* pressen; **to ~ the accelerator** Gas geben **(b)** (= *iron*) bügeln **(c)** (= *urge*) drängen; (= *harass*) bedrängen; *claim, argument* bestehen auf (+*dat*); **to ~ sb hard** jdm (hart) zusetzen; **to ~ sb for an answer** auf jds Antwort (*acc*) drängen; **to ~ the point** darauf beharren; **to ~ home an advantage** einen Vorteil ausnutzen; **to ~ money on sb** jdm Geld aufdrängen; **to be ~ed for time** unter Zeitdruck stehen **3** VI **(a)** (*lit, fig*: = *exert pressure*) drücken **(b)** (= *urge*) drängen (*for* auf +*acc*) **(c)** (= *move, push*) sich drängen; **to ~ ahead** *or* **forward (with sth)** (*fig*) (mit etw) weitermachen; (*with plans*) etw weiterführen

➤ **press on** VI weitermachen; (*with journey*) weiterfahren

press: **press agency** N Presseagentur *f*; **press box** N Pressetribüne *f*; **press-button** N = **push-button**; **press campaign** N Pressekampagne *f*; **press conference** N Pressekonferenz *f*; **press-gang** VT (*esp Brit inf*) dazu drängen; **to ~ sb into (doing) sth** jdn drängen, etw zu tun

pressing [ˈpresɪŋ] ADJ **(a)** *issue* brennend; *task* dringend **(b)** (= *insistent*) nachdrücklich

press: **press office** N Pressestelle *f*; **press officer** N Pressesprecher(in) *m(f)*; **press photographer** N Pressefotograf(in) *m(f)*; **press release** N Pressemitteilung *f*; **press report** N Pressebericht *m*; **press-up** N (*Brit*) Liegestütz *m*

pressure [ˈpreʃəʳ] N Druck *m*; **at high/full ~** (*lit, fig*) unter Hochdruck; **oil ~** Öldruck *m*; **parental ~** Druck von Seiten der Eltern; **to be/come under ~ to do sth** unter Druck (*dat*) stehen/geraten, etw zu tun; **to be under ~ from sb on sth** jdn gedrängt werden; **to put ~ on sb** jdn unter Druck (*dat*) setzen; **business ~s** geschäftliche Belastungen *pl*; **the ~s of modern life** die Belastungen *pl* des modernen Lebens

pressure: **pressure cooker** N Schnellkochtopf *m*; **pressure gauge** N Manometer *nt*; **pressure group** N Pressuregroup *f*

pressurize [ˈpreʃəraɪz] VT **(a)** *cabin, spacesuit* auf Normaldruck halten **(b)** (= *pressure*) *sb* unter Druck setzen; **to ~ sb into**

doing sth jdn so unter Druck setzen, dass er schließlich etw tut

pressurized [ˈpreʃəraɪzd] ADJ **(a)** *aircraft, container* mit Druckausgleich **(b)** *water, gas* komprimiert **(c)** (*fig*) unter Druck; **to feel ~** sich unter Druck (gesetzt) fühlen; **to feel ~ into doing sth** sich dazu gedrängt fühlen, etw zu tun

Prestel® [ˈprestel] N (*Brit Telec*) ≈ Bildschirmtext *m*

prestige [preˈstiːʒ] N Prestige *nt*; **~ value** Prestigewert *m*

prestigious [preˈstɪdʒəs] ADJ Prestige-; **a ~ job** ein Prestigeberuf *m*; **to be (very) ~** (einen hohen) Prestigewert haben

presumably [prɪˈzjuːməblɪ] ADV vermutlich; **he'll come later** er wird voraussichtlich später kommen

presume [prɪˈzjuːm] **1** VT vermuten; **~d dead** mutmaßlich verstorben; **to be ~d innocent** als unschuldig gelten; **he is ~d to be living in Spain** es wird vermutet, dass er in Spanien lebt **2** VI **(a)** (= *suppose*) vermuten; **I ~ not** ich glaube nein **(b)** (= *be presumptuous*) **I didn't want to ~** ich wollte nicht aufdringlich sein; **you ~ too much** Sie sind wirklich vermessen

presumption [prɪˈzʌmpʃən] N (= *assumption*) Vermutung *f*; **the ~ is that …** man vermutet, dass …; **~ of innocence** Unschuldvermutung *f*

presumptuous [prɪˈzʌmptjuəs] ADJ anmaßend; **it would be ~ of me to …** es wäre eine Anmaßung von mir, zu …

pre-tax [priːˈtæks] ADJ unversteuert; **~ profit** Gewinn *m* vor Abzug der Steuer

pretence, (*US*) **pretense** [prɪˈtens] N **(a)** (= *make-believe story*) erfundene Geschichte; **to make a ~ of doing sth** so tun, als ob man etw tut; **it's all a ~** das ist alles nur gespielt **(b)** (= *feigning, insincerity*) Heuchelei *f*; **his ~ of normality** seine vorgespiegelte Normalität **(c)** (= *pretext*) Vorwand *m*; **on** *or* **under the ~ of doing sth** unter dem Vorwand, etw zu tun

pretend [prɪˈtend] **1** VT so tun, als ob; (= *feign*) vorgeben; **to ~ to be interested** so tun, als ob man interessiert wäre; **to ~ to be sick** eine Krankheit vortäuschen; **to ~ to be asleep** sich schlafend stellen **2** VI so tun, als ob; (= *keep up facade*) sich verstellen; **he is only ~ing** er tut nur so (als ob); **let's stop ~ing** hören wir auf, uns (*dat*) etwas vorzumachen

pretense N (*US*) = **pretence**

pretension [prɪˈtenʃən] N **(a)** (= *claim*) Anspruch *m*; (*social, cultural*) Ambition *f* **(b)** (= *ostentation*) Prahlerei *f*; (= *affectation*) Anmaßung *f*

pretentious [prɪˈtenʃəs] ADJ anmaßend; *style, book* hochtrabend; (= *ostentatious*) angeberisch; *house, restaurant* pompös

pretentiously [prɪˈtenʃəslɪ] ADV *say, describe* hochtrabend; *decorated* pompös

pretentiousness [prɪˈtenʃəsnɪs] N Anmaßung *f*; (= *ostentatiousness*) Angeberei *f*

preterite [ˈpretərɪt] **1** ADJ *verb* im Imperfekt; (*in English*) im Präteritum; **the ~ tense** das Imperfekt **2** N Imperfekt *nt*

pretext [ˈpriːtekst] N Vorwand *m*; **on** *or* **under the ~ of doing sth** unter dem Vorwand, etw zu tun

prettily [ˈprɪtɪlɪ] ADV nett; (= *charmingly*) reizend

prettiness [ˈprɪtɪnɪs] N hübsches Aussehen; (*of place*) Schönheit *f*

pretty [ˈprɪtɪ] **1** ADJ (+*er*) **(a)** nett; *manners, compliment, speech* artig; **to be ~** (*also pej: man*) hübsch sein; **she's not just a ~ face!** (*inf*) sie hat auch Köpfchen!; **it wasn't a ~ sight** das war kein schöner Anblick **(b)** (*inf*) hübsch; **it'll cost a ~ penny** das wird eine schöne Stange Geld kosten (*inf*) **2** ADV (= *rather*) ziemlich; **~ damn** *or* **damned good** verdammt gut (*inf*); **~ nearly** *or* **well finished** so gut wie fertig (*inf*); **how's the patient? – ~ much the same** was macht der Patient? – immer noch so ziemlich gleich

prevail [prɪˈveɪl] VI **(a)** (= *gain mastery*) sich durchsetzen (*over, against* gegenüber) **(b)** (= *be widespread*) weit verbreitet sein

prevailing [prɪˈveɪlɪŋ] ADJ *fashion, conditions* derzeitig; *opinion, wind* vorherschend

prevalence [ˈprevələns] N Vorherrschen *nt*; (*of crime, disease*) Häufigkeit *f*

prevalent [ˈprevələnt] ADJ vorherschend; *opinion, attitude, custom, disease* weit verbreitet; *conditions, situation* herrschend; *fashions, style* beliebt

prevent [prɪˈvent] VT *sth* verhindern; *(through preventive measures)* vorbeugen (+*dat*); **to ~ sb (from) doing sth** jdn daran hindern, etw zu tun; **the gate is there to ~ them from falling down the stairs** das Gitter ist da, dass sie nicht die Treppe hinunterfallen; **to ~ sb from coming** jdn am Kommen hindern; **to ~ sth (from) happening** verhindern, dass etw geschieht

preventable [prɪˈventəbl] ADJ vermeidbar

prevention [prɪˈvenʃən] N Verhinderung *f*; *(through preventive measures)* Vorbeugung *f (of* gegen)

preventive [prɪˈventɪv] ADJ präventiv

preview [ˈpriːvjuː] **1** N **(a)** *(of play, film)* Vorpremiere *f*; *(of exhibition)* Vorbesichtigung *f*; **to give sb a ~ of sth (fig)** jdm eine Vorschau auf etw (*acc*) geben **(b)** *(Film, TV:* = *trailer)* Vorschau *f (of* auf +*acc*) **2** VT (= *view beforehand)* vorher ansehen; (= *show beforehand)* vorher aufführen

previous [ˈpriːvɪəs] ADJ vorherig; *page, day* vorhergehend; *year* vorangegangen; *(with indef art)* früher; **the ~ page/day/year** die Seite/der Tag/das Jahr davor; **the/a ~ holder of the title** der vorherige/ein früherer Titelträger; **in ~ years** in früheren Jahren; **he's already been the target of two ~ attacks** er war schon das Opfer von zwei früheren Angriffen; **on a ~ occasion** bei einer früheren Gelegenheit; **I have a ~ engagement** ich habe schon einen Termin; **no ~ experience necessary** Vorkenntnisse (sind) nicht erforderlich; **to have a ~ conviction** vorbestraft sein; **~ owner** Vorbesitzer(in) *m(f)*

previously [ˈpriːvɪəslɪ] ADV vorher; **he'd arrived three hours ~** er war drei Stunden zuvor angekommen

pre-war [ˈpriːˈwɔːʳ] ADJ Vorkriegs-

prey [preɪ] **1** N *(lit, fig)* Beute *f*; **bird of ~** Raubvogel *m*; **to be/ fall ~ to sb/sth** *(fig)* ein Opfer von jdm/etw werden **2** VI **to ~ (up)on** *(animals)* Beute machen auf (+*acc*); *(swindler etc)* als Opfer aussuchen an (+*dat*); *(doubts)* nagen an (+*dat*); *(anxiety)* quälen; **it ~ed (up)on his mind** es ließ ihn nicht los

price [praɪs] **1** N **(a)** Preis *m*; **the ~ of coffee** die Kaffeepreise *pl*; **~s and incomes policy** Lohn-Preis-Politik *f*; **~-earnings ratio** Kurs-Gewinn-Verhältnis *nt*; **to go up** *or* **rise/to go down** *or* **fall in ~** teurer/billiger werden; **they range in ~ from £10 to £30** die Preise dafür bewegen sich zwischen £ 10 und £ 30; **what is the ~ of that?** was kostet das?; **at a ~ of ... zum** Preis(e) von ...; **at a ~** zum entsprechenden Preis; **the ~ of victory** der Preis des Sieges; **but at what ~!** aber zu welchem Preis!; **not at any ~** um keinen Preis; **to put a ~ on sth** einen Preis für etw nennen; **to be beyond/without ~** nicht mit Geld zu bezahlen sein; **to put a ~ on sb's head** eine Belohnung auf jds Kopf *(acc)* aussetzen

(b) *(Betting:* = *odds)* Quote *f* **2** VT (= *fix* ~ *of)* den Preis festsetzen von; (= *put* ~ *label on)* auszeichnen *(at* mit); *(fig:* = *estimate value of)* schätzen; **it was ~d at £5** (= *marked £5)* es war mit £ 5 ausgezeichnet; (= *cost £5)* es kostete £ 5; **tickets ~d at £20** Karten zum Preis von £ 20; **reasonably ~d** angemessen im Preis; **to ~ oneself out of the market** sich selbst durch zu hohe Preise konkurrenzunfähig machen; **to ~ sb out of the market** jdn durch niedrigere Preise vom Markt verdrängen

price: price bracket N = **price range; price control** N Preiskontrolle *f*; **price cut** N Preissenkung *f*; **price cutting** N Preissenkungen *pl*; **price fixing** N Preisfestlegung *f*; **price-fixing method** N Preisermittlungsmethode *f*; **price freeze** N Preisstopp *m*; **price index** N Preisindex *m*

priceless [ˈpraɪslɪs] ADJ unschätzbar; *(inf) joke, film* köstlich; *person* unbezahlbar

price: price limit N Preisgrenze *f*; **price list** N Preisliste *f*; **price mechanism** N *(Econ)* Preismechanismus *m*; **price plateau** N Preisniveau *nt*; **price range** N Preisklasse *f*; **price rigging** N Preisabsprachen *pl*; **price ring** N Preiskartell *nt*; **price rise** N Preiserhöhung *f*; **price support** N *(US)* Subvention *f*; **price tag, price ticket** N Preisschild *nt*; **price war** N Preiskrieg *m*

pricing [ˈpraɪsɪŋ] N Preisgestaltung *f*

pricing policy N Preispolitik *f*

prick [prɪk] **1** N **(a)** Stich *m*; **~ of conscience** Gewissensbisse *pl* **(b)** *(sl:* = *penis)* Schwanz *m (sl)* **(c)** *(sl:* = *person)* Arsch *m (vulg)* **2** VT stechen; **to ~ one's finger** sich *(dat)* in den Finger stechen; **to ~ one's finger (on sth)** sich *(dat)* (an etw *dat)* den Finger stechen; **she ~ed his conscience** sie bereitete ihm Gewissensbisse; **to ~ one's ears** die Ohren spitzen

➤ prick up VT SEP **to prick up its/one's ears** *(lit, fig)* die Ohren spitzen

prickle [ˈprɪkl] **1** N **(a)** (= *sharp point)* Stachel *m* **(b)** (= *sensation)* Stechen *nt*; *(caused by wool etc)* Kratzen *nt*; (= *tingle, also fig)* Prickeln *nt* **2** VI stechen; *(wool, beard)* kratzen; (= *tingle, also fig)* prickeln

prickly [ˈprɪklɪ] ADJ (+ER) **(a)** *plant, animal* stach(e)lig; *beard, material* kratzig; *sensation* stechend; (= *tingling)* prickelnd *(also fig)* **(b)** *(fig) person* bissig **(c)** (= *sore) eyes* gereizt

pride [praɪd] **1** N Stolz *m*; (= *arrogance)* Hochmut *m*; **to take (a) ~ in sth** auf etw *(acc)* stolz sein; **to take (a) ~ in one's appearance** Wert auf sein Äußeres legen; **her ~ and joy** ihr ganzer Stolz; **to have** *or* **take ~ of place** den Ehrenplatz einnehmen **2** VR **to ~ oneself on sth** sich einer Sache *(gen)* rühmen

priest [priːst] N Priester(in) *m(f)*

priestess [ˈpriːstɪs] N Priesterin *f*

prim [prɪm] ADJ (+ER) *(also* ~ **and proper)** etepetete *pred (inf)*; *woman, manner* steif; *expression* verkniffen; (= *prudish)* prüde

primaeval ADJ = **primeval**

primal [ˈpraɪməl] ADJ ursprünglich, Ur-

primarily [ˈpraɪmərɪlɪ] ADV hauptsächlich

primary [ˈpraɪmərɪ] **1** ADJ Haupt-; **that is our ~ concern** das ist unser Hauptanliegen; **of ~ importance** von größter Bedeutung; **~ industries** Primärindustrien *pl* **2** N **(a)** *(esp Brit:* = ~ *school)* Grundschule *f* **(b)** *(US:* = *election)* Vorwahl *f*

primary: primary colour, *(US)* **primary color** N Grundfarbe *f*; **primary education** N Grundschul(aus)bildung *f*; **primary election** N *(US)* Vorwahl; **primary industry** N Grund(stoff)industrie *f*; *(agriculture etc)* Urindustrie *f*; (= *main industry)* Hauptindustrie *f*; **primary producer** N Lieferant(in) *m(f)* von Rohmaterial; **primary product** N Primärprodukt *nt*; (= *main product)* Hauptprodukt *nt*; **primary school** N *(esp Brit)* Grundschule *f*; **primary school teacher** N *(esp Brit)* Grundschullehrer(in) *m(f)*

prime [praɪm] **1** ADJ **(a)** Haupt-, wesentlich; *target, objective, cause* hauptsächlich; *candidate* erste(r, s); **~ suspect** Hauptverdächtige(r) *mf*; **of ~ importance** von größter Bedeutung; **my ~ concern** mein Hauptanliegen *nt* **(b)** (= *excellent)* erstklassig **2** N **in the ~ of life** in der Blüte seiner Jahre; **he is in his ~** er ist in den besten Jahren; *(singer, artist)* er ist an seinem Höhepunkt angelangt

prime costs PL *(Comm)* Selbstkosten *pl*

primed [praɪmd] ADJ *person* gerüstet; **to be ~ for the interview** für das Interview gut gerüstet sein

prime: prime minister N Premierminister(in) *m(f)*; **prime number** N *(Math)* Primzahl *f*; **prime rate** N *(Econ, Fin)* Prime Rate *f*, Vorzugszins *nt*; **prime time** N Hauptsendezeit *f*

primeval [praɪˈmiːvəl] ADJ urzeitlich, Ur-

primitive [ˈprɪmɪtɪv] ADJ primitiv

primly [ˈprɪmlɪ] ADV (= *demurely)* sittsam; (= *prudishly)* prüde

primrose [ˈprɪmrəʊz] N *(Bot)* Erdschlüsselblume *f*

primula [ˈprɪmjʊlə] N Primel *f*

prince [prɪns] N *(king's son)* Prinz *m*; (= *ruler)* Fürst *m*

princely [ˈprɪnslɪ] ADJ *(lit, fig)* fürstlich

princess [prɪnˈses] N Prinzessin *f*

principal [ˈprɪnsɪpəl] **1** ADJ Haupt-, hauptsächlich; **my ~ concern** mein Hauptanliegen *nt* **2** N **(a)** *(of school, college)* Rektor(in) *m(f)* **(b)** *(Fin) (of investment)* Kapitalsumme *f*; *(of debt)* Kreditsumme *f*

principality [ˌprɪnsɪˈpælɪtɪ] N Fürstentum *nt*

principally [ˈprɪnsɪpəlɪ] ADV in erster Linie

principle [ˈprɪnsɪpl] N Prinzip *nt*; *(no pl:* = *integrity)* Prinzipien *pl*; **in/on ~** im/aus Prinzip; **a man of ~(s)** ein Mensch mit Prinzipien; **it's a matter of ~, it's the ~ of the thing** es geht dabei ums Prinzip

principled [ˈprɪnsɪpld] ADJ mit Prinzipien

print [prɪnt] **1** N **(a)** (= *typeface, characters)* Schrift *f*; (= *printed matter)* Gedruckte(s) *nt*; **out of ~** vergriffen; **in ~** gedruckt; **to be in ~ again** wieder erhältlich sein; **in large** *or* **big ~** in Großdruck

(b) (= *picture)* Druck *m*

(c) *(Phot)* Abzug *m*; *(of cinema film)* Kopie *f*

(d) *(of foot, hand etc)* Abdruck *m*; **a thumb ~** ein Daumenabdruck *m*

2 VT **(a)** book, design, money drucken; (Comput) (aus)drucken **(b)** (= publish) veröffentlichen **(c)** (= write in block letters) in Druckschrift schreiben **3** VI **(a)** drucken; **ready to ~** book druckfertig; machine druckbereit; **the book is ~ing now** das Buch ist gerade im Druck
(b) (= write in block letters) in Druckschrift schreiben
➤ **print out** VT SEP (Comput) ausdrucken

printable ['prɪntəbl] ADJ druckfähig

print drum N (Comput) Drucktrommel f

printed ['prɪntɪd] ADJ Druck-, gedruckt; (= written in capitals) in Großbuchstaben; **~ matter/papers** Büchersendung f; **in ~ form** in gedruckter Form

printer ['prɪntə'] N Drucker m

printer driver N (Comput) Druckertreiber m

print head N (Comput) Druckkopf m

printing ['prɪntɪŋ] N (= process) Drucken nt

printing press N Druckerpresse f

print: print list N (Comput) Druckliste f; **printmaking** N Grafik f; **print menu** N (Comput) Druckmenü nt; **print-out** N (Comput) Ausdruck m; **print queue** N (Comput) Druckerwarteschlange f; **print speed** N (Comput) Druckgeschwindigkeit f; **print-through paper** N (Comput) Durchschlagpapier nt; **printwheel** ['prɪntwiːl] N (Comput) Typenrad nt

prior ['praɪə'] ADJ **(a)** vorherig; (= earlier) früher; **~ claim** Vorrecht nt (to auf +acc); **a ~ engagement** eine vorher getroffene Verabredung; **~ to sth** vor etw (dat); **~ to this/that** zuvor; **~ to going out** bevor ich/er etc ausging **(b)** (= stronger) obligation vorrangig

prioritization [praɪˌprɪtaɪˈzeɪʃən] N (= arranging in order of priority) Ordnung f nach Priorität

prioritize [praɪˈprɪtaɪz] VT **(a)** (= arrange in order of priority) der Priorität nach ordnen **(b)** (= make a priority) Priorität einräumen (+dat)

priority [praɪˈprɪtɪ] N Priorität f; (= thing having precedence) vorrangige Angelegenheit; **a top ~** eine Sache or Angelegenheit (von) höchster Priorität; **what is your top ~?** was steht bei Ihnen an erster Stelle?; **it must be given top ~** das muss vorrangig behandelt werden; **to give ~ to sth** einer Sache (dat) Priorität geben; **in strict order of ~** ganz nach Dringlichkeit; **we must get our priorities right** wir müssen unsere Prioritäten richtig setzen; **high/low on the list of priorities or the ~ list** oben/unten auf der Prioritätenliste

priority: priority share N (Fin) Vorzugsaktie f; **priority treatment** N Vorzugsbehandlung f; **to get ~** bevorzugt behandelt werden

prise, (US) **prize** [praɪz] VT **to ~ sth open** etw aufbrechen; **to ~ the lid up/off** den Deckel auf-/abbekommen; **to ~ sth out (of sth)** etw (aus etw) herausbekommen

prison ['prɪzn] **1** N (lit, fig) Gefängnis nt; **to be in ~** im Gefängnis sein; **to go to ~ for 5 years** für 5 Jahre ins Gefängnis gehen or wandern (inf); **to send sb to ~** jdn ins Gefängnis schicken **2** ATTR Gefängnis-

prisoner ['prɪznə'] N (lit, fig) Gefangene(r) mf; **to hold** or **keep sb ~** jdn gefangen halten; **to take sb ~** jdn gefangen nehmen; **~ of war** Kriegsgefangene(r) mf

prison officer N (Brit) Gefängnisaufseher(in) m(f)

pristine ['prɪstaɪn] ADJ beauty unberührt; condition makellos

privacy ['prɪvəsɪ, 'praɪvəsɪ] N Privatleben nt; **there is no ~ in these flats** in diesen Wohnungen kann man kein Privatleben führen; **in an open-plan office one has no ~** in einem Großraumbüro hat man keinen privaten Bereich; **in the ~ of one's own home** im eigenen Heim; **in the strictest ~** unter strengster Geheimhaltung

private ['praɪvɪt] **1** ADJ **(a)** privat; matter, affair vertraulich; (= secluded) place abgelegen; funeral, wedding im engsten Kreis; hearing, sitting nicht öffentlich; person reserviert; **it's just a ~ joke between us** das ist ein Privatwitz von uns; **~ and confidential** streng vertraulich; **he acted in a ~ capacity** er handelte als Privatperson; **to keep sth ~** etw für sich behalten; **his ~ life** sein Privatleben nt
(b) **~ address** Privatanschrift f; **~ car** Privatwagen m; **~ citizen** Privatperson f; **~ education** Ausbildung f in Privatschulen; **~ individual** Einzelne(r) mf; **~ limited company** ≈ Aktiengesellschaft f (die nicht an der Börse notiert ist); **~**

means Privatvermögen nt; **~ tutor** Privatlehrer(in) m(f); **~ ward** Privatstation f
2 N **(a)** (Mil) Gefreite(r) mf; **Private X** der Gefreite X
(b) **privates** PL (= genitals) Geschlechtsteile pl
(c) **in ~** privat; **we must talk in ~** wir müssen das unter uns besprechen

private: private company N Privatgesellschaft f; **private detective** N Privatdetektiv(in) m(f); **private enterprise** N Privatunternehmen nt; (= free enterprise) freies Unternehmertum; **Private Finance Initiative** N (Brit Pol) Regierungsprogramm zur Privatfinanzierung öffentlicher Projekte; **private investigator** N Privatdetektiv(in) m(f); **private liability** N (Comm) unbeschränkte Haftung

privately ['praɪvɪtlɪ] ADV **(a)** (= not publicly) privat; **the meeting was held ~** das Treffen wurde in kleinem Kreis abgehalten; **a ~ owned company** ein Unternehmen in Privatbesitz; **she is having the operation ~** sie lässt sich auf eigene Kosten operieren **(b)** (= secretly, personally, unofficially) persönlich; **but ~ he was very upset** doch innerlich war er sehr aufgebracht

private: private parts PL (= genitals) Geschlechtsteile pl; **private practice** N (Brit) Privatpraxis f; **he is in ~** er hat Privatpatienten; **private property** N Privateigentum nt; **private school** N Privatschule f; **private secretary** N Privatsekretär(in) m(f); **private sector** N privater Sektor; **private-sector company** N privatwirtschaftliches Unternehmen; **private tuition** N Privatunterricht m

privatization [praɪvətaɪˈzeɪʃən] N Privatisierung f

privatize ['praɪvətaɪz] VT privatisieren

privilege ['prɪvɪlɪdʒ] N Privileg nt, Sonderrecht nt; (= honour) Ehre f; (Parl) Immunität f

privileged ['prɪvɪlɪdʒd] ADJ person, classes privilegiert; claim, debt bevorrechtigt; **for a ~ few** für wenige Privilegierte; **to be ~ to do sth** das Privileg genießen, etw zu tun; **I was ~ to meet him** ich hatte die Ehre, ihm vorgestellt zu werden; **~ stock** Vorzugsaktien pl

Privy Council [ˌprɪvɪˈkaʊnsəl] N Geheimer Rat

prize¹ [praɪz] **1** N Preis m; **(there are) no ~s for guessing** (inf) dreimal darfst du raten **2** ADJ **(a)** entry, sheep preisgekrönt **(b)** **~ trophy** Siegestrophäe f; **~ medal** (Sieger)medaille f **(c)** (= offering a ~) **~ competition** Preisausschreiben nt **3** VT (hoch)schätzen; **to ~ sth highly** etw sehr or hoch schätzen; **to ~ sth above sth** etw über or vor etw (acc) stellen; **~d possession** wertvollster Besitz

prize² VT (US) = prise

prize: prize day N (Sch) (Tag m der) Preisverleihung f; **prize draw** N Lotterie f; **prize list** N Gewinnerliste f; **prize money** N (= cash prize) Geldpreis m; (in competition) Gewinn m; **prizewinner** N (Preis)gewinner(in) m(f); **prizewinning** ADJ preisgekrönt; **~ ticket** Gewinnlos nt

pro¹ [prəʊ] N (inf) Profi m

pro² **1** PREP (= in favour of) für **2** N **the ~s and cons** das Pro und Kontra

pro- PREF pro-, Pro-; **~-European** proeuropäisch

proactive [prəʊˈæktɪv] ADJ proaktiv

probability [prɒbəˈbɪlɪtɪ] N Wahrscheinlichkeit f; **in all ~** aller Wahrscheinlichkeit nach; **what's the ~ of that happening?** wie groß ist die Wahrscheinlichkeit, dass das geschieht?

probable ['prɒbəbl] ADJ wahrscheinlich

probably ['prɒbəblɪ] ADV wahrscheinlich; **most ~, more ~ than not** höchstwahrscheinlich; **not ~** höchstwahrscheinlich nicht

probation [prəˈbeɪʃən] N **(a)** (Jur) Bewährung f; **to put sb on ~ (for a year)** jdm (ein Jahr) Bewährung geben; **to be on ~** Bewährung haben **(b)** (of employee) Probe f; (= ~ period) Probezeit f

probationary [prəˈbeɪʃnərɪ] ADJ Probe-; **~ period** Probezeit f; (Jur) Bewährungsfrist f

probation officer N Bewährungshelfer(in) m(f)

probe [prəʊb] **1** N (= investigation) Untersuchung f (into +gen) **2** VT untersuchen; mystery ergründen **3** VI forschen (nach); **to ~ into sb's private life** in jds Privatleben (dat) herumschnüffeln

Be careful! **probe** *is not translated by the German word* **Probe**.

probing ['prəʊbɪŋ] **1** N Untersuchung *f*; **all this ~ into people's private affairs** dieses Herumschnüffeln in den privaten Angelegenheiten der Leute **2** ADJ prüfend

problem ['prɒbləm] N Problem *nt*; (= *problematic area*) Problematik *f*; **what's the ~?** wo fehlt's?; **he's got a drink(ing) ~** er trinkt (zu viel); **to have no ~ with sth** kein Problem mit etw haben; **I had no ~ in getting the money** ich habe das Geld ohne Schwierigkeiten bekommen; **no ~!** (*inf*) kein Problem!; **~ area** Problembereich *m*

problematic(al) [prɒblə'mætɪk(əl)] ADJ problematisch

problem: problem-oriented ADJ (*Comput*) problemorientiert; **problem-solving** N Problemlösung *f*

procedure [prə'siːdʒə'] N Verfahren *nt*; **parliamentary ~** parlamentarisches Verfahren; **what would be the correct ~ in such a case?** wie geht man in einem solchen Falle vor?; **business ~** geschäftliche Verfahrensweise; **rules of ~** Vorschriften *pl*; **~-oriented** (*Comput*) prozedurorientiert

proceed [prə'siːd] **1** VI (a) (*form:* = *go*) **vehicles must ~ with caution** vorsichtig fahren!; **please ~ to gate 3** begeben Sie sich zum Ausgang 3
(b) (*form:* = *go on*) weitergehen; (*vehicle, by vehicle*) weiterfahren
(c) (= *continue*) fortfahren; **can we now ~ to the next item on the agenda?** können wir jetzt zum nächsten Punkt der Tagesordnung übergehen?; **they ~ed with their plan** sie führten ihren Plan weiter; (= *start*) sie gingen nach ihrem Plan vor; **everything is ~ing smoothly** alles läuft bestens; **negotiations are ~ing well** die Verhandlungen kommen gut voran; **you may ~** (= *speak*) Sie haben das Wort
(d) (= *set about sth*) vorgehen; **our best way of ~ing would be to ask him** am besten wär es, wenn wir ihn fragten **2** VT **to ~ to do sth** (dann) etw tun

proceeding [prə'siːdɪŋ] N (a) (= *action*) Vorgehen *nt*
(b) proceedings PL (= *function*) Veranstaltung *f*
(c) proceedings PL (*esp Jur*) Verfahren *nt*; **court ~s** Gerichtsverhandlung *f*; **to take/start ~s against sb** gegen jdn gerichtlich vorgehen

proceeds ['prəʊsiːdz] PL (= *yield*) Ertrag *m*; (*from sale, raffle*) Erlös *m*; (= *takings*) Einnahmen *pl*

process ['prəʊses] **1** N Prozess *m*; (= *specific method, technique, Jur also, Ind also*) Verfahren *nt*; **in the ~** dabei; **in the ~ of doing sth** dabei sein, etw zu tun; **~ cycle** (*Ind*) Fertigungszyklus *m*; **~ planning** (*Ind*) Produktionsplanung *f* **2** VT **raw materials, data, waste** verarbeiten; *food* konservieren; *application, loan* bearbeiten; *film* entwickeln; *applicants* abfertigen

processing ['prəʊsesɪŋ] N (*of raw materials, data, waste*) Verarbeitung *f*; (*of food*) Konservierung *f*; (*of application, loan*) Bearbeitung *f*; (*of film*) Entwicklung *f*; (*of applicants*) Abfertigung *f*

processing: processing language N (*Comput*) Prozesssprache *f*; **processing plant** N Aufbereitungsanlage *f*; **processing speed** N (*Comput*) Verarbeitungsgeschwindigkeit *f*; **processing unit** N (*Comput*) Prozessor *m*

procession [prə'seʃən] N (*organized*) Umzug *m*; (= *line of people, cars etc*) Reihe *f*, Schlange *f*; **funeral/carnival ~** Trauer-/Karnevalszug *m*

processor ['prəʊsesə'] N (*Comput*) Prozessor *m*

proclaim [prə'kleɪm] VT erklären; *revolution* ausrufen; **the day had been ~ed a holiday** der Tag war zum Feiertag erklärt worden

proclamation [prɒklə'meɪʃən] N (a) (= *act*) (*of war*) Erklärung *f*; (*of laws, measures*) Verkündung *f*; (*of state of emergency*) Ausrufung *f* **(b)** (= *thing proclaimed*) Proklamation *f*

procrastinate [prəʊ'kræstɪneɪt] VI zaudern; **he always ~s** er schiebt die Dinge immer vor sich (*dat*) her

procrastination [prəʊkræstɪ'neɪʃən] N Zaudern *nt*

procreate ['prəʊkrɪeɪt] VI sich fortpflanzen

procreation [prəʊkrɪ'eɪʃən] N Fortpflanzung *f*

procure [prə'kjʊə'] VT (= *obtain*) beschaffen; (= *bring about*) herbeiführen; **to ~ sth for sb/oneself** jdm/sich etw beschaffen

prod [prɒd] **1** N (a) (*lit*) Stoß *m*; **to give sb a ~** jdm einen Stoß versetzen
(b) (*fig*) Anstoß *m*; **to give sb a ~** jdn anstoßen
2 VT (a) (*lit*) stoßen; **he ~ded the hay with his stick** er stach

mit seinem Stock ins Heu; **..., he said, ~ding the map with his finger ...**, sagte er und stieß mit dem Finger auf die Karte
(b) (*fig*) anspornen (*into sth* zu etw); **to ~ sb into action** jdm einen Stoß geben
3 VI stoßen; **he ~ded at the picture with his finger** er stieß mit dem Finger auf das Bild

prodigiously [prə'dɪdʒəslɪ] ADV *talented etc* außerordentlich

prodigy ['prɒdɪdʒɪ] N Wunder *nt*; **child *or* infant ~** Wunderkind *nt*

produce ['prɒdjuːs] **1** N, NO PL (*Agr*) Erzeugnisse *pl*; **Italian ~, ~ of Italy** italienisches Erzeugnis
2 [prə'djuːs] VT (a) (= *yield*) produzieren; *energy, heat* erzeugen; *crop* abwerfen; (= *create*) *book, article* schreiben; *painting* anfertigen; *ideas, masterpiece* hervorbringen; *interest, return on capital* abwerfen; **the sort of environment that ~s criminal types** das Milieu, das Kriminelle hervorbringt
(b) (= *bring forward, show*) *gift, wallet etc* hervorholen (*from, out of* aus); *pistol* ziehen (*from, out of* aus); *proof, results* liefern; *effect* erzielen; *witness* beibringen; *ticket, documents* vorzeigen; **if we don't ~ results soon** wenn wir nicht bald Ergebnisse vorweisen können
(c) *play* inszenieren; *film* produzieren
(d) (= *cause*) hervorrufen
3 [prə'djuːs] VI (*factory, mine*) produzieren; (*land*) Ertrag bringen; (*tree*) tragen

producer [prə'djuːsə'] N Produzent(in) *m(f)*; (*Theat*) Regisseur(in) *m(f)*; **~ goods** Produktionsgüter *pl*

-producing [-prə'djuːsɪŋ] ADJ SUF produzierend; **oil-producing country** Öl produzierendes Land; **wine-producing area** Weinregion *f*

product ['prɒdʌkt] N Produkt *nt*; **food ~s** Nahrungsmittel *pl*; **~ costs** (*Ind*) Fertigungskosten *pl*; **~ cycle** (*Ind*) Produktionszyklus *m*; **~ liability** (*Ind*) Produkthaftung *f*; **~ line** (*Ind*) Produktlinie *f*; **~ mix** (*Ind*) Sortimentsstruktur *f*, Produktpalette *f*; **~ placement** Produktplacement *nt*; **~ portfolio** (*Ind*) Produktpalette *f*; **~ range** (*Ind*) Sortiment *nt*

production [prə'dʌkʃən] N (a) Produktion *f*; (*of energy, heat*) Erzeugung *f*; (*of crop*) Anbau *m*; (*of book, article*) Schreiben *nt*; (*of painting*) Anfertigung *f*; (*of ideas, masterpiece*) Hervorbringung *f*; **to put sth into ~** die Produktion von etw aufnehmen; **when the new car goes into ~** wenn der neue Wagen in die Produktion geht; **is it still in ~?** wird das noch hergestellt?; **to take sth out of ~** etw aus der Produktion nehmen
(b) (= *bringing forward, showing*) (*of ticket, documents*) Vorzeigen *nt*; (*of proof*) Lieferung *f*; (*of witness*) Beibringung *f*; **on ~ of this ticket** gegen Vorlage dieser Eintrittskarte
(c) (*of play*) Inszenierung *f*; (*of film*) Produktion *f*

production: production capacity N Produktionskapazität *f*; **production controller** N (*Brit*) Produktionsleiter(in) *m(f)*; **production costs** PL Produktionskosten *pl*; **production department** N Produktionsabteilung *f*; **production engineer** N Betriebsingenieur(in) *m(f)*; **production line** N Fertigungsstraße *f*; **production manager** N Produktionsleiter(in) *m(f)*; **production method** N Produktionsverfahren *nt*; **production model** N (*of car*) Serienmodell *nt*; **production process** N (*Ind*) Produktionsverlauf *m*; **production run** N (*Ind*) Produktionsserie *f*

productive [prə'dʌktɪv] ADJ produktiv; *land* fruchtbar; *business, shop* rentabel; **to lead a ~ life** ein aktives Leben führen; **I don't think it would be very ~ to argue with him** ich halte es nicht für sehr lohnenswert, mit ihm zu streiten (*inf*)

productively [prə'dʌktɪvlɪ] ADV produktiv

productivity [prɒdʌk'tɪvɪtɪ] N Produktivität *f*; (*of land*) Fruchtbarkeit *f*; (*of business, shop*) Rentabilität *f*

productivity: productivity agreement N Produktivitätsvereinbarung *f*; **productivity bonus** N Leistungszulage *f*; **productivity incentive** N Leistungsanreiz *m*

profess [prə'fes] **1** VT (a) *faith, belief etc* sich bekennen zu
(b) *interest, distaste* bekunden; *belief, disbelief* kundtun; *weakness, ignorance* zugeben; **she ~es to be a good driver** sie behauptet, eine gute Fahrerin zu sein **2** VR **to ~ oneself satisfied** seine Zufriedenheit bekunden (*with über* +*acc*)

profession [prə'feʃən] N (a) Beruf *m*; **the medical/teaching ~** der Arzt-/Lehrberuf; **by ~** von Beruf **(b) the medical ~** die

Ärzteschaft; **the architectural ~** die Architekten pl; **the whole ~ was outraged** der gesamte Berufsstand war empört **(c)** (= declaration, also Eccl) Gelübde nt; **~ of faith** Glaubensbekenntnis nt; **a ~ of love** eine Liebeserklärung

professional [prəˈfeʃənl] **1** ADJ **(a)** beruflich; opinion fachlich; football, tennis professionell; **their ~ ability** ihre beruflichen Fähigkeiten; **~ army** Berufsarmee m; **his ~ life** sein Berufsleben; **our relationship is purely ~** unsere Beziehung ist rein geschäftlich(er Natur); **he's now doing it on a ~ basis** er macht das jetzt hauptberuflich; **in his ~ capacity as a doctor** in seiner Eigenschaft als Arzt; **to be a ~ singer** etc von Beruf Sänger etc sein; **the pub is used mainly by ~ men** das Lokal wird hauptsächlich von Angehörigen der gehobenen Berufe besucht; **to seek/take ~ advice** fachmännischen Rat suchen/einholen; **to turn** or **go ~** Profi werden **(b)** (= skilled) piece of work etc fachgerecht; worker, person gewissenhaft; company, approach professionell; (= expert) performance kompetent; **he handled the matter in a very ~ manner** er hat die Angelegenheit in sehr kompetenter Weise gehandhabt; **that's not a very ~ attitude to your work** das ist doch nicht die richtige Einstellung (zu Ihrem Beruf) **2** N Profi m

professionalism [prəˈfeʃnəlɪzəm] N Professionalismus m; (of job, piece of work) Perfektion f

professionally [prəˈfeʃnəlɪ] ADV beruflich; (= in accomplished manner) fachmännisch; **he sings ~** er ist ein professioneller Sänger; **now he plays ~** jetzt ist er Berufsspieler; **to know sb ~** jdn beruflich kennen

professor [prəˈfesəʳ] N Professor(in) m(f); (US: = lecturer of highest rank) Dozent(in) m(f)

proficiency [prəˈfɪʃənsɪ] N **her ~ at teaching/as a secretary** ihre Tüchtigkeit als Lehrerin/Sekretärin; **his ~ in English** seine Englischkenntnisse; **her ~ in translating** ihr Können als Übersetzerin; **level of ~** Leistungsstand m

proficient [prəˈfɪʃənt] ADJ tüchtig; **he is just about ~ in German** seine Deutschkenntnisse reichen gerade aus; **how long would it take to become ~ in Japanese?** wie lange würde es dauern, bis man Japanisch beherrscht?

profile [ˈprəʊfaɪl] **1** N Profil nt; (= picture, photograph) Profilbild nt; (= biographical ~) Porträt nt; **in ~** im Profil; **to keep a low ~** sich zurückhalten **2** VT (biographically) porträtieren

profit [ˈprɒfɪt] **1** N **(a)** (Comm) Gewinn m; **there's not much (of a) ~ in this business** dieses Geschäft wirft kaum Gewinn ab; **~ and loss account** (Brit) or **statement** (US) Gewinn-und-Verlustrechnung f; **to make a ~ (out of** or **on sth)** (mit etw) ein Geschäft machen; **to show** or **yield a ~** einen Gewinn verzeichnen; **to sell sth at a ~** etw mit Gewinn verkaufen; **the business is now running at a ~** das Geschäft rentiert sich jetzt; **~ per employee** Gewinn m pro Mitarbeiter **(b)** (fig) Nutzen m; **you might well learn something to your ~** Sie können etwas lernen, was Ihnen von Nutzen ist **2** VI profitieren (by, from von), Nutzen ziehen (by, from aus)

profitability [ˌprɒfɪtəˈbɪlɪtɪ] N Rentabilität f

profitability study N Rentabilitätsstudie f

profitable [ˈprɒfɪtəbl] ADJ (Comm) Gewinn bringend; (fig) nützlich

profitably [ˈprɒfɪtəblɪ] ADV (Comm) Gewinn bringend; (fig) nützlich

profit centre, (US) **profit center** N Profitcenter nt

profiteer [ˌprɒfɪˈtɪəʳ] N Profitmacher(in) m(f)

profiteering [ˌprɒfɪˈtɪərɪŋ] N Wucher m

profitless [ˈprɒfɪtlɪs] ADJ **(a)** (Comm) unrentabel **(b)** discussion, exercise zwecklos

profit: profit-making ADJ rentabel; (= profit-orientated) auf Gewinn gerichtet; **profit margin** N Gewinnspanne f; **profit mark-up** N (Comm) Gewinnzuschlag m; **profit-motivated** ADJ gewinnorientiert; **profit motive** N Gewinnstreben nt; **profit-oriented** N gewinnorientiert; incentive programme mit Gewinnbeteiligung; **profit-seeking** ADJ gewinnorientiert; **profit-sharing** N Gewinnbeteiligung f; **~ scheme** Gewinnbeteiligungsplan m; **profit warning** N (Comm) Gewinnwarnung f

pro forma (invoice) [ˌprəʊˈfɔːməˈ(ɪnvɔɪs)] N Pro-forma-Rechnung f

profound [prəˈfaʊnd] ADJ sorrow, love, concern tief; thought, idea tiefsinnig; book gehaltvoll; thinker, knowledge, experience, regret tief gehend; hatred, mistrust, belief, respect, ignorance tief sitzend; effect, influence, implications weit tragend; indifference völlig; changes tief greifend

profoundly [prəˈfaʊndlɪ] ADV different zutiefst; **~ deaf** vollkommen taub

profusely [prəˈfjuːslɪ] ADV bleed, sweat stark; thank, praise überschwänglich; **he apologized ~** er bat vielmals um Entschuldigung

profusion [prəˈfjuːʒən] N Überfülle f

prognosis [prɒgˈnəʊsɪs] N, pl **prognoses** [prɒgˈnəʊsiːz] Prognose f

program [ˈprəʊgræm] **1** N **(a)** (Comput) Programm nt **(b)** (US) = **programme 2** VT computer programmieren

programmable [ˈprəʊgræməbl] ADJ programmierbar

programme, (US) **program** [ˈprəʊgræm] **1** N Programm nt; **what's the ~ for tomorrow?** was steht für morgen auf dem Programm? **2** VT programmieren

programmer [ˈprəʊgræməʳ] N Programmierer(in) m(f)

programming [ˈprəʊgræmɪŋ] N Programmieren nt; **~ language** Programmiersprache f

progress [ˈprəʊgres] **1** N NO PL (= movement forwards) Vorwärtskommen nt; **we made slow ~ through the mud** wir kamen im Schlamm nur langsam vorwärts; **in ~** im Gange; **"silence please, meeting in ~"** „Sitzung! Ruhe bitte"; **the work still in ~** die noch zu erledigende Arbeit **(b)** NO PL (= advance) Fortschritt m; **to make (good/slow) ~** (gute/langsame) Fortschritte machen; **I want to see some ~!** ich möchte Fortschritte sehen! **2** [prəˈgres] VI **(a)** (= move, go forward) sich vorwärts bewegen **(b)** (in time) **as the work ~es** mit dem Fortschreiten der Arbeit; **as the game ~ed** im Laufe des Spiels; **while negotiations were actually ~ing** während die Verhandlungen im Gange waren **(c)** (= improve, make ~) Fortschritte machen; **how far have you ~ed since our last meeting?** wie weit sind Sie seit unserer letzten Sitzung gekommen?; **as you ~ through the ranks** bei Ihrem Aufstieg durch die Ränge **3** [prəˈgres] VT (esp Comm) matters etc weiterverfolgen

progression [prəˈgreʃən] N Folge f; (= development) Entwicklung f; (in taxation) Progression f; (of discount rates etc) Staffelung f; **sales have shown a continuous ~** im Absatz wurde eine stete Aufwärtsentwicklung verzeichnet; **his ~ from a junior clerk to managing director** sein Aufstieg vom kleinen Angestellten zum Direktor

progressive [prəˈgresɪv] ADJ (= increasing) zunehmend; disease, action fortschreitend; taxation progressiv

progressively [prəˈgresɪvlɪ] ADV zunehmend

progress report N Fortschrittsbericht m

prohibit [prəˈhɪbɪt] VT untersagen; **to ~ sb from doing sth** jdm untersagen, etw zu tun; **"smoking ~ed"** „Rauchen verboten"

prohibitive [prəˈhɪbɪtɪv] ADJ unerschwinglich; **the costs of producing this model have become ~** die Kosten für die Herstellung dieses Modells sind untragbar geworden

prohibitively [prəˈhɪbɪtɪvlɪ] ADV ungeheuerlich; **~ expensive** unerschwinglich (teuer)

project¹ [ˈprɒdʒekt] N Projekt nt; (= scheme) Vorhaben nt; (Sch, Univ) Referat nt; (in primary school) Arbeit f; **~ director** Projektleiter(in) m(f); **~ engineer** Projektingenieur(in) m(f)

project² [prəˈdʒekt] **1** VT **(a)** film projizieren; **to ~ one's emotions onto somebody else** seine Emotionen auf einen anderen projizieren; **to ~ one's voice** seine Stimme zum Tragen bringen **(b)** plan (voraus)planen; costs überschlagen; figures projizieren; (esp in elections) hochrechnen **(c)** (= propel) abschießen; **to ~ a missile into space** eine Rakete in den Weltraum schießen **2** VI (= jut out) hervorragen (from aus)

project-based [ˈprɒdʒektbeɪsd] ADJ projektbezogen

projection [prəˈdʒekʃən] N **(a)** (of films, guilt, feelings) Projektion f **(b)** (= estimate) (Voraus)planung f; (of cost) Überschlagung f; (of figures, esp in elections) Hochrechnung f

projectionist [prəˈdʒekʃnɪst] N Filmvorführer(in) m(f)

projector [prəˈdʒektəʳ] N (Film) Projektor m

proletarian [ˌprəʊləˈteərɪən] ADJ proletarisch

proletariat [ˌprəʊləˈteərɪət] N Proletariat nt

pro-life [ˌprəʊˈlaɪf] ADJ gegen Abtreibung pred

proliferate [prəˈlɪfəreɪt] VI *(number)* sich stark erhöhen
proliferation [prə‚lɪfəˈreɪʃən] N *(in numbers)* starke Erhöhung; *(of nuclear weapons)* Weitergabe *f*
prolific [prəˈlɪfɪk] ADJ **(a)** fruchtbar; *writer* sehr produktiv; *scorer* erfolgreich **(b)** (= *abundant*) üppig
prologue, *(US)* **prolog** [ˈprəʊlɒg] N Prolog *m*; *(of book)* Vorwort *nt*
prolong [prəˈlɒŋ] VT verlängern; *(unpleasantly)* hinauszögern; *(Fin)* draft prolongieren
prolongation [‚prəʊlɒŋˈgeɪʃən] N *(Fin: of draft)* Prolongierung *f*
prom [prɒm] N *(inf)* *(Brit* = *concert)* Konzert *nt* *(in gelockertem Rahmen); (US* = *ball)* Studenten-/Schülerball *m*

promenade [‚prɒmɪˈnɑːd] N *(esp Brit* = *esplanade)* (Strand)promenade *f*; *(US* = *ball)* Studenten-/Schülerball *m*; **~ concert** *(Brit)* Konzert *nt* *(in gelockertem Rahmen)*
prominence [ˈprɒmɪnəns] N *(of ideas, beliefs)* Beliebtheit *f*; *(of writer, politician etc)* Bekanntheit *f*; **the undisputed ~ of his position as ...** seine unbestritten führende Position als ...; **he came** *or* **rose to ~ in the Cuba affair** er wurde durch die Kuba-Affäre bekannt
prominent [ˈprɒmɪnənt] ADJ **(a)** *cheekbones, teeth* vorstehend *attr*; *crag* vorspringend *attr*; **to be ~** vorstehen/-springen **(b)** *markings* auffällig; *feature, characteristic* hervorstechend; *position, personality, publisher* prominent; **put it in a ~ position** stellen Sie es deutlich sichtbar hin **(c)** *role* führend; (= *large, significant)* wichtig
prominently [ˈprɒmɪnəntlɪ] ADV *display, place* deutlich sichtbar; **he figured ~ in the case** er spielte in dem Fall eine bedeutende Rolle
promiscuity [‚prɒmɪˈskjuːɪtɪ] N Promiskuität *f*, häufiger Partnerwechsel
promiscuous [prəˈmɪskjʊəs] ADJ *(sexually)* promisk; **to be ~** häufig den Partner wechseln; **~ behaviour** häufiger Partnerwechsel
promiscuously [prəˈmɪskjʊəslɪ] ADV *(sexually)* promisk
promise [ˈprɒmɪs] **1** N **(a)** Versprechen *nt*; **their ~ of help** ihr Versprechen zu helfen; **~ of marriage** Eheversprechen *nt*; **is that a ~?** ganz bestimmt?; **to make sb a ~** jdm ein Versprechen geben; **I'm not making any ~s** versprechen kann ich nichts; **~s, ~s!** Versprechen, nichts als Versprechen! **(b)** (= *hope, prospect)* Hoffnung *f*; **to show ~** zu den besten Hoffnungen berechtigen
2 VT versprechen; (= *forecast, augur)* hindeuten auf (+*acc*); **to ~ (sb) to do sth** (jdm) versprechen, etw zu tun; **to ~ sb sth**, **to ~ sth to sb** jdm etw versprechen; **to ~ sb the earth** jdm das Blaue vom Himmel herunter versprechen; **~ me one thing** versprich mir eins; **I won't do it again, I ~ you** ich werde es nie wieder tun, das verspreche ich Ihnen; **it ~d to be another scorching day** der Tag versprach wieder heiß zu werden
3 VR **(do you) ~?** versprichst du es?; **~!** (= *I will you ~)* versprichs mir, ehrlich?; (= *I ~)* ehrlich!; **I'll try, but I'm not promising** ich werde es versuchen, aber ich kann nichts versprechen
4 VR **to ~ oneself sth** sich (*dat*) etw versprechen; **I've ~d myself never to do it again** ich habe mir geschworen, dass ich das nicht noch einmal mache
promising ADJ, **promisingly** ADV [ˈprɒmɪsɪŋ, -lɪ] viel versprechend
promote [prəˈməʊt] VT **(a)** *(in rank)* befördern; **our team was ~d** *(Ftbl)* unsere Mannschaft ist aufgestiegen **(b)** (= *foster)* fördern **(c)** (= *advertise)* werben für; (= *put on the market)* auf den Markt bringen
promoter [prəˈməʊtəʳ] N Promoter(in) *m(f)*

promotion [prəˈməʊʃən] N **(a)** *(in rank)* Beförderung *f*; *(of football team)* Aufstieg *m*; **to get** *or* **win ~** befördert werden; *(football team)* aufsteigen **(b)** (= *fostering)* Förderung *f* **(c)** (= *advertising)* Werbung *f* *(of* für); (= *advertising campaign)* Werbekampagne *f*; (= *marketing)* Einführung *f* auf dem Markt; **~ drive** Werbekampagne *f*; **~ scheme** Werbeaktion *f*
prompt [prɒmpt] **1** ADJ (+*ER)* prompt; *action* unverzüglich; **he is always very ~** (= *on time)* er ist immer sehr pünktlich **2** ADV **at 6 o'clock ~** pünktlich um 6 Uhr **3** VT **(a)** (= *motivate)* veranlassen *(to* zu); **to ~ sb to do sth** jdn (dazu) veranlassen, etw zu tun; **what ~ed you to do it?** was hat Sie dazu veranlasst?; **he was ~ed purely by a desire to help** sein Beweggrund war einzig und allein der Wunsch zu helfen; **in the hope that this might ~ a discussion** in der Hoffnung, dass das eine Diskussion in Gang setzen wird **(b)** *memories, feelings* wecken **(c)** (= *help with speech)* vorsagen *(sb* jdm); *(Theat)* soufflieren *(sb* jdm); **the teacher had to keep ~ing him** der Lehrer musste ihm immer wieder Hilfestellung geben **4** VI *(Theat)* soufflieren **5** N **(a)** (= *reminder, encouragement)* **to give sb a ~** jdn anstoßen **(b)** *(Comput)* Prompt *m*, Eingabeaufforderung *f*
prompter [ˈprɒmptəʳ] N Souffleur *m*, Souffleuse *f*
promptly [ˈprɒmptlɪ] ADV **(a)** prompt; **of course he ~ forgot it all** er hat natürlich prompt alles vergessen; **they left ~ at 6** sie gingen Punkt 6 Uhr **(b)** (= *without further ado)* **she ~ gave him a left hook** sie versetzte ihm unverzüglich einen linken Haken
promptness [ˈprɒmptnɪs] N Promptheit *f*
prompt note N *(Comm)* Ermahnung *f*
prone [prəʊn] ADJ **(a)** (= *lying)* **to be** *or* **lie ~** auf dem Bauch liegen; **in a ~ position** in Bauchlage **(b)** (= *liable)* **to be ~ to sth** zu etw neigen; **to be ~ to do sth** dazu neigen, etw zu tun
proneness [ˈprəʊnnɪs] N Neigung *f (to* zu)
prong [prɒŋ] N Zacke *f*
-pronged [-prɒŋd] ADJ SUF -zackig; **three-pronged** dreizackig; **a three-pronged attack** ein Angriff mit drei Spitzen; **a two-pronged approach** eine zweigleisige Vorgehensweise
pronoun [ˈprəʊnaʊn] N Pronomen *nt*
pronounce [prəˈnaʊns] VT **(a)** *word etc* aussprechen; **I find Russian hard to ~** ich finde die russische Aussprache schwierig **(b)** (= *declare)* verkünden; **the doctors ~d him unfit for work** die Ärzte erklärten ihn für arbeitsunfähig; **to ~ oneself in favour of/against sth** sich für/gegen etw aussprechen; **to ~ sentence** das Urteil verkünden
pronounceable [prəˈnaʊnsəbl] ADJ aussprechbar
pronounced [prəˈnaʊnst] ADJ ausgesprochen; *accent, flavour* ausgeprägt; **he has a ~ limp** er hinkt sehr stark
pronouncement [prəˈnaʊnsmənt] N Erklärung *f*; **to make a ~** eine Erklärung abgeben
pronunciation [prə‚nʌnsɪˈeɪʃən] N Aussprache *f*
proof [pruːf] **1** N **(a)** Beweis *m (of* für); **you'll need more ~ than that** die Beweise reichen nicht aus; **as ~ of** zum Beweis für; **that is ~ that ...** das ist der Beweis dafür, dass ...; **can you give us any ~ of that?** können Sie (uns) dafür Beweise liefern?; **show me your ~** beweisen Sie (mir) das; **~ of purchase** Kaufbeleg *m* **(b)** *(of alcohol)* Alkoholgehalt *m*; **70% ~ ≈ 40 Vol-%** **2** ADJ **~ against inflation** inflationssicher
proof: **proofread** VTI Korrektur lesen; **proofreader** N Korrektor(in) *m(f)*; **proofreading** N Korrekturlesen *nt*
prop¹ [prɒp] **1** N *(lit)* Stütze *f*; *(fig)* Halt *m* **2** VT **to ~ the door open** die Tür offen halten; **to ~ oneself/sth against sth** sich/etw gegen etw lehnen
➤ **prop up** VT SEP stützen; *tunnel, wall* abstützen; *organization* unterstützen; **to prop oneself/sth up against sth** sich/etw gegen etw lehnen; **to prop oneself up on sth** sich auf etw *(acc)* stützen; **he spends most of his time propping up the bar** *(inf)* er hängt die meiste Zeit an der Bar
prop² ABBR *of* **proprietor**
propaganda [‚prɒpəˈgændə] N Propaganda *f*
propagandist [‚prɒpəˈgændɪst] ADJ propagandistisch
propagate [ˈprɒpəgeɪt] VT (= *disseminate)* verbreiten; *views* propagieren
propagation [‚prɒpəˈgeɪʃən] N (= *dissemination)* Verbreitung *f*; *(of views)* Propagierung *f*

propane ['prəʊpeɪn] N Propan nt

propel [prə'pel] VT antreiben; (fuel) betreiben

propeller [prə'pelə'] N Propeller m

proper ['prɒpə'] ADJ **(a)** (= actual) eigentlich; **is that a ~ policeman's helmet?** ist das ein richtiger Polizeihelm?; **he's never had a ~ job** er hat noch nie einen richtigen Job gehabt; **not in Berlin ~** nicht in Berlin selbst
(b) (= fitting, inf. = real, utter) richtig; (inf. = thorough) beating tüchtig (inf); **in the ~ way** richtig; **it's only right and ~** es ist nur recht und billig; **to do the ~ thing** das tun, was sich gehört; **the ~ thing to do would be to apologize** es gehört sich eigentlich, dass man sich entschuldigt; **it wasn't really the ~ thing to say** es war ziemlich unpassend, das zu sagen
(c) (= seemly) anständig; **what is ~** was sich gehört
(d) (= prim and ~) korrekt

properly ['prɒpəlɪ] ADV **(a)** (= correctly) richtig **(b)** (in seemly fashion) anständig; **to conduct oneself ~** sich korrekt verhalten **(c)** (= justifiably) zu Recht

proper name, proper noun N Eigenname m

property ['prɒpətɪ] N **(a)** (= characteristic, Philos) Eigenschaft f; **it has healing properties** es besitzt heilende Kräfte
(b) = thing owned) Eigentum nt; **government ~** Regierungseigentum nt; **common ~** (lit) gemeinsames Eigentum, (fig) Gemeingut nt; **to become the ~ of sb** in jds Eigentum (acc) übergehen
(c) (= building) Haus nt; (= office) Gebäude nt; (= land) Besitztum nt; (= estate) Besitz m; **this house is a very valuable ~** dieses Haus ist ein sehr wertvoller Besitz; **~ in London is dearer** die Preise auf dem Londoner Immobilienmarkt sind höher

property: property developer N Häusermakler(in) m(f); **property market** N Immobilienmarkt m; **property owner** N Haus- und Grundbesitzer(in) m(f); **property tax** N Vermögenssteuer f

prophecy ['prɒfɪsɪ] N Prophezeiung f

prophesy ['prɒfɪsaɪ] **1** VT prophezeien **2** VI Prophezeiungen machen

prophet ['prɒfɪt] N Prophet(in) m(f)

prophetess ['prɒfɪtɪs] N Prophetin f

prophetic ADJ, **prophetically** ADV [prə'fetɪk, -əlɪ] prophetisch

proponent [prə'pəʊnənt] N Befürworter(in) m(f)

proportion [prə'pɔːʃən] **1** N **(a)** (in number) Verhältnis nt (of x to y zwischen x und y); (in size) Proportionen pl; **~s** (= size) Ausmaß nt; (of building) Ausmaße pl; (relative to one another: of building etc) Proportionen pl; **to be in/out of ~ (to one another)** (in number) im richtigen/nicht im richtigen Verhältnis zueinander stehen; (in size, Art) in den Proportionen stimmen/nicht stimmen; (in time, effort etc) im richtigen/in keinem Verhältnis zueinander stehen; **to be in/ out of ~ to** or **with sth** im Verhältnis/in keinem Verhältnis zu etw stehen; (in size, Art) in den Proportionen zu etw passen/ nicht zu etw passen; **in direct/inverse ~ to sth** in direktem/ umgekehrtem Verhältnis zu etw; **to get sth in ~** (Art) etw proportional richtig darstellen; (fig) etw objektiv betrachten; **he has let it all get out of ~** (fig) er hat den Blick für die Proportionen verloren; **it's out of all ~!** das geht über jedes Maß hinaus!; **sense of ~** (lit, fig) Sinn m für Proportionen
(b) (= part, amount) Teil m; **a certain ~ of the population** ein bestimmter Teil der Bevölkerung; **the ~ of drinkers in our society is rising constantly** der Anteil der Trinker in unserer Gesellschaft nimmt ständig zu; **what ~ of the industry is in private hands?** wie groß ist der Anteil der Industrie, der sich in Privathand befindet?
2 VT **a nicely ~ed woman** eine wohlproportionierte Frau

proportional [prə'pɔːʃənl] ADJ proportional (to zu)

proportionally [prə'pɔːʃnəlɪ] ADV proportional; **more, less ~** entsprechend

proportional representation N (Pol) Verhältniswahlrecht nt

proportionate [prə'pɔːʃnɪt] ADJ proportional

proportionately [prə'pɔːʃnɪtlɪ] ADV proportional; **more, less ~** entsprechend

proposal [prə'pəʊzl] N **(a)** Vorschlag m (on, about zu); (= ~ of marriage) (Heirats)antrag m; **to make sb a ~** jdm einen Vorschlag/(Heirats)antrag machen; **~ form** (Insur)

Antragsformular nt **(b)** (= act of proposing: of motion) Einbringen nt

propose [prə'pəʊz] **1** VT **(a)** (= suggest) vorschlagen; motion einbringen; **to ~ marriage to sb** jdm einen (Heirats)antrag machen **(b)** (= have in mind) beabsichtigen; **how do you ~ to pay for it?** wie wollen Sie das bezahlen? **2** VI einen (Heirats)antrag machen (to +dat)

proposer [prə'pəʊzə'] N (in debate) Antragsteller(in) m(f)

proposition [prɒpə'zɪʃən] N **(a)** (= proposal) Vorschlag m; (= argument) These f; **a paying ~** ein lohnendes Geschäft
(b) (= objective) Unternehmen nt; (= prospect) Aussicht f
2 VT **he ~ed me** er hat mich gefragt, ob ich mit ihm schlafen würde

proprietary [prə'praɪətərɪ] ADJ **~ rights** Besitzrecht nt; **~ drug** Markenpräparat nt

proprietary: proprietary article N Markenartikel m; **proprietary name** N Markenname m

proprietor [prə'praɪətə'] N (of pub, hotel, patent) Inhaber(in) m(f); (of house, newspaper) Besitzer(in) m(f)

proprietress [prə'praɪətrɪs] N (of pub, hotel, patent) Inhaberin f; (of house, newspaper) Besitzerin f

propriety [prə'praɪətɪ] N (= correctness) Korrektheit f, Richtigkeit f; (= decency) Anstand m

propulsion [prə'pʌlʃən] N Antrieb m

pro rata ['prəʊ'rɑːtə] ADJ, ADV anteil(s)mäßig; **on a ~ basis** auf einer proportionalen Basis

prorate ['prəʊreɪt] VT (US) anteil(s)mäßig aufteilen

proscribe [prəʊ'skraɪb] VT (= forbid) verbieten

prose [prəʊz] N Prosa f; (= style) Stil m

prosecute ['prɒsɪkjuːt] **1** VT strafrechtlich verfolgen (for wegen); **prosecuting counsel** or **attorney** (US) Staatsanwalt m/-anwältin f; **"trespassers will be ~d"** „widerrechtliches Betreten wird strafrechtlich verfolgt" **2** VI Anzeige erstatten; **Mr Jones, prosecuting, said ...** Herr Jones, der Vertreter der Anklage, sagte ...

prosecution [prɒsɪ'kjuːʃən] N (Jur) (= act of prosecuting) strafrechtliche Verfolgung; (in court: = case, side) Anklage f (for wegen); **(the) counsel for the ~** die Anklage(vertretung); **witness for the ~** Zeuge m/Zeugin f der Anklage

prosecutor ['prɒsɪkjuːtə'] N Ankläger(in) m(f)

prospect ['prɒspekt] N **(a)** (= outlook) Aussicht f (of auf +acc); **what a ~!** (iro) das sind ja schöne Aussichten!; **a job with no ~s** eine Stelle ohne Zukunft **(b)** (= person, thing) **he's not much of a ~ for her** er hat ihr nicht viel zu bieten; **a likely ~ as a customer** ein aussichtsreicher Kunde

> Be careful! **prospect** is not translated by the German word **Prospekt**.

prospective [prə'spektɪv] ADJ ATTR (= likely to happen) voraussichtlich; (= future) son-in-law, owner zukünftig; buyer interessiert; **~ candidate** Kandidat(in) m(f); **~ earnings** voraussichtliche Einkünfte pl

prosper ['prɒspə'] VI blühen; (financially) florieren; **how's he ~ing these days?** wie geht es ihm?

prosperity [prɒs'perɪtɪ] N Wohlstand m; (of business) Prosperität f

prosperous ['prɒspərəs] ADJ person wohlhabend; business florierend; economy blühend; **those were ~ times** das waren Zeiten des Wohlstands

prosperously ['prɒspərəslɪ] ADV live im Wohlstand

prostate (gland) ['prɒsteɪt(ˌglænd)] N Prostata f

prostitute ['prɒstɪtjuːt] **1** N Prostituierte(r) mf **2** VR sich prostituieren

prostitution [prɒstɪ'tjuːʃən] N Prostitution f

prostrate ['prɒstreɪt] **1** ADJ ausgestreckt; **he was found ~ on the floor** man fand ihn ausgestreckt am Boden liegend; **~ with grief** vor Gram gebrochen **2** [prɒ'streɪt] VR sich niederwerfen (before vor +dat)

protagonist [prəʊ'tægənɪst] N (esp Liter) Protagonist(in) m(f); (= supporter) Verfechter(in) m(f)

protect [prə'tekt] VT schützen (against gegen, from vor +dat); (person, animal) sb, young beschützen (against gegen, from vor +dat); (Comput) sichern; **don't try to ~ the culprit** versuchen Sie nicht, den Schuldigen zu decken **2** VI schützen (against vor +dat)

protection [prəˈtekʃən] N Schutz *m* (*against* gegen, *from* vor +*dat*); (*of interests, rights*) Wahrung *f*; **to be under sb's ~** unter jds Schutz (*dat*) stehen

protectionism [prəˈtekʃənɪzəm] N Protektionismus *m*

protectionist [prəˈtekʃənɪst] ADJ protektionistisch

protection racket N organisiertes Erpresserunwesen

protective [prəˈtektɪv] ADJ **(a)** Schutz-; *attitude, gesture* beschützend; *equipment, layer* schützend; **~ instinct** Beschützerinstinkt *m*; **the mother is very ~ toward(s) her children** die Mutter ist sehr fürsorglich ihren Kindern gegenüber **(b)** (*Econ*) *system* protektionistisch; **~ duty** Schutzzoll *m*

protective: **protective clothing** N Schutzkleidung *f*; **protective custody** N Schutzhaft *f*

protectively [prəˈtektɪvlɪ] ADV schützend; (*with regard to people*) beschützend

protective tariff N (*Econ*) Schutzzoll *m*

protector [prəˈtektəʳ] N **(a)** (= *defender*) Beschützer(in) *m(f)* **(b)** (= *protective wear*) Schutz *m*

protégé, protégée [ˈprɒtəʒeɪ] N Schützling *m*

protein [ˈprəʊtiːn] N Protein *nt*

protest [ˈprəʊtest] **1** N Protest *m*; (= *demonstration*) Protestkundgebung *f*; **under/in ~** unter/aus Protest; **to make a/one's ~** Protest erheben; **letter of ~**, **~ letter** Protestschreiben *nt* **2** [prəˈtest] VI (*against, about* gegen) protestieren; (= *demonstrate*) demonstrieren **3** [prəˈtest] VT **(a)** *innocence* beteuern **(b)** (= *dispute*) protestieren gegen; **it's mine, he ~ed** das gehört mir, protestierte er

Protestant [ˈprɒtɪstənt] **1** ADJ protestantisch **2** N Protestant(in) *m(f)*

protestation [ˌprɒtesˈteɪʃən] N (= *protest*) Protest *m*

protester [prəˈtestəʳ] N Protestierende(r) *mf*; (*in demonstration*) Demonstrant(in) *m(f)*

protest: **protest march** N Protestmarsch *m*; **protest vote** N (*Pol*) Proteststimme *f*

protocol [ˈprəʊtəkɒl] N Protokoll *nt*

proton [ˈprəʊtɒn] N Proton *nt*

prototype [ˈprəʊtəʊtaɪp] N Prototyp *m*

protracted [prəˈtræktɪd] ADJ langwierig; *absence, dispute* längere(r, s)

protrude [prəˈtruːd] VI (*out of, from* aus) vorstehen; (*ears*) abstehen; (*eyes*) vortreten

protruding [prəˈtruːdɪŋ] ADJ vorstehend; *ears* abstehend; *eyes* vortretend; *forehead, chin* vorspringend; *ribs* hervortretend

proud [praʊd] **1** ADJ stolz (*of* auf +*acc*); **it made his parents feel very ~** das erfüllte seine Eltern mit Stolz; **~ boast** stolze Behauptung; **a ~ day for ...** ein stolzer Tag für ...; **to be ~ that ...** stolz (darauf) sein, dass ...; **to be ~ to do sth** stolz darauf sein, etw zu tun **2** ADV **to do sb/oneself ~** jdn/sich verwöhnen

proudly [ˈpraʊdlɪ] ADV stolz

prove [pruːv], *pret* **proved**, *ptp* **proved** *or* **proven 1** VT beweisen; **he ~d that she did it** er wies nach, dass sie das getan hat; **to ~ sb innocent** *or* **sb's innocence** jds Unschuld nachweisen; **whether his judgement was right remains to be ~d** *or* **~n** es muss sich erst noch erweisen, ob seine Beurteilung zutrifft; **it all goes to ~ that ...** das beweist mal wieder, dass ...; **he was ~d right in the end** er hat schließlich doch Recht behalten; **he did it just to ~ a point** er tat es nur in der Sache wegen **2** VI **to ~ (to be) hot/useful** *etc* sich als heiß/nützlich *etc* erweisen; **if it ~s otherwise** wenn sich das Gegenteil herausstellt **3** VR **(a)** (= *show one's value etc*) sich bewähren **(b)** **to ~ oneself indispensable** *etc* sich als unentbehrlich *etc* erweisen

proven [ˈpruːvən] **1** PTP *of* **prove 2** [ˈprəʊvən] ADJ bewährt

proverb [ˈprɒvɜːb] N Sprichwort *nt*

proverbial [prəˈvɜːbɪəl] ADJ (*lit, fig*) sprichwörtlich

provide [prəˈvaɪd] **1** VT (= *make available*) zur Verfügung stellen; (*agency*) *personnel* vermitteln; *money* bereitstellen; *food, records etc* sorgen für; *ideas, specialist knowledge, electricity* liefern; *light, shade* spenden; **X ~d the money and Y (~d) the expertise** X stellte das Geld bereit und Y lieferte das Fachwissen; **candidates must ~ their own pens** die

Kandidaten müssen ihr Schreibgerät selbst stellen; **to ~ sth for sb** etw für jdn stellen; (= *make available*) jdm etw zur Verfügung stellen; (= *find, supply*: *agency etc*) jdm etw besorgen; **to ~ food and clothes for one's family** für Nahrung und Kleidung seiner Familie sorgen; **it ~s a certain amount of privacy for the inhabitants** es gibt den Bewohnern eine gewisse Abgeschlossenheit; **to ~ sb with sth** with *food etc* jdn mit etw versorgen; (= *equip*) jdn mit etw ausstatten; with *excuse, idea, information* jdm etw liefern **2** VR **to ~ oneself with sth** sich mit etw ausstatten

▸ **provide against** VI +PREP OBJ vorsorgen für

▸ **provide for** VI +PREP OBJ sorgen für; **we provided for all emergencies** wir haben für alle Notfälle vorgesorgt; **we have provided for an increase in costs of 25%** wir haben eine Kostensteigerung von 25% einkalkuliert

provided (that) [prəˈvaɪdɪd(ˈðæt)] CONJ vorausgesetzt(, dass)

providence [ˈprɒvɪdəns] N die Vorsehung

provident [ˈprɒvɪdənt] **~ fund** Unterstützungskasse *f*; **~ society** private Altersversicherung

provider [prəˈvaɪdəʳ] N (*for family*) Ernährer(in) *m(f)*

providing (that) [prəˈvaɪdɪŋ(ˈðæt)] CONJ vorausgesetzt(, dass)

province [ˈprɒvɪns] N **(a)** Provinz *f* **(b)** PL **the ~s** die Provinz **(c)** (*fig*: = *area of knowledge, activity etc*) Gebiet *nt* **(d)** (= *area of authority*) Kompetenzbereich *m*; **that's not my ~** dafür bin ich nicht zuständig

provincial [prəˈvɪnʃəl] ADJ Provinz-; *custom, accent* ländlich; (*pej*) provinzlerisch; **~ capital** Provinzhauptstadt *f*

provision [prəˈvɪʒən] N **(a)** (= *act of supplying*) (*for others*) Bereitstellung *f*; (*for one's own team etc*) Beschaffung *f*; (*of food, gas, water etc*) Versorgung *f* (*of* mit, *to sb* jds) **(b)** (= *supply*) Vorrat *m* (*of* an +*dat*) **(c)** **~s** *pl* (= *food*) Lebensmittel *pl* **(d)** (= *allowance*) Berücksichtigung *f*; (= *arrangement*) Vorkehrung *f*; (= *stipulation*) Bestimmung *f*; (*Fin, Comm*) Rückstellung *f*; **with the ~ that ...** mit dem Vorbehalt, dass ...; **is there no ~ for such cases in the legislation?** sind solche Fälle im Gesetz nicht vorgesehen?; **to make ~ for sb/the future** für jdn/für die Zukunft Vorsorge treffen; **to make ~ for sth** etw vorsehen; (*in legislation, rules also*) etw berücksichtigen

provisional [prəˈvɪʒənl] ADJ provisorisch; *offer, acceptance, legislation* vorläufig; **~ driving licence** (*Brit*) vorläufige Fahrerlaubnis für Fahrschüler

provisionally [prəˈvɪʒnəlɪ] ADV vorläufig

proviso [prəˈvaɪzəʊ] N Vorbehalt *m*; (= *clause*) Vorbehaltsklausel *f*; **with the ~ that ...** unter der Bedingung, dass ...

provocation [ˌprɒvəˈkeɪʃən] N Provokation *f*; **he acted under ~** er wurde dazu provoziert; **he hit me without any ~** er hat mich geschlagen, ohne dass ich ihn dazu provoziert hätte

provocative [prəˈvɒkətɪv] ADJ provozierend; *discussion* anregend; *remark, pose, behaviour* herausfordernd

provocatively [prəˈvɒkətɪvlɪ] ADV provozierend; *say, behave* herausfordernd; **~ entitled ...** mit dem provokativen Titel ...; **~ dressed** aufreizend gekleidet

provoke [prəˈvəʊk] VT provozieren; *animal* reizen; *reaction, anger, criticism* hervorrufen; *lust, pity* erwecken, erregen; *discussion, revolt* auslösen; **to ~ a quarrel or an argument** (*person*) Streit suchen; (*action*) zu einem Streit führen; **to ~ sb into doing sth** *or* **to do sth** jdn dazu bringen, dass er etw tut; (= *taunt*) jdn dazu treiben, dass er etw tut

provoking [prəˈvəʊkɪŋ] ADJ provozierend

prow [praʊ] N Bug *m*

prowess [ˈpraʊɪs] N (= *skill*) Fähigkeiten *pl*; **his (sexual) ~** seine Manneskraft

prowl [praʊl] **1** N Streifzug *m*; **to be on the ~** (*cat, burglar*) auf Streifzug sein; (*boss*) herumschleichen **2** VI (*also* **~ about** *or* **around**) herumstreichen; (*boss*) herumschleichen; **he ~ed round the house** er schlich im Haus

prowl car N (*US*) Streifenwagen *m*

prowler [ˈpraʊləʳ] N Herumtreiber(in) *m(f)*

proximity [prɒkˈsɪmɪtɪ] N Nähe *f*; **in ~ to** in der Nähe (+*gen*); **in close ~ to** in unmittelbarer Nähe (+*gen*)

proximo [ˈprɒksɪməʊ] ADV (*Comm*) (des) nächsten Monats

proxy ['prɒksɪ] N (= *power, document*) (Handlungs)vollmacht *f*; (= *person*) Stellvertreter(in) *m(f)*; **by ~** durch einen Stellvertreter

prude [pruːd] N **to be a ~** prüde sein

prudence ['pruːdəns] N (*of person*) Umsicht *f*; (*of measure, action, decision*) Klugheit *f*

prudent ['pruːdənt] ADJ *person* umsichtig; *measure, action, decision* klug

prudently ['pruːdəntlɪ] ADV wohlweislich; *act* umsichtig; *answer* überlegt

prudish ['pruːdɪʃ] ADJ prüde; *clothes* sittsam, züchtig

prudishly ['pruːdɪʃlɪ] ADV prüde; *dress* züchtig

prune¹ [pruːn] N Backpflaume *f*

prune² VT (*also* **~ down**) beschneiden; *hedge* schneiden; (*fig*) *expenditure* kürzen; *workforce* reduzieren; *firm* schrumpfen lassen

pruning ['pruːnɪŋ] N Beschneiden *nt*; (*of hedge*) Schneiden *nt*; (*fig*) (*of expenditure*) Kürzung *f*; (*of workforce*) Reduzierung *f*; (*of firm*) Schrumpfung *f*

Prussia ['prʌʃə] N Preußen *nt*

Prussian ['prʌʃən] **1** ADJ preußisch **2** N **(a)** Preuße *m*, Preußin *f* **(b)** (*Ling*) Preußisch *nt*

pry¹ [praɪ] VI neugierig sein; (*in drawers etc*) (herum)schnüffeln (*in* in +*dat*); **I don't mean to ~, but ...** es geht mich ja nichts an, aber ...; **to ~ into sb's affairs** seine Nase in jds Angelegenheiten (*acc*) stecken

pry² VT (*US*) = **prise**

prying ['praɪɪŋ] ADJ neugierig

PS ABBR *of* **postscript** PS

psalm [sɑːm] N Psalm *m*

PSBR (*Brit*) ABBR *of* **public sector borrowing requirement**

pseudo- ['sjuːdəʊ-] PREF Pseudo-, pseudo

pseudonym ['sjuːdənɪm] N Pseudonym *nt*

PST (*US*) ABBR *of* **Pacific Standard Time** pazifische Zeit

psych [saɪk] VT (*inf: = understand*) **to ~ sb (out), to get sb ~ed (out)** jdn durchschauen

▶ **psych out** **1** VT SEP (*inf*) psychologisch fertig machen (*inf*) **2** VI (= *freak out*) ausflippen (*inf*)

▶ **psych up** VT SEP (*inf*) hochputschen (*inf*); **to psych oneself up, to get oneself psyched up** sich hochputschen (*inf*)

psychedelic [ˌsaɪkɪ'delɪk] ADJ psychedelisch

psychiatric [ˌsaɪkɪ'ætrɪk] ADJ psychiatrisch; *illness, problem* psychisch; **~ hospital** psychiatrische Klinik; **~ nurse** Psychiatrieschwester *f*

psychiatrist [saɪ'kaɪətrɪst] N Psychiater(in) *m(f)*

psychiatry [saɪ'kaɪətrɪ] N Psychiatrie *f*

psychic ['saɪkɪk] **1** ADJ **(a)** übersinnlich; *powers* übernatürlich; **you must be ~!** Sie müssen hellsehen können! **(b)** (*Psych*) psychisch **2** N Mensch *m* mit übernatürlichen Kräften

psycho ['saɪkəʊ] N (*inf*) Verrückte(r) *mf*

psychoanalyse, (*US*) **psychoanalyze** [ˌsaɪkəʊ'ænəlaɪz] VT psychoanalytisch behandeln

psychoanalysis [ˌsaɪkəʊə'nælɪsɪs] N Psychoanalyse *f*

psychoanalyst [ˌsaɪkəʊ'ænəlɪst] N Psychoanalytiker(in) *m(f)*

psychological [ˌsaɪkə'lɒdʒɪkəl] ADJ (= *mental*) psychisch; (= *concerning psychology*) psychologisch; **he's not really ill, it's all ~** er ist nicht wirklich krank, das ist alles psychisch bedingt

psychologically [ˌsaɪkə'lɒdʒɪkəlɪ] ADV (= *mentally*) psychisch; (= *concerning psychology*) psychologisch

psychological thriller N (*Film, Liter*) Psychothriller *m*

psychologist [saɪ'kɒlədʒɪst] N Psychologe *m*, Psychologin *f*

psychology [saɪ'kɒlədʒɪ] N (= *science*) Psychologie *f*; (= *make-up*) Psyche *f*

psychopath ['saɪkəʊpæθ] N Psychopath(in) *m(f)*

psychopathic [ˌsaɪkəʊ'pæθɪk] ADJ psychopathisch

psychotherapist [ˌsaɪkəʊ'θerəpɪst] N Psychotherapeut(in) *m(f)*

psychotherapy [ˌsaɪkəʊ'θerəpɪ] N Psychotherapie *f*

psychotic [saɪ'kɒtɪk] ADJ psychotisch

pt ABBR *of* **part, pint, payment, point**

PTA ABBR *of* **parent-teacher association** Lehrer-Eltern-Ausschuss *m*

pto ABBR *of* **please turn over** b.w.

pub [pʌb] N (*esp Brit*) Kneipe *f* (*inf*); (*in the country*) Gasthaus *nt*; **let's go to the ~** komm, wir gehen in die Kneipe (*inf*)

pub-crawl ['pʌbkrɔːl] N (*esp Brit inf*) Kneipenbummel *m* (*inf*); **to go on a ~** einen Kneipenbummel machen (*inf*)

puberty ['pjuːbətɪ] N die Pubertät; **to reach the age of ~** in die Pubertät kommen

pubic ['pjuːbɪk] ADJ Scham-; **~ hair** Schamhaar *nt*

public ['pʌblɪk] **1** ADJ öffentlich; **to be ~ knowledge** allgemein bekannt sein; **to become ~** publik werden; **at ~ expense** aus öffentlichen Mitteln; **~ pressure** Druck *m* der Öffentlichkeit; **he is a ~ figure** er ist eine Persönlichkeit des öffentlichen Lebens; **in the ~ eye** im Blickpunkt der Öffentlichkeit; **to make sth ~** etw publik machen; (*officially*) etw öffentlich bekannt machen; **~ image** Bild *nt* in der Öffentlichkeit; **in the ~ interest** im öffentlichen Interesse; **to go ~** (*Comm*) in eine Aktiengesellschaft umgewandelt werden **2** N SING *or* PL Öffentlichkeit *f*; **in ~** in der Öffentlichkeit; *speak also, agree, admit* öffentlich; **our** *etc* **~** unser *etc* Publikum; **the (general) ~** die (breite) Öffentlichkeit; **the viewing ~** das Fernsehpublikum; **the reading/sporting ~** die lesende/sportinteressierte Öffentlichkeit; **the great American/British ~** (*iro*) die breite amerikanische/britische Öffentlichkeit

public access channel N öffentlicher Fernsehkanal

public: **public address system** N Lautsprecheranlage *f*; **public analyst** N Analytiker(in) *m(f)* in der Öffentlichkeitsarbeit; **public assistance** N (*US*) staatliche Fürsorge

publication [ˌpʌblɪ'keɪʃən] N Veröffentlichung *f*

publication date N Erscheinungsdatum *nt*

public: **public company** N Aktiengesellschaft *f*; **public convenience** N (*Brit*) öffentliche Toilette; **public corporation** N Körperschaft *f* des öffentlichen Rechts; **public debt** N (*esp US*) Verschuldung *f* der öffentlichen Hand; (= *national debt*) Staatsverschuldung *f*; **public defender** N (*US*) Pflichtverteidiger(in) *m(f)*; **public enemy** N Staatsfeind(in) *m(f)*; **public gallery** N Besuchertribüne *f*; **public goods** PL Kollektivgüter *pl*, öffentliche Güter *pl*; **public health** N (= *health of the public*) die öffentliche Gesundheit; (= *health care*) das (öffentliche) Gesundheitswesen; **public holiday** N gesetzlicher Feiertag; **public housing** N (*US*) Sozialwohnungen *pl*; **public housing project** N (*US*) sozialer Wohnungsbau; **public inquiry** N öffentliche Untersuchung

publicist ['pʌblɪsɪst] N Publizist(in) *m(f)*

publicity [pʌb'lɪsɪtɪ] N **(a)** Publicity *f* **(b)** (*Comm*) Werbung *f*

publicity: **publicity agent** N Publicitymanager(in) *m(f)*; **publicity campaign** N Publicitykampagne *f*; (*Comm*) Werbekampagne *f*; **publicity material** N Publicitymaterial *nt*; (*Comm*) Werbematerial *nt*; **publicity stunt** N Werbegag *m*

publicize ['pʌblɪsaɪz] VT **(a)** (= *make public*) bekannt machen **(b)** *film, author, product* Werbung machen für

public: **public law** N öffentliches Recht; **public liability** N (*gesetzliche*) Haftpflicht; **public life** N öffentliches Leben; **public limited company** N Aktiengesellschaft *f*

publicly ['pʌblɪklɪ] ADV öffentlich; **~ funded** durch öffentliche Mittel finanziert; **~ accountable** der Öffentlichkeit verantwortlich; **this factory is ~ owned** diese Fabrik ist gesellschaftliches Eigentum; **~ quoted company** ≈ Aktiengesellschaft *f*

public: **public money** N öffentliche Gelder *pl*; **public opinion** N die öffentliche Meinung; **public ownership** N staatlicher

Besitz; **under** *or* **in** ~ in staatlichem Besitz; **public property** N
(a) öffentliches Eigentum **(b)** *(fig)* **intimate aspects of her
personal life had been made** ~ intime Aspekte ihres
Privatlebens waren allgemein bekannt geworden; **public
prosecutor** N Staatsanwalt *m*/-anwältin *f*; **public
prosecutor's office** N Staatsanwaltschaft *f*; **public relations**
N PL *or* SING Öffentlichkeitsarbeit *f*; ~ **campaign**
f; **public relations officer** N Öffentlichkeitsarbeiter(in) *m(f)*;
public school N *(Brit)* Privatschule *f*; *(US)* staatliche Schule;
public sector ■ N öffentlicher Sektor ■ ADJ ATTR des
öffentlichen Sektors; ~ **borrowing** staatliche
Kreditaufnahme; ~ **borrowing requirement** Kreditbedarf *m*
der öffentlichen Hand; ~ **deficit** Staatsdefizit *nt*; **public
servant** N Arbeitnehmer(in) *m(f)* im öffentlichen Dienst;
public service N *(Civil Service)* öffentlicher Dienst; *(= water,
transport etc)* öffentlicher Dienstleistungsbetrieb; **public
speaker** N Redner(in) *m(f)*; **public speaking** N Redenhalten
nt; **I'm no good at** ~ ich kann nicht in der Öffentlichkeit
reden; **public spending** N Ausgaben *pl* der öffentlichen
Hand; **public television** N *(US)* öffentliches Fernsehen;
public transport N öffentlicher Nahverkehr; **by** ~ mit
öffentlichen Verkehrsmitteln; **public utility** N öffentlicher
Versorgungsbetrieb; **public works** PL staatliche Bauvorhaben
pl

publish ['pʌblɪʃ] ■ VT veröffentlichen; ~**ed by Collins** bei
Collins erscheinen; **"~ed monthly"** „erscheint monatlich";
"just ~ed" „neu erschienen"; **who ~es that book?** in
welchem Verlag ist das Buch erschienen? ■ VI **when are we
going to ~?** *(book)* wann bringen wir das Buch heraus?;
(research) wann veröffentlichen wir die Arbeit?

publisher ['pʌblɪʃəʳ] N *(= person)* Verleger(in) *m(f)*; *(= firm: also
~s)* Verlag *m*; **who are your ~s?** wer ist Ihr Verleger?

publishing ['pʌblɪʃɪŋ] N *(= trade)* das Verlagswesen; ~ **company**
Verlagshaus *nt*

pucker ['pʌkəʳ] ■ VT *(also ~ up)* verziehen; *(for kissing)* spitzen
■ VI *(also ~ up)* *(lips)* sich verziehen; *(to be kissed)* sich
spitzen

puckered ['pʌkəd] ADJ *lips* gespitzt

pud [pʊd] N *(Brit inf)* = **pudding**

pudding ['pʊdɪŋ] N *(Brit)* **(a)** *(= dessert)* Nachtisch *m*; *(= crème
caramel, instant whip etc)* Pudding *m*; **what's for ~?** was gibt es
als Nachtisch? **(b)** black ~ ≈ Blutwurst *f*

puddle ['pʌdl] N Pfütze *f* *(also euph)*

pudgy ['pʌdʒɪ] ADJ *(+ER)* = **podgy**

Puerto Rican ['pwɜːtəʊˈriːkən] ■ ADJ puertoricanisch ■ N
Puertoricaner(in) *m(f)*

Puerto Rico ['pwɜːtəʊˈriːkəʊ] N Puerto Rico *nt*

puff [pʌf] ■ N **(a)** *(of breathing, of engine)* Schnaufen *nt no pl*;
(inf: = breath) Puste *f* *(inf)*; *(on cigarette etc)* Zug *m* *(at, of* an
+*dat)*; **a ~ of wind** ein Windstoß *m*; **a ~ of smoke** eine
Rauchwolke; **our hopes vanished in a** ~ unsere
Hoffnungen lösten sich in nichts auf; **to be out of** ~ *(Brit inf)*
außer Puste sein *(inf)*
(b) *(Cook)* **cream** ~ Windbeutel *m*
■ VT *smoke* ausstoßen; *(person)* blasen; *cigarette* paffen *(inf)*
■ VI *(person, train)* schnaufen; *(chimney, smoke)* qualmen; **to
~ (away) at** *or* **on a cigar** an einer Zigarre paffen

➤ **puff out** VT SEP **(a)** *chest* herausstrecken; *cheeks* aufblasen
(b) *(= emit)* ausstoßen **(c)** *(inf)* ALWAYS SEPARATE *(= make out of
breath)* außer Puste bringen *(inf)*

➤ **puff up** ■ VT SEP **(a)** *feathers* (auf)plustern **(b)** *(fig)* **to be
puffed up with pride** ganz aufgeblasen sein ■ VI *(eyes, face
etc)* anschwellen

puffed [pʌft] ADJ *(inf)* außer Puste *(inf)*

puffin ['pʌfɪn] N Papageientaucher *m*

puffiness ['pʌfɪnɪs] N Verschwollenheit *f*

puff pastry, *(US)* **puff paste** N Blätterteig *m*

puffy ['pʌfɪ] ADJ *(+ER)* *(= swollen)* geschwollen

puke [pjuːk] *(sl)* ■ VI kotzen *(inf)*; **he makes me** ~ er kotzt mich
an *(sl)* ■ N Kotze *f* *(vulg)*

➤ **puke up** VI *(inf)* kotzen *(inf)*

pull [pʊl] ■ N Ziehen *nt*; *(short)* Ruck *m*; *(lit, fig: = attraction)*
Anziehungskraft *f*; *(of current)* Sog *m*; **he gave her/the rope a
~** er zog sie/am Seil; **I felt a ~ at my sleeve** ich spürte, wie
mich jemand am Ärmel zog; **to be on the ~** *(Brit inf)* auf
Mädchen/Männer aus sein
■ VT **(a)** ziehen; *tooth, cork, lettuce* herausziehen; *beer*
zapfen; **to ~ a gun on sb** jdn mit der Pistole bedrohen; **he
~ed the dog behind him** er zog den Hund hinter sich *(dat)*
her; **to ~ a door shut** eine Tür zuziehen
(b) *(= tug)* *handle, rope, bell* ziehen an (+*dat*); **he ~ed her hair**
er zog sie an den Haaren; **to ~ sth to pieces** *(fig: = criticize)*
etw verreißen; **to ~ sb's leg** *(fig inf)* jdn auf den Arm nehmen
(inf); ~ **the other one(, it's got bells on)** *(Brit inf)* das glaubst
du ja selber nicht!; **she was the one ~ing the strings** sie war
es, die alle Fäden in der Hand hielt; **to ~ rank (on sb)** *(jdm
gegenüber)* den Vorgesetzten herauskehren; **when it came to
criticizing other people he didn't ~ his** *or* **any punches** wenn
es darum ging, andere zu kritisieren, zog er ganz schön vom
Leder *(inf)*
(c) *muscle* sich *(dat)* zerren
(d) *crowd* anziehen
(e) *(inf: = carry out, do)* **what are you trying to ~?** *(inf)* was
heckst du wieder aus? *(inf)*; **to ~ a stunt** Geschichten machen
(inf)
■ VI **(a)** ziehen *(on, at* an +*dat)*; **to ~ to the left/right** *(car,
brakes)* nach links/rechts ziehen; **to ~ on one's cigarette** an
seiner Zigarette ziehen; **to ~ for sb/sth** *(US inf)* jdn/etw
unterstützen
(b) *(train, car etc)* fahren; **he ~ed across to the left-hand lane**
er wechselte auf die linke Spur über; **he ~ed into the side of
the road** er fuhr an den Straßenrand; **he ~ed alongside** seitlich
heranfahren; **to ~ off the road** am Straßenrand anhalten
(c) *(Brit inf: sexually)* jemanden rumkriegen *(inf)*

➤ **pull ahead** VI *(in race, poll, contest)* Vorsprung gewinnen;
to pull ahead of sb/sth *(in race etc)* einen Vorsprung vor jdm/
etw gewinnen; *(in poll, contest)* jdm/einer Sache *(dat)*
davonziehen

➤ **pull apart** ■ VT SEP **(a)** *(= separate)* auseinander ziehen;
sheets of paper, fighting people trennen; *radio etc* auseinander
nehmen **(b)** *(fig inf)* *(= search thoroughly)* auseinander
nehmen *(inf)*; *(= criticize)* verreißen ■ VI *(through design)* sich
auseinander nehmen lassen

➤ **pull away** ■ VT SEP wegziehen; **she pulled it away from him**
sie zog es von ihm weg; *(from his hands)* sie zog es ihm aus
den Händen ■ VI *(= move off)* wegfahren; **the car pulled away
from the others** der Wagen setzte sich (von den anderen) ab

➤ **pull back** VT SEP zurückziehen

➤ **pull down** ■ VT SEP **(a)** *(= move down)* herunterziehen
(b) *buildings* abreißen **(c)** *(= weaken, make worse)* *marks,
profits, results* herunterdrücken; *company etc* mitnehmen
(d) *(US inf: = earn)* reinholen *(inf)* ■ VI *(blind etc)* sich
herunterziehen lassen

➤ **pull in** ■ VT SEP **(a)** *claws, rope, stomach etc* einziehen; *(into
room, swimming pool etc)* hineinziehen; **to pull sb/sth in(to)
sth** jdn/etw in etw *(acc)* ziehen **(b)** *crowds* anziehen **(c)** *(inf:
= earn)* kassieren *(inf)* ■ VI *(into station, harbour)* einfahren
(into in +*acc)*; *(into garage, driveway)* hineinfahren *(into* in
+*acc)*; *(= stop)* anhalten

➤ **pull off** VT SEP **(a)** *wrapping paper* abziehen; *cover*
abnehmen; *(violently)* abreißen; *clothes, shoes* ausziehen
(b) *(inf: = succeed in)* schaffen *(inf)*; *deal, coup* zuwege bringen
(inf); *order* an Land ziehen *(inf)*; *burglary* drehen *(inf)*

➤ **pull on** VT SEP *coat etc* sich *(dat)* überziehen

➤ **pull out** ■ VT SEP **(a)** *(= extract)* *(of* aus) herausziehen; *tooth*
ziehen; *page* heraustrennen; **to pull the rug out from under
sb** *(fig)* jdm den Boden unter den Füßen wegziehen
(b) *(= withdraw)* zurückziehen; *troops* abziehen
■ VI **(a)** *(= come out, become detached)* sich herausziehen
lassen; *(pages)* sich heraustrennen lassen

(b) (= *elongate*) sich ausziehen lassen
(c) (= *withdraw*) aussteigen (*of* aus); (*inf*); (*troops*) abziehen
(d) (= *move out: train etc*) herausfahren (*of* aus); **to pull out of recession** (*economy*) aus der Rezession kommen; **the car pulled out from behind the lorry** der Wagen scherte hinter dem Lastwagen aus

➤ **pull over** 〖1〗 VT SEP **(a)** (= *move over*) herüberziehen (*prep obj* über +*acc*) **(b)** (= *topple*) umreißen **(c) the police pulled him over** die Polizei stoppte ihn am Straßenrand 〖2〗 VI (*car, driver*) zur Seite fahren

➤ **pull round** (*esp Brit*) VT SEP (= *turn round*) herumdrehen

➤ **pull through** 〖1〗 VT SEP (*lit*) durchziehen; (*fig*: = *help recover, help succeed*) durchbringen; **to pull sb/sth through sth** (*lit*) jdn/etw durch etw ziehen; **to pull sb through a difficult period** jdm helfen, eine schwierige Zeit zu überstehen 〖2〗 VI (*fig*) durchkommen; **to pull through sth** (*fig*) etw überstehen

➤ **pull together** 〖1〗 VI (*fig*) am gleichen Strang ziehen 〖2〗 VR sich zusammenreißen

➤ **pull up** 〖1〗 VT SEP **(a)** (= *raise by pulling*) hochziehen **(b)** (= *uproot*) herausreißen **(c)** *chair* heranrücken **(d)** (= *stop*) anhalten 〖2〗 VI **(a)** (= *stop*) anhalten **(b)** (= *improve one's position*) aufholen

pull-down ['puldaʊn] ADJ *bed* Klapp-; **~ menu** (*Comput*) Pull-down-Menü *nt*

pulley ['pʊlɪ] N (= *wheel*) Rolle *f*; (= *block*) Flaschenzug *m*

pull: pull-out 〖1〗 N **(a)** (= *withdrawal*) Abzug *m* **(b)** (= *supplement*) heraustrennbarer Teil 〖2〗 ATTR *supplement* heraustrennbar; *table leaf, seat* ausziehbar; **pullover** N Pullover *m*

pulp [pʌlp] 〖1〗 N **(a)** (= *soft mass, paper ~, wood ~*) Brei *m*; **to beat sb to a ~** (*inf*) jdn zu Brei schlagen (*inf*) **(b)** (*of fruit, vegetable*) Fruchtfleisch *nt* 〖2〗 VT *fruit, vegetables* zerdrücken; *paper, book* einstampfen

pulpit ['pʊlpɪt] N Kanzel *f*

pulsate [pʌl'seɪt] VI (*lit, fig*) pulsieren; (*head, heart*) klopfen

pulse [pʌls] 〖1〗 N (*Anat*) Puls *m*; (*Phys*) Impuls *m*; **to feel** *or* **take sb's ~** jdm den Puls fühlen; **he still has** *or* **keeps his finger on the ~ of economic affairs** er hat in Wirtschaftsfragen immer noch den Finger am Puls der Zeit 〖2〗 VI pulsieren; (*machines*) stampfen

pulverize ['pʌlvəraɪz] VT pulverisieren; (*fig inf*) (= *defeat*) fertig machen (*inf*)

pummel ['pʌml] VT eintrommeln auf (+*acc*)

pump¹ [pʌmp] 〖1〗 N Pumpe *f*
〖2〗 VT pumpen; *stomach* auspumpen; **to ~ water out of sth** Wasser aus etw (heraus)pumpen; **to ~ sb full of drugs** jdn mit Drogen voll pumpen; **to ~ money into sth** Geld in etw (*acc*) hineinpumpen; **to ~ sb (for information)** jdn aushorchen; **to ~ iron** (*inf*) Gewichte stemmen
〖3〗 VI **(a)** pumpen; (*water, blood*) herausschießen; **the piston ~ed up and down** der Kolben ging auf und ab **(b)** (*Brit sl*: = *have sex*) poppen (*sl*)

➤ **pump in** VT SEP (*lit, fig*) hineinpumpen

➤ **pump out** VT SEP *liquid, air* herauspumpen

➤ **pump up** VT SEP **(a)** *tyre etc* aufpumpen; *prices, profits* hochtreiben **(b)** *liquid* hochpumpen

pump² N (= *gym shoe*) Turnschuh *m*; (*US*: = *court shoe*) Pumps *m*

pumpkin ['pʌmpkɪn] N Kürbis *m*

pun [pʌn] 〖1〗 N Wortspiel *nt* 〖2〗 VI Wortspiele machen

Punch [pʌntʃ] N (*Brit*) Kasper *m*; **~ and Judy show** Kasper(le)theater *nt*; **to be (as) pleased as ~** (*inf*) sich wie ein Schneekönig freuen (*inf*)

punch¹ [pʌntʃ] N **(a)** (= *blow*) Schlag *m* **(b)** NO PL (*fig*: = *vigour*) Schwung *m* 〖2〗 VT boxen; **I wanted to ~ his face** *or* **~ him in the face when he said that** als er das sagte, hätte ich ihm am liebsten ins Gesicht geschlagen

punch² 〖1〗 N (*for punching holes*) Locher *m* 〖2〗 VT *ticket etc* lochen; *holes* stechen

➤ **punch in** VT SEP (*Comput*) *data* tasten

➤ **punch out** VT SEP ausstechen

punch³ N (= *drink*) Bowle *f*; (*hot*) Punsch *m*

punch: punchbag N Sandsack *m*; **punchbowl** N Bowle *f*

punching bag ['pʌntʃɪŋ,bæg] N (*US*) Sandsack *m*

punch: punch line N Pointe *f*; **punch-up** (*Brit inf*) Schlägerei *f*

punctual ['pʌŋktjʊəl] ADJ pünktlich; **to be ~** pünktlich kommen

punctuality [,pʌŋktjʊ'ælɪtɪ] N Pünktlichkeit *f*

punctually ['pʌŋktjʊəlɪ] ADV pünktlich

punctuate ['pʌŋktjʊeɪt] VT **(a)** (*Gram*) interpunktieren **(b)** (= *intersperse*) unterbrechen

punctuation [,pʌŋktjʊ'eɪʃən] N Interpunktion *f*

puncture ['pʌŋktʃəʳ] 〖1〗 N (*in tyre, balloon etc*) Loch *nt*; (= *flat tyre*) Reifenpanne *f* 〖2〗 VT stechen in (+*acc*); *tyre, balloon* Löcher/ein Loch machen in (+*acc*)

pungency ['pʌndʒənsɪ] N (*lit, fig*) Schärfe *f*

pungent ['pʌndʒənt] ADJ (*lit, fig*) scharf; *smell* durchdringend

punish ['pʌnɪʃ] VT **(a)** bestrafen; **he was ~ed by a fine** er wurde mit einer Geldstrafe belegt; **the other team ~ed us for that mistake** die andere Mannschaft ließ uns für diesen Fehler büßen **(b)** (*fig inf*: = *drive hard, treat roughly*) strapazieren; *oneself* schinden; *opponent* zusetzen (+*dat*)

punishable ['pʌnɪʃəbl] ADJ strafbar; **this offence** (*Brit*) *or* **offense** (*US*) **is ~ by 2 years' imprisonment** dieses Verbrechen wird mit 2 Jahren Gefängnis bestraft

punishing ['pʌnɪʃɪŋ] ADJ *blow* hart; *routine, pace* strapaziös, tödlich; *workload* erdrückend

punishment ['pʌnɪʃmənt] N **(a)** (= *penalty*) Strafe *f*; (= *punishing*) Bestrafung *f*; **you know the ~ for such offences** Sie wissen, welche Strafe darauf steht; **~ beating** Bestrafungsaktion *f* **(b)** (*fig inf*) **to take a lot of ~** (*car, furniture etc*) stark strapaziert werden

Punjab ['pʌndʒɑːb] N **the ~** das Pandschab

Punjabi [pʌn'dʒɑːbɪ] 〖1〗 ADJ pandschabisch 〖2〗 N **(a)** Pandschabi *mf* **(b)** (*Ling*) Pandschabi *nt*

punk [pʌŋk] 〖1〗 N **(a)** (*also* **~ rocker**) Punker(in) *m(f)*; (*also* **~ rock**) Punkrock *m*; (= *culture*) Punk *m* **(b)** (*US inf*: = *hoodlum*) Ganove *m* (*inf*) 〖2〗 ADJ Punk-

punter ['pʌntəʳ] N **(a)** (*Brit inf*) (= *better*) Wetter(in) *m(f)*; (= *gambler*) Spieler(in) *m(f)* **(b)** (*esp Brit inf*: = *customer etc*) Kunde *m*, Kundin *f*

puny ['pjuːnɪ] ADJ (+ER) *person* schwächlich; *effort, resources* kläglich

pup [pʌp] N Junge(s) *nt*

pupil¹ ['pjuːpl] N (*Sch, fig*) Schüler(in) *m(f)*

pupil² N (*Anat*) Pupille *f*

puppet ['pʌpɪt] N Puppe *f*; (= *glove ~*) Handpuppe *f*; (= *string ~, also fig*) Marionette *f*

puppet: puppet regime N Marionettenregime *nt*; **puppet show** N Puppenspiel *nt*; (*with string puppets also*) Marionettentheater *nt*

puppy ['pʌpɪ] N junger Hund, Welpe *m*

purchase ['pɜːtʃɪs] 〖1〗 N Kauf *m*; **to make a ~** einen Kauf tätigen 〖2〗 VT kaufen

purchase: purchase allowance N (*Comm*) Preisnachlass *m* von Lieferanten; **purchase order** N Auftragsbestätigung *f*; **purchase price** N Kaufpreis *m*; **purchase returns** PL (*Comm*) Warenrücksendungen *pl*

purchaser ['pɜːtʃɪsəʳ] N Käufer(in) *m(f)*

purchase tax N (*Brit*) nach dem Großhandelspreis berechnete Kaufsteuer

purchasing ['pɜːtʃɪsɪŋ] ADJ *department, agency* Einkaufs-; *price* Kauf-

purchasing: purchasing manager N Einkaufsleiter(in) *m(f)*; **~s' index** Einkaufs(manager)index *m*; **purchasing officer** N Einkäufer(in) *m(f)*; **purchasing power** N Kaufkraft *f*

pure [pjʊəʳ] ADJ (+ER) rein; *motive* ehrlich; **she stared at him in ~ disbelief** sie starrte ihn ganz ungläubig an; **by ~ chance** durch puren Zufall, rein zufällig; **malice ~ and simple** reine Bosheit

purebred ['pjʊəbred] ADJ reinrassig

purée ['pjʊəreɪ] 〖1〗 N Püree *nt*; **tomato ~** Tomatenmark *nt* 〖2〗 VT pürieren

purely ['pjʊəlɪ] ADV rein; **~ and simply** schlicht und einfach

purgatory ['pɜːgətərɪ] N (*Rel*) das Fegefeuer

purge [pɜːdʒ] VT reinigen; (*Pol etc*) säubern (*of* von)

purification [,pjʊərɪfɪ'keɪʃən] N Reinigung *f*

purify ['pjʊərɪfaɪ] VT reinigen

puritan ['pjʊərɪtə] (*Rel: also* **Puritan**) **1** ADJ puritanisch **2** N Puritaner(in) *m(f)*

purity ['pjʊərɪtɪ] N Reinheit *f*; (*of motives*) Ehrlichkeit *f*

purple ['pɜːpl] **1** ADJ lila; *face* hochrot **2** N (= *colour*) Lila *nt*

purpose ['pɜːpəs] N **(a)** (= *intention*) Absicht *f*; (= *result aimed at, set goal*) Zweck *m*; **on ~** absichtlich; **what was your ~ in doing this?** was haben Sie damit beabsichtigt?; **to answer** *or* **serve sb's ~(s)** jds Zweck(en) dienen; **for our ~s** für unsere Zwecke; **for the ~s of this meeting** zum Zweck dieser Konferenz; **for all practical ~s** in der Praxis; **to no ~** ohne Erfolg **(b)** NO PL (= *determination*) Entschlossenheit *f*; **to have a sense of ~** zielbewusst sein; **to have no sense of ~** kein Zielbewusstsein haben

purpose: **purpose-built** ADJ (*esp Brit*) speziell angefertigt; *construction* speziell gebaut; **purpose-designed** ADJ speziell entworfen

purposeful ADJ, **purposefully** ADV ['pɜːpəsfʊl, -fəlɪ] entschlossen; *activity, life* sinnvoll

purr [pɜː] **1** VI (*cat, fig: person*) schnurren; (*engine*) surren **2** VT (= *say*) säuseln **3** N Schnurren *nt no pl*; (*of engine*) Surren *nt no pl*

purse [pɜːs] **1** N **(a)** (*for money*) Portemonnaie *nt*; **to hold the ~ strings** (*Brit fig*) über die Finanzen bestimmen **(b)** (*US*: = *handbag*) Handtasche *f* **2** VT **to ~ one's lips (up)** einen Schmollmund machen

pursue [pə'sjuː] VT verfolgen; *girl* nachlaufen (+*dat*); *pleasure, success* nachjagen (+*dat*), aus sein auf (+*acc*); *happiness* streben nach; *inquiry* durchführen; *profession, studies* nachgehen (+*dat*); *subject* weiterführen

pursuer [pə'sjuːə] N Verfolger(in) *m(f)*

pursuit [pə'sjuːt] N **(a)** (*of person*) Verfolgung *f* (*of* +*gen*); (*of knowledge, happiness*) Streben *nt* (*of* nach); (*of pleasure*) Jagd *f* (*of* nach); **he set off in ~ (of her)** er rannte/fuhr (ihr) hinterher; **to go in ~ of sb/sth** sich auf die Jagd nach jdm/ etw machen; **in hot ~ of sb** hart auf jds Fersen (*dat*); **to set off/be in hot ~ of sb/sth** jdm/einer Sache nachjagen; **in (the) ~ of his goal** in Verfolgung seines Ziels **(b)** (= *occupation*) Beschäftigung *f*; (= *hobby, pastime*) Zeitvertreib *m*

pus [pʌs] N Eiter *m*

push [pʊʃ] **1** N **(a)** Schubs *m* (*inf*); (*short*) Stoß *m*; **to give sb/ sth a ~** jdm/einer Sache einen Stoß versetzen; **to give a car a ~** einen Wagen anschieben; **he needs a little ~ now and then** (*fig*) den muss man mal ab und zu in die Rippen stoßen (*inf*); **to get the ~** (*Brit inf*) (*employee*) (raus)fliegen (*inf*) (*from* aus); (*boyfriend*) den Laufpass kriegen (*inf*); **to give sb the ~** (*Brit inf*) *employee* jdn rausschmeißen (*inf*); *boyfriend* jdm den Laufpass geben (*inf*); **at a ~** (*inf*) notfalls; **if/when ~ comes to shove** (*inf*) wenn der schlimmste Fall eintritt **(b)** (= *effort*) Anstrengung *f*; (= *sales ~*) Kampagne *f*; (*Mil*) Offensive *f*; **to make a ~** = Dampf machen (*inf*); **to have a ~ on sales** eine Verkaufskampagne führen **2** VT **(a)** (= *shove*) schieben; (*quickly, violently*) stoßen; *button, controls* drücken; **to ~ a door open/shut** eine Tür auf-/ zuschieben; (*quickly, violently*) eine Tür auf-/zustoßen; **he ~ed his way through the crowd** er drängte sich durch die Menge; **he ~ed the thought to the back of his mind** er schob den Gedanken beiseite **(b)** (*fig*) *views, claims, interests* durchzusetzen versuchen; *export side* intensiv fördern; *product* massiv Werbung machen für; *drugs* schieben (*inf*); **to ~ home one's advantage** seinen Vorteil ausnützen; **don't ~ your luck** treibs nicht zu weit!; **he's ~ing his luck trying to do that** er legt es wirklich darauf an, wenn er das versucht **(c)** (*fig*: = *put pressure on*) drängen; *athlete, employee* antreiben; **to ~ sb into doing sth** jdn dazu treiben, etw zu tun; **they ~ed him to the limits** sie trieben ihn bis an seine Grenzen; **that's ~ing it a bit** (*inf*) das ist ein bisschen übertrieben; **to be ~ed (for time)** (*inf*) mit der Zeit knapp dran sein; **to ~ oneself hard** sich schinden **3** VI (= *shove*) schieben; (*quickly, violently*) stoßen; (= *press, also in childbirth*) drücken; (*in a crowd*) drängeln (*inf*); (= *press onward*) sich (vorwärts) kämpfen; (= *apply pressure*) drängen; **"~"** (*on door*) „drücken"; (*on bell*) „klingeln"; **~ harder!** fester schieben/stoßen/drücken!

➤ **push about** VT SEP (*Brit*) = **push around**

➤ **push across** VT SEP = **push over (a)**

➤ **push ahead** VI sich ranhalten (*inf*); **to push ahead with one's plans** seine Pläne vorantreiben

➤ **push along** VT SEP vor sich (*dat*) her schieben; (*fig*: = *speed up*) *work etc* vorantreiben

➤ **push around** VT SEP **(a)** (*lit*) herumschieben; (*quickly, violently*) herumstoßen **(b)** (*fig inf*: = *bully*) *child* herumschubsen; *adult* herumkommandieren

➤ **push aside** VT SEP beiseite schieben; (*quickly, violently*) beiseite stoßen; (*fig*) *problems, suggestions* einfach abtun

➤ **push away** VT SEP wegschieben; (*quickly*) wegstoßen

➤ **push back** VT SEP *people* zurückdrängen; (*with one push*) zurückstoßen; *curtains, cover, hair* zurückschieben

➤ **push by** VI = **push past**

➤ **push down** **1** VT SEP **(a)** (= *press down*) nach unten drücken **(b)** (= *knock over*) umstoßen; *fence* niederreißen **2** VI (= *press down*) hinunterdrücken

➤ **push for** VI +PREP OBJ drängen auf (+*acc*)

➤ **push forward** **1** VI = **push ahead** **2** VT SEP (*lit*) nach vorn schieben; (*fig*) *claim* geltend machen; *ideas* hervorheben

➤ **push in** **1** VT SEP **(a)** hineinschieben; (*quickly, violently*) hineinstoßen; **to push sb/sth in(to) sth** jdn/etw in etw (*acc*) schieben/stoßen; **to push one's way in** sich hineindrängen **(b)** *sides of box* eindrücken **2** VI (*lit*: *in queue, into room etc*) sich hineindrängeln (*inf*)

➤ **push off** **1** VT SEP hinunterschieben; (*quickly, violently*) hinunterstoßen; **to push sb off sth** jdn von etw schieben/ stoßen **2** VI (*Brit inf*: = *leave*) abhauen (*inf*); **push off!** zieh ab! (*inf*)

➤ **push on** VI (*with journey*) weiterfahren; (*walking*) weitergehen; (*with job*) weitermachen

➤ **push out** VT SEP hinausschieben; (*quickly, violently*) hinausstoßen; **to push sb/sth out of sth** jdn/etw aus etw schieben/stoßen; **to push one's way out (of sth)** sich (aus etw) hinausdrängen

➤ **push over** VT SEP **(a)** (= *pass over, move over*) hinüberschieben; (*quickly, violently*) hinüberstoßen; **to push sb/sth over sth** jdn/etw über etw (*acc*) schieben/stoßen **(b)** (= *knock over*) umwerfen

➤ **push past** VI sich vorbeischieben (*prep obj* an +*dat*); (= *move violently*) sich vorbeidrängen (*prep obj* an +*dat*)

➤ **push through** **1** VT SEP **(a)** durchschieben; (*quickly, violently*) durchstoßen; **to push sb/sth through sth** jdn/etw durch etw schieben/stoßen; **she pushed her way through the crowd** sie drängte sich durch die Menge **(b)** *bill, decision* durchpeitschen (*inf*); *business* durchziehen (*inf*) **2** VI (*through crowd*) sich durchschieben; (*more violently*) sich durchdrängen

➤ **push to** VT ALWAYS SEPARATE *door* anlehnen

➤ **push up** VT SEP **(a)** (*lit*) hinaufschieben; (*quickly, violently*) hinaufstoßen; *window* hochschieben/-stoßen **(b)** (*fig*: = *raise, increase*) hoch drücken

push: **push-button** N Druckknopf *m*; **~ controls** Druckknopfsteuerung *f*; **~ telephone** Tastentelefon *nt*; **pushchair** N (*Brit*) Sportwagen *m*

pusher ['pʊʃə] N (*inf*) (*of drugs*) Pusher(in) *m(f)* (*inf*); (*small-time*) Dealer(in) *m(f)* (*inf*)

push: **pushover** ['pʊʃəʊvə] N (*inf*) (= *job etc*) Kinderspiel *nt*; (= *match also*) Geschenk *nt* (*inf*); (= *person*) leichtes Opfer; **push-start** **1** VT anschieben **2** N **to give a car a ~** ein Auto anschieben; **push-up** N (*US*) Liegestütz *m*

pushy ['pʊʃɪ] ADJ (+ER) penetrant (*pej*)

puss [pʊs] N (*inf*) Mieze *f* (*inf*)

pussy ['pʊsɪ] N **(a)** (= *cat*) Mieze *f* (*inf*) **(b)** (*sl*: = *female genitals*) Muschi *f* (*inf*)

pussycat ['pʊsɪkæt] N (*baby-talk*) Miezekatze *f* (*baby-talk*)

put [pʊt]

1 TRANSITIVE VERB	**2** PHRASAL VERBS

pret, ptp put [pʊt]

For combinations of **put** *with adverbs and prepositions, e.g.* **put in**, **put on**, **put up** *etc., see also the phrasal verbs section.*

1 TRANSITIVE VERB

(a) (= *place*) stellen, setzen; (= *lay down*) legen; (= *push in*) stecken; **you've put the picture too high up** du hast das Bild zu hoch (auf)gehängt; **put it there!** (*concluding deal*) abgemacht!; (*congratulatory*) gratuliere!

✦**to put + across** they put a plank across the stream sie legten ein Brett über den Bach

✦**to put + down** he put the corpse down the well er warf die Leiche in den Brunnen

✦**to put + in** to put sth in a drawer etw in eine Schublade legen; **he put his hand in his pocket** er steckte die Hand in die Tasche; **put the dog in the kitchen** tu den Hund in die Küche; **to put sugar in one's coffee** Zucker in den Kaffee tun; **to put sb in a good/bad mood** jdn fröhlich/missmutig stimmen

✦**to put + into** to put a lot of effort into one's work viel Mühe in seine Arbeit stecken; **to put money into sth** (sein) Geld in etw (*acc*) stecken

✦**to put + on** put the lid on the box tu *or* mach den Deckel auf die Schachtel; **he put his head on my shoulder** er legte seinen Kopf auf meine Schulter; **her aunt put her on the train** ihre Tante setzte sie in den Zug; **he put four men on the job** er setzte (für diese Arbeit) vier Leute ein; **to put money on a horse** auf ein Pferd setzen; **I'm putting my money on him to get the job** ich gehe jede Wette ein, dass er die Stelle bekommt

✦**to put + over/under** he put his rucksack over the fence er setzte seinen Rucksack über den Zaun; **to put one's hand over one's/sb's mouth** sich/jdm die Hand vor den Mund halten

✦**to put + (a)round** he put his head (a)round the door er steckte den Kopf zur Tür herein

✦**to put + through** to put one's fist through a window mit der Faust ein Fenster einschlagen; **to put a bullet through sb's head** jdm eine Kugel durch den Kopf schießen

✦**to put + to** to put a glass to one's lips ein Glas zum Mund(e) führen; **she put the shell to her ear** sie hielt (sich *dat*) die Muschel ans Ohr; **to put the children to bed** die Kinder ins Bett bringen; **to put sb to great expense** jdm große Ausgaben verursachen

✦**to put + toward(s)** we'll each put £5 toward(s) the cost of it jeder von uns gibt £ 5 (zum Betrag) dazu

✦**to put sb to do** *or* **doing sth** jdn abordnen, etw zu tun; **they put her to work on the new project** ihr wurde das neue Projekt als Arbeitsbereich zugewiesen

✦**to stay put** liegen/stehen/hängen *etc* bleiben; (*person,* = *not move*) sich nicht von der Stelle rühren; **just stay put!** bleib, wo du bist!

(b) (= *write*) schreiben; *comma, line* machen; (= *draw*) zeichnen; **to put a cross/tick against sb's name** jds Namen ankreuzen/abhaken

(c) (*case, question, proposal*) vorbringen; **to put a matter before a committee** eine Angelegenheit vor einen Ausschuss bringen; **to put sth on the agenda** etw auf die Tagesordnung setzen

✦**to put it to sb (that ...)** (= *suggest*) I put it to you that ... ich behaupte, dass ...; **it was put to me that ...** es wurde mir nahe gelegt, dass ...

(d) (= *express*) ausdrücken

✦**to put it...** that's one way of putting it so kann mans auch sagen; **as he would put it** wie er sich ausdrücken würde; **how shall I put it?** wie soll ich (es) sagen?; **to put it bluntly** um es klipp und klar zu sagen

(e) (= *rate*) schätzen (*at* auf +*acc*)

✦**to put sth above/amongst/before sth** he puts money before his family's happiness er stellt Geld über das Glück seiner Familie

2 PHRASAL VERBS

➤ **put about** VT SEP (*esp Brit*) *news, rumour* verbreiten

➤ **put across** VT SEP *ideas* verständlich machen (*to sb* jdm); *knowledge* vermitteln (*to sb* jdm); (= *promote*) an den Mann bringen (*inf*); **to put oneself across** den richtigen Eindruck von sich geben

➤ **put aside** VT SEP **(a)** *book, knitting etc* beiseite legen **(b)** (= *save for later use*) zurücklegen **(c)** (*fig:* = *forget, abandon*) ablegen; *anger, grief* begraben; *differences* vergessen

➤ **put away** VT SEP **(a)** (*in usual place*) einräumen; *toys* aufräumen; (= *tidy away*) wegräumen; **put that money away!** steck das Geld weg!; **to put the car away** das Auto wegstellen **(b)** (= *save*) zurücklegen **(c)** (*inf:* = *consume*) schaffen (*inf*) **(d)** (*in prison, mental home*) einsperren

➤ **put back** VT SEP **(a)** (= *replace*) see put 1(a) zurücksetzen/-legen/-stecken **(b)** (*esp Brit:* = *postpone*) verschieben; (= *set back*) *plans, production* zurückwerfen; *watch etc* zurückstellen

➤ **put by** VT SEP (*Brit*) zurücklegen

➤ **put down** VT SEP **(a)** (= *set down*) *object* see put 1(a) wegstellen/-legen; *surface* verlegen; **put it down on the floor** stellen Sie es auf den Boden; **I simply couldn't put that book down** ich konnte das Buch einfach nicht aus der Hand legen; **to put down the phone** (den Hörer) auflegen **(b)** *umbrella* zumachen; *lid* zuklappen **(c)** (= *land*) landen **(d)** *rebellion* niederschlagen; (= *reject, humiliate*) demütigen **(e)** (= *pay*) anzahlen; *deposit* machen **(f)** (*esp Brit*) *pet* einschläfern **(g)** (= *write down*) niederschreiben; (*on form, in register*) angeben; **to put one's name down for sth** sich *or* seinen Namen (in eine Liste) für etw eintragen; **you can put me down for £10** für mich können Sie £ 10 eintragen; **put it down to my account/my husband's account** schreiben Sie es mir/meinem Mann an; **put it down under sundries/on expenses** schreiben Sie es unter Verschiedenes auf/als Spesen an **(h)** (= *classify*) halten (*as* für) **(i)** (= *attribute*) zurückführen (*to* auf +*acc*)

➤ **put forward** VT SEP **(a)** *idea, suggestion, plan* vorbringen; *person* (*for job etc*) vorschlagen; (*as candidate*) aufstellen **(b)** (*esp Brit:* = *advance*) *date, meeting* vorverlegen (*to* auf +*acc*); *schedule* voranbringen (*by* um); *watch etc* vorstellen

➤ **put in** **1** VT SEP **(a)** (= *place in*) see put 1(a) hineinstellen/-legen/-stecken; **he opened the drawer and put his hand in** er öffnete die Schublade und griff mit der Hand hinein **(b)** (= *insert in book, speech etc*) einfügen; (= *add*) hinzufügen **(c)** *application, protest, claim* einreichen **(d)** *central heating, car radio* einbauen **(e)** (= *elect*) an die Regierung bringen **(f)** *time* zubringen (*with* mit); **could you put in a few hours' work at the weekend?** könnten Sie am Wochenende ein paar Stunden Arbeit einschieben?; **he put in a lot of hard work on the project** er hat eine Menge harter Arbeit in das Projekt gesteckt **2** VI **to put in for sth** *for job* sich um etw bewerben; *for leave, rise, house* etw beantragen

➤ **put inside** VT SEP (*inf:* *in prison*) einsperren (*inf*)

➤ **put off** VT SEP **(a)** (= *postpone, delay*) verschieben; *decision* aufschieben; *sth unpleasant* hinauszögern; **to put sth off for 10 days/until January** etw um 10 Tage aufschieben/auf Januar verschieben **(b)** (= *make excuses to, be evasive with*) hinhalten; **he's not easily put off** er lässt sich nicht so leicht beirren **(c)** (= *discourage*) die Lust nehmen (+*dat*); **to put sb off sth** jdm die Lust an etw (*dat*) nehmen; **don't let his rudeness put you off** störe dich nicht an seiner Flegelhaftigkeit; **are you trying to put me off?** versuchst du, mir das zu verleiden? *inf* **I've been put off the idea** diese Idee ist mir verleidet worden; **to put sb off doing sth** jdn davon abbringen, etw zu tun **(d)** (= *distract*) ablenken (*prep obj* von); **I'd like to watch you if it won't put you off** ich würde dir gern zusehen, wenn es dich nicht stört **(e)** (= *switch off*) ausschalten

➤ **put on** VT SEP **(a)** *coat, shoes etc* anziehen; *hat* (sich *dat*) aufsetzen; *make-up* auflegen; *(fig) accent* annehmen; *front* vortäuschen; **to put on one's make-up** sich schminken; **his sorrow is put on** sein Kummer ist bloß Schau *(inf)*
(b) (= *increase, add*) **to put on weight** zunehmen; **to put on a few pounds** ein paar Pfund zunehmen; **ten pence was put on the price of petrol** *(Brit)* **or gas** *(US)* der Benzinpreis wurde um zehn Pence erhöht
(c) *play* aufführen; *party* geben; *exhibition* veranstalten; *film* vorführen; *train, bus* einsetzen; *(fig) act, show* abziehen *(inf)*
(d) *(on telephone)* **to put sb on to sb** jdn mit jdm verbinden; **would you put him on?** könnten Sie ihn mir geben?
(e) *light, TV* einschalten; **to put the kettle on** das Wasser aufsetzen
(f) **to put sb on to sth** (= *inform about*) jdm etw vermitteln; **to put sb on to a plumber** *etc* jdm einen Installateur *etc* empfehlen

➤ **put out** VT SEP **(a)** *rubbish etc* hinausbringen; *cat* vor die Tür setzen; **to put the washing out (to dry)** die Wäsche (zum Trocknen) raushängen; **to put sb out of business** jdn aus dem Markt drängen; **that goal put them out of the competition** mit diesem Tor waren sie aus dem Wettbewerb ausgeschieden; **she could not put him out of her mind** er ging ihr nicht aus dem Sinn
(b) *hand, foot* ausstrecken; *tongue, head* herausstrecken; **to put one's head out of the window** den Kopf zum Fenster hinausstrecken
(c) *cards, dishes, cutlery* auflegen; *chessmen etc* aufstellen
(d) *propaganda* machen; *statement* abgeben; *message, appeal* durchgeben; *description* bekannt geben; *(on TV, radio)* senden; **to put money out at interest/at 12%** Geld für Zinsen/ zu 12% (Zinsen) verleihen
(e) *fire, light, candle* löschen
(f) (= *vex*) **to be put out (by sth)** (über etw *acc*) verärgert sein
(g) (= *inconvenience*) **to put sb out** jdm Umstände machen; **to put oneself out (for sb)** sich *(dat)* (wegen jdm) Umstände machen
(h) (= *dislocate*) ausrenken; *(more severely)* auskugeln; *back* verrenken
(i) (= *make inaccurate*) *instruments* ungenau machen; *(fig) calculations, figures* verfälschen

➤ **put over** VT SEP **(a)** = **put across (b)** *(esp US:* = *postpone)* verschieben *(to, until auf +acc)*

➤ **put through** VT SEP **(a)** *reform, proposal* durchbringen; *(+prep obj)* bringen durch; *claim* weiterleiten; *deal* tätigen
(b) +PREP OBJ (= *cause to undergo*) durchmachen lassen; **to put sb through a test** jdn einem Test unterziehen; **he has put his family through a lot (of suffering)** seine Familie hat seinetwegen viel durchgemacht; **they really put him through it!** *(inf)* den haben sie vielleicht durch die Mangel gedreht! *(inf)*
(c) *(by telephone) person* verbinden *(to mit)*; *call* durchstellen *(to zu)*

➤ **put together** VT SEP (= *put in same room, cage etc*) zusammentun; (= *seat together, assemble*) zusammensetzen; *essay, menu* zusammenstellen; *collection, evidence, facts* zusammentragen; **he's better than all the others put together** er ist besser als alle anderen zusammen

➤ **put up 1** VT SEP **(a)** *hand* hochheben; *car window* zumachen; *umbrella* aufklappen; *hair* hochstecken
(b) *flag, sail* hissen
(c) *picture, decorations, curtains* aufhängen; *notice* anbringen
(d) *building, fence, barrier* errichten; *ladder, scaffolding* aufstellen; *tent* aufschlagen
(e) (= *increase*) erhöhen
(f) (= *propose, nominate*) vorschlagen; *(as candidate)* aufstellen
(g) **to put sth up for sale** etw zum Verkauf anbieten; **to put one's child up for adoption** sein Kind zur Adoption freigeben; **to put up resistance (to sb)** (jdm) Widerstand leisten
(h) (= *give accommodation to*) unterbringen
(i) *capital* bereitstellen; *reward* aussetzen
(j) **to put sb up to sth** jdn zu etw anstiften
2 VI (= *stay*) wohnen; *(for one night)* übernachten

➤ **put up with** VI +PREP OBJ sich abfinden mit; **I won't put up with that** das lasse ich mir nicht gefallen

put: **put-down** N Abfuhr *f*; **put-on** *(inf)* ADJ vorgetäuscht
putrefy [ˈpjuːtrɪfaɪ] VI verwesen
putrid [ˈpjuːtrɪd] ADJ verfault; *smell* faulig
putt [pʌt] **1** N Schlag *m* *(mit dem man einlocht)* **2** VTI putten, einlochen
putter *(US)* VI = **potter²**
putty [ˈpʌtɪ] N Kitt *m*
puzzle [ˈpʌzl] **1** N (= *wordgame, mystery*) Rätsel *nt*; (= *toy*) Geduldsspiel *nt*; (= *jigsaw*) Puzzle(spiel) *nt* **2** VT
(a) verblüffen; **to be ~d about sth** sich über etw *(acc)* im Unklaren sein; **the authorities are ~d** die Behörden stehen vor einem Rätsel **(b)** **to ~ sth out** etw (her)austüfteln **3** VI **to ~ about** *or* **over sth** sich *(dat)* über etw *(acc)* den Kopf zerbrechen
puzzled [ˈpʌzld] ADJ *look, frown* verdutzt; *person* verwirrt
puzzlement [ˈpʌzlmənt] N Verwirrung *f*
puzzling [ˈpʌzlɪŋ] ADJ rätselhaft; *story, mechanism, attitude, question* verwirrend
pygmy, pigmy [ˈpɪgmɪ] **1** N **Pygmy** Pygmäe *m* **2** ADJ **Pygmy** Pygmäen-
pyjamas, *(US)* **pajamas** [pəˈdʒɑːməz] PL Schlafanzug *m*
pylon [ˈpaɪlən] N Mast *m*
pyramid [ˈpɪrəmɪd] N Pyramide *f*
pyramid selling N ≈ Schneeballsystem *nt*
pyre [ˈpaɪəʳ] N Scheiterhaufen *m*
Pyrenean [pɪrəˈniːən] ADJ pyrenäisch
Pyrenees [pɪrəˈniːz] PL Pyrenäen *pl*
Pyrex® [ˈpaɪreks] N Jenaer Glas® *nt*
python [ˈpaɪθən] N Python *m*

Qq

Q, q [kju:] N Q nt, q nt

Q and A [kju:ənðeɪ] ABBR of **questions and answers**

Qatar [kæ'tɑːʳ] N Katar nt

qtr ABBR of **quarter**

quack [kwæk] **1** N Schnattern nt no pl **2** VI (duck) schnattern

quadruple ['kwɒdrʊpl] **1** ADJ vierfach **2** VT vervierfachen **3** VI sich vervierfachen

quadruplet [kwɒ'druːplɪt] N Vierling m

quagmire ['kwægmaɪəʳ] N Sumpf m; (fig) (of vice etc) Morast m; (= difficult situation) Schlamassel m (inf)

quail [kweɪl] N (Orn) Wachtel f; **~s' eggs** Wachteleier pl

quaint [kweɪnt] ADJ (+ER) (= picturesque) idyllisch; (= charmingly old-fashioned) urig; (= pleasantly odd) idea kurios; way of speaking drollig

quaintly ['kweɪntlɪ] ADV (a) (= picturesquely) idyllisch; decorated malerisch (b) written schnurrig; dressed putzig

quaintness ['kweɪntnɪs] N (= picturesque nature) idyllischer Anblick; (= old-fashioned charm) Urigkeit f; (= oddness: of idea) Kuriosität f

quake [kweɪk] VI zittern (with vor +dat); (earth, rafters etc) beben

Quaker ['kweɪkəʳ] N Quäker(in) m(f)

qualification [ˌkwɒlɪfɪ'keɪʃən] N (a) Qualifikation f (also Sport); (= document itself) Zeugnis nt; (= ability, prerequisite) Voraussetzung f (b) (= act of qualifying) Abschluss m; **after his ~ as a doctor** nachdem er seine Ausbildung als Arzt abgeschlossen hatte (c) (= limitation) Einschränkung f; (= modification) Modifikation f

qualified ['kwɒlɪfaɪd] ADJ (a) (= having training) ausgebildet; (= with degree) Diplom-; **~ engineer** Diplomingenieur(in) m(f); **highly ~** hoch qualifiziert; **to be ~ to do sth** qualifiziert sein, etw zu tun; **he is/is not ~ to teach** er besitzt die/keine Lehrbefähigung; **he was not ~ for the job** ihm fehlte die Qualifikation für die Stelle; **to be well ~ for sth** für etw hoch qualifiziert sein; **he is fully ~** er ist voll ausgebildet (b) (= able, entitled) berechtigt; voter zugelassen; **to be ~ to vote** wahlberechtigt sein (c) (= limited) nicht uneingeschränkt; **~ acceptance** (Comm) bedingte Annahme; **~ majority** (Pol) qualifizierte Mehrheit

qualify ['kwɒlɪfaɪ] **1** VT (a) qualifizieren; (= make legally entitled) berechtigen; **to ~ sb to do sth** (= entitle) jdn berechtigen, etw zu tun (b) statement, criticism einschränken; opinion, remark modifizieren **2** VI (a) (= acquire degree etc) seine Ausbildung abschließen; **to ~ as a lawyer/doctor** sein juristisches/medizinisches Staatsexamen machen; **to ~ as a teacher** die Lehrbefähigung erhalten (b) (Sport) sich qualifizieren (for für) (c) (= fulfil required conditions) infrage kommen (for für); **does he ~ for admission to the club?** erfüllt er die Bedingungen für die Aufnahme in den Klub?

qualifying ['kwɒlɪfaɪɪŋ] ADJ adjective erläuternd; (Sport) Qualifikations-; **~ match** Qualifikationsspiel nt

quality ['kwɒlɪtɪ] **1** N (a) Qualität f; (of justice, education etc) (hoher) Stand; **of good/poor ~** von guter/schlechter Qualität; **~ matters more than quantity** Qualität geht vor Quantität; **they vary in ~** sie sind qualitativ verschieden (b) (= characteristics) Eigenschaft f (c) (= nature) Art f (d) (of voice, sound) Klangfarbe f **2** ATTR Qualitäts-; **~ goods** Qualitätsware f; **~ mark** Gütezeichen nt (b) (inf: = good) erstklassig (inf); newspaper seriös; **the ~ press** (Brit) die seriöse Presse

quality: quality assurance N (Ind) Qualitätssicherung f; **~ certificate** Qualitätszertifikat nt, Gütepass m; **quality control** N Qualitätskontrolle f; **quality controller** N (Ind) Qualitätskontrolleur(in) m(f); **quality time** N intensiv genutzte Zeit

qualm [kwɑːm] N (a) (= doubt, scruple) Skrupel m; **without a ~** ohne jeden Skrupel (b) (= misgiving) Bedenken nt

quandary ['kwɒndərɪ] N Verlegenheit f; **he was in a ~ as to or about what to do** er wusste nicht, was er tun sollte; **to put sb in a ~** jdn in Verlegenheit bringen

quango ['kwæŋgəʊ] N (Brit) ABBR of **quasi-autonomous nongovernmental organization** regierungsunabhängige Kommission

quantify ['kwɒntɪfaɪ] VT quantifizieren

quantitative ADJ, **quantitatively** ADV ['kwɒntɪtətɪv, -lɪ] quantitativ

quantity ['kwɒntɪtɪ] N (a) Quantität f; (= amount) Menge f; (= proportion) Anteil m (of an +dat); **in ~, in large quantities** in großen Mengen; **what ~ did you order?** welche Menge haben Sie bestellt?; **in equal quantities** zu gleichen Teilen (b) OFTEN PL (= large amount or number) Unmenge f (c) (Math, Phys, fig) Größe f

quantity discount N Mengenrabatt m

quantum ['kwɒntəm]: **quantum leap** N (fig) Riesenschritt m; **quantum mechanics** N SING Quantenmechanik f

quarantine ['kwɒrəntiːn] **1** N Quarantäne f; **to put sb in ~** jdn unter Quarantäne stellen **2** ATTR Quarantäne- **3** VT unter Quarantäne stellen

quarrel ['kwɒrəl] **1** N (a) Streit m; (= dispute) Auseinandersetzung f; **they have had a ~** sie haben sich gestritten (b) (cause for complaint) Einwand m (with gegen); **I have no ~ with him** ich habe nichts gegen ihn **2** VI (a) sich streiten (with mit, about, over über +acc); (more trivially) sich zanken; **to ~ over a girl** sich um ein Mädchen streiten (b) (= find fault) etwas auszusetzen haben (with an +dat); **you can't ~ with that** daran kann man doch nichts aussetzen

quarrelling, (US) **quarreling** ['kwɒrəlɪŋ] N Streiterei f

quarrelsome ['kwɒrəlsəm] ADJ streitsüchtig

quarry¹ ['kwɒrɪ] **1** N Steinbruch m; **slate etc ~** Schieferbruch etc **2** VT brechen **3** VI Steine brechen; **to ~ for sth** etw brechen

quarry² N (a) Beute f (b) (fig) (= thing) Ziel nt; (= person) Opfer nt

quarter ['kwɔːtəʳ] **1** N (a) (of amount, = district, area) Viertel nt; **to divide sth into ~s** etw in vier Teile teilen; **the bottle was a ~/three-~s full** die Flasche war viertel/drei viertel voll; **a mile and a ~** eineinviertel Meilen; **a ~ of a mile** eine Viertelmeile; **for a ~ (of) the price, for ~ the price** zu einem Viertel des Preises; **a ~ of an hour** eine Viertelstunde; **a ~ to seven, a ~ of seven** (US) (ein) Viertel vor sieben; **a ~ past six, a ~ after six** (US) (ein) Viertel nach sechs; **an hour and a ~** eineinviertel Stunden; **in these ~s** in dieser Gegend (b) (= fourth of year) Vierteljahr nt (c) (US) Vierteldollar m (d) (= direction) (Himmels)richtung f (e) (= side) Seite f; (= place) Stelle f; **he won't get help from that ~** von dieser Seite wird er keine Hilfe bekommen; **in various ~s** an verschiedenen Stellen; **at close ~s** in der Nähe; (= from nearby) aus der Nähe (f) **quarters** PL (= lodgings) Quartier nt (also Mil) (g) (= mercy in battle) Pardon m; **he gave no ~** er kannte kein Pardon **2** ADJ Viertel-; **~ pound/mile** Viertelpfund nt/-meile f; **the/a ~ part** das/ein Viertel **3** VT vierteln

quarter: **quarterback** N (*US Ftbl*) Quarterback *m*; **quarterfinal** N Viertelfinalspiel *nt*; **quarterfinalist** N Teilnehmer(in) *m(f)* am Viertelfinale

quarterly [ˈkwɔːtəlɪ] **1** ADJ, ADV vierteljährlich **2** N Vierteljahresschrift *f*

quarter: **quarter note** N (*US Mus*) Viertel(note *f*) *nt*; **quarter-pounder** N (*Cook*) Viertelpfünder *m*

quartet(te) [kwɔːˈtet] N Quartett *nt*

quartz [ˈkwɔːts] N Quarz *m*

quash [kwɒʃ] VT **(a)** (*Jur*) *verdict* aufheben **(b)** *rebellion* unterdrücken; *suggestion, objection* ablehnen

quasi- [ˈkwɑːzɪ-] PREF quasi-, quasi

quaver [ˈkweɪvəʳ] **1** N **(a)** (*esp Brit Mus*) Achtel(note *f*) *nt* **(b)** (*in voice*) Zittern *nt* **2** VI (*voice*) zittern

quavering [ˈkweɪvərɪŋ], **quavery** [ˈkweɪvərɪ] ADJ *voice* zitternd; *notes* tremolierend

quay [kiː] N Kai *m*; **alongside the** ~ am Kai

quayside [ˈkiːsaɪd] N Kai *m*

queasiness [ˈkwiːzɪnɪs] N Übelkeit *f*

queasy [ˈkwiːzɪ] ADJ (+ER) gereizt; **I feel** ~ mir ist (leicht) übel; **it makes me** ~ da wird mir übel

queen [kwiːn] N **(a)** Königin *f* **(b)** (*Cards, Chess*) Dame *f*; ~ **of spades** Pikdame *f* **(c)** (*inf*: = *homosexual*) Tunte *f* (*inf*)

queen bee N Bienenkönigin *f*

queenly [ˈkwiːnlɪ] ADJ königlich

queen mother N Königinmutter *f*

queen's [kwiːnz]: **Queen's Award** N *im Namen der Königin verliehener Preis für wirtschaftliche Leistungen*; **Queen's Counsel** N (*Brit*) Kronanwalt *m*/-anwältin *f*; **queen's English** N englische Hochsprache

Queen's Speech N Thronrede *f*

queer [kwɪəʳ] **1** ADJ (+ER) **(a)** (= *strange*) eigenartig; (= *eccentric*) komisch; **he's a bit** ~ **in the head** (*inf*) er ist nicht ganz richtig im Kopf (*inf*)
(b) (= *causing suspicion*) verdächtig; **there's something** ~ **about it** da ist etwas faul dran (*inf*)
(c) (*inf*: = *unwell*) unwohl; (= *peculiar*) komisch; **I feel** ~ (= *unwell*) mir ist nicht gut; (= *peculiar*) mir ist ganz komisch (*inf*)
(d) (*pej inf*: = *homosexual*) schwul (*inf*)
2 N (*pej inf*: = *homosexual*) Schwule(r) *mf* (*inf*)

quell [kwel] VT *fear* bezwingen; *riot* unterdrücken; *anxieties* überwinden

quench [kwentʃ] VT löschen

query [ˈkwɪərɪ] **1** N Frage *f*; (*Comput*) Abfrage *f*; ~ **language** Abfragesprache *f* **2** VT **(a)** (= *express doubt about*) bezweifeln; *statement, motives* infrage stellen; *bill, item, invoice* reklamieren **(b)** (= *check*) to ~ **sth with sb** etw mit jdm abklären **(c)** (*Comput*) abfragen

quest [kwest] N Suche *f* (*for* nach); (*for knowledge, happiness etc*) Streben *nt* (*for* nach)

question [ˈkwestʃən] **1** N **(a)** Frage *f* (*to* an +*acc*); (*Parl*) (An)frage *f* (*to* an +*acc*); **to ask sb a** ~ jdm eine Frage stellen; **don't ask so many** ~**s** frag nicht so viel; **they'll buy anything, no** ~**s asked** sie kaufen alles und stellen keine dummen Fragen; **that's another** ~ **altogether** das ist etwas völlig anderes; **it's simply a** ~ **of time** das ist einfach eine Frage der Zeit; **if it's only a** ~ **of whether ...** wenn es nur darum geht, ob ...
(b) NO PL (= *doubt*) Zweifel *m*; **beyond (all)** ~, **without** ~ ohne (jeden) Zweifel; **your sincerity is not in** ~ niemand zweifelt an Ihrer Aufrichtigkeit; **to call sth into** ~ etw infrage stellen
(c) NO PL (= *possibility, likelihood*) **there's no** ~ **of a strike** von einem Streik kann keine Rede sein; **that's out of the** ~ das kommt nicht infrage *or* in Frage; **the person in** ~ die fragliche Person
2 VT **(a)** fragen (*about* nach); (*police etc*) befragen (*about* zu);

my father started ~**ing me about where I'd been** mein Vater fing an, mich auszufragen, wo ich gewesen war; **they were** ~**ed by the immigration authorities** ihnen wurden von der Einwanderungsbehörde viele Fragen gestellt
(b) (= *express doubt about*) bezweifeln; (= *dispute, challenge*) infrage stellen

questionable [ˈkwestʃənəbl] ADJ (= *suspect*) fragwürdig; (= *open to doubt*) *statement, figures* fraglich; *advantage* zweifelhaft

questioner [ˈkwestʃənəʳ] N Frager(in) *m(f)*

questioning [ˈkwestʃənɪŋ] **1** ADJ *look* fragend **2** N Verhör *nt*; (*of candidate*) Befragung *f*; **after hours of** ~ **by the immigration authorities** nach stundenlanger Befragung durch die Einwanderungsbehörde; **they brought him in for** ~ sie holten ihn, um ihn zu vernehmen

questioningly [ˈkwestʃənɪŋlɪ] ADV fragend

question mark N Fragezeichen *nt*

questionnaire [ˌkwestʃəˈnɛəʳ] N Fragebogen *m*

queue [kjuː] **1** N (*Brit*) Schlange *f*; **to form a** ~ eine Schlange bilden; **to stand in a** ~ Schlange stehen; **to join the** ~ sich (hinten) anstellen; **a** ~ **of cars** eine Autoschlange; **a long** ~ **of people** eine lange Schlange
2 VI (*Brit: also* ~ **up**) Schlange stehen; (*people also*) anstehen; (= *form a* ~) eine Schlange bilden; (*people*) sich anstellen; **they were queuing for the bus** sie standen an der Bushaltestelle Schlange; **they were queuing for bread** sie standen nach Brot an; **people are queuing up to ...** (*fig*) die Leute schlagen sich darum, zu ...

quibble [ˈkwɪbl] **1** VI (= *be petty-minded*) kleinlich sein (*over, about* wegen); (= *argue with sb*) sich herumstreiten (*over, about* wegen); **to** ~ **over details** auf Einzelheiten herumreiten **2** N **I've got a few** ~**s about her work** ich habe ein paar Kleinigkeiten an ihrer Arbeit auszusetzen

quiche [kiːʃ] N Quiche *f*

quick [kwɪk] **1** ADJ (+ER) **(a)** schnell; **be** ~! mach schnell!; **and be** ~ **about it** aber ein bisschen dalli (*inf*); **you were/he was** ~ das war ja schnell; **he's a** ~ **worker** er arbeitet schnell; ~ **march!** (*Mil*) im Eilschritt, marsch!; **it's** ~**er by train** mit dem Zug geht es schneller; **he is** ~ **to criticize other people** er ist mit seiner Kritik schnell bei der Hand; **what's the** ~**est way to the station?** wie komme ich am schnellsten zum Bahnhof?
(b) (= *short, quickly done*) *kiss* flüchtig; *speech, synopsis, rest* kurz; **let me have a** ~ **look** lass mich mal schnell sehen; **to have a** ~ **chat (with sb)** (mit jdm) ein paar Worte wechseln; **could I have a** ~ **word?** könnte ich Sie mal kurz sprechen?; **I'll just write him a** ~ **note** ich schreibe ihm mal kurz; **time for a** ~ **beer** genügend Zeit, um ein Bierchen zu trinken; **a** ~ **one** eine(r, s) auf die Schnelle (*inf*); (*question*) eine kurze Frage
(c) (= *lively*, ~ *to understand*) *mind* wach; *person* schnell von Begriff (*inf*); *child* aufgeweckt; *temper* hitzig; *eye, ear* scharf; **he's too** ~ **for me** mit ihm komme ich nicht mit **2** ADV (+ER) schnell

quick-drying [ˈkwɪkˈdraɪɪŋ] ADJ schnell trocknend

quicken [ˈkwɪkən] **1** VT (*also* ~ **up**) beschleunigen **2** VI (*also* ~ **up**) sich beschleunigen; **the pace** ~**ed** das Tempo nahm zu

quick fix N Schnelllösung *f*

quickie [ˈkwɪkɪ] N (*inf*) (= *drink*) eine(r, s) auf die Schnelle (*inf*); (= *question*) kurze Frage; (= *sex*) Quickie *m* (*inf*)

quickly [ˈkwɪklɪ] ADV schnell

quickness [ˈkwɪknɪs] N **(a)** (= *speed*) Schnelligkeit *f* **(b)** (= *intelligence*) schnelle Auffassungsgabe

quick: **quicksand** N Treibsand *m*; **quick-tempered** ADJ hitzig; **to be** ~ leicht aufbrausen; **quick-witted** ADJ geistesgegenwärtig; *answer* schlagfertig

quid [kwɪd] N, *pl* - (*Brit inf*) Pfund *nt*; **20** - 20 Eier (*sl*)

quiet [ˈkwaɪət] **1** ADJ (+ER) **(a)** still; *neighbours, person, engine, area, time* ruhig; *footsteps, music, car, voice, smile* leise; *resentment* heimlich; **she was as** ~ **as a mouse** sie war mucksmäuschenstill (*inf*); **(be)** ~! Ruhe!; **to keep** ~ (= *not speak*) still sein; (= *not make noise*) leise sein; **keep** ~! sei still!; **that book should keep him** ~ **for a while** das Buch sollte ihn eine Weile beschäftigt halten, mit dem Buch sollte er eine Weile zu tun haben; **to keep** ~ **about sth** über etw (*acc*) nichts sagen; **to go** ~ still werden; (*music etc*) leise werden; **things are very** ~ **at the moment** im Augenblick ist nicht viel los; **business is** ~ das Geschäft ist ruhig; **I was just sitting**

there having a ~ **drink** ich saß da und habe in aller Ruhe mein Bier *etc* getrunken; **I'll have a ~ word with him** ich werde mal ein Wörtchen (im Vertrauen) mit ihm reden; **could we have a ~ word together some time?** könnten wir uns mal unter vier Augen unterhalten?; **he kept the matter ~** er behielt die Sache für sich

(b) (= *gentle*) *face, character* sanft; *child* ruhig

(c) (= *unpretentious*) *wedding, dinner* im kleinen Rahmen

(d) (= *unobtrusive, confidential*) *dinner* im kleinen Kreis; *negotiation, diplomacy* besonnen

2 N Ruhe *f*; **a period of ~** eine Zeit der Stille; **in the ~ of the night** in der Stille der Nacht; **on the ~** heimlich

3 VT = **quieten**

4 VI (*US*: = *become ~*) nachlassen

quieten ['kwaɪətn] VT (*Brit*) *sb* zum Schweigen bringen; *noisy class, dog* zur Ruhe bringen; *crying baby* beruhigen

➤ **quieten down** (*Brit*) **1** VI (= *become silent*) leiser werden; (= *become calm*) sich beruhigen; **quieten down, boys!** ein bisschen ruhiger, Jungens!; **things have quietened down a lot** es ist viel ruhiger geworden **2** VT SEP *person* beruhigen; **to quieten things down** (*situation*) die Lage beruhigen

quietly ['kwaɪətlɪ] ADV leise; (= *peacefully, making little fuss*) ruhig; (= *secretly*) still und heimlich; (= *placidly*) still; **to live ~** ruhig leben; **he's very ~ spoken** er spricht sehr leise; **to be ~ confident** insgeheim sehr sicher sein; **I was sitting here ~** sipping my wine ich saß da und trank in aller Ruhe meinen Wein; **he refused to go ~** er weigerte sich, unauffällig zu gehen; **are you going to come ~?** (*said by policeman*) kommen Sie widerstandslos mit?; **he slipped off ~** er machte sich in aller Stille davon (*inf*)

quietness ['kwaɪətnɪs] N **(a)** Stille *f*; (*of engine, car*) Geräuscharmut *f*; (*of footsteps etc*) Lautlosigkeit *f*; (*of person*) stille Art; **the ~ of her voice** ihre leise Stimme

(b) (= *peacefulness*) Ruhe *f*

quilt [kwɪlt] N (= *continental ~*) Steppdecke *f*; (*unstitched*) Federbett *nt*; (= *bedspread*) Bettdecke *f*

quintet(te) [kwɪn'tet] N (*Mus*) Quintett *nt*

quintuplet [kwɪn'tjuːplɪt] N Fünfling *m*

quip [kwɪp] **1** N witzige Bemerkung **2** VTI witzeln

quirk [kwɜːk] N Schrulle *f*; (*of nature, fate*) Laune *f*; **by a strange ~ of fate** durch eine Laune des Schicksals; **~s** (*US*: *of product*) Kinderkrankheiten *pl*, Anfangsprobleme *pl*

quirky ['kwɜːkɪ] ADJ (+ER) schrullig

quit [kwɪt], *vb: pret, ptp* **quitted** *or* **quit 1** VT **(a)** *town, army* verlassen (*also Comput*); *job* aufgeben; **I've given her notice to ~ the flat** (*form*) ich habe ihr die Wohnung gekündigt

(b) (*inf*: = *stop*) aufhören mit; **to ~ doing sth** aufhören, etw zu tun; **~ it!** hör (damit) auf!

2 VI **(a)** (= *leave one's job*) kündigen

(b) (= *go away*) weggehen; **notice to ~** Kündigung *f*

(c) (= *accept defeat*) aufgeben

(d) (*Comput*) das Programm/die Datei *etc* verlassen, aussteigen (*inf*)

quite [kwaɪt] ADV **(a)** (= *entirely*) ganz; (*emph*) völlig; **I am ~ happy where I am** ich fühle mich hier ganz wohl; **it's ~ impossible to do that** das ist völlig unmöglich; **you're being ~ impossible** du bist einfach unmöglich; **are you ~ finished?** bist du jetzt fertig?; **I ~ agree with you** ich stimme völlig mit Ihnen überein; **that's ~ another matter** das ist doch etwas

ganz anderes; **that's ~ enough for me** das reicht wirklich; **that's ~ enough of that** das reicht jetzt aber; **it was ~ some time ago** es war vor einiger Zeit; **not ~** nicht ganz; **you weren't ~ tall enough** Sie waren ein bisschen zu klein; **I don't ~ see what he means** ich verstehe nicht ganz, was er meint; **you don't ~ understand** Sie verstehen mich anscheinend nicht richtig; **it was not ~ midnight** es war noch nicht ganz Mitternacht; **sorry! – that's ~ all right** entschuldige! – das macht nichts; **I'm ~ all right, thanks** danke, mir gehts gut; **thank you – that's ~ all right** danke – bitte schön; **(so)! ~** ganz recht!

(b) (= *to some degree*) ziemlich; **~ likely/unlikely** sehr wahrscheinlich/unwahrscheinlich; **~ a few people** ziemlich viele Leute; **I ~ like this painting** dieses Bild gefällt mir ganz gut; **yes, I'd ~ like to** ja, eigentlich ganz gern

(c) (= *really, truly*) wirklich; **she's ~ a girl** *etc* sie ist ein tolles Mädchen *etc*; **it's ~ delightful** es ist entzückend; **it was ~ a shock** es war ein ziemlicher Schock; **it was ~ a party** das war vielleicht eine Party! (*inf*); **it was ~ an experience** das war schon ein Erlebnis; **he's ~ a hero now** jetzt ist er ein richtiger Held

quits [kwɪts] ADJ quitt; **to be ~ with sb** mit jdm quitt sein; **shall we call it ~?** (= *agree to stop*) lassen wirs (dabei bewenden)?; (*when owing money*) sind wir quitt?

quiver ['kwɪvəʳ] VI zittern (*with* vor +*dat*); (*lips, eyelids, heart*) zucken

quiz [kwɪz] **1** N **(a)** Quiz *nt* **(b)** (*US Sch inf*) Prüfung *f* **2** VT **(a)** ausfragen (*about* über +*acc*) **(b)** (*US Sch inf*) abfragen

quiz: **quizmaster** N Quizmaster *m*; **quiz show** N Quiz *nt*

quizzical ['kwɪzɪkəl] ADJ *air, look* fragend; *smile* zweifelnd; *face* gewitzt

quizzically ['kwɪzɪkəlɪ] ADV *look* fragend; *smile* zweifelnd

quota ['kwəʊtə] N **(a)** (*of work*) Pensum *nt* **(b)** (= *permitted amount*) Quantum *nt*; (= *share allotted*) Anteil *m*; (*of goods*) Kontingent *nt*; **the ~ of immigrants allowed into the country** die zugelassene Einwanderungsquote; **import ~** Einfuhrkontingent *nt*

quotation [kwəʊ'teɪʃən] N **(a)** (= *passage cited*) Zitat *nt* **(b)** (*Fin*) Notierung *f* **(c)** (*Comm*: = *estimate*) (Preis)angebot *nt*; (*for building work etc*) Kostenvoranschlag *m*

quotation marks PL Anführungszeichen *pl*

quote [kwəʊt] **1** VT **(a)** *author, text* zitieren; **please don't ~ me on this, but ...** (= *this isn't authoritative*) ich kann mich nicht hundertprozentig dafür verbürgen, aber ...; (= *don't repeat it*) bitte wiederholen Sie nicht, was ich jetzt sage, aber ...; **he was ~d as saying that ...** er soll gesagt haben, dass ...

(b) (= *cite*) anführen

(c) (*Comm*) *price* nennen; *reference number* angeben

(d) (*St Ex*) notieren; **the shares are ~d at £2** die Aktien werden mit £ 2 notiert; **~d price** Kursnotierung *f*

2 VI **(a)** (*from person, text*) zitieren; **to ~ from an author** einen Schriftsteller zitieren

(b) (*Comm*) ein (Preis)angebot machen; (*building firm etc*) einen Kostenvoranschlag machen; **we asked six companies to ~** wir baten sechs Firmen um Preisangaben

3 N **(a)** (*from author etc*) Zitat *nt*

(b) **in ~s** in Anführungszeichen

(c) (*Comm*) Preis *m*; (= *estimate*) Kostenvoranschlag *m*

Rr

R, r [ɑːʳ] N R nt, r nt

R (a) ABBR of **river (b)** (US Film) ABBR of **restricted** für Jugendliche nicht geeignet

rabbi ['ræbaɪ] N Rabbiner m; (as title) Rabbi m

rabbit ['ræbɪt] 🛮 N Kaninchen nt 🛮 VI (Brit inf: also ~ **on**) quasseln (inf)

rabbit IN CPDS Kaninchen-; **rabbit burrow, rabbit hole** N Kaninchenbau m

rabble ['ræbl] N (= disorderly crowd) lärmende Menge; (pej: = lower classes) Pöbel m

rabies ['reɪbiːz] N Tollwut f

RAC ABBR of **Royal Automobile Club**

raccoon N = **racoon**

race¹ [reɪs] 🛮 N Rennen nt; (swimming) Wettschwimmen nt; **100 metres** ~ 100-Meter-Lauf m; **to run a** ~ (**against sb**) (mit jdm um die Wette) laufen; **to go to the ~s** zum Pferderennen gehen; **a** ~ **against time** or **the clock** ein Wettlauf m mit der Zeit
🛮 VT um die Wette laufen/reiten/fahren/schwimmen etc mit; (Sport) laufen/reiten/fahren/schwimmen etc gegen; **I'll ~ you to school** ich mache mit dir ein Wettrennen bis zur Schule
🛮 VI (a) (= compete) laufen/reiten/fahren/schwimmen etc; **to ~ with** or **against sb** mit jdm um die Wette laufen etc **(b)** (= rush) rasen; (with work) hetzen; **to ~ about** herumrasen; **to ~ after sb/sth** hinter jdm/etw herhetzen; **he ~d through his work** er jagte durch sein Arbeitspensum; **clouds ~d across the sky** Wolken jagten über den Himmel **(c)** (engine) durchdrehen; (heart) rasen; (pulse, thoughts, mind) jagen

race² N (= ethnic group, species) Rasse f; **of mixed** ~ gemischtrassig

race: racecourse N (Brit) Rennbahn f; **race hatred** N Rassenhass m; **racehorse** N Rennpferd nt; **race relations** N PL Beziehungen pl zwischen den Rassen; **race riot** N Rassenkrawall m usu pl; **racetrack** N Rennbahn f

racial ['reɪʃəl] ADJ rassisch, Rassen-; ~ **discrimination** Rassendiskriminierung f; ~ **equality** Rassengleichheit f; ~ **harassment** rassistisch motivierte Schikanierung; ~ **minority** rassische Minderheit; ~ **violence** rassistische Gewalt

racially ['reɪʃəlɪ] ADV offensive, sensitive in Bezug auf die Rasse; abused aufgrund seiner/ihrer Rasse; diverse multikulturell; ~ **superior** rassenmäßig überlegen; **to be** ~ **motivated** (riots etc) rassistisch motiviert sein; **a** ~ **motivated attack** ein ausländerfeindlicher Angriff

racing ['reɪsɪŋ] N (= horse-~) Pferderennsport m; (= motor ~) Motorrennen nt; **he often goes** ~ er geht oft zu Pferderennen/Motorrennen

racing IN CPDS Renn-; **racing bicycle** N Rennrad nt; **racing car** N Rennwagen m; **racing driver** N Rennfahrer(in) m(f); **racing pigeon** N Brieftaube f

racism ['reɪsɪzəm] N Rassismus m

racist ['reɪsɪst] 🛮 N Rassist(in) m(f) 🛮 ADJ rassistisch

rack¹ [ræk] 🛮 N (a) (for hats, toast, pipes etc) Ständer m; (for bottles, plates) Gestell nt; (= shelves) Regal nt; (= luggage ~) Gepäcknetz nt; (on car, bicycle) Gepäckträger m **(b) to put sb on the** ~ (lit, fig) jdn auf die Folter spannen; **to be on the** ~ (fig) Folterqualen leiden 🛮 VT (a) (to cause pain, also fig) quälen **(b) to** ~ **one's brains** sich (dat) den Kopf zerbrechen

rack² N **to go to** ~ **and ruin** (person) verkommen; (country, economy) herunterkommen; (building) verfallen

racket¹ ['rækɪt] N (Sport) Schläger m

racket² N (a) (= uproar) Lärm m; **to make a** ~ Lärm machen **(b)** (inf: = dishonest business) Schwindelgeschäft nt (inf), Gaunerei f (inf); **the drugs** ~ das Drogengeschäft

racketeer [ˌrækɪ'tɪəʳ] N Gauner(in) m(f) (inf); (in serious crime) Gangster(in) m(f)

racketeering [ˌrækɪ'tɪərɪŋ] N Gaunereien pl (inf); (= organized crime) organisiertes Verbrechen

raconteur [ˌrækɒn'tɜːʳ] N Erzähler(in) m(f) von Anekdoten

racoon [rə'kuːn] N Waschbär m

racquet ['rækɪt] N (Brit Sport) Schläger m

racquetball ['rækɪtˌbɔːl] N, NO PL Racquetball m

racy ['reɪsɪ] ADJ (+ER) style schwungvoll; (= risqué) gewagt

radar ['reɪdɑːʳ] N Radar m or nt

radiance N (of sun, smile) Strahlen nt

radiant ['reɪdɪənt] ADJ (lit, fig) strahlend; colours leuchtend; **to be** ~ **with joy** vor Freude strahlen

radiantly ['reɪdɪəntlɪ] ADV **(a)** happy strahlend **(b)** (liter) shine hell

radiate ['reɪdɪeɪt] 🛮 VI Strahlen aussenden; (= emit heat) Wärme ausstrahlen; (heat, light, energy) ausgestrahlt werden 🛮 VT ausstrahlen

radiation [ˌreɪdɪ'eɪʃən] N (of heat etc) (Aus)strahlung f; (= rays) radioaktive Strahlung; **contaminated by** or **with** ~ strahlenverseucht

radiator ['reɪdɪeɪtəʳ] N (for heating) Heizkörper m; (Aut) Kühler m

radical ['rædɪkəl] 🛮 ADJ radikal; (= basic) fundamental 🛮 N (Pol) Radikale(r) mf

radically ['rædɪkəlɪ] ADV radikal

radio ['reɪdɪəʊ] 🛮 N **(a)** (= wireless) Rundfunk m; (also ~ **set**) Radio nt; **to listen to the** ~ Radio hören; **to hear sth on the** ~ etw im Radio hören; **he was on the** ~ **yesterday** er kam gestern im Radio **(b)** (in taxi etc) Funkgerät nt; **over the/by** ~ über Funk; **they don't have (a)** ~ sie haben keinen Funk 🛮 VT person über Funk verständigen; message funken 🛮 VI **to** ~ **for help** per Funk einen Hilferuf durchgeben

radio: radioactive ADJ radioaktiv; **radioactivity** N Radioaktivität f; **radio alarm (clock)** N Radiowecker m; **radio broadcast** N Radiosendung f; **radio cassette recorder** N (Brit) Radiorekorder m; **radio contact** N Funkkontakt m; **radio-controlled** ADJ ferngesteuert

radiology [ˌreɪdɪ'ɒlədʒɪ] N Radiologie f; (X-ray also) Röntgenologie f

radio: radio mast N Funkmast m; **radio programme** N Radio- or Rundfunkprogramm nt; **radio station** N Rundfunkstation f; **radiotherapy** N Röntgentherapie f

radish ['rædɪʃ] N Rettich m; (small red) Radieschen nt

radius ['reɪdɪəs] N, pl **radii** (Math) Radius m; **within a 6 km** ~ **(of Hamburg)** in einem Umkreis von 6 km (von Hamburg)

RAF ABBR of **Royal Air Force** königliche (britische) Luftwaffe

raffle ['ræfl] 🛮 N Verlosung f 🛮 VT (also ~ **off**) verlosen

raffle ticket N Los nt

raft [rɑːft] N Floß nt

rafter ['rɑːftəʳ] N (Dach)sparren m

rag [ræg] N **(a)** (= cloth) Lumpen m; (for cleaning) Lappen m; ~**s** (inf: = clothes) Klamotten pl (inf); **in** ~**s** zerlumpt; **to go from** ~**s to riches** (by luck) vom armen Schlucker zum reichen Mann/zur reichen Frau werden; (by work) vom Tellerwäscher zum Millionär werden; **to lose one's** ~ (inf) in die Luft gehen (inf) **(b)** (pej inf: = newspaper) Käseblatt nt

ragamuffin ['rægəˌmʌfɪn] N Vogelscheuche f (inf); (boy) Bengel m; (girl) Göre f; **you little** ~ du kleiner Fratz

rag: ragbag N (fig) Sammelsurium nt (inf); **rag doll** N Flickenpuppe f

rage [reɪdʒ] 🛮 N Wut f; **to be in a** ~ wütend sein; **to fly into a** ~ einen Wutanfall bekommen; **fit of** ~ Wutanfall m; **to send sb into a** ~ jdn wütend or (stronger) rasend machen; **to be (all) the** ~ (inf) der letzte Schrei sein (inf) 🛮 VI toben

ragged ['rægɪd] ADJ person, clothes zerlumpt; beard, hair zottig; coastline, rocks, hole zerklüftet; edge, cuff ausgefranst; (fig) performance stümperhaft; **to run oneself** ~ (inf) sich selbst ganz fertig machen (inf); **on the** ~ **edge** (US fig) gefährlich nah am Rande (des Abgrunds)

raggedly ['rægɪdlɪ] ADV **(a)** dress zerlumpt **(b)** (= unevenly) unregelmäßig

raging ['reɪdʒɪŋ] 🛮 ADJ person wütend; fever heftig; thirst brennend; pain, toothache rasend; storm, sea, wind tobend; **he was** ~ er tobte; **to be in a** ~ **temper** eine fürchterliche Laune haben; **to be** ~ **mad** (inf) eine Stinkwut haben (inf) 🛮 N Toben nt

raid [reɪd] **1** N Überfall *m*; (= *air* ~) Luftangriff *m*; (= *police* ~) Razzia *f*; (*by thieves*) Einbruch *m* **2** VT **(a)** (*lit*) überfallen; (*police*) eine Razzia durchführen in (+*dat*); (*thieves*) einbrechen in (+*acc*) **(b)** (*fig hum*) plündern

raider [reɪdəʳ] N (= *bandit*) Gangster(in) *m(f)*; (= *thief*) Einbrecher(in) *m(f)*; (*in bank*) Bankräuber(in) *m(f)*

rail¹ [reɪl] N **(a)** (*on bridge, stairs etc*) Geländer *nt*; (*Naut*) Reling *f*; (= *curtain* ~) Schiene *f*; (= *towel* ~) Handtuchhalter *m* **(b)** (*for train, tram*) Schiene *f*; **to go off the ~s** (*lit*) entgleisen; (*Brit fig*) (*morally*) auf die schiefe Bahn geraten; (*mentally*) zu spinnen anfangen (*inf*) **(c)** (= ~ *travel, ~way*) die (Eisen)bahn; **to travel by** ~ mit der Bahn fahren

rail² VI **to** ~ **at sb/sth** jdn/etw beschimpfen; **to** ~ **against sb/sth** über jdn/etw schimpfen

rail: railcard N (*Brit Rail*) ≈ Bahncard® *f*; **rail company** N Bahngesellschaft *f*

railing [reɪlɪŋ] N (= *rail*) Geländer *nt*; (= *fence: also* ~**s**) Zaun *m*

rail: railroad N (*US*) (Eisen)bahn *f*; ~ **car** Waggon *m*; **rail strike** N Bahnstreik *m*

railway [reɪlweɪ] N (*Brit*) (Eisen)bahn *f*; (= *track*) Gleis *nt*

railway (*Brit*): **railway carriage** N Eisenbahnwagen *m*; **railway crossing** N Bahnübergang *m*; **railway engine** N Lokomotive *f*; **railway line** N (Eisen)bahnlinie *f*; (= *track*) Gleis *nt*; **railway network** N Bahnnetz *nt*; **railway station** N Bahnhof *m*

rain [reɪn] **1** N **(a)** Regen *m*; **in the** ~ im Regen **(b)** (*fig: of bullets, blows*) Hagel *m* **2** VI IMPERS (*lit, fig*) regnen; **it is ~ing** es regnet; **it never ~s but it pours** (*Brit prov*), **when it ~s, it pours** (*US prov*) ein Unglück kommt selten allein (*prov*) **3** VT IMPERS **it's ~ing cats and dogs** (*inf*) es gießt wie aus Kübeln

➤ **rain down** VI (*blows etc*) niederprasseln (*upon* auf +*acc*)

➤ **rain off, rain out** (*US*) VT SEP **to be rained off** wegen Regen nicht stattfinden; (= *abandoned*) wegen Regen abgebrochen werden

rainbow [reɪnbəʊ] N Regenbogen *m*

rain: rain check N (*esp US*) **I'll take a** ~ **on that** (*fig inf*) das verschiebe ich auf ein andermal; **rain cloud** N Regenwolke *f*; **raincoat** N Regenmantel *m*; **raindrop** N Regentropfen *m*; **rainfall** N Niederschlag *m*; **rain forest** N Regenwald *m*; **rainout** N (*US Sport*) wegen Regens abgesagtes Spiel *nt*; **rainstorm** N schwere Regenfälle *pl*; **rainswept** [reɪnswept] ADJ ATTR regengepeitscht; **rainwater** N Regenwasser *nt*

rainy [reɪnɪ] ADJ (+ER) regnerisch, Regen-; ~ **season** Regenzeit *f*; **a** ~ **spell** ein regnerischer Abschnitt; **to keep** *or* **save sth for a** ~ **day** (*fig*) etw für schlechte Zeiten aufheben

raise [reɪz] **1** VT **(a)** *object, arm, head* heben; *blinds, eyebrow* hochziehen; (*Theat*) *curtain* hochziehen; (*Naut*) *anchor* lichten; **to** ~ **one's glass to sb** jdm zutrinken; **to** ~ **the dead** die Toten wieder zum Leben erwecken; **to** ~ **sb from the dead** jdn von den Toten erwecken; **to** ~ **one's voice** lauter sprechen; (= *get angry*) laut werden; **not a voice was ~d in protest** nicht eine Stimme des Protests wurde laut; **to** ~ **sb's/one's hopes** jdm/sich Hoffnung machen; **to** ~ **the roof** (*fig*) (*with noise*) das Haus zum Beben bringen; (*with approval*) in Begeisterungsstürme ausbrechen **(b)** (*in height or amount*) (*to* auf +*acc, by* um) erhöhen; *limit, standard, level* anheben; **to** ~ **the stakes** den Einsatz erhöhen; **to** ~ **the tone** das Niveau heben **(c)** *statue, building* errichten **(d)** *problem, question* aufwerfen; *objection* erheben; *suspicion, hope* (er)wecken; *ghosts* (herauf)beschwören; **to** ~ **a cheer** (*in others*) Beifall ernten; **to** ~ **a smile** (*in others*) ein Lächeln hervorrufen; **to** ~ **hell** (*inf*) einen Höllenspektakel machen (*inf*) **(e)** *children, animals* aufziehen; *crops* anbauen; **to** ~ **a family** Kinder großziehen **(f)** *army* aufstellen; *taxes* erheben; *funds, money* aufbringen; *loan, mortgage* aufnehmen; *capital* beschaffen **2** N (*esp US*) (*in salary*) Gehaltserhöhung *f*; (*in wages*) Lohnerhöhung *f*

➤ **raise up** VT SEP heben; **he raised himself up on his elbow** er stützte sich auf den Ellbogen

raised [reɪzd] ADJ *arm* angehoben; *voice* erhoben

raisin [reɪzən] N Rosine *f*

rake [reɪk] **1** N Harke *f* **2** VT harken; **to** ~ **sb/sth over the coals** (*US fig*) jdn/etw ordentlich runterputzen (*inf*) **3** VI **to** ~ **around** *or* **about** (herum)stöbern

➤ **rake in** VT SEP (*inf*) *money* kassieren (*inf*); **he's raking it in** er scheffelt das Geld nur so

➤ **rake over** VT SEP harken; (*fig*) *past* durchwühlen

➤ **rake up** VT SEP **(a)** *leaves* zusammenharken **(b)** (*fig*) *people, things, money* auftreiben (*inf*) **(c)** (*fig*) *quarrel* schüren; *memories, grievance* aufwärmen; **to rake up the past** in der Vergangenheit wühlen

rake-off [reɪkɒf] N (*inf*) (Gewinn)anteil *m*

rakish [reɪkɪʃ] ADJ flott

rally [rælɪ] **1** N **(a)** Versammlung *f*; (*with speaker*) Kundgebung *f*; (*Aut*) Rallye *f*; **electoral** ~ Wahlversammlung *f*; **peace** ~ Friedenskundgebung *f* **(b)** (*Tennis etc*) Ballwechsel *m* **(c)** (*St Ex*) Erholung *f* **2** VT versammeln; **to** ~ **one's strength** all seine Kräfte sammeln; **~ing call** *or* **cry** Slogan *m* **3** VI **(a)** (*sick person*) Fortschritte machen; (*St Ex*) sich erholen **(b)** (*troops, people*) sich versammeln; **~ing point** Sammelplatz *m*

➤ **rally (a)round 1** VI +PREP OBJ *leader* sich scharen um; *person in distress* sich annehmen (+*gen*) **2** VI sich seiner/ihrer *etc* annehmen

RAM [ræm] N (*Comput*) ABBR *of* **random access memory** RAM *m or nt*; **128 megabytes of** ~ 128 Megabyte RAM

ram [ræm] **1** N Widder *m* **2** VT (= *push*) stoßen; (*with great force*, = *crash into*) rammen; (= *pack*) zwängen; **to** ~ **home a message** eine Botschaft an den Mann bringen; **to** ~ **sth down sb's throat** (*inf*) jdm etw eintrichtern (*inf*); **the car ~med a lamppost** das Auto prallte gegen einen Laternenpfahl

➤ **ram down** VT SEP *earth* feststampfen

➤ **ram in** VT SEP hineinstoßen; (*with great force*) hineinrammen

ramble [ræmbl] **1** N Streifzug *m*; (*esp Brit* = *hike*) Wanderung *f*; **to go for** *or* **on a** ~ einen Streifzug/eine Wanderung machen **2** VI **(a)** (= *wander about*) Streifzüge/einen Streifzug machen; (*esp Brit*: = *go on hike*) wandern **(b)** (*in speech*) faseln (*inf*); (*pej: also* ~ **on**) schwafeln (*inf*)

rambler [ræmbləʳ] N (*esp Brit*) (= *person*) Spaziergänger(in) *m(f)*; (= *member of club*) Wanderer *m*, Wanderin *f*

rambling [ræmblɪŋ] **1** ADJ **(a)** *speech, writing* weitschweifig; *old person* faselnd (*inf*); *building, garden* weitläufig **(b)** ~ **club/ society** (*esp Brit*) Wanderklub *m*/-verein *m* **2** N **(a)** (= *wandering about*) Streifzüge *pl*; (*esp Brit*: = *hiking*) Wandern *nt*; **to go** ~ wandern gehen **(b)** (*in speech: also* ~**s**) Gefasel *nt* (*inf*)

RAM chip N (*Comput*) RAM-Chip *m*

ramification [ˌræmɪfɪˈkeɪʃən] N (*lit*) Verzweigung *f*; (*smaller*) Verästelung *f*; **the race question and its many ~s** die Rassenfrage und die damit verbundenen Probleme

ramp [ræmp] N Rampe *f*; (= *hydraulic* ~) Hebebühne *f*

rampage [ræmˈpeɪdʒ] **1** N **to be/go on the** ~ randalieren; (= *looting*) auf Raubzug sein/gehen **2** VI (*also* ~ **about** *or* **around**) herumwüten; (*angrily*) herumtoben

rampant [ræmpənt] ADJ *plants, growth* üppig, wuchernd *attr*; *evil, social injustice etc* wild wuchernd *attr*; *inflation, corruption* wuchernd; *crime* um sich greifend; **the** ~ **growth of** das Wuchern (+*gen*); **to be** ~ (*wild*) wuchern; **to run** ~ (*condition*) um sich greifen

rampart [ræmpɑːt] N Wall *m*

ramshackle [ræmʃækl] ADJ *building* baufällig; *car* klapprig; *group, movement* schlecht organisiert

ran [ræn] PRET *of* **run**

ranch [rɑːntʃ] N Ranch *f*; ~ **hand** Farmhelfer(in) *m(f)*; ~ **house** (*on* ~) Farmhaus *nt*; ~(**-style**) **house** (*US*) Bungalow *m*

rancher [rɑːntʃəʳ] N Rancher(in) *m(f)*

rancid [rænsɪd] ADJ ranzig

R & D [ɑːrənˈdiː] N ABBR *of* **research and development** Forschung und Entwicklung *f*

randiness [rændɪnɪs] N (*Brit*) Geilheit *f*

random [rændəm] **1** N **at** ~ *speak, walk, drive* aufs Geratewohl; *shoot* ziellos; (*take*) wahllos; **to hit out at** ~ ziellos um sich schlagen; **a few examples chosen** *or* **taken at** ~ ein paar willkürlich gewählte Beispiele; **I (just) chose one at** ~ ich wählte einfach irgendeine (Beliebige) **2** ADJ *selection* willkürlich; *sequence* zufällig; *inspection* stichprobenmäßig;

~ breath/drug test Stichprobe *f* auf Alkohol im Atem/auf Drogen

random (*Comput*): **random access** N wahlfreier Zugriff; **random access memory** N Direktzugriffsspeicher *m*

randomly ['rændəmlɪ] ADV wahllos

random: **random number** N Zufallszahl *f*; **random sample** N Stichprobe *f*

randy ['rændɪ] ADJ (+ER) (*Brit*) geil

rang [ræŋ] PRET of **ring**[2]

range [reɪndʒ] **1** N (a) (*of missile, telescope, gun*) Reichweite *f*; (*of vehicle*) Fahrbereich *m*; **at a ~ of** auf eine Entfernung von; **at close** *or* **short/long ~** auf kurze/große Entfernung; **to be out of ~** außer Reichweite sein; (*of gun*) außer Schussweite sein; **within (firing) ~** in Schussweite; **~ of vision** Gesichtsfeld *nt*

(b) (= *spread, selection, row*) Reihe *f*; (*of goods*) Sortiment *nt*; (*of sizes, models*) Angebot *nt* (*of* an +*dat*); (*of prices*) Bandbreite *f*; (*of interest, abilities*) Palette *f*; (= *mountain ~*) Kette *f*; **a wide ~** eine große Auswahl; **in this price ~** in dieser Preisklasse; **out of my price ~** außerhalb meiner Preisklasse; **a ~ of prices** unterschiedliche Preise *pl*; **models available in a whole ~ of prices** Modelle in unterschiedlichen Preislagen erhältlich; **we have the whole ~ of models/prices** wir führen sämtliche Modelle/Waren in allen Preislagen; **we cater for the whole ~ of customers** wir sind auf alle Kundenkreise eingestellt

(c) (= *domain, sphere*) Kompetenz *f*; (*of influence*) (Einfluss)bereich *m*

(d) (*also* **shooting ~**) (*Mil*) Schießplatz *m*; (= *rifle ~*) Schießstand *m*

(e) (= *cooking stove*) Küchenherd *m*

(f) (*US*: = *grazing land*) Weideland *nt*

2 VT (a) (= *roam over*) durchstreifen

(b) (*US*) cattle grasen lassen

(c) (*Comput*) **~d left/right** links-/rechtsbündig

3 VI (a) **to ~ (from ... to)** gehen (von ... bis); (*temperature, value*) liegen (zwischen ... und); **his interests ~ from skiing to chess** seine Interessen reichen vom Skifahren bis zum Schachspielen

(b) (= *roam*) streifen; **to ~ over the area** im Gebiet umherstreifen

ranger ['reɪndʒə] N (a) (*of forest etc*) Förster(in) (b) (*US*) (= *mounted patrolman*) Ranger *m*; (= *commando*) Überfallkommando *nt*

Rangoon [ræŋ'guːn] N Rangun *nt*

rank[1] [ræŋk] **1** N (a) (*Mil*) Rang *m*; **officer of high ~** hoher Offizier

(b) (= *class, status*) Stand *m*; **a person of ~** eine hoch gestellte Persönlichkeit

(c) (= *row*) Reihe *f*; (*Brit*: = *taxi ~*) Taxistand *m*

(d) (*Mil*: = *formation*) Glied *nt*; **to break ~(s)** aus dem Glied treten; **the ~s, other ~s** (*Brit*) die Mannschaften und die Unteroffiziere; **the ~ and file of the party** die Basis der Partei, die einfachen Parteimitglieder; **to rise from the ~s** aus dem Mannschaftsstand zum Offizier aufsteigen; (*fig*) sich hocharbeiten

2 VT **to ~ sb among the best** jdn zu den Besten zählen; **where would you ~ Napoleon among the world's statesmen?** wie würden Sie Napoleon als Staatsmann einstufen?

3 VI **to ~ among** zählen zu; **to ~ above/below sb** bedeutender/weniger bedeutend als jd sein; **to ~ high among the world's statesmen** einer der großen Staatsmänner sein; **he ~s high among her friends** er hat eine Sonderstellung unter ihren Freunden; **to ~ 6th** den 6. Rang belegen

rank[2] ADJ (+ER) (a) smell übel; drain stinkend *attr*; person vulgär; **to be ~** (drains, breath) stinken (b) *ATTR* disgrace wahr; injustice schreiend; nonsense, insolence rein; outsider absolut

rankings ['ræŋkɪŋz] PL (*Sport*) **the ~** die Plazierungen *pl*

rankle ['ræŋkl] VI **to ~ (with sb)** jdn wurmen

ransack ['rænsæk] VT room, cupboards durchwühlen; house plündern; town, region herfallen über (+*acc*)

ransom ['rænsəm] **1** N Lösegeld *nt*; (= *release*) Freilassung *f*; **to hold sb to** (*Brit*) *or* **for** (*US*) **~** (*lit*) jdn als Geisel halten; (*fig*) jdn erpressen **2** VT (= *buy free*) Lösegeld bezahlen für; (= *set free*) gegen Lösegeld freilassen

rant [rænt] **1** VI (*emotionally, angrily*) eine Schimpfkanonade loslassen (*inf*); (= *talk nonsense*) irres Zeug reden (*inf*); **to ~**

(**and rave**) herumschimpfen; **what's he ~ing (on) about?** worüber lässt er sich denn da aus? (*inf*) **2** N Schimpfkanonade *f* (*inf*)

ranting ['ræntɪŋ] N (= *outburst*) Geschimpfe *nt*; (= *incoherent talk*) irres Zeug

rap[1] [ræp] **1** N Klopfen *nt no pl*; **there was a ~ at** *or* **on the door** es hat geklopft; **to give sb a ~ on the knuckles** (*lit, fig*) jdm auf die Finger klopfen; **he got a ~ on the knuckles for that** (*lit, fig*) dafür hat er eins auf die Finger bekommen; **to take the ~** (*inf*) die Schuld zugeschoben kriegen (*inf*); **to beat the ~** (*US inf*) (von der Anklage) freigesprochen werden **2** VT table klopfen auf (+*acc*); window klopfen an (+*acc*); **to ~ sb's knuckles, to ~ sb over the knuckles** (*lit, fig*) jdm auf die Finger klopfen **3** VI klopfen; **to ~ at** *or* **on the door/window** an die Tür/ans Fenster klopfen

rap[2] (*Mus*) **1** N Rap *m* **2** VI rappen

rape[1] [reɪp] **1** N Vergewaltigung *f* **2** VT vergewaltigen

rape[2] N (= *plant*) Raps *m*

rapid ['ræpɪd] **1** ADJ schnell; decline, rise rapide; loss of heat plötzlich; river, waterfall reißend; descent steil **2** N **rapids** PL (*Geog*) Stromschnellen *pl*

rapidity [rə'pɪdɪtɪ] N Schnelligkeit *f*; (*of action, movement also*) Raschheit *f*; (*of improvement, change, spread also*) Rapidität *f*; (*of decline, rise*) Steilheit *f*

rapidly ['ræpɪdlɪ] ADV schnell; act, decline, rise rapide

rapist ['reɪpɪst] N Vergewaltiger *m*

rappel [ræ'pel] VI, N (*US*) = **abseil**

rapping ['ræpɪŋ] N (a) Klopfen *nt* (b) (*Mus*) Rappen *nt*

rapport [ræ'pɔː] N **the ~ I have with my father** das enge Verhältnis zwischen mir und meinem Vater

rapt [ræpt] ADJ interest gespannt; attention höchste(r, s); person gebannt; audience hingerissen; **~ in thought** in Gedanken versunken

rapture ['ræptʃə] N (= *delight*) Entzücken *nt*; (= *ecstasy*) Verzückung *f*; **to be in ~s** entzückt sein (*over* über +*acc*, *about* von); **to go into ~s (about sb/sth)** (über jdn/etw) ins Schwärmen geraten; **to send sb into ~s** jdn in Entzücken versetzen

rapturous ['ræptʃərəs] ADJ applause, reception stürmisch; exclamation entzückt

rapturously ['ræptʃərəslɪ] ADV applaud, receive stürmisch; exclaim entzückt

rare [rɛə] ADJ (+ER) (a) selten; **with very ~ exceptions** mit sehr wenigen Ausnahmen; **it's ~ for her to come** sie kommt nur selten (b) atmosphere dünn (c) meat roh; steak blutig (d) (*inf*: = *great*) irrsinnig (*inf*); **a person of ~ kindness** ein selten freundlicher Mensch (*inf*); **to have a ~ old time** sich selten gut amüsieren

rarefied ['rɛərɪfaɪd] ADJ atmosphere, air dünn; (*fig*) exklusiv

rarely ['rɛəlɪ] ADV selten

raring ['rɛərɪŋ] ADJ **to be ~ to go** (*inf*) in den Startlöchern sein

rarity ['rɛərɪtɪ] N Seltenheit *f*; (= *rare occurrence also*) Rarität *f*

rascal ['rɑːskəl] N Gauner *m*; (= *child*) Schlingel *m*

rash[1] [ræʃ] N (*Med*) Ausschlag *m*; **to come out** *or* **break out in a ~** einen Ausschlag bekommen

rash[2] ADJ (+ER) voreilig; person unbesonnen; **don't do anything ~** tu ja nichts Überstürztes

rasher ['ræʃə] N Streifen *m*; **~ of bacon** Speckstreifen *m*

rashly ['ræʃlɪ] ADV voreilig

rashness ['ræʃnɪs] N Voreiligkeit *f*; (*of person*) Unbesonnenheit *f*

rasp [rɑːsp] **1** N (= *tool*) Raspel *f*; (= *noise*) Kratzen *nt no pl*; (*of cough, when breathing*) Keuchen *nt no pl* **2** VT (*also* **~ out**) insults krächzen; orders schnarren **3** VI kratzen; (*breath*) rasseln

raspberry ['rɑːzbərɪ] **1** N Himbeere *f*; (= *plant: also* **~ bush** *or* **cane**) Himbeerstrauch *m*; **to blow a ~ (at sth)** (*inf*) (über etw) verächtlich schnauben **2** ADJ Himbeer-

rasping ['rɑːspɪŋ] **1** ADJ (= *sound*) kratzend; voice krächzend; cough, breath keuchend **2** N (= *sound*) Kratzen *nt*; (*of voice*) Krächzen *nt*

rat [ræt] **1** N (*Zool*) Ratte *f*; (*pej inf*: = *person*) elender Verräter (*inf*); **he's a dirty ~** (*inf*) er ist ein dreckiges Schwein (*inf*); **~s!**

(*inf: annoyance*) Mist! (*inf*) **2** VI **to ~ on sb** (*inf*) jdn verpfeifen (*inf*)

rat-a-tat [ˌrætəˈtæt], **rat-a-tat-tat** N Rattern

ratbag [ˈrætbæg] N (*Brit pej inf*) Schrulle *f* (*inf*)

ratchet up [ˌrætʃɪtˈʌp] (*esp US*) **1** VI zunehmen **2** VT SEP anheizen (*inf*); *pressure* verschärfen; *interest rates, rent* anheben

rate [reɪt] **1** N (a) (= *ratio, frequency*) Rate *f*; (= *speed*) Tempo *nt*; (*of unemployment*) Quote *f*; **the failure ~ on this course** die Durchfallrate bei diesem Kurs; **the failure ~ for small businesses** die Zahl der Konkurse bei Kleinunternehmen; **at the ~ or a ~ of 100 litres** (*Brit*) **or liters** (*US*) **an hour** (in einem Tempo von) 100 Liter pro Stunde; **~ of consumption** Verbrauch *m*; **at a great or terrific** (*inf*) **~, at a ~ of knots** (*inf*) in irrsinnigem Tempo (*inf*); **at this ~ you're going you'll be dead before long** wenn du so weitermachst, bist du bald unter der Erde; **at any ~** auf jeden Fall

(b) (*Comm, Fin*) Satz *m*; (*St Ex*) Kurs *m*; **~ of exchange** Wechselkurs *m*; **what's the ~ at the moment?** wie steht der Kurs momentan?; **what's the ~ of pay?** wie hoch ist der Satz (für die Bezahlung)?; **~ of interest** Zinssatz *m*; **~ of return** Rendite *f*; **~ of taxation** Steuersatz *m*; **postage/insurance ~s** Post-/Versicherungsgebühren *pl*; **there is a reduced ~ for children** Kinderermäßigung wird gewährt; **basic salary ~** Grundgehaltssatz *m*; **to pay sb at the ~ of £10 per hour** jdm einen Stundenlohn von £ 10 bezahlen

2 VT (a) (= *estimate value or worth of*) (ein)schätzen; **to ~ sb/ sth among ...** jdn/etw zu ... zählen or rechnen; **how does he ~ that film?** was hält er von dem Film?; **to ~ sb/sth as sth** jdn/ etw für etw halten; **he is generally ~d as a great statesman** er gilt allgemein als großer Staatsmann; **to ~ sb/sth highly** jdn/ etw hoch einschätzen

(b) (= *deserve*) verdienen

(c) (*inf* = *think highly of*) gut finden (*inf*); **I really/don't really ~ him** ich finde ihn wirklich gut/mag ihn nicht besonders

3 VI **to ~ as ...** gelten als ...; **to ~ among ...** zählen zu ...; **reading does not ~ highly among young people** vom Lesen halten die jungen Leute nicht viel

rather [ˈrɑːðər] ADV (a) (= *for preference*) lieber; **I would ~ have the blue dress** ich hätte lieber das blaue Kleid; **I would ~ be happy than rich** ich wäre lieber glücklich als reich; **I would ~ you came yourself** mir wäre es lieber, Sie kämen selbst; **I'd ~ not** lieber nicht; **I'd ~ not go** ich würde lieber nicht gehen; **I'd ~ die!** eher sterbe ich!; **he expected me to phone ~ than (to) write** er erwartete eher einen Anruf als einen Brief von mir; **it would be better to phone ~ than (to) write** es wäre besser zu telefonieren als zu schreiben

(b) (= *more accurately*) vielmehr; **he is, or ~ was, a soldier** er ist, beziehungsweise war, Soldat; **a car, or ~ an old banger** ein Auto, genauer gesagt eine alte Kiste

(c) (= *to a considerable degree*) ziemlich; (= *somewhat, slightly*) etwas; **he felt ~ better** er fühlte sich bedeutend wohler; **it's ~ more difficult than you think** es ist um einiges schwieriger, als du denkst; **it's too difficult for me** es ist etwas zu schwierig für mich; **I ~ think he's wrong** ich glaube fast, er hat Unrecht; **I've ~ got the impression ...** ich habe ganz den Eindruck, ...

ratification [ˌrætɪfɪˈkeɪʃən] N Ratifizierung *f*

ratify [ˈrætɪfaɪ] VT ratifizieren

rating [ˈreɪtɪŋ] N (a) (= *assessment*) (Ein)schätzung *f* (b) (= *category*) Klasse *f*; (*Fin: also* **credit ~**) Kreditfähigkeit *f*; **the government's low ~ in the opinion polls** die niedrigen Werte der Regierung in den Meinungsumfragen; **to boost ~s** (*TV*) die Werte stark verbessern

ratio [ˈreɪʃɪəʊ] N Verhältnis *nt*; **the ~ of men to women** das Verhältnis von Männern zu Frauen; **in the or a ~ of 100 to 1** im Verhältnis 100 zu 1 (*written:* 100:1)

ration [ˈræʃən, (*US*) ˈreɪʃən] **1** N Ration *f*; (*fig*) Quantum *nt*; **~s** (= *food*) Rationen *pl*; **~ book** Bezug(s)scheinbuch *nt*; (*for food*) ≈ Lebensmittelkarte *f* **2** VT rationieren; **he ~ed himself to five cigarettes a day** er erlaubte sich (*dat*) nur fünf Zigaretten pro Tag

➤ **ration out** VT SEP zuteilen

rational [ˈræʃənl] ADJ rational; *activity, solution* vernünftig; **it was the only ~ thing to do** es war das einzig Vernünftige

rationale [ˌræʃəˈnɑːl] N Gründe *pl*

rationality [ˌræʃəˈnælɪtɪ] N Rationalität *f*; (*of activity, solution*) Vernünftigkeit *f*

rationalization [ˌræʃnəlaɪˈzeɪʃən] N Rationalisierung *f*; (*of problem*) vernünftige Betrachtung

rationalize [ˈræʃnəlaɪz] **1** VT rationalisieren (*also Ind*); *problem* vernünftig betrachten **2** VI rationalisieren

rationally [ˈræʃnəlɪ] ADV rational

rationing [ˈræʃənɪŋ] N Rationierung *f*

rat race N ständiger Konkurrenzkampf

rattle [ˈrætl] **1** VI klappern; (*chains*) rasseln; (*bottles*) klirren; (*hailstones*) prasseln; **to ~ along** (*vehicle*) entlangrattern **2** VT (a) *box, dice, keys* schütteln; *bottles, cans* zusammenschlagen; *chains* rasseln mit; *windows* rütteln an (+*dat*); **to ~ sb's cage** (*inf*) jdn verärgern

(b) (*inf:* = *alarm*) *person* durcheinander bringen

3 N (a) (= *sound*) Klappern *nt no pl*; (*of chains*) Rasseln *nt no pl*; (*of bottles*) Klirren *nt no pl*; (*of hailstones*) Prasseln *nt no pl*

(b) (*child's*) Rassel *f*

➤ **rattle off** VT SEP herunterrasseln (*inf*)

➤ **rattle on** VI (*inf*) (unentwegt) quasseln (*inf*) (*about* über +*acc*)

➤ **rattle through** VI +PREP OBJ *speech etc* herunterrasseln; *work, music* rasen durch

rattlesnake [ˈrætlsneɪk] N Klapperschlange *f*

rattling [ˈrætlɪŋ] **1** N Klappern *nt*; (*of chains*) Rasseln *nt*; (*of bottles*) Klirren *nt*; (*of hailstones*) Prasseln *nt* **2** ADJ klappernd; *chains* rasselnd; *bottles* klirrend; *hailstones* prasselnd; **a ~ noise** ein Klappern *nt*/Rasseln *nt etc*

ratty [ˈrætɪ] ADJ (+ER) (*inf*) (a) (*Brit:* = *irritable*) gereizt (b) (*US:* = *run-down*) verlottert (*inf*)

raucous [ˈrɔːkəs] ADJ *voice, laughter, shouts* heiser; *crowd, music* lärmend; *bird cry* rau

raucously [ˈrɔːkəslɪ] ADV *laugh, shout* heiser; *sing* mit heiserer Stimme

raunchy [ˈrɔːntʃɪ] ADJ (+ER) (*inf*) *person* sexy; *film, scene, novel* erotisch; *clothing* aufreizend

ravage [ˈrævɪdʒ] **1** N **~s** (*of war*) Verheerung *f* (*of* durch); (*of disease*) Zerstörung *f* (*of* durch); **the ~s of time** die Spuren *pl* der Zeit **2** VT (= *ruin*) verwüsten

rave [reɪv] **1** VI fantasieren; (= *speak furiously*) toben; (*inf:* = *speak, write enthusiastically*) schwärmen (*about, over* von) **2** N (*Brit inf*) Rave *m* (*sl*) (*inf:* = *praise*) Schwärmerei *f*; **the play got a ~ review** (*inf*) das Stück bekam eine glänzende Kritik

raven [ˈreɪvən] N Rabe *m*; **~-black** rabenschwarz

ravenous [ˈrævənəs] ADJ ausgehungert; *appetite, hunger* gewaltig; **I'm ~** ich habe einen Bärenhunger (*inf*)

ravenously [ˈrævənəslɪ] ADV *eat* wie ein Wolf; *look* ausgehungert; **to be ~ hungry** ausgehungert sein

ravine [rəˈviːn] N Schlucht *f*

raving [ˈreɪvɪŋ] **1** ADJ (a) (= *frenzied*) verrückt; (= *delirious*) im Delirium; **a ~ lunatic** (*inf*) ein kompletter Idiot (*inf*) (b) (*inf*) *success* toll (*inf*); *beauty* hinreißend **2** ADV **~ mad** (*inf*) total verrückt (*inf*)

ravishing [ˈrævɪʃɪŋ] ADJ *woman, sight* atemberaubend; *beauty, meal* hinreißend

ravishingly [ˈrævɪʃɪŋlɪ] ADV *beautiful* hinreißend

raw [rɔː] **1** ADJ (+ER) (a) *meat, food* roh; *sewage* ungeklärt; **to give sb a ~ deal** (*inf*) jdn unfair behandeln; **to get a ~ deal** schlecht wegkommen (*inf*)

(b) *emotion, energy, ambition, facts* nackt; *talent, courage* elementar; **~ data** (*Comput*) unaufbereitete Daten *pl*

(c) *troops, recruit* neu

(d) *wound* offen; *skin* wund; *nerves* empfindlich; **red and ~** gerötet und wund

(e) (= *frank*) *account* ungeschönt

(f) (*Met*) *climate, wind* rau

(g) (*esp US:* = *coarse*) *humour, person* derb

2 in the ~ (*inf*) im Naturzustand

raw material N Rohmaterial *nt*

rawness [ˈrɔːnɪs] N (a) (*of meat, food*) Rohheit *f* (b) (= *lack of experience*) Unerfahrenheit *f* (c) (= *soreness*) Wundheit *f* (d) (*of weather*) Rauheit *f* (e) (*esp US:* = *coarseness*) Derbheit *f*

ray [reɪ] N Strahl *m*; **a ~ of hope** ein Hoffnungsschimmer or -strahl *m*; **a ~ of sunshine** (*fig*) ein kleiner Trost

raze [reɪz] VT zerstören; **to ~ sth to the ground** etw dem Erdboden gleichmachen

razor ['reɪzə^r] N Rasierapparat m; (cutthroat) Rasiermesser nt; **electric ~** Elektrorasierer m

razor: razor blade N Rasierklinge f; **razor-sharp** ADJ knife scharf (wie ein Rasiermesser); teeth rasiermesserscharf; (fig) person sehr scharfsinnig; mind, wit messerscharf

razz [ræz] VT (US inf) aufziehen (inf)

razzle-dazzle ['ræzl'dæzl], **razzmatazz** ['ræzmə'tæz] N (esp Brit inf) Rummel m

RC ABBR of **Roman Catholic** r.-k.

Rd ABBR of **Road** Str.

re [riː] PREP (Admin, Comm etc) betreffs (+gen); **re your letter of 16th June** Betr(eff): Ihr Brief vom 16. Juni

reach [riːtʃ] **1** N Reichweite f; (= sphere of action, influence) Einflussbereich m; **within/out of sb's ~** in/außer jds Reichweite (dat), in/außer Reichweite (dat); **within arm's ~** in greifbarer Nähe; **put it out of the children's ~** or **out of the ~ of the children** stellen Sie es so, dass Kinder es nicht erreichen können; **keep out of ~ of children** von Kindern fern halten; **within easy ~ of the sea** in unmittelbarer Nähe des Meers; **I keep it within easy ~** ich habe es in greifbarer Nähe; **she was beyond (the) ~ of help** für sie kam jede Hilfe zu spät **2** VT **(a)** (= arrive at) erreichen; point ankommen an (+dat); town, country ankommen in (+dat); perfection erlangen; agreement, understanding erzielen; conclusion kommen zu; **when we ~ed him he was dead** als wir zu ihm kamen, war er tot; **to ~ the terrace you have to cross the garden** um auf die Terrasse zu kommen, muss man durch den Garten gehen; **to ~ school age** das Schulalter erreichen; **this advertisement is geared to ~ a younger audience** diese Werbung soll junge Leute ansprechen; **you can ~ me at my hotel** Sie erreichen mich in meinem Hotel **(b)** (= stretch to get or touch) **to be able to ~ sth** an etw (acc) (heran)reichen können; **can you ~ it?** kommen Sie dran? **(c)** (= come up to, go down to) reichen bis zu **(d)** (inf: = get and give) langen (inf); **~ me (over) that book** lang mir das Buch (herüber) (inf) **3** VI (= stretch out hand or arm) greifen; **to ~ for sth** nach etw greifen; **can you ~?** kommen Sie dran?

▶ **reach across** VI hinübergreifen

▶ **reach down 1** VI (clothes, curtains etc) herunterreichen (to bis); (person) hinuntergreifen (for nach) **2** VT SEP herunterreichen

▶ **reach out 1** VT SEP **he reached out his hand to take the book** er streckte die Hand aus, um das Buch zu nehmen; **he reached out his hand for the cup** er griff nach der Tasse **2** VI die Hand/Hände ausstrecken; **to reach out for sth** nach etw greifen or langen (inf)

▶ **reach over** VI = **reach across**

▶ **reach up** VI **(a)** (water, level etc) (herauf)reichen (to bis) **(b)** (person) hinaufgreifen (for nach)

reachable ['riːtʃəbl] ADJ erreichbar

react [riː'ækt] VI **(a)** (= respond, Chem, Phys) reagieren (to auf +acc); **to ~ against** negativ reagieren auf (+acc) **(b)** (= have an effect) wirken (on, upon auf +acc)

reaction [riː'ækʃən] N Reaktion f (to auf +acc, against gegen); **a ~ against feminism** eine Absage an den Feminismus; **to have quick/slow ~s** schnell/langsam reagieren

reactivate [riː'æktɪveɪt] VT reaktivieren

reactor [riː'æktə^r] N (Phys) Reaktor m

read¹ [riːd], vb: pret, ptp **read** [red] **1** VT **(a)** (also Comput) lesen; (to sb) vorlesen (to +dat); words verstehen (also Telec); person einschätzen können; **I read him to sleep** las ich ihm vor, bis er einschlief; **~ my lips!** (inf) höre meine Worte!; **to take sth as read** (fig) (= as self-evident) etw als selbstverständlich voraussetzen; (= as agreed) etw für abgemacht halten; **to ~ sb's thoughts/mind** jds Gedanken lesen; **to ~ sb's palm** jdm aus der Hand lesen; **don't ~ too much into his words** interpretieren Sie nicht zu viel in seine Worte hinein; **do you ~ me?** (Telec) können Sie mich verstehen? **(b)** thermometer etc ablesen **(c)** (meter) (an)zeigen

2 VI **(a)** lesen; (to sb) vorlesen (to +dat); **to ~ aloud** or **out loud** laut lesen; **to ~ to oneself** für sich lesen **(b)** **this paragraph ~s/doesn't ~ well** dieser Abschnitt liest

sich gut/nicht gut; **this ~s like an official report** das klingt wie ein offizieller Bericht **(c)** (= have wording) lauten; **the letter ~s as follows** der Brief lautet folgendermaßen **3** N **she enjoys a good ~** sie liest gern; **this book is quite a good ~** das Buch liest sich gut

▶ **read back** VT SEP (to sb) noch einmal vorlesen

▶ **read in** VT SEP (Comput) einlesen

▶ **read off** VT SEP ablesen; (without pause) herunterlesen

▶ **read on** VI weiterlesen

▶ **read out** VT SEP vorlesen

▶ **read over** or **through** VT SEP durchlesen

▶ **read up 1** VT SEP nachlesen über (+acc), sich informieren über (+acc) **2** VI nachlesen (on über +acc)

read² [red] **1** PRET, PTP of **read¹ 2** ADJ **he is well/not very well ~** er ist sehr/wenig belesen

readable ['riːdəbl] ADJ (= legible) lesbar; (= worth reading) lesenswert

reader ['riːdə^r] N **(a)** Leser(in) m(f) **(b)** (= schoolbook) Lesebuch nt; (to teach reading) Fibel f

readership ['riːdəʃɪp] N Leser pl

read head ['riːdhed] N (Comput) Lesekopf m

readies ['redɪz] PL (Brit inf: = ready cash) Bare(s) nt (inf); **the ~** das Bare (inf)

readily ['redɪlɪ] ADV bereitwillig; (= easily) leicht; **~ available** leicht erhältlich

readiness ['redɪnɪs] N Bereitschaft f; **~ for war** Kriegsbereitschaft f; **his ~ to help** seine Hilfsbereitschaft

reading ['riːdɪŋ] N **(a)** (= action) Lesen nt **(b)** (= reading matter) Lektüre f **(c)** (= recital, excerpt) Lesung f (also Parl); **the Senate gave the bill its first ~** der Senat beriet das Gesetz in erster Lesung **(d)** (= interpretation) Interpretation f **(e)** (= variant) Version f **(f)** (from meter) Thermometer-/Zählerstand etc m; (in scientific experiment) Messwert m; **to take a ~** den Thermometerstand etc/den Messwert ablesen

reading: reading age N **a ~ of 7** die Lesefähigkeit eines 7jährigen; **reading book** N Lesebuch nt; **reading glasses** PL Lesebrille f; **reading list** N Leseliste f; **reading matter** N Lesestoff m

readjust [riːə'dʒʌst] **1** VT instrument, mechanism neu einstellen; (= correct) nachstellen; prices, salary anpassen **2** VI sich neu or wieder anpassen (to an +acc)

readjustment [riːə'dʒʌstmənt] N (of instrument, mechanism) Neueinstellung f; (= correction) Nachstellung f; (of prices, salary) Anpassung f; (of person) Wiederanpassung f

read [riːd]: **read only memory** N (Comput) Festwertspeicher m; **read-write head** N (Comput) Schreib-/Lesekopf m; **read-write memory** N (Comput) Schreib-/Lesespeicher m

ready ['redɪ] **1** ADJ **(a)** fertig; (= prepared also) bereit; answer, excuse vorformuliert; (= quick) smile rasch; supply griffbereit; market schnell; **~ to do sth** (= willing) bereit, etw zu tun; (= quick) schnell dabei, etw zu tun; **he was ~ to cry** er war den Tränen nahe; **~, willing and able (to do sth)** bereit, fertig und willens(, etw zu tun); **~ to leave** abmarschbereit; (for journey) abfahrbereit; **~ to use** or **for use** gebrauchsfertig; **~ to serve** tischfertig; **~ for action** bereit zum Angriff, klar zum Gefecht; **~ for anything** zu allem bereit; **dinner is ~** das Essen ist fertig; **"dinner's ~"** „essen kommen"; **are you ~ to go?** sind Sie so weit?; **are you ~ to order?** möchten Sie jetzt bestellen?; **well, I think we're ~** ich glaube, wir sind so weit; **I'm not quite ~ yet** ich bin noch nicht ganz fertig; **everything is ~ for his visit** alles ist für seinen Besuch vorbereitet; **the final treaty will be ~ for signing tomorrow** der endgültige Vertrag wird morgen zum Unterzeichnen fertig sein or bereitliegen; **flight 211 is now ~ for boarding** Flug 211 ist jetzt zum Einsteigen bereit; **the doctor's ~ for you now** der Doktor kann Sie jetzt sehen; **I'm ~ for him!** er soll nur kommen; **to get (oneself) ~** sich fertig machen; **to get ~ to go out** sich zum Ausgehen fertig machen; **to get ~ for sth** sich auf etw (acc) vorbereiten; **to get sth/sb ~ (for sth/to do sth)** etw/jdn fertig machen (für etw/zum Tun von etw); **~ and waiting** startbereit; **~ when you are** ich bin bereit; **~, steady, go!** (Brit) Achtung or auf die Plätze, fertig, los!

(b) (= prompt) reply prompt; wit schlagfertig **(c)** (= available) **~ money** jederzeit verfügbares Geld; **~ cash** Bargeld nt; **to pay in ~ cash** auf die Hand bezahlen **(d)** (= practical) solution sauber; **to have a ~ sale** (Comm) guten

Absatz finden **2** N **at the ~** (fig) marsch-/fahrbereit etc; **with his pen at the ~** mit gezücktem Federhalter

ready: **ready-cooked** ADJ vorgekocht; **ready-made 1** ADJ **(a)** curtains fertig; meal vorgekocht; answer, ideas vorgefertigt **(b)** (= convenient) replacement nahtlos; topic immer zur Hand; **~ solution** Patentlösung f **2** ADV komplett; **ready meal** N Fertiggericht nt; **ready-to-eat** ADJ tafelfertig; **ready-to-serve** ADJ tischfertig; **ready-to-wear** ADJ ATTR, **ready to wear** ADJ PRED Konfektions-, von der Stange (inf)

reaffirm [ˌriːəˈfɜːm] VT **(a)** (= assert again) beteuern **(b)** (= reconfirm) suspicion, doubts bestätigen; principles, wish bestärken

real [rɪəl] **1** ADJ **(a)** (= genuine, proper) echt; (= proper, complete) richtig; (= true, as opposed to apparent) wirklich; idiot, disaster komplett; (Econ) real; **you can touch it, it's ~** das können Sie anfassen, es ist wirklich da; **in ~ life** im wirklichen Leben; **the danger was very ~** das war eine ganz reale Gefahr; **it's the ~ thing** or **McCoy, this whisky!** dieser Whisky ist der echte; **it's not the ~ thing** das ist nicht das Wahre; (= not genuine) das ist nicht echt; **to keep in touch with the ~ world** auf dem Boden der Tatsachen bleiben; **get ~!** (inf) wach auf!; **it's a ~ miracle** das ist wirklich or echt (inf) ein Wunder, das ist ein wahres Wunder; **it's a ~ shame** es ist wirklich schade, es ist jammerschade; **he doesn't know what ~ contentment is** er weiß ja nicht, was Zufriedenheit wirklich ist; **that's what I call a ~ car** das nenne ich ein Auto; **I'm in ~ trouble** ich bin in großen Schwierigkeiten **(b)** (Fin) income, cost tatsächlich; **~ value** Realwert m; interest rate effektiv; **in ~ terms** effektiv **2** ADV (esp US inf) echt (inf); **~ soon** wirklich bald; **we had a ~ good laugh** wir haben so gelacht **3** N **for ~** echt (inf); **is that invitation for ~?** ist die Einladung ernst gemeint?

real: **real coffee** N Bohnenkaffee m; **real estate** N Immobilien pl; **~ developer** (US) Immobilienhändler(in) m(f); **~ agent** (US) Immobilienmakler(in) m(f)

realist [ˈrɪəlɪst] N Realist(in) m(f)

realistic [rɪəˈlɪstɪk] ADJ realistisch

realistically [rɪəˈlɪstɪkəlɪ] ADV hope for realistischerweise; **it just isn't ~ possible** es ist einfach unrealistisch

reality [riːˈælɪtɪ] N Realität f; **to become ~** sich verwirklichen; **(the) ~ is somewhat different** die Realität sieht etwas anders aus; **in ~** (= in fact) in Wirklichkeit; (= actually) eigentlich; **the realities of the situation** der wirkliche Sachverhalt

realizable [ˈrɪəlaɪzəbl] ADJ realisierbar; **net ~ value** Netto-Realisationswert m

realization [ˌrɪəlaɪˈzeɪʃən] N **(a)** (of assets) Realisation f; (of hope, plan) Realisierung f; (of potential) Verwirklichung f **(b)** (= awareness) Erkenntnis f

realize [ˈrɪəlaɪz] **1** VT **(a)** (= become aware of) erkennen; (= be aware of) sich (dat) klar sein über (+acc); (= appreciate, understand) begreifen; (= notice) (be)merken; (= discover) feststellen; **does he ~ the problems?** sind ihm die Probleme bewusst?; **he had not fully ~d that she was dead** es war ihm nicht voll bewusst, dass sie tot war; **I ~d what he meant** mir wurde klar, was er meinte; **I've just ~d I won't be here** mir ist eben klar geworden, dass ich dann nicht hier sein werde; **he didn't ~ she was cheating him** er merkte nicht, dass sie ihn betrog; **I ~d I didn't have any money on me** ich stellte fest, dass ich kein Geld dabei hatte; **I made her ~ that I was right** ich machte ihr klar, dass ich Recht hatte; **yes, I ~ that** ja, das ist mir klar; **yes, I ~ that I was wrong** ja, ich sehe ein, dass ich Unrecht hatte **(b)** hope, plan, assets realisieren; potential verwirklichen; price erzielen; interest abwerfen; (goods) einbringen **2** VI **didn't you ~?** war Ihnen das nicht klar?; (= notice) haben Sie das nicht gemerkt?; **I've just ~d** das ist mir eben klar geworden; (= noticed) das habe ich eben gemerkt; **I should have ~d** das hätte ich wissen müssen

real-life [ˈriːlˈlaɪf] ADJ situation tatsächlich; event wirklich; person real; story wahr

reallocate [riːˈæləkeɪt] VT umverteilen

really [ˈrɪəlɪ] ADV, INTERJ wirklich; **I ~ don't know what to think** ich weiß wirklich nicht, was ich davon halten soll; **I don't ~ think so** das glaube ich eigentlich nicht; **well yes, I ~ think we should** ich finde eigentlich schon, dass wir das tun sollten;

---

before he ~ understood bevor er wirklich verstand; **~ and truly** wirklich; **I ~ must say ...** ich muss schon sagen ...; **~!** (in protest, indignation) also wirklich!; **~?** wirklich?; **not ~!** ach wirklich?

realm [relm] N (liter) Königreich nt; (fig) Reich nt; **within the ~s of possibility** im Bereich des Möglichen

real (Comput): **real time** N Echtzeit f; **real-time clock** N Echtzeituhr f

realtor [ˈrɪəltɔːʳ] N (US) Grundstücksmakler(in) m(f)

reap [riːp] VT (also fig) (= cut) mähen; (= harvest) ernten; reward bekommen

reaping [ˈriːpɪŋ] N (= cutting) Mähen nt; (= harvesting) Ernten nt

reappear [ˌriːəˈpɪəʳ] VI wieder erscheinen

reappearance [ˌriːəˈpɪərəns] N Wiedererscheinen nt

reappoint [ˌriːəˈpɔɪnt] VT (to a job) wieder einstellen (to als); (to a post) wieder ernennen (to zu)

reappraisal [ˌriːəˈpreɪzəl] N Neubeurteilung f

reappraise [ˌriːəˈpreɪz] VT von neuem beurteilen

rear¹ [rɪəʳ] **1** N (= back part) hinterer Teil; (inf: = buttocks) Hintern m (inf); **in** or **at the ~** hinten (of in +dat); **to be situated at/to(wards) the ~ of the plane** hinten im Flugzeug/am hinteren Ende des Flugzeugs sein; **at** or **to the ~ of the building** (outside) hinter dem Haus; (inside) hinten im Haus; **from the ~** von hinten; **to bring up the ~** (lit, fig) die Nachhut bilden **2** ADJ **(a)** Hinter-, hintere(r, s) **(b)** (Aut) Heck-; **~ door** hintere Tür; **~ lights** Rücklichter pl; **~ wheel** Hinterrad nt

rear² **1** VT **(a)** (esp Brit) animals, family großziehen **(b)** racism **~ed its ugly head (again)** der Rassismus kam (wieder) zum Vorschein **2** VI (horse: also = up) sich aufbäumen

rearm [riːˈɑːm] **1** VT country wieder bewaffnen; forces, troops neu ausrüsten **2** VI wieder aufrüsten

rearmament [riːˈɑːməmənt] N (of country) Wiederaufrüstung f; (of forces, troops) Neuausrüstung f

rearmost [ˈrɪəməʊst] ADJ hinterste(r, s)

rearrange [ˌriːəˈreɪndʒ] VT furniture, system umstellen; plans, order, ideas ändern; meeting neu abmachen

rearrangement [ˌriːəˈreɪndʒmənt] N (of furniture, system) Umstellung f; (of plans, order, ideas) Änderung f; (of meeting) Neuabmachung f

rear-view mirror [ˈrɪəˌvjuːˈmɪrəʳ] N Rückspiegel m

reason [ˈriːzn] **1** N **(a)** (= cause, justification) Grund m (for für); **~ for living** or **being** Grund m zum Leben; **my ~ for going, the ~ for my going** (der Grund,) weshalb ich gehe/gegangen bin; **the police had no ~ to interfere** die Polizei hatte keinen Grund einzugreifen; **(but did)** die Polizei hat ohne Grund eingegriffen; **what's the ~ for this celebration?** aus welchem Anlass wird hier gefeiert?; **I want to know the ~ why** ich möchte wissen, weshalb; **and that's the ~ why ...** und deshalb ...; **I have (good) ~/every ~ to believe that ...** ich habe (guten) Grund/allen Grund anzunehmen, dass ...; **there is ~ to believe that ...** es gibt Gründe zu glauben, dass ...; **there is every ~ to believe ...** es spricht alles dafür ...; **for that very ~** eben deswegen; **without any ~** ohne jeden Grund; **for no ~ at all** ohne ersichtlichen Grund; **for no particular/apparent ~** ohne einen bestimmten/ersichtlichen Grund; **why did you do that? – no particular ~** warum haben Sie das gemacht? – einfach nur so; **for no other ~ than that ...** aus keinem anderen Grund, als dass ...; **for ~s best known to himself/myself** aus unerfindlichen/bestimmten Gründen; **all the more ~ for doing it** or **to do it** umso mehr Grund, das zu tun; **by ~ of** wegen (+gen) **(b)** NO PL (= mental faculty) Verstand m **(c)** NO PL (= common sense) Vernunft f; **to listen to ~** auf die Stimme der Vernunft hören; **he won't listen to ~** er lässt sich (dat) nichts sagen; **that stands to ~** das ist logisch; **we'll do anything within ~ to ...** wir tun alles, was in unserer Macht steht, um zu ...; **you can have anything within ~** Sie können alles haben, solange es sich in Grenzen hält **2** VI **(a)** (= think logically) vernünftig denken **(b)** (= argue) **to ~ (with sb)** vernünftig mit jdm reden **3** VT (also = out) (= deduce) schließen; (verbally) argumentieren; problem durchdenken

reasonable [ˈriːznəbl] ADJ **(a)** vernünftig; *chance* reell; *claim* berechtigt; *amount* angemessen; *excuse, offer* akzeptabel; **be ~!** sei vernünftig; **vegetables are ~ (in price) just now** Gemüse ist momentan preiswert; **to be ~ about sth** angemessen auf etw (*acc*) reagieren; **beyond (all) ~ doubt** ohne (jeden) Zweifel; **it would be ~ to assume that ...** man könnte durchaus annehmen, dass ... **(b)** (= *quite good*) ganz gut; **with a ~ amount of luck** mit einigem Glück

reasonably [ˈriːznəbli] ADV **(a)** *behave, think* vernünftig; **~ priced** preiswert **(b)** (= *quite, fairly*) ziemlich

reasoned [ˈriːznd] ADJ *argument, approach* durchdacht; *discussion* vernünftig

reasoning [ˈriːznɪŋ] N logisches Denken; (= *arguing*) Argumentation *f*

reassemble [ˌriːəˈsembl] **1** VT **(a)** *people, troops* wieder versammeln **(b)** *tool, car, machine* wieder zusammenbauen **2** VI sich wieder versammeln; (*troops*) sich wieder sammeln

reassert [ˌriːəˈsɜːt] VT mit Nachdruck behaupten; **to ~ oneself** seine Autorität wieder geltend machen

reassess [ˌriːəˈses] VT neu überdenken; *proposals, advantages* neu abwägen; (*for taxation*) neu veranlagen; *damages* neu schätzen

reassurance [ˌriːəˈʃʊərəns] N **(a)** (= *feeling of security*) Beruhigung *f*; **to give sb ~** jdn beruhigen **(b)** (= *renewed confirmation*) Bestätigung *f*; **despite his ~(s)** trotz seiner Versicherungen

reassure [ˌriːəˈʃʊə] VT **(a)** (= *relieve sb's mind*) beruhigen; (= *give feeling of security to*) das Gefühl der Sicherheit geben (+*dat*) **(b)** (*verbally*) versichern (+*dat*); **to ~ sb of sth** jdm etw versichern **(c)** = **reinsure**

reassuring ADJ, **reassuringly** ADV [ˌriːəˈʃʊərɪŋ, -lɪ] beruhigend

reawaken [ˌriːəˈweɪkən] **1** VT *person* wieder erwecken; *passion, interest* neu erwecken **2** VI wieder aufwachen; (*interest, passion*) wieder erwachen

reawakening [ˌriːəˈweɪkənɪŋ] N Wiederaufleben *nt*

rebate [ˈriːbeɪt] N (= *discount*) Rabatt *m*; (= *money back*) Rückvergütung *f*

rebel [ˈrebl] **1** N Rebell(in) *m(f)* **2** ADJ ATTR rebellisch **3** [rɪˈbel] VI rebellieren

rebellion [rɪˈbeljən] N Rebellion *f*

rebellious ADJ, **rebelliously** ADV [rɪˈbeljəs, -lɪ] rebellisch

rebirth [ˌriːˈbɜːθ] N Wiedergeburt *f*

reboot [ˌriːˈbuːt] VTI (*Comput*) rebooten

reborn [ˌriːˈbɔːn] ADJ **to be ~** wieder geboren werden; **to feel ~** sich wie neugeboren fühlen

rebound [rɪˈbaʊnd] **1** VI (*ball, bullet*) abprallen (*against, off* von); (*St Ex*) sich erholen **2** [ˈriːbaʊnd] N (*of ball, bullet*) Rückprall *m*; **she married him on the ~** sie heiratete ihn, um sich über einen anderen hinwegzutrösten

rebrand [rɪˈbrænd] VT *product* ein neues Markenimage geben (+*dat*)

rebranding [rɪˈbrændɪŋ] N **the ~ of a company** der Versuch, einer Firma ein neues Image zu geben

rebuild [ˌriːˈbɪld] VT *house, wall, country* wieder aufbauen; *society, relationship* wieder herstellen

rebuilding [ˌriːˈbɪldɪŋ] N (*of house, wall*) Wiederaufbau *m*; (*of society, relationship*) Wiederherstellung *f*

recall [rɪˈkɔːl] **1** VT **(a)** (= *summon back*) zurückrufen; (*Fin*) *capital* zurückfordern; **Ferguson was ~ed to the Scotland squad** Ferguson wurde in die schottische Mannschaft zurückgerufen **(b)** (= *remember*) sich erinnern an (+*acc*); **as I ~ ...** soweit ich mich erinnere ... **(c)** (*Comput*) *file* wieder aufrufen **2** N (= *summoning back*) Rückruf *m*; (*Fin*: *of capital*) Einzug *m*; **beyond ~** für immer vorbei

recap [ˈriːkæp] (*inf*) **1** N kurze Zusammenfassung **2** VTI rekapitulieren

recapture [ˌriːˈkæptʃə] **1** VT *animal* wieder einfangen; *prisoner* wieder ergreifen; *territory* wiedererobern; (*esp Sport*) *title etc* wiedergewinnen; (*fig*) *atmosphere, period* wieder wach werden lassen **2** N (*of animal*) Wiedereinfangen *nt*; (*of prisoner*) Wiederergreifung *f*; (*of territory*) Wiedereroberung *f*; (*esp Sport: of title etc*) Wiedererlangung *f*

recede [rɪˈsiːd] VI (*tide, price*) zurückgehen; (*fig*) sich entfernen; (*hope*) schwinden; **his hair is receding** er hat eine leichte Stirnglatze

receding [rɪˈsiːdɪŋ] ADJ *chin, forehead* fliehend; *hairline* zurückweichend; *hair* dünn

receipt [rɪˈsiːt] N **(a)** NO PL Empfang *m*; **to pay on ~ (of the goods)** bei Empfang (der Waren) bezahlen **(b)** (*Brit*: = *paper*) Quittung *f* **(c)** (*Comm, Fin*) **~s** Einnahmen *pl*

> *Be careful!* **receipt** *is not translated by the German word* **Rezept**.

receivable [rɪˈsiːvəbl] ADJ **accounts ~** (*Comm*) Außenstände *pl*; **bills ~** (*Comm*) Wechselforderungen *pl*

receive [rɪˈsiːv] **1** VT **(a)** bekommen; *refusal, setback* erfahren; *recognition* finden; (*esp Brit*) **"~d with thanks"** (*Comm*) „dankend erhalten" **(b)** *offer, news, new play etc, person into group etc* aufnehmen; **to a warm welcome** herzlich empfangen werden **(c)** (*Telec, Rad, TV*) empfangen; **are you receiving me?** hören Sie mich? **2** VI (*form*) (*Besuch*) empfangen

receiver [rɪˈsiːvə] N **(a)** (*of letter, goods*) Empfänger(in) *m(f)* **(b)** (*Fin, Jur*) **official ~** Konkursverwalter(in) *m(f)*; **to call in the ~** Konkurs anmelden **(c)** (*Telec*) Hörer *m*

receivership [rɪˈsiːvəʃɪp] N **to go into ~** in Konkurs gehen

receiving end [rɪˈsiːvɪŋend] N **to be on the ~ (of it)/of sth** derjenige sein, der es/etw abkriegt (*inf*)

recent [ˈriːsənt] ADJ kürzlich; *event, development, closure* jüngste(r, s); *news* neueste(r, s); *invention, edition, addition* neu; **the ~ improvement** die vor kurzem eingetretene Verbesserung; **their ~ loss** ihr vor kurzem erlittener Verlust; **a ~ decision** eine Entscheidung, die erst vor kurzem gefallen ist; **a ~ publication** eine Neuveröffentlichung; **his ~ arrival** seine Ankunft vor kurzem; **her ~ trip** ihre erst kurz zurückliegende Reise; **he is a ~ arrival** er ist erst kurz hier; **in ~ years** in den letzten Jahren; **in ~ times** in letzter Zeit

recently [ˈriːsəntlɪ] ADV (= *a short while ago*) vor kurzem; (= *the other day also*) neulich; (= *during the last few days or weeks*) in letzter Zeit; **~ he has been doing it differently** seit kurzem macht er das anders; **as ~ as** erst; **quite ~** erst vor kurzem, erst kürzlich

reception [rɪˈsepʃən] N, NO PL (= *receiving, welcome: of person, Rad, TV*) Empfang *m*; (*into group, of play, book etc*) Aufnahme *f*; **to give sb a warm/chilly ~** jdn herzlich/kühl empfangen; **at/to ~** (*in hotel etc*) am/zum Empfang

reception desk N Rezeption *f*

receptionist [rɪˈsepʃənɪst] N (*in hotel*) Empfangschef *m*, Empfangsdame *f*; (*with firm*) Herr *m*/Dame *f* am Empfang; (*at doctor's etc*) Sprechstundenhilfe *f*

receptive [rɪˈseptɪv] ADJ *person, mind, market* aufnahmefähig; *audience* empfänglich; **~ to** empfänglich für

receptiveness [rɪˈseptɪvnɪs] N (*of person, mind, market*) Aufnahmefähigkeit *f*; (*of audience*) Empfänglichkeit *f*; **~ to** Empfänglichkeit *f* für

recess [rɪˈses] N **(a)** (*of law courts*) Ferien *pl*; (*US Sch*) Pause *f* **(b)** (= *alcove*) Nische *f* **(c)** (= *secret place*) Winkel *m*

recession [rɪˈseʃən] N (*Econ*) Rezession *f*

recessive [rɪˈsesɪv] ADJ (*Econ*) rezessiv

recharge [ˌriːˈtʃɑːdʒ] **1** VT *battery* aufladen; **to ~ one's batteries** (*fig*) auftanken **2** VI sich wieder aufladen

recipe [ˈresɪpɪ] N Rezept *nt*; **that's a ~ for disaster** das führt mit Sicherheit in die Katastrophe; **a ~ for success** ein Erfolgsrezept *nt*

recipient [rɪˈsɪpɪənt] N Empfänger(in) *m(f)*

reciprocal [rɪˈsɪprəkəl] ADJ (= *mutual*) gegenseitig; (= *done in return*) als Gegenleistung; **~ trade** Handel *m* untereinander

reciprocate [rɪˈsɪprəkeɪt] VI sich revanchieren

recital [rɪˈsaɪtl] N (*of music, poetry*) Vortrag *m*; (= *piano ~ etc*) Konzert *nt*

recite [rɪˈsaɪt] **1** VT **(a)** *poetry* vortragen **(b)** *facts* hersagen; *details* aufzählen **2** VI vortragen

reckless [ˈreklɪs] ADJ *person, behaviour* leichtsinnig; *driver, driving* rücksichtslos; *attempt* gewagt

recklessly [ˈreklɪslɪ] ADV *behave, disregard* leichtsinnig; *drive* rücksichtslos; *attempt* gewagt

recklessness [ˈreklɪsnɪs] N (*of person*) Leichtsinn *m*; (*of behaviour*) Leichtsinnigkeit *f*; (*of driver, driving*) Rücksichtslosigkeit *f*; (*of attempt*) Gewagtheit *f*

reckon ['rekən] **1** VT **(a)** (= *calculate*) ausrechnen, berechnen; **he ~ed the cost to be £40.51** er berechnete die Kosten auf £ 40,51 **(b)** (= *judge*) zählen (*among* zu) **(c)** (= *think, suppose*) glauben; (= *estimate*) schätzen; **what do you ~?** was meinen Sie?; **I ~ he must be about forty** ich schätze, er müsste so um die vierzig sein **2** VI (= *calculate*) rechnen

➤ **reckon on** VI +PREP OBJ zählen auf (+*acc*); **you can reckon on 30** Sie können mit 30 rechnen; **I was reckoning on doing that tomorrow** ich wollte das morgen machen

➤ **reckon up 1** VT SEP zusammenrechnen **2** VI abrechnen (*with* mit)

➤ **reckon with** VI +PREP OBJ rechnen mit

➤ **reckon without** VI +PREP OBJ nicht rechnen mit

reckoning ['rekənɪŋ] N (= *calculation*) (Be)rechnung *f*; **the day of ~** der Tag der Abrechnung

reclaim [rɪ'kleɪm] **1** VT **(a)** *land* gewinnen; (*by irrigation etc*) kultivieren; *industrial landfill* rekultivieren **(b)** *rights, tax* zurückverlangen; *lost item, baggage* abholen **2** N **baggage** *or* **luggage ~** Gepäckausgabe *f*

reclaimable [rɪ'kleɪməbl] ADJ *money, tax* erstattungsfähig

recline [rɪ'klaɪn] VI (*person*) zurückliegen; (*seat*) sich verstellen lassen; **she was reclining on the sofa** sie ruhte auf dem Sofa

recluse [rɪ'kluːs] N Einsiedler(in) *m(f)*

recognition [ˌrekəg'nɪʃən] N **(a)** (= *acknowledgement, also Pol*) Anerkennung *f*; **in ~ of** in Anerkennung (+*gen*) **(b)** (= *identification*) Erkennen *nt*; **the baby's ~ of its mother** dass das Baby seine Mutter erkennt; **it has changed beyond** *or* **out of all ~** es ist nicht wieder zu erkennen

recognizable ADJ, **recognizably** ADV ['rekəgnaɪzəbl, -ɪ] erkennbar

recognize ['rekəgnaɪz] VT **(a)** (= *know again*) wieder erkennen; (= *identify, be aware*) erkennen (*by* an +*dat*); (= *be prepared to admit*) eingestehen **(b)** (= *acknowledge, also Pol*) anerkennen (*as, to be* als)

recoil [rɪ'kɔɪl] VI (*person*) (*from* vor +*dat*) zurückweichen; (*in fear*) zurückschrecken; (*in disgust*) zurückschaudern; **he ~ed from (the idea of) doing it** ihm graute davor, das zu tun; (*gun*) zurückstoßen; (*spring*) zurückschnellen

recollect [ˌrekə'lekt] **1** VT sich erinnern an (+*acc*) **2** VI sich erinnern

recollection [ˌrekə'lekʃən] N (= *memory*) Erinnerung *f* (*of* an +*acc*); **I have some/no ~ of it** ich kann mich schwach/nicht daran erinnern

recommend [ˌrekə'mend] VT **(a)** empfehlen (*as* als); **what do you ~ for a cough?** was empfehlen Sie gegen Husten?; **to ~ sb/sth to sb** jdm jdn/etw empfehlen; **to ~ against sth** von etw abraten; **to ~ doing sth/against doing sth** empfehlen/davon abraten, etw zu tun; **to come highly ~ed** wärmstens empfohlen sein **(b)** (= *make acceptable*) sprechen für; **this book has little to ~ it** das Buch ist nicht gerade empfehlenswert

recommendation [ˌrekəmen'deɪʃən] N Empfehlung *f*; **on the ~ of** auf Empfehlung von; **letter of ~** Empfehlung *f*

recommended price [ˌrekə'mendɪd'praɪs] N unverbindlicher Richtpreis

reconcile ['rekənsaɪl] VT **(a)** *people* versöhnen; *differences* beilegen; **they became** *or* **were ~d** sie versöhnten sich; **to ~ sb to sth** jdn mit etw versöhnen; **to ~ oneself to sth, to become ~d to sth** sich mit etw abfinden **(b)** *facts, ideas, principles* miteinander in Einklang bringen; *accounts* abstimmen

reconciliation [ˌrekənˌsɪlɪ'eɪʃən] N (*of persons*) Versöhnung *f*; (*of differences*) Beilegung *f*

reconsider [ˌriːkən'sɪdəʳ] **1** VT *decision, judgement* noch einmal überdenken; (= *change*) revidieren; *facts* neu erwägen; **to ~ one's position** seine Position überdenken **2** VI **there's still time to ~** es ist noch nicht zu spät, seine Meinung zu ändern

reconsideration [ˈriːkənˌsɪdəˈreɪʃən] N (*of decision, judgement*) Überdenken *nt*; (*of facts*) erneute Erwägung

reconstruct [ˌriːkən'strʌkt] VT rekonstruieren; *cities, building* wieder aufbauen

reconstruction [ˌriːkən'strʌkʃən] N Rekonstruktion *f*; (*of city, building*) Wiederaufbau *m*

record [rɪ'kɔːd] **1** VT (*person: also on cassette etc*) aufzeichnen; (*documents, diary etc*) dokumentieren; (*in register*) eintragen; *one's thoughts, feelings etc* festhalten; *protest, disapproval* zum Ausdruck bringen; **these facts are not ~ed anywhere** diese Tatsachen sind nirgends festgehalten **2** VI (Tonband)aufnahmen machen **3** ['rekɔːd] N **(a)** (= *account*) Aufzeichnung *f*; (*of meeting*) Protokoll *nt*; (= *official document*) Akte *f*; (*lit, fig: of the past etc*) Dokument *nt*; **to keep a ~ of sth** über etw (*acc*) Buch führen; (*official, registrar*) etw registrieren; **to keep a personal ~ of sth** sich (*dat*) etw notieren; **it is on ~ that ...** es gibt Belege dafür, dass ...; (*in files*) es ist aktenkundig, dass ...; **he's on ~ as having said ...** es ist belegt, dass er gesagt hat, ...; **to put** *or* **set the ~ straight** für klare Verhältnisse sorgen; **just to set the ~ straight** nur damit Klarheit herrscht; **for the ~** der Ordnung halber; **this is strictly off the ~** dies ist nur inoffizell **(b)** (= *police ~*) Vorstrafen *pl*; **~s** (= *files*) Strafregister *nt*; **he's got a ~** er ist vorbestraft

(c) (= *history*) Vorgeschichte *f*; (= *achievements*) Leistungen *pl*; **to have an excellent ~** ausgezeichnete Leistungen vorweisen können; **he has a good ~ of service** er ist ein verdienter Mitarbeiter; **to have a good safety ~** in Bezug auf Sicherheit einen guten Ruf haben

(d) (*Mus*) (Schall)platte *f*

(e) (*Sport, fig*) Rekord *m*; **to hold the ~** den Rekord halten; **~ amount** Rekordbetrag *m*

(f) (*Comput*) Datensatz *m*

record ['rekɔːd]: **record-breaking** ADJ (*Sport, fig*) rekordbrechend, Rekord-; **a ~ achievement** eine Rekordleistung; **record company** N Plattenfirma *f*

recorded [rɪ'kɔːdɪd] ADJ *music, programme* aufgezeichnet; **~ message** Ansage *f*, Bandansage *f*

recorded delivery N (*Brit*) **by ~** per Einschreiben

recorder [rɪ'kɔːdəʳ] N **(a)** **cassette ~** Kassettenrekorder *m*; **tape ~** Tonbandgerät *nt* **(b)** (*Mus*) Blockflöte *f*

record holder [rɪ'kɔːdˌhəʊldəʳ] N (*Sport*) Rekordhalter(in) *m(f)*

recording [rɪ'kɔːdɪŋ] N (*of sound*) Aufnahme *f*

record player ['rekɔːdˌpleɪəʳ] N Plattenspieler *m*

records department N Registratur *f*

recount [rɪ'kaʊnt] VT (= *relate*) erzählen

re-count 1 [ˌriː'kaʊnt] VT nachzählen **2** ['riːˌkaʊnt] N (*of votes*) Nachzählung *f*

recoup [rɪ'kuːp] VT *money, amount* wieder hereinbekommen; *losses* wieder gutmachen

recourse [rɪ'kɔːs] N Zuflucht *f*; **without ~** (*Fin*) ohne Regress; **right of ~** (*Fin*) Regressanspruch *m*

recover [rɪ'kʌvəʳ] **1** VT *sth lost* wieder finden; *one's appetite, balance* wiedergewinnen; *property, lost territory* zurückgewinnen; (*police*) *stolen/missing goods* sicherstellen; *body, wreck* bergen; *debt* eintreiben; *losses* wieder gutmachen; *expenses* decken; (*Comput*) *file* retten; **to ~ consciousness** wieder zu Bewusstsein kommen; **to ~ oneself** *or* **one's composure** seine Fassung wiedererlangen; **to be quite ~ed** sich ganz erholt haben **2** VI (*after shock etc, St Ex, Fin*) sich erholen; (*from illness also*) genesen (*geh*)

recoverable [rɪ'kʌvərəbl] ADJ (*Fin*) *debt* eintreibbar; *losses, damages* ersetzbar; *deposit* zurückzahlbar; *goods* rückgewinnbar

recovery [rɪ'kʌvərɪ] N **(a)** (*of sth lost*) Wiederfinden *nt*; (*of one's appetite also*) Wiedergewinnung *f*; (*of goods, property, lost territory*) Zurückgewinnung *f*; (*of body, wreck*) Bergung *f*; (*of debt*) Eintreibung *f*; (*of losses*) Wiedergutmachung *f*; (*of expenses*) Deckung *f* **(b)** (*after shock, illness etc, St Ex, Fin*) Erholung *f*; **to be on the road** *or* **way to ~** auf dem Weg der Besserung sein; **he is making a good ~** er erholt sich gut

recovery: **recovery service** N Abschleppdienst *m*; **recovery vehicle** N Abschleppwagen *m*

recreate [ˌriːkri'eɪt] VT *atmosphere* wieder schaffen; *scene* nachschaffen

recreation [ˌrekri'eɪʃən] N Erholung *f*; **for ~ I go fishing** zur Erholung gehe ich angeln

recreational [ˌrekri'eɪʃənəl] ADJ Freizeit-; **~ facilities** Freizeiteinrichtungen *pl*

recrimination [rɪˌkrɪmɪ'neɪʃən] N Gegenbeschuldigung *f*; **(mutual) ~s** gegenseitige Beschuldigungen *pl*

recruit [rɪ'kruːt] **1** N (*Mil*) Rekrut(in) *m(f)* (*to* +*gen*); (*to party, club*) neues Mitglied (*to* in +*dat*); (*to staff*) Neue(r) *mf* (*to* in +*dat*) **2** VT *soldier* rekrutieren; *member* werben; *staff*

einstellen 3 VT (*Mil*) Rekruten anwerben; (*organization, club*) Mitglieder werben; (*employer*) neue Leute einstellen

recruiting [rɪˈkruːtɪŋ] N (*of soldiers*) Rekrutierung f; (*of members*) Werben nt; (*of staff*) Einstellung f

recruitment [rɪˈkruːtmənt] N (*of soldiers*) Rekrutierung f; (*of members*) (An)werbung f; (*of staff*) Einstellung f

recruitment: recruitment agency N Personalagentur f; **recruitment consultant** N Personalberater(in) m(f); **recruitment drive** N Anwerbungskampagne f

rectangle [ˈrekˌtæŋgl] N Rechteck nt

rectangular [rekˈtæŋgjuləʳ] ADJ rechteckig

rectify [ˈrektɪfaɪ] VT korrigieren; *omission* nachholen; *problem, flaws* beheben

rector [ˈrektəʳ] N (*Univ*) Rektor(in) m(f)

recuperate [rɪˈkuːpəreɪt] 1 VI sich erholen 2 VT *losses* wettmachen

recuperation [rɪˌkuːpəˈreɪʃən] N Erholung f; (*of losses*) Wiedergutmachung f

recur [rɪˈkɜːʳ] VI wiederkehren; (*error, event*) sich wiederholen; (*idea, theme*) wieder auftauchen

recurrence [rɪˈkʌrəns] N Wiederkehr f; (*of error, event*) Wiederholung f; (*of problem, symptoms also*) erneutes Auftreten; (*of idea, theme*) Wiederauftauchen nt

recurrent [rɪˈkʌrənt] ADJ *idea, theme, illness, dream* (ständig) wiederkehrend attr; *error, problem* häufig (vorkommend); *event(s)* sich wiederholend attr; *expenses* regelmäßig wiederkehrend

recurring [rɪˈkɜːrɪŋ] ADJ ATTR = **recurrent**

recyclable [ˌriːˈsaɪkləbl] ADJ recycelbar

recycle [ˌriːˈsaɪkl] VT wieder verwerten, wieder aufbereiten; **~d paper** Recyclingpapier nt; **made from ~d paper** aus Altpapier (hergestellt)

recycling [ˌriːˈsaɪklɪŋ] N Recycling nt

recycling bin N Recyclingbehälter m

red [red] 1 ADJ (*also Pol*) rot; **the lights are ~** (*Aut*) es ist rot; **~ as a beetroot** rot wie eine Tomate; **to go ~ in the face** rot anlaufen; **she turned ~ with embarrassment** sie wurde rot vor Verlegenheit 2 N Rot nt; **to go through the lights on ~, to go through on ~** bei Rot über die Ampel fahren; **to be (£100) in the ~** (mit £ 100) in den roten Zahlen sein; **this pushed the company into the ~** das brachte die Firma in die roten Zahlen; **to see ~** (*fig*) rotsehen

red: red alert N Alarmstufe f rot; **to be on ~** in höchster Alarmbereitschaft sein; **red cabbage** N Rotkohl m; **red card** N (*Ftbl*) rote Karte; **to show sb the ~** (*also fig*) jdm die rote Karte zeigen; **red carpet** N (*lit, fig*) roter Teppich; **to roll out the ~ for sb, to give sb the ~ treatment** (*inf*) den roten Teppich für jdn ausrollen; **Red Cross** 1 N Rotes Kreuz 2 ATTR Rotkreuz-; **redcurrant** N (*Brit*) (rote) Johannisbeere; **red deer** N Rothirsch m; (*pl*) Rotwild nt

redden [ˈredn] 1 VT röten 2 VI (*face*) sich röten; (*person*) rot werden

reddish [ˈredɪʃ] ADJ rötlich

redecorate [ˌriːˈdekəreɪt] VTI (= *paper*) neu tapezieren; (= *paint*) neu streichen

redeem [rɪˈdiːm] VT *coupons, bill etc* einlösen (*for* gegen); (*Fin*) *debt* abzahlen; *mortgage* tilgen; *shares* verkaufen; (*US*) *banknote* wechseln (*for* in +*acc*); *failing, fault* wettmachen

redeemable [rɪˈdiːməbl] ADJ *debt* tilgbar; *coupons, bill* einlösbar; **~ against** einlösbar gegen; **~ for cash** gegen Bargeld einzulösen

redeeming [rɪˈdiːmɪŋ] ADJ *quality* ausgleichend; **~ feature** aussöhnendes Moment

redefine [ˌriːdɪˈfaɪn] VT neu definieren

redemption [rɪˈdempʃən] N (*of coupons, bill etc*) Einlösung f; (*Fin*) (*of debt*) Abzahlung f; (*of mortgage*) Tilgung f; (*of shares*) Verkauf m; (*US: of banknote*) Wechsel m; **beyond** or **past ~** (*fig*) nicht mehr zu retten; **~ date** (*St Ex*) Endfälligkeit f

redeploy [ˌriːdɪˈplɔɪ] VT *troops* umverlegen; *workers* anders einsetzen; *staff* umsetzen

redeployment [ˌriːdɪˈplɔɪmənt] N (*of troops*) Umverlegung f; (*of workers*) Einsatz m an einem anderen Arbeitsplatz; (*of staff*) Umsetzung f

redesign [ˌriːdɪˈzaɪn] VT umgestalten

redevelop [ˌriːdɪˈveləp] VT *building, area* sanieren

redevelopment [ˌriːdɪˈveləpmənt] N Sanierung f

red: red-eyed ADJ mit geröteten Augen; **red-faced** ADJ mit rotem Kopf; **red-haired** ADJ rothaarig; **red-handed** ADV **to catch sb ~** jdn auf frischer Tat ertappen; **redhead** N Rothaarige(r) mf; **red-headed** ADJ rothaarig; **red herring** N (*fig*) Ablenkungsmanöver nt; (*in thrillers etc*) falsche Spur; **red-hot** ADJ (a) (*lit*) rot glühend; (= *very hot*) glühend heiß; (*fig*) *telephone lines* heißgelaufen; **~ favourite** brandheißer Favorit (b) (*fig inf*) (= *very popular*) heiß (*inf*); (= *very skilled*) toll (*inf*); (= *very recent*) brandaktuell (c) *chilli* scharf

redial [riːˈdaɪəl] (*Telec*) 1 VTI nochmals wählen 2 N **automatic ~** automatische Wahlwiederholung

red ink N (*US*: = *losses*) rote Zahlen pl

redirect [ˌriːdaɪˈrekt] VT *letter, parcel* umadressieren; (= *forward*) nachsenden; *traffic, shipment* umleiten; *attention, efforts, resources* umverteilen

rediscover [ˌriːdɪsˈkʌvəʳ] VT wieder entdecken

rediscovery [ˌriːdɪsˈkʌvərɪ] N Wiederentdeckung f

redistribute [ˌriːdɪsˈtrɪbjuːt] VT *wealth* neu verteilen; *work* neu zuteilen

redistribution [ˌriːdɪstrɪˈbjuːʃən] N (*of wealth*) Neuverteilung f; (*of work*) Neuzuteilung f

red: red-letter day N besonderer Tag; **red light** N (*lit*) (= *warning light*) rotes Licht; (= *traffic light*) Rotlicht nt; **to go through the ~** (*Mot*) bei Rot über die Ampel fahren; **the red-light district** die Strichgegend; (*with nightclubs*) das Rotlichtviertel; **red meat** N Rind-, Lamm- und Rehfleisch

redness [ˈrednɪs] N Röte f

redo [riːˈduː] VT (a) noch einmal machen; *hair* in Ordnung bringen (b) = **redecorate**

redouble [riːˈdʌbl] 1 VT *efforts, zeal etc* verdoppeln; *attacks* verstärken 2 VI (*zeal, efforts*) sich verdoppeln; (*attacks*) sich verstärken

red rag N **it's like a ~ to a bull** das wirkt wie ein rotes Tuch

redress [rɪˈdres] 1 VT *one's errors, wrongs* wieder gutmachen; *situation* bereinigen; *grievance* beseitigen; *balance* wieder herstellen 2 N (*for errors, wrongs*) Wiedergutmachung f; (*for grievance*) Beseitigung f; **to seek ~ for** Wiedergutmachung verlangen für

red: Red Sea N Rotes Meer; **red tape** N (*fig*) Papierkrieg m (*inf*)

reduce [rɪˈdjuːs] 1 VT reduzieren; *taxes, costs* senken; *expenses, wages* kürzen; *value* mindern; (= *shorten*) verkürzen; *scale of operations* einschränken; (*in price*) heruntersetzen; **to ~ speed** (*Mot*) langsamer fahren; **it has been ~d to nothing** es ist zu nichts zusammengeschmolzen; **to ~ sb to silence/tears** jdn zum Schweigen/Weinen bringen; **to ~ sb to begging** jdn zum Betteln zwingen; **are we ~d to this!** so weit ist es also gekommen! 2 VI (*esp US*: = *slim*) abnehmen

reduced [rɪˈdjuːst] ADJ reduziert; *goods* heruntergesetzt; *scale, version* kleiner; *risk, demand, threat, role* geringer; *circumstances* beschränkt; **at a ~ price** zu einem reduzierten Preis

reduction [rɪˈdʌkʃən] N (a) NO PL (*in sth gen*) Reduzierung f; (*in taxes, costs*) Senkung f; (*in expenses, wages*) Kürzung f; (*in value*) Minderung f; (*in size*) Verkleinerung f; (= *shortening*) Verkürzung f; (*in scale of operations*) Einschränkung f; (*of goods, items*) Herabsetzung f

(b) (= *amount reduced*) (*in sth gen*) (*in pressure, temperature, output*) Rückgang m; (*of speed*) Verlangsamung f; (*in size*) Verkleinerung f; (*in length*) Verkürzung f; (*in taxes*) Nachlass m; (*in prices*) Ermäßigung f; (*Jur: of sentence*) Kürzung f; **to sell (sth) at a ~** etw zu ermäßigtem Preis verkaufen

redundancy [rɪˈdʌndənsɪ] N (*Brit Ind*) Arbeitslosigkeit f; **redundancies** Entlassungen pl

redundancy payment N (*Brit Ind*) Abfindung f

redundant [rɪˈdʌndənt] ADJ (a) überflüssig (b) (*Brit Ind*) arbeitslos; **to make sb ~** jdn entlassen; **to become/to be made ~** den Arbeitsplatz verlieren

red wine N Rotwein m

reed [riːd] N (*Bot*) Schilf(rohr) nt

re-educate [riːˈedjʊkeɪt] VT umerziehen

re-education [riːˌedjʊˈkeɪʃən] N Umerziehung f

reef [riːf] N Riff nt

reek [riːk] 1 N Gestank m 2 VI stinken (*of* nach)

reel [riːl] **1** N Spule f; (Fishing) (Angel)rolle f **2** VI (person) taumeln; **the blow made him ~** or **sent him ~ing** er taumelte unter dem Schlag; **the whole country is still ~ing from the shock** das ganze Land ist noch tief erschüttert von diesem Schock; **economic problems sent markets ~ing** Wirtschaftsprobleme brachten die Börsen ins Wanken

➤ **reel off** VT SEP list herunterrasseln (inf)

re-elect [ˌriːɪˈlekt] VT wieder wählen

re-election [ˌriːɪˈlekʃən] N Wiederwahl f

re-emerge [ˌriːɪˈmɜːdʒ] VI (object, swimmer) wieder auftauchen; (facts) (wieder) herauskommen

re-enact [ˌriːɪˈnækt] VT scene nachspielen; event, crime nachstellen

re-enactment [ˌriːɪˈnæktmənt] N (of scene) Nachspiel nt; (of event, crime) Nachstellen nt

re-enter [ˌriːˈentəʳ] **1** VI (a) (= walk in) wieder eintreten; (= drive in) wieder einfahren; (= penetrate: bullet etc) wieder eindringen; (= climb in) wieder einsteigen (b) (for race, exam etc) sich wieder melden (for zu) **2** VT (a) room wieder betreten; country wieder einreisen in (+acc); club etc wieder beitreten (+dat); society sich wieder eingliedern in (+acc); race sich wieder beteiligen an (+dat) (b) name (on list etc) wieder eintragen

re-entry [ˌriːˈentrɪ] N (also Space) Wiedereintritt m; (into country) Wiedereinreise f (into in +acc); (for exam) Wiederantritt m (for zu); **her ~ into society** ihre Wiedereingliederung in die Gesellschaft

re-establish [ˌriːɪˈstæblɪʃ] VT order wieder herstellen; control wiedererlangen; diplomatic relations, dialogue wieder aufnehmen

re-establishment [ˌriːɪˈstæblɪʃmənt] N (of order) Wiederherstellung f; (of control) Wiedererlangen nt; (of diplomatic relations, dialogue) Wiederaufnahme f; (in a position, office) Wiedereinsetzung f

re-examination [ˌriːɪɡˌzæmɪˈneɪʃən] N erneute Prüfung; (of role) genaue Überprüfung

re-examine [ˌriːɪɡˈzæmɪn] VT erneut prüfen; role nochmals genau ansehen

refer [rɪˈfɜːʳ] **1** VT matter weiterleiten (to an +acc); (to a higher court) verweisen (to an +acc); decision übergeben (to sb jdm); **I ~red him to the manager** ich verwies ihn an den Geschäftsführer; **the doctor ~red him to a specialist** der Arzt überwies ihn an einen Spezialisten; **to ~ sb to the article on ...** jdn auf den Artikel über (+acc) ... verweisen; **to ~ a cheque** (Brit) or **check** (US) **to drawer** (Comm) einen Scheck an den Aussteller zurücksenden **2** VI (a) **to ~ to** (= allude to) sprechen von; (= mention also) erwähnen; (words) sich beziehen auf (+acc); **I am not ~ring to you** ich meine nicht Sie; **what can he be ~ring to?** was meint er wohl?; **the letter ~s to you all** der Brief gilt euch allen; **~ring to your letter** (Comm) mit Bezug auf Ihren Brief (b) (= consult) **to ~ to** notes, book nachschauen in (+dat); **to person** sich wenden an (+acc)

➤ **refer back 1** VI (a) (person, remark) sich beziehen (to auf +acc) (b) (= consult again) zurückgehen (to zu) **2** VT SEP decision etc zurückgeben (to an +acc); case, matter zurückverweisen; **he referred me back to you** er hat mich an Sie zurückverwiesen

referee [ˌrefəˈriː] **1** N (a) (Ftbl, Rugby, Jur, fig) Schiedsrichter(in) m(f); (Boxing) Ringrichter(in) m(f) (b) (Brit: = person giving a reference) Referenz f **2** VT (Sport, fig) Schiedsrichter(in) sein bei **3** VI (Sport, fig) Schiedsrichter(in) sein

reference [ˈrefrəns] N (a) (= act of mentioning) Erwähnung f (to sb/sth jds/einer Sache); (= allusion) Bemerkung f (to über +acc); (indirect) Anspielung f (to auf +acc); (of letter) Bezug m; **to make (a) ~ to sth** etw erwähnen; **in** or **with ~ to** was ... anbetrifft; (Comm) bezüglich (+gen); **~ your letter ...** (Comm) mit Bezug auf Ihren Brief ... (b) (= testimonial, also **~s**) Referenz f usu pl (c) (in book, on map etc) Verweis m; (Comm) Zeichen nt (d) (esp US) = **referee 1(b)**

reference: **reference book** N Nachschlagewerk nt; **reference library** N Präsenzbibliothek f; **reference number** N Aktenzeichen nt; (of subscriber etc) Nummer f

referendum [ˌrefəˈrendəm] N, pl **referenda** [ˌrefəˈrendə] Referendum nt; **to hold a ~** ein Referendum abhalten

refill [ˌriːˈfɪl] **1** VT nachfüllen **2** [ˈriːfɪl] N (for fountain pen, lighter) Nachfüllpatrone f; (for ballpoint pen) Ersatzmine f; **would you like a ~?** (inf: = drink) darf ich nachschenken?

refillable [ˌriːˈfɪləbl] ADJ nachfüllbar

refinancing [ˌriːfaɪˈnænsɪŋ] N Neufinanzierung f

refine [rɪˈfaɪn] VT (a) metal, oil, sugar raffinieren (b) techniques, methods verfeinern

refined [rɪˈfaɪnd] ADJ (a) metal, oil raffiniert; foods veredelt; **~ products** (St Ex, Econ) raffinierte/veredelte Produkte pl (b) taste fein; person, style vornehm

refinement [rɪˈfaɪnmənt] N (a) NO PL (of person, language, style) Vornehmheit f (b) (= improvement: in technique, machine etc) Verfeinerung f (in sth gen)

refinery [rɪˈfaɪnərɪ] N (metal, oil, sugar ~) Raffinerie f

reflate [ˌriːˈfleɪt] **1** VT (Econ) ankurbeln **2** VI (economy) sich beleben

reflation [ˌriːˈfleɪʃən] N (Econ) Reflation f

reflect [rɪˈflekt] **1** VT reflektieren; (fig) views, reality etc widerspiegeln; **to be ~ed in sth** (lit, fig) sich in etw (dat) spiegeln; **I saw myself ~ed in the mirror** ich sah mich im Spiegel; **to ~ the fact that ...** die Tatsache widerspiegeln, dass ... **2** VI (= meditate) nachdenken (on, about über +acc)

➤ **reflect (up)on** VI +PREP OBJ etwas aussagen über (+acc); person also ein gutes/schlechtes Licht werfen auf (+acc)

reflection [rɪˈflekʃən] N (a) NO PL (= reflecting) Reflexion f; (by surface of lake, mirror) Spiegelung f; (fig) Widerspiegelung f (b) (= image) Spiegelbild nt; (fig) Widerspiegelung f; **to see one's ~ in a mirror** sich im Spiegel sehen (c) NO PL (= consideration) Überlegung f; (= contemplation) Reflexion f; **(up)on ~** wenn ich mir das recht überlege; **on further ~** bei genauerer Überlegung; **this is no ~ on your ability** damit soll gar nichts über Ihr Können gesagt sein

reflective [rɪˈflektɪv] ADJ person, expression nachdenklich; surface, clothing reflektierend; light reflektiert

reflex [ˈriːfleks] **1** ADJ Reflex- **2** N Reflex m

reflexive [rɪˈfleksɪv] (Gram) **1** ADJ reflexiv **2** N Reflexiv nt

refloat [ˌriːˈfləʊt] VT ship (fig) business wieder flottmachen

re-form [ˌriːˈfɔːm] **1** VT (a) (= form again) wieder bilden (b) (= give new form to) umformen, umgestalten (into zu) **2** VI sich erneut bilden

reform [rɪˈfɔːm] **1** N Reform f **2** VT reformieren; conduct, person bessern **3** VI (person) sich bessern

reformat [ˌriːˈfɔːmæt] VT (Comput) disk neu formatieren

Reformation [ˌrefəˈmeɪʃən] N **the** ~ die Reformation

reformed [rɪˈfɔːmd] ADJ reformiert; alcoholic, communist ehemalig; behaviour gebessert; **he's a ~ character** er hat sich gebessert

refrain [rɪˈfreɪn] VI **he ~ed from comment** er enthielt sich eines Kommentars; **please ~ from smoking** bitte nicht rauchen!

refresh [rɪˈfreʃ] VT (a) erfrischen; **to ~ oneself** (with drink) eine Erfrischung zu sich (dat) nehmen; (with a bath) sich erfrischen; (with rest) sich ausruhen; **to ~ one's memory** sein Gedächtnis auffrischen; **let me ~ your memory** ich will Ihrem Gedächtnis nachhelfen (b) (Comput) screen neu laden

refreshing ADJ, **refreshingly** ADV [rɪˈfreʃɪŋ, -lɪ] (lit, fig) erfrischend

refreshment [rɪˈfreʃmənt] N (a) (of mind, body) Erfrischung f (b) (light) **~s** (kleine) Erfrischungen pl

refrigerate [rɪˈfrɪdʒəreɪt] VT kühlen; **"~ after opening"** „nach dem Öffnen kühl aufbewahren"

refrigeration [rɪˌfrɪdʒəˈreɪʃən] N Kühlung f

refrigerator [rɪˈfrɪdʒəreɪtəʳ] N Kühlschrank m

refuel [ˌriːˈfjʊəl] VTI auftanken

refuge [ˈrefjuːdʒ] N (lit, fig) Zuflucht f (from vor +dat); **a ~ for battered women** ein Frauenhaus nt; **to seek ~** Zuflucht suchen; **to take ~** sich flüchten (in in +acc)

refugee [ˌrefjʊˈdʒiː] N Flüchtling m

refund [rɪˈfʌnd] **1** VT money zurückerstatten; expenses erstatten; **to ~ the difference** die Differenz erstatten **2** [ˈriːfʌnd] N (of money) Rückerstattung f; (of expenses) Erstattung f; **to get a ~ (on sth)** sein Geld (für etw) wiederbekommen; **they wouldn't give me a ~** man wollte mir das Geld nicht zurückgeben; **I'd like a ~ on this blouse, please** ich hätte gern mein Geld für diese Bluse zurück

refundable [rɪˈfʌndəbl] ADJ zurückzahlbar

refurbish [ˌriːˈfɜːbɪʃ] VT renovieren

refurnish [ˌriːˈfɜːnɪʃ] VT neu möblieren

refusal [rɪˈfjuːzəl] N Ablehnung *f*; (*of food, permission*) Verweigerung *f*; (*to do sth*) Weigerung *f*; **her ~ (of the invitation)** ihre Absage; **to meet with a ~, to get a ~** eine Absage erhalten

refuse[1] [rɪˈfjuːz] **1** VT *candidate, proposal, offer* ablehnen; *invitation* absagen; (*stronger*) zurückweisen; *permission, payment* verweigern; **to ~ to do sth** sich weigern, etw zu tun; **I ~ to be blackmailed** ich lasse mich nicht erpressen; **he was ~d entry into Germany** ihm wurde die Einreise nach Deutschland verweigert; **they were ~d permission (to leave)** es wurde ihnen nicht gestattet (wegzugehen); **his request was ~d** seine Bitte wurde abgelehnt **2** VI (*to do sth*) sich weigern

refuse[2] [ˈrefjuːs] N Müll *m*; (= *food waste*) Abfall *m*

refuse [ˈrefjuːs] IN CPDS Müll-; **refuse collection** N Müllabfuhr *f*; **refuse dump** N Müllablageplatz *m*

refute [rɪˈfjuːt] VT widerlegen

reg. [redʒ] ADJ ABBR *of* **registered**; **~ no.** amtl. Kennzeichen

regain [rɪˈɡeɪn] VT wiedererlangen; *control, confidence, title* wiedergewinnen; *territory* zurückbekommen; **to ~ consciousness** das Bewusstsein wiedererlangen, wieder zu Bewusstsein kommen; **to ~ one's strength** wieder zu Kräften kommen; **to ~ one's footing/balance** seinen Halt/das Gleichgewicht wiederfinden; **to ~ possession of sth** wieder in den Besitz einer Sache (*gen*) gelangen; **to ~ the lead** (*in sport*) wieder in Führung gehen

regal [ˈriːɡəl] ADJ königlich; (*fig*) hoheitsvoll

regale [rɪˈɡeɪl] VT (*with stories*) ergötzen (*geh*)

regally [ˈriːɡəlɪ] ADV königlich; *say* hoheitsvoll

regard [rɪˈɡɑːd] **1** VT **(a)** betrachten; **to ~ sb/sth as sth** jdn/etw für etw halten; **to be ~ed as ...** als ... angesehen werden; **we ~ it as worth doing** wir glauben, dass es sich lohnt(, das zu tun); **he is highly ~ed** er ist hoch angesehen **(b) as ~s that/your application** was das/Ihren Antrag betrifft **2** N **(a)** (= *attention, concern*) Rücksicht *f* (*for* auf +*acc*); **to have some ~ for sb/sth** auf jdn/etw Rücksicht nehmen; **to show little/no ~ for sb/sth** wenig/keine Rücksichtnahme für jdn/etw zeigen **(b) in this ~** diesbezüglich; **with** *or* **in ~ to** in Bezug auf (+*acc*) **(c)** (= *respect*) Achtung *f*; **to hold sb in high ~** jdn achten *or* sehr schätzen; **to have a great ~ for sb** jdn hoch achten **(d) regards** PL (*in message*) Gruß *m*; **to send sb one's ~s** jdn grüßen lassen; **give him my ~s** grüßen Sie ihn von mir; **(kindest) ~s, with kind ~s** mit freundlichen Grüßen

regarding [rɪˈɡɑːdɪŋ] PREP bezüglich (+*gen*)

regardless [rɪˈɡɑːdlɪs] **1** ADJ **~ of** ohne Rücksicht auf (+*acc*); **~ of what it costs** egal, was es kostet; **~ of the fact that ...** ungeachtet dessen, dass ... **2** ADV trotzdem

regenerate [rɪˈdʒenəreɪt] VT erneuern; **to be ~d** sich erneuern

regeneration [rɪˌdʒenəˈreɪʃən] N Erneuerung *f*

regenerative [rɪˈdʒenərətɪv] ADJ regenerativ

regent [ˈriːdʒənt] N Regent(in) *m(f)*

regime [reɪˈʒiːm] N (*Pol*) Regime *nt*; (*fig*) System *nt*

regiment [ˈredʒɪmənt] N (*Mil*) Regiment *nt*

region [ˈriːdʒən] N Region *f*; (*Admin*) Bezirk *m*; (*fig*) Bereich *m*; **in the ~ of 5 kg** um die 5 kg

regional [ˈriːdʒənl] ADJ regional

register [ˈredʒɪstə[r]] **1** N **(a)** (= *book*) Register *nt*; (*at school*) Namensliste *f*; (*in hotel*) Gästebuch *nt*; (*of members etc*) Mitgliedsbuch *nt*; **~ of births, deaths and marriages** Personenstandsbuch *nt*; **~ of companies** (*Brit*) Handelsregister *nt* **(b)** (*Ling*) Sprachebene *f* **2** VT registrieren; (*in book, files*) eintragen; *fact, figure* erfassen; *birth, marriage, death, company, trademark, vehicle* anmelden; *student* einschreiben; (*expression*) zum Ausdruck bringen; **he is ~ed (as) blind** er hat einen Sehbehindertenausweis **3** VI (*on electoral list etc*) sich eintragen; (*in hotel*) sich anmelden; (*student*) sich einschreiben; **to ~ with the police** sich polizeilich melden; **to ~ for a course** sich für einen Kurs anmelden; (*Univ*) einen Kurs belegen

registered [ˈredʒɪstəd] ADJ **(a)** *voter, company, name* eingetragen; *vehicle* amtlich zugelassen **(b)** (*Post*) eingeschrieben; **by ~ post** per Einschreiben

registered: **registered shareholder** N Inhaber(in) *m(f)* von Namensaktien; **Registered Trademark** N eingetragenes Warenzeichen

registrar [ˌredʒɪˈstrɑː[r]] N (*Brit Admin*) Standesbeamte(r) *m*/-beamtin *f*

registrar's office (*Brit Admin*) Standesamt *nt*

registration [ˌredʒɪˈstreɪʃən] N **(a)** (*by authorities*) Registrierung *f*; (*in books, files, of company*) Eintragung *f*; (*of fact, figure*) Erfassung *f* **(b)** (*by individual, Comm*) Anmeldung *f*; (*of student*) Einschreibung *f*; **~ fee** Anmeldegebühr *f*; (*for evening class*) Kursgebühr *f*

registration number N (*Brit Aut*) Kraftfahrzeugkennzeichen *nt*

registry [ˈredʒɪstrɪ] N Sekretariat *nt*; (*Brit*: = ~ *office*) Standesamt *nt*

registry office N (*Brit*) Standesamt *nt*; **to get married in a ~** standesamtlich heiraten

regress [rɪˈɡres] VI (*lit form*) sich rückwärts bewegen; (*fig: society*) sich rückläufig entwickeln

regression [rɪˈɡreʃən] N (*lit form*) Rückwärtsbewegung *f*; (*fig: of society*) rückläufige Entwicklung

regressive [rɪˈɡresɪv] ADJ regressiv; *trend* rückläufig

regret [rɪˈɡret] **1** VT bedauern; *one's youth, lost opportunity* nachtrauern (+*dat*); **to ~ the fact that ...** (die Tatsache) bedauern, dass ...; **I ~ to say that ...** ich muss Ihnen leider mitteilen, dass ...; **we ~ any inconvenience caused** für eventuelle Unannehmlichkeiten bitten wir um Verständnis; **you won't ~ it!** Sie werden es nicht bereuen **2** N Bedauern *nt no pl*; **much to my ~** sehr zu meinem Bedauern; **I have no ~s** ich bereue nichts; **he sends his ~s** er lässt sich entschuldigen

regretful [rɪˈɡretfʊl] ADJ bedauernd *attr*; **it is ~ that ...** es ist bedauerlich, dass ...

regretfully [rɪˈɡretfʊlɪ] ADV **(a)** (= *with regret*) mit Bedauern **(b)** (= *unfortunately*) bedauerlicherweise

regrettable [rɪˈɡretəbl] ADJ bedauerlich

regrettably [rɪˈɡretəblɪ] ADV bedauerlicherweise

regroup [ˌriːˈɡruːp] **1** VT umgruppieren **2** VI sich umgruppieren

regular [ˈreɡjʊlə[r]] **1** ADJ **(a)** regelmäßig; *footsteps, rhythm, surface* gleichmäßig; *employment* fest; *action, procedure* richtig; *size, price, time* normal; **at ~ intervals** in regelmäßigen Abständen; **on a ~ basis** regelmäßig; **to be in** *or* **to have ~ contact with sb/sth** mit jdm/etw regelmäßig in Verbindung stehen *or* Kontakt haben; **to eat ~ meals** regelmäßig essen; **to keep ~ hours** feste Zeiten haben; **he has a ~ place in the team** er ist ein ordentliches Mannschaftsmitglied; **~ customer** Stammkunde *m*/-kundin *f*; **his ~ pub** (*Brit*) seine Stammkneipe *f* **(b)** (*esp US*: = *ordinary*) gewöhnlich; **he's just a ~ guy** er ist ein ganz normaler Typ (*inf*) **2** N (*in shop etc*) Stammkunde *m*/-kundin *f*; (*in pub, hotel*) Stammgast *m*

regularity [ˌreɡjʊˈlærɪtɪ] N Regelmäßigkeit *f*; (*of rhythm, surface*) Gleichmäßigkeit *f*; (*of employment*) Festheit *f*

regularly [ˈreɡjʊləlɪ] ADV regelmäßig; (= *at evenly spaced intervals*) in gleichmäßigen Abständen

regulate [ˈreɡjʊleɪt] VT regulieren; *flow, traffic* regeln

regulation [ˌreɡjʊˈleɪʃən] N **(a)** (= *regulating*) Regulierung *f*; (*of traffic*) Regelung *f* **(b)** (= *rule*) Vorschrift *f*; **the ~s of the society** die Satzung der Gesellschaft; **according to (the) ~s** laut Vorschrift/Satzung; **to be contrary to** *or* **against (the) ~s** gegen die Vorschrift(en)/Satzung verstoßen

regulatory [reɡjʊˈleɪtər] ADJ **~ authority/body** Regulierungsbehörde *f*/-organ *nt*

regurgitate [rɪˈɡɜːdʒɪteɪt] VT wieder hochbringen; (*fig*) *facts etc* wiederkäuen

rehab [ˈriːhæb] ABBR *of* **rehabilitation**

rehabilitate [ˌriːəˈbɪlɪteɪt] VT *refugee, the disabled* (in die Gesellschaft) eingliedern; *ex-criminal* rehabilitieren; *drug addict, alcoholic* therapieren

rehabilitation [ˌriːəˌbɪlɪˈteɪʃən] N (*of refugee, the disabled*) Eingliederung *f* in die Gesellschaft; (*of ex-criminal*) Rehabilitation *f*; (*of drug addict, alcoholic*) Therapie *f*

rehearsal [rɪˈhɜːsəl] N (*Theat, Mus*) Probe *f*; **the play is in ~** das Stück wird geprobt

rehearse [rɪˈhɜːs] VTI (*Theat, Mus*) proben; **to ~ what one is going to say** einüben, was man sagen will

reheat [ˌriːˈhiːt] VT aufwärmen

rehouse [ˌriːˈhaʊz] VT unterbringen

reign [reɪn] **1** N (*lit, fig*) Herrschaft *f* **2** VI (*lit, fig*) herrschen (*over* über +*acc*)

reigning [ˈreɪnɪŋ] ADJ ATTR regierend; *champion* amtierend

reimburse [ˌriːɪmˈbɜːs] VT *person* entschädigen; *loss, expenses, costs* ersetzen

reimbursement [ˌriːɪmˈbɜːsmənt] N (*of person*) Entschädigung *f*; (*of loss*) Ersatz *m*; (*of expenses, costs*) (Rück)erstattung *f*

reimpose [ˌriːɪmˈpəʊz] VT *task, conditions* neu aufzwingen (*on sb* jdm); *sanctions, fine* erneut verhängen (*on* gegen); *one's will, authority* erneut aufzwingen (*on sb* jdm)

rein [reɪn] N (*lit, fig*) Zügel *m*; **to keep a tight ~ on sb/sth** (*lit, fig*) bei jdm/etw die Zügel kurz halten; **to give free ~ to sb/sth, to allow** *or* **give sb/sth free ~** (*fig*) jdm/einer Sache freien Lauf lassen; **to give sb free ~ to do sth** jdm freie Hand lassen, etw zu tun

➤ **rein in** VT SEP *horse, passions* zügeln; *spending, inflation* in Schranken halten

reincarnate [ˌriːɪnˈkɑːneɪt] VT reinkarnieren (*liter*); **to be ~d** wieder geboren werden

reincarnation [ˌriːɪnkɑːˈneɪʃən] N Reinkarnation *f*

reindeer [ˈreɪndɪə'] N, *pl* - Ren(tier) *nt*

reinforce [ˌriːɪnˈfɔːs] VT (*lit, fig, Psych, Mil*) verstärken; *sb's demands, belief* stärken; *evidence, statement, opinion* bestätigen; **to ~ sb's determination** jdn in seiner Absicht bestärken; **to ~ the message** der Botschaft (*dat*) mehr Nachdruck verleihen

reinforcement [ˌriːɪnˈfɔːsmənt] N (*lit, fig, Psych, Mil*) Verstärkung *f*; (*of sb's demands, beliefs*) Stärkung *f*; (*of evidence, statement, opinion*) Bestätigung *f*; **~s** (*Mil, fig*) Verstärkung *f*

reinsert [ˌriːɪnˈsɜːt] VT wieder einfügen; *coin* wieder einwerfen; *needle* wieder einstecken

reinstate [ˌriːɪnˈsteɪt] VT *person* wieder einstellen (*in* in +*acc*); *death penalty* wieder einführen

reinstatement [ˌriːɪnˈsteɪtmənt] N (*of person*) Wiedereinstellung *f*; (*of death penalty*) Wiedereinführung *f*

reinsure [ˌriːɪnˈʃʊə'] VT rückversichern

reintegrate [ˌriːˈɪntɪɡreɪt] VT wieder eingliedern (*into* in +*acc*)

reintegration [ˈriːˌɪntɪˈɡreɪʃən] N Wiedereingliederung *f*

reintroduce [ˌriːɪntrəˈdjuːs] VT *measure, death penalty* wieder einführen

reinvent [ˌriːɪnˈvent] VT **to ~ the wheel** das Rad neu erfinden; **to ~ oneself** sich (*dat*) ein neues Image geben

reinvest [ˌriːɪnˈvest] VT reinvestieren

reissue [ˌriːˈɪʃuː] **1** VT *book* neu auflegen; *stamps, recording* neu herausgeben **2** N (*of book*) Neuauflage *f*; (*of stamps, recording*) Neuausgabe *f*

reject [rɪˈdʒekt] **1** VT (a) *damaged goods etc* (*customer*) zurückweisen; (*maker, producer*) aussortieren (b) *application, request etc* ablehnen (*also* Med); (*stronger*) abweisen; *suitor, advances, plea* zurückweisen; *idea, possibility* verwerfen; *transplant* abstoßen **2** [ˈriːdʒekt] N (*Comm*) Ausschuss *m no pl*; **~ goods** Ausschussware *f*

rejection [rɪˈdʒekʃən] N (a) (*of damaged goods etc*) (*by customer*) Zurückweisung *f*; (*by maker, producer*) Aussortierung *f* (b) (*of application, request, offer etc*) Ablehnung *f* (*also* Med); (*stronger*) Abweisung *f*; (*of suitor, advances, plea*) Zurückweisung *f*; (*of idea, possibility*) Verwerfen *nt*; (*of transplant*) Abstoßung *f*

rejoice [rɪˈdʒɔɪs] VI sich freuen; (= *be jubilant*) jubeln

rejoicing [rɪˈdʒɔɪsɪŋ] N Jubel *m*

rejoin [riːˈdʒɔɪn] VT *person, regiment* sich wieder anschließen (+*dat*); *party, club* wieder eintreten in (+*acc*)

rejuvenate [rɪˈdʒuːvɪneɪt] VT verjüngen; (*fig*) erfrischen

rekindle [ˌriːˈkɪndl] VT (*fig*) *passions, love* wieder entzünden; *tensions, enmities* wieder aufflammen lassen; *hope, interest*

wieder erwecken; *debate* wieder entfachen; *affair* wieder aufleben lassen

relapse [rɪˈlæps] **1** N (*Med*) Rückfall *m*; (*fig: in economy*) Rückschlag *m* **2** VI (*Med*) einen Rückfall haben; (*economy*) einen Rückschlag erleiden

relate [rɪˈleɪt] **1** VT (a) *story* erzählen; *details* aufzählen (b) (= *associate*) in Verbindung bringen (*to, with* mit) **2** VI (a) (= *refer*) zusammenhängen (*to* mit) (b) (= *form relationship*) eine Beziehung finden (*to* zu)

related [rɪˈleɪtɪd] ADJ (a) (*in family*) verwandt (*to* mit); **~ by** *or* **through marriage** angeheiratet (b) (= *connected*) zusammenhängend; *elements, products, issues* verwandt; **to be ~ to sth** mit etw zusammenhängen, mit etw verwandt sein; **the two events are not ~** die beiden Ereignisse haben nichts miteinander zu tun; **two closely ~ questions** zwei eng miteinander verknüpfte Fragen; **health-~ problems** gesundheitliche Probleme *pl*; **earnings-~ pensions** einkommensabhängige Renten *pl*

relation [rɪˈleɪʃən] N (a) (= *person*) Verwandte(r) *mf*; **he's a/no ~ (of mine)** er ist/ist nicht mit mir verwandt (b) (= *relationship*) Beziehung *f*; **to bear no ~ to** in keinerlei Beziehung stehen zu; **to bear little ~ to** wenig Beziehung haben zu; **in ~ to** (= *as regards*) in Bezug auf (+*acc*); (= *compared with*) im Verhältnis zu (c) **relations** PL (= *dealings, ties, sexual ~s*) Beziehungen *pl*; **to have business ~s with sb** geschäftliche Beziehungen zu jdm haben

relational [rɪˈleɪʃənəl] ADJ relational; **~ database** (*Comput*) relationale Datenbank

relationship [rɪˈleɪʃənʃɪp] N (a) (*in family*) Verwandtschaft *f* (*to* mit); **what is your ~ (to** *or* **with him)?** wie sind Sie (mit ihm) verwandt? (b) (= *connection: between events etc*) Beziehung *f*; (= *relations*) Verhältnis *nt*; (*in business*) Verbindung *f*; **to have a (sexual) ~ with sb** ein Verhältnis *nt* mit jdm haben; **to have a good ~ with sb** gute Beziehungen zu jdm haben; **we have a business ~** wir haben geschäftlich miteinander zu tun

relative [ˈrelətɪv] **1** ADJ (a) (= *comparative, Sci*) relativ; **to live in ~ luxury** relativ luxuriös leben; **with ~ ease** relativ leicht; **in ~ terms** relativ gesehen (b) (= *respective*) jeweilig (c) (= *relevant*) **~ to** sich beziehend auf (+*acc*) (d) (*Gram*) Relativ- **2** N (= *person*) = **relation (a)**

relatively [ˈrelətɪvlɪ] ADV relativ

relaunch [ˌriːˈlɔːntʃ] **1** VT *organization, scheme* neu starten **2** [ˈriːlɔːntʃ] N (*of organization, scheme*) Neustart *m*

relax [rɪˈlæks] **1** VT lockern; *muscles, person, one's mind* entspannen; *attention, effort* nachlassen in (+*dat*) **2** VI (sich) entspannen; (= *rest*) sich ausruhen; (= *calm down*) sich beruhigen; **~!** immer mit der Ruhe!

relaxation [ˌriːlækˈseɪʃən] N Entspannung *f*; **reading is her form of ~** sie entspannt sich durch Lesen

relaxed [rɪˈlækst] ADJ locker; *person, voice* entspannt; *atmosphere, surroundings* zwanglos; **to feel ~** (*physically*) entspannt sein; (*mentally*) sich wohl fühlen; **to feel ~ about sth** etw ganz gelassen sehen

relaxing [rɪˈlæksɪŋ] ADJ entspannend; *climate* erholsam

relay [ˈriːleɪ] **1** N (*Sport, also* **~ race**) Staffel *f*, Staffellauf *m* **2** VT (a) (*Rad, TV etc*) (weiter) übertragen (b) *message* ausrichten (*to sb* jdm); *information, details* weiterleiten (*to sb* an jdm)

release [rɪˈliːs] **1** VT (a) *animal, person* freilassen; (*from prison*) entlassen; (*from obligation, vow*) entbinden; **to ~ tension** (*emotional*) sich abreagieren (b) (= *let go of*) loslassen; *handbrake, grip, clasp* lösen; (*Phot*) *shutter* auslösen; **to ~ one's hold** *or* **grip (on sth)** (etw) loslassen (c) (*Comm*) *film, goods, record* herausbringen (d) *news, statement* veröffentlichen (e) *gas, energy* freisetzen; *pressure, steam* ablassen (f) (*Fin*) *reserves* freigeben **2** N (a) (*of animal, person*) Freilassung *f*; (*from prison*) Entlassung *f* (b) (= *letting go*) Loslassen *nt*; (*of handbrake*) Lösen *nt*; (= *mechanism*) Auslöser *m* (c) (*Comm*) (*of film, goods, record*) Herausbringen *nt*; (= *film*) Film *m*; (= *record*) Platte *f*; **this film is now on general ~** dieser Film ist nun überall zu sehen (d) (*of news, statement*) Veröffentlichung *f*; (= *statement*) Verlautbarung *f* (e) (*of gas, energy*) Freisetzung *f*

relegate ['relɪgeɪt] VT (*lit, fig*) degradieren; (*Sport*) absteigen lassen (*to* in +*acc*); **to be ~d** (*Sport*) absteigen; **~d to second place** (*fig*) an zweite Stelle abgeschoben

relegation [relɪ'geɪʃən] N (*lit, fig*) Degradierung *f*; (*Sport*) Abstieg *m*

relent [rɪ'lent] VI (*person*) nachgeben

relentless [rɪ'lentlɪs] ADJ (a) *attitude, opposition, person* unnachgiebig (b) *pain, cold, growth* nicht nachlassend; *search* unermüdlich; *progress* unaufhaltsam (c) (= *merciless*) erbarmungslos; *person* unerbittlich

relentlessly [rɪ'lentlɪslɪ] ADV (a) *oppose, maintain* unnachgiebig (b) *hurt* unaufhörlich (c) (= *mercilessly*) erbarmungslos

relevance ['reləvəns], **relevancy** ['reləvənsɪ] N Relevanz *f*; **to be of particular ~ (to sb)** (für jdn) besonders relevant sein

relevant ['reləvənt] ADJ relevant (*to* für); *authority, person* zuständig; *time, place* betreffend; *experience* erforderlich

reliability [rɪˌlaɪə'bɪlɪtɪ] N Zuverlässigkeit *f*; (*of firm, company*) Vertrauenswürdigkeit *f*

reliable [rɪ'laɪəbl] ADJ zuverlässig; *firm, company* vertrauenswürdig

reliably [rɪ'laɪəblɪ] ADV zuverlässig; **I am ~ informed that ...** ich weiß aus zuverlässiger Quelle, dass ...

reliance [rɪ'laɪəns] N Vertrauen *nt* (*on* auf +*acc*)

reliant [rɪ'laɪənt] ADJ angewiesen (*on, upon* auf +*acc*)

relic ['relɪk] N Relikt *nt*; (*Rel*) Reliquie *f*

relief [rɪ'liːf] **1** N (a) (*from anxiety, pain*) Erleichterung *f*; **that's a ~!** mir fällt ein Stein vom Herzen; **it was a ~ to find it** ich/er *etc* war erleichtert, als ich/er *etc* es fand; **it was a ~ to get out of the office** es war eine Wohltat, aus dem Büro wegzukommen (b) (*from monotony, boredom*) Abwechslung *f* (c) (= *assistance*) Hilfe *f*; **to provide ~ for the poor** für die Armen sorgen; **to be on ~** (*US*) von der Fürsorge leben (d) (= *substitute*) Ablösung *f* **2** ATTR (a) (= *aid*) Hilfs-; **the ~ effort** die Hilfsaktion; (*in disaster*) die Rettungsaktion (b) (= *replacement*) *driver etc* zur Entlastung

relief: **relief agency** N Rettungsorganisation *f*; **relief fund** N Hilfsfonds *m*; **relief supplies** PL Hilfsgüter *pl*; **relief workers** PL Rettungshelfer *pl*; (*in disaster*) Katastrophenhelfer *pl*

relieve [rɪ'liːv] VT (a) *person* erleichtern; **to feel ~d** erleichtert sein; **to be ~d at sth** bei etw erleichtert aufatmen; **to ~ sb of sth** *of burden, pain* jdn von etw befreien; *of duty, command* jdn einer Sache (*gen*) entheben (*geh*) (b) (= *mitigate*) *anxiety* mildern; *pain* lindern; (*completely*) stillen; *tension, stress* abbauen; *pressure, symptoms* abschwächen; *monotony* (= *interrupt*) unterbrechen; (= *liven things up*) beleben; *poverty* erleichtern; **to ~ oneself** (*euph*) sich erleichtern (c) (= *take over from, also Mil*) ablösen

religion [rɪ'lɪdʒən] N Religion *f*; (= *set of beliefs*) Glaube(n) *m*; **the Christian ~** der christliche Glaube

religious [rɪ'lɪdʒəs] ADJ (a) religiös; *order* geistlich; **~ leader** Religionsführer(in) *m(f)* (b) (= *having ~ beliefs*) *person* gläubig; (= *pious*) fromm

religiously [rɪ'lɪdʒəslɪ] ADV (a) *live* fromm; *motivated* religiös (b) (*fig*: = *conscientiously*) gewissenhaft

relinquish [rɪ'lɪŋkwɪʃ] VT aufgeben; *title* ablegen; **to ~ one's hold on sb/sth** (*lit, fig*) jdn/etw loslassen

relish ['relɪʃ] **1** N (a) Gefallen *m* (*for* an +*dat*); **to do sth with (great) ~** etw mit (großem) Genuss tun (b) (*Cook*) Soße *f*; **tomato ~** Tomatenchutney *nt* **2** VT genießen; *idea, role, task* großen Gefallen finden an (+*dat*); **I don't ~ the thought of getting up at 5 a.m.** der Gedanke, um 5 Uhr aufzustehen, behagt mir gar nicht

relive [riː'lɪv] VT noch einmal durchleben

reload [riː'ləʊd] VT neu beladen; *gun* nachladen

relocate [riːləʊ'keɪt] **1** VT umsiedeln **2** VI (*individual*) umziehen; (*company*) den Standort wechseln

relocation [riːləʊ'keɪʃən] N Umzug *m*; (*of company*) Standortwechsel *m*; (*of refugees etc*) Umsiedlung *f*

reluctance [rɪ'lʌktəns] N Widerwillen *m*; **to do sth with ~** etw widerwillig *or* ungern tun

reluctant [rɪ'lʌktənt] ADJ widerwillig; **he is ~ to do it** es widerstrebt ihm, es zu tun; **he seems ~ to admit it** er scheint es nicht zugeben zu wollen

reluctantly [rɪ'lʌktəntlɪ] ADV widerwillig

rely [rɪ'laɪ] VI **to ~ (up)on sb/sth** sich auf jdn/etw verlassen; (= *be dependent on*) auf jdn/etw angewiesen sein; **I ~ on him for my income** ich bin finanziell auf ihn angewiesen

remain [rɪ'meɪn] VI bleiben; (= *be left over*) übrig bleiben; **all that ~s is for me to wish you every success** ich möchte Ihnen nur noch viel Erfolg wünschen; **that ~s to be seen** das bleibt abzuwarten; **the fact ~s that he is wrong** das ändert nichts an der Tatsache, dass er Unrecht hat; **to ~ silent** weiterhin schweigen; **it ~s the same** das bleibt sich gleich

remainder [rɪ'meɪndə^r] N (a) Rest *m* (*also Math*); **the ~** (= *remaining people*) die übrigen (Leute) (b) **remainders** PL (*Comm*) Restbestände *pl*

remaining [rɪ'meɪnɪŋ] ADJ restlich; **the ~ four, the four ~** die vier Übrigen

remains [rɪ'meɪnz] PL (*of meal*) Reste *pl*; (*of fortune, army*) Rest *m*; (= *archaeological ~*) Ruinen *pl*; **human ~** menschliche Überreste *pl*

remake [riː'meɪk], *vb*: *pret, ptp* **remade** [riː'meɪd] VT nochmals machen; (*in new form*) neu machen; **to ~ a film** ein Thema neu verfilmen

remand [rɪ'mɑːnd] **1** VT (*Jur*) **he was ~ed in custody/on bail** er blieb in Untersuchungshaft/unter Kaution **2** N **to be on ~** in Untersuchungshaft sein; (= *on bail*) auf Kaution freigelassen sein

remark [rɪ'mɑːk] **1** N Bemerkung *f* **2** VI **to ~ (up)on sth** über etw (*acc*) eine Bemerkung machen; **nobody ~ed on it** niemand hat etwas dazu gesagt

remarkable [rɪ'mɑːkəbl] ADJ (= *notable*) bemerkenswert; (= *extraordinary*) außergewöhnlich; (= *amazing*) *escape* wundersam

remarkably [rɪ'mɑːkəblɪ] ADV (= *notably*) bemerkenswert; (= *extraordinarily*) außergewöhnlich; (= *amazingly*) bemerkenswerterweise; **~ little** erstaunlich wenig

remarry [riː'mærɪ] VI wieder heiraten

remedial [rɪ'miːdɪəl] ADJ ATTR Hilfs-; (*Med*) Heil-; **~ exercises** Heilgymnastik *f*; **~ teaching** Förderunterricht *m*

remedy ['remədɪ] **1** N (*Med, fig*) Mittel *nt* (*for* gegen); (= *medication*) Heilmittel *nt* (*for* gegen) **2** VT (*fig*) *deficiency, problem* beheben; *situation* bessern

remember [rɪ'membə^r] **1** VT (a) (= *recall*) sich erinnern an (+*acc*); (= *bear in mind*) denken an (+*acc*); (= *learn*) sich (*dat*) merken; **we must ~ that he's only a child** wir sollten bedenken, dass er noch ein Kind ist; **to ~ to do sth** daran denken, etw zu tun; **I ~ doing it** ich erinnere mich daran, dass ich es getan habe; **I can't ~ the word at the moment** das Wort fällt mir im Moment nicht ein; **do you ~ when ...?** (*reminiscing*) weißt du noch, als ...?; (*asking facts*) weißt du (noch), wann ...?; **I don't ~ a thing about it** ich kann mich überhaupt nicht daran erinnern; (*about book etc*) ich weiß nichts mehr davon; **I can never ~ phone numbers** ich kann mir Telefonnummern einfach nicht merken; **~ where/who you are!** denken Sie daran, wo/wer Sie sind! (b) (*Brit*) **~ me to your mother** grüßen Sie Ihre Mutter von mir **2** VI sich erinnern; **I can't ~** ich weiß das nicht mehr; **not as far as I ~** soweit ich mich erinnere, nicht!

remembrance [rɪ'membrəns] N Erinnerung *f* (*of* an +*acc*); **in ~ of** zur Erinnerung an (+*acc*)

Remembrance Day N (*Brit*) ≈ Volkstrauertag *m*

remind [rɪ'maɪnd] VT erinnern (*of* an +*acc*); **you are ~ed that ...** wir weisen darauf hin, dass ...; **that ~s me!** da(bei) fällt mir was ein

reminder [rɪ'maɪndə^r] N Gedächtnisstütze *f*; (*letter of*) ~ (*Comm*) Mahnung *f*; **his presence was a ~ of ...** seine Gegenwart erinnerte mich/dich *etc* an (+*acc*) ...; **a gentle ~** ein zarter Wink

reminisce [remɪ'nɪs] VI sich in Erinnerungen ergehen (*about* über +*acc*)

reminiscent [remɪ'nɪsənt] ADJ **to be ~ of sth** an etw (*acc*) erinnern; **a style ~ of Shakespeare** ein an Shakespeare erinnernder Stil

remission [rɪ'mɪʃən] N (*form*) (a) (= *cancelling*: *of debt*) Erlassen *nt*; (*Brit Jur*) (Straf)erlass *m* (b) (= *sending*: *of money*) Überweisung *f* (c) (*Med*) Besserung *f*; **to be in ~** (*patient*) sich auf dem Wege der Besserung befinden; (*illness*) abklingen

remit [rɪˈmɪt] VT (*form*) **(a)** (= *cancel, pardon*) erlassen **(b)** (= *send*) *money* überweisen

remittal [rɪˈmɪtl] N = **remission (b)**

remittance [rɪˈmɪtəns] N Überweisung *f* (*to* an +*acc*)

remittance advice N Überweisungsbescheid *m*

remnant [ˈremnənt] N Rest *m*; (*fig*) Überrest *m*

remnant (*Comm*): **remnant day** N Resteverkaufstag *m*; **remnant sale** N Resteausverkauf *m*

remodel [riːˈmɒdl] VT (*also Art, Tech*) umformen; (*fig*) umgestalten

remorse [rɪˈmɔːs] N Reue *f* (*at, over* über +*acc*); **without ~** (= *merciless*) erbarmungslos

remorseful [rɪˈmɔːsfʊl] ADJ reumütig; **to feel ~** Reue spüren

remorsefully [rɪˈmɔːsfəlɪ] ADV reumütig

remorseless [rɪˈmɔːslɪs] ADJ ohne Reue; (*fig:* = *merciless*) unbarmherzig

remorselessly [rɪˈmɔːslɪslɪ] ADV ohne Reue; (*fig:* = *mercilessly*) erbarmungslos

remote [rɪˈməʊt] **1** ADJ (+ER) **(a)** *place, possibility* entfernt; (= *isolated*) entlegen; (*in time*) fern; (*Comput*) rechnerfern; *chance* gering; **in a ~ spot** an einer entlegenen Stelle **(b)** (= *aloof*) unnahbar **(c)** (= *~-controlled*) zur Fernbedienung **2** N (*Rad, TV*: = *~ control*) Fernbedienung *f*

remote: **remote access** N (*Telec, Comput*) Fernzugriff *m*; **remote control** N Fernsteuerung *f*; (*Rad, TV*) Fernbedienung *f*; **remote-controlled** ADJ *model aeroplane etc* ferngesteuert; *gates* fernbedient; **remote data entry** N (*Comput*) Datenfernverarbeitung *f*

remotely [rɪˈməʊtlɪ] ADV **(a)** **it's just ~ possible** es ist gerade eben noch möglich; **he didn't say anything ~ interesting** er sagte nichts, was im Entferntesten interessant war; **I'm not ~ interested in her** ich bin nicht im Geringsten an ihr interessiert **(b)** *situated, related* entfernt

remoteness [rɪˈməʊtnɪs] N **(a)** (*in place, time*) (= *distance*) Ferne *f*; (= *isolation*) Abgelegenheit *f* **(b)** (*of connection, relevance, possibility*) Entferntheit *f*; (*of chance*) Winzigkeit *f* **(c)** (= *aloofness*) Unnahbarkeit *f*

removable [rɪˈmuːvəbl] ADJ *cover, attachment* abnehmbar; *lining* abknöpfbar; (*from container*) herausnehmbar

removal [rɪˈmuːvəl] N **(a)** Entfernung *f* (*also Med*); (*of bandage, tie*) Abnahme *f*; (*of clothes*) Ausziehen *nt*; (*of stain, threat, problem*) Beseitigung *f*; (*of troops*) Abzug *m*; (*from container*) Herausnehmen *nt*; (*of word, item on list*) Streichen *nt*; (*of tax, restrictions*) Aufhebung *f*; (*of obstacle*) Ausräumung *f*; (*of doubt, suspicion, fear*) Zerstreuung *f* **(b)** (*form*) (= *dismissal*) Entfernung *f* **(c)** (*Brit:* = *move from house*) Umzug *m*; **"Brown & Son, ~s"** „Brown & Sohn, Umzüge"

removal (*Brit*): **removal firm** N Spedition *f*; **removal van** N Möbelwagen *m*

remove [rɪˈmuːv] VT **(a)** entfernen (*also Med*); *bandage, tie* abnehmen; *clothes* ausziehen; *stain, threat, problem* beseitigen; *lining* abknöpfen; *troops* abziehen; (*from container*) herausnehmen (*from* aus); *word, item on list* streichen; *tax, restrictions* aufheben; *obstacle* aus dem Weg räumen; *doubt, suspicion, fear* zerstreuen; **to ~ sth from sb** jdm etw wegnehmen; **to ~ one's clothes** die Kleider ablegen; **to ~ all obstacles from one's path** (*fig*) alle Hindernisse aus dem Weg räumen; **to be far ~d from ...** weit entfernt sein von ...; **a cousin once ~d** ein Cousin *m* ersten Grades **(b)** (*form:* = *dismiss*) entfernen

remunerate [rɪˈmjuːnəreɪt] VT bezahlen; (= *reward*) belohnen

remuneration [rɪˌmjuːnəˈreɪʃən] N Bezahlung *f*; (= *reward*) Belohnung *f*

remunerative [rɪˈmjuːnərətɪv] ADJ lohnend

Renaissance [rɪˈneɪsɑːns] N Renaissance *f*

rename [riːˈneɪm] VT umbenennen (*also Comput*); **Leningrad was ~d St Petersburg** Leningrad wurde in St. Petersburg umbenannt

render [ˈrendəʳ] VT **(a)** (*form*) *service, help* leisten; *explanation* abgeben; *decision, verdict* fällen; **to ~ assistance** Hilfe leisten **(b)** (*Comm*) **to ~ account** Rechnung vorlegen **(c)** (= *interpret, translate*) wiedergeben; (*in writing*) übertragen; *music, poem* vortragen **(d)** (*form:* = *make*) machen

rendering [ˈrendərɪŋ] N Wiedergabe *f*; (*in writing*) Übertragung *f*; (*of piece of music, poem*) Vortrag *m*

rendezvous [ˈrɒndɪvuː] N (= *place*) Treffpunkt *m*; (= *agreement to meet*) Rendezvous *nt*

rendition [renˈdɪʃən] N (*form*) = **rendering**

renegade [ˈrenɪgeɪd] **1** N Renegat(in) *m(f)* **2** ADJ abtrünnig

renegotiate [ˌriːnɪˈgəʊʃɪeɪt] VT neu aushandeln

renew [rɪˈnjuː] VT erneuern; *contract, passport etc* (*authority*) verlängern; (*holder*) verlängern lassen; *negotiations, diplomatic relations, attack, attempts* wieder aufnehmen; *one's strength* wieder herstellen; *fears* wieder wachrufen; *interest* wieder wecken; *supplies* auffrischen

renewable [rɪˈnjuːəbl] ADJ *contract, licence, energy, resource* erneuerbar; *passport, bill of exchange* verlängerbar

renewal [rɪˈnjuːəl] N Erneuerung *f*; (*of contract, passport etc also*) Verlängerung *f*; (*of negotiations, diplomatic relations, attack, attempts*) Wiederaufnahme *f*; (*of interest*) Wiedererwachen *nt*; (*of supplies*) Auffrischung *f*; **spiritual ~** geistige Erneuerung; **~ notice** (*Insur*) Fälligkeitsbescheid *m*

renewed [rɪˈnjuːd] ADJ erneut; **~ efforts** neue Anstrengungen; **~ strength** frische Kraft; **~ outbreaks of rioting** erneute Krawalle *pl*

renounce [rɪˈnaʊns] VT *title, right, violence* verzichten auf (+*acc*); *terrorism, devil, faith, opinions, cause, treaty* abschwören (+*dat*)

renovate [ˈrenəʊveɪt] VT *building* renovieren

renovation [ˌrenəˈveɪʃən] N (*of building*) Renovierung *f*

renown [rɪˈnaʊn] N guter Ruf; **of great ~** von hohem Ansehen

renowned [rɪˈnaʊnd] ADJ berühmt (*for* für)

rent [rent] **1** N (*for house, room*) Miete *f*; (*for farm, factory*) Pacht *f*; **for ~** (*US*) zu vermieten/verpachten **2** VT **(a)** *house, room* mieten; *farm, factory* pachten; *TV, car etc* leihen; *video* ausleihen **(b)** (*also ~ out*) vermieten; verpachten; verleihen; **3** VI (= *~ house, room*) mieten; (= *~ farm, factory*) pachten; (= *~ TV etc*) leasen; (= *~ video*) ausleihen

> *Be careful!* **rent** *is not translated by the German word* **Rente***.*

rental [ˈrentl] N (= *amount paid*) Miete *f*; (*for TV, car etc also, video*) Leihgebühr *f*; **~ car** Mietwagen *m*; **~ library** (*US*) Leihbücherei *f*

rent: **rent boy** N (*Brit inf*) Strichjunge *m* (*inf*); **rent collector** N Mietkassierer(in) *m(f)*; **rent-free** ADJ, ADV mietfrei

renunciation [rɪˌnʌnsɪˈeɪʃən] N (*of title, right, violence*) Verzicht *m* (*of* auf +*acc*); (*of terrorism*) Aufgabe *f*; (*of devil, faith*) Abschwören *nt*; (*of opinion, cause, treaty*) Leugnung *f*

reopen [ˌriːˈəʊpən] **1** VT wieder öffnen; *school, shop, hostilities* wieder eröffnen; *debate, negotiations* wieder aufnehmen; (*Jur*) *case* wieder aufrollen **2** VI wieder aufgehen; (*shop, theatre etc*) wieder eröffnen; (*negotiations*) wieder beginnen; (*case*) wieder aufgerollt werden

reopening [ˌriːˈəʊpnɪŋ] N (*of shop etc*) Wiedereröffnung *f*; (*of negotiations, debate, case*) Wiederaufnahme *f*

reorder [ˌriːˈɔːdəʳ] **1** VT **(a)** *goods, supplies* nachbestellen; (*because first order is lost etc*) neu bestellen **(b)** (= *reorganize*) neu ordnen **2** VI (= *~ goods, supplies*) nachbestellen; (*because first order is lost etc*) neu bestellen

reorganization [riːˌɔːgənaɪˈzeɪʃən] N Neuorganisation *f*; (*of furniture, books*) Umordnung *f*; (*of work, time*) Neueinteilung *f*

reorganize [riːˈɔːgənaɪz] VT neu organisieren; *furniture, books* umordnen; *work, time* neu einteilen; *essay* neu aufbauen; *company* umstrukturieren

rep [rep] (*Comm*) ABBR *of* **representative** Vertreter(in) *m(f)*; **holiday** *or* **tour** *or* **travel ~** Reiseleiter(in) *m(f)*

repaid [riːˈpeɪd] PRET, PTP *of* **repay**

repaint [ˌriːˈpeɪnt] VT neu streichen

repair [rɪˈpeəʳ] **1** VT (*lit, fig*) reparieren; *clothes* flicken; *roof, wall also, road* ausbessern; (*fig*) *damage* wieder gutmachen **2** N **(a)** (*lit*) Reparatur *f*; (*of tyre also, clothes*) Flicken *nt*; (*of roof, wall also, road*) Ausbesserung *f*; (*fig: of relationship*) Kitten *nt*; **to be under ~** (*car, ship, machine*) in Reparatur sein; **the road is under ~** an der Straße wird gerade gearbeitet; **beyond ~** nicht mehr zu reparieren/zu flicken/auszubessern; **closed for ~s** wegen Reparaturarbeiten geschlossen **(b)** NO PL **to be in good/bad ~** in gutem/schlechtem Zustand sein

repairable [rɪˈpeərəbl] ADJ (*lit, fig*) reparabel; **is that ~?** lässt sich das reparieren?

repair shop N Reparaturwerkstatt f

reparable ['repərəbl] ADJ *loss* ersetzbar

reparation [,repə'reɪʃən] N (*for damage*) Entschädigung f; (*usu pl: after war*) Reparationen pl

repartee [,repɑː'tiː] N Schlagabtausch m

repatriation ['riːˌpætrɪ'eɪʃən] N Repatriierung f

repay [riː'peɪ], *pret, ptp* **repaid** VT *money* zurückzahlen; *expenses* erstatten; *debt* abzahlen; *kindness* vergelten; *visit, compliment* erwidern; **if you lend me £2 I'll ~ it** *or* **you on Saturday** leih mir doch mal 2 Pfund, ich zahle sie dir am Samstag zurück; **to be repaid for one's efforts** für seine Mühen belohnt werden; **how can I ever ~ you?** wie kann ich das jemals wieder gutmachen?

repayable [riː'peɪəbl] ADJ rückzahlbar

repayment [,riː'peɪmənt] N (*of money*) Rückzahlung f; (*of effort, kindness*) Lohn m; **in ~** als Rückzahlung/Lohn

repayment mortgage N Tilgungshypothek f

repeal [rɪ'piːl] **1** VT *law* aufheben **2** N Aufhebung f

repeat [rɪ'piːt] **1** VT wiederholen; (= *tell to sb else*) weitersagen (*to sb* jdm); **to ~ oneself** sich wiederholen; **to ~ an order** (*Comm*) nachbestellen **2** VI wiederholen; **~ after me** sprecht mir nach **3** N (*Rad, TV*) Wiederholung f **4** ADJ **~ business** Nachfolgeaufträge pl; **~ customer** Kunde, der/Kundin, die wiederkommt

repeated ADJ, **repeatedly** ADV [rɪ'piːtɪd, -lɪ] wiederholt

repeat: repeat function N (*Comput*) Wiederholungsfunktion f; **repeat order** N (*Comm*) Nachbestellung f; **repeat performance** N (*Theat*) Wiederholungsvorstellung f; **he gave a ~** (*fig*) er machte es noch einmal; (*pej*) er machte noch einmal das gleiche Theater (*inf*); **repeat prescription** N (*Med*) erneut verschriebenes Rezept

repel [rɪ'pel] **1** VT (**a**) *attack* zurückschlagen; *insects* abwehren (**b**) (= *disgust*) abstoßen **2** VI (= *disgust*) abstoßen

repellent [rɪ'pelənt] **1** ADJ (**a**) **~ to water** Wasser abstoßend (**b**) (= *disgusting*) abstoßend; *smell* widerlich **2** N (= *insect ~*) Insektenschutzmittel nt

repent [rɪ'pent] **1** VI Reue empfinden (*of* über +*acc*) **2** VT bereuen

repentance [rɪ'pentəns] N Reue f

repentant [rɪ'pentənt] ADJ reuevoll; **he was very ~** es reute ihn sehr

repercussion [,riːpə'kʌʃən] N Auswirkung f (*on* auf +*acc*); **~s** pl (*of misbehaviour etc*) Nachspiel nt; **that is bound to have ~s** das wird Kreise ziehen; **to have ~s on sth** sich auf etw (*acc*) auswirken

repertoire ['repətwɑːʳ] N (*Theat, Mus*) Repertoire nt

repertory ['repətərɪ] N (**a**) (*also* **~ theatre**) Repertoire-Theater nt (**b**) (= *songs, plays*) Repertoire nt

repetition [,repɪ'tɪʃən] N Wiederholung f

repetitious [,repɪ'tɪʃəs] ADJ sich wiederholend

repetitive [rɪ'petɪtɪv] ADJ dauernd wiederholend; *work* monoton; **to be ~** sich dauernd wiederholen

replace [rɪ'pleɪs] VT (**a**) (= *put back*) zurücksetzen; (*on end, standing up*) zurückstellen; (*on its side, flat*) zurücklegen; **to ~ the receiver** (*Telec*) (den Hörer) auflegen (**b**) (= *provide or be substitute for*) (*temporarily*) vertreten; **the boss has ~d Smith with Jones** der Chef hat Smith durch Jones ersetzt (**c**) (= *renew*) parts ersetzen

replaceable [rɪ'pleɪsəbl] ADJ ersetzbar

replacement [rɪ'pleɪsmənt] N Ersatz m; (= *deputy*) Vertretung f; **~ part** Ersatzteil nt

replay ['riːpleɪ] (*Sport*) **1** N (= *recording*) Wiederholung f; (= *match also*) Wiederholungsspiel nt **2** [,riː'pleɪ] VT wiederholen

replenish [rɪ'plenɪʃ] VT ergänzen; (*when badly depleted*) wieder auffüllen; *glass* auffüllen; *shelves* nachfüllen

replenishment [rɪ'plenɪʃmənt] N Ergänzung f; (*when badly depleted*) Wiederauffüllen nt; (*of shelves*) Nachfüllen nt

replica ['replɪkə] N (*of painting, statue*) Reproduktion f; (*of ship, building etc*) Nachbildung f

replicate ['replɪkeɪt] VT wiederholen

reply [rɪ'plaɪ] **1** N Antwort f; **in ~** (= *as Antwort*) darauf; **in ~ to your letter** in Beantwortung Ihres Briefes (*form*); **"~ paid"** (*US: on envelope*) „Gebühr bezahlt Empfänger" **2** VT **to ~** (**to**

sb) that ... (jdm) antworten, dass ... **3** VI antworten (*to sth* auf etw +*acc*)

report [rɪ'pɔːt] **1** N (**a**) Bericht m (*on* über +*acc*); (*Press, Rad, TV*) Reportage f (*on* über +*acc*); **to give a ~ on sth** Bericht über etw (*acc*) erstatten; (*Rad, TV*) eine Reportage über etw (*acc*) machen; **an official ~ on the motor industry** ein Gutachten nt über die Autoindustrie; (*school*) ~ Zeugnis nt (**b**) (= *rumour*) **there are ~s that ...** es wird gesagt, dass ... **2** VT (**a**) *results, findings* berichten über (+*acc*); (= *announce officially*) melden; *losses* verzeichnen; (*in balance sheet*) ausweisen; **to ~ progress** einen Tätigkeitsbericht abgeben; **he is ~ed as having said ...** er soll gesagt haben ... (**b**) (*to sb* jdm) (= *notify authorities of*) *accident, crime, criminal* melden; **to ~ sb for sth** jdn wegen etw melden; **nothing to ~** keine besonderen Vorkommnisse! **3** VI (**a**) (= *announce oneself*) sich melden; **to ~ for duty** sich zum Dienst melden; **to ~ sick** sich krankmelden (**b**) (= *give a ~*) berichten (*on* über +*acc*)

➤ **report back** VI Bericht erstatten (*to sb* jdm)

➤ **report to** VI +PREP OBJ (*in organization*) unterstellt sein (+*dat*)

reported [rɪ'pɔːtɪd] ADJ gemeldet

reportedly [rɪ'pɔːtɪdlɪ] ADV angeblich

reported speech N (*Gram*) indirekte Rede

reporter [rɪ'pɔːtəʳ] N (*Press, Rad, TV*) Reporter(in) m(f); (*on the spot*) Korrespondent(in) m(f)

report generator N (*Comput*) Reportgenerator m

reposition [,riːpə'zɪʃən] VT *object* anders aufstellen; (*Comm*) *product* neu positionieren *or* platzieren; **to ~ oneself on the market** sich am Markt neu positionieren

repository [rɪ'pɒzɪtərɪ] N Lager nt

repossess [,riːpə'zes] VT wieder in Besitz nehmen

repossession [,riːpə'zeʃən] N Wiederinbesitznahme f

reprehensible [,reprɪ'hensɪbl] ADJ verwerflich

represent [,reprɪ'zent] VT (**a**) darstellen; (= *stand for*) stehen für (**b**) (= *act or speak for, Parl, Jur*) vertreten

representation [,reprɪzen'teɪʃən] N Darstellung f; (= *symbolizing*) Symbolisierung f; (= *acting or speaking for, Parl, Jur*) Vertretung f

representative [,reprɪ'zentətɪv] **1** ADJ (*of* für) repräsentativ; *attitude, game* typisch; (= *symbolic*) symbolisch; **a ~ body** eine Vertretung; **~ assembly** Abgeordnetenversammlung f **2** N (*Comm*) Vertreter(in) m(f); (*Jur*) Bevollmächtigte(r); (*US Pol*) Abgeordnete(r) mf

repress [rɪ'pres] VT unterdrücken; (*Psych*) verdrängen

repressed [rɪ'prest] ADJ unterdrückt; (*Psych*) verdrängt

repression [rɪ'preʃən] N Unterdrückung f; (*Psych*) Verdrängung f

repressive [rɪ'presɪv] ADJ repressiv

reprieve [rɪ'priːv] **1** N (*Jur*) Begnadigung f; (*fig*) Gnadenfrist f **2** VT **he was ~d** (*Jur*) er wurde begnadigt

reprimand ['reprɪmɑːnd] **1** N Tadel m; (*official*) Verweis m **2** VT tadeln

reprint ['riːprɪnt] **1** VT nachdrucken **2** [riːprɪnt] N Nachdruck m

reprisal [rɪ'praɪzəl] N Vergeltungsmaßnahme f; (*between companies, countries etc also*) Repressalie f

reproach [rɪ'prəʊtʃ] **1** N Vorwurf m; **a look of ~** ein vorwurfsvoller Blick; **above** *or* **beyond ~** über jeden Vorwurf erhaben **2** VT Vorwürfe machen (+*dat*); **to ~ sb for his mistake** jdm einen Fehler vorwerfen; **to ~ sb for having done sth** jdm Vorwürfe dafür machen, dass er etw getan hat

reproachful ADJ, **reproachfully** ADV [rɪ'prəʊtʃʊl, -fəlɪ] vorwurfsvoll

reprocess [,riː'prəʊses] VT wieder verwerten; *sewage, atomic waste, fuel* wieder aufbereiten

reprocessing plant [,riː'prəʊsesɪŋ'plɑːnt] N Wiederaufbereitungsanlage f

reproduce [,riːprə'djuːs] **1** VT (= *copy*) wiedergeben; (*mechanically, electronically*) reproduzieren; (*Typ*) abdrucken **2** VI (*Biol*) sich fortpflanzen

reproduction [,riːprə'dʌkʃən] N (**a**) (= *procreation*) Fortpflanzung f (**b**) (= *copying, copy*) Reproduktion f; (*of documents*) Vervielfältigung f; (= *photo*) Kopie f; (= *sound ~*) Wiedergabe f

reproductive [,riːprə'dʌktɪv] ADJ Fortpflanzungs-

reproving ADJ, **reprovingly** ADV [rɪ'pruːvɪŋ, -lɪ] tadelnd

reptile ['reptaɪl] N Reptil nt

republic [rɪ'pʌblɪk] N Republik f

republican [rɪ'pʌblɪkən] **1** ADJ republikanisch **2** N Republikaner(in) m(f)

republicanism [rɪ'pʌblɪkənɪzəm] N Republikanismus m

republication ['riːpʌblɪ'keɪʃən] N (of book) Wiederveröffentlichung f

republish [riː'pʌblɪʃ] VT book wieder veröffentlichen

repugnance [rɪ'pʌgnəns] N Abneigung f (towards, for gegen)

repugnant [rɪ'pʌgnənt] ADJ abstoßend; (stronger) Ekel erregend

repulse [rɪ'pʌls] VT (Mil) zurückschlagen; **sb is ~d by sth** (fig) etw stößt jdn ab

repulsion [rɪ'pʌlʃən] N (= distaste) Widerwille m (for gegen)

repulsive [rɪ'pʌlsɪv] ADJ (= loathsome) abstoßend; **to be ~ to sb** für jdn abstoßend sein

repulsively [rɪ'pʌlsɪvlɪ] ADV abstoßend

reputable ['repjʊtəbl] ADJ ehrenhaft; person angesehen; occupation ordentlich; dealer, firm seriös

reputation [ˌrepjʊ'teɪʃən] N Ruf m; (= bad ~) schlechter Ruf; **he has a ~ for being ...** er hat den Ruf, ... zu sein; **to have a ~ for honesty** als ehrlich gelten; **you don't want to get (yourself) a ~, you know** du willst dich doch sicherlich nicht in Verruf bringen

repute [rɪ'pjuːt] VT (pass only) **he is ~d to be ...** man sagt, dass er ... ist; **he is ~d to be the best** er gilt als der Beste

reputed [rɪ'pjuːtɪd] ADJ angenommen

reputedly [rɪ'pjuːtɪdlɪ] ADV wie man annimmt

request [rɪ'kwest] **1** N Bitte f; **at sb's ~** auf jds Bitte; **on/by ~** auf Wunsch; **~ for payment** Zahlungsaufforderung f **2** VT bitten um; (Rad) record sich (dat) wünschen; **to ~ sth of** or **from sb** jdn um etw bitten

requiem mass [ˌrekwɪəm'mæs] N Totenmesse f

require [rɪ'kwaɪəʳ] VT (a) (= need) benötigen; work, action erfordern; (= desire) wünschen; **it ~s great care** das erfordert große Sorgfalt; **what qualifications are ~d?** welche Qualifikationen sind erforderlich?; **if ~d** falls notwendig; **when (it is) ~d** auf Wunsch; **as and when ~d** nach Bedarf (b) (= order) verlangen; **to ~ sb to do sth** von jdm verlangen, dass er etw tut

required [rɪ'kwaɪəd] ADJ erforderlich; date vorgeschrieben; (= desired) gewünscht; **the ~ amount** die benötigte Menge

requirement [rɪ'kwaɪəmənt] N (a) (= need) Bedürfnis nt; (= desire) Wunsch m; **to meet sb's ~s** jds Wünschen (dat) entsprechen (b) (= condition, thing required) Erfordernis nt; (for job) Anforderung f; **to fit the ~s** den Erfordernissen/Anforderungen entsprechen

reran [riː'ræn] PRET of rerun

reread [riː'riːd], pret, ptp **reread** [riː'red] VT nochmals lesen

reroute [riː'ruːt] VT train, bus umleiten

rerun [riː'rʌn], vb: pret **reran**, ptp **rerun** **1** VT film wieder aufführen; tape wieder abspielen; race, elections, programme, event wiederholen **2** ['riːrʌn] N (of film) Wiederaufführung f; (of tape) Wiederabspielen nt; (of race, election, programme, event) Wiederholung f

resale ['riːseɪl] N Weiterverkauf m; **"not for ~"** „nicht zum Weiterverkauf bestimmt"; (on free sample) „unverkäufliches Muster"; **~ value** Wiederverkaufswert m

resale price maintenance N (Brit) Preisbindung f

resat [riː'sæt] PRET, PTP of resit

reschedule [riː'skedʒʊəl, esp Brit -'ʃedjuːl] VT meeting verlegen; plans ändern; production umstellen; (Econ) debts umschulden

rescue ['reskjuː] **1** N (= saving) Rettung f; (= freeing) Befreiung f; **to go/come to sb's ~** jdm zu Hilfe kommen; **it was Bob to the ~** Bob war unsere/seine etc Rettung; **~ attempt/operation** Rettungsversuch m/-aktion f **2** VT (= save) retten; (= free) erretten

rescuer ['reskjʊəʳ] N (who saves sb) Retter(in) m(f); (who frees sb) Befreier(in) m(f)

rescue services PL Rettungsdienst m

research [rɪ'sɜːtʃ] **1** N Forschung f (into, on über +acc); **to do ~** forschen; **to carry out ~ into the effects of sth** Forschungen über die Auswirkungen einer Sache (gen) anstellen; **~ and**

development Forschung und Entwicklung **2** VI forschen; **to ~ into** or **on sth** etw erforschen **3** VT erforschen

research IN CPDS Forschungs-; **research assistant** N wissenschaftlicher Assistent, wissenschaftliche Assistentin

researcher [rɪ'sɜːtʃəʳ] N Forscher(in) m(f)

resemblance [rɪ'zembləns] N Ähnlichkeit f; **to bear a strong/a faint ~ to sb/sth** starke/leichte Ähnlichkeit mit jdm/etw haben

resemble [rɪ'zembl] VT gleichen (+dat); **they ~ each other** sie gleichen sich (dat)

resent [rɪ'zent] VT remarks, behaviour übel nehmen; person ein Ressentiment haben gegen; **he ~ed her for the rest of his life** er nahm ihr das sein Leben lang übel; **he ~ed the fact that ...** er ärgerte sich darüber, dass ...; **to ~ sb's success** jdm seinen Erfolg missgönnen; **I ~ that** das gefällt mir nicht

resentful [rɪ'zentfʊl] ADJ person, look verärgert; (= jealous) voller Ressentiments (of gegen); **to be ~ at** or **about** or **of sth/of sb** über etw/jdn verärgert sein; **to feel ~ toward(s) sb for doing sth** es jdm übel nehmen, dass er/sie etc etw getan hat

resentfully [rɪ'zentfəlɪ] ADV say ärgerlich; look, behave verärgert

resentment [rɪ'zentmənt] N Ärger m no pl (of über +acc)

reservation [ˌrezə'veɪʃən] N (a) (= qualification of opinion) Vorbehalt m; **without ~** vorbehaltlos; **with ~s** unter Vorbehalt(en); **to have ~s about sb/sth** Bedenken in Bezug auf jdn/etw haben (b) (= booking) Reservierung f; **to make a ~ at the hotel** ein Zimmer im Hotel reservieren lassen; **to have a ~ (for a room)** ein Zimmer reserviert haben (c) (= area of land) Reservat nt, Reservation f

reserve [rɪ'zɜːv] **1** VT (a) (= keep) aufsparen; **to ~ judgement** mit einem Urteil zurückhalten; **to ~ the right to do sth** sich (dat) (das Recht) vorbehalten, etw zu tun (b) (= book in advance) reservieren lassen **2** N (a) (= store) (of an +dat) Vorrat m; (Fin) Reserve f; **cash ~** Barreserve f; **to have/keep sth in ~** etw in Reserve haben/halten

(b) (= reservation) **without ~** vorbehaltlos

(c) (= reserve price)

(d) (= piece of land) Reservat nt

(e) (= reticence) Zurückhaltung f

(f) (Sport) Reservespieler(in) m(f)

reserve IN CPDS Reserve-;

reserved [rɪ'zɜːvd] ADJ reserviert

reserve: reserve fund N Reservefonds m; **reserve price** N (Brit) Mindestpreis m; **reserve stock** N (Comm) Mindestbestand m

reservist [rɪ'zɜːvɪst] N (Mil) Reservist(in) m(f)

reservoir ['rezəvwɑːʳ] N (lit: for water) Reservoir nt

reset [ˌriː'set], pret, ptp **reset** VT (a) watch neu stellen (to auf +acc); (for summer time etc) umstellen (for auf +acc); dial, gauge zurückstellen (to auf +acc); machine neu einstellen; (Comput) rücksetzen; **~ switch** or **button** (Comput) Resettaste f (b) (Med) bone wieder einrichten

resettle [ˌriː'setl] VT refugees umsiedeln; land wieder besiedeln

resettlement [ˌriː'setlmənt] N (of refugees) Umsiedlung f; (of land) Neubesied(e)lung f

reshape [ˌriː'ʃeɪp] VT clay etc umformen; team umgestalten; policy umstellen

reshuffle [ˌriː'ʃʌfl] **1** VT cards neu mischen; (fig) Cabinet, board of directors umbilden **2** N (fig: of board) Umbildung f

reside [rɪ'zaɪd] VI (form) seinen Wohnsitz haben; (monarch etc) residieren

residence ['rezɪdəns] N (a) (= house) Wohnhaus nt; (for students, nurses) Wohnheim nt; (of monarch, ambassador etc) Residenz f (b) NO PL country of ~ Aufenthaltsland nt; **place of ~** Wohnort m; **after 5 years' ~ in Britain** nach 5 Jahren Aufenthalt in Großbritannien

residence permit N Aufenthaltsgenehmigung f

residency ['rezɪdənsɪ] N (a) (US) = residence (b) (b) (Brit) Residenz f

resident ['rezɪdənt] **1** N (a) Bewohner(in) m(f); (in town) Einwohner(in) m(f); (of hospital) Patient(in) m(f); (in hotel) Gast m; **"access restricted to ~s only"** „Anlieger frei" (b) (= doctor) Anstaltsarzt m/-ärztin f **2** ADJ (in country, town) wohnhaft; (= attached to institution) ansässig; **the ~ population** die ansässige Bevölkerung

residential [ˌrezɪˈdenʃəl] ADJ ~ **customer** (for utilities) Privathaushalt m; ~ **property** Wohngebäude nt; ~ **street** Wohnstraße f

residential: **residential area** N Wohngebiet nt; **residential home** N Wohnheim nt

residual [rɪˈzɪdjʊəl] ADJ restlich

residue [ˈrezɪdjuː] N Rest m; (Chem) Rückstand m

resign [rɪˈzaɪn] **1** VT (a) office, post abgeben (b) to ~ oneself to sth sich mit etw abfinden; to ~ oneself to doing sth sich damit abfinden, etw zu tun **2** VI (from public appointment, committee) zurücktreten; (employee) kündigen; to ~ from office sein Amt niederlegen; he ~ed from (his job with) "The Times" er hat (seine Stelle) bei der „Times" gekündigt

resignation [ˌrezɪgˈneɪʃən] N (a) (from public appointment, committee) Rücktritt m; (of employee) Kündigung f; (of civil servant) Amtsniederlegung f; to hand in or tender (form) one's ~ seinen Rücktritt/seine Kündigung einreichen/sein Amt niederlegen (b) (= mental state) Resignation f (to gegenüber +dat)

resigned [rɪˈzaɪnd] ADJ person resigniert; to become ~ to sth sich mit etw abfinden; to be ~ to one's fate sich in sein Schicksal ergeben haben

resignedly [rɪˈzaɪnɪdlɪ] ADV resigniert

resilience [rɪˈzɪlɪəns] N (a) (of material) Federn nt (b) (fig) (of person, nature) Unverwüstlichkeit f; (of economy) Stabilität f

resilient [rɪˈzɪlɪənt] ADJ (a) material federnd attr; to be ~ federn (b) (fig) person, nature unverwüstlich; economy stabil; market flexibel, elastisch; (Comm) performance robust

resin [ˈrezɪn] N Harz nt

resist [rɪˈzɪst] **1** VT (a) (= oppose) sich widersetzen (+dat); arrest, sb's advances, attack Widerstand leisten gegen (b) temptation, sb, urge widerstehen (+dat); I couldn't ~ (eating) another piece of cake ich konnte der Versuchung nicht widerstehen, noch ein Stück Kuchen zu essen **2** VI (a) (= be opposed) sich widersetzen; (faced with arrest, sb's advances, attack) Widerstand leisten (b) (faced with temptation, sb's charms) widerstehen

resistance [rɪˈzɪstəns] N (to gegen) Widerstand m (also Elec, Phys, Mil); ~ to heat Hitzebeständigkeit f; to meet with ~ auf Widerstand stoßen; to offer no ~ (to sb/sth) (to attacker, advances etc) (jdm/gegen etw) keinen Widerstand leisten; (to proposals) sich (jdm/einer Sache) nicht widersetzen

resistant [rɪˈzɪstənt] ADJ material, surface strapazierfähig; (Med) immun (to gegen)

resit [ˌriːˈsɪt] vb: pret, ptp resat (Brit) **1** VT exam wiederholen **2** VI die Prüfung wiederholen **3** [ˈriːsɪt] N Wiederholung(sprüfung) f

reskill [ˌriːˈskɪl] (Ind) **1** VI sich weiterbilden **2** VT weiterbilden

resolute [ˈrezəluːt] ADJ energisch; answer, refusal entschieden

resolutely [ˈrezəluːtlɪ] ADV entschieden; stare, stride entschlossen; to be ~ opposed to sth entschieden gegen etw sein

resolution [ˌrezəˈluːʃən] N (a) (= decision) Beschluss m; (esp Pol) Resolution f; (governing one's behaviour) Vorsatz m (b) NO PL (= resoluteness) Entschlossenheit f (c) NO PL (of problem, puzzle) Lösung f (d) (Comput) Auflösung f

resolve [rɪˈzɒlv] **1** VT (a) problem, conflict, crisis lösen; dispute beilegen; differences, issue klären (b) (= decide) to ~ that ... beschließen, dass ...; to ~ to do sth beschließen, etw zu tun **2** VI (= decide) to ~ (up)on sth etw beschließen **3** N, NO PL (= resoluteness) Entschlossenheit f

resolved [rɪˈzɒlvd] ADJ (fest) entschlossen

resonate [ˈrezəneɪt] VI widerhallen

resort [rɪˈzɔːt] N (a) as a last ~ als Letztes; you were my last ~ du warst meine letzte Rettung (b) (= place) Urlaubsort m; seaside ~ Seebad nt **2** VI to ~ to sth zu etw greifen; to ~ to violence gewalttätig werden; to ~ to begging sich aufs Betteln verlegen

resound [rɪˈzaʊnd] VI (wider)hallen (with von)

resounding [rɪˈzaʊndɪŋ] ADJ noise, shout widerhallend; laugh, voice schallend; (fig) triumph, victory gewaltig; success durchschlagend; defeat haushoch; ~ silence überwältigende Stille; the response was a ~ "no" die Antwort war ein überwältigendes „Nein"

resoundingly [rɪˈzaʊndɪŋlɪ] ADV defeat vernichtend; to be ~ defeated eine vernichtende Niederlage erleiden

resource [rɪˈsɔːs] **1** N resources PL Mittel pl, Ressourcen pl; financial ~s Geldmittel pl; mineral ~s Bodenschätze pl; natural ~s Rohstoffquellen pl; human ~s (= workforce) Arbeitskräfte pl **2** VT (Brit) project finanzieren; (with personnel) personell ausstatten

resourced [rɪˈsɔːst] ADJ (Brit) well-~ (with materials) gut ausgestattet; (financially) ausreichend finanziert; under-~ (with materials) unzureichend ausgestattet; (financially) unzureichend finanziert

resourceful [rɪˈsɔːsfʊl] ADJ, **resourcefully** [rɪˈsɔːsfəlɪ] ADV einfallsreich

resourcefulness [rɪˈsɔːsfʊlnɪs] N Einfallsreichtum m

respect [rɪˈspekt] **1** N (a) (= esteem) Respekt m (for vor +dat); to have/show ~ for Respekt haben/zeigen vor (+dat); the law achten; I have the highest ~ for his ability ich halte ihn für außerordentlich fähig; to hold sb in (great) ~ jdn (sehr) achten (b) (= consideration) Rücksicht f (for auf +acc); to treat with ~ person rücksichtsvoll behandeln; dangerous person etc sich in Acht nehmen vor (+dat); toys, clothes etc schonend behandeln; she has or shows no ~ for other people's feelings sie nimmt keine Rücksicht auf die Gefühle anderer; out of ~ for aus Rücksicht auf (+acc); with (due) ~, I still think that ... bei allem Respekt, meine ich dennoch, dass ... (c) (= reference) with ~ to ..., in ~ of ... was ... anbetrifft (d) (= aspect) Hinsicht f; in some/other ~s in gewisser/anderer Hinsicht; in many ~s in vieler Hinsicht; in this ~ in dieser Hinsicht (e) respects PL to pay one's ~s to sb jdm seine Aufwartung machen; to pay one's last ~s to sb jdm die letzte Ehre erweisen **2** VT respektieren; ability anerkennen; a ~ed company eine angesehene Firma

respectability [rɪˌspektəˈbɪlɪtɪ] N (= estimable quality) (of person) Ehrbarkeit f; (of life, district, club) Anständigkeit f; (= socially approved quality) (of person) Angesehenheit f; (of businessman, hotel) Seriosität f; (of clothes, behaviour) Korrektheit f

respectable [rɪˈspektəbl] ADJ (a) (= estimable) person, motives ehrbar; life, district, club anständig; (= socially approved) person angesehen; businessman, hotel seriös; clothes, behaviour korrekt; in ~ society in guter Gesellschaft; a perfectly ~ way to earn one's living eine völlig akzeptable Art und Weise, seinen Lebensunterhalt zu verdienen (b) size, income, sum ansehnlich (c) (= fairly good) advantage beträchtlich; score, lead beachtlich

respectably [rɪˈspektəblɪ] ADV dress, behave anständig

respectful [rɪˈspektfʊl] ADJ respektvoll (towards gegenüber); to be ~ of sth etw respektieren

respectfully [rɪˈspektfəlɪ] ADV respektvoll

respecting [rɪˈspektɪŋ] PREP bezüglich (+gen)

respective [rɪˈspektɪv] ADJ jeweilig; they each have their ~ merits jeder von ihnen hat seine eigenen Vorteile

respectively [rɪˈspektɪvlɪ] ADV beziehungsweise; the girls' dresses are green and blue ~ die Mädchen haben grüne beziehungsweise blaue Kleider

respiratory [rɪˈspɪrətərɪ] ADJ Atem-; infection, disease der Atemwege

respite [ˈrespaɪt] N (a) (= rest) Ruhepause f (from von); (= easing off) Nachlassen nt; without (a) ~ ohne Unterbrechung (b) (= reprieve) Aufschub m

resplendent [rɪˈsplendənt] ADJ person, face glänzend, strahlend; clothes prächtig

respond [rɪˈspɒnd] VI (a) (= reply) antworten; to ~ to a question die Frage beantworten (b) (= show reaction) (to auf +acc) reagieren; to ~ to an appeal einen Appell beantworten; to ~ to an appeal for money einem Spendenaufruf folgen; the patient did not ~ to the treatment der Patient sprach auf die Behandlung nicht an; the illness ~ed to treatment die Behandlung schlug an

response [rɪˈspɒns] N (a) (= reply) Antwort f; in ~ (to) als Antwort (auf +acc) (b) (= reaction) Reaktion f; my appeal met with no ~ meine Bitte fand keine Resonanz

responsibility [rɪˌspɒnsəˈbɪlɪtɪ] N (a) NO PL Verantwortung f; to take or assume (full) ~ (for sth) die (volle) Verantwortung (für etw) übernehmen; that's his ~ dafür ist er verantwortlich (b) (= duty, burden) Verpflichtung f (to für)

responsible [rɪ'spɒnsəbl] ADJ **(a)** (*denoting cause*, = *answerable*) verantwortlich; (= *to blame*) schuld (*for* an +*dat*); **what's ~ for the hold-up?** woran liegt die Verzögerung?; **who is ~ for breaking the window?** wer hat das Fenster eingeschlagen?; **to be directly ~ to sb** jdm unmittelbar unterstellt sein; **to hold sb ~ for sth** jdn für etw verantwortlich machen; **she is ~ for popularizing the sport** (*her task*) sie ist dafür verantwortlich, die Sportart populär zu machen; (*her merit*) es ist ihr zu verdanken, dass die Sportart populär geworden ist **(b)** (= *trustworthy*) *person, attitude* verantwortungsbewusst; *firm* seriös, zuverlässig; (= *involving responsibility*) *job* verantwortungsvoll

responsibly [rɪ'spɒnsəblɪ] ADV *act* verantwortungsbewusst; *carry out one's duties* zuverlässig

responsive [rɪ'spɒnsɪv] ADJ *person, audience* interessiert; *steering, brakes* leicht reagierend; **to be ~ to sth** auf etw (*acc*) reagieren

rest¹ [rest] **◼** N **(a)** (= *relaxation*) Ruhe *f*; (= *pause*) Pause *f*, Unterbrechung *f*; (*in ~ cure, on holiday etc*) Erholung *f*; **a day of ~** ein Ruhetag *m*; **to need ~** Ruhe brauchen; **I need a ~** ich muss mich ausruhen; (= *vacation*) ich brauche Urlaub; **to have** *or* **take a ~** (= *relax*) (sich) ausruhen; (= *pause*) (eine) Pause machen; **to have a good night's ~** sich ordentlich ausschlafen; **give it a ~!** (*inf*) hör doch auf!; **to be at ~** (= *peaceful*) ruhig sein; (*euph*: = *dead*) ruhen; **to lay to ~** (*euph*) zur letzten Ruhe betten; **to set at ~** *fears, doubts* beschwichtigen; **to put** *or* **set sb's mind at ~** jdn beruhigen; **to come to ~** (*ball, car etc*) zum Stillstand kommen; (*bird, insect*) sich niederlassen; (*gaze, eyes*) hängenbleiben (*upon* an +*dat*)
(b) (= *support*) Auflage *f*; (*of telephone*) Gabel *f*
◼ VI **(a)** (= *lie down, take ~*) ruhen (*geh*); (= *relax, be still*) sich ausruhen; (= *pause*) Pause machen; **she never ~s** sie arbeitet ununterbrochen; **to let a matter ~** eine Sache auf sich beruhen lassen; **let the matter ~!** lass es dabei!; **may he ~ in peace** er ruhe in Frieden
(b) (*decision, blame, responsibility etc*) liegen (*with* bei); **the matter must not ~ there** man kann die Sache so nicht belassen; **(you may) ~ assured that ...** Sie können versichert sein, dass ...
(c) (= *lean*) lehnen (*on* an +*dat*, *against* gegen); (*roof, eyes, gaze etc*) ruhen (*on* auf +*dat*); (*argument, case*) sich stützen (*on* auf +*acc*); (*reputation*) beruhen (*on* auf +*dat*); **his elbows were ~ing on the table** ihre Ellbogen waren auf den Tisch gestützt; **her head was ~ing on the table** ihr Kopf lag auf dem Tisch
◼ VT **(a)** *one's eyes* ausruhen; *voice* schonen; **to be ~ed** ausgeruht sein; **to feel ~ed** sich ausgeruht fühlen
(b) (= *lean*) *ladder* lehnen (*against* gegen, *on* an +*acc*); *elbow* stützen (*on* auf +*acc*); (*fig*) *theory, suspicions* stützen (*on* auf +*acc*); **to ~ one's hand on sb's shoulder** jdm die Hand auf die Schulter legen

rest² N (= *remainder*) Rest *m*; **the ~ of the boys** die übrigen Jungen; **she's no different from the ~** sie ist wie alle anderen; **all the ~ of the money** der ganze Rest des Geldes; **all the ~ of the books** alle übrigen Bücher; **for the ~** im Übrigen

rest area N (*US Aut*) Rastplatz *m*

restart [, riː'stɑːt] **◼** VT *job, activity* wieder aufnehmen; *negotiations also* wieder beginnen; *race* neu starten; *game (from beginning)* neu beginnen; (*after interruption*) fortsetzen; *engine, car* wieder anlassen; *machine* wieder anschalten; *economy* wieder ankurbeln; **to ~ work** wieder zu arbeiten anfangen
◼ VI wieder anfangen; (*race*) vom neuem beginnen; (*game*) (*from beginning*) neu beginnen; (*after interruption*) fortgesetzt werden; (*machine*) wieder starten; (*engine, car*) wieder anspringen

restate [,riː'steɪt] VT **(a)** (= *express again*) *reasons* erneut nennen; *problem, argument* erneut vortragen; *case, one's position* erneut darstellen **(b)** (= *express differently*) umformulieren; *case, one's position* neu darstellen

restatement [,riː'steɪtmənt] N **(a)** (= *expressing again*) (*of reasons*) erneute Nennung; (*of problem, argument*) erneuter Vortrag; (*of case, one's position*) erneute Darstellung **(b)** (= *expressing differently*) Umformulierung *f*; (*of case, one's position*) Neudarstellung *f*

restaurant ['restərɒnt] N Restaurant *nt*

restaurant car N (*Brit Rail*) Speisewagen *m*

restful ['restful] ADJ *occupation etc* erholsam; *atmosphere* gemütlich; *lighting* beruhigend; *colour* ruhig; *place* friedlich

rest home N Pflegeheim *nt*

restive ['restɪv] ADJ (= *restless*) rastlos

restiveness ['restɪvnɪs] N (= *restlessness*) Rastlosigkeit *f*

restless ['restlɪs] ADJ (= *unsettled*) *person, night, mind* unruhig; (= *not wanting to stay in one place*) rastlos

restlessly ['restlɪslɪ] ADV (= *in an unsettled manner*) unruhig; (= *not wanting to stay in one place*) rastlos

restlessness ['restlɪsnɪs] N (= *unsettled manner*) Unruhe *f*; (= *not wanting to stay in one place*) Rastlosigkeit *f*

restock [,riː'stɒk] VT *shelves, bar* wieder auffüllen

restoration [,restə'reɪʃən] N (= *return*) Rückgabe *f* (*to* an +*acc*); (*of confidence, order, peace*) Wiederherstellung *f*; (*to office*) Wiedereinsetzung *f* (*to* in +*acc*); (*of monument, work of art*) Restaurierung *f*

restore [rɪ'stɔː^r] VT **(a)** *sth lost, borrowed, stolen* (= *give back*) zurückgeben; (= *bring back*) zurückbringen; *confidence, order, peace* wieder herstellen; **~d to health** wieder hergestellt **(b)** (*to former post*) wieder einsetzen (*to* in +*acc*); **to ~ to power** wieder an die Macht bringen **(c)** *building, painting etc* restaurieren

restrain [rɪ'streɪn] VT *person* zurückhalten; *prisoner* mit Gewalt festhalten; *animal, unruly children, madman* bändigen; *emotions, laughter* unterdrücken; **to ~ inflation/prices** die Inflationsrate/Preisentwicklung aufhalten; **to ~ sb from doing sth** jdn davon abhalten, etw zu tun; **to ~ oneself** sich beherrschen

restrained [rɪ'streɪnd] ADJ *person, performance, response* zurückhaltend; *emotions* unterdrückt; *manner* beherrscht; *tone, colour* verhalten

restraint [rɪ'streɪnt] N **(a)** (= *restriction*) Beschränkung *f*; **without ~** unbeschränkt **(b)** (= *moderation*) Beherrschung *f*; **to show a lack of ~** wenig Beherrschung zeigen; **he said with great ~ that ...** er sagte sehr beherrscht, dass ...; **wage ~** Zurückhaltung *f* bei Lohnforderungen

restrict [rɪ'strɪkt] VT beschränken (*to* auf +*acc*); *freedom, authority* einschränken

restricted [rɪ'strɪktɪd] ADJ *view* beschränkt; *diet* eingeschränkt; (*Admin, Mil*) *information* geheim; *admission* begrenzt; **within a ~ area** (= *within limited area*) auf begrenztem Gebiet

restricted area N Sperrgebiet *nt*

restriction [rɪ'strɪkʃən] N (*on sth* etw *gen*) Beschränkung *f*; (*of freedom, authority*) Einschränkung *f*; **to place ~s on sth** etw beschränken

restrictive [rɪ'strɪktɪv] ADJ (= *limiting*) restriktiv

restrictive practices PL (*Jur, Ind*) wettbewerbsbeschränkende Geschäftspraktiken *pl*

rest room N (*US*) Toilette *f*

restructure [,riː'strʌktʃə^r] (*Comm, Ind*) **◼** VT umstrukturieren
◼ VI sich umstrukturieren

restructuring [,riː'strʌktʃərɪŋ] N (*Comm, Ind*) Umstrukturierung *f*

rest stop N (*US Aut*) (= *place*) Rastplatz *m*; (= *break in journey*) Rast *f*

result [rɪ'zʌlt] **◼** N **(a)** (= *consequence*) Folge *f*; **as a ~ he failed** folglich fiel er durch; **as a ~ this** und folglich; **as a ~ of which he ...** was zur Folge hatte, dass er ...; **to be the ~ of** resultieren aus **(b)** (*of election, exam, race, Math etc*) Resultat *nt*; **~s** (*of test, experiment*) Werte *pl*; **to get ~s** (*person*) Resultate erzielen; **as a ~ of my inquiry** auf meine Anfrage (hin); **what was the ~?** (*Sport*) wie ist es ausgegangen?
◼ VI resultieren (*from* aus)

▶ **result in** VI +PREP OBJ führen zu; **this resulted in his being late** das führte dazu, dass er zu spät kam

resume [rɪ'zjuːm] **◼** VT **(a)** (= *restart*) wieder aufnehmen; *journey* fortsetzen **(b)** *command, possession, role* wieder übernehmen **◼** VI (*classes, work etc*) wieder beginnen

résumé ['reɪzjuːmeɪ] N Zusammenfassung *f*; (*US*: = *curriculum vitae*) Lebenslauf *m*

resumption [rɪ'zʌmpʃən] N (*of activity*) Wiederaufnahme *f*; (*of command, possession*) erneute Übernahme; (*of journey*) Fortsetzung *f*; (*of classes*) Wiederbeginn *m*

resurface [,riː'sɜːfɪs] VI (*diver, fig*) wieder auftauchen

resurgence [rɪ'sɜːdʒəns] N Wiederaufleben *nt*

resurgent [rɪˈsɜːdʒənt] ADJ wieder auflebend

resurrect [ˌrezəˈrekt] VT (fig) law wieder einführen; institution wieder ins Leben rufen; custom, fashion, career wieder beleben; **to ~ the past** die Vergangenheit wieder heraufbeschwören

resurrection [ˌrezəˈrekʃən] N **(a) the Resurrection** (Rel) die Auferstehung **(b)** (fig) (of law) Wiedereinführung f; (of custom, fashion) Wiederbelebung f

resuscitate [rɪˈsʌsɪteɪt] VT (Med) wieder beleben; (fig) beleben

retail [ˈriːteɪl] **1** N Einzelhandel m **2** VT goods im Einzelhandel verkaufen **3** VI (goods) **to ~ at ...** im Einzelhandel ... kosten **4** ADV im Einzelhandel

retail IN CPDS Einzelhandels-; **retail banking** N Bankgeschäft nt; **retail business** N Einzelhandel m; (= shop) Einzelhandelsgeschäft nt

retailer [ˈriːteɪləʳ] N Einzelhändler(in) m(f)

retailing [ˈriːteɪlɪŋ] N der Einzelhandel

retail: retail park N (Brit) Shoppingcenter nt; **retail price** N Einzelhandelspreis m; **recommended ~** unverbindliche Preisempfehlung; **retail price index** N Einzelhandelspreisindex m; **retail trade** N Einzelhandel m

retain [rɪˈteɪn] VT **(a)** (= keep) behalten; money, possession zurück(be)halten; custom, flavour beibehalten; moisture speichern; **to ~ control of sth** etw weiterhin in der Gewalt haben; **~ed profits** (Comm) einbehaltene or nicht ausgeschüttete Gewinne **(b)** (= remember) sich (dat) merken; (computer) information speichern

retake [ˌriːˈteɪk], vb: pret **retook**, ptp **retaken** [ˌriːˈteɪkən] **1** VT **(a)** (Mil) zurückerobern **(b)** exam wiederholen (also Sport) **2** [ˈriːteɪk] N (of exam) Wiederholung(sprüfung) f

retaliate [rɪˈtælɪeɪt] VI Vergeltung üben; (for bad treatment, insults etc) sich revanchieren (against sb an jdm); (in battle) zurückschlagen; (Sport, in fight, with measures, in argument) kontern; **he ~d by pointing out that ...** er konterte, indem er darauf hinwies, dass ...; **then she ~d by calling him a pig** sie revanchierte sich damit, dass sie ihn ein Schwein nannte

retaliation [rɪˌtælɪˈeɪʃən] N Vergeltung f; (in fight also) Vergeltungsschlag m; (in argument, diplomacy etc) Konterschlag m; **in ~** zur Vergeltung

retard [rɪˈtɑːd] VT development verlangsamen; (Biol, Phys) retardieren

retarded [rɪˈtɑːdɪd] ADJ zurückgeblieben; growth, progress verzögert; **mentally ~** geistig zurückgeblieben

retch [retʃ] VI würgen

retell [ˌriːˈtel], pret, ptp **retold** VT wiederholen; (novelist) old legend nacherzählen

retention [rɪˈtenʃən] N **(a)** Beibehaltung f; (of possession) Zurückhaltung f; (of water) Speicherung f; (of facts) Behalten nt **(b)** (= memory) Gedächtnis nt

rethink [ˌriːˈθɪŋk], vb: pret, ptp **rethought** [ˌriːˈθɔːt] **1** VT überdenken **2** [ˈriːθɪŋk] N (inf) Überdenken nt; **we'll have to have a ~** wir müssen das noch einmal überdenken

reticence [ˈretɪsəns] N Zurückhaltung f

reticent [ˈretɪsənt] ADJ zurückhaltend

retinue [ˈretɪnjuː] N Gefolge nt

retire [rɪˈtaɪəʳ] VI **(a)** (= give up work) aufhören zu arbeiten; (civil servant, military officer) in den Ruhestand treten; (self-employed) sich zur Ruhe setzen; (singer, player etc) aufhören; **to ~ from business** sich zur Ruhe setzen, sich aus dem Geschäftsleben zurückziehen **(b)** (= withdraw) (Sport) aufgeben (Ftbl, Rugby etc) vom Feld gehen; (jury) sich zurückziehen; **to ~ from public life** sich aus dem öffentlichen Leben zurückziehen

retired [rɪˈtaɪəd] ADJ worker, employee aus dem Arbeitsleben ausgeschieden (form); civil servant, military officer pensioniert; **he is ~** er arbeitet nicht mehr; **~ people** Leute, die im Ruhestand sind; **a ~ worker/teacher** ein Rentner/pensionierter Lehrer

retirement [rɪˈtaɪəmənt] N **(a)** (= stopping work) Ausscheiden nt aus dem Arbeitsleben (form); (of civil servant, military officer) Pensionierung f; **~ at 60/65** Altersgrenze f bei 60/65; **to come out of ~** wieder zurückkommen **(b)** (Sport) Aufgabe f; (Ftbl, Rugby etc) Abgang m vom Spielfeld

retirement: retirement age N Rentenalter nt; (of civil servant) Pensionsalter nt; **retirement home** N Seniorenheim nt; **retirement pension** N Altersruhegeld nt (form)

retold [ˌriːˈtəʊld] PRET, PTP of **retell**

retook [ˌriːˈtʊk] PRET of **retake**

retrace [rɪˈtreɪs] VT past, development zurückverfolgen; **to ~ one's path** or **steps** denselben Weg zurückgehen

retract [rɪˈtrækt] **1** VT offer zurückziehen; statement zurücknehmen **2** VI einen Rückzieher machen

retraction [rɪˈtrækʃən] N (of offer) Rückzug m; (of statement) Rücknahme f; (= thing retracted) Rückzieher m

retrain [ˌriːˈtreɪn] **1** VT umschulen **2** VI sich umschulen lassen

retraining [ˌriːˈtreɪnɪŋ] N Umschulung f

retreat [rɪˈtriːt] **1** N **(a)** (Mil) Rückzug m; **the army is in ~** die Armee befindet sich or ist auf dem Rückzug; **to make** or **beat a (hasty** or **swift) ~** (fig) (schleunigst) das Feld räumen **(b)** (= place) Zufluchtsort m, Zuflucht f **2** VI **(a)** (Mil) den Rückzug antreten; (in fear) zurückweichen; **to ~ inside oneself** sich in sich selbst zurückziehen **(b)** (Chess) zurückziehen

retrench [rɪˈtrentʃ] VT expenditure kürzen

retrial [rɪˈtraɪəl] N (Jur) Wiederaufnahmeverfahren nt

retribution [ˌretrɪˈbjuːʃən] N Vergeltung f; **in ~** als Vergeltung

retrievable [rɪˈtriːvəbl] ADJ (= recoverable) zurück-/hervor-/heraus-/herunterholbar; (= rescuable) rettbar; (from wreckage etc) zu bergen; (Comput) data abrufbar; (after a crash) wiederherstellbar

retrieval [rɪˈtriːvəl] N (= recovering) Zurück-/Hervor-/Heraus-/Herunterholen nt; (= rescuing) Rettung f; (from wreckage etc) Bergung f; (Comput: of information) Abrufen nt; (after a crash) Wiederherstellen nt; (of money, investment) Wiedererlangen nt; (of loss) Wiedergutmachen nt

retrieve [rɪˈtriːv] **1** VT **(a)** (= recover) zurück-/hervor-/heraus-/herunterholen; (= rescue) retten; (from wreckage etc) bergen; (Comput) abrufen; (after a crash) wiederherstellen; honour, position, money, investment wiedererlangen; loss wieder gutmachen **(b)** (dog) apportieren **2** VI (dog) apportieren

retriever [rɪˈtriːvəʳ] N (= breed) Retriever m

retro- PREF rück-, Rück-

retroactive ADJ, **retroactively** ADV [ˌretrəʊˈæktɪv, -lɪ] rückwirkend

retrograde [ˈretrəʊɡreɪd] ADJ rückläufig; order umgekehrt; policy rückschrittlich; **~ step** Rückschritt m

retrospect [ˈretrəʊspekt] N **in ~, what would you have done differently?** was hätten Sie rückblickend anders gemacht?; **everything looks different in ~** im Nachhinein sieht alles anders aus

retrospective [ˌretrəʊˈspektɪv] ADJ rückblickend (also Admin, Jur); wisdom im Nachhinein; pay rise rückwirkend; **a ~ look (at)** ein Blick m zurück (auf +acc)

retrospectively [ˌretrəʊˈspektɪvlɪ] ADV (= in retrospect) rückblickend

return [rɪˈtɜːn] **1** VI (come back) zurückkommen; (go back) (person) zurückgehen; (vehicle) zurückfahren; (symptoms, doubts, fears) wiederkommen; **to ~ to London/the town/the group** nach London/in die Stadt/zur Gruppe zurückkehren; **to ~ to school** wieder in die Schule gehen; **to ~ to (one's) work** (after short pause) wieder an seine Arbeit gehen; **to ~ to a subject** auf ein Thema zurückkommen; **to ~ home** nach Hause kommen/gehen

2 VT **(a)** (= give back) zurückgeben (to sb jdm); (= bring or take back) zurückbringen (to sb jdm); (= put back) zurücksetzen/-stellen/-legen; (= send back) (to an +acc) letter etc zurückschicken; (= refuse) cheque nicht einlösen; compliment erwidern; **to ~ sb's (phone) call** jdn zurückrufen; **to ~ a book to the shelf/box** ein Buch auf das Regal zurückstellen/in die Kiste zurücklegen; **to ~ fire** (Mil) das Feuer erwidern

(b) (= declare) details of income angeben; **to ~ a verdict of guilty (on sb)** (Jur) (jdn) schuldig sprechen

(c) (Fin) income einbringen; profit, interest abwerfen

3 N **(a)** (= coming/going back) Rückkehr f; (of illness) Wiederauftreten nt; **on my ~** bei meiner Rückkehr; **~ home** Heimkehr f; **by ~ (of post)** (Brit) postwendend; **many happy ~s (of the day)!** herzlichen Glückwunsch zum Geburtstag!

(b) (= giving back) Rückgabe f; (= bringing or taking back) Zurückbringen nt; (= putting back) Zurücksetzen/-stellen/-legen nt; (= sending back) Zurückschicken nt

(c) (Brit: also **~ ticket**) Rückfahrkarte f

(d) *(from investments, shares) (on* aus) Einkommen *nt; (on capital)* Gewinn *m; (= product: from land, mine etc)* Ertrag *m;* **~s** *(= profits)* Gewinn *m; (= receipts)* Einkünfte *pl;* **~ on capital** *(Fin)* Kapitalertrag *m,* Rendite *f;* **~ on capital employed** Ertrag *m* aus investiertem Kapital; **~ on equity** Eigenkapitalrendite *f*

(e) *(fig)* **in ~** dafür; **in ~ for** für; **to do sb a favour** *(Brit)* **or favor** *(US)* **in ~** sich bei jdm für einen Gefallen revanchieren **(f)** *(= act of declaring)* **tax ~** Steuererklärung *f* **(g)** *(Sport) (= stroke)* Rückschlag *m; (Tennis)* Return *m; (= throw)* Rückwurf *m; (= ~ pass)* Rückpass *m* **(h)** *(Comm: = returned item)* zurückgebrachte Ware; *(= book)* Remittende *f* **(I)** *(= carriage ~, Comput)* Return *nt*

returnable [rɪˈtɜːnəbl] ADJ *(= reusable)* Mehrweg-; **~ bottle** Mehrwegflasche *f; (with deposit)* Pfandflasche *f*

return: return fare N *(Brit)* Preis *m* für eine Rückfahrkarte *or (Aviat)* ein Rückflugticket *nt;* **return flight** N *(Brit)* Rückflug *m; (both ways)* Hin- und Rückflug *m;* **return journey** N *(Brit)* Rückreise *f;* **return key** N *(Comput)* Return- or Eingabetaste *f;* **return ticket** N *(Brit)* Rückfahrkarte *f; (Aviat)* Rückflugticket *nt;* **return visit** N *(to place)* zweiter Besuch; **to make a ~** *(to a place)* (an einen Ort) zurückkehren

reunification [riːjuːnɪfɪˈkeɪʃən] N Wiedervereinigung *f*

reunion [rɪˈjuːnjən] N **(a)** *(= coming together)* Wiedervereinigung *f* **(b)** *(= gathering)* Zusammenkunft *f*

reunite [riːjuːˈnaɪt] **1** VT wieder vereinigen; **they were ~d at last** sie waren endlich wieder vereint **2** VI *(countries, parties)* sich wieder vereinigen; *(people)* wieder zusammenkommen

reusable [riːˈjuːzəbl] ADJ wieder verwertbar

reuse [riːˈjuːz] **1** VT wieder verwenden **2** [riːˈjuːs] N Wiederverwendung *f*

rev [rev] **1** VI *(driver)* den Motor auf Touren bringen; *(noisily)* den Motor aufheulen lassen; *(engine)* aufheulen **2** VT *engine* aufheulen lassen

➤ **rev up** VTI *(Aut)* = **rev**

revaluation [riːvæljuˈeɪʃən] N *(Fin)* Aufwertung *f; (= reassessment of value)* Neubewertung *f*

revalue [riːˈvæljuː] VT *(Fin)* aufwerten; *(= reassess) property* neu bewerten

revamp [riːˈvæmp] VT *(inf) book, image* aufmotzen *(inf); company* auf Vordermann bringen *(inf)*

reveal [rɪˈviːl] VT **(a)** *(= make visible)* zum Vorschein bringen; *(= show)* zeigen **(b)** *truth, facts* aufdecken; *one's/sb's identity* enthüllen; *name, details* verraten; *ignorance, knowledge* erkennen lassen; **he could never ~ his feelings for her** er konnte seine Gefühle für sie nie zeigen; **what does this ~ about the motives of the hero?** was sagt das über die Motive des Helden aus?

revealing [rɪˈviːlɪŋ] ADJ aufschlussreich; *material, skirt etc* viel zeigend

revel [ˈrevl] **1** VI **to ~ in sth** etw in vollen Zügen genießen; **to ~ in doing sth** seine wahre Freude daran haben, etw zu tun **2** N **revels** PL Feiern *nt*

revelation [revəˈleɪʃən] N Enthüllung *f*

reveller, *(US)* **reveler** [ˈrevləʳ] N Feiernde(r) *mf*

revelry [ˈrevlrɪ] N USU PL Festlichkeit *f*

revenge [rɪˈvendʒ] N Rache *f; (Sport)* Revanche *f;* **to take ~ on sb (for sth)** sich an jdm (für etw) rächen; **to get one's ~** sich rächen; *(Sport)* sich revanchieren; **in ~ for** als Rache für

revengeful [rɪˈvendʒfʊl] ADJ rachsüchtig

revenue [ˈrevənjuː] N *(of state)* öffentliche Einnahmen *pl; (= tax ~)* Steueraufkommen *nt; (of individual)* Einkünfte *pl; (= department)* Finanzbehörde *f;* **~ reserves** Gewinnrücklagen *pl*

revenue stamp N *(US)* Steuermarke *f*

reverberate [rɪˈvɜːbəreɪt] VI *(sound)* nachhallen

reverence [ˈrevərəns] N Ehrfurcht *f; (= veneration)* Verehrung *f (for* für); **to treat sb with ~** etw ehrfürchtig behandeln

reverend [ˈrevərənd] **1** ADJ **the Reverend Robert Martin** ≈ Pfarrer Robert Martin **2** N *(inf)* ≈ Pfarrer *m*

reverently [ˈrevərəntlɪ] ADV ehrfürchtig

reversal [rɪˈvɜːsəl] N **(a)** *(of order, situation, result)* Umkehren *nt; (of objects, words)* Umstellen *nt; (of verdict)* Umstoßung *f; (of*

trend, process) Umkehrung *f; (of policy)* Umkrempeln *nt; (of decision)* Rückgängigmachen *nt* **(b)** *(= setback)* Rückschlag *m*

reverse [rɪˈvɜːs] **1** ADJ *(= opposite)* umgekehrt **2** N **(a)** *(= opposite)* Gegenteil *nt;* **quite the ~!** ganz im Gegenteil!

(b) *(= back)* Rückseite *f* **(c)** *(Aut)* Rückwärtsgang *m;* **in ~** im Rückwärtsgang; **to put a/ the car into ~** den Rückwärtsgang einlegen **3** VT **(a)** *order, situation, result, verdict, trend, process* umkehren; *objects, words* vertauschen; *policy* umkrempeln; *decision* rückgängig machen; **to ~ the order of sth** etw herumdrehen; **to ~ the charges** *(Brit Telec)* ein R-Gespräch führen

(b) to ~ one's car into the garage/into a tree *(esp Brit)* rückwärts in die Garage fahren/gegen einen Baum fahren **4** VI *(esp Brit: car, driver)* zurücksetzen

reverse: reverse gear N *(Aut)* Rückwärtsgang *m;* **reverse takeover** N *(Comm)* gegenläufige Fusion

reversible [rɪˈvɜːsəbl] ADJ *decision* rückgängig zu machen *pred,* rückgängig zu machend *attr; process* umkehrbar

reversible jacket N Wendejacke *f*

reversing light [rɪˈvɜːsɪŋlaɪt] N Rückfahrscheinwerfer *m*

reversion [rɪˈvɜːʃən] N *(to former state)* Umkehr *f (to* zu); *(to bad state)* Rückfall *m (to* in +acc)

revert [rɪˈvɜːt] VI *(to former state)* zurückkehren *(to* zu); *(to bad state)* zurückfallen *(to* in +acc); *(to topic)* zurückkommen *(to* auf +acc)

review [rɪˈvjuː] **1** N **(a)** *(= look back)* Rückblick *m (of* auf +acc); *(= report)* Überblick *m (of* über +acc) **(b)** *(= re-examination)* nochmalige Prüfung; **the agreement comes up for ~ or comes under ~ next year** das Abkommen wird nächstes Jahr nochmals geprüft; **his salary is due for ~ in January** im Januar wird sein Gehalt neu festgesetzt **(c)** *(of book, film, play etc)* Kritik *f* **2** VT **(a)** *one's life, the past etc* zurückblicken auf (+acc) **(b)** *situation, case* erneut (über)prüfen **(c)** *book, play, film* besprechen **(d)** *(US: before exam)* wiederholen

reviewer [rɪˈvjuːəʳ] N Kritiker(in) *m(f)*

revise [rɪˈvaɪz] **1** VT **(a)** *(= change, correct)* revidieren **(b)** *(Brit: = learn up)* wiederholen **2** VI *(Brit)* (den Stoff) wiederholen

revised [rɪˈvaɪzd] ADJ **(a)** *(= amended)* revidiert; *offer* neu **(b)** *(Typ) edition* überarbeitet

revision [rɪˈvɪʒən] N **(a)** *(of opinion, estimate)* Revidieren *nt* **(b)** *(of proofs)* Revision *f* **(c)** *(Brit: for exam)* Wiederholung *f* (des Stoffs) **(d)** *(= revised version)* überarbeitete Ausgabe

revisit [riːˈvɪzɪt] VT wieder besuchen

revitalize [riːˈvaɪtəlaɪz] VT neu beleben

revival [rɪˈvaɪvəl] N **(a)** *(= bringing back) (of custom, usage)* Wiedererwecken *nt; (of old ideas)* Wiederaufnehmen *nt; (of play)* Wiederaufnahme *f* **(b)** *(= return: of custom, old ideas etc)* Wiederaufleben *nt;* **an economic ~** ein wirtschaftlicher Wiederaufschwung

revive [rɪˈvaɪv] **1** VT *person (from fainting, from fatigue)* (wieder or neu) beleben; *(from near death)* wieder beleben; *economy* wieder ankurbeln; *memories* wieder lebendig werden lassen; *fashion, custom, usage, fears* wieder aufleben lassen; *friendship, old habit, word, old play, talks, career* wieder aufnehmen; **to ~ interest in sth** neues Interesse an etw (*dat*) wecken **2** VI *(person) (from fainting)* wieder zu sich kommen; *(from fatigue)* wieder munter werden; *(hope, feelings)* wieder aufleben; *(business, trade)* wieder aufblühen

revoke [rɪˈvəʊk] VT *law* aufheben; *order, promise* zurückziehen; *decision* widerrufen; *licence* entziehen

revolt [rɪˈvəʊlt] **1** N Revolte *f;* **to be in ~ (against)** rebellieren (gegen) **2** VI *(= rebel)* revoltieren *(against* gegen) **3** VT abstoßen; **I was ~ed by it** es hat mich abgestoßen *inf*

revolting [rɪˈvəʊltɪŋ] ADJ *(= repulsive)* abstoßend; *meal, story* ekelhaft; *(inf: = unpleasant) colour, dress* scheußlich; *person* widerlich

revolution [revəˈluːʃən] N **(a)** *(Pol, fig)* Revolution *f* **(b)** *(= turn)* Umdrehung *f*

revolutionary [revəˈluːʃnərɪ] **1** ADJ *(lit, fig)* revolutionär; **~ government** Revolutionsregierung *f* **2** N Revolutionär(in) *m(f)*

revolutionize [revəˈluːʃənaɪz] VT revolutionieren

revolve [rɪ'vɒlv] **1** VT drehen **2** VI sich drehen

revolving [rɪ'vɒlvɪŋ] IN CPDS Dreh-; **revolving credit** N revolvierender Kredit; **revolving door** N Drehtür f

revue [rɪ'vjuː] N (Theat) Revue f; (satirical) Kabarett nt

revulsion [rɪ'vʌlʃən] N (a) (= disgust) Ekel m (at vor +dat) (b) (= reaction) Empörung f

reward [rɪ'wɔːd] **1** N Belohnung f; (= money) Entgelt nt (form); ~ offered for the return of ... Finderlohn für ...; the ~s of this job die Vorzüge dieser Arbeit **2** VT belohnen

rewarding [rɪ'wɔːdɪŋ] ADJ lohnend; task, work dankbar; relationship bereichernd; **bringing up a child is ~** ein Kind großzuziehen ist eine lohnende Aufgabe

rewind [riː'waɪnd], pret, ptp **rewound** VT thread wieder aufwickeln; watch wieder aufziehen; film, tape, video zurückspulen; ~ **button** Rückspultaste f

reword [riː'wɜːd] VT umformulieren

rewound [riː'waʊnd] PRET, PTP of **rewind**

rewrite [riː'raɪt], vb: pret **rewrote** [riː'rəʊt], ptp **rewritten** [riː'rɪtn] VT (= write out again) neu schreiben; (= recast) umschreiben; **to ~ the record books** einen neuen Rekord verzeichnen

Rhaeto-Romanic [ˈriːtəʊrəʊ'mænɪk] N Rätoromanisch nt

rhapsody [ˈræpsədɪ] N (Mus) Rhapsodie f; (fig) Schwärmerei f

Rhenish [ˈrenɪʃ] ADJ region, town rheinisch; ~ **wine** Rheinwein m

rhetoric [ˈretərɪk] N Rhetorik f; (pej) Phrasendrescherei f (pej)

rhetorical ADJ, **rhetorically** ADV [rɪ'tɒrɪkəl, -ɪ] rhetorisch

rheumatic [ruː'mætɪk] **1** N (a) (= person) Rheumatiker(in) m(f) (b) **rheumatics** SING Rheumatismus m **2** ADJ pains rheumatisch; joint rheumakrank

rheumatism [ˈruːmətɪzəm] N Rheuma nt

Rhine [raɪn] N Rhein m; ~ **wine** Rheinwein m

Rhineland [ˈraɪnlænd] N Rheinland nt

rhinoceros [raɪ'nɒsərəs] N Nashorn nt

Rhodes [rəʊdz] N Rhodos nt; **in** ~ auf Rhodos

rhododendron [ˌrəʊdə'dendrən] N Rhododendron m or nt

rhombus [ˈrɒmbəs] N Rhombus m

Rhone [rəʊn] N Rhone f

rhubarb [ˈruːbɑːb] N Rhabarber m

rhyme [raɪm] **1** N (a) (= rhyming word) Reim m; **there seems to be no ~ or reason to it, that has no ~ or reason** das hat weder Sinn noch Verstand (b) (= poem) Gedicht nt; **in** ~ in Reimen; **to put into** ~ in Reime bringen **2** VT reimen **3** VI (words) sich reimen

rhyming [ˈraɪmɪŋ] ADJ ~ **couplets** Reimpaare pl

RHYMING SLANG

Rhyming slang ist eine Sonderform des Cockney-Slangs, in dem das gemeinte Wort durch einen Ausdruck ersetzt wird, der sich darauf reimt: z. B. „apples and pears" statt stairs. Einige Ausdrücke des „rhyming slang" sind Teil der Umgangssprache geworden, z. B. „use your loaf", wobei loaf die Abkürzung von „loaf of bread" ist, das wiederum für head steht; kurz gesagt: „streng deinen Grips an". ▶ COCKNEY

rhythm [ˈrɪðm] N Rhythmus m

rhythmic(al) [ˈrɪðmɪk(əl)] ADJ, **rhythmically** [ˈrɪðmɪkəlɪ] ADV rhythmisch

rib [rɪb] **1** N (Anat, Cook) Rippe f; **to dig** (esp Brit) or **poke sb in the** ~**s** jdn in die Rippen stoßen **2** VT (inf: = tease) necken

ribbed [rɪbd] ADJ gerippt

ribbon [ˈrɪbən] N (a) (for hair, dress) Band nt; (for typewriter) Farbband nt; (fig: narrow strip) Streifen m (b) **ribbons** PL (= tatters) Fetzen pl; **to tear sth to** ~**s** etw zerfetzen; (fig) play etc etw in der Luft zerreißen

rib cage N Brustkorb m

rice [raɪs] N Reis m

rice pudding N (esp Brit) Milchreis m

rich [rɪtʃ] **1** ADJ (+ER) reich; decoration, style prächtig; food schwer; soil, land fruchtbar; colour satt; sound, voice voll; smell kräftig, stark; life erfüllt; (inf: = amusing) köstlich; **that's** ~! (iro) das ist stark (inf); **to be** ~ **in sth** in resources etc reich an etw (dat) sein; ~ **in vitamins/protein** vitamin-/eiweißreich; ~ **in minerals** reich an Bodenschätzen; **a** ~ **diet** reichhaltige Kost

2 N (a) **the** ~ pl die Reichen pl (b) **riches** PL Reichtümer pl

richly [ˈrɪtʃlɪ] ADV dress, decorate prächtig; illustrated reich; coloured, flavoured kräftig; scented intensiv; **he** ~ **deserves it** er hat es mehr als verdient; **he was** ~ **rewarded** (lit) er wurde reich belohnt; (fig) er wurde reichlich belohnt

richness [ˈrɪtʃnɪs] N Reichtum m (in an +dat); (of decoration, style) Pracht f; (of food) Schwere f; (of soil, land) Fruchtbarkeit f; (of colour) Sattheit f; (of smell) Stärke f; (of life) Erfülltheit f; **the** ~ **of his voice** seine volle Stimme

ricin [ˈraɪsɪn] N Ricin nt

rickety [ˈrɪkɪtɪ] ADJ furniture etc wack(e)lig

ricochet [ˈrɪkəʃeɪ] **1** N Abprall m **2** VI abprallen (off von)

rid [rɪd], pret, ptp **rid** or **ridded** VT **to** ~ **of** pests, disease befreien von; of bandits etc säubern von; **to** ~ **oneself of sb/sth** jdn/etw loswerden; of pests also sich von etw befreien; **to get** ~ **of sb/sth** jdn/etw loswerden; **to be** ~ **of sb/sth** jdn/etw los sein; **get** ~ **of it** sieh zu, dass du das loswirst; (= throw it away) schmeiß es weg (inf); **you are well** ~ **of him** ein Glück, dass du den los bist

riddance [ˈrɪdəns] N **good** ~ **(to bad rubbish)!** (inf) ein Glück, dass wir das/den etc los sind

ridden [ˈrɪdn] **1** PTP of **ride 2** ADJ debt-~ hoch verschuldet; disease-~ von Krankheiten befallen

riddle¹ [ˈrɪdl] VT ~d **with holes** völlig durchlöchert; ~d **with woodworm** wurmzerfressen; ~d **with corruption** von der Korruption zerfressen; ~d **with mistakes** voller Widersprüche

riddle² N Rätsel nt; **to speak in** ~s in Rätseln sprechen

ride [raɪd], vb: pret **rode**, ptp **ridden** **1** N (in vehicle, on bicycle) Fahrt f; (on horse) Ritt m; (for pleasure) Ausritt m; **to go for a** ~ eine Fahrt machen; (on horse) reiten gehen; **he gave the child a** ~ **on his back** er ließ das Kind auf den Schultern reiten; **cycle/coach** ~ Rad-/Busfahrt f; **to go for a** ~ **in the car** mit dem Auto wegfahren; **I just went along for the** ~ (fig inf) ich bin nur zum Vergnügen mitgegangen; **to take sb for a** ~ (inf: = deceive) jdn anschmieren (inf); **he gave me a** ~ **into town in his car** er nahm mich im Auto in die Stadt mit; **can I have a** ~ **on your bike?** kann ich mal mit deinem Rad fahren? **2** VI (a) (on a horse etc, Sport) reiten (on auf +dat); **to go riding** reiten gehen

(b) (= go in vehicle, by cycle etc) fahren; **he was riding on a bicycle** er fuhr mit einem Fahrrad; **to** ~ **on a bus/in a car** in einem Bus/Wagen fahren; **to** ~ **away** or **off/down** davon-/hinunterfahren

(c) (fig) **we'll just have to let the matter** or **to let things** ~ **for a while** wir müssen einfach für eine Weile den Dingen ihren Lauf lassen; **... but I'll let it** ~ ..., aber ich lasse es vorerst einmal

3 VT (a) horse etc reiten mit or auf (+dat), reiten; bicycle, motorbike fahren mit; **I have never ridden a motorbike** ich bin noch nie Motorrad gefahren; **may I** ~ **your bike?** darf ich mit deinem Fahrrad fahren?; **Jason will be ridden by H. Martin** Jason wird unter H. Martin laufen; **to** ~ **the storm** (lit, fig) den Sturm überstehen

(b) (US inf: = torment) schikanieren; **don't** ~ **him too hard** treibts nicht so toll mit ihm

▶ **ride about** (Brit) or **around** VI (on horse etc) herumreiten; (in vehicle, on motorcycle, on bicycle) herumfahren

▶ **ride behind** VI (on same horse/bicycle) hinten sitzen; (on different horse/bicycle) hinterherreiten/ fahren

▶ **ride on** VI +PREP OBJ (money, reputation) hängen an (+dat)

▶ **ride out** **1** VT SEP überstehen; **to ride out the storm** (lit, fig) den Sturm überstehen **2** VI (on horse) ausreiten

▶ **ride up** VI (skirt etc) hochrutschen

rider [ˈraɪdəʳ] N (a) (on horse) Reiter(in) m(f); (on bicycle, motorcycle) Fahrer(in) m(f) (b) (= addition) Zusatz m; (to document, will etc) Zusatzklausel f; (to bill) Allonge f

ridge [rɪdʒ] N (on fabric, cardboard etc) Rippe f; (of hills, mountains) Rücken m; (pointed, steep) Grat m; **a** ~ **of hills** eine Hügelkette; **a** ~ **of mountains** ein Höhenzug m; **a** ~ **of high pressure** (Met) ein Hochdruckkeil m

ridicule [ˈrɪdɪkjuːl] **1** N Spott m; **to hold sb/sth up to** ~ sich über jdn/etw lustig machen; **to become an object of** ~ der Lächerlichkeit preisgegeben werden **2** VT verspotten

ridiculous [rɪ'dɪkjʊləs] ADJ lächerlich; **don't be** ~ red keinen Unsinn; **to make oneself (look)** ~ sich lächerlich machen; **to be made to look** ~ der Lächerlichkeit preisgegeben werden;

to go to ~ **lengths (to do sth)** großen Aufwand betreiben(, um etw zu tun)

ridiculously [rɪˈdɪkjʊləslɪ] ADV lächerlich

riding [ˈraɪdɪŋ] N Reiten *nt*; **I enjoy ~** ich reite gern

riding IN CPDS Reit-

rife [raɪf] ADJ *disease, corruption* weit verbreitet; **to be ~** grassieren; (*rumour*) umgehen; **speculation is ~ that ...** es wird spekuliert, dass ...; **~ with** voll von, voller +*gen*; **areas ~ with unemployment** Gegenden mit hoher Arbeitslosigkeit

rifle¹ [ˈraɪfl] VT (*also ~ through*) *drawer etc* durchwühlen

rifle² N (= *gun*) Gewehr *nt* (*mit gezogenem Lauf*); (*for hunting*) Büchse *f*

rifle range N Schießstand *m*

rift [rɪft] N Spalt *m*; (*fig*) Riss *m*

rig [rɪg] **1** N (= *oil ~*) (Öl)förderturm *m*; (*offshore*) Ölbohrinsel *f* **2** VT (*fig*) *election etc* manipulieren

▶ **rig out** VT SEP (*inf*) (= *equip*) ausstaffieren (*inf*); (= *dress*) auftakeln (*inf*)

▶ **rig up** VT SEP *equipment* aufbauen; (*fig*) (= *make*) improvisieren; (= *arrange*) arrangieren

right [raɪt] **1** ADJ **(a)** richtig (= *just, fair, morally good also*), recht (*S Ger*); **he thought it ~ to warn me** er hielt es für richtig, mich zu warnen; **it seemed only ~ to give him the money** es schien richtig, ihm das Geld zu geben; **it's only ~ (and proper)** es ist nur recht und billig; **to do the ~ thing by sb** sich jdm gegenüber anständig benehmen; **to be ~** (= *correct: person*) recht haben; (*answer*) stimmen; **what's the ~ time?** wie viel Uhr ist es genau?; **you're quite ~** Sie haben ganz Recht; **how ~ you are!** (*inf*) da haben Sie ganz Recht; **you were ~ to refuse** *or* **in refusing** Sie hatten Recht, als Sie ablehnten; **let's get it ~ this time!** mach es dieses Mal richtig; (*in reporting facts etc*) sag es dieses Mal richtig; **to put** *or* **set ~** *error* korrigieren; *situation* wieder in Ordnung bringen; **I tried to put things ~ after their quarrel** ich versuchte, nach ihrem Streit wieder einzulenken; **what's the ~ thing to do in this case?** was tut man da am besten?; **to do sth the ~ way** etw richtig machen; **that is the ~ way of looking at it** das ist die richtige Einstellung; **Mr/Miss Right** (*inf*) der/die Richtige (*inf*); **we will do what is ~ for the country** wir werden tun, was für das Land gut ist; **the medicine soon put** *or* **set him ~** die Medizin hat ihn schnell wiederhergestellt; **I don't feel quite ~ today** ich fühle mich heute nicht ganz wohl; **nobody in their ~ mind would ...** kein vernünftiger Mensch würde ...; **he's not ~ in the head** (*inf*) bei ihm stimmts nicht im Oberstübchen (*inf*)

(b) (*phrases*) **~!, ~ oh!** (*Brit inf*), **~ you are!** (*Brit inf*) okay (*inf*); **~ on!** (*esp US inf*) super! (*sl*); **that's ~!** (= *correct*) das stimmt!; **so they came in the end ~ is that ~?** und so kamen sie schließlich ~ wirklich?; **~ enough!** (*das*) stimmt!

(c) (= *opposite of left*) rechte(r, s); **~ hand** rechte Hand **2** ADV **(a)** (= *straight, directly*) direkt; (= *exactly*) genau; **~ in front/ahead of you** direkt *or* genau vor Ihnen; (= *immediately*) sofort; **~ now** (= *at this very moment*) in diesem Augenblick; (= *immediately*) sofort; **~ here** genau hier; **~ in the middle** genau in der Mitte; **~ at the beginning** gleich am Anfang; **I'll be ~ back** ich bin gleich da; **it hit me ~ in the face** der Schlag traf mich voll ins Gesicht

(b) (= *completely, all the way*) ganz; **~ through** *drive, go* mitten durch

(c) (= *correctly*) richtig; **nothing goes ~ for them** nichts klappt bei ihnen (*inf*)

(d) (= *opposite of left*) rechts; **turn ~** biegen Sie rechts ab; **~, left and centre** (*Brit*) *or* **center** (*US*) überall **3** N **(a)** NO PL (*moral, legal*) Recht *nt*; **to be in the ~** im Recht sein

(b) (= *entitlement*) Recht *nt*; **(to have) a ~ to sth** einen Anspruch auf etw (*acc*) (haben); **what ~ have you to say that?** mit welchem Recht sagen Sie das?; **he is within his ~s** das ist sein gutes Recht; **by ~s** rechtmäßig; **in one's own ~** selber

(c) **rights** PL (*Comm*) Rechte *pl*; **to have the (sole) ~s to sth** die (alleinigen) Rechte an etw (*dat*) haben

(d) to put *or* **set sth to ~s** etw (wieder) in Ordnung bringen; **to put things** *or* **the world to ~s** die Welt verbessern

(e) (= *not left*) rechte Seite; **to drive on the ~** rechts fahren; **to keep to the ~** sich rechts halten; **on my ~** rechts (von mir); **on** *or* **to the ~ of the church** rechts von der Kirche; **the Right** (*Pol*) die Rechte **4** VT **(a)** (= *return to upright position*) aufrichten; **the problem**

should ~ itself (*fig*) das Problem müsste sich von selbst lösen **(b)** (= *make amends for*) *wrong* wieder gutmachen

right: right angle N rechter Winkel; **at ~s (to)** rechtwinklig (zu); **right-angled** ADJ rechtwinklig; **right-click** (*Comput*) **1** VI rechts klicken **2** VT rechts klicken auf (+*acc*)

righteous [ˈraɪtʃəs] ADJ **(a)** rechtschaffen; (*pej*) selbstgerecht (*pej*) **(b)** *indignation, anger* gerecht

righteousness [ˈraɪtʃəsnɪs] N Rechtschaffenheit *f*

rightful [ˈraɪtfʊl] ADJ rechtmäßig; *punishment* gerecht

rightfully [ˈraɪtfəlɪ] ADV rechtmäßig; **they must give us what is ~ ours** sie müssen uns geben, was uns rechtmäßig zusteht

right: right-hand ADJ **~ drive** rechtsgesteuert; **right-handed 1** ADJ *person* rechtshändig; *punch, throw* mit der rechten Hand **2** ADV rechtshändig; **right-hander** N (= *person*) Rechtshänder(in) *m(f)*; **right-hand man** N rechte Hand

rightly [ˈraɪtlɪ] ADV richtig; **quite ~** ganz recht; **they are ~ regarded as ...** sie werden zu Recht als ... angesehen; **if I remember ~** wenn ich mich recht erinnere; **~ or wrongly** ob das nun richtig ist oder nicht; **and ~ so** und zwar mit Recht

right: right-minded ADJ vernünftig; **right of way** N (*across property*) Durchgangsrecht *nt*; (*Mot*) Vorfahrt *f*

rights issue N (*St Ex*) Bezugsrechtsemission *f*

right: rightsizing N (*Comm*) Rightsizing *nt*; **right-thinking** ADJ vernünftig; **right triangle** N (*US*) rechtwinkliges Dreieck; **right wing** N (*Pol*) rechter Flügel; **right-wing** ADJ (*Pol*) rechtsgerichtet; **~ extremist** Rechtsextremist(in) *m(f)*; **right-winger** N (*Sport*) Rechtsaußen *m*; (*Pol*) Rechte(r) *mf*

rigid [ˈrɪdʒɪd] ADJ *board, material, system* starr; *character* strikt; *discipline, principles* streng; **with fear** starr vor Angst; **to be bored ~** sich zu Tode langweilen

rigidity [rɪˈdʒɪdɪtɪ] N (*of board, material, system*) Starrheit *f*; (*of character*) Striktheit *f*; (*of discipline, principles*) Strenge *f*

rigidly [ˈrɪdʒɪdlɪ] ADV **(a)** (*lit*) *stand etc* starr **(b)** (*fig*) *behave, treat, oppose* strikt

rigor N (*US*) = **rigour**

rigorous [ˈrɪɡərəs] ADJ *person, discipline, structure, method* strikt; *measures* rigoros; *analysis, tests* gründlich

rigorously [ˈrɪɡərəslɪ] ADV *enforce* rigoros; *test* gründlich; *control* streng

rigour, (*US*) **rigor** [ˈrɪɡəʳ] N **(a)** NO PL (= *strictness*) Striktheit *f* **(b) rigours** PL (*of climate etc*) Unbilden *pl*

rim [rɪm] N (*of cup, hat*) Rand *m*; (*of spectacles*) Fassung *f*; (*of wheel*) Felge *f*

rimmed [rɪmd] ADJ mit Rand; **gold-~ spectacles** Brille *f* mit Goldfassung

rind [raɪnd] N (*of cheese*) Rinde *f*; (*of bacon*) Schwarte *f*; (*of fruit*) Schale *f*

ring¹ [rɪŋ] **1** N Ring *m*; (*in tree trunk*) Jahresring *m*; (*Pol: = group*) Gruppe *f*; (*at circus*) Manege *f*; **to run ~s round sb** (*inf*) jdn in die Tasche stecken (*inf*) **2** VT (= *surround*) umringen; (= *put ~ round*) *item on list etc* einkreisen

ring² *vb*: pret **rang**, ptp **rung** **1** N **(a)** (*sound*) Klang *m* (*also fig*); (= *ringing*) (*of bell, alarm bell*) Läuten *nt*; (*of electric bell, alarm clock, phone*) Klingeln *nt*; **there was a ~ at the door** es hat geklingelt; **that has the** *or* **a ~ of truth (to** *or* **about it)** das klingt sehr wahrscheinlich

(b) (*esp Brit Telec*) Anruf *m*; **to give sb a ~** jdn anrufen **2** VI **(a)** (= *make sound*) klingen; (*bell, alarm bell*) läuten; (*electric bell, alarm clock, phone*) klingeln; **the (door)bell rang** es hat geklingelt; **to ~ for sb/sth** (nach) jdm/für etw läuten **(b)** (*esp Brit Telec*) anrufen

(c) (= *sound, resound: voice, music*) tönen; **to ~ true** wahr klingen; **my ears are ~ing** mir klingen die Ohren **3** VT **(a)** *bell* läuten; **to ~ the doorbell** (an der Tür) klingeln; **his name ~s a bell** (*fig inf*) sein Name kommt mir bekannt vor **(b)** (*esp Brit: also ~ up*) anrufen

▶ **ring back** VI, VT SEP (*esp Brit*) zurückrufen

▶ **ring in** VI (*esp Brit Telec*) sich telefonisch melden (*to* in +*dat*)

▶ **ring off** VI (*esp Brit Telec*) auflegen

▶ **ring out** VI (*bell*) ertönen; (*shot*) knallen; (= *sound above others*) herausklingen

▶ **ring up** VT SEP **(a)** (*esp Brit Telec*) anrufen **(b)** (*cashier*) eintippen; (*Comm*) *sales, profits* einnehmen

ring: ring binder N Ringbuch *nt*; **ring-fence** VT *funding, assets* reservieren

ringing ['rɪŋɪŋ] **1** ADJ *bell* läutend; *voice, tone* schallend; **~ tone** (*Brit Telec*) Rufzeichen *nt* **2** N (*of bell*) Läuten *nt*; (*of electric bell also, alarm clock, phone*) Klingeln *nt*; (*in ears*) Klingen *nt*

ring: ringleader N Anführer(in) *m(f)*; **ringmaster** N Zirkusdirektor *m*; **ring road** N (*Brit*) Umgehung(sstraße) *f*; **ring tone** N (*Telec*) Klingelton *m*

rink [rɪŋk] N Eisbahn *f*; (= *roller-skating ~*) Rollschuhbahn *f*

rinse [rɪns] **1** N Spülung *f*; (= *colorant*) Tönung *f*; **to give sth a ~** *clothes, hair* etw spülen; *plates* etw abspülen; *cup, mouth* etw ausspülen **2** VT **(a)** *clothes, hair* spülen; *plates* abspülen; *cup, mouth, basin* ausspülen **(b)** (= *colour with a ~*) *hair* tönen

➤ **rinse out** VT SEP auswaschen

Rio (de Janeiro) ['riːəʊ(dədʒə'nɪərəʊ)] N Rio (de Janeiro) *nt*

riot [raɪət] **1** N (*Pol*) Aufruhr *m no pl*; (*by mob, football fans etc*) Krawall *m*, Ausschreitungen *pl*; (*fig*) Orgie *f*; **to run ~** (*people*) randalieren; (*vegetation*) wuchern; **his imagination runs ~** seine Fantasie geht mit ihm durch; **a ~ of colour(s)** (*Brit*) *or* **color(s)** (*US*) eine Farbenexplosion **2** VI randalieren; (= *revolt*) einen Aufruhr machen

riot act N (*fig*) **to read sb the ~** jdm die Leviten lesen

rioter ['raɪətə'] N Randalierer(in) *m(f)*; (= *rebel*) Aufrührer(in) *m(f)*

rioting ['raɪətɪŋ] N Krawalle *pl*

riotous ['raɪətəs] ADJ **(a)** *person, crowd* randalierend; *behaviour* wild **(b)** (*inf*) (= *exuberant, boisterous*) wild; (= *hilarious*) urkomisch (*inf*)

rip [rɪp] **1** N Riss *m*; (*made by knife etc*) Schlitz *m* **2** VT *material* einen Riss machen in (+*acc*); (*stronger*) zerreißen; **to ~ open** aufreißen; (*with knife*) aufschlitzen **3** VI **(a)** (*cloth, garment*) reißen **(b)** (*inf*) **to let ~** loslegen (*inf*)

➤ **rip off** VT SEP **(a)** (*lit*) abreißen (*prep obj* von); *clothing* herunterreißen **(b)** (*inf*) *person* abzocken (*inf*)

➤ **rip through** VI +PREP OBJ (*explosion*) erschüttern; (*bullet*) durchbohren

➤ **rip up** VT SEP zerreißen; *road* aufreißen

ripe [raɪp] ADJ (+ER) **(a)** (*lit, fig*) reif; **to live to a ~ old age** ein hohes Alter erreichen; **to be ~ for sth** für etw reif sein; **to be ~ for the picking** pflückreif sein **(b)** (*inf*: = *pungent*) *smell* durchdringend

ripen ['raɪpən] **1** VT (*lit, fig*) reifen lassen **2** VI reifen

ripeness ['raɪpnɪs] N Reife *f*

rip-off ['rɪpɒf] N (*inf*) Wucher *m*; (= *cheat*) Schwindel *m*; (= *copy: of film, song etc*) Abklatsch *m*

ripple ['rɪpl] **1** N **(a)** (*in water*) kleine Welle **(b)** (= *noise*) Plätschern *nt*; **a ~ of laughter** ein kurzes Lachen **2** VI **(a)** (= *undulate: water*) sich kräuseln **(b)** (= *murmur: water*) plätschern **3** VT *water* kräuseln; *muscles* spielen lassen

rise [raɪz], *vb*: *pret* **rose**, *ptp* **risen 1** N **(a)** (= *increase*) (*in sth* etw *gen*) Anstieg *m*; (*in number*) Zunahme *f*; (*St Ex*) Aufschwung *m*; **a (pay) ~** (*Brit*) eine Gehaltserhöhung; **there has been a ~ in the number of participants** die Zahl der Teilnehmer ist gestiegen

(b) (*of sun*) Aufgehen *nt*; (*fig: to fame, power etc*) Aufstieg *m* (*to* zu)

(c) (= *small hill*) Erhebung *f*; (= *slope*) Steigung *f*

(d) (= *origin: of river*) Ursprung *m*; **to give ~ to sth** etw verursachen; *to speculation* zu etw führen; *to hopes, fears* etw aufkommen lassen

2 VI **(a)** (*from sitting, lying*) aufstehen; **~ and shine!** (*inf*) raus aus den Federn! (*inf*)

(b) (= *go up*) steigen; (*theatre curtain*) sich heben; (*sun, bread*) aufgehen; (*voice*) (*in volume*) sich erheben; (*in pitch*) höher werden; (*anger*) wachsen, zunehmen; **to ~ to the surface** an die Oberfläche kommen; **her spirits rose** ihre Stimmung hob sich; **to ~ to a crescendo** zu einem Crescendo anschwellen; **to ~ to fame** Berümtheit erlangen; **he rose to be President** er stieg zum Präsidenten auf

(c) (*ground*) ansteigen; (*mountains*) sich erheben

(d) (*also ~ up*) (= *revolt*) sich erheben; **to ~ (up) in protest (at sth)** protestierend gegen etw erheben

➤ **rise above** VI +PREP OBJ *level of inflation etc* ansteigen um mehr als; *insults etc* erhaben sein über (+*acc*)

➤ **rise up** VI (*person*) aufstehen; (*mountain etc*) sich erheben

risen ['rɪzn] PTP *of* **rise**

rising ['raɪzɪŋ] **1** N **(a)** (= *rebellion*) Aufstand *m* **(b)** (*of sun, star*) Aufgehen *nt*; (*of prices, river*) (An)steigen *nt*; (*of ground*)

Anstieg *m* **2** ADJ **(a)** *sun, star* aufgehend; *tide, barometer* steigend; *ground* ansteigend **(b)** (= *increasing*) steigend; *crime* zunehmend; *anger* wachsend **(c)** (*fig*) **a ~ politician** ein kommender Politiker

risk [rɪsk] **1** N Risiko *nt* (*also Insur*); (*in cpds*) -gefahr *f*; **health ~** Gesundheitsgefahr *f*; **to take** *or* **run ~s/a ~** Risiken/ein Risiko eingehen; **to take** *or* **run the ~ of doing sth** das Risiko eingehen, etw zu tun; **"cars parked at owners' ~"** „Parken auf eigene Gefahr"; **at the ~ of seeming stupid** auf die Gefahr hin, dumm zu scheinen; **some jobs are at ~** einige Stellen sind gefährdet; **to put sb at ~** jdn gefährden; **to put sth at ~** etw riskieren; **fire ~** Feuerrisiko *nt*; **to be a good (credit) ~** (*Fin*) eine gute Bonität haben

2 VT riskieren; **you'll ~ losing your job** Sie riskieren dabei, Ihre Stelle zu verlieren

risk capital N Risikokapital *nt*

riskily ['rɪskɪlɪ] ADV riskant

riskiness ['rɪskɪnɪs] N Riskantheit *f*

risk management N Absicherung *f* von Risiken

risky ['rɪskɪ] ADJ (+ER) riskant; **it's ~, it's a ~ business** das ist riskant

risqué ['riːskeɪ] ADJ gewagt

rite [raɪt] N Ritus *m*; **burial ~s** Bestattungsriten *pl*

ritual ['rɪtjʊəl] **1** ADJ **(a)** rituell **(b)** (*usu hum*) *comments, visit* üblich **2** N Ritual *nt*; **he went through the same old ~** (*fig*) er durchlief dasselbe alte Ritual

rival ['raɪvl] **1** N Rivale *m*, Rivalin *f* (*for* um, *to* für); (*Comm*) Konkurrent(in) *m(f)* **2** ADJ *groups, leaders* rivalisierend; *claims, plans, attraction* konkurrierend; **~ firm** Konkurrenzfirma *f*; **~ bid** Konkurrenzangebot *nt* **3** VT (*for affections*) rivalisieren mit; (*Comm*) konkurrieren mit; **his achievements ~ even yours** seine Leistungen können sich sogar mit deinen messen

rivalry ['raɪvlrɪ] N Rivalität *f*; (*Comm*) Konkurrenzkampf *m*

river ['rɪvə'] N Fluss *m*; (*major*) Strom *m*; **down ~** fluss-/stromabwärts; **up ~** fluss-/stromaufwärts; **the ~ Rhine** (*Brit*), **the Rhine ~** (*US*) der Rhein

river IN CPDS Fluss-; **riverbed** N Flussbett *nt*; **riverside 1** N Flussufer *nt*; **on/by the ~** am Fluss(ufer)

rivet ['rɪvɪt] **1** N Niete *f* **2** VT (*fig*) *attention* fesseln; **his eyes were ~ed to the screen** sein Blick war auf die Leinwand geheftet

riveting ['rɪvɪtɪŋ] ADJ fesselnd; **it's ~ stuff** es ist faszinierend

Riviera [rɪvɪ'eərə] N **the (French)/Italian ~** die französische/ italienische Riviera

road [rəʊd] N **(a)** Straße *f*; **by ~** (*send sth*) per Spedition; (*travel*) mit dem Bus/Auto *etc*; **she lives across the ~ (from us)** sie wohnt gegenüber (von uns); **my car is off the ~** just now ich kann mein Auto momentan nicht benutzen; **this vehicle shouldn't be on the ~** das Fahrzeug ist nicht verkehrstüchtig; **to take to the ~** sich auf den Weg machen; **to be on the ~** (= *travelling*) unterwegs sein; (*theatre company*) auf Tournee sein; (*car*) fahren; **is this the ~ to London?** geht es hier nach London?; (*signpost*) **"London ~"** „Londoner Straße"; **to have one for the ~** (*inf*) zum Abschluss noch einen trinken

(b) (*fig*) Weg *m*; **you're on the right ~** (*lit, fig*) Sie sind auf dem richtigen Weg; **on the ~ to ruin/success** auf dem Weg ins Verderben/zum Erfolg

In Großbritannien gibt es zwei Arten von Landstraßen: die wichtigeren, (man nennt sie auch **trunk roads***), tragen die Bezeichnung* **A roads***, die weniger wichtigen sind* **B roads***. Einige der* **A roads** *können mehrere Fahrbahnen für beide Fahrtrichtungen haben: Diese werden dann* **dual carriageways** *genannt. Der amerikanische Ausdruck dafür ist* **divided highway***.*

Die Benutzung des britischen Pendants zu den Autobahnen, die **motorways***, ist kostenlos. In den USA heißt dieser Straßentyp allgemein* **superhighway***, allerdings gibt es daneben noch einige ebenfalls gebräuchliche Bezeichnungen: die* **interstate highways** *verbinden mindestens zwei Staaten miteinander und sind manchmal gebührenfrei, meist kosten sie jedoch Maut, weshalb sie auch* **toll roads** *oder* **turnpikes** *heißen;* **expressways** *befinden sich normalerweise innerhalb oder in der Nähe von Städten; und* **freeways** *werden so genannt, weil sie gebührenfrei sind.*

road IN CPDS Straßen-; **road accident** N Verkehrsunfall *m*; **roadblock** N Straßensperre *f*; **road construction** N (*US*) Straßenbau *m*; **road rage** N Aggressivität *f* im Straßenverkehr; **road safety** N Verkehrssicherheit *f*; **road show** N (*Theat*) Tournee *f*; **roadside** ◼ N Straßenrand *m*; **along** *or* **by the ~** am Straßenrand ◻ ADJ *stall, pub* an der Straße; **roadsign** N (Straßen)verkehrszeichen *nt*; **road tax** N (*Brit*) Kraftfahrzeugsteuer *f*; **road transport** N Straßengüterverkehr *m*; **roadway** N Fahrbahn *f*; **roadworks** PL (*Brit*) Straßenbauarbeiten *pl*; **roadworthy** ADJ verkehrstüchtig

roam [rəʊm] ◼ VT wandern durch; **to ~ the streets** (*child, dog*) (in den Straßen) herumstreunen ◻ VI (herum)wandern

► **roam about** (*Brit*) *or* **around** ◼ VI herumwandern ◻ VI + PREP OBJ **to roam around the streets** durch die Straßen streifen

roar [rɔːʳ] ◼ VI (*person, crowd, lion, bull*) brüllen (**with** vor +*dat*); (*wind, engine*) heulen; (*sea, waterfall*) tosen; (*thunder*) toben; **to ~ at sb** jdn anbrüllen; **the car ~ed up the street** der Wagen donnerte die Straße hinauf ◻ VT (*also* ~ **out**) brüllen; **the fans ~ed their approval** die Fans grölten zustimmend ◼ N, NO PL (*of person, crowd, lion, bull*) Gebrüll *nt*; (*of wind, engine*) Heulen *nt*; (*of sea, waterfall*) Tosen *nt*; (*of thunder*) Toben *nt*; (*of traffic*) Donnern *nt*; ~**s of laughter** brüllendes Gelächter; **the ~s of the crowd/lion** das Brüllen der Menge/des Löwen

roaring [ˈrɔːrɪŋ] ◼ ADJ *person, crowd, lion, bull* brüllend; *sea, waterfall* tosend; *traffic, noise* donnernd; **a ~ success** ein voller Erfolg; **to do a ~ trade** (**in sth**) ein Riesengeschäft *nt* (mit etw) machen ◻ N = **roar 3**

roast [rəʊst] ◼ N Braten *m*; **pork ~** Schweinebraten *m* ◻ ADJ *pork, veal* gebraten; *potatoes* in Fett im Backofen gebraten; ~ **chicken** Brathähnchen *nt*; ~ **beef** Roastbeef *nt* ◼ VT *meat* braten; *coffee beans* rösten; **to ~ oneself by the fire** sich am Feuer braten lassen ◻ VI (*meat*) braten; (*inf: person*) irrsinnig schwitzen (*inf*)

roasting [ˈrəʊstɪŋ] ◼ N (a) (*lit*) Braten *nt* (b) (*inf: = criticism*) **to give sb a ~** jdm eine Standpauke halten ◻ ADJ (*inf: = hot*) knallheiß (*inf*)

roasting tin, roasting tray N Bräter *m*

rob [rɒb] VT *person* bestehlen; (*more seriously*) berauben; *shop, bank* ausrauben; **to ~ sb of sth** (*lit, fig*) jdm etw rauben; **I've been ~bed!** ich bin bestohlen worden!; (*= had to pay too much*) ich bin geneppt worden (*inf*)

robber [ˈrɒbəʳ] N Räuber(in) *m(f)*

robbery [ˈrɒbərɪ] N Raub *m* no pl; (*= burglary*) Einbruch *m* (*of* in +*acc*); **armed ~** bewaffneter Raubüberfall; **the bank ~** der Überfall auf die Bank

robe [rəʊb] N (*= garment*) Robe *f*; (*esp US: for house wear*) Morgenrock *m*

robin [ˈrɒbɪn] N Rotkehlchen *nt*

robot [ˈrəʊbɒt] N Roboter *m*

robust [rəʊˈbʌst] ADJ robust (*also Comm*); *structure* massiv; *build, constitution, flavour* kräftig; *attitude* entschieden; *speech, style* markig; *defence* stark; *exercise* hart

robustly [rəʊˈbʌstlɪ] ADV (a) (*= strongly, solidly*) robust (b) (*= determinedly*) energisch (c) *flavoured* kräftig

robustness [rəʊˈbʌstnɪs] N Robustheit *f* (*also Comm*); (*of structure*) Massivität *f*; (*of build, constitution*) Kräftigkeit *f*

rock¹ [rɒk] ◼ VT (a) (*= swing*) schaukeln; (*gently*) wiegen (b) (*= shake*) *town, building* erschüttern; (*fig inf*) **to ~ the boat** (*fig*) für Unruhe sorgen ◻ VI (a) (*gently*) schaukeln (b) (*violently*) (*building, tree*) schwanken; (*ground*) beben; **they ~ed with laughter** sie schüttelten sich *or* bebten vor Lachen ◼ N (*= pop music*) Rock *m*; (*= dance*) Rock n' Roll *m*

rock² N (a) (*= substance*) Stein *m*; (*= face*) Fels *m*; (*Geol*) Gestein *nt* (b) (*large mass*) Fels(en) *m*; (*= boulder also*) Felsbrocken *m*; (*smaller*) (großer) Stein; **the Rock (of Gibraltar)** der Felsen von Gibraltar; **as solid as a ~** *structure* massiv wie ein Fels; *firm, marriage* unerschütterlich wie ein Fels; **on the ~s** (*inf*) (*= with ice*) mit Eis; (*marriage etc*) kaputt (*inf*)

rock: **rock bottom** N der Tiefpunkt; **to be at ~** auf dem Tiefpunkt sein; **to reach** *or* **hit ~** den Tiefpunkt erreichen; **rock-bottom** ADJ (*inf*) *interest rates* niedrigste(r, s); ~ **prices** Niedrigstpreise *pl*; **rock-climber** N (Felsen)kletterer(in) *m(f)*; **rock climbing** N Klettern *nt* (im Fels)

rockery [ˈrɒkərɪ] N Steingarten *m*

rocket¹ [ˈrɒkɪt] ◼ N Rakete *f* ◻ VI (*prices*) hochschießen

rocket² N (*Cook*) Rucola *m*

rocket IN CPDS Raketen-; **rocket-propelled** ADJ mit Raketenantrieb; **rocket science** N (*lit*) Raketentechnik *f*; **it's not ~** (*inf*) dazu muss man kein Genie sein

rock: **rock face** N Felswand *f*; **rock fall** N Steinschlag *m*; **rock garden** N Steingarten *m*

Rockies [ˈrɒkɪz] PL **the ~** die Rocky Mountains *pl*

rocking [ˈrɒkɪŋ]: **rocking chair** N Schaukelstuhl *m*; **rocking horse** N Schaukelpferd *nt*

rock: **rock pool** N Wasserlache, die sich bei Ebbe zwischen Felsen bildet; **rock star** N (*Mus*) Rockstar *m*

rocky¹ [ˈrɒkɪ] ADJ (*= unsteady*) wackelig (*also fig inf*)

rocky² ADJ (+ER) *mountain* felsig; *road, path* steinig

Rocky Mountains PL **the ~** die Rocky Mountains *pl*

rod [rɒd] N Stab *m*; (*= switch*) Gerte *f*; (*in machinery*) Stange *f*; (*for punishment, fishing*) Rute *f*

rode [rəʊd] PRET *of* ride

rodent [ˈrəʊdənt] N Nagetier *nt*

roe¹ [rəʊ] N, *pl* -(**s**) (*species: also* ~ **deer**) Reh *nt*; ~**buck** Rehbock *m*; ~ **deer** (*female*) Reh *nt*, Ricke *f* (*spec*)

roe² N, *pl* - (*of fish*) Rogen *m*

rogue [rəʊg] ◼ N (*= scoundrel*) Gauner(in) *m(f)*; (*= scamp*) Schlingel *m* ◻ ADJ (a) (*= maverick*) einzelgängerisch; (*= criminal*) verbrecherisch (b) (*= abnormal, aberrant*) abnormal; *satellite* fehlgeleitet

role [rəʊl] N (*Theat, fig*) Rolle *f*

role: **role model** N (*Psych*) Rollenbild *nt*; **role-play** ◼ VI ein Rollenspiel durchführen ◻ VT als Rollenspiel durchführen; **role-playing** N Rollenspiel *nt*

roll [rəʊl] ◼ N (a) (*of paper, film, hair etc*) Rolle *f*; (*of fabric*) Ballen *m*; (*of banknotes*) Bündel *nt*; (*of flesh, fat*) Wulst *m*; **a ~ of paper** eine Rolle Papier
(b) (*Cook: also* **bread ~**) Brötchen *nt*; **cheese ~** Käsebrötchen *nt*
(c) (*of ship, thunder*) Rollen *nt*; (*of ship also*) Schlingern *nt*; (*= somersault, Aviat*) Rolle *f*; (*of drums*) Wirbel *m*; **to be on a ~** (*inf*) eine Glückssträhne haben
(d) (*= list, register*) Register *nt*; ~ **of honour** (*Brit*) Ehrenliste *f* ◻ VI (a) (*person, object*) rollen; (*ship*) schlingern; (*presses*) laufen; (*Aviat*) eine Rolle machen; **the stones ~ed down the hill** die Steine rollten den Berg hinunter; **tears were ~ing down her cheeks** Tränen rollten ihr über die Wangen; **the dog ~ed in the mud** der Hund wälzte sich im Schlamm; **he's ~ing in money or in it** (*inf*) er schwimmt im Geld (*inf*); **the words just ~ed off his tongue** die Worte flossen ihm nur so von den Lippen; **the credits ~ed** (*cine*) der Abspann lief
(b) (*= sound*) (*thunder*) grollen; (*drum*) wirbeln
(c) (*camera*) laufen ◼ VT *barrel, ball, car* rollen; *cigarette* drehen; *pastry* ausrollen; **to ~ one's eyes** die Augen rollen; **to ~ one's r's** das R rollen; **he ~ed himself in a blanket** er wickelte sich in eine Decke; **it has a kitchen and a dining room ~ed into one** es hat eine Küche und ein Esszimmer in einem

► **roll about** (*Brit*) *or* **around** VI (*balls*) herumrollen; (*ship*) schlingern; (*person, dog*) sich herumwälzen; (*inf: with laughter*) sich kugeln (vor Lachen) (*inf*)

► **roll along** ◼ VI (*ball*) entlangrollen ◻ VT SEP rollen

► **roll away** ◼ VI (*ball, vehicle*) wegrollen; (*clouds, mist*) abziehen ◻ VT SEP *trolley, table* wegrollen

► **roll back** ◼ VI zurückrollen; (*eyes*) nach innen rollen ◻ VT SEP *carpet* zurückrollen; *sheet* zurückschlagen

► **roll by** VI (*vehicle, procession*) vorbeirollen; (*clouds*) vorbeiziehen; (*time, years*) dahinziehen

► **roll down** ◼ VI hinunterrollen ◻ VT SEP *window* herunterlassen

► **roll in** ◼ VI hereinrollen; (*letters, contributions*) hereinströmen ◻ VT SEP *trolley* hereinrollen

► **roll on** VI weiterrollen; (*time*) verfliegen

► **roll out** ◼ VT SEP *barrel* hinausrollen; *pastry* ausrollen; *metal* auswalzen ◻ VI hinausrollen

► **roll over** ◼ VI herumrollen; (*vehicle*) umkippen; (*person*) sich umdrehen ◻ VT SEP umdrehen; *patient* auf die andere Seite legen

► **roll past** VI = **roll by**

➤ **roll up 1** VI **(a)** (*inf* = *arrive*) antanzen (*inf*) **(b)** (*at fairground etc*) **roll up!** treten Sie näher! **2** VT SEP *cloth, paper, map, umbrella* zusammenrollen; *sleeves, trouser legs* hochkrempeln

rolled [rəʊld] ADJ *blanket, paper etc* zusammengerollt; *tobacco* gerollt

roller ['rəʊləʳ] N Rolle *f*; (*for lawn, road, Ind*) Walze *f*; (= *hair ~*) (Locken)wickler *m*; **to put one's hair in ~s** sich (*dat*) die Haare aufdrehen

roller: Rollerblade® N Inliner *m*; **roller coaster** N Achterbahn *f*; **roller skate** N Rollschuh *m*; **roller-skate** VI Rollschuh laufen; **he ~d down the street** er fiel mit seinen Rollschuhen die Straße entlang; **roller-skating** N Rollschuhlaufen *nt*

rolling ['rəʊlɪŋ] ADJ **(a)** (= *swaying*) *motion* schwankend; *ship* schlingernd; *sea, waves* wogend; **to have a ~ gait** einen schaukelnden Gang haben **(b)** *hills* gewellt; *landscape* wellig **(c)** (= *progressing*) *plan, programme* kontinuierlich; *budget* rollend

rolling pin N Nudelholz *nt*

roll: rollneck N Rollkragen *m*; **rollneck(ed)** ADJ Rollkragen-; **roll-on** N (= *deodorant*) (Deo)roller *m*; **roll-up** N (*Brit inf*) Selbstgedrehte *f*

roly-poly ['rəʊlɪ'pəʊlɪ] ADJ (*inf*) kugelrund

ROM [rɒm] ABBR *of* read only memory ROM *m or nt*

Roman ['rəʊmən] **1** N **(a)** Römer(in) *m(f)* **(b)** (*Typ: also ~ type*) Magerdruck *m* **2** ADJ **(a)** römisch; **~ times** Römerzeit *f* **(b)** roman (*Typ*) mager

Roman: Roman Catholic 1 ADJ (römisch-)katholisch; **the ~ Church** die (römisch-)katholische Kirche **2** N Katholik(in) *m(f)*; **Roman Catholicism** N römisch-katholischer Glaube

romance [rəʊ'mæns] **1** N **(a)** (= *book*) Roman *m*; (= *love story*) Liebesgeschichte *f*; (*no pl*: = *romantic fiction*) Liebesromane *pl* **(b)** (= *love affair*) Romanze *f*; **it's quite a ~** das ist eine richtige Liebesgeschichte **(c)** NO PL (= *romanticism*) Romantik *f* **2** ADJ **Romance** *language etc* romanisch

Romanesque [,rəʊmə'nesk] ADJ romanisch

Romania [rəʊ'meɪnɪə] N Rumänien *nt*

Romanian [rəʊ'meɪnɪən] **1** ADJ rumänisch **2** N **(a)** Rumäne *m*, Rumänin *f* **(b)** (= *language*) Rumänisch *nt*

Roman: Roman nose N Römernase *f*; **Roman numeral** N römische Ziffer

Romansh [rəʊ'mænʃ] **1** ADJ romantsch **2** N Romantsch *nt*

romantic [rəʊ'mæntɪk] ADJ (*gen, Art etc: also* **Romantic**) romantisch; **they were very good friends but there was no ~ involvement** sie waren sehr enge Freunde, aber sie hatten keine Liebesbeziehung

romantically [rəʊ'mæntɪkəlɪ] ADV romantisch; **to be ~ involved with sb** eine Liebesbeziehung mit jdm haben

romanticism [rəʊ'mæntɪsɪzm] N (*Art, Liter, Mus: also* **Romanticism**) Romantik *f*

romanticize [rəʊ'mæntɪsaɪz] **1** VT romantisieren **2** VI fantasieren

Romany ['rəʊmənɪ] **1** N **(a)** Roma *mf* **(b)** (*Ling*) die Zigeunersprache, Romani *nt* **2** ADJ *language, culture* der Roma; **~ gypsy** Zigeuner(in) *m(f)*

Rome [rəʊm] N Rom *nt*; **when in ~ (do as the Romans do)** (*prov*) ≈ andere Länder, andere Sitten (*Prov*); **~ wasn't built in a day** (*Prov*) Rom ist auch nicht an einem Tag erbaut worden (*Prov*)

romp [rɒmp] **1** N Tollerei *f*; (*hum*: = *sexual intercourse*) Nümmerchen *nt* (*inf*) **2** VI (*children, puppies*) herumtollen; **to ~ home** (= *win*) spielend gewinnen; **to ~ through sth** mit etw spielend fertig werden

roof [ru:f] N Dach *nt*; (*of cave, tunnel*) Gewölbe *nt*; **the ~ of the mouth** der Gaumen; **without a ~ over one's head** ohne Dach über dem Kopf; **to live under the same ~ as sb** mit jdm unter demselben Dach wohnen; **to go through the ~** (*inf*) (*person*) an die Decke gehen (*inf*); (*prices etc*) untragbar werden

➤ **roof in** *or* **over** VT SEP überdachen

roof IN CPDS Dach-; **roof rack** N Dach(gepäck)träger *m*; **rooftop** N Dach *nt*; **to shout** *or* **scream sth from the ~s** (*fig*) etw überall herumposaunen (*inf*)

rook [rʊk] N **(a)** (= *bird*) Saatkrähe *f* **(b)** (*Chess*) Turm *m*

rookie ['rʊkɪ] N (*esp Mil sl*) Grünschnabel *m* (*inf*)

room [ru:m] **1** N **(a)** (*in house, building*) Zimmer *nt*; (= *public hall, ballroom etc*) Saal *m*; (= *office*) Büro *nt*; **the whole ~**

laughed alle im Zimmer lachten, der ganze Saal lachte **(b)** NO PL (= *space*) Platz *m*; (*fig*) Spielraum *m*; **is there (enough) ~?** ist da genügend Platz?; **there is ~ for two (people)** es ist genügend Platz für zwei (Leute); **to make ~ for sb/sth** für jdn/etw Platz machen; **there is no ~ for doubt** es kann keinen Zweifel geben; **there is ~ for improvement in your work** Ihre Arbeit könnte um einiges besser sein; **~ for manoeuvre** (*Brit*) *or* **maneuver** (*US*) Spielraum *m* **2** VI zur Untermiete wohnen

room clerk N (*US*) Empfangschef *m*, Empfangsdame *f*

-roomed [-ru:md] ADJ SUF **a 6-roomed house** ein Haus mit 6 Zimmern; **a two-roomed apartment** eine Zweizimmerwohnung

roomer ['ru:məʳ] N (*US*) Untermieter(in) *m(f)*

roomful ['ru:mfʊl] N **a ~ of people** ein Zimmer voll(er) Leute

room: roommate N (*Brit*) Zimmergenosse *m*, Zimmergenossin *f*; (*US*: = *flatmate*) Mitbewohner(in) *m(f)*; **room service** N Zimmerservice *m*; **room temperature** N Zimmertemperatur *f*

roomy ['ru:mɪ] ADJ (+ER) geräumig; *garment* weit

roost [ru:st] **1** N (= *pole*) Stange *f*; (= *henhouse*) Hühnerhaus *nt*; **to come home to ~** (*fig*) auf den Urheber zurückfallen **2** VI sich niederlassen; (= *sleep*) auf der Stange schlafen

rooster ['ru:stəʳ] N Hahn *m*

root [ru:t] **1** N **(a)** (*lit, fig*) Wurzel *f*; **~s** (*fig: of person*) Wurzeln; **by the ~s** mit der Wurzel; **to take ~** (*lit, fig*) Wurzeln schlagen; **her ~s are in Scotland** sie ist in Schottland verwurzelt; **to put down ~s in a country** in einem Land Fuß fassen; **the ~ of the matter** der Kern der Sache; **to get to the ~(s) of the problem** dem Problem auf den Grund gehen **(b)** (*Ling*) Stamm *m* **2** VI (*plants etc*) Wurzeln schlagen

➤ **root about** (*Brit*) *or* **around** VI herumwühlen (*for* nach)

➤ **root for** VI +PREP OBJ team anfeuern; **to root for sb** jdm die Daumen drücken; (*esp Sport*: = *cheer on*) jdn anfeuern

➤ **root out** VT SEP (*fig*) (= *remove*) mit der Wurzel ausreißen; (= *find*) aufspüren

root IN CPDS Wurzel-; **root beer** N (*US*) Art Limonade; **root cause** N eigentlicher Grund

rooted ['ru:tɪd] ADJ verwurzelt; **(deeply) ~** *objection, conviction etc* tief verwurzelt; **to be** *or* **stand ~ (to the spot)** wie angewurzelt dastehen

root vegetable N Wurzelgemüse *nt*

rope [rəʊp] **1** N Seil *nt*; (*Naut*) Tau *nt*; (= *hangman's ~*) Strang *m*; **to give sb more/plenty of ~** (*fig*) jdm mehr/viel Freiheit lassen; **I am at the end of my ~** (*US inf*) (= *annoyed, impatient*) mir reicht's (*inf*); (= *desperate*) ich bin am Ende; **to be on the ~s** (*inf*) in der Klemme sein; **to know the ~s** (*inf*) sich auskennen; **to show sb the ~s** (*inf*) jdn in alles einweihen; **to learn the ~s** (*inf*) sich einarbeiten **2** VT box, case verschnüren; **to ~ climbers (together)** Bergsteiger anseilen

➤ **rope in** VT SEP (*esp Brit fig*) rankriegen (*inf*); **how did you get roped into that?** wie bist du denn da reingeraten? (*inf*)

➤ **rope off** VT SEP area mit einem Seil abgrenzen

➤ **rope together** VT SEP objects zusammenbinden; climbers anseilen

rope IN CPDS Seil-; **rope ladder** N Strickleiter *f*

rosary ['rəʊzərɪ] N (*Rel*) Rosenkranz *m*

rose¹ [rəʊz] PRET *of* rise

rose² 1 N **(a)** Rose *f*; **marriage isn't all ~s** (*inf*) die Ehe hat auch ihre Schattenseiten; **everything's coming up ~s** (*inf*) alles läuft bestens (*inf*); **to come up smelling of ~s** (*inf*) gut dastehen; **that will put the ~s back in your cheeks** davon bekommst du wieder etwas Farbe im Gesicht **(b)** (= *colour*) Rosarot *nt* **2** ADJ rosarot

rosé ['rəʊzeɪ] **1** ADJ rosé **2** N Rosé *m*

rose IN CPDS Rosen-; **rosebush** N Rosenstrauch *m*; **rose-coloured**, (*US*) **rose-colored** ADJ rosarot, rosenrot; **rosehip** N Hagebutte *f*

rosemary ['rəʊzmərɪ] N Rosmarin *m*

rose petal N Rosen(blüten)blatt *nt*

rosette [rəʊ'zet] N Rosette *f*

roster ['rɒstəʳ] N Dienstplan *m*

rostrum ['rɒstrəm] N, *pl* **rostra** ['rɒstrə] Rednerpult *nt*; (*for conductor*) Dirigentenpult *nt*

rosy ['rəʊzɪ] ADJ (+ER) (= pink) rosarot; *complexion, cheeks, future* rosig; **to paint a ~ picture of sth** etw in den rosigsten Farben ausmalen

rot [rɒt] **1** N (a) (of wood) Fäulnis *f no pl*; **to stop the ~** (*lit, fig*) den Fäulnisprozess aufhalten; **then the ~ set in** (*fig*) dann setzte der Fäulnisprozess ein (b) (*inf*: = *rubbish*) Quatsch *m* (*inf*) **2** VI (*wood, material, rope*) verrotten, faulen; (*teeth, plant*) verfaulen; **to ~ in jail** im Gefängnis verrotten **3** VT verfaulen lassen

➤ **rot away** VI verfaulen

rota ['rəʊtə] N (*Brit*) Dienstplan *m*

rotary ['rəʊtərɪ] ADJ rotierend, Dreh-; **~ motion** Drehbewegung *f*

rotate [rəʊ'teɪt] **1** VT rotieren lassen; (*Comput*) rotieren; *head, body* drehen; *crops* im Wechsel anbauen; *work, jobs* turnusmäßig erledigen **2** VI rotieren; (*crops*) im Wechsel angebaut werden; (*people*: = *take turns*) sich (turnusmäßig) abwechseln

rotating [rəʊ'teɪtɪŋ] ADJ rotierend; *presidency* im Turnus wechselnd

rotation [rəʊ'teɪʃən] N Rotation *f*; (= *taking turns*) turnusmäßiger Wechsel; **in** *or* **by ~** im Turnus; **~ of crops, crop ~** Fruchtwechsel *m*

rote [rəʊt] N **by ~** *learn* auswendig; *recite, teach* mechanisch

rotten ['rɒtn] ADJ (a) faul; (*fig*: = *corrupt*) korrupt; **~ to the core** (*fig*) durch und durch verdorben; **~ apple** (*fig*) schwarzes Schaf

(b) (*inf*) (= *poor*) mies (*inf*); (= *unwell also*) elend; (= *dreadful, unpleasant*) scheußlich (*inf*); (= *mean*) gemein; (= *damned*) verdammt (*inf*); **to be ~ at sth** in etw (*dat*) schlecht sein; **I was always ~ at drawing** ich konnte noch nie gut zeichnen; **what ~ luck!** so ein Pech!; **it's a ~ business** das ist eine üble Sache; **that was a ~ trick/a ~ thing to do** das war ein übler Trick/eine Gemeinheit; **that's a ~ thing to say** es ist gemein, so etwas zu sagen; **to feel ~** sich elend fühlen; **to look ~** schlecht aussehen; **to feel ~ about doing sth** sich (*dat*) mies vorkommen, etw zu tun (*inf*); **to spoil sb ~** jdn nach Strich und Faden verwöhnen (*inf*)

rotting ['rɒtɪŋ] ADJ verfaulend; *teeth* faul; *fruit* faulig

rotund [rəʊ'tʌnd] ADJ *person* rund(lich); *object* rund

rouble, (US) ruble ['ruːbl] N Rubel *m*

rough [rʌf] **1** ADJ (+ER) (a) *ground, path* uneben; *surface, skin, cloth, voice, tone* rau; *sound, words* hart; *taste, wine* sauer

(b) (= *coarse, unrefined*) *person* ungehobelt; *manners, speech, plan, estimate* grob; **~ sketch** Faustskizze *f*; **at a ~ guess** grob geschätzt; **to give sb a ~ idea** jdm einen groben Anhaltspunkt geben; **to have a ~ idea** eine ungefähre Ahnung haben

(c) (= *violent*) *person, treatment* grob; *children's game* wild; *match, sport, work* hart; *neighbourhood, manners, pub* rau; *sea, weather, sea crossing* stürmisch; **to be ~ with sb** grob mit jdm umgehen

(d) (*inf*: = *unpleasant*) **he had a ~ time (of it)** es ging ihm ziemlich dreckig (*inf*); **to be in for a ~ time (of it)** harten Zeiten entgegensehen; **the examiners gave him a ~ time** die Prüfer haben ihn ganz schön rangenommen (*inf*); **to get a ~ ride** Schwierigkeiten bekommen; **to give sb a ~ ride** jdm die Hölle heiß machen (*inf*); **he faces a ~ ride from the media** die Medien werden es ihm nicht leicht machen; **when the going gets ~ ...** wenn es hart wird, ...; **to feel ~** sich mies fühlen (*inf*)

2 ADV *live* wüst; *play* wild; **to sleep ~** im Freien übernachten **3** N (a) **to take the ~ with the smooth** das Leben nehmen, wie es kommt

(b) (= *draft, sketch*) Rohentwurf *m*; **in (the) ~** im Rohzustand

roughage ['rʌfɪdʒ] N Ballaststoffe *pl*

rough: rough-and-ready ADJ *method, equipment, place* provisorisch; *work* zusammengehauen (*inf*); *person* rau(beinig); *measure, attitude* grob; **rough-and-tumble** N (= *play*) Balgerei *f*; (= *fighting*) Keilerei *f*; **rough copy** N Konzept *nt*; **rough draft** N Rohentwurf *m*

roughen ['rʌfn] **1** VT *skin, cloth* rau machen; *surface* aufrauhen **2** VI (*skin, voice*) rau werden

roughly ['rʌflɪ] ADV (a) (= *not gently, crudely*) grob; *play* rau (b) (= *approximately*) ungefähr; **~ (speaking)** grob gesagt; **~ half** ungefähr die Hälfte; **~ equal** ungefähr gleich; **~ similar** in etwa ähnlich

roughness ['rʌfnɪs] N (a) (of ground, road) Unebenheit *f*; (of surface, skin, cloth, voice, tone) Rauheit *f* (b) (= *coarseness*) (of person) Ungehobeltheit *f*; (of manners, speech) Grobheit *f* (c) (= *violence*) (of person) Grobheit *f*; (of treatment, match, sport) Härte *f*; (of children's game) Wildheit *f*; (of neighbourhood, manners, pub) Rauheit *f*

rough: rough paper N Konzeptpapier *nt*; **roughshod** ADV **to ride ~ over sb/sth** rücksichtslos über jdn/etw hinweggehen

roulette [ruːˈlet] N Roulett(e) *nt*

round [raʊnd] **1** ADJ (+ER) rund; **~ figure, ~ number** runde Zahl **2** ADV (*esp Brit*) **there was a wall right ~** *or* **all ~** rundherum war eine Mauer; **you can't get through here, you'll have to go ~** Sie können hier nicht durch, Sie müssen außen herum gehen; **the long way ~** der längere Weg; **~ and ~** (= *in circles, ~ field etc*) rundherum; (= *all over the place*) überall herum; **I asked him ~ for a drink** ich lud ihn auf ein Glas Wein/Bier *etc* bei mir ein; **I'll be ~ at 8 o'clock** ich werde um 8 Uhr da sein; **for the second time ~** zum zweiten Mal; **all (the) year ~** das ganze Jahr über; **all ~** (*lit*) ringsherum; (*esp Brit fig: for everyone*) für alle

3 PREP (a) (*esp Brit: of place etc*) um (... herum); **all ~ the house** (*inside*) im ganzen Haus; (*outside*) um das ganze Haus herum; **to look** *or* **see ~ a house** (*dat*) ein Haus ansehen; **to show sb ~ a town** jdm eine Stadt zeigen; **they went ~ the cafés looking for him** sie gingen in alle Cafés, um nach ihm zu suchen

(b) (= *approximately*) ungefähr; **~ (about** (*esp Brit*) **7 o'clock** ungefähr um 7 Uhr; **~ (about** (*esp Brit*) **£800** um die £ 800

4 N (a) (= *circle etc*) Kreis *m*

(b) (= *delivery ~, Sport, of election, talks*) Runde *f*; (*Showjumping*) Durchgang *m*; **~(s)** (of policeman, doctor) Runde *f*; **to be (out) on one's ~(s)** auf seiner Runde sein; **to go** *or* **do the ~s** (*visiting relatives etc*) die Runde machen; (*story etc*) reihum gehen; **he does a paper ~** (*Brit*) er trägt Zeitungen aus; **a ~ (of drinks)** eine Runde; **~ of ammunition** Ladung *f*; **10 ~s of bullets** 10 Schuss; **a ~ of applause** Applaus *m*

5 VT (a) (= *make*) ~ runden

(b) *corner, bend* gehen/fahren um; *obstacle* herumgehen/-fahren um

➤ **round down** VT SEP *price, number* abrunden

➤ **round off** VT SEP *list, series* voll machen; *speech, meal* abrunden; *debate, meeting, one's career* abschließen

➤ **round on** VI +PREP OBJ (*verbally*) anfahren; (*in actions*) herumfahren zu

➤ **round up** VT SEP (a) *people* zusammentrommeln (*inf*); *cattle* zusammentreiben; *criminals* hochnehmen (*inf*) (b) *price, number* aufrunden

➤ **round upon** VI +PREP OBJ = round on

roundabout ['raʊndəbaʊt] **1** ADJ *answer, question* umständlich; **~ route** Umweg *m*; **what a ~ way of doing things!** wie kann man nur so umständlich sein!; **by ~ means** auf Umwegen; **to say sth in a ~ way** etw auf Umwegen sagen **2** N (*Brit*) (*at fair, in playground*) Karussell *nt*; (*Mot*) Kreisverkehr *m*

rounded ['raʊndɪd] ADJ rundlich; *edges, style* abgerundet; **(well-)rounded** *bosom, figure* wohlgerundet; *sentences, style* abgerundet

roundly ['raʊndlɪ] ADV *condemn, criticize* rundum; *defeat* klar

roundness ['raʊndnɪs] N Rundheit *f*

round: round-table discussion N Diskussion *f* am runden Tisch; **round-the-clock** ADJ (*Brit*) rund um die Uhr *not attr*; **round trip** N Rundreise *f*; **round-trip ticket** N (*US*) Rückfahrkarte *f*; (*Aviat*) Hin- und Rückflugticket *nt*; **roundup** N (of cattle) Zusammentreiben *nt*; (of people) Zusammentrommeln *nt*; (of criminals) Hochnehmen *nt* (*inf*); **a ~ of today's news** eine Zusammenfassung der Nachrichten vom Tage

rouse [raʊz] VT (a) (*from sleep etc*) wecken (b) (= *stimulate*) *person* bewegen; *feeling, admiration, interest* wecken; *hatred, indignation, suspicions* erregen; **to ~ sb (to anger)** jdn reizen; **to ~ sb to action** jdn zum Handeln bewegen

rousing ['raʊzɪŋ] ADJ *speech, sermon* mitreißend; *applause* stürmisch; *music* schwungvoll; *chorus* schallend; *reception* überschwänglich

roust [raʊst] VT (*US*) (*also* **~ out**) vertreiben; (= *call out*) kommen lassen; **to ~ sb out of bed, to ~ sb out** jdn aus dem Bett holen

rout [raʊt] **1** N Schlappe *f* **2** VT in die Flucht schlagen

route [ru:t, (US) raʊt] **1** N **(a)** Strecke f; (bus service) Linie f; (fig: in planning etc) Weg m; **shipping ~s** Schifffahrtsstraßen; **what ~ does the 39 bus take?** welche Strecke fährt der 39er-Bus?; **"all ~s"** (Mot) „alle Richtungen" **(b)** (US: = delivery round) Runde f **2** VT train, bus legen; telephone call leiten; **my baggage was ~d through Amsterdam** mein Gepäck wurde über Amsterdam geschickt

routine [ru:'ti:n] **1** N **(a)** Routine f (also Comput); **as a matter of ~** routinemäßig
(b) (Dancing, Skating) Figur f; (Gymnastics) Übung f **2** ADJ Routine-, routinemäßig; **~ duties** tägliche Pflichten pl; **~ examination** Routineuntersuchung f; **~ flight** Routineflug m; **on a ~ basis** routinemäßig; **to be ~ procedure** Routine(sache) sein; **it was quite ~** es war eine reine Formsache; **reports of bloodshed had become almost ~** Berichte über Blutvergießen waren fast an der Tagesordnung

routinely [ru:'ti:nlɪ] ADV use, torture regelmäßig; test routinemäßig; describe üblicherweise

rove [rəʊv] **1** VI (person) umherwandern; (eyes) umherschweifen **2** VT countryside, streets durchwandern

roving ['rəʊvɪŋ] ADJ **he has a ~ eye** er ist riskiert gern ein Auge

row¹ [rəʊ] N Reihe f; **4 failures in a ~** 4 Misserfolge hintereinander; **arrange them in ~s** stell sie in Reihen auf

row² [rəʊ] **1** VI (in boat) rudern **2** VT rudern; **to ~ sb across** jdn hinüberrudern; **to ~ stroke** Schlagmann sein

row³ [raʊ] **1** N (esp Brit inf) (= noise) Lärm m; (= quarrel) Streit m; **to make a or kick up (inf) a ~** Krach schlagen (inf); **to have a ~ with sb** mit jdm Streit haben; **to get a ~** Krach bekommen (inf); **to give sb a ~** jdn runtermachen (inf) **2** VI (= quarrel) (sich) streiten

rowan ['raʊən] N (= tree) Vogelbeere f; **~ berry** Vogelbeere f

rowboat ['rəʊbəʊt] N (US) Ruderboot nt

rowdiness ['raʊdɪnɪs] N (= noisiness) Lärmen nt; (= disorderliness) rüpelhaftes Benehmen

rowdy ['raʊdɪ] ADJ (+ER) (= noisy) laut; football fans randalierend; behaviour grob; event, scene gewalttätig; party chaotisch

rower ['rəʊər] N Ruderer m, Ruderin f

row house ['rəʊhaʊs] N (US) Reihenhaus nt

rowing¹ ['rəʊɪŋ] N Rudern nt

rowing² ['raʊɪŋ] N (esp Brit = quarrelling) Streiterei f

rowing boat ['rəʊɪŋbəʊt] N (Brit) Ruderboot nt

royal ['rɔɪəl] **1** ADJ königlich; (fig also) fürstlich; **the ~ family** die königliche Familie; **he's a ~ pain (in the neck)** (inf) er geht einem tierisch auf die Nerven (inf) **2** N (inf) Angehörige(r) mf der königlichen Familie

royal: Royal Air Force N (Brit) Königliche Luftwaffe; **royal blue** N Königsblau nt; **royal-blue** ADJ königsblau; **Royal Highness** N **Your/His** = Eure/Seine Königliche Hoheit

royalist ['rɔɪəlɪst] **1** ADJ royalistisch **2** N Royalist(in) m(f)

royally ['rɔɪəlɪ] ADV königlich; **(right)** ~ (fig: = lavishly) fürstlich

royal: Royal Mail N (Brit) britischer Postdienst; **Royal Marines** PL (Brit) britische Marineinfanterie; **Royal Navy** (Brit) **1** N Königliche Marine **2** ATTR der Königlichen Marine

royalty ['rɔɪəltɪ] N **(a)** (= dignity, rank) das Königtum; (collectively) das Königshaus; **he's ~** er gehört zur königlichen Familie **(b) royalties** PL (on auf +acc) (from book, records) Tantiemen pl; (from patent) Lizenzgebühren pl

rpm ABBR of **revolutions per minute** U/min

RSVP ABBR of **répondez s'il vous plaît** u. A. w. g.

rub [rʌb] **1** N Reiben nt; (with duster etc) Polieren nt; **to give sth a ~** (with duster etc) etw polieren **2** VT reiben; (= polish) polieren; **to ~ lotion into sth/oneself** etw/sich mit einer Lotion einreiben; **to ~ one's hands**

(together) (in or with glee) sich (dat) (vor Freude) die Hände reiben; **to ~ sb's nose in sth** (fig) jdm etw dauernd unter die Nase reiben; **to ~ shoulders** (esp Brit) or **elbows** (esp US) **with all sorts of people** (fig) mit allen möglichen Leuten in Berührung kommen; **to ~ sb the wrong way** (US) bei jdm anecken **3** VI (thing) (against an +dat) reiben; (collar) scheuern; **the cat ~bed against my legs/the tree** die Katze strich mir um die Beine/scheuerte sich am Baum

▶ **rub down** VT SEP horse (= dry) abreiben; (= clean) striegeln; person abrubbeln (inf); wall, paintwork (= clean) abwaschen; (= sandpaper) abschmirgeln

▶ **rub in** VT SEP **(a)** oil, lotion einreiben (prep obj, -to in +acc); butter hinzureiben **(b)** (fig) **don't rub it in!** (= don't keep mentioning) reite nicht so darauf herum!; (= don't keep alluding to) musst du auch noch Salz in die Wunde streuen?

▶ **rub off 1** VT SEP dirt, paint, gold-plating abreiben; (through wear) abwetzen; (from blackboard) auswischen **2** VI (lit, fig) abgehen; **to rub off on sb** (fig) auf jdn abfärben

▶ **rub out** VT SEP stain etc herausreiben; (with eraser) ausradieren

▶ **rub up 1** VT SEP **to rub sb up the wrong way** (Brit) bei jdm anecken **2** VI **the cat rubbed up against my leg** die Katze strich mir um die Beine

rubber ['rʌbər] **1** N (= material) Gummi m; (Brit: = eraser) (Radier)gummi m; (esp US sl: = contraceptive) Gummi m (inf) **2** ADJ Gummi-

rubber: rubber band N Gummiband nt; **rubber stamp** N Stempel m; **rubber-stamp** VT (fig inf) genehmigen

rubbery ['rʌbərɪ] ADJ **(a)** material, skin gummiartig; meat zäh, wie Gummi **(b)** (= weak) gummiweich (inf)

rubbing ['rʌbɪŋ] N Reiben nt; (with towel) Frottieren nt; (= polishing) Polieren nt; (with sandpaper) Schmirgeln nt

rubbish ['rʌbɪʃ] (esp Brit) **1** N **(a)** Abfall m; (on building site) Schutt m; (fig: = trashy goods, record etc) Mist m; **household ~** Hausmüll m; **garden ~** Gartenabfälle pl
(b) (inf: = nonsense) Quatsch m (inf); **don't talk ~!** red keinen Quatsch! (inf); **he talked a lot or a load of ~** er hat eine Menge Blödsinn verzapft (inf); **(what a lot of) ~!** (so ein) Quatsch! (inf) **2** ATTR (inf) **(a)** = rubbishy
(b) **I'm ~ at ~** it ich bin zu blöd dazu (inf)

rubbish IN CPDS (esp Brit) Müll-; **rubbish bin** N Mülleimer m; **rubbish collection** N Müllabfuhr f; **rubbish dump** N Müllablageplatz m; (in garden: also **rubbish heap**) Abfallhaufen m

rubbishy ['rʌbɪʃɪ] ADJ (Brit inf) goods minderwertig; magazine, film mies (inf); ideas blödsinnig

rubble ['rʌbl] N Trümmer pl; (smaller pieces) Schutt m

ruble ['ru:bl] N (US) = **rouble**

ruby ['ru:bɪ] **1** N (= stone) Rubin m; (colour: also ~ **red**) Rubinrot nt **2** ADJ wine, lips rubinrot; (= made of rubies) Rubin-

ruby wedding (anniversary) N vierzigster Hochzeitstag, Rubinhochzeit f

ruck [rʌk] N (= wrinkle) Falte f

▶ **ruck up 1** VT SEP rug verschieben; **his shirt is all rucked up** sein Hemd hat sich hochgeschoben **2** VI (shirt etc) sich hochschieben; (rug) Falten schlagen

ruckus ['rʌkəs] N (inf) Krawall m

ruction ['rʌkʃən] N (inf) USU PL Krach m no pl; **there'll be ~s if you do that** es gibt Krach, wenn du das tust

rudder ['rʌdər] N (Naut, Aviat) Ruder nt

rudderless ['rʌdəlɪs] ADJ ohne Ruder; (fig) führungslos

ruddy ['rʌdɪ] ADJ (+ER) face, complexion rot; sky, glow rötlich

rude [ru:d] ADJ (+ER) **(a)** (= impolite) unhöflich; (stronger) unverschämt; (= rough, uncouth) grob; **to be ~ to sb** unhöflich zu jdm sein; **it's ~ to stare** es gehört sich nicht, Leute anzustarren; **don't be so ~!** so was sagt man/tut man nicht! **(b)** (= obscene, dirty) unanständig; **to make a ~ gesture at sb** jdm gegenüber eine anstößige Geste machen **(c)** shock bös, hart; reminder unsanft

rudely ['ru:dlɪ] ADV **(a)** (= impolitely) unhöflich; (stronger) unverschämt; (= roughly, uncouthly) grob; push rüde **(b)** (= obscenely) unanständig **(c)** awaken, remind, shatter unsanft

rudeness ['ruːdnɪs] N **(a)** (= *impoliteness*) Unhöflichkeit *f*; (*stronger*) Unverschämtheit *f* **(b)** (= *obscenity*) Unanständigkeit *f* **(c)** (= *harshness: of shock*) Härte *f*

rudimentary [ruːdɪ'mentərɪ] ADJ *principles* elementar; *equipment* primitiv; *language, system* rudimentär; **~ knowledge** Grundkenntnisse *pl*

rudiments ['ruːdɪmənts] PL Grundlagen *pl*

rueful ['ruːfʊl] ADJ reuig, reuevoll

ruefully ['ruːfəlɪ] ADV reuevoll

ruffian ['rʌfɪən] N Rüpel *m*; (*violent*) Schläger *m*

ruffle ['rʌfl] VT **(a)** *hair, feathers* zerzausen; *surface, water* kräuseln; *bedspread, clothes* verkrumpeln (*inf*); **the bird ~d (up) its feathers** der Vogel plusterte sich auf **(b)** (*fig*) (= *upset, disturb*) aus der Ruhe bringen; (= *annoy*) verärgern; **to ~ sb's feathers** jdn aufregen

ruffled ['rʌfld] ADJ **(a)** (= *flustered*) *person* aufgebracht; *feelings* erregt; **to smooth sb's ~ feathers** jdn besänftigen, jds erregtes Gemüt besänftigen **(b)** *bedclothes* zerwühlt; *hair* zerzaust **(c)** *shirt, skirt* gekräuselt

rug [rʌg] N **(a)** Teppich *m*; (*esp rectangular*) Läufer *m*; (*valuable*) Brücke *f*; **to pull the ~ from under sb** jdm den Boden unter den Füßen wegziehen **(b)** (= *blanket*) (Woll)decke *f*

rugby ['rʌgbɪ] N (*also ~ football*) Rugby *nt*

rugged ['rʌgɪd] ADJ rau; *cliff, mountains* zerklüftet; *ground* felsig; *features* markig; *determination* wild; *resistance* verbissen

ruggedness ['rʌgɪdnɪs] N Rauheit *f*; (*of ground*) Felsigkeit *f*; (*of features*) Markigkeit *f*

ruin ['ruːɪn] **1** N **(a)** NO PL (*of thing, person*) Untergang *m*; (*of event*) Ende *nt*; (*financial, social*) Ruin *m*; **the palace was going to ~** *or* **falling into ~** der Palast verfiel (zur Ruine); **it will be the ~ of him** das wird ihn ruinieren **(b)** (= *ruined building*) Ruine *f*; (*fig: = person*) Wrack *nt*; **~s** (*of building*) Ruinen *pl*; (*of hopes, career*) Trümmer *pl*; **to be** *or* **lie in ~s** (*lit*) eine Ruine sein; (*fig*) zerstört sein; (*life: financially, socially*) ruiniert sein **2** VT (= *destroy*) zerstören; (*financially, socially*) ruinieren; (= *spoil*) verderben

ruined ['ruːɪnd] ADJ **(a)** *building, city* in Ruinen *pred*, zerfallen **(b)** *economy, career, finances* ruiniert

ruinous ['ruːɪnəs] ADJ (*financially*) ruinös; *price* extrem

rule [ruːl] **1** N **(a)** Regel *f*; (*Admin*) Vorschrift *f*; **to play by the ~s** (*lit, fig*) die Spielregeln einhalten; **to bend** *or* **stretch the ~s** es mit den Regeln/Vorschriften nicht so genau nehmen; **running is against the ~s, it's against the ~s to run** Rennen ist nicht erlaubt; **to do sth by** ~ etw vorschriftsmäßig tun; **as a ~ of thumb** als Faustregel; **~ book** Regelheft *nt*; **as a (general) ~** in der Regel; **violence is the ~ rather than the exception** Gewalt ist eher (die) Regel als (die) Ausnahme **(b)** (= *authority, reign*) Herrschaft *f*; (= *period*) Regierungszeit *f*; **the ~ of law** die Rechtsstaatlichkeit **2** VT **(a)** (= *govern*) regieren; (*individual*) beherrschen; (*fig*) *emotions etc* beherrschen; **to ~ the roost** (*fig*) Herr im Haus sein (*inf*); **to be ~d by emotions** sich von Gefühlen beherrschen lassen; **he let his heart ~ his head** er ließ sich von seinem Herzen und nicht von seinem Verstand leiten **(b)** (*Jur, Sport, Admin*) entscheiden **(c)** *paper* linieren; *line, margin* ziehen; **~d paper** liniertes Papier **3** VI **(a)** (*lit, fig: = reign*) herrschen (*over* über +*acc*) **(b)** (*Fin: = prices*) notieren **(c)** (*Jur*) entscheiden (*against* gegen, *in favour of* für, *on* in +*dat*)

▶ **rule out** VT SEP (*fig*) ausschließen

ruler ['ruːləʳ] N **(a)** (*for measuring*) Lineal *nt* **(b)** (= *sovereign*) Herrscher(in) *m(f)*

ruling ['ruːlɪŋ] **1** ADJ **(a)** *body, elite* herrschend; **the ~ party** die Regierungspartei **(b)** (= *determining*) *factor* ausschlaggebend; (= *prevalent*) (vor)herrschend; (*Fin, St Ex*) *prices* notiert **2** N (*Admin, Jur*) Entscheidung *f*

rum [rʌm] N Rum *m*; **~ toddy** Grog *m*

Rumania *etc* [ruː'meɪnɪə] = **Romania** *etc*

rumble ['rʌmbl] **1** N (*of thunder*) Grollen *nt no pl*; (*of stomach*) Knurren *nt no pl*; (*of train, truck*) Rumpeln *nt no pl* **2** VI (*thunder*) grollen; (*stomach*) knurren; (*train, truck*) rumpeln; **to ~ past/along/off** vorbei-/entlang-/davonrumpeln

▶ **rumble on** VI (*Brit: controversy*) weiter schwelen

rumbling ['rʌmblɪŋ] N (*of thunder*) Grollen *nt no pl*; (*of stomach*) Knurren *nt no pl*; (*of train, truck*) Rumpeln *nt no pl*

ruminate ['ruːmɪneɪt] VI (*fig*) grübeln (*over, about, on* über +*acc*)

rummage ['rʌmɪdʒ] **1** N **(a) to have a good ~ in sth** etw gründlich durchwühlen **(b)** (= *jumble*) Ramsch *m* **2** VI (*also ~ about, ~ around*) herumwühlen (*among, in* in +*dat*, *for* nach)

rumour, (*US*) **rumor** ['ruːməʳ] **1** N Gerücht *nt*; **~ has it that ...** es geht das Gerücht, dass ...; **as ~ has it** wie es Gerüchten zufolge heißt; **there are ~s of war** es gehen Kriegsgerüchte um **2** VT **it is ~ed that ...** es gibt das Gerücht, dass ...; **he is ~ed to be in London** Gerüchten zufolge ist er in London; **he is ~ed to be rich** er soll angeblich reich sein

rump [rʌmp] N (*of animal*) Hinterbacken *pl*; (*inf: of person*) Hinterteil *nt*; **~ steak** Rumpsteak *nt*

rumple ['rʌmpl] VT (*also ~ up*) *clothes, paper* zerknittern; *hair* zerzausen

rumpled ['rʌmpld] ADJ *clothes, sheets* zerknittert; *person* unordentlich; *hair* zerzaust

rumpus ['rʌmpəs] N (*inf*) Krach *m* (*inf*); **to make a ~** (= *make noise*) einen Heidenlärm machen (*inf*); (= *complain*) Krach schlagen (*inf*)

rumpus room N (*US*) Spielzimmer *nt*

---

run [rʌn]

1 NOUN	**3** TRANSITIVE VERB
2 INTRANSITIVE VERB	**4** PHRASAL VERBS

---

vb: pret **ran**, *ptp* **run**

1 NOUN

(a) (= *act of running*) Lauf *m* (*also Cricket, Baseball*); **to go for a 2-km run** einen 2-km-Lauf machen; **let the dog have a run** lass den Hund laufen; **he set off at a run** er rannte los; **to break into a run** zu laufen anfangen; **to make a run for it** weglaufen; **he made a run for the door** er lief zur Tür

✦**on the run** (*from the police etc*) auf der Flucht; **at last we've got them on the run!** endlich haben wir sie in die Flucht geschlagen!; **to keep the enemy on the run** den Feind weiter zur Flucht zwingen

✦**a good run for one's money** **we'll give him a good run for his money, he'll have a good run for his money** (*inf*) wir werden ihn auf Trab halten (*inf*)

(b) (*in vehicle*) Fahrt *f*; (*for pleasure*) Ausflug *m*; (*in plane*) Flug *m*; (= *route*) Strecke *f*; **to go for a run in the car** eine Fahrt/einen Ausflug im Auto machen

✦**in the long run** auf die Dauer

✦**in the short run** fürs Nächste

(c) to have the run of a place einen Ort zur freien Verfügung haben

(d) (= *series*) Folge *f*, Serie *f*; (*Theat*) Spielzeit *f*; (*of film*) Laufzeit *f*; **the play had a long run** das Stück lief sehr lange; **a run of luck/of bad luck** eine tolle Glücks-/Pechsträhne

(e) (= *great demand*) **run on** Ansturm *m* auf (+*acc*); (*St Ex, Fin*) Run *m or* Ansturm *m* auf (+*acc*)

(f) (*of market, opinion*) Tendenz *f*; (*of events*) Lauf *m*

(g) (= *track for sledging, skiing*) Bahn *f*; **ski run** Abfahrt(sstrecke) *f*

(h) (= *animal enclosure*) Gehege *nt*; (*for chickens*) Hühnerhof *m*

(i) (= *diarrhoea*) (*inf*) **the runs** der flotte Otto (*inf*)

2 INTRANSITIVE VERB

(a) laufen, rennen; (*in race*) laufen; (= *flee*) wegrennen; **she came running out** sie kam herausgelaufen; **to run down a slope** einen Abhang hinunterlaufen; **run!** lauf!; **walk, don't run!** du sollst gehen, nicht rennen!; **he's trying to run before he can walk** (*fig*) er sollte erst einmal langsam machen; **to run for the bus** zum Bus rennen; **she ran to meet him** sie lief ihm entgegen; **she ran to help him** sie kam ihm zu Hilfe; **to run in the 100 metres** (*US*) die 100 Meter laufen; **to run for one's life** um sein Leben rennen; **run for it!** rennt, was ihr könnt!

(b) (*story, words*) gehen; **the lyrics ran through my head** der Text ging mir durch den Kopf; **he ran down the list** er ging die Liste durch; **a shiver ran down her spine** ein Schauer lief

ihr über den Rücken; **his fingers ran over the sculpture** seine Finger glitten über die Plastik
+ **to run in the family** in der Familie liegen
(c) (= *stand as candidate*) kandidieren; **to run for President** or **for the Presidency** für die Präsidentschaft kandidieren
(d) (= *be*) **I'm running a bit late** ich bin ein bisschen spät dran; **all planes are running late** alle Flugzeuge haben Verspätung; **the project is running late/to schedule** das Projekt hat sich verzögert/geht ganz nach Plan voran; **supplies are running low** Vorräte sind knapp; **his blood ran cold** das Blut fror ihm in den Adern
+ **to run dry** (*river*) austrocknen; (*resources, funds*) ausgehen
+ **to be running at** (= *stand*) betragen; **interest rates are running at record levels/15%** die Zinssätze sind auf Rekordhöhe/stehen auf 15%
(e) (= *slide*) (*drawer, curtains, rope*) gleiten; (*vehicle*) rollen
(f) (= *flow*) (*water, tears, tap, nose*) laufen; (*river, electric current, ink*) fließen; (*eyes*) tränen; (*paint, colour*) zerfließen; (*colour, dye: in washing*) färben; **let the water run hot** lass das Wasser laufen, bis es heiß kommt; **your bath is running** dein Badewasser läuft ein
+ **to be running with** **the walls were running with damp** die Wände tropften vor Feuchtigkeit
+ **to run into** **where the river runs into the sea** wo der Fluss ins Meer mündet
(g) (*play, film, contract*) laufen; (*Fin: interest rate*) gelten
+ **to run into** (*with amounts, numbers*) **the expenditure runs into thousands of pounds** die Ausgaben gehen in die tausende (von Pfund)
+ **to run and run** (*story, production*) noch lange laufen; (*debate*) noch lange fortgesetzt werden
(h) (*bus, train etc*) fahren; **the train doesn't run on Sundays** der Zug fährt sonntags nicht
(i) (= *function*) (*lit, fig*) laufen (*also* Comput); (*factory*) arbeiten; **this model runs on diesel** dieses Auto fährt mit Diesel; **the radio runs off batteries** das Radio läuft auf Batterie; **things are running smoothly** alles läuft glatt
(j) (*road*) führen; (*mountains*) sich ziehen; (*river*) fließen; **a wall runs (a)round the garden** um den Garten zieht sich eine Mauer; **the railway line runs for 300 km** die Bahnlinie ist 300 km lang; **this theme runs through all his work** dieses Thema zieht sich durch sein ganzes Werk

🖪 TRANSITIVE VERB

(a) laufen; (*distance also*) rennen; **the first race will be run at 2 o'clock** das erste Rennen findet um 2 Uhr statt; **to run errands** Botengänge machen; **to run its/their course** seinen/ihren Lauf nehmen; **to run a temperature** or **a fever** Fieber haben; (= *set in*) **to run sb off his feet** (*inf*) jdn ständig auf Trab halten (*inf*); **to run sb into debt** jdn in Schulden stürzen; **I'll run you a bath** ich lasse dir ein Bad einlaufen
(b) (*vehicle*) fahren; (*passenger also*) bringen; (*extra buses, trains*) einsetzen; **he ran the car into a tree** er fuhr das Auto gegen einen Baum; **this company runs a bus service** diese Firma unterhält einen Busdienst
(c) (*machine, engine*) betreiben; (*computer*) laufen lassen; (*software*) benutzen; (*program*) laden; (*experiment, test*) durchführen; (*person*) bedienen; **to run a radio off the mains** ein Radio ans Netz laufen lassen; **I can't afford to run a car** ich kann es mir nicht leisten, ein Auto zu unterhalten; **this car is cheap to run** dieses Auto ist billig im Unterhalt; **can you run SuperText 3 on your computer?** läuft SuperText 3 auf deinem Computer?
(d) (= *manage, be in charge of*) leiten; (*shop*) führen; (= *organize*) (*course of study, competition*) durchführen; **he runs a small hotel in the village** er hat ein kleines Hotel im Dorf; **I want to run my own life** ich möchte mein eigenes Leben leben; **she's the one who really runs everything** sie ist diejenige, die den Laden schmeißt (*inf*); **I'm running this show!** (*inf*) ich bestimme, was gemacht wird
(e) (= *move*) **to run one's fingers over the piano keys** die Finger über die (Klavier)tasten gleiten lassen; **to run one's finger down a list** mit dem Finger eine Liste durchgehen; **to run one's fingers through one's hair** sich (*dat*) mit den Fingern durch die Haare fahren; **he ran the vacuum cleaner over the carpet** er ging mit dem Staubsauger über den Teppich
(f) (*rope, road*) führen; (*piece of elastic, line, ditch*) ziehen; (*pipe, wires*) (ver)legen

(g) (*Press*) *article, series* bringen
(h) (*film*) zeigen; (*Comm*) *line* verkaufen

🖪 PHRASAL VERBS

➤ **run about** (*Brit*) or **around** VI (*lit, fig*) herumlaufen
➤ **run across** 🖪 VI **(a)** (*lit*) hinüberlaufen **(b)** (= *go to see*) kurz rübergehen (*to* zu) 🖪 VI +PREP OBJ *person* zufällig treffen; *object, reference* stoßen auf (+*acc*)
➤ **run after** 🖪 VI **to come running after** hinterherlaufen 🖪 VI +PREP OBJ nachlaufen (+*dat*)
➤ **run along** VI laufen; (= *go away*) gehen; **run along!** nun geht mal schön!
➤ **run around** VI = **run about**
➤ **run away** VI **(a)** weglaufen; **don't run away, I need your advice** (*inf*) gehen Sie nicht weg, ich möchte Sie um Rat fragen (*inf*) **(b)** (*water*) auslaufen
➤ **run away with** VI +PREP OBJ (= *steal*) durchbrennen mit (*inf*); (*Sport etc*) *race, prize* spielend gewinnen; **he lets his enthusiasm run away with him** seine Begeisterung geht leicht mit ihm durch
➤ **run back** 🖪 VI (*lit*) zurücklaufen 🖪 VT SEP **(a)** *person* zurückfahren **(b)** (= *rewind*) *tape, film* zurückspulen
➤ **run down** 🖪 VI **(a)** (*lit: person*) hinunterrennen **(b)** (*watch, clock*) ablaufen; (*battery*) leer werden; **to let stocks run down** das Lager leer werden lassen; (*deliberately*) die Vorräte abbauen 🖪 VT SEP **(a)** (= *knock down*) umfahren; (= *run over*) überfahren **(b)** *factory, shop* (allmählich) auflösen; *department, stocks, staff* abbauen; *battery* zu stark belasten **(c)** (= *disparage*) schlecht machen **(d)** *criminal, stag* zur Strecke bringen; *person* ausfindig machen
➤ **run in** VI (*lit*) hineinlaufen
➤ **run into** VI +PREP OBJ (= *meet*) zufällig treffen; (= *collide with*) rennen/fahren gegen; **to run into difficulties/trouble** Schwierigkeiten/Ärger bekommen; **to run into problems** auf Probleme stoßen
➤ **run off** 🖪 VI = **run away 1(a)** 🖪 VT SEP **(a)** *water* ablassen **(b)** (= *reproduce*) *copy* abziehen
➤ **run on** VI **(a)** (*lit*) weiterlaufen **(b)** (*fig*) **it ran on for four hours** das zog sich über vier Stunden hin **(c)** (*time*) weitergehen
➤ **run out** VI **(a)** (*person*) hinauslaufen; (*liquid*) herauslaufen; (*through leak*) auslaufen **(b)** (*contract, period of time*) ablaufen; (*money, supplies*) ausgehen
➤ **run out of** VI +PREP OBJ **he ran out of supplies/patience** ihm gingen die Vorräte/ging die Geduld aus; **she ran out of time** sie hatte keine Zeit mehr; **we're running out of time** wir haben nicht mehr viel Zeit
➤ **run over** 🖪 VI **(a)** (*to neighbour etc*) kurz hinübergehen **(b)** (= *overflow*) überlaufen **(c)** (*Rad, TV etc*) **we're running over** wir überziehen 🖪 VI +PREP OBJ *story, details* durchgehen; *text, notes* durchsehen 🖪 VT SEP (*in vehicle*) überfahren
➤ **run round** VI (*esp Brit*) kurz vorbeigehen; **to run round and see sb** kurz bei jdm vorbeigehen
➤ **run through** 🖪 VI (*lit*) durchlaufen 🖪 VI +PREP OBJ **(a)** *piece of music, play* durchspielen; *ceremony, part, list* durchgehen **(b)** (= *reproduce*) copy abziehen ... **over 2**
➤ **run to** VI +PREP OBJ **(a)** (= *afford*) **I can't run to a new car** ich kann mir kein neues Auto leisten **(b)** (= *amount to*) **the poem runs to several hundred lines** das Gedicht geht über mehrere hundert Zeilen
➤ **run up** 🖪 VI (*lit*) hinauflaufen; (= *approach quickly*) hinrennen (*to* zu); **to run up against difficulties** auf Schwierigkeiten stoßen 🖪 VT SEP **(a)** *flag* hochziehen **(b)** (= *incur*) machen; **to run up a bill** eine Rechnung zusammenkommen lassen; **to run up a debt** Schulden machen

runaround [ˈrʌnəraʊnd] N (*inf*) **to give sb the ~** jdn an der Nase herumführen (*inf*)

runaway [ˈrʌnəweɪ] 🖪 N Ausreißer(in) m(f) 🖪 ADJ **(a)** *slave* entlaufen; *person, horse* ausgerissen; **a ~ train** ein Zug, der sich selbstständig gemacht hat **(b)** (*fig*) *winner* überragend; *inflation* unkontrollierbar; **a ~ success** ein Riesenerfolg m

rundown ['rʌndaʊn] N **(a)** (of factory, shop) (allmähliche) Auflösung; (of department, stock, personnel) Abbau m **(b)** (inf: = report) Zusammenfassung f; **to give sb a ~ on sth** jdn über etw (acc) informieren

run-down [rʌn'daʊn] ADJ (= dilapidated) heruntergekommen; (= tired) abgespannt; battery leer

rung¹ [rʌŋ] PTP of **ring²**

rung² [rʌŋ] N (of ladder, also fig) Sprosse f

run-in ['rʌnɪn] N (inf) Streit m

runner ['rʌnə'] N **(a)** (= athlete) Läufer(in) m(f); (= messenger) Bote m, Botin f **(b)** (on sledge, skate) Kufe f; (for curtain) Vorhangröllchen nt; (for drawer, machine part) Laufschiene f **(c) to do a ~** (Brit inf) die Fliege machen (sl)

runner bean N (Brit) Stangenbohne f

runner-up ['rʌnər'ʌp] N Zweite(r) mf; **the runners-up** die weiteren Plätze; (in competition) die weiteren Gewinner

running ['rʌnɪŋ] **1** N **(a)** Laufen nt; **to make the ~** (lit, fig) das Rennen machen; **to be in the ~** (for sth) im Rennen (für etw) liegen; **out of the ~** aus dem Rennen
(b) (= management, being in charge) Leitung f; (of country, shop) Führung f; (= organization: of course, competition) Durchführung f
(c) (= maintenance: of machine) Unterhaltung f
2 ADJ water, stream fließend; tap, nose laufend; eyes tränend **3** ADV hintereinander; **(for) five days ~** fünf Tage hintereinander; **for the third year ~** im dritten Jahr hintereinander; **sales have fallen for the third year ~** die Verkaufszahlen sind seit drei Jahren rückläufig

running: running account N (Fin) laufendes Konto; **running battle** N (fig) Kleinkrieg m; **running commentary** N (Rad, TV) fortlaufender Kommentar; **running costs** PL Betriebskosten pl; (of car) Unterhaltskosten pl; **running mate** N (US Pol) Kandidat für die Vizepräsidentschaft; **running order** N **in ~** betriebsbereit; **running shoe** N Rennschuh m; **running total** N laufende Summe; **to keep a ~ of sth** (lit, fig) etw fortlaufend festhalten

runny ['rʌnɪ] ADJ (+ER) egg, wax flüssig; nose laufend; eyes tränend; honey, sauce, consistency dünnflüssig

run: run-of-the-mill ADJ gewöhnlich; **run-through** N Durchgehen nt; **let's have a final ~** gehen wir das noch einmal durch; **run-up** N (Sport) Anlauf m; (fig) Vorbereitungszeit f; **in the ~ to the election** in der Zeit vor der Wahl; **runway** N (Aviat) Start- und Landebahn f

rupture ['rʌptʃə'] **1** N (lit, fig) Bruch m; (Pol: of relations) Abbruch m **2** VTI brechen; **to ~ oneself** (inf) sich (dat) einen Bruch heben (inf)

ruptured ['rʌptʃəd] ADJ tank, pipe geplatzt

rural ['rʊərəl] ADJ ländlich; landscape bäuerlich; accent dörflich; poverty, crime auf dem Land; **~ land** ländlicher Raum

rural: rural life N Landleben nt; **rural population** N Landbevölkerung f

ruse [ruːz] N List f

rush [rʌʃ] **1** N **(a)** (of crowd) Andrang m; (of air) Stoß m; **they made a ~ for the door** sie drängten zur Tür; **there was a ~ for the empty seats** alles stürzte sich auf die leeren Sitze; **there's been a ~ on these goods** diese Waren sind rasend weggegangen; **we have a ~ on in the office just now** bei uns im Büro herrscht zur Zeit Hochbetrieb; **the Christmas ~** der Weihnachtsbetrieb; **we've had a ~ of orders** wir hatten eine Flut von Aufträgen; **a ~ of blood to the head** Blutandrang m im Kopf
(b) (= hurry) Eile f; (stronger) Hast f; **to be in a ~** in Eile sein; **I did it in a ~** ich habe es sehr hastig gemacht; **is there any ~ for this?** eilt das?; **it all happened in such a ~** das ging alles so plötzlich
2 VI (= hurry) eilen; (stronger) hasten; (= run) stürzen; (wind) brausen; (water) schießen; (= make rushing noise) rauschen; **they ~ed to help her** sie eilten ihr zu Hilfe; **I'm ~ing to finish it** ich beeile mich, es fertig zu machen; **don't ~, take your time** überstürzen Sie nichts, lassen Sie sich Zeit; **you shouldn't just go ~ing into things** Sie sollten die Dinge nicht so überstürzen; **to ~ through** book hastig lesen; museum, town

hetzen durch; work hastig erledigen; **to ~ past** (person) vorbeistürzen; (vehicle) vorbeischießen; **to ~ in/out/back etc** hinein-/hinaus-/zurückstürzen etc; **the ambulance ~ed to the scene** der Krankenwagen raste zur Unfallstelle; **to ~ to sb's defence** (Brit) or **defense** (US) (lit, fig) jdm zur Seite eilen; **the blood ~ed to his face** das Blut schoss ihm ins Gesicht **3** VT **(a)** (= do hurriedly) hastig machen, schnell machen; (= do badly) schludern bei (pej); (= force to hurry) hetzen; **to be ~ed off one's feet** dauernd auf Trab sein (inf); **to ~ sb into doing sth** jdn dazu treiben, etw überstürzt zu tun; **to ~ sb to hospital** jdn schnellstens ins Krankenhaus bringen; **they ~ed the bill through Parliament** sie peitschten die Gesetzesvorlage durch das Parlament
(b) (= charge at) stürmen; fence zustürmen auf (+acc)

▶ **rush about** (Brit) or **around** VI herumhasten

▶ **rush at** VI +PREP OBJ (lit) losstürzen auf (+acc)

▶ **rush down** VI (person) hinuntereilen; (very fast, also water etc) hinunterstürzen

▶ **rush out 1** VI hinauseilen; (very fast) hinausstürzen; **he rushed out and bought one** er kaufte sofort einen **2** VT SEP order eilends wegschicken; statement, book schnell(stens) veröffentlichen; troops, supplies eilends hintransportieren

▶ **rush through** VT SEP order durchjagen; goods, supplies eilends durchschleusen; legislation durchpeitschen

rushed [rʌʃt] ADJ **(a)** meal hastig; decision übereilt **(b)** (= busy) gehetzt

rush: rush hour(s) N(PL) Stoßzeit(en) f(pl); **rush-hour traffic** Stoßverkehr m; **rush job** N eiliger Auftrag; (pej: = bad work) Schluderarbeit f (inf); **rush order** N (Comm) Eilauftrag m

Russia ['rʌʃə] N Russland nt

Russian ['rʌʃən] **1** ADJ russisch **2** N **(a)** Russe m, Russin f **(b)** (Ling) Russisch nt

rust [rʌst] **1** N Rost m; (Bot) Brand m; **covered in ~** völlig verrostet **2** ADJ (also ~-coloured) rostfarben **3** VT (lit) rosten lassen **4** VI rosten

rusted ['rʌstɪd] ADJ (esp US) rostig

rustic ['rʌstɪk] ADJ (= rural) bäuerlich; furniture, style rustikal

rustiness ['rʌstɪnɪs] N Rostigkeit f; (fig) eingerostete Kenntnisse pl (of in +dat)

rustle ['rʌsl] **1** N Rascheln nt; (of foliage) Rauschen nt **2** VI (leaves, silk, papers) rascheln; (foliage, skirts) rauschen **3** VT **(a)** paper, skirt, leaves on ground etc rascheln mit **(b)** (= steal) klauen (inf)

▶ **rustle up** VT SEP (inf) meal improvisieren (inf); money auftreiben; **can you rustle up a cup of coffee?** können Sie eine Tasse Kaffee beschaffen?

rustler ['rʌslə'] N (= cattle thief) Viehdieb(in) m(f)

rustling ['rʌslɪŋ] **1** ADJ raschelnd **2** N **(a)** (of leaves, paper) Rascheln nt; (of material) Rauschen nt **(b)** (= cattle theft) Viehdiebstahl m

rustproof ['rʌstpruːf] ADJ rostfrei

rusty ['rʌstɪ] ADJ (+ER) (lit) rostig; (fig) mind, maths, language eingerostet; talent verkümmert; **I'm a bit ~** ich bin etwas aus der Übung, to get ~ (lit) verrosten; (fig: person) aus der Übung kommen

rut [rʌt] N (in track, path) Spur f; (fig) Trott m (inf); **to be in a ~** (fig) im Trott sein (inf); **to get into a ~** (fig) in einen Trott geraten (inf)

rutabaga [ruːtəˈbeɪgə] N (US) Steckrübe f

ruthless ['ruːθlɪs] ADJ person, deed rücksichtslos; cuts, treatment, self-analysis schonungslos; **you'll have to be ~** man muss hart sein; **to be ~ in doing sth** etw ohne jede Rücksicht tun

ruthlessly ['ruːθlɪslɪ] ADV suppress rücksichtslos; criticize schonungslos; **a ~ ambitious businessman** ein skrupellos ehrgeiziger Geschäftsmann

ruthlessness ['ruːθlɪsnɪs] N (of person, deed) Rücksichtslosigkeit f; (of cuts, treatment) Schonungslosigkeit f

Rwanda [rʊˈændə] N Ruanda nt

Rwandan [rʊˈændən] **1** N Ruander(in) m(f) **2** ADJ ruandisch

rye [raɪ] N (= grain) Roggen m

rye whisk(e)y N Ryewhisky m

Ss

S, s [es] N S nt, s nt

's (a) he's *etc* = he is/has; what's = what is/has/does?
(b) (*genitive*) **John's book** Johns Buch; **my brother's car** das Auto meines Bruders; **at the butcher's** beim Fleischer
(c) let's = let us

Sabbath ['sæbəθ] N Sabbat m; (*non-Jewish*) Sonntag m

saber N (*US*) = **sabre**

sabotage ['sæbətɑːʒ] **1** N Sabotage f **2** VT (*lit, fig*) sabotieren

saboteur [sæbə'tɜː'] N Saboteur(in) m(f)

sabre, (*US*) **saber** ['seɪbə'] N Säbel m

saccharin(e) ['sækərɪn] N Sa(c)charin f

sachet ['sæʃeɪ] N Beutel m; (*of powder*) Päckchen nt; (*of shampoo, cream*) Briefchen nt; (= *lavender* ~) Kissen nt

sack [sæk] **1** N (a) Sack m; **2 ~s of coal** 2 Sack Kohlen (b) (*inf*) **to get the** ~ rausfliegen (*inf*); **to give sb the** ~ jdn rausschmeißen (*inf*) (c) (*inf*: = *bed*) **to hit the** ~ sich in die Falle hauen (*sl*) **2** VT (*inf*: = *dismiss*) rausschmeißen (*inf*)

sackful ['sækfʊl] N Sack m; **two ~s of potatoes** zwei Sack Kartoffeln

sacking ['sækɪŋ] N (*inf*: = *dismissal*) Entlassung f

sacrament ['sækrəmənt] N Sakrament nt

sacred ['seɪkrɪd] ADJ heilig; *building, art, theme, rite* sakral; *music, poetry* geistlich; ~ **duty** heilige Pflicht; **is nothing ~?** (*inf*) ist denn nichts mehr heilig?

sacrifice ['sækrɪfaɪs] **1** N (*lit, fig*) Opfer nt; (= *thing sacrificed also*) Opfergabe f; **to make ~s** (*lit, fig*) Opfer bringen **2** VT opfern (*sth to sb* jdm etw)

sacrificial [sækrɪ'fɪʃl] ADJ Opfer-

sacrilege ['sækrɪlɪdʒ] N Sakrileg nt; (*fig also*) Frevel m

SAD (*Med*) ABBR *of* **seasonal affective disorder**

sad [sæd] ADJ (+ER) (a) traurig; *loss* schmerzlich; *mistake, lack* bedauerlich; **to feel** ~ traurig sein; **he was** ~ **to see her go** er war betrübt, dass sie wegging; **it makes me** ~ **to think that …** der Gedanke betrübt mich, dass …; **it's a** ~ **business** es ist eine traurige Angelegenheit (b) (*inf*: = *pathetic*) bedauernswert

sadden ['sædn] VT betrüben

saddle ['sædl] **1** N (*also of hill*) Sattel m **2** VT (a) *horse* satteln (b) (*inf*) **to** ~ **sb/oneself with sb/sth** jdm/sich jdn/etw aufhalsen (*inf*); **how did I get** ~**d with him?** wie kommt es (nur), dass ich ihn am Hals habe?

saddle: saddlebag N Satteltasche f; **saddle-sore** ADJ *person* wund geritten; **to get** ~ sich wund reiten

sad: sad-eyed ADJ traurig blickend *attr*; **sad-faced** ADJ traurig blickend *attr*

sadism ['seɪdɪzəm] N Sadismus m

sadist ['seɪdɪst] N Sadist(in) m(f)

sadistic ADJ, **sadistically** ADV [sə'dɪstɪk, -əlɪ] sadistisch

sadly ['sædlɪ] ADV (a) traurig; **she will be** ~ **missed** sie wird (uns/ihnen) allen sehr fehlen (b) (= *unfortunately*) leider (c) (= *woefully*) bedauerlicherweise; **he is** ~ **lacking in any sensitivity** ihm fehlt absolut jegliches Feingefühl; **to be** ~ **mistaken** sich sehr *or* arg täuschen

sadness ['sædnɪs] N Traurigkeit f; **our** ~ **at his death** unsere Trauer über seinen Tod

s.a.e. ABBR *of* **stamped addressed envelope**

safari [sə'fɑːrɪ] N Safari f; **to be/go on** ~ auf Safari sein/gehen

safe¹ [seɪf] N (*for valuables*) Safe m

safe² ADJ (+ER) sicher; (= *out of danger*) in Sicherheit; (= *not injured*) unverletzt; (= *not dangerous*) ungefährlich; *method, player* zuverlässig; *policy* vorsichtig; *estimate* realistisch; **to keep sth** ~ etw sicher aufbewahren; ~ **journey!** gute Fahrt/Reise!; ~ **journey home!** komm gut nach Hause!; **thank God you're** ~ Gott sei Dank ist dir nichts passiert; ~ **and sound** gesund und wohlbehalten; **the secret is** ~ **with me** bei mir ist das Geheimnis gut aufgehoben; **not** ~ gefährlich; **this car is not** ~ **to drive** das Auto ist nicht verkehrssicher; **it is** ~ **to leave it open** man kann es unbesorgt auflassen; **is it** ~ **to light a fire?** ist es auch nicht gefährlich, ein Feuer anzumachen?; **it is** ~ **to eat/drink** das kann man gefahrlos

essen/trinken; ~ **margin** Spielraum m; (*Fin also*) Reserve f; **it is** ~ **to assume** *or* **a** ~ **assumption that …** man kann mit ziemlicher Sicherheit annehmen, dass …; **I think it's** ~ **to say …** ich glaube, man kann wohl *or* ruhig sagen …; **just to be** ~ *or* **on the** ~ **side** um ganz sicher zu sein; **to follow sb at a** ~ **distance** jdm in sicherem Abstand folgen; **better** ~ **than sorry** Vorsicht ist besser als Nachsicht (*Prov*)

safe: safe area N (*Pol*) Schutzzone f; **safe-conduct** N freies Geleit; (= *document*) Geleitbrief m; **safe-deposit box** N Banksafe m *or* nt; **safeguard 1** N Schutz m; **as a** ~ **against** zum Schutz gegen **2** VT schützen (*against* vor +dat); *interests* wahrnehmen **3** VI **to** ~ **against sth** sich gegen etw absichern; **safe haven** N (*fig*) sicherer Zufluchtsort; **safe keeping** N **to give sb sth for** ~ jdm etw zur (sicheren) Aufbewahrung geben

safely ['seɪflɪ] ADV (= *unharmed*) wohlbehalten; (= *without running risks*) gefahrlos; (= *solidly, firmly*) sicher; (= *not dangerously*) ungefährlich; **she held the door open until we were all** ~ **inside** sie hielt die Tür auf, bis wir alle sicher drinnen waren; **I think I can** ~ **say …** ich glaube, ich kann ruhig sagen …; **the election is now** ~ **out of the way** die Wahlen haben wir jetzt zum Glück hinter uns; ~ **invested** sicher angelegt; **to put sth away** ~ etw an einem sicheren Ort verwahren; **he's** ~ **locked away in prison** er sitzt hinter Schloss und Riegel; **once the children are** ~ **tucked up in bed** wenn die Kinder erst mal im Bett sind

safe: safe passage N sicheres Geleit; **safe seat** N (*Pol*) ein sicherer Sitz; **safe sex** N Safer Sex m

safety ['seɪftɪ] N Sicherheit f; **for** ~**'s sake** aus Sicherheitsgründen; **for his (own)** ~ zu seiner (eigenen) Sicherheit; **to walk the streets in** ~ unbehelligt ausgehen; **(there's) in numbers** zu mehreren ist man sicherer; **to reach** ~ in Sicherheit gelangen; **when we reached the** ~ **of the opposite bank** als wir sicher das andere Ufer erreicht hatten

safety: safety belt N Sicherheitsgurt m; **safety catch** N (*on gun*) (Abzugs)sicherung f; **safety chain** N Sicherheitskette f; **safety glass** N Sicherheitsglas nt; **safety harness** N Sicherheitsgurt m; **safety island** N (*US Aut*) Verkehrsinsel f; **safety margin** N Sicherheitsmarge f; **safety measure** N Sicherheitsmaßnahme f; **safety net** N Sicherheitsnetz nt; **safety pin** N Sicherheitsnadel f; **safety precaution** N Sicherheitsvorkehrung f; **safety standards** PL Sicherheitsnormen pl

saffron ['sæfrən] **1** N Safran m **2** ADJ Safran-

sag [sæg] VI absacken; (*in the middle*) durchhängen; (*shoulders*) herabhängen; (*breasts*) schlaff herunterhängen; (*production, rate*) zurückgehen; (*price, spirit*) sinken

saga ['sɑːgə] N Saga f; (*fig*) Geschichte f

sage [seɪdʒ] N (*Bot*) Salbei m

sagely ['seɪdʒlɪ] ADV weise

sagging ['sægɪŋ] ADJ (a) *ceiling, rope* durchhängend (b) *skin* schlaff; ~ **stomach** Hängebauch m (c) (*fig*) *morale* sinkend; **a drink will revive his** ~ **spirits** ein Drink wird seine Stimmung wieder heben

saggy ['sægɪ] (+ER) ADJ *mattress* durchgelegen; *sofa* durchgesessen; *garment* ausgebeult; *bottom, breasts* schlaff

Sagittarian [sædʒɪ'teərɪən] **1** N Schütze m **2** ADJ des Schützen

Sagittarius [sædʒɪ'teərɪəs] N Schütze m; **he's (a)** ~ er ist Schütze

Sahara [sə'hɑːrə] N Sahara f; **the** ~ **Desert** die (Wüste) Sahara

said [sed] **1** PRET, PTP *of* **say 2** ADJ (*form*) besagt

sail [seɪl] **1** N (a) Segel nt; (*of windmill*) Flügel m; **to set** *or* **make** ~ **(for …)** losfahren (nach …); (*with sailing boat*) absegeln (nach …)
(b) (= *trip*) Fahrt f; **it's 3 days'** ~ **from here** von hier aus fährt *or* (*in yacht*) segelt man 3 Tage; **to go for a** ~ segeln gehen **2** VT *ship* segeln mit; *liner etc* steuern; **they** ~**ed the ship to Cadiz** sie segelten nach Cadiz; **to** ~ **the Atlantic** den Atlantik durchkreuzen
3 VI (a) (*Naut*) fahren; (*with yacht*) segeln; **are you flying?** – **no,** ~**ing** fliegen Sie? – nein, ich fahre mit dem Schiff
(b) (= *leave*) (*for* nach) abfahren; (*yacht, in yacht*) absegeln
(c) (*fig*) (*glider, swan etc*) gleiten; (*moon, clouds*) ziehen; (*ball,*

object) fliegen; **the plate ~ed past my head** der Teller segelte an meinem Kopf vorbei; **she ~ed past/out of the room** sie rauschte vorbei/aus dem Zimmer (*inf*); **she ~ed through all her exams** sie schaffte alle Prüfungen spielend

sail: sailboard ◨ N Windsurfbrett *nt* ◪ VI windsurfen; **sailboarding** N Windsurfen *nt*; **sailboat** N (*US*) Segelboot *nt*

sailing ['seɪlɪŋ] N Segeln *nt*

sailing: sailing boat N (*Brit*) Segelboot *nt*; **sailing ship** N Segelschiff *nt*

sailor ['seɪləʳ] N Seemann *m*; (*in navy*) Matrose *m*, Matrosin *f*

saint [seɪnt] N (*lit, fig*) Heilige(r) *mf*; (*before name*) (*abbr* **St**) **St John** Sankt Johannes, St. Johannes; **St Mark's (Church)** die Markuskirche

saintly ['seɪntlɪ] ADJ (+ER) heilig; (*fig pej*) *person* frömmlerisch; *smile* lammfromm

sake [seɪk] N **for the ~ of ...** willen; **for my ~ meinetwegen**; (= *to please me*) mir zuliebe; **for your own ~** dir selbst zuliebe; **for the ~ of your career** wegen deiner Karriere, deiner Karriere zuliebe; **for heaven's** *or* **Christ's ~!** (*inf*) um Gottes willen!; **for heaven's** *or* **Christ's ~ shut up** (*inf*) nun halt doch endlich die Klappe (*inf*); **for old times' ~** in Erinnerung an alte Zeiten; **for the ~ of those who ...** für diejenigen, die ...; **and all for the ~ of a few pounds** und alles wegen ein paar Pfund; **to talk for talking's ~** reden, nur damit etwas gesagt wird

salable ADJ (*US*) = **saleable**

salad ['sæləd] N Salat *m*

salad: salad bar N Salatbüffet *nt*; **salad bowl** N Salatschüssel *f*; **salad cream** N ≈ Majonäse *f*; **salad dressing** N Salatsoße *f*

salamander ['sælə,mændəʳ] N Salamander *m*

salaried ['sælərɪd] ADJ **~ post** Angestelltenposten *m*; **~ employee** Gehaltsempfänger(in) *m(f)*

salary ['sælərɪ] N Gehalt *nt*; **he earns a good ~** er hat ein gutes Gehalt; **what is his ~?** wie hoch ist sein Gehalt?

salary: salary increase N Gehaltserhöhung *f*; **salary scale** N Gehaltsskala *f*

sale [seɪl] N (**a**) (= *selling*) Verkauf *m*; (*instance*) Geschäft *nt*; (*of insurance, bulk order*) Abschluss *m*; (= *auction*) Auktion *f*; **for ~** zu verkaufen; **to put sth up for ~** etw zum Verkauf anbieten; **is it up for ~?** steht es zum Verkauf?; **not for ~** nicht verkäuflich; **to be on ~** verkauft werden; **~ or return** Kauf *m* mit Rückgaberecht; **on a ~ or return basis** auf Kommission(sbasis); **~s** *pl* (= *turnover*) der Absatz; **we've made no ~ to China** mit China haben wir keine Geschäfte abgeschlossen
(**b**) **sales** SING (= *department*) Verkaufsabteilung *f*
(**c**) (*at reduced prices*) Rabattaktion *f*; (*at end of season*) Schlussverkauf *m*; (= *clearance ~*) Räumungsverkauf *m*; **in the ~, on ~** (*US*) im (Sonder)angebot

saleable, (*US*) **salable** ['seɪləbl] ADJ (= *marketable*) absatzfähig; *skill* vermarktbar; (= *in ~ condition*) verkäuflich

sales: sales allowance N Preisnachlass *m* auf Verkäufe; **sales clerk** N (*US*) Verkäufer(in) *m(f)*; **sales department** N Verkaufsabteilung *f*; **sales figures** PL Verkaufsziffern *pl*; **sales forecast** N Absatzprognose *f*; **salesgirl**, **saleslady** N Verkäuferin *f*; **sales literature** N Werbematerial *nt*; **salesman** N Verkäufer *m*; (= *representative*) Vertreter *m*; **sales manager** N Verkaufsleiter(in) *m(f)*; **salesperson** N Verkäufer(in) *m(f)*; **sales pitch** N Verkaufstechnik *f*; **sales rep** N (*inf*), **sales representative** N Vertreter(in) *m(f)*; **sales revenue** N Verkaufserlös *m*; **sales target** N Verkaufsziel *nt*; **sales tax** N (*US*) Verkaufssteuer *f*; **sales terms** PL Geschäftsbedingungen *pl*; **sales volume** N Umsatz *m*; **saleswoman** N Verkäuferin *f*; (= *representative*) Vertreterin *f*

saline solution [,seɪlaɪnsə'luːʃən] N Salzlösung *f*

saliva [sə'laɪvə] N Speichel *m*

salivate ['sælɪveɪt] VI Speichel produzieren; (*animal*) geifern; (*old people, baby*) sabbern

sallow ['sæləʊ] ADJ bleich; *colour* fahl

salmon ['sæmən] ◨ N, *pl* - Lachs *m*; (= *colour*) Lachs(rosa) *nt* ◪ ADJ (*colour*) lachs(farben)

salmonella [,sælmə'nelə] N (*also ~ poisoning*) Salmonellenvergiftung *f*

salon ['sælɒn] N (*all senses*) Salon *m*

salt [sɔːlt] ◨ N (*Cook, Chem*) Salz *nt*; (*for icy roads*) Streusalz *nt*; **~ of the earth** (*fig*) Salz der Erde; **to take sth with a pinch** (*Brit*)

or **grain** (*US*) **of ~** (*fig*) etw nicht ganz für bare Münze nehmen; **to rub ~ into sb's wounds** (*fig*) Salz in jds Wunde streuen
◪ ADJ *air* salzig; *butter, meat* gesalzen; **~ water** Salzwasser *nt*
◫ VT (**a**) (= *cure*) einsalzen; (= *flavour*) salzen
(**b**) (= *grit*) *road* mit Salz streuen

saltcellar ['sɔːltseləʳ] N Salzfässchen *nt*; (= *shaker*) Salzstreuer *m*

salted ['sɔːltɪd] ADJ gesalzen

saltiness ['sɔːltɪnɪs] N Salzigkeit *f*

salt: salt shaker N Salzstreuer *m*; **salt water** N Salzwasser *nt*; **saltwater** ADJ **~ fish** Meeresfisch *m*; **~ lake** Salzsee *m*

salty ['sɔːltɪ] ADJ **~ water** Salzwasser *nt*

salute [sə'luːt] ◨ N Gruß *m*; (*of guns*) Salut *m*; **he raised his hand in ~** er hob seine Hand zum Gruß; **a 21-gun ~** 21 Salutschüsse ◪ VT (*Mil*) *flag etc* grüßen; *person* salutieren vor (+*dat*) ◫ VI (*Mil*) salutieren

salvage ['sælvɪdʒ] ◨ N (= *act*) Bergung *f*; (= *objects*) Bergungsgut *nt* ◪ VT bergen (*from* aus); (*fig*) retten (*from* von); **to ~ one's reputation** sich (*dat*) seinen Ruf erhalten können

salvage operation N Bergungsaktion *f*; (*fig*) Rettungsaktion *f*

salvation [sæl'veɪʃən] N (= *act of saving*) Rettung *f*; (= *state of being saved also, esp Rel*) Heil *nt*

Salvation Army ◨ N Heilsarmee *f* ◪ ATTR der Heilsarmee

salve [sælv] N Salbe *f*; (*fig liter*) Balsam *m*

Samaritan [sə'mærɪtən] N Samariter(in) *m(f)*; **good ~** (*lit, fig*) barmherziger Samariter

same [seɪm] ◨ ADJ **the ~ ...** der/die/das gleiche ...; (= *one and the ~*) der-/die-/dasselbe; **they were both wearing the ~ dress** sie hatten beide das gleiche Kleid an; **they both live in the ~ house** sie wohnen beide in demselben Haus; **they are all the ~** sie sind alle gleich; **that's the ~ tie as I've got** so eine Krawatte habe ich auch; **she just wasn't the ~ person** sie war ein anderer Mensch; **it's the ~ thing** das ist das Gleiche; **see you tomorrow, ~ time ~ place** bis morgen, gleicher Ort, gleiche Zeit; **we sat at the ~ table as usual** wir saßen an unserem üblichen Tisch; **how are you? - ~ as usual** wie gehts? - wie immer; **he is the ~ age as his wife** er ist (genau) so alt wie seine Frau; (**on**) **the very ~ day** genau am gleichen Tag; **~ difference** (*inf*) was ist der Unterschied?; **in the ~ way** (*genau*) gleich; (= *by the ~ token*) ebenso
◪ PRON (**a**) **the ~** der-/die-/dasselbe; **and I would do the ~ again** und ich würde es wieder tun; **he left and I did the ~** er ist gegangen, und ich auch; **is he that artist from New Orleans? - the very ~** ist das dieser Künstler aus New Orleans? - genau der; **another drink? - thanks, (the) ~ again** noch etwas zu trinken? - ja bitte, das Gleiche noch mal; **~ again, Joe** und noch einen, Joe; **she's much the ~** sie hat sich kaum geändert; (*in health*) es geht ihr kaum besser; **he will never be the ~ again** er wird niemals mehr derselbe sein; **frozen chicken is not the ~ as fresh** tiefgefrorene Hähnchen sind kein Vergleich zu frischen; **it's always the ~** es ist immer das Gleiche; **it comes** *or* **amounts to the ~** das kommt *or* läuft aufs Gleiche hinaus
(**b**) NO ART (*Comm*) **for repairing chair: £10, for recovering ~: £25** Stuhlreparatur: £ 10, Beziehen: £ 25
(**c**) (*in adverbial uses*) **the ~** gleich; **to pay everybody the ~** alle gleich bezahlen; **things go on just the ~ - (as always)** es ändert sich nichts; **it's not the ~ as before** es ist nicht wie früher; **I used to love you but I don't feel the ~ any more** ich habe dich mal geliebt, aber das ist jetzt anders; **I still feel the ~ about you** an meinen Gefühlen dir gegenüber hat sich nichts geändert; **if it's all the ~ to you** wenn es Ihnen egal ist; **all** *or* **just the ~** (= *nevertheless*) trotzdem; **thanks all the ~** trotzdem vielen Dank; **~ here** ich/wir auch; **~ to you** (danke) gleichfalls; **we left our country the ~ as you did** wir haben unsere Heimat verlassen, wie Sie auch

same-day ['seɪmdeɪ] ADJ *delivery* am gleichen Tag

sameness ['seɪmnɪs] N Eintönigkeit *f*

same-sex ['seɪmseks] ADJ gleichgeschlechtlich

Samoa [sə'məʊə] N Samoa *nt*

Samoan [sə'məʊən] ◨ ADJ samoanisch ◪ N Samoaner(in) *m(f)*

sample ['sɑːmpl] ◨ N (= *example*) Beispiel *nt* (*of* für); (*for tasting, fig*) Kostprobe *f*; (*Comm*) Warenprobe *f*; (*of cloth etc*) Muster *nt*; (*of commodities, urine, blood etc*) Probe *f*; **a representative ~ of the population** eine repräsentative

Auswahl aus der Bevölkerung

2 ADJ ATTR Probe-; (*esp Comm*) Muster-; **a ~ section of the population** eine Auswahl aus der Bevölkerung **3** VT *wine, food* probieren; *pleasures* kosten; *atmosphere* testen; **to ~ wines** eine Weinprobe machen

sampling [ˈsɑːmplɪŋ] N (*of food*) Kostprobe *f*; (*of wine*) Weinprobe *f*

sanatorium [ˌsænəˈtɔːrɪəm] N, *pl* **sanatoria** [ˌsænəˈtɔːrɪə] (*Brit*) Sanatorium *nt*

sanctify [ˈsæŋktɪfaɪ] VT (= *make holy*) heiligen; (= *consecrate*) weihen

sanction [ˈsæŋkʃən] **1** N (a) (= *permission*) Zustimmung *f* (b) (= *enforcing measure*) Sanktion *f* **2** VT sanktionieren; (*Pol*: = *impose sanctions on*) Sanktionen *pl* verhängen gegen

sanctity [ˈsæŋktɪtɪ] N Heiligkeit *f*; (*of rights*) Unantastbarkeit *f*

sanctuary [ˈsæŋktjʊərɪ] N (a) (= *holy place*) Heiligtum *nt* (b) (= *refuge*) Zuflucht *f* (c) (*for animals*) Schutzgebiet *nt*

sand [sænd] **1** N Sand *m no pl*; **~s** (*of desert*) Sand *m*; (= *beach*) Sandstrand *m* **2** VT (= *smooth*) schmirgeln; (= *sprinkle with ~*) streuen

➤ **sand down** VT SEP (ab)schmirgeln

sandal [ˈsændl] N Sandale *f*

sandalwood [ˈsændlwʊd] N Sandelholz *nt*

sand: sandbag N Sandsack *m*; **sandbank** N Sandbank *f*; **sandbox** N (*for playing*) Sandkasten *m*; **sand castle** N Sandburg *f*; **sand dune** N Sanddüne *f*

S & L (*US Fin*) ABBR *of* **savings and loan association** Spar- und Darlehenskasse *f*

sand: sandpaper **1** N Schmirgelpapier *nt* **2** VT schmirgeln; **sandpit** N Sandkasten *m*; **sandstone** **1** N Sandstein *m* **2** ADJ Sandstein-, aus Sandstein; **sandstorm** N Sandsturm *m*

sandwich [ˈsænwɪdʒ] **1** N Sandwich *nt*; **open ~** belegtes Brot **2** VT (*also* ~ **in**) hineinzwängen; *car* einkeilen; **~ed between two slices of bread** zwischen zwei Brotscheiben

sandwich: sandwich bar N Snackbar *f*; **sandwich board** N Reklametafel *f*

sandy [ˈsændɪ] ADJ (+ER) (a) sandig; **~ beach** Sandstrand *m* (b) (*colour*) rötlich; *hair* rotblond

sane [seɪn] ADJ (+ER) (a) (= *mentally healthy*) *person* normal; (*Med, Psych etc*) geistig gesund; *world, society etc* gesund (b) (= *sensible*) *advice, person* vernünftig

sang [sæŋ] PRET *of* **sing**

sanitarium [ˌsænɪˈtɛərɪəm] N (*US*) = **sanatorium**

sanitary [ˈsænɪtərɪ] ADJ hygienisch; *arrangements, installations* sanitär *attr*

sanitary: sanitary napkin N (*US*), **sanitary pad** N Damenbinde *f*; **sanitary protection** N Binden und Tampons *pl*; **sanitary towel** N Damenbinde *f*

sanitation [ˌsænɪˈteɪʃən] N Hygiene *f*; (= *toilets etc*) sanitäre Anlagen *pl*; (= *sewage disposal*) Kanalisation *f*

sanitation man N, *pl* **sanitation men** (*US*) Stadtreiniger *m*

sanity [ˈsænɪtɪ] N (a) (= *mental balance*) geistige Gesundheit; (*esp of individual*) gesunder Verstand; **to lose one's ~** den Verstand verlieren; **to doubt sb's ~** an jds Verstand (*dat*) zweifeln (b) (= *sensibleness*) Vernünftigkeit *f*

sank [sæŋk] PRET *of* **sink**[1]

San Marino [ˌsænməˈriːnəʊ] N San Marino *nt*

Sanskrit [ˈsænskrɪt] **1** ADJ sanskritisch **2** N Sanskrit *nt*

Santa (Claus) [ˈsæntə(ˈklɔːz)] N der Weihnachtsmann

sap[1] [sæp] N (*Bot*) Saft *m*; (*fig*) Lebenskraft *f*

sap[2] VT (*fig*) untergraben; *confidence also* schwächen; **to ~ sb's strength** jdn entkräften; jds Kräfte angreifen; **to ~ sb's enthusiasm** jdm die Begeisterung nehmen

sapling [ˈsæplɪŋ] N junger Baum

sapphire [ˈsæfaɪə] **1** N Saphir *m*; (= *colour*) Saphirblau *nt* **2** ADJ Saphir-

Sarajevo [ˌsærəˈjeɪvəʊ] N Sarajevo *nt*

sarcasm [ˈsɑːkæzəm] N Sarkasmus *m*

sarcastic [sɑːˈkæstɪk] ADJ sarkastisch; **are you being ~?** sind Sie jetzt sarkastisch?; **to be ~ about sth** über etw (*acc*) sarkastische Bemerkungen machen

sarcastically [sɑːˈkæstɪkəlɪ] ADV sarkastisch

sardine [sɑːˈdiːn] N Sardine *f*; **packed (in) like ~s** wie die Sardinen

Sardinia [sɑːˈdɪnɪə] N Sardinien *nt*

Sardinian [sɑːˈdɪnɪən] **1** ADJ sardisch **2** N Sarde *m*, Sardin *f*

sardonic ADJ, **sardonically** ADV [sɑːˈdɒnɪk, -əlɪ] süffisant

sari [ˈsɑːrɪ] N Sari *m*

sarnie [ˈsɑːnɪ] N (*Brit inf*) Sandwich *nt*

SASE N (*US*) ABBR *of* **self-addressed stamped envelope** adressierter und frankierter Rückumschlag

sash [sæʃ] N Schärpe *f*

sassy [ˈsæsɪ] ADJ (+ER) (*US inf*) frech

Sat ABBR *of* **Saturday** Sa.

sat [sæt] PRET, PTP *of* **sit**

Satan [ˈseɪtən] N Satan *m*

satanic [səˈtænɪk] ADJ satanisch; (*fig*) teuflisch

satchel [ˈsætʃəl] N Schultasche *f*

satellite [ˈsætəlaɪt] N Satellit *m*

satellite: satellite broadcasting N Satellitenfunk *m*; **satellite dish** N Satellitenantenne *f*; **satellite television** N Satellitenfernsehen *nt*; **satellite town** N Satellitenstadt *f*

satiate [ˈseɪʃɪeɪt] VT *appetite, desires etc* stillen (*geh*); *person, animal* sättigen; (*to excess*) übersättigen

satin [ˈsætɪn] **1** N Satin *m* **2** ADJ Satin-; *skin* samtig

satire [ˈsætaɪə] N Satire *f* (*on* auf +*acc*)

satirical [səˈtɪrɪkəl] ADJ *literature, film etc* satirisch; (= *mocking, joking*) ironisch

satirically [səˈtɪrɪkəlɪ] ADV satirisch; (= *mockingly, jokingly*) ironisch

satirist [ˈsætərɪst] N Satiriker(in) *m(f)*

satirize [ˈsætəraɪz] VT satirisch darstellen

satisfaction [ˌsætɪsˈfækʃən] N (a) (= *act*) (*of person, needs, creditors, curiosity etc*) Befriedigung *f*; (*of debt*) Begleichung *f*; (*of conditions, contract*) Erfüllung *f*
(b) (= *state*) Zufriedenheit *f* (*at* mit); **to feel a sense of ~ at sth** Genugtuung über etw (*acc*) empfinden; **she would not give him the ~ of seeing how annoyed she was** sie wollte ihm nicht die Genugtuung geben, ihren Ärger zu sehen; **we hope the meal was to your complete ~** wir hoffen, Sie waren mit dem Essen zufrieden; **the machine is guaranteed to give complete ~** wir garantieren mit diesem Gerät vollste Zufriedenheit; **to get ~ out of sth** Befriedigung in etw (*dat*) finden; (= *find pleasure*) Freude *f* an etw (*dat*) haben; **he gets ~ out of his job** seine Arbeit befriedigt ihn; **I get a lot of ~ out of listening to music** Musik gibt mir viel; **he proved to my ~ that ...** er hat überzeugend bewiesen, dass ...; **your son's success must be a great ~ to you** der Erfolg Ihres Sohnes muss für Sie eine große Freude sein
(c) (= *redress*) Genugtuung *f*

satisfactorily [ˌsætɪsˈfæktərɪlɪ] ADV zufrieden stellend; **does that answer your question ~?** ist damit Ihre Frage hinreichend beantwortet?; **was it done ~?** waren Sie damit zufrieden?

satisfactory [ˌsætɪsˈfæktərɪ] ADJ zufrieden stellend; (= *only just good enough*) ausreichend; *reason* einleuchtend; *excuse* angemessen; (*in exams*) befriedigend; **to be in a ~ condition** (*Med*) sich in einem zufrieden stellenden Zustand befinden; **work is proceeding at a ~ pace** die Arbeit geht zufrieden stellend voran; **this is just not ~!** das geht so nicht!; (= *not enough*) das reicht einfach nicht (aus)!; **an offer of 8% is simply not ~** ein Angebot von 8% reicht einfach nicht

satisfied [ˈsætɪsfaɪd] ADJ (= *content*) zufrieden; (= *convinced*) überzeugt; **to be ~ with sth** mit etw zufrieden sein; **you'll have to be ~ with that** Sie werden sich damit zufrieden geben müssen; **(are you) ~?** (*iro*) (bist du nun) zufrieden?; **they were not ~ with the answers** sie waren mit den Antworten nicht zufrieden

satisfy ['sætɪsfaɪ] **1** VT **(a)** befriedigen; *employer, customers etc* zufrieden stellen; *(meal) person* sättigen; *hunger* stillen; *contract, conditions* erfüllen; *requirements* genügen (+*dat*); **that won't ~ the boss** damit wird der Chef nicht zufrieden sein **(b)** (= *convince*) überzeugen; **if you can ~ him that ...** wenn Sie ihn davon überzeugen können, dass ... **(c)** *(Comm) debt* begleichen; *claims* nachkommen (+*dat*); *creditors* befriedigen **2** VR **to ~ oneself about sth** sich von etw überzeugen; **to ~ oneself that ...** sich davon überzeugen, dass ...

satisfying ['sætɪsfaɪɪŋ] ADJ befriedigend; *food, meal* sättigend; **a cool ~ beer** ein kühles, durststillendes Bier

satsuma ['sæt'suːmə] N Satsuma *f*

saturate ['sætʃəreɪt] VT **(a)** *(with liquid)* (durch)tränken; *(rain)* durchnässen; **I'm ~d** *(inf)* ich bin klatschnass *(inf)* **(b)** *(fig) market* sättigen

saturation [sætʃə'reɪʃən] N Sättigung *f*

saturation point N *(fig)* Sättigungsgrad *m*; **to have reached ~** seinen Sättigungsgrad erreicht haben

Saturday ['sætədɪ] N Samstag *m; see also* **Tuesday**

Saturn ['sætən] N *(Astron, Myth)* Saturn *m*

sauce [sɔːs] N Soße *f*; **white ~** Mehlsoße *f*

saucepan ['sɔːspən] N Kochtopf *m*

saucer ['sɔːsər] N Untertasse *f*

saucily ['sɔːsɪlɪ] ADV (= *cheekily*) frech; (= *suggestively*) aufreizend

saucy ['sɔːsɪ] ADJ (+ER) (= *cheeky*) frech; (= *suggestive*) anzüglich; *picture* aufreizend

Saudi ['saʊdɪ] **1** N *(inf)* = **Saudi Arabia 2** ADJ = **Saudi Arabian 2**

Saudi Arabia ['saʊdɪə'reɪbɪə] N Saudi-Arabien *nt*

Saudi Arabian ['saʊdɪə'reɪbɪən] **1** N Saudi(-Araber) *m*, Saudi-Araberin *f* **2** ADJ saudi-arabisch

sauna ['sɔːnə] N Sauna *f*; **to have a ~** in die Sauna gehen

saunter ['sɔːntər] **1** N Bummel *m*; **to have a ~ in the park** einen Parkbummel machen **2** VI schlendern; **he ~ed up to me** er schlenderte auf mich zu

sausage ['sɒsɪdʒ] N Wurst *f*; **not a ~** *(Brit inf)* rein gar nichts *(inf)*

sausage: sausagemeat N Wurstbrät *nt*; **sausage roll** N ≈ Bratwurst *f* im Schlafrock

sauté ['səʊteɪ] **1** ADJ **~ potatoes** Röstkartoffeln *pl* **2** VT *potatoes* rösten; (= *sear*) (kurz) anbraten

savage ['sævɪdʒ] **1** ADJ wild; *sport, fighter, revenge, conflict* brutal; *animal* gefährlich; *cuts, measures* drastisch; *criticism* schonungslos; **to make a ~ attack on sb** *(fig)* jdn scharf angreifen; **he has a ~ temper** er ist ein äußerst jähzorniger Mensch **2** N Wilde(r) *mf* **3** VT **(a)** *(animal)* anfallen; *(fatally)* zerfleischen **(b)** *(fig:* = *criticize) person also* (in der Luft) zerreißen

savagely ['sævɪdʒlɪ] ADV *attack, fight* brutal; *bite* gefährlich; *criticize* schonungslos

savageness ['sævɪdʒnɪs] N Wildheit *f*; *(of sport, fighter, revenge, conflict)* Brutalität *f*; *(of custom, war)* Grausamkeit *f*; *(of animal)* Gefährlichkeit *f*; *(of competition)* Schärfe *f*; *(of cuts, measures)* Härte *f*; *(of criticism)* Schonungslosigkeit *f*

savagery ['sævɪdʒərɪ] N **(a)** *(of tribe, people)* Wildheit *f* **(b)** (= *cruelty*) Grausamkeit *f*; *(of attack)* Brutalität *f*

save [seɪv] **1** N *(Ftbl etc)* Ballabwehr *f*; **what a ~!** eine tolle Parade!; **he made a fantastic ~** er hat den Ball prima abgewehrt **2** VT **(a)** (= *rescue, auch Rel*) retten; **to ~ sb from sth** jdn vor etw *(dat)* retten; **to ~ sb from disaster/ruin** jdn vor einer Katastrophe/dem Ruin bewahren *or* retten; **he ~d me from falling** er hat mich davor bewahrt hinzufallen; **to ~ sth from sth** etw aus etw retten; **to ~ the day** die Rettung sein; **God ~ the Queen** Gott schütze die Königin; **to be ~d by the bell** *(inf)* gerade noch einmal davonkommen; **to ~ one's neck** *or* **ass** *(US sl)* *or* **butt** *(US inf)* seinen Kopf retten; **to ~ sb's neck** *or* **ass** *(US sl)* *or* **butt** *(US inf)* jdn rauspauken *(inf)* **(b)** (= *put up, avoid using up*) aufheben; *fuel, time, space, money* sparen; *strength, battery* schonen; (= *~ up*) *strength, fuel etc* aufsparen; (= *collect*) *stamps etc* sammeln; **~ some of the cake for me** lass mir etwas Kuchen übrig; **~ me a seat** halte mir einen Platz frei; **~ it for later, I'm busy now** *(inf)* spar dirs für später auf, ich habe jetzt zu tun *(inf)*; **to ~ the best for last** das Beste bis zum Schluss aufheben; **going by plane will ~ you four hours on the train journey** der Flug spart dir vier Stunden Reisezeit im Vergleich zum Zug; **he's saving himself for the right woman** er spart sich für die Richtige auf **(c)** *(bother, trouble etc)* ersparen; **it ~d us having to do it again** das hat es uns *(dat)* erspart, es noch einmal machen zu müssen **(d)** *goal* verhindern; *shot, penalty* halten; **well ~d!** gut gehalten! **(e)** *(Comput)* sichern; **to ~ sth to disk** etw auf Diskette sichern *or* abspeichern **3** VI **(a)** *(with money)* sparen; **to ~ for sth** für *or* auf etw *(acc)* sparen **(b)** *(Comput)* **the file won't ~** die Datei lässt sich nicht sichern *or* abspeichern

➤ **save up 1** VI sparen *(for* für, auf +*acc)* **2** VT SEP (= *not spend*) sparen; (= *not use*) aufheben

saver ['seɪvər] N *(with money)* Sparer(in) *m(f)*

-saver N SUF **it is a time-/money-/space-saver** es spart Zeit/Geld/Platz; **life-saver** Lebensretter(in) *m(f)*

saving ['seɪvɪŋ] N **(a)** NO PL (= *rescue, Rel*) Rettung *f* **(b)** NO PL *(of money)* Sparen *nt* **(c)** *(of cost etc)* Einsparung *f*; (= *amount saved*) Ersparnis *f*; **how much of a ~ is there?** wie viel wird eingespart?; **we must make ~s** wir müssen sparen **(d) savings** PL Ersparnisse *pl*; (= *account*) Spareinlagen *pl*; **post-office ~s** Postsparguthaben *nt*; **~s and loan association** genossenschaftliche Bausparkasse

-saving ADJ SUF ... sparend; **time-saving** Zeit sparend

savings IN CPDS Spar-; **savings ratio** N Sparquote *f*

saviour, *(US)* **savior** ['seɪvjər] N Retter(in) *m(f)*

savour, *(US)* **savor** ['seɪvər] VT **(a)** *(form)* kosten *(geh)*; *aroma (of food)* riechen **(b)** *(fig liter)* genießen

savoury, *(US)* **savory** ['seɪvərɪ] **1** ADJ **(a)** (= *appetizing*) lecker **(b)** (= *not sweet*) pikant **(c)** *(fig)* angenehm **2** N *(Brit)* Häppchen *nt*

saw¹ [sɔː] PRET *of* **see**¹

saw² *vb: pret* **sawed**, *ptp* **sawed** *or* **sawn 1** N Säge *f* **2** VTI sägen; **to ~ sth in two** etw entzweisägen; **~ the wood into smaller logs** zersägen Sie das Holz in kleinere Scheite

➤ **saw off** VT SEP absägen

➤ **saw up** VT SEP zersägen *(into* in +*acc)*

sawdust ['sɔːdʌst] N Sägemehl *nt*

sawn [sɔːn] PTP *of* **saw**²

sawn-off, *(US)* **sawed-off** ['sɔːn'ɒf], ['sɔːd'ɒf] ADJ **~ shotgun** Gewehr *nt* mit abgesägtem Lauf

Saxon ['sæksn] **1** N **(a)** Sachse *m*, Sächsin *f*; *(Hist)* (Angel)sachse *m*/-sächsin *f* **(b)** *(Ling)* Sächsisch *nt* **2** ADJ sächsisch; *(Hist)* (angel)sächsisch

Saxony ['sæksənɪ] N Sachsen *nt*

saxophone ['sæksəfəʊn] N Saxofon *nt*

say [seɪ]	
1 TRANSITIVE/INTRANSITIVE VERB	**2** NOUN

vb: pret, ptp **said**

1 TRANSITIVE/INTRANSITIVE VERB
(a) sagen; *poem* aufsagen; *prayer, text* sprechen; (= *pronounce*) aussprechen; **he can't say his r's** er kann kein R aussprechen; **say after me ...** sprechen Sie mir nach ...; **you can say what you like (about it/me)** Sie können (darüber/über mich) sagen, was Sie wollen; **I never thought I'd hear him say that** ich hätte nie gedacht, dass er das sagen würde; **that's not for him to say** es steht ihm nicht zu, sich darüber zu äußern; (= *to decide*) das kann er nicht entscheiden; **he looks very smart, I'll say that for him** er sieht sehr schick aus, das muss man ihm lassen; **though I say it myself** wenn ich das mal selbst sagen darf; **well, all I can say is ...** na ja, da kann ich nur sagen ...; **it tastes, shall we say, interesting** das schmeckt aber, na, sagen wir mal interessant; **you'd better do it – who says?** tun Sie das lieber – wer sagt das?; **what does it mean? – I wouldn't like to say** was bedeutet das? – das kann ich auch nicht sagen; **having said that, I must point out ...** ich muss allerdings darauf hinweisen ...; **so saying, he sat down** und mit diesen Worten setzte er sich; **he said to wait here** er hat gesagt, ich soll/wir sollen *etc* hier warten

◆to say for oneself he didn't have much to say for himself er sagte nicht viel; **what have you got to say for yourself?** was haben Sie zu Ihrer Verteidigung zu sagen?

◆to say so **if you don't like it, say so** wenn Sie es nicht mögen, dann sagen Sie es doch; **do it this way – if you say so** machen Sie es so – wenn Sie meinen

(b) (= *indicate, tell*) sagen; **it says in the papers that ...** in den Zeitungen steht, dass ...; **what does this book/your horoscope** etc **say?** was steht in diesem Buch/deinem Horoskop etc?; **the rules say that ...** in den Regeln heißt es, dass ...; **what does the weather forecast say?** wie ist der Wetterbericht?; **that says a lot about his state of mind** das lässt tief auf seinen Gemütszustand schließen; **these figures say a lot about recent trends** diese Zahlen sind in Bezug auf neuere Tendenzen sehr aufschlussreich; **that's not saying much** das will nicht viel heißen; **there's no saying what might happen** was (dann) passiert, das kann keiner vorhersagen; **there's something/a lot to be said for being based in London** es spricht einiges/viel für ein Zuhause *or* (*for a firm*) für einen Sitz in London

(c) (= *suppose*) **say it takes three men to ...** angenommen, man braucht drei Leute, um zu ...; **if it happens on, say, Wednesday?** wenn es am, sagen wir mal Mittwoch, passiert?

(d) (*in suggestions*) **what would you say to a whisky?** wie wärs mit einem Whisky?; **shall we say £50?** sagen wir £ 50?; **I'll offer £500, what do you say to that?** ich biete £ 500, was meinen Sie dazu?; **let's try again, what d'you say?** (*inf*) was meinst du, versuchen wirs noch mal?; **what do you say?** was meinen Sie?; **I wouldn't say no to a cup of tea** ich hätte nichts gegen eine Tasse Tee; **he never says no to a drink** er sagt nie Nein zu einem Drink

(e) (*exclamatory*) **well, I must say!** na, ich muss schon sagen!; **say, what a great idea!** (*esp US*) Mensch, tolle Idee! (*inf*); **say, buddy!** (*esp US*) he, Mann! (*inf*); **I should say so!** das möchte ich doch meinen!; **you don't say!** (*also iro*) was du nicht sagst!; **you('ve) said it!** Sie sagen es!; **you can say that again!** das kann man wohl sagen!; **say no more!** ich weiß Bescheid!; **says you!** (*inf*) das meinst auch nur du! (*inf*); **says who?** (*inf*) wer sagt das?; **and so say all of us** und wir stimmen alle zu; **(it's) easier said than done** das ist leichter gesagt als getan; **no sooner said than done** gesagt, getan; **when all is said and done** letzten Endes; **they say ..., it is said ...** es heißt ...; **he is said to be very rich** er soll sehr reich sein; **a building said to have been built by ...** ein Gebäude, das von ... gebaut worden sein soll; **it goes without saying that ...** es versteht sich von selbst, dass ...; **that is to say** das heißt; **that's not to say that ...** das soll nicht heißen, dass ...; **to say nothing of the costs** etc von den Kosten etc mal ganz abgesehen; **enough said!** genug!

2 NOUN

(a) (= *opportunity to speak*) **let him have his say** lass ihn mal seine Meinung äußern

(b) (= *right to decide etc*) Mitspracherecht nt (*in* bei); **to have no/a say in sth** bei etw kein/ein Mitspracherecht haben; **to have the last** *or* **final say (in sth)** (etw) letztlich entscheiden

---

saying ['seɪɪŋ] N Redensart f; (= *proverb*) Sprichwort nt; **as the ~ goes** wie man so sagt, wie es so schön heißt

scab [skæb] N (*on cut*) Schorf m

scaffold ['skæfəld] N (*on building*) Gerüst nt; (*for execution*) Schafott nt

scaffolding ['skæfəldɪŋ] N Gerüst nt; **to put up ~** ein Gerüst aufbauen

scalawag ['skæləwæg] N (*US*) = **scallywag**

scald [skɔːld] **1** N Verbrühung f **2** VT verbrühen

scalding ['skɔːldɪŋ] **1** ADJ siedend; (*inf*: = *very hot*) siedend heiß **2** ADV **~ hot** siedend heiß

scale¹ [skeɪl] N (*of fish, snake*) Schuppe f; (= *kettle ~*) Kesselstein m no pl

scale² N (**pair of**) **~s** pl, (**~ form**) Waage f

scale³ N **(a)** Skala f; (= *list, table*) Tabelle f; (= *social ~*) Stufenleiter f
(b) (= *instrument*) Messgerät nt
(c) (*Mus*) Tonleiter f; **the ~ of G** die G(-Dur)-Tonleiter
(d) (*of map etc*) Maßstab m; **on a ~ of 5 km to the cm** in einem Maßstab von 5 km zu 1 cm; **(drawn/true) to ~**

maßstabgerecht
(e) (*fig*: = *size, extent*) Ausmaß nt; **to entertain on a small ~** Feste im kleineren Rahmen geben; **inflation on an unprecedented ~** Inflation von bisher nie gekanntem Ausmaß; **small in ~** von geringem Umfang; **it's similar but on a smaller ~** es ist ähnlich, nur kleiner; **on a national ~** auf nationaler Ebene

► scale down VT SEP (*lit*) verkleinern; (*fig*) verringern

► scale up VT SEP (*lit*) vergrößern; (*fig*) erhöhen

scale⁴ VT mountain, wall erklettern

scallion ['skælɪən] N (*US*) = **spring onion**

scallop ['skɒləp] N (*Zool*) Kammmuschel f, Jakobsmuschel f (*esp Cook*)

scallywag ['skælɪwæg] N (*Brit inf*) Schlingel m (*inf*)

scalp [skælp] N Kopfhaut f

scalpel ['skælpəl] N Skalpell nt

scaly ['skeɪlɪ] ADJ (+ER) schuppig

scam [skæm] N (*inf*: = *deception*) Betrug m

scamp [skæmp] N (*inf*) Frechdachs m

scamper ['skæmpəʳ] VI (*person, puppy*) tollen; (*rabbit*) hoppeln; (*squirrel, mice*) huschen

scan [skæn] **1** VT **(a)** schwenken über (+*acc*); (*person*) seine Augen wandern lassen über (+*acc*); *newspaper, book* überfliegen; *horizon* absuchen; *luggage* durchleuchten
(b) (*Med*) ein Szintigramm machen von; *pregnant woman* einen Ultraschall machen bei **2** N (*Med*) Scan m; (*in pregnancy*) Ultraschalluntersuchung f

► scan in VT SEP (*Comput*) graphics einbinden, scannen

scandal ['skændl] N **(a)** Skandal m; **to cause/create a ~** einen Skandal verursachen; (*amongst neighbours etc*) allgemeines Aufsehen erregen; **it is a ~ that ...** es ist skandalös, dass ...
(b) NO PL (= *gossip*) Skandalgeschichten pl; (= *piece of gossip*) Skandalgeschichte f; **the latest ~** der neueste Klatsch

scandalize ['skændəlaɪz] VT schockieren; **she was ~d** sie war empört (*by* über +*acc*)

scandalous ['skændələs] ADJ skandalös; **a ~ report/tale** eine Skandalgeschichte

scandalously ['skændələslɪ] ADV skandalös

Scandinavia [ˌskændɪˈneɪvɪə] N Skandinavien nt

Scandinavian [ˌskændɪˈneɪvɪən] **1** ADJ skandinavisch **2** N Skandinavier(in) m(f)

scanner ['skænəʳ] N (*Comput, Med*) Scanner m

scant [skænt] ADJ (+ER) wenig inv; *success* gering; *supply, grazing, amount* dürftig; **to pay ~ attention to sth** etw kaum beachten

scantily ['skæntɪlɪ] ADV spärlich

scanty ['skæntɪ] ADJ (+ER) *supply, information, knowledge* spärlich; *piece of clothing* knapp

scapegoat ['skeɪpɡəʊt] N Sündenbock m; **to use sb/sth as a ~, to make sb/sth one's ~** jdm/einer Sache die Schuld zuschieben

scar [skɑːʳ] **1** N (*on skin*) Narbe f; (= *scratch*) Kratzer m; (= *burn*) Brandfleck m; (*fig: emotional*) Wunde f **2** VT *furniture* (*by scratching*) zerkratzen; (*by burning*) Brandflecken hinterlassen auf (+*dat*); (*fig*) *person* zeichnen; **he was ~red for life** (*lit*) er behielt bleibende Narben zurück; (*fig*) er war fürs Leben gezeichnet; **her ~red face** ihr narbiges Gesicht **3** VI Narben/eine Narbe hinterlassen

scarce [skɛəs] ADJ (+ER) (= *in short supply*) knapp; (= *rare*) selten; *jobs* rar; **to make oneself ~** (*inf*) verschwinden (*inf*)

scarcely ['skɛəslɪ] ADV kaum; (= *not really*) wohl kaum; **~ anybody** kaum jemand; **~ anything** fast *or* beinahe nichts; **I know what to say** ich weiß nicht recht, was ich sagen soll; **you can ~ expect him to believe that** Sie erwarten doch wohl kaum, dass er das glaubt

scarceness ['skɛəsnɪs], **scarcity** ['skɛəsɪtɪ] N (= *shortage*) Knappheit f; (= *rarity*) Seltenheit f; **a scarcity of qualified people** ein Mangel m an qualifizierten Kräften

scare [skɛəʳ] **1** N (= *fright*) Schreck(en) m; (= *general alarm*) Hysterie f (*about* wegen); **to give sb a ~** jdm einen Schrecken einjagen; (= *make sb jump also*) jdn erschrecken; **to create** *or* **cause a ~** eine Panik auslösen **2** VT einen Schrecken einjagen (+*dat*); (= *worry*) Angst machen (+*dat*); (= *frighten physically*) person, animal erschrecken; *birds* aufschrecken; **to be easily ~d** sehr schreckhaft sein; (= *easily worried*) sich (*dat*) leicht Angst

machen lassen; **to ~ sb stiff** or **to death** or **out of his/her wits** (all inf) jdn zu Tode erschrecken (inf)
3 VI **I don't ~ easily** ich bekomme nicht so schnell Angst
➤ **scare away** VT SEP verscheuchen; people verjagen
➤ **scare off** VT SEP (a) = scare away (b) (= put off) abschrecken (prep obj von)

scarecrow N (lit, fig) Vogelscheuche f

scared ['skɛəd] ADJ ängstlich; **to be ~ (of sb/sth)** (vor jdm/etw) Angst haben; **to be ~ stiff** or **to death** or **out of one's wits** (all inf) Todesängste ausstehen, fürchterliche Angst haben; **to be ~ to do sth** Angst haben, etw zu tun; **she was too ~ to speak** sie konnte vor Angst nicht sprechen; **he's ~ of telling her the truth** er getraut sich nicht, ihr die Wahrheit zu sagen

scare: **scaremongering** ['skɛəmʌŋɡərɪŋ] N (esp Brit) Panikmache(rei) f (inf); **scare story** N Schauergeschichte f; **scare tactics** PL Panikmache(rei) f (inf)

scarf [skɑːf] N, pl **scarves** Schal m; (= neck ~) Halstuch nt; (= head ~) Kopftuch nt; (round the shoulders) Schultertuch nt

scarlet ['skɑːlɪt] **1** N Scharlach(rot) nt **2** ADJ (scharlach)rot; **to turn** or **go ~** rot anlaufen (inf)

scarves [skɑːvz] PL of **scarf**

scary ['skɛərɪ] ADJ (+ER) (inf) unheimlich; film grus(e)lig (inf); **it was pretty ~** da konnte man schon Angst kriegen (inf); **that's a ~ thought** das ist ein beängstigender Gedanke

scathing ['skeɪðɪŋ] ADJ bissig; attack scharf; look, criticism vernichtend; **to be ~** bissige Bemerkungen pl machen (about über +acc); **to make a ~ attack on sb/sth** jdn/etw scharf angreifen

scathingly ['skeɪðɪŋlɪ] ADV answer mit schneidendem Hohn; look vernichtend; criticize, attack scharf

scatter ['skætə'] **1** VT (a) (= distribute at random) verstreuen; seeds, gravel streuen (on, onto auf +acc); (= not group together) (unregelmäßig) verteilen; **to ~ sth around** or **about** etw überall verstreuen; **to ~ sth with sth** etw mit etw bestreuen (b) (= disperse) auseinander treiben; demonstrators zerstreuen **2** VI sich zerstreuen (to in +acc); (in a hurry, in fear) auseinander laufen

scatter: **scatterbrain** N (inf) Schussel m (inf); **scatterbrained** ['skætəbreɪnd] ADJ (inf) schuss(e)lig (inf), zerfahren

scattered ['skætəd] ADJ population weit verstreut; objects, villages verstreut; trees einzeln stehend; clouds, showers, fighting vereinzelt; **my relatives are ~ all over the country** meine Verwandten sind über das ganze Land verstreut; **the books were ~ (about) all over the room** die Bücher lagen im ganzen Zimmer verstreut

scattering ['skætərɪŋ] N (of people) vereinzeltes Häufchen; **a ~ of books** vereinzelte Bücher pl

scavenge ['skævɪndʒ] **1** VT (lit, fig) ergattern; **the tramp ~d food from the piles of litter** der Landstreicher plünderte die Abfallhaufen **2** VI (lit) Nahrung suchen; **to ~ for sth** nach etw suchen

scavenger ['skævɪndʒə'] N (= animal) Aasfresser m; (fig: = person) Aasgeier m

scenario [sɪ'nɑːrɪəʊ] N Szenarium nt; (fig) Szenario nt

scene [siːn] N (a) (= place, setting) Schauplatz m; (of play, novel) Ort m der Handlung; **the ~ of the crime** der Tatort; **to set the ~ (lit, fig)** den Rahmen geben; **a change of ~ does you good** ein Tapetenwechsel m tut dir gut; **to come** or **appear on the ~** auf der Bildfläche erscheinen; **after the accident the police were first on the ~** nach dem Unfall war die Polizei als erste zur Stelle
(b) (= description, incident, fuss, Theat) Szene f; **Act II, ~ i** Akt II, 1. Szene; **behind the ~s** (lit, fig) hinter den Kulissen; **to make a ~** eine Szene machen
(c) (= sight) Anblick m; (= landscape) Landschaft f; (= tableau) Szene f; **favourite (Brit)** or **favorite (US) Glasgow ~s** die beliebtesten Ansichten von Glasgow
(d) (inf) Szene f; **the London drug** etc **~** die Londoner Drogenszene etc; **on the fashion ~** in der Modewelt; **that's not my ~** da steh ich nicht drauf (inf)

scenery ['siːnərɪ] N (= landscape) Landschaft f; **do you like the ~?** gefällt Ihnen die Gegend? (b) (Theat) Bühnendekoration f, Kulissen pl

scenic ['siːnɪk] ADJ (= of landscape) landschaftlich; (= picturesque) malerisch; **to take the ~ route** die

landschaftlich schöne Strecke nehmen; (hum) einen kleinen Umweg machen

scent [sent] N (a) (= smell) Duft m (b) (= perfume) Parfüm nt (c) (of animal) Fährte f; **to put** or **throw sb off the ~** (lit, fig) jdn von der Fährte abbringen

scented ['sentɪd] ADJ soap, handkerchief parfümiert; flower, garden duftend; **~ candle** Duftkerze f

sceptic, (US) **skeptic** ['skeptɪk] N Skeptiker(in) m(f)

sceptical, (US) **skeptical** ['skeptɪkəl] ADJ skeptisch; **to be ~ about** or **of sth** über etw (acc) skeptisch sein

sceptically, (US) **skeptically** ['skeptɪkəlɪ] ADV skeptisch

scepticism, (US) **skepticism** ['skeptɪsɪzəm] N Skepsis f (about gegenüber)

schedule ['skedʒʊəl, (esp Brit) 'ʃedjuːl] **1** N (a) (of events) Programm nt; (of work) Zeitplan m; (of lessons) Stundenplan m; (esp US: = timetable) Fahr-/Flugplan m; **according to ~** planmäßig; **the train is behind ~** der Zug hat Verspätung; **the bus was on ~** der Bus war pünktlich; **the building will be opened on ~** das Gebäude wird wie geplant eröffnet werden; **the work is ahead of/behind ~** wir/sie etc sind (mit der Arbeit) dem Zeitplan voraus/im Rückstand; **we are working to a very tight ~** unsere Termine sind sehr eng (inf)
(b) (= insurance, mortgage ~) Urkunde f
2 VT planen; (= put on programme, timetable) ansetzen; **the work is ~d for completion in 3 months** die Arbeit soll (laut Zeitplan) in 3 Monaten fertig (gestellt) sein; **this building is ~d for demolition** es ist geplant, dieses Gebäude abzureißen; **she is ~d to speak tomorrow** ihre Rede ist für morgen geplant; **the plane is ~d to take off at 2 o'clock** planmäßiger Abflug ist 2 Uhr

scheduled ['skedʒʊəld, (esp Brit) 'ʃedjuːld] ADJ geplant; departure etc planmäßig

scheduled flight N Linienflug m

schematic ADJ, **schematically** ADV [skɪ'mætɪk, -əlɪ] schematisch

scheme [skiːm] **1** N (a) (= plan) Plan m; (= project) Projekt nt; (= insurance ~) Programm nt; (= idea) Idee f; **savings ~** Sparprogramm nt
(b) (= plot) (raffinierter) Plan; (esp political) Komplott nt; (at court, in firm etc) Intrige f
(c) (= layout) (of town centre etc) Anlage f; (of room etc) Einrichtung f; **the new road ~** das neue Straßensystem; **in the grand ~ of things** im Ganzen gesehen
2 VI Pläne schmieden; (in firm etc) intrigieren

schemer ['skiːmə'] N raffinierter Schlawiner; (in firm etc) Intrigant(in) m(f)

scheming ['skiːmɪŋ] **1** N raffiniertes Vorgehen; (of politicians, businessmen etc) Machenschaften pl; (at court, in firm etc) Intrigen pl **2** ADJ methods, businessman raffiniert; colleague intrigant; politician gewieft (inf)

schilling ['ʃɪlɪŋ] N Schilling m

schizophrenia [ˌskɪtsəʊ'friːnɪə] N Schizophrenie f

schizophrenic [ˌskɪtsəʊ'frenɪk] **1** ADJ schizophren **2** N Schizophrene(r) mf

schnap(p)s [ʃnæps] N Schnaps m

scholar ['skɒlə'] N Gelehrte(r) mf

scholarly ['skɒləlɪ] ADJ wissenschaftlich; (= learned) gelehrt; interests hochgeistig

scholarship ['skɒləʃɪp] N (a) (= learning) Gelehrsamkeit f (b) (= money award) Stipendium nt; **to win a ~ to Cambridge** ein Stipendium für Cambridge bekommen; **~ holder** Stipendiat(in) m(f)

school¹ [skuːl] N (a) Schule f; (US) (= college/university) College nt; Universität f; **at ~** in der Schule/im College/an der Universität; **to go to ~** in die Schule/ins College/zur Universität gehen; **there's no ~ tomorrow** morgen ist schulfrei (b) (Univ: = department) Fachbereich m; (of medicine, law) Fakultät f; **School of Arabic Studies** Institut nt für Arabistik

school² N (of fish) Schule f; (of herrings) Schwarm m

school IN CPDS Schul-; **school age** N Schulalter nt; **school board** N (US) Schulbehörde f; (Brit) Schulaufsichtsrat m; **schoolboy** N Schüler m; **school days** PL Schulzeit f; **school dinner** N Schulessen nt; **school fees** PL Schulgeld nt; **schoolgirl** N Schülerin f

schooling ['skuːlɪŋ] N Ausbildung f

school: **school-leaver** N (*Brit*) Schulabgänger(in) *m(f)*; **schoolmaster** N (*dated*) Lehrer *m*; **schoolmate** N (*Brit*) Schulkamerad(in) *m(f)*; **school meals** PL Schulessen *nt*; **schoolmistress** N (*dated*) Lehrerin *f*; **school report** N Schulzeugnis *nt*; **schoolroom** N Klassenzimmer *nt*; **schoolteacher** N Lehrer(in) *m(f)*; **school uniform** N Schuluniform *f*

science [ˈsaɪəns] N Wissenschaft *f*; (= *natural ~*) Naturwissenschaft *f*; **things that ~ cannot explain** Dinge, die man nicht naturwissenschaftlich erklären kann

science fiction N Sciencefiction *f*

scientific [ˌsaɪənˈtɪfɪk] ADJ naturwissenschaftlich; *apparatus, classification, methods* wissenschaftlich; **~ opinion** die wissenschaftliche Lehrmeinung; **~ management** wissenschaftliche Betriebsführung; **to be ~ about sth** etw systematisch angehen

scientifically [ˌsaɪənˈtɪfɪkəlɪ] ADV **(a)** (= *relating to natural sciences*) naturwissenschaftlich; **~ proven** wissenschaftlich erwiesen; **~ based** auf wissenschaftlicher Basis **(b)** (= *systematically, exactly*) wissenschaftlich

scientist [ˈsaɪəntɪst] N (Natur)wissenschaftler(in) *m(f)*

sci-fi [ˈsaɪfaɪ] N (*inf*) = **science fiction**

Scillies [ˈsɪlɪz], **Scilly Isles** [ˈsɪlɪˌaɪlz] PL Scillyinseln *pl*

scintillating [ˈsɪntɪleɪtɪŋ] ADJ (*fig*) *wit, performance* sprühend *attr*; *person, speech* vor Geist sprühend *attr*; (= *fascinating*) *information* faszinierend; **to be ~** sprühen; vor Geist sprühen; faszinierend sein

scissors [ˈsɪzəz] N PL Schere *f*; **a pair of ~** eine Schere

scoff¹ [skɒf] VI spotten; **to ~ at sb/sth** jdn/etw verachten; (*verbally*) sich abschätzig über jdn/etw äußern

scoff² (*Brit inf*) VT futtern (*inf*), in sich (*acc*) hineinstopfen (*inf*); **she ~ed the lot** sie hat alles verputzt (*inf*)

scold [skəʊld] **I** VT ausschimpfen (*for wegen*) **II** VI schimpfen

scolding [ˈskəʊldɪŋ] N Schelte *f no pl*; (= *act*) Schimpferei *f*

scone [skɒn] N (*Brit*) brötchenartiges Buttergebäck

scoop [skuːp] **I** N **(a)** (= *instrument*) Schaufel *f*; (*for ice cream, potatoes etc*) Portionierer *m*; (= *ball of ice cream*) Kugel *f* **(b)** (*inf*: = *lucky gain*) Fang *m* (*inf*) **(c)** (*Press*) Knüller *m* (*inf*) **II** VT **(a)** (*with ~*) schaufeln; *liquid* schöpfen **(b)** *prize, award* gewinnen

➤ **scoop out** VT SEP **(a)** (= *take out*) herausschaufeln; *liquid* herausschöpfen **(b)** *melon, marrow etc* aushöhlen; *hole* graben

➤ **scoop up** VT SEP aufschaufeln; *liquid* aufschöpfen; **she scooped the child up** sie raffte das Kind an sich (*acc*)

scooter [ˈskuːtə*r*] N (Tret)roller *m*; (= *motor ~*) (Motor)roller *m*

scope [skəʊp] N **(a)** (*of topic, investigation, knowledge*) Umfang *m*; (*of law*) Reichweite *f*; (*of sb's duties, department, tribunal*) Kompetenzbereich *m*; (*of one's pursuits, grasp*) Fassungsvermögen *nt*; **sth is within the ~ of sth** etw hält sich or bleibt im Rahmen einer Sache (*gen*); **sth is within the ~ of a department** *etc* etw fällt in den Kompetenzbereich einer Abteilung *etc*; **sth is beyond or outside the ~ of sth** etw geht über etw (*acc*) hinaus; **this project is more limited in ~** dieses Projekt ist auf einen engeren Rahmen begrenzt **(b)** (= *opportunity*) Möglichkeit(en) *f(pl)*; (*to develop one's talents*) Entfaltungsmöglichkeit *f*; (*to use one's talents*) Spielraum *m*; **there is ~ for further growth in the tourist industry** die Tourismusindustrie ist noch ausbaufähig; **there is little ~ for reducing our costs** es gibt wenig Spielraum, um die Kosten zu senken; **to give sb ~ to do sth** jdm den nötigen Spielraum geben, etw zu tun

scorch [skɔːtʃ] **I** N (*also* **~ mark**) Brandfleck *m* **II** VT versengen **III** VI **the sun ~ed down** die Sonne brannte herunter

scorching [ˈskɔːtʃɪŋ] ADJ *sun, iron* glühend heiß; *day, weather* brütend heiß; *heat* sengend

score [skɔː*r*] **I** N **(a)** (= *number of points*) (Punkte)stand *m*; (*of game, Sport*) (Spiel)stand *m*; (= *final ~*) Spielergebnis *nt*; **the ~ was Rangers 3, Celtic 0** es stand 3:0 für Rangers (gegen Celtic); (= *final ~*) Rangers schlug Celtic (mit) 3:0; **to keep (the) ~** (mit)zählen; (*officially*) Punkte zählen; (*on board*) Punkte anschreiben; **what's the ~?** wie steht es?; **he doesn't know the ~** (*fig*) er weiß nicht, was gespielt wird (*inf*) **(b)** (= *grudge*) Rechnung *f*; **to pay off or settle old ~s** alte Schulden begleichen; **to have a ~ to settle with sb** mit jdm eine alte Rechnung zu begleichen haben

(c) (*Mus*) Noten *pl*; (*esp of classical music*) Partitur *f*; (*of film, musical*) Musik *f*
(d) (= *line, cut*) Rille *f*, Kerbe *f*
(e) (= 20) zwanzig; **~s of ...** (= *many*) hunderte von ...
(f) (= *reason*) Grund *m*; **on that ~** deshalb
II VT **(a)** erzielen; **our last contestant ~d one hundred points** unser letzter Kandidat hat hundert Punkte; **each correct answer ~s five points** jede richtige Antwort zählt fünf Punkte; **to ~ a point off or over sb** (*fig*) auf jds Kosten (*acc*) glänzen
(b) (= *groove*) einkerben; (= *mark*) Kratzer/einen Kratzer machen in (+*acc*)
III VI **(a)** (= *win points etc*) einen Punkt erzielen; (*Ftbl etc*) ein Tor schießen; **to ~ well/badly** gut/schlecht abschneiden; (*in game, test etc also*) eine gute/keine gute Punktzahl erreichen **(b)** (= *keep ~*) (mit)zählen

➤ **score off** VT SEP (= *delete*) ausstreichen
➤ **score out** or **through** VT SEP durchstreichen

score: **scoreboard** N Anzeigetafel *f*; (*on TV*) Tabelle *f* der Spielergebnisse; **scorecard** N Spielprotokoll *nt*; **scorekeeper** N (= *official*) (*Sport*) Anschreiber(in) *m(f)*; (*in quiz etc*) Punktezähler(in) *m(f)*; **scoreless** ADJ (*Sport*) (= *without goals*) torlos; (= *without runs/points*) ohne dass ein Lauf/Punkt erzielt wurde

scorer [ˈskɔːrə*r*] N **(a)** (*Ftbl etc*) Torschütze *m*/-schützin *f*; **to be the top ~** die meisten Punkte machen; (*Ftbl etc*) die meisten Tore schießen **(b)** = **scorekeeper**

scoring [ˈskɔːrɪŋ] **I** N Erzielen *nt* eines Punktes; (*Ftbl etc*) Torschuss *m*; (= *scorekeeping*) Zählen *nt* **II** ADJ SUF **a low-/high-~ match** ein Spiel, in dem wenig/viele Punkte/Tore erzielt wurden

scorn [skɔːn] **I** N Verachtung *f*; **to pour** or **heap ~ on sb/sth** jdn/etw verächtlich abtun **II** VT (= *treat scornfully*) verachten; (*condescendingly*) verächtlich behandeln; *gift, advice* verschmähen

scornful [ˈskɔːnfʊl] ADJ verächtlich; *person* spöttisch; **to be ~ of sb/sth** jdn/etw verachten; (*verbally*) jdn/etw verhöhnen; **to be ~ about sb/sth** sich über jdn/etw verächtlich äußern

scornfully [ˈskɔːnfəlɪ] ADV verächtlich

Scorpio [ˈskɔːpɪəʊ] N Skorpion *m*; **he's a(n) ~** er ist Skorpion

Scot [skɒt] N Schotte *m*, Schottin *f*

Scotch [skɒtʃ] **I** ADJ schottisch **II** N (= *~ whisky*) Scotch *m*

Scotch tape® N Tesafilm® *m*

scot-free [ˈskɒtˈfriː] ADV ungeschoren; **to get off ~** ungeschoren davonkommen

Scotland [ˈskɒtlənd] N Schottland *nt*

Scots [skɒts] **I** ADJ schottisch **II** N (= *Ling*) Schottisch *nt*; **the ~** (= *people*) die Schotten *pl*

Scots: **Scotsman** N Schotte *m*; **Scotswoman** N Schottin *f*

Scottish [ˈskɒtɪʃ] **I** ADJ schottisch **II** N **(a)** (= *Ling*) Schottisch *nt* **(b) the ~** *pl* die Schotten *pl*

scoundrel [ˈskaʊndrəl] N Bengel *m*

scour¹ [ˈskaʊə*r*] VT scheuern
➤ **scour out** VT SEP *pan* ausscheuern; *borehole* durchspülen

scour² VT *area, shops* absuchen (*for nach*); *newspaper* durchkämmen (*for nach*)
➤ **scour about** (*Brit*) or **around** VI herumsuchen (*for nach*)

scourer [ˈskaʊərə*r*] N Topfkratzer *m*; (= *sponge*) Scheuerschwamm *m*

scourge [skɜːdʒ] N (*lit, fig*) Geißel *f*

scouring pad [ˈskaʊərɪŋpæd] N = **scourer**

Scouse [skaʊs] **I** ADJ Liverpooler **II** N **(a)** (= *person*) Liverpooler(in) *m(f)* **(b)** (= *dialect*) Liverpooler Dialekt *m*

scout [skaʊt] **I** N **(a)** (*Mil*) (= *person*) Kundschafter(in) *m(f)*; (= *ship, plane*) Aufklärer *m*
(b) (= *search*) Suche *f*; **to have** or **take a ~ (a)round for sth** sich um sehen
(c) Scout (= *boy ~*) Pfadfinder *m*; (*US*: = *girl ~*) Pfadfinderin *f*
(d) (= *football ~ etc*) Spion(in) *m(f)*; (= *talent ~*) Talentsucher(in) *m(f)*
II VI auskundschaften; **to ~ for sth** nach etw Ausschau halten; **he was ~ing for new talent** er war auf Talentsuche
III VT *area, country* erkunden

➤ **scout about** (*Brit*) or **around** VI sich umsehen (*for nach*)
➤ **scout out** VT SEP aufstöbern; (*Mil*) auskundschaften

scouting ['skaʊtɪŋ] **1** N **(a)** Auskundschaften nt; (Mil) Aufklärung f; (= looking) Suche f (for nach); (for talent) Talentsuche f **(b) Scouting** (= scout movement) Pfadfindertum nt **2** ADJ ATTR **Scouting** Pfadfinder-

scoutmaster ['skaʊtmɑːstə[r]] N Gruppenführer m

scowl [skaʊl] **1** N finsterer Blick **2** VI ein finsteres Gesicht machen; **to ~ at sb** jdn böse ansehen

scrabble ['skræbl] **1** VI (also **~ about** (Brit) or **around**) (herum)tasten; (among movable objects) (herum)wühlen **2** N **Scrabble®** Scrabble® nt

scraggly ['skræglɪ] ADJ (+ER) beard, hair zottig; plant kümmerlich

scraggy ['skrægɪ] ADJ (+ER) **(a)** (= scrawny) dürr; meat sehnig **(b)** hair, fur zottig

scram [skræm] VI (inf) abhauen (inf); **~!** verschwinde!

scramble ['skræmbl] **1** N **(a)** (= climb) Kletterei f **(b)** (= mad dash) Gerangel nt; **the ~ for the better-paid jobs** die Jagd nach den besser bezahlten Stellen **2** VT **(a)** pieces, letters (untereinander) mischen **(b)** eggs verquirlen **(c)** (Telec) message verschlüsseln **3** VI **(a)** (= climb) klettern; **to ~ out** herausklettern; **he ~d to his feet** er rappelte sich auf (inf); **to ~ up sth** auf etw (acc) hinaufklettern **(b)** (= struggle) **to ~ for sth** sich um etw balgen or raufen; for ball etc um etw kämpfen; for job, good site sich um etw drängeln; **to ~ to get sth** sich balgen or raufen, um etw zu bekommen; ball etc darum kämpfen, etw zu bekommen; for job, good site sich drängeln, um etw zu bekommen

scrambled egg(s) [skræmbld'eg(z)] N(PL) Rührei(er) nt(pl)

scrap [skræp] **1** N **(a)** (= small piece) Stückchen nt; (fig) bisschen no pl; (of paper, conversation, news) Fetzen m; (of truth) Spur f; **there isn't a ~ of food in the house** es ist überhaupt nichts zu essen im Haus; **his few ~s of knowledge** das bisschen Wissen, das er hat; **a few ~s of information** ein paar magere Auskünfte; **not a ~ of evidence** nicht der geringste Beweis **(b)** (usu pl: = leftover) Rest m **(c)** (= waste material) Altmaterial nt; (= metal) Schrott m; (= paper) Altpapier nt; **to sell a ship for ~** ein Schiff zum Verschrotten verkaufen **2** VT car, ship etc verschrotten; idea, plan etc fallenlassen; piece of work wegwerfen; **~ that** (inf: = forget it) vergiss es!

scrapbook ['skræpbʊk] N Sammelalbum nt

scrape [skreɪp] **1** N (= mark, graze) Schramme f **2** VT **(a)** (= make clean or smooth) potatoes etc schaben; plate, wall, shoes abkratzen; dish, saucepan auskratzen; hole scharren; **to ~ a living** gerade so sein Auskommen haben; **that's really scraping the (bottom of the) barrel** (fig) das ist wirklich das Letzte vom Letzten **(b)** (= mark, graze) car schrammen; wall, gatepost streifen; arm, knee aufschürfen **(c)** (= grate against) kratzen an (+dat) **3** VI (= make clean, grate) kratzen (against an +dat); (= rub) streifen (against +acc); **as he ~d past me** als er sich an mir vorbeizwängte; **the car just ~d past the gatepost** der Wagen fuhr um Haaresbreite am Torpfosten vorbei

➤ **scrape by** VI (lit) sich vorbeizwängen; (fig) sich durchwursteln (inf) (on mit)

➤ **scrape in** VI **he just managed to scrape in** er ist gerade noch hineingerutscht (inf)

➤ **scrape off 1** VI sich abkratzen lassen **2** VT SEP abkratzen (prep obj von)

➤ **scrape out** VT SEP auskratzen; bad parts ausschneiden

➤ **scrape through 1** VI (lit) (object) gerade so durchgehen; (person) gerade so durchkommen; (in exam) durchrutschen (inf) **2** VI +PREP OBJ narrow gap sich durchzwängen durch; exam durchrutschen durch (inf)

➤ **scrape together** VT SEP money zusammenkratzen

➤ **scrape up** VT SEP (lit) aufkratzen; money auftreiben (inf); support organisieren

scraper ['skreɪpə[r]] N (= tool) Spachtel m

scrap heap N Schrotthaufen m; **to be thrown on the ~** (thing) zum Schrott geworfen werden; (person) zum alten Eisen geworfen werden; **to end up on the ~** (person) beim alten Eisen landen

scrapings ['skreɪpɪŋz] PL (of food) Reste pl; (= potato ~) Schalen pl; (= carrot ~) Schababfälle pl; (= metal ~) Späne pl

scrap: scrap merchant N Schrotthändler(in) m(f); **scrap metal** N Schrott m

scrappy ['skræpɪ] ADJ (+ER) zusammengestückelt; knowledge lückenhaft; football match orientierungslos

scrapyard ['skræpjɑːd] N (esp Brit) Schrottplatz m

scratch [skrætʃ] **1** N (= mark) Kratzer m; (= act) **to have a ~** sich kratzen; **to start from ~** (ganz) von vorn(e) anfangen; **to start sth from ~** etw ganz von vorne anfangen; business etw aus dem Nichts aufbauen; **to learn a language from ~** eine Sprache ganz von Anfang an or von Grund auf erlernen; **to be** or **come up to ~** (inf) den Anforderungen entsprechen; **he/it is not quite up to ~ yet** (inf) er/es lässt noch zu wünschen übrig; **to bring sb up to ~** jdn auf Vordermann bringen (inf); **to ~ the surface of sth** (fig) etw oberflächlich berühren **2** VT kratzen; hole scharren; (= leave scratches on) zerkratzen; **she ~ed the dog's ear** sie kratzte den Hund am Ohr; **to ~ a living** (dat) einen kümmerlichen Lebensunterhalt verdienen; **to ~ one's head** (lit, fig) sich am Kopf kratzen; **if you ~ my back, I'll ~ yours** (fig) eine Hand wäscht die andere; **to ~ the surface of sth** (fig) etw oberflächlich berühren **3** VI kratzen; (in soil etc) scharren; (= ~ oneself) sich kratzen

➤ **scratch about** (Brit) or **around** VI (lit) herumscharren; (fig inf) sich umsehen (for nach)

➤ **scratch out** VT SEP auskratzen; (= cross out) ausstreichen

scratchcard ['skrætʃkɑːd] N (Brit: for lottery etc) Rubbellos nt

scratchiness ['skrætʃɪnɪs] N Kratzen nt

scratch: scratch pad N (US Comput) Notizblock m; **scratch paper** N (US) Notizpapier nt

scratchy ['skrætʃɪ] ADJ (+ER) sound, pen kratzend attr; record zerkratzt; feel, sweater kratzig

scrawl [skrɔːl] **1** N Krakelei f; (= handwriting) Klaue f (inf) **2** VT hinkritzeln **3** VI krakeln (inf)

scrawny ['skrɔːnɪ] ADJ (+ER) dürr

scream [skriːm] **1** N **(a)** (of tyres) Kreischen nt; (of engines) Heulen nt; **there were ~s of laughter from the audience** das Publikum kreischte vor Lachen; **to let out** or **give a ~** einen Schrei ausstoßen **(b)** (fig inf) **to be a ~** zum Schreien sein (inf) **2** VT schreien; command brüllen; (fig: headlines) ausschreien; **to ~ sth at sb** jdm etw zuschreien; **to ~ one's head off** (inf) sich (dat) die Lunge aus dem Leib or Hals schreien **3** VI (tyres) kreischen; (wind, engine) heulen; **to ~ at sb** jdn anschreien; **to ~ for sth** nach etw schreien; **to ~ in** or **with pain** vor Schmerzen schreien; **to ~ with laughter** vor Lachen kreischen

➤ **scream out 1** VI aufschreien **2** VT SEP ausschreien; (person) hinausschreien; name schreien; warning ausstoßen

screaming ['skriːmɪŋ] **1** ADJ (lit, fig) schreiend; tyres kreischend; wind, engine heulend **2** N **to have a ~ match** sich gegenseitig anbrüllen (inf)

screech [skriːtʃ] **1** N Kreischen nt no pl; (of women, tyres, brakes also) Quietschen nt no pl; (of owl) Schrei m **2** VT schreien; high notes quietschen **3** VI kreischen; **to ~ with pain** vor Schmerzen schreien; **to ~ with laughter** vor Lachen kreischen; **to ~ with delight** vor Vergnügen quietschen

screen [skriːn] **1** N **(a)** (protective) Schirm m; (for privacy etc) Wandschirm m; (as partition) Trennwand f; (against light) Verdunklungsschutz m; (fig) (for protection) Schutz m; (of trees) Wand f; (of secrecy) Schleier m; **~ of smoke** Rauchschleier m **(b)** (Film) Leinwand f; (TV, = radar =) (Bild)schirm m; **stars of the ~** Filmstars pl; **the big ~** die Leinwand; **the small ~** die Mattscheibe **(c)** (Comput) Bildschirm m; **on ~** auf Bildschirm (dat); **to work on ~** am Bildschirm arbeiten **2** VT **(a)** (= hide) verdecken; (= protect) abschirmen; (fig) schützen (from vor +dat); **he ~ed his eyes from the sun** er schützte die Augen vor der Sonne **(b)** TV programme senden; film vorführen **(c)** applicants, security risks überprüfen; calls überwachen; (Med) untersuchen **3** VI **to ~ for sth** (Med) auf etw (acc) untersuchen

➤ **screen off** VT SEP (durch einen Schirm/Vorhang/eine Wand etc) abtrennen

screenful ['skriːnfʊl] N (Comput) Bildschirm m

screening ['skriːnɪŋ] N **(a)** (of applicants, security risks) Überprüfung f **(b)** (of film) Vorführung f; (TV) Sendung f

screen: screenplay N Drehbuch nt; **screen-printing** N Siebdruck m; **screensaver** N (Comput) Bildschirmschoner m; **screen test** N Probeaufnahmen pl; **screenwriter** N Drehbuchautor(in) m(f)

screw [skru:] **■** N (a) (Mech) Schraube f; **he's got a ~ loose** (inf) bei dem ist eine Schraube locker (inf); **to put** or **turn** or **tighten the ~s on sb** (inf), **to turn the ~ on sb** (inf) jdm die Daumenschrauben anlegen
(b) (sl: = sexual intercourse) **he/she is a good ~** er/sie vögelt gut (inf); **to have a ~** vögeln (inf), bumsen (inf)
■ VT (a) (using ~s) schrauben (to an +acc, onto auf +acc); **she ~ed her handkerchief into a ball** sie knüllte ihr Taschentuch zu einem Knäuel zusammen
(b) (sl: = have intercourse with) vögeln (inf), bumsen (inf); **~ you!** (sl) leck mich am Arsch! (vulg), du kannst mich mal! (inf)
(c) (inf) (= rip off) abzocken (inf); (= cheat) bescheißen (sl)
■ VI (sl: = have intercourse) vögeln (inf), bumsen (inf)
➤ **screw down** VT SEP an- or festschrauben
➤ **screw in ■** VT SEP (hin)einschrauben (prep obj, -to in +acc) **■** VI (hin)eingeschraubt werden (prep obj, -to in +acc)
➤ **screw off ■** VT SEP abschrauben (prep obj von) **■** VI abgeschraubt werden (prep obj von)
➤ **screw on** VT SEP anschrauben (acc); **to screw sth on(to) sth** etw an etw (acc) schrauben; lid, top etw auf etw (acc) schrauben **■** VI aufgeschraubt werden (= with screws) angeschraubt werden
➤ **screw together ■** VT SEP zusammenschrauben **■** VI zusammengeschraubt werden
➤ **screw up ■** VT SEP (a) paper zusammenknüllen; eyes zusammenkneifen; face verziehen; **to screw up one's courage** seinen ganzen Mut zusammennehmen
(b) (inf: = spoil) vermasseln (inf); **he's really screwed things up** er hat da wirklich Scheiße gebaut (inf)
(c) (inf) sb neurotisch machen; **he's so screwed up** der hat einen Schaden (inf); **to be screwed up about sth** sich wegen etw ganz verrückt machen
■ VI (inf: = make a mess) Scheiße bauen (inf) (on sth bei etw)

screwdriver ['skru:draɪvəʳ] N Schraubenzieher m

scribble ['skrɪbl] **■** N Gekritzel nt no pl; **covered in ~(s)** voll gekritzelt **■** VT hinkritzeln; **to ~ sth on sth** etw auf etw (acc) kritzeln; **to ~ sth down** etw hinkritzeln **■** VI kritzeln

scribe [skraɪb] N Schreiber(in) m(f)

scrimp [skrɪmp] VI sparen, knausern; **to ~ and save** geizen und sparen

script [skrɪpt] N (a) (= style of writing) Schrift f (b) (of play) Text m; (= screenplay) Drehbuch nt; (of talk etc) (Manu)skript nt

scripture ['skrɪptʃəʳ] N **Scripture, the Scriptures** die (Heilige) Schrift

scriptwriter ['skrɪptraɪtəʳ] N Textautor(in) m(f); (of screenplay) Drehbuchautor(in) m(f); (of talk etc) Verfasser(in) m(f) des (Manu)skripts

scroll [skrəʊl] **■** N (a) Schriftrolle f; (decorative) Schnörkel m **(b)** (Comput) Scrollen nt, Blättern nt **■** VI (Comput) scrollen, blättern
➤ **scroll down** VI, VT SEP vorscrollen; (vi also) runterblättern
➤ **scroll up** VI, VT SEP zurückscrollen; (vi also) raufblättern

scroll bar N (Comput) Bildlaufleiste f

Scrooge [skru:dʒ] N Geizhals m

scrotum ['skrəʊtəm] N Hodensack m

scrounge [skraʊndʒ] (inf) **■** VTI schnorren (inf) (off, from bei) **■** N **to be on the ~** am Schnorren sein (inf)

scrounger ['skraʊndʒəʳ] N (inf) Schnorrer(in) m(f) (inf)

scrub¹ [skrʌb] N (= ~land) Gebüsch nt

scrub² **■** N Schrubben nt no pl; **to give sth a ~/a good ~** etw schrubben/gründlich abschrubben **■** VT schrubben; vegetables putzen; (inf: = cancel) abblasen (inf); idea abschreiben (inf); **to ~ oneself all over** sich von oben bis unten abschrubben **■** VI **to ~ at sth** an etw (dat) herumreiben
➤ **scrub down** VT SEP walls, person abschrubben
➤ **scrub out** VT SEP pans etc ausscheuern

scrubbing brush ['skrʌbɪŋ,brʌʃ] (Brit), **scrub brush** (US) N Scheuerbürste f

scrubland ['skrʌblænd] N see scrub¹

scruff¹ [skrʌf] N **by the ~ of the neck** am Genick

scruff² N (inf: = scruffy person) (= woman) Schlampe f (inf); (= man) abgerissener Typ (inf)

scruffily ['skrʌfɪlɪ] ADV (inf) schlampig (inf)

scruffiness ['skrʌfɪnɪs] N (inf: of person) schlampiges Aussehen (inf)

scruffy ['skrʌfɪ] ADJ (+ER) (inf) gammelig (inf); person, clothes also schlampig (inf); park, city verlottert (inf)

scrum [skrʌm] N (of reporters etc, Rugby) Gedränge nt

scrumptious ['skrʌmpʃəs] ADJ (inf) meal etc lecker

scrunch [skrʌntʃ] **■** N Knirschen nt **■** VT nose rümpfen; **to ~ sth (up) into a ball** etw zusammenknüllen **■** VI (gravel, snow) knirschen

scruple ['skru:pl] N Skrupel m; **~s** (= doubts) (moralische) Bedenken pl; **to have no ~s about sth** bei einer Sache keine Skrupel haben

scrupulous ['skru:pjʊləs] ADJ person, organization gewissenhaft; honesty unbedingt; cleanliness peinlich; account (peinlich) genau; **he is not too ~ in his business dealings** er hat keine allzu großen Skrupel bei seinen Geschäften; **she is not so ~ in matters of cleanliness** sie nimmt es mit der Sauberkeit nicht so genau; **to be ~ in doing sth** etw sehr gewissenhaft tun; **to be ~ about sth** mit etw sehr gewissenhaft sein

scrupulously ['skru:pjʊləslɪ] ADV (= honestly, conscientiously) gewissenhaft; (= meticulously) sorgfältig; exact, clean peinlich; fair, careful äußerst

scrutinize ['skru:tɪnaɪz] VT (= examine) (genau) untersuchen; (= check) genau prüfen; (= stare at) prüfend ansehen, mustern

scrutiny ['skru:tɪnɪ] N (= examination) Untersuchung f; (= checking) (Über)prüfung f; (of person) Musterung f; (= stare) prüfender or musternder Blick

SCSI ['skʌzɪ] (Comput) ABBR of **Small Computer Systems Interface** SCSI

scuba ['sku:bə]: **scuba diver** N Sporttaucher(in) m(f); **scuba diving** N Sporttauchen nt

scud [skʌd] VI flitzen; (clouds) jagen

scuff [skʌf] **■** VT abwetzen; **don't ~ your feet like that!** schlurf nicht so! **■** VI schlurfen **■** N (US: = slipper) Pantolette f

scuffle ['skʌfl] **■** N Rauferei f (inf), Handgemenge nt **■** VI (= have skirmish) sich raufen; (= make noise) poltern; **to ~ with the police** ein Handgemenge mit der Polizei haben

sculpt [skʌlpt] **■** VT = sculpture 2 **■** VI bildhauern (inf)

sculptor ['skʌlptəʳ] N Bildhauer(in) m(f)

sculptress ['skʌlptrɪs] N Bildhauerin f

sculpture ['skʌlptʃəʳ] **■** N (= art) Bildhauerkunst f; (= work) Bildhauerei f; (= object) Skulptur f, Plastik f **■** VT formen, arbeiten; (in stone) hauen; (in clay etc) modellieren

sculptured ['skʌlptʃəd] ADJ (lit) geformt; (in stone) gehauen

scum [skʌm] N (a) (on liquid) Schaum m; (= residue) Rand m; **a pond covered in green ~** ein mit einer grünen Schleimschicht bedeckter Teich **(b)** (pej inf) Abschaum m; (= one individual) Drecksau f (inf); **the ~ of the earth** der Abschaum der Menschheit

scumbag ['skʌmbæg] N (inf) Schleimscheißer m (inf)

scupper ['skʌpəʳ] VT (a) (Naut) versenken (b) (Brit inf: = ruin) zerschlagen

scurrilous ['skʌrɪləs] ADJ verleumderisch; remark, attack, story also ehrenrührig; (= indecent) unflätig

scurry ['skʌrɪ] **■** N (= hurry) Hasten nt; (= sound) Trippeln nt **■** VI (person) hasten; (with small steps) eilig trippeln; (animals) huschen; **they all scurried out of the classroom** sie hatten es alle eilig, aus dem Klassenzimmer zu kommen

'scuse [skju:z] VT (inf) = excuse 1

scuttle¹ ['skʌtl] VI (person) trippeln; (animals) hoppeln; (spiders etc) krabbeln

scuttle² VT (Naut) (a) versenken (b) (fig) agreement, talks sprengen; plans kaputtmachen

scythe [saɪð] N Sense f

SDR (Fin) ABBR of **Special Drawing Right** Sonderziehungsrecht nt

SE ABBR of **south-east** SO

sea [si:] N (a) Meer nt, See f; **by ~** auf dem Seeweg; **a town by or on the ~** eine Stadt am Meer or an der See; **(out) at ~** auf See; **to be all at ~** (fig) nicht durchblicken (with bei) (inf); **to go to ~** zur See gehen; **a ~ of flames** ein Flammenmeer

(b) (= *state of the* ~) See *f no pl*, Seegang *m*; **heavy ~s** schwere See

sea: sea air N Seeluft *f*; **sea anemone** N Seeanemone *f*; **sea battle** N Seeschlacht *f*; **seabed** N Meeresboden *m*; **sea bird** N Seevogel *m*; **seaboard** N (*US*) Küste *f*; **sea breeze** N Seewind *m*; **sea change** N totale Veränderung; **sea defences**, (*US*) **sea defenses** PL Hochwasserschutzmaßnahmen *pl*; **seafish** N Meeresfisch *m*; **seafood** N Meeresfrüchte *pl*; **~ restaurant** Fischrestaurant *nt*; **seafront** N (= *beach*) Strand *m*; (= *promenade*) Strandpromenade *f*; **sea green** N Meergrün *nt*; **sea-green** ADJ meergrün; **seagull** N Möwe *f*; **sea horse** N Seepferdchen *nt*

seal¹ [siːl] N (*Zool*) Seehund *m*

seal² ■ N **(a)** (= *impression in wax etc*) Siegel *nt*; (*against unauthorized opening*) Versiegelung *f*; (= *metal*) Plombe *f*; (= *die*) Stempel *m*; (= *decorative label*) Aufkleber *m*; **~ of quality** Gütesiegel *nt*; **to put one's** *or* **the ~ of approval on sth** einer Sache (*dat*) seine offizielle Zustimmung geben; **to set one's ~ on sth** (*lit, fig*) unter etw (*acc*) sein Siegel setzen **(b)** (= *airtight closure*) Verschluss *m*; (= *washer*) Dichtung *f* ■ VT versiegeln; *envelope, parcel also* zukleben; (*with wax*) siegeln; *border* dichtmachen; *area* abriegeln; (= *make air-* or *watertight*) abdichten; (*fig: = finalize*) besiegeln; **~ed envelope** verschlossener Briefumschlag; **my lips are ~ed** meine Lippen sind versiegelt; **this ~ed his fate** dadurch war sein Schicksal besiegelt

▸ **seal in** VT SEP einschließen

▸ **seal off** VT SEP absperren, abriegeln

▸ **seal up** VT SEP versiegeln; *parcel, letter* zukleben; *crack, windows* abdichten

sea: sea level N Meeresspiegel *m*; **above/below ~** über/unter dem Meeresspiegel; **sea lion** N Seelöwe *m*

seam [siːm] N Naht *f*; **to come** *or* **fall apart at the ~s** (*lit, fig*) aus den Nähten gehen; **to be bursting at the ~s** (*lit, fig*) aus allen Nähten platzen (*inf*)

seamless [ˈsiːmlɪs] ADJ *tube, stockings* nahtlos

seamstress [ˈsemstrɪs] N Näherin *f*

seamy [ˈsiːmɪ] ADJ (+ER) *club, person* heruntergekommen; *story, area, past* zwielichtig; *events, details* schmutzig

séance [ˈseɪɑːns] N Séance *f*

search [sɜːtʃ] ■ N (*for lost object etc*) Suche *f* (*for* nach); (*of luggage, suspect etc*) Durchsuchung *f* (*of* +*gen*); (*Comput*) Suchlauf *m*; **to go in ~ of sb/sth** auf die Suche nach jdm/etw gehen; **to carry out a ~ of a house** eine Haus(durch)suchung machen; **they arranged a ~ for the missing child** sie veranlassten eine Suchaktion nach dem vermissten Kind; **to do a ~ (and replace) for sth** (*Comput*) etw suchen (und ersetzen) ■ VT (*for* nach) durchsuchen; *records* suchen in (+*dat*); *conscience* erforschen; *memory, sb's face* durchforschen; **to ~ a place for sb/sth** einen Ort nach jdm absuchen/nach etw durch- *or* absuchen; **~ me!** (*inf*) was weiß ich? (*inf*) ■ VI (*also Comput*) suchen (*for* nach)

▸ **search about** (*Brit*) *or* **around** VI herumstöbern (*in* in +*dat*); (*in country etc*) (herum)suchen (*in* in +*dat*)

▸ **search out** VT SEP heraussuchen; *person* aufspüren; *cause* herausfinden

▸ **search through** VI +PREP OBJ durchsuchen; *papers, books* durchsehen

search engine N (*Comput*) Suchmaschine *f*

searcher [ˈsɜːtʃəʳ] N **the ~s** (= *search party*) die Suchmannschaft *f*

searching ADJ [ˈsɜːtʃɪŋ] *look* forschend; *question* bohrend

searchingly [ˈsɜːtʃɪŋlɪ] ADV *look* forschend

search: search party N Suchmannschaft *f*; **search warrant** N Durchsuchungsbefehl *m*

searing [ˈsɪərɪŋ] ADJ *heat* glühend; *pain also, attack* scharf; *grief* quälend

sea: seashell N Muschel(schale) *f*; **seashore** N Strand *m*; **on the ~** am Strand; **seasick** ADJ seekrank; **seasickness** N Seekrankheit *f*; **seaside** ■ N **at the ~** am Meer; **to go to the ~** ans Meer fahren ■ ATTR See-; *town* am Meer; **seaside resort** N Seebad *nt*

season [ˈsiːzn] ■ N **(a)** (*of the year*) Jahreszeit *f*; **rainy ~** Regenzeit *f* **(b)** (= *social ~, sporting ~ etc*) Saison *f*; **nesting/hunting ~**

Brut-/Jagdzeit *f*; **the football ~** die Fußballsaison; **strawberries are in ~/out of ~ now** für Erdbeeren ist jetzt die richtige Zeit/nicht die richtige Zeit; **their bitch is ~** ihre Hündin ist läufig; **to go somewhere out of/in ~** an einen Ort fahren *or* gehen, wenn keine Saison/wenn Saison ist; **at the height of the ~** in der *or* zur Hochsaison; **the ~ of good will** die Zeit der Nächstenliebe; **"Season's greetings"** „fröhliche Weihnachten und ein glückliches neues Jahr" **(c)** (*Theat*) Spielzeit *f*; **a Dustin Hoffman ~, a ~ of Dustin Hoffman films** eine Serie von Dustin-Hoffman-Filmen ■ VT **(a)** *food* würzen; (*fig: = temper*) durchsetzen **(b)** *wood* ablagern; (*fig: = inure*) *troops* stählen

seasonal [ˈsiːzənl] ADJ jahreszeitlich bedingt; (*Econ*) saisonbedingt; **~ fruit** Früchte *pl* der Saison

seasonally [ˈsiːzənəlɪ] ADV **~ adjusted** saisonbereinigt

seasoned [ˈsiːznd] ADJ **(a)** *food* gewürzt **(b)** *timber* abgelagert **(c)** (*fig: = experienced*) erfahren

seasoning [ˈsiːznɪŋ] N (*Cook*) Gewürz *nt*; (*fig*) Würze *f*

season ticket N (*Rail*) Zeitkarte *f*; (*Theat*) Abonnement *nt*

seat [siːt] ■ N (= *chair, country, on committee*) Sitz *m*; (= *place to sit*) (Sitz)platz *m*; (*usu pl*: = *seating*) Sitzgelegenheit *f*; (*of chair etc also*) Sitzfläche *f*; (*of trousers*) Hosenboden *m*; (= *buttocks*) Hinterteil *nt*; **to have a front ~ at the opera** in der Oper in den vorderen Reihen sitzen; **an aircraft with 250 ~s** ein Flugzeug mit 250 Plätzen; **will you keep my ~ for me?** würden Sie mir meinen Platz freihalten?; **a ~ in Parliament** ein Mandat *nt*; **to win a ~** ein Mandat gewinnen; **~ of learning** Lehrstätte *f* ■ VT *person etc* setzen; **to ~ oneself** sich setzen; **to be ~ed** sitzen; **please be ~ed** bitte, setzen Sie sich; **the table/sofa ~s 4** am Tisch/auf dem Sofa ist Platz für 4 Personen; **the hall ~s 900** die Halle hat 900 Sitzplätze

seat belt N Sicherheits- *or* Sitzgurt *m*; **to fasten one's ~, to put one's ~ on** sich anschnallen

-seater [-siːtəʳ] SUF ■ N -sitzer *m*; **two-seater** Zweisitzer *m* ■ ATTR -sitzig; **single-seater** einsitzig

seating [ˈsiːtɪŋ] N Sitzplätze *pl*

seating arrangements PL Sitzordnung *f*

sea: sea view N Seeblick *m*; **sea wall** N Deich *m*; **sea water** N Meer- *or* Seewasser *nt*; **seaweed** N (See)tang *m*; **seaworthy** ADJ seetüchtig

SEC (*US*) ABBR *of* **Securities and Exchange Commission** staatliche Börsenaufsichtsbehörde

secluded [sɪˈkluːdɪd] ADJ *spot, house* abgelegen; *life* zurückgezogen

seclusion [sɪˈkluːʒən] N Abgeschiedenheit *f*; (*of house, spot*) Abgelegenheit *f*

second¹ [ˈsekənd] ■ ADJ zweite(r, s); **the ~ floor** (*Brit*) der zweite Stock; (*US*) der erste Stock; **every ~ Thursday** jeden zweiten Donnerstag; **to be ~** Zweite(r, s) sein; **to be ~ to none** unübertroffen *or* unerreicht sein; **in ~ place** (*Sport etc*) an zweiter Stelle; **to be** *or* **lie in ~ place** auf dem zweiten Platz sein *or* liegen; **to finish in ~ place** den zweiten Platz belegen; **to be ~ in command** (*Mil*) stellvertretender Kommandeur sein; (*fig*) der zweite Mann sein; **she's like a ~ mother to me** sie ist wie eine Mutter zu mir; **will you have a ~ cup?** möchten Sie noch eine Tasse?; **I won't tell you a ~ time** ich sage dir das kein zweites Mal; **~ time around** beim zweiten Mal; **you won't get a ~ chance** die Möglichkeit kriegst du so schnell nicht wieder (*inf*) ■ ADV **(a)** (+*adj*) zweit-; (+*vb*) zweitens; **the ~ largest house** das zweitgrößte Haus; **the speaker against a motion always speaks ~** der Gegenredner spricht immer als Zweiter; **to come/lie ~** (*in race, competition*) Zweite(r) werden/sein **(b)** (= *secondly*) zweitens ■ VT *motion, proposal* unterstützen ■ N **(a)** (*of time, Math, Sci*) Sekunde *f*; (*inf*: = *short time*) Augenblick *m*; **just a ~!** (einen) Augenblick!; **it won't take a ~** es dauert nicht lange; **I'll only be a ~ (or two)** ich komme gleich; (= *back soon*) ich bin gleich wieder da **(b) the ~** (*in order*) der/die/das Zweite; (*in race, class etc*) der/die Zweite; **to come a poor/good ~** einen schlechten/guten zweiten Platz belegen **(c)** (*Aut*) (= *gear*) der zweite Gang; **to put a/the car into ~** den zweiten Gang einlegen **(d) seconds** PL (*inf*: = ~ *helping*) Nachschlag *m* (*inf*); **can I have ~s?** kann ich noch etwas nachbekommen?

(e) *(Comm)* **this is a ~** das ist zweite Wahl; **~s are much cheaper** Waren zweiter Wahl sind viel billiger

second² [sɪˈkɒnd] VT *(Brit)* abordnen

secondary [ˈsekəndərɪ] ADJ **(a)** sekundär; *industry* verarbeitend; *reason* weniger bedeutend **(b)** *education* höher; **~ school** höhere Schule; **~ teacher** Lehrer(in) *m(f)* an einer höheren Schule

second: **second best** N Zweitbeste(r, s); **I won't settle for ~** ich gebe mich nicht mit dem Zweitbesten zufrieden ADV **to come off ~** es nicht so gut haben; *(= come off badly)* den kürzeren ziehen; **second-best** ADJ zweitbeste(r, s); **she always felt she was ~** sie hatte immer das Gefühl, zweite Wahl zu sein; **second chamber** N zweite Kammer; **second class** N *(Rail, Post etc)* zweite Klasse; **second-class** ADJ **(a)** *ticket, carriage, mail* zweiter Klasse *pred*; *status, treatment* zweitklassig; **~ stamp** Briefmarke für nicht bevorzugt beförderte Briefsendungen **(b)** = **second-rate** ADV *travel* zweiter Klasse; **to send sth ~** etw mit nicht bevorzugter Post schicken; **second cousin** N Cousin *m*/Cousine *f* zweiten Grades; **second-guess** VT **(a)** *(= predict)* vorhersagen; **to ~ sb** vorhersagen, was jd machen/sagen wird **(b)** *(US = criticize)* im Nachhinein kritisieren; **second hand** N *(of watch)* Sekundenzeiger *m*; **second-hand** ADJ gebraucht; *clothes* getragen, secondhand *(esp Comm)*; *(fig)* *information* aus zweiter Hand; **a ~ car** ein Gebrauchtwagen *m*; **~ dealer** Gebrauchtwarenhändler(in) *m(f)*; **~ bookshop** Antiquariat *nt* ADV gebraucht

secondly [ˈsekəndlɪ] ADV zweitens; *(= secondarily)* an zweiter Stelle

secondment [sɪˈkɒndmənt] N *(Brit)* Abordnung *f*; **to be on ~** abgeordnet sein

second: **second name** N Familienname *m*, Nachname *m*; **second nature** N zweite Natur; **to become ~ (to sb)** (jdm) in Fleisch und Blut übergehen; **second-rate** ADJ *(pej)* zweitklassig, zweitrangig; **second sight** N das zweite Gesicht; **you must have ~** du musst hellsehen können; **second string** N *(esp US Sport)* *(= player)* Ersatzspieler(in) *m(f)*; *(= team)* Ersatzmannschaft *f*; **second-string** ADJ *(esp US Sport)* Ersatz-; **second thought** N **with hardly** *or* **without a ~** ohne lange *or* weiter darüber nachzudenken; **I didn't give it a ~** ich habe daran überhaupt keinen Gedanken verschwendet; **to have ~s about sth** sich *(dat)* etw anders überlegen; **on ~s I decided not to** dann habe ich mich doch dagegen entschieden; **on ~s maybe I'd better do it myself** vielleicht mache ich es, genau besehen, doch lieber selbst; **Second World War** N **the ~** der Zweite Weltkrieg

secrecy [ˈsiːkrəsɪ] N *(of person: = secretiveness)* Geheimnistuerei *f*; *(of event, talks)* Heimlichkeit *f*; **in ~** im Geheimen

secret [ˈsiːkrɪt] ADJ geheim; *pocket* versteckt; *drinker, admirer, ambition* heimlich; **the ~ ingredient** *(fig: of success etc)* die Zauberformel; **to keep sth ~ (from sb)** etw (vor jdm) geheim halten

N Geheimnis *nt*; **to keep sb/sth a ~ (from sb)** jdn/etw (vor jdm) geheim halten; **to tell sb a ~** jdm ein Geheimnis anvertrauen; **in ~** im Geheimen; **they always met in ~** sie trafen sich immer heimlich; **to let sb in on** *or* **into a ~** jdn in ein Geheimnis einweihen; **to keep a ~** ein Geheimnis für sich behalten; **can you keep a ~?** kannst du schweigen?; **to make no ~ of sth** kein Geheimnis aus etw machen; **the ~ of success** das Erfolgsgeheimnis

secret agent N Geheimagent(in) *m(f)*

secretarial [ˌsekrəˈtɛərɪəl] ADJ *job, qualifications* als Sekretärin/Sekretär; **to do a ~ course** einen Sekretärinnenkurs machen; **~ work** Sekretariatsarbeit *f*; **~ staff** Sekretärinnen und Schreibkräfte *pl*

secretary [ˈsekrɪtrɪ] N Sekretär(in) *m(f)*; *(of society)* Schriftführer(in) *m(f)*; *(esp US Pol: = minister)* Minister(in) *m(f)*

Secretary of State N *(Brit)* Minister(in) *m(f)*; *(US)* Außenminister(in) *m(f)*

secrete [sɪˈkriːt] VTI *(Med)* absondern

secretion [sɪˈkriːʃən] N *(Med)* *(= act)* Absonderung *f*; *(= substance)* Sekret *nt*

secretive [ˈsiːkrətɪv] ADJ *person (by nature)* verschlossen; *(in action)* geheimnistuerisch; *organization* verschwiegen; *behaviour* geheimnisvoll; **to be ~ about sth** mit etw geheimnisvoll tun

secretively [ˈsiːkrətɪvlɪ] ADV geheimnisvoll; *(= in secret)* heimlich; **to behave ~** geheimnistuerisch sein

secretly [ˈsiːkrətlɪ] ADV *(= in secrecy)* im Geheimen; *meet, marry, film* heimlich; *(= privately)* insgeheim, im Stillen

secret: **secret police** N Geheimpolizei *f*; **secret service** N Geheimdienst *m*; **secret weapon** N *(lit, fig)* Geheimwaffe *f*

sect [sekt] N Sekte *f*

section [ˈsekʃən] N **(a)** *(= part)* Teil *m*; *(= part under construction, wing of building)* Trakt *m*; *(of book, motorway)* Abschnitt *m*; *(of document, law)* Absatz *m*; *(of orange)* Stück *nt*; **the string ~** die Streicher *pl*; **the sports ~** *(Press)* der Sportteil **(b)** *(= department)* *(Mil)* Abteilung *f*; *(esp of academy etc)* Sektion *f* **(c)** *(= diagram, cutting: also Med)* Schnitt *m*; *(= Caesarean ~)* Kaiserschnitt *m*; **in ~** im Schnitt

▶ **section off** VT SEP abteilen; *(= cordon off)* absperren

sector [ˈsektə^r] N *(also Comput)* Sektor *m*

sectoral [ˈsektərəl] ADJ *(Econ)* sektorenspezifisch

secular [ˈsekjʊlə^r] ADJ weltlich, säkular; *music, art* profan; *court, education* weltlich; *state* säkular

secure [sɪˈkjʊə^r] ADJ **(+ER)** sicher; *(= solid also)* solide; *(emotionally)* geborgen; *existence, income, lock, door* gesichert; *grip, knot, tile* fest; **is the lid ~?** ist der Deckel fest drauf?; **to make a door ~** eine Tür sichern; **~ in the knowledge that ...** ruhig in dem Bewusstsein, dass ...; **to make sb feel ~** jdm das Gefühl der Sicherheit geben; **to be financially ~** finanziell abgesichert sein

VT **(a)** *(= fasten, make firm)* festmachen; *door* fest zumachen; *(with chain etc = guarantee, make safe)* sichern *(from, against* gegen*)*; *loan* (ab)sichern **(b)** *(= obtain)* sich *(dat)* sichern; *majority of votes, order* erhalten; *profits* erzielen; *share, interest in business* erwerben; *(= buy)* erstehen; **to ~ sth for sb, to ~ sb sth** jdm etw sichern; **to ~ sb's services** jdn verpflichten

securely [sɪˈkjʊəlɪ] ADV *(= firmly)* fest; *(= safely)* sicher

securities market [sɪˈkjʊərɪtɪzˈmɑːkɪt] M *(Fin)* Wertpapiermarkt *m*

security [sɪˈkjʊərɪtɪ] N **(a)** Sicherheit *f* *(also Fin)*; *(emotional)* Geborgenheit *f*; *(= ~ measures)* Sicherheitsvorkehrungen *or* -maßnahmen *pl*; *(= ~ department)* Sicherheitsdienst *m*; *(= guarantor)* Bürge *m*, Bürgin *f*; *(Ind)* Sicherheitseinrichtungen *pl*; **for ~** zur Sicherheit; **to lend money on ~** Geld gegen Sicherheit leihen; **to stand ~ for sb** für jdn Bürge/Bürgin sein **(b)** **securities** PL *(Fin)* (Wert)papiere *pl*; **securities trader** *(US)* Kursmakler(in) *m(f)*

security IN CPDS Sicherheits-; **security camera** N Überwachungskamera *f*; **security check** N Sicherheitskontrolle *f*; **security firm** N Wach- und Sicherheitsdienst *m*; **security guard** N Wache *f*; *(for security checks)* Sicherheitsbeamte(r) *m*/-beamtin *f*; **security man** N Wache *f*, Wächter *m*; **one of the security men** einer der Sicherheitsleute; **security risk** N Sicherheitsrisiko *nt*

sedan [sɪˈdæn] N **(a)** *(also ~ chair)* Sänfte *f* **(b)** *(US Aut)* Limousine *f*

sedate [sɪˈdeɪt] ADJ **(+ER)** gesetzt; *colour* ruhig; *furnishings* gediegen; *life* geruhsam; *place* beschaulich; *speed* gemächlich VT Beruhigungsmittel geben *(+dat)*; **he was heavily ~d** er stand stark unter dem Einfluss von Beruhigungsmitteln

sedately [sɪˈdeɪtlɪ] ADV **(a)** *(= gently)* gemessen, ruhig **(b)** *(= conservatively)* furnished gediegen

sedation [sɪˈdeɪʃən] N Beruhigungsmittel *pl*; **to put sb under ~** jdm Beruhigungsmittel geben

sedative [ˈsedətɪv] N Beruhigungsmittel *nt* ADJ beruhigend

sedentary [ˈsedntərɪ] ADJ sitzend *attr*; **to lead a ~ life** sehr viel sitzen

sediment [ˈsedɪmənt] N (Boden)satz *m*; *(in river)* Ablagerung *f*

seduce [sɪˈdjuːs] VT verführen; **to ~ sb into doing sth** jdn zu etw verleiten, jdn dazu verleiten, etw zu tun

seducer [sɪˈdjuːsə^r] N Verführer *m*

seduction [sɪˈdʌkʃən] N Verführung *f*

seductive [sɪˈdʌktɪv] ADJ verführerisch; *salary, offer, suggestion* verlockend

seductively [sɪ'dʌktɪvlɪ] ADV verführerisch; *offer, suggest* verlockend

seductiveness [sɪ'dʌktɪvnɪs] N verführerische Art

see¹ [siː]

1 TRANSITIVE VERB	**3** PHRASAL VERBS
2 INTRANSITIVE VERB	

pret **saw**, *ptp* **seen**

1 TRANSITIVE VERB

(a) sehen; (= *check*) nachsehen, gucken (*inf*); *film, sights* sich (*dat*) ansehen; **to see sb do sth** sehen, wie jd etw macht; **I've never seen him swim(ming)** ich habe ihn noch nie schwimmen sehen; **I saw it happen** ich habe gesehen, wie es passiert ist; **I've seen it done three times** das habe ich schon dreimal gesehen; **I don't like to see people mistreated** ich kann es nicht sehen, wenn Menschen schlecht behandelt werden; **I wouldn't like to see you unhappy** ich möchte doch nicht, dass du unglücklich bist; **see page 8** siehe Seite 8; **there was nothing to be seen** es war nichts zu sehen; **I don't know what she sees in him** ich weiß nicht, was sie an ihm findet; **we don't see much of them nowadays** wir sehen sie zurzeit nur selten; **you must be seeing things** du siehst wohl Gespenster!; **am I seeing things or is ...?** seh ich richtig, ist das nicht ...?; **worth seeing** sehenswert; **we'll see if we can help** mal sehen, ob wir helfen können; **we'll soon see who is right** wir werden ja bald sehen, wer Recht hat; **that remains to be seen** das wird sich zeigen; **let's just see what happens** wollen wir mal sehen *or* abwarten, was passiert; **I see you still haven't done that** wie ich sehe, hast du das immer noch nicht gemacht; **as I see it** so, wie ich das sehe; **this is how I see it** ich sehe das so; **try to see it my way** versuchen Sie doch einmal, es aus meiner Sicht zu sehen; **I don't see it that way** ich sehe das anders
(b) (= *visit*) besuchen; (*on business*) aufsuchen; **to call** *or* **go and see sb** jdn besuchen (gehen); **to see the doctor** zum Arzt gehen
(c) (= *meet with*) sehen; (= *talk to*) sprechen; (= *receive visit of*) empfangen; **the doctor will see you now** der Herr Doktor ist jetzt frei; **I'll have to see my wife about that** das muss ich mit meiner Frau besprechen; **have you seen Personnel yet?** waren Sie schon bei der Personalabteilung?; **I shall be seeing them for dinner** ich treffe sie beim Abendessen; **see you (soon)!** bis bald!; **be seeing you!, see you later!** bis später!
(d) (= *have relationship with*) befreundet sein mit; **I'm not seeing anyone at the moment** ich habe zurzeit keinen Freund/keine Freundin
(e) (= *accompany*) begleiten, bringen; **to see sb to the door** jdn zur Tür bringen
(f) (= *visualize*) sich (*dat*) vorstellen; **I can't** *or* **don't see that working** ich kann mir kaum vorstellen, dass das klappt; **I can't see myself in that job** ich glaube nicht, dass das eine Stelle für mich wäre; **I can't see any chance of that happening** das halte ich für unwahrscheinlich
(g) (= *experience*) erleben; **now I've seen everything!** ist das denn zu fassen?; **what impudence, I've never seen anything like it!** so eine Frechheit, so etwas habe ich ja noch nie gesehen *or* erlebt!; **it's seen a lot of hard wear** das ist schon sehr strapaziert worden
(h) (= *understand*) verstehen; (= *recognize*) einsehen; (= *realize*) erkennen; **I can see I'm going to be busy** ich sehe, ich werde viel zu tun haben; **I fail to** *or* **don't see how anyone could ...** ich begreife einfach nicht, wie jemand nur ... kann; **I don't see where the problem is** ich sehe das Problem nicht; **I see from this report that ...** ich ersehe aus diesem Bericht, dass ...; **(do you) see what I mean?** verstehst du(, was ich meine)?; (= *didn't I tell you!*) siehst dus jetzt!; **I see what you mean** ich verstehe, was du meinst; (= *you're quite right*) ja, du hast Recht; **to make sb see sth** jdm etw klarmachen; **to make sb see reason** jdn zur Vernunft bringen
(i) (= *ensure*) **see that it is done by tomorrow** sieh zu, dass es bis morgen fertig ist

2 INTRANSITIVE VERB

(a) sehen; **let me see, let's see** lassen Sie mich mal sehen; **it was so dark I couldn't see** es war so dunkel, ich konnte nichts sehen; **who was it? – I couldn't/didn't see** wer war das? – ich konnte es nicht sehen; **as far as the eye can see** so weit das Auge reicht; **see for yourself!** sieh doch selbst!; **now see here!** nun hören Sie mal her!; **will he come? – we'll soon see** kommt er? – das werden wir bald sehen *or* rausfinden (*inf*); **you'll see!** du wirst es (schon) noch sehen!
(b) (= *check, find out*) nachsehen, gucken (*inf*); **is he there? – I'll see** ist er da? – ich sehe mal nach *or* ich guck mal nach (*inf*); **see for yourself!** sieh doch selbst (nach)!
(c) (= *understand*) verstehen; **as far as I can see ...** so wie ich das sehe ...; **he's dead, don't you see?** er ist tot, begreifst du das denn nicht?; **as I see from your report** wie ich aus Ihrem Bericht ersehe; **it's too late, (you) see** (*explaining*) weißt du, es ist zu spät; (= *I told you so*) siehst du, es ist zu spät!; **(you) see, it's like this** es ist nämlich so; **I see!** aha!; (*after explanation*) ach so!; (= *I'm with you*) ja; **yes, I see** ja, aha
(d) (= *consider*) **we'll see** (wir werden *or* wollen) mal sehen; **let me see, let's see** warten Sie mal, lassen Sie mich mal überlegen

3 PHRASAL VERBS

➤ **see about** VI +PREP OBJ (= *attend to*) sich kümmern um; **he came to see about the rent** er ist wegen der Miete gekommen
➤ **see across** VT ALWAYS SEPARATE hinüberbegleiten *or* -bringen (*prep obj* über +*acc*)
➤ **see in** **1** VI hineinsehen **2** VT SEP **to see the New Year in** das neue Jahr begrüßen
➤ **see into** VI +PREP OBJ hineinsehen in (+*acc*)
➤ **see off** VT SEP **(a)** (= *bid farewell to*) verabschieden; **are you coming to see me off (at the airport** *etc*)? kommt ihr mit mir (zum Flughafen *etc*)? **(b)** (= *chase off*) Beine machen (+*dat*) (*inf*)
➤ **see out** **1** VI hinaussehen; **I can't see out of the window** ich kann nicht zum Fenster hinaussehen **2** VT SEP **(a)** (= *show out*) hinausbringen *or* -begleiten (*of* aus); **I'll see myself out** ich finde (schon) alleine hinaus **(b)** (*coat, car*) winter *etc* überdauern; (*old man, invalid*) year *etc* überleben; **to see the Old Year out** das alte Jahr verabschieden
➤ **see over** *or* **round** (*esp Brit*) VI +PREP OBJ *house etc* sich (*dat*) ansehen
➤ **see through** **1** VI (*lit*) (hin)durchsehen (*prep obj* durch) **2** VI +PREP OBJ (*fig: = not be deceived by*) durchschauen **3** VT ALWAYS SEPARATE **(a)** (= *help through difficult time*) beistehen (+*dat*); **he had £100 to see him through the term** er hatte £ 100 für das ganze Semester **(b)** *job* zu Ende bringen; (*Parl*) *bill* durchbringen
➤ **see to** VI +PREP OBJ sich kümmern um; **see to it that you don't forget** sieh zu, dass du das nicht vergisst
➤ **see up** VI + PREP OBJ (= *look up*) hinaufsehen; **I could see up her skirt** ich konnte ihr unter den Rock sehen

see² N Bistum *nt*; (*Catholic also*) Diözese *f*; (*Protestant in Germany*) Landeskirche *f*

seed [siːd] **1** N **(a)** (*Bot*) (= *one single*) Samen *m*; (*of grain etc*) Korn *nt*; (*within fruit*) (Samen)kern *m*; (*collective*) Samen *pl*; (= *grain*) Saatgut *nt*; (*fig: of unrest, idea etc*) Keim *m* (*of* zu); **to sow the ~s of doubt (in sb's mind)** (bei jdm) Zweifel säen **(b)** (*Sport*) **to be the third** – als Dritter gesetzt sein; **the number one** – der/die als Nummer eins Gesetzte **2** VT **(a)** (= *sow with* ~) besäen **(b)** (*Sport*) setzen; **~ed number one** als Nummer eins gesetzt

seedless ['siːdlɪs] ADJ kernlos

seedling ['siːdlɪŋ] N Sämling *m*

seedy ['siːdɪ] (+ER) *person, place* zwielichtig

seeing ['siːɪŋ] **1** N Sehen *nt*; **I'd never have thought it possible but ~ is believing** ich hätte es nie für möglich gehalten, aber ich habe es mit eigenen Augen gesehen **2** CONJ **~ (that** *or* **as)** da

Seeing Eye Dog N (*US*) Blindenhund *m*

seek [siːk], *pret, ptp* **sought** VT suchen; *fame, wealth* streben nach; **to ~ sb's advice** jdn um Rat fragen; **~ time** (*Comput*) Zugriffszeit *f*; **to ~ to do sth** sich bemühen, etw zu tun
➤ **seek for** VI +PREP OBJ suchen nach
➤ **seek out** VT SEP ausfindig machen

seem [siːm] VI scheinen; **he ~s (to be) honest** er scheint ehrlich zu sein; **he ~s younger than he is** er wirkt jünger, als er ist; **that makes it ~ longer** dadurch wirkt es länger; **he doesn't ~ (to be) able to concentrate** er scheint sich nicht konzentrieren zu können; **things aren't always what they ~** vieles ist anders, als es aussieht; **I ~ to have heard that before** das habe ich doch schon mal gehört; **what ~s to be the trouble?** worum geht es denn?; (*doctor*) was kann ich für Sie tun?; **it ~s to me that I'll have to do that again** mir scheint, ich muss das noch einmal machen; **we are not welcome, it ~s** wir sind anscheinend *or* scheinbar nicht willkommen; **so it ~s** es sieht (ganz) so aus; **it ~s** *or* **would ~ that he is coming after all** es sieht so aus, als ob er doch noch kommt, es scheint, er kommt doch noch; **how does it ~ to you?** meinen SIE?; **how did she ~ to you?** wie fandst du sie?; **it ~s a shame to leave it unfinished** es ist doch irgendwie *or* eigentlich schade, das nicht fertig zu machen; **it just doesn't ~ right somehow** das ist doch irgendwie nicht richtig; **I can't ~ to do it** ich kann das anscheinend *or* scheinbar *or* irgendwie nicht; **it only ~s like it** das kommt einem nur so vor; **I ~ to remember that you had that problem before** es kommt mir so vor, als hätten Sie das Problem schon einmal gehabt

seeming [ˈsiːmɪŋ] ADJ ATTR scheinbar

seemingly [ˈsiːmɪŋlɪ] ADV scheinbar, anscheinend

seen [siːn] PTP *of* **see**[1]

seep [siːp] VI sickern; **to ~ through sth** durch etw durchsickern; **to ~ into sth** in etw (*acc*) hineinsickern

➤ **seep away** VI (*water*) versickern; (*strength*) schwinden

seepage [ˈsiːpɪdʒ] N **there is an excessive amount of ~** (*Comm*) die Leckage ist zu groß

seesaw [ˈsiːsɔː] **1** N Wippe *f* **2** VI wippen; (*fig*) schwanken

seethe [siːð] VI (= *boil*) sieden; (= *surge*) schäumen; (= *be crowded*) wimmeln (*with* von); (= *be angry*) kochen (*inf*); **a seething mass of people** eine wogende Menschenmenge

see-through [ˈsiːθruː] ADJ durchsichtig

segment [ˈsegmənt] N Teil *m*; (*of orange*) Stück *nt*; (*of circle*) Abschnitt *m*; (*of market*) Segment *nt*

segregate [ˈsegrɪgeɪt] VT *individuals* absondern; *group of population* nach Rassen/Geschlechtern/Konfessionen trennen; **~d** (*racially*) *church* nur für Weiße/Schwarze; *school also* mit Rassentrennung; *society* nach Rassen getrennt

segregation [segrɪˈgeɪʃən] N Trennung *f*

seismic [ˈsaɪzmɪk] ADJ seismisch; (*fig*) *changes, events* dramatisch; *forces* ungeheuer

seize [siːz] **1** VT (*lit, fig*) packen, ergreifen; (*as hostage*) nehmen; (= *confiscate*) beschlagnahmen; *passport* einziehen; *town* einnehmen; *building* besetzen; *power* an sich (*acc*) reißen; *opportunity, initiative* ergreifen; **to ~ sb's arm, to ~ sb by the arm** jdn am Arm packen; **to ~ the day** den Tag nutzen; **to ~ control of sth** etw unter Kontrolle bringen **2** VI = **seize up**

➤ **seize on** *or* **upon** VI +PREP OBJ *idea, offer* sich stürzen auf (+*acc*); *excuse* beim Schopf packen

➤ **seize up** VI **(a)** (*engine, brakes*) sich verklemmen **(b)** (*inf*) **my back seized up** es ist mir in den Rücken gefahren (*inf*)

seizure [ˈsiːʒə^r] N **(a)** (= *confiscation*) Beschlagnahmung *f*; (*of passport*) Einzug *m*; (= *capture*) Einnahme *f*; (*of train, building*) Besetzung *f* **(b)** (*Med*) Anfall *m*; (= *apoplexy*) Schlaganfall *m*

seldom [ˈseldəm] ADV selten; **they are ~ seen** man sieht sie nur selten

select [sɪˈlekt] **1** VTI (aus)wählen; (*in buying also*) aussuchen; (*Sport*) auswählen; (*for football match etc*) aufstellen **2** ADJ (= *exclusive*) exklusiv; (= *carefully chosen*) auserwählt, auserlesen; **a ~ few** eine kleine Gruppe Auserwählter

selection [sɪˈlekʃən] N **(a)** (= *choosing*) (Aus)wahl *f*; Selektion *f* **(b)** (= *person, thing selected*) Wahl *f*; **to make one's ~** seine Wahl treffen **(c)** (= *range, assortment*) Auswahl *f* (*of* an +*dat*)

selective [sɪˈlektɪv] ADJ wählerisch; *reader* anspruchsvoll; **~ process** Auswahlverfahren *nt*; **a very ~ admission procedure** ein stark aussiebendes Aufnahmeverfahren

selectively [sɪˈlektɪvlɪ] ADV wählerisch; *read also, operate* selektiv; **to read/buy ~** beim Lesen wählerisch/beim Einkaufen kritisch sein

selector [sɪˈlektə^r] N (*Sport*) jd, der die Mannschaftsaufstellung vornimmt

self [self] **1** N, *pl* **selves** Ich *nt*, Selbst *nt no pl*; **he showed his true ~** er zeigte sein wahres Ich *or* Gesicht; **he's quite his old ~ again**, **he's back to his usual ~** er ist wieder ganz der Alte (*inf*); **back to her usual cheerful ~** wieder fröhlich wie immer **2** PRON (*Comm*) **pay ~** zahlbar an selbst; **a room for wife and ~** ein Zimmer für meine Frau und mich

self: **self-absorbed** ADJ mit sich selbst beschäftigt; **self-addressed** ADJ *envelope* adressiert; **self-addressed stamped envelope** N (*US*) frankierter Rückumschlag; **self-adhesive** ADJ selbstklebend; **self-appointed** ADJ selbst ernannt; **self-assertion** N Durchsetzungsvermögen *nt*; (*pej*) Überheblichkeit *f*; **self-assertive** ADJ selbstbewusst; (*pej*) von sich selbst eingenommen; **self-assured** ADJ selbstsicher; **self-aware** ADJ selbstbewusst; **self-awareness** N Selbsterkenntnis *f*; **self-belief** N Glaube *m* an sich (*acc*) selbst; **self-catering** (*Brit*) **1** N Selbstversorgung *f*; **to go ~** (*holidaymaker*) Urlaub *m* für Selbstversorger machen **2** ADJ für Selbstversorger; **self-centred**, (*US*) **self-centered** ADJ egozentrisch; **self-centredness**, (*US*) **self-centeredness** N Egozentrik *f*; **self-composed** ADJ ruhig, gelassen; **self-confessed** ADJ erklärt *attr*; **self-confidence** N Selbstvertrauen *nt*; **self-confident** ADJ selbstsicher; **self-conscious** ADJ befangen, gehemmt; *style etc* bewusst; **to be ~ about sth** sich (*dat*) einer Sache (*gen*) sehr bewusst sein; (= *deliberately*) bewusst; **self-consciously** ADV (= *uncomfortably*) verlegen; (= *deliberately*) bewusst; **self-consciousness** N Befangenheit *f*, Gehemmtheit *f*; (*of style etc*) Bewusstheit *f*; **self-contained** ADJ **(a)** *person* distanziert; (= *self-sufficient*) selbstgenügsam **(b)** *flat* separat; *community* eigenständig; *economy* eigenständig; *group* geschlossen; **self-contradictory** ADJ sich (*dat*) selbst widersprechend *attr*; **his argument is ~** seine Argumente widersprechen sich (*dat*); **self-control** N Selbstbeherrschung *f*; **self-controlled** ADJ selbstbeherrscht; **self-critical** ADJ selbstkritisch; **self-criticism** N Selbstkritik *f*; **self-deception** N Selbstbetrug *m*; **self-defeating** ADJ sinnlos; *argument* sich selbst widerlegend *attr*; **a ~ exercise** ein Eigentor *nt*; **self-defence**, (*US*) **self-defense** N Selbstverteidigung *f*; (*Jur*) Notwehr *f*; **to act in ~** in Notwehr handeln; **self-denial** N Selbstzucht *f*; **self-deprecating** ADJ *person* bescheiden; *remark* sich selbst herabwürdigend *attr*; **to be ~** (*person*) sich selbst abwerten; **self-destruct** **1** VI sich selbst zerstören **2** ADJ ATTR **~ button** Knopf *m* zur Selbstzerstörung; **self-destruction** N Selbstzerstörung *f*; **self-destructive** ADJ selbstzerstörerisch; **self-determination** N Selbstbestimmung *f* (*also Pol*); **self-discipline** N Selbstdisziplin *f*; **self-doubt** N Zweifel *m* an sich (*dat*) selbst; **self-drive** ADJ (*Brit*) *car* für Selbstfahrer; **self-educated** ADJ autodidaktisch; **~ person** Autodidakt(in) *m(f)*; **self-effacing** ADJ zurückhaltend; **self-employed** ADJ selbstständig; *journalist* freiberuflich; **self-esteem** N Selbstachtung *f*; **to have high/low ~** sehr/wenig selbstbewusst sein; **self-evident** ADJ offensichtlich; (= *not needing proof*) selbstverständlich; **self-evidently** ADV offensichtlich; **self-explanatory** ADJ unmittelbar verständlich; **this word is ~** das Wort erklärt sich selbst; **self-expression** N Selbstdarstellung *f*; **self-financing** ADJ selbstfinanzierend; **self-fulfilment**, (*US*) **self-fulfillment** N Erfüllung *f*; **self-governing** ADJ selbstverwaltet; **self-government** N Selbstverwaltung *f*; **self-harming** N Selbstverstümmelung *f*; **self-help** N Selbsthilfe *f*; **self-image** N Selbstbild *nt*; **self-important** ADJ aufgeblasen; **self-imposed** ADJ selbst auferlegt; **self-improvement** N Weiterbildung *f*; **self-induced** ADJ selbstverursacht *attr*; **self-indulgence** N genießerische Art; (*in eating, drinking*) Maßlosigkeit *f*; **self-indulgent** ADJ genießerisch; (*in eating, drinking*) maßlos; **self-inflicted** ADJ *wounds* sich (*dat*) selbst zugefügt *attr*; *task, punishment* sich (*dat*) freiwillig auferlegt; **self-insurance** N Eigenversicherung *f*; **self-interest** N (= *selfishness*) Eigennutz *m*; (= *personal advantage*) eigenes Interesse

selfish [ˈselfɪʃ] ADJ egoistisch; **for ~ reasons** aus selbstsüchtigen Gründen

selfishly [ˈselfɪʃlɪ] ADV egoistisch

selfishness [ˈselfɪʃnɪs] N Egoismus *m*

self: **self-justification** N Rechtfertigung *f*; **self-knowledge** N Selbsterkenntnis *f*

selfless ADJ, **selflessly** ADV [ˈselflɪs, -lɪ] selbstlos

selflessness [ˈselflɪsnɪs] N Selbstlosigkeit *f*

self: **self-made** ADJ **~ man** Selfmademan *m*; **he's a ~ millionaire** er hat es aus eigener Kraft zum Millionär gebracht; **self-**

mutilation N Selbstverstümmelung f; **self-opinionated** [ˌselfəˈpɪnjəneɪtɪd] ADJ rechthaberisch; **self-parody** N Selbstparodie f; **self-perpetuating** ADJ sich selbst erneuernd attr; **the system is ~** das System erhält sich selbst; **self-pity** N Selbstmitleid nt; **self-portrait** N Selbstporträt nt; **self-possessed** ADJ selbstbeherrscht; **self-preservation** N Selbsterhaltung f; **self-propelled** ADJ selbst angetrieben attr, mit Selbstantrieb; **self-raising**, (US) **self-rising** ADJ flour selbsttreibend, mit bereits beigemischtem Backpulver; **self-regulating** ADJ selbstregulierend attr; **this system is ~** dieses System reguliert sich selbst; **self-reliant** ADJ selbstständig; **self-reproach** N Selbstvorwurf m; **self-respect** N Selbstachtung f; **have you no ~?** schämen Sie sich gar nicht?; **self-respecting** ADJ anständig; **no ~ person would ...** niemand, der etwas auf sich hält, würde ...; **self-restraint** N Selbstbeherrschung f; **self-righteous** ADJ selbstgerecht; **self-rising** ADJ (US) = **self-raising**; **self-sacrifice** N Selbstaufopferung f; **self-sacrificing** ADJ aufopfernd; **self-satisfaction** N Selbstzufriedenheit f, (= smugness) Selbstgefälligkeit f; **self-satisfied** ADJ (= smug) selbstgefällig; **self-selection** N (Brit) Selbstbedienung f; **self-service**, (esp US) **self-serve** **1** ADJ Selbstbedienungs- **2** N Selbstbedienung f; **self-study** N Selbststudium nt; self selbst ernannt; **self-sufficiency** N (of person) Selbstständigkeit f; (of country) Autarkie f; (of community) Selbstversorgung f; **self-sufficient** ADJ person selbstständig; country autark; **they are ~ in oil** sie können ihren Ölbedarf selbst decken; **a ~ community** eine Gemeinde, die sich selbst versorgen kann; **self-supporting** ADJ person finanziell unabhängig; **the club is ~** der Klub trägt sich selbst; **self-sustaining** ADJ (Econ) development, economy nachhaltig; **self-taught** ADJ skills selbst erlernt; **he is ~** er hat sich (dat) das selbst beigebracht; (intellectually) er hat sich durch Selbstunterricht gebildet; **self-will** N Eigenwilligkeit f, Eigensinn m (pej); **self-willed** ADJ eigenwillig, eigensinnig (pej); **self-worth** N Selbstachtung f; **feeling of ~** Selbstwertgefühl nt

sell [sel], vb: pret, ptp **sold** **1** VT (a) item, goods verkaufen (sb sth, sth to sb jdm etw, etw an jdn); (business) goods auch absetzen; insurance policy abschließen (to mit); **the book sold 3,000 copies** von dem Buch wurden 3.000 Exemplare verkauft; **to ~ insurance (for a living)** Versicherungsvertreter(in) m(f) sein; **to ~ one's soul to sb/sth** jdm/einer Sache seine Seele verschreiben; **what are you ~ing it for?** wie viel verlangen Sie dafür?; **I can't remember what I sold it for** ich weiß nicht mehr, für wie viel ich es verkauft habe; **to be sold on sb/sth** (inf) von jdm/etw begeistert sein (b) (= stock) führen, haben (inf); (= deal in) vertreiben (c) (= promote the sale of) einen guten Absatz verschaffen (+dat); (inf: = gain acceptance for) schmackhaft machen (to sb jdm); **to ~ oneself** (= put oneself across) sich verkaufen (to an +acc) (d) (fig: = betray) verraten; **to ~ sb down the river** (inf) jdn ganz schön verschaukeln (inf) **2** VI (person) verkaufen (to sb an jdn); (article) sich verkaufen (lassen); **his book is ~ing well/won't ~** sein Buch verkauft sich gut/lässt sich nicht verkaufen; **what are they ~ing at or for?** wie viel kosten sie?

➤ **sell off** VT SEP verkaufen; (= get rid of quickly, cheaply) abstoßen; (at auction) versteigern

➤ **sell on** VT SEP weiterverkaufen (to an +acc)

➤ **sell out** **1** VT SEP (a) (= sell entire stock of) ausverkaufen; **we're sold out of ice cream** das Eis ist ausverkauft (b) share, interest verkaufen, abgeben (c) (inf: = betray) verraten (to an +acc) **2** VI (a) (= sell entire stock) alles verkaufen or absetzen; **this book/we sold out in two days** das Buch war/wir waren in zwei Tagen ausverkauft (b) (in business) sein Geschäft/seine Firma/seinen Anteil etc verkaufen (c) (inf: = betray) **he sold out to the enemy** er hat sich an den Feind verkauft

➤ **sell up** (esp Brit) **1** VT SEP zu Geld machen (inf); (Fin) zwangsverkaufen **2** VI sein Haus/seinen Besitz/seine Firma etc verkaufen or zu Geld machen (inf)

sell-by date [ˈselbaɪˌdeɪt] N ≈ Haltbarkeitsdatum nt; **to be past one's ~** (hum inf) seine besten Tage hinter sich (dat) haben

seller [ˈselər] N (a) Verkäufer(in) m(f) (b) (= thing sold) **big ~** Verkaufsschlager m; **this book is a good/slow ~** das Buch verkauft sich gut/schlecht

sellers' market N **it's a ~ in housing just now** zurzeit bestimmen die Verkäufer die Hauspreise

selling [ˈselɪŋ] N Verkauf m; **~ expenses** (Comm) Vertriebskosten pl

selling point N Verkaufsanreiz m

selloff [ˈselɒf] N Verkauf m

Sellotape® [ˈseləʊteɪp] (Brit) **1** N Tesafilm® m **2** VT **to sellotape (down)** mit Tesafilm® festkleben

sellout [ˈselaʊt] N (a) (inf: = betrayal) fauler Kompromiss or Handel (to mit); (of one's ideals etc) Ausverkauf m (to an +acc) (b) (Theat, Sport) ausverkauftes Haus; **to be a ~** ausverkauft sein (c) (Comm) Verkaufsschlager m

selves [selvz] PL of self

semantic ADJ, **semantically** ADV [sɪˈmæntɪk, -əlɪ] semantisch

semantics [sɪˈmæntɪks] N SING Semantik f; **it's just a question of ~** es ist nur eine Frage der Formulierung or (interpretation) Auslegung

semaphore [ˈseməfɔːr] N (= system) Signalsprache f, Winken nt

semblance [ˈsembləns] N (with def art) Anschein m (of von); (with indef art) Anflug m (of von); **he had the ~ of an experienced lawyer** er erweckte den Anschein eines erfahrenen Anwalts

semen [ˈsiːmən] N Sperma nt

semester [sɪˈmestər] N Semester nt

semi [ˈsemɪ] N (a) (Brit inf) = **semidetached** (b) (inf) = **semifinal** (c) (US inf) = **semitrailer**

semi- PREF halb-, Halb-

semi: semi-annual ADJ (US) halbjährlich; **semicircle** N Halbkreis m; **semicolon** N Semikolon nt; **semiconscious** ADJ halb bewusstlos; **semidetached** (Brit) **1** ADJ **~ house** Doppelhaushälfte f **2** N Doppelhaushälfte f; **semifinal** N Halb- or Semifinalspiel nt; **~s** Halb- or Semifinale nt; **semifinalist** N Teilnehmer(in) m(f) am Halbfinale; **semi-finished** ADJ halbfertig; **~ goods** Halbfertigwaren pl; **~ product** Halberzeugnis nt

seminar [ˈseminɑːr] N Seminar nt

seminary [ˈseminərɪ] N Priesterseminar nt

semi: semiprecious ADJ **~ stone** Halbedelstein m; **semiquaver** N (esp Brit) Sechzehntel(note f) nt; **semiskilled** ADJ worker angelernt; **~ job** Anlernberuf m; **semi-skimmed milk** N (Brit) Halbfettmilch f; **semitrailer** N (Brit) Sattelschlepper m; (= part) Sattelauflieger m

semolina [ˌseməˈliːnə] N Grieß m

sen ABBR of **senior** sen.

senate [ˈsenɪt] N Senat m

senator [ˈsenɪtər] N Senator(in) m(f)

send [send], pret, ptp **sent** VT (a) (= dispatch) schicken; letter, messenger, signal senden; (~ = off) letter abschicken; **it ~s the wrong signal or message** (fig) das könnte falsch verstanden werden; **to ~ sb to university** jdn studieren lassen; **to ~ sb for sth** jdn nach etw schicken; **she ~s her love/apologies** etc sie lässt grüßen/sich entschuldigen etc; **~ him my love/best wishes** grüßen Sie ihn von mir (b) (= propel) arrow, ball schießen; (hurl) schleudern; **he sent everything crashing to the ground** er ließ alles krachend zu Boden fallen; **the blow sent him sprawling** der Schlag schleuderte ihn zu Boden; **the decision sent shock waves through the motor industry** die Entscheidung hat die Autobranche erschüttert; **the explosion had sent the spaceship off course** die Explosion hatte das Raumschiff vom Kurs abgebracht; **this sent him into a real fury** das machte ihn fürchterlich wütend; **this sent him (off) into fits of laughter** das ließ ihn in einen Lachkrampf ausbrechen; **to ~ prices soaring** die Preise in die Höhe treiben; **to ~ shares soaring** Aktien in die Höhe schnellen lassen

➤ **send across** VT SEP hinüberschicken; (+prep obj) schicken über (+acc)

➤ **send after** VT SEP **to send sb after sb** jdn jdm nachschicken

➤ **send along** VT SEP (her-/hin)schicken

➤ **send away** **1** VT SEP (= dispatch) wegschicken; letter etc abschicken; **his parents sent him away to school** seine Eltern schickten ihn ins Internat; **to send sth away to be mended** etw zur or in die Reparatur geben or schicken **2** VI schreiben; **to send away for sth** etw anfordern

➤ **send back** VT SEP zurückschicken; *food in restaurant* zurückgehen lassen

➤ **send down** VT SEP **(a)** *temperature, prices* fallen lassen; *(gradually)* senken **(b)** *prisoner* verurteilen *(for* zu)

➤ **send for** VI +PREP OBJ **(a)** *person* kommen lassen; *doctor, police* rufen; *help* herbeirufen; *reinforcements* herbeiordern; *(person in authority) pupil, minister* zu sich bestellen; **I'll send for you/these books when I want you/them** ich lasse Sie rufen/ ich schicke nach den Büchern, wenn ich Sie/sie brauche **(b)** *copy, catalogue* anfordern

➤ **send in** VT SEP einschicken, einsenden; *person* hereinschicken; *troops* einsetzen

➤ **send off 1** VT SEP **(a)** *parcel* abschicken **(b)** *children to school* wegschicken; **he sent his son off to Paris** er schickte seinen Sohn nach Paris **(c)** *(Sport)* vom Platz stellen *(for* wegen); **send him off, ref!** Platzverweis! **(d)** (= *see off*) verabschieden **2** VI = **send away 2**

➤ **send on** VT SEP **(a)** *letter* nachschicken; *memo* weiterleiten **(b)** *(in advance) luggage etc* vorausschicken **(c)** *substitute* einsetzen

➤ **send out** VT SEP **(a)** *(out of house, room)* hinausschicken *(of* aus); **he sent me out to the post office** er hat mich zur Post geschickt; **she sent me out to buy a paper** sie hat mich losgeschickt, um eine Zeitung zu kaufen **(b)** *rays, radio signals* aussenden; *light, heat, radiation* ausstrahlen **(c)** *invitations, application forms* verschicken

➤ **send out for 1** VI +PREP OBJ holen lassen **2** VT SEP **to send sb out for sth** jdn nach etw schicken

➤ **send up** VT SEP **(a)** *rocket* hochschießen; *flare* in die Luft schießen **(b)** *prices, temperature* hoch treiben, in die Höhe treiben **(c)** *(Brit inf:* = *satirize)* verulken *(inf)*

sender ['sendə^r] N Absender(in) *m(f)*

sendoff N Verabschiedung *f*; **to give sb a good ~** jdn ganz groß verabschieden *(inf)*

Senegal [seni'gɔːl] N Senegal *nt*

Senegalese [senigə'liːz] **1** ADJ senegalesisch **2** N Senegalese *m*, Senegalesin *f*

senile ['siːnail] ADJ *person* senil; *(physically)* altersschwach

senior ['siːniə^r] **1** ADJ *(in age)* älter; *(in rank)* übergeordnet; *rank, civil servant, position* höher; *officer* ranghöher; *editor, executive etc* leitend; **he is ~ to me** *(in rank)* er ist mir übergeordnet; **the ~ management** die Geschäftsleitung; **~ consultant** Chefarzt *m*/-ärztin *f*; **my ~ officer** mein Vorgesetzter; **J. B. Schwartz, Senior** J. B. Schwartz senior **2** N *(Sch)* Oberstufenschüler(in) *m(f)*; *(US Univ)* Student(in) *m(f)* im 4./letzten Studienjahr; **he is two years my ~, he is my ~ by two years** er ist zwei Jahre älter als ich

senior citizen N älterer (Mit)bürger, ältere (Mit)bürgerin

seniority [siːnɪ'ɒrɪtɪ] N *(in age)* (höheres) Alter; *(in rank)* (höhere) Position; *(Mil)* (höherer) Rang; *(in civil service etc)* (höherer) Dienstgrad; *(by length of service)* (längere) Betriebszugehörigkeit; *(in civil service etc)* (höheres) Dienstalter

senior: senior partner N Seniorpartner(in) *m(f)*; **senior school,** *(US)* **senior high school** N Oberstufe *f*

senr ABBR *of* **senior** sen.

sensation [sen'seiʃən] N **(a)** (= *feeling)* Gefühl *nt*; *(of cold etc)* Empfindung *f*; **a/the ~ of falling** ein Gefühl *nt* der Angst, ein Angstgefühl *nt* **(b)** (= *great success)* Sensation *f*; **to cause** *or* **create a ~** (großes) Aufsehen erregen

sensational [sen'seiʃənl] ADJ **(a)** sensationell; *newspaper, book* reißerisch aufgemacht; *style* reißerisch **(b)** *(inf:* = *very good etc)* sagenhaft *(inf)*

sensationally [sen'seiʃnəlɪ] ADV (= *dramatically)* sensationell; *(inf:* = *amazingly also)* sagenhaft *(inf)*

sense [sens] **1** N **(a)** *(bodily,* = *instinct)* Sinn *m*; **~ of hearing** Gehörsinn *m*, Gehör *nt*; **~ of smell** Geruchssinn *m*; **~ of taste** Geschmack(sinn) *m*; **~ of touch** Tastsinn *m*; **~ of justice** Gerechtigkeitssinn *m* **(b) senses** PL (= *right mind)* Verstand *m*; **to bring sb to his ~s**

jdn zur Vernunft *or* Besinnung bringen; **to come to one's ~s** zur Vernunft *or* Besinnung kommen

(c) (= *feeling)* Gefühl *nt*; **to get/have a ~ that ...** das Gefühl bekommen/haben, dass ...; **~ of duty** Pflichtbewusstsein *or* -gefühl *nt*; **~ of guilt** Schuldgefühl *nt*; **a ~ of occasion** das Gefühl, dass etwas Besonderes stattfindet; **a false ~ of security** ein falsches Gefühl der Sicherheit

(d) (= *good ~)* **(common)** = gesunder Menschenverstand; **he had the (good) ~ to ...** er war so vernünftig *or* klug und ...; **what's the ~ of** *or* **in doing this?** welchen Sinn hat es denn, das zu tun?; **there is no ~ in doing that** es ist zwecklos *or* sinnlos, das zu tun; **there's some ~ in what he says** was er sagt, ist ganz vernünftig; **to talk ~** vernünftig sein; **now you're talking ~** das lässt sich schon eher hören; **to make sb see ~** jdn zur Vernunft bringen; **to make ~** (= *sentence etc)* (einen) Sinn ergeben; (= *be sensible, rational etc)* Sinn machen; **it doesn't make ~ doing it that way** es ist doch Unsinn *or* unvernünftig, es so zu machen; **it makes good financial ~ to ...** aus finanzieller Sicht gesehen ist es sehr vernünftig, zu ...; **he/his theory doesn't make ~** er/seine Theorie ist völlig unverständlich; **it all makes ~ now** jetzt wird einem alles klar; **to make ~ of sth** etw verstehen, aus etw schlau werden *(inf)*; **you're not making ~** das ist doch Unsinn; **now you're making ~** *(in explaining sth)* jetzt verstehe ich, was Sie meinen; *(in plans etc)* das ist endlich eine vernünftige Idee

(e) (= *meaning)* Sinn *m no pl*; **it has three distinct ~s** es hat drei verschiedene Bedeutungen; **in every ~ of the word** in der vollen Bedeutung des Wortes

(f) (= *way, respect)* **in a ~** in gewisser Hinsicht, gewissermaßen; **in every ~** in jeder Hinsicht; **in what ~?** inwiefern?

2 VT fühlen, spüren

senseless ['senslɪs] ADJ **(a)** (= *unconscious)* bewusstlos; **to knock sb ~** jdn bewusstlos schlagen **(b)** (= *stupid)* unsinnig; (= *futile)* sinnlos

senselessly ['senslɪslɪ] ADV (= *pointlessly)* sinnlos

senselessness ['senslɪsnɪs] N (= *stupidity)* Unsinnigkeit *f*; (= *futility)* Sinnlosigkeit *f*

sensibility [sensɪ'bɪlɪtɪ] N *(to beauty etc)* Empfindsamkeit *f*; (= *artistic* – *also)* Sensibilität *f*; **sensibilities** Zartgefühl *nt*

sensible ['sensəbl] ADJ vernünftig; **be ~ about it** seien Sie vernünftig; **that's the ~ thing to do** das ist vernünftig

sensibly ['sensəblɪ] ADV vernünftig; **he very ~ ignored the question** er hat die Frage vernünftigerweise ignoriert

sensitive ['sensɪtɪv] ADJ *(emotionally) person* sensibel, empfindsam; (= *easily upset, physically* ~) empfindlich; (= *understanding)* einfühlsam; *film, remark* einfühlend; *(fig) topic, issue* heikel; **to be ~ about sth** in Bezug auf etw *(acc)* empfindlich sein; **she is very ~ to criticism** sie reagiert sehr empfindlich auf Kritik; **~ to light** lichtempfindlich; **he has access to some highly ~ information** er hat Zugang zu streng vertraulichen Informationen

sensitively ['sensɪtɪvlɪ] ADV **(a)** (= *sympathetically)* einfühlsam **(b)** (= *tastefully)* einfühlsam

sensitivity [sensɪ'tɪvɪtɪ] N *(emotional)* Sensibilität *f*, Empfindsamkeit *f*; (= *getting easily upset, physically sensitive)* Empfindlichkeit *f*; (= *understanding)* Einfühlsamkeit *f*; *(fig: of topic, issue)* heikle Natur

sensor ['sensə^r] N Sensor *m*

sensory ['sensərɪ] ADJ sensorisch; **~ organ** Sinnesorgan *nt*

sensual ['sensjʊəl] ADJ sinnlich, wollüstig *(pej)*

sensuality [sensjʊ'ælɪtɪ] N Sinnlichkeit *f*, Wollüstigkeit *f (pej)*

sensually ['sensjʊəlɪ] ADV sinnlich, wollüstig *(pej)*

sensuous ADJ, **sensuously** ADV ['sensjʊəs, -lɪ] sinnlich

sent [sent] PRET, PTP *of* **send**

sentence ['sentəns] **1** N **(a)** *(Gram)* Satz *m*; **~ structure** Satzbau *m*; *(of particular* ~) Satzaufbau *m* **(b)** *(Jur)* Strafe *f*; **the judge gave him a 6-month ~** der Richter verurteilte ihn zu 6 Monaten Haft **2** VT *(Jur)* verurteilen; **he was ~d to life imprisonment** er wurde zu lebenslänglichem Freiheitsentzug verurteilt

sentient ['sentɪənt] ADJ empfindungsfähig

sentiment ['sentɪmənt] N **(a)** (= *feeling, emotion*) Gefühl *nt* **(b)** (= *sentimentality*) Sentimentalität *f* **(c)** (= *opinion*) Ansicht *f*, Meinung *f*; **my ~s exactly!** genau meine Ansicht *or* Meinung!

sentimental [ˌsentɪ'mentl] ADJ sentimental; *value* gefühlsmäßig; **for ~ reasons** aus Sentimentalität; **~ nonsense** Gefühlsduselei *f*

sentimentality [ˌsentɪmen'tælɪtɪ] N Sentimentalität *f*

sentimentally [ˌsentɪ'mentəlɪ] ADV *attached etc* gefühlvoll; *say, reminisce* sentimental; *sing, play music* gefühlvoll; (*pej*) sentimental

sentry ['sentrɪ] N Wache *f*; **to be on ~ duty** auf Wache sein

separable ['sepərəbl] ADJ trennbar

separate ['seprət] **1** ADJ **(a)** gesondert (*from* von); *organization, unit also* eigen *attr*; *two organizations, issues, parts also* voneinander getrennt; *regulations also* besondere(r, s) *attr*; *beds, accounts* getrennt; *entrance, toilet* separat; **that is a ~ issue** das ist eine andere Frage; **on two ~ occasions** bei zwei verschiedenen Gelegenheiten; **on a ~ occasion** bei einer anderen Gelegenheit; **they live ~ lives** sie gehen getrennte Wege; **a ~ sheet of paper** ein anderes Blatt Papier; **this is quite ~ from his job** das hat mit seinem Beruf nichts zu tun; **to keep two things ~** zwei Dinge nicht zusammentun; *questions, issues* zwei Dinge auseinander halten **(b)** (= *individual*) einzeln; **all the ~ sections/pieces** alle einzelnen Abschnitte/Teile; **everybody has a ~ task** jeder hat eine Aufgabe für sich *or* seine eigene Aufgabe **2 separates** PL Röcke, Blusen, Hosen *etc* **3** ['sepəreɪt] VT trennen; (= *divide up*) aufteilen (*into* in +*acc*); **he is ~d from his wife** er lebt von seiner Frau getrennt **4** ['sepəreɪt] VI sich trennen

➤ **separate out 1** VT SEP trennen (*from* von), absondern (*from* von) **2** VI getrennt werden

separated ['sepəreɪtɪd] ADJ getrennt; *couple* getrennt lebend *attr*; **the couple are ~** das Paar lebt getrennt

separately ['seprətlɪ] ADV gesondert, separat; *live* getrennt; (= *singly*) einzeln

separation [ˌsepə'reɪʃən] N Trennung *f*

separatist ['sepərətɪst] **1** ADJ separatistisch **2** N Separatist(in) *m(f)*

September [sep'tembəʳ] **1** N September *m*; **the first of ~** der erste September; **on 19th ~** (*written*), **on the 19th of ~** (*spoken*) am 19. September; **~ 3rd, 1990, 3rd ~ 1990** (*on letter*) 3. September 1990; **in/during ~** im September; **at the beginning/end of ~** Anfang/Ende September; **there are 30 days in ~** der September hat 30 Tage **2** ADJ ATTR September-

septic ['septɪk] ADJ vereitert, septisch; **the wound turned ~** die Wunde eiterte

septic tank N Klärbehälter *m*

sepulchre, (*US*) **sepulcher** ['sepəlkəʳ] N Grabstätte *f*

sequel ['si:kwəl] N Folge *f* (*to* von); (*of book, film*) Fortsetzung *f* (*to* von)

sequence ['si:kwəns] N **(a)** (= *order*) Folge *f*, Reihenfolge *f*; **~ of words** Wortfolge *f*; **in ~** der Reihe nach **(b)** (= *things following*) Reihe *f*, Folge *f* **(c)** (*Film*: = *dance ~*) Sequenz *f*

sequencer ['si:kwənsəʳ] N (*Comput*) Ablaufsteuerung *f*

sequential [sɪ'kwenʃəl] ADJ (*Comput*) sequenziell

sequin ['si:kwɪn] N Paillette *f*

Serb [sɜ:b] N Serbe *m*, Serbin *f*

Serbia ['sɜ:bɪə] N Serbien *nt*

Serbian ['sɜ:bɪən] **1** ADJ serbisch **2** N **(a)** Serbe *m*, Serbin *f* **(b)** (*Ling*) Serbisch *nt*

Serbo-Croat ['sɜ:bəʊ'krəʊæt] N **(a)** (*Ling*) Serbokroatisch *nt* **(b)** **the ~s** *pl* die Serben und Kroaten

serenade [ˌserə'neɪd] **1** N Serenade *f* **2** VT ein Ständchen bringen (+*dat*)

serene [sə'ri:n] ADJ gelassen; *sea* ruhig; *sky* heiter

serenely [sə'ri:nlɪ] ADV gelassen; **her face was ~ beautiful** ihr Gesicht war von einer gelassenen Schönheit

serenity [sɪ'renɪtɪ] N Gelassenheit *f*

serf [sɜ:f] N Leibeigene(r) *mf*

sergeant ['sɑ:dʒənt] N (*Mil*) Feldwebel(in) *m(f)*; (*Police*) Polizeimeister(in) *m(f)*

sergeant major N Oberfeldwebel(in) *m(f)*

serial ['sɪərɪəl] **1** ADJ Serien-; *radio/TV programme* in Fortsetzungen; (*Comput*) *interface etc* seriell; **~ drama** (*TV*) (Fernseh)serie *f* **2** N (= *novel*) Fortsetzungsroman *m*; (*in periodical, TV*) Serie *f*; (*Rad*) Sendereihe *f* (*in Fortsetzungen*); **it was published as a ~** es wurde in Fortsetzungen veröffentlicht

serial: **serial killer** N Serienmörder(in) *m(f)*; **serial killing** N Serienmord *m*; **serial number** N fortlaufende Nummer; (*on manufactured goods*) Fabrikationsnummer *f*; **serial port** N (*Comput*) serielle Schnittstelle

series ['sɪəri:z] N, *pl* - Serie *f* (*also TV*); (*of books, lectures etc also, of films, talks*) Reihe *f*; (*of events also, succession of things*) Folge *f*; (*Rad*) Sendereihe *f*; **a ~ of articles** eine Artikelserie; **in ~** der Reihe nach; (*Comm*) serienmäßig

serious ['sɪərɪəs] ADJ ernst; (= *not frivolous*) *consideration, conversation, doubts also* ernsthaft; *patient's condition also* bedenklich; *threat, lack also* ernstlich; *publication, interest also, offer, suggestion* seriös; *contender* ernst zu nehmend *attr*; *accident, loss, mistake, injury, illness* schwer; **to be ~ about doing sth** etw im Ernst tun wollen; **I'm ~ (about it)** das ist mein Ernst; **I'm deadly ~** es ist mir todernst (*inf*); **he is ~ about her** er meint es ernst mit ihr; **you can't be ~!** das kann nicht dein Ernst sein!; **to give ~ thought** *or* **consideration to sth** sich (*dat*) etw ernsthaft *or* ernstlich überlegen; **to earn ~ money** (*inf*) das große Geld verdienen; **it's ~** das ist schlimm; **it's getting ~** es wird ernst

> Be careful! The German word **seriös** is not the most common translation for **serious**.

seriously ['sɪərɪəslɪ] ADV **(a)** ernst; *talk, interested, threaten* ernsthaft; (= *not jokingly*) im Ernst; *wounded, damaged, ill* schwer; *worried* ernstlich; **to take sb/sth ~** jdn/etw ernst nehmen; **to take oneself too ~** sich selbst zu wichtig nehmen; **~ now/though ...** jetzt mal/aber mal ganz im Ernst ...; **~?** im Ernst?; **do you mean that ~?** ist das Ihr Ernst?; **the takeoff went ~ wrong** beim Start ist etwas schlimm danebengegangen; **there is something ~ wrong with that** irgendetwas ist damit überhaupt nicht in Ordnung **(b)** (*inf*: = *really*) ehrlich (*inf*); **~ rich** (*person*) schwerreich; **I was beginning to get ~ annoyed** ich wurde langsam ernsthaft sauer (*inf*)

seriousness ['sɪərɪəsnɪs] N Ernst *m*; (= *lack of frivolity*) Ernsthaftigkeit *f*; (*of offer, suggestion*) Seriosität *f*; (*of accident, loss, mistake, injury, illness*) Schwere *f*; **in all ~** ganz im Ernst

sermon ['sɜ:mən] N (*Eccl*) Predigt *f*; (= *homily*) Moralpredigt *f*; (= *scolding*) Strafpredigt *f*

serrated [se'reɪtɪd] ADJ gezackt; **~ knife** Sägemesser *nt*

servant ['sɜ:vənt] N (*lit, fig*) Diener(in) *m(f)*; (*also ~ girl*) Dienstmädchen *nt*; (*domestic*) Dienstbote *m*/-botin *f*

serve [sɜ:v] **1** VT **(a)** (= *work for*) dienen (+*dat*); (= *be of use*) dienlich sein (+*dat*), nützen (+*dat*); **he ~d his country well** er hat sich um sein Land verdient gemacht; **if my memory ~s me right** wenn ich mich recht erinnere; **to ~ its purpose** seinen Zweck erfüllen; **it ~s a variety of purposes** es hat viele verschiedene Verwendungsmöglichkeiten; **it ~s no useful purpose** es hat keinen praktischen Wert; **it has ~d us well** es hat uns gute Dienste geleistet; **his knowledge of history ~d him well** seine Geschichtskenntnisse kamen ihm sehr zugute; **(it) ~s you right!** (*inf*) das geschieht dir (ganz) recht!; **it ~s him right for being so greedy** (*inf*) das geschieht ihm ganz recht, was muss er auch so gierig sein! **(b)** (= *work out*) ableisten; *term of office* durchlaufen; *apprenticeship* durchmachen; *sentence* verbüßen **(c)** (= *supply: transport, gas etc*) versorgen **(d)** *customers, guests* bedienen; *food, drink* servieren; (= *put on plate*) aufgeben; **are you being ~d?** werden Sie schon bedient?; **I'm being ~d, thank you** danke, ich werde schon bedient *or* ich bekomme schon (*inf*); **dinner is ~d** (*host, hostess*) darf ich zu Tisch bitten? „**~s three**" (*on packet etc*) „(ergibt) drei Portionen" **(e)** (*Tennis etc*) *ball* aufschlagen **(f)** (*Jur*) zustellen (*on sb* jdm); **the landlord ~d notice (to quit) on his tenants** (*esp Brit*) der Vermieter kündigte den Mietern **2** VI **(a)** (= *do duty*) dienen (*also Mil*); **to ~ on a committee** einem Ausschuss angehören; **to ~ on the council** Ratsmitglied *nt* sein; **to ~ as, to ~ for** dienen als; **it ~s to show/explain ...** das zeigt/erklärt ...

(b) (*at table*) aufgeben; (*waiter etc*) servieren (*at table* bei Tisch)
(c) (*Tennis etc*) aufschlagen
3 N (*Tennis etc*) Aufschlag *m*

➤ **serve out** VT SEP *time in army* ableisten; *apprenticeship* abschließen; *term of office* ausüben; *sentence* absitzen

➤ **serve up** VT SEP *food* servieren

server ['sɜːvə'] N (a) (= *spoon/fork*) Vorlegelöffel *m*/-gabel *f*; **salad ~s** Salatbesteck *nt* (b) (*Tennis*) Aufschläger(in) *m(f)*
(c) (*Comput*) Server *m*

service ['sɜːvɪs] **1** N (a) Dienst *m*; (= *domestic ~ also*) Stellung *f*; **his faithful ~** seine treuen Dienste; **~s to one's country** (*of soldier etc*) Dienst an seinem Vaterland; **her ~s to industry** ihre Verdienste in der Industrie; **to be of ~** nützlich sein; **to be of ~ to sb** jdm nützen; **to be at sb's ~** jdm zur Verfügung stehen; **can I be of ~ to you?** kann ich Ihnen behilflich sein?; **out of ~** außer Betrieb; **to come into ~** (= *into operation*) in Betrieb genommen werden; **"this number is not in ~"** (*US Telec*) „kein Anschluss unter dieser Nummer"
(b) (*Mil*) Militärdienst *m*
(c) (*with adj attr.* = *branch, department etc*) -dienst *m*; **BT offers different telephone ~s** BT bietet eine Reihe von (Telekommunikations)dienstleistungen an
(d) (*to customers*) Service *m*; (*in shop etc*) Bedienung *f*
(e) (= *bus, train, plane ~ etc*) Bus-/Zug-/Flugverbindung *f*; **there's no ~ to Oban on Sundays** sonntags besteht kein Zug-/Busverkehr nach Oban
(f) (*Eccl*) Gottesdienst *m*
(g) (*of machines*) Wartung *f*; (*Aut*: = *major ~*) Inspektion *f*; **my car is in for a ~** mein Auto wird gewartet/ist zur Inspektion; **contract of ~** Wartungsvertrag *m*
(h) (= *tea or coffee set*) Service *nt*
(i) (*Tennis*) Aufschlag *m*
(j) services PL (*commercial*) Dienstleistungen *pl*; (*gas, water etc*) Versorgungsnetz *nt*
2 VT (a) *car, machine* warten; **to send a car to be ~d** ein Auto warten lassen; (*major ~*) ein Auto zur Inspektion geben
(b) *area* bedienen; *committee etc* zuarbeiten (+*dat*)
(c) (*Fin*) *loan, debt* bedienen

service: service charge N Bedienung *f*, Bedienungsgeld *nt*; (*of bank*) Bearbeitungsgebühr *f*; **service contract** N Wartungsvertrag *m*; **service department** N Kundendienstabteilung *f*; **service industry** N Dienstleistungsbranche *f*; **serviceman** N Militärangehörige(r) *m*; **service provider** N (*Comput*) Provider *m*; **service sector** N (*of economy*) Dienstleistungssektor *m*; **service station** N Tankstelle *f* (mit Reparaturwerkstatt); (*Brit*: = *service area*) Tankstelle und Raststätte *f*; **servicewoman** N Militärangehörige *f*

serviette [ˌsɜːvɪˈet] N (*Brit*) Serviette *f*

serving ['sɜːvɪŋ] **1** ADJ *politician* amtierend; (*Mil*) *officer* Dienst tuend *attr*; *man* im Dienst **2** N (= *helping of food*) Portion *f*

serving: serving dish N Servierplatte *f*; **serving spoon** N Vorlegelöffel *m*

sesame ['sesəmɪ]: **sesame oil** N Sesamöl *nt*; **sesame seed** N Sesamkorn *nt*

session ['seʃən] N Sitzung *f*; (= *discussion*) Besprechung *f*; (*Jur, Parl*) Sitzungsperiode *f*; **to be in ~** eine Sitzung abhalten; (*Jur, Pol*) tagen; **a ~ of talks/negotiations** Gespräche *pl*/Verhandlungen *pl*; **photo ~** Fotosession *f*

---

set [set]

1 NOUN	**4** INTRANSITIVE VERB
2 ADJECTIVE	**5** PHRASAL VERBS
3 TRANSITIVE VERB	

vb: pret, ptp **set**

When the verb **set** *is part of a fixed combination, eg* **to set on fire, to set one's heart on sth,** *look up the other word.*

1 NOUN
(a) (*of objects*) Satz *m*; (*of two*) Paar *nt*; (*of cutlery, furniture etc*) Garnitur *f*; (= *tea set etc*) Service *nt*; (*of tablemats etc*) Set *nt*;

(= *chess set etc, in table tennis*) Spiel *nt*; (= *chemistry set etc*) Bastelkasten *m*; (*of books*) (*on one subject*) Reihe *f*; (*by one author*) gesammelte Ausgabe; **a set of tools** Werkzeug *nt*; **a set of teeth** ein Gebiss *nt*; **he had a whole set of questions** er hatte eine ganze Reihe Fragen
(b) (= *group of people*) Kreis *m*; (*pej*) Bande *f*; **the golfing set** die Golffreunde *pl*
(c) (*Sport*) (*Tennis*) Satz *m*; (*Table Tennis*) Spiel *nt*
(d) (*Theat*) Bühnenbild *nt*; (*Film*) Szenenaufbau *m*
(e) (*TV, radio etc*) Apparat *m*; (= *headset*) Paar *nt*; **set of headphones** Kopfhörer *m*
(f) (= *position*) (*of head, shoulders*) Haltung *f*
(g) (= *hairset*) Frisur *f*; **to have a shampoo and set** sich (*dat*) die Haare waschen und legen lassen

2 ADJECTIVE
(a) (= *likely*)
➔**to be set to he is set to become the new champion** ihm werden die besten Chancen auf den Meistertitel eingeräumt; **the talks are set to continue all week** die Gespräche werden voraussichtlich die ganze Woche über andauern
(b) (= *ready*) fertig, bereit
➔**all set are we all set?** sind wir alle fertig *or* bereit?; **all set?** alles klar?; **to be all set for sth** auf etw (*acc*) vorbereitet sein; (= *mentally prepared*) auf etw (*acc*) eingestellt sein; **to be all set to do sth** sich darauf eingerichtet haben, etw zu tun; **we're all set to go** wir sind so weit *or* startklar
(c) (= *rigid*) starr; *expression* feststehend; **to be set in one's ways** in seinen Gewohnheiten festgefahren sein
(d) (= *fixed*) (*prescribed*) festgesetzt; *time, place also, task* bestimmt; *essay topic* vorgegeben; **set book(s)** Pflichtlektüre *f*; **set hours for studying** feste Zeiten zum Lernen; **set menu** Tageskarte *f*; **set lunch/meal** Tagesgericht *nt*
➔**set piece** (*in novel, play*) Standardszene *nt*
(e) (= *resolved*) entschlossen; **to be set on doing sth** entschlossen sein, etw zu tun; **to be dead set on sth/doing sth** etw auf Biegen oder Brechen haben/tun wollen; **to be (dead) set against sth/doing sth/sb doing sth** (*absolut*) gegen etw sein/dagegen sein, etw zu tun/dagegen sein, dass jd etw tut

3 TRANSITIVE VERB
(a) (= *place*) stellen; (*on its side, flat*) legen; (*deliberately, carefully*) setzen; (= *embed*) einlegen (*in* in +*acc*); (*in ground*) einlassen (*in* in +*acc*); **to set a value/price on sth** (*lit, fig*) einen Wert/Preis für etw festsetzen; **to set going/in motion** etw in Gang/Bewegung bringen; **to set sth to music** etw vertonen; **to set a dog/the police on sb** einen Hund/die Polizei auf jdn ansetzen
➔**to set free to set sb free** jdn freilassen
➔**to set right to set sth/things right** etw/die Dinge in Ordnung bringen; **to set sb right (about sth)** jdn (in Bezug auf etw *acc*) berichtigen
➔**to set straight to set sb straight** jdn berichtigen
(b) (*timer, controls*) einstellen (*at* auf +*acc*); *clock* stellen (*by* nach, *to* auf +*acc*); *trap, record* aufstellen; *fashion* bestimmen; **to set a trap for sb** (*fig*) jdm eine Falle stellen
(c) *target, limit etc* festlegen; *task, question* stellen (*sb* jdm); *homework* aufgeben; *exam* zusammenstellen; *book for exam* vorschreiben; *time, date* festsetzen; *place* bestimmen; **to set the date (of the wedding)** die Hochzeit festsetzen; **to set sb a problem** (*lit*) jdm ein Problem aufgeben; (*fig*) jdn vor ein Problem stellen; **he was set a target** ihm wurde ein Soll vorgeschrieben
(d) (*gem*) fassen (*in* in +*dat*); *piece of jewellery* besetzen (*with* mit); *table* decken
(e) (= *locate*) **a house set on a hillside** ein am Berghang gelegenes Haus; **the book is set in Rome** das Buch spielt in Rom; **he set the book in 19th century France** er wählte das Frankreich des 19. Jahrhunderts als Schauplatz für sein Buch
(f) (*bone*) (*Med*) einrichten
(g) (*hair*) legen

4 INTRANSITIVE VERB
(a) (*sun, moon*) untergehen
(b) (*jelly, cement*) hart *or* fest werden; (*jam*) gelieren; (*bone*) zusammenwachsen

5 PHRASAL VERBS

➤ **set about** VI +PREP OBJ **(a)** (= *begin*) sich machen an (+*acc*), anfangen; (= *tackle*) anfassen, anpacken (*inf*); **to set about doing sth** (= *begin*) sich daranmachen, etw zu tun **(b)** (= *attack*) herfallen über (+*acc*)

➤ **set against** VT SEP +PREP OBJ **(a)** (= *influence against*) einnehmen gegen; (= *cause trouble between*) Zwietracht säen zwischen (+*dat*) **(b)** (= *balance against*) gegenüberstellen (+*dat*)

➤ **set apart** VT SEP (= *distinguish*) abheben, unterscheiden

➤ **set aside** VT SEP *book etc* zur Seite legen; *work, money* beiseite legen; *time* einplanen; *land, room* reservieren; *plans* aufschieben; *differences, hostilities* beiseite schieben

➤ **set back** VT SEP **(a)** (= *place at a distance*) zurücksetzen; **the house is set back from the road** das Haus liegt etwas von der Straße ab **(b)** (= *retard*) verzögern, behindern; (*by a certain length of time*) zurückwerfen; **the plans have been set back (by) 2 years** die Pläne sind um 2 Jahre zurückgeworfen **(c)** (*inf*: = *cost*) kosten

➤ **set down** VT SEP **(a)** *suitcase* absetzen **(b)** (*in writing*) (schriftlich) niederlegen

➤ **set in** VI (= *start*) einsetzen; (*panic*) ausbrechen; (*night*) anbrechen; (*Med*: *complications*) sich einstellen; **the rain has set in** es hat sich eingeregnet

➤ **set off** **1** VT SEP **(a)** (= *ignite*) losgehen lassen **(b)** (= *start*) führen zu; *quarrel* auslösen; **that set us all off laughing** das brachte uns (*acc*) alle zum Lachen; **don't set him off!** lass ihn nur nicht damit anfangen! **(c)** (= *enhance*) hervorheben; **to set sth off from sth** etw von etw abheben **2** VI (= *depart*) sich auf den Weg machen, aufbrechen; (*car, in car*) losfahren; **to set off on a journey** eine Reise antreten; **to set off for Spain** nach Spanien abfahren; **the police set off in pursuit** die Polizei nahm die Verfolgung auf

➤ **set on** **1** VT SEP +PREP OBJ *dogs* ansetzen auf (+*acc*) **2** VI +PREP OBJ = **set upon**

➤ **set out** **1** VT SEP (= *display*) ausbreiten; (= *arrange*) *chess pieces* aufstellen; *essay* anlegen; (= *state*) darlegen, darstellen **2** VI **(a)** (= *depart*) = **set off 2 (b)** (= *intend*) beabsichtigen; (= *start*) sich daranmachen

➤ **set to** **1** VI (= *start working etc*) loslegen (*inf*) **2** VI +PREP OBJ **to set to work** sich an die Arbeit machen; **to set to work doing** *or* **to do sth** beginnen, etw zu tun

➤ **set up** **1** VI **to set up as a doctor** sich als Arzt niederlassen; **to set up in business** sein eigenes Geschäft aufmachen **2** VT SEP **(a)** *statue, post* aufstellen; *stall, apparatus* aufbauen; *meeting* vereinbaren; *robbery* planen; **to set sth up for sb** etw für jdn vorbereiten **(b)** (= *establish*) gründen; *school, office, system* einrichten; *inquiry* veranlassen; **to set sb up in business** jdm zu einem Geschäft verhelfen; **to be set up for life** für sein ganzes Leben ausgesorgt haben; **to set up camp** die Zelte *or* das Lager aufschlagen; **they've set up home in Spain** sie haben sich in Spanien niedergelassen **(c)** (= *restore to health*) gut tun (+*dat*) **(d)** (*inf*: = *frame*) **to set sb up** jdm etwas anhängen; **I've been set up** das will mir einer anhängen (*inf*) *or* in die Schuhe schieben

➤ **set upon** VI +PREP OBJ überfallen; (*animal*) anfallen

set: **setback** N Rückschlag *m*; **set point** N Set- *or* Satzpunkt *m*

settee [se'tiː] N Couch *f*, Sofa *nt*

setting ['setɪŋ] N **(a)** (*of sun, moon*) Untergang *m* **(b)** (= *background, atmosphere*) Rahmen *m*; (= *surroundings*) Umgebung *f*; (*of novel etc*) Schauplatz *m* **(c)** (*of jewel*) Fassung *f* **(d)** (= *position on dial etc*) Einstellung *f*

settle ['setl] **1** VT **(a)** (= *decide*) entscheiden; (= *sort out*) regeln; *problem, question* klären; *dispute, differences* beilegen; *deal* abschließen; *price, terms* aushandeln; **to ~ one's affairs** seine Angelegenheiten in Ordnung bringen; **to ~ a case out of court** einen Fall außergerichtlich klären; **that's ~d then** das ist also klar *or* geregelt; **that ~s it** damit wäre der Fall (ja wohl) erledigt; (*angry*) jetzt reichts; **I'll soon ~ his**

nonsense (*inf*) ich werde ihm schon die Flausen austreiben **(b)** *bill* begleichen, bezahlen; *account* ausgleichen; (*Insur*) regulieren **(c)** *nerves, stomach* beruhigen **(d)** (= *place carefully*) legen; (*in upright position*) stellen; **to ~ oneself comfortably in an armchair** es sich (*dat*) in einem Sessel bequem machen; **she ~d her head back against the headrest** sie lehnte ihren Kopf zurück an die Kopfstütze **(e)** (= *establish*: *in house*) unterbringen; (= *colonize*) *land* besiedeln **2** VI **(a)** (= *put down roots*) sesshaft werden; (*in country, town*) sich niederlassen; (*as settler*) sich ansiedeln; (*in house*) sich häuslich niederlassen; (= *feel at home*) (*in house, town, country*) sich einleben (*into* in +*dat*); (*in job, surroundings*) sich eingewöhnen (*into* in +*dat*) **(b)** (= *become calm*) (*child, stomach*) sich beruhigen; (= *become less excitable or restless*) zur Ruhe kommen **(c)** (= *come to rest*) (*person, bird, insect*) sich niederlassen; (*dust*) sich setzen *or* legen; (*ground, liquid, sediment*) sich setzen; **to ~ comfortably in an armchair** es sich (*dat*) in einem Sessel gemütlich *or* bequem machen; **fog ~d over the city** Nebel legte sich über die Stadt **(d)** (*Jur*) **to ~ out (of court)** sich vergleichen

➤ **settle down** **1** VI **(a)** *see* **settle 2(a)**; **it's time he settled down** es ist Zeit, dass er ein geregeltes Leben anfängt; **to marry and settle down** heiraten und sesshaft werden; **to settle down at school** sich an einer Schule einleben; **to settle down in a new job** sich in einer neuen Stellung eingewöhnen; **settle down, children!** ruhig, Kinder!; **to settle down to work** sich an die Arbeit machen; **to settle down to watch TV** es sich (*dat*) vor dem Fernseher gemütlich machen **(b)** = **settle 2(b)** **2** VT SEP **(a)** (= *calm down*) beruhigen **(b)** *baby* hinlegen; *patient* versorgen

➤ **settle for** VI +PREP OBJ sich zufrieden geben mit

➤ **settle in** VI (*in house, town*) sich einleben; (*in job, school*) sich eingewöhnen; **how are you settling in?** haben Sie sich schon eingelebt/eingewöhnt?

➤ **settle on** *or* **upon** VI +PREP OBJ sich entscheiden für; (= *agree on*) sich einigen auf (+*acc*)

➤ **settle up** VI (be)zahlen; **to settle up with sb** (*lit, fig*) mit jdm abrechnen

➤ **settle with** VI, VT SEP +PREP OBJ (*lit, fig*) abrechnen mit

settled ['setld] ADJ *weather* beständig; *way of life* geregelt; **to be ~** in geregelten Verhältnissen leben; (*in place*) sesshaft sein; (= *less restless*) ruhiger *or* gesetzter sein; **to feel ~** sich wohl fühlen

settlement ['setlmənt] N **(a)** (= *deciding*) Entscheidung *f*; (= *sorting out*) Erledigung *f*; (*of problem, question etc*) Klärung *f*; (*of dispute etc*) Beilegung *f*; (*of bill, claim*) Bezahlung *f*; (*of account*) Ausgleich *m*; (= *contract, agreement etc*) Übereinkunft *f*; **an out-of-court ~, a ~ out of court** (*Jur*) ein außergerichtlicher Vergleich; **to reach a ~** sich einigen **(b)** (= *settling of money*) Übertragung *f*, Überschreibung *f* (*on* auf +*acc*); (*esp in will*) Vermächtnis *nt*; (*of annuity, income*) Aussetzung *f* **(c)** (= *colony, village*) Siedlung *f*, Niederlassung *f*; (= *act of settling persons*) Ansiedlung *f*; (= *colonization*) Besiedlung *f* **(d)** (*US: also* **~ house**) (= *institution*) Wohlfahrtseinrichtung *f*; (= *building*) Gemeindezentrum *nt*

settlement date N (*Comm*) Zahlungstermin *m*; (*St Ex*) Erfüllungstag *m*

settler ['setlə'] N Siedler(in) *m(f)*

set-top box ['settɒp'bɒks] N (*TV*) Digitalreceiver *m*, d-box® *f*

setup ['setʌp] N **(a)** (*inf*) (= *situation*) Umstände *pl*; (= *way of organizing things*) Organisation *f*; **it's a funny ~** das sind (vielleicht) komische Zustände! **(b)** (= *equipment*) Geräte *pl*, Instrumente *pl* **(c)** (*Comput*) Setup *nt* **(d)** (*inf*: = *rigged contest*) abgekartete Sache

setup file N (*Comput*) Setupdatei *f*

seven ['sevn] **1** ADJ sieben **2** N Sieben *f*; *see also* **six**

seventeen ['sevn'tiːn] **1** ADJ siebzehn **2** N Siebzehn *f*; *see also* **sixteen**

seventeenth ['sevn'ti:nθ] **①** ADJ siebzehnte(r, s); **a ~ part** ein Siebzehntel *nt* **②** N (= *fraction*) Siebzehntel *nt*; (*of series*) Siebzehnte(r, s)

seventh ['sevnθ] **①** ADJ siebte(r, s); **a ~ part** ein Siebtel *nt* **②** N (= *fraction*) Siebtel *nt*; (*in series*) Siebte(r, s); *see also* **sixth**

seventieth ['sevntɪθ] **①** ADJ siebzigste(r, s) **②** N (= *fraction*) Siebzigstel *nt*; (*in series*) Siebzigste(r, s)

seventy ['sevntɪ] **①** ADJ siebzig **②** N Siebzig *f*

sever ['sevəʳ] **①** VT (= *cut through*) durchtrennen; (*violently*) durchschlagen; (= *cut off*) abtrennen; (*violently*) abschlagen; (*fig*) *ties* lösen; *relations, links* abbrechen; *communications* unterbrechen **②** VI (durch)reißen

several ['sevrəl] **①** ADJ (= *some*) einige, mehrere; (= *different, diverse, various*) verschiedene; **I went with ~ others** ich ging mit einigen *or* ein paar anderen zusammen; **I've seen him ~ times already** ich habe ihn schon mehrmals *or* mehrere Male gesehen; **I'll need ~ more** ich brauche noch einige **②** PRON einige; **~ of the houses** einige (der) Häuser; **~ of us** einige von uns

severe [sɪ'vɪəʳ] ADJ (+ER) *hardship, damage, blow, loss, frost, draught* schwer; *pain, storm* stark; *problem* ernsthaft; *consequence* schwerwiegend; *critic, law, punishment, test* hart; *penalty* schwer(wiegend); *reprimand, criticism* scharf; *weather* rau; *weather conditions* schwierig; *winter, manner, style* streng; *expression* ernst

severely [sɪ'vɪəlɪ] ADV *affect, damage, injure, disabled* schwer; *disrupt, limit* stark; *punish* hart; *criticize, reprimand* scharf; (= *grimly, seriously, austerely*) streng

severity [sɪ'verɪtɪ] N (*of law, winter, punishment, test*) Härte *f*; (*of illness, injury, blow, crime, storm, loss*) Schwere *f*

Seville [sə'vɪl] N Sevilla *nt*

sew [səʊ], *pret* **sewed**, *ptp* **sewn** VTI nähen; **to ~ sth on/together** etw an-/zusammennähen

➤ **sew up** VT SEP (a) (*lit*) nähen (*also Med*); *opening* zunähen (b) (*fig*) unter Dach und Fach bringen; **we've got the game all sewn up** das Spiel ist gelaufen (*inf*)

sewage ['sju:dʒ] N Abwasser *nt*

sewage works N SING *or* PL Kläranlage *f*

sewer¹ ['səʊəʳ] N Näher(in) *m(f)*

sewer² [sjʊəʳ] N (= *pipe*) Abwasserleitung *f or* -rohr *nt*; (= *main ~*) Abwasserkanal *m*

sewerage ['sjʊərɪdʒ] N Kanalisation *f*; (= *service*) Abwasserbeseitigung *f*

sewing ['səʊɪŋ] N (= *activity*) Nähen *nt*; (= *piece of work*) Näharbeit *f*

sewing machine N Nähmaschine *f*

sewn [səʊn] PTP *of* **sew**

sex [seks] **①** N (a) (*Biol*) Geschlecht *nt* (b) (= *sexuality*) Sexualität *f*, Sex *m*; (= *sexual intercourse*) Sex *m* (*inf*), Geschlechtsverkehr *m* (*form*); **to have ~** (Geschlechts)verkehr haben **②** ADJ ATTR Geschlechts-, Sexual-

sex: sex appeal N Sexappeal *m*; **sex change** N Geschlechtsumwandlung *f*; **sex discrimination** N Diskriminierung *f* aufgrund *or* auf Grund des Geschlechts; **sex drive** N Sexualtrieb *m*; **sex education** N Sexualerziehung *f*

sexily ['seksɪlɪ] ADV aufreizend, sexy (*inf*)

sexism ['seksɪzəm] N Sexismus *m*

sexist ['seksɪst] **①** N Sexist(in) *m(f)* **②** ADJ sexistisch

sex: sexless ADJ geschlechtslos; **sex life** N Geschlechtsleben *nt*; (*of people also*) Liebesleben *nt*; **sex maniac** N (= *criminal*) Triebverbrecher(in) *or* -täter(in) *m(f)*; **he/she is a ~** (*inf*) er/sie ist ganz verrückt nach Sex (*inf*); **sex offender** N Sexualtäter(in) *m(f)*; **sex scene** N (*Film, Theat*) Sexszene *f*; **sex shop** N Sexshop *m*; **sex symbol** N Sexsymbol *nt*

sextet(te) [seks'tet] N Sextett *nt*

sextuplet [seks'tju:plɪt] N Sechsling *m*

sexual ['seksjʊəl] ADJ (a) *performance, preference, violence* sexuell (b) (*Physiol*) Sexual-

sexual: sexual abuse N sexueller Missbrauch; **sexual equality** N Gleichberechtigung *f* (der Geschlechter); **sexual harassment** N sexuelle Belästigung; **sexual health** N Sexualhygiene *f*; **sexual intercourse** N Geschlechtsverkehr *m*

sexuality [seksjʊ'ælɪtɪ] N Sexualität *f*

sexually ['seksjʊəlɪ] ADV sexuell; **~ transmitted diseases** durch Geschlechtsverkehr übertragene Krankheiten; **to be ~ attracted to sb** sich zu jdm sexuell hingezogen fühlen

sexual: sexual offence, (*US*) **sexual offense** N Sexualstraftat *f*; **sexual organ** N Geschlechts- *or* Sexualorgan *nt*; **sexual partner** N Sexualpartner(in) *m(f)*; **sexual preference** N sexuelle Orientierung; **sexual reproduction** N geschlechtliche Vermehrung

sexy [seksɪ] ADJ (+ER) (*inf*) sexy *inv usu pred* (*inf*); *smile, pose also* aufreizend; *film* erotisch

sh [ʃ] INTERJ sch(t)

shabbily ['ʃæbɪlɪ] ADV (*lit, fig*) schäbig

shabbiness ['ʃæbɪnɪs] N (*lit, fig*) Schäbigkeit *f*

shabby ['ʃæbɪ] ADJ (+ER) (*lit, fig*) schäbig

shack [ʃæk] N Hütte *f*, Schuppen *m*

shackle ['ʃækl] **①** N USU PL Kette *f*, Fessel *f* (*also fig*) **②** VT in Ketten legen; **they were ~d to the wall** sie waren an die Wand (an)gekettet

shade [ʃeɪd] **①** N (a) Schatten *m*; **30° in the ~** 30 Grad im Schatten; **to give** *or* **provide ~** Schatten spenden (b) (= *lampshade*) (Lampen)schirm *m*; (= *eye ~*) Schild *nt*, Schirm *m*; (*esp US*) (= *blind*) Jalousie *f*; (= *roller blind*) Springrollo *nt*; (*outside house*) Markise *f*; **~s** (*inf*: = *sunglasses*) Sonnenbrille *f* (c) (*of colour*) (Farb)ton *m*; (*fig: of meaning*) Nuance *f*; **a brighter ~ of red** ein leuchtenderer Rotton (d) (= *small quantity*) Spur *f*; **it's a ~ too long** es ist etwas *or* eine Spur zu lang **②** VT (a) (= *cast shadow on*) Schatten werfen auf (+*acc*); (= *protect from light, sun*) abschirmen; **he ~d his eyes with his hand** er hielt die Hand vor die Augen(, um nicht geblendet zu werden) (b) (= *darken with lines*) schraffieren; **to ~ sth in** etw ausschraffieren; (= *colour in*) etw ausmalen

shadiness ['ʃeɪdɪnɪs] N Schattigkeit *f*; (*fig*) Zwielichtigkeit *f*

shading ['ʃeɪdɪŋ] N (= *shaded area*) Schraffierung *f*; (*Art*) Schattierung *f*

shadow ['ʃædəʊ] **①** N (a) (*lit, fig*) Schatten *m*; **in the ~s** im Dunkel; **sb lives under the ~ of sth** etw liegt *or* lastet wie ein Schatten auf jdm; **to be in sb's ~** (*fig*) in jds Schatten (*dat*) stehen; **to be just a ~ of one's former self** nur noch ein Schatten seiner selbst sein (b) (= *trace*) Spur *f*; **without a ~ of a doubt** ohne den geringsten Zweifel **②** ATTR (*Brit Pol*) Schatten- **③** VT (a) (= *darken*) Schatten werfen auf (+*acc*) (b) (= *follow*) beschatten (*inf*)

shadow: shadow cabinet N (*Brit Pol*) Schattenkabinett *nt*; **shadow printing** N (*Comput*) Schattendruck *m*

SHADOW CABINET

Im politischen Leben Großbritanniens spielt das **Shadow Cabinet***, das Schattenkabinett der stärksten Oppositionspartei, eine wichtige Rolle. Jeder Regierungsposten hat seine Entsprechung im Schattenkabinett. Die Schattenminister haben die Aufgabe, die Regierungspolitik in ihren jeweiligen Verantwortungsbereichen infrage zu stellen und die Politik ihrer Partei öffentlich zu vertreten* ▶ **CABINET**

shadowy ['ʃædəʊɪ] ADJ schattig; *outline, form* verschwommen; **a ~ figure** (*lit*) eine schemenhafte Gestalt; (*fig*) eine undurchsichtige Gestalt

shady ['ʃeɪdɪ] ADJ (+ER) (a) *place* schattig; *tree* Schatten spendend (b) (*inf*: = *of dubious honesty*) zwielichtig; **he has a ~ past** er hat eine dunkle Vergangenheit

shaft [ʃɑːft] **①** N (a) Schaft *m*; (*of tool etc*) Stiel *m*; (*of light*) Strahl *m*; (*Mech*) Welle *f* (b) (*of lift, mine etc*) Schacht *m* **②** VT (*sl*: = *trick, cheat*) aufs Kreuz legen (*inf*)

shag [ʃæg] (*Brit sl*) **①** N Nummer *f* (*inf*); **to have a ~** eine Nummer machen (*inf*) **②** VTI bumsen (*inf*)

shaggy ['ʃægɪ] ADJ (+ER) (= *long-haired*) zottig; (= *unkempt*) zottelig

shake [ʃeɪk], *vb: pret* **shook**, *ptp* **shaken** **①** N (a) Schütteln *nt*; **to give a rug a ~** einen Läufer ausschütteln; **a ~ of her head** mit einem Kopfschütteln; **to be no great ~s** (*inf*) nicht umwerfend sein (*at in +dat*); **the ~s** *pl* (*inf*) der Tatterich (*inf*); (*esp with fear*) das Zittern; **he's got the ~s** er hat einen

Tatterich (*inf*); (*due to alcoholism also*) er hat einen
Flattermann (*inf*); (*esp with fear*) er hat das große Zittern (*inf*)
(b) (= *milkshake*) Milchshake *m*
2 VT **(a)** *person, head, object* schütteln; *building, faith,*
(= *shock*) erschüttern; *cocktail* durchschütteln; *resolve* ins
Wanken bringen; **to ~ one's fist at sb** jdm mit der Faust
drohen; **to ~ oneself/itself free** sich losmachen; **to ~ hands**
sich (*dat*) die Hand geben; (*for longer time, in congratulations
etc*) sich (*dat*) die Hand schütteln; **to ~ hands with sb** jdm die
Hand geben/schütteln; **it was a nasty accident, he's still
rather badly ~n** es war ein schlimmer Unfall, der Schreck
sitzt ihm noch in den Knochen; **she was badly ~ by the
news** die Nachricht hatte sie sehr mitgenommen *or*
erschüttert
(b) (*inf*) = **shake off**
3 VI wackeln; (*hand, voice*) zittern; (*earth, voice*) beben; **to ~
like a leaf** zittern wie Espenlaub; **he was shaking all over** er
zitterte am ganzen Körper; **to ~ with laughter** sich vor
Lachen schütteln; **to ~ in one's shoes** das große Zittern
kriegen (*inf*); **~! (**inf*) **on it!** (*inf*) Hand drauf
➤ **shake down** VT SEP **(a)** (*US inf:* = *extort money from*)
ausnehmen (*inf*) **(b)** (*US inf:* = *search*) durchsuchen (*for* nach)
➤ **shake off** VT SEP *dust, snow, pursuer* abschütteln; *image,
illness, feeling* loswerden
➤ **shake out** VT SEP (*lit*) herausschütteln; *tablecloth, rug*
ausschütteln
➤ **shake up** VT SEP **(a)** *bottle, liquid* schütteln **(b)** (= *upset*)
erschüttern; **he was badly shaken up by the accident** der
Unfall hat ihm einen schweren Schock versetzt; **she's still a
bit shaken up** sie ist immer noch ziemlich mitgenommen
(c) *management, recruits* auf Zack bringen (*inf*); *system*
umkrempeln (*inf*); *country, industry* wachrütteln; **to shake
things up** die Dinge in Bewegung bringen
shaken [ˈʃeɪkən] PTP *of* **shake**
Shakespearean, Shakespearian [ʃeɪkˈspɪərɪən] ADJ
shakespearisch
shake-up [ˈʃeɪkʌp] N (*inf:* = *reorganization*) Umbesetzung *f*
shakily [ˈʃeɪkɪlɪ] ADV wackelig; *walk* mit wackeligen Schritten;
write, pour etc zitterig
shaking [ˈʃeɪkɪŋ] N Zittern *nt*
shaky [ˈʃeɪkɪ] ADJ (+ER) *chair, position* wackelig; *evidence*
fragwürdig; *voice, hands* zitt(e)rig; *knowledge* unsicher; **to get
off to a ~ start** (*fig*) einen unsicheren *or* holprigen Anfang
nehmen; **to be on ~ ground** (*fig*) sich auf schwankendem *or*
unsicherem Boden bewegen
shale [ʃeɪl] N Schiefer *m*
shall [ʃæl] *pret* **should** MODAL AUX VB **(a)** (*future*) **I/we ~** *or* **I'll/
we'll go to France this year** ich werde/wir werden dieses Jahr
nach Frankreich fahren, ich fahre/wir fahren dieses Jahr
nach Frankreich; **no, I ~ not** *or* **I shan't** nein, das werde ich
nicht tun *or* das tue ich nicht
(b) (*determination, obligation*) **you ~ pay for this!** dafür sollst
or wirst du büßen!; **the manufacturer ~ deliver ...** (*in contracts
etc*) der Hersteller liefert ...; **I want to go too – and so you ~**
ich will auch mitkommen – aber gewiss doch
(c) (*in questions, suggestions*) **what ~ we do?** was sollen wir
machen?, was machen wir?; **let's go in, ~ we?** komm, gehen
wir hinein!; **~ I go now?** soll ich jetzt gehen?; **I'll buy 3, ~ I?**
soll ich 3 kaufen?
shallot [ʃəˈlɒt] N Schalotte *f*
shallow [ˈʃæləʊ] **1** ADJ flach; *water also, person, novel* seicht; *soil*
dünn; *talk* oberflächlich **2** N **shallows** PL Untiefe *f*
shallowness [ˈʃæləʊnɪs] N Flachheit *f*; (*of water also, person,
novel*) Seichtheit *f*; (*of soil*) Dünne *f*
sham [ʃæm] **1** N **(a)** (= *pretence*) Heuchelei *f*; **their marriage
had become a ~** ihre Ehe war zur Farce geworden
(b) (= *person*) Scharlatan *m* **2** ADJ **a ~ marriage** eine
Scheinehe **3** VT vortäuschen, vorgeben; *illness also*
simulieren; *emotions, sympathy* heucheln **4** VI so tun; (*esp
with illness*) simulieren; (*with feelings*) heucheln; **he's just
~ming** er tut nur so
shamble [ˈʃæmbl] VI trotten; (*people also*) latschen (*inf*)
shambles [ˈʃæmblz] N SING heilloses Durcheinander; (*esp of
room etc*) Tohuwabohu *nt*; **the room was a ~** im Zimmer
herrschte das reinste Tohuwabohu; **the economy is in a ~** die
Wirtschaft befindet sich in einem Chaos; **the game was a ~**

das Spiel war das reinste Kuddelmuddel (*inf*); **he made a ~ of
that job** da hat er vielleicht einen Mist gebaut! (*inf*)
shame [ʃeɪm] **1** N **(a)** (= *feeling of ~*) Scham *f*; (= *cause of ~*)
Schande *f*; **he hung his head in ~** er senkte beschämt den
Kopf; (*fig*) er schämte sich; **to bring ~ upon sb/oneself** jdm/
sich Schande machen; **have you no ~?** schämst du dich (gar)
nicht?; **to put sb/sth to ~** (*lit*) jdm/etw Schande machen; (*fig*)
jdn/etw in den Schatten stellen; **to my (eternal) ~** zu meiner
(ewigen) Schande; **the ~ of it all** die Schande *or* Schmach;
the ~ of it! was für eine Schande!; **~ on you!** du solltest dich/
ihr solltet euch schämen!
(b) (= *pity*) **it's a ~ you couldn't come** schade, dass du nicht
kommen konntest; **what a ~!** (das ist aber) schade!; **what a ~
he ...** schade, dass er ...
2 VT Schande machen (+*dat*); (*fig: by excelling*) in den
Schatten stellen
shamefaced [ˈʃeɪmfeɪst] ADJ, **shamefacedly** [ˈʃeɪmfeɪsɪdlɪ] ADV
betreten
shameful [ˈʃeɪmfʊl] ADJ schändlich; *experience, secret* peinlich;
there is nothing ~ about it das ist doch keine Schande
shamefully [ˈʃeɪmfəlɪ] ADV schändlich; **he is ~ ignorant** es ist
eine Schande, wie wenig er weiß
shameless [ˈʃeɪmlɪs] ADJ schamlos; **he was quite ~ about it** er
schämte sich überhaupt nicht
shamelessly [ˈʃeɪmlɪslɪ] ADV schamlos
shampoo [ʃæmˈpuː] **1** N (= *liquid*) Shampoo *nt*; (= *act of
washing*) Reinigung *f*; (*of hair*) Waschen *nt*; **to have a ~ and
set** sich (*dat*) die Haare waschen und legen lassen **2** VT *hair*
waschen; *carpet, upholstery* reinigen
shamrock [ˈʃæmrɒk] N Klee *m*; (= *leaf*) Kleeblatt *nt*
shandy [ˈʃændɪ] N (*Brit*) Bier *nt* mit Limonade
shan't [ʃɑːnt] CONTR *of* **shall not**; **~!** (*inf*) will nicht! (*inf*)
shantytown [ˈʃæntɪtaʊn] N Slum(vor)stadt *f*
shape [ʃeɪp] **1** N **(a)** (= *geometrical form, outline, object*) Form *f*;
(= *unidentified figure, guise*) Gestalt *f*; **what ~ is it?** welche
Form hat es?; **it's rectangular etc in ~** es ist rechteckig *etc*; **to
knock sth out of ~** etw zerbeulen; **to take ~** (*lit*) Form
bekommen; (*fig*) Gestalt *or* Konturen annehmen; **of all ~s
and sizes, of every ~ and size** aller Art, jeder Art; **I don't
accept gifts in any ~ or form** ich nehme überhaupt keine
Geschenke an; **this may be the ~ of things to come** so könnte
das vielleicht in Zukunft sein; **in human ~** in
Menschengestalt
(b) (*fig:* = *order, condition*) **to be in good/bad ~** (*sportsman*) in
Form/nicht in Form sein; (*mentally, healthwise*) in guter/
schlechter Verfassung sein; (*things, business*) in gutem/
schlechtem Zustand sein; **to be out of ~** (*physically*) nicht in
Form sein; **to get sb/a business into ~** jdn/ein Geschäft *or*
Unternehmen auf Vordermann bringen (*inf*)
2 VT (*lit*) *stone, wood etc* bearbeiten; *clay etc* formen (*into* zu);
(*fig*) *character, ideas* prägen; *future, development, market*
gestalten; **those who have helped ~ our society** die(jenigen),
die unsere Gesellschaft mitgeformt haben
3 VI sich entwickeln
➤ **shape up** VI **to shape up well** sich gut entwickeln; **things
are shaping up well** es sieht sehr gut aus; **it's shaping up to be
a disaster** es entwickelt sich zur Katastrophe
shaped [ʃeɪpt] ADJ geformt; **an oddly ~ hat** ein Hut mit einer
komischen Form; **~ like a ...** in der Form einer/eines ...
-shaped [-ʃeɪpt] ADJ SUF -förmig
shapeless [ˈʃeɪplɪs] ADJ formlos; (= *ugly*) unförmig
shapeliness [ˈʃeɪplɪnɪs] N (*of figure*) Wohlproportiniertheit *f*;
(*of legs, bust*) Wohlgeformtheit *f*
shapely [ˈʃeɪplɪ] ADJ (+ER) *figure, woman* wohlproportioniert;
legs, bust wohlgeformt
shard [ʃɑːd] N (Ton)scherbe *f*
share [ʃɛəʳ] **1** N **(a)** Anteil *m* (*in or of* an +*dat*); **I want my fair ~**
ich will meinen (An)teil; **he didn't get his fair ~** er ist zu kurz
gekommen; **I've had more than my fair ~ of bad luck** ich habe
mehr (als mein Teil an) Pech gehabt; **I'll give you a ~ in the
profits** ich beteilige Sie am Gewinn; **he came in for his full ~
of criticism** er hat sein Teil an Kritik abbekommen; **to take
one's ~ of the blame** sich mitschuldig erklären; **to do one's
~** sein(en) Teil *or* das Seine tun *or* beitragen
(b) (*Fin*) (*general*) (Geschäfts)anteil *m*; (*in a public limited
company*) Aktie *f*

2 VT (= *divide*) teilen; (= *have in common also*) gemeinsam haben; *responsibility* gemeinsam tragen; **they ~ a room** sie teilen ein Zimmer

3 VI teilen; **to ~ and ~ alike** (brüderlich) mit (den) anderen teilen; **to ~ in sth** sich an etw (*dat*) beteiligen; *in profit* an etw (*dat*) beteiligt werden; *in enthusiasm* etw teilen; *in success, sorrow* an etw (*dat*) Anteil nehmen

➤ **share out** VT SEP verteilen

share: **share capital** N Aktienkapital *nt*; **share certificate** N Aktienzertifikat *nt*; **shareholder** N Aktionär(in) *m(f)*; **~s' funds** (*Brit*) or **equity** (*US*) Eigenkapital *nt* der Aktionäre; **shareholder value** N Shareholdervalue *m*; *observation* **share index** N Aktienindex *m*; **share issue** N (*St Ex*) Aktienemission *f*; **share option** N Aktienoption *f*; **share-out** N Verteilung *f*; (*St Ex*) (Dividenden)ausschüttung *f*; **share premium** N Agio *nt* aus Aktienemissionen

shark [ʃɑːk] N **(a)** Hai(fisch) *m* **(b)** (*inf*: = *swindler*) Schlitzohr *nt* (*inf*); **loan ~** Kreditshai *m* (*inf*)

sharp [ʃɑːp] **1** ADJ (+ER) **(a)** (*lit, fig*) scharf; *needle, point, angle etc* spitz; *sense of smell* gut, empfindlich; *observation* scharfsinnig; (= *intelligent*) schlau; *cry* durchdringend, schrill; *drop in prices* steil; *pain* heftig; *person* schroff; *temper* hitzig; **be ~ about it!** (*inf*) (ein bisschen) dalli! (*inf*)
(b) (*pej*: = *cunning*) *person, trick etc* raffiniert; **~ practice** unsaubere Geschäfte *pl*
(c) (*Mus*) *note* (= *too high*) zu hoch; (= *raised a semitone*) (um einen Halbton) erhöht; **you played F natural instead of F ~** du hast f statt fis gespielt
(d) (*inf*: = *stylish*) toll (*inf*); *piece of driving* clever (*inf*)
2 ADV (+ER) **(a)** (*Mus*) zu hoch
(b) (= *punctually*) pünktlich, genau; **at 5 o'clock ~** Punkt 5 Uhr
(c) **look ~!** dalli! (*inf*); **if you don't look ~ ...** wenn du nicht schnell machst ...; **to pull up ~** plötzlich anhalten

sharp-edged [ʃɑːpˈedʒd] ADJ *knife, outline etc* scharf; *piece of furniture etc* scharfkantig

sharpen [ʃɑːpən] VT *knife* schleifen; *pencil* spitzen; (*fig*) *appetite* anregen; *wits* schärfen

sharpener [ʃɑːpnəʳ] N Schleifgerät *nt*; (*in rod shape*) Wetzstahl *m*; (= *pencil ~*) (Bleistift)spitzer *m*

sharp-eyed [ʃɑːpˈaɪd] ADJ scharfsichtig; **to be ~** scharfe or gute Augen haben

sharpness [ʃɑːpnɪs] N **(a)** (*lit, fig*) Schärfe *f*; (*of needle, point etc*) Spitzheit *f*; (*of observation*) Scharfsinnigkeit *f*; (= *intelligence, of person*) Schläue *f* **(b)** (= *suddenness, intensity: of desire, pain*) Heftigkeit *f*; (*of temper*) Hitzigkeit *f*

sharp: **sharp-tongued** ADJ scharfzüngig; **sharp-witted** ADJ scharfsinnig

shat [ʃæt] PRET, PTP *of* shit

shatter [ʃætəʳ] **1** VT **(a)** (*lit*) zertrümmern; *hopes, dreams* zunichte machen; *nerves* zerrütten; **the blast ~ed all the windows** durch die Explosion zersplitterten alle Fensterscheiben **(b)** (*Brit fig inf*: = *exhaust*) erledigen (*inf*); (*mentally*) mitnehmen; **how are you? – ~ed!** wie gehts? – ich bin total kaputt or erledigt (*inf*) **2** VI zerbrechen, zerspringen; (*windscreen*) (zer)splittern

shattering [ʃætərɪŋ] ADJ **(a)** *blow* wuchtig; *explosion* gewaltig; *defeat* vernichtend; **it had a ~ effect on the economy** es wirkte sich verheerend auf die Wirtschaft aus (*fig inf*: = *exhausting*) erschöpfend, anstrengend; (*psychologically*) niederschmetternd; **I had a ~ day at the office** der Tag im Büro hat mich wahnsinnig geschlaucht (*inf*) **(c)** (*inf*) *news, realization* erschütternd; *effect* umwerfend (*inf*)

shave [ʃeɪv] *vb: pret* shaved, *ptp* shaved or shaven **1** N Rasur *f*; **to have a ~** sich rasieren; **that was a close ~** das war knapp **2** VT *face, legs* rasieren; *wood* hobeln **3** VI (*person*) sich rasieren; (*razor*) rasieren

➤ **shave off** VT SEP *beard* sich (*dat*) abrasieren

shaven [ʃeɪvn] ADJ *head etc* kahl geschoren

shaver [ʃeɪvəʳ] N (= *razor*) Rasierapparat *m*

shaver point, (*US*) **shaver outlet** N Steckdose *f* für Rasierapparate

shaving [ʃeɪvɪŋ] N **(a)** Rasieren *nt* **(b) shavings** PL Späne *pl*

shaving IN CPDS Rasier-

shawl [ʃɔːl] N (*round shoulders*) (Umhänge)tuch *nt*; (*tailored*) Umhang *m*; (*covering head*) (Kopf)tuch *nt*

she [ʃiː] **1** PRON sie; (*of boats, cars etc*) es; **~ who ...** (*liter*) diejenige, die ... **2** N Sie *f*

she- PREF weiblich; **~-bear** Bärin *f*

sheaf [ʃiːf] N, *pl* sheaves (*of corn*) Garbe *f*; (*of papers*) Bündel *nt*

shear [ʃɪəʳ], *pret* sheared, *ptp* shorn VT *sheep* scheren

➤ **shear off** VI (= *break off*) abbrechen

shears [ʃɪəz] PL (große) Schere; (*for hedges*) Heckenschere *f*; (*for metal*) Metallschere *f*

sheath [ʃiːθ] N (*for sword etc*) Scheide *f*; (= *contraceptive*) Kondom *m or nt*

sheathe [ʃiːð] VT *sword, knife* in die Scheide stecken; **to ~ sth in metal** etw mit Metall verkleiden

sheaves [ʃiːvz] PL *of* sheaf

shed¹ [ʃed], *pret, ptp* shed VT **(a)** *leaves, hair etc* verlieren; **to ~ its skin** sich häuten; **to ~ its load** (*lorry*) seine Ladung verlieren; **you should ~ a few pounds** Sie sollten ein paar Pfund abnehmen **(b)** *tears, blood* vergießen; **I won't ~ any tears over him** ich weine ihm keine Träne nach **(c)** *burden, reputation* loswerden; *ideas* ablegen; *jobs* abbauen **(d)** *light* verbreiten; **to ~ light on sth** (*fig*) Licht auf etw (*acc*) werfen

shed² N Schuppen *m*; (*industrial also*) Halle *f*; (= *cattle ~*) Stall *m*

she'd [ʃiːd] CONTR *of* she would, she had

sheen [ʃiːn] N Glanz *m*

sheep [ʃiːp] N, *pl -* (*lit, fig*) Schaf *nt*; **to separate the ~ from the goats** (*fig*) die Schafe von den Böcken trennen

sheepdog [ʃiːpdɒg] N Hütehund *m*

sheepish [ʃiːpɪʃ] ADJ verlegen; **I felt a bit ~ about it** das war mir ein bisschen peinlich

sheepishly [ʃiːpɪʃlɪ] ADV verlegen

sheepskin [ʃiːpskɪn] N Schaffell *nt*

sheer [ʃɪəʳ] **1** ADJ (+ER) **(a)** (= *absolute*) rein; **by ~ chance** rein zufällig; **by ~ hard work** durch nichts als harte Arbeit; **it was ~ hell** es war die (reinste) Hölle (*inf*) **(b)** *cliff, drop* steil, jäh (*geh*); **there is a ~ drop of 200 feet** es fällt 200 Fuß steil or senkrecht ab **(c)** *cloth etc* (hauch)dünn **2** ADV steil, jäh (*geh*); (= *vertically*) senkrecht

➤ **sheer away** VI (*ship, plane*) ausweichen

➤ **sheer off** VI (*ship*) ausscheren

sheet [ʃiːt] N **(a)** (*for bed*) (Bett)laken *nt*; (*for covering furniture*) Tuch *nt*; **between the ~s** (*inf*) im Bett (*inf*) **(b)** (*of paper*) Blatt *nt*; (*big, as of wrapping paper etc*) Bogen *m*; **~s** (*Brit sl*: = *money*) Kohle *f* (*inf*) **(c)** (*of plywood, metal*) Platte *f*; (*of glass*) Scheibe *f*; (*Geol*) Schicht *f*; (*of water, ice etc*) Fläche *f*; (*of flame*) Flammenmeer *nt*; **a ~ of ice covered the lake** eine Eisschicht bedeckte den See

sheet: **sheet feed** N (*Comput*) Einzelblatteinzug *m*; **sheet ice** N Glatteis *nt*

sheeting [ʃiːtɪŋ] N (= *cloth*) Leinen *nt*; (= *metal etc*) Verkleidung *f*; **plastic ~** Plastiküberzug *m*

sheet: **sheet metal** N Walzblech *nt*; **sheet music** N Notenblätter *pl*

sheik(h) [ʃeɪk] N Scheich *m*

shelf [ʃelf] N, *pl* shelves **(a)** Bord *nt*; (*for books*) Bücherbord *nt*; (*in shop*) Regal *nt*; **shelves** (= *unit of furniture*) Regal *nt*; **to buy sth off the ~** etw als Handelsware kaufen **(b)** (*on rock face*) Gesims *nt*, (Fels-)vorsprung *m*; (*under water*) (Felsen)riff *nt*

shelf life N (*lit*) Lagerfähigkeit *f*; (*fig*) Dauer *f*

shell [ʃel] **1** N **(a)** (*of egg, nut, mollusc*) Schale *f*; (*on beach*) Muschel *f*; (*of snail*) (Schnecken)haus *nt*; (*of tortoise, insect*) Panzer *m*; **to come out of one's ~** (*fig*) aus seinem Schneckenhaus kommen
(b) (= *frame*) (*of building*) Mauerwerk *nt*, Mauern *pl*; (*unfinished*) Rohbau *m*; (= *ruin*) Gemäuer *nt*; (*of car*) (*unfinished*) Karosserie *f*; (*gutted*) Wrack *nt*
(c) (*Mil*) Granate *f*; (*esp US*: = *cartridge*) Patrone *f*
2 VT **(a)** *peas etc* enthülsen; *eggs, nuts* schälen
(b) (*Mil*) (mit Granaten) beschießen

➤ **shell out** (*inf*) **1** VT SEP blechen (*inf*) **2** VI **to shell out for sth** für etw blechen (*inf*)

she'll [ʃiːl] CONTR *of* she will, she shall

shell: shell company N (*Comm*) Firmenmantel *m*; **shellfire** N Granatfeuer *nt*; **shellfish** N Schaltier(e) *nt(pl)*; (*Cook*) Meeresfrüchte *pl*

shelling ['ʃelɪŋ] N Granatfeuer *nt* (*of* auf +*acc*)

shell: shell program N (*Comput*) Shellprogramm *nt*; **shell shock** N Kriegsneurose *f*; **shell-shocked** ADJ **to be** ~ (*lit*) unter einer Kriegsneurose leiden; (*fig*) verstört sein

shelter ['ʃeltə'] **1** N (= *protection*) Schutz *m*; (= *place*) Unterstand *m*; (= *air-raid* ~) (Luftschutz)keller *or* -bunker *m*; (= *bus* ~) Wartehäuschen *nt*; (= *mountain* ~) (Berg- *or* Schutz)hütte *f*; (*for the night*) Unterkunft *f*; **a** ~ **for homeless people** ein Obdachlosenheim *nt*; **to take** ~ sich in Sicherheit bringen; (*from rain, hail etc*) sich unterstellen; **to seek** ~ Schutz suchen; **to run for** ~ Zuflucht suchen; **to provide** ~ **for sb** jdm Schutz bieten; (= *accommodation*) jdn beherbergen **2** VT schützen (*from* vor +*dat*); **criminal** verstecken; **to** ~ **sb from harm** jdn vor Schaden bewahren **3** VI **there was nowhere to** ~ man konnte nirgends Schutz finden; (*from rain etc*) man konnte sich nirgends unterstellen; **we** ~**ed in a shop doorway** wir stellten uns in einem Ladeneingang unter

sheltered ['ʃeltəd] ADJ *place* geschützt; *life* behütet; ~ **from the wind** windgeschützt

sheltered housing N (*for the elderly*) Wohnungen *pl* für Senioren; (*for the disabled*) Wohnungen *pl* für Behinderte

shelve [ʃelv] VT *problem* aufschieben; *plan* ad acta legen

shelves [ʃelvz] PL *of* **shelf**

shepherd ['ʃepəd] **1** N Schäfer *m* **2** VT führen

shepherd's pie N Auflauf aus Hackfleisch und Kartoffelbrei

sherbet ['ʃɜːbət] N (= *powder*) Brausepulver *nt*; (= *drink*) Brause *f*; (*US: = water ice*) Fruchteis *nt*

sheriff ['ʃerɪf] N Sheriff *m*; (*Scot*) Friedensrichter(in) *m(f)*

sherry ['ʃerɪ] N Sherry *m*

she's [ʃiːz] CONTR *of* **she is, she has**

Shetland ['ʃetlənd] N, **Shetland Islands** ['ʃetləndˈaɪləndz] PL, **Shetlands** ['ʃetləndz] PL Shetlandinseln *pl*

shield [ʃiːld] **1** N (*Mil, Her*) Schild *m*; (= *sporting trophy also*) Trophäe *f*; (*on machine*) Schutzschirm *or* -schild *m*; (= *eyeshield*) Schirm *m*; (*fig*) Schutz *m* **2** VT schützen (*sb from sth* jdn vor etw *dat*); **she tried to** ~ **him from the truth** sie versuchte, ihm die Wahrheit zu ersparen

shift [ʃɪft] **1** N (a) (= *change*) Änderung *f*; (*in policy, opinion also*) Wandel *m*; (*from one place to another*) Verlegung *f*; **a** ~ **in public opinion** ein Meinungsumschwung *m* in der Bevölkerung; **a** ~ **of** *or* **in emphasis** eine Gewichtsverlagerung; **a new** ~ **toward(s) liberalism** ein neuer Trend zum Liberalismus **(b)** (*Aut*: = *gear* ~) Schaltung *f* **(c)** (= *period at work, group of workers*) Schicht *f*; **to work (in)** ~**s** in Schichten arbeiten **2** VT (a) (= *move*) (von der Stelle) bewegen; *screw* loskriegen; *lid* abkriegen; *furniture* verrücken; *head, arm* wegnehmen; (*from one place to another*) verlagern, verschieben; *offices etc* verlegen; *rubble, boulder* wegräumen; **to** ~ **the blame onto somebody else** die Verantwortung auf jemand anders schieben; ~ **the table over to the wall** rück den Tisch an die Wand (rüber) **(b)** (*US Aut*) **to** ~ **gears** schalten **3** VI (a) (= *move*) sich bewegen; (*wind*) umspringen; (*from one's opinion*) ~ **over, you're taking up too much room** rück mal rüber, du nimmst zu viel Platz weg!; **he refused to** ~ (*fig*) er war nicht umzustimmen **(b)** (*Aut*) schalten

shiftily ['ʃɪftɪlɪ] ADV zwielichtig; *glance* verstohlen; *reply* ausweichend; *behave* verdächtig

shift: shift key N (*on typewriter*) Umschalttaste *f*; (*Comput*) Shifttaste *f*; **shift pay** N (*Ind*) Schichtzulage *f*; **shiftwork** N Schichtarbeit *f*; **to do** ~ Schicht arbeiten; **shiftworker** N Schichtarbeiter(in) *m(f)*

shifty ['ʃɪftɪ] ADJ (+ER) zwielichtig; *glance* verstohlen; *eyes* verschlagen; *reply* ausweichend; **there was something** ~ **about ...** mit ... war etwas faul (*inf*)

shimmer ['ʃɪmə'] **1** N Schimmer *m* **2** VI schimmern

shin [ʃɪn] **1** N Schienbein *nt*; (*of meat*) Hachse *f*; **to kick sb on the** ~ jdn vors Schienbein treten **2** VI **to** ~ **up/down** (geschickt) hinauf-/hinunterklettern

shinbone ['ʃɪnbəʊn] N Schienbein *nt*

shine [ʃaɪn] *vb*: pret, ptp **shone** **1** N Glanz *m*; **to give one's shoes a** ~ seine Schuhe polieren; **she's taken a real** ~ **to my brother** (*inf*) mein Bruder hat es ihr wirklich angetan **2** VT (a) pret, ptp *usu* **shined** (= *polish*: *also* ~ **up**) blank putzen; *shoes* polieren **(b) to** ~ **a light on sth** etw beleuchten; **don't** ~ **it in my eyes!** blende mich nicht! **3** VI leuchten; (*metal, paint, fig*: = *excel*) glänzen; (*moon, sun, lamp*) scheinen; (*glass*) blitzblank sein; **to** ~ **at/in sth** (*fig*) bei/in etw (*dat*) glänzen

➤ **shine down** VI herabscheinen (*on* auf +*acc*)

➤ **shine out** VI **the light shining out from the windows across the lawn** das durch die Fenster auf den Rasen fallende Licht; **a light (suddenly) shone out from the darkness** in der Dunkelheit blitzte (plötzlich) ein Licht auf

shingle ['ʃɪŋgl] N, NO PL (= *pebbles*) Kiesel *m*, Kieselsteine *pl*; (= *beach*) Kiesel(strand) *m*

shingles ['ʃɪŋglz] N SING (*Med*) Gürtelrose *f*

shininess ['ʃaɪnɪnɪs] N Glanz *m*

shining ['ʃaɪnɪŋ] ADJ (*lit, fig*) leuchtend; *light* strahlend; *metal, hair* glänzend; *car* blitzend; **a** ~ **light** (*fig*) eine Leuchte; **he's my knight in** ~ **armour** (*Brit*) *or* **armor** (*US*) er ist mein Märchenprinz

shiny ['ʃaɪnɪ] ADJ (+ER) glänzend; *trousers also* blank

ship [ʃɪp] **1** N Schiff *nt*; **on board** ~ an Bord; **when my** ~ **comes home** *or* **in** (*fig*) wenn ich das große Los ziehe **2** VT (= *transport*) versenden; *coal, grain etc* verfrachten; (*esp by sea*) verschiffen

➤ **ship off** VT SEP versenden; *coal, grain etc* verfrachten; (*esp by ship*) verschiffen

➤ **ship out** VT SEP versenden; *coal, grain etc* verfrachten

ship: shipbuilder N Schiffbauer(in) *m(f)*; **shipbuilding** N Schiffbau *m*; **shipmate** N Schiffskamerad(in) *m(f)*

shipment ['ʃɪpmənt] N Sendung *f*; (*of coal, grain, tractors*) Transport *m*; (= *transporting by sea*) Verschiffung *f*

shipping ['ʃɪpɪŋ] **1** N, NO PL (a) (= *ships*) Schiffe *pl* **(b)** (= *transportation*) Verschiffung *f*; (*by rail etc*) Versand *m* **2** ADJ ATTR ~ **costs** Frachtkosten *pl*; ~ **documents** Versanddokumente *pl*

shipping: shipping agent N Schiffsmakler(in) *m(f)*; (*agent for shipping company*) Reedereiagent(in) *m(f)*; **shipping company** N Reederei *f*; **shipping lane** N Schifffahrtsstraße *f*; **shipping line** N Schifffahrtslinie *f*; **shipping note** N Verladeschein *m*; **shipping route** N Schifffahrtslinie *f*

shipshape ['ʃɪpʃeɪp] ADJ, ADV tipptopp (*inf*); **to get everything** ~ alles tipptopp machen (*inf*)

ship: shipwreck **1** N Schiffbruch *m* **2** VT schiffbrüchig werden lassen; **to be** ~**ed** schiffbrüchig sein; **shipyard** N (Schiffs)werft *f*

shirk [ʃɜːk] **1** VT sich drücken vor (+*dat*) **2** VI sich drücken

shirt [ʃɜːt] N (*men's*) (Ober)hemd *nt*; (*Ftbl*) Hemd *nt*, Trikot *nt*; (*women's*) Hemdbluse *f*; **keep your** ~ **on** (*Brit inf*) reg dich nicht auf!

shirtsleeve ['ʃɜːtsliːv] **1** ADJ hemdsärmelig **2** N **shirtsleeves** PL Hemdsärmel *pl*; **in his/their** ~**s** in Hemdsärmeln

shit [ʃɪt] *vb*: pret, ptp **shat** (*sl*) **1** N (a) Scheiße *f* (*vulg*); **to have a** ~ scheißen (*vulg*); **to have the** ~**s** Dünnschiss haben (*inf*); **to be up** ~ **creek (without a paddle)** bis zum Hals in der Scheiße stecken (*vulg*); **to be in the** ~ *or* **in deep** ~ in der Scheiße stecken (*vulg*); **I don't give a** ~ das ist mir scheißegal (*inf*); **tough** ~! Scheiße auch! (*inf*) **(b)** (= *person*) Arschloch *nt* (*vulg*) **(c)** (= *nonsense*) Scheiße *f* (*inf*); **that film/idea is** ~ dieser Film/diese Idee ist totale Scheiße (*inf*) **(d) shits** PL (= *state of fear*) Schiss *m* (*sl*); **it gives me the** ~**s** da krieg ich Schiss (*sl*) **2** ADJ ATTR Scheiß- (*inf*), beschissen (*inf*) **3** VI scheißen (*vulg*) **4** VR **to** ~ **oneself** sich voll scheißen (*vulg*); (*with fear*) sich (*dat*) vor Angst in die Hosen scheißen (*vulg*) **5** INTERJ Scheiße (*inf*)

shit: shitface (*sl*), **shithead** (*sl*) N Scheißkerl *m* (*inf*), Scheißtyp *m* (*inf*); **shit-hot** ADJ (*Brit sl*) geil (*sl*), krass (*sl*); **shitless** ADJ **to be scared** ~ (*sl*) sich (*dat*) vor Angst in die Hosen scheißen (*vulg*)

shitty ['ʃɪtɪ] ADJ (+ER) (*inf*) beschissen (*inf*)

shiver [ˈʃɪvəʳ] **1** N Schauer *m*; **a ~ of cold** ein kalter Schauer; **a ~ ran down my spine** es lief mir kalt den Rücken hinunter; **his touch sent ~s down her spine** es durchzuckte sie bei seiner Berührung; **it gives me the ~s** (*fig*) ich kriege davon eine Gänsehaut **2** VI zittern (*with* vor +*dat*); (*with fear also*) schaudern

shivery [ˈʃɪvərɪ] ADJ **to feel ~** frösteln

shoal [ʃəʊl] N (*of fish*) Schwarm *m*

shock¹ [ʃɒk] **1** N **(a)** (*of explosion, impact*) Wucht *f*; (*of earthquake*) (Erd)stoß *m*
(b) (*Elec*) Schlag *m*; (*Med*) (Elektro)schock *m*; **to get a ~** einen Schlag bekommen
(c) (= *emotional disturbance*) Schock *m*; (= *state*) Schock(zustand) *m*; **to suffer from ~** einen Schock (erlitten) haben; **to be in (a state of) ~** unter Schock stehen; **a ~ to one's system** ein Kreislaufschock; **it comes as a ~ to hear that …** mit Bestürzung höre ich/hören wir, dass …; **to give sb a ~** jdn erschrecken; **it gave me a nasty ~** es hat mir einen bösen Schreck(en) eingejagt; **to get the ~ of one's life** den Schock seines Lebens kriegen; **he is in for a ~!** (*inf*) der wird sich wundern (*inf*)
2 VT (= *affect emotionally*) erschüttern, bestürzen; (= *make indignant*) schockieren; **to be ~ed by sth** über etw (*acc*) erschüttert *or* bestürzt sein; (*morally*) über etw (*acc*) schockiert sein; **to ~ sb into doing sth** jdm eine solche Angst einjagen, dass er etw tut
3 VI (*film, writer etc*) schockieren

shock² N (*also ~ of hair*) (Haar)schopf *m*

shock absorber [ˈʃɒkəbˌzɔːbəʳ] N Stoßdämpfer *m*

shocked [ʃɒkt] ADJ erschüttert, bestürzt; (= *indignant*, *outraged*) schockiert; (= *amazed*) geschockt (*inf*); **to be ~** (*Med*) unter Schock stehen

shocking [ˈʃɒkɪŋ] ADJ **(a)** (= *outrageous, upsetting*) schockierend; **the ~ truth** die grausame Wahrheit; **~ pink** knallrosa (*inf*), pink (*Fashion*) **(b)** (*inf*: = *very bad*) entsetzlich, furchtbar; **what a ~ thing to say/way to behave!** wie kann man bloß so etwas Schreckliches sagen/sich bloß so schrecklich benehmen!

shockingly [ˈʃɒkɪŋlɪ] ADV schrecklich; (= *badly also*) furchtbar; (= *extremely also*) entsetzlich; (= *disturbingly*) erschreckend; **to behave ~ (toward(s) sb)** sich (jdm gegenüber) miserabel benehmen

shock: shock tactics PL (*Mil*) Stoß- *or* Durchbruchstaktik *f*; (*fig*) Schocktherapie *f*; **shock troops** PL Stoßtruppen *pl*; **shock wave** N (*lit*) Druckwelle *f*; (*fig*) Schock *m no pl*

shod [ʃɒd] PRET, PTP *of* **shoe**

shoddy [ˈʃɒdɪ] ADJ (+ER) schäbig; **work** schludrig; **goods** minderwertig; **service** schlampig

shoe [ʃuː], *vb*: pret, ptp **shod 1** N **(a)** Schuh *m*; **I wouldn't like to be in his ~s** ich möchte nicht in seiner Haut stecken; **to put oneself in sb's ~s** sich in jds Lage (*acc*) versetzen; **to step into** *or* **fill sb's ~s** an jds Stelle (*acc*) treten *or* rücken **(b)** (= *horseshoe*) (Huf)eisen *nt* **2** VT **horse** beschlagen

shoe: shoehorn N Schuhanzieher *m*; **shoelace** N Schnürsenkel *m*; **shoemaker** N Schuster(in) *m(f)*; **shoe polish** N Schuh-creme *f*; **shoe repairer** N (= *person*) Schuster(in) *m(f)*; (= *shop*) Schuhreparaturdienst *m*; **shoe shop** N Schuhgeschäft *nt*; **shoe size** N Schuhgröße *f*; **what ~ are you?** welche Schuhgröße haben Sie?; **shoestring** N **(a)** (*US*: = *shoelace*) Schnürsenkel *m* **(b)** (*fig*) **the project is run on a ~** das Projekt wird mit ganz wenig Geld finanziert; **shoestring budget** N Minibudget *nt* (*inf*); **shoetree** N (Schuh)spanner *m*

shone [ʃɒn] PRET, PTP *of* **shine**

shoo [ʃuː] **1** INTERJ sch; (*to dog etc*) pfui; (*to child*) husch **2** VT **to ~ sb away** jdn verscheuchen

shook [ʃʊk] PRET *of* **shake**

shoot [ʃuːt], *vb*: pret, ptp **shot 1** N **(a)** (*Bot*) Trieb *m*; (*esp sprouting from seed, potato etc*) Keim *m*; (*out of ground: of bushes, trees*) Schössling *m*; (= *young branch*) Reis *nt* **(b)** (= *photographic assignment*) Fotosession *f* **2** VT **(a)** (*Mil etc, Sport*) schießen; **bullet, gun** abfeuern; (*US sl*) **craps, pool** spielen
(b) **person, animal** (= *hit*) anschießen; (= *wound seriously*) niederschießen; (= *kill*) erschießen; **to ~ sb dead** jdn erschießen; **he shot himself** er hat sich erschossen; **he shot himself in the foot** er schoss sich (*dat*) in den Fuß; (*fig inf*) er hat ein Eigentor geschossen (*inf*); **he was shot in the leg** er

wurde ins Bein getroffen; **you'll get me shot** (*fig inf*) du bringst mich um Kopf und Kragen (*inf*)
(c) (= *throw, propel*) schleudern; **to ~ a question at sb** eine Frage auf jdn abfeuern; **to ~ a glance at sb, to ~ sb a glance** jdm einen (schnellen) Blick zuwerfen; **to ~ the lights** eine Ampel (bei Rot) überfahren
(d) (*Phot*) **film, scene** drehen; **snapshot** schießen; **subject** aufnehmen
(e) (*inf*) **drug** drücken (*sl*)
3 VI **(a)** (*with gun, Sport*) schießen; (*as hunter*) jagen; **to ~ to kill** gezielt schießen; (*police*) einen gezielten Todesschuss/gezielte Todesschüsse abgeben; **don't ~!** nicht schießen!; **stop or I'll ~!** stehen bleiben oder ich schieße!; **to ~ at sb/sth** auf jdn/etw schießen; **to ~ from the hip** aus der Hüfte schießen; **to ~ at goal** aufs Tor schießen
(b) (= *move rapidly*) schießen (*inf*); **to ~ ahead/into the lead** an die Spitze vorpreschen; **he shot down the stairs** er schoss *or* jagte die Treppe hinunter; **to ~ in** (he)reingeschossen kommen; **to ~ to fame** auf einen Schlag berühmt werden; **the pain shot up his leg** der Schmerz durchzuckte sein Bein; **~ing pains** stechende Schmerzen *pl*
(c) (*Phot*) knipsen (*inf*); (*Film*) drehen
▶ **shoot away** VI **(a)** (= *move rapidly*) davonschießen **(b)** (= *shoot continuously*) schießen
▶ **shoot down** VT SEP **plane** abschießen; (*fig inf*) **person** fertig machen (*inf*); **argument** in der Luft zerreißen
▶ **shoot off 1** VI (= *rush off*) davonschießen **2** VT SEP abschießen; **to shoot one's mouth off** (*inf*) (*indiscreetly*) tratschen (*inf*); (*boastfully*) das Maul aufreißen (*inf*)
▶ **shoot out 1** VI (= *emerge swiftly*) herausschießen (*of* aus) **2** VT SEP **hand etc** blitzschnell ausstrecken
▶ **shoot up 1** VI **(a)** (*hand, prices, temperature*) in die Höhe schnellen; (= *grow rapidly*) (*children, plant*) in die Höhe schießen; (*new towns, buildings etc*) aus dem Boden schießen **(b)** (*Drugs inf*) sich (*dat*) einen Schuss setzen (*inf*) **2** VT SEP **(a) the aerodrome was shot up** das Flugfeld wurde heftig beschossen **(b)** (*inf*) **drug** drücken (*sl*)

shooting [ˈʃuːtɪŋ] N **(a)** (= *shots, Sport*) Schießen *nt*; (*by artillery*) Feuer *nt*; **was there any ~?** gab es Schießereien? **(b)** (= *murder, execution*) Erschießung *f*; **there was a ~ last night** gestern Nacht ist jemand erschossen worden **(c)** (*Hunt*) Jagd *f*; **to go ~** auf die Jagd gehen **(d)** (*Film*) Drehen *nt*

shooting: shooting gallery N Schießstand *m*; **shooting party** N Jagdgesellschaft *f*; **shooting range** N Schießplatz *m*; **shooting star** N Sternschnuppe *f*

shoot-out [ˈʃuːtaʊt] N Schießerei *f*

shop [ʃɒp] **1** N **(a)** (*esp Brit*) Geschäft *nt*, Laden *m*; (= *large store*) Kaufhaus *nt*; **I have to go to the ~s** ich muss einkaufen gehen; **to set up ~** ein Geschäft *or* einen Laden eröffnen; **to shut up** *or* **close up ~** zumachen, schließen; **to talk ~** über die Arbeit reden; (*of professional people*) fachsimpeln
(b) (= *workshop*) Werkstatt *f* **(c)** (*Brit*) **to do one's weekly ~** seinen wöchentlichen Einkauf erledigen **2** VI einkaufen; **to go ~ping** einkaufen gehen; **to ~ for fish** Fisch kaufen gehen
▶ **shop around** VI (*lit, fig*) sich umsehen (*for* nach)

shop: shop assistant N (*esp Brit*) Verkäufer(in) *m(f)*; **shop floor** N **(a)** (= *place*) Produktionsstätte *f*; (*for heavier work*) Werkstatt *f*; **on the ~** in der Werkstatt *etc*, bei *or* unter den Arbeitern **(b)** (= *workers*) Arbeiter *pl*; **shop front** N (*esp Brit*) Ladenfassade *f*; **shop hours** PL (*esp Brit*) Öffnungszeiten *pl*; **shopkeeper** N (*esp Brit*) Ladenbesitzer(in) *m(f)*, Geschäftsinhaber(in) *m(f)*; **shoplifter** N Ladendieb(in) *m(f)*; **shoplifting** N Ladendiebstahl *m*

shopper [ˈʃɒpəʳ] N Käufer(in) *m(f)*

shopping [ˈʃɒpɪŋ] N (= *act*) Einkaufen *nt*; (= *goods bought*) Einkäufe *pl*; **to do one's ~** einkaufen

shopping: shopping bag N Einkaufstasche *f*; **shopping basket** N Einkaufskorb *m*; **shopping cart** N (*US*) = **shopping trolley**; **shopping centre**, (*US*) **shopping center** N Einkaufszentrum *nt*; **shopping channel** N (*TV*) Teleshoppingsender *m*; **shopping list** N Einkaufszettel *m*; **shopping mall** N Shoppingcenter *nt*; **shopping spree** N Einkaufsbummel *m*; **shopping street** N Einkaufsstraße *f*; **shopping trolley** N (*Brit*) Einkaufswagen *m*

shop: shopsoiled ADJ (*Brit*) **clothes, furniture** angeschmutzt; **goods, material** leicht beschädigt; **shop steward** N (gewerkschaftlicher) Vertrauensmann (*im Betrieb*); **shop window** N (*lit, fig*) Schaufenster *nt*

shore[1] [ʃɔːʳ] N **(a)** (= *seashore, lake ~*) Ufer *nt*; (= *beach*) Strand *m*; **a house on the ~s of the lake** ein Haus am Seeufer **(b)** (= *land*) Land *nt*; **on** ~ an Land

shore[2] VT (*also* ~ **up**) (ab)stützen; (*fig*) stützen

shore: **shore dinner** N (*US*) Meeresfrüchte *pl*; **shoreline** N Uferlinie *f*

shorn [ʃɔːn] **1** PTP *of* **shear 2** ADJ *sheep* geschoren; *head* (kahl) geschoren

short [ʃɔːt] **1** ADJ (+ER) **(a)** kurz; *steps, person* klein; (*Ling*: = *unstressed*) unbetont; **to be in** ~ **trousers** (*fig*) ein kleiner Junge sein; **a** ~ **time ago** vor kurzem; **in a** ~ **time** *or* **while** in Kürze; **time is getting/is** ~ die Zeit wird/ist knapp; **in** ~ **order** (*US inf*) sofort; ~ **and sweet** schön kurz, kurz und ergreifend (*iro*); **in** ~ kurz gesagt; **she's called Pat for** ~ sie wird kurz *or* einfach Pat genannt; **Pat is** ~ **for Patricia** Pat ist die Kurzform von Patricia **(b)** (= *curt*) *reply* knapp; (= *rude*) barsch; *manner, person* schroff, kurz angebunden (*inf*); **to have a** ~ **temper** unbeherrscht sein; **to be** ~ **with sb** jdn schroff behandeln **(c)** (= *insufficient*) zu wenig *inv*; **to be in** ~ **supply** knapp sein; (*Comm*) beschränkt lieferbar sein; **to be** ~ (= *in* ~ *supply*) knapp sein; (*shot, throw*) nicht weit genug sein; **we are (five/ £3)** ~, **we are** ~ **(of five/£3)** wir haben (fünf/£ 3) zu wenig; **we are seven** ~ uns (*dat*) fehlen sieben; **we are not** ~ **of volunteers** wir haben genug Freiwillige; **to be** ~ **of time** wenig Zeit haben; **I'm a bit** ~ **(of cash)** (*inf*) ich bin etwas knapp bei Kasse (*inf*); **we are £2,000** ~ **of our target** wir liegen £ 2.000 unter unserem Ziel; **not far** *or* **much** ~ **of £100** nicht viel weniger als £ 100; **to be** ~ **on experience** wenig Erfahrung haben **(d)** (*Fin*) *sale* ohne Deckung, ungedeckt; *loan, bill* kurzfristig; ~ **stock** auf Baisse gekaufte Aktien

2 ADV **(a)** (= *below the expected amount*) **to fall** ~ (*arrow etc*) zu kurz landen; (*shot*) zu kurz sein; (*supplies etc*) nicht ausreichen; **to fall** ~ **of sth** etw nicht erreichen; *of expectations* etw nicht erfüllen; **it falls far** ~ **of what we require** das bleibt weit hinter unseren Bedürfnissen zurück; (*in quantity*) das bleibt weit unter unseren Bedürfnissen; **production has fallen** ~ **by 100 tons** die Produktion ist um 100 Tonnen zu niedrig; **to go** ~ **(of money/food** *etc*) zu wenig (Geld/zu essen *etc*) haben; **we are running** ~ **(of water/time)** wir haben nicht mehr viel (Wasser/Zeit); **water is running** ~ Wasser ist knapp; **to sell** ~ (*Fin*) ungedeckt *or* ohne Deckung verkaufen **(b)** (= *abruptly, suddenly*) plötzlich, abrupt; **to pull up** *or* **stop** ~ (*while driving*) plötzlich *or* abrupt anhalten; (*while walking also*) plötzlich *or* abrupt stehen bleiben; **to stop** ~ (*while talking*) plötzlich innehalten; **to stop sb** ~ jdn unterbrechen; **I'd stop** ~ **of murder** vor Mord würde ich Halt machen; **to be caught** ~ (*inf*) (= *unprepared*) überrascht werden; (= *without money, supplies*) zu knapp (dran) sein; (= *need the toilet*) dringend mal müssen (*inf*) **(c)** ~ **of** (= *except*) außer (+*dat*); **nothing** ~ **of a revolution can ...** nur eine Revolution kann ...; **it's little** ~ **of madness** das grenzt an Wahnsinn; **it's little** ~ **of murder** das ist ja schon fast Mord; ~ **of telling him a lie ...** außer ihn zu belügen ...

3 N (= ~ *circuit*) Kurzschluss *m*; (*inf*) (= ~ *drink*) Kurze(r) *m* (*inf*); (= ~ *film*) Kurzfilm *m*

shortage [ʃɔːtɪdʒ] N (*of goods, objects*) Knappheit *f no pl* (*of an* +*dat*); (*of people*) Mangel *m no pl* (*of an* +*dat*); **the housing** ~ die Wohnungsknappheit; **a** ~ **of staff** ein Personalmangel *m*; **there's no** ~ **of advice** es fehlt nicht an guten Ratschlägen

short: **shortbread** N Shortbread *nt*, ≈ Butterkeks *m*; **shortcake** N (*Brit*: = *shortbread*) Butterkeks *m*; (*US*: = *sponge*) Biskuittörtchen *nt*; **short-change** VT (*lit*) jdm zu wenig Wechselgeld geben; (*fig inf*) jdn übers Ohr hauen (*inf*); **short circuit** N Kurzschluss *m*; **short-circuit 1** VT kurzschließen; (*fig*) umgehen **2** VI einen Kurzschluss haben; **shortcoming** N (*esp pl*) Mangel *m*; (*of person*) Fehler *m*; (*of system*) Unzulänglichkeit *f*; **shortcrust** N (*also* ~ **pastry**) Mürbeteig *m*; **short cut** N Abkürzung *f*; (*fig*) Schnellverfahren *nt*; (= *easy solution*) Patentlösung *f*; **short-dated** ADJ (*Fin*) *stock* kurzfristig; *bonds, gilts* mit kurzer Laufzeit

shorten [ʃɔːtn] **1** VT verkürzen; *life, name* abkürzen; *dress, rope, book, programme etc* kürzen **2** VI (*days*) kürzer werden

short: **shortfall** N Defizit *nt*; **short-haired** ADJ kurzhaarig; **shorthand** N Stenografie *f*; **to take sth down in** ~ etw stenografieren; **short-handed** ADJ **to be** ~ zu wenig Personal haben; **shorthand typist** N Stenotypist(in) *m(f)*; **short haul** N Nahtransport *m*; **short-haul jet** N Kurzstreckenflugzeug *nt*

shortish [ʃɔːtɪʃ] ADJ ziemlich kurz; *person* ziemlich klein

short: **short list** N (*esp Brit*) Auswahlliste *f*; **to be on the** ~ in der engeren Wahl sein; **short-list** VT (*esp Brit*) **to** ~ **sb** jdn in die engere Wahl nehmen *or* ziehen; **short-lived** ADJ (*lit, fig*) kurzlebig; *protests, attempts* nicht lange andauernd; **to be** ~ (*success etc*) von kurzer Dauer sein

shortly [ʃɔːtlɪ] ADV **(a)** (= *soon*) bald, in Kürze; *after, before, afterwards* kurz **(b)** (= *curtly*) barsch

shortness [ʃɔːtnɪs] N **(a)** Kürze *f*; (*of person*) Kleinheit *f*; ~ **of breath** Kurzatmigkeit *f* **(b)** (= *curtness*) Barschheit *f*

short-range [ʃɔːtˈreɪndʒ] ADJ mit geringer *or* kurzer Reichweite; *walkie-talkie* für den Nahbereich; (*fig*) *plans* kurzfristig; ~ **missile** Kurzstreckenrakete *f*

shorts [ʃɔːts] PL **(a)** Shorts *pl*, kurze Hose(n *pl*) **(b)** (*esp US*: = *underpants*) Unterhose *f* **(c)** (*Brit St Ex*) kurzfristige Staatspapiere *pl*

short: **short-sighted** ADJ (*lit, fig*) kurzsichtig; **short-sightedness** N (*lit, fig*) Kurzsichtigkeit *f*; **short-sleeved** ADJ kurzärmelig; **short-staffed** ADJ **to be** ~ zu wenig Personal haben; **short story** N Kurzgeschichte *f*; **short-tempered** ADJ (*in general*) unbeherrscht; (*in a bad temper*) gereizt; **short term** N **for the** ~ vorläufig; **in the** ~ auf kurze Sicht; **short-term** ADJ, ADV kurzfristig; **on a** ~ **basis** kurzfristig; **short-term contract** N Kurzzeitvertrag *m*; **short-wave** ADJ *transmission* auf Kurzwelle; **a** ~ **radio** ein Kurzwellenempfänger *m*; **short weight** N Mindergewicht *nt*

shot[1] [ʃɒt] **1** PRET, PTP *of* **shoot 2** N **(a)** (*from gun, bow etc, Ftbl etc*) Schuss *m*; (= *throw*) Wurf *m*; (*Tennis, Golf*) Schlag *m*; **to take a** ~ **at goal** aufs Tor schießen; **to fire** *or* **take a** ~ **at sb/sth** einen Schuss auf jdn/ etw abfeuern; **to call the ~s** (*fig*) das Sagen haben (*inf*); **like a** ~ (*inf*) run away wie der Blitz (*inf*); do sth, agree sofort **(b)** (= *projectile*) Kugel *f*; (*no pl*: = *lead* ~) Schrot *m* **(c)** (= *person*) Schütze *m*, Schützin *f* **(d)** (= *attempt*) Versuch *m*; **to take** *or* **have a** ~ **(at it)** (= *try*) es (mal) versuchen; (= *guess*) (auf gut Glück) raten; **to give sth one's best** ~ (*inf*) sich nach Kräften um etw bemühen **(e)** (= *injection*) Spritze *f*; (= *immunization*) Impfung *f*; (*of alcohol*) Schuss *m* **(f)** (*Phot*) Aufnahme *f*; **out of** ~ nicht im Bild **(g)** (= *shot-putting*) **the** ~ (= *discipline*) Kugelstoßen *nt*; (= *weight*) die Kugel

shot[2] ADJ **(a)** (= *variegated*) durchzogen, durchschossen (*with* mit) **(b)** (= *destroyed*) **her confidence was** ~ **to pieces** ihr Vertrauen war völlig zerstört

shot: **shotgun** N Schrotflinte *f*; **shot put** N (= *event*) Kugelstoßen *nt*; (= *throw*) Wurf *m*, Stoß *m*; **shot-putter** N Kugelstoßer(in) *m(f)*

should [ʃʊd] PRET *of* **shall** MODAL AUX VB **(a)** (*expressing duty, advisability, criticism*) **I/he** ~ **do that** ich/er sollte das tun; **you** ~**n't do that** Sie sollten das nicht tun; **I** ~ **have done it** ich hätte es tun sollen *or* müssen; **which is as it** ~ **be** und so soll(te) es auch sein; **you really** ~ **see that film** den Film sollten *or* müssen Sie wirklich sehen; **you** ~ **have seen his face!** (*inf*) du hättest sein Gesicht sehen sollen!; **he's coming to apologize – I** ~ **think so** er will sich entschuldigen – das möchte ich auch meinen *or* hoffen; **... and I** ~ **know ...** und ich müsste es ja wissen; **how** ~ **I know?** woher soll ich das wissen? **(b)** (*expressing probability*) **he** ~ **be there by now** er müsste eigentlich schon da sein; **why** ~ **he suspect me?** warum sollte er mich verdächtigen?; **this book** ~ **help you** dieses Buch wird Ihnen bestimmt helfen; **this** ~ **be good!** (*inf*) das wird bestimmt gut! **(c)** (*in tentative statements*) **I** ~ **think there were about 40** ich würde schätzen, dass etwa 40 dort waren; ~ **I open the window?** soll ich das Fenster aufmachen?; **I** ~ **like to know** ich wüsste gern, ich möchte gern wissen; **I** ~ **like to apply for the job** ich würde mich gern um die Stelle bewerben

(d) (expressing surprise) **who ~ I see/~ it be but Anne!** und wen sehe ich/und wer wars? Anne!; **why ~ he want to do that?** warum will er das wohl machen?

(e) (subjunc, conditional) **I/he ~ go if ...** ich/er würde gehen, wenn ...; **it seems unbelievable that he ~ have failed** es scheint unglaublich, dass er versagt hat; **if they ~ send for me** wenn or falls sie nach mir schicken sollten; **~ it not be true, I ~n't be surprised if he comes** or **came** or **were to come** ich wäre nicht or keineswegs überrascht, wenn er kommen würde or wenn er käme; **I ~n't (do that) if I were you** ich würde das an Ihrer Stelle nicht tun

shoulder [ˈʃəʊldə*] **1** N (of person, animal) Schulter f; (of meat) Bug m; (of garment) Schulter(partie) f; **to shrug one's ~s** mit den Schultern zucken; **to cry on sb's ~** sich an jds Brust (dat) ausweinen; **a ~ to cry on** jemand, bei dem man sich ausweinen kann; **~ to ~** Schulter an Schulter
2 VT **(a)** (lit) load, case, person auf die Schulter nehmen; (fig) responsibilities, blame auf sich (acc) nehmen; expense tragen **(b)** (= push) (mit der Schulter) stoßen; **to ~ sb aside** (lit) jdn zur Seite stoßen; (fig) jdn beiseite drängen

shoulder: shoulder bag N Umhängetasche f; **shoulder blade** N Schulterblatt nt; **shoulder-length** ADJ hair schulterlang; **shoulder pad** N Schulterpolster nt; **shoulder strap** N (of satchel, bag etc) (Schulter)riemen m

shouldn't [ˈʃʊdnt] CONTR of **should not**

shout [ʃaʊt] **1** N Ruf m, Schrei m; **a ~ of protest** ein Protestruf m; **a ~ of pain** ein Freuden-/Schmerzensschrei m; **~s of laughter** Lachsalven pl; **to give a ~** einen Schrei ausstoßen; **to give sb a ~** jdn rufen; **give me a ~ when you're ready** (inf) sag Bescheid, wenn du fertig bist
2 VT schreien; (= call) rufen; order brüllen; disapproval etc laut(stark) kundtun; **to ~ abuse at sb** jdn (laut) beschimpfen; **to ~ a warning to sb** jdm eine Warnung zurufen
3 VI (= call out) rufen; (very loudly) schreien; (angrily, commanding) brüllen; **to ~ for sb/sth** nach jdm/etw rufen; **she ~ed for Jane to come** sie rief, Jane solle kommen; **to ~ at sb** mit jdm schreien; (abusively) jdn anschreien; **don't ~!** schrei nicht (so)!; **to ~ to sb** jdm zurufen; **to ~ for help** um Hilfe rufen; **it was nothing to ~ about** (inf) es war nicht umwerfend
4 VR **to ~ oneself hoarse** sich heiser schreien

➤ **shout down** VT SEP person niederbrüllen
➤ **shout out 1** VI einen Schrei ausstoßen; **to shout out in despair/pain** verzweifelt/vor Schmerz aufschreien, einen Verzweiflungs-/Schmerzensschrei ausstoßen; **shout out when you're ready** ruf, wenn du fertig bist **2** VT SEP ausrufen; order brüllen

shouting [ˈʃaʊtɪŋ] N (= act) Schreien nt; (= sound) Geschrei nt; **it's all over bar the ~** (inf) es ist so gut wie gelaufen (inf)

shove [ʃʌv] **1** N Schubs(er) m (inf), Stoß m; **to give sb a ~** jdn schubsen (inf) or stoßen; **to give sth a ~** etw rücken; door gegen etw stoßen; car etw anschieben
2 VT **(a)** (= push) schieben; (with one short push) stoßen, schubsen (inf); (= jostle) drängen; **stop shoving me** hör auf zu drängeln; **to ~ sb against a wall** jdn gegen die Wand drücken; **to ~ a door open** eine Tür aufstoßen
(b) (inf: = put) **to ~ sth on(to) sth** etw auf etw (acc) werfen (inf); **to ~ sth in(to)/between sth** etw in etw (acc)/zwischen etw (acc) stecken; **he ~d a book into my hand** er drückte mir ein Buch in die Hand
3 VI stoßen; (to move sth) schieben; (= jostle) drängeln
➤ **shove about** (Brit) or **around** VT SEP (inf) herumstoßen
➤ **shove back** VT SEP (inf) chair etc zurückschieben; sb, plate zurückstoßen; (= replace) zurücktun; (into pocket etc) wieder hineinstecken
➤ **shove off** (inf: = leave) abschieben (inf)
➤ **shove over** (inf) **1** VT SEP rüberwerfen (inf) **2** VI (also **shove up**) rutschen

shovel [ˈʃʌvl] **1** N Schaufel f; (on power ~) Löffel m **2** VT schaufeln; coal, snow also schippen

shovelful [ˈʃʌvlfʊl] N Schaufel f; **a ~ of coal** eine Schaufel Kohle

show [ʃəʊ], vb: pret **showed**, ptp **shown 1** N **(a)** (= display) **~ of force** Machtentfaltung f; **the demonstration was a ~ of sympathy** die Demonstration war eine Solidaritätsbekundung; **~ of hands** Handzeichen nt; **to put up a good/poor ~** (esp Brit inf) eine gute/schwache Leistung zeigen

(b) (= outward appearance) Schau f; (= trace) Spur f; (of hatred, affection) Kundgebung f; **it's just for ~** das ist nur zur Schau da; (= pretence) das ist nur Schau (inf); **to do sth for ~** etw tun, um Eindruck zu schinden (inf); **to make a great ~ of being impressed** sich (dat) ganz den Anschein geben, beeindruckt zu sein; **without any ~ of emotion** ohne irgendwelche Gefühle zu zeigen

(c) (= exhibition) Ausstellung f; **dog/fashion ~** Hunde-/Modenschau f; **to be on ~** ausgestellt or zu sehen sein

(d) (Theat) Aufführung f; (TV ~) Show f; (Rad) Sendung f; **to go to a ~** (esp Brit: in theatre) ins Theater gehen; (US: in movie theater) ins Kino gehen; **the ~ must go on** es muss trotz allem weitergehen; **on with the ~!** anfangen!; (= continue) weitermachen!

(e) (= undertaking, organization) Laden m (inf); **he runs the ~** er schmeißt hier den Laden (inf)
2 VT **(a)** zeigen; (at exhibition) ausstellen; film also vorführen; passport, ticket vorzeigen; (= prove) beweisen; kindness, favour erweisen; respect bezeigen; **~ me how to do it** zeigen Sie mir, wie man das macht; **it's been ~n on television** das kam im Fernsehen; **to ~ one's face** sich zeigen; **he had nothing to ~ for it** er hatte am Ende nichts vorzuweisen; **he has nothing to ~ for all his effort** seine ganze Mühe hat nichts gebracht; **I'll ~ him!** (inf) dem werd ichs zeigen! (inf); **that ~ed him!** (inf) dem habe ichs aber gezeigt! (inf); **to ~ one's gratitude** sich dankbar zeigen; **it all** or **just goes to ~ that ...** das zeigt doch nur, dass ...; **the housing market is ~ing signs of life** auf dem Immobilienmarkt tut or rührt sich (wieder) (et)was (inf); **it ~ed signs of having been used** man sah, dass es gebraucht worden war; **he's beginning to ~ his age** man sieht ihm allmählich das Alter an; **to ~ sb in/out** jdn hereinbringen/hinausbringen or -begleiten; **to ~ sb to his seat/to the door** jdn an seinen Platz/an die or zur Tür bringen; **they were ~n over** or **(a)round the factory** ihnen wurde die Fabrik gezeigt, sie wurden in der Fabrik herumgeführt

(b) (= register) (an)zeigen; loss, profit verzeichnen; rise in numbers aufzeigen; (thermometer, speedometer) stehen auf (+dat); **as ~n in the illustration** wie in der Illustration dargestellt; **the roads are ~n in red** die Straßen sind rot (eingezeichnet)
3 VI (= be visible) zu sehen sein, sichtbar sein; (film) gezeigt werden, laufen; **the dirt doesn't ~** man sieht den Schmutz nicht; **his anger ~ed in his eyes** man sah ihm seinen Ärger von den Augen ablesen; **it only ~s when ...** (= be visible) man sieht es nur, wenn ...; (= be noticed) man merkt es nur, wenn ...; **to ~ through** durchkommen; **it just goes to ~!** sieht mans mal wieder!
4 VR **to ~ oneself to be incompetent** sich (als) unfähig erweisen

➤ **show off 1** VI angeben (to, in front of vor +dat) **2** VT SEP **(a)** knowledge, medal angeben mit; new car vorführen (to sb jdm); wealth protzen mit (inf) **(b)** (= enhance) beauty, picture hervorheben; figure betonen; **to show sth off to its best advantage** etw (richtig) zur Geltung bringen
➤ **show up 1** VI **(a)** (= be seen) zu sehen or zu erkennen sein; (= stand out) hervorstechen; **to show up well/badly** (fig) eine gute/schlechte Figur machen
(b) (inf: = turn up) auftauchen, sich blicken lassen (inf) **2** VT SEP **(a)** (= highlight) (deutlich) erkennen lassen
(b) flaws, bad condition zum Vorschein bringen; sb's character, intentions deutlich zeigen
(c) (= shame) blamieren; **he always gets drunk and shows her up** er betrinkt sich immer und bringt sie dadurch in eine peinliche Situation

show: show biz N (inf) = **show business**; **show business** N Showbusiness nt, Showgeschäft nt; **to be in ~** im Showgeschäft (tätig) sein; **showcase** N Vitrine f; (fig) Schaufenster nt; **showdown** N (inf) Kraftprobe f, Show-down m (inf); **there was a ~ between the two rivals** zwischen den Rivalen kam es zur Kraftprobe

shower [ˈʃaʊə*] **1** N **(a)** (of rain etc) Schauer m; (of blows, bullets etc) Hagel m **(b)** (= ~ bath) Dusche f; **to take** or **have a ~** (sich) duschen **2** VT **to ~ sb with sth**, **to ~ sth on sb** praise, presents jdn mit etw überschütten or überhäufen **3** VI (= wash) duschen

shower: shower cap N Duschhaube f; **shower cubicle** N Duschkabine f; **shower curtain** N Duschvorhang m; **shower stall** N Duschkabine f

showery [ʃaʊərɪ] ADJ regnerisch

show home, show house N (*Brit*) Musterhaus *nt*

showing [ʃəʊɪŋ] N **(a)** (= *exhibition*) Ausstellung *f*
(b) (= *performance*) Aufführung *f*; (*of film*) Vorstellung *f*; (*of programme*) Ausstrahlung *f* **(c)** (= *standard of performance*) Leistung *f*

showing-off [ʃəʊɪŋˈɒf] N Angeberei *f*

show: show-jumper N Springreiter(in) *m(f)*; **showjumping** N Springen *nt*, Springreiten *nt*

showmanship [ʃəʊmənʃɪp] N (*of person*) Talent *nt* für effektvolle Darbietung; (*of act*) effektvolle Darbietung; (*fig*) Talent *nt* sich in Szene zu setzen

shown [ʃəʊn] PTP *of* **show**

show: show-off N (*inf*) Angeber(in) *m(f)*; **showpiece** N Schaustück *nt*; (= *fine example*) Paradestück *nt*; **showroom** N Ausstellungsraum *m*; **show stopper** N (*inf*) Publikumshit *m* (*inf*); (*fig*) Clou *m* des Abends/der Party etc; **show trial** N Schauprozess *m*

showy [ʃəʊɪ] ADJ (+ER) protzig (*inf*); *person* auffallend; *manner* theatralisch; *décor, production* bombastisch

shrank [ʃræŋk] PRET *of* **shrink**

shrapnel [ʃræpnl] N Schrapnell *nt*

shred [ʃred] **1** N (= *scrap*) Fetzen *m*; (*of paper also*) Schnipsel *m*; (*of vegetable, meat*) Stückchen *nt*; (*fig*) Spur *f*; (*of truth*) Fünkchen *nt*; **not a ~ of evidence** keinerlei Beweis; **to be** *or* **hang in ~s** zerfetzt sein; **his reputation was in ~s** sein (guter) Ruf war ruiniert; **to tear sth to ~s** etw total zerreißen, etw in Stücke reißen; (*fig*) etw verreißen; *argument* etw total zerpflücken; **to tear sb to ~s** (*fig*) keinen guten Faden an jdm lassen
2 VT **(a)** *food* zerkleinern; (= *grate*) *carrots* raspeln; *cabbage* hobeln; *paper* schnitzeln; (*in shredder*) schreddern
(b) (= *tear*) in kleine Stücke reißen; (*with claws*) zerfetzen

shredder [ʃredəʳ] N Schredder *m*; (*esp for wastepaper*) Reißwolf *m*

shrew [ʃruː] N Spitzmaus *f*; (*fig*) Xanthippe *f*

shrewd [ʃruːd] ADJ (+ER) *person, plan, move* clever (*inf*); *investment, argument* klug; *assessment, observer, mind* scharf; *smile* verschmitzt; **that was a ~ guess** das war gut geraten; **a ~ judge of character** ein guter Menschenkenner; **to have a ~ suspicion that ...** den stillen Verdacht hegen, dass ...

shrewdly [ʃruːdlɪ] ADV clever (*inf*); *look* wissend; *observe* klug

shrewdness [ʃruːdnɪs] N (*of person, play, move*) Cleverness *f* (*inf*); (*of investment, argument*) Klugheit *f*; (*of assessment*) Schärfe *f*

shriek [ʃriːk] **1** N (schriller) Schrei *m*; (*of whistle*) schriller Ton; (*of brakes*) Quietschen *nt no pl*; **a ~ of pain** ein Schmerzensschrei *m*; **~s of laughter** kreischendes Lachen; **to give a ~** einen schrillen Schrei ausstoßen **2** VT kreischen, schreien **3** VI aufschreien; **to ~ with laughter** vor Lachen quietschen

shrift [ʃrɪft] N **to give sb/sth short ~** jdn/etw kurz abfertigen

shrill [ʃrɪl] **1** ADJ (+ER) schrill; *criticism* scharf **2** VI schrillen

shrillness [ʃrɪlnɪs] N Schrillheit *f*

shrilly [ʃrɪlɪ] ADV schrill; (*fig*: = *fiercely*) lautstark

shrimp [ʃrɪmp] N Garnele *f*

shrine [ʃraɪn] N Schrein *m*; (= *sacred place also*) Heiligtum *nt*; (= *tomb*) Grabstätte *f*

shrink [ʃrɪŋk] *vb: pret* **shrank**, *ptp* **shrunk** **1** VT einlaufen lassen **2** VI **(a)** kleiner werden, schrumpfen; (*clothes etc*) einlaufen; (*wood*) schwinden; (*fig: popularity*) abnehmen; **to ~ away to nothing** auf ein Nichts zusammenschrumpfen **(b)** (*fig: = recoil*) zurückschrecken; **to ~ from doing sth** davor zurückschrecken, etw zu tun; **to ~ away from sb** vor jdm zurückweichen **3** N (*inf*) Seelenklempner(in) *m(f)* (*inf*)

shrinkage [ʃrɪŋkɪdʒ] N (*of material, clothes*) Einlaufen *nt*; (*of wood, Comm*) Schwund *m*; (*fig: of economic growth etc*) Rückgang *m*

shrink-wrap [ʃrɪŋkræp] VT einschweißen

shrivel [ʃrɪvl] **1** VT *plants* (*frost, dryness*) welk werden lassen; (*heat*) austrocknen; *skin, fruit* runzlig werden lassen **2** VI kleiner werden, schrumpfen; (*balloon*) zusammenschrumpfen; (*plants*) welk werden; (*through heat*) austrocknen; (*fruit, skin*) runzlig werden

▶ **shrivel up** VI, VT SEP = **shrivel**

shrivelled, (*US*) **shriveled** [ʃrɪvld] ADJ verwelkt; *vegetation also* verdorrt; *body part* verrunzelt, runz(e)lig; *fruit* verschrumpelt

shroud [ʃraʊd] **1** N **(a)** Leichentuch *nt* **(b)** (*fig*) Schleier *m*; **a ~ of secrecy** der Schleier eines Geheimnisses **2** VT (*fig*) hüllen; **the whole thing is ~ed in mystery** die ganze Angelegenheit ist von einem Geheimnis umgeben

Shrove Tuesday [ʃrəʊvˈtjuːzdɪ] N Fastnachtsdienstag *m*

shrub [ʃrʌb] N Busch *m*, Strauch *m*

shrubbery [ʃrʌbərɪ] N (= *shrub bed*) Strauchrabatte *f*; (= *shrubs*) Büsche *pl*, Sträucher *pl*

shrug [ʃrʌg] **1** N Achselzucken *nt no pl*; **to give a ~** mit den Schultern *or* Achseln zucken **2** VT *shoulders* zucken (mit)
▶ **shrug off** VT SEP mit einem Achselzucken abtun; *coat* abschütteln; **he simply shrugged the whole affair off** er hat die ganze Sache einfach von sich abgeschüttelt

shrunk [ʃrʌŋk] PTP *of* **shrink**

shrunken [ʃrʌŋkən] ADJ (ein)geschrumpft; *old person* geschrumpft; *profits, savings* zusammengeschrumpft

shuck [ʃʌk] (*US*) **1** N Schale *f*; (*of corn, peas*) Hülse *f* **2** VT (= *shell*) schälen; *peas* enthülsen
▶ **shuck off** VT SEP (*US inf*) *garment* abwerfen, abstreifen

shudder [ʃʌdəʳ] **1** N Schauer *m*, Schauder *m*; **to give a ~** (*person*) erschaudern (*geh*); (*ground*) beben; **a ~ ran through her** ein Schauer überlief sie; **she suddenly realized with a ~ that ...** schaudernd erkannte sie, dass ...; **a ~ of fear** ein Angstschauer *m*; **with a ~ of anticipation** zitternd *or* bebend vor Erwartung
2 VI (*person*) schaudern, schauern; (*house, ground*) beben; (*car, train*) geschüttelt werden; **the train ~ed to a halt** der Zug kam rüttelnd zum Stehen; **I ~ to think** mir graut, wenn ich nur daran denke

shuffle [ʃʌfl] **1** N **(a)** Schlurfen *nt no pl*
(b) (*Cards*) **to give the cards a ~** die Karten mischen
(c) (= *change round*) Umstellung *f*; (*of jobs*) Umbesetzung *f*
2 VT **(a)** **he sat there shuffling his feet** er saß da und scharrte mit den Füßen
(b) *cards* mischen; **he ~d the papers on his desk** er durchwühlte die Papiere auf seinem Schreibtisch
(c) (*fig*) *cabinet* umbilden; *jobs* umbesetzen
3 VI **(a)** (= *walk*) schlurfen
(b) (*Cards*) mischen
▶ **shuffle off** VT SEP *skin* abstreifen; (*fig*) *worries, fear* ablegen; *responsibility* abwälzen (*onto* auf +*acc*)

shuffling [ʃʌflɪŋ] ADJ *steps, sound* schlurfend

shun [ʃʌn] VT meiden; *publicity, light* scheuen; **to be ~ned by the world** ausgestoßen sein

shunt [ʃʌnt] **1** N Stoß *m* **2** VT **(a)** (*Rail*) rangieren **(b)** (*inf*) *person* schieben; (*out of the way*) abschieben

shush [ʃʊʃ] **1** INTERJ pst, sch **2** VT beruhigen **3** VI still sein; **oh ~, will you!** sei doch still!, pst!

shut [ʃʌt] *vb: pret, ptp* **shut** **1** VT *eyes, door, box etc* zumachen, schließen; *book, wallet* zuklappen; **they ~ the office at 6** das Büro wird um 18.00 Uhr geschlossen; **~ your eyes** mach die Augen zu; **to ~ one's ears/eyes to sth** vor etw (*dat*) die Ohren/Augen schließen; **~ your mouth** *or* **face!** (*inf*), **~ it!** (*inf*) halts Maul! (*inf*); **to ~ sb/sth in(to) sth** jdn/etw in etw (*dat*) einschließen; **to ~ one's fingers in the door** sich (*dat*) die Finger in der Tür einklemmen
2 VI schließen; (*door, window, box also*) zugehen; (*shop, factory also*) zumachen (*inf*); (*eyes*) sich schließen; **the suitcase just won't ~** der Koffer will einfach nicht zugehen; **it ~s very easily** es lässt sich ganz leicht schließen *or* zumachen
3 ADJ geschlossen, zu *pred* (*inf*); **sorry sir, we're ~** wir haben leider geschlossen; **the door swung ~** die Tür schlug zu
▶ **shut away** VT SEP (= *put away*) wegschließen; (*in sth*) einschließen (*in* in +*dat*); (= *keep locked away*) *books, papers etc* unter Verschluss halten; (*safely*) verwahren; *persons* verborgen halten; **to shut oneself away** sich zurückziehen
▶ **shut down 1** VT SEP *shop, factory* zumachen (*inf*), schließen; *reactor* abschalten; *operations* stilllegen **2** VI (*shop, factory etc*) zumachen (*inf*), schließen; (*reactor*) abschalten; (*engine*) sich ausschalten
▶ **shut in** VT SEP einschließen (*also fig*), einsperren (*inf*) (*prep obj, -to* in +*dat*)
▶ **shut off 1** VT SEP **(a)** *gas, water etc* abstellen; *light, engine* ab- *or* ausschalten; **the kettle shuts itself off** der Wasserkessel

schaltet von selbst ab **(b)** (= *isolate*) (ab)trennen; **to shut oneself off (from sth)** sich abkapseln (von etw) **2** VI abschalten

➤ **shut out** VT SEP **(a)** *person, oneself* aussperren (*of* aus); *view* versperren; *light, world* nicht hereinlassen (*of* in +*acc*); **she closed the door to shut out the noise/draught** (*Brit*) or **draft** (*US*) sie schloss die Tür, damit kein Lärm hereinkam/damit es nicht zog **(b)** (*fig*) *foreign competition* ausschalten; *memory* unterdrücken **(c)** (*US Sport*) *opponent* nicht zum Zuge kommen lassen

➤ **shut up 2** VT SEP **(a)** *house* verschließen **(b)** (= *imprison*) einsperren **(c)** (*inf*: = *silence*) zum Schweigen bringen; **that'll soon shut him up** das wird ihm schon den Mund stopfen (*inf*) **2** VI (*inf*) den Mund or die Klappe halten (*inf*); **shut up!** halt die Klappe! (*inf*)

shut: shutdown N Stilllegung *f*; (*of schools, factory*) Schließung *f*; **shut-in 1** ADJ (*US*: = *confined to the house/bed*) ans Haus/Bett gefesselt **2** N (*US*) **he is a ~** er ist ans Haus/ans Bett gefesselt

shutter ['ʃʌtəʳ] N (Fenster)laden *m*; (*Phot*) Verschluss *m*

shuttered ['ʃʌtəd] ADJ *house, room* mit geschlossenen (Fenster)läden

shutter release N (*Phot*) Auslöser *m*

shuttle ['ʃʌtl] **1** N **(a)** (*of loom*) Schiffchen *nt* **(b)** (= ~ *service*) Pendelverkehr *m*; (= *plane/train etc*) Pendelflugzeug *nt*/-zug *m etc*; (= *space* ~) Spaceshuttle *m* **(c)** (= ~*cock*) Federball *m* **2** VT *passengers, goods* hin- und hertransportieren **3** VI (*people*) pendeln; (*goods*) hin- und hertransportiert werden

shuttle: shuttle bus N Shuttlebus *m*; **shuttlecock** N Federball *m*; **shuttle service** N Pendelverkehr *m*

shy [ʃaɪ] **1** ADJ (+ER) **(a)** schüchtern; *animal* scheu; **don't be ~** nur keine Hemmungen! (*inf*); **to be ~ of/with sb** Hemmungen vor/gegenüber jdm haben; **to feel ~** schüchtern sein **(b)** (*esp US inf*) **we're 3 dollars ~** wir haben 3 Dollar zu wenig **2** VI (*horse*) scheuen (*at* vor +*dat*)

➤ **shy away** VI (*horse*) zurückscheuen; (*person*) zurückweichen; **to shy away from sb** vor jdm zurückweichen; **to shy away from sth** vor etw (*dat*) zurückschrecken

shyly ['ʃaɪlɪ] ADV schüchtern

shyness ['ʃaɪnɪs] N Schüchternheit *f*; (*esp of animals*) Scheu *f*; **her ~ of strangers** ihre Scheu vor Fremden

Siamese [ˌsaɪə'miːz] **1** ADJ siamesisch **2** N **(a)** Siamese *m*, Siamesin *f* **(b)** (*Ling*) Siamesisch *nt*

Siamese cat N Siamkatze *f*

SIB ABBR *of* **Securities and Investment Board** staatliche Börsenaufsichtsbehörde

Siberia [saɪ'bɪərɪə] N Sibirien *nt*

Siberian [saɪ'bɪərɪən] **1** ADJ sibirisch **2** N Sibirier(in) *m(f)*, Sibirer(in) *m(f)*

sibling ['sɪblɪŋ] N Geschwister *nt* (*form*)

Sicilian [sɪ'sɪlɪən] **1** ADJ sizilianisch **2** N Sizilianer(in) *m(f)*

Sicily ['sɪsɪlɪ] N Sizilien *nt*

sick [sɪk] **1** N (= *vomit*) Erbrochene(s) *nt*

2 ADJ (+ER) **(a)** (= *ill*) krank (*also fig*); **the ~** die Kranken *pl*; **to be (off) ~** (wegen Krankheit) fehlen; **to fall** or **take ~, to be taken ~** krank werden; **to call in** or **phone in** (*esp Brit*) **~** sich (telefonisch) krankmelden; **she's off ~ with tonsillitis** sie ist wegen einer Mandelentzündung krankgeschrieben **(b)** (= *vomiting* or *about to vomit*) **to be ~** brechen, sich übergeben; (*esp cat, baby, patient*) spucken; **he was ~ all over the carpet** er hat den ganzen Teppich voll gespuckt; **I think I'm going to be ~** ich glaube, ich muss mich übergeben; **I felt ~** mir war schlecht or übel; **that smell/that food makes me ~** bei dem Geruch/von dem Essen wird mir übel or schlecht; **it's enough to make you ~** (*inf*) da reicht, damit einem schlecht wird; **it makes me ~ to think that ...** (*inf*) mir wird schlecht, wenn ich daran denke, dass ...; **it makes you ~ the way he's always right** (*inf*) es ist zum Weinen, dass er immer Recht hat; **I am worried ~, I am ~ with worry** mir ist vor Sorge ganz schlecht

(c) (*inf*: = *fed up*) **to be ~ of sth/sb** etw/jdn satt haben; **to be ~ of doing sth** es satt haben, etw zu tun; **I'm ~ and tired of it** ich habe davon die Nase (gestrichen) voll (*inf*); **I'm ~ of the sight of her** ich habe ihren Anblick satt

(d) (*inf*: = *tasteless*) geschmacklos; *joke* makaber; *person* abartig, pervers

sick: sickbag N Spucktüte *f*; **sickbay** N Krankenrevier *nt*; **sickbed** N Krankenlager *nt*

sicken ['sɪkn] **1** VT (= *disgust*) anwidern; (= *turn sb's stomach also*) anekeln; (= *upset greatly*) erschüttern, krank machen (*inf*); **it ~s me the way he treats her** es macht mich krank, wie er sie behandelt (*inf*) **2** VI (= *become ill*) krank werden; **he's definitely ~ing for something** er wird bestimmt krank

sickening ['sɪknɪŋ] ADJ (*lit*) Ekel erregend; (= *upsetting*) erschütternd; (= *disgusting, annoying*) ekelhaft, zum Kotzen (*sl*); *cruelty* widerlich; **his ~ habit of always being right** seine unerträgliche Angewohnheit, immer Recht zu haben

sickeningly ['sɪknɪŋlɪ] ADV (*lit*) Ekel erregend; (*fig*) unerträglich

sickie ['sɪkɪ] N (*Brit, Austral inf*) Krankentag *m*; **to take a ~** einen Tag krankfeiern (*inf*)

sickle ['sɪkl] N Sichel *f*

sick leave N **to be on ~** krankgeschrieben sein; **employees are allowed six weeks' ~ per year** Angestellte dürfen insgesamt sechs Wochen pro Jahr wegen Krankheit fehlen

sickly ['sɪklɪ] ADJ (+ER) *person, appearance* kränklich; *smell, taste, sentimentality, colour* ekelhaft; *smile* matt; **~ sweet smell** unangenehm süßer Geruch; **~ sweet smile** übersüßes Lächeln

sickness ['sɪknɪs] N (*Med*) Krankheit *f* (*also fig*); (= *nausea*) Übelkeit *f*; (= *vomiting*) Erbrechen *nt*; (*of joke, book, film*) Geschmacklosigkeit *f*; **in ~ and in health** in guten und in schlechten Zeiten or Tagen

sickness benefit N (*Brit*) Krankengeld *nt*

sick: sick note N (*Brit inf*) Krankmeldung *f*; **sick pay** N Gehalts- or (*for workers*) Lohnfortzahlung *f* im Krankheitsfall; **~ plan** or **scheme** (*US*) Vorsorgeplan *m* zur Zahlung von Krankengeld

side [saɪd] **1** N **(a)** (*lit, fig*) Seite *f*; (*of cave, mining shaft, boat*) Wand *f*; (*of cliff, mountain*) Hang *m*; (*of business etc*) Zweig *m*; **this ~ up!** (*on parcel etc*) oben!; **right/wrong ~** (*of cloth*) rechte/linke Seite; **by/at the ~ of sth** seitlich von etw; **to drive on the left(-hand) ~** auf der linken Straßenseite fahren; **the path goes down the ~ of the house** der Weg führt seitlich am Haus entlang; **it's this/the other ~ of London** (*out of town*) es ist auf dieser/auf der anderen Seite Londons; (*in town*) es ist in diesem Teil/am anderen Ende von London; **the debit/credit ~ of an account** die Soll-/Habenseite eines Kontos; **the enemy attacked them or from all ~s** der Feind griff sie von allen Seiten an; **he moved over or stood to one ~** er trat zur Seite; **he stood to one ~ and did nothing** (*lit*) er stand daneben und tat nichts; (*fig*) er hielt sich raus; **to put sth on one ~** etw beiseite or auf die Seite legen; (*shopkeeper*) etw zurücklegen; **I'll put that issue on or to one ~** ich werde diese Frage vorerst zurückstellen; **on the other ~ of the boundary** jenseits der Grenze; **this ~ of Christmas** vor Weihnachten; **from ~ to ~** hin und her; **to shake one's head from ~ to ~** den Kopf schütteln; **by sb's ~** neben jdm; **~ by ~** nebeneinander, Seite an Seite; **to stand/sit ~ by ~ with sb** direkt neben jdm stehen/sitzen; **I'll be by your ~** (*fig*) ich werde Ihnen zur Seite stehen; **on one's father's/mother's ~** väterlicher-/mütterlicherseits; **there are always two ~s to every story** alles hat seine zwei Seiten; **let's hear your ~ of the story** erzählen Sie mal Ihre Version (der Geschichte); **to look on the bright ~** (= *be optimistic*) zuversichtlich sein; (= *look on the positive side*) die positive Seite betrachten

(b) (= *edge*) Rand *m*; **at the ~ of the road** am Straßenrand; **the body was found on the far ~ of the wood** die Leiche wurde am anderen Ende des Waldes gefunden; **at** or **on the ~ of his plate** auf dem Tellerrand

(c) **to be on the safe ~** sichergehen; **we'll take an extra £50 just to be on the safe ~** wir werden vorsichtshalber £ 50 mehr mitnehmen; **to get on the right ~ of sb** jdn für sich einnehmen; **to stay on the right ~ of sb** es (sich *dat*) mit jdm nicht verderben; **on the right ~ of the law** auf dem Boden des Gesetzes; **to make a bit (of money) on the ~** (*inf*) sich (*dat*) etwas nebenbei verdienen (*inf*); **(a bit) on the large/high etc ~** etwas groß/hoch *etc*; (*too*) etwas zu groß/hoch *etc*

(d) (= *team etc*) (*Sport, in quiz*) Mannschaft *f*; (*fig*) Seite *f*; **with a few concessions on the government ~** mit einigen Zugeständnissen vonseiten or von Seiten der Regierung; **to change ~s** sich auf die andere Seite schlagen; (*Sport*) die Seiten wechseln; **to take ~s** parteiisch sein; **to take ~s with sb** für jdn Partei ergreifen; **whose ~ are you on?** (*supporting team*) für wen sind Sie?; (*playing for team*) bei wem spielen

Sie mit?; (in argument) zu wem halten Sie eigentlich? **2** ADJ ATTR (= on one side) Seiten-; (= not main) Neben-; **~ door** Seiten-/Nebentür f; **~ road** Seiten-/Nebenstraße f **3** VI **to ~ with/against sb** Partei für/gegen jdn ergreifen

side: sideboard N Anrichte f; **sideboards** (Brit), **sideburns** PL Koteletten pl; (longer) Backenbart m

-sided [-saɪdd] ADJ SUF -seitig; **one-sided** einseitig

side: side dish N Beilage f; **side effect** N Nebenwirkung f; **side issue** N Randproblem nt; **that's just a ~** das ist Nebensache; **sidekick** N (inf) Kumpan(in) m(f) (inf), Kumpel m (inf), (= assistant) Handlanger(in) m(f) (pej); **sidelight** N (Brit Aut) Parklicht nt; (incorporated in headlight) Standlicht nt; **sideline 1** N (= extra business) Nebenerwerb m; **it's just a ~** das läuft so nebenher (inf) **2** VT **to be ~d** (Sport, fig) aus dem Rennen sein; **sidelines** PL Seitenlinien pl; **to be or stand or sit on the ~** (fig) unbeteiligter Außenstehender or Zuschauer sein; **sidelong** ADJ **a ~ glance** ein Seitenblick m; **to give sb a ~ glance** jdn kurz aus den Augenwinkeln anblicken; **side-on** ADJ **~ collision** or **crash** Seitenaufprall m; **~ view** Seitenansicht f; **side order** N (Cook) Beilage f; **side salad** N Salat m (als Beilage); **sideshow** N Nebenvorstellung f; (= exhibition) Sonderausstellung f; **side step** N Schritt m zur Seite; (Sport) Ausfallschritt m; (fig: = dodge) Ausweichmanöver nt; **sidestep 1** VT tackle, punch (seitwärts) ausweichen (+dat); person ausweichen (+dat) (also fig) **2** VI (seitwärts or zur Seite) ausweichen; (fig) ausweichen; **side street** N Seitenstraße f; **sidetrack 1** N (esp US) = **siding 2** VT ablenken; **I got ~ed onto something else** ich wurde durch irgendetwas abgelenkt; (from topic) ich wurde irgendwie vom Thema abgebracht; **side view** N Seitenansicht f; **sidewalk** N (US) Bürgersteig m; **sidewalk café** N (US) Straßencafé nt; **sidewall** N Seitenwand f; **sideward** ADJ = **sidewards 1**

sidewards ['saɪdwədz] **1** ADJ movement zur Seite; glance von der Seite **2** ADV move zur Seite, seitwärts; look at sb von der Seite

sideways ['saɪdweɪz] **1** ADJ movement zur Seite; glance von der Seite **2** ADV (a) move zur Seite, seitwärts; look at sb von der Seite; **it goes in ~** es geht seitwärts hinein (b) (= side on) sit seitlich; **~ on** seitlich (to sth zu etw) (c) (in career) **to move ~** sich auf gleichem Niveau verändern

siding ['saɪdɪŋ] N Rangiergleis nt; (= dead end) Abstellgleis nt

sidle ['saɪdl] VI (sich) schleichen; **to ~ up to sb** sich an jdn heranschleichen

siege [siːdʒ] N (of town) Belagerung f; (by police) Umstellung f; **to be under ~** belagert werden; (by police) umstellt sein; **to lay ~ to a town** eine Stadt belagern

Sierra Leone [sɪˈerəlɪˈəʊn] N Sierra Leone f

siesta [sɪˈestə] N Siesta f; **to have** or **take a ~** Siesta halten or machen

sieve [sɪv] **1** N Sieb nt **2** VT = **sift 1(a)**

sift [sɪft] **1** VT (a) (lit) **~ the sugar onto the cake** den Kuchen mit Zucker besieben (b) (fig: = search) sichten, durchgehen **2** VI (fig) sieben; **to ~ through the evidence** das Beweismaterial durchgehen

➤ **sift out** VT SEP stones, seed, applicants aussieben; (= uncover) herausfinden; (= eliminate) absondern

sigh [saɪ] **1** N (of person) Seufzer m; (of wind) (= murmur) Säuseln nt no pl; (= moan) Seufzen nt no pl (liter); **a ~ of relief** ein Seufzer m der Erleichterung **2** VI seufzen; (wind) (= murmur) säuseln; (= moan) seufzen (liter); **to ~ with relief** erleichtert aufatmen **3** VT seufzen

sighing ['saɪɪŋ] N (of person) Seufzen nt; (of wind) (= murmuring) Säuseln nt; (= moaning) Seufzen nt (liter)

sight [saɪt] **1** N (a) (= faculty) Sehvermögen nt; **the gift of ~** die Gabe des Sehens; **long/short ~** Weit-/Kurzsichtigkeit f; **to lose/regain one's ~** sein Augenlicht verlieren/ wiedergewinnen; **he has very good ~** er sieht sehr gut (b) (= glimpse, seeing) **it was my first ~ of Paris** das war das Erste, was ich von Paris gesehen habe; **to hate sb at first ~** or **on ~** jdn vom ersten Augenblick an nicht leiden können; **to shoot at** or **on ~** sofort schießen; **love at first ~** Liebe auf den ersten Blick; **to know sb by ~** jdn vom Sehen kennen; **to catch ~ of sb/sth** jdn/etw entdecken; **to lose ~ of sb/sth** (lit, fig) jdn/etw aus den Augen verlieren; **don't lose ~ of the fact that ...** Sie dürfen nicht außer Acht lassen, dass ... (c) (= sth seen) Anblick m; **the ~ of blood makes me sick** wenn ich Blut sehe, wird mir übel; **I hate** or **can't bear the ~**

of him ich kann ihn (einfach) nicht ausstehen; **what a horrible ~!** das sieht ja furchtbar aus!; **it was a ~ for sore eyes** es war eine wahre Augenweide; **you're a ~ for sore eyes** es ist schön, dich zu sehen; **to be** or **look a ~** (inf) (funny) zum Schreien aussehen (inf); (horrible) fürchterlich aussehen (d) (= range of vision) Sicht f; **to be in** or **within ~** in Sicht or in Sichtweite sein; **our goal is in ~** unser Ziel ist in greifbare Nähe gerückt; **to keep sb in ~** jdn im Auge behalten; **to keep out of ~** sich verborgen halten; **to keep sb/sth out of ~** jdn/ etw nicht sehen lassen; **keep out of my ~!** lass dich bloß bei mir nicht mehr sehen or blicken; **to be out of** or **lost to ~** nicht mehr zu sehen sein, außer Sicht sein; **when he's out of our ~** wenn wir ihn nicht sehen; **don't let the children out of your ~** lass die Kinder nicht aus den Augen; **out of ~, out of mind** (Prov) aus den Augen, aus dem Sinn (Prov) (e) (Comm) **at/after ~** bei/nach Sicht; **payable at ~** zahlbar bei Sicht; **30 days' ~** 30 Tage nach Sicht; **~ unseen** unbesehen; **we need to have ~ of the document first** das Dokument muss uns (dat) zuerst vorliegen (f) USU PL (of city etc) Sehenswürdigkeit f; **to see the ~s of a town** etc eine Stadt etc besichtigen (g) (on telescope etc) Visiereinrichtung f; (on gun) Visier nt; **to set one's ~s too high** (fig) seine Ziele zu hoch stecken; **to lower one's ~s** (fig) seine Ansprüche herabsetzen or herunterschrauben; **to set one's ~s on sth** (fig) ein Auge auf etw (acc) werfen; **to have sb/sth in** or **within one's ~s** (fig) jdn/ etw im Fadenkreuz haben (h) (inf) **a ~ cheaper** einiges billiger; **he's a damn ~ cleverer than you think** er ist ein ganzes Ende gescheiter als du meinst (inf) **2** VT (= see) sichten (also Mil); person ausmachen

sight deposit N (Brit Fin) Sichteinlage f, Tagesgeld nt

-sighted ADJ SUF (Med, fig) -sichtig

sighting ['saɪtɪŋ] N Sichten nt; **at the first ~ of land** als zum ersten Mal Land gesichtet wurde

sightless ['saɪtlɪs] ADJ person blind

sight: sight-read VTI vom Blatt spielen/lesen/singen; **sightseeing 1** N Besichtigungen pl; **I hate ~** ich hasse Sightseeing; **to go ~** auf Besichtigungstour gehen **2** ADJ **~ tour** Rundreise f; (in town) (Stadt)rundfahrt f; **sightseer** N Tourist(in) m(f)

sign [saɪn] **1** N (a) (with hand etc, = written symbol) Zeichen nt; **he nodded as a ~ of recognition** er nickte zum Zeichen, dass er mich/ihn etc erkannt hatte (b) (= indication, Med) Anzeichen nt (of für, +gen); (= evidence) Zeichen nt (of von, +gen); (= trace) Spur f; **it's a ~ of the times** es ist ein Zeichen unserer Zeit; **it's a ~ of a true expert** daran erkennt man den wahren Experten; **there is no ~ of their agreeing** nichts deutet darauf hin, dass sie zustimmen werden; **to show ~s of sth** Anzeichen von etw erkennen lassen; **he shows ~s of doing it** es sieht so aus, als ob er es tun würde; **he gave no ~ of having heard** er ließ nicht erkennen, ob er es gehört hatte; **there was no ~ of life in the village** es gab keine Spur or kein Anzeichen von Leben im Dorf; **there was no ~ of him anywhere** von ihm war keine Spur zu sehen; **is there any ~ of him yet?** ist er schon zu sehen? (c) (= road ~, shop ~) Schild nt **2** VT (a) letter, contract, cheque unterschreiben, unterzeichnen (form); picture, book signieren; **to ~ the register** sich eintragen; **~ed and sealed** (unterschrieben und) besiegelt; **~ed copy** handsigniertes Exemplar; **to ~ one's name** unterschreiben; **to ~ one's name in a book** sich in ein Buch eintragen; **he ~s himself J.G. Jones** er unterschreibt mit J. G. Jones (b) football player etc unter Vertrag nehmen **3** VI (a) (with signature) unterschreiben; **Fellows has just ~ed for United** Fellows hat gerade bei United unterschrieben (b) (= use ~ language) die Gebärdensprache benutzen

➤ **sign away** VT SEP verzichten auf (+acc)

➤ **sign for** VI +PREP OBJ den Empfang (+gen) bestätigen

➤ **sign in 1** VT SEP person eintragen **2** VI sich eintragen

➤ **sign off** VI (Rad, TV) sich verabschieden; (in letter) Schluss machen

➤ **sign on 1** VT SEP = **sign up 1 2** VI (a) = **sign up 2** (b) (Brit) **to sign on (for unemployment benefit)** (= apply) sich arbeitslos melden; **he's still signing on** er ist immer noch

arbitslos **3** VI +PREP OBJ **to sign on (the dole)** (*Brit*) sich arbeitslos melden
➤ **sign out 1** VI sich austragen **2** VT SEP austragen
➤ **sign over** VT SEP überschreiben (*to sb* jdm)
➤ **sign up 1** VT SEP (= *employ, enlist*) verpflichten; *workers, employees* anstellen **2** VI sich verpflichten; (*employees, players*) unterschreiben; (*for evening class etc*) sich einschreiben

signal ['sɪɡnl] **1** N **(a)** (= *sign*) Zeichen *nt*; (*as part of code*) Signal *nt*; (= *message*) Nachricht *f*; **to give the ~ for sth** das Zeichen/Signal zu etw geben
(b) (= *apparatus, Rail, Telec*) Signal *nt*; **the ~ is at red** das Signal steht auf Rot
2 VT (= *indicate*) anzeigen; *arrival, future event etc* ankündigen; **to ~ sb to do sth** jdm ein Zeichen geben, etw zu tun; **to ~ one's intention to do sth** anzeigen, dass man vorhat, etw zu tun
3 VI ein Zeichen geben; **he signalled** (*Brit*) *or* **signaled** (*US*) **to the waiter** er winkte dem Ober

signal: signal box N Stellwerk *nt*; **signalman** N (*Rail*) Stellwerkswärter *m*

signatory ['sɪɡnətərɪ] **1** ADJ Signatar- **2** N (= *person*) Unterzeichner(in) *m(f)*

signature ['sɪɡnətʃə'] N Unterschrift *f*; (*of artist*) Signatur *f*

significance [sɪɡˈnɪfɪkəns] N Bedeutung *f*; (*of action also*) Tragweite *f*; **what is the ~ of this?** welche Bedeutung hat das?; **of no ~** belanglos, bedeutungslos; **to attach great ~ to sth** einer Sache (*dat*) große Bedeutung beimessen

significant [sɪɡˈnɪfɪkənt] ADJ **(a)** (= *having consequence*) bedeutend; (= *important*) wichtig; **to be ~ to** *or* **for sth** eine bedeutende *or* wichtige Rolle in etw (*dat*) spielen
(b) (= *meaningful*) bedeutungsvoll; **it is ~ that ...** es ist bezeichnend, dass ...

significantly [sɪɡˈnɪfɪkəntlɪ] ADV **(a)** (= *considerably*) bedeutend; **it is not ~ different** da besteht kein wesentlicher Unterschied **(b)** (= *meaningfully*) bedeutungsvoll

signify ['sɪɡnɪfaɪ] VT **(a)** (= *mean*) bedeuten **(b)** (= *indicate*) andeuten

signing [saɪnɪŋ] N **(a)** (*of document*) Unterzeichnen *nt* **(b)** (*of football player etc*) Unterzeichnen *nt* **(b)** (*of football player etc*) Untervertragnahme *f*; (= *football player etc*) neu unter Vertrag Genommene(r) *mf*

sign: sign language N Zeichensprache *f*; (*for deaf also*) Gebärdensprache *f*; **signpost 1** N Wegweiser *m* **2** VT beschildern

Sikh [siːk] N Sikh *mf*

silence ['saɪləns] **1** N **(a)** Stille *f*; (= *quietness also*) Ruhe *f*; (= *absence of talk also, of letters etc*) Schweigen *nt*; (*on a particular subject*) (Still)schweigen *nt*; **~!** Ruhe!; **in ~** still; (= *not talking also*) schweigend; **there was a short ~** es herrschte für kurze Zeit Stille; **the conversation was full of awkward ~s** die Unterhaltung kam immer wieder ins Stocken; **to break the ~** die Stille durchbrechen
2 VT (*lit, fig*) zum Schweigen bringen

silent ['saɪlənt] ADJ **(a)** still; (= *not talking also*) schweigsam; *engine etc* ruhig; *agreement, disapproval* (still)schweigend *attr*; **to fall** *or* **become ~** still werden; (*people also, guns*) verstummen; **to keep** *or* **remain ~** still sein *or* bleiben; **be ~!** sei still!; **~ film** (*esp Brit*) *or* **movie** (*esp US*) Stummfilm *m*; **~ letter** (*Ling*) stummer Buchstabe
(b) (= *not giving comment*) **to be ~** schweigen; **to keep** *or* **remain ~** sich nicht äußern; **everyone kept ~** keiner sagte etwas; **a ~ witness** ein stummer Zeuge, eine stumme Zeugin

silently ['saɪləntlɪ] ADV lautlos; (= *without talking*) schweigend

silent partner N (*US Comm*) stiller Teilhaber *or* Gesellschafter

silhouette [ˌsɪluˈet] **1** N Silhouette *f* **2** VT **to be ~d against sth** sich (als Silhouette) gegen *or* von etw abzeichnen

silicon chip [ˌsɪlɪkənˈtʃɪp] N Siliziumchip *nt*

silicone ['sɪlɪkəʊn] N Silikon *nt*

silk [sɪlk] **1** N Seide *f* **2** ADJ Seiden-, seiden; **~ tie** Seidenkrawatte *f*

silken ['sɪlkən] ADJ seidig

silkiness ['sɪlkɪnɪs] N (= *appearance*) seidiger Glanz; (= *feeling*) seidige Weichheit

silk screen N Seidensieb *nt*; (*also* **silk-screen printing**) Seidensiebdruck *m*

silky ['sɪlkɪ] ADJ (+ER) seidig; *voice* samtig; *movements* weich; **~ smooth/soft** seidenweich

sill [sɪl] N Sims *m or nt*; (= *windowsill*) (Fenster)sims *m or nt*; (*esp of wood*) Fensterbrett *nt*; (= *doorsill*) Schwelle *f*

silliness ['sɪlɪnɪs] N Albernheit *f*

silly ['sɪlɪ] ADJ (+ER) albern, dumm, doof (*inf*); **don't be ~** (= *do ~ things*) mach keinen Quatsch (*inf*); (= *say ~ things*) red keinen Unsinn; (= *ask ~ questions*) frag nicht so dumm; **it was a ~ thing to say** es war dumm, das zu sagen; **I hope he doesn't do anything ~** ich hoffe, er macht keine Dummheiten; **he was ~ to resign** es war dumm von ihm zurückzutreten; **I feel ~ in this hat** mit diesem Hut komme ich mir albern vor; **to make sb look ~** jdn lächerlich machen; **to worry sb ~** (*inf*) jdn vor Sorge (ganz) krank machen; **to bore sb ~** (*inf*) jdn zu Tode langweilen

silt [sɪlt] **1** N Schwemmsand *m*; (= *river mud*) Schlick *m* **2** VT (*also* ~ **up**) mit Schlick/Schwemmsand füllen **3** VI (*also* ~ **up**) verschlammen

silver ['sɪlvə'] **1** N Silber *nt*; (= *coins*) Silber(geld) *nt* **2** ADJ Silber-, silbern

silver: silver birch N Weißbirke *f*; **silver foil** N (= *kitchen foil*) Alu(minium)folie *f*; (= *silver paper*) Silberpapier *nt*; **silver jubilee** N 25jähriges Jubiläum; **silver medal** N Silbermedaille *f*; **silver paper** N Silberpapier *nt*; **silversmith** N Silberschmied(in) *m(f)*; **silverware** N Silber *nt*, Silberzeug *nt* (*inf*); **silver wedding** N Silberhochzeit *f*

silvery ['sɪlvərɪ] ADJ silbern, silbrig; **~ grey** (*Brit*) *or* **gray** (*US*) silbergrau

SIM card ['sɪmˌkaːd] N (*Telec*) ABBR *of* **Subscriber Identity Module card** SIM-Karte *f*

similar ['sɪmɪlə'] ADJ ähnlich; *amount, size* fast *or* ungefähr gleich; **this is ~ to what happened before** etwas Ähnliches ist schon einmal geschehen; **she and her sister are very ~, she is very ~ to her sister** ihre Schwester und sie sind sich sehr ähnlich; **they are very ~ in character** sie ähneln sich charakterlich sehr; **~ in size** ungefähr *or* fast gleich groß; **to taste ~ to sth** ähnlich wie etw schmecken; **in a ~ way** ähnlich

similarity [ˌsɪmɪˈlærɪtɪ] N Ähnlichkeit *f* (*to* mit)

similarly ['sɪmɪləlɪ] ADV ähnlich; (= *equally*) genauso, ebenso; **~, you could maintain ...** genauso gut könnten Sie behaupten ...

simile ['sɪmɪlɪ] N Gleichnis *nt*

simmer ['sɪmə'] **1** VT auf kleiner Flamme kochen lassen **2** VI auf kleiner Flamme kochen; (*fig*) (*with rage*) kochen (*inf*); (*with excitement*) fiebern
➤ **simmer down** VI sich beruhigen, sich abregen (*inf*)

simpering ['sɪmpərɪŋ] ADJ geziert, albern

simple ['sɪmpl] ADJ (+ER) **(a)** (= *easy*) einfach; (= *unsophisticated also*) schlicht; **the camcorder is ~ to use** der Camcorder ist einfach zu bedienen; **it's as ~ as ABC** es ist kinderleicht; **"chemistry made ~"** „Chemie leicht gemacht"; **in ~ terms** in einfachen Worten; **the ~ fact** *or* **truth is ...** es ist einfach so, dass ...; **the ~ fact that ...** die schlichte Tatsache, dass...; **I'm a ~ soul** ich bin ein einfacher Mensch **(b)** (= *~-minded*) einfältig

simple-minded ['sɪmplˈmaɪndɪd] ADJ einfältig

simplicity [sɪmˈplɪsɪtɪ] N Einfachheit *f*; (= *lack of sophistication: of decor etc*) Schlichtheit *f*; **it's ~ itself** das ist die einfachste Sache der Welt

simplification [ˌsɪmplɪfɪˈkeɪʃən] N Vereinfachung *f*

simplified ['sɪmplɪfaɪd] ADJ vereinfacht

simplify ['sɪmplɪfaɪ] VT vereinfachen

simplistic [sɪmˈplɪstɪk] ADJ simpel, simplistisch (*geh*); **or am I being ~?** oder sehe ich das zu einfach?

simply ['sɪmplɪ] ADV einfach; (= *merely*) nur, bloß; **very ~, he was short of money** er war schlicht und einfach knapp bei Kasse

simulate ['sɪmjʊleɪt] VT *emotions* vortäuschen; *illness, conditions* simulieren; **to ~ sth** (*material*) etw imitieren

simulation [ˌsɪmjʊˈleɪʃən] N **(a)** (*of emotions*) Vortäuschung *f*; (= *simulated appearance*) Imitation *f* **(b)** (= *reproduction*) Simulation *f*

simultaneous ADJ, **simultaneously** ADV [ˌsɪməlˈteɪnɪəs, -lɪ] gleichzeitig, simultan (*geh*)

sin [sɪn] **1** N (*Rel, fig*) Sünde *f*; **to live in ~** (*inf*) in wilder Ehe leben; **is that your family? – yes for my ~s** (*hum*) ist das Ihre

Familie? – ja, leider **2** VI sündigen (*against* gegen, an +*dat*), sich versündigen (*against* an +*dat*)

Sinai [ˈsaɪneɪaɪ] N Sinai *m*; **Mount ~** der Berg Sinai

since [sɪns] **1** ADV (= *in the meantime*) inzwischen; (= *up to now*) seitdem; **ever ~** seither; **a long time ~, long ~** schon lange; **not long ~** erst vor kurzem; **I've never heard it before or ~** ich habe das weder vorher noch nachher je wieder gehört **2** PREP seit; **ever ~ 1900** (schon) seit 1900; **I've been coming here ~ 1992** ich komme schon seit 1992 hierher; **he left in June, ~ when we have not heard from him** er ging im Juni fort und seitdem haben wir nichts mehr von ihm gehört; **how long is it ~ the accident?** wie lange ist der Unfall schon her?; **~ when?** (*inf*) seit wann denn das? (*inf*) **3** CONJ (a) (*time*) seit(dem); **ever ~ I've known him** seit(dem) ich ihn kenne (b) (= *because*) da

sincere [sɪnˈsɪəʳ] ADJ aufrichtig; **to be ~ about sth** in Bezug auf etw (*acc*) aufrichtig sein

sincerely [sɪnˈsɪəlɪ] ADV aufrichtig; *intend also* ernsthaft; **yours ~** (*Brit*) mit freundlichen Grüßen, hochachtungsvoll (*form*)

sincerity [sɪnˈserɪtɪ] N Aufrichtigkeit *f*

sinew [ˈsɪnjuː] N Sehne *f*

sinful [ˈsɪnfʊl] ADJ sündig; *waste* sündhaft (*geh*)

sinfulness [ˈsɪnfʊlnɪs] N Sündigkeit *f*

sing [sɪŋ], *vb*: *pret* **sang**, *ptp* **sung** VTI singen; **to ~ a child to sleep** ein Kind in den Schlaf singen; **to ~ the praises of sb/sth** ein Loblied auf jdn/etw singen

➤ **sing along** VI mitsingen

➤ **sing out 1** VI laut *or* aus voller Kehle singen **2** VT SEP *words, tune* singen; **to sing one's heart out** sich (*dat*) die Seele aus dem Leib singen

Singapore [ˌsɪŋgəˈpɔːʳ] N Singapur *nt*

Singaporean [ˌsɪŋgəˈpɔːrɪən] **1** ADJ singapurisch; **he is ~** er ist Singapurer **2** N (= *person*) Singapurer(in) *m(f)*

singe [sɪndʒ] **1** VT sengen; *clothes also* versengen; (*slightly*) ansengen; *eyebrows* absengen **2** VI sengen

singer [ˈsɪŋəʳ] N Sänger(in) *m(f)*

singer-songwriter [ˌsɪŋəˈsɒŋraɪtəʳ] N Liedermacher(in) *m(f)*

Singhalese [ˌsɪŋgəˈliːz] **1** ADJ singhalesisch; **he is ~** er ist Singhalese **2** N Singhalese *m*, Singhalesin *f*

singing [ˈsɪŋɪŋ] N Singen *nt*; (*of person, bird also*) Gesang *m*; **he teaches ~** er gibt Sing- *or* Gesangstunden; **do you like my ~?** gefällt dir mein Gesang?

singing lesson N Gesangstunde *f*

single [ˈsɪŋgl] **1** ADJ (a) (= *one only*) einzige(r, s); **not a ~ one spoke up** nicht ein Einziger äußerte sich dazu; **I've missed the bus every ~ day this week** diese Woche habe ich jeden Tag den Bus verpasst; **not a ~ thing** überhaupt nichts; **in ~ figures** in einstelligen Zahlen (b) (= *not double etc*) einzeln; (*Brit*) *ticket* einfach (c) (= *not married*) unverheiratet, ledig; **marital status? – ~** Familienstand? – ledig; **~ people** Ledige *pl*, Unverheiratete *pl* **2** N (*Brit*: = *ticket*) Einzelfahrschein *m*; (= *room*) Einzelzimmer *nt*; (= *record*) Single *f*; **two ~s to Xanadu** (*Brit*) zweimal einfach nach Xanadu

➤ **single out** VT SEP (= *choose*) auswählen; *victim* sich (*dat*) herausgreifen; (= *distinguish*) herausheben (*from* über +*acc*)

single: **single bed** N Einzelbett *nt*; **single combat** N Nah- *or* Einzelkampf *m*; **single cream** N (*Brit*) Sahne *f* (*mit geringem Fettgehalt*); **single currency** N einheitliche Währung, Einheitswährung *f*; **single-density** ADJ (*Comput*) *disk* mit einfacher Dichte; **single-drive** ADJ *computer* mit Einzellaufwerk; **single-entry book-keeping** N einfache Buchführung; **Single European Act** N Einheitliche Europäische Akte; **single European market** N Europäischer Binnenmarkt; **single file** N **in ~** im Gänsemarsch; **single-handed 1** ADJ (ganz) allein *pred*; *achievement* allein *or* ohne (fremde) Hilfe vollbracht **2** ADV (*also ~ly*) ohne Hilfe, im Alleingang; **single-minded** ADJ zielstrebig; **to be ~ in *or* about doing sth** zielstrebig darin sein, etw zu tun; **single-mindedly** ADV zielstrebig; **single-mindedness** N Zielstrebigkeit *f*; **single mother** N allein erziehende Mutter; **single parent** N Alleinerziehende(r) *mf*; **single-parent** ADJ **a ~ family** eine

Einelternfamilie; **single room** N Einzelzimmer *nt*; **~ supplement** Einzelzimmerzuschlag *m*

singles [ˈsɪŋglz] N SING or PL (*Sport*) Einzel *nt*; **the ~ finals** das Finale im Einzel

singles bar N Singles-Bar *f*

single: **single-sex** ADJ **a ~ school** eine reine Jungen-/Mädchenschule; **single-sided** ADJ (*Comput*) *disk* einseitig; **single-storey**, (*US*) **single-story** ADJ einstöckig; **single supplement** N Einzelzimmerzuschlag *m*; **single-track** ADJ einspurig; (*Rail also*) eingleisig

singly [ˈsɪŋglɪ] ADV einzeln

singsong [ˈsɪŋsɒŋ] N Liedersingen *nt no indef art, no pl*; **we often have a ~ after a few drinks** nachdem wir etwas getrunken haben, singen wir oft zusammen

singular [ˈsɪŋgjʊləʳ] **1** ADJ (a) (*Gram*) im Singular; **a ~ noun** ein Substantiv *nt* im Singular (b) (= *outstanding*) einzigartig, einmalig **2** N Singular *m*; **in the ~** im Singular

singularly [ˈsɪŋgjʊləlɪ] ADV außerordentlich; *unattractive* (ganz) besonders, überaus; **he was ~ unimpressed** er war ganz und gar nicht beeindruckt

Sinhalese [ˌsɪnhəˈliːz] ADJ, N = **Singhalese**

sinister [ˈsɪnɪstəʳ] ADJ unheimlich; *person, scheme* finster; *music, look* düster; *forces* dunkel; *development, motives* unheilvoll

sink¹ [sɪŋk], *pret* **sank**, *ptp* **sunk 1** VT (a) *ship, object* versenken; **to be sunk in thought** in Gedanken versunken sein (b) (*fig*) *theory* zerstören; *hopes* zunichte machen (c) *shaft, eyes, value* senken; *hole* ausheben; **to ~ money into sth** Geld in etw (*acc*) stecken (d) *teeth, claws* schlagen; **I'd like to ~ my teeth into a juicy steak** ich möchte in ein saftiges Steak reinbeißen (*inf*) **2** VI sinken; (*sun*) versinken; (*building, land, voice*) sich senken; *person, object* untergehen; **to ~ to the bottom** auf den Grund sinken; **he sank up to his knees in the mud** er sank bis zu den Knien im Schlamm ein; **to ~ back into the cushions** in die Kissen versinken; **the sun sank beneath the horizon** die Sonne versank am Horizont; **to ~ to one's knees** auf die Knie sinken; **my spirits *or* my heart sank at the sight of the work** beim Anblick der Arbeit verließ mich der Mut; **to ~ deeper into recession** immer tiefer in die Rezession geraten

➤ **sink in** VI (a) (*into mud etc*) einsinken (*prep obj, -to* in +*acc*) (b) (*inf*: = *be understood*) kapiert werden (*inf*); **it's only just sunk in that it really did happen** ich kapiere/er kapiert *etc* erst jetzt, dass das tatsächlich passiert ist (*inf*)

sink² N Ausguss *m*

sink³ ADJ *school, estate* benachteiligt

sinking [ˈsɪŋkɪŋ] **1** N (*of ship*) Untergang *m*; (*deliberately*) Versenkung *f*; (*of shaft*) Senken *nt*; (*of well*) Bohren *nt* **2** ADJ (*Fin*) *currency* fallend; **a ~ ship** (*lit, fig*) ein sinkendes Schiff; **with (a) ~ heart** schweren Herzens; **~ feeling** flaues Gefühl (im Magen) (*inf*)

sinking fund N (*Fin*) Tilgungsfonds *m*

sinner [ˈsɪnəʳ] N Sünder(in) *m(f)*

sinuous [ˈsɪnjʊəs] ADJ (*lit, fig*) gewunden; *motion of snake* schlängelnd *attr*; *dancing etc* geschmeidig

sinuously [ˈsɪnjʊəslɪ] ADV gewunden; *dance etc* geschmeidig

sinus [ˈsaɪnəs] N (*Anat*) Sinus *m* (*spec*); (*in head*) Stirnhöhle *f*

sip [sɪp] **1** N Schluck *m*; (*very small*) Schlückchen *nt* **2** VT in kleinen Schlucken trinken; (*suspiciously, daintily*) nippen an (+*dat*); (= *savour*) schlürfen **3** VI **to ~ at sth** an etw (*dat*) nippen

siphon [ˈsaɪfən] **1** N Heber *m*; (= *soda ~*) Siphon *m* **2** VT absaugen; (*into tank*) (mit einem Heber) umfüllen

➤ **siphon off** VT SEP (a) (*lit*) absaugen; *petrol* abzapfen; (*into container*) (mit einem Heber) umfüllen *or* abfüllen (b) (*fig*) *money* abziehen; *profits* abschöpfen

sir [sɜːʳ] N (a) (*in direct address*) mein Herr (*form*), Herr X; **no, ~** nein(, Herr X); (*Mil*) nein, Herr Leutnant *etc*; **Dear Sir (or Madam), ...** Sehr geehrte (Damen und) Herren! (b) (= *knight etc*) Sir *m* (c) (*Sch inf*: = *teacher*) er (*Sch sl*); **please ~!** Herr X!

sire [ˈsaɪəʳ] VT zeugen

siren [ˈsaɪərən] N (*all senses*) Sirene *f*

sirloin [ˈsɜːlɔɪn] N (*Cook*) Lendenfilet *nt*

sirup N (*US*) = **syrup**

sissy ['sısı] (*inf*) **1** N Waschlappen *m* (*inf*), Memme *f* **2** ADJ weibisch *inf*

sister ['sıstə'] N **(a)** Schwester *f* **(b)** (= *nun*) (Ordens)schwester *f*; (*before name*) Schwester *f* **(c)** (*Brit*: = *senior nurse*) Oberschwester *f*

sister IN CPDS Schwester-; **sister city** N (*US*) Partnerstadt *f*; **sisterhood** ['sıstəhʊd] N Schwesterschaft *f*; **sister-in-law** N, *pl* **sisters-in-law** Schwägerin *f*

sit [sıt], *vb*: pret, ptp **sat** **1** VI **(a)** (= *be sitting*) sitzen (*in/on* in/ auf +*dat*); (= ~ *down*) sich setzen (*in/on* in/auf +*acc*); ~! (*to dog*) sitz!; **a place to ~** ein Sitzplatz *m*; ~ **by/with me** setz dich zu mir/neben mich; **to ~ for a painter** für einen Maler Modell sitzen; **don't just ~ there, do something!** sitz nicht nur tatenlos da (herum), tu (endlich) was!
(b) (*assembly*) tagen; (= *have a seat*) einen Sitz haben; **to ~ in parliament/on a committee** einen Sitz im Parlament/in einem Ausschuss haben
(c) (*object*: = *be placed, rest*) stehen; **the package is ~ting in the hall** das Päckchen liegt im Flur
(d) (*bird*: = *hatch*) brüten
2 VT **(a)** (*also* = *down*) setzen (*in* in +*acc*, *on* auf +*acc*); (= *place*) *object* stellen; **to ~ a child on one's knee** sich (*dat*) ein Kind auf die Knie setzen
(b) (*Brit*) *examination* ablegen (*form*), machen
3 VR **to ~ oneself down** sich gemütlich hinsetzen
➤ **sit about** (*Brit*) *or* **around** VI herumsitzen
➤ **sit back** VI (*lit, fig*) sich zurücklehnen; (*fig*: = *do nothing*) die Hände in den Schoß legen
➤ **sit by** VI (tatenlos) herumsitzen
➤ **sit down** VI (*lit*) sich (hin)setzen; **to sit down in a chair** sich auf einen Stuhl setzen
➤ **sit in** VI **(a)** **to sit in for sb** jdn vertreten **(b)** (= *attend as visitor*) dabei sein, dabeisitzen (*on sth* bei etw)
➤ **sit on** VI +PREP OBJ **(a)** *committee* sitzen in (+*dat*) **(b)** (= *not deal with*) sitzen auf (+*dat*) **(c)** (*inf*: = *suppress*) *idea, product* nicht hochkommen lassen
➤ **sit out** VT SEP **(a)** *film, meeting* bis zum Schluss *or* Ende (sitzen) bleiben bei, bis zum Schluss *or* Ende durch- *or* aushalten (*pej*); *storm* auf das Ende (+*gen*) warten; *war* durchstehen **(b)** *dance* auslassen
➤ **sit through** VI +PREP OBJ durchhalten, aushalten (*pej*)
➤ **sit up** **1** VI **(a)** (= *be sitting upright*) aufrecht sitzen; (= *action*) sich aufsetzen **(b)** (= *sit straight*) aufrecht *or* gerade sitzen; **sit up!** setz dich gerade hin!; **to make sb sit up (and take notice)** (*fig inf*) jdn aufhorchen lassen **(c)** (= *not go to bed*) aufbleiben **2** VT SEP aufsetzen; *baby* hinsetzen
➤ **sit upon** VI +PREP OBJ = **sit on**

sitcom ['sıtkɒm] N (*inf*) Situationskomödie *f*

sit-down ['sıtdaʊn] **1** N (*inf*: = *rest*) Verschnaufpause *f* (*inf*) **2** ADJ ATTR **a ~ meal** eine richtige Mahlzeit

site [saɪt] **1** N **(a)** Stelle *f*, Platz *m* **(b)** (*Archeol*) Stätte *f* **(c)** (= *building* ~) Baustelle *f* **(d)** (= *camping* ~) Campingplatz *m* **(e)** (*Comput*) Site *f* **2** VT legen, anlegen; **to be ~d** liegen, (gelegen) sein

sitter ['sıtə'] N (*Art*) Modell *nt*; (= *baby-sitter*) Babysitter(in) *m(f)*

sitting ['sıtıŋ] **1** ADJ sitzend; **to be in a ~ position** aufsitzen; **to get into a ~ position** sich aufsetzen **2** N (*of committee, parliament, for portrait*) Sitzung *f*; **they have two ~s for lunch** sie servieren das Mittagessen in zwei Schüben; **at one** *or* **a single ~** (*fig*) auf einmal

sitting: **sitting duck** N (*fig*) leichte Beute; **sitting room** N (*esp Brit*) Wohnzimmer *nt*

situate ['sıtjʊeɪt] VT legen

situated ['sıtjʊeɪtɪd] ADJ gelegen; *person* (*financially*) situiert (*geh*); **it is ~ in the High Street** es liegt an der Hauptstraße; **a pleasantly ~ house** ein Haus in angenehmer Lage

situation [sɪtjʊ'eɪʃən] N **(a)** Lage *f*; (= *state of affairs also*) Situation *f*; (*financial, marital etc also*) Verhältnisse *pl* **(b)** (= *job*) Stelle *f*; **"~s vacant"** (*Brit*) „Stellenangebote"; **"~s wanted"** (*Brit*) „Stellengesuche"

six [sıks] **1** ADJ sechs; **she is ~ (years old)** sie ist sechs (Jahre alt); **at (the age of) ~** im Alter von sechs Jahren; **it's ~ (o'clock)** es ist sechs (Uhr); **there are ~ of us** wir sind sechs; **~ and a half/quarter** sechseinhalb/-einviertel **2** N Sechs *f*; (= *bus*) Sechser *m*; (= *team of* ~) Sechsermannschaft *f*; **~ and a half/quarter** Sechseinhalb/

-einviertel *f*; **to divide sth into ~** etw in sechs Teile teilen; **they are sold in ~es** sie werden in Sechser-packungen verkauft; **to knock sb for ~** (*Brit inf*) jdn umhauen (*inf*)

six: **sixfold** **1** ADJ sechsfach **2** ADV um das Sechsfache; **six hundred** **1** ADJ sechshundert **2** N Sechshundert *f*

sixish ['sıksıʃ] ADJ um sechs herum

six: **six million** ADJ, N sechs Millionen; **six-pack** N Sechserpackung *f*

sixteen ['sıks'tiːn] **1** ADJ sechzehn **2** N Sechzehn *f*

sixteenth ['sıks'tiːnθ] **1** ADJ sechzehnte(r, s); **a ~ part** ein Sechzehntel *nt*; **a ~ note** (*esp US Mus*) eine Sechzehntelnote, ein Sechzehntel *nt* **2** N **(a)** (= *fraction*) Sechzehntel *nt*; (*in series*) Sechzehnte(r, s) **(b)** (= *date*) **the ~** der Sechzehnte

sixth [sıksθ] **1** ADJ sechste(r, s); **a ~ part** ein Sechstel *nt*; **he was** *or* **came ~** er wurde Sechster; **he was ~ from the end/left** er war der Sechste von hinten/von links **2** N **(a)** (= *fraction*) Sechstel *nt*; (*in series*) Sechste(r, s); **Charles the Sixth** Karl der Sechste
(b) (= *date*) **the ~** der Sechste; **on the ~** am Sechsten; **the ~ of September, September the ~** der sechste September **3** ADV **he did it ~** (= *the ~ person to do it*) er hat es als Sechster gemacht; (= *the ~ thing he did*) er hat es als Sechstes *or* an sechster Stelle gemacht

sixth: **sixth form** N (*Brit*) Abschlussklasse *f*, ≈ Prima *f*; **sixth grade** N (*US Sch*) sechstes Schuljahr (*unmittelbar vor Eintritt in die Junior Highschool*)

six thousand **1** ADJ sechstausend **2** N Sechstausend *f*

sixtieth ['sıkstıθ] **1** ADJ sechzigste(r, s); **a ~ part** ein Sechzigstel *nt* **2** N (= *fraction*) Sechzigstel *nt*; (*in series*) Sechzigste(r, s)

sixty ['sıkstı] **1** ADJ sechzig; **~-one** einundsechzig **2** N Sechzig *f*; **the sixties** die sechziger Jahre; **to be in one's sixties** in den Sechzigern sein; **to be in one's late/early sixties** Ende/Anfang sechzig sein; *see also* **six**

sixtyish ['sıkstıʃ] ADJ um die Sechzig (*inf*)

six-year-old ['sıksjɪərəʊld] **1** ADJ sechsjährig *attr*, sechs Jahre alt *pred*; *war* schon sechs Jahre dauernd **2** N Sechsjährige(r) *mf*

size [saɪz] N (*all senses*) Größe *f*; (*of problem, operation also*) Ausmaß *nt*; **collar/waist ~** Kragen-/Taillenweite *f*; **shoe/dress ~** Schuh-/Kleidergröße *f*; **he's about your ~** er ist ungefähr so groß wie du; **what ~ is it?** wie groß ist es?; (*clothes, shoes etc*) welche Größe ist es?; **it's quite a ~** es ist ziemlich groß; **it's two ~s too big** es ist zwei Nummern zu groß; **do you want to try it for a ~?** möchten Sie es anprobieren, ob es Ihnen passt?
➤ **size up** VT SEP abschätzen

sizeable ['saɪzəbl] ADJ ziemlich groß, größer; *sum, problem also* beträchtlich

-size(d) [-saɪzd] ADJ SUF -groß; **medium-size(d)** mittelgroß, von mittlerer Größe; **life-size(d)** lebensgroß

sizzle ['sızl] VI brutzeln

sizzling ['sızlıŋ] **1** ADJ *fat, bacon* brutzelnd; (*inf*) *temperatures* siedend **2** ADV **~ hot** kochend heiß

skate¹ [skeɪt] N (= *fish*) Rochen *m*

skate² **1** N (= *shoe*) Schlittschuh *m*; **put** *or* **get your ~s on** (*fig inf*) mach/macht mal ein bisschen dalli! (*inf*) **2** VI Schlittschuh laufen; (= *roller-skate*) Rollschuh laufen; **he ~d across the pond** er lief (auf Schlittschuhen) über den Teich
➤ **skate (a)round** *or* **over** VI +PREP OBJ links liegen lassen; *difficulty, problem* einfach übergehen

skateboard ['skeɪtbɔːd] N Skateboard *nt*

skateboarding ['skeɪtbɔːdıŋ] N Skateboardfahren *nt*

skateboard park N Skateboardanlage *f*

skater ['skeɪtə'] N (= *ice-skater*) Schlittschuhläufer(in) *m(f)*; (= *figure-skater*) Eiskunstläufer(in) *m(f)*; (= *roller-skater*) Rollschuhläufer(in) *m(f)*

skating ['skeɪtıŋ] N (= *ice-skating*) Schlittschuhlauf *m*; (= *figure-skating*) Eiskunstlauf *m*; (= *roller-skating*) Rollschuhlauf *m*

skating rink N Eisbahn *f*; (*for roller-skating*) Rollschuhbahn *f*

skeletal ['skelɪtl] ADJ *person* bis aufs Skelett abgemagert; *appearance* wie ein Skelett; *shapes of trees etc* skelettartig

skeleton ['skelɪtn] **1** N (*lit, fig*) Skelett *nt*; **a ~ in one's cupboard** (*Brit*) *or* **closet** (*US*) ein dunkler Punkt (seiner Vergangenheit); (*of public figure*) eine Leiche im Keller **2** ADJ *plan etc* provisorisch; **~ service** Notdienst *m*

skeptic (*US*) = **sceptic**

sketch [sketʃ] **1** N (*Art, Liter*) Skizze *f*; (*Theat*) Sketch *m*; (= *draft, design also*) Entwurf *m* **2** VT (*lit, fig*) skizzieren **3** VI Skizzen machen
➤ **sketch in** VT SEP (= *draw*) (grob) einzeichnen; (*verbally*) umreißen
➤ **sketch out** VT SEP (= *draw*) grob skizzieren; (= *outline also*) umreißen
sketchbook [ˈsketʃbʊk] N Skizzenbuch *nt*
sketchily [ˈsketʃɪlɪ] ADV flüchtig, oberflächlich
sketching [ˈsketʃɪŋ] N (*Art*) Skizzenzeichnen *nt*
sketch pad N Skizzenblock *m*
sketchy [ˈsketʃɪ] ADJ (+ER) *knowledge, account* flüchtig, oberflächlich; *outline* skizzenhaft; *record* bruchstückhaft
skew [skju:] VT (= *turn round*) umdrehen; (= *make crooked*) krümmen; (*fig: = distort*) verzerren
skewer [ˈskjuəʳ] **1** N Spieß *m* **2** VT aufspießen
ski [ski:] **1** N Ski *m* **2** VI Ski laufen *or* fahren; **they ~ed down the slope** sie fuhren (auf ihren Skiern) den Hang hinunter
skid [skɪd] **1** N (a) (*Aut etc*) Schleudern *nt* (b) **skids** PL (*fig*) **he was on** *or* **hit the ~s** (*inf*) es ging abwärts mit ihm **2** VI (*car, objects*) schleudern; (*person*) ausrutschen; **to ~ across the floor** über den Boden rutschen *or* schlittern
skidmark [ˈskɪdmɑ:k] N Reifenspur *f*; (*from braking*) Bremsspur *f*
skier [ˈski:əʳ] N Skiläufer(in) *m(f)*, Skifahrer(in) *m(f)*
skiing [ˈski:ɪŋ] N Skilaufen *nt*, Skifahren *nt*; **to go ~** Ski laufen *or* Ski fahren gehen
ski: **ski jump** N (= *action*) Skisprung *m*; (= *place*) Sprungschanze *f*; **ski-jumping** N Skispringen *nt*
skilful, (US) **skillful** [ˈskɪlfʊl] ADJ geschickt; *piano-playing etc* also gewandt; *sculpture etc* kunstvoll; *job* fachgerecht
skilfully, (US) **skillfully** [ˈskɪlfəlɪ] ADV geschickt; *play the piano* also gewandt; *paint, sculpt etc* kunstvoll
ski lift N Skilift *m*
skill [skɪl] N (a) NO PL (= *skilfulness*) Geschick *nt*, Geschicklichkeit *f*; (*of sculptor etc*) Kunst(fertigkeit) *f*; **his ~ at billiards** sein Geschick *nt* beim Billard (b) (= *acquired technique*) Fertigkeit *f*; (= *ability*) Fähigkeit *f*; **it's a ~ that has to be acquired** so etwas muss gelernt sein
skilled [skɪld] ADJ (= *skilful*) geschickt, gewandt (*at in +dat*); (= *trained*) ausgebildet; (= *requiring skill*) fachmännisch
skilled worker N Facharbeiter(in) *m(f)*
skillful *etc* (US) = **skilful** *etc*
skim [skɪm] VT (a) (= *remove floating matter*) abschöpfen; *milk* entrahmen; (*fig*) *profits* absahnen (*inf*) (b) (= *pass low over*) streifen *or* streichen über (+*acc*); (*fig: = touch on*) berühren (c) (= *read quickly*) überfliegen
➤ **skim off** VT SEP abschöpfen; (*fig*) absahnen
➤ **skim through** VI +PREP OBJ *book etc* überfliegen
skimmed milk [ˌskɪmd'mɪlk], (US) **skim milk** N Magermilch *f*
skimp [skɪmp] **1** VT *food, material* sparen an (+*dat*); *work* nachlässig erledigen **2** VI sparen (*on an +dat*)
skimpily [ˈskɪmpɪlɪ] ADV *dressed* spärlich
skimpy [ˈskɪmpɪ] ADJ (+ER) dürftig; *clothes* knapp
skin [skɪn] **1** N (a) Haut *f*; (= *fur*) Fell *nt*; (*of fruit etc*) Schale *f*; **to be soaked to the ~** bis auf die Haut nass sein; **that's no ~ off my nose** (*esp Brit inf*) das juckt mich nicht (*inf*); **to save one's own ~** die eigene Haut retten; **to jump out of one's ~** (*inf*) erschreckt hochfahren; **to get under sb's ~** (*inf*) (= *irritate*) jdm auf die Nerven gehen (*inf*); (= *fascinate*) (*music, voice*) jdm unter die Haut gehen; (*person*) jdn faszinieren; **to have a thick/thin ~** (*fig*) ein dickes Fell (*inf*)/eine dünne Haut haben; **by the ~ of one's teeth** (*inf*) mit Ach und Krach (*inf*) **2** VT (a) *animal* häuten; *fruit* schälen; *tomatoes* enthäuten (b) (= *graze*) abschürfen
skin: **skinflint** N (*inf*) Geizkragen *m* (*inf*); **skinhead** N Skin(head) *m*
-skinned [-skɪnd] ADJ SUF -häutig
skinny [ˈskɪnɪ] ADJ (+ER) (*inf*) dünn
skint [skɪnt] ADJ (*Brit inf*) **to be ~** pleite *or* blank sein (*inf*)
skintight [ˈskɪntaɪt] ADJ hauteng
skip¹ [skɪp] **1** N Hüpfer *m*; (*in dancing*) Hüpfschritt *m* **2** VI (a) hüpfen; (*with rope*) seilspringen (b) (= *move from subject to subject*) springen **3** VT (a) *school etc* schwänzen (*inf*); *generation, chapter etc*,

(*Comput: printer*) überspringen; **my heart ~ped a beat** mein Herzschlag setzte für eine Sekunde aus; **to ~ lunch** das Mittagessen ausfallen lassen
(b) (*US*) **to ~ rope** seilspringen
(c) (*US inf*) **to ~ town** aus der Stadt verschwinden (*inf*)
➤ **skip about** (*Brit*) *or* **around** VI (*lit*) herumhüpfen; (*fig: author, speaker*) springen
➤ **skip over** VI +PREP OBJ (= *pass over*) überspringen
➤ **skip through** VI +PREP OBJ *book* durchblättern
skip² N (*Build*) (Schutt)container *m*
ski pole N Skistock *m*
skipper [ˈskɪpəʳ] **1** N Kapitän(in) *m(f)* **2** VT anführen
skipping [ˈskɪpɪŋ] N Seilspringen *nt*
skipping rope N (*Brit*) Hüpf- *or* Sprungseil *nt*
ski resort N Skiort *m*
skirmish [ˈskɜ:mɪʃ] N (*Mil*) Gefecht *nt*; (= *scrap, fig*) Zusammenstoß *m*
skirt [skɜ:t] **1** N Rock *m* **2** VT (*also* ~ **around**) umgehen; (= *encircle*) umgeben
skirting (board) [ˈskɜ:tɪŋ(ˌbɔ:d)] N (*Brit*) Fußleiste *f*
ski: **ski run** N Skipiste *f*; **ski stick** N Skistock *m*; **ski tow** N Schlepplift *m*
skitter [ˈskɪtəʳ] VI rutschen
skittish [ˈskɪtɪʃ] ADJ *horse, investor* unruhig
skive [skaɪv] (*Brit inf*) **1** N **to have a good ~** sich (*dat*) einen schönen Tag machen (*inf*) **2** VI blaumachen (*inf*); (*from school etc*) schwänzen (*inf*)
➤ **skive off** VI (*Brit inf*) sich drücken (*inf*)
skiver [ˈskaɪvəʳ] N (*Brit inf*) fauler Bruder (*inf*), faule Schwester (*inf*)
skulduggery [skʌlˈdʌgərɪ] N (*inf*) üble Tricks *pl* (*inf*)
skulk [skʌlk] VI (= *move*) schleichen, sich stehlen; (= *lurk*) sich herumdrücken
➤ **skulk off** VI sich davonstehlen
skull [skʌl] N Schädel *m*; **~ and crossbones** Totenkopf *m*
skunk [skʌŋk] N (a) Stinktier *nt* (b) (*inf: = marijuana*) Pot *nt* (*sl*)
sky [skaɪ] N Himmel *m*; **under the open ~** unter freiem Himmel; **in the ~** am Himmel
sky: **sky-blue** ADJ himmelblau; **skycap** N (*US*) Gepäckträger(in) *m(f)*; **skydiver** N Fallschirmspringer(in) *m(f)*; **skydiving** N Fallschirmspringen *nt*; **sky-high 1** ADJ *prices* schwindelnd hoch; *confidence* unermesslich **2** ADV zum Himmel; **to blow a bridge ~** (*inf*) eine Brücke in die Luft sprengen (*inf*); **to blow a theory ~** (*inf*) eine Theorie zum Einsturz bringen; **skylight** N Oberlicht *nt*; (*in roof also*) Dachfenster *nt*; **skyline** N (= *horizon*) Horizont *m*; (*of building, hills etc*) Silhouette *f*; (*of city also*) Skyline *f*; **skyscraper** N Wolkenkratzer *m*
slab [slæb] N (*of wood etc*) Tafel *f*; (*of stone, concrete etc*) Platte *f*; (*in mortuary*) Tisch *m*; (= *slice*) dicke Scheibe; (*of cake*) großes Stück; (*of chocolate*) Tafel *f*
slack [slæk] **1** ADJ (+ER) (a) (= *not tight*) locker (b) (= *lazy*) bequem, träge; (= *negligent*) nachlässig, schlampig (*inf*) (c) (*Comm*) *market* flau; *period, season* ruhig; (*St Ex*) lustlos; **business is ~** das Geschäft geht schlecht **2** N (*of rope etc*) durchhängendes Teil (*of the Seils/Segels etc*); **to cut sb some ~** (*fig inf*) mit jdm nachsichtig sein **3** VI bummeln
➤ **slack off** VI = **slacken off**
slacken [ˈslækn] **1** VT (a) (= *loosen*) lockern (b) (= *reduce*) vermindern, verringern **2** VI (a) (= *become loose*) sich lockern (b) (*speed*) sich verringern; (*rate of development*) sich verlangsamen; (*wind, demand, market*) nachlassen
➤ **slacken off** VI (= *diminish, wind*) nachlassen; (*work, trade*) abnehmen
slackening [ˈslæknɪŋ] N (= *loosening*) Lockern *nt*; (= *reduction*) Abnahme *f*; (*of rate of development, speed*) Verlangsamung *f*; (*of efforts, market*) Abflauen *nt*
slackly [ˈslæklɪ] ADV (= *loosely*) schlaff; *hold* locker
slackness [ˈslæknɪs] N (a) (*of rope, reins*) Schlaffheit *f*, Durchhängen *nt* (b) (*of business, market etc*) Flaute *f*
slag [slæg] **1** N (a) Schlacke *f* (b) (*Brit sl: = woman*) Schlampe *f* (*inf*) **2** VT (*Brit inf: = run down*) runtermachen (*inf*)
➤ **slag off** VT SEP (*Brit inf: = run down*) runtermachen (*inf*)
slain [sleɪn] PTP *of* **slay**
slalom [ˈslɑ:ləm] N Slalom *m*

slam [slæm] **1** N (*of door etc*) Zuschlagen *nt*, Zuknallen *nt no pl*; **with a ~** mit voller Wucht
2 VT **(a)** (= *close violently*) zuschlagen, zuknallen; **to ~ the door in sb's face** jdm die Tür vor der Nase zumachen **(b)** (*inf*: = *put, throw etc with force*) knallen (*inf*); **to ~ the brakes on** (*inf*) auf die Bremse latschen (*inf*) **(c)** (*inf*: = *criticize harshly*) verreißen; *person* herunterputzen (*inf*)
3 VI (*door, window*) zuschlagen, zuknallen; **to ~ into/against sth** in etw (*acc*)/gegen etw knallen
➤ **slam down** VT SEP hinknallen (*inf*); *phone* aufknallen (*inf*); *window* zuknallen

slander ['slɑːndər] **1** N Verleumdung *f* **2** VT verleumden

slanderous ['slɑːndərəs] ADJ verleumderisch

slang [slæŋ] **1** N Slang *m*; (= *army ~, schoolboy ~ etc*) Jargon *m* **2** ADJ Slang-

slant [slɑːnt] **1** N (*lit, fig*) Neigung *f*; (= *slope also*) Schräge *f*; (= *bias, leaning also*) Tendenz *f*; (*of newspaper article*) Anstrich *m*; **to put a ~ on sth** etw biegen; **to be on a ~** sich neigen, schräg sein **2** VT verschieben; *report* färben; **the book is ~ed toward(s) women** das Buch ist auf Frauen ausgerichtet **3** VI (*road*) sich neigen

slanting ['slɑːntɪŋ] ADJ schräg

slap [slæp] **1** N Schlag *m*, Klaps *m*; **to give sb a ~** jdm einen Klaps geben; **a ~ across the face** (*lit*) eine Ohrfeige; **a ~ in the face** (*fig*) ein Schlag *m* ins Gesicht; **to give sb a ~ on the back** jdm (anerkennend) auf den Rücken klopfen; (*fig*) jdn loben; **to give sb a ~ on the wrist** (*fig inf*) jdn zurechtweisen, jdm einem Anpfiff geben (*inf*)
2 ADV (*inf*) direkt
3 VT **(a)** (= *hit*) schlagen; **to ~ sb's face, to ~ sb on** *or* **round the face** jdn ohrfeigen, jdm eine runterhauen (*inf*); **to ~ sb on the back** jdm auf den Rücken klopfen **(b)** (= *put noisily*) knallen (*on(to)* auf +*acc*)
➤ **slap down** VT SEP (*inf*) hinknallen
➤ **slap on** VT SEP (*inf*) **(a)** (= *apply carelessly*) draufklatschen (*inf*) **(b)** (*fig*) *tax, money* draufhauen (*inf*)

slap: slap-bang ADV (*esp Brit inf*) mit Karacho (*inf*); **it was ~ in the middle** es war genau in der Mitte; **to run ~ into sb/sth** mit jdm/etw zusammenknallen (*inf*); **slapdash** ADJ flüchtig, schludrig (*pej*); **slaphappy** ADJ (*inf*) unbekümmert

slapper ['slæpər] N (*Brit inf*) Flittchen *nt*

slap: slapstick N Klamauk *m* (*inf*); **~ comedy** Slapstick *m*; **slap-up meal** N (*Brit inf*) Schlemmermahl *nt* (*inf*)

slash [slæʃ] **1** N **(a)** (= *action*) Streich *m*; (= *wound*) Schnitt *m* **(b)** (*Typ*) Schrägstrich *m* **2** VT **(a)** (= *cut*) zerfetzen; *face, tyres, throat* aufschlitzen; *undergrowth* wegschlagen; **to ~ sb with a knife** jdn durch Messerstiche verletzen **(b)** (*inf*) *price* radikal herabsetzen; *estimate, budget* zusammenstreichen (*inf*) **3** VI **to ~ at sb/sth** nach jdm/etw schlagen

slat [slæt] N Leiste *f*; (*in grid etc*) Stab *m*

slate [sleɪt] **1** N **(a)** (= *rock*) Schiefer *m*; (= *roof ~*) Schieferplatte *f*; (= *writing ~*) (Schiefer)tafel *f*; **put it on the ~** (*Brit inf*) schreiben Sie es mir an; **to wipe the ~ clean** (*fig*) reinen Tisch machen **(b)** (*US Pol*) (Kandidaten)liste *f*
2 ADJ Schiefer-, schief(e)rig
3 VT **(a)** (*esp US*) (= *propose*) vorschlagen; (= *schedule*) ansetzen **(b)** (*Brit inf*: = *criticize harshly*) verreißen; *person* zusammenstauchen (*inf*)

slating ['sleɪtɪŋ] N (*Brit inf*) Verriss *m*; **to get a ~** zusammengestaucht werden (*inf*); (*play, performance etc*) verrissen werden

slaughter ['slɔːtər] **1** N (*of animals*) Schlachten *nt no pl*; (*of persons*) Gemetzel *nt no pl* **2** VT schlachten; *persons* (*lit*) abschlachten; (*fig*) fertig machen (*inf*)

slaughterhouse ['slɔːtəhaʊs] N Schlachthof *m*

Slav [slɑːv] **1** ADJ slawisch **2** N Slawe *m*, Slawin *f*

slave [sleɪv] **1** N Sklave *m*, Sklavin *f* **2** VI sich abplagen, schuften (*inf*); **to ~ (away) at sth** sich mit etw herumschlagen

slave: slave-driver N (*lit, fig*) Sklaventreiber(in) *m(f)*; **slave labour**, (*US*) **slave labor** N **(a)** (= *work*) Sklavenarbeit *f* **(b)** (= *work force*) Sklaven *pl*

slaver ['slævər] VI geifern; **the dog ~ed at the mouth** der Hund hatte Schaum vor dem Maul; **to ~ over sb/sth** nach jdm/etw geifern

slavery ['sleɪvərɪ] N Sklaverei *f*; (= *condition*) Sklavenleben *nt*

Slavic ['slɑːvɪk], **Slavonic** [sləˈvɒnɪk] **1** ADJ slawisch **2** N das Slawische

slaw [slɔː] N (*US*) Krautsalat *m*

slay [sleɪ], *pret* **slew**, *ptp* **slain** VT erschlagen; (*with gun etc, esp US*: = *kill*) ermorden

slaying ['sleɪɪŋ] N (*esp US*: = *murder*) Mord *m*

sleaze [sliːz] N (*inf*) (= *depravity*) Verderbtheit *f*; (*esp Pol*: = *corruption*) Skandalgeschichten *pl*

sleazy ['sliːzɪ] ADJ (+ER) (*inf*) schäbig

sledge [sledʒ], (*esp US*) **sled** [sled] **1** N Schlitten *m* **2** VI Schlitten fahren

sledge(hammer) ['sledʒ(ˌhæməʳ)] N Vorschlaghammer *m*

sleek [sliːk] **1** ADJ (+ER) *hair, fur* geschmeidig; (*of general appearance*) gepflegt; *car also* schnittig **2** VT glätten

sleekness ['sliːknɪs] N (*of hair, fur*) Geschmeidigkeit *f*; (*of general appearance*) Gepflegtheit *f*

sleep [sliːp], *vb: pret, ptp* **slept 1** N Schlaf *m*; **to go to ~** (*person, limb*) einschlafen; **to drop off to ~** (*person*) einschlafen; **I couldn't get to ~ last night** ich konnte letzte Nacht nicht einschlafen; **try and get some ~** versuche, etwas zu schlafen; **to have a ~** (etwas) schlafen; **to have a good night's ~** sich richtig ausschlafen; **to put sb to ~** (*person, cocoa etc*) jdn zum Schlafen bringen; (*drug*) jdn einschläfern; **to put an animal to ~** (= *euph*) ein Tier einschläfern; **that film sent me to ~** bei dem Film bin ich eingeschlafen
2 VT **(a) to ~ the day away** den ganzen Tag verschlafen **(b)** (= *accommodate*) unterbringen; **the house ~s 10** in dem Haus können 10 Leute übernachten
3 VI schlafen; **to ~ like a log** *or* **top** *or* **baby** wie ein Murmeltier schlafen; **to ~ late** lange schlafen
➤ **sleep around** VI (*inf*) mit jedem schlafen (*inf*)
➤ **sleep in** VI (= *lie in*) ausschlafen; (*inf*: = *oversleep*) verschlafen
➤ **sleep off** VT SEP (*inf*) *hangover etc* ausschlafen; **to sleep it off** seinen Rausch ausschlafen
➤ **sleep on 1** VI weiterschlafen **2** VI +PREP OBJ *problem etc* überschlafen
➤ **sleep through** VI +PREP OBJ weiterschlafen bei; **to sleep through the alarm (clock)** den Wecker verschlafen
➤ **sleep together** VI zusammen schlafen
➤ **sleep with** VI +PREP OBJ schlafen mit

sleeper ['sliːpəʳ] N **(a)** (= *person*) Schlafende(r) *mf*, Schläfer(in) *m(f)*; **to be a heavy/light ~** einen festen/leichten Schlaf haben **(b)** (*Brit Rail*: = *on track*) Schwelle *f* **(c)** (*Brit Rail*) (= *train*) Schlafwagenzug *m*; (= *coach*) Schlafwagen *m*; (= *berth*) Platz *m* im Schlafwagen **(d)** (= *agent*) Schläfer *m*

sleepily ['sliːpɪlɪ] ADV verschlafen

sleepiness ['sliːpɪnɪs] N Schläfrigkeit *f*

sleeping ['sliːpɪŋ] **1** ADJ schlafend **2** N Schlafen *nt*

sleeping: sleeping bag N Schlafsack *m*; **sleeping car** N Schlafwagen *m*; **sleeping partner** N (*Brit*) stiller Teilhaber *or* Gesellschafter; **sleeping pill** N Schlaftablette *f*; **sleeping policeman** N Bodenschwelle *f*; **sleeping quarters** PL Schlafräume *pl*, Schlafsaal *m*

sleepless ['sliːplɪs] ADJ schlaflos

sleep: sleepover N Übernachtung *f* (*bei Freunden, Bekannten etc*); **sleepwalk** VI schlafwandeln; **he was ~ing** er hat *or* ist geschlafwandelt; **sleepwalker** N Schlafwandler(in) *m(f)*

sleepy ['sliːpɪ] ADJ (+ER) **(a)** (= *drowsy*) schläfrig; (= *not yet awake*) verschlafen **(b)** *place, atmosphere* verschlafen

sleet [sliːt] **1** N Schneeregen *m* **2** VI **it was ~ing** es gab Schneeregen

sleeve [sliːv] N **(a)** (*on garment*) Ärmel *m*; **to roll up one's ~s** (*lit*) sich (*dat*) die Ärmel hochkrempeln; **to have sth up one's ~** (*fig inf*) etw in petto haben *or* auf Lager haben **(b)** (*for record, on book*) Hülle *f*

-sleeved [-sliːvd] ADJ SUF -ärmelig

sleeveless ['sliːvlɪs] ADJ ärmellos

sleigh [sleɪ] N (Pferde)schlitten *m*

slender ['slendə^r] ADJ schlank; *hand, waist also* schmal; *resources, lead, majority* knapp; *chance, hope* gering; *profit margin* dürftig

slenderize ['slendəraɪz] VT (*US*) schlank machen

slenderness ['slendənɪs] N Schlankheit *f*; (*of hand, waist also*) Schmalheit *f*; (*fig*) (*of chance, hope*) Schwäche *f*; (*of lead, majority*) Knappheit *f*

slept [slept] PRET, PTP *of* **sleep**

slew¹ [sluː], (*US also* ~ **round**) **slue 1** VT *crane, lorry* (herum)schwenken **2** VI (herum)schwenken

slew² PRET *of* **slay**

slice [slaɪs] **1** N **(a)** (*lit*) Scheibe *f*; (*of bread also*) Schnitte *f* **(b)** (*fig: of population, profits*) Teil *m*; **a ~ of luck** eine Portion Glück **(c)** (*esp Brit: = food server*) Wender *m* **2** VT **(a)** (= *cut*) durchschneiden; *bread, meat etc* (in Scheiben) schneiden **(b)** *ball* (an)schneiden **3** VI schneiden; **to ~ through sth** etw durchschneiden

➤ **slice off** VT SEP **(a)** abschneiden **(b)** *money, time* wegnehmen

sliced [slaɪst] ADJ (in Scheiben) geschnitten; *loaf, bread, sausage* (auf)geschnitten

slicer ['slaɪsə^r] N (= *cheese-~ etc*) Hobel *m*; (= *machine*) (*bread-~*) Brot(schneide)maschine *f*; (= *bacon-~*) ≈ Wurstschneidemaschine *f*

slick [slɪk] **1** ADJ (+ER) **(a)** (*often pej*: = *clever*) gewieft (*inf*), clever (*inf*); *answer* glatt; *performance, style* glatt, professionell **(b)** (*US*: = *slippery*) glatt, schlüpfrig **2** N (= *oil* ~) (Öl)teppich *m*, Schlick *nt*

➤ **slick back** VT SEP **to slick one's hair back** sich (*dat*) die Haare anklatschen (*inf*)

slicker ['slɪkə^r] N (*US*: = *coat*) Regenjacke *f*

slickly ['slɪklɪ] ADV (*often pej*: = *cleverly*) gewieft (*inf*), clever (*inf*); *answer, perform* glatt

slickness ['slɪknɪs] N (*often pej*: = *cleverness*) Gewieftheit *f* (*inf*), Cleverness *f* (*inf*); (*of performance, style*) Glattheit *f*

slide [slaɪd], *vb: pret, ptp* **slid** [slɪd] **1** N **(a)** (= *place for sliding, chute*) Rutschbahn *f*; (*in playground*) Rutsche *f* **(b)** (*fig*: = *fall, drop*) Abfall *m*; **the ~ in share prices** der Preisrutsch bei den Aktien **(c)** (*esp Brit: for hair*) Spange *f* **(d)** (*Phot*) Dia *nt*; (= *microscope* ~) Objektträger *m* **2** VT (= *push*) schieben; (= *slip*) gleiten lassen **3** VI **(a)** (= *slip*) rutschen; **suddenly it all slid into place** plötzlich passte alles zusammen; **to let things ~** (*fig*) die Dinge laufen *or* schleifen lassen **(b)** (= *move smoothly: machine part etc*) sich schieben lassen **(c)** (= *move silently*) schleichen; **he slid into the room** er kam ins Zimmer geschlichen

slide: **slide projector** N Diaprojektor *m*; **slide show** N Diavortrag *m*

sliding ['slaɪdɪŋ] ADJ *part* gleitend

sliding door N Schiebetür *f*

slight [slaɪt] **1** ADJ (+ER) **(a)** *person, build* zierlich **(b)** (= *small, trivial*) leicht; *change, possibility* geringfügig; *error, problem* klein; *pain* leicht, schwach; *acquaintance* flüchtig; **the wall's at a ~ angle** die Mauer ist leicht *or* etwas geneigt; **to have a ~ cold** eine leichte Erkältung haben; **just the ~est bit short** ein ganz kleines bisschen zu kurz; **it doesn't make the ~est bit of difference** es macht nicht den geringsten Unterschied; **I wasn't the ~est bit interested** ich war nicht im Geringsten *or* Mindesten *or* mindesten interessiert; **he is upset by at the ~est thing** er ist wegen jeder kleinsten Kleinigkeit gleich verärgert; **I don't have the ~est idea (of) what he's talking about** ich habe nicht die geringste *or* leiseste Ahnung, wovon er redet **2** N (= *affront*) Affront *m* (*on* gegen) **3** VT (= *offend*) kränken, beleidigen

slightly ['slaɪtlɪ] ADV **(a)** ~ **built** *or* **made** *person* zierlich **(b)** (= *to a slight extent*) etwas, ein klein(es) bisschen; *know* flüchtig; ~ **injured** leicht verletzt; **he hesitated ever so ~** er zögerte fast unmerklich

slim [slɪm] **1** ADJ (+ER) **(a)** schlank; *ankle, waist etc* schmal; *volume* dünn **(b)** *resources, profits* mager; *hope* schwach; *chances* gering; *majority* knapp **2** VI eine Schlankheitskur machen

➤ **slim down 1** VT SEP (*fig*) *business etc* verschlanken; *budget* kürzen **2** VI **(a)** (*person*) abnehmen, abspecken (*inf*) **(b)** (*fig: business etc*) verschlanken

sliminess ['slaɪmɪnɪs] N (*lit, fig*) Schleimigkeit *f*; (*of person also*) Öligkeit *f*; (*of stone*) Glitschigkeit *f*

slimline ['slɪmlaɪn] ADJ *diary* dünn; *mobile phone* flach; *figure* schlank

slimming ['slɪmɪŋ] **1** ADJ schlank machend *attr*; **crispbread/black is** ~ Knäckebrot/schwarz macht schlank **2** N Abnehmen *nt*; **is** ~ **really worth it?** lohnt es sich wirklich abzunehmen?

slimness ['slɪmnɪs] N Schlankheit *f*; (*of ankle, waist etc*) Schmalheit *f*; (*of volume*) Dünne *f*

slimy ['slaɪmɪ] ADJ (+ER) (*lit, fig*) schleimig; *person also* ölig; *stone* glitschig; *hands* schmierig

sling [slɪŋ], *vb: pret, ptp* **slung 1** N **(a)** Schlinge *f* (*also Med*), Schlaufe *f*; (*for baby*) (Baby)trageschlinge *f*; **to have one's arm in a** ~ den Arm in der Schlinge tragen **(b)** (= *weapon*) Schleuder *f* **2** VT (= *throw*) schleudern; (*inf*) schmeißen (*inf*); **he slung the box onto his back** er warf sich (*dat*) die Kiste auf den Rücken

➤ **sling out** VT SEP (*inf*) rausschmeißen (*inf*)

sling bag N (*US*) Schultertasche *f*

slink [slɪŋk], *pret, ptp* **slunk** VI schleichen; **to** ~ **away** *or* **off** sich davonschleichen

slinky ADJ (+ER), **slinkily** ADV ['slɪŋkɪ, -lɪ] (*inf*) aufreizend

slip [slɪp] **1** N **(a)** (= *mistake*) Ausrutscher *m*, Patzer *m*; **to make a (bad)** ~ sich (übel) vertun (*inf*); **a** ~ **of the tongue** ein Versprecher *m* **(b)** **to give sb the** ~ (*inf*: = *escape*) jdm entwischen **(c)** (= *pillow* ~) Kissenbezug *m* **(d)** (= *undergarment*) Unterrock *m* **(e)** (*of paper*) Zettel *m*; ~**s of paper** Zettel *pl* **2** VT **(a)** (= *move smoothly*) schieben; (= *slide*) gleiten *or* rutschen lassen; **she ~ped the dress over her head** sie streifte sich (*dat*) das Kleid über den Kopf; **to** ~ **a disc** (*Med*) sich (*dat*) einen Bandscheibenschaden zuziehen **(b)** (= *escape from*) sich losreißen von; **it ~ped my mind** *or* **memory** ich habe es vergessen *or* verschwitzt (*inf*) **(c)** (= *loose*) losmachen **3** VI **(a)** (= *slide*) (*person*) (aus)rutschen; (*feet, tyres*) (weg)rutschen; (= *become loose: knot, nut*) sich lösen; **the knife** ~**ped** das Messer rutschte ab; **it** ~**ped from her hand** es rutschte ihr aus der Hand; **the beads** ~**ped through my fingers** die Perlen glitten durch meine Finger; **to let sth** ~ **through one's fingers** sich (*dat*) etw entgehen lassen; **the police let the thief** ~ **through their fingers** die Polizei ließ sich (*dat*) den Dieb in letzter Minute durch die Finger schlüpfen; **to let (it)** ~ **that ...** fallen lassen, dass ... **(b)** (= *move quickly*) schlüpfen; (= *move smoothly*) rutschen **(c)** (= *decline: standards etc*) fallen; **you're** ~**ping!** (*inf*) du lässt nach (*inf*)

➤ **slip away** VI sich wegschleichen, sich wegstehlen

➤ **slip back** VI unbemerkt zurückgehen; (*quickly*) schnell zurückgehen

➤ **slip behind** VI zurückfallen

➤ **slip by** VI (*person*) sich vorbeischleichen (*prep obj* an +*dat*); (*years*) nur so dahinschwinden

➤ **slip down** VI (= *fall*) ausrutschen; (= *go down*) hinunterlaufen

➤ **slip in 1** VI (sich) hineinschleichen; (*burglar also, mistake*) sich einschleichen **2** VT SEP **(a)** **to slip sth into sb's pocket** jdm etw in die Tasche gleiten lassen **(b)** (= *mention casually*) einfließen lassen

➤ **slip off 1** VI sich wegschleichen, sich wegstehlen **2** VT SEP *clothes, shoes* abstreifen

➤ **slip on** VT SEP schlüpfen in (+*acc*); *dress, gloves also* überstreifen; *ring* aufziehen

➤ **slip out** VI **(a)** (= *leave unobtrusively*) kurz weggehen *or* rausgehen **(b)** (= *be revealed*) herauskommen; **the secret slipped out** das Geheimnis ist ihm/ihr *etc* herausgerutscht

➤ **slip past** VI = **slip by**

➤ **slip up** VI (*inf*: = *err*) sich vertun (*inf*) (*over, in* bei)

slip: **slipcover** N (*esp US*) Schonbezug *m*; **slip-ons** PL (*also* **slip-on shoes**) Slipper *pl*

slipper ['slɪpə^r] N Hausschuh *m*

slippery [ˈslɪpərɪ] ADJ **(a)** schlüpfrig; *rope, road, ground, shoes* glatt; *fish, mud* glitschig; **my hands were ~ with sweat** meine Hände waren ganz glitschig vor lauter Schweiß; **he's on the ~ slope** *(fig)* er ist auf der schiefen Bahn **(b)** *(pej inf)* person glatt, windig *(inf)*; **a ~ customer** ein aalglatter Kerl *(inf)*

slippy [ˈslɪpɪ] ADJ glatt

slip road [ˈslɪprəʊd] N *(Brit)* Zufahrtsstraße *f*; *(for entering motorway)* (Autobahn)auffahrt *f*; *(for leaving motorway)* (Autobahn)ausfahrt *f*

slipshod [ˈslɪpʃɒd] ADJ schludrig

slip-up [ˈslɪpʌp] N *(inf)* Schnitzer *m*; *(more serious)* Patzer *m*; **there's been a ~ somewhere** da muss irgendetwas schief gelaufen sein

slit [slɪt], *vb*: pret, ptp **slit** ◧ N Schlitz *m* ◨ VT (auf)schlitzen; **to ~ sb's throat** jdm die Kehle aufschlitzen

slither [ˈslɪðəʳ] VI rutschen; *(snake)* gleiten

sliver [ˈslɪvəʳ] N *(of wood, glass etc)* Splitter *m*; *(= thin slice)* Scheibchen *nt*

slob [slɒb] N *(inf)* Drecksau *f (inf)*

slobber [ˈslɒbəʳ] VI sabbeln *(also fig)*; *(dog)* geifern; **to ~ over sb** *(fig inf)* von jdm schwärmen; *(= kiss)* jdn abküssen; **to ~ over sth** *(fig inf)* etw anschmachten

slog [slɒg] *(inf)* ◧ N *(= effort)* Schinderei *f*, Plackerei *f (inf)* ◨ VI **to ~ at sth** *(= work)* an etw *(dat)* schuften *(inf)*; **to ~ away (at sth)** sich *(mit etw)* abrackern

slogan [ˈsləʊgən] N Slogan *m*; *(political also)* Parole *f*; *(= motto)* Motto *nt*

slop [slɒp] ◧ VI *(= spill)* (über)schwappen; **to ~ over (into sth)** überschwappen (in etw *acc*) ◨ VT *(= spill)* verschütten; *(= pour out)* schütten ◨ N **(a)** *(= tasteless food: also ~s)* Schlabber *m (inf)* **(b)** *(usu pl)* *(= waste)* Abwasser *nt*; *(= swill)* Schweinetrank *m*

slope [sləʊp] ◧ N **(a)** *(= angle)* Neigung *f*; *(esp downwards)* Gefälle *nt*; *(of roof)* Schräge *f* **(b)** *(= sloping ground)* (Ab)hang *m*; **on a ~** am Hang; **halfway up the ~** auf halber Höhe ◨ VT neigen, schräg (an)legen ◨ VI sich neigen; *(writing)* geneigt sein; **the picture is sloping to the left/right** das Bild hängt schief; **his handwriting ~s to the left** seine Handschrift ist nach links geneigt

➤ **slope down** VI sich neigen, abfallen

➤ **slope off** VI *(inf)* abziehen *(inf)*

➤ **slope up** VI *(road etc)* ansteigen

sloping [ˈsləʊpɪŋ] ADJ *hill, road (upwards)* ansteigend; *(downwards)* abfallend; *roof, floor* schräg; *shoulders* abfallend; *garden, field etc* am Hang; *(= not aligned)* schief

slop pail N Eimer *m* für Schmutzwasser

sloppily [ˈslɒpɪlɪ] ADV *(inf)* schlampig *(inf)*; *work* schlud(e)rig *(inf)*

sloppiness [ˈslɒpɪnɪs] N *(inf)* Schlampigkeit *f (inf)*; *(of work, writing)* Schlud(e)rigkeit *f (inf)*

sloppy [ˈslɒpɪ] ADJ (+ER) **(a)** *(= careless)* schlampig *(inf)*; *work, writing* schlud(e)rig *(inf)* **(b)** *(= sentimental)* rührselig

slosh [slɒʃ] *(inf)* ◧ VT *(= splash)* klatschen ◨ VI **to ~ (around)** *(liquid)* (herum)schwappen; **to ~ through mud/water** durch Matsch/Wasser waten

slot [slɒt] N *(= opening)* Schlitz *m*; *(= groove)* Rille *f*; *(Comput)* Steckplatz *m*; *(for aircraft to land etc)* Slot *m*; *(TV)* (gewohnte) Sendezeit *f*

➤ **slot in** ◧ VT SEP hineinstecken; **to slot sth into sth** etw in etw *(acc)* stecken ◨ VI sich einfügen lassen; **suddenly everything slotted into place** plötzlich passte alles zusammen

➤ **slot together** ◧ VI *(parts, object)* sich zusammenfügen lassen ◨ VT SEP *parts, object* zusammenfügen

slot machine N Münzautomat *m*; *(for gambling)* Spielautomat *m*

slouch [slaʊtʃ] ◧ N **(a)** *(= posture)* krumme Haltung; *(of shoulders)* Hängen *nt* **(b)** *(inf: = incompetent or lazy person)* Niete *f (inf)* ◨ VI *(= stand, sit)* herumhängen, sich lümmeln *(inf)*; *(= move)* latschen; **to ~ off** davonzockeln *(inf)*; **he was ~ed over his desk** er hing über seinem Schreibtisch

Slovak [ˈsləʊvæk] ◧ ADJ slowakisch ◨ N **(a)** Slowake *m*, Slowakin *f* **(b)** *(Ling)* Slowakisch *nt*

Slovakia [sləʊˈvækɪə] N die Slowakei

Slovak Republic N Slowakische Republik

Slovene [ˈsləʊviːn] ◧ ADJ slowenisch ◨ N **(a)** Slowene *m*, Slowenin *f* **(b)** *(Ling)* Slowenisch *nt*

Slovenia [sləʊˈviːnɪə] N Slowenien *nt*

Slovenian [sləʊˈviːnɪən] ADJ, N = **Slovene**

slovenly [ˈslʌvnlɪ] ADJ schlud(e)rig *(inf)*, schlampig *(inf)*

slow [sləʊ] ◧ ADJ (+ER) **(a)** langsam; *(= stupid)* begriffsstutzig; **it's ~ work** das braucht seine Zeit; **he's a ~ learner** er lernt langsam; **it was ~ going** es ging nur langsam voran; **to get off to a ~ start** *(race)* schlecht vom Start kommen; *(project)* nur langsam in Gang kommen; **to be ~ to do sth** sich *(dat)* mit etw Zeit lassen; **to be ~ in doing sth** sich *(dat)* Zeit damit lassen, etw zu tun; **he is ~ to make up his mind** er braucht lange, um sich zu entscheiden; **to be (20 minutes) ~** *(clock)* (20 Minuten) nachgehen

(b) *(Comm: = slack)* flau; **business is ~** das Geschäft ist flau *or* geht schlecht

(c) *(= unhurried)* ruhig

◨ ADV (+ER) langsam

◨ VI sich verlangsamen; *(= drive/walk more slowly)* langsamer fahren/gehen; *(inflation)* abnehmen

◨ VT verlangsamen

➤ **slow down** *or* **up** ◧ VI sich verlangsamen; *(= drive/walk more slowly)* langsamer fahren/gehen; **if you don't slow down** *or* **up you'll make yourself ill** Sie müssen zurückstecken, sonst werden Sie krank ◨ VT SEP *(lit)* verlangsamen; *engine* drosseln; *machine* herunterschalten; *(fig) project* verzögern; **you just slow me up** *or* **down** du hältst mich nur auf

slow: slowcoach N *(Brit inf)* Langweiler(in) *m(f)*; *(mentally)* Transuse *f (inf)*; **slowdown** N **(a)** Verlangsamung *f (in, of +gen)* **(b)** *(US: = go-slow)* Bummelstreik *m*; **slow lane** N *(Aut)* Kriechspur *f*

slowly [ˈsləʊlɪ] ADV langsam; **~ but surely** langsam aber sicher

slow: slow motion N Zeitlupe *f*; **in ~** in Zeitlupe; **slow-moving** ADJ sich (nur) langsam bewegend; *traffic* kriechend; *river* langsam fließend

slowness [ˈsləʊnɪs] N **(a)** Langsamkeit *f*; **their ~ to act** ihr Zaudern **(b)** *(= stupidity)* Begriffsstutzigkeit *f* **(c)** *(= inactivity: of party, film)* Langweiligkeit *f* **(d)** *(Comm: = slackness)* Flaute *f*

slowpoke [ˈsləʊpəʊk] N *(US inf)* = **slowcoach**

sludge [slʌdʒ] N Schlamm *m*, Matsch *m (inf)*; *(= sediment)* schmieriger Satz

slue [sluː] VTI *(US)* = **slew**[1]

slug[1] [slʌg] N Nacktschnecke *f*

slug[2] N *(inf)* **a ~ of whisky** ein Schluck *m* Whisky

sluggish [ˈslʌgɪʃ] ADJ träge *(also Med)*; *engine* lahm, langsam; *business, market, stock exchange* flau

sluggishly [ˈslʌgɪʃlɪ] ADV träge; *(Comm)* flau

sluggishness [ˈslʌgɪʃnɪs] N Trägheit *f (also Med)*; *(of engine)* Lahmheit *f*; **the ~ of the market** die Flaute am Markt

sluice [sluːs] ◧ N Schleuse *f*; *(Min)* (Wasch)rinne *f* ◨ VT ore waschen; **to ~ sth (down)** etw abspritzen ◨ VI **to ~ out** herausschießen

slum [slʌm] ◧ N *(usu pl: = area)* Slum *m*; *(= house)* Elendsquartier *nt* ◨ VTI *(inf: also ~ it)* primitiv leben; **we don't often see you (a)round here – I'm ~ming (it)** du lässt dich doch sonst kaum hier sehen! – ich will mich eben mal unters gemeine Volk mischen

slumber [ˈslʌmbəʳ] *(liter)* ◧ N Schlummer *m (geh)*, Schlaf *m* ◨ VI schlummern *(geh)*

slump [slʌmp] ◧ N *(in sth etw gen)* *(in numbers, popularity etc)* (plötzliche) Abnahme *f*; *(in production, sales)* Rückgang *m*; *(= state)* Tiefstand *m*; *(Fin)* Sturz *m*; *(of prices)* plötzliches Absinken; **~ in prices** Preissturz *m (of bei)*

◨ VI **(a)** *(also ~ off)* *(Fin, Comm)* *(prices)* stürzen, fallen; *(sales, production)* plötzlich zurückgehen; *(fig: morale etc)* sinken **(b)** *(= sink)* fallen, sinken; **he was ~ed over the wheel** er war über dem Steuer zusammengesackt; **he was ~ed on the floor** er lag in sich *(dat)* zusammengesunken auf dem Fußboden

slung [slʌŋ] PRET, PTP *of* **sling**

slunk [slʌŋk] PRET, PTP *of* **slink**

slur [slɜːʳ] ◧ N Makel *m*, Schandfleck *m*; *(= insult)* Beleidigung *f* ◨ VT undeutlich artikulieren; *words, syllable* (halb) verschlucken

slurp [slɜːp] ◧ VTI *(inf)* schlürfen ◨ N Schlürfen *nt*

slurred [slɜːd] ADJ undeutlich

slush [slʌʃ] N (Schnee)matsch m; (inf: = sentimental nonsense) Kitsch m

slushy ['slʌʃɪ] ADJ (+ER) snow matschig; (inf: = sentimental) kitschig

slut [slʌt] (inf) N (liederliche) Schlampe (inf)

sly [slaɪ] **1** ADJ (+ER) **(a)** (= cunning) schlau, gerissen **(b)** (= mischievous) look, wink verschmitzt; humour versteckt **2** N **on the ~** heimlich, still und leise (hum)

slyly ['slaɪlɪ] ADV **(a)** (= cunningly) schlau; say, look at listig **(b)** (= mischievously) verschmitzt

slyness ['slaɪnɪs] N **(a)** (= cunning) Schlauheit f, Gerissenheit f **(b)** (= mischievousness) Verschmitztheit f

smack [smæk] **1** N **(a)** (klatschender) Schlag; (= slap also) fester Klaps; (= sound) Klatschen nt; **you'll get a ~** du fängst gleich eine (inf) **(b)** (inf: = kiss) **to give sb a ~ on the cheek** jdn einen Schmatz auf die Backe geben (inf) **2** VT (= slap) knallen (inf); **to ~ a child** einem Kind eine runterhauen (inf); **I'll ~ your bottom, you'll get a ~ed bottom** ich versohl dir gleich den Hintern! (inf) **3** ADV direkt; **she ran ~ into the door** sie rannte rums! gegen die Tür (inf); **to be ~ in the middle of sth** mittendrin in etw (dat) sein; **the office was ~ in the middle of the building site** das Büro befand sich mitten auf der Baustelle

smackhead ['smækhed] N (sl) Heroinfixer(in) m(f)

small [smɔːl] **1** ADJ (+ER) klein; supply, stock gering; waist schmal; (= not much) reason, desire wenig; present, sum bescheiden; voice leise; **~ in size** von geringer Größe, klein; **a ~ number of people** eine geringe Anzahl von Leuten; **the ~est possible number of books** so wenig Bücher wie möglich; **~ shareholder** Kleinaktionär(in) m(f); **to feel ~** (fig) sich (ganz) klein und hässlich) vorkommen; **he/it made me feel pretty ~** da kam ich mir ziemlich klein vor; **a few ~ matters/problems** ein paar Kleinigkeiten **2** N **the ~ of the back** das Kreuz **3** ADV **to chop sth up ~** etw klein hacken

> Be careful! The German word **schmal** is not the most common translation for **small**.

small: **small arms** PL Handfeuerwaffen pl; **small business** N Kleinunternehmen nt; **small capitals** PL Kapitälchen pl; **small change** N Kleingeld nt; **small claims** PL (Comm, Jur) geringfügige Forderungen pl; **small claims court** N Zivilgericht nt (für Bagatellfälle); **small fry** PL (fig) kleine Fische pl (inf); **small hours** PL früher Morgen; **in the (wee) ~** in den frühen Morgenstunden

smallish ['smɔːlɪʃ] ADJ (eher) kleiner; **he is ~** er ist eher klein; **a ~ number of sth/people** eine geringe Anzahl an etw (dat)/ von Leuten

small: **small letter** N Kleinbuchstabe m; **small-minded** ADJ engstirnig

smallness ['smɔːlnɪs] N Kleinheit f; (of sum, present) Bescheidenheit f

small: **smallpox** N Pocken pl; **small print** N **the ~** das Kleingedruckte; **in ~** klein gedruckt; **small-scale** ADJ map, model in verkleinertem Maßstab; project klein angelegt; conflict begrenzt; industrialization in kleinem Rahmen; **~ enterprise** Kleinunternehmen nt; **~ integration** (Comput) niedriger Integrationsgrad; **small screen** N (TV) **on the ~** auf dem Bildschirm; **small-sized** ADJ klein; **small talk** N Smalltalk m; **to make ~** plaudern, Smalltalk machen; **small-time** ADJ (inf) mickerig; crook klein; **small-town** ADJ Kleinstadt-, kleinstädtisch

SMALL TOWN

In den USA wird mit dem Begriff **small town** jede Ortschaft mit bis zu 10.000 Einwohnern bezeichnet. Das Wort **village** wird in den Vereinigten Staaten für eine Kleinstadt selten verwendet, da der Begriff mit Europa oder eher mit der Dritten Welt assoziiert wird. Eine **small town** ist in der Vorstellung der Amerikaner normalerweise mit positiven Werten verbunden. Allerdings kann **small town** manchmal auch negative Seiten repräsentieren: so versteht man unter „small-town attitudes" vorurteilsbehaftete und engstirnige Ansichten.

smarmy ['smɑːmɪ] ADJ (+ER) (Brit inf) (= greasy) schmierig; (= ingratiating) kriecherisch (pej)

smart [smɑːt] **1** ADJ (+ER) **(a)** schick; person, clothes, car flott; society fein; appearance gepflegt; **the ~ set** die Schickeria (inf) **(b)** (= clever) clever (inf), schlau; trick raffiniert, clever (inf); (pej) person, answer superklug, neunmalklug (pej inf); (Comput, Mil) intelligent; **that wasn't very ~ (of you)** das war nicht besonders intelligent (von dir); **to get ~** (= get cheeky) frech kommen (with +dat) **(c)** (= quick) (blitz)schnell; pace, work rasch, flott (inf); work schnell, fix (inf); **and look ~ (about it)!** und zwar ein bisschen fix or plötzlich! (inf) **2** VI brennen; **to ~ from sth** from blow etc von etw brennen; (fig) unter etw (dat) leiden; **to ~ over sth** über etw (acc) gekränkt sein

smart: **smart alec(k)** N (inf) Schlauberger(in) m(f) (inf); **smartarse** ['smɑːtɑːs], (US) **smartass** ['smɑːtæs] (sl) **1** N Klugscheißer(in) m(f) (inf) **2** ADJ klugscheißerisch (inf); **smart card** N Chipkarte f; **smart drug** N bewusstseinsverändernde Droge

smarten ['smɑːtn] (also ~ up) **1** VT house, room herausputzen; appearance aufmöbeln (inf); **to ~ oneself up** (= dress up) sich in Schale werfen (inf); (= generally improve appearance) mehr Wert auf sein Äußeres legen; **you'd better ~ up your ideas** (inf) du solltest dich am Riemen reißen (inf) **2** VI (= dress up) sich in Schale werfen (inf); (= improve appearance) sich herausmachen

smartly ['smɑːtlɪ] ADV **(a)** (= elegantly) schick; dress also flott **(b)** (= cleverly) clever (inf), schlau **(c)** (= quickly) (blitz)schnell, fix (inf); walk rasch

smart money N (Fin) Investitionsgelder pl; **the ~ is on him winning** Insider setzen darauf, dass er gewinnt

smartness ['smɑːtnɪs] N **(a)** (= elegance) Schick m; (of appearance) Gepflegtheit f **(b)** (= cleverness) Cleverness f (inf), Schlauheit f

smash [smæʃ] **1** VT **(a)** (lit, fig) zerschlagen; window einschlagen; record haushoch schlagen; **I ~ed my glasses** mir ist die Brille kaputtgegangen **(b)** (= strike, also Tennis) schmettern **2** VI **(a)** (= break) zerschlagen, zerbrechen; **it ~ed into a thousand pieces** es (zer)sprang in tausend Stücke **(b)** (= crash) prallen; **the car ~ed into the wall** das Auto krachte gegen die Mauer; **the terrified animal ~ed through the fence** das verängstigte Tier durchbrach das Gatter **3** N **(a)** (= noise) Krachen nt; (of waves) Klatschen nt **(b)** (= collision) Unfall m; (esp with another vehicle) Zusammenstoß m **(c)** (= blow) Schlag m; (Tennis) Schmetterball m **(d)** (inf: also ~ hit) Riesenhit m
> **smash in** VT SEP einschlagen
> **smash up** **1** VT SEP zertrümmern; car kaputtfahren **2** VI kaputtgehen

smashed [smæʃt] ADJ PRED (inf: = drunk) total zu (inf)

smash hit N (inf) Superhit m (inf)

smashing ['smæʃɪŋ] ADJ (esp Brit inf) klasse inv, Klasse pred, dufte (all inf); **isn't it ~!** unheimlich dufte! (inf)

smattering ['smætərɪŋ] N **a ~ of French** ein paar Brocken Französisch

smear [smɪər] **1** N verschmierter Fleck; (fig) Verleumdung f; (Med) Abstrich m **2** VT **(a)** grease, ointment schmieren; (= spread) verschmieren; (= mark, make dirty) beschmieren; face, body einschmieren **(b)** (fig) person verunglimpfen; sb's name beschmutzen **3** VI (glass) verschmieren; (print) verschmiert or verwischt werden; (ballpoint pen) schmieren; (paint, ink) verlaufen

smell [smel], vb: pret, ptp **smelt** (esp Brit) or **smelled** **1** N Geruch m; (unpleasant also) Gestank m; (fragrant also) Duft m; **it has a nice ~** es riecht gut or angenehm; **there's a funny ~ in here** hier riecht es komisch; **to have** or **take a ~ at sth** an etw (acc) riechen **2** VT **(a)** (lit) riechen; **can** or **do you ~ burning?** riechst du, dass etwas brennt or (Cook) anbrennt? **(b)** (fig) danger wittern; **to ~ trouble** Ärger or Stunk (inf) kommen sehen; **to ~ a rat** (inf) Lunte or den Braten riechen **3** VI riechen; (unpleasantly also) stinken; (fragrantly also) duften; **to ~ of sth** (lit, fig) nach etw riechen; **his breath ~s** er hat Mundgeruch

smelly ['smelɪ] ADJ (+ER) übel riechend, stinkend; **it's ~ in here** hier drin stinkt es

smelt[1] [smelt] (*esp Brit*) PRET, PTP *of* **smell**

smelt[2] VT *ore* schmelzen; (= *refine*) verhütten

smile [smail] **1** N Lächeln *nt*; **to be all ~s** übers ganze Gesicht strahlen; **she gave a little ~** sie lächelte schwach; **to give sb a ~** jdm zulächeln; **take that ~ off your face!** hör auf, so zu grinsen! **2** VI lächeln; **he's always smiling** er lacht immer; **to ~ at sb** jdn anlächeln; (*cheerful person*) jdn anlachen; **to ~ at sth** über etw (*acc*) lächeln; **to ~ with relief** *etc* vor Erleichterung *etc* strahlen

smiley ['smaili] ADJ *face, person* freundlich

smiling ADJ, **smilingly** ADV ['smailiŋ, -li] lächelnd

smirk [smɜ:k] **1** N Grinsen *nt* **2** VI grinsen

smith [smiθ] N Schmied(in) *m(f)*

smithereens [ˌsmiðəˈriːnz] PL **to smash sth to ~** etw in tausend Stücke schlagen

smithy ['smiði] N Schmiede *f*

smitten ['smitn] ADJ **he's really ~ with her** (*inf*) er ist wirklich vernarrt in sie

smock [smɒk] N Kittel *m*; (*as top*) Hänger *m*

smog [smɒg] N Smog *m*

smoke [sməʊk] **1** N Rauch *m*; **to go up in ~** in Rauch (und Flammen) aufgehen; (*fig*) sich in Wohlgefallen auflösen; **to have a ~** eine rauchen **2** VT (a) *pipe, cigarette etc* rauchen (b) *bacon, fish etc* räuchern **3** VI rauchen; (*oil lamp etc*) qualmen; **do you mind if I ~?** stört es (Sie), wenn ich rauche?

smoke: **smoke alarm** N Rauchmelder *m*; **smoke bomb** N Rauchbombe *f*

smoked [sməʊkt] ADJ *bacon, fish* geräuchert

smoke: **smoke detector** N Rauchmelder *m*; **smoke-free** ['sməʊkfri:] ADJ *zone* rauchfrei

smokeless ['sməʊklɪs] ADJ *zone* rauchfrei; *fuel* rauchlos

smoker ['sməʊkə'] N Raucher(in) *m(f)*; **to be a heavy ~** stark rauchen

smoke: **smoke screen** N Rauchvorhang *m*; (*fig*) Deckmantel *m*, Vorwand *m*; **smoke signal** N Rauchzeichen *nt*; **smokestack** N Schornstein *m*

smoking ['sməʊkɪŋ] **1** ADJ rauchend **2** N Rauchen *nt*; **"no ~"** „Rauchen verboten"

smoking compartment, (*US*) **smoking car** N Raucherabteil *nt*

smoky ['sməʊkɪ] ADJ (+ER) *chimney, fire* rauchend; *room, atmosphere* verraucht; *flavour* rauchig; *colour* rauchfarben

smolder VI (*US*) = **smoulder**

smooch [smu:tʃ] (*inf*) **1** VI knutschen (*inf*) **2** N **to have a ~** rumknutschen (*inf*)

smooth [smu:ð] **1** ADJ (+ER) (a) glatt; *style of writing also* flüssig; *hair, gear change, whisky* weich; *sea* ruhig; *road, surface* eben; *outline, form* sanft; *motion, flight, crossing* ruhig; *flow* gleichmäßig; *paste* sämig; *flavour, coffee* mild; *beer* süffig; **as ~ as silk** seidenweich; **worn ~** *steps* glatt getreten; *knife* abgeschliffen; *tyre* abgefahren (b) *transition, functioning, relations* reibungslos (c) (= *polite: often pej*) *manners* glatt; *person also* aalglatt (*pej*); (= *unruffled*) kühl, cool (*inf*) **2** VT *surface* glätten, glatt machen; *dress, hair* glatt streichen; *wood* glatt hobeln; (*fig*) *feelings* beruhigen; **to ~ the way for sb/sth** jdm/einer Sache den Weg ebnen

➤ **smooth away** VT SEP glätten; (*fig*) *fears* besänftigen

➤ **smooth back** VT SEP *hair* zurückstreichen

➤ **smooth down** VT SEP glatt machen; *feathers, hair, dress* glatt streichen

➤ **smooth out** VT SEP *crease, surface* glätten; (*fig*) *difficulty* aus dem Weg räumen

➤ **smooth over** VT SEP (*fig*) *quarrel* in Ordnung bringen, geradebiegen (*inf*)

smoothly ['smu:ðlɪ] ADV *land, change gear* weich; *fit, talk* schön; *behave* aalglatt (*pej*), genau; **to run ~** (*engine*) ruhig laufen; (= *without problems*) **to go ~** glatt über die Bühne gehen; **to run ~** (*event*) reibungslos verlaufen

smoothness ['smu:ðnɪs] N (a) Glätte *f*; (*of whisky*) Weichheit *f*; (*of road, surface*) Ebenheit *f*; (*of paste*) Sämigkeit *f*; (*of coffee*) Milde *f* (b) (*of motion, flight, crossing*) Ruhe *f*; (*of takeoff, landing*) Sanftheit *f*; (*of flow*) Gleichmäßigkeit *f* (c) (*of transition, relations*) Reibungslosigkeit *f*

smooth-running ['smu:ð'rʌnɪŋ] ADJ *engine, car* ruhig laufend; *convention etc* reibungslos verlaufend

smother ['smʌðə'] **1** VT (a) *person, fire, weeds* ersticken; (*fig*) *criticism, yawn etc* unterdrücken (b) (= *cover*) bedecken, überschütten; **fruit ~ed in cream** Obst, das in Sahne schwimmt **2** VI ersticken

smoulder, (*US*) **smolder** ['sməʊldə'] VI (*lit, fig*) glimmen, schwelen; *actress* vor Sexappeal *m* ausstrahlen

smouldering, (*US*) **smoldering** ['sməʊldərɪŋ] ADJ (a) *fire, resentment* schwelend; *embers, cigarette* glimmend (b) (= *passionate*) *eyes* feurig; **a ~ look** ein glühender Blick

SMS (*Telec*) ABBR *of* **Short Message Service** SMS

smudge [smʌdʒ] **1** N Fleck *m*; (*of ink*) Klecks *m* **2** VT verwischen **3** VI verlaufen, verschmieren

smug [smʌg] ADJ (+ER) selbstgefällig; **~ satisfaction** eitle Selbstzufriedenheit

smuggle ['smʌgl] VTI (*lit, fig*) schmuggeln; **to ~ sb/sth in** jdn/ etw einschmuggeln; **to ~ sb/sth out** jdn/etw herausschmuggeln

smuggler ['smʌglə'] N Schmuggler(in) *m(f)*

smuggling ['smʌglɪŋ] N Schmuggel *m*

smugly ['smʌglɪ] ADV selbstgefällig

smugness ['smʌgnɪs] N Selbstgefälligkeit *f*

smut [smʌt] N (*fig*) Schmutz *m*

smutty ['smʌtɪ] ADJ (+ER) (*fig*) schmutzig

snack [snæk] N Imbiss *m*; **to have a ~** eine Kleinigkeit essen, einen Imbiss zu sich (*dat*) nehmen; **we just have a ~ for lunch** mittags essen wir nicht viel *or* groß (*inf*)

snack bar N Imbissstube *f*

snaffle ['snæfl] VT (*Brit inf*) sich (*dat*) unter den Nagel reißen (*inf*)

snag [snæg] **1** N (a) Haken *m*; **there's a ~** die Sache hat einen Haken; **what's the ~?** was ist das Problem?; **to run into *or* hit a ~** in Schwierigkeiten (*acc*) kommen (b) (= *flaw in clothes etc*) gezogener Faden **2** VT sich (*dat*) einen Faden ziehen; **I ~ged my tights** ich habe mir an den Strumpfhosen einen Faden gezogen

snail [sneɪl] N Schnecke *f*; **at a ~'s pace** im Schneckentempo

snail mail N (*hum*) Schneckenpost *f* (*inf*) (*im Gegensatz zur elektronischen Post*)

snake [sneɪk] N Schlange *f*

snakeskin ['sneɪkskɪn] ADJ Schlangenleder-, aus Schlangenleder

snap [snæp] **1** N (a) (= *sound*) Schnappen *nt*; (*with fingers*) Schnippen *nt*; (*of sth breaking*) Knacken *nt*; (= *click*) Klicken *nt* (b) (*Phot*) Schnappschuss *m* (c) (*Cards*) ≈ Schnippschnapp *nt* (d) **cold ~** Kälteeinbruch *m* **2** ADJ ATTR plötzlich, spontan **3** ADV **to go ~** (= *make sound*) schnapp machen; (*sth breaking*) knacken; (= *break*) (knackend) entzweibrechen **4** INTERJ **I bought a green one – ~!** (*Brit inf*) ich hab mir ein grünes gekauft – ich auch! **5** VT (a) *fingers* schnipsen mit; **to ~ a book shut** ein Buch zuklappen; **to ~ a purse shut** ein Portemonnaie zuschnappen lassen (b) (= *break*) zerbrechen; *bone* brechen (c) (*Phot*) knipsen **6** VI (a) (= *click*) (zu)schnappen, einschnappen; (= *crack, break*) zerbrechen; **to ~ shut** zuschnappen (b) (= *speak sharply*) bellen (*inf*), schnappen (*inf*); **to ~ at sb** jdn anpfeifen *or* anschnauzen (*inf*) (c) (*of dog, fish etc, fig*) schnappen (*at* nach)

(d) (*inf*: = *crack up*) durchdrehen (*inf*); **something ~ped (in him)** da hat (bei ihm) etwas ausgehakt (*inf*)

➤ **snap off** VT SEP (= *break off*) abbrechen

➤ **snap out** 🔢 VT SEP **to snap sb out of sth** jdn aus etw herausreißen 🔢 VI **to snap out of sth** sich aus etw herausreißen; **snap out of it!** reiß dich zusammen *or* am Riemen! (*inf*)

➤ **snap up** VT SEP (*lit, fig*) wegschnappen

snappy ['snæpɪ] ADJ (+ER) **(a)** (*inf*: = *quick*) flott (*inf*), zackig (*inf*); **and be ~ about it!, and make it ~!** und zwar ein bisschen flott *or* dalli! (*inf*) **(b)** (*fig*) *person* bissig **(c)** (*inf*) *phrase* zündend

snapshot ['snæpʃɒt] N Schnappschuss *m*

snare [snɛə'] N (*lit, fig*: = *trap*) Falle *f*

snarl [snɑːl] 🔢 N Knurren *nt no pl*; **..., he said with a ~ ...,** sagte er knurrend 🔢 VI knurren; **to ~ at sb** jdn anknurren

➤ **snarl up** (*inf*) VT SEP *traffic, system* durcheinander bringen; *plan also* vermasseln (*inf*)

snatch [snætʃ] 🔢 N (= *snippet*) Stück *nt*, Brocken *m*; (*of conversation*) Fetzen *m*; (*of music*) ein paar Takte 🔢 VT **(a)** (= *grab*) greifen; **to ~ sth from sb** jdm etw entreißen; **to ~ sth out of sb's hand** jdm etw aus der Hand reißen **(b)** *some sleep etc* ergattern; **to ~ a quick meal** schnell etwas essen; **to ~ defeat from the jaws of victory** einen sicheren Sieg in eine Niederlage verwandeln **(c)** (*inf*) *steal, money* klauen (*inf*); *handbag* aus der Hand reißen; (= *kidnap*) entführen 🔢 VI greifen (*at* nach); **don't ~!** nicht grapschen! (*inf*)

➤ **snatch away** VT SEP wegreißen (*sth from sb* jdm etw)

snazzy ADJ (+ER), **snazzily** ADV ['snæzɪ, -lɪ] (*dated inf*) flott

sneak [sniːk] 🔢 N Schleicher(in) *m(f)* 🔢 VT **he ~ed a cake off the counter** er klaute einen Kuchen vom Tresen (*inf*); **to ~ sth into a room** etw in ein Zimmer schmuggeln; **to ~ a look at sb/sth** auf jdn/etw schielen 🔢 VI **to ~ about** herumschleichen; **to ~ away** *or* **off** sich wegschleichen; **to ~ in** sich einschleichen; **to ~ past sb** (sich) an jdm vorbeischleichen; **to ~ up on sb** sich an jdn heranschleichen

sneakers ['sniːkəz] PL (*esp US*) Freizeitschuhe *pl*

sneaking ['sniːkɪŋ] ADJ ATTR geheim *attr*; **to have a ~ feeling that ...** ein schleichendes Gefühl haben, dass ...

sneak preview N (*of film etc*) Vorschau *f*; (*of new car etc*) Vorbesichtigung *f*

sneaky ['sniːkɪ] ADJ (+ER) (*pej inf*) gewieft (*inf*), raffiniert

sneer [snɪə'] 🔢 N (= *expression*) spöttisches *or* höhnisches Lächeln; (= *remark*) spöttische *or* höhnische Bemerkung 🔢 VI spotten; (= *look sneering*) spöttisch *or* höhnisch grinsen; **to ~ at sb** jdn verhöhnen

sneering ADJ, **sneeringly** ADV ['snɪərɪŋ, -lɪ] höhnisch, spöttisch

sneeze [sniːz] 🔢 N Nieser *m*; **~s** Niesen *nt* 🔢 VI niesen; **not to be ~d at** nicht zu verachten

snicker ['snɪkə'] N, VI = **snigger**

snide [snaɪd] ADJ abfällig

sniff [snɪf] 🔢 N Schniefen *nt no pl* (*inf*); (*disdainful*) Naserümpfen *nt no pl*; (*of dog*) Schnüffeln *nt no pl*; **have a ~ at this** riech mal hieran 🔢 VT etw riechen, schnuppern an (+*dat*) (*inf*); *air* riechen, schnuppern; *glue* schnüffeln (*inf*); *drugs* sniffen (*sl*); (*fig*: = *detect*) wittern 🔢 VI (*person*) schniefen (*inf*); (*dog*) schnüffeln; **to ~ at sth** (*lit*) an etw (*dat*) schnuppern; **not to be ~ed at** nicht zu verachten

➤ **sniff around** (*inf*) VI (*for information*) herumschnüffeln (*inf*)

➤ **sniff out** VT SEP (*lit, fig inf*) aufspüren

sniffle ['snɪfl] N, VI = **snuffle**

snigger ['snɪgə'] 🔢 N Kichern *nt*, Gekicher *nt* 🔢 VI kichern (*at, about* wegen)

snip [snɪp] 🔢 N **(a)** (= *cut, cutting action*) Schnitt *m*; (= *sound*) Schnipsen *nt no pl* **(b)** (*esp Brit inf*) **at only £2 it's a real ~** für nur £ 2 ist es unheimlich günstig 🔢 VT schnippeln (*inf*); **to ~ sth off** etw abschnippeln (*inf*) 🔢 VI **to ~ at** schnippeln an (+*dat*)

sniper ['snaɪpə'] N Heckenschütze *m*/-schützin *f*

snippet ['snɪpɪt] N Stückchen *nt*; (*of paper also*) Schnipsel *m or nt*; (*of information*) (Bruch)stück *nt*; **~s of (a) conversation** Gesprächsfetzen *pl*

snippy ['snɪpɪ] ADJ (*US inf*) *person, tone* schnippisch

---

snivel ['snɪvl] VI heulen, flennen (*inf*)

snivelling, (*US*) **sniveling** ['snɪvlɪŋ] ADJ heulend, flennend (*inf*)

snob [snɒb] N Snob *m*

snobbery ['snɒbərɪ] N Snobismus *m*

snobbish ['snɒbɪʃ] ADJ snobistisch, versnobt (*inf*); *place* für Snobs; **to be ~ about sth** bei etw wählerisch sein

snog [snɒg] (*Brit inf*) 🔢 N Knutscherei *f* (*inf*); **to have a ~ with sb** mit jdm rumknutschen (*inf*) 🔢 VI rumknutschen (*inf*) 🔢 VT abknutschen (*inf*)

snooker ['snuːkə'] N Snooker *nt*

snoop [snuːp] 🔢 N **(a)** = **snooper (b)** **I'll have a ~ around** ich gucke mich mal (ein bisschen) um 🔢 VI schnüffeln; **to ~ about** (*Brit*) *or* **around** herumschnüffeln

snooper ['snuːpə'] N Schnüffler(in) *m(f)*

snooty ['snuːtɪ] ADJ (+ER), **snootily** ['snuːtɪlɪ] ADV (*inf*) hochnäsig

snooze [snuːz] 🔢 N Schläfchen *nt*, Nickerchen *nt*; **to have a ~** ein Schläfchen machen 🔢 VI dösen, ein Nickerchen machen

snore [snɔː'] N *nt no pl* 🔢 VI schnarchen

snoring ['snɔːrɪŋ] N Schnarchen *nt*

snorkel ['snɔːkl] 🔢 N Schnorchel *m* 🔢 VI schnorcheln

snorkelling, (*US*) **snorkeling** ['snɔːkəlɪŋ] N Schnorcheln *nt*

snort [snɔːt] 🔢 N Schnauben *nt no pl*; (*of boar*) Grunzen *nt no pl*; **with a ~ of rage** wutschnaubend; **he gave a ~ of rage** er schnaubte vor Wut 🔢 VI schnauben; (*boar*) grunzen 🔢 VT **(a)** (*person*) schnauben **(b)** *drugs* sniffen (*sl*)

snot [snɒt] N (*inf*) Rotz *m* (*inf*)

snotty ['snɒtɪ] ADJ (+ER) (*inf*) (*lit, fig*) rotzig (*inf*); (= *snooty also*) pampig (*inf*); *child* rotznäsig (*inf*)

snotty-nosed ['snɒtɪnəʊzd] ADJ rotznäsig (*inf*)

snout [snaʊt] N (*of animal*) Schnauze *f*; (*of pig also, of insect*) Rüssel *m*

snow [snəʊ] 🔢 N Schnee *m*; (= *~fall*) Schneefall *m*; **as white as ~** schneeweiß 🔢 VI schneien

➤ **snow in** VT SEP (*usu pass*) **to be** *or* **get snowed in** einschneien

➤ **snow under** VT SEP (*inf: usu pass*) **to be snowed under** (*with work*) reichlich eingedeckt sein; (*with requests*) überhäuft werden

snow: snowball 🔢 N Schneeball *m* 🔢 VI eskalieren; **opposition to the referendum just ~ed** die Opposition gegen die Volksabstimmung wuchs lawinenartig an; **snow blindness** N Schneeblindheit *f*; **snowboard** 🔢 N Snowboard *nt* 🔢 VI Snowboard fahren; **snowboarding** N Snowboarding *nt*; **snowbound** ADJ eingeschneit; **snowcapped** ADJ schneebedeckt; **snow-clad** (*poet*), **snow-covered** ADJ verschneit; **snowdrift** N Schneewehe *f*; **snowdrop** N Schneeglöckchen *nt*; **snowfall** N Schneefall *m*; **snowflake** N Schneeflocke *f*; **snowman** N Schneemann *m*; **snowmobile** N Schneemobil *nt*; **snowplough**, (*US*) **snowplow** N (*also Ski*) Schneepflug *m*; **snowslide** N (*US*) Schneerutsch *m*; **snowstorm** N Schneesturm *m*; **snow-white** ADJ schneeweiß

snowy ['snəʊɪ] ADJ (+ER) **(a)** *weather, region* schneereich; *hills* verschneit **(b)** (= *white as snow*) schneeweiß

SNP ABBR *of* **Scottish National Party**

snub [snʌb] 🔢 N Brüskierung *f* 🔢 VT **(a)** *person* brüskieren; *subordinate, pupil* (*verbally*) über den Mund fahren (+*dat*); *suggestion, proposal* kurz abtun; *offer, request* ablehnen **(b)** (= *ignore*) schneiden

snub nose N Stupsnase *f*

snuff [snʌf] 🔢 N Schnupftabak *m* 🔢 VT *candle* (*also ~ out*) auslöschen; (*fig*) *revolt* ersticken

snuffle ['snʌfl] 🔢 N Schniefen *nt no pl*; **to have the ~s** (*inf*) einen leichten Schnupfen haben 🔢 VI (*person, animal*) schnüffeln; (*with cold, from crying also*) schniefen (*inf*)

snug [snʌg] ADJ (+ER) (= *cosy, comfortable*) behaglich, gemütlich; (= *cosy and warm*) behaglich warm; (= *close-fitting*) gut sitzend *attr*; (= *tight*) eng; **to be ~ in bed** es im Bett behaglich warm haben

snuggle ['snʌgl] VI sich schmiegen, sich kuscheln; **to ~ up (to sb)** sich (an jdn) anschmiegen *or* ankuscheln; **I like to ~ up with a book** ich mache es mir gern mit einem Buch gemütlich

snugly ['snʌglɪ] ADV **(a)** (= *cosily*) gemütlich, behaglich **(b)** (= *tightly*) *close* fest; *fit* gut

so [səʊ] 🔢 ADV **(a)** so; *pleased, relieved, hope, wish* sehr; *love, hate* so sehr; **so much tea** so viel Tee; **so many flies** so viele

Fliegen; **he was so stupid (that)** er war so *or* dermaßen dumm(, dass); **not so ... as** nicht so ... wie; **I am not so stupid as to believe that** *or* **that I believe that** so dumm bin ich nicht, dass ich das glaube(n würde); **would you be so kind as to open the door?** wären Sie bitte so freundlich und würden die Tür öffnen?; **how are things? – not so bad!** wie gehts? – nicht schlecht!; **that's so true** das ist ja so wahr; **I'm so very tired** ich bin ja so müde; **it would be so much better/nicer** *etc* es wäre so viel besser/netter *etc*; **so much the better (for sb)** umso besser (für jdn); **that's so kind of you** das ist wirklich sehr nett von Ihnen; **so it was that ...** so kam es, dass ...; **and so it was** und so war es auch; **by so doing he has ...** dadurch hat er ..., indem er das tat, hat er ...; **and so on** *or* **forth** und so weiter

(b) *(replacing longer sentence)* da, es; **I hope so** hoffentlich; *(emphatic)* das hoffe ich doch sehr; **I think so** ich glaube schon; **I never said so** das habe ich nie gesagt; **I told you so** ich habe es dir doch *or* ja gesagt; **why should I do it? – because I say so** warum muss ich das tun? – weil ich es sage, darum; **will you do it? – I suppose so** machen Sie es? – na ja, meinetwegen; **can I do it like that? – I suppose so** kann ich es so machen? – ich glaube schon; **so I believe** ja, ich glaube schon; **so I see** ja, das sehe ich; **it may be so** es kann schon sein; **so be it** nun gut; **if so** wenn ja; **he said he would finish it this week, and so he did** er hat gesagt, er würde es diese Woche fertig machen und das hat er auch (gemacht); **how** *or* **why did** *etc* ... – (ja) tatsächlich; **he's a nice chap – so he is** er ist ein netter Kerl – ja, wirklich

(c) *(unspecified amount)* **how high is it? – oh, about so high** *(accompanied by gesture)* wie hoch ist das? – oh, ungefähr so; **how long will it take? – a week or so** wie lange dauert das? – ungefähr eine Woche; **50 or so** etwa 50

(d) *(= likewise)* auch; **so am/would/do/could** *etc* **I** ich auch; **he's wrong and so are you** ihr irrt euch beide

(e) he walked past and didn't so much as look at me er ging vorbei, ohne mich auch nur anzusehen; **he didn't say so much as thank you** er hat nicht einmal danke gesagt; **so much for that!** *(inf)* das wärs ja wohl gewesen! *(inf)*; **so much for him** *(inf)* das war ja wohl nichts mit ihm! *(inf)*; **so much for our new car** aus der Traum vom neuen Auto; **so much for his promises** und er hat solche Versprechungen gemacht

② CONJ **(a)** *(expressing purpose)* damit; **we hurried so as not to be late** wir haben uns beeilt, um nicht zu spät zu kommen **(b)** *(= therefore in questions, exclamations)* also; **he refused to move so (that) finally the police had to carry him away** er weigerte sich wegzugehen, sodass ihn die Polizei schließlich wegtragen musste; **I told him to leave and so he did** ich habe ihm gesagt, er solle gehen und das hat er auch getan; **so you see** ... wie du siehst ...; **so you're Spanish?** Sie sind also Spanier(in)?; **so there you are!** da steckst du also!; **so what did you do?** und was haben Sie (da) gemacht?; **so (what)?** *(inf)* (na) und?; **I'm not going, so there!** *(inf)* ich geh nicht, fertig, aus!

soak [səʊk] **①** VT **(a)** *(= wet)* durchnässen **(b)** *(= steep)* einweichen *(in* in *+dat)* **②** VI **leave it to ~** weichen Sie es ein; **to ~ in a bath** sich einweichen *(inf)*; **rain has ~ed through the ceiling** der Regen ist durch die Decke gesickert; **the coffee was ~ing into the carpet** der Kaffee saugte sich in den Teppich **③** N **give the washing a good ~** lassen Sie die Wäsche gut einweichen; **I had a long ~ in the bath** ich habe lange in der Wanne gelegen

➤ **soak in** VI *(stain, dye etc)* einziehen

➤ **soak up** VT SEP *liquid, information* aufsaugen; *sunshine* genießen; *sound, money* schlucken; *atmosphere* in sich *(acc)* hineinsaugen

soaked [səʊkt] ADJ *(= drenched)* durchnässt; **her dress was ~** ihr Kleid war klatschnass *(inf)* or völlig durchnässt; **his T-shirt was ~ in sweat** sein T-Shirt war schweißgetränkt; **to be ~ to the skin, to be ~ through** bis auf die Haut nass sein

soaking [ˈsəʊkɪŋ] **①** ADJ *person* klitschnass; *object also* triefend **②** ADV **~ wet** triefend nass, klitschnass **③** N *(= steeping)* Einweichen *nt no indef art*

so-and-so [ˈsəʊənsəʊ] N *(inf)* **(a)** *(= unspecified person)* Soundso *no art*; **~ up at the shop** Herr/Frau Soundso im Laden **(b)** *(pej)* **you old ~** du bist vielleicht einer/eine

soap [səʊp] **①** N **(a)** Seife *f* **(b)** *(= ~ opera)* Seifenoper *f (inf)*, Soap *f (inf)* **②** VT einseifen

soap: soapbox N **to get up on one's ~** *(fig)* Volksreden *pl* halten; **soap opera** N *(TV, Rad: inf)* Seifenoper *f (inf)*, Soap-Opera *f (inf)*; **soap powder** N Seifenpulver *nt*

soapy [ˈsəʊpɪ] ADJ (+ER) seifig; **~ water** Seifenwasser *nt*

soar [sɔːʳ] VI **(a)** *(also ~ up)* aufsteigen **(b)** *(fig)* *(building, tower)* hochragen; *(cost, profit)* hochschnellen; *(popularity, reputation, hopes)* einen Aufschwung nehmen; *(morale, spirits)* einen Aufschwung bekommen

soaring [ˈsɔːrɪŋ] ADJ *bird, plane* aufsteigend; *imagination* hochfliegend; *popularity, reputation* schnell zunehmend; *prices* in die Höhe schnellend; *inflation* unaufhaltsam; *unemployment* hochschnellend; *hopes* wachsend

sob [sɒb] **①** N Schluchzer *m*, Schluchzen *nt no pl*; **..., he said with a ~ ...** ..., sagte er schluchzend **②** VTI schluchzen *(with vor +dat)*

➤ **sob out** VT SEP *story* schluchzend erzählen; **to sob one's heart out** sich *(dat)* die Seele aus dem Leib weinen

sobbing [ˈsɒbɪŋ] **①** N Schluchzen *nt* **②** ADJ schluchzend

sober [ˈsəʊbəʳ] ADJ *(= not drunk, advice, facts)* nüchtern; *expression, mood, occasion* ernst; *(= not bright or showy)* schlicht, dezent; *colour, suit* gedeckt

➤ **sober up** **①** VT SEP *(lit)* nüchtern machen **②** VI *(lit)* nüchtern werden

sobering [ˈsəʊbərɪŋ] ADJ ernüchternd

soberly [ˈsəʊbəlɪ] ADV nüchtern; *behave* vernünftig; *dress, furnish* schlicht, dezent

sob story N *(inf)* rührselige Geschichte *(inf)*

so-called [ˈsəʊˈkɔːld] ADJ so genannt; *(= supposed)* angeblich

soccer [ˈsɒkəʳ] N Fußball *m*; **~ player** *(US)* Fußballer(in) *m(f)*, Fußballspieler(in) *m(f)*

sociable [ˈsəʊʃəbl] ADJ *(= gregarious)* gesellig; *(= friendly)* freundlich

social [ˈsəʊʃəl] ADJ **(a)** *(= relating to community, Admin, Biol, Pol)* sozial; *structure, development, evil also, life, status, event* gesellschaftlich; *visit* privat; *behaviour* in Gesellschaft; **~ order/system** Gesellschafts- *or* Sozialordnung *f*/-system *nt*; **~ reform/policy** Sozialreform *f*/-politik *f*; **~ justice** soziale Gerechtigkeit; **to be a ~ outcast/misfit** ein sozialer Außenseiter/eine soziale Außenseiterin sein; **to be sb's ~ inferior/superior** gesellschaftlich unter/über jdm stehen; **a room for ~ functions** ein Gesellschaftsraum *m*; *(larger)* ein Saal *m* für Gesellschaften; **there isn't much ~ life around here** hier in der Gegend wird gesellschaftlich nicht viel geboten; **how's your ~ life these days?** *(inf)* und was treibst du so privat? *(inf)*; **to have an active** *or* **a good ~ life** ein ausgefülltes Privatleben haben; **to be a ~ smoker** nur in Gesellschaft rauchen; **a ~ acquaintance** ein Bekannter, eine Bekannte **(b)** *(= gregarious)* evening, person gesellig

social: social anthropology N Sozialanthropologie *f*; **social climber** N Emporkömmling *m (pej)*, sozialer Aufsteiger, soziale Aufsteigerin; **social club** N Verein *m*; **social costs** PL *(Econ)* gesamtwirtschaftliche Kosten *pl*; **social democracy** N Sozialdemokratie *f*; **social democrat** N Sozialdemokrat(in) *m(f)*; **social exclusion** N sozialer Ausschluss

socialism [ˈsəʊʃəlɪzəm] N Sozialismus *m*

socialist [ˈsəʊʃəlɪst] **①** ADJ sozialistisch **②** N Sozialist(in) *m(f)*

socialite [ˈsəʊʃəlaɪt] N *(inf)* Angehörige(r) *mf* der Schickeria *or* der feinen Gesellschaft

socialize [ˈsəʊʃəlaɪz] VI **to ~ with sb** *(= meet socially)* mit jdm gesellschaftlich verkehren; *(= chat to)* sich mit jdm unterhalten

socially [ˈsəʊʃəlɪ] ADV gesellschaftlich; *deprived etc* sozial; *meet* privat; **~ aware** sozialbewusst; **to know sb ~** jdn privat kennen

social: social science N Sozialwissenschaft *f*; **social security** N *(Brit)* Sozialhilfe *f*; *(US)* Sozialversicherungsleistungen *pl*; *(= scheme)* Sozialversicherung *f*; **to be on ~** *(Brit)* Sozialhilfeempfänger(in) sein; *(US)*

Sozialversicherungsleistungen erhalten; ~ **payments** (*Brit*) ≈ Sozialhilfe *f*; (*US*) Sozialversicherungsbezüge *pl*

social: **social services** PL Sozialdienste *pl*, soziale Einrichtungen *pl*; **social studies** N SING or PL ≈ Gemeinschaftskunde *f*; **social work** N Sozialarbeit *f*; ~ **training** Gesellschaft *f*; (*debating, dramatic etc*) (*Sch*) Sozialarbeiter(in) *m(f)*

society [sə'saɪətɪ] N (a) (= *social community, high* ~) die Gesellschaft (b) (= *club, organization*) Verein *m*; (*learned, Comm*) Gesellschaft *f*; (*debating, dramatic etc*) (*Sch*) Arbeitsgemeinschaft *f*; (*Univ*) Klub *m*

society IN CPDS Gesellschafts-

socio- [səʊsɪəʊ-] PREF sozio-

sociological ADJ [,səʊsɪə'lɒdʒɪkəl] soziologisch

sociologist [,səʊsɪ'ɒlədʒɪst] N Soziologe *m*, Soziologin *f*

sociology [,səʊsɪ'ɒlədʒɪ] N Soziologie *f*

sock[1] [sɒk] N Socke *f*; (*knee-length*) Kniestrumpf *m*; **to pull one's ~s up** (*Brit inf*) sich am Riemen reißen (*inf*); **put a ~ in it!** (*Brit inf*) hör auf damit!; **to work one's ~s off** (*inf*) bis zum Umkippen arbeiten (*inf*); **this will knock** *or* **blow your ~s off** (*inf*) das wird dich umhauen

sock[2] VT (*inf*: = *hit*) hauen (*inf*); **he ~ed her right in the eye** er verpasste ihr eine aufs Auge (*inf*)

socket ['sɒkɪt] N (a) (*of eye*) Augenhöhle *f*; (*of joint*) Gelenkpfanne *f*; **to pull sb's arm out of its ~** jdm den Arm auskugeln (b) (*Elec*) Steckdose *f*; (*Mech*) Fassung *f*

sod[1] [sɒd] N (= *turf*) Grassode *f*

sod[2] (*Brit inf*) **1** N Sau *f* (*inf*); **the poor ~s** die armen Schweine (*inf*) **2** VT ~ **it!** verdammte Scheiße! (*inf*); ~ **him** der kann mich mal (*inf*) *or* mal am Arsch lecken (*vulg*)!

➤ **sod off** VI (*Brit inf*) Leine ziehen (*inf*); **sod off!** zieh Leine, du Arsch! (*vulg*)

soda ['səʊdə] N (a) (*Chem*) Soda *nt*; (= *caustic* ~) Ätznatron *nt* (b) (= *drink*) Soda(wasser) *nt*

sod all N (*Brit inf*: = *nothing*) rein gar nichts

soda: **soda siphon** N Siphon *m*; **soda water** N Sodawasser *nt*

sodden ['sɒdn] ADJ durchnässt

sodding ['sɒdɪŋ] (*Brit inf*) **1** ADJ verflucht (*inf*), Scheiß- (*inf*); **what a ~ nuisance** verdammte Scheiße (*inf*) **2** ADV verdammt (*inf*), verflucht (*inf*)

sodium ['səʊdɪəm] N Natrium *nt*

sodium: **sodium bicarbonate** N Natron *nt*, doppeltkohlensaures Natrium; **sodium chloride** N Natriumchlorid *nt*, Kochsalz *nt*

sodomy ['sɒdəmɪ] N Analverkehr *m*

Be careful! **sodomy** *is not translated by the German word* **Sodomie**.

sofa ['səʊfə] N Sofa *nt*, Couch *f*; ~ **bed** Sofabett *nt*

soft [sɒft] **1** ADJ (+ER) (a) weich; *skin* zart; *hair* seidig; (*pej*: = *flabby*) *muscle* schlaff; *drink* alkoholfrei; ~ **cheese** Weichkäse *m*; ~ **porn film/magazine** weicher Porno (b) (= *gentle, not harsh*) sanft; *light, music* gedämpft; (= *not loud*) leise; *breeze* leicht (c) (= *weak*) *character, stocks, economy* schwach; *prices* instabil; *market* nachgiebig; *treatment* nachsichtig; *punishment* mild(e); **to be ~ with** *or* **on sb** jdm gegenüber nachgiebig sein (d) (= *not tough*) verweichlicht; *liberalism* gemäßigt (e) (= *easy*) *job, life* bequem; **that's a ~ option** das ist der Weg des geringsten Widerstands (f) (= *kind, warm*) *smile* warm; **he had another, ~er side to him** er hatte noch eine andere, gefühlvollere Seite; **to have a ~ spot for sb** (*inf*) eine Schwäche für jdn haben **2** N ~**s** (*St Ex*) Nahrungsmittel *pl*

soft: **softball** N Softball *m*; **soft-boiled** ADJ *egg* weich (gekocht); **soft-centred** ADJ mit Cremefüllung

soften ['sɒfn] **1** VT weich machen; *water also* enthärten; *light, sound, colour* dämpfen; *effect, reaction, tone* mildern; *outline* weicher machen; *image* weich zeichnen; *voice* sanfter machen; *opposition, stance* schwächen; *impact* abschwächen **2** VI (*material, person, heart*) weich werden; (*voice, look*) sanft werden; (*anger, resistance*) nachlassen; (*outlines*) weicher werden

➤ **soften up** **1** VT SEP (a) (*lit*) weich machen; *opposition* milde stimmen; (*by flattery etc*) schmeicheln (+*dat*); (*by bullying*) einschüchtern; *enemy* zermürben **2** VI (*material*) weich werden; (*person, attitude*) nachgiebiger werden

softener ['sɒfnə'] N (= *fabric* ~) Weichspüler *m*

softening ['sɒfnɪŋ] N (a) (*lit*) Weichmachen *nt* (b) (*fig*: *of person*) Erweichen *nt*; **there has been a ~ of his attitude** er ist nachgiebiger geworden

soft: **soft focus** N (*Film, Phot*) Weichzeichnung *f*; **soft fruit** N (*Brit*) Beerenobst *nt*; **soft furnishings** PL (*Brit*) Vorhänge, Teppiche, Kissen etc; **soft-hearted** ADJ weichherzig

softie ['sɒftɪ] N (*inf*) (*too tender-hearted*) gutmütiger Trottel (*inf*); (*sentimental*) sentimentaler Typ (*inf*); (*effeminate, cowardly*) Weichling *m* (*inf*)

softly ['sɒftlɪ] ADV (a) (= *gently*) sanft; (= *not loud*) leise; *rain, blow* sacht; **to be ~ spoken** eine angenehme Stimme haben; ~ **lit** gedämpft beleuchtet (b) (= *leniently*) nachsichtig

softness ['sɒftnɪs] N (a) Weichheit *f*; (*of skin*) Zartheit *f*; (*of hair*) Seidigkeit *f* (b) (= *gentleness*) Sanftheit *f*; (*of light*) Gedämpftheit *f*; (*of music*) leiser Klang

soft: **soft-spoken** ADJ *person* leise sprechend *attr*; **to be ~** eine angenehme Stimme haben; **soft target** N leichte Beute; **soft top** N (*esp US Aut*) Kabriolett *nt*; **soft toy** N (*Brit*) Stofftier *nt*; **software** N Software *f*; **software company** N Softwarehaus *nt*; **software package** N Softwarepaket *nt*

softy N (*inf*) = **softie**

sogginess ['sɒgɪnɪs] N triefende Nässe; (*of food*) Matschigkeit *f* (*inf*); (*of cake, bread*) Klitschigkeit *f*

soggy ['sɒgɪ] ADJ (+ER) durchnässt, triefnass; *soil* durchweicht; *food, vegetables* matschig (*inf*); *cake, bread* klitschig; **a ~ mess** eine Matsche

soil[1] [sɔɪl] N Erde *f*, Boden *m*; **native/British ~** heimatlicher/britischer Boden, heimatliche/britische Erde

soil[2] VT (*lit*) schmutzig machen; (*fig*) *reputation* beschmutzen

soiled [sɔɪld] ADJ schmutzig; *goods* verschmutzt; *sanitary towel* gebraucht

soiling ['sɔɪlɪŋ] N Verschmutzung *f*

solace ['sɒlɪs] N Trost *m*

solar ['səʊlə'] ADJ Sonnen-, Solar-; ~ **power/radiation** Sonnenkraft *f*/-strahlung *f*

solar: **solar eclipse** N Sonnenfinsternis *f*; **solar energy** N Sonnenenergie *f*

solarium [səʊ'lɛərɪəm] N, *pl* **solaria** [səʊ'lɛərɪə] Solarium *nt*

solar system N Sonnensystem *nt*

sold [səʊld] PRET, PTP *of* **sell**

soldier ['səʊldʒə'] N Soldat(in) *m(f)*

sole[1] [səʊl] **1** N Sohle *f* **2** VT besohlen

sole[2] N (= *fish*) Seezunge *f*

sole[3] ADJ *reason* einzig; *responsibility, owner* alleinig; *use* ausschließlich; **with the ~ exception of …** mit alleiniger Ausnahme +*gen* …; **for the ~ purpose of …** einzig und allein zu dem Zweck +*gen* …

solely ['səʊllɪ] ADV (einzig und) allein, nur

solemn ['sɒləm] ADJ feierlich; *face, mood, music also, person, plea, warning* ernst; *promise, duty* heilig

solemnity [sə'lemnɪtɪ] N Feierlichkeit *f*; (*of face, mood, music also, person, plea, warning*) Ernst *m*; (*of promise, duty*) heiliger Ernst

solemnly ['sɒləmlɪ] ADV feierlich; *walk* würdevoll; *look* ernst; *say* ernsthaft; *promise* hoch und heilig; *swear* bei allem, was einem heilig ist

sole: **sole proprietor** N (*US*) Einzelunternehmer(in) *m(f)*; **sole retailer** N (*Brit*) selbstständiger Einzelhändler; **sole rights** PL Alleinrechte *pl*; **sole trader** N (*Brit*) Einzelunternehmer(in) *m(f)*

soliciting [səˈlɪsɪtɪŋ] N Aufforderung *f* zur Unzucht

solicitor [səˈlɪsɪtə^r] N (*Jur*) (*Brit*) Rechtsanwalt *m*/-anwältin *f* (*der/die normalerweise nicht vor Gericht plädiert*); (*US*) Justizbeamte(r) *m*/-beamtin *f*

solid [ˈsɒlɪd] **1** ADJ (a) *fest*; *block, gold, oak, rock* massiv; *layer, traffic etc* dicht; *stretch, line* ununterbrochen; *week* ganz; (= *heavily-built*) *person* stämmig; *bridge, house, relationship* stabil; *furniture, piece of work, character, knowledge* solide; *business also* gesund; *grip* kraftvoll; *meal* kräftig; **to be frozen ~** hart gefroren sein; **the square was packed ~ with cars** die Autos standen an dicht auf dem Platz; **the room was ~ with people** der Raum war mit Leuten voll gedrängt; **they worked for two ~ days** sie haben zwei Tage ununterbrochen gearbeitet
(b) *reason* handfest, stichhaltig; *grounds* fundiert
(c) (= *unanimous*) *vote* einstimmig; *support* voll **2** ADV (a) (= *completely*) völlig
(b) (= *without a break*) pausenlos; **for eight hours ~** acht Stunden lang ununterbrochen
3 N (a) fester Stoff
(b) **solids** PL (= *food*) feste Nahrung *no pl*

solidarity [ˌsɒlɪˈdærɪtɪ] N Solidarität *f*

solidify [səˈlɪdɪfaɪ] VI fest werden; (*lava etc*) erstarren; (*metal also*) hart werden

solidity [səˈlɪdɪtɪ] N (a) (*of substance*) Festigkeit *f* (b) (*of bridge, house, car*) Stabilität *f*; (*of furniture also, piece of work, character*) solide Art *f* (c) (= *unanimity: of support*) Geschlossenheit *f*

solidly [ˈsɒlɪdlɪ] ADV (a) *stuck, secured* fest; **~ built** *house* solide gebaut; *person* kräftig gebaut (b) *reasoned, argued* stichhaltig (c) (= *uninterruptedly*) *work* ununterbrochen (d) (= *unanimously*) *vote* einstimmig; *support* geschlossen; **to be ~ behind sb/sth** geschlossen hinter jdm/etw stehen (e) (= *thoroughly*) Republican durch und durch

solitary [ˈsɒlɪtərɪ] **1** ADJ (a) *life, person* einsam; *place* abgelegen; **a few ~ houses** ein paar vereinzelte Häuser; **a ~ person** ein Einzelgänger *m*, eine Einzelgängerin *f* (b) *case, example, goal* einzig; **with the ~ exception of ...** mit alleiniger Ausnahme von ... **2** N (= ~ *confinement*) Einzelhaft *f*

solitary confinement N Einzelhaft *f*; **to be put/kept** *or* **held in ~** in Einzelhaft genommen/gehalten werden

solitude [ˈsɒlɪtjuːd] N Einsamkeit *f*; (*of place also*) Abgelegenheit *f*

solo [ˈsəʊləʊ] **1** N Solo *nt*; **piano ~** Klaviersolo *nt* **2** ADJ Solo-
3 ADV allein; (*Mus*) solo; **to go ~** (*musician etc*) eine Solokarriere einschlagen

soloist [ˈsəʊləʊɪst] N Solist(in) *m(f)*

Solomon [ˈsɒləmən] N Salomo(n) *m*; **the ~ Islands** die Salomonen *pl*

solstice [ˈsɒlstɪs] N Sonnenwende *f*

soluble [ˈsɒljʊbl] ADJ (a) löslich; **~ in water** wasserlöslich
(b) *problem* lösbar

solution [səˈluːʃən] N (*also Chem*) Lösung *f* (*to* +gen); (*of crime*) Aufklärung *f*

solvable [ˈsɒlvəbl] ADJ *problem* lösbar

solve [sɒlv] VT *problem, equation* lösen; *mystery* enträtseln; *crime, murder* aufklären

solvency [ˈsɒlvənsɪ] N (*Fin*) Zahlungsfähigkeit *f*, Solvenz *f*

solvent [ˈsɒlvənt] **1** ADJ (*Fin*) zahlungsfähig, solvent **2** N (*Chem*) Lösungsmittel *nt*

Somali [səˈmɑːlɪ] **1** ADJ somali; *person, culture, institution* somalisch; **he is ~** er ist Somalier **2** N Somalier(in) *m(f)*

Somalia [səˈmɑːlɪə] N Somalia *nt*

sombre, (*US*) **somber** [ˈsɒmbə^r] ADJ (= *dark*) dunkel; (= *gloomy*) düster; *prospect also* trüb; *news* traurig; *music* trist

sombrely, (*US*) **somberly** [ˈsɒmbəlɪ] ADV *say* traurig, düster; *watch* finster; *dress* trist

some [sʌm] **1** ADJ (a) (*with plural nouns*) einige; (= *a few, emph*) ein paar; (= *any: in "if" clauses, questions*) meist nicht übersetzt; **if you have ~ questions** wenn Sie Fragen haben; **did you bring ~ records?** hast du Schallplatten mitgebracht?; **~ records of mine** einige meiner Platten; **would you like ~ more biscuits?** möchten Sie noch (ein paar) Kekse?
(b) (*with singular nouns*) etwas, *meist nicht übersetzt*; (= *a little, emph also*) ein bisschen; **there's ~ ink on your shirt** Sie haben Tinte auf dem Hemd; **would you like ~ cheese?** möchten Sie

(*etwas*) Käse?; **~ more (tea)?** noch etwas (Tee)?; **leave ~ cake for me** lass mir ein bisschen *or* etwas Kuchen übrig; **did she give you ~ money?** hat sie Ihnen Geld gegeben?
(c) (= *certain, in contrast*) manche(r, s); **~ people say ...** manche Leute sagen ...; **~ people just don't care** es gibt Leute, denen ist das einfach egal; **in ~ ways** in gewisser Weise
(d) (*vague, indeterminate*) irgendein; **~ book or other** irgendein Buch; **~ woman, whose name I forget ...** eine Frau, ich habe ihren Namen vergessen, ...; **in ~ way or another** irgendwie; **or ~ such** oder so etwas Ähnliches; **or ~ such name** oder so ein ähnlicher Name; **~ time or other** irgendwann einmal; **~ other time** ein andermal; **~ day** eines Tages; **~ day next week** irgendwann nächste Woche
(e) (*intensifier*) ziemlich; (*in exclamations, iro*) vielleicht ein (*inf*); **it took ~ courage** dazu brauchte man schon (einigen) *or* ziemlichen Mut; **(that was) ~ party!** das war vielleicht eine Party! (*inf*); **this might take ~ time** das könnte einige Zeit dauern; **quite ~ time** ganz schön lange (*inf*), ziemlich lange; **to speak at ~ length** ziemlich lange sprechen; **~ help you are** du bist mir vielleicht eine Hilfe (*inf*); **~ people!** Leute gibts! **2** PRON (a) (*referring to plural nouns*) (= *a few*) einige; (= *certain ones*) manche; **in "if" clauses, questions**) welche; **~ of these books/my friends** einige dieser Bücher/meiner Freunde; **~ of them have been sold** einige sind verkauft worden; **~ ..., others ...** manche ..., andere ...; **~ of them were late** einige kamen zu spät; **they're lovely, try ~** die schmecken gut, probieren Sie mal; **I've still got ~** ich habe noch welche
(b) (*referring to singular nouns*) (= *a little*) etwas; (= *a certain amount, in contrast*) manches; (*in "if" clauses, questions*) welche(r, s); **I drank ~ of the milk** ich habe (etwas) von der Milch getrunken; **have ~!** bedienen Sie sich!; **it's lovely cake, would you like ~?** das ist ein sehr guter Kuchen, möchten Sie welchen?; **try ~ of this cake** probieren Sie doch mal diesen Kuchen; **would you like ~ money/tea?** – no, I've got ~ möchten Sie Geld/Tee? – nein, ich habe Geld/ich habe noch; **have you got money?** – no, but he has **~** haben Sie Geld? – nein, aber er hat welches; **~ of it had been eaten** einiges (davon) war gegessen worden; **he only believed ~ of it** er hat es nur teilweise geglaubt; **~ of the finest poetry in the English language** einige der schönsten Gedichte in der englischen Sprache
3 ADV (a) ungefähr, etwa, zirka
(b) (*US inf*) (= *a little*) etwas, ein bisschen; (= *a lot*) viel; **it sure bothered us ~** das hat uns ziemlich zu schaffen gemacht

somebody [ˈsʌmbədɪ] **1** PRON jemand; (*dir obj*) jemand(en); (*indir obj*) jemandem; **~ else** jemand anders; **~ or other** irgendjemand; **~ knocked at the door** es klopfte jemand an die Tür; **we need ~ German** wir brauchen einen Deutschen; **everybody needs ~ to talk to** jeder braucht einen, mit dem er sprechen kann; **you must have seen ~** Sie müssen doch irgendjemand(en) gesehen haben **2** N **to be (a) ~** etwas vorstellen, wer (*inf*) *or* jemand sein

somehow [ˈsʌmhaʊ] ADV irgendwie

someone [ˈsʌmwʌn] PRON = **somebody 1**

someplace [ˈsʌmpleɪs] ADV (*US inf*) be irgendwo; go irgendwohin; **~ else** be woanders; go woandershin

somersault [ˈsʌməsɔːlt] **1** N Purzelbaum *m*; (*Sport, fig*) Salto *m*; **to do** *or* **turn a ~** einen Purzelbaum schlagen; (*Sport*) einen Salto machen **2** VI (*person*) einen Purzelbaum schlagen; (*Sport*) einen Salto machen; (*car*) sich überschlagen

something [ˈsʌmθɪŋ] **1** PRON (a) etwas; **~ nice/serious** *etc* etwas Nettes/Ernstes *etc*; **~ or other** irgendetwas; **~ of the kind** so (et)was (Ähnliches); **there's ~ I don't like about him** irgendetwas gefällt mir an ihm nicht; **there's ~ in what you say** an dem, was du sagst, ist (schon) was dran; **well, that's ~** (das ist) immerhin etwas; **he's ~ to do with the Foreign Office** er ist irgendwie beim Außenministerium; **she's called Rachel ~** sie heißt Rachel Soundso; **three hundred and ~** dreihundert und ein paar (Zerquetschte (*inf*)); **or ~** (*inf*) oder so (was); **are you drunk or ~?** (*inf*) bist du betrunken oder was? (*inf*); **she's called Maria or ~ like that** sie heißt Maria oder so ähnlich
(b) (*inf*: = *special or unusual*) **it was ~ else** (*esp US*) *or* **quite ~** das war schon toll (*inf*)
2 N **a little ~** (= *present etc*) eine kleine Aufmerksamkeit, eine Kleinigkeit; **a certain ~** ein gewisses Etwas
3 ADV **~ over 200** etwas über 200; **~ like 200** ungefähr 200;

you look ~ **like him** du siehst ihm irgendwie ähnlich; **it's ~ of a problem** das ist schon ein Problem; **~ of a surprise** eine ziemliche Überraschung

-something [-sʌmθɪŋ] SUF **he's twenty-something** er ist in den Zwanzigern; **thirty-somethings** Leute *pl* in den Dreißigern

sometime ['sʌmtaɪm] ADV irgendwann; **~ or other it will have to be done** irgendwann muss es gemacht werden; **write to me ~ soon** schreib mir (doch) bald (ein)mal; **~ before tomorrow** bis morgen, heute noch; **~ next year** irgendwann nächstes Jahr

sometimes ['sʌmtaɪmz] ADV manchmal

someway ['sʌmweɪ] ADV (*US*) irgendwie

somewhat ['sʌmwɒt] ADV ein wenig; **the system is ~ less than perfect** das System funktioniert irgendwie nicht ganz; **~ to my surprise ...** ziemlich überraschend für mich ...

somewhere ['sʌmweəʳ] ADV **(a)** *be* irgendwo; *go* irgendwohin; **~ else** irgendwo anders, irgendwo anders hin; **to take one's business ~ else** seine Geschäfte woanders machen; **from ~** irgendwoher; **I know ~ where ...** ich weiß, wo ...; **I needed ~ to live in London** ich brauchte irgendwo in London eine Unterkunft; **we just wanted ~ to go after school** wir wollten bloß einen Ort, wo wir nach der Schule eingehen können; **~ about** *or* **around here** irgendwo hier in der Nähe; **~ nice** irgendwo, wo es nett ist; **the ideal place to go is ~ like New York** am besten fährt man in eine Stadt wie New York; **don't I know you from ~?** kenne ich Sie nicht von irgendwoher? **(b)** (*fig*) **the temperature was ~ about 40° C** die Temperatur betrug ungefähr 40° C; **~ about £50** *or* **in the region of £50** um (die) £ 50 herum; **now we're getting ~** jetzt kommen wir voran

son [sʌn] N (*lit, fig*) Sohn *m*; (*as address*) mein Junge; **Son of God/Man** Gottes-/Menschensohn *m*; **he's his father's ~** er ist ganz der Vater; **~ of a bitch** (*esp US sl*) Scheißkerl *m* (*inf*), Hurensohn *m* (*vulg*)

sonar ['səʊnɑːʳ] N Echolot *nt*

sonata [sə'nɑːtə] N Sonate *f*

song [sɒŋ] N **(a)** Lied *nt*; (*= modern folk ~, blues ~*) Song *m*; (*= singing, bird ~*) Gesang *m*; **one of Brecht's ~s** ein Brecht-Song *m*; **to burst into ~** ein Lied anstimmen **(b)** (*Brit fig inf*) **to make a ~ and dance about sth** eine Haupt- und Staatsaktion aus etw machen (*inf*); **to be on ~** (*Brit*) in Hochform sein; **it was going for a ~** das gab es für einen Apfel und ein Ei

song: songbird N Singvogel *m*; **songbook** N Liederbuch *nt*; **songwriter** N Texter(in) *m(f)* und Komponist(in) *m(f)*; (*of modern ballads*) Liedermacher(in) *m(f)*

sonic ['sɒnɪk] ADJ Schall-

sonic boom N Überschallknall *m*

son-in-law ['sʌnɪnlɔː] N, *pl* **sons-in-law** Schwiegersohn *m*

sonnet ['sɒnɪt] N Sonett *nt*

sonny ['sʌnɪ] N (*inf*) Junge *m*

sons-in-law PL *of* **son-in-law**

soon [suːn] ADV (*= in a short time from now*) bald; (*= early*) früh; (*= quickly*) schnell; **it will ~ be Christmas** bald ist Weihnachten; **~ after his death** kurz nach seinem Tode; **~ afterwards** kurz *or* bald danach; **how ~ can you be ready?** wann kannst du fertig sein?; **we got there too ~** wir kamen zu früh an; **all too ~** viel zu schnell; **as ~ as** sobald; **as ~ as possible** so schnell wie möglich; **when can I have it? – as ~ as you like** wann kann ichs kriegen? – wann du willst!; **please reply ~est** bitte antworten Sie schnellstmöglich; **I would (just) as ~ ~ you didn't tell him** es wäre mir lieber, wenn du es ihm nicht erzählen würdest

sooner ['suːnəʳ] ADV **(a)** (*time*) früher, eher; **no ~ had we arrived than ...** wir waren gerade *or* kaum angekommen, da ...; **no ~ said than done** gesagt, getan **(b)** (*preference*) lieber; **I would ~ not do it** ich würde es lieber nicht tun

soot [sʊt] N Ruß *m*; **black as ~** rußschwarz

soothe [suːð] VT beruhigen; *pain* lindern

soothing ['suːðɪŋ] ADJ beruhigend, besänftigend; (*= pain-relieving*) schmerzlindernd; *massage* wohltuend; *bath* entspannend

soothingly ['suːðɪŋlɪ] ADV *say, whisper* beruhigend, besänftigend

sop [sɒp] N (*to pacify*) Beschwichtigungsmittel *nt*

sophisticated [sə'fɪstɪkeɪtɪd] ADJ **(a)** (*= worldly*) kultiviert; *audience* anspruchsvoll; *restaurant* niveauvoll; *hairdo* elegant; *dress* raffiniert; **she thinks she looks more ~ with a cigarette holder** sie glaubt, mit einer Zigarettenspitze mehr darzustellen **(b)** (*= complex*) hoch entwickelt; *techniques* raffiniert; *method* durchdacht; *device* ausgeklügelt **(c)** (*= subtle*) subtil; *style, discussion* anspruchsvoll; *plan* raffiniert; *system, approach* komplex; *mind* differenziert

sophistication [sə,fɪstɪ'keɪʃən] N **(a)** (*= worldliness*) Kultiviertheit *f*; (*of taste also*) Feinheit *f*; (*of audience*) hohes Niveau; (*of person, restaurant also*) Gepflegtheit *f*, Eleganz *f* **(b)** (*= complexity*) hoher Entwicklungsstand *or* -grad; (*of techniques*) Raffiniertheit *f*; (*of method*) Durchdachtheit *f*; (*of device*) Ausgeklügeltheit *f* **(c)** (*= subtlety*) Subtilität *f*; (*of mind*) Differenziertheit *f*; (*of prose, style*) hohe Ansprüche *pl*; (*of discussion*) hohes Niveau; (*of plan*) Raffiniertheit *f*; (*of system, approach*) Komplexheit *f*

sophomore ['sɒfəmɔːʳ] N (*US*) Student(in) *im zweiten Jahr*

sopping ['sɒpɪŋ] ADJ (*also ~ wet*) durchnässt; *person* klitschnass

soppy ['sɒpɪ] ADJ (*Brit inf*) *book, song* schmalzig (*inf*); *person* sentimental; *look* schmachtend

soprano [sə'prɑːnəʊ] **1** N Sopran *m*; (*= person also*) Sopranist(in) *m(f)*; (*= voice also*) Sopranstimme *f*; **to sing ~** Sopran singen **2** ADJ Sopran-

sorbet ['sɔːbeɪ] N Sorbet *nt or m*

sorcerer ['sɔːsərəʳ] N Hexenmeister *m*

sorceress ['sɔːsəres] N Hexe *f*

sorcery ['sɔːsərɪ] N Hexerei *f*

sordid ['sɔːdɪd] ADJ eklig; *place, room also* heruntergekommen; *motive* niedrig; *conditions, life, story* erbärmlich; *crime* gemein; *affair* schmutzig; **spare me the ~ details** erspar mir die schmutzigen Einzelheiten

sore [sɔːʳ] **1** ADJ (+ER) **(a)** weh, schlimm (*inf*); (*= inflamed*) entzündet; **to have a ~ throat** Halsschmerzen haben; **my eyes are ~** mir tun die Augen weh; **my wrist feels ~** mein Handgelenk tut weh; **to have ~ muscles** Muskelkater haben; **to have a ~ head** (*esp US, Scot*) Kopfschmerzen haben; **I'm ~ all over** mir tut alles weh; **a ~ point** (*fig*) ein wunder Punkt; **a ~ subject** ein heikles Thema; **to be in ~ need of sth** etw unbedingt *or* dringend brauchen **(b)** (*esp US inf: = angry*) verärgert, sauer (*inf*) (*about sth* über etw *acc, at sb* über jdn) **2** N (*Med*) wunde Stelle

sorely ['sɔːlɪ] ADV *tempted* sehr; *needed* dringend; *missed* schmerzlich; **he has been ~ tested** *or* **tried** seine Geduld wurde auf eine sehr harte Probe gestellt; **to be ~ lacking** bedauerlicherweise fehlen

soreness ['sɔːnɪs] N (*= ache*) Schmerz *m*

sorority [sə'rɒrɪtɪ] N (*US Univ*) Studentinnenvereinigung *f*

sorrow ['sɒrəʊ] N (*no pl: = sadness*) Traurigkeit *f*; (*no pl: = grief*) Trauer *f*; (*= trouble, care*) Sorge *f*; (*= affliction, suffering*) Leiden *nt*; **to my (great) ~** zu meinem größten Kummer; **to drown one's ~s** seine Sorgen ertränken

sorrowful ADJ, **sorrowfully** ADV ['sɒrəʊfʊl, -fəlɪ] traurig

sorry ['sɒrɪ] ADJ (+ER) traurig; *sight, figure also* jämmerlich; *excuse* faul; **I was ~ to hear that** es tat mir Leid, das zu hören *or* das hören zu müssen; **we were ~ to hear about your mother's death** es tat uns Leid, dass deine Mutter gestorben ist; **I can't**

say I'm ~ he lost es tut mir wirklich nicht Leid, dass er verloren hat; **this work is no good, I'm ~ to say** diese Arbeit taugt nichts, das muss ich leider sagen; **to be** or **feel ~ for sb/ oneself** jdn/sich selbst bemitleiden; **I feel ~ for the child** das Kind tut mir Leid; **you'll be ~ (for this)!** das wird dir noch Leid tun!; **~! Entschuldigung!, Verzeihung!; I'm/he's ~** es tut mir/ihm Leid; **I'm so ~!** entschuldige(n Sie) bitte!; **can you lend me £5? – ~** kannst du mir £ 5 leihen? – bedaure, leider nicht; **~?** (= pardon) wie bitte?; **he's from England, ~ Scotland** er ist aus England, nein, Entschuldigung, aus Schottland; **to say ~ (to sb for sth)** sich (bei jdm für etw) entschuldigen; **I'm ~ about that vase** es tut mir Leid um die Vase; **I'm ~ about (what happened on) Thursday** es tut mir Leid wegen Donnerstag; **to be in a ~ state** (person) in einer jämmerlichen Verfassung sein; (object) in einem jämmerlichen Zustand sein

sort [sɔːt] **■** N **(a)** (= kind) Art f; (= species, type, model) Sorte f; **a ~ of** eine Art (+nom), so ein/eine; **this ~ of house** diese Art Haus, so ein Haus; **an odd ~ of novel** ein komischer Roman; **what ~ of (a) man is he?** was für ein Mensch ist er?; **he's not the ~ of man to do that** er ist nicht der Mensch, der das täte; **this ~ of thing** so etwas; **all ~s of things** alles Mögliche; **he's a painter of a ~** or **of ~s** er ist Maler, sozusagen; **it's coffee of a ~** or **of ~s** das ist Kaffee oder so etwas Ähnliches; **something of the ~** (irgend) so (et)was; **he's some ~ of administrator** er hat irgendwie in der Verwaltung zu tun; **he's got some ~ of job with ...** er hat irgendeinen Job bei ...; **you'll do nothing of the ~!** von wegen!, das wirst du schön bleiben lassen!; **that's the ~ of person I am** ich bin nun mal so!; **I'm not that ~ of girl** ich bin nicht so eine; **he's a good ~** er ist ein prima Kerl; **he's not my ~** er ist nicht mein Typ; **I don't trust his ~** solchen Leuten traue ich nicht; **your ~ never did any good** du und deinesgleichen, ihr habt noch nie etwas zustande gebracht; **it takes all ~s (to make a world)** es gibt so 'ne und solche; **to be out of ~s** (Brit) nicht ganz auf der Höhe or auf dem Damm (inf) sein

(b) (Comput) Sortiervorgang m
■ ADV **~ of** (inf) irgendwie; **is it tiring? – ~ of** ist das anstrengend? – irgendwie schon; **it's ~ of finished** es ist eigentlich schon fertig; **aren't you pleased? – ~ of** freust du dich nicht? – doch, eigentlich schon; **is this how he did it? – well, ~ of** hat er das so gemacht? – ja, so ungefähr
■ VT **(a)** (also Comput) sortieren; **to ~ sth on sth** (Comput) etw nach etw sortieren
(b) (= solve, organize) **to get sth ~ed** etw auf die Reihe bekommen; **everything is now ~ed** es ist jetzt alles (wieder) in Ordnung
■ VI **(a) to ~ through sth** etw durchsehen
(b) (Comput) sortieren

➤ **sort out** VT SEP **(a)** (= arrange) sortieren; (= select) aussortieren **(b)** muddle in Ordnung bringen; problem lösen; situation klären; **the problem will sort itself out** das Problem wird sich von selbst lösen or erledigen; **to sort oneself out** sich (dat) über sich (acc) selbst klar werden **(c)** (esp Brit inf) **to sort sb out** sich (dat) jdn vorknöpfen (inf)

sort code N (Fin) Bankleitzahl f

sorting office ['sɔːtɪŋˌɒfɪs] N (Brit) Sortierstelle f

so-so ['səʊˈsəʊ] ADJ PRED, ADV (inf) soso, so la la

sought [sɔːt] PRET, PTP of seek

sought-after ['sɔːtɑːftəʳ] ADJ begehrt; **much ~** viel begehrt; rare object gesucht

soul [səʊl] N **(a)** Seele f; **All Souls' Day** Allerheiligen nt; **God rest his ~!** Gott hab ihn selig!; **poor ~!** (inf) Ärmste(r)!; **he's a good ~** er ist ein guter Mensch; **she's a kind** or **kindly ~** sie ist eine gute Seele; **not a ~** keine Menschenseele
(b) (= inner being) Innerste(s), Wesen nt; **he loved her with all his ~** er liebte sie von ganzem Herzen; **the priest urged them to search their ~s** der Priester drängte sie, ihr Gewissen zu erforschen
(c) (= finer feelings) Herz nt, Gefühl nt
(d) (Mus) Soul m

soul-destroying ['səʊldɪˌstrɔɪɪŋ] ADJ geisttötend; factory work etc nervtötend

soulful ['səʊlfʊl] ADJ look seelenvoll

soulless ['səʊllɪs] ADJ person seelenlos; place gottverlassen; system herzlos; existence eintönig

soul: **soul mate** N Seelenfreund(in) m(f); **soul music** N Soulmusik f; **soul-searching** N Gewissensprüfung f

sound[1] [saʊnd] **■** ADJ (+ER) **(a)** constitution, lungs gesund; condition, building einwandfrei; **to be of ~ mind** (esp Jur) im Vollbesitz seiner geistigen Kräfte sein (Jur)
(b) (= good, dependable) solide; argument, analysis fundiert; economy, currency stabil; person verlässlich; idea, advice, move vernünftig
(c) (= thorough) gründlich, solide; beating gehörig; defeat vernichtend
(d) sleep tief, fest
■ ADV (+ER) **to be ~ asleep** fest schlafen

sound[2] **■** N Geräusch nt; (Phys) Schall m; (Mus, of instruments) Klang m; (verbal, TV, Rad, Film) Ton m; (of band etc) Sound m; **don't make a ~** still!; **the speed of ~** (die) Schallgeschwindigkeit; **would you still recognize the ~ of Karin's voice?** würdest du Karins Stimme immer noch erkennen?; **not a ~ was to be heard** man hörte keinen Ton; **the ~(s) of laughter** Gelächter nt; **I don't like the ~ of it** das klingt gar nicht gut; **from the ~ of it he had a hard time** es hört sich so an or es klingt, als sei es ihm schlecht gegangen
■ VT **~ your horn** hupen!; **to ~ the alarm** Alarm schlagen; (mechanism) die Alarmanlage auslösen; **to ~ the retreat** zum Rückzug blasen
■ VI **(a)** (= emit ~) erklingen, ertönen
(b) (= give impression) klingen, sich anhören; **he ~s angry** er hört sich so an, als wäre er wütend; **he ~s French (to me)** er hört sich (für mich) wie ein Franzose an; **he ~s like a nice man** er scheint ein netter Mensch zu sein; **it ~s like a sensible idea** das klingt ganz vernünftig; **how does it ~ to you?** wie findest du das?

➤ **sound off** VI (inf) sich auslassen (about über +acc)
➤ **sound out** VT SEP person aushorchen, ausfragen; opinions herausfinden; **to sound sb out about** or **on sth** bei jdm in Bezug auf etw (acc) vorfühlen

sound: **sound barrier** N Schallmauer f; **sound bite** N Soundclip m; **sound card** N (Comput) Soundkarte f; **sound effects** PL Toneffekte pl; **sound engineer** N Toningenieur(in) m(f)

sounding board ['saʊndɪŋbɔːd] N (fig) Resonanzboden m; **he used the committee as a ~ for his ideas** er benutzte den Ausschuss, um die Wirkung seiner Vorschläge zu sondieren

soundless ['saʊndlɪs] ADJ lautlos

soundlessly ['saʊndlɪslɪ] ADV move geräuschlos; weep lautlos

soundly ['saʊndlɪ] ADV built, made solide; argue, invest also vernünftig; thrash gehörig; defeat vernichtend; condemn rundum; based fest; **our team was ~ beaten** unsere Mannschaft wurde klar geschlagen; **to sleep ~** (tief und) fest schlafen

soundness ['saʊndnɪs] N **(a)** (= good condition) gesunder Zustand; (of building) guter Zustand **(b)** (= validity, dependability) Solidität f; (of argument, analysis) Fundiertheit f; (of economy, currency) Stabilität f; (of idea, advice, move, policy) Vernünftigkeit f

sound: **soundproof** ADJ schalldicht; **soundtrack** N Filmmusik f

soup [suːp] N Suppe f; **to be in the ~** (inf) in der Tinte or Patsche sitzen (inf)

soup: **soup kitchen** N Volksküche f; **soup spoon** N Suppenlöffel m

sour ['saʊəʳ] **■** ADJ (+ER) **(a)** sauer; wine, vinegar, smell säuerlich; **to go** or **turn ~** (lit) sauer werden; **to go** or **turn ~ (on sb)** (fig) (relationship, marriage) jdn anöden; (plan, investment) sich als Fehlschlag erweisen
(b) (fig) person, expression griesgrämig; **it's just ~ grapes** die Trauben sind zu sauer or hängen zu hoch
■ VT (fig) relationship, atmosphere vergiften
■ VI (fig: atmosphere, relationship) sich verschlechtern

source [sɔːs] **■** N (of river, light, information) Quelle f; (of troubles etc) Ursache f, Ursprung m; **a ~ of vitamin C** eine Vitamin-C-Quelle f; **he is a ~ of embarrassment to us** bringt uns ständig in Verlegenheit; **I have it from a good ~ that ...** ich habe es aus sicherer Quelle, dass ...; **at ~** (tax) unmittelbar; **~ of funds** (Fin) Kapitalherkunft f, Kapitalquellen pl; **~s** (in book etc) Quellen pl, Literaturangaben pl
■ VT (Comm) beschaffen

source material N Quellenmaterial *nt*

sour(ed) cream [ˌsaʊə(d)'kriːm] N saure Sahne

sour-faced ['saʊəfeɪst] ADJ (*inf*) vergrätzt (*inf*)

sourly ['saʊəlɪ] ADV (*fig*) griesgrämig

sourness ['saʊənɪs] N (*of lemon, milk*) saurer Geschmack; (*of wine, vinegar also, of smell*) Säuerlichkeit *f*; (*fig: of person, expression*) Griesgrämigkeit *f*

south [saʊθ] **1** N Süden *m*; **in the ~ of** im Süden +*gen*; **to the ~ of** im Süden *or* südlich von; **from the ~** aus dem Süden; (*wind*) aus Süden; **the wind is in the ~** es ist Südwind; **the South of France** Südfrankreich *nt*; **which way is ~?** in welcher Richtung ist Süden?; **down ~** be, live unten im Süden; *go* runter in den Süden **2** ADJ südlich; (*in names*) Süd-; **South German** süddeutsch; **South Wales** Südwales *nt* **3** ADV im Süden; (= *towards the ~*) nach Süden; (*Met*) in südliche Richtung; **to be further ~** weiter südlich sein; **~ of** südlich or im Süden von

south IN CPDS Süd-; **South Africa** N Südafrika *nt*; **South African 1** ADJ südafrikanisch; **he's ~** er ist Südafrikaner **2** N Südafrikaner(in) *m(f)*; **South America** N Südamerika *nt*; **South American 1** ADJ südamerikanisch; **he's ~** er ist Südamerikaner **2** N Südamerikaner(in) *m(f)*; **South Australia** N Südaustralien *nt*; **southbound** ADJ (in) Richtung Süden; **South Carolina** N Südkarolina *nt*; **South Dakota** N Süddakota *nt*; **southeast 1** N Südosten *m*, Südost *m* (*esp Naut*); **from the ~** aus dem Südosten; (*wind*) von Südosten **2** ADJ südöstlich; (*in names*) Südost- **3** ADV nach Südosten; **~ of** südöstlich von; **Southeast Asia** N Südostasien *nt*; **southeasterly** ADJ *direction* südöstlich; *wind also* aus Südost; **southeastern** ADJ südöstlich, im Südosten; **~ England** Südostengland *nt*

southerly ['sʌðəlɪ] ADJ südlich; *course also* nach Süden; *wind* aus Süden

southern ['sʌðən] ADJ südlich; (*in names*) Süd-; (= *Mediterranean*) südländisch; **Southern Africa** das südliche Afrika; **Southern Europe** Südeuropa *nt*; **Southern States** (*US*) Südstaaten *pl*

southerner ['sʌðənə'] N Bewohner(in) *m(f)* des Südens, Südengländer(in) *m(f)*/-deutsche(r) *mf etc*; (*US*) Südstaatler(in) *m(f)*

southernmost ['sʌðənməʊst] ADJ südlichste(r, s)

south: south-facing ADJ *wall, window* nach Süden gerichtet; *garden* nach Süden gelegen; **South Korea** N Südkorea *nt*; **South Korean 1** ADJ südkoreanisch **2** N Südkoreaner(in) *m(f)*; **South Pacific** N Südpazifik *m*; **South Pole** N Südpol *m*; **South Sea Islands** PL Südseeinseln *pl*; **South Seas** PL Südsee *f*; **south-south-east 1** ADJ südsüdöstlich **2** ADV nach Südsüdost(en); **south-south-west 1** ADJ südsüdwestlich **2** ADV nach Südsüdwest(en); **~ of** südsüdwestlich von; **southward(s)** 1 ADJ südlich 2 ADV nach Süden, südwärts; **southwest 1** N Südwesten *m*, Südwest *m* (*esp Naut*); **from the ~** aus dem Südwesten; (*wind*) von Südwesten **2** ADJ Südwest-, südwestlich **3** ADV nach Südwest(en); **~ of** südwestlich von; **southwesterly** ADJ *direction* südwestlich; *wind also* aus Südwest; **southwestern** ADJ südwestlich, im Südwesten

souvenir [ˌsuːvə'nɪə'] N Andenken *nt*, Souvenir *nt* (*of an* +*acc*)

sovereign ['sɒvrɪn] **1** N (= *monarch*) Herrscher(in) *m(f)* **2** ADJ (a) (= *supreme*) höchste(r, s), oberste(r, s); *state, power* souverän (b) (*Fin*) ~ **debt** Staatsschulden *pl*; **~ lending** staatliche Kreditaufnahme

sovereignty ['sɒvrəntɪ] N Oberhoheit *f*; (= *right of self-determination*) Souveränität *f*

soviet ['səʊvɪət] (*Hist*) **1** N Sowjet *m*; **the Soviets** (= *people*) die Sowjets **2** ADJ ATTR sowjetisch, Sowjet-

Soviet (*Hist*): **Soviet Republic** N Sowjetrepublik *f*; **Soviet Union** N Sowjetunion *f*

sow[1] [səʊ], *pret* sowed, *ptp* sown *or* sowed VT *corn, plants* säen; *seed* aussäen; **this field has been ~n with barley** auf diesem Feld ist Gerste gesät; **to ~ (the seeds of) hatred/discord** Hass/ Zwietracht säen

sow[2] [saʊ] N (= *pig*) Sau *f*; (*of wild boar*) (Wild)sau *f*

sowing ['səʊɪŋ] N (= *action*) Aussaat *f*

sown [səʊn] PTP *of* **sow**[1]

soya ['sɔɪə], **soy** [sɔɪ] N Soja *f*; **~ flour** Sojamehl *nt*

soya: soya bean N Sojabohne *f*; **soya sauce** N Sojasoße *f*

soybean ['sɔɪbiːn] N (*US*) = **soya bean**

spa [spɑː] N (= *town*) (Heil- *or* Mineral)bad *nt*, Kurort *m*

space [speɪs] **1** N (a) Raum *m* (*also Phys*); (= *outer ~*) der Weltraum, das Weltall; **to stare** *or* **gaze into ~** ins Leere starren; **to give sb some ~** (*fig*) jdm Freiraum gewähren (b) NO PL (= *room*) Platz *m*; **to take up a lot of ~** viel Platz wegnehmen; **to clear/leave some ~ for sb/sth** für jdn/etw Platz schaffen/lassen; **parking ~** Platz *m* zum Parken (c) (= *gap*) Platz *m no art*; (*between objects, words, lines*) Zwischenraum *m*; (= *parking ~*) Lücke *f*; **to leave a ~ for sb/ sth** für jdn/etw Platz lassen; **please answer in the ~ provided** bitte an der dafür vorgesehenen Stelle beantworten (d) (*of time*) Zeitraum *m*; **in a short ~ of time** in kurzer Zeit; **in the ~ of one hour** innerhalb einer Stunde **2** VT (*also ~ out*) in Abständen verteilen; *visits* verteilen; *words* Zwischenraum *or* Abstand lassen zwischen (+*dat*); **~ them out more, ~ them further out** *or* **further apart** lassen Sie etwas mehr Zwischenraum *or* Abstand (dazwischen)

space IN CPDS (Welt)raum-; **space-bar** N (*Typ*) Leertaste *f*; **spacecraft** N Raumfahrzeug *nt*; (*unmanned*) Raumkörper *m*

spaced out [ˌspeɪst'aʊt] ADJ (*inf*) (= *confused etc*) geistig weggetreten (*inf*); (= *on drugs*) high (*inf*)

space: space flight N Weltraumflug *m*; **space heater** N (*esp US*) Heizgerät *nt*; **spaceman** N (Welt)raumfahrer *m*; **space programme**, (*US*) **space program** N Raumfahrtprogramm *nt*; **space rocket** N Weltraumrakete *f*; **space-saving** ADJ *equipment etc* Platz sparend; **spaceship** N Raumschiff *nt*; **space shuttle** N Raumfähre *f*; **space station** N (Welt)raumstation *f*; **spacesuit** N Raumanzug *m*; **space travel** N die Raumfahrt; **spacewoman** N (Welt)raum-fahrerin *f*

spacing ['speɪsɪŋ] N Abstände *pl*; (*between two objects*) Abstand *m*; (*also ~ out*) Verteilung *f*; (*of payments*) Verteilung *f* über längere Zeit; **single/double ~** (*Typ*) einzeiliger/zweizeiliger Abstand

spacious ['speɪʃəs] ADJ geräumig; *garden, park* weitläufig

spaciousness ['speɪʃəsnɪs] N Geräumigkeit *f*; (*of garden, park*) Weitläufigkeit *f*

spade [speɪd] N (a) (= *tool*) Spaten *m*; (= *children's ~*) Schaufel *f* (b) (*Cards*) Pik *nt*; **the Queen/two of Spades** die Pikdame/ Pikzwei

spaghetti [spə'getɪ] N Spag(h)etti *pl*

Spain [speɪn] N Spanien *nt*

spam [spæm] (*Comput*) **1** N Spam *m* **2** VT mit Werbung bombardieren

span[1] [spæn] **1** N (a) (*of hand*) Spanne *f*; (= *wingspan, of bridge etc*) Spannweite *f*; (= *arch of bridge*) (Brücken)bogen *m*; **~ of control** (*Ind*) Weisungsbereich *m* (b) (= *time ~*) Zeitspanne *f*, Zeitraum *m*; (*of memory*) Gedächtnisspanne *f*; (*of attention*) Konzentrationsspanne *f*; (= *range*) Umfang *m* **2** VT (*rope*) sich spannen über (+*acc*); (*bridge also*) überspannen; *years, globe* umspannen; (= *encircle*) umfassen; (*in time*) sich erstrecken über (+*acc*)

span[2] [spæn] (*old*) PRET *of* **spin**

spangle ['spæŋgl] N Paillette *f*

Spaniard ['spænjəd] N Spanier(in) *m(f)*

spaniel ['spænjəl] N Spaniel *m*

Spanish ['spænɪʃ] **1** ADJ spanisch; **he is ~** er ist Spanier **2** N (a) **the ~** die Spanier *pl* (b) (*Ling*) Spanisch *nt*

spank [spæŋk] **1** N Klaps *m* **2** VT versohlen; **to ~ sb's bottom** jdm den Hintern versohlen

spanking ['spæŋkɪŋ] **1** N Tracht *f* Prügel; **to give sb a ~** jdm den Hintern versohlen **2** ADJ (a) *pace* scharf, schnell (b) (= *splendid*) **in ~ condition** in hervorragendem Zustand

spanner ['spænə'] N (*Brit*) Schraubenschlüssel *m*; **to put** *or* **throw a ~ in the works** (*fig*) jdm Knüppel *or* einen Knüppel zwischen die Beine werfen

spar [spɑː'] VI (*Boxing*) sparren; (*fig*) sich kabbeln (*inf*) (*about* um)

spare [speə'] **1** ADJ (a) den/die/das man nicht braucht, übrig *pred*; (= *surplus*) überzählig, übrig *pred*; **~ bed** Gästebett *nt*; **have you any ~ string?, have you any string ~?** kannst du mir

(einen) Bindfaden geben?; **I can give you a pencil, I have a ~ one** ich kann dir einen Bleistift geben, ich habe noch einen; **take a ~ pen in case that one doesn't work** nehmen Sie noch einen Füller mit, falls dieser nicht funktioniert; **take some ~ clothes** nehmen Sie Kleider zum Wechseln mit; **when you have a few ~ minutes** *or* **a few minutes ~** wenn Sie mal ein paar freie Minuten haben; **I still have one ~ place in the car** ich habe noch einen Platz im Auto (frei)
(b) to drive sb ~ (*inf*) jdn wahnsinnig machen (*inf*); **to go ~** durchdrehen (*inf*)
◙ N Ersatzteil *nt*; (= *tyre*) Reserverad *nt*
◙ VT **(a)** USU NEG *expense, pains, effort* scheuen; (= *use sparingly*) sparen mit; **we must ~ no effort in trying to finish this job** wir dürfen keine Mühe scheuen, um diese Arbeit zu erledigen; **no expense ~d** es wurden keine Kosten gescheut *or* gespart
(b) (= *give*) *money etc* übrig haben; *room* frei haben; *time* (übrig) haben; **to ~ sb sth** jdm etw überlassen *or* geben; *money* jdm etw geben; **can you ~ the time to do it?** haben Sie Zeit, das zu machen?; **there is none to ~** es ist keine(r, s) übrig; **to have a few minutes to ~** ein paar Minuten Zeit haben; **I got to the airport with two minutes to ~** ich war zwei Minuten vor Abflug am Flughafen
(c) (= *do without*) entbehren, verzichten auf (+*acc*); **can you ~ this for a moment?** brauchst du das gerade?; **if you can ~ it** wenn Sie es nicht brauchen; **to ~ a thought for sb/sth** an jdn/ etw denken
(d) (= *show mercy to*) verschonen; (= *refrain from upsetting*) schonen; **to ~ sb's life** jds Leben verschonen
(e) (= *save*) **to ~ sb/oneself sth** jdm/sich etw ersparen; **~ me the gory details** verschone mich mit den grausigen Einzelheiten; **he has been ~d the ordeal of seeing her again** es blieb ihm erspart, sie noch einmal sehen zu müssen

> *Be careful! The German word **sparen** is not the most common translation for **to spare**.*

spare: **spare part** N Ersatzteil *nt*; **spare room** N Gästezimmer *nt*; **spare time** N (= *leisure time*) Freizeit *f*; **spare tyre**, (*US*) **spare tire** N Ersatzreifen *m*

sparing [ˈspeərɪŋ] ADJ sparsam

sparingly [ˈspeərɪŋlɪ] ADV sparsam; *spend, drink, eat* in Maßen; **to use sth ~** mit etw sparsam umgehen

spark [spɑːk] ◙ N (*from fire, Elec*) Funke *m*; (*fig*) Fünkchen *nt*, Funke(n) *m*; **when the ~s start to fly** (*fig*) wenn die Funken anfangen zu fliegen; **a bright ~** (*iro*) ein Intelligenzbolzen *m* (*iro*) ◙ VT (*also* **~ off**) entzünden; *explosion* verursachen; (*fig*) auslösen; *quarrel* entfachen; *interest, enthusiasm* wecken ◙ VI Funken sprühen; (*Elec*) zünden

sparkle [ˈspɑːkl] ◙ N Funkeln *nt* ◙ VI funkeln (**with** vor +*dat*); (*fig: person*) vor Leben(sfreude) sprühen; (**with** wit etc) brillieren; **her eyes ~d with excitement** ihre Augen blitzten vor Erregung

sparkler [ˈspɑːklə^r] N (= *firework*) Wunderkerze *f*

sparkling [ˈspɑːklɪŋ] ADJ funkelnd; *lights also* glänzend; *wit* sprühend; *performance* brilliant; (= *witty*) voll Geist sprühend; *lemonade, wine etc* perlend; **~ (mineral) water** Selterswasser *nt*; **~ wine** (*as type*) Sekt *m*; (= *slightly ~*) Perlwein *m*; **in ~ form** in glänzender Form; **the car was ~ (clean)** das Auto blitzte vor Sauberkeit

sparkly [ˈspɑːklɪ] ADJ (*inf*) funkelnd

spark plug N Zündkerze *f*

sparring partner [ˈspɑːrɪŋpɑːtnə^r] N Sparringpartner(in) *m(f)*; (*fig also*) Kontrahent(in) *m(f)*

sparrow [ˈspærəʊ] N Sperling *m*, Spatz *m*

sparse [spɑːs] ADJ spärlich; *hair* dünn, schütter; *furnishings, data, resources* dürftig

sparsely [ˈspɑːslɪ] ADV spärlich; *wooded also, populated* dünn

sparseness [ˈspɑːsnɪs] N Spärlichkeit *f*; (*of population*) geringe Dichte

Spartan [ˈspɑːtən] ADJ (*fig: also* **spartan**) spartanisch

spasm [ˈspæzəm] N (*Med*) Krampf *m*; (*of asthma, coughing, fig*) Anfall *m*

spasmodic [spæzˈmɒdɪk] ADJ (*Med*) krampfartig; (*fig*) sporadisch; *growth* schubweise

spasmodically [spæzˈmɒdɪkəlɪ] ADV (*fig*) sporadisch, hin und wieder; *grow* in Schüben, schubweise

spastic [ˈspæstɪk] ◙ ADJ spastisch; (*pej sl*) schwach (*inf*) ◙ N Spastiker(in) *m(f)*

spat [spæt] PRET, PTP *of* **spit**[1]

spate [speɪt] N (*of river*) Hochwasser *nt*; (*fig*) (*of letters, orders etc*) Flut *f*; (*of burglaries*) Serie *f*; (*of abuse*) Schwall *m*; **the river is in (full) ~** der Fluss führt Hochwasser

spatter [ˈspætə^r] ◙ VT bespritzen; **to ~ water over sb**, **to ~ sb with water** jdn nass spritzen ◙ VI **it ~ed all over the room** es verspritzte im ganzen Zimmer; **the rain ~ed (down) on the roof** der Regen klatschte aufs Dach ◙ N (= *mark*) Spritzer *pl*; (= *sound: of rain*) Klatschen *nt*; **a ~ of rain** ein paar Tropfen Regen

spatula [ˈspætjʊlə] N Spachtel *m*; (*Med*) Spatel *m*

spawn [spɔːn] ◙ N **(a)** (*of fish, frogs*) Laich *m* **(b)** (*of mushrooms*) Fadengeflecht *nt* ◙ VI laichen ◙ VT (*fig*) hervorbringen, erzeugen

speak [spiːk], *pret* **spoke**, *ptp* **spoken** ◙ VT **(a)** (= *utter*) sagen; *one's thoughts* äußern; **to ~ one's mind** seine Meinung sagen; **nobody spoke a word** niemand sagte ein Wort
(b) *language* sprechen; **English spoken here** man spricht Englisch
◙ VI **(a)** sprechen, reden (*about* über +*acc*, von, *on* zu); (= *converse*) reden, sich unterhalten (*with* mit); (= *give one's opinion*) sich äußern (*on, to* zu); **to ~ to** *or* **with sb** mit jdm sprechen *or* reden; **did you ~?** haben Sie etwas gesagt?; **to ~ in a whisper** flüstern; **I'm not ~ing to you** mit dir rede *or* spreche ich nicht mehr; **I'll ~ to him about it** (*euph: = admonish*) ich werde ein Wörtchen mit ihm reden; **I'll have to ~ to my lawyer about it** das muss ich mit meinem Anwalt besprechen; **~ing of dictionaries ...** da *or* wo wir gerade von Wörterbüchern sprechen ...; **it's nothing to ~ of** es ist nicht weiter erwähnenswert; **no money/trees** *etc* **to ~ of** so gut wie kein Geld/keine Bäume *etc*; **to ~ ill of sb/sth** über jdn/etw schlecht reden; **to ~ well of sb/sth** jdn/etw loben; **so to ~** sozusagen, eigentlich; **roughly ~ing** grob gesagt; **strictly ~ing** genau genommen; **legally ~ing** rechtlich gesehen; **generally ~ing** im Allgemeinen; **~ing personally ...** wenn Sie mich fragen ..., was mich betrifft ...; **~ing as a member of the club I have ...** als Mitglied des Vereins habe ich ...; **to ~ in public** in der Öffentlichkeit reden; **Mr X will ~ next** als Nächster hat Herr X das Wort erteilen; **Jones ~ing!** (*hier*) Jones!; **who is that ~ing?** wer ist da, bitte?; (*on extension phone, in office*) wer ist am Apparat?
◙ N SUF **Euro-~** Eurojargon *m*

> **speak against** VI +PREP OBJ (*in debate*) sich aussprechen gegen; (= *criticize*) etwas sagen gegen

> **speak for** VI +PREP OBJ **(a)** (*in debate*) unterstützen **(b) to speak for sb** (= *on behalf of*) in jds Namen (*dat*) sprechen; **he speaks for the miners** er ist der Sprecher der Bergleute; **I know I speak for all of us** ich bin sicher, dass ich im Namen aller spreche; **speaking for myself ...** was mich angeht ...; **speak for yourself!** (= *I don't agree*) das meinst auch nur du!; (= *don't include me*) du vielleicht!; **to speak well/badly for sth** ein Beweis *m*/nicht gerade ein Beweis *m* für etw sein; **to speak for itself** (= *be obvious*) für sich sprechen

> **speak out** VI (= *give opinion*) seine Meinung deutlich vertreten; **to speak out in favour of sth** für etw eintreten; **to speak out against sth** sich gegen etw aussprechen

> **speak up** VI **(a)** (= *raise one's voice*) lauter sprechen *or* reden; **if you want anything, speak up** sag, wenn du etwas willst **(b)** (*fig*) seine Meinung sagen *or* äußern; **to speak up for sb/sth** für jdn/etw eintreten; **what's wrong? speak up!** was ist los? heraus mit der Sprache!

speaker [ˈspiːkə^r] N **(a)** (*of language*) Sprecher *m*; **all ~s of German, all German ~s** alle, die Deutsch sprechen; (*esp native speakers*) alle Deutschsprachigen
(b) (*also Parl*: **Speaker**) Sprecher(in) *m(f)*; (*in lecture, = public ~*) Redner(in) *m(f)*; **the last** *or* **previous ~** der Vorredner; **our ~ today is ...** der heutige Referent ist ...; **Mr Speaker** (*Parl*) ≈

Herr Präsident
(c) (= *loudspeaker*) Lautsprecher *m*; (*on hi-fi etc*) Box *f*

*Im britischen Parlamentssystem hat der **Speaker** die Aufgabe, im House of Commons die Ordnung aufrechtzuerhalten und zu garantieren, dass alle Mitglieder die Geschäftsordnung befolgen. Der **Speaker**, der nicht Mitglied der Regierungspartei sein muss, wird zur Eröffnung eines neuen Parlaments gewählt. Sobald er oder sie im Amt ist, spricht der **Speaker** nur noch in seiner offiziellen Funktion und muss absolut unparteiisch sein. In den Vereinigten Staaten ist der **Speaker of the House** der Vorsitzende des Repräsentantenhauses, der zudem der Vorsitzende der Partei ist, die die Mehrheit stellt. Er ist selbst Mitglied des **House of Representatives** und wird von seiner eigenen Partei gewählt. Er ist nicht nur für die Einhaltung der Geschäftsordnung zuständig, sondern fungiert zugleich als Sprecher seiner Partei. Der **Speaker of the House** steht direkt nach dem Vizepräsidenten in der Präsidentennachfolge.*

speaking ['spiːkɪŋ] **1** N Sprechen *nt*; (= *speeches*) Reden *pl* **2** ADJ ATTR **to be within ~ distance** nahe genug sein, dass man sich verständigen kann

-speaking ADJ SUF -sprechend; (*with native language also*) -sprachig; **English-speaking** englischsprachig

speaking terms PL **to be on ~ with sb** mit jdm sprechen *or* reden

spear [spɪəʳ] **1** N Speer *m* **2** VT aufspießen; (= *wound, kill*) durchbohren; (= *catch with ~*) mit Speeren fangen

spearmint ['spɪəmɪnt] N Grüne Minze; **~ chewing gum** Spearmintkaugummi *m*

spec [spek] N (*inf*) **on ~** auf gut Glück

special ['speʃəl] **1** ADJ (= *particular*) besondere(r, s); (= *out of ordinary also*) Sonder- (= *specific*) bestimmt; (= *exceptional*) friend, favour, occasion speziell; (= *~ized also*) Spezial-; **I have no ~ person in mind** ich habe eigentlich an niemanden Bestimmtes gedacht; **take ~ care of it** passen Sie besonders gut darauf auf; **nothing ~** nichts Besonderes; **he expects ~ treatment** er will besonders behandelt werden; **this is rather a ~ day for me** heute ist ein ganz besonderer Tag für mich; **he's a very ~ person to her, he's very ~ to her** er bedeutet ihr sehr viel; **what's so ~ about her?** was ist denn an ihr so besonders?; **what's so ~ about that?** na und? (*inf*), das ist doch nichts Besonderes!; **everyone has his ~ place** jeder hat seinen eigenen Platz; **to feel ~** sich als etwas ganz Besonderes vorkommen; **~ discount** Sonderrabatt *m* **2** N (*TV, Rad*) Sonderprogramm *nt*; (*Cook*) Tagesgericht *nt*; **chef's ~** Spezialität *f* des Küchenchefs

special: special agent N (= *spy*) Agent(in) *m(f)*; **special case** N (*also Jur*) Sonderfall *m*; **special character** N (*Comput*) Sonderzeichen *nt*; **special delivery** N Eilzustellung *f*; **by ~** per Eilboten

specialist ['speʃəlɪst] **1** N Spezialist(in) *m(f)*, Fachmann *m*, Fachfrau *f* (*in* für); (*Med*) Facharzt *m*/-ärztin *f* **2** ADJ ATTR Fach-

speciality [ˌspeʃɪˈælɪtɪ], (*US*) **specialty** ['speʃəltɪ] N Spezialität *f*; (= *subject also*) Spezialgebiet *nt*

specialization [ˌspeʃəlaɪˈzeɪʃən] N Spezialisierung *f* (*in* auf +*acc*); (= *special subject*) Spezialgebiet *nt*

specialize ['speʃəlaɪz] VI sich spezialisieren (*in* auf +*acc*)

specialized ['speʃəlaɪzd] ADJ spezialisiert; **a ~ knowledge of biology** Fachkenntnisse *pl* in Biologie

specially ['speʃəlɪ] ADV besonders; (= *specifically*) extra; (= *for a particular purpose also*) speziell; **I had it ~ made** ich habe es extra machen lassen; **don't go to the post office ~ for me** gehen Sie meinetwegen nicht extra zur Post

special: special needs PL (*Brit*) **children with ~, ~ children** Kinder *pl* mit Behinderungen; **special offer** N Sonderangebot *nt*; **special school** N (*Brit*) Sonderschule *f*; (*for physically handicapped*) Behindertenschule *f*

specialty ['speʃəltɪ] N (*US*) = **speciality**

species ['spiːʃiːz] N, *pl* - Art *f*; (*Biol also*) Spezies *f*

specific [spəˈsɪfɪk] **1** ADJ (= *definite*) bestimmt, speziell; (= *precise*) genau; *example* ganz bestimmt; **9.3, to be ~** 9,3, um genau zu sein; **can you be a bit more ~?** können Sie sich etwas genauer äußern?; **he was quite ~ on that point** er hat sich zu diesem Punkt recht spezifisch geäußert **2** N **specifics** PL nähere *or* genauere Einzelheiten *pl*

-specific [-spəˈsɪfɪk] ADJ SUF -spezifisch

specifically [spəˈsɪfɪkəlɪ] ADV *warn, order, mention* ausdrücklich; *designed, request* speziell; (= *precisely*) genau; (= *in particular*) im Besonderen

specification [ˌspesɪfɪˈkeɪʃən] N **(a)** (*of requirements*) genaue Angabe, Aufstellung *f*; (*for car, machine*) (detaillierter) Entwurf; (*for building*) Bauplan *m*; **to ~** nach (genauer) Angabe; **~s** *pl* genaue Angaben *pl*; (*of car, machine*) technische Daten *pl*; (*of new building*) Baubeschreibung *f* **(b)** (= *stipulation*) Bedingung *f*; (*for building*) Vorschrift *f*

specified ['spesɪfaɪd] ADJ *amount, number* bestimmt; *period* vorgeschrieben; **at a ~ time** zu einer bestimmten Zeit

specify ['spesɪfaɪ] **1** VT angeben; (= *list individually or in detail*) spezifizieren, (einzeln) aufführen; (= *stipulate*) vorschreiben; **to ~ how to do sth** genauer *or* näher ausführen, wie etw gemacht werden soll **2** VI **unless otherwise specified** wenn nicht anders angegeben

specimen ['spesɪmɪn] **1** N Exemplar *nt*; (*of urine etc*) Probe *f*; (= *sample*) Muster *nt*; **a beautiful** *or* **fine ~** ein Prachtexemplar *nt* **2** ADJ ATTR Probe-

speck [spek] N Fleck *m*; (*of dust*) Körnchen *nt*; (*of gold, colour etc*) Sprenkel *m*; **a ~ on the horizon** ein Punkt *m or* Pünktchen *nt* am Horizont

speckle ['spekl] **1** N Sprenkel *m*, Tupfer *m* **2** VT sprenkeln; **to be ~d with sth** mit etw angesprenkelt sein

specs [speks] PL (*inf*) Brille *f*

spectacle ['spektəkl] N **(a)** (= *show*) Schauspiel *nt*; **to make a ~ of oneself** unangenehm auffallen **(b) spectacles** PL (*also pair of ~s*) Brille *f*

spectacle case N Brillenetui *nt*

spectacular [spekˈtækjʊləʳ] **1** ADJ sensationell; *scenery* atemberaubend; *failure* spektakulär **2** N (*Theat*) Show *f*

spectacularly [spekˈtækjʊlɪlɪ] ADV **(a)** (= *stunningly*) überwältigend **(b)** *successful, improve, fail* sensationell; *good, bad* unglaublich; **to do ~ well** unglaublich gut abschneiden

spectate [spekˈteɪt] VI (*inf: esp Sport*) zuschauen (*at* bei)

spectator [spekˈteɪtəʳ] N Zuschauer(in) *m(f)*

specter N (*US*) = **spectre**

spectra ['spektrə] PL *of* **spectrum**

spectre, (*US*) **specter** ['spektəʳ] N Gespenst *nt*; (*fig*) (Schreck)gespenst *nt*

spectrum ['spektrəm] N, *pl* **spectra** Spektrum *nt*; (*fig: = range also*) Palette *f*

speculate ['spekjʊleɪt] VI **(a)** (= *ponder*) (nach)grübeln, nachdenken (*on* über +*acc*); (= *conjecture*) spekulieren (*about, on* über +*acc*) **(b)** (*Fin*) spekulieren (*in* mit, *on* an +*dat*)

speculation [ˌspekjʊˈleɪʃən] N (*all senses*) Spekulation *f* (*on* über +*acc*); (= *guesswork also*) Vermutung *f*

speculative ['spekjʊlətɪv] ADJ **(a)** spekulativ (*esp Philos*); *approach, suggestions* rein theoretisch **(b)** (*Fin*) Spekulations-; **~ building** Bauspekulation *f*; **~ investor** Investitions-spekulant(in) *m(f)*

speculatively [ˈspekjʊlətɪvlɪ] ADV theoretisch, spekulativ (*also Fin*); **to invest ~ in sth** mit etw spekulieren

speculator ['spekjʊleɪtəʳ] N (*also Fin*) Spekulant(in) *m(f)*

sped [sped] PRET, PTP *of* **speed**

speech [spiːtʃ] N **(a)** NO PL (= *faculty of ~*) Sprache *f*; (= *act of speaking*) Sprechen *nt*; (= *manner of speaking*) Sprechweise *f*; **his ~ was very indistinct** er sprach sehr undeutlich; **to lose/ recover the power of ~** die Sprache verlieren/ zurückgewinnen; **freedom of ~** Redefreiheit *f* **(b)** (= *oration, Theat*) Rede *f* (*on, about* über +*acc*); **to give** *or* **make a ~** eine Rede halten **(c)** (*Brit Gram*) **direct/indirect** *or* **reported ~** direkte/indirekte Rede

speech: speech bubble N Sprechblase *f*; **speech defect** N Sprachfehler *m*

speechless ['spiːtʃlɪs] ADJ sprachlos (*with* vor); *anger* stumm; **his remark left me ~** seine Bemerkung verschlug mir die Sprache

speechlessly ['spiːtʃlɪslɪ] ADV wortlos; (*from surprise, shock etc*) sprachlos

speech: speech therapist N Sprachtherapeut(in) *m(f)*, Logopäde *m*, Logopädin *f*; **speech therapy** N Sprachtherapie *f*, Logopädie *f*; (= *treatment*) logopädische Behandlung

speed [spiːd], *vb: pret, ptp* **sped** *or* **speeded** 🔟 N **(a)** (= *esp fast* ~) Schnelligkeit *f*; (*of moving object or person*) Tempo *nt*; **at** ~ äußerst schnell; **at high/low** ~ mit hoher/niedriger Geschwindigkeit; **at full** *or* **top** ~ mit Höchstgeschwindigkeit; **at a** ~ **of 50 mph** mit einer Geschwindigkeit *or* einem Tempo von 50 Meilen pro Stunde; **the** ~ **of light** die Lichtgeschwindigkeit; **to pick up** *or* **gather** ~ schneller werden; (*fig: development*) sich beschleunigen; **to bring sb up to** ~ (*inf*) jdn auf den neuesten Stand bringen; **what** ~ **were you doing?** wie schnell sind Sie gefahren?; **full** ~ **ahead!** (*Naut*) volle Kraft voraus!
(b) (*Aut, Tech:* = *gear*) Gang *m*; **three-**~ **bicycle** Fahrrad mit Dreigangschaltung
🔟 VI **(a)** *pret, ptp* **sped** (= *move quickly*) jagen, flitzen; **the years sped by** die Jahre vergingen wie im Fluge **(b)** *pret, ptp* **speeded** (*Aut:* = *exceed* ~ *limit*) die Geschwindigkeitsbegrenzung überschreiten

➤ **speed along** *pret, ptp* **speeded** *or* **sped along** 🔟 VT SEP *work etc* beschleunigen; **to speed things along** die Dinge vorantreiben 🔟 VI entlangjagen *or* -flitzen (+*prep obj* +*acc*); (*work*) vorangehen

➤ **speed off** *pret, ptp* **speeded** *or* **sped off** VI davonjagen

➤ **speed up** *pret, ptp* **speeded up** 🔟 VI (*car, driver etc*) beschleunigen; (*person*) schneller machen; (*work, production etc*) schneller werden 🔟 VT SEP beschleunigen; *person* antreiben

speed: **speedboat** N Renn- *or* Schnellboot *nt*; **speed bump** N Bodenschwelle *f*; **speed camera** N (*Police*) Blitzgerät *nt*

speedily [ˈspiːdɪlɪ] ADV schnell; *reply, return* prompt

speeding [ˈspiːdɪŋ] N Geschwindigkeitsüberschreitung *f*; **to get a** ~ **fine** eine Geldstrafe wegen Geschwindigkeitsüberschreitung bekommen

speed limit N Geschwindigkeitsbegrenzung *f*; **a 30 mph** ~ eine Geschwindigkeitsbegrenzung von 50 km/h

speedometer [spɪˈdɒmɪtə'] N Tachometer *m*

speed: **speed skater** N Eisschnellläufer(in) *m(f)*; **speed skating** N Eisschnelllauf *m*; **speed trap** N Radarfalle *f* (*inf*); **speedway** N **(a)** (*Sport*) Speedwayrennen *nt*; (= *track*) Speedwaybahn *f* **(b)** (*US*) (= *racetrack*) Rennstrecke *f*; (= *expressway*) Schnellstraße *f*

speedy [ˈspiːdɪ] ADJ (+ER) schnell; *answer, service also* prompt; **we wish Joan a** ~ **recovery** wir wünschen Joan eine rasche Genesung

spell[1] [spel] N (*lit, fig*) Zauber *m*; (= *incantation*) Zauberspruch *m*; **to be under a** ~ (*lit*) verzaubert *or* verhext sein; (*fig*) wie verzaubert sein; **to put a** ~ **on sb, to cast a** ~ **on** *or* **over sb, to put sb under a** ~ (*lit*) jdn verzaubern *or* verhexen; (*fig*) jdn in seinen Bann ziehen; **to be under sb's** ~ (*fig*) in jds Bann (*dat*) stehen; **to break the** ~ (*lit, fig*) den Zauber lösen

spell[2] N (= *period*) Weile *f*, Weilchen *nt*; **for a** ~ eine Weile, eine Zeit lang; **cold/hot** ~ Kälte-/Hitzewelle *f*; **dizzy** ~ Schwächeanfall *m*; **a short** ~ **of sunny weather** eine kurze Schönwetterperiode; **they're going through a bad** ~ sie machen eine schwierige Zeit durch

spell[3] *pret, ptp* **spelt** (*esp Brit*) *or* **spelled** 🔟 VI (*in writing*) (orthografisch) richtig schreiben; (*aloud*) buchstabieren; **she can't** ~ sie kann keine Rechtschreibung 🔟 VT **(a)** (*in writing*) schreiben; (*aloud*) buchstabieren; **how do you** ~ "**onyx**"? wie schreibt man „Onyx"?; **how do you** ~ **your name?** wie schreibt sich Ihr Name?; **what do these letters** ~? welches Wort ergeben diese Buchstaben? **(b)** (= *denote*) bedeuten

➤ **spell out** VT SEP (= *spell aloud*) buchstabieren; (= *read slowly*) entziffern; (= *explain*) verdeutlichen; **do I have to spell it out for you?** (*inf*) muss ich noch deutlicher werden?

spellbinding [ˈspelbaɪndɪŋ] ADJ fesselnd

spellbound [ˈspelbaʊnd] ADJ, ADV (*fig*) wie verzaubert, gebannt

spell: **spell-check** (*Comput*) 🔟 N Rechtschreibprüfung *f* 🔟 VT die Rechtschreibung (+*gen*) prüfen; **spellchecker** N (*Comput*) Rechtschreibprüfung *f*

speller [ˈspelə'] N **to be a good/bad** ~ in Rechtschreibung gut/schlecht sein

spelling [ˈspelɪŋ] N Rechtschreibung *f*, Orthografie *f*; (*of a word*) Schreibweise *f*; (= *activity*) Rechtschreiben *nt*

spelling mistake N (Recht)schreibfehler *m*

spelt [spelt] (*esp Brit*) PRET, PTP *of* **spell**[3]

spend [spend], *pret, ptp* **spent** 🔟 VT **(a)** *money* ausgeben (*on* für); *energy* verbrauchen; *time* brauchen; **time well spent** sinnvoll genutzte Zeit; **to** ~ **money/effort on sth** (= *devote to*) Geld/Mühe in etw (*acc*) investieren; **I spent a lot of effort on that** das hat mich viel Mühe gekostet
(b) (= *pass*) *time, holiday, evening etc* verbringen; **I spent the night in a hotel** ich habe in einem Hotel übernachtet; **he** ~**s his time reading** er verbringt seine Zeit mit Lesen
🔟 VI Geld ausgeben
🔟 N Ausgaben *pl*

> *Be careful!* **to spend** *is not translated by the German word* **spenden**.

spender [ˈspendə'] N **he is a big/free** ~ bei ihm sitzt das Geld locker

spending [ˈspendɪŋ] N, NO PL Ausgaben *pl*; **government** ~ **cuts** Kürzungen *pl* im Etat

spending: **spending money** N Taschengeld *nt*; **spending power** N Kaufkraft *f*; **spending spree** N Großeinkauf *m*; **to go on a** ~ groß einkaufen gehen

spent [spent] 🔟 PRET, PTP *of* **spend** 🔟 ADJ *cartridge, match* verbraucht; *bullets also* verschossen; *person* erschöpft; **to be a** ~ **force** nichts mehr zu sagen haben; (*movement*) sich totgelaufen haben

sperm [spɜːm] N Samenfaden *m*; (= *fluid*) Samenflüssigkeit *f*, Sperma *nt*

sperm bank N Samenbank *f*

spermicide [ˈspɜːmɪsaɪd] N Spermizid *nt*

spew [spjuː] 🔟 VI **(a)** (*inf:* = *vomit*) brechen, spucken **(b)** (*also* ~ **forth** (*form*) *or* **out**) sich ergießen (*geh*); (*esp liquid*) hervorsprudeln 🔟 VT **(a)** (*also* ~ **up**) (*inf:* = *vomit*) erbrechen, ausspucken; *blood* spucken **(b)** (*fig: also* ~ **out**) *flames* speien; *lava* auswerfen; *waste water etc* ablassen

sphere [sfɪə'] N **(a)** Kugel *f*; (= *heavenly* ~) Gestirn *nt* (*geh*); **to be a** ~ kugelförmig sein **(b)** (*fig*) Sphäre *f*, Welt *f*; (*of person, personal experience*) Bereich *m*; (*of knowledge etc*) Gebiet *nt*, Feld *nt*; (= *social etc circle*) Kreis *m*; **his** ~ **of influence** sein Einflussbereich

spherical [ˈsferɪkəl] ADJ kugelförmig

sphinx [sfɪŋks] N Sphinx *f*

spice [spaɪs] 🔟 N **(a)** Gewürz *nt* **(b)** (*fig*) Würze *f* 🔟 VT (*lit, fig*) würzen

➤ **spice up** VT (*fig*) würzen

spiced [spaɪst] ADJ (*Cook*) *savoury dish* würzig; ~ **wine** Glühwein *m*; **highly** ~ pikant (gewürzt)

spiciness [ˈspaɪsɪnɪs] N (= *quality*) Würzigkeit *f*; (= *taste*) Würze *f*; (*fig*) Pikanterie *f*

spick-and-span [ˌspɪkənˈspæn] ADJ blitzsauber

spicy [ˈspaɪsɪ] ADJ (+ER) würzig; (*fig*) *story etc* pikant

spider [ˈspaɪdə'] N Spinne *f*; ~'**s web** Spinnwebe *f*

spiderweb [ˈspaɪdəwɛb] N (*US*) Spinnwebe *f*

spidery [ˈspaɪdərɪ] ADJ *writing* krakelig

spike [spaɪk] 🔟 N (*on wall, railing etc*) Spitze *f*; (*on plant*) Stachel *m*; (*on shoe, tyre etc*) Spike *m*; (*for receipts etc*) Dorn *m* 🔟 VT **(a)** (*lit:* = *pierce*) aufspießen **(b)** *drink* einen Schuss zusetzen (+*dat*)

spiked [spaɪkt] ADJ *drink* mit Schuss; ~ **hair** Igel(schnitt) *m*

spiky [ˈspaɪkɪ] ADJ (+ER) *grass* stach(e)lig; *plant* spitzblättrig; *leaf* spitz; *hair* hoch stehend

spill [spɪl], *vb: pret, ptp* **spilt** (*esp Brit*) *or* **spilled** 🔟 N (= ~*ed liquid etc*) Lache *f*; *oil* ~ Ölkatastrophe *f* 🔟 VT verschütten; **to** ~ **the beans** alles ausplaudern; **to** ~ **the beans about sth** etw ausplaudern; **the lorry** ~**ed its load onto the road** die Ladung fiel vom Lastwagen herunter auf die Straße 🔟 VI verschüttet werden; (*large quantity*) sich ergießen; (*fig: people*) strömen

➤ **spill out** VI (*of us aus*) (*liquid*) herausschwappen; (*money, jewels*) herausfallen; (*fig: people*) (heraus)strömen

➤ **spill over** VI (*liquid*) überlaufen; (*fig*) (*population*) sich ausbreiten (*into* auf +*acc*); (*meeting*) sich hinziehen (*into* bis in +*acc*)

spillage [ˈspɪlɪdʒ] N (*act*) Verschütten *nt*; (= *quantity*) verschüttete Menge, Spillage *f* (*Comm*)

spilt [spɪlt] (*esp Brit*) PRET, PTP *of* **spill**

spin [spɪn], *vb: pret* **spun** *or* (*old*) **span**, *ptp* **spun** 🔟 N **(a)** (= *revolution*) Drehung *f*; (= *washing machine programme*)

Schleudern *nt no pl*; **to give sth a ~** etw (schnell) drehen; (*in washing machine etc*) etw schleudern; **to send sb/sth into a (flat) ~** (*Brit fig inf*) jdn/etw zum Rotieren bringen (*inf*) **(b)** (*on ball*) Drall *m*; **to put ~ on the ball** dem Ball einen Drall geben; (*with racquet*) den Ball anschneiden **(c)** (*political*) Image *nt*; **to put a new/different** *etc* **~ on sth** (= *interpretation*) etw neu/anders *etc* interpretieren **(d)** (*Aviat*) Trudeln *nt no pl*; **to go into a ~** zu trudeln anfangen **2** VT **(a)** (*person, spider*) spinnen **(b)** (= *turn*) drehen; (*fast*) herumwirbeln; (*in washing machine*) schleudern; (= *toss*) coin (hoch)werfen; (*Sport*) ball einen Drall geben (+*dat*); (*with racquet*) (an)schneiden **3** VI **(a)** (*person*) spinnen **(b)** (= *revolve*) sich drehen; (*fast*) (herum)wirbeln; (*plane etc*) trudeln; (*in washing machine*) schleudern; **to ~ round and round** sich im Kreis drehen; **the car spun out of control** der Wagen begann, sich unkontrollierbar zu drehen; **to send sb/ sth ~ning** jdn/etw umwerfen; **my head is ~ning** mir dreht sich alles

➤ **spin (a)round 1** VI (= *revolve*) sich drehen; (*very fast*) (herum)wirbeln **2** VT SEP (schnell) drehen; (*very fast*) herumwirbeln

➤ **spin out** VT SEP (*inf*) money, food strecken (*inf*); holiday, meeting in die Länge ziehen; story ausspinnen

spinach ['spɪnɪtʃ] N Spinat *m*

spinal ['spaɪnl] ADJ Rücken-, Rückgrat-

spinal: spinal column N Wirbelsäule *f*; **spinal cord** N Rückenmark *nt*

spindle ['spɪndl] N (*for spinning, Mech*) Spindel *f*

spindly ['spɪndlɪ] ADJ (+ER) spindeldürr (*inf*)

spin: spin doctor N (*Pol inf*) PR-Berater(in) *m(f)*; **spin-drier** N (*Brit*) (Wäsche)schleuder *f*; **spin-dry** VTI schleudern; **spin-dryer** N = **spin-drier**

spine [spaɪn] N **(a)** (*Anat*) Rückgrat *nt*; (*of book*) (Buch)rücken *m* **(b)** (= *spike*) Stachel *m*; (*of plant also*) Dorn *m*

spine-chilling ['spaɪntʃɪlɪŋ] ADJ schaurig, gruselig

spineless ['spaɪnlɪs] ADJ (*fig*) person ohne Rückgrat; compromise, refusal feige

spine-tingling ['spaɪntɪŋglɪŋ] ADJ (= *frightening*) schaurig, Schauder erregend

spinning IN CPDS Spinn-

spin-off ['spɪnɒf] N (= *side-product*) Nebenprodukt *nt*

spinster ['spɪnstə'] N Unverheiratete *f*, Ledige *f*; (*pej*) alte Jungfer (*pej*)

spiny ['spaɪnɪ] ADJ (+ER) stach(e)lig; plant also dornig

spiral ['spaɪərəl] **1** ADJ spiralförmig **2** N (*lit, fig*) Spirale *f*; **price/ inflationary ~** Preis-/Inflationsspirale *f* **3** VI (*also* ~ **up**) sich (hoch)winden; (*smoke also, missile etc*) spiralförmig *or* in einer Spirale aufsteigen; (*prices*) (nach oben) klettern

spiral staircase N Wendeltreppe *f*

spire [spaɪə'] N (*of church*) Turmspitze *f*, Turm *m*

spirit ['spɪrɪt] **1** N **(a)** Geist *m*; (= *mood*) Stimmung *f*; **I'll be with you in ~** im Geiste werde ich bei euch sein; **Christmas ~** (*Rel*) weihnachtlicher Geist; (= *mood*) weihnachtliche Stimmung; **a ~ of optimism** eine optimistische Stimmung; **the ~ of the age** der Zeitgeist; **to enter into the ~ of sth** bei etw mitmachen *or* dabei sein; **that's the ~!** (*inf*) so ists recht! (*inf*); **the ~ of the law** der Geist *or* Sinn des Gesetzes; **to take sth in the right/wrong ~** etw richtig/falsch auffassen **(b)** NO PL (= *courage*) Mut *m*; (= *vitality, enthusiasm*) Elan *m*, Schwung *m*; **a horse with plenty of ~** ein feuriges Pferd **(c)** **spirits** PL (= *state of mind*) Stimmung *f*, Laune *f*; (= *courage*) Mut *m*; **to be in high ~s** bester Laune sein; **to be in good/low ~s** guter/schlechter Laune sein; **to keep up one's ~s** den Mut nicht verlieren; **my ~s rose** ich bekam (neuen) Mut; **her ~s fell** ihr sank der Mut **(d)** **spirits** PL (= *alcohol*) Spirituosen *pl* **2** VT **to ~ sb/sth away** *or* **off** jdn/etw verschwinden lassen *or* wegzaubern

spirited ['spɪrɪtɪd] ADJ temperamentvoll; performance lebendig; (= *courageous*) beherzt, mutig

spirit level N Wasserwaage *f*

spiritual ['spɪrɪtjʊəl] ADJ geistig; person spirituell; expression vergeistigt; (*Eccl*) geistlich; **~ life** Seelenleben *nt*; **my ~ home** meine geistige Heimat

spirituality [spɪrɪtjʊ'ælɪtɪ] N Geistigkeit *f*

spiritually ['spɪrɪtjʊəlɪ] ADV geistig

spit¹ [spɪt], *vb: pret, ptp* **spat 1** N (= *saliva*) Spucke *f* **2** VT spucken, speien (*geh*) **3** VI spucken, speien (*geh*); (*fat*) spritzen; (*person: verbally, cat*) fauchen; **to ~ at sb** jdn anspucken, jdn anspeien (*geh*); jdn anfauchen; **it is ~ting (with rain)** (*Brit*) es tröpfelt

➤ **spit out** VT SEP ausspucken; words ausstoßen; **spit it out!** (*fig inf*) spucks aus! (*inf*), heraus mit der Sprache!

spit² N **(a)** (*Cook*) (Brat)spieß *m* **(b)** (*of land*) Landzunge *f*

spite [spaɪt] **1** N **(a)** (= *ill will*) Boshaftigkeit *f*, Gehässigkeit *f* **(b)** **in ~ of** (= *despite*) trotz (+*gen*); **it was a success in ~ of him** dennoch war es ein Erfolg; **in ~ of the fact that he ...** obwohl er ... **2** VT ärgern

spiteful ['spaɪtfʊl] ADJ boshaft, gemein; (= *gloating also*) gehässig

spitefully ['spaɪtfʊlɪ] ADV boshaft, gemein; (= *gloatingly*) gehässig

spitefulness ['spaɪtfʊlnɪs] N Boshaftigkeit *f*, Gemeinheit *f*; (= *gloating*) Gehässigkeit *f*

spitting image [spɪtɪŋ'ɪmɪdʒ] N (*inf*) Ebenbild *nt*; **to be the ~ of sb** jdm wie aus dem Gesicht geschnitten sein

spittle ['spɪtl] N Speichel *m*, Spucke *f*

splash [splæʃ] **1** N **(a)** (= *spray*) Spritzen *nt no pl*; (= *noise*) Platschen *nt no pl*; **it made a ~ as it hit the water** das Wasser spritzte nach allen Seiten, als es hineinfiel; (*noise*) es fiel platschend ins Wasser; **to make a ~** (*fig*) Furore machen; (*news*) wie eine Bombe einschlagen **(b)** (= *sth ~ed*) Spritzer *m*; (*of colour, light*) Tupfen *m*; (= *patch*) Fleck *m* **2** VT **(a)** water etc spritzen; (= *pour*) gießen; person, object besprengen **(b)** (*Press inf*) story groß rausbringen (*inf*) **3** VI (*liquid*) spritzen; (*rain, waves*) klatschen; (*when diving etc*) platschen; (*when playing*) plan(t)schen

➤ **splash about** (*Brit*) *or* **around 1** VI herumspritzen; (*in water*) herumplan(t)schen **2** VT SEP water herumspritzen mit

➤ **splash out** VI (*Brit inf*) tüchtig in die Tasche greifen (*inf*); (*on giving presents etc*) sich nicht lumpen lassen (*inf*); **to splash out on sth** sich (*dat*) etw spendieren (*inf*)

➤ **splash up 1** VT SEP spritzen **2** VI (*water, mud*) aufspritzen

splashy ['splæʃɪ] ADJ (*US inf*) protzig, auffällig

splat [splæt] N Platschen *nt*

splatter ['splætə'] **1** N Fleck *m*; (*of paint etc*) Klecks *m* **2** VI spritzen; (*paint also*) klecksen; (*rain*) prasseln **3** VT bespritzen; (*with paint etc*) beklecksen

splay [spleɪ] **1** VT legs, fingers spreizen; feet nach außen stellen **2** VI **he was ~ed out on the ground** er lag auf der Erde und hatte alle viere von sich gestreckt

spleen [spliːn] N (*Anat*) Milz *f*; (*fig*) Zorn *m*

splendid ['splendɪd] ADJ **(a)** (= *excellent*) hervorragend; rider etc, idea glänzend, ausgezeichnet **(b)** (= *magnificent*) herrlich; occasion, scale großartig

splendidly ['splendɪdlɪ] ADV **(a)** (= *magnificently*) dressed prächtig; restored herrlich **(b)** (= *excellently*) hervorragend

splendour, (*US*) **splendor** ['splendə'] N Pracht *f no pl*; (*of music, achievement*) Großartigkeit *f*

splice [splaɪs] VT ropes spleißen; (*spec*) film (zusammen)kleben; pieces of wood etc verfugen; **to ~ sth together** etw zusammenfügen

splint [splɪnt] N Schiene *f*; **to put a ~ on sth** etw schienen

splinter ['splɪntə'] **1** N Splitter *m* **2** VTI (zer)splittern; **to ~ off** absplittern

splinter group N Splittergruppe *f*

split [splɪt], *vb: pret, ptp* **split 1** N **(a)** Riss *m* (*in* in +*dat*); (*esp in wall, rock, wood*) Spalt *m* (*in* in +*dat*) **(b)** (*fig: = division*) Bruch *m* (*in* in +*dat*); (*Pol, Eccl*) Spaltung *f* (*in* +*gen*); **there is a ~ in the party over ...** die Partei ist in der Frage (+*gen*) ... gespalten; **a three-way ~ of the profits** eine Drittelung des Gewinns **(c)** (= *distinction: in meaning*) Aufteilung *f* **(d)** PL **the ~s** Spagat *m*; **to do the ~s** (einen) Spagat machen **2** ADJ gespalten (*on, over* in +*dat*) **3** VT (= *cleave*) (zer)teilen; wood, atom (= *divide*) spalten; stone zerbrechen; work, costs, etc (sich *dat*) teilen; **to ~ hairs** (*inf*) Haarspalterei treiben (*inf*); **to ~ one's sides (laughing)**

(*inf*) vor Lachen fast platzen (*inf*); **to ~ sth open** etw aufbrechen; **he ~ his head open when he fell** er hat sich (*dat*) beim Fallen den Kopf aufgeschlagen; **to ~ sth into three parts** etw in drei Teile aufteilen; **to ~ the vote** die Abstimmung zum Scheitern bringen; **they ~ the profit three ways** sie haben den Gewinn in drei Teile geteilt; **to ~ the difference** (*lit: with money etc*) sich (*dat*) die Differenz teilen **◼4** VI **(a)** (*wood, stone*) (entzwei)brechen; (*hair, Pol, Eccl*) sich spalten (*on, over* wegen); (*seam etc*) platzen; (= *divide*) sich teilen; (*people*) sich aufteilen; **to ~ open** aufplatzen, aufbrechen; **my head is ~ting** (*fig*) mir platzt der Kopf **(b)** (*inf*: = *leave*) abhauen (*inf*)

➤ **split off ◼1** VT SEP abtrennen (*prep obj* von); (= *break*) abbrechen (*prep obj* von) **◼2** VI abbrechen; (*fig*) sich trennen (*from* von)

➤ **split up ◼1** VT SEP *money, work* (auf)teilen; *party, organization* spalten; *meeting* ein Ende machen (+*dat*); *two people* trennen; *crowd* zerstreuen **◼2** VI zerbrechen; (= *divide*) sich teilen; (*meeting, crowd*) sich spalten; (*partners*) sich voneinander trennen

split: split ends PL Spliss *m*; **split screen** N (*Comput*) geteilter Bildschirm; **split second** N Bruchteil *m* einer Sekunde; **in a ~** in Sekundenschnelle; **split-second** ADJ ~ **timing** Abstimmung *f* auf die Sekunde

splitting ['splɪtɪŋ] ADJ *headache* rasend, heftig

splodge [splɒdʒ], (*US*) **splotch** [splɒtʃ] N Klecks *m*; (*of cream etc*) Klacks *m*

splurge (out) on ['splɜːdʒ('aʊt)ɒn] VI +PREP OBJ (*inf*) sich in Unkosten stürzen mit

splutter ['splʌtə'] **◼1** N (*of engine*) Stottern *nt* **◼2** VI stottern; (*person*) (= *spit*) spucken; (*fire, fat*) zischen **◼3** VT (hervor)stoßen; **that's not true, he ~ed** das ist nicht wahr, platzte er los

spoil [spɔɪl], *vb*: pret, ptp **spoilt** (*Brit*) or **spoiled ◼1** N USU PL Beute *f no pl*; (*fig*: = *profits also*) Gewinn *m*; **the ~s of war** die Kriegsbeute
◼2 VT **(a)** (= *ruin*) verderben; *town, looks etc* verschandeln; *life* ruinieren; (*Brit*) *ballot papers* ungültig machen; **to ~ the party** (*fig*) ein Spaßverderber sein; **to ~ sb's fun** jdm den Spaß verderben; **it ~ed our evening** das hat uns (*dat*) den Abend verdorben
(b) *person, children* verwöhnen; **to be ~ed for choice** die Qual der Wahl haben
◼3 VI **(a)** (*food*) verderben
(b) **to be ~ing for trouble/a fight** Ärger/Streit suchen

spoilage ['spɔɪlɪdʒ] N (*Comm*) Ausschuss *m*

spoilsport ['spɔɪlspɔːt] N (*inf*) Spielverderber(in) *m(f)* (*inf*)

spoilt [spɔɪlt] (*Brit*) **◼1** PRET, PTP of **spoil ◼2** ADJ *child* verwöhnt; *meal* verdorben; *ballot papers* ungültig

spoke¹ [spəʊk] N Speiche *f*; **to put a ~ in sb's wheel** (*Brit inf*) jdm Knüppel zwischen die Beine werfen (*inf*)

spoke² PRET of **speak**

spoken ['spəʊkən] **◼1** PTP of **speak ◼2** ADJ *language* gesprochen; **his ~ English is better than ...** er spricht Englisch besser als ...

spokesman ['spəʊksmən] N, *pl* **-men** [-mən] Sprecher *m*

spokesperson ['spəʊkspɜːsən] N Sprecher(in) *m(f)*

spokeswoman ['spəʊkswʊmən] N, *pl* **-women** [-wɪmɪn] Sprecherin *f*

sponge [spʌndʒ] **◼1** N **(a)** (*also Zool*) Schwamm *m* **(b)** (*Cook*) (*also* ~ **cake**) Rührkuchen *m*; (*fatless*) Biskuit(kuchen) *m* **◼2** VT **(a)** (= *clean*) abwischen; *wound* abtupfen **(b)** (*inf*: = *scrounge*) schnorren (*inf*) (*from* bei)

➤ **sponge down** VT SEP *person* (schnell) waschen; *walls also* abwaschen; *horse* abreiben

➤ **sponge off** VT SEP *stain, liquid* abwischen

➤ **sponge off** *or* **on** VI +PREP OBJ (*inf*) **to sponge off** *or* **on sb** jdm auf der Tasche liegen (*inf*)

sponge: sponge bag N (*Brit*) Waschbeutel *m*; **sponge cake** N Rührkuchen *m*; (*fatless*) Biskuit(kuchen) *m*; **sponge pudding** N Mehlpudding *m*

sponger ['spʌndʒə'] N (*inf*) Schmarotzer(in) *m(f)*, Schnorrer(in) *m(f)* (*inf*)

spongy ['spʌndʒɪ] ADJ (+ER) nachgiebig, weich; *skin etc* schwammig

sponsor ['spɒnsə'] **◼1** N Förderer *m*, Förderin *f*; (*for event*) Schirmherr(in) *m(f)*; (*Rad, TV, Sport etc*) Sponsor(in) *m(f)*; (*for*

fund-raising) Spender(in) *m(f)* **◼2** VT unterstützen; (*financially*) fördern; *event, programme* sponsern; **he ~ed him (at) 5p a mile** (*Brit*) er verpflichtete sich, ihm 5 Pence pro Meile zu geben

sponsored ['spɒnsəd] ADJ (*Brit: walk etc*) gesponsert

sponsorship ['spɒnsəʃɪp] N Unterstützung *f*; (*financial also*) Förderung *f*, Sponsern *nt*; (*Rad, TV, Sport*) Finanzierung *f*

spontaneity [spɒntə'neɪɪtɪ] N Spontaneität *f*; (*of style*) Ungezwungenheit *f*

spontaneous [spɒn'teɪnɪəs] ADJ spontan; *style* ungezwungen

spontaneously [spɒn'teɪnɪəslɪ] ADV spontan; (= *voluntarily also*) von sich aus, von selbst

spoof [spuːf] (*inf*) N Parodie *f* (*of auf* +*acc*)

spook [spuːk] (*inf*) **◼1** N Gespenst *nt* **◼2** VT (*esp US*: = *frighten*) einen Schrecken einjagen (+*dat*)

spooky ['spuːkɪ] ADJ (+ER) (*inf*) **(a)** gespenstisch, gruselig (*inf*) **(b)** (= *strange*) sonderbar; **it was really ~** das war wirklich ein sonderbares *or* eigenartiges Gefühl

spool [spuːl] **◼1** N (*Phot, on sewing machine*) Spule *f*; (*on fishing line, of thread*) Rolle *f*; (*for thread*) (Garn)rolle *f* **◼2** VT (*Comput*) spulen

spooler ['spuːlə'] N (*Comput*) (Drucker)spooler *m*

spoon [spuːn] **◼1** N Löffel *m* **◼2** VT löffeln

➤ **spoon out** VT SEP (löffelweise) ausschöpfen

spoon-feed ['spuːnfiːd], pret, ptp **spoon-fed** ['spuːnfed] VT *baby, invalid* füttern; (*fig*) (= *do thinking for*) gängeln; (= *supply with*) füttern (*inf*)

spoonful ['spuːnfʊl] N Löffel *m*

sporadic [spə'rædɪk] ADJ sporadisch; (= *occasional also*) gelegentlich

sporadically [spə'rædɪkəlɪ] ADV sporadisch; (= *occasionally also*) gelegentlich

sport [spɔːt] **◼1** N **(a)** Sport *m no pl*; (= *type of* ~) Sportart *f*; **to be good at ~(s)** sportlich sein; **outdoor ~s** Sport *m* im Freien; **indoor ~s** Hallensport *m*
(b) sports PL (*also* ~**s meeting**) Sportveranstaltung *f*
(c) (= *amusement*) Spaß *m*
(d) (*inf*: = *person*) feiner *or* anständiger Kerl (*inf*); **to be a (good)** ~ alles mitmachen; **be a ~!** sei kein Spielverderber!
◼2 VT *tie, dress* anhaben; *pink etc hair, beard* herumlaufen mit (*inf*)
◼3 ADJ ATTR (*US*) = **sports**

sporting ['spɔːtɪŋ] ADJ sportlich; (*fig*) *offer, solution* fair; (= *decent*) anständig; ~ **events** Wettkämpfe *pl*; ~ **editor** (*US*) Sportredakteur(in) *m(f)*; **to give sb a ~ chance** jdm eine faire Chance geben

sports [spɔːts], (*US also*) **sport** IN CPDS Sport-; **sports car** N Sportwagen *m*; **sports field, sports ground** N (*Brit*) Sportplatz *m*; **sports jacket** N Sakko *m or nt*; **sportsman** [-mən] N Sportler *m*; **sportsmanlike** [-mənlaɪk] ADJ sportlich; (*fig*) *behaviour etc* fair; **sportsmanship** [-mənʃɪp] N (= *skill*) Sportlichkeit *f*; (= *fairness also*) Fairness *f*; **sportsperson** N Sportler(in) *m(f)*; **sportswear** N (*for sport*) Sportkleidung *f*; (= *leisure wear*) Freizeitkleidung *f*; **sportswoman** N Sportlerin *f*

sporty ['spɔːtɪ] ADJ (+ER) (*inf*) *person* sportbegeistert; *clothes, car* sportlich

spot [spɒt] **◼1** N **(a)** (*lit, fig*) Punkt *m*; (*Zool, Bot*) Fleck *m*; (= *place, characteristic*) Stelle *f*; **a dress with ~s** ein gepunktetes Kleid; **~s of blood** Blutflecken *pl*; **this is the ~ where** Rizzio **was murdered** an dieser Stelle *or* hier ist Rizzio ermordet worden; **a pleasant ~** ein schönes Fleckchen (*inf*); **on the ~** (= *at the scene*) an Ort und Stelle; (= *at once*) auf der Stelle, sofort; **weak ~** schwache Stelle
(b) (*Med etc*) Fleck *m*; (= *pimple*) Pickel *m*; (= *place*) Stelle *f*; **break out** *or* **come out in ~s** Flecken/Pickel bekommen
(c) (*Brit inf*: = *small quantity*) **a ~** ~ ein/das bisschen; **we had a ~ of rain/a few ~s of rain** wir hatten ein paar Tropfen Regen; **there was a ~ of trouble/bother** es gab etwas Ärger; **we're in a ~ of bother** wir haben Schwierigkeiten
(d) (= *difficulty*) Klemme *f*; **to be in a (tight)** ~ in der Klemme sitzen (*inf*); **to put sb in a** *or* **on the** ~ jdn in Verlegenheit bringen
(e) (*in show*) Nummer *f*; (*Rad, TV*) (ein paar Minuten) Sendezeit *f*; (*for advertisement*) Werbespot *m*
(f) spots PL (*Comm*) Lokowaren *pl* (*spec*), sofort lieferbare Waren *pl*

2 VT entdecken; (= *notice also*) sehen; *signs, difference, opportunity* erkennen; *mistake, bargain* finden

spot: spot cash N sofortige Bezahlung; **spot check** N Stichprobe *f*; **spot goods** PL sofort lieferbare Waren *pl*, Lokowaren *pl* (*spec*)

spotless [ˈspɒtlɪs] ADJ tadellos sauber, pikobello (*inf*); (*fig*) *reputation* untadelig

spotlessly [ˈspɒtlɪslɪ] ADV **~ clean** blitzsauber

spot: spotlight *vb: pret, ptp* **spotlighted** **1** N (= *lamp*) (*in TV studio etc*) Scheinwerfer *m*; (*small, in room etc*) Strahler *m*; (= *light*) Scheinwerferlicht *nt*, Rampenlicht *nt* (*also fig*); **to be in the ~** (*lit*) im Scheinwerferlicht *or* Rampenlicht stehen; (*fig*) im Rampenlicht der Öffentlichkeit stehen **2** VT anstrahlen; (*fig*) aufmerksam machen auf (+*acc*); **spot-on** ADJ (*Brit inf*) exakt, haarscharf richtig (*inf*); **~!** richtig!, genau!; **spot price** N (*St Ex*) Kassapreis *m*

spotted [ˈspɒtɪd] ADJ gefleckt; (= *with dots*) getüpfelt; *material also* getupft; **~ with brown** braun gefleckt; **blue material ~ with white** blauer Stoff mit weißen Tupfen; **~ with blood** blutbespritzt; **~ with paint** mit Farbflecken

spotty [ˈspɒtɪ] ADJ (+ER) (= *stained, Med*) fleckig; (= *pimply*) pick(e)lig

spouse [spaʊs] N (*form*) Gatte *m*, Gattin *f*

spout [spaʊt] **1** N (a) Ausguss *m*, Tülle *f*; (*on teapot*) Schnabel *m*, Ausguss *m*; (*on pump, tap*) Ausflussrohr *nt*; (*on pipe*) Ausfluss *m*; (*on watering can*) Rohr *nt*; **up the ~** (*Brit inf: plans etc*) im Eimer (*inf*)
(b) (= *jet of water etc*) Fontäne *f*; (*Met: = water ~*) Wasserhose *f* **2** VT (a) (*fountain etc*) (heraus)spritzen; (*whale*) ausstoßen, spritzen; (*volcano*) speien
(b) (*inf*) *words* hervorsprudeln; *figures* herunterrasseln (*inf*); *nonsense* von sich geben **3** VI (*water etc, whale*) spritzen (*from* aus); **to ~ out (of sth)** (aus etw) hervorspritzen; (*lava*) (aus etw) ausgespien werden
(b) (*fig inf: = declaim*) palavern (*inf*), salbadern (*pej*)

sprain [spreɪn] **1** N Verstauchung *f* **2** VT verstauchen; **to ~ one's ankle** sich (*dat*) den Fuß verstauchen

sprang [spræŋ] PRET *of* **spring**

sprawl [sprɔːl] **1** N (= *posture*) Flegeln *nt no pl* (*inf*); (*of buildings etc*) Ausbreitung *f*; **urban ~** wild wuchernde Ausbreitung des Stadtgebietes **2** VI (*person*) (= *fall*) der Länge nach hinfallen; (= *lounge*) sich hinflegeln; (*town*) (wild) wuchern; **to send sb ~ing** jdn zu Boden werfen **3** VT **to be ~ed over sth/on sth** (*body*) ausgestreckt auf etw (*dat*) liegen

sprawling [ˈsprɔːlɪŋ] ADJ *city, suburbs* wildwuchernd; *house* großflächig; *grounds* ausgedehnt; *figure* hingeflegelt; *body* ausgestreckt

spray[1] [spreɪ] N (= *bouquet*) Strauß *m*

spray[2] **1** N (a) Sprühregen *m*; (*of sea*) Gischt *m*
(b) (= *implement*) Sprühdose *f*; (= *insecticide ~, for irrigation*) Sprühgerät *nt*
(c) (= *preparation, Med: hairspray etc*) Spray *m or nt*
(d) (= *act of ~ing*) (Be)sprühen *nt*; **to give sth a ~** etw besprühen; (*with insecticide*) etw spritzen; (*with hairspray etc*) etw sprayen **2** VT *plants, insects etc* besprühen; (*with insecticide, water, paint*) spritzen; *hair* sprayen; *room* aussprühen; *bullets* regnen lassen; *graffiti* sprühen; *perfume* (ver)sprühen **3** VI sprühen; (*water, mud*) spritzen

spray can N Sprühdose *f*

sprayer [ˈspreɪə(r)] N = **spray**[2] **1**(b)

spread [spred], *vb: pret, ptp* **spread** **1** N (a) (*of wings*) Spannweite *f*; (*of prices*) Spanne *f*; (*of ideas, interests*) Spektrum *nt*; **middle-age ~** Fülligkeit *f*, Altersspeck *m* (*inf*)
(b) (= *growth*) Ausbreitung *f*, Verbreitung *f*; (*spatial*) Ausdehnung *f*
(c) (*inf: of food etc*) Festessen *nt*
(d) (*for bread*) (Brot)aufstrich *m*; **anchovy ~** Sardellenpaste *f*; **cheese ~** Streichkäse *m*
(e) (*Press, Typ*) Doppelseite *f*; **a full-page/double ~** ein ganz-/zweiseitiger Bericht; (= *advertisement*) eine ganz-/zweiseitige Anzeige
2 VT (a) (= *open or lay out: also* **~ out**) *rug, hay, wings, arms* ausbreiten; *fan* öffnen; *goods* auslegen; *hands, legs* spreizen; **he was lying with his arms and legs ~ out** er lag mit ausgestreckten Armen und Beinen da
(b) *bread, canvas, surface* bestreichen; *butter, paint etc* (ver- *or*

auf)streichen; *table* decken; **~ the paint evenly** verteilen Sie die Farbe gleichmäßig; **to ~ a cloth over sth** ein Tuch über etw (*acc*) breiten
(c) (= *distribute: also* **~ out**) *forces, writing, objects, payments*, (*in time*) verteilen (*over* über +*acc*); *sand, fertilizer* streuen
(d) *news, panic, disease, rumour* **I'll ~ the news to everyone in the office** ich werde es allen im Büro mitteilen
3 VI (a) (= *extend*) (*spatially*) sich erstrecken (*over, across* über +*acc*); (*weeds, liquid, fire, smile, industry*) sich ausbreiten (*over, across* über +*acc*); (*towns*) sich ausdehnen; (*knowledge, fear, smell, disease, trouble, fire*) sich verbreiten; **to ~ to sth** erreichen; (*disease etc*) auf etw (*acc*) übergreifen
(b) (*butter etc*) sich streichen *or* schmieren (*inf*) lassen

➤ **spread about** (*Brit*) *or* **around** VT SEP *news, rumours, disease* verbreiten; *toys, seeds etc* verstreuen

➤ **spread out** **1** VT SEP = **spread 2(a, c)** **2** VI (a) (*countryside etc*) sich ausdehnen (b) (*troops, runners*) sich verteilen

spread-eagle [ˈspredˌiːgl] VT **to be** *or* **lie ~d** alle viere von sich (*dat*) strecken (*inf*)

spreadsheet [ˈspredʃiːt] N (*Comput*) Tabellenkalkulation *f*; (= *software*) Tabellenkalkulationsprogramm *nt*

spree [spriː] N **spending** *or* **shopping ~** Großeinkauf *m*; **drinking ~** Zechtour *f* (*inf*); **to go/be on a ~** (*drinking*) eine Zechtour machen; (*spending*) groß einkaufen gehen/groß einkaufen

sprig [sprɪg] N Zweig *m*

sprightly [ˈspraɪtlɪ] ADJ (+ER) *person, tune* munter, lebhaft; *old person* rüstig; *walk, dance* schwungvoll

spring [sprɪŋ], *vb: pret* **sprang** *or* (*US*) **sprung**, *ptp* **sprung** **1** N
(a) (*lit, fig liter: = source*) Quelle *f*
(b) (= *season*) Frühling *m*; **in (the) ~** im Frühling
(c) (= *leap*) Sprung *m*, Satz *m*
(d) (*Mech*) Feder *f*; (*in mattress, seat etc*) (Sprung)feder *f*
(e) NO PL (= *bounciness: of chair*) Federung *f*; **to walk with a ~ in one's step** mit federndem Schritten gehen
2 ADJ ATTR (a) (*seasonal*) Frühlings-
(b) (= *with ~s*) gefedert; **~ mattress** Federkernmatratze *f*
3 VT (= *cause to operate*) auslösen; **to ~ a leak** (*pipe*) (plötzlich) undicht werden; (*ship*) (plötzlich) ein Leck bekommen; **to ~ sth on sb** (*fig*) *idea, decision* jdn mit etw konfrontieren; **to ~ a piece of news on sb** jdn mit einer Neuigkeit überraschen
4 VI (a) (= *leap*) springen; (= *be activated*) ausgelöst werden; **to ~ at sb** jdn anspringen; **to ~ out at sb** auf jdn losspringen; **to ~ open** aufspringen; **to ~ to one's feet** aufspringen; **tears sprang to her eyes** ihr schossen die Tränen in die Augen; **to ~ into action** aktiv werden; (*police etc*) in Aktion treten; **to ~ to mind** einem einfallen; **to ~ to sb's aid/defence** jdm zu Hilfe eilen; **he sprang to fame** er wurde plötzlich berühmt; **to ~ (in)to life** (plötzlich) lebendig werden
(b) (*also* **~ forth**) (*liter*) (*water, blood*) (hervor)quellen (*from* aus); (*fire, sparks*) sprühen (*from* aus); (*fig*) (*idea*) entstehen (*from* aus); (*interest etc*) herrühren (*from* von); **where did you ~ from?** (*inf*) wo kommst du denn her?

➤ **spring up** VI (*plant*) hervorsprießen; (*weeds, building, settlement*) aus dem Boden schießen; (*person*) hoch- *or* aufspringen; (*fig: firm, magazine*) entstehen; (*problem, rumour*) auftauchen

spring: spring binder N Klemmhefter *m*; **springboard** N (*lit, fig*) Sprungbrett *nt*; **spring-clean** **1** VT gründlich putzen; **to ~ a house** (in einem Haus) Frühjahrsputz machen **2** VI Frühjahrsputz machen; **spring-cleaning** N Frühjahrsputz *m*; **spring-like** ADJ frühlingshaft; **spring-loaded** ADJ mit einer Sprungfeder; **spring onion** N (*Brit*) Frühlingszwiebel *f*; **spring roll** N Frühlingsrolle *f*; **springtime** N Frühlingszeit *f*; (*fig*) Frühling *m*; **spring water** N Quellwasser *nt*

springy [ˈsprɪŋɪ] ADJ (+ER) *step* federnd; *plank, grass also* nachgiebig; *rubber, wood etc, hair* elastisch; *bed* weich gefedert

sprinkle [ˈsprɪŋkl] VT *water* sprenkeln, sprengen; *sugar etc* streuen; *dish, cake* bestreuen; **his hair was ~d with grey** sein Haar war grau meliert; **pubs are ~d throughout the town** man findet Gasthäuser über die ganze Stadt verstreut

sprinkler [ˈsprɪŋklə(r)] N (*Hort, Agr*) Berieselungsapparat *m*; (*in garden also*) (Rasen)sprenger *m*; (*for firefighting*) Sprinkler *m*

sprinkling ['sprɪŋklɪŋ] N (*of rain, dew etc*) ein paar Tropfen; (*of sugar etc*) Prise *f*; **there was a ~ of young people** es waren ein paar vereinzelte junge Leute da

sprint [sprɪnt] **1** N Lauf *m*; (= *race, burst of speed*) Spurt *m*; **the 100-m ~** der 100-m-Lauf; **a ~ finish** ein Endspurt *m* **2** VI (*in race*) sprinten; (= *dash*) rennen

sprinter ['sprɪntə'] N Sprinter(in) *m(f)*

sprite [spraɪt] N Kobold *m* (*also Comput: icon*)

sprocket ['sprɒkɪt] N (= ~ *wheel*) Kettenrad *nt*; (*on bicycle*) Zahnkranz *m*; (*Film*) Greifer *m*

sprout [spraʊt] **1** N **(a)** (= *shoot*) (*of plant*) Trieb *m*; (*from seed*) Keim *m*
(b) (= *Brussels ~*) (Rosenkohl)röschen *nt*; **~s** *pl* Rosenkohl *m* **2** VT *leaves, shoots etc* entwickeln; *seeds etc* keimen lassen; (*inf*) *beard* sich (*dat*) wachsen lassen
3 VI **(a)** (= *grow*) wachsen, sprießen; (*seed etc*) keimen; (*potatoes etc*) Triebe *pl* bekommen
(b) (*lit, fig: also* = **up**) (*plants*) sprießen; (*new buildings*) wie die Pilze aus dem Boden schießen

spruce¹ [spruːs] N (*also* = **fir**) Fichte *f*

spruce² ADJ (+ER) *person, flower beds* gepflegt; *appearance* adrett

➤ **spruce up** VT SEP *child* herausputzen; *house, garden* auf Vordermann bringen (*inf*); *image* aufpolieren; **to spruce oneself up** (*in general*) sein Äußeres pflegen

sprung [sprʌŋ] **1** PTP *of* **spring 2** ADJ gefedert

spud [spʌd] N (*inf*) Kartoffel *f*

spun [spʌn] PRET, PTP *of* **spin**

spur [spɜː'] **1** N Sporn *m*; (*fig*) Ansporn *m*, Antrieb *m* (*to* für); **on the ~ of the moment** ganz spontan; **a ~-of-the-moment decision** ein spontaner Entschluss **2** VT **(a)** *horse* die Sporen geben (+*dat*) **(b)** (= *urge on: also* ~ **on**) (vorwärts) treiben; (*fig*) anspornen

spurious ['spjʊərɪəs] ADJ *claim, claimant* unberechtigt; *account* falsch; *interest* nicht echt; *argument* fadenscheinig

spurn [spɜːn] VT verschmähen

spurned [spɜːnd] ADJ *offer, gift* zurückgewiesen; *lover* abgewiesen; *love* verschmäht

spurt [spɜːt] **1** N **(a)** (= *flow*) Strahl *m* **(b)** (= *burst of speed*) Spurt *m*; **a final ~** (*lit, fig*) ein Endspurt *m*; **to put a ~ on** (*lit, fig*) einen Spurt vorlegen; **there was a ~ of activity** es brach plötzlich Tätigkeit aus; **to work in ~s** (nur) sporadisch arbeiten **2** VI **(a)** (= *gush: also* = **out**) (heraus)spritzen (*from* aus) **(b)** (= *run*) spurten **3** VT **the wound ~ed blood** aus der Wunde spritzte Blut

sputter ['spʌtə'] VI zischen; (*fat*) spritzen; (*engine*) stottern; (*in speech*) sich ereifern (*about* über +*acc*); **he was ~ing with rage** er geiferte (vor Zorn)

spy [spaɪ] **1** N Spion(in) *m(f)*; (= *police* ~) Spitzel *m* **2** VT sehen, erspähen (*geh*) **3** VI spionieren; **to ~ on sb** jdn bespitzeln; *on neighbours* jdm nachspionieren

➤ **spy out** VT SEP ausfindig machen; **to spy out the land** (*fig*) die Lage peilen

spy: **spy hole** N Guckloch *nt*, Spion *m*; **spy ring** N Spionagering *m*

sq ABBR *of* **square**; **sq m** qm, m²

squabble ['skwɒbl] **1** N Zank *m*, Streit *m*; **~s** Zankereien *pl*, Streitigkeiten *pl* **2** VI (sich) zanken, (sich) streiten (*about, over* um)

squabbling ['skwɒblɪŋ] N Zankerei *f*, Streiterei *f*

squad [skwɒd] N (*Mil*) Korporalschaft *f*; (= *special unit of police etc*) Kommando *nt*; (= *police department*) Dezernat *nt*; (*Sport, fig*) Mannschaft *f*

squadron ['skwɒdrən] N (*Aviat*) Staffel *f*; (*Naut*) Geschwader *nt*

squalid ['skwɒlɪd] ADJ *room, house* schmutzig und verwahrlost; *conditions* elend; *motive etc* niederträchtig; *dispute* entwürdigend; *affair* schmutzig

squalor ['skwɒlə'] N Schmutz *m*; (= *moral* ~) Verkommenheit *f*; **to live in ~** in unbeschreiblichen Zuständen leben

squander ['skwɒndə'] VT verschwenden; *opportunity* vertun

square [skwɛə'] **1** N **(a)** (= *rectangle*) Viereck *nt*; (*on chessboard etc*) Feld *nt*; (*on paper*) Kästchen *nt*; (= *check on material etc*) Karo *nt*; **cut it in ~s** schneiden Sie es quadratisch zu; **to go back to ~ one** (*fig*), **to start (again) from ~ one** (*fig*) noch einmal von vorne anfangen; **we're back to ~ one** jetzt

sind wir wieder da, wo wir angefangen haben
(b) (*in town*) Platz *m*; (*US: of houses*) Block *m*
2 ADJ (+ER) **(a)** (*in shape*) quadratisch; *picture, lawn etc also* viereckig; *block of wood etc* vierkantig; **to be a ~ peg in a round hole** am falschen Platz sein
(b) (= *forming right angle*) *angle* recht; *shoulder* eckig; *chin, jaw* kantig
(c) (*Math*) Quadrat-; **3 ~ kilometres** 3 Quadratkilometer; **3 metres ~** 3 Meter im Quadrat
(d) ATTR *meal* anständig, ordentlich
(e) *deal* gerecht, fair; **to get a ~ deal** fair behandelt werden
(f) (*fig*: = *even*) **to be ~** (*accounts etc*) in Ordnung sein; **we are (all) ~** (*Sport*) wir stehen beide/alle gleich; (*fig*) jetzt sind wir quitt
(g) (*inf*: = *conventional*) überholt; *person, ideas* spießig (*inf*); **he's ~** er ist von (vor)gestern
3 ADV (+ER) **(a)** (= *at right angles*) rechtwinklig; **~ with sth** im rechten Winkel *or* senkrecht zu etw
(b) (= *directly*) direkt, genau; **to hit sb ~ in the chest** jdn voll in die Brust treffen
(c) (= *parallel*) **to be ~ with** *or* **to sth** parallel zu etw ausgerichtet sein
4 VT **(a)** (= *make ~*) quadratisch machen; **to try to ~ the circle** die Quadratur des Kreises versuchen; **to ~ a match** in einem Spiel gleichziehen
(b) (*Math*) *number* quadrieren; **3 ~d is 9** 3 hoch 2 *or* 3 (im) Quadrat ist 9
(c) *debts* begleichen; *creditors* abrechnen mit; (= *reconcile*) in Einklang bringen; **to ~ one's accounts** abrechnen (*with* mit)

➤ **square off** VT SEP *corner* rechtwinklig machen **2** VI (*esp US*) in Kampfstellung gehen

➤ **square up** VI **(a)** (*boxers, fighters*) in Kampfstellung gehen; **to square up to sb** sich vor jdm aufpflanzen (*inf*); (*boxer, fig*) jdm die Stirn bieten; **to square up to sth** sich einer Sache (*dat*) stellen **(b)** (*lit, fig*: = *settle*) abrechnen

square bracket N eckige Klammer

squared [skwɛəd] ADJ *paper* kariert

squarely ['skwɛəlɪ] ADV (= *directly*) direkt, genau; (*fig*: = *firmly*) fest; **to hit sb ~ in the stomach** jdn voll in den Magen treffen; **to place the blame for sth ~ on sb** jdm voll und ganz die Schuld an etw (*dat*) geben; **to face sb/sth ~** jdm/einer Sache tapfer entgegentreten

square root N Quadratwurzel *f*

squash¹ [skwɒʃ] **1** N **(a)** (*Brit*) (= *fruit concentrate*) Fruchtsaftkonzentrat *nt*; (= *drink*) Fruchtsaft *m*
(b) (= *crush*) Gedränge *nt*; **it's a bit of a ~** es ist ziemlich eng **2** VT **(a)** (*also* = **up**) zerdrücken, zerquetschen; *box etc* zusammendrücken; **to be ~ed to a pulp** zu Brei zerquetscht werden
(b) (= *squeeze*) quetschen; **to be ~ed up against sb** gegen jdn gequetscht *or* gepresst werden; **to be ~ed together** eng zusammengepresst *or* -gequetscht sein
3 VI (= *squeeze*) sich quetschen; **could you ~ up?** könnt ihr etwas zusammenrücken?; (*one person*) kannst du dich etwas kleiner machen?

squash² N (*Sport*) Squash *nt*; **~ courts** *pl* Squashhalle *f*

squash³ N, NO PL (*US*) (Pâtisson)kürbis *m*

squashy ['skwɒʃɪ] ADJ (+ER) matschig; *cushion* weich

squat [skwɒt] **1** ADJ (+ER) gedrungen **2** VI **(a)** hocken; (*person also*) kauern **(b)** (*also* = **down**) sich (hin)hocken *or* (hin)kauern **(c)** (*on land*) sich (illegal) ansiedeln; **to ~ (in a house)** ein Haus besetzt haben **3** N (*inf*: = *place*) Unterschlupf *m* (*für Hausbesetzer*)

squatter ['skwɒtə'] N (*on land*) illegaler Siedler, illegale Siedlerin; (*in house*) Hausbesetzer(in) *m(f)*

squawk [skwɔːk] **1** N heiserer Schrei; **he let out a ~** er kreischte auf **2** VI schreien, kreischen

squeak [skwiːk] **1** N (*of hinge, wheel etc, shoe*) Quietschen *nt no pl*; (*of person*) Quiekser *m*; (*of small animal*) Quieken *nt no pl*; (*of mouse, bird*) Piepsen *nt no pl*; (*fig inf*: = *sound*) Pieps *m* (*inf*), Mucks *m* (*inf*) **2** VI (*door, hinge, shoes etc*) quietschen; (*person*) quieksen; (*small animal*) quieken; (*mouse, bird*) piepsen

➤ **squeak by** *or* **through** VI (*inf*: = *narrowly succeed*) gerade so durchkommen (*inf*)

squeaky ['skwiːkɪ] ADJ (+ER) quietschend; *voice* piepsig

squeaky-clean [ˌskwiːkɪ'kliːn] ADJ (*inf*) blitzsauber (*inf*)

squeal [skwiːl] **1** N Schrei *m*; (*of person, tyre, brakes*) Kreischen *nt no pl*; (*of pig*) Quieken *nt no pl*; **with a ~ of brakes** mit kreischenden Bremsen; **~s/a ~ of laughter** schrilles Gelächter **2** VI kreischen; (*person also*) schreien; (*brakes, tyres also*) quietschen; (*pig*) quieksen; **to ~ with delight** vor Wonne quietschen

squeamish ['skwiːmɪʃ] ADJ person empfindlich; **I'm not ~** (= *not easily nauseated*) mir wird nicht so schnell schlecht; (= *not easily shocked*) ich bin nicht so zart besaitet *or* empfindlich

squeamishness ['skwiːmɪʃnɪs] N (= *nausea*) Übelkeit *f*; (= *disgust*) Ekel *m*; (= *prudishness*) Zimperlichkeit *f*

squeeze [skwiːz] **1** N **(a)** (= *act of squeezing*) Drücken *nt no pl*; (= *hug*) Umarmung *f*; (*in bus etc*) Gedränge *nt*; **to give sth a ~** etw drücken; **it was a tight ~** es war fürchterlich eng; **to put a ~ on the money supply** Druck *m* auf die Geldmenge ausüben **(b)** (= *amount*) Spritzer *m* **(c)** (= *credit squeeze*) Kreditbeschränkung *f* **2** VT (*lit, fig*) drücken; *sponge, tube* ausdrücken; *orange* auspressen; (= *squash*) *person* einquetschen; (= *restrict*) *person, economy etc* unter Druck setzen; **to ~ clothes into a case** Kleider in einen Koffer zwängen; **to ~ information etc out of sb** Informationen *etc* aus jdm herausquetschen; **I'll see if we can ~ you in** vielleicht können wir Sie noch unterbringen; **we'll ~ another song in before the interval** wir schaffen vor der Pause noch ein Lied **3** VI **you should be able to ~ through** wenn du dich klein machst, kommst du durch; **to ~ in/out** sich hinein-/hinausdrängen; **to ~ past sb** sich an jdm vorbeidrücken; **to ~ onto the bus** sich in den Bus hineinzwängen; **you'll have to ~ up a bit** Sie müssen ein bisschen zusammenrücken

squelch [skwɛltʃ] **1** N quatschendes Geräusch (*inf*) **2** VI patschen, platschen; (*shoes, mud*) quatschen

squid [skwɪd] N Tintenfisch *m*

squiggle ['skwɪgl] N Schnörkel *m*

squiggly ['skwɪglɪ] ADJ (+ER) schnörkelig

squinch [skwɪntʃ] (*US*) **1** VT *eyes* zusammenkneifen **2** VI blinzeln

squint [skwɪnt] **1** N (*Med*) Schielen *nt no pl*; **to have a ~** leicht schielen **2** VI schielen; (*in strong light etc*) blinzeln; **to ~ at sb/sth** nach jdm/etw schielen **3** ADJ (= *crooked*) schief

squirm [skwɜːm] **1** N Winden *nt no pl* **2** VI sich winden; (*in distaste*) schaudern; (*with embarrassment*) sich (drehen und) winden; (*from discomfort*) hin und her rutschen; **that joke makes me ~** bei diesem Witz dreht sich in mir alles herum

squirrel ['skwɪrəl] N Eichhörnchen *nt*

squirt [skwɜːt] **1** N **(a)** Spritzer *m* **(b)** (*pej inf*: = *small person*) Pimpf *m* (*inf*) **2** VT *liquid* spritzen; *object, person* bespritzen **3** VI spritzen

squishy ['skwɪʃɪ] ADJ (+ER) (*inf*) matschig (*inf*)

Sri Lanka [srɪ'læŋkə] N Sri Lanka *nt*

Sri Lankan [srɪ'læŋkən] **1** ADJ sri-lankisch; **he is ~** er ist aus Sri Lanka **2** N Sri-Lanker(in) *m(f)*

St. **(a)** ABBR *of* **Street** Str. **(b)** ABBR *of* **Saint** hl., St.

stab [stæb] **1** N **(a)** (*with knife etc, wound, of pain*) Stich *m*; **~ wound** Stichwunde *f*; **to feel a ~ of pain** einen stechenden Schmerz empfinden; **she felt a ~ of jealousy** plötzlich durchfuhr sie Eifersucht; **a ~ in the back** (*fig*) ein Dolchstoß *m* **(b)** (*inf*: = *try*) Versuch *m*; **to have a ~ at sth** etw probieren **2** VT *person* einen Stich versetzen (+*dat*); (*several times*) einstechen auf (+*acc*); (= *wound seriously*) niederstechen; **to ~ sb (to death)** jdn erstechen; **he was ~bed through the arm/heart** der Stich traf ihn am Arm/ins Herz; **to ~ sb in the back** (*lit, fig*) jdm in den Rücken fallen

stabbing ['stæbɪŋ] **1** N Messerstecherei *f* **2** ADJ *pain* stechend

stability [stə'bɪlɪtɪ] N Stabilität *f*; (*of relationship also, of job*) Beständigkeit *f*

stabilization [steɪbəlaɪ'zeɪʃən] N Stabilisierung *f*

stabilize ['steɪbəlaɪz] **1** VT (*Fin, Naut, Aviat*) stabilisieren **2** VI sich stabilisieren

stable[1] ['steɪbl] ADJ (+ER) (*also Psych, Med*) stabil; *relationship also, job* dauerhaft; *character* gefestigt

stable[2] **1** N (= *building*) Stall *m*; **riding ~s** Reitstall *m* **2** VT (= *put in ~*) in den Stall bringen; (= *keep in ~*) im Stall halten

stablelad ['steɪbllæd] (*Brit*), **stableman** ['steɪblmən] N Stallbursche *m*

stack [stæk] **1** N **(a)** (= *pile*) Haufen *m*; (*neatly piled*) Stoß *m*, Stapel *m* **(b)** (*inf*: = *lots*) Haufen *m* (*inf*); **~s** jede Menge (*inf*); **~s of time** jede Menge (*inf*) Zeit **2** VT (= *pile up*) stapeln; *shelves* einräumen; **to ~ up** aufstapeln; **the cards** *or* **odds are ~ed against us** (*fig*) wir haben keine großen Chancen

stadium ['steɪdɪəm] N, *pl* **-s** *or* **stadia** ['steɪdɪə] Stadion *nt*

> *Be careful!* **stadium** *is not translated by the German word* **Stadium**.

staff [stɑːf] **1** N **(a)** (= *personnel*) Personal *nt*; (*Sch, Univ*) Kollegium *nt*; (*of one department, on one project*) Mitarbeiterstab *m*; **we have a large ~** wir haben viel Personal/ein großes Kollegium/einen großen Mitarbeiterstab; **we don't have enough ~ to complete the project** wir haben nicht genügend Mitarbeiter, um das Projekt zu beenden; **administrative ~** Verwaltungsstab *m*, Verwaltungspersonal *nt*; **a member of ~** ein Mitarbeiter *m*, eine Mitarbeiterin; (*Sch*) ein Kollege *m*, eine Kollegin; **to be on the ~** zum Personal/Kollegium/Mitarbeiterstab gehören **(b)** *pl* **-s** *or* (*old*) **staves** (= *stick*) Stab *m* **(c)** (*Mil*: = *general* ~) Stab *m* **2** VT *department* Mitarbeiter finden für; *hospital, shop, hotel* mit Personal besetzen; **the kitchens are ~ed by foreigners** das Küchenpersonal besteht aus Ausländern

staffed [stɑːft] ADJ **to be well ~** ausreichend Personal haben

staffing ['stɑːfɪŋ] N Stellenbesetzung *f*

staff: **staff meeting** N Personalversammlung *f*; **staff nurse** N (*Brit*) (voll)ausgebildete Krankenschwester; **staffroom** N Lehrerzimmer *nt*

stag [stæg] N (*Zool*) (= *deer*) Hirsch *m*; (= *male animal*) Bock *m*

stage [steɪdʒ] **1** N **(a)** (*Theat, fig*) Bühne *f*; **the ~** (= *profession*) das Theater, die Bühne; **to be on/go on the ~** (*as career*) beim Theater sein/zum Theater gehen; **to go on ~** (*actor*) die Bühne betreten; **to come off ~**, **to leave the ~** von der Bühne abtreten; **the ~ was set** (*fig*) alles war vorbereitet; **to set the ~ for sth** (*fig*) den Weg für etw bereiten **(b)** (= *platform in hall*) Podium *nt* **(c)** (= *point*) Stadium *nt*; (*of process, development*) Phase *f*; **at this ~ such a thing is impossible** zum gegenwärtigen Zeitpunkt ist das unmöglich; **at this ~ in the negotiations** an diesem Punkt der Verhandlungen; **in the early/final ~(s)** im Anfangs-/Endstadium; **what ~ is your thesis at?** wie weit sind Sie mit Ihrer Dissertation?; **we have reached a ~ where ...** wir sind an einem Punkt angelangt, wo ...; **to be at the experimental ~** im Versuchsstadium sein **(d)** (= *part of journey, race etc*) Etappe *f*; **in** *or* **by (easy) ~s** (*lit*) etappenweise; (*fig also*) Schritt für Schritt **2** VT *play* aufführen; *competition, event* durchführen; *accident, coup* inszenieren; *strike, protest etc* veranstalten; **to ~ a takeover bid** (*Comm*) ein Übernahmeangebot machen

stage: **stage fright** N Lampenfieber *nt*; **stage-manage** VT (*lit*) Inspizient sein bei; (*fig*) inszenieren; **stage manager** N Inspizient(in) *m(f)*; **stage set** N Bühnenbild *nt*

stagflation [stæg'fleɪʃən] N (*Econ*) Stagflation *f*

stagger ['stægə[r]] **1** VI schwanken, taumeln; (*because of weakness*) wanken; (*drunkenly*) torkeln **2** VT **(a)** (*fig*: = *amaze*) den Atem verschlagen (+*dat*), umhauen (*inf*) **(b)** *hours, holidays* staffeln; *seats, spokes* versetzen

staggered ['stægəd] ADJ **(a)** (= *amazed*) verblüfft, platt (*inf*) **(b)** *working hours etc* gestaffelt

staggering ['stægərɪŋ] ADJ **(a)** **to be a ~ blow (to sb/sth)** ein harter *or* schwerer Schlag (für jdn/etw) sein **(b)** (= *amazing*) atemberaubend, umwerfend

staggeringly ['stægərɪŋlɪ] ADV umwerfend

stagnant ['stægnənt] ADJ (= *not moving*) (still)stehend *attr*, gestaut; (= *foul, stale*) *water* abgestanden; *air* verbraucht; *trade* stagnierend; **the market is ~** der Markt stagniert

stagnate [stæg'neɪt] VI (= *not circulate, trade*) stagnieren; (= *become foul*) (*water*) abstehen; (*air*) verbraucht werden; (*person*) verdummen; (*mind*) einrosten

stagnation [stæg'neɪʃən] N Stagnieren *nt*; (*of air*) Stau *m*; (*of person*) Verdummung *f*; (*of mind*) Verlangsamung *f*

stag: **stag night** N Saufabend m (inf) des Bräutigams mit seinen Kumpeln (am Vorabend der Hochzeit); **stag party** N = **stag night**

staid [steɪd] ADJ (+ER) seriös, gesetzt; colour gedeckt

stain [steɪn] ◼◼ N (a) (lit) Fleck m; (fig) Makel m; **a blood ~** ein Blutfleck m (b) (= colorant) (Ein)färbemittel nt; (= woodstain) Beize f ◼◼ VT beflecken; (= colour) einfärben; (with woodstain) beizen ◼◼ VI (a) (= leave a stain) Flecken hinterlassen (b) (= become stained) Flecken bekommen

stained [steɪnd] ADJ fingers, teeth gefärbt; clothes, floor fleckig; glass bunt, bemalt; reputation befleckt; **~-glass window** farbiges Glasfenster; **~ with blood** blutbefleckt

stainless steel [,steɪnlɪs'stiːl] N rostfreier (Edel)stahl

stair [steəʳ] N (a) (= step) Stufe f (b) USU PL (= stairway) Treppe f; **at the top of the ~s** oben an der Treppe

stair: **staircase** N Treppe f; **stairlift** N Treppenlift m; **stairway** N Treppe f; **stairwell** N Treppenhaus nt

stake [steɪk] ◼◼ N (a) (= post) Pfosten m; (for plant) Stange f (b) (= place of execution) Scheiterhaufen m (c) (= bet) Einsatz m; (= financial interest) Anteil m; **to be at ~** auf dem Spiel stehen; **he has a lot at ~** er hat viel zu verlieren; **to have a ~ in sth** in business einen Anteil an etw (dat) haben; in the future von etw betroffen werden (d) **stakes** PL (= prize) Gewinn m; **to raise the ~s** (lit, fig) den Einsatz erhöhen ◼◼ VT (a) (also ~ up) plant hochbinden; fence abstützen (b) (= bet, risk) setzen (on auf +acc); **to ~ one's reputation on sth** sein Wort für etw verpfänden; **to ~ a/one's claim to sth** sich (dat) ein Anrecht auf etw (acc) sichern

stakeholder [steɪkhəʊldəʳ] N Teilhaber(in) m(f)

stalactite [stælaktaɪt] N Stalaktit m

stalagmite [stæləgmaɪt] N Stalagmit m

stale [steɪl] ADJ (+ER) (a) alt; cake trocken; bread altbacken; (in smell) muffig; water, beer schal; air verbraucht; cigarette smoke kalt; **to go ~** (food) verderben (b) (fig) news veraltet; idea abgegriffen; **to become ~** (relationship) an Reiz verlieren; (situation) langweilig werden

stalemate [steɪlmeɪt] N (Chess) Patt nt; (fig also) Sackgasse f; **to reach ~** (lit) ein Patt erreichen; (fig) in eine Sackgasse geraten; **to end in (a) ~** (lit) mit (einem) Patt enden; (fig) in einer Sackgasse enden

staleness [steɪlnɪs] N (lit) (of beer, water etc) Schalheit f; (of bread) Altbackenheit f; (of taste, smell) Muffigkeit f

stalk¹ [stɔːk] VT game sich anpirschen an (+acc); person sich anschleichen an (+acc); (animal) sich heranschleichen an (+acc)

stalk² N (of plant, leaf) Stiel m; (= cabbage ~) Strunk m

stalker [stɔːkəʳ] N jd, der die ständige Nähe zu einer von ihm verehrten (meist prominenten) Person sucht oder sie mit Anrufen, Briefen etc belästigt

stalking [stɔːkɪŋ] N (Jur) das Verfolgen und Belästigen einer (meist prominenten) Person

stall [stɔːl] ◼◼ N (a) (in stable) Box f, Bucht f (b) (at market etc) Stand m (c) **stalls** PL (Brit: Theat, Film) Parkett nt; **in the ~s** im Parkett ◼◼ VT (a) (Aut) abwürgen; (Aviat) überziehen (b) (also ~ off) person hinhalten; process, bill hinauszögern; talks verzögern ◼◼ VI (a) (engine) absterben; (Aviat) überziehen (b) (= delay) Zeit schinden (inf); **to ~ for time** versuchen, Zeit zu gewinnen or zu schinden (inf)

stallion [stæljən] N Hengst m

stalwart [stɔːlwət] ◼◼ ADJ supporter treu; belief unerschütterlich ◼◼ N (= supporter) (getreuer) Anhänger

stamina [stæmɪnə] N Stehvermögen nt, Durchhaltevermögen nt

stammer [stæməʳ] ◼◼ N Stottern nt; **he has a bad ~** er stottert stark ◼◼ VT (also ~ out) stammeln ◼◼ VI stottern

stammering [stæmərɪŋ] N Stottern nt

stamp [stæmp] ◼◼ N (a) (= postage ~) (Brief)marke f; (= insurance ~, revenue ~ etc) Marke f; (= trading ~) (Rabatt)marke f (b) (= rubber ~, impression) Stempel m; **to bear the ~ of authenticity** (fig) die Züge der Echtheit tragen ◼◼ VT (a) **to ~ one's foot** (mit dem Fuß) (auf)stampfen (b) (= put postage on) freimachen, frankieren; **a ~ed**

addressed envelope ein frankierter Rückumschlag (c) (with rubber ~) stempeln ◼◼ VI (= walk) sta(m)pfen; (horse) aufstampfen; **you ~ed on my foot** Sie haben mir auf den Fuß getreten

➤ **stamp on** ◼◼ VT SEP pattern, design aufprägen; **to stamp one's authority on sth** einer Sache (dat) seine Autorität aufzwingen ◼◼ VI +PREP OBJ (with foot) treten auf (+acc); (fig) im Keim ersticken

➤ **stamp out** ◼◼ VT SEP fire austreten; (fig) epidemic, crime, practice ausrotten; trouble niederschlagen ◼◼ VI heraussta(m)pfen

stamp: **stamp collection** N Briefmarkensammlung f; **stamp duty** N (Brit) Stempelgebühr f

stampede [stæm'piːd] ◼◼ N (of cattle) wilde Flucht; (of people) Massenansturm m (on auf +acc); (to escape) wilde or panikartige Flucht ◼◼ VT cattle, crowd in (wilde or helle) Panik versetzen ◼◼ VI durchgehen; (crowd) losstürmen (for auf +acc)

stamp tax N (US) Stempelgebühr f

stance [stæns] N (= posture, Sport) Haltung f; (= mental attitude also) Einstellung f; (Golf etc also) Stand m; **to take up a ~** (lit) in Stellung gehen; (fig) eine Haltung einnehmen

stand [stænd], vb: pret, ptp stood ◼◼ N (a) (= position) Platz m, Standort m; (fig) Standpunkt m, Einstellung f (on zu); **to take a ~ (on a matter)** (zu einer Angelegenheit) eine Einstellung vertreten (b) (Mil) (= resistance) Widerstand m; (= battle) Gefecht nt; **to make a ~** (lit, fig) Widerstand leisten (c) (= taxi ~, market stall etc) Stand m (d) (= lamp ~, music ~) Ständer m (e) (= band ~) Podium nt (f) (Brit Sport) Tribüne f; (US Jur) Zeugenstand m; **to take the ~** (Jur) in den Zeugenstand treten ◼◼ VT (a) (= place) stellen (b) pressure, close examination etc (object) standhalten (+dat); (person) gewachsen sein (+dat); test bestehen; climate vertragen; heat, noise ertragen, aushalten; loss, cost verkraften (c) (inf: = put up with) person, noise etc aushalten; **I can't ~ being kept waiting** ich kann es nicht leiden or ausstehen, wenn man mich warten lässt (d) **to ~ trial** vor Gericht stehen (for wegen) ◼◼ VI (a) stehen; (= get up) aufstehen; (offer, promise) gelten; (objection, contract) gültig bleiben; (fig: = remain unchanged) bestehen (bleiben); **don't just ~ there(, do something)!** stehen Sie nicht nur (dumm) rum, tun Sie was! (inf); **to ~ as a candidate** kandidieren (b) (= measure) (person) groß sein; (tree etc) hoch sein (c) (thermometer, record) stehen (at auf +dat); (sales) liegen (at bei) (d) (fig) **we ~ to gain a lot** wir können sehr viel gewinnen; **he ~s to make a lot of money** er wird wohl eine Menge Geld (dabei) verdienen; **what do we ~ to gain by it?** was springt für uns dabei heraus? (inf); **I'd like to know where I ~ (with him)** ich möchte wissen, woran ich (bei ihm) bin; **where do you ~ on this issue?** welchen Standpunkt vertreten Sie in dieser Frage?; **as things ~** nach Lage der Dinge; **as it ~s** so wie die Sache aussieht; **to ~ accused of sth** einer Sache (gen) angeklagt sein; **to ~ firm or fast** festbleiben; **to ~ together** zusammenhalten; **nothing now ~s between us** es steht nichts mehr zwischen uns

➤ **stand about** (Brit) or **around** VI herumstehen

➤ **stand apart** VI (lit) abseits stehen; (fig) sich fern halten

➤ **stand aside** VI (lit) zur Seite treten

➤ **stand back** VI (= move back) zurücktreten; (= be situated at a distance) zurückstehen; (fig: = distance oneself) Abstand nehmen

➤ **stand by** ◼◼ VI (a) (= remain uninvolved) (unbeteiligt) danebenstehen; **to stand by and do nothing** tatenlos zusehen (b) (= be on alert) sich bereithalten ◼◼ VI +PREP OBJ **stand by a promise/sb** ein Versprechen/zu jdm halten

➤ **stand down** VI (= withdraw) zurücktreten

➤ **stand for** VI +PREP OBJ (a) (= be candidate for) kandidieren für; **to stand for election** (in einer Wahl) kandidieren (b) (= represent) stehen für, bedeuten (c) (= put up with) hinnehmen, sich (dat) gefallen lassen

➤ **stand in** VI einspringen

➤ **stand out** VI **(a)** (= *project*) hervorstehen **(b)** (= *be noticeable*) hervorstechen, auffallen; **to stand out against sth** sich gegen etw *or* von etw abheben

➤ **stand over** VI +PREP OBJ (= *supervise*) auf die Finger sehen (+*dat*)

➤ **stand up** ◼ VI **(a)** (= *get up*) aufstehen; (= *be standing*) stehen; **stand up straight!** stell dich gerade hin **(b)** (= *be valid*) (*argument*) überzeugen; (*Jur*) bestehen **(c) to stand up for sb/sth** für jdn/etw eintreten; **to stand up to sth** *to test, pressure* (*object*) standhalten; (*person*) einer Sache (*dat*) gewachsen sein; **to stand up to sb** sich jdm gegenüber behaupten ◼ VT SEP **(a)** (= *put upright*) hinstellen **(b)** (*inf*) *boyfriend, sb* versetzen

stand-alone [ˈstændəlɑʊn] N (*Comput*) eigenständiges Gerät

standard [ˈstændəd] ◼ N **(a)** (= *average, established norm*) Norm *f*; (= *criterion*) Maßstab *m*; (*usu pl*: = *moral ~s*) (sittliche) Maßstäbe *pl*; **to be below** ~ unter der Norm sein *or* liegen; **to be up to** ~ den Anforderungen genügen; **he sets himself very high ~s** er stellt hohe Anforderungen an sich (*acc*) selbst; **by any ~(s)** egal, welche Maßstäbe man anlegt; **by today's ~(s)** aus heutiger Sicht **(b)** (= *degree, level*) Niveau *nt*; ~ **of living** Lebensstandard *m* **(c)** (*Measurement*) (Maß)einheit *f* **(d)** (= *flag*) Flagge *f*, Fahne *f* ◼ ADJ **(a)** (= *usual*) üblich; (*Comm*) Standard-, (handels)üblich; (= *average*) durchschnittlich; (= *widely referred to*) Standard-; ~ **discount** Standardrabatt *m*; ~ **weight** Normalgewicht *nt*; **to be** ~ **practice** üblich sein **(b)** (*Ling*) (allgemein) gebräuchlich; ~ **English** korrektes Englisch; ~ **German** Hochdeutsch *nt*

standard: standard class N (*Rail*) zweite Klasse; **standard deviation** N Standardabweichung *f*

standardization [ˌstændədaɪˈzeɪʃən] N (*of style, approach*) Vereinheitlichung *f*; (*of format, sizes*) Standardisierung *f*

standardize [ˈstændədaɪz] VT *style, approach* vereinheitlichen; *format, sizes etc* standardisieren

standard lamp N Stehlampe *f*

stand-by [ˈstændbaɪ] ◼ N **(a)** (= *person*) Ersatzperson *f*; (= *thing*) Reserve *f*; (= *ticket*) Stand-by-Ticket *nt* **(b) on** ~ in Bereitschaft; (= *ready for action*) in Einsatzbereitschaft ◼ ADJ ATTR (*Mil, Sport*) Reserve-, Ersatz-; ~ **plane** Entlastungsflugzeug *nt*; ~ **ticket** Stand-by-Ticket *nt*

stand-in [ˈstændɪn] N (*Film, Theat*) Ersatz *m*

standing [ˈstændɪŋ] ◼ N **(a)** (*social*) Rang *m*, (gesellschaftliche) Stellung; (*professional*) Position *f*; (*financial*) (finanzielle) Verhältnisse *pl*; (= *repute*) Ruf *m*, Ansehen *nt*; **of high** ~ von hohem Rang; (= *repute*) von hohem Ansehen **(b)** (= *duration*) Dauer *f*; **her husband of five years'** ~ ihr Mann, mit dem sie seit fünf Jahren verheiratet ist ◼ ADJ ATTR **(a)** (= *permanent*) ständig; *army* stehend; **it's a ~ joke** das ist schon zu einem Witz geworden **(b)** (= *from a standstill*) aus dem Stand; ~ **room only** nur Stehplätze; **to give sb a ~ ovation** jdm eine stehende Ovation darbringen

standing: standing charge N Grundgebühr *f*; **standing order** N (*Brit Fin*) Dauerauftrag *m*; **to pay sth by** ~ etw per Dauerauftrag bezahlen; **standing stone** N Menhir *m*

stand: stand-off N Patt *nt*; **standoffish** ADJ, **standoffishly** ADV [stændˈɒfɪʃ, -lɪ] (*inf*) distanziert; **standout** (*US, Austral*) ◼ N (= *person*) herausragende Größe ◼ ADJ herausragend; **standpoint** N Standpunkt *m*; **from the** ~ **of the teacher** vom Standpunkt des Lehrers (aus) gesehen; **stand rental** N Standmiete *f*; **standstill** N Stillstand *m*; **to be at a** ~ (*train*) stehen; (*machines, traffic*) stillstehen; (*factory, production*) ruhen; **to bring production to a** ~ die Produktion lahm legen *or* zum Erliegen bringen; **to come to a** ~ (*person*) stehen bleiben; (*vehicle*) zum Stehen kommen; (*traffic, machines*) zum Stillstand kommen; (*industry etc*) zum Erliegen kommen; **stand-up** ◼ ADJ ATTR ~ **comedian** Bühnenkomiker(in) *m(f)*; ~ **comedy** Stand-up Comedy *f* ◼ N (*inf*: = *comedy*) Stand-up Comedy *f*

stank [stæŋk] PRET *of* stink

staple¹ [ˈsteɪpl] ◼ N Klammer *f*; (*for paper*) Heftklammer *f* ◼ VT heften

staple² ◼ ADJ Haupt-; ~ **diet** Grund- *or* Hauptnahrung *f* ◼ N (= *main product*) Hauptartikel *m*; (= *main food*) Hauptnahrungsmittel *nt*

stapler [ˈsteɪpləʳ] N Heftgerät *nt*

star [stɑːʳ] ◼ N **(a)** Stern *m*; **the Stars and Stripes** das Sternenbanner; **you can thank your lucky ~s that ...** Sie können von Glück sagen, dass ... **(b)** (= *person*) Star *m* ◼ ADJ ATTR Haupt-; ~ **performer/player** Star *m* ◼ VT (*Film etc*) ~ **sb** jdn in der Hauptrolle zeigen; **a film ~ring Greta Garbo** ein Film mit Greta Garbo (in der Hauptrolle); ~**ring ...** in der Hauptrolle/den Hauptrollen ... ◼ VI (*Film etc*) die Hauptrolle spielen

starboard [ˈstɑːbəd] ◼ N Steuerbord *nt* ◼ ADJ Steuerbord- ◼ ADV (nach) Steuerbord

starch [stɑːtʃ] ◼ N Stärke *f* ◼ VT stärken

stardom [ˈstɑːdəm] N Berühmtheit *f*, Ruhm *m*

stare [steəʳ] ◼ N (*starrer*) Blick ◼ VT **the answer was staring us in the face** die Antwort lag klar auf der Hand; **to ~ defeat in the face** der Niederlage ins Auge blicken ◼ VI (*vacantly etc*) (vor sich hin) starren; (*madman*) stieren, glotzen (*inf*); (*in surprise*) große Augen machen; (*eyes*) weit aufgerissen sein; **to ~ at sb/sth** jdn/etw anstarren; (*madman also*) jdn/etw anstieren *or* anglotzen (*inf*); **to ~ at sb in disbelief** *etc* jdn ungläubig *etc* anstarren

➤ **stare down** *or* **out** VT SEP **the teacher just sat there and stared him down** *or* **out** der Lehrer saß da und fixierte ihn

starfish [ˈstɑːfɪʃ] N Seestern *m*

staring [ˈsteərɪŋ] ADJ starrend *attr*; ~ **eyes** starrer Blick

stark [stɑːk] ◼ ADJ (+ER) *contrast, poverty, warning* krass; *reality, terror, fact* nackt; *reminder also* überdeutlich; *choice* hart; *landscape, branches* kahl; *colour* eintönig; (= *glaring*) grell ◼ ADV ~ **raving** *or* **staring mad** (*inf*) total verrückt (*inf*); ~ **naked** splitter(faser)nackt (*inf*)

> *Be careful!* **stark** *is not translated by the German word* ***stark***.

starkly [ˈstɑːklɪ] ADV *lit* grell; *described* krass, schonungslos; *different, apparent* vollkommen; **to contrast ~ with sth** (*fig*) sich krass von etw unterscheiden

starkness [ˈstɑːknɪs] N (*of colour*) Eintönigkeit *f*; (*glaring*) Grellheit *f*; (*of truth, contrast*) Krassheit *f*; (*of landscape*) Kahlheit *f*

starlight [ˈstɑːlaɪt] N Sternenlicht *nt*

starling [ˈstɑːlɪŋ] N Star *m*

star: starlit ADJ stern(en)klar; **star prize** N (*in competition*) Hauptpreis *m*

starry [ˈstɑːrɪ] ADJ (+ER) *night* stern(en)klar; ~ **sky** Sternenhimmel *m*

star: star sign N Sternzeichen *nt*; **star-spangled banner** N the ~ das Sternenbanner; **star-studded** [ˈstɑːstʌdɪd] ADJ (*fig*) ~ **cast** Starbesetzung *f*

start¹ [stɑːt] ◼ N **to give a ~** zusammenfahren; (= ~ *up*) aufschrecken; **to give sb a ~** jdn erschrecken; **to wake with a ~** aus dem Schlaf hochschrecken ◼ VI (= *jump nervously*) zusammenfahren; (= ~ *up*) aufschrecken

start² ◼ N **(a)** (= *beginning*) Beginn *m*, Anfang *m*; (= *departure*) Aufbruch *m*; (*of race*) Start *m*; (*of trouble, journey*) Ausgangspunkt *m*; **for a** ~ (= *to begin with*) fürs Erste; (= *firstly*) zunächst einmal; **from the** ~ von Anfang an; **from ~ to finish** von Anfang bis Ende, von vorn bis hinten (*inf*); **to get off to a good** *or* **flying** ~ gut vom Start wegkommen, (*fig*) einen glänzenden Start haben; **to get sb off to a good** ~ jdm einen guten Start verschaffen; **to get sth off to a good** ~ etw gut anlaufen lassen; **to make a** ~ (**on sth**) (mit etw) anfangen; **to make a new** ~ (**in life**) (noch einmal) von vorn anfangen **(b)** (= *advantage, Sport*) Vorsprung *m* (*over* vor +*dat*) ◼ VT **(a)** (= *begin*) anfangen mit; *argument, career, new life, negotiations* beginnen, anfangen; *new job, journey* antreten; **to ~ work** anfangen zu arbeiten; **to ~ smoking** mit dem Rauchen anfangen; **he ~ed coming late** er fing an, zu spät zu kommen; **you ~ed it!** du hast angefangen! **(b)** *race, car, machine* starten; *rumour* in Umlauf setzen; *conversation, fight, war* anfangen; *engine* anlassen; *clock* in Gang setzen; *collapse, chain reaction* auslösen; (*arsonist*) legen; *enterprise, newspaper* gründen, starten (*inf*); **to ~ sb**

thinking jdn nachdenklich machen; **I don't want to ~ anything but ...** ich will keinen Streit anfangen, aber ...; **look what you've ~ed now!** da hast du was Schönes angefangen! (inf)

3 VI (= begin) anfangen, beginnen; (car, engine) anspringen, starten; (= move off) anfahren; (bus, train) abfahren; (boat) ablegen; (rumour) in Umlauf kommen; **~ing from Tuesday** ab Dienstag; **to ~ (off) with** (= at the beginning) zunächst; **what shall we have to ~ (off) with?** was nehmen wir als Vorspeise?; **I'd like soup to ~ (off) with** ich möchte erst mal eine Suppe; **to ~ after sb** jdn verfolgen; **to get ~ed** anfangen; (on journey) aufbrechen; **to ~ on a task/journey** sich an eine Aufgabe/auf eine Reise machen; **to ~ talking** or **to talk** zu sprechen beginnen or anfangen; **he ~ed by saying ...** er sagte zunächst ...; **don't you ~!** fang du nicht auch noch an!

➤ **start back** VI sich auf den Rückweg machen

➤ **start off II** VI (= begin) anfangen; (= begin talking etc also) loslegen (inf); (= begin moving: person) losgehen; (on journey) aufbrechen; (= run) loslaufen; (= drive) losfahren; (esp Sport) starten; **to start off with = start² 3**

2 VT SEP sth anfangen; **to start the baby off (crying)** das Baby zum Schreien bringen; **that started the dog off (barking)** da fing der Hund an zu bellen; **to start sb off on sth** jdn auf etw (acc) bringen; **a few stamps to start you off** ein paar Briefmarken für den Anfang

➤ **start out** VI (= begin) (zunächst) beginnen or anfangen; (= begin a journey) aufbrechen (for nach)

➤ **start over** VI (esp US) noch (ein)mal von vorn anfangen

➤ **start up** VI (= begin) anfangen; (machine) angehen (inf); (motor) anspringen; **when I started up in business** als ich als Geschäftsmann anfing **2** VT SEP (a) (= switch on) anmachen (inf); engine also anlassen; machine also anwerfen (b) (= begin) eröffnen; conversation anfangen, anknüpfen

starter ['stɑːtə'] N (a) (Sport) Starter(in) m(f) (also horse) (b) (Brit inf: = first course) Vorspeise f (c) **for ~s** (inf) für den Anfang (inf)

starter pack N (Comm) Startpaket nt

starting ['stɑːtɪŋ] IN CPDS (Sport) Start-; **starting gun** N Startpistole f; **starting point** N (lit, fig) Ausgangspunkt m

startle ['stɑːtl] VT erschrecken; animal also aufschrecken

startling ['stɑːtlɪŋ] ADJ news, clarity überraschend; (= bad) alarmierend; coincidence, resemblance, contrast, change erstaunlich; colour, originality aufregend; discovery, claim, results sensationell

startlingly ['stɑːtlɪŋlɪ] ADV simple, alike überraschend; beautiful aufregend; different verblüffend

start-up ['stɑːtʌp] N (of machine, new business) Start m; **~ capital** Start- or Anfangskapital nt; **~ costs** Startkosten pl

starvation [stɑːˈveɪʃən] N (act) Hungern nt; (= condition) Hunger m; **to die of ~** verhungern; **to live on a ~ diet** Hunger leiden

starve [stɑːv] **1** VT (a) hungern lassen; (also ~ out) aushungern; (also ~ to death) verhungern lassen; **to ~ oneself** hungern (b) (fig) **to ~ sb of sth** jdm etw vorenthalten or verweigern; **to be ~d of oxygen** Sauerstoffmangel haben; **to be ~d of capital** an akutem Kapitalmangel leiden; **to be ~d of affection** zu wenig Zuneigung erfahren **2** VI hungern; (also ~ to death) verhungern; **you must be starving!** du musst doch halb verhungert sein! (inf)

starving ['stɑːvɪŋ] ADJ (lit) hungernd attr; (fig) hungrig

stash [stæʃ] VT (inf: also ~ away) bunkern (sl); money beiseite schaffen

state [steɪt] **1** N (a) (= condition) Zustand m; **~ of health/mind/war** Gesundheits-/Geistes-/Kriegszustand m; **the ~ of the nation** die Lage der Nation; **the present ~ of the economy** die gegenwärtige Wirtschaftslage; **in a good/bad ~** in gutem/schlechtem Zustand; **he's in no (fit) ~ to do that** er ist auf gar keinen Fall in der Verfassung, das zu tun; **what a ~ of affairs!** was sind das für Zustände!; **look at the ~ of your hands!** guck dir bloß mal deine Hände an!; **the room was in a terrible ~** im Zimmer herrschte ein fürchterliches Durcheinander; **to get into a ~ (about sth)** (inf) wegen etw durchdrehen (inf); **to be in a terrible ~** (inf) in heller Aufregung or ganz durchgedreht (inf) sein; **to lie in ~** (feierlich) aufgebahrt sein

(b) (Pol) Staat m; (= federal ~) (Bundes)staat m; (in Germany, Austria) (Bundes)land nt; **the States** die (Vereinigten) Staaten; **the State of Florida** der Staat Florida

2 VT darlegen, vortragen; name, price, amount, preference, purpose angeben; intention anmelden; **to ~ that ...** feststellen or erklären, dass ...; **to ~ one's case** seine Sache vortragen; **as ~d in my letter I ...** wie in meinem Brief erwähnt, ... ich ...

state IN CPDS Staats-; control, industry staatlich; (US etc) bundesstaatlich; **state control** N staatliche Kontrolle

stated ['steɪtɪd] ADJ (a) (= declared) sum, date angegeben, genannt (b) (= fixed) times, amount fest(gesetzt)

state: State Department N (US) Außenministerium nt; **state education** N staatliche Erziehung; **state-funded** ADJ staatlich finanziert; **state funding** N staatliche Finanzierung; **statehouse** N (US) Parlamentsgebäude nt, Kapitol nt; **stateless** ADJ staatenlos

stately ['steɪtlɪ] ADJ (+ER) person, bearing würdevoll; progress gemessen; **~ home** herrschaftliches Anwesen

statement ['steɪtmənt] N (a) (of thesis etc) Darstellung f; (of problem) Darlegung f; **a clear ~ of the facts** eine klare Feststellung der Tatsachen (b) (= that said) Feststellung f; (= claim) Behauptung f; (= official, Government ~) Erklärung f; (in court, to police) Aussage f; (written also) Protokoll nt; **to make a ~ to the press** eine Presseerklärung abgeben (c) (Fin) Rechnung f; (also bank ~) Kontoauszug m

state-of-the-art [ˌsteɪtəvðiːˈɑːt] ADJ hochmodern; **~ technology** Spitzentechnologie f

STATE OF THE UNION ADDRESS

State of the Union address *ist eine Rede, die der US-Präsident jeden Januar im Kongress hält und in der er seine Sicht zur Lage der Nation und seine Pläne für die Zukunft darlegt. Die Tradition der Regierungserklärung im Kongress kurz nach dessen Zusammentreten am 3. Januar erwuchs aus einer in der Verfassung verankerten Forderung, wonach der Präsident dem Kongress Informationen über die Lage der Nation (**information on the State of the Union**) geben muss.*

state: state-owned ADJ staatseigen; **state school** N (Brit) öffentliche Schule; **state secret** N Staatsgeheimnis nt; **stateside** (US inf) **1** ADJ in den Staaten (inf); newspaper aus den Staaten (inf) **2** ADV nach Hause

statesman ['steɪtsmən] N, pl **-men** [-mən] Staatsmann m

statesmanlike ['steɪtsmənlaɪk] ADJ staatsmännisch

statesmanship ['steɪtsmənʃɪp] N Staatskunst f

stateswoman ['steɪtswʊmən] N, pl **-women** Staatsmännin f

state: state trooper N (US) Staatspolizist(in) m(f); **statewide** ADJ (US) im ganzen Bundesstaat

static ['stætɪk] **1** ADJ (also Phys) statisch; (= not moving or changing) konstant; (= stationary) feststehend attr; **~ electricity** statische Aufladung **2** N (Phys) Reibungselektrizität f; (Rad also) atmosphärische Störungen pl

station ['steɪʃən] N (a) Station f; (= police ~, fire ~) Wache f; (US) (= gas ~) Tankstelle f; (= railway ~, bus ~) Bahnhof m (b) (Rad, TV) Sender m (c) (= position) Platz m (d) (= rank) Stand m, Rang m; **~ in life** Stellung f (im Leben), Rang m; **he has got ideas above his ~** er hat Ideen, die jemandem aus seinem Stand gar nicht zukommen

station agent N (US) Bahnhofsvorsteher(in) m(f)

stationary ['steɪʃənərɪ] ADJ (= not moving) parkend attr, haltend attr; (= not movable) fest (stehend attr); **to be ~** (vehicles) stehen; (traffic, fig) stillstehen

stationer ['steɪʃənə'] N Schreibwarenhändler(in) m(f)

stationery ['steɪʃənərɪ] N (= notepaper) Briefpapier nt; (= writing materials) Schreibwaren pl; **office ~** Büromaterial nt

station: station house N (US Police) (Polizei)wache f; **stationmaster** N Bahnhofsvorsteher(in) m(f); **station wagon** N (US) Kombi(wagen) m

statistic [stəˈtɪstɪk] N Statistik f

statistical ADJ, **statistically** ADV [stəˈtɪstɪkəl, -ɪ] statistisch

statistician [ˌstætɪˈstɪʃən] N Statistiker(in) m(f)

statistics [stəˈtɪstɪks] N (a) SING Statistik f (b) PL (= data) Statistiken pl

statue ['stætjuː] N Statue f; **Statue of Liberty** Freiheitsstatue f

statuesque [ˌstætjʊˈesk] ADJ standbildhaft

stature [stætʃəʳ] N **(a)** Wuchs *m*; (*esp of man*) Statur *f*; **of short ~** von kleinem Wuchs **(b)** (*fig*) Format *nt*

status ['steɪtəs] N Stellung *f*; (= *legal ~, social ~ also*) Status *m*; **equal ~** Gleichstellung *f*; **marital ~** Familienstand *m*

status: **status line** N (*Comput*) Statuszeile *f*; **status quo** [steɪtəs'kwəʊ] N Status quo *m*; **status symbol** N Statussymbol *nt*

statute [stætjuːt] N Gesetz *nt*; (*of organization*) Satzung *f*, Statut *nt*

statute book N (*esp Brit*) Gesetzbuch *nt*; **to put sth on the ~** etw zum Gesetz machen *or* erheben

statutory ['stætjʊtərɪ] ADJ gesetzlich; (*in organization*) satzungsgemäß; *right* verbrieft; *punishment* (vom Gesetz) vorgesehen; **~ enquiry** (*Brit Jur*) Untersuchung *f*

staunch[1] [stɔːntʃ] ADJ (+ER) *ally, friend* unerschütterlich; *Catholic, loyalist etc* überzeugt; *supporter* ergeben; *support* standhaft

staunch[2] VT *flow* stauen; *bleeding* stillen

staunchly ['stɔːntʃlɪ] ADV *treu*; *oppose* entschieden; *defend* standhaft; *Catholic* streng

stave [steɪv] N **(a)** (= *stick*) Knüppel *m* **(b)** (*Mus*) Notenlinien *pl*
➤ **stave off** VT SEP *attack* zurückschlagen; *threat, crisis, cold* abwehren; *defeat, disaster* abwenden; *hunger* lindern

stay [steɪ] N Aufenthalt *m*; **come for a longer ~ next year** komm nächstes Jahr für länger
2 VT **to ~ the course** (*lit, fig*) durchhalten; **to ~ the night (with sb/in a hotel)** (bei jdm/in einem Hotel) übernachten
3 VI **(a)** (= *remain*) bleiben; **to ~ for** *or* **to supper** zum Abendessen bleiben; **is unemployment here to ~?** ist die Arbeitslosigkeit nun ein Dauerzustand?; **~ with it!** nicht aufgeben!
(b) (= *reside*) wohnen; (*at youth hostel etc*) übernachten; **to ~ at a hotel** im Hotel wohnen *or* übernachten; **I ~ed in Italy for a few weeks** ich habe mich ein paar Wochen in Italien aufgehalten; **when I was ~ing in Italy** als ich in Italien war; **where are you ~ing?** wo wohnen Sie?; **he is ~ing at Chequers for the weekend** er verbringt das Wochenende in Chequers; **we would ~ at a different resort each year** wir waren jedes Jahr an einem anderen Urlaubsort; **my brother came to ~** mein Bruder ist zu Besuch gekommen
➤ **stay away** VI (*from* von) wegbleiben; (*from person*) sich fern halten
➤ **stay behind** VI zurückbleiben; (*Sch: as punishment*) nachsitzen
➤ **stay down** VI (= *keep down*) unten bleiben; (*Sch*) wiederholen
➤ **stay in** VI (*at home*) zu Hause bleiben; (*in position*) drinbleiben
➤ **stay off** VI +PREP OBJ **to stay off work/school** nicht zur Arbeit/Schule gehen
➤ **stay on** VI (*lid etc*) draufbleiben; (*light*) anbleiben; (*people*) (noch) bleiben; **to stay on at school** (in der Schule) weitermachen
➤ **stay out** VI draußen bleiben; (*esp Brit: on strike*) weiterstreiken; (= *not come home*) wegbleiben; **to stay out of sth** sich aus etw heraushalten; **he never managed to stay out of trouble** er war dauernd in Schwierigkeiten
➤ **stay up** VI **(a)** (*person*) aufbleiben **(b)** (*tent, fence, pole*) stehen bleiben; (*picture, decorations*) hängen bleiben; **his trousers won't stay up** seine Hosen rutschen immer

staying power ['steɪɪŋˌpaʊəʳ] N Stehvermögen *nt*, Durchhaltevermögen *nt*

St Bernard [sənt'bɜːnəd] N Bernhardiner *m*

STD code [estiː'diːkəʊd] N Vorwahl(nummer) *f*

stead [sted] N **to stand sb in good ~** jdm zugute kommen

steadfast ['stedfəst] ADJ fest; *refusal also* standhaft; *belief also* unerschütterlich

steadfastly ['stedfəstlɪ] ADV fest; *adhere, refuse* standhaft, unerschütterlich; **to ~ maintain one's innocence** unerschütterlich auf seiner Unschuld beharren

steadily ['stedɪlɪ] ADV **(a)** (= *firmly*) ruhig; *gaze* fest, unverwandt **(b)** (= *constantly*) ständig; *rain* ununterbrochen; **the atmosphere in the country is getting ~ more tense** die Stimmung im Land wird immer gespannter **(c)** (= *reliably*) zuverlässig, solide **(d)** (= *regularly*) gleichmäßig, regelmäßig

steadiness ['stedɪnɪs] N (= *stability*) Festigkeit *f*; (*of hand, eye*) Ruhe *f*; (= *regularity*) Stetigkeit *f*; (*of gaze*) Unverwandtheit *f*

steady ['stedɪ] 1 ADJ (+ER) **(a)** *hand, nerves, eye* ruhig; *gaze, voice, job, boyfriend* fest; **~ on one's legs** fest *or* sicher auf den Beinen; **to hold sth ~** etw ruhig halten; *ladder* etw festhalten **(b)** *progress, demand etc* ständig, kontinuierlich, stet (*geh*); *drizzle* ununterbrochen; *income* geregelt; **at a ~ pace** in gleichmäßigem Tempo **(c)** (= *reliable*) *worker* zuverlässig
2 ADV **~!** (= *carefully*) vorsichtig!; **to go ~ (with sb)** (*inf*) mit jdm (fest) gehen (*inf*)
3 VT (= *stabilize*) *nerves, person* beruhigen; **to ~ oneself** festen Halt finden
4 VI sich beruhigen; (*person, voice*) ruhig(er) werden

steak [steɪk] N Steak *nt*; (*of fish*) Filet *nt*

steal [stiːl] *vb: pret* **stole**, *ptp* **stolen** 1 VT stehlen; **to ~ sth from sb** jdm etw stehlen; **to ~ the show** die Schau stehlen; **to ~ the limelight from sb** jdm die Schau stehlen; **to ~ a glance at sb** verstohlen zu jdm hinschauen 2 VI **(a)** (= *thieve*) stehlen **(b)** (= *move quietly etc*) sich stehlen, (sich) schleichen; **to ~ away** *or* **off** sich weg- *or* davonstehlen; **to ~ up on sb** sich an jdn heranschleichen

stealth [stelθ] N List *f*; **by ~** durch List

stealthily ['stelθɪlɪ] ADV verstohlen

stealthy ['stelθɪ] ADJ (+ER) verstohlen

steam [stiːm] 1 N Dampf *m*; **full ~ ahead** (*Naut*) volle Kraft voraus; (*fig*) mit Volldampf voraus; **to get** *or* **pick up ~** (*fig*) in Schwung kommen; **to let off ~** (*lit, fig*) Dampf ablassen; **to run out of ~** (*fig*) Schwung verlieren; **he ran out of ~** (*inf*) ihm ist die Puste ausgegangen (*inf*) 2 VT dämpfen; *food also* dünsten 3 VI dampfen
➤ **steam ahead** VI (*inf: project*) gut vorankommen
➤ **steam off** VT SEP *stamp* über Dampf ablösen
➤ **steam up** 1 VT SEP *window* beschlagen lassen; **to be (all) steamed up** (ganz) beschlagen sein; (*fig inf*) (ganz) aufgeregt sein 2 VI beschlagen

steam: **steamboat** N Dampfschiff *nt*; **steam engine** N Dampflok *f*

steamer ['stiːməʳ] N (= *ship*) Dampfer *m*; (*Cook*) Dampf(koch)topf *m*

steam: **steam iron** N Dampfbügeleisen *nt*; **steamroller** 1 N Dampfwalze *f* 2 VT *road* glatt walzen; (*fig*) überfahren; **steamship** N Dampfschiff *nt*

steamy ['stiːmɪ] ADJ (+ER) dampfig; *room, atmosphere also* voll Dampf; *jungle* dunstig; *window, mirror* beschlagen; (*fig*) *affair, novel* heiß

steel [stiːl] 1 N Stahl *m* 2 ADJ ATTR Stahl- 3 VT **to ~ oneself** sich wappnen (*for* gegen); (*physically*) sich stählen (*for* für); **to ~ oneself to do sth** allen Mut zusammennehmen, um etw zu tun; **to ~ oneself against sth** sich gegen etw hart machen *or* verhärten

steel IN CPDS Stahl-, stahl-; **steel band** N Steelband *f*; **steel manufacturing** N Stahlherstellung *f*; **steel-plated** ADJ mit Stahlüberzug; (*for protection*) stahlgepanzert

steely ['stiːlɪ] ADJ (+ER) *grip* stahlhart; *expression, gaze* hart; *determination* eisern

steep[1] [stiːp] ADJ (+ER) **(a)** steil; *fall* tief; **it's a ~ climb** es geht steil hinauf **(b)** (*fig inf*) *demand, price* unverschämt; **that's pretty ~!** das ist allerhand!

steep[2] 1 VT **(a)** (*in liquid*) eintauchen; (*in marinade*) ziehen lassen; *dried food, washing* einweichen **(b)** (*fig*) **to be ~ed in sth** von etw durchdrungen sein; **~ed in history** geschichtsträchtig 2 VI **to leave sth to ~** etw einweichen; (*in marinade*) etw ziehen lassen

steepen ['stiːpən] 1 VT steiler machen 2 VI (*slope*) steiler werden; (*ground*) ansteigen; (*fig*) *slump* zunehmen

steeple ['stiːpl] N Kirchturm *m*

steeplechase ['stiːpltʃeɪs] N (*for horses*) Hindernisrennen *nt*; (*for runners*) Hindernislauf *m*

steepness ['stiːpnɪs] N Steile *f*, Steilheit *f*

steer[1] [stɪəʳ] 1 VT (*lit, fig*) lenken; (*car also, ship*) steuern; **to ~ a course through sth** (*lit, fig*) durch etw hindurchsteuern 2 VI (*in car*) lenken; (*in ship*) steuern; **to ~ due north** Kurs nach Norden halten

steer[2] N junger Ochse

steering ['stɪərɪŋ] N (*in car etc*) Lenkung *f*

steering wheel N Steuer(rad) *nt*; (*of car also*) Lenkrad *nt*

stellar ['stelə^r] ADJ stellar

stem [stem] **1** N (*of plant, glass*) Stiel *m*; (*of woody plant, shrub, word*) Stamm *m*; (*of grain*) Halm *m*; (*of pipe*) Hals *m* **2** VT (= *stop*) aufhalten; *flow of sth, tide, flood also* eindämmen; *bleeding, decline also* zum Stillstand bringen; *inflation also, flow of words* Einhalt gebieten (+*dat*) **3** VI **to ~ from sth** (= *result from*) von etw kommen, von etw herrühren; (= *have as origin*) aus etw (her)stammen

stench [stentʃ] N Gestank *m*

stencil ['stensl] **1** N Schablone *f* **2** VT mit Schablonen zeichnen

step [step] **1** N **(a)** (= *pace, move*) Schritt *m*; (= *measure also*) Maßnahme *f*; **to take a ~** einen Schritt machen; **~ by ~** (*lit, fig*) Schritt für Schritt; **to watch one's ~** Acht geben; (*fig also*) sich vorsehen; **to be *or* stay one ~ ahead of sb** (*fig*) jdm einen Schritt voraussein; **to be in ~** (*lit*) im Gleichschritt sein; (*fig*) im Gleichklang sein; **to be out of ~** (*lit*) nicht im Tritt *or* in gleichen Schritt sein; (*fig*) nicht im Gleichklang sein; **to keep in ~** (*lit*) Tritt halten; (*fig*) Schritt halten; **the first ~ is to form a committee** als Erstes muss ein Ausschuss gebildet werden; **that would be a ~ back/in the right direction for him** das wäre für ihn ein Rückschritt/ein Schritt in die richtige Richtung; **to take ~s to do sth** Maßnahmen ergreifen, (um) etw zu tun

(b) (= *stair*) (*fig*) (*in scale*) Stufe *f*; (*in process*) Abschnitt *m*; **~s** (*outdoors*) Treppe *f*; **mind the ~** Vorsicht Stufe

(c) steps PL (*Brit*: = *~ladder*: *also* **pair of ~s**) Trittleiter *f* **2** VT **~ two paces to the left** treten Sie zwei Schritte nach links

3 VI gehen; **to ~ into/out of sth** *room, puddle* in etw (*acc*)/aus etw treten; **to ~ on(to) sth** *plane, train* in etw (*acc*) steigen; *platform* auf etw (*acc*) steigen; **to ~ on sth** auf etw (*acc*) treten; **he ~ped on my foot** er ist mir auf den Fuß getreten; **~ this way, please** hier entlang, bitte!; **he ~ped into the road** er trat auf die Straße; **he ~ped into his father's shoes** er übernahm die Stelle seines Vaters; **to ~ inside/outside** hinein-/hinaustreten; **~ on it!** (*in car*) gib Gas!

➤ **step aside** VI **(a)** (*lit*) zur Seite treten **(b)** (*fig*) Platz machen

➤ **step back** VI **(a)** (*lit*) zurücktreten **(b)** (*fig*) **to step back from sth** von etw Abstand gewinnen

➤ **step down** VI **(a)** (*lit*) hinabsteigen **(b)** (*fig*: = *resign*) zurücktreten; **to step down as president** vom Amt des Präsidenten zurücktreten

➤ **step forward** VI vortreten; (*fig*) sich melden

➤ **step in** VI **(a)** (*lit*) eintreten (*-to, +prep obj* in +*acc*) **(b)** (*fig*) eingreifen; (*interferingly*) dazwischenkommen

➤ **step off** VI +PREP OBJ (*off bus, plane, boat*) aussteigen (*prep obj* aus); **to step off the pavement** vom Bürgersteig treten

➤ **step out** VI (= *go out*) hinausgehen

➤ **step up** **1** VT SEP steigern; *efforts also, security, campaign, search, support* verstärken; *pressure also, demands, pace* erhöhen; **to step up a gear** (*fig*) eine Stufe höher schalten **2** VI (= *come forward*) vortreten; **to step up to sb** auf jdn zugehen/zukommen; **he stepped up onto the stage** er trat auf die Bühne

step- PREF Stief-; **~brother** Stiefbruder *m*

stepladder ['step,lædə^r] N Trittleiter *f*

stepping stone ['stepɪŋ,stəʊn] N (Tritt)stein *m*; (*fig*) Sprungbrett *nt*

stereo ['steriəʊ] **1** N Stereo *nt*; (= *record-player*) Stereoanlage *f*; **in ~** in Stereo **2** ADJ Stereo-

stereotype ['steriə,taɪp] **1** N (*fig*) Klischee(vorstellung *f*), Stereotyp *nt*; (= *~ character*) stereotype Figur **2** ATTR stereotyp; *ideas, thinking also* klischeehaft **3** VT (*fig*) *character* klischeehaft darstellen; **the plot of the Western has become ~d** die Handlung des Western ist zu einem Klischee geworden

stereotyped ['steriə,taɪpt] ADJ = **stereotype 2**

stereotypical [,steriə'tɪpɪkl] ADJ stereotyp

sterile ['sterail] ADJ steril; *person also, animal, soil* unfruchtbar; (= *germ-free also*) keimfrei

sterility [ste'rɪlɪti] N (*of animal, soil*) Unfruchtbarkeit *f*; (*of person also*) Sterilität *f*

sterilization [,sterilaɪ'zeɪʃən] N Sterilisation *f*

sterilize ['sterilaɪz] VT sterilisieren

sterling ['stɜːlɪŋ] **1** ADJ **(a)** (*Fin*) Sterling-; **in pounds ~** in Pfund Sterling **(b)** (*fig*) gediegen **2** N NO ART (= *money*) das Pfund Sterling; **in ~** in Pfund Sterling

stern¹ [stɜːn] N (*Naut*) Heck *nt*

stern² ADJ (+ER) (= *strict*) streng; *words also, warning* ernst; (= *tough*) *test* hart; *opposition* stark; **with a ~ face** mit strenger Miene; **made of ~er stuff** aus härterem Holz geschnitzt

sternly ['stɜːnli] ADV *say, rebuke* ernsthaft; *look* streng; **a ~ worded statement** eine streng formulierte Aussage

steroid ['stɪərɔɪd] N Steroid *nt*

stethoscope ['steθəskəʊp] N Stethoskop *nt*

stetson ['stetsən] N Stetson *m*, Texashut *m*

stew [stjuː] **1** N **(a)** Eintopf *m* **(b)** (*inf*) **to be in a ~ (over sth)** (über etw (*acc*) *or* wegen etw) (ganz) aufgeregt sein **2** VT *meat* schmoren; *fruit* dünsten **3** VI **to let sb ~** *or* **to leave sb to ~ (in his/her own juice)** jdn (im eigenen Saft) schmoren lassen

steward ['stjuːəd] N Steward *m*; (*on estate etc*) Verwalter(in) *m(f)*; (*at meeting*) Ordner(in) *m(f)*; (= *bouncer*) Türsteher(in) *m(f)*

stick¹ [stɪk] N **(a)** Stock *m*; (= *twig*) Zweig *m*; (= *hockey ~*) Schläger *m*; **to give sb/sth some/a lot of ~** (*Brit inf*) jdn/etw heruntermachen (*inf*) *or* herunterputzen (*inf*); **to get hold of the wrong end of the ~** (*fig inf*) etw falsch verstehen; **in the ~s** (= *backwoods*) in der hintersten *or* finstersten Provinz

(b) (*of celery etc, dynamite*) Stange *f*; **a ~ deodorant** (*Brit*), **a deodorant ~**, **a ~ of deodorant** ein Deostift *m*

stick² *pret, ptp* **stuck** **1** VT **(a)** (*with glue etc*) kleben; **is this glue strong enough to ~ it?** wird dieser Klebstoff das halten? **(b)** (= *pin*) stecken

(c) *knife, sword etc* stoßen; **he stuck a knife into her arm** er stieß ihr ein Messer in den Arm

(d) (*inf*: = *place, put*) tun (*inf*); (*esp in sth*) stecken (*inf*); **~ it on the shelf** tus ins Regal; **he stuck his head round the corner** er steckte seinen Kopf um die Ecke

(e) (*Brit inf*: = *tolerate*) aushalten; *pace* durchhalten; **I can't ~ him** ich kann ihn nicht ausstehen (*inf*)

2 VI **(a)** (*glue, burr etc*) kleben (*to* an +*dat*); **the name seems to have stuck** der Name scheint ihm/ihr geblieben zu sein

(b) (= *become caught, wedged etc*) stecken bleiben; (*drawer, window*) klemmen

(c) (*sth pointed*) stecken (*in* in +*dat*); **it stuck in my foot** das ist mir im Fuß stecken geblieben

(d) (= *project*) **his toes are ~ing through his socks** seine Zehen kommen durch die Socken

(e) (= *stay*) bleiben; (*slander*) haften bleiben; **to ~ in sb's mind** jdm im Gedächtnis bleiben

➤ **stick around** VI (*inf*) dableiben; **stick around!** warts ab!

➤ **stick at** VI +PREP OBJ (= *persist*) bleiben an (+*dat*) (*inf*); **to stick at it** dranbleiben (*inf*)

➤ **stick by** VI +PREP OBJ *sb* halten zu; *promise* stehen zu; *rules, principles* sich halten an

➤ **stick down** VT SEP **(a)** (= *glue*) ankleben; *envelope* zukleben **(b)** (*inf*: = *put down*) abstellen

➤ **stick in** VT SEP (= *glue, put in*) hineinstecken; *knife etc* hineinstechen; **to stick sth in(to) sth** etw in etw (*acc*) stecken; *knife, pin etc* mit etw in etw (*acc*) stechen

➤ **stick on** **1** VT SEP **(a)** *label, cover* aufkleben (*prep obj* auf +*acc*) **(b)** (= *add*) draufschlagen; (+*prep obj*) aufschlagen auf (+*acc*) **2** VI (*label etc*) kleben (*prep obj* an +*dat*)

➤ **stick out** **1** VI vorstehen; (*ears*) abstehen; (*fig*: = *be noticeable*) auffallen **2** VT SEP **(a)** herausstrecken **(b)** (= *not give up*) durchhalten

➤ **stick to** VI +PREP OBJ **(a)** (= *adhere to*) bleiben bei; *principles etc* treu bleiben (+*dat*); (= *follow*) *rules, timetable, plan, diet* sich halten an (+*acc*) **(b)** (= *persist with*) *task* bleiben an (+*dat*)

➤ **stick together** VI zusammenkleben; (*fig*: *partners etc*) zusammenhalten

➤ **stick up** **1** VT SEP **(a)** (*with tape etc*) zukleben **(b)** (*inf*) **stick 'em up!** Hände hoch!; **three pupils stuck up their hands** drei Schüler meldeten sich **2** VI (*nail etc*) vorstehen; (*hair*) abstehen; (*collar*) hochstehen

➤ **stick up for** VI +PREP OBJ eintreten für; **to stick up for oneself** sich behaupten

➤ **stick with** VI +PREP OBJ bleiben bei; (= *remain loyal to*) halten zu

sticker ['stɪkəʳ] N (= *label*) Aufkleber *m*; (= *price ~*) Klebeschildchen *nt*

stickiness ['stɪkɪnɪs] N (*lit*) Klebrigkeit *f*; (*of atmosphere, weather*) Schwüle *f*; (*of air*) Stickigkeit *f*

stickler ['stɪkləʳ] N **to be a ~ for sth** es mit etw peinlich genau nehmen

stick: stick-on ADJ zum Aufkleben; **~ label** Klebeetikett *nt*; **stick-up** N (*inf*) Überfall *m*

sticky ['stɪkɪ] ADJ (+ER) (a) klebrig; *atmosphere, weather* schwül; *air* stickig; (= *sweaty*) *hands* verschwitzt; **I'm all hot and ~** ich bin total verschwitzt; **to be ~ with blood** blutverklebt sein; **~ bun** ≈ Krapfen *m*; **~ tape** (*Brit*) Klebeband *nt* (b) (*fig inf*) *problem, person* schwierig; *situation, moment* heikel; **to go through a ~ patch** eine schwere Zeit durchmachen; **to come to a ~ end** ein böses Ende nehmen

stiff [stɪf] **1** ADJ (+ER) (*lit, fig*) steif; *corpse also* starr; *paste* fest; *resistance, opposition, drink* stark; *brush, sentence, challenge, competition* hart; *climb, test* schwierig; *punishment* schwer; *smile* kühl; *price* hoch; *door, lock, drawer* klemmend; **that's a bit ~** das ist ganz schön happig (*inf*); **to be (as) ~ as a board** *or* **poker** steif wie ein Brett sein **2** ADV steif

stiffen ['stɪfn] (*also ~ up*) **1** VT steif machen; *resistance etc* verstärken **2** VI steif werden; (*fig: resistance*) sich verhärten; **when I said this she ~ed (up)** als ich das sagte, wurde sie ganz starr

stiffly ['stɪflɪ] ADV steif

stiffness ['stɪfnɪs] N (a) (*lit, fig*) Steifheit *f*; (*of corpse also*) Starre *f*; (*of brush*) Härte *f*; (*of paste*) Festigkeit *f* (b) (*of resistance, opposition*) Stärke *f* (c) (*of door, lock, drawer*) Klemmen *nt*

stifle ['staɪfl] **1** VT (*lit, fig*) ersticken; (*fig*) *laugh, cough also, opposition* unterdrücken **2** VI ersticken

stifling ['staɪflɪŋ] ADJ (a) *fumes* erstickend; *heat* drückend; **it's ~ in here** es ist ja zum Ersticken hier drin (*inf*) (b) (*fig*) beengend; *situation* erdrückend; *atmosphere* stickig

stigma ['stɪgmə] N, *pl* **-s** Stigma *nt*

stigmatize ['stɪgmətaɪz] VT **to ~ sb as sth** jdn als etw brandmarken

stile [staɪl] N (Zaun)übertritt *m*

stiletto [stɪ'letəʊ] N (*esp Brit also* **~-heeled shoe**) Schuh *m* mit Bleistift- *or* Pfennigabsatz

still¹ [stɪl] **1** ADJ, ADV (+ER) (a) (= *motionless*) bewegungslos; *waters* ruhig; **to keep ~** stillhalten; **to hold sth ~** etw ruhig *or* still halten; **to lie ~** still *or* reglos daliegen; **my heart stood ~** mir stockte das Herz; **time stood ~** die Zeit stand still (b) (= *quiet*) still; **be ~!** (*US*) sei still! **2** ADJ *drink* ohne Kohlensäure **3** N (a) (= *~ness*) Stille *f* (b) (*Film*) Standfoto *nt* **4** VT (*liter: = calm*) beruhigen; *pain* abklingen lassen; **to ~ sb's fears** jdm die Furcht nehmen

still² **1** ADV (a) (*temporal, with comp*) noch; (*for emphasis, in exasperation, used on its own in negative statements*) immer noch; (= *now as in the past*) nach wie vor; **is he ~ coming?** kommt er noch?; **do you mean you ~ don't believe me?** willst du damit sagen, dass du mir immer noch nicht glaubst?; **it ~ hasn't come** es ist immer noch nicht gekommen; **I will ~ be here** ich werde noch da sein; **the problems were ~ to come** die Probleme sollten erst noch kommen; **there are ten weeks ~ to go** es bleiben noch zehn Wochen; **better ~, do it this way** oder noch besser, mach es so; **worse ~, ...** schlimmer noch, ...

(b) (*esp US inf: also* **~ and all** = *nevertheless*) trotzdem; **~, it was worth it** es hat sich trotzdem gelohnt; **~, he's not a bad person** na ja, er ist eigentlich kein schlechter Mensch **2** CONJ (und) dennoch

still: stillbirth N Totgeburt *f*; **stillborn** ADJ (*lit, fig*) tot geboren; **the child was ~** das Kind kam tot zur Welt; **still life** N, *pl* **still lifes** Stillleben *nt*

stillness ['stɪlnɪs] N (a) (= *motionlessness*) Unbewegtheit *f*; (*of person*) Reglosigkeit *f* (b) (= *quietness*) Stille *f*, Ruhe *f*

stilt [stɪlt] N Stelze *f*; (*Archit*) Pfahl *m*

stilted ADJ, **stiltedly** ADV ['stɪltɪd, -lɪ] gestelzt, gespreizt

stimulant ['stɪmjʊlənt] N Anregungsmittel *nt*; (*fig*) Ansporn *m*

stimulate ['stɪmjʊleɪt] VT *body, mind* anregen; (*coffee etc*) *sb* beleben; (*sexually*) *sb's interest* erregen; (*fig*) *person* animieren;

(*Med, intellectually*) *growth, production* stimulieren; *economy, sales etc* ankurbeln; **to ~ investments** Investitionen anlocken

stimulating ['stɪmjʊleɪtɪŋ] ADJ anregend; *shower, walk, music* belebend; *experience* (*physically*) erfrischend; (*mentally*) stimulierend

stimulation [stɪmjʊ'leɪʃən] N (a) (= *act*) (*physical, mental*) Anregung *f*; (*Med, intellectual*) Stimulation *f*; (*sexual*) Erregen *nt*; (= *state*) (*sexual*) Erregung *f*; (*fig: = incentive*) Anreiz *m* (b) (*of economy, sales etc*) Ankurbelung *f* (*to +gen*)

stimulus ['stɪmjʊləs] N, *pl* **stimuli** ['stɪmjʊlaɪ] Anreiz *m*, Ansporn *m*; (*Physiol*) Reiz *m*; (*Psych*) Stimulus *m*

sting [stɪŋ], *vb: pret, ptp* **stung** **1** N (a) (= *organ: of insect, fig: of remark*) Stachel *m*; (*of jellyfish*) Brennfaden *m*; (*of criticism*) Schärfe *f*; **to take the ~ out of sth** etw entschärfen; (*out of remark also*) einer Sache (*dat*) den Stachel nehmen; **to have a ~ in its tail** (*story, film*) ein unerwartet fatales Ende nehmen; (*remark*) gesalzen sein

(b) (*of insect: = act, wound*) Stich *m*; (*of nettle, jellyfish*) (= *act*) Brennen *nt*; (= *wound*) Quaddel *f*

(c) (= *pain*) (*from needle etc*) Stechen *nt*; (*of antiseptic, from nettle etc*) Brennen *nt*

2 VT (a) (*insect*) stechen; (*jellyfish*) verbrennen; **she was stung by the nettles** sie hat sich an den Nesseln verbrannt

(b) (*comments, sarcasm etc*) schmerzen; (*conscience*) quälen; **to ~ sb into doing sth** jdn antreiben, etw zu tun; **to ~ sb into action** jdn aktiv werden lassen

3 VI (a) (*insect*) stechen; (*nettle, jellyfish etc*) brennen; (= *burn: eyes, ointment etc*) brennen

(b) (*comments, sarcasm etc*) schmerzen

stinger ['stɪŋəʳ] N (*US: = insect*) stechendes Insekt

stingily ['stɪndʒɪlɪ] ADV (*inf*) knauserig (*inf*)

stinginess ['stɪndʒɪnɪs] N (*inf*) (*of person*) Knauserigkeit *f* (*inf*); (*of sum, portion*) Popeligkeit *f* (*inf*)

stinging ['stɪŋɪŋ] ADJ *pain, blow, comment* stechend; *cut, ointment* brennend; *rain* peitschend; *attack* scharf

stinging nettle N Brennnessel *f*

stingy ['stɪndʒɪ] ADJ (+ER) (*inf*) *person* knauserig (*inf*); *sum, portion* popelig (*inf*); **to be ~ with** mit etw knausern

stink [stɪŋk], *vb: pret* **stank**, *ptp* **stunk** **1** N (a) (*lit*) Gestank *m* (*of* nach); (*fig: of corruption etc*) (Ge)ruch *m* (b) (*inf: = fuss*) Knatsch (*inf*), Stunk (*inf*) *m*; **to kick up** *or* **make a ~** Stunk machen (*inf*) **2** VI (a) (*lit*) stinken (b) (*fig inf: = be bad*) sauschlecht *or* miserabel sein (*inf*); **the whole business ~s** die ganze Sache stinkt (*inf*)

➤ **stink out** VT SEP (*Brit inf*) *room* verstänkern (*inf*)

stinking ['stɪŋkɪŋ] **1** ADJ (a) (*lit*) stinkend (b) (*inf*) beschissen (*inf*); **I've got a ~ cold** ich habe eine Mordserkältung **2** ADV (*inf*) **~ rich** (*Brit*) stinkreich (*inf*)

stinky ['stɪŋkɪ] ADJ (+ER) (*inf*) stinkend

stint [stɪnt] **1** N (= *allotted amount of work*) Arbeit *f*, Aufgabe *f*; (= *share*) Anteil *m* (*of* an +*dat*); **to do one's ~** (= *daily work*) seine Arbeit leisten *or* tun; (= *share*) sein(en) Teil beitragen *or* tun; **a 2-hour ~** eine 2-Stunden Schicht; **he did a five-year ~ on the oil rigs** er hat fünf Jahre auf Ölplattformen gearbeitet; **would you like to do a ~ at the wheel?** wie wärs, wenn du auch mal fahren würdest? **2** VI **to ~ on sth** etw sparen *or* knausern

stipend ['staɪpend] N (*esp Brit: for official, clergyman*) Gehalt *nt*; (*US: for student*) Stipendium *nt*

stipulate ['stɪpjʊleɪt] VT (a) (= *make a condition*) zur Auflage machen, verlangen (b) *date, amount, price* festsetzen; *size, quantity* vorschreiben; *conditions* stellen

stipulation [stɪpjʊ'leɪʃən] N (a) (= *condition*) Auflage *f*; **with** *or* **on the ~ that ...** unter der Bedingung *or* mit der Auflage, dass ... (b) (*of date, amount, price, size*) Festsetzung *f*; (*of conditions*) Stellen *nt*

stir [stɜːʳ] **1** N (a) (*lit*) Rühren *nt*; **to give sth a ~** etw rühren; *tea etc* etw umrühren

(b) (*fig: = excitement*) Aufruhr *m*; **to cause** *or* **create a ~** Aufsehen erregen

2 VT (a) *tea, paint, soup* umrühren; *cake mixture* rühren

(b) (= *move*) bewegen; *water* kräuseln

(c) (*fig*) *emotions* aufwühlen; *imagination* anregen; *curiosity* erregen; (= *incite*) *person* anstacheln; (= *move*) *person, heart* rühren, bewegen; **to ~ sb to do sth** jdn bewegen, etw zu tun; (= *incite*) jdn dazu anstacheln, etw zu tun

3 VI (= *move*) sich regen; (*leaves, curtains, animal etc*) sich bewegen; (*anger etc*) wach werden

➤ **stir up** VT SEP **(a)** *liquid, mixture* umrühren **(b)** (*fig*) *curiosity, anger, controversy* erregen; *memories, the past* wachrufen; *opposition, discord* entfachen, erzeugen; *hatred* schüren; *revolt* anzetteln; *lazy person* aufrütteln; **to stir up trouble** Unruhe stiften; **that'll stir things up** das kann heiter werden!

stir-fry ['stɜːfraɪ] **1** N Stirfry- or Rührbratgericht *nt* **2** VT (unter Rühren) kurz anbraten

stirring ['stɜːrɪŋ] **1** ADJ bewegend; (*stronger*) aufwühlend **2** N (= *development*) **the first ~s of sth** die ersten Anzeichen *pl* von etw

stirrup ['stɪrəp] N Steigbügel *m* (*also Anat*)

stitch [stɪtʃ] **1** N **(a)** *Stich m*; (= *kind of ~*) (*in knitting etc*) Masche *f*; (= *kind of ~*) (*in knitting etc*) Muster *nt*; (*in embroidery*) Stichart *f*; **he had to have ~es** er musste genäht werden
(b) (= *pain*) Seitenstiche *pl*; **to be in ~es** (*inf: from laughing*) sich schieflachen (*inf*); **he had us all in ~es** er brachte uns alle furchtbar zum Lachen (*inf*)
2 VT (*Sew, Med*) nähen; (= *mend*) stopfen; (= *embroider*) sticken
3 VI nähen (*at* an +*dat*)

➤ **stitch on** VT SEP aufnähen; *button* annähen

➤ **stitch up** VT SEP **(a)** *seam, wound* nähen; (= *mend*) *hole etc* stopfen (*Brit inf*: = *frame*) **I've been stitched up** man hat mich reingelegt (*inf*) **(c)** (*Brit inf*) *agreement* zusammenstoppeln (*inf*)

stitching ['stɪtʃɪŋ] N (= *seam*) Naht *f*; (= *embroidery*) Stickerei *f*

stoat [stəʊt] N Wiesel *nt*

stock [stɒk] **1** N **(a)** (= *supply*) Vorrat *m* (*of* an +*dat*); (*Comm*) Bestand *m* (*of* an +*dat*); **to have sth in ~** etw vorrätig haben; **to be in ~/out of ~** vorrätig/nicht vorrätig sein; **to keep sth in ~** etw auf Vorrat haben; **to take ~ of sth** (*situation*) sich (*dat*) klar werden über etw (*acc*); *of one's life* Bilanz aus etw ziehen
(b) (= *livestock*) Viehbestand *m*
(c) (*Cook*) Brühe *f*
(d) (*Fin*) (= *capital raised by company*) Aktienkapital *nt*; (= *shares held by investor*) Anteil *m*; (= *government ~*) Staatsanleihe *f*; **to have** or **hold ~ in oil companies** Ölaktien haben; **~s and shares** (Aktien und) Wertpapiere *pl*
(e) (= *descent*) **to be** or **come of good ~** guter Herkunft sein
(f) (*Rail*) rollendes Material
2 ADJ ATTR (*Comm, fig*) Standard-
3 VT **(a)** *shop etc*) *goods* führen
(b) *cupboard* füllen; *shop, library* ausstatten

➤ **stock up** **1** VI sich eindecken (*on* mit); **I must stock up on rice, I've almost run out** mein Reis ist fast alle, ich muss meinen Vorrat auffüllen **2** VT SEP *shop, larder etc* auffüllen; *library* anreichern

stock: **stockbroker** N Börsenmakler(in) *m(f)*; **stockbroking** N Wertpapierhandel *m*; **stock certificate** N Aktienzertifikat *nt*; **stock company** N **(a)** (*Fin*) Aktiengesellschaft *f* **(b)** (*US Theat*) Repertoiretheater *nt*; **stock control** N Lager(bestands)kontrolle *f*; **stock cube** N Brühwürfel *m*; **stock exchange** N Börse *f*; **stockholder** N (*US*) Aktionär(in) *m(f)*; **stockholding** N **(a)** (*Comm*) (= *storage*) Lagerhaltung *f*; (= *stock stored*) Lagerbestand *m* **(b)** USU PL (*Fin*) Aktienbestand *m*

stockily ['stɒkɪlɪ] ADV **~ built** stämmig

stocking ['stɒkɪŋ] N Strumpf *m*; (*knee-length*) Kniestrumpf *m*; **in one's ~(ed) feet** in Strümpfen

stockist ['stɒkɪst] N (*Brit*) (Fach)händler(in) *m(f)*; (= *shop*) Fachgeschäft *nt*

stock: **stock list** N **(a)** (*Comm*) Warenliste *f* **(b)** (*Fin*) Börsenzettel *m*; **stockman** N **(a)** (*US, Austral*) Viehzüchter *m*; (= *farmhand*) Farmarbeiter *m* **(b)** (*US: in shop etc*) Lagerverwalter *m*; **stock market** N Börse *f*; **stockpile** **1** N Vorrat *m* (*of* an +*dat*); (*of weapons*) Lager *nt* **2** VT Vorräte an (+*dat*) ... anlegen; *weapons* horten; **stock room** N Lager *nt*; **stocktaking** N Inventur *f*; **stock turnover** N (*Brit*) Lagerumschlag *m*

stocky ['stɒkɪ] ADJ (+ER) stämmig

stockyard ['stɒkjɑːd] N Schlachthof *m*

stodgy ['stɒdʒɪ] ADJ (+ER) *food* pappig (*inf*), schwer; *style* schwerfällig; *subject* trocken

stoic ['stəʊɪk] **1** N Stoiker(in) *m(f)* **2** ADJ stoisch

stoical ADJ, **stoically** ADV ['stəʊɪkəl, -ɪ] stoisch

stoicism ['stəʊɪsɪzəm] N (*fig*) stoische Ruhe, Gleichmut *m*

stoke [stəʊk] VT *furnace* (be)heizen; *fire* schüren

➤ **stoke up** VT SEP *furnace* (be)heizen; *fire* schüren; (*fig*) *conflict, inflation* schüren

stole¹ [stəʊl] N Stola *f*

stole² PRET *of* **steal**

stolen ['stəʊlən] **1** PTP *of* **steal** **2** ADJ gestohlen; *pleasures* heimlich; **~ goods** gestohlene Waren *pl*, Diebesgut *nt*; **to receive ~ goods** Hehler *m* sein

stomach ['stʌmək] **1** N Magen *m*; (= *belly, paunch*) Bauch *m*; (*fig: = appetite*) Lust *f* (*for* auf +*acc*), Interesse *nt* (*for* an +*dat*); **to lie on one's ~** auf dem Bauch liegen; **to have a pain in one's ~** Magen-/Bauchschmerzen haben; **to hit sb in the ~** jdn in die Magengrube/Bauchgegend schlagen; **on an empty ~** *drink, take medicine etc* auf leeren or nüchternen Magen; **on an empty/full ~** *swim etc* mit leerem or nüchternem/vollem Magen; **I have no ~ for that** (*for party, journey etc*) mir ist nicht danach (zumute)
2 VT (*inf*) *behaviour* vertragen; *person, film etc* ausstehen

stomach IN CPDS Magen-; **stomach ache** N Magenschmerzen *pl*; **stomach upset** N Magenverstimmung *f*

stomp [stɒmp] VI stapfen

stone [stəʊn] **1** N **(a)** Stein *m*; **a ~'s throw from the station** nur einen Katzensprung vom Bahnhof entfernt; **to leave no ~ unturned** nichts unversucht lassen; **to be set** or **cast** or **carved in ~** (*fig*) in Stein gemeißelt sein
(b) (*Brit*: = *weight*) britische Gewichtseinheit = 6,35 kg
2 ADJ Stein-, aus Stein
3 VT **(a)** (= *kill*) steinigen
(b) (*esp Brit*) *fruit* entsteinen
(c) (*inf*) **to be ~d (out of one's mind)** total zu sein (*inf*)

stone: **Stone Age** N Steinzeit *f*; **stone-broke** ADJ (*US inf*) völlig abgebrannt (*inf*); **stone circle** N (*Brit*) Steinkreis *m*; **stone-cold** **1** ADJ eiskalt **2** ADV **~ sober** stocknüchtern (*inf*); **stone-dead** ADJ mausetot (*inf*); **to kill sb/sth ~** jdm/einer Sache den Garaus machen (*inf*); **stone-deaf** ADJ stocktaub (*inf*); **stonewall** VI (*fig*) (*esp Parl*) obstruieren; (*in answering questions*) ausweichen; **stonework** N Mauerwerk *nt*

stony ['stəʊnɪ] ADJ (+ER) *ground* steinig; (*fig*) *silence* steinern; *face* undurchdringlich

stony: **stony-broke** ADJ (*Brit inf*) völlig abgebrannt (*inf*); **stony-faced** ADJ mit steinerner Miene

stood [stʊd] PRET, PTP *of* **stand**

stool [stuːl] N **(a)** (= *seat*) Hocker *m*; **to fall between two ~s** sich zwischen zwei Stühle setzen **(b)** (*esp Med*: = *faeces*) Stuhl *m*

stoop¹ [stuːp] **1** N Gebeugtheit *f*; **to walk with a ~** gebeugt gehen **2** VI sich beugen or neigen (*over* über +*acc*); (*also ~ down*) sich bücken; **to ~ to sth** (*fig*) sich zu etw herablassen or hergeben

stoop² N (*US*) Treppe *f*

stop [stɒp] **1** N **(a)** (= *act of stopping*) Halt *m*, Stoppen *nt*; **to bring sth to a ~** (*lit*) etw anhalten or stoppen; *traffic* etw zum Erliegen bringen; (*fig*) *project, meeting* einer Sache (*dat*) ein Ende machen; **to come to a ~** (*car, machine*) anhalten, stoppen; (*traffic*) stocken; (*fig*) (*project*) eingestellt werden; (*conversation*) verstummen; **to make a ~** (*bus, train, tram*) (an)halten; (*plane, ship*) (Zwischen)station machen; **to put a ~ to sth** einer Sache (*dat*) einen Riegel vorschieben
(b) (= *stay*) Aufenthalt *m*; (= *break*) Pause *f*; **we had** or **made three ~s** wir haben dreimal Halt gemacht
(c) (= *stopping place*) Station *f*; (*for bus, tram, train*) Haltestelle *f*
(d) (*Mus: also* **~knob**) Registerzug *m*; **to pull out all the ~s** (*fig*) alle Register ziehen
(e) (= *stopper: for door, window*) Sperre *f*
2 VT **(a)** (= *~ when moving*) *person, vehicle, clock* anhalten; *ball* stoppen; *engine, machine etc* abstellen; (*~ from going away, from moving on*) *thief, attack, progress, traffic* aufhalten; *traffic* (= *bring to complete standstill*) zum Stehen or Erliegen bringen; (= *keep out*) *noise* auffangen; **~ thief!** haltet den Dieb!; **to ~ sb dead** or **in his tracks** jdn urplötzlich anhalten lassen; (*in conversation*) jdn plötzlich verstummen lassen
(b) *activity, rumour, crime* ein Ende machen or setzen (+*dat*); *nonsense, noise* unterbinden; *match, conversation, work* beenden; *flow of blood* stillen; *progress, inflation* hemmen;

speaker unterbrechen; production zum Stillstand bringen; (temporarily) unterbrechen

(c) (= cease) aufhören mit; **to ~ doing sth** aufhören, etw zu tun, etw nicht mehr tun; **to ~ smoking** mit dem Rauchen aufhören; **I'm trying to ~ smoking** ich versuche, das Rauchen aufzugeben; **~ saying that** nun sag das doch nicht immer; **~ it!** lass das!, hör auf!

(d) (= suspend) stoppen; payments, production, fighting einstellen; cheque, water supply, wages sperren; allowances, grant etc streichen; proceedings abbrechen; (= cancel) subscription kündigen; (temporarily) newspaper abbestellen

(e) (= prevent from happening) sth verhindern; (= prevent from doing) sb abhalten; **to ~ oneself** sich beherrschen, sich bremsen (inf); **can't you ~ him?** können Sie ihn nicht davon abhalten?; **there's no ~ping him** (inf) er ist nicht zu bremsen (inf); **there's nothing ~ping you or ~ you** es hindert Sie nichts; **to ~ sb (from) doing sth** jdn davon abhalten or (physically) daran hindern, etw zu tun; (= put a ~ to) dafür sorgen, dass jd etw nicht mehr tut or dass jd aufhört, etw zu tun; **to ~ sth (from) happening** (es) verhindern, dass etw geschieht; **that will ~ it (from) hurting** (= prevent) dann wird es nicht wehtun; (= put a ~ to) dann wird es nicht mehr wehtun; **to ~ oneself from doing sth** sich zurückhalten und etw nicht tun

(f) (= block) verstopfen; (with cork, cement etc) zustopfen (with mit); (fig) gap füllen

3 VI (a) (= halt) anhalten; (train, car) (an)halten; (traveller, driver) Halt machen; (pedestrian, clock) stehen bleiben; (engine, machine) nicht mehr laufen; **~ right there!** halt!, stopp!; **we ~ped for a drink at the pub** wir machten in der Kneipe Station, um etwas zu trinken; **to ~ at nothing (to do sth)** (fig) vor nichts Halt machen(, um etw zu tun); **to ~ dead** or **in one's tracks** plötzlich stehen bleiben

(b) (= finish, cease) aufhören; (heart) stehen bleiben; (production, payments, delivery) eingestellt werden; (programme, match, film) zu Ende sein; **to ~ doing sth** aufhören, etw zu tun; **he ~ped in mid sentence** er brach mitten im Satz ab; **I will not ~ until I find him** ich gebe keine Ruhe, bis ich ihn gefunden habe; **if you had ~ped to think** wenn du nur einen Augenblick nachgedacht hättest; **he never knows when** or **where to ~** er weiß nicht, wann er aufhören muss

(c) (Brit inf: = stay) bleiben (at in +dat, with bei)

➤ **stop by** VI kurz vorbeikommen or vorbeischauen; **to stop by sb's house** bei jdm hereinschauen (inf)

➤ **stop in** VI (Brit inf) drinbleiben (inf)

➤ **stop off** VI (kurz) Halt machen (at sb's place bei jdm); (on travels also) Zwischenstation machen (at in +dat)

➤ **stop over** VI kurz Halt machen; (on travels) Zwischenstation machen (in in +dat); (Aviat) zwischenlanden

➤ **stop up** VT SEP verstopfen; hole also zustopfen

stop: stop button N Halteknopf m; **stopcock** N Absperrhahn m; **stopgap** N (= thing) Notbehelf m; (= scheme) Notlösung f; (= person) Lückenbüßer(in) m(f); **stoplight** N (esp US) rotes Licht; **stopover** N Zwischenstation f; (Aviat) Zwischenlandung f

stoppage ['stɒpɪdʒ] N (temporary) Unterbrechung f; (in production etc: for longer time) Stopp m; (= strike) Streik m

stopper ['stɒpəʳ] N (= plug) Stöpsel m

stop: stop sign N Stoppschild nt; **stopwatch** N Stoppuhr f

storage ['stɔːrɪdʒ] N (of goods, food) Lagerung f; (of documents, in household) Aufbewahrung f; (of water, electricity, data) Speicherung f; **to put sth into ~** etw (ein)lagern

storage: storage capacity N (of computer) Speicherkapazität f; **storage device** N (Comput) Speichereinheit f; **storage heater** N (Nachtstrom)speicherofen m; **storage space** N Lagerraum m; (in house) Schränke und Abstellräume pl

store [stɔːʳ] **1 N (a)** (= stock) Vorrat m (of an +dat); (fig) Fülle f (of an +dat); **~s** pl (= supplies) Vorräte pl; **to have** or **keep sth in ~** (in shop) etw auf Lager or etw vorrätig haben; **to be in ~ for sb** jdm bevorstehen; **to have a surprise in ~ for sb** für jdn eine Überraschung auf Lager haben; **what has the future in ~ for us?** was wird uns (dat) die Zukunft bringen?

(b) (= place) Lager nt

(c) (Comput) (Daten)speicher m

(d) (= large shop, book ~) Geschäft nt; (= department ~) Kaufhaus nt; (esp US: = shop) Laden m

2 ADJ ATTR (US) clothes von der Stange; bread aus der Fabrik

3 VT lagern; documents aufbewahren; furniture unterstellen; (in depository) einlagern; information, electricity, heat speichern; (= equip, supply) larder etc auffüllen; **to ~ sth away** etw verwahren; **to ~ sth up** einen Vorrat an etw (dat) anlegen; (fig) etw anstauen

store: store detective N Kaufhausdetektiv(in) m(f); **storehouse** N Lager(haus) nt; **storekeeper** N (esp US) Ladenbesitzer(in) m(f); **storeroom** N Lagerraum m; (for food) Vorratskammer f

storey, (esp US) **story** ['stɔːrɪ] N, pl **-s** or (US) **stories** Stock m, Etage f; **a nine-~ building** ein neunstöckiges Gebäude; **he fell from the third-~ window** er fiel aus dem Fenster des dritten or (US) zweiten Stock(werk)s or der dritten or (US) zweiten Etage

-storeyed, (esp US) **-storied** [-'stɔːrɪd] ADJ SUF -stöckig

stork [stɔːk] N Storch m

storm [stɔːm] **1 N (a)** Unwetter nt; (= thunderstorm) Gewitter nt; (= strong wind) Sturm m; **there is a ~ blowing** es stürmt; **to brave the ~** dem Unwetter/Gewitter/Sturm trotzen; (fig) das Gewitter über sich (acc) ergehen lassen

(b) (fig) (of abuse) Flut f (of von); (of applause, criticism) Sturm m (of +gen); (= outcry) Aufruhr m; **~ of protest** Proteststurm m; **to take sth/sb by ~** (Mil, fig) etw/jdn im Sturm erobern

2 VT stürmen

3 VI (a) (= talk angrily) toben, wüten (at gegen)

(b) (= move violently) stürmen; **to ~ out of a room** aus einem Zimmer stürmen

storm cloud N (lit, fig) Gewitterwolke f

stormily ['stɔːmɪlɪ] ADV (lit, fig) stürmisch

storm: stormproof ADJ sturmsicher; **storm troopers** PL (Sonder)einsatzkommando nt

stormy ['stɔːmɪ] ADJ (+ER) (lit, fig) stürmisch; discussion also, temper hitzig; protests heftig

story¹ ['stɔːrɪ] **N (a)** (= tale) Geschichte f; (esp Liter) Erzählung f; (= joke) Witz m; **that's the ~ of my life** (inf) das plagt mich mein ganzes Leben lang! (inf); (said as a response) wem sagen Sie das! (inf); **the ~ goes that ...** man erzählt sich, dass ...; **I've heard his (side of the) ~** ich habe seine Version gehört; **to cut a long ~ short** um es kurz zu machen; **it's the (same) old ~** es ist das alte Lied

(b) (Press: = newspaper ~) Artikel m

(c) (= plot) Handlung f

(d) (inf: = lie) Märchen nt; **to tell stories** Märchen erzählen

story² N (US) = storey

story: storybook N Geschichtenbuch nt; **story line** N Handlung f; **storyteller** N (= narrator) Geschichtenerzähler(in) m(f); **storytelling** N, NO PL (spoken) Geschichtenerzählen nt; (written) Erzählkunst f

stout [staʊt] **1 ADJ (+ER) (a)** (= corpulent) man korpulent; woman füllig **(b)** stick, horse etc kräftig; door, rope, wall stark; shoes fest **(c)** heart, resistance tapfer; refusal entschieden; defence hartnäckig; opposition zäh **2 N** (Brit) Stout m, dunkles, obergäriges Bier; (= sweet ~) Malzbier nt

stouthearted ADJ, **stoutheartedly** ADV [staʊt'hɑːtɪd, -lɪ] tapfer, unerschrocken

stoutly ['staʊtlɪ] ADV made solide; resist, defend tapfer, beherzt; maintain fest, steif und fest (pej); resist, refuse, deny entschieden; **~ Catholic** etc gut katholisch etc

stoutness ['staʊtnɪs] **N (a)** (= corpulence) Korpulenz f; (of woman) Fülligkeit f **(b)** (of stick, horse) Kräftigkeit f; (of rope, wall) Stärke f

stove [staʊv] N Ofen m; (for cooking) Herd m; **electric/gas ~** Elektro-/Gasherd m

stow [staʊ] VT (also ~ away) verstauen (in in +dat)

➤ **stow away** VI als blinder Passagier fahren

stowaway ['staʊəweɪ] N blinder Passagier

straddle ['strædl] VT (standing) breitbeinig stehen über (+dat); (sitting) rittlings sitzen auf (+dat); (fig) two continents, border überspannen; periods gehen über; **to ~ the border** sich über beide Seiten der Grenze erstrecken

straggle ['strægl] VI (a) (houses, trees) verstreut liegen; (hair) (unordentlich) hängen; (plant) (in die Länge) wuchern **(b) to ~ behind** hinterherzockeln (inf); **stop straggling** bleibt beieinander

straggler ['strægləʳ] N Nachzügler(in) m(f)

straggling ['stræglɪŋ] ADJ *children etc* weit verteilt; *group of people* ungeordnet; (= ~ *behind*) hinterherzottelnd (*inf*)

straight [streɪt] **1** ADJ (+ER) **(a)** gerade; *shot* direkt; *answer, talking also* offen; *denial, refusal* ohne Umschweife; *stance* aufrecht; *hair* glatt; *skirt, trousers* gerade geschnitten; (= *honest*) *person, dealings* ehrlich; **to be ~ with sb** offen und ehrlich zu jdm sein; ~ **arrow** (*US inf*) biederer Mensch; (= *man also*) Biedermann *m* (*inf*); **your tie isn't ~** deine Krawatte sitzt schief; **the picture isn't ~** das Bild hängt schief; **to pull sth ~** etw geradeziehen; **is my hat on ~?** sitzt mein Hut gerade?; **to keep a ~ face, to keep one's face** ernst bleiben, das Gesicht nicht verziehen; **with a ~ face** ohne die Miene zu verziehen **(b)** (= *clear*) *thinking* klar; **to get things ~ in one's mind** sich (*dat*) der Dinge klar werden **(c)** *drink* pur; *yes or no, choice, exam pass* einfach; ~ **A's** glatte Einsen *pl*; **to have a ~ choice between …** nur die Wahl zwischen … haben **(d)** (= *continuous*) ununterbrochen; **for the third ~ day** (*US*) drei Tage ohne Unterbrechung; **our team had ten ~ wins** unsere Mannschaft gewann zehnmal hintereinander **(e)** PRED (*in order*) *house, room* ordentlich; *paperwork* in Ordnung; **to be (all)** ~ in Ordnung sein; (*fig:* = *clarified also*) (völlig) geklärt sein; **to put things ~** (= *clarify*) alles klären; **let's get this ~** das wollen wir mal klarstellen; **to put** *or* **set sb ~ about sth** jdm etw klarmachen; **if I give you a fiver, then we'll be ~** (*inf*) wenn ich dir einen Fünfer gebe, sind wir quitt **(f)** (*inf.* = *heterosexual*) hetero (*inf*) **(g)** (*Drugs inf*) clean (*inf*)

2 ADV **(a)** gerade; *leap at, aim for, above, across* direkt; ~ **through sth** glatt durch etw; **he came ~ at me** er kam direkt *or* geradewegs auf mich zu; **it went ~ up in the air** es flog senkrecht in die Luft; **to look ~ ahead** geradeaus sehen; **the airport is ~ ahead** der Flughafen ist geradeaus; **to drive ~ on** geradeaus weiterfahren; **he drove ~ into a tree** er fuhr direkt *or* voll (*inf*) gegen einen Baum; **to go ~** (*criminal*) keine krummen Sachen (mehr) machen (*inf*); **I went ~ home** ich ging direkt *or* sofort nach Hause; **to look sb ~ in the eye** jdm direkt *or* genau in die Augen sehen **(b)** (= *immediately*) sofort; ~ **after this** sofort *or* unmittelbar danach; ~ **away** *or* **off** sofort; **to come ~ to the point** sofort *or* gleich zur Sache kommen **(c)** *think, see* klar **(d)** (= *frankly*) offen, ohne Umschweife; ~ **out** (*inf*) unverblümt (*inf*) **(e)** *drink* pur

3 N (*on race track*) Gerade *f*; (*on road, Rail*) gerade Strecke; **to stay on** *or* **keep to the ~ and narrow** auf dem Pfad der Tugend bleiben

straight arrow N (*esp US*: = *person*) Musterbürger(in) *m*

straightaway [ˌstreɪtə'weɪ] (*US*) **1** N Gerade *f*; (*on road, Rail*) gerade Strecke **2** ADV = **straight 2(b)**

straighten ['streɪtn] **1** VT **(a)** *back, legs etc* gerade machen; *picture* gerade hinhängen; *road* begradigen; *hat* gerade aufsetzen; *tablecloth, clothes, tie* gerade ziehen; *hair* glätten **(b)** (= *tidy*) in Ordnung bringen **2** VI (*road etc*) gerade werden; (*person*) sich aufrichten **3** VR **to ~ oneself** sich aufrichten

➤ **straighten out** **1** VT SEP **(a)** *legs etc* gerade machen; *road* begradigen **(b)** *problem, situation* klären; *one's affairs in Ordnung bringen; *misunderstanding* (auf)klären; **to straighten oneself out** ins richtige Gleis kommen; **the problem will soon straighten itself out** das Problem wird sich bald von selbst erledigen; **to straighten things out** die Sache in Ordnung bringen; (= *clarify*) Klarheit in die Sache bringen **2** VI (*road etc*) gerade werden; (*hair*) glatt werden

➤ **straighten up** **1** VI sich aufrichten **2** VT SEP **(a)** (= *make straight*) gerade machen; *papers* ordentlich hinlegen; *picture* gerade hinhängen **(b)** (= *tidy*) aufräumen

straight: **straight-faced** ['streɪt'feɪst] **1** ADV ohne die Miene zu verziehen **2** ADJ **to be straight-faced** keine Miene verziehen; **straightforward** ADJ (= *honest*) *person* aufrichtig; *explanation* offen; (= *simple*) *question, problem, choice, instructions* einfach; *process* unkompliziert; **straightforwardly** ADV *answer* offen; *behave* aufrichtig; **straight-laced** ADJ prüde, puritanisch; **straight-line** ADJ (*Fin*) *depreciation* linear; **straight-out** ADV (*inf*) unverblümt (*inf*)

strain¹ [streɪn] **1** N **(a)** (*Mech, fig*) Belastung *f* (*on* für); (*on rope also*) Spannung *f*; (= *effort*) Anstrengung *f*; (= *pressure*) (*of job*

etc also) Beanspruchung *f* (*of* durch); (*of responsibility*) Last *f*; **can you take some of the ~?** können Sie mal mit festhalten/mit ziehen?; **to take the ~ off sth** etw entlasten; **to be under a lot of ~** großen Belastungen ausgesetzt sein; **to suffer from (nervous) ~** (*nervlich*) überlastet sein; **I find it a bit of a ~** ich finde das ziemlich anstrengend; **to put a (great) ~ on sb/sth** (*lit, fig*) jdn/etw stark belasten; **to put too great a ~ on sb/sth** (*lit, fig*) jdn/etw überlasten; **to show signs of ~** Zeichen *pl* von Überlastung *or* Überanstrengung zeigen **(b)** (= *muscle-~*) (Muskel)zerrung *f*; (*on eyes etc*) Überanstrengung *f* (*on* +*gen*); **back ~** überanstrengter Rücken

2 VT **(a)** (= *stretch*) spannen **(b)** *rope, relationship, budget* belasten; *nerves, patience, resources* strapazieren; (= *push too much* ~ *on*) überlasten; **to ~ one's ears/eyes to …** angestrengt lauschen/gucken, um zu …; **don't ~ yourself!** (*iro inf*) reiß dir bloß kein Bein aus! (*inf*) **(c)** (*Med*) *muscle* zerren; *arm, neck* verrenken; *back, eyes, voice* strapazieren; (*excessively*) überanstrengen **(d)** (= *filter*) (durch)sieben; *vegetables* abgießen

3 VI (= *exert effort*) sich anstrengen; (= *pull*) zerren, ziehen; (*fig:* = *strive*) sich bemühen; **to ~ at the leash** (*fig*) aufmüpfig werden (*inf*); **to ~ against sth** sich gegen etw stemmen

strain² N **(a)** (= *streak*) Hang *m*, Zug *m*; (*hereditary*) Veranlagung *f* **(b)** (= *breed*) (*of animal*) Rasse *f*; (*of plants*) Sorte *f*; (*of virus etc*) Art *f*

strained [streɪnd] ADJ **(a)** *expression, performance* unnatürlich, gekünstelt; *smile, conversation* gezwungen; *relationship* angespannt; *meeting* steif; *voice, relations, atmosphere, nerves* (an)gespannt **(b)** *liquids* durchgesiebt; *solids* ausgesiebt **(c)** *muscle* gezerrt; *back, eyes* strapaziert

strainer ['streɪnəʳ] N (*Cook*) Sieb *nt*

strait [streɪt] N **(a)** (*Geog*) Meerenge *f*, Straße *f*; **the ~s of Gibraltar** die Straße von Gibraltar **(b)** **straits** PL (*fig*) **to be in dire** *or* **desperate ~s** in großen Nöten sein

straitened ['streɪtnd] ADJ *circumstances* bescheiden

strait: **straitjacket** N (*lit, fig*) Zwangsjacke *f*; **strait-laced** [ˌstreɪt'leɪst] ADJ prüde, puritanisch

strand¹ [strænd] VT **to be ~ed** (*ship, fish, shipwrecked person*) gestrandet sein; **to be (left) ~ed** (*person*) festsitzen; (*without money also*) auf dem Trockenen sitzen (*inf*); **to leave sb ~ed** jdn seinem Schicksal überlassen

strand² N Strang *m*; (*of hair*) Strähne *f*; (*of thread*) Faden *m*; (*fig: in story*) Handlungsfaden *m*

stranding ['strændɪŋ] N (*of ship*) Strandung *f*

strange [streɪndʒ] ADJ (+ER) **(a)** (= *odd*) seltsam, merkwürdig; **to think/find it ~ that …** es seltsam finden, dass …; ~ **as it may seem …** so seltsam es auch scheinen mag, …; **for some ~ reason** aus irgendeinem unerfindlichen *or* seltsamen Grund; **the ~ thing is (that) …** das Seltsame ist, dass…; **he told me the ~st story** er erzählte mir eine sehr seltsame Geschichte; **I feel a bit ~** (= *odd*) mir ist etwas seltsam **(b)** (= *unfamiliar*) *surroundings* fremd; *activity* ungewohnt; **don't talk to ~ men** sprich nicht mit fremden Männern; **I felt rather ~ at first** zuerst fühlte ich mich ziemlich fremd; **I feel ~ in a skirt** ich komme mir in einem Rock komisch vor (*inf*)

strangely ['streɪndʒlɪ] ADV (= *oddly*) seltsam, merkwürdig; *also* komisch (*inf*); ~ **enough** seltsamerweise, merkwürdigerweise

strangeness ['streɪndʒnɪs] N **(a)** (= *oddness*) Seltsamkeit *f*, Merkwürdigkeit *f* **(b)** (= *unfamiliarity*) Fremdheit *f*; (*of activity*) Ungewohntheit *f*

stranger ['streɪndʒəʳ] N Fremde(r) *mf*; **I'm a ~ here myself** ich bin selbst fremd hier; **he is no ~ to London** er kennt sich in London aus; **hullo, ~!** (*inf*) hallo, lange nicht gesehen

strangle ['stræŋgl] VT erwürgen, strangulieren (*form*); (*:ig*) *cry, economy* ersticken

strangled ['stræŋgld] ADJ *voice, cry* erstickt

stranglehold ['stræŋglˌhəʊld] N (*fig*) absolute Machtposition (*on* gegenüber); **they have a ~ on us** (*fig*) sie haben uns in der Zange

strangulation [ˌstræŋgjʊ'leɪʃən] N (= *being strangled*) Ersticken *nt*; (= *act of strangling*) Erwürgen *nt*

strap [stræp] **1** N Riemen *m*; (*esp for safety*) Gurt *m*; (*in bus etc*) Schlaufe *f*; (= *watch* ~) Band *nt*; (= *shoulder* ~) Träger *m* **2** VT **(a)** festschnallen (*to* an +*dat*); **to ~ sth onto sth** etw auf etw (acc) schnallen; **to ~ sb/sth down** jdn/etw festschnallen; **to ~ sb/oneself in** (in car, plane) jdn/sich anschnallen **(b)** (Med: also ~ **up**) bandagieren; dressing festkleben **(c)** (inf) **to be ~ped (for cash)** pleite or blank sein (inf)

strapless ['stræplɪs] ADJ trägerlos, schulterfrei

strapping ['stræpɪŋ] ADJ (inf) stramm; woman also drall

Strasbourg ['stræzbɜːg] N Straßburg nt

strata ['strɑːtə] PL of **stratum**

strategic [strə'tiːdʒɪk] ADJ strategisch; (fig also) taktisch; (= strategically important) strategisch wichtig

strategically [strə'tiːdʒɪkəlɪ] ADV strategisch; (fig also) taktisch; **to be ~ placed** eine strategisch günstige Stellung haben

strategist ['strætɪdʒɪst] N Stratege m, Strategin f

strategy ['strætɪdʒɪ] N **(a)** (Mil) Strategie f; (Sport, fig also) Taktik f **(b)** (= art of ~) (Mil) Kriegskunst f; (fig) Taktieren nt

stratosphere ['strætəʊsfɪəʳ] N Stratosphäre f

stratum ['strɑːtəm] N, pl **strata** (Geol, fig) Schicht f

straw [strɔː] **1** N **(a)** (= stalk) Strohhalm m; (collectively) Stroh nt no pl; **that's the last** or **final ~!** (inf) das ist der Gipfel! (inf); **to clutch** or **grasp at ~s** sich an einen Strohhalm klammern; **to draw the short ~** den kürzeren ziehen **(b)** (= drinking ~) Trinkhalm m **2** ADJ ATTR Stroh-; basket aus Stroh

strawberry ['strɔːbərɪ] N Erdbeere f

strawberry IN CPDS Erdbeer-

straw poll, straw vote N Probeabstimmung f; (in election) Wählerbefragung f

stray [streɪ] **1** VI (also ~ **away**) sich verirren; (also ~ **about**) (umher)streunen; (fig: thoughts, speaker) abschweifen; **to ~ (away) from sth** (lit, fig) von etw abkommen **2** ADJ child, bullet, cattle verirrt; cat, dog etc streunend attr; (= ownerless) herrenlos; (= isolated) remarks, hairs vereinzelt; (= occasional) thoughts flüchtig **3** N (= dog, cat) streunendes Tier; (ownerless) herrenloses Tier

streak [striːk] **1** N Streifen m; (of light) Strahl m; (fig = trace) Spur f; (of jealousy etc) Zug m; (of madness) Anflug m; **~s** (in hair) Strähnchen pl; **~ of lightning** Blitz(strahl) m; **a winning/losing ~** eine Glücks-/Pechsträhne; **he's got a mean ~** er hat einen gemeinen Zug (an sich (dat)) **2** VT streifen; **the sky was ~ed with red** der Himmel hatte rote Streifen; **hair ~ed with grey** Haar mit grauen Strähnchen; **~ed with tears** tränenverschmiert **3** VI (lightning) zucken; (inf: = move quickly) flitzen (inf); **to ~ along/past** entlang-/vorbeiflitzen (inf) **(b)** (= run naked) flitzen

streaker ['striːkəʳ] N Flitzer(in) m(f)

streaky ['striːkɪ] ADJ (+ER) window streifig; **~ bacon** (Brit) durchwachsener Speck

stream [striːm] **1** N **(a)** (= small river) Bach m; (= current) Strömung f; **to go with/against the ~** (lit, fig) mit dem/gegen den Strom schwimmen **(b)** (of liquid, air, people, cars) Strom m; (of light) Flut f; (of words, abuse also) Schwall m **2** VI **(a)** (= flow) strömen; (liquid also) fließen; (air, sunlight also) fluten; (eyes: because of cold, gas etc) tränen; **the walls were ~ing with water** die Wände trieften vor Nässe; **her eyes were ~ing with tears** Tränen strömten ihr aus den Augen **(b)** (= wave: flag, hair) wehen

➤ **stream down** VI (liquid) in Strömen fließen; (+prep obj) herunterströmen; **tears streamed down her face** Tränen strömten or liefen über ihr Gesicht

➤ **stream in** VI hereinströmen

➤ **stream out** VI hinausströmen (of aus); (liquid also) herausfließen (of aus)

➤ **stream past** VI vorbeiströmen (prep obj an +dat); (cars) in Strömen vorbeifahren (prep obj an +dat)

streamer ['striːməʳ] N (made of paper) Luftschlange f; (made of cloth, as decoration) Band nt

streaming ['striːmɪŋ] ADJ windows triefend; eyes also tränend; **I have a ~ cold** (Brit) ich habe einen fürchterlichen Schnupfen

streamline ['striːmlaɪn] VT windschlüpfig machen; (fig) rationalisieren

streamlined ['striːmlaɪnd] ADJ wing windschlüpfig; car, plane also stromlinienförmig; (fig) rationalisiert

street [striːt] N Straße f; **in** or **on the ~** auf der Straße; **to live in** or **on a ~** in einer Straße wohnen; **it's right up my ~** (Brit fig inf) das ist genau mein Fall (inf); **to be ~s ahead of sb** (fig inf)

jdm haushoch überlegen sein (inf); **to take to the ~s** (demonstrators) auf die Straße gehen

street IN CPDS Straßen-; **streetcar** N (US) Straßenbahn f; **street cred** (Brit inf), **street credibility** N Glaubwürdigkeit f; **this jacket does nothing for my ~** dieses Jackett versaut mein ganzes Image (inf); **street lamp** N Straßenlaterne f; **street level** N **at ~** zu ebener Erde; **street light** N Straßenlaterne f; **street map** N Stadtplan m; **street party** N Straßenfest nt; **street people** PL Obdachlose pl; **street plan** N Stadtplan m; **street sweeper** N (= person) Straßenkehrer(in) m(f); (= machine) Kehrmaschine f; **streetwise** ADJ gewieft (inf), clever (inf)

strength [streŋθ] N **(a)** (lit, fig) Stärke f (also Mil); (of person, feelings) Kraft f; (of bolt, wall, market prices) Stabilität f; (of economy) Gesundheit f; (of conviction) Festigkeit f; (of imagination) Lebhaftigkeit f; (of argument, evidence) Überzeugungskraft f; (of plea, protest) Eindringlichkeit f; (= numbers) (An)zahl f; **~ of character/will** or **mind** Charakter-/Willensstärke f; **on the ~ of sth** auf Grund einer Sache (gen); **his ~ failed him** seine Kräfte versagten; **to save one's ~** mit seinen Kräften haushalten; **you don't know your own ~!** du weißt gar nicht, wie stark du bist!; **to go from ~ to ~** einen Erfolg nach dem anderen erzielen or haben; **to be at full ~** vollzählig sein; **to be up to/below** or **under ~** (die) volle Stärke/nicht die volle Stärke haben; **to turn out in ~** zahlreich erscheinen; **the police were there in ~** ein starkes Polizeiaufgebot war da **(b)** (= health, of constitution) Robustheit f; **the patient is recovering his ~** der Patient kommt wieder zu Kräften; **when she has her ~ back** wenn sie wieder bei Kräften ist **(c)** (of colour) Intensität f; (of diluted solution) Konzentration f

strengthen ['streŋθən] **1** VT stärken; material, building, grip, resolve also verstärken; muscles kräftigen; currency, market festigen **2** VI stärker werden; (wind, desire also) sich verstärken

strenuous ['strenjʊəs] ADJ **(a)** (= exhausting) anstrengend **(b)** attempt, support unermüdlich, energisch; attack, effort, denial hartnäckig; opposition, protest heftig

strenuously ['strenjʊəslɪ] ADV **(a)** exercise anstrengend **(b)** deny, oppose entschieden; object nachdrücklich

stress [stres] **1** N **(a)** Stress m; (Mech) Belastung f; (Med) Überlastung f; (= pressure) Druck m; (= tension) Spannung f; **to be under ~** großen Belastungen ausgesetzt sein; (as regards work) im Stress sein; **to put sb under great ~** jdn großen Belastungen aussetzen **(b)** (= accent) Betonung f; (fig: = emphasis) (Haupt)gewicht nt; **to put** or **lay (great) ~ on sth** einer Sache (dat) großes Gewicht beimessen; fact etw (besonders) betonen **2** VT (lit, fig: = emphasize) betonen; **good manners** großen Wert legen auf (+acc)

stressed [strest] ADJ (= under stress) gestresst, über(be)lastet

stressed out ADJ gestresst; **what are you getting so ~ about?** worüber regst du dich so auf? (inf)

stressful ['stresfʊl] ADJ anstrengend, stressig

stretch [stretʃ] **1** N **(a)** (= act of stretching) Strecken nt, Dehnen nt; **to have a ~** sich strecken or dehnen; (person also) sich recken; **to be at full ~** (lit: material) bis zum Äußersten gedehnt sein; (fig: person) mit aller Kraft arbeiten; (factory etc) auf Hochtouren arbeiten (inf); (engine, production) auf Hochtouren laufen; **by no ~ of the imagination** beim besten Willen nicht; **not by a long ~** bei weitem nicht **(b)** (= elasticity) Elastizität f, Dehnbarkeit f **(c)** (= expanse) Stück nt; (of road etc) Strecke f; (of journey) Abschnitt m; **that ~ of water is ...** dieser Gewässerlauf heißt ...; **for a long ~** über eine weite Strecke **(d)** (= ~ of time) Zeitraum m, Zeitspanne f; **for a long ~ of time** für (eine) lange Zeit, lange Zeit; **for hours at a ~** stundenlang; **three days at a ~** drei Tage an einem Stück or ohne Unterbrechung **2** ADJ ATTR dehnbar, elastisch; **~ trousers** Stretchhose f **3** VT **(a)** (lit, fig) strecken; (= widen) gloves also, elastic, shoes dehnen; (= spread) wings etc ausbreiten; (= tighten) rope, canvas spannen; (= use fully) resources voll (aus)nutzen; credit voll beanspruchen; athlete, student etc fordern; one's abilities bis zum Äußersten fordern; **to ~ sth tight** etw straffen; cover etw stramm ziehen; **to ~ one's legs** (= go for a walk) sich (dat) die Beine vertreten (inf); **to ~ sb/sth to the limit(s)** jdn/etw bis zum äußersten belasten; **to be fully ~ed** (esp Brit: person) voll

ausgelastet sein
(b) *meaning* äußerst weit fassen; *truth, law, rules* es nicht so genau nehmen mit; **that's ~ing it too far/a bit (far)** das geht zu weit/fast zu weit
4 VI *(after sleep etc)* sich strecken; (= *be elastic*) dehnbar sein; *(time, area, authority)* sich erstrecken *(to* bis, *over* über *+acc);* *(food, money)* reichen *(to* für*);* (= *become looser*) weiter werden; (= *become longer*) länger werden; **to ~ to reach sth** sich recken, um etw zu erreichen; **he ~ed across and touched her cheek** er reichte herüber und berührte ihre Wange; **the fields ~ed away into the distance** die Felder dehnten sich bis in die Ferne aus; **our funds won't ~ to that** das lassen unsere Finanzen nicht zu
5 VR **(a)** *(after sleep etc)* sich strecken
(b) (= *strain oneself*) sich verausgaben
➤ **stretch out** **1** VT SEP *arms, wings* ausbreiten; *leg, hand* ausstrecken; *foot* vorstrecken; *discussion, story* ausdehnen
2 VI sich strecken; *(inf.* = *lie down)* sich hinlegen; *(countryside)* sich ausbreiten

stretcher ['stretʃəʳ] N (Med) (Trag)bahre *f*
stretcher-bearer ['stretʃbeərəʳ] N Krankenträger(in) *m(f)*
stretchy ['stretʃi] ADJ (+ER) elastisch, dehnbar
strew [struː], *pret* **strewed,** *ptp* **strewed** *or* **strewn** [struːn] VT verstreuen; *flowers, gravel* streuen; *floor etc* bestreuen; **the floor was ~n with ... ...** lagen überall auf dem Boden verstreut
stricken ['strɪkən] ADJ *(liter)* leidgeprüft; *ship, plane* in Not; **~ with guilt etc** von Schuld *etc* erfüllt; **to be ~ by drought** von Dürre geplagt *or* heimgesucht werden
-stricken ADJ SUF *(with emotion)* -erfüllt; *(by catastrophe)* von ... heimgesucht; **grief-stricken** schmerzerfüllt; **panic-stricken** von Panik ergriffen
strict [strɪkt] ADJ (+ER) streng; *obedience* absolut; *Catholic* strenggläubig; *secrecy* absolut; **in the ~ sense of the word** genau genommen; **in (the) ~est confidence** in strengster Vertraulichkeit; **there is a ~ time limit on that** das ist zeitlich genau begrenzt
strictly ['strɪktli] ADV streng; (= *absolutely also*) absolut; (= *precisely*) genau; **smoking is ~ forbidden** Rauchen ist streng *or* strengstens verboten; **our relationship was ~ business** unser Verhältnis war rein geschäftlich; **~ personal** privat; **~ confidential** streng vertraulich; **~ speaking** genau genommen; **not ~ true** nicht ganz richtig; **~ between ourselves** ganz unter uns; **unless ~ necessary** nicht unbedingt erforderlich; **the car park is ~ for the use of residents** der Parkplatz ist ausschließlich für Anwohner vorgesehen
strictness ['strɪktnɪs] N Strenge *f*
stride [straɪd], *vb: pret* **strode,** *ptp* **stridden** ['strɪdn] **1** N (= *step*) Schritt *m*; (= *gait also*) Gang *m*; *(fig)* Fortschritt *m*; **to take sth in one's ~** *(Brit) or* **in ~** *(US)* mit etw spielend fertig werden; *exam, interview* etw spielend schaffen; **to put sb off his/her ~** jdn aus dem Konzept bringen **2** VI schreiten *(geh)*; **to ~ along** ausschreiten *(geh)*; **to ~ away** *or* **off** davonschreiten *(geh)*
strife [straɪf] N Unfriede *m*; *(in family, between friends)* Zwietracht *f (geh)*; **internal ~** innere Kämpfe *pl*; **industrial ~** Auseinandersetzungen *pl* in der Industrie
strike [straɪk], *vb: pret* **struck,** *ptp* **struck 1** N **(a)** Streik *m*; **to be on ~** streiken; **to come out on ~, to go on ~** in den Streik treten
(b) (= *discovery of oil etc)* Fund *m*; **a big oil ~** ein großer Ölfund
(c) *(Mil)* Angriff *m*
2 VT **(a)** (= *hit, sound: clock*) schlagen; *nail, table* schlagen auf *(+acc);* *(blow, bullet etc, disaster)* treffen; *(disease)* befallen; *chord, note* anschlagen; **to ~ sb/sth a blow** jdm/einer Sache einen Schlag versetzen; **who struck the first blow?** wer hat zuerst (zu)geschlagen?; **to be struck by lightning** vom Blitz getroffen werden; **to ~ the hour** die volle Stunde schlagen; **to ~ 4** 4 schlagen
(b) (= *collide with, meet*) *(person)* stoßen gegen; *(car)* fahren gegen; *ground* aufschlagen *or* auftreffen auf *(+acc);* *(ship)* auflaufen auf *(+acc);* *(sound, light, lightning) person* treffen; *tree* einschlagen in *(+acc)*
(c) (= *occur to*) in den Sinn kommen *(+dat);* **that ~s me as a good idea** das kommt mir sehr vernünftig vor; **has it ever struck you that ...?** (= *occurred to you)* haben Sie je daran

gedacht, dass ...?; (= *have you noticed)* ist Ihnen je aufgefallen, dass ...?; **it struck me how ...** (= *occurred to me)* mir ging plötzlich auf, wie ...; (= *I noticed)* mir fiel auf, wie ...
(d) (= *impress*) beeindrucken; **how does it ~ you?** wie finden Sie das?; **she struck me as being very competent** sie machte auf mich einen sehr fähigen Eindruck
(e) *coin* prägen; *(fig) agreement, truce* sich einigen auf *(+acc);* *pose* einnehmen; **to ~ a match** ein Streichholz anzünden; **to be struck dumb** mit Stummheit geschlagen werden *(geh);* **to ~ terror into sb/sb's heart** jdn mit Schrecken erfüllen
(f) *oil, correct path* finden, stoßen auf *(+acc);* **to ~ it rich** das große Geld machen; **to ~ gold** *(fig)* auf eine Goldgrube stoßen
(g) (= *remove*) streichen
3 VI **(a)** (= *hit*) treffen; *(lightning)* einschlagen; *(snake)* zubeißen; *(attack, Mil etc)* angreifen; *(disease)* zuschlagen; *(panic)* ausbrechen; **to ~ at the roots of sth** etw an der Wurzel treffen; **to be/come within striking distance of sth** einer Sache *(dat)* nahe sein; **to ~ on a new idea** eine neue Idee haben
(b) *(clock)* schlagen
(c) *(workers)* streiken
➤ **strike back** **1** VI zurückschlagen; *(fig also)* sich zur Wehr setzen **2** VT SEP zurückschlagen
➤ **strike down** VT SEP niederschlagen; **to be struck down** *(by illness)* getroffen werden
➤ **strike off** VT SEP **to be struck off** *(Brit Med, Jur)* die Zulassung verlieren
➤ **strike out** **1** VI **(a)** (= *hit out*) schlagen; **to strike out wildly** *or* **blindly** wild um sich schlagen; **to strike out at sb** *(lit, fig)* jdn angreifen **(b)** (= *set out*) sich aufmachen, losziehen *(inf)* *(for* zu); **to strike out on one's own** *(lit)* allein losziehen; *(fig)* eigene Wege gehen **2** VT SEP (aus)streichen
➤ **strike up** VT INSEP **(a)** *tune* anstimmen **(b)** *friendship* schließen; *conversation* anfangen
strike: strike ballot N Urabstimmung *f;* **strike fund** N Streikkasse *f*
striker ['straɪkəʳ] N **(a)** (= *worker*) Streikende(r) **(b)** *(Ftbl)* Stürmer(in) *m(f)*
striking ['straɪkɪŋ] ADJ *colour, resemblance etc* auffallend; *difference* erstaunlich; *person* bemerkenswert; *appearance, beauty* eindrucksvoll; **a ~ example of sth** ein hervorragendes Beispiel für etw
strikingly ['straɪkɪŋli] ADV *similar, evident* auffallend; *different* unübersehbar; *attractive* bemerkenswert; *contrast* deutlich
Strimmer® ['strɪməʳ] N Rasentrimmer *m*
string [strɪŋ], *vb: pret, ptp* **strung 1** N **(a)** Schnur *f;* (= *cord also*) Bindfaden *m;* *(on apron etc)* Band *nt;* *(on anorak)* Kordel *f;* *(of puppet)* Faden *m;* *(of people, vehicles)* Schlange *f;* *(fig:* = *series)* Reihe *f;* *(of lies, curses)* Haufen *m;* **to pull ~s** *(fig)* Beziehungen spielen lassen; **without ~s, with no ~s attached** ohne Bedingungen
(b) *(of musical instrument, tennis racquet etc)* Saite *f;* **to have two ~s** *or* **a second ~** *or* **more than one ~ to one's bow** zwei Eisen im Feuer haben
(c) strings PL (= *instruments)* **the ~s** die Streichinstrumente *pl;* (= *players)* die Streicher *pl*
(d) *(Comput: of characters)* Zeichenfolge *f*
2 VT **(a)** (= *put on ~)* aufreihen, auffädeln
(b) *violin etc, tennis racquet* (mit Saiten) bespannen
(c) (= *space out*) aufreihen
➤ **string along** *(inf)* VT SEP **to string sb along** jdn hinhalten
➤ **string out** VT SEP *washing* aufhängen; *guards* verteilen
➤ **string together** VT SEP *words, sentences* aneinander reihen; **she can't even string two sentences together** sie bringt keinen vernünftigen Satz zusammen
➤ **string up** VT SEP aufhängen; *(inf.* = *hang)* aufknüpfen *(inf)*
string bean N *(esp US)* grüne Bohne
stringed [strɪŋd] ADJ **~ instrument** Saiteninstrument *nt*
stringent ['strɪndʒənt] ADJ *standards, laws, reforms* streng; *rules, testing, training, measures* hart
string: string instrument N Saiteninstrument *nt;* **string quartet** N Streichquartett *nt;* **string vest** N Netzhemd *nt*
stringy ['strɪŋi] ADJ (+ER) *meat* sehnig, zäh; *vegetable* voller Fäden; *plant* lang und dünn; *hair* strähnig
strip [strɪp] **1** N **(a)** Streifen *m;* *(of metal)* Band *nt*
(b) *(Brit Sport)* Trikot *nt*
2 VT **(a)** (= *remove clothes etc from*) *person* ausziehen; *bed,*

wallpaper abziehen; *floor* abschleifen; *paint* abbeizen; (= *remove contents from*) ausräumen; **to ~ sth from** *or* **off sth** etw von etw entfernen **(b)** (*fig*: = *deprive of*) berauben (*of* +*gen*) **(c)** (*Tech*: = *dismantle*) zerlegen **▊** VI (= *remove clothes*) sich ausziehen; (*at doctor's*) sich freimachen; (= *perform ~tease*) strippen (*inf*); **to ~ naked** sich bis auf die Haut ausziehen

➤ **strip away** VT SEP *layer of dirt etc* ablösen; (*fig*) *pretence* über Bord werfen (*inf*)

➤ **strip down ▊** VT SEP *engine* zerlegen **▋** VI **to strip down to one's underwear** sich bis auf die Unterwäsche ausziehen

➤ **strip off ▊** VT SEP *clothes* ausziehen; *paper* abziehen (*prep obj* von); *bark* ablösen (*prep obj* von); **to strip off the leaves** die Blätter vom Zweig entfernen **▋** VI (= *take one's clothes off*) sich ausziehen; (*at doctor's*) sich freimachen; (*in striptease*) strippen (*inf*)

strip: **strip cartoon** N (*Brit*) Comic(strip) *m*; **strip club** N Stripteaseklub *m*

stripe [straɪp] N **(a)** Streifen *m* **(b)** (*US*: = *kind*) (*of politics*) Färbung *f*; (*of character, opinion*) Art *f*, Schlag *m*

striped [straɪpt] ADJ gestreift; **~ with ...** mit ... Streifen

strip: **strip lighting** N (*esp Brit*) Neonlicht *nt or* -beleuchtung *f*; **strip mine** N (*US*) Tagebau *m*; **strip mining** N (*US*) Abbau *m* über Tage

stripper [ˈstrɪpəʳ] N **(a)** (= *performer*) Stripperin *f*; **male ~** Stripper *m* **(b)** (= *paint ~*) Farbentferner *m*

strip: **strip-search ▊** N Leibesvisitation *f* **▋** VT einer Leibesvisitation (*dat*) unterziehen; **striptease ▊** N Striptease *m or nt*; **to do a ~** strippen (*inf*) **▋** ADJ ATTR **~ act** Stripteasenummer *f*

stripy [ˈstraɪpɪ] ADJ (+ER) (*inf*) gestreift

strive [straɪv], *pret* **strove**, *ptp* **striven** [ˈstrɪvn] VI **to ~ to do sth** bestrebt *or* bemüht sein, etw zu tun; **to ~ for** nach etw streben

strobe [strəʊb] N stroboskopische Beleuchtung

strode [strəʊd] PRET *of* **stride**

stroke [strəʊk] **▊** N **(a)** Schlag *m* (*also Med, Sport*); (*Swimming*) (= *movement*) Zug *m*; (= *type of ~*) Stil *m*; (*of pen, brush etc*) Strich *m*; **he doesn't do a ~** (*of work*) er tut keinen Schlag (*inf*); **to put sb off his ~** jdn aus dem Konzept bringen; **a ~ of genius** ein genialer Einfall; **a ~ of luck** ein Glücksfall *m*; **we had a ~ of luck** wir hatten Glück; **at a** *or* **one ~** mit einem Schlag; **on the ~ of twelve** Punkt zwölf (Uhr); **to have a ~** (*Med*) einen Schlag(anfall) bekommen **(b)** (= *caress*) Streicheln *nt no pl* **▋** VT streicheln; **he ~d his chin** er strich sich (*dat*) übers Kinn

stroll [strəʊl] **▊** N Spaziergang *m*; **to go for** *or* **have** *or* **take a ~** einen Spaziergang machen **▋** VI spazieren; **to ~ along/ around** herumspazieren; **to ~ around the town** durch die Stadt bummeln; **to ~ up to sb** auf jdn zuschlendern

stroller [ˈstrəʊləʳ] N (*esp US*: = *pushchair*) Sportwagen *m*

strong [strɒŋ] **▊** ADJ (+ER) **(a)** stark (*also Ling, Fin*); (*physically*) *person, grip, colour, light* kräftig; *table, bolt, wall, price* stabil; *features* ausgeprägt; *person, constitution* robust; *teeth, heart, nerves, performance* gut; *character, views* fest; *candidate, case* aussichtsreich; *influence, temptation* groß; *argument, evidence* überzeugend; *protest* energisch; *measure* drastisch; *food* deftig; (= *pungent, unpleasant*) *streng; solution* konzentriert; **when you're ~ again** wenn Sie bei Kräften sind; **to have ~ feelings/views about sth** in Bezug auf etw (*acc*) stark engagiert sein; **I didn't know you had such ~ feelings about it** ich habe nicht gewusst, dass Ihnen so viel daran liegt; (*against it*) ich habe nicht gewusst, dass Sie so dagegen sind; **his ~ point** seine Stärke; **there is a ~ possibility that ...** es ist überaus wahrscheinlich, dass ...; **a group 20** = eine 20 Mann starke Gruppe; **he is ~ in/on sth** (= *capable*) etw ist seine Stärke; **a ~ drink** ein harter Drink **(b)** (= *enthusiastic, committed*) begeistert; *supporter* überzeugt; *belief* unerschütterlich **▋** ADV (+ER) (*inf*) **to be going ~** (*old person, thing*) gut in Schuss sein (*inf*); (*party, rehearsals*) in Schwung sein (*inf*)

strong: **strong-arm** (*inf*) ADJ *tactics etc* brutal; **strongbox** N (Geld)kassette *f*; **stronghold** N (*fig*) Hochburg *f*

strongly [ˈstrɒŋlɪ] ADV stark; *grip, shine, support, built* (*person*) kräftig; *fight* heftig; *constructed* stabil; *believe* fest; *protest, defend* energisch; *sense* zutiefst; *worded* in starken Worten;

to feel ~ about sb/sth *see* **strong 1(a)**; **I ~ advise you ...** ich möchte Ihnen dringend(st) raten ...; **I feel very ~ that ...** ich vertrete entschieden die Meinung, dass ...; **to be ~ recommended** besonders *or* nachdrücklich empfohlen werden; **to be ~ in favour of sth** etw sehr *or* stark befürworten; **to be ~ opposed to** *or* **against sth** etw scharf ablehnen; **to smell/taste ~ of sth** stark nach etw riechen/ schmecken

strong-minded ADJ, **strong-mindedly** ADV [ˌstrɒŋˈmaɪndɪd, -lɪ] willensstark

strong: **strong point** N Stärke *f*; **strongroom** N Stahlkammer *f*; **strong-willed** [ˌstrɒŋˈwɪld] ADJ willensstark; (*pej*) eigensinnig

stroppy [ˈstrɒpɪ] ADJ (+ER) (*Brit inf*) fuchtig (*inf*); *answer, children* pampig (*inf*); *bouncer etc* aggressiv; **don't get ~ with me** (= *aggressive*) werd jetzt nicht pampig (*inf*)

strove [strəʊv] PRET *of* **strive**

struck [strʌk] **▊** PRET, PTP *of* **strike ▋** ADJ PRED **to be ~ with sb/ sth** (= *impressed*) von jdm/etw begeistert *or* angetan sein

structural [ˈstrʌktʃərəl] ADJ strukturell, Struktur-; (*of building*) *alterations, damage* baulich

structural: **structural engineer** N Konstrukteur(in) *m(f)*; **structural engineering** N Bautechnik *f*; **structural fault** N Konstruktionsfehler *m*

structurally [ˈstrʌktʃərəlɪ] ADV strukturell; **~ sound** sicher

structure [ˈstrʌktʃəʳ] **▊** N (= *organization*) Struktur *f*; (*Liter*) Aufbau *m*; (*Tech*: *of bridge, car etc*, = *thing constructed*) Konstruktion *f* **▋** VT strukturieren; *essay, argument* aufbauen

structured [ˈstrʌktʃəd] ADJ *programme, society* strukturiert; *approach* durchdacht; *essay* sorgfältig gegliedert

struggle [ˈstrʌɡl] **▊** N (*lit, fig*) Kampf *m* (*for* um); (*fig*: = *effort*) Anstrengung *f*; **without a ~** kampflos; **to put up a ~** sich wehren; **the ~ for survival** der Überlebenskampf; **it is/was a ~** es ist/war mühsam **▋** VI **(a)** (= *contend*) kämpfen; (*in self-defence*) sich wehren; (*financially*) in Schwierigkeiten sein; (*fig*: = *strive*) sich sehr bemühen *or* anstrengen; **to ~ for sth** um etw kämpfen, sich um etw bemühen; **to ~ with sth** *with problem* sich mit etw herumschlagen; *with injury, debts, feelings* mit etw zu kämpfen haben; *with one's conscience* mit etw ringen; *with luggage, language, subject, homework* sich mit etw abmühen; **this firm/team is struggling** diese Firma/Mannschaft hat (schwer) zu kämpfen; **are you struggling?** hast du Schwierigkeiten?; **can you manage? – I'm struggling** schaffst du's? – mit Müh und Not; **he was struggling to make ends meet** er hatte seine liebe Not durchzukommen **(b)** (= *move with difficulty*) sich quälen; **to ~ to one's feet** mühsam aufstehen *or* auf die Beine kommen; **to ~ on** (*lit*) sich weiterkämpfen; (*fig*) weiterkämpfen

struggling [ˈstrʌɡlɪŋ] ADJ *artist etc* am Hungertuch nagend *attr*

strum [strʌm] VT *tune, chord* klimpern; *guitar* klimpern auf (+*dat*)

strung [strʌŋ] PRET, PTP *of* **string**

strut¹ [strʌt] VI stolzieren

strut² N (*horizontal*) Strebe *f*; (*sloping also*) Stütze *f*; (*vertical*) Pfeiler *m*

stub [stʌb] **▊** N (*of candle, pencil, tail*) Stummel *m*; (*of cigarette also*) Kippe *f*; (*of cheque, ticket*) Abschnitt *m* **▋** VT **to ~ one's toe (on** *or* **against sth)** sich (*dat*) den Zeh (an etw *dat*) stoßen; **to ~ out a cigarette** eine Zigarette ausdrücken

stubble [ˈstʌbl] N, NO PL Stoppeln *pl*

stubbly [ˈstʌblɪ] ADJ (+ER) Stoppel-; *face* stoppelig

stubborn [ˈstʌbən] ADJ **(a)** *person, insistence* stur; *animal, child* störrisch; **to be ~ about sth** stur auf etw (*dat*) beharren **(b)** *refusal, resistance, stain, weeds, cough* hartnäckig

stubbornly [ˈstʌbənlɪ] ADV **(a)** *refuse* stur; *insist* störrisch; *say* trotzig **(b)** (= *persistently*) hartnäckig

stubbornness [ˈstʌbənnɪs] N (*of person*) Sturheit *f*; (*of animal, child*) störrische Art

stubby [ˈstʌbɪ] ADJ (+ER) *revolver etc* kurz; *tail* stummelig

stuck [stʌk] **▊** PRET, PTP *of* **stick²** **▋** ADJ **(a)** (= *baffled*) (*on, over* mit) **to be ~** nicht zurechtkommen; **to get ~** nicht weiterkommen **(b)** (= *wedged*) **to be ~** (*door etc*) verkeilt sein; **to get ~** stecken bleiben **(c)** (= *trapped, stranded*) **to be ~** festsitzen **(d)** (*inf*) **she is ~ for sth** es fehlt ihr an etw (*dat*), ihr fehlt etw;

I'm a bit ~ **for cash** ich bin ein bisschen knapp bei Kasse; **to be ~ with sb/sth** jdn/etw am Hals haben (*inf*)
(e) (*Brit inf*) **to get ~ into sb** jdn richtig in die Mangel nehmen (*inf*); **to get ~ into sth** sich in etw (*acc*) richtig reinknien (*inf*); **get ~ in!** schlagt zu! (*inf*)

stuck-up [ˌstʌkˈʌp] ADJ (*inf*) hochnäsig

stud¹ [stʌd] **1** N **(a)** (= *nail*) Beschlagnagel *m*; (*decorative*) Ziernagel *m*; (*Brit: on boots*) Stollen *m* **(b)** (= *collar ~*) Kragenknopf *m* **(c)** (= *earring*) Ohrstecker *m* **2** VT (*usu pass*) übersäen; (*with jewels*) (dicht) besetzen

stud² N (= *group of horses: for breeding*) Gestüt *nt*; (= *stallion*) (*Zucht*)hengst *m*; (*inf: = man*) Hengst *m*

student [ˈstjuːdənt] **1** N (*Univ*) Student(in) *m(f)*; (*esp US: at school, night school*) Schüler(in) *m(f)*; **he is a ~ of French** *or* a **French** ~ (*Univ*) er studiert Französisch; (*Sch*) er lernt Französisch **2** ADJ ATTR Studenten-; *activities, protest movement* studentisch; **~ nurse** Krankenpflegeschüler(in) *m(f)*; **~ teacher** N Referendar(in) *m(f)*

stud farm N Gestüt *nt*

studio [ˈstjuːdɪəʊ] N (*all senses*) Studio *nt*; (*of painter, photographer also*) Atelier *nt*; (= *broadcasting ~ also*) Senderaum *m*

studio apartment, (*Brit*) **studio flat** N Studiowohnung *f*

studious [ˈstjuːdɪəs] ADJ *person* fleißig, eifrig; *habits, appearance* gelehrsam

studiously [ˈstjuːdɪəslɪ] ADV fleißig, eifrig; (= *painstakingly*) sorgfältig; *avoid* gezielt

study [ˈstʌdɪ] **1** N **(a)** (= *studying, branch of ~*) (*esp Univ*) Studium *nt*; (*at school*) Lernen *nt*; (*of situation, evidence, case*) Untersuchung *f*; (*of nature*) Beobachtung *f*; **the ~ of cancer** die Krebsforschung; **African studies** (*Univ*) Afrikanistik *f*; **during my studies** während meines Studiums
(b) (= *piece of work*) Studie *f* (*of* über +*acc*); (*Art, Phot*) Studie *f* (*of* +*gen*); (*Liter, Sociol*) Untersuchung *f* (*of* über +*acc*)
(c) (= *room*) Arbeits- *or* Studierzimmer *nt*
2 VT studieren; (*Sch*) lernen; *nature also, stars* beobachten; *author, particular tune, text etc* sich befassen mit; (= *research into*) erforschen; (= *examine*) untersuchen; *evidence also* prüfen
3 VI studieren; (*esp Sch*) lernen; **to ~ to be a teacher/doctor** ein Lehrerstudium/Medizinstudium machen; **to ~ for an exam** sich auf eine Prüfung vorbereiten

study group N Arbeitsgruppe *or* -gemeinschaft *f*

stuff [stʌf] **1** N **(a)** (= *possessions*) Zeug *nt*; Sachen *pl*; **the ~ of tragedy** echte Tragik; **there was a lot of rough ~** es ging ziemlich rau zu; **there is some good ~ in that book** in dem Buch stecken ein paar gute Sachen; **it's poor/good** ~ das ist schlecht/gut; **this book is strong** ~ das ist Buch ist nicht starker Tobak; **I can't read his** ~ ich kann sein Zeug nicht lesen; **his later ~ is less original** seine späteren Sachen sind weniger originell; **he brought me some ~ to read** er hat mir etwas zum Lesen mitgebracht; **books and** ~ Bücher und so (*inf*); **and ~ like that** und so was (*inf*); **all that ~ about how he wants to help us** all das Gerede, dass er uns helfen will; **~ and nonsense** Quatsch *m* (*inf*), Blödsinn *m*
(b) (*inf*) **a drop of the hard** ~ ein Schluck von dem scharfen Zeug; **that's the ~!** so ists richtig!; **to do one's** ~ seine Nummer abziehen (*inf*); **go on, do your ~!** nun mach mal *or* doch! (*inf*); **to know one's** ~ wissen, wovon man redet
2 VT **(a)** *container, room, person* voll stopfen; *hole* zustopfen; *contents, object, books* (hinein)stopfen (*into* in +*acc*); (*into envelope*) stecken (*into* in +*acc*); **to ~ one's face** (*inf*) sich vollstopfen (*inf*); **to ~ sth away** etw wegstecken (*inf*); **to be ~ed up (with a cold)** verschnupft sein
(b) *cushion etc, (Cook)* füllen; *toy, dead animal* ausstopfen; **a ~ed toy** ein Stofftier *nt*
(c) (*Brit inf*) **get ~ed!** du kannst mich mal (*inf*)!; **you can ~ your job** *etc* du kannst deinen blöden Job *etc* behalten (*inf*)
3 VR **to ~ oneself (with food/on cakes)** sich (mit Essen/Kuchen) voll stopfen (*inf*)

stuffed animal N (*US*) Stofftier *nt*

stuffiness [ˈstʌfɪnɪs] N (*of room, atmosphere*) Stickigkeit *f*

stuffing [ˈstʌfɪŋ] N (*of pillow, Cook*) Füllung *f*; (*of furniture*) Polstermaterial *nt*; (*in taxidermy, toys*) Füllmaterial *nt*; **to knock the ~ out of sb** (*inf*) jdn fertig machen (*inf*)

stuffy [ˈstʌfɪ] ADJ (+ER) **(a)** *room, atmosphere* stickig **(b)** (= *narrow-minded*) spießig; (= *prudish*) prüde **(c)** *nose* verstopft

stumble [ˈstʌmbl] **1** N Stolpern *nt no pl, no indef art*; (*in speech etc*) Stocken *nt no pl, no indef art* **2** VI (*lit, fig*) stolpern; (*in speech*) stocken; **to ~ on sth** (*lit*) über etw (*acc*) stolpern; (*fig*) auf etw (*acc*) stoßen

stumbling block [ˈstʌmblɪŋblɒk] N (*fig*) **to be a ~ to sth** einer Sache (*dat*) im Weg stehen

stump [stʌmp] **1** N **(a)** (*of tree, limb*) Stumpf *m*; (*of candle, pencil, tail*) Stummel *m*
(b) (*US Pol: = platform*) Rednertribüne *f*; **to go out on the ~s** (öffentlich *or* vor Ort) als Redner auftreten
2 VT **(a)** (*fig inf*) **you've got me ~ed** da bin ich überfragt; **I'm ~ed by that problem**, that problem's got me ~ed ich bin mit meiner Weisheit *or* meinem Latein am Ende (*inf*)
(b) (*US Pol*) **to ~ the country** Wahl(kampf)reisen durch das Land machen

▶ **stump up** (*Brit inf*) **1** VT INSEP springen lassen (*inf*) **2** VI blechen (*inf*) (*for sth* für etw)

stumpy [ˈstʌmpɪ] ADJ (+ER) *person* stämmig, untersetzt; *legs* kurz

stun [stʌn] VT (= *make unconscious*) betäuben; (*noise also*: = *daze*) benommen machen; (*fig*) (= *shock*) fassungslos machen; (= *amaze*) erstaunen, verblüffen; **he was ~ned by the news** (*bad news*) er war über die Nachricht fassungslos; (*good news*) die Nachricht hat ihn überwältigt

stung [stʌŋ] PRET, PTP *of* sting

stunk [stʌŋk] PTP *of* stink

stunned [stʌnd] ADJ (= *unconscious*) betäubt; (= *dazed*) benommen; (*fig*) (= *shocked*) fassungslos; (= *amazed*) sprachlos; **there was a ~ silence** benommenes Schweigen breitete sich aus

stunning [ˈstʌnɪŋ] ADJ (*lit*) *blow* wuchtig; (*fig*) *news, victory* fantastisch, toll (*inf*); *dress, view, display, looks* atemberaubend; *defeat* überwältigend

stunningly [ˈstʌnɪŋlɪ] ADV atemberaubend, fantastisch; *beautiful* überwältigend; *simple* erstaunlich

stunt¹ [stʌnt] N Kunststück *nt*, Nummer *f*; (= *publicity ~*, *trick*) Gag *m*

stunt² VT (*lit, fig*) *growth* hemmen; *trees, mind etc* verkümmern lassen

stunted [ˈstʌntɪd] ADJ *plant* verkümmert; *child* unterentwickelt; **his ~ growth** seine Verwachsenheit

stuntman [ˈstʌntmæn] N Stuntman *m*, Double *nt*

stupefying [ˈstjuːpɪfaɪɪŋ] ADJ (*fig*: = *amazing*) verblüffend

stupendous [stjuːˈpendəs] ADJ fantastisch; *effort* enorm

stupid [ˈstjuːpɪd] **1** ADJ **(a)** dumm; (= *foolish also, boring, wretched*) blöd(e) (*inf*); **don't be ~** sei nicht so blöd (*inf*); **you ~ idiot!** du blöder Idiot!; **take that ~ look off your face** guck nicht so dumm *or* blöd (*inf*)!; **that was a ~ thing to do** das war dumm; **to make sb look ~** jdn blamieren; **to be so ~ or to be ~ enough to do sth** dumm genug sein, etw zu tun; **it is the ~est thing I've ever heard** das ist das Dümmste, was ich jemals gehört habe
(b) (= *stupefied*) benommen, benebelt; **to bore sb ~** jdn zu Tode langweilen
2 ADV (*inf*) **to talk ~** Quatsch reden (*inf*); **to act ~** sich dumm stellen

stupidity [stjuːˈpɪdɪtɪ] N Dummheit *f*; (= *silliness also*) Blödheit *f* (*inf*)

stupidly [ˈstjuːpɪdlɪ] ADV (= *unintelligently*) dumm; (= *foolishly also*) *say* dummerweise; *grin* albern; **he ~ refused** er war so dumm *or* blöd (*inf*) abzulehnen

stupor [ˈstjuːpə**ʳ**] N Benommenheit *f*; **he lay there in a ~** er lag apathisch *or* teilnahmslos da; **to be in a drunken ~** sinnlos betrunken sein

sturdily [ˈstɜːdɪlɪ] ADV stabil; **~ built** *person* kräftig *or* stämmig gebaut

sturdy [ˈstɜːdɪ] ADJ (+ER) *person, plant* kräftig, stämmig; *material* robust; *building, ship, car* stabil

sturgeon [ˈstɜːdʒən] N Stör *m*

stutter [ˈstʌtə**ʳ**] **1** N (*of person, engine*) Stottern *nt no pl*; **he has a bad ~** er stottert sehr **2** VTI stottern; **she ~ed out an apology** sie entschuldigte sich stotternd

sty [staɪ] N (*lit, fig*) Schweinestall *m*

sty(e) [staɪ] N (Med) Gerstenkorn nt

style [staɪl] **1** N (a) Stil m; **~ of painting** Malstil m; **~ of management** Führungsstil m; **he won in fine ~** er gewann souverän; **in his own inimitable ~** (iro) auf die ihm typische Art; **that house is not my ~** so ein Haus ist nicht mein Stil; **hillwalking is not his ~** Bergwanderungen liegen ihm nicht; **the man has (real) ~** der Mann hat Klasse or Format; **in ~** stilvoll; **to do things in ~** alles im großen Stil tun; **to celebrate in ~** groß feiern
(b) (= sort, type) Art f; **a new ~ of car** etc ein neuer Autotyp etc; **just the ~ of car I like** ein Auto, wie es mir gefällt
(c) (Fashion) Stil m no pl, Mode f; (= cut) Schnitt m; (= hairstyle) Frisur f; **all the latest ~s** die neue(ste) Mode
2 VT (= design) entwerfen; interior etc gestalten; hair stylen

-style [staɪl] ADJ SUF nach ... Art; **American-style fried chicken** Brathähnchen nach amerikanischer Art; **Swedish-style furniture** Möbel im schwedischen Stil; **to dress 1920s-style** sich im Stil der zwanziger Jahre kleiden

styling [staɪlɪŋ] N (of product) Gestaltung f; **~ mousse** Schaumfestiger m

stylish [staɪlɪʃ] ADJ **(a)** person elegant; car, hotel, district also vornehm; film, performer, design stilvoll; performance kunstvoll; way of life großartig **(b)** (= fashionable) clothes modisch

stylishly [staɪlɪʃlɪ] ADV **(a)** (= elegantly) elegant; furnished stilvoll **(b)** (= fashionably) dress modisch

stylishness [staɪlɪʃnɪs] N **(a)** (of person) Eleganz f; (of car, hotel, district also) Vornehmheit f; (of furnishings) stilvolle Art; (of wedding etc) groß angelegter Stil **(b)** (= fashionableness) modische Finesse

stylist [staɪlɪst] N (= hair ~) Friseur m, Friseuse f

stylized [staɪlaɪzd] ADJ stilisiert

suave ADJ, **suavely** ADV [swɑːv, -lɪ] weltmännisch, aalglatt (pej)

sub- PREF (= under, subordinate, inferior) Unter-, unter-; (esp with foreign words) Sub-, sub-; **~group** Untergruppe f

sub: subconscious **1** ADJ unterbewusst **2** N **the ~** das Unterbewusstsein; **in his ~** im Unterbewusstsein; **subconsciously** ADV im Unterbewusstsein; **subcontract** VT (vertraglich) weitervergeben (to an +acc); **subcontractor** N Subunternehmer(in) m(f); **subdivide** **1** VT unterteilen **2** VI sich aufteilen

subdue [səbˈdjuː] VT rebels, country unterwerfen; rioters überwältigen; (fig) anger, desire unterdrücken; noise, light, high spirits dämpfen

subdued [səbˈdjuːd] ADJ colour, lighting, voice, response gedämpft; manner, person ruhig, still; atmosphere gedrückt; manner, person gefügig; feelings, excitement unterdrückt

sub: subeditor N (esp Brit) Redakteur(in) m(f); **subhead** (inf), **subheading** N Untertitel m; **subhuman** ADJ unmenschlich

subject [ˈsʌbdʒɪkt] **1** N **(a)** (Pol) Staatsbürger(in) m(f); (of king etc) Untertan m, Untertanin f
(b) (Gram) Subjekt nt, Satzgegenstand m
(c) (= topic, Mus) Thema nt; **to change the ~** das Thema wechseln; **on the ~ of ...** zum Thema (+gen) ...; **while we're on the ~** da wir gerade beim Thema sind; **while we're on the ~ of mushrooms** wo wir gerade von Pilzen reden
(d) (= discipline, Sch, Univ) Fach nt
(e) (= object) Gegenstand m (of +gen); (in experiment) (= person) Versuchsperson f; (= animal) Versuchstier nt; (esp Med: for treatment) Typ m
(f) (Phot) Objekt nt
2 ADJ **~ to** (= under the control of) unterworfen (+dat); **to be ~ to sth** to law, constant change, sb's will einer Sache (dat) unterworfen sein; to illness für etw anfällig sein; to consent, approval von etw abhängig sein; **northbound trains are ~ to delays** bei Zügen in Richtung Norden muss mit Verspätung gerechnet werden; **prices are ~ to change** or **alteration without notice** Preisänderungen sind vorbehalten; **all these plans are ~ to last minute changes** all diese Pläne können in letzter Minute noch geändert werden; **~ to flooding** überschwemmungsgefährdet; **to be ~ to taxation** besteuert werden; **all offers are ~ to availability** alle Angebote nur so weit verfügbar; **"~ to status"** „Berechtigungsnachweis erforderlich"
3 [səbˈdʒekt] VT **to ~ sb to sth** to questioning, treatment, test jdn einer Sache (dat) unterziehen; to torture, heat, ridicule jdn einer Sache (dat) aussetzen; **to ~ sb to criticism** jdn kritisieren

subject index N Sachregister nt

subjective [səbˈdʒektɪv] ADJ **(a)** subjektiv **(b)** (Gram) **~ case** Nominativ m

subjectively [səbˈdʒektɪvlɪ] ADV subjektiv

subject: subject line N (of letter) Betreffzeile f; **subject matter** [ˈsʌbdʒɪktmætəʳ] N (= theme) Stoff m; (= content) Inhalt m

subjugate [ˈsʌbdʒʊɡeɪt] VT unterwerfen

subjugation [ˌsʌbdʒʊˈɡeɪʃən] N Unterwerfung f

subjunctive [səbˈdʒʌŋktɪv] **1** ADJ konjunktivisch; **the ~ mood** der Konjunktiv **2** N Konjunktiv m

sublet [ˌsʌbˈlet], pret, ptp **sublet** VTI untervermieten (to an +acc)

sublime [səˈblaɪm] ADJ **(a)** beauty, scenery, feelings erhaben; achievement also überragend; **that's going from the ~ to the ridiculous** (inf) das nenne ich tief sinken (inf) **(b)** (iro: = extreme) ignorance vollendet; indifference herablassend **(c)** (inf: = delightful) reizend

sublimely [səˈblaɪmlɪ] ADV erhaben; ignorant ergreifend (iro), vollkommen; drunk, simple unglaublich; **~ beautiful** von erhabener Schönheit

subliminal [ˌsʌbˈlɪmɪnl] ADJ (Psych) unterschwellig

submachine gun [ˌsʌbməˈʃiːnɡʌn] N Maschinenpistole f

submarine [ˌsʌbməˈriːn] N U-Boot nt

submenu [ˈsʌbˌmenjuː] N (Comput) Untermenü nt

submerge [səbˈmɜːdʒ] **1** VT untertauchen; (= flood) überschwemmen; **to ~ sth in water** etw in Wasser (ein)tauchen; **to ~ oneself in sth** (fig) ganz in etw (acc) versinken **2** VI tauchen

submerged [səbˈmɜːdʒd] ADJ rocks unter Wasser; wreck gesunken; city versunken; **the house was completely ~** das Haus stand völlig unter Wasser

submersion [səbˈmɜːʃən] N Untertauchen nt; (by flood) Überschwemmung f

submission [səbˈmɪʃən] N **(a)** **to force sb into ~** jdn zwingen, sich zu ergeben; **to starve sb into ~** jdn aushungern **(b)** (= presentation) Eingabe f

submissive [səbˈmɪsɪv] ADJ demütig, unterwürfig (pej) (to gegenüber)

submit [səbˈmɪt] **1** VT **(a)** (= put forward) vorlegen (to +dat); application, claim etc einreichen (to bei)
(b) (= refer) verweisen (to an +acc)
2 VI (= yield) sich beugen, nachgeben; **to ~ to sth** to sb's orders, judgement sich einer Sache (dat) beugen or unterwerfen; to pressure einer Sache (dat) nachgeben; **to ~ to blackmail/questioning** sich erpressen/verhören lassen
3 VR **to ~ oneself to sth** to examination, operation etc sich einer Sache (dat) unterziehen

subnormal [ˌsʌbˈnɔːməl] ADJ intelligence, temperature unterdurchschnittlich; person minderbegabt; (inf) schwachsinnig

subordinate [səˈbɔːdnɪt] **1** ADJ officer rangniedriger; rank, position, role untergeordnet; **to be ~ to sb/sth** jdm/einer Sache untergeordnet sein **2** N Untergebene(r) mf

subordinate clause N (Gram) Nebensatz m

subordination [səˌbɔːdɪˈneɪʃən] N (= subjection) Unterordnung f (to unter +acc)

subplot [ˈsʌbˌplɒt] N Nebenhandlung f

subpoena [səˈpiːnə] (Jur) **1** N Vorladung f **2** VT vorladen

sub: sub-post office N (Brit) Poststelle f; **subroutine** N (Comput) Unterprogramm nt

subscribe [səbˈskraɪb] VI **(a)** **to ~ to a magazine/mailing list** eine Zeitschrift/Mailingliste abonnieren **(b)** (= support) **to ~ to sth** to opinion, theory sich einer Sache (dat) anschließen

subscriber [səbˈskraɪbəʳ] N (to paper) Abonnent(in) m(f); (Telec) Teilnehmer(in) m(f)

subscription [səbˈskrɪpʃən] N Zeichnung f (form); (= money subscribed) Beitrag m; (to newspaper, concert etc) Abonnement nt (to +gen); **to take out a ~ to sth** etw abonnieren

subscription share N (St Ex) Subskriptionsaktie f

subsequent [ˈsʌbsɪkwənt] ADJ (nach)folgend; (in time) anschließend

subsequently [ˈsʌbsɪkwəntlɪ] ADV (= afterwards) anschließend; alter, add etc also nachträglich; (= from that time) von da an

subservient [səb'sɜːvɪənt] ADJ *(pej)* unterwürfig *(to* gegenüber); *(form)* unterworfen *(to +dat)*

subside [səb'saɪd] VI *(flood, river, fever)* sinken; *(land, building, road)* sich senken; *(storm, wind)* abflauen; *(anger, laughter, noise)* nachlassen

subsidence [səb'saɪdəns] N Senkung *f*; **there's a lot of ~ in the area** in der Gegend senkt sich das Erdreich

subsidiary [səb'sɪdɪəri] **1** ADJ untergeordnet; **~ role** Nebenrolle *f*; **~ subject** Nebenfach *nt*; **~ company** Tochtergesellschaft *f* **2** N Tochtergesellschaft *f*

subsidize ['sʌbsɪdaɪz] VT subventionieren; *housing* finanziell unterstützen

subsidized ['sʌbsɪdaɪzd] ADJ subventioniert; *housing* finanziell unterstützt

subsidy ['sʌbsɪdɪ] N Subvention *f*, Zuschuss *m*

subsist [səb'sɪst] VI *(form)* sich ernähren, leben *(on* von)

subsistence [səb'sɪstəns] N *(= living)* Leben *nt (on* von); *(= means of ~)* Existenz *f*, (Lebens)unterhalt *m*

subsistence: subsistence allowance N Unterhaltszuschuss *m*; **subsistence level** N Existenzminimum *nt*

sub: subsoil N Untergrund *m*; **subsonic** ADJ Unterschall-; **subspecies** N Unterart *f*

substance ['sʌbstəns] N **(a)** Substanz *f*, Stoff *m* **(b)** NO PL *(= essence)* Kern *m* **(c)** NO PL *(= weight, importance)* Gewicht *nt*; **the book lacks ~** das Buch hat keine Substanz; **a man of ~** ein vermögender Mann

substance abuse N Drogen- und Alkoholmissbrauch *m*

substandard [ˌsʌb'stændəd] ADJ minderwertig; *quality also, housing* unzulänglich

substantial [səb'stænʃəl] ADJ **(a)** *person* kräftig; *furniture, building, firm* solide; *book* umfangreich; *meal* reichhaltig **(b)** *income, loss, gain, amount* beträchtlich; *part, majority, contribution, improvement, difference* wesentlich **(c)** *(= weighty, important)* bedeutend; *proof* überzeugend

substantially [səb'stænʃəli] ADV **(a)** *(= solidly)* solide; *(= considerably)* beträchtlich **(b)** *(= essentially, basically)* im Wesentlichen

substantiate [səb'stænʃɪeɪt] VT erhärten

substation ['sʌbˌsteɪʃən] N *(Elec)* Umspann(ungs)werk *nt*

substitute ['sʌbstɪtjuːt] **1** N Ersatz *m no pl*; *(= representative also)* Vertretung *f*; *(Sport)* Ersatzspieler(in) *m(f)*; **to find a ~ for sb** für jdn Ersatz finden; **to use sth as a ~** etw als Ersatz benutzen **2** ADJ ATTR Ersatz-; **~ drug** Ersatzdroge *f* **3** VT **to ~ A for B** B durch A ersetzen; *(Sport also)* B gegen A auswechseln **4** VI **to ~ for sb** jdn vertreten

substitute teacher N *(US)* Aushilfslehrer(in) *m(f)*

substitution [ˌsʌbstɪ'tjuːʃən] N Ersetzen *nt (of X for Y* von Y durch X); *(Sport)* Austausch *m (of X for Y* von Y gegen X)

subterfuge ['sʌbtəfjuːdʒ] N *(= trickery)* Täuschung *f*, List *f*; *(= trick)* Trick *m*; **to resort to ~** zu einer List greifen

subterranean [ˌsʌbtə'reɪnɪən] ADJ unterirdisch

subtitle ['sʌbtaɪtl] **1** N Untertitel *m (also Film)* **2** VT *film* mit Untertiteln versehen; **the book is ~d ...** das Buch hat den Untertitel ...

subtle ['sʌtl] ADJ **(a)** *(= delicate)* fein; *perfume, flavour, hint, allusion* zart; *charm* leise, unaufdringlich **(b)** *(= not obvious) remark, point* scharfsinnig; *pressure* sanft; *design* raffiniert **(c)** *observer, critic* aufmerksam, subtil *(geh)*

subtlety ['sʌtltɪ] N **(a)** Feinheit *f*; *(of perfume, flavour also, hint, allusion)* Zartheit *f* **(b)** *(= sophistication)* *(of remark, point)* Scharfsinn(igkeit *f*) *m*; *(of design)* Raffiniertheit *f*; **his methods lack ~** seinen Methoden fehlt (die) Finesse **(c)** *(= discriminative powers: of observer, critic)* Aufmerksamkeit *f*

subtly ['sʌtlɪ] ADV fein; *flavoured also* delikat; *argue* scharfsinnig; *change* geringfügig; *imply* unterschwellig; *achieve one's ends* auf raffinierte Weise; **~ different** auf subtile Weise unterschiedlich

subtotal ['sʌbˌtəʊtl] N Zwischen- *or* Teilsumme *f*

subtract [səb'trækt] VTI abziehen, subtrahieren *(from* von)

subtraction [səb'trækʃən] N Subtraktion *f*

suburb ['sʌbɜːb] N Vorort *m*; **in the ~s** am Stadtrand

suburban [sə'bɜːbən] ADJ vorstädtisch; *(pej)* spießig, kleinbürgerlich; **~ line** *(Rail)* Vorortbahn *f*; **~ street** Vorortstraße *f*

suburbia [sə'bɜːbɪə] N *(usu pej)* die Vororte *pl*; **to live in ~** am Stadtrand wohnen

subversion [səb'vɜːʃən] N, NO PL Subversion *f*; *(of rights, freedom etc)* Unterminierung *f*

subversive [səb'vɜːsɪv] **1** ADJ subversiv, umstürzlerisch **2** N Umstürzler(in) *m(f)*

subvert [səb'vɜːt] VT *government* zu stürzen versuchen; *faith, morals etc* unterminieren; *constitution, state authority* unterwandern

subway ['sʌbweɪ] N Unterführung *f*; *(esp US Rail)* U-Bahn *f*

subzero [ˌsʌb'zɪərəʊ] ADJ unter dem Nullpunkt

succeed [sək'siːd] **1** VI **(a)** erfolgreich sein; **to ~ in business** geschäftlich erfolgreich sein; **I ~ed in doing it** es gelang mir, es zu tun; **you'll only ~ in making things worse** damit erreichst du nur, dass alles noch schlimmer wird **(b)** *(= come next)* **to ~ to the throne** die Thronfolge antreten **2** VT *(= come after, take the place of)* folgen *(+dat)*; *(person also)* Nachfolger(in) *m(f)* werden *+gen*; **to ~ sb in a post/in office** jds Stelle/Amt *(acc)* übernehmen

succeeding [sək'siːdɪŋ] ADJ folgend; **~ generations** spätere *or* nachfolgende Generationen *pl*

success [sək'ses] N Erfolg *m*; **without ~** ohne Erfolg, erfolglos; **to make a ~ of sth** mit *or* bei etw Erfolg haben; **to be a ~ with sb** bei jdm ankommen; **to meet with ~** Erfolg haben; **~ story** Erfolgsstory *f*; *(= person)* Erfolg *m*

successful [sək'sesfʊl] ADJ erfolgreich; **to be ~** erfolgreich sein, Erfolg haben *(in* mit, bei); **I was ~ in doing it** es gelang mir, es zu tun; **to be ~ at doing sth** etw erfolgreich tun; **to be ~ as a doctor** ein erfolgreicher Arzt sein

successfully [sək'sesfəli] ADV erfolgreich, mit Erfolg

succession [sək'seʃən] N **(a)** Folge *f*, Serie *f*; *(with no intervening period)* (Aufeinander)folge *f*, Kette *f*; **in ~** nacheinander, hintereinander; **in quick** *or* **rapid ~** in rascher Folge **(b)** *(to post)* Nachfolge *f*; *(to throne)* Thronfolge *f*; *(to title, estate)* Erbfolge *f*; **her ~ to the throne** ihre Thronbesteigung

successive [sək'sesɪv] ADJ aufeinander folgend *attr*; **for the third ~ time** zum dritten Mal hintereinander; **he was sacked from three ~ jobs** er wurde nacheinander *or* hintereinander aus drei verschiedenen Stellen hinausgeworfen

successively [sək'sesɪvli] ADV nacheinander, hintereinander

successor [sək'sesəʳ] N Nachfolger(in) *m(f) (to +gen)*; *(to throne)* Thronfolger(in) *m(f)*

succinct [sək'sɪŋkt] ADJ knapp, kurz und bündig *pred*

succinctly [sək'sɪŋktlɪ] ADV kurz und bündig; *write* in knappem Stil

succulence ['sʌkjʊləns] N Saftigkeit *f*

succulent ['sʌkjʊlənt] **1** ADJ saftig **2** N *(Bot)* Fettpflanze *f*

succumb [sə'kʌm] VI erliegen *(to +dat)*; *(to threats)* sich beugen *(to +dat)*

such [sʌtʃ] **1** ADJ solche(r, s); **~ a person** so *or* solch ein Mensch, ein solcher Mensch; **~ a book** so ein, ein solches Buch; **~ people/books** solche Leute/Bücher; **many/few/all ~ people/books** viele/wenige/all solche Leute/Bücher; **all ~ books are very expensive** solche Bücher sind sehr teuer; **~ a thing** so etwas, so was *(inf)*; **I said no ~ thing** das habe ich nie gesagt; **no ~ thing** nichts dergleichen; **you'll do no ~ thing** du wirst dich hüten; **there's no ~ thing as a unicorn** so etwas wie ein Einhorn gibt es nicht; **... or some ~ idea ...** oder so etwas, ... oder so was in der Richtung *(inf)*; **... or some ~ name/place** ... oder so *(ähnlich)*; **in ~ a case** in einem solchen Fall; **men/books ~ as these** Men/Bücher wie diese, solche Männer/Bücher; **writers ~ as Agatha Christie, ~ writers as Agatha Christie** (solche) Schriftsteller wie Agatha Christie; **I'm not ~ a fool as to believe that** ich bin nicht so dumm, dass ich das glaube; **he's ~ a liar** er ist so *or* solch ein Lügner; **he did it in ~ a way that ...** er machte es so, dass ...; **~ beauty!** welche Schönheit!; **he's always in ~ a hurry** er hat es immer so eilig; **his surprise was ~ that ...**, **~ was his surprise that ...** er war so überrascht, dass ...

2 ADV so, solch *(geh)*; **it's ~ a long time ago** es ist so lange her **3** PRON **~ being the case ...** in diesem Fall ...; **~ is life!** so ist das Leben!; **as ~** an sich; **as?** (wie) zum Beispiel?; **as it is** so, wie es nun mal ist

such-and-such ['sʌtʃənsʌtʃ] *(inf)* ADJ **~ a time/town** die und die Zeit/Stadt

suchlike ['sʌtʃlaɪk] *(inf)* **1** ADJ solche **2** PRON dergleichen

suck [sʌk] **1** VT saugen; *breast, straw* saugen an (+*dat*); *sweet, pastille* lutschen; *lollipop, thumb* lutschen an (+*dat*); **to ~ sb dry** (*fig*) jdn bis aufs Blut aussaugen **2** VI **(a)** (*at an* +*dat*) saugen; (*at dummy*) nuckeln (*inf*); (*at lollipop, thumb*) lutschen; (*at pipe, through straw*) ziehen **(b)** (*US inf*) **this city ~s** diese Stadt ist echt Scheiße (*inf*)
➤ **suck in** VT SEP *air* (*ventilator*) ansaugen; *cheeks, stomach* einziehen; (*fig*) *imports* anlocken
➤ **suck under** VT SEP hinunterziehen; (*completely*) verschlingen
➤ **suck up** **1** VT SEP aufsaugen **2** VI (*inf*) **to suck up to sb** vor jdm kriechen

sucker [ˈsʌkəʳ] N **(a)** (= *rubber ~, Zool*) Saugnapf *m* **(b)** (*US inf*: = *lollipop*) Lutscher *m* **(c)** (*inf*: = *fool*) Trottel *m* (*inf*); **to be a ~ for sth** (immer) auf etw (*acc*) hereinfallen; (= *be partial to*) eine Schwäche für etw haben

suckle [ˈsʌkl] **1** VT *child* stillen; *animal* säugen **2** VI saugen, trinken

sucrose [ˈsuːkrəʊz] N Sa(c)charose *f*

suction [ˈsʌkʃən] N Saugwirkung *f*

suction pump N Saugpumpe *f*

Sudan [suˈdɑːn] N **(the)** ~ der Sudan

Sudanese [ˌsuːdəˈniːz] **1** ADJ sudanesisch; **he is ~** er ist Sudanese **2** N Sudanese *m*, Sudanesin *f*

sudden [ˈsʌdn] **1** ADJ plötzlich; *bend, change of direction* unerwartet, da war eine unerwartete Kurve; **this is all so ~** das kommt alles so plötzlich **2** N **all of a ~** (ganz) plötzlich, urplötzlich (*inf*)

suddenly [ˈsʌdnlɪ] ADV plötzlich

suddenness [ˈsʌdnɪs] N Plötzlichkeit *f*

suds [sʌdz] PL Seifenwasser *nt or* -lauge *f*; (= *lather*) (Seifen)schaum *m*

sue [suː] **1** VT (*Jur*) verklagen; **to ~ sb for sth** jdn auf etw (*acc*) *or* wegen etw verklagen; **to ~ sb for divorce** gegen jdn die Scheidung einreichen **2** VI (*Jur*) klagen, Klage erheben; **to ~ for divorce** die Scheidung einreichen

suede [sweɪd] **1** N Wildleder *nt*; (*soft, fine also*) Velours(leder) *nt* **2** ADJ Wildleder-, aus Wildleder; (*of finer quality also*) Velours(leder)-, aus Velours(leder)

suet [ˈsuːɪt] N Nierenfett *nt*

Suez [ˈsuːɪz] N Suez *nt*

Suez Canal N Suezkanal *m*

suffer [ˈsʌfəʳ] **1** VT **(a)** (= *undergo, be subjected to*) erleiden; *headache, effects etc* leiden unter *or* an (+*dat*); *shock* haben; **the pound ~ed further losses** das Pfund musste weitere Einbußen hinnehmen
(b) (= *tolerate*) dulden, ertragen
2 VI (*lit, fig*) leiden (*from* unter +*dat, from illness* an +*dat*); (*as punishment, in hell etc*) büßen; **he was ~ing from shock** er hatte einen Schock (erlitten); **your work will ~** deine Arbeit wird darunter leiden; **you'll ~ for this!** das wirst du büßen!

sufferance [ˈsʌfərəns] N **on ~** (nur *or* stillschweigend) geduldet

sufferer [ˈsʌfərəʳ] N (*Med*) Leidende(r) *mf* (*from* an +*dat*); **diabetes ~s, ~s from diabetes** Diabeteskranke *pl*

suffering [ˈsʌfərɪŋ] N Leiden *nt*; (= *hardship, deprivation*) Leid *nt no pl*

suffice [səˈfaɪs] (*form*) **1** VI genügen, (aus)reichen **2** VT **~ it to say ...** es reicht wohl, wenn ich sage, ...

sufficiency [səˈfɪʃənsɪ] N (= *adequacy*) Hinlänglichkeit *f*

sufficient [səˈfɪʃənt] ADJ ausreichend; *reason, explanation* hinreichend; **is that ~ reason for his dismissal?** ist das Grund genug *or* ein ausreichender Grund, ihn zu entlassen?; **to be ~** genügen, ausreichen

sufficiently [səˈfɪʃəntlɪ] ADV genug; **~ warm** *etc* warm *etc* genug *pred*, genügend *or* ausreichend warm *etc*; **a ~ large number** eine ausreichend große Anzahl

suffix [ˈsʌfɪks] N (*Ling*) Suffix *nt*, Nachsilbe *f*

suffocate [ˈsʌfəkeɪt] VTI (*lit, fig*) ersticken; **his obsessive jealousy is suffocating me** seine krankhafte Eifersucht erdrückt mich; **he was ~d by the smoke** er erstickte am Rauch

suffocating [ˈsʌfəkeɪtɪŋ] ADJ (*lit*) erstickend *attr*; *heat* drückend *attr*; *room* stickig; (*fig*) *atmosphere* erdrückend *attr*; **it's ~ in here** es ist stickig hier drinnen

suffocation [ˌsʌfəˈkeɪʃən] N (*lit, fig*) Ersticken *nt*

suffrage [ˈsʌfrɪdʒ] N Wahl- *or* Stimmrecht *nt*

sugar [ˈʃʊgəʳ] **1** N Zucker *m* **2** VT zuckern, süßen; (*fig*) **to ~ the pill** die bittere Pille versüßen

sugar IN CPDS Zucker-; **sugar beet** N Zuckerrübe *f*; **sugar bowl** N Zuckerdose *f*; **sugar candy** N Kandis(zucker) *m*; (*US*: = *sweet*) Bonbon *nt or m*; **sugar cane** N Zuckerrohr *nt*; **sugar-coated** ADJ mit Zucker überzogen

sugared [ˈʃʊgəd] ADJ gezuckert; **~ almonds** Zuckermandeln *pl*

sugar-free ADJ ohne Zucker

sugary [ˈʃʊgərɪ] ADJ *taste* süß; (= *full of sugar*) zuckerig; (*fig pej*) *style, music etc* süßlich

suggest [səˈdʒest] **1** VT **(a)** (= *propose*) vorschlagen; **I ~ that we go, I ~ going** ich schlage vor, zu gehen *or* (dass) wir gehen; **what do you ~ we do?** was schlagen Sie vor?; **are you ~ing I should tell a deliberate lie?** soll das heißen, dass ich bewusst lügen soll?; **I am ~ing nothing of the kind** das habe ich nicht gesagt
(b) *explanation, theory* vorbringen
(c) (= *insinuate, indicate*) andeuten; (*unpleasantly*) unterstellen; (= *evoke*) (*music, poem*) denken lassen an (+*acc*); **what are you trying to ~?** was wollen Sie damit sagen? **2** VR (*idea, plan*) sich anbieten

suggestion [səˈdʒestʃən] N **(a)** (= *proposal, recommendation*) Vorschlag *m*, Anregung *f*; **my ~ is that ...** mein Vorschlag lautet ..., ich schlage vor ...; **Rome was your ~** Rom war deine Idee; **John was his ~ as candidate** er schlug John als Kandidaten vor; **I'm open to ~s** Vorschläge sind *or* jeder Vorschlag ist willkommen
(b) (= *theory, explanation*) Vermutung *f*
(c) (= *insinuation, hint*) Andeutung *f*, Anspielung *f*; (*unpleasant*) Unterstellung *f*; **there is no ~ that he was involved** (= *no indication*) es gibt keinen Hinweis darauf *or* Anhaltspunkt dafür, dass er beteiligt war
(d) (= *trace*) Spur *f*
(e) (= *impression*) Eindruck *m*, Vorstellung *f*
(f) (*also* **indecent ~**) unsittlicher Antrag

suggestive [səˈdʒestɪv] ADJ **(a)** **to be ~ of sth** auf etw (*acc*) hindeuten; (= *create impression of*) den Eindruck von etw erwecken; (= *be indicative of*) auf etw (*acc*) hindeuten **(b)** *joke, remark etc* zweideutig, anzüglich; *gesture* aufreizend

suggestively [səˈdʒestɪvlɪ] ADV viel sagend, anzüglich; *move, dance* aufreizend

suicidal [sʊɪˈsaɪdl] ADJ selbstmörderisch; **she was ~** sie war selbstmordgefährdet

suicide [ˈsʊɪsaɪd] N Selbstmord *m*; **to commit ~** Selbstmord begehen; **to contemplate ~** sich mit Selbstmordgedanken tragen

suicide note N Abschiedsbrief *m*

suit [suːt] **1** N **(a)** Anzug *m*; (*woman's*) Kostüm *nt*; **~ of clothes** Garnitur *f* (Kleider); **~ of armour** Rüstung *f*
(b) (*Jur*) Prozess *m*, Verfahren *nt*; **to bring a ~ (against sb for sth)** (wegen etw gegen jdn) Klage erheben
(c) (*Cards*) Farbe *f*; **to follow ~** (*lit*) Farbe bedienen; (*fig*) jds Beispiel (*dat*) folgen
2 VT (*arrangement, price*) passen (+*dat*); (*climate, food*) bekommen (+*dat*); (*job*) gefallen (+*dat*); (= *please*) zufrieden stellen; **~s me!** (*inf*) ist mir recht (*inf*); **that ~s me fine!** (*inf*) das ist mir recht; **that would ~ me nicely** (*arrangement*) das würde mir gut (in den Kram (*inf*)) passen; **when would it ~ you to come?** wann würde es Ihnen passen?; **to be ~ed for/to** (= *be suitable, right for*) geeignet sein für; **he is very well ~ed to the job** er eignet sich sehr gut für die Stelle; **he is not ~ed to be a doctor** er eignet sich nicht zum Arzt; **they are well ~ed (to each other)** sie passen gut zusammen; **you can't ~ everybody** man kann es nicht jedem recht machen
(b) (*clothes, hairstyle*) (gut) stehen (+*dat*), passen zu; **you ~ a beard** ein Bart steht dir gut
(c) (= *adapt*) anpassen (*to* +*dat*)
3 VR **he ~s himself** er tut, was er will *or* was ihm passt; **you can ~ yourself whether you come or not** du kannst kommen oder nicht, ganz wie du willst; **~ yourself!** wie du willst!

suitability [ˌsuːtəˈbɪlɪtɪ] N Angemessenheit *f*; (*of person for job*) Eignung *f*; **the ~ of a film for children** ob ein Film für Kinder geeignet ist

suitable [ˈsuːtəbl] ADJ geeignet, passend; (= *socially, culturally appropriate*) angemessen; **to be ~ for sb** (*date, place*) jdm passen; (*film, job*) für jdn geeignet sein; (*clothes*) das Richtige für jdn sein; **she's not ~ for him** sie passt nicht zu ihm; **to be ~ for sth** für etw geeignet sein, sich für etw eignen; (*socially*) einer Sache (*dat*) angemessen sein; **none of the dishes is ~ for freezing** keines der Rezepte eignet sich zum Einfrieren; **the most ~ man for the job** der am besten geeignete Mann für den Posten; **Tuesday is the most ~ day** Dienstag passt am besten; **animals that are ~ as pets** Tiere, die als Haustiere geeignet sind

suitably ['su:təblɪ] ADV angemessen; **he was ~ impressed** er war gehörig beeindruckt; **~ refreshed** ausreichend erfrischt; **to look ~ embarrassed** überaus verlegen aussehen

suitcase ['su:tkeɪs] N Koffer *m*

suite [swi:t] N (*of furniture*) Garnitur *f*; (= *chairs and sofa*) Sitzgarnitur *f*; (*of rooms, Mus*) Suite *f*; **3-piece ~** dreiteilige Sitzgarnitur

sulk [sʌlk] 🢒 VI schmollen, eingeschnappt sein 🢒 N **to have a ~ schmollen**; **to go into a ~** sich in den Schmollwinkel zurückziehen, einschnappen

sulkily ['sʌlkɪlɪ] ADV beleidigt

sulkiness ['sʌlkɪnɪs] N Schmollen *nt*

sulky ['sʌlkɪ] ADJ (+ER) *answer* eingeschnappt; *person, expression also* schmollend

sullen ['sʌlən] ADJ mürrisch, verdrießlich; *behaviour, silence* mürrisch

sullenly ['sʌlənlɪ] ADV mürrisch

sullenness ['sʌlənnɪs] N (*of person*) Verdrießlichkeit *f*

sulphate, (*US*) **sulfate** ['sʌlfeɪt] N Sulfat *nt*

sulphur, (*US*) **sulfur** ['sʌlfə*ʳ*] N Schwefel *m*

sulphuric acid, (*US*) **sulfuric acid** [sʌl,fjʊərɪk'æsɪd] N Schwefelsäure *f*

sultan ['sʌltən] N Sultan *m*

sultana [sʌl'tɑ:nə] N (*Brit*: = *fruit*) Sultanine *f*

sultry ['sʌltrɪ] ADJ *atmosphere* schwül; *woman* temperamentvoll; *voice, beauty, look* glutvoll

sum [sʌm] N (**a**) Summe *f*; **~ assured** (*Brit Insur*) Versicherungssumme *f* (**b**) (*esp Brit*: = *calculation*) Rechenaufgabe *f*; **to do ~s (in one's head)** (im Kopf) rechnen; **that was the ~ (total) of his achievements** das war alles, was er geschafft hatte

➤ **sum up** VT SEP (**a**) (= *summarize*) zusammenfassen (**b**) (= *evaluate rapidly*) ab- *or* einschätzen, taxieren 🢒 VI (*also Jur*) zusammenfassen, resümieren; **to sum up, we can say that ...** zusammenfassend *or* als Resümee können wir feststellen, dass ...

Sumatra [su:'mɑ:trə] N Sumatra *nt*

Sumatran [su:'mɑ:trən] 🢒 ADJ von/aus Sumatra 🢒 N Bewohner(in) *m(f)* von Sumatra

summarize ['sʌməraɪz] VT zusammenfassen

summary ['sʌmərɪ] 🢒 N Zusammenfassung *f*; (*Sci also*) Abriss *m*; **here is a ~ of the main points of the news** hier ein Überblick *m* über die wichtigsten Meldungen; **~ of contents** Inhaltsangabe *f* 🢒 ADJ (= *brief*) knapp; **in ~ form** in Zusammenfassung

summer ['sʌmə*ʳ*] 🢒 N Sommer *m*; **in (the) ~** im Sommer; **two ~s ago** im Sommer vor zwei Jahren; **a ~'s day** ein Sommertag *m* 🢒 ADJ ATTR Sommer-; **~ resort** Ferien- *or* Urlaubsort *m* (für die Sommersaison)

summer: summerhouse N Gartenhaus *nt*, (Garten)laube *f*; **summer house** N (*US*) Ferienhaus *nt*/-wohnung *f*

summersault N, VI = **somersault**

summer: summer school N Sommerkurs *m*; **summertime** N Sommer *m*, Sommer(s)zeit *f*

summery ['sʌmərɪ] ADJ sommerlich

summing-up [sʌmɪŋ'ʌp] N (*Jur*) Resümee *nt*

summit ['sʌmɪt] 🢒 N (*lit*, = ~ *conference*) Gipfel *m*; (*fig also*) Höhepunkt *m* 🢒 ADJ ATTR (*Pol*) Gipfel-

summon ['sʌmən] VT (**a**) *servant, fire brigade etc* (herbei)rufen; *help* holen; *members* zusammenrufen; *meeting* einberufen; **to ~ sb to do sth** (= *order*) jdn auffordern, etw zu tun; **to ~ the courage to do sth** den Mut aufbringen, etw zu tun (**b**) (*Jur*) vorladen

➤ **summon up** VT SEP *courage* zusammennehmen; *strength* aufbieten; *enthusiasm, energy* aufbringen; *sympathy, image* heraufbeschwören

summons ['sʌmənz] N (**a**) (*Jur*) Vorladung *f* (**b**) (= *order to appear etc*) Aufruf *m*, Aufforderung *f*

sumptuous ['sʌmptjʊəs] ADJ (= *splendid*) luxuriös; (= *costly*) aufwändig, kostspielig; *food etc* üppig

Sun ABBR *of* **Sunday** So.

sun [sʌn] N Sonne *f*; **you've caught the ~** dich hat die Sonne erwischt; **he's tried everything under the ~** er hat alles Menschenmögliche versucht

sun: sunbathe VI sonnenbaden; **sunbathing** N Sonnenbaden *nt*; **sunbeam** N Sonnenstrahl *m*; **sun bed** N Sonnenbank *f*

sun: sun block N Sonnenschutzcreme *f*; **sunburn** N Sonnenbrand *m*; **sunburnt** ADJ von der Sonne verbrannt; **to get ~** (einen) Sonnenbrand bekommen

sundae ['sʌndeɪ] N Eisbecher *m*

Sunday ['sʌndɪ] 🢒 N Sonntag *m*; *see also* **Tuesday** 🢒 ADJ ATTR Sonntags-; *trading* am Sonntag; **~ opening** verkaufsoffener Sonntag

sun: sundial N Sonnenuhr *f*; **sundown** N (*Brit*) Sonnenuntergang *m*; **at/before ~** bei/vor Sonnenuntergang; **sun-drenched** ADJ sonnenüberflutet; **sundress** N leichtes Sonnenkleid; **sun-dried** ADJ *fruit* sonnengetrocknet; **sunflower** N Sonnenblume *f*

sung [sʌŋ] PTP *of* **sing**

sun: sunglasses PL Sonnenbrille *f*; **sunhat** N Sonnenhut *m*

sunk [sʌŋk] PTP *of* **sink**[1]

sunken ['sʌŋkən] ADJ *ship* gesunken; *treasure* versunken; *garden* abgesenkt; *bath* eingelassen; *cheeks* eingefallen, hohl; *eyes* eingesunken

sun: sun lamp N Höhensonne *f*; **sunlight** N Sonnenlicht *nt*; **in the ~** in der Sonne; **sunlit** ADJ *room* sonnig; *fields etc also* sonnenbeschienen; **sun lounger** N Sonnenliege *f*

sunny ['sʌnɪ] ADJ (+ER) sonnig; (*fig*) *smile, disposition also* heiter; **to look on the ~ side (of things)** die Dinge von der angenehmen Seite nehmen

sun: sunrise N Sonnenaufgang *m*; **at ~** bei Sonnenaufgang; **sunroof** N (*of car*) Schiebedach *nt*; **sunset** N Sonnenuntergang *m*; **at ~** bei Sonnenuntergang; **sunshade** N Sonnenschirm *m*; **sunshine** N Sonnenschein *m*; **a daily average of 5 hours' ~** durchschnittlich 5 Stunden Sonne täglich; **sunstroke** N Sonnenstich *m*; **to get ~** einen Sonnenstich bekommen; **suntan** N Sonnenbräune *f*; **to get a ~** braun werden; **~ lotion/oil** Sonnenöl *nt*; **suntanned** ADJ braun gebrannt; **sunup** N (*US*) Sonnenaufgang *m*; **at ~** bei Sonnenaufgang

super ['su:pə*ʳ*] ADJ (*dated esp Brit inf*) fantastisch, klasse *inv* (*inf*); **~!** Klasse! (*inf*); **we had a ~ time** es war große Klasse (*inf*) *or* fantastisch

superabundance [,su:pərə'bʌndəns] N (*of an* +*dat*) großer Reichtum *m*; (= *excessive amount*) Überfluss *m*

superb [su:'pɜ:b] ADJ großartig; *design, painting also* meisterhaft; *quality, food also* vorzüglich

superbly [su:'pɜ:blɪ] ADV großartig; **~ fit** ungemein fit; **~ well** großartig, hervorragend

Superbowl ['su:pə,bəʊl] N (US) Superbowl m, jährlich
ausgetragenes American-Football-Turnier zwischen den
Spitzenreitern der beiden großen nationalen Ligen in den USA

supercilious ADJ, **superciliously** ADV ['su:pə'sɪlɪəs, -lɪ]
hochnäsig

super: supercomputer N Supercomputer m; **super-duper**
[,su:pə'du:pə'] ADJ (hum inf) ganz toll (inf)

superficial [,su:pə'fɪʃəl] ADJ oberflächlich; resemblance
äußerlich

superficially [,su:pə'fɪʃəlɪ] ADV oberflächlich; similar, different
äußerlich

superfluous [so'pɜ:flʊəs] ADJ überflüssig; style
verschwenderisch

super: superglue N Sekundenkleber m; **superhighway** N (US)
≈ Autobahn f; **the information ~** die Datenautobahn;
superhuman ADJ übermenschlich

superimpose [,su:pərɪm'pəʊz] VT **to ~ sth on sth** etw auf etw
(acc) legen; (Phot) etw über etw (acc) fotografieren; (fig) etw
mit etw überlagern; **the images were ~d** die Bilder hatten
sich überlagert

superintendent [,su:pərɪn'tendənt] N (US: in building)
Hausmeister(in) m(f); (of police) (Brit) ≈ Kommissar(in) m(f);
(US) ≈ Polizeipräsident(in) m(f)

superior [so'pɪərɪə'] ⬛1 ADJ (a) (= better) besser (to als); intellect,
ability überlegen (to sb/sth jdm/einer Sache); **he thinks he's so
~** er hält sich für so viel besser
(b) (= excellent) work(manship) großartig, hervorragend;
intellect überragend; **goods of ~ quality, ~ quality goods**
Waren pl bester Qualität
(c) (= higher in rank etc) höher; **~ officer** Vorgesetzte(r) mf; **to
be ~ to sb/sth** jdm/einer Sache übergeordnet sein
(d) forces stärker (to als); strength größer (to als)
(e) (= snobbish) überheblich; tone, smile überlegen; (= smart)
restaurant fein, vornehm
⬛2 N (in rank) Vorgesetzte(r) mf

superiority [so,pɪər'ɒrɪtɪ] N (a) (of cloth etc) bessere Qualität; (of
technique etc) Überlegenheit f (b) (= excellence) Großartigkeit
f (c) (in rank) höhere Stellung, höherer Rang
(d) (= conceitedness) Überheblichkeit f; (of tone, smile)
Überlegenheit f

superlative [so'pɜ:lətɪv] ⬛1 ADJ überragend, unübertrefflich;
(Gram) superlativisch ⬛2 N Superlativ m

supermarket ['su:pə,mɑ:kɪt] N Supermarkt m

supernatural [,su:pə'nætʃərəl] ⬛1 ADJ übernatürlich ⬛2 N **the ~**
das Übernatürliche

supernova [su:pə'nəʊvə] N, pl **-s** or **-e** [-'nəʊvi:] Supernova f

superpower ['su:pə,paʊə'] N (Pol) Supermacht f

superscript ['su:pə,skrɪpt] ADJ hochgestellt

supersede [,su:pə'si:d] VT ablösen

supersonic [,su:pə'sɒnɪk] ADJ Überschall-

superstar ['su:pəstɑ:'] N (Super)star m

superstition [,su:pə'stɪʃən] N Aberglaube m no pl; **this is a ~** das
ist Aberglaube

superstitious [,su:pə'stɪʃəs] ADJ abergläubisch; **to be ~ about
sth** in Bezug auf etw (acc) abergläubisch sein

superstore ['su:pəstɔ:'] N Verbrauchermarkt m

superstructure ['su:pə,strʌktʃə'] N Überbau m

supertanker ['su:pə,tæŋkə'] N Supertanker m

supervise ['su:pəvaɪz] ⬛1 VT beaufsichtigen; work also
überwachen ⬛2 VI Aufsicht führen

supervision [su:pə'vɪʒən] N Aufsicht f; (= action)
Beaufsichtigung f; (of work) Überwachung f

supervisor ['su:pəvaɪzə'] N (of work) Aufseher(in) m(f), Aufsicht
f; (Brit Univ) ≈ Tutor(in) m(f); (for PhD) Doktorvater m/
-mutter f

supervisory ['su:pəvaɪzərɪ]: **supervisory board** N (Comm, Ind)
Aufsichtsrat m; **supervisory body** N Aufsichtsgremium nt

supper ['sʌpə'] N (= evening meal) Abendessen nt, Abendbrot
nt; (= late evening snack) (später) Imbiss; **to have ~** zu Abend
essen, Abendbrot essen

suppertime ['sʌpətaɪm] N Abendessenszeit f, Abendbrotzeit f;
at ~ zur Abendbrotzeit

supplant [sə'plɑ:nt] VT ablösen, ersetzen; (forcibly) verdrängen;
(by ruse) rival ausstechen

supple [sʌpl] ADJ (+ER) geschmeidig, elastisch; person
beweglich

supplement ['sʌplɪmənt] ⬛1 N (a) Ergänzung f (to +gen); (of
book) Ergänzungsband m (to zu); (= at end of book) Anhang
m; (= food ~) Zusatz m; **a ~ to his pension** eine Aufbesserung
seiner Rente (b) (= colour ~ etc) Beilage f ⬛2 VT ergänzen;
income also aufbessern

supplementary [,sʌplɪ'mentərɪ] ADJ zusätzlich, ergänzend

suppleness ['sʌplnɪs] N Geschmeidigkeit f, Elastizität f; (of
person) Beweglichkeit f

supplier [sə'plaɪə'] N (Comm) Lieferant(in) m(f)

supply [sə'plaɪ] ⬛1 N (a) (= supplying) Versorgung f; (Comm:
= delivery, what is supplied) Lieferung f (to an +acc); (Econ)
Angebot nt; **electricity ~** Stromversorgung f; **~ and demand**
Angebot und Nachfrage (+pl vb); **to cut off the ~** (of gas,
water etc) das Gas/Wasser abstellen; **where does the badger
get its food ~?** woher bekommt der Dachs seine Nahrung?
(b) (= stock) Vorrat m; **supplies** pl (= food) Vorräte pl; (for
expedition also) Proviant m; **a good ~ of coal** ein guter
Kohlenvorrat; **to get** or **lay in supplies** or **a ~ of sth** sich (dat)
einen Vorrat an etw (dat) anlegen or zulegen; **a month's ~** ein
Monatsbedarf m; **to be in short ~** knapp sein; **to be in good
~** reichlich vorhanden sein; **medical supplies** Arzneimittel
pl; (including bandages) Ärztebedarf m
⬛2 VT (a) material, food etc sorgen für; (= deliver) goods,
information, electricity etc liefern; (= put at sb's disposal) stellen;
pens and paper are supplied by the firm Schreibmaterial wird
von der Firma gestellt
(b) (with mit) person, army, city versorgen; (Comm) beliefern
(c) (= satisfy, Comm) demand decken

supply: supply contract N Liefervertrag m; **supply industry** N
Zulieferungsindustrie f; **supply lines, supply routes** PL (Mil,
fig) Versorgungslinien pl; **supply-side** ADJ angebotsseitig;
supply-side economics N SING or PL Angebotswirtschaft f;
supply teacher N (Brit) Aushilfslehrer(in) m(f)

support [sə'pɔ:t] ⬛1 N (lit, fig: = person) Stütze f; (fig: no pl:
= moral, financial backing) Unterstützung f; **to give ~ to sb/sth**
jdn/etw stützen; **to lean on sb for ~** sich auf jdn stützen; **in
~ of** zur Unterstützung (+gen); **to speak in ~ of sb/sth** etw/jdn
unterstützen
⬛2 ATTR (Mil etc) Hilfs-
⬛3 VT (a) (lit) stützen; (= bear the weight of) tragen
(b) (fig) unterstützen (also Comput); plan, motion, sb's
application befürworten; (= give moral ~ to) beistehen (+dat);
claim, theory untermauern; (financially) family unterhalten;
party finanziell unterstützen; **he ~s Arsenal** er ist Arsenal-
Anhänger m; **which team do you ~?** für welche Mannschaft
bist du?; **without his family to ~ him** ohne die Unterstützung
seiner Familie
⬛4 VR (physically) sich stützen (on auf +acc); (financially) seinen
Unterhalt (selbst) bestreiten

support: support agency N (Fin, Pol) Sonderorganisation f;
support band N Vorgruppe f

supporter [sə'pɔ:tə'] N Anhänger(in) m(f); (of theory, cause also)
Befürworter(in) m(f); (Sport also) Fan m; **~s' club** Fanklub m

support group N Unterstützungsgruppe f

supporting [sə'pɔ:tɪŋ] ADJ (a) documents zur Unterstützung; **~
role** (lit, fig) Nebenrolle f (b) (Tech: = load-bearing) stützend,
tragend; **~ wall** Stützwand f

supporting: supporting actor N (Film, Theat) Nebendarsteller
m; **supporting actress** N (Film, Theat) Nebendarstellerin f

supportive [sə'pɔ:tɪv] ADJ stützend attr; (fig) unterstützend attr;
if his parents had been more ~ wenn seine Eltern ihn mehr
unterstützt hätten

supportiveness [sə'pɔ:tɪvnɪs] N Unterstützung f

suppose [sə'pəʊz] VT (a) (= imagine) sich (dat) vorstellen;
(= assume, believe) annehmen; **let us ~ we are living in the 8th
century** stellen wir uns einmal vor, wir lebten im 8.
Jahrhundert; **let us ~ that X equals 3** angenommen, X sei
gleich 3; **~ they could see us now!** wenn sie uns jetzt sehen
könnten!; **I ~ he'll come** ich nehme an, (dass) er kommt; **I
don't ~ he'll come** ich glaube kaum, dass er kommt; **I ~ that's
the best thing, that's the best thing, I ~** das ist or wäre
vermutlich das Beste; **you're coming, I ~?** ich nehme an, du
kommst?; **I don't ~ you could lend me a pound?** Sie könnten
mir nicht zufällig ein Pfund leihen?; **will he be coming? – I ~
so** kommt er? – ich denke or glaube schon; **you ought to be**

leaving – I ~ so du solltest jetzt gehen – stimmt wohl; **don't you agree with me? – I ~ so** bist du da nicht meiner Meinung? – na ja, schon; **I don't ~ so** ich glaube kaum; **so you see, it can't be true – I ~ not** da siehst du selbst, es kann nicht stimmen – du wirst wohl Recht haben; **he can't very well refuse, can he? – I ~ not** er kann wohl kaum ablehnen, oder? – eigentlich nicht; **he is generally ~d to be rich** er gilt als reich; **he's ~d to be coming** er soll (angeblich) kommen; **~ you have a wash?** wie wärs, wenn du dich mal wäschst? **(b)** (*modal use in pass: = ought*) **to be ~d to do sth** etw tun sollen; **he's the one who's ~d to do it** er müsste es eigentlich tun; **he isn't ~d to find out** er darf es nicht erfahren; **you're not ~d to (do that)** das darfst du nicht tun; **you're ~d to report to the police** Sie müssen sich bei der Polizei melden

supposed [səˈpəʊzd] ADJ vermutet; *date of birth, author also* mutmaßlich; *insult, glamour* angeblich

supposedly [səˈpəʊzɪdlɪ] ADV angeblich

supposing [səˈpəʊzɪŋ] CONJ angenommen; **but ~ ...** aber wenn ...; **~ he can't do it?** und wenn er es nicht schafft?; **even ~ that ...** sogar wenn ...; **always ~ ...** immer unter der Annahme, dass ...

suppository [səˈpɒzɪtərɪ] N Zäpfchen *nt*

suppress [səˈpres] VT unterdrücken; *appetite* zügeln; *information, evidence* zurückhalten

suppression [səˈpreʃən] N Unterdrückung *f*; (*of appetite*) Zügelung *f*; (*of information, evidence*) Zurückhalten *nt*

supra- [ˈsuːprə-] PREF über-; (*esp with foreign words*) supra-; **~national** supra- *or* übernational

supremacy [sʊˈpreməsɪ] N Vormachtstellung *f*; (*Pol, Eccl, fig*) Supremat *nt or m*; **air ~** Luftherrschaft *f*

supreme [sʊˈpriːm] **1** ADJ **(a)** (= *highest in authority*) höchste(r, s); *court* oberste(r, s) **(b)** *indifference etc* äußerste(r, s), größte(r, s); **to make the ~ sacrifice** das höchste Opfer bringen **2** ADV **to rule** *or* **reign ~** (*monarch*) absolut herrschen; (*champion, justice*) unangefochten herrschen

supreme commander N Oberbefehlshaber(in) *m(f)*

supremely [sʊˈpriːmlɪ] ADV confident, indifferent zutiefst; important, elegant überaus; **she does her job ~ well** sie macht ihre Arbeit außerordentlich gut

surcharge [ˈsɜːtʃɑːdʒ] **1** N Zuschlag *m* **2** VT Zuschlag erheben auf (*+acc*)

sure [ʃʊəʳ] **1** ADJ (*+ER*) sicher; *proof* eindeutig; *method, remedy* zuverlässig; **it's ~ to rain** es regnet ganz bestimmt; **be ~ to tell me** sag mir auf jeden Fall Bescheid; **be ~ to turn the gas off** vergiss nicht, das Gas abzudrehen; **be ~ to go and see her** du musst sie unbedingt besuchen; **you're ~ of a good meal** ein gutes Essen ist Ihnen sicher; **to make ~** (= *check*) nachsehen, kontrollieren; **make ~ you get the leads the right way round** achten Sie darauf, dass die Kabel richtig herum sind; **make ~ you take your keys** denk daran, deine Schlüssel mitzunehmen; **I've made ~ that there's enough coffee for everyone** ich habe dafür gesorgt, dass genug Kaffee für alle da ist; **~ thing!** (*esp US inf*) klare Sache! (*inf*); **he'll quit for ~** er kündigt ganz bestimmt; **I'll find out for ~** ich werde das genau herausfinden; **do you know for ~?** wissen Sie das ganz sicher?; **I'm ~ she's right** ich bin sicher, sie hat Recht; **do you want to see that film? – I'm not ~** willst du diesen Film sehen? – ich bin mir nicht sicher; **to be ~ about sth** sich (*dat*) einer Sache (*gen*) sicher sein; **I'm not so ~ about that** da bin ich nicht so sicher; **to be ~ of one's facts** seiner Fakten sicher sein; **to be ~ of oneself** (= *generally self-confident*) selbstsicher sein **2** ADV **(a)** (*inf*) **will you do it? – ~!** machst du das? – klar! (*inf*); **that meat was ~ tough** *or* **~ was tough** das Fleisch war vielleicht zäh!; **as ~ as ~ can be, as ~ as I'm standing here** garantiert, todsicher (*inf*) **(b)** **and ~ enough he did come** und er ist tatsächlich gekommen; **he'll come ~ enough** er kommt ganz bestimmt

sure-footed [ʃʊəˈfʊtɪd] ADJ (tritt)sicher

surely [ʃʊəlɪ] ADV **(a)** bestimmt, sicher; **~ you don't mean it?** das meinen Sie doch bestimmt *or* sicher nicht (so)?; **~ not!** das kann doch nicht stimmen!; **~ someone must know the answer** irgendjemand muss doch die Antwort wissen; **but ~ you can't expect us to believe that** Sie können doch wohl nicht erwarten, dass wir das glauben!; **~ to God** *or* **goodness** (*inf*) sicherlich **(b)** (= *inevitably, with certainty*) zweifellos

(c) (= *confidently*) mit sicherer Hand; **slowly but ~** langsam aber sicher

surety [ˈʃʊərətɪ] N **to stand ~ for sb** für jdn bürgen

surf [sɜːf] **1** N Brandung *f* **2** VI surfen **3** VT **to ~ the Net** (*inf*) im (Inter)net surfen (*inf*)

surface [ˈsɜːfɪs] **1** N **(a)** (*lit, fig*) Oberfläche *f*; (*of road*) Belag *m*; **on the ~ it seems that ...** oberflächlich sieht es so aus, als ob ...; **on the ~ he is friendly enough** nach außen hin ist er sehr freundlich **(b)** (*Min*) **at/on/up to the ~** über Tage **2** ADJ ATTR **(a)** oberflächlich **(b)** (= *not by air*) auf dem Land-/Seeweg **3** VT *road* mit einem Belag versehen **4** VI (*lit, fig*) auftauchen

surface: **surface area** N Fläche *f*; **surface mail** N **by ~** auf dem Land-/Seeweg; **surface-to-air** ADJ ATTR **~ missile** Boden-Luft-Rakete *f*

surfboard [ˈsɜːfbɔːd] N Surfbrett *nt*

surfeit [ˈsɜːfɪt] N Übermaß *nt* (*of an +dat*)

surfer [ˈsɜːfəʳ] N Surfer(in) *m(f)*

surfing [ˈsɜːfɪŋ] N Surfen *nt*

surge [sɜːdʒ] **1** N (*of sea*) Wogen *nt*; (*of floodwater*) Schwall *m*; (*Elec*) Spannungsstoß *m*; **he felt a sudden ~ of rage** er fühlte, wie die Wut in ihm aufstieg; **a ~ in demand** ein rascher Nachfrageanstieg **2** VI (*sea*) branden; (*floods, river*) anschwellen; (*demand, exports*) rasch ansteigen; **they ~d toward(s)/(a)round him** sie drängten auf ihn zu/umdrängten ihn; **people ~d in/out** eine Menschenmenge flutete herein/heraus; **to ~ ahead/forward** vorpreschen

surgeon [ˈsɜːdʒən] N Chirurg(in) *m(f)*

surgery [ˈsɜːdʒərɪ] N **(a)** Chirurgie *f*; **to have ~** operiert werden; **to need (heart) ~** (am Herzen) operiert werden müssen; **to undergo major heart ~** sich einer größeren Herzoperation unterziehen **(b)** (*Brit*) (= *room*) Sprechzimmer *nt*; (= *consultation*) Sprechstunde *f*; **~ hours** Sprechstunden *pl*

surgical [ˈsɜːdʒɪkəl] ADJ *treatment* operativ; *technique, instrument, training* chirurgisch

surgically [ˈsɜːdʒɪkəlɪ] ADV *treat, remove* operativ

surgical mask N OP-Maske *f*

surging [ˈsɜːdʒɪŋ] ADJ *water, crowd* wogend; *price, power, demand, exports* rasch ansteigend

surliness [ˈsɜːlɪnɪs] N Verdrießlichkeit *f*

surly [ˈsɜːlɪ] ADJ (*+ER*) verdrießlich

surmise [sɜːˈmaɪz] VT vermuten, mutmaßen

surmount [sɜːˈmaʊnt] VT überwinden

surname [ˈsɜːneɪm] N Nachname *m*, Familienname *m*; **what is his ~?** wie heißt er mit Nachnamen?

surpass [sɜːˈpɑːs] **1** VT **(a)** (= *be better than*) übertreffen **(b)** (= *exceed*) **to ~ all expectations** alle Erwartungen übertreffen **2** VR sich selbst übertreffen

surplus [ˈsɜːpləs] **1** N Überschuss *m* (*of an +dat*) **2** ADJ überschüssig; (*of countable objects*) überzählig; **~ capacity** Überkapazität *f*; **~ value** Mehrwert *m*; **sale of ~ stock** Verkauf *m* von Lagerbeständen; **have you any ~ sheets I could borrow?** hast du Laken übrig, die ich mir borgen könnte?

surplus: **surplus assets** PL (*Comm, Fin*) Vermögensüberschuss *m*; **surplus lines** PL (*Comm*) Überschusswaren *pl*

surprise [səˈpraɪz] **1** N Überraschung *f*; **in ~** voller Überraschung, überrascht; **it came as a ~ to us** wir waren überrascht; **to give sb a ~** jdn überraschen; **to take sb by ~** jdn überraschen; **~, ~, it's me!** rate mal, wer hier ist?; **~, ~!** (*iro*) was du nicht sagst! **2** ATTR Überraschungs-, überraschend **3** VT überraschen; **you ~ me!** (*also iro*) das überrascht mich!; **I was ~d to hear it** ich war überrascht, das zu hören; **I wouldn't be ~d if ...** es würde mich nicht wundern, wenn ...; **I'm ~d at** *or* **by his ignorance** ich bin überrascht über seine Unkenntnis; **I'm ~d you didn't think of that** es wundert mich, dass du nicht daran gedacht hast; **go on, ~ me!** ich lass mich überraschen!

surprising [səˈpraɪzɪŋ] ADJ überraschend, erstaunlich; **there's nothing ~ about that** das ist nicht weiter verwunderlich

surprisingly [səˈpraɪzɪŋlɪ] ADV überraschend; **~ (enough), he was right** er hatte erstaunlicherweise Recht; **not ~ it didn't work** wie zu erwarten (war), hat es nicht geklappt

surreal [səˈrɪəl] ADJ unwirklich

surrealism [səˈrɪəlɪzəm] N Surrealismus *m*

surrender [sə'rendə^r] **1** VI sich ergeben (*to* +*dat*); (*to police*) sich stellen (*to* +*dat*); **I ~!** ich ergebe mich! **2** VT (*Mil*) übergeben; *firearms also, control, title, lead* abgeben; *goods* ausliefern; *insurance policy* einlösen; *claim* aufgeben **3** N (**a**) (*Mil*) Kapitulation *f* (*to* vor +*dat*) (**b**) (= *handing over*) Übergabe *f* (*to* an +*acc*); (*of control, title, lead*) Abgabe *f*; (*of claim*) Aufgabe *f*

surrogate ['sʌrəgɪt] **1** N (= *substitute*) Ersatz *m* **2** ATTR Ersatz-

surrogate mother N Leihmutter *f*

surround [sə'raʊnd] **1** N (*esp Brit*) Umrandung *f*; **the ~s** die Umgebung **2** VT umgeben; (*Mil*) umzingeln

surrounding [sə'raʊndɪŋ] ADJ umliegend; **in the ~ countryside** in der Umgebung

surroundings [sə'raʊndɪŋz] PL Umgebung *f*

surtax ['sɜːtæks] N Steuerzuschlag *m*

surveillance [sɜː'veɪləns] N Überwachung *f*; **to be under ~** überwacht *or* observiert (*form*) werden; **to keep sb under ~** jdn überwachen *or* observieren (*form*)

survey ['sɜːveɪ] **1** N (**a**) (*Surv*) (*of land*) Vermessung *f*; (= *report*) (Vermessungs)gutachten *nt*; (*of house*) Begutachtung *f*; (= *report*) Gutachten *nt* (**b**) (= *inquiry*) Untersuchung *f* (*of, on* über +*acc*); (*by opinion poll etc*) Umfrage *f* (*of, on* über +*acc*) **2** [sɜː'veɪ] VT (**a**) (= *look at*) *countryside, person, prospects, plans* betrachten; **to ~ the situation** (*lit, fig*) die Lage peilen (**b**) (= *study*) *developments* untersuchen; *events, trends* einen Überblick geben über (+*acc*) (**c**) (*Surv*) *land* vermessen; *building* inspizieren

surveyor [sə'veɪə^r] N (*land* ~) Landvermesser(in) *m(f)*; (= *building* ~) Bauinspektor(in) *m(f)*

survival [sə'vaɪvəl] N Überleben *nt*; (*of customs, usages*) Weiterleben *nt*; **the ~ of the fittest** das Überleben der Stärkeren

survival kit N Überlebensausrüstung *f*

survive [sə'vaɪv] **1** VI (*person, animal etc*) überleben; (*in job*) sich halten (können); (*treasures, play*) erhalten bleiben; (*custom*) weiterleben; **only five copies ~ or have ~d** nur fünf Exemplare sind erhalten **2** VT überleben; *experience, accident also* (lebend) überstehen; (*house, objects*) *fire, flood* überstehen; (*inf*) *heat etc* aushalten

surviving [sə'vaɪvɪŋ] ADJ (**a**) (= *still living*) noch lebend (**b**) (= *remaining*) noch existierend

survivor [sə'vaɪvə^r] N Überlebende(r) *mf*; (*Jur*) Hinterbliebene(r) *mf*; (*of abuse etc*) Opfer *nt*; **he's a ~** (*fig: in politics etc*) er ist ein Überlebenskünstler

susceptible [sə'septəbl] ADJ leicht zu beeindrucken *pred*; **~ to sth** *to flattery etc* für etw empfänglich; *to suggestion, influence etc* einer Sache (*dat*) zugänglich; *to attack* einer Sache (*dat*) ausgesetzt; *to colds* für etw anfällig; **~ to pain** schmerzempfindlich

suspect ['sʌspekt] **1** ADJ verdächtig **2** ['sʌspekt] N Verdächtige(r) *mf* **3** [sə'spekt] VT (**a**) *person* verdächtigen (*of sth* einer Sache *gen*); *swindle*, (= *think likely*) vermuten; **I ~ her of having stolen it** ich habe sie im Verdacht *or* ich verdächtige sie, es gestohlen zu haben; **the ~ed bank robber etc** der mutmaßliche Bankräuber *etc*; **he ~s nothing** er ahnt nichts; **does he ~ anything?** hat er Verdacht geschöpft?; **I ~ed as much** das habe ich mir doch gedacht; **he was taken to hospital with a ~ed heart attack** er wurde mit dem Verdacht auf Herzinfarkt ins Krankenhaus eingeliefert (**b**) (= *doubt*) *truth* bezweifeln; *motive* argwöhnisch sein gegenüber

suspend [sə'spend] VT (**a**) (= *hang*) (auf)hängen (*from* an +*dat*); **to be ~ed in sth** in etw (*dat*) hängen (**b**) *publication, payment* (zeitweilig) einstellen; *talks, judgement* aussetzen; *flights* aufschieben; **he was given a ~ed sentence** eine Strafe wurde zur Bewährung ausgesetzt (**c**) *person* suspendieren; *member, student* zeitweilig ausschließen; (*Sport*) sperren; *privileges* aussetzen

suspender [sə'spendə^r] N USU PL (**a**) (*Brit: for stockings*) Strumpfhalter *m*; **~ belt** Strumpf(halter)gürtel *m* (**b**) (*US*) **suspenders** PL Hosenträger *pl*

suspense [sə'spens] N Spannung *f*; **the ~ is killing me** ich bin gespannt wie ein Flitzebogen (*hum inf*); **to keep sb in ~** jdn

auf die Folter spannen (*inf*); **to wait in ~** gespannt *or* voller Spannung warten

suspense account N Interimskonto *nt*

suspension [sə'spenʃən] N (**a**) (*of publication, payment*) zeitweilige Einstellung; (*of flights*) Aufschub *m*; (*of talks, judgement*) Aussetzung *f* (**b**) (*of person*) Suspendierung *f*; (*of member, student*) zeitweiliger Ausschluss; (*Sport*) Sperrung *f*; (*of privileges*) Aussetzen *nt* (**c**) (*Aut*) Federung *f*; (*of wheels*) Aufhängung *f*

suspension bridge N Hängebrücke *f*

suspicion [sə'spɪʃən] N Verdacht *m no pl*; **to arouse sb's ~s** jds Verdacht erregen; **I have a ~ that ...** ich habe den Verdacht *or* das Gefühl, dass ...; **to have one's ~s about sth/sb** seine Zweifel bezüglich einer Sache (*gen*)/bezüglich einer Person (*gen*) haben; **my ~s were right** mein Verdacht hat sich bestätigt; **to be under ~** unter Verdacht stehen; **to arrest sb on ~ of murder** jdn wegen Mordverdachts festnehmen

suspicious [sə'spɪʃəs] ADJ (**a**) (= *feeling suspicion*) argwöhnisch, misstrauisch (*of* gegenüber); **to be ~ about sth** etw mit Misstrauen betrachten (**b**) (= *causing suspicion*) verdächtig

suspiciously [sə'spɪʃəslɪ] ADV (**a**) (= *with suspicion*) argwöhnisch, misstrauisch (**b**) (= *causing suspicion, probably*) verdächtig; **it sounds ~ as though ...** es hört sich verdächtig danach an, als ob ...

suss [sʌs] VT (*Brit inf*) (**a**) (= *suspect*) *plan* kommen hinter (+*acc*) (*inf*); **to ~ it** dahinter kommen (*inf*) (**b**) **to ~ sb out** jdm auf den Zahn fühlen (*inf*); **I can't ~ him out** bei ihm blicke ich nicht durch (*inf*); **I've got him ~ed (out)** ich habe ihn durchschaut; **to ~ sth out** etw herausbekommen

sustain [sə'steɪn] VT (**a**) *load, weight* aushalten, tragen; *life* erhalten; *family* unterhalten; *body* bei Kräften halten; **that isn't enough food to ~ you** das wird Ihnen nicht reichen (**b**) *argument, effort, support* aufrechterhalten; *growth, position* beibehalten; (*Jur*) **objection ~ed** Einspruch stattgegeben (**c**) *injury, damage, loss* erleiden

sustainable [sə'steɪnəbl] ADJ *aufrechtzuerhalten pred*, *aufrechtzuerhaltend attr*; *development, agriculture, growth* nachhaltig; *resources* erneuerbar; *level, argument* haltbar

sustained [sə'steɪnd] ADJ anhaltend (*also Econ*); *effort etc, applause also* ausdauernd

sustenance ['sʌstɪnəns] N (= *food and drink*) Nahrung *f*

suture ['suːtʃə^r] (*Med*) **1** N Naht *f* **2** VT (ver)nähen

SUV (*esp US Aut*) ABBR *of* **sport utility vehicle** SUV *m*, Geländewagen *m*

SVGA (*Comput*) ABBR *of* **super video graphics array** SVGA *nt*

SW ABBR (**a**) *of* **south-west** SW (**b**) *of* **short wave** KW

swab [swɒb] N (*Med*) Tupfer *m*; (= *specimen*) Abstrich *m*

Swabia ['sweɪbɪə] N Schwaben *nt*

swag [swæg] N (*inf*) Beute *f*

swagger ['swægə^r] **1** N (= *gait*) Stolzieren *nt*; (= *behaviour*) Angeberei *f* **2** VI (**a**) (= *strut*) stolzieren (**b**) (= *boast*) angeben

swallow[1] ['swɒləʊ] **1** N Schluck *m* **2** VT (hinunter)schlucken; (*fig*) *story, insult* schlucken; **to ~ one's pride** seinen Stolz schlucken; **to ~ sth whole** (*lit*) etw ganz schlucken; (*fig*) etw ohne weiteres schlucken; **that's a bit hard to ~** das glaubt ja kein Mensch (*inf*) **3** VI schlucken; **to ~ hard** (*fig*) kräftig schlucken

➤ **swallow down** VT SEP hinunterschlucken

➤ **swallow up** VT SEP (*fig*) verschlingen; **I wished the ground would open and swallow me up** ich hätte vor Scham in den Boden versinken können

swallow[2] N (= *bird*) Schwalbe *f*

swam [swæm] PRET *of* **swim**

swamp [swɒmp] **1** N Sumpf *m* **2** VT (*lit, fig*) überschwemmen

swampy ['swɒmpɪ] ADJ (+ER) sumpfig

swan [swɒn] **1** N Schwan *m* **2** VI (*Brit inf*) **to ~ off** abziehen (*inf*); **to ~ around (the house)** zu Hause herumschweben (*inf*)

swanky ['swæŋkɪ] ADJ (+ER) (*esp Brit inf*) *manner, party* großspurig; *car, restaurant, house etc* protzig (*inf*); *neighbourhood* hochnäsig

swap [swɒp] **1** N Tausch *m*, Tauschhandel *m*; **to do a ~ (with sb)** (mit jdm) tauschen **2** VT *stamps, cars etc* tauschen; *stories, addresses, insults* austauschen; **to ~ sth for sth** etw für etw eintauschen; **to ~ places with sb** mit jdm tauschen; **to ~ sides** die Seiten wechseln **3** VI tauschen

swap meet N (*US Comm*) Tauschbörse *f*

swarm [swɔːm] **1** N (*of insects, birds*) Schwarm *m*; (*of people also*) Schar *f* **2** VI (*bees, people*) schwärmen; **the place was ~ing with insects/people** es wimmelte von Insekten/Leuten

swarthy ['swɔːðɪ] ADJ (+ER) *skin* dunkel; *person also* dunkelhäutig

swastika ['swɒstɪkə] N Hakenkreuz *nt*

swat [swɒt] **1** VT *fly* totschlagen; *table* schlagen auf (+*acc*) **2** VI **to ~ at a fly** nach einer Fliege schlagen **3** N (= *fly ~*) Fliegenklatsche *f*

swathe [sweɪð] VT wickeln (*in* in +*acc*); (*in bandages also*) umwickeln (*in* mit)

sway [sweɪ] **1** N (a) (= *movement: of hips*) Wackeln *nt* (b) (= *influence*) Macht *f* (*over* über +*acc*); **to hold ~ over sb/a nation** jdn/ein Volk beherrschen **2** VI (*trees*) sich wiegen; (*hanging object*) schwingen; (*building, mast etc, unsteady person*) schwanken; (*train, boat*) schaukeln; (*hips*) wackeln; (*fig*) schwenken; **she ~s as she walks** sie wiegt beim Gehen die Hüften **3** VT (a) *hips* wiegen; (*wind*) hin und her bewegen (b) (= *influence*) beeinflussen; (= *change sb's mind*) umstimmen

swear [sweəʳ], *vb: pret* **swore**, *ptp* **sworn 1** VT (a) *allegiance, love, revenge* schwören; *oath* leisten; **I ~ it!** ich kann das beschwören! (b) (*Jur*) *witness, jury* vereidigen; **to ~ sb to secrecy** jdn schwören lassen, dass er nichts verrät **2** VI (a) (= *use solemn oath*) schwören; **to ~ to sth** etw beschwören; **to ~ blind** *or* (*US*) **up and down that ...** (*inf*) Stein und Bein schwören, dass ... (*inf*) (b) (= *use swearwords*) fluchen (*about* über +*acc*); **to ~ at sb/sth** jdn/etw beschimpfen

➤ **swear by** VI +PREP OBJ (*inf*) schwören auf (+*acc*)
➤ **swear in** VT SEP *witness etc* vereidigen

swearing ['sweərɪŋ] N Fluchen *nt*

swearword ['sweəwɜːd] N Fluch *m*, Kraftausdruck *m*

sweat [swet] **1** N Schweiß *m* no *pl*; **drops/beads of ~** Schweißtropfen *pl*/-perlen *pl*; **his face was running with ~** der Schweiß rann ihm von der Stirn; **to get into a ~ about sth** (*fig*) wegen etw ins Schwitzen geraten *or* kommen; **no ~** (*inf*) kein Problem **2** VI schwitzen (*with* vor +*dat*); (*fig inf*) (= *work hard*) sich abrackern (*inf*) (*over* mit); (= *worry*) zittern, schwitzen (*inf*) (*with* vor +*dat*); **to ~ like a pig** (*inf*) wie ein Affe schwitzen (*inf*) **3** VT **to ~ buckets** (*inf*) wie ein Affe schwitzen (*inf*); **to ~ blood** (*with worry*) Blut und Wasser schwitzen; (*with effort*) sich abrackern (*inf*)

➤ **sweat out** VT SEP (a) *fever* herausschwitzen (b) **to sweat it out** (*fig inf*) durchhalten; (= *sit and wait*) abwarten

sweatband ['swetbænd] N Schweißband *nt*

sweater ['swetəʳ] N Pullover *m*

sweat: sweat pants PL (*esp US*) Jogginghose *f*; **sweatshirt** N Sweatshirt *nt*; (*Sport*) Trainingspullover *m*; **sweatshop** N (*pej, hum inf*) Ausbeuterbetrieb *m* (*pej*)

sweaty ['swetɪ] ADJ (+ER) *hands* schweißig; *body, socks* verschwitzt; *work* zum Schwitzen; *place* heiß; **to get ~** ins Schwitzen geraten; **~ feet** Schweißfüße *pl*

Swede [swiːd] N Schwede *m*, Schwedin *f*

swede [swiːd] N (*esp Brit*) Kohlrübe *f*

Sweden ['swiːdn] N Schweden *nt*

Swedish ['swiːdɪʃ] **1** ADJ schwedisch; **he is ~** er ist Schwede **2** N (a) (*Ling*) Schwedisch *nt* (b) **the ~ pl** die Schweden *pl*

sweep [swiːp], *vb: pret, ptp* **swept 1** N (a) **to give the floor a ~** den Boden kehren *or* fegen (b) (= *chimney ~*) Schornsteinfeger(in) *m(f)* (c) (*of arm*) Schwung *m*; (*of light, radar*) Strahl *m*; **in one ~** (*fig*) auf einen Schwung; **the police made a ~ of the district** die Polizei hat die Gegend abgesucht; **to make a clean ~** (*fig*) gründlich aufräumen (d) (= *curve, line, of road, river*) Bogen *m*; **a wide ~ of country** eine sich weit ausdehnende Landschaft **2** VT (a) *floor, street, chimney* fegen; *room* (aus)fegen; *dust, snow* wegfegen; **to ~ sth under the carpet** (*fig*) etw unter den Teppich kehren

(b) (= *scan*) absuchen (*for* nach)
(c) (= *move quickly over*) (*wind*) fegen über (+*acc*); (*waves, protest, violence, fashion*) überrollen; (*glance*) gleiten über (+*acc*); (*disease*) um sich greifen in (+*dat*)
(d) (= *remove with sweeping movement*) (*wave*) spülen, schwemmen; (*current*) *person* reißen; (*wind*) fegen; **to ~ sth onto the floor** etw zu Boden fegen
(e) (= *triumph*) große Triumphe feiern in (+*dat*); **to ~ the board** (*fig*) alle Preise/Medaillen gewinnen, abräumen (*inf*) **3** VI (a) (*with broom*) kehren, fegen
(b) (= *move*) (*person*) rauschen; (*vehicle, plane*) (*quickly*) schießen; (*majestically*) gleiten; (*road, river*) in weitem Bogen führen; **the disease swept through Europe** die Krankheit breitete sich in Europa aus

➤ **sweep along** VT SEP (*lit, fig*) mitreißen
➤ **sweep aside** VT SEP (*lit, fig*) wegfegen
➤ **sweep away 1** VI = **sweep off 2** VT SEP *leaves etc* wegfegen; (*storm also, avalanche*) wegreißen; (*flood etc*) wegspülen, wegschwemmen; (*fig*) *old laws* aufräumen mit; *doubts* zerstreuen; *opposition* vernichten
➤ **sweep down** VI **to sweep down on sb** über jdn herfallen
➤ **sweep off** VT SEP **to sweep sb off his/her feet** (*lit*) jdn umreißen; **he swept her off her feet** (*fig*) sie hat sich Hals über Kopf in ihn verliebt
➤ **sweep out 1** VI hinausrauschen **2** VT SEP *room* ausfegen; *dust* hinausfegen
➤ **sweep up 1** VI (a) (*with broom*) zusammenfegen; **to sweep up after sb** hinter jdm herfegen (b) (= *move*) **she swept up in a Rolls Royce** sie rollte in einem Rolls Royce vor **2** VT SEP zusammenfegen; (= *collect up*) *objects* zusammenraffen; *person* hochreißen; *hair* hochbinden

sweeper ['swiːpəʳ] N (= *carpet ~*) Teppichkehrer *m*

sweeping ['swiːpɪŋ] ADJ (a) *gesture, curve* weit ausholend; *staircase* geschwungen (b) (*fig*) *change, reduction* radikal, drastisch; *statement* pauschal; *victory* überragend

sweet [swiːt] **1** ADJ (+ER) (*lit, fig*) (= *fresh*) *food, water, air, breath* frisch; (= *kind*) lieb; **to have a ~ tooth** gern Süßes essen; **to keep sb ~** (*inf*) jdn bei Laune halten; **in his own ~ way** (*iro*) auf seine unübertroffene Art **2** N (a) (*Brit*: = *candy*) Bonbon *nt* (b) (*Brit*: = *dessert*) Nachtisch *m*, Dessert *nt*; **for ~** zum *or* als Nachtisch *or* Dessert

sweet: sweet-and-sour ADJ süßsauer; **sweetcorn** N Mais *m*

sweeten ['swiːtn] VT *coffee, sauce* süßen; *air, breath* reinigen; (*fig*) *temper* bessern; *task* versüßen; *deal* schmackhaft machen; **to ~ sb** (*inf*) jdn gnädig stimmen; **to ~ the pill** die bittere Pille versüßen

sweetener ['swiːtnəʳ] N (*Cook*) (*esp artificial*) Süßstoff *m*; (*inf*) (*to make sth more acceptable*) Anreiz *m*; (*inf*: = *bribe*) Schmiergeld *nt*

sweetheart ['swiːthaːt] N Schatz *m*, Liebste(r) *mf*

sweetish ['swiːtɪʃ] ADJ *taste, smell* süßlich

sweetly ['swiːtlɪ] ADV *sing, play* süß; *say, scented* süßlich; *smile also, answer* lieb

sweetness ['swiːtnɪs] N (*lit, fig*) Süße *f*; (*of smile, nature*) Liebenswürdigkeit *f*

sweet: sweet potato N Süßkartoffel *f*; **sweet shop** N (*Brit*) Süßwarenladen *m or* -geschäft *nt*; **sweet-smelling** ADJ süß riechend; **sweet-talk** VT (*inf*) **to ~ sb into doing sth** jdn mit süßen Worten dazu bringen, etw zu tun; **sweet-tempered** ADJ verträglich; **sweet trolley** N (*Brit*) Dessertwagen *m*

swell [swel], *vb: pret* **swelled**, *ptp* **swollen** *or* **swelled 1** N (*of sea*) Wogen *nt* no *pl* **2** ADJ (*esp US dated*: = *excellent*) klasse (*inf*), prima (*inf*) **3** VT *ankle, river, sound etc* anschwellen lassen; *stomach* (auf)blähen; *sail* blähen; *numbers* anwachsen lassen; **to be swollen with pride** stolzgeschwellt sein **4** VI (a) (*ankle, eye etc: also ~ up*) (an)schwellen; (*balloon, tyre*) sich füllen; **to ~ (up) with pride** vor Stolz anschwellen (b) (*river, lake, sound etc*) anschwellen; (*sails: also ~ out*) sich blähen; (*in size, number*) anwachsen; **the crowd ~ed to 2000** die Menschenmenge wuchs auf 2000 an

swelling ['swelɪŋ] **1** N (a) Verdickung *f*; (*Med*) Schwellung *f* (b) (*of population, debt etc*) Anwachsen *nt* **2** ADJ ATTR *ankle etc* (an)schwellend; *sails* gebläht; *sound* anschwellend; *numbers* anwachsend

swelter ['sweltəʳ] VI (*vor Hitze*) vergehen

sweltering ['sweltərɪŋ] ADJ *day* glühend heiß; *heat* glühend; **it's ~ in here** (inf) hier verschmachtet man ja! (inf)

swept [swept] PRET, PTP *of* **sweep**

swerve [swɜ:v] **1** N Bogen *m*; (*of road, coastline also*) Schwenkung *f* **2** VI einen Bogen machen; (*car, driver*) ausschwenken; (*ball*) im Bogen fliegen; **to ~ round sth** einen Bogen um etw machen; **the road ~s (round) to the right** die Straße schwenkt nach rechts; **the car ~d in and out of the traffic** der Wagen schoss im Slalom durch den Verkehrsstrom **3** VT *car etc* herumreißen; *ball* anschneiden

swift [swɪft] ADJ (+ER) schnell; *reaction also, revenge* prompt; **to take ~ action** schnell handeln; **to be ~ to do sth** etw schnell tun

swiftly ['swɪftlɪ] ADV schnell; *react* prompt; **time passes ~** die Zeit vergeht wie im Flug; **to act ~ to do sth** rasch handeln, um etw zu tun; **~ followed by ...** rasch gefolgt von ...

swiftness ['swɪftnɪs] N Schnelligkeit *f*; (*of reaction also*) Promptheit *f*; **the ~ of the current** die reißende Strömung

swig [swɪg] (inf) **1** N Schluck *m*; **to have** or **take a ~ of beer** einen Schluck Bier trinken **2** VT (*also ~ down*) herunterkippen (inf)

swill [swɪl] **1** N (a) (= *animal food*) (Schweine)futter *nt*; (= *garbage, slops*) (*solid*) Abfälle *pl*; (*liquid*) Schmutzwasser *nt*; (*fig pej*) (Schweine)fraß *m* (inf); (*liquid*) Abwaschwasser *nt* **(b)** (= *cleaning*) **to give sth a ~ (out/down) = swill 2(a) 2** VT (a) (*esp Brit: also ~ out*) ausschwenken; *cup* ausschwenken; **to ~ sth down** etw abspülen; **to ~ sth round** etw (herum)schwenken **(b)** (inf) *beer etc* kippen (inf); **he ~ed it down with beer** er hat es mit Bier runtergespült (inf)

swim [swɪm] *vb: pret* **swam**, *ptp* **swum 1** N **that was a nice ~** das (Schwimmen) hat Spaß gemacht!; **I like** or **enjoy a ~** ich schwimme gern (mal); **to have a ~** schwimmen **2** VT schwimmen; *river, Channel* durchschwimmen **3** VI schwimmen; **the room swam before my eyes** das Zimmer verschwamm vor meinen Augen; **my head is ~ming** mir dreht sich alles

swimmer ['swɪmə^r] N Schwimmer(in) *m(f)*

swimming ['swɪmɪŋ] N Schwimmen *nt*; **do you like ~?** schwimmen Sie gern?

swimming IN CPDS Schwimm-; **swimming bath** N USU PL (Brit) Schwimmbad *nt*; **swimming cap** N (Brit) Badekappe *f*, Bademütze *f*; **swimming costume** N (Brit) Badeanzug *m*; **swimming instructor** N Schwimmlehrer(in) *m(f)*; **swimming pool** N Schwimmbad *nt*; (*outdoor also*) Freibad *nt*; (*indoor also*) Hallenbad *nt*; **swimming trunks** PL (Brit) Badehose *f*

swimsuit ['swɪmsu:t] N Badeanzug *m*

swindle ['swɪndl] **1** N Schwindel *m*, Betrug *m* **2** VT *person* beschwindeln, betrügen; **to ~ sb out of sth** (= *take from*) jdm etw abschwindeln; (= *withhold from*) jdn um etw beschwindeln

swindler ['swɪndlə^r] N Schwindler(in) *m(f)*

swine [swaɪn] N (a) *pl* **-** (*old, form*) Schwein *nt* **(b)** *pl* **-s** (*pej inf*) (= *man*) (gemeiner) Hund (inf); (= *woman*) gemeine Sau (sl)

swing [swɪŋ] *vb: pret, ptp* **swung 1** N (a) Schwung *m*; (*to and fro*) Schwingen *nt*; (*fig, Pol*) (Meinungs)umschwung *m*; **to take a ~ at sb** nach jdm schlagen; **to be in ~** (*fig*) in voller Erfolg sein (inf); **to be in full ~** voll im Gang sein; **to get into the ~ of sth** *of new job etc* sich an etw (*acc*) gewöhnen; **to get into the ~ of things** (inf) reinkommen (inf) **(b)** (= *seat for swinging*) Schaukel *f*; **to have a ~** schaukeln **(c)** (*esp US: = scope, freedom*) **he was given full ~ to make decisions** man hat ihm bei allen Entscheidungen freie Hand gelassen **(d)** (Mus) Swing *m* **2** VT (a) schwingen; (*to and fro*) hin und her schwingen; (*on ~, hammock*) schaukeln; *arms* (vigorously) schwingen (mit); (= *dangle*) baumeln mit; **he swung himself over the wall/up** er schwang sich über die Mauer **(b)** *election, decision, voters* beeinflussen; *opinion* umschlagen lassen; **his speech swung the decision in our favour** seine Rede ließ die Entscheidung zu unseren Gunsten ausfallen; **to ~ it (so that ...)** (inf) es so drehen or deichseln (inf) (dass ...) **(c)** (*turn: also ~ round*) *plane, car* herumschwenken **3** VI schwingen; (*to and fro*) (hin und her) schwingen; (*on ~*) schaukeln; (*arms, legs: = dangle*) baumeln; (*into saddle etc*)

sich schwingen; **he swung at me with his axe** er schwang die Axt gegen mich; **the golfer swung at the ball** der Golfer holte aus; **to ~ open** aufschwingen; **to ~ shut** zuschlagen; **to ~ into action** in Aktion treten

➤ **swing across** VI hinüberschwingen; (*hand-over-hand*) sich hinüberhangeln

➤ **swing (a)round 1** VI (*person*) sich umdrehen; (*car, ship, plane*) herumschwenken; (*needle*) ausschlagen; (*fig: opinion*) umschwenken **2** VT SEP herumschwenken

➤ **swing back** VI zurückschwingen; (*opinion*) zurückschlagen

➤ **swing to** VI (*door*) zuschlagen

swing door N (Brit) Pendeltür *f*

swingeing ['swɪndʒɪŋ] ADJ (Brit) *cuts* extrem

swinging ['swɪŋɪŋ] ADJ **~ door** (US) Pendeltür *f*

swing: **swing shift** N (US Ind inf) Spätschicht *f*; **swing voter** N (*esp US Pol*) Wechselwähler(in) *m(f)*

swipe [swaɪp] **1** N (= *blow*) Schlag *m*; **to take** or **make a ~ at sb/ sth** nach jdm/etw schlagen **2** VT (a) *person, ball etc* schlagen **(b)** (inf: = *steal*) mopsen (inf), klauen (inf) **(c)** *credit card, entry card* durchziehen **3** VI **to ~ at sb/sth** nach jdm/etw schlagen

swipe card N Magnetstreifenkarte *f*

swirl [swɜ:l] **1** N Wirbel *m*; (= *whorl in pattern also*) Spirale *f* **2** VTI wirbeln; **to ~ around** herumwirbeln

swish [swɪʃ] **1** N (*of cane*) Zischen *nt*, Sausen *nt*; (*of skirts, water*) Rauschen *nt* **2** VT *cane* zischen or sausen lassen; *tail* schlagen mit; *skirt* rauschen mit; *water* schwenken; **she ~ed water round the bowl** sie schwenkte die Schüssel mit Wasser aus **3** VI (*cane*) zischen, sausen; (*skirts, water*) rauschen

Swiss [swɪs] **1** ADJ Schweizer, schweizerisch; **he is ~** er ist Schweizer; **the ~-German part of Switzerland** die deutsch(sprachig)e Schweiz **2** N Schweizer(in) *m(f)*; **the ~** *pl* die Schweizer *pl*

Swiss: **Swiss army knife** N Schweizermesser *nt*; **Swiss French** N (a) (= *person*) Welschschweizer(in) *m(f)* **(b)** (Ling) Schweizer Französisch *nt*; **Swiss German** N (a) (= *person*) Deutschschweizer(in) *m(f)* **(b)** (Ling) Schweizerdeutsch *nt*, Schwyzerdütsch *nt*; **Swiss roll** N (Brit) Biskuitrolle *f*

switch [swɪtʃ] **1** N (a) (*Elec etc*) Schalter *m* **(b)** (= *change*) Wechsel *m*; (*in plans, policies, opinion*) Änderung *f* (*in* +gen); (= *exchange*) Tausch *m* **(c)** (= *cane*) Rute *f*; (= *riding whip*) Gerte *f* **2** VT (a) (= *change, alter*) wechseln; *direction, plans* ändern; *allegiance* übertragen (*to* auf +*acc*); *attention, conversation* lenken (*to* auf +*acc*); **to ~ sides** die Seiten wechseln; **to ~ channels** auf einen anderen Kanal umschalten; **to ~ jobs** zu einer anderen Stelle überwechseln **(b)** (= *move*) *production* verlegen; *object* umstellen **(c)** (= *exchange*) tauschen; (*also ~ over, ~ round*) *objects, letters in word* vertauschen; **I ~ed hats with him** ich tauschte meinen Hut mit ihm; **to ~ A for B** A für or gegen B (ein)tauschen **(d)** (*Elec*) (um)schalten **3** VI (= *change: also ~ over*) (über)wechseln (*to* zu); (*Elec, TV*) umschalten (*to* auf +*acc*); (= *exchange: also ~ round, ~ over*) tauschen; **to ~ (over) from Y to Z** von Y auf Z (*acc*) (über)wechseln

➤ **switch (a)round 1** VT SEP (= *swap round*) vertauschen; (= *rearrange*) umstellen **2** VI = **switch 3(a)**

➤ **switch back 1** VI (*to original plan etc*) zum Alten zurückkehren; (*Elec, TV*) zurückschalten (*to* zu) **2** VT SEP **to switch the light back on** das Licht wieder anschalten

➤ **switch off 1** VT SEP *light* ausschalten; *radio, TV also, machine, engine* abschalten; *gas, water supply* abstellen **2** VI (*light*) ausschalten; (*radio, TV also, machine, engine, inf: person*) abschalten

➤ **switch on 1** VT SEP *gas, water* anstellen; *machine* anschalten; *radio, TV, light* einschalten; *engine* anlassen **2** VI (*machine*) anschalten; (*light*) einschalten; **the cooker will switch on at 10 o'clock** der Herd schaltet sich um 10 Uhr an or ein

➤ **switch over 1** VI = **switch 3(a) 2** VT SEP = **switch 2(c)**

switch: **switchblade** N (US) Schnappmesser *nt*; **switchboard** N (Telec) (= *exchange*) Vermittlung *f*; (*in office etc*) Zentrale *f*; **switch-over** N Wechsel *m* (*to* auf +*acc*, zu); (= *exchange*) Tausch *m*; (*of letters, figures etc*) Vertauschung *f*

Switzerland ['swɪtsələnd] N die Schweiz; **to** ~ in die Schweiz; **Italian-speaking** ~ die italienische Schweiz, die italienischsprachige Schweiz

swivel ['swɪvl] **1** N Drehgelenk *nt* **2** ATTR Dreh-; ~ **base** (*of monitor etc*) Schwenksockel *m* **3** VT (*also* ~ **round**) (herum)drehen **4** VI (*also* ~ **round**) sich drehen; (*person*) sich herumdrehen

swollen ['swəʊlən] **1** PTP *of* swell **2** ADJ (an)geschwollen; *stomach* aufgebläht; *river* angestiegen

swoon [swuːn] VI (*fig: over pop star etc*) beinahe ohnmächtig werden (*over sb/sth* wegen jdm/einer Sache)

swoop [swuːp] **1** VI (*lit: also* ~ **down**) (*bird*) herabstoßen (*on auf* +acc); (*plane*) einen Sturzflug machen; (*fig*) (*police*) einen Überraschungsangriff machen (*on auf* +acc); (*person*) sich stürzen (*on auf* +acc); **they're just waiting to** ~ die lauern nur darauf zuzuschlagen
2 N (*of bird, plane*) Sturzflug *m*; (*by police*) Razzia *f* (*on in* +dat, *on sb* bei jdm); **at** *or* **in one (fell)** ~ auf einen Schlag

swoosh [swuːʃ] **1** VI rauschen; (*air*) brausen **2** N Rauschen *nt*; (*of air*) Brausen *nt*

swop N, VTI = **swap**

sword [sɔːd] N Schwert *nt*

sword IN CPDS Schwert-; **swordfish** N Schwertfisch *m*

swore [swɔːʳ] PRET *of* swear

sworn [swɔːn] **1** PTP *of* swear **2** ADJ *enemy* eingeschworen; ~ **statement/testimony** (*Jur*) Aussage *f* unter Eid

swot [swɒt] (*Brit inf*) **1** VI büffeln (*inf*), pauken (*inf*); **to** ~ **up (on) one's maths** Mathe pauken (*inf*) **2** VT büffeln (*inf*), pauken (*inf*) **3** N (*pej: = person*) Streber(in) *m(f)*

swotting ['swɒtɪŋ] N (*Brit inf*) **to do some** ~ büffeln (*inf*), pauken (*inf*)

swum [swʌm] PTP *of* swim

swung [swʌŋ] PRET, PTP *of* swing

sycamore ['sɪkəmɔːʳ] N Bergahorn *m*; (*US: = plane tree*) nordamerikanische Platane; (*= wood*) Ahorn *m*

syllable ['sɪləbl] N Silbe *f*

syllabus ['sɪləbəs] N, *pl* **-es** *or* **syllabi** ['sɪləbaɪ] (*esp Brit: Sch, Univ*) Lehrplan *m*

symbol ['sɪmbəl] N Symbol *nt*, Zeichen *nt* (*of* für)

symbolic(al) [sɪm'bɒlɪk(əl)] ADJ symbolisch (*of* für); **to be** ~ **of sth** etw symbolisieren

symbolically [sɪm'bɒlɪkəlɪ] ADV symbolisch

symbolism ['sɪmbəlɪzəm] N Symbolik *f*

symbolize ['sɪmbəlaɪz] VT symbolisieren

symmetrical ADJ, **symmetrically** ADV [sɪ'metrɪkəl, -ɪ] symmetrisch

symmetry ['sɪmɪtrɪ] N Symmetrie *f*

sympathetic [sɪmpə'θetɪk] ADJ (**a**) (*= showing pity*) mitfühlend, teilnahmsvoll; (*= understanding*) verständnisvoll; (*= well-disposed*) wohlwollend; *look, smile* freundlich; **to be** *or* **feel** ~ **to(wards) sb** (*= showing pity*) mit jdm mitfühlen; (*= understanding*) jdm Verständnis entgegenbringen; (*= being well-disposed*) mit jdm sympathisieren; **he was most** ~ **when I told him all my troubles** er zeigte sehr viel Mitgefühl für all meine Sorgen
(**b**) (*= likeable*) sympathisch

> *Be careful! The German word **sympathisch** is not the most common translation for **sympathetic**.*

sympathetically [sɪmpə'θetɪkəlɪ] ADV (*= showing pity*) mitfühlend; (*= with understanding*) verständnisvoll; (*= well-disposed*) wohlwollend

sympathize ['sɪmpəθaɪz] VI (*= feel compassion*) Mitleid haben (*with mit*); (*= understand*) Verständnis haben (*with für*); (*= agree*) sympathisieren (*with mit*) (*esp Pol*); (*= express sympathy*) sein Mitgefühl aussprechen; **to** ~ **with sb over sth** (*= feel sorry*) mit jdm in einer Sache mitfühlen können; **to** ~ **with sb's views** jds Ansichten teilen; **I really do** ~ (*= have pity*) das tut mir wirklich Leid; (*= understand your feelings*) **I** ~ **with you** *or* **with what you say, but …** ich kann Ihnen das nachfühlen, aber …

sympathizer ['sɪmpəθaɪzəʳ] N (*with cause*) Sympathisant(in) *m(f)*

sympathy ['sɪmpəθɪ] N (**a**) (*= pity*) Mitleid *nt* (*for* mit); (*at death*) Beileid *nt*; **to feel** *or* **have** ~ **for sb** Mitleid mit jdm haben; **you have our deepest** *or* **heartfelt** ~ *or* **sympathies** wir fühlen mit Ihnen, (unser) aufrichtiges *or* herzliches Beileid; **you have my** ~! (*hum*) herzliches Beileid (*hum*); **you won't get any** ~ **from me** erwarte kein Mitleid von mir
(**b**) (*= understanding*) Verständnis *nt*; (*= agreement*) Sympathie *f*; **to be in/out of** ~ **with sb/sth** mit jdm/etw einhergehen/nicht einhergehen; **he has Democratic sympathies** er sympathisiert mit den Demokraten; **to come out** *or* **strike in** ~ (*Ind*) in Sympathiestreik treten

symphony ['sɪmfənɪ] N Sinfonie *f*

symphony orchestra N Sinfonieorchester *nt*

symptom ['sɪmptəm] N (*lit, fig*) Symptom *nt*

symptomatic [sɪmptə'mætɪk] ADJ symptomatisch (*of* für)

synagogue ['sɪnəgɒg] N Synagoge *f*

sync [sɪŋk] N (*Film, TV inf*) ABBR *of* synchronization; **in** ~ synchron; **out of** ~ nicht synchron

synchronization [sɪŋkrənaɪ'zeɪʃən] N Abstimmung *f*; (*Film*) Synchronisation *f*; (*of clocks*) Gleichstellung *f*

synchronize ['sɪŋkrənaɪz] **1** VT abstimmen (*with auf* +acc); *movements* aufeinander abstimmen; (*Film*) synchronisieren (*with mit*); *clocks* gleichstellen (*with mit*) **2** VI (*Film*) synchron sein (*with mit*); (*clocks*) gleich gehen (*with mit*); (*actions*) zusammenfallen, gleichzeitig ablaufen (*with mit*); (*movements*) in Übereinstimmung sein (*with mit*)

synchronous ['sɪŋkrənəs] ADJ (*Comput*) synchron

syndicate ['sɪndɪkɪt] N Interessengemeinschaft *f*; (*for gambling*) Wettgemeinschaft *f*; (*Comm*) Syndikat *nt*; (*of insurance companies*) Konsortium *nt*, Versicherungsgruppe *f*; (*Press*) (Presse)zentrale *f*; (*= crime* ~) Ring *m*

syndrome ['sɪndrəʊm] N (*Med*) Syndrom *nt*; (*fig, Sociol*) Phänomen *nt*

synod ['sɪnəd] N Synode *f*

synonym ['sɪnənɪm] N Synonym *nt*

synonymous [sɪ'nɒnɪməs] ADJ synonym

synopsis [sɪ'nɒpsɪs] N, *pl* **synopses** [sɪ'nɒpsiːz] Abriss *m* der Handlung; (*of article, book*) Zusammenfassung *f*

syntax ['sɪntæks] N Syntax *f*; ~ **error** (*Comput*) Syntaxfehler *m*

synthesis ['sɪnθəsɪs] N, *pl* **syntheses** ['sɪnθəsiːz] Synthese *f*; (*= artificial production also*) Synthetisieren *nt*

synthesize ['sɪnθəsaɪz] VT synthetisieren; *speech* synthetisch bilden

synthesizer ['sɪnθəsaɪzəʳ] N (*Mus*) Synthesizer *m*

synthetic [sɪn'θetɪk] **1** ADJ synthetisch; ~ **smile** künstliches *or* gekünsteltes Lächeln **2** N Kunststoff *m*; ~**s** Synthetik *f*

syphilis ['sɪfɪlɪs] N Syphilis *f*

syphon N = **siphon**

Syria ['sɪrɪə] N Syrien *nt*

Syrian ['sɪrɪən] **1** ADJ syrisch **2** N Syr(i)er(in) *m(f)*

syringe [sɪ'rɪndʒ] (*Med*) **1** N Spritze *f* **2** VT (aus)spülen

syrup, (*US also*) **sirup** ['sɪrəp] N Sirup *m* (*also Med*); (*= preservative also*) Saft *m*

syrupy, (*US also*) **sirupy** ['sɪrəpɪ] ADJ sirupartig; (*pej*) *smile, voice* zucker- *or* honigsüß; (*= sentimental*) schmalzig

system ['sɪstəm] N System *nt* (*also Comput*); **the Pitman** ~ **of shorthand** die Kurzschriftmethode nach Pitman; **digestive** ~ Verdauungsapparat *m*; **to pass through the** ~ den Körper auf natürlichem Wege verlassen; **it was a shock to his** ~ er hatte schwer damit zu schaffen; **to get sth out of one's** ~ (*fig inf*) sich (*dat*) etw von der Seele schaffen, etw loswerden (*inf*); **it's all** ~**s go!** (*inf*) jetzt heißt es: volle Kraft voraus!; **the** ~ (*= established authority*) das System; **you can't beat** *or* **buck the** ~ gegen das System kommst du *or* kommt man einfach nicht an; ~ **disk** Systemdiskette *f*; ~ **software** Systemsoftware *f*

systematic [sɪstə'mætɪk] ADJ systematisch; *liar, cruelty* ständig; **he works in a** ~ **way** er arbeitet mit System

systematically [sɪstə'mætɪkəlɪ] ADV systematisch

systematize ['sɪstəmətaɪz] VT systematisieren

systems: **systems analyst** N Systemanalytiker(in) *m(f)*; **systems disk** N (*Comput*) Systemdiskette *f*; **systems engineering** N Anlagenbau *m*, Anlagentechnik *f*; **systems manager** N Systemmanager(in) *m(f)*; **systems software** N Systemsoftware *f*

Tt

T, t [tiː] N T *nt*, t *nt*; **it suits him to a T** es ist genau das Richtige für ihn

ta [tɑː] INTERJ (*Brit inf*) danke

tab¹ [tæb] N **(a)** (= *loop on coat etc*) Aufhänger *m*; (= *name ~*) (*of owner*) Namensschild *nt*; (*of maker*) Etikett *nt*; (*on filing cards*) Reiter *m*; **to keep ~s on sb/sth** (*inf*) jdn/etw genau im Auge behalten **(b)** (*esp US inf*: = *bill*) Rechnung *f*; **to pick up the ~** (*also Brit*) die Rechnung übernehmen

tab² (*Comput etc*) **1** N Tab *m*; (*on typewriter*) Tabulator *m*; **to set the ~s** tabulieren **2** VT *columns* tabulieren

tabby ['tæbɪ] N (*also ~ cat*) getigerte Katze

tab key N Tabtaste *f*; (*on typewriter*) Tabulatortaste *f*

table ['teɪbl] **1** N **(a)** Tisch *m*; (= *banquet ~*) Tafel *f*; **at the ~** am Tisch; **at ~** bei Tisch; **to sit at ~** sich zu Tisch setzen; **to sit down at a ~** sich an einen Tisch setzen; **to drink sb under the ~** jdn unter den Tisch trinken; **the motion is on the ~** (*Brit Parl*) der Antrag liegt vor; **on the ~** (*US: = postponed*) zurückgestellt; **to turn the ~s (on sb)** (gegenüber jdm) den Spieß umdrehen **(b)** (= *people at a ~*) Tischrunde *f* **(c)** (*of figures etc, Sport*) Tabelle *f*; (**multiplication**) **~s** Einmaleins *nt*; **to say one's three times ~** das Einmaldrei aufsagen; **~ of contents** Inhaltsverzeichnis *nt* **2** VT **(a)** *motion etc* einbringen **(b)** (*US*: = *postpone*) *bill* zurückstellen

tableau ['tæblǝʊ] N, *pl* **-s** or **-x** ['tæblǝʊ(z)] (*Art, Theat*) Tableau *nt*; (*fig*) Bild *nt*, Szene *f*

table: tablecloth N Tischdecke *f* or -tuch *nt*; **table lamp** N Tischlampe *f*; **table manners** PL Tischmanieren *pl*; **tablespoon** N Esslöffel *m*; **tablespoonful** N Esslöffel *m* (voll)

tablet ['tæblɪt] N **(a)** (*Pharm*) Tablette *f* **(b)** (*of wax, clay*) Täfelchen *nt*; (*of soap*) Stückchen *nt*

table: table tennis N Tischtennis *nt*; **table top** N Tischplatte *f*; **table wine** N Tafelwein *m*

tabloid ['tæblɔɪd] N (*also ~ newspaper*) bebilderte, kleinformatige Zeitung; (*pej*) Boulevardzeitung *f*

TABLOIDS, BROADSHEETS

*In Großbritannien kann man schon an der Größe einer Zeitung deren Ausrichtung erkennen. Die größeren Exemplare, **broadsheets**, konzentrieren sich auf ernsthafte Berichterstattung und fundierte Artikel. „Daily Telegraph", „Times", „Guardian" und „Independent" sind die vier größten überregionalen **broadsheets**, die täglich erscheinen.*

Tabloids haben ein kleineres Format (ca. 30x40 cm) und zeichnen sich durch eine reißerische, prägnante Aufmachung aus. Die bekanntesten Tageszeitungen dieser Art sind „Sun", „Daily Mirror", „Daily Express" und „Daily Star".

In den USA ist der übliche Begriff für seriöse Tageszeitungen „standard-sized newspaper". Die größte überregionale Zeitung dieser Prägung ist die landesweite Ausgabe der „New York Times". Zu den bekanntesten Boulevardblättern zählen „New York Daily News" und „Chicago Sun-Times".

---

taboo, tabu [tǝ'buː] **1** N Tabu *nt*; **to be a ~** tabu sein **2** ADJ tabu

tabular ['tæbjʊlǝʳ] ADJ **in ~ form** tabellarisch

tacit ADJ, **tacitly** ADV ['tæsɪt, -lɪ] stillschweigend

taciturn ['tæsɪtɜːn] ADJ schweigsam, wortkarg

tack [tæk] **1** N **(a)** (= *nail*) kleiner Nagel; (*esp US*: = *drawing pin*) Reißzwecke *f* **(b)** (*Naut*: = *course*) Schlag *m*; **they are on a different ~** (*fig*) sie haben eine andere Richtung eingeschlagen; **to try another ~** (*fig*) es anders versuchen **(c)** (*for horse*) Sattel- und Zaumzeug *nt* **2** VT **(a)** (*with nail*) annageln (*to an +dat or acc*); (*with pin*) feststecken (*to an +dat*) **(b)** (*Brit Sew*) heften **3** VI (*Naut*) aufkreuzen

▶ **tack on** VT SEP annageln (*-to an +acc or dat*); (*with drawing pin*) anstecken (*-to an +acc or dat*); (*fig*) anhängen (*-to an +dat*)

---

tackiness ['tækɪnɪs] N (*inf*) Billigkeit *f*; (*of area, bar*) heruntergekommener Zustand; (*of clothes, colour scheme*) Geschmacklosigkeit *f*

tackle ['tækl] **1** N **(a)** (= *equipment*) Ausrüstung *f*; **fishing ~** Angelausrüstung *f* **(b)** (*Sport*) Angriff *m*, Tackling *nt* **2** VT **(a)** (*physically*) (*Sport*) angreifen; (*Rugby*) fassen; (*verbally*) zur Rede stellen (*about* wegen) **(b)** (= *undertake*) *job* in Angriff nehmen; *problem* angehen, anpacken (*inf*); (= *manage to cope with*) bewältigen; *fire* bekämpfen **3** VI angreifen

tacky¹ ['tækɪ] ADJ (+ER) klebrig

tacky² ADJ (+ER) (*inf*) billig; *area, bar* heruntergekommen; *clothes, colour scheme* geschmacklos

tact [tækt] N, NO PL Takt *m*

tactful ['tæktfʊl] ADJ taktvoll; **to be ~ about sth** etw mit Feingefühl behandeln

tactfully ['tæktfǝlɪ] ADV taktvoll

tactic ['tæktɪk] N Taktik *f*

tactical ADJ, **tactically** ADV ['tæktɪkǝl, -ɪ] (*Mil, fig*) taktisch

tactics ['tæktɪks] N SING Taktik *f*; (*fig also*) Taktiken *pl*

tactless ADJ, **tactlessly** ADV ['tæktlɪs, -lɪ] taktlos

tad [tæd] N, NO PL (*inf*) **a ~** ein bisschen, etwas

Tadjikistan [tɑːˌdʒiːkɪˈstɑːn] N = **Tajikistan**

tadpole ['tædpǝʊl] N Kaulquappe *f*

Tadzhikistan [tɑːˌdʒɪkɪˈstɑːn] N = **Tajikistan**

taffeta ['tæfɪtǝ] N Taft *m*

taffy ['tæfɪ] N (*US*) Toffee *nt*

tag [tæg] **1** N **(a)** (= *label*) Schild(chen) *nt*; (*on clothes*) (*with maker's name*) Etikett *nt*; (= *loop*) Aufhänger *m* **(b)** (*Gram*: = *question ~*) Bestätigungsfrage *f* **2** VT *specimen* mit Schildchen versehen; *garment, goods* etikettieren; (*with price*) auszeichnen

▶ **tag along** VI (*unwillingly, unwanted*) mitzockeln (*inf*); **to tag along behind sb** hinter jdm herzockeln (*inf*); **why don't you tag along?** (*inf*) warum kommst/gehst du nicht mit?

▶ **tag on** VT SEP anhängen (*to an +acc*)

tahini [tǝ'hiːnɪ] N, NO PL Sesampaste *f*

Tahiti [tɑːˈhiːtɪ] N Tahiti *nt*

Tahitian [tɑːˈhiːʃǝn] **1** ADJ tahitisch **2** N **(a)** Tahitianer(in) *m(f)* **(b)** (*Ling*) Tahitisch *nt*

tail [teɪl] **1** N **(a)** Schwanz *m*; (*of comet*) Schweif *m*; (*of shirt*) Zipfel *m*; (*of coat*) Schoß *m*; **to turn ~** die Flucht ergreifen; **he was right on my ~** er saß mir direkt im Nacken **(b)** **~s** PL (*on coin*) Rück- or Zahlseite *f* **(c)** **tails** PL (= *jacket*) Frack *m* **2** VT *person* beschatten (*inf*); *car etc* folgen (*+dat*)

▶ **tail away** VI = **tail off (a)**

▶ **tail back** VI (*Brit*: *traffic*) sich gestaut haben

▶ **tail off** VI **(a)** (= *diminish*) abnehmen; (*sounds*) schwächer werden; (*sentence*) mittendrin abbrechen **(b)** (= *deteriorate*) sich verschlechtern

tail: tailback N (*Brit*) Rückstau *m*; **tail end** N Ende *nt*; **tail-light** N (*Aut*) Rücklicht *nt*

tailor ['teɪlǝʳ] **1** N Schneider(in) *m(f)* **2** VT **(a)** *dress etc* schneidern **(b)** (*fig*) *plans, holiday, message, policy* zuschneiden (*to auf +acc*); *products, salary structure* abstimmen (*to auf +acc*)

tailor-made [ˌteɪlǝ'meɪd] ADJ (*lit, fig*) maßgeschneidert

tail: tailpipe N (*US*) Auspuffrohr *nt*; **tailwind** N Rückenwind *m*

taint [teɪnt] **1** N (*fig*) (= *blemish*) Makel *m*; (= *trace*) Spur *f* **2** VT **(a)** *food* verderben **(b)** *atmosphere* verpesten **(c)** (*fig*) *reputation* beschmutzen

tainted ['teɪntɪd] ADJ **(a)** (*fig*) *reputation* beschmutzt; **to be ~ with sth** mit etw behaftet sein **(b)** (= *contaminated*) *food* verdorben, verpestet; *air* verpestet

Taiwan [taɪ'wɑːn] N Taiwan *nt*

Taiwanese [ˌtaɪwɑː'niːz] **1** ADJ taiwanisch **2** N Taiwaner(in) *m(f)*

Tajikistan [tɑːˌdʒɪkɪˈstɑːn] N Tadschikistan *nt*

take [teɪk]

| 1 TRANSITIVE VERB | 3 NOUN |
| 2 INTRANSITIVE VERB | 4 PHRASAL VERBS |

vb: pret **took**, *ptp* **taken**

When **take** *is part of a set combination, eg* **to take sb by surprise**, **to take one's time**, **to take a bath**, *look up the other word.*

1 TRANSITIVE VERB

(a) (= *remove*) nehmen; (= *take away with one*) mitnehmen; (= *remove from its place*) wegnehmen; **to take sth from sb** jdm etw wegnehmen; **the thieves took everything** die Einbrecher haben alles mitgenommen

(b) (= *carry, transport*) bringen; (= *take along with one*) mitnehmen; **let me take your case** komm, ich nehme *or* trage deinen Koffer

✦**to take sb somewhere** I'll take you to the station ich bringe Sie zum Bahnhof; **I'll take you (with me) to the party** ich nehme dich zur Party mit; **to take sb on a trip** mit jdm eine Reise machen; **this bus will take you to the town hall** der Bus fährt zum Rathaus; **this road will take you to Paris** diese Straße führt *or* geht nach Paris; **his ability took him to the top of his profession** seine Begabung brachte ihn in seinem Beruf bis an die Spitze

(c) (= *capture*) fangen; *person* fassen; *town etc* einnehmen, erobern; **to take sb prisoner** jdn gefangen nehmen; **they took 200 prisoners** sie machten 200 Gefangene

(d) (= *accept, receive*) nehmen; *job* annehmen; *command, lead, role* übernehmen; *phone call* entgegennehmen; (= *buy regularly*) *newspaper etc* immer nehmen *or* kaufen; **take that!** da!; (= *hold that*) halt mal! halt mal!; **I won't take less than £200** ich verkaufe es nicht unter £ 200; **to take things as they come** die Dinge nehmen, wie sie kommen; **take it from me!** das können Sie mir glauben; **take it from me, he'll never ...** eines können Sie mir glauben, er wird nie ...; **the school only takes private pupils** die Schule nimmt nur Privatschüler (auf); **to take a knife by the handle** ein Messer am Griff (an)fassen; **take (the case of) England in the 17th century** nehmen Sie zum Beispiel England im 17. Jahrhundert; **let's take it from the beginning of Act 2** fangen wir mit dem Anfang vom zweiten Akt an

✦**to be taken ...** to be taken sick *or* ill krank werden

✦**take it or leave it** (you can) take it or leave it ja oder nein(, ganz wie Sie wollen); **I can take it or leave it** ich mache mir nicht besonders viel daraus

(e) (= *occupy, possess*) sich (*dat*) nehmen; **take a seat/chair!** nehmen Sie Platz!; **this seat is taken** dieser Platz ist besetzt

(f) (= *gain*) *honours etc* bekommen; **the shop takes £10,000 a week** (*Brit*) das Geschäft nimmt £ 10.000 pro Woche ein

(g) (= *do*) *test, course, subject, photo, walk* machen; *exam* ablegen; *trip* unternehmen

(h) (= *teach*) *subject, class* unterrichten, nehmen; *lesson* halten, geben; **who takes you for Latin?** (*Brit*), **who are you taking for Latin?** (*US*) wer unterrichtet *or* gibt bei euch Latein?

(i) (*census, poll*) durchführen; *church service* (ab)halten; **to take (the chair at) a meeting** den Vorsitz bei einer Versammlung führen

(j) (*taxi, train*) nehmen, fahren mit; *motorway* nehmen, fahren auf (+*dat*); *hurdle, fence* überspringen; *bend, corner* (*person*) nehmen; (*car*) fahren um; **to take the plane** fliegen; **we took a wrong turning** (*Brit*) *or* **turn** (*US*) wir sind falsch abgebogen

(k) (= *consume*) *drink, food* zu sich (*dat*) nehmen; *drugs, medicine* nehmen; (*on directions for use*) einnehmen; **to take a sip/a drink** ein Schlückchen/einen Schluck trinken; **do you take sugar?** nehmen Sie Zucker?

(l) (*letter, dictation*) aufnehmen; *address, details* (sich *dat*) aufschreiben, (sich *dat*) notieren; **to take notes** sich (*dat*) Notizen machen

(m) (*temperature, pulse*) messen; **to take the measurements of a room** ein Zimmer ausmessen; **to take sb's temperature/pulse** bei jdm Fieber/den Puls messen

(n) (= *tolerate*) sich (*dat*) gefallen lassen; *alcohol, climate* vertragen; *emotional experience, shock* verkraften; *thing, weight* aushalten; **I can take it** ich werde damit fertig; **I just can't take any more** ich bin am Ende; **I just can't take it any more** das halte ich nicht mehr aus; **I won't take any nonsense!** ich dulde keinen Unsinn!

(o) (= *respond to*) *news* aufnehmen, reagieren auf (+*acc*); *person* nehmen; **she never knows how to take him** sie weiß nie, woran sie bei ihm ist; **she took his death very badly** sein Tod hat sie sehr mitgenommen

(p) (= *understand*) auffassen, verstehen; **I would take that to mean ...** ich würde das so auffassen *or* verstehen ...

(q) (= *assume*) annehmen; **to take sb/sth for** *or* **to be ...** jdn/ etw für ... halten

(r) (= *extract*) entnehmen (*from* +*dat*); **he takes his examples from real life** seine Beispiele sind aus dem Leben gegriffen

(s) (= *require*) brauchen; *clothes size* haben; **the journey takes 3 hours** die Fahrt dauert 3 Stunden; **I took a long time over it** ich habe lange dazu gebraucht

✦**it takes** it takes five hours ... man braucht fünf Stunden ...; **it takes me five hours ...** ich brauche fünf Stunden ...; **it took ten men to complete the job** es wurden zehn Leute benötigt, um diese Arbeit zu erledigen; **it took a lot of courage** dazu gehörte viel Mut; **it takes more than that to make me angry** deswegen werde ich noch lange nicht wütend; **it takes time** es braucht (seine) Zeit; **it took a long time** es hat lange gedauert; **it took me a long time** ich habe lange gebraucht; **it won't take long** das dauert nicht lange; **that'll take some explaining** das wird schwer zu erklären sein

✦**what it takes** she's got what it takes (*inf*) sie ist nicht ohne (*inf*); **it's a difficult job but he's got what it takes** (*inf*) es ist eine schwierige Arbeit, aber er hat das Zeug dazu

(t) (= *have capacity or room for*) Platz haben für

(u) (*Math*) (= *subtract*) abziehen (*from* von)

(v) (*Gram*) stehen mit; (*preposition*) *case* gebraucht werden mit; **verbs that take "haben"** Verben, die mit „haben" konjugiert werden

2 INTRANSITIVE VERB (= *take hold*) (*fire*) angehen; (*dye, perm, graft*) angenommen werden; (*plant*) anwachsen

3 NOUN

(a) (*Film*) Aufnahme *f*

(b) (= *takings*) (*US inf*) Einnahmen *pl*

4 PHRASAL VERBS

➤ **take aback** VT SEP überraschen; **I was completely taken aback** ich war völlig perplex

➤ **take after** VI +PREP OBJ nachschlagen (+*dat*); (*in looks*) ähnlich sein (+*dat*)

➤ **take along** VT SEP mitnehmen

➤ **take apart** VT SEP (*lit, fig inf*) auseinander nehmen; (*lit:* = *dismantle also*) zerlegen

➤ **take (a)round** VT SEP mitnehmen; (= *show around*) herumführen

➤ **take aside** VT SEP beiseite nehmen

➤ **take away** 1 VI to take away from sth etw schmälern; *from worth* etw mindern; *from pleasure etc* etw beeinträchtigen
2 VT SEP **(a)** (= *subtract*) abziehen; **6 take away 2** 6 weniger 2
(b) (= *remove*) wegnehmen (*from sb* jdm); (*from school etc*) nehmen (*from* aus); (= *lead, transport, carry away*) weg- *or* fortbringen (*from* von); **to take sb/sth away (with one)** jdn/ etw mitnehmen; **to take away sb's freedom** *etc* jdm die Freiheit *etc* nehmen; **they've come to take him away** sie sind da, um ihn abzuholen
(c) *food* mitnehmen; **pizza to take away** Pizza zum Mitnehmen

➤ **take back** VT SEP **(a)** (= *reclaim, get back*) sich (*dat*) zurückgeben lassen; *toy etc* wieder wegnehmen; (*fig:* = *retract*) zurücknehmen **(b)** (= *return*) zurückbringen; **to take sb back to his childhood** jdn in seine Kindheit zurückversetzen; **that takes me back** das ruft Erinnerungen wach **(c)** (= *agree to receive again*) *thing* zurücknehmen; *employee* wieder einstellen; *husband* wieder aufnehmen

➤ **take down** VT SEP **(a)** (*lit:* = *off high shelf etc*) herunternehmen; *curtains, decorations* abnehmen; *picture* abhängen; **to take one's trousers down** seine Hose herunterlassen **(b)** *scaffolding, tent etc* abbauen **(c)** (= *write* *down*) (sich *dat*) notieren *or* aufschreiben; *notes* (sich *dat*) machen; *letter* aufnehmen; **take this down please** notieren Sie bitte

➤ **take home** VT SEP *£400 per week* netto verdienen *or* bekommen

➤ **take in** VT SEP **(a)** (= *bring in*) hereinbringen *or* -nehmen; *harvest* einbringen; **I'll take the car in(to work) on Monday** ich fahre am Montag mit dem Auto (zur Arbeit) **(b)** *refugee* (bei sich) aufnehmen; *stray dog* zu sich nehmen; (*for payment*) **she takes in lodgers** sie vermietet (Zimmer) **(c)** (= *receive*) *money* einnehmen **(d)** (= *make narrower*) *dress* enger machen **(e)** (*usu insep*: = *include, cover*) einschließen **(f)** (= *note visually*) *surroundings, contents* wahrnehmen, registrieren (*inf*); *room* überblicken; (= *understand*) *meaning* begreifen; *sights etc, situation* erfassen; **the children were taking it all in** die Kinder haben alles mitbekommen *or* mitgekriegt (*inf*); **his death was so sudden that she couldn't take it in** sein Tod kam so plötzlich, dass sie es gar nicht fassen konnte **(g)** (= *deceive*) hereinlegen; **to be taken in** hereingelegt werden; **to be taken in by sb/sth** auf jdn/etw hereinfallen

➤ **take off** ■ VI **(a)** (*plane*) starten; (*fig*) (*project, sales*) anlaufen; (*film, product*) ankommen; (*career*) abheben **(b)** (*inf*: = *leave*) sich davonmachen (*inf*) ■ VT SEP **(a)** *beard, hat, lid* abnehmen (*prep obj* von); *tablecloth* herunternehmen (*prep obj* von); *pillowcases etc, detective etc from job*, (= *deduct*) abziehen (*prep obj* von); (*from price*) 5%, 50p nachlassen; *coat, gloves etc* (sich *dat*) ausziehen; (= *withdraw*) *play* absetzen; *food from menu, bus* streichen (*prep obj* von); *service, tax* abschaffen; **to take sth off sb** jdm etw abnehmen; **to take the receiver off (the hook)** den Hörer abnehmen; **he took her dress off** er zog ihr das Kleid aus; **he took his/her clothes off** er zog sich/sie aus; **would you like to take your coat off?** möchten Sie ablegen?; **the barber took too much off** der Friseur hat zu viel abgeschnitten; **to take sb's mind off sth** jdn von etw ablenken; **to take the weight off one's feet** seine Beine ausruhen; **to take sb/sth off sb's hands** jdm jdn/etw abnehmen **(b)** (= *lead away*) mitnehmen; (*under arrest etc*) abführen; **he was taken off to hospital** er wurde ins Krankenhaus gebracht **(c)** (= *have free*) *week, Monday* freinehmen; **to take time off (work)** sich (*dat*) freinehmen **(d)** (*Brit*: = *imitate*) nachahmen

➤ **take on** VT SEP **(a)** *job* annehmen; *responsibility* übernehmen; *colour, aspect* bekommen; (= *employ*) einstellen; **when he married her he took on more than he bargained for** als er sie heiratete, hat er sich (*dat*) mehr aufgeladen, als er gedacht hatte **(b)** (*Sport etc*: = *accept as opponent*) antreten gegen; *union* sich anlegen mit **(c)** *passengers* (*train etc*) aufnehmen; (*plane, ship*) an Bord nehmen; *cargo* laden

➤ **take out** VT SEP **(a)** (= *bring or carry out*) (hinaus)bringen (*of* aus); (*for drive etc*) wegfahren mit **(b)** (*to theatre etc*) ausgehen mit; **to take the dog out (for a walk)** mit dem Hund spazieren gehen; **to take sb out to** *or* **for dinner/to the opera** jdn zum Essen/in die Oper einladen **(c)** (= *pull out, extract*) herausnehmen; *stain* entfernen; *tooth* ziehen; *nail* herausziehen (*of* aus); **to take sth out of sth** etw aus etw (heraus)nehmen; **take it out of the housekeeping** nimm es vom Haushaltsgeld; **to take time out from sth** von etw (eine Zeit lang) Urlaub nehmen; **to take time out from doing sth** etw eine Zeit lang nicht tun; **to take sth out on sb** (*inf*) etw an jdm auslassen (*inf*); **to take it out on sb** sich an jdm abreagieren; **to take it/a lot out of sb** (= *tire*) jdn ziemlich/sehr schlauchen (*inf*) **(d)** (= *withdraw from bank etc*) abheben **(e)** (= *procure*) *insurance* abschließen; *mortgage* aufnehmen **(f)** (*US*) = **take away 2(c)**

➤ **take over** ■ VI (= *assume government*) an die Macht kommen; (*military junta etc*) die Macht ergreifen; (*party*) an die Regierung kommen; (*new boss etc*) die Leitung übernehmen; (*in a place: tourists etc*) sich breit machen (*inf*); **to take over (from sb)** jdn ablösen; **he's ill so I have to take over** da er krank ist, muss ich (für ihn) einspringen ■ VT SEP **(a)** (= *take control or possession of*) übernehmen; **tourists take Edinburgh over in the summer** im Sommer machen sich die Touristen in Edinburgh breit (*inf*)

(b) (= *escort or carry across*) *person* hinüberbringen; (+*prep obj*) bringen über (+*acc*); (*to visit town etc*) mitnehmen (*to* nach, *to sb* zu jdm)

➤ **take round** VT SEP (*esp Brit*) **(a)** **I'll take it round (to her place** *or* **to her)** ich bringe es zu ihr **(b)** (= *show round*) führen (*prep obj* durch)

➤ **take to** VI +PREP OBJ **(a)** *person* sympathisch finden; **sb takes to a subject/place** ein Fach/Ort sagt jdm zu; **I don't know how she'll take to him** ich weiß nicht, wie sie auf ihn reagieren wird; **I don't take kindly to that** ich kann das nicht leiden; **to take to doing sth** anfangen, etw zu tun; **to take to drink** zu trinken anfangen **(b)** (= *escape to*) *woods, hills* sich flüchten in (+*acc*)

➤ **take up** ■ VI (= *continue*) (*person*) weitermachen ■ VT SEP **(a)** aufnehmen; *carpet, floorboards* hochnehmen; *road* aufreißen; *dress* kürzen; *conversation* weiterführen; (= *join in*) *chorus* einstimmen in (+*acc*) **(b)** (= *lead or carry upstairs etc*) *child* hinaufbringen; *visitor* (mit) hinaufnehmen; *thing* hinauftragen **(c)** *time, attention* in Anspruch nehmen; *space* einnehmen **(d)** *matter, point* (= *raise*) zur Sprache bringen; (= *go into*) eingehen auf (+*acc*) **(e)** *photography* zu seinem Hobby machen; *a hobby* sich (*dat*) zulegen; *a language* (anfangen zu) lernen; **to take up painting** anfangen zu malen **(f)** (= *adopt*) *cause* sich einsetzen für, verfechten; **to take up a position** (*lit*) eine Stellung einnehmen; **to be taken up with sb/sth** (= *busy*) mit jdm/etw sehr beschäftigt sein **(g)** *challenge, invitation, job, employment* annehmen; *new job, post* antreten; *career* einschlagen; **he left to take up a job as a headmaster** er ist gegangen, um eine Stelle als Schulleiter zu übernehmen; **to take up residence** sich niederlassen (*at, in* in +*dat*); (*in house*) einziehen (*in* in +*acc*); **to take sb up on his/her invitation/offer** von jds Einladung/Angebot Gebrauch machen; **I'll take you up on that** ich werde davon Gebrauch machen; (*on promise etc*) ich nehme Sie beim Wort **(h)** (= *question, argue with*) **I would like to take you up on that** ich möchte gern etwas dazu sagen; **he took me up on that point** dagegen hatte er etwas einzuwenden **(i)** (*Fin*) *to take up an option* Bezugsrecht ausüben; **to take up a bill** einen Wechsel einlösen; **to take up shares** Aktien beziehen

➤ **take upon** VT +PREP OBJ **he took that job upon himself** er hat das völlig ungebeten getan; **he took it upon himself to answer for me** er meinte, er müsse für mich antworten

➤ **take up with** VI +PREP OBJ *person* sich anfreunden mit

take: **takeaway** (*esp Brit*) ■ N **(a)** (= *meal*) Essen *nt* zum Mitnehmen; **let's get a ~** wir können uns ja etwas (zu essen) holen *or* mitnehmen **(b)** (= *restaurant*) Imbissstube *f* ■ ADJ ATTR *food* zum Mitnehmen; **take-home pay** N Nettolohn *m*

taken ['teɪkən] ■ PTP *of* **take** ■ ADJ **to be ~ with sb/sth** (= *attracted by*) von jdm/etw angetan sein

take: **takeoff** N **(a)** (*Aviat*) Start *m*; (= *moment of leaving ground*) Abheben *nt*; **the plane was ready for ~** das Flugzeug war startbereit **(b)** (*Brit*: = *imitation*) Parodie *f*; **to do a ~ of sb** jdn nachahmen; **takeover** N (*Comm*) Übernahme *f*; **takeover bid** N Übernahmeangebot *nt*

taker ['teɪkəʳ] N **any ~s?** (*fig*) wer ist daran interessiert?; **there were no ~s** (*fig*) niemand war daran interessiert

taking ['teɪkɪŋ] N **(a)** **it's yours for the ~** das können Sie (umsonst) haben **(b)** **takings** PL (*Comm*) Einnahmen *pl*

talc [tælk], **talcum** ['tælkəm], **talcum powder** N Talkumpuder *m*

tale [teɪl] N **(a)** Geschichte *f*; (*Liter*) Erzählung *f*; **he had quite a ~ to tell** er hatte einiges zu erzählen; **at least he lived to tell the ~** zumindest hat er die Sache überlebt; **thereby hangs a ~** das ist eine lange Geschichte **(b)** **to tell ~s** petzen (*inf*) (*to* +*dat*); (*dated*: = *fib*) flunkern (*inf*); **to tell ~s about sb** jdn verpetzen (*inf*) (*to* bei)

talent ['tælənt] N **(a)** Begabung *f*, Talent *nt*; **to have a ~ for drawing/mathematics** Begabung *f* zum Zeichnen/für Mathematik haben **(b)** (= *talented people*) Talente *pl* **(c)** (*inf*) (= *girls*) Bräute *pl* (*sl*); (= *boys*) Typen *pl* (*sl*), Jungs *pl* (*inf*)

talented ['tæləntɪd] ADJ begabt, talentiert

talisman ['tælɪzmən] N, *pl* **-s** Talisman *m*

talk [tɔ:k] **1** N **(a)** Gespräch nt (also Pol); (= conversation also) Unterhaltung f; (esp heart-to-heart) Aussprache f; **to have a ~** ein Gespräch führen/sich unterhalten/sich aussprechen (with sb about sth mit jdm über etw acc); **could I have a ~ with you?** könnte ich Sie mal sprechen?; **to hold** or **have ~s** Gespräche führen; **I have enjoyed our ~** ich habe mich gern mit Ihnen unterhalten

(b) NO PL (= talking) Reden nt, Rederei f; (= rumour) Gerede nt; **he's all ~** (and no action) der führt bloß große Reden; **there is some ~ of his returning** es heißt, er kommt zurück; **it's the ~ of the town** es ist Stadtgespräch

(c) (= lecture) Vortrag m; **to give a ~** einen Vortrag halten (on über +acc); **a series of ~s** eine Vortragsreihe

2 VI **(a)** reden (of von, about über +acc); (= speak, mention) sprechen (of von, about über +acc); (= have conversation) sich unterhalten (of, about über +acc); **to ~ to** or **with sb** mit jdm sprechen or reden (about über +acc); (= converse also) sich mit jdm unterhalten (about über +acc); (= reprimand also) mit jdm ein ernstes Wort reden; **could I ~ to Mr Smith please?** kann ich bitte Herrn Smith sprechen?; **it's easy** or **all right for you to ~** (inf) du hast gut reden (inf); **don't (you) ~ to me like that!** wie redest du denn mit mir?; **that's no way to ~ to your parents** so redet man doch nicht mit seinen Eltern!; **~ to me!** erzähl mir was!; **to get/be ~ing to sb** mit jdm ins Gespräch kommen/im Gespräch sein; **I'm not ~ing to you** (= we're on bad terms) mit dir spreche ich nicht mehr; **you can ~!** (inf) du kannst gerade reden!; **to keep sb ~ing** jdn (mit einem Gespräch) hinhalten; **to ~ to oneself** Selbstgespräche führen; **now you're ~ing!** das lässt sich schon eher hören!; **he's been ~ing of going abroad** er hat davon gesprochen or geredet, dass er ins Ausland fahren will; **~ing of films ...** da or wo (inf) wir gerade von Filmen sprechen ...; **~ about rude!** so was von unverschämt! (inf); **to make sb ~** (= reveal secret) jdn zum Reden bringen; **we're ~ing about at least £2,000** es geht um mindestens £ 2.000

(b) (= chatter) schwatzen; **stop ~ing!** sei/seid ruhig!

(c) (= gossip) klatschen; **everyone was ~ing about them** sie waren in aller Munde; (because of scandal also) alle haben über sie geredet or geklatscht

3 VT **(a)** (= speak) a language sprechen; nonsense reden; politics, business reden über (+acc) or von; **~ sense!** red keinen solchen Unsinn!; **we're ~ing big money** etc **here** (inf) hier gehts um große Geld etc (inf); **we have to ~ business for a while** wir müssen mal kurz etwas Geschäftliches besprechen; **to ~ sb/oneself into doing sth** jdn überreden or jdn/sich dazu bringen, etw zu tun; (against better judgement) jdm/sich einreden, dass man etw tut; **to ~ sb out of sth/doing sth** jdn von etw abbringen/davon abbringen, etw zu tun, jdm etw ausreden/jdm ausreden, etw zu tun; **he ~ed himself out of trouble** er redete sich (geschickt) heraus; **he ~ed himself into this situation** er hat sich selbst durch sein Reden in diese Lage gebracht

➤ **talk away** VI ununterbrochen reden, schwatzen
➤ **talk back** VI (= be cheeky) frech antworten (to sb jdm)
➤ **talk down** VI **to talk down to sb** mit jdm herablassend reden or sprechen
➤ **talk on** VI weiterreden
➤ **talk out** VT SEP (= discuss) ausdiskutieren
➤ **talk over** VT SEP problem besprechen
➤ **talk round 1** VT ALWAYS SEPARATE (Brit) umstimmen **2** VI +PREP OBJ (esp Brit) problem, subject herumreden um
➤ **talk through** VT SEP besprechen; (= explain also) durchsprechen; **to talk sb through sth** jdm etw erklären

talkative ['tɔ:kətɪv] ADJ gesprächig, redselig
talked-of ['tɔ:ktɒv] ADJ **much ~** berühmt; plans also viel besprochen
talker ['tɔ:kə'] N Redner(in) m(f)
talking ['tɔ:kɪŋ] N Reden nt, Sprechen nt; **no ~ please!** bitte Ruhe!, Sprechen verboten!; **his constant ~ will drive me mad** sein dauerndes Gerede or Geschwätz macht mich noch verrückt
talking: **talking point** N Gesprächsthema nt; **talking-to** N (inf) Standpauke f (inf); **to give sb a good ~** jdm eine Standpauke halten (inf)
talk show N Talkshow f
tall [tɔ:l] ADJ (+ER) **(a)** person groß; **how ~ are you?** wie groß sind Sie?; **he is 6 ft ~** er ist 1,80 m groß; **to walk ~** stolz einhergehen **(b)** building, tree, grass, glass hoch **(c)** (inf) that's

a ~ order das ist ganz schön viel verlangt; **a ~ story** or **tale** ein Märchen nt (inf)
tallish ['tɔ:lɪʃ] ADJ person ziemlich groß; building ziemlich hoch
tallness ['tɔ:lnɪs] N (of person) Größe f
tally ['tælɪ] **1** N **(a)** (= count, account) **to keep a ~ of** Buch führen über (+acc) **(b)** (= number) (An)zahl f **2** VI übereinstimmen; (reports etc also) sich decken **3** VT (also ~ up) zusammenrechnen or -zählen
talon ['tælən] N (lit, fig) Kralle f; (of animal also) Klaue f
tambourine [tæmbəˈri:n] N Tamburin nt
tame [teɪm] **1** ADJ (+ER) **(a)** animal zahm **(b)** (= dull) adventure, story, joke etc lahm (inf) **2** VT animal, person zähmen; passion zügeln; inflation, unions unter Kontrolle bringen
tamely ['teɪmlɪ] ADV (= meekly) zahm; agree, surrender lahm
Tampax® ['tæmpæks] N Tampon m
➤ **tamper with** VI +PREP OBJ herumhantieren an (+dat); (with evil intent) sich (dat) zu schaffen machen an (+dat); plan, system herumpfuschen an (+dat) (inf); evidence verfälschen
tampon ['tæmpɒn] N Tampon m
tan [tæn] **1** N **(a)** (= suntan) Bräune f; **to get a ~** braun werden; **she's got a lovely ~** sie ist schön braun **(b)** (= colour) Hellbraun nt **2** ADJ hellbraun **3** VT **(a)** skins gerben **(b)** (sun) body etc bräunen **4** VI braun werden
tandem ['tændəm] N (= cycle) Tandem nt; **in ~ (with)** (fig) zusammen (mit)
tang [tæŋ] N (= smell) scharfer Geruch; (= taste) starker Geschmack
tangent ['tændʒənt] N **to go off at a ~** (fig) (plötzlich) vom Thema abschweifen
tangerine [ˌtændʒəˈri:n] N Mandarine f
tangible ['tændʒɪbl] ADJ (fig) result greifbar; proof handfest; **~ assets** Sachanlagen pl
Tangier(s) [tænˈdʒɪə(z)] N Tanger nt
tangle ['tæŋgl] **1** N (lit) Gewirr nt; (fig: = muddle) Wirrwarr m, Durcheinander nt; **to get into a ~** (lit, fig) sich verheddern **2** VT (lit, fig) verwirren, durcheinander bringen; string also verheddern; **to get ~d** (lit, fig) sich verheddern; (ropes) sich verknoten
➤ **tangle up** VT SEP (lit, fig) verwirren, durcheinander bringen; string also verheddern; **to get tangled up** durcheinander geraten; (wool etc also) sich verheddern; (ropes) sich verknoten; (person) (in explaining etc) sich verstricken; (= become involved) verwickelt or verstrickt werden
tango ['tæŋgəʊ] **1** N Tango m **2** VI Tango tanzen
tangy ['tæŋɪ] ADJ (+ER) taste scharf, streng; smell also durchdringend
tank [tæŋk] N **(a)** (= container) Tank m; (esp for water) Wasserspeicher m; (= oxygen ~) Flasche f **(b)** (Mil) Panzer m
➤ **tank up** VI, VT SEP voll tanken
tankard ['tæŋkəd] N (esp Brit) Humpen m
tanker ['tæŋkə'] N **(a)** (= boat) Tanker m, Tankschiff nt **(b)** (= vehicle) Tankwagen m
tankful ['tæŋkfʊl] N Tank m (voll)
tank top N Pullunder m
tanned [tænd] ADJ person braun (gebrannt)
tannin ['tænɪn] N Tannin nt
Tannoy® ['tænɔɪ] N Lautsprecheranlage f
tantalize ['tæntəlaɪz] VT reizen; (= torment also) quälen
tantalizing ['tæntəlaɪzɪŋ] ADJ verführerisch
tantrum ['tæntrəm] N Wutanfall m, Koller m (inf); **to have** or **throw a ~** einen Koller or Wutanfall bekommen
Tanzania [ˌtænzəˈnɪə] N Tansania nt
Tanzanian [ˌtænzəˈnɪən] **1** ADJ tansanisch **2** N Tansanier(in) m(f)
Taoiseach ['ti:ʃæx] N (Ir) Premierminister(in) m(f)
tap¹ [tæp] **1** N (esp Brit) Hahn m; **the hot ~** der Heißwasserhahn; **on ~** (lit) (beer etc) vom Fass; (fig) zur Hand **2** VT (fig) resources, market erschließen; **to ~ telephone wires** Telefonleitungen anzapfen
➤ **tap into** VI +PREP OBJ system anzapfen; (= exploit) fear ausnutzen
tap² **1** N **(a)** (= light knock) Klopfen nt **(b)** (= light touch) Klaps m, leichter Schlag **2** VTI klopfen; **he ~ped me on the shoulder**

er klopfte mir auf die Schulter; **to ~ in a nail** einen Nagel einschlagen; **he ~ped his fingers impatiently on the table** er trommelte ungeduldig (mit den Fingern) auf den Tisch; **to ~ on** or **at the door** sachte an die Tür klopfen

➤ **tap out** VT SEP *rhythm* klopfen

tap: tap-dance VI steppen; **tap-dancer** N Stepptänzer(in) *m(f)*; **tap-dancing** N Steppen *nt*

tape [teɪp] **1** N **(a)** Band *nt*; (= *sticky paper*) Klebeband *nt*; (= *Sellotape ® etc*) Kleb(e)streifen *m*; (*Sport*) Zielband *nt* **(b)** (*magnetic*) (Ton)band *nt*; **on ~** auf Band; **to put** or **get sth on ~** etw auf Band aufnehmen; **to make a ~ of sth** etw auf Band aufnehmen **2** VT **(a)** *parcel* (mit Kleb(e)streifen/Klebeband) verkleben or zukleben **(b)** (= *~-record*) (auf Band) aufnehmen; (= *video-~*) (auf Video) aufnehmen

➤ **tape down** VT SEP (mit Kleb(e)streifen/Klebeband) festkleben

➤ **tape over** (*Recording*) **1** VI +PREP OBJ überspielen **2** VT SEP **to tape A over B** B mit A überspielen

➤ **tape up** VT SEP *sth broken* mit Kleb(e)streifen/Klebeband zusammenkleben; *parcel* mit Kleb(e)streifen/Klebeband verkleben

tape: tape deck N Tapedeck *nt*; **tape measure** N Maßband *nt*

taper ['teɪpə'] **1** N (= *candle*) (dünne) Kerze **2** VT zuspitzen **3** VI sich zuspitzen; (*trousers*) nach unten enger werden

➤ **taper off** VI (*fig*) langsam aufhören; (*numbers*) langsam zurückgehen; (*production*) langsam auslaufen

tape: tape reader N (*Comput*) Lochstreifenleser *m*; **tape-record** VT auf Band aufnehmen; **tape recorder** N Tonbandgerät *nt*; (= *cassette recorder*) Kassettenrekorder *m*; **tape recording** N Bandaufnahme *f*; **tape streamer** N (*Comput*) Streamer *m*

tapestry ['tæpɪstrɪ] N Wand- or Bildteppich *m*

tapeworm ['teɪpwɜːm] N Bandwurm *m*

tapioca [ˌtæpɪ'əʊkə] N Tapioka *f*

tap water N Leitungswasser *nt*

tar [tɑː'] **1** N Teer *m* **2** VT teeren

tarantula [tə'ræntjʊlə] N Tarantel *f*

tardy ['tɑːdɪ] ADJ (+ER) **(a)** (= *belated*) *reply, offer to help* (reichlich) spät **(b)** (*US*: = *late*) **to be ~** (*person*) zu spät kommen; (*train etc*) Verspätung haben

target ['tɑːgɪt] **1** N Ziel *nt*; (*Sport, fig: of joke, criticism etc*) Zielscheibe *f*; (*in production*) (Plan)soll *nt*; **his shot was off/on ~** (*Mil*) sein Schuss ist danebengegangen/hat getroffen; (*Ftbl etc*) sein Schuss war ungenau/sehr genau; **production is above/on/below ~** das Produktionssoll ist überschritten/ erfüllt/nicht erfüllt; **the government met its ~ for reducing unemployment** die Regierung hat mit der Abnahme der Arbeitslosigkeit ihren Plan erfüllt; **we set ourselves the ~ of £10,000** wir haben uns £ 10.000 zum Ziel gesetzt; **to be on ~** auf Kurs sein; **the project is on ~ for completion** das Projekt ist auf dem besten Weg, planmäßig fertig zu werden; **to be behind ~** hinter dem Soll zurückliegen **2** VT sich (*dat*) zum Ziel setzen; *group, audience* als Zielgruppe haben; *area, resources* abzielen auf (+*acc*)

target: target cost N Richtkosten *pl*; **target figure** N Richtsumme *f*; **target group** N Zielgruppe *f*; **target price** N Richtpreis *m*

tariff ['tærɪf] N **(a)** (*esp Brit*) (Gebühren)tarif *m*; (*in hotels*) Preisliste *f* **(b)** (*Econ*) (= *tax*) Zoll *m*; (= *table*) Zolltarif *m*

tariff: tariff reform N (*Econ*) Zolltarifreform *f*; **tariff walls** PL (*Econ*) Zollschranken *pl*

tarmac ['tɑːmæk] **1** N Tarmac® Makadam *m*; (*generally*) Asphalt *m* **2** VT (*generally*) asphaltieren

tarnish ['tɑːnɪʃ] **1** VT **(a)** *metal* stumpf werden lassen **(b)** (*fig*) *reputation* beflecken; *ideals, image* trüben **2** VI (*metal*) anlaufen

tarot card ['tærəʊkɑːd] N Tarockkarte *f*

tarpaulin [tɑː'pɔːlɪn] N Plane *f*; (*Naut*) Persenning *f*

tarragon ['tærəgən] N Estragon *m*

tart[1] [tɑːt] ADJ (+ER) **(a)** *flavour, wine* herb, sauer (*pej*); *fruit* sauer **(b)** (*fig*) *remark* scharf; *person* schroff

tart[2] N (*Cook*) Obstkuchen *m*; (*individual*) Obsttörtchen *nt*; **apple ~** Apfelkuchen *m*/-törtchen *nt*

tart[3] N (*Brit inf*) (= *prostitute*) Nutte *f* (*inf*); (= *loose woman*) Flittchen *nt* (*pej inf*)

➤ **tart up** VT SEP (*esp Brit inf*) aufmachen (*inf*); *oneself* aufdonnern (*inf*)

tartan ['tɑːtən] **1** N (= *pattern*) Schottenkaro *nt*; (= *material*) Schottenstoff *m* **2** ADJ im Schottenkaro

tartar sauce [ˌtɑːtə'sɔːs] N ≈ Remouladensoße *f*

task [tɑːsk] **1** N Aufgabe *f*; **to set** or **give sb a ~** jdm eine Aufgabe stellen or geben; **to take sb to ~** jdn ins Gebet nehmen (*for, about* wegen) **2** VT = **tax 2(b)**

task: task force N Sondereinheit *f*; **taskmaster** N **he's a hard ~** er ist ein strenger Meister

Tasmania [tæz'meɪnɪə] N Tasmanien *nt*

Tasmanian [tæz'meɪnɪən] **1** ADJ tasmanisch **2** N Tasmanier(in) *m(f)*

Tasman Sea [ˌtæzmən'siː] N Tasmansee *f*

tassel ['tæsəl] N Quaste *f*, Troddel *f*

taste [teɪst] **1** N (*lit, fig*) Geschmack *m*; (= *sense*) Geschmack(sinn) *m*; (= *small amount*) Kostprobe *f* (*also fig*); (*of sth in the future*) Vorgeschmack *m*; **I don't like the ~** das schmeckt mir nicht; **her cooking has no ~** ihr Essen schmeckt nach nichts; **a ~ of onions** ein Zwiebelgeschmack; **would you like some? – just a ~** möchten Sie etwas? – nur eine Idee; **to have a ~ (of sth)** (*lit*) (etw) probieren or kosten; (*fig*) eine Kostprobe (von etw) bekommen; **to acquire** or **develop a ~ for sth** Geschmack an etw (*dat*) finden; **it's an acquired ~** das ist etwas für Kenner; **my ~ in music has changed over the years** mein musikalischer Geschmack hat sich mit der Zeit geändert; **to be to sb's ~** nach jds Geschmack sein; **it is a matter of ~** das ist Geschmack(s)sache; **her novels are too violent for my ~** ihre Romane enthalten für meinen Geschmack zu viel Gewalt; **she has very good ~ in furniture** was Möbel anbelangt, hat sie einen sehr guten Geschmack; **a man of ~** ein Mann mit Geschmack; **in good ~** geschmackvoll; **in bad ~** geschmacklos **2** VT **(a)** (= *perceive flavour of*) schmecken; **wait till you ~ this** warten Sie mal, bis Sie das probiert haben **(b)** (= *take a little*) probieren, kosten **(c)** (= *test*) *wine* verkosten; *food products* probieren; (*official*) prüfen; **~ the sauce before adding salt** schmecken Sie die Soße ab, bevor Sie Salz beigeben **(d)** (*fig*) *power, freedom etc* erfahren, erleben **3** VI schmecken; **to ~ good** or **nice** (gut) schmecken; **it ~s all right to me** ich schmecke nichts; (= *I like it*) ich finde, das schmeckt nicht schlecht; **to ~ of sth** nach etw schmecken

---

Be careful! **taste** *is not translated by the German word* **Taste***.*

---

tasteful ADJ, **tastefully** ADV ['teɪstfʊl, -fəlɪ] geschmackvoll

tasteless ['teɪstlɪs] ADJ (*lit, fig*) geschmacklos; *food also* fade

taster ['teɪstə'] N **(a)** (*of wine*) Prüfer(in) *m(f)*, Probierer(in) *m(f)* **(b)** (*esp Brit fig*) Vorgeschmack *m*

taste test N Geschmackstest *m*

tasty ['teɪstɪ] ADJ (+ER) *dish* schmackhaft; **his new girlfriend is very ~** (*inf*) seine neue Freundin ist zum Anbeißen (*inf*)

ta-ta [tæ'tɑː] INTERJ (*Brit inf*) tschüss (*inf*)

tattered ['tætəd] ADJ *clothes* zerlumpt; *book, sheet* zerfleddert; (*fig*) *pride, reputation* angeschlagen

tatters ['tætəz] PL Lumpen *pl*, Fetzen *pl*; **to be in ~** in Fetzen sein or hängen; **his confidence was in ~** sein Selbstbewusstsein war sehr angeschlagen

tattoo [tə'tuː] **1** VT tätowieren **2** N Tätowierung *f*

tatty ['tætɪ] ADJ (+ER) (*esp Brit inf*) schmuddelig; *clothes* schäbig

taught [tɔːt] PRET, PTP of **teach**

taunt [tɔːnt] **1** N Spöttelei *f* **2** VT verspotten, aufziehen (*inf*) (*about* wegen)

taunting ADJ, **tauntingly** ADV ['tɔːntɪŋ, -lɪ] spöttisch

Taurus ['tɔːrəs] N (*Astron, Astrol*) Stier *m*; **he's a ~** er ist Stier

taut [tɔːt] ADJ (+ER) **(a)** *rope* straff (gespannt); *skin, body* straff; *muscles* stramm, gestrafft; **to pull sth ~** etw stramm ziehen **(b)** (*fig*: = *tense*) angespannt; *look* gespannt

tauten ['tɔːtn] **1** VT *rope* spannen; *muscle, body* anspannen **2** VI sich spannen or straffen

tautly ['tɔːtlɪ] ADV straff

tautness ['tɔːtnɪs] N (*of muscles*) Strammheit *f*

tavern ['tævən] N (*old*) Taverne *f*, Schänke *f*

tawny ['tɔːnɪ] ADJ (+ER) goldbraun

tax [tæks] **1** N (Fin, Econ) Steuer *f*; (*on a company's profit*) Abgabe *f*; (= *import ~*) Gebühr *f*; **before ~** brutto; **after ~** netto; **profits before/after ~** Brutto-/Nettoverdienst *m*; **to put a ~ on sb/sth** jdn/etw besteuern; **the ~ on alcohol** *etc* die Getränkesteuer *etc* **2** VT **(a)** (*Fin, Econ*) besteuern **(b)** (*fig*) *brain, patience etc* strapazieren; *strength* stark beanspruchen; *resources* angreifen

taxable ['tæksəbl] ADJ *person* steuerpflichtig; *goods* besteuert, abgabenpflichtig; **~ income** zu versteuerndes Einkommen

tax: tax adviser N Steuerberater(in) *m(f)*; **tax allowance** N Steuervergünstigung *f*; (= *tax-free income*) Steuerfreibetrag *m*; **tax arrears** PL Steuerrückstände *pl*

taxation [tæk'seɪʃən] N Besteuerung *f*; (= *taxes also*) Steuern *pl*; **exempt from ~** nicht besteuert; *goods, income also* steuerfrei; **subject to ~** steuerpflichtig

tax: tax avoidance N Steuerumgehung *f*; **tax base** N (*Brit*) Besteuerungsgrundlage *f*; **tax bill** N Steuerbescheid *m*; **tax bracket** N Steuergruppe *f or -klasse f*; **tax break** N Steuerentlastung *f*; **tax burden** N Steuerlast *f*; **tax code** N (*Brit*) Steuernummer *f*; **tax collector** N Finanz- *or* Steuerbeamte(r) *m/-beamtin f*; **tax credit** N Steuervergünstigung *f*; **tax cut** N Steuerkürzung *f*; **tax-deductible** ADJ (steuerlich) absetzbar; **tax demand** N Steuerbescheid *m*; **tax disc** N (*Brit: on vehicle*) Steuermarke *f or -plakette f*; **tax evasion** N Steuerhinterziehung *f*; (*by going abroad*) Steuerflucht *f*; **tax-exempt** ADJ (*US*) *person* steuerbefreit; *business* abgabenfrei; *income, status* steuerfrei; **tax exemption** N Steuerbefreiung *f*; **tax exile** N Steuerexil *nt*; (= *person*) Steuerflüchtling *m*; **tax-free** ADJ, ADV steuerfrei; **tax haven** N Steuerparadies *nt*; **tax holiday** N zeitweilige Steuerbefreiung

taxi ['tæksɪ] **1** N Taxi *nt*; **to go by ~** mit dem Taxi fahren **2** VI (*Aviat*) rollen

taxicab ['tæksɪkæb] N (*esp US*) Taxi *nt*

taxidermist ['tæksɪdɜːmɪst] N Tierausstopfer(in) *m(f)*

taxi driver N Taxifahrer(in) *m(f)*

tax: tax incentive N Steueranreiz *m*; **tax inspector** N (*Brit*) Finanzbeamte(r) *mf*

taxi rank (*Brit*), **taxi stand** (*esp US*) N Taxistand *m*

tax: tax liability N Steuerpflicht *f*; **tax loophole** N Steuerschlupfloch *nt*; **taxman** N Steuer- *or* Finanzbeamte(r) *m*; **the ~ gets 35%** das Finanzamt bekommt 35%; **taxpayer** N Steuerzahler(in) *m(f)*; **tax rebate** N Steuererstattung *f*; **tax refund** N Steuerrückerstattung *f*; **tax relief** N Steuervergünstigung *f*; **it qualifies for ~** das ist steuerbegünstigt; **tax return** N Steuererklärung *f*; **tax revenue** N Steueraufkommen *nt*; **tax shelter** N Steuerbegünstigung *f*; **tax system** N Steuerwesen *nt*; **tax year** N Steuerjahr *nt*

TB ABBR *of* **tuberculosis** Tb *f*, Tbc *f*

tbc ABBR *of* **to be confirmed** noch zu bestätigen

T-bill ['tiːbɪl] N (*US Fin*) Schatzwechsel *m*

tea [tiː] N **(a)** Tee *m*; **a cup of ~** eine Tasse Tee **(b)** (*also ~ plant*) Tee(strauch) *m* **(c)** (*Brit*) (= *afternoon ~*) ≈ Kaffee und Kuchen; (= *meal*) Abendbrot *nt*

tea: tea bag N Teebeutel *m*; **tea break** N (*esp Brit*) Pause *f*; **tea caddy** N (*esp Brit*) Teedose *f*; **teacake** N (*Brit*) Rosinenbrötchen *nt*

teach [tiːtʃ] *vb: pret, ptp* **taught** **1** VT *subject, person* unterrichten, lehren (*geh*); *animal* abrichten; **to ~ sth to sb**, **to ~ sb sth** jdm etw beibringen; (*teacher*) jdn in etw (*dat*) unterrichten; **to ~ sb to do sth** jdm beibringen, etw zu tun; **the accident taught me to be careful** durch diesen Unfall habe ich gelernt, vorsichtiger zu sein; **who taught you to drive?** bei wem haben Sie Fahren gelernt?; **to ~ school** (*US*) Lehrer(in) sein/werden; **to ~ oneself sth** sich (*dat*) etw beibringen; **make her pay, that'll ~ her** lass sie bezahlen, das wird ihr eine Lehre sein; **that'll ~ you to break the speed limit** das hast du (nun) davon, dass du die Geschwindigkeitsbegrenzung überschritten hast **2** VI unterrichten, Unterricht geben; **he can't ~** (= *no ability*) er gibt keinen guten Unterricht

teacher ['tiːtʃə'] N Lehrer(in) *m(f)*; **~s of English, English ~s** Englischlehrer *pl*

teacher-training [ˌtiːtʃə'treɪnɪŋ] N Lehrer(aus)bildung *f*; **~ college** (*for primary teachers*) pädagogische Hochschule; (*for secondary teachers*) Studienseminar *nt*

tea chest N (*Brit*) Kiste *f*

teaching ['tiːtʃɪŋ] N **(a)** das Unterrichten *or* Lehren (*geh*); (*as profession*) der Lehrberuf; **she enjoys ~** sie unterrichtet gern **(b)** (= *doctrine: also ~s*) Lehre *f*

teaching aid N Lehr- *or* Unterrichtsmittel *nt*

tea: tea cloth N (*Brit*) Geschirrtuch *nt*; **tea cosy**, (*US*) **tea cozy** N Teewärmer *m*; **teacup** N Teetasse *f*

teak [tiːk] N (= *wood*) Teak(holz) *nt*

tea leaf N Teeblatt *nt*

team [tiːm] N **(a)** Team *nt*; (*Sport*) Mannschaft *f*; **football ~** Fußballmannschaft *f* **(b)** (*of horses etc*) Gespann *nt*

➤ **team up** VI (*people*) sich zusammentun (*with* mit); (= *join group*) sich anschließen (*with sb* jdm, an jdn)

team: team effort N Teamarbeit *f*; **team game** N Mannschaftsspiel *nt*; **team-mate** N Mannschaftskamerad(in) *m(f)*; **team member** N Teammitglied *nt*; (*Sport also*) Mannschaftsmitglied *nt*; **team player** N (*fig*) Teamplayer(in) *m(f)*; **team spirit** N Gemeinschaftsgeist *m*; (*Sport*) Mannschaftsgeist *m*

teamster ['tiːmstə'] N (*US*: = *truck driver*) Lastwagenfahrer(in) *m(f)*

teamwork ['tiːmwɜːk] N Teamgemeinschaftsarbeit *f*, Teamwork *nt*

tea: tea party N Teegesellschaft *f*; **teapot** N Teekanne *f*

tear¹ [tɛə'] *vb: pret* **tore**, *ptp* **torn** **1** VT *material, paper* zerreißen; (= *pull away*) *hole* reißen; **to ~ sth in two** etw (in zwei Stücke *or* Hälften) zerreißen, etw in der Mitte durchreißen; **to ~ sth to pieces** etw in Stücke reißen; **the critics tore the play to pieces** die Kritiker haben das Stück total verrissen; **to ~ sth open** etw aufreißen; **to ~ one's hair (out)** sich (*dat*) die Haare raufen; **to be torn between two things** (*fig*) zwischen zwei Dingen hin und her gerissen sein; **she was completely torn** (*fig*) sie war innerlich zerrissen **2** VI **(a)** (*material etc*) (zer)reißen; **~ along the dotted line** an der gestrichelten Linie abtrennen **(b)** (= *move quickly*) rasen; **to ~ past** vorbeirasen **3** N (*in material etc*) Riss *m*

➤ **tear along** VI entlanggrasen

➤ **tear apart** VT SEP *place, house* völlig durcheinander bringen; *country* zerreißen; **it tore me apart to leave you** es hat mir schier das Herz zerrissen, dich zu verlassen

➤ **tear at** VI +PREP OBJ zerren an (+*dat*)

➤ **tear away 1** VI davonrasen **2** VT SEP *wrapping* abreißen (*from* von); **if you can tear yourself away from the paper** wenn du dich von der Zeitung losreißen kannst

➤ **tear down 1** VI hinunterrasen (*prep obj* +*acc*) **2** VT SEP *poster* herunterreißen; *house* abreißen

➤ **tear into** VI +PREP OBJ **(a)** (*shell*) ein Loch reißen in (+*acc*); *food* sich hermachen über (+*acc*) **(b)** (= *attack verbally*) abkanzeln; (*critic*) keinen guten Faden lassen an (+*dat*)

➤ **tear off 1** VI **(a)** (= *rush off*) wegrasen **(b) the carbon tears off** die Durchschrift lässt sich abtrennen **2** VT SEP *label, wrapping, calendar leaf* abreißen; *cover* wegreißen; *clothes* herunterreißen

➤ **tear out 1** VI hinausrasen, wegrasen **2** VT SEP (her)ausreißen (*of* aus)

➤ **tear up 1** VI **he tore up the road** er raste die Straße entlang **2** VT SEP **(a)** *paper etc* zerreißen **(b)** (*fig*) *contract* aufkündigen **(c)** (= *pull from ground*) *post, plant* (her)ausreißen **(d)** (= *break surface of*) *ground* aufwühlen; *road* aufreißen

tear² [tɪə'] N Träne *f*; **in ~s** in Tränen aufgelöst; **there were ~s in her eyes** ihr standen Tränen in den Augen; **the news brought ~s to her eyes** als sie das hörte, stiegen ihr die Tränen in die Augen; **the ~s were running down her cheeks** ihr Gesicht war tränenüberströmt

tearaway ['tɛərəweɪ] N (*Brit inf*) Rabauke *m* (*inf*)

tearful ['tɪəfʊl] ADJ *look* tränenfeucht; *face* tränenüberströmt; *farewell, reunion* tränenreich; **to become ~** zu weinen anfangen

tearfully ['tɪəfəlɪ] ADV *look* mit Tränen in den Augen; *say* unter Tränen

tear gas N Tränengas *nt*

tearoom ['tiːruːm] N (*Brit*) Teestube *f*, Café *nt*

tear-stained ['tɪəsteɪnd] ADJ verweint, verheult (*pej inf*)

tease [ti:z] **1** VT **(a)** person necken; animal reizen; (= torment) quälen; (= make fun of) hänseln (about wegen); (= pull leg, have on) auf den Arm nehmen (inf) **(b)** hair toupieren **2** VI (= joke) Spaß machen **3** N (inf: = person) Scherzbold m (inf); **she's/he's just a ~** (sexually) sie/er geilt einen nur auf (inf)
► **tease out** VT SEP fibres kardieren; tangles auskämmen

teaser ['ti:zə'] N **(a)** (= difficult question) harte Nuss (inf); (= riddle) Denksportaufgabe f **(b)** (= person) Schäker(in) m(f) (inf)

tea: tea service, tea set N Teeservice nt; **teashop** N Teestube f

teasing ['ti:zɪŋ] ADJ voice, manner neckend; expression, smile neckisch; (= making fun) hänselnd

teasingly ['ti:zɪŋlɪ] ADV **(a)** (= provocatively) herausfordernd **(b)** (= playfully) neckend **(c)** (sexually) verführerisch

tea: teaspoon N **(a)** Teelöffel m **(b)** (also ~ful) Teelöffel m (voll); **tea strainer** N Teesieb nt

teat [ti:t] N (of animal) Zitze f; (Brit: on baby's bottle) (Gummi)sauger m

tea: teatime N (Brit) (for afternoon tea) Teestunde f; (= mealtime) Abendessen nt; **I'll meet you at ~** ich treffe Sie am späten Nachmittag; **tea towel** N (Brit) Geschirrtuch nt; **tea trolley**, (US) **tea wagon** N Teewagen m

technical ['teknɪkəl] ADJ **(a)** (= concerning technology and technique) technisch **(b)** (of particular branch) fachlich, Fach-; problems, vocabulary fachspezifisch; details formal; **~ dictionary** Fachwörterbuch nt; **~ term** Fachausdruck m; **am I getting too ~ for you?** benutze ich zu viele Fachausdrücke?

technical: technical college N (esp Brit) technische Fachschule; **technical drawing** N technische Zeichnung

technicality [teknɪ'kælɪtɪ] N (= technical detail, difficulty) technische Einzelheit; (fig, Jur) Formsache f; **because of a ~** aufgrund einer Formsache

technically ['teknɪkəlɪ] ADV **(a)** technisch **(b)** (= concerned with specialist field) vom Fachlichen her gesehen **(c)** (= strictly speaking) **~ you're right** genau genommen haben Sie recht; **~ speaking** (= strictly speaking) streng genommen

technical: technical school N (US) technische Fachschule; **technical support** N (Comput) (technischer) Support, technische Unterstützung

technician [tek'nɪʃən] N Techniker(in) m(f)

technique [tek'ni:k] N Technik f; (= method) Methode f

technological [teknə'lɒdʒɪkəl] ADJ technologisch; details, information technisch

technologically [teknə'lɒdʒɪklɪ] ADV technologisch

technologist [tek'nɒlədʒɪst] N Technologe m, Technologin f

technology [tek'nɒlədʒɪ] N Technologie f; **computer/communications ~** Computer-/Kommunikationstechnik f

teddy (bear) ['tedɪ(ˌbeə')] N Teddy(bär) m

tedious ['ti:dɪəs] ADJ langweilig, öde; behaviour ermüdend

tediously ['ti:dɪəslɪ] ADV langweilig

tedium ['ti:dɪəm] N Lang(e)weile f

tee [ti:] N (Golf) Tee nt
► **tee off** VI einen Ball vom (ersten) Abschlag spielen

teem [ti:m] VI **(a)** (with people, insects etc) wimmeln (with von); (with mistakes, information etc) strotzen (with vor) **(b)** **it's ~ing with rain** es regnet or gießt (inf) in Strömen

teeming ['ti:mɪŋ] ADJ **(a)** streets von Menschen wimmelnd; crowd wuselnd **(b)** rain strömend

teen [ti:n] ADJ (esp US) movie, magazine für Teenager; boy, girl, pregnancy im Teenageralter; **~ crime** Jugendkriminalität f

teenage ['ti:neɪdʒ] ADJ Teenager-; son, boy, girl im Teenageralter; pregnancy unter Teenagern

teenaged ['ti:neɪdʒd] ADJ im Teenageralter; **~ boy/girl** Teenager m

teenager ['ti:nˌeɪdʒə'] N Teenager m

teens [ti:nz] PL **(a)** Teenageralter nt; **to be in one's ~** im Teenageralter sein **(b)** (inf: = teenagers) Teenager pl

teeny(weeny) ['ti:nɪ('wi:nɪ)] ADJ (inf) klitzeklein (inf)

tee shirt N = **T-shirt**

teeter ['ti:tə'] VI **(a)** taumeln, schwanken; **to ~ on the brink** or **edge of sth** (lit) am Rand von etw taumeln; (fig) am Rand von etw sein **(b)** (US: = seesaw) wippen

teeth [ti:θ] PL of **tooth**

teethe [ti:ð] VI zahnen

teething ['ti:ðɪŋ]: **teething ring** N Beißring m; **teething troubles** PL (Brit fig) Kinderkrankheiten pl

teetotal [ti:'təʊtl] ADJ person abstinent; party etc ohne Alkohol

teetotaller, (US) **teetotaler** [ti:'təʊtlə'] N Abstinenzler(in) m(f), Antialkoholiker(in) m(f)

TEFL ABBR of **Teaching of English as a Foreign Language**

tel ABBR of **telephone (number)** Tel.

telebanking ['telɪˌbæŋkɪŋ] N Telebanking nt

telecommunications [telɪkəmju:nɪ'keɪʃənz] N **(a)** PL Fernmeldewesen nt **(b)** SING (= science) Fernmeldetechnik f

telegram ['telɪgræm] N Telegramm nt

telegraph ['telɪgrɑ:f] **1** N (= message) Telegramm nt **2** VT telegrafisch übermitteln; person telegrafieren (+dat) **3** VI telegrafieren

telegraph pole N (Brit) Telegrafenmast m

teleordering ['telɪˌɔ:dərɪŋ] N Teleordern nt

telepathic [telɪ'pæθɪk] ADJ telepathisch; **you must be ~!** du musst ja ein Hellseher sein!; **I'm not ~!** ich kann doch keine Gedanken lesen! (inf)

telepathy [tɪ'lepəθɪ] N Telepathie f

telephone ['telɪfəʊn] **1** N Telefon nt; **there's somebody on the ~ for you, you're wanted on the ~** Sie werden am Telefon verlangt; **are you on the ~?** (Brit) **have you got a ~?** haben Sie Telefon?; (= can you be reached by ~?) sind Sie telefonisch zu erreichen?; **he's on the ~** (= is using the ~) er telefoniert gerade; (= wants to speak to you) er ist am Telefon; **by ~** telefonisch; **I've just been on the ~ to him** ich habe eben mit ihm telefoniert; **I'll get on the ~ to her** ich werde sie anrufen; **to shout down the ~** ins Telefon brüllen **2** VT anrufen; message, reply telefonisch übermitteln **3** VI anrufen, telefonieren; (= make ~ call) telefonieren; **to ~ for an ambulance** einen Krankenwagen rufen

telephone IN CPDS Telefon-; **telephone banking** N Telefonbanking nt; **telephone box**, (US) **telephone booth** N Telefonzelle f; **telephone call** N Telefongespräch nt, Telefonanruf m; **telephone customer** N (US) Telefonkunde m, Telefonkundin f; **telephone directory** N Telefonbuch nt; **telephone exchange** N (esp Brit) Fernsprechamt nt; **telephone kiosk** N Telefonzelle f; **telephone line** N Telefonleitung f; **telephone number** N Telefonnummer f; **telephone operator** N (esp US) Telefonist(in) m(f); **telephone pole** N (US) Telegrafenmast m

telephoto (lens) ['telɪˌfəʊtəʊ('lenz)] N Teleobjektiv nt

telesales ['teliseɪlz] N SING or PL Verkauf m per Telefon

telescope ['telɪskəʊp] N Teleskop nt, Fernrohr nt

telescopic [telɪ'skɒpɪk] ADJ aerial etc ausziehbar, zusammenschiebbar; view teleskopisch

telescopic lens N Fernrohrlinse f

Teletext® ['telɪtekst] N Videotext m

televangelist [telɪ'vændʒəlɪst] N (esp US) Fernsehevangelist(in) m(f)

televise ['telɪvaɪz] VT (im Fernsehen) senden or übertragen; **~d debate** Fernsehdebatte f

television ['telɪˌvɪʒən] N Fernsehen nt; (= set) Fernseher m; **to watch ~** fernsehen; **to be on ~** im Fernsehen kommen; **what's on ~ tonight?** was gibt es heute Abend im Fernsehen?

television IN CPDS Fernseh-; **television camera** N Fernsehkamera f; **television licence** N (Brit) Bescheinigung f über die Entrichtung der Fernsehgebühren; **television rights** PL Übertragungsrechte pl, Fernsehrechte pl; **television screen** N Bildschirm m, Mattscheibe f (inf); **television set** N Fernseher m

teleworker ['telɪwɜːkəʳ] N Telearbeiter(in) m(f)

telex ['teleks] **1** N Telex nt; (= message also) Fernschreiben nt **2** VT message per Telex mitteilen; person ein Telex schicken (+dat)

tell [tel], pret, ptp **told** **1** VT (a) (= relate) story erzählen (sb sth, sth to sb jdm etw acc); (= inform, say, order) sagen (sb sth jdm etw acc); **to ~ lies** lügen; **to ~ tales** petzen (inf); **to ~ sb's fortune** jdm wahrsagen; **to ~ sb a secret** jdm ein Geheimnis anvertrauen or (give away) verraten; **to ~ sb about** or **of sth** jdm von etw erzählen; **I can't ~ you how pleased I am** ich kann Ihnen gar nicht sagen, wie sehr ich mich freue; **you can't ~ her anything** (= she can't keep a secret) man kann ihr (aber auch) nichts sagen or anvertrauen; **could you ~ me the way to the station, please?** könn(t)en Sir mir bitte sagen, wie ich zum Bahnhof komme?; **(I'll) ~ you what, let's go to the cinema** weißt du was, gehen wir doch ins Kino!; **don't ~ me you can't come!** sagen Sie bloß nicht, dass Sie nicht kommen können!; **I won't do it, I ~ you!** und ich sage dir, das mache ich nicht!; **I told you so** ich habe es (dir) ja gesagt; **we were told to bring sandwiches with us** es wurde uns gesagt, dass wir belegte Brote mitbringen sollten; **don't you ~ me what to do!** Sie haben mir nicht zu sagen, was ich tun soll!; **do as** or **what you are told!** tu, was man dir sagt!

(b) (= distinguish, discern) erkennen; **to ~ the time** die Uhr kennen; **to ~ the difference** den Unterschied sehen/fühlen/ schmecken etc; **you can ~ that he's clever** man sieht or merkt, dass er intelligent ist; **you can't ~ whether it's moving** man kann nicht sagen or sehen, ob es sich bewegt; **it was impossible to ~ where the bullet had entered** es war unmöglich festzustellen, wo die Kugel eingetreten war; **to ~ sb/sth by sth** jdn/etw an etw (dat) erkennen; **I can't ~ butter from margarine** ich kann Butter nicht von Margarine unterscheiden; **to ~ right from wrong** Recht von Unrecht unterscheiden

(c) (= know, be sure) wissen; **how can I ~ that?** wie soll ich das wissen?; **how could I ~ that?** wie hätte ich das wissen können?; **how can I ~ that he will do it?** wie kann ich sicher sein, dass er es tut?

2 VI +INDIR OBJ es sagen (+dat); **I won't ~ you again** ich sage es dir nicht noch einmal; **you know what? – don't ~ me, let me guess** weißt du was? – sags mir nicht, lass mich raten; **you're ~ing me!** wem sagen Sie das!

3 VI (a) (= discern, be sure) wissen; **as** or **so far as one can ~** soweit man weiß; **who can ~?** wer weiß?; **you never can ~, you can never ~** man kann nie wissen

(b) (= talk, ~ tales of) sprechen; **that would be ~ing!** das kann ich nicht verraten; **promise you won't ~** du musst versprechen, dass du nichts sagst

➤ **tell off** VT SEP (inf) ausschimpfen, schelten (for wegen); **he told me off for being late** er schimpfte (mich aus), weil ich zu spät kam

➤ **tell on** VI +PREP OBJ (a) (inf: = inform on) verpetzen (inf) (b) (= have a bad effect on) sich bemerkbar machen bei

teller ['teləʳ] N (in bank) Kassierer(in) m(f)

telling ['telɪŋ] **1** ADJ (= effective) wirkungsvoll; blow (lit, fig) empfindlich; (= revealing) aufschlussreich **2** N (a) (= narration) Erzählen nt (b) **there is no ~ what he may do** man kann nicht sagen or wissen, was er tut

telling-off ['telɪŋ'ɒf] N (Brit inf) Standpauke f (inf); **to give sb a good ~** jdm eine (kräftige) Standpauke halten (inf)

telltale ['telteɪl] **1** N (Brit) Petze f **2** ADJ ATTR verräterisch

telly ['telɪ] N (Brit inf) Fernseher m, Glotze f (inf); **on ~** im Fernsehen; **to watch ~** fernsehen; see also **television**

temerity [tɪ'merɪtɪ] N Kühnheit f, Unerhörtheit f (pej)

temp [temp] **1** N Aushilfskraft m **2** VI als Aushilfskraft arbeiten

temper ['tempəʳ] N (= disposition) Wesen nt, Naturell nt; (= angry mood) Wut f; ~ **tantrum** Wutanfall m; **to be in a ~** wütend sein; **to be in a good/bad ~** guter/schlechter Laune sein; **he was not in the best of ~s** er war nicht gerade bester Laune; **she's got a quick ~** sie kann sehr jähzornig sein; **she's**

got a terrible ~ sie kann sehr unangenehm werden; **to be in a (bad) ~ with sb/over** or **about sth** auf jdn/wegen einer Sache (gen) wütend sein; **to lose one's ~** die Beherrschung verlieren (with sb bei jdm); **to keep one's ~** sich beherrschen (with sb bei jdm); **to fly into a ~** einen Wutanfall bekommen; **he has quite a ~** er kann ziemlich aufbrausen

temperament ['temprəmənt] N (= disposition) Veranlagung f; (of a people) Temperament nt; **he has an artistic ~** er ist eine Künstlernatur; **their ~s are quite different** sie sind völlig unterschiedlich veranlagt

temperamental [temprə'mentl] ADJ (a) temperamentvoll, launenhaft (pej) (b) machine, car launisch (hum)

temperate ['tempərɪt] ADJ climate gemäßigt

temperature ['temprɪtʃəʳ] N Temperatur f; (Med: above normal – also) Fieber nt; **to take sb's ~** bei jdm Fieber messen; **he has a ~** er hat Fieber; **he has a slight/high ~, he's running a slight/high ~** er hat erhöhte Temperatur/hohes Fieber; **he has a ~ of 39° C** er hat 39° Fieber

-tempered [-'tempəd] ADJ SUF ... gelaunt

tempestuous [tem'pestjʊəs] ADJ (fig) stürmisch; argument heftig; speech leidenschaftlich

template, templet ['templɪt] N Schablone f

temple¹ ['templ] N (Rel) Tempel m

temple² N (Anat) Schläfe f

tempo ['tempəʊ] N (Mus, fig) Tempo nt

temporarily ['tempərərɪlɪ] ADV vorübergehend

temporary ['tempərərɪ] ADJ vorübergehend; job also befristet; arrangement also, building, road surface provisorisch; licence zeitlich begrenzt; address vorläufig; **she is a ~ resident here** sie wohnt hier nur vorübergehend; ~ **worker** Zeitarbeiter(in) m(f)

tempt [tempt] VT in Versuchung führen; (successfully) verführen; **to ~ sb to do** or **into doing sth** jdn dazu verführen, etw zu tun; **don't ~ me** bring or führ mich nicht in Versuchung!; **one is ~ed to believe that ...** man möchte fast glauben, dass ...; **I am very ~ed to accept** ich bin sehr versucht anzunehmen; **may I ~ you to have a little more wine?** kann ich Sie noch zu etwas Wein überreden?; **to ~ fate** or **providence** (fig) sein Schicksal herausfordern; (in words) den Teufel an die Wand malen

temptation [temp'teɪʃən] N Versuchung f (also Rel), Verlockung f; **to yield to** or **to give way to ~** der Versuchung erliegen

tempting ADJ, **temptingly** ADV ['temptɪŋ, -lɪ] verlockend, verführerisch

ten [ten] **1** ADJ zehn **2** N Zehn f; ~**s** (Math) Zehner pl; see also **six**

tenacious [tɪ'neɪʃəs] ADJ zäh, hartnäckig; character, person also beharrlich

tenacity [tɪ'næsɪtɪ] N Zähigkeit f, Hartnäckigkeit f; (of character, person also) Beharrlichkeit f

tenancy ['tenənsɪ] N conditions of ~ Mietbedingungen pl; (of farm) Pachtbedingungen pl; **during his ~** während er (dort) Mieter/Pächter ist/war

tenant ['tenənt] N Mieter(in) m(f); (of farm) Pächter(in) m(f)

tend¹ [tend] VT sich kümmern um; sheep hüten; machine bedienen

tend² VI (a) **to ~ to be/do sth** gewöhnlich or gern etw sein/ tun; (person also) dazu neigen, etw zu sein/tun; **the lever ~s to stick** der Hebel bleibt oft hängen; **that would ~ to suggest that ...** das würde gewissermaßen darauf hindeuten, dass ... (b) **to ~ toward(s)** (= be directed, lead) (measures etc) führen zu, anstreben; (= incline, person, views etc) neigen or tendieren zu

tendency ['tendənsɪ] N Tendenz f (geh); (= physical predisposition) Neigung f; **artistic tendencies** künstlerische Neigungen pl; **to have a ~ to be/do sth** gern or gewöhnlich etw sein/tun; (person also) dazu neigen or tendieren, etw zu sein/zu tun; **there is a ~ for prices to rise in autumn** gewöhnlich steigen die Preise im Herbst; **a strong upward ~** (St Ex) eine stark steigende Tendenz

tender¹ ['tendəʳ] **1** VT money, services, shares (an)bieten; apology aussprechen; resignation einreichen **2** VI (Comm) sich bewerben (for um) **3** N (Comm) Angebot nt; **to invite ~s for a job** Angebote pl für eine Arbeit einholen; **to put work**

out to ~ Arbeiten *pl* ausschreiben; **we won the** ~ wir haben die Ausschreibung gewonnen; ~ **price** Angebotspreis *m*

tender² ADJ **(a)** *spot, bruise* empfindlich; *skin, plant, meat* zart; *(fig) subject* heikel; **at the** ~ **age of 7** im zarten Alter von 7 Jahren; **cook the carrots until** ~ die Möhren kochen bis sie weich sind **(b)** (= *affectionate*) *person, look* liebevoll; *kiss, embrace* zärtlich; ~ **loving care** Liebe und Zuneigung *f*; **in sb's** ~ **care** in jds Obhut

tenderhearted [ˌtendəˈhaːtɪd] ADJ gutherzig

tendering [ˈtendərɪŋ] N, NO PL *(Comm)* Angebotsabgabe *f*

tenderly [ˈtendəlɪ] ADV liebevoll

tenderness [ˈtendənɪs] N **(a)** (= *soreness*) Empfindlichkeit *f* **(b)** (*of meat*) Zartheit *f* **(c)** (= *affection*) (*of person, look*) Zärtlichkeit *f*; (*of heart*) Güte *f*

tendon [ˈtendən] N Sehne *f*

tendril [ˈtendrɪl] N Ranke *f*

Tenerife [ˌtenəˈriːf] N Teneriffa *nt*

tenfold [ˈtenfəʊld] **1** ADJ zehnfach **2** ADV um das Zehnfache; **to increase** ~ sich verzehnfachen

tennis [ˈtenɪs] N Tennis *nt*

tennis IN CPDS Tennis-; **tennis court** N Tennisplatz *m*; **tennis racket, tennis racquet** N Tennisschläger *m*

tenor [ˈtenə] **1** N Tenor *m* **2** ADJ *(Mus)* Tenor-

tenpin bowling [ˌtenpɪnˈbəʊlɪŋ], (*US*) **tenpins** [ˈtenpɪnz] N Bowling *nt*

tense¹ [tens] N *(Gram)* Zeit *f*; **present** ~ Gegenwart *f*; **past** ~ Vergangenheit *f*; **future** ~ Zukunft *f*

tense² **1** ADJ (+ER) *rope, silence, atmosphere* gespannt; *muscles, situation* (an)gespannt; *neck* verspannt; *relations, person, expression* (*through stress etc*) angespannt; (*through nervousness, fear etc*) verkrampft; *voice* nervös; *time, negotiations, scene* spannungsgeladen; **to grow** *or* **become** *or* **get** ~ (*person*) nervös werden; **to make sb** ~ jdn in Anspannung versetzen **2** VT anspannen **3** VI sich (an)spannen, sich straffen

➤ **tense up** **1** VI sich anspannen **2** VT SEP anspannen

tension [ˈtenʃən] N (*lit*) Spannung *f*; (*of muscle*) Anspannung *f*; (= *nervous strain also*) nervliche Belastung *f*; (*in relationship*) Spannungen *pl*

tent [tent] N Zelt *nt*

tentacle [ˈtentəkl] N *(Zool)* Tentakel *m or nt* (*spec*)

tentative [ˈtentətɪv] ADJ (= *not definite*) vorläufig; *offer* unverbindlich; (= *hesitant*) *conclusion, suggestion* vorsichtig; *smile* zögernd; **we've a** ~ **arrangement to play tennis tonight** wir haben halb abgemacht, heute Abend Tennis zu spielen

tentatively [ˈtentətɪvlɪ] ADV (= *hesitantly*) *smile* zögernd; (= *gingerly*) vorsichtig; (= *provisionally*) *agree* vorläufig

tenterhooks [ˈtentəhʊks] PL **to be on** ~ wie auf glühenden Kohlen sitzen (*inf*); **to keep sb on** ~ jdn zappeln lassen

tenth [tenθ] **1** ADJ (*in series*) zehnte(r, s); **a** ~ **part** ein Zehntel *nt* **2** N (= *fraction*) Zehntel *nt*; (*in series*) Zehnte(r, s); (*Mus*) Dezime *f*; *see also* **sixth**

tent peg N Zeltpflock *m*, Hering *m*

tenuous [ˈtenjʊəs] ADJ (*fig*) *connection etc* schwach; *position* unsicher; **to have a** ~ **grasp of sth** etw nur ansatzweise verstehen

tenure [ˈtenjʊə] N **(a)** (= *holding of office*) Anstellung *f*; (= *period of office*) Amtszeit *f* **(b)** (*of property*) **during her** ~ **of the farm** während sie die Farm innehatte

tepid [ˈtepɪd] ADJ (*lit, fig*) lau(warm)

tequila [tɪˈkiːlə] N Tequila *m*

term [tɜːm] **1** N **(a)** (= *period of time*) Dauer *f*, Zeitraum *m*; (*of contract*) Laufzeit *f*; (= *limit*) Frist *f*; ~ **of government/office** Regierungs-/Amtszeit *f*; ~ **of imprisonment** Gefängnisstrafe *f*; **elected for a three-year** ~ auf *or* für drei Jahre gewählt; **in the long/short** ~ auf lange/kurze Sicht; **at** ~ (*Fin*) bei Fälligkeit **(b)** (*Sch*) (*three in one year*) Trimester *nt*; (*two in one year*) Halbjahr *nt*; (*Univ*) Semester *nt* **(c)** (= *expression*) Ausdruck *m*; **in simple** ~**s** in einfachen Worten; **a contradiction in** ~**s** ein Widerspruch in sich **(d)** (*Math, Logic*) Term *m*; **in** ~**s of production we are doing well** was die Produktion betrifft, stehen wir gut da; **in** ~**s of money** finanziell **(e) terms** PL (= *conditions*) Bedingungen *pl*; ~**s of surrender/payment** Kapitulations-/Zahlungsbedingungen *pl*; ~**s of**

delivery/trade Liefer-/Handelsbedingungen *pl*; **on what** ~**s?** zu welchen Bedingungen?; **not on any** ~**s** unter gar keinen Umständen; **to accept sb on his/her own** ~**s** jdn nehmen, wie er/sie ist; **on equal** ~**s** auf gleicher Basis; **to come to** ~**s (with sb)** sich (mit jdm) einigen **(f) terms** PL (= *relations*) **to be on good/bad** ~**s with sb** gut/nicht (gut) mit jdm auskommen; **to be on friendly** ~**s with sb** auf freundschaftlichem Fuß mit jdm stehen; **they are not on speaking** ~**s** sie reden nicht miteinander **2** VT nennen, bezeichnen

term deposit N (*Brit*) Termineinlage *f*, Festgeld *nt*

terminal [ˈtɜːmɪnl] **1** ADJ (= *final*) End-; (*Med*) unheilbar; (= *dire*) *problem* fatal; ~ **stage** Endstadium *nt*; **to be in** ~ **decline** in unaufhaltsamem Niedergang befinden **2** N **(a)** (*Rail*) Endbahnhof *m*; (*for tramway, buses*) Endstation *f*; **air** *or* **airport** ~ (Flughafen)terminal *m*; **ferry** ~ Fährterminal *m*; **railway** (*Brit*) *or* **railroad** (*US*) ~ Zielbahnhof *m* **(b)** (*Elec*) Pol *m* **(c)** (*Comput*) Terminal *nt*

terminal bonus N (*Insur*) Zusatzdividende *f* (*fällig bei Vertragsablauf*)

terminally [ˈtɜːmɪnlɪ] ADV ~ **ill** unheilbar krank

terminal station N (*Rail*) Endbahnhof *m*

terminate [ˈtɜːmɪneɪt] **1** VT beenden; *contract etc* lösen; *pregnancy* unterbrechen; *employment* kündigen **2** VI enden; (*contract, lease*) ablaufen

termination [ˌtɜːmɪˈneɪʃən] N Ende *nt*; (= *bringing to an end*) Beendigung *f*; (*of contract etc*) (= *expiry*) Ablauf *m*; (= *cancellation*) Lösung *f*; ~ **of pregnancy** Schwangerschaftsabbruch *m*

terminology [ˌtɜːmɪˈnɒlədʒɪ] N Terminologie *f*; **all the technical** ~ **in the article** all die Fachausdrücke in dem Artikel

terminus [ˈtɜːmɪnəs] N (*Rail, bus*) Endstation *f*

termite [ˈtɜːmaɪt] N Termite *f*

term: **term life insurance** N Risikolebensversicherung *f*; **term loan** N Kredit *m* mit fester Laufzeit

terrace [ˈterəs] N **(a)** Terrasse *f* **(b)** (*Brit*: = *row of houses*) Häuserreihe *f*

terraced [ˈterəst] ADJ **(a)** *hillside etc* terrassenförmig *or* stufenförmig angelegt; *garden* in Terrassen angelegt **(b)** (*esp Brit*) ~ **house** Reihenhaus *nt*

terrain [teˈreɪn] N Terrain *nt* (*esp Mil*), Gelände *nt*; (*fig*) Boden *m*

terrapin [ˈterəpɪn] N Sumpfschildkröte *f*

terrestrial [tɪˈrestrɪəl] ADJ terrestrisch

terrible [ˈterəbl] ADJ schrecklich, furchtbar; **he is** ~ **at golf** er spielt schrecklich (*inf*) *or* furchtbar schlecht Golf; **I feel** ~ (= *feel ill*) mir ist fürchterlich schlecht; (= *feel guilty*) es ist mir furchtbar peinlich

terribly [ˈterəblɪ] ADV schrecklich; *disappointed, sorry, suffer* furchtbar; *play, sing* fürchterlich; *important, difficult* schrecklich (*inf*); **I'm not** ~ **good with money** ich kann nicht besonders gut mit Geld umgehen

terrier [ˈterɪə] N Terrier *m*

terrific [təˈrɪfɪk] ADJ *nuisance, shock* unheimlich (*inf*); *person, success, idea, party also* sagenhaft (*inf*); *speed, heat* unwahrscheinlich (*inf*); **that's** ~ **news** das sind tolle Nachrichten (*inf*); **to have a** ~ **time** viel Spaß haben; ~! (*also iro*) prima! (*inf*)

terrified [ˈterɪfaɪd] ADJ verängstigt; *look also* angstvoll; **to be** ~ **of sth** vor etw schreckliche Angst haben; **he was** ~ **in case ...** er hatte fürchterliche Angst davor, dass ...

terrify [ˈterɪfaɪ] VT in Angst *or* Schrecken versetzen

terrifying [ˈterɪfaɪɪŋ] ADJ *film, story* Grauen erregend; *thought, sight* entsetzlich; *speed* Angst erregend

territorial [ˌterɪˈtɔːrɪəl] ADJ territorial; ~ **rights** Hoheitsrechte *pl*

Territorial Army N (*Brit*) Territorialheer *nt*

TERRITORIAL ARMY

*Die **Territorial Army** (abgekürzt auch **TA**) ist eine britische Organisation freiwilliger Armeereservisten. Die Mitglieder sind Zivilisten, die in ihrer Freizeit Militärübungen absolvieren und in Kriegs- oder Krisenzeiten zur Unterstützung der regulären Armee zur Verfügung stehen.*

territory ['terɪtərɪ] N Territorium *nt*; (*of animals*) Revier *nt*; (*fig also*) Gebiet *nt*; (*Comm: of agent etc*) Bezirk *m*; **that comes** *or* **goes with the ~** das gehört einfach dazu

terror ['terə'] N (**a**) NO PL (= *great fear*) panische Angst (*of* vor +*dat*); **the IRA ~ campaign** die Terrorkampagne der IRA (**b**) (= *cause of ~, terrible event*) Schrecken *m* (**c**) (*inf*) (= *person*) Teufel *m*; (= *child*) Ungeheuer *nt*

terrorism ['terərɪzəm] N Terrorismus *m*; (= *acts of ~*) Terror *m*; **an act of ~** ein Terrorakt *m*

terrorist ['terərɪst] **1** N Terrorist(in) *m(f)* **2** ADJ ATTR terroristisch; **~ attack** Terroranschlag *m*

terrorize ['terəraɪz] VT terrorisieren

terse [tɜːs] ADJ (+ER) knapp; **he was very ~** er war sehr kurz angebunden

tersely ['tɜːslɪ] ADV knapp, kurz; *say, answer* kurz (angebunden)

tertiary ['tɜːʃərɪ] ADJ tertiär; **~ education** (*Brit*) Universitätsausbildung *f*

TESL ABBR *of* **Teaching of English as a Second Language** *see* **TEFL**

TESOL ABBR *of* **Teaching of English as a Second or Other Language** *see* **TEFL**

test [test] **1** N Test *m*; (= *chemical ~ also*) Untersuchung *f*; (*Sch*) Klassenarbeit *f*; (*Univ*) Klausur *f*; (*short*) Kurzarbeit *f*; (= *driving ~*) (Fahr)prüfung *f*; (= *check*) Untersuchung *f*; **he gave them a vocabulary ~** er ließ eine Vokabelarbeit schreiben; (*orally*) er hat sie Vokabeln abgefragt; **to put sb/ sth to the ~** jdn/etw auf die Probe stellen; **to stand the ~ of time** die Zeit überdauern; **that was a real ~ of character** das war eine wirkliche Charakterprüfung für ihn; **the samples were sent for ~s** die Proben wurden zur Untersuchung geschickt
2 ADJ ATTR Test-
3 VT (**a**) testen; (= *examine, check also, Sch*) prüfen; (*orally*) abfragen; (*fig*) auf die Probe stellen; **to ~ sb/sth for accuracy** jdn/etw auf Genauigkeit prüfen
(**b**) (*chemically*) *water etc* untersuchen; **to ~ sth for sugar** etw auf seinen Zuckergehalt untersuchen; **the blood samples were sent for ~ing** *or* **to be ~ed** die Blutproben wurden zur Untersuchung geschickt
4 VI Tests/einen Test machen; (*chemically also*) untersuchen (*for* auf +*acc*)
➤ **test out** VT SEP ausprobieren (*on* bei *or* an +*dat*)

testament ['testəmənt] N (*Bibl*) **Old/New Testament** Altes/Neues Testament

test: **test ban** N Versuchsverbot *nt*; **test bay, test-bed** N Prüfstand *m*; **test case** N Musterfall *m*; **test drive** N Probefahrt *f*; **test-drive** VT probefahren

tester ['testə'] N (*of product etc*) Prüfer(in) *m(f)*

test flight N Test- *or* Probeflug *m*

testicle ['testɪkl] N Testikel *m*, Hoden *m*

testify ['testɪfaɪ] **1** VT **to ~ that ...** (*Jur*) bezeugen, dass ... **2** VI (*Jur*) aussagen; **to ~ against/for sb** gegen/für jdn aussagen

testily ['testɪlɪ] ADV *say* unwirsch, gereizt

testimonial [testɪ'məʊnɪəl] N (**a**) (= *character recommendation*) Referenz *f* (**b**) (*Sport*) Gedenkspiel *nt*

testimony ['testɪmənɪ] N Aussage *f*; **he gave his ~** er machte seine Aussage; **to bear ~ to sth** etw bezeugen

testing ['testɪŋ] ADJ hart

testing ground N Test- *or* Versuchsgebiet *nt*; (*fig*) Versuchsfeld *nt*

testosterone [te'stɒstərəʊn] N Testosteron *nt*

test: **test piece** N (*of handwork*) Prüfungsstück *nt*; **test pilot** N Testpilot(in) *m(f)*; **test results** PL (*Med etc*) Testwerte *pl*; **test tube** N Reagenzglas *nt*; **test-tube baby** N Retortenbaby *nt*

testy ['testɪ] ADJ (+ER) unwirsch, gereizt

tetanus ['tetənəs] N Tetanus *m*

tetchy, techy ['tetʃɪ] ADJ (+ER) (*esp Brit inf*) (*on particular occasion*) gereizt; (*generally*) reizbar

tête-à-tête [teɪtɑː'teɪt] **1** ADJ, ADV unter vier Augen **2** N Tête-a-tete *nt*

tether ['teðə'] **1** N (*lit*) Strick *m*; (= *chain*) Kette *f*; **he was at the end of his ~** (*Brit fig inf*) (= *annoyed*) ihm hats gereicht (*inf*); (= *desperate*) er war am Ende (*inf*) **2** VT (*also* **up**) anbinden

Teutonic [tjuː'tɒnɪk] ADJ (*Hist, hum*) teutonisch

Texas ['teksəs] N Texas *nt*

text [tekst] **1** N Text *m* **2** VT **to ~ sb** (*on mobile phone*) jdm eine Textnachricht *or* eine SMS schicken

textbook ['tekstbʊk] **1** N Lehrbuch *nt* **2** ADJ **~ case** Paradefall *m*; **~ landing** Bilderbuchlandung *f*

text editor N (*Comput*) Texteditor *m*

textile ['tekstaɪl] **1** ADJ Textil- **2** N Stoff *m*; **~s** Textilien *pl*

text (*Comput*): **text input** N Texteingabe *f*; **text message** N Textnachricht *f*, SMS *f*; **text messaging** N (*Telec*) SMS-Messaging *nt*, SMS-Versand *m*; **text processing** N Textverarbeitung *f*; **text processor** N Textverarbeitungssystem *nt*

textual ['tekstjʊəl] ADJ Text-; **~ analysis** Textanalyse *f*

texture ['tekstʃə'] N (stoffliche) Beschaffenheit, Textur *f*; (*of dough also*) Konsistenz *f*; (*of food*) Substanz *f*; (*of material, paper*) Griff *m* und Struktur; (*fig: of music etc*) Gestalt *f*; **the ~ of velvet** wie sich Samt anfühlt

textured ['tekstʃəd] ADJ strukturiert

Thai [taɪ] **1** ADJ thailändisch **2** N (**a**) Thailänder(in) *m(f)* (**b**) (= *language*) Thai *nt*; (= *language family*) Tai *nt*

Thailand ['taɪlænd] N Thailand *nt*

Thames [temz] N Themse *f*

than [ðæn, (*weak form*) ðən] CONJ als; **I'd rather do anything ~ that** das wäre das Letzte, was ich tun wollte; **no sooner had I sat down ~ he began to talk** kaum hatte ich mich hingesetzt, als er auch schon anfing zu reden; **who better to help us ~ he?** wer könnte uns besser helfen als er?

thank [θæŋk] VT danken (+*dat*), sich bedanken bei; **he won't ~ you for it** er wird es Ihnen nicht danken; **he has his brother/ he only has himself to ~ for this** das hat er seinem Bruder zu verdanken/sich selbst zuzuschreiben; **~ you** danke (schön); **~ you very much** vielen Dank; **no ~ you** nein, danke; **yes, ~ you** ja, bitte *or* danke; **~ you for coming – not at all, ~ YOU!** vielen Dank, dass Sie gekommen sind – ICH habe zu danken; **to say ~ you** danke sagen (*to sb* jdm); **~ goodness** *or* **heavens** *or* **God** (*inf*) Gott sei Dank! (*inf*)

thankful ['θæŋkfʊl] ADJ dankbar (*to sb* jdm); **to be ~ to sb for sth** jdm für etw dankbar sein

thankfully ['θæŋkfəlɪ] ADV dankbar; **~, no real harm has been done** zum Glück ist kein wirklicher Schaden entstanden

thankless ['θæŋklɪs] ADJ undankbar

thanks [θæŋks] **1** PL Dank *m*; **to accept sth with ~** etw dankend *or* mit Dank annehmen; **and that's all the – I get** und das ist jetzt der Dank dafür; **to give ~ to God** Gott danksagen; **~ to** wegen (+*gen*); (*with positive cause also*) dank (+*gen*); **it's all ~ to you that we're so late** bloß deinetwegen kommen wir so spät; **it was no ~ to him that ...** ich hatte/wir hatten *etc* es nicht ihm zu verdanken, dass ...
2 INTERJ (*inf*) danke (*for* für); **many ~** vielen *or* herzlichen Dank (*for* für); **~ a lot** *or* **a million** vielen *or* tausend Dank; (*iro*) (*na,*) vielen Dank (*inf*); **~ for nothing!** (*iro*) vielen Dank auch!; **will you have some more? – no ~/yes, ~** etwas mehr? – nein/ ja, danke

Thanksgiving (Day) ['θæŋksɡɪvɪŋ(deɪ)] N (*US*) Thanksgiving Day *m*

THANKSGIVING

Thanksgiving Day oder auch einfach nur *Thanksgiving* ist ein Feiertag in den USA, der auf den vierten Donnerstag im November fällt. Er erinnert an das erste Erntedankfest der Pilgrim Fathers, als diese im Jahre 1621 ihre erste erfolgreiche Ernte auf amerikanischem Boden feierten. Deshalb darf bei keinem traditionellen Thanksgiving-Festessen der Truthahnbraten und der Kürbiskuchen fehlen. Bei einem solchen Essen versammelt sich häufig die gesamte Familie.

In Kanada gibt es am zweiten Montag im Oktober einen ähnlichen Feiertag. ▶ PILGRIM FATHERS

---

thank you N Dankeschön *nt*; **thank-you letter** Dankschreiben *nt*

that¹ [ðæt, (*weak form*) ðət] **1** DEM PRON, *pl* **those** (**a**) das; **what is ~?** was ist das?; **they all say ~** das sagen alle; **~ is Joe (over there)** das (dort) ist Joe; **who is ~ ~ speaking?** wer spricht (denn) da?; (*on phone*) wer ist am Apparat?; **if she's as stupid** *etc* **as (all) ~** wenn sie so *or* derart dumm *etc* ist; **I didn't think she'd get/be as angry as ~** ich hätte nicht gedacht, dass sie sich so ärgern würde; **... and all ~** ... und so (*inf*); **like ~** so; **with luck like ~ ...** bei solchem *or* so einem (*inf*) Glück ...; **just**

like ~ einfach so; **~'s got ~/him out of the way** so, das wäre geschafft/den wären wir los; **~ is (to say)** das heißt; **oh well, ~'s ~** nun ja, damit ist der Fall erledigt; **you can't go and ~'s ~** du darfst nicht gehen, und damit hat sichs *or* und damit basta (*inf*); **well, ~'s ~ then** das wärs dann also; **so ~ was ~** damit hatte sichs; **~'s it!** das ist es!; (= *the right way*) gut so!; (= *the last straw*) jetzt reichts!; **after/before/below/over ~** danach/davor/darunter/darüber; **and ... at ~** und dabei ...; **you can get it in any supermarket and quite cheaply at ~** man kann es in jedem Supermarkt, und zwar ganz billig, bekommen; **what do you mean by ~?** (*not understanding*) was wollen Sie damit sagen?; (*amazed, annoyed*) was soll (denn) das heißen?; **as for ~** was das betrifft *or* angeht; **if it has come to ~** wenn es (schon) so weit gekommen ist
(b) (*opposed to "this" and "these"*) das (da), jenes (*old, geh*); **~'s the one I like, not this one** das (dort) mag ich, nicht dies (hier)
(c) (*followed by rel pron*) **this theory is different from ~ which ...** diese Theorie unterscheidet sich von derjenigen, die ...; **~ which we call ...** das, was wir ... nennen

▨ DEM ADJ, *pl* **those** der/die/das, jene(r, s); **what was ~ noise?** was war das für ein Geräusch?; **~ dog!** dieser Hund!; **~ poor girl!** das arme Mädchen!; **I only saw him on ~ one occasion** ich habe ihn nur bei dieser einen Gelegenheit gesehen; **~ morning I had put on my green dress** an jenem Morgen hatte ich mein grünes Kleid an(gezogen); **I like ~ one** ich mag da da; **I'd like ~ one, not this one** ich möchte das da, nicht dies hier; **she was rushing this way and ~** sie rannte hierhin und dorthin; **~ dog of yours!** Ihr Hund, dieser Hund von Ihnen (*inf*)

▨ DEM ADV (*inf*) so; **it's not ~ good** *etc* SO gut *etc* ist es auch wieder nicht; **he was ~ angry** er hat sich DERart(ig) geärgert

that² REL PRON (*after def art*) der/die/das; **all/nothing** *etc* **~ ...** alles/nichts *etc*, was ...; **the best** *etc* **~ ...** das Beste *etc*, das *or* was ...; **the girl ~ I told you about** das Mädchen, von dem ich Ihnen erzählt habe; **no-one has come ~ I know of** soviel ich weiß, ist niemand gekommen; **the day ~ we spent on the beach was one of the hottest** der Tag, den wir am Strand verbrachten, war einer der heißesten; **the day ~ ...** an dem Tag, als ...

that³ CONJ dass; **she promised ~ she would come** sie versprach zu kommen; **he said ~ it was wrong** er sagte, es sei *or* wäre (*inf*) falsch, er sagte, dass es falsch sei *or* wäre (*inf*); **~ things *or* it should come to this!** dass es so weit kommen konnte!

thatched [θætʃt] ADJ (*with straw*) strohgedeckt; (*with reeds*) reetgedeckt; **~ roof** Stroh-/Reetdach *nt*

Thatcherism [ˈθætʃərɪzəm] N Thatcherismus *m*

thaw [θɔː] ▨ VT auftauen (lassen); *snow also* tauen lassen ▨ VI (*lit, fig*) auftauen; (*snow*) tauen; **it is -ing** es taut ▨ N (*lit, fig*) Tauwetter *nt*

➤ **thaw out** ▨ VI (*lit, fig*) auftauen ▨ VT SEP (*lit*) *frozen food etc* auftauen (lassen)

the [ðə, (*before vowels, stressed also*) ðiː] ▨ DEF ART **(a)** der/die/das; **in ~ room** im *or* in dem Zimmer; **on ~ edge** am *or* an dem Rand; **to play ~ piano** Klavier spielen; **all ~ windows** all die *or* alle Fenster; **have you invited ~ Browns?** haben Sie die Browns *or* (*with children*) die Familie Brown eingeladen?; **Henry ~ Eighth** Heinrich der Achte; **by ~ hour** pro Stunde; **the car does thirty miles to ~ gallon** das Auto verbraucht 11 Liter auf 100km; **it's THE restaurant in this part of town** das ist DAS Restaurant in diesem Stadtteil
(b) (*with adj used as n*) das, die; (*with comp or superl*) der/die/das; **~ poor** die Armen *pl*
▨ ADV (*with comp adj or adv*) **all ~ more/better** umso mehr/besser; **~ more he has ~ more he wants** je mehr er hat, desto mehr will er

theatre, (*US*) **theater** [ˈθɪətəʳ] N **(a)** Theater *nt*; **to go to the ~** ins Theater gehen; **what's on at the ~?** was wird im Theater gegeben? **(b)** (*Brit: = operating ~*) Operationssaal *m* **(c)** (= *scene of events*) Schauplatz *m*

theatre, (*US*) **theater**: **theatre company** N Theaterensemble *nt*; (*touring*) Schauspieltruppe *f*; **theatregoer**, (*US*) **theatergoer** N Theaterbesucher(in) *m(f)*

theatrical [θɪˈætrɪkəl] ADJ **(a)** Theater- **(b)** (*pej*) *behaviour etc* theatralisch

theatrically [θɪˈætrɪkəlɪ] ADV (*pej*) *behave, speak* theatralisch

theft [θeft] N Diebstahl *m*

their [ðɛəʳ] POSS ADJ **(a)** ihr **(b)** (*inf: = belonging to him or her*) seine(r, s); *see also* **my**

theirs [ðɛəz] POSS PRON **(a)** ihre(r, s) **(b)** (*inf: = belonging to him or her*) seine(r, s); *see also* **mine¹**

them [ðem, (*weak form*) ðəm] PERS PRON PL (*dir obj, with prep +acc, emph*) sie; (*indir obj, with prep +dat*) ihnen; **both of ~ saw me** beide haben mich gesehen; **neither of ~ saw me** keiner von beiden hat mich gesehen; **give me a few of ~** geben Sie mir ein paar davon; **none of ~** keiner/keinen von ihnen; **he's one of ~** das ist einer von ihnen; **~ and us** (*inf*) sie *or* die (*inf*) und wir; **it's ~** sie sinds

thematic ADJ, **thematically** ADV [θɪˈmætɪk, -əlɪ] thematisch

theme [θiːm] N **(a)** Thema *nt* (*also Mus*) **(b)** (*US Sch: = essay*) Aufsatz *m*

theme: **theme music** N (*Film*) Titelmusik *f*; (*TV*) Erkennungsmelodie *f*; **theme park** N Themenpark *m*; **theme tune** N = **theme music**

themselves [ðəmˈselvz] PERS PRON PL **(a)** (*reflexive*) sich **(b)** (*emph*) selbst; *see also* **myself**

then [ðen] ▨ ADV **(a)** (= *next, afterwards, in that case*) dann; (= *furthermore also*) außerdem; **and ~ what happened?** und was geschah dann?; **I don't want that - ~ what DO you want?** ich will das nicht – was willst du denn?; **what are you going to do, ~?** was wollen Sie dann tun?; **but ~ that means that ...** das bedeutet ja aber dann, dass ...; **all right, ~** also *or* dann meinetwegen; **(so) I was right ~** ich hatte also Recht; **(and) ~ there's my aunt** und dann ist da noch meine Tante; **but ~ ...** aber ... auch; **but ~ again he is my friend** aber andererseits ist er mein Freund; **now ~, what's the matter?** na, was ist denn los?; **come on ~** nun komm doch
(b) (= *at this particular time*) da; (= *in those days*) damals; **I will be in Paris ~** ich werde da in Paris sein; **he did it ~ and there** *or* **there and ~** er hat es auf der Stelle getan; **from ~ on(wards)** von da an; **before ~** vorher, zuvor; **but they had gone by ~** aber da waren sie schon weg; **we'll be ready by ~** bis dahin sind wir fertig; **since ~** seitdem, seit der Zeit; **(up) until ~ I had never tried it** bis dahin hatte ich es nie versucht
▨ ADJ ATTR damalig

theologian [θɪəˈləʊdʒən] N Theologe *m*, Theologin *f*

theological [θɪəˈlɒdʒɪkəl] ADJ theologisch

theology [θɪˈɒlədʒɪ] N Theologie *f*

theoretic(al) [θɪəˈretɪk(əl)] ADJ, **theoretically** [θɪəˈretɪkəlɪ] ADV theoretisch

theorize [ˈθɪəraɪz] VI theoretisieren

theory [ˈθɪərɪ] N Theorie *f*; **in ~** theoretisch; **~ of evolution** Evolutionstheorie *f*; **he has a ~ that ...** er hat die Theorie, dass ...

therapeutic(al) [θerəˈpjuːtɪk(əl)] ADJ therapeutisch; **to be therapeutic** therapeutisch wirken

therapist [ˈθerəpɪst] N Therapeut(in) *m(f)*

therapy [ˈθerəpɪ] N Therapie *f*; **to be in ~** sich einer Therapie unterziehen

there [ðɛəʳ] ▨ ADV dort, da (*also fig*); (*with movement*) dorthin, dahin; **look, ~'s Joe/~'s Joe coming** guck mal, da ist/kommt Joe; **it's under/over/in ~** es liegt dort *or* da drunter/drüben/drin; **put it under/in/on ~** stellen Sie es dort *or* da drunter/rein *or* hinein/drauf *or* hinauf; **let's stop ~** hören wir doch da auf; (*travelling*) halten wir doch da *or* dort an; **~ and back** hin und zurück; **so ~ we were** da waren wir nun also; **is Gordon ~ please?** (*on telephone*) ist Gordon da?; **you've got me ~** da bin ich überfragt; **~ is/are** es *or* da ist/sind; (= *~ exists/exist also*) es gibt; **~ were three of us** wir waren zu dritt; **~ is a mouse in the room** es ist eine Maus im Zimmer; **~ was once a castle here** hier war *or* stand einmal eine Burg; **is a chair in the corner** in der Ecke steht ein Stuhl; **is ~ any beer?** ist Bier da?; **~ afterwards ~ was coffee** anschließend gab es Kaffee; **is ~ any wine left? - well, ~ was** ist noch Wein da? – gerade war noch welcher da; **~ isn't any food/time/point, is ~? - yes ~ is** es gibt wohl nichts zu essen/dazu haben wir wohl keine Zeit/das hat wohl keinen Sinn, oder? – doch!; **~ seems to be no-one at home** es scheint keiner zu Hause zu sein; **~ comes a time when ...** es kommt eine Zeit, wo ...; **hi ~!** hallo!; **~ you go again** (*inf*) jetzt gehts schon wieder los; **now ~'s a real woman** das ist eine richtige Frau; **so ~!** ätsch!; **~ you are** (*giving sb sth*) hier(, bitte)!; (*on finding sb*) da sind Sie ja!; **~ you *or* we are, you see, I knew he'd say that** na, sehen Sie, ich habe es ja gewusst, dass er das sagen würde

2 INTERJ ~! ~! na, na!; **stop crying now, ~'s a good boy** hör auf zu weinen, na komm; **now ~'s a good boy, don't tease your sister** komm, sei ein braver Junge und ärgere deine Schwester nicht; **hey, you ~!** (*inf*) he, Sie da!; **~! I knew it would break!** da! ich habs ja gewusst, dass es kaputtgehen würde!

thereabouts [‚ðɛərə'baʊts] ADV **fifteen or ~** so um fünfzehn (herum)

thereby [‚ðɛə'baɪ] ADV dadurch, damit

therefore ['ðɛəfɔ:ʳ] ADV deshalb, daher; (*as logical consequence*) also; **so ~ I was wrong** ich hatte also Unrecht

there's [ðɛəz] CONTR *of* **there is, there has**

thereupon [‚ðɛərə'pɒn] ADV (= *then*) darauf(hin)

thermal ['θɜ:məl] **1** ADJ (a) (*Phys*) Wärme- (b) *clothing* Thermo-; **~ blanket** Aluminiumdecke *f* **2** N **thermals** PL (*inf*: = ~ **underwear**) Thermounterwäsche *f*

thermal: **thermal baths** PL Thermalbäder *pl*; **thermal printer** N (*Comput*) Thermodrucker *m*; **thermal spring** N Thermalquelle *f*

thermometer [θə'mɒmɪtəʳ] N Thermometer *nt*

Thermos® ['θɜ:məs] N (*also* **~ flask** *or* (*US*) **bottle**) Thermosflasche *f*

thermostat ['θɜ:məstæt] N Thermostat *m*

thesaurus [θɪ'sɔ:rəs] N Thesaurus *m*

these [ði:z] ADJ, PRON *see* **this**

thesis ['θi:sɪs] N, *pl* **theses** ['θi:si:z] (*Univ*) (*for PhD*) Dissertation *f*, Doktorarbeit *f* (*inf*); (*for diploma*) Diplomarbeit *f*

thespian ['θespɪən] (*liter, hum*) **1** ADJ dramatisch **2** N Mime *m*, Mimin *f*

they [ðeɪ] PERS PRON PL (a) sie; **~ are very good people** es sind sehr gute Leute; **~ who** diejenigen, die *or* welche, wer (+*sing vb*) (b) (= *people in general*) **~ say that ...** man sagt, dass ...; **~ are going to build a new road** man will *or* sie wollen eine neue Straße bauen; **~ are thinking of changing the law** es ist beabsichtigt, das Gesetz zu ändern; **if anyone looks at this closely, ~ will notice ...** (*inf*) wenn sich das jemand näher ansieht, wird er bemerken ...

they'd [ðeɪd] CONTR *of* **they had, they would**

they'd've [ðeɪdəv] CONTR *of* **they would have**

they'll [ðeɪl] CONTR *of* **they will**

they're [ðeəʳ] CONTR *of* **they are**

they've [ðeɪv] CONTR *of* **they have**

thick [θɪk] **1** ADJ (+ER) (a) dick; *thread, legs* stark; *lips* voll; *hair, fog, smoke, forest, hedge* dicht; *liquid, syrup etc* dick(flüssig); *air* schlecht, dick (*inf*); (= *airless*) *atmosphere* schwer; (= *unclear*) *voice* träge; *accent* breit; **a wall three feet ~** eine drei Fuß starke Wand; **they are ~ on the ground** (*inf*) die gibt es wie Sand am Meer (*inf*); **the air is ~ with rumours** Gerüchte liegen in der Luft

(b) (*Brit inf*: = *stupid*) *person* dumm, doof (*inf*); **to get sth into** *or* **through sb's ~ head** etw in jds dicken Schädel bekommen (*inf*)

2 N **to be in the ~ of the fighting** im dicksten Kampfgetümmel stecken; **in the ~ of it** mittendrin; **he likes to be in the ~ of things** er ist gern bei allem voll dabei; **to stick together through ~ and thin** zusammen durch dick und dünn gehen

3 ADV (+ER) *spread, lie, cut* dick; *grow* dicht; **the snow lay ~** es lag eine dichte Schneedecke; **offers of help poured in ~ and fast** es kam eine Flut von Hilfsangeboten; **the jokes came ~ and fast** die Witze kamen Schlag auf Schlag; **that's laying it on a bit ~** (*inf*) das ist ja wohl etwas übertrieben

thicken ['θɪkən] **1** VT *sauce etc* eindicken **2** VI (a) (*fog, crowd, forest*) dichter werden; (*smoke*) sich verdichten; (*sauce, mixture*) dick werden (b) (*fig: plot, mystery*) undurchsichtiger werden; **aha, the plot ~s!** aha, jetzt wirds interessant!

thicket ['θɪkɪt] N Dickicht *nt*

thickhead ['θɪkhed] N (*inf*) Dummkopf *m*

thickly ['θɪklɪ] ADV *spread, cut, lie* dick; *populated, wooded* dicht; **to be ~ covered with sth** dick mit etw bedeckt sein

thickness ['θɪknɪs] N (a) Dicke *f*; (*of wall, thread, legs also*) Stärke *f*; (*of forest, hedge*) Dichte *f*; (*of liquid, syrup etc*) Dickflüssigkeit *f*; (*of accent*) Stärke *f* (b) (= *layer*) Schicht *f*

thick: **thickset** ADJ gedrungen; **thick-skinned** ADJ (*lit*) dickhäutig; (*fig*) dickfellig

thief [θi:f] N, *pl* **thieves** [θi:vz] Dieb(in) *m(f)*; **to be as thick as thieves** (*Brit*) dicke Freunde sein (*inf*)

thieve [θi:v] VTI stehlen

thigh [θaɪ] N (Ober)schenkel *m*

thigh: **thighbone** N Oberschenkelknochen *m*; **thigh-length** ADJ *boots* übers Knie reichend; *coat* kurz

thimble ['θɪmbl] N Fingerhut *m*

thimble printer N (*Comput*) Thimbledrucker *m*

thin [θɪn] **1** ADJ (+ER) (a) dünn; *liquid* dünn(flüssig); (= *narrow*) *column* schmal; *fog* leicht; *hair, eyebrows* schütter; *vegetation* spärlich; *crowd* klein, kümmerlich (*pej*); **as ~ as a rake** (*Brit*) *or* **rail** (*US*) dünn wie eine Bohnenstange; **he's a bit ~ on top** bei ihm lichtet es sich oben schon ein wenig; **to be ~ on the ground** (*fig*) dünn gesät sein; **to vanish into ~ air** (*fig*) sich in Luft auflösen; **to appear out of ~ air** aus dem Nichts auftauchen

(b) (*fig*) *smile, excuse, plot* schwach; *profits* gering; **a ~ majority** eine knappe Mehrheit

2 ADV (+ER) *spread, cut* dünn; *lie* spärlich

3 VT *paint, sauce* verdünnen; *trees, ranks* lichten; *hair* ausdünnen; *blood* dünner werden lassen

4 VI (*fog, crowd*) sich lichten; (*hair also*) schütter werden; (*ozone layer*) dünner werden

➤ **thin down** VT SEP *paint, sauce* verdünnen

➤ **thin out 1** VI (*crowd*) kleiner werden; (*hair*) schütter werden; **the trees started thinning out** die Bäume lichteten sich **2** VT SEP *hair* ausdünnen; *seedlings also* verziehen; *forest* lichten

thing [θɪŋ] N (a) Ding *nt*; **a ~ of beauty** etwas Schönes; **she likes sweet ~s** sie mag Süßes; **what's that ~?** was ist das?; **I don't have a ~ to wear** ich habe nichts zum Anziehen; **poor little ~** das arme (kleine) Ding!; **you poor ~!** du Arme(r)!; **lucky ~!** der/die Glückliche/du Glückliche(r)!

(b) **things** PL (= *equipment, belongings*) Sachen *pl*; **have you got your swimming ~s?** hast du dein Badezeug *or* deine Badesachen dabei?

(c) (*non material*: = *affair, subject*) Sache *f*; **the odd ~ about it is ...** das Seltsame daran ist, ...; **it's a good ~ I came** nur gut, dass ich gekommen bin; **to make a big ~ of** *or* **about sth** viel Lärm um etw machen; **he's on to** *or* **onto a good ~** (*inf*) er hat da was Gutes aufgetan (*inf*); **what a (silly) ~ to do** wie kann man nur so was (Dummes) tun!; **there is one/one other ~ I want to ask you** eines/und noch etwas möchte ich Sie fragen; **the ~ you say!** was du so sagst!; **I must be hearing ~s!** ich glaube, ich höre nicht richtig!; **all the ~s I meant to say** alles, was ich sagen wollte; **to expect great ~s of sb/sth** Großes *or* große Dinge von jdm/etw erwarten; **I must think ~s over** ich muss mir die Sache *or* das überlegen; **~s are going from bad to worse** es wird immer schlimmer; **as ~s stand at the moment, as ~s are ...** so wie die Dinge im Moment liegen; **how are ~s (with you)?** wie gehts (bei) Ihnen?; **~s aren't what they used to be** es ist alles nicht mehr so wie früher; **it's been one ~ after the other (going wrong)** es kam eins zum anderen; **if it's not one ~ it's the other** es ist immer irgendetwas; **(what) with one ~ and another I haven't had time to do it yet** ich bin einfach noch nicht dazu gekommen; **it's neither one ~ nor the other** es ist weder das eine noch das andere; **~ led to another** eins führte zum anderen; **for one ~ it doesn't make sense** erst einmal ergibt das überhaupt keinen Sinn; **not to understand a ~** (*absolut*) nichts verstehen; **to tell sb a ~ or two** jdm einiges erzählen; **he knows a ~ or two about cars** er kennt sich mit Autos aus; **it's just one of those ~s** so was kommt eben vor (*inf*); **that's just the ~ for me** das ist genau das Richtige für mich; **that's not the ~ to do** so was macht *or* tut man nicht; **the latest ~ in ties** der letzte Schrei in der Krawattenmode; **the ~ to do now would be ...** was wir jetzt machen sollten, wäre ...; **I'm not at my best first ~ in the morning** so früh am Morgen bin ich nicht gerade in Hochform; **I'll do that first ~ in the morning** ich werde das gleich *or* als Erstes morgen früh tun; **last ~ at night** vor dem Schlafengehen; **the ~ is to know when ...** man muss wissen, wann ...; **yes, but the ~ is ...** ja, aber ...; **the ~ is we haven't got enough money** die Sache ist die, wir haben nicht genug Geld; **to do one's own ~** (*inf*) tun, was man will; **she's got this ~ about Sartre** (*inf*) (= *can't stand*) sie kann Sartre einfach nicht ausstehen; (= *is fascinated by*) sie hat einen richtigen Sartrefimmel (*inf*); **she's got a ~ about spiders** (*inf*) bei Spinnen dreht sie durch (*inf*); **(all)** ~**s mechanical** alles Mechanische

thingummybob [ˈθɪŋəmɪˌbɒb], **thingamajig** [ˈθɪŋəmɪˌdʒɪg], **thingummy** [ˈθɪŋəmɪ] N Dings(da) *nt* or (*for people*) *mf*, Dingsbums *nt* or (*for people*) *mf*

think [θɪŋk], *vb*: pret, ptp **thought** ▉ VI denken; **to ~ to oneself** sich (*dat*) denken; ~ **before you speak** denk nach or überleg, bevor du sprichst; **to act without ~ing** unüberlegt handeln; (= *stupidly also*) unbedacht handeln; ~ **again!** denk noch mal nach; **it makes you ~** es macht or stimmt einen nachdenklich; **I need time to ~** ich brauche Zeit zum Nachdenken; **it's so noisy you can't hear yourself ~** bei so einem Lärm kann doch kein Mensch denken; **now let me ~** lass (mich) mal überlegen or nachdenken; **it's a good idea, don't you ~?** es ist eine gute Idee, findest or meinst du nicht auch?; **just ~** stellen Sie sich (*dat*) bloß mal vor; **listen, I've been ~ing, ...** hör mal, ich habe mir überlegt ...; **sorry, I just wasn't ~ing** Entschuldigung, da habe ich geschlafen (*inf*); **you just didn't ~, did you?** da hast du dir nichts gedacht, oder?; **you just don't ~, do you?** (*about consequences*) was denkst du dir eigentlich?

▉ VT **(a)** (= *believe*) denken; (= *be of opinion also*) glauben, meinen; **I ~ you'll find I'm right** ich glaube or denke, Sie werden zu der Überzeugung gelangen, dass ich Recht habe; **well, I THINK it was there!** nun, ich glaube zumindest, dass es da war!; **and what do you ~?** asked the interviewer und was meinen Sie? fragte der Interviewer; **I ~ you'd better go** ich denke, Sie gehen jetzt besser; **I ~ so** ich denke or glaube (schon); **I ~ so too** das meine or denke ich auch; **I don't ~ so, I shouldn't ~ so, I ~ not** ich denke or glaube nicht; **I should ~ so!** das will ich (aber) auch gemeint haben; **I should ~ not!** das will ich auch nicht hoffen; **I hardly ~ that ...** ich glaube kaum, dass ...; **one would have thought there was an easier answer** man sollte eigentlich meinen, dass es da eine einfachere Lösung gäbe; **what do you ~ I should do?** was soll ich Ihrer Meinung nach tun?; **I ~ I'll go for a walk** ich glaube, ich mache einen Spaziergang; **do you ~ you can manage?** glauben Sie, dass Sie es schaffen?; **I was ~ing (to myself) how ill he looked** ich dachte mir (im Stillen), dass er sehr krank aussah; **I never thought to ask you** ich hätte gar nicht daran gedacht, Sie zu fragen; **I didn't ~ to see you here** ich hätte nicht gedacht or erwartet, Sie hier zu treffen; **I thought as much, I thought so** das habe ich mir schon gedacht

(b) (= *consider*) **you must ~ me very rude** Sie müssen mich für sehr unhöflich halten; **I wouldn't have thought it possible** das hätte ich nicht für möglich gehalten

(c) (= *imagine*) sich (*dat*) denken, sich (*dat*) vorstellen; **I don't know what to ~** ich weiß nicht, was ich davon halten soll; **that's what you ~!** denkste! (*inf*); **that's what he ~s** hat der eine Ahnung! (*inf*); **who do you ~ you are!** für wen hältst du dich eigentlich?; **anyone would ~ he was dying** man könnte beinahe glauben, er läge im Sterben; **who would have thought it?** wer hätte das gedacht?; **to ~ that she's only ten!** wenn man bedenkt, dass sie erst zehn ist

▉ N **have a ~ about it and let me know** denken Sie mal darüber nach, und geben Sie mir dann Bescheid; **to have a good ~** gründlich nachdenken

➤ **think about** VI +PREP OBJ **(a)** (= *reflect on*) nachdenken über (+*acc*); **OK, I'll think about it** okay, ich überlege es mir; **what are you thinking about?** woran denken Sie gerade?; **it's worth thinking about** das wäre zu überlegen; **to think twice about sth** sich (*dat*) etw zweimal überlegen; **that'll give him something to think about** das wird ihm zu denken geben **(b)** (*in progressive tenses*: = *half intend to*) daran denken, vorhaben **(c)** *see* **think** of (a, d)

➤ **think ahead** VI vorausdenken

➤ **think back** VI sich zurückversetzen (*to* in +*acc*)

➤ **think of** VI +PREP OBJ **(a)** denken an (+*acc*); **I've enough things to think of as it is** ich habe sowieso schon genug um die Ohren (*inf*); **he has his family to think of** er muss an seine Familie denken; **he thinks of nobody but himself** er denkt bloß an sich; **what was I thinking of!** (*inf*) was habe ich mir da(bei) bloß gedacht?; **come to think of it** wenn ich es mir recht überlege; **I can't think of her name** ich komme nicht auf ihren Namen; **she'd never think of getting married** sie denkt gar nicht daran zu heiraten; **he'd never think of such a thing** so etwas würde ihm nicht im Traum einfallen

(b) (= *imagine*) sich (*dat*) vorstellen, sich (*dat*) denken **(c)** (= *devise, suggest*) solution, idea sich (*dat*) ausdenken; **who thought of that idea?** wer ist auf diese Idee gekommen?; **what will they think of next!** was sie sich wohl (nächstens) noch alles einfallen lassen! **(d)** (= *have opinion of*) halten von; **to think well** or **highly of sb/sth** viel von jdm/etw halten; **to think little** or **not to think much of sb/sth** wenig or nicht viel von jdm/etw halten; **I told him what I thought of him** ich habe ihm gründlich die or meine Meinung gesagt

➤ **think out** VT SEP *plan* durchdenken

➤ **think over** VT SEP nachdenken über (+*acc*), sich (*dat*) überlegen

➤ **think through** VT SEP (gründlich) durchdenken

➤ **think up** VT SEP sich (*dat*) ausdenken; **who thought up that idea?** wer ist auf die Idee gekommen?

thinker [ˈθɪŋkəʳ] N Denker(in) *m(f)*

thinking [ˈθɪŋkɪŋ] ▉ ADJ denkend; **to put one's ~ cap on** scharf überlegen or nachdenken ▉ N **to my way of ~** meiner Meinung nach; **this calls for some quick ~** hier muss eine schnelle Lösung gefunden werden

think-tank [ˈθɪŋktæŋk] N Expertenkommission *f*

thinly [ˈθɪnlɪ] ADV **(a)** dünn; *wooded, attended* spärlich **(b)** (*fig*) *disguised* kaum, dürftig; *smile* schwach

thinner [ˈθɪnəʳ] N Verdünnungsmittel *nt*

thinness [ˈθɪnnɪs] N **(a)** Dünnheit *f*; (*of material*) Leichtheit *f*; (*of liquid*) Dünnflüssigkeit *f*; (*of paper, line*) Feinheit *f*; (*of person*) Magerkeit *f*

thin-skinned [ˈθɪnskɪnd] ADJ (*fig*) empfindlich

third [θɜːd] ▉ ADJ **(a)** (*in series*) dritte(r, s); **to be ~** Dritte(r, s) sein; **in ~ place** (*Sport etc*) an dritter Stelle; **~ time around** beim dritten Mal; **she was** or **came ~ in her class** sie war die Drittbeste in der Klasse; **he was** or **came ~ in the race** er machte or belegte den dritten Platz beim Rennen; **~ time lucky** beim dritten Anlauf gelingts! **(b)** (*of fraction*) **a ~ part** ein Drittel *nt* ▉ N **(a)** (*of series*) Dritte(r, s); (= *fraction*) Drittel *nt*; *see also* **sixth** **(b)** (*Aut*: = ~ *gear*) dritter Gang

third: **third-class** ADV, ADJ dritter Klasse; **~ degree** (*Brit Univ*) Abschluss *m* mit „Befriedigend"; **third country** N Drittland *nt*; **third degree** **to give sb the ~** (*fig*) jdn in die Zange nehmen

thirdly [ˈθɜːdlɪ] ADV drittens

third: **third-party** (*Brit*) ADJ ATTR Haftpflicht-; ~ **insurance** Haftpflichtversicherung *f*; **third person** ▉ ADJ in der dritten Person ▉ N **the ~ singular** (*Gram*) die dritte Person Singular; **third-rate** ADJ drittklassig; **Third World** ▉ N Dritte Welt ▉ ATTR der Dritten Welt

thirst [θɜːst] ▉ N Durst *m*; **to die of ~** verdursten ▉ VI (*fig*) **to ~ for revenge** *etc* nach Rache *etc* dürsten

thirstily [ˈθɜːstɪlɪ] ADV durstig

thirsty [ˈθɜːstɪ] ADJ (+*ER*) **(a)** durstig; **to be/feel ~** Durst haben; ~ **for revenge/knowledge** nach Rache/Wissen dürstend; **it's ~ work** diese Arbeit macht durstig **(b)** (*fig inf*) *car* durstig (*inf*)

thirteen [θɜːˈtiːn] ▉ ADJ dreizehn ▉ N Dreizehn *f*

thirteenth [θɜːˈtiːnθ] ▉ ADJ (*in series*) dreizehnte(r, s); **a ~ part** ein Dreizehntel *nt* ▉ N (*in series*) Dreizehnte(r, s); (= *fraction*) Dreizehntel *nt*; *see also* **sixth**

thirtieth [ˈθɜːtɪɪθ] ▉ ADJ (*in series*) dreißigste(r, s); **a ~ part** ein Dreißigstel *nt* ▉ N (*in series*) Dreißigste(r, s); (= *fraction*) Dreißigstel *nt*; *see also* **sixth**

thirty [ˈθɜːtɪ] ▉ ADJ dreißig; ~-**two** zweiunddreißig; **a ~-second note** (*US Mus*) ein Zweiunddreißigstel *nt* ▉ N Dreißig *f*; **the thirties** (= *era*) die dreißiger Jahre or Dreißigerjahre; **one's thirties** (= *age*) die Dreißiger; *see also* **sixty**

this [ðɪs] ▉ DEM PRON, pl **these** dies, das; **what is ~?** was ist das (hier)?; **who is ~?** wer ist das?; **~ is John** das ist John; **these are my children** das sind meine Kinder; **~ is where I live** hier wohne ich; **do you like ~?** gefällt dir das?; **under/in front of** *etc* **~** darunter/davor *etc*; **it ought to have been done before ~** es hätte schon vorher getan werden sollen; **what's all ~?** was soll das?; **what's all ~ I hear about your new job?** was höre ich da so (alles) über deine neue Stelle?; **~ and that** mancherlei; **we were talking of ~ and that** wir haben über dies und das geredet; **~, that and the other** alles Mögliche;

will you take ~ or that? nehmen Sie dieses hier oder das da?; **it was like ~** es war so; **and now ~!** und jetzt (auch noch) das!; **~ is Mary (speaking)** hier (ist) Mary; **~ is what I mean!** das meine ich (ja)!; **~ is it!** (= *now*) jetzt!; (*showing sth*) das da!, das ist er/sie/es!; (= *exactly*) genau!

2 DEM ADJ, *pl* these diese(r, s); **~ month** diesen Monat; **~ evening** heute Abend; **~ time last week** letzte Woche um diese Zeit; **~ time** diesmal, dieses Mal; **these days** heutzutage; **to run ~ way and that** hin und her rennen; **I met ~ guy who ...** (*inf*) ich habe (so) einen getroffen, der ...; **~ friend of hers** dieser Freund von ihr (*inf*), ihr Freund

3 DEM ADV SO; **it was ~ long** es war so lang; **~ far** (*time*) bis jetzt; (*place*) so weit, bis hierher

thistle ['θɪsl] N Distel *f*

tho' [ðəʊ] ABBR *of* though

thong [θɒŋ] N (a) (= *fastening*) Lederriemen *m* (b) (*US*: = *flip-flop*) Badelatsche *f* (*inf*), Gummilatsche *f* (*inf*) (c) (= *G-string*) Tangaslip *m* (d) **thongs** (*US, Austral*: = *flip-flops*) Gummisandalen *pl*

thorn [θɔːn] N Dorn *m*; **to be a ~ in sb's flesh** *or* **side** (*fig*) jdm ein Dorn im Auge sein

thorny ['θɔːnɪ] ADJ (+ER) (*lit*) dornig; (*fig*) haarig

thorough ['θʌrə] ADJ gründlich; *knowledge also* umfassend; *contempt also* bodenlos; *success* voll, durchschlagend; **to do a ~ job** gründliche Arbeit leisten; **to get a ~ grounding in sth** eine solide Basis in etw bekommen; **she's a ~ nuisance** sie ist wirklich eine Plage

thorough: thoroughbred 1 N reinrassiges Tier; (= *horse*) Vollblut(pferd) *nt* **2** ADJ reinrassig; **~ horse** Vollblut(pferd) *nt*; **thoroughfare** N Durchfahrts- *or* Durchgangsstraße *f*

thoroughly ['θʌrəlɪ] ADV (a) gründlich (b) (= *extremely*) durch und durch, von Grund auf; *convinced* völlig; **we ~ enjoyed our meal** wir haben unser Essen von Herzen genossen; **I ~ enjoyed myself** es hat mir aufrichtig Spaß gemacht; **I ~ agree** ich stimme voll und ganz zu; **I'm ~ ashamed** ich schäme mich zutiefst

thoroughness ['θʌrənɪs] N Gründlichkeit *f*

those [ðəʊz] PL *of* that **1** DEM PRON das (da) *sing*; **what are ~?** was ist das (denn) da?; **whose are ~?** wem gehören diese da?; **~ are my suggestions** das sind meine Vorschläge; **above ~** darüber; **~ who want to go, may** wer möchte, kann gehen; **one of ~ who ...** einer/eine von denen *or* denjenigen, die ...; **there are ~ who say ...** einige sagen ...

2 DEM ADJ diese *or* die (da), jene (*old, liter*); **on ~ two occasions** bei diesen beiden Gelegenheiten; **it was just one of ~ days/things** das war wieder so ein Tag/so eine Sache; **he is one of ~ people who ...** er ist einer von den Leuten *or* von denjenigen, die ...; **~ sons of yours!** also, deine Söhne!

though [ðəʊ] **1** CONJ obwohl, obgleich, obschon; **even ~** obwohl *etc*; **strange ~ it may seem ...** so seltsam es auch scheinen mag ...; **~ I say it** *or* **so myself** auch wenn ich es selbst sage; **as ~** als ob **2** ADV (a) (= *nevertheless*) doch; **he didn't do it ~** er hat es aber (doch) nicht gemacht; **nice day – rather windy ~** schönes Wetter! – aber ziemlich windig! (b) (= *really*) but will he ~? tatsächlich?, wirklich?

thought [θɔːt] **1** PRET, PTP *of* think **2** N (a) NO PL Denken *nt*; **to be lost in ~** ganz in Gedanken sein

(b) (= *idea, opinion*) Gedanke *m*; (*sudden*) Einfall *m*; **that's a ~!** (= *amazing*) man stelle sich das mal vor!; (= *problem to be considered*) das ist wahr!; (= *good idea*) das ist eine (gute) Idee *or* ein guter Gedanke; **don't give it another ~** machen Sie sich (*dat*) keine Gedanken darüber; (= *forget it*) denken Sie nicht mehr daran; **it's the ~ that counts, not how much you spend** es kommt nur auf die Idee an, nicht auf den Preis

(c) NO PL (= *care, consideration*) Nachdenken *nt*, Überlegung *f*; **to give some ~ to sth** sich (*dat*) Gedanken über etw (*acc*) machen; **after much ~** nach langer Überlegung *or* langem Überlegen; **I never gave it a moment's ~** ich habe mir nie darüber Gedanken gemacht

thoughtful ['θɔːtfʊl] ADJ (a) (= *full of thought*) *expression, person* nachdenklich; *remark, book* gut durchdacht; *present* gut ausgedacht (b) (= *considerate*) rücksichtsvoll; (= *attentive, helpful*) aufmerksam; **to be ~ of/toward(s) sb** jdm gegenüber aufmerksam/rücksichtsvoll sein

thoughtfully ['θɔːtfəlɪ] ADV (a) *say, look* nachdenklich (b) (= *with much thought*) mit viel Überlegung; **a ~ written**

book ein wohl durchdachtes Buch (c) (= *considerately*) rücksichtsvoll; (= *attentively*) aufmerksam; **she ~ provided rugs** sie war so aufmerksam, Decken bereitzustellen

thoughtfulness ['θɔːtfʊlnɪs] N (a) (*of expression, person*) Nachdenklichkeit *f* (b) (= *consideration*) Rücksicht(nahme) *f*; (= *attentiveness*) Aufmerksamkeit *f*

thoughtless ['θɔːtlɪs] ADJ (= *inconsiderate*) rücksichtslos

thoughtlessly ['θɔːtlɪslɪ] ADV (= *inconsiderately*) rücksichtslos

thoughtlessness ['θɔːtlɪsnɪs] N (= *lack of consideration*) Rücksichtslosigkeit *f*

thought-provoking ['θɔːtprəvəʊkɪŋ] ADJ zum Nachdenken anregend

thousand ['θaʊzənd] **1** ADJ tausend; **a ~** (ein)tausend; **two ~** zweitausend; **a ~ times** tausendmal; **a ~ and one** tausend(und)eins; **I have a ~ and one (different) things to do** (*inf*) ich habe tausend Dinge zu tun **2** N Tausend *nt*; **the ~s** (*Math*) die Tausender *pl*; **people arrived in their ~s** die Menschen kamen zu tausenden

thousandth ['θaʊzəntθ] **1** ADJ (*in series*) tausendste(r, s); **a** *or* **one ~ part** ein Tausendstel *nt* **2** N (*in series*) Tausendste(r, s); (= *fraction*) Tausendstel *nt*; *see also* **sixth**

thrash [θræʃ] **1** VT (a) (= *beat*) verprügeln; *donkey etc* einschlagen auf (+*acc*) (b) (*Sport inf*) *opponent* (vernichtend) schlagen (c) *arms* fuchteln mit; *legs* strampeln mit **2** VI **to ~ about** *or* **around** um sich schlagen; (*in bed*) sich herumwerfen; (*fish*) zappeln

thrashing ['θræʃɪŋ] N (= *beating*) Prügel *pl*; **to give sb a good ~** jdm eine ordentliche Tracht Prügel verpassen

thread [θred] **1** N (a) (*of cotton etc*) Faden *m*; (*Sew*) Garn *nt*; (= *strong ~*) Zwirn *m*; **to hang by a ~** (*fig*) an einem (seidenen *or* dünnen) Faden hängen

(b) (*fig: of story*) (roter) Faden; **to follow the ~ of a conversation** dem Gedankengang eines Gespräches folgen; **he lost the ~ of what he was saying** er hat den Faden verloren (c) (*E-mail*) Subject *m*

2 VT (a) *needle* einfädeln; *beads* auffädeln (*on* auf +*acc*) (b) **to ~ one's way through the crowd** *etc* sich durch die Menge *etc* hindurchschlängeln

threadbare ['θredbeə] ADJ abgewetzt; *clothes also* abgetragen; *carpet also* abgelaufen

threat [θret] N (a) Drohung *f*; **to make a ~** drohen (*against sb* jdm); **under ~ of sth** unter Androhung von etw (b) (= *danger*) Bedrohung (*to* +*gen*), Gefahr *f* (*to* für)

threaten ['θretn] **1** VT bedrohen; *person also* drohen (+*dat*); *revenge, violence* androhen; **don't you ~ me!** von Ihnen lasse ich mir nicht drohen!; **to ~ to do sth** (an)drohen, etw zu tun; **to ~ sb with sth** jdm etw androhen; **the rain ~ed to spoil the harvest** der Regen drohte, die Ernte zu zerstören; **it's ~ing to rain** es sieht (bedrohlich) nach Regen aus **2** VI (*danger, storm etc*) drohen, im Anzug sein

threatened ['θretnd] ADJ (a) **he felt ~** er fühlte sich bedroht (b) (= *under threat*) gefährdet

threatening ['θretnɪŋ] ADJ drohend; *clouds also, situation* bedrohlich; **a ~ letter** ein Drohbrief *m*; **~ behaviour** Drohungen *pl*

three [θriː] **1** ADJ drei **2** N Drei *f*; **~'s a crowd** drei Leute sind schon zu viel; *see also* **six**

three: three-D 1 N **to be in ~** dreidimensional sein **2** ADJ (*also* **three-dimensional**) dreidimensional; **three-dimensional** ADJ dreidimensional; (= *realistic*) ausgereift; **threefold** ADJ, ADV dreifach; **three-fourths** N (*US*) = **three-quarters**; **three-piece suit** N (*man's*) Anzug *m* mit Weste; **three-piece suite** N (*esp Brit*) dreiteilige Polster- *or* Sitzgarnitur; **three-ply** ATTR *wood* dreischichtig; **three-quarter** ATTR dreiviertel-; **three-quarters 1** N drei Viertel *pl*; **~ of an hour** eine Dreiviertelstunde **2** ADV drei viertel; **threesome** N Trio *nt*; **in a ~** zu dritt; **three-way** ADJ *discussion* mit drei Parteien; **a ~ split** eine Dreiteilung

---

THREE Rs

Die **three Rs** *sind „reading, writing and arithmetic" - Lesen, Schreiben, Rechnen - die allgemein wichtigsten Fähigkeiten, die man durch Erziehung und Bildung erlernen kann.*

---

thresh [θreʃ] VTI dreschen

threshing machine ['θreʃɪŋməʃiːn] N Dreschmaschine *f*

threshold ['θreʃhəʊld] N (*lit, fig, Psych*) Schwelle *f*; (*of door also*) Türschwelle *f*; **on the ~** an der Schwelle

threw [θruː] PRET *of* **throw**

thrift [θrɪft] N Sparsamkeit *f*

thrifty ['θrɪftɪ] ADJ (+ER) (a) sparsam, wirtschaftlich (b) (*US: = thriving*) blühend

thrill [θrɪl] **1** N Erregung *f*; **it gave me quite a ~, it was quite a ~ for me** es war ein richtiges Erlebnis; **what a ~!** wie aufregend!; **that's how he gets his ~s** das erregt ihn **2** VT *person* (*story, crimes*) mitreißen, fesseln; (*experience*) eine Sensation sein für; **I was ~ed to get your letter** ich habe mich riesig über deinen Brief gefreut; **the thought of going to America ~ed her** der Gedanke an eine Amerikareise versetzte sie in freudige Erregung; **to be ~ed to bits** (*inf*) sich freuen wie ein Kind; (*esp child*) ganz aus dem Häuschen sein vor Freude **3** VI **she ~ed to his touch** ein freudiger Schauer durchlief sie, bei seiner Berührung

thriller ['θrɪləʳ] N Reißer *m* (*inf*); (= *whodunnit*) Krimi *m*, Thriller *m*

thrilling ['θrɪlɪŋ] ADJ aufregend; *book, film* spannend, fesselnd; *sensation, experience, victory* überwältigend

thrive [θraɪv] VI (= *be in good health*) (gut) gedeihen; (*child also*) sich gut entwickeln; (= *do well, business*) blühen

➤ **thrive on** VI +PREP OBJ **the baby thrives on milk** mit Milch gedeiht das Baby prächtig; **he thrives on praise** Lob bringt ihn erst zur vollen Entfaltung

thriving ['θraɪvɪŋ] ADJ *plant* prächtig gedeihend; *person, city, community, business, nightlife* blühend; *child* gut gedeihend; **he's ~!** ihm gehts prächtig!; (*child*) er blüht und gedeiht!

thro' [θruː] ABBR *of* **through**

throat [θrəʊt] N (*external*) Kehle *f*; (*internal*) Rachen *m*; **to cut sb's ~** jdm die Kehle *or* Gurgel durchschneiden; **the doctor looked down her ~** der Arzt sah ihr in den Hals; **to clear one's ~** sich räuspern; **to ram** *or* **force one's ideas down sb's ~** (*inf*) jdm seine eigenen Ideen aufzwingen; **the words stuck in my ~** die Worte blieben mir im Halse stecken

throaty ADJ (+ER), **throatily** ADV ['θrəʊtɪ, -ɪlɪ] kehlig, rau

throb [θrɒb] VI klopfen; (*painfully: wound*) pochen; (*very strongly*) hämmern; (*fig: with life, activity*) pulsieren (*with* vor +*dat*, mit); **my head is ~bing** ich habe rasende Kopfschmerzen

throbbing ['θrɒbɪŋ] **1** N (*of engine*) Klopfen *nt*; (*of heart, pulse*) Pochen *nt* **2** ADJ (a) *pain, place, nightlife* pulsierend; *headache* pochend (b) *music* hämmernd

throes [θrəʊz] PL (*fig*) **to be in the final ~ of sth** in den letzten Zügen einer Sache (*gen*) liegen; **we are in the ~ of moving** wir stecken mitten im Umzug

thrombosis [θrɒm'bəʊsɪs] N Thrombose *f*

throne [θrəʊn] N Thron *m*; **to come to the ~** den Thron besteigen

throng [θrɒŋ] **1** N (*of people*) Scharen *pl* **2** VI sich drängen; **to ~ round sb/sth** sich um jdn/etw drängen *or* scharen **3** VT belagern; **people ~ed the streets** die Menschen drängten sich in den Straßen; **to be ~ed with** wimmeln von *or* mit

throttle ['θrɒtl] **1** VT (a) (*lit*) *person* erwürgen (b) (*fig*) *opposition* ersticken; *economy* drosseln **2** N (*on engine*) Drossel *f*; (*Aut etc: = lever*) Gashebel *m*; **at full ~** mit Vollgas

through, (*US*) **thru** [θruː] **1** PREP (a) durch; **he couldn't get ~ the hedge** er konnte nicht durch die Hecke durchkommen; **he went right ~ the red light** er ist bei Rot einfach durchgefahren; **he has come ~ many hardships** er hat viel Schweres durchgemacht; **to be halfway ~ a book** ein Buch halb *or* zur Hälfte durchhaben (*inf*); **that happens halfway ~ the book** das passiert in der Mitte des Buches; **all ~ his life** sein ganzes Leben lang; **he won't live ~ the night** er wird die Nacht nicht überleben; **he slept ~ the film** er hat den ganzen Film über *or* lang geschlafen; **~ the post** (*Brit*) *or* **mail** (*US*) mit der Post, per Post; **to act ~ fear** aus Angst handeln (b) (*US: = up to and including*) bis (einschließlich); **Monday ~ Friday** von Montag bis (einschließlich) Freitag **2** ADV durch; **he's a gentleman ~ and ~** er ist durch und durch ein Gentleman; **to sleep all night ~** die ganze Nacht durchschlafen; **did you stay right ~?** (*Brit*) sind Sie bis zum Schluss geblieben?; **to let sb ~** jdn durchlassen; **to be wet ~** durch und durch *or* bis auf die Haut nass sein; **to read sth ~**

etw durchlesen; **he's ~ in the other office** er ist (drüben) im anderen Büro **3** ADJ PRED (a) (= *finished*) **to be ~ with sb/sth** mit jdm/etw fertig sein (*inf*); **we're ~** (= *have finished relationship*) es ist (alles) aus zwischen uns; (= *have finished job*) wir sind fertig; **I'm ~ with him** der ist für mich gestorben *or* erledigt *inf* (b) (*Brit Telec*) **to be ~ (to sb/London)** mit jdm/London verbunden sein; **to get ~ (to sb/London)** zu jdm/nach London durchkommen

through: through flight N Direktflug *m*; **through-hole** ADJ (*Comput*) durchkontaktiert

throughout [θruː'aʊt] **1** PREP (a) (*place*) überall in (+*dat*); **~ the world** in der ganzen Welt (b) (*time*) den ganzen/die/das ganze ... hindurch *or* über; **~ his life** sein ganzes Leben lang **2** ADV (a) (= *in every part*) **the house is carpeted ~** das Haus ist ganz mit Teppichboden ausgelegt; **a block of flats with water and gas ~** ein Wohnblock mit Wasser und Gas in allen Wohnungen (b) (*time*) die ganze Zeit hindurch *or* über

through: throughput N (*Ind, Comput*) Durchsatz *m*; **through ticket** N **can I get a ~ to London?** kann ich bis London durchlösen?; **through traffic** N Durchgangsverkehr *m*; **throughway** N (*US*) Schnellstraße *f*

throw [θrəʊ], *vb: pret* **threw**, *ptp* **thrown** **1** N (a) (*of ball, javelin, dice*) Wurf *m*; **it's your ~** du bist dran; **have another ~** werfen Sie noch einmal (b) (*for covering furniture*) Überwurf *m* **2** VT (a) (*lit, fig*) werfen; *rider* abwerfen; *opponent* zu Boden werfen; *water* schütten; **to ~ the dice** würfeln; **to ~ sth to sb** jdm etw zuwerfen; **~ me those keys** werfen Sie mir die Schlüssel herüber; **to ~ sth at sb** etw nach jdm werfen; *paint etc* jdn mit etw bewerfen; **to ~ a ball 20 metres** einen Ball 20 Meter weit werfen; **to ~ sth across the room** etw (quer) durchs Zimmer werfen; **to ~ oneself at sb** (*physically*) sich auf jdn werfen; (*fig*) sich jdm an den Hals werfen *or* schmeißen (*inf*); **to ~ oneself into the job** sich in die Arbeit stürzen (*inf*); **to ~ a glance at sb/sth** einen Blick auf jdn/etw werfen; **to ~ an angry look at sb/sth** jdm/einer Sache einen wütenden Blick zuwerfen; **to ~ doubt on sth** etw in Zweifel ziehen (b) *switch, lever* betätigen (c) (*inf: = disconcert*) aus dem Konzept bringen (d) *party* geben, schmeißen (*inf*); *fit* bekommen, kriegen (*inf*) (e) (*inf: = deliberately lose*) *game* absichtlich verlieren **3** VI werfen; (= *~ dice*) würfeln

➤ **throw about** (*Brit*) *or* **around** VT ALWAYS SEPARATE (a) (= *scatter*) verstreuen; (*fig*) *money* um sich werfen mit (b) (= *toss*) herumwerfen; **to throw oneself around** sich hin und her werfen

➤ **throw away** VT SEP (a) (= *discard*) wegwerfen (b) (= *waste*) verschenken; *money* verschwenden (*on sth* auf *or* für etw, *on sb* an jdn)

➤ **throw back** VT SEP zurückwerfen; *curtains* aufreißen; **to throw oneself back** zurückweichen; **to be thrown back upon sth** (*fig*) auf etw (*acc*) zurückgreifen müssen; **I don't want you throwing that back at me** (*fig*) ich möchte nicht, dass du mir meine eigenen Worte/Taten wieder vorhältst

➤ **throw down** VT SEP (*from a roof etc*) herunterwerfen; **to throw oneself down on the sofa** sich aufs Sofa fallen lassen; **it's throwing it down** (*inf: = raining*) es gießt (in Strömen)

➤ **throw in** VT SEP (a) *extra* (gratis) dazugeben (b) (*fig*) **to throw in the sponge** (*Brit*) *or* **towel** das Handtuch werfen (*inf*) (c) (= *say casually, Sport*) einwerfen (*to in* +*acc*)

➤ **throw off** VT SEP *clothes* abwerfen; *disguise, habits* ablegen; *pursuer* abschütteln; *cold* loswerden

➤ **throw on** VT SEP *clothes* sich (*dat*) überwerfen

➤ **throw open** VT SEP *door, window* aufreißen; *arms* ausbreiten

➤ **throw out** VT SEP (a) *rubbish etc* wegwerfen (b) (= *reject*) *suggestion, bill* (*Parl*) ablehnen; *case* verwerfen (c) *person* hinauswerfen, rauswerfen (*inf*) (*of aus*) (d) *calculations etc* über den Haufen werfen (*inf*)

➤ **throw together** VT SEP (a) *ingredients* zusammenwerfen; *clothes* zusammenpacken; (= *make quickly*) hinhauen (b) *people* (*fate etc*) zusammenführen

➤ **throw up** **1** VI (*inf*) sich übergeben; **it makes you want to throw up** da kann einem schlecht werden **2** VT SEP (a) *ball, hands* hochwerfen; *dust* aufwirbeln; *stones* aufspritzen lassen (b) (= *abandon*) *job* aufgeben; *opportunity etc* verschenken (c) (= *vomit up*) von sich (*dat*) geben, ausbrechen (d) (= *produce*) hervorbringen; *problems, questions* aufwerfen

throw: **throwaway** ADJ **(a)** *remark* achtlos gemacht
(b) (= *disposable*) Wegwerf-, zum Wegwerfen; **throwback** N
(*fig*) (= *return*) Rückkehr *f* (*to* zu); (= *revival*) Neubelebung *f* (*to*
gen)

thrower [ˈθrəʊəʳ] N Werfer(in) *m(f)*

thrown [θrəʊn] PTP *of* **throw**

thru PREP, ADV, ADJ (*US*) = **through**

thrush¹ [θrʌʃ] N (*Orn*) Drossel *f*

thrush² N (*Med*) Schwämmchen *nt*; (*of vagina*) Pilzkrankheit *f*

thrust [θrʌst], *vb*: pret, ptp **thrust** **1** N **(a)** Stoß *m*; (*of knife*)
Stich *m*
(b) (*Tech*) Druckkraft *f*; (*in rocket*) Schubkraft *f*
(c) (*fig*: *of speech etc*) Tenor *m*
2 VT **(a)** stoßen; **to ~ one's hands into one's pockets** die
Hände in die Tasche stecken
(b) (*fig*) **I had the job ~ upon me** die Arbeit wurde mir
aufgedrängt; **to ~ one's way through a crowd** sich durch die
Menge drängen *or* schieben
3 VI stoßen (*at* nach); (*with knife*) stechen (*at* nach)
➤ **thrust aside** VT SEP beiseite schieben; (*fig*) *objection also*
zurückweisen
➤ **thrust out** VT SEP *leg* ausstrecken; *hand also* hinstrecken;
chest wölben

thruway [ˈθruːweɪ] N (*US*) Schnellstraße *f*

thud [θʌd] **1** N dumpfes Geräusch; **he fell to the ground with
a ~** er fiel mit einem dumpfen Aufschlag zu Boden **2** VI
dumpf aufschlagen; (= *move heavily*) stampfen; **with ~ding
heart** mit pochendem Herzen

thug [θʌɡ] N Schlägertyp *m*

thumb [θʌm] **1** N Daumen *m*; **to be under sb's ~** unter jds
Pantoffel (*dat*) stehen; **she has him under her ~** sie hat ihn
unter ihrer Fuchtel; **he gave me the ~s up/down** er gab mir zu
verstehen, dass alles in Ordnung war/dass es nicht in
Ordnung war; **the idea was given the ~s up/down** für den
Vorschlag wurde grünes/rotes Licht gegeben **2** VT **to ~ a ride**
or **lift** (*inf*) per Anhalter fahren; **to ~ one's nose at sb/sth** auf
jdn/etw pfeifen
➤ **thumb through** VI +PREP OBJ *book* durchblättern

thumb: **thumb index** N Daumenregister *nt*; **thumbtack** N (*US*)
Reißzwecke *f*

thump [θʌmp] **1** N (= *blow*) Schlag *m*; (= *noise*) (dumpfes)
Krachen
2 VT *table* klopfen *or* schlagen auf (+*acc*); *door* klopfen *or*
schlagen an (+*acc*); (*esp Brit inf*) *person* verhauen (*inf*); **he ~ed
his fist on the desk** er donnerte die Faust auf den Tisch; **he
~ed the box down on my desk** er knallte die Schachtel auf
meinen Tisch
3 VI (*person*) schlagen; (*heart*) heftig schlagen *or* pochen;
(= *move heavily*) stapfen; (= *fall loudly*) plumpsen (*inf*); **he ~ed
on the door/table** er schlug gegen *or* an die Tür/auf den
Tisch

thunder [ˈθʌndəʳ] **1** N **(a)** Donner *m* **(b)** (*fig*: *of cannons*)
Donnern *nt*; (*of waves*) Tosen *nt* **2** VI (*lit*, *fig*) donnern;
(*applause also*) brausen; (*waves*) tosen **3** VT (= *shout*) brüllen,
donnern
➤ **thunder past** VI (*train, traffic*) vorbeidonnern

thunder: **thunderbolt** N (*lit*) Blitz *m*, Blitz und Donner; **the
news came like a ~** (*fig*) die Nachricht schlug wie der Blitz ein
or kam wie ein Donnerschlag; **thunderclap** N Donnerschlag
m; **thundercloud** N Gewitterwolke *f*

thunderous [ˈθʌndərəs] ADJ stürmisch; *voice, explosion*
donnernd

thunder: **thunderstorm** N Gewitter *nt*; **thunderstruck** ADJ (*fig*)
wie vom Donner gerührt

Thurs ABBR *of* **Thursday** Do.

Thursday [ˈθɜːzdɪ] N Donnerstag *m*; *see also* **Tuesday**

thus [ðʌs] ADV **(a)** (= *in this way*) so, auf diese Art; **~ it was
that ...** so kam es, dass ... **(b)** (= *consequently*) folglich, somit
(c) (+ptp or adj) **~ far** so weit

thwack [θwæk] **1** N (= *blow*) Schlag *m*; (= *noise*) Klatschen *nt*
2 VT schlagen **3** VI schlagen (*against* gegen); (*cane*)
klatschen

thwart [θwɔːt] VT vereiteln; *plan also* durchkreuzen; *robbery,
attack also* verhindern

thyme [taɪm] N Thymian *m*

thyroid [ˈθaɪrɔɪd] N (*also* **~ gland**) Schilddrüse *f*

tiara [tɪˈɑːrə] N Diadem *nt*

Tibet [tɪˈbet] N Tibet *nt*

Tibetan [tɪˈbetən] **1** ADJ tibetanisch; **he is ~** er ist Tibeter **2** N
Tibeter(in) *m(f)*

tic [tɪk] N (*Med*) Tick *m*

tick¹ [tɪk] **1** N **(a)** (*of clock etc*) Ticken *nt* **(b)** (*Brit inf*:
= *moment*) Augenblick *m*, Sekunde *f*; **I'll be ready in a ~** *or* **two
~s** bin sofort fertig (*inf*) **(c)** (*esp Brit*: = *mark*) Häkchen *nt*,
Haken *m* **2** VI **(a)** (*clock*) ticken **(b)** (*inf*) **what makes him ~?**
was geht in ihm vor? **3** VT (*Brit*) *name* abhaken; *box, answer*
ankreuzen
➤ **tick off** VT SEP (*Brit*) **(a)** *name etc* abhaken **(b)** (*inf*: = *scold*)
ausschimpfen (*inf*)
➤ **tick over** VI **(a)** (*engine*) im Leerlauf sein **(b)** (*fig*: *business
etc*) ganz ordentlich laufen; (*pej*) auf Sparflamme sein (*inf*)

tick² N (*Zool*) Zecke *f*

ticker tape [ˈtɪkəteɪp] N Lochstreifen *m*; **~ parade**
Konfettiparade *f*

ticket [ˈtɪkɪt] N **(a)** (= *rail ~, bus ~*) Fahrkarte *f*; (= *plane ~*)
Ticket *nt*, Flugschein *m*; (*Theat, for football match etc*)
(Eintritts)karte *f*; (= *cloakroom ~*) Garderobenmarke *f*; (*for dry
cleaner's etc*) Abschnitt *m*; (= *raffle ~*) Los *nt*; (= *lottery ~*)
Lottoschein *m*; (= *price ~*) Preisschild *nt*; (*for car park*)
Parkschein *m* **(b)** (*US Pol*) Wahlliste *f* **(c)** (*Jur*) Strafzettel *m*

ticket: **ticket agency** N (*Theat*) Vorverkaufsstelle *f*; (*Rail etc*)
Verkaufsstelle *f*; **ticket collector** N (*on train*) Schaffner(in)
m(f); **ticket inspector** N (Fahrkarten)kontrolleur(in) *m(f)*;
ticket machine N (*public transport*) Fahrkartenautomat *m*; (*in
car park*) Parkscheinautomat *m*; **ticket office** N (*Rail*)
Fahrkartenschalter *m*; (*Theat*) Kasse *f*

ticking [ˈtɪkɪŋ] N (*of clock*) Ticken *nt*

ticking-off [ˌtɪkɪŋˈɒf] N (*Brit inf*) Rüffel *m*, Anpfiff *m* (*inf*)

tickle [ˈtɪkl] **1** VT **(a)** (*lit*) kitzeln; **to ~ sb's toes** jdn an den
Zehen kitzeln **(b)** (*fig inf*) (= *please*) schmeicheln (+*dat*) und
freuen; (= *amuse*) amüsieren; **to be ~d** sich gebauchpinselt
fühlen (*inf*); **that story really ~d me** diese Geschichte fand ich
wirklich köstlich **2** VI kitzeln; (*wool*) kratzen **3** N Kitzeln *nt*;
to have a ~ in one's throat einen Hustenreiz haben

ticklish [ˈtɪklɪʃ] ADJ (*lit*) kitz(e)lig; (*fig*) *situation also* heikel; **~
cough** Reizhusten *m*

tidal [ˈtaɪdl] ADJ Gezeiten-; *waters* den Gezeiten unterworfen

tidal wave N (*lit*) Flutwelle *f*

tidbit [ˈtɪdbɪt] N (*US*) = **titbit**

tiddly [ˈtɪdlɪ] ADJ (+ER) (*Brit inf*) **(a)** (= *tiny*) klitzeklein (*inf*)
(b) (= *tipsy*) angesäuselt (*inf*)

tiddlywinks [ˈtɪdlɪwɪŋks] N Floh(hüpf)spiel *nt*

tide [taɪd] N **(a)** (*lit*) Gezeiten *pl*; **(at) high ~** (bei) Flut *f*; **(at) low
~** (bei) Ebbe *f*; **the ~ is in/out** es ist Flut/Ebbe; **the ~ comes in
very fast** die Flut kommt sehr schnell **(b)** (*fig*) **the ~ of public
opinion** der Trend der öffentlichen Meinung; **to go** *or* **swim
against/with the ~** gegen den/mit dem Strom schwimmen;
the ~ has turned das Blatt hat sich gewendet
➤ **tide over** VT ALWAYS SEPARATE **is that enough to tide you
over?** reicht Ihnen das vorläufig?

tidily [ˈtaɪdɪlɪ] ADV ordentlich

tidiness [ˈtaɪdɪnɪs] N (*of person*) Ordentlichkeit *f*; (*of
appearance*) Gepflegtheit *f*; (*of room*) Aufgeräumtheit *f*; (*of
desk*) Ordnung *f*

tidy [ˈtaɪdɪ] **1** ADJ (+ER) **(a)** (= *orderly*) ordentlich; *appearance*
gepflegt; *room* aufgeräumt; **to look ~** (*person*) gepflegt
aussehen; (*room*) ordentlich aussehen; **to keep sth ~** etw in
Ordnung halten **(b)** (*inf*: = *considerable*) ordentlich (*inf*),
ganz schön (*inf*) **2** VT *hair* in Ordnung bringen; *room also,
drawer, desk* aufräumen
➤ **tidy away** VT SEP wegräumen, aufräumen
➤ **tidy out** VT SEP entrümpeln, ausmisten (*inf*)
➤ **tidy up** **1** VI Ordnung machen **2** VT SEP aufräumen; *piece
of work* in Ordnung bringen; **to tidy oneself up** sich
zurechtmachen

tie [taɪ] **1** N **(a)** (*esp US: also* **neck ~**) Krawatte *f*, Schlips *m* (*inf*)
(b) (*fig*: = *bond*) Beziehung *f*, (Ver)bindung *f*; **~s of friendship**
freundschaftliche Beziehungen *pl*; **family ~s** familiäre
Bindungen *pl*
(c) (= *hindrance*) Belastung *f* (*on* für)
(d) (*Sport etc*) (= *result*) Unentschieden *nt*; (= *match etc ending
in draw*) unentschiedenes Spiel; **there was a ~ for second**

place es gab zwei zweite Plätze

2 VT **(a)** binden (*to an* +*acc*); (= *fasten*) befestigen (*to an* +*dat*); **to ~ a knot in sth** einen Knoten in etw (*acc*) machen; **my hands are ~d** (*fig*) mir sind die Hände gebunden

(b) (*fig:* = *unite, link*) verbinden

(c) (*Sport*) **the match was ~d** das Spiel ging unentschieden aus

3 VI **(a)** (*ribbon etc*) **it ~s at the back** es wird hinten (zu)gebunden

(b) (*Sport*) unentschieden spielen; (*in competition, vote*) gleich stehen; **they ~d for first place** (*Sport, competition*) sie teilten sich den ersten Platz

➤ **tie back** VT SEP zurückbinden

➤ **tie down** VT SEP **(a)** (*lit*) festbinden (*to an* +*dat*); *tents* verankern (*to in* +*dat*) **(b)** (*fig:* = *restrict*) binden (*to an* +*acc*); **to tie oneself down to doing sth** sich verpflichten, etw zu tun

➤ **tie in 1** VI dazu passen; **to tie in with sth** zu etw passen **2** VT SEP *plans* verbinden, in Einklang bringen

➤ **tie on** VT SEP anbinden, festbinden; **to tie sth on(to) sth** etw an etw (*dat*) anbinden

➤ **tie up** VT SEP **(a)** *parcel* verschnüren; *shoelaces* binden **(b)** *boat* festmachen; *animal* festbinden, anbinden (*to an* +*dat*); *prisoner, hands etc* fesseln **(c)** (= *settle*) *deal etc* unter Dach und Fach bringen **(d)** (*Fin*) *capital* (fest) anlegen **(e)** (= *link*) **to be tied up with sth** mit etw zusammenhängen **(f)** (= *keep busy*) beschäftigen; *machines* auslasten **(g)** (= *obstruct, hinder*) *production etc* stilllegen

tie: **tie-break, tie-breaker** N (*Tennis, in quiz etc*) Tiebreak *m*; **tie-dye** VT nach dem Bindebatikverfahren färben; **tie-in 1** N **(a)** (= *connection*) Verbindung *f*, Beziehung *f* **(b)** (*US:* = *sale*) Kopplungsgeschäft *nt* **2** ATTR **~ edition** (*of book*) Begleitbuch *nt*; **~ sale** (*US*) Kopplungsgeschäft *nt*; **tiepin** N Krawattennadel *f*, Schlipsnadel *f* (*inf*)

tier [tɪəʳ] N (*of cake*) Etage *f*; (*Theat, of stadium*) Rang *m*; (*fig: in hierarchy etc*) Stufe *f*; **a three-~ hierarchy** eine dreigestufte Hierarchie

tie-up [ˈtaɪʌp] N (*US:* = *stoppage*) Stillstand *m*

tiff [tɪf] N (*inf*) Krach *m* (*inf*)

tiger [ˈtaɪgəʳ] N Tiger *m*

tight [taɪt] **1** ADJ (+ER) **(a)** *clothes, bend, community, space* eng; *join* dicht; **~ curls** kleine Locken

(b) (= *stiff*) festsitzend, unbeweglich; (= *firm*) *screw* fest angezogen; *tap, window* dicht; *lid, embrace* fest; *control, discipline, security* streng; **to have/keep a ~ hold of sth** (*lit*) etw gut festhalten; **the bolt is (too) ~** der Bolzen sitzt fest

(c) (= *taut*) *rope, skin* straff; *knot* fest (angezogen)

(d) *timing etc, race, budget, money* knapp; *schedule* knapp bemessen

(e) (= *difficult*) *situation* schwierig; **in a ~ corner** *or* **spot** (*fig*) in der Klemme (*inf*)

(f) (= *tense*) *voice* fest; *smile* verkrampft; *throat* zusammengeschnürt; *muscle* verspannt; *chest* zusammengeschnürt

(g) (*inf:* = *miserly*) knick(e)rig (*inf*)

2 ADV (+ER) *hold, shut, fasten* fest; *stretch* straff; **to hold sb/sth ~** jdn/etw festhalten; **to do sth up ~** etw festmachen *or* gut befestigen; **to pull sth ~** etw festziehen *or* stramm ziehen; **to sit ~** sich nicht rühren; **sleep ~!** schlaf(t) gut!; **hold ~!** festhalten!

3 ADJ SUF **-dicht**; **watertight** wasserdicht

tighten [ˈtaɪtn] (*also ~ up*) **1** VT **(a)** *knot* fester machen; *screw* anziehen; (= *re-tighten*) nachziehen; *muscles* anspannen; *rope* straffen; (= *stretch tighter*) straffer spannen; **to ~ one's grip on sth** etw fester halten; (*fig*) etw besser unter Kontrolle bringen **(b)** (*fig*) *rules, security* verschärfen **2** VI (*rope*) sich straffen; (*knot*) sich zusammenziehen

➤ **tighten up 1** VI **(a)** = **tighten 2 (b)** (*in discipline*) strenger werden; **they've tightened up on security** sie haben die Sicherheitsvorkehrungen verschärft **2** VT SEP **(a)** = **tighten 1(a) (b)** *organization, procedure* straffen

tight: **tightfisted** [ˌtaɪtˈfɪstɪd] ADJ knick(e)rig (*inf*); **tight-fitting** ADJ eng anliegend; **tightknit** ADJ *community* eng (miteinander) verbunden; **tight-lipped** ADJ **(a)** (*lit*) mit schmalen Lippen; (= *silent*) verschwiegen **(b)** (= *angry*) *person* verbissen; *expression* abweisend; *smile* verkniffen

tightly [ˈtaɪtlɪ] ADV **(a)** fest; *wrapped* eng; *stretch* straff; **~ fitting** eng anliegend **(b)** (= *compactly*) dicht; **~ packed** dicht gedrängt **(c)** (= *rigorously*) scharf, streng

tightness [ˈtaɪtnɪs] N **(a)** (*of clothes*) enges Anliegen **(b)** (= *tautness, of rope, skin*) Straffheit *f* **(c)** (*in chest*) Beengtheit *f*

tightrope [ˈtaɪtrəup] N Seil *nt*; **to walk a ~** (*fig*) einen Balanceakt vollführen

tightrope walker N Seiltänzer(in) *m(f)*

tights [taɪts] PL (*Brit*) Strumpfhose *f*; **a pair of ~** eine Strumpfhose

tile [taɪl] **1** N (*on roof*) (Dach)ziegel *m*; (= *ceramic ~*) Fliese *f*; (*on wall*) Kachel *f*; (= *lino ~, cork ~ etc*) Platte *f*; (= *carpet ~*) (Teppich)fliese *f* **2** VT *roof* (mit Ziegeln) decken; *floor* mit Fliesen/Platten auslegen; *wall, bathroom* kacheln

tiled [taɪld] ADJ *floor* gefliest; *path* mit Platten ausgelegt; *wall, room* gekachelt; **~ roof** Ziegeldach *nt*

till¹ [tɪl] PREP, CONJ = **until**

till² N (*Brit*) (= *cash register*) Kasse *f*; (= *drawer*) (*in bank*) Geldkasse *f*; (*in shop*) Ladenkasse *f*

tilt [tɪlt] **1** N (= *slope*) Neigung *f*; **to have a ~** sich neigen **2** VT (*lit, fig*) kippen; *head* (seitwärts) neigen; **to ~ the balance of power toward(s)/against sb** das Kräftegleichgewicht zugunsten/zuungunsten von jdm verschieben **3** VI sich neigen

➤ **tilt back 1** VI sich nach hinten neigen **2** VT SEP nach hinten neigen; *chair also* nach hinten kippen

➤ **tilt forward 1** VI sich nach vorne neigen **2** VT SEP nach vorne neigen; *chair also* nach vorne kippen

➤ **tilt up 1** VI nach oben kippen **2** VT SEP *bottle* kippen

timber [ˈtɪmbəʳ] N **(a)** Holz *nt*; (*for building*) (Bau)holz *nt*; **~!** Baum fällt! **(b)** (= *beam*) Balken *m*

timbered [ˈtɪmbəd] ADJ **~ house** Fachwerkhaus *nt*

timber-framed [ˈtɪmbəˈfreɪmd] ADJ Fachwerk-; **~ house** Fachwerkhaus *nt*

---

time [taɪm]	
1 NOUN	**2** TRANSITIVE VERB

1 NOUN

(a) Zeit *f*; **how time flies!** wie die Zeit vergeht!; **only time will tell whether ...** es muss sich erst herausstellen, ob ...; **it takes time to do that** das erfordert *or* braucht (seine) Zeit; **to take (one's) time (over sth)** sich (*dat*) (bei etw) Zeit lassen; **(in the course of) time** mit der Zeit; **in (next to) no time** im Nu, im Handumdrehen; **at this (present) point** *or* **moment in time** zu diesem *or* zum gegenwärtigen Zeitpunkt; **to have a lot of/no time for sb/sth** viel/keine Zeit für jdn/etw haben; (*fig:* = *be for/against*) viel/nichts für jdn/etw übrig haben; **to make time (for sb/sth)** sich (*dat*) Zeit (für jdn/etw) nehmen; **in** *or* **given time** mit der Zeit; **in one's own/the company's time** *or* während der Freizeit/Arbeitszeit; **don't rush, do it in your own time** nur keine Hast, tun Sie es, wie Sie es können; **for some time past** seit einiger Zeit; **I don't know what she's saying half the time** (*inf*) meistens verstehe ich gar nicht, was sie sagt; **in two weeks' time** in zwei Wochen; **for a time** eine Zeit lang; **not before time** (*Brit*) das wurde auch (langsam) Zeit; **there's a time and a place for everything** alles zu seiner Zeit; **this is hardly the time or the place to ...** dies ist wohl kaum die rechte Zeit oder der rechte Ort, um ...; **this is no time for quarrelling** *or* **to quarrel** jetzt ist nicht die Zeit, sich zu streiten; **there are times when ...** es gibt Augenblicke, wo *or* da (*geh*) ...; **at the** *or* **that time** damals, zu der Zeit, seinerzeit; **at this (particular) time, at the present time** zurzeit; **sometimes ..., (at) other times ...** (manch)mal ..., (manch)mal ...; **this time last year** letztes Jahr um diese Zeit; **my time is (almost) up** meine *or* die Zeit ist (gleich) um; **in my time** zu meiner Zeit; **it happened before my time** das war vor meiner Zeit; **of all time** aller Zeiten; **he is ahead of his time** *or* **before his time** er ist seiner Zeit (weit) voraus; **in Victorian times** im Viktorianischen Zeitalter; **times are hard** die Zeiten sind hart *or* schwer; **times are changing** es kommen andere Zeiten

◆**the times** **to be behind the times** rückständig sein; (= *be out of touch*) nicht auf dem Laufenden sein

◆ **all the time** (= *always*) immer; (= *all along*) die ganze Zeit

◆ **in good time to be in good time** rechtzeitig dran sein; **all in good time** alles zu seiner Zeit

◆ **in one's own good time** he'll let you know in his own good time er wird Ihnen Bescheid sagen, wenn er so weit ist

◆ **a long time** (for) a long time lange; **rhythm) I'm going away for a long time** ich fahre für *or* auf längere Zeit weg; **it's a long time (since ...)** es ist schon lange her(, seit ...)

◆ **a short time** (for) a short time kurz; **a short time later** kurz darauf; **a short time ago** vor kurzem

◆ **for the time being** (= *provisionally*) vorläufig; (= *temporarily*) vorübergehend

◆ **time + come** the time has come (to do sth) es ist an der Zeit(, etw zu tun); **the time has come for us to leave** es ist Zeit für uns zu gehen; **when the time comes** wenn es so weit ist

◆ **at + times** manchmal; **at all times** jederzeit, immer

◆ **by the time** by the time it had finished als es zu Ende war; **by the time we arrive, there's not going to be anything left** bis wir ankommen, ist nichts mehr übrig

◆ **by that time** by that time we knew da *or* inzwischen wussten wir es; **by that time we'll know** dann *or* bis dahin wissen wir es

◆ **by this time** inzwischen; **by this time tomorrow** morgen um diese Zeit

◆ **from time to time** von Zeit zu Zeit

◆ **such time** until such time as ... so lange bis ...

◆ **time of** this time of the year diese Jahreszeit; **at this time of the month** zu diesem Zeitpunkt des Monats

◆ **time to** now's the time to do it jetzt ist der richtige Zeitpunkt *or* die richtige Zeit, es zu tun
  (b) (*by clock*) **what time is it?, what's the time?** wie spät ist es?, wie viel Uhr ist es?; **what time do you make it?** wie spät haben Sie?; **the time is 2.30** es ist 2.30 Uhr; **it's 2 o'clock local time** es ist 2.00 Uhr Ortszeit; **the winning time was ...** die Zeit des Siegers war ...; **it's time (for me/us etc) to go, it's time I was/we were etc going, it's time I/we etc went** es wird Zeit, dass ich gehe/wir gehen *etc*

◆ **to tell the time** (*person*) die Uhr kennen; **can you tell the time?** kennst du die Uhr?

◆ **to make good time** gut *or* schnell vorankommen

◆ **about time** it's about time he was here (*he has arrived*) es wird (aber) auch Zeit, dass er kommt; (*he has not arrived*) es wird langsam Zeit, dass er kommt; **(and) about time too!** das wird aber auch Zeit!

◆ **ahead of time** zu früh; **we are ahead of time** wir sind früh dran

◆ **behind time** zu spät; **we are behind time** wir sind spät dran

◆ **at + time** at any time during the day zu jeder Tageszeit; **not at this time of night!** nicht zu dieser nachtschlafenden Zeit *or* Stunde!; **at one time** früher, einmal; **at any time** jederzeit; **at no time** niemals; **at the same time** (*lit*) gleichzeitig; **they arrived at the same time as us** sie kamen zur gleichen Zeit an wie wir; **but at the same time, you must admit that ...** aber andererseits müssen Sie zugeben, dass ...

◆ **in/on time** rechtzeitig; **to be in time for sth** rechtzeitig zu etw kommen; **on time** pünktlich
  (c) (= *occasion*) **this time** diesmal, dieses Mal; **every** *or* **each time** jedes Mal; **many a time, many times** viele Male; **for the last time** zum letzten Mal; **and he's not very bright at the best of times** und er ist ohnehin *or* sowieso nicht sehr intelligent; **the time before** das letzte *or* vorige Mal; **time and (time) again, time after time** immer wieder; **I've told you a dozen times ...** ich habe dir schon x-mal gesagt ...; **nine times out of ten ...** neun von zehn Malen ...; **she comes three times a week** sie kommt dreimal pro Woche *or* in der Woche

◆ **at a time** they came in one/three *etc* at a time sie kamen einzeln/immer zu dritt *etc* herein; **four at a time** vier auf einmal; **for weeks at a time** wochenlang

◆ **(the) next time** nächstes Mal, das nächste Mal

◆ **(the) last time** letztes Mal, das letzte Mal
  (d) (*Math*) **2 times 3 is 6** 2 mal 3 ist 6; **it was ten times as big as** *or* **ten times the size of ...** es war zehnmal so groß wie ...
  (e) (= *experience*) **to have the time of one's life** sich glänzend amüsieren; **what time we had** *or* **that was!** das war eine Zeit!; **to have an easy/a hard time** es leicht/schwer haben; **to have**

a bad/rough time viel mitmachen; **to give sb a bad/rough** *etc* **time (of it)** jdm das Leben schwer machen

◆ **a good time** we had a good time es war (sehr) schön, es hat uns (*dat*) gut gefallen; **have a good time!** viel Vergnügen *or* Spaß!
  (f) (= *rhythm*) Takt *m*; **(to be) in time (with)** im Takt (sein) (mit); **(to be) out of time** aus dem Takt (sein); **3/4 time** Dreivierteltakt *m*; **to keep time** (= *beat time*) den Takt angeben *or* schlagen

2 TRANSITIVE VERB
  (a) (= *choose time of*) **to time sth perfectly** genau den richtigen Zeitpunkt für etw wählen; **he timed his arrival to coincide with ...** er legte seine Ankunft so, dass sie mit ... zusammenfiel
  (b) (*with stopwatch*) stoppen; *speed* messen; **to time sb (over 1000 metres)** jdn (auf 1000 Meter) stoppen; **time how long it takes you, time yourself** sieh auf die Uhr, wie lange du brauchst; (*with stopwatch*) stopp, wie lange du brauchst

time: **time bomb** N (*lit, fig*) Zeitbombe *f*; **time-consuming** ADJ zeitraubend; **time delay** N (*gen, Telec*) Zeitverzögerung *f*; (*in bank*) Zeitschloss *nt*; **time deposit** N (*Fin*) Termingeld *nt*; **time difference** N Zeitunterschied *m*; **time frame, timeframe** N Zeitrahmen *m*, zeitlicher Rahmen; **time-honoured**, (*US*) **time-honored** ADJ althergebracht; **time-lag** N Zeitverschiebung *f*; **time-lapse** ADJ **~ photography** Zeitraffertechnik *f*

timeless [ˈtaɪmlɪs] ADJ zeitlos; (= *everlasting*) immer während

timelessly [ˈtaɪmlɪslɪ] ADV zeitlos; (= *eternally*) immerfort

timelessness [ˈtaɪmlɪsnɪs] N Zeitlosigkeit *f*; (= *eternal nature*) Unvergänglichkeit *f*

time limit N zeitliche Begrenzung; (*for the completion of a job*) Frist *f*; **to put a ~ on sth** etw befristen

timeline N Zeitlinie *f*

timely [ˈtaɪmlɪ] ADJ rechtzeitig; **~ advice** ein Rat zur rechten Zeit

time: **time machine** N Zeitmaschine *f*; **time-out** N (*US*)
  (a) (*Ftbl, Basketball*) Auszeit *f* (b) (= *break*) **to take ~** Pause machen

timer [ˈtaɪməʳ] N Zeitmesser *m*; (= *switch*) Schaltuhr *f*

time: **time-saving** ADJ Zeit sparend; **timescale** N (*in drama etc*) zeitlicher Rahmen; (= *perception of time*) Zeitmaßstab *m*; **timeshare** **1** N Wohnung *f*/Haus *nt etc* auf Timesharingbasis **2** ADJ ATTR Timesharing-; **time sheet** N Stundenzettel *m*; **time signal** N (*Brit*) Zeitzeichen *nt*; **time signature** N Taktvorzeichnung *f*; **time span** N Zeitspanne *f*; **time switch** N Schaltuhr *f*; **timetable** N (*Transport*) Fahrplan *m*; (*Brit Sch*) Stundenplan *m*; **to have a busy ~** ein volles Programm haben; **time travel** N Zeitreise *f*; **time warp** N (*Sci-Fi, fig*) Zeitverzerrung *f*; **time zone** N Zeitzone *f*

timid [ˈtɪmɪd] ADJ scheu, ängstlich; *person, behaviour, words also* schüchtern, zaghaft; **to be ~ about doing sth** etw nur zögernd tun

timidly [ˈtɪmɪdlɪ] ADV *say, ask* zaghaft; *enter, approach* schüchtern

timing [ˈtaɪmɪŋ] N (= *choice of time*) Wahl *f* des richtigen Zeitpunkts (*of* für), Timing *nt* (*also Tennis, Ftbl*); **perfect ~, I'd just opened a bottle** ihr kommt gerade richtig, ich habe eben eine Flasche aufgemacht; **the ~ of the statement was wrong/excellent** die Erklärung kam zum falschen/genau zum richtigen Zeitpunkt

tin [tɪn] N (a) Blech *nt*; (*Chem*: = *metal*) Zinn *nt* (b) (*esp Brit*: = *can*) Dose *f*; **a ~ of beans** eine Dose Bohnen

tin can N (Blech)dose *f*

tinder [ˈtɪndəʳ] N Zunder *m*

tinfoil [ˈtɪnfɔɪl] N (= *wrapping*) Stanniolpapier *nt*; (= *aluminium foil*) Aluminiumfolie *f*

tinge [tɪndʒ] **1** N (*lit, fig*) Spur *f*; (*of colour*) Hauch *m*; **a ~ of red** ein (leichter) Rotstich **2** VT (a) (= *colour*) (leicht) tönen
  (b) (*fig*) **to ~ sth with sth** einer Sache (*dat*) eine Spur von etw geben; **~d with ...** mit einer Spur von ...

tingle [ˈtɪŋgl] **1** VI prickeln, kribbeln (*inf*) (*with* vor +*dat*) **2** N Prickeln *nt*, Kribbeln *nt* (*inf*); **she felt a ~ of excitement** sie war ganz kribbelig (*inf*)

tingling ['tɪŋglɪŋ] **1** N Prickeln *nt*, Kribbeln *nt* (*inf*) **2** ADJ (*with cold, excitement*) prickelnd

tingly ['tɪŋglɪ] ADJ prickelnd; **my arm feels (all)** ~ mein Arm kribbelt (*inf*); **I feel ~ all over** es kribbelt mich überall (*inf*); (*with excitement*) ich bin ganz kribbelig (*inf*)

tinker ['tɪŋkəʳ] **1** N (*Brit pej*) Kesselflicker *m*; **you little ~!** (*inf*) du kleiner Stromer! (*inf*) **2** VI **(a)** (*also* ~ **about**) herumbasteln (*with, on* an +*dat*) **(b)** (*unskilfully*) **to** ~ **with sth** an etw (*dat*) herumpfuschen

tinkle ['tɪŋkl] **1** VT zum Klingen bringen **2** VI **(a)** (*bells etc*) klingen, bimmeln (*inf*); (*breaking glass*) klirren **(b)** (*inf*: = *to urinate*) pinkeln (*inf*) **3** N Klingen *nt no pl*, Bimmeln *nt no pl* (*inf*); (*of breaking glass*) Klirren *nt no pl*

tinkling ['tɪŋklɪŋ] **1** N (*of bells etc*) Klingen *nt*, Bimmeln *nt* (*inf*); (*of broken glass*) Klirren *nt* **2** ADJ *bells* klingend, bimmelnd (*inf*); *broken glass* klirrend

tinned [tɪnd] ADJ (*esp Brit*) *peas etc* aus der Dose; ~ **food** Dosennahrung *f*; ~ **meat** Dosenfleisch *nt*

tinny ['tɪnɪ] ADJ (+ER) *sound* blechern

tin: **tin-opener** N (*esp Brit*) Dosenöffner *m*; **tin plate** N Zinnblech *nt*

tinsel ['tɪnsəl] N Girlanden *pl* aus Rauschgold *etc*

tint [tɪnt] **1** N Ton *m*; (= *product for hair*) Tönung(smittel *nt*) *f*; ~**s of purple** Violetttöne *pl* **2** VT *hair* tönen

tinted ['tɪntɪd] ADJ getönt

tiny ['taɪnɪ] ADJ (+ER) winzig; *baby, child* sehr *or* ganz klein; ~ **little** winzig klein

tip¹ [tɪp] **1** N Spitze *f*; (*of cigarette*) Filter *m*; **to stand on the ~s of one's toes** auf Zehenspitzen stehen; **it's on the ~ of my tongue** es liegt mir auf der Zunge; **it's just the ~ of the iceberg** (*fig*) das ist nur die Spitze des Eisbergs **2** VT **copper-/ steel-~ped** mit Kupfer-/Stahlspitze; ~**ped** *cigarette* mit Filter

tip² **1** N **(a)** (= *gratuity*) Trinkgeld *nt* **(b)** (= *advice*) Tipp *m* (*also Racing*) **2** VT **(a)** (= *give gratuity to*) Trinkgeld geben (+*dat*) **(b)** (*Racing*) setzen auf (+*acc*); **to be ~ped for success** (*Brit*) als sicherer Erfolgskandidat gelten; **they are ~ped to win the election** (*Brit fig*) sie sind die Favoriten in der Wahl **3** VI **Americans ~ better** Amerikaner geben mehr Trinkgeld
➤ **tip off** VT SEP einen Tipp *or* Wink geben +*dat* (*about* über +*acc*)

tip³ **1** VT (= *tilt*) kippen; (= *pour also, empty*) *load, rubbish* schütten; *books, clothes etc* schmeißen (*inf*); (= *overturn*) umkippen; **to** ~ **sth backwards/forwards** etw nach hinten/ vorne kippen; **it ~ped the scales in his favour** (*fig*) das hat für ihn den Ausschlag gegeben; **to** ~ **the balance** (*fig*) den Ausschlag geben; ~ **the case upside down** dreh die Kiste um **2** VI (= *incline*) kippen; (= *dump rubbish*) Schutt abladen **3** N (*Brit*) (*for rubbish*) Müllkippe *f*; (*for coal*) Halde *f*; (*inf*: = *untidy place*) Saustall *m* (*inf*)
➤ **tip back 1** VI (*chair, person*) nach hinten (weg)kippen **2** VT SEP nach hinten kippen; *head* nach hinten neigen
➤ **tip out 1** VT SEP auskippen; *liquid, sand also* ausschütten; *load, objects, rubbish* abladen **2** VI herauskippen; (*liquid*) herauslaufen; (*sand*) herausrutschen; (*load, objects, rubbish also*) herausfallen
➤ **tip over** VI, VT SEP (= *overturn*) umkippen
➤ **tip up** VI, VT SEP (= *tilt*) kippen; (= *overturn*) umkippen; (*folding seat*) hochklappen

tip-off ['tɪpɒf] N (*inf*) Tipp *m*, Wink *m*

Tipp-Ex® ['tɪpeks] **1** N Tipp-Ex® *nt* **2** VT **to** ~ (**out**) mit Tipp-Ex® löschen

tipple ['tɪpl] (*esp Brit inf*) **1** N **he enjoys a** ~ er trinkt ganz gerne mal einen; **gin is his** ~ er trinkt am liebsten Gin

tippy-toe ['tɪpɪtəʊ] VI, N (*US inf*) = **tiptoe**

tipsy ['tɪpsɪ] ADJ (+ER) beschwipst, angesäuselt (*inf*)

tip: **tiptoe 1** VI auf Zehenspitzen gehen **2** N **on** ~ auf Zehenspitzen; **tip-up lorry** (*Brit*), **tip-up truck** N Kipplaster *m*

tirade [taɪ'reɪd] N Schimpfkanonade *f*

tire¹ [taɪəʳ] **1** VT müde machen **2** VI müde werden; **to** ~ **of sb/ sth** jdn/etw satt haben; **she never** ~**s of talking about her son** sie wird es nie müde, über ihren Sohn zu sprechen
➤ **tire out** VT SEP (völlig) erschöpfen

tire² N (*US*) = **tyre**

tired ['taɪəd] ADJ müde; *cliché* abgegriffen; (*pej*: = *boring, stale*) langweilig; ~ **out** völlig erschöpft; **to be** ~ **of sb/sth** jdn/etw

satt haben; **to get** ~ **of sb/sth** jdn/etw satt bekommen; **I'm** ~ **of telling you** ich habe es satt, dir das zu sagen; **a** ~ **lettuce leaf** ein schlaffes Salatblatt

tiredly ['taɪədlɪ] ADV müde

tiredness ['taɪədnɪs] N Müdigkeit *f*

tireless ['taɪəlɪs] ADJ unermüdlich; *patience also* unerschöpflich

tirelessly ['taɪəlɪslɪ] ADV *work, campaign* unermüdlich

tiresome ['taɪəsəm] ADJ (= *irritating*) lästig; (= *boring*) langweilig

tiring ['taɪərɪŋ] ADJ anstrengend, ermüdend

Tirol [tɪ'rəʊl] N = **Tyrol**

tissue ['tɪʃuː] N **(a)** (*Anat, Bot, fig*) Gewebe *nt* **(b)** (= *handkerchief*) Papier(taschen)tuch *nt* **(c)** (*also* ~ **paper**) Seidenpapier *nt*

tit¹ [tɪt] N (= *bird*) Meise *f*

tit² N ~ **for tat** wie du mir, so ich dir

tit³ N (*sl*: = *breast*) Titte *f* (*sl*); **he gets on my ~s** er geht mir auf den Sack (*sl*)

titanic [taɪ'tænɪk] ADJ (= *huge*) gigantisch

titbit ['tɪtbɪt], (*US*) **tidbit** ['tɪdbɪt] N **(a)** Leckerbissen *m* **(b)** (= *piece of information*) Pikanterie *f*

titillate ['tɪtɪleɪt] VT *person, senses* anregen; *interest* erregen

title ['taɪtl] N Titel *m* (*also Sport*); (*of chapter*) Überschrift *f*; (*Film*) Untertitel *m*; (= *form of address*) Anrede *f*

titled ['taɪtld] ADJ *person, classes* mit (Adels)titel

title: **title deed** N Eigentumsurkunde *f*; **titleholder** N (*Sport*) Titelträger(in) *m(f)*; **title page** N (*Typ*) Titelseite *f*; **title role** N (*Theat, Film*) Titelrolle *f*

titter ['tɪtəʳ] **1** VTI kichern **2** N Kichern *nt*, Gekicher *nt*

tittle-tattle ['tɪtl,tætl] N Geschwätz *nt*; (= *gossip also*) Klatsch *m*, Tratsch *m* (*inf*)

tizzy ['tɪzɪ], **tizwoz** ['tɪzwɒz] N (*inf*) **to be in a** ~ höchst aufgeregt sein; **to get into a** ~ sich schrecklich aufregen

T-junction ['tiː,dʒʌŋkʃən] N (*Brit*) T-Kreuzung *f*

TM ABBR *of* **trademark** Wz

to [tuː]	
1 PREPOSITION	**3** ADVERB
2 ADJECTIVE	

1 PREPOSITION

(a) (= *in direction of, towards*) zu; **to go to the station** zum Bahnhof gehen; **to go to the doctor('s)** *etc* zum Arzt *etc* gehen; **to go to the opera** *etc* in die Oper *etc* gehen; **to go to France/London** nach Frankreich/London fahren; **to the left** nach links; **to the west** nach Westen; **he came up to where I was standing** er kam dahin *or* zu der Stelle, wo ich stand; **to turn one's face to the wall** sich mit dem Gesicht zur Wand drehen; **hold it up to the light** halte es gegen das Licht; **I have never been to Brussels/India** (= *been in*) ich war noch nie in Brüssel/Indien

(b) (= *as far as, until*) bis; **to count (up) to 20** bis 20 zählen; **it's 90 kms to Paris** nach Paris sind es 90 km; **8 years ago to the day** auf den Tag genau vor 8 Jahren; **to this day** bis auf den heutigen Tag

(c) (= *secure to*) **he nailed it to the wall/floor** *etc* er nagelte es an die Wand/auf den Boden *etc*; **they tied him to the tree** sie banden ihn am Baum fest

(d) (*with indirect object*) **to give sth to sb** jdm etw geben; **I said to myself ...** ich habe mir gesagt ...; **he was muttering to himself** er murmelte vor sich hin; **what is it to you?** was geht dich das an?; **he is kind to everyone** er ist zu allen freundlich; **it's a great help to me** das ist eine große Hilfe für mich; **he has been a good friend to us** er war uns (*dat*) ein guter Freund; **to Lottie** (*toast*) auf Lottie (*acc*); **to drink to sb** jdm zutrinken; **to drink to sb's health** auf jds Wohl (*acc*) trinken

(e) (= *next to*) (*with position*) **close to sb/sth** nahe bei jdm/ etw; **at right angles to the wall** im rechten Winkel zur Wand; **to the west (of)/the left (of)** westlich/links (von)

(f) (*with expressions of time*) vor; **20 (minutes) to 2** 20 (Minuten) vor 2; **at (a) quarter to 2** um Viertel vor 2; **25 to 3** 5 (Minuten) nach halb 3

(g) (= *in relation to*) zu; **they won by 4 goals to 2** sie haben mit 4:2 (*spoken*: vier zu zwei) Toren gewonnen; **3 to the 4th, 3 to the power of 4** 3 hoch 4

(h) (= per) pro; (in recipes, when mixing) auf (+acc)

(I) (phrases) **what would you say to a beer?** was hältst du von einem Bier?; **there's nothing to it** (= it's very easy) es ist nichts dabei; **that's all there is to it** das ist alles; **to the best of my knowledge** nach bestem Wissen; **it's not to my taste** das ist nicht nach meinem Geschmack; **to dance to a band** zu den Klängen or der Musik eines Orchesters tanzen; **ambassador to America** Botschafter in Amerika; **secretary to the director** Sekretärin des Direktors; **to everyone's surprise** zu jedermanns Überraschung

(j) (infinitive) **to begin to do sth** anfangen, etw zu tun; **he decided to come** er beschloss zu kommen; **I want to do it** ich will es tun; **I want him to do it** ich will, dass er es tut; **to work to live** arbeiten, um zu leben; **to get to the point, ...** um zur Sache zu kommen, ...; **I arrived to find she had gone** als ich ankam, war sie weg

(k) (omitting verb) **I don't want to** ich will nicht; **I'll try to** ich werde es versuchen; **you have to** du musst; **I'd love to** sehr gerne; **we didn't want to but we were forced to** wir wollten nicht, aber wir waren dazu gezwungen; **buy it, it would be silly not to** kaufe es, es wäre dumm, es nicht zu tun

(l) (set structures)

✦**noun/pronoun + to + infinitive** **I have done nothing to deserve this** ich habe nichts getan, womit ich das verdient hätte; **there's no-one to help us** es ist niemand da, der uns helfen könnte; **who is he to order you around?** wer ist er denn, dass er dich so herumkommandiert?; **he was the first to arrive** er kam als Erster an; **who was the last to see her?** wer hat sie zuletzt gesehen?; **what is there to do here?** was gibt es hier zu tun?

✦**adjective + to + infinitive** **to be ready to do sth** (= willing) bereit sein, etw zu tun; **it's hard to understand** es ist schwer zu verstehen; **it's impossible to believe** das kann man einfach nicht glauben; **you are foolish to try it** du bist dumm, das überhaupt zu versuchen

2 ADJECTIVE door (= shut) zu

3 ADVERB **to and fro** hin und her; walk auf und ab

---

toad [təʊd] N Kröte f; (fig: = repulsive person) Ekel nt

toadstool [ˈtəʊdstuːl] N (nicht essbarer) Pilz

toady [ˈtəʊdɪ] **1** N (pej) Speichellecker(in) m(f) **2** VI Rad fahren (pej inf); **to ~ to sb** vor jdm kriechen

toast¹ [təʊst] **1** N Toast m; **a piece of ~** ein Toast m; **on ~** auf Toast **2** VT toasten; (on open fire) rösten; **to ~ one's feet by the fire** sich (dat) die Füße am Feuer wärmen

toast² **1** N Toast m, Trinkspruch m; **to drink a ~ to sb** auf jdn trinken; **to propose a ~** einen Toast or Trinkspruch ausbringen (to auf +acc); **she was the ~ of the town** sie war der gefeierte Star der Stadt **2** VT **to ~ sb/sth** auf jds Wohl or jdn/ etw trinken

toaster [ˈtəʊstəʳ] N Toaster m

toast rack N Toastständer m

tobacco [təˈbækəʊ] N Tabak m

tobacconist [təˈbækənɪst] N Tabak(waren)händler(in) m(f); (= shop) Tabak(waren)laden m

to-be [təˈbiː] ADJ zukünftig; **the bride-~** die zukünftige Braut; **the mother-~** die werdende Mutter

toboggan [təˈbɒɡən] **1** N Schlitten m **2** VI **to go ~ing** Schlitten fahren, rodeln

today [təˈdeɪ] ADV, N **(a)** heute; **a week/fortnight ~** heute in einer Woche/zwei Wochen; **a year ago ~** heute vor einem Jahr; **from ~** von heute an, ab heute; **later ~** später (am Tag); **~'s paper** die Zeitung von heute; **what's ~'s date?** welches Datum ist heute?, der Wievielte ist heute?; **~'s rate** (Fin) der Tageskurs; **here ~ and gone tomorrow** (fig) heute hier und morgen da

(b) (= these days) heutzutage; **the world/youth of ~** die Welt/ Jugend von heute; **~'s youth** die Jugend von heute

toddle [ˈtɒdl] VI **(a)** (child) wackelnd laufen **(b)** (inf) (= walk) gehen; (= leave: also **~ off**) abzwitschern (inf)

toddler [ˈtɒdləʳ] N Kleinkind nt

toddy [ˈtɒdɪ] N Grog m

to-do [təˈduː] N (inf) Theater nt (inf)

---

toe [təʊ] **1** N Zehe f, Zeh m; (of sock, shoe) Spitze f; **to tread or step on sb's ~s** (lit) jdm auf die Zehen treten; (fig) jdm ins Handwerk pfuschen (inf); **to be on one's ~s** (fig) auf Zack sein (inf); **to keep sb on his ~s** (fig) jdn auf Zack halten (inf) **2** VT (fig) **to ~ the line** sich einfügen, spuren (inf)

TOEFL ABBR of **Test of English as a Foreign Language** TOEFL-Test m, englische Sprachprüfung für ausländische Studenten

toe: toehold N Halt m für die Fußspitzen; (fig) Einstieg m; **toenail** N Zehennagel m

toff [tɒf] N (Brit inf) feiner Pinkel (inf)

toffee [ˈtɒfɪ] N (Brit) (= substance) (Sahne)karamell m; (= sweet) Toffee nt

tofu [ˈtɒfuː] N Tofu nt

toga [ˈtəʊɡə] N Toga f

together [təˈɡeðəʳ] **1** ADV zusammen; **to do sth ~** etw zusammen tun; (= with one another) discuss, play etc also etw miteinander tun; (= jointly) try, achieve etc also etw gemeinsam tun; **to sit** etc **~** zusammensitzen etc; **to be (all) ~** (people) (alle) zusammen or beisammen sein; **to tie/glue** etc **two things ~** zwei Dinge zusammenbinden/-kleben etc; **we're in this ~** wir hängen da alle or (two people) beide zusammen drin (inf); **they were both in it ~** sie waren beide zusammen daran beteiligt; **to go ~** (= match) zusammenpassen; **all ~ now** jetzt alle zusammen; **~ with** (zusammen) mit **2** ADJ (inf) cool (inf)

toggle [ˈtɒɡl] **1** N Knebel m; (on clothes) Knebelknopf m; (on tent) Seilzug m **2** VI (Comput) hin- und herschalten

toggle: toggle key N (Comput) Umschalttaste f; **toggle switch** N Kipp(hebel)schalter m

Togo [ˈtəʊɡəʊ] N Togo nt

togs [tɒɡz] PL (inf) Sachen pl, Klamotten pl (inf)

toil [tɔɪl] **1** VI **(a)** (liter: = work) sich plagen (at, over mit) **(b)** (= move with effort) sich schleppen **2** N (liter) Plage f (geh)

toilet [ˈtɔɪlɪt] N Toilette f; **to go to the ~** (esp Brit) auf die Toilette gehen; **she's in the ~/~s** sie ist auf or in der Toilette

toilet IN CPDS Toiletten-; **toilet bag** N (Brit) Kulturbeutel m; **toilet paper** N Toilettenpapier nt

toiletries [ˈtɔɪlɪtrɪz] PL Toilettenartikel pl

toilet: toilet roll N Rolle f Toilettenpapier; **toilet seat** N Toilettensitz m; **toilet tissue** N Toilettenpapier nt; **toilet training** N Erziehung f zur Sauberkeit; **toilet water** N Eau de Toilette nt

to-ing and fro-ing [ˌtuːɪŋənˈfrəʊɪŋ] N (esp Brit) Hin und Her nt

token [ˈtəʊkən] **1** N **(a)** (= sign) Zeichen nt; **as a ~ of, in ~ of** als or zum Zeichen (+gen); **by the same ~** ebenso; (with neg) aber auch

(b) (for gambling etc) Spielmarke f

(c) (Brit: = voucher, gift token) Gutschein m

2 ATTR Schein-, pro forma; **~ gesture** leere Geste; **it was just a ~ offer** das hat er/sie etc nur so zum Schein angeboten; **~ payment** symbolische Bezahlung; **the one ~ woman** die Alibifrau

Tokyo [ˈtəʊkɪəʊ] N Tokio nt

told [təʊld] PRET, PTP of **tell**

tolerable [ˈtɒlərəbl] ADJ (lit) erträglich; (fig also) annehmbar, passabel (inf)

tolerance [ˈtɒlərəns] N (also Med, Tech) Toleranz f (of, for, towards gegenüber); (towards children) Nachsicht f (of mit); **racial ~** Toleranz in Rassenfragen

tolerant [ˈtɒlərənt] ADJ **(a)** (of, towards, with gegenüber) tolerant; (towards children) nachsichtig **(b)** (Tech) **to be ~ of heat** hitzebeständig sein; **to be ~ to light** Licht vertragen können

tolerate [ˈtɒləreɪt] VT **(a)** pain, noise etc ertragen; drug vertragen **(b)** person, abuse tolerieren; behaviour, injustice etc also dulden

toleration [ˌtɒləˈreɪʃən] N Duldung f, Tolerierung f

toll¹ [təʊl] **1** VTI läuten **2** N Läuten nt; (= single stroke) Glockenschlag m

toll² N **(a)** (= bridge ~, road ~) Maut f, Zoll m; **~ charge** Maut f **(b)** (= deaths, loss etc) **the ~ on the roads** die Zahl der Verkehrsopfer

toll: tollbooth N Mautstelle f; **toll bridge** N Mautbrücke f; **toll call** N (US) Ferngespräch nt; **toll-free** (US Telec) ADJ, ADV gebührenfrei; **toll road** N Mautstraße f

Tom [tɒm] N **you don't have to invite every ~, Dick and Harry** (*inf*) du brauchst ja nicht gerade Hinz und Kunz einzuladen (*inf*)

tomato [təˈmɑːtəʊ, (*US*) təˈmeɪtəʊ] N, *pl* **-es** Tomate *f*

tomato IN CPDS Tomaten-; **tomato ketchup** N (Tomaten)ket(s)chup *m or nt*; **tomato puree** N Tomatenmark *nt*

tomb [tuːm] N (= *grave*) Grab *nt*; (= *building*) Grabmal *nt*

tombola [tɒmˈbəʊlə] N Tombola *f*

tomboy [ˈtɒmbɔɪ] N Wildfang *m*

tombstone [ˈtuːmstəʊn] N Grabstein *m*

tomcat [ˈtɒmkæt] N Kater *m*

tome [təʊm] N Wälzer *m* (*inf*)

tomfoolery [tɒmˈfuːlərɪ] N Blödsinn *m*, Unsinn *m*

tomorrow [təˈmɒrəʊ] ADV, N morgen; (= *future*) Morgen *nt*; **~ week, a week ~** morgen in einer Woche; **a fortnight ~** morgen in zwei Wochen; **a year ago ~** morgen vor einem Jahr; **the day after ~** übermorgen; **~ morning/lunchtime/ evening** morgen früh/Mittag/Abend; **late/early ~** morgen spät/früh; **(as) from ~** ab morgen, von morgen an; **see you ~!** bis morgen!; **~'s paper** die Zeitung von morgen; **will ~ do?** (*early enough*) reicht es noch bis morgen?; (*convenient*) ist es morgen recht?; **~ is another day** (*prov*) morgen ist auch noch ein Tag (*prov*); **who knows what ~ will bring?** wer weiß, was das Morgen bringt?; **the stars of ~** die Stars von morgen

ton [tʌn] N **(a)** (britische) Tonne; **it weighs a ~** (*fig inf*) das wiegt ja eine Tonne **(b) tons** PL (*inf*: = *lots*) jede Menge (*inf*)

tone [təʊn] 🟦 N (*lit, fig*) Ton *m* (*also Mus*); (*US*: = *note*) Note *f*; (*of colour*) (Farb)ton *m*; (= *quality of sound*) Klang *m*; **the soft ~s of her voice** der sanfte Klang ihrer Stimme; **... he said in a friendly ~ ...** sagte er in freundlichem Ton; **the new people have lowered the ~ of the neighbourhood** die neuen Leute haben dem Ruf des Viertels geschadet 🟦 VT *body, muscles* in Form bringen

➤ **tone down** VT SEP (*lit, fig*) abmildern; *colour also* abschwächen; *criticism also, language, demands* mäßigen

➤ **tone up** VT SEP *muscles* kräftigen; *person, body* in Form bringen

tone-deaf [təʊnˈdef] ADJ nicht in der Lage, Tonhöhen zu unterscheiden; **he's ~** er hat kein Gehör für Tonhöhen

toneless [ˈtəʊnlɪs] ADJ tonlos; *music* eintönig

tonelessly [ˈtəʊnlɪslɪ] ADV *reply* tonlos; *sing* eintönig

toner [ˈtəʊnəʳ] N **(a)** (*for printer, copier*) Toner *m* **(b)** (= *cosmetic*) Tönung *f*

toner cartridge N Tonerpatrone *f*

tongs [tɒŋz] PL Zange *f*; (*electric*) Lockenstab *m*; **a pair of ~** eine Zange

tongue [tʌŋ] N Zunge *f*; (*of land*) (Land)zunge *f*; **to put** *or* **stick one's ~ out at sb** jdm die Zunge herausstrecken; **to hold one's ~** den Mund halten; **to have a sharp ~** eine scharfe Zunge haben; **I can't get my ~ round it** dabei breche ich mir fast die Zunge ab

tongue: tongue-in-cheek ADJ ATTR, **tongue in cheek** ADJ PRED *humour* ironisch; *remark* ironisch gemeint; **tongue in cheek** ADV nicht ganz ernst gemeint; **tongue-tied** ADJ **to be ~** keinen Ton herausbringen; **tongue twister** N Zungenbrecher *m*

tonic [ˈtɒnɪk] N **(a)** (*Med*) Tonikum *nt*; (= *hair ~*) Haarwasser *nt* **(b)** (= *water*) Tonic(water) *nt*; *gin* and ~ Gin *m* (mit) Tonic

tonight [təˈnaɪt] 🟦 ADV (= *this evening*) heute Abend; (= *during the coming night*) heute Nacht; **see you ~!** bis heute Abend! 🟦 N (= *this evening*) der heutige Abend; (= *the coming night*) die heutige Nacht; **~'s party** die Party heute Abend; **~ is the night we've been looking forward to** heute ist der Abend, auf den wir uns gefreut haben; **~'s paper** die Abendzeitung von heute

tonnage [ˈtʌnɪdʒ] N Tonnage *f*

tonne [tʌn] N Tonne *f*

tonsil [ˈtɒnsl] N Mandel *f*

tonsillitis [ˌtɒnsɪˈlaɪtɪs] N Mandelentzündung *f*

tony [ˈtəʊnɪ] ADJ (*US inf*: = *classy*) schick

too [tuː] ADV **(a)** (+*adj or adv*, = *very*) zu; **~ much** zu viel *inv*; **~ many** zu viele; **he's had ~ much to drink** er hat zu viel getrunken; **you can have ~ much of a good thing** allzu viel ist ungesund (*prov*); **don't worry ~ much** mach dir nicht zu viel

Sorgen; **~ right!** (*inf*) das kannste laut sagen (*inf*); **all ~ ...** allzu ...; **only ~ ...** nur zu ...; **none ~ ...** gar nicht ..., keineswegs ...; **not ~ ...** nicht zu ...; **he wasn't ~ interested** er war nicht allzu interessiert; **I'm not/none ~ sure** ich bin nicht ganz/gar nicht *or* keineswegs sicher; **(that's) ~ kind of you** (*iro*) (das ist) wirklich zu nett von Ihnen; **all ~ soon** allzu früh **(b)** (= *also*) auch

(c) (= *moreover, into the bargain*) auch noch

took [tʊk] PRET *of* **take**

tool [tuːl] N Werkzeug *nt*; (= *gardening ~*) (Garten)gerät *nt*; **~s** Werkzeuge *pl*; (= *set*) Werkzeug *nt*; **that's one of the ~s of the trade** das gehört zum Handwerkszeug

tool: toolbox, tool chest N Werkzeugkasten *m*; **toolkit** N Werkzeug(ausrüstung) *f nt*; **tool shed** N Geräteschuppen *m*

toot [tuːt] 🟦 VT **to ~ a horn** (*in car*) hupen 🟦 VI (*in car*) hupen; (*train*) pfeifen; (*ship*) tuten 🟦 N (*in car*) Hupen *nt*; (*of train*) Pfiff *m*, Pfeifsignal *nt*

tooth [tuːθ] N, *pl* **teeth** Zahn *m*; (*of comb*) Zinke *f*; **to have a ~ out** sich (*dat*) einen Zahn ziehen lassen; **to get one's teeth into sth** (*fig*) sich in etw (*dat*) festbeißen; **to fight ~ and nail** bis aufs Blut kämpfen; **to lie through** *or* **in one's teeth** das Blaue vom Himmel herunterlügen; **I'm fed up to the (back) teeth with that** (*inf*) *or* **sick to the (back) teeth of that** (*inf*) hängt mir zum Hals heraus (*inf*); **selling a car these days is like pulling teeth** (*esp US*) ein Auto zu verkaufen ist heutzutage ein mühsames Geschäft

tooth IN CPDS Zahn-; **toothache** N Zahnschmerzen *pl*; **toothbrush** N Zahnbürste *f*; **tooth decay** N Karies *f*; **toothless** ADJ zahnlos; **toothpaste** N Zahnpasta *or* -creme *f*; **toothpick** N Zahnstocher *m*

tootle [ˈtuːtl] (*esp Brit inf*) VI **(a)** (*on whistle etc: also* **~ away**) vor sich hin dudeln (*inf*) **(b)** (= *drive*) juckeln (*inf*); (= *go*) trotten

top¹ [tɒp] 🟦 N **(a)** (= *highest part*) oberer Teil; (*of spire, cone etc, fig: of league, company etc*) Spitze *f*; (*of mountain*) Gipfel *m*; (*of tree*) Krone *f*; (*of branch, road, beach*) oberes Ende; (*of carrots*) Ende *nt*; (= *leafy part*) Kraut *nt*; (= *detachable part: of cupboard etc*) Aufsatz *m*; (= *head end: of table, sheet*) Kopfende *nt*; **which is the ~?** wo ist oben?; **the ~ of the tree/page** *etc* **is ...** der Baum/die Seite *etc* ist oben ...; **at the ~** oben; **at the ~ of the page/list** oben auf der Seite/Liste; **at the ~ of the league/ pile** oben in der Tabelle/im Stapel; **at the ~ of the stairs/hill** oben an der Treppe/am Berg; **at the ~ of the table** am oberen Ende des Tisches; **to be (at the) ~ of the class** Klassenbeste(r) *or* -erste(r) sein; **near the ~** (ziemlich) weit oben; **five lines from the ~** in der fünften Zeile von oben; **from ~ to toe** von Kopf bis Fuß; **from ~ to bottom** von oben bis unten; **to scream at the ~ of one's voice** aus vollem Hals *or* aus Leibeskräften brüllen; **they were talking at the ~(s) of their voices** sie haben sich in voller Lautstärke unterhalten; **to be at the ~ of the ladder** *or* **the tree** (*fig*) auf dem Gipfel (des Erfolgs) sein; **off the ~ of my head** (*fig*) grob gesagt; (*with figures*) über den Daumen gepeilt (*inf*); **to go over the ~** (= *exaggerate*) zu viel des Guten tun; **that's a bit over the ~** das geht ein bisschen zu weit; **I find him a bit over the ~** ich finde, er übertreibt es ein bisschen; **in ~** (*Aut: also* **in ~ gear**) im höchsten Gang

(b) (= *upper surface*) Oberfläche *f*; **to be on ~** oben sein *or* liegen; (*fig*) obenauf sein; **it was on ~ of/on the ~ of the cupboard** *etc* es war auf/oben auf dem Schrank *etc*; **on ~ of** (*in addition to*) zusätzlich zu; **things are getting on ~ of me** die Dinge wachsen mir über den Kopf; **then, on ~ of all that ...** und dann, um das Maß voll zu machen ...; **and, on ~ of that ...** und außerdem ...; **it's just one thing on ~ of another** es kommt eines zum anderen; **he didn't see it until he was right on ~ of it** er sah es erst, als er ganz nah dran war; **he felt he was on ~ of the situation** er hatte das Gefühl, die Situation unter Kontrolle zu haben; **to come out on ~** sich durchsetzen; (*over rival*) die Oberhand gewinnen

(c) (*inf: of body*) Oberkörper *m*; **to blow one's ~** in die Luft *or* an die Decke gehen (*inf*)

(d) (= *working surface*) Arbeitsfläche *f*

(e) (= *bikini ~*) Oberteil *nt*; (= *blouse*) Top *nt*

(f) (= *lid*) (*of jar, suitcase*) Deckel *m*; (*of bottle*) Verschluss *m*; (*of pen*) Hülle *f*; (*of car*) Dach *nt*

🟦 ADJ (= *upper*) oberste(r, s); (= *highest*) oberste(r, s); *branches, note, honours, price* höchste(r, s); (= *best*) Spitzen-, Top-; *pupil, school, marks* beste(r, s); **~ athlete** Spitzenathlet(in) *m(f)*; **~ job** Spitzenjob *m*; **today's ~ story** die wichtigste Meldung von heute; **on the ~ floor** im obersten Stockwerk; **the ~ end of the market** das obere Marktsegment; **at ~ speed** mit Höchstgeschwindigkeit; **in ~ form** in Höchstform; **the ~ men in the party/firm** die Partei-/Unternehmensspitze; **the ~ people** (*in a company*) die Leute an der Spitze

3 ADV **(a) to come ~** (= *Sch*) Beste(r) werden

(b) ~s (*inf*) höchstens, maximal

4 VT **(a)** (= *cover, cap*) bedecken; **fruit ~ped with cream** Obst mit Sahne darauf

(b) (= *be at ~ of*) **his name ~ped the list** sein Name stand ganz oben auf der Liste

(c) (= *be higher than, fig*: = *surpass*) übersteigen; **that ~s the lot** (*inf*) das übertrifft alles; **and to ~ it all ...** (*inf*) und um das Maß voll zu machen

➤ **top off** VT SEP **(a)** abrunden **(b)** (*US*) = **top up**

➤ **top up** VT SEP (*Brit*) auffüllen; *pension, income* ergänzen; **can I top you up?** (*inf*) darf ich dir nachschenken?

top² N Kreisel *m*

top: top dog N (*fig*) **he always has to be ~** er muss immer das Sagen haben; **top-flight** ADJ Spitzen-, erstklassig; **top gear** N höchster Gang; **to be in ~** (*lit*) im höchsten Gang sein; (*fig*) auf Hochtouren sein; **top hat** N Zylinder *m*; **top-heavy** ADJ (*lit, fig*) kopflastig

topic ['tɒpɪk] N Thema *nt*; **~ of conversation** Gesprächsthema *nt*

topical ['tɒpɪkəl] ADJ aktuell; **he made a few ~ remarks** er ging kurz auf aktuelle Geschehnisse ein

top: topless **1** ADJ oben ohne, Oben-ohne-; **~ model** Oben-ohne-Modell *nt* **2** ADV oben ohne; **top-level** ADJ Spitzen-; *inquiry, negotiations* auf höchster Ebene; **~ meeting** Spitzentreffen *nt*; **top management** N Spitzenmanagement *nt*; **topmost** ADJ oberste(r, s); **top-notch** ADJ (*inf*) eins a (*inf*); **top-of-the-range, top-of-the-line** ADJ ATTR Spitzen-, der Spitzenklasse; **~ model** Spitzenmodell *nt*

topographic(al) [tɒpə'græfɪk(əl)] ADJ topografisch

topping ['tɒpɪŋ] N (*Cook*) **with a ~ of cream** *etc* mit Sahne *etc* (oben) darauf

topple ['tɒpl] **1** VI wackeln; (= *fall*) fallen **2** VT umwerfen; (*from a height*) hinunterkippen *or* -werfen; (*fig*) *government etc* stürzen; **to ~ sb from power** jdn stürzen *or* entmachten

➤ **topple down** VI (*group of objects*) runterpurzeln; (*from top of stairs etc*) herunterfallen; (*+prep obj*) hinunterfallen

➤ **topple over** VI schwanken und fallen (*prep obj* über +*acc*)

top: top-ranked ADJ ATTR (*Sport*) Spitzen-; **top-ranking** ADJ von hohem Rang; *civil servant, officer also* hohe(r); *tennis player etc* der Spitzenklasse; **~ author** Spitzenautor(in) *m(f)*; **top-rated** ADJ ATTR führend

tops [tɒps] ADJ (*Brit sl*) **to be ~** cool sein (*sl*)

top: top-secret ADJ streng geheim; **topsoil** N (*Agr*) Ackerkrume *f*

topsy-turvy [tɒpsɪ'tɜːvɪ] (*inf*) ADJ (*lit*) (= *upside down*) umgedreht; (= *in disorder*) kunterbunt durcheinander *pred*; (*fig*) auf den Kopf gestellt

top-up ['tɒpʌp] (*Brit*) **1** N (*inf*) **would you like a ~?** darf man dir noch nachschenken? **2** ADJ Zusatz-

torch [tɔːtʃ] N (*lit, fig*) Fackel *f*; (*Brit*: = *flashlight*) Taschenlampe *f*

tore [tɔːʳ] PRET *of* tear¹

torment ['tɔːment] **1** N Qual *f*; **to be in ~, to suffer ~(s)** Qualen leiden **2** [tɔː'ment] VT quälen; (= *annoy, tease*) plagen

tormentor [tɔː'mentəʳ] N Peiniger(in) *m(f)*

torn [tɔːn] PTP *of* tear¹

tornado [tɔː'neɪdəʊ] N, *pl* **-es** Tornado *m*

torpedo [tɔː'piːdəʊ] **1** N, *pl* **-es** Torpedo *m* **2** VT torpedieren

torpor ['tɔːpəʳ] N (= *lethargy*) Trägheit *f*; (= *apathy*) Abgestumpftheit *f*

torrent ['tɒrənt] N reißender Strom; (*fig*: *of words, insults*) Schwall *m*; **a ~ of abuse** ein Schwall *m* von Beschimpfungen

torrential [tə'renʃəl] ADJ *rain* sintflutartig

torso ['tɔːsəʊ] N Körper *m*; (*Art*) Torso *m*

tortoise ['tɔːtəs] N Schildkröte *f*

tortoiseshell ['tɔːtəʃel] N Schildpatt *m*

tortuous ['tɔːtjʊəs] ADJ (*lit*) *path* gewunden; (*fig*) verwickelt; *methods also, journey* umständlich

---

torture ['tɔːtʃəʳ] **1** N Folter *f*; (*fig*) Qual *f* **2** VT **(a)** (*lit*) foltern **(b)** (*fig*: = *torment*) quälen

torture chamber N Folterkammer *f*

torturer ['tɔːtʃərəʳ] N (*lit*) Folterknecht *m*; (*fig*: = *tormentor*) Peiniger(in) *m(f)*

torturous ['tɔːtʃərəs] ADJ qualvoll

Tory ['tɔːrɪ] (*Brit Pol*) **1** N Tory *m*, Konservative(r) *mf* **2** ADJ konservativ, Tory-

toss [tɒs] **1** N **(a)** (= *throw*) Wurf *m*

(b) (*of coin*) Münzwurf *m*; **to win/lose the ~** (*esp Sport*) die Seitenwahl gewinnen/verlieren

2 VT **(a)** (= *throw*) werfen; *salad* anmachen; *pancake* wenden (*durch Hochwerfen*); *rider* abwerfen; **to ~ sth to sb** jdm etw zuwerfen; **to ~ sth aside** etw zur Seite werfen; **to ~ sb aside** jdn fallen lassen; **to ~ a coin** eine Münze (zum Losen) hochwerfen; **to ~ sb for sth** mit jdm (durch Münzenwerfen) um etw knobeln; **I'll ~ you for it** lass uns darum knobeln

(b) (= *move*) schütteln, zerren an (+*dat*); **to ~ one's head** den Kopf zurückwerfen *or* hochwerfen

3 VI **(a)** (*ship*) rollen; **to ~ and turn (in bed)** sich (im Bett) hin und her wälzen

(b) (*with coin*) (durch Münzenwerfen) knobeln; **to ~ for sth** um etw knobeln

➤ **toss about** (*Brit*) *or* **around** **1** VI sich heftig hin und her bewegen; (*person*) sich hin und her werfen **2** VT (= *move*) durchschütteln; *boat* schaukeln; (= *throw*) *ball* herumwerfen; (*fig*) *ideas* zur Debatte stellen

➤ **toss away** VT SEP wegwerfen

➤ **toss back** VT SEP *head* zurückwerfen; *drink* hinunterstürzen

➤ **toss out** VT SEP *rubbish* wegwerfen; *person* hinauswerfen; *idea* verwerfen

➤ **toss up** VT SEP werfen; **to toss sth up (into the air)** etw in die Luft werfen

toss-up ['tɒsʌp] N **it was a ~ whether ...** (*inf*) es war völlig offen, ob ...

tot [tɒt] N **(a)** (= *child*: *also* **tiny ~**) Steppke (*inf*), Knirps (*inf*) *m*

(b) (*esp Brit*: *of alcohol*) Schlückchen *nt*

➤ **tot up** VT SEP (*esp Brit inf*) zusammenzählen

total ['təʊtl] **1** ADJ (= *complete*) völlig, absolut; (= *comprising the whole*) Gesamt-; *eclipse* total; **~ sum/amount** Gesamtsumme *f*; **the ~ cost** die Gesamtkosten *pl*; **what is the ~ number of rooms you have?** wie viele Zimmer haben Sie (insgesamt)?; **a ~ stranger** ein völlig Fremder; **to be in ~ ignorance (of sth)** (von etw) überhaupt nichts wissen

2 N Gesamtmenge *f*; (= *money, figures*) Endsumme *f*; **a ~ of 50 people** insgesamt 50 Leute; **this brings the ~ to £100** das bringt die Gesamtsumme auf £ 100; **in ~** (= *in all*) insgesamt

3 VT **(a)** (= *amount to*) sich belaufen auf (+*acc*)

(b) (= *add*: *also* **~ up**) zusammenzählen

totalitarian [ˌtəʊtælɪ'teərɪən] ADJ totalitär

totally ['təʊtəlɪ] ADV völlig, total

tote bag ['təʊtbæg] N (*US*) (Einkaufs)tasche *f*

totem pole ['təʊtəmpəʊl] N Totempfahl *m*

totter ['tɒtəʳ] VI (= *wobble before falling, fig*) schwanken; (= *stagger*) taumeln; (*old man, baby*) tapsen; (*economy*) kränkeln

touch [tʌtʃ] **1** N **(a)** (= *sense of ~*) (Tast)gefühl *nt*; **to be cold to the ~** sich kalt anfühlen

(b) (= *act of touching*) Berühren *nt*, Berührung *f*; (*of typist, typewriter*) Anschlag *m*; **it opens at a ~** es öffnet sich auf Fingerdruck; **at the ~ of a button** auf Knopfdruck

(c) (= *skill*) Hand *f*; (= *style*) Stil *m*; **it has the professional ~** es hat etwas Professionelles *or* einen professionellen Anstrich; **he's losing his ~** er wird langsam alt; **a personal ~** eine persönliche Note

(d) (= *stroke*) (*Art*) Strich *m*; (*fig*) Einfall *m*; **a nice ~** eine hübsche Note; (*gesture*) eine nette Geste; **to put the final** *or* **finishing ~es to sth** letzte Hand an etw (*acc*) legen

(e) (= *small quantity*) Spur *f*; (*esp of irony etc*) Anflug *m*; **a ~ of flu** eine leichte Grippe

(f) (= *communication*) **to be in (constant) ~ with sb** mit jdm in (ständiger) Verbindung stehen; **to be/keep in ~ with (political) developments** (politisch) auf dem Laufenden sein/bleiben; **I'll be in ~!** ich melde mich!; **keep in ~!** lass wieder einmal von dir hören!; **to be completely out of ~ (with sth)** (in Bezug auf etw *acc*) überhaupt nicht auf dem Laufenden sein; **you can get in ~ with me at this number** Sie

können mich unter dieser Nummer erreichen; **you ought to get in ~ with the police** Sie sollten sich mit der Polizei in Verbindung setzen; **to lose ~ (with sb)** den Kontakt (zu jdm) verlieren; **to lose ~ (with sth)** (in Bezug auf etw acc) nicht mehr auf dem Laufenden sein; **I'll put you in ~ with Mr Brown** ich werde Sie mit Herrn Brown in Verbindung bringen **(g)** (Ftbl) Aus nt; **in ~** im Aus
(h) (inf) **to be an easy** or **soft ~** leicht anzupumpen (inf) sein 🔁 VT **(a)** (= concern) betreffen; (= get hold of) anfassen; (= press lightly) piano keys anschlagen; (= strike lightly) streichen über (+acc); (= brush against) streifen; **she was so happy, her feet hardly ~ed the ground** (fig) sie war so glücklich, dass sie in den Wolken schwebte; **his hair was ~ed with grey** sein Haar war von Grau durchzogen
(b) criminal, food, drink, problem anrühren; capital herankommen an (+acc) (inf); (= use) antasten; **the police can't ~ me** die Polizei kann mir nichts anhaben; **everything he ~es turns to gold** ihm gelingt einfach alles; **I wouldn't ~ those shares** ich würde meine Finger von den Aktien lassen
(c) (= equal) herankommen an (+acc), erreichen
(d) (= move emotionally) rühren, bewegen; (= affect) berühren; (= wound) pride treffen
🔁 VI sich berühren; **don't ~!** Finger weg!; **"please do not ~"** „bitte nicht berühren"
➤ **touch up** VT SEP colour, make-up auffrischen; picture, paintwork ausbessern; photo retuschieren
➤ **touch (up)on** VI +PREP OBJ subject antippen; **he barely touched on the question** er hat die Frage kaum berührt
touch-and-go [ˈtʌtʃənˈgəʊ] ADJ **to be ~** riskant sein; **it's ~ whether ...** es steht auf des Messers Schneide, ob ...; **it's ~ if we'll make it** es ist noch nicht vollkommen offen, ob wir es schaffen; **after his operation it was ~** nach der Operation hing sein Leben an einem Faden
touchdown [ˈtʌtʃdaʊn] N **(a)** (Aviat, Space) Aufsetzen nt **(b)** (US Ftbl) Versuch m, Niederlegen des Balles im Malfeld des Gegners
touched [tʌtʃt] ADJ PRED **(a)** (= moved) gerührt, bewegt **(b)** **to be a bit ~** (inf: = mad) einen leichten Stich haben (inf)
touching ADJ, **touchingly** ADV [ˈtʌtʃɪŋ, -lɪ] rührend, bewegend
touch: **touchline** N (esp Brit Sport) Seitenlinie f; **touchpaper** N Zündpapier nt; **touch-sensitive** ADJ berührungsempfindlich; **~ screen** Touch-Screen m; **~ switch** Kontaktschalter m; **touchstone** N (fig) Prüfstein m; **touch-tone** ADJ telephone Tonwahl-; **touch-type** VI blind schreiben
touchy [ˈtʌtʃɪ] ADJ empfindlich (about in Bezug auf +acc); (= irritable also) leicht reizbar; subject heikel
touchy-feely [ˈtʌtʃɪˈfiːlɪ] ADJ (pej) sentimental
tough [tʌf] 🔁 ADJ (+ER) zäh; (= resistant) widerstandsfähig; cloth strapazierfähig; (towards others) bargaining, opponent, fight, problem, controls hart; city rau; journey anstrengend; choice schwierig; **(as) ~ as old boots** (Brit hum inf) or **shoe leather** (US hum inf) zäh wie Leder (inf); **he'll get over it, he's pretty ~** er wird schon darüber hinwegkommen, er ist hart im Nehmen (inf); **to get ~ (with sb)** (fig) hart durchgreifen (gegen jdn); **~ guy** (inf) (knall)harter Kerl or Bursche (inf); **it was ~ going** (lit, fig) es war eine Strapaze; **to have a ~ time of it** nichts zu lachen haben; **I had a ~ time controlling my anger** es fiel mir schwer, meinen Zorn unter Kontrolle zu halten; **it's ~ when you have kids** es ist schwierig, wenn man Kinder hat; **she's a ~ customer** sie ist zäh wie Leder (inf); **it was ~ on the others** (inf) das war hart für die andern; **~ (luck)!** (inf) Pech!; **~ luck on Taylor** (inf) Pech für Taylor
🔁 ADV (+ER) (inf) **to act ~** hart durchgreifen
toughen [ˈtʌfn] 🔁 VT **(a)** glass, metal härten **(b)** (fig) rules, terms verschärfen; **they will have to ~ their policy** sie müssen einen härteren politischen Kurs einschlagen 🔁 VI (attitude) sich verhärten
➤ **toughen up** 🔁 VT SEP person stählen (geh); muscles trainieren; sportsman also fit machen; regulations verschärfen 🔁 VI hart or zäh werden; (attitude) sich verhärten; **to toughen up on sth** härter gegen etw vorgehen
tough-minded [tʌfˈmaɪndɪd] ADJ störrisch
toughness [ˈtʌfnɪs] N (of meat etc) Zähheit f; (of person) Zähigkeit f; (= resistance) Widerstandsfähigkeit f; (of bargaining, opponent, fight, controls) Härte f
toupee [ˈtuːpeɪ] N Toupet nt
tour [tʊəʳ] 🔁 N **(a)** Tour f; (by bus, car etc also) Reise f; (of town, building, exhibition etc) Rundgang m (of durch); (also guided

~) Führung f (of durch); (by bus) Rundfahrt f (of durch); **to go on a ~ of Scotland** auf eine Schottlandreise gehen
(b) (also ~ **of inspection**) Runde f (of durch); (esp on foot) Rundgang m (of durch)
(c) (Sport, Theat) Tournee f (of durch); **to take a play on ~** mit einem Stück auf Gastspielreise or Tournee gehen
🔁 VT **(a)** country etc fahren durch; (= travel around) bereisen; **to ~ the world** um die Welt reisen
(b) town, building, exhibition einen Rundgang machen durch; (by bus etc) eine Rundfahrt machen durch
(c) (Theat, Sport) eine Tournee machen durch
🔁 VI **(a)** (on holiday) eine Reise or Tour machen; **we're ~ing (around)** wir reisen herum
(b) (Theat, Sport) eine Tournee machen; **to be ~ing** auf Tournee sein
tour de force [tʊədəˈfɔːs] N Glanzleistung f
tour guide N Reiseleiter(in) m(f)
touring [ˈtʊərɪŋ] N (Herum)reisen nt
touring: **touring company** N (Theat) Tourneetheater nt; **touring holiday** N (Brit) Reiseurlaub m; **touring party** N Reisegruppe f
tourism [ˈtʊərɪzəm] N Fremdenverkehr m, Tourismus m
tourist [ˈtʊərɪst] 🔁 N Tourist(in) m(f); (Sport) Gast m 🔁 ATTR Touristen-; **~ season** Reisesaison or -zeit f
tourist: **tourist class** 🔁 N Touristenklasse f 🔁 ADV in der Touristenklasse; **tourist-class** ADJ der Touristenklasse; **tourist guide** N Fremdenführer(in) m(f); **tourist information centre** N (Brit) Touristen-Informationsbüro nt; **tourist office** N Fremdenverkehrsbüro nt
touristy [ˈtʊərɪstɪ] ADJ (pej) auf Tourismus getrimmt; resorts, shops, souvenirs für Touristen
tournament [ˈtʊənəmənt] N (Sport etc, also Hist) Turnier nt
tourniquet [ˈtʊənɪkeɪ] N Aderpresse f
tour operator N Reiseveranstalter m
tousle [ˈtaʊzl] VT zerzausen
tousled [ˈtaʊzld] ADJ hair zerzaust, wuschelig (inf)
tout [taʊt] (inf) 🔁 N (= ticket ~) (Karten)schwarzhändler(in) m(f); (for business) Kundenfänger(in) m(f) 🔁 VT (also ~ **around**) tickets schwarz verkaufen (inf); goods (den Leuten) aufschwatzen (inf) 🔁 VI **to ~ for business** (aufdringlich) Reklame machen; **to ~ for customers** auf Kundenfang sein (inf)
tow [təʊ] 🔁 N **to take a car in ~** ein Auto abschleppen; **to give sb/a car a ~** (in car) jdn/ein Auto abschleppen; **in ~** (fig) im Schlepptau 🔁 VT boat schleppen; car also abschleppen; trailer, caravan ziehen
➤ **tow away** VT SEP car (gebührenpflichtig) abschleppen
toward(s) [təˈwɔːd(z)] PREP **(a)** (= in direction of) (with verbs of motion) auf (+acc) ... zu; **we sailed ~ China** wir segelten in Richtung China; **it's further north, ~ Dortmund** es liegt weiter im Norden, Richtung Dortmund; **~ the south** nach Süden; **he turned ~ her** er wandte sich ihr zu; **with his back ~ the wall** mit dem Rücken zur Wand; **on the side (facing) ~ the sea** zum Meer hin; **they are working ~ a solution** sie arbeiten auf eine Lösung hin; **~ a better understanding of ...** zum besseren Verständnis von ...; **I gave him some money ~ a car** ich gab ihm etwas Geld als Beitrag zu seinem Auto
(b) (= in relation to) ... (dat) gegenüber; **what are your feelings ~ him?** was empfinden Sie für ihn?
(c) **~ ten o'clock** gegen zehn Uhr; **~ the end of the year** gegen Ende des Jahres
towbar [ˈtəʊbaːʳ] N Anhängerkupplung f
towel [ˈtaʊəl] 🔁 N Handtuch nt 🔁 VT (mit einem Handtuch) (ab)trocknen
➤ **towel down** VT SEP (ab)trocknen
towelling [ˈtaʊəlɪŋ] N Frottee(stoff) m
tower [ˈtaʊəʳ] 🔁 N **(a)** Turm m **(b)** (fig) **a ~ of strength** ein starker (Rück)halt **(c)** (Comput) Tower m 🔁 VI ragen
➤ **tower above** or **over** VI +PREP OBJ **(a)** (buildings etc) emporragen über (+acc) **(b)** (lit, fig: people) überragen
tower block N (Brit) Hochhaus nt
towering [ˈtaʊərɪŋ] ADJ **(a)** building hochragend **(b)** (fig) achievement, presence überragend; performance hervorragend
tower system N (Comput) Towersystem nt
towline [ˈtəʊlaɪn] N (Aut) Abschleppseil nt

town [taʊn] N Stadt f; **the ~ of Brighton** (die Stadt) Brighton; **to go into** or **down ~** in die Stadt gehen; **guess who's in ~?** raten Sie mal, wer zurzeit hier (in der Stadt) ist?; **he's out of ~** er ist nicht in der Stadt, er ist außerhalb; **to have a night on the ~** (inf) die Nacht durchmachen; **you didn't know? but it's all over ~** du hattest keine Ahnung? das ist doch stadtbekannt; **to go to ~ on sth** (fig inf: = go to great trouble with) sich (dat) bei etw einen abbrechen (inf); **John's really gone to ~ on his new house** John hat bei seinem neuen Haus wirklich keine Kosten gescheut

town: town centre, (US) **town center** N Stadtmitte f, (Stadt)zentrum nt; **town council** N Stadtrat m; **town councillor**, (US) **town councilor** N Stadtrat m, Stadträtin f; **town hall** N Rathaus nt; **town house** N Stadthaus nt; (= type of house) Reihenhaus nt; **town planner** N Stadtplaner(in) m(f); **town planning** N Stadtplanung f

townsfolk [ˈtaʊnzfəʊk] PL Stadtmenschen pl; (= citizens) Bürger pl

township [ˈtaʊnʃɪp] N (Stadt)gemeinde f; (US) Verwaltungsbezirk m; (in South Africa) Township f

townspeople [ˈtaʊnzpiːpl] PL Städter pl, Stadtmenschen pl; (= citizens) Bürger pl

tow: towpath N Treidelpfad m; **towrope** N (Aut) Abschleppseil nt; **tow truck** N (US) Abschleppwagen m

toxic [ˈtɒksɪk] ADJ giftig, Gift-; effects schädlich; **to be ~ to sb/sth** für jdn/etw schädlich sein

toxic waste N Giftmüll m

toxin [ˈtɒksɪn] N Giftstoff m

toy [tɔɪ] **1** N Spielzeug nt; **~s** Spielsachen pl, Spielzeug nt; (in shops also) Spielwaren pl **2** VI **to ~ with an idea** etc mit einer Idee etc spielen; **to ~ with one's food** mit dem Essen (herum)spielen

toy IN CPDS Spielzeug-; **toy boy** N (inf) jugendlicher Liebhaber; **toy car** N Spielzeugauto nt; **toy dog** N Zwerghund m; (made of material) Stoffhund m; **toyshop** N Spielzeug- or Spielwarenladen m

trace [treɪs] **1** N Spur f; (of irony etc also) Hauch m; **I can't find any ~ of your file** Ihre Akte ist spurlos verschwunden; **there's no ~ of it** keine Spur davon; **to sink without ~** spurlos versinken; (fig also) sang- und klanglos untergehen; **to lose all ~ of sb/sth** jdn/etw aus den Augen verlieren **2** VT (a) (= draw) zeichnen; (= copy) nachziehen; (with tracing paper) durchpausen

(b) trail, progress verfolgen; steps folgen (+dat); **to ~ a phone call** einen Anruf zurückverfolgen; **she was ~d to a house in Soho** ihre Spur führte zu einem Haus in Soho

(c) (= find) ausfindig machen, auffinden; **I can't ~ your file** ich kann Ihre Akte nicht finden

▶ **trace back** VT SEP descent zurückverfolgen; rumour auf seinen Ursprung zurückverfolgen; problem etc zurückführen (to auf +acc); **he can trace his family back to Henry VIII** seine Familie lässt sich bis zu Heinrich VIII. zurückverfolgen

trace element, trace mineral N Spurenelement nt

tracing paper [ˈtreɪsɪŋpeɪpə˞] N Pauspapier nt

track [træk] **1** N (a) Spur f; (of tyres) (Fahr)spur f; **to be on sb's ~** jdm auf der Spur sein; **to keep ~ of sb/sth** (= watch, follow) jdn/etw im Auge behalten; (= keep up to date with) über jdn/etw auf dem Laufenden bleiben; **how do you keep ~ of the time without a watch?** wie können Sie wissen, wie spät es ist, wenn Sie keine Uhr haben?; **I can't keep ~ of your girlfriends** du hast so viele Freundinnen, da komme ich nicht mit (inf); **no-one can keep ~ of the situation** niemand hat mehr einen Überblick über die Lage; **to lose ~ of sb/sth** (= lose contact with) über jdn/etw nicht mehr auf dem Laufenden sein (= not be up to date with) über jdn/etw nicht mehr auf dem Laufenden sein; **we lost ~ of time** wir haben die Zeit ganz vergessen; **he lost ~ of what he was saying** er hat den Faden verloren

(b) (fig) **we must be making ~s** (inf) wir müssen uns auf die Socken (inf) or auf den Weg machen; **to make ~s for home** sich auf den Nachhauseweg machen; **he stopped dead in his ~s** er blieb abrupt stehen; **to stop sb (dead) in his/her ~s** jdn abrupt zum Stillstand bringen; **to cover (up) one's ~s** seine Spuren verwischen

(c) (= path, of storm) Weg m; **to be on ~** (fig) auf Kurs sein; **to be on the right ~** (fig) auf der richtigen Spur sein; **to be on the wrong ~** (fig) auf dem Holzweg sein (inf); **to get the economy back on ~** die Wirtschaft wieder auf Kurs bringen

(d) (Rail) Gleise pl; (US: = platform) Bahnsteig m; **double/single ~ line** zwei-/eingleisige Strecke

(e) (Sport) Rennbahn f; (Athletics) Bahn f; (Motorsport) Piste f; (= circuit) Rennstrecke f; (Cycling) Radrennbahn f

(f) (on tape, diskette, CD) Spur f; (= song etc) Stück nt **2** VT (a) person, animal verfolgen; movements folgen (+dat)

(b) (US) **the children ~ed dirt all over the carpet** die Kinder hinterließen überall auf dem Teppich Schmutzspuren

▶ **track down** VT SEP aufspüren (to in +dat); thing aufstöbern; reference ausfindig machen

track: track-and-field ADJ Leichtathletik-; **trackball** N (Comput) (in laptop) Trackball m; (in mouse) Rollkugel f

tracker dog [ˈtrækədɒg] N Spürhund m

track: track event N Laufwettbewerb m; **track record** N (fig) **what's his ~?** was hat er vorzuweisen?; **to have a good/poor ~** gute/schlechte Leistungen vorweisen können; **tracksuit** N Trainingsanzug m

traction engine [ˈtrækʃənendʒɪn] N Zugmaschine f

tractor [ˈtræktə˞] N Traktor m

tractorfeed [ˈtræktəfiːd] N (Comput) Traktor m

trade [treɪd] **1** N (a) Gewerbe nt; (= commerce) Handel m; (= turnover: of shop, hotel etc) die Geschäfte pl; **he used to be in ~** er war Geschäftsmann; **how's ~?** wie gehen die Geschäfte?; **to do ~ with sb** mit jdm Handel treiben; **to do a good ~** gute Geschäfte machen

(b) (= line of business) Branche f; **he's in the wool ~** er ist in der Wollbranche; **he's in the ~** er ist in der Branche

(c) (= job) Handwerk nt; **he's a bricklayer by ~** er ist Maurer von Beruf

(d) (= people) Geschäftsleute pl, Branche f; **to sell to the ~** an Gewerbetreibende verkaufen

(e) (= exchange) Tauschgeschäft nt **2** VT tauschen; **to ~ sth for sth else** etw gegen etw anderes (ein)tauschen

3 VI (a) Handel treiben, handeln; **to ~ in sth** mit etw handeln; **to ~ with sb** mit jdm Geschäfte machen or Handel treiben

(b) (US inf) einkaufen (at bei)

▶ **trade in** VT SEP in Zahlung geben (for für)

trade: trade association N Unternehmerverband m; **trade balance** N Handelsbilanz f; **trade barrier** N Handelsschranke f; **trade buyer** N Facheinkäufer(in) m(f); **trade deficit** N Handelsdefizit nt; **trade directory** N Branchenverzeichnis nt; **trade discount** N Händlerrabatt m; **trade fair** N Handelsmesse f; **trade figures** PL Handelsziffern pl; **trade gap** N Außenhandelsdefizit nt; **trade-in** N **1** Altgerät nt; (= car) in Zahlung gegebenes Auto; **we will take your old car as a ~** wir nehmen Ihren alten Wagen in Zahlung **2** ATTR **~ value** Gebrauchtwert m; **trade journal** N Branchenblatt nt; **trademark** N (lit) Warenzeichen nt; **trade name** N Handelsname m; **trade-off** N **there's always a ~** etwas geht immer verloren; **trade official** N Handelsbeamte(r) m, Handelsbeamtin f; **trade price** N Großhandelspreis m

trader [ˈtreɪdə˞] N Händler(in) m(f)

trade: trade-related ADJ handelsbezogen; **~ intellectual property rights** Rechte pl am geistigen Eigentum; **trade route** N Handelsweg m; **trade school** N Gewerbe- or Berufsschule f; **trade secret** N (lit, fig) Betriebsgeheimnis nt

trades: tradesman N (= delivery man) Lieferant m; (= shopkeeper) Ladenbesitzer m; (= plumber etc) Handwerker m; **tradespeople** PL Geschäftsleute pl, Händler pl; **trades union** N (Brit) = trade union; **trade surplus** N Handelsüberschuss m; **tradeswoman** N (= shopkeeper) Ladenbesitzerin f; (= electrician etc) Handwerkerin f

trade: trade union N (Brit) Gewerkschaft f; **trade unionist** N (Brit) Gewerkschaft(l)er(in) m(f); **trade war** N Handelskrieg m

trading [ˈtreɪdɪŋ] N Handel m, Handeln m (in mit); **there was heavy ~ in ...** ... wurde(n) verstärkt gehandelt

trading IN CPDS Handels-; **trading account** N Geschäftskonto nt; **trading estate** N Industriegelände nt; **trading floor** N (St Ex) Börsenparkett m; **trading links** PL Handelsverbindungen pl; **trading loss** N Betriebsverlust m; **trading partner** N Handelspartner(in) m(f); **trading profits** PL Geschäfts- or Handelsgewinn m; **trading results** PL Betriebsergebnis nt; **trading volume** N (St Ex) Geschäftsvolumen nt

tradition [trəˈdɪʃən] N Tradition f; **village ~s** Dorfbräuche pl or -traditionen pl; **according to ~ he ...**, **~ has it that he ...** es ist überliefert, dass er ...

traditional [trəˈdɪʃənl] ADJ traditionell; story, custom also alt; **it's ~ for us to spend New Year's Day at my mother's** es ist bei uns Brauch, dass wir den Neujahrstag bei meiner Mutter verbringen; **in the ~ way** auf traditionelle Weise

traditionalist [trəˈdɪʃənəlɪst] N Traditionalist(in) m(f)

traditionally [trəˈdɪʃənəlɪ] ADV traditionell; (= customarily) üblicherweise; **turkey is ~ eaten at Christmas** es ist Tradition or ein Brauch, Weihnachten Truthahn zu essen

traffic [ˈtræfɪk] ◼ N **(a)** Verkehr m; (Aviat) Flug- or Luftverkehr m **(b)** (= business: of port, airport) Umschlag m; **freight ~** Frachtumschlag m **(c)** (usu pej) (= trading) Handel m (in mit); (in illegal alcohol) Schieberei f (in von) ◼ VI (usu pej) handeln (in mit); (in drugs also) dealen (inf) (in mit); (in illegal alcohol) verschieben (in acc)

traffic: **traffic circle** N (US) Kreisverkehr m; **traffic cop** N (US inf) Verkehrspolizist(in) m(f); **traffic hold-up** N = traffic jam; **traffic island** N Verkehrsinsel f; **traffic jam** N Verkehrsstockung or -stauung f

trafficker [ˈtræfɪkəʳ] N (usu pej) Händler(in) m(f), Schieber(in) m(f) (pej); (in drugs also) Dealer(in) m(f) (inf)

trafficking [ˈtræfɪkɪŋ] N Handel m (in mit); (in illegal alcohol) Schieberei f (in von)

traffic: **traffic lights** PL, (US) **traffic light** N Verkehrsampel f; **traffic police** PL Verkehrspolizei f; **traffic policeman** N Verkehrspolizist m; **traffic signals** PL = traffic lights; **traffic warden** N (Brit) ≈ Verkehrspolizist(in) m(f) ohne polizeiliche Befugnisse; (woman) ≈ Politesse f

tragedy [ˈtrædʒɪdɪ] N Tragödie f; (Theat also) Trauerspiel nt; (no pl: = tragic quality) Tragische(s) nt; **it is a ~ that ...** es ist (wirklich) tragisch or ein Unglück, dass ...

tragic [ˈtrædʒɪk] ADJ tragisch

tragically [ˈtrædʒɪkəlɪ] ADV **her career ended ~ at the age of 19** ihre Karriere endete tragisch, als sie 19 Jahre alt war; **her husband's ~ early death** der tragisch frühe Tod ihres Mannes; **the operation went ~ wrong** die Operation nahm einen tragischen Verlauf

trail [treɪl] ◼ N **(a)** Spur f; **~ of blood** Blutspur f; **~ of smoke** Rauchfahne f; **the hurricane left a ~ of destruction** der Hurrikan hinterließ eine Spur der Verwüstung; **hot on the ~** dicht auf den Fersen; **the police are on his ~** die Polizei ist ihm auf der Spur
(b) (= path) Weg m, Pfad m; (= nature ~ etc) (Wander)weg m ◼ VT **(a)** (esp Brit: = follow) verfolgen
(b) (= drag) schleppen; (US: = tow) ziehen
(c) team, rival zurückliegen hinter (+dat) ◼ VI **(a)** (on floor) schleifen
(b) (= walk) zuckeln, trotten
(c) (in competition etc) weit zurückliegen; (Sport) weit zurückgefallen sein; **our team is ~ing by 3 points** unsere Mannschaft ist mit 3 Punkten im Rückstand
➤ **trail along** ◼ VI entlangzuckeln; **the child trailed along behind his mother** das Kind trottete or zuckelte hinter der Mutter her ◼ VT entlangschleppen; **the child trailed his coat along behind him** das Kind schleppte seinen Mantel hinter sich (dat) her
➤ **trail away** or **off** VI (voice) sich verlieren (into in +dat)
➤ **trail behind** ◼ VI hinterhertrotten or -zuckeln (+prep obj hinter +dat); (in competition etc) zurückgeblieben sein (+prep obj hinter +acc) ◼ VT SEP hinter sich (dat) herziehen

trailblazer [ˈtreɪlbleɪzəʳ] N (fig) Wegbereiter(in) m(f), Bahnbrecher(in) m(f)

trailer [ˈtreɪləʳ] N **(a)** (Aut) Anhänger m; (esp US: of lorry) Sattelauflieger m **(b)** (US) Wohnwagen m **(c)** (Film, TV) Trailer m

train¹ [treɪn] N **(a)** (Rail) Zug m; **to go/travel by ~** mit dem Zug or der (Eisen)bahn fahren/reisen; **a ~ journey** eine Bahn- or Zugfahrt; **to take** or **catch** or **get the 11 o'clock ~** den Elfuhrzug nehmen; **to change ~s** umsteigen; **on the ~** im Zug
(b) (= line) Kolonne f; (of people) Schlange f; (of camels) Karawane f
(c) (of events) Folge f; **he interrupted my ~ of thought** er unterbrach meinen Gedankengang
(d) (of dress) Schleppe f

train² ◼ VT **(a)** person ausbilden; staff weiterbilden; child erziehen; animal abrichten; (Sport) trainieren; **to ~ sb as sth** jdn als or zu etw ausbilden; **to ~ an animal to do sth** ein Tier dazu abrichten, etw zu tun; **this dog has been ~ed to kill** dieser Hund ist aufs Töten abgerichtet
(b) (= aim) gun, telescope richten (on auf +acc)
(c) plant wachsen lassen (over über +acc) ◼ VI **(a)** (esp Sport) trainieren (for für)
(b) (= study) ausgebildet werden; **he ~ed as a teacher** er hat eine Lehrerausbildung gemacht

train driver N Zug- or Lokführer(in) m(f)

trained [treɪnd] ADJ worker gelernt; nurse, teacher, voice ausgebildet; animal dressiert; eye geschult; **to be highly/specially ~** hoch qualifiziert/speziell ausgebildet sein

trainee [treɪˈniː] N Auszubildende(r) mf; (academic, technical) Praktikant(in) m(f); (management) Trainee m

trainee: **trainee manager** N Managementtrainee m; **trainee mechanic** N Schlosserlehrling m; **trainee teacher** N (in primary school) ≈ Praktikant(in) m(f); (in secondary school) ≈ Referendar(in) m(f)

trainer [ˈtreɪnəʳ] N **(a)** (Sport) Trainer(in) m(f); (of animals) Dresseur,(in) m(f) **(b)** (Brit: = shoe) Turnschuh m

training [ˈtreɪnɪŋ] N **(a)** Ausbildung f (also Mil); (of staff) Schulung f; (of animal) Dressur f, Abrichten nt **(b)** (Sport) Training nt; **to be in ~** im Training stehen or sein

training: **training centre**, (US) **training center** N Lehr- or Ausbildungszentrum nt; **training college** N (for teachers) pädagogische Hochschule; **training course** N Ausbildungskurs m; **training ground** N (Sport, fig) Trainingsgelände nt; **training manager** N (Brit) Ausbildungsleiter(in) m(f); **training scheme** N Ausbildungsprogramm nt; **training shoes** PL (Brit) Turnschuhe pl

train: **trainload** N (of goods) Zugladung f; **~s of holidaymakers** (Brit) or **vacationers** (US) ganze Züge voller Urlauber; **train service** N Zugverkehr m; (between two places) (Eisen)bahnverbindung f; **train set** N (Spielzeug)eisenbahn f; **trainspotting** N Hobby, bei dem die Züge begutachtet und deren Nummern notiert werden

traipse [treɪps] (inf) VI latschen (inf); **to ~ (a)round the shops** in den Geschäften rumlatschen (inf)

trait [treɪt, treɪ] N Eigenschaft f; (of particular person also) Charakter- or Wesenszug m

traitor [ˈtreɪtəʳ] N Verräter(in) m(f)

trajectory [trəˈdʒektərɪ] N Flugbahn f

tram [træm] N (esp Brit) Straßenbahn f; **to go by ~** mit der Straßenbahn fahren

tram: **tram driver** N (esp Brit) Straßenbahnfahrer(in) m(f); **tramline** N (esp Brit: = track) Straßenbahnschiene f

tramp [træmp] ◼ VI **(a)** (= walk heavily) stapfen **(b)** (= hike) marschieren, wandern ◼ VT **(a)** (= spread by walking) herumtreten; **don't ~ that mud into the carpet** tritt den Dreck nicht in den Teppich **(b)** (= walk) streets latschen durch (inf) ◼ N **(a)** (= vagabond) Landstreicher(in) m(f); (in town) Stadtstreicher(in) m(f) **(b)** (= sound) Stapfen nt **(c)** (inf: = loose woman) Flittchen nt (pej)
➤ **tramp down** VT SEP feststampfen

trample [ˈtræmpl] VT niedertrampeln; **to ~ sth underfoot** (lit, fig) auf etw (dat) herumtrampeln; **he was ~d to death by a bull** er wurde von einem Bullen zu Tode getrampelt
➤ **trample down** VT SEP niedertreten
➤ **trample on** VI +PREP OBJ herumtreten auf (+dat); **several children were trampled on** mehrere Kinder wurden getreten; **to trample on sb's feelings** (fig) jds Gefühle mit Füßen treten

trampoline [ˈtræmpəlɪn] N Trampolin nt

trance [trɑːns] N (Med) tiefe Bewusstlosigkeit; **to go into a ~** in Trance verfallen

tranquil [ˈtræŋkwɪl] ADJ ruhig, still; life friedlich; music sanft

tranquillity, (US) **tranquility** [træŋˈkwɪlɪtɪ] N Ruhe f, Stille f

tranquillize, (US) **tranquilize** [ˈtræŋkwɪlaɪz] VT beruhigen

tranquillizer, (US) **tranquilizer** [ˈtræŋkwɪlaɪzəʳ] N Beruhigungsmittel nt

trans- [trænz-] PREF trans-, Trans-

transact [trænˈzækt] VT abwickeln; business also, deal abschließen

transaction [trænˈzækʃən] N **(a)** (= *act*) Abwicklung *f*; (= *deal*) Abschluss *m* **(b)** (= *piece of business*) Geschäft *nt*; (*Fin, St Ex*) Transaktion *f*

transatlantic [ˈtrænsətˈlæntɪk] ADJ transatlantisch, Transatlantik-; (= *American*) amerikanisch; (= *British*) britisch; ~ **flight** Transatlantikflug *m*

transcend [trænˈsend] VT übersteigen, überschreiten

transcribe [trænˈskraɪb] VT *manuscripts* transkribieren; *speech, interview etc* niederschreiben

transcript [ˈtrænskrɪpt] N **(a)** (*of court proceedings*) Protokoll *nt*; (*of tapes*) Niederschrift *f*; (= *copy*) Abschrift *f* **(b)** (*US*: = *academic record*) Abschrift *f* (Studienunterlagen)

transfer [trænsˈfɜːʳ] **1** VT übertragen (*to* auf +*acc*) (*also Jur*); *prisoner* überführen (*to* in +*acc*); *premises, account* verlegen (*to* in +*acc, to town* nach); *soldier, employee* versetzen (*to* in +*acc, to town, country* nach); *stocks, player* transferieren (*to* zu); *funds, money* überweisen (*to* auf +*acc*); **he ~red his capital into gold shares** er investierte sein Kapital in Goldaktien; **he ~red the money from the box to his pocket** er nahm das Geld aus der Schachtel und steckte es in die Tasche
2 VI **(a)** (= *move*) überwechseln (*to* zu); (*to new system*) umstellen (*to* auf +*acc*)
(b) (*Fin*) umsteigen (*into* auf +*acc*)
(c) (*in travelling*) umsteigen (*to* in +*acc*)
3 [ˈtrænsfɜːʳ] N Übertragung *f* (*also Jur*); (*of prisoner*) Überführung *f*; (*of premises, account*) Verlegung *f*; (*of employee*) Versetzung *f*; (*of stocks, player*) Transfer *m*; (*of funds, money*) Überweisung *f*; **automatic** ~ (*US Fin*) Dauerauftrag *m*; **he's a ~ from Chelsea** er ist von Chelsea hierher gewechselt

transferable [trænsˈfɜːrəbl] ADJ übertragbar; *money, stocks* transferierbar

transfer: **transfer desk** N (*Aviat*) Transitschalter *m*; **transfer list** (*Ftbl*) **1** N Transferliste *f* **2** VT auf die Transferliste setzen; **transfer pricing** (*Comm*) Transferpreissystem *nt*; **transfer rate, transfer speed** N (*Comput*: *of data*) Übertragungsgeschwindigkeit *f*

transfix [trænsˈfɪks] VT (*fig*) **he stood as though ~ed (to the ground)** er stand da wie angewurzelt

transform [trænsˈfɔːm] VT umwandeln, umformen (*into* zu); *ideas, views* (von Grund auf) verändern; *person, life, country, caterpillar* verwandeln; **when she came out of the hairdresser's she was ~ed** sie sah aus dem Friseursalon kam, sah sie wie umgewandelt aus

transformation [trænsfəˈmeɪʃən] N Umwandlung *f*, Umformung *f*; (*of ideas, views etc*) (grundlegende) Veränderung; (*of person, caterpillar etc*) Verwandlung *f*

transfusion [trænsˈfjuːʒən] N (*also* **blood** ~) (Blut)transfusion *f*; **(blood)** ~ **service** Blutspendedienst *m*

transgression [trænsˈgreʃən] N **(a)** (*of law*) Verstoß *m*, Verletzung *f* **(b)** (= *sin*) Sünde *f*

transient [ˈtrænzɪənt] **1** ADJ **(a)** *life* kurz; *grief, pleasure* vorübergehend; *interest* flüchtig **(b)** (*US*) ~ **population** nichtansässiger Teil der Bevölkerung eines Ortes **2** N (*US*) Durchreisende(r) *mf*

transistor [trænˈzɪstəʳ] N (*Elec*) Transistor *m*

transit [ˈtrænzɪt] N Durchfahrt *f*, Transit *m*; (*of goods*) Transport *m*; **the books were damaged in** ~ die Bücher wurden auf dem Transport beschädigt

transit camp N Durchgangslager *nt*

transition [trænˈzɪʃən] N Übergang *m* (*from* ... *to* von ... zu); **period of** ~, ~ **period** Übergangsperiode *or* -zeit *f*

transitional [trænˈzɪʃənl] ADJ Übergangs-; (= *provisional*) vorläufig; ~ **government** Übergangsregierung *f*

transitive [ˈtrænzɪtɪv] ADJ transitiv

transitory [ˈtrænzɪtərɪ] ADJ *life* kurz; *grief, joy* vorübergehend; *interest* flüchtig; **the** ~ **nature of sth** die Kurzlebigkeit von etw

transit: **Transit (van)**® N (*Brit*) Transporter *m*; **transit visa** N Transitvisum *nt*

translatable [trænzˈleɪtəbl] ADJ übersetzbar

translate [trænzˈleɪt] **1** VT **(a)** (*lit*) übersetzen; **to** ~ **a text from German (in)to English** einen Text aus dem Deutschen ins Englische übersetzen; **it is ~d as** ... es wird mit ... übersetzt **(b)** (*fig*) übertragen; **could you** ~ **that into cash terms?** lässt sich das geldmäßig ausdrücken?
2 VI **(a)** (*lit*) übersetzen; **it ~s well (into English)** es lässt sich

gut (ins Englische) übersetzen *or* übertragen
(b) (*fig*) übertragbar sein; **how does that** ~ **into cash?** was kommt geldmäßig dabei heraus?

translation [trænzˈleɪʃən] N Übersetzung *f* (*from* aus); (*of work of literature also, fig*) Übertragung *f*; **to do a** ~ **of sth** von etw eine Übersetzung machen *or* anfertigen; **it loses (something) in** ~ es verliert (etwas) bei der Übersetzung; ~ **table** (*Comput*) Umsetzungs- *or* Übersetzungstabelle *f*

translator [trænzˈleɪtəʳ] N Übersetzer(in) *m(f)*

translucent [trænzˈluːsnt], **translucid** [trænzˈluːsɪd] ADJ *glass etc* lichtdurchlässig; *skin* durchsichtig

transmission [trænzˈmɪʃən] N **(a)** (= *transmitting*) Übertragung *f*; (*of news*) Übermittlung *f*; (*of heat*) Leitung *f*; (= *programme*) Sendung *f* **(b)** (*Aut*) Getriebe *nt*

transmit [trænzˈmɪt] **1** VT *message* übermitteln; *information, knowledge* vermitteln; *illness* übertragen; *heat etc* leiten; *radio/TV programme* senden **2** VI senden

transmitter [trænzˈmɪtəʳ] N (*Tech*) Sender *m*

transnational [trænzˈnæʃənəl] ADJ multinational

transparency [trænsˈpærənsɪ] N **(a)** Transparenz *f*, Durchsichtigkeit *f* **(b)** (*of lies etc*) Durchschaubarkeit *f* **(c)** (*Phot*) Dia(positiv) *nt*

transparent [trænsˈpærənt] ADJ **(a)** durchsichtig, transparent **(b)** (*fig*) *lie, intentions* durchschaubar; *guilt, meaning* offensichtlich; **you're so** ~ du bist so leicht zu durchschauen

transpire [trænˈspaɪəʳ] VI **(a)** (= *become clear*) sich herausstellen **(b)** (= *happen*) passieren (*inf*)

transplant [trænsˈplɑːnt] **1** VT **(a)** (*Hort*) umpflanzen **(b)** (*Med*) transplantieren (*spec*) **(c)** (*fig*) *people* verpflanzen **2** [ˈtrɑːnsplɑːnt] N Transplantation *f*

transport [ˈtrænspɔːt] **1** N **(a)** (*of goods*) Transport *m*, Beförderung *f*; **road** ~ Straßentransport *m*; **rail** ~ Beförderung *f or* Transport *m* per Bahn; **Ministry of Transport** (*Brit*) Verkehrsministerium *nt*; **have you got your own** ~? bist du motorisiert?; **public** ~ öffentliche Verkehrsmittel *pl*; ~ **will be provided** für An- und Abfahrt wird gesorgt
(b) (*US*: = *shipment*) (Schiffs)fracht *f*, Ladung *f*
2 [trænˈspɔːt] VT befördern; *goods also* transportieren

transportation [ˌtrænspɔːˈteɪʃən] N Beförderung *f*, Transport *m*; (= *means*) Beförderungsmittel *nt*; (*public*) Verkehrsmittel *nt*; **Department of Transportation** (*US*) Verkehrsministerium *nt*; ~ **by road** (*US*) Straßentransport *m*

transportation document N Beförderungspapier *nt*

transport café N (*Brit*) Fernfahrerlokal *nt*

transporter [trænˈspɔːtəʳ] N (*Brit*: = *car* ~) Transporter *m*

transport: **transport insurance** N Transportversicherung *f*; **transport plane** N Transportflugzeug *nt*; **transport system** N Verkehrswesen *nt*

transputer [trænsˈpjuːtəʳ] N (*Comput*) Transputer *m*

transsexual [trænzˈseksjʊəl] N Transsexuelle(r) *mf*

transverse [ˈtrænzvɜːs] ADJ Quer-; ~ **section** Querschnitt *m*

transvestite [trænzˈvestaɪt] N Transvestit(in) *m(f)*

trap [træp] **1** N **(a)** (*for animal, fig*) Falle *f*; **to set a** ~ **for sb** (*fig*) jdm eine Falle stellen; **to fall into a** ~ in die Falle gehen; **to fall into the** ~ **of doing sth** den Fehler begehen, etw zu tun **(b)** (*inf*: = *mouth*) **shut your** ~! (halt die) Klappe! (*inf*)
2 VT **(a)** *animal* (mit einer Falle) fangen
(b) (*fig*) *person* in die Falle locken; **he realized he was ~ped** er merkte, dass er in der Falle saß; **to** ~ **sb into saying sth** jdn dazu bringen, etw zu sagen
(c) (= *leave no way of escape*) in die Enge treiben; **the miners are ~ped** die Bergleute sind eingeschlossen; **to be ~ped in the snow** im Schnee festsitzen; **my arm was ~ped behind my back** mein Arm war hinter meinem Rücken eingeklemmt
(d) (= *catch*) *ball* stoppen; **to** ~ **one's finger in the door** sich (*dat*) den Finger in der Tür einklemmen
(e) *gas, liquid* stauen

trap door N Falltür *f*; (*Theat*) Versenkung *f*

trapeze [trəˈpiːz] N Trapez *nt*

trapper [ˈtræpəʳ] N Fallensteller(in) *m(f)*

trappings [ˈtræpɪŋz] PL **(a)** (*of chieftain etc*) Rangabzeichen *pl*; (*of horse*) Schmuck *m* **(b)** (*fig*) äußere Aufmachung; ~ **of office** Amtsinsignien *pl*

trash [træʃ] **1** N **(a)** (*US*: = *refuse*) Abfall *m* **(b)** (= *poor quality item*) Schund *m*; (= *pop group etc*) Mist *m* (*inf*) **(c)** (*pej inf*:

= *people*) Gesindel *nt*, Pack *nt*; **he is ~** er taugt nichts **2** VT **(a)** (*inf*) *place* verwüsten; *car* (= *crash*) zu Schrott fahren; (= *vandalize*) kaputt machen (*inf*) **(b)** (*esp US inf*: = *criticize*) verreißen

trash can N (*US*) Abfalleimer *m*

trashy ['træʃɪ] ADJ (+ER) *goods* minderwertig; *pop group* billig; *place* schäbig; **~ novel** Schundroman *m*

trauma ['trɔːmə] N (*Psych*) Trauma *nt*

traumatic [trɔːˈmætɪk] ADJ traumatisch

traumatize ['trɔːmətaɪz] VT (*Med, Psych*) traumatisieren

travel ['trævl] **1** VI **(a)** (= *make a journey*) reisen; **they have travelled** (*Brit*) or **traveled** (*US*) **a lot** sie sind viel gereist; **he ~s to work by car** er fährt mit dem Auto zur Arbeit; **she is travelling** (*Brit*) or **traveling** (*US*) **to London tomorrow** sie fährt morgen nach London; **they have travelled** (*Brit*) or **traveled** (*US*) **a long way** sie haben eine weite Reise hinter sich (*dat*); **to ~ (a)round the world** eine Reise um die Welt machen; **to ~ around a country** ein Land bereisen **(b)** (= *go, move*) sich bewegen; (*sound, light*) sich fortpflanzen; **we were travelling** (*Brit*) or **traveling** (*US*) **at 80 kph** wir fuhren 80 km/h; **the parts ~ along the conveyor belt** die Teile werden vom Förderband weiterbefördert; **the electricity ~s along the wire** der Strom fließt durch den Draht; **some wines do not ~ well** manche Weine vertragen den Transport nicht; **his eye travelled** (*Brit*) or **traveled** (*US*) **over the scene** seine Augen wanderten über die Szene **(c)** (*Tech*) sich hin- und herbewegen **2** VT *area* bereisen; *distance* zurücklegen; *route* fahren **3** N **(a)** NO PL (= *~ling*) Reisen *nt* **(b) travels** PL (*in country*) Reisen *pl*; (*hum: in town, building*) Ausflüge *pl*, Gänge *pl*; **if you meet him on your ~s** wenn Sie ihm auf einer Ihrer Reisen begegnen; **he's off on his ~s again tomorrow** er verreist morgen wieder

travel: travel agency N Reisebüro *nt*; **travel agent** N Reisebürokaufmann *m*/-kauffrau *f*; (*of package tours*) Reiseveranstalter(in) *m(f)*; **~('s)** (= *travel agency*) Reisebüro *nt*; **travel brochure** N Reiseprospekt *m*; **travel insurance** N Reiseversicherung *f*

travelled, (*US*) **traveled** ['trævld] ADJ **well-~** *person* weit gereist; *route* viel befahren; **widely ~** weit gereist

traveller, (*US*) **traveler** ['trævlə'] N **(a)** Reisende(r) *mf* **(b)** (*also* **commercial ~**) Vertreter(in) *m(f)*

traveller's cheque, (*US*) **traveler's check** N Reisescheck *m*

travelling, (*US*) **traveling** ['trævlɪŋ] N Reisen *nt*; **I hate ~** ich hasse das Reisen

travelling, (*US*) **traveling: travelling bag** N Reisetasche *f*; **travelling exhibition** N Wanderausstellung *f*; **travelling expenses** PL Reisekosten *pl*; (*on business*) Reisespesen *pl*; **travelling salesman** N Vertreter *m*

travel: travel-sick ADJ reisekrank; **travel-sickness** N Reisekrankheit *f*

traverse ['trævɜːs] VT *land* durchqueren; (*bridge, person*) *water* überqueren; **to ~ the globe** den Erdball bereisen

travesty ['trævɪstɪ] N (*Liter*) Travestie *f*; **a ~ of justice** ein Hohn *m* auf die Gerechtigkeit

trawl [trɔːl] **1** VI **(a)** (= **~ for fish**) mit dem Schleppnetz fischen; (*US*) mit einer Grundleine fischen **(b)** (*esp Brit*) **to ~ for players** Spieler fischen **2** VT **(a) they ~ed the sea-bottom** sie fischten mit Schleppnetzen auf dem Meeresboden **(b)** (*esp Brit*) *streets, Internet etc* durchkämmen

trawler ['trɔːlə'] N (= *boat*) Trawler *m*

tray [treɪ] N Tablett *nt*; (= *tea ~*) Servierbrett *nt*; (= *baking ~*) (Back)blech *nt*; (*for pencils etc*) (Feder)schale *f*; (*for papers, mail*) Ablage *f*; (= *drawer*) (Schub)fach *nt*

treacherous ['tretʃərəs] ADJ **(a)** *person, action* verräterisch **(b)** (= *unreliable*) *weather conditions, ice* trügerisch; (= *dangerous*) *corner* gefährlich; *journey* gefahrvoll

treacherously ['tretʃərəslɪ] ADV **(a)** (= *disloyally*) verräterisch **(b)** (= *unreliably*) trügerisch **(c)** (= *dangerously*) tückisch

treachery ['tretʃərɪ] N Verrat *m*; (*of weather*) Tücke *f*

treacle ['triːkl] N (*Brit*) Sirup *m*

tread [tred], *vb*: *pret* **trod**, *ptp* **trodden** **1** N **(a)** (= *gait, noise*) Schritt *m*, Tritt *m*; **I could hear his ~ on the stairs** ich konnte seine Schritte auf der Treppe hören **(b)** (*of stair*) Stufe *f* **(c)** (*of shoe, tyre*) Profil *nt*

---

2 VI **(a)** (= *walk*) gehen **(b)** (= *bring foot down*) treten (*on* auf +*acc*); **he trod on my foot** er trat mir auf den Fuß; **to ~ on sb's heels** (*lit*) jdm auf die Fersen treten; (*fig*) an jds Fersen (*dat*) hängen; **to ~ softly** or **lightly** leise or leicht auftreten; **to ~ carefully** (*lit*) vorsichtig gehen; (*fig*) vorsichtig vorgehen **3** VT *path* (= *make*) treten; (= *follow*) gehen; **to ~ a fine line between ...** sich vorsichtig zwischen ... bewegen; **it got trodden underfoot** es wurde zertreten; **to ~ water** Wasser treten; (*fig*) auf der Stelle treten

► **tread down** or **in** VT SEP festtreten

► **tread out** VT SEP *fire, cigarette* austreten

treadle ['tredl] N (*of sewing machine*) Pedal *nt*; (*of lathe also*) Fußhebel *m*

treadmill ['tredmɪl] N (*lit*) Tretwerk *nt*; (*fig*) Tretmühle *f*; (*in gym*) Laufband *nt*

treason ['triːzn] N Verrat *m* (*to* an +*dat*); **an act of ~** Verrat *m*

treasure ['treʒə'] **1** N (*lit, fig*) Schatz *m*; **many ~s of modern art** viele moderne Kunstschätze **2** VT zu schätzen wissen; **I shall ~ this memory** ich werde in dieser Erinnerung behalten

treasure: treasure chest N (*lit*) Schatztruhe *f*; (*fig*) Fundgrube *f*; **treasure hunt** N Schatzsuche *f*

treasurer ['treʒərə'] N (*of club*) Kassenwart(in) *m(f)*; (= *city ~*) Stadtkämmerer *m*/-kämmerin *f*

treasure trove N Schatzfund *m*; (= *market*) Fundgrube *f*; (= *collection, source*) Schatzhöhle *f*

treasury ['treʒərɪ] N **(a)** (*Pol*) **the Treasury** (*Brit*), **the Treasury Department** (*US*) das Finanzministerium **(b)** (*of society*) Kasse *f* **(c)** (= *anthology*) Schatzkästlein *nt*

Treasury bill N kurzfristiger Schatzwechsel

treat [triːt] **1** VT **(a)** behandeln (*also Med*); (= *handle*) *books* umgehen mit; *sewage* klären; *wastepaper* verarbeiten; **the doctor is ~ing him for nervous exhaustion** er ist wegen Nervenüberlastung in Behandlung **(b)** (= *consider*) betrachten (*as* als); **you should ~ your work more seriously** Sie sollten Ihre Arbeit ernster nehmen **(c)** (= *pay for, give*) einladen; **to ~ sb to sth** jdm etw spendieren; **to drink, ice cream** *also* jdm etw ausgeben; **to ~ oneself to sth** sich (*dat*) etw gönnen **2** N (= *special outing, present*) besondere Freude; **I thought I'd give myself a ~** ich dachte, ich gönne mir mal etwas; **I'm taking them to the circus as** or **for a ~** ich mache ihnen eine Freude und lade sie in den Zirkus ein; **it's my ~** das geht auf meine Kosten or Rechnung, ich lade Sie ein; **there's a ~ in store** es gibt etwas, worauf wir uns noch freuen können

treatise ['triːtɪz] N Abhandlung *f* (*on* über +*acc*)

treatment ['triːtmənt] N Behandlung *f* (*also Med*); (*of sewage*) Klärung *f*; (*of wastepaper*) Verarbeitung *f*; **their ~ of foreigners** ihre Art, Ausländer zu behandeln; **there are many ~s for ...** es gibt viele Heilverfahren für ...; **to be having ~ for sth** wegen etw in Behandlung sein

treaty ['triːtɪ] N Vertrag *m*; **the Treaty of Rome** die Römischen Verträge *pl*

treble¹ ['trebl] **1** ADJ dreifach **2** ADV **clothes are ~ the price** Kleider kosten dreimal so viel **3** VT verdreifachen **4** VI sich verdreifachen

treble² **1** N (*Mus*) (= *boy's voice*) (Knaben)sopran *m*; (= *highest part*) Oberstimme *f*; (*of piano*) Diskant *m* **2** ADJ **~ voice** (Knaben)sopranstimme *f*

treble clef N (*Mus*) Violinschlüssel *m*

tree [triː] N **(a)** Baum *m*; **an oak ~** eine Eiche; **a cherry ~** ein Kirschbaum *m*; **money doesn't grow on ~s** das Geld fällt nicht vom Himmel; **he's at the top of the ~** (*fig inf*) er ist ganz oben (an der Spitze) **(b)** (= *family ~*) Stammbaum *m* **(c)** (= *shoe ~*) Leisten *m*

tree: **tree-covered** ADJ baumbestanden; **tree house** N Baumhaus *nt*; **treeless** ADJ baumlos; **tree line** N Baumgrenze *f*; **tree-lined** ADJ baumbestanden; **tree structure** N (*Comput*) Baumstruktur *f*; **treetop** N Baumkrone *f*; **tree trunk** N Baumstamm *m*

trek [trek] **1** VI trecken; (*inf*) latschen (*inf*); **they ~ked across the desert** sie zogen durch die Wüste **2** N Treck *m*; (*inf*) anstrengender Weg *or* Marsch

trekking ['trekɪŋ] N Trekking *nt*

trellis ['trelɪs] N Gitter *nt*; (*for plants also*) Spalier *nt*

tremble ['trembl] VI (*person, hand etc*) zittern (**with** vor); (*voice, ground, building also*) beben (**with** vor)

trembling ['tremblɪŋ] **1** ADJ *hands* zitternd; *voice, lip also* bebend **2** N (*of person, hand*) Zittern *nt*; (*of voice, ground, building also*) Beben *nt*

tremendous [trə'mendəs] ADJ **(a)** gewaltig; *size, number, crowd* riesig; **a ~ success** ein Riesenerfolg *m* **(b)** (= *very good*) prima (*inf*), toll (*inf*); **she has done a ~ job** sie hat fantastische Arbeit geleistet

tremendously [trə'mendəslɪ] ADV sehr; *relieved, upset, grateful, dangerous, intelligent, difficult* äußerst; **they enjoyed themselves ~** sie haben sich prächtig *or* prima amüsiert (*inf*)

tremor ['tremə^r] N Zittern *nt*, Beben *nt*; (*Med*) Tremor *m*; (= *earth ~*) Beben *nt*

tremulous ['tremjʊləs] ADJ (= *trembling*) zitternd; *voice also* bebend; (= *timid*) schüchtern

trench [trentʃ] N Graben *m*; (*Mil*) Schützengraben *m*

trench warfare N Stellungskrieg *m*

trend [trend] N **(a)** (= *tendency*) Tendenz *f*, Richtung *f*; **upward ~** Aufwärtstrend *m*; **the downward ~ in the birth rate** die Rückläufigkeit *or* der Abwärtstrend der Geburtenrate; **the ~ away from materialism** die zunehmende Abkehr vom Materialismus; **to set a ~** richtungweisend sein **(b)** (= *fashion*) Mode *f*, Trend *m*; **that is the ~/the latest ~ among young people** das ist bei jungen Leuten jetzt Mode/ der letzte Schrei (*inf*)

trendily ['trendɪlɪ] ADV modern; **to dress ~** sich nach der neuesten Mode kleiden

trendiness ['trendɪnɪs] N (*of person*) Modebewusstsein *nt*; (*of ideas etc*) Modernität *f*; **the ~ of her clothes** ihre modische Kleidung

trendsetter ['trendsetə^r] N Trendsetter(in) *m(f)*

trendy ['trendɪ] **1** ADJ (+ER) modern, in *pred* (*inf*); *image* modisch, schick; **to be ~** große Mode sein; **it's no longer ~ to smoke** Rauchen ist nicht mehr in (*inf*); **this is a ~ club** dieser Klub ist zur Zeit in (*inf*) **2** N (*inf*) Schickimicki *m* (*inf*); **the trendies** die Schickeria *sing*

trepidation [trepɪ'deɪʃən] N Bangigkeit *f*, Ängstlichkeit *f*; **full of ~ he knocked on the door** voll ängstlicher Erwartung klopfte er an die Tür

trespass ['trespəs] **1** VI (*on property*) unbefugt betreten (**on** *sth* etw *acc*); **"no ~ing"** „Betreten verboten"; **you're ~ing** Sie dürfen sich hier nicht aufhalten; **to ~ (up)on sb's rights** in jds Rechte eingreifen **2** N (*Jur*) unbefugtes Betreten

trespasser ['trespəsə^r] N Unbefugte(r) *mf*; **"~s will be prosecuted"** „widerrechtliches Betreten wird strafrechtlich verfolgt"

trestle table [tresl'teɪbl] N auf Böcken stehender Tisch

trial ['traɪəl] N **(a)** (*Jur*) (Gerichts)verfahren *nt*, Prozess *m*; (= *actual hearing*) (Gerichts)verhandlung *f*; **to be on ~ for theft** des Diebstahls angeklagt sein; **to stand ~ (for sth)** (wegen etw) vor Gericht stehen; **at the ~** bei *or* während der Verhandlung; **to bring sb to ~** jdn vor Gericht stellen; **~ by jury** Schwurgerichtsverfahren *nt* **(b)** (= *test*) Versuch *m*, Probe *f*; **~s** (*of machine*) Test(s) *m(pl)*; **to give sth a ~** etw ausprobieren; **to take sb/sth on ~** jdn/etw zur Probe nehmen; **to be on ~** (*new product etc*) getestet werden; **the new clerk is on ~** der neue Büroangestellte ist auf Probe eingestellt; **~ of strength** Kraftprobe *f*; **by ~ and error** durch Ausprobieren

(c) (= *hardship*) Widrigkeit *f*; (= *nuisance*) Plage *f* (**to** für); **~s and tribulations** Schwierigkeiten *pl*

trial: **trial lawyer** N (*US Jur*) Prozessanwalt *m*, Prozessanwältin *f*; **trial offer** N Einführungsangebot *nt*; **trial period** N (*for people*) Probezeit *f*; (*for goods*) Zeit, die man etw zur Probe oder Prüfung hat; **trial run** N Generalprobe *f*; (*of machine*) Probelauf *m*

triangle ['traɪæŋgl] N Dreieck *nt*; (*Mus*) Triangel *m*

triangular [traɪ'æŋgjʊlə^r] ADJ **(a)** (*Math*) dreieckig **(b)** **~ relationship** Dreiecksverhältnis *nt*

tribal ['traɪbəl] ADJ Stammes-; **~ region** Stammessiedlung *f*

tribe [traɪb] N **(a)** Stamm *m* **(b)** (*fig inf*) Korona *f*

tribulation [trɪbjʊ'leɪʃən] N Kummer *m no pl*; **~s** Sorgen *pl*; (*less serious*) Kümmernisse *pl*

tribunal [traɪ'bjuːnl] N Gericht *nt*; (= *inquiry*) Untersuchungsausschuss *m*; (*held by revolutionaries etc, fig*) Tribunal *nt*

tribune ['trɪbjuːn] N (= *platform*) Tribüne *f*

tributary ['trɪbjʊtərɪ] **1** ADJ **~ river** Nebenfluss *m*; **~ valley** Seitental *nt* **2** N Nebenfluss *m*

tribute ['trɪbjuːt] N Tribut *m*; **to pay ~ to sb/sth** jdm/einer Sache (den schuldigen) Tribut zollen; **after her performance ~s came flooding in** nach ihrer Vorstellung wurde sie mit Ehrungen überschüttet; **to be a ~ to one's parents** seinen Eltern (alle) Ehre machen

trice [traɪs] N (*Brit*) **in a ~** im Handumdrehen, im Nu

triceps ['traɪseps] N, *pl* **-(es)** Trizeps *m*

trick [trɪk] **1** N **(a)** (= *ruse*) Trick *m*; **be careful, it's a ~** pass auf, das ist eine Falle!; **it's a ~ of the light** da täuscht das Licht **(b)** (= *mischief*) Streich *m*; **to play a ~ on sb** jdm einen Streich spielen; **unless my eyes are playing ~s on me** wenn meine Augen mich nicht täuschen; **he's up to his (old) ~s again** jetzt macht er wieder seine (alten) Mätzchen (*inf*) **(c)** (= *skilful act*) Kunststück *nt*; **that should do the ~** (*inf*) das müsste eigentlich hinhauen (*inf*) **(d)** (= *habit*) Eigenart *f*; **to have a ~ of doing sth** die Eigenart haben, etw zu tun **2** ATTR *cigar, spider, glass* als Scherzartikel **3** VT hereinlegen (*inf*); **I've been ~ed!** ich bin hereingelegt *or* übers Ohr gehauen (*inf*) worden!; **to ~ sb into doing sth** jdn (mit einem Trick *or* mit List) dazu bringen, etw zu tun; **to ~ sb out of sth** jdm etw abtricksen (*inf*)

trickery ['trɪkərɪ] N Tricks *pl* (*inf*)

trickiness ['trɪkɪnɪs] N Schwierigkeit *f*

trickle ['trɪkl] **1** VI **(a)** (*liquid*) tröpfeln; **tears ~d down her cheeks** Tränen kullerten ihr über die Wangen; **the sand ~d through his fingers** der Sand rieselte ihm durch die Finger **(b)** (*fig*) **people began to ~ in/out** die Leute begannen, vereinzelt herein-/hinauszukommen; **donations are beginning to ~ in** so langsam trudeln die Spenden ein (*inf*) **2** N **(a)** (*of liquid*) Tröpfeln *nt*; (= *stream*) Rinnsal *nt* **(b)** (*fig*) **a steady ~ of people** gradually filled the lecture hall der Hörsaal füllte sich langsam aber stetig mit Leuten; **news reports have dwindled to a mere ~** Berichte *pl* kommen nur noch ganz selten durch

trickle-down ['trɪkldaʊn] N (*Econ*) Wirtschaftstheorie, nach der sich der Reichtum einiger positiv auf die Gesamtgesellschaft auswirkt

trick: **trick or treat** N Spiel zu Halloween, bei dem Kinder von Tür zu Tür gehen und von den Bewohnern entweder Geld oder Geschenke erhalten oder ihnen einen Streich spielen; **trick photography** N Trickfotografie *f*; **trick question** N Fangfrage *f*

tricky ['trɪkɪ] ADJ (+ER) **(a)** (= *difficult*) schwierig; (= *fiddly*) knifflig; **it is going to be ~ explaining** *or* **to explain his absence** es wird nicht einfach sein, seine Abwesenheit zu erklären **(b)** (= *requiring tact*) *situation, problem* heikel **(c)** (= *sly, crafty*) *person, plan* gerissen; **a ~ customer** ein schwieriger Typ

tricycle ['traɪsɪkl] N Dreirad *nt*

tried-and-tested ['traɪdənd'testɪd], **tried and tested** ADJ bewährt; *method also* erprobt; *recipe, technology* ausgereift; *product* getestet

trifle ['traɪfl] N **(a)** Kleinigkeit *f*; (= *trivial matter*) Lappalie *f* (*inf*); **a ~ hot** *etc* ein bisschen heiß *etc* **(b)** (*Brit Cook*) Trifle *nt*

➤ **trifle with** VI +PREP OBJ *person* zu leicht nehmen; *affections* spielen mit; **he is not a person to be trifled with** mit ihm ist nicht zu spaßen

trifling ['traɪflɪŋ] ADJ unbedeutend, geringfügig

trigger ['trɪgər] **1** N (*of gun*) Abzug(shahn) *m*; (*of machine*) Auslöser *m*; **to pull the ~** abdrücken **2** VT (*also ~ off*) auslösen; *bomb* zünden

trigonometry [trɪgə'nɒmɪtrɪ] N Trigonometrie *f*

trilingual [traɪ'lɪŋgwəl] ADJ dreisprachig

trill [trɪl] **1** N (a) (*of bird*) Trillern *nt*; (*of voice*) Tremolo *nt* (b) (*Mus*) Triller *m* (c) (*Phon*) rollende Aussprache **2** VT (*person*) trällern **3** VI (*bird*) trillern; (*person*) trällern

trillion ['trɪljən] N Billion *f*; (*dated Brit*) Trillion *f*

trilogy ['trɪlədʒɪ] N Trilogie *f*

trim [trɪm] **1** ADJ (+ER) (a) sauber; *appearance, hair* gepflegt (b) (= *slim*) *person* schlank; *waist* schmal; **to stay ~** in Form bleiben
2 N (a) (*Brit*) (= *condition*) Zustand *m*; (= *fitness*) Form *f*; **to get into ~** sich trimmen
(b) **to give sth a ~** etw schneiden; *hedge, beard also* etw stutzen; **just a ~, please** nur etwas kürzen *or* nachschneiden, bitte
(c) (= *edging*) Rand *m*; (= *decoration*) Bordüre *f*
3 VT (a) *hair* nachschneiden; *beard, hedge* stutzen; *dog* trimmen; *wick, roses* beschneiden
(b) (*fig*) *budget, essay* kürzen; *interest rates* (etwas) senken; *staff* reduzieren
(c) (= *decorate*) *dress* besetzen; *Christmas tree* schmücken

➤ **trim away** VT SEP weg- *or* abschneiden

➤ **trim back** VT SEP *hedge, roses* zurückschneiden; *costs* senken; *staff* reduzieren

➤ **trim down** VT SEP *budget, essay* kürzen (*to* auf +*acc*)

➤ **trim off** VT SEP *bits of beard, ends of branch* abschneiden; *fat also* wegschneiden

trimester [trɪ'mestər] N Trimester *nt*

trimmings ['trɪmɪŋz] PL (= *accessories*) Zubehör *nt*; **roast beef with all the ~** Roastbeef mit allen Beilagen

Trinidad ['trɪnɪdæd] N Trinidad *nt*

Trinity ['trɪnɪtɪ] N Dreieinigkeit *f*

trinket ['trɪŋkɪt] N Schmuckstück *nt*; (= *ornament*) Schmuckgegenstand *m*

trio ['triːəʊ] N Trio *nt*

trip [trɪp] **1** N (a) (= *journey*) Reise *f*; (= *excursion*) Ausflug *m*; (*esp shorter*) Trip *m*; **let's go on a ~ to the seaside** machen wir doch einen Ausflug ans Meer!; **that's his fifth ~ to the bathroom already!** er geht jetzt schon zum fünften Mal auf die Toilette! (*inf*); **he is away on a ~** er ist verreist; **to take a ~ (to)** eine Reise machen (nach)
(b) (*inf: on drugs*) Trip *m* (*inf*)
(c) (= *stumble*) Stolpern *nt*
2 VI (a) (= *stumble*) stolpern (*on, over* über +*acc*)
(b) (*fig*) sich vertun
(c) (= *skip*) trippeln; **to ~ in/out** hinein-/hinaustrippeln; **a phrase which ~s off the tongue** ein Ausdruck, der einem leicht von der Zunge geht
3 VT (a) (= *make fall*) stolpern lassen; (*deliberately*) ein Bein stellen (+*dat*)
(b) (*Mech*) *lever* betätigen; *mechanism* auslösen

➤ **trip over** VI stolpern (+*prep obj* über +*acc*)

➤ **trip up** **1** VI (a) (*lit*) stolpern (b) (*fig*) sich vertun **2** VT SEP (a) (= *make fall*) stolpern lassen; (*deliberately*) zu Fall bringen (b) (*fig*: = *cause to make a mistake etc*) eine Falle stellen (+*dat*)

tripartite [traɪ'pɑːtaɪt] ADJ dreiseitig

tripe [traɪp] N (a) (*Cook*) Kaldaunen *pl* (b) (*fig inf*) Quatsch *m*, Stuss *m* (*inf*)

triple ['trɪpl] **1** ADJ dreifach **2** ADV dreimal so viel **3** VT verdreifachen **4** VI sich verdreifachen

triple: triple crown N (a) (*of pope*) Tiara *f* (b) (*Rugby*) Triple Crown *f*, Siegestrophäe im Wettkampf zwischen England, Schottland, Wales und Irland; **triple jump** N Dreisprung *m*

triplet ['trɪplɪt] N Drilling *m*

triplicate ['trɪplɪkɪt] **1** N **in ~** in dreifacher Ausfertigung **2** ADJ in dreifacher Ausfertigung

tripod ['traɪpɒd] N (*Phot*) Stativ *nt*

trip: trip switch N (*Elec*) Sicherheitsschalter *m*; **tripwire** N Stolperdraht *m*

triumph ['traɪʌmf] **1** N Triumph *m*; **in ~** triumphierend **2** VI den Sieg davontragen (*over* über +*acc*); **to ~ over sb/sth** über jdn/etw triumphieren

triumphal [traɪ'ʌmfəl] ADJ triumphal

triumphant [traɪ'ʌmfənt] ADJ (= *victorious*) siegreich; (= *rejoicing*) triumphierend; *moment* triumphal; **to be ~ (over sth)** triumphieren (über etw *acc*); **to emerge ~** triumphieren

triumphantly [traɪ'ʌmfəntlɪ] ADV triumphierend

trivia ['trɪvɪə] PL belangloses Zeug

trivial ['trɪvɪəl] ADJ trivial; *loss, details, matters, mistake* belanglos

triviality [trɪvɪ'ælɪtɪ] N Trivialität *f*; (*of loss, details, matters also*) Belanglosigkeit *f*

trivialize ['trɪvɪəlaɪz] VT trivialisieren

trod [trɒd] PRET *of* **tread**

trodden ['trɒdn] PTP *of* **tread**

trolley ['trɒlɪ] N (a) (*Brit*: = *cart*) (*four wheels*) (*in supermarket*) Einkaufswagen *m*; (*in station*) (*for passengers*) Kofferkuli *m*; (*two wheels*) (*for golf clubs*) Caddy *m*; (*in station, factory etc*) Sackkarre *f*; (*Brit*: = *tea* ~) Teewagen *m* (c) (= *passenger vehicle*) Obus *m*; (*US*: = ~ *car*) Straßenbahn *f*

trolley: trolleybus N Obus *m*; **trolley car** N (*US*) Straßenbahn *f*

trombone [trɒm'bəʊn] N (*Mus*) Posaune *f*

troop [truːp] **1** N (a) (*Mil*) (*of cavalry*) Trupp *m*; (= *unit*) Schwadron *f* (b) (*Mil*) **troops** PL (*Mil*) Truppen *pl*; **200 ~s** 200 Soldaten (c) (*of Scouts*) Stamm *m* (d) (*of people*) Horde *f* (*pej*), Schar *f* **2** VI **to ~ out/in** hinaus-/hineinströmen; **to ~ past sth** an etw (*dat*) vorbeiziehen; **to ~ away** *or* **off** abziehen (*inf*)

troop carrier ['truːpˌkærɪər] N Truppentransporter *m*

trooper ['truːpər] N (*Mil*) Kavallerist *m*; (*US*: = *state* ~) Staatspolizist(in) *m(f)*

troopship ['truːpʃɪp] N (Truppen)transportschiff *nt*

trophy ['trəʊfɪ] N (*Hunt, Mil, Sport*) Trophäe *f*

tropic ['trɒpɪk] N (a) Wendekreis *m*; **Tropic of Cancer/Capricorn** Wendekreis *m* des Krebses/Steinbocks (b) **tropics** PL Tropen *pl*

tropical ['trɒpɪkəl] ADJ tropisch, Tropen-; **~ diseases** Tropenkrankheiten *pl*

tropical rainforest N tropischer Regenwald

trot [trɒt] **1** N (a) (= *pace*) Trab *m*; **to go at a ~** traben (b) (*inf*) **for five days on the ~** fünf Tage lang in einer Tour; **he won three games on the ~** er gewann drei Spiele hintereinander **2** VI (*horse, person*) traben; (*small child*) trippeln

➤ **trot along** VI (*horse, person*) traben; (*small child*) trippeln; **to trot along behind sb** hinter jdm hertraben *etc*

➤ **trot away** *or* **off** VI *see* **trot 2** davon- *or* wegtraben/-trippeln

➤ **trot out** VT SEP *excuses, names* aufwarten *or* kommen mit

trotter ['trɒtər] N (*of animal*) Fuß *m*

trouble ['trʌbl] **1** N (a) Schwierigkeiten *pl*; (*bothersome*) Ärger *m*; **to be in ~** in Schwierigkeiten sein; **to be in ~ with sb** mit jdm Schwierigkeiten *or* Ärger haben; **to get into ~** in Schwierigkeiten geraten; (*with authority*) Schwierigkeiten *or* Ärger bekommen (*with* mit); **to get sb into ~** jdn in Schwierigkeiten bringen (*with* mit); **to get out of ~** aus den Schwierigkeiten herauskommen; **to keep** *or* **stay out of ~** nicht in Schwierigkeiten kommen; **to make ~** (= *cause a row etc*) Krach schlagen (*inf*); **that's/you're asking for ~** das kann ja nicht gut gehen; **to look for ~, to go around looking for ~** sich (*dat*) Ärger einhandeln; **there'll be ~ if he finds out** wenn er das erfährt, gibts Ärger; **what's the ~?** was ist los?; (*to sick person*) wo fehlts?; **the ~ is that ...** das Problem ist, dass ...; **family/money ~s** Familien-/Geldsorgen *pl*; **the child is nothing but ~ to his parents** das Kind macht seinen Eltern nur Sorgen; **he's been no ~ at all** (*of child*) er war ganz lieb (b) (= *bother, effort*) Mühe *f*; **it's no ~ (at all)!** das mache ich doch gern; **thank you – (it was) no ~** vielen Dank – (das ist) gern geschehen; **it's not worth the ~** das ist nicht der Mühe wert; **it's more ~ than it's worth** es macht mehr Ärger *or* Umstände als es wert ist; **nothing is too much ~ for her** nichts ist ihr zu viel; **to go to the ~ (of doing sth), to take the ~ (to do sth)** sich (*dat*) die Mühe machen(, etw zu tun); **to go to** *or* **take a lot of ~ (over** *or* **with sth)** sich (*dat*) (mit etw) viel Mühe geben; **to put sb to a lot of ~** jdm viel Mühe machen (c) (*Med*: = *illness*) Leiden *nt*; (*fig*) Schaden *m*; **heart ~** Herzleiden *nt*; **my back is giving me ~** mein Rücken macht mir zu schaffen; **engine ~** (ein) Motorschaden *m* (d) (= *unrest, upheaval*) Unruhe *f*; **there's ~ at the factory/in**

Iran in der Fabrik/im Iran herrscht Unruhe; **he caused/made ~ between them** er hat Unruhe zwischen ihnen gestiftet **2** VT **(a)** (= *worry*) beunruhigen; (= *disturb, grieve*) bekümmern; **to be ~d by sth** wegen etw besorgt *or* beunruhigt/bekümmert sein
(b) (= *bother*) bemühen, belästigen; **I'm sorry to ~ you, but could you tell me if ...** entschuldigen Sie die Störung, aber könnten Sie mir sagen, ob ...; **may I ~ you for a light?** darf ich Sie um Feuer bitten?; **I shan't ~ you with the details** ich werde Ihnen die Einzelheiten ersparen; **to ~ to do sth** sich bemühen, etw zu tun

troubled ['trʌbld] ADJ **(a)** unruhig; (= *grieved*) bekümmert; *mind, conscience* aufgewühlt; *relationship* gestört **(b)** (*Ind, Fin*) in Schwierigkeiten *pred*

trouble: **trouble-free** ADJ *period, process, car* problemlos; *area* ruhig; *machine* störungsfrei; **troublemaker** N Unruhestifter(in) *m(f)*; **troubleshooter** N Störungssucher(in) *m(f)*; (*Pol, Ind*: = *mediator*) Vermittler(in) *m(f)*; **troublesome** ADJ (= *bothersome*) lästig; *person, problem* schwierig; **trouble spot** N Unruheherd *m*; (*in system*) Störung *f*

trough [trɒf] N Trog *m* (*also Met*); (= *depression*) Furche *f*, Rille *f*; (*on graph*) Tal *nt*

trounce [traʊns] VT verprügeln; (*Sport*) vernichtend schlagen

troupe [truːp] N (*Theat*) Truppe *f*

trouser ['traʊzə'] (*esp Brit*): **trouser leg** N Hosenbein *nt*; **trouser press** N Hosenpresse *f*

trousers ['traʊzəz] PL (*esp Brit*) (*also pair of ~*) Hose *f*; **she was wearing ~** sie hatte Hosen *or* eine Hose an; **to wear the ~** (*fig inf*) die Hosen anhaben (*inf*)

trouser suit N (*Brit*) Hosenanzug *m*

trout [traʊt] N Forelle *f*

trove [trəʊv] N = **treasure trove**

trowel ['traʊəl] N Kelle *f*

truancy ['truːənsɪ] N (*Schule*)schwänzen *nt*

truant ['truːənt] **1** N (*Schul*)schwänzer(in) *m(f)*; **to play ~ (from sth)** (etw) schwänzen (*inf*) **2** VI schwänzen (*inf*)

truce [truːs] N (*Mil, fig*) Waffenstillstand *m*; (*Mil: interrupting fighting*) Waffenruhe *f*; **~!** Friede!

truck [trʌk] **1** N **(a)** (*esp Brit Rail*) Güterwagen *m* **(b)** (= *lorry*) Last(kraft)wagen *m*; (= *van, pick-up*) Lieferwagen *m* **2** VT (*US*) transportieren

truck: **truck cab** N (*US*) Führerhaus *nt*; **truck driver** N Lastwagenfahrer(in) *m(f)*

trucker ['trʌkə'] N (*esp US*) (= *truck driver*) Lastwagenfahrer(in) *m(f)*; (= *haulage contractor*) Spediteur(in) *m(f)*

truck (*US*): **truck farm** N Gemüsefarm *f*; **truck farmer** N Gemüsegärtner(in) *m(f)*

trucking ['trʌkɪŋ] N (*esp US*) Spedition *f*, Transport *m*; **~ company** Fuhrunternehmen *nt*

truck: **truckload** N Wagenladung *f*; **truckstop** N (*US*) Fernfahrerlokal *nt*

trudge [trʌdʒ] **1** VI **to ~ in/out/along** *etc* hinein-/hinaus-/entlangtrotten *etc*; **to ~ through the mud** durch den Matsch stapfen; **we ~d (a)round the shops** wir sind durch die Geschäfte getrottet *or* gelatscht (*inf*) **2** N mühseliger Marsch

true [truː] **1** ADJ **(a)** wahr; (= *genuine*) echt; **to come ~** (*dream, wishes*) wahr werden; (*prophecy*) sich verwirklichen; (*fears*) sich bewahrheiten; **it is ~ that ...** es stimmt, dass ...; **that's ~** das stimmt; **it is ~ to say that ...** es ist richtig, dass ...; **~!** richtig!; **too ~!** (das ist nur) zu wahr!; **we mustn't generalize, (it's) ~, but ...** wir sollten natürlich nicht verallgemeinern, aber ...; **the reverse is ~** ganz im Gegenteil; **he's got so much money it's not ~!** (*inf*) es ist unfassbar, wie viel Geld er hat!; **the frog is not a ~ reptile** der Frosch ist kein echtes Reptil; **spoken like a ~ football fan** so spricht ein wahrer Fußballfan; **~ love** die wahre Liebe; (= *person*) Schatz *m*; **to be ~ for sb/sth** für jdn/etw wahr sein; **to be ~ of sb/sth** auf jdn/etw zutreffen; **the same is** *or* **holds ~ for ...** dasselbe gilt auch für ...

(b) (= *accurate*) *description, account* wahrheitsgetreu; *likeness* (lebens)getreu; *aim* genau; **the ~ meaning of** die wahre Bedeutung (+*gen*); **in the ~ sense (of the word)** im wahren Sinne (des Wortes)

(c) (= *faithful*) treu; **to be ~ to sb** jdm treu sein/bleiben; **to be ~ to one's word** (treu) zu seinem Wort stehen; **~ to life** lebensnah; (*Art*) lebensecht; **the horse ran ~ to form** das Pferd

lief erwartungsgemäß; **~ to type** erwartungsgemäß **(d)** *wall, surface* gerade; *join* genau; *circle* rund **(e)** (*Phys*) tatsächlich; **~ north** der tatsächliche *or* geografische Norden **(f)** (*Mus*) *note* richtig; *voice* rein **2** N **out of ~** upright, beam, wheels schief; *join* verschoben **3** ADV *aim* genau; *sing* richtig

true-life ['truːlaɪf] ADJ ATTR aus dem Leben gegriffen

truffle ['trʌfl] N Trüffel *f or m*

truly ['truːlɪ] ADV **(a)** wirklich, wahrhaftig; **(really and) ~?** wirklich und wahrhaftig?; **the only man she had ever ~ loved** der einzige Mann, den sie je wahrhaft geliebt hat; **I am ~ sorry** es tut mir aufrichtig Leid; **~ amazing** wirklich erstaunlich **(b)** (= *faithfully*) *serve, love* treu

trump [trʌmp] **1** N (*Cards, fig*) Trumpf *m*; **spades are ~s** Pik ist Trumpf; **to hold all the ~s** (*fig*) alle Trümpfe in der Hand halten; **to come** *or* **turn up ~s** (*Brit inf*) sich als Sieger erweisen **2** VT (*Cards*) stechen; (*fig*) übertrumpfen

trump card N (*Cards*) Trumpfkarte *f*; (*fig*) Trumpf *m*; **to play one's ~** (*lit, fig*) seinen Trumpf ausspielen

trumped-up ['trʌmptʌp] ADJ *charge* erfunden

trumpet ['trʌmpɪt] **1** N (*Mus*) Trompete *f* **2** VI (*elephant*) trompeten

trumpeter ['trʌmpɪtə'] N Trompeter(in) *m(f)*

truncate [trʌŋ'keɪt] VT kürzen; (*Comput*) *number* abschneiden; *process* abbrechen

truncated [trʌŋ'keɪtɪd] ADJ *tree* gestutzt; *article, speech, version* gekürzt; *presidency* verkürzt

truncheon ['trʌntʃən] N (Gummi)knüppel *m*; (*esp of riot police*) Schlagstock *m*

trundle ['trʌndl] **1** VT (= *push*) rollen; (= *pull*) ziehen **2** VI **to ~ in/along/down** hinein-/entlang-/hinunterzockeln

trunk [trʌŋk] N **(a)** (*of tree*) Stamm *m*; (*of body*) Rumpf *m* **(b)** (*of elephant*) Rüssel *m* **(c)** (= *case*) Schrankkoffer *m* **(d)** (*US Aut*) Kofferraum *m* **(e)** **trunks** PL (*for swimming*) Badehose *f*; **a pair of ~s** eine Badehose

trunk: **trunk call** N (*Brit Telec*) Ferngespräch *nt*; **trunk road** N (*Brit*) Fernstraße *f*

truss [trʌs] **1** N (*Med*) Bruchband *nt* **2** VT (*Cook*) *chicken etc* dressieren

➤ **truss up** VT SEP (*Cook*) *chicken etc* dressieren; (*inf*) *person* fesseln

trust [trʌst] **1** N **(a)** Vertrauen *nt* (*in* zu); **I have every ~ in him** ich habe volles Vertrauen zu ihm; **to put** *or* **place one's ~ in sb** Vertrauen in jdn setzen; **to take sth on ~** etw einfach glauben; **to give sb sth on ~** (= *without payment*) jdm etw im guten Glauben geben; **position of ~** Vertrauensstellung *f* **(b)** (= *charge*) Verantwortung *f* **(c)** (*Jur, Fin*) Treuhand(schaft) *f*; (= *property*) Treuhandeigentum *nt*; (= *charitable fund*) Stiftung *f*; **to hold sth in ~ for sb** etw für jdn treuhänderisch verwalten **(d)** (*Comm: also* = **company**) Trust *m* **2** VT **(a)** trauen (+*dat*); *person* (ver)trauen (+*dat*); **to ~ sb to do sth** (= *believe him honest etc*) jdm vertrauen, dass er etw tut; (= *believe him capable*) jdm zutrauen, dass er etw tut; **to ~ sb with sth, to ~ sth to sb** jdm etw anvertrauen; **can he be ~ed not to lose it?** kann man sich darauf verlassen, dass er es nicht verliert? **(b)** (*iro inf*) **~ you/him!** typisch!; **~ him to break it!** er muss es natürlich kaputtmachen **(c)** (= *hope*) hoffen; **I ~ not** hoffentlich nicht **3** VI vertrauen; **to ~ in sb** auf jdn vertrauen; **to ~ to luck** *or* **chance** sich auf sein Glück verlassen

trusted ['trʌstɪd] ADJ *method* bewährt; *friend, servant* getreu

trustee [trʌs'tiː] N **(a)** (*of estate*) Treuhänder(in) *m(f)* **(b)** (*of institution*) Verwalter(in) *m(f)*; **~s** Vorstand *m*

trusteeship [trʌs'tiːʃɪp] N Treuhandschaft *f*

trust fund N Treuhandvermögen *nt*

trusting ['trʌstɪŋ] ADJ *person, nature* gutgläubig; *relationship* vertrauensvoll; *face* arglos

trustworthiness ['trʌst,wɜːðɪnɪs] N (*of person*) Vertrauenswürdigkeit *f*

trustworthy ['trʌst,wɜːðɪ] ADJ *person* vertrauenswürdig

trusty ['trʌstɪ] ADJ (+ER) (*liter, hum*) getreu (*liter*)

truth [truːθ] N, *pl* **~s** [truːðz] NO PL Wahrheit *f*; **to tell the ~ ..., ~ to tell ...** um ehrlich zu sein ...; **the ~ of it** *or* **the matter is**

that ... die Wahrheit ist dass ...; **there's no ~** or or **not a word of ~ in what he says** es ist kein Wort wahr von dem, was er sagt; **there's some ~ in that** da ist etwas Wahres dran (inf); **in ~** in Wahrheit

truthful [ˈtruːθfʊl] ADJ person ehrlich; statement wahrheitsgetreu

truthfully [ˈtruːθfəlɪ] ADV ehrlich; answer, say also, explain wahrheitsgemäß

truthfulness [ˈtruːθfʊlnɪs] N Ehrlichkeit f, Aufrichtigkeit f; (of statement) Wahrheit f

try [traɪ] **1** N Versuch m; **to have a ~** es versuchen; **let me have a ~** lass mich mal versuchen!; **to have a ~ at doing sth** (sich daran) versuchen, etw zu tun; **I'll give it a ~** (= will attempt it) ich werde es mal versuchen; (= will test it out) ich werde es ausprobieren; **it was a good ~** das war schon ganz gut **2** VT **(a)** (= attempt) versuchen; **to ~ one's hardest** or **one's best** sein Bestes tun or versuchen; **I've given up ~ing to help him** ich habe es aufgegeben, ihm helfen zu wollen; **to ~ one's hand at sth** etw probieren; **I'll ~ anything once** ich probiere alles einmal; **just you ~ it!** (= you dare) versuchs bloß!

(b) (= ~ out) ausprobieren; glue, aspirin es versuchen mit; newsagent es versuchen (bei); **I can't shut this case – ~ sitting on it** ich kriege diesen Koffer nicht zu – setz dich doch mal drauf! (inf); **you could ~ seeing whether John would help** Sie könnten doch John mal um Hilfe angehen; **~ this for size** probieren Sie mal, ob dieser/diese etc passt

(c) (= sample, taste) beer, olives probieren

(d) courage, patience auf die Probe stellen; **(just) ~ me!** (inf) wetten dass?; **these things are sent to ~ us** ja, ja, das Leben ist nicht so einfach

(e) (Jur) person vor Gericht stellen; case verhandeln; **he is being tried for theft** er steht wegen Diebstahls vor Gericht **3** VI versuchen; **~ and arrive on time** versuch mal, pünktlich zu sein; **as he might, he didn't succeed** sosehr er es auch versuchte, er schaffte es einfach nicht; **he didn't even ~** er hat sich (dat) überhaupt keine Mühe gegeben; (= didn't attempt it) er hat es überhaupt nicht versucht

➤ **try for** VI +PREP OBJ sich bemühen um

➤ **try on** VT SEP **(a)** clothes anprobieren; hat aufprobieren **(b)** (fig inf) **to try it on with sb** probieren, wie weit man bei jdm gehen kann

➤ **try out** VT SEP ausprobieren (on bei, an +dat); person eine Chance geben (+dat), einen Versuch machen mit

trying [ˈtraɪɪŋ] ADJ anstrengend; work, day, time also aufreibend; experience schwer

tsar [zɑːʳ] N **(a)** Zar m **(b)** (Pol) alcohol/tobacco ~ Regierungsbeauftragte(r) m(f) (für Maßnahmen zur Regulierung des Alkohol-/Tabakkonsums)

T-shirt [ˈtiːʃɜːt] N T-Shirt nt

tsp(s) ABBR of teaspoonful(s), teaspoon(s) Teel.

tub [tʌb] N **(a)** Kübel m; (for rainwater) Tonne f; (for washing) Bottich m; (of ice cream, margarine) Becher m **(b)** (esp US inf: = bath ~) Wanne f

tuba [ˈtjuːbə] N Tuba f

tubby [ˈtʌbɪ] ADJ (+ER) (inf) dick; woman mollig; child pummelig; man rundlich

tube [tjuːb] N **(a)** (= pipe) Rohr nt; (of rubber, plastic) Schlauch m **(b)** (of toothpaste, paint, glue) Tube f; (of sweets) Rolle f **(c)** (Brit: = London underground) U-Bahn f; **to travel by ~** mit der U-Bahn fahren **(d)** (Anat, Elec, TV, US Rad) Röhre f; **the ~** (US inf) die Röhre (inf)

tuber [ˈtjuːbəʳ] N (Bot) Knolle f

tuberculosis [tjuːˌbɜːkjʊˈləʊsɪs] N Tuberkulose f

tube station N (Brit) U-Bahnstation f

tubing [ˈtjuːbɪŋ] N Schlauch m

tubular [ˈtjuːbjʊləʳ] ADJ röhrenförmig

TUC (Brit) ABBR of Trades Union Congress ≈ DGB m

tuck [tʌk] N (Sew) Saum m **2** VT (= put) stecken; **he ~ed his umbrella under his arm** er steckte sich (dat) den Regenschirm unter den Arm; **the bird's head was ~ed under its wing** der Vogel hatte den Kopf unter den Flügel gesteckt; **she sat with her feet ~ed under her** sie saß mit untergeschlagenen Beinen da

➤ **tuck away** VT SEP (= hide) wegstecken; **he tucked it away in his pocket** er steckte es in die Tasche; **the hut is tucked away among the trees** die Hütte liegt versteckt zwischen den Bäumen

➤ **tuck in 1** VI (Brit inf) zulangen, reinhauen (inf); **tuck in!** langt zu!, haut rein! (inf); **to tuck into sth** sich (dat) etw schmecken lassen **2** VT SEP flap etc hineinstecken, reinstecken (inf); **to tuck one's shirt in(to) one's trousers, to tuck one's shirt in** das Hemd in die Hose stecken; **to tuck sb in** (in bed) jdn zudecken

➤ **tuck up** VT SEP (Brit) **to tuck sb up (in bed)** jdn zudecken

tucker [ˈtʌkəʳ] VT (US inf) fertig machen (inf)

tuck shop N (Brit) Bonbonladen m

Tudor [ˈtjuːdəʳ] **1** ADJ Tudor- **2** N Tudor mf

Tue(s) ABBR of Tuesday Di.

Tuesday [ˈtjuːzdɪ] N Dienstag m; **on ~** (am) Dienstag; **on ~s, on a ~** dienstags; **I met her on a ~** ich habe sie an einem Dienstag kennen gelernt; **on ~ morning/evening** (am) Dienstag Morgen/Abend; **on ~ mornings** dienstags or Dienstag morgens; **last/next/this ~** letzten/nächsten/diesen Dienstag; **a year (ago) last ~** letzten Dienstag vor einem Jahr; **~'s newspaper** die Zeitung vom Dienstag; **our ~ meeting** (this week) unser Treffen am Dienstag; (every week) unser dienstägliches Treffen; **~ December 5th** (in letter) Dienstag, den 5. Dezember

tuft [tʌft] N Büschel nt; **a ~ of hair** ein Haarbüschel nt

tug [tʌg] **1** VT zerren, ziehen; vessel (ab)schleppen; **she ~ged his sleeve** sie zog an seinem Ärmel **2** VI ziehen, zerren (at an +dat) **3** N **(a)** **to give sth a ~** etw (dat) ziehen; **I felt a ~ on my sleeve** ich spürte, wie mich jemand am Ärmel zog **(b)** (also **~boat**) Schleppkahn m

tug: **tug-of-love** N Tauziehen um das Kind/die Kinder bei einer Ehescheidung; **tug-of-war** N (Sport, fig) Tauziehen nt

tuition [tjʊˈɪʃən] N Unterricht m

tulip [ˈtjuːlɪp] N Tulpe f

tumble [ˈtʌmbl] **1** N (= fall) Sturz m; **to take a ~** stürzen, straucheln; (fig) fallen **2** VI (= fall) straucheln, (hin)fallen; (= move quickly) stürzen; (fig: prices) fallen; **he ~d off his bicycle** er stürzte vom Fahrrad; **to ~ over sth** über etw (acc) stolpern

➤ **tumble about** (Brit) or **around** VI durcheinanderpurzeln; (children, kittens etc) herumpurzeln

➤ **tumble down** VI (= fall down) (person) hinfallen, stürzen; (object) herunterfallen; **to tumble down the stairs** die Treppe hinunterfallen

➤ **tumble over** VI umfallen, umkippen

tumble: **tumbledown** ADJ verfallen, baufällig; **tumble drier, tumble dryer** N Wäschetrockner m

tumbler [ˈtʌmbləʳ] N (= glass) (Becher)glas nt

tummy [ˈtʌmɪ] N (inf) Bauch m, Bäuchlein nt (baby-talk)

tumour, (US) **tumor** [ˈtjuːməʳ] N Tumor m; **a ~ on the brain, brain ~** ein Gehirntumor m

tumult [ˈtjuːmʌlt] N Tumult m; **his mind was in a ~** sein Inneres befand sich in Aufruhr

tumultuous [tjʊˈmʌltjʊəs] ADJ stürmisch

tuna (fish) [ˈtjuːnə(ˈfɪʃ)] N T(h)unfisch m

tundra [ˈtʌndrə] N Tundra f

tune [tjuːn] **1** N **(a)** (= melody) Melodie f; **to change one's ~** (fig) seine Meinung ändern; **to dance to sb's ~** (fig) nach jds Pfeife tanzen; **to call the ~** (fig) den Ton angeben; **to the ~ of £100** in Höhe von £ 100

(b) (= pitch) **to sing in ~/out of ~** richtig/falsch singen; **the piano is out of ~** das Klavier ist verstimmt; **to be in/out of ~ with sb/sth** (fig) mit jdm/etw harmonieren/nicht harmonieren **2** VT **(a)** (Mus) instrument stimmen **(b)** (Rad, TV, Aut) einstellen

➤ **tune in 1** VI (Rad) einschalten; **to tune in to Radio London** Radio London hören **2** VT SEP (a) radio einschalten (to +acc); **you are tuned in to Radio 2** Sie hören or hier ist Radio 2 **(b)** **to be tuned in to sth** to feelings etc auf etw (acc) eingestellt sein

➤ **tune up** VI (Mus) (sein Instrument) stimmen

tuneful ADJ, **tunefully** ADV [ˈtjuːnfʊl, -fəlɪ] melodisch

tuneless ADJ, **tunelessly** ADV [ˈtjuːnlɪs, -lɪ] unmelodisch

tune-up [ˈtjuːnʌp] N (Aut) **the car needs/has had a ~** das Auto muss getunt werden/ist getunt worden

tungsten [ˈtʌŋstən] N Wolfram nt

tunic ['tjuːnɪk] N Kasack m, Hemdbluse f; (of uniform) Uniformrock m

tuning fork ['tjuːnɪŋfɔːk] N (Mus) Stimmgabel f

Tunisia [tjuːˈnɪzɪə] N Tunesien nt

Tunisian [tjuːˈnɪzɪən] **1** N Tunesier(in) m(f) **2** ADJ tunesisch; **he is ~** er ist Tunesier

tunnel ['tʌnl] **1** N Tunnel m; (under road, railway also) Unterführung f; (Min) Stollen m; **at last we can see the light at the end of the ~** (fig) endlich sehen wir wieder Licht **2** VI (into in +acc, through durch) einen Tunnel bauen; (mole) Gänge pl graben **3** VT **they tunnelled** (Brit) or **tunneled** (US) **a road through the mountain** sie bauten einen Straßentunnel durch den Berg; **to ~ one's way through** sich durch etw hindurchgraben

tunnel vision N (Med) Gesichtsfeldeinengung f; (fig) Engstirnigkeit f

tuppence ['tʌpəns] N (Brit) zwei Pence

Tupperware® ['tʌpəweəʳ] **1** N Tupperware f **2** ADJ Tupperware-

turban ['tɜːbən] N Turban m

turbine ['tɜːbaɪn] N Turbine f

turbo-charged ['tɜːbəʊˌtʃɑːdʒd] ADJ mit Turboaufladung

turbot ['tɜːbət] N Steinbutt m

turbulence ['tɜːbjʊləns] N (of person, crowd) Wildheit f; (of emotions) Aufgewühltheit f; (of career, period) Turbulenz f; **air ~** Turbulenzen pl

turbulent ['tɜːbjʊlənt] ADJ stürmisch; person, crowd wild; emotions aufgewühlt; career, period, world turbulent

turd [tɜːd] N (sl) Kacke f (vulg), Scheiße f no pl (vulg); (single) Haufen m (inf)

tureen [təˈriːn] N (Suppen)terrine f

turf [tɜːf] N, pl **-s** or **turves** (a) (no pl: = lawn) Rasen m; (= square of grass) Sode f (b) (no pl) (= peat) Torf m; (= square of peat) Torfsode f

➤ **turf out** VT SEP (Brit inf) person rauswerfen, rausschmeißen (inf); (= throw away) wegschmeißen (inf)

turgid ['tɜːdʒɪd] ADJ (fig) schwülstig

Turk [tɜːk] N Türke m, Türkin f

Turkey ['tɜːkɪ] N die Türkei

turkey ['tɜːkɪ] N Truthahn m/-henne f; (esp Cook) Puter m, Pute f

Turkish ['tɜːkɪʃ] **1** ADJ türkisch; **she is ~** sie ist Türkin **2** N (Ling) Türkisch nt

Turkish delight N Lokum nt

Turkmenistan ['tɜːkmenɪsˌtɑːn] N Turkmenistan nt

turmeric ['tɜːmərɪk] N Kurkuma f, Gelbwurz f

turmoil ['tɜːmɔɪl] N Aufruhr m; (= confusion) Durcheinander nt; **everything is in a ~** alles ist in Aufruhr; **her mind was in a ~** sie war völlig verwirrt

---

turn [tɜːn]

1 NOUN	**3** INTRANSITIVE VERB
2 TRANSITIVE VERB	**4** PHRASAL VERBS

1 NOUN
(a) (= movement) Drehung f; **six turns of the wheel** sechs Umdrehungen des Rades; **to give sth a turn** etw drehen; **give the handle another turn** dreh den Griff noch einmal herum
(b) (= change of direction) (in road) Kurve f; (Sport) Wende f; **take the left-hand turn** biegen Sie links ab; **"no left turn"** „Linksabbiegen verboten"

✦**to take a turn (for)** things took a turn for the better/the worse die Dinge wendeten sich zum Guten/zum Schlechten; **the patient took a turn for the worse/the better** das Befinden des Patienten wendete sich zum Schlechteren/zum Besseren

✦**turn of + noun** at the turn of the century um die Jahrhundertwende; **I'm very upset by the turn of events** ich bin über den Verlauf der Dinge sehr beunruhigt; **turn of phrase** Ausdrucksweise f; **to have a good turn of speed** (car) sehr schnell fahren; (horse, athlete) sehr schnell sein; **the turn of the tide** der Gezeitenwechsel

✦**at every turn** (fig) he was thwarted at every turn ihm wurde auf Schritt und Tritt ein Strich durch die Rechnung gemacht
(c) (in game, queue, series) **it's your turn** du bist an der Reihe, du bist dran; **it's your turn to wash the dishes** du bist mit (dem) Abwaschen an der Reihe or dran; **it's my turn next** ich komme als Nächste(r) an die Reihe or dran; **wait your turn** warten Sie, bis Sie an der Reihe sind; **to miss a turn** eine Runde aussetzen; **your turn will come** du kommst auch noch mal dran; **to take turns to do sth** or **at doing sth** etw abwechselnd tun; **to take it in turn(s) to do sth** etw abwechselnd tun

✦**in turn** he told a colleague, who in turn told a reporter er sagte es einem Kollegen, der es wiederum einem Reporter erzählte; **they answered in turn** sie antworteten der Reihe nach; (2 people only) sie antworteten abwechselnd

✦**by turn(s)** abwechselnd

✦**out of turn** außer der Reihe; **my secretary was speaking out of turn** es stand meiner Sekretärin nicht zu, sich darüber zu äußern

✦**turn and turn about** abwechselnd
(d) (= service)

✦**a good/bad turn** to do sb a good/bad turn jdm einen guten/schlechten Dienst erweisen; **one good turn deserves another** (Prov) eine Hand wäscht die andere (prov)
(e) (= attack) (Brit inf) he had one of his (funny) turns last night er hatte letzte Nacht wieder einen Anfall
(f) (Theat etc) Nummer f

2 TRANSITIVE VERB
(a) (= rotate) drehen; wood drechseln; **to turn the key in the lock** den Schlüssel im Schloss herumdrehen; **he turned his head toward(s) me** er wandte mir den Kopf zu; **he turned his back to the wall** er kehrte den Rücken zur Wand; **as soon as his back is turned** sobald er den Rücken kehrt; **the sight of all that food quite turned my stomach** beim Anblick des vielen Essens drehte sich mir regelrecht der Magen um; **without turning a hair** ohne mit der Wimper zu zucken; **she can still turn a few heads** die Leute schauen sich immer noch nach ihr um; **he can turn his hand to anything** er kann alles, er ist sehr geschickt
(b) (= turn over/round) wenden; page umblättern; chair, picture etc umdrehen
(c) (= direct) **to turn one's thoughts/attention to sth** seine Gedanken/Aufmerksamkeit einer Sache (dat) zuwenden; **to turn a gun on sb** ein Gewehr auf jdn richten
(d) (= transform, make become) verwandeln (in(to) in +acc); **the shock turned his hair white overnight** durch den Schock bekam er über Nacht weiße Haare; **to turn the lights down low** das Licht herunterdrehen; **his goal turned the game** sein Tor gab dem Spiel eine andere Wendung; **to turn a profit** (esp US) einen Gewinn machen

✦**to turn sth into ...** the play was turned into a film das Stück wurde verfilmt

✦**to turn sb loose** jdn loslassen or laufen lassen

3 INTRANSITIVE VERB
(a) (= rotate, move round) sich drehen; **he turned to me and smiled** er drehte sich mir zu und lächelte; **this key won't turn** dieser Schlüssel lässt sich nicht drehen; **to turn upside down** umkippen
(b) (= change direction) (to one side) (person, car) abbiegen; (plane, boat) abdrehen; (= turn around) wenden; (person) (on the spot) sich umdrehen; (tide) wechseln; **to turn and go back** umkehren; **to turn (to the) left** links abbiegen
(c) (= go) **I don't know which way** or **where to turn for help/money** ich weiß nicht, an wen ich mich um Hilfe wenden kann/wen ich um Geld bitten kann; **I don't know which way to turn** ich weiß nicht, was ich machen soll; **to turn to sb** sich an jdn wenden; **our thoughts turn to those who ...** wir gedenken derer, die ...; **to turn to sth** sich einer Sache (dat) zuwenden; **turn to page 306** gehen or blättern Sie weiter bis Seite 306; **the conversation turned to the accident** das Gespräch kam auf den Unfall
(d) (= change) (leaves) sich (ver)färben; (milk) sauer werden; (weather) umschlagen; **to turn to stone** zu Stein werden; **his admiration turned to scorn** seine Bewunderung verwandelte sich in Verachtung

✦to turn into sth sich in etw (acc) verwandeln; (= develop into) sich zu etw entwickeln; **the whole thing turned into a nightmare** die ganze Sache wurde zum Albtraum **(e)** (= become) werden; **Paul Crooks, an actor turned director, ...** der Regisseur Paul Crooks, ein ehemaliger Schauspieler, ...; **to turn violent** gewalttätig werden; **to turn red** (leaves etc) sich rot färben; (person) rot werden; (traffic lights) auf Rot umspringen; **he has just turned 18** er ist gerade 18 geworden; **it has turned 2 o'clock** es ist 2 Uhr vorbei

4 PHRASAL VERBS

➤ **turn against 1** VI +PREP OBJ sich wenden gegen **2** VT SEP +PREP OBJ **they turned him against his parents** sie brachten ihn gegen seine Eltern auf; **they turned his argument against him** sie verwendeten sein Argument gegen ihn

➤ **turn around 1** VT SEP **(a)** (lit, fig) wenden; argument umdrehen; country, economy, company aus der Krise führen; **he turned himself around** er wandte sich um **(b)** ship etc abfertigen; goods fertig stellen **2** VI +PREP OBJ corner biegen um **3** VI (person) sich umdrehen; (car, boat, driver etc) wenden; **we had to turn around and go home** wir mussten umkehren (und nach Hause gehen)

➤ **turn away 1** VI sich abwenden **2** VT SEP **(a)** head, gun abwenden **(b)** (= send away) person abweisen; business ablehnen

➤ **turn back 1** VI **(a)** umkehren; (= look back) sich umdrehen; **we can't turn back now, there's no turning back now** (fig) jetzt gibt es kein Zurück mehr **(b)** (in book) zurückblättern (to auf +acc) **2** VT SEP **(a)** bedclothes zurück- or aufschlagen **(b)** (= send back) person zurückschicken; **they were turned back at the frontier** sie wurden an der Grenze zurückgewiesen **(c)** clock zurückstellen; **to turn the clock back fifty years** (fig) die Uhr um fünfzig Jahre zurückdrehen

➤ **turn down 1** VT SEP **(a)** bedclothes zurück- or aufschlagen; collar, brim herunterklappen; corner of page umknicken **(b)** gas, heat kleiner stellen; volume leiser stellen; lights herunterdrehen **(c)** candidate, novel, offer etc ablehnen; suitor abweisen; invitation ausschlagen **2** VI +PREP OBJ **he turned down a side street** er bog in eine Seitenstraße ab

➤ **turn in 1** VI **(a)** the car turned in at the top of the drive das Auto bog in die Einfahrt ein **(b)** (inf: = go to bed) sich hinhauen (inf) **2** VT SEP **(a)** (inf: to police) **to turn sb in** jdn anzeigen or verpfeifen (inf); **to turn oneself in** sich (der Polizei) stellen **(b)** (esp US inf: = give back) equipment zurückgeben; weapons (to police) abgeben (to bei)

➤ **turn into** VTI +PREP OBJ = **turn** 2(d), 3(d)

➤ **turn off 1** VI abbiegen (for nach, prep obj von) **2** VT SEP **(a)** light, radio ausmachen; gas abdrehen; tap zudrehen; TV programme abschalten; water, electricity, engine, machine abstellen **(b)** (inf) **to turn sb off** (= disgust) jdn anwidern; (= put off) jdm die Lust verderben

➤ **turn on 1** VT SEP **(a)** gas, heat, engine, machine anstellen; radio, television, the news einschalten; light anmachen; tap, central heating aufdrehen; **to turn on the charm** seinen (ganzen) Charme spielen lassen **(b)** (inf: = appeal to) **sth turns sb on** jd steht auf etw (acc) (sl); **whatever turns you on** wenn du das gut findest (inf); **he doesn't turn me on** er lässt mich kalt (also sexually) **(c)** (inf: sexually) anmachen (inf); **she really turns me on** auf sie kann ich voll abfahren (inf) **2** VI +PREP OBJ (= turn against) sich wenden gegen; (= attack) angreifen

➤ **turn out 1** VI **(a)** (= appear, attend) erscheinen, kommen **(b)** (firemen, police) ausrücken **(c)** the car turned out of the drive das Auto bog aus der Einfahrt **(d)** (= transpire) sich herausstellen; **he turned out to be the murderer** es stellte sich heraus, dass er der Mörder war **(e)** (= develop, progress) sich entwickeln, sich machen (inf); **how did it turn out?** (= what happened?) was ist daraus geworden?; (cake etc) wie ist er etc geworden?; **as it turned out** wie sich herausstellte; **everything will turn out all right** es wird sich schon alles ergeben; **it turned out nice in the afternoon** (Brit) am Nachmittag wurde es noch schön **2** VT SEP **(a)** light ausmachen; gas abstellen **(b)** (= produce) produzieren; novel etc schreiben **(c)** (= expel) vertreiben (of aus), hinauswerfen (inf) (of aus);

tenant kündigen (+dat) **(d)** (Cook: = tip out) cake stürzen **(e)** (= empty) pockets (aus)leeren **(f)** (usu pass: = dress) **well turned-out** gut gekleidet

➤ **turn over 1** VI **(a)** (person, stomach) sich umdrehen; (car, plane etc) sich überschlagen; (boat) kentern; **he turned over on(to) his stomach** er drehte sich auf den Bauch **(b)** please turn over (with pages) bitte wenden **(c)** (Aut: engine) laufen **(d)** (TV, Rad) umschalten (to auf +acc) **2** VT SEP **(a)** umdrehen; patient, mattress, steak wenden; (= turn upside down) umkippen; page umblättern; soil umgraben; **to turn an idea over in one's mind** sich (dat) eine Idee durch den Kopf gehen lassen **(b)** (= hand over) übergeben (to dat) **(c)** (Comm) goods umsetzen; **to turn over £500 a week** einen Umsatz von £ 500 in der Woche haben

➤ **turn round** (esp Brit) **1** VI **(a)** (= face other way) sich umdrehen; (= go back) umkehren **(b)** (inf) **one day she'll just turn round and leave you** eines Tages wird sie dich ganz einfach verlassen **2** VI +PREP OBJ **we turned round the corner** wir bogen um die Ecke **3** VT SEP **(a)** head drehen; box umdrehen **(b)** (= process) job etc bearbeiten **(c)** ship abfertigen; goods fertig stellen **(d)** = **turn around** 1(a)

➤ **turn to** VI +PREP OBJ **(a)** to turn to sb/sth see **turn** 3(c) **(b)** after a short rest, they turned to their work again nach einer kurzen Pause machten sie sich wieder an die Arbeit

➤ **turn up 1** VI **(a)** (= arrive) erscheinen, auftauchen (inf); **I was afraid you wouldn't turn up** ich hatte Angst, du würdest nicht kommen **(b)** (= be found) sich (an)finden; (esp smaller things) zum Vorschein kommen **(c)** (= happen) **something is sure to turn up** irgendetwas passiert schon **(d)** (= point up) **he has a turned-up nose** er hat eine Stupsnase; **to turn up at the ends** sich an den Enden hochbiegen **2** VT SEP **(a)** collar hochklappen; hem umnähen; **to turn up one's nose at sth** (fig) die Nase über etw (acc) rümpfen **(b)** heat, gas, volume aufdrehen; radio lauter drehen; light heller machen; pressure erhöhen **(c)** (= find) finden, entdecken

turnaround ['tɜːnəraʊnd], **turnround** ['tɜːnraʊnd] N **(a)** (also **turnabout**: in position, fig: in opinion etc) Kehrtwendung f **(b)** (also ~ **time**) Bearbeitungszeit f; (= production time) Fertigstellungszeit f **(c)** (of situation, company) Umschwung m, Wende f

turncoat ['tɜːnkəʊt] N Überläufer(in) m(f)

turning ['tɜːnɪŋ] N (in road) Abzweigung f; **take the second ~ on the left** nimm die zweite Abfahrt links

turning point N Wendepunkt m

turnip ['tɜːnɪp] N Rübe f; (= swede) Steckrübe f

turn: turn-off N **(a)** Abzweigung f; (on motorway) Abfahrt f **(b)** (inf) **it was a real ~** das hat einem die Lust verdorben; **hairy armpits are the ultimate ~ for me** bei Haaren unter den Achseln hörts bei mir auf (inf); **turn-on** N (inf) **she finds his accent a real ~** sie fährt voll auf seinen Akzent ab (inf)

turnout ['tɜːnaʊt] N **(a)** (= attendance) Teilnahme f, Beteiligung f; **in spite of the rain there was a good ~** (for a match etc) trotz des Regens war das Spiel gut besucht; (in election) trotz des Regens war die Wahlbeteiligung gut or hoch **(b)** (Comm: = output) Produktion f

turnover ['tɜːnəʊvə'] N (= total business) Umsatz m; (Comm, Fin: of capital) Umlauf m; (Comm) (of stock) (Lager)umschlag m; (of staff) Fluktuation f

turn: turnpike N (US) gebührenpflichtige Autobahn; **turnround** N = **turnaround**; **turn signal** N (US Aut) Fahrtrichtungsanzeiger m; **turnstile** N Drehkreuz nt; **turntable** N Drehscheibe f; (on record player) Plattenteller m; **turn-up** N (Brit) **(a)** (on trousers) Aufschlag m **(b)** (inf) **that was a ~ for the books** das war eine (echte) Überraschung

turpentine ['tɜːpəntaɪn] N Terpentin(öl) nt

turquoise ['tɜːkwɔɪz] **1** N **(a)** (= gem) Türkis m **(b)** (= colour) Türkis nt **2** ADJ türkis(farben)

turret ['tʌrɪt] N (Archit) Mauer- or Eckturm m; (on tank) Turm m

turtle ['tɜːtl] N (Wasser)schildkröte f; (*US also*) (Land)schildkröte f

turtle: turtledove N (*lit, fig inf*) Turteltaube f; **turtleneck (pullover)** N Pullover m mit Stehkragen

turves [tɜːvz] PL *of* **turf**

Tuscany ['tʌskənɪ] N die Toskana

tusk [tʌsk] N (*of elephant*) Stoßzahn m

tussle ['tʌsl] **1** N (*lit, fig*) Gerangel nt **2** VI sich rangeln (*with sb for sth* mit jdm um etw)

tut [tʌt] INTERJ, VI *see* **tut-tut**

tutor ['tjuːtəʳ] **1** N (a) (= *private teacher*) Privatlehrer(in) m(f) (b) (*Brit Univ*) Tutor(in) m(f) **2** VT (*as private teacher*) privat unterrichten; (= *give extra lessons to*) Nachhilfe(unterricht) geben (+*dat*)

tutorial [tjuːˈtɔːrɪəl] **1** N (*Brit Univ*) Kolloquium nt **2** ADJ Tutoren-; **group** Seminargruppe f

tut-tut ['tʌt'tʌt] **1** INTERJ (*in disapproval*) na, na **2** VI **she ~ted in disapproval** na, na!, sagte sie missbilligend

tutu ['tuːtuː] N Tutu nt

tux [tʌks] (*inf*), **tuxedo** [tʌkˈsiːdəʊ] N (*esp US*) Smoking m

TV [tiːˈviː] N (*inf*) ABBR *of* **television** Fernsehen nt; (= *set*) Fernseher m (*inf*); **on TV** im Fernsehen; **TV channel** (*Brit*) or **station** (*US*) Fernsehsender m; **TV programme** (*Brit*) or **program** (*US*) Fernsehsendung f; *see also* **television**

twang [twæŋ] **1** N (a) (*of wire, guitar string*) Doing nt (b) (*of voice*) näselnder Tonfall m **2** VT zupfen; *guitar also* klimpern auf (+*dat*) (b) VI (*guitar, string etc*) einen scharfen Ton von sich geben; (*rubber band*) pitschen (*inf*)

tweak [twiːk] **1** VT (a) (= *pull gently*) kneifen; **to ~ sb's nose** (*lit*) jdn an der Nase ziehen; (*fig*) jdm eins auswischen (*inf*) (b) (*inf*) *rules, schedule, text* herumdoktern an (+*dat*) (*inf*) **2** N (a) (= *gentle pull*) **to give sth a ~** an etw (*dat*) (herum)zupfen; **to give sb's nose a ~** jdn an der Nase ziehen (b) (*inf: to rules, schedule, text*) **to give sth a ~** an etw (*dat*) herumdoktern (*inf*)

twee [twiː] ADJ (+ER) (*Brit inf*) niedlich, putzig (*inf*)

tweed [twiːd] **1** N (= *cloth*) Tweed m **2** ADJ Tweed-; **jacket** Tweedjacke f

tweet [twiːt] **1** N (*of birds*) Piepsen nt no pl; **~ ~** pieps, pieps **2** VI piepsen

tweezers ['twiːzəz] PL (*also* **pair of ~**) Pinzette f

twelfth [twelfθ] **1** ADJ zwölfte(r, s); **a ~ part** ein Zwölftel nt **2** N (*in series*) Zwölfte(r, s); (= *fraction*) Zwölftel nt; *see also* **sixth**

Twelfth Night N Dreikönige; (= *evening*) Dreikönigsabend m

twelve [twelv] **1** ADJ zwölf; **~ noon** zwölf Uhr (mittags) **2** N Zwölf f; *see also* **six**

twentieth ['twentɪɪθ] **1** ADJ zwanzigste(r, s); **a ~ part** ein Zwanzigstel nt **2** N (*in series*) Zwanzigste(r, s); (= *fraction*) Zwanzigstel nt; *see also* **sixth**

twenty ['twentɪ] **1** ADJ zwanzig **2** N Zwanzig f; (= *banknote*) Zwanziger m; *see also* **sixty**

twerp [twɜːp] N (*inf*) Einfaltspinsel m (*inf*)

twice [twaɪs] ADV zweimal; **~ as much/many** doppelt or zweimal so viel/so viele; **~ as much bread** doppelt so viel or zweimal so viel Brot; **~ as long as ...** doppelt or zweimal so lange wie ...; **~ 2 is 4** zweimal 2 ist 4; **~ weekly**, **~ a week** zweimal wöchentlich; **I'd think ~ before trusting him with it** ihm würde ich das nicht so ohne weiteres anvertrauen

twiddle ['twɪdl] **1** VT herumdrehen an (+*dat*); **to ~ one's thumbs** (*lit, fig*) Däumchen drehen **2** N **he gave the knob a ~** er drehte den Knopf herum

twig [twɪg] N Zweig m

twilight ['twaɪlaɪt] N (= *time*) Dämmerung f; (= *semi-darkness also*) Dämmer- or Zwielicht nt; **at ~** in der Dämmerung; **the ~ of his life, his ~ years** sein Lebensabend m

twin [twɪn] **1** N Zwilling m; **her ~** (= *sister*) ihre Zwillingsschwester; (= *brother*) ihr Zwillingsbruder m **2** ADJ ATTR (a) Zwillings-; (*fig*) genau gleiche(r, s); **~ boys/girls** Zwillingsjungen pl/-mädchen pl (b) (= *double*) **~ towers** Zwillingstürme pl; **~ peaks** Doppelgipfel pl **3** VT (*Brit*) **town** verschwistern; **Oxford was ~ned with Bonn** Oxford und Bonn wurden zu Partnerstädten/waren Partnerstädte

twin: twin beds PL zwei (gleiche) Einzelbetten pl; **twin brother** N Zwillingsbruder m

twine [twaɪn] **1** N Schnur f, Bindfaden m **2** VT winden **3** VI (*around* um +*acc*) sich winden; (*plants also*) sich ranken

twinge [twɪndʒ] N Zucken nt; **a ~ of pain** ein zuckender Schmerz; **a ~ of conscience** Gewissensbisse pl

twinkle ['twɪŋkl] **1** VI funkeln; (*eyes also*) blitzen; (*stars also*) glitzern **2** N (*of stars, lights*) Funkeln nt, Glitzern nt; **no, he said with a ~ (in his eye)** nein, sagte er augenzwinkernd

twinkling ['twɪŋklɪŋ] N **in the ~ of an eye** im Nu, im Handumdrehen

twin: twinset N (*Brit*) Twinset nt; **twin sister** N Zwillingsschwester f; **twin town** N (*Brit*) Partnerstadt f; **twin-track** ADJ *approach, process* zweigleisig; **twin-tub** (*washing machine*) N Waschmaschine f mit getrennter Schleuder

twirl [twɜːl] **1** VT (*herum*)wirbeln; *glass* drehen; *moustache* zwirbeln **2** VI wirbeln **3** N Wirbel m; (*in dance*) Drehung f; (*in writing*) Schnörkel m; **give us a ~** dreh dich doch mal

twist [twɪst] **1** N (a) (= *action*) **to give sth a ~** etw (herum)drehen; **to do the ~** (= *dance*) Twist tanzen (b) (= *bend*) Kurve f; (*fig: in story etc*) Wendung f; **by** or **in a cruel ~ of fate** durch eine grausame Laune des Schicksals (c) (= *coiled shape*) **salt in little ~s of paper** in kleine Papierstückchen eingewickeltes Salz (d) (*Brit inf*) **to go round the ~** verrückt werden; **she's driving me round the ~!** sie macht mich wahnsinnig! **2** VT (a) (= *wind, turn*) drehen; (= *coil*) wickeln (*into* zu +*dat*); **to ~ the top off a jar** den Deckel von einem Glas abdrehen; **to ~ sth (a)round sth** etw um etw (*acc*) wickeln (b) (= *bend, distort*) *rod, key* verbiegen; *part of body, meaning, words* verdrehen; **to ~ sth out of shape** etw verbiegen; **she had to ~ my arm to get me to do it** (*fig*) sie musste mich sehr überreden, bis ich es tat; **to ~ one's ankle** sich (*dat*) den Fuß vertreten; **his face was ~ed with pain** sein Gesicht war verzerrt vor Schmerz **3** VI (= *wind*) sich drehen; (*plant*) sich ranken; (*road, river*) sich schlängeln; **the kite strings have ~ed (a)round the pole** die Drachenschnüre haben sich um den Pfahl verwickelt

➤ **twist about** (*Brit*) or **around** VT SEP = **twist round 2**

➤ **twist off** **1** VI **the top twists off** der Deckel lässt sich abschrauben **2** VT SEP abdrehen; *lid* abschrauben

➤ **twist round** (*esp Brit*) **1** VI sich umdrehen; (*road etc*) eine Biegung machen **2** VT SEP herumdrehen

➤ **twist up** VT SEP *ropes, wires* verwickeln

twisted ['twɪstɪd] ADJ *wires, rope* (zusammen)gedreht; (= *bent*) verbogen; (= *tangled, fig pej*: = *warped*) verdreht; *ankle* verrenkt; (= *disfigured*) *limbs* verwachsen; **bitter and ~** verbittert und verwirrt

twister ['twɪstəʳ] N (*US inf*) Tornado m

twit [twɪt] N (*esp Brit inf*) Trottel m (*inf*)

twitch [twɪtʃ] **1** N (a) (= *tic*) Zucken nt; (= *individual spasm*) Zuckung f (b) (= *pull*) Ruck m (*of an* +*dat*) **2** VI (*face, muscles*) zucken **3** VT *tail, ears, nose* zucken mit (b) (= *pull*) zupfen

twitter ['twɪtəʳ] **1** VI (*lit, fig*) zwitschern **2** N (a) (*of birds*) Zwitschern nt (b) (*inf*) **to be all of a ~** ganz aufgeregt or aufgelöst sein

two [tuː] **1** ADJ zwei; **to cut sth in ~** etw in zwei Teile schneiden; **~ by ~**, **in ~s** zu zweien; **in ~s and threes** immer zwei oder drei (Leute) auf einmal; **to put ~ and ~ together** (*fig*) zwei und zwei zusammenzählen; **~'s company, three's a crowd** ein Dritter stört nur; **~ can play at that game** (*inf*) den Spieß kann man auch umdrehen; *see also* **six** **2** N Zwei f; **just the ~ of us/them** nur wir beide/die beiden

two: two-bit ADJ (*US inf*) mies (*inf*); **two-cycle** ADJ (*US*) = **two-stroke**; **two-dimensional** ADJ zweidimensional; (*fig:* = *superficial*) flach; **two-door** ADJ zweitürig; **two-edged** ADJ (*fig*) zweideutig; **a ~ sword** or **weapon** (*fig*) ein zweischneidiges Schwert; **two-faced** ADJ (*fig*) falsch; **twofold** **1** ADJ zweifach, doppelt; **a ~ increase** ein Anstieg um das Doppelte; **the advantages of this method are ~** diese Methode hat einen doppelten or zweifachen Vorteil **2** ADV **to increase** ~ um das Doppelte steigern; **two-handed** ADJ beidhändig; **two-legged** ADJ zweibeinig; **a ~ animal** ein Zweibeiner m; **two-percent milk** N (*US*) Halbfettmilch f; **two-piece** **1** ADJ zweiteilig **2** N (= *suit*) Zweiteiler m; **two-pin plug** N Stecker m mit zwei Kontakten; **two-seater** **1** ADJ zweisitzig **2** N (= *car, plane*) Zweisitzer m; **twosome** N (= *people*) Paar nt; **two-star** ADJ Zweisterne-; **two-storey**, (*US*) **two-story** ADJ zweistöckig; **two-stroke** (*Brit*) ADJ Zweitakt-;

two-time VT (*inf*) *boyfriend* betrügen; **two-timing** ADJ (*inf*) falsch; **two-tone** ADJ (*in colour*) zweifarbig; **two-way** ADJ *trade, relationship* wechselseitig; ~ **traffic** Gegenverkehr *m*; **two-way mirror** N Spion(spiegel) *m*; **two-way radio** N Funksprechgerät *nt*

tycoon [taɪˈkuːn] N Magnat(in) *m(f)*

type[1] [taɪp] N **(a)** (= *kind*) Art *f*; (*of produce, plant*) Sorte *f*; (*esp of people*: = *character*) Typ *m*; **different ~s of roses** verschiedene Rosensorten *pl*; **what ~ of car is it?** was für ein Auto(typ) ist das?; **Cheddar-~ cheese** eine Art Cheddar; **they're totally different ~s of person** sie sind vom Typ her völlig verschieden; **a man of this ~** ein Mann dieser Art *or* dieses Schlages; **that ~ of behaviour** (*Brit*) *or* **behavior** (*US*) ein solches Benehmen; **it's not my ~ of film** diese Art Film gefällt mir nicht; **he's not my ~** er ist nicht mein Typ
(b) (*inf*: = *man*) Typ *m*; **a strange ~** ein komischer Typ (*inf*)

type[2] 🯱 N (*Typ*) Type *f*; **large/small ~** große/kleine Schrift; **printed in italic ~** kursiv gedruckt 🯲 VT tippen, (mit der Maschine) schreiben 🯳 VI Maschine schreiben, tippen (*inf*)
➤ **type in** VT SEP eintippen; (*esp Comput*) eingeben; (*with typewriter*) mit Schreibmaschine ausfüllen
➤ **type out** VT SEP *letter etc* schreiben, tippen (*inf*)
➤ **type up** VT SEP auf der Maschine zusammenschreiben

type: **typecast** VT IRREG (*Theat*) (auf eine bestimmte Rolle) festlegen; **to be ~ as a villain** auf die Rolle des Schurken festgelegt werden/sein; **typeface** N Schrift *f*; **typescript** N Typoskript *nt* (*geh*); **typeset** VT setzen; **typewriter** N Schreibmaschine *f*; **typewritten** ADJ maschinegeschrieben

typhoid [ˈtaɪfɔɪd] N (*also ~ fever*) Typhus *m*
typhoon [taɪˈfuːn] N Taifun *m*
typhus [ˈtaɪfəs] N Fleckfieber *nt*
typical [ˈtɪpɪkəl] ADJ typisch (*of* für); **that's ~ of him** das ist typisch für ihn; **~ male!** typisch Mann!
typically [ˈtɪpɪkəlɪ] ADV typisch; **~, he insisted on getting there early** er wollte natürlich unbedingt früh hingehen, typisch
typing [ˈtaɪpɪŋ] N Tippen *nt* (*inf*); (*with typewriter*) Maschinenschreiben *nt*
typing: **typing error** N Tippfehler *m*; **typing pool** N Schreibzentrale *f*; **typing speed** N Schreibgeschwindigkeit *f*
typist [ˈtaɪpɪst] N (*professional*) Schreibkraft *f*, Stenotypist(in) *m(f)*
typographic(al) [taɪpəˈɡræfɪk(əl)] ADJ typografisch; **typographical error** Druckfehler *m*
typography [taɪˈpɒɡrəfɪ] N Typografie *f*
tyrannic(al) ADJ, **tyrannically** ADV [tɪˈrænɪk(əl), tɪˈrænɪkəlɪ] tyrannisch
tyrannize [ˈtɪrənaɪz] VT (*lit, fig*) tyrannisieren
tyranny [ˈtɪrənɪ] N (*lit, fig*) Tyrannei *f*
tyrant [ˈtaɪərənt] N (*lit, fig*) Tyrann(in) *m(f)*
tyre, (*US*) **tire** [taɪə] N Reifen *m*
tyre pressure N Reifendruck *m*
Tyrol [tɪˈroʊl] N **the ~** Tirol *nt*
Tyrrhenian Sea [tɪˈriːnɪənˈsiː] N Tyrrhenisches Meer
tzar N = tsar

Uu

U, u [juː] N U nt, u nt

U-bend [ˈjuːbend] N U-Bogen m

ubiquitous [juːˈbɪkwɪtəs] ADJ allgegenwärtig

udder [ˈʌdəʳ] N Euter nt

UFO [ˈjuːfəʊ] ABBR of **unidentified flying object** Ufo nt

Uganda [juːˈgændə] N Uganda nt

Ugandan [juːˈgændən] **1** ADJ ugandisch; **he is ~** er ist Ugander **2** N Ugander(in) m(f)

ugh [ɜːh] INTERJ i, igitt

ugliness [ˈʌglɪnɪs] N Hässlichkeit f; (of situation) Ekelhaftigkeit f

ugly [ˈʌglɪ] ADJ (+ER) person, face, rumour, scenes hässlich; (= unpleasant, nasty) übel; wound schlimm; situation, sky bedrohlich; **to cut up** or **grow** or **turn ~** (inf) gemein or fies (inf) werden

UHT ABBR of **ultra heat treated** ultrahocherhitzt; **~ milk** H-Milch f

UK ABBR of **United Kingdom** Vereinigtes Königreich

Ukraine [juːˈkreɪn] N **the ~** die Ukraine

Ukrainian [juːˈkreɪnɪən] **1** ADJ ukrainisch; **he is** ~ er ist Ukrainer **2** N Ukrainer(in) m(f)

ukulele, ukelele [juːkəˈleɪlɪ] N Ukulele f

ulcer [ˈʌlsəʳ] N (Med) Geschwür nt; (= stomach ~) Magengeschwür nt

ulcerated [ˈʌlsəreɪtɪd] ADJ geschwürig; wound vereitert; **an ~ stomach** ein Magengeschwür nt

Ulster [ˈʌlstəʳ] N Ulster nt

ulterior [ʌlˈtɪərɪəʳ] ADJ purpose verborgen; **~ motive** Hintergedanke m

ultimata [ʌltɪˈmeɪtə] PL of ultimatum

ultimate [ˈʌltɪmɪt] **1** ADJ (a) (= final) letzte(r, s); solution, decision endgültig; control oberste(r, s); authority höchste(r, s); **~ goal** or **aim** Endziel nt; **what is your ~ ambition in life?** was streben Sie letzten Endes im Leben an? **(b)** (= perfect) vollendet, perfekt; **the ~ insult** der Gipfel der Beleidigung; **the ~ sin** die schlimmste Sünde; **the ~ weapon** (fig) das letzte und äußerste Mittel **2** N Nonplusultra nt; **that is the ~ in comfort** das ist das Höchste an Komfort

ultimately [ˈʌltɪmɪtlɪ] ADV (= in the end) letztlich, letzten Endes; (= eventually) schließlich

ultimatum [ʌltɪˈmeɪtəm] N, pl **-s** or **ultimata** (Mil, fig) Ultimatum nt; **to deliver** or **issue an ~ to sb** jdm ein Ultimatum stellen

ultra- [ˈʌltrə-] PREF ultra-; **ultrahigh frequency** N Ultrahochfrequenz f; **ultramodern** ADJ ultra- or hypermodern; **ultrasound** N Ultraschall m; (= scan) Ultraschalluntersuchung f; **ultrasound picture** N Ultraschallbild nt or -aufnahme f; **ultraviolet** ADJ ultraviolett

ultra vires [ˈʌltrə-ˈvaɪriːz] (Jur) **1** ADJ die Befugnisse überschreitend attr **2** ADV über die Befugnisse hinaus

um [əm] INTERJ äh; (in decision, answering) hm

umbilical cord [ʌmˌbɪlɪkəlˈkɔːd] N Nabelschnur f

umbrella [ʌmˈbrelə] N (Regen)schirm m; (= sun ~) (Sonnen)schirm m

umbrella organization N Dachorganisation f

umpire [ˈʌmpaɪəʳ] **1** N Schiedsrichter(in) m(f) **2** VT (Sport) Schiedsrichter(in) sein bei **3** VI (in bei) Schiedsrichter(in) sein

umpteen [ˈʌmpˈtiːn] ADJ (inf) zig (inf), x (inf); **I've told you ~ times** ich habe dir zigmal or x-mal gesagt (inf)

umpteenth [ˈʌmpˈtiːnθ] ADJ (inf) x-te(r, s); **for the ~ time** zum x-ten Mal

UN ABBR of **United Nations** UNO f, UN pl

un- [ʌn-] PREF (before adj, adv) un-, nicht; (before n) Un-

unabated [ʌnəˈbeɪtɪd] ADJ unvermindert; **the storm continued ~** der Sturm ließ nicht nach

unable [ʌnˈeɪbl] ADJ PRED **to be ~ to do sth** etw nicht tun können

unabridged [ʌnəˈbrɪdʒd] ADJ ungekürzt

unacceptable [ʌnəkˈsɛptəbl] ADJ plans, terms unannehmbar; excuse, offer, behaviour nicht akzeptabel; standard, working conditions untragbar; **it's quite ~ that we should be expected to ...** es kann doch nicht von uns verlangt werden, dass ...; **it's quite ~ for young children to ...** es kann nicht zugelassen werden, dass kleine Kinder ...

unacceptably [ʌnəkˈsɛptɪblɪ] ADV untragbar; high unannehmbar; poor, bad unzumutbar

unaccompanied [ʌnəˈkʌmpənɪd] ADJ person, child, singing ohne Begleitung; bag, suitcase (= travelling separately) aufgegeben

unaccountable [ʌnəˈkaʊntəbl] ADJ (a) (= inexplicable) unerklärlich (b) (= not answerable) person niemandem unterstellt

unaccountably [ʌnəˈkaʊntəblɪ] ADV unerklärlicherweise; disappear auf unerklärliche Weise

unaccounted for [ʌnəˈkaʊntɪdˈfɔːʳ] ADJ ungeklärt; **£30 is still ~** es ist noch ungeklärt, wo die £ 30 geblieben sind; **three of the passengers are still ~** drei Passagiere werden noch vermisst

unaccustomed [ʌnəˈkʌstəmd] ADJ (a) (= unusual) ungewohnt (b) (of person: = unused) **to be ~ to sth** etw nicht gewohnt sein; **to be ~ to doing sth** nicht gewohnt sein, etw zu tun

unacquainted [ʌnəˈkweɪntɪd] ADJ PRED **to be ~ with poverty** die Armut nicht kennen; **to be ~ with the facts** mit den Tatsachen nicht vertraut sein

unadulterated [ʌnəˈdʌltəreɪtɪd] ADJ (a) unverfälscht; wine rein, ungepan(t)scht; (hum) whisky unverdünnt (b) (fig) nonsense schier; bliss ungetrübt

unadventurous [ʌnədˈventʃərəs] ADJ time, life wenig abenteuerlich, ereignislos; tastes bieder; style einfallslos; person wenig unternehmungslustig

unaffected [ʌnəˈfektɪd] ADJ (a) (= sincere) ungekünstelt, natürlich (b) (= not damaged) nicht angegriffen (also Med); (= not influenced) unbeeinflusst; (= not involved) nicht betroffen; (= unmoved) ungerührt; **he remained quite ~ by all the noise** der Lärm berührte or störte ihn überhaupt nicht

unafraid [ʌnəˈfreɪd] ADJ unerschrocken, furchtlos; **to be ~ of sb/sth** vor jdm/etw keine Angst haben

unaided [ʌnˈeɪdɪd] **1** ADV ohne fremde Hilfe **2** ADJ **~ by sb** ohne jds Hilfe; **~ by sth** ohne Zuhilfenahme von etw

unalike [ʌnəˈlaɪk] ADJ PRED unähnlich, ungleich

unallocated [ʌnˈæləkeɪtɪd] ADJ funds nicht zugewiesen or zugeteilt; **~ tickets** Karten im freien Verkauf

unalterable [ʌnˈɒltərəbl] ADJ decision, fact unabänderlich; laws unveränderlich

unaltered [ʌnˈɒltəd] ADJ unverändert

unambiguous, unambiguously [ʌnæmˈbɪgjʊəs, -lɪ] eindeutig, unzweideutig

unambitious [ʌnæmˈbɪʃəs] ADJ person, plan nicht ehrgeizig (genug); theatrical production anspruchslos

unamused [ʌnəˈmjuːzd] ADJ **she was ~ (by this)** sie fand es or das überhaupt nicht lustig

unanimous [juːˈnænɪməs] ADJ einmütig; decision also (Jur) einstimmig; **they were ~ in their condemnation of him** sie haben ihn einmütig verdammt; **by a ~ vote** einstimmig

unanimously [juːˈnænɪməslɪ] ADV einmütig; vote einstimmig

unannounced [ʌnəˈnaʊnst] ADJ, ADV unangemeldet

unanswered [ʌnˈɑːnsəd] ADJ unbeantwortet

unapologetic [ʌnəˌpɒləˈdʒetɪk] ADJ unverfroren, dreist; **he was so ~ about it** es schien ihm überhaupt nicht Leid zu tun

unappealing [ʌnəˈpiːlɪŋ] ADJ nicht ansprechend; person also unansehnlich; prospect, sight nicht verlockend

unappetizing [ʌnˈæpɪtaɪzɪŋ] ADJ unappetitlich; prospect, thought wenig verlockend

unappreciated [ʌnəˈpriːʃɪeɪtɪd] ADJ nicht geschätzt or gewürdigt; **she felt she was ~ by him** sie hatte den Eindruck, dass er sie nicht zu schätzen wusste

unappreciative [ʌnəˈpriːʃɪətɪv] ADJ undankbar; audience verständnislos

unapproachable [ʌnəˈprəʊtʃəbl] ADJ place unzugänglich; person also unnahbar

unarguably [ʌn'ɑːgjʊəblɪ] ADV unbestreitbar, zweifellos

unarmed [ʌn'ɑːmd] ADJ, ADV unbewaffnet

unashamed [ʌnə'ʃeɪmd] ADJ schamlos; *admirer, reactionary* unverhohlen; **to be ~ to do sth** keine Hemmungen haben, etw zu tun

unashamedly [ʌnə'ʃeɪmɪdlɪ] ADV unverschämt; *say, admit* ohne Scham; *romantic, in favour of, partisan* unverhohlen

unasked-for [ʌn'ɑːsktfɔːʳ] ADJ ungewünscht, unwillkommen

unassisted [ʌnə'sɪstɪd] ADJ, ADV = **unaided**

unassuming [ʌnə'sjuːmɪŋ] ADJ bescheiden

unattached [ʌnə'tætʃt] ADJ **(a)** (= *not fastened*) unbefestigt **(b)** (*emotionally*) ungebunden

unattainable [ʌnə'teɪnəbl] ADJ unerreichbar

unattended [ʌnə'tendɪd] ADJ *children* unbeaufsichtigt; *car park, car, luggage* unbewacht; **to leave sth ~** *car, luggage* etw unbewacht lassen; *shop* etw unbeaufsichtigt lassen; **to leave sb/sth ~ (to)** (= *not deal with*) *guests, problem* sich nicht um jdn/etw kümmern; *patient* jdn nicht behandeln; *customer* jdn nicht bedienen; **to be** *or* **go ~ to** (*wound, injury*) nicht behandelt werden

unattractive [ʌnə'træktɪv] ADJ *sight, place* unschön, wenig reizvoll; *offer, woman* unattraktiv; *character* unsympathisch

unauthorized [ʌn'ɔːθəraɪzd] ADJ unbefugt, unberechtigt

unavailable [ʌnə'veɪləbl] ADJ nicht erhältlich; *person* nicht zu erreichen *pred*; **the minister was ~ for comment** der Minister lehnte eine Stellungnahme ab

unavoidable [ʌnə'vɔɪdəbl] ADJ unvermeidlich; *conclusion, consequence* zwangsläufig

unavoidably [ʌnə'vɔɪdəblɪ] ADV notgedrungen; **to be ~ detained** verhindert sein

unaware [ʌnə'weəʳ] ADJ PRED **to be ~ of sth** sich (*dat*) einer Sache (*gen*) nicht bewusst sein; **I was ~ of his presence** ich hatte ihn nicht bemerkt, dass er da war; **I was ~ that there was a meeting going on** ich wusste nicht, dass da gerade eine Besprechung stattfand

unawares [ʌnə'weəz] ADV (= *by surprise*) unerwartet; (= *without knowing*) unwissentlich; **to catch** *or* **take sb ~** jdn überraschen

unbalance [ʌn'bæləns] VT (*physically, mentally*) aus dem Gleichgewicht bringen

unbalanced [ʌn'bælənst] ADJ **(a)** *painting, diet, economy* unausgewogen; *report* einseitig **(b)** *mind* unstet; (*also* **mentally ~** = *slightly crazy*) nicht ganz normal **(c)** *account, budget* nicht ausgeglichen

unbearable ADJ, **unbearably** ADV [ʌn'beərəbl, -lɪ] unerträglich

unbeatable [ʌn'biːtəbl] ADJ unschlagbar; *army also* unbesiegbar

unbeaten [ʌn'biːtn] ADJ ungeschlagen; *army also* unbesiegt; *record* ungebrochen

unbecoming [ʌnbɪ'kʌmɪŋ] ADJ *behaviour, language etc* unschicklich, unziemlich (*geh*); *clothes* unvorteilhaft

unbeknown(st) [ʌnbɪ'nəʊn(st)] ADV ohne dass es jemand wusste; **~ to me** ohne mein Wissen; **~ to his father** ohne Wissen seines Vaters

unbelievable [ʌnbɪ'liːvəbl] ADJ unglaublich; **he has so much talent it's ~** es ist unglaublich, wie begabt er ist

unbelievably [ʌnbɪ'liːvəblɪ] ADV unglaublich; *good, pretty etc also* sagenhaft (*inf*)

unbeliever [ʌnbɪ'liːvəʳ] N Ungläubige(r) *mf*

unbending [ʌn'bendɪŋ] ADJ *person* unnachgiebig; *determination* unbeugsam; *commitment* unerschütterlich

unbias(s)ed [ʌn'baɪəst] ADJ unvoreingenommen; *opinion, report also* unparteiisch

unbleached [ʌn'bliːtʃt] ADJ ungebleicht

unblemished [ʌn'blemɪʃt] ADJ (*lit, fig*) makellos; *reputation also* unbescholten; *skin also* tadellos

unblinkingly [ʌn'blɪŋkɪŋlɪ] ADV *stare* starr, stoisch

unblock [ʌn'blɒk] VT freimachen; *sink, pipe* die Verstopfung in (+*dat*) beseitigen; *chimney* ausputzen

unbolt [ʌn'bəʊlt] VT aufriegeln; **he left the door ~ed** er verriegelte die Tür nicht

unborn [ʌn'bɔːn] ADJ ungeboren; **generations yet ~** kommende Generationen

unbound [ʌn'baʊnd] ADJ *hair* gelöst; *book* ungebunden

unbounded [ʌn'baʊndɪd] ADJ grenzenlos; (*fig also*) unermesslich

unbowed [ʌn'baʊd] ADJ (*fig*) ungebrochen; *pride* ungebeugt

unbreakable [ʌn'breɪkəbl] ADJ *glass, toy* unzerbrechlich; *record* nicht zu brechen *pred*; *rule, law* unumstößlich

unbridgeable [ʌn'brɪdʒəbl] ADJ unüberbrückbar

unbridled [ʌn'braɪdld] ADJ *lust, passion* ungezügelt; *tongue* lose; *capitalism* ungehemmt

unbroken [ʌn'brəʊkən] ADJ **(a)** (= *intact*) unbeschädigt; *promise* nicht gebrochen **(b)** (= *continuous*) ununterbrochen; **an ~ night's sleep** eine ungestörte Nacht **(c)** (= *unbeaten*) *record* ungebrochen **(d)** *pride* ungebeugt; **his spirit remained ~** er war ungebrochen

unbuckle [ʌn'bʌkl] VT aufschnallen

unbundle [ʌn'bʌndl] VT **(a)** (*US*: = *itemize*) aufschlüsseln **(b)** (*Comm*: = *asset-strip*) finanziell gefährdete Firmen aufkaufen und anschließend deren Vermögenswerte veräußern

unbundling [ʌn'bʌndlɪŋ] N (*Comm*) Aufkauf finanziell gefährdeter Firmen und anschließende Veräußerung ihrer Vermögenswerte

unburden [ʌn'bɜːdn] VT (*fig*) *conscience* erleichtern; **to ~ oneself/one's heart/one's soul to sb** jdm sein Herz ausschütten

unbusinesslike [ʌn'bɪznɪslaɪk] ADJ wenig geschäftsmäßig; **the firm handled the transaction in such an ~ way** die Firma hat die Transaktion so ungeschäftsmäßig abgewickelt

unbutton [ʌn'bʌtn] VT aufknöpfen

uncalled-for [ʌn'kɔːldfɔːʳ] ADJ (= *unjustified*) ungerechtfertigt; (= *unnecessary*) unnötig; (= *rude*) deplatziert

uncannily [ʌn'kænɪlɪ] ADV unheimlich; **to look ~ like sb/sth** jdm/einer Sache auf unheimliche Weise ähnlich sehen

uncanny [ʌn'kænɪ] ADJ unheimlich; **to bear an ~ resemblance to sb** jdm auf unheimliche Weise ähnlich sehen

uncapped [ʌn'kæpt] ADJ (*Brit Sport*) **~ player** Spieler, der/ Spielerin, die noch nie in der Nationalmannschaft gespielt hat

uncared-for [ʌn'keədfɔːʳ] ADJ *garden, hands* ungepflegt; *child* vernachlässigt

uncaring [ʌn'keərɪŋ] ADJ gleichgültig, teilnahmslos; *parents* lieblos

unceasing ADJ, **unceasingly** ADV [ʌn'siːsɪŋ, -lɪ] unaufhörlich

uncensored [ʌn'sensəd] ADJ unzensiert

unceremonious [ʌnserɪ'məʊnɪəs] ADJ *dismissal, manner* brüsk, barsch; *reply* unverblümt; *departure* überstürzt; *haste* unfein

unceremoniously [ʌnserɪ'məʊnɪəslɪ] ADV (= *abruptly, rudely*) ohne Umschweife, kurzerhand

uncertain [ʌn'sɜːtn] ADJ **(a)** (= *unsure, unsteady*) unsicher; **to be ~ whether ...** sich (*dat*) nicht sicher sein, ob ...; **to be ~ of** *or* **about sth** sich (*dat*) einer Sache (*gen*) nicht sicher sein **(b)** (= *unknown*) *date, result* ungewiss; *origins* unbestimmt **(c)** (= *unreliable*) *weather, prices* unbeständig; *temper* unberechenbar **(d)** (= *unclear*) vage; **in no ~ terms** klar und deutlich

uncertainly [ʌn'sɜːtnlɪ] ADV *say* unbestimmt; *look, move* unsicher; *smile* zögernd

uncertainty [ʌn'sɜːtntɪ] N (= *state*) Ungewissheit *f*; (= *indefiniteness*) Unbestimmtheit *f*; (= *doubt*) Zweifel *m*, Unsicherheit *f*; **there is still some ~ as to whether ...** es besteht noch Ungewissheit, ob ...

unchallenged [ʌn'tʃælɪndʒd] ADJ unangefochten; **the record was** *or* **went ~ for several years** der Rekord wurde jahrelang nicht überboten

unchanged [ʌn'tʃeɪndʒd] ADJ unverändert

unchanging [ʌn'tʃeɪndʒɪŋ] ADJ unveränderlich

uncharacteristic [ʌnkærəktə'rɪstɪk] ADJ uncharakteristisch, untypisch (*of* für); **with ~ modesty** mit (für ihn/sie *etc*) völlig untypischer Bescheidenheit

uncharacteristically [ʌnkærəktə'rɪstɪklɪ] ADV auf uncharakteristische *or* untypische Weise

uncharitable [ʌn'tʃærɪtəbl] ADJ *remark* unfreundlich; *view, person* herzlos; *attitude* hartherzig

uncharted [ʌn'tʃɑːtɪd] ADJ nicht verzeichnet *or* eingezeichnet; **to enter ~ waters** *or* **territory** (*fig*) sich in unbekanntes Terrain begeben

unchecked [ʌnˈtʃekt] ADJ **(a)** (= *unrestrained*) ungehemmt; **to go ~** (*abuse*) geduldet werden; (*advance*) nicht gehindert werden; (*inflation*) nicht eingedämmt werden; **if left ~, the fungus can spread extensively** wenn der Pilzbefall nicht unter Kontrolle gebracht wird, kann er sich weit ausbreiten **(b)** (= *not verified*) ungeprüft

unchristian [ʌnˈkrɪstjən] ADJ unchristlich

uncivil [ʌnˈsɪvɪl] ADJ unhöflich

uncivilized [ʌnˈsɪvɪlaɪzd] ADJ unzivilisiert; (*inf*) *habit* barbarisch

unclaimed [ʌnˈkleɪmd] ADJ *prize* nicht abgeholt; *property also* herrenlos; *right, inheritance* nicht geltend gemacht; *social security etc* nicht beansprucht; **to go ~** (*prize*) nicht abgeholt werden

unclasp [ʌnˈklɑːsp] VT *necklace* lösen; *hands* voneinander lösen; **he ~ed her hand** er löste ihre Hand

unclassified [ʌnˈklæsɪfaɪd] ADJ **(a)** (= *not arranged*) nicht klassifiziert *or* eingeordnet **(b)** (= *not secret*) nicht geheim

unclassified road N (*Brit*) *schlecht ausgebaute Landstraße*

uncle [ˈʌŋkl] N Onkel *m*; **Uncle Sam** Uncle *or* Onkel Sam; **to say** *or* **cry ~** (*US*) aufgeben

unclean [ʌnˈkliːn] ADJ unsauber (*also Bibl*); (*fig:* = *contaminated*) schmutzig

unclear [ʌnˈklɪəʳ] ADJ unklar; **to be ~ about sth** sich (*dat*) über etw (*acc*) im Unklaren *or* nicht im Klaren sein

unclog [ʌnˈklɒg] VT die Verstopfung in (+*dat*) beseitigen

unclothed [ʌnˈkləʊðd] ADJ unbekleidet

uncluttered [ʌnˈklʌtəd] ADJ schlicht, einfach; *desk, room* nicht überfüllt *or* überladen

uncoil [ʌnˈkɔɪl] **1** VT abwickeln **2** VIR (*snake*) sich langsam strecken; (*person*) sich ausstrecken; (*wire etc*) sich abwickeln

uncollected [ʌnkəˈlektd] ADJ *rubbish* nicht abgeholt; *tax* nicht eingezogen

uncombed [ʌnˈkəʊmd] ADJ ungekämmt

uncomfortable [ʌnˈkʌmfətəbl] ADJ **(a)** unbequem; **it feels ~** es ist unbequem **(b)** (= *uneasy*) *feeling* ungut; *silence* (= *awkward*) peinlich; (= *nerve-racking*) beklemmend; **to feel ~** sich unbehaglich fühlen; **I felt ~ about it/about doing it** ich hatte ein ungutes Gefühl dabei, mir war ich nicht wohl dabei; **they make me feel ~** in ihrer Gegenwart fühle ich mich unbehaglich; **to put sb in an ~ position** jdn in eine heikle Lage bringen **(c)** (= *unpleasant*) *fact, time, position* unerfreulich

uncomfortably [ʌnˈkʌmfətəblɪ] ADV **(a)** unbequem **(b)** (= *uneasily*) unbehaglich, unruhig **(c)** (= *unpleasantly*) unangenehm

uncommitted [ʌnkəˈmɪtɪd] ADJ nicht engagiert; *party* neutral; **we want to remain ~ till we get a full report** wir wollen uns nicht festlegen, bevor wir einen ausführlichen Bericht haben

uncommon [ʌnˈkɒmən] ADJ **(a)** (= *unusual*) ungewöhnlich; **it is not ~ for her to be late** es ist nichts Ungewöhnliches, dass sie zu spät kommt; **a not ~ problem** ein nicht ganz ungewöhnliches Problem **(b)** (= *outstanding*) außergewöhnlich

uncommonly [ʌnˈkɒmənlɪ] ADV **(a)** (= *unusually*) ungewöhnlich **(b)** (= *exceptionally*) außergewöhnlich

uncommunicative [ʌnkəˈmjuːnɪkətɪv] ADJ (*by nature*) verschlossen; (*temporarily*) schweigsam

uncompetitive [ʌnkəmˈpetɪtɪv] ADJ *industry* nicht wettbewerbsfähig; *price* nicht konkurrenzfähig

uncomplaining [ʌnkəmˈpleɪnɪŋ] ADJ duldsam

uncomplicated [ʌnˈkɒmplɪkeɪtɪd] ADJ unkompliziert

uncomplimentary [ʌnkɒmplɪˈmentərɪ] ADJ unschmeichelhaft; **to be ~ about sb/sth** sich nicht sehr schmeichelhaft über jdn/etw äußern

uncomprehending ADJ, **uncomprehendingly** ADV [ʌnkɒmprɪˈhendɪŋ, -lɪ] verständnislos

uncompromising [ʌnˈkɒmprəmaɪzɪŋ] ADJ kompromisslos; *dedication, honesty* rückhaltlos; *commitment* hundertprozentig

uncompromisingly [ʌnˈkɒmprəmaɪzɪŋlɪ] ADV unerbittlich

unconcealed [ʌnkənˈsiːld] ADJ *delight etc* offen, unverhüllt; *distaste, anger etc also* unverhohlen

unconcern [ʌnkənˈsɜːn] N (= *lack of worry*) Unbekümmertheit *f*; (= *indifference*) Gleichgültigkeit *f*

unconcerned [ʌnkənˈsɜːnd] ADJ (= *unworried*) unbekümmert; (= *indifferent*) gleichgültig; **to be ~ about sth** sich nicht um etw kümmern; **to be ~ by sth, to be ~ at sth** von etw unberührt sein

unconditional [ʌnkənˈdɪʃənl] ADJ vorbehaltlos; *surrender, love* bedingungslos; *support* uneingeschränkt

unconfirmed [ʌnkənˈfɜːmd] ADJ unbestätigt

unconnected [ʌnkəˈnektɪd] ADJ (= *unrelated*) nicht miteinander in Beziehung stehend *attr; fact* losgelöst; *several facts* unzusammenhängend; **the two events are ~** es besteht keine Beziehung zwischen den beiden Ereignissen; **to be ~ with** *or* **to sth** zu *or* mit etw nicht in Beziehung stehen

unconquered [ʌnˈkɒŋkəd] ADJ *army* unbesiegt; *mountain* unbezwungen; *spirit* ungebrochen

unconscious [ʌnˈkɒnʃəs] **1** ADJ **(a)** (*Med*) bewusstlos; **the blow knocked him ~** durch den Schlag wurde er bewusstlos **(b)** PRED (= *unaware*) **to be ~ of sth** sich (*dat*) einer Sache (*gen*) nicht bewusst sein; **I was ~ of the fact that …** ich war mir *or* es war mir nicht bewusst, dass … **(c)** (= *unintentional*) *insult, allusion etc* unbeabsichtigt **(d)** (*Psych*) unbewusst; **at** *or* **on an ~ level** auf der Ebene des Unbewussten **2** N (*Psych*) **the ~** das Unbewusste

unconsciously [ʌnˈkɒnʃəslɪ] ADV unbewusst

unconsciousness [ʌnˈkɒnʃəsnɪs] N (*Med*) Bewusstlosigkeit *f*

unconsidered [ʌnkənˈsɪdəd] ADJ (= *rash*) *action etc* unüberlegt

unconstitutional ADJ, **unconstitutionally** ADV [ʌnkɒnstɪˈtjuːʃnəl, -lɪ] verfassungswidrig

unconstructive [ʌnkənˈstrʌktɪv] ADJ nicht konstruktiv

uncontaminated [ʌnkənˈtæmɪneɪtɪd] ADJ nicht verseucht; *people* (*fig*) unverdorben

uncontested [ʌnkənˈtestɪd] ADJ unbestritten; *divorce* unangefochten; *election, seat* ohne Gegenkandidat

uncontrollable [ʌnkənˈtrəʊləbl] ADJ unkontrollierbar; *child* nicht zu bändigend *attr*, nicht zu bändigen *pred*; *car, horse, dog* nicht unter Kontrolle zu bringend *attr*, nicht unter Kontrolle zu bringen *pred*; *rage, laughter* unbezähmbar; *desire, urge* unwiderstehlich

uncontrollably [ʌnkənˈtrəʊləblɪ] ADV unkontrollierbar; *weep* hemmungslos; *laugh* unkontrolliert

uncontrolled [ʌnkənˈtrəʊld] ADJ ungehindert; *behaviour* undiszipliniert

uncontroversial [ʌnkɒntrəˈvɜːʃəl] ADJ unverfänglich

unconventional [ʌnkənˈvenʃənl] ADJ unkonventionell; *weapons* nicht konventionell

unconventionally [ʌnkənˈvenʃənəlɪ] ADV unkonventionell

unconvinced [ʌnkənˈvɪnst] ADJ nicht überzeugt (*of* von); *look* wenig überzeugt; **his arguments leave me ~** seine Argumente überzeugen mich nicht; **I remain ~** ich bin noch immer nicht überzeugt

unconvincing [ʌnkənˈvɪnsɪŋ] ADJ nicht überzeugend; **rather ~** wenig überzeugend

unconvincingly [ʌnkənˈvɪnsɪŋlɪ] ADV wenig überzeugend

uncooked [ʌnˈkʊkt] ADJ ungekocht, roh

uncool [ʌnˈkuːl] ADJ (*inf*) nicht (sehr) cool (*sl*)

uncooperative [ʌnkəʊˈɒpərətɪv] ADJ *attitude* stur, wenig entgegenkommend; *witness, colleague* wenig hilfreich; **if the prisoner is still ~** wenn sich der Gefangene weiterhin weigert, mit uns zusammenzuarbeiten; **why are you being so ~?** warum helfen Sie denn nicht mit?

uncoordinated [ʌnkəʊˈɔːdɪneɪtɪd] ADJ unkoordiniert

uncork [ʌnˈkɔːk] VT entkorken

uncorroborated [ʌnkəˈrɒbəreɪtɪd] ADJ unbestätigt; *evidence* nicht bekräftigt

uncorrupted [ʌnkəˈrʌptɪd] ADJ nicht korrumpiert; *person also* rechtschaffen

uncouple [ʌnˈkʌpl] VT abkoppeln

uncouth [ʌnˈkuːθ] ADJ *person* ungehobelt; *behaviour* unflätig

uncover [ʌnˈkʌvəʳ] VT (*lit, fig*) aufdecken; *ancient ruins etc* zum Vorschein bringen

uncritical ADJ, **uncritically** ADV [ʌnˈkrɪtɪkəl, -lɪ] unkritisch (*of, about* in Bezug auf +*acc*)

uncross [ʌnˈkrɒs] VT **he ~ed his legs** er nahm das Bein vom Knie; **she ~ed her arms** sie löste ihre verschränkten Arme

uncrowded [ʌn'kraʊdɪd] ADJ nicht überlaufen

uncrowned [ʌn'kraʊnd] ADJ (lit, fig) ungekrönt

uncultivated [ʌn'kʌltɪveɪtɪd] ADJ unkultiviert; land also unbebaut

uncurl [ʌn'kɜːl] **1** VT auseinander rollen; **to ~ oneself** sich strecken **2** VI glatt werden; (cat, snake) sich langsam strecken

uncut [ʌn'kʌt] ADJ (a) ungeschnitten; stone unbehauen; **~ diamond** Rohdiamant m (b) (= unabridged) ungekürzt

undamaged [ʌn'dæmɪdʒd] ADJ unbeschädigt; (fig) reputation makellos

undaunted [ʌn'dɔːntɪd] ADJ (= not discouraged) unverzagt; (= fearless) unerschrocken; **~ by these threats ...** nicht eingeschüchtert von diesen Drohungen ...

undead [ʌn'ded] N **the ~** pl die Untoten pl

undecided [ʌndɪ'saɪdɪd] ADJ person unentschlossen; **he is ~ as to whether he should go or not** er ist (sich) noch unschlüssig, ob er gehen soll oder nicht; **to be ~ about sth** sich (dat) über etw (acc) im Unklaren sein

undeclared [ʌndɪ'kleəd] ADJ love, candidate unerklärt; interest uneingestanden; **~ income** nicht angegebenes Einkommen

undefeated [ʌndɪ'fiːtɪd] ADJ army, team unbesiegt; champion, record ungeschlagen; spirit ungebrochen

undefended [ʌndɪ'fendɪd] ADJ unverteidigt

undefined [ʌndɪ'faɪnd] ADJ nicht definiert; (= vague) undefinierbar

undelete ['ʌndɪ'liːt] VT (Comput) **to ~ sth** das Löschen von etw rückgängig machen

undelivered ['ʌndɪ'lɪvəd] ADJ mail unzustellbar

undemanding [ʌndɪ'mɑːndɪŋ] ADJ anspruchslos; task wenig fordernd

undemocratic ADJ, **undemocratically** ADV [ʌndemə'krætɪk, -əlɪ] undemokratisch

undemonstrative [ʌndɪ'mɒnstrətɪv] ADJ reserviert, zurückhaltend

undeniable [ʌndɪ'naɪəbl] ADJ unbestreitbar

undeniably [ʌndɪ'naɪəblɪ] ADV zweifellos; successful, proud unbestreitbar

under ['ʌndə'] **1** PREP (a) unter (+dat); (with motion) unter (+acc); **~ it** darunter; **to come out from ~ the bed** unter dem Bett hervorkommen; **it's ~ there** es ist da drunter (inf); **it took ~ an hour** es dauerte weniger als eine Stunde; **there were ~ 50 of them** es waren weniger als 50, es waren unter 50; **he had 50 men ~ him** er hatte 50 Männer unter sich; **to study ~ sb** bei jdm studieren; **he died ~ the anaesthetic** (Brit) or **anesthetic** (US) er starb in der Narkose; **~ construction** im Bau; **the matter ~ discussion** der Diskussionsgegenstand; **to be ~ the doctor** in (ärztlicher) Behandlung sein; **you'll find the number ~ "garages"** Sie finden die Nummer unter „Werkstätten"; **~ sentence of death** zum Tode verurteilt; **~ an assumed name** unter falschem Namen; **the house is ~ threat of demolition** das Haus ist vom Abbruch bedroht (b) (= according to) nach (+dat), gemäß (+dat), laut (+dat); **~ the terms of the contract** nach or gemäß den Vertragsbedingungen

2 ADV (a) (= beneath) unten; (= unconscious) bewusstlos; **he came to the fence and crawled ~** er kam zum Zaun und kroch darunter durch; **to go ~** untergehen; **to get out from ~** (fig inf) wieder Licht sehen (inf) (b) (= less) darunter

under- PREF (a) (in rank) Unter-; **for the ~-twelves/-eighteens/ -forties** für Kinder unter zwölf/Jugendliche unter achtzehn/ Leute unter vierzig (b) (= insufficiently) zu wenig, ungenügend

under: underachiever N **Johnny is an ~** Johnnys Leistungen bleiben hinter den Erwartungen zurück; **underage** ADJ ATTR minderjährig; **underarm** **1** ADJ (a) Unterarm- (b) throw von unten **2** ADV von unten; **underbid** pret, ptp underbid VT (Comm) unterbieten; **underbrush** N = undergrowth; **undercapitalized** ADJ (Fin) unterkapitalisiert; **undercarriage** N (Aviat) Fahrwerk nt; **undercharge** **1** VI zu wenig berechnen **2** VT **he ~d me by 50p** er berechnete mir 50 Pence zu wenig; **underclass** N Unterklasse f; **underclothes** PL, **underclothing** N Unterwäsche f; **undercoat** N (= paint) Grundierfarbe f; (= coat) Grundierung f; **undercook** VT nicht durchgaren; **undercover** **1** ADJ geheim; **~ agent** Geheimagent(in) m(f)

2 ADV **to work ~** undercover arbeiten; (with police) als verdeckter Ermittler/verdeckte Ermittlerin arbeiten; **undercurrent** N (lit, fig) Unterströmung f; (in speech, attitude) Unterton m; **undercut** pret, ptp undercut VT competitor, fare (im Preis) unterbieten; **underdeveloped** ADJ unterentwickelt; **underdog** N (in society) Benachteiligte(r) mf, Underdog m; (in game also) sicherer Verlierer, sichere Verliererin; **underdone** ADJ nicht gar; (deliberately) steak nicht durchgebraten; **underemployed** ADJ nicht ausgelastet; person also unterbeschäftigt; **underestimate** [ʌndər'estɪmeɪt] **1** VT unterschätzen **2** [ʌndər'estɪmɪt] N Unterschätzung f; **underestimation** N Unterschätzung f; **underfed** ADJ unterernährt; **underfinanced** ADJ unterfinanziert; **underfoot** ADV am Boden; **it is wet ~** der Boden ist nass; **to trample sb/ sth ~** (lit, fig) auf jdm/etw herumtrampeln; **underfunded** ADJ unterfinanziert; **underfunding** N Unterfinanzierung f; **undergo** pret underwent, ptp undergone VT suffering, process durchmachen; training mitmachen; change also erleben; test, treatment, operation sich unterziehen (+dat); (machine) test unterzogen werden (+dat); **to ~ repairs** in Reparatur sein; **undergrad** (inf), **undergraduate** **1** N Student(in) m(f) **2** ATTR class, course für nichtgraduierte Studenten

underground ['ʌndəɡraʊnd] **1** ADJ (a) explosion, lake, passage unterirdisch; **~ cable** Erdkabel nt (b) (fig: = secret) Untergrund-; **~ movement** Untergrundbewegung f (c) (= alternative) Underground- **2** ADV (a) unterirdisch; (Min) unter Tage; **3 m ~** 3 m unter der Erde (b) (fig) **to go ~** untertauchen **3** N (a) (Brit Rail) U-Bahn f, Untergrundbahn f (b) (= movement) Untergrundbewegung f; (= subculture) Underground m

underground station N (Brit Rail) U-Bahnhof m

under: undergrowth N Gestrüpp nt; (under trees) Unterholz nt; **underhand, underhanded** ADJ hinterhältig; **underinsurance** N Unterversicherung f; **underinsure** VT unterversichern; **underinvestment** N mangelnde or unzureichende Investitionen pl; **industry is suffering from ~** die Industrie leidet unter Investitionsmangel; **underlie** pret underlay, ptp underlain VT (fig: = be basis for or cause of) zugrunde liegen (+dat); **underline** VT (lit, fig) unterstreichen; **underlying** ADJ (a) soil, rocks tiefer liegend (b) cause eigentlich; (= deeper) tiefer; problem, message zugrunde liegend; tension unterschwellig; **the ~ cause of all this** was all dem zugrunde liegt (c) (Econ) **~ rate of inflation** Basis-Inflationsrate f; **undermanned** ADJ unterbesetzt; **undermentioned** ADJ unten genannt; **undermine** VT (a) (= weaken) schwächen; (sea) cliffs unterhöhlen (b) (fig: = weaken) unterminieren; health angreifen

underneath [ʌndə'niːθ] **1** PREP (place) unter (+dat); (direction) unter (+acc); **~ it** darunter; **the cat came out from ~ the table** die Katze kam unter dem Tisch hervor **2** ADV darunter; **the ones ~** die darunter **3** N Unterseite f

under: undernourished ADJ unterernährt; **underpaid** ADJ unterbezahlt; **underpants** PL Unterhose(n) f(pl); **a pair of ~** eine Unterhose; **underpass** N Unterführung f; **underpay** pret, ptp underpaid VT unterbezahlen; **underpin** VT (fig) argument, claim untermauern; economy, market etc (ab)stützen; **underplay** VT significance, role herunterspielen; **underpopulated** ADJ unterbevölkert; **underprice** VT zu billig or unter Preis anbieten; **underprivileged** **1** ADJ unterprivilegiert **2** N **the ~** pl die Unterprivilegierten pl; **underqualified** ADJ unterqualifiziert; **underrate** VT (= underestimate) unterschätzen; (= undervalue) unterbewerten; **underrated** ADJ unterschätzt; **underscore** VT = underline; **undersea** ADJ Unterwasser-; **undersell** pret, ptp undersold VT (a) (= sell at lower price) unter Preis verkaufen, verschleudern (b) (= not publicize) nicht gut verkaufen; **he tends to ~ himself** er kann sich normalerweise nicht verkaufen; **undershirt** N (US) Unterhemd nt; **undershorts** PL (US) Unterhose(n) f(pl); **underside** N Unterseite f; **undersigned** **1** ADJ (form) unterzeichnet **2** N **we the ~** wir, die Unterzeichneten; **undersized** ADJ klein; (= less than proper size) zu klein; **underskirt** N Unterrock m; **undersold** PRET, PTP of undersell; **underspend** vb: pret, ptp underspent **1** VI zu wenig ausgeben (on für) **2** N zu geringe Ausgaben pl; **understaffed** ADJ office unterbesetzt; prison, hospital mit zu wenig Personal; **we are very ~ at the moment** wir haben momentan zu wenig Leute

understand [ˌʌndəˈstænd], *pret, ptp* **understood** ◼ VT
(a) (= *comprehend*) verstehen; *action, event, person, difficulty also* begreifen; **I don't ~ Russian** ich verstehe *or* kann kein Russisch; **I can't ~ his agreeing to do it** ich kann nicht verstehen, warum er sich dazu bereit erklärt hat; **what do you ~ by "pragmatism"?** was verstehen Sie unter „Pragmatismus"?
(b) (= *believe*) **I ~ that you are going to Australia** ich höre, Sie gehen nach Australien; **I ~ that you've already met her** Sie haben sich, soviel ich weiß, schon kennen gelernt; **I understood (that) he was abroad** ich dachte, er sei im Ausland; **am I/are we to ~ that ...?** soll das etwa heißen, dass ...?; **as I ~ it,** ... soweit ich weiß, ...; **I was given to ~ that ...** man hat mir bedeutet, dass ...; **I understood from his speech that ...** ich schloss aus seiner Rede, dass ...
◼ VI **(a)** (= *comprehend*) verstehen; **(do you) ~?** (hast du/haben Sie das) verstanden?; **you don't ~!** du verstehst mich nicht!; **but you don't ~, I must have the money now** aber verstehen Sie doch, ich brauche das Geld jetzt!; **I quite ~** ich verstehe schon
(b) (= *believe*) **so I ~** es scheint so; **he was, I ~, a widower** wie ich hörte, war er Witwer

understandable [ˌʌndəˈstændəbl] ADJ verständlich; (= *natural also*) begreiflich

understandably [ˌʌndəˈstændəblɪ] ADV verständlicherweise

understanding [ˌʌndəˈstændɪŋ] ◼ ADJ verständnisvoll
◼ N **(a)** (= *intelligence*) Auffassungsgabe *f*; (= *knowledge*) Kenntnisse *pl*; (= *comprehension, sympathy*) Verständnis *nt*; **her ~ of children** ihr Verständnis *nt* für Kinder; **my ~ of the situation is that ...** ich verstehe die Situation so, dass ...; **it was my ~ that ...** ich nahm an *or* ich war der Meinung, dass ...; **he has a good ~ of the problem** er kennt sich mit dem Problem gut aus
(b) (= *agreement*) Abmachung *f*, Vereinbarung *f*; **to come to** *or* **reach an ~ with sb** eine Abmachung *or* Vereinbarung mit jdm treffen; **Susie and I have an ~** Susie und ich haben unsere Abmachung
(c) (= *assumption*) Voraussetzung *f*; **on the ~ that ...** unter der Voraussetzung, dass ...

understate [ˌʌndəˈsteɪt] VT herunterspielen

understated [ˌʌndəˈsteɪtɪd] ADJ *film etc* subtil; *music, colours* gedämpft; *clothes* unaufdringlich; *performance, manner* zurückhaltend

understatement [ˈʌndəˌsteɪtmənt] N Untertreibung *f*, Understatement *nt*

understood [ˌʌndəˈstʊd] ◼ PRET, PTP *of* **understand** ◼ ADJ
(a) (= *clear*) klar; **to make oneself ~** sich verständlich machen; **do I make myself ~?** ist das klar?; **~! gut!; I thought that was ~!** ich dachte, das sei klar **(b)** (= *believed*) angenommen; **he is ~ to have left** es heißt, dass er gegangen ist

understudy [ˈʌndəˌstʌdɪ] N (*Theat*) zweite Besetzung

undertake [ˌʌndəˈteɪk], *pret* **undertook** [ˌʌndəˈtʊk], *ptp* **undertaken** [ˌʌndəˈteɪkn] VT **(a)** *job, responsibility* übernehmen; *risk* eingehen; *research, reform* durchführen **(b)** (= *agree, promise*) sich verpflichten

undertaker [ˈʌndəˌteɪkəʳ] N (Leichen)bestatter(in) *m(f)*; (= *company*) Bestattungs- *or* Beerdigungsinstitut *nt*

undertaking [ˌʌndəˈteɪkɪŋ] N **(a)** (= *enterprise*) Vorhaben *nt*; (*esp Comm:* = *project*) Projekt *nt* **(b)** (= *promise*) Zusicherung *f*, Wort *nt*; **I can give no such ~** das kann ich nicht versprechen

under: **under-the-counter** ADJ *see* counter; **undertone** N **(a)** (*of voice*) **in an ~** mit gedämpfter Stimme **(b)** (*fig: of discontent*) Unterton *m*; **an ~ of racism** ein rassistischer Unterton; **undertook** PRET *of* undertake; **undertow** N (*lit, fig*) Unterströmung *f*; **underused** ADJ Land nicht voll genutzt; *resources, facilities also* unausgeschöpft; **undervalue** VT *antique, artist* unterbewerten, unterschätzen; *assets, shares* zu niedrig schätzen; *person* zu wenig schätzen; **underwater** ◼ ADJ Unterwasser- ◼ ADV unter Wasser; **underwear** N Unterwäsche *f*; **underweight** ADJ untergewichtig; **to be (2 kg) ~** (2 kg) Untergewicht haben; **underwent** PRET *of* undergo; **underworld** N (= *criminals, Myth*) Unterwelt *f*; **underwrite** pret **underwrote**, *ptp* **underwritten** VT (= *finance*) tragen,

garantieren; (= *guarantee*) bürgen für; (= *insure*) versichern; (*St Ex*) *shares, issue* zeichnen; **underwriter** N (*Insur.:* = *company*) Versicherungsgeber *m*

undeserved [ˌʌndɪˈzɜːvd] ADJ unverdient

undeservedly [ˌʌndɪˈzɜːvɪdlɪ] ADV unverdient(ermaßen)

undeserving [ˌʌndɪˈzɜːvɪŋ] ADJ unwürdig

undesirable [ˌʌndɪˈzaɪərəbl] ◼ ADJ *policy, effect* unerwünscht; *influence, characters, area* übel; **an ~ person to have as a manager** kein wünschenswerter Manager; **~ elements** unerwünschte Elemente *pl* ◼ N (= *person*) unerfreuliches Element

undetected [ˌʌndɪˈtektɪd] ADJ unentdeckt; **to go ~** nicht entdeckt werden; **to remain ~** unentdeckt bleiben

undetermined [ˌʌndɪˈtɜːmɪnd] ADJ unbestimmt

undeterred [ˌʌndɪˈtɜːd] ADJ keineswegs entmutigt; **the teams were ~ by the weather** das Wetter schreckte die Mannschaften nicht ab

undeveloped [ˌʌndɪˈveləpt] ADJ unentwickelt; *land, resources* ungenutzt

undiagnosed [ˌʌndaɪəgˈnəʊzd] ADJ *disease* unerkannt

undid [ʌnˈdɪd] PRET *of* undo

undies [ˈʌndɪz] PL (*inf*) (Unter)wäsche *f*

undignified [ʌnˈdɪgnɪfaɪd] ADJ *person, behaviour* würdelos; (= *inelegant*) *way of sitting etc* unelegant

undiluted [ˌʌndaɪˈluːtɪd] ADJ unverdünnt; (*fig*) *truth, version* unverfälscht; *pleasure* rein, voll

undiminished [ˌʌndɪˈmɪnɪʃt] ADJ *enthusiasm* unvermindert; *strength, courage also* unbeeinträchtigt

undiplomatic ADJ, **undiplomatically** ADV [ˌʌndɪpləˈmætɪk, -əlɪ] undiplomatisch

undischarged [ˌʌndɪsˈtʃɑːdʒd] ADJ (*Fin*) *debt* unbezahlt, unbeglichen; *bankrupt* nicht entlastet

undisciplined [ʌnˈdɪsɪplɪnd] ADJ *mind, person* undiszipliniert; *imagination* zügellos

undisclosed [ˌʌndɪsˈkləʊzd] ADJ geheim gehalten; *fee, reason, number* ungenannt

undiscovered [ˌʌndɪsˈkʌvəd] ADJ unentdeckt

undisguised [ˌʌndɪsˈgaɪzd] ADJ ungetarnt; (*fig*) *truth* unverhüllt; *dislike, affection* unverhohlen

undisposed [ˌʌndɪsˈpəʊzd] ADJ **~ of** (*Comm*) unverkauft

undisputed [ˌʌndɪsˈpjuːtɪd] ADJ unbestritten

undisturbed [ˌʌndɪsˈtɜːbd] ADJ (= *untouched*) *papers, dust, village* unberührt; (= *uninterrupted*) *person, sleep etc* ungestört

undivided [ˌʌndɪˈvaɪdɪd] ADJ *opinion, attention* ungeteilt; *support* voll; *loyalty* absolut; *love* uneingeschränkt

undo [ʌnˈduː], *pret* **undid**, *ptp* **undone** ◼ VT **(a)** (= *unfasten*) aufmachen; *button, dress, parcel* öffnen; *knot* lösen; *sewing* auftrennen **(b)** (= *reverse*) *wrong* ungeschehen machen; *decision* rückgängig machen; *work* ruinieren; (*Comput*) *command* rückgängig machen ◼ VI aufgehen

undoing [ʌnˈduːɪŋ] N Ruin *m*, Verderben *nt*

undone [ʌnˈdʌn] ◼ PTP *of* undo ◼ ADJ **(a)** (= *unfastened*) offen; **to come ~** aufgehen **(b)** (= *neglected*) *task* unerledigt; **to leave sth ~** etw ungetan lassen

undoubted [ʌnˈdaʊtɪd] ADJ unbestritten; *success also* unzweifelhaft

undoubtedly [ʌnˈdaʊtɪdlɪ] ADV zweifellos, ohne Zweifel

undreamt-of [ʌnˈdremtɒv], (*US*) **undreamed-of** [ʌnˈdriːmdɒv] ADJ ungeahnt

undress [ʌnˈdres] ◼ VT ausziehen; **to get ~ed** sich ausziehen ◼ VI sich ausziehen

undressed [ʌnˈdrest] ADJ **(a)** *person* (*still*) (noch) nicht angezogen; (*already*) (schon) ausgezogen **(b)** (*Cook*) *salad* nicht angemacht; *wound* unverbunden

undrinkable [ʌnˈdrɪŋkəbl] ADJ ungenießbar

undue [ʌnˈdjuː] ADJ (= *excessive*) übertrieben, übermäßig; (= *improper*) ungebührlich

undulating [ˈʌndjʊleɪtɪŋ] ADJ *movement, line* wellenförmig; *countryside* hügelig; *hills* sanft; *path* auf und ab führend

unduly [ʌnˈdjuːlɪ] ADV übermäßig; *optimistic, pessimistic, lenient* zu; **you're worrying ~** Sie machen sich (*dat*) unnötige Sorgen

undying [ʌnˈdaɪɪŋ] ADJ *love* unsterblich, ewig

unearned income N Kapitalertrag *m*

unearth [ʌnˈɜːθ] VT ausgraben; (fig) book etc aufstöbern; evidence, talent zutage bringen

unearthly [ʌnˈɜːθlɪ] ADJ calm gespenstisch, unheimlich; beauty überirdisch; (inf: = awful) racket schauerlich; **at the ~ hour of 5 o'clock** (inf) zu nachtschlafender Stunde um 5 Uhr

unease [ʌnˈiːz] N Unbehagen nt

uneasily [ʌnˈiːzɪlɪ] ADV sit unbehaglich; smile, listen etc also beklommen; sleep unruhig

uneasiness [ʌnˈiːzɪnɪs] N (= awkwardness) Beklommenheit f; (= anxiety) Unruhe f

uneasy [ʌnˈiːzɪ] ADJ sleep, night unruhig; conscience schlecht; laugh, look beklommen; silence unbehaglich; peace, balance unsicher; alliance, relationship instabil; feeling beunruhigend, beklemmend; **to be ~** (= ill at ease) beklommen sein; (= worried) beunruhigt sein; **I am** or **feel ~ about it** mir ist nicht wohl dabei; **to make sb ~** jdn beunruhigen; **to grow** or **become ~ about sth** sich über etw (acc) beunruhigen

uneconomic [ʌnˌiːkəˈnɒmɪk] ADJ unwirtschaftlich

uneconomical [ʌnˌiːkəˈnɒmɪkəl] ADJ unwirtschaftlich; style of running unökonomisch

uneducated [ʌnˈedjʊkeɪtɪd] ADJ ungebildet

unemotional [ʌnɪˈməʊʃənl] ADJ person, approach, voice nüchtern; reaction also unbewegt; (= without passion) leidenschaftslos, kühl (pej)

unemployable [ʌnɪmˈplɔɪəbl] ADJ als Arbeitskraft nicht brauchbar

unemployed [ʌnɪmˈplɔɪd] **1** ADJ person arbeitslos, erwerbslos; (Fin) capital tot, brachliegend **2** PL **the ~ pl** die Arbeitslosen pl, die Erwerbslosen pl

unemployment [ʌnɪmˈplɔɪmənt] N Arbeitslosigkeit f, Erwerbslosigkeit f

unemployment: **unemployment benefit**, (US) **unemployment compensation** N Arbeitslosenunterstützung f; **unemployment figures** PL Arbeitslosenziffer f; **unemployment line** N (US) **to be in the ~** arbeitslos sein, stempeln gehen (inf); **unemployment rate** N Arbeitslosenquote f

unending [ʌnˈendɪŋ] ADJ (= everlasting) ewig, nie endend attr; stream nicht enden wollend attr; (= incessant) endlos

unenterprising [ʌnˈentəpraɪzɪŋ] ADJ ohne Unternehmungsgeist

unenthusiastic [ʌnɪnθuːzɪˈæstɪk] ADJ kühl, wenig begeistert; **he was ~ about it** er war wenig begeistert davon

unenthusiastically [ʌnɪnθuːzɪˈæstɪkəlɪ] ADV ohne Begeisterung

unenviable [ʌnˈenvɪəbl] ADJ wenig beneidenswert

unequal [ʌnˈiːkwəl] ADJ ungleich; standard unterschiedlich; **~ in length** unterschiedlich lang; **to be ~ to a task** einer Aufgabe (dat) nicht gewachsen sein

unequalled, (US) **unequaled** [ʌnˈiːkwəld] ADJ unübertroffen; skill, record also unerreicht; beauty also, stupidity beispiellos

unequivocal [ʌnɪˈkwɪvəkəl] ADJ (a) unmissverständlich, eindeutig; proof unzweifelhaft (b) (= categorical) support rückhaltlos

unequivocally [ʌnɪˈkwɪvəkəlɪ] ADV unmissverständlich; state, answer also eindeutig; support rückhaltlos

unerring [ʌnˈɜːrɪŋ] ADJ judgement, accuracy, ability unfehlbar; instinct untrüglich; aim treffsicher

unethical [ʌnˈeθɪkəl] ADJ unmoralisch; (in more serious matters) unethisch

uneven [ʌnˈiːvən] ADJ surface uneben; line, number ungerade; thickness, contest ungleich; pace, colour, distribution ungleichmäßig; quality unterschiedlich

unevenly [ʌnˈiːvənlɪ] ADV move, spread unregelmäßig; share ungleichmäßig

unevenness [ʌnˈiːvənnɪs] N (of surface) Unebenheit f; (of pace, colour, distribution) Ungleichmäßigkeit f; (of quality) Unterschiedlichkeit f; (of contest, competition) Ungleichheit f

uneventful [ʌnɪˈventfʊl] ADJ day, meeting ereignislos; life ruhig, eintönig (pej)

uneventfully [ʌnɪˈventfəlɪ] ADV ereignislos

unexceptional [ʌnɪkˈsepʃənl] ADJ alltäglich, durchschnittlich

unexciting [ʌnɪkˈsaɪtɪŋ] ADJ nicht besonders aufregend; (= boring) langweilig

unexpected [ʌnɪkˈspektɪd] ADJ unerwartet; arrival, result, development also unvorhergesehen

unexpectedly [ʌnɪkˈspektɪdlɪ] ADV unerwartet; arrive, happen also unvorhergesehen

unexplained [ʌnɪkˈspleɪnd] ADJ nicht geklärt, ungeklärt; mystery unaufgeklärt; absence unbegründet; **for some ~ reason** aus unerklärlichen Gründen

unexploited [ʌnɪkˈsplɔɪtɪd] ADJ resources ungenutzt; market (noch) nicht erschlossen; talent also brachliegend attr

unexplored [ʌnɪkˈsplɔːd] ADJ mystery unerforscht; territory also unerschlossen

unexpressed [ʌnɪkˈsprest] ADJ sorrow, wish unausgesprochen

unfailing [ʌnˈfeɪlɪŋ] ADJ zeal, interest, source unerschöpflich; optimism, humour also unbezwinglich; support, generosity, regularity, accuracy beständig

unfair [ʌnˈfeəʳ] ADJ unfair; decision, remark, criticism also ungerecht; **to be ~ to sb** jdm gegenüber unfair sein; **~ competition** or **trading** (Comm) unlauterer Wettbewerb

unfair dismissal N ungerechtfertigte Entlassung

unfairly [ʌnˈfeəlɪ] ADV unfair; treat, criticize etc also ungerecht; accuse, punish, dismissed zu Unrecht

unfairness [ʌnˈfeənɪs] N Ungerechtigkeit f

unfaithful [ʌnˈfeɪθfʊl] ADJ (a) wife, husband, lover untreu; friend, servant treulos (b) translation, description ungenau

unfaithfulness [ʌnˈfeɪθfəlnɪs] N (of wife, husband, lover) Untreue f; (of friend, servant) Treulosigkeit f

unfaltering [ʌnˈfɔːltərɪŋ] ADJ step, voice fest; courage unerschütterlich

unfamiliar [ʌnfəˈmɪljəʳ] ADJ experience, taste, sight, surroundings ungewohnt; subject, person fremd, unbekannt; **~ territory** (fig) Neuland nt; **to be ~ with sth** mit etw nicht vertraut sein; with machine etc sich mit etw nicht auskennen

unfamiliarity [ʌnfəmɪlɪˈærɪtɪ] N (of surroundings) Ungewohntheit f; (of subject, person) Fremdheit f, Unbekanntheit f; **because of my ~ with ...** wegen meiner mangelnden Vertrautheit mit ...

unfashionable [ʌnˈfæʃnəbl] ADJ unmodern; district wenig gefragt; hotel, subject nicht in Mode

unfashionably [ʌnˈfæʃnəblɪ] ADV dressed unmodern

unfasten [ʌnˈfɑːsn] **1** VT aufmachen; (= detach) tag, horse etc losbinden; hair, bonds lösen **2** VI aufgehen

unfavourable, (US) **unfavorable** [ʌnˈfeɪvərəbl] ADJ outlook, weather, result ungünstig; conditions also widrig; reaction negativ; trade balance passiv; **on ~ terms** zu ungünstigen Bedingungen; **to show sb/sth in an ~ light** jdn/etw in einem ungünstigen Licht darstellen

unfavourably, (US) **unfavorably** [ʌnˈfeɪvərəblɪ] ADV compare unvorteilhaft; react ablehnend; review negativ; regard ungünstig; **to compare ~ with sth** im Vergleich mit etw schlecht abschneiden

unfeasible [ʌnˈfiːzəbl] ADJ nicht machbar

unfeeling [ʌnˈfiːlɪŋ] ADJ gefühllos; response also herzlos

unfeminine [ʌnˈfemɪnɪn] ADJ unweiblich

unfilled [ʌnˈfɪld] ADJ ungefüllt; job offen; seat (= not taken) leer; (Pol) unbesetzt; **~ vacancies** offene Stellen pl

unfinished [ʌnˈfɪnɪʃt] ADJ (a) unfertig; work of art unvollendet; **~ business** unerledigte Geschäfte pl (b) (Tech) unbearbeitet; **~ product** Rohprodukt nt

unfit [ʌnˈfɪt] ADJ (a) (= unsuitable) ungeeignet, untauglich; (= incompetent) unfähig; **to be ~ to do sth** (physically) nicht fähig sein, etw zu tun; (mentally) außer Stande sein, etw zu tun; **~ to drive** fahruntüchtig; **he is ~ to be a lawyer** er ist als Jurist untauglich; **to be ~ for (human) consumption** nicht zum Verzehr geeignet sein; **~ to eat** ungenießbar; **road ~ for lorries** für Lastkraftwagen nicht geeignete Straße (b) (Sport: = injured) nicht fit; (in health) schlecht in Form; **(for military service)** (dienst)untauglich; **to be ~ for work** arbeitsunfähig sein

unfitness [ʌnˈfɪtnɪs] N (= unhealthiness) mangelnde Fitness

unfitting [ʌnˈfɪtɪŋ] ADJ behaviour unschicklich

unflagging [ʌnˈflægɪŋ] ADJ person, patience unermüdlich; enthusiasm unerschöpflich; devotion, interest unverändert stark

unflappable [ʌnˈflæpəbl] ADJ (inf) unerschütterlich; **to be ~** die Ruhe weghaben (inf)

unflattering [ʌnˈflætərɪŋ] ADJ portrait, comments wenig schmeichelhaft; dress, hairstyle, light also unvorteilhaft; **to**

portray sb/sth in an ~ light jdn/etw in einem wenig schmeichelhaften Licht erscheinen lassen

unflinching [ʌnˈflɪntʃɪŋ] ADJ unerschrocken; *support* unbeirrbar; *gaze* unbeirrt

unfocus(s)ed [ʌnˈfəʊkəst] ADJ *eyes* unkoordiniert; *debate* weitschweifig; *campaign* zu allgemein angelegt

unfold [ʌnˈfəʊld] **1** VT *paper, cloth* auseinander falten; *wings* ausbreiten; *arms* lösen; *chair* aufklappen **2** VI *(story, plot)* sich abwickeln

unforced [ʌnˈfɔːst] ADJ ungezwungen, natürlich

unforeseeable [ʌnfɔːˈsiːəbl] ADJ unvorhersehbar

unforeseen [ʌnfɔːˈsiːn] ADJ unvorhergesehen; **due to ~ circumstances** aufgrund unvorhergesehener Umstände

unforgettable [ʌnfəˈgetəbl] ADJ unvergesslich

unforgivable ADJ, **unforgivably** ADV [ʌnfəˈgɪvəbl, -ɪ] unverzeihlich

unforgiving [ʌnfəˈgɪvɪŋ] ADJ unversöhnlich

unformatted [ʌnˈfɔːmætɪd] ADJ *(Comput)* unformatiert

unformed [ʌnˈfɔːmd] ADJ *clay, foetus* ungeformt; *character, idea* unfertig

unforthcoming [ʌnfɔːˈθkʌmɪŋ] ADJ nicht sehr mitteilsam; **to be ~ about sth** sich nicht zu etw äußern wollen

unfortunate [ʌnˈfɔːtʃnɪt] ADJ unglücklich; *person* glücklos; *event, error* unglückselig; *turn of phrase* ungeschickt; *time* ungünstig; **to be ~** *(person)* Pech haben; **it is most ~ that ...** es ist höchst bedauerlich, dass ...

unfortunately [ʌnˈfɔːtʃnɪtlɪ] ADV leider; *worded* ungeschickt; **~ for you** bedauerlicherweise für Sie; **~ not** leider nicht

unfounded [ʌnˈfaʊndɪd] ADJ unbegründet; *rumour also, allegations* aus der Luft gegriffen

unfreeze [ʌnˈfriːz], *pret* **unfroze**, *ptp* **unfrozen** VT *(Fin)* freigeben

unfriendliness [ʌnˈfrendlɪnɪs] N Unfreundlichkeit *f*; *(of country, inhabitants also)* Feindseligkeit *f*

unfriendly [ʌnˈfrendlɪ] ADJ unfreundlich *(to sb* zu jdm); *natives, country* feindselig; *(Fin) takeover* feindlich

unfroze [ʌnˈfrəʊz] PRET *of* **unfreeze**

unfrozen [ʌnˈfrəʊzn] **1** PTP *of* **unfreeze** **2** ADJ *assets, prices* freigegeben; *(= not yet frozen)* frei

unfruitful [ʌnˈfruːtfʊl] ADJ *discussion* unfruchtbar; *attempt* fruchtlos

unfulfilled [ʌnfʊlˈfɪld] ADJ unerfüllt; *person, life* unausgefüllt

unfunded [ʌnˈfʌndɪd] ADJ *(Fin)* unfundiert

unfunny [ʌnˈfʌnɪ] ADJ *(inf)* (gar) nicht komisch

unfurl [ʌnˈfɜːl] **1** VT *flag* aufrollen; *sail* losmachen **2** VI sich entfalten; *(flag, sails also)* sich aufrollen

unfurnished [ʌnˈfɜːnɪʃt] ADJ unmöbliert

ungainly [ʌnˈgeɪnlɪ] ADJ *animal, movement* unbeholfen; *appearance* unschön

ungenerous [ʌnˈdʒenərəs] ADJ kleinlich

unglazed [ʌnˈgleɪzd] ADJ *window* unverglast; *pottery* unglasiert

ungodly [ʌnˈgɒdlɪ] ADJ gottlos; *(inf) noise, hour* unchristlich *(inf)*

ungraceful [ʌnˈgreɪsfʊl] ADJ nicht anmutig; *movement* plump, ungelenk

ungracious [ʌnˈgreɪʃəs] ADJ unhöflich; *(= gruff) grunt, refusal* schroff; *answer* rüde

ungraciously [ʌnˈgreɪʃəslɪ] ADV *say, respond* schroff

ungrammatical ADJ, **ungrammatically** ADV [ʌngrəˈmætɪkəl, -ɪ] grammatikalisch falsch

ungrateful ADJ, **ungratefully** ADV [ʌnˈgreɪtfʊl, -fəlɪ] undankbar *(to* gegenüber)

ungrudging [ʌnˈgrʌdʒɪŋ] ADJ *help, support* bereitwillig; *admiration* neidlos; *(= generous) person* großzügig; *praise* von ganzem Herzen kommend *attr*

unguarded [ʌnˈgɑːdɪd] ADJ **(a)** *(= undefended)* unbewacht **(b)** *(fig: = careless)* unvorsichtig, unachtsam; **in an ~ moment he ...** als er einen Augenblick nicht aufpasste, ... er ...

unhampered [ʌnˈhæmpəd] ADJ ungehindert; **~ by regulations** ohne den Zwang von Bestimmungen

unhappily [ʌnˈhæpɪlɪ] ADV *(= unfortunately)* leider, unglücklicherweise; *(= miserably)* unglücklich

unhappiness [ʌnˈhæpɪnɪs] N Traurigkeit *f*; *(= discontent)* Unzufriedenheit *f*

unhappy [ʌnˈhæpɪ] ADJ **(+ER) (a)** unglücklich; *look, voice, state of affairs* traurig; **an ~ choice** keine gute Wahl **(b)** *(= not pleased)* unzufrieden *(about* mit), nicht glücklich *(about* über +*acc*); *(= uneasy)* unwohl; **to be ~ with sb/sth** mit jdm/etw unzufrieden sein; **to be ~ at work** unzufrieden mit der Arbeit sein; **to be ~ about** *or* **at doing sth** nicht glücklich darüber sein, etw zu tun; **if you feel ~ about it** *(= worried)* wenn Ihnen dabei nicht wohl ist; **I feel ~ about letting him go** ich lasse ihn nur ungern gehen

unharmed [ʌnˈhɑːmd] ADJ *person* unverletzt; *thing* unbeschädigt; *reputation* ungeschädigt

unhealthy [ʌnˈhelθɪ] ADJ **(a)** *person* nicht gesund; *climate, place, life, complexion* ungesund; *(Econ: = weak)* kränkelnd **(b)** *curiosity, interest* krankhaft; *influence* schädlich; **it's an ~ relationship** das ist eine verderbliche Beziehung

unheard [ʌnˈhɜːd] ADJ **to go ~** *(lit)* ungehört bleiben; *(fig also)* unbeachtet bleiben

unheard-of [ʌnˈhɜːdɒv] ADJ *(= unknown)* gänzlich unbekannt; *(= unprecedented)* einmalig, noch nicht da gewesen; *(= outrageous)* unerhört

unheeded [ʌnˈhiːdɪd] ADJ **to go ~** auf taube Ohren stoßen

unhelpful [ʌnˈhelpfʊl] ADJ *person* nicht hilfreich; *advice, book* wenig hilfreich; **you are being very ~** du bist aber wirklich keine Hilfe

unhelpfully [ʌnˈhelpfəlɪ] ADV wenig hilfreich

unhesitating [ʌnˈhezɪteɪtɪŋ] ADJ *answer, offer* prompt; *help also, generosity* bereitwillig

unhesitatingly [ʌnˈhezɪteɪtɪŋlɪ] ADV ohne Zögern

unhindered [ʌnˈhɪndəd] ADJ *(by clothes, luggage etc)* unbehindert, nicht behindert; *(by regulations)* ungehindert, nicht gehindert

unhitch [ʌnˈhɪtʃ] VT *horse (from post)* losbinden; *(from wagon)* ausspannen; *caravan, engine* abkoppeln

unholy [ʌnˈhəʊlɪ] ADJ **(+ER)** *(Rel) place* ungeweiht; *delight* diebisch *(inf); alliance* übel; *mess* heillos; *noise, hour* unchristlich *(inf)*

unhook [ʌnˈhʊk] **1** VT *latch, gate* loshaken; *dress* aufhaken; *(= free)* losmachen **2** VI sich aufhaken lassen

unhurried [ʌnˈhʌrɪd] ADJ *pace, person* gelassen; *steps, movement* gemächlich; *meal, journey* gemütlich

unhurriedly [ʌnˈhʌrɪdlɪ] ADV gemächlich, in aller Ruhe

unhurt [ʌnˈhɜːt] ADJ unverletzt

unhygienic [ʌnhaɪˈdʒiːnɪk] ADJ unhygienisch

unicorn [ˈjuːnɪkɔːn] N Einhorn *nt*

unicycle [ˈjuːnɪsaɪkl] N Einrad *nt*

unidentifiable [ˈʌnaɪdentɪfaɪəbl] ADJ *object, smell, sound* unidentifizierbar; *body* nicht identifizierbar

unidentified [ˌʌnaɪˈdentɪfaɪd] ADJ unbekannt; *body* nicht identifiziert; *belongings* herrenlos

unification [ˌjuːnɪfɪˈkeɪʃən] N *(of country)* Einigung *f*; *(of system)* Vereinheitlichung *f*

uniform [ˈjuːnɪfɔːm] **1** ADJ **(a)** *length, colour, tax, treatment* einheitlich; *temperature, pace* gleich bleibend; *life, thinking* gleichförmig; **~ in shape/size** von gleicher Form/Größe **(b)** *(Mil, Sch etc)* Uniform-; **~ jacket** Uniformjacke *f* **2** N Uniform *f*; **in ~** in Uniform; **out of ~** in Zivil

uniformed [ˈjuːnɪfɔːmd] ADJ uniformiert; *person also* in Uniform

uniformity [ˌjuːnɪˈfɔːmɪtɪ] N *(of length, colour)* Einheitlichkeit *f*; *(of treatment also)* Gleichheit *f*; *(of temperature, pace)* Gleichmäßigkeit *f*

uniformly [ˈjuːnɪfɔːmlɪ] ADV *measure, paint, tax* einheitlich; *heat* gleichmäßig; *treat* gleich; *(pej)* einförmig *(pej)*

uniform resource locator N *(Comput)* URL-Adresse *f*

unify [ˈjuːnɪfaɪ] VT einigen; *theories, systems* vereinheitlichen

unifying [ˈjuːnɪfaɪɪŋ] ADJ verbindend

unilateral [ˌjuːnɪˈlætərəl] ADJ einseitig; *(Jur)* einseitig; *(Pol also)* unilateral

unilaterally [ˌjuːnɪˈlætərəlɪ] ADV einseitig; *(Pol auch)* unilateral

unimaginable [ˌʌnɪˈmædʒɪnəbl] ADJ unvorstellbar

unimaginative ADJ, **unimaginatively** ADV [ˌʌnɪˈmædʒɪnətɪv, -lɪ] fantasielos

unimpaired [ˌʌnɪmˈpeəd] ADJ unbeeinträchtigt; *eyesight, mental powers also* unvermindert; **to be ~** nicht gelitten haben

unimpeachable [ʌnɪmˈpiːtʃəbl] ADJ *reputation, character* untadelig; *proof, honesty* unanfechtbar; *person* über jeden Zweifel erhaben

unimpeded [ʌnɪmˈpiːdɪd] ADJ ungehindert

unimportant [ʌnɪmˈpɔːtənt] ADJ unwichtig, unbedeutend; *detail also* unwesentlich

unimposing [ʌnɪmˈpəʊzɪŋ] ADJ unscheinbar; *building also* wenig beeindruckend

unimpressed [ʌnɪmˈprest] ADJ unbeeindruckt; **I was ~ by his story** seine Geschichte hat mich überhaupt nicht beeindruckt

unimpressive [ʌnɪmˈpresɪv] ADJ wenig beeindruckend; *person also* unscheinbar; *performance also, speaker* wenig überzeugend

uninformed [ʌnɪnˈfɔːmd] ADJ (= *not knowing*) nicht informiert (*about* über +acc); (= *ignorant also*) unwissend; *criticism* blindwütig; *comment, rumour* unfundiert; **to be ~ about sth** über etw (acc) nicht Bescheid wissen

uninhabitable [ʌnɪnˈhæbɪtəbl] ADJ unbewohnbar

uninhabited [ʌnɪnˈhæbɪtɪd] ADJ unbewohnt

uninhibited [ʌnɪnˈhɪbɪtɪd] ADJ *person* ohne Hemmungen; *greed, laughter* hemmungslos

uninitiated [ʌnɪˈnɪʃɪeɪtɪd] ■ ADJ nicht eingeweiht ② N **the ~** *pl* Nichteingeweihte *pl*

uninjured [ʌnˈɪndʒəd] ADJ *person* unverletzt; *arm etc also* heil

uninspired [ʌnɪnˈspaɪəd] ADJ *performance* fantasielos; *book* einfallslos

uninspiring [ʌnɪnˈspaɪərɪŋ] ADJ trocken; *suggestion, idea* nicht gerade aufregend

uninstall [ʌnɪnˈstɔːl] VT (*Comput*) deinstallieren

uninsurable [ʌnɪnˈʃʊərəbl] ADJ nicht versicherbar

uninsured [ʌnɪnˈʃʊəd] ADJ nicht versichert

unintelligent [ʌnɪnˈtelɪdʒənt] ADJ unintelligent

unintelligible [ʌnɪnˈtelɪdʒɪbl] ADJ *person* nicht zu verstehen; *speech, writing* unverständlich

unintended [ʌnɪnˈtendɪd], **unintentional** [ʌnɪnˈtenʃənl] ADJ unbeabsichtigt, unabsichtlich; *joke also* unfreiwillig

unintentionally [ʌnɪnˈtenʃnəlɪ] ADV unabsichtlich, unbeabsichtigt; *funny* unfreiwillig

uninterested [ʌnˈɪntrɪstɪd] ADJ desinteressiert; **to be ~ in sth** an etw (dat) nicht interessiert sein

uninteresting [ʌnˈɪntrɪstɪŋ] ADJ uninteressant

uninterrupted [ʌnɪntəˈrʌptɪd] ADJ *line* ununterbrochen; *noise, rain also* anhaltend; *rest, view* ungestört; **to continue ~** ungestört fortfahren

uninvited [ʌnɪnˈvaɪtɪd] ADJ *guest* ungeladen, ungebeten; *criticism* unerwünscht; *sexual advances* unwillkommen

uninviting [ʌnɪnˈvaɪtɪŋ] ADJ *atmosphere* nicht (gerade) einladend; *prospect* nicht (gerade) verlockend; *smell, food, sight* unappetitlich

union [ˈjuːnjən] ■ N (= *act, association*) Vereinigung f; (*Pol also*, = *customs ~*) Union f; (= *trade ~*) Gewerkschaft f; (= *students' ~*) Studentenklub m; **the Union** (*US*) die Vereinigten Staaten; (*in civil war*) die Unionsstaaten *pl* ② ADJ ATTR (= *trade ~*) Gewerkschafts-; **~ contract** Tarifvertrag *m*

unionist [ˈjuːnjənɪst] ■ N **(a)** (= *trade ~*) Gewerkschaftler(in) *m(f)* **(b)** (*Pol*) Unionist(in) *m(f)* ② ADJ (*Pol*) unionistisch

Union Jack N Union Jack *m*

unique [juːˈniːk] ADJ einzig *attr*; (= *outstanding*) einzigartig, einmalig (*inf*); **such cases are not ~ to Britain** solche Fälle sind nicht nur auf Großbritannien beschränkt

uniquely [juːˈniːklɪ] ADV (= *solely*) einzig und allein, nur; (= *outstandingly*) einmalig (*inf*); **~ suited** außergewöhnlich geeignet

unisex [ˈjuːnɪseks] ADJ für Männer und Frauen; (*Fashion also*) Unisex-

unison [ˈjuːnɪzn] N (*Mus*) Gleichklang *m*, Einklang *m* (*also fig*); **in ~** unisono (*geh*), einstimmig; **to act in ~ with sb** (*fig*) in Übereinstimmung mit jdm handeln

unit [ˈjuːnɪt] N Einheit *f* (*also Mil*); (= *set of equipment*) Anlage *f*; (*of furniture*) Element *nt*; (*of machine*) Teil *nt*; (*of organization*) Abteilung *f*; (*of course book*) Lektion *f*; **power ~** Aggregat *nt*; **the family as the basic ~** die Familie als Grundelement; **~ of length** Längeneinheit *f*

unit cost N (*Fin*) Stückkosten *pl*

unite [juːˈnaɪt] ■ VT vereinigen, verbinden; *party, country* (*treaty etc*) (ver)einigen; (*ties, loyalties*) (ver)einen ② VI sich zusammenschließen; **to ~ in doing sth** gemeinsam etw tun; **to ~ in grief/opposition to sth** gemeinsam trauern/gegen etw Opposition machen

united [juːˈnaɪtɪd] ADJ verbunden; *group, nation, front* geschlossen; (= *unified*) *people, nation* einig; **a ~ Ireland** ein vereintes *or* vereinigtes Irland; **to be ~ in the** *or* **one's belief that ...** einig sein in seiner Überzeugung, dass ...

United: United Arab Emirates PL Vereinigte Arabische Emirate *pl*; **United Arab Republic** N Vereinigte Arabische Republik; **United Kingdom** N Vereinigtes Königreich (*Großbritannien und Nordirland*); **United Nations (Organization)** N Vereinte Nationen *pl*; **United States (of America)** PL Vereinigte Staaten *pl* (von Amerika)

unit: unit-linked ADJ (*Insur*) fondsgebunden; **unit price** N (= *price per unit*) Preis *m* pro Einheit; (= *inclusive price*) Pauschalpreis *m*; **unit trust** N (*Brit Fin*) Unit Trust *m*; (= *share*) Unit-Trust-Papiere *pl*

unity [ˈjuːnɪtɪ] N Einheit *f*; (= *harmony*) Einmütigkeit *f*; **national ~** (nationale) Einheit

universal [juːnɪˈvɜːsəl] ADJ *phenomenon, remedy* universell; *truth, rule also* allgemein gültig; *custom, game* allgemein *or* überall verbreitet; (= *general*) *approval, peace* allgemein; **~ language** Weltsprache *f*

universally [juːnɪˈvɜːsəlɪ] ADV allgemein

universal: universal product code N (*US*: = *bar code*) Barkode *m*; **universal suffrage** N allgemeines Wahlrecht

universe [ˈjuːnɪvɜːs] N Universum *nt*

university [juːnɪˈvɜːsɪtɪ] ■ N Universität *f*; **which ~ does he go to?** wo studiert er?; **to be at/go to ~** studieren; **to be at/go to London University** in London studieren ② ADJ ATTR Universitäts-; *education* akademisch; **~ teacher** Hochschullehrer(in) *m(f)*

unjust [ʌnˈdʒʌst] ADJ ungerecht (*to* gegen)

unjustifiable [ʌnˈdʒʌstɪfaɪəbl] ADJ nicht zu rechtfertigend *attr*, nicht zu rechtfertigen *pred*

unjustifiably [ʌnˈdʒʌstɪfaɪəblɪ] ADV *expensive, critical, act* ungerechtfertigt; *criticize, dismiss* zu Unrecht

unjustified [ʌnˈdʒʌstɪfaɪd] ADJ ungerechtfertigt

unjustly [ʌnˈdʒʌstlɪ] ADV zu Unrecht; *judge, treat* ungerecht

unkempt [ʌnˈkempt] ADJ ungepflegt; *hair* ungekämmt

unkind [ʌnˈkaɪnd] ADJ (+ER) (= *not nice*) unfreundlich; (= *cruel*) gemein; (= *harsh*) *climate* schlecht (*to* für); **don't be (so) ~!** das ist aber gar nicht nett (von dir)!; **she never has an ~ word to say about anyone** von ihr ist niemals ein unfreundliches *or* böses Wort über irgendjemanden zu hören; **fate has been very ~ to him** das Schicksal hat ihn grausam behandelt

unkindly [ʌnˈkaɪndlɪ] ADV unfreundlich; (= *cruelly*) gemein; **how ~ fate had treated her** wie grausam das Schicksal ihr mitgespielt hatte

unkindness [ʌnˈkaɪndnɪs] N Unfreundlichkeit *f*; (= *cruelty*) Gemeinheit *f*

unknowingly [ʌnˈnəʊɪŋlɪ] ADV unwissentlich

unknown [ʌnˈnəʊn] ■ ADJ unbekannt; **the ~ soldier** *or* **warrior** der Unbekannte Soldat; **~ territory** (*lit, fig*) Neuland *nt* ② N (= *person*) Unbekannte(r) *mf*; (= *factor*) Unbekannte *f*; **the ~** das Unbekannte; **a journey into the ~** (*lit, fig*) eine Fahrt ins Ungewisse ③ ADV **~ to me** *etc* ohne dass ich *etc* es wusste

unladylike [ʌnˈleɪdɪlaɪk] ADJ nicht damenhaft

unlawful [ʌnˈlɔːfʊl] ADJ gesetzwidrig; *means, imprisonment, act* ungesetzlich

unlawfully [ʌnˈlɔːfəlɪ] ADV gesetzwidrig, illegal; *imprison* ungesetzlich

unleaded [ʌnˈledɪd] ■ ADJ bleifrei ② N bleifreies Benzin

unleash [ʌnˈliːʃ] VT (*fig*) *anger, war* entfesseln

unleavened [ʌnˈlevnd] ADJ ungesäuert

unless [ənˈles] CONJ es sei denn; (*at beginning of sentence*) wenn ... nicht; **don't do it ~ I tell you to** mach das nicht, es sei denn, ich sage es dir; **~ I tell you to, don't do it** wenn ich es dir nicht sage, mach das nicht; **~ I am mistaken ...** wenn *or* falls ich mich nicht irre ...; **~ there is an interruption** vorausgesetzt, alles läuft ohne Unterbrechung

unlicensed [ʌnˈlaɪsənst] ADJ *car, TV* nicht angemeldet; *premises* ohne Lizenz *or* (Schank)konzession; *software* nicht lizenziert

unlike [ʌnˈlaɪk] **1** ADJ unähnlich, nicht ähnlich **2** PREP **(a)** im Gegensatz zu, anders als **(b)** (= *uncharacteristic of*) **to be quite ~ sb** jdm (gar) nicht ähnlich sehen **(c)** (= *not resembling*) **this house is ~ their former one** dieses Haus ist ganz anders als ihr früheres

unlikeable [ʌnˈlaɪkəbl] ADJ unsympathisch

unlikely [ʌnˈlaɪklɪ] ADJ (+ER) *explanation* unwahrscheinlich; (= *odd also*) unglaubwürdig; *friendship* merkwürdig; *candidate* unpassend; **it is (most) ~/not ~ that ...** es ist (höchst) unwahrscheinlich/es kann durchaus sein, dass ...; **she is ~ to come** sie kommt höchstwahrscheinlich nicht; **it looks an ~ place for mushrooms** es sieht mir nicht nach der geeigneten Stelle für Pilze aus; **he's ~ to be chosen** es ist unwahrscheinlich, dass er gewählt wird; **in the ~ event of war** im unwahrscheinlichen Fall eines Krieges

unlimited [ʌnˈlɪmɪtɪd] ADJ *wealth, time* unbegrenzt; *power also* schrankenlos; *patience* unendlich; *access, use* uneingeschränkt

unlimited: **unlimited company** N (*Fin*) Gesellschaft *f* mit unbeschränkter Haftung; **unlimited liability** N (*Comm, Jur*) unbeschränkte Haftung

unlisted [ʌnˈlɪstɪd] ADJ *company, items* nicht verzeichnet; *bonds, stock* nicht notiert; **the number is ~** (*US Telec*) die Nummer steht nicht im Telefonbuch

unlisted securities market N Freiverkehr *m*

unlit [ʌnˈlɪt] ADJ *road* unbeleuchtet; *lamp* nicht angezündet; *fire, cigarette* unangezündet

unload [ʌnˈləʊd] **1** VT **(a)** *ship, gun* entladen; *boot, luggage, car* ausladen; *cargo* löschen; *passengers* absetzen **(b)** (*inf*: = *get rid of*) (*Fin*) *shares* abstoßen; *problem* abladen (*on(to)* bei) **2** VI (*ship*) löschen; (*truck*) abladen

unlock [ʌnˈlɒk] VT *door etc* aufschließen; (*fig*) *heart, secret* offenbaren; **the door is ~ed** die Tür ist nicht abgeschlossen; **to leave a door ~ed** eine Tür nicht abschließen

unloved [ʌnˈlʌvd] ADJ ungeliebt

unluckily [ʌnˈlʌkɪlɪ] ADV zum Pech; **~ for him** zu seinem Pech

unlucky [ʌnˈlʌkɪ] ADJ (+ER) *person, object, action, place* unglückselig; *defeat, loser, victim, coincidence* unglücklich; **to be ~** Pech haben; (= *not succeed*) keinen Erfolg haben; (= *bring bad luck*) Unglück *or* Pech bringen; **it was ~ for her that she was seen** Pech für sie, dass man sie gesehen hat; **how ~ for you!** was für ein Pech!; **~ number** Unglückszahl *f*

unmanageable [ʌnˈmænɪdʒəbl] ADJ (= *unwieldy*) *vehicle* schwer zu manövrieren; *size* unhandlich; *problem* nicht zu bewältigen; (= *uncontrollable*) *animal, person, hair* widerspenstig; *situation* unkontrollierbar

unmanly [ʌnˈmænlɪ] ADJ unmännlich

unmanned [ʌnˈmænd] ADJ *spacecraft, level crossing* unbemannt; *vehicle* fahrerlos; (= *lacking crew*) *telephone exchange* nicht besetzt

unmarked [ʌnˈmɑːkt] ADJ **(a)** (= *unstained*) ohne Flecken *or* Spuren; (= *without marking*) *face* ungezeichnet (*also fig*); *banknotes* unmarkiert; *boxes etc* ohne Namen *or* Adresse; *police car* nicht gekennzeichnet; *grave* anonym **(b)** (*Sport*) *player* ungedeckt **(c)** (*Sch*) *papers* unkorrigiert

unmarketable [ʌnˈmɑːkɪtəbl] ADJ schlecht *or* nicht zu verkaufen

unmarried [ʌnˈmærɪd] ADJ unverheiratet; **~ mother** ledige Mutter

unmask [ʌnˈmɑːsk] VT (*lit*) demaskieren; (*fig*) entlarven

unmatched [ʌnˈmætʃt] ADJ einmalig, unübertroffen (*for* in Bezug auf +*acc*); **~ by anyone** von niemandem übertroffen

unmentionable [ʌnˈmenʃnəbl] ADJ tabu *pred*; *word also* unaussprechlich; **to be ~** tabu sein

unmerciful ADJ, **unmercifully** ADV [ʌnˈmɜːsɪfʊl, -fəlɪ] unbarmherzig, erbarmungslos

unmetered [ʌnˈmiːtəd] ADJ **(a)** *water* ohne Messung durch Wasserzähler **(b)** (*Telec*) *Internet access* zeitlich unbeschränkt

unmissable [ʌnˈmɪsəbl] ADJ (*Brit inf*) **to be ~** ein Muss sein; **this ~ conference** diese Konferenz, die man sich nicht entgehen lassen sollte

unmistak(e)able [ʌnmɪˈsteɪkəbl] ADJ unverkennbar; (*visually*) nicht zu verwechseln

unmistak(e)ably [ʌnmɪˈsteɪkəblɪ] ADV unverkennbar

unmitigated [ʌnˈmɪtɪgeɪtɪd] ADJ (*inf*) *disaster* vollkommen; *success* total

unmotivated [ʌnˈməʊtɪveɪtɪd] ADJ unmotiviert; *attack also* grundlos

unmourned [ʌnˈmɔːnd] ADJ unbeweint

unmoved [ʌnˈmuːvd] ADJ *person* ungerührt; **they were ~ by his playing** sein Spiel(en) ergriff sie nicht

unnamed [ʌnˈneɪmd] ADJ (= *anonymous*) ungenannt

unnatural [ʌnˈnætʃrəl] ADJ unnatürlich; (= *abnormal also*) *relationship, crime* widernatürlich; **to die an ~ death** keines natürlichen Todes sterben; **it is ~ for him to be so rude** normalerweise ist er nicht so grob

unnaturally [ʌnˈnætʃrəlɪ] ADV unnatürlich; (= *extraordinarily also*) *loud, anxious* ungewöhnlich

unnecessarily [ʌnˈnesɪsərɪlɪ] ADV unnötigerweise; *strict, serious* unnötig

unnecessary [ʌnˈnesɪsərɪ] ADJ unnötig; (= *superfluous also*) überflüssig; (= *not requisite*) nicht notwendig *or* nötig; **no, you needn't bother thanks, that's quite ~** nein, machen Sie sich keine Umstände, das ist wirklich nicht nötig

unnerve [ʌnˈnɜːv] VT entnerven; (*gradually*) zermürben; (= *discourage*) entmutigen; **~d by their reaction** durch ihre Reaktion aus der Ruhe gebracht

unnerving [ʌnˈnɜːvɪŋ] ADJ *experience* entnervend; *silence also* zermürbend; (= *discouraging also*) entmutigend

unnoticed [ʌnˈnəʊtɪst] ADJ unbemerkt

unobservant [ʌnəbˈzɜːvənt] ADJ unaufmerksam; **to be ~** ein schlechter Beobachter sein

unobserved [ʌnəbˈzɜːvd] ADJ unbemerkt

unobstructed [ʌnəbˈstrʌktɪd] ADJ *view* ungehindert

unobtainable [ʌnəbˈteɪnəbl] ADJ nicht erhältlich; *goal* unerreichbar

unobtrusive ADJ, **unobtrusively** ADV [ʌnəbˈtruːsɪv, -lɪ] unauffällig

unoccupied [ʌnˈɒkjʊpaɪd] ADJ *person* unbeschäftigt; *house* leer stehend; *seat, table* frei

unofficial [ʌnəˈfɪʃəl] ADJ inoffiziell; (= *unconfirmed also*) nicht amtlich

unofficially [ʌnəˈfɪʃəlɪ] ADV inoffiziell

unopened [ʌnˈəʊpənd] ADJ ungeöffnet

unopposed [ʌnəˈpəʊzd] ADJ **they marched on ~** sie marschierten weiter, ohne auf Widerstand zu treffen; **~ by the committee** ohne Widerspruch seitens des Ausschusses

unorganized [ʌnˈɔːgənaɪzd] ADJ unsystematisch; *person also* unmethodisch; *life* ungeregelt

unoriginal [ʌnəˈrɪdʒɪnəl] ADJ wenig originell

unorthodox [ʌnˈɔːθədɒks] ADJ unkonventionell, unorthodox

unpack [ʌnˈpæk] VTI auspacken

unpaid [ʌnˈpeɪd] ADJ unbezahlt

unpalatable [ʌnˈpælɪtəbl] ADJ *food, drink* ungenießbar; (*fig*) *truth* schwer zu verdauen

unparalleled [ʌnˈpærəleld] ADJ einmalig, beispiellos; (= *unprecedented also*) noch nie da gewesen; **an ~ success** ein Erfolg ohnegleichen

unpardonable [ʌnˈpɑːdnəbl] ADJ unverzeihlich

unpatriotic [ʌnpætrɪˈɒtɪk] ADJ unpatriotisch

unpaved [ʌnˈpeɪvd] ADJ nicht gepflastert

unperfumed [ʌnˈpɜːfjuːmd] ADJ nicht parfümiert

unperturbed [ʌnpəˈtɜːbd] ADJ nicht beunruhigt (*by* von, durch)

unpick [ʌnˈpɪk] VT auftrennen; (*Brit fig*) *plan, policy* auseinander nehmen

unpin [ʌnˈpɪn] VT *dress, hair* die Nadeln entfernen aus

unplanned [ʌnˈplænd] ADJ ungeplant

unplayable [ʌnˈpleəbl] ADJ unspielbar; *pitch* unbespielbar

unpleasant [ʌnˈpleznt] ADJ unangenehm; *experience, situation also* unerfreulich; *person, smile, remark* unfreundlich; **to be ~ to sb** unfreundlich zu jdm sein

unpleasantly [ʌnˈplezntlɪ] ADV *reply* unfreundlich; *warm, smell* unangenehm; **he was getting ~ close to the truth** es war unangenehm, wie nah er an der Wahrheit war

unpleasantness [ʌnˈplezntnɪs] N **(a)** (= *quality*) Unangenehmheit *f*; (*of experience, situation also*)

Unerfreulichkeit f; (of person, smile, remark) Unfreundlichkeit f **(b)** (= bad feeling, quarrel) Unstimmigkeit f

unplug [ʌn'plʌg] VT radio, lamp, plug rausziehen; ~ **it first** zieh zuerst den Stecker raus

unpolished [ʌn'pɒlɪʃt] ADJ **(a)** unpoliert; stone ungeschliffen **(b)** (fig) manners ungehobelt; performance unausgefeilt; style holprig

unpolluted [ˌʌnpə'luːtɪd] ADJ sauber, unverschmutzt

unpopular [ʌn'pɒpjʊləʳ] ADJ person unbeliebt (with sb bei jdm); decision, measures, tax unpopulär

unpopularity [ʌnˌpɒpjʊ'lærɪtɪ] N Unbeliebtheit f; (of decision, move) geringe Popularität

unpractical [ʌn'præktɪkəl] ADJ unpraktisch

unprecedented [ʌn'presɪdəntɪd] ADJ noch nie da gewesen; success also beispiellos; profit, step unerhört; **this event is** ~ dieses Ereignis ist bisher einmalig; **on an** ~ **scale** in einem noch nie da gewesenen Ausmaß

unpredictable [ˌʌnprɪ'dɪktəbl] ADJ unvorhersehbar; result nicht vorherzusagen pred, nicht vorherzusagend attr; behaviour, person, weather unberechenbar

unprejudiced [ʌn'predʒʊdɪst] ADJ (= impartial) objektiv, unparteiisch; (= not having prejudices) vorurteilslos

unprepared [ʌnprɪ'peəd] ADJ unvorbereitet; **to be** ~ **for sth** für etw nicht vorbereitet sein; (= be surprised) auf etw (acc) nicht vorbereitet or gefasst sein

unprepossessing [ʌnpriːpə'zesɪŋ] ADJ wenig einnehmend; building, room wenig ansprechend

unpretentious [ʌnprɪ'tenʃəs] ADJ schlicht, bescheiden; style, book einfach, nicht schwülstig

unpretentiously [ʌnprɪ'tenʃəslɪ] ADV schlicht, bescheiden, einfach; speak natürlich; write in einfachen Worten

unpriced [ʌn'praɪst] ADJ ohne Preisschild

unprincipled [ʌn'prɪnsɪpld] ADJ skrupellos; person also charakterlos

unprintable [ʌn'prɪntəbl] ADJ nicht druckfähig; **his answer was** ~ seine Antwort war nicht druckreif

unproductive [ʌnprə'dʌktɪv] ADJ capital nicht gewinnbringend; discussion, meeting unergiebig; factory unproduktiv

unprofessional [ʌnprə'feʃnl] ADJ unprofessionell; work also unfachmännisch; conduct berufswidrig

unprofitable [ʌn'prɒfɪtəbl] ADJ (financially) keinen Profit bringend or abwerfend; activities, business etc unrentabel; (fig) nutzlos; **the company was** ~ die Firma machte keinen Profit or warf keinen Profit ab

unpromising [ʌn'prɒmɪsɪŋ] ADJ nicht sehr viel versprechend; start also wenig erfolgversprechend; **to look** ~ nicht sehr hoffnungsvoll or gut aussehen

unprompted [ʌn'prɒmptɪd] ADJ spontan; ~ **by me** unaufgefordert

unpronounceable [ʌnprə'naʊnsɪbl] ADJ unaussprechbar; **that word is** ~ das Wort ist nicht auszusprechen

unprotected [ʌnprə'tektɪd] ADJ schutzlos; machine, skin, eyes ungeschützt; ~ **by** nicht geschützt durch

unprotected sex N ungeschützter Sex

unproven [ʌn'pruːvən], **unproved** [ʌn'pruːvd] ADJ allegation unbewiesen

unprovoked [ʌnprə'vəʊkt] ADJ grundlos

unpublished [ʌn'pʌblɪʃt] ADJ unveröffentlicht

unpunctual [ʌn'pʌŋktjʊəl] ADJ unpünktlich

unpunished [ʌn'pʌnɪʃt] ADJ unbestraft; **to go** ~ ohne Strafe bleiben

unqualified [ʌn'kwɒlɪfaɪd] ADJ **(a)** unqualifiziert; **to be** ~ **(for a job)** (für eine Arbeit) nicht qualifiziert sein; **he is** ~ **to do it** er ist dafür nicht qualifiziert **(b)** delight, praise uneingeschränkt; success voll(ständig)

unquenchable [ʌn'kwentʃəbl] ADJ thirst, desire unstillbar; optimism unerschütterlich

unquestionable [ʌn'kwestʃənəbl] ADJ authority unbestritten; evidence, fact unbezweifelbar; honesty fraglos; **a man of** ~ **courage** ein zweifellos or fraglos mutiger Mann

unquestionably [ʌn'kwestʃənəblɪ] ADV fraglos, zweifellos

unquestioned [ʌn'kwestʃənd] ADJ unbestritten; **to be** ~ (honesty etc) außer Frage stehen; (social order etc) nicht infrage gestellt werden

unquestioning [ʌn'kwestʃənɪŋ] ADJ bedingungslos; belief, faith also blind

unquestioningly [ʌn'kwestʃənɪŋlɪ] ADV accept bedingungslos; obey blind

unquoted [ʌn'kwəʊtɪd] ADJ (St Ex) nicht notiert

unravel [ʌn'rævəl] **1** VT knitting aufziehen; (lit, fig: = untangle) entwirren; mystery lösen **2** VI (knitting) sich aufziehen; (fig) sich entwirren; (mystery) sich lösen; (plan, system) aufdecken

unreadable [ʌn'riːdəbl] ADJ **(a)** writing unleserlich; book schwer lesbar **(b)** (Comput) data nicht lesbar **(c)** (liter: = impenetrable) undurchdringlich

unready [ʌn'redɪ] ADJ (noch) nicht fertig

unreal [ʌn'rɪəl] ADJ unwirklich; **this is just** ~! (inf: = unbelievable) das gibts doch nicht! (inf); **he's** ~ er ist unmöglich

unrealistic [ʌnrɪə'lɪstɪk] ADJ unrealistisch

unrealistically [ʌnrɪə'lɪstɪkəlɪ] ADV high, low unrealistisch; optimistic unangemessen

unreality [ʌnrɪ'ælɪtɪ] N Unwirklichkeit f; **extreme exhaustion gives a feeling of** ~ extreme Erschöpfung lässt alles unwirklich erscheinen

unrealized [ʌn'rɪəlaɪzd] ADJ unverwirklicht; (Fin) assets unverwertet; profit nicht realisiert

unreasonable [ʌn'riːznəbl] ADJ unzumutbar; demand, price also, expectations übertrieben; person uneinsichtig; **to be** ~ **about sth** (= be overdemanding) in Bezug auf etw (acc) zu viel verlangen; **it is** ~ **to …** es ist zu viel verlangt, zu …; **it is** ~ **to expect children to keep quiet** man kann doch von Kindern nicht verlangen, ruhig zu sein; **you are being very** ~! das ist wirklich zu viel verlangt!; **an** ~ **length of time** übermäßig or übertrieben lange

unreasonably [ʌn'riːznəblɪ] ADV long, strict etc übertrieben; **you must prove that your employer acted** ~ Sie müssen nachweisen, dass Ihr Arbeitgeber ungerechtfertigt gehandelt hat; **not** ~ nicht ohne Grund

unreceptive [ʌnrɪ'septɪv] ADJ unempfänglich (to für); audience also unaufgeschlossen

unrecognizable [ʌn'rekəgnaɪzəbl] ADJ nicht wieder zu erkennen pred, nicht wieder zu erkennend attr; **to be** ~ **to sb** für jdn nicht zu erkennen sein

unrecognized [ʌn'rekəgnaɪzd] ADJ unerkannt; (= not acknowledged) genius, talent also ungewürdigt; **to go** ~ (person, talent, achievement) nicht gewürdigt or anerkannt werden

unrecorded [ʌnrɪ'kɔːdɪd] ADJ (in documents) nicht festgehalten

unredeemed [ʌnrɪ'diːmd] ADJ pledge (from pawn) uneingelöst; mortgage, debt ungetilgt

unrefined [ʌnrɪ'faɪnd] ADJ petroleum etc nicht raffiniert; person unkultiviert; manners unfein

unregarded [ʌnrɪ'gɑːdɪd] ADJ unbeachtet; **to go** ~ unbeachtet bleiben

unregistered [ʌn'redʒɪstəd] ADJ birth nicht gemeldet; car, firearm nicht angemeldet; voter nicht (im Wähler-verzeichnis) eingetragen; trademark nicht gesetzlich geschützt; letter nicht eingeschrieben; taxi, agent nicht zugelassen

unregulated [ʌn'regjʊleɪtɪd] ADJ unkontrolliert

unrehearsed [ʌnrɪ'hɜːst] ADJ (= spontaneous) spontan

unrelated [ʌnrɪ'leɪtɪd] ADJ (= unconnected) ohne Beziehung (to zu); (by family) nicht verwandt; **the two events are** ~ die beiden Ereignisse stehen in keinem Zusammenhang miteinander

unrelenting [ʌnrɪ'lentɪŋ] ADJ pressure unablässig; opposition, attack, struggle unerbittlich; violence, criticism, pain, pace, severity unvermindert; determination hartnäckig; (= not merciful) person, heat unbarmherzig

unreliability ['ʌnrɪˌlaɪə'bɪlɪtɪ] N Unzuverlässigkeit f

unreliable [ʌnrɪ'laɪəbl] ADJ unzuverlässig

unremarkable [ʌnrɪ'mɑːkəbl] ADJ nicht sehr bemerkenswert

unremitting [ʌnrɪ'mɪtɪŋ] ADJ efforts, toil unaufhörlich, unablässig; zeal unermüdlich; hatred unversöhnlich

unrepeatable [ʌnrɪ'piːtəbl] ADJ words, views nicht wiederholbar; offer, chance einmalig

unrepentant [ˌʌnrɪ'pentənt] ADJ reu(e)los

unreported [ˌʌnrɪ'pɔːtɪd] ADJ *events* nicht berichtet; *crime* nicht angezeigt

unrepresentative [ˌʌnreprɪ'zentətɪv] ADJ *minority, sample etc* nicht repräsentativ; **~ of sth** nicht repräsentativ für etw

unrepresented [ˌʌnreprɪ'zentɪd] ADJ nicht vertreten

unrequited [ˌʌnrɪ'kwaɪtɪd] ADJ *love* unerwidert

unreserved [ˌʌnrɪ'zɜːvd] ADJ *approval, apology, support* uneingeschränkt; *praise, admiration* rückhaltlos

unreservedly [ˌʌnrɪ'zɜːvɪdlɪ] ADV *speak* freimütig, offen; *approve, recommend* uneingeschränkt; *condemn* rückhaltlos

unresolved [ˌʌnrɪ'zɒlvd] ADJ *difficulty* ungelöst

unresponsive [ˌʌnrɪ'spɒnsɪv] ADJ *(physically)* nicht reagierend *attr; (emotionally, intellectually)* unempfänglich; **to be ~** nicht reagieren *(to* auf *+acc); (to pleas, request also)* nicht empfänglich sein *(to* für); **an ~ audience** ein Publikum, das nicht mitgeht; **I suggested it but he was fairly ~** ich habe es vorgeschlagen, aber er zeigte sich nicht sehr interessiert

unrest [ʌn'rest] N Unruhen *pl; (= discontent)* Unzufriedenheit *f*

unrestrained [ˌʌnrɪ'streɪnd] ADJ uneingeschränkt, unkontrolliert; *feelings* ungehemmt; *joy, enthusiasm* ungezügelt; *behaviour* unbeherrscht; *laughter, violence* hemmungslos

unrestricted [ˌʌnrɪ'strɪktɪd] ADJ **(a)** *power, use, growth* uneingeschränkt; *travel, access* ungehindert **(b)** *(= unobstructed) view* ungehindert

unrewarded [ˌʌnrɪ'wɔːdɪd] ADJ unbelohnt; **to go ~** unbelohnt bleiben

unrewarding [ˌʌnrɪ'wɔːdɪŋ] ADJ *work* undankbar

unripe [ʌn'raɪp] ADJ unreif

unrivalled, *(US)* **unrivaled** [ʌn'raɪvəld] ADJ unerreicht, unübertroffen

unroll [ʌn'rəʊl] **1** VT aufrollen **2** VI *(carpet etc)* sich aufrollen

unromantic [ˌʌnrə'mæntɪk] ADJ unromantisch

unruffled [ʌn'rʌfld] ADJ *person* gelassen; *calm* unerschütterlich; **she was** *or* **remained quite ~** sie blieb ruhig und gelassen

unruly [ʌn'ruːlɪ] ADJ (+ER) *child, behaviour* wild; *elements, crowd also* tobend

unsaddle [ʌn'sædl] VT *horse* absatteln

unsafe [ʌn'seɪf] ADJ *ladder, machine, car, person* nicht sicher; *(= dangerous) journey, toy, wiring, street, activity* gefährlich; *drug* gesundheitsschädigend; **this is ~ to eat/drink** das ist nicht genießbar/trinkbar; **it is ~ to walk there at night** es ist gefährlich, dort nachts spazieren zu gehen; **to feel ~** sich nicht sicher fühlen

unsafe sex N ungeschützter Sex

unsaid [ʌn'sed] ADJ **to leave sth ~** etw unausgesprochen lassen

unsalaried [ʌn'sælərɪd] ADJ ehrenamtlich

unsaleable, *(US)* **unsalable** [ʌn'seɪləbl] ADJ unverkäuflich; **to be ~** sich nicht verkaufen lassen

unsanitary [ʌn'sænɪtrɪ] ADJ unhygienisch

unsatisfactory [ˌʌnsætɪs'fæktərɪ] ADJ unbefriedigend; *profits, figures* nicht ausreichend; *service* unzulänglich; *(Sch)* mangelhaft, ungenügend; **this is highly ~** das lässt sehr zu wünschen übrig

unsatisfied [ʌn'sætɪsfaɪd] ADJ *person* unzufrieden; *(= not convinced)* nicht überzeugt; *desire, need, curiosity* unbefriedigt; **the book's ending left us ~** wir fanden den Schluss des Buches unbefriedigend

unsatisfying [ʌn'sætɪsfaɪɪŋ] ADJ unbefriedigend; *meal* unzureichend

unsaturated [ʌn'sætʃəreɪtɪd] ADJ *(Chem)* ungesättigt

unsavoury, *(US)* **unsavory** [ʌn'seɪvərɪ] ADJ *(= unpleasant) smell, sight* widerwärtig; *appearance (= repulsive)* abstoßend; *(= dishonest etc)* fragwürdig; *subject, details, rumours* unerfreulich; *district* übel; *characters* zwielichtig; *reputation* zweifelhaft

unscathed [ʌn'skeɪðd] ADJ *(lit)* unverletzt, unversehrt; *(fig)* unbeschadet; *relationship* heil

unscented [ʌn'sentɪd] ADJ geruchlos

unscheduled [ʌn'ʃedjuːld] ADJ *stop, flight etc* außerfahrplanmäßig; *meeting, visit* außerplanmäßig

unscientific [ˌʌnsaɪən'tɪfɪk] ADJ unwissenschaftlich

unscramble [ʌn'skræmbl] VT entwirren; *(Telec) message, signal* entschlüsseln

unscrew [ʌn'skruː] VT losschrauben; *plate, lid also* abschrauben; **to come ~ed** sich lösen

unscrupulous [ʌn'skruːpjʊləs] ADJ skrupellos, gewissenlos

unseal [ʌn'siːl] VT öffnen

unsealed [ʌn'siːld] ADJ offen, unverschlossen

unseasonable [ʌn'siːznəbl] ADJ nicht der Jahreszeit entsprechend *attr*

unseasonably [ʌn'siːznəblɪ] ADV (für die Jahreszeit) ungewöhnlich *or* außergewöhnlich

unseat [ʌn'siːt] VT *rider* abwerfen; *person (from office)* seines Amtes entheben

unsecured [ˌʌnsɪ'kjʊəd] ADJ *(Fin) loan, bond* ohne Sicherheit(en); **~ debenture** ungesicherte Schuldverschreibung

unseeded [ʌn'siːdɪd] ADJ unplatziert

unseeing [ʌn'siːɪŋ] ADJ *(lit, fig)* blind; *gaze* leer; **to stare at sb/sth with ~ eyes** jdn/etw mit leerem Blick anstarren

unseemly [ʌn'siːmlɪ] ADJ ungebührlich

unseen [ʌn'siːn] ADJ ungesehen; *(= invisible)* unsichtbar; *(= unobserved) escape* unbemerkt

unselfconscious ADJ, **unselfconsciously** ADV [ˌʌnself'kɒnʃəs, -lɪ] unbefangen

unselfish ADJ, **unselfishly** ADV [ʌn'selfɪʃ, -lɪ] uneigennützig, selbstlos

unsentimental [ˌʌnsentɪ'mentl] ADJ unsentimental

unsettle [ʌn'setl] VT *(= throw off balance, confuse)* aus dem Gleichgewicht bringen; *(= agitate, upset)* aufregen; *person (news)* beunruhigen; *(failure, criticism) market* verunsichern

unsettled [ʌn'setld] ADJ **(a)** *(= unpaid)* unbezahlt, unbeglichen; *(= undecided) question* ungeklärt, offen; **the question remains ~** die Frage bleibt ungelöst **(b)** *(= changeable) weather, market* unbeständig; *life, character* unstet, unruhig; **to be ~** durcheinander sein; *(= thrown off balance)* aus dem Gleis geworfen sein; **to feel ~** sich nicht wohl fühlen

unsettling [ʌn'setlɪŋ] ADJ *change, pace of life* aufreibend; *time also* aufregend; *defeat, knowledge* verunsichernd; *thought, news, book, atmosphere* beunruhigend

unsexy [ʌn'seksɪ] ADJ *(inf)* nicht sexy *(inf)*

unshak(e)able ADJ, **unshak(e)ably** ADV [ʌn'ʃeɪkəbl, -ɪ] unerschütterlich

unshaken [ʌn'ʃeɪkən] ADJ unerschüttert; **he was ~ by the accident** der Unfall erschütterte ihn nicht

unshaven [ʌn'ʃeɪvn] ADJ unrasiert

unshockable [ʌn'ʃɒkəbl] ADJ durch nichts zu schockieren

unsightly [ʌn'saɪtlɪ] ADJ unansehnlich; *(stronger)* hässlich

unsigned [ʌn'saɪnd] ADJ *painting* unsigniert; *letter* nicht unterzeichnet

unsinkable [ʌn'sɪŋkəbl] ADJ unsinkbar; *battleship* unversenkbar

unskilful, *(US)* **unskillful** [ʌn'skɪlfʊl] ADJ *(= inexpert)* ungeschickt; *(= clumsy)* unbeholfen

unskilled [ʌn'skɪld] ADJ **(a)** *work, worker* ungelernt; **to be ~ in sth** ungeübt in etw *(dat)* sein; **~ labour** *(Brit)* or **labor** *(US)* *(= workers)* Hilfsarbeiter *pl* **(b)** *(= inexperienced)* unerfahren

unskillful *etc (US)* = **unskilful** *etc*

unsociable [ʌn'səʊʃəbl] ADJ ungesellig

unsocial [ʌn'səʊʃəl] ADJ **to work ~ hours** außerhalb der normalen Arbeitszeiten arbeiten

unsold [ʌn'səʊld] ADJ unverkauft; **to go** *or* **be left** *or* **remain ~** nicht verkauft werden

unsolicited [ˌʌnsə'lɪsɪtɪd] ADJ unerbeten

unsolved [ʌn'sɒlvd] ADJ *crossword, problem etc* ungelöst; *mystery also, crime* unaufgeklärt

unsophisticated [ˌʌnsə'fɪstɪkeɪtɪd] ADJ **(a)** *(= simple) person* einfach; *style also* natürlich; *tastes* schlicht; *film, machine also* unkompliziert; *technique also* simpel **(b)** *(= crude) method* grob(schlächtig)

unsound [ʌn'saʊnd] ADJ **(a)** *timber* morsch; *construction, design* unsolide; *foundations, finances* unsicher; **structurally ~ building** bautechnische Mängel aufweisend *attr* **(b)** *argument* nicht stichhaltig; *advice* unvernünftig; *judgement* unzuverlässig; *policy, move* unklug; *(Jur) conviction* ungesichert; **of ~ mind** (*Jur*) unzurechnungsfähig; **ecologically ~** ökologisch nicht vertretbar; **environmentally ~** umweltschädlich; **~ banking procedures** heikle Bankgeschäfte *pl*; **the company is ~** die Firma steht auf schwachen Füßen; **our financial position is ~** unsere Finanzlage ist heikel

unsparing [ʌnˈspɛərɪŋ] ADJ **(a)** (= *lavish*) großzügig, verschwenderisch; **to be ~ in one's efforts** keine Kosten und Mühen scheuen **(b)** (= *unmerciful*) *criticism* schonungslos; **the report was ~ in its criticism** der Bericht übte schonungslos Kritik

unspeakable ADJ, **unspeakably** ADV [ʌnˈspiːkəbl, -ɪ] unbeschreiblich

unspecified [ʌnˈspɛsɪfaɪd] ADJ *time, amount* nicht genau angegeben; *location* unbestimmt

unspectacular [ʌnspɛkˈtækjʊləʳ] ADJ wenig eindrucksvoll; *career* wenig Aufsehen erregend

unspoiled [ʌnˈspɔɪld], **unspoilt** [ʌnˈspɔɪlt] ADJ (*by tourism, civilization*) unberührt

unspoken [ʌnˈspəʊkən] ADJ *words, thoughts* unausgesprochen; *agreement, consent* stillschweigend

unsporting [ʌnˈspɔːtɪŋ], **unsportsmanlike** [ʌnˈspɔːtsmənlaɪk] ADJ unsportlich, unfair

unstable [ʌnˈsteɪbl] ADJ instabil (*also Chem, Phys*); *foundations also, area* unsicher; *government, country* instabil; *economy, prices* schwankend; (*Psych: mentally*) labil

unstatesmanlike [ʌnˈsteɪtsmənlaɪk] ADJ unstaatsmännisch

unsteadily [ʌnˈstɛdɪlɪ] ADJ *rise, walk* schwankend, unsicher

unsteady [ʌnˈstɛdɪ] ADJ *hand, legs, steps* unsicher; *ladder* wack(e)lig; *voice, economy* schwankend; *progress* ungleichmäßig; *growth* unregelmäßig; **the pound is still ~** das Pfund schwankt noch

unstinting [ʌnˈstɪntɪŋ] ADJ *person* großzügig; *kindness, support* uneingeschränkt; *work* unermüdlich; **to be ~ in one's efforts** keine Kosten und Mühen scheuen

unstoppable [ʌnˈstɒpəbl] ADJ nicht aufzuhalten

unstructured [ʌnˈstrʌktʃəd] ADJ unstrukturiert, nicht strukturiert

unstuck [ʌnˈstʌk] ADJ **to come ~** (*stamp, notice*) sich lösen; (*inf*) (*plan*) schief gehen (*inf*); (*speaker, actor*) stecken bleiben; **where they came ~ was ...** sie sind daran gescheitert, dass ...

unsubsidized [ʌnˈsʌbsɪdaɪzd] ADJ unsubventioniert

unsubstantial [ʌnsəbˈstænʃəl] ADJ *structure, meal* leicht; *evidence* nicht überzeugend; *claim* ungerechtfertigt

unsubstantiated [ʌnsəbˈstænʃɪeɪtɪd] ADJ *accusation, testimony, rumour* unbegründet; *gossip* unbestätigt; **these reports remain ~** diese Berichte sind weiterhin unbestätigt

unsubtle [ʌnˈsʌtl] ADJ plump; **how ~ can you get!** plumper gehts nicht!

unsuccessful [ʌnsəkˈsɛsfʊl] ADJ erfolglos; *venture, visit, meeting, person etc also* ergebnislos; *candidate* abgewiesen; *attempt* vergeblich; *marriage, outcome* unglücklich; **to be ~ in doing sth** keinen Erfolg damit haben, etw zu tun; **to be ~ in one's efforts to do sth** erfolglos in seinem Bemühen sein, etw zu tun

unsuccessfully [ʌnsəkˈsɛsfəlɪ] ADV erfolglos; *try* vergeblich; *apply* ohne Erfolg

unsuitability [ʌnsuːtəˈbɪlɪtɪ] N Ungeeignetsein *nt*; **his ~ for the job** seine mangelnde Eignung für die Stelle; **their ~ as partners is clear** es ist klar, dass sie keine geeigneten Partner füreinander sind

unsuitable [ʌnˈsuːtəbl] ADJ unpassend; *moment, clothes, colour also, candidate, land* ungeeignet; **this film is ~ for children** dieser Film ist für Kinder ungeeignet *or* nicht geeignet; **she is ~ for him** sie ist nicht die Richtige für ihn

unsuitably [ʌnˈsuːtəblɪ] ADV *dressed* (*for weather conditions*) unzweckmäßig; (*for occasion*) unpassend

unsuited [ʌnˈsuːtɪd] ADJ **to be ~ for** *or* **to sth** für etw ungeeignet *or* untauglich sein; **to be ~ to sb** nicht zu jdm passen

unsupported [ʌnsəˈpɔːtɪd] ADJ *roof, person* ungestützt; *claim, theory* ohne Beweise; *statement* unbestätigt

unsure [ʌnˈʃʊəʳ] ADJ *person* unsicher; **to be ~ of oneself** unsicher sein; **to be ~ (of sth)** sich (*dat*) (einer Sache *gen*) nicht sicher sein; **I'm ~ of him** ich bin mir bei ihm nicht sicher

unsurpassed [ʌnsəˈpɑːst] ADJ unübertroffen

unsurprising ADJ, **unsurprisingly** ADV [ʌnsəˈpraɪzɪŋ, -lɪ] wenig überraschend

unsuspected [ʌnsəˈspɛktɪd] ADJ *coal deposits, causes* unvermutet; *wealth, powers* ungeahnt

unsuspecting ADJ, **unsuspectingly** ADV [ʌnsəˈspɛktɪŋ, -lɪ] ahnungslos, nichts ahnend

unsweetened [ʌnˈswiːtnd] ADJ ungesüßt

unswerving [ʌnˈswɜːvɪŋ] ADJ *resolve, loyalty* unerschütterlich, unbeirrbar

unsympathetic [ʌnsɪmpəˈθɛtɪk] ADJ **(a)** (= *unfeeling*) gefühllos; *attitude, response* abweisend **(b)** (= *unlikeable*) unsympathisch

unsympathetically [ʌnsɪmpəˈθɛtɪkəlɪ] ADV ohne Mitgefühl; *say also* gefühllos

unsystematic ADJ, **unsystematically** ADV [ʌnsɪstɪˈmætɪk, -əlɪ] planlos, unsystematisch

untainted [ʌnˈteɪntɪd] ADJ einwandfrei, tadellos; *person* unverdorben

untalented [ʌnˈtæləntɪd] ADJ unbegabt

untamed [ʌnˈteɪmd] ADJ *animal* ungezähmt; *jungle, landscape, beauty* wild

untangle [ʌnˈtæŋgl] VT (*lit, fig*) entwirren

untapped [ʌnˈtæpt] ADJ *resources, source of wealth, talent* ungenutzt; *market* unerschlossen

untarnished [ʌnˈtɑːnɪʃt] ADJ (*lit, fig*) makellos; *silver also* nicht angelaufen

untaught [ʌnˈtɔːt] ADJ nicht ausgebildet

untaxed [ʌnˈtækst] ADJ *goods, income* steuerfrei; *car* unversteuert

untenable [ʌnˈtɛnəbl] ADJ (*lit, fig*) unhaltbar

untenanted [ʌnˈtɛnəntɪd] ADJ *house* unbewohnt

untended [ʌnˈtɛndɪd] ADJ *patient* unbehütet, unbewacht; *garden* vernachlässigt

untested [ʌnˈtɛstɪd] ADJ *person* unerprobt; *theory, product also* ungetestet

unthinkable [ʌnˈθɪŋkəbl] ADJ undenkbar; (= *too horrible*) unvorstellbar

unthinking [ʌnˈθɪŋkɪŋ] ADJ (= *thoughtless*) unbedacht, gedankenlos; (= *uncritical*) bedenkenlos, blind

unthinkingly [ʌnˈθɪŋkɪŋlɪ] ADV (= *thoughtlessly*) unbedacht, gedankenlos; *assume* ohne nachzudenken

untidily [ʌnˈtaɪdɪlɪ] ADV unordentlich

untidiness [ʌnˈtaɪdɪnɪs] N (*of room*) Unordnung *f*; (*of person*) Unordentlichkeit *f*

untidy [ʌnˈtaɪdɪ] ADJ (+ER) unordentlich

untie [ʌnˈtaɪ] VT *knot* lösen; *string, tie, shoelaces also* aufbinden; *parcel* aufknoten; *person, animal, hands, apron* losbinden

until [ənˈtɪl] **1** PREP bis; **from morning ~ night** von morgens bis abends; **~ now** bis jetzt; **~ then** bis dahin; **not ~** (*in future*) nicht vor (+*dat*); (*in past*) erst; **I didn't leave him ~ the following day** ich bin bis zum nächsten Tag bei ihm geblieben

2 CONJ bis; **wait ~ I come** warten Sie, bis ich komme; **not ~** (*in future*) nicht bevor, erst wenn; (*in past*) erst als; **he won't come ~ you invite him** er kommt erst, wenn Sie ihn einladen; **they did nothing ~ we came** bis wir kamen, taten sie nichts

untimely [ʌnˈtaɪmlɪ] ADJ (= *premature*) *death* vorzeitig; *end also* verfrüht; (= *inopportune*) *development, occurrence, visit* ungelegen; **to come to** *or* **meet an ~ end** ein vorzeitiges Ende finden

untiring ADJ, **untiringly** ADV [ʌnˈtaɪərɪŋ, -lɪ] unermüdlich

untitled [ʌnˈtaɪtld] ADJ *painting* ohne Titel

untold [ʌnˈtəʊld] ADJ *story* nicht erzählt; *wealth, damage, suffering* unermesslich; *agony, delights* unsäglich; *losses* unzählig; **this story is better left ~** über diese Geschichte schweigt man besser; **~ thousands** unzählig viele

untouchable [ʌnˈtʌtʃəbl] ADJ unantastbar

untouched [ʌnˈtʌtʃt] ADJ **(a)** (= *unhandled, unused*) unberührt, unangetastet; *bottle etc* nicht angebrochen; **~ by human hand** nicht von Menschenhand berührt **(b)** (= *unharmed*) heil, unversehrt

untoward [ʌntəˈwɔːd] ADJ (= *unseemly*) unpassend, ungehörig

untrained [ʌn'treɪnd] ADJ *person, teacher* unausgebildet; *voice, mind* ungeschult; *animal* undressiert; **to the ~ eye** dem ungeschulten Auge

untranslatable [ˌʌntrænz'leɪtəbl] ADJ unübersetzbar

untreated [ʌn'triːtɪd] ADJ unbehandelt

untried [ʌn'traɪd] ADJ (= *not tested*) *person* unerprobt; *product, method* ungetestet; (= *not attempted*) unversucht

untroubled [ʌn'trʌbld] ADJ *appearance* unbekümmert; *sleep* ungestört; *period, person* friedlich, ruhig; **to be ~ by the news** eine Nachricht gleichmütig hinnehmen; **the children seemed ~ by the heat** die Hitze schien den Kindern nichts auszumachen; **to be ~ by injury** von Verletzungen verschont bleiben; **to be ~ by the police** von der Polizei nicht belästigt werden

untrue [ʌn'truː] ADJ (= *false*) unwahr, falsch

untrustworthy [ʌn'trʌst,wɜːðɪ] ADJ (= *not reliable*) unzuverlässig; (= *not worthy of confidence*) nicht vertrauenswürdig

untruthful [ʌn'truːθfʊl] ADJ *statement* unwahr; *person* unaufrichtig

untruthfully [ʌn'truːθfəlɪ] ADV fälschlich; **he said, quite ~, that ...** er sagte, und das war nicht die Wahrheit, dass ...

untypical [ʌn'tɪpɪkl] ADJ untypisch (*of* für)

unusable [ʌn'juːzəbl] ADJ unbrauchbar

unused¹ [ʌn'juːzd] ADJ (= *new*) unbenutzt, ungebraucht; (= *not made use of*) ungenutzt; (= *no longer used*) nicht mehr benutzt *or* gebraucht

unused² [ʌn'juːst] ADJ **to be ~ to sth** etw (*acc*) nicht gewohnt sein; **to be ~ to doing sth** es nicht gewohnt sein, etw zu tun

unusual [ʌn'juːʒʊəl] ADJ (= *uncommon*) ungewöhnlich; (= *exceptional*) außergewöhnlich; **it's ~ for him to be late** er kommt normalerweise nicht zu spät; **that's ~ for him** das ist sonst nicht seine Art; **that's not ~ for him** das wundert mich überhaupt nicht; **how ~!** das kommt selten vor; (*iro*) welch Wunder!

unusually [ʌn'juːʒʊəlɪ] ADV ungewöhnlich; **~ for her, she was late** ganz gegen ihre Gewohnheit kam sie zu spät; **~ for a big city, it has no cinema** obwohl das für eine Großstadt ungewöhnlich ist, gibt es hier/dort kein Kino

unvarnished [ʌn'vɑːnɪʃt] ADJ unlackiert

unvarying [ʌn'vɛərɪɪŋ] ADJ gleich bleibend, unveränderlich

unveil [ʌn'veɪl] VT *statue, plan* enthüllen; (*Comm*) *car* vorstellen

unveiling [ʌn'veɪlɪŋ] N (*lit, fig*) Enthüllung *f*

unverifiable [ʌn'verɪfaɪəbl] ADJ nicht beweisbar

unverified [ʌn'verɪfaɪd] ADJ unbewiesen

unwaged [ʌn'weɪdʒd] ADJ ohne Einkommen

unwanted [ʌn'wɒntɪd] ADJ (a) (= *unwelcome, unplanned*) unerwünscht (b) (= *superfluous*) überflüssig

unwarranted [ʌn'wɒrəntɪd] ADJ ungerechtfertigt

unwary [ʌn'wɛərɪ] ADJ unvorsichtig, unachtsam

unwashed [ʌn'wɒʃt] ADJ ungewaschen; *dishes* ungespült

unwavering [ʌn'weɪvərɪŋ] ADJ *faith, resolve* unerschütterlich; *gaze, voice* fest; *course* beharrlich

unwaveringly [ʌn'weɪvərɪŋlɪ] ADV *gaze, aim* fest; *support, oppose* beharrlich

unwelcome [ʌn'welkəm] ADJ *visitor* unerwünscht; *news, memories* unerfreulich; *side effect, surprise* unangenehm; *reminder, change, publicity, advances* unwillkommen; **to make sb feel ~** sich jdm gegenüber abweisend verhalten

unwelcoming [ʌn'welkəmɪŋ] ADJ *manner* abweisend, unfreundlich; *host also, place* ungastlich

unwell [ʌn'wel] ADJ PRED unwohl, nicht wohl; **I am afraid he's rather ~ today** es geht ihm heute leider gar nicht gut

unwholesome [ʌn'həʊlsəm] ADJ ungesund; *influence* ungut; *appearance, character* schmierig; *food* minderwertig; *desire, thoughts* schmutzig; **to have an ~ interest in sb/sth** ein perverses Interesse an jdm/etw haben

unwieldy [ʌn'wiːldɪ] ADJ *tool* unhandlich; *object also* sperrig; (= *clumsy*) *body* schwerfällig, unbeholfen; *system, bureaucracy* schwerfällig

unwilling [ʌn'wɪlɪŋ] ADJ *helper, pupil* widerwillig; *accomplice* unfreiwillig; **to be ~ to do sth** nicht bereit *or* gewillt sein, etw zu tun; **to be ~ for sb to do sth** nicht wollen, dass jd etw tut

unwillingly [ʌn'wɪlɪŋlɪ] ADV widerwillig

unwillingness [ʌn'wɪlɪŋnɪs] N Widerwillen *nt*; **their ~ to compromise** ihre mangelnde Kompromissbereitschaft

unwind [ʌn'waɪnd], *pret, ptp* **unwound** ◨ VT *thread, tape* abwickeln ◪ VI (a) (*lit*) sich abwickeln; (*fig: story, plot*) sich entwickeln (b) (*inf: = relax*) abschalten (*inf*)

unwise [ʌn'waɪz] ADJ unklug

unwisely [ʌn'waɪzlɪ] ADV unklug; **rather ~ the Government agreed** die Regierung hat unklugerweise zugestimmt

unwitting [ʌn'wɪtɪŋ] ADJ *accomplice* unbewusst, unwissentlich; *victim* ahnungslos; *involvement* unabsichtlich

unwittingly [ʌn'wɪtɪŋlɪ] ADV unbewusst

unworkable [ʌn'wɜːkəbl] ADJ *scheme, idea* undurchführbar; *law* nicht durchsetzbar

unworkmanlike [ʌn'wɜːkmənlaɪk] ADJ *job* unfachmännisch

unworldly [ʌn'wɜːldlɪ] ADJ *life* weltabgewandt

unworried [ʌn'wʌrɪd] ADJ unbekümmert, sorglos; **he was ~ by my criticism** meine Kritik (be)kümmerte ihn nicht

unworthiness [ʌn'wɜːðɪnɪs] N Unwürdigkeit *f*

unworthy [ʌn'wɜːðɪ] ADJ nicht wert (*of* +*gen*); **this is ~ of you** das ist unter deiner Würde

unwound [ʌn'waʊnd] PRET, PTP *of* **unwind**

unwounded [ʌn'wuːndɪd] ADJ unverwundet

unwrap [ʌn'ræp] VT auspacken, auswickeln

unwritten [ʌn'rɪtn] ADJ *story, constitution* ungeschrieben; *agreement* stillschweigend

unwritten law N (*Jur, fig*) ungeschriebenes Gesetz

unyielding [ʌn'jiːldɪŋ] ADJ *substance* unnachgiebig; (*fig*) *person, demand* also hart

unzip [ʌn'zɪp] VT *zip* aufmachen; *dress, trousers, case* den Reißverschluss aufmachen an (+*dat*)

---

up [ʌp]	
◨ ADVERB	◪ ADJECTIVE
◩ PREPOSITION	◫ TRANSITIVE VERB
◪ NOUN	◬ INTRANSITIVE VERB

◨ ADVERB

(a) (= *in high or higher position*) oben; (= *higher position*) nach oben; **up there** dort oben; **on your way up (to see them)** auf dem Weg (zu ihnen) hinauf; **he climbed all the way up (to them)** er ist den ganzen Weg (zu ihnen) hochgeklettert; **to stop halfway up** auf halber Höhe anhalten; **5 floors up** 5 Stockwerke hoch; **I looked up (above)** ich schaute nach oben; **this side up** diese Seite oben!; **a little further up** ein bisschen weiter oben; **to go a little further up** ein bisschen höher (hinauf)gehen; **stick the notice up here** häng den Anschlag hier hin; **from up on the hill** vom Berg oben; **up on top of the cupboard** ganz oben (auf dem Schrank); **up in the mountains/sky** oben in den Bergen/am Himmel; **the temperature was up in the thirties** die Temperatur war über dreißig Grad; **the sun is up** die Sonne ist aufgegangen; **with his collar up** mit hochgeschlagenem Kragen; **the road is up** (*Brit*) die Straße ist aufgegraben; **to move up into the lead** nach vorn an die Spitze kommen; **then up jumps Richard and says ...** dann springt Richard auf und sagt ...; **up with Spurs!** Spurs hoch!; **up yours!** (*inf*) du kannst mich mal (*inf*)
(b) (= *installed, built*) **to be up** (*building*) stehen; (*tent also*) aufgeschlagen sein; (*scaffolding*) aufgestellt sein; (*notice*) angeschlagen sein; (*shelves, wallpaper, curtains, picture*) hängen; **the new houses went up very quickly** die neuen Häuser sind sehr schnell gebaut *or* hochgezogen (*inf*) worden

+**to be up and running** laufen; (*committee etc*) in Gang sein
+**to get sth up and running** etw zum Laufen bringen; *committee etc* etw in Gang setzen

(c) (= *not in bed*) auf; **to be up and about** auf sein; (*after illness also*) auf den Beinen sein
(d) (= *north*) oben; **up in Inverness** in Inverness oben, oben in Inverness; **we are going up to Aberdeen** wir fahren nach Aberdeen (hinauf); **to live up north** im Norden wohnen; **to go up north** in den Norden fahren
(e) (*in price, value*) gestiegen (*on* gegenüber); **my shares are up 70p** meine Aktien sind um 70 Pence gestiegen
(f) (*in score*) **to be 3 goals up** mit 3 Toren führen *or* vorn

liegen (*on* gegenüber); **the score was 9 up** (*US*) es stand 9 beide; **we were £100 up on the deal** wir haben bei dem Geschäft £ 100 gemacht; **to be one up on sb** jdm um einen Schritt voraus sein

(g) (= *wrong*) (*inf*) **what's up?** was ist los?; **something is up** (= *wrong*) da stimmt irgendetwas nicht; (= *happening*) da ist irgendetwas im Gange

(h) (= *knowledgeable*) firm, beschlagen (*in, on* +*dat*); **he's well up on foreign affairs** in außenpolitischen Fragen kennt er sich aus

(i) (= *finished*) **time's up** die Zeit ist um; **to eat/use sth up** etw aufessen/aufbrauchen

(j) (*set structures*)

◆**up against** it was up against the wall es war an die Wand gelehnt; **to be up against an opponent** einem Gegner gegenüberstehen; **I fully realize what I'm up against** mir ist völlig klar, womit es hier zu tun habe; **they were really up against it** sie hatten wirklich schwer zu schaffen

◆**up and down** auf und ab; **to walk up and down** auf und ab gehen

◆**up before** the matter is up before the committee die Sache ist vor dem Ausschuss

◆**up for** to be up for sale zu verkaufen sein; **to be up for discussion** zur Diskussion stehen; **to be up for election** (*candidate*) zur Wahl aufgestellt sein; (*candidates*) zur Wahl stehen

◆**up to** (= AS FAR AS) bis; **up to now/here** bis jetzt/hier; **to count up to 100** bis 100 zählen; **up to £100** bis zu £ 100; **I'm up to here in debt** (*inf*) ich stecke bis hier in Schulden; **what page are you up to?** bis zu welcher Seite bist du gekommen? (= EQUAL TO) **I don't feel up to it** ich fühle mich dem nicht gewachsen; (= *not well enough*) ich fühle mich nicht wohl genug dazu; **it isn't up to much** damit ist nicht viel los (*inf*); **he isn't up to running the company by himself** er hat nicht das Zeug dazu, die Firma allein zu leiten; **it isn't up to his usual standard** das ist nicht sein sonstiges Niveau

◆**to be up to sb** (= DEPEND ON) **it's up to us to help him** wir sollten ihm helfen; **if it were up to me** wenn es nach mir ginge; **it's up to you whether you go or not** es bleibt dir überlassen, ob du gehst oder nicht; **I'd like to accept, but it isn't up to me** ich würde gerne annehmen, aber das hängt nicht von mir ab; **shall I take it? – that's entirely up to you** soll ich es nehmen? – das müssen Sie selbst wissen; **what colour shall I choose? – (it's) up to you** welche Farbe soll ich nehmen? – das ist deine Entscheidung (= BE DUTY OF) **it's up to the government to put this right** es ist Sache der Regierung, das richtig zu stellen

◆**to be up to sth** (*inf*) **what's he up to?** (= *actually doing*) was macht er da?; (= *planning etc*) was hat er vor?; (*suspiciously*) was führt er im Schilde?; **what have you been up to?** was hast du angestellt?; **he's up to no good** er führt nichts Gutes im Schilde

2 PREPOSITION oben auf (+*dat*); (*with movement*) hinauf (+*acc*); **further up the page** weiter oben auf der Seite; **to live up the hill** am Berg wohnen; **to go up the hill** den Berg hinaufgehen; **they live further up the hill/street** sie wohnen weiter oben am Berg/weiter die Straße entlang; **he lives up a dark alley** er wohnt am Ende einer dunklen Gasse; **up the road from me** (von mir) die Straße entlang; **he went off up the road** er ging (weg) die Straße hinauf; **the water goes up this pipe** das Wasser geht durch dieses Rohr; **as I travel up and down the country** wenn ich so durchs Land reise; **to go up to sb** auf jdn zugehen

3 NOUN

◆**ups and downs** gute und schlechte Zeiten *pl*; (*of life*) Höhen und Tiefen *pl*

◆**to be on the up and up** (*inf*) auf dem aufsteigenden Ast sein (*inf*); **he is on the up and up** (*inf*) mit ihm geht es aufwärts

4 ADJECTIVE *escalator* nach oben

5 TRANSITIVE VERB (*inf*) *price, offer* hinaufsetzen; *production* ankurbeln; *bet* erhöhen (*to* auf +*acc*)

6 INTRANSITIVE VERB (*inf*) **she upped and left him** sie verließ ihn ganz plötzlich *or* Knall auf Fall (*inf*)

up-and-coming [ˈʌpənˈkʌmɪŋ] ADJ *city* aufstrebend; **an ~ star** ein Star, der im Kommen ist

up-and-down [ˈʌpənˈdaʊn] ADJ **(a)** (*lit*) ~ **movement** Auf- und Abbewegung *f* **(b)** (*fig*) *career, period etc* wechselhaft

up arrow N (*Comput*) Aufwärtspfeil *m*

upbeat [ˈʌpbiːt] ADJ (*inf*) (= *cheerful*) fröhlich; (= *optimistic*) optimistisch; **to be ~ about sth** über etw (*acc*) optimistisch gestimmt sein

upbringing [ˈʌpbrɪŋɪŋ] N Erziehung *f*; (= *manners also*) Kinderstube *f*; **we had a strict ~** wir hatten (als Kinder) eine strenge Erziehung

update [ʌpˈdeɪt] **1** VT aktualisieren; *file, book also, person* auf den neuesten Stand bringen; **to ~ sb on sth** jdn über etw (*acc*) auf den neuesten Stand bringen **2** [ˈʌpdeɪt] N Aktualisierung *f*; (= *progress report*) Bericht *m*

upend [ʌpˈend] VT *box, sofa* hochkant stellen; *person, animal* umdrehen

upfront [ˈʌpˈfrʌnt] **1** ADJ **(a)** *person* offen; **to be ~ about sth** sich offen über etw (*acc*) äußern **(b) an ~ fee** eine Gebühr, die im Voraus zu entrichten ist **2** ADV **(a)** *pay, charge* im Voraus; **we'd like 20%** ~ wir hätten gern 20% (als) Vorschuss **(b)** (*esp US*: = *openly*) offen

upgrade [ˈʌpˌɡreɪd] **1** N **(a)** (= *improved version*) verbesserte Version; (*Comput*) Upgrade *nt* **(b)** (*US*) Steigung *f* **2** [ʌpˈɡreɪd] VT *employee* befördern; *job* anheben; (= *improve*) verbessern; (= *expand*) *computer system etc* nachrüsten

upgrad(e)able [ʌpˈɡreɪdəbl] ADJ *computer system etc* ausbaufähig (*to* auf +*acc*), nachrüstbar (*to* auf +*acc*)

upheaval [ʌpˈhiːvəl] N (*fig*) Aufruhr *m*; **emotional ~** Aufruhr *m* der Gefühle; **social/political ~s** soziale/politische Umwälzungen *pl*

upheld [ʌpˈheld] PRET, PTP *of* **uphold**

uphill [ˈʌpˈhɪl] **1** ADV bergauf; **to go ~** bergauf gehen; (*road also*) bergauf führen; (*car*) den Berg hinauffahren **2** ADJ *road* bergauf (führend); (*fig*) *work, struggle* mühsam

uphold [ʌpˈhəʊld], *pret, ptp* **upheld** VT *tradition, principle* wahren; *the law* hüten; *right, values* schützen; (= *support*) *person, decision* (unter)stützen; *complaint* anerkennen; (*Jur*) *verdict, appeal* bestätigen

upholster [ʌpˈhəʊlstəʳ] VT polstern; (= *cover*) beziehen; **~ed furniture** Polstermöbel *pl*

upholstery [ʌpˈhəʊlstərɪ] N (= *padding and springs*) Polsterung *f*; (= *cover*) Bezug *m*

upkeep [ˈʌpkiːp] N (= *running*) Unterhalt *m*; (= *maintenance*) Instandhaltung *f*; (= *maintenance cost*) Instandhaltungskosten *pl*; (*of public gardens etc*) Pflege *f*

upland [ˈʌplənd] **1** N (*usu pl*) Hochland *nt no pl* **2** ADJ Hochland-

uplift [ˈʌplɪft] **1** N (= *exaltation*) Erhebung *f*; **an ~ in the economy** ein Wirtschaftsaufschwung *m* **2** [ʌpˈlɪft] VT *heart* erheben; *person* erbauen; **with ~ed arms** mit erhobenen Armen; **to feel ~ed** sich erbaut fühlen

uplifting [ʌpˈlɪftɪŋ] ADJ *experience* erhebend; *music, story* erbaulich

upload [ˈʌpləʊd] VT (*Comput*) uploaden

up-market [ˈʌpˈmɑːkɪt] **1** ADJ *customer* anspruchsvoll; *person* vornehm; *image, version, hotel* exklusiv **2** ADV *sell* an anspruchsvollere Kunden; **his shop has gone ~** in seinem Laden verkauft er jetzt Waren der höheren Preisklasse

upon [əˈpɒn] PREP = **on**

upper [ˈʌpəʳ] **1** ADJ obere(r, s); (*in rank, importance also*) höhere(r, s); (*Anat, Geog*) Ober-; **temperatures in the ~ thirties** Temperaturen hoch in den dreißig; ~ **body** Oberkörper *m*; **the ~ Loire** die obere Loire; **Upper Rhine** Oberrhein *m*; **the ~ ranks of the Civil Service** das gehobene Beamtentum **2** N **uppers** PL (*of shoe*) Obermaterial *nt*

upper: **upper case** N (*Typ: also* **upper-case letter**) Großbuchstabe *m*; **upper-case** ADJ groß; **upper circle** N (*Brit Theat*) zweiter Rang; **upper class** N obere Klasse, Oberschicht *f*; **the ~es** die Oberschicht; **upper-class** ADJ *accent, person* vornehm; *sport, attitude* der Oberschicht; **upperclassman** N

(US) Mitglied einer High School oder eines College; **Upper Egypt** N Oberägypten nt; **Upper House** N (Parl) Oberhaus nt

uppermost [ˈʌpəˈməʊst] **1** ADJ oberste(r, s); (fig) ambition größte(r, s); **safety should be ~ in your minds** Sicherheit sollte für Sie an erster Stelle stehen **2** ADV **face ~** mit dem Gesicht nach oben

upper school N Oberschule f

uppity [ˈʌpɪtɪ] ADJ (inf) hochnäsig (inf); woman also schnippisch; **to get ~ with sb** jdm frech kommen

upright [ˈʌpraɪt] **1** ADJ (lit, fig) aufrecht; (= honest) rechtschaffen; (= vertical) post senkrecht; **~ freezer** Gefrierschrank m **2** ADV (= erect) aufrecht, gerade; (vertical) senkrecht; **to pull sb/oneself ~** jdn/sich aufrichten **3** N (= post) Pfosten m

uprising [ˈʌpraɪzɪŋ] N Aufstand m

upriver [ˈʌpˈrɪvəʳ] ADV flussaufwärts

uproar [ˈʌprɔːʳ] N Aufruhr m, Tumult m; **the whole room was in ~** der ganze Saal war in Aufruhr

uproarious [ʌpˈrɔːrɪəs] ADJ meeting tumultartig; crowd lärmend; laughter brüllend; success, welcome spektakulär

uproariously [ʌpˈrɔːrɪəslɪ] ADV lärmend; laugh brüllend

uproot [ʌpˈruːt] VT plant entwurzeln; (fig) evil ausmerzen; **he ~ed his whole family (from their home) and moved to New York** er riss seine Familie aus ihrer gewohnten Umgebung und zog nach New York

upset [ʌpˈset], vb: pret, ptp upset **1** VT **(a)** (= knock over) umstoßen, umwerfen
(b) (= make sad: news, death) bestürzen; (question, insolence etc) aus der Fassung bringen; (divorce, experience, accident etc) mitnehmen (inf); (= distress, excite) aufregen; (= offend: unkind words etc) wehtun (+dat); (= annoy) ärgern; **don't ~ yourself** regen Sie sich nicht auf; **there's no point in ~ting yourself** es hat doch keinen Zweck, das so tragisch zu nehmen
(c) calculations, balance, plan etc durcheinander bringen; **the rich food ~ his stomach** das schwere Essen ist ihm nicht bekommen
2 ADJ **(a)** (about divorce, accident, dismissal etc) mitgenommen (inf) (about von); (about death, bad news etc) bestürzt (about über +acc); (= sad) betrübt (about über +acc); (= distressed, worried) aufgeregt (about wegen); child durcheinander pred; (= annoyed) aufgebracht (about über +acc); (= hurt) gekränkt (about über +acc); **she was pretty ~ about it** das ist ihr ziemlich nahe gegangen; (= distressed, worried) sie hat sich deswegen ziemlich aufgeregt; (= annoyed) das hat sie ziemlich geärgert; (= hurt) das hat sie ziemlich gekränkt; **she was ~ about something** irgendetwas hatte sie aus der Fassung gebracht; **she was ~ about the news/ that he'd left her** es hat sie ziemlich mitgenommen, als sie das hörte/dass er sie verlassen hat (inf); **would you be ~ if I decided not to go after all?** wärst du traurig, wenn ich doch nicht ginge?; **to get ~** sich aufregen (about über +acc); (= hurt) gekränkt or verletzt werden; **don't get ~ about it, you'll find another** nimm das doch nicht so tragisch, du findest bestimmt einen anderen; **to feel ~** gekränkt sein; **to sound/look ~** verstört klingen/aussehen
(b) [ˈʌpset] stomach verstimmt, verdorben attr; **to have an ~ stomach** (dat) den Magen verdorben haben
3 [ˈʌpset] N (= disturbance) Störung f; (emotional) Aufregung f; (inf) (= quarrel) Verstimmung f, Ärger m; (= unexpected defeat etc) unliebsame or böse Überraschung f; **stomach ~** Magenverstimmung f

upset price [ˈʌpsetpraɪs] N (esp US Comm) Mindestpreis m

upsetting [ʌpˈsetɪŋ] ADJ (= saddening) traurig; (stronger) bestürzend; (= disturbing) störend; situation schwierig; (= annoying) ärgerlich; **that must have been very ~ for you** das war bestimmt nicht einfach für Sie; **it is ~ (for them) to see such terrible things** es ist schlimm (für sie), so schreckliche Dinge zu sehen; **the divorce was very ~ for the child** das Kind hat unter der Scheidung sehr gelitten

upshot [ˈʌpʃɒt] N (= result) Ergebnis nt; **the ~ of it all was that ...** es lief darauf hinaus, dass ...

upside down [ˈʌpsaɪdˈdaʊn] ADV verkehrt herum; **to turn sth ~** (lit) etw umdrehen; (fig) etw auf den Kopf stellen (inf)

upside-down [ˈʌpsaɪdˈdaʊn] ADJ **to be ~** (picture) verkehrt herum hängen; (world) kopfstehen

upstage [ʌpˈsteɪdʒ] VT **to ~ sb** (fig) jdm die Schau stehlen (inf)

upstairs [ʌpˈsteəz] **1** ADV oben; (with movement) nach oben; **the people ~** die Leute über uns **2** ADJ window im oberen Stock(werk); room also obere(r, s) **3** N oberes Stockwerk

upstanding [ʌpˈstændɪŋ] ADJ (= strong) kräftig; (= honourable) rechtschaffen

upstart [ˈʌpstɑːt] **1** N Emporkömmling m **2** ADJ rival, company emporgekommen

upstate [ˈʌpsteɪt] (US) **1** ADJ im Norden (des Bundesstaates); **to live in ~ New York** im Norden des Staates New York wohnen **2** ADV im Norden (des Bundesstaates); (with movement) in den Norden (des Bundesstaates)

upstream [ˈʌpstriːm] **1** ADV flussaufwärts **2** ADJ flussaufwärts gelegen

upstretched [ʌpˈstretʃt] ADJ arms ausgestreckt

upsurge [ˈʌpsɜːdʒ] N Zunahme f; (of fighting) Eskalation f (pej)

upswing [ˈʌpswɪŋ] N (lit, fig) Aufschwung m

uptake [ˈʌpteɪk] N (inf) **to be quick on the ~** schnell verstehen; **to be slow on the ~** eine lange Leitung haben (inf)

uptight [ˈʌptaɪt] ADJ (inf) (= nervous) nervös; (= inhibited) verklemmt (inf); (= angry) sauer (inf); **to get ~ (about sth)** sich (wegen etw) aufregen; (auf etw acc) verklemmt reagieren (inf); (wegen etw) sauer werden (inf)

up-to-date [ˈʌptəˈdeɪt] ADJ ATTR, **up to date** ADJ PRED auf dem neusten Stand; fashion also, book, news, information aktuell; person, method also up to date pred (inf); **to keep ~ with the news** mit den Nachrichten auf dem Laufenden bleiben; **to keep sb/sth/oneself up to date** jdn/etw/sich auf dem Laufenden halten; **would you bring me up to date on developments?** würden Sie mich über den neusten Stand der Dinge informieren?

up-to-the-minute [ˈʌptəðəˈmɪnɪt] ADJ news, reports allerneuste(r, s); style also hochmodern

uptown [ˈʌptaʊn] (US) **1** ADJ (= in northern part of town) im Norden (der Stadt); (= in residential area) im Villenviertel; person anspruchsvoll; bar, theatre, store vornehm; **~ New York** der Norden von New York **2** ADV im Norden der Stadt; im Villenviertel; (with movement) in den Norden der Stadt; ins Villenviertel

uptrend [ˈʌptrend] N (Econ) Aufwärtstrend m

upturn [ˈʌptɜːn] N (fig) Aufschwung m

upturned [ʌpˈtɜːnd] ADJ boat, table, box etc umgedreht; face nach oben gewandt; collar aufgeschlagen; **~ nose** Stupsnase f

upward [ˈʌpwəd] **1** ADJ Aufwärts-, nach oben **2** ADV (esp US) upwards

upwards [ˈʌpwədz] ADV (esp Brit) **(a)** move aufwärts, nach oben; **to look ~** nach oben sehen; face ~ mit dem Gesicht nach oben **(b)** (with numbers) prices from £4 ~ Preise ab £ 4; **and ~** und darüber; **~ of 3000** über 3000

upwind [ˈʌpwɪnd] ADJ, ADV im Aufwind; **to be/stand ~ of sb** gegen den Wind zu jdm sein/stehen

Ural [ˈjuːrəl] N **the ~ Mountains, the ~s** der Ural

uranium [jʊəˈreɪnɪəm] N Uran nt

Uranus [ˈjʊəˈreɪnəs] N (Astron) Uranus m

urban [ˈɜːbən] ADJ städtisch; life also in der Stadt; **~ decay** Verfall m der Städte

urban development N Stadtentwicklung f

urbanization [ɜːbənaɪˈzeɪʃən] N Urbanisierung f, Verstädterung f (pej)

urbanize [ˈɜːbənaɪz] VT urbanisieren, verstädtern (pej)

urban: urban planning N Stadtplanung f; **urban renewal** N Stadterneuerung f

urchin [ˈɜːtʃɪn] N Gassenkind nt; (mischievous) Range f

Urdu [ˈʊəduː] N Urdu nt

urge [ɜːdʒ] **1** N (= need) Verlangen nt, Bedürfnis nt; (= drive) Drang m no pl; (physical, sexual) Trieb m; **to feel the ~ to do sth** das Bedürfnis verspüren, etw zu tun; **I resisted the ~ to (= contradict him)** ich habe mich beherrscht (und ihm nicht widersprochen)
2 VT **(a) to ~ sb to do sth** (= plead with) jdn eindringlich bitten, etw zu tun; (= earnestly recommend) darauf dringen, dass jd etw tut; **to ~ sb to accept** jdn drängen, anzunehmen; **to ~ sb onward** jdn vorwärts treiben or weitertreiben
(b) (= advocate) measure etc, acceptance drängen auf (+acc); **to ~ caution** zur Vorsicht mahnen

➤ **urge on** VT SEP (*lit, fig*) antreiben; *horse, troops also* vorwärts treiben; *team* anfeuern

urgency ['ɜːdʒənsɪ] N Dringlichkeit *f*; (*of tone of voice, pleas also*) Eindringlichkeit *f*; **it's a matter of ~** das ist dringend

urgent ['ɜːdʒənt] ADJ dringend; **is it ~?** (= *important*) ist es dringend?; (= *needing speed*) eilt es?; **the letter was marked "~"** der Brief trug einen Dringlichkeitsvermerk

urgently ['ɜːdʒəntlɪ] ADV *required* dringend; *requested also* dringlich; *talk* eindringlich; **he is ~ in need of help** er braucht dringend Hilfe

urinal [jʊə'raɪnl] N (= *room*) Pissoir *nt*; (= *vessel*) Urinal *nt*

urinate ['jʊərɪneɪt] VI Wasser lassen, urinieren (*geh*)

urine ['jʊərɪn] N Urin *m*, Harn *m*

URL (*Comput*) ABBR *of* **uniform resource locator** URL-Adresse *f*

urn [ɜːn] N (a) Urne *f* (b) (*also* **tea ~, coffee ~**) Kessel *m*

Uruguay ['jʊərəgwaɪ] N Uruguay *nt*

Uruguayan [jʊərə'gwaɪən] **1** N (= *person*) Uruguayer(in) *m(f)* **2** ADJ uruguayisch

US ABBR *of* **United States** USA *pl*

us [ʌs] PERS PRON (*dir and indir obj*) uns; **give it (to) us** gib es uns; **who, us?** wer, wir?; **younger than us** jünger als wir; **it's us** wir sinds; **this table shows us the tides** auf dieser Tafel sieht man die Gezeiten; **us and them** wir und die

USA ABBR *of* **United States of America** USA *pl*

usable ['juːzəbl] ADJ verwendbar; *suggestion, ideas* brauchbar; **to be no longer ~** nicht mehr zu gebrauchen sein

usage ['juːzɪdʒ] N (a) (= *custom, practice*) Brauch *m*, Sitte *f*; **it's common ~** es ist allgemein üblich (b) (*Ling*) Gebrauch *m no pl*, Anwendung *f*

use¹ [juːz] **1** VT (a) benutzen; *suggestion, idea* verwenden; *word, intelligence* gebrauchen; *method, technique, force, trickery, one's abilities, powers of persuasion* anwenden; *tact, care* walten lassen; *drugs* einnehmen; **I have to ~ the toilet before I go** ich muss noch einmal zur Toilette, bevor ich gehe; **to ~ sth for sth** etw zu etw verwenden; **what did you ~ the money for?** wofür haben Sie das Geld verwendet?; **what sort of fuel do you ~?** welchen Treibstoff verwenden Sie?; **why don't you ~ a hammer?** warum nehmen Sie nicht einen Hammer dazu?; **to ~ sb's name** jds Namen verwenden *or* benutzen; (*as reference*) jds Namen angeben; **~ your imagination!** zeig mal ein bisschen Fantasie!; **we can ~ the extra staff to do this** dafür können wir das übrige Personal einsetzen; **I'll have to ~ some of your men** ich brauche ein paar Ihrer Leute; **I could ~ a drink** (*inf*) ich könnte etwas zu trinken (ge)brauchen *or* vertragen (*inf*)
(b) (= *make ~ of, exploit*) *information, one's training, talents, resources, opportunity* (aus)nutzen; *advantage* nutzen; *waste products* verwerten; **you can ~ the leftovers to make a soup** Sie können die Reste zu einer Suppe verwerten
(c) (= *up, consume*) verbrauchen
(d) (*pej* = *exploit*) ausnutzen; **I feel (I've just been) ~d** ich habe das Gefühl, man hat mich ausgenutzt; (*sexually*) ich komme mir missbraucht vor
2 [juːs] N (a) Benutzung *f*; (*of calculator, word, style*) Gebrauch *m*; (*of method, technique, force*) Anwendung *f*; (*of personnel, truncheons etc*) Einsatz *m*; (*of drugs*) Einnahme *f*; **directions for ~** Gebrauchsanweisung *f*; **for the ~ of** für; **for external ~** zur äußerlichen Anwendung; **ready for ~** gebrauchsfertig; *machine* einsatzbereit; **to make ~ of sth** von etw Gebrauch machen; **can you make ~ of that?** können Sie das brauchen?; **in ~/out of ~** in *or* im/außer Gebrauch; *machines also* in/außer Betrieb; **to be no longer in ~** nicht mehr benutzt *or* verwendet *or* gebraucht werden
(b) (= *exploitation, making ~ of*) Nutzung *f*; (*of waste products, leftovers etc*) Verwertung *f*; (= *way of using*) Verwendung *f*; **to make ~ of sth** etw nutzen; **to put sth to ~** etw benutzen; **to put sth to good ~/make good ~ of sth** etw gut nutzen; **it has many ~s** es ist vielseitig verwendbar; **to find a ~ for sth** für etw Verwendung finden; **to have no ~ for** (*lit, fig*) keine Verwendung haben für; **to have no further ~ for sb/sth** keine Verwendung mehr haben für jdn/etw
(c) (= *usefulness*) Nutzen *m*; **to be of ~ to sb** für jdn von Nutzen sein *or* nützlich sein; **this is no ~ any more** das ist zu nichts mehr zu gebrauchen; **is this (of) any ~ to you?** können Sie das brauchen?; **it has its ~s** das ist ganz nützlich; **you're no ~ to me if you can't spell** du nützt mir nichts, wenn du keine Rechtschreibung kannst; **he's no ~ as a goalkeeper** er

ist als Torhüter nicht zu gebrauchen; **it's no ~ you** *or* **your protesting** es hat keinen Sinn *or* es nützt nichts, wenn du protestierst; **what's the ~ of telling him?** was nützt es, wenn man es ihm sagt?; **what's the ~ in trying?** wozu überhaupt versuchen?; **it's no ~** es hat keinen Zweck; **ah, what's the ~!** ach, was solls!
(d) (= *right*) Nutznießung *f* (*Jur*); **to have the ~ of a car** ein Auto zur Verfügung haben; **to give sb the ~ of sth** jdn etw benutzen lassen; *of car also* jdm etw zur Verfügung stellen; **to have lost the ~ of one's arm** seinen Arm nicht mehr benutzen können

➤ **use up** VT SEP verbrauchen; (= *finish also*) aufbrauchen; *scraps etc* verwerten; **the butter is all used up** die Butter ist alle (*inf*) *or* aufgebraucht

use² [juːs] VB AUX **I didn't ~ to smoke** ich habe früher nicht geraucht

use-by-date ['juːzbaɪdeɪt] N Mindesthaltbarkeitsdatum *nt*

used¹ [juːzd] ADJ (= *second-hand*) gebraucht; (= *soiled*) *towel etc* benutzt; *stamp* gestempelt

used² [juːst] VB AUX (*only in past*) **I ~ to swim every day** ich bin früher täglich geschwommen; **he ~ to play golf, didn't he?** er hat doch früher Golf gespielt, nicht wahr?; **he ~ to be a well-known singer** er war einmal ein bekannter Sänger; **there ~ to be a field here** hier war (früher) einmal ein Feld; **things aren't what they ~ to be** es ist alles nicht mehr (so) wie früher; **life is more hectic than it ~ to be** das Leben ist hektischer als früher

used³ [juːst] ADJ **to be ~ to sb** an jdn gewöhnt sein; **to be ~ to sth** etw gewohnt sein; **to be ~ to doing sth** es gewohnt sein, etw zu tun; **to be ~ to sb** *or* **sb's doing sth** daran gewöhnt sein, dass jd etw tut; **I'm not ~ to it** ich bin das nicht gewohnt; **to get ~ to sb/sth** sich an jdn/etw gewöhnen; **to get ~ to doing sth** sich daran gewöhnen, etw zu tun; **you might as well get ~ to it!** (*inf*) daran wirst du dich gewöhnen müssen!

useful ['juːsfʊl] ADJ (a) nützlich; (= *handy*) *tool, language* praktisch; *person, contribution, addition* wertvoll; *discussion* fruchtbar; *life, employment* nutzbringend; **to make oneself ~** sich nützlich machen; **he likes to feel ~** er hat gern das Gefühl, nützlich zu sein; **thank you, you've been very ~** vielen Dank, Sie haben mir/uns *etc* sehr geholfen; **to come in ~** sich als nützlich erweisen; **he's a ~ man to know** es ist sehr nützlich ihn zu kennen; **that advice was most ~** to me der Rat hat mir sehr genützt; **that's a ~ thing to know** es ist gut das zu wissen; **to prove ~** sich als nützlich erweisen
(b) (*inf* = *capable*) *player* brauchbar, fähig; (= *creditable*) *score* wertvoll; **he's quite ~ with a gun** er kann ziemlich gut mit der Pistole umgehen

usefulness ['juːsfʊlnɪs] N Nützlichkeit *f*; (*of person, contribution also*) Wert *m*

useless ['juːslɪs] ADJ (a) nutzlos; (= *unusable*) *manager, player* unbrauchbar; **to be ~ to sb** für jdn nutzlos *or* ohne Nutzen sein; **to prove ~** sich als nutzlos erweisen; (*machine, object*) sich als unbrauchbar erweisen; **to be worse than ~** völlig nutzlos sein; **it is ~ (for you) to complain** es hat keinen Sinn, sich zu beschweren; **he's ~ as a goalkeeper** er ist als Torwart nicht zu gebrauchen; **to be ~ at doing sth** unfähig dazu sein, etw zu tun; **I'm ~ at languages** Sprachen kann ich überhaupt nicht; **to feel ~** sich unnütz fühlen
(b) (= *pointless*) zwecklos, sinnlos

uselessly ['juːslɪslɪ] ADV nutzlos

uselessness ['juːslɪsnɪs] N (a) (= *worthlessness*) Nutzlosigkeit *f*; (*of sth unusable, manager, player*) Unbrauchbarkeit *f*
(b) (= *pointlessness*) Zwecklosigkeit *f*, Sinnlosigkeit *f*

user ['juːzəʳ] N Benutzer(in) *m(f)*; (*of machines also*) Anwender(in) *m(f)*

user: **user-definable** ADJ (*Comput*) *keys* frei definierbar; **user-defined** ADJ (*Comput*) *keys* frei definiert; **user-friendly** ADJ benutzer- *or* anwenderfreundlich; **user group** N Nutzergruppe *f*; (*Comput*) Anwendergruppe *f*; **user identification** N (*Comput*) Benutzerkode *m*; **user-interface** N (*esp Comput*) Benutzerschnittstelle *f*; **user language** N (*Comput*) Benutzersprache *f*; **user software** N (*Comput*) Anwendersoftware *f*; **user support** N (*esp Comput*) Benutzerunterstützung *f*

usher [ˈʌʃəʳ] **1** N (*Theat, at wedding etc*) Platzanweiser(in) *m(f)* **2** VT **to ~ sb into a room/to his seat** jdn in ein Zimmer/zu seinem Sitz bringen

➤ **usher in** VT SEP *people* hineinführen *or* -bringen

usherette [ʌʃəˈret] N Platzanweiserin *f*

USM ABBR *of* **unlisted securities market**

USP ABBR *of* **unique selling proposition** (einzigartiges) verkaufsförderndes Merkmal

usual [ˈjuːʒʊəl] **1** ADJ (= *customary*) üblich; (= *normal*) gewöhnlich, normal; **beer is his ~ drink** er trinkt gewöhnlich Bier; **when shall I come? – oh, the ~ time** wann soll ich kommen? – oh, zur üblichen Zeit; **as is ~ with second-hand cars** wie gewöhnlich bei Gebrauchtwagen; **the ~ stuff** (*inf*) das Übliche; **with his ~ tact** (*iro*) taktvoll wie immer; **it wasn't ~ for him to arrive early** es war nicht typisch für ihn, zu früh da zu sein; **to do sth in the** *or* **one's ~ way** *or* **manner** etw auf die einem übliche Art und Weise tun; **as ~, as per ~** (*inf*) wie üblich, wie gewöhnlich; **business as ~** normaler Betrieb; (*in shop*) Verkauf geht weiter; **to carry on as ~** weitermachen wie immer; **later/less than ~** später/weniger als sonst **2** N (*inf*) der/die/das Übliche; **what sort of mood was he in? – the ~** wie war er gelaunt? – wie üblich

usually [ˈjuːʒʊəlɪ] ADV gewöhnlich, normalerweise; **is he ~ so rude?** ist er sonst auch so unhöflich?; **he's not ~ late** er kommt sonst *or* normalerweise nicht zu spät

usurp [juːˈzɜːp] VT sich (*dat*) widerrechtlich aneignen; *power, inheritance also* an sich (*acc*) reißen; *throne* sich bemächtigen (+*gen*) (*geh*); *role* sich (*dat*) anmaßen; *person* verdrängen

usurper [juːˈzɜːpəʳ] N unrechtmäßiger Machthaber, unrechtmäßige Machthaberin; (*fig*) Eindringling *m*

usury [ˈjuːʒʊrɪ] N Wucher *m*; **to practise** (*Brit*) *or* **practice** (*US*) **~** Wucher treiben; **32% interest is ~** 32% Zinsen sind *or* ist Wucher

utensil [juːˈtensl] N Gerät *nt*, Utensil *nt*

uterus [ˈjuːtərəs] N Gebärmutter *f*

utility [juːˈtɪlɪtɪ] N (a) **public ~** (= *company*) Versorgungsbetrieb *m*; (= *service*) Leistung *f* der Versorgungsbetriebe (b) (*Comput*) Hilfsprogramm *nt*

utility: **utility company** N Versorgungsbetrieb *m*; **utility program** N (*Comput*) Hilfsprogramm *nt*; **utility room** N Allzweckraum *m*; **utility software** N (*Comput*) Hilfssoftware *f*

utilization [juːtɪlaɪˈzeɪʃən] N Verwendung *f*; (*of materials, resources*) Verwertung *f*

utilize [ˈjuːtɪlaɪz] VT verwenden; (= *make sth new*) *wastepaper etc* verwerten

utmost [ˈʌtməʊst] **1** ADJ *ease, danger* größte(r, s); *caution* äußerste(r, s); **with the ~ speed** so schnell wie nur möglich; **it is of the ~ importance that ...** es ist äußerst wichtig, dass ...; **a matter of (the) ~ urgency** ein Fall von äußerster Dringlichkeit; **~ good faith** (*Insur*) höchster guter Glaube **2** N **to do one's ~ (to do sth)** sein Möglichstes *or* Bestes tun(, um etw zu tun); **we have done our ~ to help him** wir haben unser Bestmöglichstes *or* Äußerstes getan, um ihm zu helfen

Utopia [juːˈtəʊpɪə] N Utopia *nt*

utter¹ [ˈʌtəʳ] ADJ total, vollkommen; *disgust, misery* grenzenlos; **a complete and ~ waste of time** eine totale Zeitverschwendung; **what ~ nonsense!** so ein totaler Blödsinn! (*inf*)

utter² VT von sich (*dat*) geben; *word* sagen; *word of complaint* äußern; *cry, sigh, threat* ausstoßen

utterly [ˈʌtəlɪ] ADV total, völlig; *depraved also, despise* zutiefst

uttermost [ˈʌtəməʊst] N, ADJ = **utmost**

U-turn [ˈjuːtɜːn] N (*lit, fig*) Wende *f*; **no ~s** Wenden verboten!; **to do a ~** (*fig*) seine Meinung völlig ändern

Uzbek [ˈʊzbek] **1** ADJ usbekisch; **he is ~** er ist Usbeke **2** N Usbeke *m*, Usbekin *f*

Uzbekistan [ʌzbekɪˈstɑːn] N Usbekistan *nt*

V, v [viː] N V *nt*, v *nt*

V, v ABBR *of* versus

vacancy ['veɪkənsɪ] N **(a)** *(in boarding house)* (freies) Zimmer; **have you any vacancies for August?** haben Sie im August noch Zimmer frei?; **"no vacancies"** „belegt"; **"vacancies"** „Zimmer frei" **(b)** *(= job)* offene *or* freie Stelle; **we have a ~ in our personnel department** in unserer Personalabteilung ist eine Stelle zu vergeben; **we have a ~ for an editor** wir suchen einen Redakteur/eine Redakteurin; **vacancies** *pl* offene Stellen *pl*

vacant ['veɪkənt] ADJ **(a)** *post* offen; *WC, seat, hotel room, parking space* frei; *house* leer stehend; **~ lot** unbebautes Grundstück **(b)** *mind, stare* leer

vacate [vəˈkeɪt] VT *seat* freimachen; *post* aufgeben; *presidency etc* niederlegen; *room, premises* räumen

vacation [vəˈkeɪʃən] **1** N **(a)** *(Univ)* Semesterferien *pl* **(b)** *(US)* Ferien *pl*, Urlaub *m*; **on ~** im *or* auf Urlaub; **to take a ~** Urlaub machen; **where are you going for your ~?** wohin fahren Sie in Urlaub?; **to go on ~** auf Urlaub *or* in die Ferien gehen **2** VI *(US)* Urlaub *or* Ferien machen

vacationer [veɪˈkeɪʃənəʳ], **vacationist** [veɪˈkeɪʃənɪst] N *(US)* Urlauber(in) *m(f)*

vaccinate ['væksɪneɪt] VT impfen

vaccination [ˌvæksɪˈneɪʃən] N (Schutz)impfung *f*

vaccine ['væksiːn] N Impfstoff *m*

vacillate ['væsɪleɪt] VI *(lit, fig)* schwanken

vacuum ['vækjʊəm] N, *pl* **-s** *or* **vacua** *(form)* **1** N **(a)** *(Phys, fig)* Vakuum *nt* **(b)** *(= ~ cleaner)* Staubsauger *m* **2** VT (staub)saugen

vacuum: vacuum bottle N *(US)* Thermosflasche *f*; **vacuum cleaner** N Staubsauger *m*; **vacuum flask** N *(Brit)* Thermosflasche *f*; **vacuum-packed** ADJ vakuumverpackt

vagabond ['vægəbɒnd] N Vagabund *m*

vagina [vəˈdʒaɪnə] N Scheide *f*, Vagina *f*

vagrancy ['veɪgrənsɪ] N Land-/Stadtstreicherei *f* *(also Jur)*

vagrant ['veɪgrənt] N Landstreicher(in) *m(f)*; *(in town)* Stadtstreicher(in) *m(f)*

vague [veɪg] ADJ (+ER) **(a)** *(= not clear)* vage; *report, question* ungenau; *outline, shape* verschwommen; **I haven't the ~st idea** ich habe nicht die leiseste Ahnung; **there's a ~ resemblance** es besteht eine entfernte Ähnlichkeit; **I had a ~ idea she would come** ich hatte so eine (dunkle) Ahnung, dass sie kommen würde; **a ~ sense of unease** ein leichtes Unbehagen

(b) *(= absent-minded)* geistesabwesend; **do you really understand, you look rather ~?** verstehst du das wirklich, du siehst so verwirrt aus?

vaguely ['veɪglɪ] ADV vage; *remember also* dunkel; *understand* in etwa; *interested* flüchtig; *embarrassed, disappointed, surprised* leicht; **to be ~ aware of sth** ein dunkles *or* vages Bewusstsein von etw haben; **to be ~ aware that ...** sich dunkel *or* vage bewusst sein, dass ...; **they're ~ similar** sie haben eine entfernte Ähnlichkeit; **it sounded ~ familiar** es kam einem irgendwie bekannt vor; **there's something ~ sinister about it** es hat so etwas Düsteres an sich

vain [veɪn] ADJ **(a)** (+ER) *(about looks)* eitel; *(about qualities)* eingebildet **(b)** *(= useless, empty)* eitel *(liter)*; *attempt also* vergeblich; *promises, words also, threat* leer; *hope also* töricht; **in the ~ hope that ...** in der vergeblichen Hoffnung, dass ...; **in ~** umsonst, vergeblich

vainly ['veɪnlɪ] ADV *(= to no effect)* vergeblich, vergebens

valediction [ˌvælɪˈdɪkʃən] N *(form)* *(= act)* Abschied *m*; *(= speech)* Abschiedsrede *f*; *(US Sch)* Entlassungsrede *f*

valedictory [ˌvælɪˈdɪktərɪ] **1** ADJ *(form)* Abschieds-; **speech** Abschiedsrede *f* **2** N *(US Sch)* Entlassungsrede *f*

valentine ['væləntaɪn] N **~ (card)** Valentinskarte *f*; **St Valentine's Day** Valentinstag *m*

valet ['væleɪ] N Kammerdiener *m*; **~ service** Reinigungsdienst *m*

valiant ['væljənt] ADJ **she made a ~ effort to smile** sie versuchte tapfer zu lächeln; **never mind, it was a ~ attempt** machen Sie sich nichts draus, es war ein löblicher Versuch

valid ['vælɪd] ADJ *ticket, passport* gültig; *(Jur)* *document* (rechts)gültig; *contract* bindend; *claim, objection* berechtigt; *argument, interpretation* stichhaltig; *excuse, reason* einleuchtend; **this argument isn't ~** *(in itself)* dieses Argument ist nicht stichhaltig; *(= not relevant)* dieses Argument ist nicht zulässig; **that's a very ~ point** das ist ein sehr wertvoller Hinweis

validate ['vælɪdeɪt] VT *document* *(= check validity)* für gültig erklären; *(with stamp, signature)* (rechts)gültig machen; *claim, theory* bestätigen

validity [vəˈlɪdɪtɪ] N *(Jur etc: of document)* (Rechts)gültigkeit *f*; *(of ticket etc)* Gültigkeit *f*; *(of claim)* Berechtigung *f*; *(of argument)* Stichhaltigkeit *f*; *(of excuse etc)* Triftigkeit *f*

valley ['vælɪ] N Tal *nt*; *(big and flat)* Niederung *f*; **to go up/down the ~** talaufwärts/talabwärts gehen/fließen *etc*; **the Upper Rhine ~** die Oberrheinische Tiefebene

valour, *(US)* **valor** ['væləʳ] N *(liter)* Heldenmut *m* *(liter)*

valuable ['væljʊəbl] **1** ADJ wertvoll; *time* kostbar; *help, advice* nützlich **2** N **valuables** PL Wertsachen *pl*

valuation [ˌvæljʊˈeɪʃən] N Schätzung *f*

value ['væljuː] **1** N **(a)** Wert *m*; *(= usefulness)* Nutzen *m*; **to be of ~** wertvoll/nützlich sein; **to put a ~ on sth** etw schätzen *or* bewerten; **of little ~** wert wenig wertvoll/nützlich; **of no ~** wert-/nutzlos; **of great ~** sehr wertvoll; **what's the ~ of your house?** wie viel ist Ihr Haus wert?; **to gain/lose (in) ~** im Wert steigen/fallen; **it's good ~** es ist preisgünstig; **in our restaurant you get ~ for money** in unserem Restaurant bekommen Sie etwas für Ihr Geld *(inf)*; **this TV was good ~** dieser Fernseher ist sein Geld wert; **goods to the ~ of £500** Waren im Wert von £ 500; **shock/novelty ~** Schock-/Neuigkeitswert *m*

(b) values PL *(= moral standards)* (sittliche) Werte *pl*, Wertwelt *f*

2 VT schätzen; *friendship, person* (wert)schätzen; **the property was ~d at £100,000** das Grundstück wurde auf £ 100.000 geschätzt; **I ~ her (highly)** ich weiß sie (sehr) zu schätzen; **if you ~ your life, you'll stay away** bleiben Sie weg, wenn Ihnen Ihr Leben lieb ist

value added N Mehrwert *m*

value-added tax [ˌvæljuːˈædɪdtæks] N *(Brit)* Mehrwertsteuer *f*

valued ['væljuːd] ADJ (hoch) geschätzt; *friend also* lieb; *contribution* geschätzt; **he is a ~ colleague** er ist als Kollege hoch geschätzt; **as a ~ customer** als (ein) geschätzter Kunde

valuer ['væljʊəʳ] N *(Brit)* Schätzer(in) *m(f)*

valve [vælv] N *(Anat)* Klappe *f*; *(Tech: in pipe system)* Absperrhahn *m*

vampire ['væmpaɪəʳ] N *(lit, fig)* Vampir(in) *m(f)*

van [væn] N **(a)** *(Brit Aut)* Transporter *m* **(b)** *(Brit Rail)* Wag(g)on *m*

vandal ['vændəl] N *(fig)* Vandale *m*, Vandalin *f*; **it was damaged by ~s** es ist mutwillig beschädigt worden

vandalism ['vændəlɪzəm] N Vandalismus *m*; *(Jur)* mutwillige Beschädigung (fremden Eigentums); **destroyed by an act of ~** mutwillig zerstört

vandalize ['vændəlaɪz] VT *painting etc* mutwillig beschädigen; *building* verwüsten; *(= wreck)* demolieren

vanguard ['vængɑːd] N *(Mil, Naut)* Vorhut *f*; *(fig also)* Spitze *f*, Führung *f*

vanilla [vəˈnɪlə] **1** N Vanille *f* **2** ADJ Vanille-

vanish ['vænɪʃ] VI verschwinden; *(traces also)* sich verlieren; *(hopes)* schwinden

vanity ['vænɪtɪ] N **(a)** *(concerning looks)* Eitelkeit *f*; *(concerning own value)* Einbildung *f* **(b)** *(US: = dressing table)* Frisiertisch *m*

vanity: **vanity case** N Schmink- *or* Kosmetikkoffer *m*; **vanity plates** PL (*US Aut*) Nummernschild mit persönlicher Note

vantage point ['vɑːntɪdʒpɔɪnt] N (*Mil*) (günstiger) Aussichtspunkt; **our window is a good ~ for watching the procession** von unserem Fenster aus hat man einen guten Blick auf die Prozession

vapour, (*US*) **vapor** ['veɪpə'] N Dunst *m*; (*Phys also*) Gas *nt*; (*steamy*) Dampf *m*

variability [ˌveərɪə'bɪlɪtɪ] N (*of weather, mood*) Unbeständigkeit *f*; (*of costs*) Schwankung(en) *f(pl)*

variable ['veərɪəbl] **1** ADJ **(a)** veränderlich, variabel (*also Math*); *weather, mood* unbeständig; **his work is very ~** er arbeitet sehr unterschiedlich **(b)** *speed* regulierbar **2** N (*Chem, Math, Phys, Comput*) Variable *f*; (*fig also*) veränderliche Größe

variable: **variable cost** N variable Kosten *pl*; **variable rate** N (*Fin*) variabler Zinssatz; **~ mortgage** Hypothek *f* mit variablem Zinssatz

variance ['veərɪəns] N **(a)** **to be at ~ with sb** anderer Meinung sein als jd (*about* hinsichtlich +*gen*); **this is at ~ with what he said earlier** dies stimmt nicht mit dem überein, was er vorher gesagt hat **(b)** (= *difference*) Unterschied *m*; (*Fin*) Abweichung *f*

variant ['veərɪənt] **1** N Variante *f* **2** ADJ (= *alternative*) andere(r, s); **there are two ~ spellings (of his name)** es gibt zwei verschiedene Schreibweisen (für seinen Namen)

variation [ˌveərɪ'eɪʃən] N **(a)** (= *varying*) Veränderung *f*; (*of temperature*) Schwankung(en) *f(pl)*; (*of prices*) Schwankung *f* **(b)** (= *different form*) Variation *f*, Variante *f*; **this is a ~ on that** das ist eine Variation dessen *or* davon

varicose veins [ˌværɪkəʊs'veɪnz] PL Krampfadern *pl*

varied ['veərɪd] ADJ unterschiedlich; *career, life* bewegt; *selection* reichhaltig; *interests* vielfältig; *diet, work* abwechslungsreich; **a ~ group of people** eine gemischte Gruppe

variety [və'raɪətɪ] N **(a)** (= *diversity*) Abwechslung *f*; **to add ~ to sth** Abwechslung in etw (*acc*) bringen; **a job with a lot of ~** eine sehr abwechslungsreiche Arbeit **(b)** (= *assortment*) Vielfalt *f*; (*Comm*) Auswahl *f* (*of* an +*dat*); **in a ~ of colours** (*Brit*) *or* **colors** (*US*) in den verschiedensten Farben *pl*; **for a ~ of reasons** aus verschiedenen Gründen; **a wide ~ of birds** eine große Vielfalt an Vogelarten **(c)** (= *type*) Art *f* (*also Biol, Bot*); (*of cigarette, potato*) Sorte *f*; **a new ~ of potato** eine neue Kartoffelsorte

variety show N (*Theat*) Varietee- *or* Varietévorführung *f*; (*TV*) Fernsehshow *f*; (*Rad, TV*) Unterhaltungssendung *f*

various ['veərɪəs] ADJ **(a)** (= *different*) verschieden; **his excuses are many and ~** seine Entschuldigungen sind zahlreich und vielfältig **(b)** (= *several*) mehrere, verschiedene

variously ['veərɪəslɪ] ADV verschiedentlich

varnish ['vɑːnɪʃ] **1** N (*lit*) Lack *m*; (*on furniture also, on painting*) Firnis *m* **2** VT lackieren; *floorboards also* versiegeln; *painting* firnissen

varnished ['vɑːnɪʃt] ADJ lackiert; *floorboards also* versiegelt

vary ['veərɪ] **1** VI **(a)** (= *diverge, differ*) sich unterscheiden, abweichen (*from* von); **opinions ~ on this point** in diesem Punkt gehen die Meinungen auseinander **(b)** (= *be different*) unterschiedlich sein; **the price varies from shop to shop** der Preis ist von Geschäft zu Geschäft verschieden; **it varies** es ist unterschiedlich **(c)** (= *change, fluctuate*) sich (ver)ändern; (*pressure, prices*) schwanken; **prices that ~ with the season** saisonbedingte Preise *pl* **2** VT (= *alter*) verändern, abwandeln; (= *give variety*) abwechslungsreich(er) gestalten

varying ['veərɪɪŋ] ADJ (= *changing*) veränderlich; (= *different*) unterschiedlich; **with ~ degrees of success** mit unterschiedlichem Erfolg; **of ~ sizes/abilities** unterschiedlich groß/begabt

vase [vɑːz, (*US*) veɪz] N Vase *f*

vasectomy [væ'sektəmɪ] N Sterilisation *f* (*des Mannes*)

vassal ['væsəl] N (*lit, fig*) Vasall *m*

vast [vɑːst] ADJ (+ER) gewaltig, riesig; *knowledge* enorm; *majority* überwältigend; *wealth, powers* unermesslich; **a ~ expanse** eine weite Ebene; **to a ~ extent** in sehr hohem Maße; **at ~ expense** zu enormen Kosten; **to be a ~ improvement on sth** eine enorme Verbesserung gegenüber etw sein

vastly ['vɑːstlɪ] ADV erheblich, wesentlich; *experienced* äußerst; **it is ~ different** da besteht ein erheblicher *or* wesentlicher Unterschied; **he is ~ superior to her** er ist ihr haushoch überlegen

vastness ['vɑːstnɪs] N (*of size*) riesiges *or* gewaltiges Ausmaß; (*of ocean, plane, area*) riesige Weite; (*of knowledge, wealth*) gewaltiger Umfang

VAT ['viːer'tiː, væt] (*Brit*) ABBR *of* **value-added tax** Mehrwertsteuer *f*, MwSt.

vat [væt] N Fass *nt*; (*without lid*) Bottich *m*

Vatican ['vætɪkən] N Vatikan *m*

Vatican City N Vatikanstadt *f*

VAT (*Brit*): **VAT number** N Mehrwertsteueridentifikationsnummer *f*; **VAT-registered** ADJ zur Mehrwertsteuer veranlagt; **VAT return** N Mehrwertsteuerausgleich *m*

vault[1] [vɔːlt] N **(a)** (= *cellar*) (Keller)gewölbe *nt*; (= *tomb*) Gruft *f*; (*in bank*) Tresor(raum) *m* **(b)** (*Archit*) Gewölbe *nt*

vault[2] **1** N Sprung *m* **2** VI springen **3** VT springen über (+*acc*), überspringen

vaunt [vɔːnt] VT **much-~ed** viel gepriesen

VCR ABBR *of* **video cassette recorder** Videorekorder *m*

VD ABBR *of* **venereal disease** Geschlechtskrankheit *f*

VDU ABBR *of* **visual display unit**

veal [viːl] N Kalbfleisch *nt*; **~ cutlet** Kalbsschnitzel *nt*

veer [vɪə'] VI (*wind*) (sich) drehen (*im Uhrzeigersinn*) (*to* nach); (*ship*) abdrehen; (*car*) ausscheren; (*road*) scharf abbiegen; **the car ~ed to the left** das Auto scherte nach links aus; **the car ~ed off the road** das Auto kam von der Straße ab; **to ~ off course** vom Kurs abkommen; **he ~ed away from the subject** er kam (völlig) vom Thema ab

veg [vedʒ] (*esp Brit*) N, NO PL ABBR *of* **vegetable**

vegan ['viːgən] **1** N Veganer(in) *m(f)* **2** ADJ veganisch; **to be ~** Veganer(in) *m(f)* sein

vegetable ['vedʒtəbl] N Gemüse *nt*; **with fresh ~s** mit frischem Gemüse; (*on menu*) mit frischen Gemüsen; **what ~s do you grow in your garden?** welche Gemüsesorten hast du in deinem Garten?; **she's become a ~** (*fig pej*) sie vegetiert nur noch dahin

vegetable: **vegetable garden** N Gemüsegarten *m*; **vegetable knife** N kleines Küchenmesser; **vegetable oil** N pflanzliches Öl; (*Cook*) Pflanzenöl *nt*

vegetarian [ˌvedʒɪ'teərɪən] **1** N Vegetarier(in) *m(f)* **2** ADJ vegetarisch; **~ cheese** Käse *m* für Vegetarier; **to go** *or* **become ~** Vegetarier(in) *m(f)* werden

vegetate ['vedʒɪteɪt] VI (*fig*) dahinvegetieren

vegetation [ˌvedʒɪ'teɪʃən] N Vegetation *f*

veggie ['vedʒɪ] (*inf*) **1** N **(a)** (= *vegetarian*) Vegetarier(in) *m(f)* **(b)** **veggies** *pl* (*US*) = **veg 2** ADJ (= *vegetarian*) vegetarisch

vehemence ['viːɪməns] N Vehemenz *f* (*geh*); (*of feelings also*) Heftigkeit *f*; (*of protests also*) Schärfe *f*

vehement ['viːɪmənt] ADJ vehement (*geh*); *attack also* heftig; *critic, opponent, opposition, protest* scharf; *dislike* stark; *supporter, speech* leidenschaftlich

vehemently ['viːɪməntlɪ] ADV vehement (*geh*), heftig; *love, hate also* leidenschaftlich; *protest also* mit aller Schärfe; *attack* scharf

vehicle ['viːɪkl] N **(a)** Fahrzeug *nt*; **~ excise duty** (*Brit*) Kraftfahrzeugsteuer *f*; **~ insurance** Kraftfahrzeugversicherung *f* **(b)** (*fig: = medium*) Mittel *nt*;

this paper is a ~ of right-wing opinions diese Zeitung ist ein Sprachrohr *nt* der Rechten

vehicular [vɪ'hɪkjʊlə'] ADJ Fahrzeug-

veil [veɪl] **1** N Schleier *m*; **to draw** *or* **throw a ~ over sth** den Schleier des Vergessens über etw (*acc*) breiten; **under a ~ of secrecy** unter dem Mantel der Verschwiegenheit **2** VT (*fig*) **the town was ~ed by mist** die Stadt lag in Nebel gehüllt

veiled [veɪld] ADJ *criticism, threat etc* versteckt

vein [veɪn] N **(a)** (*Anat, Bot, Min*) Ader *f*; **~s and arteries** Venen und Arterien *pl*; **a creative ~** eine künstlerische Ader; **the ~ of humour** (*Brit*) *or* **humor** (*US*) **which runs through the book** ein humorvoller Zug, der durch das ganze Buch geht **(b)** (*fig: = mood*) Stimmung *f*, Laune *f*; **in the same ~** in derselben Art

Velcro® [velkrəʊ] N Klettband *nt*

velocity [və'lɒsɪtɪ] N Geschwindigkeit *f*

velvet [velvɪt] **1** N Samt *m* **2** ADJ Samt-

vend [vend] VT verkaufen

vendetta [ven'detə] N Fehde *f*; (*of gangsters*) Vendetta *f*; **to carry on a ~ against sb** mit jdm in Fehde liegen

vending machine [vendɪŋmə'ʃi:n] N Automat *m*

vendor [vendɔ:'] N (*esp Jur*) Verkäufer(in) *m(f)*; **street ~** Straßenhändler(in) *m(f)*

veneer [və'nɪə'] N (*lit*) Furnier *nt*; (*fig*) Politur *f*; **he had a ~ of respectability** nach außen hin machte er einen sehr ehrbaren Eindruck

venerable [venərəbl] ADJ ehrwürdig

venerate [venəreɪt] VT verehren; *sb's memory* ehren

venereal disease [vɪ'nɪərɪəldɪ,zi:z] N Geschlechtskrankheit *f*

Venetian [vɪ'ni:ʃən] ADJ venezianisch

Venetian blind N Jalousie *f*

Venezuela [,vene'zweɪlə] N Venezuela *nt*

Venezuelan [,vene'zweɪlən] **1** ADJ venezolanisch **2** N Venezolaner(in) *m(f)*

vengeance [vendʒəns] N Vergeltung *f*, Rache *f*; **with a ~** (*inf*) gewaltig (*inf*)

vengeful [vendʒfʊl] ADJ rachsüchtig

Venice [venɪs] N Venedig *nt*

venison [venɪsən] N Reh(fleisch) *nt*

venom [venəm] N (*lit*) Gift *nt*; (*fig*) Gehässigkeit *f*; **he spoke with real ~ in his voice** er sprach mit hasserfüllter Stimme

venomous [venəməs] ADJ (*lit, fig*) giftig; *tone also* gehässig; *attack* scharf; **~ snake** Giftschlange *f*

vent [vent] **1** N (*for gas, liquid*) Öffnung *f*; (*in chimney*) Abzug *m*; (*for feelings*) Ventil *nt*; **to give ~ to sth** (*fig*) einer Sache (*dat*) Ausdruck verleihen; **to give ~ to one's feelings** seinen Gefühlen freien Lauf lassen **2** VT *feelings, anger* abreagieren (*on an +dat*); **to ~ one's spleen** sich (*dat*) Luft machen

ventilate [ventɪleɪt] VT (*= control air flow*) belüften; (*= let fresh air in*) lüften

ventilated [ventɪleɪtɪd] ADJ *room, building* belüftet

ventilation [,ventɪ'leɪʃən] N (*= control of air flow*) Belüftung *f*; (*= letting fresh air in*) Lüften *nt*

ventilation shaft N Luftschacht *m*

ventilator [ventɪleɪtə'] N **(a)** Ventilator *m* **(b)** (*Med*) Beatmungsgerät *nt*; **to be on a ~** künstlich beatmet werden

ventriloquist [ven'trɪləkwɪst] N Bauchredner(in) *m(f)*

venture [ventʃə'] **1** N Unternehmung *f*, Unterfangen *nt*; **mountain-climbing is his latest ~** seit neuestem hat er sich aufs Bergsteigen verlegt; **this was a disastrous ~ for the company** dieses Projekt war für die Firma ein Fiasko; **he made a lot of money out of his ~s in the world of finance** er verdiente bei seinen Spekulationen in der Finanzwelt viel Geld; **his purchase of stocks was his first ~ into the world of finance** mit dem Erwerb von Aktien wagte er sich zum ersten Mal in die Finanzwelt; **the astronauts on their ~ into the unknown** die Astronauten auf ihrer abenteuerlichen Reise ins Unbekannte **2** VT **(a)** *life, reputation, money* aufs Spiel setzen, riskieren (*on* bei) **(b)** *guess, explanation* wagen; *opinion* zu äußern wagen; **I would ~ to say that ...** ich wage sogar zu behaupten, dass ... **3** VI sich wagen; **to ~ out of doors** sich vor die Tür wagen; **they lost money when they ~d into book publishing** sie verloren Geld bei ihrem Versuch, Bücher zu verlegen

▶ **venture forth** VI (*liter*) sich hinauswagen; **the astronauts ventured forth into the unknown** die Astronauten wagten sich ins Unbekannte

▶ **venture on** VI +PREP OBJ sich wagen an (*+acc*); **they ventured on a programme** (*Brit*) *or* **program** (*US*) **of reform** sie wagten sich an ein Reformprogramm heran

▶ **venture out** VI = **venture forth**

venture: venture capital N Risikokapital *nt*; **venture capitalist** N Risikokapitalgeber(in) *m(f)*; **~s** Kapitalbeteiligungsgesellschaft *f*

venue [venju:] N (*= meeting place*) Treffpunkt *m*; (*Sport*) Austragungsort *m*; (*Jur*) Gerichtsstand *m*

Venus [vi:nəs] N Venus *f*

veracity [və'ræsɪtɪ] N (*of person*) Ehrlichkeit *f*; (*of report, evidence*) Richtigkeit *f*

veranda(h) [və'rændə] N Veranda *f*

verb [vɜ:b] N Verb *nt*

verbal [vɜ:bəl] ADJ **(a)** *agreement* mündlich; **~ abuse** Beschimpfung *f*; **~ attack** Verbalattacke *f* **(b)** (*= of words*) *error, skills* sprachlich

verbally [vɜ:bəlɪ] ADV mündlich; *threaten* verbal; **to ~ abuse sb** jdn beschimpfen; **~ abusive** ausfällig

verbatim [vɜ:'beɪtɪm] **1** ADJ wörtlich **2** ADV wortwörtlich

verbose [vɜ:'bəʊs] ADJ wortreich, langatmig

verdant [vɜ:dənt] ADJ (*liter*) grün

verdict [vɜ:dɪkt] N Urteil *nt* (*also Jur*); **a ~ of guilty/not guilty** ein Schuldspruch *m*/Freispruch *m*; **what's the ~?** wie lautet das Urteil?; **what's your ~ on this wine?** wie beurteilst du diesen Wein?; **to give one's ~ about** *or* **on sth** sein Urteil über etw (*acc*) abgeben

verge [vɜ:dʒ] N (*fig, Brit lit*) Rand *m*; **to be on the ~ of ruin/war** am Rande des Ruins/eines Krieges stehen; **to be on the ~ of tears** den Tränen nahe sein; **to be on the ~ of doing sth** im Begriff sein, etw zu tun

▶ **verge on** VI +PREP OBJ grenzen an (*+acc*); **she was verging on madness** sie stand am Rande des Wahnsinns

verifiable [verɪfaɪəbl] ADJ nachprüfbar, verifizierbar (*geh*)

verification [,verɪfɪ'keɪʃən] N (*= check*) Überprüfung *f*; (*= confirmation*) Bestätigung *f*; (*= proof*) Nachweis *m*

verify [verɪfaɪ] VT (*= check up*) (über)prüfen; (*= confirm*) bestätigen; *theory* beweisen

veritable [verɪtəbl] ADJ (*hum*) *genius* wahr; **a ~ disaster** die reinste Katastrophe; **a ~ miracle** das reinste Wunder

vermin [vɜ:mɪn] N, NO PL (*= animal*) Schädling *m*; (*= insects*) Ungeziefer *nt*; (*pej: = people*) Pack *nt*

vermouth [vɜ:məθ] N Wermut *m*

vernacular [və'nækjʊlə'] **1** N (*= dialect*) Mundart *f*; (*= not Latin, not official language*) Landessprache *f* **2** ADJ **~ language** mundartliche Sprache

verruca [ve'ru:kə] N Warze *f*

versatile [vɜ:sətaɪl] ADJ vielseitig

versatility [,vɜ:sə'tɪlɪtɪ] N Vielseitigkeit *f*

verse [vɜ:s] N **(a)** (*= stanza*) Strophe *f* **(b)** NO PL (*= poetry*) Poesie *f*, Dichtung *f*; **in ~** in Versform **(c)** (*of Bible, Koran*) Vers *m*

versed [vɜ:st] ADJ (*also* **well ~**) bewandert, beschlagen (*in* +*dat*); **he's well ~ in the art of judo** er beherrscht die Kunst des Judos; **I'm not very well ~ in ...** ich verstehe nicht viel *or* ich habe wenig Ahnung von ...

version [vɜ:ʃən] N Version *f*; (*of text*) Fassung *f*

versus [vɜ:səs] PREP gegen (*+acc*)

vertebra [vɜ:tɪbrə] N, *pl* **-e** [vɜ:tɪbri:] Rückenwirbel *m*

vertebrate [vɜ:tɪbrət] N Wirbeltier *nt*; **the ~s** die Wirbeltiere

vertical [vɜ:tɪkəl] ADJ senkrecht; (*Comm, Econ*) vertikal; **~ cliffs** senkrecht abfallende Klippen; **~ axis** y-Achse *f*; **~ stripes** Längsstreifen *pl*; **there is a ~ drop from the cliffs into the sea below** die Klippen fallen steil *or* senkrecht ins Meer ab

vertically [vɜ:tɪkəlɪ] ADV senkrecht, vertikal; **stand it ~ or it'll fall over** stell es aufrecht hin, sonst fällt es um; **~ integrated** (*Comm*) vertikal integriert

vertigo [vɜ:tɪgəʊ] N Schwindel *m*; (*Med*) Gleichgewichtsstörung *f*; **he suffers from ~** ihm wird leicht schwindlig

verve [vɜːv] N Schwung *m*; (*of person also*) Elan *m*; (*of performance also*) Ausdruckskraft *f*

very ['verɪ] **1** ADV **(a)** sehr; **it's ~ well written** es ist sehr gut geschrieben; **I'm ~ sorry** es tut mir sehr Leid; **that's not ~ funny** das ist überhaupt nicht lustig; **I'm not ~ good at maths** ich bin in Mathe nicht besonders gut; **he is so ~ lazy** er ist SO faul; **how ~ odd** wie eigenartig; **~ little** sehr wenig; **~ much** sehr; **thank you ~ much** vielen Dank; **I liked it ~ much** es hat mir sehr gut gefallen; **~ much bigger** sehr viel größer; **he doesn't work ~ much** er arbeitet nicht sehr viel; **~ much so** sehr (sogar)
(b) (= *absolutely*) aller-; **~ best quality** allerbeste Qualität; **~ last** allerletzte(r, s); **~ first** allererste(r, s); **at the ~ latest** allerspätestens; **to do one's ~ best** sein Äußerstes tun; **at the ~ most** allerhöchstens; **at the ~ least** allerwenigstens; **to be in the ~ best of health** bei bester Gesundheit erfreuen; **they are the ~ best of friends** sie sind die dicksten Freunde
(c) (*for emphasis*) **he fell ill and died the ~ same day** er wurde krank und starb noch am selben Tag; **he died the ~ same day as Kennedy** er starb genau am selben Tag wie Kennedy; **the ~ same hat** genau der gleiche Hut; **we met again the ~ next day** wir trafen uns am nächsten Tag schon wieder; **the ~ next day he was tragically killed** schon einen Tag später kam er unter tragischen Umständen ums Leben; **my ~ own car** mein eigenes Auto; **a house of your ~ own** ein eigenes Häuschen; **~ well, if that's what you want** nun gut, wenn du das willst; **I couldn't ~ well say no** ich konnte schlecht Nein sagen
2 ADJ **(a)** (= *precise, exact*) genau; **that ~ day/moment** genau an diesem Tag/in diesem Augenblick; **at the ~ heart of the organization** direkt im Zentrum der Organisation; **those were his ~ words** genau das waren seine Worte; **before my ~ eyes** direkt vor meinen Augen; **you are the ~ person I want to speak to** mit IHNEN wollte ich sprechen; **the ~ thing/man I need** genau das, was/genau der Mann, den ich brauche; **the ~ thing!** genau das Richtige!
(b) (= *extreme*) äußerste(r, s); **in the ~ beginning** ganz am Anfang; **at the ~ end** ganz am Ende; **at the ~ back/front** ganz hinten/vorn(e); **go to the ~ end of the road** gehen Sie die Straße ganz entlang *or* durch
(c) (= *mere*) **the ~ thought of it** allein schon der Gedanke daran; **the ~ idea!** nein, so etwas!

vessel ['vesl] N **(a)** (*Naut*) Schiff *nt* **(b)** (*form*: = *receptacle*) Gefäß *nt*; **drinking ~** Trinkgefäß *nt*

vest¹ [vest] N **(a)** (*Brit*) Unterhemd *nt* **(b)** (*US*) Weste *f*

vest² VT (*form*) **the rights ~ed in the Crown** die der Krone zustehenden Rechte; **the authority ~ed in me** die mir verliehene Macht; **he has ~ed interests in the oil business** er ist (finanziell) am Ölgeschäft beteiligt; **he has a ~ed interest in the play** (*fig*) er hat ein persönliches Interesse an dem Stück

vestibule ['vestɪbjuːl] N Vorhalle *f*; (*of hotel*) Foyer *nt*

vestige ['vestɪdʒ] N Spur *f*; **the ~ of a moustache** (*Brit*) *or* **mustache** (*US*) der Anflug eines Schnurrbarts

vestment ['vestmənt] N (*of priest*) Ornat *m*; (= *ceremonial robe*) Robe *f*

vestry ['vestrɪ] N Sakristei *f*

vet [vet] **1** N ABBR *of* **veterinary surgeon**, **veterinarian** Tierarzt *m*/-ärztin *f* **2** VT überprüfen

veteran ['vetərən] N (*Mil, fig*) Veteran(in) *m(f)*; **a ~ golfer** ein (alt)erfahrener Golfspieler; **a ~ actor** ein Veteran *m* der Schauspielkunst

veterinary ['vetərɪnərɪ] ADJ Veterinär-; *training* tierärztlich; *school, college* für Tierärzte

veterinary: **veterinary medicine** N Veterinärmedizin *f*; **veterinary practice** N Tierarztpraxis *f*; **veterinary surgeon** N Tierarzt *m*/-ärztin *f*

veto ['viːtəʊ] **1** N, *pl* **-es** Veto *nt*; **power of ~** Vetorecht *nt*; **to use one's ~** von seinem Vetorecht Gebrauch machen **2** VT sein Veto einlegen gegen; **if they ~ it** wenn sie ihr Veto einlegen

vetting ['vetɪŋ] N Überprüfung *f*

vex [veks] VT ärgern, irritieren

vexed [vekst] ADJ *question* viel diskutiert, schwierig

vexing ['veksɪŋ] ADJ ärgerlich, irritierend; *problem* verzwickt

VHF (*Rad*) ABBR *of* **very high frequency** UKW

---

via [ˈvaɪə] PREP über (+*acc*); (*with town names also*) via; **they got in ~ the window** sie kamen durchs Fenster herein

viability [ˌvaɪəˈbɪlɪtɪ] N (*of plan, project*) Durchführbarkeit *f*, Realisierbarkeit *f*; (*of firm*) Rentabilität *f*

viable [ˈvaɪəbl] ADJ *company* rentabel; *economy* lebensfähig; *suggestion* brauchbar; *plan, project* machbar; *alternative, solution* gangbar; *option* realisierbar; **the company is not economically ~** die Firma ist unrentabel; **a ~ form of government** eine funktionsfähige Regierungsform

viaduct [ˈvaɪədʌkt] N Viadukt *m*

vial [ˈvaɪəl] N Fläschchen *nt*

vibes [vaɪbz] PL (*inf*) **what sort of ~ do you get from him?** wie wirkt er auf dich?; **this town is giving me bad ~** diese Stadt macht mich ganz fertig (*inf*)

vibrant [ˈvaɪbrənt] ADJ **(a)** *personality etc* dynamisch; *voice* volltönend; *city, community, culture* lebendig; *economy* boomend; **the shipyard was ~ with activity** auf der Werft herrschte emsiges Treiben **(b)** *colour* leuchtend

vibrate [vaɪˈbreɪt] **1** VI (*lit, fig*) zittern, beben (*with* vor +*dat*); (*machine, string, air*) vibrieren; (*notes*) schwingen; **Glasgow's West End ~s with activity** im Glasgower West End pulsiert das Leben **2** VT zum Vibrieren bringen; *string* zum Schwingen bringen

vibration [vaɪˈbreɪʃən] N (*of string, sound waves*) Schwingung *f*; (*of machine*) Vibrieren *nt*

vibrator [vaɪˈbreɪtəʳ] N Vibrator *m*

vicar [ˈvɪkəʳ] N Pfarrer(in) *m(f)*

vicarage [ˈvɪkərɪdʒ] N Pfarrhaus *nt*

vicarious [vɪˈkɛərɪəs] ADJ *pleasure, enjoyment* indirekt, mittelbar; *experience* ersatzweise

vice¹ [vaɪs] N Laster *nt*; **his main ~ is laziness** sein größter Fehler ist die Faulheit

vice² (*US*) **vise** N Schraubstock *m*

vice- PREF Vize-; **vice-chairman** N stellvertretender Vorsitzender; **vice-chairwoman** N stellvertretende Vorsitzende; **vice chancellor** N (*Brit Univ*) ≈ Rektor(in) *m(f)*; **vice president** N Vizepräsident(in) *m(f)*

vice versa [ˌvaɪsɪˈvɜːsə] ADV umgekehrt

vicinity [vɪˈsɪnɪtɪ] N Umgebung *f*; **in the ~** in der Nähe (*of* von, *gen*); **in the ~ of £500** um die £ 500 (herum)

vicious [ˈvɪʃəs] ADJ **(a)** *animal* bösartig; *blow, gang, attack, crime* brutal; **to have a ~ temper** jähzornig sein **(b)** (= *nasty*) gemein, boshaft; *remark* gehässig; *look* böse **(c)** (*inf*) *headache* fies (*inf*), gemein (*inf*)

vicious circle N Teufelskreis *m*

viciously [ˈvɪʃəslɪ] ADV (= *violently*) bösartig; *murder* auf grauenhafte Art; **the dog ~ attacked him** der Hund fiel wütend über ihn her

victim [ˈvɪktɪm] N Opfer *nt*; **he was the ~ of a practical joke** ihm wurde ein Streich gespielt; **to fall (a) ~ to sth** einer Sache (*dat*) zum Opfer fallen; **to fall ~ to sb's charms** jds Charme (*dat*) erliegen

victimization [ˌvɪktɪmaɪˈzeɪʃən] N ungerechte Behandlung; (= *harassment*) Schikanierung *f*

victimize [ˈvɪktɪmaɪz] VT ungerecht behandeln; (= *pick on*) schikanieren

victor [ˈvɪktəʳ] N Sieger(in) *m(f)*

Victoria Falls [vɪkˈtɔːrɪəˈfɔːlz] PL Viktoriafälle *f*

Victorian [vɪkˈtɔːrɪən] **1** N Viktorianer(in) *m(f)* **2** ADJ viktorianisch; (*fig*) (sitten)streng

---

VICTORIAN

*Das Adjektiv **Victorian**, viktorianisch, wird für das Großbritannien, seine Bevölkerung und Kultur unter der Regentschaft von Königin Viktoria (1837 - 1901) verwendet.*

Mit **Victorian** kann man aber auch die vorherrschenden Meinungen und gesellschaftlichen Vorstellungen jener Epoche in ihrem negativen wie positiven Sinn bezeichnen. Unangenehme viktorianische Eigenschaften sind das äußerste Bedachtsein auf den gesellschaftlichen Ruf, repressiv strenge Moralvorstellungen, Humorlosigkeit, Bigotterie und Heuchelei.

Dagegen lieben es britische Politiker, die viktorianischen Tugenden hervorzuheben, wie das Streben nach Weiterbildung und gesellschaftlichem Aufstieg, Anstand, Respekt vor der Autorität und Familiensinn.

victorious [vɪk'tɔːrɪəs] ADJ *army, allies* siegreich; *battle, campaign* erfolgreich; **to be ~ over sb/sth** jdn/etw besiegen; **to be ~ in the struggle against …** siegen im Kampf gegen …

victory ['vɪktərɪ] N Sieg *m*; **to gain** *or* **win a ~ over sb/sth** einen Sieg über jdn/etw erringen

video ['vɪdɪəʊ] **1** N (**a**) (= *film*) Video *nt*; (= *recorder*) Videorekorder *m* (**b**) (*US*) Fernsehen *nt*; **on ~** im Fernsehen **2** VT (auf Video) aufnehmen

video: **video camera** N Videokamera *f*; **video cassette** N Videokassette *f*; **video conferencing** N Videokonferenzschaltung *f*; **video disc** N Bildplatte *f*; **video disc player** N Bildplattenspieler *m*; **video game** N Telespiel *nt*; **video library** N Videothek *f*; **videophone** N Fernsehtelefon *nt*; **video recorder** N Videorekorder *m*; **video-recording** N Videoaufnahme *f*; **video rental** N Videoverleih *m*; **~ shop** (*esp Brit*) *or* **store** Videothek *f*; **video shop** N Videothek *f*; **video tape** N Videoband *nt*; **video-tape** VT (auf Video) aufzeichnen

vie [vaɪ] VI wetteifern; (*Comm*) konkurrieren; **to ~ with sb for sth** mit jdm um etw wetteifern; **to ~ with sb to do sth** mit jdm darum wetteifern, etw zu tun

Vienna [vɪ'enə] **1** N Wien *nt* **2** ADJ Wiener

Vietnam [ˌvjet'næm] N Vietnam *nt*

Vietnamese [ˌvjetnə'miːz] **1** ADJ vietnamesisch **2** N Vietnamese *m*, Vietnamesin *f*

view [vjuː] **1** N (**a**) (= *range of vision*) Sicht *f*; **in full ~ of thousands of people** vor den Augen von tausenden *or* Tausenden von Menschen; **the magician placed the box in full ~ of the audience** der Zauberer stellte die Kiste so auf, dass das ganze Publikum sie sehen konnte; **the ship came into ~** das Schiff kam in Sicht; **to keep sth in ~** etw im Auge behalten; **the house is within ~ of the sea** vom Haus aus ist das Meer zu sehen; **hidden from ~** verborgen, versteckt; **the house is hidden from ~ from the main road** das Haus ist von der Hauptstraße aus nicht zu sehen; **on ~** (*for purchasing*) zur Ansicht; (*of exhibits*) ausgestellt
(**b**) (= *prospect, sight*) Aussicht *f*; **a ~ over …** ein Blick *m* über … (*acc*); **a good ~ of the sea** ein schöner Blick auf das Meer; **a room with a ~** ein Zimmer mit schöner Aussicht; **he stood up to get a better ~** er stand auf, um besser sehen zu können
(**c**) (= *photograph etc*) Ansicht *f*
(**d**) (= *opinion*) Ansicht *f*, Meinung *f*; **in my ~** meiner Ansicht *or* Meinung nach; **to have** *or* **hold ~s on sth** Ansichten über etw (*acc*) haben; **what was his ~s on this problem?** was meint er zu diesem Problem?; **I have no ~s on that** ich habe keine Meinung dazu; **to take the ~ that …** die Ansicht vertreten, dass …; **an idealistic ~ of the world** eine idealistische Welt(an)sicht; **an overall ~ of a problem** ein umfassender Überblick über ein Problem; **in ~ of** wegen (+*gen*), angesichts (+*gen*)
(**e**) (= *intention, plan*) Absicht *f*; **with a ~ to doing sth** mit der Absicht, etw zu tun; **with this in ~** im Hinblick darauf **2** VT (**a**) (= *see*) betrachten
(**b**) (= *examine*) *house* besichtigen
(**c**) (= *consider*) *problem etc* sehen **3** VI (= *watch television*) fernsehen

viewer ['vjuːəʳ] N (**a**) (*TV*) Zuschauer(in) *m(f)* (**b**) (*for slides*) Diaor Bildbetrachter *m*

viewfinder ['vjuːˌfaɪndəʳ] N Sucher *m*

viewing ['vjuːɪŋ] N (**a**) (*of house etc*) Besichtigung *f* (**b**) (*TV*) Fernsehen *nt*; **tennis makes compulsive ~** Tennis macht die Fernsehzuschauer süchtig

viewing figures PL (*TV*) Zuschauerzahlen *pl*

viewpoint ['vjuːpɔɪnt] N (**a**) Standpunkt *m*; **from the ~ of economic growth** unter dem Gesichtspunkt des

Wirtschaftswachstums; **to see sth from sb's ~** etw aus jds Sicht sehen (**b**) (*for scenic view*) Aussichtspunkt *m*

vigil ['vɪdʒɪl] N (Nacht)wache *f*; **to keep ~ over sb** bei jdm wachen

vigilance ['vɪdʒɪləns] N Wachsamkeit *f*

vigilant ['vɪdʒɪlənt] ADJ wachsam; **to be ~ about sth** auf etw (*acc*) achten; **the customs officers are ever ~ for drug traffickers** die Zollbeamten haben stets ein wachsames Auge auf Drogenhändler

vigilante [ˌvɪdʒɪ'læntɪ] **1** N *Mitglied einer Selbstschutzorganisation* **2** ADJ ATTR Selbstschutz-

vigor N (*US*) = **vigour**

vigorous ['vɪgərəs] ADJ energisch; (= *powerful also*) kräftig; *walk* forsch; *activity* dynamisch; *opponent, advocate* engagiert

vigorously ['vɪgərəslɪ] ADV energisch; *shake hands* kräftig; *defend, campaign* engagiert; *oppose* heftig

vigour, (*US*) **vigor** ['vɪgəʳ] N Kraft *f*, Energie *f*; **youthful ~** jugendliche Spannkraft

Viking ['vaɪkɪŋ] **1** N Wikinger(in) *m(f)* **2** ADJ Wikinger-

vile [vaɪl] ADJ abscheulich; *mood, smell, habit also, conditions* übel; *thoughts* niedrig; *language* unflätig; *weather, food* scheußlich; **that was a ~ thing to say** es war eine Gemeinheit, so etwas zu sagen

villa ['vɪlə] N Villa *f*

village ['vɪlɪdʒ] N Dorf *nt*

village IN CPDS Dorf-; **village green** N Dorfwiese *f or* -anger *m*; **village hall** N Gemeindesaal *m*

villager ['vɪlɪdʒəʳ] N Dörfler(in) *m(f)*, Dorfbewohner(in) *m(f)* (*also Admin*)

villain ['vɪlən] N (= *scoundrel*) Schurke *m*, Schurkin *f*; (*inf*) (= *criminal*) Verbrecher(in) *m(f)*, Ganove *m* (*inf*); (*in drama, novel*) Bösewicht *m*; **he's the ~ of the piece** (*inf*) er ist der Übeltäter

villainy ['vɪlənɪ] N Gemeinheit *f*, Niederträchtigkeit *f*

vim [vɪm] N (*inf*) Schwung *m*; **full of ~ and vigour** (*Brit*) *or* **vigor** (*US*) voller Schwung und Elan

vinaigrette [ˌvɪnɪ'gret] N Vinaigrette *f* (*Cook*); (*for salad*) Salatsoße *f*

vindicate ['vɪndɪkeɪt] VT (**a**) *opinion, action, decision* rechtfertigen (**b**) (= *exonerate*) rehabilitieren

vindication [ˌvɪndɪ'keɪʃən] N (**a**) (*of opinion, action, decision*) Rechtfertigung *f* (**b**) (= *exoneration*) Rehabilitation *f*

vindictive [vɪn'dɪktɪv] ADJ rachsüchtig; *mood* nachtragend, unversöhnlich; **he is not a ~ person** er ist nicht nachtragend

vindictiveness [vɪn'dɪktɪvnɪs] N Rachsucht *f*; (*of mood*) Unversöhnlichkeit *f*

vine [vaɪn] N (= *grapevine*) Rebe *f*; (= *similar plant*) Rebengewächs *nt*

vinegar ['vɪnɪgəʳ] N Essig *m*

vine: **vine leaf** N Rebenblatt *nt*; **vineyard** ['vɪnjəd] N Weinberg *m*

vintage ['vɪntɪdʒ] **1** N (*of wine, fig*) Jahrgang *m*; (*of car*) Baujahr *nt*; **the 1984 ~** der Jahrgang 1984 **2** ADJ ATTR (= *old*) uralt; (= *high quality*) glänzend, hervorragend; **this typewriter is a ~ model** diese Schreibmaschine hat Museumswert

vintage: **vintage car** N Vorkriegsmodell *nt*; **vintage wine** N edler Wein; **vintage year** N **a ~ for wine** ein besonders gutes Weinjahr

vinyl ['vaɪnɪl] N Vinyl *nt*

viola [vɪ'əʊlə] N (*Mus*) Bratsche *f*

violate ['vaɪəleɪt] VT (**a**) *treaty* brechen; (*partially*) verletzen; *law, rule* verstoßen gegen; *rights, airspace* verletzen (**b**) *holy place* entweihen; *peacefulness* stören; **to ~ sb's privacy** in jds Privatsphäre eindringen

violation [ˌvaɪə'leɪʃən] N (**a**) (*of law, rule*) Verstoß *m* (*of gegen*); (*of rights*) Verletzung *f*; **a ~ of a treaty** ein Vertragsbruch *m*; (*partial*) eine Vertragsverletzung; **traffic ~** Verkehrsvergehen *nt* (**b**) (*of holy place*) Entweihung *f*; (*of peacefulness*) Störung *f*; (*of privacy*) Eingriff *m* (*of in* +*acc*)

violence ['vaɪələns] N (**a**) (= *forcefulness, strength*) Heftigkeit *f*; (*of protest*) Schärfe *f* (**b**) (= *brutality*) Gewalt *f*; (*of people*) Gewalttätigkeit *f*; (*of actions*) Brutalität *f*; **act of ~** Gewalttat *f*; **to use ~ against sb** Gewalt gegen jdn anwenden; **was there any ~?** kam es zu Gewalttätigkeiten?; **outbreak of ~** Ausbruch *m* von Gewalttätigkeiten

violent [ˈvaɪələnt] ADJ *person, nature, action, sport, game* brutal; *crime* Gewalt-; *times* voller Gewalt; *attack, blow, protest, argument, opposition* heftig; *death* gewaltsam; *film, book* gewalttätig; *impact* gewaltig; *wind, storm, pain, dislike* stark; *contrast* krass; *change* tief greifend; *feeling, affair, speech* leidenschaftlich; *colour* grell; **to have a ~ temper** jähzornig sein; **to turn ~** gewalttätig werden; **to get** *or* **become ~** gewalttätig werden

violently [ˈvaɪələntlɪ] ADV *kick, beat, attack, react* brutal; *push, hurl* kräftig; *tremble, shake* heftig; *swerve, brake* abrupt; *speak* leidenschaftlich; *disagree* scharf; *blush* tief, heftig; *fall in love* unsterblich; **to be ~ ill** *or* **sick** sich furchtbar übergeben; **he was ~ angry** er war außer sich (*dat*) vor Wut; **to cough ~** gewaltig husten; **red and pink clash ~** Rot und Rosa beißen sich

violet [ˈvaɪəlɪt] **1** N (*Bot*) Veilchen *nt*; (= *colour*) Violett *nt* **2** ADJ violett

violin [ˌvaɪəˈlɪn] N Geige *f*, Violine *f*

violinist [ˌvaɪəˈlɪnɪst], **violin player** N Geiger(in) *m(f)*

VIP N VIP *m*, Promi *m* (*hum inf*); **he got/we gave him ~ treatment** er wurde/wir haben ihn als Ehrengast behandelt

viral [ˈvaɪərəl] ADJ Virus-; **~ infection** Virusinfektion *f*

virgin [ˈvɜːdʒɪn] **1** N Jungfrau *f*; **the Virgin Mary** die Jungfrau Maria; **he's still a ~** er ist noch unschuldig **2** ADJ (*fig*) *forest etc* unberührt; **~ olive oil** natives Olivenöl

Virginia [vəˈdʒɪnɪə] N (= *state*) Virginia *nt*

Virgin Isles N **the ~** die Jungferninseln *pl*

virginity [vəˈdʒɪnɪtɪ] N Unschuld *f*; (*of girls also*) Jungfräulichkeit *f*; **to take sb's ~** jds Unschuld rauben

Virgo [ˈvɜːgəʊ] N Jungfrau *f*; **he's (a) ~** er ist Jungfrau

virile [ˈvɪraɪl] ADJ (*lit*) männlich; (*fig*) ausdrucksvoll, kraftvoll

virility [vɪˈrɪlɪtɪ] N (*lit*) Männlichkeit *f*; (= *sexual power*) Potenz *f*; (*fig*) Ausdruckskraft *f*

virtual [ˈvɜːtjʊəl] ADJ ATTR **(a)** *certainty, impossibility* fast völlig; **it led to the ~ collapse of the economy** es führte dazu, dass die Wirtschaft fast so gut wie zusammenbrach; **she was a ~ prisoner** sie war so gut wie eine Gefangene; **he is the ~ leader** er ist quasi der Führer; **it was a ~ admission of guilt** es war praktisch ein Schuldgeständnis **(b)** (*Comput*) virtuell; **~ address** (*Comput*) virtuelle Adresse

virtually [ˈvɜːtjʊəlɪ] ADV **(a)** praktisch; *blind, lost also* fast, nahezu; **to be ~ certain** sich (*dat*) so gut wie sicher sein **(b)** (*Comput*) virtuell

virtual (*Comput*): **virtual memory** N virtueller Speicher; **virtual reality** N virtuelle Realität; **~ computer** virtueller Computer

virtue [ˈvɜːtjuː] N **(a)** (= *moral quality*) Tugend *f* **(b)** (= *chastity*) Keuschheit *f* **(c)** (= *advantage, point*) Vorteil *m*; **what's the ~ of that?** welchen Vorteil hat das? **(d)** (= *healing power*) Heilkraft *f*; **in** *or* **by ~ of** aufgrund +*gen*

virtuoso [ˌvɜːtjʊˈəʊzəʊ] **1** N (*esp Mus*) Virtuose *m*, Virtuosin *f* **2** ADJ meisterhaft, virtuos

virtuous [ˈvɜːtjʊəs] ADJ **(a)** tugendhaft **(b)** (*pej*: = *self-satisfied*) selbstgerecht

virtuously [ˈvɜːtjʊəslɪ] ADV (*pej*: = *self-righteously*) selbstgerecht

virulent [ˈvɪrʊlənt] ADJ **(a)** (*Med*) bösartig; *poison* stark **(b)** (*fig*) *attack, speech, opponent* scharf; *hatred* unversöhnlich

virus [ˈvaɪərəs] N (*Med, Comput*) Virus *nt* *or* *m*; **polio ~** Polioerreger *m*; **the AIDS ~** das Aidsvirus; **she's got** *or* **caught a ~** (*inf*: = *flu etc*) sie hat sich (*dat*) was geholt *or* eingefangen (*inf*); **~-infected** (*Comput*) virenbefallen

visa [ˈviːzə] N Visum *nt*; (= *stamp also*) Sichtvermerk *m*

vis-à-vis [ˌviːzɑːˈviː] **1** PREP in Anbetracht (+*gen*) **2** ADV gegenüber

visceral [ˈvɪsərəl] ADJ (*fig*) *hatred* tief sitzend

viscose [ˈvɪskəʊs] N Viskose *f*

viscount [ˈvaɪkaʊnt] N Viscount *m*

viscountess [ˈvaɪkaʊntɪs] N Viscountess *f*

viscous [ˈvɪskəs] ADJ (*form*) zähflüssig; (*Phys*) viskos

vise [vaɪs] N (*US*) = **vice²**

visibility [ˌvɪzɪˈbɪlɪtɪ] N **(a)** Sichtbarkeit *f* **(b)** (*Met*) Sichtweite *f*; **poor/good ~** schlechte/gute Sicht

visible [ˈvɪzəbl] ADJ **(a)** sichtbar; **~ to the naked eye** mit dem bloßen Auge zu erkennen; **the house is ~ from the road** das Haus ist von der Straße aus zu sehen; **there is no ~ difference**

man kann keinen Unterschied erkennen; **with a ~ effort** mit sichtlicher Mühe **(b)** (= *obvious*) sichtlich; (= *prominent*) *person* eminent, herausragend; **at management level women are becoming increasingly ~** auf Führungsebene treten Frauen immer deutlicher in Erscheinung

visible (*Econ*): **visible exports** PL Warenausfuhren *pl*; **visible imports** PL Wareneinfuhren *pl*

visibly [ˈvɪzəblɪ] ADV sichtbar, sichtlich; *deteriorate, decay* zusehends

vision [ˈvɪʒən] N **(a)** (= *power of sight*) Sehvermögen *nt*; **within/beyond the range of ~** in/außer Sichtweite **(b)** (= *foresight*) Weitblick *m* **(c)** (*in dream, trance*) Vision *f* **(d)** (= *image*) Vorstellung *f*; **Orwell's ~ of the future** Orwells Zukunftsvision *f*

visionary [ˈvɪʒənərɪ] **1** ADJ *idea, writer, artist* visionär **2** N Visionär(in) *m(f)*

visit [ˈvɪzɪt] **1** N Besuch *m*; (= *stay also*) Aufenthalt *m*; (*of doctor*) Hausbesuch *m*; **I felt better after a ~ to the doctor's** nachdem ich beim Arzt gewesen war, ging es mir besser; **to pay sb/sth a ~** jdn/etw besuchen; **to pay a ~** (= *euph*) mal verschwinden (müssen); **to have a ~ from sb** von jdm besucht werden; **we're expecting a ~ from the police any day** wir rechnen jeden Tag mit dem Besuch der Polizei; **to be on a ~ to London** zu einem Besuch in London sein; **to be on a private/official ~** inoffiziell/offiziell da sein **2** VT **(a)** besuchen; *doctor, solicitor* aufsuchen; **you never ~ us these days** Sie kommen uns ja gar nicht mehr besuchen **(b)** (= *inspect*) inspizieren, besichtigen **3** VI **(a)** einen Besuch machen; **come and ~ some time** komm mich mal besuchen; **I'm only ~ing here** ich bin nur auf Besuch hier **(b)** (*US inf*: = *chat*) ein Schwätzchen halten

➤ visit with VI +PREP OBJ (*US*) schwatzen mit

visiting [ˈvɪzɪtɪŋ] ADJ *scholar, expert* Gast-; *dignitary, monarch* der/die zu Besuch ist

visiting: **visiting hours** PL Besuchszeiten *pl*; **visiting professor** N Gastprofessor(in) *m(f)*; **visiting team** N **the ~** die Gäste *pl*; **visiting time** N Besuchszeit *f*

visitor [ˈvɪzɪtəʳ] N Besucher(in) *m(f)*; (*in hotel*) Gast *m*; **to have ~s/a ~** Besuch haben; **~s' book** Gästebuch *nt*

visor [ˈvaɪzəʳ] N (*on helmet*) Visier *nt*; (*on cap*) Schirm *m*; (*Aut*) Blende *f*; **sun ~** Schirm *m*; (*Aut*) Sonnenblende *f*

vista [ˈvɪstə] N Aussicht *f*, Blick *m*

visual [ˈvɪzjʊəl] ADJ Seh-; *image, memory, depiction, joke* visuell

visual: **visual aids** PL Anschauungsmaterial *nt*; **visual arts** N **the ~** die darstellenden Künste *pl*; **visual display unit** N Sichtgerät *nt*

visualize [ˈvɪzjʊəlaɪz] VT sich (*dat*) vorstellen

visually [ˈvɪzjʊəlɪ] ADV visuell; **~ attractive** attraktiv anzusehen

visually handicapped, visually impaired ADJ sehbehindert

vital [ˈvaɪtl] ADJ **(a)** (= *of life, lively*) vital; (= *necessary for life*) lebenswichtig **(b)** (= *essential*) unerlässlich; **of ~ importance** von größter Wichtigkeit; **this is ~** das ist unbedingt notwendig; **your support is ~ to us** wir brauchen unbedingt Ihre Unterstützung; **how ~ is this?** wie wichtig ist das? **(c)** (= *critical*) *argument, issue* entscheidend; *error* schwerwiegend

vitality [vaɪˈtælɪtɪ] N (= *energy*) Energie *f*, Vitalität *f*; (*of language*) Lebendigkeit *f*; (*of companies*) Dynamik *f*

vitally [ˈvaɪtəlɪ] ADV *important* äußerst; *necessary, needed* dringend

vital: **vital parts** PL wichtige Teile *pl*; **vital signs** PL (*Med*) Lebenszeichen *pl*; **vital statistics** PL Bevölkerungsstatistik *f*; (*inf: of woman*) Maße *pl*

vitamin [ˈvɪtəmɪn] N Vitamin *nt*; **~ A** Vitamin A

viticulture [ˈvɪtɪkʌltʃəʳ] N Weinbau *m*

vitriol [ˈvɪtrɪəl] N (*fig*) Bissigkeit *f*

vitriolic [ˌvɪtrɪˈɒlɪk] ADJ (*fig*) *remark, criticism* beißend; *attack, speech* hasserfüllt

vitro [ˈviːtrəʊ] ADJ, ADV *see* **in vitro**

viva [ˈvaɪvə] N (*Brit*) = **viva voce**

vivacious [vɪˈveɪʃəs] ADJ lebhaft; *character, person also* temperamentvoll; *smile, laugh* munter

vivaciously [vɪˈveɪʃəslɪ] ADV *say, laugh* munter

viva voce [ˌvaɪvəˈvəʊtʃɪ] N (*Brit*) mündliche Prüfung

vivid [ˈvɪvɪd] ADJ *light* hell; *colour* kräftig; *imagination, recollection* lebhaft; *description, image* lebendig, anschaulich; *emotions* stark; *example, contrast* deutlich; **a ~ blue dress** ein leuchtend blaues Kleid; **in ~ detail** in allen plastischen Einzelheiten; **the memory of that day is still quite ~** der Tag ist mir noch in lebhafter Erinnerung; **to be a ~ reminder of sth** lebhaft an etw (*acc*) erinnern

vividly [ˈvɪvɪdlɪ] ADV *coloured, remember* lebhaft; *shine* leuchtend; *describe, illustrate, portray* anschaulich; *demonstrate* klar und deutlich; **the red stands out ~ against its background** das Rot hebt sich stark vom Hintergrund ab

vividness [ˈvɪvɪdnɪs] N (*of colour, imagination, memory*) Lebhaftigkeit *f*; (*of light*) Helligkeit *f*; (*of style*) Lebendigkeit *f*; (*of description, image*) Anschaulichkeit *f*

vivisection [ˌvɪvɪˈsekʃən] N Vivisektion *f*

vixen [ˈvɪksn] N (*Zool*) Füchsin *f*; (*fig*) zänkisches Weib

viz [vɪz] ADV nämlich

V-J Day N *Tag des Sieges gegen Japan im 2. Weltkrieg*

VLSI ABBR *of* **very large scale integration** Höchst- *or* Größtintegration *f*, VLSI *f*

V: V-neck N V-Ausschnitt *m*; **V-necked** ADJ mit V-Ausschnitt

vocabulary [vəʊˈkæbjʊlərɪ] N Wortschatz *m*, Vokabular *nt* (*geh*); **~ test** (*Sch*) Vokabelarbeit *f*

vocal [ˈvəʊkəl] **1** ADJ (a) (= *using voice*) Stimm-; **~ style** Singstil *m*; **~ range** Stimmumfang *m*; **best male ~ performer** bester Vokalsänger; **~ group** Gesangsgruppe *f*
(b) *communication* mündlich
(c) (= *voicing one's opinions*) lautstark; **to be/become ~** sich zu Wort melden; **to be ~ in sth** etw deutlich zum Ausdruck bringen; **to be ~ in demanding sth** etw laut fordern
2 N **~s: Van Morrison** Gesang: Van Morrison; **featuring Madonna on ~s** mit Madonna als Sängerin; **backing ~s** Hintergrundgesang *m*; **lead ~s ...** Leadsänger(in) *m(f)* ...

vocal cords PL Stimmbänder *pl*

vocalist [ˈvəʊkəlɪst] N Sänger(in) *m(f)*

vocalize [ˈvəʊkəlaɪz] VT *thoughts* aussprechen, Ausdruck verleihen (+*dat*); *feelings* zum Ausdruck bringen

vocation [vəʊˈkeɪʃən] N (a) (*Rel etc*) Berufung *f*; (*form: = profession*) Beruf *m* (b) (= *aptitude*) Begabung *f*, Talent *nt*

vocational [vəʊˈkeɪʃənl] ADJ Berufs-; *qualifications* beruflich; **~ course** Weiterbildungskurs *m*; **~ training** Berufsausbildung *f*

vocational school N (*US*) ≈ Berufsschule *f*

vociferous [vəʊˈsɪfərəs] ADJ *class, audience* laut; *demands, protest, opponent* lautstark

vociferously [vəʊˈsɪfərəslɪ] ADV lautstark

vodka [ˈvɒdkə] N Wodka *m*

vogue [vəʊɡ] N Mode *f*; **the ~ for jeans** die Jeansmode; **to be the ~ or in ~** (in) Mode sein

voice [vɔɪs] **1** N (a) (*lit, fig*) Stimme *f*; **I've lost my ~** ich habe keine Stimme mehr; **to be in good ~** gut bei Stimme sein; **in a deep ~** mit tiefer Stimme; **in a low ~** mit leiser Stimme; **to like the sound of one's own ~** sich gern(e) reden hören; **his ~ has broken** er hat den Stimmbruch hinter sich; **tenor ~** Tenor *m*; **with one ~** einstimmig; **to give ~ to sth** einer Sache (*dat*) Ausdruck verleihen; **we have a/no ~ in the matter** wir haben in dieser Angelegenheit ein/kein Mitspracherecht
(b) (*Gram*) Aktionsart *f*, Genus (verbi) *nt*; **the active/passive ~** das Aktiv/Passiv
2 VT *feelings, opinion* zum Ausdruck bringen

-voiced ADJ SUF mit ... Stimme; **soft-voiced** mit sanfter Stimme

voice: voiceless ADJ (a) stumm (b) (= *having no say*) ohne Mitspracherecht; **voice mail** N Voicemail *f*; **voice-operated** ADJ sprachgesteuert; **voice-over** N Filmkommentar *m*; **voice recognition** N Spracherkennung *f*; **voice synthesizer** N Sprachsynthesizer *m*

void [vɔɪd] **1** N (*lit, fig*) Leere *f* **2** ADJ (a) (= *empty*) leer; **~ of any sense of decency** ohne jegliches Gefühl für Anstand *geh*
(b) (*Jur*) ungültig, nichtig

voidable [ˈvɔɪdəbl] ADJ (*Jur*) anfechtbar

vol ABBR *of* **volume** Bd

volatile [ˈvɒlətaɪl] ADJ (a) (*Chem*) flüchtig (b) *person* (*in moods*) impulsiv; (*in interests*) sprunghaft; *relationship* wechselhaft; *political situation* brisant; (*St Ex*) unbeständig (c) (*Comput*) **~ memory** flüchtiger Speicher

volatility [ˌvɒləˈtɪlɪtɪ] N (*of political situation*) Brisanz *f*; (*of stock market*) Unbeständigkeit *f*

vol-au-vent [ˈvɒləʊvɑː] N (Königin)pastetchen *nt*

volcanic [vɒlˈkænɪk] ADJ (*lit*) Vulkan-; *rock, dust, activity* vulkanisch; **~ activity** Vulkantätigkeit *f*; **~ eruption** Vulkanausbruch *m*

volcano [vɒlˈkeɪnəʊ] N Vulkan *m*

vole [vəʊl] N Wühlmaus *f*; (= *common ~*) Feldmaus *f*

Volga [ˈvɒlɡə] N Wolga *f*

volition [vəˈlɪʃən] N Wille *m*; **of one's own ~** aus freiem Willen

volley [ˈvɒlɪ] **1** N (a) (*of shots*) Salve *f*; (*of arrows, stones*) Hagel *m*; (*fig*) (*of insults*) Flut *f* (b) (*Tennis*) Volley *m* **2** VT **to ~ a ball** (*Tennis*) einen Volley spielen *or* schlagen **3** VI (*Tennis*) einen Volley schlagen

volleyball [ˈvɒlɪ,bɔːl] N Volleyball *m*

volt [vəʊlt] N Volt *nt*

voltage [ˈvəʊltɪdʒ] N Spannung *f*

voluble [ˈvɒljʊbl] ADJ *speaker* redegewandt, redselig (*pej*); *protest* wortreich

volume [ˈvɒljuːm] **1** N (a) Band *m*; **a six-~ dictionary** ein sechsbändiges Wörterbuch; **that speaks ~s** (*fig*) das spricht Bände (*for* für)
(b) (= *space occupied by sth*) Volumen *nt*
(c) (= *size, amount*) Umfang *m*, Ausmaß *nt* (*of* an +*dat*); **a large ~ of sales/business** ein großer Umsatz; **the ~ of traffic** das Verkehrsaufkommen
(d) (= *sound*) Lautstärke *f*; **turn the ~ up/down** (*Rad, TV*) stell (das Gerät) lauter/leiser
2 ATTR **~ discount** Mengenrabatt *m*; **~ sales** Mengenabsatz *m*

volume control N (*Rad, TV*) Lautstärkeregler *m*

voluminous [vəˈluːmɪnəs] ADJ voluminös (*geh*); *figure also* üppig; *skirts, shirt* wallend

voluntarily [ˈvɒləntərɪlɪ] ADV freiwillig; (= *unpaid*) *work* ehrenamtlich

voluntary [ˈvɒləntərɪ] ADJ (a) freiwillig; **~ code** (*Comm*) freiwilliger Verhaltenskodex; **~ worker** freiwilliger Helfer, freiwillige Helferin; (*overseas*) Entwicklungshelfer(in) *m(f)*
(b) (= *supported by charity*) *body* karitativ; **a ~ organization for social work** ein freiwilliger Wohlfahrtsverband

voluntary: voluntary manslaughter N (*US Jur*) vorsätzliche Tötung; **voluntary redundancy** N freiwilliges Ausscheiden; **to take ~** sich abfinden lassen

volunteer [ˌvɒlənˈtɪəʳ] **1** N (*also Mil*) Freiwillige(r) *mf*; **any ~s?** wer meldet sich freiwillig?
2 VT *help, services* anbieten; *information* geben, herausrücken mit (*inf*); **we didn't ask you to ~ any advice** wir haben Sie nicht um Rat gebeten
3 VI (a) sich freiwillig melden; **to ~ for sth** sich freiwillig für etw zur Verfügung stellen; **to ~ to do sth** sich anbieten, etw zu tun; **who will ~ to clean the windows?** wer meldet sich freiwillig zum Fensterputzen?
(b) (*Mil*) sich freiwillig melden (*for* zu, *for places* nach)

voluptuous [vəˈlʌptjʊəs] ADJ *mouth, woman* sinnlich; *body* verlockend

voluptuousness [vəˈlʌptjʊəsnɪs] N (*of woman*) Sinnlichkeit *f*; (*of body*) verlockende Formen *pl*

vomit [ˈvɒmɪt] **1** N Erbrochene(s) *nt* **2** VT (*lit, fig*) spucken; *food* erbrechen **3** VI sich übergeben

voodoo [ˈvuːduː] N Voodoo *m*

voracious [vəˈreɪʃəs] ADJ *person* gefräßig; *collector* besessen; **she is a ~ reader** sie verschlingt die Bücher geradezu; **to be a ~ eater** Unmengen vertilgen; **to have a ~ appetite** einen Riesenappetit haben

voraciously [vəˈreɪʃəslɪ] ADV *eat* gierig; **to read ~** die Bücher nur so verschlingen

vortex [ˈvɔːteks] N, *pl* **-es** *or* **vortices** [ˈvɔːtɪsiːz] (*lit*) Wirbel *m*, Strudel *m* (*also fig*)

vote [vəʊt] **1** N Stimme *f*; (= *act of voting*) Abstimmung *f*, Wahl *f*; (= *result*) Abstimmungs- *or* Wahlergebnis *nt*; (= *franchise*) Wahlrecht *nt*; **to put sth to the ~** über etw (*acc*) abstimmen lassen; **to take a ~ on sth** über etw (*acc*) abstimmen; **the ~ for/against the change surprised him** dass für/gegen den Wechsel gestimmt wurde, erstaunte ihn; **the ~ was 150 to 95** das Abstimmungsergebnis war 150 zu 95; **we would like to offer a ~ of thanks to Mr Smith** wir möchten Herrn Smith unseren aufrichtigen Dank aussprechen; **a**

photo of the Prime Minister casting his ~ ein Foto des Premierministers bei der Stimmabgabe; **he won by 22 ~s** er gewann mit einer Mehrheit von 22 Stimmen; **the Labour ~** die Labourstimmen *pl*; **the Labour ~ has increased** der Stimmenanteil von Labour hat sich erhöht

2 VT **(a)** (= *elect*) wählen; **he was ~d chairman** er wurde zum Vorsitzenden gewählt; **to ~ Labour** Labour wählen **(b)** (*inf*: = *judge*) wählen zu; **I ~ we go back** ich schlage vor, dass wir umkehren **(c)** (= *approve*) bewilligen

3 VI wählen; **to ~ for/against sth** für/gegen etw stimmen; **~ for Clark!** wählen Sie Clark!; **to ~ with one's feet** mit den Füßen abstimmen

➤ **vote down** VT SEP *proposal* niederstimmen

➤ **vote in** VT SEP *law* beschließen; *person* wählen

➤ **vote on** VI +PREP OBJ abstimmen über (+*acc*)

➤ **vote out** VT SEP abwählen; *amendment* ablehnen

voter ['vəʊtəʳ] N Wähler(in) *m(f)*

voting ['vəʊtɪŋ] N Wahl *f*; **a system of ~** ein Wahlsystem *nt*; **~ was heavy** die Wahlbeteiligung war hoch

voting: **voting booth** N Wahlkabine *f*; **voting machine** N (*US*) Wahlmaschine *f*; **voting paper** N Stimmzettel *m*; **voting precinct** N (*US Pol*) Wahlbezirk *m*; **voting right** N Stimmrecht *nt*

vouch [vaʊtʃ] VI **to ~ for sb/sth** sich für jdn/etw verbürgen; (*legally*) für jdn/etw bürgen

voucher ['vaʊtʃəʳ] N Gutschein *m*; (= *receipt*) Beleg *m*

vow [vaʊ] **1** N Gelöbnis *nt*; (*Rel*) Gelübde *nt*; **to make a ~ to do sth** geloben, etw zu tun; **to take one's ~s** sein Gelübde ablegen **2** VT geloben; **he is ~ed to silence** er hat Schweigen gelobt

vowel ['vaʊəl] N Vokal *m*, Selbstlaut *m*; **~ sound** Vokal(laut) *m*

voyage ['vɔɪdʒ] N Reise *f*, Fahrt *f*; (*esp by sea*) Seereise *f*; **to go on a ~** auf eine Reise *etc* gehen; **~ of discovery** (*fig*) Entdeckungsreise *f*

voyager ['vɔɪədʒəʳ] N Passagier(in) *m(f)*

voyeur [vwaː'jɜːʳ] N Voyeur(in) *m(f)*

voyeurism [vwaː'jɜːrɪzəm] N Voyeurismus *m*

voyeuristic [vwaː'jɜːrɪstɪk] ADJ voyeuristisch

vs ABBR *of* **versus**

V-sign ['viːsaɪn] N (*Brit*) (*victory*) Victoryzeichen *nt*; (*rude*) ≈ Stinkefinger *m* (*inf*); **he gave me the ~** ≈ er zeigte mir den Stinkefinger (*inf*)

vulgar ['vʌlgəʳ] ADJ (*pej*) (= *unrefined*) vulgär; *clothes, joke* ordinär; (= *tasteless*) geschmacklos; **it is ~ to talk about money** es ist unfein, über Geld zu reden

vulgarity [vʌl'gærɪtɪ] N Vulgarität *f*; (*of gesture, joke also*) Anstößigkeit *f*; (*of colour, tie etc*) Geschmacklosigkeit *f*

vulnerability [ˌvʌlnərə'bɪlɪtɪ] N Verwundbarkeit *f*; (= *susceptibility*) Verletzlichkeit *f*; (*fig*) Verletzbarkeit *f*; (*of troops, fortress*) Ungeschütztheit *f*; **the ~ of the young fish to predators** die Wehrlosigkeit der jungen Fische gegen Raubtiere

vulnerable ['vʌlnərəbl] ADJ verwundbar; (= *exposed*) verletzlich; (*fig*) verletzbar; *troops, fortress* ungeschützt; **to feel ~** sich verwundbar fühlen; **she is at a very ~ age** sie ist in einem sehr schwierigen Alter; **to be ~ to disease** anfällig für Krankheiten sein; **the turtle on its back is completely ~** auf dem Rücken liegend ist die Schildkröte völlig wehrlos; **to be ~ to attack** Angriffen schutzlos ausgesetzt sein; **a ~ point in our argument** ein schwacher *or* wunder Punkt unseres Arguments; **economically ~** wirtschaftlich wehrlos; **hotels are acutely ~ to recession** Hotels sind äußerst rezessionsanfällig

vulture ['vʌltʃəʳ] N (*lit, fig*) Geier *m*

vulva ['vʌlvə] N (weibliche) Scham, Vulva *f* (*geh*)

Ww

W, w [ˈdʌblju:] N W *nt*, w *nt*

W ABBR *of* **west** W

wacky [ˈwækɪ] ADJ (+ER) (*inf*) verrückt (*inf*)

wad [wɒd] **1** N (= *compact mass*) Knäuel *m or nt*; (*of cotton wool etc*) Bausch *m*; (*of papers, banknotes*) Bündel *nt* **2** VT (= *secure, stuff*) stopfen; (= *squeeze*) zusammenknüllen

wadding [ˈwɒdɪŋ] N (*for packing*) Material *nt* zum Ausstopfen

waddle [ˈwɒdl] **1** N Watscheln *nt* **2** VI watscheln

wade [weɪd] **1** VT durchwaten **2** VI waten
➤ **wade in** VI (a) (*lit*) hineinwaten (b) (*fig inf*) sich hineinknien (*inf*)
➤ **wade into** VI +PREP OBJ (*fig inf*: = *attack*) **to wade into sb** auf jdn losgehen; **to wade into sth** etw in Angriff nehmen
➤ **wade through** VI +PREP OBJ (a) (*lit*) waten durch (b) (*fig*) sich (durch)kämpfen durch

waders [ˈweɪdəz] PL (= *boots*) Watstiefel *pl*

wading pool [ˈweɪdɪŋpuːl] N (*US*) Plan(t)schbecken *nt*

wafer [ˈweɪfə] N (a) (= *biscuit*) Waffel *f* (b) (*Eccl*) Hostie *f*

wafer-thin [ˈweɪfəˈθɪn] ADJ hauchdünn

waffle[1] [ˈwɒfl] N (*Cook*) Waffel *f*

waffle[2] (*Brit inf*) **1** N Geschwafel *nt* (*inf*) **2** VI (*also ~ on*) schwafeln (*inf*)

waffle iron N Waffeleisen *nt*

waft [wɑːft] **1** N Hauch *m*; **a ~ of cool air** ein kühler Lufthauch **2** VTI wehen; **a delicious smell ~ed up from the kitchen** ein köstlicher Geruch zog aus der Küche herauf

wag[1] [wæg] **1** N **with a ~ of its tail** mit einem Schwanzwedeln **2** VT *tail* wedeln mit; **to ~ one's finger at sb** jdm mit dem Finger drohen **3** VI (*tail*) wedeln; **to stop the tongues ~ging** (*inf*) um dem Gerede ein Ende zu machen; **that'll set the tongues ~ging** (*inf*) dann gibt das Gerede los

wag[2] N (= *wit, clown*) Witzbold *m* (*inf*)

wage[1] [weɪdʒ] N USU PL Lohn *m*

wage[2] VT *war, campaign* führen; **to ~ war against sth** (*fig*) gegen etw einen Feldzug führen

wage IN CPDS Lohn-; **wage bargaining** N, NO PL Tarifverhandlung *f*; **wage claim** *or* **demand** N Lohnforderung *f*; **wage earner** N (*esp Brit*) Lohnempfänger(in) *m(f)*; **wage increase** N Lohnerhöhung *f*; **wage packet** N (*esp Brit*) Lohntüte *f*

wager [ˈweɪdʒə] N Wette *f* (*on* auf +*acc*); **to make a ~** eine Wette abschließen

wages [ˈweɪdʒɪz] PL Lohn *m*; **~ office** Lohnbuchhaltung *f*

wage: **wage settlement** N Tarifabschluss *m*; **wage structure** N Lohngefüge *nt*; **wage worker** N (*US*) Lohnempfänger(in) *m(f)*

waggle [ˈwægl] **1** VT wackeln mit; *tail* wedeln mit **2** VI wackeln; (*tail*) wedeln

waggon N [ˈwægən] (*Brit*) = **wagon**

wagon [ˈwægən] N (a) (*horse-drawn*) Fuhrwerk *nt*; (= *covered ~*) Planwagen *m* (b) (*Brit Rail*) Wag(g)on *m* (c) (*inf*) **I'm on the ~** ich trinke nichts

wagonload [ˈwægənləʊd] N Wagenladung *f*; **prisoners arrived by the ~** ganze Wagenladungen von Gefangenen kamen an

waif [weɪf] N obdachloses *or* heimatloses Kind; (= *animal*) herrenloses Tier; **~s and strays** (= *children*) obdachlose *or* heimatlose Kinder *pl*; (= *animals*) herrenlose Tiere *pl*

wail [weɪl] **1** N (*of baby*) Geschrei *nt*; (*of mourner, music*) Klagen *nt*; (*of sirens, wind*) Heulen *nt*; **a great ~/a ~ of protest went up** es erhob sich lautes Wehklagen/Protestgeheul **2** VI (*baby, cat*) schreien; (*mourner, music*) klagen; (*siren, wind*) heulen

waist [weɪst] N Taille *f*; **stripped to the ~** mit nacktem *or* bloßem Oberkörper

waist: **waistband** N Rock-/Hosenbund *m*; **waistcoat** N (*Brit*) Weste *f*; **waist-deep** ADJ hüfthoch; **we stood in ... wir standen bis zur Hüfte in ...; **waist-high** ADJ hüfthoch; **waistline** N Taille *f*

wait [weɪt] **1** N (a) warten (*for* auf +*acc*); **to ~ for sb to do sth** darauf warten, dass jd etw tut; **it was definitely worth ~ing for** es hat sich wirklich gelohnt, darauf zu warten; **well, what are you ~ing for?** worauf wartest du denn (noch)?; **this stamp is worth, ~ for it, £10,000** diese Briefmarke kostet sage und schreibe £ 10.000; **can't it ~?** kann das nicht warten?; **this work is still ~ing to be done** diese Arbeit muss noch gemacht *or* erledigt werden; **~ a minute** *or* **moment** *or* **second** (einen) Augenblick *or* Moment (mal); **(just) you ~!** warte nur ab!; (*threatening*) warte nur!; **I can't ~** ich kanns kaum erwarten; (*out of curiosity*) ich bin gespannt; **I can't ~ to see his face** da bin ich (aber) auf sein Gesicht gespannt; **I can't ~ to try out my new boat** ich kann es kaum noch erwarten, bis ich mein neues Boot ausprobiere; **"repairs while you ~"** „Sofortreparaturen"; **~ and see!** abwarten und Tee trinken! (*inf*)
(b) **to ~ at table** (*Brit*) servieren, bedienen **2** VT (a) **to ~ one's turn** (ab)warten, bis man an der Reihe ist; **to ~ one's moment** *or* **chance** eine günstige Gelegenheit abwarten
(b) (*US*) **to ~ a table** bedienen **3** N Wartezeit *f*; **did you have a long ~?** mussten Sie lange warten?; **to lie in ~ for sb/sth** jdm/einer Sache auflauern
➤ **wait about** (*Brit*) *or* **around** VI warten (*for* auf +*acc*)
➤ **wait behind** VI zurückbleiben
➤ **wait on** VI +PREP OBJ (a) (*also* **wait upon**: = *serve*) bedienen (b) (*US*) **to wait on table** servieren, bei Tisch bedienen (c) (= *wait for*) warten auf (+*acc*)
➤ **wait out** VT SEP das Ende (+*gen*) abwarten; **to wait it out** abwarten
➤ **wait up** VI (a) aufbleiben (*for* wegen, für) (b) (*esp US inf*) **wait up!** langsam!

waiter [ˈweɪtə] N Kellner *m*, Ober *m*; **~!** (Herr) Ober!

waiting [ˈweɪtɪŋ] N Warten *nt*; **all this ~ (around)** diese ewige Warterei (*inf*); **no ~** Halteverbot *nt*

waiting: **waiting list** N Warteliste *f*; **waiting room** N Warteraum *m*; (*at doctor's*) Wartezimmer *nt*; (*in railway station*) Wartesaal *m*

waitress [ˈweɪtrɪs] **1** N Kellnerin *f*, Serviererin *f*; **~!** Fräulein! **2** VI kellnern

waitressing [ˈweɪtrɪsɪŋ] N Kellnern *nt*

wait state N (*Comput*) Wartezyklus *m*; **with zero ~s** ohne Wartezyklen

waive [weɪv] VT *rights, fee* verzichten auf (+*acc*); *principles, rules etc* außer Acht lassen; *objection* abtun

waiver [ˈweɪvə] N (*Jur*) Verzicht *m* (*of* auf +*acc*); (= *document*) Verzichterklärung *f*; (*of law, contract, clause*) Außerkraftsetzung *f*

wake[1] [weɪk] N (*Naut*) Kielwasser *nt*; **in the ~ of** (*fig*) im Gefolge (+*gen*); **to follow in sb's ~** in jds Kielwasser segeln; **X follows in the ~ of Y** Y bringt X mit sich; **X brings Y in its ~** X bringt Y mit sich; **X leaves Y in its ~** X hinterlässt Y

wake[2] *pret* **woke**, *ptp* **woken** *or* **waked** **1** VT (auf)wecken; (*fig*) wecken **2** VI aufwachen; **he woke to find himself in prison** als er aufwachte, fand er sich im Gefängnis wieder
➤ **wake up** **1** VI (*lit, fig*) aufwachen; **to wake up to sth** (*fig*) sich (*dat*) einer Sache (*gen*) bewusst werden **2** VT SEP (*lit*) aufwecken; (*fig*: = *rouse from sloth*) wach- *or* aufrütteln

waken [ˈweɪkən] **1** VT (auf)wecken **2** VI (*liter, Scot*) erwachen (*geh*)

wake-up call [ˈweɪkʌpkɔːl] N (a) (*Telec*) Weckruf *m* (b) (*esp US*: = *warning*) Warnsignal *nt*

waking [ˈweɪkɪŋ] ADJ **one's ~ hours** von früh bis spät; **~ dream** Wachtraum *m*

Wales [weɪlz] N Wales *nt*; **Prince of ~** Prinz *m* von Wales

walk [wɔːk] **1** N (a) (= *stroll*) Spaziergang *m*; (= *hike*) Wanderung *f*; (*Sport*) Gehen *nt*; **it's only 10 minutes' ~** es sind nur 10 Minuten zu Fuß; **it's a long/short ~ to the shops** zu den Läden ist es weit/nicht weit zu Fuß; **that's quite a ~** das ist ganz schön weit zu laufen (*inf*); **to go for a ~, to have** *or* **take a ~** einen Spaziergang machen; **to take sb/the dog for a ~** mit jdm/dem Hund spazieren gehen
(b) (= *gait*) Gang *m*; **he ran for a bit, then slowed to a ~** er rannte ein Stück und ging dann im Schritttempo weiter
(c) (= *route*) Weg *m*; (*signposted etc*) Wander-/Spazierweg *m*; **he knows some good ~s in the Lake District** er kennt ein paar

gute Wanderungen im Lake District

(d) ~ **of life** Milieu *nt*; **people from all ~s of life** Leute aus allen Schichten und Berufen

2 VT (= *lead*) *person, horse* (spazieren) führen; *dog* ausführen; (= *ride at a* ~) im Schritt gehen lassen; *distance* laufen, gehen; **to** ~ **sb home/to the bus** jdn nach Hause/zum Bus bringen; **to** ~ **the streets** (*prostitute*) auf den Strich gehen (*inf*); (*aimlessly*) durch die Straßen streichen

3 VI **(a)** gehen, laufen; **to learn to** ~ laufen lernen; **to** ~ **in one's sleep** schlaf- *or* nachtwandeln; **to** ~ **with a stick** am Stock gehen

(b) (= *not ride*) zu Fuß gehen, laufen (*inf*); (= *stroll*) spazieren gehen; (= *hike*) wandern; **you can** ~ **there in 5 minutes** da ist man in 5 Minuten zu Fuß; **to** ~ **home** nach Hause laufen (*inf*)

(c) (*inf*: = *disappear*) Beine bekommen (*inf*)

➤ **walk about** (*Brit*) or **around** **1** VI herumlaufen (*inf*) **2** VT SEP (= *lead*) *person, horse* auf und ab führen; (= *ride at a walk*) im Schritt gehen lassen

➤ **walk away** VI weg- *or* davongehen; **he walked away from the crash unhurt** er ist bei dem Unfall ohne Verletzungen davongekommen; **you can't just walk away from ten years of marriage** du kannst doch zehn Jahre Ehe nicht einfach so abschreiben; **to walk away with a prize** *etc* einen Preis *etc* kassieren

➤ **walk in** VI hereinkommen; (*casually*) hereinspazieren (*inf*)

➤ **walk in on** VI +PREP OBJ hereinplatzen bei (*inf*)

➤ **walk into** VI +PREP OBJ *room* hereinkommen in (+*acc*); *person* anrempeln; *wall* laufen gegen; **to walk into a trap** in eine Falle gehen; **he just walked into the first job he applied for** er hat gleich die erste Stelle bekommen, um die er sich beworben hat; **to walk right into sth** (*lit*) mit voller Wucht gegen etw rennen

➤ **walk off** **1** VT SEP *pounds* ablaufen (*inf*); **we walked off our lunch with a stroll in the park** nach dem Mittagessen haben wir einen Verdauungsspaziergang im Park gemacht **2** VI weggehen; **he walked off in the opposite direction** er ging in die andere Richtung davon

➤ **walk off with** VI +PREP OBJ (*inf*) **(a)** (= *take*) (*unintentionally*) abziehen mit (*inf*); (*intentionally*) abhauen mit (*inf*) **(b)** (= *win easily*) *prize* kassieren, einstecken (*inf*)

➤ **walk on** **1** VI +PREP OBJ *grass etc* betreten **2** VI (= *continue walking*) weitergehen

➤ **walk out** VI **(a)** (= *quit*) gehen; **to walk out of a meeting** eine Versammlung verlassen; **to walk out on sb** jdn verlassen; *girlfriend etc* jdn sitzen lassen (*inf*); **to walk out on sth** aus etw aussteigen (*inf*) **(b)** (= *strike*) streiken

➤ **walk over** VI +PREP OBJ **to walk all over sb** (*inf*) (= *dominate*) jdn unterbuttern (*inf*); (= *treat harshly*) jdn fertig machen (*inf*)

➤ **walk through** VI +PREP OBJ (*Theat*) *part* durchgehen

➤ **walk up** VI **(a)** (= *go up, ascend*) hinaufgehen **(b)** (= *approach*) zugehen (*to* auf +*acc*); **a man walked up to me/her** ein Mann kam auf mich zu/ging auf sie zu

walk: walkabout N (*esp Brit: by king etc*) Rundgang *m*; **the Queen went (on a)** ~ die Königin nahm ein Bad in der Menge; **walkaway** N (*US*) = **walkover**

walker ['wɔːkə^r] N **(a)** (= *stroller*) Spaziergänger(in) *m(f)*; (= *hiker*) Wanderer *m*, Wanderin *f*; (*Sport*) Geher(in) *m(f)*; **to be a fast/slow** ~ schnell/langsam gehen **(b)** (*for baby, invalid*) Gehhilfe *f*; (*US*: = *Zimmer* ®) Gehwagen *m*

walkie-talkie ['wɔːkɪ'tɔːkɪ] N Sprechfunkgerät *nt*

walk-in ['wɔːkɪn] **1** ADJ **a** ~ **cupboard** begehbarer Wandschrank **2** N (*US*) (= *cupboard*) begehbarer Wandschrank; (= *victory*) spielender Sieg

walking ['wɔːkɪŋ] **1** N Gehen *nt*; (*as recreation*) Spazierengehen *nt*; (= *hiking*) Wandern *nt*; **we did a lot of** ~ **while we were in Wales** als wir in Wales waren, sind wir viel gewandert **2** ADJ ATTR *miracle etc* wandelnd; **at (a)** ~ **pace** im Schritttempo; **the** ~ **wounded** die leicht Verwundeten *pl*; **it's within** ~ **distance** dahin kann man laufen *or* zu Fuß gehen

walking: walking boots PL Wanderstiefel *pl*; **walking frame** N Gehhilfe *f*; **walking holiday** N (*Brit*) Wanderferien *pl*; **walking shoes** PL Wanderschuhe *pl*; **walking stick** N Spazierstock *m*

Walkman ® ['wɔːkmən] N Walkman ® *m*

walk: walk-on ADJ ~ **part/role** (*Theat*) Statistenrolle *f* **2** N Statistenrolle *f*; **walkout** N (= *strike*) Streik *m*; **to stage a** ~ (*from conference etc*) demonstrativ den Saal verlassen;

walkover N (*Sport*) Walkover *m*; (= *easy victory*) spielender Sieg; (*fig*) Kinderspiel *nt*; **walk-up** N (*US inf*) Haus *nt* ohne Fahrstuhl; **walkway** N Fußweg *m*

wall [wɔːl] N (*outside*) Mauer *f*; (*inside*) Wand *f*; **the Great Wall of China** die Chinesische Mauer; **a** ~ **of fire** eine Feuerwand; **a** ~ **of troops** eine Mauer von Soldaten; **to go up the** ~ (*inf*) die Wände hochgehen (*inf*); **I'm climbing the ~s** (*inf*) ich könnte die Wände hochgehen (*inf*); **he drives me up the** ~ (*inf*) er bringt mich auf die Palme (*inf*); **this constant noise is driving me up the** ~ (*inf*) bei diesem ständigen Lärm könnte ich die Wände hochgehen (*inf*); **to go to the** ~ (*inf: firm etc*) kaputtgehen (*inf*)

➤ **wall in** VT SEP mit einer Mauer/von Mauern umgeben

➤ **wall off** VT SEP (= *cut off*) durch eine Mauer (ab)trennen; (= *separate into different parts*) unterteilen

➤ **wall up** VT SEP zumauern

wallaby ['wɒləbɪ] N Wallaby *nt*

wall: wall calendar N Wandkalender *m*; **wall chart** N Plantafel *f*; **wall clock** N Wanduhr *f*; **wall cupboard** N Wandschrank *m*

walled [wɔːld] ADJ von Mauern umgeben

wallet ['wɒlɪt] N Brieftasche *f*

Walloon [wɒ'luːn] **1** N **(a)** Wallone *m*, Wallonin *f* **(b)** (*dialect*) Wallonisch *nt* **2** ADJ wallonisch

wallop ['wɒləp] **1** N (*inf*) Schlag *m*; **to give sb/sth a** ~ jdm/einer Sache einen Schlag versetzen **2** VT (*esp Brit inf*) (= *hit*) schlagen; (= *punish*) verdreschen (*inf*); (= *defeat*) fertig machen (*inf*)

wallow ['wɒləʊ] VI **(a)** (*lit: animal*) sich suhlen **(b)** (*fig*) **to** ~ **in self-pity** *etc* im Selbstmitleid *etc* schwelgen

wall: wall painting N Wandmalerei *f*; **wallpaper** **1** N **(a)** Tapete *f* **(b)** (*Comput*) Bildschirmhintergrund *m*, Wallpaper *nt* **2** VT tapezieren; **wall socket** N Steckdose *f*; **Wall Street** N Wall Street *f*; **wall-to-wall** ADJ ~ **carpeting** Teppichboden *m*

wally ['wɒlɪ] N (*Brit inf*) Trottel *m* (*inf*)

walnut ['wɔːlnʌt] N (= *nut*) Walnuss *f*; (= ~ *tree*) (Wal)nussbaum *m*; (= *wood*) Nussbaumholz *nt*

walrus ['wɔːlrəs] N Walross *nt*

waltz [wɔːls] **1** N Walzer *m* **2** VI **(a)** Walzer tanzen; **they ~ed across the ballroom** sie walzten durch den Ballsaal **(b)** (*inf*: = *move, come etc*) walzen (*inf*); **he came ~ing up** er kam angetanzt (*inf*)

➤ **waltz in** VI (*inf*) hereintanzen (*inf*); **to come waltzing in** angetanzt kommen (*inf*)

➤ **waltz off** VI (*inf*) abtanzen (*inf*)

➤ **waltz off with** VI +PREP OBJ (*inf*) *prizes* abziehen mit (*inf*)

➤ **waltz through** VI +PREP OBJ (*fig inf*) spielend bewältigen

waltz music N Walzermusik *f*

wan [wɒn] ADJ bleich; *light, smile, look* matt

wand [wɒnd] N (= *magic* ~) Zauberstab *m*

Be careful! **wand** *is not translated by the German word* **Wand**.

---

wander ['wɒndə^r] **1** N Spaziergang *m*; (*through town, park also*) Bummel *m*; **I'm going for a** ~ **(a)round the shops** ich mache einen Ladenbummel

2 VT *hills* durchstreifen (*geh*); **to** ~ **the streets** durch die Straßen wandern

3 VI **(a)** herumlaufen; (*more aimlessly*) umherwandern (*through, about* in +*dat*); (*leisurely*) schlendern; (*to see the shops*) bummeln; **he ~ed past me in a dream** sie ging wie im Traum an mir vorbei; **he ~ed over to speak to me** er kam zu mir herüber, um mit mir zu reden; **the river ~ed through the valley** der Fluss zog sich durch das Tal; **to** ~ **from the path** vom Wege *or* Pfad abkommen; **the cattle must not be allowed to** ~ das Vieh darf nicht einfach so herumlaufen; **the children had ~ed out onto the street** die Kinder waren auf die Straße gelaufen

(b) (*fig: thoughts, eye*) schweifen, wandern; **to let one's mind** ~ seine Gedanken schweifen lassen; **during the lecture his mind ~ed a bit** während der Vorlesung schweiften seine Gedanken ab; **to** ~ **off the subject** vom Thema abschweifen *or* abkommen

➤ **wander about** (*Brit*) or **around** VI umherziehen, umherwandern

➤ **wander back** VI (*cows, strays*) zurückkommen *or* -wandern
➤ **wander in** VI ankommen (*inf*), anspazieren (*inf*)
➤ **wander off** VI weggehen; **he must have wandered off somewhere** er muss (doch) irgendwohin verschwunden sein

wanderer ['wɒndərə'] N Wandervogel *m*

wandering ['wɒndərɪŋ] ADJ *tribesman, refugees* umherziehend; *thoughts* (ab)schweifend; *gaze* schweifend; *path* gewunden; **to have ~ hands** (*hum*) seine Finger nicht bei sich (*dat*) behalten können

wanderlust ['wɒndəlʌst] N Fernweh *nt*

wane [weɪn] **1** N **to be on the ~** (*fig*) im Schwinden sein **2** VI (*moon*) abnehmen; (*fig*) (*influence, strength*) schwinden; (*reputation*) verblassen

wangle ['wæŋgl] (*inf*) VT *job, ticket etc* organisieren (*inf*); **to ~ money out of sb** jdm Geld abluchsen (*inf*); **we ~d an extra day off** wir haben noch einen zusätzlichen freien Tag rausgeschlagen (*inf*)

wannabe ['wɒnəbi:] (*inf*) **1** N Möchtegern *m* (*inf*) **2** ADJ Möchtegern- (*inf*)

want [wɒnt] **1** N **(a)** (= *lack*) Mangel *m* (*of* an +*dat*); **for ~ of** aus Mangel an (+*dat*); **though it wasn't for ~ of trying** nicht, dass er sich/ich mich *etc* nicht bemüht hätte
(b) (= *need*) Bedürfnis *nt*; (= *wish*) Wunsch *m*; **to be in ~ of sth** etw brauchen *or* benötigen; **to be in ~ of repair** reparaturbedürftig sein
2 VT **(a)** (= *wish, desire*) wollen; (*more polite*) mögen; **to ~ to do sth** etw tun wollen; **I ~ you to come here** ich will *or* möchte, dass du herkommst; **I ~ it done now** ich will *or* möchte das sofort erledigt haben; **I was ~ing to leave the job next month** ich hätte gerne nächsten Monat mit der Arbeit aufgehört; **what does he ~ with me?** was will er von mir?; **I don't ~ strangers coming in** ich wünsche *or* möchte nicht, dass Fremde (hier) hereinkommen
(b) (= *need, require*) brauchen; **you ~ to see a lawyer** Sie sollten zum Rechtsanwalt gehen; **he ~s to be more careful** (*inf*) er sollte etwas vorsichtiger sein; **that's the last thing I ~** (*inf*) alles, bloß das nicht (*inf*); **"~ed"** „gesucht"; **he's a ~ed man** er wird (polizeilich) gesucht; **to feel ~ed** das Gefühl haben, gebraucht zu werden; **you're ~ed on the phone** Sie werden am Telefon verlangt *or* gewünscht; **all the soup ~s is a little salt** das Einzige, was an der Suppe fehlt, ist etwas Salz
3 VI **(a)** (= *wish, desire*) wollen; (*more polite*) mögen; **you can go if you ~ (to)** wenn du willst *or* möchtest, kannst du gehen; **I don't ~ to** ich will *or* möchte nicht; **do as you ~** tu, was du willst; **he said he'd do it, but does he really ~ to?** er sagte, er würde es machen, aber will er es wirklich?
(b) **they ~ for nothing** es fehlt *or* mangelt (*geh*) ihnen an nichts

want ad N Kaufgesuch *nt*

wanting ['wɒntɪŋ] ADJ fehlend; **it's a good novel, but there is something ~** der Roman ist gut, aber irgendetwas fehlt; **he is ~ in confidence** *etc* es fehlt *or* mangelt (*geh*) ihm an Selbstvertrauen *etc*; **his courage was found ~** sein Mut war nicht groß genug

wanton ['wɒntən] ADJ *cruelty, destruction* mutwillig; *disregard, negligence* sträflich

WAP [wæp] N (*Comput*) ABBR *of* **Wireless Application Protocol** WAP *nt*

war [wɔ:'] **1** N Krieg *m*; **this is ~!** (*fig*) das bedeutet Krieg!; **the ~ against disease** der Kampf gegen die Krankheit; **~ of nerves** Nervenkrieg *m*; **~ of words** Wortgefecht *nt*; **to be at ~** sich im Krieg(szustand) befinden; **to declare ~** den Krieg erklären (*on* +*dat*); (*fig also*) den Kampf ansagen (*on* +*dat*); **to go to ~** (= *start*) (einen) Krieg anfangen (*against* mit); **to make** *or* **wage ~** Krieg führen (*on, against* gegen); **I hear you've been in the ~s recently** (*inf*) ich höre, dass du zur Zeit ganz schön angeschlagen bist (*inf*)
2 VI sich bekriegen; (*fig*) ringen (*geh*) (*for* um)

warble ['wɔ:bl] **1** N Trällern *nt* **2** VTI trällern

war: **war correspondent** N Kriegsberichterstatter(in) *m(f)*; **war crime** N Kriegsverbrechen *nt*; **war criminal** N Kriegsverbrecher(in) *m(f)*; **war cry** N Kriegsruf *m*; (*fig*) Schlachtruf *m*

ward [wɔ:d] N **(a)** (*part of hospital*) Station *f*; (= *room*) (*small*) (Kranken)zimmer *nt*; (*large*) (Kranken)saal *m* **(b)** (*Jur*: = *person*) Mündel *nt*; **~ of court** Mündel *nt* unter

Amtsvormundschaft **(c)** (*Admin*) Stadtbezirk *m*; (= *election* ~) Wahlbezirk *m*
➤ **ward off** VT SEP abwehren; *danger also* abwenden; *depression* nicht aufkommen lassen

warden ['wɔ:dn] N (*of youth hostel*) Herbergsvater *m*, Herbergsmutter *f*; (= *game* ~) Jagdaufseher(in) *m(f)*; (= *traffic* ~) ≈ Verkehrspolizist *m*, ≈ Politesse *f*; (*of museum etc*) Aufseher(in) *m(f)*; (= *head* ~) Kustos *m*; (*Univ*) Heimleiter(in) *m(f)*; (*US: of prison*) Gefängnisdirektor(in) *m(f)*

warder ['wɔ:də'] N (*Brit*) Wärter(in) *m(f)*

wardress ['wɔ:drɪs] N (*Brit*) Wärterin *f*

wardrobe ['wɔ:drəʊb] N **(a)** (*esp Brit*: = *cupboard*) (Kleider)schrank *m* **(b)** (= *clothes*) Garderobe *f* **(c)** (*Theat*: = *room*) Kleiderkammer *f*

-ward(s) [-wəd(z)] ADV SUF -wärts; **southward(s)** südwärts; **townward(s)** in Richtung Stadt; **in a homeward(s) direction** Richtung Heimat

-ware [-weə'] N SUF -waren *pl*; **glassware** Glaswaren *pl*; **kitchenware** Küchenutensilien *pl*

warehouse ['weəhaʊs] N Lager(haus) *nt*

warehouse: **warehouse club** N (*esp US Comm*) Geschäft, in dem Waren zu Großhandelspreisen an Mitglieder verkauft werden; **warehouseman** N, *pl* **-men** Lagerarbeiter *m*; **warehouse manager** N Lagerleiter(in) *m(f)*

wares [weəz] PL N Waren *pl*

warfare ['wɔ:feə'] N Krieg *m*; (= *techniques*) Kriegskunst *f*

war: **war game** N Kriegsspiel *nt*; **warhead** N Sprengkopf *m*; **war hero** N Kriegsheld *m*; **warhorse** N (*lit, fig*) Schlachtross *nt*

warily ['weərɪlɪ] ADV vorsichtig; (= *suspiciously*) misstrauisch, argwöhnisch; **to tread ~** (*lit, fig*) sich vorsehen

wariness ['weərɪnɪs] N Vorsicht *f*; (= *mistrust*) Misstrauen *nt*, Argwohn *m*

war: **warlike** ADJ kriegerisch; *tone, speech* militant; **warlord** N Kriegsherr *m*

warm [wɔ:m] **1** ADJ (+ER) **(a)** warm; (= *hearty*) herzlich; **I am** *or* **feel ~** mir ist warm; **come to the fire and get ~** komm ans Feuer und wärm dich; **~ start** (*Comput*) Warmstart *m*
(b) (*in party games*) **am I ~?** ist es (hier) warm?; **you're getting ~** es wird schon wärmer; **you're very ~!** heiß!
2 N **we were glad to get into the ~** wir waren froh, dass wir ins Warme kamen; **to give sth a ~** etw wärmen
3 VT wärmen; **it ~s my heart to ...** mir wird (es) ganz warm ums Herz, wenn ...
4 VI **the milk was ~ing on the stove** die Milch wurde auf dem Herd angewärmt; **I ~ed to him** er wurde mir sympathischer; **he spoke hesitantly at first but soon ~ed to his subject** anfangs sprach er noch sehr zögernd, doch dann fand er sich in sein Thema hinein

➤ **warm over** VT SEP (*esp US*) **(a)** *food* aufwärmen **(b)** (*inf*) *idea* (wieder) aufwärmen

➤ **warm up** **1** VI (*lit, fig*) warm werden; (*game, speaker*) in Schwung kommen; (*Sport*) sich aufwärmen; **things are warming up** es kommt Schwung in die Sache **2** VT SEP *engine* warm laufen lassen; *food etc* aufwärmen; (*fig*) *party* in Schwung bringen; *audience* in Stimmung bringen

warm-blooded ['wɔ:m'blʌdɪd] ADJ warmblütig

warm-hearted ['wɔ:m'hɑ:tɪd] ADJ *person* warmherzig; *action, gesture* großzügig

warmish ['wɔ:mɪʃ] ADJ ein bisschen warm; **~ weather** ziemlich warmes Wetter

warmly ['wɔ:mlɪ] ADV warm; *welcome* herzlich; *recommend* wärmstens

warmth [wɔ:mθ] N Wärme *f*; (*fig also*) Herzlichkeit *f*

warm-up ['wɔ:mʌp] N (*Sport*) Aufwärmen *nt*; **the teams had a ~ before the game** die Mannschaften wärmten sich vor dem Spiel auf

warn [wɔ:n] VT warnen (*of, about, against* vor +*dat*); (*police etc*) verwarnen; **to ~ sb not to do sth** jdn davor warnen, etw zu tun; **I'm ~ing you** ich warne dich!; **you have been ~ed!** sag nicht, ich hätte dich nicht gewarnt; **to ~ sb that ...** (= *inform*) jdn darauf aufmerksam machen *or* darauf hinweisen, dass ...; **you might have ~ed us that you were coming** du hättest uns ruhig vorher Bescheid sagen können, dass du kommst

➤ **warn off** VT SEP warnen; **to warn sb off doing sth** jdn (davor) warnen, etw zu tun; **he warned me off** er hat mich davor gewarnt

warning ['wɔːnɪŋ] **1** N Warnung f; (*from police, judge etc*) Verwarnung f; **without** ~ ohne Vorwarnung; **they had no** ~ **of the enemy attack** der Feind griff sie ohne Vorwarnung an; **he had plenty of** ~ er ist oft *or* häufig genug gewarnt worden; (*early enough*) er wusste früh genug Bescheid; **to give sb a** ~ jdn warnen; (*police etc*) jdm eine Verwarnung geben; **let this be a** ~ **to you** lassen Sie sich (*dat*) das eine Warnung sein!; **they gave us no** ~ **of their arrival** sie kamen ohne Vorankündigung; **please give me a few days'** ~ bitte sagen *or* geben Sie mir ein paar Tage vorher Bescheid **2** ADJ Warn-; *look, tone* warnend; **a** ~ **sign** (*fig*) ein Warnzeichen *nt*

warning light N Warnleuchte f

warningly ['wɔːnɪŋlɪ] ADV warnend

warp [wɔːp] **1** VT *wood* wellen; *character* entstellen; *judgement* verzerren **2** VI (*wood*) sich wellen, sich verziehen

war: **war paint** N (*lit, fig inf*) Kriegsbemalung f; **warpath** N **on the** ~ auf dem Kriegspfad

warped [wɔːpt] ADJ **(a)** (*lit*) verzogen, wellig **(b)** (*fig*) *sense of humour, character* abartig; *judgement* verzerrt; **he has a** ~ **mind** er hat eine abartige Fantasie

warrant ['wɒrənt] **1** N (= *search* ~) Durchsuchungsbefehl *m*; (= *death* ~) Hinrichtungsbefehl *m*; **a** ~ **of arrest** Haftbefehl *m* **2** VT **(a)** (= *justify*) *action etc* rechtfertigen; **to** ~ **sb doing sth** jdn dazu berechtigen, etw zu tun **(b)** (= *merit*) verdienen **(c)** (= *guarantee*) gewährleisten; **these goods are** ~**ed for three months by the manufacturers** für diese Waren übernimmt der Hersteller eine Garantie von drei Monaten

warranted ['wɒrəntɪd] ADJ (= *justifiable*) berechtigt

warranty ['wɒrəntɪ] N (*Comm*) Garantie f; **it's still under** ~ darauf ist noch Garantie

warren ['wɒrən] N (= *rabbit* ~) Kaninchenbau *m*; (*fig*) Labyrinth *nt*

warring ['wɔːrɪŋ] ADJ *parties, sides* gegnerisch; *nations* Krieg führend; *factions* sich bekriegend

warrior ['wɒrɪəʳ] N Krieger(in) *m(f)*

Warsaw ['wɔːsɔː] N Warschau *nt*; ~ **Pact** Warschauer Pakt *m*

warship ['wɔːʃɪp] N Kriegsschiff *nt*

wart [wɔːt] N Warze f

war: **wartime 1** N Kriegszeit f; **in** ~ in Kriegszeiten **2** ADJ Kriegs-; ~ **atrocities** Kriegsgräuel *pl*; **in** ~ **England** in England während des Krieges; **wartorn** ADJ vom Krieg erschüttert; **war widow** N Kriegswitwe f; **war-wounded** PL **the** ~ die Kriegsversehrten *pl*

wary ['wɛərɪ] ADJ (+ER) vorsichtig; (= *looking and planning ahead*) umsichtig; *look* misstrauisch; **to be** ~ **of** *or* **about sb/sth** vor jdm/einer Sache auf der Hut sein; **to be** ~ **of** *or* **about doing sth** seine Zweifel *or* Bedenken haben, ob man etw tun soll; **be** ~ **of talking to strangers** hüte dich davor, mit Fremden zu sprechen

war zone N Kriegsgebiet *nt*

was [wɒz] PRET **of be**

wash [wɒʃ] **1** N **(a)** (= *act of washing*) **sb/sth needs a** ~ jd/etw muss gewaschen werden; **to give sb/sth a (good)** ~ jdn/etw (gründlich) waschen; **to have a** ~ sich waschen **(b)** (= *laundry*) Wäsche f **2** VT **(a)** *car, hair, clothes etc* waschen; *dishes* abwaschen; *floor* aufwaschen; *parts of body* sich (*dat*) waschen; **to** ~ **one's hands of sb/sth** mit jdm/etw nichts mehr zu tun haben wollen; **to** ~ **sth clean** etw rein waschen **(b)** (*sea etc*) umspülen; *wall, cliffs etc* schlagen gegen **(c)** (*river, sea*: = *carry*) spülen; **the body was** ~**ed downstream** die Leiche wurde flussabwärts getrieben; **to** ~ **ashore** anschwemmen **3** VI **(a)** (= *have a* ~) sich waschen **(b)** (= *do the laundry etc*) waschen; (*Brit*: = ~ *up*) abwaschen; **a material that** ~**es well** ein Stoff, der sich gut wäscht **(c)** (*sea etc*) schlagen; **the sea** ~**ed over the promenade** das Meer überspülte die Strandpromenade

➤ **wash away** VT SEP (*lit*) (hin)wegspülen

➤ **wash down** VT SEP **(a)** *walls, deck* abwaschen **(b)** *meal, food* runterspülen (*inf*)

➤ **wash off 1** VI sich rauswaschen lassen **2** VT SEP abwaschen; **wash that grease off your hands** wasch dir die Schmiere von den Händen (ab)!

➤ **wash out 1** VI sich (r)auswaschen lassen **2** VT SEP **(a)** (= *clean*) auswaschen; *mouth* ausspülen **(b)** (= *stop, cancel*) *game etc* ins Wasser fallen lassen (*inf*)

➤ **wash over** VI +PREP OBJ **he lets everything just wash over him** er lässt alles einfach ruhig über sich ergehen

➤ **wash up 1** VI **(a)** (*Brit*: = *clean dishes*) abwaschen **(b)** (*US*: = *have a wash*) sich waschen **2** VT SEP **(a)** (*Brit*) *dishes* abwaschen **(b)** (*sea etc*) anschwemmen **(c)** **that's/we're all washed up** (*fig inf*: = *finished*) das ist gelaufen (*inf*)

washable ['wɒʃəbl] ADJ waschbar

wash: **washbag** N (*US*) Kulturbeutel *m*; **washbasin** N Waschbecken *nt*; **washcloth** N (*US*) Waschlappen *m*

washed out ADJ PRED, **washed-out** ADJ ATTR [wɒʃt'aʊt] (*inf*) erledigt (*inf*), schlapp (*inf*); **to look** ~ mitgenommen aussehen

washer ['wɒʃəʳ] N **(a)** (*Tech*) Dichtungsring *m* **(b)** (= *washing machine*) Waschmaschine f

washing ['wɒʃɪŋ] N Waschen *nt*; (= *clothes*) Wäsche f; **many boys dislike** ~ viele Jungen waschen sich nicht gerne; **to do the** ~ Wäsche waschen; **to take in** ~ (für Kunden) waschen

washing: **washing line** N Wäscheleine f; **washing machine** N Waschmaschine f; **washing powder** N Waschpulver *nt*; **washing-up** N (*Brit*) Abwasch *m*; **to do the** ~ den Abwasch machen; **washing-up liquid** N (*Brit*) Spülmittel *nt*

wash: **washout** N (*inf*) Reinfall *m* (*inf*); **washrag** N (*US*) Waschlappen *m*; **washroom** N Waschraum *m*

wasn't ['wɒznt] CONTR **of was not**

WASP [wɒsp] (*US*) ABBR **of White Anglo-Saxon Protestant** weißer angelsächsischer Protestant

wasp [wɒsp] N Wespe f

wastage ['weɪstɪdʒ] N Schwund *m*; (= *action*) Verschwendung f; (= *amount also*) Materialverlust *m*; (*unusable products etc also*) Abfall *m*

waste [weɪst] **1** ADJ (= *superfluous*) überschüssig, überflüssig; (= *left over*) ungenutzt; *land* brachliegend; ~ **food** Abfall *m*; ~ **material/matter** Abfallstoffe *pl* **2** N **(a)** Verschwendung f; **it's a** ~ **of time/money** es ist Zeit-/Geldverschwendung; **it's a** ~ **of effort** das ist nicht der Mühe (*gen*) wert; **to go to** ~ (*food*) umkommen; (*training, money, land*) ungenutzt sein/bleiben; (*talent etc*) verkümmern **(b)** (= ~ *material*) Abfallstoffe *pl*; (*in factory*) Schwund *m*; (= *rubbish*) Abfall *m* **(c)** (= *land, expanse*) Wildnis f *no pl*; **the snowy** ~**s of Siberia** die Schneewüsten *pl* Sibiriens **3** VT verschwenden (*on* an +acc, für); *life, time* vergeuden, *opportunity* vertun; **you're wasting your time** das ist reine Zeitverschwendung; **don't** ~ **my time** stiehl mir nicht meine Zeit; **you didn't** ~ **much time getting here!** (*inf*) da bist du ja schon, das hat ja nicht gerade getrödelt! (*inf*); **all our efforts were** ~**d** all unsere Bemühungen waren umsonst *or* vergeblich; **I wouldn't** ~ **my breath talking to him** ich würde doch nicht für den meine Spucke vergeuden! (*inf*); **Beethoven/your joke is** ~**d on him** Beethoven/dein Witz ist an den verschwendet *or* vergeudet

➤ **waste away** VI (*physically*) dahinschwinden (*geh*)

wastebasket ['weɪstbɑːskɪt], **wastebin** ['weɪstbɪn] N (*esp US*) Papierkorb *m*

wasted ['weɪstɪd] ADJ **(a)** **I've had a** ~ **journey** ich bin umsonst hingefahren; **a vote for him is a** ~ **vote** ihn zu wählen heißt eine Stimme verschenken **(b)** (= *emaciated*) geschwächt

waste: **waste disposal** N Abfallentsorgung f; **waste disposal unit** N Müllschlucker *m*

wasteful ['weɪstfʊl] ADJ verschwenderisch; *method, process* aufwändig

wastefully ['weɪstfʊlɪ] ADV verschwenderisch

wastefulness ['weɪstfʊlnɪs] N (*of person*) verschwenderische Art; (*in method, organization, of process etc*) Aufwändigkeit f

waste: **wasteland** N Ödland *nt*; (*fig*) Einöde f; **waste minimization** N Abfallminimierung f; **wastepaper** N Papierabfall *m*; **wastepaper basket** N Papierkorb *m*; **they go straight into the** ~ die wandern sofort in den Papierkorb; **waste pipe** N Abflussrohr *nt*; **waste product** N Abfallprodukt *nt*

waster [ˈweɪstəʳ] N **it's a real time-/money-~** das ist wirklich Zeit-/Geldverschwendung

waste: **waste reduction** N Abfallverringerung f; **waste water** N Abwasser nt

watch¹ [wɒtʃ] N (Armband)uhr f

watch² **1** N Wache f; **to be on the ~ for sb/sth** nach jdm/etw Ausschau halten; **to keep ~** Wache halten; **to keep a close ~ on sb/sth** jdn/etw scharf bewachen; **to keep ~ over sb/sth** bei jdm/etw wachen or Wache halten

2 VT (a) (= guard) aufpassen auf (+acc); (police etc) überwachen

(b) (= observe) beobachten; match zusehen or zuschauen bei; film, play, programme on TV sich (dat) ansehen; **to ~ TV** fernsehen; **to ~ sb doing sth** jdm bei etw zusehen or zuschauen; **I'll come and ~ you play** ich komme und sehe dir beim Spielen zu; **he just stood there and ~ed her drown** er stand einfach da und sah zu, wie sie ertrank; **I ~ed her coming down the street** ich habe sie beobachtet, wie or als sie die Straße entlang kam; **~ the road in front of you** pass auf die Straße auf!; **now ~ this closely** passen Sie mal genau auf!; **~ this!** pass auf!; **~ this space** warten Sie ab, demnächst mehr; **just ~ me!** guck or schau mal, wie ich das mache!; **we are being ~ed** wir werden beobachtet; **I can't stand being ~ed** ich kann es nicht aushalten, wenn mir ständig einer zusieht (c) (= be careful of) Acht geben or aufpassen auf (+acc); time achten auf (+acc); **(you'd better) ~ it!** (inf) pass (bloß) auf! (inf); **~ yourself** sieh dich vor!; **~ your language!** drück dich bitte etwas gepflegter aus!; **~ him, he's crafty** sieh dich vor or pass auf, er ist raffiniert; **~ where you put your feet** pass auf, wo du hintrittst; **~ how you drive, the roads are icy** fahr vorsichtig, die Straßen sind vereist!; **~ how you go!** machs gut!; (on icy surface etc) pass beim Laufen/Fahren auf!

3 VI (a) (= observe) zusehen, zuschauen; **to ~ for sb/sth** nach jdm/etw Ausschau halten or ausschauen; **they ~ed for a signal from the soldiers** sie warteten auf ein Signal von den Soldaten; **to ~ for sth to happen** darauf warten, dass etw geschieht

(b) (= keep ~) Wache halten

➤ **watch out** VI (a) (= look carefully) Ausschau halten, ausschauen (for sb/sth nach jdm/etw) (b) (= be careful) aufpassen, Acht geben (for auf +acc); **watch out!** Achtung!, Vorsicht!; **you'd better watch out!** (threat) pass bloß auf!

➤ **watch over** VI +PREP OBJ wachen über (+acc)

watch: **watchband** N (US) Uhrarmband nt; **watchdog** N (lit) Wachhund m; (fig) Aufpasser m (inf)

watchful [ˈwɒtʃfʊl] ADJ wachsam; **to keep a ~ eye on sb/sth** ein wachsames Auge auf jdn/etw werfen

watchfulness [ˈwɒtʃfʊlnɪs] N Wachsamkeit f

watch: **watchmaker** N Uhrmacher(in) m(f); **watchman** N (in bank, factory etc) Wächter(in) m(f); (also **night ~**) Nachtwächter(in) m(f); **watchstrap** N Uhrarmband nt; **watchtower** N Wachtturm m; **watchword** N Parole f

water [ˈwɔːtəʳ] **1** N (a) Wasser nt; **the field is under (two feet of) ~** das Feld steht (zwei Fuß) unter Wasser; **to take in** or **make ~** (ship) lecken; **to hold ~** wasserdicht sein; **by ~** auf dem Wasserweg, zu Wasser (geh); **we spent an afternoon on the ~** wir verbrachten einen Nachmittag auf dem Wasser; **~s** Gewässer pl; **to pass ~** Wasser lassen; **the ~s** (at spa) die Heilquelle; **to drink** or **take the ~s** eine Kur machen; (drinking only) eine Trinkkur machen; rose etc ~ Rosenwasser nt etc (b) (fig phrases) **to keep one's head above ~** sich über Wasser halten; **to pour cold ~ on sb's idea** jds Idee mies machen (inf); **to get (oneself) into deep ~(s)** ins Schwimmen kommen; **a lot of ~ has flowed under the bridge since then** seitdem ist so viel Wasser den Berg or den Bach hinuntergeflossen; **to be in/get into hot ~** (inf) in Schwierigkeiten or in (des) Teufels Küche (inf) sein/geraten (over wegen +gen)

2 VT (a) garden, lawn sprengen; field bewässern; plant (be)gießen

(b) horses, cattle tränken

(c) **to ~ capital** (Fin) Aktienkapital verwässern

3 VI (mouth) wässern; (eye) tränen; **the smoke made his eyes ~** ihm tränten die Augen vom Rauch; **my mouth ~ed** mir lief das Wasser im Mund zusammen; **to make sb's mouth ~** jdm den Mund wässerig machen

➤ **water down** VT SEP (lit, fig) verwässern; liquids (mit Wasser) verdünnen

water: **water bed** N Wasserbett nt; **waterborne** ADJ **a ~ disease** eine Krankheit, die durch das Wasser übertragen wird; **water bottle** N Wasserflasche f; (for troops etc) Feldflasche f; **water butt** N Regentonne f; **water cannon** N Wasserwerfer m; **water closet** N (abbr WC) (esp Brit) Wasserklosett nt; **watercolour**, (US) **watercolor** **1** N (= picture) Aquarell nt **2** ATTR Aquarell-; **a ~ painting** ein Aquarell nt; **watercourse** N (= stream) Wasserlauf m; (= bed) Flussbett nt; (artificial) Kanal m; **watercress** N (Brunnen)kresse f; **water damage** N Wasserschaden m

watered-down [ˌwɔːtədˈdaʊn] ADJ (lit, fig) verwässert

water: **waterfall** N Wasserfall m; **waterfowl** N Wasservogel m; (pl) Wassergeflügel nt; **waterfront** **1** N Hafenviertel nt; **we drove along the ~/down to the ~** wir fuhren am Wasser entlang/hinunter zum Wasser **2** ATTR am Wasser; **water gun** N (esp US) = water pistol; **water heater** N Heißwassergerät nt; **water hole** N Wasserloch nt

watering [ˈwɔːtərɪŋ]: **watering can** N Gießkanne f; **watering hole** N (for animals) Wasserstelle f; (fig hum: = pub) Kneipe f (inf); **watering place** N (for animals) Wasserstelle f

water: **water jump** N Wassergraben m; **water level** N Wasserstand m; (= measured level: of river etc also) Pegelstand m; (= surface of water) Wasserspiegel m; **water lily** N Seerose f; **water line** N Wasserlinie f; **waterlogged** ADJ **the fields are ~** die Felder stehen unter Wasser; **to get ~** sich voll Wasser saugen; **water main** N Haupt(wasser)leitung f; (= pipe) Hauptwasserrohr nt; **watermark** N (a) (on wall) Wasserstandsmarke f (b) (on paper) Wasserzeichen nt; **watermelon** N Wassermelone f; **water meter** N Wasseruhr f; **water mill** N Wassermühle f; **water pistol** N Wasserpistole f; **water polo** N Wasserball m; **waterproof** **1** ADJ watch wasserdicht; clothes, roof wasserundurchlässig; make-up, paint wasserfest **2** N **~s** (esp Brit) Regenhaut® f **3** VT wasserundurchlässig machen; material also wasserdicht machen; **water-repellent** ADJ wasserabstoßend; **water-resistant** ADJ wasserbeständig; sunscreen wasserfest; **watershed** N (fig) Wendepunkt m; **waterside** **1** N Ufer nt; (at sea) Strand m **2** ATTR am Wasser; **water-ski** **1** N Wasserski m **2** VI Wasserski laufen; **water-skiing** N Wasserskilaufen nt; **water-soluble** ADJ wasserlöslich; **water sports** PL Wassersport m; **water supply** N Wasserversorgung f; **water table** N Grundwasserspiegel m; **water tank** N Wassertank m; **watertight** ADJ (lit also) wasserdicht; (fig also) hieb- und stichfest; **water tower** N Wasserturm m; **waterway** N Wasserstraße f; (= channel) Fahrrinne f; **water wings** PL Schwimmflügel pl; **waterworks** N SING or PL Wasserwerk nt

watery [ˈwɔːtərɪ] ADJ soup, colour etc wäss(e)rig; eye tränend; sun blass

watt [wɒt] N Watt nt

wave [weɪv] **1** N (a) (of water, Phys, Rad, in hair, fig) Welle f; **a ~ of strikes** eine Streikwelle; **a ~ of enthusiasm** eine Welle der Begeisterung; **during the first ~ of the attack** in der ersten Angriffswelle; **to make ~s** (fig inf) Unruhe stiften (b) (= movement of hand) **to give sb a ~** jdm (zu)winken; **with a ~ of his hand** mit einer Handbewegung

2 VT (as sign or greeting) winken mit (at, to sb jdm); (= ~ about) schwenken; (gesticulating, in a dangerous manner) herumfuchteln mit; **to ~ sb goodbye**, **to ~ goodbye to sb** jdm zum Abschied winken; **he ~d his hat** er schwenkte seinen Hut; **he ~d the ticket under my nose** er fuchtelte mir mit der Karte vor der Nase herum; **he ~d the children across the road** er winkte die Kinder über die Straße; **he ~d me over** er winkte mich zu sich herüber

3 VI (a) (person) winken; **to ~ at** or **to sb** jdm (zu)winken (b) (flag) wehen; (branches) sich hin und her bewegen; (corn) wogen

➤ **wave aside** VT SEP (fig) suggestions etc ab- or zurückweisen

➤ **wave down** VT SEP anhalten, stoppen

➤ **wave on** VT SEP **the policeman waved us on** der Polizist winkte uns weiter

wavelength [ˈweɪvleŋθ] N (Rad) Wellenlänge f; **we're not on the same ~** (fig) wir haben nicht dieselbe Wellenlänge

waver [ˈweɪvəʳ] VI (a) (light, flame, eyes) flackern; (voice) zittern (b) (courage) wanken; (support) nachlassen (c) (= hesitate) schwanken (between zwischen +dat)

wavering [ˈweɪvərɪŋ] **1** ADJ (a) voice bebend (b) loyalty unsicher; courage, determination wankend; support

(= *hesitating*) wechselhaft; (= *decreasing*) nachlassend **2** N (= *hesitation*) Schwanken *nt*

wavy [ˈweɪvɪ] ADJ (+ER) *hair, surface* wellig, gewellt; ~ **line** Schlangenlinie *f*

wax¹ [wæks] **1** N Wachs *nt*; (= *ear* ~) Ohrenschmalz *nt* **2** ADJ Wachs-; ~ **crayon** Wachsmalstift *m* **3** VT *car, furniture* wachsen; *floor* bohnern; *legs* mit Wachs behandeln

wax² VI (a) (*moon*) zunehmen; **to** ~ **and wane** (*fig*) kommen und gehen (b) (*liter.* = *become*) werden

wax: **wax museum** N (*esp US*) Wachsfigurenkabinett *nt*; **waxworks** N SING or PL Wachsfigurenkabinett *nt*

way [weɪ]	
1 NOUN	**2** ADVERB

1 NOUN
(a) (= *road, route*) Weg *m*; **across** or **over the way** gegenüber; (*motion*) rüber; **to fall by the way** (*fig*) auf der Strecke bleiben; **to ask the way** nach dem Weg fragen; **you'll learn new skills along the way** Sie werden nebenbei auch neue Fertigkeiten erlernen; **to go the wrong way** sich verlaufen; (*in car*) sich verfahren; **to go down the wrong way** (*food, drink*) in die falsche Kehle kommen; **there's no way out** (*fig*) es gibt keinen Ausweg; **to find a way in** hineinfinden; **the way up/down** der Weg nach oben/unten; **the way there/back** der Hin-/Rückweg; **prices are on the way up/down** die Preise steigen/fallen; **the way forward** der Weg vorwärts or in die Zukunft; **to bar** or **block the way** den Weg ab- or versperren; **love will find a way** die Liebe überwindet jedes Hindernis or alle Schwierigkeiten

✦**in the/sb's way** **to be in sb's way** jdm im Weg stehen or sein; (*fig also*) jdn stören; **to get in the way** in den Weg kommen; (*fig*) stören; **her job gets in the way of her leisure interests** ihr Beruf stört sie nur bei ihren Freizeitvergnügungen; **to stand in sb's way** (*lit, fig*) jdm im Weg stehen or sein; **he lets nothing stand in his way** er lässt sich durch nichts aufhalten or beirren

✦**out of the/sb's way** **get out of the/my way!** (*geh*) aus dem Weg!; **to get sb out of the way** (= *get rid of*) jdn loswerden (*inf*); (= *remove*: *lit, fig*) jdn aus dem Wege räumen; **to get sth out of the way** *work* etw hinter sich (*acc*) bringen; *difficulties, problems etc* etw aus dem Weg räumen; **to keep** or **stay out of sb's/the way** (= *not get in the way*) jdm nicht in den Weg kommen; (= *avoid*) (jdm) aus dem Weg gehen; **keep** or **stay out of my way!** komm mir nicht mehr über den Weg!

✦**to make way for sb/sth** (*lit, fig*) für jdn/etw Platz machen

✦**the way to** **the way to the station** der Weg zum Bahnhof; **can you tell me the way to the town hall, please?** können Sie mir bitte sagen, wie ich zum Rathaus komme?

✦**on the/one's way (to)** **the shop is on the/your way** der Laden liegt auf dem/deinem Weg; **to stop on the way** unterwegs anhalten; **on the way (here)** auf dem Weg (hierher); **they're on their way now** sie sind jetzt auf dem Weg or unterwegs; **he's on the way to becoming an alcoholic** er ist dabei or auf dem besten Weg, Alkoholiker zu werden

✦**out of the/sb's way** **if it is out of your way** wenn es ein Umweg für Sie ist; **to go out of one's way to do sth** (*fig*) sich besonders anstrengen, um etw zu tun; **please, don't go out of your way for us** (*fig*) machen Sie sich (*dat*) bitte unsertwegen keine Umstände

✦**under way** **to get under way** in Gang kommen, losgehen (*inf*); **to be (well) under way** im Gang/in vollem Gang sein; (*with indication of place*) unterwegs sein

✦**the/one's way in** **the way in** der Eingang; **on the way in** beim Hereingehen

✦**the/one's way out** **the way out** der Ausgang; **please show me the way out** bitte zeigen Sie mir, wie ich hinauskomme *inf* **can you find your own way out?** finden Sie selbst hinaus?; **on the way out** beim Hinausgehen; **to be on the way out** (*fig inf*) am Aussterben sein

✦*verb* + **the/one's way** **I know my way around the town** ich kenne mich in der Stadt aus; **can you find your way home?** finden Sie nach Hause?; **to make one's way to somewhere** sich an einen Ort or irgendwohin begeben; **can you make your own way to the restaurant?** kannst du allein zu dem

Restaurant kommen?; **to make one's way home** nach Hause gehen; **to make/push one's way through the crowd** sich einen Weg durch die Menge bahnen; **to go one's own way** (*fig*) eigene Wege gehen; **they went their separate ways** (*lit, fig*) ihre Wege trennten sich; **to pay one's way** für sich selbst bezahlen; (*company, project, machine*) sich rentieren
(b) (= *direction*) Richtung *f*; **which way are you going?** in welche Richtung or wohin gehen Sie?; **look both ways** schau nach beiden Seiten; **to look the other way** (*fig*) wegschauen, wegsehen; **if a good job comes my way** wenn ein guter Job für mich auftaucht; **we'll split it three/ten ways** wir werden es dritteln/in zehn Teile (auf)teilen; **it's the wrong way up** es steht verkehrt herum or auf dem Kopf (*inf*); **"this way up"** „hier oben"; **it's the other way (a)round** es ist (genau) umgekehrt; **put it the right way up/the other way (a)round** stellen Sie es richtig (herum) hin/andersherum hin

✦**this way** **this way, please** hier entlang, bitte; **look this way** schau hierher!

✦**that way** **he went that way** er ging in diese Richtung

✦**this way and that** hierhin und dorthin

✦**every which way** ungeordnet, durcheinander
(c) (= *distance*) Weg *m*, Strecke *f*; **a little/good way away** or **off** nicht/weit weit weg or entfernt

✦**all the way** **it rained all the way there** es hat auf der ganzen Strecke geregnet; **I'm behind you all the way** (*fig*) ich stehe voll (und ganz) hinter Ihnen; **I haven't read it all the way through yet** ich habe es noch nicht ganz gelesen

✦**a long way** **that's a long way away** bis dahin ist es weit or (*time*) noch lange; **a long way out of town** weit von der Stadt weg; (*live also*) weit draußen or außerhalb; **he's come a long way since then** (*fig*) er hat sich seitdem sehr gebessert; **he'll go a long way** (*fig*) er wird es weit bringen; **to have a long way to go** (*lit, fit*) weit vom Ziel entfernt sein; (*with work*) bei weitem nicht fertig sein; **it should go a long way toward(s) solving the problem** das sollte or müsste bei dem Problem schon ein gutes Stück weiterhelfen; **a little goes a long way** ein kleines bisschen reicht sehr lange; **that's a long way from the truth** das ist weit von der Wahrheit entfernt; **not by a long way** bei weitem nicht
(d) (= *manner*) Art *f*, Weise *f*; **that's his way of saying thank you** das ist seine Art, sich zu bedanken; **the French way of doing it** (die Art,) wie man es in Frankreich macht; **to learn the hard way** aus dem eigenen Schaden lernen; **way of thinking** Denkweise *f*; **to my way of thinking** meiner Meinung nach; **what a way to live!** (= *unpleasant*) so möchte ich nicht leben; **to get** or **have one's (own) way** seinen Willen durchsetzen or bekommen; **have it your own way!** wie du willst!

✦**one way or another/the other** so oder so; **it does not matter (to me) one way or the other** es macht (mir) so oder so nichts aus

✦**either way** so oder so

✦**no way** (*inf*) **no way!** ausgeschlossen!; **there's no way I'm going to agree** auf keinen Fall werde ich zustimmen; **there's no way that's a Porsche** ausgeschlossen, dass das ein Porsche ist; **that's no way to speak to your mother** so spricht man nicht mit seiner Mutter

✦**have/want it both ways** **you can't have it both ways** du kannst nicht beides haben; **he wants it both ways** er will das eine haben und das andere nicht lassen

✦**this way** (= *like this*) so, auf diese (Art und) Weise; **this way he need never know** auf diese Weise muss er es nie erfahren

✦**that way** (= *like that*) in dieser Hinsicht

✦**the way (that) …** (= HOW) wie; **the way she walks** (so) wie sie geht; **I don't like the way (that) he's looking at you** ich mag nicht, wie er dich ansieht; **that's not the way we do things here** so or auf die Art machen wir das hier nicht; **you could tell by the way he was dressed** das merkte man schon an seiner Kleidung; **that's the way it goes!** so ist das eben; **the way things are** so, wie es ist or wie die Dinge liegen; **the way things are going** so, wie die Dinge sich entwickeln (= EXACTLY AS) so, wie; **it was all the way you said it would be** es war alles so, wie du (es) gesagt hattest; **do it the way I do (it)** machen Sie es so or auf dieselbe Art und Weise wie ich (es mache)

✦**the way to do sth** **to show sb the way to do sth** jdm zeigen, wie or auf welche Art und Weise etw gemacht wird; **show me the way to do it** zeig mir, wie (ich es machen soll); **that's not** the right way to do it so geht das nicht; **what's the best way to do it?** wie macht man das am besten?

◆**ways and means** Mittel und Wege *pl*
(e) (= *method, habit*) Art *f*; **there are many ways of solving the problem** es gibt viele Wege *or* Möglichkeiten, das Problem zu lösen; **the best way is to put it in the freezer for ten minutes** am besten legt man es für zehn Minuten ins Gefrierfach; **he has a way with children** er versteht es, mit Kindern umzugehen; **it is not/only his way to ...** es ist nicht/ eben seine Art, zu ...; **the way of the world** der Lauf der Welt *or* der Dinge; **as is the way with ...** wie das mit ... so ist; **way of life** Lebensstil *m*; (*of nation*) Lebensart *f*
(f) (= *respect*) Hinsicht *f*; **in a way** in gewisser Hinsicht *or* Weise; **in no way** in keiner Weise; **in many/some ways** in vieler/gewisser Hinsicht; **in more ways than one** in mehr als nur einer Hinsicht
(g) (= *state*) Zustand *m*; **he's in a bad way** er ist in schlechter Verfassung

2 ADVERB (*inf*) **way over/up** weit drüben/oben; **it's way too big** das ist viel zu groß

◆**way back** that was way back das ist schon lange her
◆**way out** he was way out with his guess er hatte weit gefehlt *or* er lag weit daneben (*inf*) mit seiner Annahme; **his guess was way out** seine Annahme war weit gefehlt

way: **waybill** N Frachtbrief *m*; **waylay** *pret, ptp* **waylaid** VT (= *ambush*) überfallen; (= *stop*) abfangen; **way-out** ADJ (*inf*) extrem (*dated sl*); **wayside 1** N (*of path, track*) Wegrand *m*; (*of road*) Straßenrand *m*; **by the ~** am Weg(es)-/Straßenrand; **to fall** *or* **go by the ~** (*fig*) auf der Strecke bleiben **2** ADJ *café* am Weg/an der Straße gelegen; **way station** N (*US*) Zwischenstation *f*

wayward ['weɪwəd] ADJ (= *self-willed*) eigensinnig; **their ~ son** ihr ungeratener Sohn

WC (*esp Brit*) ABBR *of* **water closet** WC *nt*

we [wiː] PRON wir

weak [wiːk] ADJ (+ER) schwach; *character* labil; *tea, solution etc* dünn; **he was ~ from hunger** ihm war schwach vor Hunger; **to go/feel ~ at the knees** weiche Knie haben/bekommen; **the dollar is ~ against the pound** der Dollar steht schwach zum Pfund; **what are his ~ points?** wo liegen seine Schwächen?

weaken ['wiːkən] **1** VT (*lit, fig*) schwächen; *influence also, control etc* verringern; *argument also* entkräften; *walls, foundations* angreifen; *hold* lockern **2** VI (*lit, fig*) schwächer werden, nachlassen; (*person*) schwach werden; (*foundations*) nachgeben; (*defence*) erlahmen; (*dollar*) nachlassen

weakling ['wiːklɪŋ] N Schwächling *m*

weakly ['wiːklɪ] ADV schwach

weak-minded ['wiːk'maɪndɪd] ADJ **(a)** (= *feeble-minded*) schwachsinnig **(b)** (= *weak-willed*) willensschwach

weakness ['wiːknɪs] N (*all senses*) Schwäche *f*; (= *weak point*) schwacher Punkt; **to have a ~ for sth** für etw eine Schwäche *or* Vorliebe haben

weak-willed ['wiːk'wɪld] ADJ willensschwach

wealth [welθ] N **(a)** Reichtum *m*; (= *private fortune*) Vermögen *nt* **(b)** (*fig*) Fülle *f*

wealthy ['welθɪ] **1** ADJ (+ER) wohlhabend, reich; (= *having a private fortune also*) vermögend **2** N **the ~** *pl* die Reichen *pl*

wean [wiːn] VT entwöhnen; **to ~ sb from** *or* **off sb/sth** jdn jdm/ einer Sache entwöhnen (*geh*)

weapon ['wepən] N (*lit, fig*) Waffe *f*

weaponry ['wepənrɪ] N Waffen *pl*

wear [weəʳ], *vb: pret* **wore**, *ptp* **worn 1** N **(a)** (= *use*) **I've had a lot of/I haven't had much ~ out of** *or* **from this jacket** ich habe diese Jacke viel/wenig getragen; **there isn't much ~/there is still a lot of ~ left in this carpet** dieser Teppich hält nicht mehr lange/hält noch lange; **for casual/evening/everyday ~** für die Freizeit/den Abend/jeden Tag
(b) (= *clothing*) Kleidung *f*
(c) (= *damage through use: also* **~ and tear**) Abnutzung *f*, Verschleiß *m*; **to show signs of ~** (*lit*) anfangen, alt auszusehen; (*fig*) angegriffen aussehen; **to look the worse for ~** (*lit*) (*curtains, carpets etc*) verschlissen aussehen; (*clothes*) abgetragen aussehen; (*furniture etc*) abgenutzt aussehen; (*fig*) verbraucht aussehen; **I felt a bit the worse for ~** (*inf*) ich

fühlte mich etwas angeknackst (*inf*)
2 VT **(a)** *clothing, spectacles, beard etc* tragen; **what shall I ~?** was soll ich anziehen?; **I haven't a thing to ~!** ich habe nichts anzuziehen; **to ~ white** *etc* Weiß *etc* tragen; **he wore a big smile** er strahlte über das ganze Gesicht
(b) (= *reduce to a worn condition*) abnutzen; *clothes* abtragen; *sleeve, knee etc* durchwetzen; *steps* austreten; *tyres* abfahren; *engine* kaputtmachen; **to ~ holes in sth** etw durchwetzen; *in shoes* etw durchlaufen; **to ~ smooth** (*by handling*) abgreifen; (*by walking*) austreten; *pattern* angreifen; *sharp edges* glatt machen; **centuries of storms had worn the inscription smooth** die Inschrift war durch die Stürme im Laufe der Jahrhunderte verwittert
3 VI **(a)** (= *last*) halten; **she has worn well** (*inf*) sie hat sich gut gehalten (*inf*)
(b) (= *become worn*) kaputtgehen; (*engine, material*) sich abnutzen; **to ~ smooth** (*by water*) glatt gewaschen sein; (*by weather*) verwittern; (*pattern*) abgegriffen sein; **the sharp edges will ~ smooth with use** die scharfen Kanten werden sich im Gebrauch abschleifen; **my patience is ~ing thin** meine Geduld ist langsam erschöpft *or* geht langsam zu Ende

➤ **wear away 1** VT SEP *steps* austreten; *rock* abtragen; *inscription* verwischen **2** VI (*rocks, rough edges etc*) sich abschleifen; (*inscription*) verwittern; (*pattern*) verwischen

➤ **wear down 1** VT SEP **(a)** (*lit*) abnutzen; *heel* ablaufen; *tyre tread* abfahren **(b)** (*fig*) *opposition, strength etc* zermürben; *person* fix und fertig machen (*inf*) **2** VI sich abnutzen; (*heels*) sich ablaufen; (*tyre tread*) sich abfahren

➤ **wear off** VI **(a)** (= *diminish*) nachlassen; **don't worry, it'll wear off!** keine Sorge, das gibt sich **(b)** (= *disappear: paint*) abgehen

➤ **wear on** VI sich hinziehen; (*year*) voranschreiten; **as the evening** *etc* **wore on** im Laufe des Abends *etc*

➤ **wear out 1** VT SEP **(a)** (*lit*) kaputtmachen; *carpet* abtreten; *clothes, shoes* kaputttragen; *record, machinery* abnutzen **(b)** (*fig: = exhaust*) (*physically*) erschöpfen, erledigen (*inf*); (*mentally*) fertig machen (*inf*); **to be worn out** erschöpft *or* erledigt sein; (*mentally*) am Ende sein (*inf*); **to wear oneself out** sich überanstrengen, sich kaputtmachen (*inf*) **2** VI kaputtgehen; (*clothes, curtains, carpets*) verschleißen

➤ **wear through 1** VT SEP durchwetzen; *elbows, trousers also* durchscheuern; *soles of shoes* durchlaufen **2** VI sich durchwetzen; (*elbows, trousers also*) sich durchscheuern; (*soles of shoes*) sich durchlaufen

wearable ['weərəbl] ADJ (= *not worn out etc*) tragbar; **fashionable clothes which are also very ~** modische Kleidung, die man auch gut trägt

wearer ['weərəʳ] N Träger(in) *m(f)*

wearily ['wɪərɪlɪ] ADV *say* müde; *smile, gaze, nod, sigh* matt

weariness ['wɪərɪnɪs] N (*physical*) Müdigkeit *f*; (*mental*) Lustlosigkeit *f*

wearing ['weərɪŋ] ADJ (= *exhausting*) anstrengend; (= *boring*) ermüdend

weary ['wɪərɪ] ADJ (+ER) müde; (= *fed up*) lustlos; *smile* matt; **to feel** *or* **be ~** müde sein; **to be/grow ~ of sth** etw leid sein/ werden

weasel ['wiːzl] N Wiesel *nt*

weather ['weðəʳ] **1** N Wetter *nt*; (*in ~ reports*) Wetterlage *f*; (= *climate*) Witterung *f*; **in cold ~** bei kaltem Wetter; **what's the ~ like?** wie ist das Wetter?; **in all ~s** bei jedem Wetter; **to be** *or* **feel under the ~** (*inf*) angeschlagen sein (*inf*)
2 VT **(a)** (*storms, winds etc*) angreifen; *skin* gerben
(b) (= *expose to ~*) *wood* ablagern
(c) (*also* **~ out**) *crisis* überstehen; **to ~ (out) the storm** (*lit, fig*) den Sturm überstehen
3 VI (*rock etc*) verwittern; (*paint etc*) verblassen; (= *become seasoned: wood*) ablagern

weather: **weather-beaten** ADJ *face* vom Wetter gegerbt; *house, stone* verwittert; **weather bureau** N Wetteramt *nt*; **weathercock** N Wetterhahn *m*

weathered ['weðəd] ADJ verwittert; *skin* wettergegerbt

weather: **weather forecast** N Wettervorhersage *f*; **weatherman** N Wettermann *m* (*inf*); **weatherproof** ADJ wetterfest; **weather report** N Wetterbericht *m*; **weather vane** N Wetterfahne *f*

weave [wiːv], *vb: pret* **wove**, *ptp* **woven** 🔳 N (= *patterns of threads*) Webart *f*; (= *loosely etc woven fabric*) Gewebe *nt* 🔳 VT **(a)** *thread, cloth etc* weben (*into* zu); *cane, garland* flechten (*into* zu)
(b) (*fig*) *plot, story* erfinden; *details* einflechten (*into* in +*acc*)
(c) *pret also* **weaved** (= *wind*) **to ~ one's way through the traffic** sich durch den Verkehr schlängeln
🔳 VI **(a)** (*lit*) weben
(b) *pret also* **weaved** (= *twist and turn*) sich schlängeln

weaver ['wiːvəʳ] N Weber(in) *m(f)*

web [web] N **(a)** (*lit, fig*) Netz *nt* **(b)** (*Comput*) **the Web** das (World Wide) Web

webbed [webd] ADJ **~ feet** Schwimmfüße *pl*

web (*Comput*): **web browser** N Browser *m*; **webcam** N Webcam *f*; **webcast** (*Comput*) 🔳 N Webcast *m*, Internetübertragung *m* 🔳 VT im Internet übertragen; **webmaster** N Webmaster(in) *m(f)*; **web page** N Web-Seite *f*; **website** N Web-Site *f*; **webspace** N Webspace *m*; **webzine** N Onlinemagazin *nt*

Wed ABBR *of* **Wednesday** Mittw.

wed [wed] (*old*), *pret, ptp* **wed** *or* **wedded** 🔳 VI heiraten 🔳 VT **(a)** (*bride, bridegroom*) ehelichen (*form*); (*priest*) trauen
(b) (*fig*) (= *combine*) paaren; **to be ~ded to sth** (= *devoted*) mit etw verheiratet sein

we'd [wiːd] CONTR *of* **we would**, **we had**

wedding ['wedɪŋ] N Hochzeit *f*; (= *ceremony*) Trauung *f*; **to have a registry office** (*Brit*)/**church ~** sich standesamtlich/kirchlich trauen lassen; **to go to a ~** zu einer *or* auf eine Hochzeit gehen

wedding IN CPDS Hochzeits-; **wedding anniversary** N Hochzeitstag *m*; **wedding cake** N Hochzeitskuchen *m*; **wedding day** N Hochzeitstag *m*; **wedding dress** N Hochzeitskleid *nt*; **wedding reception** N Hochzeitsempfang *m*; **wedding ring** N Trauring *m*, Ehering *m*; **wedding vows** PL Ehegelübde *nt*

wedge [wedʒ] 🔳 N **(a)** (*of wood etc, fig*) Keil *m*; **rubber ~** Gummibolzen *m* **(b)** (*of cake etc*) Stück *nt*; (*of cheese*) Ecke *f* 🔳 VT verkeilen; **to ~ a door open/shut** eine Tür festklemmen *or* verkeilen **(b)** (*fig*) **to ~ oneself/sth** sich/etw zwängen (*in* in +*acc*); **to be ~d between two people** zwischen zwei Personen eingekeilt sein
➤ **wedge in** VT SEP (*lit*) *post* festkeilen; **to be wedged in** (*car, person etc*) eingekeilt sein

Wednesday ['wenzdɪ] N Mittwoch *m*; *see also* **Tuesday**

Weds ABBR *of* **Wednesday** Mittw.

wee¹ [wiː] ADJ (+ER) (*inf*) winzig; (*Scot*) klein

wee² (*Brit inf*) 🔳 N **to have** *or* **do/need a ~** Pipi machen/machen müssen (*inf*) 🔳 VI Pipi machen (*inf*)

weed [wiːd] 🔳 N **(a)** Unkraut *nt no pl* **(b)** (*inf*: = *person*) Schwächling *m* 🔳 VTI jäten
➤ **weed out** VT SEP (*fig*) aussondern

weeding ['wiːdɪŋ] N Unkrautjäten *nt*; **to do some ~** Unkraut *nt* jäten

weedkiller ['wiːdkɪləʳ] N Unkrautvernichter *m*

weedy ['wiːdɪ] ADJ (+ER) (*inf*) *person* schmächtig

week [wiːk] N Woche *f*; **it'll be ready in a ~** in einer Woche *or* in acht Tagen ist es fertig; **my husband works away during the ~** mein Mann arbeitet die Woche über auswärts; **~ in, ~ out** Woche für Woche; **twice/£15 a ~** zweimal/£ 15 in der Woche *or* pro Woche; **a ~ today** heute in einer Woche *or* in acht Tagen; **a ~ tomorrow/on Tuesday** morgen/Dienstag in einer Woche *or* in acht Tagen; **a ~ (ago) last Monday** letzten Montag vor einer Woche; **for ~s** wochenlang; **a ~'s/a two-~ holiday** (*Brit*) *or* **vacation** (*US*) ein einwöchiger/zweiwöchiger Urlaub; **he works a 40-hour ~** er hat eine Vierzigstundenwoche; **two ~s' holiday** (*Brit*) *or* **vacation** (*US*) zwei Wochen Ferien; **that is a ~'s work** das ist eine Woche Arbeit

week: **weekday** 🔳 N Wochentag *m* 🔳 ATTR *morning* eines Werktages; *routine* an Werktagen *or* Wochentagen; **weekend** 🔳 N Wochenende *nt*; **to go/be away for the ~** am Wochenende verreisen/nicht da sein; **at** (*Brit*) *or* **on** (*esp US*) **the ~** am Wochenende; **to take a long ~** ein langes Wochenende machen 🔳 ATTR Wochenend-; **~ bag** Reisetasche *f*

weekly ['wiːklɪ] 🔳 ADJ Wochen-; *wage also, meeting* wöchentlich; *visit* allwöchentlich; **~ newspaper**

Wochenzeitung *f* 🔳 ADV wöchentlich; **twice ~** zwei Mal die Woche 🔳 N Wochenzeitschrift *f*

weep [wiːp], *vb: pret, ptp* **wept** 🔳 VTI weinen (*over* über +*acc*); **to ~ with** *or* **for joy** vor *or* aus Freude weinen 🔳 N **to have a good/little ~** tüchtig/ein bisschen weinen

weepie N (*inf*) = **weepy 2**

weepy ['wiːpɪ] (*inf*) 🔳 ADJ (+ER) *person* weinerlich; (*inf*) *film* rührselig 🔳 N (*inf*: = *film etc*) Schmachtfetzen *m* (*inf*)

weigh [weɪ] 🔳 VT **(a)** (*lit*) wiegen; **could you ~ these bananas for me?** könnten Sie mir diese Bananen abwiegen? **(b)** (*fig*) *words, merits etc* abwägen 🔳 VI **(a)** (*lit*) wiegen **(b)** (*fig*: = *be a burden*) lasten (*on* auf +*dat*) **(c)** (*fig*: = *be important*) gelten; **his age ~ed against him** sein Alter wurde gegen ihn in die Waagschale geworfen
➤ **weigh down** VT SEP **(a)** niederbeugen; **she was weighed down with packages** sie war mit Paketen überladen **(b)** (*fig*) niederdrücken
➤ **weigh in** VI **(a)** (*Sport*) sich (vor dem Kampf/Rennen) wiegen lassen; **he weighed in at 70 kilos** er brachte 70 Kilo auf die Waage **(b)** (*fig inf*: = *join in*) zu Hilfe kommen; (= *interfere*) sich einschalten
➤ **weigh out** VT SEP abwiegen
➤ **weigh up** VT SEP abwägen; *person* einschätzen

weighing scales PL Waage *f*

weight [weɪt] 🔳 N **(a)** Gewicht *nt* (*also Phys*); (*Sport, esp Boxing*) Gewichtsklasse *f*; (*of cloth*) Schwere *f*; **3 kilos in ~** 3 Kilo Gewicht; **a blow without much ~ behind it** ein Schlag ohne viel Kraft dahinter; **the branches broke under the ~ of the snow** die Zweige brachen unter der Schneelast; **to gain** *or* **put on ~** zunehmen; **to lose ~** abnehmen; **it's worth its ~ in gold** das ist Gold(es) wert; **to lift ~s** Gewichte heben; **the doctor warned him not to lift heavy ~s** der Arzt warnte ihn davor, schwere Lasten zu heben; **she's quite a ~** sie ist ganz schön schwer
(b) (*fig*: = *burden*) Last *f*; **the ~ of evidence** die Beweislast; **that's a ~ off my mind** mir fällt ein Stein vom Herzen
(c) (*fig*: = *importance*) Bedeutung *f*, Gewicht *nt*; **he carries no ~** seine Stimme hat kein Gewicht; **those arguments carry great ~** diesen Argumenten wird großes Gewicht beigemessen; **to add ~ to sth** einer Sache (*dat*) zusätzliches Gewicht geben *or* verleihen; **to pull one's ~** seinen Beitrag leisten; **to throw** *or* **chuck** (*inf*) **one's ~ about** (*Brit*) *or* **around** seinen Einfluss geltend machen
🔳 VT **(a)** (= *make heavier*) beschweren
(b) (*fig*) **to be ~ed in favour** (*Brit*) *or* **favor** (*US*) **of sb/sth** so angelegt sein, dass es zugunsten einer Person/Sache ist
➤ **weight down** VT SEP *person* (*with parcels etc*) überladen; *corpse* beschweren; (*fig*) belasten

weighted ['weɪtɪd] ADJ (*Econ*) gewogen

weightlessness ['weɪtlɪsnɪs] N Schwerelosigkeit *f*

weight: **weightlifter** N Gewichtheber(in) *m(f)*; **weightlifting** N Gewichtheben *nt*; **weight loss** N, NO PL Gewichtsverlust *m*; **weight training** N Krafttraining *nt*

weighty ['weɪtɪ] ADJ (+ER) (*fig*) *argument* gewichtig; *responsibility* schwerwiegend

weir [wɪəʳ] N **(a)** (= *barrier*) Wehr *nt* **(b)** (= *fish trap*) Fischreuse *f*

weird [wɪəd] ADJ (+ER) (= *eerie*) unheimlich; (*inf*: = *odd*) seltsam

weirdly ['wɪədlɪ] ADV (= *eerily*) unheimlich; (*inf*: = *oddly*) seltsam

weirdo ['wɪədəʊ] N (*inf*) verrückter Typ (*inf*)

welcome ['welkəm] 🔳 N Willkommen *nt*; **to give sb a hearty** *or* **warm ~** jdm einen herzlichen Empfang bereiten; **to receive a cold ~** kühl empfangen werden
🔳 ADJ willkommen; *visitor also* gern gesehen attr; *news* angenehm; **the money is very ~ just now** das Geld kommt gerade jetzt sehr gelegen; **to make sb ~** jdn sehr freundlich aufnehmen; **to make sb feel ~** jdm das Gefühl geben, ein willkommener *or* gern gesehener Gast zu sein; **you're ~!** nichts zu danken!, bitte sehr!; (*iro*) von mir aus gerne!; **you're ~ to use my room** Sie können gerne mein Zimmer benutzen; **you're ~ to it!** (*iro*) von mir aus herzlich gerne! 🔳 VT (*lit, fig*) begrüßen; **they ~d him home with a big party** sie veranstalteten zu seiner Heimkehr ein großes Fest 🔳 INTERJ **~ home/to Scotland/on board!** willkommen daheim/in Schottland/an Bord!; **~ back!** willkommen zurück!

welcoming ['welkəmɪŋ] ADJ zur Begrüßung; *smile, gesture, house, room* einladend

weld [weld] **1** VT **(a)** (*Tech*) schweißen; **to ~ parts together** Teile zusammenschweißen **(b)** (*fig: also* **~ together**) zusammenschmieden (*into* zu) **2** N Schweißnaht *f*

welder ['weldə^r] N (= *person*) Schweißer(in) *m(f)*

welfare ['welfeə^r] N **(a)** (= *wellbeing*) Wohl *nt* **(b)** (= ~ *work*) Fürsorge *f*; **social** ~ soziale Fürsorge **(c)** (*US:* = *social security*) Sozialhilfe *f*; **to be on** ~ Sozialhilfeempfänger(in) *m(f)* sein

welfare: welfare benefits PL (*US*) Sozialhilfe *f*; **welfare check** N (*US*) Sozialhilfeüberweisung *f*; **welfare services** PL soziale Einrichtungen *pl*; **welfare state** N Wohlfahrtsstaat *m*

well¹ [wel] **1** N **(a)** (= *water* ~) Brunnen *m*; (= *oil* ~) Ölquelle *f*; (*drilled*) Bohrloch *nt*; (*fig: = source*) Quelle *f* **(b)** (= *shaft*) (*for lift*) Schacht *m*; (*for stairs*) Treppenschacht *m*; (*down centre of staircase*) Treppenhaus *nt* **2** VI quellen; **tears ~ed in her eyes** Tränen stiegen *or* schossen ihr in die Augen

➤ **well up** VI (*water, liquid*) emporsteigen, emporquellen; (*fig*) aufsteigen; (*noise*) anschwellen; **tears welled up in her eyes** Tränen stiegen *or* schossen ihr in die Augen

well² *comp* **better**, *superl* **best** **1** ADV **(a)** gut; **he did it as ~ as he could/as I could have done** er machte es so gut er konnte/ ebenso gut, wie ich es hätte machen können; **he's doing ~ at school** er ist gut in der Schule; **he did ~ in the history exam** er hat in der Geschichtsprüfung gut abgeschnitten; **his business is doing ~** sein Geschäft geht gut; **the patient is doing ~** dem Patienten geht es gut; **if you do ~ you'll be promoted** wenn Sie sich bewähren, werden Sie befördert; ~ **done!** gut gemacht!, sehr gut!; ~ **played!** gut gespielt!; **everything went ~/quite ~** es ging alles gut *or* glatt (*inf*)/recht *or* ganz gut; **to speak/think ~ of sb** von jdm positiv sprechen/ denken; **to do ~ out of sth** von etw ganz schön *or* ordentlich profitieren; **you might as ~ go** du könntest eigentlich geradeso gut *or* ebenso gut (auch) gehen; **are you coming? – I might as ~** kommst du? – ach, könnte ich eigentlich (auch) (*inf*) *or* ach, warum nicht; **shake the bottle ~** (*on medicine*) Flasche kräftig *or* gut schütteln; **we were ~ beaten** wir sind gründlich geschlagen worden; **all *or* only too ~** nur (all)zu gut; ~ **and truly** (ganz) gründlich; **settled in** ganz richtig; (*iro also*) fest; **he sat ~ forward in his seat** er saß weit vorne auf seinem Sitz; **it was ~ worth the trouble** das hat sich *or* sehr gelohnt; ~ **out of sight** weit außer Sichtweite; ~ **within ...** durchaus in ... (*dat*); ~ **past midnight** lange nach Mitternacht; **it continued ~ into 1996/the night** es zog sich bis weit ins Jahr 1996/in die Nacht hin; **he's ~ over fifty** er ist weit über fünfzig

(b) (= *probably, reasonably*) ohne weiteres, gut, wohl; **I may ~ be late** es kann leicht *or* ohne weiteres sein, dass ich spät komme; **it may ~ be that ...** es ist gut *or* ohne weiteres möglich, dass ...; **you may ~ be right** Sie mögen wohl Recht haben; **you may ~ ask!** (*iro*) das kann man wohl fragen; **I couldn't very ~ stay** ich konnte schlecht bleiben

(c) (= *in addition*) **as** ~ auch; **if he comes as** ~ wenn er auch kommt; **x as ~ as y** x sowohl als auch y

2 INTERJ **(a)** (= *in good health*) gesund; **get ~ soon!** gute Besserung; **are you ~?** geht es Ihnen gut?; **I'm very ~, thanks** danke, es geht mir sehr gut; **she's not been ~ lately** ihr ging es in letzter Zeit (gesundheitlich) gar nicht gut; **I don't feel at all ~** ich fühle mich gar nicht gut *or* wohl

(b) (= *satisfactory, desirable*) gut; **that's all very ~, but ...** das ist ja alles schön und gut, aber ...; **it's all very ~ for you to suggest ...** Sie können leicht vorschlagen ...; **it's all very ~ for you, you don't have to ...** Sie haben gut reden, Sie müssen ja nicht ...; **it would be as ~ to ask first** es wäre wohl besser, sich erst mal zu erkundigen; **it's just as ~ he came** es ist (nur *or* schon) gut, dass er gekommen ist; **you're ~ out of that** seien Sie froh, dass Sie damit nichts mehr zu tun haben; **all's ~ that ends** ~ Ende gut, alles gut

3 INTERJ also; (*expectantly also*) na; (*doubtfully*) na ja; ~, ~!, ~ **I never (did)!** also, so was!; ~ **now** also; ~ **then?** also (gut); (*in question*) na?, also?; **very ~ then!** also gut!; (*indignantly*) also bitte (sehr)!; **oh ~, never mind** macht nichts; ~, **that's a relief!** na (also), das ist ja eine Erleichterung!

4 N Gute(s) *nt*; **to wish sb ~** (*in general*) jdm alles Gute wünschen; (*in an attempt, also iro*) jdm Glück wünschen (*in* bei)

we'll [wi:l] CONTR *of* **we shall**, **we will**

well IN CPDS gut; **well-adjusted** ADJ ATTR, **well adjusted** ADJ PRED (*Psych*) gut angepasst; **well-advised** ADJ ATTR, **well advised** ADJ PRED **to be well advised to ...** wohl *or* gut beraten sein zu ...;

well-appointed ADJ ATTR, **well appointed** ADJ PRED gut ausgestattet; **well-balanced** ADJ ATTR, **well balanced** ADJ PRED **(a)** *person, mind* ausgeglichen **(b)** *budget, diet* (gut) ausgewogen; **well-behaved** ADJ ATTR, **well behaved** ADJ PRED *child* artig, wohlerzogen; *animal* gut erzogen; **wellbeing** N Wohl *nt*; **well-bred** ADJ ATTR, **well bred** ADJ PRED *person* wohlerzogen; **well-built** ADJ ATTR, **well built** ADJ PRED *house* gut *or* solide gebaut; *person* kräftig; **well-chosen** ADJ ATTR, **well chosen** ADJ PRED *remarks* gut *or* glücklich gewählt; **well-connected** ADJ ATTR, **well connected** ADJ PRED **to be well connected** Beziehungen zu *or* in höheren Kreisen haben; **well-deserved** ADJ ATTR, **well deserved** ADJ PRED wohlverdient; **well-developed** ADJ ATTR, **well developed** ADJ PRED *market, industry, muscle* gut entwickelt; *sense* (gut) ausgeprägt; *system* ausgereift; **well-disposed** ADJ ATTR, **well disposed** ADJ PRED **to be well disposed toward(s) sb/sth** jdm/einer Sache gewogen sein *or* freundlich gesonnen sein; **well-done** ADJ ATTR, **well done** ADJ PRED *steak* durchgebraten, durch *inv*; **well-dressed** ADJ ATTR, **well dressed** ADJ PRED gut angezogen *or* gekleidet; **well-earned** ADJ ATTR, **well earned** ADJ PRED wohlverdient; **well-educated** ADJ ATTR, **well educated** ADJ PRED gebildet; **well-equipped** ADJ ATTR, **well equipped** ADJ PRED *office, studio* gut ausgestattet; *army* gut ausgerüstet; **well-established** ADJ ATTR, **well established** ADJ PRED *practice, custom* fest; *pattern also* klar; *company, player* bekannt; **well-fed** ADJ ATTR, **well fed** ADJ PRED wohl genährt; **well-founded** ADJ ATTR, **well founded** ADJ PRED wohl begründet; **the warnings proved (to be) well founded** die Warnungen erwiesen sich als begründet; **well-informed** ADJ ATTR, **well informed** ADJ PRED gut informiert; *sources also* wohl unterrichtet

wellington (boot) ['welɪŋtən('bu:t)] N (*Brit*) Gummistiefel *m*

well: well-intentioned ADJ ATTR, **well intentioned** ADJ PRED wohlmeinend; **well-kept** ADJ ATTR, **well kept** ADJ PRED *garden, hair etc* gepflegt; *secret* streng gehütet; **well-known** ADJ ATTR, **well known** ADJ PRED bekannt; *fact also* wohl bekannt; **it's well known that ...** es ist allgemein bekannt, dass ...; **to be well known for sth** für etw bekannt sein; **to be well known to sb** jdm bekannt sein; **well-loved** ADJ ATTR, **well loved** ADJ PRED viel geliebt; **well-mannered** ADJ ATTR, **well mannered** ADJ PRED mit guten Manieren; **well-meaning** ADJ ATTR, **well meaning** ADJ PRED wohlmeinend; **well-meant** ADJ ATTR, **well meant** ADJ PRED gut gemeint; **well-nigh** ADV **this is ~ impossible** das ist nahezu *or* beinahe unmöglich; **well-off** ADJ ATTR, **well off** ADJ PRED (= *affluent*) reich, begütert; **to be well off** (= *fortunate*) gut daran sein; **well-paid** ADJ ATTR, **well paid** ADJ PRED gut bezahlt; **well-preserved** ADJ ATTR, **well preserved** ADJ PRED gut erhalten; *person also* wohl erhalten; **well-read** ADJ ATTR, **well read** ADJ PRED belesen; **well-spoken** ADJ ATTR, **well spoken** ADJ PRED mit gutem Deutsch/Englisch *etc*; **to be well spoken** gutes Deutsch/Englisch *etc* sprechen; **well-stocked** ADJ ATTR, **well stocked** ADJ PRED gut bestückt; (*Comm also*) mit gutem Sortiment; *larder, shelves also* gut gefüllt; *library also* umfangreich; **well-thought-of** ADJ angesehen; **well-timed** ADJ ATTR, **well timed** ADJ PRED zeitlich günstig; **well-to-do** ADJ wohlhabend, reich; *district also* vornehm; **well-trodden** ADJ ATTR, **well trodden** ADJ PRED (*lit*) viel begangen; **a ~ path** (*fig*) eine beliebte Methode; **well-wisher** N **cards from ~s** Karten von Leuten, die ihm/ihr *etc* alles Gute wünschten; **well-worn** ADJ ATTR, **well worn** ADJ PRED *garment* abgetragen; *carpet etc* abgelaufen; *path* ausgetreten; *saying, subject etc* abgedroschen

welly ['welɪ] N (*Brit inf*) Gummistiefel *m*

Welsh [welʃ] **1** ADJ walisisch **2** N **(a)** (*Ling*) Walisisch *nt* **(b)** **the** PL die Waliser *pl*

Welsh: Welshman N Waliser *m*; **Welsh rabbit, Welsh rarebit** N überbackene Käseschnitte; **Welshwoman** N Waliserin *f*

welter ['weltə^r] N Unzahl *f*; (*of blood, cheers*) Meer *nt*; (*of emotions*) Sturm *m*

wend [wend] VT **to ~ one's way home/to the bar** *etc* sich auf den Heimweg/zur Bar *etc* begeben

went [went] PRET *of* **go**

wept [wept] PRET, PTP *of* **weep**

were [wɜ:] 2ND PERS SING, 1ST, 2ND, 3RD PERS PL PRET *of* **be**

we're [wɪə^r] CONTR *of* **we are**

weren't [wɜ:nt] CONTR *of* **were not**

werewolf ['wɪəwʊlf] N Werwolf *m*

west [west] **1** N **the ~, the West** (*also Pol*) der Westen; **in the ~** im Westen; **to the ~** nach Westen; **to the ~ of** westlich von; **he comes from the ~ (of Ireland)** er kommt aus dem Westen (von Irland); **the wind is coming from the ~** der Wind kommt von West(en) **2** ADJ West-; **the ~ coast** die Westküste; **Salford West** Salford West **3** ADV nach Westen, westwärts; **it faces ~** es geht nach Westen; **~ of** westlich von

west IN CPDS West-; **West Africa** N Westafrika *nt*; **West Bank** N (*in Middle East*) Westjordanland *nt*, West Bank *f*; **West Berlin** N Westberlin *nt*; **westbound** ['westbaʊnd] ADJ (*traffic etc*) (in) Richtung Westen; **to be ~** nach Westen unterwegs sein; **West End** N **the ~** (*in London*) das Westend

westerly ['westəlɪ] ADJ westlich; **~ wind** Westwind *m*; **in a ~ direction** in westlicher Richtung

western ['westən] **1** ADJ westlich; **on the Western front** an der Westfront; **Western Europe** Westeuropa *nt*; **the Western Sahara** die Westsahara **2** N Western *m*

Western Australia N Westaustralien *nt*

westerner ['westənə^r] N (*US*) Weststaatler(in) *m(f)*

Western Isles *pl* **the ~** die Hebriden *pl*

westernize ['westənaɪz] VT die westliche Zivilisation/Kultur einführen in (+*dat*); (*pej*) verwestlichen

westernized ['westənaɪzd] ADJ westlich ausgerichtet; (*pej*) verwestlicht

westernmost ['westənməʊst] ADJ westlichste(r, s)

Western Samoa [ˌwestənsə'məʊə] N Westsamoa *nt*

west: West Germany N Westdeutschland *nt*, Bundesrepublik *f* (Deutschland); **West Indian 1** ADJ westindisch **2** N Westindier(in) *m(f)*; **West Indies** PL Westindische Inseln *pl*

Westphalia [west'feɪlɪə] N Westfalen *nt*

westward ['westwəd], **westwardly** ['westwədlɪ] **1** ADJ *direction* westlich; *route* nach Westen **2** ADV (*also* **westwards**) westwärts, nach Westen

wet [wet], *vb: pret, ptp* **wet** *or* **wetted 1** ADJ (+ER) **(a)** nass; *climate* feucht; **to be ~** (*paint, ink*) nass *or* feucht sein; **to be ~ through** völlig durchnässt sein; **~ with tears** tränenfeucht; **her eyes were ~ with tears** sie hatte Tränen in den Augen; **"~ paint"** (*esp Brit*) „Vorsicht, frisch gestrichen"; **to be ~ behind the ears** (*inf*) noch feucht *or* nicht trocken hinter den Ohren sein (*inf*); **the ~ season** die Regenzeit; **it's been ~ all week** es war die ganze Woche (über) regnerisch; **you're all ~** (*US inf* = *wrong*) da liegst du völlig falsch (*inf*) **(b)** (*Brit inf* = *weak, spiritless*) weichlich **2** N **(a)** (= *moisture*) Feuchtigkeit *f* **(b)** (= *rain*) Nässe *f* **(c)** (*Brit inf* = *person*) Waschlappen *m* (*inf*) **3** VT nass machen; *lips, washing* befeuchten; **to ~ the bed/ one's pants/oneself** das Bett/seine Hosen/sich nass machen; **I nearly ~ myself** (*inf*) ich habe mir fast in die Hose gemacht (*inf*)

wet: wet blanket N (*inf*) Miesmacher(in) *m(f)* (*inf*); **wet-look** ADJ *material* (hoch)glänzend; *hair* (vor Gel) glänzend

wetness ['wetnɪs] N Nässe *f*; (*of climate, paint, ink*) Feuchtigkeit *f*

wet: wet nurse N Amme *f*; **wet rot** N Nassfäule *f*; **wet suit** N Neoprenanzug *m*

we've [wiːv] CONTR *of* **we have**

whack [wæk] **1** N **(a)** (*inf* = *blow*) (knallender) Schlag; **to give sth a ~** auf etw (*acc*) schlagen **(b)** (*esp Brit inf* = *share*) (An)teil *m* **2** VT (*inf* = *hit*) schlagen, hauen (*inf*)

whacked [wækt] ADJ (*Brit inf* = *exhausted*) kaputt (*inf*)

whacking ['wækɪŋ] ADJ (*Brit inf*) Mords- (*inf*); **~ great** riesengroß; **he earns a ~ £100,000 a year** (*also US*) er verdient mordsmäßige £ 100.000 pro Jahr (*inf*)

whacky ['wækɪ] ADJ (+ER) (*inf*) = **wacky**

whale [weɪl] N **(a)** Wal *m* **(b)** (*inf*) **to have a ~ of a time** sich prima amüsieren

whaling ['weɪlɪŋ] N Wal(fisch)fang *m*; **to go ~** auf Walfang gehen

wham [wæm], **whang** [wæŋ] INTERJ wumm

wharf [wɔːf] N, *pl* **-s** *or* **wharves** [wɔːvz] Kai *m*

what [wɒt] **1** PRON **(a)** (*interrog*) was; **~ is this called?** wie heißt das?; **~'s the weather like?** wie ist das Wetter?; **you need (a) ~?** WAS brauchen Sie?; **~ is it now?**, **~ do you want now?** was ist denn?; **~?** (= *pardon?*) was?; **~'s that (you etc said)?** WAS hast du *etc* da gerade gesagt?; **~'s that to you?** was geht dich

das an?; **~ for?** wozu?, wofür?; **~'s that tool for?** wofür ist das Werkzeug?; **~ did he agree to?** wozu hat er zugestimmt?; **~ did he object to?** wogegen *or* gegen was hat er Einwände erhoben?; **~ did you do that for?** warum hast du denn das gemacht?; **~ about ...?** wie wärs mit ...?; **you know that restaurant? – ~ about it?** kennst du das Restaurant? – was ist damit?; **~ of or about it?** na und? (*inf*); **~ if ...?** was ist, wenn ...?; **so ~?** (*inf*) ja *or* na und?; **~ does it matter?** was macht das schon?; **you ~?** (*inf*) wie bitte?; **~-d'you(-ma)-call-him/-it** (*inf*) wie heißt er/es gleich *or* schnell

(b) (*rel*) was; **that is not ~ I asked for** danach habe ich nicht gefragt; **that's exactly ~ I want/said** genau das möchte ich/habe ich gesagt; **do you know ~ you are looking for?** weißt du, wonach du suchst?; **he agreed to ~ we suggested** er stimmte unseren Vorschlägen zu; **he didn't know ~ he was objecting to** er wusste nicht, was er ablehnte; **she fell in with ~ everyone else wanted** sie schloss sich den Wünschen der Allgemeinheit an; **come ~ may** komme was wolle; **~ I'd like is a cup of tea** was ich jetzt gerne hätte, (das) wäre ein Tee; **~ with work and the new baby, life's been very hectic** die ganze Arbeit, das Baby ist da - es ist alles sehr hektisch; **~ with one thing and the other** wie das so ist *or* geht; **and ~'s more** und außerdem; **he knows ~'s ~** (*inf*) der weiß Bescheid (*inf*); **(I'll) tell you ~** (*inf*) weißt du was?

2 ADJ **(a)** (*interrog*) welche(r, s), was für (ein/eine) (*inf*); **~ age is he?** wie alt ist er?; **~ good would that be?** (*inf*) wozu sollte das gut sein?; **~ sort of** was für ein/eine; **~ else** was noch; **~ more could a girl ask for?** was könnte sich ein Mädchen sonst noch wünschen

(b) (*rel*) der/die/das; **~ little I had** das wenige, das ich hatte; **buy ~ food you like** kauf das Essen, das du willst

(c) (*in interj, also iro*) was für (ein/eine); **~ luck!** was für ein Glück, so ein Glück; **~ a fool I've been/I am!** ich Idiot!

3 INTERJ was; (*dated: = isn't it/he etc also*) wie; **is he good-looking, or ~?** sieht der aber gut aus! (*inf*)

whatever [wɒt'evə^r] **1** PRON was (auch) (immer); (= *no matter what*) egal was, ganz gleich was; **~ you like** was (immer) du (auch) möchtest; **shall we go home now? – ~ you like** *or* **say** gehen wir jetzt nach Hause? – ganz wie du willst; **~ it's called** egal wie es heißt; **... or ~ they're called** ... oder wie sie sonst heißen; **or ~** oder sonst (so) etwas; **~ does he want?** was will er wohl?; (*impatiently*) was, zum Kuckuck, will er denn?; **~ do you mean?** was meinst du denn bloß?

2 ADJ **(a)** egal welche(r, s), welche(r, s) (auch) (immer); **~ book you choose** welches Buch Sie auch wählen; **~ else you do** was immer du *or* egal was du auch sonst machst; **~ else will he do?** was wird er nur *or* bloß *or* wohl noch alles machen?

(b) (*with neg*) überhaupt, absolut; **it's of no use ~** es hat überhaupt *or* absolut keinen Zweck

what's [wɒts] CONTR *of* **what is**, **what has**

whatsit ['wɒtsɪt] N (*inf*) Dingsbums *nt* (*inf*), Dingsda *nt* (*inf*)

whatsoever [ˌwɒtsəʊ'evə^r] PRON, ADJ = **whatever**

wheat [wiːt] N Weizen *m*

wheat germ N Weizenkeim *m*

wheedle ['wiːdl] VT **to ~ sth out of sb** jdm etw abschmeicheln

wheel [wiːl] **1** N **(a)** Rad *nt*; (= *steering ~*) Lenkrad *nt*; (*Naut*) Steuer(rad) *nt*; (= *potter's ~*) (Töpfer)scheibe *f*; **at the ~** (*lit*) am Steuer; (*fig also*) am Ruder **(b) wheels** PL (*inf*: = *car*) fahrbare(r) Untersatz (*hum inf*) **2** VT **(a)** (= *push*) schieben; (= *pull*) ziehen; (*invalid*) wheelchair fahren **(b)** (= *cause to turn*) drehen **3** VI (= *turn*) drehen; (*birds, planes*) kreisen

► **wheel (a)round** VI sich (rasch) umdrehen

wheel: wheelbarrow N Schubkarre *f*; **wheelchair** N Rollstuhl *m*; **wheel clamp** N (*Brit*) (Park)kralle *f*

-wheeled ADJ SUF **-räd(e)rig**; **four-wheeled** vierräd(e)rig

wheeler-dealer ['wiːlə'diːlə^r] N (*inf*) Schlitzohr *nt* (*inf*); (*in finance also*) Geschäftemacher(in) *m(f)*

wheeling and dealing ['wiːlɪŋən'diːlɪŋ] N Gemauschel *nt* (*inf*); (*in business*) Geschäftemacherei *f*

wheeze [wiːz] **1** N (*of person*) pfeifender Atem *no pl*; (*of machine*) Fauchen *nt no pl* **2** VI pfeifend atmen; (*machines, asthmatic*) keuchen

wheezy ['wiːzɪ] ADJ (+ER) *old man* mit pfeifendem Atem; *voice, cough* keuchend

whelk [welk] N Wellhornschnecke *f*

when [wen] **1** ADV **(a)** wann; **say ~!** (inf) sag halt!
(b) (rel) **on the day ~** an dem Tag, an dem or als
2 CONJ **(a)** wenn; (with past reference) als; **you can go ~ I have finished** du kannst gehen, sobald or wenn ich fertig bin
(b) (+gerund) beim; (= at or during which time) wobei; **be careful ~ crossing the road** seien Sie beim Überqueren der Straße vorsichtig
(c) (= although, whereas) wo ... doch; **why do you do it that way ~ it would be much easier like this?** warum machst du es denn auf die Art, wo es doch so viel einfacher wäre?

whenever [wen'evə'] ADV **(a)** (= each time) jedes Mal wenn
(b) (= at whatever time) wann (auch) immer; (= as soon as) sobald; **~ you like!** wann du willst!; **we'll leave ~ he's ready** wir brechen auf, sobald er fertig ist; **tomorrow, or ~** (inf) morgen, oder wann auch immer

where [weə'] ADV, CONJ wo; (= in the place ~) da, wo ...; **~ (to)** wohin, wo ... hin; **~ ... from** woher, wo ... her; **~ are you going (to)?** wohin gehst du?, wo gehst du hin?; **~ are you from?** woher kommen Sie?, wo kommen Sie her?; **from ~ I'm sitting I can see the church** von meinem Platz aus kann ich die Kirche sehen; **go ~ you like** geh, wohin du willst; **the bag is ~ you left it** die Tasche ist da, wo du sie liegen gelassen hast; **that's ~ I used to live** hier or da habe ich (früher) gewohnt; **we carried on from ~ we left off** wir haben da weitergemacht, wo wir vorher aufgehört haben; **this is ~ we got to** soweit or bis hierhin sind wir gekommen; **you can trust him ~ money is concerned** in Geldsachen können Sie ihm trauen

Be careful! **where** *is not translated by the German word* **wer**.

whereabouts [,weərə'bauts] **1** ADV wo, in welcher Gegend **2** ['weərəbauts] N SING or PL Verbleib m; (of people also) Aufenthaltsort m

whereas [weər'æz] CONJ (= whilst) während; (= while on the other hand) wohingegen

wherever [weər'evə'] **1** CONJ **(a)** (= no matter where) egal wo, wo (auch) immer; **~ it came from** egal, woher es kommt **(b)** (= anywhere, in or to whatever place) wohin; **he comes from Bishopbriggs, ~ that is** or **may be** er kommt aus Bishopbriggs, wo auch immer das sein mag **(c)** (= everywhere) überall wo **2** ADV wo nur, wo bloß; **~ did you get that hat?** wo haben Sie nur or bloß diesen Hut her?; **in London or Liverpool or ~** in London oder Liverpool oder sonstwo

whet [wet] VT **appetite etc** anregen

whether [weðə'] CONJ ob; (= no matter ~) egal or ganz gleich, ob; **I am not certain ~ they're coming or not** or **~ or not they're coming** ich bin nicht sicher, ob sie kommen oder nicht

which [wɪtʃ] **1** ADJ welche(r, s); **~ one?** welche(r, s)?; (of people also) wer?; **I can't tell ~ key is ~** ich kann die Schlüssel nicht auseinander halten; **... by ~ time I was asleep** ... und zu dieser Zeit schlief ich (bereits)
2 PRON **(a)** (interrog) welche(r, s); **~ of the children** welches Kind; **~ is ~?** (of people) wer ist wer?; (of things) welche(r, s) ist welche(r, s)?
(b) (rel) (with n antecedent) der/die/das, welche(r, s) (geh); (with clause antecedent) was; **the bear – I saw** der Bär, den ich sah; **it rained hard, ~ upset her plans** es regnete stark, was ihre Pläne durcheinander brachte; **~ reminds me ...** dabei fällt mir ein, ...; **the shelf on ~ I put it** das Brett, auf das or worauf ich es gelegt habe

whichever [wɪtʃ'evə'] **1** ADJ welche(r, s) auch immer; (= no matter which) ganz gleich or egal welche(r, s) **2** PRON welche(r, s) auch immer; **~ (of you) has the most money** wer immer (von euch) das meiste Geld hat

whiff [wɪf] N Hauch m; (pleasant) Duft m; (fig: = trace) Spur f

while [waɪl] **1** N Weile f; **for a ~** (für) eine Weile, eine Zeitlang; (= a short moment) (für) einen Augenblick or Moment; **a good** or **long ~** eine ganze Weile, eine ganze Zeit lang; **for/after quite a ~** ziemlich or recht lange; **a little** or **short ~** ein Weilchen (inf), kurze Zeit; **it'll be ready in a short ~** es wird bald fertig sein; **a little ~ ago** vor kurzem; **a long ~ ago** vor einer ganzen Weile; **to be worth (one's) ~ to ...** sich (für jdn) lohnen, zu ...; **we'll make it worth your ~** es soll ihr Schaden nicht sein
2 CONJ während; (= as long as) solange; **she fell asleep ~ reading** sie schlief beim Lesen ein; **he became famous ~ still young** er wurde berühmt, als er noch jung war; **~ one must**

admit there are difficulties ... (= although) man muss zwar zugeben, dass es Schwierigkeiten gibt, trotzdem ...
➤ **while away** VT SEP **time** sich (dat) vertreiben

whilst [waɪlst] CONJ = **while 2**

whim [wɪm] N Laune f; **her every ~** jede ihrer Launen; **at** or **on ~, at** or **on a ~** aus Jux und Tollerei (inf)

whimper ['wɪmpə'] **1** N (of dog) Winseln nt no pl; (of person) Wimmern nt no pl **2** VI (dog) winseln; (person) wimmern **3** VT **person** wimmern

whimsical ['wɪmzɪkəl] ADJ wunderlich; **look, remark** neckisch; **smile** verschmitzt; **idea, tale** schnurrig

whine [waɪn] **1** N Heulen nt no pl; (of dog) Jaulen nt no pl **2** VI heulen; (dog) jaulen; (person: = speak, complain) jammern; (child) quengeln

whinge [wɪndʒ] (Brit inf) **1** VI jammern, meckern (inf); (baby) plärren **2** N **to have a ~** meckern (inf), jammern

whining ['waɪnɪŋ] **1** N (of dog) Gejaule nt; (= complaining) Gejammer nt **2** ADJ **(a)** (= complaining) **voice** weinerlich **(b)** **sound** wimmernd; (of machine) schrillend; **dog** jaulend

whinny ['wɪnɪ] **1** N Wiehern nt no pl **2** VI wiehern

whip [wɪp] **1** N Peitsche f; (= riding ~) Reitgerte f
2 VT **(a)** **people** auspeitschen; **horse** peitschen; (with stick etc, Cook) schlagen; **to ~ sb/sth into shape** (fig) jdn/etw zurechtschleifen
(b) (fig) **he ~ped the book off the desk** er schnappte sich (dat) das Buch vom Schreibtisch; **he ~ped his hand out of the way** er zog blitzschnell seine Hand weg
3 VI (= move quickly: person) schnell (mal) laufen; **the car ~ped past** das Auto brauste vorbei
➤ **whip off** VT SEP **clothes** herunterreißen; **tablecloth** wegziehen
➤ **whip out** VT SEP **gun, camera etc** zücken; **they whipped out his tonsils** (inf) sie haben ihm schnell die Mandeln entfernt
➤ **whip up** VT SEP (inf) **meal** hinzaubern; (fig) **interest** entfachen; **support** finden; **audience** mitreißen

whiplash ['wɪplæʃ] N (Med: also ~ **injury**) Peitschenschlagverletzung f

whipped cream [wɪpt'kri:m] N Schlagsahne f

whir [wɜː'] N, VI = **whirr**

whirl [wɜːl] **1** N (= spin) Wirbeln nt no pl; (of dust etc, also fig) Wirbel m; (of cream etc) Tupfer m; **to give sth a ~** (fig inf: = try out) etw ausprobieren **2** VT wirbeln; **to ~ sb/sth round** jdn/etw herumwirbeln **3** VI wirbeln; (water) strudeln; **to ~ (a)round** herumwirbeln; (water) strudeln; (person: = turn round quickly) herumfahren; **my head is ~ing** mir schwirrt der Kopf

whirlpool ['wɜːlpuːl] N Strudel m; (in health club) ≈ Kneippbecken nt

whirlwind ['wɜːlwɪnd] N Wirbelwind m; (fig) Trubel m, Wirbel m; **a ~ romance** eine stürmische Romanze

whirr, whir [wɜː'] **1** N (of wings) Schwirren nt; (of camera, machine) (quiet) Surren nt; (louder) Brummen nt **2** VI (wings) schwirren; (camera, machine) (quietly) surren; (louder) brummen

whisk [wɪsk] **1** N (Cook) Schneebesen m; (electric) Rührgerät nt **2** VT **(a)** (Cook) schlagen; **eggs** verquirlen **(b)** **she ~ed the book out of my hand** sie riss mir das Buch aus der Hand
➤ **whisk away** or **off** VT SEP **the magician whisked away the tablecloth** der Zauberer zog das Tischtuch schnell weg; **he whisked her away to the Bahamas** er entführte sie auf die Bahamas

whisker ['wɪskə'] N Schnurrhaar nt; (of person) Barthaar nt; **~s** (= moustache, Zool) Schnurrbart m; (= side whiskers) Backenbart m; **to miss sth by a ~** etw um Haaresbreite verpassen

whisky, (US, Ir) whiskey ['wɪskɪ] N Whisky m

whisper ['wɪspə'] **1** N **(a)** Geflüster nt no pl, Flüstern nt no pl; (of leaves) Wispern nt no pl; **they were talking in ~s** sie sprachen im Flüsterton **(b)** (= rumour) Gerücht nt **2** VT flüstern; **to ~ sth to sb** jdm etw zuflüstern; (secretively) jdm etw zuraunen **3** VI flüstern, wispern (also fig); (secretively) raunen; (schoolchildren) tuscheln

whispering ['wɪspərɪŋ] N Geflüster nt no pl, Flüstern nt no pl; (poet: of wind) Säuseln nt no pl; (of schoolchildren) Tuscheln nt no pl; (fig) Gemunkel nt no pl

whist [wɪst] N Whist nt

whistle ['wɪsl] **1** N **(a)** (= sound) Pfiff m; (of wind) Pfeifen nt; **to give a ~** einen Pfiff ausstoßen **(b)** (= instrument) Pfeife f; **to blow a/one's ~** pfeifen **2** VTI pfeifen; **to ~ sb back/over** etc jdn zurück-/herüberpfeifen etc; **the boys ~d at her** die Jungen pfiffen ihr nach; **he ~d for a taxi** er pfiff nach einem Taxi

whistle-stop ['wɪslstɒp] ATTR **~ tour** (Pol) Wahlreise f; (fig) Reise mit Kurzaufenthalten an allen Orten

white [waɪt] **1** ADJ (+ER) weiß; (with fear, exhaustion etc also) blass, kreidebleich; **as ~ as a sheet** or **ghost** leichenblass; **~r than ~** (lit, fig) weißer als weiß **2** N (= colour) Weiß nt; (= person) Weiße(r) mf; (of egg) Eiweiß nt; (of eye) Weiße(s) nt; **~s** (Brit) (household) Weißwäsche f; (Sport) weiße Kleidung; (also ~ **wine**) Weißwein m

white: **white blood cell** N weißes Blutkörperchen; **white coffee** N (Brit) Kaffee m mit Milch; **white-collar** ADJ **~ worker** Schreibtischarbeiter(in) m(f); **~ job** Schreibtisch- or Büroposten m; **white flag** N (Mil, fig) weiße Fahne; **to raise** or **wave the ~** sich geschlagen geben; **white goods** PL (Comm) weiße Ware, Haushaltsgeräte pl; **white-haired** ADJ weißhaarig; **Whitehall** N (= British government) Whitehall no art; **if ~ decides ...** wenn London beschließt ...; **white-hot** ADJ weiß glühend; (fig) brennend, glühend; **White House** N **the ~** das Weiße Haus; **white knight** N (St Ex) weißer Ritter; **white lie** N Notlüge f; **white meat** N helles Fleisch

whiten ['waɪtn] **1** VT weiß machen **2** VI weiß werden

whiteness ['waɪtnɪs] N Weiße f; (of skin) Helligkeit f

white: **White Nile** N **the ~** der Weiße Nil; **white noise** N weißes Rauschen; **White-Out®** N (US) Tipp-Ex® nt; **whiteout** N starkes Schneegestöber; **White Pages** PL (US Telec) Telefonverzeichnis nt, Weiße Seiten pl; **white paper** N (Pol) Weißbuch nt (on zu); **White Russia** N Weißrussland nt; **White Russian** N Weißrusse m, Weißrussin f; **white sauce** N helle Soße; **White Sea** N **the ~** das Weiße Meer; **white spirit** N (Brit) Terpentinersatz m; **white stick** N Blindenstock m; **white tie** N **a ~ occasion** eine Veranstaltung mit Frackzwang; **white trash** N (US pej inf) weißes Pack (pej inf)

WHITE TRASH

White trash ist ein abfälliger amerikanischer Ausdruck für arme, ungebildete Weiße, vor allem für die in den Südstaaten. Sie werden als die unterste gesellschaftliche Schicht von Weißen angesehen, gelten als dumm, schmutzig und faul und haben einen ebenso schweren Stand wie ihre gleichfalls armen schwarzen, hispanischen oder indianischen Mitbürger.

white: **whitewash** **1** N Tünche f; (fig) Augenwischerei f **2** VT walls tünchen; (fig) schönfärben; opponent zu null schlagen; **white-water rafting** N Rafting nt, Wildwasserfahren nt; **white wedding** N Hochzeit f in Weiß; **white wine** N Weißwein m

whiting ['waɪtɪŋ] N, pl - Weißling m

whitish ['waɪtɪʃ] ADJ weißlich

Whit Monday [wɪt'mʌndɪ] N (Brit) Pfingstmontag m

Whitsun ['wɪtsən] (Brit) N Pfingsten nt

Whit Sunday [wɪt'sʌndɪ] N (Brit) Pfingstsonntag m

Whitsuntide ['wɪtsəntaɪd] N (Brit) Pfingstzeit f

whittle ['wɪtl] VT schnitzen

➤ **whittle away** VT SEP (= gradually reduce) allmählich abbauen; rights, power etc nach und nach beschneiden

➤ **whittle down** VT SEP (= reduce) kürzen, reduzieren, stutzen (to auf +acc); gap, difference verringern

whiz(z) [wɪz] **1** N (inf) Kanone f (inf); **a computer ~** ein Computergenie nt (inf) **2** VI (arrow) schwirren, sausen

whiz(z) kid N (inf: in career) Senkrechtstarter(in) m(f); **financial ~** Finanzgenie nt or -größe f

who [huː] PRON **(a)** (interrog) wer; (acc) wen; (dat) wem; **~ do you think you are?** für wen hältst du dich eigentlich?; **~ are you looking for?** wen suchen Sie?; **~ did you stay with?** bei wem haben Sie gewohnt? **(b)** (rel) der/die/das, welche(r, s); **any man ~ ...** jeder (Mensch), der ...; **anyone ~ wishes** or **those ~ wish to go ...** wer gehen will ...

Be careful! **who** *is not translated by the German word* **wo***.*

who'd [huːd] CONTR of **who had**, **who would**

whoever [huː'evəʳ] PRON wer (auch immer); (acc) wen (auch immer); (dat) wem (auch immer); (= no matter who) ganz gleich or egal (inf) wer/wen/wem

whole [həʊl] **1** ADJ ganz; truth voll; **the ~ lot** das Ganze; (of people) alle, der ganze Verein (inf); **a ~ lot better** (inf) ein ganzes Stück besser (inf); **let's forget the ~ thing** vergessen wir das Ganze; **the figures don't tell the ~ story** die Zahlen sagen nicht alles; **a ~ new wardrobe** eine völlig neue Garderobe **2** N Ganze(s) nt; **the ~ of the month** der ganze or gesamte Monat; **the ~ of the time** die ganze Zeit; **the ~ of his savings** seine gesamten or sämtlichen Ersparnisse; **the ~ of London** ganz London; **as a ~** als Ganzes; **these people, as a ~, are ...** diese Leute sind in ihrer Gesamtheit ...; **on the ~** im Großen und Ganzen

whole: **wholefood** ADJ ATTR (esp Brit) Vollwert(kost)-; **~ shop** Bioladen m; **wholehearted** ADJ völlig, uneingeschränkt; **wholeheartedly** ADV voll und ganz; **wholemeal** (Brit) ADJ Vollkorn-; **~ bread** Vollkornbrot nt

wholesale ['həʊlseɪl] **1** N Großhandel m **2** ADJ ATTR **(a)** (Comm) Großhandels-; **~ dealer** Großhändler(in) m(f) **(b)** (fig) (= widespread) umfassend, massiv; **~ redundancies** Massenentlassungen pl **3** ADV **(a)** im Großhandel **(b)** (fig) in Bausch und Bogen; (= in great numbers) massenhaft

wholesale: **wholesale business** N Großhandel m; **wholesale price index** N Großhandelspreisindex m

wholesaler ['həʊlseɪləʳ] N Großhändler(in) m(f)

wholesale trade N Großhandel m

wholesaling ['həʊlseɪlɪŋ] N Großhandel m

wholesome ['həʊlsəm] ADJ **(a)** gesund **(b)** (= moral) entertainment erbaulich; person mustergültig

whole-wheat ['həʊlwiːt] N Voll(korn)weizen m

who'll [huːl] CONTR of **who will**, **who shall**

wholly ['həʊlɪ] ADV völlig, gänzlich; **~ owned** im Alleinbesitz

whom [huːm] PRON **(a)** (interrog) (acc) wen; (dat) wem **(b)** (rel) (acc) den/die/das; (dat) dem/der/dem; **..., all/both of ~ were drunk** ..., die alle/beide betrunken waren; **none/all of ~** von denen keine(r, s)/alle

whoop [huːp] **1** N Ruf m, Schrei m **2** VI rufen, schreien; (with joy) jauchzen

whooping cough ['huːpɪŋkɒf] N Keuchhusten m

whoops [wʊps] INTERJ hoppla

whoosh [wʊʃ] **1** N (of water) Rauschen nt; (of air) Zischen nt **2** VI rauschen; (air) zischen

whopper ['wɒpəʳ] N (inf) (= sth big) Brocken m (inf), Apparat m (inf); (= lie) faustdicke Lüge

whopping ['wɒpɪŋ] ADJ (inf) Mords- (inf), Riesen-; **a ~ big fish** ein Monstrum nt von einem Fisch (inf)

whore [hɔːʳ] N Hure f

whorehouse ['hɔːhaʊs] N (inf) Bordell nt

whorl [wɜːl] N Kringel m; (of shell) (Spiral)windung f

who's [huːz] CONTR of **who has**, **who is**

whose [huːz] POSS PRON **(a)** (interrog) wessen; **~ is this?** wem gehört das?; **~ car did you go in?** bei wem sind Sie gefahren? **(b)** (rel) dessen; (after f and pl) deren

why [waɪ] **1** ADV warum, weshalb; (asking for the purpose) wozu; (= how come that ...) wieso; **~ not ask him?** warum fragst du/fragen wir etc ihn nicht?; **~ wait?** warum or wozu (noch) warten?; **~ do it this way?** warum denn so?; **that's ~** darum, deshalb **2** INTERJ **~, of course, that's right!** ja doch, das stimmt so!; **are you sure? ~ ~ yes (of course/I think so)** sind Sie sicher? – aber ja doch; **~, if it isn't Charles!** na so was, das ist doch (der) Charles!

wick [wɪk] N Docht m

wicked ['wɪkɪd] ADJ böse; (= immoral) schlecht; satire boshaft; smile, look, grin frech; (inf) price etc hanebüchen (inf), unverschämt; **that was a ~ thing to do** das war aber gemein (von dir/ihm etc); **it's ~ to tell lies** Lügen ist hässlich; **he has a ~ temper** er ist jähzornig

wickedly ['wɪkɪdlɪ] ADV smile, look, grin frech

wickedness ['wɪkɪdnɪs] N **(a)** (of person) Schlechtigkeit f; (= immorality) Verderbtheit f **(b)** (= mischievousness) Boshaftigkeit f

wicker ['wɪkəʳ] ADJ ATTR Korb-

wicker: **wicker basket** N (Weiden)korb m; **wickerwork** **1** N (= articles) Korbwaren pl **2** ADJ Korb-

wide [waɪd] **1** ADJ (+ER) **(a)** road, gap, knowledge, range breit; skirt, trousers weit; eyes, difference, variety, circulation groß; experience, choice reich; interests vielfältig; network weit verzweigt; **it is three feet ~** es ist drei Fuß breit; (material) es liegt drei Fuß breit; (room) es ist drei Fuß in der Breite; **the big ~ world** die (große) weite Welt
(b) (missing the target) daneben pred, gefehlt; **it was ~ of the target** es verpasste das Ziel, es ging daneben
2 ADV **(a)** weit; **they are set ~ apart** sie liegen weit auseinander; **open ~!** bitte weit öffnen; **the writer left himself ~ open to attack** der Verfasser hat sich (überhaupt) nicht gegen Angriffe abgesichert; **the law is ~ open to abuse** das Gesetz öffnet dem Missbrauch Tür und Tor
(b) (= far from the target) daneben; **to go ~ of sth** an etw (dat) vorbeigehen

-wide [-waɪd] ADJ SUF in dem/der gesamten, (country-wide etc) -weit; **Europe-wide** europaweit

wide: **wide-angle (lens)** N (Phot) Weitwinkel(objektiv nt) m; **wide area network** N (Comput) Weitverkehrsnetz nt; **wide-awake** ADJ ATTR, **wide awake** ADJ PRED hellwach; **wide-bodied** ADJ (Aviat) mit breitem Rumpf; **wide-eyed** ADJ mit großen Augen

widely [waɪdlɪ] ADV weit; (= by or to many people) überall, allgemein; vary stark; differing völlig; available fast überall; **his remarks were ~ publicized** seine Bemerkungen fanden weite Verbreitung; **a ~ read student** ein sehr belesener Student

widen [waɪdn] **1** VT road verbreitern; passage, scope, knowledge erweitern; circle of friends vergrößern; appeal erhöhen **2** VI breiter werden; (interests etc) sich ausweiten
➤ **widen out** VI (river, valley etc) sich erweitern (into zu)

wideness [waɪdnɪs] N (of road, gap) Breite f

wide: **wide-open** ADJ ATTR, **wide open** ADJ PRED **(a)** (= fully open) door, window weit or sperrangelweit (inf) offen; eyes weit aufgerissen **(b)** contest etc völlig offen; **wide-ranging, wide-reaching** ADJ weitreichend; **wide-screen** ADJ (Film) Breitwand-; **in ~ format** im Breitwandformat; **television set** Breitbildfernseher m; **widespread** ADJ weitverbreitet attr; **to become ~** weite Verbreitung erlangen

widow [wɪdəʊ] **1** N Witwe f **2** VT zur Witwe/zum Witwer machen; **she was twice ~ed** sie ist zweimal verwitwet

widowed [wɪdəʊd] ADJ verwitwet

widower [wɪdəʊəʳ] N Witwer m

width [wɪdθ] N Breite f; (of skirts etc) Weite f; **six feet in ~** sechs Fuß breit; **what is the ~ of the material?** wie breit liegt dieser Stoff?

widthways [wɪdθweɪz] ADV der Breite nach

wield [wiːld] VT pen, sword führen; axe schwingen; power, influence ausüben

wife [waɪf] N, pl **wives** Frau f; **businessmen who take their wives with them on their trips** Geschäftsleute, die ihre (Ehe)frauen mit auf Geschäftsreise nehmen

wig [wɪg] N Perücke f

wiggle [wɪgl] **1** N Wackeln nt no pl **2** VT wackeln mit; eyebrows zucken mit **3** VI wackeln; (eyebrows) zucken

wiggly [wɪglɪ] ADJ wackelnd; **~ line** Schlangenlinie f; (drawn) Wellenlinie f

wigwam [wɪgwæm] N Wigwam m

wild [waɪld] **1** ADJ (+ER) **(a)** (= not domesticated, not civilized) wild; people unzivilisiert; garden, wood verwildert; flowers wild wachsend; ~ animals Tiere pl in freier Wildbahn; **a lion is a ~ animal** der Löwe lebt in freier Wildbahn
(b) weather, sea rau, stürmisch
(c) (= excited, frantic, riotous) wild (with vor +dat); hair wirr, unordentlich; desire unbändig; **to be ~ about sb/sth** (inf) auf jdn/etw wild or scharf (inf) sein
(d) (inf: = angry) wütend (with, at mit, auf +acc), rasend; **it drives or makes me ~** das macht mich ganz wild or rasend
(e) (= rash, extravagant) verrückt; exaggeration maßlos; allegation wild; fluctuations stark; imagination kühn; **never in my ~est dreams** auch in meinen kühnsten Träumen nicht
(f) (= wide of the mark, erratic) Fehl-; **~ throw** Fehlwurf m; **it was just a ~ guess** es war nur so (wild) drauflosgeraten
(g) (inf: = fantastic, great) toll (inf)
2 ADV grow wild; run frei; **to let one's imagination run ~** seiner Fantasie (dat) freien Lauf lassen; **he lets his kids run ~** (pej) er lässt seine Kinder auf der Straße aufwachsen; **in the country the kids can run ~** auf dem Land kann man die Kinder einfach laufen lassen
3 N Wildnis f; **in the ~** in freier Wildbahn; **the ~s** die Wildnis

wild: **wild card** (Comput) N Wildcard f; **wildcat** N (Zool) Wildkatze f; **wildcat strike** N wilder Streik

wildebeest [wɪldəbiːst] N Gnu nt

wilderness [wɪldənɪs] N Wildnis f; (fig) Wüste f

wild: **wild-eyed** ADJ person wild dreinblickend attr; look wild; **wildfire** N **to spread like ~** sich wie ein Lauffeuer ausbreiten; **wildfowl** N, NO PL Wildgeflügel nt; **wild-goose chase** N fruchtloses Unterfangen; **wildlife** N die Tierwelt; **~ sanctuary or park** Wildschutzgebiet nt

wildly [waɪldlɪ] ADV wild; (= violently also) heftig; (= excitedly, distractedly) aufgeregt; (= in disorder) wirr; guess drauflos; exaggerated maßlos; different völlig

wildness [waɪldnɪs] N Wildheit f; (of storm etc) Stärke f

wile [waɪl] N USU PL List f, Schliche pl

wilful, (US) **willful** [wɪlfʊl] ADJ **(a)** (= self-willed) eigensinnig **(b)** neglect, damage mutwillig; disobedience wissentlich

will[1] [wɪl], pret **would** **1** MODAL AUX VB **(a)** (future) werden; **I'm sure that he ~ come** ich bin sicher, dass er kommt; **you ~ come to see us, won't you?** Sie kommen uns doch besuchen, ja?; **I'll be right there** komme sofort!; **I ~ have finished by Tuesday** bis Dienstag bin ich fertig; **you won't lose it, ~ you?** du wirst es doch nicht verlieren, oder?; **you won't insist on that, ~ you? – oh yes, I ~** Sie bestehen doch nicht darauf, oder? – o doch!
(b) (emphatic, expressing determination, compulsion etc) **~ you be quiet!** willst du jetzt wohl ruhig sein!; **he says he ~ go and I say he won't** er sagt, er geht, und ich sage, er geht nicht; **he ~ interrupt all the time** er muss ständig dazwischenreden
(c) (expressing willingness, capability) wollen; **he won't sign** er unterschreibt nicht; **he wouldn't help me** er wollte or mochte mir nicht helfen; **wait a moment, ~ you?** warten Sie einen Moment, ja bitte?; (impatiently) jetzt warte doch mal einen Moment!; **the car won't start** das Auto springt nicht an; **the door won't open** die Tür lässt sich nicht öffnen or geht nicht auf (inf)
(d) (in questions) **~ you have some more tea?** möchten Sie noch Tee?; **~ you accept these conditions?** akzeptieren Sie diese Bedingungen?; **won't you have a seat?** wollen or möchten Sie sich nicht setzen?; **there isn't any tea, ~ coffee do?** es ist kein Tee da, darf es auch Kaffee sein?
(e) (assumption) **he'll be there by now** jetzt ist er schon da, jetzt dürfte er schon da sein; **was that the doorbell? that ~ be for you** hats geklingelt? – das ist bestimmt für dich
(f) (tendency) **sometimes he ~ sit in his room for hours** manchmal sitzt er auch stundenlang in seinem Zimmer
2 VI wollen; **say what you ~** du kannst sagen, was du willst; **as you ~!** wie du willst!

will[2] **1** N **(a)** Wille m; **to have a ~ of one's own** einen eigenen Willen haben; (hum) so seine Mucken haben (inf); **the ~ to live** der Wille, zu leben, der Lebenswille; **(to go) against one's/sb's ~** gegen seinen/jds Willen (handeln); **at ~** nach Lust und Laune, beliebig; **of one's own free ~** aus freien Stücken, aus freiem Willen; **with the best ~ in the world** beim or mit (dem) (aller)besten Willen
(b) (= testament) letzter Wille, Testament nt
2 VT (durch Willenskraft) erzwingen; **to ~ sb to do sth** jdn durch die eigene Willensanstrengung dazu bringen, dass er etw tut; **he ~ed himself to stay awake** er hat sich (dazu) gezwungen, wach zu bleiben

willful etc (US) = **wilful** etc

willie [wɪlɪ] N (Brit inf: = penis) Pimmel m (inf)

willies [wɪlɪz] PL (inf) **it/he gives me the ~** da/bei dem wird mir ganz anders (inf)

willing [wɪlɪŋ] ADJ **(a)** (= prepared) **to be ~ to do sth** bereit or gewillt (geh) sein, etw zu tun; **he was ~ for me to take it** es war ihm recht, dass ich es nahm; **he was not ~ for us to go** er war nicht gewillt, uns gehen zu lassen **(b)** workers, helpers bereitwillig; sacrifice willentlich

willingly [wɪlɪŋlɪ] ADV bereitwillig, gerne

willingness [wɪlɪŋnɪs] N Bereitschaft f

willow [wɪləʊ] N (also ~ **tree**) Weide f

willpower [wɪlpaʊəʳ] N Willenskraft f

willy [wɪlɪ] N (Brit inf) = **willie**

willy-nilly ['wɪlɪ'nɪlɪ] ADV **(a)** *choose, allocate* aufs Geratewohl; *accept* wahllos **(b)** (= *willingly or not*) wohl oder übel

wilt [wɪlt] VI **(a)** (*flowers*) welken, verwelken **(b)** (*person*) matt werden; (*after physical exercise*) schlapp werden

wily ['waɪlɪ] ADJ (+ER) listig, hinterlistig (*pej*)

wimp [wɪmp] N Waschlappen *m* (*inf*)

win [wɪn], *vb: pret, ptp* **won** ◨ N Sieg *m* ◨ VT gewinnen; *scholarship, contract* bekommen; *victory* erringen; **to ~ sb's heart/love/hand** jds Herz gewinnen ◨ VI gewinnen, siegen; **OK, you ~, I was wrong** okay, du hast gewonnen, ich habe mich geirrt; **whatever I do, I just can't ~** egal, was ich mache, ich machs immer falsch

➤ **win back** VT SEP zurück- *or* wiedergewinnen

➤ **win over** VT SEP für sich gewinnen

➤ **win round** VT SEP (*esp Brit*) = **win over**

➤ **win through** VI **to win through to the finals** das Finale schaffen; **we'll win through in the end** wir werden es schon schaffen (*inf*)

wince [wɪns] VI zusammenzucken

winch [wɪntʃ] ◨ N Winde *f* ◨ VT winschen

➤ **winch up** VT SEP hochwinschen

wind¹ [wɪnd] ◨ N **(a)** Wind *m*; **the ~ is from the east** der Wind kommt aus dem Osten; **a ~ of change** (*fig*) ein frischer(er) Wind; **to put the ~ up sb** (*Brit inf*) jdn ins Bockshorn jagen; **to see which way the ~ blows** (*fig*) sehen, woher der Wind weht; **to get ~ of sth** (*lit, fig*) von etw Wind bekommen; **to the four ~s** in alle (vier) Winde; **to throw caution to the ~s** Bedenken in den Wind schlagen **(b)** (*from bowel, stomach*) Wind *m*, Blähung *f*; **to break ~** einen Wind streichen lassen **(c)** (= *breath*) Atem *m*, Luft *f* (*inf*); **to get one's ~ back** wieder Luft bekommen
◨ VT (*Brit*: = *knock breathless*) den Atem nehmen (+*dat*); **he was ~ed by the ball** der Ball nahm ihm den Atem

wind² [waɪnd], *vb: pret, ptp* **wound** ◨ VT **(a)** *wool, bandage* wickeln; *turban etc* winden; (*on to a reel*) spulen **(b)** *handle* kurbeln; *clock, clockwork toy* aufziehen **(c)** **to ~ one's way** sich schlängeln ◨ VI (*river etc*) sich winden

➤ **wind around** ◨ VT SEP +PREP OBJ wickeln um; **wind it twice around the post** wickele es zweimal um den Pfosten; **to wind itself around sth** sich um etw schlingen ◨ VI (*road*) sich winden ◨ VI +PREP OBJ (*road*) sich schlängeln durch; (*procession*) sich winden durch

➤ **wind back** VT SEP *film, tape* zurückspulen

➤ **wind down** ◨ VT SEP **(a)** *car window etc* herunterdrehen *or* -kurbeln **(b)** *operations* reduzieren; *production* zurückschrauben ◨ VI (*inf:* = *relax*) entspannen

➤ **wind forward** *or* **on** VT SEP *film* weiterspulen

➤ **wind round** VTI SEP (*esp Brit*) = **wind around**

➤ **wind up** ◨ VT SEP **(a)** *car window* hinaufkurbeln *or* -drehen **(b)** *clock, mechanism* (*Brit fig inf*) *person* aufziehen; **to be wound up about sth** (*fig*) über etw (*acc*) *or* wegen einer Sache (*gen*) erregt sein **(c)** (= *close, end*) beschließen, zu Ende bringen; *company* auflösen; *service, series* auslaufen lassen ◨ VI (*inf:* = *end up*) enden; **to wind up in hospital** im Krankenhaus landen; **to wind up doing sth** am Ende etw tun

wind ['wɪnd]: **windbreak** N Windschutz *m*; **Windbreaker®** (*US*), **windcheater** (*Brit*) N Windjacke *f*; **wind-chill factor** N Wind-Kälte-Faktor *m*

winded ['wɪndɪd] ADJ atemlos, außer Atem

windfall ['wɪndfɔːl] N Fallobst *nt*; (*fig*) unerwartetes Geschenk

windfall tax N (*Econ*) Spekulationssteuer *f*

wind farm ['wɪndfɑːm] N Windfarm *f*

winding ['waɪndɪŋ] ADJ gewunden; *road also* kurvenreich

winding: **winding staircase** N Wendeltreppe *f*; **winding-up** N (*of project*) Abschluss *m*; (*of company, society*) Auflösung *f*

wind ['wɪnd]: **wind instrument** N Blasinstrument *nt*; **windmill** N Windmühle *f*

window ['wɪndəʊ] N (*also Comput*) Fenster *nt*; (= *shop ~*) (Schau)fenster *nt*; (*of bank*) Schalter *m*; (*Comm inf*: = *opportunity*) Gelegenheit *f*

window: **window box** N Blumenkasten *m*; **windowcleaner** N Fensterputzer(in) *m(f)*; **window display** N (Schaufenster)auslage *f*; **window-dressing** N Auslagen- *or*

Schaufensterdekoration *f*; (*fig*) Mache *f*, Schau *f* (*inf*); **that's just ~** das ist alles nur Mache

windowing ['wɪndəʊɪŋ] N (*Comput*) Fenstertechnik *f*

window: **window ledge** N = **windowsill**; **windowpane** N Fensterscheibe *f*; **window-shopping** N **to go ~** einen Schaufensterbummel machen; **windowsill** N Fensterbank *f or* -brett *nt*; (*outside also*) Fenstersims *m*

wind ['wɪnd]: **windpipe** N Luftröhre *f*; **wind power** N Windkraft *f*; **windscreen**, (*US*) **windshield** N Windschutzscheibe *f*; **windscreen washer**, (*US*) **windshield washer** N Scheibenwaschanlage *f*; **windscreen wiper**, (*US*) **windshield wiper** N Scheibenwischer *m*; **windsurf** VI windsurfen; **windsurfer** N (= *person*) Windsurfer(in) *m(f)*; (= *board*) Windsurfbrett *nt*; **windsurfing** N Windsurfen *nt*; **windswept** ADJ *beach, field* über den/die/das der Wind fegt; *person, hair* (vom Wind) zerzaust; **wind tunnel** N Windkanal *m*

wind-up ['waɪndʌp] N **(a)** (*US*) = **winding-up** **(b)** (*Brit inf:* = *joke*) Witz *m*

Windward Islands ['wɪndwəd'aɪləndz] PL **the Windward islands** die Inseln *pl* über dem Winde (*von Dominica bis Grenada*)

windy ['wɪndɪ] ADJ (+ER) windig

wine [waɪn] ◨ N Wein *m*; **cheese and ~ party** Party, bei der Wein und Käse gereicht wird ◨ VT **to ~ and dine sb** jdn zu einem guten Abendessen einladen ◨ ADJ (*colour*) burgunderrot

wine: **wine bar** N Weinlokal *nt*; **wine bottle** N Weinflasche *f*; **wine cellar** N Weinkeller *m*; **wineglass** N Weinglas *nt*; **wine growing** ADJ Wein(an)bau-; **~ region** Wein(an)baugebiet *nt*; **wine list** N Weinkarte *f*; **wine merchant** N Weinhändler(in) *m(f)*

winery ['waɪnərɪ] N (*US*) (Wein)kellerei *f*

wine: **wine tasting** N Weinprobe *f*; **wine waiter** N (*Brit*) Weinkellner *m*

wing [wɪŋ] ◨ N **(a)** Flügel *m* (*also Mil, Pol, Sport*); (*Brit Aut*) Kotflügel *m*; **to take sb under one's ~** (*fig*) jdn unter seine Fittiche nehmen; **to spread one's ~s** (*fig*) flügge werden; **to play on the (left/right) ~** (*Sport*) auf dem (linken/rechten) Flügel spielen **(b) wings** PL (*Theat*) Kulisse *f*; **to wait in the ~s** (*lit, fig*) in den Kulissen warten ◨ VT **to ~ one's way** (= *fly*) fliegen ◨ VI fliegen

winger ['wɪŋə'] N (*Sport*) Flügelspieler(in) *m(f)*

wing: **wing nut** N Flügelmutter *f*; **wingspan** N Flügelspannweite *f*

wink [wɪŋk] ◨ N (*with eye*) Zwinkern *nt*, Blinzeln *nt*; **I didn't get a ~ of sleep, I didn't sleep a ~** (*inf*) ich habe kein Auge zugetan ◨ VT blinzeln, zwinkern mit (+*dat*) ◨ VI (*meaningfully*) zwinkern, blinzeln; (*light, star etc*) blinken, funkeln; **to ~ at sb** jdm zuzwinkern *or* zublinzeln

winkle ['wɪŋkl] N (*Brit*) Strandschnecke *f*

winner ['wɪnə'] N (*in race, competition*) Sieger(in) *m(f)*; (*of bet, pools etc*) Gewinner(in) *m(f)*; (*inf:* = *sth successful*) Renner *m* (*inf*); **to be onto a ~** (*inf*) das große Los gezogen haben (*inf*)

winning ['wɪnɪŋ] ◨ ADJ **(a)** (= *successful*) *person, entry* der/die gewinnt; *horse, team* siegreich; *goal* Sieges-; **the ~ time** die beste Zeit **(b)** *smile, ways* gewinnend, einnehmend ◨ N **winnings** PL Gewinn *m*

winning post N Zielpfosten *m*

wino ['waɪnəʊ] N (*inf*) Saufbruder *m* (*inf*)

winter ['wɪntə'] ◨ N (*lit, fig*) Winter *m* ◨ ADJ ATTR Winter- ◨ VI überwintern

winterize ['wɪntəraɪz] VT (*US*) winterfest machen

winter: **Winter Olympics** PL Winterolympiade *f*; **winter sports** PL Wintersport *m*; **wintertime** N Winter *m*

wintery ['wɪntərɪ], **wintry** ['wɪntrɪ] ADJ winterlich

wipe [waɪp] ◨ N **(a)** Wischen *nt*; **to give sth a ~** etw abwischen **(b)** (= *cloth*) Wischtuch *nt*; (*for face, hands*) Erfrischungstuch *nt*
◨ VT wischen; *floor* aufwischen; *window* überwischen; *hands, feet* abwischen; **to ~ sb/sth dry** jdn/etw abtrocknen; **to ~ sb/sth clean** jdn/etw sauber wischen; **to ~ sth with/on a cloth** etw mit/an einem Tuch abwischen; **to ~ one's eyes** sich (*dat*) die Augen wischen; **to ~ one's nose** sich (*dat*) die Nase putzen; **to ~ one's feet** sich (*dat*) die Füße *or* Schuhe abtreten; **to ~ one's bottom** sich (*dat*) den Hintern abputzen; **to ~ the floor with sb** (*fig inf*) jdn fertigmachen (*inf*)

➤ **wipe away** VT SEP (*lit, fig*) wegwischen; *tears also* abwischen

➤ **wipe off** VT SEP weg- or abwischen; (from blackboard also) ab- or auslöschen; **wipe that smile off your face** (inf) hör auf zu grinsen (inf); **to be wiped off the map** or **the face of the earth** von der Landkarte or Erdoberfläche getilgt werden; **millions were wiped off share values yesterday** gestern kam es zu Aktienverlusten in Millionenhöhe

➤ **wipe out** VT SEP **(a)** bowl auswischen **(b)** memory, sth on blackboard (aus)löschen **(c)** debt bereinigen; gain, benefit zunichte machen **(d)** disease, village, race ausrotten; enemy, battalion aufreiben

➤ **wipe up** 🛈 VT SEP liquid aufwischen; dishes abtrocknen 🞥 VI abtrocknen

wire [waɪəʳ] 🛈 N **(a)** Draht m; (for electricity supply) Leitung f; (= insulated flex) (for home appliance etc) Schnur f; (for television) Fernsehkabel nt; **you've got your ~s crossed there** (inf) Sie verwechseln da etwas
(b) (Telec) Telegramm nt
(c) (= microphone) Wanze f (inf)
🞥 VT **(a)** plug anschließen; house die (elektrischen) Leitungen verlegen in (+dat); (= connect to electricity) (an das Stromnetz) anschließen
(b) (Telec) telegrafieren
(c) (= fix with ~) mit Draht zusammen- or verbinden

➤ **wire up** VT SEP lights, battery, speakers anschließen; house elektrische Leitungen or den Strom verlegen in (+dat)

wire: **wire brush** N Drahtbürste f; **wire cutters** PL Drahtschere f

wireless [ˈwaɪəlɪs] 🛈 N (esp Brit dated) **(a)** (also ~ **set**) Radio nt **(b)** (= radio) Rundfunk m 🞥 ADJ station, programme Radio-; data, technology, network drahtlos

Wireless Application Protocol N (Comput) WAP-Protokoll nt

wire: **wire netting** N Maschendraht m; **wiretap** VT phone, conversation abhören; building abhören in (+dat); **wiretapping** [ˈwaɪətæpɪŋ] N Abhören nt; **wire wool** N Stahlwolle f

wiring [ˈwaɪərɪŋ] N elektrische Leitungen pl

wiry [ˈwaɪərɪ] ADJ (+ER) drahtig; hair also borstig

wisdom [ˈwɪzdəm] N Weisheit f; (= prudence) Einsicht f

wisdom tooth N Weisheitszahn m

wise [waɪz] ADJ (+ER) weise; move, step etc klug, vernünftig; **a ~ choice** eine kluge or gute Wahl; **the Three Wise Men** die drei Weisen; **I'm none the ~r** (inf) ich bin nicht klüger als vorher; **nobody will be any the ~r** (inf) niemand wird das spitzkriegen (inf); **you'd be ~ to ...** du tätest gut daran, ...; **it would be ~ to accept the offer** es wäre klug, das Angebot anzunehmen; **to get ~ to sb/sth** (inf) jd/etw spitzkriegen (inf); **to be ~ to sb/sth** (inf) jdn/etw kennen; **he fooled her twice, then she got ~ to him** zweimal hat er sie hereingelegt, dann ist sie ihm auf die Schliche gekommen

➤ **wise up** (inf) VI if he doesn't wise up soon to what's going on ... wenn er nicht bald dahinter kommt, was da gespielt wird ...

-wise ADV SUF -mäßig, in Bezug auf (+acc)

wise: **wisecrack** N Witzelei f; (pej) Stichelei f; **to make a ~ (about sb/sth)** witzeln (über jdn/etw); **wise guy** N (inf) Klugscheißer m

wisely [ˈwaɪzlɪ] ADV weise; (= sensibly) klugerweise

wish [wɪʃ] 🛈 N Wunsch m (for nach); **I have no great ~ to see him** ich habe kein Bedürfnis or keine große Lust, ihn zu sehen; **to make a ~** sich (dat) etwas wünschen; **you can make three ~es** du hast drei Wünsche; **with best ~es** mit den besten Wünschen or Grüßen, alles Gute; **he sends his best ~es** er lässt (vielmals) grüßen
🞥 VT wünschen; **he ~es to be alone** er möchte allein sein; **how he ~ed that his wife was** or **were there** wie sehr er sich (dat) wünschte, dass seine Frau hier wäre; **~ you were here** ich wünschte or wollte, du wärest hier; **to ~ sb well/ill** jdm Glück or alles Gute/Schlechtes or Böses wünschen; **to ~ sb good luck** jdm viel Glück or alles Gute wünschen; **to ~ sb merry Christmas** jdm frohe Weihnachten wünschen; **he ~ed himself anywhere but there** er wünschte sich nur möglichst weit weg
🞧 VI (= make a ~) sich (dat) etwas wünschen

➤ **wish for** VI +PREP OBJ **to wish for sth** sich (dat) etw wünschen; **what more could you wish for?** etwas Besseres kann man sich doch gar nicht wünschen

➤ **wish on** or **upon** VT SEP +PREP OBJ (inf: = foist) **to wish sb/sth on** or **upon sb** jdn jdm/jdm etw aufhängen (inf); **I would not wish that on** or **upon my worst enemy!** das würde ich meinem ärgsten Feind nicht wünschen

wishful [ˈwɪʃfʊl] ADJ **that's just ~ thinking** das ist reines Wunschdenken

wishy-washy [ˈwɪʃɪˌwɒʃɪ] ADJ coffee, soup wässrig; person farblos; colour verwaschen; argument schwach (inf)

wisp [wɪsp] N (of straw, hair etc) kleines Büschel; (of cloud) Fetzen m; (of smoke) Wölkchen nt

wispy [ˈwɪspɪ] ADJ (+ER) grass dürr, fein; ~ **clouds** Wolkenfetzen pl; ~ **hair** dünne Haarbüschel

wistful [ˈwɪstfʊl] ADJ, **wistfully** [ˈwɪstfəlɪ] ADV wehmütig

wit [wɪt] N **(a)** (= understanding) Verstand m; **a battle of ~s** ein geistiges Kräftemessen; **to be at one's ~s' end** mit seinem Latein am Ende sein (hum inf); **to be frightened** or **scared out of one's ~s** zu Tode erschreckt sein; **to have** or **keep one's ~s about one** seine (fünf) Sinne zusammen- or beisammenhaben **(b)** (= humour, wittiness) Geist m, Witz m; **full of ~** geistreich **(c)** (= person) geistreicher Kopf

witch [wɪtʃ] N (lit, fig) Hexe f

witch: **witchcraft** N Hexerei f; **witch doctor** N Medizinmann m

witch-hunt [ˈwɪtʃhʌnt] N (lit, fig) Hexenjagd f

with [wɪð, wɪθ] PREP **(a)** mit; **are you pleased ~ it?** bist du damit zufrieden?; **bring a book ~ you** bring ein Buch mit; ~ **no ...** ohne ...; **to walk ~ a stick** am or mit einem Stock gehen; **put it ~ the rest** leg es zu den anderen; **how are things ~ you?** wie gehts?; **it varies ~ the temperature** es verändert sich je nach Temperatur; **wine improves ~ age** Wein wird mit zunehmendem Alter immer besser; **is he ~ us or against us?** ist er für oder gegen uns?
(b) (= at house of, in company of etc, on person) bei; (= in the case of) mit; (= in spite of) trotz; **I'll be ~ you in a moment** einen Augenblick bitte, ich bin gleich da; **10 years ~ the company** 10 Jahre bei or in der Firma; **it's always the same ~ you** es ist (doch) immer dasselbe mit dir; **the trouble ~ him is that he ...** die Schwierigkeit bei or mit ihm ist (die), dass er ...
(c) (cause) vor (+dat); **to shiver ~ cold** vor Kälte zittern; **the hills are white ~ snow** die Berge sind weiß vom Schnee; **to be ill ~ measles** die Masern haben
(d) (= while sb/sth is) wo; **you can't go ~ your mother ill in bed** wo deine Mutter krank im Bett liegt, kannst du nicht gehen; **to quit ~ the job half-finished** von der halb fertigen Arbeit weglaufen; ~ **the window open** bei offenem Fenster
(e) (inf: expressing comprehension) **are you ~ me?** kapierst du? (inf), kommst du mit? (inf); **I'm not ~ you** da komm ich nicht mit (inf); **to be ~ it** (= alert) bei der Sache sein; (= fashionable) im Trend liegen (inf)

withdraw [wɪθˈdrɔː], pret **withdrew**, ptp **withdrawn** 🛈 VT object, motion, charge, offer zurückziehen; troops also abziehen; coins, stamps einziehen; (from bank) money abheben; words, comment widerrufen; privileges entziehen; **she withdrew her hand from his** sie entzog ihm ihre Hand 🞥 VI sich zurückziehen; (Sport also) zurücktreten (from von); (= move away) zurücktreten or -gehen

withdrawal [wɪθˈdrɔːəl] N (of objects, charge) Zurückziehen nt; (of coins, stamps) Einziehen nt; (of money) Abheben nt; (of words) Zurücknehmen nt; (of troops) Rückzug m; (= withdrawing) Abziehen nt; (in sport) Abzug m; (from drugs) Entzug m; **to make a ~ from a bank** von einer Bank Geld abheben

withdrawn [wɪθˈdrɔːn] 🛈 PTP of **withdraw** 🞥 ADJ person verschlossen; manner also zurückhaltend

withdrew [wɪθˈdruː] PRET of **withdraw**

wither [ˈwɪðəʳ] 🛈 VT plants etc verdörren 🞥 VI **(a)** (lit) verdorren, ausdorren; (limb) verkümmern **(b)** (fig) welken

➤ **wither away** VI = **wither 2**

withered [ˈwɪðəd] ADJ verdorrt

withering [ˈwɪðərɪŋ] ADJ heat ausdörrend; criticism, look, tone vernichtend

withhold [wɪθˈhəʊld], pret, ptp **withheld** [wɪθˈheld] VT vorenthalten; truth also verschweigen; (= refuse) verweigern; **to ~ sth from sb** jdm etw vorenthalten/verweigern

withholding tax [wɪθˈhəʊldɪŋtæks] N (US) (vom Arbeitgeber) einbehaltene Steuer

within [wɪð'ɪn] **1** PREP innerhalb (+*gen*); (*temporal also*) binnen (+*dat or* (*geh*) +*gen*); **we were ~ 100 feet of the finish** wir waren auf den letzten 100 Fuß vor dem Ziel; **we came ~ 50 feet of the summit** wir kamen bis auf 50 Fuß an den Gipfel heran; **~ his power** in seiner Macht **2** ADV (*old, liter*) innen; **from ~** von drinnen; (= *on the inside*) von innen

without [wɪð'aʊt] **1** PREP ohne; **~ a tie/passport** ohne Krawatte/(einen) Pass; **~ speaking** ohne zu sprechen, wortlos; **~ my noticing it** ohne dass ich es bemerkte; **to be ~ sth** etw nicht haben **2** ADV (*old, liter*) außen; **from ~** von draußen; (= *on the outside*) von außen

without-profits [wɪð'aʊt,prɒfɪts] ADJ *policy etc* ohne Gewinnbeteiligung

with-profits [wɪð,prɒfɪts] ADJ *policy etc* mit Gewinnbeteiligung

withstand [wɪθ'stænd], *pret, ptp* **withstood** [wɪθ'stʊd] VT standhalten (+*dat*); *climate, attack also* trotzen (+*dat*); *loss* verkraften

witless [wɪtlɪs] ADJ **to be scared ~** zu Tode erschreckt sein

witness [wɪtnɪs] **1** N **(a)** (= *person*: *Jur, fig*) Zeuge *m*, Zeugin *f*; **~ for the defence** (*Brit*) or **defense** (*US*) Zeuge *m*/Zeugin *f* der Verteidigung **(b)** (= *evidence*) Zeugnis *nt*; **to bear ~ to sth** (*lit, fig*) Zeugnis über etw (*acc*) ablegen; (*actions, events also*) von etw zeugen **2** VT **(a)** *accident* Zeuge/Zeugin sein bei or (+*gen*); *scenes* (mit)erleben; *changes* erleben **(b)** (= *testify*) bezeugen **(c)** (= *attest by signature*) *signature, will* bestätigen

witness box, (*US*) **witness stand** N Zeugenstand *m*

-witted [-wɪtɪd] ADJ SUF **dull-witted** geistig träge; **quick-witted** geistig rege

witticism [wɪtɪsɪzəm] N geistreiche Bemerkung

wittily [wɪtɪlɪ] ADV witzig, geistreich

witty [wɪtɪ] ADJ (+ER) witzig, geistreich

wives [waɪvz] PL *of* **wife**

wizard [wɪzəd] N **(a)** Zauberer *m* **(b)** (*inf*) Genie *nt*, Leuchte *f* (*inf*); **a financial ~** ein Finanzgenie *nt*

wizened [wɪznd] ADJ verschrumpelt

wk ABBR *of* **week** Wo.

WMD ABBR *of* **weapons of mass destruction**

wobble [wɒbl] **1** N Wackeln *nt* **2** VI wackeln; (*tightrope walker, dancer also, cyclist*) schwanken; (*voice, hand*) zittern; (*wheel*) eiern (*inf*); (*chin, jelly etc*) schwabbeln **3** VT rütteln an (+*dat*)

wobbly [wɒblɪ] ADJ (+ER) wackelig; *voice, notes also, hand* zitterig; *jelly* (sch)wabbelig; *wheel* eiernd; **to feel ~** wackelig auf den Beinen sein (*inf*)

woe [wəʊ] N **(a)** (*liter, hum*: *sorrow*) Jammer *m*; **~ (is me)!** weh mir!; **~ betide him who ...!** wehe dem, der ...! **(b)** (*esp pl*: = *trouble, affliction*) Kummer *m*

woeful [wəʊfʊl] ADJ (= *sad*) traurig; *neglect also, ignorance, lack* bedauerlich

wok [wɒk] N (*Cook*) Wok *m*

woke [wəʊk] PRET *of* **wake**

woken [wəʊkn] PTP *of* **wake**

wolf [wʊlf] **1** N, *pl* **wolves** Wolf *m*; **to cry ~** blinden Alarm schlagen; **to keep the ~ from the door** sich über Wasser halten **2** VT (*inf: also* **~ down**) *food* hinunterschlingen

wolf whistle (*inf*) **1** N bewundernder Pfiff **2** VI nachpfeifen

wolves [wʊlvz] PL *of* **wolf**

woman [wʊmən] **1** N, *pl* **women** Frau *f*; (= *girlfriend*) Mädchen *nt*; (= *mistress*) Geliebte *f*; **cleaning ~** Putzfrau *f*; **the little ~** (*inf*: = *wife*) die or meine Frau **2** ADJ ATTR **~ doctor** Ärztin *f*; **~ teacher** Lehrerin *f*; **~ driver** Frau *f* am Steuer

womanhood [wʊmənhʊd] N (= *women in general*) alle Frauen, die Frauen *pl*; **to reach ~** (zur) Frau werden

womanize [wʊmənaɪz] VI hinter den Frauen her sein

womanizer [wʊmənaɪzə] N Schürzenjäger *m*

womb [wuːm] N Mutterleib *m*, Gebärmutter *f* (*Med*); (*fig*) Schoß *m*

women [wɪmɪn] PL *of* **woman**

women's lib [wɪmɪnz] N (*inf*) Frauen(rechts)bewegung *f*; **women's libber** [wɪmɪnz'lɪbə'] N (*inf*) Frauenrechtlerin *f*; **women's refuge** N Frauenhaus *nt*; **women's room** N (*US*) Damentoilette *f*

won [wʌn] PRET, PTP *of* **win**

wonder [wʌndə'] **1** N **(a)** (= *feeling*) Staunen *nt*, Verwunderung *f*; **in ~** voller Staunen **(b)** (= *object or cause of ~*) Wunder *nt*; **it is a ~ that ...** es ist ein Wunder, dass ...; **no ~** (**he refused**)! kein Wunder, dass er abgelehnt hat)!; **to do** or **work ~s** Wunder wirken; **~s will never cease!** es geschehen noch Zeichen und Wunder! **2** VT **I ~ what he'll do now** ich bin gespannt, was er jetzt tun wird (*inf*); **I ~ why he did it** ich möchte (zu gern) wissen or ich wüsste (zu) gern, warum er das getan hat; **I was ~ing if you'd like to come too** möchten Sie nicht vielleicht auch kommen?; **I was ~ing when you'd realize that** ich habe mich (schon) gefragt, wann du das merkst **3** VI **(a)** (= *ask oneself, speculate*) **why do you ask? – oh, I was just ~ing** warum fragst du? – ach, nur so; **what will happen next, I ~?** ich frage mich or ich bin gespannt, was als Nächstes kommt; **I was ~ing about that** ich habe mir darüber schon Gedanken gemacht; **I expect that will be the end of the matter – I ~!** ich denke, damit ist die Angelegenheit erledigt – da habe ich meine Zweifel; **I'm ~ing about going to the party** ich habe daran gedacht, vielleicht auf die Party zu gehen; **John, I've been ~ing, is there really any point?** John, ich frage mich, ob es wirklich (einen) Zweck hat **(b)** (= *be surprised*) sich wundern; **I ~ (that) he didn't tell me** es wundert mich, dass er es mir nicht gesagt hat; **to ~ at sth** sich über etw (*acc*) wundern, über etw (*acc*) erstaunt sein

wonder IN CPDS Wunder-

wonderful ADJ, **wonderfully** ADV [wʌndəfəl, -ɪ] wunderbar

wonderland [wʌndəˌlænd] N (= *fairyland*) Wunderland *nt*; (= *wonderful place*) Paradies *nt*

wonderment [wʌndəmənt] N = **wonder 1(a)**

wondrous [wʌndrəs] (*old, liter*) ADJ wunderbar; *ways also* wundersam

wonky [wɒŋkɪ] ADJ (+ER) (*Brit inf*) *chair, marriage, grammar* wackelig; *machine* nicht (ganz) in Ordnung; **your collar's all ~** dein Kragen sitzt ganz schief

won't [wəʊnt] CONTR *of* **will not**

woo [wuː] VT *person* umwerben; (*fig*) *stardom, sleep etc* suchen; *audience etc* für sich zu gewinnen versuchen

wood [wʊd] **1** N **(a)** (= *material*) Holz *nt*; **touch ~!** (*esp Brit*), **knock on ~!** (*esp US*) dreimal auf Holz geklopft! **(b)** (= *small forest: also* **~s**) Wald *m*; **we're not out of the ~s yet** (*fig*) wir sind noch nicht über den Berg or aus dem Schneider (*inf*); **he can't see the ~ for the trees** (*Brit: prov*) er sieht den Wald vor (lauter) Bäumen nicht (*prov*) **2** ADJ ATTR (= *made of ~*) Holz-; **~ floor** Holzboden *m*

wood: wood carving N (Holz)schnitzerei *f*; **woodcutter** N Holzfäller(in) *m(f)*; (*of logs*) Holzhacker(in) *m(f)*

wooded [wʊdɪd] ADJ bewaldet

wooden [wʊdn] ADJ **(a)** Holz-; **~ chair** Holzstuhl *m*; **the ~ horse** das hölzerne Pferd **(b)** (*fig*) *expression, performance* hölzern

wooden spoon N (*lit*) Holzlöffel *m*; (*fig*) Trostpreis *m*

wood: woodland N Waldland *nt*; **woodpecker** N Specht *m*; **woodpile** N Holzhaufen *m*; **woodshed** N Holzschuppen *m*; **woodwind** N Holzblasinstrument *nt*; **the ~(s), the ~ section** die Holzbläser *pl*; **woodwork** N **(a)** Holzarbeit *f*, (= *craft*) Tischlerei *f* **(b)** (= *wooden parts*) Holzteile *pl*; **to come out of the ~** (*fig*) aus dem Unterholz or der Versenkung hervorkommen; **woodworm** N Holzwurm *m*

woody [wʊdɪ] ADJ (+ER) **(a)** (= *wooded*) waldig, bewaldet **(b)** (= *like wood in texture*) holzig

woof [wʊf] **1** N (*of dog*) Wuff *nt* **2** VI kläffen; **~, ~!** wau, wau!

wool [wʊl] **1** N Wolle *f*; (= *cloth*) Wollstoff *m*; **to pull the ~ over sb's eyes** (*inf*) jdm Sand in die Augen streuen (*inf*) **2** ADJ Woll-; (= *made of wool also*) aus Wolle; **~ coat** Wollmantel *m*

woollen, (*US*) **woolen** [wʊlən] **1** ADJ Woll-; (= *made of wool also*) wollen, aus Wolle; **~ blanket** Wolldecke *f* **2** N **woollens** PL (= *garments*) Wollsachen *pl*; (= *fabrics, blankets*) Wollwaren *pl*

woolly, (*US*) **wooly** [wʊlɪ] **1** ADJ (+ER) **(a)** wollig; (= *soft also*) flauschig **(b)** (*fig pej*) *thinking, idea* verworren **2** N (*inf*: = *sweater etc*) Pulli *m* (*inf*); **winter woollies** (*esp Brit*: = *sweaters etc*) dicke Wollsachen *pl* (*inf*); (*esp US*: = *underwear*) Wollene *pl* (*inf*)

woozy [wuːzɪ] ADJ (+ER) (*inf*) duselig (*inf*)

word [wɜːd] **1** N **(a)** Wort nt; ~s Wörter pl; (in meaningful sequence, remarks) Worte pl; **foreign** ~s Fremdwörter pl; **for** ~ Wort für Wort; (= exactly also) wortwörtlich; **cold isn't the** ~ **for it** kalt ist gar kein Ausdruck (dafür); ~s **cannot describe it** so etwas kann man nicht beschreiben; **too funny for** ~s unbeschreiblich komisch; **to put one's thoughts into** ~s seine Gedanken in Worte fassen; **in a** ~ mit einem Wort, kurz gesagt; **(not) in so many** ~s (nicht) direkt or ausdrücklich; **in other** ~s mit anderen Worten; **in one's own** ~s mit eigenen Worten; **the last** ~ (fig) der letzte Schrei (in an +dat); **a** ~ **of advice** ein Rat(schlag) m; **a** ~ **of warning** eine Warnung; **I can't get a** ~ **out of him** ich kann kein Wort aus ihm herausbekommen; **by** ~ **of mouth** durch mündliche Überlieferung; **to say a few** ~s ein paar Worte sprechen; **to be lost** or **at a loss for** ~s nicht wissen, was man sagen soll; **to take sb at his** ~ jdn beim Wort nehmen; **to have a** ~ **with sb (about sth)** (= talk to) mit jdm (über etw) sprechen; **to have a** ~ **with sb** (= reprimand, discipline) jdn ins Gebet nehmen; **John, could I have a** ~? John, kann ich dich mal sprechen?; **(could I have) a** ~ **in your ear?** kann ich Sie bitte allein or unter vier Augen sprechen?; **you took the** ~s **out of my mouth** du hast mir das Wort aus dem Mund genommen; **to put in** or **say a (good)** ~ **for sb** für jdn ein gutes Wort einlegen; **nobody had a good** ~ **to say for him** niemand wusste etwas Gutes über ihn zu sagen; **without a** ~ ohne ein Wort; **don't say** or **breathe a** ~ **about it** sag aber bitte keinen Ton or kein Sterbenswörtchen (inf) davon; **to have** ~s **with sb** (= quarrel) mit jdm eine Auseinandersetzung haben; ~ **of honour** (Brit) or **honor** (US) Ehrenwort nt; **a man of his** ~ ein Mann, der zu seinem Wort steht; **to keep one's** ~ sein Wort halten; **I give you my** ~ ich gebe dir mein (Ehren)wort; **to break one's** ~ sein Wort brechen; **take my** ~ **for it** das kannst du mir glauben; **it's his** ~ **against mine** Aussage steht gegen Aussage; **to give the** ~ **(to do sth)** (Mil) das Kommando geben(, etw zu tun); **just say the** ~ sag nur ein Wort **(b) words** PL (= text, lyrics) Text m

(c) NO PL (= message, news) Nachricht f; ~ **went round that ...** es ging die Nachricht um, dass ...; **is there any** ~ **from John yet?** schon von John gehört?; **to send** ~ Nachricht geben; **to send** ~ **to sb** jdn benachrichtigen; **to spread the** ~ **(around)** (inf) es allen sagen (inf); **the** ~ **on the street is ...** man sagt, ... **2** VT (in Worten) ausdrücken, formulieren; speech abfassen

word: wordcount N (Comput) Wortzählung f; **wordcrunch** VT (Comput inf) text (nach Wörtern) analysieren; **word game** N Buchstabenspiel nt

wording [ˈwɜːdɪŋ] N Formulierung f

word: word order N Satzfolge f; **word-perfect** ADJ sicher im Text; **to be** ~ den Text perfekt beherrschen; **wordplay** N Wortspiel nt; **word processing** N Textverarbeitung f; **word-processing** ADJ, ATTR Textverarbeitungs-; **word processor** N (= machine) Text(verarbeitungs)system nt; (= software) Text(verarbeitungs)programm nt; **wordwrap** N (Comput) (automatischer) Zeilenumbruch

wordy [ˈwɜːdɪ] ADJ (+ER) wortreich, langatmig (pej)

wore [wɔː] PRET of **wear**

work [wɜːk] **1** N **(a)** Arbeit f; (Art, Liter. = product) Werk nt; **have you got any** ~ **for me?** haben Sie was für mich zu tun?; (= employment) haben Sie Arbeit für mich?; **he doesn't like** ~ er arbeitet nicht gern; **that's a good piece of** ~ das ist gute Arbeit; **is this all your own** ~? haben Sie das alles selbst gemacht?; **when** ~ **begins on the new bridge** wenn die Arbeiten an der neuen Brücke anfangen; **to be at** ~ **(on sth)** (an etw dat) arbeiten; **to do a good day's** ~ ein schönes Stück Arbeit leisten; **nice** or **good** ~! gut or super (inf) gemacht!; **we've a lot of** ~ **to do before this choir can give a concert** wir haben noch viel zu tun, ehe dieser Chor ein Konzert geben kann; **you need to do some more** ~ **on your accent** Sie müssen noch an Ihrem Akzent arbeiten; **to get** or **set to** ~ **on sth** sich an etw (acc) machen; **I've been trying to get some** ~ **done** ich habe versucht zu arbeiten; **to put a lot of** ~ **into sth** eine Menge Arbeit in etw (acc) stecken; **to get on with one's** ~ sich (wieder) an die Arbeit machen; **to make short** or **quick** ~ **of sb/sth** mit jdm/etw kurzen Prozess machen; **to be (out) at** ~ arbeiten sein; **to go out to** ~ arbeiten gehen; **to be out of** ~ arbeitslos sein; **to have an** ~ eine Stelle haben; **how long does it take you to get to** ~? wie lange brauchst du, um zu deiner Arbeitsstelle zu kommen?; **at** ~ am Arbeitsplatz; **to be off** ~ (am Arbeitsplatz) fehlen; **a** ~ **of art** ein Kunstwerk nt; **a**

~ **of literature** ein literarisches Werk; **a fine piece of** ~ eine schöne Arbeit

(b) works SING or PL (Brit: = factory) Betrieb m, Fabrik f; **gas/ steel** ~s Gas-/Stahlwerk nt; ~s **manager** Werks- or Betriebsleiter(in) m(f)

(c) (inf) **the works** PL alles Drum und Dran; **we had fantastic food, wine, brandy, the** ~s es gab tolles Essen, Wein, Kognak, alle Schikanen (inf)

2 VI **(a)** person arbeiten (at an +dat); **to** ~ **toward(s)/for sth** auf etw (acc) hin/für etw arbeiten; **to** ~ **for better conditions** etc sich für bessere Bedingungen etc einsetzen; **these factors which** ~ **in our favour** (Brit) or **favor** (US) diese Faktoren, die zu unseren Gunsten arbeiten

(b) (= function, operate) funktionieren, klappen (inf); (medicine, spell) wirken; (= be successful) klappen (inf); **it won't** ~ das klappt nicht; **to get sth** ~**ing** etw in Gang bringen

(c) (= move gradually) **to** ~ **loose** sich lockern; **to** ~ **along** sich entlangarbeiten; **OK, I'm** ~**ing (a)round to it** okay, das mache ich schon noch

3 VT **(a)** employees, students arbeiten lassen, heranziehen (inf); muscles trainieren; **to** ~ **oneself/sb hard** sich/jdn nicht schonen

(b) (= operate) machine bedienen; lever, brake betätigen

(c) change, cure bewirken, herbeiführen; **to** ~ **it (so that ...)** (inf) es so deichseln(, dass ...) (inf)

(d) wood, metal, land bearbeiten; dough, clay also kneten; mine ausbeuten; ~ **the flour in gradually** mischen Sie das Mehl allmählich unter

(e) (= move gradually) **to** ~ **one's hands free** seine Hände freibekommen; **to** ~ **sth loose** etw losbekommen; **to** ~ **one's way to the top** sich nach oben arbeiten or kämpfen; **to** ~ **one's way up from nothing** sich von ganz unten hocharbeiten; **he** ~**ed his way across the rock face/through the tunnel** er überquerte die Felswand/kroch durch den Tunnel

➤ **work in 1** VT SEP **(a)** (= rub in) einarbeiten **(b)** (in book, speech) reference etc einbauen (into in +acc) **(c)** (in schedule etc) einschieben **2** VI (= fit in) passen (with in +acc)

➤ **work off** VT SEP debts, fat abarbeiten; energy loswerden

➤ **work on 1** VT SEP lid, washer darauf bringen **2** VI +PREP OBJ **(a)** car, book, subject, accent arbeiten an (+dat); **who's working on this case?** wer bearbeitet diesen Fall?; **we haven't solved it yet but we're still working on it** wir haben es noch nicht gelöst, aber wir sind dabei; **if we work on him a little longer we might persuade him** wenn wir ihn noch ein Weilchen bearbeiten, können wir ihn vielleicht überreden **(b)** evidence, assumption ausgehen von; principle (person) ausgehen von; (machine) arbeiten nach

➤ **work out 1** VI **(a)** (puzzle, sum etc) aufgehen **(b)** (= amount to) **that works out at £105** das macht £ 105; **it works out more expensive in the end** am Ende kommt or ist es teurer **(c)** (= succeed) funktionieren, klappen (inf); **things didn't work out at all well for him** es ist ihm alles schief gegangen; **things didn't work out that way** es kam ganz anders **(d)** (in gym etc) trainieren **2** VT SEP **(a)** (= solve, calculate) herausbringen; mathematical problem lösen; problem fertig werden mit; sum ausrechnen; **you can work that out for yourself** das kannst du dir (doch) selbst denken; **things will always work themselves out** Probleme lösen sich stets von selbst **(b)** (= devise) scheme (sich dat) ausdenken; (in detail) ausarbeiten **(c)** (= understand) schlau werden aus (+dat); **can you work out where we are on the map?** kannst du herausfinden, wo wir auf der Karte sind?; **I can't work out why it went wrong** ich kann nicht verstehen, wieso es nicht geklappt hat

➤ **work through** VI +PREP OBJ sich (durch)arbeiten durch

➤ **work up** VT SEP **(a)** enthusiasm (in oneself) aufbringen; appetite sich (dat) holen; courage sich (dat) machen; **to work one's way up (through the ranks)** von der Pike auf dienen; **to work up a sweat** richtig ins Schwitzen kommen; **to be worked up** aufgeregt sein; **to get worked up** sich aufregen; **to work oneself up** sich erhitzen **(b)** lecture, theme, notes ausarbeiten

➤ **work up to** VI +PREP OBJ proposal etc zusteuern auf (+acc)

workable [ˈwɜːkəbl] ADJ plan, system, agreement durchführbar; solution, alternative machbar; relationship funktionierend

workaholic [ˌwɜːkəˈhɒlɪk] N (inf) Arbeitswütige(r) mf, Arbeitstier nt

work: **workbench** N Werkbank f; **workbook** N Arbeitsheft nt; **workday** N (esp US) Arbeitstag m; (= weekday) Werktag m; **work environment** N Arbeitsumfeld nt

worker [ˈwɜːkə] N Arbeiter(in) m(f); ~ **representation** Arbeitnehmervertretung f; ~ **representative** Arbeitnehmervertreter(in) m(f)

work: **work ethic** N Arbeitsmoral f; **workforce** N Arbeitskräfte pl; **workhorse** N (lit, fig) Arbeitspferd nt; **workhouse** N (Brit Hist) Armenhaus nt

working [ˈwɜːkɪŋ] **1** ADJ (a) population berufstätig; (Comm) partner aktiv; ~ **man** Arbeiter m; ~ **woman** berufstätige Frau **(b)** (= spent in or used for ~, provisional) Arbeits-; majority arbeitsfähig; ~ **hours** Arbeitszeit f; **during ~ hours** während der Arbeitszeit; **your order will be sent within three ~ days** ihre Bestellung wird innerhalb von drei Werktagen geschickt; **in ~ order** funktionsfähig; **in good/perfect ~ order** voll funktionsfähig; ~ **knowledge** Grundkenntnisse pl **(c)** farm, mill, steam train in Betrieb **2** N **workings** PL (= way sth works) Arbeitsweise f, Funktionsweise f; **in order to understand the ~s of this machine** um zu verstehen, wie die Maschine funktioniert

working: **working capital** N Betriebskapital nt; **working class** N (also **-es**) Arbeiterklasse f; **working-class** ADJ der Arbeiterklasse; (pej) proletenhaft; **to be ~** zur Arbeiterklasse gehören; **working environment** N Arbeitsumfeld nt; **working life** N (of machine part) Lebensdauer f; (of person) Berufsleben nt; **working lunch** N Arbeitsessen nt; **working memory** N (Comput) Arbeitsspeicher m; **working party** N (Arbeits)ausschuss m; **working relationship** N Zusammenarbeit f; **to have a good ~ with sb** mit jdm gut zusammenarbeiten

work: **work-in-progress** N (Fin) laufende Arbeiten pl; **workload** N Arbeit(slast) f; **workman** N Handwerker m; **workmanship** [ˈwɜːkmənʃɪp] N Arbeit(squalität) f; **workmate** N (inf) (Arbeits)kollege m, (Arbeits)kollegin f; **work-out** N (Sport) Training nt; **work permit** N Arbeitserlaubnis f; **workplace** N Arbeitsplatz m; **in** or **at the ~** am Arbeitsplatz; **workroom** N Arbeitszimmer nt

works [wɜːks] PL = **work** 1(b, c)

works council, works committee N (esp Brit) Betriebsrat m

work: **worksheet** N Arbeitsblatt nt; **workshop** N Werkstatt f; **a music ~** ein Musik-Workshop m; **work station** N Arbeitsplatz m; (Comput) Arbeitsplatzstation f; **work surface** N Arbeitsfläche f; **worktable** N Arbeitstisch m; **worktop** N (Brit) Arbeitsfläche f; **work-to-rule** N Dienst m nach Vorschrift; **workweek** N (esp US) Arbeitswoche f

world [wɜːld] N Welt f; **in the ~** auf der Welt; **all over the ~** auf der ganzen Welt; **he jets all over the ~** er jettet in der Weltgeschichte herum; **to go (a)round the ~** eine Weltreise machen; **to feel** or **be on top of the ~** munter und fidel sein; **it's not the end of the ~!** (inf) davon geht die Welt nicht unter! (inf); **it's a small ~** wie klein doch die Welt ist; **to live in a ~ of one's own** in seiner eigenen (kleinen) Welt leben; **the New/Third World** die Neue/Dritte Welt; **the business ~** die Geschäftswelt; **the animal ~** die Tierwelt; **woman of the ~** Frau f von Welt; **to come** or **go down in the ~** herunterkommen; **to go up** or **to rise in the ~** es (in der Welt) zu etwas bringen; **he had the ~ at his feet** die ganze Welt lag ihm zu Füßen; **to lead the ~ in sth** in etw (dat) führend sein; **to come into the ~** zur Welt kommen; **to have the best of both ~s** das eine tun und das andere nicht lassen; **out of this ~** (inf) fantastisch; **to bring sb into the ~** jdn zur Welt bringen; **to be (all) alone in the ~** allein auf der Welt sein; **nothing in the ~** nichts auf der Welt; **what/who in the ~** was/wer in aller Welt; **it did him a ~ of good** es hat ihm (unwahrscheinlich) gut getan; **they're ~s apart** sie sind total verschieden; **for all the ~ like …** beinahe wie …; **to mean the ~ to sb** jdm alles bedeuten; **to think the ~ of sb** große Stücke auf jdn halten

world IN CPDS Welt-; **world-beater** N (Brit inf) **to be a ~** unschlagbar sein; **world champion** N Weltmeister(in) m(f); **world championship** N Weltmeisterschaft f; **world-class** ADJ Weltklasse-, der Weltklasse; **world-famous** ADJ weltberühmt; **world leader** N (a) (Pol) **the ~s** die führenden Regierungschefs der Welt **(b)** (Comm: = company) weltweiter Marktführer

worldly [ˈwɜːldlɪ] ADJ (+ER) **(a)** (= material) success, ambition materiell **(b)** weltlich; person weltlich gesinnt; (= sophisticated) manner weltmännisch

world: **world music** N Weltmusik f; **world picture** N Weltbild nt; **world power** N Weltmacht f; **world rankings** PL Weltrangliste f; **world record** N Weltrekord m; **world record holder** N Weltrekordinhaber(in) m(f); **world's champion** N (US) Weltmeister(in) m(f); **world's record** N (US) Weltrekord m; **world-view** N Weltbild nt; **World War One, World War I** N Erster Weltkrieg; **World War Two, World War II** N Zweiter Weltkrieg; **world-weary** ADJ lebensmüde; **worldwide** ADJ, ADV weltweit; **World Wide Web** N World Wide Web nt

worm [wɜːm] **1** N (lit, fig inf) Wurm m; (= wood ~) Holzwurm m; ~**s** (Med) Würmer pl; **to open a can of ~s** in ein Wespennest stechen **2** VT (= wriggle) zwängen; **to ~ one's way along/through/into sth** sich an etw (dat) entlangdrücken/durch etw (acc) durchschlängeln/in etw (acc) hineinzwängen; **to ~ one's way into a group** sich in eine Gruppe einschleichen; **to ~ one's way into sb's affection** sich bei jdm einschmeicheln; **to ~ sth out of sb** jdm etw entlocken

worn [wɔːn] **1** PTP of **wear** **2** ADJ (a) (= ~-out) coat abgetragen; carpet abgetreten; tyre abgefahren **(b)** (= weary) smile müde; person angegriffen

worn-out [ˈwɔːnaʊt] ADJ ATTR, **worn out** ADJ PRED carpet abgetreten; person erschöpft

worried [ˈwʌrɪd] ADJ besorgt (about, by wegen); (= anxious also) beunruhigt; **to be ~ sick** krank vor Sorge(n) sein (inf)

worriedly [ˈwʌrɪdlɪ] ADV besorgt; (= anxiously also) beunruhigt

worrier [ˈwʌrɪə] N **she's a great ~** sie macht sich (dat) immerzu Sorgen

worry [ˈwʌrɪ] **1** N Sorge f; **I know it's a ~ for you** ich weiß, es macht dir Sorgen; **that's the least of my worries** das macht mir noch am wenigsten Sorgen; **no worries!** (inf) kein Problem! **2** VT **(a)** (= cause concern) beunruhigen, Sorgen machen (+dat); **it worries me** es macht mir Sorgen; **to ~ oneself sick** or **silly (about** or **over sth)** (inf) sich krank machen vor Sorge (um or wegen etw) (inf) **(b)** (= bother) stören; **to ~ sb with sth** jdn mit etw stören **3** VI sich sorgen, sich (dat) Sorgen machen (about, over um, wegen); **he worries a lot** er macht sich immer so viel Sorgen; **don't ~!, not to ~!** keine Angst or Sorge!; **don't ~, I'll do it** lass mal, das mach ich schon; **don't ~ about letting me know** es macht nichts, wenn du mich nicht benachrichtigen kannst

worrying [ˈwʌrɪɪŋ] **1** ADJ problem beunruhigend, Besorgnis erregend; **it's very ~** es macht mir große Sorge **2** N ~ **won't help** sich nur Sorgen machen, nützt nichts

worse [wɜːs] **1** ADJ COMP of **bad** schlechter; (morally, with bad consequences) schlimmer; **the patient is getting ~** der Zustand des Patienten verschlechtert sich; **and to make matters ~** und zu allem Übel; **his "corrections" only made it ~** er hat alles nur verschlimmbessert; **it could have been ~** es hätte schlimmer kommen können; ~ **luck!** (so ein) Pech!; **he's none the ~ for it** es ist ihm nichts dabei passiert **2** ADV COMP of **badly** schlechter; **to be ~ off than …** schlechter dran sein als … (inf); **I could do a lot ~ than accept their offer** es wäre bestimmt kein Fehler, wenn ich das Angebot annähme **3** N Schlechtere(s) nt; (morally, with regard to consequences) Schlimmere(s) nt; **there is ~ to come** es kommt noch schlimmer; **it's changed for the ~** es hat sich zum Schlechteren gewendet

worsen [ˈwɜːsn] **1** VT verschlechtern **2** VI sich verschlechtern

worship [ˈwɜːʃɪp] **1** N **(a)** (of God, person etc) Verehrung f; **place of ~** Andachtsstätte f; (non-Christian) Kultstätte f **(b)** (Brit) **Your Worship** (to judge) Euer Ehren/Gnaden; (to mayor) (verehrter or sehr geehrter) Herr Bürgermeister **2** VT anbeten; **he ~ped the ground she walked on** er betete den Boden unter ihren Füßen an **3** VI (Rel) den Gottesdienst abhalten; (RC) die Messe feiern

worst [wɜːst] **1** ADJ SUPERL of **bad** schlechteste(r, s); (morally, with regard to consequences) schlimmste(r, s); **the ~ possible time** die ungünstigste Zeit **2** ADV SUPERL of **badly** am schlechtesten **3** N **the ~ is over** das Schlimmste ist vorbei; **at (the) ~** schlimmstenfalls; **if the ~ comes to the ~, if ~ comes to ~** (US) wenn alle Stricke reißen (inf)

worst-case scenario [wɜːstkeɪsrˈnɑːrɪəʊ] N Schlimmstfall m

worth [wɜːθ] **1** ADJ wert; **it's ~ £5** es ist £ 5 wert; **it's not ~ £5** es ist keine £ 5 wert; **what's this ~?** was or wie viel ist das wert?; **it's ~ a great deal to me** (sentimentally) es bedeutet mir sehr viel; **will you do this for me? – what's it ~ to you?** tust du das für mich? – was ist es dir wert?; **he's ~ all his brothers put together** er ist so viel wert wie alle seine Brüder zusammen; **for all one is ~** so sehr man nur kann; **you need to exploit the idea for all it's ~** du musst aus der Idee machen, was du nur kannst; **for what it's ~, I personally don't think ...** wenn mich einer fragt, ich persönlich glaube nicht, dass ...; **to be ~ it** sich lohnen; **to be ~ sth** etw wert sein; **it's not ~ the trouble** es ist der Mühe nicht wert; **the museum is ~ a visit** das Museum ist einen Besuch wert; **life isn't ~ living** das Leben ist nicht lebenswert; **is there anything ~ seeing in this town?** gibt es in dieser Stadt etwas Sehenswertes?; **hardly ~ mentioning** kaum der Rede wert; **it's not ~ having** es ist nichts; **if a thing's ~ doing, it's ~ doing well** wennschon, dennschon

2 N Wert m; **hundreds of pounds' ~ of books** Bücher im Werte von hunderten von Pfund; **to show one's true ~** zeigen, was man wirklich wert ist

worthiness [ˈwɜːðɪnɪs] N (of charity, cause etc) Wert m; (of person) Ehrenhaftigkeit f

worthless [ˈwɜːθlɪs] ADJ wertlos; person also nichtsnutzig

worthwhile [ˈwɜːθˈwaɪl] ADJ lohnend attr; **to be ~** sich lohnen; (= worth the trouble also) der Mühe (gen) wert sein

worthy [ˈwɜːðɪ] ADJ (+ER) **(a)** ehrenwert; opponent würdig; cause löblich **(b)** PRED wert, würdig; **to be ~ of sb/sth** jds/einer Sache würdig sein (geh)

would [wʊd] PRET of will[1] MODAL AUX VB **(a)** (conditional) **if you asked him he ~ do it** wenn du ihn fragtest, würde er es tun; **if you had asked him he ~ have done it** wenn du ihn gefragt hättest, hätte er es getan; **I thought you ~ want to know** ich dachte, du wüsstest es gerne or du würdest es gerne wissen; **if I were you, I ~ ...** wenn ich du wäre, würde ich ...; **you ~ think ...** man sollte meinen ...; **she said she ~ come** sie sagte, sie würde kommen or sie käme; **I said I ~, so I will** ich habe gesagt, ich würde es tun und ich werde es auch tun **(b)** (emph) **I ~n't know** keine Ahnung; **you ~!** das sieht dir ähnlich!; **he ~ have to come right now** ausgerechnet jetzt muss er kommen; **you ~ say that, ~n't you!** von dir kann man ja nichts anderes erwarten; **it ~ have to rain** es muss auch ausgerechnet regnen! **(c)** (insistence) **he ~n't listen** er wollte partout nicht zuhören; **he ~n't be told** er wollte sich (dat) einfach nichts sagen lassen **(d)** (conjecture) **it ~ seem so** es sieht wohl so aus; **it ~ have been about 8 o'clock** es war (wohl) so ungefähr 8 Uhr; **you ~n't have a cigarette, ~ you?** Sie hätten nicht zufällig eine Zigarette? **(e)** (= wish) möchten; **what ~ you have me do?** was soll ich tun? **(f)** (in questions) **~ he come?** würde er vielleicht kommen?; **~ he have come?** wäre er gekommen?; **~ you mind closing the window?** würden Sie bitte das Fenster schließen?; **~ you care for some tea?** hätten Sie gerne etwas Tee? **(g)** (habit) **he ~ paint it each year** er strich es jedes Jahr

would-be [ˈwʊdbiː] ADJ ATTR **~ poet** jemand, der gerne (ein) Dichter würde; (pej) Möchtegerndichter(in) m(f)

wouldn't [ˈwʊdnt] CONTR of would not

wound[1] [wuːnd] **1** N (lit) Wunde f; (fig also) Kränkung f; **to open** or **re-open old ~s** (fig) alte Wunden öffnen **2** VT (lit) verwunden; (fig) verletzen **3** N **the ~ed** pl die Verwundeten pl

wound[2] [waʊnd] PRET, PTP of wind[2]

wove [wəʊv] PRET of weave

woven [ˈwəʊvən] PTP of weave

wow [waʊ] INTERJ hui (inf), Mann (inf)

WPC (Brit) N ABBR of Woman Police Constable Polizistin f

wrack [ræk] N, VT = rack[1], rack[2]

wrangle [ˈræŋgl] **1** N Gerangel nt no pl **2** VI streiten, rangeln (about um)

wrap [ræp] **1** N **(a)** (= garment) Umhangtuch nt **(b)** **under ~s** (lit) verhüllt; car, weapon getarnt; (fig) geheim **2** VT einwickeln; **shall I ~ it for you?** soll ich es Ihnen einwickeln?; **to ~ sth (a)round sth** etw um etw wickeln; **to ~ one's arms**

(a)round sb jdn in die Arme schließen; **to be ~ped in sth** (fig) in etw gehüllt sein **3** VI (Comput) **the lines ~ automatically** der Zeilenumbruch erfolgt automatisch

▶ **wrap up 1** VT SEP **(a)** (lit, fig) einpacken, einwickeln **(b)** (inf) deal unter Dach und Fach bringen; **that just about wraps things up for today** das wärs (dann wohl) für heute **(c)** **to be wrapped up in sb/sth** in jdm/etw aufgehen **2** VI (= dress warmly) sich warm einpacken (inf)

wrapper [ˈræpər] N Verpackung f; (of sweets) Papier(chen) nt; (of book) (Schutz)umschlag m

wrapping [ˈræpɪŋ] N Verpackung f (round +gen, von)

wrapping paper N Packpapier nt; (decorative) Geschenkpapier nt

wrath [rɒθ] N Zorn m; (liter: of storm) Wut f

wreak [riːk] VT destruction anrichten; chaos also stiften

wreath [riːθ] N, pl **-s** [riːðz] Kranz m

wreathe [riːð] VT (= encircle) (um)winden; (clouds, mist) umhüllen; (= entwine) flechten

wreck [rek] **1** N (= wrecked ship etc, fig inf = person) Wrack nt; (fig inf: = old bicycle, furniture etc) Trümmerhaufen m; **he was killed in a car ~** (US) er kam bei einem Autounfall ums Leben; **I'm a ~, I feel a ~** ich bin ein (völliges) Wrack; (= exhausted) ich bin vollkommen fertig or erledigt **2** VT **(a)** ship, train, plane einen Totalschaden verursachen an (+dat); car zu Schrott fahren (inf); machine, mechanism kaputtmachen (inf); furniture, house zerstören **(b)** (fig) hopes, plans, chances zunichte machen; marriage zerrütten; career, health, sb's life ruinieren; party, holiday verderben

wreckage [ˈrekɪdʒ] N (lit, fig) Trümmer pl; (of ship also) Wrackteile pl; (of house, town) Ruinen pl

wrecker [ˈrekər] N **(a)** (US = breaker, salvager) Schrotthändler(in) m(f); (for buildings) Abbrucharbeiter(in) m(f) **(b)** (US: = breakdown van) Abschleppwagen m

wren [ren] N Zaunkönig m

wrench [rentʃ] **1** N **(a)** (= tug) Ruck m; **he gave his shoulder a nasty ~** er hat sich (dat) die Schulter schlimm verrenkt; **to be a ~** (fig) wehtun **(b)** (= tool) Schraubenschlüssel m **2** VT **(a)** (= tug) winden; **to ~ sth (away) from sb** jdm etw entwinden; **to ~ a door open** eine Tür aufzwingen **(b)** (Med) **to ~ one's ankle** sich (dat) den Fuß verrenken **(c)** (fig) reißen

wrest [rest] VT **to ~ sth from sb/sth** jdm/einer Sache etw abringen; leadership, title jdm etw entreißen

wrestle [ˈresl] **1** VT ringen mit; (Sport also) einen Ringkampf bestreiten gegen **2** VI **(a)** (lit) ringen (for sth um etw) **(b)** (fig: with problem, conscience etc) ringen, kämpfen (with mit)

wrestler [ˈreslər] N Ringkämpfer m; (modern) Ringer(in) m(f)

wrestling [ˈreslɪŋ] N Ringen nt

wretch [retʃ] N **(a)** (miserable) armer Schlucker (inf) **(b)** (= nuisance) Blödmann m (inf); (= child) Schlingel m

wretched [ˈretʃɪd] ADJ **(a)** elend; conditions, life erbärmlich; (= unhappy) (tod)unglücklich **(b)** weather, novel, player miserabel (inf); (inf: = damned) verflixt (inf), Mist- (inf)

wriggle [ˈrɪgl] **1** N Schlängeln nt no pl; (of child, fish) Zappeln nt no pl **2** VT toes, ears wackeln mit; **to ~ one's way through sth** sich durch etw (hin)durchwinden or -schlängeln **3** VI (also ~ about or around) (worm, snake) sich schlängeln; (fish) sich winden, zappeln; (person) (restlessly, excitedly) zappeln; (in embarrassment) sich winden; **to ~ along/down** sich vorwärts/nach unten schlängeln; **she managed to ~ free** es gelang ihr, sich loszuwinden

▶ **wriggle out** VI (lit) sich herauswinden (of aus); (fig also) sich herausmanövrieren (of aus); **he's wriggled (his way) out of it** er hat sich gedrückt

wring [rɪŋ] vb: pret, ptp **wrung** VT **(a)** (also ~ out) clothes etc auswringen; **to ~ sth out of from sb** etw aus jdm herausquetschen **(b)** hands (in distress) ringen; **to ~ a duck's neck** einer Ente (dat) den Hals umdrehen; **I could have wrung his neck** ich hätte ihm den Hals umdrehen können

wringing [ˈrɪŋɪŋ] ADJ (also ~ wet) tropfnass; person also patschnass (inf)

wrinkle [ˈrɪŋkl] **1** N (in clothes, paper) Knitter m; (on skin, in stocking) Falte f **2** VT verknittern; **to ~ one's nose** die Nase rümpfen; **to ~ one's brow** die Stirne runzeln **3** VI (sheet, material) (ver)knittern; (stockings) Falten schlagen; (skin etc) faltig werden

wrinkled [ˈrɪŋkld] ADJ sheet, skirt, paper zerknittert; skin faltig; brow gerunzelt; apple, old man/woman schrumpelig

wrinkly [ˈrɪŋklɪ] ADJ (+ER) schrumpelig; fabric zerknittert

wrist [rɪst] N Handgelenk nt

wrist: wristband [ˈrɪstˌbænd] N Armband nt; (Sport) Schweißband nt; **wrist rest** N (Comput) Handballenauflage f; **wristwatch** N Armbanduhr f

writ [rɪt] N (Jur) Verfügung f; **to issue a ~** eine Verfügung herausgeben

write [raɪt], pret **wrote** or (obs) **writ** [rɪt], ptp **written** or (obs) **writ** [rɪt] **1** VT (also Comput) schreiben; cheque ausstellen; notes sich (dat) machen; **he wrote me a letter** er schrieb mir einen Brief; **he wrote himself a note so that he wouldn't forget** er machte sich (dat) eine Notiz, um sich zu erinnern; **how is that written?** wie schreibt man das?; **to ~ sth to disk** etw auf Diskette schreiben; **it was written all over his face** es stand ihm im or auf dem Gesicht geschrieben
2 VI schreiben; **to ~ to sb** jdm schreiben; **we ~ to each other** wir schreiben uns; **that's nothing to ~ home about** (inf) das ist nichts Weltbewegendes

➤ **write away** VI schreiben; **to write away for sth** etw anfordern

➤ **write back** VI zurückschreiben

➤ **write down** VT SEP **(a)** (= make a note of) aufschreiben; (= record, put in writing) niederschreiben **(b)** (Comm, Fin) abschreiben

➤ **write in** **1** VT SEP **(a)** correction etc hineinschreiben (prep obj in +acc) **(b)** condition, provision aufnehmen **2** VI schreiben (to an +acc); **to write in for sth** etw anfordern

➤ **write off** **1** VI = **write away 2** VT SEP **(a)** (Fin, fig) abschreiben **(b)** car etc (driver) zu Schrott fahren (inf)

➤ **write out** VT SEP **(a)** (in full) notes ausarbeiten; name etc ausschreiben **(b)** cheque, prescription ausstellen **(c)** actor, character einen Abgang schaffen (+dat)

➤ **write up** VT SEP **(a)** notes ausarbeiten; report, diary schreiben **(b)** (Comm, Fin) höher bewerten or ansetzen

write-off N **(a)** (= car etc) Totalschaden m; (inf: = holiday, picnic etc) Katastrophe f (inf) **(b)** (Comm) Abschreibung f

write-protected [ˈraɪtprəˌtektɪd] ADJ (Comput) schreibgeschützt

writer [ˈraɪtə'] N Schreiber(in) m(f); (of report etc also) Autor(in) m(f); (as profession) Schriftsteller(in) m(f); **he's a very poor ~** er schreibt sehr schlecht

write-up [ˈraɪtʌp] N Pressebericht m; (of play, film) Kritik f

writhe [raɪð] VI sich krümmen, sich winden (with, in vor +dat)

writing [ˈraɪtɪŋ] N Schrift f; (= act, profession) Schreiben nt; (= inscription) Inschrift f; **in ~** schriftlich; **permission in ~** schriftliche Genehmigung; **this is a fantastic piece of ~** das ist fantastisch geschrieben; **his ~s** seine Werke or Schriften; **the ~ is on the wall for them** ihre Stunde hat geschlagen

writing IN CPDS Schreib-; **writing desk** N Schreibtisch m; **writing pad** N Schreib- or Notizblock m

written [ˈrɪtn] **1** PTP of **write 2** ADJ examination, statement, evidence schriftlich; language Schrift-; word geschrieben; constitution schriftlich niedergelegt

wrong [rɒŋ] **1** ADJ **(a)** falsch; **to be ~** nicht stimmen; (answer also) falsch sein; (person) Unrecht haben; (watch) falsch gehen; **it's all ~** das ist völlig verkehrt or falsch; (= not true) das stimmt alles nicht; **I was ~ about him** ich habe mich in ihm getäuscht; **you were ~ in thinking he did it** du hast Unrecht gehabt, als du dachtest, er sei es gewesen; **I took a ~ turning** ich habe eine verkehrte or falsche Abzweigung genommen; **to say/do the ~ thing** das Falsche sagen/tun; **the ~ side of the fabric** die linke Seite des Stoffes; **you live in the ~ part of town** du wohnst nicht im richtigen Stadtteil; **you've come to the ~ man or person/place** da sind Sie an den Falschen/an die Falsche/an die falsche Adresse geraten; **to do sth the ~ way** etw falsch or verkehrt machen; **something is ~** (irgend)etwas stimmt nicht (with mit); (suspiciously) irgendetwas stimmt da nicht or ist da faul (inf); **is anything or something ~?** ist was? (inf); **there's nothing ~** (es ist) alles in Ordnung; **what's ~?** was ist los?; **what's ~ with you?** was fehlt Ihnen?; **I hope there's nothing ~ at home** ich hoffe, dass zu Hause alles in Ordnung ist
(b) (morally) schlecht, unrecht; (= unfair) ungerecht, unfair; **it's ~ to steal** es ist unrecht zu stehlen; **that was very ~ of you** das war absolut nicht richtig von dir; **it's ~ that he should have to ask** es ist unrecht or falsch, dass er überhaupt fragen muss; **what's ~ with working on Sundays?** was ist denn schon dabei, wenn man sonntags arbeitet?; **I don't see anything ~ in or with that** ich finde nichts daran auszusetzen
2 ADV falsch; **to get sth ~** sich mit etw vertun; **he got the answer ~** er hat die falsche Antwort gegeben; (Math) er hat sich verrechnet; **I think you got things a bit ~** ich glaube, Sie sehen die Sache or das nicht ganz richtig; **you've got him (all) ~** (= he's not like that) Sie haben sich in ihm getäuscht; **to go ~** (on route) falsch gehen/fahren; (in calculation) einen Fehler machen; (plan etc) schief gehen; **you can't go ~** du kannst gar nichts verkehrt machen
3 N Unrecht nt no pl; **to be in the ~** im Unrecht sein; **he can do no ~** er macht natürlich immer alles richtig
4 VT **to ~ sb** jdm unrecht tun; **to be ~ed** ungerecht behandelt werden

wrong-foot [ˌrɒŋˈfʊt] VT (Sport, fig) auf dem falschen Fuß erwischen

wrongful [ˈrɒŋfʊl] ADJ ungerechtfertigt

wrongfully [ˈrɒŋfəlɪ] ADV zu Unrecht

wrongly [ˈrɒŋlɪ] ADV (= unjustly, improperly) unrecht; (= incorrectly) falsch, verkehrt; punished, accused, maintain zu Unrecht; believe fälschlicherweise

wrote [rəʊt] PRET of **write**

wrought [rɔːt] VT **the accident ~ havoc with his plans** der Unfall durchkreuzte alle seine Pläne; **the storm ~ great destruction** der Sturm richtete große Verheerungen an

wrought-iron [ˌrɔːtˈaɪən] ADJ schmiedeeisern attr, aus Schmiedeeisen; **~ gate** schmiedeeisernes Tor

wrung [rʌŋ] PRET, PTP of **wring**

wry [raɪ] ADJ (= ironical) ironisch; joke, sense of humour etc trocken

WTO ABBR of **World Trade Organization** Welthandelsorganisation f

Xx

X, x [eks] N **(a)** X *nt*, x *nt* **(b)** (*Math*, *fig*) x; **Mr X** Herr X; **X marks the spot** die Stelle ist mit einem Kreuzchen gekennzeichnet

xenophobia [zenəˈfəʊbɪə] N Fremdenfeindlichkeit *f*

xenophobic [zenəˈfəʊbɪk] ADJ fremdenfeindlich

Xerox® [ˈzɪərɒks] **1** N (= *copy*) Xerokopie *f*; (= *process*) Xeroxverfahren *nt* **2** VT xerokopieren

XL ABBR *of* **extra large**

Xmas [ˈeksməs, ˈkrɪsməs] N = **Christmas** Weihnachten *nt*

X-ray [ˈeksˈreɪ] **1** N Röntgenstrahl *m*; (*also* ~ **photograph**) Röntgenaufnahme *f or* -bild *nt*; **to take an ~ of sth** etw röntgen **2** VT *person* röntgen; *envelope*, *baggage* durchleuchten

X-ray IN CPDS Röntgen-

xylophone [ˈzaɪləfəʊn] N Xylophon *nt*

Yy

Y, y [waɪ] N Y *nt*, y *nt*

yacht [jɒt] **1** N Jacht *f* **2** VI segeln; **to go ~ing** segeln gehen

yachting ['jɒtɪŋ] N Segeln *nt*

yachtsman ['jɒtsmən] N, *pl* **-men** [-mən] Segler *m*

yachtswoman ['jɒtswʊmən] N, *pl* **-women** [-wɪmɪn] Seglerin *f*

yak¹ [jæk] N (*Zool*) Jak *m*

yak² VI (*inf*) schnattern (*inf*), quasseln (*inf*)

Yale lock® ['jeɪlˌlɒk] N Sicherheitsschloss *nt*

yam [jæm] N Süßkartoffel *f*

yammer ['jæmə*r*] VI (*inf*: = *moan*) jammern

Yank [jæŋk] (*inf*) **1** N Ami *m* (*inf*) **2** ADJ ATTR Ami- (*inf*)

yank [jæŋk] **1** N Ruck *m* **2** VT **to ~ sth** mit einem Ruck an etw (*dat*) ziehen

➤ **yank out** VT SEP ausreißen; *tooth* ziehen

Yankee ['jæŋkɪ] (*inf*) **1** N Yankee *m* (*inf*); (*Hist auch*) Nordstaatler(in) *m(f)* **2** ADJ ATTR Yankee- (*inf*)

yap [jæp] **1** VI (*dog*) kläffen; (= *talk noisily*) quatschen (*inf*) **2** N (*of dog*) Kläffen *nt*

yapping ['jæpɪŋ] N (*of dog*) Kläffen *nt*

yard¹ [jɑːd] N (*Measure*) Yard *nt* (*0.91 m*); **to buy cloth by the ~** ≈ Stoff meterweise *or* im Meter kaufen

yard² N **(a)** (*of farm, prison, house etc*) Hof *m*; **in the ~** auf dem Hof **(b)** (= *worksite*) Werksgelände *nt*; **builder's ~** Bauhof *m*; **shipbuilding ~** Werft *f*; **naval (dock)yard, navy ~** (*US*) Marinewerft *f*; **goods ~, freight ~** (*US*) Güterbahnhof *m* **(c)** (*US*: = *garden*) Garten *m*

yardstick ['jɑːdstɪk] N (*fig*) Maßstab *m*

yarn [jɑːn] N **(a)** (*Tex*) Garn *nt* **(b)** (= *tale*) Seemannsgarn *nt*; **to spin a ~** Seemannsgarn spinnen

yawn [jɔːn] **1** VTI gähnen **2** N (*of person*) Gähnen *nt*; **to give a ~** gähnen

yawning ['jɔːnɪŋ] **1** ADJ *chasm etc* gähnend **2** N Gähnen *nt*

yawp [jɔːp] (*US*) **1** N **(a)** (*inf*: = *yelp*) Aufschrei *m*; **to give a ~** aufschreien **(b)** (*inf*: = *chatter*) Geschwätz *nt*; **to have a ~** schwatzen **2** VI **(a)** (*inf*: = *yelp*) aufschreien **(b)** (*inf*: = *chatter*) schwatzen

yeah [jɛə] ADV (*inf*) ja

year [jɪə*r*] N **(a)** Jahr *nt*; **this/last ~** dieses/letztes Jahr; **every other ~** jedes zweite Jahr; **three times a ~** dreimal pro *or* im Jahr; **in the ~ 1989** im Jahr(e) 1989; **~ after ~** Jahr für Jahr; **~ by ~, from ~ to ~** von Jahr zu Jahr; **~ in, ~ out** jahrein, jahraus; **all (the) ~ round** das ganze Jahr über *or* hindurch; **as (the) ~s go by** mit den Jahren; **~s (and ~s) ago** vor (langen) Jahren; **~ a ~ last January** (im) Januar vor einem Jahr; **it'll be a ~ in** *or* **next January** (*duration*) es wird nächsten Januar ein Jahr sein; (*point in time*) es wird nächsten Januar ein Jahr her sein; **a ~ from now** nächstes Jahr um diese Zeit; **a hundred-~-old tree** ein hundert Jahre alter Baum; **he is six ~s old** *or* **six ~s of age** er ist sechs Jahre (alt); **he is in his fortieth ~** er ist im vierzigsten Lebensjahr; **I haven't laughed so much in ~s** ich habe schon lange nicht mehr so gelacht; **~ under review** (*Comm, Fin*) Berichtsjahr *nt*; **well advanced** *or* **well on in ~s** in vorgerücktem Alter; **to get on in ~s** in die Jahre kommen **(b)** (*Univ, Sch*: *of coin, stamp, wine*) Jahrgang *m*; **the 2001/02 academic ~** das akademische Jahr 2001/02; **first-~ student, first ~ student** Student(in) *m(f)* im ersten Jahr; (= *first term student*) Student(in) *m(f)* im ersten Semester; **she was in my ~ at school** sie war im selben Schuljahrgang wie ich

year: yearbook N Jahrbuch *nt*; **year-end** N Jahresende *nt*; **~ report** Jahresbericht *m*

yearling ['jɪəlɪŋ] **1** N (= *animal*) Jährling *m*; (= *racehorse also*) Einjährige(r) *mf* **2** ADJ einjährig

yearlong ['jɪə'lɒŋ] ADJ einjährig

yearly ['jɪəlɪ] **1** ADJ jährlich **2** ADV jährlich, einmal im Jahr; **twice ~** zweimal jährlich *or* im Jahr

yearn [jɜːn] VI sich sehnen (*after, for* nach); **to ~ to do sth** sich danach sehnen, etw zu tun

yearning ['jɜːnɪŋ] N Sehnsucht *f*, Verlangen *nt* (*for* nach)

year-round ['jɪə'raʊnd] ADJ, ADV das ganze Jahr über

yeast [jiːst] N, NO PL Hefe *f*

yell [jel] **1** N Schrei *m*; **to let out** *or* **give a ~** einen Schrei ausstoßen, schreien; **could you give me a ~ when we get there?** könnten Sie mich rufen, wenn wir da sind? **2** VTI (*also ~ out*) schreien, brüllen (*with* vor +*dat*); **he ~ed at her** er schrie *or* brüllte sie an; **just ~ if you need help** ruf, wenn du Hilfe brauchst; **he ~ed abuse at the teacher** er beschimpfte den Lehrer wüst

yellow ['jeləʊ] **1** ADJ (+ER) **(a)** gelb; **to go** *or* **turn ~** gelb werden; (*paper*) vergilben **(b)** (*inf*: = *cowardly*) feige **2** N Gelb *nt* **3** VT gelb färben; **the sunlight had ~ed the pages** die Sonne hatte die Seiten vergilben lassen **4** VI gelb werden; (*pages*) vergilben

yellow: yellow card N (*Ftbl*) gelbe Karte; **yellow fever** N Gelbfieber *nt*

yellowish ['jeləʊɪʃ] ADJ gelblich

yellow: yellow line N (*Brit*) Halteverbot *nt*; **double ~** absolutes Halteverbot; **to be parked on a (double) ~** im (absoluten) Halteverbot stehen; **Yellow Pages®** N SING **the ~** die Gelben Seiten *pl*; **Yellow River** N Gelber Fluss; **Yellow Sea** N Gelbes Meer

yellowy ['jeləʊɪ] ADJ gelblich

yelp [jelp] **1** N (*of animal*) Jaulen *nt no pl*; (*of person*) Aufschrei *m*; **to give a ~** (*animal*) (auf)jaulen; (*person*) aufschreien **2** VI (*animal*) (auf)jaulen; (*person*) aufschreien

yelping ['jelpɪŋ] N (*of animal*) Jaulen *nt*

Yemen ['jemən] N **the ~** der Jemen

Yemeni ['jemənɪ] **1** N Jemenit(in) *m(f)* **2** ADJ jemenitisch

yen [jen] N (*Fin*) Yen *m*

yep [jep] ADV (*inf*) ja; **is he sure? – ~!** ist er sicher? – klar!

yes [jes] **1** ADV **(a)** (*answering question*) ja; **to say ~** Ja sagen; **he said ~ to all my questions** er hat alle meine Fragen bejaht *or* mit Ja beantwortet; **if they say ~ to an increase** wenn sie eine Lohnerhöhung bewilligen; **I'd say ~ to 35%, no to 32%** ich würde 35% akzeptieren, 32% nicht; **she says ~ to everything** sie kann nicht Nein sagen; **waiter! – ~ sir?** Herr Ober! – ja, bitte?; **~ indeed** o ja, allerdings **2** N Ja *nt*

yes man N Jasager *m*

yesterday ['jestədeɪ] **1** N Gestern *nt* **2** ADV (*lit, fig*) gestern; **~ morning/evening** gestern Morgen/Abend; **he was at home all (day) ~** er war gestern den ganzen Tag zu Hause; **the day before ~** vorgestern; **a week ago ~** gestern vor einer Woche

yes woman N Jasagerin *f*

yet [jet] **1** ADV **(a)** (= *still*) noch; (= *thus far*) bis jetzt, bisher; **they haven't ~ returned** *or* **returned ~** sie sind noch nicht zurückgekommen; **as ~** (*with present tenses*) bis jetzt, bisher; (*with past*) bis dahin; **no, not ~** nein, noch nicht; **not just ~** jetzt noch nicht; **we've got ages ~** wir haben noch viel Zeit; **I've ~ to learn how to do it** ich muss erst noch lernen, wie man es macht; **(and) ~ again** und wieder, und noch einmal; **another arrived and ~ another** es kam noch einer und noch einer; **I may ~ go to Italy** ich fahre vielleicht noch nach Italien; **I'll do it ~** ich schaffe es schon noch **(b)** (*with interrog*: = *so far, already*) schon; **has he arrived ~?** ist er schon angekommen?; **do you have to go just ~?** müssen Sie jetzt schon gehen? **2** CONJ doch, trotzdem

yeti ['jetɪ] N Yeti *m*

yew [juː] N (*also ~ tree*) Eibe *f*; (= *wood*) Eibe(nholz *nt*) *f*

Y-fronts® ['waɪfrʌnts] PL (*esp Brit*) (Herren-)Slip *m*

Yiddish ['jɪdɪʃ] **1** ADJ jiddisch **2** N (*Ling*) Jiddisch *nt*

yield [jiːld] **1** VT **(a)** (land) crop hervorbringen; (tree) fruit tragen; (mine, oil well) bringen; interest, profit abwerfen; result (hervor)bringen; opportunity, clue ergeben; **this ~ed a weekly increase of 20%** das brachte eine wöchentliche Steigerung von 20%

(b) (= surrender, concede) aufgeben; **to ~ sth to sb** etw an jdn abtreten; **to ~ ground to sb** vor jdm zurückstecken

2 VI (lit, fig) nachgeben; **they ~ed to us** (Mil) sie haben sich uns (dat) ergeben; (general) sie haben nachgegeben; **at last she ~ed to his charm** schließlich erlag sie seinem Charme doch; **he ~ed to her requests** er gab ihren Bitten nach; **to ~ to temptation** der Versuchung erliegen; **to ~ under pressure** (fig) dem Druck weichen; (Mot) **to ~ to oncoming traffic** den Gegenverkehr vorbeilassen; **"~"** (US, Ir) „Vorfahrt beachten!"

3 N (of land, tree, shares, business) Ertrag m; (of work also) Ergebnis nt; (of mine, well) Ausbeute f; (of industry) (= goods) Produktion f; (= profit) Gewinne pl

yob [jɒb], **yobbo** [ˈjɒbəʊ] N (Brit inf) Halbstarke(r) m, Rowdy m

yodel [ˈjəʊdl] VTI jodeln

yodelling, (US) **yodeling** [ˈjəʊdlɪŋ] N Jodeln nt

yoga [ˈjəʊgə] N Joga m or nt

yoghourt, yog(h)urt [ˈjɒgət] N Jog(h)urt m or nt

yoke [jəʊk] N (lit, fig) Joch nt; (for carrying pails) (Trag)joch nt; (= pair of oxen) Gespann nt; **to throw off the ~** das Joch abschütteln

yokel [ˈjəʊkəl] N (pej) Bauerntölpel m

yolk [jəʊk] N (of egg) Eigelb nt

you [juː] PRON **(a)** (German familiar form) (sing) (nom) du; (acc) dich; (dat) dir; (pl) (nom) ihr; (acc, dat) euch; (German polite form: sing, pl) (nom, acc) Sie; (dat) Ihnen; **all of ~** (pl) ihr alle/Sie alle; **if I were ~** wenn ich du/Sie wäre, an deiner/Ihrer Stelle; **~ Germans** ihr Deutschen; **two/three wait here!** ihr beide/drei wartet hier; **is that ~?** bist dus/seid ihrs/sind Sies?; **it's ~** du bist es/ihr seids/Sie sinds; **now there's a woman for ~!** das ist mal eine (tolle) Frau!; **just ~ dare!** untersteh dich!; **that hat just isn't ~** (inf) der Hut passt einfach nicht zu dir/zu Ihnen

(b) (indef) (nom) man; (acc) einen; (dat) einem; **~ never know, ~ never can tell** man kann nie wissen; **it's not good for ~** es ist nicht gut

you'd [juːd] CONTR of **you would** of **you had**

you'd've [ˈjuːdəv] CONTR of **you would have**

you'll [juːl] CONTR of **you will**, **you shall**

young [jʌŋ] **1** ADJ (+ER) jung; wine, grass also neu; **~ people** junge Leute pl; **they have a ~ family** sie haben kleine Kinder; **he is ~ at heart** er ist innerlich jung geblieben; **at a ~ age** in frühen Jahren; **I'm not getting any ~er** ich werde auch nicht jünger; **you ~ rascal!** (inf) du kleiner Schlingel!; **~ Mr Brown** der junge Herr Brown; **he's a very ~ forty** er ist ein sehr jung gebliebener Vierziger

2 ADV marry, have children jung

3 PL **(a)** (= people) **the ~** die Jugend, die jungen Leute; **~ and old** jung und alt

(b) (= animals) Junge pl

youngest [ˈjʌŋgɪst] **1** ADJ ATTR SUPERL of **young** jüngste(r, s) **2** N **the ~** der/die/das Jüngste; (pl) die Jüngsten pl; **the ~ of four children** das jüngste von vier Kindern

youngish [ˈjʌŋɪʃ] ADJ ziemlich jung

young offender N jugendlicher Straftäter

youngster [ˈjʌŋstəʳ] N (= boy) Junge m; (= child) Kind nt; **he's just a ~** er ist eben noch jung or ein Kind

your [jɔːʳ, jəʳ] POSS ADJ (German familiar form) (sing) dein/deine/dein; (pl) euer/eure/euer; (German polite form: sing, pl) Ihr/Ihre/Ihr; **one of ~ friends** einer deiner/Ihrer Freunde, einer von deinen/Ihren Freunden; **the climate here is bad for ~ health** das Klima hier ist ungesund

you're [jʊəʳ, jɔːʳ] CONTR of **you are**

yours [jɔːz] POSS PRON (German familiar form) (sing) deiner/deine/deins; (pl) euer/eure/euers; (German polite form: sing, pl) Ihrer/Ihre/Ihr(e)s; **this is my book and that is ~** dies ist mein Buch und das (ist) deins/Ihres; **the idea was ~** es war deine/Ihre Idee, die Idee stammt von dir/Ihnen; **she is a cousin of ~** sie ist deine Kusine, sie ist eine Kusine von dir; **that is no business of ~** das geht dich/Sie nichts an; **~** (in letter-writing) Ihr/Ihre; **~ faithfully, ~ truly** (Brit: on letter) mit freundlichem Gruß, mit freundlichen Grüßen, hochachtungsvoll (form)

yourself [jɔːˈself, jəˈself] PRON, pl **yourselves** [jɔːˈselvz, jəˈselvz] **(a)** (reflexive) (German familiar form) (sing) (acc) dich; (dat) dir; (pl) euch; (German polite form: sing, pl) sich; **have you hurt ~?** hast du dir/haben Sie sich wehgetan?; **you never speak about ~** du redest nie über dich (selbst)/Sie reden nie über sich (selbst)

(b) (emph) selbst; **you ~ told me, you told me ~** du hast/haben mir selbst gesagt; **you are not quite ~ today** du bist heute gar nicht du selbst; **you will see for ~** du wirst/Sie werden selbst sehen; **did you do it by ~?** hast du/haben Sie das allein gemacht?

youth [juːθ] N **(a)** NO PL Jugend f; **in (the days of) my ~** in meiner Jugend(zeit) **(b)** pl **-s** [juːðz] (= young man) junger Mann, Jugendliche(r) m **(c)** **youth** PL (= young men and women) Jugend f; **she likes working with (the) ~** sie arbeitet gerne mit Jugendlichen

youth club N Jugendklub m

youthful [ˈjuːθfʊl] ADJ jugendlich; **he's a ~ 65** er ist ein jugendlicher Fünfundsechziger

youthfulness [ˈjuːθfʊlnɪs] N Jugendlichkeit f

youth: **youth hostel** N Jugendherberge f; **youth worker** N Jugendarbeiter(in) m(f)

you've [juːv] CONTR of **you have**

yowl [jaʊl] **1** N (of person) Heulen nt no pl; (of dog) Jaulen nt no pl; (of cat) klägliches Miauen no pl **2** VI (person) heulen; (dog) jaulen; (cat) kläglich miauen

yo-yo [ˈjəʊjəʊ] N Jo-Jo nt

yucca [ˈjʌkə] N Yucca f

yuck [jʌk] INTERJ (inf) i, igitt

Yugoslav [ˈjuːgəʊslɑːv] **1** ADJ jugoslawisch **2** N Jugoslawe m, Jugoslawin f

Yugoslavia [ˈjuːgəʊslɑːvɪə] N Jugoslawien nt; **the former ~** das ehemalige Jugoslawien

Yugoslavian [ˈjuːgəʊslɑːvɪən] ADJ jugoslawisch

yuk [jʌk] INTERJ (inf) i, igitt

yukky [ˈjʌkɪ] ADJ (+ER) (inf) eklig, fies (inf)

Yuletide N [ˈjuːltaɪd] Weihnachtszeit f

yummy [ˈjʌmɪ] (inf) ADJ (+ER) food lecker; man toll

yum yum [ˈjʌmˈjʌm] INTERJ lecker, jamjam (inf)

yuppie, yuppy [ˈjʌpɪ] **1** N Yuppie m **2** ADJ yuppiehaft; **~ car** Yuppieauto nt

Zz

Z, z [(Brit) zed, (US) ziː] N Z nt, z nt
Zaire [zɑːˈɪəʳ] N (Hist) Zaire nt
Zambesi, Zambezi [zæmˈbiːzɪ] N Sambesi m
Zambia [ˈzæmbɪə] N Sambia nt
zany [ˈzeɪnɪ] ADJ (+ER) verrückt; *person also* irrsinnig komisch
Zanzibar [ˈzænzɪbɑːʳ] N Sansibar nt
zap [zæp] (*inf*) **1** VT **(a)** (*Comput*: = *delete*) löschen **(b)** (*inf*) (= *kill*) abknallen (*inf*); (= *destroy*) kaputtmachen (*inf*) **2** VI (*inf*: = *change channel*) umschalten
zeal [ziːl] N, NO PL Eifer m; **to work with great ~** mit Feuereifer arbeiten
zealot [ˈzelət] N Fanatiker(in) m(f); (*religious also*) (Glaubens)eiferer(in) m(f)
zealous ADJ, **zealously** ADV [ˈzeləs, -lɪ] eifrig
zebra [ˈzebrə] N Zebra nt
zebra crossing N (*Brit*) Zebrastreifen m
zenith [ˈzenɪθ] N (*Astron, fig*) Zenit m
zero [ˈzɪərəʊ] **1** N, *pl* **-(e)s** Null f; (= *point on scale*) Nullpunkt m; **15 degrees below ~** 15 Grad unter null; **the needle is at** *or* **on ~** der Zeiger steht auf null **2** ADJ **~ degrees** null Grad; **~ growth** Nullwachstum nt
➤ **zero in** VI (*Mil*) sich einschießen (*on* auf +*acc*); **to zero in on sb/sth** (*fig*) on core of problem jdn/etw einkreisen; *on difficulty* sich (*dat*) etw herausgreifen; *on opportunity* sich auf etw (*acc*) stürzen

zero: **zero-coupon bond** N (*St Ex*) Zero Bond m, Nullkupon-Anleihe f; **zero-emission** ADJ emissionsfrei; **zero gravity** N Schwerelosigkeit f; **zero hour** N (*Mil, fig*) die Stunde X; **zero-rated** ADJ (*Brit: for VAT*) mehrwertsteuerfrei; **zero rating** N (*for VAT*) Befreiung f von der Mehrwertsteuer; **zero tolerance** N Nulltoleranz f
zest [zest] N **(a)** (= *enthusiasm*) Begeisterung f; **~ for life** Lebensfreude f **(b)** (*in style, of food etc*) Pfiff m (*inf*), Schwung m (c) (= *lemon etc peel*) Zitronen-/Orangenschale f
zigzag [ˈzɪgzæg] **1** N Zickzack m *or* nt; **in a ~** im Zickzack **2** ADJ Zickzack-; *road, path* zickzackförmig; **~ line** Zickzacklinie f **3** ADV im Zickzack **4** VI im Zickzack laufen/fahren *etc*
zilch [zɪltʃ] N (*inf*) nix (*inf*)
zillion [ˈzɪljən] (*US inf*) **1** N **~s of dollars** zig Milliarden Dollar (*inf*) **2** ADJ **I've told you a ~ times …** ich hab dir hunderttausendmal *or* zigmal gesagt … (*inf*)
Zimbabwe [zɪmˈbɑːbwɪ] N Simbabwe nt

Zimbabwean [zɪmˈbɑːbwɪən] **1** ADJ simbabwisch **2** N Simbabwer(in) m(f)
Zimmer® [ˈzɪməʳ] N (*Brit: also* ~ **frame**) Gehgerät nt
zinc [zɪŋk] N Zink nt
Zionism [ˈzaɪənɪzəm] N Zionismus m
Zionist [ˈzaɪənɪst] **1** ADJ zionistisch **2** N Zionist(in) m(f)
zip [zɪp] **1** N **(a)** (*Brit*: = *fastener*) Reißverschluss m **(b)** (*inf*: = *energy*) Schwung m **(c)** (*inf*: = *nothing*) nichts, nix (*inf*) **2** VT **to ~ a dress** den Reißverschluss eines Kleides zumachen *or* zuziehen **3** VI (*car*) flitzen (*inf*); (*person also*) wetzen (*inf*); **to ~ past/along** *etc* vorbei-/daherflitzen *etc* (*inf*)
➤ **zip up** **1** VT SEP **to zip up a dress** den Reißverschluss eines Kleides zumachen; **will you zip me up please?** kannst du mir bitte den Reißverschluss zumachen? **2** VI **it zips up** es hat einen Reißverschluss; **it zips up at the back** der Reißverschluss ist hinten
zip: **zip code** N (*US*) Postleitzahl f; **zip fastener** N (*Brit*) Reißverschluss m

zipper [ˈzɪpəʳ] N (*US*) Reißverschluss m
zit [zɪt] N (*inf*: = *spot*) Pickel m
zither [ˈzɪðəʳ] N Zither f
zodiac [ˈzəʊdɪæk] N Tierkreis m; **signs of the ~** Tierkreiszeichen pl
zombie [ˈzɒmbɪ] N (*fig*) Idiot(in) m(f) (*inf*), Schwachkopf m (*inf*); **like ~s/a ~** wie im Tran
zone [zəʊn] N (*Geog*) (*fig*) Zone f; (*US:* = *postal ~*) Post(zustell)bezirk m; **no-parking ~** Parkverbot nt; **time ~** Zeitzone f
zonked [zɒŋkt] ADJ (*inf*) (= *drunk, high*) breit (*sl*), zu (*inf*); (= *exhausted*) total geschafft (*inf*)
zoo [zuː] N Zoo m
zoo keeper N Tierpfleger(in) m(f)
zoological [zʊəˈlɒdʒɪkəl] ADJ zoologisch; **~ gardens** zoologischer Garten
zoologist [zʊˈɒlədʒɪst] N Zoologe m, Zoologin f
zoology [zʊˈɒlədʒɪ] N Zoologie f
zoom [zuːm] **1** N (*Phot: also* ~ **lens**) Zoom(objektiv) nt **2** VI **(a)** (*inf*) sausen (*inf*); **we were ~ing along at 90** wir sausten mit 90 daher (*inf*); **he ~ed through it so quickly he can't possibly have read it properly** er war in null Komma nichts damit fertig, er kann das unmöglich gründlich gelesen haben (*inf*) **(b)** (*Aviat: plane, rocket*) steil (auf)steigen; **the rocket ~ed up into the sky** die Rakete schoss in den Himmel
➤ **zoom in** VI (*Phot*) hinzoomen; **to zoom in on sth** etw heranholen; **he zoomed in on the problem** (*inf*) er kam direkt auf das Problem zu sprechen
zucchini [zuːˈkiːnɪ] N (*esp US*) Zucchini pl
Zulu [ˈzuːluː] **1** ADJ Zulu-, der Zulus; **the ~ people** die Zulus pl **2** N Zulu mf
Zululand [ˈzuːluːlænd] N Kwazulu nt
zwieback [ˈzwiːbæk] N (*US*) Zwieback m